Clerical Directory 1998/99

Crockford's Clerical Directory

1998/99

Ninety-fifth edition

First issue 1858

A Directory of the Clergy
of the Church of England
the Church in Wales
the Scottish Episcopal Church
the Church of Ireland

Published for The Church Commissioners for England
and The Central Board of Finance of The Church of England
by Church House Publishing

Crockford's Clerical Directory
95th edition (1998/99) © The Church Commissioners for England and
The Central Board of Finance of The Church of England 1997

All rights reserved. No part of this publication may be reproduced, stored or transmitted in any form or by any means, electronic or mechanical, including photocopying, recording, or any information storage and retrieval system, without permission in writing from the copyright owners.

Published December 1997 by
Church House Publishing
Church House
Great Smith Street
London SW1P 3NZ

ISBN 0 7151 8093 2 (hardback)
0 7151 8094 0 (paperback)

Jacket and cover design by Drummond and Peggy Chapman

Typeset, printed and bound by
Page Bros
Mile Cross Lane
Norwich NR6 6SA

CONTENTS

Index to advertisements *6*
Introduction *51*
John Crockford *53*
A user's guide to *Crockford* *54*
How to address the clergy *58*
Abbreviations *61*

Biographies of clergy and deaconesses
Clergy of the Church of England, the Church in Wales, the Scottish Episcopal Church and the Church of Ireland 1
Deaconesses of the Church of England, the Church in Wales, the Scottish Episcopal Church and the Church of Ireland 792

Indexes
Bishops in England, Wales, Scotland and Ireland 794
Bishops in the House of Lords 797
Historical succession of archbishops and bishops 798
Cathedrals 829
Royal Peculiars, clergy of the Queen's household, etc. 831
Diocesan offices 832
Archdeaconries, deaneries and rural deans of the Church of England and the Church in Wales 835
English benefices and churches 843
Welsh benefices and churches 1016
Scottish incumbencies 1032
Irish benefices and churches 1036
The Diocese of Gibraltar in Europe 1050
Chaplains to Her Majesty's Services 1052
Prison chaplains 1054
Hospital chaplains 1056
Hospice chaplains 1063
Educational chaplains 1064
Theological colleges and courses 1068

The Anglican Communion
Bishops of Anglican dioceses overseas 1069
Bishops of united churches 1081
Provincial offices 1083
Directories of the Anglican provinces 1084

Supplementary information
Addresses unknown 1085
Ordinations to the diaconate at Michaelmas 1997 1086
Clergy who have died since the last edition 1088

Maps
Scotland 1093
England and Wales 1094
Ireland 1096

INDEX TO ADVERTISEMENTS

Advertisements can be found on the following pages

BELLFOUNDERS

John Taylor Bellfounders Ltd, *32*
Whitechapel Bell Foundry, *19*

CHURCH AND BENEVOLENT SOCIETIES

Additional Curates Society, *8*
Anglican Stewardship Association, *49*
Bromley & Sheppard's Colleges, *45*
CCPAS, *35*
Central Board of Finance, *34*
The Children's Society, *36*
Christians Aware, *35*
Church of England Pensions Board, *40*
Church Lads' and Church Girls' Brigade, *42*
Church Society, *39*
Church Society Trust, *45*
Church Union, *22*
College of St Barnabas, *38*
Corporation of the Sons of the Clergy, *18*
Corrymeela Link, *20*
The English Clergy Association, *37*
The Friends of the Clergy Corporation, *8*
London City Mission, *12*
The Missions to Seamen, *27*
The Mothers' Union, *10*
The Prayer Book Society, *7*
St Luke's Hospital for the Clergy, *41*
Tear Fund, *28*
Trinity Care, *20*

CHURCH FURNISHERS, SUPPLIERS AND ROBES

James Chase & Son (Furnishings) Ltd, *15*
F A Dumont Ltd, *16*
Charles Farris Ltd, *38*
Pruden & Smith Silversmiths, *24*
St Martin Vestment Ltd, *22*
ST Churchware, *46*
The House of Vanheems Ltd, *9*
Vanpoulles Ltd, *17*
Watts & Company Ltd, *26*
J Wippell & Co Ltd, *11*

CARS

Autosave (UK) Ltd, *33*

HEATING

Dunphy Ecclesiastical Heating, *12*
Emberheat, *31*
Multibeton Ltd, *43*

FINANCE AND INSURANCE

Church Finance Supplies Ltd, *14*
Ecclesiastical, *13*
Lockie Envelopes, *14*

PASTORAL REORGANISATION, TRAINING AND PLANNING

Christian Research, *30*
Decade Ministries, *49*
David E Gillman, *35*

PUBLICITY

John Hart Publicity Ltd, *43*

PUBLISHERS, PUBLICATIONS AND BOOKSELLERS

Anglicanite Directory, *49*
Canterbury Press Norwich, *25*
Chansitor Publications, *30*
Church House Bookshop, *50*
Churchman, *46*
Church of England Newspaper, *47*
Church Pulpit Year Book, *30*
Church Times, *48*
An English Prayer Book, *39*
FW Sermons, *46*
John Pendlebury Bookseller, *24*

SCHOOLS AND COLLEGES

Dean Close School, Cheltenham, *38*
Liverpool Hope University College, *44*
Marlborough College, *29*
St Lawrence College, Ramsgate, *29*
St Mary's Hall, Brighton, *10*

STAINED GLASS AND ORGANS

Copeman Hart & Co Ltd, *23*
Clifford Durant, *10*

TRAVEL AND HOLIDAYS

Christian Tours (UK) Ltd, *42*
Highway Journeys, *42*
Maranatha Tours, *21*
SN Industries, *24*

The inclusion of an advertisement is for purposes of information and is not to be taken as implying acceptance of the objects of the advertiser by the publishers or proprietors.

THE PRAYER BOOK SOCIETY

Registered Charity 1001783

SAINT JAMES GARLICKHYTHE
GARLICK HILL
LONDON EC4

President: The Rt Hon Lord Charteris of Amisfield, G.C.B., G.C.V.O., P.C.

Ecclesiastical Patron:
The Rt Revd and Rt Hon Richard Chartres, Lord Bishop of London

Lay Patron: The Rt Hon The Lord Sudeley, F.S.A.

Vice Presidents:
The Rt Hon Lord Glenamara, C.H., P.C.
The Rt Hon Viscount Cranborne, P.C.
The Rt Hon Frank Field, M.P., Andrew Hunter, Esq, M.P.
The Rt Hon Baroness James of Holland Park, O.B.E.
The Rt Hon Lord Morris of Castle Morris, The Revd Dr Roger Beckwith
Roger Evans, Esq

Chairman: C. A. Anthony Kilmister, Esq

Deputy-Chairman: Colonel John Hall

Vice Chairmen: Professor the Revd Raymond Chapman and Neil Inkley, Esq

Hon Secretary: Miss Nada Pobjoy Hon Treasurer: John Service, Esq

The Book of Common Prayer

contains some of the most majestic and beautiful prose into the English language. Over the centuries it has been the repository of doctrine from which Anglican beliefs could be learned. A devotional power-house, the Book of Common Prayer is a deeply valued means of communication with our Maker.

The Prayer Book Society

★ seeks to defend and uphold that doctrine and to promote the worship enshrined in the Book of Common Prayer

★ does NOT propagate Prayer Book fundamentalism but believes a modest amount of flexibility in usage is both sensible and to be desired

The Prayer Book Society aims

★ to encourage the use of the Book of Common Prayer for the training of Ordinands and Confirmands

★ to spread knowledge of the Book of Common Prayer and the doctrine contained therein

★ to encourage use of the Book of Common Prayer for public worship.

ARE YOU A REGULAR READER OF THE SOCIETY'S TWO MAGAZINES?

ISSUES OF "*FAITH AND HERITAGE*" ALTERNATE WITH "*FAITH AND WORSHIP*"

Please support

THE PRAYER BOOK SOCIETY

write now to:

PBS OFFICE, ST JAMES GARLICKHYTHE
GARLICK HILL, LONDON EC4V 2AL

Additional Curates Society

gives grants for assistant priests in poor and populous parishes and fosters vocations to the priesthood.
Every penny donated to A.C.S. is used to provide parishes with priests

Donations and enquiries to:
The General Secretary
The Reverend Stephen Leach
ADDITIONAL CURATES SOCIETY
Gordon Browning House, 8 Spitfire Road, Birmingham B24 9PB
Tel: 0121 382 5533 Fax: 0121 382 6999

Registered Charity No. 209448

Founded 1837

Patron: Her Most Excellent Majesty The Queen

Holidays – Clothing – Essentials – Emergencies

'..often, something as simple as a family holiday can lift a seemingly insupportable burden of strain..'

We help Anglican clergy and their families when they are in financial need or other distress. We make cash grants for a wide variety of needs, giving special consideration to the provision of holidays for those in stressful circumstances.

Please help us with a regular subscription (ideally, covenanted), with a donation or through Gift Aid.

And please remember us in your Will!

If you can help – or if you need us – please contact The Secretary.

THE FRIENDS OF THE CLERGY CORPORATION

27 Medway Street, Westminster, London SW1P 2BD. Telephone 0171–222 2288. *Registered Charity 264724.*

THE HOUSE OF VANHEEMS LTD

BROOMFIELD WORKS, 6 BROOMFIELD PLACE, EALING, LONDON W13 9LB

Established 1793

ROBEMAKERS, CLERICAL TAILORS & CHURCH OUTFITTERS

Clerical Tailoring
Clergy Cassocks, Surplices,
Cloaks, Hoods, Scarves,
Vestments, etc. Cassock-Albs

Cut and made on the premises;
first class materials and workmanship,
at keenly competitive prices

Academic Gowns & Hoods,
Preaching Gowns, Clerical Collars,
Stocks, Shirts and Ready Made Suits

Choir Robes
Cassocks, Surplices, Gowns and
Cassock-Albs

Church Outfitting
Altar Frontals, Altar Cloths,
Communion Linens, Pulpit Falls,
Hassocks, Flags, etc.
Materials by the metre

**Catalogue and fabric samples
upon request**

Church Silverware
Chalices, Ciboria,
Communion Sets, Wafer Boxes,
Cruets, Flagons

Please write for details
stating your interests

**BROOMFIELD WORKS, BROOMFIELD PLACE, EALING,
LONDON, W13 9LB. Telephone 0181 567 7885**

CLIFFORD G. DURANT

STAINED GLASS ARTIST

ESTABLISHED 1972

THE GLASSHOUSE STUDIO
NEW STREET, HORSHAM
SUSSEX, ENGLAND RH13 5DU

This conservation practice is included on the Register maintained by The Conservation Unit of the Museum & Galleries Commission

Telephone
Horsham
(01403)
264607

FINE GLASS PAINTING
COMMISSION DESIGNS

RESTORATION & CONSERVATION WORK

STAINED GLASS PROTECTION

WINDOW GUARDS

'BSMGP Accredited Conservation Studio, Category 4'

Phone for a brochure of recent works

Independent Church of England School for Girls

St Mary's Hall

Brighton

Substantial Clergy Bursaries and uniform grant

Quality education in a warm family atmosphere

Boarding and Day School

Scholarships and Music Scholarships also available to other applicants

Come and spend a day with us

Tel: 01273 606061
Fax: 01273 620782

A registered charity providing quality education

THE MOTHERS' UNION

(Incorporated by Royal Charter)

The Mothers' Union (MU) is an Anglican organisation which promotes the well-being of families worldwide.

We achieve this by developing prayer and spiritual growth in families, studying and reflecting on family life and its place in society, and resourcing our members to take practical action to improve conditions for families, both nationally and in the communities in which they live.

If you would like further information about the MU, please contact:

Communications Organiser
The Mothers' Union
Mary Sumner House
24 Tufton Street
London SW1P 3RB
Tel 0171 222 5533
Fax 0171 222 1591

(Reg Charity No 240531)

Clergy Cassocks

This double breasted cassock is one of a variety of styles available from any of the addresses below. Enquiries or personal calls are always welcome.

Wippells also stock a wide range of clerical and academic wear, including:–

Surplices
for clergy, choir and organists
Albs and Tunics
for choir and servers
Cloaks
for clergy winter wear
Choir Robes
Readers' Robes
Preaching Gowns

also

Church Furnishings * Stained Glass * Altar Wines * Textiles * Metalwork * Church Furniture

For further information on any of the above, please write or call

WIPPELL'S

Exeter 88 Buller Rd. EX4 1DQ Tel. 01392 254234. Fax. 01392 250868
London 11 Tufton St. SW1P 3QB Tel. 0171-222 4528 Fax. 0171-976 7536
Manchester 9-21 Princess St., M2 4DN Tel. 0161-834 7967 Fax. 0161-835 1652

London's own Mission needs your help

The London City Mission was founded in 1835 and exists for the spiritual and social uplift of the people of London – mainly by house-to-house visitation and evangelism in industry.

We support 100 full-time Missionaries (as well as an ever-changing army of part-time volunteers) serving in the London churches; in the docks, on the railways, in the markets and the hospitals – wherever people live and work – listening, comforting, giving practical help wherever possible, running playschools and recreation centres; and always relating the problems of daily life to the Gospel message of harmony and Salvation.

We depend on voluntary contributions and legacies to maintain this vital work. Please ask your clients to remember the work of the Mission when drawing up their Wills. Latest Report gladly sent on request.

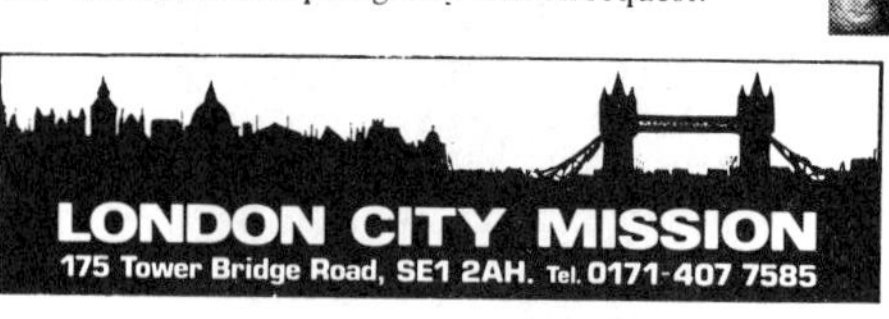

LONDON CITY MISSION
175 Tower Bridge Road, SE1 2AH. Tel. 0171-407 7585

Reg'd Charity No. 247186

THE TRUTH ABOUT CHURCH HEATING

Dunphy Ecclesiastical Heating can give you the whole truth about church heating. We do not manufacture, so we can design and install all types of system and advise you with complete impartiality. Our service is professional and personal and comes completely free of charge.

**FREE ADVICE, FREE SURVEY,
FREE QUOTATION**

CALL US NOW FREE ON 0800 614 100

OR FREEPOST OL 5557 ROCHDALE

THE NATIONS LEADERS IN CHURCH HEATING

My, how you've grown.

Thanks to a group of churchmen, Ecclesiastical was born back in 1887. At the end of 1996 our Group's assets exceeded £817 million. (You could say we've shot up). We still insure 93% of the Anglican churches in the UK and donate all available profits to the Church and charities. Our Parish Voucher Scheme is an innovative vehicle for boosting the funds of churches at the local level. We make regular charitable grants to dioceses too, in fact over the last 5 years, we contributed a total of £11.2 million making us the 24th largest corporate giver to charity in the UK and we're still an ethical organisation, run on Christian principles.

Looking after the Church and its members.

But there's another side to Ecclesiastical. We also offer a wide range of personal insurances and investment products. These include:

- Competitive, household and motor insurance that combines excellent cover with friendly service.
- A wide range of investment products including bonds, PEPs, endowments, unit trusts and ethical investments.
- Protection insurance such as critical illness cover and life assurance.

Our friendly knowledgeable staff will be delighted to discuss any of these services with you.

Call **01452 528533** to find out more, or email on: **gbeigmkg@ibmmail**

Beaufort House, Brunswick Road, Gloucester GL1 1JZ

Written details of any of the above products can be obtained by contacting us at the address above. The value of units can fall as well as rise. Investment products are provided by Ecclesiastical Marketing Group, members of which are regulated by the Personal Investment Authority and IMRO. A representative of the company may call. Any recommendations you may receive will relate only to the products of Ecclesiastical. Not available in Northern Ireland.

REGULAR GIVING ENVELOPES

- Choice of Weekly & Monthly styles in cartons or booklets
- Various colours and designs
- Special occasion envelopes
- Childrens envelopes
- Supporting supplies

Thousands of Churches benefit from using our envelopes, can WE help YOU. Contact us on 01235 524488 *or write to*

CHURCH FINANCE SUPPLIES LTD
FREEPOST
ABINGDON, OXON OX14 3BR
(No stamp required)

We can help to improve the level of your Fund raising

Lockie Envelopes

manufacture envelopes specifically for fund raising, together with a full range of stationery designed to simplify the job of accounting & recording

01942 726146

Fax: 01942 271220

38 HIGH STREET, GOLBORNE,
Nr. WARRINGTON, WA3 3BG

It's comforting to know who you can rely on

The 4000 Chair

The Abbey Lectern

The Kelso Stacking Chair

Our customers have the peace of mind in knowing that we are renowned for our commitment to only using the best raw materials and the highest standards of production in our furniture. Quality of service and product has been our priority since James Chase & Son was established in 1931.

ASK FOR OUR BROCHURE NOW
0345 125488
Calls charged at local rate

We have over thirty years experience as Church Furnishings specialists, so you will be in good hands. Our chairs are in over 5,000 places of worship throughout the UK, so you will be in good company too. If you do need someone to rely on, call us and we will be delighted to discuss your requirements.

OUR RANGE INCLUDES

CHAIRS • TABLES • PULPITS • ALTARS • KNEELERS
SILVERWARE • VESTMENTS

191 Thornton Rd, Bradford BD1 2JT. Telephone: 01274 738282 Fax: 01274 737836

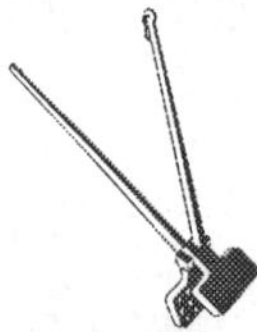

F. A. Dumont Altar Breads

Serving the religious community worldwide

F.A. Dumont offers by far the finest altar bread available today. Our breads are baked daily using only the purest ingredients and are made strictly without additives.

Dumont breads are offered in a number of styles and sizes including our single-cross bread which has a carefully moulded sealed edge to prevent crumbs. And when supplied in our new roll package, pictured below, you can be assured that our breads will arrive free of damage.

Altar Breads available include:

- **People's**
- **Priest's**
- **Concelebration**

in white and wholemeal

For a pack including our brochure, free samples, and details of your local supplier, please call or write to us today.

F. A. Dumont ~ High Street ~ Lyminge ~ Folkestone ~ Kent CT18 8EL
FREEPHONE: 0800 413401 Telephone: 01303 863193 Fax: 01303 863700

VANPOULLES

Church furnishers
~ EST 1908 ~

Vanpoulles Limited
1 Old Lodge Lane, Purley, Surrey, CR8 4DG.
Tel : 0181-668 6266. Fax : 0181-668 1033.
E-mail: sales@vanpoulles.co.uk
http://www.vanpoulles.co.uk

A complete range of church furnishings is available - please see our catalogues:

Part One - for all your textile and clothing requirements, including: Vestments, Copes, Frontals, Albs, Shirts & Cassocks etc.

Part Two - for Silverware, Brassware and woodwork, including: Chalices, Ciboria, Pyxes, Candlesticks, Crucifixes, Tabernacles, Mass Kits, Chairs, Lecterns, Altars, Statuary & Devotional items etc.

Candle List - for your candles and related consumables, including: Altar Candles, Paschal Candles, Oil Candles, Wine, Wafers & Incense etc.

Slabbinck Brochure - for a range of items of more modern design in textiles, clothing and silverware.

We hold very large stocks of the majority of our lines which enables us to offer a 'by return' service on a very wide range of products. Vanpoulles Ltd is able to offer the personal service of a family business with over 89 years experience in supplying Church Furnishings. Telephone, write, fax, e-mail or visit us at our showrooms where a range of our goods are on display.

Office & Showroom hours :
9.00 am to 5.00 pm Monday to Friday

Access, Mastercard and Switch cards accepted for your convenience.

CORPORATION OF THE

SONS OF THE CLERGY

Founded A.D. 1655 Incorporated by Royal Charter 1678

For assisting Clergymen of the Anglican Church and their Widows and Dependants, and for providing Grants for Education, Maintenance or Apprenticeship of Children of the Clergy of the Dioceses of the United Kingdom, Ireland and the Mission field.

Office; 1 DEAN TRENCH STREET, WESTMINSTER LONDON SW1P 3HB

Telephone: 0171-799 3696 & 0171-222 5887

(Charity registration number: 207736)

THE COURT OF ASSISTANTS

President:
THE ARCHBISHOP OF CANTERBURY

Vice President:
LORD LLOYD OF BERWICK, D.L.

TREASURERS:
Mr L H G TRIMM
Mr T D BAXENDALE
THE REVEREND D BURGESS

ASSISTANTS

The Archbishop of Armagh
Mr R J Askwith
Rear Admiral D W Bazalgette CB
Dr J A Birch
Mr P W Boorman JP
Alderman D W Brewer JP
The Reverend P Buckler
Mr C B Byford CBE
Mr C P G Chavasse
Viscount Churchill
Major Sir Peter Clarke KCVO
Mr B W Derbyshire
The Bishop of Edinburgh and Primus
The Right Reverend D J Farmbrough
The Venerable K Gibbons
Professor A H P Gillett
Mr T D D Hoffman
Mr N J R James JP
The Venerable F Johnston CB
Mr Sheriff S K Knowles
Mr P Locke
Mr I S Lockhart
The Bishop of London
Lord Luke of Pavenham DL
The Right Reverend L E Luscombe
Mrs J C Manual JP
The Venerable J A Morrison
Major General J I H Owen OBE
Canon J Robinson
Mrs D M Stanesby
Mr D N Vermont
The Archbishop of Wales
Alderman Sir Christopher Walford
Dr E M Webb
Mrs C White
Mr A E Woodall
The Archbishop of York

The Corporation distributed over £1,208,000 in 1996 by way of grants to 2500 clergymen, their widows and dependents. Education and maintenance help was given to 200 ordinands and 500 boys and girls.

The ANNUAL FESTIVAL SERVICE in St Paul's Cathedral is held in May and tickets may be obtained from the Registrar at the address given above.

Donors of not less than £100 may be elected to be Governors of the Corporation.

SUBSCRIPTIONS, DONATIONS, CHURCH and SCHOOL COLLECTIONS, and LEGACIES, in aid of funds or towards the extension of any of the above branches of work, are requested, and will be gratefully acknowledged by the Registrar, who will provide any information required.

R C F LEACH, Registrar

Bells bring people together!

Their call to worship proclaims the Christian message to the world. And the bellringers themselves, developing their skills, become united as a team.

The team that works at the Whitechapel Bell Foundry, casting and tuning, installing and restoring church bells of every kind, is deploying skills that have been developed over four hundred years. Today, our technical expertise, and our reputation for the highest standards of craftsmanship and service, stand unrivalled.

Bells and bellringers make an important contribution to the Church's witness in the world. We are proud to be a part of it.

The World's most famous

WHITECHAPEL

Bellfoundry

32 & 34 Whitechapel Road, London E1 1DY.
Tel. 0171-247 2599. *Fax.* 0171-375 1979.

CORRYMEELA

BUILDING FOR PEACE IN NORTHERN IRELAND
Working to heal the hurts of 31 years of violence

CORRYMEELA is a dispersed Christian community which feels itself called to be an instrument of God's peace. It works to break down barriers and build bridges between individuals and groups: 'If Christianity has nothing to say about reconciliation then it has nothing to say' (The Revd Dr R R Davey, OBE, founder of Corrymeela).

CORRYMEELA LINK, based in Great Britain, seeks to spread the vision and support the work of the Corrymeela Community: it needs your help if this aim is to be realised.

PLEASE support us with your prayers especially on CORRYMEELA SUNDAY which is held annually on the Sunday before St Patrick's Day.

Information and donations:
Corrymeela Link (C)
PO Box 118, Reading RG1 1SL
Tel: 01734 589800

Charity No. XN 48052A

corry

What could be better than her own home?

Right now, nothing

Your own home is where you are independent. You have dignity, choice and memories.

Which makes 'right now' the perfect time to start thinking positively about the future. Not when weakening health makes decisions urgent or stressful, but now while you can discuss with your family and friends what the next secure move should be.

Later, Trinity Care

Trinity Care Christian nursing homes are a natural and secure extension to people's lives. They are beautifully run, their values are Christian and the staff are there to serve the whole person, respecting all of her – or his – needs. **What could be better than your own home? One day, Trinity Care.**

Call FREEPHONE 0800 163216 for a copy of our video and information on Trinity Care Homes.

TRINITY CARE
caring for the whole person

15 Musters Road, West Bridgford, Nottingham NG2 7PP
Tel: 0800 163216 Fax: 0115 982 1919

Care Homes in the following locations :
Cheshire, East Sussex, Hampshire, Kent, Merseyside, Nottinghamshire, Shropshire, Somerset, South & West Yorkshire, Worcestershire

Visiting The Biblical World

Tailor-made itineraries for group visits to

THE HOLY LAND

Jordan - Egypt - Syria - Turkey - Greece - Italy

RKK93©

Trafalgar House, Horton, Berks SL3 9NU
Tel: 01753-689568 / Fax: 01753-689768
E-Mail 100566,471@Compuserve.Com

Eastertide/Ascensiontide frontal at St. Mary's, Pinchbeck

* ALTAR FRONTALS AND FALLS
* VESTMENTS AND COPES
* CASSOCKS AND SURPLICES
* CASSOCK – ALBS
* CLERICAL SHIRTS
* BANNERS
* CHOIR REGALIA
* FABRICS AND TRIMMINGS

St. Martin Vestment Ltd.

LUTTON, SPALDING, LINCS. PE12 9LR

Tel: Holbeach (01406) 362386

We also offer a design service and will be pleased to send Fabric samples and colour brochure if you let us know your needs.

THE CHURCH UNION & FAITH HOUSE BOOKSHOP

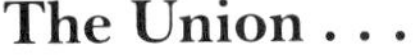

The Union . . .

Founded in 1859, at the time of the 'Oxford Movement', to promote catholic faith and order, it continues this work today by providing support and encouragement to those lay people and priests who wish to see catholic faith, order, morals and spirituality maintained and upheld, and who wish to promote catholic unity. The Union runs Faith House Bookshop (Christian books and cards, sacristy supplies), publishes books, tracts and a biannual theological journal, 'The Tufton Review', produces a quarterly magazine, the 'Church Observer', and has full-time staff who can advise on matters liturgical, legal and musical. President: The Rt Revd Eric Kemp, Bishop of Chichester. Chairman: the Rt Revd Lindsay Urwin, Bishop of Horsham.

The Bookshop

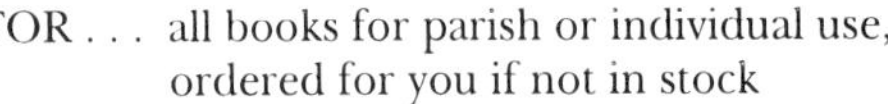

FOR . . . all books for parish or individual use, ordered for you if not in stock
FOR . . . confirmation, Advent and Lent courses and all parish stationery and registers
FOR . . . candles, wafers, incense and charcoal
FOR . . . crosses, crucifixes, ikons, rosaries etc.
FOR . . . cards and certificates for all occasions

We will always try to give helpful and informed advice if you have a question, or offer assistance if you do not know exactly what you want.

We operate a world-wide mail-order service and accept all major credit/debit cards
Open: 9.30am – 5.00pm Mon – Fri (10.00am opening on Thursday)

THE CHURCH UNION AND FAITH HOUSE BOOKSHOP
7 Tufton Street, Westminster, London SW1P 3QN

Telephone 0171-222 6952 Fax 0171-976 7180

Nearest Underground: St James's Park

CH COPEMAN HART
THE ORGAN BUILDERS

For four decades the most realistic and musical electronic substitute for the pipe organ

- **MADE IN BRITAIN**
  Every organ is completely custom built in Irthlingborough.
- **SUPERB VOICING**
  We use extremely sophisticated 'real-time' computing hardware and software, and every organ is properly voiced and finished on site.
- **CONTINUOUS SUPPORT**
  We look after your organ and have an enviable record for permanent on-going care and attention.
- **NEVER OBSOLETE**
  Every Copeman Hart organ is built to last, using only the highest quality materials. No organ need become obsolete, but it is the preferred policy of importers and agents to sell new organs rather than update existing instruments.

". . . the dedication service of the Copeman Hart organ represented the zenith of musical achievement and experience in the life of the Chapel."
Marcus Jeffrey, St Edmund's School, Canterbury

"We have now had our organ for almost ten years, and I am as excited about its performance now as I was when it was installed. I continue to be astonished by the flexibility of the Copeman Hart system which allows software updates and any desired voicing changes to be made, keeping the instrument always up-to-date."
Jack Levett, Master of the Music, St Luke's Parish Church, Chelmsford

". . . this instrument has surpassed my wildest hopes. Not only does the console look, feel and act just like a pipe organ, the sound is exciting, believable . . . many of our students and faculty have been fooled."
Mary Jean Hackett, Director of Chapel Music, and Organist
St Paul's School, Concord, New Hampshire, USA

". . . a totally conventional console in the English style. We now have a superb instrument, the voicing and tonality of which has surpassed our expectations, and which can be regularly updated and maintained at minimal cost because of the unique Copeman Hart design and software concepts. We have a truly magnificent pipe sound and a very much more versatile organ than could have been even remotely considered via the conventional pipe route, and which has already delighted our organists and singers. Visitors have been amazed to find out that this is an electronic system."
Peter Palles-Clark, All Saints Parish Church, Lindfield, West Sussex

COPEMAN HART & COMPANY LTD

FINEDON ROAD, IRTHLINGBOROUGH, NORTHAMPTONSHIRE, ENGLAND NN9 5TZ
TEL 01933 652600 INTERNATIONAL +44 1933 652600 FAX 01933 652288
EMAIL info@copemanhart.co.uk WEB SITE http://www.copemanhart.co.uk

FROM THE

HOLY LAND

TO YOUR HOME

Our service includes first hand knowledge on the famous biblical sites and the hidden places, new discoveries, documents, people, and researches of your request.

Also the growing catalogue of the

HOLY LAND CHRISTIAN RESOURCES

Take part in the **biblical competition** and win the

FIRST PRIZE OF HOLY LAND PILGRIMAGE

For more information contact:

P.O. Box 629 Netanya 42106 ISRAEL
Tel: 972 - 9 - 86 16 904
Fax: 972 - 9 - 83 57 946
E Mail:authentic@inter.net.il

Visit our web site:
http://www.authentic.co.il

SN INDUS

SILVERWARE

Third generation silversmiths producing individually designed, hand-made contemporary silverware for clients that include Ampleforth Abbey & Durham Cathedral. Chalice commissions a specialty. Figurative work by Dunstan Pruden.

Turner Dumbrell Workshops,
North End, Ditchling,
East Sussex BN6 8TD.
Telephone: 01273 846338
Fax: 01273 846684 Tuesday to Saturday 10am to 6pm
Registered with the Council for the care of Churches

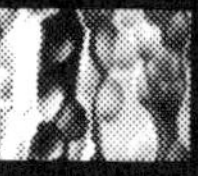

PRUDEN & SMITH
silversmiths

Secondhand Theological books

BIBLICAL, LITURGICAL, HISTORICAL, PASTORAL

Largest stock in England
Catalogues issued
Collection arranged
Open daily 10-5
Ample parking
Secular books also bought

Well worth a visit

Pendleburys Bookshop

Tel/Fax: 0181 809 4922

Church House, Portland Avenue,
Stamford Hill, London N16 6HJ

CANTERBURY
PRESS
Norwich

POSITIVELY SERVING THE CHURCH

A superb range of music, liturgy, resources for the 3-year Lectionary and books for the spiritual life.

Please send for our complete catalogue and enquire about grants to churches for hymn and service books.

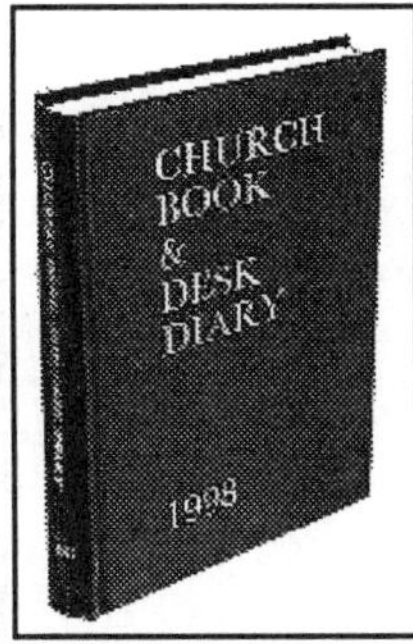

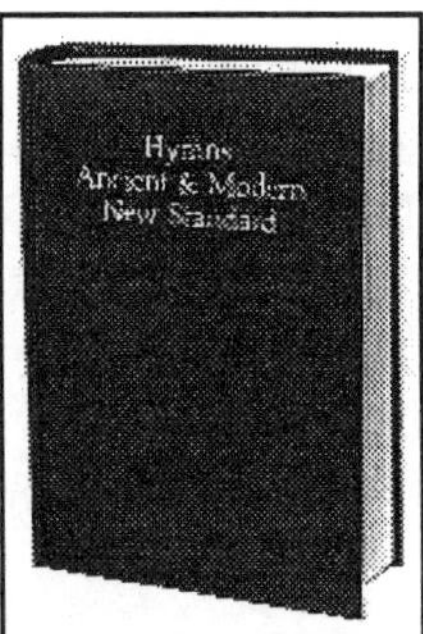

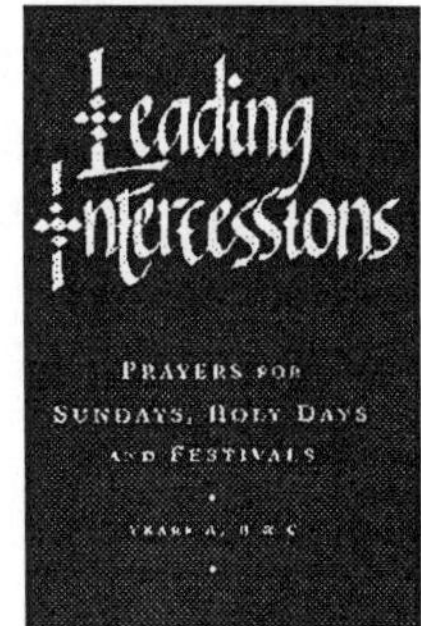

Canterbury Press Norwich

St Mary's Works, St Mary's Plain, Norwich, Norfolk NR3 3BH.
Tel. 01603 612914. *Fax.* 01603 624483.
The publishing imprint of Hymns Ancient & Modern Ltd, a Registered Charity.

BY APPOINTMENT TO H.M. THE QUEEN
ECCLESIASTICAL FURNISHERS

Messrs. WATTS & Co. Ltd.

ECCLESIASTICAL FURNISHERS
&
CLERICAL OUTFITTERS

ESTABLISHED FOR OVER 100 YEARS AND
FAMOUS FOR FINE VESTMENTS AND
QUALITY FURNISHINGS

7 TUFTON STREET, LONDON, SW1P 3QE
TELEPHONE: 0171 222-7169/1978
FACSIMILE: 0171 233-1130

"..I was a stranger and you welcomed me.." Matthew 25.v35

THE MISSIONS TO SEAMEN GIVES A WELCOME TO SEAFARERS AROUND THE WORLD

Being a seafarer means being a stranger in foreign ports.The Missions to Seamen, which carries out the Anglican Church's ministry to seafarers, gives a welcome to people of all races and creeds. We share our faith by offering friendship, comfort in times of distress, aid in emergencies, spiritual support, counselling to those with problems and help in cases of injustice.

Please help us to continue the Church's ministry to seafarers.

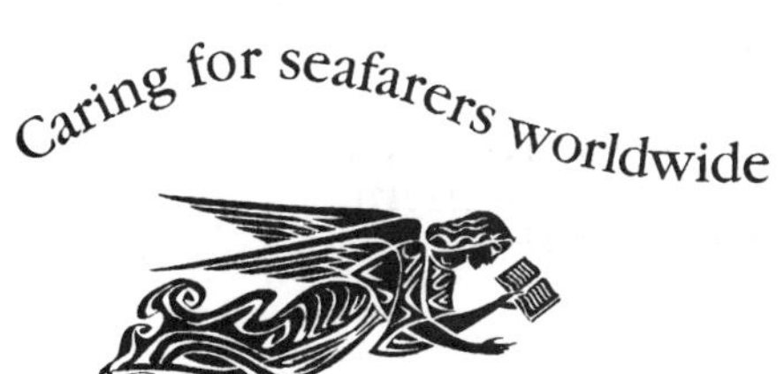

THE MISSIONS TO SEAMEN

ST. MICHAEL PATERNOSTER ROYAL
COLLEGE HILL, LONDON EC4R 2RL
TELEPHONE: 0171 248 5202

Charity No.212432

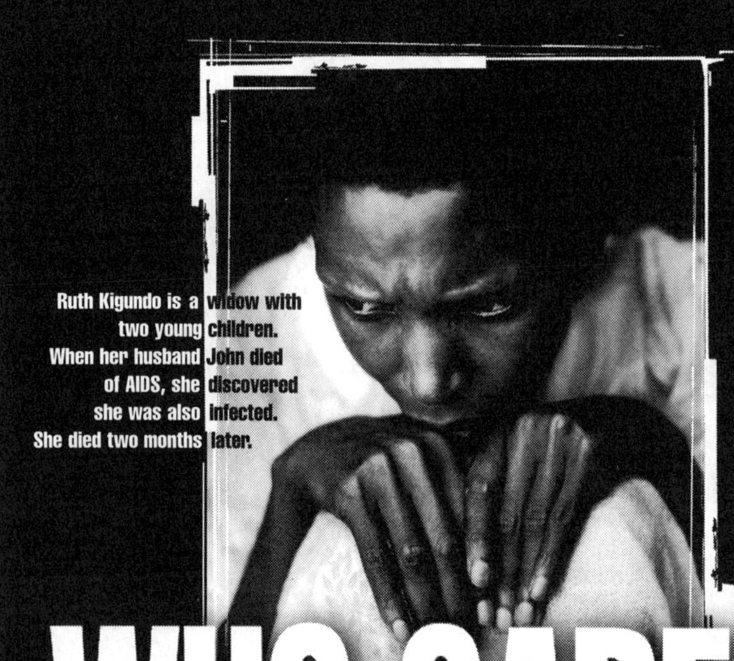

WHO CARES?

If you do, help us to.

Thousands of churches, voluntary reps and individuals in the UK help us care - bringing good news to the poor through a global network of evangelical partners.

Why not join us today in caring for the poor? Together we can make a difference.

100 Church Road, Teddington, Middlesex TW11 8QE **Tel : 0181 977 9144**
Challenge House, 29 Canal Street, Glasgow G4 0AD **Tel : 0141 332 3621**
23 University Street, Belfast BT7 1FY **Tel : 01232 324940**

Registered Charity No 265464

Tear Fund is a Christian relief and development charity which enables evangelical partners in over 100 countries to bring help and spiritual hope to people in need.

MARLBOROUGH COLLEGE

Assistance with Fees for Children of Clergy

Marlborough College was founded in 1843 and is now **fully co-educational.** There is an entry each year at age 13 of some 150 boys and girls, and at age 16 of 35 girls direct to the Sixth Form. There are also Sixth Form places for boys. **The basic fee** for children of Clergy is 85% of the full fee. In addition, the **Children of Clergy Fund** exists to provide further assistance as financially appropriate. Most Clergy children are admitted for substantially less than the 85% basic fee, and where family circumstances make a boarding school especially important the fee can sometimes be very small indeed. Marlborough also offers Open Scholarships and Exhibitions (academic, art and music), for which Clergy children are eligible to compete.

For a Prospectus, and further details, please contact The Senior Admissions Tutor
Marlborough College, Marlborough, Wilts, SN8 1PA
Tel: 01672 892300 Fax: 01672 892307

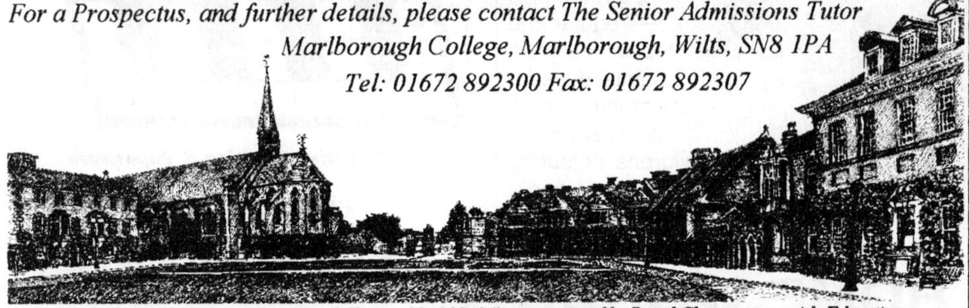

Marlborough College is a Registered Charity (No 309486) incorporated by Royal Charter to provide Education

ST LAWRENCE COLLEGE IN THANET

Ramsgate, Kent CT11 7AE

Junior School
IAPS
3 - 13

Boys and Girls
Boarding and Day

Senior School
HMC
11 - 19

BURSARIES OF 30% FOR CHILDREN OF CLERGY AND MISSIONARIES

- Excellent Academic Standards
- A Church of England Foundation 1879
- On the Threshold of Mainland Europe

Visitor: The Rev. & Right Hon. The Lord Coggan, PC. DD.

For a Prospectus and any further information, please contact:

Tel: (01843) 867125 Fax: (01843 851123

St. Lawrence College exists to provide education for children.
Charity number 307 921

ADDED VALUE

FOR YOUR PARISH MAGAZINE

Why not use a parish magazine insert to improve the content of your own publication? We have two to choose from.

THE SIGN

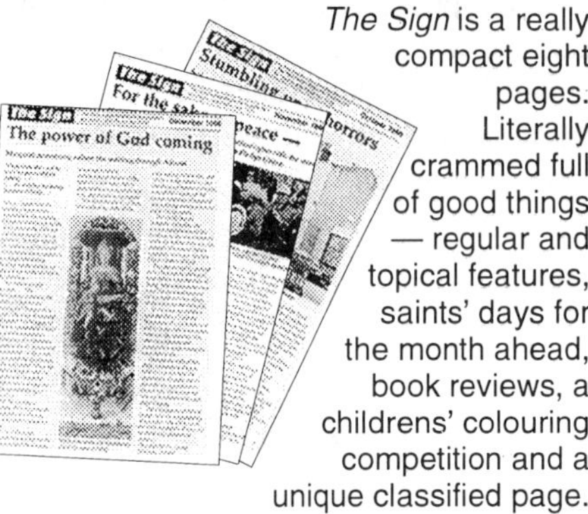

The Sign is a really compact eight pages. Literally crammed full of good things — regular and topical features, saints' days for the month ahead, book reviews, a childrens' colouring competition and a unique classified page.

OR

HOME WORDS

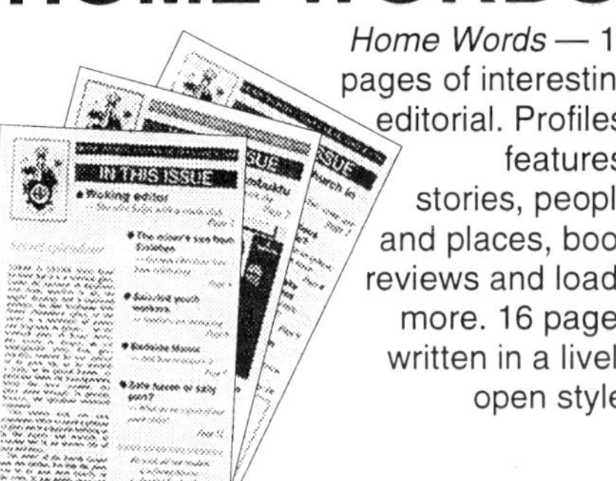

Home Words — 16 pages of interesting editorial. Profiles, features, stories, people and places, book reviews and loads more. 16 pages written in a lively open style.

Special sample packs are available for either, or both, publications.

Simply write or call:

The Subscription Office, 16 Blyburgate, Beccles, Suffolk NR34 9TB
Tel: 01502-711231 or 711171

For advice on advertisements — booking and copy — contact:

Stephen Dutton, c/o *Church Times*, 33 Upper Street, London N1 0PN
Tel: 0171-359 4570 Fax: 0171-226 3051

The Sign and *Home Words* are published by
CHANSITOR PUBLICATIONS LTD
(A wholly owned subsidiary of Hymns Ancient & Modern Limited, a Registered Charity)

PARISH2

SHORT SEMINARS for BUSY LEADERS

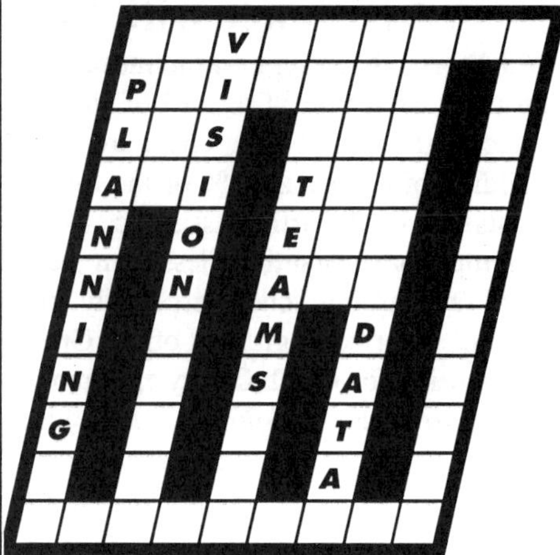

Priorities Planning & Paperwork
1998 3-4 April, 6-7 October
1999 8-9 June

Vision Building & Strategic Planning
1998 24-25 February
1999 24-25 February

Know Yourself Know Your Team
1998 28-29 April, 29-30 September
1999 27-28 April, 26-27 November

Info Outflow - Interpretation of Data
To be arranged

For further information phone Pam Poynter 0181 294 1989 Quote Crockford's

CHURCH PULPIT YEAR BOOK

Published *every* October

A complete set of expository sermon outlines for all Sundays of the year plus Saints' Days and special occasions.

Two outlines are given for each Sunday. Usually based on the ASB readings for the day - but in many cases they suit also, or can be adapted to the BCP readings. Can be taken as they stand, or adapted to suit your congregation's particular needs.

Invaluable aid to the hard-pressed parish priest, deacon or reader.

CHANSITOR PUBLICATIONS
Subscriptions Office;
16 Blyburgate, Beccles
Suffolk, NR34 9TB
Tel. (01502) 711231

EMBERHEAT

HEATING ENGINEERS
of Distinction

Sympathetic, Affordable, Efficient Church heating systems designed by experts.

FAST HEAT UP FROM COLD

EXCELLENT HEAT DISTRIBUTION

LOW CAPITAL & RUNNING COSTS

QUIET IN OPERATION

DISCREET AND SYMPATHETIC TO CHURCH'S APPEARANCE

St. Anne's Limehouse by Nicholas Hawksmoor 1714
Heating system by EMBERHEAT 1991

Site survey and advice is freely given
THE HEATING CENTRE 324 BATTERSEA PARK ROAD
LONDON SW11 3BY TEL: 0171 223 5944 FAX: 0171 223 7118

The Founding Principles

Bell founding has altered little through the centuries and the principles of quality and craftsmanship are preserved at Taylors, the world's largest and most successful bellfoundry.

For single bells, peals, chimes, carillons and handbells, new bells or the restoration of existing bells, ring the master craftsmen.

(01509) 212241

Fax (01509) 263305

Bellfounding since 1784

The Bellfoundry, Freehold Street,
Loughborough, Leics. LE11 1AR

AUTOSAVE

The best way to buy your next car

Unique suppliers to clergy, churches and charities

Autosave has developed a special scheme to research the motor car market and negotiate special prices for our customers. By constant reference to the fluctuations in price we are able to secure the best deals on a day to day basis.

- **Exceptional discounts on all makes and models**
- **Extended warranty plans**
- **Competitive insurance cover**
- **Part exchange without affecting your discount**
- **Special finance rates**
- **Substantial used car stocks**

USED CAR LOCATION SCHEME

Autosave has developed a unique search and locate scheme for clients wishing to buy a used car. **FREE OF CHARGE** we will scan the used car market for a vehicle to **YOUR** specification. We have access to huge stocks of 1982-1994 registered vehicles including very high quality ex-demonstration cars.

BUT IT'S MORE THAN JUST SELLING YOU A USED CAR!

★ AA/R.A.C. Inspection standard on all vehicles

★ All cars carry an RAC 3 months parts and labour warranty - extendible up to 36 months **AND** any claims necessary can be made via a local garage

★ Your old vehicle is welcomed as a part-exchange payment

★ Delivery of vehicles is by Autosave personnel - nationwide

★ Autosave are licensed credit brokers offering very competitive finance rates

DO YOU HAVE DIFFICULTY SELLING YOUR OLD CAR?

Autosave will give you a telephone valuation and if it is acceptable we will collect your car, FREE OF CHARGE from anywhere in the U.K.

NEW and USED VEHICLES

AUTOSAVE (UK) LIMITED
IVY HOUSE
THE DALE
SHEFFIELD S8 0PG
Telephone: (0114) 255 4040
Facsimile: (0114) 255 4949

AUTOSAVE

OF SHEFFIELD Dedicated to the church market

Please send me a FREE copy of the Motor Information Pack

Name ....

Address ....

....

..............................Tel: ....

For the nation-wide work of the Church of England

The Central Church Fund is unique. It is the *only* fund available for the general purposes of the Church of England as a whole.

It helps parishes and dioceses with imaginative and innovative projects of all kinds – and especially those that meet the needs of local communities.

It provides for training for ministry in the Church (donations and bequests can be directed specifically for this purpose).

It makes money available for those unexpected and urgent needs which cannot be budgeted for.

As a general purpose Fund, its flexibility allows it to provide, without delay, for a host of needs that no other fund is geared to cope with, and its value in this way to the Church of England is incalculable.

There are inevitably many calls upon it and funds are always urgently needed. Please help with your donation, covenanted subscription or bequest – or find out more from the Secretary.

Charity No. 248711

The Central Church Fund

The Central Board of Finance of the Church of England, Church House, Great Smith Street, Westminster, London SW1P 3NZ. Tel: 0171-222 9011.

An international and ecumenical movement. Its main aim is to develop multi cultural understanding and friendship locally, nationally and internationally,

conferences, work-camps, international exchanges local community work.

Christians Aware recognises the importance of openness, adaptability and faith in the future.

FOR PEOPLE WHO WANT TO SHARE WAYS AND WISDOMS

CHARITY NO. 328322
10 SPRINGFIELD ROAD, LEICESTER, LE2 3BD
TEL. 0116 270 8831 FAX. 0116 2703288

PASTORAL REORGANIZATON ADVISORY SERVICE

* A confidential independent professional service covering all aspects of Pastoral Reorganisation
* Supportive advice available to interested parties to Pastoral and Redundancy Schemes at all stages of evolution
* Church redundancy perspectives (including research on prospective Judicial Appeals under 1983 Pastoral Measure) an acknowledged speciality
* Over 20 years' extensive nationwide experience of Anglican and Nonconformist reorganization cases
* Research-trained in Ecclesiastical Law & Procedure

Written enquiries to:

DAVID E. GILLMAN, B.Sc, B. Phil., 18 West Avenue, Clarendon Park, Leicester LE2 1TR

The Churches' Child Protection Advisory Service

Offers Churches, Children's and Counselling Organisations:

- Child protection training through half-day and evening seminars (available at 50 centres throughout the British Isles over a year)
- Help in developing child protection policies
- Supporting leaders in responding to specific cases of abuse, etc

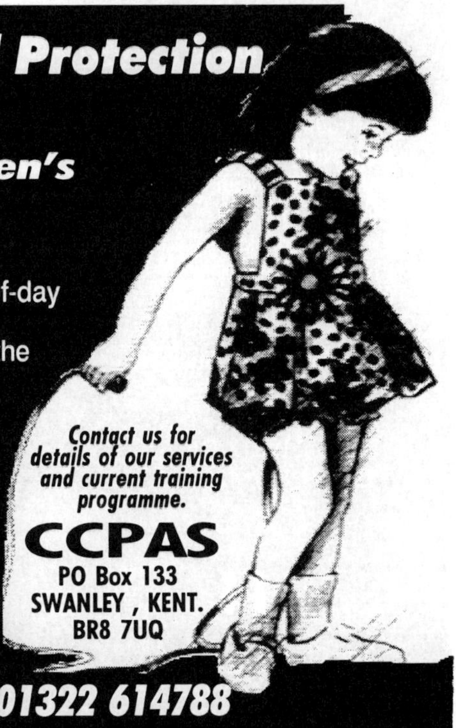

Contact us for details of our services and current training programme.

CCPAS
PO Box 133
SWANLEY , KENT.
BR8 7UQ

CCPAS

Tel: 01322 667207 Fax: 01322 614788

A project of PCCA Christian Child Care. Charity No: 1004490

Just for a change
WE'RE SUPPORTING
YOU

We are proud of our links with the Church and are grateful for your faithful support. It is only because of your prayers and fundraising that we can continue our work with some of Britain's most vulnerable children and young people.

Your dedication means that we can carry on our pioneering work - reaching out to child runaways, offering support to young families in crisis and opening new horizons for children with disabilities.

Please let us support you in spreading the news about our work and with your prayers. For your free information and resource pack, including the Cycle of Prayer, please contact:

The Children's Society,
Edward Rudolf House,
Margery Street,
London. WC1X OJL
☎0171 837 4299

The Children's Society
MAKING LIVES WORTH LIVING

Charity Registration No. 221124

AP9037

THE ENGLISH

CLERGY ASSOCIATION

Patron: The Worshipful Chancellor June Rodgers
Chancellor of the Diocese of Gloucester.
Parliamentary Vice-President: Sir Patrick Cormack, , F.S.A., M.P.

Vice-Presidents: Sir William Dugdale, Bt., C.B.E., M.C., J.P., D.L.;
The Rt. Hon. Sir Robin Dunn, M.C., P.C.;
The Very Revd. Derek Hole, Provost of Leicester;
The Very Revd. Dr. Peter Moore, O.B.E., M.A., D.Phil., F.S.A.;
The Most Hon. The Marquess of Salisbury;
Dr. D. M. Tyrrell, B.D., M.A., Ph.D., A.C.I.S., A.C.A.;
The Venerable Tom Walker, M.A.;
The Rt. Hon. The Lady Willoughby de Eresby.

THE ASSOCIATION supports the integrity of traditional parish and cathedral ministry alongside modern developments, particularly asserting in broad terms the value of the ***patronage system and the parson's freehold*** within the abiding worth of the Ministry of the Church of England as by Law Established.

PARSON & PARISH, free to Members of the Association, is presently published twice a year: Membership is £10 p.a., £5 to the retired and to ordinands.

HOLIDAY GRANTS of a discretionary kind are made to Church of England clergy upon written application by the form in use to the Hon. Almoner.

LEGACIES & DONATIONS are especially welcome at a time of low interest-rates. P.C.C.s can become Corporate Members.

Chairman: The Revd. J. W. Masding, M.A., LL.M.
E.C.A. Office: The Old School, Norton Hawkfield
Pensford, Bristol BS18 4HB
Telephone: (+44) Chew Magna (01275) 83 0017

Deputy Chairman: Colonel John Hall; Vice-Chairman: The Revd. A. E. Harvey, M.Sc.
Treasurer: J. M. Hanks, Esq., LL.M., A.C.A.
Honorary Almoner: The Revd. J. D. Thompstone, M.A.
Editor of *Parson & Parish*: The Revd. M. G. Smith, M.A., B.D. (Oxon.)
Clerk to the Trustees & Hon. Secretary to the Council: J. H. Wearing, Esq., LL.B.

Benefit Fund Registered Charity No.: 258559.
Bankers: Coutts & Co., St. Martin's Office, Strand, London; Bank of Scotland, Birmingham.

BY APPOINTMENT
TO HER MAJESTY
QUEEN ELIZABETH II
CHANDLERS
BY APPOINTMENT
TO H.M. QUEEN ELIZABETH
THE QUEEN MOTHER
CANDLEMAKERS
Farris
CANDLEMAKERS

Est. 1845

QUALITY CHURCH CANDLES AND REQUISITES

Since 1845 Charles Farris has offered a comprehensive range of quality products for the church

CANDLES • PALMS
ADVENT PRODUCTS
HANDMADE CANDLES
BAPTISM CANDLES
WINE • INCENSE
ALTAR BREADS
METAL RESTORATION

We also take pride in providing high standards of service at all times. For further information please contact us on:

Tel: 0171 924 7544
Fax: 0171 738 0197
(24 hour Answer service)

Charles Farris Limited
Belmont Works, 110 York Road
Battersea, London SW11 3RU

DEAN CLOSE SCHOOL and DEAN CLOSE JUNIOR SCHOOL

Cheltenham

(Church of England Foundation)

Dean Close School offers independent, co-educational, boarding and day education from 2½-7 in the Pre-Preparatory School, 7-13 in the Junior School and 13-18 in the Senior School.

The School prides itself on a friendly, family atmosphere where everyone is known and all have a place. Old fashioned standards of work, discipline and personal involvement are maintained without a great deal of pressure, by means of the co-operative spirit that prevails. Much of the above is engendered by the Christian heart of the School. Worship is central to the corporate life and there are many voluntary Christian activities.

Generous academic and music scholarships are available at 11, 13 and Sixth Form. There is an automatic Clergy Bursary and Scholarships dedicated to the children of the Clergy.

Pupils are prepared for GCSE and A-levels and for Oxbridge and other universities' Entrance and Scholarship examinations. Our excellent facilities provide for many forms of physical and cultural recreation. Music and drama play and important part in the life of the School.

Further details may be obtained from:

The Registrar, Dean Close School
Cheltenham, Glos. GL51 6HE
Tel: 01242 522640 or Fax: 01242 258003
e-mail: dcscomp@rmplc.co.uk

The College of

ST. BARNABAS

for RETIRED CLERGY
(Regd. Charity No. 205220)
Library, Common Room, Refectory, Chapel, nursing for those who fall ill.

PLEASE HELP US MEET EVER RISING COSTS by legacies, covenants, donations . . . .

Particulars: The Warden
College of St. Barnabas,
Lingfield, Surrey RH7 6NJ
Tel: 01342-870366

CHURCH SOCIETY

FOR BIBLE, CHURCH AND NATION

The Church of England is

• Protestant • Reformed • Bible based

Its beliefs are set out in the Thirty Nine Articles of Religion.

Its official liturgy is the Book of Common Prayer.

More and more, the Church of England is forsaking its Protestant heritage in favour of a broad theology and liturgy which are meant to appeal to everybody but in reality satisfy no-one and disappoint many.

Church Society works to defend our Church's established values and standards. It campaigns for the orthodox faith of the Church of England which believes that only the Word of God has the power to save. It contends for the true Gospel of the Lord Jesus Christ.

Join us if you share our concern for the future of the Church of England.

For more information contact the Director, Dean Wace House, 16 Rosslyn Road, Watford, Herts, WD1 7EY.
Tel: 01923-235111. Fax: 01923-800362.
e-mail: 106522.1537@compuserve.com

Registered Charity No 249594

A Classical Prayer Book in Contemporary English

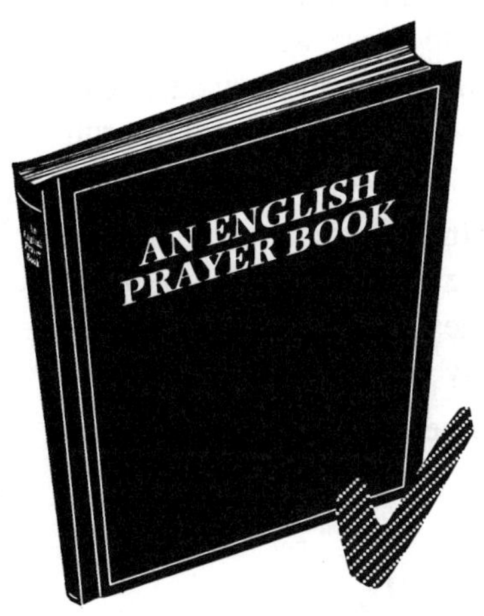

- ✓ conforms to the doctrine of the 39 Articles and the Book of Common Prayer of 1662.
- ✓ contains all the normal services associated with the Book of Common Prayer and the 39 Articles in original and modern language.
- ✓ Is a compact, slender volume, in a durable binding, it measures less than 5 x 7 inches and is about half an inch thick. It is clearly printed and is comfortable to hold.
- ✓ is available to all at the very economical price of £6.99. However, churches initially ordering more than 30 copies will receive a 25% discount.

An English Prayer Book is published jointly by The Church Society and Oxford University Press. For further information contact:

Church Society, Dean Wace House, 16 Rosslyn Road, Watford, Herts WD1 7EY
Telephone: 01923 235111 Fax: 01923 800362

OUR WORK IS CARING . . .

The Church of England Pensions Board offers support to retired clergy and their spouses, the widows or widowers of clergy, and church workers retired from full time ministry.

Our greatest concern is for the welfare of our older pensioners, who because of age or infirmity need sheltered accommodation and some special care. The Pensions Board runs nine residential and nursing homes offering security and peace of mind to those who have given their lives towards helping others in the name of Christ. Assistance can also be given towards the fees payable for accommodation in homes run by other organisations.

The Board receives no help from central Church funds towards the cost of its residential and nursing care, and must rely on support from donations, deeds of covenant, and legacies in order to continue this much needed work. Please help us in any way you can.

For further information about ways to help, a form of words for inclusion in a Will, or more details about our work, please write to:

The Secretary, Freepost CD,
The Church of England Pensions Board
7 LITTLE COLLEGE STREET
WESTMINSTER, LONDON SW1P 3SF

Reg. Charity No. 236627

No change at St Luke's

– IT'S STILL FREE!

IN OVER 100 YEARS St Luke's has seen many changes, not least the recent rebuilding and modernisation which makes it now one of the most up-to-date acute hospitals in the country.

But one thing has NOT changed. The unsurpassed standards of care for which the hospital has always been famous are still available to the clergy ***with no charges of any kind*** – either to them or, save in cases where referral to another hospital is necessary, their local GP's practice.

Free treatment

Those eligible for free treatment (including outpatient psychiatric support which is available countrywide) are: Church of England ordained ministers, their spouses and dependent children (up to and including university education); Ordinands accepted by a bishop for ordination training, and their spouses; Monks and Nuns of the Anglican Communion; Church Army Officers; Overseas Missionaries, and Priests from Anglican churches abroad.

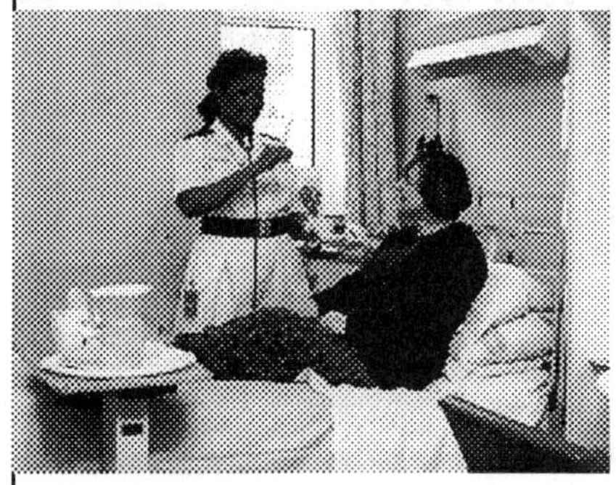

If you are eligible and need a consultation with a Consultant Surgeon or Physician, then nothing more is needed than a letter of referral from your GP. ***The consultation, and any subsequent treatment at St Luke's, are entirely free.***

Outreach

In addition, St Luke's helps to care for the laity through the St Luke's Healthcare Scheme, which provides lay church members with treatment at greatly reduced fees, as well as through Couples Counselling services, and Courses on Stress Management.

Find out more by writing to the General Secretary, or ring us on 0171–388 4954.

And if you, or your parish, would like to join our family of supporters by sponsoring a patient for an hour (£15) or a day (£350), your gift will be most welcome!

St Luke's

HOSPITAL FOR THE CLERGY

Caring for those who care for others

14 Fitzroy Square, London W1P 6AH.

Tel. 0171–388 4954. *Fax.* 0171–383 4812. *Reg. Charity* 209236

"Come and See the Place"!

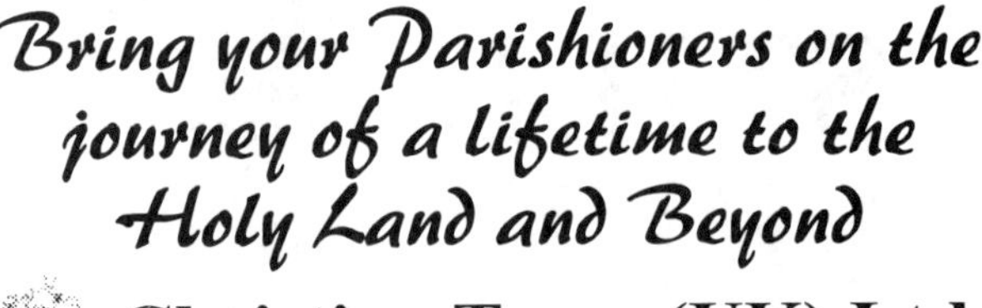
Bring your Parishioners on the journey of a lifetime to the Holy Land and Beyond

MOUNT OF THE BEATITUDES GALILEE

Christian Tours (UK) Ltd.

for the Advice, Care and Value for your Group Pilgrimage

TAILOR MADE PILGRIMAGE TOURS for GROUPS to the **HOLY LAND** FROM ONLY £398

ATOL
4030

Group Leaders: call us FREE on 0800 137928 for details or write to us at:

Lombard House, 12-17 Upper Bridge Street, Canterbury, Kent CT1 2NF

Highway Journeys can take you off the beaten track . . . interested?

Discover and experience from a new perspective, the lands, sights and sounds of different cultures. Meet the local people, the 'Living Stones', make new friends and and return home with a fresh insight, physically and spiritually refreshed.

Highway Journeys to the Holy Land and many other countries

For brochures please tel 01256 895966

Highway Journeys, 3 Winchester Street
Whitchurch, HampshireRG28 7AH

HIGHWAY
HIGHWAY
Journeys
ATOL
89
Encouraging physical, emotional & spiritual refreshment

The Church Lads' and Church Girls' Brigade

Registered Charity No. 276821

A parish based Anglican voluntary organisation for boys and girls between the ages of 5 and 21. With fun and friendship at its heart it offers an extensive range of youthful activities appropriate to age.

Mission: To advance the development of members as confident Christians in a modern society.

For further details contact:

The Church Lads' and Church Girls' Brigade
2 Barnsley Road, Wath-upon-Dearne, Rotherham S63 6PY
Telephone: Rotherham (01709) 876535 Fax: (01709) 878089

Empathy

The ability to mentally relate with, and comprehend, another's situation

There is much to be gained from using the services of an advertising agency that understands the problems of charities with limited budgets.

We have been specialising in this field for most of our 118 years.

So we already know most of the problems — and some of the answers.

Now part of the *Hymns Ancient and Modern* group of companies, our client list includes a significant number of religious charities — including 9 within the Anglican communion.

If your organisation needs a sypathetic and informed approach to advertising by people who really know and understand your market, then write or call us straight away.

John Hart Publicity Ltd

Bridge House, 181 Queen Victoria St, London EC4V 4DD
Tel. 0171-248 4759 Fax: 0171-329 0575

HART2

MULTIBETON LTD

UNDERFLOOR HEATING SYSTEMS
EMBEDDED RADIANT HEATING SYSTEMS

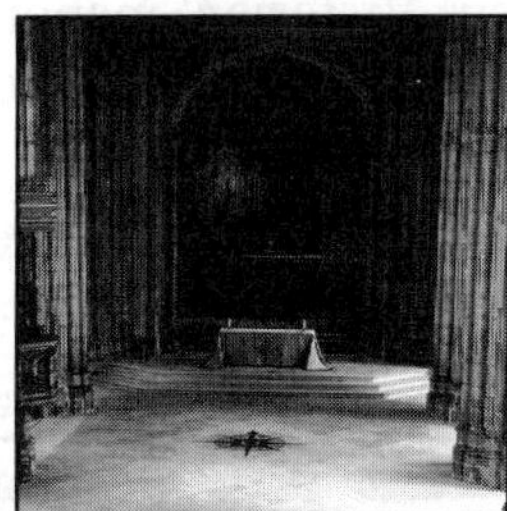

The ideal heating system for Churches whereby the occupied zone is heated and not the total volume. Suitable for all churches, both existing and new build.

Substantial savings on running costs over comparable radiator and warm air systems.

A complete design and installation service is offered, through-out the U.K. and each system is covered by the Multibeton 30 year warranty.

MULTIBETON LTD

15 Oban Court, Hurricane Way, Wickford Business Park, Wickford, Essex SS11 8YB
Tel No: 01268 561688 Fax No: 01268 561690

Famous for faith & friendliness, Liverpool Hope is a University College with over 150 years of history on Merseyside. With a shared Anglican and Catholic foundation, it welcomes those of all faiths and beliefs.

The history of Liverpool Hope goes right back to 1844 when the Church of England founded a women's teacher training college in Warrington, giving women an equal opportunity to study for a profession. The College now continues that commitment of opening access to education and maintains its strong reputation for teacher training. A wide range of degree courses is now studied by over 4000 undergraduate and postgraduate students, in this the only ecumenical University College in Britain.

The College is located in Hope Park, a pleasant green, thirty-acre landscaped campus, set beneath the blue suburban skies four miles south of Liverpool city centre. Hope Park is the perfect setting for conferences or other activities. Its facilities can be used for a variety of events: seminars, conferences, business meetings, exhibitions, even weddings. For example, The Sheppard-Worlock Library, named after our Chairs of Governing Council in recent years, is a truly distinctive venue.

'Hope on the Waterfront' is an excellent alternative. Located in the superb setting of Liverpool's Albert Dock, it is one of the most prestigious and desirable conference locations in the North West. With its videowall, excellent multimedia and AVA facilities, Hope on the Waterfront is ideal for all your conferencing needs. Plas Caerdeon, our Victorian manor house in Snowdonia, is ideal for outdoor pursuits and can be booked by groups for residential visits and retreats.

For further information about Liverpool Hope please contact:

Hope Park, Liverpool L16 9JD
Tel: 0151 291 3000 Fax: 0151 291 3100

Educating the whole person in mind, body and spirit.

SHELTERED HOUSING AT

BROMLEY & SHEPPARD'S COLLEGES

Registered Charity No.210337

The Colleges exist to provide sheltered housing for Clerks in Holy Orders and certain relatives in accordance with the Will of John Warner, Bishop of Rochester 1638–1666, subsequent benefactions and the provisions of Charity Commission Schemes.

Bromley College was founded in 1666 and Sheppard's College in 1840. The original foundations provided housing for widows of Church of England Clergy and unmarried daughters of former residents of Bromley College. The Colleges now provide modernised, unfurnished self-contained flats, mainly two bedrooms, all centrally heated with an emergency call system, and are available to retired clergy (married or single), widows or widowers, divorced or separated spouses of the Church of England, the Church in Wales, the Scottish Episcopal Church or the Church of Ireland.

Unmarried daughters or stepdaughters of a deceased former resident of Bromley College may also apply.

The Colleges occupy a delightful 3 acre site in Bromley, Kent, close to the town centre with excellent rail access to London and the South East.

Enquiries to the Chaplain & Clerk to the Trustees, Chaplain's House Bromley College, London Road, Bromley, Kent BR1 1PE
Tel: 0181 460 4712

DONATIONS AND BEQUESTS ALWAYS WELCOME

CHURCH SOCIETY TRUST

FOR BIBLE, CHURCH AND NATION

The Church of England is

- **Protestant**
- **Reformed**
- **Bible based**

Its beliefs are set out in the Thirty Nine Articles of Religion.
Its official liturgy is the Book of Common Prayer.

Church Society works to defend our Church's established values and standards. It campaigns for the orthodox faith of the Church of England which believes that only the Word of God has the power to save.

Church Society is the patron of around 120 parishes either on our own or jointly. As well as finding the right man for the right place, we aim to give support and help in the form of prayer, letters, grants for training, legal advice, etc.

If you would like to be considered for one of our livings, please contact:

THE SECRETARY, CHURCH SOCIETY TRUST,
Dean Wace House, 16 Rosslyn Road, Watford, Herts, WD1 7EY.
Tel: 01923-235111. Fax: 01923-800362.

S.T. CHURCHWARE

WE OFFER A COMPREHENSIVE SERVICE TO THE CHURCH

Church Plate, Carved wood, Candles, Vestments and Linens, Hassocks, Kneelers and Pew Cushions, Wine

We give a personal service and we will gladly call at your request, without obligation or charge, to discuss your needs

S.T. CHURCHWARE
176 Short Heath Road, Erdington,
Birmingham B23 6JX
Telephone: 0121 350 6177/693 6277
Fax: 0121 350 6177

SERMONS

FOR THE CHRISTIAN YEAR

(NEW 3 YEAR LECTIONARY)

Also Sermons for special Services:

Harvest, Holy Week,
Family/Parade,
Christmas, Weddings, Funerals.

Other sermons also available.

For full details please send a self addressed, stamped envelope to:

F W SERMONS
Dept CR, PO Box 28
Barnstaple, Devon EX31 2PU

CHURCHMAN

A Quarterly Journal of Anglican Theology

GOOD WRITERS • John Richardson, Jim Packer, Wallace Benn, Iain Murray, Roger Beckwith, Alec Motyer, Alistair Campbell

RELEVANT ARTICLES ON ALL ASPECTS OF CHURCH LIFE:
The Trial of Bishop Righter in the USA
The Place of the Christian at Work
Is Worship Biblical? - The Discernment of Signs
Revising the Revision (the place of liturgy in worship)
The Turnbull Report - The Toronto Blessing

THOUGHT PROVOKING EDITORIALS • EXTENSIVE REVIEWS

"A must if you want to know where modern evangelical thinking is going." Gerald Bray, Editor

Contact Church Society, Dean Wace House, 16 Rosslyn Road, Watford, Herts, WD1 7EY (01923-235111) for a free sample copy.

The world is our parish.
But your parish is our world

The CHURCH OF ENGLAND Newspaper

For almost two centuries *The Church of England Newspaper* has been keeping people informed about their faith.
Now you need never feel out of touch with the news.
For just 45p a week you can keep up to date with news in the church and further afield.
For a free sample copy of *The Church of England Newspaper* write to Judith Watsham,
The Church of England Newspaper,
10 Little College Street,
London SW1P 3SH
Or call her on: 0171 878 1510

Britain's oldest church newspaper

UPDATE YOUR CROCKFORD EVERY WEEK

Our two-page Gazette section each week lists all the clergy moves

The *Church Times* is the leading newspaper reporting on the Church of England and Anglican issues in the world at large

If you would like to see a FREE copy of the *Church Times* simply complete the coupon.

To The Subscriptions Manager, *Church Times*,
16 Blyburgate, Beccles, Suffolk NR34 9TB

Please send me a free sample copy of the *Church Times*

Name ....

Address ....

....

.... Poscode ....

Ours, Lord, is the smallest, the weakness, the dullness, the failure and the mediocrity.

Do you long for deeper worship, stronger community, realistic giving — a more faithful response in your Church?

You need a

***FULL* MEASURE PROJECT**

by the Anglican Stewardship Association

For details contact:

General Secretary

Brian Hargreaves
'Weatherbury'
Stoner Hill Road
Steep, Petersfield
GU32 1AG

Tel: 01730 261196

WANT TO SELL TO THE HUGE RELIGIOUS MARKET IN AMERICA?

The Anglicanite Directory is poised to help you advertise your goods and services to the faithful in America's annual billion dollar retail market to Churches, clergy, and laity.

For information plus advertisement rates, phone or fax

The Anglicanite Directory on **01.228.466.2767** or write:

Father Monty, Anglican Church House, 312 Union Street
Bay Saint Louis, MS 39520-4447, USA

Decade Ministries

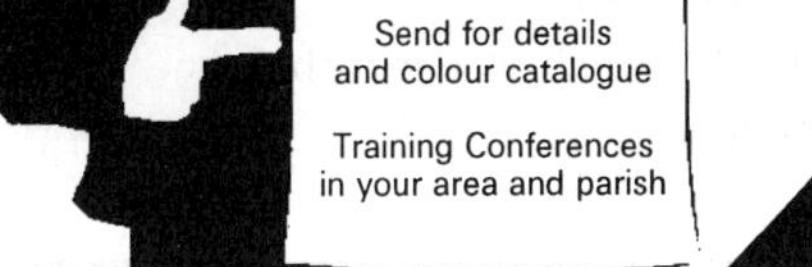

For clergy, readers, teachers, leaders and parish administrators
Send for details and colour catalogue
Training Conferences in your area and parish

- Conferences
- Clipart packs
- All-age visuals
- Wallplanners
- Posters

Decade Ministries

Rev Roy Weaver

Grove House : Limetrees
CHILTON ; Oxon
OX11 OHY : 01235 833030

Church House Bookshop is one of the largest religious booksellers in the UK.
Its stock has been carefully chosen to meet the needs of ordained and lay members of the Anglican church including:

- the complete range of books, stationery and other items produced by Church House Publishing
- an extremely wide selection of other books, newspapers, magazines, software, stationery items, posters and gifts produced by other publishers

Any religious book in print can be supplied by mail order

Based at the Church of England's administrative headquarters in London, Church House Bookshop is fully equipped to provide you with a fast, efficient mail order service – whatever your requirements, and wherever you live.

Church House Bookshop
31 Great Smith Street
London SW1P 3BN
Tel: 0171-340 0276/0277
Fax: 0171-340 0278/0281
Email: mclifford@chb.u-net.com
Internet: http://www.herald.co.uk/clients/C/Church_House/chb.html
Credit cards accepted

INTRODUCTION

This, the ninety-fifth edition of *Crockford's Clerical Directory*, provides details as at 31 July 1997 of more than 25,000 clergy and deaconesses in the Church of England (including the Diocese of Gibraltar in Europe), the Church in Wales, the Scottish Episcopal Church and the Church of Ireland.

Some of the more observant users of *Crockford* may have noticed a break in chronology between the new *1998/99* edition and its predecessor, which was known as the *1995/96* edition. Our thinking behind the change was that, if the old chronology had been retained, and we had described this edition as referring to 1997/98, those who were to consult the directory in 1999 might be in some doubt whether or not they were using the latest edition. We have therefore decided that it would be more helpful for the date to reflect accurately the period of time during which an edition of *Crockford* is current.

This is the seventh edition for which the Central Board of Finance and the Church Commissioners have had joint responsibility. As in previous years, the clergy payroll continues to be the bedrock on which *Crockford* rests, with any changes to the central payroll details of clergy (for example, when they move or retire) being automatically reflected on the *Crockford* database. It is this link between the payroll and *Crockford* systems which enables the Church to have access to detailed records of its clergy at a reasonable price without the need for any subsidy from central Church funds.

Production of a reference book of this size depends very much on partnerships. In addition to that between Church House Publishing and the Commissioners, mention must also be made of the vital partnership between the *Crockford* section and the dioceses, without which it would not be possible to provide details for the approximately 7,000 clergy not on the central payroll. In maintaining records on these clergy (principally non-stipendiary ministers, those engaged in some form of ministry outside the parochial system and those serving in Wales, Scotland or Ireland), we rely greatly on assistance from bishops' secretaries and diocesan offices and information contained in diocesan directories and year books, the *Church Times* and *The Church of England Newspaper*. We also receive considerable assistance from the Ministry of Defence, the Hospital Chaplaincies Council, and the central authorities of the Church in Wales, the Scottish Episcopal Church and the Church of Ireland.

In many ways, a publication's most vital partnership is the one that it has with its readers. We are particularly grateful to all those users of *Crockford* who have taken the trouble to provide us with information. Whilst it is not possible for *Crockford* to include all the details that clergy request us to publish, we are always glad to be given the opportunity to correct in future editions the omissions and errors that are, unfortunately, inevitable in a volume of this size.

Previous editions produced under the auspices of the CBF and the Commissioners have (much to our regret) not been able to include all appointments for clergy pensioners. We have attempted to include complete biographies of all clergy in this edition, and welcome the opportunity to pay tribute to the vital contribution to the Church's mission being made by clergy who have retired from the stipendiary ministry. Researching and inputting this additional data onto the *Crockford* computer system has been an enormous task, and special thanks should be recorded to Richard Christmas and Frances Garratt, who have been responsible for most of the work in compiling the directory.

As well as keeping an eye on the past, we are also looking to the future and new media of communication. For the first time, this edition includes clergy e-mail addresses. Every effort has been made to include as many e-mail addresses as possible, but those clergy whose e-mail addresses are not included are encouraged to let us know (if they wish, by e-mail at trish.hetherington@chucomm.org.uk)

For archival information from previous editions of *Crockford*, please write to the Church of England Record Centre, 15 Galleywall Road, London SE16 3PB (tel 0171-231 1251). Corrections, together with any comments and suggestions on how *Crockford* might be improved, are always welcomed by the Crockford Working Party, Church Commissioners, 1 Millbank, London SW1P 3JZ.

Church Commissioners
1 Millbank
London SW1P 3JZ

Central Board of Finance
Church House
Great Smith Street
London SW1P 3NZ

September 1997

JOHN CROCKFORD

John Crockford, publisher (?1823–1865) is best remembered for his association with the clerical directory that bears his name. His origins and parentage are obscure. No baptism can be traced, though his marriage certificate records him as the son of John Crockford, schoolmaster. By his early twenties he was in business as a printer and publisher at 29 Essex Street, Strand; and it was from that address that *Crockford* was first published in 1858. On 6 December of the same year, John Crockford moved to new business premises at 346 Strand and 19 Wellington Street North.

His private address at that time was 16 Oakley Square, Hampstead Road; though by 1865 he had moved to 10 Park Road, Haverstock Hill.

Crockford's business association of more than two decades with Edward William Cox (1809–1879) had begun in 1843, when the *Law Times* first appeared. Both men are claimed as publisher – Crockford by Boase in *Modern English Biography*; Cox by the *Athenaeum* and by *Notes and Queries*. There is similar lack of agreement over other publications, such as the ill-fated *Critic*. "[Crockford] tried to establish a literary paper, the *Critic*. To this he brought all his great ability, but after fifteen years he gave it up in despair" (*Notes and Queries*): whereas the *Dictionary of National Biography* has it that Cox became "proprietor of . . . two other papers called respectively 'The Critic' and 'The Royal Exchange'."

The truth appears to be that the two men, who shared the same business address in Essex Street, were joint founders of a number of projects. Cox – the elder, more established and richer man – was often the financier and named publisher, with Crockford as the manager of the undertaking. Each had his own specialities: Cox, called to the bar in 1843, and successively Recorder of Helston & Falmouth (1857–1868) and of Portsmouth (1868–1879) was no doubt the leader in the establishment of the *Law Times*, to which, in *DNB*'s words, he "thenceforth devoted . . . the larger portion of his time and attention." But the legend which has arisen that Cox, restrained by professional ethics from using his own name, chose, almost at random, the name of one of his clerks to bear the title of his new clerical directory in 1858 – thus, in the words of the first postwar editor (probably Newman) bestowing "a more than tomb-stone meed of remembrance" – cannot be substantiated. As the jubilee account of the *Field* notes, Crockford was an equal partner in the success of the joint enterprises: "It was John Crockford who purchased the paper for Mr Cox. He obtained it from Mr Benjamin Webster for a trifling sum . . . In a short time the net profits amounted to 20,000*l*. a year. The management was placed under Crockford's control. He was a splendid man of business" (*Notes and Queries*).

The first *Clerical Directory* (1858), "A Biographical and Statistical Book of Reference for facts relating to the clergy and the Church", seems to have been assembled in a very haphazard fashion, with names added "as fast as they could be obtained", out of alphabetical order and with an unreliable index. By 1860 the *Directory* had become a very much more useful work of reference; and by 1917, with the absorption of its only serious rival, the *Clergy List*, reigned supreme.

No more than glimpses survive of Crockford's personality, and those mostly from the account of him given by John C. Francis, in the *Field* jubilee article already referred to. "I had occasion to call upon him a short time before his death, when we joined in a hearty laugh over his former furious attacks upon the *Athenaeum*. 'Dilke's Drag' he used to call it, and would accuse it of 'vulgar insolence and coxcombry' and 'the coarsest vulgarity'. As we parted he said, 'You have the *Athenaeum* to be proud of, and we have the *Field*.' "

John Crockford died suddenly at his home on 13 January 1865, at the age of 41. He left a widow, Annie (née Ellam) whom he married on 24 December 1847 at St Pancras Old Church. No children are recorded. His very brief will, proved 6 February 1865 at the Principal Probate Registry, left everything to his widow. His personal effects were valued at less than £1,000, but the family must have lived in some style, since one of the witnesses to the will was the resident coachman.

BRENDA HOUGH

A request from the *Dictionary of National Biography* for a notice of the life of John Crockford led to the preparation of this article, a shorter version of which appeared in *The Dictionary of National Biography: Missing Persons*, 1993.

A USER'S GUIDE TO *CROCKFORD*

Who is included in *Crockford?*
Crockford includes details of over 25,000 clergy and deaconesses of the Church of England, the Church in Wales, the Scottish Episcopal Church and the Church of Ireland. Clergy currently serving overseas qualify for inclusion if they have trained or have been licensed in this country (see **Overseas clergy**). Clergy who have died since the last edition are listed on p.1088. Generally, clergy who have resigned their offices (but not their orders) are included unless they are known to have been received into another Church. A small number of clergy are excluded at their own request.

Readers and lay workers are not included: please consult diocesan directories. The *Who's Who* section of *The Church of England Year Book* (published annually by Church House Publishing and covering most aspects of the life and institutions of the Church of England) lists members of General Synod and principal members of staff of the Church's central organisations.

Addressing the clergy
See p.*58*.

Appointment details in the *Biographies* section
These reflect the legal pastoral situation prevailing at 31 July 1997, the date of the compilation of this edition of *Crockford*. Conventional districts, proprietary chapels and local ecumenical projects are also recorded. Benefice names are only recorded once in a biographical entry when they apply to successive appointments.

Crockford does not record group ministries, informal local arrangements, areas of special responsibility, emeritus appointments (except as reflected in the style of address), licence or permission to officiate when held in conjunction with another appointment from the same diocese, commissary appointments, examining chaplaincies, or secular appointments (except for educational or charitable posts).

Appointments before ordination are not included (apart from service as a deaconess) unless they straddle the date of ordination.

Archdeaconries
See *Archdeaconries, deaneries and rural deans* on p.835.

Archdeacons
Look up the place name in *Biographies*: this is cross-referenced to a personal name.

Bishops (diocesan, area, suffragan, and provincial episcopal visitors)
Look up the place name in *Biographies*: this is cross-referenced to a personal name. See also p. 794, which lists the diocesan, area, suffragan and assistant bishops by diocese, as well as provincial episcopal visitors.

Bishops (assistant)
See *Bishops in England, Wales, Scotland and Ireland* on p.794.

Bishops in the House of Lords
See p. 797.

Bishops overseas
See *Bishops of Anglican dioceses overseas* on p.1069, and Bishops of united churches on p.1081. Further information about the Anglican Communion can be found in *The Church of England Year Book*.

Bishops and archbishops, former
A list of former archbishops and bishops (diocesan and suffragan) will be found on p.798.

Boundaries, provincial and diocesan
Maps of England and Wales, Scotland and Ireland, showing provincial and diocesan boundaries and cathedral cities, will be found on p.1094.

Cathedral clergy
See *Cathedrals* on p.829 for full-time cathedral clergy. The list does not include honorary appointments.

Chapel Royal
See *Royal Peculiars* on p.831.

Christian names
The name by which a person prefers to be known, if not the first Christian name, is underlined (e.g. David John Smith prefers to be called John). Names 'in religion' or names not part of a person's legal name are shown in parentheses.

Church: how to find the names of clergy responsible for a particular church
Look up the place name in the appropriate *Benefices and churches* section, see pp.843–1049: if the entry is in bold type, the names of all clergy are listed and can be cross-referenced in the *Biographies* section; if the place name is not in bold type, the name of the benefice is given where the names of all clergy will be found.

Church: how to find the names of clergy responsible for a particular church when there is a vacancy
If the benefice is vacant, the telephone number of the clergy house is usually given in the appropriate *Benefices and churches* section to enable contact to be made with a new incumbent or priest-in-charge. The deanery reference (e.g. *Guildf 2*) following the benefice name cross-refers to *Archdeaconries, deaneries and rural deans* on p.835 by means of which the name of the rural dean responsible for the vacant benefice can be found.

College chaplains
See p.1064 for chaplains at universities, colleges of further education, colleges of higher education, and schools.

Corrections
Please send notice of any corrections to: *Crockford, 1 Millbank, London SW1P 3JZ*
Tel 0171-222 7010 Fax 222 0653 E-mail trish.hetherington@chucomm.org.uk

Crockford
The full title is *Crockford's Clerical Directory*. *Crockford* (not *Crockford's*) is an accepted abbreviation. See also the biography of John Crockford on p.53.

Deaconesses
See separate section on p.792.

Deacons
See *Biographies* section.

Deaneries
See rural or area deans below.

Deans
Look up the place name in *Biographies*: this is cross-referenced to a personal name. See also *Cathedrals* on p.829, and *Royal Peculiars* on p.831.

Diocesan offices
Details of the diocesan offices in England, Wales, Scotland and Ireland can be found on p.832.

E-mail addresses
These are provided where known. See after the telephone and/or fax number.

Europe, chaplains in
See *Chaplains of the Diocese of Gibraltar in Europe* on p.1050.

Fax numbers
The exchange number is only given if different from that of the preceding telephone number.

Hospital chaplains
Whole-time and part-time hospital chaplains at their base hospitals (as defined by the Hospital Chaplaincies Council) are listed on p.1056.

Lay workers
Lay workers are not included in *Crockford*: please consult diocesan directories.

London churches
See *English benefices and churches* on p.843. City and Guild churches are listed under LONDON CITY CHURCHES and LONDON GUILD CHURCHES. In other cases, see under church name (e.g. LANGHAM PLACE (All Souls), WESTMINSTER (St Matthew)).

Married or single?
Crockford does not provide information on marital status. However, where a woman priest, deacon or deaconess has requested the form of address Miss, Mrs or Ms, this is included. Where there has been a change of surname following marriage, a cross-reference may be found from the previous name.

Non-stipendiary clergy
Non-stipendiary clergy are listed in the main *Biographies* section.

Ordination courses
See *Theological colleges and courses* on p.1068.

Overseas clergy
Clergy who are on the *Crockford* database and who are currently serving overseas qualify for inclusion. Service overseas has in the past been recorded simply by country, though higher office (e.g. as bishop or archdeacon) has also been noted. Other eligible appointments are now being added on request.

Overseas addresses and telephone numbers are given as required by a user in the UK. Where area codes are not applicable (e.g. France), the country code is given. In other cases, the area code is listed and the country code will need to be obtained from international directory enquiries (telephone 153). The international access code (00 when dialling from the U.K.) will be required in all cases.

Patronage
The patron of each benefice is listed under the benefice name in *English benefices and churches* on p.843.

Prison chaplains
See p.1054.

Proprietary chapels
See *English benefices and churches* on p.843.

Provincial episcopal visitors
Look up the place name in *Biographies*: this is cross-referenced to a personal name. See also p. 794, which lists the diocesan, area, suffragan and assistant bishops and provincial episcopal visitors.

Provosts
Look up the place name in *Biographies*: this is cross-referenced to a personal name. See also *Cathedrals* on p.829.

Queen's Chaplains
See *Royal Peculiars* on p.831.

Readers
Readers are not included in *Crockford*: please consult diocesan directories.

Religious orders
For members of religious orders where the Christian name alone is commonly used (e.g. Brother Aidan) a cross-reference is provided to the surname. Names 'in religion' not forming part of a person's legal name will be shown in parentheses. Details of religious communities are provided in *The Church of England Year Book*.

Retired clergy
The description 'rtd' does not imply that ministry has ceased, only that clergy so described are now in receipt of a pension. All eligible appointments are now recorded.

Rural or area deans
See *Archdeaconries, deaneries and rural deans* on p.835. To find who is the rural dean of a particular church, look up the place or benefice name in the appropriate *Benefices* section: the deanery reference (e.g. *Guildf 2*) following the benefice name cross-refers to *Archdeaconries, deaneries and rural deans on* p.835 where the name of the rural dean responsible can be found.

School chaplains
See p.1066 for chaplains in schools.

Service chaplains
See p.1052.

Theological colleges and courses
See p.1068.

University chaplains
See p.1064.

HOW TO ADDRESS THE CLERGY

In offering the advice below, we do not intend to imply that other practices are necessarily to be discouraged (for example, the use of Father as in 'Father Smith'). A good deal depends on circumstances, and, where a personal preference is known, it is usually good practice to follow it.

The following notes show acceptable current usage

(a) on an envelope or formal listing
(b) in starting a social letter or in speech, and
(c) when referring to a member of the clergy

Category (a) is not open to much variation, owing to the formality of the context, but categories (b) and (c) will often vary according to circumstances. It is always acceptable to use the appropriate Christian name in place of initials (for example, the Revd Alice Smith). In the absence of any style or title conferred by a post, all deacons and priests are styled 'The Reverend', and all who have been consecrated bishop are styled 'The Right Reverend'.

For abbreviations, see paragraph 12 below.

1 **Deacons and Priests**

(a) The Reverend A B Smith
(b) Mr/Mrs/Miss/Ms Smith (unless it is known that some other style is preferred–the title Vicar or Rector is acceptable only if the person so addressed really is the incumbent of the parish where you live or worship)
(c) The Reverend A B Smith at the first mention, and Mr/Mrs/Miss/Ms Smith thereafter

Notes 1 The form 'Reverend Smith' or 'The Reverend Smith' should *never* be used this side of the Atlantic. If the Christian name or initials are not known, the correct forms are
(a) The Reverend—Smith, *or* The Reverend Mr/Mrs/Miss/Ms Smith
(b) Mr/Mrs/Miss/Ms Smith
(c) The Reverend Mr/Mrs/Miss/Ms Smith at the first mention, and Mr/Mrs/Miss/Ms Smith thereafter

2 There is no universally accepted way of addressing an envelope to a married couple of whom both are in holy orders. We recommend the style 'The Reverend A B and the Reverend C D Smith'.

2 **Prebendaries**

(a) The Reverend Prebendary A B Smith
(b) Prebendary Smith
(c) Prebendary Smith

3 **Canons (both Residentiary and Honorary)**

(a) The Reverend Canon A B Smith
(b) Canon Smith
(c) Canon Smith

4 **Archdeacons**

(a) The Venerable the Archdeacon of X
(b) Archdeacon, *or more formally* Mr Archdeacon
(c) The Archdeacon of X at the first mention, and the Archdeacon thereafter

Notes 1 In the case of an archdeacon (or dean/provost, bishop, or archbishop) in office, the style above is to be preferred. The personal name should be used only for the purpose of identification.

2 For an archdeacon emeritus, the correct forms are
(a) The Venerable A B Smith
(b) Archdeacon
(c) Archdeacon Smith

5 **Deans and Provosts**

(a) The Very Reverend the Dean/Provost of X
(b) Dean/Provost, *or more formally* Mr Dean/Provost
(c) The Dean/Provost of X at the first mention, and the Dean thereafter (see also note 1 to paragraph 4 above)

6 **Bishops, Diocesan and Suffragan**

(a) The Right Reverend the Bishop of X, *or* The Right Reverend the Lord Bishop of X
(b) Bishop, *or more formally* My Lord
(c) The Bishop of X at the first mention, and the Bishop thereafter (see also note 1 to paragraph 4 above)

Notes 1 The use of 'Lord' before 'Bishop' is diminishing. It is a matter of individual preference whether it should be used.
2 The Bishop of London is a Privy Councillor, and has the style 'The Right Reverend and Right Honourable the Lord Bishop of London'.
3 The Bishop of Meath and Kildare is styled 'The Most Reverend'.

7 **Assistant and Retired Bishops**

(a) The Right Reverend A B Smith
(b) Bishop
(c) Bishop Smith

8 **Archbishops**

(a) The Most Reverend the Lord Archbishop of X
(b) Archbishop, *or more formally* Your Grace
(c) The Archbishop of X at the first mention, and the Archbishop thereafter (see also note 1 to paragraph 4 above)

Notes 1 The Archbishops of Canterbury and York, being Privy Councillors, also have 'Right Honourable' included in their style (for example, The Most Reverend and Right Honourable the Lord Archbishop of Canterbury).
2 The presiding bishop of the Scottish Episcopal Church is the Primus, and the correct forms are
(a) The Most Reverend the Primus
(b) Primus
(c) Primus
3 Retired archbishops properly revert to the status of bishop, but may be given as a courtesy the style of an archbishop.

9 **Chaplains to the Armed Services**

(a) The Reverend A B Smith RN (*or* CF *or* RAF)
(b) Padre, *or* Padre Smith
(c) The Padre, *or* Padre Smith

10 **Ordained Members of Religious Orders**

(a) The Reverend Alan/Alice Smith XYZ; The Reverend Brother Alan/Sister Alice XYZ
(b) Father, Father Smith, *or* Father Alan; Brother Alan/Sister Alice
(c) The Reverend Alan/Alice Smith; Father Alan Smith; Father Smith; Brother Alan/Sister Alice

Notes 1 A name 'in religion', shown in parentheses in the biographical entry, should be used in preference to the baptismal name or initials. Sometimes the surname is not used. In this Directory, however, the entry will be found under the surname, whether it is normally used or not, and, if appropriate, a cross-reference is given under the Christian name.
2 Some orders use 'Brother' and 'Sister' for lay and ordained members without distinction, along with Christian names.
3 It is customary to specify the religious order by giving the appropriate letters after the name.

11 Academics

When a member of the clergy holds more than one title, the ecclesiastical one is normally used.

Professor also Canon	(a) The Reverend Canon A B Smith (b) Canon Smith, *or* Professor Smith, according to context (c) Canon Smith, *or* Professor Smith, according to context
Canon also Doctor	(a) The Reverend Canon A B Smith (degree) (b) Canon Smith, *or* Dr Smith, according to context (c) Canon Smith, *or* Dr Smith, according to context

12 Abbreviations

The following abbreviations are in common use

Reverend:	Revd *or* Rev
Father:	Fr
Right Reverend:	Rt Revd *or* Rt Rev
Prebendary:	Preb
Venerable:	Ven

Reverend, Right Reverend, Very Reverend, Most Reverend and Venerable, whether abbreviated or not, should always be preceded by the definite article.

ABBREVIATIONS USED IN CROCKFORD'S CLERICAL DIRECTORY

A

AAAI	Associate of the Institute of Administrative Accountants
AACCA	Associate of the Association of Certified and Corporate Accountants (see ACCA)
AB	Bachelor of Arts (USA)
ABAF	Associate of the British Academy of Fencing
ABIA	Associate of the Bankers' Institute of Australasia
ABIPP	Associate of the British Institute of Professional Photographers
ABIST	Associate of the British Institute of Surgical Technology
ABM	Advisory Board of Ministry (formerly ACCM and CACTM)
ABPsS	Associate of the British Psychological Society (now see AFBPsS)
ABSM	Associate of the Birmingham and Midland Institute School of Music
ACA	Associate of the Institute of Chartered Accountants
ACC	Anglican Consultative Council
ACCA	Associate of the Chartered Association of Certified Accountants (formerly AACCA)
ACCM	Advisory Council for the Church's Ministry (formerly CACTM; now see ABM)
ACCS	Associate of the Corporation of Secretaries
ACF	Army Cadet Force
ACGI	Associate of the City and Guilds of London
ACIArb	Associate of the Chartered Institute of Arbitrators
ACIB	Associate of the Chartered Institute of Bankers (formerly AIB)
ACII	Associate of the Chartered Insurance Institute
ACIPA	Associate of the Chartered Institute of Patent Agents
ACIS	Associate of the Institute of Chartered Secretaries and Administrators
ACIT	Associate of the Chartered Institute of Transport
ACMA	Associate of the Institute of Cost and Management Accountants (formerly ACWA)
ACORA	Archbishops' Commission on Rural Areas
ACP	Associate of the College of Preceptors
ACS	Additional Curates Society
ACSM	Associate of Camborne School of Mines
ACT	Australian Capital Territory Australian College of Theology
ACTVR	Advanced Certificate in Television and Radio
ACUPA	Archbishops' Commission on Urban Priority Areas
ACWA	Associate of the Institute of Cost and Works Accountants (now see ACMA)
ACertCM	Archbishop of Canterbury's Certificate in Church Music
ACertEd	Advanced Certificate of Education
AD	Area Dean
ADB	Associate of the Drama Board
ADC	Advanced Diploma in Counselling
ADCM	Archbishop of Canterbury's Diploma in Church Music
ADEDC	Advanced Diploma in Education of the Deaf and Partially Hearing Children
ADEd	Advanced Diploma in Education
ADME	Advanced Diploma in Maths Education
ADMT	Advanced Diploma in Ministerial Theology
ADPS	Advanced Diploma in Pastoral Studies
ADipR	Archbishop's Diploma for Readers
ADipRE	Advanced Diploma in Religious Education
ADipTh	Advanced Diploma in Theology
AEdRD	Associateship in Educational Research and Development
AFAIM	Associate Fellow of the Australian Institute of Management
AFBPsS	Associate Fellow of the British Psychological Society (formerly ABPsS)
AFC	Air Force Cross
AFIMA	Associate Fellow of the Institute of Mathematics and its Applications
AGSM	Associate of the Guildhall School of Music and Drama
AHSM or AHA	Associate of the Institute of Health Service Management (formerly Administrators)
AIA	Associate of the Institute of Actuaries
AIAS	Associate of the Incorporated Association of Architects and Surveyors
AIAT	Associate of the Institute of Animal Technicians
AIB	Associate of the Institute of Bankers (now see ACIB)
AIDS	Acquired Immunity Deficiency Syndrome
AIFST	Associate of the Institute of Food Science and Technology
AIGCM	Associate of the Incorporated Guild of Church Musicians
AIIM	Associate of the Institute of Investment Management
AIL	Associate of the Institute of Linguists
AIMLS	Associate of the Institute of Medical Laboratory Sciences
AIMarE	Associate of the Institute of Marine Engineering
AIPM	Associate of the Institute of Personnel Management
AITI	Associate of the Institute of Taxation in Ireland
AKC	Associate of King's College, London
ALA	Associate of the Library Association
ALAM	Associate of the London Academy of Music
ALBC	Associate of the London Bible College
ALCD	Associate of the London College of Divinity
ALCM	Associate of the London College of Music
ALSM	Associate of the Lancashire School of Music
AM	Albert Medal Auxiliary Minister Master of Arts (USA)
AMA	Associate of the Museums Association
AMBIM	Associate Member of the British Institute of Management (later MBIM; now see FBIM)
AMCST	Associate of the Manchester College of Science and Technology
AMCT	Associate of the Manchester College of Technology
AMGAS	Associate Member of the Group-Analytic Society
AMIBF	Associate Member of the Institute of British Foundrymen
AMIC	Associate Member of the Institute of Counselling
AMICE	Associate Member of the Institution of Civil Engineers (now see MICE)
AMIDHE	Associate Member of the Institute of Domestic Heating Engineers
AMIEE	Associate Member of the Institution of Electrical Engineers (now see MIEE)
AMIEHO	Associate Member of the Institution of Environmental Health Officers
AMIM	Associate Member of the Institute of Metals
AMIMechE	Associate of the Institution of Mechanical Engineers (now see MIMechE)
AMIMinE	Associate Member of the Institute of Mining Engineers
AMITD	Associate Member of the Institute of Training and Development
AMIWO	Associate Member of the Institute of Welfare Officers
AMInstTA	Associate Member of the Institute of Transport Administration
AMP	Advanced Management Program
AMRSH	Associate Member of the Royal Society of Health
AMSIA	Associate Member of the Society of Investment Analysts
AMusTCL	Associate in Music of Trinity College of Music, London
ANCA	Advanced National Certificate in Agriculture
AP	Assistant Priest
APM	Auxiliary Pastoral Minister (or Ministry)
APhS	Associate of the Philosophical Society of England
ARAM	Associate of the Royal Academy of Music
ARCA	Associate of the Royal College of Art
ARCIC	Anglican-Roman Catholic International Commission
ARCM	Associate of the Royal College of Music
ARCO	Associate of the Royal College of Organists
ARCS	Associate of the Royal College of Science
ARCST	Associate of the Royal College of Science and Technology (Glasgow)
ARCT	Associate of the Royal Conservatory of Music, Toronto

ARCUK	Architects' Registration Council of the United Kingdom
ARHistS	Associate of the Royal Historical Society
ARIBA	Associate of the Royal Institute of British Architects (now see RIBA)
ARIC	Associate of the Royal Institute of Chemistry (later MRIC; now see MRSC)
ARICS	Associate of the Royal Institution of Chartered Surveyors
ARMCM	Associate of the Royal Manchester College of Music
ARSM	Associate of the Royal School of Mines
AS	Associate in Science (USA)
ASCA	Associate of the Society of Company and Commercial Accountants
ASCAT	All Souls' College of Applied Theology
ASEEDip	Association of Supervising Electrical Engineers Diploma
ATC	Air Training Corps
ATCL	Associate of Trinity College of Music, London
ATD	Art Teacher's Diploma
ATI	Associate of the Textile Institute
ATII	Associate Member of the Institute of Taxation
ATPL	Airline Transport Pilot's Licence
ATV	Associated Television
ATh(SA)	Associate in Theology (South Africa)
AV	Associate Vicar
AVCM	Associate of the Victoria College of Music
Ab	(Diocese of) Aberdeen and Orkney
Aber	Aberdeen
Abp	Archbishop
Abth	Aberystwyth
AcDipEd	Academic Diploma in Education
Admin	Administration Administrative Administrator
Adn	Archdeacon
Adnry	Archdeaconry
Adv	Adviser Advisory
AdvDipCrim	Advanced Diploma in Criminology
Agric	Agricultural Agriculture
Aid	Aidan Aidan's
alt	alternate
Andr	Andrew Andrew's Andrews
Angl	Anglican Anglicans
Ant	Anthony Anthony's
Appt	Appointment
Arg	(Diocese of) Argyll and The Isles
Arm	(Diocese of) Armagh
Assn	Association
Assoc	Associate
Asst	Assistant
Aug	Augustine Augustine's
Aus	Australia Australian
Aux	Auxiliaries Auxiliary

B

b	Born
B & W	(Diocese of) Bath and Wells
B or Bapt	Baptist Baptist's
BA	Bachelor of Arts
BA(Econ)	Bachelor of Arts in Economics
BA(Ed)	Bachelor of Arts in Education
BA(Theol)	Bachelor of Arts in Theology
BAC Acc	Accredited Counsellor (British Association for Counselling)
BAC Accred	British Accreditation Council Accredit
BAI	Bachelor of Engineering (also see BE and BEng)
BAO	Bachelor of Obstetrics
BAOR	British Army of (formerly on) the Rhine
BASc	Bachelor of Applied Science
BAdmin	Bachelor of Administration
BAgr	Bachelor of Agriculture
BArch	Bachelor of Architecture
BBA	Bachelor of Business Administration
BBC	British Broadcasting Corporation
BBS	Bachelor of Business Studies
BC	British Columbia (Canada)
BCC	British Council of Churches (now see CCBI)
BCL	Bachelor of Civil Law
BCMS	Bible Churchmen's Missionary Society (now Crosslinks)
BCh or BChir	Bachelor of Surgery (also see BS and ChB)
BCom	Bachelor of Commerce
BCombStuds	Bachelor of Combined Studies
BD	Bachelor of Divinity
BDQ	Bachelor of Divinity Qualifying Examination
BDS	Bachelor of Dental Surgery
BDip	Bible Diploma
BE	Bachelor of Engineering (also see BAI and BEng)
BEM	British Empire Medal
BEcon	Bachelor of Economics (USA)
BEd	Bachelor of Education
BEng	Bachelor of Engineering (also see BAI and BE)
BFBS	British and Foreign Bible Society
BFPO	British Forces Post Office
BIE	Bachelor of Industrial Engineering (USA)
BL	Bachelor of Law
BLitt	Bachelor of Letters
BM	Bachelor of Medicine (also see MB)
BMMF	Bible and Medical Missionary Fellowship (now Intersave)
BMU	Board for Mission and Unity
BMedSci	Bachelor of Medical Science
BMet	Bachelor of Metallurgy
BMin	Bachelor of Ministry
BMus	Bachelor of Music (also see MusB or MusBac)
BMusEd	Bachelor of Music Education
BN	Bachelor of Nursing
BNC	Brasenose College
BPaed	Bachelor of Paediatrics
BPh or BPhil	Bachelor of Philosophy
BPharm	Bachelor of Pharmacy
BPhil(Ed)	Bachelor of Philosophy (Education)
BRE	Bachelor of Religious Education (USA)
BRF	Bible Reading Fellowship
BS	Bachelor of Science (also see BSc) Bachelor of Surgery (also see BCh, BChir and ChB)
BSA	Bachelor of Scientific Agriculture
BSB	Brotherhood of St Barnabas
BSE	Bachelor of Science in Engineering (also see BScEng)
BSEd	Bachelor of Science in Education (USA)
BSP	Brotherhood of St Paul
BSSc	Bachelor of Social Science (also see BSocSc)
BSW	Bachelor of Social Work
BSc	Bachelor of Science (also see BS)
BSc(Econ)	Bachelor of Science in Economics
BSc(Soc)	Bachelor of Science (Sociology)
BScAgr	Bachelor of Science in Agriculture
BScEng	Bachelor of Science in Engineering (also see BSE)
BScFor	Bachelor of Science in Forestry
BScTech	Bachelor of Technical Science
BSocAdmin	Bachelor of Social Administration
BSocSc	Bachelor of Social Science (also see BSSc)
BSocStuds	Bachelor of Social Studies
BT	Bachelor of Teaching
BTA	British Tuberculosis Association Certificate
BTEC HNC	Business and Technician Education Council Higher National Certificate
BTEC NC	Business and Technician Education Council National Certificate
BTEC ND	Business and Technician Education Council National Diploma
BTS	Bachelor of Theological Studies
BTech	Bachelor of Technology
BTh	Bachelor of Theology (also see STB)
BVSc	Bachelor of Veterinary Science
BVetMed	Bachelor of Veterinary Medicine (also see VetMB)
Ball	Balliol
Ban	(Diocese of) Bangor
Barn	Barnabas Barnabas's
Bart	Bartholomew Bartholomew's
Bd	Board
Bedf	Bedford
Beds	Bedfordshire
Belf	Belfast
Berks	Berkshire
BesL	Bachelier es Lettres
Bibl	Biblical
Birkb	Birkbeck
Birm	(Diocese of) Birmingham
Blackb	(Diocese of) Blackburn
Boro	Borough
Bp	Bishop
Br	British
Bradf	(Diocese of) Bradford
Bre	(Diocese of) Brechin
Brig	Brigadier
Bris	(Diocese of) Bristol
Bt	Baronet
Buckm	Buckingham
Bucks	Buckinghamshire

C

C	Curate
c	Consecrated
C & O	(Diocese of) Cashel and Ossory (united dioceses of Cashel, Waterford, Lismore, Ossory, Ferns and Leighlin)
C of E	Church of England
C of S	Church of Scotland
C&G	City and Guilds
C, C & R	(Diocese of) Cork, Cloyne and Ross
C-in-c	Curate-in-charge

c/o .... Care of
CA.................. Church Army
Member of the Institute of Chartered Accountants of Scotland
CA(Z).............. Member of the Institute of Chartered Accountants of Zimbabwe
CACP.............. Certificate in Advanced Counselling Practice
CACTM .... Central Advisory Council for the Ministry (later ACCM; now see ABM)
CANDL........... Church and Neighbourhood Development in London
CANP .... Certificate in Advanced Nursery Practices
CAP................ Certificat d'aptitude de la Prêtrise
CARA............ Care and Resources for people affected by AIDS/HIV
CARE .... Christian Action Research and Education
CASA.............. Anglican Church of the Southern Cone of America
CASS .... Certificate in Applied Social Studies
CB.................. Companion of the Bath
CBE................ Commander of the Order of the British Empire
CBIM.............. Companion of the British Institute of Management
CBTS .... Certificate in Biblical and Theological Studies
CBiol............... Chartered Biologist
CCBI............... Council of Churches for Britain and Ireland (formerly BCC)
CCC................ Corpus Christi College
Council for the Care of Churches
CCCS.............. Commonwealth and Continental Church Society
CCSk .... Certificate in Counselling Skills
CCT................ Certificate in Clinical Teaching
CChem .... Chartered Chemist
CCouns............ Certificate in Counselling
CD .... Canadian Forces Decoration
Conventional District (also see ED)
CD (US Air)..... Commercial Diver (US Air Force)
CDRS .... Certificate in Divinity and Religious Studies
CDipAF........... Certified Diploma in Accounting and Finance
CECD .... Church of England Council for the Deaf
CECM............. Certificate of Education for the Church's Ministry
CECS .... Church of England Children's Society (now known as the Children's Society)
CEIR .... Certificate in Economics and Industrial Relations
CEMS .... Church of England Men's Society
CES .... Certificate in Ecumenical Studies
CEng................ Chartered Engineer
CEurStuds........ Certificate in European Studies
CF.................. Chaplain to the Forces
CFTV.............. Certificate in Film and Television
CGA .... Community of the Glorious Ascension
CIO .... Church Information Office
CIPFA............. Chartered Institute of Public Finance and Accountancy
CITC............... Church of Ireland Theological College
CJGS .... Community of the Companions of Jesus the Good Shepherd
CLHist .... Certificate in Local History
CLJ................ Commander of the Order of St Lazarus of Jerusalem
CLRHist .... Certificate in Local and Regional History
CM................. Carnegie Medal
CMBHI .... Craft Member of the British Horological Institute
CMD .... Cambridge Mission to Delhi (now see USPG)
CME............... Continuing Ministerial Education
CMG .... Companion of St Michael and St George
CMJ................ Church's Ministry among Jewish People
CMM.............. Certificate in Ministry and Mission
CMS .... Church Mission Society
Church Missionary Society
CMT............... Certificate in Ministerial Theology
CMinlEd.......... Certificate in Ministerial Education
CMinlStuds ...... Certificate in Ministerial Studies
CNAA............. Council for National Academic Awards
COPEC............ Conference on Politics, Economics and Community
CORAT........... Christian Organizations Research and Advisory Trust
CORE .... City Outreach through Renewal Evangelism
CP.................. Community Priest
CPA................ Chartered Patent Agent (formerly FCIPA)
CPAS .... Church Pastoral Aid Society
CPC................ Certificate of Professional Competence (Road Transport)
CPES .... Certificate in Post Excavation Studies
CPM .... Colonial Police Medal
CPPS............... Certificate of Proficiency in Pastoral Studies
CPS .... Certificate in Pastoral Studies
CPSS............... Certificate in Pastoral and Social Studies
CPT................ Certificate in Pastoral Theology
CPTS .... Certificate in Pastoral and Theological Studies
CPhys.............. Chartered Physicist of the Institute of Physics
CPsychol.......... Chartered Psychologist
CQSW............. Certificate of Qualification in Social Work
CR.................. Community of the Resurrection (Mirfield)
CSA................ Community of St Andrew
CSD................ Co-operative Societies' Diploma
CSF .... Community of St Francis
CSG................ Company of the Servants of God
CSMV............. Community of St Mary the Virgin
CSS................. Certificate in Social Service
CSSM.............. Children's Special Service Mission
CSWG............. Community of the Servants of the Will of God
CSocSc .... Certificate in Social Science
CSocStuds .... Certificate in Social Studies
CSpPastCat ...... Certificate in Special Pastoral Catechesis
CStJ................ Commander, the Most Venerable Order of the Hospital of St John of Jerusalem
CTM............... Certificate in Theology and Mission
CTMin .... Certificate in Theology and Ministry
CTOSc............. Certificate in the Teaching of Science
CTPS .... Certificate in Theological and Pastoral Studies
CTUS.............. Certificate in Trades Union Studies
CUF .... Church Urban Fund
CVO .... Commander of the Royal Victorian Order
CWME............ Commission on World Mission and Evangelism
CWWCh.......... Certificate of Women's Work in the Church
CYCW .... Certificate in Youth and Community Work
CYFA .... Church Youth Fellowships Association
CYPECS.......... Christian Youth Fellowship, Pathfinders, Explorers, Climbers and Scramblers
Cam................ Cambridge
Cambs............. Cambridgeshire
Can................. Canon
Cand .... Candidate
Candidate's
Candidates'
Cant................ (Diocese of) Canterbury
Capt................ Captain
Carl .... (Diocese of) Carlisle
Cath................ Catharine/Catherine
Catharine's/Catherine's
Cathl............... Cathedral
Cdre................ Commodore
Cen................. Centre
Center
Central
Cert .... Certificat(e)
CertAnPsych..... Certificate in Analytical Psychology
CertBS............. Certificate in Bible Studies
CertCC .... Certificate of Child Care
CertCEd........... Certificate for Leadership in Christian Education
CertCS............. Certificate in Christian Studies
CertCT .... Certificate in Ceramic Technology
CertComp .... Certificate in Computing
CertDiv............ Certificate in Divinity
CertEd............. Certificate of Education
CertEdD .... Certificate in the Education of the Deaf
CertFAI........... Certificate in French, Arabic and Islamic Studies
CertFE .... Certificate of Further Education
CertFSW.......... Certificate in Family Social Work of the NSPCC
CertFT .... Certificate in Family Therapy
CertHE............ Certificate in Health Education
CertHist........... Certificate in History
CertJourn......... Certificate in Journalism
CertMBiol........ Certificate of Microbiology
CertMS............ Certificate in Management Studies
CertPsych......... Certificate in Psychology
CertRE............ Certificate in Religious Education
CertRK............ Certificate in Religious Knowledge
CertRS .... Certificate in Religious Studies
CertSc .... Certificate of Science
CertTESLA ...... Certificate in Teaching English as a Second Language to Adults
CertTESOL ...... Certificate in Teaching English to Speakers of Other Languages
CertTS............. Certificate in Timber Surveying
CertYS .... Certificate in Youth Service
Ch.................. Christ
Christ's
Church
Ch Ch .... Christ Church
ChB .... Bachelor of Surgery (also see BCh, BChir and BS)
ChStJ .... Chaplain, the Most Venerable Order of the Hospital of St John of Jerusalem
Chan .... Chancellor

Chapl	Chaplain
	Chaplaincies
	Chaplaincy
Chas	Charles
	Charles's
Chelmsf	(Diocese of) Chelmsford
Ches	(Diocese of) Chester
Chich	(Diocese of) Chichester
Chmn	Chairman
	Chairwoman
Chpl	Chapel
Chr	Christian
	Christians
Chris	Christopher
	Christopher's
Chrys	Chrysostom
	Chrysostom's
Chu	Churchill
Cl-in-c	Cleric-in-charge
Clem	Clement
	Clement's
Cllr	Councillor
Clogh	(Diocese of) Clogher
Co	Company
	County
	Counties
Co-ord	Co-ordinator
	Co-ordinating
Col	Colonel
Coll	College
Colleg	Collegiate
Comdr	Commander
Commn	Commission
Commr	Commissioner
Comp	Comprehensive
Conf	Confederation
	Conference
Congr	Congregation
	Congregational
Conn	(Diocese of) Connor
Corp	Corporation
Coun	Council
Cov	(Diocese of) Coventry
Cttee	Committee
Cust	Custodian
	Custody
Cuth	Cuthbert
	Cuthbert's
Cypr	Cyprian
	Cyprian's

D

d	Ordained Deacon
D & D	(Diocese of) Down and Dromore
D & G	(Diocese of) Dublin and Glendalough
D & R	(Diocese of) Derry and Raphoe
D&C	Dean and Chapter
DA	Diploma in Anaesthetics (England)
	Diploma in Art (Scotland)
DAA	Diploma in Archive Administration
DAC	Diploma in Adult Counselling
DAES	Diploma in Advanced Educational Studies
DAM	Diploma in Archives Management
DAPC	Diploma in Advanced Psychological Counselling
DASAE	Diploma of Advanced Study in Adult Education
DASE	Diploma in the Advanced Study of Education
DASHE	Diploma in Advance Studies in Higher Education
DASS	Diploma in Applied Social Studies
DASSc	Diploma in Applied Social Science
DATh	Diploma of the Arts in Theology
DAVM	Diploma in Audio Visual Media
DB	Bachelor of Divinity (USA)
DBF	Diocesan Board of Finance
DBMS	Diploma in Biblical and Mission Studies
DBO	Diploma of the British Orthoptic Society
DBP	Diocesan Board of Patronage
DBRS	Diploma in Biblical and Religious Studies
DBS	Diploma in Biblical Studies
DC	Diocesan Certificate
	District of Columbia (USA)
DCAe	Diploma of the College of Aeronautics
DCC	Diploma in Crisis Counselling of the Institute of Counselling
DCE	Diploma in Careers Education
DCEG	Diploma in Careers Education and Guidance
DCEd	Diploma in Community Education
DCG	Diploma in Careers Guidance
DCH	Diploma in Child Health
DCHospC	Diploma in Counselling and Hospital Chaplaincy
DCL	Doctor of Civil Law
DCM	Diploma in Christian Ministry
DCMus	Diploma in Church Music
DCR	Diploma of the College of Radiographers
DCR, MU	Diploma of the College of Radiographers in Medical Ultra Sound
DCS	Diploma in Community Studies
DCTM	Diploma in Christian Theology and Ministry
DCYW	Diploma in Community and Youth Work
DChCD	Diploma in Church Community Development
DChemEng	Diploma in Chemical Engineering
DCnL	Doctor of Canon Law
DCouns	Diploma in Counselling
DD	Doctor of Divinity
DDEd	Diploma in Distance Education
DDW	Diploma in Deaf Welfare
DEd	Doctor of Education (also see EdD)
DEdin Cert	Duke of Edinburgh's Awards Certificate of Recognition
DFC	Distinguished Flying Cross
DFM	Distinguished Flying Medal (Canada)
DFStuds	Diploma in French Studies
DGA	Diploma in Government Administration
DHA	District Health Authority
DHL	Doctor of Humane Letters
DHRK	Diploma in Humanities and Religious Knowledge
DHSA	Diploma in Health Services Administration
DHistA	Diploma in the History of Art
DIC	Diploma of Imperial College
DIH	Diploma in Industrial Health
DIL	Diploma of the Institute of Linguists
DIM	Diploma in Industrial Management
DIS	Diploma in Industrial Studies
DIT	Diploma in Interpreting and Translating
DL	Deputy Lieutenant
DLC	Diploma of Loughborough College
DLIS	Diploma in Library and Information Studies
DLLP	Diploma in Law and Legal Practice
DLO	Diploma in Laryngology and Otology
DLSc	Doctor of Legal Science
DLitt	Doctor of Letters (also see LittD)
DLitt et Phil	Doctor of Letters and Philosophy
DM	Diploma in Management
DMA	Diploma in Municipal Administration
DMEd	Diploma of Management in Education
DMS	Diploma in Management Studies
DMS(Ed)	Diploma in Management Studies (Education)
DMSchM	Diploma of the Mission School of Medicine, London
DMin	Doctor of Ministry
DMinlStuds	Diploma in Ministerial Studies
DMinlTh	Diploma in Ministerial Theology
DMusEd	Diploma in Music Education
DN	Diploma in Nursing
DNEd	Diploma in Nursery Education
DNM	Diploma in Nuclear Medicine
DOE	Department of the Environment
DOMS	Diploma in Ophthalmic Medicine and Surgery
DON	Diploma in Ophthalmic Nursing
DObstRCOG	Diploma in Obstetrics, Royal College of Obstetricians and Gynaecologists
DPA	Diploma in Public Administration
DPEd	Diploma in Primary Education
DPH	Diploma in Public Health
DPM	Diploma in Psychological Medicine
DPMSA	Diploma in Philosophy of Medicine, Society of Apothecaries
DPS	Diploma in Pastoral Studies
DPSE	Diploma in Professional Studies in Education
DPSN	Diploma in Professional Studies in Nursing
DPST	Diploma in Pastoral and Social Theology
DPT	Diploma in Pastoral Theology
DPastMin	Diploma in Pastoral Ministry
DPhil	Doctor of Philosophy (also see PhD)
DRBS	Diploma in Religious and Biblical Studies
DRCOG	Diploma of the Royal College of Obstetricians and Gynaecologists
DRI	Diploma in Radionuclide Imaging
DRS	Diploma in Rural Studies
DRSS	Diploma in Religious and Social Studies
DSA	Diploma in Social Administration
DSC	Distinguished Service Cross
DSCE	Diploma in Social and Community Education
DSM	Distinguished Service Medal
DSMS	Diploma in Sales Management Studies
DSO	Companion of the Distinguished Service Order
DSPT	Diploma in Social and Pastoral Theology
DSRS	Diploma in Social and Religious Studies
DST	Doctor of Sacred Theology (also see STD)
DSc	Doctor of Science (also see ScD)
DSocSc	Doctor of Social Science
DSocStuds	Diploma in Social Studies

DSpEd .... Diploma in Special Education
DTEd .... Diploma in Tertiary Education
DTI .... Department of Trade and Industry
DTM .... Diploma in Tropical Medicine
DTM&H .... Diploma in Tropical Medicine and Hygiene
DTPH .... Diploma in Tropical Public Health
DTPS .... Diploma in Theological and Pastoral Studies
DTS .... Diploma in Theological Studies
DTechM .... Diploma in Technical Mining
DTh .... Doctor of Theology (also see ThD)
DUP .... Docteur de l'Université de Paris
DUniv .... Doctor of the University
Darw .... Darwin
Dav .... David
David's
Dep .... Deputy
Dept .... Department
DesL .... Docteur es Lettres
Det .... Detention
Dio .... Diocese
Dioc .... Diocesan
Dip .... Diploma
DipA&CE .... Diploma in Adult and Continuing Education
DipAD .... Diploma in Art and Design
DipADO .... Diploma of the Association of Dispensing Opticians
DipAE .... Diploma in Adult Education
DipAI .... Diploma in Artificial Insemination
DipAct .... Diploma in Acting
DipAdEd .... Diploma in Advanced Education
DipAgr .... Diploma in Agriculture
DipAnChem .... Diploma in Analytical Chemistry
DipAnPsych .... Diploma in Analytical Psychology
DipAnth .... Diploma in Anthropology
DipApEc .... Diploma in Applied Economics
DipApSc .... Diploma of Applied Science
DipApTh .... Diploma in Applied Theology
DipArch .... Diploma in Architecture
DipBA .... Diploma in Business Administration
DipBBSS .... Diploma in Bilingual Business and Secretarial Studies
DipBS .... Diploma in Business Studies
DipC .... Diploma in Counselling
DipC&G .... Diploma in Counselling and Guidance
DipC&S .... Diploma in Counselling and Supervision
DipCD .... Diploma in Church Development
DipCH .... Diploma in Clinical Hypnotherapy
DipCK .... Diploma in Christian Knowledge
DipCL .... Diploma in Christian Leadership
DipCMus .... Diploma in Church Music
DipCOT .... Diploma of the College of Occupational Therapists
DipCSM .... Diploma of the Cork School of Music
DipChD .... Diploma of Chaplains to the Deaf
DipCivEng .... Diploma in Civil Engineering
DipCombStuds .... Diploma in Combined Studies
DipContEd .... Diploma in Continuing Education
DipDA .... Diploma in Dramatic Art
DipDiet .... Diploma in Dietetics
DipEEngD .... Diploma in Environmental Engineering and Design
DipEH .... Diploma in Environmental Health
DipEM .... Diploma in Estate Management
DipEcon .... Diploma in Economics
DipEcum .... Diploma in Ecumenicalism
DipEd .... Diploma in Education
DipEdG .... Diploma in Educational Guidance
DipEdHChild .... Diploma in the Education of Handicapped Children
DipEdMan .... Diploma in Educational Management
DipEvang .... Diploma in Evangelism
DipFD .... Diploma in Funeral Directing
DipFE .... Diploma in Further Education
DipFL .... Diploma in Foreign Languages
DipG&C .... Diploma in Guidance and Counselling
DipGD .... Diploma in Graphic Design
DipGL .... Diploma in German Language
DipGeochem .... Diploma in Geochemistry
DipHCM .... Diploma in Hotel and Catering Management
DipHE .... Diploma in Higher Education
DipHP .... Diploma in Human Purposes
DipHRel .... Diploma in Human Relations
DipHV .... Diploma in Health Visiting
DipHort .... Diploma in Horticulture
DipHums .... Diploma in Humanities
DipHyp .... Diploma in Hypnotherapy
DipIR .... Diploma in Industrial Relations
DipInstAM .... Diploma of the Institute of Administrative Management
DipInstBM .... Diploma of the Institution of Merchanting (Builders)
DipInstHSM .... Diploma of the Institute of Health Service Management
DipInstM .... Diploma of the Institute of Marketing
DipL&A .... Diploma in Liturgy and Architecture
DipLib .... Diploma of Librarianship
DipLit .... Diploma in Liturgy
DipM .... Diploma in Marketing
DipMA .... Diploma of the Museums Association
DipMM .... Diploma in Mission and Ministry
DipMan .... Diploma for Management
DipMathEd .... Diploma in Maths Education
DipMaths .... Postgraduate Diploma in Mathematics
DipMechEng .... Diploma in Mechanical Engineering
DipMentH .... Diploma in Mental Health
DipMin .... Diploma in Ministry
DipMiss .... Diploma in Mission
DipMus .... Diploma in Music
DipNCTD .... Diploma of the National College of Teachers of the Deaf
DipNuc .... Diploma in Nuclear Technology
DipOAS .... Diploma in Oriental and African Studies
DipOH&S .... Diploma in Occupational Health and Safety
DipOT .... Diploma in Occupational Therapy
DipP&C .... Diploma in Psychology and Counselling
DipPC .... Diploma in Pastoral Counselling
DipPE .... Diploma in Physical Education
DipPM .... Diploma in Personnel Management
DipPSA .... Diploma in Public and Social Administration
DipPSE .... Diploma in Personal and Social Education
DipPTh .... Diploma in Practical Theology
DipPastS .... Diploma Pastoral Studies
DipPh .... Diploma in Physiotherapy
DipPhil .... Diploma in Philosophy
DipPs .... Diploma in Psychotherapy
DipPsych .... Diploma in Psychology
DipRCM .... Diploma of the Royal College of Music
DipRD .... Diploma in Reading Development
DipRE .... Diploma in Religious Education
DipREM .... Diploma in Rural Estate Management
DipRIPH&H .... Diploma of the Royal Institute of Public Health and Hygiene
DipRJ .... Diploma of Retail Jewellery
DipRK .... Diploma in Religious Knowledge
DipRS .... Diploma in Religious Studies
DipRSAMDA .... Diploma of the Royal Scottish Academy of Music and Dramatic Art
DipS&PT .... Diploma in Social and Pastoral Theology
DipSC .... Diploma in Student Counselling
DipSM .... Diploma in Sales Marketing of the Managing and Marketing Sales Association
DipSMan .... Diploma in School Management
DipSoc .... Diploma in Sociology
DipSocAnth .... Diploma in Social Anthropology
DipSocSc .... Diploma in Social Sciences
DipSocWork .... Diploma in Social Work
DipSurg .... Diploma in Surgery
DipT .... Diploma in Teaching
DipTE .... Diploma in Transportation Engineering
DipTHPsych .... Diploma in Therapeutic Hypnosis and Psychology
DipTLSA .... Diploma in Teaching Literacy Skills to Adults
DipTM .... Diploma in Training Management
DipTP .... Diploma in Town Planning
DipTS .... Diploma in Transport Studies
DipTSM .... Diploma in the Techniques of Safety Management
DipTh .... Diploma in Theology
DipThPS .... Diploma in Theological and Pastoral Studies
DipThe .... Diploma in Theatre
DipVG .... Diploma in Vocational Guidance
DipYESTB .... Diploma of the Youth Employment Service Training Board
DipYL .... Diploma in Youth Leadership
DipYW .... Diploma in Youth Work
Dipl-Reg .... Diplom-Regiesseur für Musiktheater
Dir .... Director
Distr .... District
Div .... Divinity
Div Test .... Divinity Testimonium
Dn-in-c .... Deacon-in-charge
Dom .... Domestic
Down .... Downing
Dr .... Doctor
DrTheol .... Doctor of Theology (Germany)
Dss .... Deaconess
dss .... Admitted Deaconess
Dub .... Dublin
Dur .... (Diocese of) Durham

E

E .... East
Eastern

EAMTC .... East Anglian Ministerial Training Course
EC .... Emergency Commission
ED .... Ecclesiastical District (also see CD)
Efficiency Decoration
EKD .... Evangelische Kirche Deutschland
EMMTC .... East Midlands Ministry Training Course
EN(G) .... Enrolled Nurse (General)
EN(M) .... Enrolled Nurse (Mental)
ERD .... Emergency Reserve Decoration
ESC .... Ecole Superieure de Commerce
ESMI .... Elderly, Sick and Mentally Infirm
Ecum .... Ecumenical
Ecumenics
Ecumenism
Ed .... Editor
Editorial
EdD .... Doctor of Education (also see DEd)
Edin .... (Diocese of) Edinburgh
Edm .... Edmund
Edmund's
Educn .... Education
Educational
Edw .... Edward
Edward's
Eliz .... Elizabeth
Elizabeth's
Em .... Emmanuel
Emb .... Embassy
EngTech .... Engineering Technician
Episc .... Episcopal
Episcopalian
Esq .... Esquire
etc .... et cetera
Eur .... (Diocese of) Gibraltar in Europe
Europe
European
Ev .... Evangelist
Evangelists
Evangelist's
Evang .... Evangelical
Evangelism
Ex .... (Diocese of) Exeter
Ex-paroch .... Extra-parochial
Exam .... Examining
Exec .... Executive
Exors .... Executors
Exper .... Experimental
Ext .... Extension

F

F&HE .... Further and Higher Education
FAA .... Fellow of the Institution of Administrative Accountants
FACC .... Fellow of the American College of Cardiology
FACCA .... Fellow of the Association of Certified and Corporate Accountants (now see FCCA)
FACOG .... Fellow of the American College of Obstetricians and Gynaecologists
FAEB .... Fellow of the Academy of Environmental Biology (India)
FAIW .... Fellow of the Australian Institute of Welfare and Community Workers
FASI .... Fellow of the Architects' and Surveyors' Institute
FBA .... Fellow of the British Academy
FBCO .... Fellow of the British College of Ophthalmic Opticians (Optometrists)
FBCS .... Fellow of the British Computer Society
FBDO .... Fellow of the Association of British Dispensing Opticians
FBIM .... Fellow of the British Institute of Management (formerly MBIM)
FBIS .... Fellow of the British Interplanetary Society
FBOA .... Fellow of the British Optical Association
FBPICS .... Fellow of the British Production and Inventory Control Society
FBPsS .... Fellow of the British Psychological Society
FCA .... Fellow of the Institute of Chartered Accountants
FCCA .... Fellow of the Chartered Association of Certified Accountants (formerly FACCA)
FCFI .... Fellow of the Clothing and Footwear Institute
FCIArb .... Fellow of the Chartered Institute of Arbitrators
FCIB .... Fellow of the Corporation of Insurance Brokers
FCII .... Fellow of the Chartered Insurance Institute
FCILA .... Fellow of the Chartered Institute of Loss Adjusters
FCIM .... Fellow of the Chartered Institute of Marketing (formerly FInstM)
FCIPA .... Fellow of the Chartered Institute of Patent Agents (now see CPA)
FCIS .... Fellow of the Institute of Chartered Secretaries and Administrators
FCIT .... Fellow of the Chartered Institute of Transport
FCMA .... Fellow of the Institute of Cost and Management Accountants
FCO .... Foreign and Commonwealth Office
FCP .... Fellow of the College of Preceptors
FCollP .... Ordinary Fellow of the College of Preceptors
FDS .... Fellow in Dental Surgery
FDSRCS .... Fellow in Dental Surgery of the Royal College of Surgeons of England
FE .... Further Education
FEPA .... Fellow of the Evangelical Preachers' Association
FETC .... Further Education Teacher's Certificate
FEng .... Fellow of the Royal Academy (formerly Fellowship) of Engineering
FFARCS .... Fellow of the Faculty of Anaesthetists, Royal College of Surgeons of England
FFChM .... Fellow of the Faculty of Church Music
FFPHM .... Fellow of the Faculty of Public Health Medicine
FFS .... Full Faith Society
FGA .... Fellow of the Gemmalogical Association
FGS .... Fellow of the Geological Society of London
FHSM or FHA .... Fellow, Institute of Health Service Management (formerly Administrators)
FIA .... Fellow of the Institute of Actuaries
FIBD .... Fellow of the Institute of British Decorators
FIBMS .... Fellow of the Institute of Bio-Medial Sciences
FIBiol .... Fellow of the Institute of Biology
FICE .... Fellow of the Institution of Civil Engineers
FICM .... Fellow of the Institution of Commercial Managers
FIChemE .... Fellow of the Institution of Chemical Engineers
FIDiagE .... Fellow of the Institute of Diagnostic Engineers
FIED .... Fellow of the Institution of Engineering Designers
FIEE .... Fellow of the Institution of Electrical Engineers (formerly FIERE)
FIEEE .... Fellow of the Institute of Electrical and Electronics Engineers (NY)
FIERE .... Fellow of the Institution of Electronic and Radio Engineers (now see FIEE)
FIFireE .... Fellow of the Institution of Fire Engineers
FIHospE .... Fellow of the Institute of Hospital Engineering
FIIM .... Fellow of the Institution of Industrial Managers (formerly FIPlantE)
FIL .... Fellow of the Institute of Linguists
FILEx .... Fellow of the Institute of Legal Executives
FIMA .... Fellow of the Institute of Mathematics and its Applications
FIMEMME .... Fellow of the Institution of Mining Electrical and Mining Mechanical Engineers
FIMI .... Fellow of the Institute of the Motor Industry
FIMLS .... Fellow of the Institute of Medical Laboratory Sciences
FIMM .... Fellow of the Institution of Mining and Metallurgy
FIMS .... Fellow of the Institute of Management Specialists
FIMSSA .... Fellow of the Institute of Mine Surveyors of South Africa
FIMarE .... Fellow of the Institute of Marine Engineers
FIMechE .... Fellow of the Institution of Mechanical Engineers
FIMgt .... Fellow of the Institute of Management
FIPD .... Fellow of the Institute of Personnel and Development
FIPEM .... Fellow of the Institute of Physics and Engineering in Medicine
FIPM .... Fellow of the Institute of Personnel Management
FIPlantE .... Fellow of the Institution of Plant Engineers (now see FIIM)
FIQA .... Fellow of the Institute of Quality Assurance
FIST .... Fellow of the Institute of Science and Technology
FIStructE .... Fellow of the Institution of Structural Engineers
FITD .... Fellow of the Institute of Training and Development
FIWSc .... Fellow of the Institute of Wood Science
FInstD .... Fellow of the Institute of Directors
FInstE .... Fellow of the Institute of Energy
FInstFF .... Fellow of the Institute of Freight Forwarders Limited
FInstM .... Fellow of the Institute of Marketing (now see FCIM)
FInstP .... Fellow of the Institute of Physics
FInstSMM .... Fellow of the Institute of Sales and Marketing Management
FKC .... Fellow of King's College, London
FLA .... Fellow of the Library Association
FLAME .... Family Life and Marriage Education
FLAS .... Fellow of the Chartered Land Agents' Society (now see FRICS)
FLCM .... Fellow of the London College of Music
FLIA .... Fellow of the Life Insurance Association

FLS .... Fellow of the Linnean Society
FMA .... Fellow of the Museums Association
FNI .... Fellow of the Nautical Institute
FPACert .... Family Planning Association Certificate
FPS .... Fellow of the Pharmaceutical Society of Great Britain
FPWI .... Fellow of the Permanent Way Institute
FPhS .... Fellow of the Philosophical Society of England
FRACI .... Fellow of the Royal Australian Chemical Institute
FRAI .... Fellow of the Royal Anthropological Institute
FRAM .... Fellow of the Royal Academy of Music
FRAS .... Fellow of the Royal Asiatic Society
Fellow of the Royal Astronomical Society
FRAeS .... Fellow of the Royal Aeronautical Society
FRCGP .... Fellow of the Royal College of General Practitioners
FRCM .... Fellow of the Royal College of Music
FRCO .... Fellow of the Royal College of Organists
FRCOG .... Fellow of the Royal College of Obstetricians and Gynaecologists
FRCOpth .... Fellow of the Royal College of Opthalmologists
FRCP .... Fellow of the Royal College of Physicians, London
FRCPEd .... Fellow of the Royal College of Physicians, Edinburgh
FRCPGlas .... Fellow of the Royal College of Physicians and Surgeons, Glasgow (also see FRCSGlas)
FRCPath .... Fellow of the Royal College of Pathologists
FRCPsych .... Fellow of the Royal College of Psychiatrists
FRCR .... Fellow of the Royal College of Radiologists
FRCS .... Fellow of the Royal College of Physicians and Surgeons of England
FRCSE or FRCSEd Fellow of the Royal College of Surgeons of Edinburgh
FRCSGlas .... Fellow of the Royal College of Physicians and Surgeons, Glasgow (also see FRCPGlas)
FRCVS .... Fellow of the Royal College of Veterinary Surgeons
FRGS .... Fellow of the Royal Geographical Society
FRHS .... Fellow of the Royal Horticultural Society
FRHistS .... Fellow of the Royal Historical Society
FRIAS .... Fellow of the Royal Incorporation of Architects of Scotland
FRIBA .... Fellow of the Royal Institute of British Architects
FRIC .... Fellow of the Royal Institute of Chemistry (now see FRSC)
FRICS .... Fellow of the Royal Institution of Chartered Surveyors (formerly FLAS and FSI)
FRIN .... Fellow of the Royal Institute of Navigation
FRINA .... Fellow of the Royal Institution of Naval Architects
FRIPHH .... Fellow of the Royal Institute of Public Health and Hygiene
FRMetS .... Fellow of the Royal Meteorological Society
FRS .... Fellow of the Royal Society
FRSA .... Fellow of the Royal Society of Arts
FRSC .... Fellow of the Royal Society of Canada
Fellow of the Royal Society of Chemistry (formerly FRIC)
FRSE .... Fellow of the Royal Society of Edinburgh
FRSH .... Fellow of the Royal Society for the Promotion of Health
FRSL .... Fellow of the Royal Society of Literature
FRSM .... Fellow of the Royal Society of Medicine
FRTPI .... Fellow of the Royal Town Planning Institute
FSA .... Fellow of the Society of Antiquaries
FSAScot .... Fellow of the Royal Society of Antiquaries of Scotland
FSCA .... Fellow of the Royal Society of Company and Commercial Accountants
FSI .... Fellow of the Chartered Surveyors' Institution (now see FRICS)
FSJ .... Fellowship of St John the Evangelist
FSMC .... Freeman of the Spectacle-Makers' Company
FSR .... Fellowship Diploma of the Society of Radiographers
FSS .... Fellow of the Royal Statistical Society
FTC .... Flying Training Command
Full Technological Certificate, City and Guilds of the London Institute
FTCD .... Fellow of Trinity College, Dublin
FTCL .... Fellow of Trinity College of Music, London
FTII .... Fellow of the Institute of Taxation
FTSC .... Fellow of the Tonic sol-fa College
FVCM .... Fellow of the Victoria College of Music
FWeldI .... Fellow of the Institute of Welding
Fell .... Fellow
Fitzw .... Fitzwilliam
Foundn .... Foundation
Fran .... Francis
Francis's

G

G&C .... Gonville and Caius
GB .... Great Britain
GBSM .... Graduate of the Birmingham School of Music
GCMG .... Knight Grand Cross of the Order of St Michael and St George
GCVO .... Knight Grand Cross of the Royal Victorian Order
GDip .... Gemmology Diploma
GDipGP .... Graduate Diploma in Gestalt Psychotherapy
GDipP .... Graduate Diploma in Physiotherapy
GFS .... Girls' Friendly Society
GGSM .... Graduate Diploma of the Guildhall School of Music and Drama
GIBiol .... Graduate of the Institute of Biology
GIFireE .... Graduate of the Institute of Fire Engineers
GIMechE .... Graduate of the Institution of Mechanical Engineers
GIPE .... Graduate of the Institution of Production Engineers
GLCM .... Graduate Diploma of the London College of Music
GM .... George Medal
GNSM .... Graduate of the Northern School of Music
GRIC .... Graduate Membership of the Royal Institute of Chemistry
GRNCM .... Graduate of the Royal Northern College of Music
GRSC .... Graduate of the Royal School of Chemistry
GRSM .... Graduate of the Royal Schools of Music
GSM .... (Member of) the Guildhall School of Music and Drama
GSSR .... Graduate of the Scottish School of Reflexology
GTCL .... Graduate Diploma of Trinity College of Music, London
Gabr .... Gabriel
Gabriel's
Gd .... Good
Gen .... General
Geo .... George
George's
Gib .... Gibraltar
Glam .... Glamorgan
Glas .... (Diocese of) Glasgow and Galloway
Glasgow
Glos .... Gloucestershire
Glouc .... (Diocese of) Gloucester
Golds .... Goldsmiths'
Gov .... Governor
Gp .... Group
Gr .... Grammar
Grad LI .... Graduate of the Landscape Institute
GradCertEd(FE) Graduate Certificate in Education (Further Education)
GradDipEd .... Postgraduate Diploma of Education (Australia)
GradIEE .... Graduate of the Institution of Electrical Engineers
GradIMI .... Graduate of the Institute of the Motor Industry
GradIPM .... Graduate of the Institute of Personnel Management
GradIT .... Graduate of the Institute of Transport
Greg .... Gregory
Gregory's
Gt .... Great
Gtr .... Greater
Guildf .... (Diocese of) Guildford

H

H .... Holy
H&FE .... Higher and Further Education
HA .... Health Authority
HDipABiol .... Higher Diploma in Applied Biology
HDipEd .... Higher Diploma in Education
HDipHV .... Higher Diploma in Health Visit Studies
HDipRE .... Higher Diploma in Religious Education
HE .... Higher Education
HIV .... Human Immunodeficiency Virus
HM .... Her (or His) Majesty
HMI .... Her (or His) Majesty's Inspector (or Inspectorate)
HMS .... Her (or His) Majesty's Ship
HNC .... Higher National Certificate
HND .... Higher National Diploma
HND(IMechE) .. Higher National Diploma, Institution of Mechanical Engineers
HQ .... Headquarters
HTC .... Higher Technical Certificate
HTV .... Harlech Television

HVCert .... Health Visitor's Certificate
Hants .... Hampshire
Hatf .... Hatfield
Hd .... Head
Heref .... (Diocese of) Hereford
Hertf .... Hertford
Herts .... Hertfordshire
Hist .... Historical
History
Ho .... House
Hon .... Honorary
Honourable
Hon RCM .... Honorary Member of the Royal College of Music
HonDLaws .... Honorary Doctor of Laws
HonFChS .... Honorary Fellow of the Society of Chiropodists
HonLMStJ .... Honorary Life Member of the St John's Ambulance Association
Hosp .... Hospital
HospCC .... Hospital Chaplaincy Certificate
Hunts .... Huntingdonshire

I

I .... Incumbent
IAAP .... International Association for Analytical Psychology
IBA .... Independent Broadcasting Authority
ICF .... Industry Churches Forum (formerly Industrial Christian Fellowship)
ICM .... Irish Church Missions
ICS .... Intercontinental Church Society
IDC .... Inter-Diocesan Certificate
IDWAL .... Inter-Diocesan West African Link
IEng .... Incorporated Engineer (formerly TEng(CEI))
IGAP .... Independent Group of Analytical Psychology
ILEA .... Inner London Education Authority
IMinE .... Institution of Mining Engineers
IPFA .... Member of the Chartered Institute of Public Finance and Accountancy
ISM .... Imperial Service Medal
ISO .... Imperial Service Order
ITV .... Independent Television
IVF .... Inter-Varsity Fellowship of Evangelical Unions (now see UCCF)
IVS .... International Voluntary Service
Imp .... Imperial
Inc .... Incorporated
Ind .... Industrial
Industry
Info .... Information
Insp .... Inspector
Inst .... Institute
Institution
Intercon .... Intercontinental
Internat .... International
Interpr .... Interpretation
Is .... Island
Islands
Isle
Isles

J

JCL .... Licentiate in Canon Law
JD .... Doctor of Jurisprudence
JEM .... Jerusalem and the East Mission (now see JMECA)
JMECA .... Jerusalem and Middle East Church Association (formerly JEM)
JP .... Justice of the Peace
Jas .... James
James's
Jes .... Jesus
Jo .... John
John's
Jos .... Joseph
Joseph's
Jt or jt .... Joint
Jun .... Junior

K

K .... King
King's
K, E & A .... (Diocese of) Kilmore, Elphin and Ardagh
KBE .... Knight Commander of the Order of the British Empire
KCB .... Knight Commander of the Order of the Bath
KCMG .... Knight Commander of the Order of St Michael and St George
KCT .... Knight Commander of the Order of the Templars
KCVO .... Knight Commander of the Royal Victorian Order
KIAD .... Kent Institute of Art and Design
KLJ .... Knight of the Order of St Lazarus of Jerusalem
KPM .... King's Police Medal
KStJ .... Knight of the Most Venerable Order of the Hospital of St John of Jerusalem
Kath .... Katharine/Katherine
Katharine's/Katherine's
Kt .... Knight

L

L & K .... (Diocese of) Limerick and Killaloe (united dioceses of Limerick, Ardfert, Aghadoe, Killaloe, Kilfenora, Clonfert, Kilmacduagh and Emly)
LASI .... Licentiate of the Ambulance Service Institute
LBIPP .... Licentiate of the British Institute of Professional Photography
LCC .... London County Council
LCP .... Licentiate of the College of Preceptors
LCST .... Licentiate of the College of Speech Therapists
LDS .... Licentiate in Dental Surgery
LDSRCSEng .... Licentiate in Dental Surgery of the Royal College of Surgeons of England
LDiv .... Licentiate in Divinity
LEA .... Local Education Authority
LEP .... Local Ecumenical Project
LGCM .... Lesbian and Gay Christian Movement
LGSM .... Licentiate of the Guildhall School of Music and Drama
LHSM .... Licentiate of the Institute of Health Services Management
LICeram .... Licentiate of the Institute of Ceramics
LLA .... Lady Literate in Arts
LLAM .... Licentiate of the London Academy of Music and Dramatic Art
LLB .... Bachelor of Laws
LLCM .... Licentiate of the London College of Music
LLD .... Doctor of Laws
LLM .... Master of Laws
LMH .... Lady Margaret Hall
LMPA .... Licentiate Master of the Photographers' Association
LNSM .... Local Non-stipendiary Minister (or Ministry)
LOROS .... Leicestershire Organization for the Relief of Suffering
LRAM .... Licentiate of the Royal Academy of Music
LRCP .... Licentiate of the Royal College of Physicians
LRCPI .... Licentiate of the Royal College of Physicians of Ireland
LRSC .... Licentiate of the Royal Society of Chemistry
LSE .... London School of Economics and Political Science
LSHTM .... London School of Hygiene and Tropical Medicine
LSIAD .... Licentiate of the Society of Industrial Artists and Designers
LSMF .... Licentiate of the State Medical Faculty
LST .... Licentiate in Theology (also see LTh)
LTCL .... Licentiate of the Trinity College of Music, London
LTh .... Licentiate in Theology (also see LST)
LVCM .... Licentiate of the Victoria College of Music
LVO .... Lieutenant of the Royal Victorian Order
LWCMD .... Licentiate of the Welsh College of Music and Drama
Lamp .... Lampeter
Lanc .... Lancaster
Lancs .... Lancashire
Laur .... Laurence
Laurence's
Lawr .... Lawrence
Lawrence's
Ld .... Lord
Ldr .... Leader
Lect .... Lecturer
Leic .... (Diocese of) Leicester
Leics .... Leicestershire
Leon .... Leonard
Leonard's
LesL .... Licencie es Lettres
Lib .... Librarian
Library
Lic .... Licence
Licensed
Licentiate
LicIM&C .... Licentiate of the Institute of Measurement and Control
LicSTh .... Licentiate in Sacred Theology
LicScCat .... Licence en Sciences Catechetiques
LicTh .... Licence in Theology
Lich .... (Diocese of) Lichfield
Linc .... (Diocese of) Lincoln
Lincs .... Lincolnshire
Lit .... Literature
LittD .... Doctor of Letters (also see DLitt)
Liturg .... Liturgical
Liv .... (Diocese of) Liverpool
Llan .... (Diocese of) Llandaff
Lon .... (Diocese of) London
Loughb .... Loughborough
Lt .... Lieutenant
Little
Ltd .... Limited
Luth .... Lutheran

M

M & K .... (Diocese of) Meath and Kildare
MA .... Master of Arts
MA(Ed) .... Master of Arts in Education
MA(Theol) .... Master of Arts in Theology
MAAIS .... Member of the Association of Archaeological Illustrators and Surveyors
MAAR .... Member of the American Academy of Religion
MAAT .... Member of the Association of Accounting Technicians
MACC .... Member of the Australian College of Chaplains

MACE............ Member of the Australian College of Education
MACT............ Member of the Association of Corporate Treasurers
MAJA............ Member of the Association of Jungian Analysts
MAMIT........... Member of the Associate of Meat Inspectors Trust
MAOT............ Member of the Association of Occupational Therapists (now see MBAOT)
MAPCC........... Member of the Association for Pastoral Care and Counselling
MASCH........... Member of the Australian Society of Clinical Hypnotherapists
MATA............ Member of the Animal Technicians' Association
MATCA........... Member of the Air Traffic Control Association
MArch............ Master of Architecture
MB............... Bachelor of Medicine (also see BM)
MB,BS or MB,ChB.......... Conjoint degree of Bachelor of Medicine, Bachelor of Surgery
MBA.............. Master of Business Administration
MBAC............ Member of the British Association for Counselling
MBAOT........... Member of the British Association of Occupational Therapists (formerly MAOT)
MBAP............ Member of the British Association of Psychotherapists
MBASW........... Member of the British Association of Social Workers
MBATOD.......... Member of the British Association of Teachers of the Deaf
MBC.............. Metropolitan (or Municipal) Borough Council
MBCS............ Member of the British Computer Society
MBE.............. Member of the Order of the British Empire
MBHI............ Member of the British Horological Institute
MBIM............ Member of the British Institute of Management (formerly AMBIM; now see FBIM)
MBKSTS.......... Member of the British Kinematograph, Sound and Television Society
MBPsS........... Member of the British Psychological Society
MBTI............. Licensed Administrator of the Myers Briggs Type Indicator
MC............... Military Cross
MCA.............. Member of the Institute of Chartered Accountants
MCB.............. Master in Clinical Biochemistry
MCBiblAA........ Member of the Catholic Biblical Association of America
MCCEd........... Member of the Craft College of Education
MCD............. Master of Civic Design
MCE.............. Master of Civil Engineering
MCIBSE.......... Member of the Chartered Institute of Building Service Engineers
MCIM............ Member of the Chartered Institute of Marketing (formerly MInstM)
MCIMA........... Member of the Chartered Institute of Management Accountants
MCIOB........... Member of the Chartered Institute of Building
MCIT............. Member of the Chartered Institute of Transport
MCS.............. Master of Christian Studies
MCSD............ Member of the Chartered Society of Designers

MCSP............ Member of the Chartered Society of Physiotherapy
MCST............ Member of the College of Speech Therapists
MCThA........... Member of the Clinical Theology Association
MChS............. Member of the Society of Chiropodists
MChemA......... Master in Chemical Analysis
MCollP........... Member of the College of Preceptors
MCom............ Master of Commerce
MD............... Doctor of Medicine
MDCT............ Manager's Diploma in Ceramic Technology
MDiv............. Master of Divinity
MEHS............ Member of the Ecclesiastical History Society
MESB............ Member of the English Speaking Board
MEd.............. Master of Education
MEng............. Master of Engineering
MFA.............. Master of Fine Art
MFBA............ Member of the Freshwater Biological Association
MFCM............ Member of the Faculty of Community Medicine
MHCIMA......... Member of the Hotel, Catering and Institutional Management Association
MHSA............ Member of the Hymn Society of America
MHSGBI......... Member of the Hymn Society of Great Britain and Ireland
MHums........... Master of Humanities
MIA.............. Malawi Institute of Architects
MIAAP........... Member of the International Association for Analytical Psychology
MIAAS........... Member of the Incorporated Association of Architects and Surveyors
MIBC............. Member of the Institute of Business Counsellors
MIBCO........... Member of the Institution of Building Control Officers
MIBF............. Member of the Institute of British Foundrymen
MIBiol............ Member of the Institute of Biology
MICA............. Member of the International Cartographic Association
MICE............. Member of the Institution of Civil Engineers (formerly AMICE)
MICFM........... Member of the Institute of Charity Fundraising Managers
MICFor.......... Member of the Institute of Chartered Foresters
MICS............. Member of the Institute of Chartered Shipbrokers
MIChemE........ Member of the Institution of Chemical Engineers
MICorrST........ Member of the Institution of Corrosion Science and Technology
MIDPM........... Member of the Institute of Data Processing Management
MIE.............. Member of the Institute of Engineers and Technicians
MIEE............. Member of the Institution of Electrical Engineers (formerly AMIEE & MIERE)
MIEEE............ Member of the Institute of Electrical and Electronics Engineers (NY)
MIEH............. Member of the Institute of Environmental Health
MIERE............ Member of the Institution of Electronic and Radio Engineers (now see MIEE)

MIElecIE......... Corporate Member of the Institution of Electrical and Electronics Incorporated Engineers
MIEx............. Member of the Institute of Export
MIGasE.......... Member of the Institution of Gas Engineers
MIH.............. Member of the Institute of Housing
MIHE............. Member of the Institute of Health Education
MIHEEM......... Member of the Institute of Healthcare Engineering and Estate Management
MIHT............. Member of the Institution of Highways and Transportation
MIHospE......... Member of the Institute of Hospital Engineers
MIIExE........... Member of the Institute of Incorporated Executive Engineers
MIIM............. Member of the Institution of Industrial Managers
MIL.............. Member of the Institute of Linguists
MIM.............. Member of the Institute of Metals (formerly Institution of Metallurgists)
MIMA............ Member of the Institute of Management Accountants
MIMC............ Member of the Institute of Management Consultants
MIMI............. Member of the Institute of the Motor Industry
MIMM........... Member of the Institution of Mining and Metallurgy
MIMarE.......... Member of the Institute of Marine Engineers
MIMechE......... Member of the Institution of Mechanical Engineers (formerly AMIMechE)
MIMfgE.......... Member of the Institution of Manufacturing Engineers
MIMgt........... Member of the Institute of Management
MIMunE.......... Member of the Institution of Municipal Engineers
MINucE.......... Member of the Institute of Nuclear Engineers
MIOSH........... Member of the Institution of Occupational Safety and Health
MIOT............. Member of the Institute of Operating Theatre Technicians
MIPD............. Member of the Institute of Personnel and Development
MIPI.............. Member of the Institute of Private Investigators
MIPR............. Member of the Institute of Public Relations
MIProdE......... Member of the Institution of Production Engineers
MIQA............ Member of the Institute of Quality Assurance
MISE............. Member of the Institute of Sales Engineers
MISM............ Member of the Institute of Supervisory Management
MISW............ Member of the Institute of Social Welfare
MIStructE....... Member of the Institute of Structural Engineers
MITD............ Member of the Institute of Training and Development
MITE............. Member of the Institution of Electrical and Electronics Technician Engineers
MITMA.......... Member of the Institute of Trade Mark Agents
MITSA........... Member of the Institute of Trading Standards Administration
MIWEM......... Member of the Institution of Water and Environmental Management

MInstAM .... Member of the Institute of Administrative Management
MInstC(Glas) .... Member of the Institute of Counselling (Glasgow)
MInstE .... Member of the Institute of Energy
MInstGA .... Member of the Institute of Group Analysis
MInstM .... Member of the Institute of Marketing (now see MCIM)
MInstP .... Member of the Institute of Physics
MInstPC .... Member of the Institute of Psychotherapy and Counselling
MInstPS .... Corporate Member of the Institute of Purchasing and Supply
MInstPkg .... Member of the Institute of Packaging
MLS .... Master of Library Studies
MLawSoc .... Member of the Law Society
MLitt .... Master of Letters
MM .... Military Medal
MMCET .... Martyrs' Memorial and Church of England Trust
MMS .... Member of the Institute of Management Services
MMin .... Master of Ministry
MMus .... Master of Music (also see MusM)
MNAAL .... Member of the North American Academy of Liturgy
MNACH .... Member of the National Association of Clergy Hypnotherapists
MNFSH .... Member of the National Federation of Spiritual Healers
MOD .... Ministry of Defence
MPS .... Member of the Pharmaceutical Society (now see MRPharmS)
MPhil .... Master of Philosophy
MPsychSc .... Master of Psychological Science
MRAC .... Member of the Royal Agricultural College
MRAeS .... Member of the Royal Aeronautical Society
MRCGP .... Member of the Royal College of General Practitioners
MRCO .... Member of the Royal College of Organists
MRCOG .... Member of the Royal College of Obstetricians and Gynaecologists
MRCP .... Member of the Royal College of Physicians
MRCPath .... Member of the Royal College of Pathologists
MRCPsych .... Member of the Royal College of Psychiatrists
MRCS .... Member of the Royal College of Surgeons
MRCSE .... Member of the Royal College of Surgeons of Edinburgh
MRCVS .... Member of the Royal College of Veterinary Surgeons
MRHS .... Member of the Royal Horticultural Society
MRIA .... Member of the Royal Irish Academy
MRIC .... Member of the Royal Institute of Chemistry (formerly ARIC; now see MRSC)
MRIN .... Member of the Royal Institute of Navigation
MRINA .... Member of the Royal Institution of Naval Architects
MRIPHH .... Member of the Royal Institute of Public Health and Hygiene
MRPharmS ...... Member of the Royal Pharmaceutical Society (formerly MPS)
MRSC .... Member of the Royal Society of Chemistry (formerly MRIC)
MRSH .... Member of the Royal Society for the Promotion of Health
MRSL .... Member of the Order of the Republic of Sierra Leone
MRST .... Member of the Royal Society of Teachers
MRTPI .... Member of the Royal Town Planning Institute
MRTS .... Member of the Royal Television Society
MS .... Master of Science (USA)
Master of Surgery
MSAICE .... Member of the South African Institution of Civil Engineers
MSAPP .... Member of the Society of Advanced Psychotherapy Practitioners
MSAnPsych ...... Member of the Society of Analytical Psychology
MSBC .... Member of the Society of British Cartographers
MSBiblLit .... Member of the Society of Biblical Literature
MSE .... Minister (or Ministers) in Secular Employment
MSERT .... Member of the Society of Electronic and Radio Technicians
MSHAA .... Member of the Society of Hearing Aid Audiologists
MSIAD .... Member of the Society of Industrial Artists and Designers
MSLS .... Member of the Society of Liturgical Study
MSOSc .... Member of the Society of Ordained Scientists
MSOTS .... Member of the Society for Old Testament Study
MSR .... Member of the Society of Radiographers
MSSCLE .... Member of the Society for the Study of the Crusades and the Latin East
MSSCh .... Member of the School of Surgical Chiropody
MSSTh .... Member of the Society for the Study of Theology
MSTSD .... Member of the Society of Teachers of Speech and Drama
MSUC .... Member of the Society of (University) Cartographers
MSW .... Master of Social Work
MSacMus .... Master of Sacred Music
MSc .... Master of Science
MSc(Econ) .... Master of Science in Economics
MSocSc .... Master of Social Sciences
MSocWork .... Master of Social Work (USA)
MSt .... Master of Studies
MTD .... Master of Transport Design
Midwife Teacher's Diploma
MTS .... Master of Theological Studies
MTech .... Master of Technology
MTh or MTheol Master of Theology (also see STM and ThM)
MU .... Mothers' Union
MVI .... Member of the Victoria Institute
MVO .... Member of the Royal Victorian Order
MYPS .... Member of the Yorkshire Philosophical Society
Magd .... Magdalen/Magdalene
Magdalen's/Magdalene's
Man .... (Diocese of) Manchester
Man Dir .... Managing Director
Mansf .... Mansfield
Marg .... Margaret
Margaret's
Mass .... Massachusetts (USA)
Matt .... Matthew
Matthew's
Mert .... Merton
MesL .... Lettres Modernes
Meth .... Methodist
Metrop .... Metropolitan
Mich .... Michael
Michael's
Michael and All Angels
Middlesb .... Middlesbrough
Middx .... Middlesex
Midl .... Midlands
Mil .... Military
Min .... Minister
Ministries
Ministry
Minor
Minl .... Ministerial
Miss .... Mission
Missions
Missionary
Missr .... Missioner
Mon .... (Diocese of) Monmouth
Mor .... (Diocese of) Moray, Ross and Caithness
Mt .... Mount
MusB or MusBac .... Bachelor of Music (also see BMus)
MusD or MusDoc .... Doctor of Music
MusM .... Master of Music (also see MMus)

N

N .... North
Northern
NACRO .... National Association for the Care and Rehabilitation of Offenders
NC(BS) .... National Certificate in Business Studies (Irish Republic)
NCA .... National Certificate in Agriculture
NCEC .... National Christian Education Council
NCTJ .... National Certificate for the Training of Journalists
NDA .... National Diploma in Agriculture
NDAD .... National Diploma in Art and Design
NDD .... National Diploma in Design
NDFOM .... National Diploma in Farm Organisation and Management
NDH .... National Diploma in Horticulture
NDN .... National District Nurse Certificate
NDTJ .... National Diploma in the Training of Journalists
NE .... North East
NHS .... National Health Service
NIDA .... National Institute of Dramatic Art
NNEB .... National Nursery Examination Board
NRD .... National Registered Designer
NS .... Nova Scotia (Canada)
NSM .... Non-stipendiary Minister (or Ministry)
NSPCC .... National Society for the Prevention of Cruelty to Children
NSW .... New South Wales (Australia)
NT .... New Testament
NTMTC .... North Thames Ministerial Training Course
NUI .... National University of Ireland
NUU .... New University of Ulster
NW .... North West/Northwestern
NWT .... North West Territories (Canada)
NY .... New York (USA)
NZ .... New Zealand
Nat .... National

Nath .... Nathanael/Nathaniel
Nathanael's/Nathaniel's
née .... Maiden name
Newc .... (Diocese of) Newcastle
Nic .... Nicholas/Nicolas
Nicholas's/Nicolas's
Nor .... (Diocese of) Norwich
Northants .... Northamptonshire
Northd .... Northumberland
Northn .... Northampton
Nottm .... Nottingham
Notts .... Nottinghamshire
Nuff .... Nuffield

O

OBE .... (Officer of) the Order of the British Empire
OBI .... Order of British India
OCF .... Officiating Chaplain to the Forces
OGS .... Oratory of the Good Shepherd
OHP .... Order of the Holy Paraclete
OM .... Order of Merit
OM(Ger) .... Order of Merit of Germany
OMF .... Overseas Missionary Fellowship
ONC .... Ordinary National Certificate
OND .... Ordinary National Diploma
OSB .... Order of St Benedict
OSJM .... (Prelate of) the Order of St John of Malta
OSP .... Order of St Paul
OStJ .... (Officer of) the Order of the Hospital of St John of Jerusalem
OT .... Old Testament
Offg .... Officiating
Offic .... Officiate
Or .... Oriel
Ord .... Ordained
Ordinands
Ordination
Org .... Organizer
Organizing
Ox .... (Diocese of) Oxford
Oxon .... Oxfordshire

P

P .... Patron(s)
Priest
p .... Ordained Priest
P in O .... Priest in Ordinary
P-in-c .... Priest-in-charge
PACTA .... Professional Associate of the Clinical Theology Association
PBS .... Pengeran Bintang Sarawak (Companion of the Order of the Star, Sarawak)
PC .... Perpetual Curate
Privy Counsellor
PCC .... Parochial Church Council
PCVG .... Postgraduate Certificate of Vocational Guidance
PEV .... Provincial Episcopal Visitor
PGCE .... Postgraduate Certificate in Education
PGDE .... Postgraduate Diploma in Education
PGDHE .... Postgraduate Diploma in Healthcare Ethics
PM .... Priest Missioner
PO .... Post Office
PPAC .... Post Professional Award in Counselling
PQCSW .... Post-Qualifying Certificate in Social Work
PV .... Priest Vicar
Par .... Parish
Parishes
Paroch .... Parochial
Past .... Pastoral
Patr .... Patrick
Patrick's
Patronage
Pb .... Presbyterian
Pemb .... Pembroke
Penn .... Pennsylvania (USA)
Perm .... Permission
Pet .... (Diocese of) Peterborough
Peter
Peter's
Peterho .... Peterhouse
PhC .... Pharmaceutical Chemist
PhD .... Doctor of Philosophy (also see DPhil)
PhL .... Licentiate of Philosophy
Phil .... Philip
Philip's
plc .... public limited company
Poly .... Polytechnic
Portsm .... (Diocese of) Portsmouth
Preb .... Prebendary
Prec .... Precentor
Prep .... Preparatory
Pres .... President
Prin .... Principal
Pris .... Prison
Prisons
Prof .... Professor
Professorial
Progr .... Programme
Programmes
Prop .... Proprietary
Prov .... Province
Provincial
Pt .... Point

Q

QC .... Queen's Counsel
QFSM .... Queen's Fire Service Medal for Distinguished Service
QGM .... Queen's Gallantry Medal
QHC .... Queen's Honorary Chaplain
QN .... Queen's Nurse
QPFF .... Qualified Professional Fire-Fighter
QPM .... Queen's Police Medal
QSM .... Queen's Service Medal
QUB .... The Queen's University of Belfast
QVO .... Queen's Service Order (NZ)
Qu .... Queen
Queen's
Queens'

R

R .... Rector
Royal
R and D .... Research and Development
R of O .... Reserve of Officers
R&SChTrust .... Rochester and Southwark Church Trust
RAAF .... Royal Australian Air Force
RAChD .... Royal Army Chaplains' Department
RAD or RADD. Royal Association in Aid of Deaf People (formerly Deaf and Dumb)
RAEC .... Royal Army Educational Corps
RAF .... Royal Air Force
RAFVR .... Royal Air Force Volunteer Reserve
RAM .... (Member of) the Royal Academy of Music
RC .... Roman Catholic
RCA .... Royal College of Art
RCAF .... Royal Canadian Air Force
RCM .... Royal College of Music
RCN .... Royal Canadian Navy
Royal College of Nursing
RCS .... Royal College of Surgeons of England
RCSE .... Royal College of Surgeons of Edinburgh
RD .... Royal Navy Reserve Decoration
Rural Dean
RE .... Religious Education
RGN .... Registered General Nurse
RHV .... Registered Health Visitor
RIA .... Royal Irish Academy
RIBA .... (Member of) the Royal Institute of British Architects (formerly ARIBA)
RM .... Registered Midwife
RMA or RMC .. Royal Military Academy (formerly College), Sandhurst
RMCM .... Royal Manchester College of Music
RMCS .... Royal Military College of Science, Shrivenham
RMN .... Registered Mental Nurse
RN .... Registered Nurse (Canada)
Royal Navy
RNIB .... Royal National Institute for the Blind
RNLI .... Royal National Lifeboat Institution
RNR .... Royal Naval Reserve
RNT .... Registered Nurse Tutor
RNVR .... Royal Naval Volunteer Reserve
RS .... Religious Studies
RSCM .... Royal School of Church Music
RSCN .... Registered Sick Children's Nurse
RTC .... Religious Teaching Certificate
RTE .... Radio Telefis Eireann
RVC .... Royal Veterinary College
RVO .... Royal Victorian Order
Reg .... Registered
Relig .... Religious
Relns .... Relations
Rem .... Remand
Rep .... Representative
Res .... Residence
Resident
Residential
Residentiary
Resp .... Responsibility
Resurr .... Resurrection
Revd .... Reverend
Rich .... Richard
Richard's
Rob .... Robinson
Roch .... (Diocese of) Rochester
Rt .... Right
Rtd or rtd .... Retired

S

S .... South
Southern
S & B .... (Diocese of) Swansea and Brecon
S & M .... (Diocese of) Sodor and Man
S'wark .... (Diocese of) Southwark
S'well .... (Diocese of) Southwell
SA .... Salvation Army
SACert .... Social Administration Certificate
SAMS .... South American Mission Society
SBStJ .... Serving Brother, the Most Ven Order of the Hospital of St John of Jerusalem
SCM .... State Certified Midwife
Student Christian Movement
SDES .... Special Diploma in Educational Studies
SE .... South East
SEAN .... Study by Extension to All Nations
SEITE .... South East Institute for Theological Education
SEN .... State Enrolled Nurse
SHARE .... Shelter Housing and Renewal Experiment
SMF .... Society for the Maintenance of the Faith

SOAS .... School of Oriental and African Studies
SOMA............. Sharing of Ministries Abroad
SOSc............... Society of Ordained Scientists
SPCK.............. Society for Promoting Christian Knowledge
SPG................ Society for the Propogation of the Gospel (now see USPG)
SRD................ State Registered Dietician
SRN................ State Registered Nurse
SRP................ State Registered Physiotherapist
SS.................. Saints
Saints'
Sidney Sussex
SSC................ Secretarial Studies Certificate
Societas Sanctae Crucis (Society of the Holy Cross)
Solicitor before the Supreme Court (Scotland)
SSF................ Society of St Francis
SSJ................. Society of St John of Jerusalem
SSJE............... Society of St John the Evangelist
SSM................ Society of the Sacred Mission
STB................ Bachelor of Theology (also see BTh)
STD................ Doctor of Sacred Theology (also see DST)
STDip............. Sister-Tutor's Diploma
STL................ Reader (or Professor) of Sacred Theology
STM............... Master of Theology (also see MTh or MTheol and ThM)
STV................ Scottish Television
STh................ Scholar in Theology (also see ThSchol)
SW................. South West
SWJ................ Servants with Jesus
Sacr................ Sacrist
Sacristan
Sarum.............. (Diocese of) Salisbury
Sav................. Saviour
Saviour's
ScD................. Doctor of Science (also see DSc)
Sch................. School
Sec.................. Secretary
Selw................ Selwyn
Sem................. Seminary
Scn................. Senior
Sheff............... (Diocese of) Sheffield
Shep................ Shepherd
So................... Souls
Souls'
Soc................. Social
Society
Southn............. Southampton
Sqn Ldr........... Squadron Leader
St................... Saint
St Alb.............. (Diocese of) St Albans
St Alban
St Alban's
St And............. (Diocese of) St Andrews, Dunkeld and Dunblane
St As............... (Diocese of) St Asaph
St D................ (Diocese of) St Davids
St E................ (Diocese of) St Edmundsbury and Ipswich
Staffs............... Staffordshire
Ste.................. Sainte
Steph............... Stephen
Stephen's
Sub................. Substitute
Succ................ Succentor
Suff................. Suffragan
Supt................ Superintendent
Switz............... Switzerland
Syn................. Synod

T

T, K & A......... (Diocese of) Tuam, Killala and Achonry
TA.................. Territorial Army
TAVR............. Territorial and Army Volunteer Reserve
TC.................. Technician Certificate
TCD............... Trinity College, Dublin
TCert.............. Teacher's Certificate
TD.................. Territorial Efficiency Decoration
TDDSc............ Technical Diploma in Domestic Science
TDip............... Teacher's Diploma
TEAR............. The Evangelical Alliance Relief
TEM............... Territorial Efficiency Medal
TEng............... Senior Technician Engineer
TEng(CEI)........ Technician Engineer (now see IEng)
TM................. Team Minister (or Ministry)
TNC............... Thoracic Nursing Certificate
TP.................. Team Priest
TR.................. Team Rector
TS.................. Training Ship
TSB................ Trustee Savings Bank
TV.................. Team Vicar
Television
TVS................ Television South
Tech................ Technical
Technology
temp................ temporarily
Th.................. Theologian
Theological
Theology
ThA................ Associate of Theology
ThB................ Bachelor of Theology (USA)
ThD................ Doctorate in Theology (also see DTh)
ThDip............. Theology Diploma (Australia)
ThL................ Theological Licentiate
ThM............... Master of Theology (also see MTh or MTheol and STM)
ThSchol........... Scholar in Theology (also see STh)
Thos................ Thomas
Thomas's
Tim................. Timothy
Timothy's
Tr................... Trainer
Training
TransDip.......... Translator's Diploma
Treas............... Treasurer
Treasurer's
Trin................ Trinity

U

UAE............... United Arab Emirates
UCCF............. Universities and Colleges Christian Fellowship of Evangelical Unions (formerly IVF)
UCD............... University College, Dublin
UEA............... University of East Anglia
UK................. United Kingdom
UKRC............. United Kingdom Register of Counsellors
UMCA............ Universities' Mission to Central Africa (now see USPG)
UMIST............ University of Manchester Institute of Science and Technology
UNISA............ University of South Africa
UPA............... Urban Priority Area (or Areas)
URC............... United Reformed Church
US or USA....... United States (of America)
USCL............. United Society for Christian Literature
USPG............. United Society for the Propagation of the Gospel (formerly SPG, UMCA, and CMD)
UWE.............. University of the West of England
UWIST............ University of Wales Institute of Science and Technology
Univ................ University

V

V.................... Vicar
Virgin
Virgin's
VRD............... Royal Naval Volunteer Reserve Officers' Decoration
Ven................. Venerable
VetMB............. Bachelor of Veterinary Medicine (also see BVetMed)
Vin................. Vincent
Vincent's
Voc................. Vocational
Vocations

W

W................... West
Western
w.................... with
W/Cdr............. Wing Commander
WCC.............. World Council of Churches
WEC.............. Worldwide Evangelism Crusade
WMMTC......... West Midlands Ministerial Training Course
WRAF............ Women's Royal Air Force
Wadh.............. Wadham
Wakef.............. (Diocese of) Wakefield
Warks.............. Warwickshire
Warw.............. Warwick
Westf............... Westfield
Westmr............ Westminster
Wilts............... Wiltshire
Win................. (Diocese of) Winchester
Wm................. William
Wolfs.............. Wolfson
Wolv............... Wolverhampton
Worc............... (Diocese of) Worcester
Worcs.............. Worcestershire

Y

YMCA............ Young Men's Christian Association
YOI................ Young Offender Institution

A

AAGAARD, Angus Robert. b 64. Moray Ho Coll of Educn CQSW86 DipSocWork86. Ripon Coll Cuddesdon BTh93. **d** 93 **p** 94. C Taunton St Andr *B & W* 93-97; TV Southampton (City Cen) *Win* from 97. *St Augustine's Vicarage, 27 Parsonage Road, Northam, Southampton SO14 0PQ* Tel (01703) 493880

ABAYOMI-COLE, Bimbisara Alfred (Bimbi). b 58. CCC Ox BA80 MA85. Trin Coll Bris BA94. **d** 94 **p** 95. C Deptford St Pet *S'wark* from 94. *31A Crescent Way, London SE4 1QL* Tel 0181-469 0898

ABBEY, Canon Anthony James. b 36. Selw Coll Cam BA59 MA63 ARCO61. Ely Th Coll 59. **d** 61 **p** 62. C Wanstead St Mary *Chelmsf* 61-63; C Laindon w Basildon 63-67; R Sandon 67-76; V Epping St Jo 76-92; Hon Can Chelmsf Cathl from 85; P-in-c Doddinghurst and Mountnessing from 92. *The Rectory, Church Lane, Doddinghurst, Brentwood, Essex CM15 0NJ* Tel (01277) 821366

ABBOTT, Barry Ingle. b 31. Sarum Th Coll 65. **d** 67 **p** 68. C Wootton Bassett *Sarum* 67-69; C Broad Town 67-69; C Wilton w Netherhampton 69-71; V Warminster Ch Ch 71-76; Lic to Offic 76-77; P-in-c Figheldean w Milston 77-79; P-in-c Bulford 77-79; Lic to Offic *B & W* 79-88; Lic to Offic *Ex* 80-88; Perm to Offic *Sarum* from 88; rtd 91. *Fern Cottage, Berwick Lane, Steeple Langford, Salisbury SP3 4NB* Tel (01722) 790348

ABBOTT, Barry Joseph. b 59. MIEH Newc Coll of Arts DipEH81 DipOH&S83 DipTSM83. NE Ord Course 89. **d** 92 **p** 93. NSM Bishopwearmouth Ch Ch *Dur* from 92. *3 Greetlands Road, Sunderland SR2 9EB* Tel 0191-520 0577

ABBOTT, Charles Peter. b 25. Maryland Univ 60. Pecusa Ord Course. **d** 62 **p** 62. USA 62-66; C Oxhey St Matt *St Alb* 66-70; Asst Chapl Alleyn's Foundn Dulwich 70-72; C Dulwich St Barn *S'wark* 70-72; V Southway *Ex* 72-78; V Whitgift w Adlingfleet and Eastoft *Sheff* 78-79; rtd 86. *21 Lychgates Close, Bexhill-on-Sea, E Sussex TN40 2EW*

ABBOTT, Christopher Ralph (Chris). b 38. Univ of Wales (Lamp) BA59. Wells Th Coll 59. **d** 61 **p** 62. C Camberwell St Giles *S'wark* 61-67; C Portsea St Mary *Portsm* 67-70; V Portsea St Cuth 70-87; P-in-c Gt Milton *Ox* 87-88; P-in-c Lt Milton 87-88; R Gt w Lt Milton and Gt Haseley 88-93; R Chailey *Chich* from 93. *Chailey Rectory, East Grinstead Road, North Chailey, Lewes, E Sussex BN8 4DA* Tel (01825) 722286

ABBOTT, David John. b 52. CertEd. St Jo Coll Nottm LTh. **d** 87 **p** 88. C Biddulph *Lich* 87-90; C Tunbridge Wells St Jas *Roch* 90-92; TV Tunbridge Wells St Jas w St Phil from 92. *St Philip's House, Birken Road, Tunbridge Wells, Kent TN2 3TE* Tel (01892) 531031

ABBOTT, David Robert. b 49. Edin Univ BD72 Birm Univ DipTh73. Qu Coll Birm 72. **d** 74 **p** 75. C Kirkby *Liv* 74-78; C Ditton St Mich 78-80; R Ashton-in-Makerfield H Trin from 80. *The Rectory, North Ashton, Wigan, Lancs WN4 0QF* Tel (01942) 727241

ABBOTT, Miss Geraldine Mary. b 33. SRN55 SCM58 Open Univ BA77 Lon Univ MTh85. Oak Hill Th Coll BA82. **dss** 86 **d** 87 **p** 94. Tutor Oak Hill Th Coll from 86; St Alb St Paul *St Alb* 86-87; Hon Par Dn 87-94; Hon C from 94. *2 Wheatleys, St Albans, Herts AL4 9UE* Tel (01727) 860869 Fax 0181-441 5996

ABBOTT, Michael Reginald. b 40. Hull Univ BSc64. Cuddesdon Coll 64. **d** 66 **p** 67. C Workington St Jo *Carl* 66-68; C Ambleside w Rydal and Brathay 68-70; Hong Kong 70-71; Chapl RN 71-72; C Dalton-in-Furness *Carl* 72-73; V Stanbridge w Tilsworth *St Alb* 73-78; TV Dunstable 78-83; TR Chambersbury (Hemel Hempstead) 83-97; V Eaton Bray w Edlesborough from 97. *The Vicarage, High Street, Eaton Bray, Dunstable, Beds LU6 2DN* Tel (01525) 220261

ABBOTT, Canon Nigel Douglas Blayney. b 37. Open Univ BA87. Bps' Coll Cheshunt 58. **d** 61 **p** 62. C Northampton St Mich *Pet* 61-64; C Wanstead St Mary *Chelmsf* 64-66; Chapl St Jo Sch Tiffield 66-69; V Earls Barton *Pet* 69-73; V Cov H Trin *Cov* 73-80; Provost St Jo Cathl Oban *Arg* 80-86; R Oban St Jo 80-86; TR Hemel Hempstead *St Alb* 86-96; RD Hemel Hempstead 94-96; Chmn BSR from 94; R Much Hadham from 96; Hon Can St Alb from 96. *The Rectory, High Street, Much Hadham, Herts SG10 6DA* Tel (01279) 842609

ABBOTT, Peter John. b 48. Gwent Coll of HE DipSocWork86 S Glam Inst HE CQSW86. St Mich Coll Llan DPT94. **d** 96 **p** 97. C Neath w Llantwit *Llan* from 96. *18 Woodland Road, Neath SA11 3AL* Tel (01639) 635738

ABBOTT, Stephen Anthony. b 43. K Coll Cam BA65 MA69 Edin Univ BD68 Harvard Univ ThM69. Edin Th Coll 65. **d** 69 **p** 70. C Deal St Leon *Cant* 69-72; Chapl K Coll Cam 72-75; C Cambridge St Matt *Ely* 75-76; Asst Chapl Bris Univ *Bris* 77-80; Hon C Clifton St Paul 77-80; Perm to Offic from 81. *29 Withleigh Road, Knowle, Bristol BS4 2LG* Tel 0117-977 9270

ABBOTT, Stephen John. b 62. Qu Mary Coll Lon LLB83. Linc Th Coll BTh92. **d** 92 **p** 93. C E Dereham and Scarning *Nor* 92-95; TV Penistone and Thurlstone *Wakef* 95-97; R Brandon and Santon Downham w Elveden *St E* from 97. *The Rectory, 40 London Road, Brandon, Suffolk IP27 0EL* Tel (01842) 811907 Mobile 0378-068008

ABDY, John Channing. b 38. Nottm Univ BA63. Cuddesdon Coll 63. **d** 65 **p** 66. C Leagrave *St Alb* 65-69; C N Mymms 69-72; V Kings Walden 72-79; V S Woodham Ferrers *Chelmsf* 79-85; V Walthamstow St Pet 85-91; V Burrington and Churchill *B & W* from 91. *The Parsonage, Bristol Road, Langford, Bristol BS18 7JE* Tel (01934) 852295

ABEL, David John. b 31. S'wark Ord Course 71. **d** 74 **p** 75. NSM Crowhurst *S'wark* 74-85; NSM Lingfield and Crowhurst 85-92; Perm to Offic from 92. *Tye Copse Cottage, South Park Lane, Bletchingley, Redhill, Surrey RH1 4NF* Tel (01883) 743370

ABELL, Brian. b 37. Nottm Univ BA61 DipEd. Cuddesdon Coll 61. **d** 63 **p** 64. C Lightcliffe *Wakef* 63-66; C-in-c Mixenden CD 66-68; Lect Linc Coll of Tech 68-69; Chapl Trent Coll Nottm 70-74; V Thorner *Ripon* 74-82; V Far Headingley St Chad 82-86; Deputation Appeals Org CECS 86-89; V Masham and Healey *Ripon* from 89. *The Vicarage, Rodney Terrace, Masham, Ripon, N Yorkshire HG4 4JA* Tel (01765) 689255 Fax as telephone

ABELL, George Derek. b 31. Selw Coll Cam BA54 MA68. Qu Coll Birm 54. **d** 56 **p** 57. C Stoke upon Trent *Lich* 56-60; C Wolverhampton 60-64; R Bridgnorth St Mary *Heref* 64-70; P-in-c Oldbury 64-70; Australia 70-73; R Withington w Westhide and Weston Beggard *Heref* 73-81; R Withington w Westhide 81-83; P-in-c Sutton St Nicholas w Sutton St Michael 76-81; R 81-83; Preb Heref Cathl 82-83; V Basing *Win* 83-88; rtd 88; Perm to Offic *Heref* from 88. *51 Buckfield Road, Leominster, Herefordshire HR6 8SF* Tel (01568) 614564

ABELL, Peter John. b 45. Chich Th Coll 67. **d** 70 **p** 71. C Churchdown St Jo *Glouc* 70-74; Chapl RAF from 74. *Chaplaincy Services (RAF), HQ, Personnel and Training Command, RAF Innsworth, Gloucester GL3 1EZ* Tel (01452) 712612 ext 5164 Fax 510828

ABERDEEN AND ORKNEY, Bishop of. *See* CAMERON, The Rt Revd Andrew Bruce

ABERDEEN AND ORKNEY, Dean of. *See* STRANRAER-MULL, The Very Revd Gerald Hugh

ABERDEEN, Provost of. *See* WIGHTMAN, The Very Revd William David

ABERNETHY, Alan Francis. b 57. QUB BA78. CITC 81. **d** 81 **p** 82. C Dundonald *D & D* 81-84; C Lecale Gp 84-86; I Helen's Bay 86-90; I Ballyholme from 90. *Ballyholme Rectory, 3 Ward Avenue, Bangor, Co Down BT20 5JW* Tel (01247) 274912 or 274901

ABERNETHY, David Terence Phillips (Terry). b 42. St D Coll Lamp 61. **d** 65 **p** 66. C Abergele *St As* 65-72; Bermuda 72-84; V Beaulieu and Exbury and E Boldre *Win* from 84. *The Vicarage, Palace Lane, Beaulieu, Hants SO4 7YG* Tel (01590) 612242

ABINGTON, David John Barringer. b 48. EAMTC 91. **d** 94 **p** 95. C Newport w Longford and Chetwynd *Lich* 94-96; C Newport w Longford, Chetwynd and Forton from 96. *9 Mere Close, Newport, Shropshire TF10 7SL* Tel (01952) 825209

ABLETT, Edwin John. b 37. Clifton Th Coll 64. **d** 67 **p** 68. C Sneinton St Chris w St Phil *S'well* 67-70; R High and Gd Easter w Margaret Roding *Chelmsf* 70-73; Chile 73-75; C Gt Baddow *Chelmsf* 75-78; V Newchapel *Lich* 78-82; V S Westoe *Dur* 82-86; V Tibshelf *Derby* from 86. *The Vicarage, 67 High Street, Tibshelf, Alfreton, Derbyshire DE55 5NU* Tel (01773) 872243

ABLEWHITE, John Leslie Charles. b 43. K Coll Lon BA66. Coll of Resurr Mirfield 84. **d** 86 **p** 87. C E Dereham *Nor* 86-88; C E Dereham and Scarning 89; P-in-c S Lynn 89-95; V New Brompton St Luke *Roch* from 95. *St Luke's Vicarage, Sidney Road, Gillingham, Kent ME7 1PA* Tel (01634) 853060 Fax as telephone

ABLEWHITE, Stanley Edward. b 30. Birm Univ BSocSc59 LSE CASS60. Tyndale Hall Bris 64 Wycliffe Hall Ox 73. **d** 73 **p** 74. C Much Woolton *Liv* 73-77; V Brough w Stainmore *Carl* 77-84; Min Aldridge *Lich* 84-90; P-in-c Swindon 90-96; P-in-c Himley 90-96; rtd 96. *33 Paddock Lane, Aldridge, Walsall WS9 0BP* Tel (01922) 58710

ABRAHAM, Canon David Alexander. b 37. AKC61. **d** 62 **p** 63. C Oswestry St Oswald *Lich* 62-63; C Gt Wyrley 65-65; C Sprowston *Nor* 65-67; V Ormesby w Scratby 67-81; R Oxborough w Foulden and Caldecote 81-87; R Cockley Cley w Gooderstone 81-87; V Didlington 81-87; R Gt and Lt Cressingham w Threxton 81-87; R Hilborough w Bodney 81-87; P-in-c Nor St Giles 87-96; Chapl Asst Norfolk and Nor Hosp 87-91; Hon Can Nor Cathl *Nor* from 95; V Thorpe St Matt from 96. *St Matthew's Vicarage, Albert Place, Norwich NR1 4JL* Tel (01603) 620820

ABRAHAM, Canon John Collis Harford. b 31. Univ of W Aus BA52. Westcott Ho Cam 53. **d** 55 **p** 56. C Wigan St Anne *Liv* 55-57; Australia 57-67 and from 68; Lic to Offic *Birm* 67-68; Can Perth 71-84; Can Bunbury 92-94; rtd 94. *Unit 10, Royston Park, Pioneer Street, Albany, W Australia 6330* Tel Albany (98) 411809

ABRAHAM, Richard James. b 42. Liv Univ BA63. Ridley Hall Cam 64. **d** 66 **p** 67. C Warrington St Ann *Liv* 66-70; C Golborne 70-73; V Bickershaw 73-78; V Ewerby w Evedon *Linc* 78-82; R Kirkby Laythorpe w Asgarby 78-82; R Kirkby Laythorpe from 82. *The Rectory, Kirkby Laythorpe, Sleaford, Lincs NG34 9NY* Tel (01529) 304804

ABRAHAMS, Peter William. b 42. Southn Univ BA77. Sarum Th Coll 77. **d** 78 **p** 79. C Bitterne Park *Win* 78-82; C Old Brumby *Linc* 82-84; V Mitcham Ascension *S'wark* 84-91; TV Riverside *Ox* from 91. *The Vicarage, Mill Street, Colnbrook, Slough SL3 0JJ* Tel (01753) 682156 Fax as telephone

ABRAM, Paul Robert Carrington. b 36. Keble Coll Ox BA62 MA65. Chich Th Coll 60. **d** 62 **p** 63. C Redcar *York* 62-65; CF 65-89; V Salcombe *Ex* 89-96; Miss to Seamen 89-96; rtd 96. *1 The Green, HM Tower of London, London EC3 4AB*

ABRAM, Steven James. b 50. Lon Univ DipTh74 BD76. Oak Hill Th Coll 71. **d** 76 **p** 77. C Biddulph *Lich* 76-79; C Heatherlands St Jo *Sarum* 79-83; Libya 83-84; C Stratford-on-Avon w Bishopton *Cov* 84; V Alderholt *Sarum* 84-90; V Daubhill *Man* from 90. *St George's Vicarage, Roseberry Street, Bolton BL3 4AR* Tel (01204) 61067

ABREY, Mark Evans John. b 66. Ripon Coll Cuddesdon BTh93. **d** 93 **p** 94. C W Derby St Mary *Liv* 93-97; P-in-c Anfield St Marg from 97; Chapl Alder Hey Hosp Liv from 97. *St Margaret's Vicarage, Rocky Lane, Liverpool L6 4BA* Tel 0151-263 3118

ABREY, Philip James. b 51. N Ord Course 82. **d** 85 **p** 86. NSM Hindley All SS *Liv* 85-90; C Caversham and Mapledurham *Ox* from 90; Min Caversham Park LEP from 90; Co Ecum Officer (Berks) from 96. *51 Galsworthy Drive, Caversham Park, Reading RG4 0PR* Tel 0118-947 5152

ABSALOM, Alexander James David Edward (Alex). b 69. St Jo Coll Dur BA91. Cranmer Hall Dur DMinlStuds94. **d** 94 **p** 95. C Cranham *Chelmsf* from 94. *72 Marlborough Gardens, Upminster, Essex RM14 1SG* Tel (01708) 225604

ABSALOM, Hugh Pryse. b 10. Fitzw Ho Cam BA31 MA36 Lon Univ BD56. **d** 36 **p** 37. C Abergavenny H Trin *Mon* 36-39; C Torquay St Luke *Ex* 39-43; Chapl RAFVR 43-49; Canada 49-52; C Brixham *Ex* 52-53; V Friday Bridge *Ely* 53-57; V Coldham 53-57; V Lucton w Eyton *Heref* 57-61; C-in-c Croft w Yarpole 57-61; Chapl and Master Lucton Sch 57-61; Chapl St Hild Coll Dur 61-73; Chapl and Sen Lect St Hild's Tr Coll Dur 61-73; R Walton W w Talbenny and Haroldston W *St D* 73-77; rtd 77. *34 Ruther Park, Haverfordwest SA61 1DH* Tel (01437) 765950

ABSOLON, Michael John. b 33. St Jo Coll Cam BA54 MA59 Lon Hosp BChir57 MB57 FRCS FRCOPhth. Wycliffe Hall Ox 95. **d** 96 **p** 97. NSM Micheldever and E Stratton, Woodmancote etc *Win* from 96. *Cheniston, Compton Street, Compton, Winchester, Hants SO21 2AS* Tel (01962) 715097 Fax 713816

ABSOLON, Canon Peter Chambers. b 27. St Jo Coll Cam BA50 MA55. Linc Th Coll 50. **d** 53 **p** 54. C Yate *Glouc* 53-56; C Belvedere All SS *Roch* 56-60; Ind Chapl 60-67; C Erith Ch Ch 60-61; V 61-67; TV Strood 67-80; Hon Can Roch Cathl 79-91; C Strood St Nic w St Mary 80-81; V Gillingham H Trin 81-91; RD Gillingham 90-91; rtd 91; Perm to Offic *Glouc* from 91. *Holly Tree Cottage, 1 Itlay, Daglingworth, Cirencester, Glos GL7 7HZ* Tel (01285) 654225

ACHESON, James Malcolm. b 48. BNC Ox BA70 MA73. Sarum & Wells Th Coll 83. **d** 85 **p** 86. C Highgate St Mich *Lon* 85-88; TV Tisbury *Sarum* 88-94; Offg Chapl RAF from 88; R Storrington *Chich* from 94. *The Rectory, Storrington, Pulborough, W Sussex RH20 4EF* Tel (01903) 742888

ACHESON, Canon Russell Robert. b 16. Univ Coll Ox BA39 MA45 DipTh47. Wells Th Coll 45. **d** 47 **p** 48. C Bedminster Down *Bris* 47-49; Youth Chapl 49-54; Chapl Bris Univ 55-66; V Clifton St Paul 57-66; Hon Can Bris Cathl 64-66; V Much Wenlock w Bourton *Heref* 66-79; P-in-c Hughley w Church Preen 69-79; RD Condover 72-78; P-in-c Harley w Kenley 73-75; Preb Heref Cathl 74-79; P-in-c Shipton 76-79; P-in-c Easthope w Long Stanton 76-79; Warden of Readers 78-83; Can Res Heref Cathl 79-83; rtd 83; Perm to Offic *Heref* from 83. *1 Penras Terrace, Newborough, Llanfairpwllgwyngyll LL61 6RS* Tel (01248) 440325

ACHONRY, Dean of. *Vacant*

ACKERLEY, Glyn James. b 57. HNC83. Cranmer Hall Dur 84. **d** 87 **p** 88. C Tonbridge SS Pet and Paul *Roch* 87-90; R Willingham *Ely* 90-94; R Rampton 90-94; V Chatham St Phil and St Jas *Roch* from 94. *The Vicarage, 139 Sussex Drive, Walderslade, Chatham, Kent ME5 0NE* Tel (01634) 862498 or 302075 Fax 862498 E-mail glynackerley@cableinet.co.uk

ACKERLEY, Herbert. b 20. St Deiniol's Hawarden 60. **d** 61 **p** 63. C Atherton *Man* 61-64; R Ardwick St Matt 64-68; P-in-c Longsight St Clem 67-68; R Longsight St Matt w St Clem 68-71; R Longsight St Luke 71-85; rtd 85; Perm to Offic *Man* from 85; Perm to Offic *Ches* from 86. *42 Newboult Road, Cheadle, Cheshire SK8 2AH* Tel 0161-428 5801

ACKLAM, Leslie Charles. b 46. Birm Univ BEd71. Ripon Coll Cuddesdon 78. **d** 80 **p** 81. C Chingford St Anne *Chelmsf* 80-83; C Spalding *Linc* 83-85; V Spalding St Paul 85-93; P-in-c Linc St Faith and St Martin w St Pet from 93; Chapl Lincs and Humberside Univ *York* from 96. *165C Carholme Road, Lincoln LN1 1RU* Tel (01522) 531477

ACKLAND, John Robert Warwick. b 47. **d** 82 **p** 83. Lic to Offic *S'wark* 82-88; Hon C Mottingham St Andr 88-94; Hon C Woolwich St Thos 94-96; Hon C Bellingham St Dunstan from 96. *Priory Cottage, 39 Upton Road, Bexleyheath, Kent DA6 8LW* Tel 0181-301 0718 Fax as telephone

ACKROYD, David Andrew. b 66. Coll of Ripon & York St Jo BA90. Cranmer Hall Dur BA97. **d** 97. C Lilleshall and Sheriffhales *Lich* from 97. *16 Thornton Park Avenue, Muxton, Telford TF2 8RF* Tel (01952) 603447

ACKROYD, Dennis. b 36. Cranmer Hall Dur 67. **d** 70 **p** 71. C Newcastle w Butterton *Lich* 70-73; C Horsell *Guildf* 73-77; P-in-c Moreton and Woodsford w Tincleton *Sarum* 77-82; R 82-86; RD Dorchester 79-85; R Ewhurst *Guildf* 86-94; V Cleckheaton St Luke and Whitechapel *Wakef* from 94. *The Vicarage, 62 Whitcliffe Road, Cleckheaton, W Yorkshire BD19 3BY* Tel (01274) 873964

ACKROYD, Eric. b 29. Leeds Univ BA51 Liv Univ MA71 Leic Univ MA(Ed)86. St Jo Coll Dur DipTh54. **d** 55 **p** 56. C Newland St Jo *York* 55-58; Succ Birm Cathl *Birm* 58-60; Chapl K Sch Bruton 61-66; Lect Kirkby Fields Tr Coll Liv 67-72; Sen Lect Nene Coll of HE Northn 72-85; rtd 85. *1 Beech Avenue, Northampton NN3 2HE* Tel (01604) 717848

ACKROYD, John Michael. b 32. Lon Univ BSc53. Ripon Hall Ox 71. **d** 73 **p** 74. C Keighley *Bradf* 73-76; TV 76-81; V Keighley All SS 81; V Whalley *Blackb* from 81; Chapl Calderstones Hosp Blackb from 81. *The Vicarage, 40 The Sands, Whalley, Clitheroe, Lancs BB7 9TL* Tel (01254) 823943 or 823249

ACKROYD, Peter Michael. b 60. Jes Coll Cam BA82 MA86 Fontainebleau MBA87. Wycliffe Hall Ox BA93 DipTh94. **d** 94 **p** 95. C Denton Holme *Carl* 94-97; Sec Proclamation Trust from 97; Perm to Offic *Lon* from 97. *16 Delamere Road, London SW20 8PS* Tel 0181-626 6989 or 946 2277 Fax 283 9985

ACKROYD, Prof Peter Runham. b 17. Down Coll Cam BA38 Trin Coll Cam MA42 PhD45 Lon Univ MTh42 DD70 FKC69 St Andr Univ Hon DD70. Westcott Ho Cam 57. **d** 57 **p** 58. Lect Div Cam Univ 52-61; Hon C Cambridge H Trin *Ely* 57-61; Prof OT Studies Lon Univ 61-82; Select Preacher Ox Univ 62 and 81; rtd 82; Perm to Offic *St E* from 86. *Lavender Cottage, Middleton, Saxmundham, Suffolk IP17 3NQ* Tel (01728) 73458

ACKROYD, William Lancelot. b 1900. Egerton Hall Man 31. **d** 33 **p** 34. C Salford Ch Ch *Man* 33-35; C Pendlebury St Jo 35-37; R Ardwick St Thos 37-42; V Bolton SS Simon and Jude 42-45; Gen Sec BFBS 45-47; R Old Trafford St Jo *Man* 47-53; V S Petherwin w Trewen *Truro* 53-60; V St Germans 60-64; V Eastleach w Southrop *Glouc* 64-68; rtd 68; C Stokenham w Sherford *Ex* 69-71; Perm to Offic *Truro* from 72. *2 Trelawney Road, Callington, Cornwall PL17 7EE* Tel (01579) 83150

ACLAND, Simon Henry Harper. b 41. Westcott Ho Cam 65. **d** 67 **p** 68. C Prestwich St Marg *Man* 67-69; New Zealand 69-71 and 75-85; Singapore 71-74; C Kensington St Mary Abbots w St Geo *Lon* 85-87; C Chelsea Ch Ch 87; C Chelsea St Luke and Ch Ch 87-93; Dir Post-Ord Tr 87-94; C Kensington St Mary Abbots w St Geo 93-94. *87 Kennington Park Road, London SE11 4JJ* Tel 0171-735 5898

ACOTT, David. b 32. Clifton Th Coll 54. **d** 58 **p** 59. C Streatham Park St Alb *S'wark* 58-60; C Maidstone St Faith *Cant* 60-64; R Pettaugh and Winston *St E* 64-76; R Pettaugh and Winston w Framsden 76-77; Area Sec (Dios Cant and Roch) CMS 77-85; C-in-c Hove H Trin CD *Chich* 86-93; TV Hove from 93. *Holy Trinity Parsonage, Blatchington Road, Hove, E Sussex BN3 3TA* Tel (01273) 739870

ACREMAN, John. b 53. Oak Hill Th Coll 86. **d** 88 **p** 89. C Iver *Ox* 88-92; R Hook Norton w Gt Rollright, Swerford etc from 92. *Hook Norton Rectory, Banbury, Oxon OX15 5QQ* Tel (01608) 737223

ACWORTH, Oswald Roney. b 10. SS Coll Cam BA33 MA37. Westcott Ho Cam. **d** 46 **p** 47. C Ipswich St Aug *St E* 46-48; V Chobham *Guildf* 48-56; V Chobham w Valley End 56-79; rtd 79; Perm to Offic *B & W* from 82; Perm to Offic *Sarum* from 82. *Farrs, Chapel Lane, Zeals, Warminster, Wilts BA12 6NP* Tel (01747) 840128

ACWORTH, The Ven Richard Foote (Dick). b 36. SS Coll Cam BA62 MA65. Cuddesdon Coll 61. **d** 63 **p** 64. C Fulham

St Etheldreda *Lon* 63-64; C Langley All SS and Martyrs *Man* 64-66; C Bridgwater St Mary w Chilton Trinity *B & W* 66-69; V Yatton 69-81; V Yatton Moor 81; P-in-c Taunton St Jo 81-84; P-in-c Taunton St Mary 81-85; V 85-93; Preb Wells Cathl 87-93; Adn Wells, Can Res and Preb Wells Cathl from 93. *The Old Rectory, The Crescent, Croscombe, Wells, Somerset BA5 3QN* Tel (01749) 342242 Fax 330060

ACWORTH, Richard John Philip. b 30. Ch Ch Ox BA52 MA56 Paris Univ DesL70. **d** 63 **p** 63. In RC Ch 63-67; C Walthamstow St Mary w St Steph *Chelmsf* 68-70; P-in-c Lt Sampford 70-76; P-in-c Gt Sampford 74-76; Lect Bath Coll of HE 76-77; Lect Th Derby Lonsdale Coll *Derby* 77-83; Derbyshire Coll of HE 83-88; P-in-c Newton Tracey, Alverdiscott, Huntshaw etc *Ex* 88-96; TR Newton Tracey, Horwood, Alverdiscott etc from 96; RD Torrington from 94. *The Rectory, Newton Tracey, Barnstaple, Devon EX31 3PL* Tel (01271) 858292

ADAIR, Raymond (Ray). b 33. Ripon Hall Ox 70. **d** 72 **p** 73. C Knottingley *Wakef* 72-75; C Sandal St Helen 75-77; V Sandal St Cath 77-87; V Brownhill from 87. *The Vicarage, 24 Intake Lane, Batley, W Yorkshire WF17 0QQ* Tel (01924) 471999

ADAIR, William Matthew. b 52. Open Univ BA. CITC 77. **d** 77 **p** 78. C Portadown St Mark *Arm* 77-78; Asst Chapl Miss to Seamen 78-80; C Lisburn Ch Ch Cathl *Conn* 80-84; I Kildress w Altedesert *Arm* 84-92; I Portadown St Columba from 92. *St Columba's Rectory, 81 Loughgall Road, Portadown, Craigavon, Co Armagh BT62 4EG* Tel (01762) 332746

ADAM, Canon David. b 36. Kelham Th Coll 54. **d** 59 **p** 60. C Auckland St Helen *Dur* 59-63; C Owton Manor CD 63-67; V Danby *York* 67-90; Can and Preb York Minster 89-90; V Holy Is *Newc* from 90. *The Vicarage, Holy Island, Berwick-upon-Tweed TD15 2RX* Tel (01289) 89216

ADAM, Canon John Marshall William. b 09. Or Coll Ox BA31 MA36. Wycliffe Hall Ox 31. **d** 33 **p** 34. C Endcliffe *Sheff* 33-35; Chapl Sheff Cathl 35-36; India 36-39; Chapl Sheff Cathl *Sheff* 39-42; V Paddock *Wakef* 42-46; Home Sec Miss Coun of Ch Assembly 46-55; R Friern Barnet St Jas *Lon* 55-63; V Preston St Jo *Blackb* 63-69; Hon Can Blackb Cathl 64-74; RD Preston 67-70; V Broughton 69-74; rtd 74; Lic to Offic *Blackb* from 74. *7 Caton Green Road, Brookhouse, Lancaster LA2 9JL* Tel (01524) 770030

ADAM, Lawrence (Lawrie). b 38. N Ord Course 82. **d** 82 **p** 83. C Thornton-le-Fylde *Blackb* 82-86; Dioc Video Production Co-ord 85-97; P-in-c Scorton 86-91; C W Burnley 91-97; P-in-c Ashton St Jas *Man* from 97. *The Vicarage, Union Street, Ashton-under-Lyne, Lancs OL6 9NQ* Tel 0161-330 2771

ADAM, Michael MacIntosh (Mike). b 48. Sarum & Wells Th Coll. **d** 84 **p** 85. C Stamford Hill St Thos *Lon* 84-87; rtd 88; Perm to Offic *Lon* from 88. *Flat 1, 112 Millfields Road, London E5 0AP*

ADAM, Peter James Hedderwick. b 46. Lon Univ BD73 MTh76 Ridley Coll Melbourne ThL69. **d** 70 **p** 71. Australia 70-75 and from 82; Perm to Offic *Lon* 72-75; Tutor St Jo Coll Dur 75-81. *235 Palmerston Street, Carlton, Victoria, Australia 3053* Tel Melbourne (3) 9347 7493 Fax 9349 1508

ADAM, William Jonathan (Will). b 69. Man Univ BA91. Westcott Ho Cam 92 Bossey Ecum Inst Geneva CES94. **d** 94 **p** 95. C Beaconsfield *Ox* 94-97; C Witney from 97. *The Vicarage, 292 Thorney Leys, Witney, Oxon OX8 7YN* Tel (01993) 773281

✠**ADAMS, The Rt Revd Albert James.** b 15. K Coll Lon 39. St Andr Whittlesford 41. **d** 42 **p** 43 **c** 75. C Walkley *Sheff* 42-44; Succ Sheff Cathl 44; Prec 45-47; Chapl Bermondsey Medical Miss 47-55; R Bermondsey St Mary w St Olave and St Jo *S'wark* 47-55; RD Bermondsey 55; R Stoke Damerel *Ex* 55-63; R Wanstead St Mary *Chelmsf* 63-71; Adn W Ham 71-75; Suff Bp Barking 75-83; rtd 83; C Ridgeway *Sarum* 84-87. *89 Hardens Mead, Chippenham, Wilts SN15 3AQ* Tel (01249) 660728

ADAMS, Anthony John. b 42. St Jo Coll Nottm 83. **d** 85 **p** 86. C Wellesbourne *Cov* 85-89; R Weddington and Caldecote from 89. *The Rectory, Weddington, Nuneaton, Warks CV10 0EX* Tel (01203) 353400

ADAMS, Brian Hugh. b 32. Pemb Coll Ox BA54 MA57 Lon Univ DipTh56. Sarum & Wells Th Coll 77. **d** 79 **p** 80. Hon C Crediton *Ex* 79-81; Chapl St Brandon's Sch Clevedon 81-85; C Street w Walton *B & W* 86-88; RD Glastonbury 86-92 and 93-97; V Baltonsborough w Butleigh and W Bradley 88-97; rtd 97. *Manor Cottage, Weir Lane, Yeovilton, Yeovil, Somerset BA22 8EU* Tel (01935) 840462

ADAMS, Brian Peter. b 47. FInstD FRSA Avery Hill Coll CertEd70 Lon Univ CertRS92 DipRS93. S'wark Ord Course 90. **d** 93 **p** 94. NSM Tonbridge SS Pet and Paul *Roch* from 93. *16 Dry Hill Road, Tonbridge, Kent TN9 1LX* Tel (01732) 350053 Fax 362600

ADAMS, Mrs Celia. b 39. R Holloway Coll Lon BSc60 Cam Univ CertEd61. Sarum & Wells Th Coll 86. **d** 88 **p** 94. NSM Canley *Cov* 88-91; NSM Cov N Deanery 91-92; C Coventry Caludon 92-97; Asst to Dioc Dir of Educn 92-93; Asst Chapl Geo Eliot Hosp NHS Trust Nuneaton from 97; Perm to Offic *Cov* from 97. *St Mary's Abbey Vicarage, 99 Bottrill Street, Nuneaton, Warks CV11 5JB* Tel (01203) 382936

ADAMS, The Ven Charles Alexander. b 29. MBE73 CBE82 JP. AKC59. **d** 60 **p** 61. C Bishopwearmouth St Mich w St Hilda *Dur* 60-63; C Ox SS Phil and Jas *Ox* 63-66; C Tunbridge Wells St Barn *Roch* 66-68; St Vincent from 68; Miss to Seamen from 68; Can Kingstown Cathl from 73; Adn St Vincent & The Grenadines from 76. *St Mary's Rectory, Bequia, Northern Grenadines, Windward Islands* Tel St Vincent (1809) 458-3234

ADAMS, David James. b 58. Trin Coll Bris 95. **d** 97. C Wirksworth *Derby* from 97. *57 Yokecliffe Drive, Wirksworth, Matlock, Derbyshire DE4 4DJ* Tel (01629) 822536

ADAMS, David John Anthony. b 46. BSc. Bris Sch of Min. **d** 84 **p** 85. NSM Sea Mills *Bris* from 84. *31 Elberton Road, Bristol BS9 2PZ* Tel 0117-968 4625

ADAMS, Denis Leslie. b 23. Ox NSM Course 78. **d** 81 **p** 82. NSM Reading All SS *Ox* 81-82; C Wargrave 82-83; C Skegness and Winthorpe *Linc* 83-85; V Gainsborough St Jo 85-89; rtd 89; Perm to Offic *Linc* from 89. *4 Collum Gardens, Ashby, Scunthorpe, S Humberside DN16 2SY* Tel (01724) 842554

ADAMS, Donald John. b 46. St Jo Coll Nottm 86. **d** 88 **p** 89. C Byfleet *Guildf* 88-93; P-in-c E Molesey St Mary from 93; Perm to Offic *S'wark* from 96. *The Vicarage, St Mary's Road, East Molesey, Surrey KT8 0ST* Tel 0181-979 1441

ADAMS, Douglas George. b 39. ALBC65 St Luke's Coll Ex CertEd69 MEd87. SW Minl Tr Course 86. **d** 89 **p** 90. NSM Bude Haven and Marhamchurch *Truro* 89-93; P-in-c St Mewan from 93; Chapl Mt Edgcumbe Hospice from 93. *The Rectory, St Mewan, St Austell, Cornwall PL26 7DP* Tel (01726) 72679

ADAMS, George Ernest. b 12. Sarum Th Coll 37. **d** 39 **p** 40. C Fordington *Sarum* 39-42; P-in-c Stevenage H Trin *St Alb* 42-43; R Belchamp Otten *Chelmsf* 45-56; R Bulmer w Belchamp Walter 45-56; Chapl RAF 56-59; R Wrestlingworth *St Alb* 60-66; V Dunton 60-66; V Arlesey w Astwick 66-70; R Gillingham w Geldeston and Stockton *Nor* 70-80; rtd 80; Perm to Offic *Nor* from 82; Perm to Offic *St E* from 87. *4 Malthouse Court, London Road, Harleston, Norfolk IP20 9BU* Tel (01379) 853445

ADAMS, Gillian. *See* WILTON, Mrs Gillian Linda

ADAMS, Godfrey Bernard. b 47. Local Minl Tr Course. **d** 93 **p** 94. NSM Saddleworth *Man* from 93. *11 Springmeadow Lane, Uppermill, Oldham OL3 6EP* Tel (01457) 875126

ADAMS, Ian Robert. b 57. R Holloway Coll Lon BA79. Ridley Hall Cam 95. **d** 97. C Thame w Towersey *Ox* from 97. *8 Victoria Road, Thame, Oxon OX9 3HY* Tel (01844) 218832

ADAMS, James Michael. b 49. LLB. St Jo Coll Nottm DipTh CertEd. **d** 82 **p** 83. C Luton St Mary *St Alb* 82-85; TV Cove St Jo *Guildf* 85-92; V Chislehurst Ch Ch *Roch* from 92. *Christ Church Vicarage, 62 Lubbock Road, Chislehurst, Kent BR7 5JX* Tel 0181-467 3185

ADAMS, John. b 38. Lon Univ DipEd66 Open Univ BA79. Linc Th Coll 68. **d** 70 **p** 71. C Skipton H Trin *Bradf* 70-72; C Bassingham *Linc* 72-73; Chapl St Piers Hosp Sch Lingfield 73-74; Hon C Keighley *Bradf* 76-79; P-in-c Bredenbury and Wacton w Grendon Bishop *Heref* 79-84; P-in-c Edwyn Ralph and Collington w Thornbury 79-84; P-in-c Pencombe w Marston Stannett and Lt Cowarne 79-84; V Macclesfield St Jo *Ches* 84-87; R Wimblington *Ely* 87-90; V Manea 87-90; R Hallaton w Horninghold, Allexton, Tugby etc *Leic* 90-96; P-in-c Moulton *Linc* 96-97; V Moulton from 97. *All Saints' Vicarage, Church Lane, Moulton, Spalding, Lincs PE12 6NP* Tel (01406) 370791

ADAMS, John David Andrew. b 37. TCD BA60 Div Test61 MA64 BD69 Reading Univ MEd74. **d** 62 **p** 63. C Belfast St Steph *Conn* 62-65; Teacher 65-74; Hd Master St Paul's Secondary Sch Addlestone 74-82; Weydon Secondary Sch Farnham from 82; NSM Bourne *Guildf* 80-85; Chapl to The Queen from 94. *Brookside Farm, Oast House Crescent, Farnham, Surrey GU9 0NP* Tel (01252) 726888

ADAMS, John Peter. b 42. Lon Univ BD69. Oak Hill Th Coll 65. **d** 70 **p** 71. C Whitnash *Cov* 70-73; Hon Asst Chapl Basle *Eur* 73-74; Chapl Davos 74-75; Chapl Düsseldorf 75-76; C Gt Baddow *Chelmsf* 77-80; Miss Eur Chr Miss 80-91; Perm to Offic *Chelmsf* 80-91; Hon Asst Chapl Vienna *Eur* 90-91; Asst Chapl Zurich 91-95; P-in-c Harmondsworth *Lon* from 95. *St Mary's Vicarage, High Street, Harmondsworth, West Drayton, Middx UB7 0AQ* Tel 0181-897 2385 Fax as telephone

ADAMS, John Richard. b 38. St D Coll Lamp BA62 Lich Th Coll 62. **d** 64 **p** 65. C Falmouth K Chas *Truro* 64-68; C Bath Twerton-on-Avon *B & W* 68-72; C Milton *Win* 72-79; P-in-c Weymouth St Edm *Sarum* 79-90; V 90-95; Chapl Westhaven Hosp Weymouth 79-94; P-in-c The Winterbournes and Compton Valence from 95. *The Rectory, Martinstown, Dorchester, Dorset DT2 9JZ* Tel (01305) 588241

ADAMS, Jonathan Henry. b 48. St Andr Univ MA73. Cranmer Hall Dur 73. **d** 76 **p** 77. C Upperby St Jo *Carl* 76-78; C Sunderland St Chad *Dur* 78-82; Soc Resp Officer 83-91; TV Willington Team *Newc* 91-96; Local Min Development Officer 91-96; P-in-c Byker St Silas from 96. *26 Crompton Road, Heaton, Newcastle upon Tyne NE6 5QL*

ADAMS, Margaret Anne. *See* FREEMAN, Mrs Margaret Anne

ADAMS, Martin Philip. b 57. Sarum & Wells Th Coll 88. **d** 90 **p** 91. C Sandringham w W Newton *Nor* 90-93; P-in-c Docking w The Birchams and Stanhoe w Barwick 93-95; V Docking, The Birchams, Stanhoe and Sedgeford from 95. *The Vicarage, Sedgeford Road, Docking, King's Lynn, Norfolk PE31 8PN* Tel (01485) 518247

ADAMS, Michael John. b 48. St Jo Coll Dur BA77. Ripon Coll Cuddesdon 77. **d** 79 **p** 80. C Falmouth K Chas *Truro* 79-81; C St Buryan, St Levan and Sennen 81-83; P-in-c Lanlivery w Luxulyan 83-84; V 84-88; V St Agnes from 88; RD Powder 90-96; Perm to Offic *Ex* from 94. *The Vicarage, Trevaunance Road, St Agnes, Cornwall TR5 0SE* Tel (01872) 552328

ADAMS, Nigel David. b 40. Sarum & Wells Th Coll 86. **d** 88 **p** 89. C Tile Hill *Cov* 88-91; C Coventry Caludon 91-92; TV 92-97; Asst Chapl HM Young Offender Inst Onley 92-95; Sub-Chapl HM Pris Birm from 95; P-in-c Nuneaton St Mary *Cov* from 97. *St Mary's Abbey Vicarage, 99 Bottrill Street, Nuneaton, Warks CV11 5JB* Tel (01203) 382936

ADAMS, Peter. Bris Univ CertEd52 Lon Univ ADEd81. Oak Hill Th Coll. **d** 91 **p** 92. NSM Towcester w Easton Neston *Pet* 91-95; Perm to Offic *Ex* from 95. *3 Copperwood Close, Ashburton, Newton Abbot, Devon TQ13 7JQ* Tel (01364) 654261

ADAMS, Peter. b 37. Trin Coll Cam MA70. AKC65 St Boniface Warminster 65. **d** 66 **p** 67. C Clapham H Trin *S'wark* 66-70; Chapl Trin Coll Cam 70-75; Warden Trin Coll Cen Camberwell 75-83; V Camberwell St Geo *S'wark* 75-83; RD Camberwell 80-83; V W Dulwich All SS and Em 83-92; V Addington from 92. *Addington Vicarage, Spout Hill, Croydon CR0 5AN* Tel (01689) 842167 or 841838

ADAMS, Peter Anthony. b 48. K Coll Lon BD70 AKC70 MTh72. **d** 72 **p** 74. Lic to Offic *Eur* 72-73; C Ashford *Cant* 73-79; P-in-c Ramsgate H Trin 79-86; P-in-c Ramsgate St Geo 84-86; R Ramsgate H Trin and St Geo from 86. *Holy Trinity Rectory, Winterstoke Way, Ramsgate, Kent CT11 8AG* Tel (01843) 593593

ADAMS, Peter Harrison. b 41. Tyndale Hall Bris 63. **d** 68 **p** 69. C Kendal St Thos *Carl* 68-71; C W Bromwich Gd Shep w St Jo *Lich* 71-75; R Aldham *Chelmsf* 76-81; R Marks Tey 76-81; R Marks Tey w Aldham and Lt Tey 81-85; NSM Colchester St Jo from 85; Dioc Missr from 85. *4 St Jude's Gardens, St John's Estate, Colchester CO4 4PP* Tel (01206) 854041

ADAMS, Canon Raymond Michael (Ray). b 41. Lon Univ BD67. ALCD66. **d** 67 **p** 68. C Old Hill H Trin *Worc* 67-73; TR Ipsley from 73; Hon Can Worc Cathl from 84. *The Rectory, Icknield Street, Ipsley, Redditch, Worcs B98 0AN* Tel (01527) 523307

ADAMS, Raymond William. b 58. Reading Univ BA79. Oak Hill Th Coll BA85. **d** 85 **p** 86. C Blackpool St Thos *Blackb* 85-88; C Padiham 88-90; TV Rodbourne Cheney *Bris* from 90; RD Cricklade from 97. *The Vicarage, 54 Furlong Close, Haydon Wick, Swindon SN2 3QP* Tel (01793) 726378

ADAMS, Robin Thomas. b 54. QUB BSc76. Oak Hill Th Coll BA79. **d** 79 **p** 80. C Magheralin *D & D* 79-82; C Coleraine *Conn* 82-86; I Belfast St Aid 86-89; USA from 89. *332 North Union Street, Tecumseh, Michigan, 49286, USA* Tel Tecumseh (517) 423-3233

ADAMS, Roger Charles. b 36. Em Coll Cam BA60 MA64. Tyndale Hall Bris 60. **d** 62 **p** 63. C Longfleet *Sarum* 62-65; C Uphill *B & W* 66-71; R Ramsden Crays w Ramsden Bellhouse *Chelmsf* 71-78; SW Area Sec BFBS 78-84; P-in-c Plymouth St Aug *Ex* 84-85; TV Plymouth Em w Efford 85-90; V Paignton Ch Ch from 90. *Christ Church Vicarage, 133 Torquay Road, Paignton, Devon TQ3 2AG* Tel (01803) 556311

ADAMS, Ms Ruth Helen. b 73. St Jo Coll Dur BA94 CITC BTh97. **d** 97. C Drumragh w Mountfield *D & R* from 97. *12 Crevenagh Way, Omagh, Co Tyrone BT8 4JF* Tel (01662) 247200 E-mail ruth@sackbutt.demon.co.uk

ADAMS, Stephen Paul. b 56. Ex Univ BSc78. Sarum & Wells Th Coll 85. **d** 87 **p** 88. C Swansea St Nic *S & B* 87-88; C Llwynderw 88-91; R Badby w Newham and Charwelton w Fawsley etc *Pet* from 91. *The Vicarage, Vicarage Hill, Badby, Daventry, Northants NN11 6AP* Tel (01327) 310239

ADAMSON, Anthony Scott (Tony). b 49. Newc Univ BA70. St Jo Coll Dur 75. **d** 78 **p** 79. C High Elswick St Paul *Newc* 78-86; C Benwell Team 86-92; V Tweedmouth from 92; Miss to Seamen from 92. *The Vicarage, Main Street, Tweedmouth, Berwick-upon-Tweed TD15 2AW* Tel (01289) 306409

ADAMSON, Arthur John. b 38. Keble Coll Ox BA61 MA65. Tyndale Hall Bris 61. **d** 63 **p** 64. C Redhill H Trin *S'wark* 63-66; Chapl Trent Park Coll of Educn 66-69; C Enfield Ch Ch Trent Park *Lon* 66-70; Ind Chapl *S'wark* 70-74; V Battersea St Geo w St Andr 70-74; R Reedham *Nor* 74-80; Min Beighton and Moulton 75-80; P-in-c Cantley w Limpenhoe and Southwood 77-80; R Oulton St Mich 80-90; Chapl Lothingland Hosp 80-90; R Laceby *Linc* from 90. *The Rectory, 4 Cooper Lane, Laceby, Grimsby, S Humberside DN37 7AX* Tel (01472) 870884

ADAMSON, Paul. b 35. Leeds Univ BA58. Coll of Resurr Mirfield. **d** 60 **p** 61. C Southwick St Columba *Dur* 60-63; Br Guiana 63-66; Guyana 66-75; C Benwell St Jas *Newc* 75-77; V Cowgate 77-83; V Prudhoe 83-93; TV N Tyne and Redesdale Team from 93. *Falstone Rectory, Hexham, Northd NE48 1AE* Tel (01434) 240213

ADAMSON, Richard Edwin Aidan. b 56. Pepperdine Univ BA76 Hamburg Univ Dipl-Reg86. Coll of Resurr Mirfield 89 Sarum & Wells Th Coll 90. **d** 91 **p** 92. C Reddish *Man* 91-93; Chapl Bryanston Sch Dorset from 93. *Bryanston School, Blandford Forum, Dorset DH11 0PX* Tel (01258) 452411

ADAMSON, Warren Joseph. b 43. St Jo Coll Nottm. **d** 82 **p** 83. C S Croydon Em *Cant* 82-85; TV Folkestone H Trin and St Geo w Ch Ch 85-90; R Folkestone St Geo 90-91; V Douglas St Ninian *S & M* 91-93; V Potters Green *Cov* from 93. *St Philip's Vicarage, Ringwood Highway, Coventry CV2 2GF* Tel (01203) 617568

ADDENBROOKE, Peter Homfray. b 38. Trin Coll Cam BA59 MA. Lich Th Coll 61. **d** 63 **p** 64. C Bakewell *Derby* 63-67; C Horsham *Chich* 67-73; P-in-c Colgate 73-96; Adv for Past Care and Counselling from 73; C Rusper w Colgate from 96. *The Vicarage, Colgate, Horsham, W Sussex RH12 4SZ* Tel (01293) 851362

ADDINGTON HALL, Canon Gerald Richard. b 38. Qu Coll Ox BA62 MA67 Birm Univ MA69. Qu Coll Birm 62. **d** 65 **p** 66. C Leeds St Sav *Ripon* 65-69; Tanzania 69-75; V Ipswich St Fran *St E* 75-81; V Pakenham w Norton and Tostock 81-91; V Charsfield w Debach, Monewden, Hoo etc from 91; Warden of Readers from 91; Hon Can St E Cathl from 95. *The Vicarage, Charsfield, Woodbridge, Suffolk IP13 7PY* Tel (01473) 37740

ADDIS, Arthur Lewis. b 11. TD. Worc Ord Coll 62. **d** 64 **p** 65. C Highcliffe w Hinton Admiral *Win* 64-66; R W Dean w E Grimstead *Sarum* 66-70; V Stratford sub Castle 70-79; rtd 79. *78 Park Street, Salisbury SP1 3AU* Tel (01722) 500328

ADDISON, Bernard Michael Bruce. b 31. Cam Univ MA73. St Steph Ho Ox 58. **d** 61 **p** 62. C Paddington St Sav *Lon* 61-64; C Primrose Hill St Mary w Avenue Road St Paul 64-66; S Africa 66-69; Australia 70-72; C Catford St Andr *S'wark* 72-73; Chapl Ch Coll Cam 73-78; Chapl Bonn w Cologne *Eur* 79-82; R Kegworth *Leic* 82-89; V Market Harborough 89-94; rtd 94; Spain from 94. *Calle Madrid 28, Piso 4, PTA 8, 46700 Gandia, Valencia, Spain*

ADDISON, David John Frederick. b 37. DipMA73 K Coll Dur BA60 DipEd62 Birm Univ MA79 Bris Univ MLitt93. Wells Th Coll 64. **d** 66 **p** 71. C Rastrick St Matt *Wakef* 66-67; Perm to Offic *Bradf* 67-71; Hon C Manningham St Luke 71-73; Perm to Offic *Glouc* 77-79; Hon C Bisley w Oakridge 79-81; V Newland and Redbrook w Clearwell from 81; Chapl R Forest of Dean Coll from 89. *The Vicarage, Newland, Coleford, Glos GL16 8NP* Tel (01594) 833777

ADDISON, Philip Ives. b 29. Dur Univ 49. Ely Th Coll 59. **d** 61 **p** 62. C Waltham Cross *St Alb* 61-64; C Bedford St Paul 64-66; Chapl RN 66-70; V Foleshill St Laur *Cov* 70-74; P-in-c Halsham *York* 74-78; V Owthorne and Rimswell w Withernsea from 74. *The Vicarage, 28 Park Avenue, Withernsea, N Humberside HU19 2JU* Tel (01964) 613598

ADDISON SMITH, Canon Anthony Cecil. b 18. Keble Coll Ox BA48 MA53. Linc Th Coll 48. **d** 49 **p** 50. C Berwick H Trin *Newc* 49-52; V Middlesbrough St Chad *York* 52-58; V Saltburn-by-the-Sea 58-64; R Long Marston 64-66; V Easingwold w Raskelfe 66-78; RD Easingwold 70-77; Can and Preb York Minster 76-83; V Selby Abbey 78-83; rtd 83; Perm to Offic *Ox* 83-85 and from 87; C Cookham 85-86; C Hambleden Valley 87. *5 Tierney Court, Marlow, Bucks SL7 2BL* Tel (01628) 483288

ADDLEY, David Bernard. b 41. St Paul's Cheltenham CertEd64 Leic Univ DipEd69 Bradf Univ MSc73. Ox Min Course 91. **d** 92 **p** 93. NSM Claydon w Mollington *Ox* 92-96; NSM Shires' Edge from 96; NSM Ironstone from 94; Perm to Offic *Pet* from 95. *66 Main Road, Middleton Cheney, Banbury, Oxon OX17 2LT* Tel (01295) 710313 Fax (01608) 662180

ADENEY, Dr Harold Walter. b 14. OBE76. Qu Coll Cam BA35 MB BChir38 MA53. Trin Coll Bris. **d** 75 **p** 76. Burundi 75-82; Perm to Offic *St Alb* from 83; Perm to Offic *Nor* from 92. *5 Coles Way, Reepham, Norwich NR10 4LW* Tel (01603) 871932

ADENEY, Canon Ronald Edward. b 19. OBE79. Qu Coll Cam BA40 MA44 Birm Univ PGCE71. Ridley Hall Cam 41. **d** 42 **p** 43. C Fulham St Matt *Lon* 42-46; Jerusalem 47-73 and 75-80; Perm to Offic *Birm* 73-75; Hon Can Jerusalem 77-80; P-in-c Fulmer *Ox* 81-85; rtd 85; Perm to Offic *Ox* 85-87; Perm to Offic Jerusalem 86-92. *28 Trafford Road, Oxford OX3 8BE* Tel (01865) 68538

ADEY, John Douglas. b 33. Man Univ BSc54. Coll of Resurr Mirfield 56. **d** 58 **p** 59. C Forton *Portsm* 58-64; C Northolt St Mary *Lon* 64-67; V Snibston *Leic* 67-72; V Outwood *Wakef* 72-78; V Clifton 78; V Upton Priory *Ches* 79-81; V Hyde St Thos 81-82; V Newton in Mottram 82-89; R Roos and Garton in Holderness w Tunstall etc *York* 89-92; C Woodchurch *Ches* 92-95; C Coppenhall from 95. *149 Broad Street, Crewe CW1 3UD* Tel (01270) 505537

ADFIELD, Richard Ernest. b 31. Oak Hill Th Coll 62. **d** 64 **p** 65. C Bedworth *Cov* 64-67; V Whitehall Park St Andr Hornsey Lane *Lon* 67-77; V Kensington St Helen w H Trin 77-86; V Turnham Green Ch Ch 86-92; rtd 92; Perm to Offic *Chich* from 92. *363 Hangleton Road, Hove, E Sussex BN3 7LQ* Tel (01273) 732538

✠**ADIE, The Rt Revd Michael Edgar.** b 29. CBE94. St Jo Coll Ox BA52 MA56. Westcott Ho Cam 52. **d** 54 **p** 55 **c** 83. C Pallion *Dur* 54-57; Abp's Dom Chapl *Cant* 57-60; V Sheff St Mark Broomhall *Sheff* 60-69; RD Hallam 66-69; R Louth w Welton-le-Wold *Linc* 69-75; P-in-c N w S Elkington 69-75; TR Louth 75-76; V Morton w Hacconby 76-83; Adn Linc 77-83; Can and Preb Linc Cathl 77-83; Bp Guildf 83-94; rtd 95. *Greenslade, Froxfield, Petersfield, Hants GU32 1EB* Tel (01730) 827266

ADKINS, Canon Harold. b 20. Lon Univ BA41. Wycliffe Hall Ox. **d** 43 **p** 44. C Hugglescote w Donington *Leic* 43-45; C Loughborough All SS 45-47; Lebanon 47-54; Jerusalem 54-73; Hon Can Jerusalem 63-65; Can Res Jerusalem 65-70; Dean Jerusalem 70-73; V Barkby *Leic* 74-83; RD Goscote II 82-84; V Barkby and Queniborough 83-85; rtd 85; Perm to Offic *Leic* from 85. *14 Spinney Drive, Quorn, Loughborough, Leics LE12 8HB* Tel (01509) 416080

ADKINS, Peter Vincent Alexander (Alex). b 44. Lon Univ DipTh68 Lanc Univ BA71 Lon Inst of Educn CertEd78. Kelham Th Coll 63. **d** 69 **p** 70. SSM 67-73; Tutor Kelham Th Coll 71-73; Jerusalem 73-75; Hon C Cambridge St Giles w St Pet *Ely* 76-78; Hon C Northolt St Mary *Lon* 81-83; P-in-c Hanworth St Geo 83-86; R 86-88; Adult Educn Officer 83-86; Priory of Our Lady Burford 89-93; Perm to Offic *Ox* 89-93; Warden Edw K Ho *Linc* from 93; Gen Preacher from 93. *Edward King House, The Old Palace, Lincoln LN2 1PU* Tel (01522) 528778 Fax 527308

ADLER, Thomas Payne. b 07. Selw Coll Cam BA29 MA36. Wells Th Coll 29. **d** 30 **p** 31. C New Humberstone *Leic* 30-34; C Hinckley St Mary 34-36; V Rothwell w Orton *Pet* 36-47; CF 39-45; R Castor *Pet* 47-74; R Marholm 47-74; rtd 74; Perm to Offic *Glouc* 75-94; Perm to Offic *Worc* from 85. *Hill Cottage, Cottons Lane, Ashton-under-Hill, Evesham, Worcs WR11 6SS* Tel (01386) 881431

ADLEY, Ernest George. b 38. Leeds Univ BA61. Wells Th Coll 62. **d** 64 **p** 65. C Bideford *Ex* 64-67; C Yeovil St Mich *B & W* 67-70; V Taunton Lyngford 70-79; R Skegness and Winthorpe *Linc* 79-91; R Wantage Downs *Ox* from 91. *The Rectory, Church Street, East Hendred, Wantage, Oxon OX12 8LA* Tel (01235) 833235

ADLINGTON, David John. b 51. AKC73. **d** 74 **p** 75. C Clapham St Paul *S'wark* 74-77; C Bethnal Green St Matt *Lon* 77-80; P-in-c Stepney St Pet w St Benet 80-84; Succ S'wark Cathl *S'wark* 84-87; Min Llan w Capel Llanilltern *Llan* 88-91; PV and Succ Llan Cathl 88-91; Dioc Dir of Educn from 91; V St Hilary 91-94; TV Cowbridge 94-95; C Whitchurch from 95. *Pendinas, The Cathedral Green, Llandaff, Cardiff CF5 2EB* Tel (01222) 562649 or 578899

ADNETT, Roy Gumley. b 14. Tyndale Hall Bris 39. **d** 42 **p** 43. C Blackb Ch Ch *Blackb* 42-44; C Denton Holme *Carl* 44-46; V Constable Lee *Man* 46-49; R Peldon w Gt and Lt Wigborough *Chelmsf* 49-55; V Chilcompton *B & W* 55-80; RD Midsomer Norton 78-81; R Chilcompton w Downside and Stratton on the Fosse 80-81; rtd 81; Perm to Offic *Leic* 81-96. *Bosbury, St James Close, Pangbourne, Reading RG8 7AP* Tel 0118-984 3781

ADOYO, Miss Eugeniah Ombwayo. b 54. Lon Bible Coll 84 Westmr Coll Ox BA86 MPhil90. **dss** 82 **d** 91 **p** 91. Kenya 82-94; Internat Sec Crosslinks from 94; NSM Hatcham St Jas *S'wark* from 94. *12 Redstart Close, Southern Gateway, London SE14 6DE* Tel 0181-469 3840 or 691 6111

ADU-BOACHIE, Francis. b 60. Oak Hill Th Coll DipTh95. **d** 95 **p** 96. C Stonebridge St Mich *Lon* from 95. *3 Alric Avenue, London NW10 8RB*

AEGEAN AND THE DANUBE, Archdeacon of the. *See* PEAKE, The Ven Simon Jeremy Brinsley

ÆLRED, Brother. *See* ARNESEN, Raymond Halfdan

AFFLECK, John. b 20. Liv Univ LLB48. K Coll Lon 68 St Aug Coll Cant 71. **d** 71 **p** 72. C Hutton *Chelmsf* 71-74; P-in-c Hawkchurch, Fishpond, Bettiscombe, Marshwood etc *Sarum* 74-80; R Marshwood Vale 80-86; rtd 86; Perm to Offic *Sarum* from 86. *23 St Nicholas Hospital, St Nicholas Road, Salisbury SP1 2SW*

AFFLECK, Stuart John. b 47. AKC69. St Aug Coll Cant. **d** 70 **p** 71. C Prittlewell St Mary *Chelmsf* 70-75; Asst Chapl Charterhouse Godalming 75-78; Chapl 78-80; Warden Pilsdon Community 80-94. *Address temp unknown*

AGAR, George. b 40. Edin Univ BSc63 Ox Univ PGCE64. N Ord Course 92. **d** 94 **p** 95. NSM Sandbach *Ches* from 94; Head Buddulph High Sch Stoke-on-Trent from 94. *128 Middlewich Road, Sandbach, Cheshire CW11 9EA* Tel (01270) 760191

AGASSIZ, David John Lawrence. b 42. St Pet Hall Ox BA64 MA68 Imp Coll Lon PhD94. Ripon Hall Ox 64. **d** 66 **p** 67. C Southampton St Mary Extra *Win* 66-71; V Enfield St Jas *Lon* 71-80; P-in-c Grays Thurrock *Chelmsf* 80-83; P-in-c Grays All SS 81-84; P-in-c Lt Thurrock St Mary 81-84; P-in-c W Thurrock 81-83; P-in-c Grays SS Pet and Paul, S Stifford and W Thurrock 83-84; TR Grays Thurrock 84-90; Hon Can Chelmsf Cathl 90-93; Dioc Development Rep 90-93; Perm to Offic 93-94. *23 St James's Road, Gravesend, Kent DA11 0HF* Tel (01474) 332193

AGBELUSI, Dele Omotayo. b 51. Ahmadu Bello Univ Zaria MSc81. Immanuel Coll Ibadan DipTh85. **d** 86 **p** 87. Nigeria 86-96; C Edmonton All SS w St Mich *Lon* from 97. *60 Tillotson Road, London N9 9AH* Tel 0181-350 7069

AGGETT, Miss Vivienne Cecilia. b 33. Sarum & Wells Th Coll 86. **d** 88 **p** 94. C Binley *Cov* 88-91; C Hednesford *Lich* 91-96; rtd 96; Greece from 96. *Balsi, Andros, Greece 84503*

AGGREY, Solomon Samuel. b 49. BSc76. Immanuel Coll Ibadan MA84. **d** 80 **p** 82. Nigeria 80-88; Miss Partner CMS from 88; C Gorton Em *Man* 93-95; C Gorton St Jas 93-95. *58 Darras Road, Gorton, Manchester M18 7PA* Tel 0161-231 4094

AGNEW, Kenneth David. b 33. Jes Coll Cam BA58 MA62. Clifton Th Coll 58. **d** 60 **p** 61. C Lozells St Silas *Birm* 60-63; C Skellingthorpe *Linc* 63-68; C Birchwood 68-72; R Willand *Ex* from 72; RD Cullompton 89-95. *Willand Rectory, Cullompton, Devon EX15 2RH* Tel (01884) 32247

AGNEW, Kevin Raymond Christopher. b 59. Chich Th Coll. **d** 94 **p** 95. C Eastbourne St Mary *Chich* from 94. *6 Bay Pond Road, Eastbourne, E Sussex BN21 1HX* Tel (01323) 728680

AGNEW, Stephen Mark. b 54. Univ of Wales BSc76 Southn Univ BTh81. Sarum & Wells Th Coll 76. **d** 79 **p** 80. C Wilmslow *Ches* 79-84; V Crewe St Jo 84-90; Chapl Bromsgrove Sch from 90. *Willow Cottage, 14 Ednall Lane, Bromsgrove, Worcs B60 2BZ* Tel (01527) 575048

AHRENS, Dr Irene Karla Elisabeth. b 40. Berlin Univ Bonn Univ PhD69 Lon Bible Coll BA92 K Coll Lon MTh93. SE Inst for Th Educn 93. **d** 95 **p** 96. NSM Kew St Phil and All SS w St Luke *S'wark* from 95. *18 Taylor Avenue, Kew, Richmond, Surrey TW9 4ED*

AIDAN, Brother. *See* THOMPSON, Barry

AIKEN, Nicholas John. b 58. Sheff Univ BA. Wycliffe Hall Ox 80. **d** 82 **p** 83. C Ashtead *Guildf* 82-86; Dioc Youth Officer 86-93; R Wisley w Pyrford from 93. *The Rectory, Aviary Road, Woking, Surrey GU22 8TH* Tel (01932) 352914

AIKEN, Simon Mark. b 62. St Andr Univ MTh85. Ripon Coll Cuddesdon 86. **d** 88 **p** 89. C Burnley (Habergham Eaves) St Matt w H Trin *Blackb* 88-91; C Heyhouses on Sea 91-94; V Musbury from 94. *St Thomas's Vicarage, 1 Flaxmoss Close, Haslingden, Rossendale, Lancs BB4 4PX* Tel (01706) 213302

AIKMAN, Michael Alexander. b 64. St Andr Univ MA85 Rolle Coll PGCE86. Linc Th Coll BTh94. **d** 94 **p** 95. C Andover w Foxcott *Win* from 94. *2 Madrid Road, Andover, Hants SP10 1JR* Tel (01264) 359625

AINGE, Canon David Stanley. b 47. Brasted Place Coll 68 Lon Univ DipTh74. Oak Hill Th Coll 70. **d** 73 **p** 74. C Bitterne *Win* 73-77; C Castle Church *Lich* 77-79; P-in-c Becontree St Alb *Chelmsf* 79-89; P-in-c Becontree St Jo 85-89; TR Becontree S 89-91; RD Barking and Dagenham 86-91; V Leyton St Mary w St Edw 91-96; P-in-c Leyton St Luke 91-96; V Leyton St Mary w St Edw and St Luke from 96; RD Waltham Forest from 94; Can Chelmsf Cathl from 97. *St Mary's Vicarage, 4 Vicarage Road, London E10 5EA* Tel 0181-539 7882

AINSCOUGH, Malcolm Ralph. b 52. Liv Univ BEd76 Liv Inst of Educn DASE85 Univ of Wales (Cardiff) DipTh87. St Mich Coll Llan 85. **d** 87 **p** 88. C Fleur-de-Lis *Mon* 87-90; C Chepstow 90-91; TV Cwmbran 91-95; V Newport St Steph and H Trin from 95. *St Stephen's Vicarage, Adeline Street, Newport NP9 2HA* Tel (01633) 265192

AINSLEY, Canon Anthony Dixon. b 29. Or Coll Ox BA52 MA57 Univ of S Africa BA74. St Steph Ho Ox 53. **d** 55 **p** 56. C Burnley St Cath *Blackb* 55-60; S Africa 60-80; Adn All SS 73-80; Can St Jo Cathl Umtata 73-80; Hon Can from 81; Chapl Bordeaux w Riberac, Cahors, Duras etc *Eur* 81; V Blackpool St Steph *Blackb* 81-94; rtd 94; Perm to Offic *Bradf* from 94. *The Reader's House, Slaidburn Road, Waddington, Clitheroe, Lancs BB7 3JO*

AINSLEY, John Alwyn. b 32. Univ of Wales (Lamp) BA53. St Mich Coll Llan 53. **d** 55 **p** 56. C Merthyr Tydfil Ch Ch *Llan* 55-57; C Roath St Marg 57-62; V Sandbach Heath *Ches* 62-64; Youth Chapl *Pet* 64-69; Dir Lay Tr & Community Service Worcs 72-76; Officer Gen Syn Bd of Educn 69-72; Dioc Youth and Community Officer *Ox* 76-90; rtd 94. *Cleeve Cottage, 8 Lower Downside, Shepton Mallet, Somerset BA4 4JP* Tel (01749) 330046

AINSLEY, Peter Dixon. b 32. OBE87. St Steph Ho Ox 58. **d** 60 **p** 61. C Bury St Thos *Man* 60-62; Chapl RN 62-87; Chapl HM Pris Liv 87-88; Chapl HM Pris Garth 88-95; rtd 95; Perm to Offic *Blackb* from 95; Perm to Offic *Liv* from 95. *21 Ridge Close, Southport, Merseyside PR9 8JU*

AINSWORTH, Canon David Lawrence. b 28. AKC54. **d** 55 **p** 56. C Friern Barnet St Jas *Lon* 55-58; C Harrow Weald All SS 58-63; R Northrepps *Nor* 63-93; R Sidestrand 63-93; P-in-c Roughton 75-79; Hon Can Nor Cathl 92-93; rtd 93; Perm to Offic *Nor* from 93. *36 Vicarage Street, North Walsham, Norfolk NR28 9DQ* Tel (01692) 405501

AINSWORTH, Mark John. b 64. Lon Univ MTh92. Wycliffe Hall Ox 86. **d** 89 **p** 90. C Chipping Barnet w Arkley *St Alb* 89-93; USA from 93. *8020 St Martins Lane, Philadelphia PA 19118, USA* Tel Philadelphia (215) 247 3775

AINSWORTH, Michael Ronald. b 50. K Coll Lon LLB71 LLM72 Trin Hall Cam BA74 MA79. Westcott Ho Cam 72. **d** 75 **p** 76. C Scotforth *Blackb* 75-78; Chapl St Martin's Coll of Educn 78-82; Chapl N Ord Course 82-89; R Withington St Chris *Man* 89-94; TR Worsley from 94. *The Rectory, Walkden Road, Worsley, Manchester M28 2WH* Tel 0161-790 2362 Fax as telephone

AINSWORTH, Paul Henry. b 46. JP. Man Poly BA81. N Ord Course 85. **d** 88 **p** 89. NSM Salterhebble All SS *Wakef* 88-92; C Golcar 92-96; TV Moor Allerton *Ripon* from 96. *St Stephen's Vicarage, Cranmer Road, Moortown, Leeds LS17 5DR* Tel 0113-268 7338

AINSWORTH, Peter. b 34. Lon Univ BD57. Coll of Resurr Mirfield 69. **d** 70 **p** 71. C Leeds St Wilfrid *Ripon* 70-74; TV Tong *Bradf* 74-77; V Fairweather Green 77-94; rtd 94; Perm to Offic

Wakef from 94. *21 Park Avenue, Royston, Barnsley, S Yorkshire S71 4AD* Tel (01226) 726435

AINSWORTH-SMITH, Canon Ian Martin. b 41. Selw Coll Cam BA64 MA68. Westcott Ho Cam 64. **d** 66 **p** 67. C Mill Hill Jo Keble Ch *Lon* 66-69; USA 69-71; C Purley St Mark Woodcote *S'wark* 71-73; Chapl Atkinson Morley Hosp Lon from 73; Chapl St Geo Hosp Lon 73-94; Chapl St Geo's Healthcare NHS Trust Lon from 94; Hon Can S'wark Cathl *S'wark* from 95. *107 West Side, London SW4 9AZ* Tel 0171-223 5302 or 0181-672 1255

AIRD, Donald Allan Ross. b 33. BSc84. AKC55. **d** 56 **p** 57. C N Wembley St Cuth *Lon* 56-59; C Sidmouth, Woolbrook and Salcombe Regis *Ex* 59-62; Youth Chapl *Ely* 62-68; V Swaffham Bulbeck 62-69; V Preston Ascension *Lon* 69-79; V St Marylebone St Mark Hamilton Terrace 79-95; rtd 95. *1 Mews Cottages, 81 Albert Road South, Malvern, Worcs WR14 3DX* Tel (01684) 569603

AIRD, Robert Malcolm. b 31. Lon Univ BSc54. Westcott Ho Cam 75. **d** 77 **p** 78. C Burnham *B & W* 77-79; P-in-c Taunton Lyngford 79-84; V 84-87; R Dulverton and Brushford 87-94; rtd 96. *Arran Cottage, East Street, Chulmleigh, Devon EX18 7DD* Tel (01769) 581042

AIREY, Simon Christopher. b 60. Trin Coll Bris BA87. **d** 87 **p** 88. C Wilton *B & W* 87-90; Chapl Scargill Ho 90-93; TV Kingswood *Bris* 93-96; Perm to Offic *Newc* from 96; Asst P Nether Springs Northumbria Community from 96. *Nether Springs, Hetton Hall, Chatton, Alnwick, Northd NE66 5SD* Tel (01289) 388242

AISBITT, Joanne. *See* LISTER, Mrs Joanne

AISBITT, Michael. b 60. St Pet Coll Ox BA81 MA84. Westcott Ho Cam 81. **d** 84 **p** 85. C Norton St Mary *Dur* 84-87; C Kirkleatham *York* 87-90; V S Bank 90-96; R Whitby from 96. *The Rectory, Chubb Hill Road, Whitby, N Yorkshire YO21 1JP* Tel (01947) 602590

AISBITT, Osmond John. b 35. St Chad's Coll Dur BA57 DipTh61. **d** 61 **p** 62. C Ashington *Newc* 61-64; C Blyth St Mary 64-68; V Cleckheaton St Jo *Wakef* 68-75; V Horbury 75-78; V Horbury w Horbury Bridge from 78. *St Peter's Vicarage, Horbury, Wakefield, W Yorkshire WF4 6AS* Tel (01924) 273477

AISH, Canon Norman Cyril Roslyn. b 20. St Steph Ho Ox 52. **d** 54 **p** 55. C Wyken *Cov* 54-57; C Southbourne St Kath *Win* 57-59; Adv Chr Stewardship 59-62; V Hyde Common 62-73; Adv Soc Resp 73-85; Hon Can Win Cathl 83-85; rtd 85; Perm to Offic *Win* from 85. *51 Pearce Avenue, Poole, Dorset BH14 8EL* Tel (01202) 742077

AITCHISON, Charles Baillie. b 45. ACP69 Bede Coll Dur TCert67 Newc Univ DAES74 New Coll Dur BEd85. LNSM course 85. **d** 93 **p** 93. NSM Peebles *Edin* from 93; NSM Innerleithen from 93. *Milestone Cottage, Princes Street, Innerleithen, Peeblesshire EH44 6JT* Tel (01896) 831491

AITKEN, Christopher William Mark. b 53. Dur Univ BA75. Westcott Ho Cam 76. **d** 79 **p** 80. C Finchley St Mary *Lon* 79-82; C Radlett *St Alb* 82-85; V Sprowston *Nor* 85-90; R Beeston St Andr 85-90; R Sprowston w Beeston 90-93; Chapl Sherborne Sch from 93. *Rosslyn House, Acreman Street, Sherborne, Dorset DT9 3NU* Tel (01935) 813846

AITKEN, Leslie Robert. b 19. MBE76. St Aid Coll Dur. **d** 46 **p** 47. C Wakef St Andr *Wakef* 46-48; C Kingston upon Hull H Trin *York* 48-52; V Burley *Ripon* 52-56; R S Normanton *Derby* 56-58; V Audenshaw St Steph *Man* 58-63; V Stambermill *Worc* 63-68; R Alvechurch 68-84; rtd 84; Perm to Offic *Cant* from 84. *36 Ethelbert Road, Birchington, Kent CT7 9PY* Tel (01843) 841877

AITKEN, Leslie St John Robert. b 41. Open Univ BA75. Cranmer Hall Dur 62. **d** 65 **p** 66. C Worc St Barn w Ch Ch *Worc* 65-69; C Halesowen 69-73; P-in-c Wyche 73-80; R Blackley St Pet *Man* from 80; Chapl Booth Hall Hosp Man 80-89. *St Peter's Rectory, 1161 Rochdale Road, Manchester M9 2FP* Tel 0161-740 2124

AITKEN, William Stuart. b 35. FCFI MSIAD CertEd. Cant Sch of Min 79. **d** 82 **p** 83. NSM Roch 82-86; C Orpington All SS 86-88; R Burham and Wouldham 88-96; Dioc Communications Officer 88-96; rtd 96; Perm to Offic *Roch* from 96. *18 Commissioners Road, Rochester, Kent ME2 4EB* Tel (01634) 715892

AITON, Robert Neilson (Bob). b 36. Univ of Wales BA59 DipEd60. Chich Th Coll 74. **d** 76 **p** 77. C E Grinstead St Swithun *Chich* 76-83; R Lavant 83-90; V Durrington from 90; Chapl St Barn Hospice Worthing from 90. *The Vicarage, Bramble Lane, Worthing, W Sussex BN13 3JE* Tel (01903) 693499

AIZLEWOOD, Geoffrey Rymer. b 27. St Aid Birkenhead. **d** 61 **p** 62. C W Derby St Luke *Liv* 61-65; C Ashton-in-Makerfield St Thos 65-69; PC Liv St Mark Edge Lane 69-75; rtd 75. *c/o Mrs L Threlfall, 20 Brereton Avenue, Wavertree, Liverpool L15 6TJ* Tel 0151-733 8583

AJETUNMOBI, Jacob Ademola. b 48. Igbaja Sem Nigeria BTh73 Lon Bible Coll BA80. **d** 83 **p** 83. Nigeria 83-89; Chapl to Nigerian Students in UK (CMS) from 89; Miss Partner CMS from 89. *82 Keslake Road, London NW6 6DG* Tel 0181-969 2379 or 0171-793 8257 Fax 0171-401 3215

AKEHURST, Peter Russell. b 16. Reading Univ BSc38 Trin Hall Cam. Wycliffe Hall Ox. **d** 48 **p** 49. C Tonbridge SS Pet and Paul *Roch* 48-51; C Kennington St Mark *S'wark* 51; S Africa 51-70; R Didsbury St Jas *Man* 70-74; V Totland Bay *Portsm* 75-81; rtd 81; Perm to Offic *Bris* 86-89; Perm to Offic *Ox* 89-90. *20 Emmbrook Court, Woolacombe Drive, Reading RG6 5TZ* Tel 0118-986 2946

AKERMAN, Roy. b 37. ALCD63. **d** 63 **p** 64. C E Ham St Paul *Chelmsf* 63-67; C Hornchurch St Andr 67-69; Area Sec (Dios Ox and Win) CMS 69-75; V Ollerton *S'well* 75-79; V Boughton 76-79; V N and S Leverton from 79. *The Vicarage, South Gore Lane, North Leverton, Retford, Notts DN22 0AA* Tel (01427) 880882

AKIN-FLENLEY, Kenneth Bernard. b 17. TD62 and Bar 69. St Pet Hall Ox BA41 MA43. Wycliffe Hall Ox 44. **d** 45 **p** 46. C Widnes St Paul *Liv* 45-46; C Keynsham w Queen Charlton *B & W* 46-50; CF (TA) 49-80; V Bathford *B & W* 50-79; Perm to Offic from 79; rtd 82. *Mudros, 85 Dovers Park, Bathford, Bath BA1 7UE* Tel (01225) 858763

AKKER, Derek Alexander. b 46. Bradf Univ MA83. N Ord Course 85. **d** 88 **p** 89. C Mossley *Man* 88-90; C Bury St Pet 90-92; V Lever Bridge 92-97; TV Wolstanton *Lich* from 97. *St Barnabas' Vicarage, Old Castle Avenue, Bradwell, Newcastle, Staffs ST5 8QG* Tel (01782) 635978

ALAN, Brother. *See* MILLER, Alan James

ALBAN-JONES, Timothy Morris. b 64. Warw Univ BA85. Ripon Coll Cuddesdon 85. **d** 88 **p** 89. C Tupsley *Heref* 88-93; P-in-c Weston-under-Penyard w Hope Mansel and The Lea 93; TV Ross w Brampton Abbotts, Bridstow, Peterstow etc from 93. *The Rectory, Weston under Penyard, Ross-on-Wye, Herefordshire HR9 7QA* Tel (01989) 62926

ALBANY, John Brian. b 10. ALCD40. **d** 40 **p** 41. C Forest Gate St Jas *Chelmsf* 40-42; P-in-c 42-44; R Farnham 44-49; Dioc Insp of RE 47-49; Australia from 49; Hon Can Perth 76-78; rtd 79. *48 Parry House, Lesmurdie, W Australia 6076* Tel Perth (9) 291 7177

ALBIN, Colin Leslie. b 51. Cov Poly BA75 DCG78. Cranmer Hall Dur 89. **d** 91 **p** 92. C Chadderton Ch Ch *Man* 91-94; V Witton *Blackb* from 94; Bp's Adv on Inter-Faith Relns from 94. *St Mark's Vicarage, Buncer Lane, Blackburn BB2 6SY* Tel (01254) 676615

ALBON, Lionel Frederick Shapland. b 31. CEng MIMechE60. St Alb Minl Tr Scheme 80. **d** 83 **p** 84. NSM Bromham w Oakley *St Alb* 83-88; NSM Bromham w Oakley and Stagsden 88-89; Ind Chapl 89-96; rtd 96. *Greenways, 43 High Street, Stagsden, Bedford MK43 8SG* Tel (01234) 825754

ALBY, Harold Oriel. b 45. Witwatersrand Univ BA68 MA77. Sarum Th Coll 68. **d** 71 **p** 72. S Africa 71-89; P-in-c Forton *Portsm* 89-96; V Milton from 96. *St James's Vicarage, 287 Milton Road, Southsea, Hants PO4 8PG* Tel (01705) 732786

ALCOCK, Edwin James. b 31. AKC57. **d** 58 **p** 59. C Old St Pancras w Bedford New Town St Matt *Lon* 58-62; C Hillingdon St Andr 62-81; V N Acton St Gabr from 81. *The Vicarage, 15 Balfour Road, London W3 0DG* Tel 0181-992 5938

ALDCROFT, Malcolm Charles. b 44. Lon Univ DSocSc68 Liv Univ DASS71 Leeds Univ MA94. N Ord Course 79. **d** 82 **p** 83. NSM Alverthorpe *Wakef* 82-85; NSM Horbury Junction 85-93; Perm to Offic from 93; Sub Chapl HM Pris New Hall 94-97; Sub Chapl HM Pris Wakef 96-97; R Cupar *St And* from 97; R Ladybank from 97. *St James's Rectory, 33 Millbank, Cupar, Fife KY15 5DP* Tel (01334) 653548

ALDER, Eric Reginald Alfred. b 23. St Luke's Coll Ex 47 Lon Univ BA55 Cam Inst of Educn 64. Chich Th Coll 70. **d** 71 **p** 72. C Deal St Leon w Sholden *Cant* 71-80; P-in-c Woodnesborough 80-83; P-in-c Worth 80-83; P-in-c Staple 80-83; V Woodnesborough w Worth and Staple 83-90; rtd 90; Perm to Offic *Cant* from 90. *3 Hackington Terrace, Canterbury, Kent CT2 7HE* Tel (01227) 766783

ALDER, William. b 09. Ripon Hall Ox. **d** 55 **p** 56. C Fareham H Trin *Portsm* 55-59; R Silchester *Win* 59-81; rtd 81; Perm to Offic *Ox* from 81. *17 Isis Close, Long Hanborough, Oxford OX8 8JN* Tel (01993) 882198

ALDERMAN, John David. b 49. Man Univ BA71 Selw Coll Cam BA79. Ridley Hall Cam 77. **d** 80 **p** 81. C Hartley Wintney, Elvetham, Winchfield etc *Win* 80-83; V Bursledon 83-92; R Dibden from 92. *The Rectory, Beaulieu Road, Dibden Purlieu, Southampton SO45 4PT* Tel (01703) 843204

ALDERSLEY, Ian. b 42. FIBMS68. Wycliffe Hall Ox 89. **d** 91 **p** 92. C Allestree *Derby* 91-94; R Brailsford w Shirley and Osmaston w Edlaston from 94. *The Rectory, Church Lane, Brailsford, Derby DE6 3BX* Tel (01335) 360362

ALDERSON, Albert George. b 22. K Coll Lon 46. **d** 50 **p** 51. C Whitworth w Spennymoor *Dur* 50-54; V S Shields St Fran 54-69; P-in-c 69-72; V S Shields St Jude 69-72; R Penshaw 72-79; P-in-c Bilsdale Midcable *York* 79-80; P-in-c Hawnby w Old Byland 79-80; P-in-c Scawton w Cold Kirby 79-80; R Upper Ryedale 80-91; rtd 91; Perm to Offic *York* from 91. *11 Bells Court, Helmsley, York YO6 5BA* Tel (01439) 712631

ALDERSON, Christopher Derek. b 21. AKC55. **d** 55 **p** 56. C Goring-by-Sea *Chich* 55-59; V Gt Bentley *Chelmsf* 59-67; R Lt Bentley 60-67; V Dunster *B & W* 67-82; P-in-c Brompton Regis w Upton and Skilgate 82-83; R 83-86; rtd 86; Perm to Offic *B & W* 86-90. *377 Old Commercial Road, Portsmouth PO1 4QL* Tel (01705) 821032

ALDERSON, Mrs Maureen. b 40. WMMTC 90. **d** 93 **p** 94. NSM Yardley St Cypr Hay Mill *Birm* 93-96; P-in-c from 96. *The*

Vicarage, 7 The Fordrough, Haymills, Birmingham B25 8DL Tel 0121-773 1278

ALDERSON, Roger James. b 47. Lon Univ BD70 AKC71. **d** 71 **p** 72. C Lawton Moor *Man* 71-75; C Barton w Peel Green 75-76; R Heaton Norris St Thos 76-85; V Bedford Leigh 85-92. *St Joseph's College Farm, Stony Brow, Roby Mill, Upholland, Skelmersdale, Lancs WN8 0QD* Tel (01695) 627474

ALDERTON-FORD, Jonathan Laurence. b 57. Nottm Univ BTh85. St Jo Coll Nottm 82. **d** 85 **p** 86. C Gaywood, Bawsey and Mintlyn *Nor* 85-87; C Herne Bay Ch Ch *Cant* 87-90; Min Bury St Edmunds St Mary *St E* 90-91; Min Moreton Hall Estate CD 91-94; V Bury St Edmunds Ch Ch from 94. *18 Heldhaw Road, Bury St Edmunds, Suffolk IP32 7ER* Tel (01284) 769956

ALDIS, Canon John Arnold. b 43. Univ of Wales BA65 Lon Univ BD67. Clifton Th Coll 68. **d** 69 **p** 70. C Tonbridge SS Pet and Paul *Roch* 69-72; C St Marylebone All So w SS Pet and Jo *Lon* 72-77; Overseas Service Adv and Under Sec CMS 77-80; C Welling *Roch* 77-80; V Leic H Trin w St Jo *Leic* 80-89; Hon Can Leic Cathl 88-89; Hong Kong from 89. *St Andrew's Church, 138 Nathan Road, Tsim Sha Tsui, Kowloon, Hong Kong* Tel Hong Kong (852) 367-1478 Fax 367-6562

ALDIS, Preb John Steadman. b 07. Magd Coll Cam BA28 MA42. Cuddesdon Coll 42. **d** 43 **p** 44. C Newport Pagnell *Ox* 43-47; C Aylesbury 47-49; V Wood Green St Mich *Lon* 49-68; RD Tottenham 62-67; RD E Haringey 67-68; Preb St Paul's Cathl 63-75; Chapl Vienna w Budapest and Prague *Eur* 68-71; Hon Can Gib Cathl 75-85; Chapl to Bp Edmonton *Lon* 71-75; Hon C Edmonton All SS 76-80; Hon C Edmonton St Mary w St Jo from 76; rtd 75; Perm to Offic *Chich* from 92. *College of St Barnabas, Blackberry Lane, Lingfield, Surrey RH7 6NJ*

ALDOUS, Alexander Charles Victor. b 56. Southn Univ BA81 K Alfred's Coll Win PGCE83. S Dios Minl Tr Scheme 91. **d** 94 **p** 95. Chapl Oundle Sch from 94. *Oundle School, New Street, Oundle, Peterborough PE8 4EN* Tel (01832) 273536

ALDOUS, John Herbert. b 37. Portsm Poly CQSW83. Bp Otter Coll 94. **d** 96. NSM Gosport Ch Ch *Portsm* from 96. *20 Church Path, Gosport, Hants PO12 1NR* Tel (01705) 501204

ALDRIDGE, Christopher John. b 35. Trin Hall Cam BA57 MA61. Ripon Hall Ox 59. **d** 60 **p** 61. C Coalville *Leic* 60-64; P-in-c Clifton St Fran *S'well* 64-72; V Gospel Lane St Mich *Birm* 72-90; V Selly Oak St Mary from 90. *St Mary's Vicarage, Bristol Road, Birmingham B29 6ND* Tel 0121-472 0250

ALDRIDGE, Harold. b 35. Keble Coll Ox BA61 MA71. Chich Th Coll 60. **d** 62 **p** 63. C Notting Hill All SS w St Columb *Lon* 62-65; C Kensington St Mary Abbots w St Geo 65-69; Chapl Beech Hill Sch Macclesfield 69-82; TV Staveley and Barrow Hill *Derby* 82-86; P-in-c Longford 86-89; P-in-c Radbourne 86-89; P-in-c Dalbury, Long Lane and Trusley 86-89; V Braddan *S & M* 89-94. *21 Windermere Drive, Onchan, Douglas, Isle of Man IM3 2DN* Tel (01624) 626201

ALDRIDGE, Harold John. b 42. Lon Univ DipTh67. Oak Hill Th Coll 65. **d** 69 **p** 70. C Rawtenstall St Mary *Man* 69-76; CMJ 72-76; C Woodford Wells *Chelmsf* 76-79; TV Washfield, Stoodleigh, Withleigh etc *Ex* 79-86; V Burton *Ches* 86-90; Chapl Clatterbridge Hosp Wirral from 86; P-in-c Shotwick *Ches* 90; V Burton and Shotwick from 91; Dioc Clergy Widows and Retirement Officer from 91; RD Wirral S from 96. *The Vicarage, Vicarage Lane, Burton, South Wirral L64 5TJ* Tel 0151-336 4070

ALDRIDGE, Mark Richard. b 58. Oak Hill Th Coll BA89. **d** 89 **p** 90. C Combe Down w Monkton Combe and S Stoke *B & W* 89-90; C Woodside Park St Barn *Lon* 90-94; P-in-c Cricklewood St Gabr and St Mich from 94. *St Gabriel's Vicarage, 156 Anson Road, London NW2 6BH* Tel 0181-452 6305

ALEXANDER, David Graham. b 61. Ridley Hall Cam 87. **d** 89 **p** 90. C New Barnet St Jas *St Alb* 89-93; C Northwood H Trin *Lon* 93-95; V Stopsley *St Alb* from 95. *The Vicarage, 702 Hitchin Road, Luton LU2 7UJ* Tel (01582) 29194

ALEXANDER, Douglas Keith. b 45. Ripon Coll Cuddesdon 87. **d** 89 **p** 90. C Thorpe St Matt *Nor* 89-92; P-in-c Lakenham St Alb from 92; Chapl Nor City Coll of F&HE from 92. *St Alban's Vicarage, Eleanor Road, Norwich NR1 2RE* Tel (01603) 621843

ALEXANDER, Hugh Crighton. b 03. Qu Coll Cam BA24 MA30. Ridley Hall Cam 29. **d** 30 **p** 31. C Sparkhill St Jo *Birm* 30-33; C Henbury *Bris* 33-37; V Plymouth St Aug *Ex* 37-46; V Uffculme 46-58; RD Cullompton 51-54; C Salisbury St Fran *Sarum* 58-64; R Hazelbury Bryan w Stoke Wake etc 64-71; R Mappowder 64-71; rtd 71. *The Vicarage Flat, 99 Water Lane, Oakington, Cambridge CB4 5AL* Tel (01223) 232396

ALEXANDER, James Crighton. b 43. Qu Coll Cam BA65 MA69. Cuddesdon Coll 68. **d** 68 **p** 69. C Much Wenlock w Bourton *Heref* 68-72; V Oakington *Ely* from 72; P-in-c Dry Drayton 85-95. *The Vicarage, 99 Water Lane, Oakington, Cambridge CB4 5AL* Tel (01223) 232396

ALEXANDER, Canon James Douglas (Jim). b 27. Linc Th Coll 57. **d** 58 **p** 59. C Frodingham *Linc* 58-61; V Alvingham w N and S Cockerington 61-65; V Keddington 61-65; R Gunhouse w Burringham 65-70; R Peterhead *Ab* 70-76; R Aberdeen St Mary 76-96; Miss to Seamen 76-96; Can St Andr Cathl *Ab* from 79; Chapl HM Pris Aber from 82; P-in-c Cove Bay *Ab* 85-90; rtd 95. *25 Belrorie Circle, Dyce, Aberdeen AB21 7LT* Tel (01224) 723574

ALEXANDER, Jane Louise. *See* MACLAREN, Mrs Jane Louise

ALEXANDER, Julius Erik Louis. b 66. Guildf Co Coll of Tech BTEC NC84 BTEC HNC86. Wycliffe Hall Ox 89. **d** 92 **p** 93. C Hoole *Ches* 92-94; C Offerton from 94. *11 Martham Drive, Offerton, Stockport, Cheshire SK2 5XZ* Tel 0161-487 2861

ALEXANDER, Michael George. b 47. Open Univ BA90 DipEd91. Sarum & Wells Th Coll 74. **d** 77 **p** 78. C Wednesfield *Lich* 77-80; C Tettenhall Wood 80-83; Distr Min Tettenhall Wood 83-85; Dioc Adv in Adult and Youth Educn *Derby* 85-89; V Hazelwood 85-89; V Turnditch 85-89; Par Educn Adv (Laity Development) 89-96; Dioc Laity Development Adv from 96; Dioc Dir Studies Bp's Centres of Learning from 96. *14 Chevin Road, Duffield, Belper, Derbyshire DE56 4DS* Tel (01332) 840817

ALEXANDER, Norman William. b 27. Chich Th Coll 54. **d** 56 **p** 57. C Hatcham St Cath *S'wark* 56-59; C Horley 59-61; V Markington and S Stainley *Ripon* 61-69; R Mutford w Rushmere w Gisleham w N Cove w Barnby *Nor* 69-74; R W Winch 74-81; V Frensham *Guildf* 81-84; V Hemsby *Nor* 84-89; RD Flegg (Gt Yarmouth) 87-89; rtd 89. *12 Planters Grove, Oulton Broad, Lowestoft, Suffolk NR33 9QL* Tel (01502) 562144

ALEXANDER, Peter John. b 36. CQSW73 DMA74. Oak Hill Th Coll 92. **d** 95 **p** 96. NSM Aspenden, Buntingford and Westmill *St Alb* from 95. *14 Meadow View, Buntingford, Herts SG9 9SQ* Tel (01763) 272882

ALEXANDER, Robert. b 37. Lon Univ LLB60 St Cath Coll Ox BA62. St Steph Ho Ox 60. **d** 63 **p** 64. C Kensington St Mary Abbots w St Geo *Lon* 63-68; C Notting Hill 71-74; TV 74-79; Australia from 79. *5/31 Alexandra Street, Drummoyne, NSW, Australia 2047* Tel Sydney (2) 232-3592

ALEXANDER, Wilfred Robert Donald. b 35. TCD BA58 MA80. **d** 63 **p** 63. C Raheny w Coolock *D & G* 63-67; Min Can St Patr Cathl Dublin 65-67; Hon C Herne Hill St Paul *S'wark* 68-70; Asst Master Gosforth Gr Sch 71-76; Hon C Long Benton St Mary *Newc* 74-76; Chapl Sch of St Mary and St Anne Abbots Bromley 76-80; V Cauldon *Lich* 80-83; V Waterfall 80-83; P-in-c Calton 80-83; P-in-c Grindon 80-83; V Blackb St Luke w St Phil *Blackb* 83-89; V Rainhill *Liv* 89-92; R Croft w Southworth from 92. *The Rectory, 76 New Lane, Croft, Warrington WA3 0ES* Tel (01925) 762294

ALFLATT, Malcolm Edward. b 35. FBA68 Bp's Univ Lennoxville BA64 Lon Univ BD69 Univ of New Brunswick MA74. Wells Th Coll 64. **d** 66 **p** 68. C Leeds St Marg *Ripon* 66-67; Canada 67-81; C Sheff St Oswald *Sheff* 81-83; V Sheff Abbeydale St Pet 83-93. *1 Farndon Cottages, Romanby, Northallerton, N Yorkshire DL7 8HE* Tel (01609) 771637

ALFORD, John. b 35. Nottm Univ BSc58 NDA59 DipEd76. Qu Coll Birm 74. **d** 77 **p** 78. NSM Edgmond *Lich* 77-87; C Cheadle 87-88; C Cheadle w Freehay 88-89; Chapl to RD Alcester 89-95; P-in-c Wootton Wawen *Cov* 89-95; P-in-c Ellington *Ely* from 95; P-in-c Grafham from 95; P-in-c Easton from 95; P-in-c Spaldwick w Barham and Woolley from 95. *The Vicarage, Parson's Drive, Ellington, Huntingdon, Cambs PE18 0AB* Tel (01480) 891695

ALGAR, John Herbert. b 29. Tyndale Hall Bris 54. **d** 57 **p** 58. C Stapenhill w Cauldwell *Derby* 57-61; C Willesborough w Hinxhill *Cant* 61-69; V Tipton St Martin *Lich* 69-89; P-in-c Tipton St Paul 86-89; V Tipton St Martin and St Paul from 89. *St Martin's Vicarage, Tipton, W Midlands DY4 7PR* Tel 0121-557 1902

ALKER, Adrian. b 49. Wadh Coll Ox BA70 Lanc Univ MA71. Ripon Coll Cuddesdon 77. **d** 79 **p** 80. C W Derby St Mary *Liv* 79-83; Dioc Youth Officer *Carl* 83-88; V Sheff St Mark Broomhill *Sheff* from 88; Dioc Dir of In-Service Tr from 90. *St Mark's Vicarage, 4 St Mark's Crescent, Sheffield S10 2SG* Tel 0114-267 0362

ALLABY, Miss Mary Dorothea. b 60. Bedf Coll Lon BA82 W Sussex Inst of HE PGCE83. Trin Coll Bris DipHE90 ADPS92. **d** 92 **p** 94. Par Dn Ipsley *Worc* 92-94; C 94-96; TV Bloxwich *Lich* from 96. *9 Sanstone Road, Bloxwich, Walsall WS3 3SJ* Tel (01922) 479160

ALLABY, Simon Arnold Kenworthy. b 65. St Chad's Coll Dur BA88. Trin Coll Bris 88. **d** 90 **p** 91. C Preston on Tees *Dur* 90-93; C Chester le Street from 93. *16 Park Road North, Chester le Street, Co Durham DH3 3SD* Tel 0191-388 6801

ALLAIN CHAPMAN, Ms Justine Penelope Heathcote. b 67. K Coll Lon BA88 PGCE89 Nottm Univ MDiv93. Linc Th Coll 91. **d** 93 **p** 94. Par Dn Forest Hill *S'wark* 93-94; C 94-96; TV Clapham TM from 96. *St Paul's Vicarage, Rectory Grove, London SW4 0DX* Tel 0171-622 2128

ALLAN, Andrew John. b 47. Westcott Ho Cam 76. **d** 79 **p** 80. C Whitstable All SS w St Pet *Cant* 79-84; C Whitstable 84-86; P-in-c Littlebourne 86-87; P-in-c Ickham w Wickhambreaux and Stodmarsh 86-87; R Littlebourne and Ickham w Wickhambreaux etc from 87. *The Vicarage, Church Road, Littlebourne, Canterbury, Kent CT3 1UA* Tel (01227) 721233

ALLAN, Canon Archibald Blackie. b 35. Edin Th Coll 57. **d** 60 **p** 61. C Aberdeen St Jo *Ab* 60-63; R from 82; Chapl St Paul's Cathl Dundee *Bre* 63-68; P-in-c Aberdeen St Clem *Ab* 68-76; Vice-

Provost St Andr Cathl 76-82; Can St Andr Cathl from 88. *15 Ashley Road, Aberdeen AB10 6RU* Tel (01224) 591527

ALLAN, Donald James. b 35. Sarum & Wells Th Coll 63. **d** 65 **p** 66. C Royton St Paul *Man* 65-71; V Middleton Junction 71-78; P-in-c Finmere w Mixbury *Ox* 78-83; R Finmere w Mixbury, Cottisford, Hardwick etc 83; Chapl Westcliff Hosp 83-87; V Westcliff St Andr *Chelmsf* 83-87; R Goldhanger w Lt Totham from 87. *The Rectory, Church Street, Goldhanger, Maldon, Essex CM9 8AR* Tel (01621) 88740

ALLAN, Jeanette Winifred. b 40. ALA63. St And Dioc Tr Course 79. **dss** 81 **d** 86 **p** 94. Hillfoot's Team Min 81-86; NSM Bridge of Allan *St And* 86-88; NSM Dunblane from 88. *Pernettya, Sinclairs Street, Dunblane, Perthshire FK15 0AH* Tel (01786) 822037

ALLAN, John William. b 58. St Olaf Coll Minnesota BA80 Bris Univ PhD90. Trin Luth Sem Ohio MDiv84 Qu Coll Birm 90. **d** 91 **p** 92. In Luth Ch (USA) 84-86; C Newport w Longford and Chetwynd *Lich* 91-94; P-in-c Longdon from 94; Lich Local Min Adv from 94. *The Vicarage, Longdon, Rugeley, Staffs WS15 4PS* Tel (01543) 490307

ALLAN, Peter Burnaby. b 52. Clare Coll Cam BA74 MA78 St Jo Coll Dur BA82. Cranmer Hall Dur 80. **d** 83 **p** 84. C Chaddesden St Mary *Derby* 83-86; C Brampton St Thos 86-89; TV Halesworth w Linstead, Chediston, Holton etc *St E* 89-94; TR Trunch *Nor* from 94. *The Rectory, 1 Gimingham Road, Mundesley, Norwich NR11 8DG* Tel (01263) 720520

ALLAN, Peter George. b 50. Wadh Coll Ox BA72 MA76 Leeds Univ DipTh74. Coll of Resurr Mirfield 72. **d** 75 **p** 76. C Stevenage St Geo *St Alb* 75-78; Chapl Wadh Coll Ox 78-82; C Ox St Mary V w St Cross and St Pet *Ox* 78-82; CR from 85. *House of the Resurrection, Mirfield, W Yorkshire WF14 0BN* Tel (01924) 494318

ALLANDER, William Edward Morgell Kidd. b 15. TCD BA37 MA40. CITC 37. **d** 38 **p** 39. C Knock *D & D* 38-43; Hd of Trin Coll Miss Belf 43-46; Lic to Offic *Lon* 46-51; C Foleshill St Laur *Cov* 53-55; P-in-c Wood End 55-57; V 57-64; V Atherstone 64-73; I Rathcooney Union *C, C & R* 73-88; rtd 88. *12 Richmond Estate, Blackrock, Cork, Irish Republic* Tel Cork (21) 293352

ALLARD, John Ambrose. b 30. Bps' Coll Cheshunt 63. **d** 65 **p** 66. C Leigh-on-Sea St Marg *Chelmsf* 65-69; P-in-c Rawreth w Rettendon 69-70; R 70-72; V Barkingside St Fran 73-84; V E Ham St Geo 84-86; V St Osyth 86-95; rtd 95; Perm to Offic *Nor* from 97. *3 John Shepherd Road, Fressingfield, Eye, Suffolk IP21 5SW* Tel (01379) 586627

ALLARD, Roy Frank. b 38. EAMTC 86. **d** 89 **p** 90. NSM Ipswich All Hallows *St E* from 89. *6 Mandy Close, Ipswich IP4 5JE* Tel (01473) 724470

ALLARD, Victor James. b 13. S'wark Ord Course 65. **d** 68 **p** 69. Hd Master Isleworth C of E Primary Sch 59-73; C Isleworth All SS *Lon* 68-73; C Stansted Mountfitchet *Chelmsf* 73-80; C Mayfield *Chich* 80-83; rtd 83; Perm to Offic *Leic* from 83. *1 Oakley Close, Shepshed, Loughborough, Leics LE12 9AS* Tel (01509) 502745

ALLARDICE, Alexander Edwin. b 49. SRN. Chich Th Coll 73. **d** 76 **p** 77. C Rugeley *Lich* 76-79; C Felixstowe St Jo *St E* 79-81; TV Ipswich St Fran 81-87; C Lostwithiel *Truro* 87-90; C Boconnoc w Bradoc 87-90; C St Veep 87-90; C St Winnow 87-90; R Lostwithiel, St Winnow w St Nectan's Chpl etc 90-97; R Mevagissey and St Ewe from 97. *The Rectory, School Hill, Mevagissey, St Austell, Cornwall PL26 6TQ* Tel (01726) 842488

ALLBERRY, William Alan John. b 49. Ch Coll Cam BA70 MA71. Ripon Coll Cuddesdon 84. **d** 86 **p** 87. C Brixton St Matt *S'wark* 86-90; V Wandsworth St Paul from 90. *St Paul's Vicarage, Augustus Road, London SW19 6EW* Tel 0181-788 2024

ALLCHIN, Canon Arthur Macdonald (Donald). b 30. Ch Ch Ox BA51 MA55 BLitt56 Univ of Wales 93. Bucharest Th Inst Hon DD77 Cuddesdon Coll 54. **d** 56 **p** 57. C Kensington St Mary Abbots w St Geo *Lon* 56-60; Lib Pusey Ho 60-69; Warden Community of Sisters of the Love of God Ox 68-73; Can Res and Lib Cant Cathl *Cant* 73-87; Dir St Theosevia Cen for Chr Spirituality 87-94; Hon Prof Univ of N Wales Ban from 93; rtd 94; Lic to Offic *Cant* from 94. *1 Trem Y Wyddfa, Bangor LL57 2ER* Tel (01248) 353744

ALLCHIN, Miss Maureen Ann. b 50. Edge Hill Coll of HE CertEd71 Sussex Univ MA93. S Dios Minl Tr Scheme 88. **d** 91 **p** 94. Hd of Faculty Steyning Gr Sch 79-92; NSM Southwick *Chich* 91-92; C Storrington 93-95; TV Bridport *Sarum* from 95. *The Vicarage, King's Head Hill, Bridport, Dorset DT6 3DZ* Tel (01308) 458788

ALLCOCK, Jeremy Robert. b 63. Trin Coll Bris BA92. **d** 92 **p** 93. C Walthamstow St Luke *Chelmsf* 92-96; V E Ham St Paul from 96. *St Paul's Vicarage, 227 Burges Road, London E6 2EU* Tel 0181-472 5531

ALLCOCK, Peter Michael. b 37. Oak Hill Th Coll 65. **d** 68 **p** 69. C Upper Tulse Hill St Matthias *S'wark* 68-71; C Dunkeswell and Dunkeswell Abbey *Ex* 71-72; P-in-c Luppitt 72-75; P-in-c Monkton 72-75; V Okehampton w Inwardleigh 75-80; TV Solihull *Birm* 80-85; V Highbury New Park St Aug *Lon* from 85. *St Augustine's Vicarage, 108 Highbury New Park, London N5 2DR* Tel 0171-226 6870

ALLDRIT, Nicolas Sebastian Fitz-Ansculf. b 41. St Edm Hall Ox BA63 MA69 DPhil69. Cuddesdon Coll 72. **d** 72 **p** 73. C Limpsfield and Titsey *S'wark* 72-81; Tutor Linc Th Coll 81-96; Sub-Warden 88-96; R Witham Gp *Linc* from 97. *The Rectory, 15 Hillview Road, South Witham, Grantham, Lincs NG33 5QB* Tel (01572) 767240

ALLEN, Andrew Stephen. b 55. MPS Nottm Univ BPharm77. St Steph Ho Ox 78. **d** 81 **p** 82. C Gt Ilford St Mary *Chelmsf* 81-83; C Luton All SS w St Pet *St Alb* 83-86; TV Chambersbury (Hemel Hempstead) 86-91; TV Brixham w Churston Ferrers and Kingswear *Ex* from 91. *The Vicarage, 41 Greenway Road, Galmpton, Brixham, Devon TQ5 0LZ* Tel (01803) 846127

ALLEN, Ms Beverley Carole. b 52. Ch Ch Coll Cant CertEd74 Open Univ BA91. Sarum Th Coll 93. **d** 96 **p** 97. NSM Ruislip Manor St Paul *Lon* from 96. *81 Blossom Way, West Drayton, Middx UB7 9HG* Tel (01895) 445407

ALLEN, Brian. b 58. Oak Hill NSM Course 90. **d** 93 **p** 94. Hon C Norwood St Luke *S'wark* 93-94; Hon C W Norwood St Luke from 94. *11A Queen Mary Road, London SE19 3NN* Tel 0181-670 2227

ALLEN, Brian Stanley. b 24. Roch Th Coll 65. **d** 67 **p** 68. C Roch 67-74; P-in-c Drypool St Jo *York* 74-80; TV Drypool 80; V Marlpool *Derby* 80-87; rtd 87; Perm to Offic *York* from 90. *22 Sycamore Terrace, York YO3 7DN* Tel (01904) 653418

ALLEN, Christopher Dennis. b 50. Fitzw Coll Cam BA73 MA77. Cuddesdon Coll 74. **d** 76 **p** 77. C Kettering St Andr *Pet* 76-79; C Pet H Spirit Bretton 79-82; R Bardney *Linc* 82-87; V Knighton St Mary Magd *Leic* from 87. *The Vicarage, Church Lane, Knighton, Leicester LE2 3WG* Tel 0116-270 5730

ALLEN, Christopher Leslie. b 56. Leeds Univ BA78. St Jo Coll Nottm 79. **d** 80 **p** 81. C Birm St Martin *Birm* 80-85; Tr and Ed Pathfinders 85-89; Hd 89-92; Midl Youth Dept Co-ord CPAS 85-89; Hon C Selly Park St Steph and St Wulstan *Birm* 86-92; V Hamstead St Bernard 92-95. *33 Endwood Court, Handsworth Wood Road, Birmingham B20 2RZ* Tel 0121-515 2959

ALLEN, David. b 38. Llan Dioc Tr Scheme. **d** 76 **p** 77. C Fairwater *Llan* 76-84; Lic to Offic from 84; Chapl The Bp of Llan High Sch from 84. *16 Restways Close, Llandaff, Cardiff CF5 2SB* Tel (01222) 554334

ALLEN, David Edward. b 70. Van Mildert Coll Dur BSc91. Ripon Coll Cuddesdon BA94. **d** 95 **p** 96. C Grantham *Linc* from 95. *26 Castlegate, Grantham, Lincs NG31 6SW* Tel (01476) 564351

ALLEN, Derek Milton. b 45. Bradf Univ BTech67 Man Univ BD80. Oak Hill Th Coll 80. **d** 81 **p** 82. C Chadderton Ch Ch *Man* 81-84; V Roundthorn 84-94. *47 Malvern Avenue, Redcar, Cleveland TS10 4AJ* Tel (01642) 488023

ALLEN, Preb Donovan Bawden. b 14. Keble Coll Ox BA36 MA40. Westcott Ho Cam 36. **d** 38 **p** 39. C Whitchurch *Lich* 38-42; Chapl RNVR 42-46; C S Shore H Trin *Blackb* 47-49; R Mucklestone *Lich* 49-57; R Bridgnorth w Tasley *Heref* 57-68; P-in-c Astley Abbotts w Linley 61-68; Chapl Cross Ho Hosp Shropshire 68-80; R Berrington and Betton Strange 68-80; Preb Heref Cathl 73-80; rtd 80; Perm to Offic *Lich* from 80; Perm to Offic *Heref* from 81. *13 Swan Hill, Shrewsbury SY1 1NL* Tel (01743) 352412

ALLEN, Edward Charles. b 16. Bps' Coll Cheshunt 47. **d** 50 **p** 51. C Plymouth St Andr *Ex* 50-52; C Epsom St Martin *Guildf* 52-57; C Burgh Heath 57-60; V E Molesey St Mary 60-87; rtd 87; Perm to Offic *Chich* from 87. *11 Cootham Green, Storrington, Pulborough, W Sussex RH20 4JW* Tel (01903) 745932

ALLEN, Canon Francis Arthur Patrick. b 26. Em Coll Saskatoon Div Test52. **d** 51 **p** 52. Canada 51-57; C Bishopwearmouth St Nic *Dur* 57-59; Japan 59-63; Hon Can Kobe from 63; V Kingston upon Hull St Matt *York* 63-67; Australia from 67; rtd 91. *PO Box 396, St Helens, Tasmania, Australia 7216*

ALLEN, Frank Brian. b 47. K Coll Lon BD AKC71. **d** 71 **p** 72. C Leam Lane *Dur* 71-74; C Tynemouth Ch Ch *Newc* 74-78; Chapl Newc Poly 78-84; V Newc St Hilda 84-88; Chapl Nottm Mental Illness and Psychiatric Unit 88-89; Chapl St Nic Hosp Newc 89-94; Chapl Newc City Health NHS Trust from 94; Chapl Newc Mental Health Unit from 89. *43 Cherryburn Gardens, Newcastle upon Tyne NE4 9UQ* Tel 0191-274 9335 or 213 0151

ALLEN, Frank John. b 17. FRIC58 Aston Univ BSc66 Birm Univ DipTh75. Qu Coll Birm 75. **d** 76 **p** 76. NSM Hobs Moat *Birm* 76-79; Perm to Offic *Heref* from 79. *Haresfield, Luston, Leominster, Herefordshire HR6 0EB* Tel (01568) 615735

ALLEN, The Ven Geoffrey Gordon. b 39. Sarum Th Coll 64. **d** 66 **p** 67. C Langley Marish *Ox* 66-70; Miss to Seamen from 70; Chapl Rotterdam w Schiedam *Eur* 78-82; Asst Chapl The Hague 84-93; Chapl Voorschoten 84-93; Can Brussels Cathl from 89; Chapl E Netherlands from 93; Adn NW Eur from 93; Chapl Haarlem from 95. *IJsselsingel 86, 6991 ZT Rheden, The Netherlands* Tel Rheden (26) 495-3800 Fax 495-4922

ALLEN, Giles David. b 70. BMus91. Coll of Resurr Mirfield 92. **d** 95 **p** 96. C Palmers Green St Jo *Lon* from 95. *19 Pembroke Road, London N13 5NR* Tel 0181-807 4283

ALLEN, Gordon Richard. b 29. St Jo Coll Dur BA54 DipTh55 MA58. **d** 55 **p** 56. C N Meols *Liv* 55-58; Uganda 58-63; V Lathom *Liv* 64-68; USA from 68; rtd 94. *237 Emery's Bridge Road, South Berwick, Maine 03908, USA*

ALLEN, Hugh Edward. b 47. Sarum & Wells Th Coll 79. **d** 81 **p** 82. C Frome St Jo *B & W* 81-85; R Old Cleeve, Leighland and Treborough 85-97; RD Exmoor 92-97; P-in-c The Stanleys *Glouc* from 97. *The Vicarage, Leonard Stanley, Stonehouse, Glos GL10 3NP* Tel (01453) 823161

ALLEN, John Catling. b 25. Leeds Univ BA50. Coll of Resurr Mirfield 50. **d** 52 **p** 53. C Knowle H Nativity *Bris* 52-54; C De Beauvoir Town St Pet *Lon* 54-57; C Beckenham St Barn *Roch* 57-60; V Orpington St Andr 60-66; V Linc St Jo *Linc* 66-84; C Tynemouth Ch Ch w H Trin *Newc* 85-87; C N Shields 87-89; rtd 89. *St Giles's House, Little Torrington, Devon EX38 8PS* Tel (01805) 622497

ALLEN, John Clement. b 32. K Coll Lon 54. **d** 58 **p** 59. C Middlesbrough St Martin *York* 58-60; C Northallerton w Kirby Sigston 60-64; V Larkfield *Roch* 64-70; R Ash 70-79; R Ridley 70-79; RD Cobham 76-79; R Chislehurst St Nic 79-97; rtd 97. *The Peppergarth, 9 Lane Fox Terrace, Penny Street, Sturminster Newton, Dorset DT10 1DE*

ALLEN, The Very Revd John Edward. b 32. Univ Coll Ox BA56 MA63 Fitzw Coll Cam BA68. Westcott Ho Cam 66. **d** 68 **p** 69. C Deal St Leon *Cant* 68-71; P-in-c Clifton St Paul *Bris* 71-78; Chapl Bris Univ 71-78; P-in-c Chippenham St Andr w Tytherton Lucas 78-82; Provost Wakef 82-97; rtd 97. *The Glebe Barn, Main Street, Sawdon, Scarborough, N Yorkshire YO13 9DY* Tel (01723) 859854

ALLEN, John Michael. b 27. Cuddesdon Coll 71. **d** 72 **p** 73. C Shrewsbury St Giles *Lich* 72-75; V Hengoed w Gobowen 75-82; V Burghill *Heref* 82-85; RD Heref Rural 83-85; TV Bracknell *Ox* 85-92; rtd 92; Perm to Offic *Heref* from 93. *15 Mill Street, Ludlow, Shropshire SY8 1BE* Tel (01584) 877679

ALLEN, Mrs Kathleen. b 46. N Ord Course 88. **d** 91 **p** 94. NSM Colne H Trin *Blackb* from 91. *St Mary's Vicarage, Burnley Road, Trawden, Colne, Lancs BB8 8PN* Tel (01282) 864046

ALLEN, Malcolm. b 60. Hatfield Poly HND82. Trin Coll Bris 94. **d** 96 **p** 97. C Skirbeck H Trin *Linc* from 96. *43 Spilsby Road, Boston, Lincs PE21 9NX* Tel (01205) 368721

ALLEN, Michael Edward Gerald. b 26. Selw Coll Cam BA50 MA53. Chich Th Coll 50. **d** 52 **p** 53. C Farncombe *Guildf* 52-56; R Bentley 56-60; V Baswich *Lich* 60-75; V Highbrook and W Hoathly *Chich* 75-91; RD Cuckfield 77-88; rtd 91; Perm to Offic *Chich* from 91. *Michell House, 6 Chatsworth Gardens, Eastbourne, E Sussex BN20 7JP* Tel (01323) 638688

ALLEN, Michael Stephen. b 37. Nottm Univ BA60. Cranmer Hall Dur 60. **d** 62 **p** 63. C Sandal St Helen *Wakef* 62-66; Hon C Tile Cross *Birm* 66-70; V 72-84; Hon C Bletchley *Ox* 70-72; Vice-Prin Aston Tr Scheme 84-91; Hon C Boldmere *Birm* 85-91; P-in-c Easton w Colton and Marlingford *Nor* 91-93; Local Min Officer 91-93; Dioc Adv in Adult Educn *S'well* from 93. *8 Grenville Rise, Arnold, Nottingham NG5 8EW* Tel 0115-981 4504

ALLEN, Michael Tarrant. b 30. St Cath Coll Cam BA56 MA61. Ely Th Coll 56. **d** 58 **p** 59. C Portslade St Nic *Chich* 58-64; C Folkestone St Sav *Cant* 64-65; V Harston w Hauxton *Ely* 65-91; rtd 91; Perm to Offic *Ely* from 91. *13 Church End, Rampton, Cambridge CB4 4QA* Tel (01945) 250434

ALLEN, Noel Stephen (Brother Noel). b 38. Kelham Th Coll. **d** 63 **p** 64. C Nuneaton St Mary *Cov* 63-67; Australia from 67; Can Adelaide 86-89. *23 Scott Avenue, Flinders Park, S Australia 5025* Tel Adelaide (8) 340 3231 or 222 6000

ALLEN, Peter Henry. b 34. Nottm Univ BA66. Kelham Th Coll 58. **d** 66 **p** 67. C Salisbury St Martin *Sarum* 66-70; C Melksham 70-73; C Paignton Ch Ch *Ex* 73-76; P-in-c W Holloway St Dav *Lon* 76-77; V Barnsbury St Dav w St Clem 77-84; P-in-c Brentford St Faith 84-87; TV Brentford 87-91; TV Catford (Southend) and Downham *S'wark* from 91. *St Luke's House, Northover, Bromley BR1 5JR* Tel 0181-698 1354

ALLEN, Peter John. b 34. HNC72 Leic Coll of Educn CertEd74 Leic Univ BEd75 MA79. EAMTC 89. **d** 92 **p** 93. NSM Ketton w Tinwell *Pet* 92-94; NSM Easton on the Hill, Collyweston w Duddington etc 94-96; Chapl St Pet Vina del Mar Chile from 96. *Casilla 676, Vina del Mar, Chile*

ALLEN, Peter John Douglas. b 35. Jes Coll Cam BA61 MA64. Westcott Ho Cam 60. **d** 62 **p** 63. C Wyken *Cov* 62-65; USA 65-66; Chapl Jes Coll Cam 66-72; Chapl K Sch Cant 72-87; Hon Min Can Cant Cathl *Cant* 73-87; Second Master and Sen Chapl Sedbergh Sch Cumbria 87-93; P-in-c Edin St Ninian *Edin* from 93; Prec and Can St Mary's Cathl from 94; Tutor Edin Th Coll from 94. *147 Comely Bank Road, Edinburgh EH4 1BH* Tel 0131-332 6226

ALLEN, Philip Gerald. b 48. Lon Univ DipTh71. Trin Coll Bris 71. **d** 73 **p** 74. C Portsea St Luke *Portsm* 73-75; C-in-c 75-79; C Southsea St Jude 75-79; P-in-c Gatten St Paul 79-85; V from 85. *St Paul's Vicarage, St Paul's Crescent, Shanklin, Isle of Wight PO37 7AW* Tel (01983) 862027

ALLEN, Richard James. b 46. Wells Th Coll 69. **d** 71 **p** 72. C Upholland *Liv* 71-75; TV 76-79; TV Padgate 79-85; V Weston-super-Mare St Andr Bournville *B & W* 85-93; V Williton from 93. *The Vicarage, 16 Bridge Street, Williton, Taunton, Somerset TA4 4NR* Tel (01984) 632626

ALLEN, Richard Lee. b 41. Liv Inst of Educn TCert67. N Ord Course 80. **d** 83 **p** 84. NSM Colne Ch Ch *Blackb* 83-90; P-in-c Trawden from 91. *The Vicarage, Burnley Road, Trawden, Colne, Lancs BB8 8PN* Tel (01282) 864046

ALLEN, Richard Walter Hugh. b 48. Linc Th Coll 75. **d** 77 **p** 78. C Plymstock *Ex* 77-80; C Leckhampton SS Phil and Jas w Cheltenham St Jas *Glouc* 80; C Shepton Mallet *B & W* 80-81; C Shepton Mallet w Doulting 81-83; V Newport St Matt *Mon* 83-91; P-in-c Telford Park St Thos *S'wark* 91; V Cwmtillery and Six Bells *Mon* 91-94; C Coity w Nolton *Llan* from 95. *Y Lletty, Heol yr Ysgol, Coity, Bridgend CF35 6BL* Tel (01656) 652540

ALLEN, Roger Charles Brews. b 44. Solicitor 77 Loughb Univ BTech66. LNSM course 89. **d** 92 **p** 93. NSM S Elmham and Ilketshall *St E* 92-93; NSM Wainford from 93. *The Old Rectory, Ilketshall St Mary, Bungay, Suffolk NR35 1QZ* Tel (01986) 781429

ALLEN, Roy Vernon. b 43. Open Univ BA81 Birm Univ MA84. Sarum Th Coll 67. **d** 70 **p** 71. C Hall Green Ascension *Birm* 70-74; V Temple Balsall 74-78; P-in-c Smethwick St Steph 78-81; V Smethwick St Mich 78-81; V Smethwick SS Steph and Mich 81-86; V Marston Green from 86. *The Vicarage, Elmdon Road, Birmingham B37 7BT* Tel 0121-779 2492

ALLEN, Samuel Joseph. b 25. CITC. **d** 65 **p** 66. C Bray *D & G* 65-75; P-in-c Carbury *M & K* 75-84; rtd 84. *2 Coastguard Terrace, Putland Road, Bray, Co Wicklow, Irish Republic* Tel Dublin (1) 282 8476

ALLEN, Canon Stanley Leonard Sidney. b 26. K Coll Lon BD52 AKC52. **d** 53 **p** 54. C Friern Barnet St Jas *Lon* 53-55; Canada 55-58; Chapl K Coll Newcastle-upon-Tyne 58-61; P-in-c Woburn Square Ch Ch *Lon* 61-66; Chapl Gt Ormond Street Hosp for Sick Children Lon 61-66; Warden Roch Th Coll 66-70; Can Res Roch Cathl *Roch* 66-70; Hon Can Roch Cathl 70-95; V Sidcup St Jo 70-95; Chapl Qu Mary's Hosp Sidcup 70-95; RD Sidcup *Roch* 75-93; rtd 95; Perm to Offic *Nor* from 96. *55 Manor Road, Dersingham, King's Lynn, Norfolk PE31 6LH* Tel (01485) 543425

ALLEN, Steven. b 49. Nottm Univ BA73. St Jo Coll Nottm 73. **d** 75 **p** 76. C Gt Horton *Bradf* 75-80; V from 89; V Upper Armley *Ripon* 80-89. *The Vicarage, 30 Bartle Close, Bradford, W Yorkshire BD7 4QH* Tel (01274) 521456

ALLEN, Mrs Susan Rosemary (Sue). b 47. Warw Univ BSc68 Trevelyan Coll Dur PGCE69. Sarum Th Coll 93. **d** 96 **p** 97. C Goldsworth Park *Guildf* from 96. *3 Thornash Road, Horsell, Woking, Surrey GU21 4UW* Tel (01483) 760225

ALLEN, Thomas Davidson. b 49. Greenwich Univ MA BTh QUB BA. **d** 84 **p** 85. C Magheralin w Dollingstown *D & D* 84-86; I Kilwarlin Upper w Kilwarlin Lower 86-91; I Maghera w Killelagh *D & R* from 91. *20 Church Street, Maghera, Co Londonderry BT46 5EA* Tel (01648) 42252

ALLEN, Thomas Henry (Tom). b 42. N Ord Course 87. **d** 90 **p** 91. C Upholland *Liv* 90-93; TV Walton-on-the-Hill from 93. *51 Queens Drive, Walton, Liverpool L4 6SF* Tel 0151-521 5276

ALLEN, William Charles Ralph. b 09. Clifton Th Coll 46. **d** 47 **p** 48. C Bris St Mich *Bris* 47-51; C Bishopston 51-53; V Bris St Leon Redfield 53-74; rtd 74; Perm to Offic *Bris* 74-94. *17 Creswicke Avenue, Bristol BS15 3HD* Tel 0117-967 0955

ALLEN, Zachary Edward. b 52. Warw Univ BA74. Ripon Coll Cuddesdon 78. **d** 81 **p** 82. C Bognor *Chich* 81-84; C Rusper 84-86; C Roughey 84-86; TV Carl H Trin and St Barn *Carl* 86-90; Chapl Strathclyde Ho Hosp Carl 86-90; V Findon w Clapham and Patching *Chich* from 90. *The Vicarage, School Hill, Findon, Worthing, W Sussex BN14 0TR* Tel (01903) 873601

ALLEYNE, Sir John Olpherts Campbell, Bt. b 28. Jes Coll Cam BA50 MA55. **d** 55 **p** 56. C Southampton St Mary w H Trin *Win* 55-58; Chapl Cov Cathl *Cov* 58-62; Chapl Clare Hall Cam 62-66; Chapl Bris Cathl *Bris* 66-68; Area Sec (SW England) Toc H 68-71; V Speke All SS *Liv* 71-73; TR Speke St Aid 73-76; R Win St Matt *Win* 76-93; rtd 93; Perm to Offic *Guildf* from 93. *2 Ash Grove, Guildford, Surrey GU2 5UT* Tel (01483) 573824

ALLFORD, Judith Mary. b 55. Sheff Univ BA Lon Univ BD. Trin Coll Bris 77. **dss** 86 **d** 87 **p** 94. Par Dn Deptford St Jo w H Trin *S'wark* 87-91; Asst Chapl Dulwich Hosp 91-93; Asst Chapl K Coll Hosp Lon 91-95; Asst Chapl King's Healthcare NHS Trust 93-95; Chapl St Pet's Hosp NHS Trust Chertsey from 95. *St Peter's Hospital, Guildford Road, Chertsey, Surrey KT16 0PZ* Tel (01932) 872000

ALLIN, Philip Ronald. b 43. Lich Th Coll 71. **d** 71 **p** 72. C Sutton in Ashfield St Mary *S'well* 71-74; Chapl to Sutton Cen 74-76; Lic to Offic 74-76; P-in-c Grove 76-77; R Ordsall 76-80; V Mansfield St Mark 81-83; TR Hermitage and Hampstead Norreys, Cold Ash etc *Ox* 83-96; OCF 83-96; Chapl Nine O'Clock Service *Sheff* from 96. *352 Crookesmoor Road, Sheffield S10 1BH*

ALLINGTON, Andrew William. b 57. ACA81 Sheff Univ BA78. Cranmer Hall Dur BA95. **d** 95 **p** 96. C Clifton *York* from 95. *5 Manor Park Close, Rawcliffe, York YO3 6UZ* Tel (01904) 624241

ALLINGTON-SMITH, Canon Richard. b 28. Lon Univ BA49 MA52. Wells Th Coll 54. **d** 56 **p** 57. C Milton next Gravesend Ch Ch *Roch* 56-61; R Cuxton 61-67; V Rainham 67-79; V Gt Yarmouth *Nor* 79-89; TR 89-91; Hon Can Nor Cathl from 86; rtd 91; P-in-c Nor St Andr *Nor* from 91. *14 Yare Court, Yarmouth Road, Norwich NR7 0EJ* Tel (01603) 37185

ALLINSON, Capt Paul Timothy. b 63. Edin Th Coll 89. **d** 91 **p** 92. C Peterlee *Dur* 91-94; Dio Children's Adv from 94; C Shadforth from 94; C Sherburn w Pittington from 94. *The Rectory, 1 Rectory View, Shadforth, Durham DH6 1LF* Tel 0191-372 0223

ALLISON, Elliott Desmond. b 36. Univ of S Africa BA64 K Coll Lon MTh74. S Africa Federal Th Coll. **d** 69 **p** 70. *294 Reinwood Road, Huddersfield HD3 4DS* Tel (01484) 461109

ALLISON, James Timothy. b 61. Man Univ BSc83. Oak Hill Th Coll BA89. **d** 89 **p** 90. C Walkden Moor *Man* 89-93; Chapl Huddersfield Univ *Wakef* from 93. *85 New North Road, Huddersfield HD1 5ND* Tel (01484) 530655 or 422288 E-mail j.t.allison@hud.ac.uk

ALLISON, Keith. b 34. Dur Univ BA59. Ely Th Coll 59. **d** 61 **p** 62. C Sculcoates *York* 61-64; C Stainton-in-Cleveland 64-65; C Leeds St Pet *Ripon* 65-70; V Micklefield *York* 70-74; V Appleton-le-Street w Amotherby 74-78; P-in-c Barton le Street 77-78; P-in-c Salton 77-80; R Amotherby w Appleton and Barton-le-Street 78-82; Chapl Lister Hosp Stevenage 82-90; P-in-c St Ippolyts *St Alb* 82-85; V 85-90; Chapl Hitchin Hosp 86-90; Chapl Shotley Bridge Gen Hosp 90-94; Chapl Dur HA 90-94; Chapl N Dur Acute Hosps NHS Trust from 94. *Chaplain's Office, General Hospital, Shotley Bridge, Consett, Co Durham DH8 0NB* Tel (01207) 503456 or 503863

ALLISON, Canon Roger Grant. b 10. MBE54. Jes Coll Cam BA33 MA36. Ridley Hall Cam 32. **d** 34 **p** 35. C New Wortley St Mary w Armley Hall *Ripon* 34-37; C Upper Tulse Hill St Matthias *S'wark* 37-39; CMJ 39-75; Poland 39; Romania 39-40; Jerusalem 41; Haifa 42-46; Tel Aviv and Jaffa 46-68; R Jerusalem Ch Ch 68-75; Hon Can Jerusalem 68-75; rtd 75; Perm to Offic *Chich* from 76. *11 Gloucester Avenue, Bexhill-on-Sea, E Sussex TN40 2LA* Tel (01424) 218786

ALLISTER, Donald Spargo. b 52. Peterho Cam BA74 MA77. Trin Coll Bris 74. **d** 76 **p** 77. C Hyde St Geo *Ches* 76-79; C Sevenoaks St Nic *Roch* 79-83; V Birkenhead Ch Ch *Ches* 83-89; R Cheadle from 89. *The Rectory, 1 Depleach Road, Cheadle, Cheshire SK8 1DZ* Tel 0161-428 3440

ALLISTON, Cyril John. b 11. Fitzw Ho Cam BA33 MA37. Cuddesdon Coll 33. **d** 35 **p** 36. C Boyne Hill *Ox* 35-37; C Hessle *York* 37-39; S Africa 40-50; Sarawak 50-52; Borneo 52-59; R Somersham w Pidley and Colne *Ely* 60-63; V Penponds *Truro* 63-70; S Africa from 71; rtd 76. *14 Three Sisters, Sixth Street, Kleinmond, 7195 South Africa*

ALLMAN, Mrs Susan. b 56. Bris Univ BA. W of England Minl Tr Course. **d** 96. Hon C Henleaze *Bris* from 96. *32 Oakwood Road, Bristol BS9 4NR* Tel 0117-962 0394

ALLON-SMITH, Roderick David. b 51. Leic Univ BA PhD Cam Univ MA. Ridley Hall Cam 79. **d** 82 **p** 83. C Kinson *Sarum* 82-86; V Westwood *Cov* 86-96; RD Cov S 92-96; P-in-c Radford Semele and Ufton from 96. *The Vicarage, 7 Church Lane, Leamington Spa, Warks CV31 1TA* Tel (01926) 427374

ALLPORT, David Jack. b 55. Ox Univ BA Birm Univ DPS. Qu Coll Birm 78. **d** 80 **p** 81. C Abingdon w Shippon *Ox* 80-83; C-in-c Woodgate Valley CD *Birm* 83-91; Perm to Offic *Lich* from 91. *122 Cherry Tree Avenue, Walsall, W Midlands WS5 4JL* Tel 0121-353 2292

ALLRED, Frank. b 23. Tyndale Hall Bris 62. **d** 64 **p** 65. C Halliwell St Pet *Man* 64-67; V Ravenhead *Liv* 67-75; R Chadwell *Chelmsf* 75-82; TV Heworth *York* 82-86; rtd 87; Perm to Offic *York* from 87. *12 Viking Road, Bridlington, N Humberside YO16 5TW* Tel (01262) 677321

ALLSOP, Anthony James. b 37. AKC62. **d** 63 **p** 64. C Leytonstone St Marg w St Columba *Chelmsf* 63-68; V Gt Ilford St Alb 68-80; V Gainsborough St Jo *Linc* 80-85; V Hockerill *St Alb* from 85; Chapl Herts and Essex Hosp Bp's Stortford from 85. *Hockerill Vicarage, All Saints' Close, Bishop's Stortford, Herts CM23 2EA* Tel (01279) 834407

ALLSOP, Patrick Leslie Fewtrell. b 52. Fitzw Coll Cam BA74 MA78. Ripon Coll Cuddesdon BA78 MA83. **d** 79 **p** 80. C Barrow St Matt *Carl* 79-82; Chapl Eton Coll 82-88; Chapl K Sch Roch from 89; Hon PV Roch Cathl *Roch* from 89. *49 Holcombe Road, Rochester, Kent ME1 2HX* Tel (01634) 400184

ALLSOP, Peter William. b 33. Kelham Th Coll 58. **d** 58 **p** 59. C Woodford St Barn *Chelmsf* 58-61; C Upholland *Liv* 61-65; V Wigan St Geo 65-71; P-in-c Marham *Ely* 71-72; TV Fincham 72-76; V Trawden *Blackb* 76-90; C Marton 90-92; C S Shore H Trin from 92. *31 Lomond Avenue, Blackpool FY3 9QL* Tel (01253) 696624

ALLSOPP, Mrs Christine. b 47. Aston Univ BSc68. S Dios Minl Tr Scheme 86. **d** 89 **p** 94. C Caversham and Mapledurham *Ox* 89-94; C Bracknell 94; TV from 94. *St Paul's Vicarage, 58 Harmanswater Road, Bracknell, Berks RG12 9PT* Tel (01344) 422819

ALLSOPP, Mark Dennis. b 66. Cuddesdon Coll 93. **d** 96 **p** 97. C Hedworth *Dur* from 96. *112 Hedworth Lane, Boldon Colliery, Tyne & Wear NE35 9HZ* Tel 0191-536 7903

ALLSOPP, Dr Stephen Robert. b 50. BSc71 MSc72 PhD75. Mon Dioc Tr Scheme 81. **d** 84 **p** 85. NSM Trevethin *Mon* 84-88; Asst Chapl K Sch Roch from 88; Hon PV Roch Cathl *Roch* from 89. *33 St Margarets Street, Rochester, Kent ME1 1UF* Tel (01634) 409878

ALLSWORTH, Peter Thomas. b 44. St Mich Coll Llan DMinlStuds93. **d** 93 **p** 94. C Prestatyn *St As* 93-96; V Esclusham from 96. *The Vicarage, Vicarage Hill, Rhostyllen, Wrexham LL14 4AR* Tel (01978) 354438

ALLTON, Canon Paul Irving. b 38. Man Univ BA60 Dur Univ DipTh62. **d** 63 **p** 64. C Kibworth Beauchamp *Leic* 63-66; C Reading St Mary V *Ox* 66-70; R Caston *Nor* 70-75; R Caston w Griston, Mert and Thompson 70-75; P-in-c Sturston w Thompson and Tottington 70-75; V Holme-next-the-Sea 75-80; V Hunstanton St Mary w Lt Ringstead 75-80; V Hunstanton St Mary w Ringstead Parva, Holme etc 80-85; RD Heacham and Rising 81-85; Hon Can Nor Cathl 85-93; TR Lowestoft and Kirkley 85-93; TR Keynsham *B & W* 93-96; TR Gaywood St Faith *Nor* from 96. *The Rectory, Gayton Road, King's Lynn, Norfolk PE30 4DZ* Tel (01553) 774662

ALLUM, Jeremy Warner. b 32. Wycliffe Hall Ox 60. **d** 62 **p** 63. C Hornchurch St Andr *Chelmsf* 62-67; P-in-c W Derby St Luke *Liv* 67-69; V 69-75; P-in-c Boulton *Derby* 75-90; RD Melbourne 86-90; V Hathersage from 90. *The Vicarage, Hathersage, Sheffield S30 1AB* Tel (01433) 650215

ALLUM, Peter Drage. b 11. Univ Coll Dur LTh35 BA36 MA42. Sarum Th Coll 32. **d** 36 **p** 37. C Moulsecoomb *Chich* 36-41; C Fort William *Arg* 41-43; C Annan *Glas* 43-46; P-in-c Clonfadfornan w Castletown *M & K* 46-48; I 48-51; V Sheepscombe *Glouc* 51-77; rtd 77; Perm to Offic *Glouc* from 78; Perm to Offic *Heref* 82-94 and from 96. *Rose Cottage, Kempley, Dymock, Glos GL18 2BN* Tel (01531) 890571

ALLWRIGHT, Mrs Janet Margaret. b 40. Oak Hill Th Coll 87. **d** 90 **p** 94. NSM Galleywood Common *Chelmsf* 90-93; NSM Downham w S Hanningfield from 93. *26 Chaplin Close, Chelmsford CM2 8QW* Tel (01245) 265499

ALMOND, Kenneth Alfred. b 36. EMMTC 76 Linc Th Coll 78. **d** 79 **p** 80. C Boston *Linc* 79-82; V Surfleet 82-87; RD Elloe W 86-96; V Spalding St Jo w Deeping St Nicholas from 87. *St John's Vicarage, 66A Hawthorn Bank, Spalding, Lincs PE11 1JQ* Tel (01775) 722816

ALPIAR, Ronald. b 29. Pemb Coll Cam BA52. Ely Th Coll 52. **d** 54 **p** 55. C Plaistow St Andr *Chelmsf* 54-56; SSF 54-57; rtd 79. *84 Dudsbury Road, Ferndown, Dorset BH22 8RG* Tel (01202) 590314

ALSBURY, Colin. b 56. Ch Ch Ox BA77 MA81. Ripon Coll Cuddesdon 77. **d** 80 **p** 81. C Oxton *Ches* 80-84; V Crewe All SS and St Paul 84-92; Ind Chapl 92-95; V Kettering St Andr *Pet* from 95. *25 St Mary's Road, Kettering, Northants NN15 7BP* Tel (01536) 513858 E-mail alsbury@internetaddress.com

ALSOP, Eric George. b 12. Dorchester Miss Coll 34. **d** 37 **p** 38. C Grimsby All SS *Linc* 37-39; Chapl RAF 39-67; Hon Chapl to The Queen 65-66; V Over *Ely* 67-69; P-in-c Bodiam *Chich* 69-72; V Burwash Weald 72-77; rtd 77; Perm to Offic *Chich* from 77; Perm to Offic *Cant* from 90. *Jacob's Well Farm House, 125 London Road, Hurst Green, Etchingham, E Sussex TN19 7PN* Tel (01580) 860591

ALTHAM, Donald. b 40. Liv Univ BA62. N Ord Course 87. **d** 90 **p** 91. NSM Ramsbottom St Jo and St Paul *Man* 90-96; Chapl Asst Rossendale Gen Hosp from 93; Lic Preacher *Man* from 96. *387 Whalley Road, Ramsbottom, Bury, Lancs BL0 0ER* Tel (01706) 822025

ALWAY, Cecil William. b 24. Glouc Th Course 67. **d** 69 **p** 70. C Wotton-under-Edge *Glouc* 69-73; P-in-c Pauntley w Upleadon 74-76; V Quinton w Marston Sicca 76-82; P-in-c Lower Cam 82-83; V Lower Cam w Coaley 83-90; rtd 90; Lic to Offic *Glouc* from 90; Clergy Widows Officer Adnry Glouc from 94. *Middlecot, 116A Parklands, Wotton-under-Edge, Glos GL12 7NR* Tel (01453) 844346

AMBANI, Stephen Frederick. b 45. Univ of Wales (Lamp) BA90. St Jo Coll Nottm 86 CA Tr Coll Nairobi 70. **d** 83 **p** 83. Kenya 83-93; C Glan Ely *Llan* 93-95; C Whitchurch from 95. *3 Lon Ganol, Rhiwbina, Cardiff CF4 6EB* Tel (01222) 627531

AMBROSE, Edgar. b 22. N Ord Course 80. **d** 81 **p** 82. NSM Broughton *Blackb* 81-94; Perm to Offic from 94. *76 Conway Drive, Fulwood, Preston PR2 3EQ* Tel (01772) 717530

AMBROSE, Canon Frederick Lee Giles. b 12. Kelham Th Coll 28. **d** 36 **p** 37. C Nottingham St Geo w St Jo *S'well* 36-39; S Africa 39-63 and from 70; Lic to Offic *S'well* 63-70; Hon Can Pretoria from 92. *PO Box 11026, Queenswood, Pretoria, 0121 South Africa* Tel Pretoria (12) 731379

AMBROSE, James Field. b 51. Newc Univ BA73. Cranmer Hall Dur DipTh80. **d** 80 **p** 81. C Barrow St Geo w St Luke *Carl* 80-83; C Workington St Jo 83-85; Ch Radio Officer BBC Radio Shropshire 85-88; R Montford w Shrawardine and Fitz *Lich* 85-88; Chapl RAF 88-92; Voc and Min Adv CPAS from 92; Perm to Offic *Cov* from 92. *CPAS, Athena Drive, Tachbrook Park, Warwick CV34 6NG* Tel (01926) 334242 Fax 337613

AMBROSE, John George. b 30. Ox Univ PGCE Lon Univ BD. **d** 74 **p** 75. C Rayleigh *Chelmsf* 74-79; V Hadleigh St Barn 79-95; rtd 95; Perm to Offic *Chelmsf* from 95. *9 Fairview Gardens, Leigh-on-Sea, Essex SS9 3PD* Tel (01702) 74632

AMBROSE, Dr Thomas (Tom). b 47. Sheff Univ BSc69 PhD73 Em Coll Cam BA77. Westcott Ho Cam 75. **d** 78 **p** 79. C Morpeth *Newc* 78-81; C N Gosforth 81-84; R March St Jo *Ely* 84-93; RD March 89-93; P-in-c Witchford w Wentworth from 93; Dioc Dir of Communications from 93; Chapl K Sch Ely from 94. *The Vicarage, Main Street, Witchford, Ely, Cambs CB6 2HQ* Tel (01353) 669420 Fax 669609

AMES, Jeremy Peter. b 49. K Coll Lon BD71 AKC71. **d** 72 **p** 73. C Kennington St Jo *S'wark* 72-75; Chapl RN from 75; RN Engineering Coll from 86; RN Dir of Studies RAF Chapl Sch from 89; USA 91-93; Naval Base Chapl Portsmouth 96. *Royal Naval Chaplaincy Service, Room 203, Victory Building, HM Naval Base, Portsmouth PO1 3LS* Tel (01705) 727903 Fax 727112

AMES, Reginald John. b 27. Bps' Coll Cheshunt 51. **d** 54 **p** 55. C Edmonton St Alphege *Lon* 54-58; C Mill Hill Jo Keble Ch 58-60; P-in-c Northwood Hills St Edm 61-64; V 64-92; rtd 92; Hon C Moffat *Glas* from 92. *Oakbank, Lochwood, Beattock, Moffat, Dumfriesshire DG10 9PS* Tel (01683) 300381

AMES-LEWIS, Richard. b 45. Em Coll Cam BA66 MA70. Westcott Ho Cam 76. **d** 78 **p** 79. C Bromley St Mark *Roch* 78-81; C Edenbridge 81-84; V 84-91; P-in-c Crockham Hill H Trin 84-91; P-in-c Barnes St Mary *S'wark* from 91; RD Richmond and Barnes from 94. *The Rectory, 25 Glebe Road, London SW13 0DZ* Tel 0181-878 6982 or 741 5422

AMEY, Graham George. b 44. Lon Univ BD70. Tyndale Hall Bris 67. **d** 71 **p** 72. C Hornsey Rise St Mary *Lon* 71-74; C St Helens St Helen *Liv* 74-79; V Liv All So Springwood 79-91; V Whiston from 91. *The Vicarage, 90 Windy Arbor Road, Prescot, Merseyside L35 3SG* Tel 0151-426 6329

AMIS, Ronald. b 37. Linc Th Coll 74. **d** 76 **p** 77. C Grantham w Manthorpe *Linc* 76-78; C Grantham 78-79; P-in-c Holbeach Hurn 79-81; V Long Bennington w Foston 81-91; V Corby Glen 91-93; RD Grantham 90-92; rtd 93; Perm to Offic *Pet* from 93. *2 Manor Cottages, Stamford Road, Marholm, Peterborough PE6 7HY*

AMOR, Peter David Card. b 28. AKC53. **d** 54 **p** 55. C St Margarets on Thames *Lon* 54; C Leighton Buzzard *St Alb* 54-58; C Toxteth Park St Agnes *Liv* 58-62; C-in-c Aldershot Ascension CD *Guildf* 62-65; V Bingley H Trin *Bradf* 65-72; V The Collingbournes *Sarum* 72-75; R The Collingbournes and Everleigh 75-77; V Thorpe *Guildf* 77-85; P-in-c Monks Risborough *Ox* 85-89; R 89-94; rtd 94. *1 Murren Croft, Crowmarsh Gifford, Wallingford, Oxon OX10 8EZ* Tel (01491) 826580

AMOS, Alan John. b 44. OBE79. K Coll Lon BD66 AKC67 MTh67. St Steph Ho Ox 68. **d** 69 **p** 70. C Hoxton H Trin w St Mary *Lon* 69-72; Lebanon 73-82; Lect Liturg Studies Westcott Ho Cam 82-85; Vice-Prin 85-89; Prin Cant Sch of Min 89-94; Co-Prin SEITE 94-96; Chapl Medway NHS Trust from 96. *Medway Hospital, Windmill Road, Gillingham, Kent ME7 5NY* Tel (01634) 830000 Fax 815811

AMOS, Brother. *See* YONGE, James Mohun

AMOS, Colin James. b 62. Univ of Wales (Lamp) BA83 Univ of Wales (Cardiff) CQSW85 DipSocWork85. Ridley Hall Cam CTMin93. **d** 93 **p** 94. C Aberdare St Jo *Llan* 93-96; V Port Talbot St Theodore from 96. *St Theodore's Vicarage, Talbot Road, Port Talbot SA13 1LB* Tel (01639) 883935

AMOS, Gerald. b 31. St Mich Coll Llan. **d** 58 **p** 62. C Rhosymedre *St As* 58-59; C Peckham St Andr w All SS *S'wark* 62-65; C Walworth 65-72; C S Wimbledon H Trin 72-74; C S Wimbledon H Trin and St Pet 74-75; C Warlingham w Chelsham and Farleigh 75-78; TV Speke St Aid *Liv* 78-88; P-in-c Fazakerley St Nath 88-92; TV Walton-on-the-Hill 92-96; rtd 96. *6 Church Walk, Colwyn Bay LL29 9RU*

AMOS, Patrick Henry. b 31. Roch Th Coll 63. **d** 65 **p** 66. C Strood St Nic *Roch* 65-68; C Polegate *Chich* 68-71; V Horam 71-83; R Chiddingly w E Hoathly 83-93; rtd 93; Clergy Widows Officer Maidstone Adnry *Cant* from 95; Perm to Offic from 93; Perm to Offic *Roch* from 93. *20 Fauchons Close, Bearsted, Maidstone, Kent ME14 4BB* Tel (01622) 736725

AMYS, Richard James Rutherford. b 58. Trin Coll Bris BA90. **d** 90 **p** 91. C Whitnash *Cov* 90-93; P-in-c Gravesend H Family w Ifield *Roch* 93-95; R from 95. *The Rectory, 2 Wilberforce Way, Gravesend, Kent DA12 5DQ* Tel (01474) 363038

ANCRUM, John. b 28. Clifton Th Coll 55. **d** 58 **p** 59. C Branksome St Clem *Sarum* 58-61; C Sparkhill St Jo *Birm* 61-63; V Tibshelf *Derby* 63-70; Canada 70-74; P-in-c Salwarpe *Worc* 74-75; P-in-c Tibberton w Bredicot and Warndon 75-76; P-in-c Hadzor w Oddingley 76-78; Lic to Offic *Chelmsf* 78-81; Chapl HM Pris Stafford 81-82; Chapl HM Pris Dartmoor 82-89; Lic to Offic *Ex* from 88; rtd 89. *14 Merrivale View Road, Dousland, Yelverton, Devon PL20 6NS* Tel (01822) 853909

ANDERS, Jonathan Cyril. b 36. Wycliffe Hall Ox 69. **d** 71 **p** 72. C Prescot *Liv* 71-74; C-in-c 74-76; R Wavertree St Mary 76-81; V Aigburth from 81. *St Anne's Vicarage, 389 Aigburth Road, Liverpool L17 6BH* Tel 0151-727 1101

ANDERS, Roger John. b 38. Man Univ LLB61. Nor Ord Course 91. **d** 94 **p** 95. NSM New Mills *Derby* from 94. *Bowden Head Farmhouse, Bowden Lane, Chapel-en-le-Frith, Stockport, Cheshire SK12 6QP* Tel (01298) 813332

ANDERS-RICHARDS, Dr Donald. b 28. Dur Univ BA60 MA62 Leic Univ MEd72 Sheff Univ PhD76. Coll of Resurr Mirfield 60. **d** 62 **p** 63. C Bournemouth St Fran *Win* 62-64; C Kenton *Lon* 64-68; Lic to Offic *Derby* from 68; Sen Lect Sheff Poly 75-88; rtd 88; Perm to Offic *Lich* from 88. *Laburnum Cottage, Gwern-y-Brenin, Oswestry, Shropshire SY10 8AS* Tel (01691) 653528

ANDERSEN, Paul John. b 49. **d** 77 **p** 83. USA 77-82; Belize 82-84; Zagreb *Eur* 84-85; Belgrade 85-86; USA 86-89; India 89-91; Sierra Leone 92-93; Valletta *Eur* 94-96; Kopje from 96. *c/o US Embassy, Ilindenska BB, 91000 Skopje, Macedonia* Tel Skopje (91) 116180 or 115231 Fax 117103

ANDERSON, Albert Geoffrey (Geoff). b 42. Ex Univ BA65 MA67. Qu Coll Birm DipTh75. **d** 75 **p** 76. C Helsby and Ince *Ches* 75-77; C Helsby and Dunham-on-the-Hill 77-78; TV Gleadless *Sheff* 78-85; V Thorpe Hesley 85-92; R Ribbesford w Bewdley and Dowles *Worc* from 92. *The Rectory, 57 Park Lane, Bewdley, Worcs DY12 2HA* Tel (01299) 402275

ANDERSON, Alice Calder. b 50. Moray Ho Coll of Educn DipEd76. Local Minl Tr Course 90. **d** 93 **p** 95. NSM Edin St Barn *Edin* from 93. *54 Eldinlean Terrace, Bonnyrigg, Midlothian EH19 2HQ* Tel 0131-663 3371

ANDERSON, Brian Arthur. b 42. Sarum Th Coll 75. **d** 78 **p** 79. C Plymouth St Jas Ham *Ex* 78-80; Org Sec (Dios B & W, Ex and Truro) CECS 80-89; Perm to Offic *B & W* from 86; TV Saltash *Truro* 89-94; RD E Wivelshire 91-94; P-in-c St Breoke and Egloshayle 94-97; R from 97. *The Rectory, 31 Trevanion Road, Wadebridge, Cornwall PL27 7NZ* Tel (01208) 812460

ANDERSON, Brian Glaister (Jeremy). b 35. SSF. K Coll Lon 57. **d** 79 **p** 79. Chapl St Fran Sch Hooke 79; C Croydon *Cant* 80-83; Asst Chapl HM Youth Cust Cen Glen Parva 83-84; Chapl HM Young Offender Inst Hewell Grange 84-89; Chapl HM Rem Cen Brockhill 84-89; Chapl HM Pris Parkhurst 89-96; rtd 96. *The Garden Flat, 126A High Street, Portsmouth PO1 2HW* Tel (01705) 821101

ANDERSON, David. b 19. Selw Coll Cam BA41 MA45. Wycliffe Hall Ox 47. **d** 49 **p** 50. C Bishopwearmouth St Gabr *Dur* 49-52; Tutor St Aid Birkenhead 52-56; Chapl Heswall Nautical Sch 52-53; Nigeria 56-62; Prin Wycliffe Hall Ox 62-69; Sen Lect Wall Hall Coll Aldenham 70-74; Prin Lect 74-84; rtd 84; Perm to Offic *Dur* from 84. *6 Flassburn Road, Durham DH1 4LX* Tel 0191-384 3063

ANDERSON, David Graham. b 33. MICE MIStructE. St Mich Coll Llan 85. **d** 88 **p** 89. C Llanishen and Lisvane *Llan* 88-90; C Fazeley *Lich* 90-94; Perm to Offic *Heref* from 96. *Buddleia, Wrigglesbrook Lane, Kingsthorne, Hereford HR2 8AD* Tel (01981) 540424

ANDERSON, Digby Carter. b 44. PhD. **d** 85 **p** 86. NSM Luton St Sav *St Alb* from 85. *17 Hardwick Place, Woburn Sands, Milton Keynes MK17 8QQ* Tel (01908) 584526

ANDERSON, Donald Whimbey. b 31. Trin Coll Toronto BA54 LTh57 STB57 MA58 ThD71. **d** 56 **p** 57. Canada 57-59 and 75-88; Japan 59-74; The Philippines 74-75; Assoc Sec Ecum Affairs ACC from 88. *c/o ACC, Partnership House, 157 Waterloo Road, London SE1 8UT* Tel 0171-620 1110

ANDERSON, Francis Hindley. b 20. Ch Coll Cam BA43 MA47. Wycliffe Hall Ox. **d** 44 **p** 45. C Surbiton St Matt *S'wark* 44-48; C Loughborough All SS *Leic* 48-50; C Pimlico St Pet w Westmr Ch Ch *Lon* 50-59; V Upper Chelsea St Sav 59-91; rtd 92; P-in-c Linchmere *Chich* 93-96; C Lynchmere and Camelsdale 96-97; Perm to Offic *Guildf* from 96. *35 Oaklands, Haslemere, Surrey GU27 3RD* Tel (01428) 642133

ANDERSON, Canon Gordon Fleming. b 19. TCD BA41 MA46. **d** 42 **p** 43. C Drumholm *D & R* 42-46; C Clooney 46-47; I Termonamongan 47-57; P-in-c Cumber Lower 57-61; I 61-72; I Cumber Lower w Banagher 72-94; Can Derry Cathl 76-94; Preb Howth St Patr Cathl Dublin 86-94; rtd 94. *Silversprings, 85 Dunboe Road, Ardiclave, Coleraine, Co Londonderry BT51 4JR*

ANDERSON, Gordon Roy. b 30. FCA58. Ox NSM Course 83. **d** 86 **p** 87. NSM Beaconsfield *Ox* from 86. *9 Mynchen Road, Beaconsfield, Bucks HP9 2AS* Tel (01494) 676617

ANDERSON, Gordon Stuart. b 49. St Jo Coll Nottm. **d** 82 **p** 83. C Hattersley *Ches* 82-86; C Dagenham *Chelmsf* 86-91; TV Mildenhall *St E* from 91. *The Rectory, 8 Church Walk, Mildenhall, Bury St Edmunds, Suffolk IP28 7ED* Tel (01638) 718840

ANDERSON, Hugh Richard Oswald. b 35. Roch Th Coll 68. **d** 70 **p** 71. C Minehead *B & W* 70-76; C Darley w S Darley *Derby* 76-80; R Hasland 80-94; V Temple Normanton 80-94; rtd 94; Perm to Offic *Derby* from 94. *32 Barry Road, Brimington, Chesterfield, Derbyshire S43 1PX* Tel (01246) 551020

ANDERSON, James Frederick Wale. b 34. G&C Coll Cam BA58 MA62. Cuddesdon Coll 60. **d** 62 **p** 63. C Leagrave *St Alb* 62-65; C Eastleigh *Win* 65-70; R Sherfield-on-Loddon 70-86; P-in-c Stratfield Saye w Hartley Wespall 75-86; R Sherfield-on-Loddon and Stratfield Saye etc 86-87; R Newton Valence, Selborne and E Tisted w Colemore from 87. *The Vicarage, The Plestor, Selborne, Alton, Hants GU34 3JQ* Tel (01420) 511242

ANDERSON, Canon James Raffan. b 33. FRSA90 Edin Univ MA54. Edin Th Coll 56. **d** 58 **p** 59. Chapl St Andr Cathl *Ab* 58-59; Prec St Andr Cathl 59-62; CF (TA) 59-67; Chapl Aber Univ *Ab* 60-62; Chapl Glas Univ *Glas* 62-69; Chapl Lucton Sch Herefordshire 69-71; Chapl Barnard Castle Sch 71-74; Asst Dir of Educn *Blackb* 74-78; P-in-c Whitechapel 74-78; Bp's Officer for Min *Cov* 78-87; Hon Can Cov Cathl 83-87; Miss Sec Gen Syn Bd for Miss and Unity 87-92; rtd 92. *15 Cotswold Drive, Coventry CV3 6EZ* Tel (01203) 411985

ANDERSON (née FLAHERTY), Mrs Jane Venitia. b 68. Oak Hill Th Coll DipHE91 BA92. **d** 93 **p** 94. C Timperley *Ches* 93-97; C

Cheshunt *St Alb* from 97. *156 Churchgate, Cheshunt, Herts EN8 9DY* Tel (01992) 620659

ANDERSON, Jeremy Dudgeon. b 41. Edin Univ BSc63. Trin Coll Bris 75. **d** 77 **p** 78. C Bitterne *Win* 77-81; TV Wexcombe *Sarum* 81-91; Evang Enabler (Reading Deanery) *Ox* 91-96; V Epsom Common Ch Ch *Guildf* from 96. *Christ Church Vicarage, 20 Christ Church Road, Epsom, Surrey KT19 8NE* Tel (01372) 720302

ANDERSON, Mrs Joanna Elisabeth. b 53. St Andr Univ MTh75. EMMTC 85. **d** 88 **p** 95. Par Dn Crosby *Linc* 88-92; Warden Iona Community *Arg* 92-95; R Filby, Thrigby, Mautby, Stokesby, Runham etc *Nor* from 95. *The Rectory, Rollesby, Great Yarmouth, Norfolk NR29 5HJ* Tel (01493) 740323

ANDERSON, John Michael. b 17. Madras Univ BA38. St Aug Coll Cant 59. **d** 60 **p** 61. C Smethwick St Alb *Birm* 60-62; C Stockland Green 62-65; C Braunstone *Leic* 65-69; Trinidad and Tobago 69-73; V Leic St Sav *Leic* 74-82; rtd 82; Perm to Offic *Leic* from 82. *4 Cooden Avenue, West End, Leicester LE3 0JS* Tel 0116-255 7112

ANDERSON, Canon Keith Bernard. b 36. Qu Coll Cam BA60 MA64. Tyndale Hall Bris 60. **d** 62 **p** 63. C Bootle St Leon *Liv* 62-65; Burundi 66-74; Kenya 74-83; Hon Can Mt Kenya E from 82; P-in-c Doddington w Wychling *Cant* 83-88; P-in-c Newnham 83-88; Chapl Cannes w Grasse *Eur* 88-94; Dir and Chapl Mulberry Ho High Ongar 94-95; TV Horley *S'wark* from 96. *St Wilfrid's Vicarage, Horley Row, Horley, Surrey RH6 8DF* Tel (01293) 771869

ANDERSON, Keith Edward. b 42. MRCS83 Fitzw Coll Cam BA77 MA83. Ridley Hall Cam 74. **d** 77 **p** 78. C Goodmayes All SS *Chelmsf* 77-80; Lic to Offic *Truro* 80-87; Chapl Coll of St Mark and St Jo Plymouth *Ex* 80-87; RD Plymouth Moorside 83-86; V Northampton H Sepulchre w St Andr and St Lawr *Pet* from 87; RD Northn from 92. *The Vicarage, Campbell Square, Northampton NN1 3EB* Tel (01604) 230563

ANDERSON, Kenneth. b 38. G&C Coll Cam BA62 MA66. Westcott Ho Cam 63. **d** 65 **p** 66. C Nor St Steph *Nor* 65-68; Chapl Norfolk and Nor Hosp 65-68; C Wareham w Arne *Sarum* 68-71; Chapl Sherborne Sch 71-83; Zimbabwe 83-94; Chapl Van Mildert Coll *Dur* from 95; Chapl Trevelyan Coll from 95. *Trevelyan College, Elvet Hill Road, Durham DH1 3LN* Tel 0191-374 3770 Fax 374 3789 E-mail kenneth.anderson @durham.ac.uk

ANDERSON, Canon Michael Garland. b 42. Clifton Th Coll 62. **d** 66 **p** 67. C Fareham St Jo *Portsm* 66-69; C Worting *Win* 69-74; V Hordle from 74; RD Lyndhurst from 82; Hon Can Win Cathl from 92. *The Vicarage, Stopples Lane, Hordle, Lymington, Hants SO41 0HX* Tel (01425) 614428

ANDERSON, Michael John Austen. b 35. AKC60. **d** 66 **p** 67. C Southall Ch Redeemer *Lon* 66-69; C Hampstead Garden Suburb 69-73; V S Mimms St Giles 73-80; V S Mymms *St Alb* 80; V The Brents and Davington w Oare and Luddenham *Cant* 80-86; V Margate All SS from 86. *All Saints' Vicarage, All Saints' Avenue, Margate, Kent CT9 5QL* Tel (01843) 220795

ANDERSON, Nicholas Patrick. b 53. BA. **d** 81 **p** 82. In RC Ch 81-89; C Gt Crosby St Faith *Liv* 89-92; C Walton-on-the-Hill 92-95; V Pemberton St Fran Kitt Green from 95. *The Vicarage, 42 Sherbourne Road, Kitt Green, Wigan, Lancs WN5 0JA* Tel (01942) 213227

ANDERSON, Olaf Emanuel. b 64. Queensland Univ BA88. St Fran Coll Queensland 84. **d** 87 **p** 88. Australia 87-90; C Petersfield *Portsm* 91-93; C Buriton from 91. *42 Heath Road, Petersfield, Hants GU31 4EH* Tel (01730) 263190

ANDERSON, Mrs Pearl Ann. b 46. MIPM74 St Andr Univ MA68. Cant Sch of Min 90. **d** 93. Par Dn Epping St Jo *Chelmsf* 93-95; Adv to Coun for Soc Resp (Dios Cant and Roch) *Cant* from 95; Perm to Offic *Roch* from 95. *1 Gibbs Hill, Headcorn, Ashford, Kent TN27 9UD* Tel (01622) 890043 or 755014

ANDERSON, Peter John. b 44. Nottm Univ BA65 BA73. St Jo Coll Nottm DPS. **d** 74 **p** 75. C Otley *Bradf* 74-77; TV Marfleet *York* 77-84; V Greasbrough *Sheff* 84-95; I Clonmel Union *C, C & R* from 95; I Rathcooney Union from 95. *Ardeevan, Lake Road, Cobh, Co Cork, Irish Republic* Tel Cork (21) 811790

ANDERSON, Peter Scott. b 49. Nottm Univ BTh72 CertEd. Kelham Th Coll 68. **d** 74 **p** 75. C Sheff Parson Cross St Cecilia *Sheff* 74-77; C Leytonstone St Marg w St Columba *Chelmsf* 77-81; P-in-c Forest Gate St Edm 81-89; V 89-90; P-in-c Plaistow 90-94; V Willesden Green St Andr and St Fran of Assisi *Lon* from 94. *The Clergy House, St Andrew's Road, London NW10 2QS* Tel 0181-459 2670

ANDERSON, Canon Dr Roderick Stephen (Rod). b 43. Cant Univ (NZ) BSc63 PhD67 New Coll Ox BA72. Wycliffe Hall Ox 70. **d** 73 **p** 74. C Bradf Cathl *Bradf* 73-75; C Allerton 76-78; V Cottingley 78-94; RD Airedale 88-95; Hon Can Bradf Cathl from 94; V Heaton St Barn from 94. *The Vicarage, Parsons Road, Heaton, Bradford, W Yorkshire BD9 4AY* Tel (01274) 496712

ANDERSON, Canon Rosemary Ann. b 36. Ex Univ BA59. N Ord Course 83. **dss** 86 **d** 87 **p** 94. Oldham St Paul *Man* 86-87; Hon Par Dn 87-89; Bp's Adv for Women's Min from 88; Par Dn Roughtown 93-94; P-in-c from 94; Hon Can Man Cathl from 96. *St John's Vicarage, Carrhill Road, Mossley, Ashton-under-Lyne, Lancs OL5 0BL* Tel (01457) 832250

ANDERSON, Stuart. b 31. Dur Univ BA52. Linc Th Coll 52. **d** 54 **p** 55. C Billingham St Cuth *Dur* 54-57; C Fulham St Etheldreda *Lon* 57-61; New Zealand from 61. *3 Arataki Road, Havelock North, Hawkes Bay, New Zealand* Tel Hastings (6) 877 8567

ANDERSON, Timothy George. b 59. Ealing Coll of HE BA82. Wycliffe Hall Ox 83. **d** 86 **p** 87. C Harold Wood *Chelmsf* 86-90; C Whitfield *Derby* 90-95; P-in-c Wolverhampton St Luke *Lich* from 95. *St Luke's Vicarage, 122 Goldthorn Hill, Wolverhampton WV2 3HQ* Tel (01902) 340261

ANDERSON, Timothy James Lane. b 59. Pemb Coll Ox BA80 MA90. St Jo Coll Nottm DTS92. **d** 93 **p** 94. C Reigate St Mary *S'wark* 93-95. *81A Bramcote Drive, Beeston, Nottingham NG9 1AR* Tel 0115-922 4773

ANDERTON, Frederic Michael. b 31. IAAP IGAP Pemb Coll Cam MA57 Jung Institut Zurich DipAnPsych86. Westcott Ho Cam 64. **d** 66 **p** 67. C St Jo Wood *Lon* 66-69; C All Hallows by the Tower etc 70-77; C St Giles Cripplegate w St Bart Moor Lane etc 77-82; C Zurich *Eur* 82-86; Perm to Offic *Lon* from 94; rtd 96. *100 Harvist Road, London NW6 6HZ* Tel 0171-960 4780

ANDERTON, Peter. b 45. Sarum & Wells Th Coll 80. **d** 82 **p** 83. C Adel *Ripon* 82-86; P-in-c Dacre w Hartwith 86-90; P-in-c Thornthwaite w Thruscross and Darley 88-90; V Dacre w Hartwith and Darley w Thornthwaite 90-91; V Owton Manor *Dur* from 91. *The Vicarage, 18 Rossmere Way, Hartlepool, Cleveland TS25 5EF* Tel (01429) 290278

ANDREW, Brian. b 31. Oak Hill Th Coll 75. **d** 77 **p** 78. C Broadwater St Mary *Chich* 77-81; R Nettlebed w Bix and Highmore *Ox* 81-87; V Shenstone *Lich* 87-96; rtd 96. *96 Langlands Road, Cullompton, Devon EX15 1JB* Tel (01884) 38279

ANDREW, Dr David Neil. b 62. Down Coll Cam BA83 MA87 PhD88. Ridley Hall Cam CTMin93. **d** 93 **p** 94. C Heatherlands St Jo *Sarum* from 93. *91 Churchill Road, Poole, Dorset BH12 2LR* Tel (01202) 748754

ANDREW, Donald. b 35. Tyndale Hall Bris 63. **d** 66 **p** 67. C Croydon Ch Ch Broad Green *Cant* 66-69; C Ravenhead *Liv* 69-72; Scripture Union 72-77; V Rushen *S & M* 77-82; TR Heworth *York* from 82. *Heworth Rectory, Melrosegate, York YO3 0RP* Tel (01904) 422958

ANDREW, Frank. b 17. St D Coll Lamp BA49 Ely Th Coll 50. **d** 51 **p** 52. C Howden *York* 51-55; V Mosborough *Sheff* 55-59; C-in-c Greenhill CD 59-65; V Greenhill 65-69; R March St Jo *Ely* 69-77; R March St Mary 71-77; RD March 73-77; R Catworth Magna 77-83; R Covington 77-83; R Tilbrook 77-83; rtd 83; Perm to Offic *Chich* from 83. *11 Romney Close, Seaford, E Sussex BN25 3TR* Tel (01323) 897352

ANDREW, Canon John Gerald Barton. b 31. OBE. Keble Coll Ox BA55 MA58 Cuttington Univ Coll Liberia Hon DD76 Kentucky Sem Hon DD76 Nashotah Ho Wisconsin Hon DD77 Gen Th Sem NY Hon DD96. Cuddesdon Coll 54. **d** 56 **p** 57. C Redcar *York* 56-59; USA 59-60 and 72-96; Abp's Dom Chapl *York* 60-61; Abp's Dom Chapl *Cant* 61-65; Abp's Sen Chapl 65-69; Six Preacher Cant Cathl 67-72; V Preston St Jo *Blackb* 69-72; RD Preston 70-72; R St Thos Fifth Avenue 72-96; rtd 96. *93 Sydney Place, Bath BA2 6NE* Tel (01225) 422783

ANDREW, Michael Paul. b 51. SSC Leic Univ CertEd73. Chich Th Coll 80. **d** 83 **p** 84. C Par *Truro* 83-86; Hon Chapl Miss to Seamen 86; P-in-c Salford Ordsall St Clem *Man* 86-91; P-in-c Hammersmith St Jo *Lon* from 91. *St John's Vicarage, Iffley Road, London W6 0PA* Tel 0181-748 0079 Fax 741 1825 or 741 8933

ANDREW, Ronald Arthur. b 27. Sarum Th Coll 64. **d** 65 **p** 66. C Darwen St Cuth *Blackb* 65-69; C Padiham 69-71; V Colne H Trin 71-76; V Adlington 76-85; V Goosnargh w Whittingham 85-92; rtd 92; Perm to Offic *Blackb* from 92. *7 Windsor Gardens, Garstang, Preston PR3 1EG* Tel (01995) 600273

ANDREW, Sydney William. b 55. Cranmer Hall Dur 82. **d** 85 **p** 86. C Horncastle w Low Toynton *Linc* 85-88; V Worlaby 88-93; V Bonby 88-93; V Elsham 88-93; rtd 93; Lic to Offic *Linc* 93-95; Hon C Brocklesby Park from 95; Hon C Croxton from 96. *10 Bentley Lane, Grasby, Barnetby, S Humberside DN38 6AW* Tel (01652) 62586

ANDREW, Canon William Hugh (Bill). b 32. Selw Coll Cam BA56 MA60. Ridley Hall Cam 56. **d** 58 **p** 59. C Woking St Mary *Guildf* 58-61; C Farnborough 61-64; V Gatten St Paul *Portsm* 64-71; R Weymouth St Mary *Sarum* 71-76; V Heatherlands St Jo 76-82; Can and Preb Sarum Cathl 81-86; R Alderbury and W Grimstead 82-86; Perm to Offic *Bris* 86-88; Communications Dir Bible Soc 86-94; Communications Consultant from 94; Hon C The Lydiards *Bris* 88-94; C W Swindon and the Lydiards 94-96; rtd 96; Hon C W Swindon and the Lydiards *Bris* from 96. *20 Chudleigh, Freshbrook, Swindon SN5 8NQ* Tel (01793) 695313

ANDREWES, Nicholas John. b 64. Southn Univ BA87 La Sainte Union Coll PGCE88. Cranmer Hall Dur BTh93 DMS93. **d** 96 **p** 97. C Dovecot *Liv* from 96. *8B Grant Road, Dovecot, Liverpool L14 0LQ* Tel 0151-489 2163

ANDREWES UTHWATT, Henry. b 25. Jes Coll Cam BA49 MA51. Wells Th Coll 49. **d** 51 **p** 52. C Fareham H Trin *Portsm* 51-55; C Haslemere *Guildf* 55-59; C Wimbledon *S'wark* 59-61; V W Wimbledon Ch Ch 61-73; V Yeovil St Jo w Preston Plucknett

B & W 73-76; TR Yeovil 76-82; V Burrington and Churchill 82-90; RD Locking 87-90; rtd 90; Perm to Offic *B & W* from 90; Chapl Partis Coll Bath from 91; Chapl St Martin's Hosp Bath from 91. *71 Mount Road, Bath BA2 1LJ* Tel (01225) 482220

ANDREWS, Canon Alan Robert Williams. b 14. AKC37. **d** 37 **p** 38. C Milton next Gravesend Ch Ch *Roch* 37-40; C Stratfield Mortimer *Ox* 40-45; C Heanor *Derby* 45-47; R Whittington 47-58; V Quarndon 58-79; Hon Can Derby Cathl 77-79; rtd 79; Perm to Offic *Derby* from 79. *33 Waterpark Road, Doveridge, Ashbourne, Derbyshire DE6 5NU* Tel (01889) 565223

ANDREWS, Anthony Brian. b 33. Lon Univ BA54 AKC58. Coll of Resurr Mirfield 56. **d** 58 **p** 59. C Haggerston St Columba *Lon* 58-60; C N Hammersmith St Kath 60-63; V Goldthorpe *Sheff* 63-74; V Notting Hill St Mich and Ch Ch *Lon* from 74. *St Michael's Vicarage, 35 St Lawrence Terrace, London W10 5SR* Tel 0181-969 0776

ANDREWS, Anthony Bryan de Tabley. b 20. K Coll Lon BA42. Linc Th Coll 42. **d** 44 **p** 45. C Hutton *Chelmsf* 44-48; C St Marylebone All SS *Lon* 48-57; Chapl to Ho of SS Mary and Jo Holyrood Witney 57-59; C Ox St Barn *Ox* 57-59; V Babbacombe *Ex* 59-75; R Worth *Chich* 75-82; RD E Grinstead 77-82; P-in-c Exton and Winsford and Cutcombe w Luxborough *B & W* 82-83; R 83-85; rtd 85; Perm to Offic *Ex* from 86. *Cordwainers, Iddesleigh, Winkleigh, Devon EX19 8BG* Tel (01837) 810116

ANDREWS, Anthony Frederick. b 25. K Coll Lon 54. **d** 55 **p** 56. C Kentish Town St Jo *Lon* 55-58; C Belmont 58-60; R Evershot, Frome St Quinton, Melbury Bubb etc *Sarum* 60-66; CF 66-69; C Bridgwater St Mary w Chilton Trinity *B & W* 69-70; R Cossington 70-73; C Highworth w Sevenhampton and Inglesham etc *Bris* 75-84; P-in-c Bishopstone w Hinton Parva 84-88; rtd 88. *Burford House, Highworth, Swindon SN6 7AD* Tel (01793) 762796

ANDREWS, Anthony John. b 35. S'wark Ord Course 75. **d** 80 **p** 81. NSM Cheam *S'wark* 80-83; C Epsom St Martin *Guildf* 83-86; V Barton *Portsm* 86-89; Chapl Northwick Park and St Mark's NHS Trust Harrow from 90. *Northwick Park Hospital, Watford Road, Harrow, Middx HA1 3UJ* Tel 0181-869 3923

ANDREWS, Canon Brian Keith. b 39. Keble Coll Ox BA62 MA69. Coll of Resurr Mirfield 62. **d** 64 **p** 65. C Is of Dogs Ch Ch and St Jo w St Luke *Lon* 64-68; C Hemel Hempstead *St Alb* 68-71; TV 71-79; V Abbots Langley from 79; RD Watford 88-94; Hon Can St Alb from 94. *The Vicarage, High Street, Abbots Langley, Herts WD5 0AS* Tel (01923) 263013 or 261795 Fax 261795

ANDREWS, Christopher Paul. b 47. Fitzw Coll Cam BA70 MA73. Westcott Ho Cam 69. **d** 72 **p** 73. C Croydon *Cant* 72-75; C Gosforth All SS *Newc* 75-79; TV Newc Epiphany 80-87; RD Newc Cen 82-87; V Alnwick St Mich and St Paul 87-96; Chapl Alnwick Infirmary 87-96; TR Grantham *Linc* from 96. *The Rectory, Church Street, Grantham, Lincs NG31 6RR* Tel (01476) 563710

ANDREWS, Clive Francis. b 50. K Coll Lon BD72 AKC72. **d** 73 **p** 74. C Clapham H Trin *S'wark* 73-75; C Kidbrooke St Jas 76-78; Youth Officer 79-84; V Forest Hill St Aug 84-89; Perm to Offic *Sarum* from 89. *Cross River Cottage, Donhead St Andrew, Shaftesbury, Dorset SP7 9EQ* Tel (01747) 828126

ANDREWS, Clive Frederick. b 43. St Jo Coll Nottm 81. **d** 83 **p** 84. C Leic St Jas *Leic* 83-86; Ind Chapl 86-90; Hon TV Melton Gt Framland 89-90; TV Clifton *S'well* 90-92; P-in-c Elkesley w Bothamsall 92-94; P-in-c Gamston w Eaton and W Drayton 92-94; R from 94. *The Vicarage, 3 Maple Drive, Elkesley, Retford, Notts DN22 8AX* Tel (01777) 838293

ANDREWS, Edward Robert. b 33. St Mich Coll Llan 62. **d** 64 **p** 65. C Kingswinford St Mary *Lich* 64-69; Chapl RAF 69-88; R St Just in Roseland w Philleigh *Truro* from 88. *The Rectory, St Just in Roseland, Truro, Cornwall TR2 5JD* Tel (01326) 270248

ANDREWS, Eric Charles. b 17. AKC41. **d** 41 **p** 42. C W Derby (or Tuebrook) St Jo *Liv* 41-44; C Kettering All SS *Pet* 44-46; C Letchworth *St Alb* 46-54; V Hastings All So *Chich* 54-63; V Eastbourne St Andr 63-73; R E Blatchington 73-83; rtd 83; Perm to Offic *Chich* from 83. *3 The Spinney, Bexhill-on-Sea, E Sussex TN39 3SW* Tel (01424) 843864

ANDREWS, Eric Keith. b 11. Tyndale Hall Bris 36. **d** 38 **p** 39. C Fulham St Mary N End *Lon* 38-40; P-in-c Kensal Town St Thos 40-42; C Worthing H Trin *Chich* 42-47; R Newick 47-56; R Pembridge *Heref* 56-66; S Africa 61-62; Kenya 66-70; R Stanton *St E* 70-76; rtd 76; Perm to Offic *Heref* from 76. *79 Bearcroft, Weobley, Hereford HR4 8TD* Tel (01544) 318114

ANDREWS, Frances. b 24. EMMTC 73. **dss** 78 **d** 87 **p** 94. Porchester *S'well* 78-86; Asst Chapl Nottm City Hosp 86-88; Hon C Gedling *S'well* 88-92; NSM Epperstone 92-95; NSM Gonalston 92-95; NSM Oxton 92-95; rtd 95. *1 Cromford Avenue, Nottingham NG4 3RU* Tel 0115-961 3857

ANDREWS, John Colin. b 47. Sarum & Wells Th Coll 78. **d** 80 **p** 81. C Burnham *B & W* 80-84; V Williton 84-92; P-in-c Ashwick w Oakhill and Binegar from 92; Dioc Communications Officer from 92. *The Rectory, Fosse Road, Oakhill, Bath BA3 5HU* Tel (01749) 841341 Fax 841098

ANDREWS, Preb John Douglas. b 19. Keble Coll Ox BA39 MA44. Chich Th Coll 40. **d** 42 **p** 43. C S Bermondsey St Aug *S'wark* 42-44; C Lambeth St Jo w All SS 44-46; C Towcester w Easton Neston *Pet* 46-50; C Shrewsbury H Cross *Lich* 50-52; V Ettingshall 52-59; V Walsall St Andr 59-68; V Penkhull 68-80; P-in-c Ellenhall w Ranton 80-86; P-in-c Chebsey 80-86; Preb Lich Cathl 81-86; rtd 86; Perm to Offic *Heref* from 86; Perm to Offic *Lich* from 86. *The Bungalow, 1 Belgrave Place, Shrewsbury SY2 5LT* Tel (01743) 240270

ANDREWS, John Elfric. b 35. Ex Coll Ox BA59 MA63. Wycliffe Hall Ox 59. **d** 61 **p** 62. C Cheltenham All SS *Glouc* 61-66; Cand Sec Lon City Miss 66-92; Lic to Offic *S'wark* 66-92; R Kingham w Churchill, Daylesford and Sarsden *Ox* from 92. *The Rectory, 6 The Moat, Kingham, Oxford OX7 4XZ* Tel (01608) 658230

ANDREWS, John Francis. b 34. Jes Coll Cam BA58 MA62. S'wark Ord Course 78. **d** 81 **p** 82. NSM Norwood All SS *Cant* 81-82; NSM Upper Norwood All SS w St Marg 82-85; NSM Upper Norwood All SS *S'wark* 85-87; NSM Dulwich St Barn 89-92; NSM S Dulwich St Steph 92-95; Perm to Offic from 95. *46 Cypress Road, London SE25 4AU* Tel 0181-653 5620

ANDREWS, John George William. b 42. Qu Coll Birm 65. **d** 68 **p** 69. C Smethwick St Matt w St Chad *Birm* 68-71; CF 71-97; P-in-c Lyme Regis *Sarum* from 97. *The Vicarage, West Hill Road, Lyme Regis, Dorset DT7 3LW* Tel (01297) 443134

ANDREWS, John Viccars. b 31. St Edm Hall Ox BA55. St Steph Ho Ox 55. **d** 58 **p** 59. C Clerkenwell H Redeemer w St Phil *Lon* 58-63; C Tilehurst St Mich *Ox* 63-69; P-in-c Abingdon w Shippon 69-76; R Cranwich *Nor* 76-86; R Ickburgh w Langford 76-86; R Mundford w Lynford 76-86; R Seaton Ross Gp of Par *York* 86-96; RD S Wold 90-96; rtd 96. *11 St Mary's Close, Beverley, N Humberside HU17 7AY*

ANDREWS, Keith. b 47. St Mich Coll Llan 79. **d** 81 **p** 82. C Penarth w Lavernock *Llan* 81-85; V Nantymoel w Wyndham 85-91; RD Bridgend 89-93; R Coychurch w Llangan and St Mary Hill from 91. *The Rectory, Church Terrace, Coychurch, Bridgend CF35 5HF* Tel (01656) 860785

ANDREWS, Major Paul Rodney Gwyther. b 16. GM41. Mon Dioc Tr Scheme 74. **d** 77 **p** 78. NSM Goetre w Llanover and Llanfair Kilgeddin *Mon* 77-80; Lic to Offic *S & B* from 81. *Bromelys, Llangorse, Brecon LD3 7UG* Tel (01874) 84296

ANDREWS, Peter Alwyne. b 44. Lon Univ BSc67. Westcott Ho Cam 70. **d** 73 **p** 74. C Barnoldswick w Bracewell *Bradf* 73-76; C Maltby *Sheff* 76-78; V Bradf St Oswald Chapel Green *Bradf* 78-85; V Hanwell St Thos *Lon* from 85. *St Thomas's Vicarage, 182 Boston Road, London W7 2AD* Tel 0181-567 5280

ANDREWS, Peter Douglas. b 52. SEN72 SRN78. St Steph Ho Ox 86. **d** 88 **p** 89. C Perry Barr *Birm* 88-92; TV Swindon New Town *Bris* from 92. *St Saviour's Vicarage, 6 Hillcrest Close, Hillside Avenue, Swindon SN1 4LX* Tel (01793) 617681

ANDREWS, Richard John. b 57. Bris Univ BA78 CertEd79. Ripon Coll Cuddesdon 82. **d** 84 **p** 85. C Kidderminster St Mary and All SS, Trimpley etc *Worc* 84-87; Hon C Derby Cathl *Derby* 87-89; Chapl Derbyshire Coll of HE 87-89; V Chellaston *Derby* 89-93; V Spondon from 93. *St Werburgh's Vicarage, Gascoigne Drive, Spondon, Derby DE21 7GL* Tel (01332) 673573

ANDREYEV, Michael. b 62. Hatf Coll Dur BA85. Wycliffe Hall Ox BA91. **d** 96. C Surbiton Hill Ch Ch *S'wark* from 96. *19A Dennan Road, Surbiton, Surrey KT6 7RY* Tel 0181-390 2256

ANGEL, Gervais Thomas David. b 36. Ch Ch Ox BA59 MA62 Bris Univ MEd78. **d** 61 **p** 62. C Aberystwyth St Mich *St D* 61-65; Tutor Clifton Th Coll 65-72; Dean Studies Trin Coll Bris 72-81; Dir Studies 81-90; Hon C Clifton H Trin, St Andr and St Pet *Bris* 82-90; Area Sec (W England) SAMS from 90; Th Consultant SAMS from 90; Perm to Offic *Ex* from 90; NSM Stoke Gifford *Bris* from 92; Perm to Offic *B & W, Truro* and *Heref* from 92. *82 Oak Close, Little Stoke, Bristol BS12 6RD* Tel (01454) 618081 Fax 0117-923 6053

ANGEL, Robin Alan. b 41. St Mich Coll Llan. **d** 89 **p** 90. C Whitchurch *Llan* 89-94; V Aberpergwm and Blaengwrach from 94. *The Vicarage, 11 Roberts Close, Glynneath, Neath SA11 5HR* Tel (01639) 721964

ANGELO, Brother. *See* DEACON, Donald

ANGLE, John Edwin George. b 42. Liv Univ ADEd73 Univ of Wales MEd75 Univ of the W of England, Bris DipEdMan85. Lon Bible Coll BD65 W of England Minl Tr Course 92. **d** 94 **p** 95. NSM Clevedon St Andr and Ch Ch *B & W* 94-97; NSM Worle from 97. *19 Pyne Point, Clevedon, Avon BS21 7RL* Tel (01275) 872630 Fax as telephone

ANGOVE, Ms Helen Teresa. b 71. Bath Univ BEng93. Ripon Coll Cuddesdon BTh94. **d** 97. C Bridgwater St Mary, Chilton Trinity and Durleigh *B & W* from 97. *11 Alexandra Road, Bridgwater, Somerset TA6 7HU* Tel (01278) 429565

ANGUS, Edward. b 39. Man Univ BA60. Qu Coll Birm DipTh61. **d** 62 **p** 63. C Chorley St Geo *Blackb* 62-65; C S Shore H Trin 65-68; R Bretherton 68-76; V Altham w Clayton le Moors 76-90; V Preesall from 90. *St Oswald's Vicarage, Lancaster Road, Poulton-le-Fylde, Lancs FY6 0DU* Tel (01253) 810297

ANGWIN, Richard Paul. b 25. ACA49 FCA60 AKC56. **d** 56 **p** 57. C Clacton St Jas *Chelmsf* 56-59; V Brightlingsea 59-69; V Wanstead H Trin Hermon Hill 69-75; Chapl Wanstead Hosp Lon 69-75; Chapl Halstead Hosp 75-87; V Halstead St Andr *Chelmsf* 75-78; P-in-c Greenstead Green 75-78; V Halstead St Andr w H Trin 78-79; V Halstead St Andr w H Trin and

Greenstead Green 79-87; RD Halstead and Coggeshall 84-87; rtd 87; Perm to Offic *Lich* from 91. *2 Seckham Road, Lichfield, Staffs WS13 7AN* Tel (01543) 250848

ANIDO, John David Forsdyke. b 16. Ox Univ BA38 MA41 McGill Univ Montreal PhD75. Westcott Ho Cam 39. **d** 40 **p** 41. C Stoke Newington St Mary *Lon* 40-45; C Cobham *Guildf* 45-47; R Harbledown *Cant* 52-57; Canada 47-51 and 57-76; V Auckland St Andr and St Anne *Dur* 76-83; rtd 83; Perm to Offic *York* from 83. *The Spinney, 2 Park Road, Malton, N Yorkshire YO17 9EA* Tel (01653) 696338

ANKER, George William. b 10. AKC51. **d** 51 **p** 52. C Richmond H Trin and Ch Ch *S'wark* 51-54; C Battersea St Pet 54-57; C Shere *Guildf* 57-62; C Leatherhead 62-68; V Brockley Hill St Sav *S'wark* 68-72; C Sanderstead All SS 72-76; rtd 76; Perm to Offic *S'wark* from 76. *The College of St Barnabas, Blackberry Lane, Lingfield, Surrey RH7 6NJ* Tel (01342) 870260

ANKER, Malcolm. b 39. Univ of Wales BA61. Bps' Coll Cheshunt 61. **d** 63 **p** 64. C Marfleet *York* 63-66; C Cottingham 66-69; V Skirlaugh w Long Riston 69-74; V Elloughton and Brough w Brantingham 74-84; V Tadcaster 84-86; V Tadcaster w Newton Kyme 86-91; V Oatlands *Guildf* from 91. *The Vicarage, 5 Beechwood Avenue, Weybridge, Surrey KT13 9TE* Tel (01932) 847963

ANKER-PETERSEN, Robert Brian. b 52. Aber Univ MTh88. Wycliffe Hall Ox BA79 MA88. **d** 93 **p** 94. C Perth St Ninian *St And* 93-96; Bp's Researcher on Ch's Min of Healing from 93. *Blackruthven House, Tibbermore, Perth PH1 1PY* Tel (01738) 583238

ANKERS, Charles William (<u>Bill</u>). b 42. FIMI. NE Ord Course 89. **d** 93 **p** 95. NSM York St Luke *York* 93-95; C Kexby w Wilberfoss from 95; Asst Chapl HM Pris Full Sutton from 95. *85 Burton Stone Lane, York YO3 6BZ* Tel (01904) 634145

ANKETELL, Jeyarajan. b 41. MInstP Lon Univ BSc62 PhD67. Coll of Resurr Mirfield 69. **d** 73 **p** 74. Asst Chapl Newc Univ *Newc* 73-75; Asst Chapl Lon Univ *Lon* 75-77; Teacher from 78; Lic to Offic *S'wark* 81-83; Chasetown High Sch from 85; NSM Lich St Mary w St Mich *Lich* 86-96; NSM Lich St Mich w St Mary and Wall from 96. *7 Wissage Lane, Lichfield, Staffs WS13 6DQ* Tel (01543) 262032

ANNACEY, Felix. b 62. Hull Univ DipTh87. **d** 87 **p** 88. C Fenton *Lich* 87-88; Ghana from 88. *PO Box 248, Koforidua, Ghana*

ANNAS, Geoffrey Peter. b 53. Sarum & Wells Th Coll. **d** 83 **p** 84. C S'wark H Trin w St Matt *S'wark* 83-87; TV Walworth 87-94; Warden Pemb Coll Miss Walworth 87-94; V Southampton Thornhill St Chris *Win* from 94. *St Christopher's Vicarage, 402 Hinkler Road, Southampton SO19 6DF* Tel (01703) 448537

ANNEAR, Hubert Tours. b 24. Dur Univ BA49 Leeds Univ MA58. Linc Th Coll 49. **d** 51 **p** 52. C Holbeck St Matt *Ripon* 51-55; C Adel 55-57; V Middleton St Mary 57-64; UMCA 64-65; USPG 65-71; V Bierley *Bradf* 71-76; V Morley St Paul *Wakef* 76-87; rtd 88; Perm to Offic *Wakef* from 88. *112 Asquith Avenue, Morley, Leeds LS27 9QN* Tel 0113-253 7880

ANNET, John Thomas. b 20. TD66. Selw Coll Cam BA49 MA53. Westcott Ho Cam 49. **d** 51 **p** 52. C Chorlton-cum-Hardy St Clem *Man* 51-54; C Ashton Ch Ch 54-56; V Hindsford 56-66; R Didsbury Ch Ch 66-75; V Gt Budworth *Ches* 75-86; rtd 86; Perm to Offic *Ex* from 86. *58 Lydgates Road, Seaton, Devon EX12 2BX* Tel (01297) 23495

ANNIS, Herman North. b 28. Lich Th Coll 62. **d** 64 **p** 65. C Kilburn St Aug *Lon* 64-67; C Toxteth Park St Agnes *Liv* 67-70; V 70-82; V Hempton and Pudding Norton *Nor* 82-84; P-in-c Sculthorpe w Dunton and Doughton 82-84; V Northampton H Trin *Pet* 84-95; rtd 95; NSM Brighton St Bart *Chich* from 95. *45 Orchard Avenue, Worthing, W Sussex BN14 7PY* Tel (01903) 205683

ANNIS, Jennifer Mary. b 49. **d** 95. NSM Digswell and Panshanger *St Alb* from 95. *261 Knightsfield, Welwyn Garden City, Herts AL8 7RA* Tel (01707) 329599

ANNIS, Rodney James. b 43. Ex Univ BA75 MA79 PhD86. Ripon Coll Cuddesdon 75. **d** 76 **p** 77. C Brixham *Ex* 76-77; Asst Chapl Ex Univ 77-80; Chapl Ex Sch 77-80; C Boston *Linc* 80-84; Chapl Trin Hall Cam 84-87; Chapl St Edw K and Martyr Cam *Ely* 84-87; V Bush Hill Park St Steph *Lon* from 87. *St Stephen's Vicarage, Village Road, Bush Hill Park, Enfield, Middx EN1 2ET*

ANNS, Pauline Mary. *See* HIGHAM, Mrs Pauline Mary

ANSAH, Kwesi Gyebi Ababio (<u>George</u>). b 54. DipSM87. Simon of Cyrene Th Inst 90 Oak Hill Th Coll DipHE93 BTh97. **d** 93 **p** 94. C Peckham St Mary Magd *S'wark* 93-96; V W Dulwich Em from 96. *Emmanuel Vicarage, 94 Clive Road, London SE21 8BU* Tel 0181-670 2793

ANSCOMBE, John Thomas. b 51. Ex Univ BA72. Cranmer Hall Dur DipTh73. **d** 74 **p** 75. C Upper Armley *Ripon* 74-77; C Leeds St Geo 78-81; Exec Producer Scripture Union from 81; Hon C Beckenham Ch Ch *Roch* from 82. *26 Wimborne Way, Beckenham, Kent BR3 4DJ* Tel 0181-658 4037 or 0171-782 0013 Fax 0171-782 0014

ANSCOMBE, Canon Thomas. b 15. Qu Coll Cam BA37 MA41. Ridley Hall Cam 37. **d** 39 **p** 40. C Lenton *S'well* 39-45; V Becontree St Mary *Chelmsf* 45-52; R Nottingham St Nic *S'well* 52-57; Prin Clifton Th Coll 57-64; R Kirkheaton *Wakef* 64-80; Hon Can Wakef Cathl 77-80; rtd 80; Perm to Offic *Bradf* from 80; Perm to Offic *Wakef* 80-92. *Milton House Nursing Home, Gargrave, Skipton, N Yorkshire BD23 3NN* Tel (01756) 749289

ANSDELL-EVANS, Peter. b 25. Liv Univ BArch51. S'wark Ord Course 89. **d** 91 **p** 92. NSM Kennington St Jo w St Jas *S'wark* from 91. *9 Dalmore Road, London SE21 8HD* Tel 0181-670 8046

ANSELL, Antony Michael. b 40. St Jo Coll Nottm 78. **d** 80 **p** 81. C Harrow Weald St Mich *Lon* 80-84; C Harrow Trin St Mich 84; Hon C Ches Square St Mich w St Phil 86-88; Hon C Mayfair Ch Ch from 88. *10 Durand Gardens, London SW9 0PP* Tel 0171-587 0997

ANSELL, Howard. b 36. St Jo Coll Cam BA59 MA62. NW Ord Course 73. **d** 76 **p** 77. C Chapeltown *Sheff* 76-79; V Worsbrough St Thos and St Jas 79-83; R Lt Waltham *Chelmsf* from 83; P-in-c Gt Leighs from 92; P-in-c Lt Leighs from 95. *The Rectory, Brook Hill, Little Waltham, Chelmsford CM3 3LJ* Tel (01245) 360241

ANSELL, John Christopher. b 49. DipAD. Sarum & Wells Th Coll 79. **d** 81 **p** 82. C Dartford St Alb *Roch* 81-84; C Leybourne 84-88; C Larkfield 84-88; TV Mortlake w E Sheen *S'wark* from 88. *17 Sheen Gate Gardens, London SW14 7PD* Tel 0181-876 5002

ANSELL, Philip Harding. b 67. LMH Ox BA89 Rob Coll Cam BA92. Ridley Hall Cam CTM93. **d** 93 **p** 94. C Rainham w Wennington *Chelmsf* from 93. *34 Warwick Road, Rainham, Essex RM13 9XU* Tel (01708) 555810

ANSELL, Stuart Adrian. b 59. Ripon Coll Cuddesdon DipMin95 St Alb Minl Tr Scheme 81. **d** 97. C Cheadle w Freehay *Lich* from 97. *3 Byron Close, Cheadle, Stoke-on-Trent ST10 1XB* Tel (01538) 756166

ANSELM, Brother. *See* SMYTH, Robert Andrew Laine

ANSON (née DRAX), Mrs Elizabeth Margaret (<u>Liz</u>). b 57. St Jo Coll Nottm DipMin93. **d** 94 **p** 95. C Kimberworth *Sheff* 94-95; C Doncaster St Mary 95-97; rtd 97. *164 Park Avenue, Princes Avenue, Hull HU5 3EY* Tel (01482) 343169

ANSON, Harry. b 35. FInstFF79. St Jo Coll Nottm 83. **d** 88. NSM Ayr *Glas* 88-93; Miss to Seamen 91-93. *Bridgend House, Patna, Ayr KA6 7LP* Tel (01292) 531238

ANSTEY, Nigel John. b 55. Cranmer Hall Dur 84. **d** 87 **p** 88. C Plumstead St Jo w St Jas and St Paul *S'wark* 87-91; TV Ipswich St Fran *St E* 91-97; TV Walthamstow St Luke *Chelmsf* 97; TV Walthamstow from 97. *St Luke's Vicarage, 17A Greenleaf Road, London E17 6QQ* Tel 0181-520 2885

ANSTICE, John Neville. b 39. Lon Univ BSc63. Cuddesdon Coll 69. **d** 71 **p** 72. C Stonebridge St Mich *Lon* 71-74; Chapl Woodbridge Sch 74-76; TV Droitwich *Worc* 76-80; P-in-c Salwarpe 76-79; Perm to Offic *Chich* from 80. *Address temp unknown*

ANTHONY, Charles William. b 15. St Cath Coll Cam BA38 MA42 Leeds Univ DipEd. Ely Th Coll 38. **d** 39 **p** 40. C Battyeford *Wakef* 39-41; C York St Lawr w St Nic *York* 43-45; C Stocksbridge *Sheff* 55-59; P-in-c Airmyn 59-78; V Hook 60-78; V Hook w Airmyn 78-86; rtd 86; Perm to Offic *Sheff* from 86; Perm to Offic *S'well* from 87. *The Old Rectory, Top Street, North Wheatley, Retford, Notts DN22 9OA* Tel (01427) 880959

ANTHONY, Gerald Caldecott. b 18. Down Coll Cam BA41 MA44. Wycliffe Hall Ox 41. **d** 43 **p** 44. C Roxeth Ch Ch *Lon* 43-47; C Harlington 47-49; R Grays Inn Road St Bart 49-51; P-in-c Ernesettle *Ex* 51-55; V S Lambeth All SS and St Barn *S'wark* 55-58; Chapl Parkstone Sea Tr Sch Poole 58-64; Chapl HMS Ganges 64-65; P-in-c Bulmer *York* 65-66; R 66-72; V Broughton-in-Furness w Woodland *Carl* 72-75; P-in-c Seathwaite w Ulpha 73-75; V Broughton and Duddon 75-83; rtd 83; Perm to Offic *Worc* from 83. *2 Coppice Close, Malvern, Worcs WR14 1LE* Tel (01886) 832930

ANTHONY, Ian Charles. b 47. NW Ord Course 76. **d** 79 **p** 80. NSM Lt Lever *Man* from 79. *36 Meadow Close, Little Lever, Bolton BL3 1LG* Tel (01204) 791437

ANTONY-ROBERTS, Gelert Roderick. b 43. Southn Univ BEd78 Reading Univ MA84. Sarum & Wells Th Coll. **d** 90 **p** 91. C Alton St Lawr *Win* 90-94. *11 Jubilee Court, North Street, Salisbury SP2 7TA* Tel (01722) 338399

ap GWILYM, Gwynn. b 50. Univ of Wales (Ban) BA71 MA76. Wycliffe Hall Ox BA84 MA89. **d** 84 **p** 85. C Ynyscynhaearn w Penmorfa and Porthmadog *Ban* 84-86; R Penegoes and Darowen w Llanbryn-Mair 86-97; R Mallwyd w Cemais, Llanymawddwy, Darowen etc from 97. *The Rectory, Penegoes, Machynlleth SY20 8LW* Tel (01654) 703214

ap IORWERTH, Geraint. b 50. Univ of Wales (Lamp) DipTh72 Univ of Wales (Cardiff) DPS73 MPhil90 Open Univ BA78. Burgess Hall Lamp 69 Westmr Past Foundn 73 St Mich Coll Llan 73. **d** 74 **p** 75. C Holyhead w Rhoscolyn *Ban* 74-78; R Pennal w Corris and Esgairgeiliog from 78; Founder and Ldr Order of Sancta Sophia from 87. *The Rectory, Pennal, Machynlleth SY20 9JS* Tel (01654) 791216

APPELBE, Frederick Charles. b 52. TCD DipTh87. CITC 87. **d** 87 **p** 88. C Waterford w Killea, Drumcannon and Dunhill *C & O* 87-90; C Taney *D & G* 90-92; I Rathmichael from 92. *Rathmichael Rectory, Shankill, Co Dublin, Irish Republic* Tel Dublin (1) 282 2803 Fax as telephone

APPLEBY, Anthony Robert Nightingale (<u>Tony</u>). b 40. K Coll Lon AKC62. St Boniface Warminster 62. **d** 63 **p** 64. C Cov St Mark *Cov* 63-67; CF 67-95; R Dulverton and Brushford *B & W* from

95. *The Vicarage, High Street, Dulverton, Somerset TA22 9DW* Tel (01398) 323425

APPLEBY, Miss Janet Mohr (Jan). b 32. Lon Univ TCert53 BA79 Sussex Univ MA(Ed)74. Chich Th Coll 90. **d** 91 **p** 95. NSM Rottingdean *Chich* 91-95; NSM Stantonbury and Willen *Ox* from 95. *28 Lodge Gate, Great Linford, Milton Keynes MK14 5EW* Tel (01908) 676993

APPLEFORD, Kenneth Henry (Ken). b 30. ISM90. Portsm Dioc Tr Course 91. **d** 92. NSM Portsea St Mary *Portsm* from 92. *124 Stride Avenue, Portsmouth PO3 6HN* Tel (01705) 814685

APPLEFORD, Canon Patrick Robert. b 25. Trin Coll Cam BA49 MA54. Chich Th Coll 50. **d** 52 **p** 53. C Poplar All SS w St Frideswide *Lon* 52-58; Chapl Bps' Coll Cheshunt 58-61; Educn Sec USPG 61-66; Dean Lusaka Cath 66-72; P-in-c Sutton St Nicholas w Sutton St Michael *Heref* 73-75; Dir of Educn *Chelmsf* 75-90; Can Chelmsf Cathl 78-90; rtd 90; Perm to Offic *Chelmsf* from 90. *35 Sowerberry Close, Chelmsford, Essex CM1 4YB* Tel (01245) 443508

APPLEGARTH, Anthony Edgar (Tony). b 44. Chich Th Coll 82. **d** 84 **p** 85. C Cannington, Otterhampton, Combwich and Stockland *B & W* 84-86; C Bridgwater St Mary, Chilton Trinity and Durleigh 86-89; R Stogursey w Fiddington from 89. *The Rectory, High Street, Stogursey, Bridgwater, Somerset TA5 1PL* Tel (01278) 732884

APPLEGATE, John. b 56. Bris Univ BSc75. Trin Coll Bris DipHE PhD. **d** 84 **p** 85. C Collyhurst *Man* 84-87; C Broughton 87-92; C Higher Broughton 87-92; C Lower Broughton St Clem w St Matthias 87-92; C Broughton St Jas w St Clem and St Matthias 92-94; R Broughton 94-96; TR Broughton from 96. *237 Great Clowes Street, Salford M7 9DZ* Tel 0161-792 9161

APPLETON, Mrs Bonita (Bonnie). b 55. St Jo Coll Nottm DCM93. **d** 93 **p** 94. C Camberley St Paul *Guildf* 93-96; TV Cove St Jo from 96. *Southwood Vicarage, 15 The Copse, Southwood, Farnborough, Hants GU14 0QD* Tel (01252) 513422

APPLETON, John Bearby. b 42. Linc Th Coll 74. **d** 76 **p** 77. C Selby Abbey *York* 76-79; C Epsom St Barn *Guildf* 79-82; V Linc All SS *Linc* 82-94. *33 South End, Osmotherley, Northallerton, N Yorkshire DL6 3BN*

APPLETON, Canon Paul Valentine. b 19. LRAM ARCM K Coll Cam BA42 MA46. Lich Th Coll 42. **d** 44 **p** 45. C Shrewsbury St Chad *Lich* 44-46; C Stafford St Mary 46-48; V Rangemore 48-60; V Dunstall 52-60; Hd Master Linc Cathl Sch 60-70; Succ Linc Cathl *Linc* 60-85; V Owmby w Normanby 70-75; P-in-c Spridlington w Saxby and Firsby 73-90; R Owmby and Normanby w Glentham 75-90; Can and Preb Linc Cathl 77-90; rtd 90; Perm to Offic *Linc* from 90. *2 Eastfield Lane, Welton, Lincoln LN2 3NA* Tel (01673) 860667

APPLETON, Canon Ronald Percival. b 15. St Pet Hall Ox BA36 MA40. Ridley Hall Cam 36. **d** 38 **p** 39. C Hunsingore w Cowthorpe *Ripon* 38-39; C High Harrogate Ch Ch 39-42; C Bromley SS Pet and Paul *Roch* 42-44; R Knockholt 44-53; V Bromley Common St Luke 53-62; V Winchcombe, Gretton, Sudeley Manor etc *Glouc* 62-86; RD Winchcombe 63-86; Hon Can Glouc Cathl 80-86; rtd 86; Perm to Offic *Glouc* from 86. *1 Abbey Croft, Pershore, Worcs WR10 1JQ* Tel (01386) 553023

APPLETON, Stanley Basil. b 04. Wycliffe Hall Ox 66. **d** 66 **p** 66. Lic to Offic *Ox* 66-74; Hon C Welford w Wickham and Gt Shefford 74-86; Hon C Welford w Wickham and Gt Shefford, Boxford etc 86-94. *Leigh Cottage, Wickham, Newbury, Berks RG16 8HD* Tel (01488) 38239

APPLETON, Dr Timothy Charles. b 36. Selw Coll Cam BA60 MA65 K Coll Lon PhD67 Cam Univ DSc81. S'wark Ord Course 69. **d** 72 **p** 73. NSM Harston w Hauxton *Ely* 72-76; Lect Cam Univ 73-88; Lic to Offic *Ely* 76-79 and from 84; P-in-c Gt w Lt Eversden 79-84; Chapl and Counsellor Bourn Hall Clinic from 88. *44 Eversden Road, Harlton, Cambridge CB3 7ET* Tel (01223) 262226

APPLEYARD, Edward. b 19. OBE75 RD68. Kelham Th Coll 37. **d** 43 **p** 44. C Middlesbrough St Aid *York* 43-46; C-in-c Horton Bank Top CD *Bradf* 46-47; Chapl RN 47-49; Chapl RAF 49-53; V Swine *York* 53-56; Chapl Wm Baker Tech Sch Dr Barnado's Homes 56-58; V Flamborough 60-68; V Gt Ayton w Easby and Newton in Cleveland 68-78; RD Stokesley 70-77; P-in-c Middlesbrough St Columba w St Paul 78-84; rtd 84; Perm to Offic *York* from 84; Dioc Rtd Clergy and Widows Officer from 87. *16 Linden Road, Great Ayton, Middlesbrough, Cleveland TS9 6AN* Tel (01642) 722488

APPLIN, David Edward. b 39. Oak Hill Th Coll 63. **d** 65 **p** 66. C Ox St Clem *Ox* 65-69; C Felixstowe SS Pet and Paul *St E* 69-71; Lic to Offic *Win* 71-91; Travelling Sec Rwanda Miss 71-74; Home Sec 74-77; Gen Sec 77-81; Dir Overseas Personnel Dept TEAR Fund 82-87; Overseas Dir 87-92; Hon C Kempshott *Win* 91-92; R Awbridge w Sherfield English from 92-97; Exec Dir Samaritan's Purse Internat from 95. *Flat 4, 25 Christchurch Road, St Cross, Winchester, Hants SO23 9SU* Tel (01962) 865678

APPS, Anthony Howard. b 22. Ch Coll Cam BA47 MA51. **d** 49 **p** 50. C Poplar All SS w St Frideswide *Lon* 49-55; V Mile End Old Town H Trin 55-66; V Myddleton Square St Mark 66-82; rtd 82; Perm to Offic *York* from 82. *18 Longworth Way, Guisborough, Cleveland TS14 6DG* Tel (01287) 637939

APPS, Bryan Gerald. b 37. Univ of Wales (Lamp) BA59 St Cath Coll Ox BA61 MA65. Wycliffe Hall Ox 59. **d** 61 **p** 62. C Southampton St Alb *Win* 61-65; C Andover w Foxcott 65-69; P-in-c Freemantle 69-72; R 73-78; V Pokesdown All SS from 78. *All Saints' Vicarage, 14 Stourwood Road, Bournemouth BH6 3QP* Tel (01202) 423747

APPS, David Ronald. b 34. Univ of Wales (Lamp) BA57. Sarum Th Coll 57. **d** 59 **p** 60. C Southbourne St Chris *Win* 59-62; C Weeke 62-67; V Alton All SS 67-80; V Charlestown *Truro* 80-97; Miss to Seamen 80-97. *Blue Haze, 154 Goodrington Road, Paignton, Devon TQ4 7HX* Tel (01726) 812824

APPS, Canon Michael John (Brother Bernard). b 28. Pemb Coll Cam BA52 MA56. Cuddesdon Coll 53. **d** 55 **p** 56. C Spalding *Linc* 55-58; SSF from 58; Perm to Offic *Chelmsf* 59-63 and 67-69; P-in-c Plaistow 63-67; Australia 69-75; Guardian St Nic Friary Harbledown 77-78; Guardian Hilfield Friary Dorchester 78-89; Can and Preb Sarum Cathl *Sarum* 81-89. *10 Halcrow Street, London E1 2EP* Tel 0171-247 6233

APTHORP, The Ven Arthur Norman. b 24. Pemb Coll Cam BA47 MA50. Chich Th Coll 48. **d** 50 **p** 51. C Henfield *Chich* 50-52; C Hove All SS 52-56; Australia from 56; Hon Can Perth 73-77 and 79-89; Adn of the Country (Perth) 82-89; rtd 89. *2 Brookton Highway, Brookton, W Australia 6306* Tel Brookton (96) 421046

ARBER, Gerald Kenneth. b 37. Open Univ BA87. Oak Hill NSM Course. **d** 84 **p** 85. NSM Romford St Edw *Chelmsf* 84-95; NSM Cranham from 95. *5 Hill Grove, Romford RM1 4JP* Tel (01708) 750070

ARBERY, Canon Richard Neil. b 25. AKC49. **d** 50 **p** 51. C Pemberton St Jo *Liv* 50-55; V Roundthorn *Man* 55-59; V Hindley All SS *Liv* 59-78; RD Wigan 75-89; Hon Can Liv Cathl 77-92; V Wigan St Andr 78-92; rtd 92; Asst Chapl HM Young Offender Inst Hindley from 92; Perm to Offic *Liv* from 92. *11 Gillan Road, Wigan, Lancs WN6 7HQ* Tel (01942) 491734 or 866255 Fax 867442

ARBUCKLE, Canon James Hugh. b 19. AKC49. **d** 49 **p** 50. C Seaford w Sutton *Chich* 49-52; C Crosby *Linc* 52-54; V Barnetby le Wold 54-76; P-in-c Bigby 64-76; Can and Preb Linc Cathl from 70; RD Yarborough 70-76; P-in-c Somerby w Humby 74-76; Sec Linc Dioc Syn and Past Cttee 76-84; rtd 85. *26 St Clare's Walk, Brigg, S Humberside DN20 8JS* Tel (01652) 655594

ARBUTHNOT, Andy. b 26. S'wark Ord Course 71. **d** 74 **p** 75. NSM Mortlake w E Sheen *S'wark* 74-77; Lic to Offic *Guildf* 77-83; Missr Lon Healing Miss from 83. *20 Dawson Place, London W2 4TJ* Tel 0171-229 3641

ARBUTHNOT, Canon James. b 19. QUB BA42. CITC 44. **d** 44 **p** 45. C Belfast St Aid *Conn* 44-47; C Belfast St Simon 47-51; I Ardglass w Dunsford *D & D* 51-60; I Belfast St Phil *Conn* 60-70; I Belfast St Paul 70-87; Can Conn Cathl 83-87; rtd 87. *20 St Colman's Crescent, Carrickfergus, Co Antrim BT38 7XN* Tel (01960) 359226

ARCHER, Alan Robert. b 38. AKC56. Lich Th Coll 65. **d** 68 **p** 69. C Lower Mitton *Worc* 68-71; C Foley Park 71-74; V Warndon 74-79; P-in-c Clifton upon Teme 79-81; P-in-c Lower Sapey 79-81; P-in-c The Shelsleys 79-81; V Malvern Wells and Wyche 81-83; TV Braunstone *Leic* 83-91; P-in-c Bemerton *Sarum* from 91; Dioc Link Officer for ACUPA 92-94. *St Michael's Rectory, St Michael's Road, Salisbury SP2 9EQ* Tel (01722) 333750

ARCHER, Frederick John. b 06. Clifton Th Coll 29. **d** 33 **p** 38. Trinidad and Tobago 33-35; Perm to Offic *Lich* 35-38; C Aldridge 38-39; C Bucknall and Bagnall 39-40; C Bedworth *Cov* 40-44; V Kenilworth St Jo 44-53; V Dunton *St Alb* 53-58; R Wrestlingworth 53-58; R Woolstone w Gotherington and Oxenton *Glouc* 58-61; V Corse and Staunton 61-73; rtd 73; Perm to Offic *Glouc* from 75. *c/o 194 Silverdale Road, Earley, Reading RG6 2NB* Tel 0118-926 4494

ARCHER, Graham John. b 58. Lanc Univ BSc79. St Jo Coll Nottm DipTh. **d** 85 **p** 86. C Ipswich St Matt *St E* 85-89; C Walton 89-95; P-in-c from 95; Chapl E Suffolk Local Health Services NHS Trust from 96. *2 Blyford Way, Felixstowe, Suffolk IP11 8FW* Tel (01394) 282204

ARCHER, John Thomas. b 28. Birm Coll of Commerce GIMechE68 Birm Poly CQSW83. EMMTC 79. **d** 80 **p** 81. NSM Derby St Thos *Derby* 80-86; V Edlington *Sheff* from 87. *The Vicarage, Broomhouse Lane, Edlington, Doncaster, S Yorkshire DN12 1LN* Tel (01709) 863148

ARCHER, Keith Malcolm. b 40. Man Univ BA61 MA80 Magd Coll Cam BA67 MA72. Ridley Hall Cam 66. **d** 68 **p** 69. C Newland St Jo *York* 68-72; Hon C Kersal Moor *Man* 72-79; Ind Chapl 72-93; V Weaste from 93. *The Vicarage, Derby Road, Salford M6 5BA* Tel 0161-736 5819

ARCHER, Michael James (Mike). b 67. St Jo Coll Dur BA90. Ridley Hall Cam CTM92. **d** 94 **p** 95. C Littleover *Derby* from 94. *4 Merridale Road, Littleover, Derby DE23 7DJ* Tel (01332) 763263

ARCHER, Michael John. b 37. Trin Coll Bris 76. **d** 78 **p** 79. C Kinson *Sarum* 78-81; C Harpenden St Nic *St Alb* 81-88; P-in-c Rashcliffe and Lockwood *Wakef* from 88. *The Vicarage,*

42 Beaumont Park Road, Huddersfield HD4 5JS Tel (01484) 514968

ARCHER, Stanley Edwin. b 21. St Jo Coll Dur 80. **d** 81 **p** 82. C Upper Nidderdale *Ripon* 81-83; P-in-c Wensley 83-89; P-in-c W Witton 83-89; rtd 89. *40 The Oaks, Masham, Ripon, N Yorkshire HG4 4DT* Tel (01765) 689685

ARCUS, Jeffrey. b 40. NW Ord Course 72. **d** 75 **p** 76. C Halliwell St Thos *Man* 75-78; C Walmsley 78-81; P-in-c Bury Ch King 81-82; TV Bury Ch King w H Trin 82-93; V Ramsbottom St Jo and St Paul from 93. *St Paul's Vicarage, Maple Grove, Ramsbottom, Bury, Lancs BL0 0AN* Tel (01706) 821036

ARDAGH-WALTER, Christopher Richard. b 35. Univ of Wales (Lamp) BA58. Chich Th Coll 58. **d** 60 **p** 61. C Heavitree *Ex* 60-64; C Redcar *York* 64-67; C King's Worthy *Win* 67-69; C-in-c Four Marks CD 70-73; V Four Marks 73-76; P-in-c Eling, Testwood and Marchwood 76-78; TR Totton 76-84; R The Sherbornes w Pamber 84-88; V Froyle and Holybourne 88-95; C Verwood *Sarum* from 95. *The Parsonage, 2 Saints Close, Three Legged Cross, Wimborne, Dorset BH21 6UJ* Tel (01202) 826752

✠**ARDEN, The Rt Revd Donald Seymour.** b 16. CBE81. Leeds Univ BA37. Coll of Resurr Mirfield 37. **d** 39 **p** 40 **c** 61. C Hatcham St Cath *S'wark* 39-40; C Potten End w Nettleden *St Alb* 41-43; S Africa 44-61; Can Zululand 59-61; Bp Nyasaland 61-64; Bp Malawi 64-71; Bp S Malawi and Abp Cen Africa 71-80; Asst Bp Willesden *Lon* 81-94; Asst Bp Lon from 94; P-in-c Uxbridge St Marg 81-86; rtd 86; Hon C N Harrow St Alb *Lon* from 86. *6 Frobisher Close, Pinner, Middx HA5 1NN* Tel 0181-866 6009 Fax as telephone

ARDFERT AND AGHADOE, Archdeacon of. *See* SHANNON, The Ven Malcolm James Douglas

ARDILL, Dr Robert William Brian. b 40. QUB BSc63 PhD67 SOSc. Ox NSM Course 80 St Jo Coll Nottm DipTh85. **d** 83 **p** 85. NSM Sunninghill *Ox* 83-84; Chapl R Holloway Coll *Lon* 83-84; C Lenton *S'well* 85-87; NSM Loughborough Em *Leic* 92-94; Perm to Offic 94-95; C Harpenden St Nic *St Alb* from 95. *10 Cross Way, Harpenden, Herts AL5 4RA* Tel (01582) 713007

ARDING, Richard. b 52. ACIB84. Oak Hill Th Coll DipHE92. **d** 92 **p** 93. C Bromley Common St Aug *Roch* 92-96; V Wilmington from 96. *The Vicarage, Church Hill, Wilmington, Dartford DA2 7EH* Tel (01322) 220561

ARDIS, The Very Revd Edward George. b 54. Dur Univ BA76. CITC 76. **d** 78 **p** 79. C Dublin Drumcondra w N Strand and St Barn *D & G* 78-81; C Dublin St Bart w Leeson Park 81-84; I Ardamine w Kiltennel, Glascarrig etc *C & O* 84-89; Can Tuam Cathl *T, K & A* from 89; Dean Killala from 89; I Killala w Dunfeeny, Crossmolina etc 89-94; I Killala w Dunfeeny, Crossmolina, Kilmoremoy etc from 94; Dir of Ords from 95. *The Rectory, Ballina, Co Mayo, Irish Republic* Tel Ballina (96) 216547

ARDLEY, Canon John Owen. b 39. Lon Univ BD70. S'wark Ord Course 70. **d** 72 **p** 73. C Caterham Valley *S'wark* 72-76; V Abbey Wood 76-84; Sub-Dean Woolwich 77-84; P-in-c Lower Sydenham St Mich 84-95; P-in-c Sydenham All SS 84-95; V from 95; RD W Lewisham from 87; Hon Can S'wark Cathl from 95. *All Saints' Vicarage, 41 Trewsbury Road, London SE26 5DP* Tel 0181-778 3065

ARGUILE, Roger Henry William. b 43. Dur Univ LLB64 Keble Coll Ox BA70 MA75. Ripon Hall Ox 70. **d** 71 **p** 72. C Walsall *Lich* 71-76; TV Blakenall Heath 76-83; TV Stafford 83-95; P-in-c St Neots *Ely* 95-97; V from 97. *The Vicarage, Church Street, St Neots, Huntingdon, Cambs PE19 2BU* Tel (01480) 472297

ARGYLE, Douglas Causer. b 17. St Jo Coll Cam BA39 MA43. Ridley Hall Cam 39. **d** 41 **p** 42. C Somercotes *Derby* 41-44; CF (EC) 44-47; Chapl Repton Sch Derby 47-59; Chapl Gresham's Sch Holt 59-74; P-in-c Eastleach w Southrop *Glouc* 74-82; rtd 82; Perm to Offic *Glouc* from 82. *East Lynn, London Road, Fairford, Glos GL7 4AR* Tel (01285) 713235

ARGYLE, Canon Edward Charles. b 55. ACT DipTh80. **d** 80 **p** 80. Australia 80-83; C Gt Yarmouth *Nor* 83-85; I Kilcooley w Littleon, Crohane and Fertagh *C & O* 85-94; Preb Ossory and Leighlin Cathls 92-94; rtd 94. *The Rectory, Grange Barna, Thurles, Co Tipperary, Irish Republic* Tel Thurles (56) 34147

ARGYLL AND THE ISLES, Bishop of. *See* CAMERON, The Rt Revd Douglas MacLean

ARGYLL AND THE ISLES, Dean of. *See* MACLEAY, The Very Revd John Henry James

ARIES, William Albert. b 28. ACT ThL61 Bps' Coll Cheshunt 59. **d** 60 **p** 61. C Nuneaton St Mary *Cov* 60-63; C Chandler's Ford *Win* 63-66; C-in-c Ringwood St Ive and St Leon CD 66-70; V St Leonards and St Ives 70-75; V Bournemouth St Clem 75-91; rtd 92; Perm to Offic *Win* 92-95. *Avon View, 15 Beatty Road, Bournemouth BH9 3RG* Tel (01202) 351128

ARKELL, Kevin Paul. b 53. Preston Poly DipSocWork81 BTh86. Sarum & Wells Th Coll 84. **d** 86 **p** 87. C S Petherton w the Seavingtons *B & W* 86-88; P-in-c Gt Harwood St Bart *Blackb* 88-90; V 90-95; TR Darwen St Pet w Hoddlesden from 95. *The Rectory, St Peter's Close, Darwen, Lancs BB3 2EA* Tel (01254) 702411

ARLOW, Canon William James. b 26. Edin Th Coll 59. **d** 59 **p** 60. C Ballymacarrett St Patr *D & D* 59-61; Cen Adv on Chr Stewardship to Ch of Ireland 61-66; I Newry St Patr 66-70; I Belfast St Donard 70-74; Dep Sec Irish Coun of Chs 74-75; Sec 75-79; Can for Ecum Affairs Belf Cathl from 79; Treas 85-89; P-in-c Ballyphilip w Ardquin 86-89; rtd 89; Lic to Offic *D & D* from 90. *13 Ashford Park, Bangor, Co Down BT19 6DD* Tel (01247) 469758

ARMAGH, Archbishop of. *See* EAMES, The Most Revd Robert Henry Alexander

ARMAGH, Archdeacon of. *See* HOEY, The Ven Raymond George

ARMAGH, Dean of. *See* CASSIDY, The Very Revd Herbert

ARMAN, Brian Robert. b 54. St Jo Coll Dur BA77 LTh78. Cranmer Hall Dur 74. **d** 78 **p** 79. C Lawrence Weston *Bris* 78-82; C Bishopston 82-88; R Filton from 88. *The Rectory, Station Road, Bristol BS12 7BX* Tel 0117-979 1128

ARMES, John Andrew. b 55. SS Coll Cam BA77 MA81. Sarum & Wells Th Coll 77. **d** 79 **p** 80. C Walney Is *Carl* 79-82; Chapl to Agric 82-86; TV Greystoke, Matterdale and Mungrisdale 82-86; TV Watermillock 84-86; TV Man Whitworth *Man* 86-88; TR 88-94; Chapl Man Univ 86-94; P-in-c Goodshaw and Crawshawbooth from 94; AD Rossendale from 94. *Goodshaw Vicarage, Goodshawfold Road, Rossendale, Lancs BB4 8QN* Tel (01706) 213969

ARMFELT, Julian Roger. b 31. K Coll Cam BA53. Wells Th Coll 54. **d** 56 **p** 58. C Stocksbridge *Sheff* 56-57; C Cantley 57-59; P-in-c Clayton w Frickley 59-61; C Eglingham *Newc* 61-63; V Alkborough w Whitton *Linc* 63-64; C Corringham 69-73; TV Fincham *Ely* 73-75; V Freckleton *Blackb* 75-79; P-in-c Sherburn *York* 79-80; P-in-c W and E Heslerton w Knapton 79-80; P-in-c Yedingham 79-80; R Sherburn and W and E Heslerton w Yedingham 80-83; TV York All SS Pavement w St Crux and St Martin etc 83-84; P-in-c York St Mary Bishophill Junior w All SS 83-84; C Howden TM 84-86; P-in-c Laughton w Throapham *Sheff* 86-88; rtd 88. *Meadow Haven Cottage, Pier Road, Berwick-upon-Tweed TD15 1JB* Tel (01289) 307241

ARMITAGE, Bryan Ambrose. b 28. K Coll Lon AKC55 BD58. **d** 56 **p** 57. C High Harrogate St Pet *Ripon* 56-59; S Africa 59-61; Uganda 61-73; Chapl Sutton Valence Sch Kent 73-75; Chapl Qu Ethelburga's Sch Harrogate 76-91; V Weaverthorpe w Helperthorpe, Luttons Ambo etc *York* from 91. *The Vicarage, Helperthorpe, Malton, N Yorkshire YO17 8TJ* Tel (01944) 738213

ARMITAGE, Michael Stanley. b 45. Jes Coll Cam BA67 MA71. Cuddesdon Coll 67. **d** 69 **p** 70. C Sanderstead All SS *S'wark* 69-70; C Battersea St Mary 70-71; Hon C Kingston St Jo 72-73; Chapl Kingston Poly 72-73; V Angell Town St Jo from 73. *St John's Vicarage, Wiltshire Road, London SW9 7NF* Tel 0171-733 0585

ARMITAGE, Richard Norris. b 51. AKC. St Aug Coll Cant 73. **d** 74 **p** 75. C Chapelthorpe *Wakef* 74-77; C W Bromwich All SS *Lich* 77-82; P-in-c Ketley 82-83; V Oakengates 82-83; V Ketley and Oakengates 83-89; V Evesham *Worc* 89-96; V Evesham w Norton and Lenchwick from 96. *The Vicarage, 5 Croft Road, Evesham, Worcs WR11 4NE* Tel (01386) 446219

ARMITAGE, Susan. b 46. **d** 92. S Africa 92-97; C Fawley *Win* from 97. *15 Long Lane Close, Fawley, Southampton SO45 2LE* Tel (01703) 591809

ARMSON, Canon John Moss. b 39. Selw Coll Cam BA61 MA64 St Andr Univ PhD65. Coll of Resurr Mirfield 64. **d** 66 **p** 67. C Notting Hill St Jo *Lon* 66-69; Chapl Down Coll Cam 69-73; Fell 70-73; Chapl Westcott Ho Cam 73-76; Vice-Prin 76-82; Prin Edin Th Coll 82-89; Can St Mary's Cathl *Edin* 82-89; Can Res Roch Cathl *Roch* from 89. *Easter Garth, King's Orchard, Rochester, Kent ME1 1SX* Tel (01634) 406992

ARMSTEAD, Geoffrey Malcolm. b 32. K Coll Lon BD56 AKC56 Nottm Univ ADEd73. St Boniface Warminster 56. **d** 57 **p** 57. C Weymouth H Trin *Sarum* 57-60; C Mortlake w E Sheen *S'wark* 60-63; Chapl Em Sch Wandsworth 63-74; Dep Hd Master Harriet Costello Sch 74-91; Acting Hd Master 91-92; Perm to Offic *Win* 74-92; V Win St Bart from 92. *Hyde Vicarage, 1 Abbey Hill Close, Winchester, Hants SO23 7AZ* Tel (01962) 852032

ARMSTEAD, Gordon. b 33. Oak Hill Th Coll DPS74. **d** 74 **p** 75. C Woodside *Ripon* 74-76; C Heaton Ch Ch *Man* 76-79; Australia 79-81; R Levenshulme St Mark *Man* 81-86; V Borth and Eglwys-fach w Llangynfelyn *St D* 86-92; rtd 93; Perm to Offic *Blackb* from 93. *27 Parkside Road, St Annes, Lytham St Annes, Lancs FY8 3SZ* Tel (01253) 727647

ARMSTRONG, Dr Adrian Christopher. b 48. LSE BSc70 K Coll Lon PhD80. EAMTC 84. **d** 87 **p** 88. NSM Linton *Ely* 87-95; P-in-c N and S Muskham *S'well* from 95; P-in-c Averham w Kelham from 95. *St Wilfrid's Vicarage, Marsh Lane, North Muskham, Newark, Notts NG23 6HG* Tel (01636) 702655

ARMSTRONG, Alexander Milford. b 57. Local Minl Tr Course 87 96. **d** 95 **p** 95. NSM Livingston LEP *Edin* 95-97; C Cleator Moor w Cleator *Carl* from 97; C Frizington and Arlecdon from 97. *The Vicarage, Arlecdon, Frizington, Cumbria CA26 3UB* Tel (01946) 861353 Fax as telephone

ARMSTRONG, Christopher John. b 47. Nottm Univ BTh75. Kelham Th Coll 72. **d** 76 **p** 76. C Maidstone All SS w St Phil and H Trin *Cant* 76-79; Chapl St Hild and St Bede Coll *Dur* 79-84; Dir of Ords *York* 85-91; Abp's Dom Chapl 85-91; V Scarborough St Martin from 91. *St Martin's Vicarage, Craven Street, Scarborough, N Yorkshire YO11 2BY* Tel (01723) 360437

ARMSTRONG, Christopher John Richard. b 35. Fribourg Univ LTh60 Ch Coll Cam BA64 MA68 PhD79. Edin Th Coll 74. **d** 59 **p** 59. In RC Ch 59-71; Lect Aber Univ 68-74; C Ledbury *Heref* 74-76; P-in-c Bredenbury and Wacton w Grendon Bishop 76-79; P-in-c Edwyn Ralph and Collington w Thornbury 76-79; P-in-c Pencombe w Marston Stannett and Lt Cowarne 76-79; R Cherry Burton *York* 79-80; Tutor Westcott Ho Cam 80-85; V Bottisham *Ely* 85-89; P-in-c Lode and Longmeadow 85-89; P-in-c Cropthorne w Charlton *Worc* 89-93; Dioc Local Min Sec 89-93; R Aberdaron w Rhiw and Llanfaelrhys etc *Ban* from 93. *The Rectory, Llangwnnadl, Pwllheli LL53 8NU* Tel (01758) 770250

ARMSTRONG, Colin John. b 32. St Cath Soc Ox BA59 MA65. Wells Th Coll 59. **d** 61 **p** 62. C Acomb St Steph *York* 61-64; C Newland St Jo 64-67; Chapl and Tutor All SS Coll Tottenham 67-78; Chapl and Tutor Middx Poly 78-85; rtd 97. *Mead House, The Street, Preston St Mary, Sudbury, Suffolk CO10 9NQ* Tel (01787) 248218

ARMSTRONG, Edwin. b 23. TCD BA45 MA69. **d** 46 **p** 47. C Belfast Trin Coll Miss *Conn* 46-49; C Donaghadee *D & D* 49-57; I Gilford 57-85; rtd 85. *Malone Nursing Home, 1 Deramore Park South, Belfast BT9 5JY*

ARMSTRONG, Eileen. d 95 **p** 96. NSM *M & K* from 95. *Hennigan, Nobber, Co Meath, Irish Republic* Tel Navan (46) 52314

ARMSTRONG, Canon George. b 09. Clifton Th Coll 29. **d** 32 **p** 33. C Fazakerley Em *Liv* 32-37; C Winwick 37-40; CF 41-46; R Layer Marney *Chelmsf* 46-82; R Gt w Lt Birch and Layer Breton 47-82; RD Coggeshall and Tey 68-79; Hon Can Chelmsf Cathl 77-82; rtd 82; Perm to Offic *Chelmsf* from 82; Perm to Offic *St E* from 82. *11 The Westerings, Nayland, Colchester CO6 4LJ* Tel (01206) 262952

ARMSTRONG, Guy Lionel Walter. b 18. OBE93. Wycliffe Hall Ox 60. **d** 61 **p** 62. C Caversham *Ox* 61-65; V Bagshot *Guildf* 65-73; V Ripley 73-77; rtd 77; Perm to Offic *Portsm* from 81. *The Briary, 3 Wood Street, Ryde, Isle of Wight PO33 2DH* Tel (01983) 562454

ARMSTRONG, John Edwin. b 51. Leic Univ CertEd73 BEd74 Homerton Coll Cam AEdRD87. Ridley Hall Cam CTM93. **d** 93 **p** 94. C Gt Wilbraham *Ely* 93-96; P-in-c Bassingbourn from 96; P-in-c Whaddon from 96. *The Vicarage, 21 North End, Bassingbourn, Royston, Herts SG8 5NZ* Tel (01763) 243119

ARMSTRONG, John Gordon. b 64. Man Poly BSc86 MSc91. Wycliffe Hall Ox 95. **d** 97. C Pennington *Man* from 97. *11 Ruby Grove, Leigh, Lancs WN7 4JW* Tel (01942) 260988

ARMSTRONG, Canon John Hammond. b 24. Dur Univ BA47 DipTh49. **d** 49 **p** 50. C Bishopwearmouth St Gabr *Dur* 49-52; C Cockfield w Staindrop 52-54; V Skipwith *York* 54-59; V Thorganby 54-59; V N Ferriby 59-63; R Sutton upon Derwent 63-71; Dioc Stewardship Adv 63-75; P-in-c York All SS and St Crux w St Sav etc 71-72; R 72-76; Can and Preb York Minster from 72; P-in-c York St Denys 74-76; RD City of York 76-86; TR York All SS Pavement w St Crux and St Denys 76-77; TR York All SS Pavement w St Crux and St Martin etc 77-91; rtd 91. *20 Hempland Avenue, Stockton Lane, York YO3 0DE* Tel (01904) 421312

ARMSTRONG, John James. b 15. TCD BA38 MA42 Div Test40. **d** 40 **p** 41. C Ballymacarrett St Patr *D & D* 40-46; C Neasden cum Kingsbury St Cath *Lon* 46-49; Ceylon 49-52; C St Marylebone St Mary *Lon* 52-55; Hd of Trin Coll Miss Belfast 55-58; Miss to Seamen 58-77; Sudan 58-59; Dunkirk 60-62; Belfast 75-77; C Derriaghy *Conn* 62-71; C Seagoe *D & D* 71-73; Hd of S Ch Miss Belfast 73-75; C Belfast St Simon w St Phil *Conn* 77-80; rtd 80. *60 The Green, Dunmurry, Belfast BT17 0QA* Tel (01232) 623032

ARMSTRONG, Mrs Margaret Betty. b 48. Westcott Ho Cam 89. **d** 92 **p** 94. NSM Linton *Ely* 92-95; NSM Shudy Camps 92-95; NSM Castle Camps 92-95; NSM Bartlow 92-95; NSM N and S Muskham *S'well* from 95; NSM Averham w Kelham from 95. *St Wilfrid's Vicarage, Marsh Lane, North Muskham, Newark, Notts NG23 6HG* Tel (01636) 702655

ARMSTRONG, Maurice Alexander. b 62. Ulster Poly BA84 TCD DipTh87. CITC 84. **d** 87 **p** 88. C Portadown St Mark *Arm* 87-90; I Sixmilecross w Termonmaguirke 90-95; I Richhill from 95. *The Rectory, 15 Annareagh Road, Richhill, Armagh BT61 9JT* Tel (01762) 871232

ARMSTRONG, Nicholas Paul (Nick). b 58. Bris Univ BSc79. Trin Coll Bris DipHE93. **d** 93 **p** 94. C Filey *York* 93-97; P-in-c Alveley and Quatt *Heref* from 97. *The Vicarage, Alveley, Bridgnorth, Shropshire WV15 6ND* Tel (01746) 780326

ARMSTRONG, Canon Robert Charles (Robin). b 24. TCD BA46 HDipEd52 MA57. CITC 47. **d** 47 **p** 48. C Belfast St Luke *Conn* 48-50; Warden Gr Sch Dub 50-59; Succ St Patr Cathl Dublin 50-59; I Dublin Finglas *D & G* 59-67; I Dun Laoghaire 67-94; RD Newcastle 71-76; Dir of Ords (Dub) 74-84; USPG Area Sec 77-94; Can Ch Ch Cathl Dublin 84-88; Treas 88-94; rtd 94. *1 Glenageary Terrace, Dun Laoghaire, Co Dublin, Irish Republic* Tel Dublin (1) 284 6941

ARMSTRONG, Ronald. b 09. St Jo Coll Dur BA38 MA42. **d** 38 **p** 39. C Pudsey St Lawr *Bradf* 38-41; C Chester le Street *Dur* 41-43; Nigeria 43-52; C Bridport *Sarum* 53-54; P-in-c 54; Min Hartcliffe St Andr CD *Bris* 54-59; V Beckermet St Bridget w Ponsonby *Carl* 59-60; V Penrith Ch Ch 60-63; V Leyton Em *Chelmsf* 63-65; Chapl Whipps Cross Hosp Lon 65-79; Public Preacher *Chelmsf* 74-80; rtd 79. *Nether Barr, Newton Stewart, Wigtownshire DG8 6AU* Tel (01671) 402236

ARMSTRONG, Samuel David. b 48. BD MTh. **d** 86 **p** 87. C Cambridge H Trin w St Andr Gt *Ely* 86-89; V Cambridge St Martin from 89. *33 Rustat Road, Cambridge CB1 3QR* Tel (01223) 248648

ARMSTRONG, Samuel George (Sammie). b 39. Ox Univ Inst of Educn TCert65 CYCW65 ACertEd71 Open Univ BA72 Reading Univ MSc89. S Dios Minl Tr Scheme 90. **d** 93 **p** 94. NSM N Tadley St Mary *Win* from 93. *The Cedars, Blakes Lane, Tadley, Basingstoke, Hants RG26 6PU* Tel 0118-981 6593

ARMSTRONG, William. b 29. Sarum Th Coll 52. **d** 54 **p** 55. C Hebburn St Cuth *Dur* 54-55; C Ferryhill 55-57; C Gateshead H Trin 57-60; V Cassop cum Quarrington 60-66; Australia 66-81; Asst Dir of Educn *Liv* 81-90; V Aintree St Pet 81-88; TV Speke St Aid 88-90; rtd 90. *10 Blenheim Court, Horn Lane, Woodford Green, Essex IG8 9AQ* Tel 0181-504 1874

ARMSTRONG-MacDONNELL, Mrs Vivienne Christine. b 42. Open Univ BA89. Ripon Coll Cuddesdon 88. **d** 90 **p** 94. C Crediton and Shobrooke *Ex* 90-93; Dioc Adv in Adult Tr from 93. *Strand House, Woodbury, Exeter EX5 1LZ* Tel (01395) 232790

ARNAUD, John Charles Stanley. b 23. Aber Univ MA48 DipEd49. **d** 78 **p** 79. Hon C Huntly *Mor* 78-91; Hon C Aberchirder 78-91; Hon C Keith 78-91; rtd 91; Perm to Offic *Mor* from 91. *Rosemount, 19 Kynoch Terrace, Keith, Banffshire AB5 3EX*

ARNESEN, Christopher Paul. b 48. Lon Univ BA70. Sarum & Wells Th Coll 78. **d** 80 **p** 81. C Dalton-in-Furness *Carl* 80-83; C Ranmoor *Sheff* 83-86; R Distington *Carl* 86-93; TV Sheff Manor *Sheff* from 93. *St Paul's Vicarage, East Bank Road, Sheffield S2 2AD* Tel 0114-239 8533

ARNESEN, Raymond Halfdan (Brother Ælred). b 25. Qu Coll Cam BA49 MA54. Linc Th Coll 50. **d** 52 **p** 53. C Newc St Fran *Newc* 52-55; SSF 55-66; Cistercian Monk from 66; Ewell Monastery from 66; rtd 95. *Ewell Monastery, Water Lane, West Malling, Maidstone, Kent ME19 6HH* Tel (01732) 843089

ARNOLD, Alan Roy. b 33. Lon Univ BD79. S'wark Ord Course 75. **d** 78 **p** 79. C Fleet *Guildf* 78-81; V Hinchley Wood 81-84; C Cobham 84-89; C Addlestone 89-92; rtd 93; Perm to Offic *Guildf* 92-94; Perm to Offic *Win* from 94. *Flat 9, 68 West Cliff Road, Bournemouth BH4 8BE* Tel (01202) 752018

ARNOLD, Arthur Philip. b 46. Em Coll Cam BA67 MA71. Qu Coll Birm DipTh69. **d** 70 **p** 71. C Failsworth H Family CD *Man* 70-74; Asst Chapl Hurstpierpoint Coll Hassocks 74-77; Chapl K Coll Cam 77-80; Chapl St Chad's Coll Dur 80-82; Chapl Plymouth Coll 83-96; Lic to Offic *Ex* from 83; C Rawmarsh w Parkgate *Sheff* from 96. *117 Hague Avenue, Rawmarsh, Rotherham, S Yorkshire S62 7PT* Tel (01709) 710056

ARNOLD, Brother. *See* NODDER, Thomas Arthur

ARNOLD, Elisabeth Anne Truyens. b 44. TCert66. LNSM course 88. **d** 91 **p** 94. NSM Ipswich St Thos *St E* from 91. *66 Bromeswell Road, Ipswich IP4 3AT* Tel (01473) 257406

ARNOLD, Ernest Stephen. b 27. **d** 64 **p** 65. C Aberavon *Llan* 64-68; V Ferndale 68-74; Cyprus 81-85; rtd 94; Perm to Offic *Portsm* from 94. *Barn Cottage, Apse Manor Road, Shanklin, Isle of Wight PO37 7PN* Tel (01983) 866324

ARNOLD, George Innes. b 22. Roch Th Coll. **d** 61 **p** 62. C Cullercoats St Geo *Newc* 61-64; C Benwell St Jas 64-68; Egypt 68-70; V Croydon St Jas *Cant* 71-80; P-in-c Dullingham *Ely* 80-91; P-in-c Stetchworth 80-91; RD Linton 81-88; rtd 91; Perm to Offic *Chich* from 91. *5 Bridge Place, Rye, E Sussex TN31 7LN* Tel (01797) 224509

ARNOLD, Graham Thomas. b 62. S Kent Coll of Tech OND80. Aston Tr Scheme 87 Ripon Coll Cuddesdon 89. **d** 92 **p** 93. C Margate St Jo *Cant* 92-95; TV Whitstable from 95. *Swalecliffe Rectory, Swalecliffe Court Drive, Whitstable, Kent CT5 2LZ* Tel (01227) 792826

ARNOLD, The Very Revd John Robert. b 33. SS Coll Cam BA57 MA61. Westcott Ho Cam 58. **d** 60 **p** 61. C Millhouses H Trin *Sheff* 60-63; Chapl and Lect Southn Univ *Win* 63-72; Gen Sec Gen Syn Bd for Miss and Unity 72-78; Hon Can Win Cathl *Win* 74-78; Dean Roch 78-89; Dean Dur from 89. *The Deanery, The College, Durham DH1 3EQ* Tel 0191-384 7500

✠**ARNOLD, The Rt Revd Keith Appleby.** b 26. Trin Coll Cam BA50 MA55. Westcott Ho Cam 50. **d** 52 **p** 53 **c** 80. C Haltwhistle *Newc* 52-55; C Edin St Jo *Edin* 55-61; R 61-69; CF (TA) 58-62; V Kirkby Lonsdale w Mansergh *Carl* 69-73; RD Berkhamsted *St Alb* 73-80; TR Hemel Hempstead 73-80; Suff Bp Warw *Cov* 80-90; Hon Can Cov Cathl 80-90; rtd 90. *9 Dinglederry, Olney, Bucks MK46 5ES* Tel (01234) 713044

ARNOLD, Richard Nicholas. b 54. AKC76. S'wark Ord Course 76. **d** 77 **p** 78. C Nunhead St Antony *S'wark* 77-80; C Walworth 80-82; P-in-c Streatham Hill St Marg 82-84; V 84-89; P-in-c Oseney Crescent St Luke *Lon* 89-93; P-in-c Kentish Town St Jo 89-93; P-in-c Kentish Town St Benet and All SS 89-93; V Kentish Town from 93. *Kentish Town Vicarage, 43 Lady Margaret Road, London NW5 2NH* Tel 0171-485 4231 Mobile 0802-730974 Fax 482 7222 E-mail fr_arnold@compuserve.com

ARNOLD, Canon Roy. b 36. St D Coll Lamp BA62 DipTh63. **d** 63 **p** 64. C Brislington St Luke *Bris* 63-66; C Ches St Mary *Ches*

67-70; V Brinnington w Portwood 71-75; V Sale St Paul 75-82; R Dodleston 82-84; V Sheff St Oswald *Sheff* 84-90; Dioc Communications Officer 84-97; Chapl w the Deaf 90-97; Hon Can Sheff Cathl 95-97; rtd 97. *10 Devonshire Road, Sheffield S17 3NT* Tel 0114-236 1972 Fax 262 1189

ARNOLD, Victor Norman. b 45. Oak Hill Th Coll 91. **d** 94 **p** 95. NSM Chigwell and Chigwell Row *Chelmsf* from 94. *Spring Cottage, 6 Spring Grove, Loughton, Essex IG10 4QA* Tel 0181-508 6572

ARNOTT, David. b 44. Em Coll Cam BA66. Qu Coll Birm 68. **d** 69 **p** 70. C Charlton St Luke w St Paul *S'wark* 69-73; C S Beddington St Mich 73-78; Chapl Liv Poly *Liv* 78-82; V Bridgwater St Fran *B & W* from 86. *The Vicarage, Saxon Green, Bridgwater, Somerset TA6 4HZ* Tel (01278) 422744

ARNOTT, Eric William. b 12. Cranmer Hall Dur 67. **d** 68 **p** 69. C Gosforth St Nic *Newc* 68-71; C Wooler 71-74; TV Wooler Gp 74-78; rtd 78. *Forge Cottage, Hoopers Lane, Puncknowle, Dorchester, Dorset DT2 9BE* Tel (01308) 897768

ARNOTT, Thomas Grenfell. b 11. Solicitor. NE Ord Course 61 Cranmer Hall Dur 68. **d** 68 **p** 69. C Ryton *Dur* 68-71; V Weston-super-Mare Em *B & W* 71-73; R Brandesburton *York* 73-78; RD N Holderness 76-78; rtd 78; Perm to Offic *York* from 78. *1 Mulrany Manor, 2 Graham Crescent, Scarborough, N Yorkshire YO12 5DG* Tel (01723) 363133

ARRAND, The Ven Geoffrey William. b 44. K Coll Lon BD66 AKC66. **d** 67 **p** 68. C Washington *Dur* 67-70; C S Ormsby w Ketsby, Calceby and Driby *Linc* 70-73; TV Gt Grimsby St Mary and St Jas 73-79; TR Halesworth w Linstead and Chediston *St E* 79-80; TR Halesworth w Linstead, Chediston, Holton etc 80-85; R Hadleigh w Layham and Shelley 85-94; Dean Bocking 85-94; RD Hadleigh 86-94; Hon Can St E Cathl from 91; Adn Suffolk from 94. *38 Saxmundham Road, Aldeburgh, Suffolk IP15 5JE* Tel (01728) 454034 Fax as telephone

ARRANDALE, Richard Paul Matthew. b 63. BA87. Chich Th Coll 87. **d** 90 **p** 91. C E Grinstead St Swithun *Chich* 90-94; C Crawley 94. *6 Main Drive, Bognor Regis, W Sussex PO22 7TN*

ARRANTASH, Canon Reginald Thomas. b 12. Linc Th Coll 33. **d** 36 **p** 37. C Kennington St Jo *S'wark* 36-37; Australia 37-48 and from 52; R Kenchester and Bridge Sollers *Heref* 48-52; R Bishopstone 48-52; rtd 83. *51 Sundowner Centre, 416 Stirling Highway, Cottesloe, W Australia 6011* Tel Perth (9) 385 2318

ARRIDGE, Leonard Owen. b 22. Univ of Wales (Ban) BA51. St Deiniol's Hawarden 64. **d** 67 **p** 68. Tutor Ches Coll of FE 67-79; Hon C Hope *St As* 67-69; Hon C Wrexham 69-79; Min Can Ban Cathl *Ban* 79-87; C Ban Cathl Par 79-87; rtd 87; Lic to Offic *Ban* from 87. *8 Ffordd Islwyn, Bangor LL57 1AR* Tel (01248) 362233

ARSCOTT, Barry James. b 36. AKC59. **d** 60 **p** 61. C Walthamstow St Andr *Chelmsf* 60-65; P-in-c Leyton St Luke 65-67; V 67-77; P-in-c Lt Ilford St Barn 77-86; R from 86. *St Barnabas' Vicarage, Browning Road, London E12 6PB* Tel 0181-472 2777

ARTHINGTON, Sister Muriel. b 23. **dss** 67 **d** 87. St Etheldreda's Children's Home Bedf 64-84; Hon Par Dn Bedford St Paul *St Alb* 87-94; Perm to Offic from 94; rtd 97. *12 Christie House, Newnham Road, Bedford MK40 3NZ*

ARTHUR, Graeme Richard. b 52. Univ of NSW BCom78. Linc Th Coll CMinlStuds93. **d** 93 **p** 94. C Witney *Ox* from 93. *111 Thorney Leys, Witney, Oxon OX8 7AY* Tel (01993) 772191

ARTHUR, Ian Willoughby. b 40. Lon Univ BA63 BA66 PGCE64. Ripon Coll Cuddesdon 78. **d** 80 **p** 81. C Kempston Transfiguration *St Alb* 80-83; R Potton w Sutton and Cockayne Hatley 83-96; P-in-c Sharnbrook and Knotting w Souldrop from 96. *The Rectory, 81 High Street, Sharnbrook, Bedford MK44 1PE* Tel (01234) 781444

ARTISS, Joseph Sturge. b 28. Dur Univ BSc52. Cranmer Hall Dur DipTh67. **d** 67 **p** 68. C Dur St Cuth *Dur* 67-68; C Chester le Street 68-70; V Walsall St Pet *Lich* 71-94; rtd 94. *89 Bloxwich Road, Walsall WS2 8BP* Tel (01922) 23995

ARTLEY, Clive Mansell. b 30. St Jo Coll Dur BA56. Cranmer Hall Dur DipTh58. **d** 58 **p** 59. C Eston *York* 58-61; R Burythorpe w E Acklam and Leavening 61-64; CF 64-73; Teacher 73-93; Perm to Offic *York* from 73; rtd 93. *56 High Street, Castleton, Whitby, N Yorkshire YO21 2DA* Tel (01287) 660470

ARTLEY, Harold Leslie. b 37. N Ord Course 79. **d** 82 **p** 83. NSM Flamborough *York* 82-89; R Bainton w N Dalton, Middleton-on-the-Wolds etc from 89; RD Harthill from 97. *The New Rectory, West End, Bainton, Driffield, N Humberside YO25 9NR* Tel (01377) 217622

ARTUS, Stephen James. b 60. Man Poly BA82 W Midl Coll of Educn PGCE84. St Jo Coll Nottm MA95. **d** 95 **p** 96. C Altrincham St Geo *Ches* from 95. *18 Hawarden Road, Altrincham, Cheshire WA14 1NG* Tel 0161-928 5897

ARUNDEL, Canon Michael. b 36. Qu Coll Ox BA60 MA64. Linc Th Coll 60. **d** 62 **p** 63. C Hollinwood *Man* 62-65; C Leesfield 65-69; R Newton Heath All SS 69-80; RD N Man 75-80; P-in-c Eccles St Mary 80-81; TR Eccles 81-91; Hon Can Man Cathl from 82; R Man St Ann from 91. *The Rectory, 449 Wilbraham Road, Chorlton-cum-Hardy, Manchester M21 1US* Tel 0161-881 1229

ARVIDSSON, Karl Fredrik. b 66. Independent Bible Coll DipTh91. **d** 92 **p** 93. OSB from 92; C Southsea H Spirit *Portsm* 92-94; C Botley 94-96; C Curdridge 94-96; C Durley 94-96; P-in-c Ringwould w Kingsdown *Cant* from 96. *The Rectory, Upper Street, Kingsdown, Deal, Kent CT14 8BJ* Tel (01304) 373951

ASBRIDGE, Preb John Hawell. b 26. Dur Univ BA47. Bps' Coll Cheshunt 47. **d** 49 **p** 50. C Barrow St Geo *Carl* 49-52; C Fort William *Arg* 52-54; C Lon Docks St Pet w Wapping St Jo *Lon* 54-55; C Kilburn St Aug 55-59; V Northolt Park St Barn 59-66; V Shepherd's Bush St Steph w St Thos 66-96; Preb St Paul's Cathl 89-96; rtd 96. *Crystal Glen, The Old Mineral Line, Roadwater, Watchet, Somerset TA23 0RL* Tel (01984) 640211

ASBRIDGE, Nigel Henry. b 58. Bris Univ BA80. Chich Th Coll 87. **d** 89 **p** 90. C Tottenham St Paul *Lon* 89; C W Hampstead St Jas 89-94; P-in-c Hornsey H Innocents from 94. *99 Hillfield Avenue, London N8 7DG* Tel 0171-340 1300

ASH, Arthur Edwin. b 44. St Jo Coll Nottm 85. **d** 87 **p** 88. C Attleborough *Cov* 87-91; V Garretts Green *Birm* from 91. *The Vicarage, 112 Rotherfield Road, Birmingham B26 2SH* Tel 0121-743 2971

ASH, Brian John. b 32. ALCD62. **d** 62 **p** 63. C Plymouth St Andr *Ex* 62-66; Area Sec (Dios Cant and Roch) CMS 66-73; V Bromley Common St Aug *Roch* from 73. *St Augustine's Vicarage, Southborough Lane, Bromley BR2 8AT* Tel 0181-467 1351

ASH, Christopher Brian Garton. b 53. Trin Hall Cam MA76. Wycliffe Hall Ox BA92. **d** 93 **p** 94. C Cambridge H Sepulchre *Ely* 93-97; P-in-c Lt Shelford from 97. *The Rectory, 2 Manor Road, Little Shelford, Cambridge CB2 5HF* Tel (01223) 843710

ASH, Nicholas John. b 59. Bath Univ BSc81 Nottm Univ BTh88. Linc Th Coll 85. **d** 88 **p** 89. C Hersham *Guildf* 88-93; P-in-c Flookburgh *Carl* from 93; Dioc Officer for Stewardship 94-97; Dir of Ords from 97. *The Vicarage, Station Road, Flookburgh, Grange-over-Sands, Cumbria LA11 7JY* Tel (01539) 558245

ASHBURNER, David Barrington. b 26. Ch Coll Cam BA51 MA55. Wycliffe Hall Ox 51. **d** 53 **p** 54. C Coalville *Leic* 53-56; C Leic H Apostles 56-58; V Bucklebury w Marlston *Ox* 58-70; V Belton *Leic* 70-75; P-in-c Osgathorpe 73-75; R Belton and Osgathorpe 75-79; V Frisby-on-the-Wreake w Kirby Bellars 79-82; V Uffington w Woolstone and Baulking *Ox* 82-91; P-in-c Shellingford 83-91; RD Vale of White Horse 87-91; rtd 91; Perm to Offic *Glouc* from 91; Perm to Offic *Ox* from 91. *Buckleberry, 188 Fosseway Avenue, Moreton-in-Marsh, Glos GL56 0EH* Tel (01608) 650347

ASHBY, Eric. b 37. EMMTC 78. **d** 81 **p** 82. C Hucknall Torkard *S'well* 81-85; V Lowdham 85-93; V Lowdham w Caythorpe, and Gunthorpe from 93. *The Vicarage, Lowdham, Notts NG14 7BU* Tel 0115-966 3069

✠**ASHBY, The Rt Revd Godfrey William Ernest Candler.** b 30. Lon Univ AKC54 BD54 PhD69. **d** 55 **p** 56 **c** 80. C St Helier *S'wark* 55-57; S Africa 57-88 and from 95; Can Grahamstown Cathl 69-75; Dean and Adn Grahamstown 75-80; Bp St John's 80-85; Prof Div Witwatersrand Univ 85-88; Asst Bp Johannesburg 85-88; Asst Bp Leic 88-95; P-in-c Newtown Linford 92-95; Hon Can Leic Cathl 93-95; rtd 95; Asst Bp George from 95. *PO Box 2685, Knysna, 6570 South Africa* Tel Knysna (445) 21857 Fax as telephone

ASHBY, John Robert Patrick. b 36. Lon Univ BSc57. Coll of Resurr Mirfield 58. **d** 60 **p** 61. C Northolt St Mary *Lon* 60-64; Tanzania 64-66; C W Brompton St Mary *Lon* 66-68; V N Acton St Gabr 68-80; R Arlington, Folkington and Wilmington *Chich* 80-88; V Willingdon from 88. *The Vicarage, 35A Church Street, Willingdon, Eastbourne, E Sussex BN20 9HR* Tel (01323) 502079

ASHBY, Kevin Patrick. b 53. Jes Coll Ox BA76 MA80. Wycliffe Hall Ox 76. **d** 78 **p** 79. C Market Harborough *Leic* 78-82; C Horwich H Trin *Man* 82-84; C Horwich 84; TV 84-90; R Billing *Pet* from 90. *The Rectory, 25 Church Walk, Great Billing, Northampton NN3 4ED* Tel (01604) 784870

ASHBY, Norman. b 13. Man Egerton Hall. **d** 39 **p** 40. C Farnworth St Jo *Man* 39-41; C Ross *Heref* 41-43; C Hove All SS *Chich* 43-44; CF (EC) 44-48; Clerical Org Sec Dr Barnardo's Homes 49; CF (TA) from 49; Iraq 50-52; Warden Ripon Dioc Retreat Ho 62-70; P-in-c Pickhill *Ripon* 70-72; V 72-84; R Kirkby Wiske 77-84; rtd 84; Perm to Offic *York* from 90. *8 Southolme Drive, York YO3 6RL* Tel (01904) 638422

ASHBY, Peter George. b 49. Univ of Wales (Cardiff) BSc(Econ)70 Nottm Univ DipTh71. Linc Th Coll 70. **d** 73 **p** 74. C Bengeo *St Alb* 73-75; Chapl Hatf Poly 76-79; C Apsley End 80; TV Chambersbury (Hemel Hempstead) 80-82; Zimbabwe 82-87; Adn N Harare 84-87; V Eskdale, Irton, Muncaster and Waberthwaite *Carl* 87-93; V Sedgley All SS *Lich* 93; TR Sedgley All SS *Worc* from 93. *All Saints' Vicarage, Vicar Street, Sedgley, Dudley, W Midlands DY3 3SD* Tel (01902) 883255

ASHCROFT, Mrs Ann Christine. b 46. Cov Coll of Educn TCert68. N Ord Course 82. **d** 87 **p** 94. Chapl Trin High Sch Man 86-91; Burnage St Nic *Man* 86-87; Hon Par Dn 87-95; Dio Adv Man Coun for Educn 91-95; TV Wareham *Sarum* from 95; Chapl Purbeck Sch Wareham from 95. *St Martin's Vicarage, Keysworth Road, Sandford, Wareham, Dorset BH20 7DD* Tel (01929) 552756

ASHCROFT, Mark David. b 54. Worc Coll Ox BA77 MA82 Fitzw Coll Cam BA81. Ridley Hall Cam 79. **d** 82 **p** 83. C Burnage

St Marg *Man* 82-85; CMS 86-96; Kenya 86-96; R Harpurhey Ch Ch *Man* from 96; R Harpurhey St Steph from 96. *95 Church Lane, Harpurhey, Manchester M9 5BG* Tel 0161-205 4020

ASHDOWN, Andrew William Harvey. b 64. K Coll Lon BD88 AKC88. Sarum & Wells Th Coll 88. **d** 90 **p** 91. C Cranleigh *Guildf* 90-94; V Ryhill *Wakef* from 94. *The Vicarage, 20 School Lane, Ryhill, Wakefield, W Yorkshire WF4 2DW* Tel (01226) 722363

ASHDOWN, Anthony Hughes. b 37. AKC63. **d** 64 **p** 65. C Tettenhall Regis *Lich* 64-67; P-in-c Bassaleg *Mon* 67-70; Rhodesia 70-77; P-in-c Longton St Jas *Lich* 77-78; P-in-c Longton St Jo 77-78; R Longton 78-80; TR Cove St Jo *Guildf* 80-87; Chapl Lisbon *Eur* 87-90; V Wanstead H Trin Hermon Hill *Chelmsf* from 90. *Holy Trinity Vicarage, Hermon Hill, London E18 1QQ* Tel 0181-989 0912

ASHDOWN, Barry Frederick. b 42. St Pet Coll Ox BA65 MA69. Ridley Hall Cam 66. **d** 68 **p** 69. C Shipley St Pet *Bradf* 68-71; C Rushden w Newton Bromswold *Pet* 71-74; R Haworth *Bradf* 74-82; V Ore Ch Ch *Chich* 82-87; C Southwick 91-93. *47 Kipling Court, Bradford, W Yorkshire BD10 9BQ* Tel (01274) 617484

ASHDOWN, Dr Philip David. b 57. ARCS79 AFIMA87 Imp Coll Lon BSc79 NW Univ Chicago MS80 Cranfield Inst of Tech PhD85. Ripon Coll Cuddesdon DipMin93. **d** 93 **p** 94. C Houghton le Spring *Dur* 93-96; C Stockton from 96; Chapl Univ Coll Stockton from 96. *St Mark's Vicarage, 76 Fairfield Road, Stockton-on-Tees, Cleveland TS19 7BP* Tel (01642) 581591

ASHE, Francis John. b 53. Sheff Univ BMet74. Ridley Hall Cam 77. **d** 79 **p** 80. C Ashtead *Guildf* 79-82; S Africa 82-87; R Wisley w Pyrford *Guildf* 87-93; V Godalming from 93; RD Godalming from 96. *The Vicarage, Westbrook Road, Godalming, Surrey GU7 1ET* Tel (01483) 414135

ASHE, Francis Patrick Bellesme. b 15. St Jo Coll Cam BA37 MA41. Westcott Ho Cam 37. **d** 40 **p** 41. C Woolwich St Mary w H Trin *S'wark* 40-44; Greece 44-46; Youth Chapl *S'wark* 46-50; V Blindley Heath 50-56; V Otley *Bradf* 56-64; V Leamington Priors St Mary *Cov* 64-72; R Church Stretton *Heref* 72-74; Chmn Admin Project Vietnam Orphanage 75-81; rtd 80; Perm to Offic *Guildf* from 81. *62 Busbridge Lane, Godalming, Surrey GU7 1QQ* Tel (01483) 422435

ASHENDEN, Gavin Roy Pelham. b 54. Bris Univ LLB76 Heythrop Coll Lon MTh89. Oak Hill Th Coll BA80. **d** 80 **p** 81. C Bermondsey St Jas w Ch Ch *S'wark* 80-83; TV Sanderstead All SS 83-89; Chapl and Lect Sussex Univ *Chich* from 89. *42 New Road, Shoreham-by-Sea, W Sussex BN43 6RA* Tel (01273) 606755 or 453277 Fax 453277 E-mail g.ashenden@sussex.ac.uk

ASHFORD, The Ven Percival Leonard. b 27. Tyndale Hall Bris 49. **d** 54 **p** 55. C Ilfracombe SS Phil and Jas *Ex* 54-56; C Walton H Trin *Ox* 56-59; V Poughill *Truro* 59-65; Asst Chapl HM Pris Wormwood Scrubs 65-66; Chapl HM Rem Cen Risley 66-69; Chapl HM Pris Dur 69-71; Chapl HM Pris Wandsworth 71-75; Chapl HM Pris Win 75-85; SW Regional Chapl of Pris and Borstals 77-81; Chapl Gen of Pris 81-85; Chapl to The Queen from 82; V Hambledon *Portsm* 85-87; rtd 87; Chmn Selectors ACCM 87-88. *45 Windsor Way, Alderholt, Fordingbridge, Hants SP6 3BN* Tel (01425) 655493

ASHFORTH, David Edward. b 37. ARCS59 Lon Univ BSc Birm Univ DipTh61. Qu Coll Birm. **d** 61 **p** 62. C Scarborough St Columba *York* 61-65; C Northallerton w Kirby Sigston 65-67; V Keyingham 67-73; Chapl Imp Coll *Lon* 73-89; V Balderstone *Blackb* from 89; Dir of Post-Ord Tr from 89. *The Vicarage, Commons Lane, Balderstone, Blackburn BB2 7LL* Tel (01254) 812232

ASHLEY, Brian. b 36. S'wark Ord Course 75. **d** 77 **p** 78. NSM Horsell *Guildf* from 77. *Starston, Church Hill, Horsell, Woking, Surrey GU21 4QE* Tel (01483) 761232

ASHLEY, Brian Christenson. b 33. Roch Th Coll 68. **d** 70 **p** 71. C New Sleaford *Linc* 70-72; Min Basegreen CD 72-74; TV Gleadless *Sheff* 74-77; R Dinnington 77-85; RD Laughton 82-85; V Mosborough 85-88; P-in-c Curbar and Stoney Middleton *Derby* 88-91; rtd 91; Perm to Offic *Pet* from 95. *15 Eliot Close, Saxon Fields, Kettering, Northants NN16 9XR* Tel (01536) 524457

ASHLEY, Clive Ashley. b 54. SRN80 RGN81 Croydon Coll of Art and Design LSIAD75 E Ham Coll of Tech FETC82 NE Lon Poly NDN83. Aston Tr Scheme 81 Cranmer Hall Dur 84. **d** 86 **p** 87. C Withington St Paul *Man* 86-89; Asst Chapl Freeman Hosp Newc 89-92; Chapl St Rich Hosp Chich 92-94; Chapl Graylingwell Hosp Chich from 92; Chapl R W Sussex Hosp Chich 92-94; Chapl Chich Priority Care Services NHS Trust from 94; Chapl R W Sussex NHS Trust from 94. *St Richard's Hospital, Spitalfield Lane, Chichester, W Sussex PO19 4SE* Tel (01243) 788122

ASHLEY, John Michael. b 28. Worc Coll Ox BA51 MA54. Linc Th Coll 50. **d** 54 **p** 55. Australia 54-60; C Anderby w Cumberworth *Linc* 60-66; P-in-c Huttoft 60-61; V 61-66; R Woolsthorpe 66-93; R W w E Allington and Sedgebrook 66-93; CF (TAVR) 79-93; rtd 93; Perm to Offic *Linc* from 93. *35 Gregory Close, Harlaxton, Grantham, Lincs NG32 1JG* Tel (01476) 561846

ASHLEY-ROBERTS, James. b 53. Lon Univ BD77. Oak Hill Th Coll 75 Wycliffe Hall Ox 79. **d** 80 **p** 81. C Gt Warley Ch Ch *Chelmsf* 80-83; C E Ham St Paul 83-85; TV Holyhead w Rhoscolyn w Llanfair-yn-Neubwll *Ban* 85-88; R 88-91; V Penrhyndeudraeth w Llanfrothen w Beddgelert from 91. *The Vicarage, Penrhyndeudraeth LL48 6LG* Tel (01766) 770677

ASHLING, Raymond Charles. b 32. Dur Univ BA58. Linc Th Coll 58. **d** 60 **p** 61. C Halifax St Aug *Wakef* 60-63; C Farlington *Portsm* 63-65; Rhodesia 65-71; Chapl Rishworth Sch Ripponden 71-75; Lesotho 75-85; V Somercotes *Linc* 85-88; Ethiopia 88-89; R Gt w Lt Snoring w Kettlestone and Pensthorpe *Nor* 89-94; rtd 94. *14 Abbey Court, Norwich NR1 2AW*

ASHMAN, Peter Nicholas. b 52. CSS81 SEN73. Sarum & Wells Th Coll 87. **d** 89 **p** 90. C Stafford *Lich* 89-93; R Dymchurch w Burmarsh and Newchurch *Cant* from 93. *The New Rectory, 135 High Street, Dymchurch, Romney Marsh, Kent TN29 0LD* Tel (01303) 872150

ASHTON, Anthony Joseph. b 37. Oak Hill Th Coll 62. **d** 65 **p** 66. C Crookes St Thos *Sheff* 65-68; C Heeley 68-73; V Bowling St Steph *Bradf* 73-78; R Chesterfield H Trin *Derby* 78-92; rtd 93; Perm to Offic *Derby* from 93. *118 Newbold Road, Chesterfield, Derbyshire S41 7BG* Tel (01246) 279604

ASHTON, Canon Cyril Guy. b 42. Lanc Univ MA86. Oak Hill Th Coll 64. **d** 67 **p** 68. C Blackpool St Thos *Blackb* 67-70; Voc Sec CPAS 70-74; V Lancaster St Thos 74-91; Lanc Almshouses 76-90; Dioc Dir of Tr *Blackb* from 91; Hon Can Blackb Cathl from 91. *1 Piccadilly Grove, Scotforth, Lancaster LA1 4PP* Tel (01524) 841495 E-mail ministry@blackburn.anglican.org.uk

ASHTON, David. b 52. Sarum Th Coll 93. **d** 96 **p** 97. NSM St Leonards Ch Ch and St Mary *Chich* from 96. *67 The Ridge, Hastings, E Sussex TN34 2AB* Tel (01424) 436384

ASHTON, David William. b 51. Reading Univ BA74 Lanc Univ PGCE75. Wycliffe Hall Ox 79. **d** 82 **p** 83. C Shipley St Pet *Bradf* 82-85; C Tadley St Pet *Win* 85-88; V Sinfin *Derby* 88-91; Chapl Sophia Antipolis *Eur* 91-94; P-in-c Swanwick and Pentrich *Derby* from 95; RD Alfreton from 95. *The Vicarage, 4 Broom Avenue, Broadway, Swanwick, Alfreton, Derbyshire DE55 1DQ* Tel (01773) 602684 or 541458 Fax 602684

✠ASHTON, The Rt Revd Jeremy Claude. b 30. Trin Coll Cam BA53 MA57. Westcott Ho Cam 53. **d** 55 **p** 56 **c** 76. C Bury St Mary *Man* 55-60; CF (TA) 57-60; CF (TA - R of O) 60-70; Papua New Guinea 60-86; Asst Bp Papua 76-77; Bp Aipo Rongo 77-86; rtd 86; Australia from 86. *PO Box 113, Maldon, Victoria 3463, or 19 Glyndon Avenue, Merlynston, Victoria, Australia 3058* Tel Melbourne (3) 9350 4819

ASHTON, Miss Joan Elizabeth. b 54. Eaton Hall Coll of Educn CertEd76. Cranmer Hall Dur CTMin93. **d** 93 **p** 94. Par Dn Darnall-cum-Attercliffe *Sheff* 93-94; C Hillsborough and Wadsley Bridge 94-96; P-in-c Stainforth from 96. *The Vicarage, Field Road, Stainforth, Doncaster, S Yorkshire DN7 5AQ* Tel (01302) 841295

ASHTON, Joseph Patrick Bankes (Pat). b 27. Jes Coll Cam BA49 MA52. Wells Th Coll 53. **d** 55 **p** 56. C Cheadle *Lich* 55-59; C Caverswall 59-61; C-in-c Werrington CD 61-64; I 64-66; R Eyke w Bromeswell and Rendlesham *St E* 66-76; R Eyke w Bromeswell, Rendlesham, Tunstall etc 76-86; Chapl Seckford Foundn 86-92; Hon C Woodbridge St Mary 86-92; rtd 92. *Drift Cottage, Church Lane, Rendlesham, Woodbridge, Suffolk IP12 2SF* Tel (01394) 461511

✠ASHTON, The Rt Revd Leonard James. b 15. CB70. Tyndale Hall Bris 40. **d** 42 **p** 43 **c** 74. C Cheadle *Ches* 42-45; Chapl RAF 45-62; Asst Chapl-in-Chief RAF 62-65; Chapl St Clem Danes (RAF Ch) 65-69; Chapl-in-Chief RAF 69-73; QHC 67-83; Can and Preb Linc Cathl *Linc* 69-73; Asst Bp Jerusalem 74-76; Can from 76; Bp Cyprus and the Gulf 76-83; rtd 83; Asst Bp Ox from 84; Can Cyprus from 89. *60 Lowndes Avenue, Chesham, Bucks HP5 2HJ* Tel (01494) 782952

ASHTON, Mrs Margaret Lucie. b 40. St Jo Coll Nottm DPS79. **dss** 83 **d** 87 **p** 94. Billericay and Lt Burstead *Chelmsf* 83-87; NSM from 87. *The Rectory, 40 Laindon Road, Billericay, Essex CM12 9LD* Tel (01277) 622837

ASHTON, Mark Hewett. b 48. Ch Ch Ox BA70 MA74 Trin Coll Cam BA72. Ridley Hall Cam 71. **d** 73 **p** 74. C Beckenham Ch Ch *Roch* 73-77; Win Coll 78-81; Lic to Offic *S'wark* 81-87; Hd of CYFA (CPAS) 81-87; V Cambridge H Sepulchre w All SS *Ely* 87-92; V Cambridge H Sepulchre from 92. *The Vicarage, Manor Street, Cambridge CB1 1LQ* Tel (01223) 518218 Fax 327331

ASHTON, Neville Anthony. b 45. Sarum & Wells Th Coll 78. **d** 80 **p** 81. C Hattersley *Ches* 80-82; C Lancaster Ch Ch w St Jo and St Anne *Blackb* 82-84; R Church Kirk from 84. *Church Kirk Rectory, 434 Blackburn Road, Accrington, Lancs BB5 0DE* Tel (01254) 236946

ASHTON, Nigel Charles. b 49. SW Minl Tr Course. **d** 78 **p** 79. NSM St Stephen by Saltash *Truro* 78-94; Lic to Offic *Ex* from 94. *9 Bunn Road, Exmouth, Devon EX8 5PP* Tel (01395) 224345

ASHTON, Canon Peter Donald. b 34. Lon Univ BD62. ALCD61. **d** 62 **p** 63. C Walthamstow St Mary *Chelmsf* 62-68; V Girlington *Bradf* 68-73; Dir Past Studies St Jo Coll Nottm 73-80; TR Billericay and Lt Burstead *Chelmsf* from 80; Chapl Mayflower Hosp Billericay from 80; Chapl St Andr Hosp Billericay from 80; RD Basildon *Chelmsf* from 89; Hon Can Chelmsf Cathl from 92. *The Rectory, 40 Laindon Road, Billericay, Essex CM12 9LD* Tel (01277) 622837

ASHTON, Preb Samuel Rupert. b 42. Sarum & Wells Th Coll. **d** 83 **p** 84. C Ledbury w Eastnor *Heref* 83-86; R St Weonards w Orcop, Garway, Tretire etc from 86; RD Ross and Archenfield 91-95 and from 96; Preb Heref Cathl from 97. *The Vicarage, St Weonards, Hereford HR2 8NU* Tel (01981) 580307

ASHTON, Stephen Robert. b 55. BA BPhil. Sarum & Wells Th Coll. **d** 84 **p** 85. C Penzance St Mary w St Paul *Truro* 84-86; C Tewkesbury w Walton Cardiff *Glouc* 86-89; P-in-c Newton Heath St Wilfrid and St Anne *Man* 89-92; V Breage w Germoe *Truro* 92-94. *20 Tregarrick Close, Helston, Cornwall TR13 8YA* Tel (01326) 573449

ASHTON, Thomas Eyre Maunsell (Tom). b 13. St Edm Hall Ox BA36 MA39. Wycliffe Hall Ox 36. **d** 38 **p** 39. C Shirley *Win* 38-41; Chapl RAFVR 41-46; V Derringham Bank *York* 46-47; V Kingston upon Hull St Martin 47-54; V Crewkerne *B & W* 54-67; R Lee St Marg *S'wark* 67-75; Chapl Morden Coll Blackheath 75-83; rtd 83; Perm to Offic *S'wark* from 83. *7 The Quadrangle, Morden College, London SE3 0PW* Tel 0181-853 1576

ASHTON, William Grant. b 57. St Chad's Coll Dur BA79. Oak Hill Th Coll BA85. **d** 85 **p** 86. C Lancaster St Thos *Blackb* 85-89; CF from 89. *MOD Chaplains (Army), Trenchard Lines, Upavon, Pewsey, Wilts SN9 6BE* Tel (01980) 615804 Fax 615800

ASHWELL, Anthony John. b 42. CChem74 MRSC74 St Andr Univ BSc65. Sarum & Wells Th Coll 86. **d** 88 **p** 89. C Plymstock *Ex* 88-91; C Axminster, Chardstock, Combe Pyne and Rousdon 91-92; TV 92-95; C Crediton and Shobrooke 95-97; TV Bride Valley *Sarum* from 97. *The Vicarage, Litton Cheney, Dorchester, Dorset DT2 9AG* Tel (01308) 482302

ASHWIN, Vincent George. b 42. Worc Coll Ox BA65. Coll of Resurr Mirfield 65. **d** 67 **p** 68. C Shildon *Dur* 67-70; V 79-85; C Newc St Fran *Newc* 70-72; Swaziland 72-79; V Fenham St Jas and St Basil *Newc* 85-97; RD Newc W 89-97; V Haydon Bridge and Beltingham w Henshaw from 97; RD Hexham from 97. *The Vicarage, Station Yard, Haydon Bridge, Hexham, Northd NE47 6LL* Tel (01434) 684307

ASHWORTH, Canon David. b 40. Nottm Univ BPharm62. Linc Th Coll 63. **d** 65 **p** 66. C Halliwell St Thos *Man* 65-69; C Heywood St Jas 69-72; C-in-c Heywood St Marg CD 72-78; V Hale *Ches* 78-87; V Hale and Ashley 87-96; RD Bowdon 87-95; Hon Can Ches Cathl from 94; V Prestbury from 96. *The Vicarage, Prestbury, Macclesfield, Cheshire SK10 4DG* Tel (01625) 829288 or 827625

ASHWORTH, Edward James. b 33. Clifton Th Coll 60. **d** 63 **p** 64. C Spitalfields Ch Ch w All SS *Lon* 63-65; C Pennycross *Ex* 65-69; C Blackb Ch Ch *Blackb* 69-72; V Camerton H Trin W Seaton *Carl* 72-79; V Tunstead *Man* 79-97; rtd 97. *The Vicarage, 33 Booth Road, Bacup, Lancs OL13 0QP* Tel (01706) 874508

ASHWORTH, James Nigel. b 55. York Univ BA77. Cranmer Hall Dur CTMin93. **d** 93 **p** 94. C Rothwell *Ripon* 93-96; Chapl Campsfield Ho Oxon from 96; C Akeman *Ox* from 96. *The Rectory, Troy Lane, Kirtlington, Kidlington, Oxon OX5 3HA* Tel (01869) 350224

ASHWORTH, John Russell. b 33. Lich Th Coll 57. **d** 60 **p** 61. C Castleford All SS *Wakef* 60-62; C Luton St Sav *St Alb* 63-67; V Clipstone *S'well* 67-70; V Bolton-upon-Dearne *Sheff* 70-82; V Thornhill Lees *Wakef* from 82. *The Vicarage, Thornhill Lees, Dewsbury, W Yorkshire WF12 9PD* Tel (01924) 461269

ASHWORTH, Keith Benjamin. b 33. NW Ord Course 76. **d** 79 **p** 80. C Pennington *Man* 79-83; P-in-c Bolton St Bede 83-88; V 88-95; V Hillock from 95. *St Andrew's Vicarage, Mersey Drive, Whitefield, Manchester M45 8LA* Tel 0161-766 1635

ASHWORTH, Martin. b 41. AKC63. **d** 64 **p** 65. C-in-c Wythenshawe Wm Temple Ch CD *Man* 64-71; R Haughton St Anne 71-83; V Prestwich St Marg from 83. *St Margaret's Vicarage, St Margaret's Road, Prestwich, Manchester M25 5QB* Tel 0161-773 2698

ASHWORTH, Timothy (Tim). b 52. Worc Coll of Educn CertEd74. Trin Coll Bris DipHE79 Oak Hill Th Coll BA81. **d** 82 **p** 83. C Tonbridge St Steph *Roch* 82-85; C-in-c Whittle-le-Woods *Blackb* 85-90; Chapl Scargill Ho 90-96; V Ingleton w Chapel le Dale *Bradf* from 96. *St Mary's Vicarage, Main Street, Ingleton, Carnforth, Lancs LA6 3HF* Tel (01524) 241440

ASHWORTH, Mrs Vivien (Viv). b 52. Worc Coll of Educn CertEd73. Trin Coll Bris DipHE81 Oak Hill Th Coll BA82. **dss** 82 **d** 87 **p** 94. Tonbridge St Steph *Roch* 82-85; Whittle-le-Woods *Blackb* 85-90; Hon Par Dn 87-90; Chapl Scargill Ho 90-96; Hon C Ingleton w Chapel le Dale *Bradf* from 96; Dioc Youth Adv from 96. *St Mary's Vicarage, Main Street, Ingleton, Carnforth, Lancs LA6 3HF* Tel (01524) 241440

ASKE, Sir Conan, Bt. b 12. Ball Coll Ox BA33 MA39. Wycliffe Hall Ox 69. **d** 70 **p** 71. C Hagley *Worc* 70-72; C St Jo in Bedwardine 72-80; rtd 80; Perm to Offic *Worc* from 80. *167 Malvern Road, Worcester WR2 4NN* Tel (01905) 422817

ASKEW, Miss Alison Jane. b 57. Dur Univ BA78 PGCE79. S Dios Minl Tr Scheme DipTh96. **d** 95 **p** 96. NSM Kingsclere *Win* from 95; Asst Chapl Loddon Trust Hants from 95; Asst Chapl N Hants Hosps NHS Trust from 95. *6 Worcester Block, North Hampshire Hospital, Basingstoke, Hants RG24 9NA*

ASKEW, Canon Dennis. b 30. Open Univ BA76. Kelham Th Coll 45 Lich Th Coll 55. **d** 58 **p** 59. C Garforth *Ripon* 58-61; C Seacroft 61-64; V Holland Fen *Linc* 64-69; R Folkingham w Laughton 69-77; V Aswarby w Swarby 69-77; R Osbournby w Scott Willoughby 69-77; R Pickworth w Walcot 69-77; V Threckingham 69-77; P-in-c Newton w Haceby 72-77; P-in-c Aunsby w Dembleby 72-77; R S Lafford 77-87; Can and Preb Linc Cathl 86-96; R Ruskington 87-96; rtd 96; Perm to Offic *Linc* from 96. *Langford House, 4 Hereford Close, Sleaford, Lincs NG34 8TP* Tel (01529) 305645

ASKEW, Canon Reginald James Albert. b 28. CCC Cam BA51 MA55. Linc Th Coll 55. **d** 57 **p** 58. C Highgate St Mich *Lon* 57-61; Lect and Vice-Prin Wells Th Coll 61-69; PV Wells Cathl *B & W* 61-69; V Paddington Ch Ch *Lon* 69-73; Member Corrymeela Community from 71; Prin Sarum & Wells Th Coll 73-87; Chmn S Dios Minl Tr Scheme 73-87; Can and Preb Sarum Cathl *Sarum* 75-87; Dean K Coll Lon 88-93; rtd 93; Perm to Offic *B & W* from 93; Perm to Offic *Lon* from 93. *Carters Cottage, North Wootton, Shepton Mallet, Somerset BA4 4AF* Tel (01749) 890728

ASKEW, Preb Richard George. b 35. BNC Ox BA59 MA63. Ridley Hall Cam 62. **d** 64 **p** 65. C Chesham St Mary *Ox* 64-66; C Mossley Hill St Matt and St Jas *Liv* 66-67; Chapl Ox Pastorate 67-72; Asst Chapl BNC Ox 67-71; R Ashtead *Guildf* 72-83; RD Leatherhead 80-83; Can Res and Treas Sarum Cathl *Sarum* 83-90; Dioc Adv on Miss and Min *B & W* 83-90; R Bath Abbey w St Jas from 90; Preb Wells Cathl from 92. *The Abbey Rectory, Redwood House, Trossachs Drive, Bath BA2 6RP* Tel (01225) 464930 or 422462 Fax 429990

ASKEW, Sydney Derek. b 29. Roch Th Coll 66. **d** 68 **p** 69. C Kirkstall *Ripon* 68-73; V Markington w S Stainley and Bishop Thornton 73-94; rtd 94. *6 Mallorie Close, Ripon, N Yorkshire HG4 2QE* Tel (01765) 603309

ASKEY, Gary Simon. b 64. St Steph Ho Ox 88. **d** 91 **p** 92. SSM from 87; Prior from 96; C Middlesbrough All SS *York* 91-94; Sub-Chapl HM Pris Holme Ho 92-94; C Whitby 94-96; Missr Whitby Miss and Seafarer's Trust 94-96; Lic to Offic *S'wark* from 96. *SSM Priory, 90 Vassall Road, London SW9 6JA* Tel 0171-582 2162

ASKEY, John Stuart. b 39. Chich Th Coll 63. **d** 66 **p** 67. C Feltham *Lon* 66-69; C Epsom Common Ch Ch *Guildf* 69-72; C Chesterton Gd Shep *Ely* 72-74; R Stretham w Thetford 74-93; Dioc Youth Officer from 80; P-in-c Brinkley, Burrough Green and Carlton from 93; P-in-c Westley Waterless from 93; P-in-c Dullingham from 93; P-in-c Stetchworth from 93. *The Rectory, Brinkley, Newmarket, Suffolk CB8 0SE* Tel (01638) 507263

ASKEY, Thomas Cyril. b 29. Sheff Univ BSc50 Man Univ MTh81 ACIPA58 MITMA76. NW Ord Course 70. **d** 73 **p** 74. NSM Gawsworth *Ches* 73-76; Perm to Offic 76-80; rtd 81. *Park Cottage, Nether End, Baslow, Bakewell, Derbyshire DE45 1SR* Tel (01246) 583780 Fax 583008

ASLACHSEN, Grosvenor Trevelyan. b 03. Lich Th Coll 24. **d** 28 **p** 29. C Roch St Marg *Roch* 28-35; C Speldhurst w Groombridge 35-40; R Halstead 40-68; rtd 68. *c/o Dawson Hart Solicitors, The Old Grammar School, Church Street, Uckfield, E Sussex TN22 1BH* Tel (01825) 762281

ASPDEN, Peter George. b 28. Univ of Wales (Lamp) BA50. Ely Th Coll 52. **d** 53 **p** 54. C Morecambe St Barn *Blackb* 53-55; C Marton 55-58; V Tockholes 58-63; C St Annes 63-66; V St Annes St Marg 66-75; V Lancaster Ch Ch 75-79; R Eccleston 79-94; rtd 94; Perm to Offic *Liv* from 94. *21 Glencoyne Drive, Southport, Merseyside PR9 9TS* Tel (01704) 214066

ASPINALL, Philip Norman. b 51. Cam Univ MA ATI. WMMTC 86. **d** 89 **p** 90. NSM Cov E *Cov* from 89. *139 Wiltshire Court, Nod Rise, Mount Nod, Coventry CV5 7JP* Tel (01203) 467509 E-mail phil.n.aspinall@corp.courtaulds.co.uk

ASQUITH, Eric Lees. b 24. St Aid Birkenhead 55. **d** 56 **p** 57. C Hanging Heaton *Wakef* 56-59; V Netherthong 59-68; rtd 89. *15 Heycroft Way, Nayland, Colchester CO6 4LN* Tel (01206) 262593

ASQUITH, Michael John. b 60. St D Coll Lamp BA82 MPhil91 Ch Ch Coll Cant PGCE83. Cant Sch of Min 91. **d** 94 **p** 95. C S Ashford Ch Ch *Cant* from 94. *112 Beaver Road, Ashford, Kent TN23 7SR* Tel (01233) 620600

ASSON, Geoffrey Ormrod. b 34. Univ of Wales (Ban) BA54 St Cath Coll Ox BA56 MA61. St Steph Ho Ox 54. **d** 57 **p** 58. C Aberdare St Jo *Llan* 57-59; C Roath St Marg 59-61; R Hagworthingham w Asgarby and Lusby *Linc* 61-65; P-in-c Mavis Enderby w Raithby 62-65; V Friskney 65-69; R S Ormsby w Ketsby, Calceby and Driby 69-74; R Harrington w Brinkhill 69-74; R Oxcombe 69-74; R Ruckland w Farforth and Maidenwell 69-74; R Somersby w Bag Enderby 69-74; R Tetford and Salmonby 69-74; P-in-c Belchford 71-74; P-in-c W Ashby 71-74; V Riverhead w Dunton Green *Roch* 75-80; R Kington w Huntington *Heref* 80-82; RD Kington and Weobley 80-86; P-in-c Almeley 81-82; P-in-c Knill 81-82; P-in-c Old Radnor 81-82; R Kington w Huntington, Old Radnor, Kinnerton etc 82-86; V Mathry w St Edren's and Grandston etc *St D* from 86; Bp's Rural Adv and Tourist Officer 91-95; rtd 96. *The Rectory, St Nicholas, Goodwick SA64 0LG* Tel (01348) 891230

ASTILL, Cyril John. b 33. Lon Univ DipTh64. Oak Hill Th Coll 62. **d** 65 **p** 66. C Carl St Jo *Carl* 65-68; C St Helens St Helen *Liv* 68-71; V Blackb Sav *Blackb* 71-85; P-in-c Blackb Ch Ch w

St Matt 81-83; TR N Ferriby *York* from 85. *The Rectory, 20 Aston Hall Drive, North Ferriby, N Humberside HU14 3EB* Tel (01482) 631306

ASTIN, Alfred Ronald. b 18. St Pet Hall Ox BA43 MA45. Ridley Hall Cam. **d** 47 **p** 48. C Weaste *Man* 47-50; C Harpurhey Ch Ch 50-51; V Leesfield 51-57; V Earlham St Anne *Nor* 57-70; V Sheringham 70-84; rtd 84; Perm to Offic *Nor* from 84. *1 Cromer Road, Overstrand, Cromer, Norfolk NR27 0NU* Tel (01263) 78201

ASTIN, Howard Keith. b 51. Warw Univ LLB DipHE. Trin Coll Bris 83. **d** 83 **p** 84. C Kirkheaton *Wakef* 83-88; V Bowling St Jo *Bradf* from 88. *St John's Vicarage, 96 Lister Avenue, Bradford, W Yorkshire BD4 7QS* Tel (01274) 720660

ASTIN, Mrs Moira Anne Elizabeth. b 65. Clare Coll Cam BA86 MA90. Wycliffe Hall Ox BA94 DipMin95. **d** 95 **p** 96. C Newbury *Ox* from 95. *10 Braunfels Walk, Newbury, Berks RG14 5NQ* Tel (01635) 582006

ASTIN, Dr Timothy Robin. b 58. St Edm Hall Ox BA79 Darw Coll Cam PhD82. Ox Min Course CBTS93. **d** 93 **p** 94. NSM Reading St Jo *Ox* from 93. *10 Braunfels Walk, Newbury, Berks RG14 5NQ* Tel (01635) 582006

ASTLEY, Dr Jeffrey. b 47. Down Coll Cam BA68 MA72 Birm Univ DipTh69 Dur Univ PhD79. Qu Coll Birm 68. **d** 70 **p** 71. C Cannock *Lich* 70-73; Lect and Chapl St Hild Coll Dur 73-75; Sen Lect and Chapl SS Hild and Bede Coll Dur 75-77; Prin Lect & Hd Relig Studies Bp Grosseteste Coll 77-81; Lic to Offic *Linc* 78-81; Dir N England Inst for Chr Educn from 81. *Carter House, Pelaw Leazes Place, Durham DH1 1TB* Tel 0191-384 1034 or 386 4466 Fax 384 7529

ASTON, Glyn. b 29. Univ of Wales (Abth) BA54. **d** 79 **p** 80. Hon C Maindee *Mon* 79-85; C 85-86; P-in-c Llangwm Uchaf w Llangwm Isaf w Gwernesney etc 86; V from 86. *The Rectory, Gwernesney, Usk NP5 1HF* Tel (01291) 672518

ASTON, John Bernard. b 34. Leeds Univ BA55 PGCE56. Qu Coll Birm 72. **d** 75 **p** 76. NSM Shenstone *Lich* from 75; Chapl HM Young Offender Inst Swinfen Hall from 90. *21 Wordsworth Close, Lichfield, Staffs WS14 9BY* Tel (01543) 264960 Fax 480138

ASTON, John Leslie. b 47. Oak Hill Th Coll 77. **d** 80 **p** 81. C Trentham *Lich* 80-83; C Meir Heath 83-85; V Upper Tean 85-91; CF from 91. *MOD Chaplains (Army), Trenchard Lines, Upavon, Pewsey, Wilts SN9 6BE* Tel (01980) 615804 Fax 615800

ASTON SMITH, Dr Anthony. b 29. CEng MIM FIDiagE MICorrST AMIMechE Trin Coll Cam BA52 MA56 PhD56. Ox NSM Course 86. **d** 93 **p** 94. NSM Ox St Giles and SS Phil and Jas w St Marg *Ox* from 93. *32 Chalfont Road, Oxford OX2 6TH* Tel (01865) 57090

ASTON, Archdeacon of. *See* BARTON, The Ven Charles John Greenwood

ASTON, Suffragan Bishop of. *See* AUSTIN, The Rt Revd John Michael

ATACK, John Philip. b 49. Lanc Univ MA91. Linc Th Coll 86. **d** 88 **p** 89. C Cleveleys *Blackb* 88-92; V Appley Bridge 92-96. *7 Second Avenue, Warboys, Huntingdon, Cambs PE17 2SP* Tel (01487) 822095

ATFIELD, Gladys. Univ Coll Lon BSc53 DipTh76. Gilmore Course. **dss** 79 **d** 87 **p** 94. Bexley St Mary *Roch* 79-87; Hon C from 87. *7 Clarendon Mews, High Street, Bexley, Kent DA5 1JS* Tel (01322) 551741

ATHERFOLD, Mrs Evelyne Sara (Eve). b 43. Leeds Inst of Educn CertEd64. N Ord Course 82. **dss** 85 **d** 92 **p** 94. Kirk Sandall and Edenthorpe *Sheff* 85-87; Fishlake w Sykehouse, Kirk Bramwith, Fenwick etc 87-92; NSM from 92. *Padley House, Hawkeshouse Green, Moss, Doncaster, S Yorkshire DN6 0DL* Tel (01302) 700452 Fax 707221

ATHERLEY, Keith Philip. b 56. St Steph Ho Ox 77. **d** 80 **p** 81. C Armley w New Wortley *Ripon* 80-82; C Harrogate St Wilfrid and St Luke 82-85; V Forcett and Stanwick w Aldbrough 85-89; CF from 89. *MOD Chaplains (Army), Trenchard Lines, Upavon, Pewsey, Wilts SN9 6BE* Tel (01980) 615804 Fax 615800

ATHERSTONE, Castell Hugh. b 45. Natal Univ BA67 St Chad's Coll Dur DipTh69 MA79. **d** 70 **p** 70. S Africa 70-83; Dioc Stewardship Adv *Ely* 83-87; P-in-c Doddington w Benwick 83-87; R Frant w Eridge *Chich* 87-95; RD Rotherfield 90-94; V Seaford w Sutton from 95. *The Vicarage, Sutton Road, Seaford, E Sussex BN25 1SH* Tel (01323) 893508

ATHERTON, Albert. b 26. CQSW71. St Aid Birkenhead 60. **d** 62 **p** 63. C Northenden *Man* 62-64; C Newall Green CD 64-66; V Patricroft 66-70; Lic to Offic 71-72; V Mossley 77-83; V Ockbrook *Derby* 83-86; P-in-c Newall Green *Man* 86-91; V 91-94; rtd 94; Perm to Offic *Man* from 94. *50 Belmont Drive, Bury, Lancs BL8 2HU* Tel 0161-764 8397

ATHERTON, Graham Bryson. b 47. GRSM69 FTCL69. Edin Th Coll 77. **d** 79 **p** 80. C Orford St Marg *Liv* 79-82; V Warrington St Barn 82-88; V Leeds Halton St Wilfrid *Ripon* 88-95; RD Whitkirk 92-95; TR Guiseley w Esholt *Bradf* from 95. *The Rectory, The Green, Guiseley, Leeds LS20 9BT* Tel (01943) 874321

ATHERTON, Henry Anthony. b 44. FGS68 Univ of Wales BSc67 DipEd68 Fitzw Coll Cam BA72 MA75. Westcott Ho Cam 70. **d** 72 **p** 73. C Leamington Priors All SS *Cov* 72-75; C Orpington All SS *Roch* 75-78; V Gravesend St Mary 78-87; Chapl St Jas Hosp Gravesend 82-87; V Bromley St Andr *Roch* from 87. *The Vicarage, 1 Lake Avenue, Bromley BR1 4EN* Tel 0181-460 0481

ATHERTON, Canon John Robert. b 39. Lon Univ BA60 Man Univ MA74 PhD79. Coll of Resurr Mirfield 60. **d** 62 **p** 63. C Aberdeen St Marg *Ab* 62-64; C Bury St Mark *Man* 64-67; P-in-c Glas St Marg *Glas* 67-68; R Hulme St Geo *Man* 68-74; Ind Chapl 68-74; Asst Dir Wm Temple Foundn 74-79; Dir from 79; Lic to Offic 74-84; Can Res Man Cathl from 84. *Latham, Myrtle Grove, Whitefield, Manchester M25 7RR* Tel 0161-766 9296 or 833 2220

ATHERTON, Lionel Thomas. b 45. Univ of Wales (Ban) BA74 St Luke's Coll Ex. St Steph Ho Ox 74. **d** 76 **p** 77. C Chenies and Lt Chalfont *Ox* 76-79; C Fleet *Guildf* 79-84; V S Farnborough 84-89; TR Alston Team *Newc* 89-96; V Chorley St Pet *Blackb* from 96. *St Peter's Vicarage, Harpers Lane, Chorley, Lancs PR6 0HT* Tel (01257) 263423

ATHERTON, Paul Christopher. b 56. Chich Th Coll. **d** 82 **p** 83. C Orford St Marg *Liv* 82-86; Chapl Univ of Wales (Cardiff) *Llan* 88-89; TV Walton St Mary *Liv* 89-92; C Westmr St Matt *Lon* 92-96; C Somers Town St Mary 96-97; V Bush Hill Park St Mark from 97. *St Mark's Vicarage, St Mark's Road, Bush Hill Park, Enfield, Middx EN1 1BE* Tel 0181-363 2780

ATHERTON, Percy Francis. b 22. Man Univ BA47 PGCE48 Univ of Minnesota MA56. Seabury-Western Th Sem 52. **d** 52 **p** 53. USA 52-57; Asst Chapl Rishworth Sch Halifax 57-61; Chapl Bretton Hall Coll of Educn 62-66; Lic to Offic *Ex* 66-75; HMI of Schs 70-75; Peru 75-76; Singapore 76-77; P-in-c Zeal Monachorum *Ex* 78-79; R Bow w Broad Nymet 78-79; V Colebrooke 78-79; Perm to Offic from 79; Algeria 80-81; rtd 89. *The Old Dame's Cottage, Cove, Tiverton, Devon EX16 7RX* Tel (01398) 331489

ATHERTON, Philip Andrew. b 51. Wycliffe Hall Ox. **d** 84 **p** 85. C Ox St Clem *Ox* 84-87; Lic Preacher *Man* from 87; Ind Missr from 87. *192 Windsor Road, Oldham OL8 1RG* Tel 0161-652 2684

ATKIN, Arthur Courtney Qu'appelle. b 19. Dur Univ BA44. Lich Th Coll 59. **d** 59 **p** 60. Chapl Bromsgrove Jun Sch 59-64; C Kidderminster St Geo *Worc* 59-60; C Bromsgrove All SS 60-64; Chapl RN 64-69; Chapl R Hosp Sch Holbrook 69-72; P-in-c Brixham *Ex* 72-74; Chapl Colston's Sch Bris 74-79; P-in-c Pitcombe w Shepton Montague and Bratton St Maur *B & W* 79-85; rtd 86; Perm to Offic *B & W* 86-93; Perm to Offic *Heref* from 93. *26 Queen's Court, Ledbury, Herefordshire HR8 2AL* Tel (01531) 634526

ATKIN, John Anthony. b 33. Glouc Th Course 70. **d** 72 **p** 73. NSM Leamington Priors All SS *Cov* 72-77; NSM Barford 77-78; NSM Barford w Wasperton and Sherbourne 78-80; P-in-c Exford w Exmoor *B & W* 80-82; P-in-c Hawkridge w Withypool 80-82; P-in-c Exford, Exmoor, Hawkridge and Withypool 82-83; R 83-92; RD Exmoor 86-92; rtd 93; Perm to Offic *B & W* from 93. *Halsgrove Farm, Withypool, Minehead, Somerset TA24 7RX* Tel (01643) 83388

ATKIN, Mrs Stephanie. b 23. **d** 87. Boreham Wood St Mich *St Alb* 78-79; Borehamwood 79-81; Dunstable 81-87; Par Dn 87-90; rtd 90; Perm to Offic *Linc* from 95. *11 Mount Street, Lincoln LN1 3JE* Tel (01522) 560428

ATKINS, Anthony John. b 58. Nottm Univ BSc80 SS Paul & Mary Coll Cheltenham PGCE82. Cranmer Hall Dur 87. **d** 90 **p** 91. C Shipley St Paul and Frizinghall *Bradf* 90-92; C Baildon 92-93; Chapl Asst Hope Hosp Salford 93-95; Chapl Asst Ladywell Hosp 93-95; Chapl Rotherham Gen Hosps NHS Trust from 96. *Rotherham District Hospital, Moorgate Road, Rotherham, S Yorkshire S60 2UD* Tel (01709) 820000

ATKINS, Austen Shaun. b 55. St Pet Coll Ox MA82 Selw Coll Cam MA85. Ridley Hall Cam 79. **d** 82 **p** 83. C S Mimms Ch Ch *Lon* 82-86; C Fulham St Matt 86-91; P-in-c Fulham St Dionis Parson's Green from 91. *St Dionis' Vicarage, 18 Parson's Green, London SW6 4UH* Tel 0171-736 2585

ATKINS, Christopher Leigh. b 33. Keble Coll Ox BA55 MA58. Wells Th Coll 57. **d** 59 **p** 60. C Foley Park *Worc* 59-62; C Eastleigh *Win* 62-69; TV Lord's Hill 69-81; V 81-85; R Church Oakley and Wootton St Lawrence 85-96; rtd 96; Hon C Portswood St Denys *Win* from 97. *60 Kent Road, St Denys, Southampton SO17 2LH* Tel (01703) 581473

ATKINS, David John. b 43. Lon Univ DipTh68. Kelham Th Coll 64. **d** 68 **p** 69. C Lewisham St Mary *S'wark* 68-72; Min Motspur Park 72-77; P-in-c Mitcham Ascension 77-82; V 82-83; P-in-c Downham w S Hanningfield *Chelmsf* 83-88; R from 88; Asst RD Chelmsf 88-93; RD Chelmsf S from 93; P-in-c W Hanningfield 90-93. *The Rectory, Castledon Road, Billericay, Essex CM11 1LD* Tel (01268) 710370

ATKINS, Dean John. b 70. Univ of Wales (Cardiff) BD93. St Steph Ho Ox 93. **d** 95 **p** 96. C Merthyr Dyfan *Llan* from 95. *18 Woodlands Court, Barry CF62 8DR* Tel (01446) 746235

ATKINS, Mrs Diana. b 31. K Coll Lon BD54 DipEd55. Qu Coll Birm 81. **dss** 83 **d** 87. De Beauvoir Town St Pet *Lon* 83-85; Gleadless *Sheff* 85-87; Par Dn 87-93; rtd 93; Perm to Offic *Sheff* from 93. *27 Stannington Glen, Sheffield S6 6NA* Tel 0114-234 0543

ATKINS, Forrest William (Bill). b 59. Ch Coll Cam MA85 Lon Univ BD84. Ridley Hall Cam 83. **d** 86 **p** 87. C Normanton *Derby*

86-90; C Stratford St Jo and Ch Ch w Forest Gate St Jas *Chelmsf* 90-97; Chapl Dubai and Sharjah w N Emirates from 97. *PO Box 7415, Dubai, UAE* Tel Dhayd (6) 357530 Fax as telephone

ATKINS, Francis John. b 47. CEng MIStructE. S Dios Minl Tr Scheme. **d** 89 **p** 90. NSM Studley *Sarum* 89-92; Lic to RD Bradford from 92. *Church Cottage, 344 Frome Road, Trowbridge, Wilts BA14 0EF* Tel (01225) 761757

ATKINS, Graham Anthony Hazlewood. b 28. Selw Coll Cam BA52 MA57. Coll of Resurr Mirfield 52. **d** 54 **p** 55. C St Marychurch *Ex* 54-57; Chapl Prestfelde Sch Shrewsbury 58-76; P-in-c Ash *Lich* 76-77; P-in-c Tenbury St Mich *Heref* 77-84; R Hinstock and Sambrook *Lich* 85-94; rtd 94. *The Rectory, Ellerton Road, Hinstock, Market Drayton, Shropshire TF9 0NH* Tel (01952) 550783

ATKINS, Canon John Hamilton. b 15. AKC42. **d** 42 **p** 43. C Lewisham St Jo Southend *S'wark* 42-46; C Hayes St Mary *Lon* 46-51; C-in-c Badshot Lea CD *Guildf* 51-55; V Addlestone 55-63; V Cuddington 63-72; Hon Can Guildf Cathl 71-80; R Walton-on-the-Hill 72-80; rtd 80; Perm to Offic *Sarum* from 81; Perm to Offic *B & W* from 86. *1 Elizabeth Court, High Street, Bembridge, Isle of Wight PO35 5SN* Tel (01983) 873008

ATKINS, Nicholas Steven (Nick). b 60. Oak Hill Th Coll BA88. **d** 88 **p** 89. C Shepton Mallet w Doulting *B & W* 88-91; C Combe Down w Monkton Combe and S Stoke 91-93; TV N Wingfield, Clay Cross and Pilsley *Derby* from 93. *The Vicarage, Stretton Road, Clay Cross, Chesterfield, Derbyshire S45 9AQ* Tel (01246) 866908

ATKINS, Canon Paul Henry. b 38. Univ of Wales DipTh65. St Mich Coll Llan 62. **d** 65 **p** 66. C Sheringham *Nor* 65-68; V Southtown 68-84; RD Flegg (Gt Yarmouth) 78-84; R Aylmerton w Runton from 84; RD Repps 86-95; Hon Can Nor Cathl from 88. *The Rectory, West Runton, Cromer, Norfolk NR27 9QT* Tel (01263) 837279

ATKINS, Peter. b 29. Edin Univ MA52. Edin Th Coll 52. **d** 54 **p** 55. C Edin Old St Paul *Edin* 54-59; P-in-c Edin St Dav 59-64; Chapl Fulbourn Hosp Cam 64-66; R Galashiels *Edin* 66-69; Perm to Offic 69-72; Divisional Dir Soc Services Brighton 72-83; Asst Dir Soc Services E Sussex from 83. *11 South Street, Lewes, E Sussex BN7 2BT* Tel (01273) 476230

ATKINS, Roger Francis. b 30. AKC54. **d** 55 **p** 56. C Bromley All Hallows *Lon* 55-58; C Eastleigh *Win* 58-62; Australia 62-71; V Wolverley *Worc* 71-76; V S Hackney St Mich w Haggerston St Paul *Lon* 76-85; TV Gleadless *Sheff* 85-93; rtd 93; Perm to Offic *Sheff* from 93. *27 Stannington Glen, Sheffield S6 6NA* Tel 0114-234 0543

ATKINS, Timothy David. b 45. Ridley Hall Cam 71. **d** 74 **p** 75. C Stoughton *Guildf* 74-79; C Chilwell *S'well* 79-84; R Eastwood 84-91; V Finchley Ch Ch *Lon* from 91; Chapl Finchley Memorial Hosp from 92. *Christ Church Vicarage, 616 High Road, London N12 0AA* Tel 0181-445 2377 or 445 2532

ATKINS, Timothy James (Tim). b 38. Worc Coll Ox BA62. Cuddesdon Coll 62. **d** 64 **p** 65. C Stafford St Mary *Lich* 64-67; C Loughborough St Pet *Leic* 67-69; C Usworth *Dur* 69-71; Lic to Offic *Newc* 71-76; P-in-c Slaley 76-87; P-in-c Shotley from 87. *St John's Vicarage, Snods Edge, Consett, Co Durham DH8 9TL* Tel (01207) 55665

ATKINS, Timothy Samuel. b 22. DSC44. Em Coll Cam BA46 MA52. Ridley Hall Cam 47. **d** 49 **p** 50. C Melton Mowbray w Burton Lazars, Freeby etc *Leic* 49-51; C Preston St Jo *Blackb* 51-54; V Baxenden 54-58; R Mildenhall *St E* 58-63; V Bunbury *Ches* 63-87; RD Malpas 85-87; rtd 87; Perm to Offic *Ches* from 87. *Lime Tree Cottage, Barton Road, Farndon, Chester CH3 6NL* Tel (01829) 270183

ATKINS, Preb William Maynard. b 11. FSA TCD BA33 MA41. **d** 35 **p** 36. C Dundalk *Arm* 35-40; I Clonfeacle 40-46; Dep Min Can St Paul's Cathl *Lon* 46-49; Min Can 49-55; Hon Min Can from 55; C St Sepulchre w Ch Ch Greyfriars etc 49-55; Chapl Mercers' Sch Holborn 54-59; R Hanover Square St Geo *Lon* 55-74; Chapl City of Lon Sch 62-67; P-in-c N Audley Street St Mark *Lon* 68-74; R Hanover Square St Geo w St Mark from 74; Preb St Paul's Cathl from 96. *St George's Vestry, 2A Mill Street, London W1R 9LB* Tel 0171-629 0874

ATKINSON, Albert Edward. b 35. St Deiniol's Hawarden 79. **d** 79 **p** 80. C Ellesmere Port *Ches* 79-81; TV 81-84; P-in-c Kirkby Malzeard w Grewelthorpe and Mickley etc *Ripon* 84-88; P-in-c Fountains 88-90; R Fountains Gp 90-92; V Aysgarth and Bolton cum Redmire 92-96; rtd 96. *79 Hillshaw Park Way, Ripon, N Yorkshire HG4 1JU* Tel (01765) 607964

ATKINSON, Brian Colin. b 49. Sarum & Wells Th Coll 85. **d** 87 **p** 88. C Up Hatherley *Glouc* 87-90; R Upper Stour *Sarum* 90-95; TR Trowbridge H Trin from 95. *Holy Trinity Rectory, 2B Broadmead, Trowbridge, Wilts BA14 9AA* Tel (01225) 753326

ATKINSON, Christopher John (Chris). b 57. Man Univ BA80 DipTh84. Qu Coll Birm 82. **d** 85 **p** 86. C Stalybridge *Man* 85-88; P-in-c Westhall w Brampton and Stoven *St E* 88-89; P-in-c Sotterley, Willingham, Shadingfield, Ellough etc 88-90; P-in-c Hundred River Gp of Par 90-92; R Hundred River from 92. *The Rectory, Moll's Lane, Brampton, Beccles, Suffolk NR34 8DB* Tel (01502) 575859

ATKINSON, Canon Christopher Lionel Varley. b 39. K Coll Lon 63. Chich Th Coll 65. **d** 67 **p** 68. C Sowerby Bridge w Norland *Wakef* 67-70; P-in-c Flushing *Truro* 70-73; Dioc Adv in RE 70-73; Perm to Offic *Worc* 74-78; TR Halesowen 78-88; RD Dudley 79-87; Hon Can Worc Cathl 83-88; V Cartmel *Carl* from 88; RD Windermere from 94; Hon Can Carl Cathl from 94. *Priory Vicarage, Cartmel, Grange-over-Sands, Cumbria LA11 6PU* Tel (015395) 36261

ATKINSON, Clive James. b 68. QUB BA90. CITC 90. **d** 93 **p** 94. C Belfast H Trin and Ardoyne *Conn* 93-97; I Belfast Upper Falls from 97. *31 Dunmurry Lane, Dunmurry, Belfast BT17 9RP* Tel (01232) 622400

ATKINSON, Canon David James. b 41. Lon Univ BD AKC63 Selw Coll Cam BA65 MA72. Linc Th Coll 65. **d** 66 **p** 67. C Linc St Giles *Linc* 66-70; Asst Chapl Newc Univ *Newc* 70-73; Adult Educn Officer *Lich* 73-75; P-in-c Adbaston 73-80; Dir of Educn 75-82; Preb Lich Cathl 79-82; Chapl Hull Univ *York* 82-87; Dir of Educn *Linc* 87-94; Can and Preb Linc Cathl from 89; P-in-c Bishop Norton, Wadingham and Snitterby from 94. *The Rectory,Church Road, Waddingham, Gainsborough, Lincs DN21 4SU* Tel (01673) 818551

ATKINSON, The Ven David John. b 43. MSOSc K Coll Lon BSc65 AKC65 PhD69 Bris Univ DipTh70 MLitt73 Ox Univ MA85. Trin Coll Bris and Tyndale Hall Bris 69. **d** 72 **p** 73. C Halliwell St Pet *Man* 72-74; C Harborne Heath *Birm* 74-77; Lib Latimer Ho Ox 77-80; Chapl and Lect CCC Ox 80-93; Fell from 84; Visiting Lect Wycliffe Hall Ox 84-93; Can Res and Chan S'wark Cathl *S'wark* 93-96; Adn Lewisham from 96. *3A Court Farm Road, London SE9 4JH* Tel 0181-857 7982 Fax 249 0350

ATKINSON, Derek Arthur. b 31. K Coll Lon BD59 AKC59. **d** 60 **p** 61. C Ashford *Cant* 60-64; C Deal St Leon 64-68; R E w W Ogwell *Ex* 68-81; Asst Dir of RE 68-78; Dep Dir and Children's Adv 78-88; R Ogwell and Denbury 81-84; R Kenton w Mamhead and Powderham 84-88; rtd 88; Perm to Offic *Ex* from 88. *6 Hudson Close, Harthill, Sheffield S31 8WB* Tel (01909) 771149

ATKINSON, Ian. b 33. BNC Ox BA58 MA63. Coll of Resurr Mirfield 56. **d** 58 **p** 59. C Welling *S'wark* 58-62; C Camberwell St Giles 62-63; V Wandsworth Common St Mary 63-67; S Africa 67-68; C Oxted *S'wark* 68-69; Asst Chapl Ch Hosp Horsham 70-85; NSM Dalmahoy *Edin* 85-91; Asst Master Clifton Hall Sch 85-91; NSM Dunkeld *St And* from 92. *Dalbeathie House, Dunkeld, Perthshire PH8 0JA* Tel (01350) 727230

ATKINSON, Canon Prof James. b 14. St Jo Coll Dur BA36 MA39 MLitt50 Univ of Munster DTh55 Hull Univ Hon DD97. **d** 37 **p** 38. C Newc H Cross *Newc* 37-41; Succ Sheff Cathl *Sheff* 41-42; Prec 42-44; V Shiregreen St Jas and St Chris 44-51; Fell Sheff Univ from 51; Can Th Leic Cathl *Leic* 54-70; Lect Th Hull Univ 56-64; Reader 64-67; Prof Bibl Studies Sheff Univ 67-79; Lic to Offic *Sheff* from 68; Can Th Sheff Cathl 70-93; rtd 79; Latimer Ho Ox 81-84. *Leach House, Leadmill Bridge, Hathersage, Hope Valley, Derbyshire S32 1BA* Tel (01433) 650570

ATKINSON, John Dudley. b 38. ACA60 FCA71. Qu Coll Birm 63. **d** 66 **p** 67. C Bishop's Stortford St Mich *St Alb* 66-70; C Norton 70-73; V Markyate Street 73-80; R Baldock w Bygrave 80-94; RD Stevenage 83-89; TR Bride Valley *Sarum* from 94. *The Rectory, Church Street, Burton Bradstock, Bridport, Dorset DT6 4QS* Tel (01308) 897359

ATKINSON, Ms Judith Angela. b 70. Leeds Univ BA92 Fitzw Coll Cam BA95. Ridley Hall Cam CTM93. **d** 96 **p** 97. C Chester le Street *Dur* from 96. *The Kepier Flat, Church Street, Houghton-le-Spring, Tyne & Wear DH4 4DN* Tel 0191-584 8970

ATKINSON (formerly BIGWOOD), Mrs Kate Bigwood. b 56. Cranmer Hall Dur 94. **d** 96 **p** 97. C Woking St Jo *Guildf* from 96. *13 Ashley Road, Woking, Surrey GU21 1SR* Tel (01483) 723878 Fax as telephone

ATKINSON, Kenneth. b 24. Qu Coll Birm 74. **d** 77 **p** 77. C Olton *Birm* 77-82; Perm to Offic *York* 83-93; Perm to Offic *Birm* from 93. *98 Fabian Crescent, Shirley, Solihull, W Midlands B90 2AB* Tel 0121-744 4044

ATKINSON, Lewis Malcolm. b 34. St Jo Coll Dur. **d** 82 **p** 83. C Chapeltown *Sheff* 82-85; V Sheff St Paul Wordsworth Avenue 85-93; Ind Chapl from 85; RD Ecclesfield 90-93; V Oughtibridge from 93; RD Tankersley from 96. *The Vicarage, Church Street, Oughtibridge, Sheffield S30 3FU* Tel 0114-286 2317

ATKINSON, Marianne Rose. b 39. Girton Coll Cam BA61 CertEd62 MA64. Linc Th Coll 86. **d** 88 **p** 94. C S w N Hayling *Portsm* 88-91; C Rainham *Roch* 91-92; Asst Chapl Salford R Hosps NHS Trust 92-97; Hon C Prestwich St Marg *Man* 94-97; Chapl R United Hosp Bath NHS Trust from 97. *Royal United Hospital, Combe Park, Bath BA1 3NG, or 5 The Linleys, Weston Park, Bath BA1 2XE* Tel (01225) 428331 or 316572

ATKINSON, Michael Hubert. b 33. Qu Coll Ox BA57 MA60. Ripon Hall Ox 56. **d** 58 **p** 59. C Attercliffe w Carbrook *Sheff* 58-60; Ind Chapl 60-66; C Sheff Sharrow 60-66; Ind Chapl *Pet* 66-71; Sen Ind Chapl *Cant* 71-79; Research Officer Gen Syn Bd for Soc Resp 79-87; Representation Sec USPG 88-92; TV High Wycombe *Ox* 92-97; Chapl Bucks Coll of HE from 94. *7 Birch Court, Old Bridge Rise, Ilkley, W Yorkshire LS29 9HH* Tel (01943) 609891

ATKINSON, Michael James. b 38. AKC62. **d** 63 **p** 64. C Leeds Halton St Wilfrid *Ripon* 63-65; C Luton St Hugh Lewsey CD *St Alb* 65-67; V Luton Lewsey St Hugh 67-71; C Caversham *Ox*

71-73; P-in-c N Woolwich *Chelmsf* 73-74; V N Woolwich w Silvertown 74-78; V Clavering w Langley and Arkesden 78-89; V Chelmsf All SS 89-92; P-in-c Gt and Lt Bardfield 92-94; V Gt and Lt Bardfield w Gt and Lt Saling from 94. *The Vicarage, Braintree Road, Great Bardfield, Braintree, Essex CM7 4RN* Tel (01371) 810267

ATKINSON, Nigel Terence. b 60. Sheff Univ BA82. Westmr Th Sem (USA) MDiv87 Cranmer Hall Dur 87. **d** 89 **p** 90. C Oakwood St Thos *Lon* 89-92; P-in-c Dolton *Ex* 92-95; P-in-c Iddesleigh w Dowland 92-95; P-in-c Monkokehampton 92-95; Warden Latimer Ho Ox from 95. *Latimer House, 131 Banbury Road, Oxford OX2 7AJ* Tel (01865) 513879

ATKINSON, Mrs Patricia Anne. b 47. LNSM course. **d** 89. NSM Nor St Steph *Nor* 89-94; Lic to Offic from 94. *32 Berryfields, Brundall, Norwich NR13 5QE* Tel (01603) 714720

ATKINSON, Peter Duncan. b 41. Univ Coll Dur BA62. Linc Th Coll 63. **d** 65 **p** 66. C Beckenham St Geo *Roch* 65-69; C Caversham *Ox* 69-75; P-in-c Millfield St Mark *Dur* 76-86; V Dedworth *Ox* 86-93; TV Aylesbury w Bierton and Hulcott from 93. *4 Cubb Field, Aylesbury, Bucks HP21 8SH* Tel (01296) 25008

ATKINSON, Peter Geoffrey. b 50. Sarum & Wells Th Coll 81. **d** 83 **p** 84. C Aylesbury *Ox* 83-86; C Dorchester 86-87; TV 87-91; V Cropredy w Gt Bourton and Wardington 91-96; V Shires' Edge from 96. *The Vicarage, High Street, Cropredy, Banbury, Oxon OX17 1NG* Tel (01295) 750799

ATKINSON, Canon Peter Gordon. b 52. St Jo Coll Ox BA74 MA78. Westcott Ho Cam 77. **d** 79 **p** 80. C Clapham Old Town *S'wark* 79-83; P-in-c Tatsfield 83-90; R Bath H Trin *B & W* 90-91; Prin Chich Th Coll 91-94; Can and Preb Chich Cathl *Chich* 91-97; R Lavant 94-97; Can Res and Chan Chich Cathl from 97. *The Residentiary, Canon Lane, Chichester, W Sussex PO19 1PX* Tel (01243) 782961

ATKINSON, Philip Charles. b 50. Hull Univ BA71 PhD76 Chorley Coll of Educn CertEd77. N Ord Course 81. **d** 84 **p** 85. NSM Bolton SS Simon and Jude *Man* 84-87; Chapl R Wolv Sch from 87. *5A Claremont Road, Wolverhampton WV3 0EA* Tel (01902) 330706

ATKINSON, Philip Stephen. b 58. K Coll Lon BD80 AKC80. Ridley Hall Cam. **d** 83 **p** 84. C Barrow St Matt *Carl* 83-86; C Kirkby Lonsdale 86-89; R Redmarshall *Dur* 89-95; V Bishopton w Gt Stainton 89-95; C Kirkby Lonsdale *Carl* from 95; Chapl Casterton Sch Lancs from 95. *Beckside, Casterton, Kirkby Lonsdale, Carnforth, Lancs LA6 2SB* Tel (01524) 271731

ATKINSON, Richard William Bryant. b 58. Magd Coll Cam MA. Ripon Coll Cuddesdon. **d** 84 **p** 85. C Abingdon w Shippon *Ox* 84-87; TV Sheff Manor *Sheff* 87-91; TR 91-96; V Rotherham from 96. *The Vicarage, 2 Heather Close, Rotherham, S Yorkshire S60 2TQ* Tel (01709) 364341

ATKINSON, Canon Samuel Charles Donald. b 30. TCD BA54. **d** 55 **p** 56. C Belfast St Simon *Conn* 55-62; I Ballynaclough *L & K* 62-68; I Cloughjordan w Modreeny 68-87; Dioc Youth Adv (Killaloe) 75-83; Dioc Info Officer 76-88; Can Killaloe Cathl 76-82; Chan 82-96; I Cloughjordan w Borrisokane etc 87-96; rtd 96. *Dromore Lodge, Rockcorry, Co Monaghan, Irish Republic* Tel Dundalk (42) 42356

ATKINSON, Simon James. b 71. St Chad's Coll Dur BA93. St Steph Ho Ox 93. **d** 95 **p** 96. C Norton St Mary *Dur* 95-96; C Hartlepool H Trin from 96. *43 Alderwood Close, Hartlepool, Cleveland TS27 3QR* Tel (01429) 862539

ATKINSON, Terence Harry. b 52. Coll of Resurr Mirfield 88. **d** 90 **p** 91. C Bottesford w Ashby *Linc* 90-93; TV Cleethorpes from 93. *St Francis House, Sandringham Road, Cleethorpes, S Humberside DN35 9HA* Tel (01472) 691215

ATKINSON, Wendy Sybil. b 53. Man Univ BA95. N Ord Course 95. **d** 97. NSM Brinnington w Portwood *Ches* from 97. *8 Freshfield Close, Marple Bridge, Stockport, Cheshire SK6 5ES* Tel 0161-427 5612

ATTAWAY, Mrs Elizabeth Ann. b 36. Herts Coll CertEd56. Cant Sch of Min 93 Bp Otter Coll 57. **d** 96. NSM Maidstone St Paul *Cant* from 96. *18 Norman Close, Maidstone, Kent ME14 5HT* Tel (01622) 762656

ATTFIELD, David George. b 31. Magd Coll Ox BA54 MA58 BD61 K Coll Lon MPhil72 Dur Univ MA81. Westcott Ho Cam 57. **d** 58 **p** 59. C Edgbaston St Aug *Birm* 58-61; C Ward End 61-62; Lect Div St Kath Coll Tottenham 62-64; All SS Coll Tottenham 64-68; Sen Lect St Bede Coll Dur 68-75; St Hild and St Bede Coll 75-80; TV Drypool *York* 80-86; R Newton Heath All SS *Man* 86-96; rtd 97. *19 Laburnum Avenue, Durham DH1 4HA* Tel 0191-383 0509

ATTLEY, Ronald (Ron). b 46. Open Univ BA87 Dur Univ CCSk90. Chich Th Coll 68. **d** 70 **p** 71. C Heworth St Mary *Dur* 70-73; C Hulme Ascension *Man* 73-75; Belize 76-79; V Leadgate *Dur* 79-84; Chapl HM Rem Cen Ashford 84-87; Chapl HM Pris Ashwell and Stocken 87-89; Chapl HM Pris Frankland 89-92; Chapl HM Young Offender Inst Deerbolt 92-96; V Bath St Barn w Englishcombe *B & W* from 96. *The Vicarage, Mount View, Southdown, Bath BA2 1JX* Tel (01225) 421838

ATTRILL, Norman Edmund Charles. b 16. K Coll Lon BA37. Wm Temple Coll Rugby 65 Ripon Hall Ox 67. **d** 68 **p** 69. C Portsea St Mary *Portsm* 68-72; V Sea View 72-80; rtd 81; Perm to Offic *Ox* from 83. *27 Church Street, Henley-on-Thames, Oxon RG9 1SE* Tel (01491) 574268

ATTWATER, Mrs Sallyanne (Sally). b 48. S Dios Minl Tr Scheme 86. **d** 94 **p** 95. Chapl Asst Eastbourne Distr Gen Hosp 94-95; Asst Chapl Princess Alice Hosp and All SS Hosp 94-95; C E Grinstead St Swithun *Chich* from 95. *11 Garden House Lane, East Grinstead, W Sussex RH19 4JT* Tel (01342) 328306

ATTWATER, Stephen Philip. b 47. ALCM67. Linc Th Coll 85. **d** 87 **p** 88. C Warrington St Elphin *Liv* 87-90; P-in-c Eccleston St Thos 90-94; V from 94. *St Thomas' Vicarage, 21 St George's Road, St Helens, Merseyside WA10 4LH* Tel (01744) 22295

ATTWOOD, Anthony Norman (Tony). b 47. Univ of Wales (Abth) BSc(Econ)69 Birm Univ DipTh71 Hull Univ MA82. Qu Coll Birm 69. **d** 72 **p** 73. C Greenhill *Sheff* 72-75; V Elsecar 76-81; Ind Missr 81-95; TV Maltby 81-86; Ind Chapl 86-96; RD Adwick 89-95; Teesside Ind Miss *Dur* from 95. *5 The Close, Long Newton, Stockton-on-Tees, Cleveland TS21 1DW* Tel (01642) 570878

ATTWOOD, Preb Carl Norman Harry. b 53. Bris Univ BA74 Ox Univ BA76 MA80. Cuddesdon Coll 74. **d** 77 **p** 78. C Tupsley *Heref* 77-82; R Colwall w Upper Colwall and Coddington from 82; Bp's Voc Officer 83-89; Chapl St Jas Sch Malvern from 86; RD Ledbury *Heref* 90-96; Preb Heref Cathl from 97. *The Rectory, Walwyn Road, Colwall, Malvern, Worcs WR13 6EG* Tel (01684) 540330 Fax 540083

ATTWOOD, David John Edwin. b 51. Dur Univ BA76 Em Coll Cam BA73 MA74. Cranmer Hall Dur 74. **d** 77 **p** 78. C Rodbourne Cheney *Bris* 77-79; C Lydiard Millicent w Lydiard Tregoz 79-85; Lect Trin Coll Bris from 85. *13 St Andrews Road, Bristol BS19 3NR* Tel (01275) 463864

ATWELL, The Very Revd James Edgar. b 46. Ex Coll Ox BA68 MA73 BD94 Harvard Univ ThM70. Cuddesdon Coll 68. **d** 70 **p** 71. C E Dulwich St Jo *S'wark* 70-74; C Cambridge Gt St Mary w St Mich *Ely* 74-77; Chapl Jes Coll Cam 77-81; V Towcester w Easton Neston *Pet* 81-95; RD Towcester 83-91; Provost St E from 95. *The Provost's House, Bury St Edmunds, Suffolk IP33 1RS* Tel (01284) 754852

ATWELL, Brother Robert Ronald. b 54. St Jo Coll Dur BA75 Dur Univ MLitt79. Westcott Ho Cam 76. **d** 78 **p** 79. C Mill Hill Jo Keble Ch *Lon* 78-81; Chapl Trin Coll Cam 81-87; OSB from 87; Lic to Offic *Ox* from 87. *Burford Priory, Priory Lane, Burford, Oxford OX18 4SQ* Tel (01993) 823605

AUBREY, Canon John Watkin. b 17. Ch Coll Cam BA39 MA43. Westcott Ho Cam 39. **d** 40 **p** 41. C Romsey *Win* 40-43; Chapl RNVR 43-48; S Africa 48-76; Prec St Geo Cathl Cape Town 48-51; R Claremont St Sav 51-64; Can Cape Town 58-64; Hon Can 64-66; St Paul's Coll Grahamstown 64-65; Hd Master St Andr Coll Grahamstown 65-72; R Fish Hoek 62-76; R Collyweston w Duddington and Tixover *Pet* 76-82; rtd 82. *St Barnabas, Beauchamp Community, The Quadrangle, Newland, Malvern, Worcs WR13 5AX* Tel (01684) 892187

AUCHMUTY, John Robert. b 67. ACCA Athlone Regional Tech Coll NC(BS)89. CITC 89. **d** 92 **p** 93. C Dundela *D & D* 92-96; I Eglish w Killylea *Arm* from 96. *154 Killylea Road, Armagh BT60 4LN* Tel (01861) 568320

AUCKLAND, Canon Allan Frank. b 13. K Coll Lon 49. **d** 49 **p** 50. C Kennington Cross St Anselm *S'wark* 49-52; C Peckham St Jo 52-56; V Hatcham St Cath 56-74; RD Greenwich and Deptford 61-65; RD Lewisham 65-70; Hon Can S'wark Cathl 67-81; R Burstow 74-81; rtd 81; Perm to Offic *Cant* from 81. *14 The Pavement, Front Road, Woodchurch, Ashford, Kent TN26 3QE* Tel (01233) 861231

AUCKLAND, Archdeacon of. *See* GIBSON, The Ven George Granville

AUDEN, Lawson Philip. b 45. Qu Coll Birm 73. **d** 78 **p** 81. C Spalding *Linc* 78-81; TV Wordsley *Lich* 81-82; TV Kidderminster St Mary and All SS, Trimpley etc *Worc* 82-87; Ind Chapl 82-87; Perm to Offic *Worc* and *Cov* from 87; *Birm* and *Lich* from 90; *Glouc* from 94. *Willowbrook, Willersley Fields, Badsey, Evesham, Worcs WR11 5HF* Tel (01386) 858263

AUGUSTINE, Brother. *See* MORRIS, David Freestone

AULD, Mrs Sheila Edith. b 38. Newc Poly BA87. NE Ord Course 91. **d** 94 **p** 95. NSM Newc St Gabr *Newc* from 94. *5 Plessey Terrace, Newcastle upon Tyne NE7 7DJ* Tel 0191-281 8647

AUST, Arthur John. b 14. St Aug Coll Cant 62. **d** 63 **p** 64. C Dagenham *Chelmsf* 63-65; Kenya 65-67; P-in-c Skidbrooke *Linc* 67-69; R Theddlethorpe w Mablethorpe 67-71; Nigeria 71-74; S Africa 74-77; TV Clyst St George, Aylesbeare, Clyst Honiton etc *Ex* 79-81; rtd 81; Perm to Offic *Cant* from 81. *Overhill House, Upper Street, Kingsdown, Deal, Kent CT14 8DR* Tel (01304) 361583

AUSTEN, Glyn. b 54. UEA BA MPhil Ox Univ MA. Ripon Coll Cuddesdon 79. **d** 82 **p** 83. C Newport w Longford and Chetwynd *Lich* 82-85; C Hawley H Trin *Guildf* 85-87; R Barnack w Ufford and Bainton *Pet* from 87. *The Rectory, Millstone Lane, Barnack, Stamford, Lincs PE9 3ET* Tel (01780) 740234

AUSTEN, John. b 46. St Cath Coll Cam BA69 MA72. Qu Coll Birm DipTh70. **d** 71 **p** 72. C Thornaby on Tees *York* 71-74; C Aston St Jas *Birm* 74-82; Chapl Aston Univ 82-88; C Handsworth St Andr from 88. *151 Church Lane, Birmingham B20 2RU* Tel 0121-554 8882

AUSTEN, Simon Neil. b 67. Warw Univ BSc88. Wycliffe Hall Ox BA93 DipMin94. **d** 94 **p** 95. C Gt Chesham *Ox* from 94. *31 Chapmans Crescent, Chesham, Bucks HP5 2QT* Tel (01494) 783629

AUSTERBERRY, Preb David Naylor. b 35. Birm Univ BA58. Wells Th Coll 58. **d** 60 **p** 61. C Leek St Edw *Lich* 60-63; Iran 64-70; Chapl CMS Foxbury 70-73; V Walsall Pleck and Bescot *Lich* 73-82; R Brierley Hill 82-88; R Kinnerley w Melverley and Knockin w Maesbrook from 88; RD Oswestry 92-95; Preb Lich Cathl from 96. *The Rectory, Vicarage Lane, Kinnerley, Oswestry, Shropshire SY10 8DE* Tel (01691) 682233

AUSTERBERRY, John Maurice. b 62. Birm Univ BA83. Sarum & Wells Th Coll 84. **d** 86 **p** 87. C Clayton *Lich* 86-89; Asst Chapl Withington Hosp Man 89-95; Chapl Tameside and Glossop NHS Trust from 95. *The Chaplain's Office, Tameside General Hosp, Fountain Street, Ashton-under-Lyne, Lancs OL6 9RW, or 5 Warley Road, Manchester M16 0HX* Tel 0161-331 5151, 331 5333 or 286 2389

AUSTIN, Alfred George. b 36. Ridley Coll Melbourne 59. **d** 61 **p** 62. Australia 61-77; C Dartford St Alb *Roch* 77-79; Australia from 79. *1 Marco Polo Street, Essendon, Victoria, Australia 3040* Tel Launceston (03) 9379 2770

AUSTIN, The Ven George Bernard. b 31. St D Coll Lamp BA53 Chich Th Coll 53. **d** 55 **p** 56. C Chorley St Pet *Blackb* 55-57; C Notting Hill St Clem *Lon* 57-60; Asst Chapl Lon Univ 60-61; C Dunstable *St Alb* 61-64; V Eaton Bray 64-70; V Bushey Heath 70-88; Hon Can St Alb 78-88; Adn York from 88; Can and Preb York Minster from 88. *North Back House, 3B Main Street, Wheldrake, York YO4 6AG* Tel (01904) 448509

AUSTIN, Canon Jane. b 43. SRN64 SCM66. Trin Coll Bris DipTh81. **dss** 81 **d** 87 **p** 94. Tonbridge SS Pet and Paul *Roch* 81-87; Par Dn 87-94; C from 94; Hon Can Roch Cathl from 96. *48 Longmead Way, Tonbridge, Kent TN10 3TG* Tel (01732) 367765

✠**AUSTIN, The Rt Revd John Michael.** b 39. St Edm Hall Ox BA63. St Steph Ho Ox 62. **d** 64 **p** 65 **c** 92. C E Dulwich St Jo *S'wark* 64-68; USA 68-69; Warden Pemb Ho and Missr Walworth St Chris CD *S'wark* 69-76; TV Walworth 75-76; Soc Resp Adv *St Alb* 76-84; Dir Dioc Bd for Soc Resp *Lon* 84-92; Preb St Paul's Cathl 89-92; Suff Bp Aston *Birm* from 92. *Strensham House, 8 Strensham Hill, Birmingham B13 8AG* Tel 0121-449 0675 Fax 428 1114

AUSTIN, Leslie Ernest. b 46. Trin Coll Bris 72. **d** 74 **p** 75. C Paddock Wood *Roch* 74-79; C Upper Armley *Ripon* 79-81; V Horton *Bradf* 81-85; V Long Preston w Tosside 85-97; TR Shirwell, Loxhore, Kentisbury, Arlington, etc *Ex* from 97. *The Rectory, 2 Barnfield, Mill Lane, Bratton Fleming, Barnstaple, Devon EX31 4RT* Tel (01598) 710807

AUSTIN, Canon Michael Ridgwell. b 33. FRHistS Lon Univ BD57 PhD69 Birm Univ MA66. Lon Coll of Div ALCD56 LTh. **d** 57 **p** 58. C Ward End *Birm* 57-60; PC Derby St Andr *Derby* 60-66; Lect Th Derbyshire Coll of HE 66-73; Chapl Derby Cathl *Derby* 66-81; Prin Lect 73-85; Can Res Derby Cathl 81-85; Bp's Tr Adv *S'well* 85-88; Dir of Post-Ord Tr 86-94; Can Res S'well Minster 88-94; Dioc Dir of Tr 88-94; Abps' Adv for Bps' Min *Cant* from 94. *22 Marlock Close, Fiskerton, Southwell, Notts NG25 0UB* Tel (01636) 830074

AUSTIN, Raymond Charles. b 23. St Edm Hall Ox BA48 MA53 Lon Univ BD70 DipEd74. Linc Th Coll 48. **d** 50 **p** 51. C Norton St Mich *Dur* 50-53; C Wolverhampton St Pet *Lich* 53-57; V Chapel-en-le-Frith *Derby* 57-66; RD Buxton 64-66; Perm to Offic *Mon* 66-84; V Llantilio Crossenny w Penrhos, Llanvetherine etc 84-91; rtd 88. *Glanmor, Hardwick Hill, Chepstow NP6 5PN* Tel (01291) 620079

AUSTIN, Ronald Glyn. b 52. Llan Dioc Tr Scheme 88. **d** 90 **p** 91. C Llangynwyd w Maesteg *Llan* 90-91; C Barry All SS 91-93; V Nantymoel w Wyndham 93-97; V Pontyclun w Talygarn from 97. *The Vicarage, Heol Miskin, Pontyclun CF72 9AJ* Tel (01443) 225477

AUSTIN, Mrs Susan Frances. b 47. Open Univ BA81. Cant Sch of Min 87. **d** 92 **p** 94. Chapl Ch Ch High Sch Ashford 90-94; C Gt Chart *Cant* 92-94; C Ashford 92-94; C Estover *Ex* 94-96; V Stevenage All SS Pin Green *St Alb* from 96. *All Saints' Vicarage, 100 Derby Way, Stevenage, Herts SG1 5TJ* Tel (01438) 318706

AUTTON, Canon Norman William James. b 20. Selw Coll Cam BA42 MA46. St Mich Coll Llan 42. **d** 44 **p** 45. C Merthyr Tydfil *Llan* 44-49; C Newcastle 49-52; C Hillingdon St Jo *Lon* 52-54; Asst Chapl Guild of Health 54-56; Chapl Deva Hosp Cheshire 56-61; Chapl St Geo Hosp Lon 61-67; Dir of Tr Gen Syn Hosp Chapls Coun 67-72; Chapl Univ Hosp of Wales Cardiff 72-85; Can Llan Cathl *Llan* 77-85; Chan 85-92; rtd 85; Perm to Offic *Llan* from 85. *112 St Anthony Road, Cardiff CF4 4DJ* Tel (01222) 625788

AVANN, Canon Penelope Joyce (Penny). b 46. Trin Coll Bris DipTh71. **dss** 83 **d** 87. Southborough St Pet w Ch Ch and St Matt *Roch* 83-89; Par Dn 87-89; Warden Past Assts from 89; Par Dn Beckenham St Jo 89-94; C from 94; Hon Can Roch Cathl from 94. *21 Glanfield Road, Beckenham, Kent BR3 3JS* Tel 0181-650 4061

AVENT, Raymond John. b 28. St D Coll Lamp BA55 Coll of Resurr Mirfield 55. **d** 57 **p** 58. C Bury H Trin *Man* 57-60; C Holborn St Alb w Saffron Hill St Pet *Lon* 60-66; C Munster Square St Mary Magd 66-67; V Tottenham St Paul 67-77; RD E Haringey 73-77; V Kilburn St Aug w St Jo 77-87; AD Westmr Paddington 79-84; R St Vedast w St Mich-le-Querne etc 87-94; rtd 94; Perm to Offic *Lon* from 94. *124 Midhurst Road, London W13 9TP* Tel 0181-567 8964

AVERY, Richard Julian. b 52. Keble Coll Ox BA73. St Jo Coll Nottm 74. **d** 77 **p** 78. C Macclesfield St Mich *Ches* 77-80; Canada 82-83 and 87-97; C Becontree St Mary *Chelmsf* 84-87; TV Cheltenham St Mark *Glouc* from 97. *St Silas' Vicarage, Chesters Way Lane, Cheltenham, Glos GL51 0LB* Tel (01242) 580496

AVERY, Robert Edward. b 69. Magd Coll Cam BA90. Ripon Coll Cuddesdon 90. **d** 93 **p** 94. C Cen Telford *Lich* 93-96; C Cambridge Gt St Mary w St Mich *Ely* from 96. *31A Shelford Road, Cambridge CB2 2LZ* Tel (01223) 512165

AVERY, Russell Harrold. b 46. JP74. ACT ThDip75 Moore Th Coll Sydney 66. **d** 77 **p** 77. Australia 77-78 and from 88; C Prenton *Ches* 78-79; Egypt 79-82; Chapl Maisons-Laffitte *Eur* 82-88. *The Rectory, 6 Finlayson Street, Lane Cove, NSW, Australia 2066* Tel Sydney (2) 427 6569 or 427 1163 Fax 427 1163

AVES, John Albert. b 51. K Coll Lon AKC73 BD74 CertEd79 MA82. **d** 75 **p** 76. C Plaistow St Andr *Chelmsf* 75-77; Perm to Offic *Lon* 77-79; C Nor St Pet Mancroft *Nor* 79-82; R Attleborough w Besthorpe from 82. *The Rectory, Surrogate Street, Attleborough, Norfolk NR17 2AW* Tel (01953) 453185

AVES, Peter Colin. b 57. Qu Mary Coll Lon BSc79 CertEd80. Wycliffe Hall Ox 85. **d** 88 **p** 89. C Thames Ditton *Guildf* 88-90; C Chertsey 90-93; R Stockbridge and Longstock and Leckford *Win* from 93. *The Rectory, 11 Trafalgar Way, Stockbridge, Hants SO20 6ET* Tel (01264) 810810

AVESON, Ian Henry. b 55. Jes Coll Ox BA77 MA81 Univ Coll Dur PGCE78 Birkb Coll Lon MSc85. St Mich Coll Llan BD97. **d** 97. C Penarth All SS *Llan* from 97. *84 Coleridge Avenue, Penarth CF64 2SR* Tel (01222) 708044

AVEYARD, Ian. b 46. Liv Univ BSc68. ALCD72 St Jo Coll Nottm 71. **d** 71 **p** 72. C Bradley *Wakef* 71-74; C Knowle *Birm* 74-79; P-in-c Cofton Hackett 79; P-in-c Barnt Green 79; V Cofton Hackett w Barnt Green 80-94; Dioc Dir of Reader Tr 85-94; Dioc Warden of Readers 91-94; Course Leader St Jo Coll Nottm from 96. *19 Darley Avenue, Beeston, Nottingham NG9 6JP* Tel 0115-973 1367

AVIS, Preb Paul David Loup. b 47. Lon Univ BD70 PhD76. Westcott Ho Cam 73. **d** 75 **p** 76. C S Molton, Nymet St George, High Bray etc *Ex* 75-80; V Stoke Canon, Poltimore w Huxham and Rewe etc from 80; Preb Ex Cathl from 92. *The Vicarage, Stoke Canon, Exeter EX5 4AS* Tel (01392) 841583

AWRE, Richard William Esgar. b 56. Univ of Wales BA78. Wycliffe Hall Ox 78. **d** 81 **p** 82. C Blackpool St Jo *Blackb* 81-84; Asst Dir of Ords and Voc Adv 84-89; C Altham w Clayton le Moors 84-89; V Longridge from 89. *The Vicarage, Church Street, Longridge, Preston PR3 3WA* Tel (01772) 783281

AXFORD, Robert Henry. b 50. CEng85 Univ of Wales BEng72. Sarum & Wells Th Coll 89. **d** 91 **p** 92. C Castle Cary w Ansford *B & W* 91-95; P-in-c Queen Camel w W Camel, Corton Denham etc from 95. *The Rectory, Englands Lane, Queen Camel, Yeovil, Somerset BA22 7NN* Tel (01935) 850326

AXTELL, Ronald Arthur John. b 33. Lon Univ BSc54 St Cath Soc Ox BA58 MA62. Wycliffe Hall Ox 56. **d** 58 **p** 59. C Walton Breck *Liv* 58-61; Iran 63-78; Chr Witness to Israel Miss in Man 78-82; Perm to Offic *Man* 79-82; TV Man Resurr 82; TV Man Gd Shep 82-88; R Levenshulme St Pet from 88. *29A Ardwick Green North, Manchester M12 6FZ* Tel 0161-273 5020

AYAD, Dr Karl. b 25. Cairo Univ BSc48 Lon Univ MSc53 PhD55. St Steph Ho Ox 80. **d** 81 **p** 82. C Allerton *Liv* 81-83; V Knowsley 83-90; rtd 90; Perm to Offic *Ches* from 90; Perm to Offic *Liv* from 90. *2 Stanley House, 46 Stanley Road, Hoylake, Wirral, Merseyside L47 1HY* Tel 0151-632 5519

AYERS, Canon John. b 40. FCollP Bris Univ BEd75 Newton Park Coll Bath MEd89 FRSA94. **d** 77 **p** 78. NSM Corsham *Bris* 77-79; NSM Gtr Corsham 79-88; NSM Ditteridge 88-92; NSM Box w Hazlebury and Ditteridge from 93; Hon Can Bris Cathl from 94. *Toad Hall, Middlehill, Box, Corsham, Wilts SN13 8QP* Tel (01225) 742123

AYERS, Paul Nicholas. b 61. St Pet Coll Ox BA82 MA86. Trin Coll Bris 83. **d** 85 **p** 86. C Clayton *Bradf* 85-88; C Keighley St Andr 88-91; V Wrose 91-97; V Pudsey St Lawr and St Paul from 97. *The Vicarage, Vicarage Drive, Pudsey, W Yorkshire LS28 7RL* Tel 0113-257 7843

AYERST, Edward Richard. b 25. Leeds Univ BA51. Coll of Resurr Mirfield 51. **d** 53 **p** 54. C Bethnal Green St Jo w St Simon *Lon* 53-57; C Hayes St Mary 58-60; V Edmonton St Mary w St Jo 60-66; R Whippingham w E Cowes *Portsm* 66-77; V Bridgwater St Mary w Chilton Trinity *B & W* 77-84; V Durleigh 77-84; V Bridgwater St Mary, Chilton Trinity and Durleigh 84-90; Chapl to The Queen from 87; rtd 90; Perm to Offic *B & W* from 90. *56 Maple Drive, Burham-on-Sea, Somerset TA8 1DH* Tel (01278) 780701

AYKROYD, Harold Allan. b 22. DFC. Man Univ BA48. Qu Coll Birm 73. **d** 76 **p** 76. NSM Moseley St Agnes *Birm* 76-82; NSM

Bournville 82-96; Perm to Offic from 96. *108 Middleton Hall Road, Birmingham B30 1DG* Tel 0121-451 1365 or 569 4687

AYLEN, George Richard. b 24. Chich Th Coll 48. **d** 52 **p** 53. C Cant St Greg *Cant* 52-55; C Margate All SS 55-58; V Spring Park 58-61; V Newington 61-67; V Whitstable St Pet 67-75; R Petham w Waltham and Lower Hardres w Nackington 75-78; rtd 78; Perm to Offic *Cant* from 80. *20 Seymour Place, Canterbury, Kent CT1 3SF* Tel (01227) 456243

AYLETT, Graham Peter. b 59. Qu Coll Cam BA81 MA84 PhD85 St Jo Coll Dur BA88. Cranmer Hall Dur 86 All Nations Chr Coll 96. **d** 90 **p** 91. C Wilton *B & W* 90-94; C Runcorn All SS *Ches* 94-96. *2A Musley Lane, Ware, Herts SG12 7EN* Tel (01920) 463856

AYLETT, Mrs Nicola Jane. b 63. St Anne's Coll Ox BA84 St Jo Coll Dur BA89. Cranmer Hall Dur 87 All Nations Chr Coll 96. **d** 90 **p** 94. C Wilton *B & W* 90-94; NSM Runcorn All SS *Ches* 94-96. *2A Musley Lane, Ware, Herts SG12 7EN* Tel (01920) 463856

AYLING, Arnold Paul. b 38. Ball Coll Ox BA61. Wells Th Coll 65. **d** 67 **p** 68. C Weymouth H Trin *Sarum* 67-70; Chapl K Alfred Coll *Win* 70-73; Miss to Seamen 73-84; Dunkirk 73; Nigeria 74-82; S Africa 82-84; Perm to Offic *Sarum* 85-86; Perm to Offic *Chich* from 85; Distr Chapl Tunbridge Wells HA 86-94; Chapl Kent and Sussex Weald NHS Trust from 94. *Pembury Hospital, Pembury, Tunbridge Wells, Kent TN2 4QJ* Tel (01892) 824954 or 823535 Mobile 0468-132403 Fax 824267 E-mail pgzl@englandmail.com

AYLING, Preb John Charles. b 02. St Jo Coll Dur BA29. **d** 29 **p** 30. C Gravesend St Jas *Roch* 29-32; C Heigham St Thos *Nor* 32-35; V Walsall St Paul *Lich* 35-43; Chapl Manor Hosp and Beacon Lodge 35-43; V Bilston St Leon 43-59; R Myddle 59-70; V Broughton 59-70; P-in-c Grinshill 59-65; Dioc Dir RE 59-75; Preb Lich Cathl 61-75; rtd 70. *10 Church Close, Bicton, Shrewsbury SY3 8EN* Tel (01743) 850491

AYLING, John Michael. b 37. St Cath Coll Cam BA60 MA64. Linc Th Coll 60. **d** 62 **p** 63. C Stoke upon Trent *Lich* 62-66; C Codsall 66-67; Australia 67-71; Solomon Is 71-72; Lic to Offic *St Alb* 72-91; TR Boscastle w Davidstow *Truro* from 91. *The Rectory, Boscastle, Cornwall PL35 0DJ* Tel (01840) 250359

AYLMER-KELLY, Aylmer William Brendan. b 40. Birm Univ BSc63 Southn Univ PhD73 CChem76 FRSC76 Coll of Ripon & York St Jo MA97. Nor Ord Course 93. **d** 96 **p** 97. NSM Monk Fryston and S Milford *York* from 96. *23A Springfield Road, Sherburn in Elmet, Leeds LS25 6BU* Tel (01977) 684774

AYLWARD, James Gareth. b 45. St Cath Coll Cam BA68 MA72. St As Minl Tr Course 94. **d** 97. NSM Wrexham *St As* from 97. *11 Spring Road, Wrexham LL11 2LU* Tel (01978) 350083

AYNSLEY, Ernest Edgar. b 02. FRIC Dur Univ BSc23 MSc24 PhD34 DSc62. Westcott Ho Cam 42. **d** 42 **p** 43. Hon C Long Benton St Mary *Newc* 42-54; Hon C Newc St Barn and St Jude 54-57; Hon C Gosforth St Nic 57-62; Lic to Offic 63-95; Prof Chemistry Newc Univ 63-67; rtd 67. *7 Manor Court, Ulgham, Morpeth, Northd NE61 3BG* Tel (01670) 790197

AYOK-LOEWENBERG, Joseph. b 60. DipEd91. Trin Coll Bris 85. **d** 88 **p** 89. C Swanage and Studland *Sarum* 88-90; Cam Univ Miss Bermondsey 90; C Barnes St Mary *S'wark* 91-92; CMS 92-95; Uganda 92-95; P-in-c Symondsbury and Chideock *Sarum* from 96. *The Rectory, Shutes Lane, Symondsbury, Bridport, Dorset DT6 6HF* Tel (01308) 422145

AYRES, Anthony Lawrence. b 47. Trin Coll Bris 69. **d** 73 **p** 74. C Plumstead All SS *S'wark* 73-77; Hon C from 77; Member of Counselling Team CA from 83. *37 Donaldson Road, London SE18 4JZ* Tel 0181-856 1542

B

BAAR, Canon William Henry. b 19. Yale Univ BA42 BD45 MA48 PhD53 STM55 DD77. Seabury-Western Th Sem. **d** 54 **p** 54. USA 54-86 and from 93; Chapl Venice w Trieste *Eur* 86-93; Can Malta Cathl 89-93. *114 Briarwood Lakes, Oak Brook, Illanois, USA*

BABB, Charles Thomas. b 47. Newfoundland Univ BA70. Qu Coll Newfoundland 64. **d** 70 **p** 72. Canada 70-80; Miss to Seamen 80-94; Chapl Antwerp Seafarers' Cen *Eur* 80-94; Chapl Hull Miss to Seamen from 94. *Hull Missions to Seamen, 900 Hendon Road, Hull HU9 5LZ* Tel (01482) 76322

BABB, Canon Geoffrey. b 42. Man Univ BSc64 MA74 Linacre Coll Ox BA67. Ripon Hall Ox 65. **d** 68 **p** 69. C Heywood St Luke *Man* 68-71; P-in-c Loundsley Green Ascension CD *Derby* 71-76; TV Old Brampton and Loundsley Green 76-77; TV Stafford St Mary and St Chad *Lich* 77-79; TV Stafford 79-88; Soc Resp Officer 77-88; Preb Lich Cathl 87-88; P-in-c Salford Sacred Trin *Man* from 88; Dir of Continuing Min Educn from 88; Hon Can Man Cathl from 89. *197A Lancaster Road, Salford M6 8NB* Tel 0161-788 7077 or 832 5785

BABBAGE, Canon Stuart Barton. b 16. St Jo Coll Auckland 35 Univ of NZ BA35 MA36 K Coll Lon PhD42. Tyndale Hall Bris 37. **d** 39 **p** 40. C Havering-atte-Bower *Chelmsf* 39-41; Chapl-in-Chief RAF 42-46; Australia from 46. *46 St Thomas Street, Waverley, NSW, Australia 2024* Tel Sydney (2) 665 1882

BABINGTON, Canon Gervase Hamilton. b 30. Keble Coll Ox BA57 MA57. Wells Th Coll 55. **d** 57 **p** 58. C Sheff St Geo and St Steph *Sheff* 57-60; P-in-c Manor Park CD 60-65; R Waddington *Linc* 65-81; RD Graffoe 74-81; Can and Preb Linc Cathl 77-95; V Gainsborough All SS 81-90; RD Corringham 82-87; R Walesby 90-95; rtd 95; Perm to Offic *Linc* from 95. *15 Highfields, Nettleham, Lincoln LN2 2ST* Tel (01522) 595702

BACH, Frances Mary. b 48. Open Univ BA AIL. CITC BTh. **d** 94 **p** 95. NSM Ballynure and Ballyeaston *Conn* 94-96; C Larne and Inver from 96; C Glynn w Raloo from 96. *70 Hopefield Avenue, Portrush, Co Antrim BT56 8HE, or 57 Sallagh Park Central, Larne, Co Antrim BT40 1NU* Tel (01265) 823348 or (01574) 275196

BACH, John Edward Goulden. b 40. JP. Dur Univ BA66 DipTh69. Cranmer Hall Dur 66. **d** 69 **p** 70. C Bradf Cathl *Bradf* 69-72; Chapl and Lect NUU 73-84; Chapl and Lect Ulster Univ from 84. *The Anglican Chaplaincy, 70 Hopefield Avenue, Portrush, Co Antrim BT56 8HE* Tel (01265) 823348, 324652 or 324549 Fax 324904

BACHE, Edward Cyril Forbes. b 07. Dur Univ BA33 MA56. **d** 34 **p** 35. C Temple Fortune St Barn *Lon* 34-35; C Tottenham St Hilda 35-36; Kenya 36-39; Chapl RAF 39-46; C St Alb St Paul *St Alb* 46-48; Chapl K Alfred Sch BOAR 48-53; R Ufton *Cov* 53-57; Dir Relig Educn 53-57; V Husborne Crawley *St Alb* 57-66; P-in-c Ridgmont 61-66; R Husborne Crawley w Ridgmont 66-71; Chapl St Felix Sch Southwold 71-74; TV Halesworth w Linstead and Chediston *St E* 76-77; rtd 77; C Hardwick w Tusmore *Ox* 77-80; C Cottisford 77-80; Perm to Offic *St E* from 81. *Brook Cottage, Newbourn, Woodbridge, Suffolk IP12 4NY* Tel (01473) 736702

BACHELL, Kenneth George. b 22. Lon Univ BD49. K Coll Lon 55. **d** 56 **p** 57. C Bitterne Park *Win* 56-60; C-in-c Andover St Mich CD 60-64; V Andover St Mich 64-68; V Southampton St Alb 68-76; Warden Dioc Conf Ho Crawshawbooth *Man* 76-79; P-in-c Crawshawbooth 76-79; V Holdenhurst *Win* 79-83; V Froyle and Holybourne 83-87; rtd 87; Perm to Offic *Blackb* from 88. *8 Hazelwood, Silverdale, Carnforth, Lancs LA5 0TQ* Tel (01524) 701181

BACHMANN, Paul Douglas. b 45. **d** 79 **p** 80. USA 75-77 and from 79; C Alverstoke *Portsm* 77-79. *102 Heron Drive, Mankato, Minnesota 56001-5707, USA*

BACK, Edward James. b 24. Regent Street Poly Lon BScEng49 MIEE53 CEng85. ALCD65. **d** 65 **p** 66. C Northwood Em *Lon* 65-69; Teacher Rutland Ho Sch Uxbridge 69-70; Lect Harrow Coll Middx 70-89; rtd 94. *8 Wolsey Road, Northwood, Middlesex HA6 2HW* Tel (01923) 825332

BACK, Esther Elaine. *See* McCAFFERTY, Mrs Esther Elaine

BACKHOUSE, Alan Eric. b 37. Keble Coll Ox BA61 MA67. Tyndale Hall Bris 61. **d** 64 **p** 65. C Burnage St Marg *Man* 64-67; C Cheadle Hulme St Andr *Ches* 67-70; V Buglawton 70-80; V New Ferry 80-87; V Tarvin 87-93; V Knypersley *Lich* from 93. *St John's Vicarage, 62 Park Lane, Knypersley, Stoke-on-Trent ST8 7AU* Tel (01782) 512240

BACKHOUSE, Colin. b 41. MCSD82 Birm Poly BA67. Oak Hill Th Coll DipHE87. **d** 87 **p** 88. C Branksome St Clem *Sarum* 87-91; P-in-c Bluntisham cum Earith w Colne and Woodhurst *Ely* 91-92; R from 92. *The Rectory, Bluntisham, Huntingdon, Cambs PE17 3LN* Tel (01487) 740456

BACKHOUSE, John. b 30. Univ Coll Southn BA50. Wycliffe Hall Ox 51. **d** 53 **p** 54. C Eccleston St Luke *Liv* 53-55; C Maghull 55-58; V Lathom 58-64; Area Sec CMS 64-78; Dios Linc and Ely 64-71; Leic 72-78; Pet 72-75; Cov 75-78; V Thorpe Acre w Dishley *Leic* 78-83; R Ab Kettleby Gp 83-89; P-in-c Bitteswell 89-94; RD Guthlaxton II 90-94; rtd 94; Perm to Offic *Leic* from 94. *29 Peashill Close, Sileby, Loughborough, Leics LE12 7PT* Tel (01509) 812016

BACON, David Gary. b 62. Leic Univ BA83 Southn Univ BTh88. Sarum & Wells Th Coll 85. **d** 88 **p** 89. C Bromley St Mark *Roch* 88-92; C Lynton, Brendon, Countisbury, Lynmouth etc *Ex* 92; TV 92-95; P-in-c Lapford, Nymet Rowland and Coldridge from 95. *The Rectory, Lapford, Crediton, Devon EX17 6PX* Tel (01363) 83321

BACON, Derek Robert Alexander. b 44. Birkb Coll Lon DAC87 CACP89 BA92 MSc94. TCD Div Sch 69. **d** 71 **p** 72. C Templemore *D & R* 71-73; V Choral Derry Cathl 72-73; C Heeley *Sheff* 74-76; V Sheff Abbeydale St Pet 76-82; Chapl Gt Ormond Street Hosp for Children NHS Trust 82-95; Visiting Fell Ulster Univ from 95. *14A Heathmount, Portstewart, Co Londonderry BT55 7AP* Tel (01265) 834987

BACON, Eric Arthur. b 23. Qu Coll Birm 68. **d** 69 **p** 70. C Linc St Pet-at-Gowts and St Andr *Linc* 69-71; C Asterby Gp 71-74; V Anwick 74-78; V S Kyme 74-78; P-in-c Kirkby Laythorpe w Asgarby 76-78; P-in-c Ewerby w Evedon 76-78; P-in-c Burton Pedwardine 76-78; V Messingham 78-89; rtd 89; Perm to Offic

Linc from 89. *23 Londesborough Way, Metheringham, Lincoln LN4 3HW* Tel (01526) 320418

BACON, John Martindale. b 22. St Aid Birkenhead 54. **d** 57 **p** 58. C Bury St Paul *Man* 57-59; C-in-c Clifton Green St Thos CD 59-71; V Astley Bridge 71-87; rtd 87; Perm to Offic *Man* from 87; Perm to Offic *Blackb* from 91. *21 Lichen Close, Charnock Richard, Chorley, Lancs PR7 5TT* Tel (01257) 792535

BACON, Lionel William Rupert. b 06. OBE95. Univ Coll Dur LTh31 BA32 MA40. St Paul's Coll Burgh 27. **d** 33 **p** 34. C Auckland St Pet *Dur* 33-35; Argentina 35-39; Hon C Kentish Town St Martin w St Andr *Lon* 39-40; Hon C Castle Bromwich SS Mary and Marg *Birm* 40-41; Org Sec (SW Area) CCCS 41-47; Kenya 47-52; R Whitfield *Newc* 53-55; V Ninebanks 53-55; PC Carshield 53-55; R Laceby *Linc* 55-59; V Irby on Humber 55-59; V Ancaster 59-73; V Honington 59-73; rtd 73; Perm to Offic *Chich* from 77. *Lomas House, 43 Wordsworth Road, Worthing, W Sussex BN11 3JA* Tel (01903) 213667

BADDELEY, The Ven Martin James. b 36. Keble Coll Ox BA60 MA64. Linc Th Coll 60. **d** 62 **p** 63. C Stretford St Matt *Man* 62-64; Lic to Offic *Linc* 65-69; Lect Linc Th Coll 65-66; Tutor 66-69; Chapl 68-69; Chapl Fitzw Coll and New Hall Cam 69-74; Can Res Roch Cathl *Roch* 74-80; Hon Can 80-96; Prin S'wark Ord Course 80-94; Co-Prin SEITE 94-96; Adn Reigate *S'wark* from 96. *89 Nutfield Road, Merstham, Redhill RH1 3HD* Tel (01737) 462375 E-mail martinbaddeley@dswark.org.uk

BADDELEY, The Very Revd William Pye. b 14. St Chad's Coll Dur BA40. Cuddesdon Coll 40. **d** 41 **p** 42. C Camberwell St Luke *S'wark* 41-44; C Wandsworth St Anne 44-46; C Bournemouth St Steph *Win* 46-49; V St Pancras *Lon* 49-54; V St Pancras w St Jas and Ch Ch 54-58; Dean Brisbane 58-67; R Westmr St Jas *Lon* 67-80; ChStJ from 70; RD Westmr St Marg *Lon* 74-80; Visiting Chapl Westmr Abbey from 80; rtd 80; Perm to Offic *St E* from 81. *Cumberland House, 17 Cumberland Street, Woodbridge, Suffolk IP12 4AH* Tel (01394) 384104

BADEJO, The Ven Erasmus Victor. b 21. JP. Lon Univ BSc54. Immanuel Coll Ibadan 70. **d** 71 **p** 73. Ethiopia 71-74; Hon C Wembley St Jo *Lon* 75-76; C W Dulwich All SS and Em *S'wark* 76-78; C Cheam 79-83; Nigeria from 83; Adn Benin S from 83; rtd 88. *Cathedral Church of Christ, PO Box 726, Lagos, Nigeria*

BADEN, Peter Michael. b 35. CCC Cam BA59 MA62. Cuddesdon Coll 58. **d** 60 **p** 61. C Hunslet St Mary and Stourton *Ripon* 60-63; Lic to Offic *Wakef* 63-64; C E Grinstead St Swithun *Chich* 65-68; V Brighton St Martin 68-74; TR Brighton Resurr 74-76; R Westbourne 76-84; V Stansted 76-84; V Copthorne 84-91; V Clifton *Carl* from 91; R Dean from 91. *The Vicarage, 1 Clifton Gardens, Great Clifton, Workington, Cumbria CA14 1TT* Tel (01900) 603886

BADGER, Canon Edwin. b 09. Bris Univ BA32 MA86 Lon Univ BD57. St Boniface Warminster 28. **d** 34 **p** 35. C Kidderminster St Jo *Worc* 34-36; Australia from 36; Hon Can Wangaratta 69-76; rtd 76. *Providence Village, Griffiths Street, Bacchus Marsh, Victoria, Australia 3340* Tel Ballarat (53) 672316

BADGER, Mark. b 65. Qu Coll Birm 93. **d** 96 **p** 97. C Barbourne *Worc* from 96. *5 Keats Avenue, Worcester WR3 8DU*

BADHAM, Prof Paul Brian Leslie. b 42. Jes Coll Ox BA65 MA69 Jes Coll Cam BA68 MA72 Birm Univ PhD73. Westcott Ho Cam 66. **d** 68 **p** 69. C Edgbaston St Bart *Birm* 68-69; C Rubery 69-73; Lic to Offic *St D* from 73; Lect Th Univ of Wales (Lamp) 73-83; Sen Lect 83-88; Reader 88-91; Prof Th from 91. *St David's University College, Lampeter SA48 7ED* Tel (01570) 422351

BAELZ, The Very Revd Peter Richard. b 23. Ch Coll Cam BA44 MA48 BD71 Ox Univ DD79 Dur Univ Hon DD93. Westcott Ho Cam 44. **d** 47 **p** 50. C Bournville *Birm* 47-50; C Sherborne w Castleton and Lillington *Sarum* 50-52; Asst Chapl Ripon Hall Ox 52-53; R Wishaw *Birm* 53-56; V Bournville 56-60; Dean Jes Coll Cam 60-72; Lic to Offic *Ely* 61-72; Lect Th Cam Univ 66-72; Can Res Ch Ch *Ox* 72-79; Regius Prof Moral and Past Th Ox Univ 72-79; Dean Dur 80-88; rtd 88; Perm to Offic *S & B* from 88. *36 Brynteg, Llandrindod Wells LD1 5NB* Tel (01597) 825404

BAGGALEY, Canon Dennis. b 31. Dur Univ BA53 Liv Univ MA79. St Jo Coll Dur DipTh56. **d** 56 **p** 57. C Pennington *Man* 56-59; C N Meols *Liv* 59-60; V Bacup Ch Ch *Man* 60-65; R Burnage St Nic 65-71; V Onchan *S & M* 71-96; Can St German's Cathl 80-89; RD Douglas 82-86; rtd 96; Perm to Offic *S & M* from 96. *45 High Street, Port St Mary, Isle of Man IM9 5DN* Tel (01624) 835388

BAGGALEY, John Roger Pocklington. b 14. MC45. Keble Coll Ox BA36 MA45. Westcott Ho Cam. **d** 47 **p** 48. C Bishopwearmouth St Mich *Dur* 47-50; CF 50-69; R Badger *Lich* 69-83; R Ryton 69-83; R Beckbury 69-83; rtd 83. *21 Swanston Drive, Fairmilehead, Edinburgh EH10 7BP* Tel 0131-445 1331

BAGGOTT, Michael. b 30. FVCM91 ADipR92. Chich Th Coll DipTh94. **d** 94 **p** 95. NSM Southbourne w W Thorney *Chich* from 94. *14 Orchard Lane, Hermitage, Emsworth, Hants PO10 8BH* Tel (01243) 377778

BAGLEY, Canon John Marmaduke Erskine. b 08. G&C Coll Cam BA30 MA36. Ely Th Coll 30. **d** 32 **p** 33. C Swindon New Town *Bris* 32-36; C Cambridge St Mary Less *Ely* 36-38; Chapl Jubbulpore Ch Ch 38-44; C Littleham w Exmouth *Ex* 44-46; R Huntingdon All SS w St Jo *Ely* 46-63; Chapl HM Borstal Gaynes Hall 52-55; V Ely 63-74; Chapl Ely Cathl 63-74; RD Ely 66-71; Hon Can Ely Cathl 68-74; P-in-c Chettisham 68-74; rtd 74; Perm to Offic *St E* 74-77; Perm to Offic *Ely* from 77; Perm to Offic *Nor* from 91. *Old House Cottage, Church Road, Aylmerton, Norwich NR11 8PZ* Tel (01263) 837685

BAGLEY, Richard Alexander. b 25. New Coll Ox BA51 MA55 K Coll Cam MA57. Cuddesdon Coll 51. **d** 53 **p** 54. C Cambridge St Mary Less *Ely* 53-58; Hon C Pimlico St Mary Graham Terrace *Lon* 58-64. *Flat 2, 73 Sinclair Road, London W14 0NR* Tel 0171-602 1951

BAGNALL, Harry. b 30. OBE82. S'wark Ord Course 64. **d** 67 **p** 68. C Goole *Sheff* 67-70; C Doncaster St Leon and St Jude 70-72; C-in-c New Cantley CD 72-79; Falkland Is 79-86; V Hook w Airmyn *Sheff* 86-95; rtd 95; Perm to Offic *Sheff* from 95. *33 Stone Font Grove, Cantley, Doncaster, S Yorkshire DN4 6UQ* Tel (01302) 573028

BAGNALL, Roger. b 15. St Edm Hall Ox BA37 MA41. Linc Th Coll 37. **d** 39 **p** 40. C Hitchin St Mary *St Alb* 39-44; Chapl RNVR 44-46; C Kempston *St Alb* 47-51; V Blackfordby *Leic* 51-55; V Smisby *Derby* 52-55; V Elvaston 55-66; R Shardlow 56-66; V Ticknall 66-84; RD Melbourne 68-78; V Smisby 69-84; P-in-c Stanton-by-Bridge and Swarkestone 80-84; V Ticknall, Smisby and Stanton by Bridge 84-86; rtd 86. *12 Berkeley Drive, Beverley, N Humberside HU17 8UE* Tel (01482) 872260

BAGOTT, Paul Andrew. b 61. Leeds Univ BA85. Westcott Ho Cam 86. **d** 88 **p** 89. C Chingford SS Pet and Paul *Chelmsf* 88-91; C Pimlico St Sav *Lon* 91-95; P-in-c Clerkenwell H Redeemer and St Mark from 95. *Holy Redeemer Clergy House, 24 Exmouth Market, London EC1R 4QE* Tel 0171-837 1861

BAGOTT, Robert Blakeway. b 25. St Aid Birkenhead 51. **d** 54 **p** 55. C Gt Malvern St Mary *Worc* 54-56; C Bexleyheath Ch Ch *Roch* 56-59; V Paddock Wood 59-66; R Luton Ch Ch 66-77; Chapl All SS Hosp Chatham 70-77; R Dowlishwake w Chaffcombe, Knowle St Giles etc *B & W* 77-82; R E w W Harptree and Hinton Blewett 82-90; Co-ord Retirement Officer 89-96; rtd 90; Perm to Offic *B & W* from 90. *12 Hawkers Lane, Wells, Somerset BA5 3JL* Tel (01749) 674086

BAGSHAW, Paul Stanley. b 55. Selw Coll Cam BA78 MA81 Man Univ CQSW80. N Ord Course 85. **d** 88 **p** 89. Ind Missr *Sheff* 86-90; C Handsworth Woodhouse 88-90; NSM 91-93; C Newark *S'well* 93-96; P-in-c Ordsall from 96. *The Rectory, All Hallows Street, Retford, Notts DN22 7TP* Tel (01777) 702515

BAGSHAWE, John Allen. b 45. Dur Univ BA70 DipTh71. Cranmer Hall Dur 67. **d** 71 **p** 72. C Bridlington Priory *York* 71-75; C N Ferriby 75-79; V Kingston upon Hull St Matt w St Barn from 79. *St Matthew's Vicarage, Boulevard, Hull HU3 2TA* Tel (01482) 26573

BAGULEY, Henry. b 23. Qu Coll Birm 55. **d** 58 **p** 59. C Wilmslow *Ches* 58-61; V Kelsall 61-75; V New Brighton St Jas 75-88; rtd 88; Perm to Offic *Ches* from 88; Perm to Offic *Lich* from 93. *The Meadows, Nantwich Road, Whitchurch, Shropshire SY13 4AA* Tel (01948) 662692

BAILES, Dr Kenneth. b 35. Dur Univ BA69 DipTh71 DPhil. **d** 71 **p** 72. C Redcar *York* 71-73; TV Redcar w Kirkleatham 73-74; P-in-c Appleton Roebuck w Acaster Selby 74-80; P-in-c Sutton on the Forest 80-82; R Stamford Bridge Gp of Par 82-90; V Healaugh w Wighill, Bilbrough and Askham Richard 90-95; rtd 95. *7 Pear Tree Lane, Dunnington, York YO1 5QG*

BAILEY, Adrian Richard. b 57. St Jo Coll Dur 89. **d** 91 **p** 92. C Oswestry St Oswald *Lich* 91-94; C Shobnall from 94; Town Cen Chapl from 94. *114 Shobnall Road, Burton-on-Trent, Staffs DE14 2BB* Tel (01283) 530910

BAILEY, Alan George. b 40. Ripon Hall Ox 62. **d** 64 **p** 65. C Formby H Trin *Liv* 64-67; C Upholland 67-70; P-in-c Edge Hill St Dunstan 70-74; V 74-81; RD Toxteth 78-81; Perm to Offic 81-83; Asst Chapl Liv Cathl 83-85; C Liv Our Lady and St Nic w St Anne 85-89; V Waddington *Bradf* from 89. *The Vicarage, Waddington, Clitheroe, Lancs BB7 3JQ* Tel (01200) 423589

BAILEY, Andrew Henley. b 57. AKC78. Sarum & Wells Th Coll 79. **d** 80 **p** 81. C Romsey *Win* 80-83; V Bournemouth St Alb 83-93; R Milton from 93. *The Rectory, New Milton, Hants BH25 6QN* Tel (01425) 615150

BAILEY, Andrew John. b 37. Trin Coll Cam BA61 MA. Ridley Hall Cam 60. **d** 63 **p** 64. C Drypool *York* 63-66; C Melton Mowbray w Thorpe Arnold *Leic* 66-69; C-in-c Skelmersdale Ecum Cen *Liv* 69-79; V Langley Mill *Derby* 79-90; V Gt Faringdon w Lt Coxwell *Ox* from 90. *The Vicarage, Coach Lane, Faringdon, Oxon SN7 8AB* Tel (01367) 240106

BAILEY, Ms Angela. b 61. Kent Univ BA82. Qu Coll Birm 83. **dss** 85 **d** 87 **p** 94. Reculver and Herne Bay St Bart *Cant* 85-88; Par Dn 87-88; Asst Chapl Hull Univ *York* 88-92; Sen Chapl from 94; Perm to Offic 92-94. *Kingston, 21 Southwood Road, Cottingham, N Humberside HU15 5AE* Tel (01482) 847151

BAILEY, Anthony. b 27. Univ of Wales (Lamp) BA51. Ely Th Coll 51. **d** 53 **p** 54. C Barkingside H Trin *Chelmsf* 53-55; Chapl W Buckland Sch Barnstaple 55-59; R Machen *Mon* 59-66; Min Can Bris Cathl *Bris* 66-84; Chapl Bris Cathl Sch 66-84; Succ Bris Cathl *Bris* 68-82; P-in-c Maenclochog w Henry's Moat and Mynachlogddu etc *St D* 83-90; V 90-92; rtd 92; P-in-c Llandysilio w Egremont and Llanglydwen etc *St D* from 96. *The Village Stores, Charing Cross, Llangolman, Clunderwen SA66 7XN* Tel (01991) 532430

BAILEY, Bertram Arthur. b 20. Tyndale Hall Bris 65. **d** 67 **p** 68. C Bath St Luke *B & W* 67-72; C Bickenhill w Elmdon *Birm* 72-73; R N Tawton *Ex* 73-79; R N Tawton and Bondleigh 79-87; rtd 87; Perm to Offic *B & W* 87-89; Clergy Retirement and Widows' Officer from 89. *4 Uphill Road South, Uphill, Weston-super-Mare, Avon BS23 4SD* Tel (01934) 633552

BAILEY, Brendan John. b 61. Strathclyde Univ BSc83. Ripon Coll Cuddesdon BTh93. **d** 94 **p** 95. C Purley *Ox* from 94. *10 Knowsley Road, Tilehurst, Reading RG3 6FA* Tel 0118-945 1411 E-mail brendan.bailey@kcl.ac.uk

BAILEY, Brian Constable. b 36. AKC62. **d** 63 **p** 64. C Mill Hill Jo Keble Ch *Lon* 63-66; C Gt Stanmore 66-69; C Gt Marlow *Ox* 69-72; R Burghfield 72-81; R Wokingham All SS 81-96; Hon Can Ch Ch 94-96; TV Pinhoe and Broadclyst *Ex* from 96. *The Vicarage, Broadclyst, Exeter, Devon EX5 3EW* Tel (01392) 461280

BAILEY, Darren Stephen. b 65. Wales Poly BA87 Sheff Poly CertTESOL89 Nottm Univ BTh. Linc Th Coll. **d** 95 **p** 96. C Mexborough *Sheff* from 95. *49 Tennyson Avenue, Mexborough, S Yorkshire S64 0AX* Tel (01709) 582675

BAILEY, David Charles. b 52. Linc Coll Ox BA75 MA78 MSc77. St Jo Coll Nottm BA79. **d** 80 **p** 81. C Worksop St Jo *S'well* 80-83; C Edgware *Lon* 83-87; V S Cave and Ellerker w Broomfleet *York* from 87; RD Howden from 91. *The Vicarage, 10 Station Road, South Cave, Brough, N Humberside HU15 2AA* Tel (01430) 423693

BAILEY, Dennis. b 53. Man Univ BEd74 BMus74. St Jo Coll Nottm BTh79. **d** 79 **p** 80. C Netherley Ch Ch CD *Liv* 79-83; S Africa from 83. *PO Box 635, Hilton, 3245 South Africa*

BAILEY, Derek Gilbert. b 42. Div Hostel Dub 65. **d** 68 **p** 69. C Cork St Luke w St Ann *C, C & R* 68-72; CF from 72; rtd 97. *MOD Chaplains (Army), Trenchard Lines, Upavon, Pewsey, Wilts SN9 6BE* Tel (01980) 615804 Fax 615800

BAILEY, Derek William. b 39. Lon Univ DipTh64. Cranmer Hall Dur 64. **d** 67 **p** 68. C Sutton *Liv* 67-69; C Chapel-en-le-Frith *Derby* 69-73; V Hadfield 73-90; R Collyhurst *Man* 90-95; V Chaddesden St Mary *Derby* from 95. *The Vicarage, 133 Chaddesden Lane, Chaddesden, Derby DE21 6LL* Tel (01332) 672336

BAILEY, Canon Dr Edward Ian. b 35. CCC Cam BA59 MA63 Bris Univ MA69 PhD77. United Th Coll Bangalore 59 Westcott Ho Cam 61. **d** 63 **p** 64. C Newc St Jo *Newc* 63-65; Asst Chapl Marlborough Coll 65-68; Perm to Offic *Bris* 69-70; R Winterbourne from 70; P-in-c Winterbourne Down 75-81; RD Stapleton 77-83; Hon Can Bris Cathl from 84. *The Rectory, 58 High Street, Winterbourne, Bristol BS17 1JQ* Tel (01454) 772131 or 776518

BAILEY, Edward Peter. b 35. Nottm Univ MA93. Qu Coll Birm. **d** 62 **p** 63. C Ordsall *S'well* 62-66; C Clifton w Glapton 66-71; V Lady Bay 71-83; Relig Affairs Adv to Radio Trent 83-85; C Gedling 86-89; C Bilborough St Jo from 89. *32 Crosslands Meadow, Colwick, Nottingham NG4 2DJ* Tel 0115-940 1074

BAILEY, Mrs Elizabeth Carmen. b 45. EAMTC 89. **d** 93 **p** 94. Hon C Roughton and Felbrigg, Metton, Sustead etc *Nor* 93-95; Hon C Cromer from 95. *5 Warren Road, Southrepps, Norwich NR11 8UN* Tel (01263) 833785

BAILEY, Eric Arthur. b 14. AKC37. **d** 37 **p** 38. C S'wark St Geo *S'wark* 37-39; C Waltham Cross *St Alb* 39-41; C Diss *Nor* 41-42; Chapl CF (EC) 42-43; C Kingsbury *Birm* 44-45; V Dordon 45-52; R Londesborough *York* 52-60; P-in-c Nunburnholme 53-54; R 54-60; P-in-c Burnby 53-54; R 54-60; V Gt w Lt Ouseburn *Ripon* 60-65; V Stonegate *Chich* 65-79; rtd 79; Perm to Offic *St E* 81-88. *Hill End, Sapiston, Bury St Edmunds, Suffolk IP31 1RR* Tel (01359) 269638

BAILEY, Frederick Hugh. b 18. Keble Coll Ox BA40. Linc Th Coll 40. **d** 42 **p** 43. C Boultham *Linc* 42-49; Chapl Rauceby Hosp Lincs from 49; R Quarrington w Old Sleaford *Linc* 49-84; R Silk Willoughby 57-84; rtd 84; Perm to Offic *Linc* from 84. *1 Willow Close, Scopwick, Lincoln LN4 3PJ* Tel (01522) 321127

BAILEY, Canon Ivan John. b 33. Keble Coll Ox BA57 MA65. St Steph Ho Ox DipTh59. **d** 59 **p** 60. C Ipswich All Hallows *St E* 59-62; Clerical Sec CEMS 62-66; V Cringleford *Nor* 66-81; RD Humbleyard 73-81; R Colney 80-81; Relig Adv Anglia TV 81-91; P-in-c Kirby Bedon w Bixley and Whitlingham *Nor* 81-92; Hon Can Nor Cathl from 84; Chapl St Andr Hosp Norwich 92-94; Chapl Mental Health Unit Nor HA 92-94; Chapl Norfolk Mental Health Care NHS Trust from 94. *21 Cranleigh Rise, Norwich NR4 6PQ, or Hellesdon Hospital, Drayton High Road, Norwich NR6 5BE* Tel (01603) 53565 or 421421

BAILEY, John Ernest. b 32. Leeds Univ BA57. Coll of Resurr Mirfield 57. **d** 59 **p** 60. C Newbury St Nic *Ox* 59-62; Australia 62-63; V Uffington w Woolstone and Baulking *Ox* 63-70; P-in-c Gt w Lt Oakley *Pet* 70-72; TV Corby SS Pet and Andr w Gt and Lt Oakley 70-72; Chapl Cen Hosp Warw 72-94; Chapl Cen Weston and Abbeyfields 82-90; Chapl Cen Weston 90-94; Chapl S Warks Mental Health Services NHS Trust 94-96; rtd 96. *22 Hill Wootton Road, Leek Wootton, Warwick CV35 7QL* Tel (01926) 853528

BAILEY, John Robert. b 40. St Jo Coll Cam BA62 MA66 Nottm Univ MEd77. S'wark Ord Course 68. **d** 69 **p** 70. NSM Plumstead Wm Temple Ch Abbey Wood CD *S'wark* 69-70; Lon Sec Chr Educn Movement 69-71; NSM Markyate Street *St Alb* 70-71; RE Adv *Linc* 72-80; Perm to Offic *Man* 80-83; Perm to Offic *St Alb* 84-92; Perm to Offic *Linc* from 92. *Juniper Cottage, Vicarage Lane, Wellingore, Lincoln LN5 0JP* Tel (01522) 810317

✠**BAILEY, The Rt Revd Jonathan Sansbury.** b 40. Trin Coll Cam BA61 MA65. Ridley Hall Cam 62. **d** 65 **p** 66 **c** 92. C Sutton *Liv* 65-68; C Warrington St Paul 68-71; Warden Marrick Priory *Ripon* 71-76; V Wetherby 76-82; Adn Southend *Chelmsf* 82-92; Suff Bp Dunwich *St E* 92-95; Bp Derby from 95. *Bishop's House, 6 King Street, Duffield, Belper, Derbyshire DE56 4EU* Tel (01332) 840132 or 346744 Fax 295810

BAILEY, Joyce Mary Josephine. *See* OUTEN, Mrs Joyce Mary Josephine

BAILEY, Justin Mark. b 55. Birm Univ BA77 Wolv Poly PGCE78. Ripon Coll Cuddesdon 90. **d** 92 **p** 93. C Oakdale *Sarum* 92-96; P-in-c Milton Abbas, Hilton w Cheselbourne etc from 96. *The Rectory, Ansty, Dorchester, Dorset DT2 7PX* Tel (01258) 880372

BAILEY, Mark David. b 62. Ripon Coll Cuddesdon 87. **d** 90 **p** 91. C Leigh Park *Portsm* 90-93; C Fleet *Guildf* 93-95; TV Basingstoke *Win* from 95. *The Vicarage, 75 Cumberland Avenue, Basingstoke, Hants RG22 4BQ* Tel (01256) 465666

BAILEY, Mark Robert. b 60. Trin Coll Bris BA89. **d** 89 **p** 90. C Heigham H Trin *Nor* 89-94; TV Cheltenham St Mary, St Matt, St Paul and H Trin *Glouc* from 94. *100 Hewlett Road, Cheltenham, Glos GL52 6AR* Tel (01242) 582396

BAILEY, Martin Tristram. b 57. BA79. Oak Hill Th Coll DipHE91. **d** 91 **p** 92. C Brundall w Braydeston and Postwick *Nor* 91-95; TV Plymouth St Andr and St Paul Stonehouse *Ex* from 95. *88 Durnford Street, Plymouth PL1 3QW* Tel (01752) 228114

BAILEY, Nicholas Andrew. b 55. Nottm Univ CertEd80 Open Univ BA84. Ripon Coll Cuddesdon 88. **d** 90 **p** 91. C Guisborough *York* 90-92; Chapl Foremark Prep Sch Derby from 92. *Sycamore Cottage, Foremark, Milton, Derby DE65 6TB* Tel (01283) 703558

BAILEY, Norman Gerald. b 25. **d** 83 **p** 84. Hon C Kingswood *Bris* 83-90; Hon C E Bris from 90. *71 Lincombe Road, Bristol BS16 5LL* Tel 0117-957 2822

BAILEY, Canon Peter Robin. b 43. St Jo Coll Dur BA64. Trin Coll Bris 72. **d** 74 **p** 75. C Corby St Columba *Pet* 74-77; C Bishopsworth *Bris* 77-82; V Sea Mills 82-97; RD Westbury and Severnside 91-97; P-in-c Bishopston from 97; P-in-c Bris St Andr w St Bart from 97; Hon Can Bris Cathl from 97. *The Vicarage, Walsingham Road, St Andrews, Bristol BS6 5BT* Tel 0117-924 8683

BAILEY, Richard William. b 38. Man Univ BSc59. Ripon Hall Ox 63. **d** 65 **p** 66. C Tonge *Man* 65-68; C Stretford St Matt 68-71; R Abbey Hey 71-80; V E Crompton 80-86; V Chadderton St Matt from 86. *St Matthew's Vicarage, Mill Brow, Chadderton, Oldham OL1 2RT* Tel 0161-624 8600

BAILEY, Richard William. b 47. All Nations Chr Coll DBMS75 Oak Hill Th Coll BA84. **d** 84 **p** 85. C Huyton St Geo *Liv* 84-87; V Wombridge *Lich* from 87. *Wombridge Vicarage, Wombridge Road, Telford, Shropshire TF2 6HT* Tel (01952) 613334

BAILEY, Robert William. b 49. Lich Th Coll 69. **d** 72 **p** 73. C Stoke *Cov* 72-75; Chapl RAF from 75. *Chaplaincy Services (RAF), HQ, Personnel and Training Command, RAF Innsworth, Gloucester GL3 1EZ* Tel (01452) 712612 ext 5164 Fax 510828

BAILEY, Ronald William. b 12. Linc Coll Ox BA35 BSc36 MA45. Ripon Hall Ox 57. **d** 58 **p** 59. C N Stoneham *Win* 58-61; V Lamberhurst *Roch* 61-77; rtd 77. *Tamarisk, Wagg Drove, Huish Episcopi, Langport, Somerset TA10 9ER* Tel (01458) 250103

BAILEY, Simon. b 56. Man Univ MusB Nottm Univ BCombStuds. Linc Th Coll. **d** 83 **p** 84. C Armley w New Wortley *Ripon* 83-86; C Harrogate St Wilfrid and St Luke 86-90; R Harby, Long Clawson and Hose *Leic* 90-94; V Woodhall *Bradf* from 94. *St James's Vicarage, Galloway Lane, Pudsey, W Yorkshire LS28 8JR* Tel (01274) 662735

BAILEY, Stephen. b 39. Leic Univ BA61. Clifton Th Coll 61. **d** 62 **p** 63. C Wellington w Eyton *Lich* 62-66; C Rainham *Chelmsf* 66-69; V Ercall Magna *Lich* 69-75; V Rowton 69-75; RD Wrockwardine 72-75; V W Bromwich Gd Shep w St Jo 75-83; P-in-c W Bromwich St Phil 80-81; V 81-83; R Chadwell *Chelmsf* 83-96; Area Warden Ords Brentwood, Basildon and Thurrock 91-96; RD Thurrock 92-96; V Galleywood Common from 96. *Galleywood Vicarage, 450 Beehive Lane, Chelmsford CM2 8RN* Tel (01245) 353922

BAILEY, Stephen John. b 57. NE Surrey Coll of Tech HNC78. Sarum & Wells Th Coll 88. **d** 90 **p** 91. C Redhill H Trin *S'wark* 90-95; Chapl E Surrey Coll 91-93; P-in-c Betchworth *S'wark* from 95; P-in-c Buckland from 95. *The Vicarage, Old Reigate Road, Betchworth, Surrey RH3 7DE* Tel (01737) 842102

BAILEY, Mrs Susan Mary. b 40. F L Calder Coll Liv CertEd61. EAMTC 89. **d** 92 **p** 94. NSM Chelmsf Cathl *Chelmsf* 92-93; NSM Needham Market w Badley *St E* 93-95; NSM Belper *Derby* from 96. *Bishop's House, 6 King Street, Duffield, Belper, Derbyshire DE56 4EU* Tel (01332) 840132 Fax 842743

BAILLIE, Alistair Hope Pattison. b 50. Loughb Univ BSc73 Ox Univ DipTh. Ripon Coll Cuddesdon 73. **d** 76 **p** 77. C Aylestone *Leic* 76-79; C Leic All SS 79-82; C Leic H Spirit 82-83; TV

Heavitree w Ex St Paul *Ex* 83-84; C 84-86; Asst Chapl N Gen Hosp Sheff 86-88; C Sheff St Cuth *Sheff* 86-88; Chapl Broadgreen Hosp Liv 88-94; Chapl Broadgreen Hosp NHS Trust Liv from 94. *Broadgreen Hospital, Thomas Drive, Liverpool L14 3LB* Tel 0151-228 4878 or 228 1616

BAILLIE, Canon Frederick Alexander. b 21. FRGS Open Univ BA75 QUB MA86 PhD87. CITC 53. **d** 55 **p** 56. C Belfast St Paul *Conn* 55-59; C Dunmurry 59-61; I Eglantine 61-69; I Belfast Whiterock 69-74; Hd of S Ch Miss Ballymacarrett 74-79; I Magheraculmoney *Clogh* 79-87; Dioc Info Officer 80-86; RD Kesh 85-87; Can Clogh Cathl 85-87; rtd 87. *2 St Elizabeth's Court, Ballyregan Road, Dundonald, Belfast BT16 0HX* Tel (01232) 487642

BAILLIE, Iain Robert Cullen. b 28. St Pet Hall Ox BA54 MA58. Wycliffe Hall Ox 54. **d** 56 **p** 57. C Penge Lane H Trin *Roch* 56-58; CF 58-83; Perm to Offic *Cant* from 92. *8 The Precincts, Canterbury, Kent CT1 2EE* Tel (01227) 768206

BAILLIE, Terence John. b 46. New Coll Ox BA69 MA78 Man Univ MSc72. St Jo Coll Nottm 74. **d** 77 **p** 78. C Chadwell *Chelmsf* 77-80; C Bickenhill w Elmdon *Birm* 80-84; V Bedminster St Mich *Bris* 84-96; V Clevedon St Andr and Ch Ch *B & W* from 96. *The Vicarage, 10 Coleridge Road, Clevedon, Avon BS21 7TB* Tel (01275) 872982

BAILY, Canon Robert Spencer Canning. b 21. G&C Coll Cam BA42 MA46. Westcott Ho Cam 42. **d** 44 **p** 45. C Sherborne w Castleton and Lillington *Sarum* 44-46; C Heacham *Nor* 46-47; C Bedford All SS *St Alb* 48-50; C-in-c Hayes St Edm CD *Lon* 50-56; R Blofield w Hemblington *Nor* 56-69; P-in-c Perlethorpe *S'well* 69-87; Dir of Educn 69-87; Hon Can S'well Minster 80-87; rtd 87; Perm to Offic *Linc* from 87. *17 Ravendale Close, Grantham, Lincs NG31 8BS* Tel (01476) 568614

BAIN, Alan. b 48. Thames Poly BSc72. St Jo Coll Nottm DipTh75. **d** 77 **p** 78. C Wakef St Andr and St Mary *Wakef* 77-81; V Bath Odd Down *B & W* 81-82; P-in-c Combe Hay 81-82; V Bath Odd Down w Combe Hay from 82. *The Vicarage, 39 Frome Road, Bath BA2 2QF* Tel (01225) 832838

BAIN, Andrew John. b 55. Newc Poly BA77 Edin Univ MTh89. Edin Th Coll 86. **d** 88 **p** 89. Chapl St Mary's Cathl *Edin* 88-91; C Edin St Mary 88-91; R Edin St Jas from 91; P-in-c Edin St Marg from 93; Dioc Dir of Ords from 95. *71 Restalrig Road, Edinburgh EH6 8BG* Tel 0131-554 3520

BAIN, David Roualeyn Findlater (Roly). b 54. Bris Univ BA75. Ripon Coll Cuddesdon 76. **d** 78 **p** 79. C Perry Hill St Geo *S'wark* 78-81; Chapl Asst Guy's Hosp Lon 81-84; Succ S'wark Cathl *S'wark* 81-84; V Streatham St Paul 84-90; Perm to Offic *Bris* from 90; Perm to Offic *Lon* from 90. *285 North Street, Bedminster, Bristol BS3 1JP* Tel 0117-963 6490

BAIN, John Stuart. b 55. Van Mildert Coll Dur BA77. Westcott Ho Cam 78. **d** 80 **p** 81. C Washington *Dur* 80-84; C Dunston 84-86; V Shiney Row 86-92; V Herrington 86-92; P-in-c Whitworth w Spennymoor 92-97; P-in-c Merrington 94-97; RD Auckland from 96; V Spennymoor, Whitworth and Merrington from 97. *The Vicarage, Horswell Gardens, Spennymoor, Co Durham DL16 7AA* Tel (01388) 814522

BAINBRIDGE, Ms Christine Susan. b 48. St Aid Coll Dur BA70. SEITE 93. **d** 96. C S'wark H Trin w St Matt *S'wark* from 96. *1 St Matthew's Court, Meadow Row, London SE1 6RG* Tel 0171-403 1946

BAINBRIDGE, David George. b 42. Wadh Coll Ox BA63 MA67 Lon Univ CertEd67. Ridley Hall Cam 84. **d** 86 **p** 87. C Downend *Bris* 86-90; TV Yate New Town from 90. *The Vicarage, 57 Brockworth, Yate, Bristol BS17 4SJ* Tel (01454) 322921

BAINBRIDGE, Mrs Jean Waite. b 29. ALA54 Birm Univ BA77 DipL&A79. Qu Coll Birm 78. **dss** 79 **d** 87 **p** 94. Worc St Barn w Ch Ch *Worc* 79-82; Catshill and Dodford 82-87; Par Dn 87-90; rtd 90; Hon Par Dn Hallow *Worc* 90-94; Hon C Worc St Wulstan from 94. *26 Barley Crescent, Long Meadow, Worcester WR4 0HW* Tel (01905) 748593

BAINBRIDGE, John Richard. b 35. Pemb Coll Cam BA59 MA63. Clifton Th Coll 65. **d** 67 **p** 68. C Ex St Leon w H Trin *Ex* 67-70; P-in-c Penge St Paul *Roch* 70-73; Chapl Uppingham Sch Leics 73-87; Lic to Offic *Pet* 73-87; V Stevenage St Nic *St Alb* from 87. *St Nicholas House, 2A North Road, Stevenage, Herts SG1 4AT* Tel (01438) 354355

BAINBRIDGE, Norman Harold. b 15. St Jo Coll Dur LTh38. ALCD38. **d** 38 **p** 39. C Morden *S'wark* 38-46; CF (EC) 43-46; V Bayswater *Lon* 46-58; V Muswell Hill St Jas 58-66; V Boscombe St Jo *Win* 66-80; rtd 80; Perm to Offic *Sarum* 81-93; Perm to Offic *Win* 81-93; Perm to Offic *Ex* 95-96. *Manormead, Tilford Road, Hindhead, Surrey GU26 6RA*

BAINBRIDGE, Richard Densham. b 49. Ch Coll Cam BA71 MA75 Edge Hill Coll of HE PGCE72 Roehampton Inst DipC&CD91. S'wark Ord Course 91. **d** 94 **p** 95. C Bermondsey St Jas w Ch Ch *S'wark* from 94. *1 St Matthew's Court, Meadow Row, London SE1 6RG* Tel 0171-403 1946 or 394 0993

BAINES, Alan William. b 50. S Bank Poly BSc72. Trin Coll Bris DipHE94. **d** 94 **p** 95. C Chenies and Lt Chalfont, Latimer and Flaunden *Ox* from 94. *St George's Parsonage, White Lion Road, Amersham, Bucks HP7 9LW* Tel (01494) 763244

BAINES, Bernard Frederick. b 20. JP. ACP. St Jo Coll Nottm 83. **d** 84 **p** 85. NSM Nottingham All SS *S'well* 84-90; rtd 90; Perm to Offic *S'well* from 90. *18 Forest Road East, Nottingham NG1 4HH* Tel 0115-978 4191

BAINES, John Edmund. b 22. Down Coll Cam BA47 MA50 Lon Univ BD51. New Coll Lon. **d** 58 **p** 59. C Penistone w Midhope *Wakef* 58-60; V Batley St Thos 60-69; V Cawthorne 69-89; rtd 89; Perm to Offic *Wakef* from 90. *3 Huskar Close, Silkstone, Barnsley, S Yorkshire S75 4SX* Tel (01226) 791088

BAINES, Nicholas. b 57. Bradf Univ BA80. Trin Coll Bris BA87. **d** 87 **p** 88. C Kendal St Thos *Carl* 87-91; C Leic H Trin w St Jo *Leic* 91-92; V Rothley from 92; RD Goscote from 96. *The Vicarage, 128 Hallfields Lane, Rothley, Leicester LE7 7NG* Tel 0116-230 2241

BAINES, Noel Edward (Ted). b 29. St Jo Coll Dur BSc52 DipTh54 MA62. **d** 54 **p** 55. C Rainham *Chelmsf* 54-58; C Surbiton Hill Ch Ch *S'wark* 58-61; V Southborough St Matt *Roch* 61-67; V Beckenham St Jo 67-74; Hd RE Taunton Manor High Sch Caterham 74-83; Keston Coll 85-91; Perm to Offic *Roch* 74-91; Hon C Bromley Ch Ch from 91; rtd 94. *10 Bromley Avenue, Bromley BR1 4BQ* Tel 0181-460 8256

BAINES, Canon Roger Holford. b 07. St Jo Coll Cam BA29 MA32. Westcott Ho Cam 29. **d** 30 **p** 31. C Chilvers Coton *Cov* 30-33; C Rugby St Andr 33-35; Uganda 35-39; P-in-c Leeds Gipton Epiphany *Ripon* 39-43; V Beeston 43-47; V High Harrogate St Pet 47-66; RD Knaresborough 54-66; Hon Can Ripon Cathl 55-66; Lic to Offic *Heref* from 68; rtd 72. *Barn House, Ashford Bowdler, Ludlow, Shropshire SY8 4DJ* Tel (01584) 74602

BAIRD, Agnes Murry (Nancy). Man Univ CertEd70. St Jo Coll Nottm DipPC92 EAMTC 93. **d** 96 **p** 97. NSM Bramford *St E* from 96. *14 Ballater Close, Ipswich IP1 6LL* Tel (01473) 741722

BAIRD, Dr Edward Simpson. b 17. Lon Univ BD58 MLitt65 DLitt68 Newc Univ 62. Yorkshire United Th Coll 42 Selly Oak Coll 47 Sarum Th Coll 54. **d** 55 **p** 56. C S Westoe *Dur* 55-58; V Swalwell 58-66; R Harrington *Carl* 66-75; V Barton w Peel Green *Man* 75-80; R Jarrow Grange *Dur* 80-83; rtd 83. *5 Hemsley Road, South Shields, Tyne & Wear N34 6HW* Tel 0191-456 1389

BAIRD, Paul Drummond. b 48. Newc Univ CertEd71 Open Univ BA85. Ripon Coll Cuddesdon 88. **d** 90 **p** 91. C Chandler's Ford *Win* 90-93; V Hythe from 93. *The Vicarage, 14 Atheling Road, Hythe, Southampton SO45 6BR* Tel (01703) 842461

BAIRD, Robert Douglas. b 21. ERD56. Cam Univ MA64. Ripon Coll Cuddesdon. **d** 85 **p** 86. NSM Charlbury w Shorthampton *Ox* 85-87; Asst Chapl HM Pris Grendon and Spring Hill 85; Lic to Offic *Ox* from 87. *Glebe House, Ibstone, High Wycombe, Bucks HP14 3XZ* Tel (01491) 638642

BAIRD, Canon William Stanley. b 33. TCD BA54 Div Test. **d** 56 **p** 57. C Carlow *C & O* 56-59; I Dunganstown *D & G* 59-64; C Knock *D & D* 64-69; P-in-c Kilwarlin Upper w Kilwarlin Lower 69-71; I 71-72; Warden Ch Min of Healing (Ireland) 72-79; I Dublin Drumcondra w N Strand *D & G* 79-91; Dir of Ords (Dub) from 84; Can Ch Ch Cathl Dublin 88-92; Preb from 92; I Swords w Donabate and Killsallaghan from 91. *The Rectory, Church Road, Swords, Co Dublin, Irish Republic* Tel Dublin (1) 840 2308

BAISLEY, Canon Barbara Pauline. b 47. DipAD69. S Dios Minl Tr Scheme 79. **dss** 82 **d** 87 **p** 94. Glouc St Geo w Whaddon *Glouc* 82-83; Welford w Weston and Clifford Chambers 83-87; Chapl Warw Univ *Cov* 87-94; Dioc Adv for Women's Min 90-96; Hon C Kenilworth St Nic 93-95; Hon C Berkswell from 95; Voc Development Adv from 96; Hon Can Cov Cathl from 96. *The Rectory, Meriden Road, Berkswell, Coventry CV7 7BE* Tel (01676) 533605 Fax as telephone E-mail rev@baisley.u-net.com

BAISLEY, George. b 45. Sarum & Wells Th Coll 78. **d** 80 **p** 81. C Glouc St Geo w Whaddon *Glouc* 80-83; R Welford w Weston and Clifford Chambers 83-87; Chapl Myton Hamlet Hospice from 87; Chapl Warw Univ *Cov* 87-91; R Berkswell from 91. *The Rectory, Meriden Road, Berkswell, Coventry CV7 7BE* Tel (01676) 533605

BAKER, Alan. b 42. Liv Univ BA64. Carl Dioc Tr Inst 93. **d** 96. NSM Cartmel *Carl* from 96. *1 Church View, Priest Lane, Cartmel, Grange-over-Sands, Cumbria LA11 6PU* Tel (01539) 536551

BAKER, Albert George. b 30. Qu Coll Birm. **d** 61 **p** 62. C Merton St Mary *S'wark* 61-64; C Limpsfield and Titsey 64-65; C Chapel-en-le-Frith *Derby* 65-68; R Odd Rode *Ches* 68-76; V Holme Cultram St Mary *Carl* 76-78; R Blofield w Hemblington *Nor* 78-94; rtd 94. *240 Raedwald Drive, Bury St Edmunds, Suffolk IP32 7DN* Tel (01284) 701802

BAKER, Angela. b 42. **d** 91. Par Dn Battersea St Sav and St Geo w St Andr *S'wark* 91-94; C 94-96; C Battersea Fields from 96. *St George's House, 11 Patmore Street, London SW8 4JD* Tel 0171-622 4244

BAKER, Anne-Marie Clare. *See* BIRD, Mrs Anne-Marie Clare

BAKER, Anthony Peter (Tony). b 38. Hertf Coll Ox BA59 MA63. Clifton Th Coll 60. **d** 63 **p** 64. C Ox St Ebbe w St Pet *Ox* 63-66; C Welling *Roch* 66-70; V Redland *Bris* 70-79; Lect Tyndale Hall Bris 70-71; Lect Trin Coll Bris 71-77; V Beckenham Ch Ch *Roch* 79-94; Chapl Beckenham Hosp 79-94; V Hove Bp Hannington Memorial Ch *Chich* from 94. *82 Holmes Avenue, Hove, E Sussex BN3 7LD* Tel (01273) 732821

BAKER, Miss Barbara Ann. b 36. Linc Th Coll 85. **d** 87 **p** 94. Par Dn Hornchurch St Andr *Chelmsf* 87-94; C 94-97; rtd 97; Perm to Offic *Chelmsf* from 97. *St Matthew's Bungalow, 55A Chelmsford Drive, Upminster, Essex RM14 2PH* Tel (01708) 452705

BAKER, Canon Bernard George Coleman. b 36. Lon Univ BD61. Oak Hill Th Coll 61. **d** 63 **p** 64. C Broadwater St Mary *Chich* 63-66; Tanzania 66-84; Hon Can Morogoro from 77; C-in-c Ryde St Jas Prop Chpl *Portsm* 84-96; Crosslinks from 96. *c/o Crosslinks, 251 Lewisham Way, London SE4 1XF* Tel 0181-691 6111

BAKER, Brian Ernest Harry. b 38. Sarum & Wells Th Coll 74. **d** 76 **p** 77. C Cannock *Lich* 76-79; C Penkridge w Stretton 79-80; C Dunston w Coppenhall 79-80; P-in-c Earl Stonham w Stonham Parva and Creeting St Pet *St E* 80-89; V Staincliffe *Wakef* 89-93. *3 Lansdowne Close, Batley, W Yorkshire WF17 0EZ* Tel (01924) 473214

BAKER, Charles Edward. b 47. **d** 87 **p** 88. NSM Dublin Clontarf *D & G* 87-90; NSM Delgany 90-94; NSM Dublin Sandford w Milltown from 94. *12 Aranleigh Vale, Rathfarnham, Dublin 14, Irish Republic* Tel Dublin (1) 494 6465

BAKER, Christopher James. b 54. MRAeS83 MICE83 CEng83 St Cath Coll Cam BA75 MA78 PhD78. EMMTC 85. **d** 88 **p** 89. NSM Matlock Bath *Derby* 88-95; NSM Matlock Bath and Cromford 95. *54A Park Road, Chilwell, Beeston, Nottingham NG9 4DD* Tel (0115) 925 7345

BAKER, Christopher Richard (Chris). b 61. Man Univ BA83 Southn Univ BTh90 Heythrop Coll Lon MTh92. Sarum & Wells Th Coll 86. **d** 89 **p** 93. C Dulwich St Barn *S'wark* 89-92; Tutor Sarum & Wells Th Coll 92-94; Dir Chr Tr Milton Keynes *Ox* from 94; Stantonbury and Willen from 95. *The Vicarage, 2 Hooper Gate, Willen, Milton Keynes MK15 9JR* Tel (01908) 662092 Fax 233638

BAKER, David Ayshford. b 66. St Aid Coll Dur BA88 Univ of Wales (Cardiff) Dip Journalism 89. Wycliffe Hall Ox BTh94. **d** 97. C Chadwell Heath *Chelmsf* from 97. *3 St Chad's Road, Chadwell Heath, Romford RM6 6JB* Tel 0181-597 2811

BAKER, David Clive. b 47. Sarum & Wells Th Coll 76. **d** 78 **p** 79. C Shirley *Birm* 78-82; P-in-c Croft *Linc* 82-83; R Wainfleet All SS w St Thos 82-83; P-in-c Wainfleet St Mary 82-83; R The Wainfleets and Croft 83-86; V Stirchley *Birm* 86-96; Perm to Offic from 97. *28 Minton Road, Minton Gardens, Coventry CV2 2XQ*

BAKER, David Frederick. b 32. Clifton Th Coll 67. **d** 69 **p** 70. C Bilton *Ripon* 69-71; C Heworth w Peasholme St Cuth *York* 71-75; V Sand Hutton w Gate and Upper Helmsley 75-77; P-in-c Bossall w Buttercrambe 75-77; V Sand Hutton 77-80; R Preston in Holderness 80; P-in-c Sproatley 80; R Preston and Sproatley in Holderness 80-89; C Topcliffe w Dalton and Dishforth 89; V Baldersby w Dalton, Dishforth etc 89-96; rtd 96. *Chinkoa, 15 Williamson Gardens, Ripon, N Yorkshire HG4 2QB*

BAKER, David John. b 27. LRAM50 GRSM51. Ely Th Coll 53. **d** 55 **p** 56. C Swanley St Mary *Roch* 55-58; C Guildf St Nic *Guildf* 58-63; Prec St Alb Abbey *St Alb* 63-67; P-in-c Colney St Pet 67-68; V 68-73; V Tattenham Corner and Burgh Heath *Guildf* 73-84; R Fetcham 84-96; rtd 96; Perm to Offic *Guildf* from 96. *1 Terra Cotta Court, Quennels Hill, Wrecclesham, Farnham, Surrey GU10 4SL* Tel (01252) 734202

BAKER, David Jordan. b 35. Univ of Wales (Lamp) BA59. Ely Th Coll 59. **d** 61 **p** 62. C Spalding *Linc* 61-66; C Gainsborough All SS 66-69; V Wrawby 69-78; V Melton Ross w New Barnetby 70-78; V Linc St Pet-at-Gowts and St Andr 78-94. *Fartherwell, The Paddock, Canwick, Lincoln LN4 2RX* Tel (01522) 526903

BAKER, Elsie. b 13. **dss** 38 **d** 87 **p** 94. Blackheath Ascension *S'wark* 68-83; NSM Lewisham St Swithun from 87. *24 Princes Rise, London SE13 7PP* Tel 0181-852 2169

BAKER, Frank Thomas. b 36. Selw Coll Cam BA61. Coll of Resurr Mirfield. **d** 63 **p** 64. C Mackworth St Fran *Derby* 63-66; C Leeds St Pet *Ripon* 66-73; P-in-c Stanley *Dur* 73-74; R Crook 73-74; Chapl Bucharest *Eur* 74-75; C Tewkesbury w Walton Cardiff *Glouc* 75-81; Min Can Windsor 81-86; rtd 86; Perm to Offic *Ox* from 86. *St Anne's House, Hatch Lane, Windsor, Berks SL4 3QP* Tel (01753) 865757

BAKER, Frederick Peter. b 24. Bps' Coll Cheshunt 58. **d** 60 **p** 61. C Peckham St Jude *S'wark* 60-63; C Mitcham St Mark 63-66; C Northampton St Pet w Upton *Pet* 66-69; P-in-c Northampton St Lawr 69-71; V Northampton St Edm 71-78; V Spratton 78-83; R Walgrave w Hannington and Wold 83-89; rtd 89. *1A Malvern Close, Bournemouth BH9 3BN* Tel (01202) 512862

BAKER, Geoffrey Gorton. b 26. Chich Th Coll 63. **d** 65 **p** 66. C Jersey St Mark *Win* 65-66; V 66-73; Lic to Offic from 73; Chapl HM Pris Jersey 80-91; rtd 91. *La Rousse, Le Bourg, St Clement, Jersey, Channel Islands JE2 6SP* Tel (01534) 854735

BAKER, Canon Gerald Stothert. b 30. Univ of NZ MA54. St Jo Coll Auckland LTh56. **d** 56 **p** 57. New Zealand 56-87 and from 92; Hon Can Wellington 80-87; TV Kidderminster St Mary and All SS w Trimpley etc *Worc* 87-92; rtd 95. *83 Kuratawhiti Street, Greytown, New Zealand* Tel Greytown (6) 304 8367

BAKER, Gillian Devonald. b 40. S Dios Minl Tr Scheme 88. **d** 91 **p** 94. NSM Redhorn *Sarum* from 91; Chapl HM Young Offender Inst Erlestoke Ho from 94. *11 The Street, Chirton, Devizes, Wilts SN10 3QS* Tel (01380) 848170

BAKER, The Very Revd Graham Brinkworth. b 26. AKC54. **d** 55 **p** 56. C Wandsworth St Anne *S'wark* 55-58; Canada from 58. *1280 Tracksell Avenue, Victoria, British Columbia, Canada, V8P 2C9*

BAKER, Harry Hallas. b 16. Bps' Coll Cheshunt 51. **d** 53 **p** 54. C Killingworth *Newc* 53-58; V Mickley 58-63; V Howdon Panns 63-73; C Alnwick St Mich 73-74; C Alnwick St Mich and St Paul 74-84; rtd 84. *16 Canongate, Alnwick, Northd NE66 1NE* Tel (01665) 604716

BAKER, Mrs Heather Elizabeth. b 48. W of England Minl Tr Course 94. **d** 97. NSM Ewyas Harold w Dulas, Kenderchurch etc *Heref* from 97. *Park Lodge, Rowlstone, Hereford HR2 0HE* Tel (01981) 240503 E-mail richard@parklodge.com

BAKER, Henry Blandford Benedict. b 26. Univ of NZ BA49 MA50. Coll of Resurr Mirfield 51. **d** 53 **p** 54. C New Mills *Derby* 53-56; New Zealand 56-57; CSWG 57-66; Father Superior 65-66; Perm to Offic *Chich* 81-86; R Beckington w Standerwick, Berkley, Rodden etc *B & W* 86-92; rtd 92. *Coed Glas, Talgarth Road, Bronllys, Brecon LD3 0HN* Tel (01874) 711964

BAKER, Henry Edward (Ted). b 09. Bris Univ BA31. Sarum Th Coll 31. **d** 32 **p** 33. C Swindon St Aug *Bris* 32-35; C Bedminster Down 35-38; V Hullavington 38-51; V Fishponds All SS 51-59; V Neston 59-66; V Bitton 66-69; C Kingswood 69-74; rtd 74. *26 Henley Court, Spencer Road, Lichfield, Staffs WS14 9AT* Tel (01543) 256520

BAKER, Ms Hilary Mary (Dilly). b 61. Man Univ BA83 Univ of Wales (Cardiff) CQSW86. Sarum & Wells Th Coll 86. **d** 89 **p** 94. Par Dn E Dulwich St Jo *S'wark* 89-92; Tutor Sarum & Wells Th Coll 92-94; TV Stantonbury and Willen *Ox* from 94. *The Vicarage, 2 Hooper Gate, Willen, Milton Keynes MK15 9JR* Tel (01908) 662092

BAKER, Hugh Crispin. b 58. Open Univ BA92. Linc Th Coll CMinlStuds95. **d** 95 **p** 96. C Birstall and Wanlip *Leic* from 95. *33 Walker Road, Birstall, Leicester LE4 4DJ* Tel 0116-267 7572

BAKER, Hugh John. b 46. Birm Univ BSocSc68 Nottm Univ DipTh69. Cuddesdon Coll 69. **d** 71 **p** 72. C Binley *Cov* 71-74; C Pemberton St Mark Newtown *Liv* 74-78; TV Sutton 78-90; V Fazeley *Lich* from 90; R Drayton Bassett from 90; V Canwell from 90; P-in-c Hints from 90. *St Paul's Vicarage, 9 West Drive, Bonehill, Tamworth, Staffs B78 3HR* Tel (01827) 287701

BAKER, Ivon Robert. b 28. St Aug Coll Cant 59. **d** 60 **p** 61. C Sutton in Ashfield St Mary *S'well* 60-62; V Gringley-on-the-Hill 62-94; Chapl HM Young Offender Inst Gringley 82-91; RD Bawtry *S'well* 85-90; rtd 94; Perm to Offic *York* from 94. *2 Willowgate, Pickering, N Yorkshire YO18 7BE*

BAKER, Canon James Henry. b 39. Lon Univ DipTh66. Kelham Th Coll 62. **d** 67 **p** 68. C Sheff Arbourthorne *Sheff* 67-70; C Pemberton St Jo *Liv* 70-71; Chapl and Prec St Mary's Cathl *Edin* 71-74; R Lochgelly *St And* 74-84; P-in-c Rosyth 76-84; P-in-c Inverkeithing 76-84; Can St Ninian's Cathl Perth 83-84; V Whitehaven *Carl* from 84; RD Calder from 96; Hon Can Carl Cathl from 96. *The Vicarage, Oakbank, Whitehaven, Cumbria CA28 6HY* Tel (01946) 692630 or 62572

BAKER, Jean Margaret. b 47. Sheff Univ BSc69 DipEd70 Lon Univ DipTh75 BD78. All Nations Chr Coll 75 Gilmore Course 81. **dss** 82 **d** 87 **p** 97. Liv Our Lady and St Nic w St Anne *Liv* 82-87; Chapl Huyton Coll 87; Chapl Sch of St Mary and St Anne Abbots Bromley 87-91; Chapl Howell's Sch Denbigh from 91. *9 Woodcroft Lane, Bebington, Wirral, Merseyside L63 8NL* Tel 0151-645 7934

BAKER, John Albert. b 29. St Edm Hall Ox BA52 MA56 Lon Univ BSc68 S Bank Poly MSc76. Cuddesdon Coll 52. **d** 54 **p** 55. C Battersea St Luke *S'wark* 54-58; Hon C from 84; C Richmond St Mary 58-62; V Battersea Park All SS 62-83; Tutor Roehampton Inst 83-91; rtd 94. *44 Wroughton Road, London SW11 6BG* Tel 0171-585 2492

✠**BAKER, The Rt Revd John Austin.** b 28. Or Coll Ox BA52 MA55 BLitt55 MLitt. Lambeth DD91 Cuddesdon Coll 52. **d** 54 **p** 55 **c** 82. C Cuddesdon *Ox* 54-57; Tutor Cuddesdon Coll 54-57; C Hatch End St Anselm *Lon* 57-59; Lect K Coll Lon 57-59; Chapl CCC Ox 59-73; Lect Th Ox Univ 59-73; Can Westmr Abbey 73-82; Sub-Dean Westmr 78-82; R Westmr St Marg 78-82; Chapl to Speaker of Ho of Commons 78-82; Bp Sarum 82-93; Can and Preb Sarum Cathl 82-93; rtd 93. *4 Mede Villas, Kingsgate Road, Winchester, Hants SO23 9QQ* Tel (01962) 861388

BAKER, John Carl. b 55. Chich Th Coll 77. **d** 80 **p** 81. C Wigan St Andr *Liv* 80-83; V Hollinfare 83-85; TV Seacroft *Ripon* 85-89; TV Bottesford w Ashby *Linc* 89-94; V Liv St Paul Stoneycroft *Liv* from 94. *St Paul's Vicarage, Carlton Lane, Liverpool L13 6QS* Tel 0151-228 1041

BAKER, John Reginald. b 62. Hatf Coll Dur BSc83. Wycliffe Hall Ox 86. **d** 89 **p** 90. C Amersham *Ox* 89-92; C Greenford H Cross *Lon* from 92. *St Edward's House, Medway Drive, Greenford, Middx UB6 8LN* Tel 0181-997 4953

BAKER, Jonathan Mark Richard. b 66. St Jo Coll Ox BA88 MPhil90. St Steph Ho Ox BA92. **d** 93 **p** 94. C Ascot Heath *Ox* 93-96; C Reading St Mark 96; P-in-c from 96. *Holy Trinity Presbytery, 31 Baker Street, Reading RG1 7XY* Tel 0118-957 2650

BAKER, Jonathan William. b 61. SS Coll Cam MA85. Wycliffe Hall Ox BA91. **d** 92 **p** 93. C Sanderstead All SS *S'wark* 92-96; P-in-c Scalby w Ravenscar and Staintondale *York* 96-97; P-in-c Hackness w Harwood Dale 96-97; V Scalby from 97; V Hackness w Harwood Dale from 97. *The Vicarage, Scalby, Scarborough, N Yorkshire YO13 0PS* Tel (01723) 362740

BAKER, Kenneth William. b 38. Nottm Univ DipThPS95. EMMTC 92. **d** 96 **p** 97. NSM Welford w Sibbertoft and Marston Trussell *Pet* from 96. *Homestead, The Green, Lilbourne, Rugby, Warks CV23 0SR* Tel (01788) 860120

BAKER, Canon Michael Robert Henry. b 39. Keele Univ MA88. Lich Th Coll 63. **d** 66 **p** 67. C Wellingborough All SS *Pet* 66-68; C Pet All SS 68-73; V Earls Barton 73-87; RD Wellingborough 76-87; P-in-c Gt Doddington 77-82; Can Pet Cathl from 85; TR Kingsthorpe w Northn St Dav 87-95; V Towcester w Easton Neston from 95. *The Vicarage, Towcester, Northants NN12 6AB* Tel (01327) 350459

BAKER, Michael William. b 38. Roch Th Coll 68. **d** 70 **p** 71. C Woodmansterne *S'wark* 70-75; TV Danbury *Chelmsf* 75-78; P-in-c Barrington *Ely* 78-90; V from 90; P-in-c Shepreth 78-90; V from 90. *The Vicarage, 4 Church Road, Shepreth, Royston, Herts SG8 6RG* Tel (01763) 260172

BAKER, Canon Neville Duff. b 35. St Aid Birkenhead 60. **d** 63 **p** 64. C Stranton *Dur* 63-66; C Houghton le Spring 66-68; V Tudhoe Grange from 68; RD Auckland 83-94; Hon Can Dur Cathl from 90; P-in-c Merrington 91-94. *St Andrew's Vicarage, Tudhoe Grange, Spennymoor, Co Durham DL16 6NE* Tel (01388) 814817

BAKER, Noel Edward Lloyd. b 37. Sarum & Wells Th Coll 73. **d** 75 **p** 76. C Charlton Kings St Mary *Glouc* 75-79; V Clearwell 79-81; R Eastington and Frocester 81-97; RD Stonehouse 90-94; P-in-c Eastington and Frocester from 97; P-in-c Standish w Haresfield and Moreton Valence etc from 97. *The Rectory, Mill End Lane, Eastington, Stonehouse, Glos GL10 3SG* Tel (01453) 822437

BAKER, Paul Anthony. b 64. St Chad's Coll Dur BA85. St Steph Ho Ox BA88. **d** 89 **p** 90. C Hartlepool St Aid *Dur* 89-93; TV Jarrow from 93. *St Mark's House, Randolph Street, Jarrow, Tyne & Wear NE32 3AQ* Tel 0191-483 2092

BAKER, Peter Colin. b 43. Sarum & Wells Th Coll. **d** 82 **p** 83. C Bridgemary *Portsm* 82-86; V Ash Vale *Guildf* from 86. *The Vicarage, 203 Vale Road, Ash Vale, Aldershot, Hants GU12 5JE* Tel (01252) 25295

BAKER, Peter Graham. b 55. MA PhD. St Steph Ho Ox. **d** 82 **p** 83. C Ches H Trin *Ches* 82-86; C Holborn St Alb w Saffron Hill St Pet *Lon* 86-91; V Golders Green 91-94; V Golders Green from 94; AD W Barnet from 95. *The Vicarage, 3 St Alban's Close, London NW11 7RA* Tel 0181-455 4525

BAKER, Canon Peter Malcolm. b 21. Lich Th Coll 40. **d** 43 **p** 45. C Bedminster St Aldhelm *Bris* 43-47; C Charlton Kings H Apostles *Glouc* 47-49; C Halesowen *Worc* 49-53; CF (TA) 53-75; V Dudley St Luke *Worc* 53-59; R Hindlip w Martin Hussingtree 59-67; V Inkberrow 67-75; P-in-c Kington w Dormston 74-75; R Inkberrow w Cookhill and Kington w Dormston 75-77; P-in-c Wilden 77-80; R Mamble w Bayton 80-82; RD Stourport 80-88; R Teme Valley N 82-88; Hon Can Worc Cathl 84-88; Perm to Offic *Heref* from 88; rtd 88. *The Ryelands, Menith Wood, Worcester WR6 6UG* Tel (01584) 881227

BAKER, Robert John Kenneth. b 50. MICE79 Southn Univ BSc71. Oak Hill Th Coll 88. **d** 90 **p** 91. C Cromer *Nor* 90-94; P-in-c Pakefield 94; R from 94. *The Rectory, Pakefield, Lowestoft, Suffolk NR33 0JZ* Tel (01502) 574040

BAKER, Canon Robert Mark. b 50. Bris Univ BA73. St Jo Coll Nottm 74. **d** 76 **p** 77. C Portswood Ch Ch *Win* 76-80; R Witton w Brundall and Braydeston *Nor* 80-89; P-in-c Buckenham w Hassingham and Strumpshaw 80-86; R Brundall w Braydeston and Postwick from 89; RD Blofield 89-94; Hon Can Nor Cathl from 93. *The Rectory, 73 The Street, Brundall, Norwich NR13 5LZ* Tel (01603) 715136

BAKER, Canon Robin Henry. b 31. Man Univ BA52. Cuddesdon Coll 54. **d** 56 **p** 57. C Swinton St Pet *Man* 56-59; C Birch St Jas 59-61; R Stretford All SS 61-66; Chapl High Royds Hosp Menston 66-72; P-in-c Simpson w Woughton on the Green *Ox* 72-73; P-in-c Woughton 74; TR 74-79; RD Milton Keynes 78-86; C-in-c Milton Keynes City Cen 79-80; V Milton Keynes 80-86; Hon Can Ch Ch 84-91; TR Banbury 86-91; P-in-c Scorton *Blackb* 91-96; Bp's Adv on Healing 91-96; rtd 96. *5 Calluna Mews, Palantine Road, Manchester M20 3BF* Tel 0161-446 1268

BAKER, Ronald Harry. b 21. Ely Th Coll 62. **d** 64 **p** 65. C Crediton *Ex* 64-66; R Thornbury 66-73; R Bradford 67-73; R Black Torrington, Bradf and Thornbury 73-77; P-in-c Broadhempston and Woodland 77-78; P-in-c Lt Hempston 77-78; P-in-c Berry Pomeroy 77-78; V Broadhempston, Woodland, Berry Pomeroy etc 78-86; rtd 86; Chapl Marseille w St Raphael Aix-en-Provence etc *Eur* 87-88; Perm to Offic *Ex* from 88. *95 Barton Avenue, Paignton, Devon TQ3 3HY* Tel (01803) 557462

BAKER, Ronald Kenneth (<u>Ron</u>). b 43. Open Univ BA80 LTh. St Jo Coll Nottm 85. **d** 87 **p** 88. C Paddock Wood *Roch* 87-90; V Ramsgate St Mark *Cant* 90-95; P-in-c Ewhurst *Chich* from 95; P-in-c Bodiam from 95. *The Rectory, Ewhurst Green, Robertsbridge, E Sussex TN32 5TB* Tel (01580) 830268

BAKER, Roy David. b 36. Lon Univ DipTh61. St Aid Birkenhead 59. **d** 62 **p** 63. C Garston *Liv* 62-64; C N Meols 64-68; V Newton-le-Willows 68-73; V Crossens 73-82; V Blundellsands St Nic from 82. *St Nicholas' Vicarage, Nicholas Road, Blundellsands, Liverpool L23 6TS* Tel 0151-924 3551

BAKER, Simon Nicholas Hartland. b 57. K Coll Lon BD78 Trin Hall Cam DipTh79. Qu Coll Birm 79. **d** 81 **p** 82. C Tupsley *Heref* 81-85; V Shinfield *Ox* from 85; Prin Berks Chr Tr Scheme from 93. *The Vicarage, Church Lane, Shinfield, Reading RG2 9BY* Tel 0118-988 3363

BAKER, Stephen Anthony. b 55. St Luke's Coll Ex BEd80. Sarum & Wells Th Coll 88. **d** 91 **p** 92. C Guildf H Trin w St Mary *Guildf* 91-97; Chapl Guildf Coll of Tech 91-97; Chapl Eliz Coll Guernsey from 97. *Elizabeth College, Grange Road, St Peter Port, Guernsey GY1 2PY* Tel (01481) 726544

BAKER, Stuart. b 44. MATA63 AIAT65. Spurgeon's Coll DipTh71 Bapt Tr Coll DipMin75 Ripon Coll Cuddesdon 92. **d** 93 **p** 94. C Whitchurch *Bris* 93-97; R Brightling, Dallington, Mountfield etc *Chich* from 97. *The Rectory, Brightling, Robertsbridge, E Sussex TN32 5HE* Tel (01424) 838281

BAKER, The Very Revd Thomas George Adames. b 20. Ex Coll Ox BA43 MA50. Linc Th Coll 43. **d** 44 **p** 45. C Kings Heath *Birm* 44-47; V Edgbaston St Jas 47-54; Sub-Warden Linc Th Coll 54-60; Lic to Offic *Linc* 54-60; Can Th Leic Cathl *Leic* 59-66; Preb Wells Cathl *B & W* 60-71; Prin Wells Th Coll 60-71; Adn Bath and Preb Wells Cathl *B & W* 71-75; Dean Worc 75-86; rtd 86; Perm to Offic *B & W* 86-94. *Charterhouse, Charterhouse Square, London EC1M 6AN* Tel 0171-250 3578

BAKER, Walter Donald. b 06. FRSA LTCL. St Aid Birkenhead 42. **d** 44 **p** 45. C Preston St Thos *Blackb* 44-46; R Elsing w Bylaugh *Nor* 46-50; R Lammas w Lt Hautbois 50-54; V Scottow 50-54; R Blankney *Linc* 54-58; V Old Ford St Paul w St Steph *Lon* 58-64; R Hanwell St Mary 64-68; V Upper Holloway St Steph 69-80; rtd 80; Hon C St Jas Garlickhythe w St Mich Queenhithe etc *Lon* from 80. *Charterhouse, Charterhouse Square, London EC1M 6AH* Tel 0171-253 2728

BAKER, William Alfred Douglas. b 21. Lon Univ BSc52 MSc56. Qu Coll Birm 72. **d** 75 **p** 76. Hon C Bridgnorth w Tasley *Heref* 75-78; Hon C Bridgnorth, Tasley, Astley Abbotts, Oldbury etc from 78. *Oaklea, Astley Abbotts, Bridgnorth, Shropshire WV16 4SW* Tel (01746) 762980

BAKER, William Douglas Willson. b 19. Linc Th Coll 79. **d** 80 **p** 81. NSM Mablethorpe w Trusthorpe *Linc* 80-84; NSM Sutton le Marsh 84-90; NSM Sutton, Huttoft and Anderby 90-94; Perm to Offic from 94. *7 Grove Road, Sutton-on-Sea, Mablethorpe, Lincs LN12 2LP* Tel (01507) 441506

BAKER, William George. b 07. St Cath Coll Ox BA37 MA42. **d** 38 **p** 42. C Swinton *Sheff* 38-42; C Mount Pellon *Wakef* 42-45; C Sutton in Ashfield St Mary *S'well* 45-47; C Kirkburton *Wakef* 47-53; V Moreton *Lich* 53-76; rtd 76. *Fidelis, 39 Lime Tree Road, Matlock, Derbyshire DE4 3EJ* Tel (01629) 582717

BAKER, William John (<u>Bill</u>). b 45. FCII80. Cranmer Hall Dur 87. **d** 89 **p** 90. C Sale St Anne *Ches* 89-93; V Crewe St Andr 93-94; P-in-c Crewe St Jo 93-94; V Crewe St Andr w St Jo from 94. *St John's Vicarage, 14 Dane Bank Avenue, Crewe CW2 8AA* Tel (01270) 69000

BAKERE, The Very Revd Ronald Duncan. b 35. TCD BA58 HDipEd60 MA61 BD62 Ch Ch Ox MA66 FRSA68 FBIM79. CITC 59. **d** 59 **p** 60. C Knockbreda *D & D* 59-61; C Dublin Zion Ch *D & G* 61-63; Min Can St Patr Cathl Dublin 62-64; CF (TA) 65-67; Lect Th Plymouth Univ 67-72; Nigeria 73-77; Cen Org Ex Red Cross 78-81; Perm to Offic *Ex* 82-85; P-in-c Chew Magna w Dundry *B & W* 86-87; Hd Relig Studies Sir Jo Cass Foundn Lon 88-93; Perm to Offic *Lon* 88-93; Dean Port Moresby 93-96; ChStJ from 95; rtd 96. *12 Dumbarton Road, London SW2 5LU* Tel 0171-265 0296

BALCH, John <u>Robin</u>. b 37. Lon Univ BSc61 Bris Univ CertEd62. ALCD68. **d** 68 **p** 69. C Bath Walcot *B & W* 68-71; C Fulwood *Sheff* 71-76; V Erith St Paul *Roch* 76-93; RD Erith 90-93; P-in-c Fairlight *Chich* 93-94; R Fairlight, Guestling and Pett from 94. *The Rectory, Pett, Hastings, E Sussex TN35 4HG* Tel (01424) 813234

BALCHIN, Michael John. b 38. Selw Coll Cam BA60 MA64. Wells Th Coll 60. **d** 62 **p** 63. C Bournemouth H Epiphany *Win* 62-65; C Bris St Mary Redcliffe w Temple etc *Bris* 65-69; R Norton sub Hamdon *B & W* 69-70; P-in-c Chiselborough w W Chinnock 69-70; R Norton sub Hamdon w Chiselborough 70-77; P-in-c Chipstable w Huish Champflower and Clatworthy 77-82; R 82-88; Rural Affairs Officer 87-88; Perm to Offic *Ban* from 88. *Glyntwymyn, Commins Coch, Machynlleth SY20 8LS* Tel (01650) 511659

BALDOCK, Charles William Martin. b 52. Nottm Univ BPharm73. St Jo Coll Nottm LTh. **d** 85 **p** 86. C Nailsea Ch Ch *B & W* 85-89; V Brampton Bierlow *Sheff* from 89; RD Wath from 95. *The Vicarage, Christchurch Road, Wath-upon-Dearne, Rotherham, S Yorkshire S63 6NW* Tel (01709) 873210

BALDOCK, Canon Norman. b 29. K Coll Lon BD52 AKC52. **d** 53 **p** 54. C Cant St Pet w H Cross *Cant* 53-54; C Thornton Heath St Jude 54-58; V Ash w W Marsh 58-67; V Sheerness H Trin w St Paul 67-75; V Margate St Jo 75-94; RD Thanet 80-86; Hon Can Cant Cathl 82-94; Chapl Margate Gen Hosp 82-94; rtd 94;

Lic to Offic *Cant* from 94. *9 Beach Avenue, Birchington, Kent CT7 9VS* Tel (01843) 841173

BALDOCK, Reginald David. b 48. Oak Hill Th Coll 72. **d** 75 **p** 76. C Plymouth St Jude *Ex* 75-79; C Ardsley *Sheff* 79-85; V Rawthorpe *Wakef* 85-96; C Salterhebble All SS from 96. *41 Gibraltar Road, Halifax, W Yorkshire HX1 4HE* Tel (01422) 354448

BALDRY, John Netherway. b 19. Lon Univ BA53. **d** 79 **p** 80. Hon C Brighton St Paul *Chich* from 79. *26 Braybon Avenue, Brighton BN1 8HG* Tel (01273) 501268

BALDRY, Ralph Yorke. b 18. St Jo Coll Ox BA40 MA44. Wycliffe Hall Ox 40. **d** 41 **p** 42. C Southall H Trin *Lon* 41-45; C Oakwood St Thos 45-47; V Clay Hill St Jo 47-52; V Stonebridge St Mich 52-58; V Finchley St Luke 64-72; V Golders Green St Alb 72-80; P-in-c Golders Green St Mich 77-80; V Golders Green 80-83; rtd 84; Perm to Offic *Lon* from 84. *159 Falloden Way, London NW11 6LG* Tel 0181-455 6926

BALDWICK, Frank Eric. b 24. Ripon Hall Ox 54. **d** 55 **p** 56. C Newark Ch Ch *S'well* 55-58; C Hawton 55-58; C W Bridgford 58-60; V Oldham St Barn *Man* 60-65; R Gt Lever 65-78; V Hindsford 78-81; TV Clifton *S'well* 81-89; rtd 89; Perm to Offic *S'well* from 89. *35 Ladybay Road, Nottingham NG2 5BJ* Tel 0115-982 1273

BALDWIN, David Frederick Beresford. b 57. Wolv Univ 91. Ripon Coll Cuddesdon DipMin95. **d** 95 **p** 96. C Uttoxeter w Bramshall *Lich* 95-97; C Uttoxeter Area from 97. *5 Beech Close, Uttoxeter, Staffs ST14 7DZ* Tel (01889) 567677

BALDWIN, Derek Wilfred Walter. b 23. Lon Univ LTh74. ALCD56. **d** 52 **p** 53. C Sheff Sharrow *Sheff* 52-54; C Woodlands 54-56; V Shepley *Wakef* 56-59; V Earl's Heaton 59-66; Org Sec (Dios B & W, Ex and Truro) CECS 66-72; Lic to Offic *Ex* 67-72; R Morchard Bishop 72-73; Org Sec (Dios St Alb and Ox) CECS 73-77; C Portishead *B & W* 77-79; R Wymondham w Edmondthorpe *Leic* 79-80; P-in-c St Mewan *Truro* 80-81; V Crowan w Godolphin 81-83; C Cockington *Ex* 83-87; rtd 87; Perm to Offic *Ex* from 90. *Belfry Cottage, Sidmouth, Devon EX10 8SY*

BALDWIN, Dr John Charles. b 39. FBCS CEng Bris Univ BSc61 Sussex Univ DPhil65. St Steph Ho Ox 82. **d** 83 **p** 84. C Llan w Capel Llanilltern *Llan* 83-90; R Ewenny w St Brides Major 90-92; Lic to Offic from 92; Hon Chapl Llan Cathl from 96. *39 Cathedral Road, Cardiff CF1 9XF, or 60 Llantrisant Road, Llandaff, Cardiff CF5 2PX* Tel (01222) 231638 or 560081 Fax 387835 E-mail johnbaldwin@rb.churchinwales.org.uk

BALDWIN, Jonathan Michael. b 58. Chich Th Coll 92. **d** 94 **p** 95. C Crawley *Chich* 94-96; C New Shoreham from 96; C Old Shoreham from 96. *17 Colvill Avenue, Shoreham-by-Sea, W Sussex BN43 5WN* Tel (01273) 464528

BALDWIN, Peter Alan. b 48. Bede Coll Dur BA70 Birm Univ DipTh72. Qu Coll Birm 72. **d** 73 **p** 74. C Hartlepool St Oswald *Dur* 73-75; C Darlington H Trin 75-78; OGS from 77; C-in-c Bishop Auckland Woodhouse Close CD *Dur* 78-82; V Ferryhill 82-88; P-in-c Charlestown *Man* 88-89; V Pendleton St Thos 88-89; TR Pendleton St Thos w Charlestown 89-90; TR Newton Aycliffe *Dur* 90-96; TR Gt Aycliffe 96-97; RD Sedgefield from 96; V The Trimdons from 97. *The Vicarage, Trimdon Grange, Trimdon Station, Co Durham TS29 6EX* Tel (01429) 880872

BALDWIN, William. b 48. RMN73 FRSH83. NW Ord Course 75. **d** 78 **p** 79. C Royton St Anne *Man* 78-82; V Halliwell St Thos 82-87; TR Atherton from 87; OStJ from 88. *Atherton Rectory, Bee Fold Lane, Atherton, Manchester M29 0BL* Tel (01942) 874666

BALE, Edward William Carre. b 22. ABAF74 AKC55 Leic Univ DSRS67. **d** 55 **p** 56. C Mansfield St Pet *S'well* 55-59; C Corby St Jo *Pet* 59-61; R Corby SS Pet and Andr 61-69; V Wollaston and Strixton 69-87; rtd 88; Perm to Offic *Ox* from 88; Perm to Offic *Pet* 89-94. *27 The Crescent, Haversham, Milton Keynes MK19 7AN* Tel (01234) 391443

BALE, James Henry. b 30. St Pet Hall Ox BA53 DipEd54 MA57. Oak Hill Th Coll 56. **d** 58 **p** 59. C Walcot St Sav *B & W* 58-61; C Kinson *Sarum* 61-64; Ethiopia 65-71; Hon C Taunton H Trin *B & W* 71-72; Kingsmead Sch Hoylake 72-75; Hon C Upton (Overchurch) *Ches* 72-75; Dep Hd Thornton Sch Ayrshire 76-89; Hon C Prestwick *Glas* 76-89; Brazil 89-95; rtd 95; Perm to Offic *Glas* from 96. *Flat 3, 16 Ardayre Road, Prestwick, Ayrshire KA9 1QL* Tel (01292) 474880

BALE, Kenneth John. b 34. Univ of Wales (Lamp) BA58. Qu Coll Birm DipTh60. **d** 60 **p** 61. C Mitcham St Olave *S'wark* 60-63; C Warlingham w Chelsham and Farleigh 63-67; V Battersea Rise St Mark 67-85; Perm to Offic 85-88; Hon C Balham St Mary and St Jo 88-90; V S Wimbledon All SS from 90; Dioc Adv Min of Healing from 91. *All Saints' Vicarage, De Burgh Road, London SW19 1DX* Tel 0181-542 5514

BALFOUR, Andrew Crispin Roxburgh. b 49. Coll of Resurr Mirfield 93. **d** 95 **p** 96. C S Lafford *Linc* from 95. *The Vicarage, 1 The Drove, Osbournby, Sleaford, Lincs NG34 0DH* Tel (01529) 455630

BALFOUR, Hugh Rowlatt. b 54. SS Coll Cam BA76. Ridley Hall Cam 78. **d** 81 **p** 82. C Bedford Ch Ch *St Alb* 81-86; P-in-c Camberwell Ch Ch *S'wark* 86-90; V from 90. *Christ Church Vicarage, 79 Asylum Road, London SE15 2RJ* Tel 0171-639 5662

BALFOUR, Mrs Penelope Mary (Penny). b 47. St Andr Univ MA69 St Jo Coll York DipEd72. Coates Hall Edin 89 St Jo Coll Nottm 84. **d** 88 **p** 95. C Dundee St Marg *Bre* 88-94; Dioc AIDS Officer 90-94; NSM Invergowrie 94-96; Chapl Abertay Univ from 94; C Dundee St Marg from 96. *10 Strathaird Place, Dundee DD2 4TN* Tel (01382) 643114

BALKWILL, Michael Robert. b 67. Univ of Wales (Lamp) BD89 Univ of Wales (Cardiff) DPS90 MTh92. St Mich Coll Llan 89 Bp Tucker Coll Mukono 91. **d** 91 **p** 92. C Llanrhos *St As* 91-97; Dioc RE Adv from 94; R Llanfyllin and Bwlchycibau from 97. *The Rectory, Coed Llan Lane, Llanfyllin SY22 5BW* Tel (01691) 648306

BALKWILL, Roger Bruce. b 41. Univ of Wales DipTh64 DPS66. St Mich Coll Llan 61. **d** 64 **p** 65. C Llantrisant *Llan* 64-68; C Caerphilly 68-73; Rhodesia 73-76; P-in-c Ilam w Blore Ray and Okeover *Lich* 76-81; P-in-c Albrighton 81-82; V from 82; P-in-c Beckbury 89-90; P-in-c Badger 89-90; P-in-c Ryton 89-90; P-in-c Kemberton, Sutton Maddock and Stockton 89-90; RD Shifnal from 89. *The Vicarage, High Street, Albrighton, Wolverhampton WV7 3EQ* Tel (01902) 372701

BALL, Alan. b 26. Qu Coll Birm 72. **d** 75 **p** 75. NSM Hamstead St Paul *Birm* 75-93; rtd 93. *23 Tebourba Drive, Sovereign Green, Alverstoke, Gosport, Hants PO12 2NT* Tel (01705) 601694

BALL, Andrew Thomas. b 54. K Coll Lon BD75 AKC75. Sarum & Wells Th Coll 76. **d** 77 **p** 78. C Ribbleton *Blackb* 77-80; C Sedgley All SS *Lich* 80-84; V Pheasey 84-90; Chapl Gd Hope Distr Gen Hosp Sutton Coldfield 90-94; Chapl Gd Hope Hosp NHS Trust Sutton Coldfield from 94. *Chaplain's Office, Good Hope Hospital, Rectory Road, Sutton Coldfield, W Midlands B75 7RR* Tel 0121-378 2211

BALL, Anthony Charles. b 46. Lon Univ BD71. Chich Th Coll 72. **d** 73 **p** 74. C Heref St Martin *Heref* 73-76; C Ealing St Pet Mt Park *Lon* 76-82; V Ruislip Manor St Paul from 82. *St Paul's Vicarage, Thurlstone Road, Ruislip, Middx HA4 0BP* Tel (01895) 633499

BALL, Anthony Michael (Tony). b 46. Kelham Th Coll 66. **d** 70 **p** 71. C Kingswinford St Mary *Lich* 70-74; C W Bromwich All SS 74-76; P-in-c Priorslee 76-80; V 80-82; Asst Chapl HM Pris Liv 82-83; Chapl 88-95; Chapl HM Pris Lewes 83-88; Chapl HM Pris Featherstone from 95. *HM Prison, New Road, Featherstone, Wolverhampton WV10 7PN* Tel (01902) 790991

BALL, Christopher Rowland. b 40. Wycliffe Hall Ox. **d** 82 **p** 83. C Heysham *Blackb* 82-86; TV Swanborough *Sarum* 86-90; R Llanyblodwel and Trefonen *Lich* from 90. *The Rectory, School Lane, Trefonen, Oswestry, Shropshire SY10 9DY* Tel (01691) 654184

BALL, Canon Frank. b 21. Leeds Univ BA47. Coll of Resurr Mirfield 46. **d** 48 **p** 49. C Shiregreen St Hilda *Sheff* 48-50; C Attercliffe w Carbrook 50-53; V Handsworth Woodhouse 53-61; V Sheff Norwood St Leon 61-87; RD Ecclesfield 80-87; Hon Can Sheff Cathl 85-93; rtd 87; Gov and Chapl Shrewsbury Hosp Sheff 87-93; Perm to Offic *Sheff* from 93. *40 Seagrave Road, Sheffield S12 2JS* Tel 0114-264 4931

BALL, Geoffrey Williams. b 32. FLIA80 FInstSMM81. SW Minl Tr Course 82. **d** 85 **p** 86. NSM Sampford Spiney w Horrabridge *Ex* 85-87; TV Yelverton, Meavy, Sheepstor and Walkhampton 87-91; V Marystowe, Coryton, Stowford, Lewtrenchard etc from 91. *The Rectory, Lewdown, Okehampton, Devon EX20 4NU* Tel (01566) 783493

BALL, George Raymond. b 15. Univ of Wales (Lamp) BA40. St Mich Coll Llan 40. **d** 42 **p** 43. C Llansamlet *S & B* 42-46; C Swansea St Nic 46-50; R Bosherston w St Twynells *St D* 50-85; rtd 85. *1 Meadow Bank, St Twynnells, Pembroke SA71 5HZ* Tel (01646) 661432

BALL, Glynne Howell James. b 47. ACIS DMA. Llan Dioc Tr Scheme. **d** 90 **p** 91. NSM Llangynwyd w Maesteg *Llan* 90-95; NSM Tonyrefail w Gilfach Goch 96; C 96-97; C Tonyrefail w Gilfach Goch and Llandyfodwg from 97. *The Vicarage, 102 High Street, Gilfach Goch, Porth CF39 8SN*

BALL, Ian Raymond. b 45. CertEd Univ of Wales MPhil. Glouc Th Course 81. **d** 85 **p** 87. NSM Churchstoke w Hyssington and Sarn *Heref* from 85; Lic to Bp Ludlow from 87; Lic to Offic *St As* from 93. *Bachaethlon Cottage, Sarn, Newtown SY16 4HH* Tel (01686) 670505 Fax as telephone

BALL, John Kenneth. b 42. Lon Univ BSc64 AKC64. Linc Th Coll 69. **d** 71 **p** 72. C Garston *Liv* 71-74; C Eastham *Ches* 74-75; C Barnston 75-77; V Over St Jo 77-82; V Helsby and Dunham-on-the-Hill 82-94; RD Frodsham 88-94; P-in-c Alvanley 92-94; V Hoylake from 94. *The Vicarage, Stanley Road, Hoylake, Wirral, Merseyside L47 1HW* Tel 0151-632 3897

✠**BALL, The Rt Revd John Martin.** b 34. Univ of Wales BA55. Tyndale Hall Bris. **d** 59 **p** 60 **c** 95. C Blackb St Jude *Blackb* 59-63; Kenya 63-79; Dep Gen Sec BCMS 79-81; Gen Sec 81-93; Gen Sec Crosslinks 93-95; Hon C Sidcup Ch Ch *Roch* 81-95; Hon Can Karamoja from 88; Asst Bp Tanzania from 95. *PO Box 15, Dodoma, Tanzania* Tel Dodoma (61) 23025 or 21777

BALL, John Roy. b 47. Fitzw Coll Cam MA71. Wycliffe Hall Ox 83. **d** 85 **p** 86. C Stockport St Mary *Ches* 85-88; C Fazeley *Lich* 88-94; Res Min Drayton Bassett 89-94; Chapl Grenoble *Eur* from 94. *34 Quai de France, 3800 Grenoble, France* Tel France (33) 76 85 46 07

BALL, Jonathan. b 63. BNC Ox BA85 Leeds Univ BA87. Coll of Resurr Mirfield 85. **d** 88 **p** 89. C Blakenall Heath *Lich* 88-92; TV Rugeley 92-96; CF from 96. *MOD Chaplains (Army), Trenchard Lines, Upavon, Pewsey, Wilts SN9 6BE* Tel (01980) 615804 Fax 615800

BALL, Kevin Harry. b 55. Linc Th Coll 92. **d** 94 **p** 95. C New Mills *Derby* 94-96; C Walthamstow St Sav *Chelmsf* from 96. *212 Markhouse Road, London E17 8EP* Tel 0181-556 4912

✠**BALL, The Rt Revd Michael Thomas.** b 32. Qu Coll Cam BA55 MA59. **d** 71 **p** 71 **c** 80. CGA from 60; Prior Stroud Priory 64-76; C Whiteshill *Glouc* 71-76; Lic to Offic 76; P-in-c Stanmer w Falmer *Chich* 76-80; Chapl Sussex Univ 76-80; Suff Bp Jarrow *Dur* 80-90; Angl Adv Tyne Tees TV 84-90; Bp Truro 90-97; rtd 97. *Southdowns, King Harry Road, Feock, Truro, Cornwall TR3 6HD*

BALL, Nicholas Edward. b 54. Man Univ BA75 Ox Univ MA85. Ripon Coll Cuddesdon 79. **d** 80 **p** 81. C Yardley Wood *Birm* 80-83; C Moseley St Mary 83-86; Chapl Cen 13 83-85; V Bartley Green 86-95; P-in-c Hall Green St Pet 95-97. *St Peter's Vicarage, 33 Paradise Lane, Birmingham B28 0DY* Tel 0121-777 1935

BALL, Norman. b 41. Liv Univ BA63. Cuddesdon Coll 67. **d** 68 **p** 69. C Broseley w Benthall *Heref* 68-72; Lic to Offic *Ches* 72-75; V Plemstall w Guilden Sutton 75-79; Perm to Offic 79-88; NSM Dodleston 88-94; TV Hawarden *St As* from 94. *White Cottage, Lower Mountain Road, Penyffordd, Chester CH4 0EX* Tel (01244) 661132

BALL, Peter Edwin. b 44. Lon Univ BD65 DipEd. Wycliffe Hall Ox 75. **d** 77 **p** 78. C Prescot *Liv* 77-80; R Lawford *Chelmsf* from 80; RD Harwich 91-96. *The Rectory, Church Hill, Lawford, Manningtree, Essex CO11 2JX* Tel (01206) 392659

✠**BALL, The Rt Revd Peter John.** b 32. Qu Coll Cam BA54 MA58. Wells Th Coll 54. **d** 56 **p** 57 **c** 77. C Rottingdean *Chich* 56-58; Novice SSM 58-60; CGA from 60; Prior CGA 60-77; Lic to Offic *Birm* 65-66; P-in-c Hoar Cross *Lich* 66-69; Lic to Offic *B & W* 69-77; Suff Bp Lewes *Chich* 77-84; Area Bp Lewes 84-92; Can and Preb Chich Cathl 78-92; Bp Glouc 92-93; rtd 93. *Southdowns, King Harry Road, Feock, Truro, Cornwall TR3 6HD*

BALL, Canon Peter Prior. b 25. St Jo Coll Ox BA50 MA55. Ridley Hall Cam 51. **d** 53 **p** 54. C Gt Baddow *Chelmsf* 53-56; C Farnborough *Guildf* 56-60; Chapl RN 60-76; Chapl Cannes *Eur* 76-80; Visiting Chapl (Eur & N Africa) Intercon Ch Soc 80-86; Eur Rep SOMA from 86; rtd 90; Hon Can Malta Cathl *Eur* from 91. *Chateau d'Azur, 44 Boulevard d'Italie, Monte Carlo MC98000, Monaco* Tel Monaco (3393) 303079

BALL, Canon Peter William. b 30. Worc Coll Ox BA53 MA57. Cuddesdon Coll 53. **d** 55 **p** 56. C Poplar All SS w St Frideswide *Lon* 55-61; V Preston Ascension 61-68; R Shepperton 68-84; RD Staines 72-74; RD Spelthorne 74-83; Preb St Paul's Cathl 76-84; Can Res and Chan 84-90; Perm to Offic *Sarum* from 90; rtd 95. *Whittonedge, Whittonditch Road, Ramsbury, Marlborough, Wilts SN8 2PX* Tel (01672) 20259

BALL, Philip John. b 52. Bris Univ BEd75. Ripon Coll Cuddesdon 79. **d** 82 **p** 83. C Norton St Mich *Dur* 82-84; C Greenford H Cross *Lon* 84-88; V Hayes St Edm from 88; AD Hillingdon from 94. *St Edmund's Vicarage, 1 Edmund's Close, Hayes, Middx UB4 0HA* Tel 0181-573 6913

BALL, Timothy William. b 60. Trin Coll Bris 96. **d** 96 **p** 97. C Harlow St Mary and St Hugh w St Jo the Bapt *Chelmsf* from 96. *134 East Park, Harlow, Essex CM17 0SR* Tel (01279) 427357

BALL, Vernon. b 34. Ox Min Course 87. **d** 90 **p** 91. NSM Banbury *Ox* from 90. *15 Crouch Street, Banbury, Oxon OX16 9PP* Tel (01295) 259839

BALLAMAN, Ms Pauline Margaret. b 54. Golds Coll Lon BA89 Lon Univ MA90. Oak Hill Th Coll 93 Ridley Hall Cam CTM95. **d** 95 **p** 96. C New Addington *S'wark* from 95. *126 Fairchildes Avenue, New Addington, Croydon CR0 0AN*

BALLANTINE, Peter Sinclair. b 46. Nottm Univ MTh85. K Coll Lon BA68 AKC68 St Jo Coll Nottm 70 Lon Coll of Div ALCD71 BD73 LTh74. **d** 73 **p** 74. C Rainham *Chelmsf* 73-77; C Wennington 73-77; TV Barton Mills *St E* 77-80; TV Barton Mills, Beck Row w Kenny Hill etc 80-82; Chapl Liv Poly *Liv* 83-86; Tr Officer Rugby Deanery *Cov* 86-97; P-in-c Churchover w Willey 86-97; P-in-c Clifton upon Dunsmore and Newton 86-97; Dir Buckm Adnry Chr Tr Sch *Ox* from 97. *175 Dashwood Avenue, High Wycombe, Bucks HP12 3DB* Tel (01494) 474996

BALLANTINE, Roderic Keith. b 44. Chich Th Coll 66. **d** 69 **p** 70. C Nunhead St Antony *S'wark* 69-72; C S Hackney St Jo w Ch Ch *Lon* 72-75; P-in-c Kensal Town St Thos w St Andr and St Phil 75-79; V Stoke Newington St Andr from 79. *St Andrew's Vicarage, 106 Bethune Road, London N16 5DU* Tel 0181-800 2900

BALLANTYNE, Jane Elizabeth. *See* KENCHINGTON, Mrs Jane Elizabeth Ballantyne

BALLARD, Andrew Edgar. b 44. Dur Univ BA66. Westcott Ho Cam 66. **d** 68 **p** 69. C St Marylebone St Mary *Lon* 68-72; C Portsea St Mary *Portsm* 72-76; V Haslingden w Haslingden Grane *Blackb* 76-82; V Walkden Moor *Man* 82-93; TR Walkden Moor w Lt Hulton from 93; Chapl Salford Coll 82-92; AD Farnworth *Man* from 90. *St Paul's Vicarage, Manchester Road, Worsley, Manchester M28 5LN* Tel 0161-790 2483

BALLARD, Miss Anne Christina. b 54. LRAM76 Hon RCM93 ARAM94. Wycliffe Hall Ox 82. **dss** 85 **d** 87 **p** 94. Hove Bp Hannington Memorial Ch *Chich* 85-87; Chapl St Mich Sch Burton Park 87-89; Chapl RCM *Lon* 89-93; Chapl Imp Coll 89-93; Prec Ch Ch *Ox* from 93. *Christ Church, Oxford OX1 1DP* Tel (01865) 276214 Fax as telephone

BALLARD, Anthony James. EMMTC 86. **d** 89 **p** 90. Hon Chapl Woodbank Gr Sch Leic from 89; Hon C Clarendon Park St Jo w Knighton St Mich *Leic* from 89. *Flat 7, 51 Evington Road, Leicester LE2 1QG* Tel 0116-255 8086

BALLARD, Charles Martin. b 29. Jes Coll Cam BA52 MA56. **d** 58 **p** 59. C Doncaster St Geo *Sheff* 58-61; V Balne 61-62; rtd 94. *35 Abbey Road, Cambridge CB5 8HH*

BALLARD, Canon Michael Arthur. b 44. Lon Univ BA66. Westcott Ho Cam 68. **d** 70 **p** 71. C Harrow Weald All SS *Lon* 70-73; C Aylesbury *Ox* 73-78; V Eastwood *Chelmsf* 78-90; RD Hadleigh 83-90; Hon Can Chelmsf Cathl from 89; R Southchurch H Trin from 90; RD Southend-on-Sea from 94. *The Rectory, 8 Pilgrims Close, Southend-on-Sea SS2 4XF* Tel (01702) 466423

BALLARD, Nigel Humphrey. b 48. Linc Th Coll 92. **d** 94 **p** 95. C Old Brumby *Linc* 94; C Bottesford w Ashby from 94. *111 Ashby High Street, Scunthorpe, S Humberside DN16 2JX* Tel (01724) 860573

BALLARD, Peter James. b 55. SS Hild & Bede Coll Dur BEd78 Lon Univ DipTh85. Sarum & Wells Th Coll 85. **d** 87 **p** 88. C Grantham *Linc* 87-90 and 91; Australia 90; V Lancaster Ch Ch w St Jo and St Anne *Blackb* from 91; RD Lancaster from 94. *Christ Church Vicarage, 1 East Road, Lancaster LA1 3EE* Tel (01524) 34430

BALLARD, Richard Ernest. b 37. Linc Coll Ox BA60 MA66 Lon Univ BD68. Wells Th Coll 60. **d** 62 **p** 63. C Farnham *Guildf* 62-67; Chapl Pierrepont Sch Frensham 67-69; Asst Chapl Eton Coll 69-74; P-in-c Fiddington *B & W* 74-76; P-in-c Stogursey 74-76; R Stogursey w Fiddington 76-78; R Trull w Angersleigh 78-80; Chapl Qu Coll Taunton 78-80; Chapl Wells Cathl Sch 81-86; Chapl Haileybury Coll Herts 86-91; Lic to Offic *Lon* from 91; Chapl Westmr Sch from 91; PV Westmr Abbey from 91; Hon C Westmr St Matt *Lon* from 94. *8 Gayfere Street, London SW1P 3HN* Tel 0171-799 2620 or 222 2831

BALLARD, Steven Peter. b 52. Man Univ BA73 MA74. St Steph Ho Ox 76. **d** 78 **p** 79. C Lancaster St Mary *Blackb* 78-81; C Blackpool St Mich 81-84; V Brierfield 84-94; Perm to Offic *Carl* from 95. *1 St Catherine's Court, Drover's Lane, Penrith, Cumbria CA11 9EF* Tel (01768) 890976

BALLENTINE, Ian Clarke. b 46. Aston Univ BSc71 CEng. BTh. **d** 91 **p** 92. C Lurgan St Jo *D & D* 91-95; I Mallusk *Conn* from 95. *The Rectory, Carwood Drive, Glengormley, Newtownabbey, Co Antrim BT36 5LP* Tel (01232) 833773

BALLENTYNE, Fiona Virginia Grace. **d** 97. NSM Halesworth w Linstead, Chediston, Holton etc *St E* from 97. *64 Old Station Road, Halesworth, Suffolk IP19 8JQ* Tel (01986) 874480

BALLEY, John Frederick. b 05. ALCD41. **d** 41 **p** 42. C Illogan *Truro* 41-44; V Gt w Lt Abington *Ely* 44-49; P-in-c Hildersham 47-48; R 48-49; V Brixton Hill St Sav *S'wark* 49-56; V Richmond H Trin 56-65; Lic to Offic *Ex* 65-70; Chapl Torbay Hosp Torquay 65-70; rtd 70; Perm to Offic *Ex* 70-73; Perm to Offic *Ox* 73-78. *Hornsey Rise Memorial Home, Main Road, Wellsborough, Nuneaton, Warks CV13 6PA* Tel (01455) 290219

BALLINGER, Francis James. b 43. AKC70. **d** 71 **p** 85. C Weston-super-Mare St Sav *B & W* 71-72; Dir Bd Soc Resp *Leic* 85-88; Hon C Bringhurst w Gt Easton 85-88; TV Melksham *Sarum* 88-93; P-in-c Spernall, Morton Bagot and Oldberrow *Cov* from 93; P-in-c Coughton from 93; Dioc Rural Adv from 93. *The Parsonage, Sambourne Lane, Sambourne, Redditch, Worcs B96 6PA* Tel (01527) 892372

BALMER, Walter Owen. b 30. N Ord Course 83. **d** 86 **p** 87. NSM Gateacre *Liv* 86-91; NSM Hale from 91. *38 Grangemeadow Road, Liverpool L25 4SU* Tel 0151-421 1189

BALMFORTH, The Ven Anthony James. b 26. BNC Ox BA50 MA51. Linc Th Coll 50. **d** 52 **p** 53. C Mansfield St Pet *S'well* 52-55; V Skegby 55-61; V Kidderminster St Jo *Worc* 61-65; V Kings Norton *Birm* 65-72; TR 73-79; RD Kings Norton 73-79; Hon Can Birm Cathl 75-79; Hon Can Bris Cathl *Bris* 79-90; Adn Bris 79-90; rtd 90; Perm to Offic *Glouc* from 90. *Slipper Cottage, Stag Hill, Yorkley, Lydney, Glos GL15 4TB* Tel (01594) 564016

BAMBER, David Beverley. b 51. Univ of Wales (Lamp) BA75. St Steph Ho Ox 75. **d** 77 **p** 78. C Altrincham St Geo *Ches* 77-80; C Oxton 80-81; Perm to Offic *Derby* 85-87; C Staveley and Barrow Hill 87-88; C W Retford *S'well* 89-90; C E Retford 89-90 and 91-92. *97 Grove Lane, Retford, Notts DN22 6ND* Tel (01777) 701317

BAMFORD, Mrs Marion. b 35. K Coll Lon BA56 AKC56. N Ord Course 81. **dss** 84 **d** 90 **p** 94. Baildon *Bradf* 84-85; S Kirkby *Wakef* 85-90; Chapl Pontefract Gen Infirmary Wakef 89-96; D-in-c Brotherton *Wakef* 90-94; P-in-c 94-96; rtd 96; Perm to Offic *Wakef* from 96. *170 Warren Lane, Eldwick, Bingley, W Yorkshire BD16 3BY* Tel (01274) 564925

BAMFORTH, Marvin John. b 48. N Ord Course 78. **d** 81 **p** 82. C Barnoldswick w Bracewell *Bradf* 81-84; V Cullingworth 84-88; New Zealand 88-89; V Thornton in Lonsdale w Burton in Lonsdale *Bradf* from 89; Dioc Chapl MU from 91; P-in-c

Bentham St Jo from 93. *The Vicarage, Low Street, Burton in Lonsdale, Carnforth, Lancs LA6 3LF* Tel (015242) 61579

BAMFORTH, Stuart Michael. b 35. Hertf Coll Ox BA58 MA61. Sarum Th Coll 60. **d** 62 **p** 63. C Adel *Ripon* 62-67; V Hempton and Pudding Norton *Nor* 67-71; V Toftrees w Shereford 67-71; P-in-c Pensthorpe 67-71; P-in-c Colkirk 69-70; Lic to Offic *Derby* 72-77; Lic to Offic *Ripon* from 77; rtd 95. *36 Gainsborough Avenue, Leeds LS16 7PQ*

BANBURY, David Paul. b 62. Coll of Ripon & York St Jo BA84. Ridley Hall Cam 85. **d** 88 **p** 89. C Blackb St Jas *Blackb* 88-90; C Preston St Cuth 90-95; P-in-c Bradf St Clem *Bradf* from 95. *St Clement's Vicarage, 294A Barkerend Road, Bradford, W Yorkshire BD3 9DF* Tel (01274) 665109

BANFIELD, Andrew Henry. b 48. AKC71. St Aug Coll Cant 72. **d** 73 **p** 74. C Crayford *Roch* 73-76; Youth Chapl *Glouc* 77-89; Soc Services Development Officer Glos Co Coun from 89. *Rosemary Cottage, Oakwood Close, Bream, Lydney, Glos GL15 6HS*

BANFIELD, The Ven David John. b 33. ALCD56. **d** 57 **p** 58. C Middleton *Man* 57-62; Chapl Scargill Ho 62-65; Asst Warden 65-67; V Addiscombe St Mary *Cant* 67-80; V Luton St Mary *St Alb* 80-90; Hon Can St Alb 89-90; RD Luton 89-90; Adn Bris from 90. *10 Great Brockeridge, Westbury-on-Trym, Bristol BS9 3TY* Tel 0117-962 2438 Fax as telephone

BANGAY (formerly REAST), Mrs Eileen Joan. b 40. Open Univ BA93. EMMTC 81. **dss** 84 **d** 87 **p** 94. Linc St Mary-le-Wigford w St Benedict etc *Linc* 80-87; C 87-90; C Stamford All SS w St Jo 90-93; NSM Walesby 93-95; P-in-c Sutton Bridge from 95. *The Vicarage, 79 Bridge Road, Sutton Bridge, Spalding, Lincs PE12 9SD* Tel (01406) 351503

BANGERT, Harry Alfred. b 07. ALCD33. **d** 33 **p** 34. C Ramsgate Ch Ch *Cant* 33-35; C Harlington *Lon* 35-37; C Sprowston *Nor* 37-39; R Gimingham 39-43; V Bamford *Man* 43-50; Chapl Bromsgrove Gp Hosps 50-67; Chapl Knowle Hosp Fareham 67-75; rtd 76; Hon C E Preston w Kingston *Chich* 76-80. *Davenham, 148 Graham Road, Malvern, Worcs WR14 2HY* Tel (01684) 567179

BANGOR, Archdeacon of. *See* ROBERTS, The Ven Elwyn

BANGOR, Bishop of. *See* MORGAN, The Rt Revd Barry Cennydd

BANGOR, Dean of. *See* EDWARDS, The Very Revd Thomas Erwyd Pryse

BANISTER, Jane Catherine. b 67. Man Univ BA90. Westcott Ho Cam BA96 CTM97. **d** 97. C Addington *S'wark* from 97. *56 Viney Bank, Court Wood Lane, Croydon CR0 9JT* Tel 0181-657 2478

BANISTER, Martin John. b 39. Worc Coll Ox BA62 MA68. Chich Th Coll 62. **d** 64 **p** 65. C Wellingborough All Hallows *Pet* 64-67; C Heene *Chich* 67-70; V Denford w Ringstead *Pet* 70-78; P-in-c Wilshamstead *St Alb* 78-80; P-in-c Houghton Conquest 78-80; V Wilshamstead and Houghton Conquest 80-89; RD Elstow 86-89; V Waltham Cross from 89. *The Vicarage, 5 Longlands Close, Waltham Cross, Herts EN8 8LW* Tel (01992) 633243

BANKS, Aleck George. b 18. Lon Univ BD42 AKC42. **d** 42 **p** 43. C Colchester St Jas, All SS, St Nic and St Runwald *Chelmsf* 42-45; C Leigh St Clem 45-51; V Bradfield 51-56; PC Becontree St Geo 56-61; V S Benfleet 61-83; rtd 83; Perm to Offic *Chelmsf* from 83; Perm to Offic *St E* from 85. *5 Gosford Close, Clare, Sudbury, Suffolk CO10 8PT* Tel (01787) 277088

BANKS, Brian William Eric. b 35. Lon Univ DipTh65 BD69 Birm Univ DPS70. Wycliffe Hall Ox 63. **d** 65 **p** 66. C Swindon Ch Ch *Bris* 65-68; C Halesowen *Worc* 68-71; R Wychbold and Upton Warren 71-77; V Bengeworth 77-87; RD Evesham 81-86; R Freshwater *Portsm* from 87; P-in-c Yarmouth from 95; R from 96. *The Rectory, Afton Road, Freshwater, Isle of Wight PO40 9TS* Tel (01983) 752010

BANKS, Ernest Leslie. b 10. Oak Hill Th Coll 53. **d** 55 **p** 56. C St Alb Ch Ch *St Alb* 55-58; C Attenborough w Bramcote *S'well* 58-60; R Kimberley 60-83; rtd 83; Perm to Offic *Derby* from 83. *32 King's Drive, Littleover, Derby DE23 6EY* Tel (01332) 360706

BANKS, Geoffrey Alan. b 43. St Andr Univ MA66. N Ord Course 84. **d** 87 **p** 88. NSM Shelley and Shepley *Wakef* 87-89; C Halifax 89-91; V Holmfield from 91. *St Andrew's Vicarage, Beechwood Road, Holmfield, Halifax, W Yorkshire HX2 9AR* Tel (01422) 244586

BANKS, John Alan. b 32. Hertf Coll Ox BA54 MA58. Westcott Ho Cam 56. **d** 58 **p** 59. C Warsop *S'well* 58-61; C Ox St Aldate w H Trin *Ox* 61-64; V Ollerton *S'well* 64-75; V Boughton 64-75; R Wollaton 75-83; RD Beeston 77-81; Lic to Offic 83-85; C Bramcote 85-86; C Arnold 86-95; rtd 95. *247 Oxclose Lane, Nottingham NG5 6FB* Tel 0115-926 6814

BANKS, Joseph. b 23. CEng65 MIMechE65 FBIM70. **d** 80 **p** 81. NSM Bollington St Jo *Ches* 80-84; R New Galloway *Glas* 84-93; rtd 93. *Castlebank House, Castlebank Road, Cupar, Fife KY15 4HL* Tel (01334) 654090

BANKS, Michael Lawrence. b 40. Open Univ BA72 Brunel Univ MA82. Westcott Ho Cam 84. **d** 86 **p** 87. C Cheshunt *St Alb* 86-89; Chapl HM Pris Blundeston 89-90; V Leagrave *St Alb* 90-94; Asst RD Luton 91-94; V Hatfield Hyde from 95. *Church House, Hollybush Lane, Welwyn Garden City, Herts AL7 4JS* Tel (01707) 322313

BANKS, Canon Michael Thomas Harvey. b 35. Ushaw Coll Dur 58 Open Univ BA75. **d** 63 **p** 64. In RC Ch 63-69; C Winlaton *Dur* 69-71; P-in-c Bishopwearmouth Gd Shep 71-75; TV Melton Mowbray w Thorpe Arnold *Leic* 75-80; TR Loughborough Em 80-88; Dir of Ords 83-87; Hon Can Leic Cathl 83-87; Can Res and Chan from 87; RD Christianity S 93-95. *Chancellor's House, 3 Morland Avenue, Leicester LE2 2PF* Tel 0116-270 8078

BANKS, Norman. b 54. Or Coll Ox BA76 MA80. St Steph Ho Ox 79. **d** 82 **p** 83. C Newc Ch Ch w St Ann *Newc* 82-87; P-in-c 87-90; V Tynemouth Cullercoats St Paul from 90. *The Vicarage, 53 Grosvenor Drive, Whitley Bay, Tyne & Wear NE26 2JR* Tel 0191-252 4916

BANKS, Philip Charles. b 61. ARICS87 NE Lon Poly BSc85 Nottm Univ BTh93. Linc Th Coll 90. **d** 93 **p** 94. C Chelmsf Ascension *Chelmsf* 93-94; C Brentwood St Thos from 94. *25 St Thomas Road, Brentwood, Essex CM14 4DS* Tel (01277) 210323

BANKS, Susan Angela. *See* GRIFFITHS, Mrs Susan Angela

BANNARD-SMITH, Dennis Ronald. b 22. Birm Univ BSc42. St Alb Minl Tr Scheme. **d** 83 **p** 84. NSM Pavenham *St Alb* 83-88; NSM Odell and Pavenham from 88. *Goodly Heritage, 10 The Bury, Pavenham, Bedford MK43 7PX* Tel (01234) 822992

BANNER, John William. b 36. Open Univ BA78. Tyndale Hall Bris 61. **d** 64 **p** 65. C Bootle St Leon *Liv* 64-66; C Wigan St Jas 66-69; C Stapleton *Bris* 69-70; Australia 70-72; V Liv Ch Ch Norris Green *Liv* 72-82; V Tunbridge Wells H Trin w Ch Ch *Roch* from 82. *The Vicarage, 63 Claremont Road, Tunbridge Wells, Kent TN1 1TE* Tel (01892) 526644

BANNER, Prof Michael Charles. b 61. Ball Coll Ox BA83 MA86 DPhil87. **d** 86 **p** 87. Fell St Pet Coll Ox 85-88; Dean Peterho Cam 88-94; Prof Moral and Soc Th K Coll Lon from 94. *King's College, Strand, London WC2R 2LS* Tel 0171-873 2073 Fax 873 2255

BANNISTER, Preb Anthony Peter. b 40. Ex Univ BA62. Clifton Th Coll 63. **d** 65 **p** 66. C Uphill *B & W* 65-69; C Hove Bp Hannington Memorial Ch *Chich* 69-74; V Wembdon *B & W* 74-91; Youth Chapl 80-83; RD Bridgwater 80-89; V Taunton St Jas from 91; Preb Wells Cathl from 97. *St James's Vicarage, 3 Richmond Road, Taunton, Somerset TA1 1EN* Tel (01823) 333194

BANNISTER, Clifford John. b 53. Hatf Coll Dur BA76. Ripon Coll Cuddesdon 84. **d** 86 **p** 87. C Weymouth H Trin *Sarum* 86-89; TV Basingstoke *Win* 89-94; V Hedge End from 94. *The Vicarage, Vicarage Drive, Hedge End, Southampton SO30 4DF* Tel (01489) 782288

BANNISTER, Edward. b 06. Lich Th Coll 27. **d** 29 **p** 30. C Patricroft *Man* 29-32; India 32-35; C Moss Side Ch Ch *Man* 35-37; Min Can Win Cathl *Win* 37-38 and 51-56; C Rickmansworth *St Alb* 38-43; V High Wych 43-51; V Sparsholt w Lainston *Win* 56-73; Hon Min Can Win Cathl 60; rtd 73; Warden Morley Coll 76-95. *c/o E A Bannister Esq, 19A Adam and Eve Mews, London W8 6UG* Tel 0171-938 1636

BANNISTER, Grattan Eric McGillycuddy Colm Brendon. b 01. TCD BA50 MA53. **d** 52 **p** 57. C Rainbow Hill St Barn *Worc* 57-58; C Cork St Luke *C, C & R* 61-63; P-in-c Schull 63-75; rtd 75. *Ballydehob, Co Cork, Irish Republic*

BANNISTER, John. b 24. Westcott Ho Cam 68. **d** 69 **p** 70. Hon C Rye *Chich* 69-73; Hon C Playden w E Guldeford 69-73; Hon C Rye w Rye Harbour and Playden 73-79; Hon C Rye, Rye Harbour and Playden and Iden 79-80; Hon C Rye 80-94; rtd 94; Perm to Offic *Chich* from 94. *Wynfields, Grove Lane, Iden, Rye, E Sussex TN31 7PX* Tel (01797) 280229

BANNISTER, Peter Edward. b 38. Leeds Univ BSc60. Linc Th Coll 72. **d** 74 **p** 75. C Norbury St Steph *Cant* 74-77; C Allington and Maidstone St Pet 77-80; R Temple Ewell w Lydden 80-86; TV Bracknell *Ox* 86-93; P-in-c Swallowfield from 93. *The Vicarage, Swallowfield Street, Swallowfield, Reading RG7 1QY* Tel 0118-988 3786

BANNISTER, Canon Simon Monro. b 38. St Jo Coll Ox BA62 MA69. Linc Th Coll 61. **d** 63 **p** 64. C Prestwich St Marg *Man* 63-66; C Farnborough *Roch* 66-70; V Bury St Mark *Man* 70-78; V Oldham St Mary w St Pet 78; TR Oldham 78-87; Hon Can Man Cathl 81-87; V Hatfield Hyde *St Alb* 87-94; P-in-c Brasted *Roch* from 94; Dioc Adv on Continuing Minl Educn from 94. *The Rectory, Brasted, Westerham, Kent TN16 1NH* Tel (01959) 563491

BANNOCKS, David George. b 64. Trin Coll Bris DipHE84 Lon Bible Coll BA85 Dur Univ MA94. Cranmer Hall Dur 88. **d** 90 **p** 91. C Stapleford *S'well* 90-93; C Southport Ch Ch *Liv* 93-95; Chapl R Coll of Art from 95; Chapl Imp Coll *Lon* from 95. *1 Porchester Gardens, London W2 3LA* Tel 0171-229 5089

BANNON, Canon Richard Babington. b 20. TCD BA42 MA47. CITC 48. **d** 48 **p** 49. I Ardclinis w Tickmacrevan *Conn* 55-86; Can Belf Cathl 85-86; rtd 86. *Dean's Cottage, 7 Whin Road, Ballygally, Larne, Co Antrim BT40 2QJ* Tel (01574) 583230

BANTING, David Percy. b 51. Magd Coll Cam MA74. Wycliffe Hall Ox MA79. **d** 80 **p** 81. C Ox St Ebbe w H Trin and St Pet *Ox* 80-83; Min St Jos Merry Hill CD *Lich* 83-90; V Chadderton Ch Ch *Man* from 90. *Christ Church Vicarage, Block Lane, Chadderton, Oldham OL9 7QB* Tel 0161-624 2326

BANTING, The Ven Kenneth Mervyn Lancelot Hadfield. b 37. Pemb Coll Cam BA61 MA65. Cuddesdon Coll 64. **d** 65 **p** 66. Asst Chapl Win Coll 65-70; C Leigh Park *Portsm* 70-72; TV Hemel Hempstead *St Alb* 73-79; V Goldington 79-88; P-in-c Renhold 80-82; RD Bedford 84-87; V Portsea St Cuth *Portsm* 88-96; RD Portsm 94-96; Hon Can Portsm Cathl 95-96; Adn Is of Wight from 96. *5 The Boltons, Kite Hill, Wootton Bridge, Ryde, Isle of Wight PO33 4PB* Tel (01983) 884432

BANYARD, Douglas Edward. b 21. S'wark Ord Course 69. **d** 71 **p** 72. NSM Selsdon St Jo w St Fran *Cant* 71-77; Perm to Offic *Portsm* from 77; Perm to Offic *Chich* from 77. *22 Lower Wardown, Petersfield, Hants GU31 4NY* Tel (01730) 261004

BANYARD, Peter Vernon. b 35. Sarum Th Coll 57. **d** 59 **p** 60. C Southampton Maybush St Pet *Win* 59-63; C Tilbury Docks *Chelmsf* 63-65; Miss to Seamen 63-65; Namibia 65-68; V Chesterfield St Aug *Derby* 68-74; TV Grantham w Manthorpe *Linc* 74-78; TV Grantham 78-79; Chapl Warminster Sch 79-85; V Hykeham *Linc* 85-88; rtd 88; Perm to Offic *Linc* from 88. *56 Western Avenue, Lincoln LN6 7SY*

BANYARD (or BRUNSKILL), Ms Sheila Kathryn. b 53. Univ of Wales (Ban) BA75 K Coll Lon MA83. Cranmer Hall Dur 76. **dss** 82 **d** 92 **p** 94. Sunbury *Lon* 82-85; Asst Chapl Ch Hosp Horsham 85-90; Chapl Malvern Girls' Coll 90-95; TV Droitwich Spa *Worc* from 95. *The Vicarage, 205 Worcester Road, Droitwich, Worcs WR9 8AS* Tel (01905) 773134

BARBER, Charles William Walters. b 60. Pemb Coll Cam BA81 MA85. Wycliffe Hall Ox 83. **d** 86 **p** 87. C Wolverhampton St Matt *Lich* 86-90; C Hornsey Rise Whitehall Park Team *Lon* 90-94; Sub Chapl HM Prison Holloway 95; V Bowling St Steph *Bradf* from 96. *St Stephen's Vicarage, 48 Newton Street, Bradford, W Yorkshire BD5 7BH* Tel (01274) 720784

BARBER, Canon Christopher Albert (Chris). b 33. Ch Coll Cam BA53 MA57. Coll of Resurr Mirfield 56. **d** 58 **p** 59. C Cov St Pet *Cov* 58-61; C Stokenchurch and Cadmore End *Ox* 61-64; V Royton St Paul *Man* 64-70; V Stapleford *Ely* 70-80; RD Shelford 76-80; V Cherry Hinton St Andr 80-88; Hon Can Ely Cathl from 88; R Cottenham 88-92; RD N Stowe 90-92; V Terrington St John from 92; V Tilney All Saints from 92. *The Vicarage, Church Road, Terrington St John, Wisbech, Cambs PE14 7SA* Tel (01945) 880259

BARBER, Garth Antony. b 48. FRAS MSOSc Southn Univ BSc69 Lon Univ MSc79. St Jo Coll Nottm LTh76. **d** 76 **p** 77. C Hounslow H Trin *Lon* 76-79; Chapl City of Lon Poly 79-86; P-in-c Twickenham All Hallows from 86; Chapl Richmond Coll from 87. *All Hallows' Vicarage, 138 Chertsey Road, Twickenham TW1 1EW* Tel 0181-892 1322

BARBER, Geoffrey Thomas. b 23. Univ of Wales (Lamp) BA51. Ridley Hall Cam 51. **d** 53 **p** 54. C Walthamstow St Mary *Chelmsf* 53-55; C Woking St Pet *Guildf* 56-57; V Chelsea St Jo *Lon* 57-66; V Rushden St Pet 66-75; V Leyton Em *Chelmsf* 75-81; rtd 81. *22 Longacre Drive, Ferndown, Dorset BH22 9EE* Tel (01202) 873626

BARBER, Hilary John. b 65. Aston Tr Scheme 92 Sarum Th Coll 94. **d** 96 **p** 97. C Moston St Jo *Man* from 96. *38 Ilkley Street, Manchester M10 9PD* Tel 0161-688 7654

BARBER, John Eric Michael. b 30. Wycliffe Hall Ox 63. **d** 65 **p** 66. C Lupset *Wakef* 65-68; C Halifax St Jo Bapt 68-70; V Dewsbury St Matt and St Jo 70-80; V Perry Common *Birm* 80-95; rtd 95. *21A Westhill Road, Weymouth, Dorset DT4 9NB* Tel (01305) 786553

BARBER, Mrs Margaret Ann. b 31. GTCL52. Dalton Ho Bris 55 Sarum & Wells Th Coll 82. **dss** 83 **d** 87 **p** 94. Wimborne Minster and Holt *Sarum* 83-90; Par Dn 87-90; rtd 90; Hon Par Dn Hampreston *Sarum* 90-94; Hon C from 94. *22 Longacre Drive, Ferndown, Dorset BH22 9EE* Tel (01202) 873626

BARBER, Martin John. b 35. Univ Coll Lon BA61. Linc Th Coll 61. **d** 63 **p** 64. C Stepney St Dunstan and All SS *Lon* 63-67; Chapl K Sch Bruton 67-93; rtd 93; Lic to Offic *B & W* from 93. *1 Plox Green, Bruton, Somerset BA10 0EY* Tel (01749) 812290

BARBER, Michael. b 40. Open Univ BA83. Oak Hill Th Coll 69. **d** 71 **p** 72. C Rothley *Leic* 71-74; C Leic Martyrs 74-76; V Queniborough 76-82; V Monkwearmouth All SS *Dur* 82-92; V Mirehouse *Carl* from 92. *The Vicarage, Hollins Close, Mirehouse, Whitehaven, Cumbria CA28 8EX* Tel (01946) 693565

✠**BARBER, The Rt Revd Paul Everard.** b 35. St Jo Coll Cam BA58 MA66. Wells Th Coll 58. **d** 60 **p** 61 **c** 89. C Westborough *Guildf* 60-66; V York Town St Mich 66-73; V Bourne 73-80; RD Farnham 74-79; Hon Can Guildf Cathl 80-89; Adn Surrey 80-89; Suff Bp Brixworth *Pet* from 89. *4 The Avenue, Dallington, Northampton NN5 7AN* Tel (01604) 759423 Fax 750925

BARBER, Philip Kenneth. b 43. St Jo Coll Dur BA65. NW Ord Course 74. **d** 76 **p** 77. NSM Burscough Bridge *Liv* 76-84; P-in-c Brigham *Carl* 84-85; V 85-89; P-in-c Mosser 84-85; V 85-89; P-in-c Borrowdale 89-94; Chapl Keswick Sch 89-94; P-in-c Beetham *Carl* from 94; Educn Adv from 94. *The Old Parsonage, Stanley Street, Beetham, Milnthorpe, Cumbria LA7 7AL* Tel (015395) 62216

BARBER, Royston Henry (Roy). b 38. Univ of Wales (Abth) BD86. United Th Coll Abth 83. **d** 86 **p** 87. NSM Tywyn w Aberdyfi *Ban* 86-92; NSM Cannington, Otterhampton, Combwich and Stockland *B & W* from 93. *2 Slewton Crescent, Whimple, Exeter EX5 2QA* Tel (01404) 823343

BARBER, William Ewart Worsley. b 15. Leeds Univ BA38. Coll of Resurr Mirfield 38. **d** 40 **p** 41. C Auckland St Helen *Dur* 40-41; C Heworth St Mary 41-44; C Winlaton 44-47; C Cov H Trin *Cov* 47-53; V Dean Forest H Trin *Glouc* 53-59; V Sandhurst 59-64; Asst Youth Chapl 60-64; Min Lower Tuffley St Geo CD 64-67; V Tuffley 67-74; R Huntley 74-79; Hon C Bromsberrow 79-90; rtd 79; Hon C Redmarley D'Abitot, Bromesberrow w Pauntley etc *Glouc* from 79. *37 St Mary's Square, Gloucester GL1 2QT* Tel (01452) 330842

BARBOUR, Mrs Jennifer Louise. b 32. JP67. Barrister-at-Law 55 St Hugh's Coll Ox BA54 MA57. Gilmore Course 80. **dss** 81 **d** 87 **p** 94. Bray and Braywood *Ox* 81-84; Hermitage and Hampstead Norreys, Cold Ash etc 84-87; Chapl Leeds Poly *Ripon* 87-92; Chapl Leeds Metrop Univ 92-95; rtd 95; NSM Shipton Moyne w Westonbirt and Lasborough *Glouc* from 95; Perm to Offic *Bris* from 95. *The Rectory, Shipton Moyne, Tetbury, Glos GL8 8PW* Tel (01666) 880244

BARBOUR, Walter Iain. b 28. FICE65 Pemb Coll Cam BA48 MA53. Ox NSM Course 78. **d** 81 **p** 82. NSM Bray and Braywood *Ox* 81-84; NSM Thatcham 84-87; TV Moor Allerton *Ripon* 87-95; rtd 95; NSM Shipton Moyne w Westonbirt and Lasborough *Glouc* from 95; Perm to Offic *Bris* from 95. *The Rectory, Shipton Moyne, Tetbury, Glos GL8 8PW* Tel (01666) 880244

BARBY, Canon Sheana Braidwood. b 38. Bedf Coll Lon BA59. EMMTC 81. **dss** 84 **d** 87 **p** 94. Derby St Paul *Derby* 84-87; NSM Derby Cathl from 87; Dioc Dir of Female Ords from 90; Par Educn Adv from 93; Hon Can Derby Cathl from 96. *2 Margaret Street, Derby DE1 3FE* Tel (01332) 383301

BARCLAY, Ian Newton. b 33. Clifton Th Coll 58. **d** 61 **p** 62. C Cullompton *Ex* 61-63; C Ashill w Broadway *B & W* 63-66; V Chatham St Phil and St Jas *Roch* 66-69; C St Helen Bishopsgate w St Martin Outwich *Lon* 70-73; V Prestonville St Luke *Chich* 73-81; Lic to Offic 82-93; rtd 93. *35 Marine Avenue, Hove, E Sussex BN3 4LH* Tel (01273) 421628

BARCLAY, Mrs Susan Molly. **d** 87. Hon Par Dn March St Wendreda *Ely* from 87. *42 Greystoke Road, Cambridge CB1 4DS* Tel (01223) 246877

BARCROFT, Ambrose William Edgar. b 17. TCD BA40 MA46. TCD Div Sch Div Test41. **d** 41 **p** 42. C Drumachose *D & R* 41-46; Chapl RN 46-70; R Pitlochry *St And* 70-82; rtd 82; Perm to Offic *St And* from 82. *The Old School House, Calvine, Pitlochry, Perthshire PH18 5UD* Tel (01796) 483224

BARCROFT, Ian David. b 60. UMIST BSc83 Edin Univ BD88. Edin Th Coll 85. **d** 88 **p** 89. Prec St Ninian's Cathl Perth *St And* 88-92; Min Perth St Ninian 88-92; P-in-c Aberdeen St Clem *Ab* 92-97; R Hamilton *Glas* from 97. *The Rectory, 4C Auchingramont Road, Hamilton, Lanarkshire ML3 6JT* Tel (01698) 429895

BARD, Christopher Frederick Jesse (Chris). b 52. AKC75 Open Univ BA88. St Aug Coll Cant 75. **d** 76 **p** 77. C Billingham St Cuth *Dur* 76-79; Chapl to Arts and Recreation 79-81; C Egglescliffe 79-81; P-in-c Epping Upland *Chelmsf* 81-95; Dioc Communications Officer 81-91; BBC Essex Relig Producer from 89; Bp's Adv on Satellite Broadcasting from 91; TV Epping Distr from 95. *The Vicarage, Epping Green, Epping, Essex CM16 6PN* Tel (01992) 572949 Fax 578892

BARDELL, Alan George. LNSM course. **d** 92 **p** 93. NSM Addlestone *Guildf* from 92; NSM Byfleet from 92. *14 Dickens Drive, Addlestone, Surrey KT15 1AW* Tel (01932) 847524

BARDSLEY, Warren Nigel Antony. b 52. AKC74. St Aug Coll Cant 74. **d** 75 **p** 76. C Leeds St Aid *Ripon* 75-78; C Cov St Jo *Cov* 78-80; P-in-c Stoke Golding w Dadlington *Leic* 80-89; TV Swinton and Pendlebury *Man* 90-94. *68 High Road, Wortwell, Harleston, Norfolk IP20 2EF* Tel (01986) 788365

BARDWELL, Edward Mercer. b 12. ALCD41 LTh74. **d** 41 **p** 43. C Leic H Apostles *Leic* 41-46; C Dudley St Fran *Worc* 46-49; C Southsea St Simon *Portsm* 49-51; V Battersea Park St Sav *S'wark* 51-59; R Cranworth w Letton and Southbergh *Nor* 59-78; rtd 79; Perm to Offic *Ely* from 79; Perm to Offic *St E* from 89. *6 Cromwell Road, Weeting, Brandon, Suffolk IP27 0QT* Tel (01842) 810582

BARDWELL, Mrs Elaine Barbara. b 60. K Coll Lon BA81 AKC81. St Steph Ho Ox BA85 MA90. **dss** 86 **d** 87 **p** 95. Heref H Trin *Heref* 86-89; C 87-89; Dir Past Studies St Steph Ho Ox 89-96; V New Marston *Ox* from 96. *The Vicarage, 8 Jack Straws Lane, Headington, Oxford OX3 0DL* Tel (01865) 798186 or 242803

BARDWELL, John Edward. b 53. Jes Coll Cam BA75 MA79 Ox Univ BA85 MA90. St Steph Ho Ox 83. **d** 86 **p** 87. C Heref H Trin *Heref* 86-89; Perm to Offic *Ox* 90-96. *The Vicarage, 8 Jack Straws Lane, Headington, Oxford OX3 0DL* Tel (01865) 798186

BAREHAM, Miss Sylvia Alice. b 36. Hockerill Coll Cam CertEd59 Open Univ BA83 Ox Univ DipEd84. Ox Min Course 86. **d** 89 **p** 94. NSM N Leigh *Ox* 89-93; NSM Bampton w Clanfield 93-95; NSM Kedington *St E* from 95; NSM Hundon w Barnardiston from 95; NSM Haverhill w Withersfield, the Wrattings etc from 95. *The Stone Cottage, Little Wratting, Haverhill, Suffolk CB9 7UQ* Tel (01440) 762303

BARFETT, The Ven Thomas. b 16. Keble Coll Ox BA38 MA42. Wells Th Coll 38. **d** 39 **p** 40. C Gosport Ch Ch *Portsm* 39-44; C Gladstone Park St Fran *Lon* 44-47; C St Andr Undershaft w St Mary Axe 47-49; V Penzance St Paul *Truro* 49-55; R Falmouth K Chas 55-77; Asst ChStJ 63-71; Sub Chapl 71-95; Chapl from 95; Chapl to The Queen 75-86; Adn Heref 77-82; Can Res and Treas Heref Cathl 77-82; rtd 82; Bermuda 84; Chapl Menton w San Remo *Eur* 86; Perm to Offic *Truro* from 86. *Treberveth, 57 Falmouth Road, Truro, Cornwall TR1 2HL* Tel (01872) 73726

BARFF, John Robert. b 43. Ch Coll Cam BA66 MA70 K Coll Lon MTh69. ALCD68. **d** 69 **p** 70. C Fulham St Mary N End *Lon* 69-73; CMS 73-83; Sudan 75-83; P-in-c Compton Greenfield *Bris* 83-85; P-in-c Pilning 83-85; V Pilning w Compton Greenfield 85-92; rtd 92; Perm to Offic *Bris* from 92. *10 Cote Park, Stoke Bishop, Bristol BS9 2AD* Tel 0117-968 5889

BARGE, Mrs Ann Marina. b 42. **d** 96 **p** 97. C Ludlow, Ludford, Ashford Carbonell etc *Heref* from 96. *8 Old Street, Ludlow, Shropshire SY8 1NP* Tel (01584) 877307

BARGE, David Robert. b 45. S Dios Minl Tr Scheme 92. **d** 95 **p** 96. NSM Westfield *B & W* from 95. *Westhill House, Wells Road, Radstock, Bath BA3 3SA* Tel (01761) 433787

BARGH, George Edward Norman. b 25. St Jo Coll Cam BA48 MA53 Leeds Univ LLB51. Carl Dioc Tr Course 80. **d** 83 **p** 84. NSM Ulverston St Mary w H Trin *Carl* 83-86; P-in-c Egton w Newland 86-87; P-in-c Blawith w Lowick 86-87; P-in-c Egton-cum-Newland and Lowick 87-89; rtd 90; Perm to Offic *Carl* from 90. *1 Willowdene Gardens, Old Hall Road, Ulverston, Cumbria LA12 7WD* Tel (01229) 588051

BARHAM, Ian Harold. b 40. Clifton Th Coll 64. **d** 66 **p** 67. C Broadwater St Mary *Chich* 66-69 and 72-76; Burundi 71-72; R Beyton and Hessett *St E* 76-79; Perm to Offic 79-81; Hon C Bury St Edmunds St Mary 81-84; Chapl St Aubyn's Sch Tiverton 84-96; Chapl Lee Abbey from 96; Lic to Offic *Ex* from 84. *Lee Abbey Fellowship, Lynton, Devon EX35 6JJ* Tel (01598) 752621 Fax 752619

BARHAM, Mrs Jennifer Mary (Jen). b 43. RN65. Oak Hill Th Coll 92. **d** 95 **p** 96. NSM Leigh-on-Sea St Aid *Chelmsf* from 95. *47 Walker Drive, Leigh-on-Sea, Essex SS9 3QT* Tel (01702) 558766

✠**BARHAM, The Rt Revd Kenneth Lawrence (Ken).** b 36. Clifton Th Coll BD63. **d** 63 **p** 64 **c** 93. C Worthing St Geo *Chich* 63-65; C Sevenoaks St Nic *Roch* 65-67; C Cheltenham St Mark *Glouc* 67-70; V Maidstone St Luke *Cant* 70-79; S Area Sec Rwanda Miss 79-84; P-in-c Ashburnham w Penhurst *Chich* from 84; Asst Bp Cyangugu (Rwanda) from 93. *Rosewood, Canadia Road, Battle, E Sussex TN33 0LR* Tel (01424) 773073 Fax as telephone

BARHAM, Peter. b 62. Selw Coll Cam MA83. Linc Th Coll BTh94. **d** 94 **p** 95. C Fornham All SS and Fornham St Martin w Timworth *St E* 94-97; P-in-c Cockfield w Bradfield St Clare, Felsham etc from 97. *The Rectory, Howe Lane, Cockfield, Bury St Edmunds, Suffolk IP30 0HA* Tel (01284) 828385

BARKER, Arthur John Willoughby. b 10. Lon Coll of Div 46. **d** 48 **p** 49. C Addiscombe St Mary *Cant* 48-53; V Westgate St Jas 53-58; Warden Scargill Ho 58-61; V Dent w Cowgill *Bradf* 61-76; rtd 76; Perm to Offic *Bradf* from 76. *West Banks, Dent, Sedbergh, Cumbria LA10 5QT* Tel (015396) 25355

BARKER, Arundel Charles. b 24. Tyndale Hall Bris 54. **d** 56 **p** 57. C Rodbourne Cheney *Bris* 56-58; V Islington St Steph w St Bart and St Matt *Lon* 58-65; R Passenham *Pet* 65-90; P-in-c Cosgrove 65-66; rtd 90; Perm to Offic *Derby* from 90. *7 Bull Farm Mews, Bull Lane, Matlock, Derbyshire DE4 5NB* Tel (01629) 580321

BARKER, Brian Wallwork. b 26. G&C Coll Cam BA50 MA55. Wells Th Coll 51. **d** 52 **p** 53. C Bradford cum Beswick *Man* 52-55; Singapore 55-61; Malaya 62-63; Malaysia 63-64; V Ashton St Jas *Man* 65-71; R Burnage St Nic 71-85; R Heaton Reddish 85-91; rtd 91; Perm to Offic *Man* from 91; Perm to Offic *Ches* from 91. *105 Crossfield Road, Cheadle Hulme, Cheadle, Cheshire SK8 5PD* Tel 0161-486 0334

BARKER, Cameron Timothy. b 62. Rhodes Univ BL83. St Jo Coll Nottm 94. **d** 96 **p** 97. C W Streatham St Jas *S'wark* from 96. *171 Mitcham Lane, London SW16 6NA* Tel 0181-769 0695

BARKER, Charles Gordon. b 19. St Aug Coll Cant 60. **d** 61 **p** 62. C Bridgnorth w Tasley *Heref* 61-64; R Hope w Shelve 64-68; P-in-c Middleton 64-69; P-in-c Hope w Shelve 68-69; V Marton 68-69; V Chirbury 68-69; P-in-c Trelystan 68-69; Lic to Offic 70-78; P-in-c Hopesay w Edgton 78-80; P-in-c Lydbury N 78-80; rtd 83. *South Lodge, Dinham, Ludlow, Shropshire SY8 2JE* Tel (01584) 877225

✠**BARKER, The Rt Revd Clifford Conder.** b 26. TD71. Or Coll Ox BA50 MA55. St Chad's Coll Dur DipTh52. **d** 52 **p** 53 **c** 76. C Falsgrave *York* 52-55; C Redcar 55-57; V Sculcoates 57-63; CF (TA) 58-74; P-in-c Sculcoates St Silas *York* 59-61; V Rudby in Cleveland w Middleton 63-70; RD Stokesley 65-70; V York St Olave w St Giles 70-76; RD City of York 71-75; Can and Preb York Minster 73-76; Suff Bp Whitby 76-83; Suff Bp Selby 83-91; rtd 91; Asst Bp York from 95. *15 Oak Tree Close, Strensall, York YO3 5TE* Tel (01904) 490406

BARKER, David Robert. b 45. Worc Coll Ox BA67 MA70. Virginia Th Sem BD72. **d** 72 **p** 73. C Roehampton H Trin *S'wark* 72-75; Chapl Golds Coll Lon 75-79; Min Tr Officer *Cov* 79-85; Selection Sec ACCM 85-90; Sec for Continuing Minl Educn ACCM 85-90; V Sutton Valence w E Sutton and Chart Sutton *Cant* from 90. *The Vicarage, Chart Road, Sutton Valence, Maidstone, Kent ME17 3AW* Tel (01622) 843156

BARKER, Francis Howard. b 41. St Deiniol's Hawarden. **d** 84 **p** 85. NSM Capesthorne w Siddington and Marton *Ches* 84-86; NSM Wilmslow 86-93; C 93-96; P-in-c Woodford from 96. *The Vicarage, Wilmslow Road, Woodford, Stockport, Cheshire SK7 1RH* Tel 0161-439 2286

BARKER, Mrs Gillian Ann (Gill). b 52. Portsm Dioc Tr Course 91. **d** 92. NSM Alverstoke *Portsm* 92-95; NSM Bridgemary 95-96; Asst Chapl Portsm Hosps NHS Trust from 96. *Queen Alexandra Hospital, Cosham, Portsmouth PO6 3LY* Tel (01705) 286408 or 286000

BARKER, Gordon. **d** 94 **p** 95. NSM Malew *S & M* from 94. *Ingleton House, Shore Road, Castletown, Isle of Man IM9 1BF* Tel (01624) 822941

BARKER, Canon Hugh Remington. b 19. Pemb Coll Cam BA41 MA45. Chich Th Coll 41. **d** 43 **p** 44. C Mill Hill St Mich *Lon* 43-48; C Welling *S'wark* 48-51; V Walworth All SS and St Steph 51-62; V Wisbech St Mary *Ely* 62-75; RD Wisbech 72-75; P-in-c Walpole St Andrew 75-77; V 77-84; P-in-c Walpole St Peter 75-77; R 77-84; RD Lynn Marshland 76-84; Hon Can Ely Cathl 81-84; rtd 84; Perm to Offic *Ely* from 84. *39 Dowgate Road, Leverington, Wisbech, Cambs PE13 5DJ* Tel (01945) 585385

BARKER, James Gavin. b 33. Kelham Th Coll 54. **d** 58 **p** 59. C Greenford H Cross *Lon* 58-61; C Bournemouth St Clem w St Mary *Win* 61-66; C Pokesdown St Jas 66-70; V Stanmore 70-77; Chapl Besselsleigh Sch Abingdon 77-86; Hon C S Hinksey *Ox* 77-79; Hon C Wootton (Boars Hill) 79-86; V Southbourne St Chris *Win* from 86. *St Christopher's Vicarage, 81 Watcombe Road, Bournemouth BH6 3LX* Tel (01202) 424886

BARKER, Canon John Howard. b 36. Southn Univ BA58. Ripon Coll Cuddesdon 80. **d** 82 **p** 83. C W Leigh *Portsm* 82-84; V Cosham 84-88; Bp's Dom Chapl 88-96; Hon Can Portsm Cathl from 93; V St Helens from 96; V Sea View from 96. *The Vicarage, Eddington Road, Seaview, Isle of Wight PO34 5EF* Tel (01983) 875190

BARKER, John Lawrence. b 26. Middx Poly BA74 NE Lon Poly MSc84. Oak Hill NSM Course 86. **d** 88 **p** 89. NSM Prittlewell *Chelmsf* 88-91; Perm to Offic *Linc* from 91. *Rose Cottage, Back Lane, Bilsby, Alford, Lincs LN13 9PT* Tel (01507) 462644

BARKER, John Stuart. b 30. Keele Univ BA55. Wells Th Coll 55. **d** 57 **p** 58. C Oswestry St Oswald *Lich* 57-60; C Portishead *B & W* 60-63; V Englishcombe 63-69; R Priston 63-69; V Chew Magna w Dundry 70-85; rtd 94. *9 West Street, Axbridge, Somerset BS26 2AA* Tel (01934) 732740

BARKER, Jonathan. b 55. Hull Univ BA79. Westcott Ho Cam 79. **d** 83 **p** 84. C Swetty *S & B* 83-86; Chapl Sport & Leisure 83-86; C Swansea St Mary w H Trin 85-86; Bermuda 86-90; TV Liv Our Lady and St Nic w St Anne *Liv* 90-93; P-in-c S Shore St Pet *Blackb* from 93; Chapl Qu Victoria's Hosp Morecambe from 93. *St Peter's Vicarage, 19 Windermere Road, Blackpool FY4 2BX* Tel (01253) 41231

BARKER, Julian Roland Palgrave. b 37. Magd Coll Cam BA61 MA65. Westcott Ho Cam 61. **d** 63 **p** 64. C Stafford St Mary *Lich* 63-66; Chapl Clare Hall Cam 66-69; Chapl Clare Coll Cam 66-70; Lic to Offic *Cant* 70-71; Tutor St Aug Coll Cant 70-71; TV Raveningham *Nor* 71-78; TR 78-82; V Foremark *Derby* from 82; V Repton from 82; RD Repton 91-95. *St Wystan's Vicarage, Repton, Derby DE65 6FH* Tel (01283) 703317

BARKER, Leonard Ralph. b 11. ALCD39. **d** 39 **p** 40. C Leic H Apostles *Leic* 39-41; Chapl RNVR 41-46; R Nether Broughton *Leic* 46-48; R Nuthall *S'well* 48-63; R Linby w Papplewick 63-78; rtd 78; Perm to Offic *Linc* from 78. *53 Lancaster Drive, Long Sutton, Spalding, Lincs PE12 9BD* Tel (01406) 363422

BARKER, Canon Leonard Roy. b 24. Selw Coll Cam BA49 MA53. Ridley Hall Cam 49. **d** 51 **p** 52. C Harrogate St Luke *Ripon* 51-53; Succ Bradf Cathl *Bradf* 53-54; V Eccleston St Luke *Liv* 55-62; V Upton (Overchurch) *Ches* 62-80; Hon Can Ches Cathl 78-80; Dir Past Studies Ridley Hall Cam 80-84; Dir of Ords *Ches* 84-90; Can Res Ches Cathl 84-89; rtd 90; Perm to Offic *Ches* from 90. *6 Dee Hills Park, Chester CH3 5AR* Tel (01244) 344104

BARKER, Mark. b 62. ACIB90. St Jo Coll Nottm BTh95. **d** 95 **p** 96. C Barking St Marg w St Patr *Chelmsf* from 95. *48 Sunningdale Avenue, Barking, Essex IG11 7QF*

BARKER, Neil Anthony. b 52. St Andr Univ BSc73. Ridley Hall Cam 74. **d** 77 **p** 78. C Leic H Apostles *Leic* 77-81; C Camberley St Paul *Guildf* 81-86; R Bradfield *Ox* 86-88; P-in-c Stanford Dingley 88; R Bradfield and Stanford Dingley 88-92; R Woodmansterne *S'wark* from 92; Chapl Mother's Union from 96. *The Rectory, Woodmansterne, Banstead, Surrey SM7 3NL* Tel (01737) 352849

BARKER, Nicholas John Willoughby (Nick). b 49. Or Coll Ox BA73 BTh75 MA77. Trin Coll Bris 75. **d** 77 **p** 78. C Watford *St Alb* 77-80; TV Didsbury St Jas and Em *Man* 80-86; TR Kidderminster St Geo *Worc* from 86. *The Rectory, 30 Leswell Street, Kidderminster, Worcs DY10 1RP* Tel (01562) 822131

BARKER, Canon Roy Thomas. b 33. K Coll Lon BD57 AKC57. **d** 58 **p** 59. C Headingley *Ripon* 58-62; C Hawksworth Wood

62-66; S Africa 66-92; Sub-Dean Cape Town Cathl 73-80; Can 74-80; Dean and Adn Grahamstown 80-92; Hon Can from 92; V Southmead *Bris* from 92. *St Stephen's Vicarage, Wigton Crescent, Bristol BS10 6DR* Tel 0117-950 7164

BARKER, Stephen Luke Remington. b 20. Cant Sch of Min. **d** 82 **p** 83. NSM Cranbrook *Cant* 82-90; rtd 90; Perm to Offic *Cant* from 91. *St Damian's, High Street, Cranbrook, Kent TN17 3LH* Tel (01580) 712048

BARKER, Timothy Reed (Tim). b 56. Qu Coll Cam BA79 MA82. Westcott Ho Cam 78. **d** 80 **p** 81. C Nantwich *Ches* 80-83; V Norton 83-88; V Runcorn All SS 88-94; Urban Officer 88-90; Dioc Communications Officer from 91; Bp's Chapl from 94; Hon P Asst Ches Cathl from 94. *11 Abbey Street, Chester CH1 2JF* Tel (01244) 347811 or 350864 Fax 347823

BARKER, Walter Frederick. b 25. Lon Univ BD48 ALCD48. St Jo Coll Lon 44. **d** 51 **p** 52. C Worthing St Geo *Chich* 51-53; C Leeds St Geo *Ripon* 53-56; V Tollington Park St Anne *Lon* 56-63; V Tollington Park St Mark 56-63; Midl Sec CMJ 63-66; Home Sec CMJ 66-71; Gen Sec CMJ 71-86; Min at Large CMJ 86-89; rtd 89. *72 Lime Grove, Ruislip, Middx HA4 8RY* Tel 0181-866 6941

BARKER, William Edward. b 28. Kelham Th Coll 49. **d** 54 **p** 55. C Warsop *S'well* 54-55; C Bawtry w Austerfield 55-57; V Frizington *Carl* 57-64; V Barrow St Jas 64-70; V Applethwaite 70-93; P-in-c Troutbeck 78-93; rtd 93; Perm to Offic *Carl* from 93. *114 Burneside Road, Kendal, Cumbria LA9 4RZ* Tel (01539) 734787

BARKING, Area Bishop of. *See* SAINSBURY, The Rt Revd Roger Frederick

BARKS, Jeffrey Stephen. b 45. Cranmer Hall Dur 66. **d** 71 **p** 72. C Wootton *St Alb* 71-74; C Boscombe St Jo *Win* 74-76; C Ringwood 76-80; P-in-c Spaxton w Charlynch *B & W* 80; P-in-c Enmore w Goathurst 80; P-in-c Spaxton w Goathurst, Enmore and Charlynch 80-81; R 81-92; RD Bridgwater 89-94; V Wembdon from 92. *The Vicarage, 12 Greenacre, Wembdon, Bridgwater, Somerset TA6 7RD* Tel (01278) 423468

BARLEY, Ann Christine. b 47. LNSM course 91. **d** 93 **p** 94. NSM Walton *St E* from 93. *Carmel, 143 Melford Way, Felixstowe, Suffolk IP11 8UH* Tel (01394) 283752

BARLEY, Christopher James. b 56. St Steph Ho Ox DipMin93. **d** 93 **p** 94. C Upton cum Chalvey *Ox* 93-96; TV High Wycombe from 96. *The Vicarage, Rutland Avenue, High Wycombe, Bucks HP12 3XA* Tel (01494) 471545

BARLEY, Ivan William. b 48. CEng74 MIEE74 Suffolk Poly DMS80. LNSM course 91. **d** 93 **p** 94. NSM Walton *St E* from 93. *Carmel, 143 Melford Way, Felixstowe, Suffolk IP11 8UH* Tel (01394) 283752

BARLEY (née LAWSON), Mrs Lynda Mary. b 53. York Univ BA74 PGCE75 Lon Univ MSc76 FSS. S'wark Ord Course 93. **d** 96. NSM Lower Nutfield *S'wark* from 96. *Pilgrim Cottage, Church Lane, Godstone, Surrey RH9 8BL* Tel (01883) 742232

BARLING, Michael Keith. b 38. Oak Hill Th Coll 63. **d** 66 **p** 67. C Portman Square St Paul *Lon* 66-70; C Enfield Ch Ch Trent Park 70-74; V Sidcup St Andr *Roch* 74-78; Dir Fountain Trust 78-81; Lic to Offic *Guildf* 78-81; Chapl Bethany Fellowship and Roffey Place 81-88; Lic to Offic *Chich* 81-88; Hon C Kennington St Mark *S'wark* 88-89; Prin Kingdom Faith Bible Coll from 89. *Kingdom Faith Ministries, Foundry Lane, Horsham, W Sussex RH13 5PX* Tel (01403) 211505 Fax 218463

BARLOW, Alan David. b 36. Worc Coll Ox BA59 MA65. Wycliffe Hall Ox 59. **d** 61 **p** 62. C Wealdstone H Trin *Lon* 61-67; V Neasden cum Kingsbury St Cath 67-73; Chapl Cranleigh Sch Surrey 73-81; Chapl Cheltenham Ladies' Coll from 82. *22 Moorend Road, Leckhampton, Cheltenham, Glos GL53 0EU* Tel (01242) 584668

BARLOW, Canon Charles William Moore. b 32. ALCM50 Man Univ BA57. Cuddesdon Coll 56. **d** 58 **p** 59. C Atherton *Man* 58-61; C Swinton St Pet 61-64; V Dobcross 64-76; V Dobcross w Scouthead from 76; Hon Can Man Cathl from 96; AD Saddleworth from 97. *The Vicarage, Woods Lane, Dobcross, Oldham OL3 5AN* Tel (01457) 872342

BARLOW, Clive Christopher. b 42. Linc Th Coll 67. **d** 70 **p** 71. C Surbiton St Mark *S'wark* 70-74; C Spring Park *Cant* 74-77; V Ash w Westmarsh 77-92; RD E Bridge 86-92; R Chartham from 92; RD W Bridge from 95. *The Rectory, The Green, Chartham, Canterbury, Kent CT4 7JW* Tel (01227) 738256

BARLOW, David. b 50. Leeds Univ BA71 MA. Wycliffe Hall Ox 71. **d** 73 **p** 74. C Horninglow *Lich* 73-75; C Wednesfield St Thos 75-77; C Bloxwich 77-78; Chapl RN from 78. *Royal Naval Chaplaincy Service, Room 203, Victory Building, HM Naval Base, Portsmouth PO1 3LS* Tel (01705) 727903 Fax 727112

BARLOW, Canon Edward Burnley. b 29. St Aid Birkenhead 56. **d** 58 **p** 59. C Lenton Abbey *S'well* 58-61; C Ipswich All SS *St E* 61-63; R Fishtoft *Linc* 63-76; V Linc St Giles 76-96; Can and Preb Linc Cathl from 92; rtd 96; Perm to Offic *Linc* from 96. *8 Pynder Close, Washingborough, Lincoln LN4 1EX* Tel (01522) 527655

BARLOW, Paul Andrew. b 59. Imp Coll Lon BSc80 UMIST PhD84 Bolton Inst of HE PGCE85. Aston Tr Scheme 89 Chich Th Coll 91. **d** 93 **p** 94. C Hale *Guildf* 93-97; C Christchurch *Win* from 97. *St George's House, Jumpers Road, Christchurch, Dorset BH23 2JR* Tel (01202) 486248

BARLOW, Paul Benson. b 31. Fitzw Coll Cam BA73 MA77 FRSA94. **d** 64 **p** 65. C Bath Abbey w St Jas *B & W* 64-74; Dep Hd Master Leys High Sch Redditch 74-81; Hd Master Jo Kyrle High Sch Ross-on-Wye from 82; Perm to Offic *Heref* 82-85; Lic to Offic 85-92; NSM Walford and St John w Bishopswood, Goodrich etc from 92. *The Coach House, Hentland, Ross-on-Wye, Herefordshire HR9 6LP*

BARLOW, Robert Mark. b 53. St Jo Coll Nottm. **d** 86 **p** 87. C Colwich w Gt Haywood *Lich* 86-91; R Crick and Yelvertoft w Clay Coton and Lilbourne *Pet* from 91. *The Rectory, Crick, Northants NN6 7TU* Tel (01788) 822147

BARLOW, Thomas Frank. b 24. WMMTC. **d** 84 **p** 85. NSM Dudley St Jas *Worc* 84-88; NSM Belbroughton w Fairfield and Clent 88-93; Perm to Offic from 93. *30 The Glebe, Belbroughton, Stourbridge, W Midlands DY9 9TH* Tel (01562) 730426

BARLOW, Timothy David. b 46. Univ Coll Ox BA67 MA71 Lon Univ BD71. Oak Hill Th Coll 71. **d** 71 **p** 72. C Marple All SS *Ches* 71-74; C Northwood Em *Lon* 74-78; Chapl Vevey w Château d'Oex and Villars *Eur* 78-84; Switzerland 84-89; V Chadkirk *Ches* from 89. *St Chad's Vicarage, Chadkirk Road, Romiley, Stockport, Cheshire SK6 3JY* Tel 0161-430 4652

BARLOW, William George. b 40. Liv Univ BSc62 Univ of Wales BD65. St Mich Coll Llan 76. **d** 76 **p** 77. C Roath St Marg *Llan* 76-79; TV Cyncoed *Mon* 79-83; R Radyr *Llan* from 83; RD Llan from 95. *The Rectory, Radyr, Cardiff CF4 8DY* Tel (01222) 842417

BARNACLE, Ronald William. b 20. Wells Th Coll 66. **d** 66 **p** 67. C Emscote *Cov* 66-67; C Nuneaton St Nic 67-69; C Camp Hill w Galley Common 69-70; R Etton w Dalton Holme *York* 70-76; R Hinderwell w Roxby 76-78; P-in-c Buckland Newton *Sarum* 78-80; P-in-c Wootton Glanville and Holnest 78-80; P-in-c Pulham 78-80; R Radwinter w Hempstead *Chelmsf* 80-83; V Blackfordby *Leic* 83-84; rtd 84; Perm to Offic *Worc* 84-92; Perm to Offic *Cov* from 87. *12 Larch Close, Bilton, Rugby CV22 7PJ* Tel (01788) 810390

BARNARD, Canon Anthony Nevin. b 36. St Jo Coll Cam BA60 MA64. Wells Th Coll 61. **d** 63 **p** 64. C Cheshunt *St Alb* 63-65; Tutor Wells Th Coll 65-66; Chapl 66-69; Vice-Prin 69-71; Dep Prin Sarum & Wells Th Coll 71-77; Dir S Dios Minl Tr Scheme 74-77; Can Res and Chan Lich Cathl *Lich* from 77; Warden of Readers 77-91; Dir of Tr 86-91. *13 The Close, Lichfield, Staffs WS13 7LD* Tel (01543) 255168 or 250300

BARNARD, Catherine Elizabeth. b 54. York Univ BA76 Dur Univ BA79. Cranmer Hall Dur 77. **dss** 80 **d** 87 **p** 94. Mexborough *Sheff* 80-83; Sheff Manor 83-90; Hon Par Dn 87-90; Hon Par Dn Bolsterstone 90-94; C from 94. *The Vicarage, Stonemoor Road, Bolsterstone, Sheffield S30 5ZN* Tel 0114-288 2149

BARNARD, Canon John Stuart. b 19. Em Coll Cam BA41 MA45. Ridley Hall Cam 41. **d** 43 **p** 44. C Erith St Jo *Roch* 43-46; C Tonbridge SS Pet and Paul 46-49; C Ox St Aldate *Ox* 49-53; C Bromley Common St Aug *Roch* 53-58; V 58-73; Hon Can Roch Cathl 70-82; V Seal St Pet 73-82; Perm to Offic *Chich* from 82; rtd 84. *3 Chanctonbury Close, Rustington, Littlehampton, W Sussex BN16 2JB* Tel (01903) 771351

BARNARD, Jonathan Dixon. b 46. St Cath Coll Cam BA68. Cuddesdon Coll 69. **d** 71 **p** 72. C Silksworth *Dur* 71-74; C Hatfield Hyde *St Alb* 74-78; TV Hitchin 78-86; TR Penrith w Newton Reigny and Plumpton Wall *Carl* 86-91; rtd 91. *4 Hallin Croft, Penrith, Cumbria CA11 8AA* Tel (01768) 63000

BARNARD, Kevin James Frodo. b 52. Keble Coll Ox BA77 MA79. Cranmer Hall Dur 77. **d** 79 **p** 80. C Swinton *Sheff* 79-83; TV Sheff Manor 83-90; V Bolsterstone from 90; Bp's Adv on Issues Relating to Ageing from 94. *The Vicarage, Stonemoor Road, Bolsterstone, Sheffield S30 5ZN* Tel 0114-288 2149

BARNARD, Leslie William. b 24. St Cath Coll Ox BA50 MA55 Southn Univ PhD70. Cuddesdon Coll 51. **d** 51 **p** 52. C Portswood Ch Ch *Win* 51-55; V Shaw and Whitley *Sarum* 55-61; R Chilcomb w Win All SS and Chesil *Win* 61-68; Sen Lect Leeds Univ 69-83; Dioc Dir of Tr *Ripon* 70-76; Chapl Harrogate Gen Hosp 83-89; rtd 89. *68 Park Place, Park Parade, Harrogate, N Yorkshire HG1 4NS* Tel (01423) 560038

BARNARD, Robert James. b 15. Lich Th Coll 54. **d** 55 **p** 56. C Wisbech SS Pet and Paul *Ely* 55-58; V Holbrooke *Derby* 58-65; R Clenchwarton *Ely* 65-77; P-in-c Hinxton 77-80; rtd 80; Perm to Offic *Roch* 80-95. *Flat 23, Bromley College, London Road, Bromley BR1 1PE* Tel 0181-290 1280

BARNARD, Canon William Henry (Bill). b 09. Dorchester Miss Coll 37. **d** 39 **p** 40. C Leic St Paul *Leic* 39-43; C Brighton All So *Chich* 43-51; C Barrowhill *Derby* 51-52; C Newbold w Dunston 51-53; R Hinton Martel *Sarum* 53-93; RD Wimborne 75-79; Can and Preb Sarum Cathl 79-93; rtd 93; Perm to Offic *B & W* from 94. *Halcyon, 94 Park Road, Congresbury, Bristol BS19 5HH*

BARNES, Alan Duff. b 42. St Steph Ho Ox 75. **d** 77 **p** 78. C Wanstead H Trin Hermon Hill *Chelmsf* 77-80; C Clacton St Jas 80-82; R Cranham 82-89; V Calcot *Ox* from 89. *St Birinus' House, Langley Hill, Reading RG3 5QX* Tel 0118-942 2828

BARNES, Brian. b 42. Sussex Univ MA82. Cant Sch of Min 79. **d** 82 **p** 83. NSM Maidstone All SS and St Phil w Tovil *Cant* 82-89; C 89-92; FE Adv Gen Syn Bd of Educn 86-92; R Staplehurst *Cant* from 92; RD W Charing from 95. *The Rectory, Frittenden*

Road, Staplehurst, Tonbridge, Kent TN12 0DH Tel (01580) 891258

BARNES, Brian. b 49. St Mich Coll Llan DMinlStuds93. **d** 93 **p** 94. C Betws w Ammanford *St D* 93-96; V Llanwnda, Goodwick, w Manorowen and Llanstinan from 96. *The Vicarage, Dyffryn, Goodwick SA64 0AN* Tel (01348) 873758

BARNES, Canon Bryan Peter. b 24. Leeds Univ BA50. Coll of Resurr Mirfield 50. **d** 52 **p** 53. C Swindon New Town *Bris* 52-59; S Rhodesia 59-65; Rhodesia 65-66; V Moorfields *Bris* 66-71; P-in-c Winterbourne Down 71-75; V Fishponds St Mary 75-87; Hon Can Bris Cathl 84-87; rtd 87; NSM Duloe w Herodsfoot *Truro* 91-95; Warden Jes Hosp Cant from 95. *The Warden's Lodge, Jesus Hospital, Canterbury, Kent CT1 1BS* Tel (01227) 463771

BARNES, Canon Charles Peter Kentish. b 19. Ch Coll Cam BA40 MA44. Ridley Hall Cam 40. **d** 42 **p** 43. C Reading St Jo *Ox* 42-45; C Sutton Coldfield H Trin *Birm* 45-49; Sub-Dean Cairo Cathl Egypt 49-52; R Wavertree St Mary *Liv* 52-56; R Maghull 56-69; R Stratford-on-Avon w Bishopton *Cov* 69-75; TR 75-81; Hon Can Cov Cathl 75-84; V Priors Hardwick, Priors Marston and Wormleighton 81-84; rtd 84; Perm to Offic *Cov* from 84; Perm to Offic *Glouc* from 84. *5 Willow Bank, Welford on Avon, Stratford-upon-Avon, Warks CV37 8HB* Tel (01789) 750780

BARNES, Colin. b 33. St Jo Coll York CertEd58. St Aid Birkenhead 61. **d** 64 **p** 65. C Eccles St Mary *Man* 64-66; C Barrow St Geo w St Luke *Carl* 66-68; V Goodshaw *Man* 68-80; P-in-c Wythenshawe St Martin 80-83; New Zealand from 83. *St Matthew's Vicarage, 16 Pearce Crescent, Taita, Lower Hutt, New Zealand* Tel Wellington (4) 567 7655

BARNES, The Very Revd Cyril Arthur. b 26. Edin Th Coll 47. **d** 50 **p** 51. C Aberdeen St Jo *Ab* 50-53; R Forres *Mor* 53-55; C Darrington w Wentbridge *Wakef* 55-58; V Ripponden 58-67; V Thorpe 66-67; R Huntly *Mor* 67-83; R Aberchirder 67-83; Hon Can St Andr Cathl Inverness 71-80; Dioc Sec 71-83; R Keith 74-83; Syn Clerk 77-80; Dean Mor 80-83; rtd 83; Perm to Offic *Ab* from 83; Perm to Offic *Mor* from 90. *Tillytarmont Cottage, Bridge of Isla, Huntly, Aberdeenshire AB54 4SP* Tel (01466) 711370 Fax as telephone

BARNES, David John. b 37. Lon Univ DipRS65 Kent Univ MA96. Chich Th Coll 65. **d** 68 **p** 69. C Crayford *Roch* 68-71; Chapl RAF 71-75; Chapl Sutton Valence Sch Kent 75-87; C Minster in Sheppey *Cant* 87-93; V Ash w Westmarsh from 93. *The Vicarage, Queen's Road, Ash, Canterbury, Kent CT3 2BG* Tel (01304) 812296

BARNES, David Keith. b 53. Linc Th Coll. **d** 89 **p** 90. C E Crompton *Man* 89-93; V Belfield from 93. *St Ann's Vicarage, 310 Milnrow Road, Rochdale, Lancs OL16 5BT* Tel (01706) 46173

BARNES, Derek Ian. b 44. Leeds Univ BA66. Westcott Ho Cam 66. **d** 68 **p** 69. C Far Headingley St Chad *Ripon* 68-71; Chapl Qu Eliz Coll *Lon* 72-77; Warden Lee Abbey Internat Students' Club Kensington 77-81; Hon C Willesden Green St Gabr *Lon* 81-83; P-in-c Southall H Trin from 84; P-in-c Southall St Geo 89-92. *Holy Trinity Vicarage, 41 Park View Road, Southall, Middx UB1 3HJ* Tel 0181-574 3762

BARNES, Preb Donald Edward. b 26. K Coll Lon BD51 AKC51. **d** 52 **p** 53. C Willesden St Matt *Lon* 52-59; V Cricklewood St Pet 59-79; Lect Bps' Coll Cheshunt 63-68; V Belsize Park *Lon* 79-96; Preb St Paul's Cathl 84-96; AD N Camden (Hampstead) 83-88; rtd 96; Perm to Offic *Lon* from 96. *94 Hamilton Road, London NW11 9DY* Tel 0181-731 9860

BARNES, Duncan Christopher. b 64. Warw Univ BA90. Trin Coll Bris BA93. **d** 93 **p** 94. C Hornchurch St Andr *Chelmsf* from 93. *49 Burnway, Hornchurch, Essex RM11 3SN* Tel (01708) 443358

✠**BARNES, The Rt Revd Edwin Ronald.** b 35. Pemb Coll Ox BA58 MA62. Cuddesdon Coll 58. **d** 60 **p** 61 **c** 95. C Portsea N End St Mark *Portsm* 60-64; C Woodham *Guildf* 64-67; R Farncombe 67-78; V Hessle *York* 78-87; AD W Hull 85-87; Prin St Steph Ho Ox 87-95; Hon Can Ch Ch *Ox* 94-95; Suff Bp Richborough (PEV) *Cant* from 95; Hon Can St Alb *St Alb* from 96. *14 Hall Place Gardens, St Albans, Herts AL1 3SP* Tel (01727) 857764 Fax 763025

BARNES, Mrs Enid Mabel. b 38. Homerton Coll Cam DipT58. WMMTC 87. **d** 90 **p** 94. Par Dn Walsall St Paul *Lich* 90-94; C 94-96; TV Chell from 96. *110 Sprinkbank Road, Stoke-on-Trent ST6 6HZ* Tel (01782) 839334

BARNES, Esdaile Lenox. b 13. ALCD40. **d** 40 **p** 41. C Street *B & W* 40-43; R Priston 43-45; V Upper Tulse Hill St Matthias *S'wark* 45-52; V Maidenhead St Andr and St Mary *Ox* 52-60; Australia 61-72 and from 75; V Uralla 61-65; V Moree 65-69; C-in-c Tamworth St Jas 69-70; C St Pet Cathl Armidale 70-71; C Folkestone H Trin w Ch Ch *Cant* 72-74; R Grimston w Congham *Nor* 74-75; R Roydon All SS 74-75; V Greenacre 76-78; V Beverly Hills 78-83; Perm to Offic Sydney from 83. *84 Upper Street, Tamworth, NSW, Australia 2340* Tel Tamworth (67) 669808

BARNES, James Barrie. b 27. Bps' Coll Cheshunt 51. **d** 53 **p** 54. C Leic St Phil *Leic* 53-59; V Blackfordby 59-76; V Smisby *Derby* 59-69; RD Akeley W *Leic* 69-76; V Broom Leys 76-92; rtd 93. *15 Diamond Avenue, Sherwood Park, Rainsworth, Mansfield, Notts NG21 0FF* Tel (01623) 796601

BARNES, Jennifer (Jenny). b 45. AdvDipCrim. N Ord Course 94. **d** 96 **p** 97. C Thorne *Sheff* from 96. *The Rectory, Church Street, Armthorpe, Doncaster, S Yorkshire DN3 3AD* Tel (01302) 831231

BARNES, Canon John Barwick. b 32. AKC58. **d** 59 **p** 60. C Brentwood St Thos *Chelmsf* 59-65; R Arkesden w Wicken Bonhunt 65-71; V Gt Ilford St Mary from 71; Hon Can Chelmsf Cathl from 95. *26 South Park Road, Ilford, Essex IG1 1SS* Tel 0181-478 0546

BARNES, John Christopher. b 43. MA ATI DMS. Linc Th Coll 78. **d** 80 **p** 81. C Guiseley *Bradf* 80-83; TV Guiseley w Esholt 83-86; V Rawdon 86-92; R Armthorpe *Sheff* from 92; RD Doncaster from 96. *The Rectory, Church Street, Armthorpe, Doncaster, S Yorkshire DN3 3AD* Tel (01302) 831231

BARNES, John Seymour. b 30. Qu Coll Birm 58. **d** 61 **p** 62. C Bromsgrove St Jo *Worc* 61-64; C Kingsthorpe *Pet* 64-66; C Styvechale *Cov* 66-69; P-in-c Avon Dassett w Farnborough 69-75; P-in-c Cov St Alb 75-84; R Weddington and Caldecote 84-89; P-in-c Wilnecote *Lich* 89-90; V Bentley 90-96; rtd 96; Perm to Offic *Lich* from 96. *The Vicarage, 110 Sprinkbank Road, Chell Heath, Stoke-on-Trent ST6 6HZ* Tel (01782) 839334

BARNES, Katrina Crawford. b 52. Oak Hill NSM Course 90. **d** 93 **p** 94. NSM Bromley H Trin *Roch* from 93. *39 The Fairway, Bromley BR1 2JZ* Tel 0181-467 0338

BARNES, Matthew John. b 68. St Jo Coll Nottm BA93. **d** 96 **p** 97. C Stanley *Wakef* from 96. *33 Noon Close, Stanley, Wakefield, W Yorkshire WF3 4PT* Tel (01924) 828480

BARNES, Dr Neal Duncan. b 63. Leeds Univ BSc84 Cranfield Inst of Tech PhD92. Oak Hill Th Coll DipHE95. **d** 95 **p** 96. C Biggleswade *St Alb* from 95. *46 Wilsheres Road, Biggleswade, Beds SG18 0DN* Tel (01767) 314240

BARNES, Canon Neil. b 42. Kelham Th Coll 61 Bps' Coll Cheshunt 65. **d** 68 **p** 69. C Poulton-le-Fylde *Blackb* 68-72; C Ribbleton 72-75; V Knuzden 75-81; Chapl Prestwich Hosp Man 81-88; Chapl Salford Mental Health Services NHS Trust from 88; Hon Can Man Cathl *Man* from 96. *Mental Health Services of Salford, Bury New Road, Prestwich, Manchester M25 3BL* Tel 0161-772 3675 or 773 9121

BARNES, Paul Nicholas. b 58. Qu Coll Birm 89. **d** 91 **p** 92. C Weymouth H Trin *Sarum* 91-95; P-in-c Studley from 95. *The Vicarage, 340 Frome Road, Trowbridge, Wilts BA14 0ED* Tel (01225) 753162

BARNES, Peter Frank. b 52. St Jo Coll Nottm LTh81. **d** 81 **p** 82. C Colne St Bart *Blackb* 81-83; C Melton Mowbray w Thorpe Arnold *Leic* 83-86; P-in-c Barlestone 86-89; V Broughton and Duddon *Carl* from 89. *The Vicarage, Broughton-in-Furness, Cumbria LA20 6HS* Tel (01229) 716305

BARNES, Ms Sheena Elizabeth. b 56. Reading Univ MFA Cant Coll of Art BA78 Ox Univ BA85. Ripon Coll Cuddesdon 83. **dss** 86 **d** 87. Westmr St Jas *Lon* 86-89; Par Dn 87-89; rtd 89. *14H Sussex Street, London SW1V 4RS* Tel 0171-931 8318

BARNES, Stephen. b 46. Hull Univ BA69 Bris Univ DipTh71. Clifton Th Coll 69. **d** 72 **p** 73. C Girlington *Bradf* 72-74; TV Glyncorrwg w Afan Vale and Cymmer Afan *Llan* 74-79; R 79-86; V Aberavon from 86. *The Vicarage, 68 Pentyla Baglan Road, Aberavon, Port Talbot SA12 8AD* Tel (01639) 883824

BARNES, Stephen John. b 59. Univ of Wales (Cardiff) BSc80. Chich Th Coll 83. **d** 86 **p** 87. C Neath w Llantwit *Llan* 86-89; C Coity w Nolton 89-95; V Troedyrhiw w Merthyr Vale from 95. *The Vicarage, Nixonville, Merthyr Vale, Merthyr Tydfil CF48 4RF* Tel (01443) 690249

BARNES, Stephen William. b 53. Man Univ BSc. St Jo Coll Nottm DipTh82. **d** 83 **p** 84. C Chadwell Heath *Chelmsf* 83-87; C Becontree St Alb 88-89; Deanery Youth Chapl 88-91; C Becontree S 89-91; TV Worth *Chich* from 91. *St Barnabas's Vicarage, 2 Crawley Lane, Crawley, W Sussex RH10 4EB* Tel (01293) 513398

BARNES, Mrs Sylvia Frances (Sally). b 43. Shoreditch Coll Lon CertEd75. S Tr Scheme 92. **d** 96 **p** 97. Hon C Cusop w Clifford, Hardwicke, Bredwardine etc *Heref* from 96. *Pwll Cwm, Arthur's Stone Lane, Dorstone, Hereford HR3 6AY* Tel (01981) 500252

BARNES, William (Billy). b 54. RGN89 St Andr Univ MTh84. Westcott Ho Cam CTM92. **d** 92 **p** 93. C S Bank *York* 92-95; C Northallerton w Kirby Sigston 95-97; V Dormanstown from 97. *All Saints' Vicarage, South Avenue, Redcar, Cleveland TS10 5LL* Tel (01642) 478334

BARNES, William Thomas. b 39. Dur Univ BA60. Wycliffe Hall Ox 60. **d** 62 **p** 63. C Scotforth *Blackb* 62-66; C Cleveleys 66-67; V Colne Ch Ch 67-74; V Bamber Bridge St Sav from 74. *St Saviour's Vicarage, Bamber Bridge, Preston PR5 6AJ* Tel (01772) 35374

BARNES-CEENEY, Brian. b 35. St Aid Birkenhead 59. **d** 62 **p** 63. C Plaistow St Andr *Chelmsf* 62-64; C Waltham Abbey 64-66; V Falfield *Glouc* 66-71; R Rockhampton 66-71; Chapl HM Det Cen Eastwood Park 68-71; Chapl HM Youth Cust Cen Everthorpe 71-76; Chapl HM Pris Coldingley 76-79; Chapl HM Pris Bris 79-87; Chapl HM Pris Ford from 87. *HM Prison, Arundel, W Sussex BN18 0BX* Tel (01903) 717261 Fax 726060

BARNES-CLAY, Peter John Granger. b 43. MCollP Cam Univ CertEd69. Chich Th Coll 72. **d** 75 **p** 82. C Earlham St Anne *Nor* 75-76; Asst Master Hewett Sch Nor 76-83; Hon C Eaton 81-83; C 83-87; R Winterton w E and W Somerton and Horsey 87-92; R

Weybourne Gp from 92; RD Holt from 95. *The Rectory, The Street, Weybourne, Holt, Norfolk NR25 7SY* Tel (01263) 588268

BARNETT, Alec James Leon. b 44. Em Coll Cam BA66 MA70. Cuddesdon Coll. **d** 69 **p** 70. C Preston St Jo *Blackb* 69-72; Asst Chapl Uppingham Sch Leics 72-80; Hd of RE 73-80; Dir of Farmington/Ampleforth Project 79-83; C Witney *Ox* 80-84; P-in-c Lt Compton w Chastleton, Cornwell etc 84-88; Prin Ox Chr Tr Scheme 84-88; P-in-c St Michael Penkevil *Truro* 88-95; P-in-c Lamorran and Merther 88-95; Dioc Tr Officer 88-95; Chapl Strasbourg *Eur* from 95; Perm to Offic *Truro* from 95. *16 rue Riehl, 67100 Strasbourg-Neuhof, France* Tel France (33) 88 40 36 15 Fax 88 39 07 58

BARNETT, David John. b 33. Magd Coll Ox BA56 BTh58 MA61. St Steph Ho Ox 56. **d** 59 **p** 60. C Styvechale *Cov* 59-62; S Africa 62-69; Rhodesia 70-76; V Colindale St Matthias *Lon* 77-90; R Finchley St Mary from 90. *St Mary's Rectory, Rectory Close, London N3 1TS* Tel 0181-346 4600

BARNETT, Dudley Graham. b 36. Ch Ch Ox BA62 MA65. St Steph Ho Ox 62. **d** 64 **p** 65. C Abbey Hey *Man* 64-68; V Swinton H Rood 68-90; R Old Trafford St Hilda from 90. *St Hilda's Rectory, 255 Kings Road, Manchester M16 0JD* Tel 0161-881 9332

BARNETT, Miss Jessica Dorothy Anne. b 18. St Paul's Coll Limuru. **dss** 69 **d** 87. Halifax St Jo Bapt *Wakef* 72-80; rtd 80; Perm to Offic *Ox* 80-96. *Cotswold Cottage, Thames Street, Charlbury, Chipping Norton, Oxon OX7 3QL* Tel (01608) 810234

BARNETT, John Raymond. b 51. Lon Univ LLB74 BD86. Westcott Ho Cam 74. **d** 77 **p** 78. C Northfield *Birm* 77-81; V Hamstead St Bernard 81-91; R The Quinton from 91. *The Rectory, 773 Hagley Road West, Birmingham B32 1AJ* Tel 0121-422 2031

BARNETT, John Richard. b 28. FCIS72. Portsm Dioc Tr Course 86. **d** 88. NSM Droxford *Portsm* 88-91; NSM Meonstoke w Corhampton cum Exton 88-91; NSM W Meon and Warnford from 91. *Pinfarthings, Coombe Lane, West Meon, Petersfield, Hants GU32 1NB* Tel (01730) 829380

BARNETT, Canon Norman. b 19. Univ of Wales BA41. St Mich Coll Llan 41. **d** 43 **p** 44. C Roath St German *Llan* 43-49; Chapl Llan Cathl 49-53; R Liss *Portsm* 53-85; RD Petersfield 70-75; Hon Can Portsm Cathl 76-85; rtd 85. *Banbury House, Burton Street, Marnhull, Sturminster Newton, Dorset DT10 1PS* Tel (01258) 820260

BARNETT, Miss Patricia Ann. b 38. Whitelands Coll Lon CertEd. St Jo Coll Dur 75. **dss** 78 **d** 87 **p** 94. Gateacre *Liv* 78-82; Litherland St Paul Hatton Hill 82-87; Par Dn 87-88; Par Dn Platt Bridge 88-94; C 94-95; V Skelmersdale Ch at Cen from 95. *10 Ferndale, Skelmersdale, Lancs WN8 6PZ*

BARNETT, Peter Geoffrey. b 46. AKC71. St Aug Coll Cant 71. **d** 72 **p** 73. C Wolverhampton *Lich* 72-77; P-in-c Caldmore 77-83; TR Bris St Agnes and St Simon w St Werburgh *Bris* 83-87; P-in-c Bris St Paul w St Barn 83-87; TR Bris St Paul's 87-94; Warden Pilsdon Community from 94. *Pilsdon Manor, Pilsdon, Bridport, Dorset DT6 5NZ* Tel (01308) 868308

BARNETT, Peter John. b 36. N Ord Course 82. **d** 85 **p** 86. C New Bury *Man* 85-87; TV 87-94; P-in-c Clifton from 94. *St Anne's Vicarage, Manchester Road, Manchester M27 6PP* Tel 0161-794 1939

BARNETT, Preb Raymond Michael. b 31. Man Univ BA54. Wells Th Coll 54. **d** 56 **p** 57. C Fallowfield *Man* 56-59; Madagascar 59-60; V Blackrod *Man* 60-67; V Woolavington *B & W* 67-76; RD Bridgwater 72-76; V St Decumans 76-96; RD Quantock 78-86 and 93-95; Preb Wells Cathl 89-96; rtd 96; Perm to Offic *B & W* from 96. *4 Foster Close, Wells, Somerset BA5 3NB* Tel (01749) 672983

BARNETT, Russell Scott. b 20. Oak Hill Th Coll 56. **d** 58 **p** 59. C Ulverston St Mary *Carl* 58-61; V Kirkdale St Paul N Shore *Liv* 61-67; V Salterhebble All SS *Wakef* 67-77; R Aikton *Carl* 77-85; R Orton St Giles 77-85; rtd 86; Perm to Offic *Carl* from 86. *8 Jackson Road, Houghton, Carlisle CA3 0NW* Tel (01228) 31721

BARNEY, Michael Frank. b 29. New Coll Ox BA53 MA58. Chich Th Coll 53. **d** 55 **p** 56. C Hampstead St Jo *Lon* 55-59; C Wilton Place St Paul 59-68; C Kensington St Mary Abbots w St Geo 68-75; V Chiswick St Mich 75-93; rtd 94; Perm to Offic *Lon* from 95; Perm to Offic *S'wark* from 95. *58 Deanhill Court, Upper Richmond Road West, London SW14 7DL* Tel 0181-878 2668

BARNFATHER, Thomas Fenwick. b 52. Linc Th Coll 86. **d** 88 **p** 89. C Sedgefield *Dur* 88-91; TV E Darlington 91-92; CF 92-96; V Heybridge w Langford *Chelmsf* from 96. *The Vicarage, 1A Crescent Road, Heybridge, Maldon, Essex CM9 4SJ* Tel (01621) 842245

BARNSLEY, Mrs Angela Vera. b 47. St Hild Coll Dur BA70. St Alb Minl Tr Scheme 90. **d** 93. NSM Codicote *St Alb* 93-94. *1 Marquis Close, Weymouth, Dorset DT4 9TA* Tel (01305) 770406

BARNSLEY, Melvyn. b 46. Dur Univ BA67 DipTh69 CertEd. St Chad's Coll Dur 64. **d** 71 **p** 72. C Cov St Thos *Cov* 71-74; C Cov St Jo 71-75; V New Bilton 75-82; R Stevenage St Andr and St Geo *St Alb* from 82; RD Stevenage from 89. *The Rectory, Cuttys Lane, Stevenage, Herts SG1 1UP* Tel (01438) 351631

BARNSLEY, Mrs Valerie Anne. b 48. Sussex Univ BEd71. WMMTC 91. **d** 94 **p** 95. NSM Tettenhall Regis *Lich* from 94. *3 Highlands Road, Finchfield, Wolverhampton WV3 8AG* Tel (01902) 344115

BARNSTAPLE, Archdeacon of. *See* LLOYD, The Ven Bertram Trevor

BARON, Noel Spencer Peter. b 15. K Coll Cam BA39 MA42. Linc Th Coll 40. **d** 41 **p** 42. C Welwyn Garden City *St Alb* 41-43; C Welwyn 43-48; V Holcombe Rogus w Hockworthy *Ex* 48-52; V W Malvern *Worc* 52-83; rtd 83; Perm to Offic *Heref* from 85. *Brindley, 21 The Crescent, Colwall, Malvern, Worcs WR13 6QN* Tel (01684) 40477

BARON, Peter Murray. b 56. New Coll Ox MA78. Cranmer Hall Dur 91. **d** 93 **p** 94. C Monkseaton St Pet *Newc* 93-95; C Guildf St Sav *Guildf* from 96. *16 Cunningham Avenue, Guildford GU1 2PE* Tel (01483) 562332

BARON, Thomas Michael. b 63. St Steph Ho Ox 85. **d** 88 **p** 89. C Hartlepool St Paul *Dur* 88-92; Chapl Asst Hartlepool Gen Hosp 89-92; Asst Chapl Whittington Hosp Lon 92-95; Chapl Chase Farm Hosps NHS Trust Enfield from 95; Chapl Enfield Community Care Trust from 95. *Chase Farm Hospital, 127 The Ridgeway, Enfield, Middx EN2 8JL* Tel 0181-366 6600

BARON, Mrs Vanessa Lilian. b 57. SRN79 City Univ BSc79 Fitzw Coll Cam MA85. Ridley Hall Cam 83. **dss** 86 **d** 87 **p** 94. Roxbourne St Andr *Lon* 86-89; Par Dn 87-89; NSM Roxeth 94-95; Lic to Offic from 95; Asst Chapl Harrow Sch from 95. *3 High Street, Harrow, Middx HA1 3HT* Tel 0181-869 1254 Fax as telephone

BARR, Canon David James Osborne (Ossie). b 23. TCD BA45 MA. CITC 46. **d** 46 **p** 47. C Derriaghy *Conn* 46-48; C Dublin Donnybrook *D & G* 48-51; C Dublin St Ann 51-57; I Dublin St Mark 57-65; I Dublin Booterstown 65-92; RD Monkstown 83-92; Can Ch Ch Cathl Dublin 84-92; rtd 92. *26 Woodlands Avenue, Stillorgan, Co Dublin, Irish Republic* Tel Dublin (1) 288 4275 Fax as telephone

BARR, John Gourlay Crichton. b 23. Edin Univ BL46. Edin Dioc NSM Course 81. **d** 84 **p** 85. NSM Edin St Mark *Edin* 84-91; rtd 91; Perm to Offic *Bre* from 91. *Grove House, 22 St Andrew Street, Brechin, Angus DD9 6JJ* Tel (01356) 624412

BARR (née HAYTER), Dr Mary Elizabeth. b 58. Jes Coll Ox BA80 CertEd81 MA84 DPhil85. Ridley Hall Cam 84. **dss** 86 **d** 87 **p** 94. Chapl Cam Univ Pastorate 86-91; Cambridge H Trin w St Andr Gt *Ely* 86-87; Par Dn 87-91; Perm to Offic 91-92; Perm to Offic *Ex* 92-94; NSM Torquay St Luke from 94. *St Luke's Vicarage, 1 Mead Road, Torquay TQ2 6TE* Tel (01803) 605097

BARR, Michael John Alexander. b 60. Qu Coll Ox BA82 MA86 Pemb Coll Cam BA86 MA90. Ridley Hall Cam 84. **d** 87 **p** 88. C Earley St Pet *Ox* 87-89; C Cambridge Gt St Mary w St Mich *Ely* 89-92; Chapl Girton Coll Cam 90-92; P-in-c Torquay St Luke *Ex* 92-97; Dioc Communications Officer 92-97; P-in-c Gt Malvern St Mary from 97. *Priory Vicarage, Clarence Road, Malvern, Worcs WR14 3EN* Tel (01684) 563707

BARR, The Very Revd William Norman Cochrane. b 20. TCD BA44 MA50 BD50. CITC 45. **d** 46 **p** 46. C Ballymena *Conn* 46-52; C Belf Cathl 52-54; R Duneane w Ballyscullion 54-58; Bp's Dom Chapl 56-71; P-in-c Belfast Whiterock 58-61; I Derriaghy w Colin 61-90; RD Derriaghy 72-82; Can Conn Cathl 80-82; Dean Conn 82-90; rtd 90. *45 Killeaton Crescent, Dunmurry, Belfast BT17 9HB* Tel (01232) 621746

BARRACLOUGH, Dennis. b 35. LCP62 FCP74 CertEd58. Lambeth STh68 Ripon Hall Ox 66. **d** 68 **p** 69. C Woodhouse *Wakef* 68-71; V Gildersome 71-83; V Kirkburton from 83; RD Kirkburton from 92. *The Vicarage, 3B Shelley Lane, Kirkburton, Huddersfield HD8 0SJ* Tel (01484) 602188

BARRACLOUGH, Canon Owen Conrad. b 32. Pemb Coll Cam BA55 MA59. Westcott Ho Cam 56. **d** 57 **p** 58. C Chippenham St Andr w Tytherton Lucas *Bris* 57-62; V Harringay St Paul *Lon* 62-70; Bp's Chapl for Community Relns *Cov* 70-77; P-in-c Baginton 72-77; V Swindon Ch Ch *Bris* from 77; Chapl Princess Marg Hosp Swindon 77-89; Hon Can Bris Cathl *Bris* from 87. *Christ Church Vicarage, 26 Cricklade Street, Swindon SN1 3HG* Tel (01793) 522832

BARRALL, John Henry. b 31. BEd. Bps' Coll Cheshunt. **d** 61 **p** 62. C Digswell *St Alb* 61-65; C Aldershot St Mich *Guildf* 65-70; TV Hemel Hempstead *St Alb* 70-82; Perm to Offic 83-91; R Meppershall w Campton and Stondon from 91. *The Rectory, Church Road, Meppershall, Shefford, Beds SG17 5NA* Tel (01462) 813334

BARRATT, The Ven Anthony John. b 19. Glas Univ MRCVS. Bible Churchmen's Coll. **d** 49 **p** 50. C Slough *Ox* 49-52; SAMS Miss Cholchol Falkland Is 52-64; Hon Can Port Stanley 57-64; SAMS Miss Asuncion Paraguay 64-70; Argentina 70-84; Adn Tucuman 73-84; rtd 84. *Couchill Villa, Couchill Farm Lane, Seaton, Devon EX12 3AL* Tel (01297) 21118

BARRATT, Mrs Elizabeth June. b 32. ACP65. Trin Coll Bris 75. **dss** 78 **d** 87 **p** 94. W Kilburn St Luke w St Simon and St Jude *Lon* 78-87; Par Dn 87-94; C from 94. *Flat 1, St Luke's Church Centre, Fernhead Road, London W9 3EH* Tel 0181-969 9338

BARRATT, Peter. b 29. Down Coll Cam BA53 MA57. Ridley Hall Cam 53. **d** 55 **p** 56. C Bebington *Ches* 55-58; C-in-c Cam St Martin CD *Ely* 58-61; V Cambridge St Martin 61-68; V

Rawtenstall St Mary *Man* 68-83; AD Rossendale 80-83; V Bosley and N Rode w Wincle and Wildboarclough *Ches* 83-94; rtd 94; Perm to Offic *Ches* from 94. *10 Snab Wood Close, Little Neston, South Wirral L64 0UP* Tel 0151-336 6641

BARRATT, Philip Norman. b 62. Aston Tr Scheme 87 St Steph Ho Ox 89 Coll of Resurr Mirfield 90. **d** 92 **p** 93. C Heywood St Luke w All So *Man* 92-96; V Thornham St Jas from 96. *St James's Vicarage, 120 Shaw Road, Rochdale, Lancs OL16 4SQ* Tel (01706) 45256

BARRETT, Alan. b 48. Southn Univ BA69. Wycliffe Hall Ox 74. **d** 77 **p** 78. C Conisbrough *Sheff* 77-80; C Lower Homerton St Paul *Lon* 80-81; C Homerton St Barn w St Paul 81; C-in-c Hounslow Gd Shep Beavers Lane CD 81-87; R Langdon Hills *Chelmsf* from 87. *The Rectory, 105A Berry Lane, Langdon Hills, Basildon, Essex SS16 6AP* Tel (01268) 542156

BARRETT, Christopher Paul. b 49. AKC71 St Aug Coll Cant 71. **d** 72 **p** 73. C Tupsley *Heref* 72-75; C Ex St Thos *Ex* 75-79; R Atherington and High Bickington 79-83; V Burrington 79-83; Asst Dir of Educn 79-87; P-in-c Sticklepath 83-85; P-in-c Barnstaple 83-85; TV 85-90; V Whipton from 90. *The Vicarage, 19 The Mede, Exeter EX4 8ED* Tel (01392) 467552

BARRETT, Clive. b 55. MA CertEd. St Steph Ho Ox. **d** 83 **p** 84. C Wakef Cathl *Wakef* 83-87; Chapl Leeds Univ *Ripon* from 87; Dioc Development Rep from 89. *81 Becketts Park Drive, Leeds LS6 3PJ* Tel 0113-275 5497 or 233 5071

BARRETT, Dr David Brian. b 27. Clare Coll Cam BA48 MA50 BD69 Columbia Univ (NY) PhD65. Union Th Sem (NY) STM63 PhD65 Ridley Hall Cam 52. **d** 54 **p** 55. Succ Bradf Cathl *Bradf* 54-56; CMS 57-92; Kenya 57-62 and 65-85; USA 62-63; Guatemala 63-65; Research Sec ACC 70-87; Lic to Offic *Lon* 70-87; USA from 87; rtd 92. *2503 Prestwick Circle, Richmond, Virginia 23294, USA* Tel Richmond (804) 747-7455 Fax 358-0504

BARRETT, Canon Derek Leonard. b 25. St Fran Coll Brisbane ThL57. **d** 57 **p** 58. Australia 57-63; C Ramsgate St Geo *Cant* 64-65; C Putney St Mary *S'wark* 65-67; V Kidderminster St Jo *Worc* 67-77; V Stourbridge St Thos 77-90; RD Stourbridge 83-89; Hon Can Worc Cathl 87-90; rtd 90; Perm to Offic *Glouc* from 90. *Barton Cottage, Bourton-on-the-Water, Glos GL54 2AR* Tel (01451) 821777

BARRETT, Gary John. b 46. Sarum & Wells Th Coll 87. **d** 90 **p** 91. NSM Guernsey St Peter Port *Win* 90-97; Chapl Eliz Coll Guernsey 93-97; P-in-c Westham *Chich* from 97. *The Vicarage, 6 Rattle Road, Westham, Pevensey, E Sussex BN24 5DE* Tel (01323) 762294

BARRETT, Graham Crichton. b 51. IEng76 FIMEMME78. Linc Th Coll 88. **d** 90 **p** 91. C Torpoint *Truro* 90-94; Dio Youth and Voc Officer 94-95; C St Columb Major w St Wenn 94-95; P-in-c St Issey w St Petroc Minor from 95; Dioc Children's Adv from 95. *The Rectory, St Issey, Wadebridge, Cornwall PL27 7QB* Tel (01841) 540314

BARRETT, John Joseph James. b 38. Lon Univ BD65. Sarum & Wells Th Coll. **d** 78 **p** 78. C Danbury *Chelmsf* 78-80; Ind Chapl 80-89; C Dovercourt 80-83; TV Dovercourt and Parkeston 83-89; V Rubery *Birm* from 89. *St Chad's Vicarage, 160A New Road, Rednal, Birmingham B45 9JA* Tel 0121-453 3255

BARRETT, Kenneth. b 42. Univ of Wales (Lamp) BA64. St Steph Ho Ox 65. **d** 67 **p** 68. C Poulton-le-Fylde *Blackb* 67-69; C S Shore H Trin 69-72; V Brierfield 72-83; V Chorley St Geo from 83. *St George's Vicarage, Letchworth Place, Chorley, Lancs PR7 2HJ* Tel (01257) 263064

BARRETT, Kenneth Arthur Lambart. b 60. CITC BTh94. **d** 97. NSM Seagoe *D & D* from 97. *71 Seagoe Road, Portadown, Craigavon, Co Armagh BT63 5HS* Tel (01762) 331015

BARRETT, Canon Kenneth Sydney. b 26. Roch Th Coll 60. **d** 62 **p** 63. C Wollaton *S'well* 62-65; C Hucknall Torkard 65-67; Australia from 67; Can Bunbury 76-92; rtd 92. *PO Box 818, 2 Loxton Street, Mandurah, W Australia 6210* Tel Mandurah (9) 581 2519

BARRETT, Mrs Marion Lily. b 54. SRN75. SW Minl Tr Course 91. **d** 94 **p** 95. C St Mawgan w St Ervan and St Eval *Truro* from 94. *The Rectory, St Issey, Wadebridge, Cornwall PL27 7QB* Tel (01841) 540314

BARRETT, Peter Francis. b 56. TCD BA78 MA81 DipTh81 MPhil84. CITC. **d** 81 **p** 82. C Drumachose *D & R* 81-83; C Dublin St Ann *D & G* 83-85; I Conwal Union w Gartan *D & R* 85-90; RD Kilmacrenan E and W 88-90; I Belfast St Geo *Conn* 90-94; Chapl Actors' Ch Union from 93; Chapl TCD from 94; Min Can St Patr Cathl Dublin 94-96; Treas V 96-97; Succ from 97. *The Chaplaincy, 27 Trinity College, Dublin 2, Irish Republic* Tel Dublin (1) 608 1402 Fax 679-0335 E-mail pebarrett@tcd.ie

BARRETT, Philip Leslie Sibborn. b 47. Ex Coll Ox BA68 MA72 BD90 Univ of Wales (Cardiff) LLM95 FSA96 FRHistS88. Cuddesdon Coll 68. **d** 70 **p** 71. C Pershore w Wick *Worc* 70-73; C Bournemouth St Pet w St Swithun, H Trin etc *Win* 74-76; V Choral Heref Cathl *Heref* 76-86; P-in-c Otterbourne *Win* 86-87; R Compton and Otterbourne from 87; Hon Chapl Win Cathl from 90. *The Rectory, Kiln Lane, Otterbourne, Winchester, Hants SO21 2EJ* Tel (01962) 713400

BARRETT, Mrs Rachel Jeanne Alexandra. b 56. Ex Univ BA78 PGCE79. SW Minl Tr Course 92. **d** 95 **p** 96. NSM Ex St Mark *Ex* 95-96; NSM Ex St Mark, St Sidwell and St Matt from 96. *The Vicarage, 19 The Mede, Exeter EX4 8ED* Tel (01392) 467552

BARRETT, Raymond William. b 23. St Mich Coll Llan 72. **d** 73 **p** 74. C Cheltenham St Luke and St Jo *Glouc* 73-75; P-in-c Holbeach Hurn *Linc* 75-78; V Baston 78-83; rtd 83; Perm to Offic *Glouc* from 83. *2 Millhouse Drive, Wymans Brook, Cheltenham, Glos GL50 4RG* Tel (01242) 575434

BARRETT, Ronald Reginald. b 30. Roch Th Coll 61. **d** 64 **p** 65. C Spring Park *Cant* 64-66; C Thornton Heath St Jude 66-68; V Greengates *Bradf* 68-73; V Shelf 73-79; V Embsay w Eastby 79-87; V Farndon and Coddington *Ches* 87-92; rtd 92; Perm to Offic *Bradf* from 92. *12 Craigmore Drive, Ben Rhydding, Ilkley, W Yorkshire LS29 8PG* Tel (01943) 609713

BARRETT, Stephen David Norman. b 54. Aber Univ BSc75 Edin Univ BD78. Edin Th Coll 75. **d** 78 **p** 79. C Ardrossan *Glas* 78-80; R Peterhead *Ab* 80-81; Chapl HM Pris Peterhead 80-81; R Renfrew *Glas* 81-87; R Bishopbriggs 87-94; Chapl HM Pris Glas (Barlinnie) from 87; Chapl Stobhill Gen Hosp from 87; P-in-c Port Glas from 94. *The Rectory, Bardrainney Avenue, Port Glasgow, Renfrewshire PA14 6HB* Tel (01475) 707444

BARRETT, Mrs Thelma. b 29. S'wark Ord Course 80. **dss** 82 **d** 87 **p** 94. Newington St Mary *S'wark* 82-84; Chapl Asst St Pet Hosp Chertsey 84-90; Chertsey *Guildf* 84-87; C 87-90; rtd 91; Perm to Offic *Guildf* from 91; NSM Worplesdon 94-95. *9 Danses Close, Guildford, Surrey GU4 7EE* Tel (01483) 505215

BARRETT, Wilfred. b 19. Dur Univ BA46 MA49. Wycliffe Hall Ox 55. **d** 57 **p** 58. C Erith St Paul *Roch* 57-60; V Wilmington 60-72; Perm to Offic *Chelmsf* from 76; rtd 84. *204 Hockley Road, Rayleigh, Essex SS6 8EU* Tel (01268) 770364

BARRIBAL, Richard James Pitt. b 45. Trin Coll Bris DipTh80. **d** 80 **p** 81. C Northampton St Giles *Pet* 80-82; V Long Buckby w Watford 82-86; Perm to Offic from 86. *5 The Green, Great Bowden, Market Harborough, Leics LE16 7EW* Tel (01858) 468852

BARRIE, John Arthur. b 38. K Coll Lon 58 Bps' Coll Cheshunt 59. **d** 63 **p** 64. C Southgate St Mich *Lon* 63-66; CF 66-88; Sen CF 88-93; QHC 91-93; P-in-c Heref H Trin *Heref* 93-96; P-in-c Breinton 95-96; V St Marylebone St Mark Hamilton Terrace *Lon* from 96. *St Mark's Vicarage, 114 Hamilton Terrace, London NW8 9UT* Tel 0171-328 4373

BARRINGTON, Dominic Matthew Jesse. b 62. Hatf Coll Dur BA84 MSc85. Ripon Coll Cuddesdon BA94 Ch Div Sch of Pacific MTS95. **d** 95 **p** 96. C Mortlake w E Sheen *S'wark* from 95. *5 Vernon Road, London SW14 8NH* Tel 0181-876 6364 Fax 878 5064 E-mail dominic@mortlake.sonnet.co.uk

✠**BARRINGTON-WARD, The Rt Revd Simon.** b 30. Magd Coll Cam BA53 MA57. Wycliffe Coll Toronto Hon DD Westcott Ho Cam 54. **d** 56 **p** 57 **c** 85. Chapl Magd Coll Cam 56-60; Nigeria 60-63; Fell and Dean of Chpl Magd Coll Cam 63-69; Prin Crowther Hall CMS Tr Coll Selly Oak 69-74; Gen Sec CMS 75-85; Hon Can Derby Cathl *Derby* 75-85; Chapl to The Queen 84-85; Bp Cov 85-97; rtd 97. *4 Searle Street, Cambridge CB4 3DB* Tel (01223) 573099

BARRODALE, George Bryan. b 44. Univ of Wales (Ban) DipTh DipMin88. St Mich Coll Llan 67. **d** 69 **p** 70. C Maindee *Mon* 69-72; TV Merthyr Tydfil and Cyfarthfa *Llan* 72-76; R Cotgrave *S'well* from 76; P-in-c Owthorpe from 76; CF (TA) 76-86; RD Bingham *S'well* from 94. *The Rectory, Thurman Drive, Cotgrave, Nottingham NG12 3HT* Tel 0115-989 2223

BARRON, Kurt Karl. b 60. Chich Th Coll BTh92. **d** 92 **p** 93. C Bulwell St Mary *S'well* 92-97; TV Southend *Chelmsf* from 97. *39 St John's Road, Westcliff-on-Sea, Essex SS0 7JY* Tel (01702) 433327

BARRON, Leslie Gill. b 44. ACII69. Lich Th Coll 67. **d** 70 **p** 71. C Bishopwearmouth Ch Ch *Dur* 70-72; C Bishopwearmouth St Mary V w St Pet CD 72-75; C Harton 75-77; V Lumley 77-88; P-in-c Hendon and Sunderland 88-90; R Hendon 90-94; P-in-c Ushaw Moor 94-95; TR Bearpark and Ushaw Moor from 95. *The Vicarage, 8 Woodland Close, Bearpark, Durham DH7 7EB* Tel 0191-373 3886

BARRON, Richard Davidson. b 51. Lon Univ BSc74. Trin Coll Bris 75. **d** 78 **p** 79. C Bradley *Wakef* 78-81; C Heworth *York* 81-82; TV 82-89; Chapl York Distr Hosp 82-86; R Greenhithe St Mary *Roch* from 89. *The Rectory, Mounts Road, Greenhithe, Kent DA9 9ND* Tel (01322) 842031

BARRON, Victor Robert. b 45. Ex Univ CertEd70. Trin Coll Bris 76. **d** 78 **p** 79. C Rainham *Chelmsf* 78-81; V Easton H Trin w St Gabr and St Lawr *Bris* 81-82; V Easton H Trin w St Gabr and St Lawr and St Jude 82-89; TR Kinson *Sarum* from 89; RD Poole from 94. *St Andrew's Rectory, 51 Millhams Road, Bournemouth BH10 7LJ* Tel (01202) 571996

BARROW, Sqn Ldr Wilfrid Edward Lewis. b 10. Worc Ord Coll 60. **d** 62 **p** 63. C Boreham Wood All SS *St Alb* 62-66; V Heath and Reach 66-86; rtd 86; Perm to Offic *Ox* 86-96; Perm to Offic *St Alb* 86-95. *High Tree House, 5 Leopold Road, Leighton Buzzard, Beds LU7 7QU* Tel (01525) 377122

BARRY, Colin Lionel. **d** 96 **p** 97. C Arbory *S & M* from 96. *80 Ballanorris Crescent, Friary Park, Ballabeg, Isle of Man IM9 4ER* Tel (01624) 823080

BARRY, Herbert Brian. b 25. QUB 46. Edin Th Coll 46. **d** 48 **p** 49. C Edin Old St Paul *Edin* 48-52; R Burntisland *St And* 52-55; C Hayes St Anselm *Lon* 56-63; C Hayes St Mary 56-63; R Edin St Salvador *Edin* 63-68; C Northolt Park St Barn *Lon* 69-72; P-in-c S Acton All SS 72-82; V Acton Green St Alb 75-82; V Acton St Alb w All SS 82-88; V Acton Green 88-90; Sub-Warden Guild of St Raphael from 85; rtd 90; Perm to Offic *Ex* from 90; Perm to Offic *Truro* from 90. *4 Hendra Close, Truro, Cornwall TR1 3SL* Tel (01872) 260076

BARRY, Canon John. b 15. TCD BA38 MA41. CITC 38. **d** 38 **p** 39. C Belfast St Matt *Conn* 38-41; C Dundela *D & D* 41-45; I Dunluce *Conn* 45-49; I Hillsborough *D & D* 49-83; Can Belf Cathl 56-83; Chan Down Cathl *D & D* 64-73; Preb St Patr Cathl Dublin 73-83; rtd 83. *16 West Park, Lisburn, Co Antrim BT28 2BQ* Tel (01846) 670664

BARRY, Jonathan Peter Oulton. b 47. TCD BA70 MA73 Hull Univ BA73 QUB PhD84. Ripon Hall Ox 73. **d** 74 **p** 75. C Dundela *D & D* 74-79; I Ballyphilip w Ardquin 79-85; Dioc Info Officer 80-90; I Comber from 85. *12 Windmill Hill, High Street, Comber, Newtownards, Co Down BT23 5WH* Tel (01247) 872283 E-mail jpobarry@compuserve.com

BARRY, Keith Gordon. b 67. TCD BA92. CITC 92. **d** 94 **p** 95. C Templemore *D & R* 94-97; V Choral Derry Cathl 94-97; CF from 97. *MOD Chaplains (Army), Trenchard Lines, Upavon, Pewsey, Wilts SN9 6BE* Tel (01980) 615804 Fax 615800

BARRY, Nicholas Brian Paul. b 61. Leic Univ BA83. St Steph Ho Ox 84. **d** 87 **p** 88. C St Jo Wood *Lon* 87-90; Chapl RAF from 90. *Chaplaincy Services (RAF), HQ, Personnel and Training Command, RAF Innsworth, Gloucester GL3 1EZ* Tel (01452) 712612 ext 5164 Fax 510828

BARSLEY, Anthony Noel. b 11. St Aid Birkenhead 46. **d** 47 **p** 48. C Hindley All SS *Liv* 47-50; C Penn *Lich* 50-53; V Gailey-cum-Hatherton 53-59; V Lower Gornal 59-61; V Chebsey 61-76; rtd 76. *5 Brookside Close, Bedale, N Yorkshire DL8 2DR* Tel (01677) 422087

BARSLEY, Ms Margaret Ann. b 39. Totley Hall Coll CertEd60. EMMTC 79. **dss** 83 **d** 87 **p** 94. Kirton in Holland *Linc* 83-87; NSM 87-89; NSM Skirbeck Quarter 89-96; P-in-c Swineshead from 96; RD Holland W from 97. *The Vicarage, Church Lane, Swineshead, Boston, Lincs PE20 3JA* Tel (01205) 820271

BARTER, Christopher Stuart. b 49. Chich Th Coll. **d** 84 **p** 85. C Margate St Jo *Cant* 84-88; R Whitwood *Wakef* 88-95; Chapl Castleford, Normanton & Distr Hosp 88-95; AIDS Counsellor W Yorkshire Health Authority from 95; P-in-c Ravensthorpe *Wakef* from 95. *St Saviour's Vicarage, Church Street, Ravensthorpe, Dewsbury, W Yorkshire WF13 3LA* Tel (01924) 465959

BARTER, The Very Revd Donald. b 34. St Fran Coll Brisbane ThL69 ACT ThSchol74. **d** 69 **p** 70. Australia 69-90 and from 93; Adn of the W 81-86; Dean Townsville 86-90; Appeals Dir SPCK 90-93; Lic to Offic *Leic* 90-93. *6 Sixth Avenue, South Townsville, Queensland, Australia 4810* Tel Townsville (077) 727036 Fax as telephone

BARTER, Geoffrey Roger. b 41. Bris Univ BSc63. Clifton Th Coll 65. **d** 67 **p** 68. C Normanton *Derby* 67-70; C Rainham *Chelmsf* 70-75; V Plumstead St Jo w St Jas and St Paul *S'wark* 75-82; V Frogmore *St Alb* from 82. *Holy Trinity Vicarage, 39 Frogmore, St Albans, Herts AL2 2JU* Tel (01727) 872172

BARTER, Leonard. d 95. NSM St Stythians w Perranarworthal and Gwennap *Truro* from 95. *c/o The Vicarage, Old Vicarage Close, Stithians, Truro, Cornwall TR3 7DZ*

BARTHOLOMEW, David Grant. b 50. Univ of Wales (Lamp) BA77 Brighton Poly DMS78. Chich Th Coll 91. **d** 93 **p** 94. C Petersfield *Portsm* 93-96; R Etton w Helpston and Maxey *Pet* from 96. *The Rectory, Golden Drop, Helpston, Peterborough PE6 7DW* Tel (01733) 253456

BARTLAM, Alan Thomas. b 51. Bris Univ BEd74. Linc Th Coll 88. **d** 90 **p** 91. C Longdon-upon-Tern, Rodington, Uppington etc *Lich* 90-92; C Tilstock and Whixall 92-95; V Tilstock, Edstaston and Whixall from 95. *The Vicarage, Tilstock, Whitchurch, Shropshire SY13 3JL* Tel (01948) 880552

BARTLAM, Graham Frederick. b 37. Lon Univ BA63. Oak Hill Th Coll 59. **d** 64 **p** 65. C Hawkwell *Chelmsf* 64-68; C Gt Warley Ch Ch 68-74; R High and Gd Easter w Margaret Roding 74-96; rtd 96. *23 Tyrells Close, Chelmsford CM2 6BT* Tel (01245) 355179

BARTLE, Alan. b 45. Ridley Hall Cam 82. **d** 84 **p** 85. C Ely 84-88; V 87-93; V Chettisham 87-93; V Prickwillow 87-93; P-in-c Thorney Abbey 93-95. *54 Munnion Road, Ardingly, Haywards Heath, W Sussex RH17 6RP*

BARTLE, Canon David Colin. b 29. Em Coll Cam BA53 MA57. Ridley Hall Cam 53. **d** 55 **p** 56. C Birm St Martin *Birm* 55-57; C Boscombe St Jo *Win* 57-60; V Lowestoft St Jo *Nor* 60-70; P-in-c Thetford St Cuth w H Trin 70-72; TR Thetford 72-75; P-in-c Kilverstone 70-75; P-in-c Croxton 70-75; Teacher Bournemouth Sch 75-83; R Brantham w Stutton *St E* 83-90; RD Samford 86-90; P-in-c Roxwell *Chelmsf* 90-93; Dioc Dir of Ords 90-93; Dioc Lay Min Adv 90-93; Hon Can Chelmsf Cathl 91-93; rtd 93. *8 River Way, Christchurch, Dorset BH23 2QW* Tel (01202) 482919

BARTLE, Reginald Stephen. b 24. K Coll Lon AKC51 BD52. **d** 52 **p** 53. C Penge Ch Ch w H Trin *Roch* 52-55; SAMS 55-79; Chile 55-70; Adn Chile and Can St Andr Cathl Santiago 64-70; C Tunbridge Wells St Jas *Roch* 80-83; rtd 83; Perm to Offic *St D* 84-94; Perm to Offic *Chelmsf* from 94. *28 Blacksmith Close, Pump Lane, Chelmsford CM1 5SY* Tel (01245) 462249

BARTLE-JENKINS, Canon Leonard Christmas. b 13. Univ of Wales (Lamp) BA35. Lich Th Coll 35. **d** 38 **p** 39. C Fleur-de-Lis *Mon* 38-41; C Trevethin 41-47; V Llangattock-vibon-Avel 48-55; V Bassaleg 55-73; Can St Woolos Cathl 64-82; RD Bassaleg 67-82; R Michaelston-y-Fedw and Rudry 74-82; rtd 82; Lic to Offic *Mon* from 85; Perm to Offic *Llan* from 85. *3 St Teilo's Court, Sturminster Road, Roath, Cardiff CF2 5AX* Tel (01222) 489378

BARTLE-JENKINS, Paul. b 43. Bris & Glouc Tr Course. **d** 84 **p** 86. NSM Bris St Agnes and St Simon w St Werburgh *Bris* 84-87; NSM Bris St Paul's from 87. *51 Henleaze Park Drive, Westbury-on-Trym, Bristol BS9 4LN* Tel 0117-962 4689

✠**BARTLEET, The Rt Revd David Henry.** b 29. St Pet Hall Ox BA55 MA61. Westcott Ho Cam 55. **d** 57 **p** 58 **c** 82. C Ipswich St Mary le Tower *St E* 57-60; C Doncaster St Geo *Sheff* 60-64; V Edenbridge *Roch* 64-73; V Bromley SS Pet and Paul 73-82; Hon Can Roch Cathl 79-93; Suff Bp Tonbridge 82-93; rtd 93. *21 Lee Road, Aldeburgh, Suffolk IP15 5EY* Tel (01728) 452724

BARTLES-SMITH, The Ven Douglas Leslie. b 37. St Edm Hall Ox BA61 MA65. Wells Th Coll 61. **d** 63 **p** 64. C Westmr St Steph w St Jo *Lon* 63-68; P-in-c Camberwell St Mich w All So w Em *S'wark* 68-72; V 72-75; V Battersea St Luke 75-85; RD Battersea 81-85; Adn S'wark from 85; Chapl to The Queen from 96. *1A Dog Kennel Hill, London SE22 8AA* Tel 0171-274 6767

BARTLETT, Alan. b 38. Qu Coll Birm. **d** 79 **p** 80. Hon C Perry Beeches *Birm* 79-81; Hon C Kingstanding St Mark from 82. *43 Delhurst Road, Birmingham B44 9UT* Tel 0121-360 7878

BARTLETT, Dr Alan Bennett. b 58. G&C Coll Cam BA81 MA85 Birm Univ PhD87 St Jo Coll Dur BA90. Cranmer Hall Dur 88. **d** 91 **p** 92. C Newc H Cross *Newc* 91-94; C Newburn 94-96; Tutor Cranmer Hall Dur from 96. *Cranmer Hall, St John's College, 3 South Bailey, Durham DH1 3RJ* Tel 0191-374 3579 Fax 374 3573

BARTLETT, Alban Denys. b 26. St Jo Coll Ox BA50 MA55. St Mich Coll Llan and St D Coll Lamp 50. **d** 52 **p** 53. C Neath w Llantwit *Llan* 52-54; C Newport St Mark *Mon* 54-57; CF 57-81; Chapl R Hosp Chelsea 81-91; rtd 91. *17 Henley Close, Saxmundham, Suffolk IP17 1EY* Tel (01728) 604418

BARTLETT, Anthony Martin. b 43. Cranmer Hall Dur 74. **d** 77 **p** 78. C Heworth St Mary *Dur* 77-80; V Cleadon 80-84; CF (TA) 81-90; Prec Dur Cathl *Dur* 85-87; V Harton 87-95; P-in-c Hendon 95-96; R from 96. *St Ignatius Rectory, Bramwell Road, Sunderland SR2 8BY* Tel 0191-567 5575

BARTLETT, Basil Gordon. b 11. Selw Coll Cam BA34 MA38. Wells Th Coll 34. **d** 36 **p** 37. C Llansamlet *S & B* 36-39; Chapl RAF 39-46; TR Sheff Manor *Sheff* 46-51; Chapl and Prin R Sch for the Blind Leatherhead 50-76; rtd 76; Perm to Offic *B & W* from 76; Perm to Offic *Ex* from 76. *Meadow Cottage, North Wootton, Shepton Mallet, Somerset BA4 4AQ* Tel (01749) 890547

BARTLETT, Clifford William Tudor. b 15. ALCD38. **d** 38 **p** 39. C Holloway Em w Hornsey Road St Barn *Lon* 38-41; C Havering-atte-Bower *Chelmsf* 41-44; CF 44-47; C Rothbury *Newc* 47-49; V Otterburn 49-60; V Horsley and Burness 53-60; V Ovingham 60-80; rtd 80; Lic to Offic *Newc* from 85; Perm to Offic *Dur* from 81. *69 Rectory Lane, Winlaton, Blaydon-on-Tyne, Tyne & Wear NE21 6PJ* Tel 0191-414 4236

BARTLETT, Canon David Blandford. b 24. Cam Univ BA49 MA50. Sarum Th Coll. **d** 51 **p** 52. C Brighouse *Wakef* 51-54; Tanganyika 54-64; Tanzania 64-90; Chan and Can Zanzibar 73-88; rtd 91; P-in-c Heptonstall *Wakef* 91-94; Perm to Offic *Nor* from 94. *25 Simpson Close, North Walsham, Norfolk NR28 0HZ* Tel (01692) 405304

BARTLETT, David John. b 36. Pemb Coll Ox BA61. Linc Th Coll 63. **d** 65 **p** 66. C Wollaton *S'well* 65-70; V Woodthorpe 70-83; P-in-c Kirklington w Hockerton from 83; V Farnsfield from 83; RD S'well 83-93. *The Vicarage, Beck Lane, Farnsfield, Newark, Notts NG22 8ER* Tel (01623) 882247

BARTLETT, David William. b 59. Trin Coll Bris 89. **d** 91 **p** 92. C Frinton *Chelmsf* 91-95; TV Eston w Normanby *York* 95-96; C Worksop St Jo *S'well* from 96. *5 Windermere Close, Worksop, Notts S81 7QE* Tel (01909) 472397

BARTLETT, Canon Prof John Raymond. b 37. FSA88 BNC Ox BA59 MA62 BLitt62 TCD MA70 LittD. Linc Th Coll 61. **d** 63 **p** 64. C W Bridgford *S'well* 63-66; Lect Div TCD 66-86; Assoc Prof Bibl Studies 86-90; Prin CITC from 89; Prof Past Th from 90; Treas Ch Ch Cathl Dublin *D & G* 86-88; Prec from 88. *CITC, Braemor Park, Rathgar, Dublin 14, Irish Republic* Tel Dublin (1) 492 3506 or 492 3274 Fax 492 3082

BARTLETT, Kenneth Vincent John. b 36. OBE93. Or Coll Ox BA61 BTh63. Ripon Hall Ox. **d** 63 **p** 64. C Paddington St Jas *Lon* 63-67; Lic to Offic from 67. *13 Shaa Road, London W3 7LN* Tel 0181-743 3989

BARTLETT, Canon Maurice Edward. b 33. G&C Coll Cam BA59 MA63. Wells Th Coll 59. **d** 60 **p** 61. C Batley All SS *Wakef* 60-64; Bp's Dom Chapl 64-66; Dir of Ords 64-66; Asst Chapl HM Pris Wakef 64-66; V Allerton *Liv* 66-81; V Lancaster St Mary *Blackb*

from 81; Sub-Chapl HM Pris Lanc from 81; Hon Can Blackb Cathl from 87. *The Vicarage, Priory Close, Lancaster LA1 1YZ* Tel (01524) 63200

BARTLETT, Michael Fredrick. b 52. Ex Univ BA74 Liv Univ BPhil75 Ox Univ BA79 MA. Ripon Coll Cuddesdon 76 Ven English Coll Rome 78. **d** 79 **p** 80. C Kirkby *Liv* 79-82; C Wordsley *Lich* 82-83; Chapl Wordsley Hosp 82-88; TV Wordsley *Lich* 83-88; TV Redditch, The Ridge *Worc* from 88. *St Peter's House, Littlewoods, Crabbs Cross, Redditch, Worcs B97 5LB* Tel (01527) 545709

BARTLETT, Preb Michael George. b 35. S Dios Minl Tr Scheme 84. **d** 87 **p** 88. NSM Wimborne Minster and Holt *Sarum* 87-90; C Charlestown *Truro* 90-91; R St Endellion w Port Isaac and St Kew from 91; Preb St Endellion from 91. *The Rectory, St Endellion, Port Isaac, Cornwall PL29 3TP* Tel (01208) 880442

BARTLETT, Richard Charles. b 68. St Kath Coll Liv BA90. Westcott Ho Cam CTM94. **d** 94 **p** 95. C Wareham *Sarum* from 94. *110 Northmoor Way, Wareham, Dorset BH20 4ET* Tel (01929) 552607

BARTON, Dr Andrew Edward. b 53. MRSC St Jo Coll Ox MA77 DPhil80. Ridley Hall Cam 87. **d** 90 **p** 91. C Ringwood *Win* 90-95; R Baughurst, Ramsdell, Wolverton w Ewhurst etc from 95. *The Rectory, Wolverton, Basingstoke, Hants RG26 5RU* Tel (01635) 298008

BARTON, Canon Arthur Michael. b 33. CCC Cam BA57 MA61. Wycliffe Hall Ox 57. **d** 59 **p** 60. Min Can Bradf Cathl *Bradf* 59-61; C Maltby *Sheff* 61-63; V Silsden *Bradf* 63-70; V Moor Allerton *Ripon* 70-81; TR 81-82; V Wetherby from 82; Chapl HM Young Offender Inst Wetherby 82-89; RD Harrogate *Ripon* 88-95; Hon Can Ripon Cathl from 89. *The Vicarage, Parsons Green, Wetherby, W Yorkshire LS22 6RQ* Tel (01937) 582423

BARTON, Mrs Caroline Janet (Carrie). b 61. Ex Univ BA83 Lon Univ 86. Westcott Ho Cam 93. **d** 96 **p** 97. C Ivybridge w Harford *Ex* from 96. *12 Buddle Close, Ivybridge, Devon PL21 0JU* Tel (01752) 690797

BARTON, The Ven Charles John Greenwood. b 36. ALCD63. **d** 63 **p** 64. C Cant St Mary Bredin *Cant* 63-66; V Whitfield w W Langdon 66-75; V S Kensington St Luke *Lon* 75-83; AD Chelsea 80-83; Chief Broadcasting Officer for C of E 83-90; Lic to Offic *Lon* 84-90; Adn Aston and Can Res Birm Cathl *Birm* from 90. *26 George Road, Birmingham B15 1PJ* Tel 0121-454 5525 Fax 455 6085

BARTON, Canon Cyril Albert. b 28. St Pet Hall Ox BA50 MA54. Ridley Hall Cam. **d** 52 **p** 53. C Maghull *Liv* 52-55; Min Can Bradf Cathl *Bradf* 55-58; V Oldham St Paul *Man* 58-68; V Norbury *Ches* 68-90; Hon Can Ches Cathl 85-95; R Aldford and Bruera 90-95; rtd 95; Perm to Offic *Ches* from 95. *5 Calder Close, Bollington, Macclesfield, Cheshire SK10 5LJ* Tel (01625) 572601

BARTON, Dale. b 49. Selw Coll Cam BA71 MA76. Linc Th Coll 71. **d** 73 **p** 74. C Gosforth All SS *Newc* 73-77; Lesotho 77-81; Dep Warden CA Hostel Cam 82-83; C Shepton Mallet w Doulting *B & W* 83-88; TV Preston St Jo *Blackb* 88-96; V Preston St Steph from 96. *St Stephen's Vicarage, 60 Broadgate, Preston PR1 8DU* Tel (01772) 555762

BARTON, David Gerald Story. b 38. Selw Coll Cam BA62 MA66. Cuddesdon Coll 63. **d** 65 **p** 66. C Cowley St Jas *Ox* 65-67; C Hambleden 67-70; Hon C Hammersmith St Jo *Lon* 72-77; Hon C Paddington St Jas 77-81; Hd Master Soho Par Sch 81-88; Hon C Westmr St Jas 81-92; RE Project Officer Lon Dioc Bd for Schs 88-92; Dioc Schs Adv *Ox* from 93; NSM Iffley from 93. *12 Parker Street, Oxford OX4 1TD* Tel (01865) 240059

BARTON, Edward. b 23. **d** 75 **p** 76. C Budock *Truro* 75-79; P-in-c St Stithians w Perranarworthal 79-80; V St Stythians w Perranarworthal and Gwennap 80-82; rtd 88. *Riverside, 5 Riviera Terrace, Malpas, Truro TR1 1SR* Tel (01872) 71686

BARTON, Eric Alfred. b 13. Clifton Th Coll 38. **d** 40 **p** 41. C Stratford New Town St Paul *Chelmsf* 40-42; C Barnet Ch Ch *Lon* 42-44; V Islington St Barnabas w St Mary Magd 44-48; V Ripon H Trin *Ripon* 48-53; V Clifton *York* 53-59; R Haworth *Bradf* 59-61; V Buttershaw St Paul 61-70; V Nailsea Ch Ch *B & W* 70-82; rtd 82; Perm to Offic *Ex* from 82. *22 Woolbrook Rise, Sidmouth, Devon EX10 9UD* Tel (01395) 514841

BARTON, Canon Geoffrey. b 27. Or Coll Ox BA48 MA52. Chich Th Coll 49. **d** 51 **p** 52. C Arnold *S'well* 51-53; C E Retford 53-54; V Mirfield Eastthorpe St Paul *Wakef* 54-60; V Boroughbridge w Roecliffe *Ripon* 60-73; V Aldborough w Boroughbridge and Roecliffe 73; P-in-c Farnham w Scotton and Staveley and Copgrove 73-74; R 74-77; Chapl Roundway Hosp Devizes 77-92; Can and Preb Sarum Cathl *Sarum* 86-92; rtd 92. *4B Willow House, Downlands Road, Devizes, Wilts SN10 5EA* Tel (01380) 725311

BARTON, Canon John. b 25. MBE91. Keble Coll Ox BA48 MA50. Ely Th Coll 48. **d** 50 **p** 51. C Worksop St Anne *S'well* 50-53; C Harrogate St Wilfrid *Ripon* 53-56; V Beeston Hill H Spirit 56-60; Chapl Stanley Royd & Pinderfields Hosps Wakef 60-72; RD Wakef 68-72; Chapl Jo Radcliffe Hosp & Radcliffe Infirmary 72-90; Chapl Chu Hosp Ox 72-89; Hon Can Ch Ch *Ox* 77-90; RD Cowley 89-94; rtd 90. *212 Headington Road, Oxford OX3 7PS* Tel (01865) 63918

BARTON, Canon Dr John. b 48. Keble Coll Ox BA69 MA73 Mert Coll Ox DPhil74 St Cross Coll Ox DLitt88. **d** 73 **p** 73. Lect St Cross Coll Ox 74-89; Fell 74-91; Chapl 79-91; Reader in Bibl Studies 89-91; Prof and Fell Oriel Coll Ox from 91; Can Th Win Cathl *Win* from 91. *11 Withington Court, Abingdon, Oxon OX14 3QA* Tel (01235) 525925

BARTON, Canon John Christopher Peter. b 28. Trin Hall Cam BA51 MA56. Ridley Hall Cam 51. **d** 53 **p** 54. C Erith St Paul *Roch* 53-56; C Cockfosters Ch Ch CD *Lon* 56-64; V Welling *Roch* 64-75; P-in-c Malmesbury w Westport *Bris* 75-84; P-in-c Charlton w Brokenborough and Hankerton 80-84; V Malmesbury w Westport and Brokenborough 84-94; Hon Can Kigezi from 92; rtd 94; Perm to Offic *B & W* from 94. *Orchard House, Orchard Road, Crewkerne, Somerset TA18 7AF* Tel (01460) 72536

BARTON, Canon John Michael. b 40. TCD BA62 Div Test. **d** 63 **p** 64. C Coleraine *Conn* 63-68; C Portadown St Mark *Arm* 68-71; I Carnteel and Crilly 71-83; I Derryloran from 83; Preb Arm Cathl from 94. *Derryloran Rectory, 13 Loy Street, Cookstown, Co Tyrone BT80 8PZ* Tel (01648) 762261

BARTON, Dr Margaret Anne. b 54. St Anne's Coll Ox MA80 DPhil81 Selw Coll Cam BA89. Ridley Hall Cam 87. **d** 90 **p** 94. Par Dn Burley Ville *Win* 90-94; C 94; Chapl K Alfred Coll from 94. *King Alfred's College, Sparkford Road, Winchester, Hants SO22 4NR* Tel (01962) 841515 E-mail anneba@wkac.ac.uk or andrewba@patrol.i-way.co.uk

BARTON, Samuel David. b 45. DipTh. **d** 84 **p** 85. C Ballywillan *Conn* 84-86; I Aghadowey w Kilrea *D & R* 86-92; Bp's C Fahan Lower and Upper from 92; Dio Educn Co-ord from 94. *Fahan Lower Rectory, Church Street, Buncrana, Co Donegal, Irish Republic* Tel Buncrana (77) 61154

BARTON, Dr Stephen Christian. b 52. Macquarie Univ (NSW) BA75 DipEd75 Lanc Univ MA78 K Coll Lon PhD92. Cranmer Hall Dur 91. **d** 93 **p** 94. NSM Neville's Cross St Jo CD *Dur* from 93. *33 Nevilledale Terrace, Durham DH1 4QG* Tel 0191-386 4983

BARTON, Stephen William. b 50. St Jo Coll Cam BA73 MA76 Leeds Univ MPhil81. Coll of Resurr Mirfield 75. **d** 77 **p** 78. C Horton *Bradf* 77-80; USPG 80-92; Bangladesh 81-92; TV Southampton (City Cen) *Win* from 92. *St Matthew's Vicarage, 12-14 King's Park Road, Southampton SO15 2AT* Tel (01703) 224588

BARTON, Timothy Charles. b 47. Sarum & Wells Th Coll 73. **d** 76 **p** 77. C Upholland *Liv* 76-80; V Dalton from 80. *88 Lyndhurst Avenue, Skelmersdale, Lancs WN8 6UH* Tel (01695) 33148

BARTON, Trevor James. b 50. St Alb Minl Tr Scheme 79. **d** 87 **p** 88. NSM Hemel Hempstead *St Alb* from 87. *46 Crossfell Road, Hemel Hempstead, Herts HP3 8RQ* Tel (01442) 251537

BARWELL, Brian Bernard Beale. b 30. Preston Poly CertEd79. AKC59 St Boniface Warminster 59. **d** 60 **p** 61. C Heywood St Jas *Man* 60-63; V Smallbridge 63-69; V Farington *Blackb* 69-72; C-in-c Blackb St Luke w St Phil 72-75; C Standish 75-76; Lic to Offic 76-92; rtd 92; Perm to Offic *Blackb* from 92. *70 Claytongate, Coppull, Chorley, Lancs PR7 4PS* Tel (01257) 794251

BARWOOD, Frederick James. b 05. Selw Coll Cam BA30 MA34. Ely Th Coll 33. **d** 34 **p** 35. C Redhill St Matt *S'wark* 34-37; C Mortlake w E Sheen 37-39; V Gt Cornard *St E* 39-49; P-in-c Lt Cornard 44-49; V Weaste *Man* 49-51; R Odell *St Alb* 51-61; V Pavenham 54-61; RD Felmersham 54-61; P-in-c Felmersham 60-61; V Hordle *Win* 61-74; rtd 74; Perm to Offic *Win* 75-95. *94 Manor Road, New Milton, Hants BH25 5EJ* Tel (01425) 616150

BARZEY, Ms Michele Alison Lesley. b 63. Trin Coll Bris BA94. **d** 94. C Gravelly Hill *Birm* 94-96. *40 Holly Park Drive, Birmingham B24 9LQ*

BASFORD HOLBROOK, Colin Eric. b 42. St Steph Ho Ox 73. **d** 75 **p** 76. C Dovecot *Liv* 75-78; V Hollinfare 79-83; CMS 83-88; Cyprus 83-91; Chapl Athens, Kifissia, Patras, Thessaloniki etc *Eur* 91-93; Chapl Athens w Patras, Thessaloniki and Voula 93-94. *18 Shorwell Close, Great Sankey, Warrington WA5 3JZ*

BASH, Dr Anthony. b 52. Bris Univ LLB73 LLM76 Glas Univ BD89 Clare Hall Cam PhD96. Westcott Ho Cam CTM94. **d** 96 **p** 97. C Kingston upon Hull H Trin *York* from 96. *1 Ha'penny Bridge Way, Hull HU9 1HD* Tel (01482) 224299

BASHFORD, Richard Frederick. b 36. Lon Univ DipTh68. Clifton Th Coll. **d** 68 **p** 69. C Bedworth *Cov* 68-71; C Lower Homerton St Paul *Lon* 71-75; V Bordesley Green *Birm* 75-81; R Birm Bishop Latimer w All SS from 81. *The Vicarage, 28 Handsworth New Road, Birmingham B18 4PT* Tel 0121-554 2221

BASHFORD, Robert Thomas. b 49. Ch Coll Cam BA70 CertEd72 MA74 Lon Univ BD84 MPhil89. Oak Hill Th Coll 86. **d** 88 **p** 89. C Frinton *Chelmsf* 88-91; C Galleywood Common 91-96; V Clapham *St Alb* from 96. *The Vicarage, Green Lane, Clapham, Bedford MK41 6ER* Tel (01234) 352814

BASHFORTH, Alan George. b 64. Cuddesdon Coll BTh93. **d** 96 **p** 97. C Calstock *Truro* from 96. *Lara, Rising Sun, Callington, Cornwall PL17 8GE* Tel (01579) 350662

BASIL, Brother. *See* FARRANT, Jonathan

BASINGSTOKE, Archdeacon of. *See* KNIGHT, The Ven Alexander Francis

BASINGSTOKE, Suffragan Bishop of. *See* ROWELL, The Rt Revd Douglas Geoffrey

BASKERVILLE, John. b 45. Open Univ BA78. Sarum & Wells Th Coll 92. **d** 93 **p** 94. C Wanstead St Mary w Ch Ch *Chelmsf* 93-96; C Chingford SS Pet and Paul from 96. *2 Church Path, London E11 2SS* Tel 0181-530 6875

BASKERVILLE, Philip Duncan. b 58. St Chad's Coll Dur BSc79 Or Coll Ox PGCE80. Trin Coll Bris BA87. **d** 88 **p** 89. C Roby *Liv* 88-93; Kenya from 93. *St Paul's Theological College, PO Box 18, Kapsabet, Kenya* Tel Kenya (254) 326-2053 Fax 2451

BASON, Brian Vaudrey. b 27. Leeds Univ BA49 Lon Univ BD69. Coll of Resurr Mirfield 49. **d** 51 **p** 52. C Haggerston St Aug w St Steph *Lon* 51-55; C Bow w Bromley St Leon 55-56; V Audenshaw St Hilda *Man* 56-89; Perm to Offic *Ches* from 89; Perm to Offic *Man* from 89; Audenshaw High Sch 89-92; rtd 92. *78 Windsor Road, Denton, Manchester M34 2HE* Tel 0161-320 8455

BASS, Colin Graham. b 41. Liv Univ BSc62 Fitzw Ho Cam BA64 MA68. Ox NSM Course 84. **d** 87 **p** 88. Dir of Studies Leighton Park Sch Reading 87-97; NSM Earley St Pet *Ox* 87-92; NSM Reading Deanery from 92. *9 Bramley Close, Reading RG6 7PL* Tel 0118-966 3732

BASS, George Michael. b 39. Ely Th Coll 62. **d** 65 **p** 66. C Romaldkirk *Ripon* 65-68; C Kenton Ascension *Newc* 68-71; CF 71-94; Chapl N Tyneside Healthcare NHS Trust from 94. *North Tyneside General Hospital, Rake Lane, North Shields, Tyne & Wear NE29 8NH* Tel 0191-259 6660

BASS, Mrs Rosemary Jane. b 38. Linc Th Coll 76. **dss** 79 **d** 87 **p** 94. Bedford All SS *St Alb* 79-84; Leavesden All SS 84-87; Par Dn 87-94; C 94-95; V Luton St Andr from 95. *St Andrew's Vicarage, 11 Blenheim Crescent, Luton LU3 1HA* Tel (01582) 32380

BASSETT, Abner Gerwyn. b 25. Univ of Wales (Lamp) BA48 LTh50. **d** 50 **p** 51. C Henfynyw w Aberaeron *St D* 50-53; C Betws w Ammanford 53-58; P-in-c Llanfair-ar-y-Bryn 58-73; V Llandysilio w Egremont and Llanglydwen etc 73-91; rtd 91. *1 Ger-y-Llan, The Parade, Carmarthen SA31 1LY* Tel (01267) 235284

BASSETT, John Edmund. b 33. St Aid Birkenhead 63. **d** 66 **p** 67. C Guiseley *Bradf* 66-67; C Stechford *Birm* 67-71; C Ross *Heref* 71-72; P-in-c Brampton Abbotts 73-75; P-in-c Weston under Penyard 73-75; P-in-c Hope Mansell 73-75; TR Halesworth w Linstead and Chediston *St E* 75-78; P-in-c Irby on Humber *Linc* 78; R Laceby 78-83; V Sale St Paul *Ches* 83-88; P-in-c Southport All SS *Liv* 88-94; P-in-c Southport All So 88-94; V Southport All SS and All So from 94. *All Saints' Vicarage, 1 Park Avenue, Southport, Merseyside PR9 9LS* Tel (01704) 533336

BASTEN, Richard Henry. b 40. Codrington Coll Barbados 60. **d** 63 **p** 64. Br Honduras 63-67; Barbados 68-72; C Hartlepool H Trin *Dur* 72-73; Chapl Bedstone Coll 73-88; C Clun w Chapel Lawn *Heref* 73-77; P-in-c Clungunford 77-78; R Clungunford w Clunbury and Clunton, Bedstone etc 78-88; R Rowde and Poulshot *Sarum* 88-95; rtd 95; Perm to Offic *Glouc* from 95. *41 Bewley Way, Churchdown, Gloucester GL3 2DU* Tel (01452) 859738

BASTIDE, Derek. b 44. Dur Univ BA65 Reading Univ DipEd66 Sussex Univ MA77. Chich Th Coll 76. **d** 77 **p** 78. Hon C Lewes All SS, St Anne, St Mich and St Thos *Chich* 77-84; Prin Lect Brighton Poly 80-92; Prin Lect Brighton Univ from 92; P-in-c Hamsey *Chich* from 84. *The Rectory, Offham, Lewes, E Sussex BN7 3PX* Tel (01273) 474356

BASTOCK, Kenneth William. b 22. Launde Abbey 75. **d** 76 **p** 77. C Glen Parva and S Wigston *Leic* 76-80; V Orton-on-the-Hill w Twycross etc 80-92; rtd 92; Perm to Offic *Leic* from 92. *18 Beech Road, Oadby, Leicester LE2 5QL* Tel 0116-271 0454

BASTON, Mrs Caroline. b 56. Birm Univ BSc78 CertEd79. Ripon Coll Cuddesdon 87. **d** 89 **p** 94. Par Dn Southampton Thornhill St Chris *Win* 89-94; C 94-95; R Win All SS w Chilcomb and Chesil from 95; Dioc Communications Officer from 95. *All Saints' Rectory, 19 Petersfield Road, Winchester, Hants SO23 0JD* Tel (01962) 853777

BATCHELOR, Alan Harold. b 30. Bris Univ BA54 Hull Univ MA63 DipPM68 LSE. Linc Th Coll 54. **d** 56 **p** 57. C Kingston upon Hull St Alb *York* 56-60; C Attercliffe w Carbrook *Sheff* 60-62; India 63-87; Ind Chapl *Ripon* 87-95; C Kirkstall 92-95; rtd 95. *16 Moor Grange Rise, Leeds LS16 5BP* Tel 0113-275 6553

BATCHELOR, John Millar. b 35. CITC 76. **d** 78 **p** 79. C Belfast All SS *Conn* 78-80; I Eglish w Killylea *Arm* 80-96; I Ballyhalbert w Ardkeen *D & D* from 96. *Ballyeasboro Rectory, 187 Main Road, Portavogie, Newtownards, Co Down BT22 1DA* Tel (01247) 771234

BATCHELOR, Martin John. b 67. Plymouth Poly BSc91. St Jo Coll Nottm DTS94 MA95. **d** 95 **p** 96. C Brecon St Mary and Battle w Llanddew *S & B* 95-97; Min Can Brecon Cathl 95-97; C Sketty from 97. *10 Sketty Park Close, Sketty, Swansea SA2 8LR* Tel (01792) 204086

BATCOCK, Neil Gair. b 53. UEA BA74. Westcott Ho Cam CTM96. **d** 96 **p** 97. C Barton upon Humber *Linc* from 96. *7 West Grove, Barton-upon-Humber, S Humberside DN18 5AG* Tel (01652) 632697

BATE, Dylan Griffin. b 48. Glam Poly HNC71. Mon Dioc Tr Scheme 91. **d** 94 **p** 95. NSM Fleur-de-Lis *Mon* 94-96; NSM Bedwellty 96-97; C Pontypool from 97. *St Luke's Vicarage, Freeholdland Road, Pontnewynydd, Pontypool NP4 8LW* Tel (01495) 763019

BATE, Lawrence Mark. b 40. Univ Coll Ox BA63. Coll of Resurr Mirfield 65. **d** 67 **p** 68. C Benwell St Jas *Newc* 67-69; C Monkseaton St Pet 69-72; TV Withycombe Raleigh *Ex* 72-84; RD Aylesbeare 81-84; R Alphington from 84; RD Christianity from 95. *The Rectory, Alphington, Exeter EX2 8XJ* Tel (01392) 437662

BATE, Michael Keith. b 42. Lich Th Coll 67. **d** 69 **p** 70. C W Bromwich St Jas *Lich* 69-73; C Thornhill *Wakef* 73-76; V Wrenthorpe 76-82; V Upper Gornal *Lich* 82-93; V Upper Gornal *Worc* from 93; Chapl Burton Rd Hosp Dudley 82-94; Chapl Dudley Priority Health NHS Trust from 94. *St Peter's Vicarage, 35 Eve Lane, Upper Gornal, Dudley, W Midlands DY1 3TY* Tel (01902) 883467

BATEMAN, Alfred Neville. b 39. MIMI83. Oak Hill Th Coll 87. **d** 89 **p** 90. C Pendlebury St Jo *Man* 89-92; P-in-c Lt Hulton 92-93; TV Walkden Moor w Lt Hulton from 93. *St John's Vicarage, Algernon Road, Worsley, Manchester M28 5RD* Tel 0161-790 2338

BATEMAN, James Edward (Jim). b 44. Lon Univ BSc65 Bris Univ DipTh74. Trin Coll Bris 71. **d** 74 **p** 75. C Woodlands *Sheff* 74-77; C Rushden w Newton Bromswold *Pet* 77-84; R Vange *Chelmsf* 84-94; V Southminster from 94. *The Vicarage, Burnham Road, Southminster, Essex CM0 7ES* Tel (01621) 772300

BATEMAN, Kenneth William. b 34. ACII58. N Ord Course 85. **d** 88 **p** 89. Hon C Pilling *Blackb* 88-91; Chapl Lanc Moor Hosp 88-95; C Kirkby Lonsdale *Carl* 91-95; rtd 95; NSM Kirkby Lonsdale *Carl* from 95. *Greenside, Barbon, Carnforth, Lancs LA6 2LT*

BATEMAN, Martyn Henry. b 31. Jes Coll Cam BA54 MA58. Clifton Th Coll 54. **d** 56 **p** 57. C Heatherlands St Jo *Sarum* 56-59; C New Malden and Coombe *S'wark* 59-60; Iran 60-62; V Charsfield *St E* 62-69; R Monewden and Hoo 62-69; V Wickham Market 69-82; Hon Can St E Cathl 80-85; V Felixstowe SS Pet and Paul 82-85; TR Lydford, Brent Tor, Bridestowe and Sourton *Ex* 85-92; RD Tavistock 90-92; rtd 92. *Ardochy, Whitebridge, Inverness IV1 2UR* Tel (01456) 486273

BATEMAN, Richard George. b 46. St Jo Coll Dur. **d** 82 **p** 83. C Wolviston *Dur* 82-85; C Greenside 85-87; V Newburn *Newc* from 87. *The Vicarage, Newburn, Newcastle upon Tyne NE15 8LQ* Tel 0191-229 0522

BATEMAN, Richard William. b 36. AKC61. **d** 62 **p** 63. C Pennywell St Thos and Grindon St Oswald CD *Dur* 62-66; Trinidad and Tobago 66-70; R Etherley *Dur* 70-77; Ind Chapl *Roch* 77-83; Hon C Chatham St Steph 78-83; Chapl RN 79-83; V Kemsing w Woodlands *Roch* 83-90; P-in-c Petham and Waltham w Lower Hardres etc *Cant* from 90. *Stoneyridge, Waddem Hall Lane, Petham, Canterbury, Kent CT4 5PX* Tel (01227) 709318 or 700440

BATEMAN-CHAMPAIN, John Nicholas. b 30. G&C Coll Cam BA53 DipRS85. S'wark Ord Course 85. **d** 85 **p** 86. CStJ from 80; C Harpenden St Jo *St Alb* 85-88; V Northaw 88-97. *Littleworth, Surrey Gardens, Effingham, Leatherhead, Surrey KT24 5HF* Tel (01483) 282461

BATES, Cecil Robert. b 48. Coll of Resurr Mirfield. **d** 96 **p** 97. C Hartlepool St Oswald *Dur* from 96. *52 Brecongill Close, Hartlepool, Cleveland TS24 8PH* Tel (01429) 269968

BATES, David William. b 25. Cranmer Hall Dur 59. **d** 61 **p** 62. C Lt Coates *Linc* 61-63; V Wrawby 63-68; V Melton Ross w New Barnetby 65-68; V Linc St Pet-at-Gowts and St Andr 68-77; V Metheringham 77-81; V Metheringham w Blankney 81-91; rtd 91; Perm to Offic *Linc* from 91. *11 Neustadt Court, Danes Terrace, Lincoln LN2 1PG* Tel (01522) 545207

BATES, Derek Alvin. b 27. St Mich Coll Llan 57. **d** 59 **p** 60. C Bishop's Cleeve *Glouc* 59-63; V Shebbear *Ex* 67-71; R Buckland Filleigh 67-71; R Highampton w Sheepwash 71; R Coates *Ely* 72-80; R Clovelly *Ex* 80-92; V Woolfardisworthy and Buck Mills 80-92; rtd 92; Perm to Offic *Ex* from 92. *Jorejoder, 10 J H Taylor Drive, Laurel Park, Northam, Bideford, Devon EX39 1TU*

✠**BATES, The Rt Revd Gordon.** b 34. Kelham Th Coll 54. **d** 58 **p** 59 **c** 83. C New Eltham All SS *S'wark* 58-62; Asst Youth Chapl *Glouc* 62-64; Youth Chapl *Liv* 65-69; Chapl Liv Cathl 65-69; V Huyton St Mich 69-73; Can Res and Prec Liv Cathl 73-83; Dir of Ords 73-83; Suff Bp Whitby *York* from 83. *Handyside, 60 West Green, Stokesley, Middlesbrough, Cleveland TS9 5BD* Tel (01642) 710390 Fax 710685

BATES, James. b 46. Linc Th Coll 73. **d** 75 **p** 76. C Ewell *Guildf* 75-77; C Farncombe 77-80; V Pet St Mary Boongate *Pet* 80-92; V Kingston All SS w St Jo *S'wark* from 92. *All Saints' Vicarage, 15 Woodbine Avenue, Kingston upon Thames KT1 2AZ* Tel 0181-546 2644

BATES, Michael. b 33. Dur Univ BSc57 Hull Univ ADME84. Clifton Th Coll 57. **d** 59 **p** 60. C Drypool St Columba w St Andr and St Pet *York* 59-62; C Cheadle *Ches* 62-67; V Newbottle *Dur* 67-75; Chapl Nat Coal Bd 68-75; Teacher Bilton Grange High Sch Hull 76-88; Tutor Wilberforce Coll Hull 88-94; Hon C Kingston upon Hull H Trin *York* 81-96; rtd 96. *5 Fernland Close, Brough, N Humberside HU15 1DQ* Tel (01482) 669023

BATES, Canon Paul Spencer. b 40. CCC Cam BA62 MA66. Linc Th Coll 63. **d** 65 **p** 66. C Bris St Andr Hartcliffe *Bris* 65-69; Chapl Win Coll 69-80; Dir of Tr *Win* 80-90; Hon Can Win Cathl 87-90; Can Westmr Abbey 90-95; Steward Westmr Abbey 90-95. *Address temp unknown*

BATES, Miss Phyllis Edith. b 29. S'wark Ord Course 80. **dss** 83 **d** 87 **p** 94. Registrar S'wark Ord Course 83-89; Fulham St Dionis Parson's Green *Lon* 83-87; Hon Par Dn 87-94; rtd 89; NSM Hammersmith St Paul *Lon* from 94; Perm to Offic *S'wark* from 89. *26 St Dionis Road, London SW6 4TT* Tel 0171-731 6935

BATES, Mrs Rosemary Eileen Hamilton. b 45. Ripon Coll Cuddesdon 87. **d** 89 **p** 94. Par Dn Brackley St Pet w St Jas *Pet* 89-94; C 94-95; P-in-c N Hinksey and Wytham *Ox* from 95. *The Vicarage, 81 West Way, Oxford OX2 9JY* Tel (01865) 242345

BATES, Stuart Geoffrey. b 61. Univ of Wales (Lamp) BA82. St Steph Ho Ox 83. **d** 85 **p** 86. C Bromley St Mark *Roch* 85-88; C Westmr St Matt *Lon* 88-89; C Gt Ilford St Mary *Chelmsf* 89-95; V Crofton Park St Hilda w St Cypr *S'wark* from 95. *St Hilda's Vicarage, 35 Buckthorne Road, London SE4 2DG* Tel 0181-699 1277

BATES, Vincent. b 24. **d** 65 **p** 65. Kenya 65-66; Perm to Offic *Bris* 66-76; Perm to Offic *Ox* 68-72; C Yarlington *B & W* 72-76; Lic to Offic *Ox* 76-95. *6 Nursery Gardens, Earl Shilton, Leicester LE9 7JE* Tel (01455) 841936

BATES, William Frederic. b 49. St Jo Coll Dur BSc72 BA74. Cranmer Hall Dur DipTh75. **d** 75 **p** 76. C Knutsford St Jo and Toft *Ches* 75-78; C Ripley *Derby* 78-80; R Nether and Over Seale 81-93; V Lullington 81-93; V Allestree St Nic from 93. *The Vicarage, 4 Lawn Avenue, Allestree, Derby DE22 2PE* Tel (01332) 550224

BATES, William Hugh. b 33. Keble Coll Ox BA56 MA59. Westcott Ho Cam 59. **d** 60 **p** 61. C Horsforth *Ripon* 60-63; Tutor St Chad's Coll Dur 63-70; V Bishop Wilton *York* 70-76; RD Pocklington 74-76; V Pickering 76-82; Tutor NE Ord Course 79-94; P-in-c Crayke w Brandsby and Yearsley 82-94; P-in-c Stillington and Marton w Moxby 82-94; rtd 94; Perm to Offic *York* from 94. *Jessibrook, Main Street, Bugthorpe, York YO4 1QG* Tel (01759) 368402

BATESON, Canon Geoffrey Frederick. b 27. K Coll Lon BD51 AKC51. **d** 52 **p** 53. C Tynemouth Cullercoats St Paul *Newc* 52-56; C Gosforth All SS 56-60; V Monkseaton St Pet 60-68; V Newc St Geo 68-77; RD Newc 75-77; Chapl St Geo and Cottage Hosp Morpeth 77-89; R Morpeth *Newc* 77-89; Hon Can Newc Cathl 80-89; rtd 89; Perm to Offic *York* from 91. *1 Netherby Close, Sleights, Whitby, N Yorkshire YO22 5HD* Tel (01947) 810997

BATESON, James Howard. b 36. CEng64 FIMM88 MSOSc88 Qu Mary Coll Lon BSc57. EMMTC 85. **d** 87 **p** 88. NSM W Bridgford *S'well* 87-88; NSM Wilford Hill 88-95; Dioc Officer for NSMs from 94; P-in-c Staunton w Flawborough from 96; P-in-c Kilvington from 96. *45 Stamford Road, Nottingham NG2 6GD* Tel 0115-923 1820

BATEY, Canon Herbert Taylor. b 22. Qu Coll Ox BA46 MA48. Linc Th Coll 48. **d** 48 **p** 49. C Dalton-in-Furness *Carl* 48-50; C Egremont 50-52; V Cleator Moor w Cleator 52-59; Chapl St Bees Sch Cumbria 59-64; Chapl Culham Coll Abingdon 64-68; Prin Lect 68-75; P-in-c Culham *Ox* 68-75; Vice-Prin Coll of Ripon and York St Jo from 75; Hon Can Ripon Cathl *Ripon* 85-92; rtd 87. *29 College Road, Ripon, N Yorkshire HG4 2HE* Tel (01765) 607096

BATEY, William Abbott. b 20. Cranmer Hall Dur 62. **d** 63 **p** 64. C Appleby and Murton cum Hilton *Carl* 63-66; R Moresby 66-77; P-in-c Arnside 77-85; V 85-90; rtd 90; Perm to Offic *Carl* from 90. *33 Greengate, Levens, Kendal, Cumbria LA8 8NF* Tel (015395) 66791

BATH, David James William. b 43. Oak Hill NSM Course 87. **d** 89 **p** 90. NSM Henley *Ox* 89-90; Gen Manager Humberside Gd News Trust 90-96; NSM Anlaby St Pet *York* from 96. *24 Lawnswood, Hessle, N Humberside HU13 0PT* Tel (01482) 844734

BATH, Edward Nelson. b 16. Bps' Coll Cheshunt 55. **d** 57 **p** 58. C Norwood All SS *Cant* 57-60; R Allington 60-67; V Charing Heath w Egerton 67-82; P-in-c Pluckley w Pevington 78-82; rtd 82; Perm to Offic *Cant* from 82. *10 Win Pine House, Lyell Close, Hythe, Kent CT21 5JD* Tel (01303) 261630

BATH AND WELLS, Bishop of. *See* THOMPSON, The Rt Revd James Lawton

BATH, Archdeacon of. *See* EVENS, The Ven Robert John Scott

BATSLEER, Canon Albert. b 21. Selw Coll Cam BA46 MA54. Cuddesdon Coll 46. **d** 48 **p** 49. C Leic St Phil *Leic* 48-50; C Hope St Jas *Man* 50-52; V Heap Bridge 52-56; V Glossop *Derby* 56-65; R Staveley 65-72; V Riddings 72-81; RD Alfreton 76-81; V New Mills 81-85; RD Glossop 81-83; Hon Can Derby Cathl 81-85; rtd 85; Perm to Offic *Pet* from 95. *2 Slade Valley Avenue, Rothwell, Kettering, Northants NN14 6HR* Tel (01536) 711612

BATSON, David Frederick Edward. b 38. K Coll Lon BD69. AKC61. **d** 62 **p** 63. C Southport H Trin *Liv* 62-64; Asst Chapl Hurstpierpoint Coll Hassocks 64-65; C Cleator Moor w Cleator *Carl* 65-66; Asst Master K Geo V Sch Southport 66-67; NSM Leigh w Bransford *Worc* 68-79; Hon Asst Chapl Convent of H Name Malvern Link 68-72; Prin Soc Work Tr Dept Dumfries and Galloway Coun 84-94; Lect and Tutor Langside Coll Glas 95-97; Lect Soc Studies Dumfries and Galloway Coll from 96. *Connelcraig, Dalswinton, Dumfries DG2 0XY* Tel (01387) 740589

BATSON, John Gordon Kemp. b 38. Kelham Th Coll 60 Bps' Coll Cheshunt 64. **d** 65 **p** 66. C Lamorbey H Redeemer *Roch* 65-69; Trinidad and Tobago 69-74; V Borough Green *Roch* 74-83; V Perry Street 83-92; V Yalding w Collier Street 92-97; V Woodnesborough w Worth and Staple *Cant* from 97. *The Vicarage, The Street, Woodnesborough, Sandwich, Kent CT13 0NQ* Tel (01304) 613056

BATSON, William Francis Robert. b 43. Nottm Univ DipTP69 St Jo Coll Dur BA72. **d** 73 **p** 74. C Eastwood *S'well* 73-77; R Long Marton w Dufton and w Milburn *Carl* 77-79; V Flimby 79-85; TR Raveningham *Nor* 85-91; R Kinver and Enville *Lich* from 91. *The Vicarage, Kinver, Stourbridge, W Midlands DY7 6HJ* Tel (01384) 872556

BATT, Joseph William. b 39. Keele Univ BA62. Ripon Hall Ox 63. **d** 64 **p** 65. C Bushbury *Lich* 64-68; C Walsall 68-71; Nigeria 71-75; Area Sec (Dios Guildf and Chich) CMS 75-84; V Ottershaw *Guildf* from 84. *Christ Church Vicarage, Coach Road, Ottershaw, Chertsey, Surrey KT16 0PA* Tel (01932) 873160

BATT, Kenneth Victor. b 41. Wycliffe Hall Ox 68. **d** 71 **p** 72. C Yateley *Win* 71-76; R The Candover Valley 76-82; R Durrington *Sarum* 82-89; V Kempshott *Win* from 89. *The Vicarage, 171 Kempshott Lane, Kempshott, Basingstoke, Hants RG22 5LF* Tel (01256) 56400

BATTE, Mrs Kathleen (Kath). b 47. Homerton Coll Cam TCert68. NE Ord Course 91. **d** 94 **p** 95. NSM Newc St Gabr *Newc* 94-96; NSM Wilford Hill *S'well* from 96. *10 Bracey Rise, West Bridgford, Nottingham NG2 7AX* Tel 0115-923 5054

BATTEN, George William John. b 34. Bris & Glouc Tr Course 76. **d** 80 **p** 81. NSM Dean Forest St Paul *Glouc* 80-96. *39 Bells Place, Coleford, Glos GL16 8BX* Tel (01594) 832291

BATTEN, Graham John. b 39. Open Univ BA81 Univ of Wales (Cardiff) DipTh65. St D Coll Lamp 65. **d** 66 **p** 67. C Llangynwyd w Maesteg *Llan* 66-70; C St Andrew's Major and Michaelston-le-Pit 70-72; Chapl RN 72-91; Asst Chapl Fleet 91-94; V Dover St Mary *Cant* from 94. *The Vicarage, Taswell Street, Dover, Kent CT16 1SE* Tel (01304) 206842

BATTEN, Thomas Cyril. b 10. St Jo Coll Dur BA37 DipTh38 MA40. **d** 38 **p** 39. C Thornton-le-Fylde *Blackb* 38-40; C Marton 40-42; V Preston St Oswald 42-59; Chapl Deepdale Hosp 42-59; V Mellor 59-70; rtd 70; Lic to Offic *Blackb* from 70. *40 Belgrave Avenue, Penwortham, Preston PR1 0BH* Tel (01772) 746473

BATTERSBY, David George Sellers. b 32. AKC57. St Boniface Warminster 57 Lambeth STh80. **d** 58 **p** 59. C Glas St Marg *Glas* 58-60; C Burnley St Pet *Blackb* 60-62; V Warton St Paul 62-71; Chapl K Wm's Coll Is of Man 71-91; C Ashchurch *Glouc* 91-97; rtd 97. *The Old Stables, Back Lane, Beckford, Tewkesbury, Glos GL20 7AF* Tel (01386) 881137

BATTERSBY, Harold. b 16. **d** 79 **p** 80. Hon C Werneth *Ches* 79-84; V 84-88; rtd 89; Perm to Offic *Ches* from 89; Perm to Offic *Derby* from 89. *3 Cote Green Lane, Marple Bridge, Stockport, Cheshire SK1 5DZ* Tel 0161-427 1789

BATTERSBY, Paul Clifford. b 49. Bede Coll Dur TCert70 St Jo Coll Dur BA74. Cranmer Hall Dur DipTh75. **d** 75 **p** 76. C Sunderland St Chad *Dur* 75-78; Argentina 78-81; P-in-c Holme *Carl* 81-85; Dioc Youth Officer 81-85; Nat Officer for Youth Work Gen Syn Bd of Educn 85-92; TR Darwen St Pet w Hoddlesden *Blackb* 92-94; Soc Resp Officer from 95. *7 Billinge Close, Blackburn BB2 6SB* Tel (01254) 53442

BATTIN (née WEBB), Mrs Frances Mary. b 52. W of England Minl Tr Course 92. **d** 95 **p** 96. NSM Inkberrow w Cookhill and Kington w Dormston *Worc* from 95. *Collitts Forge, Upper Moor, Pershore, Worcs WR10 2JR* Tel (01386) 860467

BATTLE, Dean of. *See* CUMMINGS, The Very Revd William Alexander Vickery

BATTMAN, John Brian. b 37. ALCD61. **d** 61 **p** 62. C Fulham Ch Ch *Lon* 61-64; Argentina 64-69; Paraguay 69-76; Adn Paraguay 70-76; Ext Sec SAMS 77-80; V Romford Gd Shep Collier Row *Chelmsf* 80-92; V Werrington *Pet* from 92. *The Vicarage, 51 The Green, Werrington, Peterborough PE4 6RT* Tel (01733) 571649

BATTY, John Ivan. b 35. Clifton Th Coll 59. **d** 62 **p** 63. C Clayton *Bradf* 62-67; V Toxteth Park St Clem *Liv* 67-73; R Darfield *Sheff* 73-90; Chapl Düsseldorf *Eur* 90-95; V The Marshland *Sheff* from 95. *The Vicarage, Kings Causeway, Swinefleet, Goole, N Humberside DN14 8DH* Tel (01405) 704643 Fax as telephone

BATTY, Mark Alan. b 56. BSc. Ripon Coll Cuddesdon. **d** 82 **p** 83. C Bottesford w Ashby *Linc* 82-86; V Scunthorpe All SS 86-95; P-in-c N Wolds Gp 95-97; V from 97. *The Vicarage, Barnetby, S Humberside DN38 6JL* Tel (01652) 688182

BATTY, Stephen Roy. b 58. Chich Th Coll 88. **d** 90 **p** 91. C Wimborne Minster and Holt *Sarum* 90-94; P-in-c Yetminster w Ryme Intrinseca and High Stoy from 94. *The Rectory, Church Street, Yetminster, Sherborne, Dorset DT9 6LG* Tel (01935) 872237

BATTYE, Canon John Noel. b 42. TCD BA64 MA73. CITC 66. **d** 66 **p** 67. C Drumglass *Arm* 66-69; C Ballynafeigh St Jude *D & D* 70-73; Chapl Pemb Coll Cam 73-78; Bp's C Knocknagoney *D & D* 78-80; I Cregagh from 80; Preb Castleknock St Patr Cathl

Dublin from 94. *St Finnian's Rectory, 3 Upper Knockbreda Road, Belfast BT6 9QH* Tel (01232) 793822

BATY, Dr Edward. b 30. ARICS59 Open Univ BA77 UEA PhD88. St Aid Birkenhead 60. **d** 62 **p** 63. C Acomb St Steph *York* 62-64; Succ Chelmsf Cathl *Chelmsf* 64-67; V Becontree St Cedd 67-71; R Hope Bowdler w Eaton-under-Heywood *Heref* 71-79; R Rushbury 71-79; P-in-c Cardington 71-79; R Fincham *Ely* 79-82; OCF 79-94; R Long Stanton w St Mich *Ely* 82-94; P-in-c Lolworth 85-88; CF(V) 86-95; rtd 95; Perm to Offic *Guildf* from 95. *25 Martindale Avenue, Camberley, Surrey GU15 1BB* Tel (01276) 20315

BATY, Ernest John. b 20. Univ of Wales BA42. St Mich Coll Llan 42. **d** 44 **p** 45. C Swansea St Thos and Kilvey *S & B* 44-47; C Defynnog w Rhydybriw and Llandeilo'r Fan 47-49; C Caerphilly *Llan* 49-52; V Huyton St Geo *Liv* 53-56; C Wigan St Cath 53; V Pemberton St Mark Newtown 56-62; V Lydiate 62-67; Hon C Sefton 69-85; rtd 85. *7 Delph Park Avenue, Ormskirk, Lancs L39 5DE* Tel (01695) 423711

BAUERSCHMIDT, John Crawford. b 59. Kenyon Coll Ohio BA81. Gen Th Sem (NY) MDiv84. **d** 84 **p** 85. USA 84-87; Lib Pusey Ho from 87; Lic to Offic *Ox* from 88. *Pusey House, Oxford OX1 3LZ* Tel (01865) 278415

BAUGHEN, Andrew Jonathan. b 64. Lon Guildhall Univ BA87. Wycliffe Hall Ox BTh94. **d** 94 **p** 95. C Battersea Rise St Mark *S'wark* from 94. *24 Parma Crescent, London SW11 1LT* Tel 0171-223 9341

✠**BAUGHEN, The Rt Revd Michael Alfred.** b 30. Lon Univ BD55. Oak Hill Th Coll 51. **d** 56 **p** 57 **c** 82. C Hyson Green *S'well* 56-59; C Reigate St Mary *S'wark* 59-61; Ord Cand Sec CPAS 61-64; R Rusholme H Trin *Man* 64-70; TV St Marylebone All So w SS Pet and Jo *Lon* 70-75; R 75-82; AD Westmr St Marylebone 78-82; Preb St Paul's Cathl 79-82; Bp Ches 82-96; rtd 96; Perm to Offic *S'wark* from 97. *99 Brunswick Quay, London SE16 1PX* Tel 0171-237 0167

BAULCOMB, Geoffrey Gordon. b 46. K Coll Lon BD86 AKC68. **d** 69 **p** 70. C Crofton Park St Hilda w St Cypr *S'wark* 69-74; TV Padgate *Liv* 74-79; R Whitton and Thurleston w Akenham *St E* from 79. *The Rectory, Whitton Church Lane, Ipswich IP1 6LT* Tel (01473) 741389

✠**BAVIN, The Rt Revd Timothy John.** b 35. Worc Coll Ox BA59 MA61. Cuddesdon Coll 59. **d** 61 **p** 62 **c** 74. S Africa 61-69 and 73-85; C Uckfield *Chich* 69-71; V Brighton Gd Shep Preston 71-73; Dean and Adn Johannesburg 73-74; Bp Johannesburg 74-85; Bp Portsm 85-95; OGS from 87; Community of Our Lady and St John from 96; Perm to Offic *Win* from 96. *Alton Abbey, Abbey Road, Beech, Alton, Hants GU34 4AP* Tel (01420) 562145 or 563575 Fax 561691

BAWTREE, Andrew James. b 66. Univ of Wales BD91 Ch Ch Coll Cant PGCE92. St Jo Coll Nottm 94. **d** 96. C Hoddesdon *St Alb* from 96. *St Catherine's House, Paul's Lane, Hoddesdon, Herts EN11 8TS* Tel (01992) 443724

BAWTREE, Robert John. b 39. Oak Hill Th Coll 62. **d** 67 **p** 68. C Foord St Jo *Cant* 67-70; C Boscombe St Jo *Win* 70-73; C Kinson *Sarum* 73-75; TV Bramerton w Surlingham *Nor* 76-82; R Arborfield w Barkham *Ox* 82-91; V Hildenborough *Roch* from 91; RD Tonbridge from 95. *The Vicarage, 194 Tonbridge Road, Hildenborough, Tonbridge, Kent TN11 9HR* Tel (01732) 833596

BAXANDALL, Peter. b 45. Tyndale Hall Bris 67. **d** 70 **p** 72. C Kidsgrove *Lich* 70-71; C St Helens St Mark *Liv* 71-75; C Ardsley *Sheff* 76-77; Rep Leprosy Miss E Anglia 77-86; P-in-c March St Wendreda *Ely* 86-87; R from 87; RD March from 93. *St Wendreda's Rectory, 21 Wimblington Road, March, Cambs PE15 9QW* Tel (01354) 53377

BAXENDALE, John Richard. b 48. Cranmer Hall Dur 89. **d** 91 **p** 92. C Carl St Jo *Carl* 91-94; C Dalston 94-95; P-in-c Monton *Man* 95-96; TV Eccles from 96. *The Vicarage, 3 Egerton Road, Monton, Eccles, Manchester M30 9LR* Tel 0161-789 2420

BAXENDALE, Paul Gordon. b 70. Leeds Univ BA91. Ridley Hall Cam 93. **d** 96 **p** 97. C Kendal St Thos *Carl* from 96. *6 Caroline Street, Kendal, Cumbria LA9 4SH* Tel (01539) 728482

BAXENDALE, Rodney Douglas. b 45. Ex Univ BA66 Nottm Univ DipTh79. Linc Th Coll 78. **d** 80 **p** 81. C Maidstone All SS and St Phil w Tovil *Cant* 80-83; Chapl RN from 83. *Royal Naval Chaplaincy Service, Room 203, Victory Building, HM Naval Base, Portsmouth PO1 3LS* Tel (01705) 727903 Fax 727112

BAXTER, Brian Raymond. b 31. Tyndale Hall Bris. **d** 58 **p** 59. C Heworth H Trin *York* 58-61; C Belper *Derby* 61-65; R Leverton *Linc* 65-67; C Mile Cross *Nor* 74-76; C Farnborough *Guildf* 76-79; Ldr Southgate Chr Project Bury St Edmunds 79-84; Chapl W Suffolk Hosp 79-81; R Ringsfield w Redisham, Barsham, Shipmeadow etc *St E* 82-88; V Nor Heartsease St Fran *Nor* 88-91; rtd 91; Perm to Offic *Nor* from 91. *104 Welsford Road, Norwich NR4 6QJ*

BAXTER, David Norman. b 39. Open Univ BA87. Kelham Th Coll 59. **d** 64 **p** 65. C Tonge Moor *Man* 64-68; Chapl RN 68-84; P-in-c Becontree St Pet *Chelmsf* 84-85; TV Becontree W 85-86; TR 86-94; Spain from 94. *C/ Card Vidal i Barraquer, 10, Escalera B, 1er, 2a, 08870 Sitges, Barcelona, Spain* Tel Barcelona (3) 894-6151 Fax as telephone

BAXTER, Mrs Elizabeth Mary. b 49. Coll of Ripon & York St Jo CCouns91 Leeds Poly DipHE91 Leeds Metrop Univ BA93. N Ord Course 81. **dss** 84 **d** 87 **p** 94. Leeds St Marg *Ripon* 84-87; Chapl Abbey Grange High Sch 85-93; Leeds All Hallows w Wrangthorn 85-87; Par Dn Leeds St Marg and All Hallows 87-93; Par Dn Topcliffe *York* 93-94; C 94-96; Jt Dir N of England Chr Healing Trust from 93; Jt Dir Cen for Spirituality, Past Care and Healing from 95; Perm to Offic *Ripon* from 93; Perm to Offic *Dur* and *Newc* from 94; Perm to Offic *Bradf* from 95; C Thirsk *York* from 96. *Holy Rood House, 10 Sowerby Road, Sowerby, Thirsk, N Yorkshire YO7 1HX* Tel (01845) 525591 or 522580

BAXTER, Harold Leslie. b 11. Roch Th Coll 62. **d** 64 **p** 65. C Corsham *Bris* 64-67; C Bath Lyncombe *B & W* 67-70; V Shapwick w Ashcott 70-88; P-in-c Burtle 75-88; V Shapwick w Ashcott and Burtle 88-95; rtd 96. *Tredole, Prussia Cove Lane, Rosudgeon, Penzance, Cornwall TR20 9AX*

BAXTER, Peter James. b 29. St Chad's Coll Dur BA53 DipTh55. **d** 55 **p** 56. C Stanground *Ely* 55-58; C Paddington St Mich w All SS *Lon* 58; C Woodston *Ely* 59-62; R Eynesbury 62-89; rtd 89. *15 Bromley College, London Road, Bromley BR1 1PE*

BAXTER, Canon Richard David. b 33. Kelham Th Coll 53. **d** 57 **p** 58. C Carl St Barn *Carl* 57-59; C Barrow St Matt 59-64; V Drighlington *Wakef* 64-73; V Penistone 73-80; V Carl St Aid and Ch Ch *Carl* 80-86; Perm to Offic from 86; Can Res Wakef Cathl *Wakef* 86-97; Prec from 86; Vice-Provost 92-97; rtd 97; Perm to Offic *Carl* from 97. *20 Summerfield, Dalston, Carlisle CA5 7NW* Tel (01228) 710496 Fax as telephone

BAXTER, Stanley Robert. b 31. AMIWO69 Leeds Univ MA90 FRSA96. Chich Th Coll 79. **d** 80 **p** 81. C Far Headingley St Chad *Ripon* 80-82; P-in-c Leeds St Marg and All Hallows 82-87; P-in-c Leeds All Hallows w Wrangthorn 85-87; P-in-c Leeds St Marg and All Hallows 87-93; Dir Leeds Cen for Urban Th Studies 88-93; Assoc Chapl Leeds Univ 91-93; Perm to Offic from 93; P-in-c Topcliffe *York* 93-95; Jt Dir N of England Chr Healing Trust from 93; NSM Topcliffe *York* 95-96; NSM Thirsk from 96; Jt Dir N of England Chr Healing Trust from 93; Perm to Offic *Dur* and *Newc* from 94; Perm to Offic *Bradf* from 95. *Holy Rood House, 10 Sowerby Road, Sowerby, Thirsk, N Yorkshire YO7 1HX* Tel (01845) 525591 or 522580

BAXTER, Stuart. b 43. Liv Univ BA65 Nottm Univ PGCE66. Cuddesdon Coll 66. **d** 70 **p** 71. C Kirkby *Liv* 70-73; C Ainsdale 73-76; Sierra Leone 77-83; CMS 83-84; V Nelson in Lt Marsden *Blackb* 84-92; V Lostock Hall from 92. *St James's Vicarage, 76A Brownedge Road, Lostock Hall, Preston PR5 5AD* Tel (01772) 35366

BAXTER, Terence Hugh (Terry). b 48. Leeds Poly BSc74. N Ord Course 89. **d** 92 **p** 93. NSM Guiseley w Esholt *Bradf* from 92. *2 Flatfield Cottage, Kelcliffe Lane, Guiseley, Leeds LS20 9DD* Tel (01943) 875170 Fax as telephone

BAYCOCK, Philip Louis. b 33. Wells Th Coll 64. **d** 66 **p** 67. C Kettering SS Pet and Paul *Pet* 66-68; C St Peter-in-Thanet *Cant* 68-72; V Bobbing w Iwade 72-73; Perm to Offic 73-76; V Thanington w Milton 77-84; R Chagford w Gidleigh and Throwleigh *Ex* from 84. *The Rectory, Chagford, Newton Abbot, Devon TQ13 8BW* Tel (01647) 432265

BAYES, Frederick Alan. b 60. Imp Coll Lon BSc81. St Jo Coll Dur BA92 Cranmer Hall Dur DMinlStuds93. **d** 93 **p** 94. C Talbot Village *Sarum* 93-97; Chapl St Hild and St Bede Coll *Dur* from 97. *3 Ravensworth Terrace, Durham DH1 1QP* Tel 0191-374 7853

BAYES, Paul. b 53. Birm Univ BA75 DipTh78. Qu Coll Birm 76. **d** 79 **p** 80. C Tynemouth Cullercoats St Paul *Newc* 79-82; Chapl Qu Eliz Coll *Lon* 82-87; Chapl Chelsea Coll 85-87; TV High Wycombe *Ox* 87-90; TR 90-94; TR Totton *Win* from 95. *Testwood Rectory, 92 Salisbury Road, Totton, Southampton SO40 3JA* Tel (01703) 865103

BAYFORD, Mrs Daphne Jean. b 32. Lon Univ TCert53. Qu Coll Birm 84. **d** 87 **p** 94. NSM Brinklow *Cov* 87-95; NSM Harborough Magna 87-95; NSM Monks Kirby w Pailton and Stretton-under-Fosse 87-95; Perm to Offic from 95. *Warwick House, 36 Lutterworth Road, Pailton, Rugby, Warks CV23 0QE* Tel (01788) 832797

BAYLEY, Albert William David. b 15. Lon Coll of Div 66. **d** 68 **p** 69. C Denham *Ox* 68-71; C St Giles-in-the-Fields *Lon* 71-78; rtd 78; Perm to Offic *St Alb* from 82. *25 Belper Road, Luton LU4 8RG* Tel (01582) 598196

BAYLEY, Dr Anne Christine. b 34. OBE86. MB, ChB58 FRCS66 FRCSEd86 Girton Coll Cam BA55. St Steph Ho Ox 90. **d** 91 **p** 94. NSM Wembley Park St Aug *Lon* from 91. *8 Winthrop Walk, Wembley, Middx HA9 7TT* Tel 0181-904 6621

BAYLEY, Canon John Benson. b 39. K Coll Cam BA60 MA64. Qu Coll Birm 61. **d** 63 **p** 64. C Clee *Linc* 63-68; V Gainsborough H Trin 68-73; P-in-c Linc St Mich 73-75; P-in-c Linc St Pet in Eastgate w St Marg 73-75; P-in-c Linc St Mary Magd w St Paul 73-75; R Linc Minster Gp from 75; Can and Preb Linc Cathl from 75; Hon PV from 77. *St Peter's Vicarage, Lee Road, Lincoln LN2 4BH* Tel (01522) 525741

BAYLEY, Dr Michael John. b 36. CCC Cam BA60 MA64 Sheff Univ DSocStuds67 PhD73. Linc Th Coll 60. **d** 62 **p** 63. C Leeds Gipton Epiphany *Ripon* 62-66; NSM Sheff St Mark Broomhill *Sheff* 67-93; C Sheff St Mary w Highfield Trin 93-95; C Sheff St Mary Bramhall Lane from 95. *27 Meadowbank Avenue, Sheffield S7 1PB* Tel 0114-258 5248

BAYLEY, Oliver James Drummond. b 49. Mansf Coll Ox MA PGCE. St Jo Coll Nottm 81. **d** 83 **p** 84. C Bath Weston St Jo w Kelston *B & W* 83-88; P-in-c Bathampton 88-93; P-in-c Claverton 92-93; R Bathampton w Claverton 93-96; Chapl Dauntsey's Sch Devizes from 96. *Dauntsey's School, West Lavington, Devizes, Wilts SN10 4HE* Tel (01380) 812446

BAYLEY, Dr Raymond. b 46. Keble Coll Ox BA68 MA72 Dur Univ DipTh69 Ex Univ PhD86. St Chad's Coll Dur 68. **d** 69 **p** 70. C Mold *St As* 69-74; C Llan w Capel Llanilltern *Llan* 74; PV Llan Cathl 74-77; V Cwmbach 77-80; Dir Past Studies St Mich Coll Llan 80-84; V Ynysddu *Mon* 84-86; V Griffithstown 86-92; V Rhosymedre *St As* 92-96; Dir Post-Ord Tr from 94; R Ruthin w Llanrhydd from 96. *The Cloisters, School Road, Ruthin LL15 1BL* Tel (01824) 702068

BAYLOR, Nigel Peter. b 58. NUI BA80 TCD DipTh84 MPhil88. **d** 84 **p** 86. C Carrickfergus *Conn* 84-87; C Dundela *D & D* 87-89; I Galloon w Drummully *Clogh* 89-94; Adult Educn Adv 91-94; I Carnmoney *Conn* from 94. *Coole Glebe, 20 Glebe Road, Carnmoney, Newtownabbey, Co Antrim BT36 6UW* Tel (01232) 844981

BAYLY, Samuel Niall Maurice. b 36. TCD BA64 MA. CITC Div Test65. **d** 65 **p** 66. C Belfast St Matt *Conn* 65-68; Miss to Seamen 68-69; C Belfast St Pet *Conn* 69-74; I Belfast Ch Ch from 74. *25 Beechlands, Malone Road, Belfast BT9 5HU* Tel (01232) 668732

BAYNE, David William. b 52. St Andr Univ MA75. Edin Th Coll 88. **d** 90 **p** 91. C Dumfries *Glas* 90-92; P-in-c 92-93; R from 93. *The Rectory, 8 Newall Terrace, Dumfries DG1 1LW* Tel (01387) 254126

BAYNE, Mrs Felicity Meriel. b 47. WMMTC 91. **d** 94 **p** 95. NSM Cheltenham Ch Ch *Glouc* from 94. *Hamfield House, Ham, Charlton Kings, Cheltenham, Glos GL52 6NG* Tel (01242) 237074

BAYNES, Matthew Thomas Crispin. b 62. UEA BA83. Westcott Ho Cam BA86. **d** 87 **p** 88. C Southgate Ch Ch *Lon* 87-90; C Gt Berkhamsted *St Alb* 90-95; V Coseley *Worc* from 95. *The Vicarage, Church Road, Coseley, Bilston, W Midlands WV14 8YB* Tel (01902) 353551

BAYNES, Simon Hamilton. b 33. New Coll Ox BA57 DipTh58 MA62. Wycliffe Hall Ox 57. **d** 59 **p** 60. C Rodbourne Cheney *Bris* 59-62; Japan 63-80; C Keynsham *B & W* 80-84; P-in-c Winkfield *Ox* 84-85; V Winkfield and Cranbourne from 85. *The Vicarage, Winkfield Street, Winkfield, Windsor, Berks SL4 4SW* Tel (01344) 882322

BAYNES, Timothy Francis de Brissac. b 29. Ely Th Coll 59. **d** 61 **p** 62. C Hockerill *St Alb* 61-65; C Mansfield Woodhouse *S'well* 65-67; Ind Chapl *Man* 67-94; P-in-c Miles Platting St Jo 67-72; rtd 94; Perm to Offic *Man* from 94. *5 Stainbank Green, Brigsteer Road, Kendal, Cumbria LA9 5RP* Tel (01539) 740605

BAYNES, William Hendrie (Will). b 39. Adelaide Univ BA60. S'wark Ord Course 77. **d** 79 **p** 80. C Notting Hill All SS w St Columb *Lon* 79-85; Perm to Offic 86-88; C Paddington St Sav from 88. *39E Westbourne Gardens, London W2 5NR* Tel 0171-727 9522 Fax as telephone E-mail will.baynes@dlondon.org.uk

BAYNHAM, Canon George Thorp. b 19. TCD BA41. **d** 42 **p** 43. C Dunboyne w Moyglare, Kilcock and Maynooth *M & K* 42-44; C Dublin St Cath *D & G* 44-52; I Castlemacadam 52-89; I Kilbride (Arklow) 64-73; Can Ch Ch Cathl Dublin 71-89; I Castlemacadam w Ballinaclash, Aughrim etc 73-89; rtd 89. *2 St Peter's Place, Drogheda, Co Louth, Irish Republic* Tel Drogheda (41) 36260

BAYNHAM, Matthew Fred. b 57. BA. Wycliffe Hall Ox 80. **d** 83 **p** 84. C Yardley St Edburgha *Birm* 83-87; TV Bath Twerton-on-Avon *B & W* 87-93; V Reddal Hill St Luke *Worc* from 93. *St Luke's Vicarage, Upper High Street, Cradley Heath, Warley, W Midlands B64 5HX* Tel (01384) 569940

BAYNHAM, William Benjamin. b 11. Fitzw Ho Cam BA34 MA37. Cuddesdon Coll 34. **d** 35 **p** 36. C Maidstone All SS *Cant* 35-37; CR from 44; rtd 81. *House of the Resurrection, Mirfield, W Yorkshire WF14 0BN* Tel (01924) 494318

BAZELY, William Francis (Bill). b 53. Sheff Univ BEng75. St Jo Coll Nottm DipTh79 DPS. **d** 81 **p** 82. C Huyton St Geo *Liv* 81-84; TV Netherthorpe *Sheff* 84-92; Chapl W Lambeth Community Care Trust from 92; Chapl Tooting Bec Hosp Lon from 92; Chapl SW Hosp Lon from 92. *4-5 Voss Court, London SW16 3BS, or 5 Glenhurst Rise, London SE19 3XN* Tel 0181-771 9781 or 765 0699

✠**BAZLEY, The Rt Revd Colin Frederick.** b 35. St Pet Coll Ox MA57. Tyndale Hall Bris 57. **d** 59 **p** 60 **c** 69. C Bootle St Leon *Liv* 59-62; SAMS from 62; Chile from 62; Asst Bp Cavtin and Malleco 69-75; Asst Bp Santiago 75-77; Bp Chile from 77; Primate CASA 77-83 and 89-95. *Iglesia Anglicana del Chile, Casilla 50675, Correo Central, Santiago, Chile* Tel Santiago (2) 821-2478 or 383009

BAZLINTON, Stephen Cecil. b 46. MRCS Lon Univ BDS LDS. Ridley Hall Cam 78. **d** 85 **p** 86. NSM Stebbing w Lindsell *Chelmsf* from 85. *St Helens, High Street, Stebbing, Dunmow, Essex CM6 3SE* Tel (01371) 856495

BEACH, Jonathan Mark. b 67. Essex Univ BSc89. Trin Coll Bris BA94. **d** 94 **p** 95. C Oulton Broad *Nor* from 94. *3 Windward Way, Lowestoft, Suffolk NR33 9HF* Tel (01502) 582083

BEACH, Mark Howard Francis. b 62. Kent Univ BA83. St Steph Ho Ox 85. **d** 87 **p** 88. C Beeston *S'well* 87-90; C Hucknall Torkard 90-93; R Gedling from 93; R Netherfield from 96. *The Rectory, Rectory Drive, Gedling, Nottingham NG4 4BG* Tel 0115-961 3214 E-mail markb@innotts.co.uk

BEACH, Stephen John. b 58. Man Univ BA81 BD88 Didsbury Coll of Educn PGCE82. N Ord Course 92. **d** 93 **p** 94. NSM Harwood *Man* 93; C 93-97; TV Westhoughton and Wingates from 97. *The Vicarage, 91 Chorley Road, Westhoughton, Bolton BL5 3PG* Tel (01942) 812119

BEACHAM, Ian William Henry. b 17. Dur Univ LTh41. ALCD41. **d** 41 **p** 42. C Twerton *B & W* 41-48; P-in-c Westfield 48-53; V 53-58; Asst Master and Chapl Wells Cathl Sch 52-58; V Kidlington *Ox* 58-70; R Hampton Poyle 58-70; V Banbury 70-74; TR 74-82; Chapl Horton Gen Hosp 70-82; rtd 82. *11 West Lea Road, Weston, Bath BA1 3RL* Tel (01225) 421682

BEACHAM, Peter Martyn. b 44. Ex Coll Ox BA65 MA70 Lon Univ MPhil67. Sarum Th Coll 70. **d** 73 **p** 74. NSM Ex St Martin, St Steph, St Laur etc *Ex* 73-74; NSM Cen Ex 74-90. *Bellever, Barrack Road, Exeter EX2 6AB* Tel (01392) 35074

BEACOM, Canon Thomas Ernest. b 12. TCD BA33 MA40 BD40. **d** 36 **p** 36. C Limerick St Lawr w H Trin and St Jo *L & K* 36-38; C Seapatrick *D & D* 38-44; P-in-c Belfast St Kath *Conn* 44-58; I 58-82; RD N Belfast 54-65; Dioc Registrar 63-82; Can Belf Cathl 66-82; rtd 82. *4955-41 Avenue, Drayton Valley, Alberta, Canada, T7A 1V4* Tel Edmonton (403) 542 3488

BEACON, Canon Ralph Anthony. b 44. Univ of Wales (Ban) DipTh70. St Mich Coll Llan 70. **d** 71 **p** 72. C Neath w Llantwit *Llan* 71-74; TV Holyhead w Rhoscolyn *Ban* 74-78; R Llanenddwyn w Llanddwywe, Llanbedr w Llandanwg from 78; RD Ardudwy from 89; Hon Can Ban Cathl from 91. *The Rectory, Dyffryn Ardudwy LL44 2EY* Tel (01341) 247207

BEACON, Stephanie. b 49. **d** 96 **p** 97. NSM Llanenddwyn w Llanddwywe, Llanbedr w Llandanwg *Ban* from 96. *The Rectory, Dyffryn Ardudwy LL44 2EY* Tel (01341) 247207

BEADLE, David Alexander. b 37. St And Dioc Tr Course. **d** 88 **p** 89. NSM St Andrews St Andr *St And* from 88. *48 Clayton Caravan Park, St Andrews, Fife KY16 9YB* Tel (01334) 870001

BEADLE, Ms Janet Mary. b 52. Philippa Fawcett Coll CertEd74. EAMTC 91. **d** 94 **p** 95. C Kingston upon Hull H Trin *York* from 94. *The Clergy House, 67 Adelaide Street, Hull HU3 2EZ* Tel (01482) 215665

BEADLE, Mrs Lorna. b 40. NE Ord Course DipHE95. **d** 95 **p** 96. C Ashington *Newc* from 95. *9 Arundel Square, Ashington, Northd NE63 8AW* Tel (01670) 816467

✠**BEAK, The Rt Revd Robert Michael Cawthorn.** b 25. OBE90. Lon Bible Coll DipTh51. **d** 53 **p** 54 **c** 84. C Tunbridge Wells St Jo *Roch* 53-55; BCMS 55-56 and 84-89; Kenya 56-69 and 84-89; R Heanton Punchardon *Ex* 70-84; Offg Chapl RAF 70-80; RD Barnstaple *Ex* 77-81; R Heanton Punchardon w Marwood 79-84; Preb Ex Cathl 82-84; Asst Bp Mt Kenya E 84-89; rtd 90; Asst Bp Derby from 91. *Hillcrest, Newton Road, Tibshelf, Alfreton, Derbyshire DE55 5PA* Tel (01773) 872154

BEAK, Stephen Robert (Steve). b 64. City Univ BSc86 MBCO87. Wycliffe Hall Ox BTh94. **d** 94 **p** 95. C Lache cum Saltney *Ches* 94-97; C Howell Hill *Guildf* from 97. *18 Nonsuch Walk, Cheam, Surrey SM2 7NG* Tel 0181-393 4019

BEAKE, Christopher Martyn Grandfield. b 36. K Coll Lon BA60 AKC60. **d** 61 **p** 62. C Berwick H Trin *Newc* 61-66; V Tynemouth H Trin W Town 66-78; V Hanslope w Castlethorpe *Ox* from 78. *The Vicarage, Park Road, Hanslope, Milton Keynes MK19 7LT* Tel (01908) 510542

BEAKE, Canon Kenneth George. b 37. Ripon Coll Cuddesdon 75. **d** 77 **p** 78. C Guisborough *York* 77-80; V Kingston upon Hull St Martin 80-84; V Hull St Martin w Transfiguration 84-88; P-in-c Gt Wishford *Sarum* 88-91; P-in-c S Newton 88-91; Dir of Ords 88-91; Dioc Dir of Ords *Nor* from 91; P-in-c Nor St Steph from 91; Hon Brigade Chapl to Norfolk Co Fire Service from 91; Hon Can Nor Cathl from 97. *12 The Crescent, Norwich NR2 1SA* Tel (01603) 623045

BEAKE, Stuart Alexander. b 49. Em Coll Cam BA72 MA76. Cuddesdon Coll 72. **d** 74 **p** 75. C Hitchin St Mary *St Alb* 74-76; C Hitchin 77-79; TV Hemel Hempstead 79-85; Bp's Dom Chapl *S'well* 85-87; V Shottery St Andr *Cov* from 87; RD Fosse from 93; Dioc Dir of Ords from 96. *The Vicarage, Church Lane, Stratford-upon-Avon, Warks CV37 9HQ* Tel (01789) 293381

BEAKEN, Robert William Frederick. b 62. SS Paul & Mary Coll Cheltenham BA83 Lambeth STh90. Ripon Coll Cuddesdon 85 Ven English Coll and Pontifical Gregorian Univ Rome 87. **d** 88 **p** 89. C Forton *Portsm* 88-92; C Shepshed *Leic* 92-94; V Colchester St Barn *Chelmsf* from 94. *The Vicarage, 13 Abbot's Road, Colchester CO2 8BE* Tel (01206) 797481

BEAL, David Michael. b 61. Nottm Univ BTh89. St Jo Coll Nottm 86. **d** 89 **p** 90. C Marton *Blackb* 89-92; C Darwen St Pet w Hoddlesden 92-93; TV 93-97; R Itchingfield w Slinfold *Chich* from 97. *The Rectory, The Street, Slinfold, Horsham, W Sussex RH13 7RR* Tel (01403) 790197

BEAL, Malcolm. b 31. Bris Univ BA52. Ridley Hall Cam 57. **d** 59 **p** 60. C Keynsham w Queen Charlton *B & W* 59-62; C Speke All SS *Liv* 62-65; Uganda 65-74; V Salford Priors *Cov* 74-83; R Jersey St Clem *Win* 83-97; rtd 97. *3 Redwoods Close, Hemyock, Cullompton, Devon EX15 3QQ* Tel (01823) 680853

BEAL, Royston David. b 35. K Coll Lon BD60 AKC60. **d** 61 **p** 62. C Chesterfield St Mary and All SS *Derby* 61-64; C Chiswick St Nic w St Mary *Lon* 64-70; V Kensal Green St Jo from 70. *St John's Vicarage, Kilburn Lane, London W10 4AA* Tel 0181-969 2615

BEALE, Wilfred Henry Ellson. b 11. FCCA FCIS. **d** 69 **p** 71. Hon C Northwood H Trin *Lon* 69-82; Perm to Offic from 82. *23 Woodridge Way, Northwood, Middx HA6 2BE* Tel (01923) 826301

BEALE, William Edgar. b 11. K Coll Lon 37. Bps' Coll Cheshunt 40. **d** 42 **p** 43. C Sawbridgeworth *St Alb* 42-45; Chapl Pishiobury Sch Sawbridgeworth 45-48; Chapl LCC Res Sch Hutton 48-51; Chapl LCC Res Sch Banstead 51-52; C Felixstowe St Jo *St E* 52-53; V Lakenheath 53-56; Ceylon 56-64; R Kedington *St E* 64-72; C Brighton St Paul *Chich* 72-73; C Bingley All SS *Bradf* 73-77; rtd 77. *The Charterhouse, Charterhouse Square, London EC1M 6AN*

BEALES, Christopher Leader Day. b 51. St Jo Coll Dur BA72. Cranmer Hall Dur DipTh75. **d** 76 **p** 77. C Upper Armley *Ripon* 76-79; Ind Chapl 76-79; Ind Chapl *Dur* 79-84; Sen Chapl 82-84; Sec Ind Cttee of Gen Syn Bd for Soc Resp 85-91; Sec Inner Cities Relig Coun (DOE) 92-94; Dir NE Churches' Regional Commn *Dur* from 94. *12 Castle View, Chester le Street, Co Durham DH3 3XA* Tel 0191-388 9941 Fax as telephone

BEALES, John David. b 55. SS Hild & Bede Coll Dur BA77 Univ of W Aus DipEd79 Nottm Univ DipTh82. St Jo Coll Nottm DPS83. **d** 83 **p** 84. Australia 83-89; Dir Educn and Tr Philo Trust 89-90; NSM Nottingham St Nic *S'well* 89-95; Australia from 95. *73 Belford Road, Kew East, Victoria, Australia 3102* Tel Melbourne (3) 9859 7774

BEALING, Andrew John. b 42. Sarum Th Coll 67. **d** 69 **p** 70. C Auckland St Andr and St Anne *Dur* 69-73; P-in-c Eastgate 73-76; P-in-c Rookhope 73-76; V Frosterley 76-85; V Rekendyke from 85; Chapl S Tyneside Distr Hosp from 90. *The Vicarage, St Jude's Terrace, South Shields, Tyne & Wear NE33 5PB* Tel 0191-455 2338

BEALING, Mrs Patricia Ramsey. b 39. Lightfoot Ho Dur IDC63. **dss** 63 **d** 87 **p** 94. Rekendyke *Dur* 85-87; Par Dn 87-94; C from 94; Chapl S Tyneside Distr Hosp from 88. *The Vicarage, St Jude's Terrace, South Shields, Tyne & Wear NE33 5PB* Tel 0191-455 2338

BEAMENT, Owen John. b 41. Bps' Coll Cheshunt 61. **d** 64 **p** 65. C Deptford St Paul *S'wark* 64-68; C Peckham St Jo 69-73; C Vauxhall St Pet 73-74; V Hatcham Park All SS from 74. *All Saints Vicarage, 22 Erlanger Road, London SE14 5TG* Tel 0171-639 3497

BEAMER, Neville David. b 40. Univ of Wales (Lamp) BA62 Jes Coll Ox BA65 MA70. Wycliffe Hall Ox 64. **d** 65 **p** 66. C Hornchurch St Andr *Chelmsf* 65-68; C Warwick St Mary *Cov* 68-72; V Holton-le-Clay *Linc* 72-75; P-in-c Stoneleigh w Ashow *Cov* 75-79; P-in-c Baginton 77-79; V Fletchamstead 79-86; Warden Whatcombe Ho Blandford Forum 86-90; V Jersey Millbrook St Matt *Win* 90-95; R Jersey St Lawr 90-95; V Yateley from 95; RD Odiham from 95. *The Vicarage, 99 Reading Road, Yateley, Camberley, Surrey GU17 7LR* Tel (01252) 873133

BEAMISH, Canon Frank Edwin. b 28. TCD BA49 MA. **d** 50 **p** 52. C Templecorran *Conn* 50-53; C Drumglass *Arm* 53-61; I Caledon w Brantry 61-94; Preb Arm Cathl from 88; Treas Arm Cathl from 92; rtd 94. *214 Killylea Road, Caledon, Co Tyrone BT68 4TN* Tel (01861) 568609

BEAN, Alan Evison. b 13. Ch Coll Cam BA35 MA39. Ely Th Coll 35. **d** 36 **p** 37. C Hendon St Ignatius *Dur* 36-40; Perm to Offic *Ox* 41-50; CF 42-45; SSJE from 47; India 50-55 and 57-64; Lic to Offic *Ox* from 55; rtd 83. *SSJE Priory, 228 Iffley Road, Oxford OX4 1SE* Tel (01865) 248116

BEAN, Douglas Jeyes Lendrum. b 25. Worc Coll Ox BA50 MA53. Ely Th Coll 50. **d** 51 **p** 52. C Croydon Woodside *Cant* 51-54; Min Can Windsor 54-59; V Reading St Laur *Ox* 59-68; Chapl HM Borstal Reading 61-68; RD Reading *Ox* 65-68; Min Can St Paul's Cathl *Lon* 68-72; Hon Min Can from 72; V St Pancras w St Jas and Ch Ch 72-93; PV Westmr Abbey 75-80; rtd 93. *3 Bishop Street, London N1 8PH* Tel 0171-226 8340

BEAN, Canon John Victor. b 25. Down Coll Cam BA47 MA51. Sarum Th Coll 48. **d** 50 **p** 51. C Milton *Portsm* 50-55; C Fareham SS Pet and Paul 55-59; V St Helens 59-66; V Cowes St Mary 66-91; RD W Wight 68-72; Hon Can Portsm Cathl 70-91; P-in-c Cowes St Faith 77-80; C-in-c Gurnard All SS CD 78-91; Chapl to The Queen from 80; rtd 91. *Magnolia, 23 Seldon Avenue, Ryde, Isle of Wight PO33 1NS* Tel (01983) 812516

BEAN, Kevin Douglas. b 54. Edin Univ BD78. Edin Th Coll 75. **d** 81 **p** 82. USA 81-88 and from 89; C Edin St Marg *Edin* 88-89; C Edin Old St Paul 88-89. *1625 North Rodney Street, Wilmington, Delaware 19806, USA*

BEANEY, John. b 47. Trin Coll Bris DipHE79. **d** 79 **p** 80. C Bromley Ch Ch *Roch* 79-84; V Broadheath *Ches* from 84; Chapl Altrincham Gen Hosp from 91. *The Vicarage, Lindsell Road, West Timperley, Altrincham, Cheshire WA14 5NX* Tel 0161-928 4820

BEARCROFT, Bramwell Arthur. b 52. Homerton Coll Cam BEd82. EAMTC 87. **d** 90 **p** 91. Chapl and Hd Relig Studies Kimbolton Sch Cambs from 88; NSM Tilbrook *Ely* from 90; NSM Covington from 90; NSM Catworth Magna from 90; NSM Keyston and Bythorn from 90. *White House, High Street, Kimbolton, Huntingdon, Cambs PE18 0HB* Tel (01480) 860469

BEARD, Christopher Robert (Chris). b 47. Chich Th Coll 81. **d** 83 **p** 84. C Chich St Paul and St Pet *Chich* 83-86; TV Ifield 86-91; V Haywards Heath St Rich from 91. *St Richard's Vicarage, Queen's Road, Haywards Heath, W Sussex RH16 1EB* Tel (01444) 413621

BEARD, Laurence Philip (Laurie). b 45. Lon Univ BA68. Trin Coll Bris 88. **d** 90 **p** 91. C Trentham *Lich* 90-94; V Wolverhampton St Matt from 94. *St Matthew's Vicarage, 14 Sydenham Road, Wolverhampton WV1 2NY* Tel (01902) 453300

BEARD, Peter Harley. b 39. Coll of Resurr Mirfield 60. **d** 71 **p** 72. S Africa 71-75; Miss to Seamen 75-82; V St Osyth *Chelmsf* 81-86; P-in-c Wellington Ch Ch *Lich* 86-95; V Pelsall 95-97; rtd 97. *The Vicarage, 39 Hall Lane, Pelsall, Walsall WS3 4JN* Tel (01922) 682098

BEARD, Robert John Hansley. b 61. St Andr Univ BD85. Ripon Coll Cuddesdon 86 Ch Div Sch of the Pacific (USA) 87. **d** 88 **p** 89. C Sheff Manor *Sheff* 88-91; C Rotherham 91-94; V Sheff Abbeydale St Pet from 94; Chapl Sheff Hallam Univ from 95. *St Peter's Vicarage, Ashland Road, Sheffield S7 1RH* Tel 0114-250 9716

BEARDALL, Raymond. b 32. St Jo Coll Nottm 70. **d** 72 **p** 73. C Ilkley All SS *Bradf* 72-74; C Seasalter *Cant* 74-79; V Farndon *S'well* 79-84; R Thorpe 79-84; V Blidworth from 84. *2 Kirk's Croft, Wain Street, Mansfield, Notts NG21 0QH* Tel (01623) 792306

BEARDMORE, John Keith. b 42. FCP85 Bris Univ BEd74 K Coll Lon MA90. **d** 77 **p** 78. NSM Maindee *Mon* from 77. *16 Hove Avenue, Newport NP9 7QP* Tel (01633) 263272

BEARDSHAW, David. b 37. JP. DPS. Wells Th Coll 65. **d** 67 **p** 68. C Wood End *Cov* 67-69; C Stoke 70-73; V Whitley 73-77; Dioc Educn Officer 77-87; P-in-c Offchurch 87-93; Warden Offa Retreat Ho 87-93; rtd 93. *180 Ashington Grove, Coventry CV3 4DB*

BEARDSLEY, Christopher (Chris). b 51. Sussex Univ BA73. Westcott Ho Cam 76. **d** 78 **p** 79. C Portsea N End St Mark *Portsm* 78-85; V Catherington and Clanfield from 85. *The Vicarage, 330 Catherington Lane, Catherington, Waterlooville, Hants PO8 0TD* Tel (01705) 593139

BEARDSLEY, Daniel Graham Richard. b 55. Liv Univ BA86. St Steph Ho Ox 90. **d** 92 **p** 93. C Stanley *Liv* 92-95; V Dovecot from 95. *Holy Spirit Vicarage, Dovecot Avenue, Liverpool L14 7QJ* Tel 0151-220 6611

BEARDSMORE, Alan. b 45. Wycliffe Hall Ox 67. **d** 70 **p** 71. C Prittlewell St Mary *Chelmsf* 70-72; C Epsom St Martin *Guildf* 72-78; P-in-c Burbage and Savernake Ch Ch *Sarum* 78-79; P-in-c E Grafton, Tidcombe and Fosbury 78-79; TV Wexcombe 79-80; Chapl RN 80-83; TV Haverhill w Withersfield, the Wrattings etc *St E* 83-87; V Gt Barton 87-95; V Eaton *Nor* from 95. *The Vicarage, 210 Newmarket Road, Norwich NR4 7LA* Tel (01603) 250915

BEARDSMORE, John. b 19. Kelham Th Coll 46. **d** 51 **p** 51. C Caldmore *Lich* 51-53; C Otley *Bradf* 53-55; V Burley in Wharfedale 55-69; V Bromley H Trin *Roch* 69-70; V Buttershaw St Paul *Bradf* 70-88; rtd 88; Perm to Offic *Bradf* from 88. *41 Nab Wood Grove, Shipley, W Yorkshire BD18 4HR* Tel (01274) 596197

BEARE, Canon William. b 33. TCD BA58 DipCSM77. **d** 59 **p** 60. C Waterford St Patr *C & O* 59-62; C Cork H Trin w Shandon St Mary *C, C & R* 62-64; I Rathcormac 64-68; I Marmullane w Monkstown 68-76; Dioc C 76-82; I Stradbally w Ballintubbert, Coraclone etc *C & O* from 82; Preb Ossory and Leighlin Cathls 88-90; Chan 90-92; Prec from 92; Preb Stagonil St Patr Cathl Dublin from 95. *The Rectory, Church Lane, Stradbally, Laois, Irish Republic* Tel Portlaoise (502) 25173

BEARMAN, Leslie Raymond Livingstone. b 09. ALCD35. **d** 35 **p** 36. C Walthamstow St Luke *Chelmsf* 35-38; C Bedford St Cuth *St Alb* 38-40; C Bedford Ch Ch 38-40; Public Preacher 40-43; Chapl HM Pris Bedf 43-45; R Clophill *St Alb* 45-51; Chapl Bedford Modern Sch 51-61; Public Preacher *St Alb* 51-61; R Sherington w Chicheley *Ox* 61-74; RD Newport 70-73; R N Crawley and Astwood w Hardmead 73-75; rtd 74; Perm to Offic *Pet* from 75. *395A Kettering Road, Northampton NN3 6QT* Tel (01604) 462326

BEARN, Hugh William. b 62. Man Univ BA84. Cranmer Hall Dur 86. **d** 89 **p** 90. C Heaton Ch Ch *Man* 89-92; Chapl RAF Coll Cranwell 92-96; V Tottington *Man* from 96. *St Anne's Vicarage, Chapel Street, Tottington, Bury, Lancs BL4 8AP* Tel (01204) 883713

BEARPARK, Canon John Michael. b 36. Ex Coll Ox BA59 MA63. Linc Th Coll 59. **d** 61 **p** 62. C Bingley H Trin *Bradf* 61-64; C Baildon 64-67; V Fairweather Green 67-77; Chapl Airedale Gen Hosp 77-94; V Steeton *Bradf* 77-94; Hon Can Bradf Cathl from

89; V Bentham St Marg from 94; RD Ewecross from 94. *St Margaret's Vicarage, 27 Station Road, High Bentham, Lancaster LA2 7LH* Tel (015242) 61321

BEASLEY, Canon Arthur James. b 12. Hertf Coll Ox BA33 MA38. Ridley Hall Cam 34. **d** 36 **p** 37. C Harpurhey Ch Ch *Man* 36-39; C Flixton St Mich 39-42; P-in-c Stand 42-43; R Moss Side Ch Ch 43-48; Chapl Man R Infirmary 43-48; V Heaton Ch Ch *Man* 48-81; Hon Can Man Cathl 72-81; rtd 81; Perm to Offic *Man* from 81. *40 Chorley New Road, Lostock, Bolton BL6 4AL* Tel (01204) 494450

BEASLEY, Bernard Robinson. b 07. OBE56. Leeds Univ BA30 MA45. Coll of Resurr Mirfield 25. **d** 31 **p** 32. C Vauxhall St Pet *S'wark* 31-34; Chapl RN 34-62; QHC 60; V Easebourne *Chich* 62-72; RD Midhurst 64-72; rtd 72. *Agra Cottage, Worton, Devizes, Wilts SN10 5SE* Tel (01380) 723383

BEASLEY, Michael John. b 41. Dur Univ BA63. Sarum Th Coll 63. **d** 65 **p** 66. C Weston St Jo *B & W* 65-67; C Pinner *Lon* 67-69; C E Grinstead St Swithun *Chich* 69-72; Chapl St Mary's Hosp and Qu Hosp Croydon 72-77; Mayday Hosp Thornton Heath 72-77; TV Swanborough *Sarum* 77-82; V Stourbridge St Mich Norton *Worc* from 82. *St Michael's House, Westwood Avenue, Stourbridge, W Midlands DY8 3EN* Tel (01384) 393647

BEASLEY, Canon Walter Sydney. b 33. Nottm Univ BA57. Linc Th Coll 57. **d** 59 **p** 60. C Harworth *S'well* 59-64; V Forest Town 64-70; R Bulwell St Mary from 70; Hon Can S'well Minster from 85. *The Rectory, Station Road, Bulwell, Nottingham NG6 9AA* Tel 0115-927 8468

BEATER, David MacPherson. b 41. Chich Th Coll 66. **d** 69 **p** 70. C Withington St Crispin *Man* 69-72; C Lightbowne 72-74; V Prestwich St Hilda 74-81; V Northfleet *Roch* 81-85; C Bickley 86-90; TV Stanley *Dur* 90-97; SSF from 97. *Friary of St Francis, Hilfield, Dorchester, Dorset DT2 7BE* Tel (01300) 341345

BEATSON, Christine. b 32. Wolv Teacher Tr Coll TCert68. W of England Minl Tr Course. **d** 96. NSM Huntley and Longhope *Glouc* from 96. *High Orchard, Old Hill, Longhope, Glos GL17 0PF* Tel (01452) 830921

BEATTIE, Margaret. *See* BREWSTER, Margaret

BEATTIE, Noel Christopher. b 41. TCD BTh65 Cranfield Inst of Tech MSc86. **d** 68 **p** 69. C Belfast H Trin *Conn* 68-70; C Belfast St Bart 70-73; C Doncaster St Mary *Sheff* 73-77; TV Northampton Em *Pet* 77-88; Ind Chapl 85-88; Ind Chapl *Linc* 88-92; Ind Chapl *Roch* from 92. *181 Maidstone Road, Chatham, Kent ME4 6JG* Tel (01634) 844867 Fax as telephone

BEATTY, Robert Harold. b 27. W Ontario Univ BA48 Keble Coll Ox BA55 MA58 McGill Univ Montreal PhD62. **d** 51 **p** 52. Canada 51, 55-57 and 58-67; Perm to Offic *Ox* 52-55; Tutor Bps' Coll Cheshunt 57-58; C W Byfleet *Guildf* 67-71; C Oseney Crescent St Luke w Camden Square St Paul *Lon* 71-72; R Cosgrove *Pet* 72-83; V Hebburn St Oswald *Dur* 83-93; rtd 93; Perm to Offic *Dur* from 93. *60 Briarwood Avenue, Gosforth, Newcastle-upon-Tyne NE3 5DB* Tel 0191-285 2429

BEAUCHAMP, Anthony Hazlerigg Proctor. b 40. MICE68 Trin Coll Cam BA62 MA66. St Jo Coll Nottm 73. **d** 75 **p** 76. C New Humberstone *Leic* 75-77; C-in-c Polegate *Chich* 77-80; Chapl Bethany Sch Goudhurst 80-86; Chapl Luckley-Oakfield Sch Wokingham 86-88; Chapl Clayesmore Sch Blandford 89-93; R Kirby-le-Soken w Gt Holland *Chelmsf* from 93. *The Rectory, 18 Thorpe Road, Kirby Cross, Frinton-on-Sea, Essex CO13 0LT* Tel (01255) 675997

BEAUCHAMP, Gerald Charles. b 55. Hull Univ BA78. Coll of Resurr Mirfield 78. **d** 80 **p** 81. C Hatcham St Cath *S'wark* 80-83; S Africa 83-86; C Ealing St Steph Castle Hill *Lon* 86-88; P-in-c Brondesbury St Anne w Kilburn H Trin 88-89; V 89-93; Chapl Kilburn Coll 88-93; C Chelsea St Luke and Ch Ch *Lon* 93-96; V W Brompton St Mary w St Pet from 96. *The Vicarage, 24 Fawcett Street, London SW10 9EZ* Tel 0171-351 4204 or 373 2810

BEAUCHAMP, John Nicholas. b 57. Wycliffe Hall Ox 92. **d** 94 **p** 95. C Ipswich St Jo *St E* from 94. *2A Norbury Road, Ipswich IP4 4RQ* Tel (01473) 710025

BEAUMONT, Arthur Ralph. b 37. Open Univ BA82 Salford Univ MSc86. Ely Th Coll 61. **d** 64 **p** 87. C Grimsby All SS *Linc* 64-65; Perm to Offic *S'well* 70-72; NSM Addingham, Edenhall, Langwathby and Culgaith *Carl* from 87. *Brookside, Melmerby, Penrith, Cumbria CA10 1HF* Tel (01768) 881270

BEAUMONT, Canon Brian Maxwell. b 34. Nottm Univ BA56. Wells Th Coll 58. **d** 59 **p** 60. C Clifton *S'well* 59-62; C E Stoke w Syerston 62; C Edgbaston St Geo *Birm* 62-65; V Smethwick St Alb 65-70; Asst Dir RE *Blackb* 70-73; V Blackb H Trin 70-77; Hon Can Blackb Cathl 73-77 and from 92; Can Res 77-92; Dir RE 73-92; V Goosnargh w Whittingham from 92; Bp's Adv for Rural Areas from 92. *The Vicarage, Goosnargh Lane, Goosnargh, Preston PR3 2BN* Tel (01772) 865274

BEAUMONT, Canon John Philip. b 32. Leeds Univ BA55. Coll of Resurr Mirfield 55. **d** 57 **p** 58. C Leeds St Marg *Ripon* 57-60; C Wellingborough All Hallows *Pet* 60-64; Chapl HM Borstal Wellingborough 64-70; V Wellingborough St Andr *Pet* 64-70; V Finedon 70-96; Can Pet Cathl 80-96; RD Higham 83-87; rtd 96. *9 Warren Bridge, Oundle, Peterborough PE8 4DQ* Tel (01832) 273863

BEAUMONT, John William. b 19. MBE48. RMC 38. Qu Coll Birm 48. **d** 51 **p** 52. C Portsea N End St Mark *Portsm* 51-54; C-in-c Leigh Park St Fran CD 54-59; V S w N Hayling 59-74; R Droxford 74-86; R Meonstoke w Corhampton cum Exton 78-86; rtd 86; Perm to Offic *Portsm* from 86. *134 The Dale, Widley, Waterlooville, Hants PO7 5DF* Tel (01705) 377492

BEAUMONT, Stephen Martin. b 51. K Coll Lon BD73 AKC74. St Aug Coll Cant 73. **d** 74 **p** 75. C Benwell St Jas *Newc* 74-77; Asst Chapl Marlborough Coll 77-81; R Ideford, Luton and Ashcombe *Ex* 81-84; Bp's Dom Chapl 81-84; Chapl Taunton Sch 85-91; Chapl Haileybury Coll Herts from 92. *Haileybury College, Heathgate, College Road, Hertford Heath, Hertford SG13 7PU* Tel (01992) 462000

BEAUMONT, Terence Mayes. b 41. Lon Univ BA63 Nottm Univ DipTh69. Linc Th Coll 68. **d** 71 **p** 72. C Hitchin St Mary *St Alb* 71-74; C Harpenden St Nic 75-79; V Stevenage St Pet Broadwater 79-87; V St Alb St Mich from 87. *St Michael's Vicarage, St Michael's Street, St Albans, Herts AL3 4SL* Tel (01727) 835037

BEAUMONT, Mrs Veronica Jean. b 38. Ox Min Course CBTS93. **d** 93 **p** 94. NSM High Wycombe *Ox* from 93. *Edgehill, Upper Stanley Road, High Wycombe, Bucks HP12 4DB* Tel (01494) 523697

BEAUMONT of Whitley, The Revd and Rt Hon Lord (Timothy Wentworth). b 28. Ch Ch Ox BA52 MA56. Westcott Ho Cam 54. **d** 55 **p** 56. Asst Chapl Hong Kong Cathl 55-59; Hon C Westmr St Steph w St Jo *Lon* 60-63; Lic to Offic 63-73; Hon C Balham Hill Ascension *S'wark* 85-86; P-in-c Richmond St Luke 86-87; P-in-c N Sheen St Phil and All SS 86-87; V Kew St Phil and All SS w St Luke 87-91; Perm to Offic from 91; rtd 93. *40 Elms Road, London SW4 9EX* Tel 0171-498 8664

BEAVAN, Charles Kenneth. b 15. JP63. Lon Univ BA49. St Deiniol's Hawarden 66. **d** 67 **p** 68. Hd Master Meole Brace Sch 53-76; Hon C Meole Brace *Lich* 67-71; P-in-c Shrewsbury St Alkmund 71-89; Perm to Offic from 89. *School House, 5 Vicarage Road, Shrewsbury SY3 9EZ* Tel (01743) 344172

BEAVAN, Edward Hugh. b 43. Ex Coll Ox BA70 MA74. Cuddesdon Coll 69. **d** 71 **p** 72. C Ashford St Hilda *Lon* 71-74; C Newington St Mary *S'wark* 74-76; R Sandon *Chelmsf* 76-86; V Thorpe Bay from 86. *The Vicarage, 86 Tyrone Road, Southend-on-Sea, Essex SS1 3HB* Tel (01702) 587597

BEAVER, Christopher Martin. b 31. AKC56. **d** 60 **p** 61. C Leek All SS *Lich* 60-64; C Uttoxeter w Bramshall 64-67; V Normacot 67-77; V Pheasey 77-83; V Dordon *Birm* 83-89; V Langley St Mich 89-94; rtd 94; Perm to Offic *Lich* 94-97. *70 Filance Lane, Penkridge, Stafford ST19 5JT* Tel (01785) 715834

BEAVER, William Carpenter. b 45. Colorado Coll BA Wolfs Coll Ox DPhil. Ox NSM Course. **d** 82 **p** 83. NSM Kennington St Jo w St Jas *S'wark* 82-95; Hon P-in-c Avonmouth St Andr *Bris* 96-97; NSM Bris St Mary Redcliffe w Temple etc from 95; Dir Communications for C of E from 97. *Church House, Great Smith Street, London SW1P 3NZ* Tel 0171-222 9011 Fax 222 6672

BEAZLEY, Prof John Milner. b 32. DRCOG59 MRCOG62 FRCOG73 FACOG89 Man Univ MB, ChB57 MD64. St Deiniol's Hawarden 83. **d** 86 **p** 87. NSM W Kirby St Bridget *Ches* 86-89; NSM Newton 89-92; NSM Aspatria w Hayton *Carl* from 92. *High Rigg, Faugh, Heads Nook, Carlisle CA4 9EA* Tel (01228) 70353

BEAZLEY, Miss Margaret Sheila Elizabeth Mary. b 32. Nor City Coll CertEd59. St Alb Minl Tr Scheme 86. **d** 89 **p** 94. NSM Ware St Mary *St Alb* from 89. *38 Fanshawe Crescent, Ware, Herts SG12 0AS* Tel (01920) 462349

BEBBINGTON, Myles. b 35. Kelham Th Coll 56. **d** 61 **p** 62. C Horbury *Wakef* 61-64; C Ardwick St Benedict *Man* 64-66; V Cudworth *Wakef* 66-73; P-in-c Kensington St Jo *Lon* 73-78; P-in-c Walthamstow St Mich *Chelmsf* 78-80; V 80-89; V Sunderland Red Ho *Dur* 89-95; P-in-c S Moor from 95. *St George's Vicarage, South Moor, Stanley, Co Durham DH9 7EN* Tel (01207) 232564

BECK, Alan. b 28. AKC50. **d** 53 **p** 54. C N Harrow St Alb *Lon* 53-56; C Northolt St Mary 56-59; C Loughborough All SS *Leic* 59-61; V Crookham *Guildf* 61-69; V Puriton *B & W* 69-78; P-in-c Pawlett 74-78; V Puriton and Pawlett 78-79; P-in-c Staplegrove 79-84; R 84-88; rtd 88; Perm to Offic *B & W* from 88. *Redwing, Creech Heathfield, Taunton, Somerset TA3 5EG* Tel (01823) 443030

BECK, Amanda Ruth. b 68. Liv Univ BA91 Birm Univ BD93. Qu Coll Birm 91. **d** 94 **p** 95. C W Derby Gd Shep *Liv* from 94. *345 Utting Avenue East, Liverpool L11 1DF* Tel 0151-256 0510

BECK, Mrs Gillian Margaret. b 50. Sheff Univ CertEd71 Nottm Univ BTh78. Linc Th Coll 74. **dss** 78 **d** 87. Gt Grimsby St Mary and St Jas *Linc* 78-83; St Paul's Cathl *Lon* 84-87; Hon Par Dn St Botolph Aldgate w H Trin Minories 87-88; Par Dn Monkwearmouth St Andr *Dur* 88-94; C 94-96; NSM Eppleton and Hetton le Hole from 96. *The Rectory, Houghton Road, Hetton-le-Hole, Tyne & Wear DH5 9PH* Tel 0191-526 3198

BECK, John Edward. b 28. ARCM52 FRCO59 St Jo Coll Ox BA56 MA59. Wells Th Coll 56. **d** 58 **p** 59. C Dursley *Glouc* 58-61; C Glouc St Paul 61-63; S Rhodesia 63-65; Rhodesia 65-70; C Cheltenham Ch Ch *Glouc* 70-77; C Cirencester 77-93; rtd 93;

Perm to Offic *Glouc* from 93. *25 Bowling Green Road, Cirencester, Glos GL7 2HD* Tel (01285) 653778

BECK, Michael Leonard. b 50. K Coll Lon BD77 AKC77. Linc Th Coll 77. **d** 78 **p** 79. C Gt Grimsby St Mary and St Jas *Linc* 78-83; Min Can and Succ St Paul's Cathl *Lon* 83-88; V Monkwearmouth St Andr *Dur* 88-96; TR Monkwearmouth 97; R Eppleton and Hetton le Hole from 97; RD Houghton from 97. *The Rectory, Houghton Road, Hetton-le-Hole, Houghton le Spring, Tyne & Wear DH5 9PH* Tel 0191-526 3198

BECK, Peter George Cornford. b 36. Dur Univ BA61. Ridley Hall Cam 61. **d** 63 **p** 64. C Slade Green *Roch* 63-65; C Aylesford 65-68; C-in-c Brampton St Mark CD *Derby* 68-70; V Brampton St Mark 71-75; P-in-c Alvaston 75-89. *Mixon Mines Farm, Onecote, Leek, Staffs ST13 7SH*

BECK, Peter John. b 48. Mert Coll Ox BA69 MA75. Sarum Th Coll 69. **d** 72 **p** 73. C Banbury *Ox* 72-75; TV 75-78; Dioc Youth and Community Officer 75-78; P-in-c Linc St Mary-le-Wigford w St Benedict etc *Linc* 78-81; New Zealand from 81; Adn Waitemata 87-93. *21 Hepburn Street, Ponsonby, Auckland, New Zealand* Tel Auckland (9) 376 2411 or 379 0625 Fax 303 1302

BECK, Roger William. b 48. Chich Th Coll 79. **d** 81 **p** 82. C St Marychurch *Ex* 81-85; TV Torre 85-88; V Torquay St Jo and Ellacombe 88-94; C Plympton St Mary from 94. *27 Pinewood Close, Plympton, Plymouth PL7 2DW* Tel (01752) 336393

BECK, Canon Stephen. b 16. St Pet Hall Ox BA44 MA45. Westcott Ho Cam 45. **d** 47 **p** 48. C Portsea N End St Mark *Portsm* 47-56; RAChD 56-59; V Moseley St Agnes *Birm* 59-83; RD Moseley 71-81; Hon Can Birm Cathl 76-83; rtd 83; Perm to Offic *Ban* from 83. *Artro View, Llanbedr LL45 2DQ* Tel (01341) 23545

BECKERLEG, Barzillai. b 20. Selw Coll Cam BA43 MA46. Westcott Ho Cam 42. **d** 44 **p** 45. C Golders Green St Alb *Lon* 44-48; Chapl St Jo Coll Dur 48-52; Lic to Offic *Dur* 49-52; V Battersea St Mary *S'wark* 52-58; V Wentworth *Sheff* 58-59; Hd Master Newc Cathl Choir Sch 59-62; Prec Newc Cathl *Newc* 59-62; R Duncton *Chich* 62-64; R Burton w Coates 62-64; V Kippington *Roch* 64-75; R E Bergholt *St E* 75-79; Chapl St Mary's Sch Wantage 79-85; rtd 85; Perm to Offic *Roch* 86-93; Perm to Offic *Chich* from 93. *3 April Close, Horsham, W Sussex RL12 2LL* Tel (01403) 240867

BECKETT, George. b 26. Scawsby Coll of Educn CertEd76 Sheff Univ BEd77 Hull Univ MEd84. **d** 91 **p** 92. NSM Hatfield *Sheff* from 91. *10 Norman Drive, Hatfield, Doncaster, S Yorkshire DN7 6AQ* Tel (01302) 841091

BECKETT, Michael Shaun. b 55. ACA79. Oak Hill Th Coll BA88. **d** 88 **p** 89. C Cambridge St Barn *Ely* 88-93; P-in-c Cambridge St Paul 93-94; V from 94. *St Paul's Vicarage, 15 St Paul's Road, Cambridge CB1 2EZ* Tel (01223) 354186

BECKETT, Canon Stanley. b 20. Linc Th Coll. **d** 64 **p** 65. C Barnston *Ches* 64-71; V Daresbury 71-87; Hon Can Ches Cathl 82-87; P-in-c Aston by Sutton 86-87; Hon C 87-90; rtd 87; Hon C Grappenhall *Ches* from 90. *13 Wilson Close, Thelwall, Warrington WA4 2ET* Tel (01925) 663639

BECKHAM, John Francis. b 25. Bps' Coll Cheshunt 65. **d** 67 **p** 68. C Leytonstone St Jo *Chelmsf* 67-70; C Colchester St Mary V 70-73; R Lawford 73-80; V Gt w Lt Chesterford 80-90; rtd 90; Perm to Offic *St E* from 91. *Eastwood, Walberswick, Southwold, Suffolk IP18 6UN* Tel (01502) 724919

BECKINSALE, Mrs Pamela Rachel. b 46. Man Univ BSc69. Cant Sch of Min 88. **d** 91 **p** 94. NSM Sittingbourne St Mich *Cant* 91-96; Perm to Offic from 96. *8 Glovers Crescent, Bell Road, Sittingbourne, Kent ME10 4DU* Tel (01795) 471632

BECKLEY, Peter William. b 52. Lon Univ BSc73 CertEd. Trin Coll Bris 76. **d** 79 **p** 80. C Plymouth St Jude *Ex* 79-83; C Ecclesall *Sheff* 83-88; V Greystones from 88. *The Vicarage, 1 Cliffe Farm Drive, Sheffield S11 7JW* Tel 0114-266 7686

BECKLEY, Simon Richard. b 38. Lon Univ BA61. Oak Hill Th Coll 58. **d** 63 **p** 64. C Watford St Luke *St Alb* 63-67; C New Ferry *Ches* 67-70; C Chadderton Ch Ch *Man* 70-73; V Friarmere 73-80; V Tranmere St Cath *Ches* from 80. *St Catherine's Vicarage, 9 The Wiend, Birkenhead, Merseyside L42 6RY* Tel 0151-645 4533

BECKWITH, Ian Stanley. b 36. Nottm Univ BA58 Selw Coll Cam CertEd59 Westmr Coll Ox MTh96. Linc Th Coll 78. **d** 79 **p** 80. NSM Linc Cathl *Linc* 79-85; Sen Lect Bp Grosseteste Coll Linc 80-86; NSM Wallingford w Crowmarsh Gifford etc *Ox* 91-97; LNSM Tr Officer (Berks) from 96; P-in-c Gt Coxwell w Buscot, Coleshill & Eaton Hastings from 97. *The Vicarage, Great Coxwell, Faringdon, Oxon SN7 7NG* Tel (01367) 240665

BECKWITH, Canon John Douglas. b 33. AKC57. **d** 58 **p** 65. C Streatham St Leon *S'wark* 58-59; Lic to Offic *Ripon* 59-60; Nigeria 60-62; C Bedale *Ripon* 62-63; C Mottingham St Andr *S'wark* 64-69; Chapl Gothenburg w Halmstad and Jönköping *Eur* 69-70; Chapl to Suff Bp Edmonton 70-77; Lic to Offic *Lon* 70-77; Dir of Ords 70-77; V Brookfield St Anne, Highgate Rise 77-88; Can Gib Cathl *Eur* 84-88; Hon Can Gib Cathl from 88; P-in-c Bladon w Woodstock *Ox* 88-93; P-in-c Wootton by Woodstock 88; P-in-c Kiddington w Asterleigh 88; C Kidlington w Hampton Poyle 93-94; Lic to Offic *Lon* from 94. *1-16 Northwood Hall, Hornsey Lane, London N6 5PG* Tel 0181-340 0626

BECKWITH, Dr Roger Thomas. b 29. St Edm Hall Ox BA52 MA56 BD85 Lambeth DD92. Ripon Hall Ox 51 Tyndale Hall Bris 52 Cuddesdon Coll 54. **d** 54 **p** 55. C Harold Wood *Chelmsf* 54-57; C Bedminster St Luke w St Silas *Bris* 57-59; Tutor Tyndale Hall Bris 59-63; Lib Latimer Ho Ox 63-73 and from 94; Warden 73-94; Lect Wycliffe Hall Ox 71-94; Hon C Wytham *Ox* 88-90; Hon C N Hinksey and Wytham 90-96; rtd 94. *Latimer House, 131 Banbury Road, Oxford OX2 7AJ* Tel (01865) 557340 Fax 556706

BEDDINGTON, Peter Jon. b 36. ACP68 DipEd81. NW Ord Course 71. **d** 74 **p** 75. C Bury St Pet *Man* 74-77; Hon C Bury Ch King 77-82; Hon C Elton All SS from 82. *18 Throstle Grove, Bury, Lancs BL8 1EB* Tel 0161-764 3292

BEDDOES, The Very Revd Ronald Alfred. b 12. St Chad's Coll Dur BA35 MA50. **d** 36 **p** 37. C Dawdon *Dur* 36-39; P-in-c Grindon 39-40; V Greatham 40-44; V Easington Colliery 44-53; Provost Derby 53-80; V Derby All SS 53-80; P-in-c Beeley and Edensor 80-97; rtd 97. *Grafton Cottage, Calton Lees, Beeley, Matlock, Derbyshire DE4 2NX* Tel (01629) 732177

BEDDOW, Arthur Josiah Comyns. b 13. Ch Coll Cam BA35 MA41. Linc Th Coll 38. **d** 40 **p** 41. C Sherborne w Castleton and Lillington *Sarum* 40-46; C Bideford *Ex* 46-54; R Nymet Rowland w Coldridge 54-63; Dioc Youth Officer and Asst Dir Relig Educn 56-62; R Bere Ferrers 63-78; rtd 78; Perm to Offic *Sarum* from 79; Perm to Offic *B & W* from 84. *Flat 5, Hillside, South Street, Sherborne, Dorset DT9 3NH* Tel (01935) 815134

BEDDOW, Nicholas Mark Johnstone-Wallace. b 47. Birm Univ BA69. Qu Coll Birm 69. **d** 71 **p** 72. C Blackheath *Birm* 71-75; Zambia 75-80; V Escomb *Dur* from 80; V Witton Park from 80; Bp's Dom Chapl 80-85. *The Vicarage, Escomb, Bishop Auckland, Co Durham DL14 7ST* Tel (01388) 602861

BEDELL, Anthony Charles. b 59. Worc Coll Ox BA81. Linc Th Coll 87. **d** 90 **p** 91. C Newbold w Dunston *Derby* 90-94; C Bedford Leigh *Man* from 94. *30 Carisbrook Road, Leigh, Lancs WN7 2XA* Tel (01942) 607893

BEDFORD, Colin Michael. b 35. ALCD60. **d** 61 **p** 62. C Woking St Mary *Guildf* 61-63; C Guildf St Sav 63-65; C Morden *S'wark* 65-69; V Toxteth Park St Philemon *Liv* 69-75; P-in-c Toxteth Park St Gabr 69-75; P-in-c Toxteth Park St Jas and St Matt 69-75; P-in-c Prince's Park St Paul 70-75; P-in-c Toxteth Park St Cleopas 73-78; TR Toxteth St Philemon w St Gabr 75-89; TR Toxteth St Philemon w St Gabr and St Cleopas 89-91; R Edgware *Lon* from 91. *The Rectory, Rectory Lane, Edgware, Middx HA8 7LG* Tel 0181-952 1081

BEDFORD, Norman Stuart. b 28. Oak Hill Th Coll 66. **d** 68 **p** 69. C Iver *Ox* 68-71; V Warfield 71-75; V Southwold *St E* 75-83; V Dedham *Chelmsf* 83-93; rtd 93; Perm to Offic *Chelmsf* from 93. *28 Hadleigh Road, Frinton-on-Sea, Essex CO13 9HU* Tel (01255) 672752

BEDFORD, Richard Derek Warner. b 27. Clare Coll Cam BA52. ALCD54. **d** 54 **p** 55. C Wallington H Trin *S'wark* 54-57; C Sanderstead All SS 57; C Weybridge *Guildf* 57-59; C Addlestone 59-62; C-in-c New Haw CD 62-66; V Epsom Common Ch Ch 66-81; R Walton-on-the-Hill 81-87; Asst Chapl Burrswood Home of Healing 87-92; rtd 92; Perm to Offic *Chich* from 92; Perm to Offic *Roch* from 92. *2 Lealands Close, Groombridge, Tunbridge Wells, Kent TN3 9ND* Tel (01892) 864550

BEDFORD, Archdeacon of. *See* LESITER, The Ven Malcolm Leslie

BEDFORD, Suffragan Bishop of. *See* RICHARDSON, The Rt Revd John Henry

BEDLOE, Horace Walter. b 11. Keble Coll Ox 33. Sarum Th Coll 34. **d** 37 **p** 38. C Gillingham St Barn *Roch* 37-41; P-in-c Chatham St Steph 41-45; V Kingsclere *Win* 45-49; Jamaica 49-56, 60-69 and 72-75; V Perry Street *Roch* 56-60; Can Res Bradf Cathl *Bradf* 70-71; P-in-c Brighton St Jo *Chich* 76-78; rtd 78; Chapl Malaga w Almunecar and Nerja *Eur* 81-83; Perm to Offic *S'wark* 83-94; Perm to Offic *Chich* from 83; Perm to Offic *Roch* 84-95; Perm to Offic *Guildf* from 94. *Manormead Residential Home, Tilford Road, Hindhead, Surrey GU26 6RA* Tel (01428) 607506

BEDWELL, Stanley Frederick. b 20. MPS42. Ox NSM Course 77. **d** 80 **p** 81. NSM Farnham Royal *Ox* 80-81; NSM Farnham Royal w Hedgerley from 81. *18 Ingleglen, Farnham Common, Slough SL2 3QA* Tel (01753) 644522

BEEBY, Lawrence Clifford. b 28. S'wark Ord Course 70. **d** 73 **p** 74. C Notting Hill St Jo *Lon* 73-74; C Sunbury 74-76; C-in-c Hounslow Gd Shep Beavers Lane CD 76-80; Chapl Botleys Park Hosp Chertsey 80-96; rtd 96. *54 Bingley Road, Sunbury-on-Thames, Middx TW16 7RB* Tel (01932) 788922

BEECH, Miss Ailsa. b 44. N Co Coll Newc TDip65. Trin Coll Bris DipHE80. **dss** 80 **d** 87 **p** 94. Pudsey St Lawr *Bradf* 80-82; Pudsey St Lawr and St Paul 82-87; Par Dn 87-88; C Attleborough *Cov* 88-89; Par Dn Cumnor *Ox* 89-92; Asst Chapl Walsgrave Hosp Cov 92-94; Asst Chapl Walsgrave Hosp NHS Trust Cov from 94. *48 Fulstaff Close, Nuneaton, Warks CV11 6FB* Tel (01203) 532290 or 538950

BEECH, Frank Thomas. b 36. Tyndale Hall Bris 64. **d** 66 **p** 67. C Penn Fields *Lich* 66-70; C Attenborough w Chilwell *S'well* 70-74; P-in-c 74-75; P-in-c Attenborough 75-76; V 76-84; V Worksop St Anne from 84; Chapl Welbeck Coll from 84. *The Vicarage, 11 Poplar Close, Worksop, Notts S80 3BZ* Tel (01909) 472069

BEECH, Canon Harold. b 17. Univ of Wales BA39. Chich Th Coll 39. **d** 41 **p** 42. C Abertillery *Mon* 41-51; P-in-c Abercwmboi *Llan* 51-56; V 56-59; Chapl Cell Barnes Hosp and Hill End Hosp St Alb 59-82; Hon Can St Alb *St Alb* 77-83; rtd 82; Perm to Offic *St Alb* from 83. *Milfraen House, 32 Campfield Road, St Albans, Herts AL1 5JA* Tel (01727) 863608

BEECH, John. b 41. St Jo Coll Nottm. **d** 83 **p** 83. C York St Paul *York* 83-84; P-in-c Bubwith w Ellerton and Aughton 84-85; P-in-c Thorganby w Skipwith and N Duffield 84-85; V Bubwith w Skipwith 85-87; V Acomb H Redeemer from 87. *The Vicarage, 108 Boroughbridge Road, York YO2 6AB* Tel (01904) 798593

BEECH, John Thomas. b 38. St Aid Birkenhead 64. **d** 67 **p** 68. C Burton St Paul *Lich* 67-70; Chapl RN 70-85; V Ellingham and Harbridge and Ibsley *Win* 85-94; Chapl Whiteley Village *Guildf* from 94. *The Chaplaincy, Whiteley Village, Walton-on-Thames, Surrey KT12 4EJ* Tel (01932) 848260

BEECH, Peter John. b 34. Bps' Coll Cheshunt 58. **d** 61 **p** 62. C Fulham All SS *Lon* 61-64; S Africa 64-67; V S Hackney St Mich *Lon* 68-71; P-in-c Haggerston St Paul 68-71; V S Hackney St Mich w Haggerston St Paul 71-75; V Wanstead H Trin Hermon Hill *Chelmsf* 75-89; P-in-c St Mary-at-Latton 89-90; V from 90. *St Mary-at-Latton Vicarage, The Gowers, Harlow, Essex CM20 2JP* Tel (01279) 424005

BEECHAM, Clarence Ralph. b 35. S'wark Ord Course. **d** 83 **p** 84. NSM Leigh-on-Sea St Jas *Chelmsf* from 83. *27 Scarborough Drive, Leigh-on-Sea, Essex SS9 3ED* Tel (01702) 574923

BEEDELL, Trevor Francis. b 31. ALCD65. **d** 65 **p** 66. C Walton *St E* 65-68; R Hartshorne *Derby* 68-79; RD Repton 74-79; V Doveridge 79-86; Chapl HM Det Cen Foston Hall 79-80; Dioc Dir of Chr Stewardship *Derby* from 79. *1 River View, Milford, Belper, Derbyshire DE56 0QR* Tel (01332) 842381

BEEDON, David Kirk. b 59. Birm Univ BA89 MPhil93. Qu Coll Birm 86. **d** 89 **p** 90. C Cannock *Lich* 89-92; V Wednesbury St Bart from 92. *The Vicarage, Little Hill, Wednesbury, W Midlands WS10 9DE* Tel 0121-556 0378 E-mail d.beedon-st.barts @dial.pipex.com

BEEK, Canon Michael Peter. b 27. Em Coll Cam BA50 MA55. Linc Th Coll 50. **d** 52 **p** 53. C Mitcham St Barn *S'wark* 52-55; C Talbot Village *Sarum* 55-58; V Higham and Merston *Roch* 58-66; R Gravesend St Geo 66-74; R Gravesend St Jas 66-74; RD Gravesend 70-74; Hon Can Roch Cathl 73-92; RD Tunbridge Wells 74-83; R Speldhurst w Groombridge 74-77; P-in-c Ashurst 77; R Speldhurst w Groombridge and Ashurst 77-83; V Bromley SS Pet and Paul 83-92; rtd 92; Perm to Offic *Nor* from 92; RD Hartismere *St E* from 93. *18 Henry Ward Road, Harleston, Norfolk IP20 9EZ* Tel (01379) 854003

BEER, Mrs Janet Margaret. b 43. Golds Coll Lon CertEd64. Oak Hill Th Coll 83. **dss** 86 **d** 87 **p** 94. Colney St Pet *St Alb* 86-87; Hon C from 87; Chapl St Alb High Sch for Girls 87-89; Chapl Middx Univ *Lon* from 94. *The Vicarage, Riverside, London Colney, St Albans, Herts AL2 1QX* Tel (01727) 769797

BEER, The Ven John Stuart. b 44. Pemb Coll Ox BA65 MA70 Fitzw Coll Cam MA78. Westcott Ho Cam 69. **d** 71 **p** 72. C Knaresborough St Jo *Ripon* 71-74; Chapl Fitzw Coll and New Hall Cam 74-80; Fell Fitzw Coll 77-80; P-in-c Toft w Caldecote and Childerley *Ely* 80-83; R 83-87; P-in-c Hardwick 80-83; R 83-87; V Grantchester 87-97; Dir of Ords, Post-Ord Tr and Student Readers from 88; Hon Can Ely Cathl from 89; Adn Huntingdon from 97. *The Vicarage, 44 High Street, Grantchester, Cambridge CB3 9NF* Tel (01223) 840460

BEER, Michael Trevor. b 44. Chich Th Coll 66. **d** 69 **p** 70. C Leagrave *St Alb* 69-73; St Vincent 73-74; C Thorley w Bishop's Stortford H Trin *St Alb* 74-80; V Colney St Pet from 80. *The Vicarage, Riverside, London Colney, St Albans, Herts AL2 1QX* Tel (01727) 769797

BEER, Nigel David. b 62. Portsm Poly BSc84. St Jo Coll Nottm DTS92 MA93. **d** 93 **p** 94. C Rastrick St Matt *Wakef* 93-96; C Bilton *Ripon* from 96. *59 Coppice Way, Harrogate, N Yorkshire HG1 2DT* Tel (01423) 522194

BEER, William Barclay. b 43. ACT ThA68 St Steph Ho Ox. **d** 71 **p** 72. C St Marychurch *Ex* 71-76; V Pattishall w Cold Higham *Pet* 76-82; V Northampton St Benedict 82-85; V Chislehurst Annunciation *Roch* from 85. *The Vicarage, 2 Foxhome Close, Chislehurst, Kent BR7 5XT* Tel 0181-467 3606

BEESLEY, Michael Frederick. b 37. K Coll Cam BA59. Westcott Ho Cam 60. **d** 61 **p** 64. C Eastleigh *Win* 61-69. *42 Highland Road, Parkstone, Poole, Dorset BH14 0DX* Tel (01202) 730497

BEESLEY, Ramon John. b 27. Magd Coll Ox BA51 MA55. Wycliffe Hall Ox 51. **d** 53 **p** 56. C Gerrards Cross *Ox* 53-54; Asst Chapl Embley Park Sch Romsey 54-58; Perm to Offic *Guildf* 59-63; Perm to Offic *Win* from 63; Hd Master Bellemoor Sch Southn from 74. *Wayfarers, Burley, Ringwood, Hants BH24 4HW* Tel (01425) 402284

BEESLEY, Symon Richard. b 27. Bris Univ BA53. Tyndale Hall Bris 47. **d** 53 **p** 54. C Mile Cross *Nor* 53-55; Tanganyika 55-60; Chapl Sutton Valence Sch Kent 60-64; V Leic H Trin *Leic* 64-72; Chapl HM Pris Leic 64-69; Dep Chapl HM Pris Leic 69-72; Jt Gen Sec CCCS 72-76; Lic to Offic *Lon* 73-76; P-in-c St Leonards St Leon *Chich* 76-77; R 77-82; Kenya 82-84; V Roby *Liv* 84-89; rtd 89. *8 Shales Road, Bitterne, Southampton SO18 5RN* Tel (01703) 463671

BEESON, Christopher George. b 48. Man Univ BSc70. Qu Coll Birm 72. **d** 75 **p** 76. C Flixton St Mich *Man* 75-78; C Newton Heath All SS 78-80; R Gorton St Jas 80-90; Dioc Communications Officer *Blackb* 91-92; C Ribbleton 92-93; rtd 93; Perm to Offic *Blackb* from 93. *24 Arnold Close, Ribbleton, Preston PR2 6DX* Tel (01772) 702675

BEESON, The Very Revd Trevor Randall. b 26. OBE97. K Coll Lon MA76 FKC87. **d** 51 **p** 52. C Leadgate *Dur* 51-54; C Norton St Mary 54-56; C-in-c Stockton St Chad CD 56-60; V Stockton St Chad 60-65; C St Martin-in-the-Fields *Lon* 65-71; V Ware St Mary *St Alb* 71-76; Can Westmr Abbey 76-87; Treas 78-82; R Westmr St Marg 82-87; Chapl to Speaker of Ho of Commons 82-87; Dean Win 87-96; rtd 96. *69 Greatbridge Road, Romsey, Hants SO51 8FE* Tel (01794) 514627

BEETHAM, Anthony (Tony). b 32. Lon Univ BSc53. Ox NSM Course. **d** 75 **p** 76. NSM Ox St Clem *Ox* from 75; Dir Chr Enquiry Agency from 88. *44 Rose Hill, Oxford OX4 4HS, or Inter-Church House, 31-35 Lower Marsh, London SE1 7RL* Tel (01865) 770923 or 0171-620 4444 Fax 0171-928 0010

BEETON, David Ambrose Moore. b 39. Chich Th Coll 62. **d** 65 **p** 66. C Forest Gate St Edm *Chelmsf* 65-71; V Rush Green 71-81; V Coggeshall w Markshall from 81. *The Vicarage, 4 Church Green, Coggeshall, Colchester CO6 1UD* Tel (01376) 561234

BEETY, Arthur Edward. b 38. Sheff Univ BA60. Cant Sch of Min 92. **d** 95 **p** 96. NSM Cobham w Luddesdowne and Dode *Roch* from 95. *The Old Forge, 4 The Street, Cobham, Gravesend, Kent DA12 3BN*

BEEVER, Miss Alison Rosemary. b 59. Man Univ BA80. Linc Th Coll 88. **d** 90 **p** 94. Par Dn Watford Ch Ch *St Alb* 90-94; C 94-96; V Tilehurst St Cath *Ox* from 96. *The Vicarage, Wittenham Avenue, Tilehurst, Reading RG3 5LN* Tel 0118-942 7786

BEEVERS, Dr Colin Lionel. b 40. CEng70 MIEE70 MBIM73 K Coll Lon BSc62 PhD66 DMS72. Sarum & Wells Th Coll 87. **d** 89 **p** 90. C Ledbury w Eastnor *Heref* 89-93; C Lt Marcle 89-93; Asst Dir of Tr 92-96; P-in-c Kimbolton w Hamnish and Middleton-on-the-Hill 93-96; P-in-c Bockleton w Leysters 93-96; P-in-c Ledbury w Eastnor from 96; P-in-c Much Marcle from 96; RD Ledbury from 96. *The Rectory, Worcester Road, Ledbury, Herefordshire HR8 1PL* Tel (01531) 632571

BEEVERS, Reginald (Reggie). b 22. Dur Univ BA48. Qu Coll Birm 48. **d** 50 **p** 51. C Stockton H Trin *Dur* 50-52; C Esh 52-53; C-in-c Peterlee CD 53-57; V Peterlee 57-60; Chapl Worc R Infirmary 60-63; Lic to Offic *Man* 63-65; Chapl Hulme Gr Sch Oldham 63-65; Chapl Guy's Hosp Lon 65-70; Chapl Liv Coll 70-81; R Hatch Beauchamp w Beercrocombe, Curry Mallet etc *B & W* 81-88; rtd 88; P-in-c Oare w Culbone *B & W* 90-93; Perm to Offic from 93. *18 Abbey Close, Curry Rivel, Langport, Somerset TA10 0EL* Tel (01458) 253676

BEGBIE, Jeremy Sutherland. b 57. ARCM LRAM MSSTh Edin Univ BA Aber Univ BD PhD. Ridley Hall Cam. **d** 82 **p** 83. C Egham *Guildf* 82-85; Chapl Ridley Hall Cam 85-87; Dir Studies 87-92; Vice-Prin from 92. *Ridley Hall, Cambridge CB3 9HG* Tel (01223) 60995 Fax 301287

BEGGS, Norman Lindell. b 32. CertFSW69 N Lon Poly CQSW77 DipSocWork77. S Dios Minl Tr Scheme 86. **d** 89 **p** 90. NSM Milborne St Andrew w Dewlish *Sarum* 89-92; C 92-95; C Piddletrenthide w Plush, Alton Pancras etc 92-95; C Puddletown and Tolpuddle 92-95; rtd 95. *Wallingford House, Dewlish, Dorchester, Dorset DT2 7LX* Tel (01258) 837320

BEGLEY, Frank William. b 18. Univ of Wales (Lamp) BA48. **d** 49 **p** 50. C Ebbw Vale *Mon* 49-55; C Richmond St Jo *S'wark* 55-57; Tanganyika 57-63; C-in-c Boxmoor St Fran Hammerfield CD *St Alb* 64-66; Guyana 66-70; C Roath St Marg *Llan* 70-74; V Cardiff St Dyfrig and St Samson 74-83; R Llanwenarth Ultra *Mon* 83-87; rtd 87; Perm to Offic *Llan* from 87. *24 St Teilo's Court, Church Terrace, Cardiff CF2 5AX* Tel (01222) 489375

BEGLEY, Mrs Helen. b 59. Kingston Poly BA81. N Ord Course 87. **d** 89 **p** 94. Par Dn Leeds H Trin *Ripon* 89-90; Chapl to the Deaf 89-96; Par Dn Leeds City 91-94; C 94-96; Chapl to the Deaf (Wilts) *Sarum* from 96. *129 Avon Road, Devizes, Wilts SN10 1PY* Tel (01380) 724929

BEHENNA, Miss Gillian Eve. b 57. CertEd78. St Alb Minl Tr Scheme 82. **dss** 85 **d** 87 **p** 94. Chapl to the Deaf *Sarum* 85-90; Chapl to the Deaf *Ex* from 90. *16 Mayflower Avenue, Pennsylvania, Exeter EX4 5DS* Tel (01392) 215174 or 427227 Fax 427227

BEHEYDT, Gregory S. b 47. **d** 74 **p** 75. In RC Ch 74-84; Chapl Tangier *Eur* 93-97; Chapl Milan w Genoa and Varese from 97. *All Saints Church, via Solferino 17, 20121 Milan, Italy* Tel Milan (2) 655 2258

BEHREND, Michael Christopher. b 60. St Jo Coll Cam BA82 PGCE83 Cam Univ MA86. Oak Hill Th Coll DipHE95. **d** 97. C Hensingham *Carl* from 97. *13 West View, Hensingham, Whitehaven, Cumbria CA28 8QY* Tel (01946) 67030

BELBEN, Kenneth Frank. b 30. TD77. Cranmer Hall Dur 51. **d** 55 **p** 56. C Plaistow St Mary *Chelmsf* 55-58; C Chadwell Heath 58-60; C-in-c Marks Gate 60-64; V Gt w Lt Maplestead 64-76; CF (TA) 65-95; P-in-c Gestingthorpe *Chelmsf* 75-76; V Gt and Lt Maplestead w Gestingthorpe 76-95; ChStJ from 77; rtd 95; Perm to Offic *Chelmsf* from 95. *69 Hunt Road, Earls Colne, Colchester CO6 2NY* Tel (01787) 224094

BELCHER, David John. b 44. Ch Ch Ox BA65 MA69. Cuddesdon Coll 68. **d** 70 **p** 71. C Gateshead St Mary *Dur* 70-73; C Stockton St Pet 73-76; Lic to Offic *Lich* 76-81; P-in-c W Bromwich Ch Ch 81-85; P-in-c W Bromwich Gd Shep w St Jo 85-89; V 89-95; RD W Bromwich 90-94; R Bratton, Edington and Imber, Erlestoke etc *Sarum* from 95. *The Rectory, Upper Garston Lane, Bratton, Westbury, Wilts BA13 4SN* Tel (01380) 830374

BELCHER, Derek George. b 50. MRSH73 MBIM82 DipDiet Lon Univ PGCE82 Univ of Wales MEd86. Chich Th Coll 74. **d** 77 **p** 78. C Newton Nottage *Llan* 77-81; V Llan w Capel Llanilltern 81; PV Llan Cathl 81-87; V Margam from 87. *The Vicarage, 59A Bertha Road, Margam, Port Talbot SA13 2AP* Tel (01639) 891067 or 891548

BELCHER, Frederick William (Fred). b 30. Kelham Th Coll 50 Chich Th Coll 53. **d** 54 **p** 55. C Catford St Laur *S'wark* 54-58; C-in-c Plumstead Wm Temple Ch Abbey Wood CD 58-62; V Eltham Park St Luke 62-64; Lic to Offic 65-81; NSM Charminster and Stinsford *Sarum* 88-94; Perm to Offic from 94; rtd 95. *Little Mead, North Street, Charminster, Dorchester, Dorset DT2 9QZ* Tel (01305) 260688

BELCHER, Nicholas Arthur John. b 59. Oak Hill Th Coll BA89. **d** 89 **p** 90. C Danbury *Chelmsf* 89-92; C Barnston *Ches* from 92. *8 Antons Road, Pensby, Wirral, Merseyside L61 9PT* Tel 0151-648 1512

BELFAST, Dean of. *See* SHEARER, The Very Revd John

BELHAM, John Edward. b 42. K Coll Lon BSc65 AKC65 PhD70. Oak Hill Th Coll 69. **d** 72 **p** 73. C Cheadle Hulme St Andr *Ches* 72-75; C Cheadle 75-83; R Gressenhall w Longham w Wendling etc *Nor* from 83. *The Rectory, Bittering Street, Gressenhall, Dereham, Norfolk NR20 4EB* Tel (01362) 860211

BELHAM, Michael. b 23. Lon Univ BScEng50. **d** 67 **p** 68. C Northwood Hills St Edm *Lon* 67-69; C Hendon St Mary 69-73; V Tottenham H Trin 73-78; V Hillingdon St Jo 78-85; P-in-c Broughton *Ox* 85; R Broughton w N Newington and Shutford 85-90; Chapl Horton Gen Hosp 85-90; rtd 90; Perm to Offic *Pet* from 90; Sec DBP *Ox* from 95. *6 Blackwood Place, Bodicote, Banbury, Oxon OX15 4BE* Tel (01295) 253923

BELING, David Gibson. b 30. Fitzw Ho Cam BA54 MA58. **d** 56 **p** 57. C Radipole *Sarum* 56-59; C Broadwater St Mary *Chich* 59-61; R W Knighton w Broadmayne *Sarum* 61-73; V Paignton St Paul Preston *Ex* 73-91; rtd 91; Perm to Offic *Ex* from 91. *51 Manor Road, Paignton, Devon TQ3 2HZ*

BELITHER, John Roland. b 36. Oak Hill Th Coll 83. **d** 86 **p** 87. NSM Bushey Heath *St Alb* 86-91; V Marsh Farm from 91. *The Vicarage, 40 Purway Close, Marsh Farm, Luton LU3 3RT* Tel (01582) 575757

BELL, Adrian Christopher. b 48. AKC70. St Aug Coll Cant 70. **d** 71 **p** 72. C Sheff St Aid w St Luke *Sheff* 71-74; C Willesborough w Hinxhill *Cant* 74-78; P-in-c Wormshill 78; P-in-c Hollingbourne w Hucking 78-82; P-in-c Leeds w Broomfield 79-82; V Hollingbourne and Hucking w Leeds and Broomfield 82-84; V Herne Bay Ch Ch 84-91; R Washingborough w Heighington and Canwick *Linc* from 91. *The Rectory, Church Hill, Washingborough, Lincoln LN4 1EJ* Tel (01522) 794056

BELL, Alan. b 29. Handsworth Coll Birm 55 Linc Th Coll 64. **d** 65 **p** 65. C Spilsby w Hundleby *Linc* 65-67; R Ludford Magna w Ludford Parva 67-76; V Burgh on Bain 68-76; V Kelstern, Calcethorpe and E Wykeham 68-76; Clerical Org Sec CECS 76-78; rtd 94. *116 The Birches, Crawley, W Sussex RH10 1RZ* Tel (01293) 407195

BELL, Alan John. b 47. Liv Univ BA68. Ridley Hall Cam 69. **d** 72 **p** 73. C Speke St Aid *Liv* 72-77; P-in-c Halewood 77-81; R Wavertree St Mary 81-88; Chapl Mabel Fletcher Tech Coll Liv 81-88; Chapl Olive Mt Hosp 81-88; R Fakenham w Alethorpe *Nor* from 88; RD Burnham and Walsingham from 92. *The Rectory, Gladstone Road, Fakenham, Norfolk NR21 9BZ* Tel (01328) 862268

BELL, Allan McRae. b 49. Moray Ho Teacher Tr Coll Edin CertEd80 E Lon Poly BA90. S'wark Ord Course 86. **d** 92 **p** 95. NSM Bow H Trin and All Hallows *Lon* 91-93; NSM R Foundn of St Kath in Ratcliffe 93-95; USA 95-97; Chapl Univ of California 95-96; P-in-c Bolinas St Aidan 96-97. *c/o Motture, Apt 1, 177 Well Street, London E9 6QU*

BELL, Andrew Thomas. b 58. Ripon Coll Cuddesdon 93. **d** 95 **p** 96. C Leighton Buzzard w Eggington, Hockliffe etc *St Alb* from 95. *138 Brooklands Drive, Leighton Buzzard, Beds LU7 8PG* Tel (01525) 850204

BELL, Anthony Lawson. b 47. AKC72. St Aug Coll Cant 71. **d** 72 **p** 73. C Peterlee *Dur* 72-77; C-in-c Stockton St Jas CD 82-89; P-in-c Byers Green 89-96; Ind Chapl Teesside 89-96; P-in-c Ault Hucknall *Derby* from 96. *The Vicarage, 59 The Hill, Glapwell, Chesterfield, Derbyshire S44 5LX* Tel (01246) 850371

BELL, Antony Fancourt. b 28. Magd Coll Ox BA51 MA58. Wells Th Coll 54. **d** 56 **p** 57. C Clapham H Trin *S'wark* 56-59; C Gillingham *Sarum* 59-61; R Stanway *Chelmsf* 61-94; RD Dedham and Tey 81-91; rtd 94. *Walsingham House, Ilchester Road, Charlton Mackrell, Somerton, Somerset TA11 6AN* Tel (01458) 223657

BELL, Arthur Francis. b 17. Leeds Univ BA39. Bps' Coll Cheshunt 40. **d** 41 **p** 42. C Bedford H Trin *St Alb* 41-43; C Chesterfield St Mary and All SS *Derby* 43-45; C Barrowhill 45-46; C Westbury-on-Trym H Trin *Bris* 46-48; C Knowle H Nativity 48-50; R Priston *B & W* 50-61; V Englishcombe 55-61; R Charlcombe 61-85; rtd 85; Perm to Offic *B & W* from 86. *31 New Road, Bradford-on-Avon, Wilts BA15 1AR* Tel (01225) 867624

BELL, Arthur James. b 33. Ch Coll Cam BA55 MA60. Coll of Resurr Mirfield 57. **d** 59 **p** 60. C New Cleethorpes *Linc* 59-63; C Upperby St Jo *Carl* 63-66; Canada 67-72 and 77-83; Perm to Offic *Ely* 73-75; Lic to Offic *Carl* 75-76; Warden Retreat of the Visitation Rhandirmwyn from 83. *Nantymwyn, Retreat of the Visitation, Rhandirmwyn, Llandovery SA20 0NR* Tel (01550) 760247

BELL, Brian Thomas. b 64. Newc Poly BA87 Newc Univ PGCE88 MA93. Coll of Resurr Mirfield BA95. **d** 97. C Tynemouth Cullercoats St Paul *Newc* from 97. *14 Naters Street, Whitley Bay, Tyne & Wear NE26 2PG* Tel 0191-297 1967

BELL, Bryan Bland. b 07. Wadh Coll Ox BA30. Tyndale Hall Bris 38. **d** 40 **p** 41. C Braintree *Chelmsf* 40-42; C New Milverton *Cov* 42-44; CF (EC) 44-46; R Wickhambreaux and Stodmarsh *Cant* 46-50; V Mile Cross *Nor* 50-54; R Barnwell *Pet* 54-60; R Poole *Sarum* 60-68; R Nedging w Naughton *St E* 68-72; rtd 72; P-in-c Chawleigh w Cheldon *Ex* 78-81; Perm to Offic from 81. *Address temp unknown*

BELL, Miss Catherine Ann. b 63. Trin Coll Bris BA88. **d** 89 **p** 94. Par Dn Southsea St Jude *Portsm* 89-94; C from 94. *45 Great South Street, Southsea, Hants PO5 3BY* Tel (01705) 863056

BELL, Charles William. b 43. TCD BA66 MA69. **d** 67 **p** 68. C Newtownards *D & D* 67-70; C Larne and Inver *Conn* 70-74; C Ballymena w Ballyclug 74-80; Bp's C Belfast Ardoyne 80-88; RD M Belfast 86-89; Bp's C Belfast Ardoyne w H Redeemer 88-89; I Eglantine from 89; Dioc Info Officer from 89. *All Saints' Rectory, 16 Eglantine Road, Lisburn, Co Antrim BT27 5RQ* Tel (01846) 662634

BELL, Colin Ashworth. b 52. FCCA83. Westcott Ho Cam 89. **d** 91 **p** 92. C Lytham St Cuth *Blackb* 91-93; C Whittle-le-Woods from 93. *61 Cliff Drive, Whittle-le-Woods, Chorley, Lancs PR6 7HT* Tel (01257) 268440

BELL, Colin Douglas. b 65. QUB DipTh90 BTh94 TCD MPhil96. CITC 94. **d** 96 **p** 97. C Dundonald *D & D* from 96. *6 Mount Regan Avenue, Dundonald, Belfast BT16 0JA* Tel (01232) 485557

BELL, Cyril John. b 22. Hull Univ BA48. Wycliffe Hall Ox 52. **d** 53 **p** 54. C Monkwearmouth St Pet *Dur* 53-56; India 56-60; Hon C Westlands St Andr *Lich* 66-71; Lic to Offic *Ches* 71-82; Perm to Offic 82-90; Perm to Offic *Lich* 90-97. *32 Summerhill Gardens, Market Drayton, Shropshire TF9 1BQ* Tel (01630) 654196

BELL, David James. b 62. QUB BSc84 BTh. **d** 91 **p** 92. C Ballyholme *D & D* 91-94; C Coleraine *Conn* from 94. *19 Adelaide Avenue, Coleraine, Co Londonderry BT52 1LT* Tel (01265) 43474

BELL, Canon David Owain. b 49. Dur Univ BA69 Nottm Univ DipTh70 Fitzw Coll Cam BA72 MA80. Westcott Ho Cam 70. **d** 72 **p** 73. C Houghton le Spring *Dur* 72-76; C Norton St Mary 76-78; P-in-c Worc St Clem *Worc* 78-84; R 84-85; R Old Swinford Stourbridge 85-97; RD Stourbridge 90-96; Hon Can Worc Cathl from 96; TR Kidderminster St Mary and All SS w Trimpley etc from 97. *The Vicarage, 22 Roden Avenue, Kidderminster, Worcs DY10 2RF* Tel (01562) 823265

BELL, Donald John. b 50. Sarum & Wells Th Coll 73. **d** 76 **p** 77. C Jarrow St Paul *Dur* 76-77; C Jarrow 77-80; C Darlington St Cuth w St Hilda 80-83; V Wingate Grange 83-89; V Sherburn w Pittington 89-95; RD Dur from 93; R Shadforth 94-95; P-in-c Dur St Cuth 95-97; V from 97. *St Cuthbert's Vicarage, 1 Aykley Court, Durham DH1 4NW* Tel 0191-386 4526

BELL, Edwin Lucius Wyndham. b 19. Worc Coll Ox BA41 MA45. Westcott Ho Cam 41. **d** 43 **p** 44. C Croydon *Cant* 43-50; CF 50-54; V Bapchild w Tonge and Rodmersham *Cant* 54-63; P-in-c Murston 54-56; V Maidstone St Paul 63-78; P-in-c Nonington w Barfreystone 78-85; P-in-c Womenswold 78-85; rtd 85; Perm to Offic *Cant* from 85. *2 Boarley Court, Sandling Lane, Maidstone, Kent ME14 2NL* Tel (01622) 756924

BELL, Edwin Ray. b 23. Clifton Th Coll 60. **d** 62 **p** 63. C Madeley *Heref* 62-65; V Rashcliffe *Wakef* 65-76; V Holmebridge 76-89; rtd 89; Perm to Offic *Blackb* from 93. *10 Hill Walk, Leyland, Preston PR5 1NY* Tel (01772) 432774

BELL, Canon Francis William Albert. b 28. TCD BA52 MA57 BD57. **d** 53 **p** 54. C Belfast St Mich *Conn* 53-55; C Belfast All SS 55-61; C Ballynafeigh St Jude *D & D* 61-63; P-in-c Ballyhalbert 63-71; P-in-c Ardkeen 67-71; I Ballyhalbert w Ardkeen 71-95; Miss to Seamen 71-95; RD Ards *D & D* 73-95; Can Belf Cathl 89-95; rtd 95. *Stationbanks, 18 Kilmore Road, Crossgar, Downpatrick, Co Down BT30 9HJ* Tel (01396) 831665

BELL, Godfrey Bryan. b 44. Oak Hill Th Coll 72. **d** 75 **p** 76. C Penn Fields *Lich* 75-79; R Dolton *Ex* 79-89; R Iddesleigh w Dowland 79-89; R Monkokehampton 79-89; R Tollard Royal w Farnham, Gussage St Michael etc *Sarum* 89-96; TV Washfield, Stoodleigh, Withleigh etc *Ex* from 96. *The Vicarage, 3 Court Gardens, Stoodleigh, Tiverton, Devon EX16 9PL* Tel (01398) 351373

BELL, Graham Dennis Robert. b 42. ALCM K Coll Lon BSc63 AKC63 Nottm Univ MTh73. Tyndale Hall Bris 65. **d** 68 **p** 69. C Stapleford *S'well* 68-71; C Barton Seagrave *Pet* 71-73; C Barton

Seagrave w Warkton 73-76; Perm to Offic *Nor* 76-82; V Wickham Market *St E* 82-86; V Wickham Market w Pettistree and Easton from 86. *The Vicarage, Crown Lane, Wickham Market, Woodbridge, Suffolk IP13 0SA* Tel (01728) 746314

BELL, Canon Jack Gorman. b 23. Lon Univ BSc48. Oak Hill Th Coll 51. **d** 53 **p** 54. C Blackpool Ch Ch *Blackb* 53-55; C Chadderton Ch Ch *Man* 55-59; R Man St Jerome w Ardwick St Silas 59-69; V Mosley Common 69-89; Hon Can Man Cathl 87-89; rtd 89; Perm to Offic *Carl* from 89. *36 Sandgate, Kendal, Cumbria LA9 6HT* Tel (01539) 725807

BELL, Canon James Harold. b 50. St Jo Coll Dur BA72 St Pet Hall Ox BA74 MA78. Wycliffe Hall Ox 72. **d** 75 **p** 76. Hon C Ox St Mich w St Martin and All SS *Ox* 75-76; Chapl and Lect BNC Ox 76-82; Lic to Offic 76-82; R Northolt St Mary *Lon* 82-93; AD Ealing 91-93; Adv for Min Willesden 93-97; Dioc Dir of Tr *Ripon* from 97; Can Res Ripon Cathl from 97. *12 Clotherholme Road, Ripon, N Yorkshire HG4 2DA* Tel (01765) 604835

BELL, James Samuel. b 40. MBE71. St Chad's Coll Dur BA69. Coll of Resurr Mirfield 71. **d** 72 **p** 73. C Lambeth St Phil *S'wark* 72-74; P-in-c St Ninian Invergordon 74-77; C N Lambeth 74; P-in-c Dornoch *Mor* 74-77; P-in-c Brora 74-77; V Pet H Spirit Bretton *Pet* 77-83; P-in-c Marholm 82-83; Chapl Tonbridge Sch from 83. *High Trees, 8 Bourne Lane, Tonbridge, Kent TN9 1LG* Tel (01732) 352802

BELL, Jeffrey William. b 37. Sarum Th Coll 60. **d** 63 **p** 64. C Northampton St Matt *Pet* 63-66; C Portishead *B & W* 66-68; C Digswell *St Alb* 68-72; V Pet St Jude *Pet* 72-79; V Buckingham *Ox* 79-93; RD Buckingham 84-88 and 89-90; V Portsea N End St Mark *Portsm* from 93. *The Vicarage, 3A Wadham Road, Portsmouth PO2 9ED* Tel (01705) 662500 or 662753

BELL, Jeremy Aidan. b 46. DipHE. Oak Hill Th Coll 80. **d** 82. C St Paul's Cray St Barn *Roch* 82-83; Perm to Offic *Ex* from 83. *Address temp unknown*

BELL, John Alfred Collingwood. b 23. Fitzw Coll Cam BA47 MA52 St Jo Coll Dur DipTh51 DipEd59. **d** 51 **p** 52. C Beverley Minster *York* 74-77; R Castle Douglas *Glas* 85-88; rtd 88; Perm to Offic *Ely* from 97. *18 Holme Close, Oakington, Cambridge CB4 5AP* Tel (01223) 235918

BELL, Canon John Christopher. b 33. TCD BA56 MA66. TCD Div Sch Div Test. **d** 56 **p** 57. C Newtownards *D & D* 56-59; C Willowfield 59-62; I Carrowdore 62-70; I Drumbo from 70; Chapl Young Offender Cen Belf from 79; RD Hillsborough *D & D* from 81; Can Down Cathl from 87; Treas from 91. *The Rectory, 5 Pinehill Road, Drumbo, Ballylesson, Belfast BT8 8LA* Tel (01232) 826225

BELL, John Edward. b 34. Cranmer Hall Dur. **d** 67 **p** 68. C Harraby *Carl* 67-70; C Dalton-in-Furness 70-72; V Pennington 72-75; V Carl St Herbert w St Steph 75-84; V Wreay 84-85. *189 Brampton Road, Carlisle CA3 9AX* Tel (01228) 22746

BELL, John Holmes. b 50. Sheff City Coll of Educn CertEd71. Oak Hill Th Coll DipHE79 BA80. **d** 80 **p** 81. C Leic St Phil *Leic* 80-83; C Portswood Ch Ch *Win* 83-86; TV S Molton w Nymet St George, High Bray etc *Ex* from 86. *The Rectory, Kings Nympton, Umberleigh, Devon EX37 9ST* Tel (01769) 80457

BELL, Joseph William. b 30. St Cath Coll Ox BA53 Pemb Coll Cam MA57. Wycliffe Hall Ox 53. **d** 55 **p** 56. C Blundellsands St Nic *Liv* 55-58; CF 58-68; V Roby *Liv* 68-70; CF 70-86; P-in-c Fovant, Sutton Mandeville and Teffont Evias etc *Sarum* 86-89; Perm to Offic from 89; rtd 95. *61 St Ann's Place, Salisbury SP1 2SU* Tel (01722) 322576

BELL, Judith Margaret. *See* GRIEVE, Mrs Judith Margaret

BELL, Karl Edwin. b 33. Minnesota Univ BA56. Seabury-Western Th Sem MDiv61. **d** 61 **p** 62. USA 61-71 and 76-92; Venezuela 71-76; Chapl Wiesbaden *Eur* from 92. *c/o St Augustine of Canterbury, Frankfurterstrasse 3, 65189 Wiesbaden, Germany* Tel Wiesbaden (611) 306674 Fax 372270

BELL, Kenneth Murray. b 30. Sarum & Wells Th Coll 75. **d** 74 **p** 76. Perm to Offic *Guildf* 74-76; C Hartley Wintney and Elvetham *Win* 76-77; C Hartley Wintney, Elvetham, Winchfield etc 77-80; V Fair Oak 80-95; rtd 96. *12 Hill Meadow, Overton, Basingstoke, Hants RG25 3JD* Tel (01256) 770890

BELL, Kevin David. b 58. Newc Univ MA93. Selly Oak Coll CPS87 Aston Tr Scheme 78 Sarum & Wells Th Coll 80. **d** 83 **p** 84. C Weoley Castle *Birm* 83-87; C Acocks Green 87-89; CF from 89. *MOD Chaplains (Army), Trenchard Lines, Upavon, Pewsey, Wilts SN9 6BE* Tel (01980) 615804 Fax 615800

BELL, Nicholas Philip Johnson. b 46. St Jo Coll Dur BSc69 Nottm Univ DipTh72. St Jo Coll Nottm 70. **d** 73 **p** 74. C Chadderton Ch Ch *Man* 73-77; C Frogmore *St Alb* 77-81; V Bricket Wood 81-91; RD Aldenham 87-91; V Luton St Mary from 91. *The Vicarage, 48 Crawley Green Road, Luton LU2 0QX* Tel (01582) 28925 or 21867

BELL, Paul Joseph. b 35. Dur Univ BA56 DipEd57. Trin Coll Bris 77. **d** 77 **p** 78. CMS 77-82; C Highbury Ch Ch w St Jo and St Sav Lon 82-85; V Middleton w E Winch *Nor* 85-95; P-in-c Barningham w Matlaske w Baconsthorpe etc from 95. *The Rectory, The Street, Matlaske, Norwich NR11 7AQ* Tel (01263) 577420

BELL, Philip Harold. b 19. Leeds Univ BA45. Coll of Resurr Mirfield 38. **d** 44 **p** 45. C Barrow St Matt *Carl* 44-49; C Lewisham St Jo Southend *S'wark* 50-56; Tristan da Cunha 56-61; R Crawley w Littleton *Win* 61-72; V Holdenhurst 72-78; P-in-c Hilperton w Whaddon *Sarum* 78-84; P-in-c Staverton 78-84; R Hilperton w Whaddon and Staverton etc 85-86; rtd 86. *31 Duxford Close, Larksfield, Bowerhill, Melksham, Wilts SN12 6XN* Tel (01225) 709732

BELL, Reginald Leslie (Reg). b 13. Trin Coll Bris 72. **d** 74 **p** 75. NSM Stoke Bishop *Bris* 74-75 and 78-94; NSM Horfield H Trin 75-77; Perm to Offic from 94. *September Cottage, 14 Pitch and Pay Lane, Bristol BS9 1NH* Tel 0117-968 1510

BELL, Dr Richard Herbert. b 54. Univ Coll Lon BSc75 PhD79 Tubingen Univ DrTheol91. Wycliffe Hall Ox BA82 MA87. **d** 83 **p** 84. C Edgware *Lon* 83-86; W Germany 86-90; Lect Th Nottm Univ from 90. *14 Anderson Crescent, Beeston, Nottingham NG9 2PT* Tel 0115-922 2036

BELL, Robert Clarke. b 30. Roch Th Coll 63. **d** 65 **p** 66. C Leeds All SS *Ripon* 65-67; C Claxby w Normanby-le-Wold *Linc* 67-69; R Newark St Leon *S'well* 69-71; V Gosberton Clough *Linc* 71-74; P-in-c Quadring 73-74; Chapl to the Deaf 74-85; V Harmston 85-94; V Coleby 85-94; RD Graffoe 92-94; rtd 94; Perm to Offic *Blackb* from 94; Perm to Offic *Carl* from 94. *33 Mill Lane, Bolton le Sands, Carnforth, Lancs LA5 8EZ*

BELL, Robert Mason. b 35. Lon Coll of Div 66. **d** 68 **p** 69. C Burgess Hill St Andr *Chich* 68-78; R Lewes St Jo sub Castro from 78. *St John's Rectory, 1 The Avenue, Lewes, E Sussex BN7 1BA* Tel (01273) 473080

BELL, Ross. b 64. Bradf and Ilkley Coll BA87. Aston Tr Scheme 89 Westcott Ho Cam 91. **d** 94 **p** 95. C W Bromwich All SS *Lich* from 94. *50 Wilford Road, West Bromwich, W Midlands B71 1QN* Tel 0121-588 3440

BELL, Simon Barnaby. b 48. Bris Univ CertEd70. Sarum & Wells Th Coll 87. **d** 89 **p** 90. C Ewyas Harold w Dulas *Heref* 89-90; C Ewyas Harold w Dulas, Kenderchurch etc 90-93; P-in-c Clungunford w Clunbury and Clunton, Bedstone etc from 93. *The Rectory, Clungunford, Craven Arms, Shropshire SY7 0PN* Tel (01588) 660342

BELL, Stuart Rodney. b 46. Ex Univ BA67. Tyndale Hall Bris 69. **d** 71 **p** 72. C Henfynyw w Aberaeron and Llanddewi Aberarth *St D* 71-74; V 81-88; V Llangeler 74-80; R Aberystwyth from 88; Chapl Univ of Wales (Abth) from 94; Ev St Teilo Trust from 95. *The Rectory, Laura Place, Aberystwyth SY23 2AU* Tel (01970) 617184 or 625080 Fax 617184

BELL, Terrance James. b 63. **d** 97. C Wedmore w Theale and Blackford *B & W* from 97. *27 St Medard Road, Wedmore, Somerset BS28 4AY* Tel (01934) 712221

BELL-RICHARDS, Douglas Maurice. b 23. St Steph Ho Ox 59. **d** 61 **p** 62. C Chipping Campden *Glouc* 61-62; C Thornbury 62-67; V Dymock w Donnington 67-75; V Fairford 75-91; rtd 91. *5 Palace Yard, Hereford HR4 9BJ* Tel (01432) 341070

BELLAMY, Charles Gordon. b 15. St Chad's Coll Dur BA42. St Deiniol's Hawarden 36. **d** 42 **p** 43. C Howdon Panns *Newc* 42-44; C Byker St Ant 44-46; C Horton 46-50; C Sighill 50-56; V Burnley (Habergham Eaves) St Matt w H Trin *Blackb* 56-67; V Overton 67-80; rtd 80; Hon C Monkseaton St Mary *Newc* 80-94; Hon C Tynemouth Cullercoats St Paul from 94. *60 Davison Avenue, Whitley Bay, Tyne & Wear NE26 1SH* Tel 0191-251 3355

BELLAMY, David Quentin. b 62. Univ of Wales (Cardiff) BMus84. Ripon Coll Cuddesdon 87 Ch Div Sch of the Pacific (USA). **d** 90 **p** 91. C Rhyl w St Ann *St As* 90-94; V Llay from 94. *The Vicarage, First Avenue, Llay, Wrexham LL12 0TN* Tel (01978) 832262

BELLAMY, Mrs Dorothy Kathleen. b 33. Gilmore Course 74. **dss** 82 **d** 87 **p** 94. Feltham *Lon* 82-84; Twickenham St Mary 84; Hampton St Mary 84-85; Hampton Wick 85-87; Par Dn 87-88; Par Dn Teddington St Mark and Hampton Wick St Jo 88-90; Par Dn Westbury *Sarum* 90-94; C 94-96; rtd 97; NSM Freshwater *Portsm* from 97; NSM Yarmouth from 97. *Easterholme, Tennyson Road, Yarmouth, Isle of Wight PO41 0PR* Tel (01983) 760657

BELLAMY, John Stephen. b 55. Jes Coll Ox BA77 MA81 DipTh82 DPS84. St Jo Coll Nottm. **d** 84 **p** 85. C Allerton *Liv* 84-87; C Southport Ch Ch 87-89; Bp's Dom Chapl 89-91; V Birkdale St Jas from 91. *St James's Vicarage, 26 Lulworth Road, Southport, Merseyside PR8 2BQ* Tel (01704) 66255

BELLAMY, Mervyn Roger Hunter. b 47. Sussex Univ CertEd. St Mich Coll Llan DipTh81. **d** 81 **p** 82. C Frecheville and Hackenthorpe *Sheff* 81-85; V Shiregreen St Hilda 85-94; RD Ecclesfield 93-94; R Rawmarsh w Parkgate from 94. *The Rectory, High Street, Rawmarsh, Rotherham, S Yorkshire S62 6NE* Tel (01709) 527160

BELLAMY, Peter Charles William. b 38. Birm Univ MA70 PhD79 AKC61. **d** 62 **p** 63. C Allestree *Derby* 62-65; Chapl All SS Hosp Birm 65-73; Chapl St Pet Coll of Educn Saltley 73-78; Lic to Offic *Birm* 78-90; Chapl Qu Eliz Psychiatric Hosp Birm 78-90; Manager HIV Services Birm Cen HA 90-92; Perm to Offic *Birm* from 90. *51 St Denis Road, Selly Oak, Birmingham B29 4JY* Tel 0121-475 6363 or 627 2052

BELLAMY, Robert John. b 40. Ripon Hall Ox 64. **d** 66 **p** 67. C Fishponds St Jo *Bris* 66-70; C Oldland 70-74; P-in-c Coalpit Heath 74-76; TV Cannock *Lich* 90-96; Chapl Chase Hosp Cannock 90-96; Perm to Offic *Lich* from 96. *10 Meadowlark*

Close, Hednesford, Cannock, Staffs WS12 5UE Tel (01543) 876809

BELLENES, Peter Charles. b 49. Pontifical Univ Salamanca DipPhil68 Thurrock Coll Essex CQSW72 DipSocWork72. Linc Th Coll 79. **d** 81 **p** 90. C Penistone *Wakef* 81-82; Hon C Liskeard, St Keyne, St Pinnock, Morval etc *Truro* 89-92; Hon C Menheniot from 92. *Fernlea, Beneathway, Dobwalls, Liskeard, Cornwall PL14 6JN* Tel (01579) 20031

BELLINGER, Canon Denys Gordon. b 29. Sheff Univ BA49. Westcott Ho Cam 51. **d** 53 **p** 54. C Ribbleton *Blackb* 53-56; C Lancaster St Mary 56-58; V Colne H Trin 58-68; V Scotforth 68-93; RD Lancaster 82-89; Hon Can Blackb Cathl 86-93; rtd 93; Perm to Offic *Blackb* from 93. *40 Yewlands Drive, Garstang, Preston PR3 1JP*

BELLINGER, Richard George. b 47. Univ of Wales (Abth) BSc(Econ)69. S Dios Minl Tr Scheme 91. **d** 94 **p** 95. SSF from 94; NSM Guernsey St Steph *Win* 94-96; NSM Guernsey St Martin from 96. *La Maison des Vinaires, Rues des Vinaires, St Peter's, Guernsey, Channel Islands GY7 9EZ* Tel (01481) 63203

BELOE, Robert Francis. b 39. Sarum Th Coll. **d** 65 **p** 71. C Nor Heartsease St Fran *Nor* 65-66; C Edmonton St Mary w St Jo *Lon* 68-70; C St Marylebone Ch Ch w St Paul 70-74; P-in-c Wicken *Ely* 74-76; V from 76. *The Vicarage, Wicken, Ely, Cambs CB7 5XT* Tel (01353) 720243

BEMAN, Donald Oliver. b 37. Southn Univ BA58. Coll of Resurr Mirfield 58. **d** 60 **p** 65. C Forton *Portsm* 60-61; Hon C Hound *Win* 64-68; Lic to Offic 69-82. *8 Avon Court, Netley Abbey, Southampton SO31 5BU* Tel (01703) 453239

BEMENT, Peter James. b 43. Univ of Wales (Cardiff) BA64 PhD69. Wycliffe Hall Ox 92. **d** 94 **p** 95. C Hubberston *St D* 94-97; V Llandeilo and Taliaris from 97. *The Vicarage, 10 Carmarthen Road, Llandeilo SA19 6RS* Tel (01558) 822421

BENBOW, Susan Catherine. *See* TURNER, Mrs Susan Catherine

BENCE, Canon Graham Edwin. b 16. Lon Univ BA54. Sarum Th Coll 64. **d** 65 **p** 66. C Clacton St Jas *Chelmsf* 65-68; R Barlborough *Derby* 68-86; RD Bolsover 70-73; RD Bolsover and Staveley 73-78; Hon Can Derby Cathl 78-86; rtd 86; Perm to Offic *Lich* from 87. *Flat 3, 4 Quarry Place, Shrewsbury SY1 1JN* Tel (01743) 233533

BENCE, Helen Mary. b 44. Leic Univ BA65 PGCE66. EMMTC 93. **d** 97. NSM Humberstone *Leic* from 97. *The Grange, 126 Shanklin Drive, Leicester LE2 3QB* Tel 0116-270 7820

BENCE, Norman Murray. b 34. Ripon Hall Ox 63. **d** 63 **p** 64. C Eling *Win* 63-66; Australia 66 and 75; Lic to Offic *Win* 67-74 and 75-81; NSM Iford from 81. *72 Corhampton Road, Bournemouth BH6 5PB* Tel (01202) 421992

BENCE, Roy. b 21. Chich Th Coll 55. **d** 57 **p** 58. C Stepney St Dunstan and All SS *Lon* 57-60; V Notting Hill St Mark 61-66; Chapl Zurich w St Gallen and Winterthur *Eur* 66-68; V Bethnal Green St Jas the Gt w St Jude *Lon* 69-72; V Bush Hill Park St Mark 72-79; V Highgate St Aug 79-86; rtd 87; Perm to Offic *Lon* from 87. *5 St James's Close, Bishop Street, London N1 8PH* Tel 0171-359 0885

BENDELL, David James. b 38. S'wark Ord Course. **d** 87 **p** 88. NSM Surbiton Hill Ch Ch *S'wark* from 87. *3 Pine Walk, Surbiton, Surrey KT5 8NJ* Tel 0181-399 7143

BENDING, Richard Clement. b 47. Southn Univ BSc68. Ridley Hall Cam 87. **d** 89 **p** 90. Par Dn St Neots *Ely* 89-92; V Buckden from 92. *The Vicarage, Buckden, St Neots, Huntingdon, Cambs PE18 9TL* Tel (01480) 810371

BENEDICT, Brother. *See* WINSPER, Arthur William

BENFIELD, Gordon. b 29. OBE95. Lon Univ BD60 STh79 Birm Univ MA81 LGSM Leeds Univ 60. **d** 80 **p** 81. NSM Warwick *Cov* 80-85; Prin Westhill Coll of HE Birm 85-90; Perm to Offic *Birm* 85-90; Chmn Ch Educn Movement 86-96; R Barford w Wasperton and Sherbourne *Cov* 90-96; rtd 96. *Ivy Cottage, Butlers Marston, Warwick CV35 0NG* Tel (01926) 640758

BENFIELD, Paul John. b 56. Barrister-at-Law (Lincoln's Inn) 78 Newc Univ LLB77 Southn Univ BTh89. Chich Th Coll 86. **d** 89 **p** 90. C Shiremoor *Newc* 89-92; C Hexham 92-93; TV Lewes All SS, St Anne, St Mich and St Thos *Chich* 93-97; R Pulborough from 97. *The Rectory, 2 London Road, Pulborough, W Sussex RH20 1AP* Tel (01798) 875773 Fax as telephone

BENFORD, Brian. b 47. Sheff Univ BA Hull Univ MEd PhD88. N Ord Course 82. **d** 85 **p** 86. NSM Stocksbridge *Sheff* 85-90; NSM Gawber *Wakef* from 90. *9 Midhope Way, Pogmoor, Barnsley, S Yorkshire S75 2LS* Tel (01226) 291407

BENGE, Charles David. b 40. Cranmer Hall Dur 63. **d** 68 **p** 69. C Millfield St Mark *Dur* 68-72; C Hensingham *Carl* 72-74; TV Maghull *Liv* 75-82; V Bootle St Leon 82-97; NSM Ormskirk from 97. *26 Drummersdale Lane, Scarisbrick, Ormskirk, Lancs L40 9RB*

BENIAMS, Alec Charles. b 28. AKC52. **d** 53 **p** 54. C Gosforth All SS *Newc* 53-56; C Cullercoats St Geo 56-58; C Eltham St Jo *S'wark* 58-59; C-in-c Lynemouth St Aid CD *Newc* 59-61; CF (TA) 60-67; V Lynemouth *Newc* 61-63; V Whittingham 63-67; V Willington 67-71; CF (TA - R of O) from 67; V Haydon Bridge *Newc* 71-85; R Yardley Hastings, Denton and Grendon etc *Pet* 85-90; rtd 90. *12 Dickson Drive, Highford Park, Hexham, Northd NE46 2RB* Tel (01434) 600226

BENIANS, Martin Ackland. b 19. St Jo Coll Cam BA41 MA45. Ridley Hall Cam 59. **d** 59 **p** 60. C Headstone St Geo *Lon* 59-62; R Rackheath *Nor* 62-89; V Salhouse 62-89; rtd 89; Perm to Offic *Nor* from 89. *26 Victoria Street, Sheringham, Norfolk NR26 8JZ* Tel (01263) 822563

BENISON, Brian. b 41. K Coll Lon 61. Bps' Coll Cheshunt 63. **d** 66 **p** 67. C Tynemouth Ch Ch *Newc* 66-70; C Gosforth All SS 70-72; TV Cullercoats St Geo 73-81; V Denton 81-93; V Blyth St Mary from 93; Chapl Blyth Community Hosp Northd from 93. *St Mary's Vicarage, 51 Marine Terrace, Blyth, Northd NE24 2JP* Tel (01670) 353417

BENJAMIN, Adrian Victor. b 42. Wadh Coll Ox BA66 MA68. Cuddesdon Coll 66. **d** 68 **p** 69. C Gosforth All SS *Newc* 68-71; C Stepney St Dunstan and All SS *Lon* 71-75; V Friern Barnet All SS from 75; Relig Ed ITV Oracle from 83. *14 Oakleigh Park South, London N20 9JU* Tel 0181-445 4645 or 445 6831

✠**BENN, The Rt Revd Wallace Parke.** b 47. UCD BA69 Lon Univ DipTh71. Trin Coll Bris 69. **d** 72 **p** 73 **c** 97. C New Ferry *Ches* 72-76; C Cheadle 76-82; V Audley *Lich* 82-87; V Harold Wood *Chelmsf* 87-97; Chapl Harold Wood Hosp Chelmsf 87-96; Area Bp Lewes *Chich* from 97. *Bishop's Lodge, 16A Prideaux Road, Eastbourne, E Sussex BN21 2NB*

BENNELL, Canon Richard. b 25. Leeds Univ BA45 DipEd45. Coll of Resurr Mirfield 46. **d** 48 **p** 49. C Bedminster *Bris* 48-51; C Brislington St Anne 51-56; V Fishponds St Jo 56-68; V Knowle St Martin 68-73; TR Knowle 73-80; RD Brislington 73-79; Hon Can Bris Cathl 76-91; Chapl St Monica Home Bris 80-91; rtd 91; Perm to Offic *Bris* from 91. *1B Cooper Road, Bristol BS9 3QZ* Tel 0117-962 2364

BENNET, Gordon Duncan Affleck. b 31. Lon Univ BSc(Econ)55. Clifton Th Coll 55. **d** 57 **p** 58. C Carl St Jo *Carl* 57-60; C W Kilburn St Luke w St Simon and St Jude *Lon* 60-63; C-in-c Dallam CD *Liv* 63-69; Lic to Offic *Man* 69-75; NW Area Sec CPAS 69-75; R Edgware *Lon* 75-91; V Walton le Soken *Chelmsf* from 91. *The Vicarage, Martello Road, Walton on the Naze, Essex CO14 8TA* Tel (01255) 675452

BENNETT, Alan Robert. b 31. Roch Th Coll 62. **d** 64 **p** 65. C Asterby w Goulceby *Linc* 64-67; C St Alb St Pet *St Alb* 67-70; R Banham *Nor* 70-72; CF 72-77; P-in-c Colchester St Mary Magd *Chelmsf* 77; TV Colchester St Leon, St Mary Magd and St Steph 77-81; R Colne Engaine 81-88; P-in-c Stoke Ferry w Wretton *Ely* 88-89; V 89-96; V Whittington 88-96; rtd 96. *34 West Way, Wimbotsham, King's Lynn, Norfolk PE34 3PZ*

BENNETT, Alan William. b 42. Sarum Th Coll 65. **d** 68 **p** 69. C Fareham H Trin *Portsm* 68-71; C Brighton St Matthias *Chich* 71-73; C Stanmer w Falmer and Moulsecoomb 73-75; C Moulsecoomb 76; V Lower Sandown St Jo *Portsm* 76-80; V Soberton w Newtown 80-87; R Aston Clinton w Buckland and Drayton Beauchamp *Ox* from 87; RD Wendover from 94. *The Rectory, New Road, Aston Clinton, Aylesbury, Bucks HP22 5JD* Tel (01296) 631626

BENNETT, Alexander Steven Frederick. b 69. Hull Univ BA91. Westcott Ho Cam CTM95. **d** 95 **p** 96. C Whitton and Thurleston w Akenham *St E* from 95. *530 Norwich Road, Ipswich IP1 6JR* Tel (01473) 463676

BENNETT, Anthony. b 31. Qu Coll Birm 72. **d** 74 **p** 74. C Hobs Moat *Birm* 74-76; C Hill 76-79; R Grendon 79-82; R Upwell Ch Ch *Ely* 82-86; R Welney 82-86; P-in-c Coates 86-88; R 88-93; rtd 93; Perm to Offic *Ely* from 93. *77 Snoots Road, Whittlesey, Peterborough PE7 1NN* Tel (01733) 208214

BENNETT, Arnold Ernest. b 29. K Coll Lon BD59 AKC53. **d** 54 **p** 55. C S w N Hayling *Portsm* 54-59; C Stevenage *St Alb* 59-64; R N w S Wootton *Nor* 64-74; V Hykeham *Linc* 74-85; V Heckfield w Mattingley and Rotherwick *Win* from 85. *The Vicarage, Mattingley, Basingstoke, Hants RG27 8LF* Tel (0118) 932 6385

BENNETT, Arthur Harling. b 22. Ripon Hall Ox 70. **d** 71 **p** 72. C Standish *Blackb* 71-74; TV Darwen St Pet w Hoddlesden 75-79; V Whitechapel 79-89; V Whitechapel w Admarsh-in-Bleasdale 89-90; rtd 90; Perm to Offic *Blackb* from 90. *1 Eden Gardens, Mersey Street, Longridge, Preston PR3 3WF* Tel (01772) 784924

BENNETT, Bernard Michael. b 27. Leeds Univ CertEd52 DipPE54. St Aid Birkenhead 55. **d** 58 **p** 59. C Hemsworth *Wakef* 58-60; C Chapelthorpe 60-62; V Birkenhead St Bede w All SS *Ches* 62-71; V Latchford St Jas 71-75; Chapl HM Pris Appleton Thorn 75-82; V Appleton Thorn and Antrobus *Ches* 75-86; Chapl HM Rem Cen Risley 81-84; rtd 86; Perm to Offic *Ches* from 86; Perm to Offic *Blackb* from 91. *7 Montpelier Avenue, Blackpool FY2 9AE* Tel (01253) 51139

BENNETT, Bryan James. b 39. Tyndale Hall Bris 64. **d** 67 **p** 68. C Consett *Dur* 67-70; CF 70-84; R Leadenham *Linc* 84-91; R Welbourn 84-91; R Castle Bytham w Creeton from 91. *The Rectory, Holywell Road, Castle Bytham, Grantham, Lincs NG33 4SL* Tel (01780) 410166

BENNETT, Charles William. b 38. **d** 63 **p** 64. New Zealand 63-80 and from 81; C N Walsham w Antingham *Nor* 80. *59 McGrath Street, Napier, New Zealand* Tel Levin (6) 835 9924 Fax 835 9920

BENNETT, Clifford Orford. b 32. St Mich Coll Llan 73. **d** 75 **p** 76. C Holywell *St As* 75-79; V Pontblyddyn from 79. *The Vicarage,*

Wrexham Road, Pontblyddyn, Mold CH7 4HG Tel (01352) 771489

BENNETT, David Edward. b 35. Fitzw Ho Cam BA56 MA60 Lon Univ PGCE. Wells Th Coll 58. **d** 60 **p** 61. C Lightcliffe *Wakef* 60-62; NE Area Sec Chr Educn Movement 62-68; Lic to Offic *S'well* 68-71; Gen Insp RE Nottm Co Coun from 68; Hon C Holme Pierrepont w Adbolton 71-85; NSM Radcliffe-on-Trent and Shelford etc from 85. *The Old Farmhouse, Main Street, Gunthorpe, Nottingham NG14 7EY* Tel 0115-966 3451

BENNETT, David Lawrence. b 38. Liv Univ BA61. Ripon Hall Ox 61. **d** 63 **p** 64. C Harlington *Lon* 63-66; Zambia from 67. *c/o University of Zambia, PO Box 2379, Lusaka, Zambia*

BENNETT, David Satterly. b 37. Lanc Univ BA79 Linc Coll Ox CertEd80. English Coll Valladolid 57. **d** 62 **p** 63. In RC Ch 63-72; RAChD 72-75; RE 77-84; NSM Alresford *Chelmsf* 83-84; C Chandler's Ford *Win* 84-89; C Bitterne Park 89-94; C W End from 94. *8 Bassett Close, Southampton SO16 7PE* Tel (01703) 769404

BENNETT, Donovan Harry (Don). b 27. Qu Mary Coll Lon BScEng52 FGS61 AMICE61 CEng61 FICE72. Moray Ord Course 88. **d** 92 **p** 93. Hon C Dingwall *Mor* 92-93; Hon C Strathpeffer 92-93; Hon C Inverness St Mich 93-95; P-in-c Grantown-on-Spey from 96. *St Columba's Rectory, Grant Road, Grantown-on-Spey, Morayshire PH26 3LD* Tel (01479) 872866

BENNETT, Edwin James. b 23. St Barn Coll Adelaide ThL47 STh52. **d** 47 **p** 48. Australia 47-74; V Oldham St Barn *Man* 74-78; V Alderney *Win* 78-84; V Hatherden w Tangley, Weyhill and Penton Mewsey 84-89; rtd 89. *35 Charlton Village, Andover, Hants SP10 4AP* Tel (01264) 356358

BENNETT, Garry Raymond. b 46. K Coll Lon 66. **d** 70 **p** 71. C Mitcham St Mark *S'wark* 70-73; C Mortlake w E Sheen 73-75; TV 76-78; V Herne Hill St Paul 78-88; V Herne Hill 89; P-in-c Ruskin Park St Sav and St Matt 82-88; Sen Dioc Stewardship Adv *Chelmsf* 89-94; TR Southend from 94. *144 Alexandra Road, Southend-on-Sea, Essex SS1 1HB* Tel (01702) 342687

BENNETT, Geoffrey Kenneth. b 56. Oak Hill Th Coll. **d** 89 **p** 90. C Ipswich St Matt *St E* 89-92; R St Ruan w St Grade and Landewednack *Truro* from 92. *The Rectory, Church Cove, The Lizard, Helston, Cornwall TR12 7PQ* Tel (01326) 290713

BENNETT, George Darley. b 21. ACIS47. **d** 66 **p** 67. Zambia 66-76; R Hulland, Atlow and Bradley *Derby* 76-78; P-in-c Hulland, Atlow, Bradley and Hognaston 76-78; R 78-86; RD Ashbourne 81-86; rtd 87; Perm to Offic *Derby* from 87. *11 Freemantle Road, Mickleover, Derby DE3 5HW* Tel (01332) 510212

BENNETT, George Edward. b 51. Univ of Wales (Abth) BA72. St Steph Ho Ox 73. **d** 76 **p** 77. C Clifton All SS w Tyndalls Park *Bris* 76-78; C Clifton All SS w St Jo 78-82; Chapl Newbury and Sandleford Hosps 82-93; TV Newbury *Ox* 82-93; V Llwynderw *S & B* from 93. *Llwynderw Vicarage, Fairwood Road, West Cross, Swansea SA3 5JP* Tel (01792) 401903

BENNETT, Graham Eric Thomas. b 53. Sarum & Wells Th Coll 88. **d** 90 **p** 91. C Baswich *Lich* 90-94; C Codsall from 94. *Church House, Bilbrook Road, Bilbrook, Wolverhampton WV8 1EU* Tel (01902) 842912

BENNETT, Guy. b 33. St Edm Hall Ox BA56. Wells Th Coll 56. **d** 58 **p** 59. C Norbury St Phil *Cant* 58-61; C Minehead *B & W* 61-63; Chapl Butlin's Clacton-on-Sea 63; C Raynes Park St Sav *S'wark* 63-66; C Motspur Park H Cross CD 66-72; R Oxted 72-97; R Oxted and Tandridge from 97. *The Rectory, 29 Chichele Road, Oxted, Surrey RH8 0AE* Tel (01883) 712955

BENNETT, Handel Henry Cecil. b 33. MCIM. Cant Sch of Min 79. **d** 82 **p** 83. NSM St Margarets-at-Cliffe w Westcliffe etc *Cant* 82-85; Dir Holy Land Chr Tours 85-94; Holy Land Consultant F T Tours 95-96; Sen Travel Consultant Raymond Cook Chr Tours from 96; Perm to Offic *St Alb* from 85. *23 The Marsh, Carlton, Bedford MK43 7JU* Tel (01234) 720745 Mobile 0374-981569 Fax as telephone

BENNETT, Harold Archibald Timson. b 11. Keble Coll Ox BA33 MA45. St Steph Ho Ox 34. **d** 35 **p** 36. C Beckenham St Jas *Roch* 35-38; C Small Heath St Greg *Birm* 38-39; P-in-c 39-45; R Wootton by Woodstock *Ox* 45-52; V Cropredy w Gt Bourton 52-65; V Kennington 65-79; rtd 79; C Ox St Mary Magd *Ox* 79-87; Perm to Offic from 87. *St John's Home, St Mary's Road, Oxford OX4 1QE* Tel (01865) 246937

BENNETT, Canon Ian Frederick. b 30. Ch Coll Cam BA54 MA62. Westcott Ho Cam 61. **d** 63 **p** 64. C Hemel Hempstead *St Alb* 63-68; Asst Chapl Man Univ *Man* 69-73; Sen Chapl 73-79; C Chorlton upon Medlock 69-73; P-in-c 73-79; TR Man Whitworth 79; Dioc Tr Officer *Birm* 79-88; Hon Can Birm Cathl 86-88; Can Res Newc Cathl *Newc* from 88; Dioc Dir of Min and Tr from 90; Dir Post-Ord Tr from 97. *21 Otterburn Avenue, Gosforth, Newcastle upon Tyne NE3 4RR* Tel 0191-285 1967 or 226 0622

BENNETT, James Kenneth Bretherton. b 11. St Jo Coll Ox BA33 DipTh34 MA37. Wycliffe Hall Ox 33. **d** 35 **p** 36. C Leic H Apostles *Leic* 35-38; C-in-c Westwood and Wingfield *Sarum* 38-40; RAChD 40-46; V Lythe *York* 46-49; V Bainton 49-57; V N Dalton 49-57; Chapl Glebe Ho Sch Hunstanton 57-59; Hd Master 59-67; Lic to Offic *Nor* 57-67; Asst Master Loretto Sch Musselburgh 67-73; Chapl Caldicott Sch Farnham Royal 73-76; rtd 76. *2 Elmfields Gate, Winslow, Buckingham MK18 3JG* Tel (01296) 712725

BENNETT, John David. b 58. Ox Univ BA79 MA83. Westcott Ho Cam 81. **d** 83 **p** 84. C Taunton St Andr *B & W* 83-86; Chapl Trowbridge Coll *Sarum* 86-90; AP Studley 86-90; V Yeovil H Trin *B & W* 90-95; R Yeovil H Trin w Barwick from 95. *The Rectory, 24 Turners Barn Lane, Yeovil, Somerset BA20 2LM* Tel (01935) 23774

BENNETT, John Walker. b 09. Hatf Coll Dur BA39 LTh39 MA41. St Aug Coll Cant 35. **d** 39 **p** 40. C Buckhurst Hill *Chelmsf* 39-42; C Seaham w Seaham Harbour *Dur* 42-44; V Gateshead St Geo 44-48; Australia 48-53; V Kingsbury *Birm* 53-64; PC Dosthill and Wood End 53-59; R Bradfield St Geo w Rushbrooke *St E* 64-77; R Bradfield St Clare 64-77; rtd 77; Perm to Offic *St E* from 77. *5 Orchard Way, Barrow, Bury St Edmunds, Suffolk IP29 5BX* Tel (01284) 810617

BENNETT, Dr Joyce Mary. b 23. OBE79. Westf Coll Lon BA44 DipEd45 K Coll Lon DipTh61 Hon DSocSc84. **d** 62 **p** 71. Hong Kong 62-83; NSM St Martin-in-the-Fields *Lon* 84-87; Perm to Offic *Ox* from 87; Perm to Offic *Lon* from 87. *The Cornerstone, 72 The Crescent, High Wycombe, Bucks HP13 6JP* Tel (01494) 539016

BENNETT, Mark Ian. b 61. K Coll Cam BA83 MA86. Trin Coll Bris BA94. **d** 94 **p** 95. C Selly Park St Steph and St Wulstan *Birm* 94-97; C Harrow Trin St Mich *Lon* from 97. *74 Bishop Ken Road, Harrow Weald, Harrow, Middx HA3 7HR* Tel 0181-861 1710

BENNETT, Canon Michael Edgar. b 32. Keble Coll Ox BA53 MA58 DipEd. Wells Th Coll 59. **d** 61 **p** 62. C Calne and Blackland *Sarum* 61-64; C Tewkesbury w Walton Cardiff *Glouc* 64-69; R Swindon w Uckington and Elmstone Hardwicke 69-92; Ed Glouc Dioc Gazette from 73; Chapl Sue Ryder Home Cheltenham 80-92; R Toddington, Stanton, Didbrook w Hailes etc from 92; Hon Can Glouc Cathl from 96. *The Rectory, Church Lane, Toddington, Cheltenham, Glos GL52 5DQ* Tel (01242) 620126

BENNETT, Michael John. b 43. AKC66. St Boniface Warminster. **d** 67 **p** 68. C Chester le Street *Dur* 67-71; C Portland All SS w St Pet *Sarum* 71-74; Chapl Portland Hosp Weymouth 74-85; V Portland St Jo *Sarum* 74-85; R Alveley and Quatt *Heref* 85-92; Dep Chapl HM Young Offender Inst Glen Parva 93-95; TV Wrexham *St As* from 95. *St Mark's Vicarage, Menai Road, Queens Park, Wrexham LL13 9LB* Tel (01978) 356647

BENNETT, Nigel John. b 47. Lon Univ DipTh69. Oak Hill Th Coll 66. **d** 71 **p** 72. C Tonbridge St Steph *Roch* 71-75; C Heatherlands St Jo *Sarum* 75-79; P-in-c Kingham w Churchill, Daylesford and Sarsden *Ox* 79; R 80-85; Chapl Blue Coat Sch Reading from 85. *13 Wilmington Close, Woodley, Reading RG5 4LR* Tel 0118-969 9223

BENNETT, Osmond Shirley. b 36. Or Coll Ox BA67. Ripon Hall Ox 64. **d** 68 **p** 69. C Stocking Farm *Leic* 68-71; C Thurcaston 71-72; V Leic St Marg 72-82; V Leic St Marg and All SS 83-89; R Houghton-on-the-Hill, Keyham and Hungarton from 89. *The Rectory, 16 Main Street, Houghton-on-the-Hill, Leicester LE7 9GD* Tel 0116-241 2226

BENNETT, Paul. b 55. Southn Univ BTh94. St Steph Ho Ox 95. **d** 97. C Willingdon *Chich* from 97. *11 Winchester Way, Willingdon, Eastbourne, E Sussex BN22 0JP* Tel (01323) 520928

BENNETT, Paul John. b 47. Univ of Wales (Cardiff) DPS89. St Mich Coll Llan 88 Llan Dioc Tr Scheme 79. **d** 85 **p** 86. NSM Ystrad Rhondda w Ynyscynon *Llan* 85-89; C Tylorstown w Ynyshir 89-93; V Llanwynno from 93. *The Vicarage, 40 Hoel-y-Plwyf, Ynysybwl, Pontypridd CF37 3HU* Tel (01443) 790340

BENNETT, Paul Jonathan. b 61. **d** 87 **p** 88. C Henleaze *Bris* 87-91; P-in-c Swindon All SS 91-94; V Swindon All SS w St Barn 94-96; V Patrick *S & M* from 96; V Foxdale from 96; V German St Jo from 96. *The Vicarage, Patrick, Peel, Isle of Man IM5 1AW* Tel (01624) 842637

BENNETT, Paul William. b 61. DCR92. Linc Th Coll CMinlStuds95. **d** 95 **p** 96. C Thornton-le-Fylde *Blackb* from 95. *6 Waring Drive, Thornton-Cleveleys, Blackpool FY5 2SP* Tel (01253) 855103

BENNETT, Peter Hugh. b 22. K Coll Lon 46. **d** 50 **p** 51. C Newington Transfiguration *York* 50-53; C Bottesford *Linc* 53-57; V Tile Hill *Cov* 58-64; V Hillmorton 64-76; R Beaudesert w Henley-in-Arden 76-81; P-in-c Ullenhall cum Aspley 76-81; R Beaudesert and Henley-in-Arden w Ullenhall 81-87; rtd 87; Perm to Offic *Cov* from 87. *20 Avon Crescent, Stratford-upon-Avon, Warks CV37 7EY* Tel (01789) 296278

BENNETT, Reginald George. b 11. K Coll Lon 32. **d** 35 **p** 36. C Grimsbury *Ox* 35-37; C Batsford w Moreton-in-Marsh *Glouc* 37-40; CF (EC) 40-46; V Aldsworth *Glouc* 46-52; V Morville w Aston Eyre *Heref* 52-57; V Acton Round 52-57; R Todenham w Lower Lemington *Glouc* 57-61; V Kirtlington *Ox* 61-83; P-in-c Weston on the Green 76-83; rtd 83; Perm to Offic *Ox* from 83. *13 Kennett Road, Headington, Oxford OX3 7BH* Tel (01865) 750826

BENNETT, Richard Edward Stuart. b 24. St Jo Coll Ox BA49 MA55. Wells Th Coll 50. **d** 51 **p** 52. C Twerton *B & W* 51-56; V Gt Staughton *Ely* 56-63; Chapl HM Youth Cust Cen Gaynes Hall 56-63; R Camerton *B & W* 63-80; R Dunkerton 63-80; R

Camerton w Dunkerton, Foxcote and Shoscombe 80-88; RD Midsomer Norton 86-88; rtd 88; Perm to Offic *B & W* 88-94. *Xlendi, 21 Kings Oak Meadow, Clutton, Bristol BS18 4SU* Tel (01761) 453586

BENNETT, Roger Sherwood. b 35. Nottm Univ BA56. Wells Th Coll 58. **d** 59 **p** 60. C Mansfield Woodhouse *S'well* 59-60; C Spalding *Linc* 60-63; V Gedney 63-69; Chapl RNR 65-68; Chapl RN 69-90; V Amport, Grateley, Monxton and Quarley *Win* 90-95; rtd 96. *Le Reduit, School Lane, Nether Wallop, Andover, Hants SO20 8EH* Tel (01264) 782336

BENNETT, Roy Donald. b 40. St Jo Coll Nottm 78. **d** 80 **p** 81. C Fletchamstead *Cov* 80-83; C Bedworth 83-87; P-in-c Studley 87-93; Chapl Univ Hosp Nottm 93-96; Chapl Qu Medical Cen Nottm 94-96; Chapl Bassetlaw Hosp and Community Services NHS Trust from 96. *Bassetlaw Hospital, Kilton Road, Worksop, Notts S81 0BD, or 51 Blyth Road, Worksop, Notts S81 0JJ* Tel (01909) 500990 or 472925

BENNETT, Ms Toni Elizabeth. b 56. Worc Coll of Educn BA81 Sheff Poly 87. St Jo Coll Nottm MA94. **d** 96 **p** 97. C Heanor *Derby* from 96. *143 Ray Street, Heanor, Derbyshire DE75 7GF* Tel (01773) 534276

BENNETT, William Leslie. b 52. TCD Div Sch DipTh90. **d** 90 **p** 91. C Carrickfergus *Conn* 90-93; I Lisnaskea *Clogh* from 93. *The Rectory, Castlebalfour Road, Lisnaskea, Enniskillen, Co Fermanagh BT92 0GJ* Tel (01365) 721237

✠**BENNETTS, The Rt Revd Colin James.** b 40. Jes Coll Cam BA63 MA67. Ridley Hall Cam 63. **d** 65 **p** 66 **c** 94. C Tonbridge St Steph *Roch* 65-69; Chapl Ox Pastorate 69-79; C Ox St Aldate w H Trin *Ox* 69-73; Lic to Offic 73-78; Asst Chapl Jes Coll Ox 73-75; Chapl 75-78; P-in-c Ox St Andr *Ox* 79; V 80-90; RD Ox 84-89; Can Res Ches Cathl and Dioc Dir of Ords *Ches* 90-94; Area Bp Buckingham *Ox* from 94. *Sheridan, Grimms Hill, Great Missenden, Bucks HP16 9BD* Tel (01494) 862173 Fax 890508

BENNETTS, Gordon Vivian. b 15. TD62. Open Univ BA78. **d** 77 **p** 78. NSM Phillack w Gwithian and Gwinear *Truro* 77-79; NSM Redruth 79-80; NSM Redruth w Lanner 80-82; Chapl Tehidy Hosp Camborne 82-87; Lic to Offic *Truro* from 82; Chapl Duchy Hosp Truro from 87. *66 Tregolls Road, Truro, Cornwall TR1 1LD* Tel (01872) 41857

BENNETTS, John Barrington. b 32. LNSM course 85. **d** 92 **p** 93. NSM Falmouth K Chas *Truro* from 92. *39 Budock Terrace, Falmouth, Cornwall TR11 3NE* Tel (01326) 314961 or 312111

BENNETTS, William Rawling. b 28. Univ of W Aus BSc48 BA54 Adelaide Univ DipEd56. Cuddesdon Coll 56. **d** 58 **p** 59. C Portsea St Mary *Portsm* 58-60; Australia from 60; rtd 93. *8 Kapok Court, Parkwood, W Australia 6147* Tel Perth (9) 354 3536

BENNIE, Stanley James Gordon. b 43. Edin Univ MA65. Coll of Resurr Mirfield 66. **d** 68 **p** 69. C Ashington *Newc* 68-70; Prec St Andr Cathl Inverness *Mor* 70-74; Itinerant Priest 74-81; R Portsoy *Ab* 81-84; R Buckie 81-84; R Stornoway *Arg* from 84; R Eorrapaidh from 84; Miss to Seamen from 84. *St Peter's House, 10 Springfield Road, Stornoway, Isle of Lewis PA87 2PT* Tel (01851) 703609 E-mail stanley_bennie@msn.com

BENNISON, Philip Owen. b 42. Dur Univ BA64. Coll of Resurr Mirfield. **d** 66 **p** 67. C Guisborough *York* 66-67; C S Bank 67-71; C Thornaby on Tees St Paul 71-72; TV Thornaby on Tees 72-74; R Skelton in Cleveland 74-78; R Upleatham 75-78; Chapl Freeman Hosp Newc 78-84; V Ashington *Newc* 84-93; Chapl N Tees Health NHS Trust Stockton-on-Tees from 93; Perm to Offic *York* from 95. *North Tees General Hospital, Hardwick Road, Stockton-on-Tees, Cleveland TS19 8PE* Tel (01642) 617617

BENNISON, Timothy Paul. b 63. Aber Univ BD94 PhD98. Edin Th Coll 95. **d** 97. C St Andr Cathl *Ab* from 97; Asst Chapl Aberdeen Univ from 97. *21 College Bounds, Aberdeen AB24 3DX* Tel (01224) 492835 Mobile 0421-635889 Fax 492835

BENOY, Stephen Michael. b 66. Clare Coll Cam BA87 MA90. Trin Coll Bris BA93. **d** 96 **p** 97. C New Malden and Coombe *S'wark* from 96. *12 Rosebery Avenue, New Malden, Surrey KT3 4JS* Tel 0181-942 2523

BENSON, Christopher Hugh. b 53. Bath Academy of Art BA75 Keble Coll Ox BA78 MA87. Chich Th Coll 78. **d** 80 **p** 81. C Heavitree w Ex St Paul *Ex* 80-83; P-in-c Broadclyst 83-85; TV Pinhoe and Broadclyst 85-90; V Kingsteignton from 90; Chapl Plymouth Univ from 92. *The Vicarage, Daws Meadow, Kingsteignton, Newton Abbot, Devon TQ12 3UA* Tel (01626) 54915

BENSON, Donald. b 26. NW Ord Course 75. **d** 78 **p** 79. NSM Edge Hill St Dunstan *Liv* 78-84; NSM Liv St Paul Stoneycroft from 84. *114 Claremont Road, Liverpool L13 3HL* Tel 0151-733 8706

BENSON, Douglas Arthur Terrell. b 08. St Jo Coll Dur BA36. Lon Coll of Div 32. **d** 36 **p** 37. C Wolverhampton St Luke *Lich* 36-39; C Cheadle *Ches* 39-42 and 43-44; C New Ferry 42-43; P-in-c Stockton St Jas *Dur* 44-48; V Clapham *St Alb* 48-76; rtd 76; Perm to Offic *Ox* 76-91. *2 Beech Court, Tower Street, Taunton, Somerset TA1 4BH* Tel (01823) 337963

BENSON, Gareth Neil. b 47. HNC71 Jordan Hill Coll Glas FETC80. St And NSM Tr Scheme 77. **d** 81 **p** 82. NSM Glenrothes *St And* 81-88; NSM Kinghorn from 88; NSM Kirkcaldy from 88. *129 Waverley Drive, Glenrothes, Fife KY6 2LZ* Tel (01592) 759278

BENSON, George Patrick (Paddy). b 49. Ch Ch Ox BA70 Lon Univ BD77. All Nations Chr Coll 78 St Jo Coll Nottm 89. **d** 91 **p** 92. C Upton (Overchurch) *Ches* 91-95; V Barnston from 95. *The Vicarage, Barnston, Wirral, Merseyside L61 1BW* Tel 0151-648 1776

BENSON, Mrs Hilary Christine. b 51. Man Univ BA72 St Hugh's Coll Ox PGCE73. Trin Coll Bris DipHE83. **dss** 84 **d** 87 **p** 94. Starbeck *Ripon* 84-86; Birm St Martin w Bordesley St Andr *Birm* 86-87; NSM 87-91; NSM Brandwood from 91; Chapl Birm Univ from 92. *77 Doversley Road, Birmingham B14 6NN* Tel 0121-624 0217

BENSON, James Christopher Reginald. b 14. TCD BA35 MA60. **d** 37 **p** 38. C Belfast St Andr *Conn* 37-38; C Ballinderry 38-39; Dioc C *Clogh* 40-41; P-in-c Inishmacsaint 41-44; P-in-c Tempo 44-47; P-in-c Lack 47-51; P-in-c Derrybrusk 51-53; I Trillick 53-57; I Mullaghdun 57-61; rtd 61. *4 Morston Avenue, Bangor, Co Down BT20 3ES* Tel (01247) 461049

BENSON, John David. b 36. Lon Univ DipTh61 Hull Univ DipTh82. St Aid Birkenhead 58. **d** 61 **p** 62. C Kingston upon Hull St Martin *York* 61-65; C Marfleet 65-68; V Ingleby Greenhow 68-72; P-in-c Kildale 68-72; Asst Youth Chapl 68-72; Youth Chapl *Sheff* 72-78; V Thorne 78-91; V Totley from 91. *All Saints' Vicarage, 37 Sunnyvale Road, Sheffield S17 4FA* Tel 0114-236 2322

BENSON, John Patrick. b 51. Univ of Wales (Ban) BSc72. Trin Coll Bris 83. **d** 85 **p** 86. C Stoke Damerel *Ex* 85-88; P-in-c Petrockstowe, Petersmarland, Merton and Huish 88; TV Shebbear, Buckland Filleigh, Sheepwash etc 89-94; RD Torrington 93-94; P-in-c Newport, Bishops Tawton and Tawstock from 94. *The Vicarage, 40 Chichester Road, Newport, Barnstaple, Devon EX32 9EH* Tel (01271) 72733

BENSON, John Patrick. b 52. Ch Coll Cam BA73 MA76 PhD76. Trin Coll Bris 78. **d** 81 **p** 82. C Walmley *Birm* 81-84; C Chadkirk *Ches* 84-86; Singapore from 87. *St George's Church, Minden Road, Singapore 1024*

BENSON, Nicholas Henry. b 53. Trin Coll Bris. **d** 84 **p** 85. C Starbeck *Ripon* 84-86; C Birm St Martin w Bordesley St Andr *Birm* 86-91; Chapl to the Markets 86-91; V Brandwood from 91. *The Vicarage, 77 Doversley Road, Birmingham B14 6NN* Tel 0121-444 4631

BENSON, Peter Leslie. b 60. Leeds Univ BA81. Westcott Ho Cam 81. **d** 85 **p** 86. C Kippax w Allerton Bywater *Ripon* 85-88; C Potternewton 88-91; Asst Chapl St Jas Univ Hosp Leeds 91-94; Chapl Dewsbury Health Care NHS Trust from 94. *Dewsbury and District Hospital, Healds Road, Dewsbury, W Yorkshire WF13 4HS* Tel (01924) 465105

BENSON, Philip Steven. b 59. ACertCM79 LLCM80 Ulster Univ BSc81. S Dios Minl Tr Scheme 88. **d** 92 **p** 93. Producer Relig Broadcasting Dept BBC 91-94; NSM W Ealing St Jo w St Jas *Lon* 92-94; Lic to Offic *Ches* from 94; Relig Progr Producer BBC Man from 94. *4 Cranford Avenue, Knutsford, Cheshire WA16 0EB* Tel (01565) 652513

BENSON, Mrs Rachel Candia. b 43. JP76. TCD MA66 Lon Univ PGCE67 DipRS87. S'wark Ord Course 84. **d** 87 **p** 94. NSM Putney St Marg *S'wark* from 87. *34 St John's Avenue, London SW15 6AN* Tel 0181-788 3828

BENSON, Richard Edmund Miller. b 12. TCD BA35 MA50. **d** 36 **p** 37. C Tralee *L & K* 36-39; Dioc C Ardfert and Aghadoe 36-39; P-in-c Garvary *Clogh* 39-44; I Donagh 44-47; I Dromore 47-51; C Portadown St Mark *Arm* 51-52; I Sixmilecross w Termonmaguirke 69-76; rtd 76. *14 Dellmount Park, Bangor, Co Down BT20 4UA* Tel (01247) 455175

BENSON, Richard John. b 55. Birm Coll of Educn CertEd78. Ripon Coll Cuddesdon DipMin94. **d** 94 **p** 95. C Alford w Rigsby *Linc* from 94. *Bilsby Vicarage, Alford Road, Bilsby, Alford, Lincs LN13 9PY* Tel (01507) 462770

BENSON, Preb Riou George. b 14. QGM79. Linc Th Coll 38. **d** 39 **p** 40. C Penistone w Midhope *Wakef* 39-44; V Goff's Oak St Jas *St Alb* 44-50; V Burghill *Heref* 50-61; Chapl St Mary's Hosp Burghill 50-61; V Clun w Chapel Lawn *Heref* 61-79; Chapl St Cath Hosp Clun 61-75; V Bettws-y-Crwyn w Newcastle 63-79; P-in-c Clungunford 63-79; Preb Heref Cathl 65-91; P-in-c Bedstone w Hopton Castle 65-79; P-in-c Llanfair Waterdine w Stowe 73-79; P-in-c Clunbury 75-79; RD Clun Forest 68-72; V Clun w Chapel Lawn, Bettws-y-Crwyn and Newcastle 79; rtd 79; Perm to Offic *Heref* from 91. *Maiden Hill Wood, All Stretton, Church Stretton, Shropshire SY6 6LA* Tel (01694) 723610

BENSON, Roy William. b 32. Em Coll Saskatoon LTh76 MDiv76. **d** 76 **p** 77. Canada 76-79 and 80-83; C E Wickham *S'wark* 79-80; V Southea w Murrow and Parson Drove *Ely* 83-85; P-in-c Guyhirn w Ring's End 83-84; V 84-85; Canada from 85; rtd 97. *Box 594, Wakan, Saskatchewan, Canada*

BENSON, Terence Edward Benjamin. b 17. TCD BA37. **d** 41 **p** 42. Dioc C (Cork) *C, C & R* 41-42; P-in-c Corbally *L & K* 42-44 and 49-52; I Templeharry 44-46; Hd Master Killaloe Dioc Sch 46-52; I Brinny *C, C & R* 52-56; Perm to Offic *Clogh* from 56; rtd 79. *30 Willoughby Place, Enniskillen, Co Fermanagh BT74 7EX* Tel (01365) 322817

BENSON, William George. b 26. Lon Univ BA51 CertEd52 Ex Univ BA56. Sarum & Wells Th Coll 76. **d** 79 **p** 80. Hon C Heanton Punchardon w Marwood *Ex* 79-88; TR Newport, Bishops Tawton and Tawstock 88-94; rtd 94; Perm to Offic *Ex* from 94. *7 Brynsworthy Park, Roundswell, Barnstaple, Devon EX31 3RB* Tel (01271) 23547

BENSON, Canon William John Robinson. b 02. QUB BA25 DipHE40. **d** 26 **p** 27. C Belfast St Mich *Conn* 26-31; I 31-40; C Belfast St Mary Magd 31; I 40-56; I Belfast St Donard *D & D* 56-62; I Coleraine *Conn* 62-76; Preb Clonmethan St Patr Cathl Dublin 63-76; rtd 76. *16 Ratheane Avenue, Mountsandel Road, Coleraine, Co Londonderry BT52 1JH* Tel (01265) 51922

BENT, David Michael. b 55. Leeds Univ BSc77. Trin Coll Bris BA94. **d** 96 **p** 97. C Gorleston St Andr *Nor* from 96. *2 Elmgrove Road, Gorleston, Great Yarmouth, Norfolk NR31 7PP* Tel (01493) 659410

BENT, James. b 31. St Deiniol's Hawarden 79. **d** 81 **p** 82. C Prenton *Ches* 81-84; V W Derby St Jas *Liv* 84-88; NSM Newchurch and Glazebury 93-94; NSM Glazebury w Hollinfare 94-96; rtd 96. *133 Bright Street, Leigh, Lancs WN7 5QN* Tel (01942) 601065

BENT, Canon Michael Charles. b 31. Kelham Th Coll 51. **d** 55 **p** 56. C Wellingborough St Mary *Pet* 55-60; New Zealand 60-85 and from 89; Adn Taranaki 76-85; Dean H Trin Cathl Suva Fiji 85-89; Can St Pet Cathl Hamilton from 90. *34 Brooklands Road, New Plymouth, New Zealand* Tel Te Awamutu (7) 871-4627

BENTALL, Mrs Jill Margaret. b 44. MCSP66. S Dios Minl Tr Scheme 91. **d** 94 **p** 95. NSM W Andover *Win* 94-95; NSM Knights Enham from 95. *Old Farm Cottage, 102 Charlton, Andover, Hants SP10 4AN* Tel (01264) 365643

BENTHAM, John William. b 58. Loughb Univ BSc80 Nottm Univ LTh. St Jo Coll Nottm 82. **d** 85 **p** 86. C Burmantofts St Steph and St Agnes *Ripon* 85-88; C Horsforth 88-90; P-in-c Nottingham St Sav *S'well* 90-92; V from 92. *St Saviour's Vicarage, Arkwright Walk, The Meadow, Nottingham NG2 2JU* Tel 0115-986 4046

BENTHAM, Philip John (Ben). b 55. Hull Univ BA83 PGCE85. Trin Coll Bris 94. **d** 96 **p** 97. C Wrockwardine Deanery *Lich* from 96. *The Parsonage, Upton Magna, Shrewsbury SY4 4TZ* Tel (01743) 709283

✠**BENTLEY, The Rt Revd David Edward.** b 35. Leeds Univ BA56. Westcott Ho Cam 58. **d** 60 **p** 61 **c** 86. C Bris St Ambrose Whitehall *Bris* 60-62; C Guildf H Trin w St Mary *Guildf* 62-66; R Headley All SS 66-73; R Esher 73-86; RD Emly 77-82; Hon Can Guildf Cathl 80-86; Chmn Dioc Coun Soc Resp 80-86; Suff Bp Lynn *Nor* 86-93; Chmn Cand Cttee ACCM 87-91; ABM 91-93; Bp Glouc from 93. *Bishopscourt, Pitt Street, Gloucester GL1 2BQ* Tel (01452) 524598 Fax 310025 E-mail bshpglos@star.co.uk

BENTLEY, Edward John. b 35. Bris Univ BA61. Tyndale Hall Bris 58. **d** 63 **p** 64. C Wolverhampton St Luke *Lich* 63-66; BCMS 66-72; C Cheltenham St Mark *Glouc* 72-78; V Wallasey St Nic *Ches* from 78. *St Nicholas' Vicarage, 22 Groveland Road, Wallasey, Merseyside L45 8JY* Tel 0151-639 3589

BENTLEY, Frank Richard. b 41. K Coll Lon BD67 AKC67. **d** 68 **p** 69. C Feltham *Lon* 68-72; P-in-c Bethnal Green St Bart 72-77; R Bow w Bromley St Leon 77-88; P-in-c Mile End Old Town H Trin 77-88; P-in-c Bromley All Hallows 77-88; AD Tower Hamlets 83-88; TR E Ham w Upton Park St Alb *Chelmsf* 88-97; P-in-c Petersham *S'wark* from 97; Chapl HM Pris Latchmere Ho from 97. *99 Barnfield Avenue, Kingston upon Thames, Surrey KT2 5RG* Tel 0181-547 0923

BENTLEY, The Ven Frank William Henry. b 34. AKC57. **d** 58 **p** 59. C Shepton Mallet *B & W* 58-62; R Kingsdon w Podymore-Milton 62-66; P-in-c Yeovilton 62-66; P-in-c Babcary 64-66; V Wiveliscombe 66-76; RD Tone 73-76; V St Jo in Bedwardine *Worc* 76-84; RD Martley and Worc W 80-84; Hon Can Worc Cathl 81-84; P-in-c Worc St Mich 82-84; Adn Worc and Can Res Worc Cathl from 84; Chapl to The Queen from 94. *The Archdeacon's House, 56 Battenhall Road, Worcester WR5 2BQ* Tel (01905) 764446 Fax 612302

BENTLEY, Graham John. b 29. S'wark Ord Course 77. **d** 80 **p** 81. NSM Merton St Mary *S'wark* 80-83; C Balham St Mary 83-84; C Wimbledon 85-86; V Raynes Park St Sav 86-95; rtd 95; Perm to Offic *Guildf* from 95. *61 Clarence Road, Fleet, Aldershot, Hants GU13 9RY* Tel (01252) 628771

BENTLEY, Ian Robert. b 55. Sheff Univ BA76 Sheff City Poly PGCE78. St Jo Coll Dur CTMin95. **d** 95 **p** 96. C Mattishall w Mattishall Burgh, Welborne etc *Nor* from 95. *1 Robert Key Drive, Mattishall, Dereham, Norfolk NR20 3RW* Tel (01362) 858071

BENTLEY, Ian Ronald. b 51. BA79. Oak Hill Th Coll 76. **d** 79 **p** 80. C Northwood Em *Lon* 79-85; C St Marylebone All So w SS Pet and Jo 85-88; C Langham Place All So 88-91; V Eynsham and Cassington *Ox* from 91. *The Vicarage, 45 Acre End Street, Eynsham, Witney, Oxon OX8 1PF* Tel (01865) 881323

BENTLEY, James. b 37. TD. Mert Coll Ox BA59 BTh61 MA63 BD75 Sussex Univ DPhil80. St Steph Ho Ox 59. **d** 62 **p** 63. C Elton St Steph *Man* 62-64; C Swinton St Pet 64-66; CF (TA) 65-82; R Stretford All SS *Man* 66-73; V Oldham St Mary w St Pet 73-77; Sen Chapl Eton Coll 79-82. *6 Arborfield Close, Slough, Berks SL1 2JW* Tel (01753) 573522

BENTLEY, Mrs Lesley. b 55. RMN80 Univ of Wales (Lamp) BA76 Nottm Univ MTh82. St Jo Coll Nottm DPS83. **dss** 82 **d** 87 **p** 94. Mickleover St Jo *Derby* 82-84; Thornton *Liv* 84-87; Par Dn 87-89; Dir Diaconal Mins 89-92; Par Dn Farnworth 92-94; C 94-95; V Westbrook St Phil from 95. *St Philip's Vicarage, 89 Westbrook Crescent, Warrington WA5 5TE* Tel (01925) 574932

BENTLEY, Paul. b 48. Sarum & Wells Th Coll DipTh93. **d** 93 **p** 94. C Ex St Dav *Ex* 93-96; P-in-c Marlpool *Derby* from 96; Chapl Heanor, Langley Mill and District Hosps from 96. *Marlpool Vicarage, 85 Ilkeston Road, Heanor, Derbyshire DE75 7BP* Tel (01773) 712097

BENTLEY, William. Univ Coll Dur BA39 DipTh40 MA42. St Andr Whittlesford 40. **d** 41 **p** 42. C Chester le Street *Dur* 41-46; C Bishopwearmouth St Mich 46-49; V Auckland St Pet 49-59; R Hartlepool St Hilda 59-82; Chapl St Hilda's Hosp Hartlepool 59-82; rtd 82. *4 Lindisfarne, High Shincliffe, Durham DH1 2PH* Tel 0191-384 9876

BENTON, John Anthony. b 27. Ex Coll Ox BA48 MA52. Sarum Th Coll 49. **d** 50 **p** 51. C N Keyham *Ex* 50-52; C Tavistock and Gulworthy 52-55; C Heavitree 55-56; R Lower Gravenhurst *St Alb* 56-61; V Silsoe 56-61; V Upper Gravenhurst 56-61; S Africa 61-68; R Moretonhampstead *Ex* 68-74; RD Moreton 73-74; R Holsworthy w Cookbury and Hollacombe 74-80; TR Withycombe Raleigh 80-92; RD Aylesbeare 84-89; rtd 92; Perm to Offic *Ex* from 92. *38 Wreford's Close, Exeter EX4 5AY* Tel (01392) 211428

BENTON, Canon Michael John. b 38. Lon Univ BSc60 FRSA93 MSOSc. Sarum & Wells Th Coll 72. **d** 74 **p** 74. Hon C Weeke *Win* 74-76; Sen Lect K Alfred Coll Win 74-76; C Bursledon 76-78; R Over Wallop w Nether Wallop 78-83; Dir of Educn 79-96; R Win St Lawr and St Maurice w St Swithun 83-90; Hon Can Win Cathl from 89; P-in-c Kingsclere from 96. *The Vicarage, Fox's Lane, Kingsclere, Newbury, Berks RG15 8SL* Tel (01635) 298272

BENWELL, John Desmond. Jes Coll Cam BA54 MA58 Sheff Univ DSocStuds58 Lon Univ CASS59. St Jo Coll Nottm CertCS89. **d** 89 **p** 89. Somalia 89-90; Chapl Fontainebleau *Eur* 91-93; Hon C Portswood Ch Ch *Win* from 93. *14 Furzedown Road, Southampton SO17 1PN* Tel (01703) 557622

BENWELL, Dr Michael Patrick. b 55. Jes Coll Cam BA77 Glas Univ PhD80. Sarum & Wells Th Coll BTh92. **d** 92 **p** 93. C Eastleigh *Win* 92-95; Chapl Leeds Metrop Univ *Ripon* from 95. *10 St Chad's Rise, Leeds LS6 3QE* Tel 0113-275 8229 E-mail m.benwell@lmu.ac.uk

✠**BENZIES, The Rt Revd Keith John.** b 38. OBE93. Glas Univ MA60. Sarum Th Coll 60. **d** 62 **p** 63 **c** 82. C Kingston upon Hull St Nic *York* 62-66; Madagascar from 66; Prin Ambatoharanana Th Coll 66-79; Bp Antsiranana from 82. *Misiona Anglikana, BP 278, 201 Antsiranana, Madagascar* Tel Diego Suarez (8) 22650

BENZIES, Neil Graham. Bede Coll Dur. Cranmer Hall Dur. **d** 95 **p** 96. NSM Stockton St Pet *Dur* from 95. *62 Fairwell Road, Stockton-on-Tees, Cleveland TS19 7HX* Tel (01642) 582322

BERDINNER, Clifford. b 24. SS Mark & Jo Coll Plymouth BA88. **d** 64 **p** 65. C Leic St Pet *Leic* 64-67; R Heather 67-72; NSM Totnes and Berry Pomeroy *Ex* 86-91; NSM Totnes, Bridgetown and Berry Pomeroy etc 91-94; rtd 89; Perm to Offic *Ex* from 89. *Hilltop Cottage, Ashprington, Totnes, Devon TQ9 7UW* Tel (01803) 732518

BERESFORD, Charles Edward. b 45. St Jo Coll Nottm. **d** 86 **p** 87. C Bushbury *Lich* 86-90; TV Glascote and Stonydelph from 90. *The New Vicarage, Bamford Street, Tamworth, Staffs B77 2AS* Tel (01827) 62612

BERESFORD, Eric Brian. b 57. Liv Univ BSc78 Ox Univ BA82 MA86. Wycliffe Hall Ox. **d** 82 **p** 83. C Upton (Overchurch) *Ches* 82-85; Canada from 85; Asst Prof Ethics McGill Univ Montreal from 88. *600 Jarvis Street, Toronto, Ontario, Canada M4Y 2J6*

BERESFORD, Mrs Florence. b 33. Cranmer Hall Dur 75. **dss** 78 **d** 87 **p** 94. Eighton Banks *Dur* 78-86; Lobley Hill 86-87; Par Dn 87-90; Par Dn Chester le Street 90-91; rtd 91. *Gilead, 39 Picktree Lodge, Chester-le-Street, Co Durham DH3 4DH* Tel 0191-388 7425

BERESFORD, Peter Marcus de la Poer. b 49. Cranmer Hall Dur 74. **d** 77 **p** 78. C Walney Is *Carl* 77-80; C Netherton 80-83; TV Wednesfield *Lich* 83-88; TV Rugby St Andr *Cov* from 88. *The Vicarage, St Johns Avenue, Hillmorton, Rugby, Warks CV22 5HR* Tel (01788) 577331

BERESFORD-DAVIES, Thomas. b 14. Univ of Wales (Lamp) BD67. **d** 42 **p** 43. C Glouc St Mary de Lode and St Nic *Glouc* 42-46; C Langley Marish *Ox* 46; C Glouc St Jas *Glouc* 46-48; V Church Honeybourne w Cow Honeybourne 48-51; P-in-c Pauntley w Upleadon 51-62; V Twigworth w Down Hatherley 63-85; rtd 85; P-in-c Glouc St Mark *Glouc* 86-87; Perm to Offic from 87. *Islwyn, Tewkesbury Road, Twigworth, Gloucester GL2 9PQ* Tel (01452) 730362

BERESFORD-PEIRSE, Mark de la Poer. b 45. Qu Coll Birm 73. **d** 76 **p** 77. C Garforth *Ripon* 76-79; C Beeston 79-83; V Barton and Manfield w Cleasby 83-90; V Pannal w Beckwithshaw from 90; Dioc Chapl MU from 91. *The Vicarage, 21 Crimple Meadows, Pannal, Harrogate, N Yorkshire HG3 1EL* Tel (01423) 870202

BERG, John Russell. b 36. MBE78. Sarum Th Coll 57. **d** 60 **p** 61. C Ipswich St Aug *St E* 60-64; C Whitton and Thurleston w Akenham 64-65; Miss to Seamen from 65; Hong Kong 65-72; Japan from 72. *Port PO Box 139, Naka-ku, Yokohama 231-91, Japan* Tel Yokohama (45) 662-1871 Fax 641-5772

BERG, Canon Paul Michael. b 31. Lon Univ BA53. Oak Hill Th Coll 54. **d** 56 **p** 57. C Woodford Wells *Chelmsf* 56-60; V Tittensor *Lich* 60-65; V Rainham *Chelmsf* 65-74; R Wennington 65-74; V Clifton Ch Ch w Em *Bris* 74-97; Hon Can Bris Cathl 82-97; RD Clifton 87-93; rtd 97. *32 Old Farm Road, Nether Stowey, Bridgwater, Somerset TA5 1PE* Tel (01278) 733032

BERGER, Otto. b 19. CEng FIMechE. Oak Hill Th Coll. **d** 83 **p** 84. NSM Dovercourt and Parkeston *Chelmsf* 83-93; Perm to Offic from 93. *35 Gordon Road, Dovercourt, Harwich, Essex CO12 3TL* Tel (01255) 502806

BERGQUIST, Canon Anders Karim. b 58. Peterho Cam BA79 MA83 PhD90. St Steph Ho Ox BA85 MA90. **d** 86 **p** 87. C Abbots Langley *St Alb* 86-89; C Cambridge St Mary Less *Ely* 89; Hon C 89-97; Tutor Westcott Ho Cam 89-95; Vice-Prin 95-97; Minl Development Officer *St Alb* from 97; Can Res St Alb from 97. *7 Corder Close, St Albans, Herts AL3 4NH* Tel (01727) 841116

BERKSHIRE, Archdeacon of. *See* HILL, The Ven Michael Arthur

BERMUDA, Archdeacon of. *See* HOLLIS, The Ven Arnold Thaddeus

BERMUDA, Bishop of. *See* RATTERAY, The Rt Revd Alexander Ewen

BERNARD, Brother. *See* APPS, Canon Michael John

BERNARDI, Frederick John. b 33. JP75 KCT89. Chich Th Coll 55. **d** 58 **p** 59. C Blackb St Luke *Blackb* 58-60; C Ribbleton 60-63; V Brinsley w Underwood *S'well* 63-66; Barbados 67-71; V Sparkbrook St Agatha *Birm* 71-77; P-in-c Sparkbrook Ch Ch 73-75; V Haywards Heath St Wilfrid *Chich* 77-80; TR 80-87; Chapl Madrid *Eur* 87-90; NSM Tooting All SS *S'wark* 90-91; V Hanger Hill Ascension and W Twyford St Mary *Lon* 91-95; rtd 95; Perm to Offic *Chich* from 95. *13 Kingmere, South Terrace, Littlehampton, W Sussex BN17 5LD* Tel (01903) 713543

BERNERS-WILSON (or SILLETT), Mrs Angela Veronica Isabel. b 54. St Andr Univ MTh76 St Jo Coll Dur DipTh78. **dss** 79 **d** 87 **p** 94. Southgate Ch Ch *Lon* 79-82; St Marylebone Ch Ch 82-84; Ind Chapl 82-84; Chapl Thames Poly *S'wark* 84-91; Chapl Bris Univ *Bris* 91-95; C Bris St Mich and St Paul 94-95; P-in-c Colerne w N Wraxall from 95. *The Rectory, Market Place, Colerne, Chippenham, Wilts SN14 8DF* Tel (01225) 742742

BERNERS-WILSON, Daniel Downing. b 10. ALCD37. **d** 36 **p** 37. C Southsea St Jude *Portsm* 36-38; C Cambridge H Trin *Ely* 38-39; Perm to Offic *Portsm* 39-44; Lic to Offic *Lon* 44-53; Chapl RAFVR 41-44; Officer for Relig Tr Nat Assn of Boys' Clubs 45-46; Warden Ford Castle Nat Assn of Boys' Clubs 45-48; Chapl Eton Coll 49-53; R Frant *Chich* 53-72; rtd 72. *Hamstede, Parkham Hill, Rotherfield, Crowborough, E Sussex TN6 3HR*

BERRETT, Paul Graham. b 49. St Chad's Coll Dur BA70. St Steph Ho Ox 71. **d** 74 **p** 75. C Hockerill *St Alb* 74-77; C Leighton Buzzard 77-81; C Leighton Buzzard w Eggington, Hockliffe etc 81-83; V Bournemouth St Fran *Win* from 83. *St Francis's Clergy House, Charminster Road, Bournemouth BH8 9SH* Tel (01202) 529336

BERRIDGE, Grahame Richard. b 38. S'wark Ord Course 71. **d** 72 **p** 73. NSM Beddington *S'wark* 72-75; NSM Merton St Jas 75-81; Perm to Offic from 81. *11 Cedar Walk, Kingswood, Tadworth, Surrey KT20 6HW* Tel (01737) 358882

BERRIMAN, Gavin Anthony. b 60. S'wark Ord Course 87. **d** 90 **p** 91. C Greenwich St Alfege w St Pet and St Paul *S'wark* 90-94; V Lee St Aug from 94. *St Augustine's Vicarage, 336 Baring Road, London SE12 0DU* Tel 0181-857 4941

BERROW, Philip Rees. b 36. St D Coll Lamp 58. **d** 62 **p** 63. C Neath w Llantwit *Llan* 62-66; CF 67-87; R Welford w Weston and Clifford Chambers *Glouc* 87-94; P-in-c Badminton w Lt Badminton, Acton Turville etc from 94. *The Vicarage, Badminton, Avon GL9 1ET* Tel (01454) 218427

BERRY, Adrian Charles. b 50. Mert Coll Ox BA71 MA. Cuddesdon Coll 72. **d** 75 **p** 76. C Prestbury *Glouc* 75-79; C Cirencester 79-83; V Cam w Stinchcombe 83-88; Dioc Ecum Officer 83-95; P-in-c Twyning 88-95; R Leckhampton St Pet from 95. *The Rectory, Leckhampton, Cheltenham, Glos GL51 5XX* Tel (01242) 513647

BERRY, Alan Peter. b 36. NW Ord Course 74. **d** 77 **p** 78. NSM Headingley *Ripon* 77-78; NSM Chapel Allerton 78-91; Perm to Offic from 91. *17 High Street, Spofforth, Harrogate, N Yorkshire HG3 1BQ* Tel (01937) 590503

BERRY, Anthony Nigel. b 53. Lon Bible Coll BA80 Sarum & Wells Th Coll 84. **d** 87 **p** 88. NSM Howell Hill *Guildf* 87-90; C 90; C Farnham 90-93; R Abinger cum Coldharbour from 93. *The Rectory, Abinger Common, Dorking, Surrey RH5 6HZ* Tel (01306) 730746

BERRY, David Llewellyn Edward. b 39. St Jo Coll Cam BA61 MA65. Wells Th Coll 64. **d** 66 **p** 67. C Poplar All SS w St Frideswide *Lon* 66-69; C Ellesmere Port *Ches* 69-73; V Brafferton w Pilmoor and Myton on Swale *York* 73-79; P-in-c Thormanby 78-79; R Skelton in Cleveland 79; R Skelton w Upleatham 79-87; V Barrow St Aid *Carl* 87-97; Chapl Rotterdam w Schiedam *Eur* from 97. *Bolkruid 41, 3068 DJ, Rotterdam, The Netherlands* Tel Rotterdam (10) 330 2474 or 476 4043

BERRY, Geoffrey Wilbur Ronald. b 22. Ridley Hall Cam 54. **d** 56 **p** 57. C Northwood Em *Lon* 56-59; V Poplar St Matthias 59-70; V Westacre *Nor* 70-79; R Gayton Thorpe w E Walton 71-79; P-in-c Maresfield *Chich* 79; R 79-87; P-in-c Nutley 79; V 79-87; rtd 87; Perm to Offic *Bris* from 87. *13 Manor Park, Great Somerford, Chippenham, Wilts SN15 5EQ* Tel (01249) 720530

BERRY, Graham Renwick (Silvanus). b 24. Univ of NZ BA54. Coll of Resurr Mirfield 55. **d** 57 **p** 58. C Earl's Court St Cuth w St Matthias *Lon* 57-61; Lic to Offic *Wakef* from 63; CR from 64; Prior 75-87; Superior from 87; Lic to Offic *Ripon* 68-75; rtd 94. *House of the Resurrection, Mirfield, W Yorkshire WF14 0BN* Tel (01924) 494318 Fax 492738

BERRY, John. b 41. Dur Univ BA62. Oak Hill Th Coll 63. **d** 65 **p** 66. C Burnage St Marg *Man* 65-68; C Middleton 68-70; Travelling Sec IVF 70-73; V Derby St Pet *Derby* 73-76; P-in-c Derby Ch Ch and H Trin 73-76; V Derby St Pet and Ch Ch w H Trin 76-81; Bp's Officer for Evang *Carl* 81-86; P-in-c Bampton and Mardale 81-86; TR N Wingfield, Pilsley and Tupton *Derby* 86-89; Evang Sec Evang Alliance 89-92; V Guernsey H Trin *Win* from 92. *Holy Trinity Vicarage, Brock Road, St Peter Port, Guernsey, Channel Islands GY1 1RS* Tel (01481) 724382

BERRY, Michael. b 22. Ex Coll Ox BA49 DipEd53 MA54. Westcott Ho Cam 69. **d** 71 **p** 72. C Didcot *Ox* 71-75; R Farthinghoe w Hinton-in-the-Hedges w Steane *Pet* 75-96; rtd 96. *5 Park Road, Aldeburgh, Suffolk IP15 5EX*

BERRY, Paul Edward. b 56. N Ord Course 91. **d** 94 **p** 95. C Halliwell St Luke *Man* from 94. *7 Russell Close, Bolton BL1 4BL* Tel (01204) 527319

BERRY, The Very Revd Peter Austin. b 35. Keble Coll Ox BA59 BTh61 MA63. St Steph Ho Ox 59. **d** 62 **p** 63. C Cov St Mark *Cov* 62-66; Dioc Community Relns Officer 64-70; C Cov Cathl 66-73; Can Res Cov Cathl 73-86; Vice-Provost Cov Cathl 77-86; Bp's Adv for Community Relns 77-86; Provost Birm from 86. *The Provost's House, 16 Pebble Mill Road, Birmingham B5 7SA* Tel 0121-472 0709 or 236 4333 Fax 212 0868

BERRY, Phillipa Raines. b 51. Man Univ BA72 Univ of Wales (Cardiff) CertEd73. St Jo Coll Nottm 82. **d** 95 **p** 96. NSM Leic H Apostles *Leic* from 95. *273 Fosse Road South, Leicester LE3 1AE* Tel 0116-291 8272

BERRY, Miss Susan Patricia (Sue). b 49. Bris Univ BA70 Hughes Hall Cam PGCE72. Qu Coll Birm 77. **dss** 86 **d** 87 **p** 94. Chapl Barn Fellowship Whatcombe Ho 86-89; Chapl Lee Abbey 89-91; Lic to Offic *Ex* 89-91; Perm to Offic *Ox* 93; NSM Thatcham 93-95; Community of St Fran from 95. *The Community of St Francis, Compton Durville, South Petherton, Somerset TA13 5ES* Tel (01460) 240473

BERRY, Timothy Hugh. b 50. Reading Univ BA72. Oak Hill NSM Course 81. **d** 84 **p** 85. NSM Swanley St Paul *Roch* 84-88; Perm to Offic *S'wark* 86-88; C Gorleston St Andr *Nor* 88-93; V Grain w Stoke *Roch* 93-95; rtd 95. *39 Claremont Road, Swanley, Kent BR8 7RF* Tel (01332) 662716

BERRY, William James. b 25. Bps' Coll Cheshunt 62. **d** 63 **p** 64. C Redbourn *St Alb* 63-65; C Hatfield Hyde 65-67; V Lidlington 67-72; R Dunton w Wrestlingworth and Eyeworth 72-83; V Earby *Bradf* 83-89; rtd 89; Perm to Offic *Heref* from 91. *34 Severn Way, Cressage, Shrewsbury SY5 6DS* Tel (01952) 510462

BERRYMAN, William Arthur David. b 47. Lon Univ BD69 St Pet Coll Ox CertEd71. Sarum & Wells Th Coll 75. **d** 76 **p** 77. Asst Master Preston Sch Yeovil 76-80; Hon C Yeovil St Mich *B & W* 76-80; C Ex St Dav *Ex* 80-83; Chapl Ex Coll 80-83; Chapl RN 83-89; V Highertown and Baldhu *Truro* 89-95; TR Cov E *Cov* 95-97; TR The Abbey Leicester *Leic* from 97; P-in-c Leic St Paul from 97. *1 Finch Way, Narborough, Leicester LE9 5TP* Tel 0116-286 5503

BERSON, Alan Charles. b 31. Univ of Michigan BA52 MA53 Lon Univ PhD62. St Steph Ho Ox 63. **d** 65 **p** 66. C Leeds St Pet *Ripon* 65-68; C St Giles-in-the-Fields *Lon* 68; Lic to Offic 69-80; Perm to Offic 80-88; rtd 96. *74 Ridgmount Gardens, London WC1E 7AX* Tel 0171-636 1990

BERSWEDEN, Judith Anne. b 63. St Jo Coll Dur BA84. Ripon Coll Cuddesdon BA92. **d** 92 **p** 94. Par Dn Mirfield *Wakef* 92-94; NSM Roberttown from 94. *The Vicarage, Church Road, Liversedge, W Yorkshire WF15 7PF* Tel (01924) 404743

BERSWEDEN, Nils Herry Stephen. b 57. Newc Univ BSc78. Ripon Coll Cuddesdon 88. **d** 90 **p** 91. C Mirfield *Wakef* 90-93; P-in-c Purlwell 93-94; P-in-c Roberttown from 94. *The Vicarage, Church Road, Liversedge, W Yorkshire WF15 7PF* Tel (01924) 404743

BERTRAM, Preb Richard Henry. b 27. TCD BA50 MA64. CITC 50. **d** 53 **p** 54. C Sligo Cathl *K, E & A* 53-56; C Dublin Booterstown *D & G* 56-58; I Stranorlar w Meenglas and Kilteevogue *D & R* 58-65; I Dublin St Cath w St Jas *D & G* 65-73; I Dublin Irishtown 73-74; I Dublin Irishtown w Donnybrook from 74; Can Ch Ch Cathl Dublin 86-92; Preb from 92; Treas from 95. *4 Ailesbury Grove, Dublin 4, Irish Republic* Tel Dublin (1) 269 2090

BESSANT, Brian Keith. b 32. Roch Th Coll 65. **d** 67 **p** 68. C Chatham St Wm *Roch* 67-70; C Cove St Jo *Guildf* 71-74; V

Frimley Green from 74. *The Vicarage, 37 Sturt Road, Frimley Green, Camberley, Surrey GU16 6HY* Tel (01252) 835179

BESSANT, Idwal Brian. b 39. Cardiff Coll of Art NDD61 ATD62 Univ of Wales DipTh68. St Mich Coll Llan 65. **d** 68 **p** 69. C Llantwit Major and St Donat's *Llan* 68-73; C Llangammarch w Garth, Llanlleonfel etc *S & B* 73-77; C Crickhowell 77-78; CMS Miss 78-83; Cyprus 80-83; V Crickhowell w Cwmdu and Tretower *S & B* 83-91; RD Crickhowell 86-91; V Llanwrtyd w Llanddulas in Tir Abad etc from 91. *The Vicarage, Llanwrtyd Wells LD5 4SA* Tel (01591) 3231

BESSANT, Simon David. b 56. Sheff Univ BMus77. St Jo Coll Nottm DipTh79. **d** 81 **p** 82. C Litherland St Jo and St Jas *Liv* 81-84; C Holloway Em w Hornsey Road St Barn *Lon* 84-86; C Holloway St Mark w Em 86-91; V Blackb Redeemer *Blackb* from 91; Acting RD Blackb from 97. *The Redeemer Vicarage, 200 Old Bank Lane, Blackburn BB1 2HU* Tel (01254) 52782 E-mail s.d.bessant@dial.pipex.com

BESSENT, Stephen Lyn. b 53. Bris Univ BA75. Wycliffe Hall Ox 75. **d** 77 **p** 78. C Patchway *Bris* 77-80; TV Swindon St Jo and St Andr 80-83; TV Eston w Normanby *York* 83-90; V Cogges *Ox* 90-94; P-in-c S Leigh 90-94; V Cogges and S Leigh from 94. *Cogges Priory, Church Lane, Witney, Oxon OX8 6LA* Tel (01993) 702155

BEST, Miss Karen Belinda. b 62. Qu Coll Birm 92. **d** 94 **p** 95. C Southall Green St Jo *Lon* 94-97; C Northolt Park St Barn from 97. *3 Vernon Rise, Greenford, Middx UB6 0EQ* Tel 0181-723 8140

BEST, Canon Raymond. b 42. Sarum & Wells Th Coll 71. **d** 74 **p** 75. C Whorlton *Newc* 74-78; C Seaton Hirst 78-83; C Benwell St Jas 83-85; TV Benwell Team 85-89; V Walker from 89; P-in-c Byker St Martin from 96; Hon Can Newc Cathl from 97. *Walker Vicarage, Middle Street, Newcastle upon Tyne NE6 4BX* Tel 0191-262 3666

BESTELINK, William Meindert Croft. b 48. Hull Univ BA70. Cuddesdon Coll 71. **d** 73 **p** 74. C Holt *Nor* 73-74; C E Dereham w Hoe 74-76; C Nor St Andr 76-80; R Colby w Banningham and Tuttington 80-90; R Felmingham 80-90; R Suffield 80-90; P-in-c Roydon St Remigius from 90. *The Rectory, High Road, Roydon, Diss, Norfolk IP22 3RD* Tel (01379) 642180

BESTLEY, Peter Mark. b 60. Qu Coll Cam MA Univ of Wales (Cardiff) MPhil92. St Mich Coll Llan 89. **d** 92 **p** 93. C Hampton All SS *Lon* 92-95; Chapl W Middx Univ Hosp NHS Trust from 95. *The Chaplain's Office, West Middlesex University Hospital, Twickenham Road, Isleworth, Middx TW7 6AF* Tel 0181-560 2121

BESWETHERICK, Andrew Michael. b 55. SS Mark & Jo Coll Plymouth BEd80. S'wark Ord Course 87. **d** 90 **p** 91. Dep Hd Maze Hill Sch Greenwich from 88; NSM Blackheath St Jo *S'wark* from 90. *112 Charlton Road, London SE7 7EY* Tel 0181-853 0853

BESWICK, Canon Colin Edward. b 28. Leeds Univ BA51 Ex Univ MA75. Sarum Th Coll 58. **d** 60 **p** 61. C Shrewsbury St Mary *Lich* 60-63; Min Can Worc Cathl *Worc* 63-73; Hon Can Worc Cathl 78-84; R Bredon w Bredon's Norton 73-79; RD Pershore 76-79; Dir of Min 79-84; P-in-c Overbury w Alstone, Teddington and Lt Washbourne 81-84; Can Res Nor Cathl *Nor* 84-93; P-in-c Nor St Mary in the Marsh 84-87; rtd 93. *Medhurst, Peasmarsh Road, Rye, E Sussex TN31 7UL* Tel (01797) 226817

BESWICK, Canon Gary Lancelot. b 38. ALCD63. **d** 63 **p** 64. C Walthamstow St Mary *Chelmsf* 63-67; C Laisterdyke *Bradf* 67-70; V Idle H Trin 70-78; Area Sec (NW England) SAMS 78-92; Area Sec (N Thames) from 92; Lic to Offic *Man* 78-92; Lic to Offic *St Alb* from 92; Hon Can N Argentina from 87; Perm to Offic *Chelmsf* from 92. *10 Valeside, Hertford SG14 2AR* Tel (01992) 553274

BESWICK, Jonathan Warwick. b 67. Westcott Ho Cam. **d** 95 **p** 96. C Dudley St Fran *Worc* 95-96; C Brookfield St Anne, Highgate Rise *Lon* from 96; C Brookfield St Mary from 96. *106 Highgate West Hill, London N6 6AP* Tel 0181-340 5190

BESWICK, Dr Joseph Hubert. b 25. Birm Univ MB, ChB48 Lon Univ DipTh58. **d** 59 **p** 60. Lic to Offic *S'well* from 59. *38 Hallams Lane, Beeston, Nottingham NG9 5FH* Tel 0115-925 6719

BESWICK, Canon Walter. b 13. St Aid Birkenhead 46. **d** 48 **p** 49. C Acomb St Steph *York* 48-52; R Bulmer 52-64; R Dalby w Whenby 64-85; R Terrington 64-85; RD Malton 75-80; Can and Preb York Minster 79-95; rtd 85; Perm to Offic *York* from 85. *23 Princess Court, Princess Road, Malton, N Yorkshire YO17 0HL* Tel (01653) 696128

BETSON, Stephen. b 53. Sarum & Wells Th Coll 89. **d** 91 **p** 92. C Sittingbourne St Mich *Cant* 91-95; V Fairweather Green *Bradf* from 95. *St Saviour's Vicarage, Ings Way, Bradford, W Yorkshire BD8 0LU* Tel (01274) 544807

BETTELEY, John Richard. b 46. Sarum & Wells Th Coll 81. **d** 83 **p** 84. C Auchterarder *St And* 83-85; C Dunblane 83-85; Chapl RAF 85-89; R Callander *St And* 89-94; P-in-c Aberfoyle 89-94; P-in-c Doune 89-94; R Ballachulish *Arg* from 94; R Glencoe from 94; R Onich from 94. *The Rectory, Glencoe, Argyll PA39 4HP* Tel (01855) 811335

BETTIS, Canon Margaret Jean. b 42. Gilmore Ho 72. **dss** 77 **d** 87 **p** 94. Kenya 77-79; Tutor Crowther Hall CMS Tr Coll Selly Oak 79-82; Hodge Hill *Birm* 82-87; Par Dn 87; Par Dn Flitwick *St Alb* 87-93; P-in-c Westoning w Tingrith 93-94; V from 94; Hon Can St Alb from 97. *The Vicarage, Church Road, Westoning, Bedford MK45 5JW* Tel (01525) 713703

BETTRIDGE, Canon Graham Winston. b 39. Kelham Th Coll 60. **d** 65 **p** 66. C Burley in Wharfedale *Bradf* 65-67; C Baildon 67-70; V Harden and Wilsden 70-81; TR Kirkby Lonsdale *Carl* from 81; Hon Can Carl Cathl from 89; Chapl Cumbria Constabulary from 96. *The Rectory, Vicarage Lane, Kirkby Lonsdale, Carnforth, Lancs LA6 2BA* Tel (015242) 71320

BETTS, Alan John. b 55. Portsm Poly BSc77 St Martin's Coll Lanc PGCE81. St Jo Coll Nottm DTS93. **d** 93 **p** 94. C Cannock *Lich* from 93. *9 Condor Grove, Heath Hayes, Cannock, Staffs WS12 5YB* Tel (01543) 270107

BETTS, Anthony Clive (Tony). b 40. Wells Th Coll 63. **d** 65 **p** 66. C Leeds All Hallows w St Simon *Ripon* 65-67; C Wetherby 67-70; C Adel 70-73; V Leeds All SS 73-79; V Leeds Richmond Hill 79-84; R Knaresborough from 84; Chapl Knaresborough Hosp from 84; RD Harrogate *Ripon* from 95. *The Rectory, High Bond End, Knaresborough, N Yorkshire HG5 9BT* Tel (01423) 865273

BETTS, Canon Anthony Percy. b 26. Lon Univ BD52. ALCD52. **d** 52 **p** 53. C Guildf St Sav *Guildf* 52-56; C Hanworth St Geo *Lon* 56-59; V Derby St Aug *Derby* 59-74; RD Derby 71-74; V Bracebridge *Linc* 74-83; P-in-c Fenny Bentley, Thorpe and Tissington *Derby* 83; P-in-c Kniveton w Hognaston 83; R Fenny Bentley, Kniveton, Thorpe and Tissington 83-91; RD Ashbourne 86-91; Hon Can Derby Cathl 87-91; rtd 91; Perm to Offic *Derby* from 91. *Otterbourne House, Windley, Belper, Derbyshire DE56 2LP* Tel (01773) 550677

BETTS, David John. b 38. Lon Univ BSc61. Oak Hill Th Coll 63. **d** 65 **p** 66. C Slough *Ox* 65-70; C Welling *Roch* 70-75; V Swanley St Paul 75-93; R Nottingham St Nic *S'well* from 93. *18 Lenton Road, The Park, Nottingham NG7 1DU* Tel 0115-941 1383

BETTS, Edmund John. b 51. St Chad's Coll Dur BA72 Lanc Univ MA81. Qu Coll Birm DipTh75 DPS76. **d** 76 **p** 77. C Leagrave *St Alb* 76-79; Asst Chapl R Albert Hosp Lanc 79-81; Chapl Lea Castle Hosp and Kidderminster Gen Hosp 81-86; Prov Officer Educn for Min Ch in Wales 86-88; Exec Sec for Min 88-90; TR Haverhill w Withersfield, the Wrattings etc *St E* from 90; RD Clare from 91. *The Rectory, 10 Hopton Rise, Haverhill, Suffolk CB9 7FS* Tel (01440) 708768

BETTS, George William John. b 23. Ex Univ BA51. Westcott Ho Cam 51. **d** 53 **p** 54. C Wallsend St Luke *Newc* 53-54; C Benwell St Jas 54-56; C Plumstead St Jas w St Jo *S'wark* 56; C Peckham St Andr w All SS 56; C Eltham St Jo 57-60; C Findon *Chich* 60-67; Rhodesia 67-68; C Sherborne w Castleton and Lillington *Sarum* 68-69; C Brookfield St Anne, Highgate Rise *Lon* 69; rtd 88. *72 Westmount Road, London SE9 1JE* Tel 0181-850 2116

BETTS, Ivan Ringland. b 38. TCD BA61 MA67. **d** 62 **p** 63. C Ballyholme *D & D* 62-65; C Dundela 65-69; Miss to Seamen 69-73; Sudan 69-71; Trinidad and Tobago 71-73; C Drumglass *Arm* 73-81; I Augher w Newtownsaville and Eskrahoole *Clogh* 81-86; Bp's C Ballymacarrett St Martin *D & D* from 86. *7 Greenwood Park, Belfast BT4 3NJ* Tel (01232) 658659

BETTS, Mrs Patricia Joyce (Pat). b 43. St Kath Coll Lon CertEd64 DipTLSA85 FRSA. S Dios Minl Tr Scheme 90. **d** 96 **p** 97. NSM Bath Widcombe *B & W* from 96. *Hunters Lodge, North Road, Bath BA2 6HP* Tel (01225) 464918

BETTS, Paul Robert. b 31. Lon Univ BSc51. Oak Hill Th Coll 53. **d** 56 **p** 57. C Plymouth St Jude *Ex* 56-59; C Cheltenham St Mark *Glouc* 59-63; V Finchley St Paul Long Lane *Lon* 63-76; Warden St Columba Cen Cam 76-79; R Datchworth w Tewin *St Alb* 79-96; rtd 96; Perm to Offic *Ex* from 96. *2 Penny Close, Exminster, Exeter EX6 8SU* Tel (01392) 824403

BETTS, Richard Alan. b 56. ACA83 UEA BA77. Sarum & Wells Th Coll DCTM93. **d** 93 **p** 94. C Mile Cross *Nor* from 93. *140 Mile Cross Road, Norwich NR3 2LD* Tel (01603) 425493

✠**BETTS, The Rt Revd Stanley Woodley.** b 12. CBE67. Jes Coll Cam MA37. Ridley Hall Cam 33. **d** 35 **p** 36 **c** 56. C Cheltenham St Paul *Glouc* 35-38; Chapl RAF 38-47; Chapl Clare Coll Cam 47-49; V Cambridge H Trin *Ely* 49-57; Suff Bp Maidstone *Cant* 56-66; Abp's Rep w HM Forces 57-66; Dean Roch 66-77; rtd 77. *2 Kings Houses, Pevensey, E Sussex BN24 5JR* Tel (01323) 762421

BETTS, Steven James. b 64. York Univ BSc86. Ripon Coll Cuddesdon 87. **d** 90 **p** 91. C Bearsted w Thurnham *Cant* 90-94; Bp's Chapl *Nor* from 94. *The Vicarage, St Martin at Palace Plain, Norwich NR3 1RW* Tel (01603) 614172 Fax 761613

BEUKES, Douglas. b 22. Oak Hill Th Coll 45. **d** 51 **p** 52. C Walthamstow St Andr *Chelmsf* 51-53; C E Barnet *St Alb* 53-55; Chapl RAF 55-58; Utrecht w Arnhem, Zwolle, Amersfoort etc *Eur* 59-90; rtd 90. *Vogelzanglaan 6, 3571 ZM Utrecht, The Netherlands*

BEVAN, Alan John. b 29. Bris Univ BA54. Oak Hill Th Coll 54. **d** 56 **p** 59. C Penn Fields *Lich* 56-57; C Corsham *Bris* 58-61; C Wath-upon-Dearne w Adwick-upon-Dearne *Sheff* 61-68; C Darfield 68-71; C Drypool St Columba w St Andr and St Pet *York* 71-79; Chapl HM Pris Wandsworth 79-83; Chapl HM Pris Kirkham 83-86; rtd 86; Perm to Offic *Ex* from 86. *41 Bellever Close, Princetown, Yelverton, Devon PL20 6RT* Tel (01822) 890625

BEVAN, Bryan David. Lon Univ BD60 MA70 CertEd65 DipEd66 MPhil84. Lambeth STh62 St Aug Coll Cant 62. **d** 64 **p** 66. C E Dereham w Hoe *Nor* 64-65; C Hove All SS *Chich* 65-67; Lect St Mich Coll Salisbury 67-70; The Coll Bedf from 70. *4A De Parys Lodge, De Parys Avenue, Bedford MK40 2TZ* Tel (01234) 343622

BEVAN, Canon Charles Joseph Godfrey. b 22. TCD BA44 MA52. **d** 45 **p** 46. C Dublin St Geo *D & G* 45-49; I Rathvilly *C & O* 49-59; I Carbury *M & K* 59-64; I Drogheda St Pet w Ballymakenny, Beaulieu etc *Arm* 64-90; I Drogheda w Ardee, Collon and Termonfeckin from 90; Miss to Seamen from 64; Can Arm Cathl *Arm* from 83; Chan 88-92; Prec from 92; RD Creggan and Louth from 90. *St Peter's Rectory, Drogheda, Co Louth, Irish Republic* Tel Drogheda (41) 38441

BEVAN, David Graham. b 34. Univ of Wales (Lamp) BA54 LTh56. Gen Th Sem (NY) MDiv57. **d** 57 **p** 58. C Llanelli *St D* 57-60; CF 60-76. *148 Bromley Heath Road, Downend, Bristol BS16 6JJ* Tel 0117-956 0946

BEVAN, Dennis Butler. b 24. Bris Univ BA51. St Mich Coll Llan 53. **d** 54 **p** 55. C Canton St Cath *Llan* 54-56; C Llangynwyd w Maesteg 56-59; C Porthkerry 59-67; C Barry All SS 59-67; V Cymmer and Porth 67-79; V St Brides Major 79-89; rtd 89; Perm to Offic *Llan* from 89. *Glenside, 50 Allen Street, Mountain Ash CF45 4BB* Tel (01443) 477585

BEVAN, Gordon Richard. b 26. NW Ord Course. **d** 75 **p** 76. C Spondon *Derby* 75-80; R Upper Langwith w Langwith Bassett etc 80-87; P-in-c Scarcliffe 82-87; R Upper Langwith w Langwith Bassett etc 87-94; TV E Scarsdale 94-96; rtd 96; Perm to Offic *Derby* from 96. *8 Whaley Common, Langwith, Mansfield, Notts NG20 9HY* Tel (01623) 742413

BEVAN, Herbert Richard. b 28. Birm Univ DipTh56 MA67. **d** 57 **p** 58. C Sutton Coldfield H Trin *Birm* 57-60; C Chelsea All SS *Lon* 60-62; R Abberley *Worc* 62-92; RD Mitton 72-74; P-in-c Pensax 80-84; rtd 92. *Redlake Reach, Bridgend, Bucknell, Shropshire SY7 0AL* Tel (01547) 4427

BEVAN, Hubert Basil Henry. b 24. Univ of Wales (Lamp) BA52 LTh54 MTh77 PhD78. **d** 54 **p** 55. C Knighton and Heyope *S & B* 54-60; C Toxteth Park St Marg *Liv* 60-61; V Walsall St Mary and All SS Palfrey *Lich* 61-64; R Sunderland *Dur* 64-66; V Hendon St Paul 64-66; V Gilfach Goch w Llandyfodwg *Llan* 66-73; R Cregina *S & B* 73-78; V Bettws Disserth w Llansantffraed in Elwell 73-78; V Glascwm and Rhulen 76-78; R Llanferres, Nercwys and Eryrys *St As* 78-80; Tutor St Deiniol's Lib Hawarden 79-89; V Treuddyn and Nercwys and Eryrys *St As* 80-85; R Llanfynydd 85-89; rtd 89. *Creiglys, Bangor Road, Caernarfon LL55 1LR* Tel (01286) 672874

BEVAN, John Vernon. b 16. Univ of Wales BA38. St Mich Coll Llan 38. **d** 39 **p** 40. C Llangeinor *Llan* 39-43; C Cardiff St Jo 43-50; R Newton Nottage 50-57; R Enmore w Goathurst *B & W* 57-71; V Carhampton 71-81; rtd 82; Perm to Offic *B & W* 84-91. *12 Spring Gardens, Alcombe, Minehead, Somerset TA24 6BH* Tel (01643) 702897

BEVAN, Noel Haden. b 34. St Aid Birkenhead 61. **d** 63 **p** 64. C Girlington *Bradf* 63-66; C Worksop St Jo *S'well* 66-68; V Everton w Mattersey 68-70; R Everton and Mattersey w Clayworth 70-77; TV Barton Mills *St E* 77-80; TV Barton Mills, Beck Row w Kenny Hill etc 80-85; TV Mildenhall 85-86; P-in-c Sternfield w Benhall and Snape 86-89; R from 89. *The Rectory, Benhall Green, Benhall, Saxmundham, Suffolk IP17 1HT* Tel (01728) 603825

BEVAN, Paul John. b 49. Bris Sch of Min 84. **d** 87 **p** 88. NSM Bishopsworth *Bris* 87-96; NSM Bishopsworth and Bedminster Down from 97. *10 Brookdale Road, Headley Park, Bristol BS13 7PZ* Tel 0117-964 6330

BEVAN, Peter John. b 54. K Coll Lon BA76 AKC76 MA86. St Steph Ho Ox BA79. **d** 80 **p** 81. C Brighouse *Wakef* 80-83; C Chapelthorpe 83-86; V Scholes 86-95; V Potters Bar *St Alb* from 95. *The Vicarage, 15 The Walk, Potters Bar, Herts EN6 1QN* Tel (01707) 644539 or 645080

BEVAN, Philip Frank. b 41. Chich Th Coll 65. **d** 67 **p** 68. C Walton St Mary *Liv* 67-71; Bahamas from 71. *c/o N-963, Nassau, Bahamas*

BEVAN, Canon Richard Justin William. b 22. LTh42 St Chad's Coll Dur BA45 DTh72 PhD80. St Aug Coll Cant 39. **d** 45 **p** 46. C Stoke upon Trent *Lich* 45-49; Chapl Aberlour Orphanage 49-51; Lic to Offic *Mor* 49-51; Lic to Offic *Blackb* 51-52; C Church Kirk 52-56; C Whalley 56-61; R Dur St Mary le Bow w St Mary the Less *Dur* 61-64; Chapl Dur Univ 61-74; V Dur St Oswald 64-74; P-in-c Dur St Mary le Bow w St Mary the Less 64-67; R 67-74; R Grasmere *Carl* 74-82; Can Res, Lib and Treas Carl Cathl 82-89; Vice-Dean Carl 86-89; Chapl to The Queen 86-93; rtd 89; Perm to Offic *Carl* from 89. *Beck Cottage, West End, Burgh-by-Sands, Carlisle CA5 6BT* Tel (01228) 576781

BEVER, Canon Michael Charles Stephen. b 44. Selw Coll Cam BA66 MA70. Cuddesdon Coll. **d** 69 **p** 70. C Steeton *Bradf* 69-72; C Northampton St Mary *Pet* 72-74; Niger 75-79; P-in-c Elmstead *Chelmsf* 80-83; V 83-85; Hon Can Awka from 83; V Bocking St Pet *Chelmsf* 85-96; P-in-c Odiham *Win* from 96. *The Vicarage, The Bury, Odiham, Hook, Hants RG29 1ND* Tel (01256) 703896

BEVERIDGE, Mrs Freda Joy. b 38. Qu Mary Coll Lon BA59 Lon Inst of Educn PGCE60. Ripon Coll Cuddesdon 83. **dss** 85 **d** 87 **p** 94. Ox St Giles and SS Phil and Jas w St Marg *Ox* 85-87; Par Dn 87-88; Par Dn Woughton 88-94; C 94-95; TR from 95. *The Rectory, 10 Forest Rise, Milton Keynes MK6 5EU* Tel (01908) 670070

BEVERIDGE, Simon Alexander Ronald. b 61. Nottm Univ BA84. Chich Th Coll 84. **d** 87 **p** 88. C Braunton *Ex* 87-90; TV N Creedy 90-93; Chapl RN from 93. *Royal Naval Chaplaincy Service, Room 203, Victory Building, HM Naval Base, Portsmouth PO1 3LS* Tel (01705) 727903 Fax 727112

BEVERIDGE, Wilbert Esler. b 16. AFBPsS TCD BA38 Div Test 40 MLitt60 Lon Univ MA64. **d** 40 **p** 41. C Belfast St Mary *Conn* 40-42; CF (EC) 43-47; C St Alb St Paul *St Alb* 47-48; C Greenhill St Jo *Lon* 48-50; Min Preston Ascension CD 51-57; V Preston Ascension 57-61; Sen Ind Chapl 61-69; Prin Lect Middx Poly 69-81; rtd 81; Perm to Offic *Win* from 83. *33 Harewood Avenue, Boscombe, Bournemouth BH7 6NJ* Tel (01202) 420463

BEVERLEY, Canon Arthur Leslie. b 14. Dur Univ BA37. Ely Th Coll 37. **d** 39 **p** 40. C Featherstone *Wakef* 39-43; V Brothertoft *Linc* 43-48; V Skirbeck Quarter 48-59; R Ruskington 59-78; V Dorrington 59-78; Can and Preb Linc Cathl 72-79; RD Lafford 73-78; C Linc St Nic w St Jo Newport 78-79; rtd 79; Perm to Offic *Linc* from 79. *3 Middleton's Field, Lincoln LN2 1QP* Tel (01522) 523637

BEVERLEY, David John. b 46. Univ of Wales (Lamp) BA68. Linc Th Coll 71. **d** 73 **p** 74. C Cov E *Cov* 73-76; C Immingham *Linc* 76-84; V Bracebridge Heath 84-86; Ind Chapl from 86. *161 Ashby Road, Scunthorpe, S Humberside DN16 2AQ* Tel (01724) 844606

BEVERLEY, Suffragan Bishop of (Provincial Episcopal Visitor). *See* GAISFORD, The Rt Revd John Scott

BEVINGTON, Canon Colin Reginald. b 36. ALCD63. Lon Coll of Div 63. **d** 63 **p** 64. C Devonport St Budeaux *Ex* 63-65; C Attenborough w Chilwell *S'well* 65-68; R Benhall w Sternfield *St E* 68-74; P-in-c Snape w Friston 73-74; V Selly Hill St Steph *Birm* 74-81; P-in-c Selly Oak St Wulstan 80-81; V Selly Park St Steph and St Wulstan 81-88; Dioc Ecum Officer and Adv on Miss *St E* from 88; Hon Can St E Cathl from 93; Bp's Dom Chapl from 95. *44 Thorney Road, Capel St Mary, Ipswich IP9 2LH* Tel (01473) 310069

BEVINGTON, David John. b 51. Ch Coll Cam BA72 MA76. Trin Coll Bris 73. **d** 76 **p** 77. C Tulse Hill H Trin *S'wark* 76-79; C Galleywood Common *Chelmsf* 79-82; TV Hanley H Ev *Lich* 82-90; TV Hemel Hempstead *St Alb* from 90. *6 Arkley Road, Woodhall Farm, Hemel Hempstead, Herts HP2 7JT* Tel (01442) 248008

BEVIS, Anthony Richard (Tony). b 34. Chich Th Coll 87. **d** 87 **p** 89. NSM Hamble le Rice *Win* 87-94; Chapl Moorgreen Hosp W End Southn from 90; NSM Woolston *Win* from 94; Chapl Western Community Hosp from 96. *Lynwood, High Street, Hamble, Southampton SO31 4HA* Tel (01703) 453102

BEVIS, Derek Harold. FCIS. **d** 90 **p** 91. NSM Guildf Ch Ch *Guildf* from 90. *94 Wodeland Avenue, Guildford, Surrey GU2 5LD* Tel (01483) 61968

BEWES, Emmanuel John. b 21. Edin Th Coll 49. **d** 52 **p** 53. C Walney Is *Carl* 52-55; C Workington St Jo 55-60; V Hesket in the Forest 60-76; V Hesket-in-the-Forest and Armathwaite 76-87; rtd 87; Perm to Offic *Carl* from 87. *5 St Andrews Close, Carlisle CA1 2SG* Tel (01228) 37279

BEWES, Preb Richard Thomas. b 34. Em Coll Cam BA58 MA61. Ridley Hall Cam 57. **d** 59 **p** 60. C Beckenham Ch Ch *Roch* 59-65; V Harold Wood *Chelmsf* 65-74; V Northwood Em *Lon* 74-83; R St Marylebone All So w SS Pet and Jo 83-88; P-in-c Portman Square St Paul 87-88; R Langham Place All So from 88; Preb St Paul's Cathl from 88. *12 Weymouth Street, London W1N 3FB* Tel 0171-580 6029 or 580 4357 Fax 436 3019

BEWLEY, Albert Latham. b 38. Leeds Univ BA61. Ely Th Coll 61. **d** 63 **p** 64. C Wigan St Mich *Liv* 63-65; C Caister *Nor* 65-69; R W Lynn 69-76; V Lakenham St Jo from 76. *Old Lakenham Vicarage, Harwood Road, Norwich NR1 2NG* Tel (01603) 625678

BEXON, Miss Mavis Adelaide. b 31. St Mich Ho Ox. **d** 87 **p** 94. Bestwood St Matt *S'well* 77-86; Chaddesden St Mary *Derby* 86-87; Par Dn 87-91; rtd 91; Perm to Offic *S'well* from 91. *1 Dover Street, Southwell, Notts NG5 0EZ* Tel (01636) 815976

BEYNON, Malcolm. b 36. Univ of Wales (Lamp) BA56 Univ of Wales (Swansea) DipSocSc59 Univ of Wales (Cardiff) PGCE71. St Mich Coll Llan 56. **d** 59 **p** 60. C Aberavon *Llan* 59-62; C Whitchurch 63-68; V Llanwynno 68-73; Chapl Old Hall Sch Wellington Shropshire 74-75; Perm to Offic *Leic* 75-82; Chapl Nevill Holt Sch Market Harborough 75-82; Chapl Denstone Coll Prep Sch Uttoxeter 82-93; V Dale and St Brides w Marloes *St D* from 93. *The Vicarage, Castle Way, Dale, Haverfordwest SA62 3RN* Tel (01646) 636255

BEYNON, Nigel David. b 68. Collingwood Coll Dur BSc90. Ridley Hall Cam BA94. **d** 95 **p** 96. C Fulham St Matt *Lon* from 95. *2A Clancarthy Road, London SW6 3AB* Tel 0171-736 4421

BEYNON, Vincent Wyn. b 54. CertEd76 Univ of Wales DipTh81 Lambeth STh97. St Mich Coll Llan 78. **d** 81 **p** 82. C Llantrisant *Llan* 81-83; C Caerphilly 84-85; R Gelligaer 85-88; TV Gtr Corsham *Bris* 88-97; R Potton w Sutton and Cockayne Hatley

St Alb from 97. *The Rectory, Hatley Road, Potton, Sandy, Beds SG19 2DX* Tel (01767) 260782 E-mail 106056.2062 @compuserve.com

BIANCHI, Mrs Margaret Ruth. b 56. St Mary's Coll Dur BA77. Cranmer Hall Dur 78. **dss** 80 **d** 91 **p** 94. Chester le Street *Dur* 80-83; W Pelton 83-91; NSM 91-95; Perm to Offic from 95. *Flat 2, Woodland Surgery, Vigo Lane, Rickleton, Washington, Tyne & Wear NE38 9ET*

BIANCHI, Robert Frederick (Rob). b 56. St Jo Coll Dur BA77. Cranmer Hall Dur 78. **d** 80 **p** 81. C Chester le Street *Dur* 80-83; C W Pelton 83-86; P-in-c 86-95; Perm to Offic from 95. *Flat 2, Woodland Surgery, Vigo Lane, Rickleton, Washington, Tyne & Wear NE38 9ET*

BIBBY, Canon Frank. b 37. ACP60 K Coll Lon BD64 AKC64. **d** 65 **p** 66. C Upholland *Liv* 65-67; Lect Birm Coll of Educn 67-72; V Prestwich St Gabr *Man* 72-76; Dir of Ords 72-76; V Hope St Jas 76-86; AD Salford 82-86; R Prestwich St Mary from 86; Hon Can Man Cathl from 96. *The Rectory, Church Lane, Prestwich, Manchester M25 5AN* Tel 0161-773 2912

BIBBY, Paul Benington. b 27. Magd Coll Cam BA51 MA56. Westcott Ho Cam 55. **d** 57 **p** 58. C Flixton St Mich *Man* 57-60; C Woolwich St Mary w H Trin *S'wark* 60-62; V Hurst *Man* 62-69; Hd of Cam Ho Camberwell 69-76; R Shepton Mallet *B & W* 76-81; P-in-c Doulting w E and W Cranmore and Downhead 78-81; R Shepton Mallet w Doulting 81-82; Sen Chapl Eton Coll 82-87; R Hambleden Valley *Ox* 87-93; rtd 93; Perm to Offic *Nor* from 94. *Vine Cottage, Cross Lane, Stanhoe, King's Lynn, Norfolk PE31 8PS* Tel (01485) 518291

BICK, David Jim. b 33. ALCD59 LTh74. **d** 59 **p** 60. C Glouc St Cath *Glouc* 59-61; C Coleford w Staunton 61-63; R Blaisdon w Flaxley 63-72; V Coaley 72-83; P-in-c Arlingham 80-83; P-in-c Frampton on Severn 80-83; Hon C Saul w Fretherne and Framilode 83-84; Perm to Offic from 84. *St Joseph's, Prinknash Park, Cranham, Glos GL4 8EX* Tel (01452) 812973

BICKERDYKE, James Clifford. b 17. St Jo Coll Dur BA42 MA45. Oak Hill Th Coll LTh41. **d** 42 **p** 43. C Stockport St Geo *Ches* 42-43; C Cannock *Lich* 43-45; Normanton Sch Buxton 45-48; Chadderton Gr Sch 48-51; CF 51-67; Launceston Coll 67-75; Grove Sch Hindhead 75-81. *Lonningarth, Hawkshead, Ambleside, Cumbria LA22 0PU* Tel (015394) 36100

BICKERSTETH, Anthony Cyril. b 33. K Coll Lon 54. Bps' Coll Cheshunt 55. **d** 58 **p** 59. C Middlesbrough St Oswald *York* 58-61; S Africa 61-64; V Stillington w Marton and Farlington *York* 64-68; V Stoke Newington Common St Mich *Lon* 68-74; V Nayland w Wiston *St E* 74-82; R Tolleshunt Knights w Tiptree *Chelmsf* 82-87; R Tolleshunt Knights w Tiptree and Gt Braxted 87; rtd 87; Perm to Offic *Chelmsf* 87-90. *Lanreath, 125 Woodland Avenue, Hove, E Sussex BN3 6BJ* Tel (01273) 564663

BICKERSTETH, David Craufurd. b 50. Wycliffe Hall Ox 71. **d** 75 **p** 76. C Beverley Minster *York* 75-79; C Farnborough *Guildf* 79-81; P-in-c Dearham *Carl* 81-85; V 85-86; R Gosforth w Nether Wasdale and Wasdale Head 86-93; P-in-c Harraby from 93. *St Elizabeth's Vicarage, Arnside Road, Carlisle CA1 3QA* Tel (01228) 596429 E-mail dcbickersteth@msn.com

BICKERSTETH, Edward Piers. b 56. ARICS80. Wycliffe Hall Ox 89. **d** 91 **p** 92. NSM Bebington *Ches* 91-92; C 92-94; Perm to Offic *Lon* from 94. *The Proclamation Trust, St Peter's Church, Cornhill, London EC3V 3PD* Tel 0171-626 6989

✠**BICKERSTETH, The Rt Revd John Monier.** b 21. KCVO89. Ch Ch Ox BA49 MA53. Wells Th Coll 48. **d** 50 **p** 51 **c** 70. C Moorfields *Bris* 50-54; C-in-c Hurst Green CD *S'wark* 54-62; V Chatham St Steph *Roch* 62-70; Hon Can Roch Cathl 68-70; Suff Bp Warrington *Liv* 70-75; Bp B & W 75-87; ChStJ and Sub-Prelate from 77; Clerk of the Closet 79-89; rtd 87. *Beckfords, Newtown, Tisbury, Salisbury SP3 6NY* Tel (01747) 870479

BICKLEY, John. b 12. Magd Coll Ox BA34 MA38. Sarum Th Coll 35. **d** 36 **p** 37. C Tunstall Ch Ch *Lich* 36-40; C Tettenhall Regis 40-45; V Goldenhill 45-52; V Newborough w Ch Ch on Needwood 52-53; V Mossley *Man* 53-61; V Preston St Jo *Blackb* 61-63; V Colne Ch Ch 63-67; R Slimbridge *Glouc* 67-70; R Huntingfield w Cookley *St E* 70-77; rtd 77; Perm to Offic *St E* from 77. *Breckland Cottage, Santon Downham, Brandon, Suffolk IP27 0TQ* Tel (01842) 810497

BICKNELL (née RIDING), Mrs Pauline Alison. b 61. SEN82. Oak Hill Th Coll BA90. **d** 90. Par Dn Moor Allerton *Ripon* 90-93; Par Dn Leeds St Aid 93-94; C 94-96; C Rothwell from 96. *6 Sandy Grove, Rothwell, Leeds LS26 0UF* Tel 0113-282 7237

BIDDELL, Canon Christopher David. b 27. Ch Coll Cam BA48 MA52. Ridley Hall Cam 51. **d** 51 **p** 52. C Hornchurch St Andr *Chelmsf* 51-54; Succ S'wark Cathl *S'wark* 54-56; P-in-c Wroxall *Portsm* 56-61; R Bishops Waltham 62-75; RD Bishops Waltham 69-74; V Stockport St Geo *Ches* 75-86; Hon Can Ches Cathl 81-86; Can Res 86-93; RD Stockport 85-86; Vice-Dean Ches 91-93; rtd 93; P-in-c Duncton *Chich* from 95; P-in-c Tillington from 95; P-in-c Up Waltham from 95. *3 Park Terrace, Tillington, Petworth, W Sussex GU28 9AE* Tel (01798) 342008

BIDDELL, John Herman. b 15. Worc Coll Ox BA38 MA45. Wells Th Coll 38. **d** 47 **p** 48. C Basingstoke *Win* 47-51; V Pennington 51-58; R Merstham and Gatton *S'wark* 58-65; V Milverton *B & W* 65-80; R Fitzhead 77-80; rtd 80; Perm to Offic *B & W* from 81. *Snape Cottage, Wiltown, Curry Rivel, Langport, Somerset TA10 0JF* Tel (01458) 251435

BIDDER, John. b 19. Cuddesdon Coll. **d** 62 **p** 63. C Birstall *Leic* 62-65; R Croft 65-71; R Witcham w Mepal *Ely* 71-80; R Coates 80-85; rtd 85; Perm to Offic *Blackb* from 86. *Carinya, 83 Main Street, Nether Kellett, Carnforth, Lancs LA6 1EF* Tel (01524) 734993

BIDDINGTON, Dr Terence Eric. b 56. MCollP83 Hull Univ BA77 Trin & All SS Coll Leeds PGCE78 Leeds Univ PhD86 Nottm Univ BTh88 Man Univ MA(Theol)96. Linc Th Coll 85. **d** 88 **p** 89. C Harpenden St Jo *St Alb* 88-90; Chapl Keele Univ *Lich* 90-93; Freelance Th Educator and Asst Lect Keele Univ from 94; Assoc Min Betley and Keele from 90; Asst Dir Cornerstone St Aug Manchester from 96. *22 Water Street, Bollington, Macclesfield, Cheshire SK10 5PB* Tel (01625) 576886

BIDDLE, Rodney William Dennis. b 44. St Jo Coll Nottm. **d** 85 **p** 86. C Penn *Lich* 85-89; P-in-c Shrewsbury St Geo 89-90; V from 90; P-in-c Montford w Shrawardine and Fitz 89; Chapl HM Pris Shrewsbury 90-96; RD Shrewsbury *Lich* from 91; P-in-c Bicton, Montford w Shrawardine and Fitz from 97. *The Vicarage, St George's Street, Shrewsbury SY3 8QA* Tel (01743) 235461

BIDDLE, Miss Rosemary. b 44. CertEd67. St Jo Coll Dur 76. **dss** 79 **d** 87 **p** 94. Sheldon *Birm* 79-83; Burntwood *Lich* 83-87; Par Dn 87-89; Par Dn Gt Wyrley 89-94; C from 94. *46 Gorsey Lane, Great Wyrley, Walsall WS6 6EX*

BIDDLECOMBE, Francis William. b 30. St Mich Coll Llan 57. **d** 59 **p** 60. C Llangynwyd w Maesteg *Llan* 59-62; C Roath St Marg 62-65; V Llanddewi Rhondda w Bryn Eirw 65-71; V Berse and Southsea *St As* 71-79; P-in-c Teme Valley S *Worc* 79-85; rtd 92; Perm to Offic *Heref* from 92. *Four Winds, New Road, Highley, Bridgnorth, Shropshire WV16 6NN* Tel (01746) 861746

BIDDLESTONE, Joseph. b 15. Wycliffe Hall Ox 67. **d** 68 **p** 68. C Woodley St Jo the Ev *Ox* 68-71; P-in-c Dunsden 71-77; P-in-c Kiddington w Asterleigh 77-85; P-in-c Wootton by Woodstock 77-85; rtd 85; Perm to Offic *Ox* from 85. *6 Dashwood Rise, Duns Tew, Oxford OX6 4JQ* Tel (01869) 40350

BIDE, Mrs Mary Elizabeth. b 53. St Anne's Coll Ox BA74 MA78. S Dios Minl Tr Scheme 91. **d** 94 **p** 95. NSM Gt Bookham *Guildf* 94-95; C from 95. *19 The Lorne, Bookham, Leatherhead, Surrey KT23 4JY* Tel (01372) 453729

BIDE, Peter William. b 12. St Cath Soc Ox BA39 MA45. Wells Th Coll 38. **d** 49 **p** 50. C Portslade St Nic *Chich* 49-55; PC Hangleton 55-57; V Goring-by-Sea 57-59; Asst Gen Sec BCC 59-61; R Lt Hadham *St Alb* 61-64; V Battersea St Luke *S'wark* 64-68; Chapl LMH Ox 68-80; Fell 78-80; rtd 80; Prec Ch Ch *Ox* 80-82; Perm to Offic *Portsm* 84-88; Perm to Offic *Chich* from 80. *Meadow Corner, The Street, Boxgrove, Chichester, W Sussex PO18 0DY* Tel (01243) 774134

BIDEN, Neville Douglas. b 31. Lon Univ DipRS80. S'wark Ord Course 76. **d** 79 **p** 80. C Ash *Guildf* 79-82; NSM Surbiton St Andr and St Mark *S'wark* 87-91; Chapl Asst Long Grove Hosp Epsom 90-91; Perm to Offic *Guildf* 90-91; C Coulsdon St Jo *S'wark* 91-96; rtd 96; Perm to Offic *Heref* 95-97; Perm to Offic *Guildf* from 97. *8 Waddington Avenue, Thames Ditton, Surrey CR5 1QE* Tel (01737) 556043

BIENFAIT, Alexander (Alex). b 61. Hatf Poly BSc86. Sarum & Wells Th Coll BTh94. **d** 94 **p** 95. C Battersea St Luke *S'wark* 94-96; C Clapham TM from 96. *The Glebe House, 6 Rectory Grove, London SW4 0DZ* Tel 0171-720 3370

BIERLEY, George Leslie. b 11. Worc Ord Coll 58. **d** 60 **p** 61. C Clee *Linc* 60-63; R Gt Coates 63-71; R N Thoresby 71-82; R Grainsby 71-82; V Waithe 71-82; rtd 82; Perm to Offic *Linc* 82-94. *57 Brackenborough Road, Louth, Lincs LN11 0AD* Tel (01507) 602516

BIGG, Howard Clive. b 40. Jes Coll Cam BA68 MA72. Ridley Hall Cam 73. **d** 74 **p** 75. C Worksop St Jo *S'well* 74-76; Min Can St Alb 76-77; Perm to Offic *Ches* 78-82; Perm to Offic *Ely* from 82; Vice-Prin Romsey Ho Cam 86-89. *55 Hemingford Road, Cambridge CB1 3BY* Tel (01223) 410810

BIGGAR, Dr Nigel John. b 55. Worc Coll Ox BA76 MA88 Chicago Univ PhD86 AM81. **d** 90 **p** 91. Lib Latimer Ho Ox from 85; Asst Lect in Chr Ethics Wycliffe Hall Ox from 87; Chapl Or Coll Ox from 90. *The Chaplain's Office, Oriel College, Oxford OX1 4EW* Tel (01865) 276580 Fax 791823

BIGGIN, Ronald. b 20. NW Ord Course 70. **d** 73 **p** 74. C Thelwall *Ches* 73-79; V 79-87; rtd 87; NSM Lt Leigh and Lower Whitley *Ches* from 90. *44 Richmond Avenue, Grappenhall, Warrington, Cheshire WA4 2ND* Tel (01925) 261531

BIGGS, David James. b 55. St Jo Coll Auckland LTh82. **d** 81 **p** 82. New Zealand 81-86; C Stevenage St Andr and St Geo *St Alb* 86-89; TV Moulsecoomb *Chich* from 89. *Barn Lodge, Norwich Drive, Brighton BN2 4LA* Tel (01273) 602325

BIGGS, George Ramsay. b 45. Liv Univ BA67 Qu Coll Cam BA73. Westcott Ho Cam 72. **d** 74 **p** 75. C Lee St Aug *S'wark* 74-78; TV Eling, Testwood and Marchwood *Win* 78; TV Totton 78-93; V Wellow from 93. *Wellow Vicarage, 1 The Beeches, Slab Lane, West Wellow, Romsey, Hants SO51 6RN* Tel (01794) 323356

BIGGS, Canon Ivan Richard. b 22. Edgehill Th Coll Belf 49. **d** 73 **p** 73. Bp's C Killea *C & O* 73-82; I Kiltoghart w Drumshambo, Annaduff and Kilronan *K, E & A* 82-91; Preb Elphin Cathl

84-91; Dioc Sec (Elphin and Ardagh) from 87; Glebes Sec and Dioc Info Officer 87-91; rtd 91. *Carrowkeel Lodge, Castlebaldwin, Co Sligo, Irish Republic* Tel Castlebaldwin (79) 66015 Fax as telephone

BIGGS, Laurence John. b 60. Leeds Univ BSc81. Trin Coll Bris DipHE94. **d** 94 **p** 95. C St Alb St Paul *St Alb* from 94. *46 Brampton Road, St Albans, Herts AL1 4PT* Tel (01727) 841245

BIGGS, Laurence Walter. b 23. ACT DipTh73 Roch Th Coll 64. **d** 66 **p** 67. C Cleethorpes *Linc* 66-69; C St Germans *Truro* 69-70; Australia from 70; rtd 88. *Lamport Lane, Old Sale Road, Brandy Creek, via Warragal, Victoria, Australia 3820* Tel Brandy Creek (56) 268454

BIGGS, Philip John. b 51. Ripon Hall Ox 74 Ripon Coll Cuddesdon 75. **d** 77 **p** 78. C Maidstone All SS w St Phil and H Trin *Cant* 77-80; Dioc Youth Officer *Truro* 80-84; Australia from 84; Hon Chapl Miss to Seamen from 84. *22 Monument Street, Mosman Park, W Australia 6012* Tel Perth (9) 384 0108 or 383 2620

BIGMORE, Graeme Paul. b 57. Univ of Wales (Cardiff) BTh95. St Mich Coll Llan DipTh92. **d** 92 **p** 93. C Cardiff St Jo *Llan* 92-96; Cardiff City Cen Chapl 94-96; C Rhondda from 96. *The Vicarage, Graig Road, Ynyshir, Porth CF39 0NS* Tel (01443) 684148

BIGNELL, Alan Guy. b 39. Lon Univ BA64. Ox NSM Course. **d** 81 **p** 82. NSM Upton cum Chalvey *Ox* 81-90; NSM Burnham and Slough Deanery from 90. *Little Gidding, 2 Wheatlands Road, Slough SL3 7PB* Tel (01753) 523005

BIGNELL, David Charles. b 41. EMMTC 76. **d** 79 **p** 80. C Porchester *S'well* 79-82; V Awsworth w Cossall 82-86; Bp's Ecum Officer from 84; V Edwalton from 86. *The Vicarage, Edwalton, Notts NG12 4AB* Tel 0115-923 2034

BIGWOOD, Kate Elizabeth. *See* ATKINSON, Mrs Kate Bigwood

BILES, David George. b 35. AKC58 Open Univ BA75 Lambeth STh91 Leeds Univ MA96. **d** 59 **p** 60. C Cockerton *Dur* 59-62; C Winlaton 62-67; P-in-c Dipton 67-74; R Wolviston 74-89; P-in-c Thirkleby w Kilburn and Bagby *York* 89-90; V from 90; RD Thirsk 90-91; RD Mowbray from 91. *The Vicarage, Kilburn, York YO6 4AH* Tel (01347) 868234

BILES, Canon Timothy Mark Frowde. b 35. Univ of Wales DipTh64. St Mich Coll Llan 60. **d** 64 **p** 66. C Middleton St Cross *Ripon* 64-66; Chapl St Fran Sch Hooke 66-72; P-in-c Toller Porcorum w Hooke *Sarum* 72-79; P-in-c Melplash w Mapperton 74-79; P-in-c Beaminster 77-79; TR Beaminster Area from 79; Can and Preb Sarum Cathl from 83; RD Beaminster 84-89. *The Rectory, Barnes Lane, Beaminster, Dorset DT8 3BU* Tel (01308) 862150 Fax 863662

BILL, Alan. b 29. K Coll Lon BD66 AKC66. **d** 67 **p** 68. C Gt Burstead *Chelmsf* 67-70; TV Thornaby on Tees *York* 71-76; R E Gilling 76-81; V Ormesby 81-91; rtd 91. *13 Wilmington Close, Tudor Grange, Newcastle upon Tyne NE3 2SF* Tel 0191-271 3556

BILL, Denis Aubrey. b 20. Coll of Resurr Mirfield 48. **d** 50 **p** 51. C Shieldfield Ch Ch *Newc* 50-59; V Cambois 59-64; V Holy Is 64-89; rtd 89. *The Annexe, Etal Manor, Berwick-upon-Tweed TD15 2PU* Tel (01890) 820378

BILL, Herbert Sydney. b 12. Keble Coll Ox BA34 DipTh35. Wells Th Coll 35. **d** 36 **p** 37. C Upper Chelsea St Sav *Lon* 36-39; C Acton Green St Pet 39-41; Acting C Hampstead Garden Suburb 41-43; Min Northolt Wood End CD 43-45; V Washwood Heath *Birm* 45-52; V Dudley St Aug Holly Hall *Worc* 52-60; Dioc Missr 54-82; R Feckenham w Bradley 60-82; rtd 82; Perm to Offic *Worc* from 82. *31 Tredington Close, Woodrow, Redditch, Worcs B98 7UR*

BILL, Thomas Andrew Graham. b 47. Dur Univ BA76 DipTh78. Cranmer Hall Dur 78. **d** 77 **p** 78. C Penwortham St Mary *Blackb* 77-80; C Torrisholme 80-82; P-in-c Accrington St Pet 82-89; P-in-c Haslingden St Jo Stonefold 82-89; V Skerton St Chad from 89. *St Chad's Vicarage, 1 St Chad's Drive, Lancaster LA1 2SE* Tel (01524) 63816

BILLETT, Anthony Charles. b 56. Bris Univ BEd. Wycliffe Hall Ox 82. **d** 85 **p** 86. C Waltham Abbey *Chelmsf* 85-88; C Nor St Pet Mancroft w St Jo Maddermarket *Nor* 88-91; V Stalham and E Ruston w Brunstead from 91. *The Vicarage, Stalham, Norwich NR12 9DT* Tel (01692) 580250

BILLINGHAM, Canon Peter Charles Geoffrey. b 34. Leeds Univ BA56. Westcott Ho Cam 61. **d** 62 **p** 63. C Halesowen *Worc* 62-66; R Addingham *Bradf* 66-70; R Droitwich St Nic w St Pet *Worc* 70-72; TR Droitwich 72-83; P-in-c Salwarpe 76-80; RD Droitwich 78-83; P-in-c Gt Malvern H Trin 83; P-in-c W Malvern 83; V Malvern H Trin and St Jas from 84; RD Malvern from 92; Hon Can Worc Cathl from 93. *The Vicarage, 2 North Malvern Road, Malvern, Worcs WR14 4LR* Tel (01684) 574380

BILLINGHURST, Richard George. b 48. FIA76 St Jo Coll Cam BA70 MA74. Ridley Hall Cam 76. **d** 79 **p** 80. C Caverswall *Lich* 79-81; C Cullompton *Ex* 81-84; R Redgrave cum Botesdale w Rickinghall *St E* 84-92; R Skellingthorpe w Doddington *Linc* from 92; RD Graffoe from 94. *The Rectory, 50 Lincoln Road, Skellingthorpe, Lincoln LN6 5UY* Tel (01522) 682520

BILLINGS, Dr Alan Roy. b 42. Em Coll Cam BA65 MA69 Bris Univ PGCE66 Leic Univ MEd75. NY Th Sem DMin87 Linc Th Coll 66. **d** 68 **p** 69. C Knighton St Mary Magd *Leic* 68-72; P-in-c Sheff Gillcar St Silas *Sheff* 72-76; V Beighton 76-77; Head RE Broadway Sch Barnsley 77-81; Perm to Offic 77-81; V Walkley 81-86; Perm to Offic *Ox* 86-92; Dir Ox Inst for Ch and Soc 86-92; Vice-Prin Ripon Coll Cuddesdon 88-92; Prin WMMTC 92-94; V Kendal St Geo *Carl* from 94. *St George's Vicarage, 3 Firbank, Sedbergh Road, Kendal, Cumbria LA9 6BE* Tel (01539) 723039

BILLINGS, Derek Donald. b 30. Fitzw Ho Cam BA54 MA59. Tyndale Hall Bris 55. **d** 56 **p** 57. C Attenborough w Bramcote and Chilwell *S'well* 56-58; R Ashley w Silverley *Ely* 59-66; V Bottisham 66-80; R Houghton w Wyton from 80. *The Rectory, 3 Rectory Lane, Wyton, Huntingdon, Cambs PE17 2AQ* Tel (01480) 462499

BILLINGS, Roger Key. b 41. AIB. Oak Hill Th Coll BA80. **d** 80 **p** 81. C Tunbridge Wells St Jas *Roch* 80-84; V Chatham St Paul w All SS 84-95; V Carterton *Ox* from 95. *St John's Vicarage, Burford Road, Carterton, Oxon OX8 3AA* Tel (01993) 842429

BILLINGSLEY, Raymond Philip. b 48. FCMA80. Qu Coll Birm 87. **d** 89 **p** 90. C Yardley St Edburgha *Birm* 89-92; V Ward End 92-96; V Brymbo *St As* from 96. *The Vicarage, Vicarage Road, Brymbo, Wrexham LL11 5LF* Tel (01978) 758107

BILLINGTON, Charles Alfred. b 30. Leeds Univ BA55. Coll of Resurr Mirfield 53. **d** 55 **p** 56. C Carl H Trin *Carl* 55-59; CR 59-64; Lic to Offic *Wakef* 60-64; R Man St Aid *Man* 64-66; V Gt Crosby St Faith *Liv* 66-72; R Harrold and Carlton w Chellington *St Alb* 72-80; R Tintinhull w Chilthorne Domer, Yeovil Marsh etc *B & W* 80-81; Chapl Leybourne Grange Hosp W Malling 81-85; Lic to Offic *Roch* 81-85; V Walsden *Wakef* 85-88; R Llanfair Talhaearn and Llansannan etc *St As* 88-97; rtd 97. *27 Lon-y-Mes, Abergele LL22 7JG* Tel (01745) 824563

BILLINGTON, George. b 45. St Jo Coll Nottm DipThMin94. **d** 94 **p** 95. C Accrington St Jo w Huncoat *Blackb* from 94. *21 Ambleside Close, Huncoat, Accrington, Lancs BB5 6HY* Tel (01254) 301297

BILLINGTON, John Keith. b 16. **d** 61 **p** 62. C Ovenden *Wakef* 61-63; C Pontefract St Giles 63-64; V Shepley 64-68; C-in-c Seacroft CD *Ripon* 68-73; rtd 73; Perm to Offic *Bradf* from 86. *9 The Lawns, Skipton Road, Ilkley, W Yorkshire LS29 9EW* Tel (01943) 602732

BILLOWES, David. b 20. Chich Th Coll. **d** 76 **p** 77. NSM Cowes St Mary *Portsm* 76-91; Chapl St Mary's Hosp Newport 82-91; rtd 91; Perm to Offic *Portsm* from 91. *45 Solent View Road, Gurnard, Cowes, Isle of Wight PO31 8JZ* Tel (01983) 297366

BILLS, Reginald. b 18. TCert47. Lich Th Coll 68 Wm Temple Coll Rugby DipTh68. **d** 70 **p** 71. C Wednesfield St Thos *Lich* 70-73; C Wolverhampton St Pet 73-79; Chapl St Pet Colleg Sch 73-79; C Wolverhampton St Andr 79-81; P-in-c Brockmoor 81-87; rtd 87. *43 Kewstoke Road, Willenhall, W Midlands WV12 5DY* Tel (01922) 405049

BILNEY, Kenneth Henry. b 25. FBCS. St Deiniol's Hawarden 75. **d** 75 **p** 76. Hon C Knighton St Mary Magd *Leic* 75-78; C Leic St Jas 78-80; R Leire w Ashby Parva and Dunton Bassett 80-90; rtd 90; Perm to Offic *Leic* from 90. *20 Ferndale Road, Leicester LE2 6GN* Tel 0116-257 0436

BILSTON, Barbara Bradley. **d** 97. NSM Bacton w Wyverstone and Cotton *St E* from 97. *Boy's Hall, Ward Green, Old Newton, Stowmarket, Suffolk IP14 4EZ* Tel (01449) 781253

BILTON, Paul Michael. b 52. AKC74. St Aug Coll Cant 74. **d** 75 **p** 76. C Skipton Ch Ch *Bradf* 75-79; Ind Chapl *Worc* 79-81; V Greetland and W Vale *Wakef* 81-88; R Mablethorpe w Trusthorpe *Linc* 88-91; V Bradf St Wilfrid Lidget Green *Bradf* from 91. *St Wilfrid's Vicarage, Lidget Green, Bradford, W Yorkshire BD7 2LU* Tel (01274) 572504

BINDOFF, Stanley. b 54. Sarum & Wells Th Coll 79. **d** 82 **p** 83. C Thirsk *York* 82-86; Chapl HM Young Offender Inst Northallerton 85-89; P-in-c Rounton w Welbury *York* 86-89; Chapl HM Pris Gartree 89-92; Chapl HM Pris Frankland 92-96; Chapl HM Young Offender Inst Deerbolt from 96. *HM YOI Deerbolt, Bowes Road, Barnard Castle, Co Durham DL12 9BG* Tel (01833) 37561 Fax 31736

BINDON, David Charles. b 33. Ex Univ DipT57 Lon Univ BSc58. Sarum & Wells Th Coll 77. **d** 79 **p** 80. C Yeovil *B & W* 79-83; R Kilmersdon w Babington 83-89; R Radstock w Writhlington 83-89; Chapl St Swithun's Sch Win 89-95; rtd 95; Hon C Wittersham w Stone-in-Oxney and Ebony *Cant* from 95. *The Rectory, The Street, Wittersham, Tenterden, Kent TN30 7EA* Tel (01797) 270227

BINDON, Joan Vereker. b 19. K Coll Lon DipTh47. St Chris Coll Blackheath 47. **dss** 67 **d** 73. New Zealand from 67; rtd 79. *3/149 Church Street, Onehunga, Auckland 1006, New Zealand* Tel Auckland (9) 634 3920

BING, Alan Charles. b 56. St Edm Hall Ox BA78 DipInstM83. Oak Hill Th Coll DipHE91. **d** 91 **p** 92. C Fremington *Ex* 91-94; C-in-c Roundswell CD from 94. *16 Mulberry Way, Roundswell, Barnstaple, Devon EX31 3QZ* Tel (01271) 75877

BINGHAM, Mrs Marie Joyce Phyllis. b 27. Glouc Sch of Min 80. **dss** 84 **d** 87 **p** 94. Glouc St Mary de Crypt w St Jo and Ch Ch *Glouc* 84-85; Glouc St Mary de Lode and St Nic 85-87; Hon C 87-95; Hon C Glouc St Mary de Crypt w St Jo and Ch Ch 94-95; Hon C Glouc St Mary de Crypt w St Jo, Ch Ch etc from 95.

Hazel Cottage, Sandhurst, Gloucester GL2 9NP Tel (01452) 730285

BINGHAM, Norman James Frederick. b 26. Lon Univ BSc51. Tyndale Hall Bris 61. **d** 63 **p** 64. C Chell *Lich* 63-67; C Macclesfield St Mich *Ches* 67-71; P-in-c Macclesfield St Pet 71-73; V Leyton St Mary w St Edw *Chelmsf* 73-91; RD Waltham Forest 81-86; P-in-c Leyton St Luke 82-91; rtd 91. *97 Monks Walk, Buntingford, Herts SG9 9DP* Tel (01763) 272275

BINKS, Canon Edmund Vardy. b 36. FRSA89 K Coll Lon BD61 AKC61. **d** 62 **p** 63. C Selby Abbey *York* 62-65; Asst Chapl Univ Coll of Ripon and York St Jo 65-83; Prin St Kath Coll Liv 83-87; Prin Ches Coll *Ches* from 87; Hon Can Ches Cathl from 95. *Chester College, Cheyney Road, Chester CH1 4BJ* Tel (01244) 375444 Fax 373379

BINLEY, Miss Teresa Mary. b 37. Dalton Ho Bris 61. **d** 87 **p** 94. Par Dn Ashton on Mersey St Mary *Ches* 87-92; Bp's Officer for Women in Min 87-92; C Chaddesden St Mary *Derby* from 92. *24 Ordish Avenue, Chaddesden, Derby DE21 6QF* Tel (01332) 662420

BINNEY, Mark James Gurney. b 58. K Coll Lon BD80. Qu Coll Birm 84. **d** 86 **p** 87. C Hornchurch St Andr *Chelmsf* 86-89; C Hutton 89-91; V Pheasey *Lich* 91-96; TV Wombourne w Trysull and Bobbington from 96. *The Vicarage, School Lane, Trysull, Wolverhampton WV5 7HR* Tel (01902) 892647

BINNIAN, Mrs Jennifer Ann. b 34. Qu Coll Birm 81. **dss** 84 **d** 87 **p** 94. Chaddesley Corbett and Stone *Worc* 84-85; Bewdley Far Forest 85-87; Chapl Kemp Hospice 87-96; Chapl Asst Kidderminster Gen Hosp 87-94; rtd 96. *Bodenham Farm, Wolverley, Kidderminster, Worcs DY11 5SY* Tel (01562) 850382

BINNIE, Alexander David. b 22. Ripon Hall Ox 67. **d** 68 **p** 69. C Sutton Coldfield H Trin *Birm* 68-72; V Dosthill 72-88; C-in-c Wood End St Mich CD 72-83; rtd 88; Perm to Offic *Lich* from 88; Perm to Offic *Birm* from 88. *3 Walkers Croft, Lichfield, Staffs WS13 6TR* Tel (01543) 254250

BINNS, Dr John Richard. b 51. Cam Univ MA76 Lon Univ PhD89. Coll of Resurr Mirfield 74. **d** 76 **p** 77. C Clapham H Trin *S'wark* 76-78; C Clapham Old Town 78-80; TV Mortlake w E Sheen 80-87; V Upper Tooting H Trin 87-94; V Cambridge Gt St Mary w St Mich *Ely* from 94. *Great St Mary's Vicarage, 39 Madingley Road, Cambridge CB3 0EL* Tel (01223) 355285

BINNS, Peter Rodney. b 44. St Andr Univ MA66. Ox NSM Course 72. **d** 75 **p** 76. NSM Amersham on the Hill *Ox* 75-90; NSM Wingrave w Rowsham, Aston Abbotts and Cublington from 90; NSM Hawridge w Cholesbury and St Leonard from 90. *16 Turnfurlong Row, Turnfurlong Lane, Aylesbury, Bucks HP21 7FF* Tel (01296) 22705

BINNY, John Wallace. b 46. Univ of Wales (Lamp) BA70. St Mich Coll Llan 69. **d** 71 **p** 72. C Llantrisant *Llan* 71-77; V Troedrhiwgarth 77-82; R Eglwysbrewis w St Athan, Flemingston, Gileston 82-95; R Eglwysbrewis w St Athan w Gileston from 95. *The Rectory, Rectory Drive, St Athan, Barry CF62 4PD* Tel (01446) 750540

BIRBECK, Anthony Leng (Tony). b 33. MBE90. Linc Coll Ox BA59 MA61. Linc Th Coll 58. **d** 60 **p** 61. C Redcar *York* 60-74; Chapl Teesside Ind Miss 62-74; Can Res and Treas Wells Cathl *B & W* 74-78; NSM Wells St Thos w Horrington from 78. *4 Mount Pleasant Avenue, Wells, Somerset BA5 2JQ* Tel (01749) 673246 Fax 679485

BIRBECK, John Trevor. b 49. AIB77. St Jo Coll Nottm 86. **d** 88 **p** 89. C Eccleshill *Bradf* 88-92; V Hurst Green and Mitton from 92. *The Vicarage, Hurst Green, Clitheroe, Lancs BB7 9QR* Tel (01254) 826686

BIRCH, Arthur James Fleet. b 14. Univ Coll Dur BA36 MA39. **d** 37 **p** 38. C W Bromwich Ch Ch *Lich* 37-41; C Wroxeter 41-43; C Crewe St Jo *Ches* 43-46; V Lostock Gralam 46-55; V Plemstall w Guilden Sutton 55-59; V Hooton 59-70; R Lymm 70-79; rtd 79; Perm to Offic *Ches* from 79. *21 Arran Drive, Frodsham, Warrington WA6 6AL* Tel (01928) 733709

BIRCH, Arthur Kenneth. b 15. Qu Coll Birm 46. **d** 48 **p** 49. C St Alb St Paul *St Alb* 48-50; Area Sec (Dios Ely, Nor and St E & I) CMS 50-55; V New Catton Ch Ch *Nor* 55-60; V Buxton w Oxnead 60-71; R Lammas w Lt Hautbois 60-71; Uganda 71-75; V Fence in Pendle *Blackb* 75-76; C Bollington St Jo *Ches* 77-79; R Church Lawton 79-81; rtd 81; Perm to Offic *Sarum* 81-95; Perm to Offic *Nor* from 95. *26 Smugglers Lane, Reepham, Norfolk NR10 4QT* Tel (01603) 871405

BIRCH, Derek. b 31. Univ of Wales (Lamp) BA58. Coll of Resurr Mirfield 58. **d** 60 **p** 61. C S Elmsall *Wakef* 60-62; C Penistone w Midhope 62-66; V Silkstone 66-89; Chapl Stainborough 76-89; P-in-c Hoyland Swaine 85-89; V Hoylandswaine and Silkstone w Stainborough from 89. *The Vicarage, 12 High Street, Silkstone, Barnsley, S Yorkshire S75 4JN* Tel (01226) 790232

BIRCH, Graham James. b 62. N Ord Course BTh94. **d** 97. C Southport St Phil and St Paul *Liv* from 97. *63 Belmont Street, Southport, Merseyside PR8 1JH* Tel (01704) 531615

BIRCH, Henry Arthur. b 24. St Jo Coll Dur BA48. Tyndale Hall Bris 48. **d** 49 **p** 50. C Edin St Thos *Edin* 49-51; C Surbiton Hill Ch Ch *S'wark* 51-54; R Uphill *B & W* 54-69; Australia 69-81 and from 84; S Africa 81-84; rtd 90. *9/87 Yathong Road, Caringbah, NSW, Australia 2229* Tel Sydney (2) 525 1763

BIRCH, Janet Ann. St Alb Minl Tr Scheme 77. **dss** 80 **d** 87 **p** 94. Luton St Mary *St Alb* 80-87; Par Dn Streatley 87-91; rtd 91; NSM Aldeburgh w Hazlewood *St E* from 91. *3 Market Cross House, Wentworth Road, Aldeburgh, Suffolk IP15 5BJ* Tel (01728) 453371

BIRCH, Shirley Anne. b 34. EMMTC 88. **d** 91 **p** 94. Hon Par Dn Melton Gt Framland *Leic* 91-93; Hon C Melton Mowbray from 93. *16 Weaver Green, Melton Mowbray, Leics LE13 0UH* Tel (01664) 69883

BIRCHALL, Maurice Molyneux. b 11. Dur Univ LTh41 BA45. Edin Th Coll 36. **d** 39 **p** 40. C Burntisland *St And* 39-42; C Falkirk *Edin* 42-43; Chapl RAF 43-44; Chapl St Chad's Coll *Dur* 44-45; C Cullercoats St Geo *Newc* 45-46; C Penrith St Andr *Carl* 46-48; V Castle Sowerby 48-56; V Sowerby *Wakef* 56-65; V Thorpe 56-65; Clerical Org Sec CECS 65-73; P-in-c Ightenhill St Oswald Burnley 73-77; rtd 77. *33 South Avenue, Morecambe, Lancs LA4 5RJ* Tel (01524) 414136

BIRCHALL, Robert Gary. b 59. Sheff Univ BA81. St Jo Coll Nottm 85. **d** 88 **p** 89. C Manston *Ripon* 88-91; C Leic Martyrs *Leic* 91-94; C New Humberstone 94-95; V Burnopfield *Dur* from 95. *The Vicarage, Front Street, Burnopfield, Newcastle upon Tyne NE16 6HQ* Tel (01207) 270261

BIRCHARD, Canon Thaddeus Jude. b 45. Louisiana State Univ BA66 Nottm Univ DipTh68. Kelham Th Coll 66. **d** 70 **p** 71. C Devonport St Mark Ford *Ex* 70-73; C Southend St Jo w St Mark, All SS w St Fran etc *Chelmsf* 73-76; TV Poplar *Lon* 76-80; V Paddington St Jo w St Mich from 80; Hon Can Louisiana from 90. *18 Somers Crescent, London W2 2PN* Tel 0171-262 1732

BIRCHBY, Martin Cecil. b 17. Worc Ord Coll 66. **d** 68 **p** 69. C Bromyard *Heref* 68-70; P-in-c Bredenbury and Wacton w Grendon Bishop 70-75; P-in-c Edwyn Ralph and Collington w Thornbury 71-75; P-in-c Pembridge 75-80; P-in-c Shobdon 79-80; R Pembridge w Moor Court and Shobdon 80-83; P-in-c Staunton-on-Arrow w Byton 81-83; R Pembridge w Moorcourt, Shobdon, Staunton etc 83-85; rtd 85; Perm to Offic *Heref* from 85. *Cornerways, 9 Bearcroft, Weobley, Hereford HR4 8TA* Tel (01544) 318185

BIRCHMORE, Brian Leonard. b 35. ALCD59. **d** 59 **p** 60. C Rusthall *Roch* 59-62; C Rainham 62-64; C Belvedere All SS 64-66; V Meopham 66-74; R Chatham St Mary w St Jo 74-75; Perm to Offic *Chelmsf* 81-83; Ind Chapl Harlow from 83; P-in-c Bush End 83-89; P-in-c Hatfield Broad Oak 83-89; P-in-c Greenstead juxta Colchester from 89. *The Rectory, 74 Howe Close, Greenstead, Colchester CO4 3XD* Tel (01206) 865762

BIRCHNALL, Canon Simeon Robert. b 18. St Jo Coll Dur BA42 MA45 DipTh43. **d** 43 **p** 44. C Pitsmoor w Wicker *Sheff* 43-46; C Conisbrough 46-47; C Clifton St Jas 47-50; C Chingford SS Pet and Paul *Chelmsf* 50-53; C-in-c Chingford St Anne 53-55; V 56-64; R Woodford St Mary 64-71; R Woodford St Mary w St Phil and St Jas 71-97; Hon Can Chelmsf Cathl 76-97; RD Redbridge 77-90; P-in-c Barkingside St Cedd 83-90; rtd 97. *2 Brodie Road, London E4 7HF* Tel 0181-524 9908

BIRD, Alfred. b 10. Keble Coll Ox BA32 MA39. Melbourne Coll of Div MTh75 Bps' Coll Cheshunt 33. **d** 34 **p** 35. C Carl St Aid and Ch Ch *Carl* 34-38; Chapl Asst St Thos Hosp Lon 38-41; Lic to Offic *S'wark* 38-41; C Cockington *Ex* 41-42; Chapl RNVR 42-46; Australia 46-48; Chapl Eastbourne Coll 48-51; Australia from 51; rtd 75. *Unit 19, Pittwater Village, Brinawa Street, Mona Vale, NSW, Australia 2103* Tel Sydney (2) 9998 0119

BIRD (née BAKER), Mrs Anne-Marie Clare. b 56. Wye Coll Lon BSc78 Glas Univ MSc80. St Jo Coll Nottm 88. **d** 90 **p** 94. Par Dn Levenshulme St Pet *Man* 90-94; C 94-95; P-in-c Crumpsall from 95. *St Matthew's Rectory, 30 Cleveland Road, Manchester M8 6QU* Tel 0161-795 4376

BIRD, Dr Anthony Peter. b 31. St Jo Coll Ox BA54 BTh55 MA57 Birm Univ MB, ChB70. Cuddesdon Coll 55. **d** 57 **p** 58. C Stafford St Mary *Lich* 57-60; Chapl Cuddesdon Coll 60-61; Vice-Prin 61-64; C Selly Oak St Wulstan *Birm* 64-68; Lic to Offic 68-79; Prin Qu Coll Birm 74-79; Perm to Offic *Birm* from 85; rtd 96. *93 Bournbrook Road, Birmingham B29 7BX*

BIRD, The Ven Colin Richard Bateman. b 33. Selw Coll Cam BA56 MA61. Cuddesdon Coll 56. **d** 58 **p** 59. S Africa 58-70; C Limpsfield and Titsey *S'wark* 70-75; V Hatcham St Cath 75-88; RD Deptford 80-85; Hon Can S'wark Cathl 82-88; Adn Lambeth from 88; P-in-c Brixton Hill St Sav 91-94. *7 Hoadly Road, London SW16 1AE* Tel 0181-769 4384 or 392 3742 Fax 392 3743

BIRD, David John. b 46. Univ of Wales (Lamp) BA70 Pittsburgh Univ PhD87. Gen Th Sem (NY) STM74. **d** 70 **p** 71. C Kidderminster St Geo *Worc* 70-72; USA from 72. *Grace Church, 1041 Wisconsin Avenue, Northwest, Georgetown, Washington DC 20007, USA* Tel Washington DC (202) 333-7100

BIRD, David Ronald. b 55. York Univ BA76. St Jo Coll Nottm 83. **d** 86 **p** 87. C Kinson *Sarum* 86-90; R Thrapston *Pet* from 90; P-in-c Islip 94-95; RD Higham from 94. *The Rectory, Thrapston, Kettering, Northants NN14 4PD* Tel (01832) 732393

BIRD, Donald Wilfred Ray. b 27. Dur Univ BA52. Linc Th Coll 61. **d** 63 **p** 64. C E w W Barkwith *Linc* 63-65; Rhodesia 66-80; R Scotter w E Ferry *Linc* 80-92; rtd 92; Zimbabwe 94. *Bryn Hyfryd,*

25 Mersey Street, Borth y Gest, Porthmadog LL49 9UB Tel (01766) 514265

BIRD, Douglas Norman. b 38. LNSM course 89. **d** 92 **p** 93. NSM New Bury *Man* from 92. *14 Tudor Avenue, Farnworth, Bolton BL4 9RH* Tel (01204) 861167

BIRD, Canon Frederick Hinton. b 38. St Edm Hall Ox BA62 MA66 Univ of Wales MEd81 PhD86. St D Coll Lamp BD65. **d** 65 **p** 66. C Mynyddislwyn *Mon* 65-67; Min Can St Woolos Cathl 67-70; Chapl Anglo-American Coll Farringdon 70-71; Perm to Offic *Ox* 70-78; Perm to Offic *Cant* 72-78; Perm to Offic *Mon* 76-82; V Rushen *S & M* from 82; Can St German's Cathl from 93. *Kirk Rushen Vicarage, Port St Mary, Isle of Man IM9 5LP* Tel (01624) 832275

BIRD, Canon Geoffrey Neville. b 22. AKC48. St Boniface Warminster 48. **d** 49 **p** 50. C Berkeley *Glouc* 49-53; C Malden St Jo *S'wark* 53-54; C Glouc St Aldate *Glouc* 54-56; R Edge w Pitchcombe 56-82; P-in-c Brookthorpe w Whaddon and Harescombe 76-82; R The Edge, Pitchcombe, Harescombe and Brookthorpe 82-90; Hon Can Glouc Cathl 83-90; RD Bisley 84-90; rtd 90; Perm to Offic *Glouc* from 90. *Ivy Croft, Winstone, Cirencester, Glos GL7 7JZ* Tel (01285) 821664

BIRD, Henry John Joseph. b 37. ARCO58 Qu Coll Cam BA59 MA63. Linc Th Coll 62. **d** 64 **p** 65. C Harbledown *Cant* 64-68; C Skipton H Trin *Bradf* 68-70; V Oakworth 70-81; Chapl Abingdon Sch 81-82; P-in-c Doncaster St Geo *Sheff* 82-85; V from 85. *The Vicarage, 98 Thorne Road, Doncaster, S Yorkshire DN2 5BJ* Tel (01302) 368796 or 323748

BIRD, Dr Hugh Claud Handley. b 24. FRCGP SS Coll Cam MA MB BCh. Ridley Hall Cam. **d** 86 **p** 86. NSM Coxheath w E Farleigh, Hunton and Linton *Roch* 86-95; Perm to Offic *Cant* from 95. *The Slate Farm, Seamark Road, Brooksend, Birchington, Kent CT7 0JL* Tel (01843) 846619

BIRD, Jeffrey David. b 54. Nottm Univ BCombStuds85. Linc Th Coll 82. **d** 85 **p** 86. C Frome St Jo *B & W* 85-88; Asst Chapl HM Pris Pentonville 88-89; Chapl HM Pris Dartmoor 89-95; Chapl HM Pris Albany from 95. *HM Prison Albany, 55 Parkhurst Road, Newport, Isle of Wight PO30 5RS* Tel (01983) 524055 Fax 825827

BIRD, Jeremy Paul. b 56. Ex Univ BSc77 DipTh78 Hull Univ MA88. Sarum Th Coll 78. **d** 80 **p** 81. C Tavistock and Gulworthy *Ex* 80-83; Chapl Teesside Poly *York* 83-88; R Chipstable w Huish Champflower and Clatworthy *B & W* 88-93; Rural Affairs Officer 88-93; V Uffculme *Ex* from 93. *The Vicarage, Uffculme, Cullompton, Devon EX15 3AX* Tel (01884) 841001

BIRD, Maurice Pidding. b 19. Linc Coll Ox BA40 MA44. Cuddesdon Coll 40. **d** 42 **p** 43. C Malden St Jo *S'wark* 42-43; C Headington *Ox* 43-46; C Eastney *Portsm* 47-55; Chapl Hostel of God Clapham 55-59; R Winterton w E Somerton *Nor* 59-71; V Heigham St Barn 71-75; V Heigham St Barn w St Bart 75-82; P-in-c Edington and Imber *Sarum* 82-83; P-in-c Erlestoke and Gt Cheverell 82-83; P-in-c Edington and Imber, Erlestoke and E Coulston 83-88; rtd 88; Perm to Offic *Wakef* from 88. *61 Beechwood, Woodlesford, Leeds LS26 8PQ* Tel 0113-282 0865

BIRD, Norman David. b 32. CQSW73. Coll of Resurr Mirfield 87. **d** 89 **p** 90. NSM Willesden Green St Andr and St Fran of Assisi *Lon* 89-92; NSM Preston Ascension from 93. *5 Oldfield Road, London NW10 9UD* Tel 0181-451 4160 or 459 2670

BIRD, Peter Andrew. b 40. Wadh Coll Ox BA62 MA68. Ridley Hall Cam 63. **d** 65 **p** 66. C Keynsham w Queen Charlton *B & W* 65-68; C Strood St Nic *Roch* 68-72; TV Strood 72-79; V S Gillingham 79-89; V Westerham from 89. *The Vicarage, Borde Hill, Vicarage Hill, Westerham, Kent TN16 1TL* Tel (01959) 563127

BIRD, Rex Alan. b 30. Trin Coll Bris 54. **d** 57 **p** 58. C Wellington Ch Ch *Lich* 57-59; C St Alb St Paul *St Alb* 59-61; V Rainham *Chelmsf* 61-65; R Wennington 61-65; R Lavenham *St E* 65-75; CF (TA) from 65; RD Lavenham *St E* 72-75; Dean Battle *Chich* 75-84; V Battle 75-84; V Castle Hedingham *Chelmsf* 84-91; R Monks Eleigh w Chelsworth and Brent Eleigh etc *St E* 91-96; R Monks Eleigh w Chelsworth and Brent Eleigh etc from 96. *The Rectory, High Street, Monks Eleigh, Ipswich IP7 7AU* Tel (01449) 740244

BIRD, Canon Roger Alfred. b 49. AKC72. St Aug Coll Cant 72. **d** 73 **p** 74. C Prestatyn *St As* 73-78; R Llandysilio and Penrhos and Llandrinio etc 78-92; Dioc RE Adv from 84; Dioc Dir of Educn from 89; R Guilsfield 92-97; R Guilsfield w Pool Quay from 97; Hon Can St As Cathl from 93; RD Pool from 96. *The Vicarage, Guilsfield, Welshpool SY21 9NF* Tel (01938) 554245

BIRDSEYE, Miss Jacqueline Ann. b 55. Sussex Univ BEd78 Southn Univ BTh88 K Coll Lon MTh93. Sarum & Wells Th Coll 85. **d** 88 **p** 94. C Egham Hythe *Guildf* 88-91; C Fleet 91-92; C Shottermill 92-95; C Leavesden All SS *St Alb* from 95. *49 Ross Crescent, Garston, Watford WD2 6DA* Tel (01923) 673129

BIRDWOOD, William Halhed. b 51. St Jo Coll Dur BA73. Sarum & Wells Th Coll 76. **d** 78 **p** 79. C Royston *St Alb* 78-82; C Thorley w Bishop's Stortford H Trin 82-89; Chapl HM Pris Ex 89-95; Chapl HM Pris Dartmoor from 95; Lic to Offic *Ex* from 89. *HM Prison Dartmoor, Princetown, Yelverton, Devon PL20 6RR* Tel (01822) 890261 Fax 890679

BIRKENHEAD, Suffragan Bishop of. *See* LANGRISH, The Rt Revd Michael Laurence

BIRKET, Cyril. b 28. ACIS70. NW Ord Course 71. **d** 74 **p** 75. C Broughton *Blackb* 74-79; V Wesham 79-86; V Overton 86-96; rtd 96; Perm to Offic *Bradf* from 96; Perm to Offic *Blackb* from 96. *61 Twemlow Parade, Morecambe, Lancs LA3 2AL*

BIRKETT, Mrs Joyce. b 38. WMMTC 84. **d** 87 **p** 94. Par Dn Hill *Birm* 87-91; Asst Chapl Highcroft Hosp Birm 87-91; Par Dn Rowley Regis *Birm* 91-94; C 94-96; V Londonderry from 96. *The Vicarage, 15 St Mark's Road, Smethwick, Warley, W Midlands B67 6QF* Tel 0121-429 1149

BIRKETT, Neil Warren. b 45. Lanc Univ BEd74 Southn Univ MA84. Kelham Th Coll 65. **d** 77 **p** 77. NSM Win St Matt *Win* from 77. *Corrymeela, 132 Teg Down Meads, Winchester, Hants SO22 5NS* Tel (01962) 864910

BIRKETT, Peter. b 13. Univ Coll Dur BA35 MA39. **d** 36 **p** 37. C Boxley *Cant* 36-38; C Birchington w Acol 38-40; Chapl RAFVR 40-46; V Charing *Cant* 46-51; R Crowcombe *B & W* 51-64; P-in-c Bicknoller 60-62; V Castle Cary w Ansford 64-69; R Holford w Dodington 69-77; rtd 78; Perm to Offic *B & W* 82-87. *14 Long Street, Williton, Taunton, Somerset TA4 4NQ* Tel Williton (01984) 632220

BIRKIN, Mrs Elspeth Joyce (Joy). b 36. CertEd58. W of England Minl Tr Course 95. **d** 96 **p** 97. NSM Hanley Castle, Hanley Swan and Welland *Worc* from 96. *111 Cowleigh Road, Malvern, Worcs WR14 1QW* Tel (01684) 569493

BIRKINSHAW, Ian George. b 58. Pemb Coll Ox BA81 Sheff Univ PGCE82 Leeds Univ MA97. N Ord Course 93. **d** 96 **p** 97. NSM Chapeltown *Sheff* from 96. *69 Willow Crescent, Chapeltown, Sheffield S35 1QS* Tel 0114-245 4708

BIRLEY, John Lindsay. b 19. Kelham Th Coll 37. **d** 43 **p** 44. C Coulsdon St Andr *S'wark* 43-46; Asst Chapl Wellingborough Sch 46-48; Asst Master Choristers' Sch Ex 48-50; Chapl Reed's Sch Cobham 50-54; Asst Chapl St Jo Sch Leatherhead 54-64; Asst Master Wellington Coll Berks 64-76; rtd 76. *Abtei Himmerod, D 54534 Grosslittgen, Germany* Tel Grosslittgen (6575) 96075

BIRMINGHAM, Archdeacon of. *See* DUNCAN, The Ven John Finch

BIRMINGHAM, Bishop of. *See* SANTER, The Rt Revd Mark

BIRMINGHAM, Provost of. *See* BERRY, The Very Revd Peter Austin

BIRT, David Edward. b 26. St Steph Ho Ox 86. **d** 86 **p** 87. NSM Ealing Ch the Sav *Lon* from 86. *10 Manor Court Road, London W7 3EL* Tel 0181-579 4871

BIRT, Malcolm Douglas. b 33. Trin Coll Cam BA56 MA60. Ridley Hall Cam 56. **d** 58 **p** 59. C Barrow St Mark *Carl* 58-60; C Tunbridge Wells St Jo *Roch* 60-63; V Constable Lee *Man* 63-72; V Anslow *Lich* from 72; R Rolleston from 72. *The Rectory, Rolleston, Burton-on-Trent, Staffs DE13 9BE*

BIRT, Patrick. b 34. Glouc Th Course 71. **d** 75 **p** 75. NSM Bisley *Glouc* 75-76; NSM Whiteshill 76-81; C Stroud H Trin 81; R Ruardean 81-86; V Newbridge-on-Wye and Llanfihangel Brynpabuan *S & B* 86-88; TV Gillingham *Sarum* from 88. *The Vicarage, Stour Provost, Gillingham, Dorset SP8 5RU* Tel (01747) 838216

BIRT, Richard Arthur. b 43. Ch Ch Ox BA66 MA69. Cuddesdon Coll 67. **d** 69 **p** 70. C Sutton St Mich *York* 69-71; C Wollaton *S'well* 71-75; R Kirkby in Ashfield 75-80; P-in-c Duxford *Ely* 80-87; R 87-88; P-in-c Hinxton 80-87; V 87-88; P-in-c Ickleton 80-87; V 87-88; V Weobley w Sarnesfield and Norton Canon *Heref* from 88; P-in-c Letton w Staunton, Byford, Mansel Gamage etc from 88. *The Vicarage, Church Road, Weobley, Hereford HR4 8SD* Tel (01544) 318415

BIRT, The Ven William Raymond. b 11. Ely Th Coll 55. **d** 56 **p** 57. C Caversham *Ox* 56-59; C Newbury St Jo 59-63; V Newbury St Geo Wash Common 63-71; P-in-c Enbourne w Hampstead Marshall 68-70; RD Newbury 70-73; R W Woodhay 71-81; Adn Berks 73-77; Hon Can Ch Ch 79-82; rtd 81; C W Woodhay w Enborne, Hampstead Marshall etc *Ox* 81-91. *1 The Old Bakery, George Street, Kingsclere, Newbury, Berks RG15 8NQ* Tel (01635) 297426 Fax as telephone

BIRTWISTLE, Canon James. b 33. FCA66. Ely Th Coll 57. **d** 59 **p** 60. C Southport St Luke *Liv* 59-63; V Cleator Moor w Cleator *Carl* 63-70; R Letchworth *St Alb* 70-73; P-in-c Wareside 73-80; Dep Dir of Educn 77-80; Dioc Dir of Educn from 80; Hon Can St Alb from 85; P-in-c Hertingfordbury from 88. *St Mary's Rectory, Hertingfordbury, Herts SG14 2LE* Tel (01992) 554450 Fax (01707) 373089

BISCOE, Clive. b 45. St Deiniol's Hawarden 85. **d** 86 **p** 87. C Llansamlet *S & B* 86-90; V Landore 90-91. *6 Hazelwood Row, Cwmavon, Port Talbot SA12 9DP*

BISH, Donald. b 26. Ripon Hall Ox. **d** 75 **p** 75. C S Gillingham *Roch* 75-79; R Wateringbury w Teston and W Farleigh 79-92; rtd 92; Perm to Offic *Cant* from 92; Perm to Offic *Roch* from 92. *5 Eynesford Road, Allington, Maidstone, Kent ME16 0TD* Tel (01622) 661847

BISHOP, Mrs Alice Margaret Marion. b 67. Newnham Coll Cam BA89 MA93 Lon Univ MTh92. St Steph Ho Ox 92. **d** 94. C Stepney St Dunstan and All SS *Lon* from 94. *St Faith's House, Shandy Street, London E1 4ST* Tel 0171-790 9961

BISHOP, Andrew Scott. b 70. Leeds Univ BA93. St Steph Ho Ox BTh93. **d** 96 **p** 97. C Westmr St Steph w St Jo *Lon* from 96. *St Faith's House, Shandy Street, London E1 4ST* Tel 0171-790 9961

BISHOP, Anthony John (Tony). b 43. G&C Coll Cam BA66 MA69 Lon Univ MTh69. ALCD67. **d** 69 **p** 70. C Eccleston St Luke *Liv* 69-73; C Gt Baddow *Chelmsf* 73-77; Nigeria 77-84; Lect Lon Bible Coll 84-85; TV Chigwell *Chelmsf* 85-93; P-in-c Walthamstow St Jo from 93. *St John's Vicarage, 18 Brookscroft Road, London E17 4LH* Tel 0181-531 6249

BISHOP, Anthony Peter. b 46. FRSA87. St Jo Coll Nottm LTh74 MPhil84 ALCD71. **d** 71 **p** 72. C Beckenham St Geo *Roch* 71-75; Chapl RAF 75-91; Asst Chapl-in-Chief RAF from 91. *Chaplaincy Services (RAF), HQ, Personnel and Training Command, RAF Innsworth, Gloucester GL3 1EZ* Tel (01452) 712612 ext 5164 Fax 510828

BISHOP, Miss Cecil Marie. b 18. Lon Univ DipTh48. St Chris Coll Blackheath 46 Gilmore Ho 56. **dss** 57 **d** 87. Jamaica 57-74; Gambia 74-76; Lic to Offic *Ex* 76-87; rtd 78; Hon Par Dn Paignton St Jo *Ex* 87-94; Perm to Offic from 94. *Flat 5, Lancaster House, Belle Vue Road, Paignton, Devon TQ4 6HD* Tel (01803) 523522

BISHOP, Christopher (Chris). b 48. K Coll Lon. St Aug Coll Cant 71. **d** 72 **p** 73. C Gt Ilford St Mary *Chelmsf* 72-75; C Upminster 75-78; Adn's Youth Chapl 77-80; Dioc Youth Officer 80-86; Chapl Stansted Airport from 86; P-in-c Manuden w Berden from 86; RD Newport and Stansted from 89. *24 Mallows Green Road, Manuden, Bishop's Stortford, Herts CM23 1DG* Tel (01279) 812228

BISHOP, Canon David Harold. b 28. ARIBA53 FRSA75 DipArch. Westcott Ho Cam 55. **d** 57 **p** 58. C Cannock *Lich* 57-61; C Gt Barr 61-67; V All Hallows Lon Wall *Lon* 67-80; Architectural Adv CCC 67-80; Can Res Nor Cathl *Nor* 80-92; Vice-Dean 84-92; rtd 92. *Coneycote, 6 Coneygar Park, Bridport, Dorset DT6 3BA* Tel (01308) 424673

BISHOP, David Henry Ryder. b 27. R Agric Coll Cirencester MRAC50. Tyndale Hall Bris DipTh57. **d** 57 **p** 58. C Sevenoaks St Nic *Roch* 57-59; C Branksome St Clem *Sarum* 59-63; Uganda 64-67; Dep Sec CCCS 68; R Ox St Clem *Ox* 69-91; Zimbabwe 91-93; rtd 93. *38 Sandfield Road, Headington, Oxford OX3 7RT* Tel (01865) 60099

BISHOP, Donald. b 22. Lon Univ BSc48. Qu Coll Birm 56. **d** 57 **p** 58. C Trowbridge H Trin *Sarum* 57-60; CF (TA) 58-68; V Bodicote *Ox* 60-87; P-in-c Broughton 71-85; rtd 87; Perm to Offic *Cov* from 87. *66 Hanson Avenue, Shipston-on-Stour, Warks CV36 4HS* Tel (01608) 663431

BISHOP, Huw Daniel. b 49. Univ of Wales (Lamp) BA71 DipTh73. Bp Burgess Hall Lamp CPS73. **d** 73 **p** 74. C Carmarthen St Pet *St D* 73-77; Prov Youth Chapl Wales 77-79; V Llanybydder and Llanwenog w Llanwnnen 79-80; Youth and Community Officer 80-81; Hd of Relig Studies Carre's Gr Sch Sleaford 81-85; Hd of Relig Studies K Sch Pet 85-92; Lic to Offic *Linc* 83-95; CF (TA) from 85; Perm to Offic *Pet* 86-92; Perm to Offic *Lich* from 92. *5 Shaw Hall Lane, Coven Heath, Wolverhampton WV10 7EH*

BISHOP, Ian Gregory. b 62. ARICS87 Portsm Poly BSc84. Oak Hill Th Coll BA91. **d** 91 **p** 92. C Purley Ch Ch *S'wark* 91-95; P-in-c Saxlingham Nethergate and Shotesham *Nor* from 95. *The Rectory, Church Hill, Tasburgh, Norwich NR15 1NB* Tel (01508) 470656

BISHOP, Jeremy Simon. b 54. Nottm Univ BSc75 Yonsei Univ S Korea 84. All Nations Chr Coll 82 Wycliffe Hall Ox 89. **d** 91 **p** 92. C Macclesfield Team Par *Ches* from 91. *7 Brocklehurst Way, Macclesfield, Cheshire SK10 2HY* Tel (01625) 617680

BISHOP, John Baylis. b 32. Selw Coll Cam BA54 MA58. Cuddesdon Coll 54. **d** 56 **p** 57. C Middlesbrough St Oswald *York* 56-59; C Romsey *Win* 59-62; Chapl RN 62-66; P-in-c Linc St Mary-le-Wigford w St Martin *Linc* 66-67; V Linc St Faith 66-68; V Linc St Faith and St Martin w St Pet 69-71; Lic to Offic *Bris* 72-84; C Henbury 84-87; TV Bris St Agnes and St Simon w St Werburgh 87; TV Bris St Paul's 87-92; P-in-c Barrow Gurney *B & W* from 92; P-in-c Flax Bourton from 92; Asst Resources Adv 92-94. *The Rectory, Main Road, Flax Bourton, Bristol BS19 3QJ* Tel (01275) 462582

BISHOP, John Charles Simeon. b 46. Chich Th Coll 77. **d** 79 **p** 79. SSF 66-86; P-in-c Edin St Dav *Edin* 82-86; Chapl to the Deaf *Birm* from 86. *135 Wellman Croft, Birmingham B29 6NS* Tel 0121-471 3314 or 455 0601

BISHOP, John David. b 36. Liv Univ BEng MIMechE. EMMTC. **d** 85 **p** 86. NSM Ockbrook *Derby* from 85. *143 Victoria Avenue, Borrowash, Derby DE7 3HF* Tel (01332) 663828

BISHOP, John Harold. b 09. Univ Coll Dur BA31 MA45. Cuddesdon Coll 34. **d** 35 **p** 36. C Glouc St Steph *Glouc* 35-37; India 37-51; V Hugglescote w Donington *Leic* 51-60; R Singleton *Chich* 60-79; V E Dean 60-79; V W Dean 75-79; RD Westbourne 73-78; rtd 80; Perm to Offic *Chich* from 80. *6 Tregarth Road, Chichester, W Sussex PO19 4QU* Tel (01243) 527612

BISHOP, Michael George. b 27. Wycliffe Hall Ox 63. **d** 65 **p** 66. C Cheltenham St Mary *Glouc* 65-68; P-in-c Edale *Derby* 68-71; V Doveridge 71-79; Chapl HM Det Cen Foston Hall 73-79; V Cotmanhay *Derby* 79-81; Chapl Ilkeston Gen Hosp 79-81; USA 81-89; Perm to Offic *Chich* from 89; rtd 92. *Kingsley, 50 Filsham Road, St Leonards-on-Sea, E Sussex TN38 0PA* Tel (01424) 423539

BISHOP, Philip Michael. b 47. Lon Univ BD69 AKC69. St Aug Coll Cant 70. **d** 71 **p** 72. C Mansfield Woodhouse *S'well* 71-76; C Liscard St Mary w St Columba *Ches* 76-78; V Thornton le Moors w Ince and Elton 78-90; V Sutton w Carlton and Normanton upon Trent etc *S'well* 90-96; P-in-c Ch Broughton w Barton Blount, Boylestone etc *Derby* from 96. *The Vicarage, Chapel Lane, Church Broughton, Derby DE6 5BB* Tel (01283) 585296

BISHOP, Phillip Leslie. b 44. K Coll Lon BD66 AKC66. **d** 67 **p** 68. C Albrighton *Lich* 67-70; C St Geo-in-the-East St Mary *Lon* 70-71; C Middlesbrough Ascension *York* 71-73; P-in-c Withernwick 73-77; Ind Chapl 73-82; V Gt Ayton w Easby and Newton in Cleveland 82-89; RD Stokesley 85-89; R Guisborough from 89. *The Rectory, Guisborough, Cleveland TS14 6BS* Tel (01287) 632588

BISHOP, Stephen John. b 62. Hull Univ BA84 PGCE86. Ripon Coll Cuddesdon 90 Ch Div Sch of the Pacific (USA) 90. **d** 92 **p** 93. C Syston *Leic* 92-93; C Syston TM 93-95; C Market Harborough from 95. *The Vicarage, 49 Burnmill Road, Market Harborough, Leics LE16 7JF* Tel (01858) 463441

BISHOP, Thomas Harold. b 21. Ridley Hall Cam 60. **d** 61 **p** 62. C Wavertree H Trin *Liv* 61-64; V Wavertree St Bridget 64-69; V Rainford 69-87; rtd 87; Perm to Offic *Liv* from 87. *14 Keswick Road, Liverpool L18 9UH* Tel 0151-724 6647

BISHOP, Thomas Harveyson. b 25. Coll of Resurr Mirfield 54. **d** 56 **p** 57. S Africa 56-79 and from 87; Lic to Offic *Lon* 79-87; Lon Sec USPG 79-87; rtd 91. *c/o R C Bishop Esq, PO Box 4438, Cape Town, 8000 South Africa*

BISHOP, Miss Waveney Joyce. b 38. Westf Coll Lon BSc60. Cranmer Hall Dur DipTh72. **dss** 82 **d** 87 **p** 94. Leyton St Mary w St Edw *Chelmsf* 82-84; Bishopsworth *Bris* 84-87; Hon Par Dn 87-94; Hon C 94-96; rtd 96; Perm to Offic *Bris* from 96. *2 Bishop's Cove, Bishopsworth, Bristol BS13 8HH* Tel 0117-964 2588

BISHTON, Gerald Arthur (Gerry). b 32. MRSH76 Ruskin Coll Ox DipEcon56 St Pet Hall Ox BA59 MA63. Qu Coll Birm 60. **d** 61 **p** 62. C Forest Gate St Edm *Chelmsf* 61-64; Asst Chapl Lon Univ *Lon* 64-67; Chapl NE Lon Poly 68-73; Sen Lect 73-80; Chapl St Mary's Hosp Gt Ilford 68-80; Ind Chapl *Chelmsf* from 80; P-in-c Shopland 80-89; P-in-c Sutton 80-89; P-in-c Sutton w Shopland from 89. *The Rectory, Sutton Road, Rochford, Essex SS4 1LQ* Tel (01702) 544587

BISSET, Canon Robert McBain. b 05. Glas Univ MA30. Edin Th Coll 30. **d** 32 **p** 33. C Glas Ch Ch *Glas* 32-37; I Glas St Luke 37-41; R Lanark 41-47; R Bearsden 47-73; R Milngavie 56-73; Can St Mary's Cathl 62-73; rtd 73; Hon Can St Mary's Cathl *Glas* from 77. *Rannoch Lodge, Rannoch Drive, Cumbernauld, Glasgow G67 4EP* Tel (01236) 729273

BISSEX, Mrs Janet Christine Margaret. b 50. Westhill Coll Birm CertEd72. Trin Coll Bris 76. **dss** 86 **d** 87 **p** 94. Toxteth Park St Bede *Liv* 86-93; Par Dn 87-93; D-in-c Kirkdale St Mary and St Athanasius 93-94; P-in-c from 94. *St Athanasius Vicarage, 54 Fonthill Road, Liverpool L4 1QQ* Tel 0151-933 6860

BLACK, Canon Alexander Stevenson. b 28. Glas Univ MA53. Edin Th Coll 53. **d** 55 **p** 56. C Dumfries *Glas* 55-58; Chapl Glas Univ 58-61; C Glas St Mary 58-61; P-in-c E Kilbride 61-69; R Edin St Columba *Edin* 69-79; TV Edin St Jo 79-83; R Haddington 83-93; R Dunbar 83-93; Can St Mary's Cathl from 88; rtd 93. *3 Bass Rock View, Canty Bay, North Berwick, East Lothian EH39 5PJ* Tel (01620) 894771

BLACK, Douglas John. b 58. Middx Poly BA80 CertMS84. Ridley Hall Cam 89. **d** 91 **p** 92. C Wrexham *St As* from 91; Chapl NE Wales Inst HE from 93. *16 Foster Road, Wrexham LL11 2LT* Tel (01978) 365841

BLACK, Mrs Elizabeth Anne. b 47. Qu Coll Birm 80 Cranmer Hall Dur 81. **dss** 82 **d** 87. Cleadon *Dur* 82-85; S Westoe 85-88; Par Dn 87-88; Par Dn Chester le Street 88-92; Emmaus Chr Healing Trust from 93; Perm to Offic *Dur* from 95. *King's House Christian Healing Resource Centre, 29 Keppel Street, Dunston, Gateshead, Tyne & Wear NE11 9AR* Tel 0191-460 7404

BLACK, Ian Christopher. b 62. Kent Univ BA85 Nottm Univ MDiv93. Linc Th Coll 91. **d** 93 **p** 94. C Maidstone All SS and St Phil w Tovil *Cant* 93-96; P-in-c The Brents and Davington w Oare and Luddenham from 96. *The Vicarage, Brent Hill, Faversham, Kent ME13 7EF* Tel (01795) 533272

BLACK, Ian Forbes. b 29. St Aid Birkenhead 55. **d** 58 **p** 59. C Bramhall *Ches* 58-61; C Witton 61-63; P-in-c Prestonpans *Edin* 63-68; R Edin Ch Ch-St Jas 68-71; Asst Chapl HM Pris Liv 71-72; Chapl HM Pris Haverigg 72-73; R Bootle w Corney *Carl* 73-75; P-in-c Whicham w Whitbeck 73-75; R Bootle, Corney, Whicham and Whitbeck 75-86; P-in-c Orton St Giles 86-89; R 89-94; P-in-c Aikton 86-89; R 89-94; rtd 94. *Solwayside, Fort Carlisle, Carlisle CA5 5BU* Tel (016973) 51964

BLACK, Canon Leonard Albert (Len). b 49. Edin Th Coll 69. **d** 72 **p** 73. C Aberdeen St Marg *Ab* 72-75; Chapl St Paul's Cathl Dundee *Bre* 75-77; P-in-c Aberdeen St Ninian *Ab* 77-80; Miss to Seamen from 80; R Inverness St Mich *Mor* from 80; P-in-c Balloch New Town Distr 80-87; R Inverness St Jo 80-87; Relig

Progr Producer Moray Firth Radio from 87; Syn Clerk *Mor* from 92; Can St Andr Cathl Inverness from 92. *St Michael's Rectory, 28 Abban Street, Inverness IV3 6HH* Tel (01463) 233797 or 224433 Mobile 0836-365719 Fax (01463) 233797

BLACK, Canon Neville. b 36. MBE97. DMS86 DASHE97. Oak Hill Th Coll 61. **d** 64 **p** 65. C Everton St Ambrose w St Tim *Liv* 64-69; P-in-c Everton St Geo 69-71; V 71-81; P-in-c Everton St Benedict 70-72; P-in-c Everton St Chad w Ch Ch 70-72; Nat Project Officer Evang Urban Tr Project 74-81; P-in-c Edge Hill St Nath 81; TR St Luke in the City from 81; Chapl Liv Women's Hosp from 82; Tutor N Ord Course 82-89; Dir Gp for Urban Min and Leadership *Liv* 84-95; Hon Can Liv Cathl from 87. *445 Aigburth Road, Liverpool L19 3PA* Tel 0151-427 9803 Pager 01399-727640 Fax 0151-494 0736

BLACK, Canon Robert John Edward Francis Butler. b 41. TCD BA65 HDipEd70 DipG&C80 MA85. CITC 66. **d** 66 **p** 67. C Jordanstown *Conn* 66-68; C Dublin St Steph and St Ann *D & G* 68-73; C Stillorgan w Blackrock 73-85; Hd Master Dundalk Gr Sch *Arm* 85-96; Lic to Offic from 85; Hd Master Kilkenny Coll *C & O* from 96; Preb Ossory Cathl from 96. *Kilkenny College, Kilkenny, Co Kilkenny, Irish Republic* Tel Kilkenny (56) 61544 or 22213 Fax 70918

BLACK, Samuel James. b 38. CITC. **d** 68 **p** 69. C Cloughfern *Conn* 68-72; C Lisburn St Paul 72-78; I Rasharkin w Finvoy 78-82; I Belfast Upper Malone (Epiphany) 82-95; I Ballymore *Arm* from 95. *The Rectory, Glebe Hill Road, Tandragee, Craigavon, Co Armagh BT62 2EP* Tel (01762) 840234

BLACK, William H. d 88 **p** 89. NSM Malahide w Balgriffin *D & G* 88-89; NSM Dublin St Ann and St Steph 89-94; C from 94; Asst Hon Chapl Miss to Seamen from 89. *27 Greendale Avenue, Dublin 5, Irish Republic* Tel Dublin (1) 832 3141

BLACKALL, Mrs Margaret Ivy. b 38. St Kath Coll Lon CertEd58. EAMTC 82. **dss** 86 **d** 87 **p** 94. NSM Wickham Market w Pettistree and Easton *St E* 86-88; Par Dn Leiston 88-92; Par Dn Gt and Lt Glemham, Blaxhall etc 92-94; P-in-c 94-96; R from 96. *The Rectory, Stratford St Andrew, Saxmundham, Suffolk IP17 1LJ* Tel (01728) 603180

BLACKALL, Robin Jeremy McRae. b 35. Ridley Hall Cam 67. **d** 69 **p** 70. C Stowmarket *St E* 69-72; R Stanstead w Shimplingthorne and Alpheton 72-77; R Bradwell on Sea *Chelmsf* 77-79; R St Lawrence 77-79; Warden Bede Ho Staplehurst 79-81; Chapl HM Det Cen Blantyre Ho 81-82; R Edith Weston w N Luffenham and Lyndon w Manton *Pet* 86-95; P-in-c Upwell St Pet *Ely* from 95; P-in-c Outwell from 95. *The Rectory, 5 New Road, Upwell, Wisbech, Cambs PE14 9AB* Tel (01945) 772213

BLACKBURN, David James. b 45. Hull Univ BA67. Trin Coll Bris DipHE87. **d** 87 **p** 88. C Bromsgrove St Jo *Worc* 87-90; V Cradley from 90. *34 Beecher Road, Halesowen, W Midlands B63 2DJ* Tel (01384) 566928

BLACKBURN, Frederick John Barrie. b 28. TD73. Lich Th Coll 52. **d** 55 **p** 56. C Hebburn St Cuth *Dur* 55-58; C Bishopwearmouth St Mary V w St Pet CD 58-61; V Hunwick 61-64; CF (TA) 61-87; V Eighton Banks *Dur* 64-75; R Stella 75-87; TV Bellingham/Otterburn Gp *Newc* 87-89; rtd 89. *47 Coldstream Road, Newcastle upon Tyne NE15 7BY* Tel 0191-274 7851

BLACKBURN, John. b 47. Univ of Wales (Cardiff) DipTh69 DPS71 Open Univ BA88. St Mich Coll Llan 66. **d** 71 **p** 72. C Risca *Mon* 71-76; CF (TA) 73-76; CF from 76. *MOD Chaplains (Army), Trenchard Lines, Upavon, Pewsey, Wilts SN9 6BE* Tel (01980) 615804 Fax 615800

BLACKBURN, Keith Christopher. b 39. K Coll Lon BD63 AKC63. St Boniface Warminster 63. **d** 64 **p** 65. C Surbiton St Andr *S'wark* 64-66; C Battersea St Mary 67-70; Teacher Sir Walter St Jo Sch Battersea 67-70; Hon C Eltham H Trin 70-76; Hd of Ho Crown Woods Sch Eltham 70-76; Dep Hd Master Altwood C of E Sch 76-82; Lic to Offic *Ox* 76-82; Chapl and Hd Master St Geo Sch Gravesend 83-93; Hon C Fawkham and Hartley *Roch* 83-93; V Seal St Pet from 93. *The Vicarage, Church Street, Seal, Sevenoaks, Kent TN15 0AR* Tel (01732) 762955

BLACKBURN, Peter James Whittaker. b 47. Sydney Univ BA69. Coll of Resurr Mirfield DipTh71. **d** 72 **p** 73. C Felixstowe St Jo *St E* 72-76; C Bournemouth St Pet w St Swithun, H Trin etc *Win* 76-79; R Burythorpe, Acklam and Leavening w Westow *York* 79-85; Chapl Naples Ch Ch *Eur* 85-91; Chapl Algarve 91-97. *Casa Sao Vicente, Apartado 135, Boliqueime, 8100 Loule, Algarve, Portugal* Tel Loule (89) 366720

BLACKBURN, Richard Finn. b 52. St Jo Coll Dur BA74. Westcott Ho Cam 81. **d** 83 **p** 84. C Stepney St Dunstan and All SS *Lon* 83-87; P-in-c Isleworth St Jo 87-92; V Mosborough *Sheff* from 92; RD Attercliffe from 96. *The Vicarage, Duke Street, Mosborough, Sheffield S19 5DG* Tel 0114-248 6518

BLACKBURN, Archdeacon of. *See* MARSH, The Ven Francis John

BLACKBURN, Bishop of. *See* CHESTERS, The Rt Revd Alan David

BLACKBURN, Provost of. *See* FRAYNE, The Very Revd David

BLACKER, Herbert John. b 36. Bris Univ BSc59. Cranmer Hall Dur DipTh61. **d** 61 **p** 62. C Wednesbury St Bart *Lich* 61-63; C Chasetown 63-65; C Chigwell *Chelmsf* 65-69; TV Barnham Broom w Kimberley, Bixton etc *Nor* 69-76; R Burgh Parva w Briston 76-92; P-in-c Melton Constable w Swanton Novers 86-92; R Briston w Burgh Parva and Melton Constable from 92. *The Vicarage, Grange Close, Briston, Melton Constable, Norfolk NR24 2LY* Tel (01263) 860280

BLACKETT, James Gilbert. b 27. Tyndale Hall Bris 52. **d** 55 **p** 56. C Heworth H Trin *York* 55-57; C Newburn *Newc* 57-58; C Newc St Barn and St Jude 58-61; V Broomfleet *York* 61-67; V Ledsham 67-74; V Burton All SS *Lich* 74-82; V Burton All SS w Ch Ch 82-92; rtd 92; Perm to Offic *Pet* from 92. *103 Milford Avenue, Stony Stratford, Milton Keynes MK11 1EZ* Tel (01908) 265149

BLACKETT, Robert Peter. b 63. Dur Univ BSc85. Ripon Coll Cuddesdon BTh95. **d** 95 **p** 96. C Wigton *Carl* from 95. *8B Longthwaite Crescent, Wigton, Cumbria CA7 9JN* Tel (01697) 345937

BLACKFORD, David Walker. b 25. Univ of Wales DipTh69. **d** 70 **p** 71. C Holyhead w Rhoscolyn w Llanfair-yn-Neubwll *Ban* 70-72; Lic to Offic *Blackb* 72-80; Hon C Bassaleg *Mon* 80-85; V Treuddyn and Nercwys and Eryrys *St As* 85-90; rtd 90. *11 Whitechapel Walk, Undy, Magor, Newport NP6 3NS* Tel (01633) 880507

BLACKHAM, Paul. d 97. C Langham Place All So *Lon* from 97. *20 Holcroft Court, Clipstone Street, London W1P 7DL*

BLACKIE, Richard Footner (Brother Edmund). b 37. St Cath Coll Cam BA59 MA63 Worc Coll Ox BA59 BSc61. Ely Th Coll 60. **d** 62 **p** 63. C Saffron Walden *Chelmsf* 62-65; SSF from 66. *St Francis House, 75 Deerpark House, Belfast BT14 7PW* Tel (01232) 351480

BLACKLEDGE, David John. b 51. Oak Hill Th Coll 89. **d** 92 **p** 93. NSM Woodford Wells *Chelmsf* from 92. *Hornbeam, 143 Monkhams Lane, Woodford Green, Essex IG8 0NW* Tel 0181-505 3554

BLACKMAN, Brian David Eric. b 38. Ox NSM Course 82. **d** 85 **p** 86. NSM Reading St Luke *Ox* 85-86; NSM Reading St Luke w St Bart from 86. *13 Avebury Square, Reading RG1 6ET* Tel 0118-926 0345

BLACKMAN, Clive John. b 51. Hull Univ BSc73 MSc74 Birm Univ DipTh77. Qu Coll Birm 75. **d** 78 **p** 79. C Folkestone St Sav *Cant* 78-81; Chapl Birm Univ *Birm* 81-86; V Thorpe St Matt *Nor* 86-94; R Cringleford w Colney and Bawburgh from 94. *The Vicarage, Cringleford, Norwich NR4 6VE* Tel (01603) 54424

BLACKMAN, James Bentley. b 57. SS Hild & Bede Coll Dur BEd80 Nottm Univ BTh88. Linc Th Coll 85. **d** 88 **p** 89. C Nether Hoyland St Pet *Sheff* 88-91; C Harrogate St Wilfrid and St Luke *Ripon* 91-94; V Leyburn w Bellerby from 94. *The Vicarage, Bellerby Road, Leyburn, N Yorkshire DL8 5JF* Tel (01969) 22251

BLACKMAN, John Franklyn. b 34. LRAM70 DipRS75. S'wark Ord Course 72. **d** 75 **p** 76. NSM Cov H Trin *Cov* 75-81; Succ Cov Cathl 81-95; TV Cov E 88-95. *86A St George's Terrace, Jesmond, Newcastle-upon-Tyne NE2 2DL* Tel 0191-281 5267

BLACKMAN, Michael Orville. b 46. Univ of W Ontario BMin80 Univ of W Indies LTh70. Codrington Coll Barbados 67. **d** 71 **p** 71. Antigua 71-73; Barbados 73-78 and 80-86 and 91-97; Canada 78-80; TV E Ham w Upton Park St Alb *Chelmsf* 86-91; V Dalton *Sheff* from 97. *The Vicarage, 2 Vicarage Close, Dalton, Rotherham, S Yorkshire S65 3QL* Tel (01709) 850377

BLACKMAN, Peter Richard. b 28. Sarum Th Coll 52. **d** 55 **p** 56. C Aylestone *Leic* 55-60; V Ratby w Groby 60-84; TR 84-93; rtd 93; Perm to Offic *Chich* from 93. *25 Turnbull Road, Chichester, W Sussex PO19 4LY* Tel (01243) 787299

BLACKMORE, Cuthbert. b 17. Qu Coll Birm 57. **d** 59 **p** 60. C Acomb St Steph *York* 59-62; V Hackness w Harwood Dale 62-66; V Seamer w E Ayton 66-83; rtd 84. *85 West Garth, Cayton, Scarborough, N Yorkshire YO11 3SD* Tel (01723) 585156

BLACKMORE, Frank Ellis. b 43. Univ of Wales (Lamp) BA66. Wells Th Coll 65. **d** 67 **p** 68. C S'wark St Geo *S'wark* 67-70; Hon C Camberwell St Giles 70-79; NSM Paddington St Sav *Lon* from 79. *65 Sutherland Avenue, London W9 2HF* Tel 0171-289 3020

BLACKMORE, Robert Ivor. b 37. Univ of Wales (Lamp) 59 Open Univ BA78. **d** 62 **p** 63. C Llangynwyd w Maesteg *Llan* 62-65; C Dowlais 65-67; C Neath w Llantwit 67-71; V Pontlottyn 71-73; V Troedrhiwgarth 73-80; V Seven Sisters from 80. *The Vicarage, Church Road, Seven Sisters, Neath SA10 9DT* Tel (01639) 700286

BLACKMORE, Vernon John. b 50. Southn Univ BSc Man Univ MSc Lon Univ DipTh K Coll Lon MTh. Oak Hill Th Coll DipHE. **d** 82 **p** 83. C Ecclesall *Sheff* 82-87; Bp's Adv on Youth 85-87; Ed Lion Publishing 87-90; Dir Par Resources CPAS from 90; Perm to Offic *Cov* from 90. *CPAS, Athena Drive, Tachbrook Park, Warwick CV34 6NG* Tel (01926) 334242 Fax 337613

BLACKSHAW, Alfred. b 14. St Jo Coll Dur BA39 DipTh40 MA42. **d** 40 **p** 41. C Darwen St Barn *Blackb* 40-43; C Crookes St Thos *Sheff* 43-44; R Collyhurst *Man* 44-48; V Haydock St Mark *Liv* 48-55; V Blackpool Ch Ch *Blackb* 55-66; V Chesham Ch Ch *Ox* 66-72; V Copp *Blackb* 72-79; rtd 79; Perm to Offic *Blackb* from 79. *10 Denebank, All Hallows Road, Bispham, Blackpool FY2 0AS* Tel (01253) 596284

BLACKSHAW, Brian Martin. b 43. Lanc Univ MA74 Ch Ch Ox BA95 MA96. Ox NSM Course 87. **d** 90 **p** 91. NSM Amersham

Ox 90-93; C Hatch End St Anselm *Lon* 93-95; V Cheshunt *St Alb* from 96. *The Vicarage, Churchgate, Cheshunt, Herts EN8 9DY* Tel (01992) 623121

BLACKSHAW, Trevor Roland. b 36. GIMechE59. Lon Coll of Div 67. **d** 69 **p** 70. C New Catton St Luke *Nor* 69-73; C Luton Lewsey St Hugh *St Alb* 73-78; V Llandinam w Trefeglwys w Penstrowed *Ban* 78-85; Youth Chapl 82-83; Dioc Dir of Adult Educn 84-85; Consultant Dir Wholeness Through Ch Min 85-92; Midl Regional Co-ord BCMS 92-93; Crosslinks 93-97; Dir Perm to Offic *Linc* from 95; Warden Divine Healing Miss Crowhurst from 97. *The Old Rectory, Crowhurst, Battle, E Sussex TN33 9AD* Tel (01424) 830204

BLACKTOP, Graham Leonard. b 33. St Alb Minl Tr Scheme. **d** 85 **p** 86. NSM Rickmansworth *St Alb* 85-92; Perm to Offic *Sarum* from 92. *Dairy House, Wolfeton, Dorchester, Dorset DT2 9QN* Tel (01305) 262184

BLACKWALL, David D'Arcy Russell. b 35. Southn Univ BSc60 Imp Coll Lon DIC62. Wycliffe Hall Ox 63. **d** 65 **p** 66. C Southampton Thornhill St Chris *Win* 65-68; V Long Sutton 69-72; Chapl Ld Wandsworth Coll Hants 69-74; Hon C Odiham w S Warnborough *Win* 72-75; Chapl and Hd Jun Sch St Lawr Coll Ramsgate from 75; Lic to Offic *Cant* from 75. *Kerrison Cottage, Felderland Lane, Worth, Deal, Kent CT14 0BN* Tel (01304) 617708

BLACKWELL, Geoffrey Albert. b 27. Lon Coll of Div 62. **d** 65 **p** 66. C Clifton *York* 65-69; Chapl RN 69-73; Warden St Mich Home of Healing Cleadon 73-75; V S Hetton *Dur* 75-82; rtd 82; CSWG 89-95; NSM Burpham *Chich* 95-96; Perm to Offic from 96. *1 Highfield Gardens, Rustington, Littlehampton, W Sussex BN16 2PZ* Tel (01903) 782219

BLACKWELL, Geoffrey David. b 34. Jes Coll Ox BA57 MA61. Chich Th Coll 57. **d** 59 **p** 60. C Romford St Edw *Chelmsf* 59-62; S Africa 62-68; Chapl Westcott Ho Cam 68-73; V Forest Gate St Edm *Chelmsf* 73-81; Pilsdon Community 83-95; rtd 94; Perm to Offic *Pet* from 94. *15 Chatsfield, Werrington, Peterborough PE4 5DJ* Tel (01733) 324278

BLACKWELL, Nicholas Alfred John. b 54. St Jo Coll Nottm BTh85. **d** 85 **p** 86. C Birkenhead Priory *Ches* 85-88; C Stratford-on-Avon w Bishopton *Cov* 88-91; TV Cov E from 91. *St Anne's Vicarage, 129A London Road, Coventry CV1 2JQ* Tel (01203) 223381

BLACKWELL-SMYTH, Dr Charles Peter Bernard. b 42. TCD BA64 MA71 MB73. Gen Th Sem (NY) MDiv65. **d** 65 **p** 66. C Bangor Abbey *D & D* 65-67; C Dublin Ch Ch Leeson Park *D & G* 67-69; P-in-c Carbury *M & K* 73-75; Hon C St Stephen in Brannel *Truro* 87-94; Perm to Offic from 94. *Parcgwyn, Rectory Road, St Stephen, St Austell, Cornwall PL26 7RL* Tel (01726) 822465

BLACOE, Canon Brian Thomas. b 36. Open Univ DipEH BA. Oak Hill Th Coll 63. **d** 66 **p** 67. C Dundonald *D & D* 66-69; C Drumcree *Arm* 69-74; I Ardtrea w Desertcreat 74-78; I Annalong *D & D* 78-95; Can Dromore Cathl from 93; I Knocknamuckley from 95. *30 Mossbank Road, Ballynagarrick, Portadown, Co Armagh BT63 5SL* Tel (01762) 831227

BLADE, Brian Alan. b 24. ACCS55 ASCA66. Roch Th Coll 67. **d** 69 **p** 70. C Barnehurst *Roch* 69-71; C Crayford 71-76; V Buttershaw St Aid *Bradf* 76-80; R Etton w Helpston *Pet* 80-86; V Hardingstone and Horton and Piddington 86-90; rtd 90; Perm to Offic *Cant* from 90; Perm to Offic *Roch* from 90. *25 Dan Drive, Faversham, Kent ME13 7SW* Tel (01795) 531842

BLADON, Ernest Albert. b 19. Ex Univ DipEd58. Glouc Sch of Min 75. **d** 78 **p** 78. Hon C Cinderford St Jo *Glouc* 78-89; rtd 89; Perm to Offic *Glouc* 89-94. *Valista, Grange Road, Littledean, Cinderford, Glos GL14 3NJ* Tel (01594) 822702

BLAGDON-GAMLEN, Peter Eugene. b 20. KLJ. SSC. AKC48 St Boniface Warminster 48. **d** 49 **p** 50. C Wellington w W Buckland *B & W* 49-51; C Torquay St Martin Barton *Ex* 51-52; C Evesham *Worc* 52-53; V Swinefleet *Sheff* 53-56; PC Derby St Bart 56-64; CF (R of O) 59-75; R Harrold and Carlton w Chellington *St Alb* 64-68; R & V Eastchurch *Cant* 68-71; R & V Eastchurch w Leysdown and Harty 71-87; CF (TA) 78-85; rtd 87; Perm to Offic *Ex* 87-93; Perm to Offic *Pet* from 93; Perm to Offic *Leic* from 96. *Blagdon House, 110 Neale Avenue, Kettering, Northants NN16 9HD* Tel (01536) 484885

BLAGG, Colin. b 31. Leeds Univ BA57. Coll of Resurr Mirfield 57. **d** 59 **p** 60. C Edin Old St Paul *Edin* 59-63; R Gourock *Glas* 63-68; Chapl to the Deaf RADD Lon 68-74; Hon C Stoke Newington St Olave *Lon* 73-74; Chapl to the Deaf *Chich* 74-80; V Shoreham Beach 80-96; rtd 97; Perm to Offic *Chich* from 97. *55 Roedean Road, Worthing, W Sussex BN13 2BT* Tel (01903) 695321

BLAIR, John Wallace. b 48. Lon Univ BSc70. Qu Coll Birm 79. **d** 81 **p** 82. C Chorlton-cum-Hardy St Werburgh *Man* 81-83; CF 83-97; rtd 97. *MOD Chaplains (Army), Trenchard Lines, Upavon, Pewsey, Wilts SN9 6BE* Tel (01980) 615804 Fax 615800

BLAIR, The Very Revd Patrick Allen. b 31. Trin Coll Cam BA54 MA58. Ridley Hall Cam 54. **d** 56 **p** 57. C Harwell *Ox* 56-59; Chapl Oundle Sch 59-64; Jerusalem 64-66; Sudan 67-71; Provost Khartoum 67-71; R Chester le Street *Dur* 71-77; TR Barking St Marg w St Patr *Chelmsf* 77-87; Chapl Barking Hosp 77-87; Tunisia 87-91; Cyprus 91-96; Provost Nicosia 91-96; rtd 96. *Grace Cottage, Pilley Green, Boldre, Lymington, Hants SO41 5QG* Tel (01596) 677015

BLAIR, Philip Hugh. b 39. St Edm Hall Ox BA62 MA67. Ridley Hall Cam 62. **d** 64 **p** 65. C Camborne *Truro* 64-68; C Kenwyn 68-70; Sudan 70-73 and from 78; P-in-c St Enoder *Truro* 73-76; Tutor Ex Univ *Ex* 76-77. *PO Box 322, Khartoum, Sudan*

BLAIR-BROWN, Dennis. b 17. Em Coll Saskatoon LTh52. **d** 56 **p** 56. Canada 56-63; C Lymington *Win* 63-70; V Wellow 70-93; rtd 93. *135 The Close, Salisbury SP1 2EY* Tel (01722) 334008

BLAIR-FISH, Canon John Christopher. b 20. Linc Coll Ox BA46 MA47. Cuddesdon Coll 48. **d** 49 **p** 50. C Mottingham St Andr *S'wark* 49-51; C Warlingham w Chelsham 51-55; V Surbiton St Mark 55-72; R Chipstead 73-89; Hon Can S'wark Cathl 79-88; rtd 89; Perm to Offic *Chich* from 93. *39 Beehive Lane, Ferring, Worthing, W Sussex BN12 5NR* Tel (01903) 241480

BLAKE, Colin David. b 52. CertEd BEd BD. Trin Coll Bris 81. **d** 84 **p** 85. C Hucclecote *Glouc* 84-88; C Patchway *Bris* from 88. *106 Cooks Close, Bradley Stoke, Bristol BS12 0BB* Tel (01454) 617569

BLAKE, Derek Gordon. b 10. St Jo Coll Dur 32. **d** 36 **p** 37. C Bermondsey St Crispin *S'wark* 36-39; C Plumstead St Marg 39-42; V Maryport *Carl* 42-57; V Carl St Aid and Ch Ch 57-69; V Holme Cultram St Cuth 69-88; P-in-c Allonby 77-81; rtd 89; Perm to Offic *Carl* 89-95. *The Mount, Moor Road, Great Broughton, Cockermouth, Cumbria CA13 0YT* Tel (01900) 827483

BLAKE, Ian Martyn. b 57. BA79. Oak Hill Th Coll 76. **d** 80 **p** 81. C Widford *Chelmsf* 80-84; C Barton Seagrave w Warkton *Pet* 84-90; V Sneinton St Chris w St Phil *S'well* from 90. *St Christopher's Vicarage, 180 Sneinton Boulevard, Nottingham NG2 4GL* Tel 0115-950 5303

BLAKE, Mrs Margaret. b 48. Open Univ BA87. S'wark Ord Course 92. **d** 95 **p** 96. NSM Farnham *Guildf* 95-96; C from 96. *6 High Park Road, Farnham, Surrey GU9 7JL* Tel (01252) 25020

BLAKE, Preb Patrick John. b 30. Univ of Wales BA51 St Edm Hall Ox BA54 MA58. St Mich Coll Llan 54. **d** 55 **p** 56. C Buckley *St As* 55-59; C Oystermouth *S & B* 59-63; V Cleeve *B & W* 63-71; R Bruton w Lamyatt, Wyke and Redlynch 71-83; Dioc Ecum Officer 79-84; Preb Wells Cathl from 79; TR Yeovil 83-88; R Yeovil w Kingston Pitney 88; P-in-c Backwell 88-89; R 89-92; R Backwell w Chelvey and Brockley 92-95; RD Portishead 92-95; rtd 95; Clergy Retirement and Widows' Officer *B & W* from 96. *The Firs, 47 Lower Street, Merriott, Somerset TA16 5NN* Tel (01460) 78932

BLAKE, Peta Ruth. b 44. Lambeth STh89 Episc Div Sch Cam Mass MA89 DMin90 Trin Coll Bris 82. **dss** 83 **d** 87. New Swindon St Barn Gorse Hill *Bris* 83-87; Par Dn 87-88; Perm to Offic from 88. *10 Elmer Close, Malmesbury, Wilts SN16 9UE* Tel (01666) 823722

BLAKE, Canon Peter Douglas Stuart. b 27. BNC Ox BA52 MA57. Westcott Ho Cam 52. **d** 54 **p** 55. C Armley St Bart *Ripon* 54-58; N Rhodesia 58-64; Zambia 64-65; V Cropthorne w Charlton *Worc* 65-69; V Leek St Edw *Lich* 70-76; P-in-c Hartfield *Chich* 76-78; R Hartfield w Coleman's Hatch 78-87; rtd 87; P-in-c Breamore *Win* 89-90; Perm to Offic *Glas* from 91. *Holmhouse Cottage, Tynron, Thornhill, Dumfriesshire DG3 4LE* Tel (01848) 200417

BLAKE, Philip Charles. b 29. FAIW88 MACC88 Lon Univ DipTh57 Mitchell Coll (USA) BA80 Macquarie Univ (NSW) MA86 PhD91. Melbourne Coll of Div DipRE76 DPS80 Oak Hill Th Coll 54. **d** 57 **p** 58. C Slough *Ox* 57-60; C Uphill *B & W* 60-62; V Branston *Lich* 62-69; Australia from 69; rtd 91. *Shalom, Bridgenorth Road, Bridgenorth, Tasmania, Australia 7277* Tel Launceston (03) 301663 or 314896

BLAKE, Canon Roy Harold David. b 25. Chich Th Coll 54. **d** 57 **p** 58. C Westbury-on-Trym H Trin *Bris* 57-61; C Bishopston 61-65; V Bris St Agnes w St Simon 65-72; TR Bris St Agnes and St Simon w St Werburgh 72-74; RD Bris City 73-74; V Purton 74-93; RD Cricklade 76-82; Hon Can Bris Cathl 77-93; rtd 93. *10 Elmer Close, Malmesbury, Wilts SN16 9UE* Tel (01666) 823722

BLAKE, William Cornford. b 18. Ripon Hall Ox. **d** 67 **p** 68. C Putney St Mary *S'wark* 67-73; C Diss *Nor* 73-76; C Roydon St Remigius 73-76; P-in-c 76-79; R 79-85; rtd 85; Perm to Offic *Derby* from 85. *4 Farnway, Darley Abbey, Derby DE22 2BN* Tel (01332) 550431

BLAKELEY, Julian Graham. b 60. Oak Hill Th Coll BA88. **d** 88 **p** 89. C Bedworth *Cov* 88-91; C Harlow St Mary and St Hugh w St Jo the Bapt *Chelmsf* 91-95; R Darfield *Sheff* from 95. *The Rectory, Church Street, Darfield, Barnsley, S Yorkshire S73 9JX* Tel (01226) 752236

BLAKELEY, Robert Daniel. b 29. Saskatchewan Univ BA63 St Pet Coll Ox BA66 MA70. Em Coll Saskatchewan LTh56. **d** 56 **p** 57. Canada 56-59; USA 59-68; C High Wycombe *Ox* 68-71; USA 71-75; C St Marylebone St Mary *Lon* 75-82; Chapl Hill Ho Sch Knightsbridge 75-82; P-in-c Tasburgh *Nor* 82-85; P-in-c Tharston 82-85; P-in-c Forncett St Mary w St Pet 82-85; P-in-c Flordon 82-85; Hd Master and Chapl Corona Ravenscourt Sch Lon 85-92; rtd 92. *c/o Mr & Mrs N Bhoola, 40 St Mary's Crescent, Osterley, Middx*

BLAKELY, Miss Denise Irene. b 69. QUB BD91 PGCE92. CITC DPS95. **d** 95 **p** 96. C Holywood *D & D* from 95. *51 Princess Gardens, Holywood, Co Down BT18 0PN* Tel (01232) 424554

BLAKEMAN, Mrs Janet Mary. b 36. Man Univ BA57 CertEd58. Carl Dioc Tr Course 87. **d** 90. NSM Wetheral w Warw *Carl* 90-97; NSM Thornthwaite cum Braithwaite and Newlands from 97. *Langstrath, Greenfield Lane, Brampton, Cumbria CA8 1AU* Tel (016977) 2008

BLAKEMAN, Walter John. b 37. Qu Coll Birm 74. **d** 76 **p** 77. C Gnosall *Lich* 76-83; C Cheadle 83-86; Res Min Hednesford 86-90; Min Roundshaw LEP *S'wark* 90-94; C Pleasley *Derby* 94; TV E Scarsdale from 94. *The Rectory, 57 Newboundmill Lane, Pleasley, Mansfield, Notts NG19 7PT* Tel (01623) 810775

BLAKESLEY, Ms Christine Marilyn. b 50. St Hugh's Coll Ox BA73 MA75 PGCE74. NE Ord Course 93. **d** 95 **p** 96. C Darlington H Trin *Dur* from 95. *12 Vane Terrace, Darlington, Co Durham DL3 7AT* Tel (01325) 353326

BLAKESLEY, John. b 50. Keble Coll Ox BA72 MA76. St Steph Ho Ox 72. **d** 74 **p** 75. C Egremont *Carl* 74-77; C Doncaster Ch Ch *Sheff* 77-79; V Auckland St Helen *Dur* 79-94; Lect Th Dur Univ 91-94. *46 Northumberland Avenue, Bishop Auckland, Co Durham DL14 6NP* Tel (01388) 605227

BLAKEWAY-PHILLIPS, Richard John. b 19. St Chad's Coll Dur BA43. **d** 43 **p** 44. C Ledbury *Heref* 43-45; C Cirencester *Glouc* 45-50; C Lydney w Aylburton 50-52; R Dumbleton w Wormington 52-58; V Crawley Down All SS *Chich* 58-69; V Arrington *Ely* 69-77; R Orwell 69-77; R Wimpole 69-77; P-in-c Gt w Lt Abington 77-86; P-in-c Hildersham 77-86; rtd 86; Perm to Offic *Heref* from 86. *Church Cottage, Clun, Craven Arms, Shropshire SY7 8JW* Tel (01588) 640494

BLAKEY, Cedric Lambert. b 54. Fitzw Coll Cam BA76 MA80. St Jo Coll Nottm 77. **d** 79 **p** 80. C Cotmanhay *Derby* 79-83; C-in-c Blagreaves St Andr CD 83-89; P-in-c Sinfin Moor 84-89; V Heanor from 89; RD Heanor from 94. *The Vicarage, 1A Mundy Street, Heanor, Derbyshire DE75 7EB* Tel (01773) 719800

BLAKEY, William George. b 51. Southn Univ BSc72 PGCE73. Oak Hill Th Coll BA82. **d** 82 **p** 83. C Cheltenham St Mark *Glouc* 82-85; P-in-c Parkham, Alwington, Buckland Brewer etc *Ex* 85-86; R 86-94; TR from 94; RD Hartland 89-96; P-in-c Lundy Is from 92. *The Rectory, Parkham, Bideford, Devon EX39 5PL* Tel (01237) 451204

BLAKISTON, Patrick. b 14. Magd Coll Cam BA36 MA42. Linc Th Coll 36. **d** 39 **p** 40. C Gainsborough All SS *Linc* 39-42; C Corbridge *Newc* 42-45; V Cambo 45-50; R Middle w E Claydon *Ox* 50-52; R Halesowen *Worc* 52-59; R Alvechurch 59-68; V Whittingham *Newc* 68-79; rtd 80. *8 Paradise Court, Paradise Street, Cambridge CB1 1DR* Tel (01223) 311967

BLAMIRE-BROWN, Charles Richard. b 21. St Cath Soc Ox BA49 MA53. Cuddesdon Coll 49. **d** 51 **p** 52. C Bedale *Ripon* 51-53; C Welwyn *St Alb* 53-58; P-in-c Tewin 58-67; R 67-75; RD Hatfield 71-75; V Chipperfield St Paul 75-86; rtd 86; Perm to Offic *Cov* from 87. *7 Willoughby Avenue, Kenilworth, Warks CV8 1DG* Tel (01926) 50808

BLANCH, Paul Frederick. b 56. Dur Univ BA97. Chich Th Coll. **d** 86 **p** 87. C Chaddesden St Phil *Derby* 86-88; C Auckland St Andr and St Anne *Dur* 88-91; P-in-c Hunwick 91-94. *3 Beechcroft Avenue, Brandon, Durham DH7 8TF* Tel 0191-378 1533

BLANCHARD, Christopher John. b 46. Univ of Wales (Lamp) BA70. St Mich Coll Llan 86. **d** 79 **p** 80. NSM Chepstow *Mon* 79-81; NSM Itton and St Arvans w Penterry and Kilgwrrwg etc 81-86; C Ebbw Vale 87-88; R 88-89; V Llangenni and Llanbedr Ystrad Yw w Patricio *S & B* from 89. *The Rectory, Llangenny, Crickhowell NP8 1HD* Tel (01873) 810348

BLANCHARD, Ernest Desmond. b 26. St Jo Coll Dur BA55 DipTh56. **d** 56 **p** 57. C Bedlington *Newc* 56-60; R Salford St Bart *Man* 60-66; V Ashton Ch Ch 66-83; RD Ashton-under-Lyne 74-83; Hon Can Man Cathl 78-83; V Kettlewell w Conistone and Hubberholme *Bradf* 83-84; P-in-c Arncliffe w Halton Gill 83-84; V Kettlewell w Conistone, Hubberholme etc 84-91; rtd 91. *15 Castle Street, Morpeth, Northd NE61 1UM* Tel (01670) 503550

BLANCHARD, Frank Hugh. b 30. St Jo Coll Dur BA54 DipTh55 MA62. **d** 55 **p** 56. C Bottesford *Linc* 55-58; CMS 58-65; C Kirby Grindalythe *York* 65-67; V 67-71; C N Grimston w Wharram Percy and Wharram-le-Street 65-67; V 67-71; P-in-c Thorpe Bassett 67-71; P-in-c Settrington 67-68; V Scarborough St Jas 71-79; P-in-c Scarborough H Trin 78-79; V Scarborough St Jas and H Trin 79-86; R Stockton-on-the-Forest w Holtby and Warthill 87-94; rtd 94; P-in-c Rothesay *Arg* 94-96. *The Vicarage, Bridekirk, Cockermouth, Cumbria CA13 0PE* Tel (01900) 826557

BLANCHARD, Mrs Jean Ann. b 43. St Alb Minl Tr Scheme 79. **dss** 85 **d** 87 **p** 94. Mill End and Heronsgate w W Hyde *St Alb* 85-87; Hon Par Dn 87-92; Par Dn Luton All SS w St Pet 92-94; C 94-95; P-in-c Skirbeck Quarter *Linc* 96-97; V from 97. *St Thomas's Vicarage, 2 Linley Drive, Boston, Lincs PE21 7EJ* Tel (01205) 367380

BLANCHARD, Canon Lawrence Gordon. b 36. Edin Univ MA60. Linc Th Coll 63. **d** 65 **p** 66. C Woodhouse *Wakef* 65-67; C Cannock *Lich* 67-70; Swaziland 70-76; TV Raveningham *Nor* 76-80; V Ancaster *Linc* 80-87; Dir LNSM 80-87; Can and Preb Linc Cathl 85-88; Dir of Tr CA 88-93; V Roxton w Gt Barford *St Alb* from 93. *The Vicarage, High Street, Great Barford, Bedford MK44 3JJ* Tel (01234) 870363

BLAND, Albert Edward. b 14. St Mich Coll Llan. **d** 62 **p** 63. C Darwen St Cuth *Blackb* 62-65; P-in-c Over Darwen St Jo 65-66; V 66-67; V Feniscowles 67-84; rtd 85; Perm to Offic *Blackb* from 85. *Flat 18, Royal Oak Place, Matlock Street, Bakewell, Derbyshire DE45 1EE* Tel (01629) 813370

BLAND, Jean Elspeth. b 42. K Coll Lon BA63. Glouc Sch of Min 87. **d** 90 **p** 94. Par Dn Cen Telford *Lich* 90-94; C 94; Asst Chapl HM Pris Shrewsbury 92-94; Chapl HM Pris Doncaster from 94. *HM Prison Doncaster, Marshgate, Doncaster, S Yorkshire DN5 8UX* Tel (01302) 760870

BLAND, Thomas. b 12. Clifton Th Coll 39. **d** 42 **p** 43. C Bishopston *Bris* 42-44; C Styvechale *Cov* 44-45; V 45-61; V Stratford-on-Avon 61-63; R Stratford-on-Avon w Bishopton 63-69; Hon Can Cov Cathl 67-69; rtd 77. *1 Costard Avenue, Shipston-on-Stour, Warks CV36 4HW* Tel (01608) 663284

BLANDFORD-BAKER, Neil James. b 64. Dundee Univ BSc86 Nottm Univ BTh92. St Jo Coll Nottm DipMM93. **d** 93 **p** 94. C The Quinton *Birm* 93-96; V E Acton St Dunstan w St Thos *Lon* from 96. *The Vicarage, 54 Perryn Road, London W3 7NA* Tel 0181-743 4117

BLANEY, Laurence (Laurie). b 41. Lon Univ DipTh69 Open Univ BA85 Essex Univ MA88. Oak Hill Th Coll 66. **d** 69 **p** 70. C Leyton St Mary w St Edw *Chelmsf* 69-73; P-in-c Wimbish w Thunderley 73-77; P-in-c Steeple 77-82; P-in-c Mayland 77-82; R Pitsea 82-95; R Pitsea w Nevendon 95-96; P-in-c Mayland from 96; P-in-c Steeple from 96. *The Vicarage, 31 Imperial Avenue, Mayland, Essex CM3 6AH* Tel (01621) 740943

BLANKENSHIP, Charles Everett. b 42. Santa Clara Univ BA64. Cuddesdon Coll 71. **d** 74 **p** 75. C Catford (Southend) and Downham *S'wark* 74-78; P-in-c Battersea St Phil w St Bart 78-83; V 83-85; TV Wimbledon 85-91; P-in-c Welling 91-92; V from 92. *St Mary's Vicarage, Sandringham Drive, Welling, Kent DA16 3QU* Tel 0181-856 0684

BLANKLEY, Roger Henry. b 32. ARICS60. Clifton Th Coll 62. **d** 66 **p** 67. C Peckham St Mary Magd *S'wark* 66-69; SAMS 70-74; Brazil 74-80; R Gillingham w Geldeston, Stockton, Ellingham etc *Nor* 80-91; P-in-c Charmouth and Catherston Leweston *Sarum* from 91. *The Rectory, 5 Georges Close, Charmouth, Bridport, Dorset DT6 6RU* Tel (01297) 560409

BLANT, Edgar. b 18. St Chad's Coll Dur BA47 DipTh48. **d** 48 **p** 49. C Meir *Lich* 48-54; Antigua 55-85; St Kitts-Nevis 60-85; Adn St Kitts 78-85; rtd 86; Perm to Offic *Lich* from 86. *326 Sandon Road, Stoke-on-Trent ST3 7EB* Tel (01782) 398300

BLATCHLY, Owen Ronald Maxwell. b 30. Bps' Coll Cheshunt 62. **d** 64 **p** 65. C Boxmoor St Jo *St Alb* 64-67; C Boreham Wood All SS 67-69; C Frimley *Guildf* 69-77; V Manaccan w St Anthony-in-Meneage *Truro* 77-82; R Binfield *Ox* 82-97; rtd 97. *1 Rose Cottages, East Road, Stithians, Truro, Cornwall TR3 7BD*

BLATHWAYT, Canon Linley Dennys. b 16. Qu Coll Cam BA38 MA44. Wells Th Coll 38. **d** 40 **p** 41. C Halifax St Jo Bapt *Wakef* 40-45; C Tynemouth Ch Ch *Newc* 45-48; V Bywell St Pet 48-56; V Monkseaton St Pet 56-59; V Shalbourne w Ham *Sarum* 59-66; R Ballachulish *Arg* 66-69; R Glencoe 66-69; R Gussage St Michael and Gussage All Saints *Sarum* 69-71; R Corscombe 71-75; P-in-c Frome St Quintin w Evershot and Melbury Bubb 71-75; R Evershot, Frome St Quinton, Melbury Bubb etc 75-79; TR Melbury 79-81; RD Beaminster 75-81; Can and Preb Sarum Cathl 79-81; rtd 81. *50 Wentworth Park, Allendale, Hexham, Northd NE47 9DR* Tel (01434) 683448

BLATHWAYT, Canon Wynter. b 18. St Pet Hall Ox BA40 MA44. Ripon Hall Ox 40. **d** 41 **p** 42. C Herne Bay Ch Ch *Cant* 41-46; C Earlham St Anne *Nor* 46-48; R Chedgrave w Hardley and Langley 48-56; V Nor St Andr 56-66; R Nor St Mich at Plea and St Pet Hungate 56-66; CF (TA) 60-67; V Horning *Nor* 66-85; P-in-c Beeston St Laurence w Ashmanhaugh 78-85; Hon Can Nor Cathl 81-85; rtd 85; Perm to Offic *Nor* from 85. *155 Sir William Close, Aylsham, Norwich NR11 6AY* Tel (01263) 734502

BLAY, Ian. b 65. Man Univ BA88. Westcott Ho Cam 89. **d** 91 **p** 92. C Withington St Paul *Man* 91-94; C Elton All SS 94-96; R Droylsden St Andr from 96. *St Andrew's Rectory, Merton Drive, Droylsden, Manchester M35 6BH* Tel 0161-370 3242

BLEAKLEY, Melvyn Thomas. b 43. K Coll Lon BD66 AKC66. **d** 67 **p** 68. C Cross Heath *Lich* 67-70; TV High Wycombe *Ox* 70-77; Perm to Offic from 77. *294 Hughenden Road, High Wycombe, Bucks HP13 5PE* Tel (01494) 529315

BLEASE, John Thomas. b 19. Edin Th Coll 41. **d** 43 **p** 44. C Edin St Paul and St Geo *Edin* 43-45; C Greenock *Glas* 45-46; Hon C Carl St Aid and Ch Ch *Carl* 46-47; Chapl RN 47-74; rtd 74. *180 Manor Road North, Thames Ditton, Surrey KT7 0BQ* Tel 0181-398 5117

BLEE, Peter Michael. b 64. St Jo Coll Cam BA86. St Steph Ho Ox BTh94. **d** 94 **p** 95. C Guildf St Nic *Guildf* from 94. *St Catherine's House, 72 Wodeland Avenue, Guildford GU2 5LA* Tel (01483) 67633

BLENCOE, Charles Dennis. b 17. Lon Univ BA38. Bps' Coll Cheshunt 38. **d** 41 **p** 42. C Sutton in Ashfield St Mary *S'well* 41-43; Chapl RAF 43-61; Canada from 61. *526 Bay View Place, Duncan, British Columbia, Canada, V9L 1M3*

BLENKIN, Hugh Linton. b 16. Trin Coll Cam BA39 MA43. Lambeth STh56 Westcott Ho Cam 39. **d** 40 **p** 41. C Hitchin St Mary *St Alb* 40-43; Prec St Alb Abbey 43-48; Chapl and Lect Hockerill Coll Bp's Stortford 48-66; Lect St Mich Coll Salisbury 66-78; Lect Sarum Th Coll 78-83; rtd 81. *31 Abbey Mews, Amesbury, Salisbury SP4 7EX* Tel (01980) 624813

BLENNERHASSETT, Canon Richard Noel Rowland. b 09. TCD BA33 MA52. **d** 33 **p** 34. C Clonmel *C & O* 33-37; I Kilrossanty 37-39; I Kilrossanty w Stradbally and Monksland 39-45; I Knappagh *T, K & A* 45-47; I Aughaval w Burrishoole 47-68; I Aughaval w Burrishoole w Achill w Dugort 68-69; Dom Chapl to Bp Tuam 51-57; Can Tuam Cathl 52-69; Adn Tuam 56-69; Preb Kilmactalway St Patr Cathl Dublin 60-67; I Timoleague *C, C & R* 69-73; rtd 73. *The Moorings, Fenit, Tralee, Co Kerry, Irish Republic* Tel Tralee (66) 36198

BLENNERHASSETT, Canon Thomas Francis. b 15. TCD BA37 BD43 HDipEd56 MA68. **d** 39 **p** 40. C Dublin St Geo *D & G* 39-43; C Dublin Booterstown w Carysfort 43-47; I Balbriggan w Balrothery 47-58; I Howth 58-90; Can Ch Ch Cathl Dublin from 76; rtd 90; C Dalkey St Patr *D & G* from 90. *25 Bayside Square West, Sutton, Dublin 13, Irish Republic* Tel Dublin (1) 832 3720

BLEWETT, Roy. b 32. K Coll Lon BSc54 MPhil74 Leeds Inst of Educn 66 Newc Univ DipRS81. Edin Th Coll 81. **d** 82 **p** 83. C Newc St Fran *Newc* 82-85; P-in-c Cornhill w Carham 85-91; P-in-c Branxton 85-91; rtd 92; Perm to Offic *Truro* from 92. *Bryn Mawr, Lower Broad Lane, Redruth, Cornwall TR15 3HT* Tel (01209) 313152

BLEWETT, Timothy John (Tim). b 67. Surrey Univ BA88. Westcott Ho Cam 89. **d** 92 **p** 93. C Knaresborough *Ripon* 92-95; V Hanmer, Bronington, Bettisfield, Tallarn Green *St As* from 95. *The Vicarage, Hanmer, Whitchurch, Shropshire SY13 3DE* Tel (01948) 830468

BLIGH, Peter Alan. b 27. NE Ord Course 78. **d** 81 **p** 82. NSM Thornaby on Tees *York* 81; NSM Stockton *Dur* 87-95; rtd 95; Perm to Offic *Dur* from 95. *52 Cambridge Road, Thornaby, Stockton-on-Tees, Cleveland TS17 6LR* Tel (01642) 612700

BLIGH, Philip Hamilton. b 36. MInstP75 Lon Univ BSc57 PhD61 MEd79 St Cath Coll Ox BA63. S'wark Ord Course 86. **d** 88 **p** 89. C Abington *Pet* 88-90; V Bozeat w Easton Maudit from 90. *The Vicarage, Hensmans Lane, Bozeat, Wellingborough, Northants NN9 7NY* Tel (01933) 663216

BLISS, Allan Ernest Newport. b 29. K Coll Lon AKC50. St Boniface Warminster 54. **d** 54 **p** 57. C Wooburn *Ox* 54-56; C Whitley Ch Ch 56-58; C Hatcham Park All SS *S'wark* 63-68; C Sundon w Streatley *St Alb* 68-73; P-in-c Caldecote All SS 74-78; V 78-91; V Old Warden 81-91; Perm to Offic from 91; rtd 94. *6 Jubilee Gardens, Biggleswade, Beds SG18 0JW* Tel (01767) 313797

BLISS, David Charles. b 52. Aston Univ BSc75 Cranfield Inst of Tech MSc82. St Jo Coll Nottm 87. **d** 89 **p** 90. C Burntwood *Lich* 89-93; P-in-c Todwick *Sheff* 93; TV Aston cum Aughton w Swallownest, Todwick etc from 93; Chapl w the Deaf from 97. *The Vicarage, 15 Rectory Gardens, Todwick, Sheffield S31 0JU* Tel (01909) 770283

BLISS, John Derek Clegg. b 40. Sarum Th Coll. **d** 68 **p** 69. C Wymondham *Nor* 68-73; V Easton 73-80; R Colton 73-80; USA from 80. *4 Edgewater Hillside, Westport, Connecticut 06880, USA*

BLISS, Neil Humberstone. b 29. TCD BA54 MA59. Coll of Resurr Mirfield 55. **d** 57 **p** 58. C N Keyham *Ex* 57-60; Swaziland 61-65 and 68-80; S Africa 65-67; P-in-c Osmington w Poxwell *Sarum* 80-81; TV Preston w Sutton Poyntz and Osmington w Poxwell 81-84; V Ernesettle *Ex* 84-88; R S Tawton and Belstone 88-93; rtd 94. *Jordan House, Jordan, Lyme Regis, Dorset DT7 3AQ* Tel (01297) 445189

BLISS, Rupert Geoffrey. b 05. MIMechE27 K Coll Cam BA31 MA45. Ridley Hall Cam 32. **d** 50 **p** 50. C Bromley Ch Ch *Roch* 50-55; Area Sec (Dios Lon and S'wark) CMS 52-55; Prin Dunford Coll Midhurst 55-64; P-in-c Heyshott *Chich* 64-66; P-in-c Melbury Abbas *Sarum* 66-73; rtd 73; Perm to Offic *Sarum* 73-81; Perm to Offic *S'wark* 81-82; Perm to Offic *Lon* 82-86; Perm to Offic *Guildf* 86-92. *32 York Road, Broadstone, Dorset BH18 8ET* Tel (01202) 692673

BLISSARD-BARNES, Christopher John. b 36. ARCO55 Linc Coll Ox BA61 MA64. Ridley Hall Cam 61. **d** 63 **p** 64. C Woking St Paul *Guildf* 63-67; C Orpington Ch Ch *Roch* 67-71; P-in-c Heref St Jas *Heref* 71-78; Chapl Heref Gen Hosp 71-78; R Hampreston *Sarum* 78-88; TR 88-89; RD Wimborne 80-85; P-in-c Hambledon *Guildf* 89-94; R Newdigate from 94. *The Rectory, Church Road, Newdigate, Dorking, Surrey RH5 5DL* Tel (01306) 631469

BLOCK, Robert Allen. b 62. Univ of Wales (Lamp) BA84. Coll of Resurr Mirfield 86. **d** 88 **p** 89. C Hampton *Worc* 88-91; C Notting Hill St Mich and Ch Ch *Lon* 91-96; P-in-c Hammersmith St Luke from 96; C-in-c Hammersmith SS Mich and Geo White City Estate CD from 96. *The Parsonage, 1 Commonwealth Avenue, London W12 7QR* Tel 0181-743 7100

BLOFELD, Thomas Guest. *See* GUEST-BLOFELD, Thomas

BLOGG, Kevin Derek. b 55. Ch Ch Coll Cant BSc82 PGCE87. Franciscan Ho of Studies. **d** 84 **p** 85. NSM Eythorne and Elvington w Waldershare etc *Cant* 89-92; Orchard Sch Cant 89-90; Harbour Sch Dover 92-93; NSM Colkirk w Oxwick w Pattesley, Whissonsett etc *Nor* from 95; Sidestrand Hall Sch Nor from 94. *Meadow House, School Road, Brisley, Dereham, Norfolk NR20 5LH* Tel (01362) 668689

BLOOD, David John. b 36. G&C Coll Cam BA60 MA64. Westcott Ho Cam 64. **d** 62 **p** 63. C Rushmere *St E* 62-66; C Harringay St Paul *Lon* 66-71; Lic to Offic 71-81. *33 Rosebery Gardens, London N8 8SH* Tel 0181-340 3312

BLOOD, Canon Michael William. b 44. AKC67. **d** 69 **p** 70. C Moseley St Agnes *Birm* 69-75; V Cotteridge from 75; Relig Progr Producer BBC Radio W Midl from 76; Hon Can Birm Cathl from 97. *118 Northfield Road, Birmingham B30 1DX* Tel 0121-458 2815

BLOOD, Stephen John. b 28. Keble Coll Ox BA53 MA58. Coll of Resurr Mirfield 53. **d** 55 **p** 56. C Greenford H Cross *Lon* 55-58; C Forest Gate St Edm *Chelmsf* 58-61; C-in-c Ashford St Hilda CD *Lon* 61-73; V Ashford St Hilda from 73. *St Hilda's Vicarage, 8 Station Crescent, Ashford, Middx TW15 3HH* Tel (01784) 254237

BLOOMER, Ms Sherry Lesley. b 50. TD. Liv Jo Moores Univ BA91 Lon Univ DipNursing82 Wolv Poly CertEd83 RN73 RM74 RHV78 DipHV78. Westcott Ho Cam 95. **d** 97. C Llangollen w Trevor and Llantysilio *St As* from 97. *Homelea, Aber Adda, Hill Street, Llangollen LL20 8EU* Tel (01978) 861768

BLOOMFIELD, Mrs Gillian. b 38. Leeds Univ BA59. WMMTC 84. **d** 87 **p** 94. Par Dn Highters Heath *Birm* 87-89; TD Chelmsley Wood 89-94; TV 94-95; Chapl Chelmsley Hosp Birm 89-95; Chapl Marston Green Hosp Birm 89-95; P-in-c Pattingham w Patshull *Lich* from 95. *20 Dartmouth Avenue, Pattingham, Wolverhampton WV6 7DP*

BLOOMFIELD, Harry. b 29. Chich Th Coll 57. **d** 60 **p** 61. C Brighton St Mich *Chich* 60-64; C Wantage *Ox* 64-84; V Kennington from 84. *The Vicarage, Kennington, Oxford OX1 5PG* Tel (01865) 735135

BLOOMFIELD, John Michael. b 35. Univ of Wales (Lamp) BA57. Sarum Th Coll 59. **d** 61 **p** 62. C Fordington *Sarum* 61-64; C Branksome St Aldhelm 64-66; Youth Chapl *Win* 66-69; R Win All SS w Chilcomb and Chesil 71-79; P-in-c Corsley *Sarum* 79-81; C Swanage and Studland 83-86; Chapl HM Pris Dorchester 87-89; C Dorchester *Sarum* 87-89; Chapl HM Pris The Verne from 89. *The Chaplain's Office, HM Prison, The Verne, Portland, Dorset DT5 1EG* Tel (01305) 820124 Fax 823724

BLOOMFIELD, John Stephen. b 56. Southn Univ. Chich Th Coll 83. **d** 86 **p** 87. C Chich St Paul and St Pet *Chich* 86-89; TV Littlehampton and Wick from 89. *12 Cornwall Road, Littlehampton, W Sussex BN17 6EE*

BLOOMFIELD, Canon Peter Grayson. b 19. ACIS50 K Coll Lon BD60 AKC61. **d** 61 **p** 61. S Rhodesia 61-65; Rhodesia 65-78; Can Matabeleland 75-78; P-in-c Chideock *Sarum* 78-83; P-in-c Symondsbury 78-83; P-in-c Winterbourne Came w Whitcombe etc 83; Perm to Offic from 84; rtd 85. *Batchfoot Country House, 181 Church Street, Weymouth, Dorset DT3 5QE*

BLORE, John Francis. b 49. Jes Coll Ox BA72 MA76. Wycliffe Hall Ox 73. **d** 75 **p** 76. C Waltham Abbey *Chelmsf* 75-78; C E Ham St Geo 78-81; R Colchester St Mich Myland from 81; Chapl Oxley Parker Sch Colchester from 81. *Myland Rectory, Rectory Close, Colchester, Essex CO4 5DN* Tel (01206) 853076

BLOUNT, Robin George. b 38. Lon Univ DipTh68. Lon Coll of Div 61 Wycliffe Hall Ox 67. **d** 68 **p** 69. C Bletchley *Ox* 68-71; C Washington *Dur* 71-74; TV Chelmsley Wood *Birm* 74-76; Ind Chapl *Worc* 76-89; AP Dudley St Jo 76-89; AP Dudley St Thos and St Luke 88-89; Ind Chapl (Eurotunnel Development) *Cant* from 89; Lic to Offic from 89. *Rivendell, School Lane, Newington, Folkestone, Kent CT18 8AY* Tel (01303) 279222 Fax 273595

BLOWERS, Canon Ralph Barrie. b 28. Fitzw Ho Cam BA50 MA61. Ridley Hall Cam 51. **d** 53 **p** 54. C Higher Openshaw *Man* 53-56; R Man Albert Memorial Ch 56-68; RD Cheetham 63-69; R Man Albert Memorial Ch w Newton Heath 68-69; V Normanton *Derby* 69-93; RD Derby 74-79; RD Derby S 79-89; Hon Can Derby Cathl 85-93; rtd 93; Perm to Offic *Derby* from 93. *8 Portland Close, Mickleover, Derby DE3 5BQ* Tel (01332) 517114

BLOWS, Canon Derek Reeve. b 26. MSAnPsych75 Linc Coll Ox BA50 MA52. Cuddesdon Coll 50. **d** 52 **p** 53. C Cov St Mark *Cov* 52-56; SSF 56-58; Hon Can S'wark Cathl *S'wark* 72; Lic to Offic *Sarum* 56-58; Chapl Warlingham Park Hosp Croydon 58-65; V Purley St Mark Woodcote *S'wark* 65-70; Dir Past Care and Counselling 70-80; Dir Westmr Past Foundn 80-91; Perm to Offic *Roch* from 80; rtd 91. *2 Blackmoor House, Four Elms, Edenbridge, Kent TM8 6PG* Tel (01732) 700770

BLOXAM-ROSE, Canon Simon Franklyn. b 61. Southn Univ BTh MA Hon FLCM88. Chich Th Coll 85. **d** 88 **p** 89. C Bassaleg *Mon* 88-89; Chapl Aldenham Sch Herts 89-94; Perm to Offic *Ex* from 90; Chapl (Sen) Millfield Sch Somerset from 94; Can St Jo Pro-Cathl Katakwa from 95. *Orchard Leigh, Millfield, Street, Somerset BA16 0DA* Tel (01458) 841125 or 42291 Fax 47276

BLOXHAM, Oliver. b 27. Ely Th Coll 60. **d** 62 **p** 63. C Newc H Cross *Newc* 62-65; C Ponteland 65-69; V Dudley 69-79; P-in-c Balkwell 79-81; V 81-92; rtd 92. *23 Lambley Avenue, North Shields, Tyne & Wear NE30 3SL* Tel 0191-926 1785

BLOY, Philip Penrose. b 19. Ox Univ MA49 Lanc Univ MA71. Wells Th Coll 49. **d** 51 **p** 53. Asst Ind Missr *Sheff* 51-60; N Rhodesia 60-64; Zambia 64-70; C-in-c Bris St Geo *Bris* 72-73; Chapl Gatwick Airport *Chich* 73-88; Can and Preb Chich Cathl 86-88; rtd 89; Perm to Offic *B & W* from 96. *Old Orchard, Blackford Road, Charlton Horethorne, Sherborne, Dorset DT9 4NS* Tel (01963) 220418

BLUNDELL, Canon Derek George. b 32. Tyndale Hall Bris 58. **d** 61 **p** 62. C Fazakerley Em *Liv* 61-64; C-in-c Bath Odd Down *B & W* 64-69; V 69-74; V Tulse Hill H Trin *S'wark* 74-81; Org and Admin African Pastor Fund from 81; Perm to Offic *Cov* from 81; Hon Can Mityana from 90. *12 Ibex Close, Coventry CV3 2FB* Tel (01203) 448068 Fax as telephone

BLUNDELL, Peter Grahame. b 61. Ealing Coll of Educn BA83. Oak Hill NSM Course 91. **d** 94 **p** 95. NSM Kensington St Barn *Lon* 94-97; Zimbabwe from 97. *Address temp unknown*

BLUNDEN, Jacqueline Ann. *See* MILLER, Mrs Jacqueline Ann

BLUNSUM, Charles Michael. b 28. ACIB51 MBIM86. **d** 74 **p** 75. C Stoke Bishop *Bris* 74-79; Chapl Brunel Manor Chr Cen Torquay from 79. *5 Merrivale Close, Torquay TQ2 8PZ* Tel (01803) 326089 or 329333

BLUNT, Paul David. b 44. Lon Univ BSc65 Leeds Univ DipTh70. Coll of Resurr Mirfield 67. **d** 70 **p** 71. C Norbury St Steph *Cant* 70-73; Canada from 73. *1234 Prestone Drive, Orleans, Ontario, Canada, K1E 3X6*

BLYDE, Ian Hay. b 52. Liv Univ BSc74 Edin Univ BD80. Edin Th Coll 77. **d** 80 **p** 81. C Ainsdale *Liv* 80-83; Chapl Birkenhead Sch Merseyside 83-90; Perm to Offic *Ches* 83-90; V Over St Chad 90-93; Chapl Ex Sch from 93; Chapl St Marg Sch Ex from 93. *2 Hulham Road, Exmouth, Devon EX8 3HR* Tel (01395) 264339

BLYTH, Bryan Edward Perceval. b 22. Linc Coll Ox BA49 MA52. Wells Th Coll 48. **d** 50 **p** 51. C Timperley *Ches* 50-52; C Talbot Village *Sarum* 52-55; C-in-c Weymouth St Edm 55; P-in-c 56-63; Asst Dir of Educn *Chelmsf* 64-67; Hon C Mountnessing 67-68; Hon C Ingatestone w Buttsbury 67-68; Teacher Ingatestone Sec Modern Sch 67-68; Teacher Westwood Co Jun Sch 68-72; Dep Hd 72-87; Hon C Thundersley 80-84; rtd 87. *Church Cottage, Chettle, Blandford Forum, Dorset DT11 8DB* Tel (01258) 830396

BLYTH, Canon Drummond Gwyn. b 26. K Coll Lon 53. **d** 54 **p** 55. C N Lynn w St Marg and St Nic *Nor* 54-59; C Sheff Parson Cross St Cecilia *Sheff* 59-62; R Carlton Colville *Nor* 62-70; V Stalham w Brunstead 70-77; P-in-c E Ruston 76-77; RD Waxham 77-89; V Stalham and E Ruston w Brunstead 77-91; Hon Can Nor Cathl 87-91; rtd 91; Perm to Offic *Nor* from 91. *Pegg's Close, 6 St Nicholas Close, Sheringham, Norfolk NR26 8LE* Tel (01263) 822611

BLYTH, Mrs Geraldine Anne. b 50. Llan Dioc Tr Scheme 90. **d** 94 **p** 97. C Llantrisant *Llan* from 94. *1 Heol-y-Fro, Upper Church Village, Pontypridd CF38 1UD* Tel (01443) 201761

BLYTH, John Reddie. b 25. Wadh Coll Ox BA48 MA50. Ridley Hall Cam 48. **d** 50 **p** 51. C Southport Ch Ch *Liv* 50-52; C Enfield Ch Ch Trent Park *Lon* 52-55; V Plymouth St Jude *Ex* 55-63; E Midl Area Sec CPAS 63-70; V Parkstone St Luke *Sarum* 70-90; Chapl Uplands Sch Parkstone 70-73; rtd 90; Perm to Offic *Chich* from 90. *5 Powell Road, Newick, E Sussex BN8 4LS* Tel (01825) 722011

BLYTH, John Stuart. b 36. Lon Univ BD64 DipTh Ox Brookes Univ MA95. Lich Th Coll 63. **d** 65 **p** 66. C Knowle St Barn *Bris* 65-68; C Whitchurch *B & W* 68-70; P-in-c Sutton St Nicholas w Sutton St Michael *Heref* 70-73; Dioc RE Adv 70-73; Chapl RAF 73-77; P-in-c Launton *Ox* 77-84; TV Bicester w Bucknell, Caversfield and Launton 79-84; P-in-c Hanborough 84-86; R Hanborough and Freeland 86-89; Perm to Offic from 89; rtd 96. *9 Green Ridges, Headington, Oxford OX3 8PL* Tel (01865) 62691

BLYTH, Kenneth Henry. b 35. Lon Univ DipTh60. Oak Hill Th Coll 58. **d** 61 **p** 62. C St Alb St Paul *St Alb* 61-65; P-in-c Aspenden and Layston w Buntingford 65-66; R 66-72; R Washfield, Stoodleigh, Withleigh etc *Ex* 72-82; P-in-c Cruwys Morchard 72-74; RD Tiverton 76-82; V Eastbourne H Trin *Chich* from 82. *Holy Trinity Vicarage, Trinity Trees, Eastbourne, E Sussex BN21 3BE* Tel (01323) 729046

BLYTH, Dr Michael Graham. b 53. Jes Coll Ox BA75 MA78 Dur Univ PhD79. Qu Coll Birm 82. **d** 84 **p** 85. C Nantwich *Ches* 84-86; C Coppenhall 86-88; TV Southend *Chelmsf* 88-95; P-in-c Danbury from 95. *St John's Rectory, 55 Main Road, Danbury, Chelmsford CM3 4NG* Tel (01245) 223140

BOADEN, John Edward. b 15. Down Coll Cam BA41 MA45. Ridley Hall Cam 41. **d** 43 **p** 44. C Southall H Trin *Lon* 43-47; C E Twickenham St Steph 47-50; R Openshaw *Man* 50-56; V Bitterne *Win* 56-67; R Blackley St Andr *Man* 67-77; P-in-c Parkfield in Middleton 77-81; rtd 81; Hon C Constable Lee *Man* 81-83; Perm to Offic from 83. *11 Horncliffe Close, Rawtenstall, Rossendale, Lancs BB4 6EE* Tel (01706) 223696

BOAG, David. b 46. Edin Th Coll 69. **d** 72 **p** 73. C Edin Old St Paul *Edin* 72-75; P-in-c Edin St Andr and St Aid 75-88; Lic to Offic from 88. *26 Noble Place, Edinburgh EH6 8AX* Tel 0131-554 7876

BOAK, Canon Donald Kenneth. b 30. MBAOT53. S'wark Ord Course DipRS85. **d** 85 **p** 86. C Tulse Hill H Trin and St Matthias *S'wark* 85-88; C Surbiton St Matt 88-91; Intercon Ch Soc, SAMS and Miss to Seamen 91-95; Peru 91-95; Dean Lima 93-95; rtd 95; Hon Can Peru from 95; Hon C Bournemouth St Andr *Win* from 96. *96 Shelley Road East, Boscombe, Bournemouth BH7 6HB* Tel (01202) 303706

BOAKE, Canon Henry Vaux. b 16. TCD BA38 MA52. CITC 38. **d** 39 **p** 40. C Tralee *L & K* 39-43; Dioc C (Ardfert and Aghadoe) 39-43; C Wexford St Iberius *C & O* 43-44; P-in-c Kilscoran 44-46; I Crosspatrick Gp 46-79; Can Ferns Cathl 62-69; Treas 69-71; Chan 71-79; rtd 79. *Little Orton, Rutland, Palatine, Carlow, Irish Republic* Tel Carlow (503) 43065

BOAKES, Norman. b 50. Univ of Wales (Swansea) BA71 Univ of Wales (Lamp) LTh73 Ox Univ MTh96. Bp Burgess Hall Lamp 71. **d** 73 **p** 74. C Swansea St Mary w H Trin *S & B* 73-78; Chapl Univ of Wales (Swansea) 76-78; Chapl K Alfred Coll *Win* 78-82; V Colbury 82-91; Chapl Ashurst Hosp 82-91; Chapl Mental Handicap Services Unit 82-91; V Southampton Maybush St Pet *Win* from 91. *Maybush Vicarage, Sedbergh Road, Southampton SO16 9HJ* Tel (01703) 703443

BOAR, Alan Bennett. b 23. Sarum Th Coll 56. **d** 58 **p** 59. C E Dereham w Hoe *Nor* 58-60; C Gorleston St Andr 60-63; V Tibenham 63-67; P-in-c Tivetshall 64-67; R Beeston St Laurence w Ashmanhaugh and Hoveton 67-78; P-in-c Tunstead w Sco' Ruston 67-78; P-in-c Marsham 78-89; P-in-c Burgh 78-89; rtd 89; Perm to Offic *Nor* from 89. *20 Emelson Close, Dereham, Norfolk NR19 2ES* Tel (01362) 698944

BOARDMAN, Dr Frederick Henry. b 25. Liv Univ BSc46 St Cath Soc Ox BA49 MA54 Birm Univ MEd71 PhD77. Wycliffe Hall Ox 47. **d** 50 **p** 51. C Bootle Ch Ch *Liv* 50-52; C-in-c Netherton CD 52-57; V Stechford *Birm* 57-63; Lic to Offic 63-69; Lic to Offic *Liv* from 71; Hon C Sutton 76-89; Hon C Burtonwood from 89; rtd 90. *Woodside, Burtonwood Road, Great Sankey, Warrington WA5 3AN* Tel (01925) 635079

BOARDMAN, John Frederick. b 37. Bolton Coll of Art NDD57 Leeds Univ ATD58 AKC64. **d** 65 **p** 66. C Harrogate St Wilfrid *Ripon* 65-68; C Fleetwood *Blackb* 68-71; C Cen Torquay *Ex* 71-77; Chapl S Devon Tech Coll Torbay 71-77; P-in-c Ellacombe *Ex* 76-77; V Milber 77-95; rtd 95; Perm to Offic *Ex* from 95. *St Benedict's House, 61 Priory Road, St Marychurch, Torquay TQ1 4NH* Tel (01803) 327276

BOARDMAN, Jonathan. b 63. Magd Coll Cam BA89 Magd Coll Ox MA90. Westcott Ho Cam 87. **d** 90 **p** 91. C W Derby St Mary *Liv* 90-93; Prec St Alb Abbey *St Alb* 93-96; TR Catford (Southend) and Downham *S'wark* from 96. *St John's Rectory, 353 Bromley Road, London SE6 2RP* Tel 0181-698 3898

BOARDMAN, Ms Philippa Jane. b 63. Jes Coll Cam BA85 MA89. Ridley Hall Cam 87. **d** 90 **p** 94. Par Dn Walthamstow St Mary w St Steph *Chelmsf* 90-93; C Hackney Wick St Mary of Eton w St Aug *Lon* 93-96; Dean of Women's Min Stepney Area from 94; P-in-c Old Ford St Paul and St Mark from 96. *The Vicarage, St Stephen's Road, London E3 5JL* Tel 0181-980 9020

BOASE, David John. b 49. St Jo Coll Dur BA71 Trin Coll Ox PGCE73. Cuddesdon Coll 71. **d** 73 **p** 74. C Penrith *Carl* 73-76; Tutor Greystoke Coll Carl 76-78; Prec Gib Cathl *Eur* 78-80; Miss to Seamen 78-80; Chapl Gothenburg w Halmstad and Jonkoping *Eur* 80-82; TV Thornaby on Tees *York* 82-88; V Kirkby-in-Cleveland from 88; Resp for Clergy In-Service Tr Cleveland W from 88. *3 Holmemead, The Holme, Great Broughton, Middlesbrough TS9 7HQ* Tel (01642) 710005 Fax 713953

BOCKING (Essex), Dean of. *See* NEED, Philip Alan

BOCKING (Suffolk), Dean of. *See* MORRIS, The Very Revd Stuart Collard

BODDINGTON, Canon Alan Charles Peter. b 37. Lon Univ DipTh65. Oak Hill Th Coll 63. **d** 66 **p** 67. C Bedworth *Cov* 66-69; Bp's Officer for Min 69-75; Bp's Chapl for Miss 69-73; P-in-c Wroxall 72-75; P-in-c Honiley 72-75; V Westwood 75-85; Asst Chapl Warw Univ 78-85; TR N Farnborough *Guildf* from 85; RD Aldershot 88-93; Hon Can Guildf Cathl from 92. *The Rectory, 66 Church Avenue, Farnborough, Hants GU14 7AP* Tel (01252) 544754

BODDINGTON, Clive Frederick Malcolm. b 35. Qu Coll Cam BA59 MA63. Ridley Hall Cam 59. **d** 61 **p** 62. C Tonbridge SS Pet and Paul *Roch* 61-64; C St Leonards St Leon *Chich* 64-66; Kenya 67-94; rtd 95. *Coopers Bridge Farm, Bramshott, Liphook, Hants GU30 7RF* Tel (01428) 722007

BODDINGTON, John Slater. b 17. Wells Th Coll 63. **d** 64 **p** 65. C Harrow St Pet *Lon* 64-68; C Roxbourne St Andr 68-71; V W Acton St Martin 71-85; rtd 85; Perm to Offic *Ban* from 85; Perm to Offic *St As* from 85. *Lane End, Aber Place, Llandudno LL30 3AR* Tel (01492) 547080

BODDY, Alan Richard. b 47. Ripon Coll Cuddesdon. **d** 84 **p** 85. C Eastcote St Lawr *Lon* 84-87; C Kensington St Mary Abbots w St Geo 87-90; Chapl HM Pris Brixton 90-91; Chapl HM Pris Send and Downview 91-92; Chapl HM Pris Highdown from 92. *HM Prison Highdown, Sutton Lane, Sutton, Surrey SM2 5PJ* Tel 0181-643 0063

BODDY, David. b 57. SSF. Linc Th Coll CMinlStuds92. **d** 92 **p** 93. C Peterlee *Dur* 92-95; C Penshaw 95; C 95-97; C Shiney Row 95; P-in-c from 95; C Herrington 95; P-in-c from 95. *The Vicarage, Shiney Row, Houghton le Spring, Tyne & Wear DH4 4JU* Tel 0191-385 7271

BODKIN, Thomas Patrick Joseph (Tom). b 45. Richmond Fellowship Coll DipHRel78 Open Univ BA77 BA90. St Hyacinth's Coll and RC Sem Mass 64 Franciscan Ho of Studies DipPhil67 DipTh70. **d** 80 **p** 80. In RC Ch 80-86; NSM Littlehampton and Wick *Chich* 91-93; Visiting Tutor Moral Th Chich Th Coll from 92; TV Aldrington from 93. *St Leonard's Vicarage, 18 Amesbury Crescent, Hove, E Sussex BN3 5RD* Tel (01273) 328973 Fax as telephone

BODMIN, Archdeacon of. *See* WHITEMAN, The Ven Rodney David Carter

BODY, Andrew. b 46. Pemb Coll Cam BA68 MA71. Ridley Hall Cam 68. **d** 70 **p** 71. C New Bury *Man* 70-73; TV Droylsden St Mary 73-78; V Low Harrogate St Mary *Ripon* 78-92; Trustee FLAME from 90; TR Redhorn *Sarum* 92-97; V Chobham w Valley End *Guildf* from 97. *Chobham Vicarage, Bagshot Road, Chobham, Woking, Surrey GU24 8BY* Tel (01276) 858197

BODY, Richard Sidney. b 25. CEng FIEE55 FIHospE72 BSc46 CertRS88. S'wark Ord Course 86. **d** 88 **p** 89. Hon C Chelsfield *Roch* from 88. *Beechwood, 96 Goddington Lane, Orpington, Kent BR6 9DY* Tel (01689) 829990

BODYCOMBE, Stephen John. b 58. Lanchester Poly BA. St Mich Coll Llan DipTh83. **d** 83 **p** 84. C Cardiff St Jo *Llan* 83-86; V Dinas and Penygraig w Williamstown from 86. *The Vicarage, 1 Llanfair Road, Penygraig, Tonypandy CF40 1TA* Tel (01443) 422677

BOFF, Charles Roy. b 31. Pemb Coll Ox BA57 MA60. Clifton Th Coll 55. **d** 57 **p** 58. C Plumstead All SS *S'wark* 57-61; V Gipsy Hill Ch Ch 61-68; V Felbridge 68-79; V Steyning *Chich* 79-84; R Ashurst 79-84; RD Storrington 81-84; R Romaldkirk w Laithkirk *Ripon* 84-94; RD Richmond 90-93; rtd 94; Perm to Offic *Carl* from 94. *Laithkirk, Aikton, Wigton, Cumbria CA7 0HY* Tel (016973) 45563

BOFFEY, Ian. b 40. Glas Univ MA63. Glas NSM Course 75. **d** 75 **p** 78. Hon C Dalry *Glas* 75-78; P-in-c from 78. *2 Kinloch Avenue, Stewarton, Kilmarnock, Ayrshire KA3 3HF* Tel (01560) 482586

BOGGIS, Miss Christine Louise. b 38. R Holloway Coll Lon BA60 Cam Univ CertEd61 Hull Univ BTh94. EMMTC DTPS94. **d** 94 **p** 95. NSM Scartho *Linc* from 94. *90 Waltham Road, Grimsby, S Humberside DN33 2NA* Tel (01472) 822108

BOGGUST, Mrs Patricia Anne. Portsm Dioc Tr Course. **d** 90. NSM Hook w Warsash *Portsm* 90-94; NSM Locks Heath from 94. *21 Beverley Close, Park Gate, Southampton SO31 6QU* Tel (01489) 573586

BOGLE, Ms Elizabeth. b 47. York Univ BA68 Leeds Univ PGCE69. S'wark Ord Course 93. **d** 96. NSM E Greenwich *S'wark* from 96. *8 Waller Road, London SE14 5LA* Tel 0171-732 9420

BOGLE, James Main Lindam Linton. b 33. Peterho Cam BA56 MA60. Wells Th Coll 59. **d** 61 **p** 62. C Bermondsey St Anne *S'wark* 61-65; Chapl York Univ *York* 65-72; V Brayton 72-76; V Forest Hill St Aug *S'wark* 76-83; C Hatcham St Cath 83-85; NSM from 91; C Herne Hill St Paul 86-87; rtd 87. *8 Waller Road, London SE14 5LA* Tel 0171-732 9420

BOHUN, Roger Alexander. b 32. Lon Univ BSc58. Cuddesdon Coll 65. **d** 68 **p** 69. C Rugby St Andr *Cov* 68-74; SSF from 74; Perm to Offic *Sarum* 74-76; Perm to Offic *Newc* 76-78; Tanzania 78-86; Zimbabwe 86-88. *The Friary, Hilfield, Dorchester, Dorset DT2 7BE* Tel (01300) 341345

BOIT, Mervyn Hays. b 38. Univ of Wales (Lamp) BA59. St Mich Coll Llan 59. **d** 61 **p** 62. C Roath St German *Llan* 61-63; C Skewen 63-69; V Pontycymer and Blaengarw from 69. *The Vicarage, St David Street, Pontycymer, Bridgend CF32 8LT* Tel (01656) 870280

BOLAND, Geoffrey. b 56. DipHE89. Oak Hill Th Coll 87. **d** 89 **p** 90. C Ormskirk *Liv* 89-94; C Woodside Park St Barn *Lon* from 94. *13 Chislehurst Avenue, London N12 0HU* Tel 0181-346 0777

BOLD, Dr Peter Edward. b 64. Sheff Univ BEng86 PhD90. Cranmer Hall Dur BA94 DMS95. **d** 95 **p** 96. C Grenoside *Sheff* from 95. *49 Denistone Road, Grenoside, Sheffield S30 3QH* Tel 0114-240 1381

BOLE, Malcolm Dennis. b 30. Oak Hill Th Coll 65. **d** 67 **p** 68. C Bridlington Priory *York* 67-70; Rwanda 71-73; P-in-c Combe Hay *B & W* 74-81; V Bath Odd Down 74-81; P-in-c Taunton St Jas 81-84; V 84-90; R Bicknoller w Crowcombe and Sampford Brett from 90. *The Rectory, 11 Trendle Lane, Bicknoller, Taunton, Somerset TA4 4EG* Tel (01984) 56262

BOLLARD, Canon Richard George. b 39. Fitzw Ho Cam BA61 MA65 K Coll Lon BD63 AKC63. **d** 64 **p** 65. C Southampton Maybush St Pet *Win* 64-68; Chapl Aston Univ *Birm* 68-74; TR Chelmsley Wood 74-82; V Coleshill from 82; V Maxstoke from 82; RD Coleshill 82-92; Hon Can Birm Cathl from 85; Dioc Ecum Officer from 97. *The Vicarage, High Street, Coleshill, Birmingham B46 3BP* Tel (01675) 462188

BOLLEN, Bryan Hayward. b 26. **d** 77 **p** 78. NSM Chippenham St Pet *Bris* 77-94; Perm to Offic from 94. *27 The Tinings, Chippenham, Wilts SN15 3LY* Tel (01249) 652515

BOLLEY, Michael Francis. b 55. St Cath Coll Ox BA76 MSc77. Ripon Coll Cuddesdon MA92. **d** 92 **p** 93. C Pinner *Lon* 92-95; C Eastcote St Lawr from 95. *163 Pine Gardens, Eastcote, Ruislip, Middx HA4 9TE* Tel 0181-866 1676

BOLSTER, David Richard. b 50. BA. St Jo Coll Nottm. **d** 84 **p** 85. C Luton Lewsey St Hugh *St Alb* 84-87; V Woodside w E Hyde from 87. *The Vicarage, Church Road, Slip End, Luton LU1 4BJ* Tel (01582) 424363

BOLT, David Dingley. b 18. St Jo Coll Cam LLB58 LLM85. Westcott Ho Cam 66. **d** 68 **p** 69. Malawi 68-70; C Chesterton Gd Shep *Ely* 70-71; P-in-c Gt Wilbraham 71-74; V 74-86; P-in-c Lt Wilbraham 71-74; R 74-86; RD Quy 75-81; rtd 86; Perm to Offic *Ely* from 86. *24 Warwick Road, Cambridge CB4 3HN* Tel (01223) 66361

BOLT, George Henry. b 34. MInstP75 CPhys75 Lon Univ BSc60 Bath Univ MSc75. S Dios Minl Tr Scheme 85. **d** 88 **p** 89. NSM Oldbury *Sarum* 88-89; Chapl Chippenham Tech Coll 89-90; C Kington *Bris* 90-92; P-in-c Aldenham *St Alb* from 92; Chapl Herts Univ from 96. *The Vicarage, Church Lane, Aldenham, Watford WD2 8BE* Tel (01923) 855905

BOLT, Mrs Mary Veronica. b 36. S Dios Minl Tr Scheme 90. **d** 93 **p** 94. NSM Aldenham *St Alb* from 93; Sub-Chapl HM Pris The Mount from 93; Chapl Herts Univ from 96. *The Vicarage, Church Lane, Aldenham, Watford WD2 8BE* Tel (01923) 855905

BOLT, Philip John Mitchell. b 15. Bps' Coll Cheshunt 49. **d** 52 **p** 53. C Carnforth *Blackb* 52-56; C-in-c Burnley St Mark CD 56-59; P-in-c Burnley St Mark 59-65; R Nunney *B & W* 65-74; P-in-c Wanstrow w Cloford 72-74; R Nunney w Wanstrow and Cloford 74-80; V Rotherham Ferham Park *Sheff* 80-84; rtd 84; Hon C Stoke Lacy, Moreton Jeffries w Much Cowarne etc *Heref* 87-90. *192 Berrow Road, Burnham-on-Sea, Somerset TA8 2JF* Tel (01278) 793094

BOLTON, Christopher Leonard. b 60. St Mich Coll Llan DipTh83. **d** 83 **p** 84. C Lampeter *St D* 83-86; P-in-c Llanarth and Capel Cynon w Talgarreg etc 86-87; V from 87. *The Vicarage, Llanarth SA47 0NJ* Tel (01545) 580745

BOLTON, Mrs Jane Elizabeth. b 53. Leic Univ BA75. Ripon Coll Cuddesdon DipMin95. **d** 97. C Sheff St Mark Broomhill *Sheff* from 97. *9 Betjeman Gardens, Endcliffe Vale Road, Sheffield S10 3FW* Tel 0114-266 4343

BOLTON, John. b 43. SS Paul & Mary Coll Cheltenham DipEd64. Trin Coll Bris 83. **d** 85 **p** 86. C Minehead *B & W* 85-89; R Winford w Felton Common Hill from 89. *The Rectory, 4 Parsonage Lane, Winford, Bristol BS18 8DG* Tel (01275) 474636

BOLTON, Peter Richard Shawcross. b 58. Warw Univ BA79. Sarum & Wells Th Coll 80. **d** 83 **p** 84. C Beckenham St Jas *Roch* 83-86; C Bedford Leigh *Man* 86-88; V Royton St Paul 88-94; AD Tandle 93-94; P-in-c Lower Broughton Ascension from 95. *Ascension Rectory, Duke Street, Salford M7 1PR* Tel 0161-834 4370

BOLTON, Richard David Edward. b 52. MA. St Steph Ho Ox 79. **d** 81 **p** 82. C Rawmarsh w Parkgate *Sheff* 81-84; Chapl Wellingborough Sch 85-92; Lic to Offic *Pet* 85-92; Chapl Merchant Taylors' Sch Northwood from 91; P in O from 96. *1 Askew Road, Sandy Lodge, Northwood, Middx HA6 2JE* Tel (01923) 821136 or 820644

BOLTON, Sidney Robert. b 15. Dur Univ LTh45. Edin Th Coll 42. **d** 44 **p** 45. C Cowley St Jas *Ox* 44-47; C Wolverton St Geo 47-50; Toc H Padre (SW Region) 50-53; Toc H Padre (Lincs) 53-58; P-in-c Ermington *Ex* 51-53; R Nettleton *Linc* 53-58; V Stainton-by-Langworth 58-59; V Bloxham and Milcombe *Ox* 59-81; V Bloxham w Milcombe and S Newington 81-84; rtd 84; Perm to Offic *Ox* from 84. *Finches, 1 Brookside, Hook Norton, Banbury, Oxon OX15 5NS* Tel (01608) 737153

BOLTON, Archdeacon of. *See* DAVIES, The Ven Lorys Martin

BOLTON, Suffragan Bishop of. *See* BONSER, The Rt Revd David

BOMFORD, Canon Rodney William George. b 43. BNC Ox BA64 DipTh66 MA68. Coll of Resurr Mirfield 67 Union Th Sem (NY) STM69. **d** 69 **p** 70. C Deptford St Paul *S'wark* 69-77; V Camberwell St Giles w St Matt from 77; RD Camberwell from 87; Hon Can S'wark Cathl from 93. *St Giles's Vicarage, Benhill Road, London SE5 8RB* Tel 0171-703 4504

BOMYER, Julian Richard Nicholas Jeffrey. b 55. AKC78 Sarum & Wells Th Coll 78. **d** 79 **p** 80. C Rugby St Andr *Cov* 79-84; TV 85-88; P-in-c Clifton upon Dunsmore w Brownsover 84-85; Prec Ch Ch *Ox* 88-93; V Hampton *Worc* from 93; Chapl Evesham Coll from 93. *St Andrew's Vicarage, Pershore Road, Evesham, Worcs WR11 6PQ* Tel (01386) 446381

BOND, Alan Richard. b 49. Lon Univ BSc71 Imp Coll Lon ARCS71 Portsm Poly DMS74 MIMgt75 AFIMA75. S Dios Minl Tr Scheme 80. **d** 83 **p** 84. NSM Westbourne *Chich* 83-86. *14 Fraser Gardens, Southbourne, Emsworth, Hants PO10 8PY*

BOND, Arthur Edward Stephen. b 44. St Steph Ho Ox 66. **d** 69 **p** 69. S Africa 69-70; OGS 70-73; C Hendon St Alphage *Lon* 70-73; OSB 74-95; Asst Sec ACS 75-95; Hon C Sparkbrook St Agatha w Balsall Heath St Barn *Birm* 86-92; Hon C Washwood Heath 92-95. *58 rue Albert Vincon, Certe, 44570 Trignac, Loire Atlantique, France* Tel France (33) 40 45 92 17 Fax 40 45 92 18

✠**BOND, The Rt Revd Charles Derek.** b 27. AKC51. **d** 52 **p** 53 **c** 76. C Friern Barnet St Jas *Lon* 52-56; Lic to Offic *Birm* 56-58; Midl

Sch Sec SCM 56-58; V Harringay St Paul *Lon* 58-62; V Harrow Weald All SS 62-72; P-in-c Pebmarsh *Chelmsf* 72-73; Adn Colchester 72-76; Suff Bp Bradwell 76-84; Area Bp Bradwell 84-92; rtd 92; Asst Bp Worc from 92. *Ambleside, 14 Worcester Road, Evesham, Worcs WR11 4JU* Tel (01386) 446156

BOND, Charles Robert. b 25. Trin Coll Bris DipHE80. **d** 80 **p** 81. C Wythenshawe Wm Temple Ch *Man* 80-82; TV Cwmbran *Mon* 82-88; Chapl Corfu *Eur* 88-91; Chapl Playa de Las Americas Tenerife 91-93; rtd 93. *Urbanizacion Club Miraverde, Apartment 1, Edifico Iris, 38660 Playa de Las Americas, Tenerife, Canary Islands* Tel Tenerife (22) 791082

BOND, Clifford Frank. b 24. St Aid Birkenhead 60. **d** 62 **p** 63. C Kirkham *Blackb* 62-64; C Wallingford St Mary w All Hallows and St Leon *Ox* 64-69; PM Reading St Barn CD 69-73; R Reading St Barn 73-95; rtd 95. *Devonia, St James's Close, Pangbourne, Reading RG8 7AP* Tel (0118) 984 3793

BOND, David. b 36. Oak Hill Th Coll 72. **d** 74 **p** 75. C Leyton St Mary w St Edw *Chelmsf* 74-78; C Slough *Ox* 78-80; V Selby St Jas *York* 80-93; P-in-c Wistow 80-82; V 82-93; RD Selby 89-93; P-in-c Northiam *Chich* 93-94; R from 94. *The Rectory, 24 High Meadow, Rye, E Sussex TN31 6GA* Tel (01797) 253118

BOND, David Matthew. b 38. Leic Univ BA59 Nottm Univ MA85. Sarum Th Coll 59. **d** 61 **p** 62. C Leic St Anne *Leic* 61-64; Hon C Nor St Pet Mancroft *Nor* 64-67; E England Sec SCM from 64; Sen Lect Pet Regional Coll from 67; Hon C Stamford All SS w St Pet *Linc* 74-81; Hon C Stamford All SS w St Jo from 81; Perm to Offic *Pet* from 85. *2 The Courtyard, Cotterstock, Peterborough PE8 5HB* Tel (018326) 255

BOND, David Warner. b 32. MA BSc(Econ). Cant Sch of Min. **d** 82 **p** 83. NSM Otham w Langley *Cant* from 82. *6 Denton Close, Maidstone, Kent ME15 8ER* Tel (01622) 202239 Fax 205149

BOND, Douglas Gregory. b 39. Edin Th Coll 74. **d** 76 **p** 77. NSM Edin St Paul and St Geo *Edin* 76-83; P-in-c Abthorpe w Slapton *Pet* 83-84; P-in-c Silverstone and Abthorpe w Slapton 84; R 84-89; V Pet St Jude 89-95; R Kislingbury and Harpole from 95. *The Rectory, School Lane, Harpole, Northampton NN7 4DR* Tel (01604) 830322

BOND, Gordon. b 44. Chich Th Coll 68. **d** 71 **p** 72. C Wisbech St Aug *Ely* 71-74; C Wembley Park St Aug *Lon* 74-77; C York Town St Mich *Guildf* 77-80; C Haywards Heath St Wilfrid *Chich* 80; TV 80-82; V Lower Beeding 82-86; V E Grinstead St Mary from 86. *The Vicarage, Windmill Lane, East Grinstead, W Sussex RH19 2DS* Tel (01342) 323439

BOND, Canon John Albert. b 35. St Cath Soc Ox BA61 MA65 MPhil77 LRAM55 GGSM56. Wycliffe Hall Ox 58 Seabury-Western Th Sem BD62. **d** 62 **p** 63. C Chelmsf Cathl *Chelmsf* 62-63; Succ Chelmsf Cathl 63-64; Prec 64-66; Lect St Osyth Coll Clacton-on-Sea 66-69; Lic to Offic 66-69; Lect Ch Ch Coll Cant 69-73; Sen Lect 73-85; Prin Lect and Hd Relig Studies from 85; Hon Min Can Cant Cathl *Cant* 70-85; Hon Can from 85; Lic to Offic from 85. *St Lawrence Priory, 136 Old Dover Road, Canterbury, Kent CT1 3NX* Tel (01227) 765575

BOND, Canon John Frederick Augustus. b 45. Open Univ BA75. CITC 64. **d** 67 **p** 69. C Lisburn St Paul *Conn* 67-70; C Finaghy 70-77; I Ballynure and Ballyeaston from 77; Can Conn Cathl from 96. *The Rectory, 11 Church Road, Ballynure, Ballyclare, Co Antrim BT39 9UF* Tel (01960) 322350 Mobile 0411-285728 Fax as telephone

BOND, Kim Mary. *See* BURGESS, Mrs Kim Mary

BOND, Lawrence (Laurie). b 53. ACIB77. Sarum & Wells Th Coll CMinlStuds92. **d** 92 **p** 93. C Saffron Walden w Wendens Ambo and Littlebury *Chelmsf* 92-95; TV from 96. *The Vicarage, Church Walk, Littlebury, Saffron Walden, Essex CB11 4TT* Tel (01799) 523130

BOND, Mark Francis Wilson. b 53. Sarum & Wells Th Coll 89. **d** 91 **p** 92. C Taunton Lyngford *B & W* 91-95; V Highbridge from 95. *The Vicarage, 81A Church Street, Highbridge, Somerset TA9 3HS* Tel (01278) 783671

BOND, Norman. b 23. Wycliffe Hall Ox. **d** 70 **p** 71. C Warrington St Ann *Liv* 70-73; P-in-c 73-77; P-in-c Warrington St Pet 73-77; V Wigan St Cath 77-88; rtd 88; Perm to Offic *Carl* from 88; Perm to Offic *Liv* from 88. *Bridge House, Old Hutton, Kendal, Cumbria LA8 0NH* Tel (01539) 722293

BOND, Paul Maxwell. b 36. TD73. ACIB56. Oak Hill Th Coll 76. **d** 79 **p** 80. Hon C Wisley w Pyrford *Guildf* 79-91; Deputation Appeals Org Children's Soc 88-91; C Egham *Guildf* 91-93; V Rockfield and St Maughen's w Llangattock etc *Mon* from 94. *The Vicarage, Rockfield, Monmouth NP5 3QB* Tel (01600) 712003

BOND, Richard Jack. b 16. Lich Th Coll 38. **d** 41 **p** 42. C Filton *Bris* 41-44; C Chippenham St Andr w Tytherton Lucas 44-46; Chapl St Mich Coll Bexley and Lon Choir Sch 46-47; Chapl RAF 47-50; C Bris St Mary Redcliffe w Temple *Bris* 50-53; C Newc St Andr *Newc* 64-66; C-in-c Balkwell CD 66-68; V Balkwell 68-78; R Allendale 78-79; R Allendale w Whitfield 79-83; rtd 83. *82 Brantwood Avenue, Whitley Bay, Tyne & Wear NE25 8NL* Tel 0191-252 9798

BOND, The Ven Thomas James. b 18. TCD BA41 MA68. CITC 41. **d** 42 **p** 43. C Annagh w Drumaloor and Cloverhill *K, E & A* 42-44; C Sligo Cathl 44-47; I Kilgobbin *L & K* 47-49; I Bourney w Dunkerrin 49-52; I Kilkeevin w Kiltullagh *K, E & A* 52-55; I Bailieborough 55-60; I Templemichael w Clongish, Clooncumber etc 60-91; Preb Elphin Cathl 67-91; Adn Elphin and Ardagh 78-91; rtd 91. *Halstow, Drumelis, Cavan, Co Cavan, Irish Republic* Tel Cavan (49) 61812

BOND-THOMAS, David Harradence. b 23. Ch Coll Cam BA44 MA51. **d** 59 **p** 60. C Langley Marish *Ox* 59-62; C Earley St Pet 62-71; P-in-c Middleton Stoney 71-77; P-in-c Bucknell 71-76; P-in-c Weston on the Green 72-76; P-in-c Chesterton w Wendlebury 76-77; V Chesterton w Middleton Stoney and Wendlebury 77-89; rtd 89; Perm to Offic *Glouc* from 89. *35 Greet Road, Winchcombe, Cheltenham, Glos GL54 5JT* Tel (01242) 603150

✠**BONE, The Rt Revd John Frank Ewan.** b 30. St Pet Coll Ox BA54 MA59 Whitelands Coll Lon PGCE71. Ely Th Coll 54. **d** 56 **p** 57 **c** 89. C Pimlico St Gabr *Lon* 56-60; C Henley *Ox* 60-63; V Datchet 63-76; RD Burnham 74-77; R Upton cum Chalvey 76-78; Adn Buckingham 77-89; Area Bp Reading 89-96; rtd 97. *4 Grove Road, Henley-on-Thames, Oxon RG9 1DH* Tel (01491) 413482

BONE, Michael Thomas. b 33. ACMA62 Open Univ BA82. Brechin NSM Ord Course 79. **d** 83 **p** 84. Chapl Dundee Inst of Tech 83-93; Hon C Broughty Ferry *Bre* 83-84; Hon C Arbroath 84-87; Hon C Auchmithie 84-87; Hon C Dundee St Mary Magd from 87; Hon C Arbroath from 95. *5 Roxburgh Terrace, Dundee DD2 1NZ* Tel (01382) 566897

BONE, Noel Francis. b 18. TD64. Clifton Th Coll. **d** 59 **p** 60. C W Hampstead St Cuth *Lon* 59-61; V Ryarsh *Roch* 61-69; Lic to Offic *Lon* 69-71; V Boxmoor St Jo *St Alb* 71-72; V Aston w Benington 72-83; C St Giles-in-the-Fields *Lon* 83; rtd 83; Perm to Offic *St Alb* 84-94; Chapl St Jo Hosp Win 84-86; Perm to Offic *Nor* 87-95. *10 Livingstone Court, Christchurch Lane, Barnet, Herts EN5 4PL*

BONHAM, Frederick Thomas (Fred). b 37. St Deiniol's Hawarden 70. **d** 72 **p** 73. C Northwood Hills St Edm *Lon* 72-75; C Clewer St Andr *Ox* 75-90; V Reading H Trin 90-93; TV Newbury from 93. *Saint Mary's Vicarage, 14 Strawberry Hill, Newbury, Berks RG13 1XJ* Tel (01635) 40889

BONHAM-CARTER, Gerard Edmund David. b 31. Lon Univ BSc53 DCAe55. S'wark Ord Course. **d** 87 **p** 88. NSM Wandsworth St Paul *S'wark* from 87; Perm to Offic *St E* from 87; Chapl R Hosp and Home Putney from 92. *85 Victoria Drive, London SW19 6HW* Tel 0181-788 1230

BONIFACE, Lionel Ernest George. b 36. Lon Coll of Div ALCD63 BD64. **d** 64 **p** 65. C Attenborough w Chilwell *S'well* 64-69; C Farndon 69-71; C Thorpe 69-71; P-in-c Mansfield St Aug 71-77; V Oughtibridge *Sheff* 77-92; Ind Chapl 79-81; P-in-c Treeton 92-93; TV Brinsworth w Catcliffe and Treeton from 93. *The Rectory, Church Lane, Treeton, Rotherham, S Yorkshire S60 5QZ* Tel 0114-269 6542

BONIWELL, Timothy Richard. b 51. AKC73. St Aug Coll Cant 74. **d** 75 **p** 76. C Walthamstow St Mich *Chelmsf* 75-78; C Wigmore Abbey *Heref* 78-83; C Studley *Sarum* 83-86; Chapl Trowbridge Coll 83-86; V Bath St Barn w Englishcombe *B & W* 86-95; R Tintinhull w Chilthorne Domer, Yeovil Marsh etc from 95. *The Rectory, Vicarage Street, Tintinhull, Yeovil, Somerset BA22 8PY* Tel (01935) 822655

BONNER, David Robert. b 28. ASCA66 FCIS72 FCIB74 Lon Univ DipRS78. S'wark Ord Course 74. **d** 77 **p** 78. NSM Hampton All SS *Lon* 77-84; P-in-c Twickenham All SS 84-91; rtd 91; Perm to Offic *Lon* from 91. *17 St James's Road, Hampton Hill, Hampton, Middx TW12 1DH* Tel 0181-979 1565

BONNER, Frederick Charles. b 10. Worc Ord Coll 63. **d** 65 **p** 66. C Hungerford and Denford *Ox* 65-69; R W Ilsley w Farnborough 69-75; P-in-c E Ilsley 70-74; rtd 75. *4 Ham View, Upton-upon-Severn, Worcester WR8 0QE* Tel (01684) 592087

BONNER, James Maxwell Campbell. Sydney Univ BSc48 DipEd49 Lon Univ BD59. Oak Hill Th Coll. **d** 60 **p** 61. C Walthamstow St Mary *Chelmsf* 60-63; C Morden *S'wark* 63-65; Australia from 65; rtd 94. *13 Waratah Street, Croydon Park, NSW, Australia 2133* Tel Sydney (2) 744 9832

BONNET, Tom. b 51. Univ of Wales (Ban) DipTh89 Univ of Wales (Cardiff) BTh90. St Mich Coll Llan 90. **d** 90 **p** 91. C Criccieth w Treflys *Ban* 90-91; C Denio w Abererch 91-93; R Llanfachraeth 93-94; P-in-c Valley w Llanfachraeth 94; R from 94. *The Rectory, London Road, Valley, Holyhead LL65 3DP* Tel (01407) 741242

BONNEY, Mark Philip John. b 57. St Cath Coll Cam BA78 MA82. St Steph Ho Ox BA84 MA89. **d** 85 **p** 86. C Stockton St Pet *Dur* 85-88; Chapl St Alb Abbey *St Alb* 88-90; Prec 90-92; V Eaton Bray w Edlesborough 92-96; R Gt Berkhamsted from 96. *The Rectory, Berkhamsted, Herts HP4 2DH* Tel (01442) 864194

BONNEY, Richard John. **d** 96 **p** 97. NSM Knighton St Mary Magd *Leic* from 96. *7 Carisbrooke Park, Carisbrooke Road, Leicester LE2 3PQ*

BONNEY, Stuart Campbell. b 51. Edin Univ BD83. Edin Th Coll 81. **d** 83 **p** 84. C Edin St Luke *Edin* 83-86; C Edin St Martin 83-86; P-in-c Auchterarder *St And* 86-90; P-in-c Muthill 86-90; Dep Chapl HM Pris Leeds 90-91; Chapl HM Pris Moorland 91-96; P-in-c Bathgate *Edin* from 96; P-in-c Linlithgow from 96. *St Peter's Rectory, 85 Acredales, Linlithgow, West Lothian EH49 6JA* Tel (01506) 842384

BONNEYWELL, Miss Christine Mary. b 57. Univ of Wales (Lamp) BA78 LTh80. Sarum & Wells Th Coll 80. **d** 81 **p** 94. C Swansea St Pet *S & B* 81-84; C Llangyfelach 84-86; Chapl Univ of Wales (Lamp) *St D* 86-90; Educn Officer Wells Cathl *B & W* 90-95; C Yeovil H Trin w Barwick 95-97; Chapl Yeovil Distr Hosp 95-97; Chapl Pilgrim Health NHS Trust Boston from 97. *The Chaplaincy, Pilgrim Hospital, Sibsey Road, Boston, Lincs PE21 9QT, or 4 Hospital Lane, Boston, Lincs PE21 9BY* Tel (01205) 364801 or 355151 Fax 354395

BONSALL, Charles Henry Brash. b 42. Ex Univ BA66. Ridley Hall Cam 66. **d** 68 **p** 69. C Cheltenham St Mary *Glouc* 68-72; Sudan 72-77 and 79-83; Perm to Offic *Nor* 78; Development and Miss Sec Intercon Ch Soc 83-93; Perm to Offic *Birm* from 91; rtd 93. *3 Pakenham Road, Birmingham B15 2NE* Tel 0121-440 6143

✠**BONSER, The Rt Revd David.** b 34. Man Univ MA75 AKC61. **d** 62 **p** 63 **c** 91. C Heckmondwike *Wakef* 62-65; C Sheff St Geo *Sheff* 65-68; R Chorlton-cum-Hardy St Clem *Man* 68-82; Bp's Ecum Adv 73-81; Hon Can Man Cathl 81-82; AD Hulme 81-82; Adn Rochdale 82-91; TR Rochdale 82-91; Suff Bp Bolton from 91. *4 Sandfield Drive, Lostock, Bolton BL6 4DU* Tel (01204) 843400 Fax 849652

BONSEY, Hugh Richmond Lowry. b 49. Sarum & Wells Th Coll 74. **d** 76 **p** 77. C Bris St Mary Redcliffe w Temple etc *Bris* 76-80; TV Sutton *Liv* 80-88; P-in-c Yatton Keynell *Bris* 88-89; P-in-c Biddestone w Slaughterford 88-89; P-in-c Castle Combe 88-89; P-in-c W Kington 88-89; P-in-c Nettleton w Littleton Drew 88-89; C Westbury-on-Trym H Trin 89-90; V Peasedown St John w Wellow *B & W* from 90. *The Vicarage, 18 Church Road, Peasedown St John, Bath BA2 8AA* Tel (01761) 432293

BONSEY, Thory Richmond. b 18. St Chad's Coll Dur 37. Cuddesdon Coll 46. **d** 47 **p** 48. C Salisbury St Martin *Sarum* 47-50; C Kingsthorpe *Pet* 50-53; PC Ashwick w Oakhill *B & W* 53-57; V Desborough *Pet* 57-61; R Teigh w Whissendine 61-67; R Ecton 67-73; V Ketton 73-77; Australia from 77; rtd 83. *21/167 La Perouse Street, Red Hill, ACT, Australia 2603* Tel Canberra (6) 295 2316

BONTING, Sjoerd Lieuwe. b 24. Amsterdam Univ BSc44 MSc50 PhD52 Lon Univ BD58. Washington Dioc Course 63. **d** 63 **p** 64. USA 63-80 and from 85; Chapl Nijmegen, Eindhoven, Arnhem, and Twenthe *Eur* 80-85. *1006 East Evelyn Avenue, Sunnyvale, California 94086, USA* Tel Sunnyvale (408) 7380259 or 7364155

BOOCOCK, John Walter. b 31. Wells Th Coll 63. **d** 65 **p** 66. C Guisborough *York* 65-67; C Bottesford *Linc* 67-73; TV Bottesford w Ashby 73-74; V Riddlesden *Bradf* 74-83; V Darlington H Trin *Dur* 83-91; P-in-c Ingleton w Denton 91-96; Dioc Par Development Officer 91-95; rtd 96; Perm to Offic *Wakef* from 96. *3 Wellhouse Lane, Mirfield, W Yorkshire WF14 0PN* Tel (01924) 496449

BOOKER, Gerald Dennis. b 30. St Pet Coll Ox BA52 MA56. Ridley Hall Cam 53 Oak Hill Th Coll 80. **d** 81 **p** 82. Hon C Hertford All SS *St Alb* 81-83; R Bramfield w Stapleford and Waterford 83-96; Chapl Herts Univ 90-96; rtd 96. *The Garden House, Churchfields, Hertford SG13 8AE* Tel (01992) 583939

BOOKER, James Howard (Jim). b 57. CD (US Air)83. Edin Th Coll 88. **d** 90 **p** 91. C Peterhead *Ab* 90-92; C Old Deer 90-92; C Longside 90-92; C Strichen 90-92; Bp's Chapl Peterhead 92-93; Miss to Seamen from 92; R Peterhead *Ab* from 93; Chapl HM Pris Peterhead from 93. *19 York Street, Peterhead, Aberdeenshire AB42 6SN* Tel (01779) 472217 or 478626 Pager 01426-947418

BOOKER, Mrs Margaret Katharine. b 20. MCSP42. Westcott Ho Cam 82. **dss** 83 **d** 87 **p** 94. Stansted Mountfitchet *Chelmsf* 83-95; Par Dn 87-90; NSM 90-95; rtd 90; Perm to Offic *Ely* from 95. *49 Home Farm Road, Houghton, Huntingdon, Cambs PE17 2BN* Tel (01480) 469167

BOOKER, Michael Charles. b 36. LLCM57 ARCO58. Lon Coll of Div LTh63. **d** 63 **p** 64. C Royston *St Alb* 63-66; C Mildenhall *St E* 66-68; Min Can St E Cathl 68-83; Prec St E Cathl 70-83; Chapl Framlingham Coll Suffolk from 84. *29 The Mowbrays, Framlingham, Woodbridge, Suffolk IP13 9DL* Tel (01728) 723122

BOOKER, Michael Paul Montague. b 57. Jes Coll Ox BA79 Bris Univ CertEd80. Trin Coll Bris 84. **d** 87 **p** 88. C Cant St Mary Bredin *Cant* 87-91; V Leamington Priors St Mary *Cov* 91-96; Dir Miss and Past Studies Ridley Hall Cam from 96. *Ridley Hall, Sidgwick Avenue, Cambridge CB3 9HG* Tel (01223) 353040 Fax 301287

BOOKLESS, Andrew Pitcairn. b 63. Sheff Univ BA85. St Jo Coll Nottm DipMM92. **d** 92 **p** 93. C Llantrisant *Llan* 92-95; C Llangynwyd w Maesteg from 95. *10 Upper Street, Maesteg, Bridgend CF34 9DU* Tel (01656) 736858

BOOKLESS, David John Charles. b 62. Jes Coll Cam MA83 PGCE. Trin Coll Bris DipHE90 MA91. **d** 91 **p** 92. C Southall Green St Jo *Lon* from 91. *St George's Vicarage, 1 Lancaster Road, Southall, Middx UB1 1NP* Tel 0181-574 1876

BOOKLESS, John Guy. b 19. Clare Coll Cam BA40 MA46 Serampore Univ MTh72. Ridley Hall Cam 47. **d** 49 **p** 50. C Toxteth Park Ch Ch *Liv* 49-50; C Fazakerley Em 50-51; Tutor Ridley Hall Cam 51-52; India 53-72; C St Alb St Mich *St Alb* 73-76; C Harlow New Town w Lt Parndon *Chelmsf* 76-78; TV 78-79; P-in-c Widmerpool *S'well* 79-85; V Willoughby-on-the-Wolds w Wysall 79-85; V Willoughby-on-the-Wolds w Wysall and Widmerpool 85; rtd 85; Perm to Offic *S'well* from 85; Perm to Offic *Leic* from 85. *84 Kirkstone Drive, Loughborough, Leics LE11 3RW* Tel (01509) 263650

BOOKLESS, Mrs Rosemary. b 26. Westf Coll Lon BA47 DipEd49 Serampore Univ BD72. St Mich Ho Ox 56. **dss** 80 **d** 91 **p** 94. Willoughby-on-the-Wolds w Wysall and Widmerpool *S'well* 80-85; rtd 85; Perm to Offic *Leic* 85-89; Loughborough Em 89-91; NSM 91-95; NSM Loughborough Em and St Mary in Charnwood from 95. *84 Kirkstone Drive, Loughborough, Leics LE11 3RW* Tel (01509) 263650

BOON, Nigel Francis. b 39. St Jo Coll Nottm. **d** 83 **p** 84. C St Helens St Helen *Liv* 83-86; V Kirkdale St Lawr 86-92; V Huyton Quarry from 92. *St Gabriel's Vicarage, 2 St Agnes Road, Huyton, Liverpool L36 5TA* Tel 0151-489 2688

BOON, William John. b 54. Glouc Sch of Min 84. **d** 88 **p** 89. Hon C Matson *Glouc* 88-91; NSM Gt Witcombe 91; C 91-95; C Brockworth 91-96; P-in-c Sharpness w Purton and Brookend from 96; P-in-c Slimbridge from 97. *The Vicarage, Sanigar Lane, Newtown, Berkeley, Glos GL13 9NF* Tel (01453) 811360

BOOT, Felicity Olivia. S Tr Scheme. **d** 97. NSM Lyndhurst and Emery Down *Win* from 97. *Pikes Hill Cottage, Pikes Hill Avenue, Lyndhurst, Hants SO43 7AX* Tel (01703) 282616

BOOTES, Michael Charles Edward. b 35. ACP70. Sarum Th Coll 58. **d** 61 **p** 62. C Winchmore Hill St Paul *Lon* 61-64; Switzerland 64-67; C St Marylebone All SS *Lon* 67-68; OGS from 68; Chapl Kingsley St Mich Sch W Sussex 69-75; V Brandon *Dur* 75-78; Chapl Shoreham Gr Sch 78-79; C Clayton w Keymer *Chich* 80-84; TV Ovingdean w Rottingdean and Woodingdean 84-85; TR Ovingdean 85-88; V Lundwood *Wakef* 88-92; C Pontefract St Giles 92-95; P-in-c Kellington w Whitley from 95. *The Vicarage, 1 Manor Farm Close, Kellington, Goole, N Humberside DN14 0PF* Tel (01977) 662876 E-mail mbogs @msn.com

BOOTH, Charles Robert. b 48. Leeds Univ CertEd75. N Ord Course 79. **d** 82 **p** 83. C Eccleshill *Bradf* 82-84; C Jersey St Brelade *Win* 84-88; Australia 88-90 and from 93; V Blurton *Lich* 90-93. *5 Royce Street, Singleton, W Australia 6175, or PO Box 687, Mandurah, W Australia 6210* Tel Perth (9) 537 3215 or 581 6777 Fax 581 6323

BOOTH, David. b 44. Coll of Resurr Mirfield 72. **d** 74 **p** 75. C Osmondthorpe St Phil *Ripon* 74-77; C Armley w New Wortley 77-79; V Leeds St Wilfrid 79-95; V Royton St Paul *Man* from 95. *St Paul's Vicarage, 2 Low Meadows, Royton, Oldham OL2 6YB* Tel 0161-624 2388

BOOTH, Derek. b 36. LTCL ALCM AKC61. **d** 62 **p** 63. C Woodchurch *Ches* 62-65; C Penrith St Andr *Carl* 65-67; C Tranmere St Paul *Ches* 67-70; C Wilmslow 70-72; V Micklehurst 73-97; C Staveley and Barrow Hill *Derby* from 97. *191 Middlecroft Road, Staveley, Chesterfield, Derbyshire S43 3NQ* Tel (01426) 472724

BOOTH, Eric James. b 43. Open Univ BA84. N Ord Course 86. **d** 89 **p** 90. NSM Nelson St Phil *Blackb* 89-93; NSM Fence and Newchurch-in-Pendle 93-97; NSM Padiham from 97. *5 Round Hill Place, Park Road, Cliviger, Burnley, Lancs BB10 4UA* Tel (01282) 450708

BOOTH, Ewart Charles. b 67. LTCL85 K Coll Lon LLB88. Sarum & Wells Th Coll BTh93. **d** 93 **p** 95. NSM Tadley St Pet *Win* 93-95; C Highcliffe w Hinton Admiral from 95. *14 Lakewood Road, Christchurch, Dorset BH23 5NX* Tel (01425) 273456

BOOTH, George Kenneth. b 12. Pemb Coll Ox BA37 MA40. Wells Th Coll 37. **d** 39 **p** 50. C Portsea St Sav *Portsm* 39-40; C Portchester 40-41; Asst Master Epsom Coll 41-46; Felsted Sch Essex 46; Ho Master Fettes Coll Edin 47-59; C Edin St Ninian *Edin* 50-55; Chapl St Luke's Coll Ex 59-78; rtd 78. *Furcroft, Rock, Wadebridge, Cornwall PL27 6LD* Tel (01208) 2476

BOOTH, Graham Richard. b 55. Birm Univ BSocSc75. St Jo Coll Nottm 89. **d** 91 **p** 92. C Woodthorpe *S'well* 91-96; P-in-c Trowell from 96. *The Rectory, Nottingham Road, Trowell, Nottingham NG9 3PF* Tel 0115-932 1474

BOOTH, Ian George. b 64. Chich Th Coll 85 Linc Th Coll 87. **d** 88 **p** 89. C Pet St Mary Boongate *Pet* 88-90; C Hawley H Trin *Guildf* 90-94; V Willesden St Mary *Lon* from 94. *Willesden Vicarage, 18 Neasden Lane, London NW10 2TT* Tel 0181-459 2167

BOOTH, James Roger. b 46. Keble Coll Ox BA71 MA74 BTh77. Wycliffe Hall Ox 75. **d** 78 **p** 79. C Bridlington Priory *York* 78-83; V Nafferton w Wansford from 83. *The Vicarage, Nafferton, Driffield, N Humberside YO25 0JS* Tel (01377) 44372

BOOTH, Jon Alfred. b 42. Nottm Univ BA64 Lon Univ MPhil72. Coll of Resurr Mirfield 78. **d** 80 **p** 81. C Elland *Wakef* 80-84; C Royston from 84. *The Vicarage, Church Street, Royston, Barnsley, S Yorkshire S71 4QZ* Tel (01226) 722410

BOOTH, Kenneth Neville. b 41. Otago Univ BA62 MA63 BD66 MTh69 St Andr Univ PhD74. **d** 65 **p** 66. C Dundee St Paul *Bre* 65-69; Perm to Offic *Mor* 70-71; New Zealand 72-80 and from 81; Perm to Offic *Ox* 80-81. *The Vicarage, 373 Highgate, Roslyn, Dunedin, New Zealand* Tel Christchurch (3) 464 0240 Fax as telephone E-mail ken.booth@nevill.earthlight.co.nz

BOOTH, Leonard William. b 46. K Coll Lon BD70 AKC70. **d** 71 **p** 72. C Cockerton *Dur* 72-75; C Hove St Barn *Chich* 75-77; TV Brighton Resurr 77-78; C E Grinstead St Mary 78-81; USA from

81. *254 St Joseph Avenue, Long Beach, California 90803, USA* Tel Long Beach (213) 433-6531

BOOTH, Michael Kevin. b 47. Louvain Univ Belgium BA. St Jo Coll Nottm 88 Oscott Coll (RC) 65. **d** 71 **p** 72. In RC Ch 71-87; C N Reddish *Man* 88-89; R Heaton Norris Ch w All SS from 89. *The Rectory, 6 Glenfield Road, Stockport, Cheshire SK4 2QP* Tel 0161-432 6838

BOOTH, Paul Harris. b 49. St Jo Coll Nottm LTh79. **d** 79 **p** 80. C Thorpe Edge *Bradf* 79-82; P-in-c Frizinghall 82-83; TV Shipley St Paul and Frizinghall 83-97; rtd 97. *3 Gilstead Court, Gilstead, Bingley, W Yorkshire BD16 3LA* Tel (01274) 551071

BOOTH, Wallace. b 14. **d** 62 **p** 63. C Croydon Woodside *Cant* 62-66; V Woodnesborough 66-79; P-in-c Staple 77-79; rtd 79; Perm to Offic *Chich* from 87. *3 St Augustine's Close, Bexhill-on-Sea, E Sussex TN39 3AZ* Tel (01424) 214524

BOOTH, William James. b 39. TCD BA60 MA75. **d** 62 **p** 63. C Belfast St Luke *Conn* 62-64; Chapl Cranleigh Sch Surrey 65-74; Chapl Westmr Sch 74-91; Lic to Offic *Lon* 74-93; P in O 76-93; PV Westmr Abbey 87-93; Sub Dean HM Chpls Royal and Dep Clerk of the Closet from 91; Sub Almoner and Dom Chapl to The Queen from 91. *Marlborough Gate, St James's Palace, London SW1A 1BG* Tel 0171-930 6609

BOOTHBY, Frank. b 29. St D Coll Lamp 56. **d** 58 **p** 59. C Maghull *Liv* 58-61; C N Meols 61-64; Miss to Seamen 64; rtd 94. *7 Belsfield Drive, Hesketh Bank, Preston PR4 6YB*

BOOTHMAN, Ms Olive. b 31. TCD BA. **d** 94 **p** 95. NSM Clondalkin w Rathcoole *D & G* from 94. *Miley Hall, Blessington, Co Wicklow, Irish Republic* Tel Wicklow (45) 865119

BOOTHMAN, Canon Samuel. b 09. TCD BA34 Div Test35 MA37. **d** 35 **p** 35. C Enniskillen and Trory *Clogh* 35-37; C Win St Thos and St Clem w St Mich etc *Win* 37-40; CF (EC) 40-46; Hon CF 46; R Farley Chamberlayne w Braishfield *Win* 46-81; RD Romsey 71-79; Hon Can Win Cathl 73-81; R Michelmersh, Timsbury, Farley Chamberlayne etc 81; rtd 81; Perm to Offic *Win* from 81. *Boldbrook Lodge, Pound Lane, Ampfield, Romsey, Hants SO51 9BP* Tel (01794) 368143

BOOTS, Claude Donald Roy. b 26. Roch Th Coll 67. **d** 69 **p** 70. C Midsomer Norton *B & W* 69-73; V Westfield 73-80; P-in-c Hambridge w Earnshill and Isle Brewers 80; R Ilton w Hambridge, Earnshill, Isle Brewers etc 80-91; rtd 91; Perm to Offic *B & W* from 91. *41 Furlong Close, Midsomer Norton, Bath BA3 2PR* Tel (01761) 419263

BOOYS, Mrs Susan Elizabeth (Sue). b 56. Bris Univ BA78 LMH Ox PGCE79. St Alb and Ox Min Course 92. **d** 95 **p** 96. C Kidlington w Hampton Poyle *Ox* from 95. *4 Court Close, Kidlington, Oxford OX5 2DG* Tel (01865) 374021

BOREHAM, Harold Leslie (Harry). b 37. S'wark Ord Course. **d** 72 **p** 73. C Whitton and Thurleston w Akenham *St E* 72-77; R Saxmundham 77-85; V Felixstowe SS Pet and Paul 85-96; Chapl Felixstowe Hosp 85-96; Chapl Bartlet Hosp Felixstowe 95-96; P-in-c Ramsgate St Mark *Cant* from 96. *St Mark's Vicarage, 198 Margate Road, Ramsgate, Kent CT12 6AQ* Tel (01843) 581042

BORRETT, The Ven Charles Walter. b 16. Em Coll Cam BA39 MA43. Ridley Hall Cam 39. **d** 41 **p** 43. C Newmarket All SS *St E* 41-45; C Wolverhampton St Paul *Lich* 45-48; C Tettenhall Regis 48-49; V 49-70; RD Trysull 58-70; Preb Lich Cathl 64-71; Adn Stoke 70-82; P-in-c Sandon 76-82; Chapl to The Queen 80-86; rtd 82; Perm to Offic *St E* from 82. *34 Queensway, Mildenhall, Bury St Edmunds, Suffolk IP28 7JL* Tel (01638) 712718

BORRILL, John. b 19. Lon Univ BD41 AKC41. Westcott Ho Cam 41. **d** 42 **p** 43. C Hanwell St Thos *Lon* 42-45; C Ealing St Pet Mt Park 45-48; New Zealand 48-49; Lon Dioc Home Missr Whitton St Aug *Lon* 49-51; P-in-c 51-58; V 58-59; V St Pancras w St Jas and Ch Ch 59-71; Chapl Elizabeth Garrett Anderson Hosp 62-71; Nat Temperance Hosp 62-71; Lon Ho Meckleburgh 62-63; V Hendon St Mary 71-82; Chapl Puerto de la Cruz Tenerife *Eur* 82-84; rtd 84; Hon C Tenerife *Eur* 84-87; Perm to Offic *Chich* from 87. *Loganberry Cottage, Strand Hill, Winchelsea, E Sussex TN36 4JT* Tel (01797) 226489

BORROWDALE, Geoffrey Nigel. b 61. Southn Univ BSc83. Chich Th Coll 87. **d** 90. C Tilehurst St Mich *Ox* 90-91; Perm to Offic *Chich* from 93. *Ruskins, 2 High Street, Chichester, W Sussex PO20 6DD* Tel (01243) 789269

BORSBEY, Alan. b 38. Linc Th Coll 71. **d** 73 **p** 73. C Bardsley *Man* 73-75; C Elton All SS 75-78; V Bury St Paul 78-96; P-in-c Bolton St Bede from 96. *St Bede's Vicarage, 92 Normanby Street, Bolton BL3 3QR* Tel (01204) 61496

BORTHWICK, Alexander Heywood (Sandy). b 36. MBPsS90 Open Univ BA80 Surrey Univ MSc89. Lich Th Coll 57. **d** 60 **p** 61. C Glas Ch Ch *Glas* 60-62; C Landore *S & B* 62-64; C Swansea St Thos and Kilvey 64-65; Br Guiana 65-66; Guyana 66-70; C Oystermouth *S & B* 70-71; Lic to Offic *Man* 71-76; Area Sec (Dios Man and Liv) USPG 71-76; Area Sec (Dios Blackb and S & M) 73-76; Sch and Children's Work Sec 76-83; Chapl Tooting Bec Hosp Lon 83-91; Chapl Charing Cross Hosp Lon 92-94; Chapl Hammersmith Hosps NHS Trust from 94. *The Chaplain's Office, Charing Cross Hospital, Fulham Palace Road, London W6 8RF* Tel 0181-846 1040 or 846 1234

BOSHER, Philip Ross. b 61. Sarum & Wells Th Coll 84. **d** 87 **p** 88. C Warminster St Denys *Sarum* 87-90; P-in-c Farley w Pitton and W Dean w E Grimstead 90-91; TV Alderbury Team 91-96; CF from 96. *c/o MOD Chaplains (Army), Bagshot Park, Bagshot, Surrey GU19 5PL* Tel Bagshot (01276) 71717

BOSSOM, Peter Emery. b 28. St D Dioc Tr Course. **d** 82 **p** 83. NSM Llandysilio w Egremont and Llanglydwen etc *St D* 82-86; rtd 86; Lic to Offic *St D* 86-90. *Glyn-y-Fran, Eglwyswrw, Crymych SA41 3SN* Tel (01239) 831347

BOSTOCK, Canon Geoffrey Kentigern. b 30. OGS. Sarum Th Coll 66. **d** 68 **p** 69. SSF 50-60; C Shrewsbury St Chad *Lich* 68-72; C Hanley w Hope 72-74; P-in-c Wednesbury St Jo 74-79; V Dudley St Aug Holly Hall *Worc* 79-80; V Sheff Parson Cross St Cecilia *Sheff* 80-92; V Bilham from 92. *Bilham Vicarage, Churchfield Road, Clayton, Doncaster, S Yorkshire DN5 7DH* Tel (01977) 643756

BOSTOCK, Peter Anthony. b 64. Nottm Univ BA85 Fitzw Coll Cam BA89. Westcott Ho Cam 87. **d** 90 **p** 91. C Brighton St Matthias *Chich* 90-94; C Leytonstone St Marg w St Columba *Chelmsf* from 94. *The Presbytery, 16 Terling Close, London E11 3NP* Tel 0181-519 9252

BOSTOCK, Canon Peter Geoffrey. b 11. Qu Coll Ox BA33 MA37. Wycliffe Hall Ox 33. **d** 35 **p** 37. Kenya 35-59; Hon Can Mombasa 52-59; Adn and V Gen Mombasa 55-59; Adn Doncaster *Sheff* 59-67; R Melton on the Hill 59-67; Asst Sec Miss and Ecum Coun of Ch Assembly 67-70; Dep Sec Bd Miss and Unity Gen Syn 71-73; Clergy Appts Adv 74-76; rtd 77; Perm to Offic *Ox* from 77. *6 Moreton Road, Oxford OX2 7AX* Tel (01865) 515460

BOSTON, Jonathan Bertram. b 40. Ely Th Coll 61. **d** 64 **p** 65. C Eaton *Nor* 64-70; Sen Chapl ACF Norfolk from 70; V Horsham St Faith w Newton St Faith 70-90; V Horsford 71-90; V Horsford and Horsham w Newton St Faith from 90. *The Vicarage, Horsford, Norwich NR10 3DB* Tel (01603) 898266

BOSWELL, Colin John Luke. b 47. Sarum & Wells Th Coll 72. **d** 74 **p** 75. C Upper Tooting H Trin *S'wark* 74-78; C Sydenham St Phil 78-79; C St Helier 80-83; P-in-c Caterham 83-95; P-in-c Chaldon 85-95; RD Caterham 85-95; V Croydon St Jo from 95. *Croydon Vicarage, 22 Bramley Hill, Croydon CR2 6LT* Tel 0181-688 1387

BOTHAM, Norman. Nottm Univ MPhil80 Lon Univ CertEd55 DBRS66 MRTS84. S'wark Ord Course 63. **d** 66 **p** 67. Lect Coll SS Mark & Jo Chelsea 66-69; C Englefield Green *Guildf* 66-69; Sen Lect Shoreditch Coll Egham 69-74; C Bagshot 69-73; C-in-c Bath H Trin *B & W* 74; Asst Dir RE 74; Sen Lect Doncaster Inst of HE 74-82; Public Preacher *S'well* from 75; Perm to Offic *Sheff* 75; Hon AP Bawtry w Austerfield and Misson 75-85; Offg Chapl RAF from 85; rtd 94. *Rufford, Mattersey Road, Ranskill, Retford, Notts DN22 8NF* Tel (01777) 818234

BOTT, Dr Theodore Reginald. b 27. CEng58 FIChemE68 Birm Univ BSc52 PhD68 DSc84. WMMTC 85. **d** 86 **p** 87. NSM Harborne St Faith and St Laur *Birm* from 86. *17 Springavon Croft, Harborne, Birmingham B17 9BJ* Tel 0121-427 4209

BOTTERILL, David Darrell. b 45. Open Univ BA. Sarum & Wells Th Coll. **d** 83 **p** 84. C Blandford Forum and Langton Long etc *Sarum* 83-86; TV Shaston from 86; Chapl HM Young Offender Inst Guys Marsh 89-91. *St James's Vicarage, 34 Tanyard Lane, Shaftesbury, Dorset SP7 8HW* Tel (01747) 852193

BOTTING, Canon Michael Hugh. b 25. K Coll Lon BSc51 AKC K Coll Lon PGCE52. Ridley Hall Cam 54. **d** 56 **p** 57. C Onslow Square St Paul *Lon* 56-61; V Fulham St Matt 61-72; RD Hammersmith 67; V Leeds St Geo *Ripon* 72-84; RD Headingley 81-84; Hon Can Ripon Cathl 82-84; R Aldford and Bruera *Ches* 84-90; rtd 90; Jt Dir Lay Tr *Ches* 90-95; Perm to Offic from 95. *25 Woodfield Grove, Hoole, Chester CH2 3NY* Tel (01244) 321133

BOTTING, Paul Lloyd. b 43. Brasted Th Coll 67 St Mich Coll Llan 69. **d** 71 **p** 72. C Hucknall Torkard *S'well* 71-74; C Cen Torquay *Ex* 74-76; P-in-c Sutton in Ashfield St Mich *S'well* 76; V 77-88; Chapl King's Mill Hosp Sutton-in-Ashfield 85-88; Perm to Offic *Leic* from 95; NSM Vale of Belvoir Gp 95-97; C High Framland Parishes from 97. *High Framland Rectory, Harston, Grantham, Lincs NG32 1PP* Tel (01476) 870329

BOTTOMLEY, George Edward. b 06. St Jo Coll Dur LTh34. Bible Churchmen's Coll 30. **d** 35 **p** 36. C Upper Holloway St Jo *Lon* 35-37; C Marple All SS *Ches* 37-40; Jt Sec ICM 40-42; R Bucknall and Bagnall *Lich* 42-50; V Wolverhampton St Luke 50-54; Lic to Offic *Glas* 54-61; V Cheltenham St Mark *Glouc* 61-76; rtd 76; Hon C Camborne *Truro* from 77. *Salem, Reskadinnick Road, Camborne, Cornwall TR14 7LR* Tel (01209) 713028

BOTTOMLEY, Gordon. b 31. Oak Hill Th Coll 51. **d** 55 **p** 56. C Kinson *Sarum* 55-58; Lic to Offic *Man* 58-63; N Area Sec BCMS 58-63; V Hemswell w Harpswell *Linc* 63-72; V Glentworth 63-72; Chapl RAF 63-71; R Bucknall and Bagnall *Lich* 72-80; TR 80-82; P-in-c Worthing H Trin *Chich* 82-88; V Camelsdale 88-96; rtd 96. *6 Jay Close, Fareham, Hants PO14 3TA*

BOTTOMLEY, Philip. b 45. Cranmer Hall Dur BA67 DipTh69. **d** 70 **p** 71. C Harlow New Town w Lt Parndon *Chelmsf* 70-74; C W Kilburn St Luke w St Simon and St Jude *Lon* 74-78; Midl Sec CMJ 78-84; Hon C Selly Park St Steph and St Wulstan *Birm* 81-84; USA from 84. *211 Elizabeth, Avalon, Pennsylvania 15202, USA*

BOTWRIGHT, Adrian Paul. b 55. St Jo Coll Ox MA PGCE. Westcott Ho Cam 80. **d** 82 **p** 83. C Chapel Allerton *Ripon* 82-85; Chapl Chapel Allerton Hosp 82-85; C Bourne *Guildf* 85-88; V Weston 88-94; R Skipton H Trin *Bradf* from 94. *The Rectory, Rectory Lane, Skipton, N Yorkshire BD23 1ER* Tel (01756) 793622

BOUCHER, Brian Albert. b 39. Univ of Wales (Lamp) BA61. Chich Th Coll 61. **d** 63 **p** 64. C Hoxton H Trin w St Mary *Lon* 63-67; Chapl RN 67-68; Asst Chapl Harrow Sch 68-73; Chapl 73-86; P-in-c Clerkenwell H Redeemer w St Phil *Lon* 86-91; P-in-c Myddleton Square St Mark 86-91; Chapl Hurstpierpoint Coll Hassocks 92-96; rtd 96. *20 Summervale Close, Tunbridge Wells, Kent TN4 8JB* Tel (01892) 530342

BOUCHER, Geoffrey John Geoff. b 61. Warw Univ BA82 K Coll Lon 94. Ridley Hall Cam 94. **d** 96 **p** 97. C Tavistock and Gulworthy *Ex* from 96. *32 Plym Crescent, Tavistock, Devon PL19 9HX* Tel (01822) 615501

BOUGHEY, Richard Keith. b 26. Man Univ MEd71. Qu Coll Birm 77. **d** 80 **p** 82. NSM Upper Tean *Lich* 80-81; NSM Stoke-upon-Trent 80-81; NSM Uttoxeter w Bramshall 82-88; rtd 88; Perm to Offic *Lich* from 88. *Kontokali, The Old Lane, Checkley, Stoke-on-Trent ST6 8TG* Tel (01538) 722013

BOUGHTON, Mrs Elisabeth Mary Victoria. b 66. St Anne's Coll Ox BA87. Ridley Hall Cam 89. **d** 91 **p** 94. C Guildf Ch Ch *Guildf* 91-95; Chapl St Cath Sch Bramley from 92. *The Rectory, 10A The Ridgeway, Fetcham, Leatherhead, Surrey KT22 9AZ* Tel (01372) 372598

BOUGHTON, Michael John. b 37. Kelham Th Coll 57. **d** 62 **p** 63. C Grantham St Wulfram *Linc* 62-66; C Kingsthorpe *Pet* 66-68; C Linc St Nic w St Jo Newport *Linc* 68-72; V Scunthorpe All SS 72-79; V Crowle 79-89; R Epworth 80-89; TR Bottesford w Ashby from 89. *St Paul's Rectory, Ashby, Scunthorpe, S Humberside DN16 3DL* Tel (01724) 856863

BOUGHTON, Paul Henry. b 55. ACA80 Imp Coll Lon BScEng77 ARSM77. Ridley Hall Cam 89. **d** 91 **p** 92. C Guildf Ch Ch *Guildf* 91-96; R Fetcham from 96. *The Rectory, 10A The Ridgeway, Fetcham, Leatherhead, Surrey KT22 9AZ* Tel (01372) 372598

BOULCOTT, Thomas William. b 16. Bps' Coll Cheshunt 47. **d** 49 **p** 50. C Hitchin St Mary *St Alb* 49-51; C Kempston 51-54; Chapl Bedf Gen Hosp 52-54; V Newfoundpool *Leic* 54-61; V N Evington 61-73; Chapl Leic Gen Hosp 62-73; V Loppington w Newtown *Lich* 73-85; RD Wem and Whitchurch 83-85; rtd 85; Perm to Offic *Lich* 85-94. *Silver Birch, Tilley Road, Wem, Shrewsbury SY4 5HA* Tel (01939) 233602

BOULD, Preb Arthur Roger. b 32. Selw Coll Cam BA54 MA58 Wadh Coll Ox BA55 DipTh56 DipEd57 MA58. St Steph Ho Ox 54. **d** 57 **p** 58. C Wednesfield St Thos *Lich* 57-64; V Wellington Ch Ch 64-71; R Cheadle 71-88; P-in-c Freehay 84-88; R Cheadle w Freehay 88-91; Chapl Cheadle Hosp 71-91; Chapl HM Pris Moorcourt 72-82; RD Cheadle 72-91; Preb Lich Cathl from 83; Asst to Bp Wolv 91-97; Bp Lich's Past Aux from 97. *4 Mansell Close, Stafford ST16 1AG* Tel (01785) 220860 Fax as telephone

BOULD, Stephen Frederick. b 49. K Coll Lon BD78 AKC78. Sarum & Wells Th Coll 78. **d** 79 **p** 80. C Cantril Farm *Liv* 79-82; AV Hindley St Pet 82-85; C Wigan All SS 85; Hon C Leic H Spirit *Leic* 85-88; Chapl Leic Univ 85-88; V Leic St Pet 88; P-in-c Leic St Sav 88; V Leic Ch Sav 88-96; P-in-c New Humberstone 94-96; TR Leic Presentation from 96. *St Saviour's Rectory, Woodhill, Leicester LE5 3JB* Tel 0116-251 3396 Fax 262 3240

BOULLIER, Kenneth John (Ken). b 51. Lon Bible Coll 79 Trin Coll Bris DipHE84. **d** 84 **p** 85. C Heref St Pet w St Owen and St Jas *Heref* 84-87; V Nutley *Chich* 88-93; R Maresfield 88-93; New Zealand from 93. *The Vicarage, 47 Church Road, Kaitaia 0500, Northland, New Zealand* Tel Auckland (9) 408 0528 Fax as telephone E-mail 100405.25417@compuserve.com

BOULNOIS, Linda Dianne. b 59. Trin Coll Bris 92. **d** 96 **p** 97. C Brampton Bierlow *Sheff* from 96. *52 Rotherham Road, Wath-upon-Dearne, Rotherham, S Yorkshire S63 6AE*

BOULSOVER, Philip John. b 16. ACT ThL55 Kelham Th Coll 34. **d** 40 **p** 41. C Middlesbrough St Cuth *York* 40-41; C Northallerton 41-43; C Bexhill St Pet *Chich* 43-51; Australia from 51; rtd 81. *21 Chillagoe Street, Fisher, Canberra, Australia 2611* Tel Canberra (6) 288 7589

BOULT, Audrey. Qu Coll Birm. **dss** 85 **d** 87 **p** 94. Sheldon *Birm* 85-87; NSM 87-96; Perm to Offic from 96. *17 Fulford Grove, Sheldon, Birmingham B26 3XX* Tel 0121-743 9993

BOULT, Geoffrey Michael. b 56. Southn Univ BTh88 Bris Univ MA90 Birm Univ MSc97. Sarum & Wells Th Coll 77. **d** 80 **p** 81. C Newark w Hawton, Cotham and Shelton *S'well* 80-83; TV Melksham *Sarum* 83-90; P-in-c Charminster and Stinsford 90-95; Perm to Offic *Birm* 95-96; Perm to Offic *Sarum* from 95. *2B Cairns Court, Cairns Road, Redland, Bristol BS6 7TL* Tel 0117-924 8428

BOULTBEE, John Michael Godolphin. b 22. Oak Hill Th Coll 66. **d** 68 **p** 69. C Hawkwell *Chelmsf* 68-71; C St Keverne *Truro* 71-73; V Constantine 74-79; P-in-c St Merryn 79-81; V 81-87; rtd 87; Perm to Offic *Ex* from 87. *July Cottage, 8 Williams CLose, Dawlish, Devon EX7 9SP* Tel (01626) 865761

BOULTER, Michael Geoffrey. b 32. Lon Univ BD56. Tyndale Hall Bris 53. **d** 57 **p** 58. C Tranmere St Cath *Ches* 57-60; R Cheetham Hill *Man* 60-65; R Tollard Royal w Farnham *Sarum* 65-66; Chapl Alderney Hosp Poole 66-96; V Branksome St Clem *Sarum* 66-96; rtd 96. *5 Curzon Court, 11 Portarlington Road, Bournemouth BH4 8BU* Tel (01202) 768718

BOULTER, Robert George. b 49. Man Univ BA90. St Aug Coll Cant 72. **d** 75 **p** 76. C Langley All SS and Martyrs *Man* 75-80; V Lower Kersal 80-84; Oman 84-86; Slough Community Chapl *Ox* 86-87; R Whalley Range St Marg *Man* from 87. *St Margaret's Rectory, Rufford Road, Whalley Range, Manchester M16 8AE* Tel 0161-226 1289

BOULTON, Christopher David. b 50. Keble Coll Ox BA71 MA80. Cuddesdon Coll 71. **d** 74 **p** 75. C Harlow St Mary and St Hugh w St Jo the Bapt *Chelmsf* 74-77; C Shrub End 77-80; P-in-c Gt Bentley 80-83; V 83-89; V Cherry Hinton St Andr *Ely* from 89; P-in-c Teversham from 90. *Cherry Hinton Vicarage, Fulbourn Old Drift, Cambridge CB1 4LR* Tel (01223) 247740

BOULTON, Canon Peter Henry. b 25. St Chad's Coll Dur BA49. Ely Th Coll 49. **d** 50 **p** 51. C Coppenhall *Ches* 50-54; C Mansfield St Mark *S'well* 54-55; V Clipstone 55-60; V Carlton 60-67; Chapl Victoria Hosp Worksop 67-87; V Worksop Priory *S'well* 67-87; Hon Can S'well Minster 75-92; Dir of Educn 87-92; Chapl to The Queen from 91; rtd 92; Perm to Offic *Ches* from 92. *3 Grasmere Drive, Holmes Chapel, Crewe CW4 7JT*

BOULTON, Preb Thomas Oswald. b 10. Keble Coll Ox BA35 MA39. Wycliffe Hall Ox 35. **d** 36 **p** 37. C Oswestry St Oswald *Lich* 36-39; C Garston *Liv* 39; CF (EC) 39-45; V Shobnall *Lich* 45-48; V Penn 48-60; RD Oswestry 60-76; V Oswestry St Oswald 60-76; Preb Lich Cathl 67-76. *21 Rayleigh Road, Harrogate, N Yorkshire HG2 8QR* Tel (01423) 871753

BOULTON, Wallace Dawson. b 31. Lon Coll of Div 65. **d** 67 **p** 68. C Bramcote *S'well* 67-71; Dioc Public Relns Officer 69-71; Hon C St Bride Fleet Street w Bridewell etc *Lon* 71-86; Publicity Sec CMS 71-79; Media Sec 79-86; Lic to Offic *Chich* from 84; Guild Chapl 86-96; Ed C of E Newspaper 86-88; rtd 96. *44 Winterbourne Close, Hastings, E Sussex TN34 1XQ* Tel (01424) 713743

BOULTON-LEA, Peter John. b 46. St Jo Coll Dur BA68. Westcott Ho Cam 69. **d** 71 **p** 72. C Farlington *Portsm* 72-75; C Darlington St Jo *Dur* 75-77; R E and W Horndon w Lt Warley *Chelmsf* 77-82; V Hersham *Guildf* 82-91; R Kirk Sandall and Edenthorpe *Sheff* 91-96; RD Doncaster 95-96; V Campsall from 96. *The Vicarage, Church Hill Cottage, High Street, Campsall, Doncaster, S Yorkshire DN6 9AD* Tel (01302) 700286

BOULTON-REYNOLDS, Mrs Jean. b 49. Sarum Th Coll 93. **d** 96 **p** 97. C Harnham *Sarum* from 96. *87 Netherhampton Road, Salisbury SP2 8NA* Tel (01722) 323259

BOUNDY, David. b 34. Kelham Th Coll 55. **d** 59 **p** 60. C Stirchley *Birm* 59-64; Chapl E Birm Hosp 64-74; V Bordesley St Oswald 64-70; V S Yardley St Mich 70-74; R Bideford *Ex* 74-82; RD Hartland 80-82; R Northfield *Birm* 82-88; P-in-c Penzance St Mary w St Paul *Truro* 88-90; V 90-94; rtd 94; Chapl Convent of St Mary at the Cross Edgware from 94. *St John's House, 27 High View Avenue, Edgware, Middx HA8 9TX* Tel 0181-958 8980

BOUNDY, Canon Gerald Neville. b 36. BA. Linc Th Coll. **d** 65 **p** 66. C Bris St Mary Redcliffe w Temple etc *Bris* 65-70; P-in-c Southmead 70-72; V 72-81; V Cotham St Sav w St Mary from 81; Hon Can Bris Cathl from 96. *182 St Michael's Hill, Cotham, Bristol BS2 8DE* Tel 0117-974 3198 or 973 3395

BOURDEAUX, Canon Michael Alan. b 34. St Edm Hall Ox BA57 MA61 BD68 Lambeth DD96. Wycliffe Hall Ox 57. **d** 60 **p** 61. C Enfield St Andr *Lon* 60-64; C Charlton St Luke w St Paul *S'wark* 65-66; Lic to Offic *Roch* 66-70; Gen Dir Keston Coll from 70; Hon Can Roch Cathl *Roch* from 90. *Keston Research, PO Box 276, Oxford OX2 6BQ* Tel (01865) 311022 Fax 311280

BOURKE, The Very Revd Francis Robert. b 16. TCD BA40 BD46 PhD61. CITC 41. **d** 42 **p** 42. Dean Kilfenora *L & K* 72-86; Dean Killaloe 72-86; I Killaloe 72-76; I Killaloe w Abington, Kiltinanlea etc 76-86; Can Killaloe Cathl 72-86; rtd 86. *Tinnaview, Inchanore, Ballina, Killaloe, Co Clare, Irish Republic* Tel Killaloe (61) 376461

✠**BOURKE, The Rt Revd Michael Gay.** b 41. CCC Cam BA63 MA67. Cuddesdon Coll 65. **d** 67 **p** 68 **c** 93. C Gt Grimsby St Jas *Linc* 67-71; C Digswell *St Alb* 71-73; C-in-c Panshanger CD 73-78; Course Dir St Alb Minl Tr Scheme 75-87; V Southill 78-86; Adn Bedford 86-93; Area Bp Wolverhampton *Lich* from 93. *61 Richmond Road, Wolverhampton WV3 9JH* Tel (01902) 23008 Fax 25443

BOURKE, Ronald Samuel James. b 50. MA HDipEd. **d** 79 **p** 80. C Portadown St Mark *Arm* 79-83; I Carnteel and Crilly 83-90; I Mountmellick w Coolbanagher, Rosenallis etc *M & K* 90-97; I Kingscourt w Drumconrath, Syddan and Moybologue from 97. *St Ernan's Rectory, Kingscourt, Co Cavan, Irish Republic* Tel Dundalk (42) 56255 Fax 67947

BOURKE, Stanley Gordon. b 48. CITC 78. **d** 78 **p** 79. C Dundonald *D & D* 78-80; C Lurgan Ch Ch 81-82; I Dungiven w Bovevagh *D & R* 82-89; I Lurgan St Jo *D & D* from 89. *St John's Rectory, Sloan Street, Lurgan, Craigavon, Co Armagh BT66 8NT* Tel (01762) 322770

BOURNE, David George. b 67. Coll of Ripon & York St Jo BA91. Coll of Resurr Mirfield BA93. **d** 94 **p** 95. C Portsea St Mary

Portsm from 94. *1 Glebe Flats, Nutfield Place, Portsmouth PO1 4JF* Tel (01705) 830154

BOURNE, David James. b 54. Reading Univ BA76. Trin Coll Bris 77. **d** 79 **p** 80. C W Bromwich Gd Shep w St Jo *Lich* 79-84; V Riseley w Bletsoe *St Alb* from 84. *The Vicarage, Church Lane, Riseley, Bedford MK44 1ER* Tel (01234) 708234

BOURNE, Canon Dennis John. b 32. Loughb Coll of Educn DLC55. Ridley Hall Cam 58. **d** 60 **p** 61. C Gorleston St Andr *Nor* 60-64; Min Gorleston St Mary CD 64-79; V Costessey 79-86; R Hingham w Wood Rising w Scoulton 86-97; RD Hingham and Mitford 90-95; Hon Can Nor Cathl 93-97; rtd 97; Perm to Offic *Nor* from 97. *Amron, Star Lane, Long Stratton, Norwich NR15 2XH* Tel (01508) 850863

BOURNE, Mrs Diana Mary. b 46. St Jo Coll York BEd68. S Dios Minl Tr Scheme 92. **d** 95 **p** 96. C Pinner *Lon* from 95. *58 Cannonbury Avenue, Pinner, Middx HA5 1TS* Tel 0181-866 5604

BOURNE, Henry. b 34. Spurgeon's Coll 55. **d** 64 **p** 65. C Handsworth St Mary *Birm* 64-67; Chapl RAF 67-85; Asst Chapl-in-Chief RAF 85-87; P-in-c Bourn *Ely* 87-88; V 88-89; P-in-c Kingston 87-88; R 88-89; V Caxton 88-89; R Bourn and Kingston w Caxton and Longstowe 89-91; rtd 91; Perm to Offic *Truro* from 95. *Newlyn Cottage, The Coombe, Newlyn, Penzance, Cornwall TR18 5HS*

BOURNE, John Mark. b 49. Cant Sch of Min 88. **d** 91 **p** 92. C Allington and Maidstone St Pet *Cant* 91-94; V Marden from 94; Chapl HM Pris Blantyre Ho from 94. *The Vicarage, Haffenden Close, Marden, Tonbridge, Kent TN12 9DR* Tel (01622) 831379

BOURNE, Nigel Irvine. b 60. St Jo Coll Ox BA82 MA86. Trin Coll Bris BA92. **d** 92 **p** 93. C Bedhampton *Portsm* 92-94; C Newport St Jo from 94. *7 College Road, Newport, Isle of Wight PO30 1HB* Tel (01983) 825030

BOURNE, Philip John. b 61. Sussex Univ BEd83 Aber Univ MLitt86 Ex Univ MEd96. Cranmer Hall Dur 85. **d** 87 **p** 88. C Gildersome *Wakef* 87-89; Chapl Ex Univ *Ex* 89-93; Lic to Offic 89-93; Assoc Chapl The Hague and Voorschoten *Eur* 94-95; Chapl Voorschoten from 96. *Chopinlaan 17, 2253 BS Voorschoten, The Netherlands* Tel Leiden (71) 561 2762 Fax 572 2780

BOURNER, Paul. b 48. CA Tr Coll. **d** 90 **p** 91. CA from 79; C Ipswich St Mary at Stoke w St Pet *St E* 90-93; R Ufford w Bredfield and Hasketon from 93. *The Rectory, School Lane, Ufford, Woodbridge, Suffolk IP13 6DX* Tel (01394) 460935

BOURNON, Dennis Harry. b 20. St Cuth Soc Dur LTh48 BA49. Oak Hill Th Coll 46. **d** 49 **p** 50. C Heworth H Trin *York* 49-51; C Bebington *Ches* 51-54; V Everton St Jo *Liv* 54-58; R Gunton St Pet *Nor* 58-65; R Eastrop *Win* 65-80; R Nursling and Rownhams 80-85; rtd 85. *17 Wessex Avenue, New Milton, Hants BH25 6NG* Tel (01425) 614016

BOURNON, Canon John Raymond. b 18. St Cath Soc Ox BA48 MA52. Oak Hill Th Coll 48. **d** 50 **p** 51. C Wellington w Eyton *Lich* 50-53; V Wombridge 53-60; V Ware Ch Ch *St Alb* 60-85; RD Hertford 71-77; Hon Can St Alb 80-85; rtd 85; Perm to Offic *Linc* from 86; Perm to Offic *Pet* from 87. *Hawkesbury, 14 Cambridge Road, Stamford, Lincs PE9 1BN* Tel (01780) 54394

BOUTAN, Marc Robert. b 53. Univ of Iowa BA74. Fuller Th Sem California MD87 Virginia Th Sem 90. **d** 91 **p** 92. USA 91-96; Asst Chapl Brussels *Eur* from 96. *Pro-Cathedral of the Holy Trinity, 29 rue Capitaine Crespel, 1050 Brussels, Belgium* Tel Brussels (2) 511 7183 Fax 511 1028 E-mail info@htb.ontonet.be

BOUTLE, David Francis. b 44. Leeds Univ BSc67 Lon Univ DipTh72. Cuddesdon Coll 69. **d** 72 **p** 73. C Boston *Linc* 72-77; C Waltham 77-80; P-in-c Morton 80-81; V 81-94; Chapl Jo Coupland Hosp Gainsborough from 80; Local Mental Health Chapl from 88; P-in-c Heckington *Linc* from 94. *The Vicarage, Heckington, Sleaford, Lincs NG34 9RW* Tel (01529) 60302

BOVEY, Denis Philip. b 29. Ely Th Coll 50. **d** 53 **p** 54. C Southwick St Columba *Dur* 53-57; Perm to Offic *Ox* 57-59; Lic to Offic *Chich* 62-64; C W Hartlepool St Aid *Dur* 64-66; R Aberdeen St Jas *Ab* 66-74; R Old Deer 74-89; R Longside 74-89; R Strichen 74-89; Can St Andr Cathl 75-88; Syn Clerk 78-83; Dean Ab 83-88; R Alford 89-94; R Auchindoir 89-94; R Inverurie 89-94; P-in-c Dufftown 89-94; P-in-c Kemnay 89-94; rtd 94. *15 Loskin Drive, Glasgow GL22 7QV* Tel 0141-772 2825

BOVILL, Francis William. b 34. Lon Univ DipTh58. St Aid Birkenhead 55. **d** 58 **p** 59. C Bispham *Blackb* 58-61; C Crosthwaite Keswick *Carl* 61-64; V Radcliffe St Andr *Man* 64-68; P-in-c Woodside St Steph *Glouc* 68; V 69-73; V Scotby *Carl* 73-96; P-in-c Cotehill and Cumwhinton 94-96; rtd 96; Perm to Offic *Carl* from 96. *16 Summerfields, Dalston, Carlisle CA5 7NW* Tel (01228) 716682

BOWDEN, Andrew David. b 59. Newc Univ BA80 BArch83. Cranmer Hall Dur 95. **d** 97. C Monkseaton St Pet *Newc* from 97. *30 Paignton Avenue, Monkseaton, Whitley Bay, Tyne & Wear NE25 8SY* Tel 0191-251 7587

BOWDEN, John Stephen. b 35. CCC Ox BA59 MA62 Edin Univ Hon DD81 Lambeth DD96. Linc Th Coll 59. **d** 61 **p** 62. C Nottingham St Mary *S'well* 61-64; Lect Nottm Univ 64-66; Ed and Managing Dir SCM Press from 66; Hon C Highgate All SS *Lon* from 66; Hon C Brentford St Faith 80-87; Hon C Brentford from 87. *20 Southwood Avenue, London N6 5RZ, or 26 Tottenham Road, London N1 4BZ* Tel 0181-340 7548 or 249 7262 Fax 249 3776

BOWDEN, John-Henry David. b 47. MIL78 Magd Coll Cam BA69 MA73 Man Poly DMS77. S Dios Minl Tr Scheme 81. **d** 84 **p** 85. NSM Redlynch and Morgan's Vale *Sarum* 84-88; NSM Cuckfield *Chich* 88-92; Perm to Offic from 92; NSM St Mary le Bow w St Pancras Soper Lane etc *Lon* from 92. *Dene House, South Chailey, Lewes, E Sussex BN8 4AB* Tel (01273) 401076

BOWDEN, Canon Robert Andrew. b 38. Worc Coll Ox BA62 DipTh63 MA67 BDQ68. Cuddesdon Coll 63. **d** 65 **p** 66. C Wolverhampton St Geo *Lich* 65-69; C Duston *Pet* 69-72; R Byfield 72-79; Chapl R Agric Coll Cirencester 79-93; R Coates, Rodmarton and Sapperton etc *Glouc* from 79; Bp's Adv on Rural Soc 81-93; Hon Can Glouc Cathl from 90; Chapl to The Queen from 92; Local Min Officer *Glouc* from 93. *Coates Rectory, Cirencester, Glos GL7 6NR* Tel (01285) 770235

BOWDER, Reginald William Maxwell (Bill). b 46. TCD BA68 MA81 Kent Univ DipSocWork71. S'wark Ord Course 78. **d** 80 **p** 81. C Bush Hill Park St Steph *Lon* 81-84; I Fiddown w Clonegam, Guilcagh and Kilmeaden *C & O* 84-87; I Lismore w Cappoquin, Kilwatermoy, Dungarvan etc 87-89; Dean Lismore 87-89; Chapl Kent Univ and KIAD *Cant* 90-97; I Donoughmore and Donard w Dunlavin *D & G* from 97. *The Rectory, Donard, Dunlavin, Co Wicklow, Irish Republic* Tel Naas (45) 404631

BOWDLER, Ernest Roy. b 10. Lich Th Coll 32. **d** 34 **p** 36. C Sedgley St Mary *Lich* 34-38; C Goldenhill 38-40; V Smallthorne 40-50; Chapl RNVR 43-46; V Coseley St Chad *Lich* 50-57; V Wolverhampton Ch Ch 57-71; Chapl CGA 71-73; C Langley Marish *Ox* 73-76; rtd 75; Hon C Worc St Martin w St Pet *Worc* 76-85; Hon C Walsall Pleck and Bescot *Lich* 85-88; Perm to Offic 87-94. *47 Melton Road, Wymondham, Norfolk NR28 0DE*

BOWEN, Colin Wynford. b 48. St D Coll Lamp DipTh71. **d** 71 **p** 72. C Hubberston w Herbrandston and Hasguard etc *St D* 71-75; R Cosheston w Nash and Upton 75-77; V Carew and Cosheston w Nash and Upton 77-85; V Pembroke St Mary and St Mich from 85. *The Vicarage, 18 Grove Hill, Pembroke SA71 5PT* Tel (01646) 682710

BOWEN, Daniel Austin. b 11. St D Coll Lamp BA33 St Steph Ho Ox 33. **d** 35 **p** 36. C Llanelli *St D* 35-41; R Puncheston w Lt Newcastle 41-48; V Llandyfriog w Llanfair-Trelygen 48-58; V Llanfihangel Aberbythych 58-67; V Monkton 67-78; rtd 78; Perm to Offic *Chich* 78-95. *30 Old School Close, Stokenchurch, High Wycombe, Bucks HP14 3RB* Tel (01494) 483871

BOWEN, David Gregory. b 47. Lanchester Poly BSc69. Cuddesdon Coll 70. **d** 74 **p** 75. C Rugby St Andr *Cov* 74-77; C Charlton St Luke w H Trin *S'wark* 78-80; TV Stantonbury *Ox* 80-82; Perm to Offic *B & W* from 89. *17 Chapel Hill, Clevedon, Avon BS21 7NL* Tel (01275) 878962

BOWEN, David John. b 46. Glouc Th Course 83. **d** 86 **p** 88. NSM Ross w Brampton Abbotts, Bridstow and Peterstow *Heref* 86-88; C Kingstone w Clehonger, Eaton Bishop etc 88-93; P-in-c Lugwardine w Bartestree and Weston Beggard 93-94; V Lugwardine w Bartestree, Weston Beggard etc from 94. *The Vicarage, Lugwardine, Hereford HR1 4AE* Tel (01432) 850244

BOWEN, Mrs Delyth. b 54. St D Coll Lamp BA90. St Mich Coll Llan 90. **d** 91 **p** 97. C Llandybie *St D* 91-95; P-in-c Llanllwni 95-97; V Llanybydder and Llanwenog w Llanllwni from 97. *The Vicarage, Llanllwni, Pencader SA39 9DR* Tel (01559) 395413

BOWEN, Gwyn Humphrey. b 21. Univ of Wales (Lamp) BA54. **d** 56 **p** 57. C Penarth w Lavernock *Llan* 56-63; C Pontycymer and Blaengarw 63-65; V Cwmaman 65-91; rtd 91; Perm to Offic *Llan* from 91. *18 St Luke's Avenue, Penarth CF64 3PS*

BOWEN, Miss Jennifer Ethel. b 46. Liv Univ BSc68 CertEd69. N Ord Course 80. **dss** 83 **d** 87 **p** 94. Blundellsands St Nic *Liv* 83-86; W Derby St Mary 86-87; Par Dn 87-94; C from 94. *4 The Armoury, West Derby, Liverpool L12 5EL* Tel 0151-256 6600

BOWEN, John. b 39. Univ of Wales DipTh63 Aus Nat Univ BA88. St Mich Coll Llan 60. **d** 68 **p** 69. C Aberavon *Llan* 68-73; Australia from 73. *3 Sculptor Street, Giralang, ACT, Australia 2617* Tel Bruce (6) 241 5716 or 234 2252

BOWEN, John Roger. b 34. St Jo Coll Ox BA59 MA62. Tyndale Hall Bris 59. **d** 61 **p** 62. C Cambridge St Paul *Ely* 61-65; Tanzania 65-76; Kenya 76-80; Lic to Offic *S'well* from 80; Dir Past Studies St Jo Coll Nottm 80-85; Tutor from 85. *St John's College, Bramcote, Nottingham NG9 3DS* Tel 0115-922 4086 or 925 1114 Fax 922 0134 or 943 6438

BOWEN, Lionel James. b 16. S'wark Ord Course 63. **d** 64 **p** 65. C Vauxhall St Pet *S'wark* 64-67; C Sanderstead All SS 67-74; V Pill *B & W* 74-79; Perm to Offic *Chich* from 79; rtd 81. *43 Sussex Court, Eaton Road, Hove, E Sussex BN3 3AS* Tel (01273) 775945

BOWEN, Roger William. b 47. Magd Coll Cam BA69 MA73 Hatf Poly Cert Counselling 91. St Jo Coll Nottm 69 Selly Oak Coll 76. **d** 72 **p** 73. C Rusholme H Trin *Man* 72-75; Rwanda Miss 75-84; Burundi 77-84; Tutor and Lect All Nations Chr Coll Ware 85-91; Hon C Ware Ch Ch *St Alb* 86-91; Gen Sec Mid-Africa Min (CMS) 91-97; V Lt Amwell *St Alb* from 97. *The Vicarage, 17 Barclay Close, Hertford Heath, Hertford SG13 7RW* Tel (01992) 589140

BOWEN, Stephen Allan. b 51. Leic Univ BA72. Glouc Sch of Min 88. **d** 91 **p** 92. NSM Bream *Glouc* 91-92; NSM Tidenham w Beachley and Lancaut 91-94; C Glouc St Jas and All SS from 94. *16 Derby Road, Gloucester GL1 4AE* Tel (01452) 308951

BOWEN, Stephen Guy. b 47. Qu Coll Cam BA68 MA72 Bris Univ MA72. Clifton Th Coll 69. **d** 71 **p** 72. C Chelsea St Jo *Lon* 71-73; C Chelsea St Jo w St Andr 73; C Guildf St Sav *Guildf* 73-76; C Guildf St Sav w Stoke-next-Guildford 76-77; C Wallington H Trin *S'wark* 77-79; V Felbridge from 79. *The Vicarage, The Glebe, Felbridge, East Grinstead, W Sussex RH19 2QT* Tel (01342) 321524

BOWEN, Thomas Raymond. b 20. Univ of Wales (Lamp) BA42. **d** 48 **p** 49. C Monkton *Cant* 48-52; C Haverfordwest St Martin w Lambston *St D* 52; Chapl RAF 53-75; Chapl Gresham's Sch Holt 75-83; rtd 83; Perm to Offic *St D* from 83. *35 Gail Rise, Llangwm, Haverfordwest SA62 4HJ* Tel (01437) 891179

BOWEN, Vincent Paul. b 26. Qu Coll Cam BA50 MA55. Ely Th Coll 51. **d** 53 **p** 54. C Cowley St Jo *Ox* 53-56; C Brentwood St Thos *Chelmsf* 56-61; R Cranham 61-71; R Wanstead St Mary 71-91; rtd 91; Perm to Offic *Cant* from 92. *44 Nunnery Fields, Canterbury, Kent CT1 3JT* Tel (01227) 472036

BOWER, Brian Mark. b 60. QUB BA DipTh. **d** 85 **p** 86. C Orangefield w Moneyreagh *D & D* 85-87; I Inver w Mountcharles, Killaghtee and Killybegs *D & R* 87-93; Miss to Seamen from 87; I Augher w Newtownsaville and Eskrahoole *Clogh* from 93. *16 Knockmay Road, Augher, Co Tyrone BT77 0DF* Tel (01662) 548008 Fax as telephone

BOWER, James Hugh Marsh. b 17. St Chad's Coll Dur BA39 DipTh40 MA43. **d** 40 **p** 41. C Shrewsbury St Mary *Lich* 40-41; C Rugeley 41-42; C Wolverhampton St Pet 42-48; V Northwood 48-54; V Caldmore 54-58; V Wolverhampton St Andr 58-74; R Cavendish *St E* 74-83; P-in-c Stansfield 78-83; RD Clare 82-83; rtd 83; Perm to Offic *St E* from 83; Perm to Offic *Chelmsf* from 83. *142 Melford Road, Sudbury, Suffolk CO10 6JZ* Tel (01787) 372683

BOWERING, John Anthony (Tony). b 34. SS Coll Cam BA57 MA. Wycliffe Hall Ox 57. **d** 59 **p** 60. C Hornchurch St Andr *Chelmsf* 59-62; Succ Chelmsf Cathl 62; Prec 63; V Brampton Bierlow *Sheff* 64-70; V Norton Woodseats St Paul 70-80; V Tickhill w Stainton 80-97; RD W Doncaster 87-92; rtd 97. *Linthwaite Cottage, Main Street, Kirklington, Newark, Notts NG22 8ND* Tel (01636) 816995

BOWERING, The Ven Michael Ernest. b 35. Kelham Th Coll 55. **d** 59 **p** 60. C Middlesbrough St Oswald *York* 59-62; C Huntington 62-64; V Brayton 64-72; RD Selby 71-72; V Saltburn-by-the-Sea 72-81; Can Res York Minster 81-87; Sec for Miss and Evang 81-87; Adn Lindisfarne *Newc* from 87. *12 Rectory Park, Morpeth, Northd NE61 2SZ* Tel (01670) 513207

BOWERS, David. b 55. Man Univ BA79. Wycliffe Hall Ox 82. **d** 84 **p** 85. C Lawton Moor *Man* 84-87; C Walmsley 87-93; V Milnrow from 93. *The Vicarage, 40 Eafield Avenue, Milnrow, Rochdale, Lancs OL16 3UN* Tel (01706) 42988

BOWERS, Francis Malcolm. b 44. Chan Sch Truro 79. **d** 82 **p** 83. NSM Penzance St Mary w St Paul *Truro* 82-83; C 86-88; NSM Madron 83-86; TV Redruth w Lanner and Treleigh 88-91; V St Blazey from 91; RD St Austell from 96. *The Vicarage, St Blazey, Par, Cornwall PL24 2NG* Tel (01726) 812113

BOWERS, Canon John Edward. b 23. TD68. AKC50. **d** 51 **p** 52. C Leic St Pet *Leic* 51-55; Sacr S'wark Cathl *S'wark* 55-57; CF (TA) 56-67; V Loughborough St Pet *Leic* 57-63; V Ashby-de-la-Zouch St Helen w Coleorton 63-88; CF (R of O) 67-78; RD Akeley W *Leic* 76-88; Hon Can Leic Cathl 78-88; rtd 88; Perm to Offic *Derby* 88-94; Perm to Offic *Leic* 88-94; Chapl High Sheriff of Derbyshire 89-90; Perm to Offic *Ely* from 94. *13 Bathurst, Orton Goldhay, Peterborough PE2 5QH* Tel (01733) 361834

BOWERS, Canon John Edward William. b 32. St Aid Birkenhead 60. **d** 63 **p** 64. C Bromborough *Ches* 63-68; Ind Chapl 68-74; P-in-c Crewe St Pet 69-71; V Crewe St Mich 71-74; TR Ellesmere Port 74-79; V Hattersley 79-91; Hon Can Ches Cathl from 80; RD Mottram 88-91; V Bunbury and Tilstone Fearnall from 91. *The Vicarage, Vicarage Lane, Bunbury, Tarporley, Cheshire CW6 9PE* Tel (01829) 260991

BOWERS, Julian Michael. b 48. Edin Th Coll 69. **d** 72 **p** 73. C Chippenham St Andr w Tytherton Lucas *Bris* 72-74; C Henbury 74-77; Sri Lanka 77-82; P-in-c Evercreech w Chesterblade and Milton Clevedon *B & W* 82-83; V 83-89; V Enfield St Jas *Lon* from 89. *St James's Vicarage, 144 Hertford Road, Enfield, Middx EN3 5AY* Tel 0181-804 1966

BOWERS, Michael Charles. b 52. Sarum & Wells Th Coll 89. **d** 91 **p** 92. C St Peter-in-Thanet *Cant* 91-95; V Reculver and Herne Bay St Bart from 95. *The Vicarage, 29 Burlington Drive, Herne Bay, Kent CT6 6PG* Tel (01227) 375154

BOWERS, Peter. b 47. Linc Th Coll 72. **d** 76 **p** 77. C Mackworth St Fran *Derby* 76-78; C Maidstone St Martin *Cant* 78-83; V Elmton *Derby* 83-89; V Swimbridge and W Buckland *Ex* from 89. *The Rectory, Barnstaple Hill, Swimbridge, Barnstaple, Devon EX32 0PH* Tel (01271) 830068

BOWERS, Peter William Albert. b 36. K Coll Lon BD61 AKC61. **d** 62 **p** 63. C Chorley St Pet *Blackb* 62-64; C New Sleaford *Linc* 64-67; C Folkestone H Trin w Ch Ch *Cant* 67-72; V Deal St Geo 72-80; Dir Galilee Community 80-85; R River from 86; RD Dover from 93. *The Vicarage, 23 Lewisham Road, Dover, Kent CT17 0QG* Tel (01304) 822037

BOWERS, Raymond Franklin. b 16. Lon Univ BD40. ALCD40. **d** 40 **p** 41. C Neasden cum Kingsbury St Cath *Lon* 40-43; CF (EC) 43-47; C Stonebridge St Mich *Lon* 47; Uganda 47-60; Home Educn Sec CMS 61-66; V Bath St Steph *B & W* 66-76; RD Bath 71-76; P-in-c Gosforth *Carl* 76-78; P-in-c Wasdale Head and Nether Wasdale 76-78; R Gosforth w Nether Wasdale and Wasdale Head 78-80; rtd 81; Perm to Offic *Carl* from 81. *Brow House, Blackbeck, Egremont, Cumbria CA22 2NY* Tel (01946) 841345

BOWERS, Stanley Percival. b 20. Lon Univ BD45 AKC45. Hartley Victoria Coll 40 Wells Th Coll 66. **d** 66 **p** 66. In Meth Ch 45-66; C Lawrence Weston *Bris* 66-69; V Two Mile Hill St Mich 69-91; rtd 91; Perm to Offic *Bris* from 91; Perm to Offic *B & W* 91-95. *1 Windsor Road, Longwell Green, Bristol BS15 6AF* Tel 0117-932 4051

BOWES, Mrs Beryl Sylvia. b 48. SRN70 RSCN71 Hull Univ BTh89. NE Ord Course 89. **d** 91 **p** 94. NSM Kirk Ella *York* from 91; Chapl R Hull Hosps NHS Trust from 93. *236 West Ella Road, West Ella, Hull HU10 7SF* Tel (01482) 656392, 328541 or 674427

BOWES, Ernest Ward. b 04. Trin Coll Cam BA27 MA30. Ridley Hall Cam 27. **d** 29 **p** 30. C Bowling St Steph *Bradf* 29-33; C Hampstead Em W End *Lon* 34-41; Area Sec CMS 41-49; CMS Publicity Field Org 49-52; V Weston-super-Mare Em *B & W* 52-70; rtd 70; Perm to Offic *Chich* 70-93. *6 Capel Court, The Burgage, Prestbury, Cheltenham, Glos GL52 3EL* Tel (01242) 235637

BOWES, John Anthony Hugh. b 39. Ch Ch Ox BA62 DipTh63 MA65. Westcott Ho Cam 63. **d** 65 **p** 66. C Langley All SS and Martyrs *Man* 65-68; Asst Chapl Bris Univ *Bris* 68-73; TV Cramlington *Newc* 73-76; P-in-c Oldland *Bris* 76-80; TR 80-84; V Westbury-on-Trym St Alb from 84. *St Alban's Vicarage, 21 Canowie Road, Bristol BS6 7HR* Tel 0117-973 5844

BOWES-SMITH, Edward Michael Crispin. b 67. K Coll Lon LLB89 AKC89 Solicitor 90 Selw Coll Cam BA96. Ridley Hall Cam 94. **d** 97. C Combe Down w Monkton Combe and S Stoke *B & W* from 97. *13A Fox Hill, Combe Down, Bath BA2 5QL* Tel (01225) 836092

BOWETT, Richard Julnes. b 45. EAMTC 86. **d** 89 **p** 90. C Hunstanton St Mary w Ringstead Parva, Holme etc *Nor* 89-93; C King's Lynn St Marg w St Nic 93-95; V Watton w Carbrooke and Ovington from 95. *The Vicarage, Norwich Road, Watton, Thetford, Norfolk IP25 6DB* Tel (01953) 881439

BOWIE, Dr Michael Nicholas Roderick. b 59. Sydney Univ BA78 CCC Ox DPhil90. St Steph Ho Ox MA90. **d** 91 **p** 92. C Swanley St Mary *Roch* 91-93; C Penarth w Lavernock *Llan* 93-96; Australia from 96. *The Clergy House, 507 Pitt Street, Sydney, NSW, Australia 2000*

BOWKER, Archibald Edward. b 18. Univ of Manitoba BA52. St Jo Coll Winnipeg LTh51. **d** 51 **p** 52. Canada 51-59; C Monkwearmouth All SS *Dur* 59-61; V Blackhill 61-79; rtd 80. *19 Greenside, Greatham, Hartlepool, Cleveland TS25 2HS* Tel (01429) 871973

BOWKER, Prof John Westerdale. b 35. Worc Coll Ox BA58. Ripon Hall Ox. **d** 61 **p** 62. C Endcliffe *Sheff* 61-62; Fell Lect and Dir of Studies CCC Cam 62-74; Lect Div Cam Univ 70-74; Prof of Relig Studies Lanc Univ 74-86; Hon Can Cant Cathl *Cant* from 85; Dean of Chpl Trin Coll Cam 86-91; rtd 91; Lic to Offic *Cant* from 91; Perm to Offic *Ely* from 94. *14 Bowers Croft, Cambridge CB1 4RP*

BOWKETT, Canon Cyril Edward Vivian. b 11. St Jo Coll Dur LTh38 BA39 MA68. Clifton Th Coll 35. **d** 39 **p** 40. C Bris St Mich *Bris* 39-42; C Knowle St Barn 42-47; R S'wark St Geo *S'wark* 47-82; Hon Can S'wark Cathl 66-82; P-in-c S'wark St Jude 75-82; rtd 82; Perm to Offic *B & W* from 82. *The Lookout, Warren Road, Brean, Burnham-on-Sea, Somerset TA8 2RP* Tel (01278) 751517

✠**BOWLBY, The Rt Revd Ronald Oliver.** b 26. Trin Coll Ox BA50 MA54. Westcott Ho Cam 50. **d** 52 **p** 53 **c** 73. C Pallion *Dur* 52-56; C Billingham St Cuth 56-57; C-in-c Billingham St Aid CD 57-60; V Billingham St Aid 60-66; V Croydon *Cant* 66-73; Hon Can Cant Cathl 70-73; Bp Newc 73-80; Bp S'wark 80-91; rtd 91; Asst Bp Lich from 91. *4 Uppington Avenue, Shrewsbury SY3 7JL* Tel (01743) 244192

BOWLER, Christopher William. *See* JAGE-BOWLER, Christopher William

BOWLER, David Henderson. b 54. Kent Univ BA75. St Jo Coll Nottm 75. **d** 78 **p** 79. C Bramcote *S'well* 78-82; TV Kirby Muxloe *Leic* 82-88; V Quorndon from 88. *Quorn Vicarage, 6 Loughborough Road, Quorn, Loughborough, Leics LE12 8DX* Tel (01509) 412593

BOWLER, Denis Charles Stanley. b 16. **d** 66 **p** 67. C Bishop's Cleeve *Glouc* 66-69; C Coleford w Staunton 69-72; V Coney Hill 72-77; V Lydbrook 77-82; rtd 82; Perm to Offic *Glouc* 82-96. *22 Harpfield Road, Bishops Cleeve, Cheltenham, Glos GL52 4EB* Tel (01242) 674307

BOWLER, Frederick Wallace. b 11. MBE46. AKC34. **d** 34 **p** 35. C Walworth St Jo *S'wark* 34-37; C Scarborough St Mary *York*

37-39; CF (EC) 40-46; Hon CF from 51; V Woburn Sands *St Alb* 46-50; Borneo 51-55; R Marston Magna w Rimpton *B & W* 55-58; V Westfield 58-66; V Alcombe 66-71; rtd 72. *The Manor Nursing Home, Bishop's Hull, Taunton, Somerset TA1 5EB* Tel (01823) 336633

BOWLER, Preb Kenneth Neville. b 37. K Coll Lon 57. **d** 61 **p** 62. C Buxton *Derby* 61-67; R Sandiacre 67-75; V E Bedfont *Lon* 75-87; AD Hounslow 82-87; Preb St Paul's Cathl from 85; V Fulham All SS from 87. *All Saints' Vicarage, 70 Fulham High Street, London SW6 3LG* Tel 0171-736 6301

BOWLER, Roy Harold. b 27. Wadh Coll Ox BA48 MA57. Wells Th Coll 52. **d** 53 **p** 54. C Clerkenwell H Redeemer w St Phil *Lon* 53-55; C Tottenham All Hallows 55-57; Lic to Offic *Cant* 57-61; S Rhodesia 61-65; Rhodesia 65-80; Zimbabwe from 80. *Box 537, Mutare, Zimbabwe*

BOWLES, Arthur William. b 36. Loughb Coll of Educn DLC59. LNSM course 94. **d** 96. NSM Gt Yarmouth *Nor* from 96. *Gables Farmhouse, Scratby Road, Scratby, Great Yarmouth, Norfolk NR29 3NL* Tel (01493) 732107

✠**BOWLES, The Rt Revd Cyril William Johnston.** b 16. Em Coll Cam Jes Coll Cam BA38 MA41. Ridley Hall Cam 37. **d** 39 **p** 40 **c** 69. C Barking St Marg *Chelmsf* 39-41; Chapl Ridley Hall Cam 42-44; Vice-Prin 44-51; Prin 51-63; Hon Can Ely Cathl *Ely* 59-63; Adn Swindon *Bris* 63-69; Hon Can Bris Cathl 63-69; Bp Derby 69-87; rtd 87. *Rose Lodge, Tewkesbury Road, Stow on the Wold, Cheltenham, Glos GL54 1EN* Tel (01451) 831965

BOWLES, David Anthony. b 44. Kelham Th Coll 63. **d** 68 **p** 69. C Bilborough w Strelley *S'well* 68-72; C Beeston 72-75; Ascension Is 75-77; V Wellingborough St Mark *Pet* 77-83; P-in-c Wilby 78-83; R Burton Latimer 83-90; V Sheff St Oswald *Sheff* 90-91; Perm to Offic *Derby* 94-96; Perm to Offic *Roch* from 96. *18B The Pleasaunce, Rockdale Road, Sevenoaks, Kent TN13 1JT* Tel (01732) 742380

BOWLES, John. b 32. N Ord Course. **d** 89 **p** 90. NSM Stockport St Mary *Ches* from 89. *Brockra, Bosden Hall Road, Hazel Grove, Stockport, Cheshire SK7 4JJ* Tel 0161-483 9566

BOWLES, Preb Michael Hubert Venn. b 36. Selw Coll Cam BA59 MA63. Ridley Hall Cam 59. **d** 61 **p** 62. C Woodside Park St Barn *Lon* 61-64; C Swanage *Sarum* 64-67; Lect St Mich Coll Llan 67-72; Chapl 67-70; Lib 70-72; Lect Th Univ of Wales (Cardiff) 67-72; R Gt Stanmore *Lon* from 72; Preb St Paul's Cathl from 85. *The Rectory, Rectory Lane, Stanmore, Middx HA7 4AQ* Tel 0181-954 0276

BOWLES, Peter John. b 39. Lon Univ BA60. Linc Th Coll 71. **d** 73 **p** 74. C Clay Cross *Derby* 73-76; C Boulton 76-79; R Brailsford w Shirley 79-85; P-in-c Osmaston w Edlaston 81-85; R Brailsford w Shirley and Osmaston w Edlaston 85-89; TR Old Brampton and Loundsley Green from 89. *The Rectory, 25 Oldridge Close, Chesterfield, Derbyshire S40 4UF* Tel (01246) 236663

BOWLES, Ronald Leonard. b 24. K Coll Lon BD52 AKC52. **d** 53 **p** 54. C Berwick H Trin *Newc* 53-56; C Christchurch *Win* 56-60; R Nursling and Rownhams 60-66; V Woolston 66-75; V Moordown 75-89; rtd 89. *25 Cherry Tree Avenue, Cowplain, Waterlooville, Hants PO8 8BA* Tel (01705) 267376

BOWLEY, John Richard Lyon. b 46. MRTPI76 Dur Univ BA68 QUB MSc72. CITC. **d** 79 **p** 80. C Knock *D & D* 79-81; Bp's C Knocknagoney 81-90; I Ballywalter w Inishargie from 90; RD Ards from 95. *The Vicarage, 2 Whitechurch Road, Ballywalter, Newtownards, Co Down BT22 2JY* Tel (01247) 758416

BOWLZER, Ronald. b 41. CEng69 MIMechE69. **d** 84 **p** 84. NSM Rosyth *St And* 84-85; NSM Lochgelly 84-85; NSM Inverkeithing 84-85; NSM Dunfermline 85-89; C Whitehaven *Carl* 89-91; P-in-c Netherton 91-97; Chapl to the Deaf and Hard of Hearing from 95; P-in-c Cleator Moor w Cleator from 97; P-in-c Frizington and Arlecdon from 97. *The Vicarage, Trumpet Road, Cleator, Cumbria CA23 3EF* Tel (01946) 810510

BOWMAN, Miss Alison Valentine. b 57. St Andr Univ MA79. St Steph Ho Ox 86. **d** 89 **p** 94. Par Dn Peacehaven *Chich* 89-94; C 94-95; Chapl to Area Bp Lewes 93-95; TV Rye from 95. *St Michael's House, 21 Fair Meadow, Rye, E Sussex TN31 7NL* Tel (01797) 225769

BOWMAN, Clifford William. b 57. St Jo Coll Dur BA78 Nottm Univ MA96. Ridley Hall Cam. **d** 82 **p** 83. C Sawley *Derby* 82-85; C Hucknall Torkard *S'well* 85-89; R Warsop from 89. *The Rectory, Church Road, Warsop, Mansfield, Notts NG20 0SL* Tel (01623) 843290

BOWMAN, John. b 06. Glas Univ MA38 BD41 Ch Ch Ox DPhil45. **d** 50 **p** 54. Hon C Leeds St Geo *Ripon* 51-53; Hon C Kirkstall 53-54; Perm to Offic *York* 54-59; Australia from 59; rtd 73. *15 Haines Street, North Melbourne, Victoria, Australia 3051* Tel Melbourne (3) 9329 0794

BOWMAN-EADIE, Russell Ian. b 45. ACP68 K Coll Lon BD71 AKC71. St Aug Coll Cant 71. **d** 72 **p** 73. C Hammersmith St Pet *Lon* 72-74; V Leic St Nic *Leic* 74-81; Chapl Leic Univ 74-81; Adult Educn Adv *Dur* 81-84; Dir of Tr *B & W* from 84; Preb Wells Cathl from 90. *2 The Liberty, Wells, Somerset BA5 2SU* Tel (01749) 674702

BOWN, Francis Adrian Charles Simon. b 48. Jes Coll Cam BA72 MA74 Jes Coll Ox BA75 MA78 Hull Univ MA88. Linc Th Coll 76. **d** 77 **p** 78. C Howden *York* 77-79; C Howden TM 80; P-in-c Hull St Steph Sculcoates 80-85; V from 85. *St Stephen's Presbytery, 29 Westbourne Avenue, Hull HU5 3HN* Tel (01482) 46075

BOWN, Canon John Frederick Olney. b 13. TD50. BA36 MA70. Cuddesdon Coll 36. **d** 37 **p** 38. C Prittlewell St Mary *Chelmsf* 37-39; CF (TA) 39-44; CF 44-70; V Dover St Mary *Cant* 44-45; Hon Chapl Edin St Mary *Edin* 53-55; Can Mombasa 56-58; QHC 67-70; R Fordingbridge w Ibsley *Win* 70-79; RD Christchurch 74-78; rtd 79; Hon P-in-c Longstock w Leckford *Win* 79-87. *Dawlish House, 7 Trafalgar Way, Stockbridge, Hants SO20 6ET* Tel (01264) 810672

BOWNESS, William Gary. b 48. Warw Univ BSc69. Ripon Coll Cuddesdon 80. **d** 82 **p** 83. C Lancaster St Mary *Blackb* 82-86; V Lostock Hall 86-91; V Whittington w Arkholme and Gressingham from 91; RD Tunstall from 93. *The Vicarage, Arkholme, Carnforth, Lancs LA6 1AX* Tel (015242) 21359

BOWRING, Stephen John. b 55. R Holloway Coll Lon BMus77 St Mary's Coll Twickenham PGCE78. EMMTC 89. **d** 92 **p** 93. C Thurmaston *Leic* 92-95; V Shepshed from 95. *The Vicarage, 36 Church Street, Shepshed, Loughborough, Leics LE12 9RH* Tel (01509) 502255

BOWRON, Hugh Mark. b 52. Cant Univ (NZ) BA74 MA76 Leeds Univ DipTh78. Coll of Resurr Mirfield 76. **d** 79 **p** 80. C Northampton St Mary *Pet* 79-82; New Zealand from 82. *3 Macfarlane Mews, Mount Victoria, Wellington, New Zealand* Tel Wellington (4) 384 3250 or 382 8486

BOWSER, Alan. b 35. Univ of Wales (Lamp) BA60 DipTh63. **d** 63 **p** 64. C Gateshead St Chad Bensham *Dur* 63-67; C Owton Manor CD 67-72; V Horden from 72. *The Vicarage, Horden, Peterlee, Co Durham SR8 4JF* Tel 0191-586 4423

BOWSHER, Andrew Peter (Andii). b 59. Reading Univ BA81 Nottm Univ DipTh84. St Jo Coll Nottm DPS86. **d** 86 **p** 87. C Grenoside *Sheff* 86-89; C Darfield 89-91; P-in-c Halifax All So *Wakef* 91-96; V Bradf St Aug Undercliffe *Bradf* from 96. *St Augustine's Vicarage, Undercliffe Lane, Bradford, W Yorkshire BD3 0DW* Tel (01274) 408520

BOWSKILL, Robert Preston (Bob). b 48. S Dios Minl Tr Scheme 88. **d** 91 **p** 92. NSM Eastrop *Win* 91-94; NSM Winklebury from 94. *Old Sarum, 1 Camfield Close, Basingstoke, Hants RG21 3AQ* Tel (01256) 27301

BOWTELL, Paul William. b 47. Lon Univ BSc68. St Jo Coll Nottm. **d** 82 **p** 83. C Gorleston St Andr *Nor* 82-85; TV Forest Gate St Sav w W Ham St Matt *Chelmsf* 85-91; R Spitalfields Ch Ch w All SS *Lon* from 91. *The Rectory, 2 Fournier Street, London E1 6QE* Tel 0171-247 7202

BOWYER, Frank. b 28. Man Univ BA49 BD56. Oak Hill Th Coll 53. **d** 55 **p** 56. C Halliwell St Paul *Man* 55-57; C Crosthwaite Keswick *Carl* 57-59; V Thornham w Gravel Hole *Man* 59-63; R Burnage St Marg 63-81; R Gosforth w Nether Wasdale and Wasdale Head *Carl* 81-85; R Holcombe *Man* 85-93; rtd 93; Perm to Offic *Man* from 93. *43 New Church Road, Bolton BL1 5QQ* Tel (01204) 844547

BOWYER, Geoffrey Charles. b 54. ACA79 ATII82 Lanc Univ BA76. St Jo Coll Nottm 85. **d** 87 **p** 88. C Walton *St E* 87-89; C Macclesfield Team Par *Ches* 89-91; V Cinderford St Steph w Littledean *Glouc* 91-95; V Brockenhurst *Win* from 95. *The Vicarage, Meerut Road, Brockenhurst, Hants SO42 7TD* Tel (01590) 622150

BOWYER, Dr Richard Astley. b 55. Jes Coll Ox MA Ex Univ PhD. Chich Th Coll 82. **d** 84 **p** 85. C Ex St Jas *Ex* 84-87; TV Ex St Thos and Em 87-95; USA from 95. *Address temp unknown*

BOX, David Norman. b 28. K Coll Lon BD48 AKC48. **d** 51 **p** 52. C Grays Thurrock *Chelmsf* 51-53; Hon C Aldershot St Mich *Guildf* 53-55; Asst Master St Benedict's Sch Aldershot 53-55; C Weston 55-58; C Camberley St Paul 58-61; V Blackheath and Chilworth 61-69; V Allerton *Bradf* 69-75; R Exford w Exmoor *B & W* 75-80; V Castle Cary w Ansford 80-90; P-in-c Childe Okeford, Manston, Hammoon and Hanford *Sarum* 90-91; R Childe Okeford, Okeford Fitzpaine, Manston etc 91-94; rtd 94; Perm to Offic *Carl* from 94. *Granary House, 1 Castle Street, Hilton, Appleby-in-Westmorland, Cumbria CA16 6LX* Tel (017683) 52689

BOX, Reginald Gilbert (Brother Reginald). b 20. Lon Univ BD41 AKC41 Em Coll Cam BA52 MA57 Lambeth STh91. Westcott Ho Cam 41. **d** 43 **p** 44. C Chingford SS Pet and Paul *Chelmsf* 43-47; Chapl Bps' Coll Cheshunt 47-50; SSF from 51; Lic to Offic *Ely* 51-55; Lic to Offic *Sarum* 55-61; C Cambridge St Benedict *Ely* 61-67; Chapl Coll of SS Mark and Jo Chelsea 67-69; New Zealand, Australia and Melanesia 69-84; Perm to Offic *Sarum* from 84; Perm to Offic *Ely* from 85; rtd 90; Chapl Chich Th Coll 90-93. *The Friary, Hilfield, Dorchester, Dorset DT2 7BE* Tel (01300) 341345 Fax 341293

BOXALL, David John. b 41. Dur Univ BA63 DipTh65. Sarum Th Coll 65. **d** 66 **p** 67. C Ipswich St Aug *St E* 66-69; C Bourne *Linc* 69-71; C Woodside Park St Barn *Lon* 71-72; C Thundersley *Chelmsf* 72-76; P-in-c Farcet *Ely* 76-77; TV Stanground and Farcet 77-85; V Guyhirn w Ring's End 85-90; V Southea w Murrow and Parson Drove 85-90; P-in-c Fletton 90-94; Perm to Offic from 94. *Melrose Cottage, Euximoor Drive, Christchurch, Wisbech, Cambs PE14 8DF*

BOXALL, Keith Michael. b 37. Trin Coll Bris. **d** 82 **p** 83. C Staines St Pet *Lon* 82-83; C Staines St Mary and St Pet 83-85; C Lydiard

Millicent w Lydiard Tregoz *Bris* 85-86; TV The Lydiards 86-93; V Mangotsfield from 93. *The Vicarage, St James Place, Mangotsfield, Bristol BS17 3JA* Tel 0117-956 0510

BOXALL, Canon Martin Alleyne. b 37. Wells Th Coll 65. **d** 67 **p** 68. C Crowthorne *Ox* 67-70; C Tilehurst St Mich 70-76; V Tilehurst St Cath 76-78; V Padstow *Truro* from 78; Miss to Seamen from 78; RD Pydar *Truro* 93; Hon Can Truro Cathl from 93. *The Vicarage, 46 Treverbyn Road, Padstow, Cornwall PL28 8DN* Tel (01841) 532224

BOXALL, Simon Roger. b 55. St Jo Coll Cam BA76. Ridley Hall Cam 77. **d** 79 **p** 80. C Eaton *Nor* 79-82; SAMS from 82; Brazil from 82. *Igreja Episcopal do Brasil, Caixa Postal 380, 96 400 970 Bage, RS Brasil*

BOXLEY, Christopher. b 45. K Coll Lon BD68 AKC68 Southn Univ CertEd73 Reading Univ MA84. **d** 69 **p** 70. C Bitterne Park *Win* 69-73; Perm to Offic *Chich* 73-78; Hd of Relig Studies Midhurst Gr Sch from 73; Dir Midhurst and Petworth Relig Studies Cen from 78; P-in-c Heyshott from 78. *The Rectory, Heyshott, Midhurst, W Sussex GU29 0DH* Tel (01730) 814405

BOYCE, Canon Brian David Michael. b 32. Fitzw Ho Cam BA55 MA62. Wells Th Coll 55. **d** 57 **p** 58. C Tavistock and Gulworthy *Ex* 57-60; C Paignton St Jo 60-62; S Africa 62-97; rtd 97. *Flat 6, The Judges Lodging, 19 New Street, Wells, Somerset BA5 2LD*

BOYCE, Christopher Allan. b 44. ARIBA69 Brighton Coll of Art DipArch66. S Dios Minl Tr Scheme 84. **d** 87 **p** 88. NSM Eastbourne All SS *Chich* 87-93; C Upton (Overchurch) *Ches* 93-96; V New Brighton St Jas w Em from 96. *The Vicarage, 14 Albion Street, Wallasey, Merseyside L45 9LF* Tel 0151-639 5844

BOYCE, John Frederick. b 33. ALCD57. **d** 57 **p** 58. C Earlsfield St Andr *S'wark* 57-60; C Westerham *Roch* 60-63; C Farnborough 63-66; V Sutton at Hone 66-73; P-in-c Chiddingstone 73-74; R Chiddingstone w Chiddingstone Causeway 74-84; V Brenchley from 84. *The Vicarage, 8 Broadoak, Brenchley, Tonbridge, Kent TN12 7NN* Tel (01892) 722140

BOYCE, Kenneth Albert (Ken). b 51. St Edm Hall Ox BA72 MA76 Selw Coll Cam BA75 MA79. Westcott Ho Cam 73. **d** 75 **p** 76. C Evington *Leic* 75-78; P-in-c Gt Bowden w Welham 78-81; Dioc Stewardship Adv 78-81; Chapl Leic Poly 81-86; TV Leic H Spirit 82-86; Chapl to the Deaf *Worc* 86-93; P-in-c Astwood Bank 86-93; R Fladbury, Wyre Piddle and Moor from 93; P-in-c Cropthorne w Charlton from 94; RD Pershore from 97. *The Rectory, Station Road, Fladbury, Pershore, Worcs WR10 2QW* Tel (01386) 860356

BOYCE, Robert Albert Wright. b 19. BA. St Alb Minl Tr Scheme. **d** 82 **p** 83. NSM Hatfield *St Alb* 82-89; Perm to Offic from 89; rtd 90. *92 Park Meadow, Hatfield, Herts AL9 5HE* Tel (01707) 267531

BOYD, Alan McLean. b 50. St Jo Coll Nottm BTh79. **d** 79 **p** 80. C Bishops Waltham *Portsm* 79-83; Chapl Reading Univ *Ox* 83-88; Chapl E Birm Hosp 88-94; Chapl Solihull Distr Hosp from 94. *Solihull Hospital, Lode Lane, Solihull, W Midlands B91 2JL* Tel 0121-711 4455

BOYD, Alexander Jamieson. b 46. MIBiol FSAScot St Chad's Coll Dur BSc68 Nottm Univ PGCE69. Coll of Resurr Mirfield 69. **d** 79 **p** 80. NSM Musselburgh *Edin* 79-83; CF from 83. *MOD Chaplains (Army), Trenchard Lines, Upavon, Pewsey, Wilts SN9 6BE* Tel (01980) 615804 Fax 615800

BOYD, Allan Gray. b 41. St Jo Coll Nottm 84. **d** 87 **p** 88. Hon Chapl Miss to Seamen from 87; NSM Glas St Gabr *Glas* 87-93; NSM Greenock 93-96; NSM Paisley St Barn from 96; NSM Paisley H Trin from 96. *47 Holms Crescent, Erskine, Renfrewshire PA8 6DJ* Tel 0141-812 2754

BOYD, Allan Newby. b 31. MInstM73 Ball Coll Ox MA. St Alb Minl Tr Scheme 81. **d** 84 **p** 85. NSM Watford St Luke *St Alb* 84-88; C Ardsley *Sheff* 88-91; V Barrow St Jo *Carl* 91-94; rtd 94. *Bishop Fold, Thoralby, Leyburn, N Yorkshire DL8 3SH* Tel Leyburn (0969) 663474

BOYD, David Anthony. b 42. Sarum & Wells Th Coll 72. **d** 75 **p** 76. C Ches H Trin *Ches* 75-79; R 85-93; V Congleton St Jas 79-85; V Farndon and Coddington from 93. *The Vicarage, Farndon, Chester CH3 6QD* Tel (01829) 270270

BOYD, David George. b 37. Cant Univ (NZ) BSc62 BTh64. St Aug Coll Cant. **d** 63 **p** 64. New Zealand 63-66; St Aug Coll Cant 66-67; Chapl RAF 67-71; New Zealand from 71; Adn Mid-Canterbury (NZ) 92-96. *14 Te Ara Crescent, RD1 Lyttelton, New Zealand* Tel Christchurch (3) 329 4270 or 379 3749 Fax 329 4270 E-mail dgb@terrier.chch.planet.org.nz

BOYD, Michael Victor. b 33. St Chad's Coll Dur BA57 DipAdEd69 MEd77 PhD81. Coll of Resurr Mirfield 57. **d** 59 **p** 60. C Warsop *S'well* 59-61; Chapl St Geo Coll Quilmes Argent 62-63; Chapl Wolsingham Sch 63-67; Lect St Hild Coll Dur 67-75; Lect SS Hild and Bede Dur 75-79; Lect Dur Univ 79-84. *4 Aykley Green, Whitesmocks, Durham DH1 4LN* Tel 0191-384 9473

BOYD, Robert Henry. b 36. **d** 66 **p** 67. C Drumcree *Arm* 66-69; I Annaghmore 69-83; Bp's C Lissan 83-90; I from 90. *The Rectory, 150 Moneymore Road, Cookstown, Co Tyrone BT80 8PY* Tel (01648) 766112

BOYD, Samuel Robert Thomas. b 62. **d** 90 **p** 91. NSM Derryloran *Arm* 90-95; C from 95. *51 Oldtown Street, Cookstown, Co Tyrone BT80 8EE* Tel (01648) 766046

BOYD, Canon William John Peter. b 28. Lon Univ BA48 BD53 PhD77 Birm Univ MA60. **d** 57 **p** 58. C Aston SS Pet and Paul *Birm* 57-60; V W Smethwick 60-63; V St Breward *Truro* 63-68; Adult Educn Chapl 64-85; Dioc Ecum Officer 65-83; R St Ewe 68-73; Preb St Endellion 73-85; V St Kew 73-77; R Falmouth K Chas 77-85; RD Carnmarth S 84-85; Dir of Tr 85-93; Prin SW Minl Tr Course 85-93; Can Res and Chan Truro Cathl *Truro* 85-93; rtd 93; Perm to Offic *Truro* from 93. *7 Chapel Crescent, Zelah, Truro, Cornwall TR4 9HN*

BOYD, William Thomas. b 15. TCD BA38 MA43. **d** 39 **p** 40. C Carrickfergus *Conn* 39-42; Chapl RAFVR 42-46; I Mullavilly *Arm* 46-51; Chapl RAF 51-70; Asst Chapl-in-Chief RAF 65-70; Hon Chapl to The Queen 68-70; R W Parley *Sarum* 70-76; rtd 76. *Turlough, 4 Heath Farm Close, Ferndown, Dorset BH22 8JP* Tel (01202) 892055

BOYD-WILLIAMS, Anthony Robert. b 46. Univ of Wales (Cardiff) DPS88. St Mich Coll Llan 86. **d** 88 **p** 89. C Tonyrefail w Gilfach Goch *Llan* 88-91; V Treharris w Bedlinog 91-96; V Ocker Hill *Lich* from 96. *St Mark's Vicarage, Ocker Hill Road, Tipton, W Midlands DY4 0XE* Tel 0121-556 0678

BOYDEN, Peter Frederick. b 41. Lon Univ BSc62 AKC62 Em Coll Cam BA64 MA68 MLitt69. Ridley Hall Cam 63. **d** 66 **p** 67. C Chesterton St Andr *Ely* 66-68; C Wimbledon *S'wark* 68-72; Chapl K Sch Cant 72-89; Chapl Radley Coll Oxon from 89. *Radley College, Abingdon, Oxon OX13 2HR* Tel (01235) 530750

BOYES, Canon David Arthur Stiles. b 30. Lon Coll of Div 62. **d** 63 **p** 64. C Islington St Mary *Lon* 63-71; V Canonbury St Steph 71-75; V St Paul's Cray St Barn *Roch* 75-85; P-in-c Earl Soham w Cretingham and Ashfield cum Thorpe *St E* 85-96; Dioc Development Officer 86-92; RD Loes 91-95; Hon Can St E Cathl 95-96; rtd 96. *13 Magdalen Drive, Woodbridge, Suffolk IP12 4EF* Tel (01394) 383389

BOYES, Michael Charles. b 27. Lon Univ BA53 BD58. Wells Th Coll 53. **d** 55 **p** 56. C Heavitree *Ex* 55-61; C Exwick 61-68; V Broadclyst 68-83; RD Aylesbeare 77-81; TV Sampford Peverell, Uplowman, Holcombe Rogus etc 83-85; TR Sampford Peverell, Uplowman, Holcombe Rogus etc 85-92; rtd 92; Perm to Offic *Ex* from 92. *Southdown, Burlescombe, Tiverton, Devon EX16 7LB* Tel (01884) 840492

BOYLAND, David Henry. b 58. TCD BA79 BAI79. **d** 91 **p** 92. C Seapatrick *D & D* 91-94; I Celbridge w Straffan and Newcastle-Lyons *D & G* from 94. *The Rectory, Maynooth Road, Celbridge, Co Kildare, Irish Republic* Tel Dublin (1) 628 8231

BOYLAND, Henry Hubert. b 23. DipMan. CITC. **d** 84 **p** 85. NSM Dunboyne w Kilcock, Maynooth, Moyglare etc *M & K* 84-87; Bp's C Carrickmacross w Magheracloone *Clogh* 87-90; I 90-93; rtd 93. *18 The Nurseries, Forest Road, Swords, Co Dublin, Irish Republic* Tel Dublin (1) 840 8810

BOYLE, Andrew McKenzie. b 45. Down Coll Cam BA67 MA71 CEng72 MICE72. WMMTC 82. **d** 85 **p** 86. NSM Woodthorpe *S'well* 85-87; Perm to Offic *Roch* 88-90; 91-96; Hon C Sevenoaks St Luke CD 90-91; NSM Sundridge w Ide Hill from 96. *31 Lambarde Drive, Sevenoaks, Kent TN13 3HX* Tel (01732) 456546

BOYLE, Canon Christopher John. b 51. AKC75. St Aug Coll Cant 75. **d** 76 **p** 77. C Wylde Green *Birm* 76-80; Bp's Dom Chapl 80-83; R Castle Bromwich SS Mary and Marg from 83; RD Coleshill from 92; P-in-c Shard End from 96; Hon Can Birm Cathl from 96. *The Rectory, Rectory Lane, Birmingham B36 9DH* Tel 0121-747 2281

BOYLE, Canon Richard Henry. b 08. TCD BA30 LLB37 MA47. **d** 45 **p** 46. C Killermogh *C & O* 45-47; P-in-c Kilmacshalgan *T, K & A* 47-50; I Skreen w Kilmacshalgan and Dromard 50-60; I Banagher *M & K* 60-82; Can Meath 69-82; rtd 82. *Shannon Cottage, West End, Banagher, Birr, Co Offaly, Irish Republic* Tel Banagher (509) 51134

BOYLES, Peter John. b 59. Univ of Wales (Lamp) BA84. Sarum & Wells Th Coll 86. **d** 88 **p** 89. C Ches St Mary *Ches* 88-91; C Neston 91-95; R Lavendon w Cold Brayfield, Clifton Reynes etc *Ox* from 95. *The New Rectory, 7A Northampton Road, Lavendon, Olney, Bucks MK46 4EY* Tel (01234) 712647

BOYLING, Canon Denis Hudson. b 16. Keble Coll Ox BA38 DipTh39 MA42. Cuddesdon Coll 39. **d** 40 **p** 41. C Sheff St Cuth *Sheff* 40-46; Chapl K Coll Hosp Lon 46-49; Chapl United Sheff Hosps 49-57; V Endcliffe *Sheff* 57-68; Hon Can Sheff Cathl 58-68; V Almondbury *Wakef* 68-75; RD Almondbury 68-75; Hon Can Wakef Cathl 72-75; Can Res Wakef Cathl 75-82; rtd 82; Perm to Offic *Heref* from 82. *7 St Mary's Close, Tenbury Wells, Worcs WR15 8ES* Tel (01584) 810360

BOYLING, Canon Mark Christopher. b 52. Keble Coll Ox BA74 BA76 MA78. Cuddesdon Coll 74. **d** 77 **p** 78. C Kirkby *Liv* 77-79; P-in-c 79-80; TV 80-85; Bp's Dom Chapl 85-89; V Formby St Pet 89-94; Can Res and Prec Liv Cathl from 94. *3 Cathedral Close, Liverpool L1 7BR* Tel 0151-708 0934

BOYNS, Martin Laurence Harley. b 26. St Jo Coll Cam BA49 MA51. Ridley Hall Cam 50. **d** 52 **p** 53. C Woodmansterne *S'wark* 52-55; C Folkestone H Trin w Ch Ch *Cant* 55-58; V Duffield *Derby* 58-71; V Rawdon *Bradf* 71-76; Chapl Woodlands Hosp

Rawdon 71-76; R Melton *St E* 76-85; R Gerrans w St Antony in Roseland *Truro* 85-92; Miss to Seamen 85-92; rtd 92; Perm to Offic *Truro* from 92. *Bojunda, Boscaswell Village, Pendeen, Penzance, Cornwall TR19 7EP* Tel (01736) 788390

BOYNS, Timothy Martin Harley. b 58. Warw Univ BA80 Nottm Univ BCombStuds84. Linc Th Coll 81. **d** 84 **p** 85. C Oxhey St Matt *St Alb* 84-87; TV Solihull *Birm* 87-94; V Lillington *Cov* from 94. *The Vicarage, Lillington, Leamington Spa, Warks CV32 7RH* Tel (01926) 424674

BOYS, Mrs Margaret Ann. b 34. Lon Univ TCert56 Liv Univ DipPE59. Oak Hill Th Coll 91. **d** 94 **p** 95. NSM Hadleigh St Barn *Chelmsf* from 94. *10 Seymour Road, Westcliff-on-Sea, Essex SS0 8NJ* Tel (01702) 75997

BOYSE, Felix Vivian Allan. b 17. LVO78. CCC Cam BA39 MA42. Cuddesdon Coll 39. **d** 40 **p** 41. C New Mills *Derby* 40-43; P-in-c 43-45; Lic to Offic *Ox* 46-51; V Kingswood *S'wark* 51-58; V St Mary Abchurch *Lon* 58-61; Prin St Geo Coll Jersey 61-64; Select Preacher Cam Univ 60 and 67; Chapl Chpl Royal Hampton Court Palace 65-82; Preacher Lincoln's Inn from 82; rtd 83; Perm to Offic *Chich* from 83. *Rose Cottage, Rookwood Road, West Wittering, Chichester, W Sussex PO20 8LT* Tel (01243) 514320

BOZON, David Hamish. b 28. Fitzw Ho Cam BA52 MA56. Linc Th Coll 53. **d** 55 **p** 56. C Baswich *Lich* 55-58; S Rhodesia 58-64; C Westbury-on-Trym H Trin *Bris* 64-65; Chapl to the Deaf 66-68; Info Officer RADD 68-84; Lic to Offic *Chelmsf* 74-84; R Sundridge w Ide Hill *Roch* 84-92; rtd 92. *22 Birch Close, Liss, Hants GU33 7HS* Tel (01730) 895525

BRACE, Dr Alistair Andrew. b 53. Newc Univ MB, BS76 DRCOG77. WMMTC 90. **d** 94 **p** 97. NSM Broseley w Benthall, Jackfield, Linley etc *Heref* from 94. *58 Spout Lane, Benthall, Shropshire TF12 1QY* Tel (01952) 884031

BRACE, Stuart. b 49. Bp Burgess Hall Lamp DipTh74. **d** 74 **p** 75. C Llanelli Ch Ch *St D* 74-76; C Tenby w Gumfreston 76-77; V Ystradmeurig and Strata Florida 77-79; CF 79-86; Chapl HM Youth Cust Cen Everthorpe 86-88; Chapl HM Pris Stafford 88-93; Chapl HM Pris Long Lartin 93-95. *HM Prison Long Lartin, South Littleton, Evesham, Worcs WR11 5TZ* Tel (01386) 830101 Fax 832834

BRACEGIRDLE, Christopher Andrew. b 56. Dur Univ BEd79 St Edm Ho Cam BA84 MA89. Ridley Hall Cam 82. **d** 85 **p** 86. C Livesey *Blackb* 85-88; TV E Farnworth and Kearsley *Man* 88-92; V Astley from 92. *St Stephen's Vicarage, 7 Holbeck, Astley, Tyldesley, Manchester M29 7DU* Tel (01942) 883313

BRACEGIRDLE, Mrs Cynthia Wendy Mary. b 52. LMH Ox BA73 MA77 Liv Univ DipAE82. N Ord Course. **d** 87 **p** 94. Chapl Asst Man R Infirmary 85-88; Dir Dioc LNSM Scheme *Man* from 89. *The Rectory, Parsonage Close, Salford M5 3GT* Tel 0161-872 0800 or 832 5785 Fax 832 1466

BRACEGIRDLE, Robert Kevin Stewart. b 47. Univ Coll Ox BA69 MA73. St Steph Ho Ox 70. **d** 73 **p** 74. C Dorchester *Sarum* 73-75; C Woodchurch *Ches* 75-78; V Bidston 78-82; P-in-c Salford St Ignatius *Man* 82-86; R Salford St Ignatius and Stowell Memorial from 86. *The Rectory, Parsonage Close, Salford M5 3GT* Tel 0161-872 0800

BRACEWELL, David John. b 44. Leeds Univ BA66 Man Univ MA82. Tyndale Hall Bris 67. **d** 69 **p** 70. C Tonbridge St Steph *Roch* 69-72; C Shipley St Pet *Bradf* 72-75; V Halliwell St Paul *Man* 75-84; R Guildf St Sav *Guildf* from 84. *St Saviour's Rectory, Wharf Road, Guildford, Surrey GU1 4RP* Tel (01483) 577811

BRACEWELL, Howard Waring. b 35. FRGS73. Tyndale Hall Bris. **d** 63 **p** 63. Canada 63-72; Travel Missr World Radio Miss Fellowship 72-77; P-in-c Ashill *Nor* 72-74; Hon C Bris St Phil and St Jacob w Em *Bris* 77-84; Perm to Offic *St Alb* 84-86; R Odell 86-88; V Pavenham 86-88; rtd 88; Lic to Offic *Man* from 88. *13 Ashbee Street, Asterley Bridge, Bolton, Manchester BL1 6NT* Tel (01204) 597576

BRACEY, David Harold. b 36. AKC63. **d** 64 **p** 65. C Westleigh St Pet *Man* 64-67; C Dunstable *St Alb* 67-70; V Benchill *Man* 70-76; V Elton St Steph 76-87; V Howe Bridge from 87. *The Vicarage, Leigh Road, Atherton, Manchester M29 0PH* Tel (01942) 883359

BRACHER, Paul Martin. b 59. Solicitor 84 Ex Univ LLB80. Trin Coll Bris BA90. **d** 90 **p** 91. C Sparkhill St Jo *Birm* 90; C Sparkhill w Greet and Sparkbrook 90-93; Chapl Birm Women's Health Care NHS Trust from 92; P-in-c Lea Hall *Birm* from 93. *St Richard's Vicarage, Hallmoor Road, Birmingham B33 9QY* Tel 0121-783 2319

BRACK, Edward James (Ted). b 37. Sarum Th Coll 67. **d** 69 **p** 70. C Gravesend St Aid *Roch* 69-73; C Woodside Park St Barn *Lon* 73-77; C Wood Green St Mich 77-80; V Whitton SS Phil and Jas 80-83; TV Bethnal Green St Jo w St Bart 83-86; TV St Jo on Bethnal Green 87-94; C W Hackney St Barn 94-96; rtd 96. *8 Surrey Gardens, Hermitage Road, London N4 1UD*

BRACKENBURY, The Ven Michael Palmer. b 30. Linc Th Coll 64. **d** 66 **p** 67. C S Ormsby w Ketsby, Calceby and Driby *Linc* 66-69; V Scothern w Sudbrooke 69-77; RD Lawres 73-78; Bp's Personal Asst 77-88; Dioc Dir of Ords 77-87; Can and Preb Linc Cathl 79-95; Dioc Lay Min Adv 86-87; Adn Linc 88-95; rtd 95. *18 Lea View, Ryhall, Stamford, Lincs PE9 4HZ* Tel (01780) 52415

✠**BRACKLEY, The Rt Revd Ian James.** b 47. Keble Coll Ox BA69 MA73. Cuddesdon Coll 69. **d** 71 **p** 72 **c** 96. C Bris Lockleaze St Mary Magd w St Fran *Bris* 71-74; Asst Chapl Bryanston Sch Dorset 74-77; Chapl 77-80; V E Preston w Kingston *Chich* 80-88; RD Arundel and Bognor 82-87; TR Haywards Heath St Wilfrid 88-96; RD Cuckfield 89-95; Suff Bp Dorking *Guildf* from 96. *13 Pilgrim's Way, Guildford, Surrey GU4 8AD* Tel (01483) 570829 Fax 67268

BRACKLEY, Mark Ozanne. b 53. Boro Road Teacher Tr Coll CertEd75. S'wark Ord Course 90. **d** 93 **p** 94. C Hampstead St Steph w All Hallows *Lon* 93-97; V W Green Ch Ch w St Pet from 97. *Christ Church Vicarage, Waldeck Road, London N15 3EP* Tel 0181-889 9677

BRADBERRY, John. b 20 Clifton Th Coll 46. **d** 47 **p** 48. C Hinckley H Trin *Leic* 47-50; C Earlham St Anne *Nor* 50-51; V Leyton Ch Ch *Chelmsf* 51-55; Argentina 55-61; V Siddal *Wakef* 61-72; R Bentham St Jo *Bradf* 72-85; rtd 85; Perm to Offic *Wakef* from 85; Perm to Offic *Bradf* from 86. *18 Moor Bottom Road, Halifax, W Yorkshire HX2 9SR* Tel (01422) 244944

BRADBERRY, John Stephen. b 47. Hull Univ BSc70 Leeds Univ CertEd71 MEd86. NW Ord Course 76. **d** 79 **p** 80. NSM Warley *Wakef* from 79. *129 Paddock Lane, Halifax, W Yorkshire HX2 0NT* Tel (01422) 358282

BRADBROOK, Mrs Averyl. b 46. Girton Coll Cam BA67 MA88 Man Univ PGCE69. N Ord Course 90. **d** 93 **p** 94. C Heaton Ch Ch *Man* 93-96; P-in-c Elton St Steph from 96. *St Stephen's Vicarage, 44 Peers Street, Bury, Lancs BL9 2QF* Tel 0161-764 1775

BRADBROOK, Peter David. b 33. Kelham Th Coll 54. **d** 60 **p** 61. C Ches St Oswald St Thos *Ches* 60-63; C Fulham St Etheldreda *Lon* 64-65; V Congleton St Jas *Ches* 65-79; V Wheelock 79-92; V Crewe All SS and St Paul from 92. *All Saints' Vicarage, 79 Stewart Street, Crewe CW2 8LX* Tel (01270) 60310

BRADBURY, George Graham. b 35. AKC58. **d** 59 **p** 60. C Portsea St Mary *Portsm* 59-62; C Melksham *Sarum* 62-64; R Winfrith Newburgh w Chaldon Herring 64-68; CF 68-71. *16 Bread Street, Warminster, Wilts BA12 8DF* Tel (01985) 213179

BRADBURY, Canon Herbert Cedric. b 30. FPS Man Univ PhC53. Linc Th Coll 64. **d** 66 **p** 67. C Blackpool St Steph *Blackb* 66-71; TV Hempnall *Nor* 71-75; TR 75-81; R Fritton w Morningthorpe w Shelton and Hardwick 74-77; RD Depwade 77-81; V Wroxham w Hoveton 81; P-in-c Belaugh 81; R Wroxham w Hoveton and Belaugh 81-92; RD Tunstead 83-91; Hon Can Nor Cathl 90-97; R Gt and Lt Massingham and Harpley 92-97; P-in-c South Raynham, E w W Raynham, Helhoughton, etc 94-97; rtd 97; Perm to Offic *Nor* from 97. *Morningthorpe, 66 Grove Lane, Holt, Norfolk NR25 6ED*

BRADBURY, Julian Nicholas Anstey. b 49. BNC Ox BA71 MA75 Birm Univ MA84. Cuddesdon Coll 71. **d** 73 **p** 74. C S'wark H Trin *S'wark* 73-76; USA 76-79; V Tottenham H Trin *Lon* 79-85; Dir Past Th Sarum & Wells Th Coll 85-90; P-in-c Yatton Keynell *Bris* 90-97; P-in-c Biddestone w Slaughterford 90-97; P-in-c Castle Combe 90-97; P-in-c W Kington 90-97; P-in-c Nettleton 90-97; R Horfield H Trin from 97. *The Rectory, Wellington Hill, Bristol BS7 8ST* Tel 0117-924 6185

BRADBURY, Kenneth James Frank. b 23. Qu Coll Birm 72. **d** 75 **p** 76. NSM Cen Telford *Lich* 75-77; C 77-80; V Chirbury *Heref* 80-88; V Marton 80-88; V Trelystan 80-88; rtd 88; Perm to Offic *Heref* from 90. *The Glebe, Rodington, Shrewsbury SY4 4QX* Tel (01952) 770312

BRADBURY, Norman Lunn. b 15. K Coll Lon BA36 AKC36. N Ord Course 76. **d** 77 **p** 78. NSM Paddock *Wakef* 77-81; NSM Rashcliffe and Lockwood 81-84; Perm to Offic from 84. *23 Springwood Hall Gardens, Huddersfield HD1 4HA* Tel (01484) 427548

BRADBURY, Robert Douglas. b 50. Ripon Coll Cuddesdon 75. **d** 76 **p** 77. C Harlescott *Lich* 76-81; V Ruyton 81-88; P-in-c Gt w Lt Ness 84-88; V Ruyton XI Towns w Gt and Lt Ness from 88. *The Vicarage, The Village, Ruyton Eleven Towns, Shrewsbury SY4 1LQ* Tel (01939) 260254

BRADBURY, Roy Albert. b 30. Chich Th Coll 72. **d** 74 **p** 75. C Earlsdon *Cov* 74-76; C Coventry Caludon 76-78; P-in-c Calow *Derby* 78-82; V Pensnett *Lich* 82-90; V Pattingham w Patshull 90-94; V Ocker Hill 94-95; rtd 95; Perm to Offic *Derby* from 95. *2 Stretton Close, Mickleover, Derby DE3 5NW* Tel (01332) 513380

BRADDICK-SOUTHGATE, Charles Anthony Michael. b 70. Univ Coll Lon BD92. Chich Th Coll MTh95. **d** 94 **p** 95. C Catford St Laur *S'wark* from 94. *33 Bromley Road, London SE6 2TS* Tel 0181-461 5542

BRADDOCK, Arthur Derek. b 25. Bolton Inst of Educn BA90. Lich Th Coll 56. **d** 59 **p** 60. C Droylsden St Mary *Man* 59-61; C New Bury 61-65; V Kearsley Moor 65-79; C Ellesmere Port *Ches* 79-85; rtd 85; Perm to Offic *Man* from 85. *1 Corrie Drive, Kearsley, Bolton BL4 8RG* Tel 0161-794 8953

BRADFORD, John. b 34. FRSA FRGS Lon Univ BA60 Birm Univ MEd81 Ox Univ ACertEd70. Oak Hill Th Coll 55. **d** 60 **p** 61. C Walcot *B & W* 60-64; Ass Master Wendover C of E Primary Sch 64-65; Hd RE Dr Challoner's High Sch Lt Chalfont 65-69; Perm to Offic *Ox* 66-70; Lect St Pet Coll of Educn Saltley 70-77; Perm to Offic *Birm* 70-71; Lic to Offic from 71; Perm to

Offic *Cov* from 77; Nat Chapl-Missr CECS from 77; Gen Perm to Offic Ch in Wales from 89. *27 Marsh Lane, Solihull, W Midlands B91 2PG* Tel 0121-704 9895 or 0171-837 4299

BRADFORD, Peter. b 38. Sarum Th Coll 69. **d** 70 **p** 71. C Holdenhurst *Win* 70-73; C Stanmore 73-77; P-in-c Eling, Testwood and Marchwood 77-78; R Marchwood 78-86; C Christchurch 86-90; C Andover w Foxcott 90-92; V E and W Worldham, Hartley Mauditt w Kingsley etc from 92. *The Vicarage, East Worldham, Alton, Hants GU34 3AS* Tel (01420) 82392

BRADFORD, Archdeacon of. *See* SHREEVE, The Ven David Herbert

BRADFORD, Bishop of. *See* SMITH, The Rt Revd David James

BRADFORD, Provost of. *See* RICHARDSON, The Very Revd John Stephen

BRADLEY, Andrew Robert. b 65. Clare Coll Cam BA88. St Jo Coll Nottm DTS93 MA94. **d** 94 **p** 95. C Burnage St Marg *Man* from 94. *29 Bournlea Avenue, Manchester M19 1AE* Tel 0161-431 7272

BRADLEY, Anthony David. b 56. Wye Coll Lon BSc76. St Jo Coll Nottm DPS88. **d** 88 **p** 89. C Southchurch Ch Ch *Chelmsf* 88-91; C Cov H Trin *Cov* from 91; Dioc Lay Tr Adv from 93. *466 Tile Hill Lane, Coventry CV4 9DY* Tel (01203) 471047

BRADLEY, Brian Hugh Granville. b 32. Lon Coll of Div 59. **d** 62 **p** 63. C E Twickenham St Steph *Lon* 62-65; C Herne Bay Ch Ch *Cant* 65-69; Miss to Seamen Teesside 69-71; Ceylon 71-72; Sri Lanka 72-74; Chapl Amsterdam w Haarlem and Den Helder *Eur* 75-79; Chapl Lyon w Grenoble and Aix-les-Bains 79-85; TV Bucknall and Bagnall *Lich* 87-93; Assoc Chapl Dubai and Sharjah w N Emirates 93-97; rtd 97. *7 Clos d'Eglise, rue de la Cache, St Andrew's, Guernsey GY6 8TQ* Tel (01481) 56348

BRADLEY, Canon Cecil Robert Jones. b 23. TCD BA47 MA50. CITC 48. **d** 48 **p** 49. C Clooney *D & R* 48-50; C Derry Cathl 50-67; Dean's V St Patr Cathl Dublin 67-96; Preb Maynooth St Patr Cathl Dublin 81-96; rtd 96. *The Vicarage, St Patrick's Close, Dublin 8, Irish Republic* Tel Dublin (1) 475 4817 Fax 454 6374

BRADLEY, Clifford David. b 36. Lon Univ BA60. St Aid Birkenhead 60. **d** 62 **p** 63. C Stoneycroft All SS *Liv* 62-65; C Chipping Sodbury and Old Sodbury *Glouc* 65-68; Br Honduras 68-70; C Leckhampton SS Phil and Jas *Glouc* 70-71; V Badgeworth w Shurdington 71-79; Dioc Missr *S & M* 79-84; V Santan 79-84; V Braddan 79-84; Bp's Dom Chapl 81-84; V Stroud and Uplands w Slad *Glouc* 84-89; C Shepshed *Leic* 90-92; R Leire w Ashby Parva and Dunton Bassett from 92. *The Rectory, Dunton Road, Leire, Lutterworth, Leics LE17 5HD* Tel (01455) 209421

BRADLEY, Canon Colin John. b 46. Edin Univ MA69 Hertf Coll Ox 71. Sarum & Wells Th Coll 72. **d** 75 **p** 76. C Easthampstead *Ox* 75-79; V Shawbury *Lich* 79-90; R Moreton Corbet 80-90; P-in-c Stanton on Hine Heath 81-90; Can Res Portsm Cathl *Portsm* from 90; Dir of Ords from 90. *61 St Thomas Street, Portsmouth PO1 2EZ* Tel (01705) 824621 Fax 821356

BRADLEY, Connla John Osman. b 08. Bible Churchmen's Coll. **d** 47 **p** 47. C Tunbridge Wells H Trin *Roch* 47-49; V Camberwell Ch Ch *S'wark* 49-55; V Frogmore *St Alb* 55-68; V Havering-atte-Bower *Chelmsf* 68-76; rtd 76; Perm to Offic *Chich* 76-88. *57 Davis Court, Marlborough Road, St Albans, Herts AL1 3XU* Tel (01727) 846795

BRADLEY, Canon Donald John Walter. b 19. Em Coll Cam BA40 MA44. Westcott Ho Cam 40. **d** 42 **p** 43. C Purley St Mark Woodcote *S'wark* 42-44; Succ S'wark Cathl 44-48; V Battersea St Luke 53-63; Lic to Offic *Birm* 63-70; Hon Can Birm Cathl 70-84; V Edgbaston St Geo 71-84; RD Edgbaston 77-84; rtd 84. *32 St Mark's Road, Salisbury SP1 3AZ* Tel (01722) 334653

BRADLEY (née DRAPER), Mrs Elizabeth Ann. b 38. Nottm Univ BTh75 Birm Univ DipTh77. Linc Th Coll 71. **dss** 84 **d** 87 **p** 94. Ind Chapl *Linc* 84-91; Bracebridge 84-91; Hon C 87-91; GFS Ind Chapl *Lon* 91-96; Hon Chapl GFS from 96; Riverside Chapl *S'wark* 96. *The Vicarage, 26 Dew Pond Road, Flitwick, Bedford MK45 1RT* Tel (01525) 712369

BRADLEY, Gary Scott. b 53. Lon Univ LLB75. Ripon Coll Cuddesdon 75. **d** 78 **p** 79. C St Jo Wood *Lon* 78-83; V Paddington St Sav from 83; P-in-c Paddington St Mary from 95. *6 Park Place Villas, London W2 1SP* Tel 0171-262 3787

BRADLEY, Miss Hazel. b 61. N Lon Poly BA85 Loughb Univ MSc87. Ripon Coll Cuddesdon 89. **d** 92 **p** 94. Par Dn Thurnby Lodge *Leic* 92-94; C 94-95; C Aylestone St Andr w St Jas from 95. *St James's Vicarage, 38 Park Hill Drive, Leicester LE2 8HR* Tel 0116-283 2458

BRADLEY, John Owen. b 30. Jes Coll Ox BA55 MA56. St Mich Coll Llan 52. **d** 56 **p** 57. C Cardiff St Mary *Llan* 56-59; Lect St Mich Coll Llan 59-61; C Caerau w Ely *Llan* 60; C Newton Nottage 61-64; V Aberavon H Trin 65-69; Lic to Offic *Cov* 70-76; C W Kirby St Bridget *Ches* 76-79; TV Knowle *Bris* 79-80; TR 80-91; RD Brislington 83-89; Chapl St Monica Home Westbury-on-Trym from 91. *St Augustine, Cote Lane, Westbury-on-Trym, Bristol BS9 3UL* Tel 0117-949 4019 or 949 4020 Fax 949 4044

BRADLEY, Ms Joy Elizabeth. b 63. Sheff Univ BA85 Fitzw Coll Cam BA91. Ridley Hall Cam CTM92. **d** 92 **p** 94. Par Dn Wadsley *Sheff* 92-94; C 94-96; C Mosborough from 96. *29 Mosborough Hall Drive, Halfway, Sheffield S19 5UA* Tel 0114-248 7729

BRADLEY, Kenneth Sutton. b 08. ALCD39. **d** 38 **p** 39. C Parkstone St Luke *Sarum* 38-41; C Portland All SS w St Pet 41-43; Chapl RAFVR 43-47; R Ellisfield and Farleigh Wallop *Win* 47-53; R Preston Candover w Nutley and Bradley 47-53; R Dogmersfield w Winchfield 53-72; Chapl Winchfield Hosp 53-73; rtd 73. *12 Mildway Court, Odiham, Hook, Hants RG29 1AX* Tel (01256) 704897

BRADLEY, Michael Frederick John. b 44. Qu Coll Birm 76. **d** 77 **p** 78. C Sheff St Cuth *Sheff* 77-78; C Alford w Rigsby *Linc* 78-83; V Bracebridge 83-90; V Flitwick *St Alb* from 90. *The Vicarage, 26 Dew Pond Road, Flitwick, Bedford MK45 1RT* Tel (01525) 712369

BRADLEY, Peter David Douglas. b 49. Nottm Univ BTh79. Linc Th Coll 75. **d** 79 **p** 80. C Upholland *Liv* 79-83; TR from 94; V Dovecot 83-94; Dir Continuing Minl Educn from 89. *The Rectory, 1A College Road, Upholland, Skelmersdale, Lancs WN8 0PY* Tel (01695) 622936

BRADLEY, Peter Edward. b 64. Trin Hall Cam BA86 Trin Coll Cam MA90. Ripon Coll Cuddesdon 86. **d** 88 **p** 89. C Northampton St Mich w St Edm *Pet* 88-91; Chapl G&C Coll Cam 91-95; TV Abingdon *Ox* from 95. *The Vicarage, Farringdon Road, Abingdon, Oxon OX14 1BG* Tel (01235) 520297

BRADLEY, Ronald Percival. b 25. ACP51 FRSA52 TCert49. Ex & Truro NSM Scheme 80. **d** 83 **p** 84. C Honiton, Gittisham, Combe Raleigh, Monkton etc *Ex* 83-86; P-in-c Halberton 86-87; rtd 90. *Haddon House, 20 Moorland Road, Plympton, Plymouth PL7 2BH* Tel (01752) 337667

BRADNUM, Canon Ella Margaret. b 41. CertEd64 St Hugh's Coll Ox MA65. **dss** 69 **d** 87 **p** 94. Illingworth *Wakef* 69-72; Batley All SS 72-73; Lay Tr Officer 77-82; Min Tr Officer 82-88; Warden of Readers from 88; Sec Dioc Bd of Min from 88; Co-ord Lay Tr from 88; Hon Can Wakef Cathl from 94; Prin Wakef Min Scheme from 97. *13 Boothtown Road, Halifax, W Yorkshire HX3 6EU* Tel (01422) 321740

BRADNUM, Richard James (Dick). b 39. Pemb Coll Ox BA62 MA67. Ridley Hall Cam 62. **d** 64 **p** 65. C Birm St Martin *Birm* 64-68; C Sutton St Jas *York* 68-69; Perm to Offic *Wakef* 71-72; C Batley All SS 72-74; V Gawthorpe and Chickenley Heath 74-86; V Mixenden 86-97; rtd 97. *13 Boothtown Road, Halifax, W Yorkshire HX3 6EU*

BRADSHAW, Charles Anthony. b 44. Birm Univ MA76. Qu Coll Birm DipTh74. **d** 75 **p** 76. C Whickham *Dur* 75-78; C Bilton *Cov* 78-81; TV Coventry Caludon 81-89; V Birstall and Wanlip *Leic* from 89. *The Rectory, 251 Birstall Road, Birstall, Leicester LE4 4DJ* Tel 0116-267 4517

BRADSHAW, Denis Matthew. b 52. Chich Th Coll 77. **d** 80 **p** 81. C Ruislip St Martin *Lon* 80-84; C Northolt Park St Barn 84-86; V Northolt W End St Jos from 86; C-in-c Hayes St Nic CD from 94. *St Joseph's Vicarage, 430 Yeading Lane, Northolt, Middx UB5 6JS* Tel 0181-845 6161

BRADSHAW, George Henry. b 28. Wycliffe Hall Ox. **d** 62 **p** 63. C Thame *Ox* 62-65; Chapl RAF 65-84; R Wittering w Thornhaugh and Wansford *Pet* 65-84; Ascension Is 84-85; V The Suttons w Tydd *Linc* 85-87; rtd 87; Perm to Offic *Linc* from 87. *42 Welland Mews, Stamford, Lincs PE9 2LW* Tel (01780) 56070

BRADSHAW, Graham. b 58. Edin Univ BD86. Edin Th Coll 83. **d** 86 **p** 87. C Thornton-le-Fylde *Blackb* 86-89; C Kirkby Lonsdale *Carl* 89-91; V Langford *St Alb* 91-97; Papua New Guinea from 97. *c/o Mrs D Bradshaw, 70 Preston Street, Fleetwood, Lancs FY7 6LA*

BRADSHAW, Miss Jennie McNeille. b 47. UEA BA69. Cranmer Hall Dur 85. **d** 90 **p** 94. Par Dn Herne *Cant* 90-94; C 94-95; P-in-c Claybrooke cum Wibtoft and Frolesworth *Leic* 95-96; R from 96. *The Rectory, Lutterworth Road, Bitteswell, Lutterworth, Leics LE17 4RX* Tel (01455) 556367

BRADSHAW (née DAY), Mrs Jennifer Ann. b 67. Aber Univ BSc89. Wycliffe Hall Ox BTh95. **d** 95 **p** 96. C Whitburn *Dur* from 95. *Stier House, St Gabriel's Avenue, Sunderland SR4 7TF* Tel 0191-564 0563

BRADSHAW, Jolyon Anthony. b 51. St Jo Coll Dur BA73. Trin Coll Bris 73. **d** 76 **p** 77. C Normanton *Wakef* 76-82; TV Wreningham *Nor* 82-89; P-in-c Bermondsey St Mary w St Olave, St Jo etc *S'wark* 89-96; R from 96. *The Rectory, 193 Bermondsey Street, London SE1 3UW* Tel 0171-407 5273

BRADSHAW, Kenneth Allan. b 23. Roch Th Coll 60. **d** 62 **p** 63. C Cheam Common St Phil *S'wark* 62-65; C Portslade St Nic *Chich* 65-67; C Preston 67-71; C Haywards Heath St Wilfrid 71-82; C Sidley 82-88; rtd 88; Lic to Offic *Llan* from 88. *The Cottage, 115A Splott Road, Cardiff CF2 2BY* Tel (01222) 465998

BRADSHAW, Malcolm McNeille. b 45. Lon Univ DipTh69. Kelham Th Coll 65. **d** 70 **p** 71. C New Addington *Cant* 70-76; Chapl Milan w Cadenabbia, Varese and Lugano *Eur* 77-82; V Boxley w Detling *Cant* from 82. *The Vicarage, Boxley, Maidstone, Kent ME14 3DX* Tel (01622) 758606

BRADSHAW, Canon Prof Paul Frederick. b 45. Clare Coll Cam BA66 MA70 K Coll Lon PhD71 FRHistS91 Ox Univ DD94. Westcott Ho Cam 67. **d** 69 **p** 70. C W Wickham St Jo *Cant* 69-71; C Cant St Martin and St Paul 71-73; Tutor Chich Th Coll 73-78; V Flamstead *St Alb* 78-82; Dir of Minl Tr Scheme 78-82; Vice-

Prin Ripon Coll Cuddesdon 83-85; USA 85-95; Prof Th Notre Dame Univ from 85; Hon Can N Indiana from 90; PV Westmr Abbey from 95. *Notre Dame London Centre, 7 Albemarle Street, London W1X 4NB* Tel 0171-493 2951 Fax 493 3978

BRADSHAW, Philip Hugh. b 39. Qu Coll Ox BA64 MA67 Lon Univ DipRS91. S'wark Ord Course 88. **d** 91 **p** 92. NSM Bletchingley *S'wark* from 91; Ldr Community of Celebration from 91. *Community of Celebration, Berry House, 58 High Street, Bletchingley, Redhill RH1 4PA* Tel (01883) 743911

BRADSHAW, Richard Gordon Edward (Dick). b 66. Southn Univ LLB90. Wycliffe Hall Ox BTh94. **d** 97. C Bishopwearmouth St Gabr *Dur* from 97. *Stier House, St Gabriel's Avenue, Sunderland SR4 7TF* Tel 0191-529 3572

BRADSHAW, Roy John. b 49. Sarum & Wells Th Coll 85. **d** 87 **p** 88. FSJ from 84; C Gainsborough All SS *Linc* 87-90; V New Waltham 90-94; R Killamarsh *Derby* from 94. *The Rectory, Sheepcote Road, Killamarsh, Sheffield S31 8BN* Tel 0114-248 2769

BRADSHAW, Dr Timothy (Tim). b 50. PhD Keble Coll Ox BA72 MA78. St Jo Coll Nottm BA75. **d** 76 **p** 77. C Clapton Park All So *Lon* 76-79; Lect Trin Coll Bris 80-91; Hon C Sea Mills *Bris* 83-91; Tutor Regent's Park Coll Ox from 91; NSM Ox St Aldate w St Matt *Ox* 91-94; NSM Ox St Aldate from 95. *54 St Giles, Oxford OX1 3LU* Tel (01865) 288147

BRADSHAW (née STUART-BLACK), Mrs Veronica. b 52. St Jo Coll Dur BA75. Cranmer Hall Dur. **dss** 82 **d** 87. Borehamwood *St Alb* 82-84; Watford Ch Ch 84-85; Stevenage St Mary Shephall 85-87; Par Dn Stevenage St Mary Sheppall w Aston 87-88. *31 Harefield, Shephall, Stevenage, Herts SG2 9NG* Tel (01438) 365714

BRADWELL, Area Bishop of. *See* GREEN, The Rt Revd Laurence Alexander

BRADY, Canon Ernest William. b 17. Dur Univ LTh42. Edin Th Coll 39. **d** 42 **p** 43. C Glas Ch Ch *Glas* 42-46; C Hendon St Alphage *Lon* 46-48; R Buckie *Ab* 49-57; R Edin All SS *Edin* 57-71; R Edin St Mich and All SS 65-71; Can St Mary's Cathl 67-83; Syn Clerk 69-76; Dioc Supernumerary 71-74 and 82-90; P-in-c S Queensferry 74-82; Dean Edin 76-82 and 85-86; rtd 82; Hon Can St Mary's Cathl *Edin* 83-85 and from 86. *44 Glendevon Place, Edinburgh EH12 5UJ* Tel 0131-337 9528

BRADY, Mrs Madalaine Margaret. b 45. Univ of Wales (Ban) BD88 CertEd91 MA92. **d** 89 **p** 97. Asst Chapl Univ of Wales (Ban) *Ban* from 89; Dioc Comm Officer from 94; C Arllechwedd 96-97; P-in-c Llanfaelog from 97. *The Rectory, Station Road, Rhosneigr LL64 5JX* Tel (01407) 810412

BRAGGER, Martin James. b 47. CEng72 MICE72 Sheff Univ BEng68. Ridley Coll Melbourne ThL90. **d** 90 **p** 90. Australia from 90. *6 Burke Road, Ferntree Gully, Victoria, Australia 3156* Tel Melbourne (3) 9758 1068

BRAILSFORD, Matthew Charles. b 64. Newc Univ BSc86. Cranmer Hall Dur BA95. **d** 95 **p** 96. C Hull Newland St Jo *York* from 95. *St Faith's House, Dunswell Lane, Dunswell, Hull HU6 0AG* Tel (01482) 854526

BRAIN, George. b 19. St Chad's Coll Dur BA41 DipTh43 MA44. **d** 43 **p** 44. C Haydock St Jas *Liv* 43-44; C Wigan St Anne 44-47; C Leic St Pet *Leic* 47-50; C Whitwick St Jo the Bapt 50-54; V Leic St Leon 54-81; Perm to Offic from 81; rtd 84. *1 Steyning Crescent, Glenfield, Leicester LE3 8PL* Tel 0116-287 8451

BRAIN, Michael Charles. b 39. ACP65 Culham Coll Ox 59 Ox Univ Inst of Educn TCert61. Lich Th Coll 68. **d** 70 **p** 71. C Stone St Mich *Lich* 70-73; C Harlescott 73-76; C Longton St Jas 76-77; P-in-c Dudley St Edm *Worc* 77-79; V from 79; Chapl Dudley Coll of Tech from 77. *St Edmund's Vicarage, 9 Ednam Road, Dudley, W Midlands DY1 1JX* Tel (01384) 252532

BRAIN, Vernon Roy. b 15. St D Coll Lamp BA38 Ripon Hall Ox 41. **d** 42 **p** 43. C Bistre *St As* 42-45; C Almondbury *Wakef* 45-50; V Gomersal 50-53; Area Sec (Dios Dur and Newc) CMS 53-61; V Seaham w Seaham Harbour *Dur* 61-80; rtd 80. *61 Vicarage Close, Silksworth, Sunderland SR3 1JF* Tel 0191-521 0847

BRAITHWAITE, Albert Alfred. b 24. Clifton Th Coll. **d** 59 **p** 60. C Bestwood St Matt *S'well* 59-62; Chapl RN 62-81; QHC from 77; C Southsea St Jude *Portsm* 82-90; Lic to Offic from 90; rtd 90. *3 Lorne Road, Southsea, Hants PO5 1RR* Tel (01705) 738753

BRAITHWAITE, Canon Michael Royce. b 34. Linc Th Coll 71. **d** 73 **p** 74. C Barrow St Geo w St Luke *Carl* 73-77; V Kells 77-88; RD Calder 84-88; V Lorton and Loweswater w Buttermere from 88; Ldr Rural Life and Agric Team 93-96; Member Rural Life and Agric Team from 96; RD Derwent from 94; Hon Can Carl Cathl from 94. *The Vicarage, Loweswater, Cockermouth, Cumbria CA13 0RU* Tel (01900) 85237

BRAITHWAITE, Canon Roy. b 34. Dur Univ BA56. Ridley Hall Cam 58. **d** 60 **p** 61. C Blackb St Gabr *Blackb* 60-63; C Burnley St Pet 63-66; V Accrington St Andr 66-74; V Blackb St Jas 74-95; RD Blackb 86-91; Hon Can Blackb Cathl from 93; V Garstang St Helen Churchtown from 95; Dioc Ecum Officer from 95. *St Helen's Vicarage, 6 Vicarage Lane, Churchtown, Preston PR3 0HW* Tel (01995) 602294

BRAITHWAITE, Wilfrid. b 14. St Chad's Coll Dur BA41 MA44. **d** 42 **p** 43. C Harrington *Carl* 42-45; C Kendal H Trin 45-46; R Soulby w Crosby Garrett 46-51; V Ireleth w Askam 51-62; V Lanercost w Kirkcambeck 62-79; P-in-c Walton 78-79; rtd 79; Perm to Offic *Carl* from 82. *Brougham Lodge, Eamont Bridge, Penrith, Cumbria CA10 2BZ* Tel (01768) 862939

BRALESFORD, Nicholas Robert. b 53. St Jo Coll Nottm LTh79 BTh79. **d** 79 **p** 80. C Leic St Chris *Leic* 79-82; C Heeley *Sheff* 82-85; TV Kings Norton *Birm* 85-90; V Chapel-en-le-Frith *Derby* from 90. *The Vicarage, 71 Manchester Road, Chapel-en-le-Frith, Stockport, Cheshire SK23 9TH* Tel (01298) 812134

BRALEY, Robert James. b 57. Ch Ch Ox BA82 Down Coll Cam BA83 MA87. Ridley Hall Cam 81. **d** 84 **p** 85. C Thames Ditton *Guildf* 84-87; C Gravesend St Geo *Roch* 87-91; Perm to Offic *Blackb* 92-95; Perm to Offic *S'wark* from 95. *1 Glebe House, Waynflete Street, London SW18 3QG* Tel 0181-946 0616

BRAMELD, Peter John. b 40. AKC62. **d** 63 **p** 64. C Hucknall Torkard *S'well* 63-66; C Ordsall 66-70; C Carlton 70-74; C Colwick 70-74; P-in-c Overton w Fyfield and E Kennett *Sarum* 74-75; TV Upper Kennet 75-80; R Hickling w Kinoulton and Broughton Sulney *S'well* 80-94; RD Bingham S 86-91. *108 Westgate, Southwell, Notts NG25 0LT* Tel (01636) 816226

BRAMHALL, Eric. b 39. St Cath Coll Cam BA61 MA65. Tyndale Hall Bris 61. **d** 63 **p** 64. C Eccleston St Luke *Liv* 63-66; C Bolton Em *Man* 66-69; Perm to Offic *Ches* 70-74; Chapl Ormskirk Hosp Liv from 75; V Aughton Ch Ch *Liv* 75-92; V Childwall All SS from 92. *All Saints' Vicarage, Childwall Abbey Road, Liverpool L16 0JW* Tel 0151-737 2169

BRAMLEY, Thomas Anthony. **d** 96 **p** 97. NSM Penicuik *Edin* from 96; NSM W Linton from 96. *44 Bavelaw Crescent, Penicuik, Midlothian EH26 9AT* Tel (01968) 675240

BRAMMER, Charles Harold. b 08. Ripon Hall Ox 54. **d** 54 **p** 55. C Wythenshawe St Martin CD *Man* 54-56; V Smallbridge 56-63; V Hindley Green *Liv* 63-65; V St Cleer *Truro* 65-75; rtd 75; Perm to Offic *Liv* 75-85; Perm to Offic *Man* 85-90. *20 The Windrush, Rochdale, Lancs OL12 6DY* Tel (01706) 342818

BRAMPTON, Ms Fiona Elizabeth Gordon. b 56. St Jo Coll Dur BA78. Cranmer Hall Dur BA83. **dss** 84 **d** 87 **p** 94. Bris St Andr Hartcliffe *Bris* 84-87; Par Dn 87-90; C Orton Waterville *Ely* 90-96; C-in-c Orton Goldhay CD 90-96; TV The Ortons, Alwalton and Chesterton from 96. *5 Riseholme, Orton Goldhay, Peterborough PE2 5SP* Tel (01733) 238691

BRANCHE, Brian Maurice. b 37. Chich Th Coll 73. **d** 75 **p** 76. C Brighton Resurr *Chich* 75-78; C Upper Norwood St Jo *Cant* 78-81; P-in-c Croydon St Martin 81-84; V Croydon St Martin *S'wark* 85-88; V St Helier 88-93; V New Eltham All SS from 93. *All Saints' Vicarage, 22 Bercta Road, London SE9 3TZ* Tel 0181-850 9894

BRAND, Frank Ronald Walter. b 25. Lon Coll of Div ALCD56 LTh74. **d** 56 **p** 57. C Brondesbury St Anne w Kilburn H Trin *Lon* 56-58; Br Guiana 58-66; Guyana 66-67; V N Greenford All Hallows *Lon* 67-91; rtd 91; Perm to Offic *B & W* from 91. *23 Hawthorn Grove, Combe Down, Bath BA2 5QA* Tel (01225) 834572

BRAND, Peter John. b 32. Lon Univ BSc54. Edin Dioc NSM Course 75. **d** 83 **p** 84. NSM Edin St Jo *Edin* from 83. *24 Drum Brae Park, Edinburgh EH12 8TF* Tel 0131-339 4406

BRAND, Richard Harold Guthrie. b 65. Dur Univ BA87. Ripon Coll Cuddesdon 87. **d** 89 **p** 90. C N Lynn w St Marg and St Nic *Nor* 89-92; C King's Lynn St Marg w St Nic 92-93; C Croydon St Jo *S'wark* 93-96; New Zealand from 96. *118A Kauri Street, Riccarton, Christchurch 4, New Zealand* Tel Christchurch (3) 348 8611 or 351 7064 Fax 348 8611

BRAND, Stuart William. b 30. Leeds Univ BSc53. Coll of Resurr Mirfield 53. **d** 55 **p** 56. C Stepney St Dunstan and All SS *Lon* 55-59; C Acton Green St Pet 59-60; C-in-c Godshill CD *Portsm* 60-63; Malawi 63-67; V Widley w Wymering *Portsm* 67-72; Chapl Fieldhead Hosp Wakef 72-80; Chapl Pinderfields & Stanley Royd Hosps Wakef 72-80; Chapl Brook Gen Hosp Lon 80-95; Chapl Greenwich Distr Hosp Lon 80-95; rtd 95; Perm to Offic *S'wark* from 95. *53 Bullingdon Road, Oxford OX4 1QJ* Tel (01865) 249524

BRANDES, Simon Frank. b 62. Univ of Wales (Ban) BA83. Edin Th Coll 83. **d** 85 **p** 86. C Barton w Peel Green *Man* 85-88; Asst Dioc Youth Officer from 88; C Longsight St Jo w St Cypr 88-90; R 90-94; V Lt Lever from 94. *The Vicarage, Market Street, Little Lever, Bolton BL3 1HH* Tel (01204) 700936

BRANDIE, Canon Beaumont Lauder (Beau). b 40. K Coll Lon AKC64 BD66. **d** 65 **p** 66. C Whitton St Aug *Lon* 65-71; C Portsea St Mary *Portsm* 71-77; TR Brighton Resurr *Chich* from 77; Can and Preb Chich Cathl from 87; RD Brighton from 97. *St Martin's Rectory, Upper Wellington Road, Brighton BN2 3AN* Tel (01273) 604687

BRANDON, Miss Vera Eileen. b 12. Univ of Wales (Abth) CertEd35 BSc40 Lon Univ DipEd42 BD53. St Mich Ho Ox 51. **dss** 60 **d** 87. Lect and Tutor St Mich Ho Ox 51-61; Rushden St Pet 61-63; Tutor CA Wilson Carlile Coll of Evang 64-74; Community of the Word of God from 75; Lower Homerton St Paul *Lon* 75-80; Clapton Park All So 75-80; Hanger Lane St Ann 80-83; rtd 83; Tunbridge Wells St Pet *Roch* 83-87; Hon Par Dn 87-89; Perm to Offic from 89. *Florence Balls House, Trinity Close, Tunbridge Wells, Kent TN2 3PP* Tel (01892) 522430

BRANNAGAN, Alan McKenzie. b 34. Chich Th Coll 66. **d** 68 **p** 69. C N Hull St Mich *York* 68-70; C Dunstable *St Alb* 70-75; R E w

W Rudham *Nor* 75-81; V Houghton 75-81; TV Wolverhampton *Lich* 81-87; R W Felton 87-96; Chapl Ypres *Eur* 96-97. *8 Park Lane, Blunham, Bedford MK44 3NH*

BRANSCOMBE, Michael Peter. b 65. Cranmer Hall Dur BA95. **d** 95 **p** 96. C Ogley Hay *Lich* from 95. *50 Lichfield Road, Brownhills, Walsall WS8 6HT* Tel (01543) 378542 E-mail rev.mike@dial.pipex.com

BRANSON, Robert David. b 46. Linc Th Coll 74. **d** 77 **p** 78. C Kempston Transfiguration *St Alb* 77-80; C Goldington 80-82; V Marsh Farm 82-91; V Aylsham *Nor* from 91. *The Vicarage, 64 Holman Road, Aylsham, Norwich NR11 6BZ* Tel (01263) 733871

BRANT, Anthony Richard. b 44. S Dios Minl Tr Scheme. **d** 82 **p** 83. NSM Felpham w Middleton *Chich* 82-84; C Clymping 84-85; NSM 85-87; Perm to Offic from 88. *6 Elm Cottages, Nyton Road, Aldingbourne, Chichester, W Sussex PO20 6UL* Tel (01243) 544735

BRANT, Anthony William. b 31. TD67. Linc Th Coll 73. **d** 75 **p** 76. C Cove St Jo *Guildf* 75-79; P-in-c Puttenham and Wanborough 79-83; V Lightwater 83-93; rtd 93; Perm to Offic *Chich* from 93. *1 Phoenix House, Ferring Grange Gardens, Ferring, Worthing, W Sussex BN12 5HU* Tel (01903) 244772

BRANT, Leslie Harold. b 11. **d** 71 **p** 72. C Lower Sandown St Jo *Portsm* 71-74; P-in-c Newchurch 75-80; rtd 80; Perm to Offic *Portsm* from 82. *Seaspray, 22 The Esplanade, Ryde, Isle of Wight PO33 2DZ* Tel (01983) 564054

BRANWELL, Edward Bruce. b 20. St Cath Coll Cam BA42 MA46. Linc Th Coll 42. **d** 44 **p** 45. C S Hampstead St Sav *Lon* 44-46; Trinidad and Tobago 46-49; C Rugby St Andr *Cov* 49-51; V Glossop *Derby* 51-56; Area Sec (SE England) UMCA 56-57; V Lavender Hill Ascension *S'wark* 58-64; Chapl Aldenham Sch Herts 64-70; Asst Master Burlington Sch Lon 70-77; Perm to Offic *St Alb* 81-84; Perm to Offic *Ches* from 84; rtd 85. *16 King's Crescent West, Chester CH3 5TQ* Tel (01244) 313641

BRASIER, Ralph Henry (Jim). b 30. Cant Sch of Min 82. **d** 85 **p** 86. C S Ashford Ch Ch *Cant* 85-89; V Pembury *Roch* 89-95; rtd 95. *72 Jenkyns Close, Botley, Southampton SO30 2UU* Tel (01489) 788332

BRASSELL, Canon Kenneth William. b 23. Kelham Th Coll 46. **d** 50 **p** 51. C Woodbridge St Mary *St E* 50-53; C-in-c Bury St Edmunds All SS CD 53-57; V Ipswich St Thos 57-63; V Beckenham St Jas *Roch* 63-88; P-in-c Beckenham St Aug 66-77; P-in-c Beckenham St Mich 77-78; P-in-c Beckenham St Mich w St Aug 77-78; Hon Can Roch Cathl 82-88; rtd 88; Perm to Offic *Glouc* from 88. *20 College Green, Gloucester GL1 2LR* Tel (01452) 309080

BRATLEY, David Frederick. b 42. Linc Th Coll 80. **d** 82 **p** 83. C Holbeach *Linc* 82-85; R Fleet w Gedney from 85. *The Rectory, Fleet, Spalding, Lincs PE12 8NQ* Tel (01406) 23795

BRATTON, Mark Quinn. b 62. Barrister 87 Lon Univ BA84 City Univ DipLaw85. Wycliffe Hall Ox BA94 DipMin94. **d** 94 **p** 95. C W Ealing St Jo w St Jas *Lon* from 94. *41 Leighton Road, London W13 9EL* Tel 0181-566 2512

BRAUN, Dr Thom. b 53. St Jo Coll Ox BA76 MA76 Univ Coll Lon PhD80. S'wark Ord Course 89. **d** 92 **p** 93. Hon C Surbiton St Andr and St Mark *S'wark* from 92. *8 Kings Drive, Surbiton, Surrey KT5 8NG* Tel 0181-399 6898

BRAUND, George Basil. b 26. SS Coll Cam BA50 MA54. Ely Th Coll 51. **d** 53 **p** 54. OGS from 52; Superior OGS 69-75; C Chesterton St Luke *Ely* 53-60; Chapl SS Coll Cam 60-68; Lic to Offic *Ely* 60-68; Lic to Offic *Lon* 68-69; Travel Missr USPG 68-73; Overseas Sec USPG 73-79; Lic to Offic *Ox* 69-88; Assoc Sec Miss and Ecum Affairs ACC 79-88; Co Sec Angl Reformed Internat Commn 80-86; TV Wallingford w Crowmarsh Gifford etc *Ox* 88-93; rtd 93. *40 Warmans Close, Wantage, Oxon OX12 9XT* Tel (01235) 767761

BRAVINER, William Edward (Bill). b 66. Leic Poly BSc88 ACA91. Cranmer Hall Dur BA94 DMS95. **d** 95 **p** 96. C Royton St Anne *Man* from 95. *387 Middleton Road, Royton, Oldham OL2 5EH* Tel 0161-626 5986

BRAY, Anthony Markham. b 16. Magd Coll Cam BA37 MA43. Cuddesdon Coll 38. **d** 39 **p** 40. C Dur St Oswald *Dur* 39-42; C E Dulwich St Jo *S'wark* 42-46; C Kingswood 46-53; V Crediton *Ex* 53-75; V Posbury Chap Ex 53-75; P-in-c Colebrooke 65-68; P-in-c Hittisleigh 65-68; RD Cadbury 56-65; P-in-c Otterton 76-80; rtd 81; Lic to Offic *Ex* from 81. *Quince, King Street, Colyton, Devon EX13 6LA* Tel (01297) 553149

BRAY, Christopher Laurence. b 53. Leeds Univ BSc74 Qu Univ Kingston Ontario MSc76. St Jo Coll Nottm DipTh79 DPS81. **d** 81 **p** 82. C Aughton Ch Ch *Liv* 81-84; Hon C Scarborough St Mary w Ch Ch and H Apostles *York* 84-88; Chapl Scarborough Coll 84-88; V St Helens St Matt Thatto Heath *Liv* from 88. *The Vicarage, St Matthew's Grove, St Helens, Merseyside WA10 3SE* Tel (01744) 24644

BRAY, David Charles. b 39. MIMechE. Ripon Coll Cuddesdon 94. **d** 96 **p** 97. NSM N Stoneham *Win* from 96. *43 Holly Hill, Bassett, Southampton SO16 7ES* Tel (01703) 768004 Fax as telephone

BRAY, Gerald Lewis. b 48. McGill Univ Montreal BA69. Ridley Hall Cam 76. **d** 78 **p** 79. C Canning Town St Cedd *Chelmsf* 78-80; Tutor Oak Hill NSM Course 80-92; Lic to Offic *Lon* 81-92; Ed Churchman from 93. *Church Society, Dean Wace House, 16 Rosslyn Road, Watford WD1 7EY* Tel (01923) 235111 Fax as telephone

BRAY, Jason Stephen. b 69. SS Hild & Bede Coll Dur BA90 MA91 Fitzw Coll Cam PhD96 DipTh96. Westcott Ho Cam 95. **d** 97. C Abergavenny St Mary w Llanwenarth Citra *Mon* from 97. *12A Park Court, Abergavenny NP7 5SR* Tel (01873) 852407

BRAY, Jeremy Grainger. b 40. Man Univ BA62. Wells Th Coll 62. **d** 64 **p** 65. C Bris St Andr w St Bart *Bris* 64-67; C Bris H Cross Inns Court 67-71; C-in-c Stockwood CD 71-73; V Bris Ch the Servant Stockwood 73-83; RD Brislington 79-83; P-in-c Chippenham St Pet 83-88; V 88-93; V Fishponds St Jo from 93. *St John's Vicarage, Mayfield Park, Bristol BS16 3NW* Tel 0117-965 4130

BRAY, Joyce. b 32. CA Tr Coll. **dss** 80 **d** 87 **p** 94. Bloxwich *Lich* 80-84; Derringham Bank *York* 84-87; Par Dn 87-94; Hon C from 94; rtd 94. *413 Willerby Road, Hull HU5 5JD* Tel (01482) 502193

BRAY, Kenneth John. b 31. St Mich Coll Llan 65. **d** 67 **p** 72. C Killay *S & B* 67-68; C S Harrow St Paul *Lon* 71-73; C Hillingdon St Jo 73-76; C Chipping Sodbury and Old Sodbury *Glouc* 76-79; C Worle *B & W* 79-80; Lic to Offic *Ches* 80-83; TV Wrexham *St As* 83-85; V Llay 85-94; rtd 94. *21 Glenthorn Road, Bexhill-on-Sea, E Sussex TN39 3QH* Tel (01424) 213965

BRAY, Richard. b 29. Linc Th Coll 55. **d** 57 **p** 58. C Lt Ilford St Barn *Chelmsf* 57-62; R Tye Green w Netteswell 62-93; rtd 93; Perm to Offic *Chelmsf* from 93. *14 The Wayback, Saffron Walden, Essex CB10 2AX* Tel (01799) 526901

BRAY, Thomas Chadwick. b 08. Qu Coll Birm 46. **d** 48 **p** 49. C Gnosall w Knightley *Lich* 48-51; C Shifnal 51-55; R Ryton 55-69; P-in-c Badger 55-56; R 56-69; P-in-c Beckbury 55-56; R 56-69; RD Shifnal 65-69; V Bolam *Newc* 69-74; rtd 74. *33 Heron Way, Newport, Shropshire TF10 8QF* Tel (01952) 825872

BRAYBROOKE, Marcus Christopher Rossi. b 38. Magd Coll Cam BA62 MA65 Lon Univ MPhil68. Wells Th Coll 63. **d** 64 **p** 65. C Highgate St Mich *Lon* 64-67; C Frindsbury w Upnor *Roch* 67-72; TV Strood St Fran 72-73; P-in-c Swainswick w Langridge and Woolley *B & W* 73-76; R 76-79; Dir of Tr 79-84; Hon C Bath Ch Ch Prop Chpl 84-91; Exec Dir Coun of Chrs and Jews 84-87; rtd 88; Perm to Offic *Bris* 88-93; Preb Wells Cathl *B & W* 90-93; Chapl Bath St Mary Magd Holloway 92-93; Perm to Offic 93; NSM Dorchester *Ox* from 93. *The Rectory, Marsh Baldon, Oxford OX44 9LS* Tel (01865) 343215 Fax 343575

BRAZELL, Denis Illtyd Anthony. b 42. Trin Coll Cam BA64 MA68. Wycliffe Hall Ox 78. **d** 80 **p** 81. C Cheltenham Ch Ch *Glouc* 80-84; V Reading St Agnes w St Paul *Ox* 84-96; Perm to Offic *Guildf* from 96; Warden and Chapl Acorn Chr Healing Trust from 97. *Acorn Christian Healing Trust, Whitehill Chase, High Street, Bordon, Hants GU35 0AP* Tel (01420) 478121 Fax 478122

BRAZELL, Mrs Elizabeth Jane. b 44. LRAM64 ARCM65 GGSM65 AGSM65. Wycliffe Hall Ox 85. **dss** 86 **d** 87 **p** 94. Reading St Agnes w St Paul *Ox* 86-96; Par Dn 87-94; C 94-96; Perm to Offic *Guildf* from 96. *Acorn Christian Healing Trust, Whitehill Chase, High Street, Bordon, Hants GU35 0AP* Tel (01420) 478121 Fax 478122

BRAZIER, Eric James Arthur. b 37. Qu Coll Birm 84. **d** 86 **p** 87. C Lighthorne *Cov* 86-89; P-in-c 89-92; P-in-c Chesterton 89-92; P-in-c Newbold Pacey w Moreton Morrell 89-92; R Astbury and Smallwood *Ches* from 92. *The Rectory, Astbury, Congleton, Cheshire CW12 4RQ* Tel (01260) 272625

BRAZIER, Canon Raymond Venner (Ray). b 40. Wells Th Coll 68. **d** 71 **p** 72. C Horfield St Greg *Bris* 71-75; P-in-c Bris St Nath w St Kath 75-79; V 79-84; P-in-c Kingsdown 80-84; V Bris St Matt and St Nath from 84; RD Horfield 85-91; P-in-c Bishopston 93-97; Hon Can Bris Cathl from 94. *The Vicarage, 11 Glentworth Road, Bristol BS6 7EG* Tel 0117-942 4186

BREADEN, The Very Revd Robert William. b 37. Edin Th Coll 58. **d** 61 **p** 62. C Broughty Ferry *Bre* 61-65; R from 72; R Carnoustie 65-72; Can St Paul's Cathl Dundee from 77; Dean Bre from 84. *46 Seafield Road, Broughty Ferry, Dundee DD5 3AN* Tel (01382) 477477

BREADMORE, Martin Christopher. b 67. Lon Univ LLB89. Wycliffe Hall Ox BTh93. **d** 93 **p** 94. C Herne Bay Ch Ch *Cant* 93-97; C Camberley St Paul *Guildf* from 97. *Cornerways, 3 Upper Gordon Road, Camberley, Surrey GU15 2AD* Tel (01276) 504103

BREAR, Alvin Douglas. **d** 87 **p** 96. NSM Leic H Spirit *Leic* 87-88; NSM Leic Ch Sav 88-96; NSM Leic Presentation from 96. *84 Parkland Drive, Oadby, Leicester LE2 4DG* Tel 0116-271 4137

BREARLEY, Mrs Janet Mary. b 48. Cranmer Hall Dur 88. **d** 90 **p** 94. C Prudhoe *Newc* 90-91; C Fenham St Jas and St Basil 91-95; V Warkworth and Acklington from 95. *The Vicarage, 11 Dial Place, Warkworth, Morpeth, Northd NE65 0UR* Tel (01665) 711217

BREBNER, Martin James. b 47. ARCS68 Imp Coll Lon BSc68. St Alb Minl Tr Scheme 87. **d** 90 **p** 91. Hon C Letchworth St Paul w Willian *St Alb* 90-94; Perm to Offic 95; Hon C St Ippolyts from 95. *42 Farthing Drive, Letchworth, Herts SG6 2TR* Tel (01462) 67919

BRECHIN, Mrs Valerie Becky Allan (Val). b 43. Ridley Hall Cam CTMin93. **d** 93 **p** 94. C Ipswich All Hallows *St E* 93-96; P-in-c Bottisham and Lode w Long Meadow *Ely* from 96. *The Vicarage, 86 High Street, Bottisham, Cambridge CB5 9BA* Tel (01223) 812367

BRECHIN, Bishop of. *See* CHAMBERLAIN, The Rt Revd Neville

BRECHIN, Dean of. *See* BREADEN, The Very Revd Robert William

BRECKLES, Robert Wynford. b 48. St Edm Hall Ox BA72 MA74 CertEd. St Jo Coll Dur DipTh79. **d** 79 **p** 80. C Bulwell St Mary *S'well* 79-84; P-in-c Lady Bay 84; V from 84. *The Vicarage, 121 Holme Road, Nottingham NG2 5AG* Tel 0115-981 3565

BRECKNELL, David Jackson. b 32. Keble Coll Ox BA53 MA57. St Steph Ho Ox 56. **d** 58 **p** 59. C Streatham St Pet *S'wark* 58-62; C Sneinton St Steph w St Alb *S'well* 62-64; C Solihull *Birm* 64-68; V Streatham St Paul *S'wark* 68-75; R Rumboldswyke *Chich* 75-81; P-in-c Portfield 79-81; R Whyke w Rumboldswhyke and Portfield 81-95; rtd 95; Perm to Offic *Chich* from 95. *8 Priory Close, Boxgrove, Chichester, W Sussex PO18 0EA* Tel (01243) 784841

BRECKWOLDT, Peter Hans. b 57. Man Poly BA79. Oak Hill Th Coll BA88. **d** 88 **p** 89. C Knutsford St Jo and Toft *Ches* 88-92; V Moulton *Pet* from 92. *The Vicarage, 30 Cross Street, Moulton, Northampton NN3 1RZ* Tel (01604) 491060

BRECON, Archdeacon of. *See* JAMES, The Ven David Brian

BRECON, Dean of. *See* HARRIS, The Very Revd John

BREED, Kenneth Wilfred. b 11. Leeds Univ BA33. Coll of Resurr Mirfield 33. **d** 35 **p** 36. C Cov H Trin *Cov* 35-37; C Parkstone St Pet w Branksea *Sarum* 37-43; Chapl RNVR 43-46; C Eastleigh *Win* 46-49; C Cheam *S'wark* 49-51; V Shirley *Birm* 51-77; rtd 77; Hon C St Andr Holborn *Lon* 77-79; Perm to Offic *Sarum* 80-97; Perm to Offic *B & W* 86-94. *4 Yard Court, East Street, Warminster, Wilts BA12 9NY* Tel (01985) 213230

BREEDS, Christopher Roger. b 51. LGSM83 ACertCM87 Lon Univ CertEd73. Chich Th Coll 84. **d** 87 **p** 88. C E Grinstead St Swithun *Chich* 87-90; TV Aldrington 90-92; P-in-c Hove St Andr Old Ch 92-93; TV Hove from 93. *The Vicarage, 17 Vallance Gardens, Hove, E Sussex BN3 2DB* Tel (01273) 734859

BREEN, Michael James. b 58. Oak Hill Th Coll BA79 MA85 LTh Cranmer Hall Dur 81. **d** 83 **p** 84. C Cambridge St Martin *Ely* 83-87; V Clapham Park All SS *S'wark* 87-92; USA 92-94; TR Crookes St Thos *Sheff* from 94. *The Rectory, 18A Hallam Gate Road, Sheffield S10 5BT* Tel 0114-268 6362

BREENE, Timothy Patrick Brownell. b 59. Kent Univ BA81 CCC Cam BA89. Ridley Hall Cam 87. **d** 90 **p** 93. C Hadleigh w Layham and Shelley *St E* 90-95; C Martlesham w Brightwell from 95. *4 Sadlers Place, Martlesham Heath, Ipswich IP5 7SS* Tel (01473) 625433

BREFFITT, Geoffrey Michael. b 46. CChem MRIC72 Trent Poly CertEd77 DipPSE82. Qu Coll Birm 87. **d** 89 **p** 90. C Prenton *Ches* 89-92; V Frankby w Greasby from 92. *The Vicarage, 14 Arrowe Road, Greasby, South Wirral L49 1RA* Tel 0151-678 6155

BRENCHLEY, Miss Joy Pamela. b 40. **d** 91. NSM Ramsgate St Luke *Cant* from 91. *37 Pysons Road, Ramsgate, Kent CT12 6TU* Tel (01843) 587124

BRENDON-COOK, John Lyndon. b 37. FRICS. SW Minl Tr Course. **d** 81 **p** 82. NSM Bodmin *Truro* 81-82; NSM St Breoke and Egloshayle 82-90; NSM Helland 90-94; P-in-c from 94; NSM Cardynham 90-94. *Treworder Byre, 119 Egloshayle Road, Wadebridge, Cornwall PL27 6AG* Tel (01208) 812488

BRENNAN, Dr John Lester. b 20. MRCP51 FRCPath77 Barrister-at-Law (Middle Temple) 71 Lon Univ MB, BS44 DipTh47 MD52 LLM86. St Aug Coll Cant 54. **d** 55 **p** 56. India 55-65; Hon C Woodside Park St Barn *Lon* 65-69; Lic to Offic *Lich* 69-88; P-in-c Chrishall *Chelmsf* 88-89; Hon C 89-91; Hon C Heydon, Gt and Lt Chishill, Chrishall etc 91-93; Perm to Offic *St Alb* from 93. *16 Butterfield Road, Wheathampstead, Herts AL4 8PU* Tel (01582) 832230

BRENNAN, Samuel James. b 16. St Aid Birkenhead. **d** 57 **p** 58. C Magheralin *D & D* 57-60; C Down H Trin 60-63; Min Can Down Cathl 60-63; I Scarva 63-69; I Aghalee 69-84; RD Shankill 77-84; rtd 84. *71 Bangor Road, Newtownards, Co Down BT23 3BZ* Tel (01247) 819139

BRENNEN, Canon Colin. b 15. Lon Univ BA47 BD56 Dur Univ PhD88. Linc Th Coll 46. **d** 48 **p** 49. C Seaton Hirst *Newc* 48-50; C Bishopwearmouth Ch Ch *Dur* 50-52; V Grangetown 52-58; V Whitworth w Spennymoor 58-78; RD Auckland 74-82; Hon Can Dur Cathl 78-93; V Hamsterley 78-82; rtd 82. *13 Springwell Road, Durham DH1 4LR* Tel 0191-386 9386

BRENT, Philip. b 68. K Coll Lon BD89. Cuddesdon Coll 94. **d** 96 **p** 97. C Sawbridgeworth *St Alb* from 96. *St Mary's Lodge, Knight Street, Sawbridgeworth, Herts CM21 9AX* Tel (01279) 726696

BRENTNALL, David John. b 53. UEA BA75 MPhil82. Ridley Hall Cam 84. **d** 86 **p** 87. C Eaton *Nor* 86-90; V Stevenage St Pet Broadwater *St Alb* 90-96; V St Alb St Pet from 96. *The Vicarage, 23 Hall Place Gardens, St Albans, Herts AL1 3SB* Tel (01727) 851464

BRENTON, Basil. b 28. Sarum Th Coll. **d** 55 **p** 56. C Kensington St Mary Abbots w St Geo *Lon* 55-59; CF 59-62; Chapl Sliema *Eur* 62-65; C-in-c Hayes St Edm CD *Lon* 65-68; V Cowfold *Chich* 68-94; rtd 94; Perm to Offic *Chich* from 95. *74 Silver Lane, Billingshurst, W Sussex RH14 9QB* Tel (01403) 783604

BRETEL, Keith Michael. b 51. St Mich Coll Llan 79. **d** 81 **p** 82. C Thundersley *Chelmsf* 81-84; CF from 84. *MOD Chaplains (Army), Trenchard Lines, Upavon, Pewsey, Wilts SN9 6BE* Tel (01980) 615804 Fax 615800

BRETHERTON, Donald John. b 18. Lon Univ BD57. Handsworth Coll Birm 38 Headingley Coll Leeds 38 St Aug Coll Cant 59. **d** 60 **p** 61. C Cant St Martin w St Paul *Cant* 60-62; In Meth Ch 42-59; V Thornton Heath St Jude 62-70; V Herne 70-82; RD Reculver 74-80; rtd 82; Perm to Offic *Cant* 84-92. *Martin's, The Green, Chartham, Canterbury, Kent CT4 7JW* Tel (01227) 731666

BRETHERTON, Canon William Alan. b 22. St Cath Coll Cam BA43 MA47. Lon Coll of Div BD49 ALCD49. **d** 49 **p** 50. C Fazakerley Em *Liv* 49-52; V Everton St Chrys 52-65; V Ince Ch Ch 65-72; V Kirkdale St Mary 72-73; V Kirkdale St Mary and St Athanasius 73-87; RD Liv 81-87; Hon Can Liv Cathl 81-87; rtd 87; Perm to Offic *Liv* from 87. *3 Bradville Road, Liverpool L9 9BH* Tel 0151-525 0866

BRETHERTON-HAWKSHEAD-TALBOT, Richard Dolben. b 11. Trin Coll Cam BA32 MA56. Ely Th Coll 32. **d** 34 **p** 35. C Ryhope *Dur* 34-38; C Whitby *York* 39-40; V E Boldon *Dur* 40-47; C Eccleston *Blackb* 47-58; R 58-78; rtd 78; Lic to Offic *Blackb* from 79. *The Delph, 71 Marsh Lane, Longton, Preston PR4 5ZL* Tel (01772) 612893

BRETT, Dennis Roy Anthony. b 46. Sarum & Wells Th Coll 86. **d** 88 **p** 89. C Bradford-on-Avon *Sarum* 88-92; P-in-c Bishopstrow and Boreham from 92; Chapl Warminster Hosp from 92. *The Rectory, 8 Rock Lane, Warminster, Wilts BA12 9JZ* Tel (01985) 213000

BRETT, Canon Paul Gadsby. b 41. St Edm Hall Ox BA62 MA66. Wycliffe Hall Ox 64. **d** 65 **p** 66. C Bury St Pet *Man* 65-68; Asst Ind Chapl 68-72; Ind Chapl *Worc* 72-76; Asst Sec Ind Cttee of Gen Syn Bd for Soc Resp 76-84; Dir Soc Resp *Chelmsf* 85-94; Can Res Chelmsf Cathl 85-94; R Shenfield from 94. *The Rectory, 41 Worrin Road, Shenfield, Brentwood, Essex CM15 8DH* Tel (01277) 220360

BRETT, Canon Peter Graham Cecil. b 35. Em Coll Cam BA59 MA63. Cuddesdon Coll 59. **d** 61 **p** 62. C Tewkesbury w Walton Cardiff *Glouc* 61-64; C Bournemouth St Pet *Win* 64-66; Chapl Dur Univ *Dur* 66-72; R Houghton le Spring 72-83; RD Houghton 80-83; Can Res Cant Cathl *Cant* from 83. *22 The Precincts, Canterbury, Kent CT1 2EP* Tel (01227) 459757

BRETTELL, Robert Michael. b 20. St Cath Soc Ox BA49 MA54. Lon Coll of Div 46 Wycliffe Hall Ox 47. **d** 49 **p** 50. C Blackheath St Jo *S'wark* 49-51; C Norbiton 51-53; V Woking St Mary *Guildf* 53-62; V Clifton Ch Ch w Em *Bris* 62-73; V Eastbourne H Trin *Chich* 73-82; V Bexhill St Steph 82-86; rtd 86; Perm to Offic *Chich* from 86. *229 Little Ridge Avenue, St Leonards-on-Sea, E Sussex TN37 7HN* Tel (01424) 752035

BREW, William Kevin Maddock. b 49. BA MSc. **d** 78 **p** 79. C Raheny w Coolock *D & G* 78-80; Bp's C Dublin Finglas 80-83; I Mountmellick w Coolbanagher, Rosenallis etc *M & K* 83-89; I Ahoghill w Portglenone *Conn* from 89. *42 Church Street, Ahoghill, Ballymena, Co Antrim BT42 2PA* Tel (01266) 871240

BREW, William Philip. b 43. FCollP84 Derby Coll of Educn CertEd64 Liv Univ DSpEd72. N Ord Course 84. **d** 87 **p** 88. Hd Master Birtenshaw Sch 78-90; NSM Holcombe *Man* 87-90; TV Horwich 91-93; TV Horwich and Rivington from 93. *St Elizabeth's Vicarage, Cedar Avenue, Horwich, Bolton BL6 6HT* Tel (01204) 669120

BREWER, Barry James. b 44. Oak Hill Th Coll 72. **d** 75 **p** 76. C Hove Bp Hannington Memorial Ch *Chich* 75-78; C Church Stretton *Heref* 78-81; TV Bishopsnympton, Rose Ash, Mariansleigh etc *Ex* 81-87; R Swynnerton and Tittensor *Lich* from 87. *3 Rectory Gardens, Swynnerton, Stone, Staffs ST15 0RT* Tel (0178135) 564

BREWER, Canon John Herbert. b 13. DDEd. St Steph Ho Ox 37. **d** 39 **p** 40. C Finsbury St Clem *Lon* 39-40; C Bethnal Green St Jas the Gt w St Jude 40-42; C Ealing Ch the Sav 42-48; CF (EC) 44-47; Hon CF from 47; Ghana 48-60; V Notting Hill All SS w St Columb *Lon* 61-66; V Isleworth St Fran 66-78; rtd 78; Lic to Offic *Nor* 78-86; Perm to Offic from 86. *36 Cleaves Drive, Walsingham, Norfolk NR22 6EQ* Tel (01328) 820579

BREWIN, Dr David Frederick. b 39. Leic Poly BSc PhD. Lich Th Coll 63. **d** 66 **p** 67. C Shrewsbury H Cross *Lich* 66-69; C Birstall *Leic* 69-73; V Eyres Monsell 73-79; V E Goscote 79-82; V E Goscote w Ratcliffe and Rearsby 82-90; R Thurcaston 90-91; R Thurcaston w Cropston from 92. *The Rectory, 74 Anstey Lane, Thurcaston, Leicester LE7 7JA* Tel 0116-236 2525

BREWIN, Donald Stewart (Don). b 41. Ch Coll Cam BA62 MA66. Ridley Hall Cam 68. **d** 71 **p** 72. C Ecclesall *Sheff* 71-75; V Anston 75-81; V Walton H Trin *Ox* 81-89; TR 89-94; RD Aylesbury 90-94; Nat Dir SOMA from 94. *Wickham Cottage, Gaddesden Turn, Billington, Leighton Buzzard, Beds LU7 9BW* Tel (01525) 373644 Fax 853787

BREWIN, Canon Eric Walter. b 16. Hertf Coll Ox BA38 MA42. Ripon Hall Ox 38. **d** 40 **p** 41. C Leic St Marg *Leic* 40-42; Ind Sec SCM 42-46; C Ox St Mary V *Ox* 46-48; Sub-Chapl Nuff Coll Ox

46-48; V Coleford w Staunton *Glouc* 48-70; RD Forest S 57-70; Hon Can Glouc Cathl 65-81; R Leckhampton St Pet 70-81; rtd 81; Perm to Offic *Glouc* from 82. *The Pleck, Llangrove, Ross-on-Wye, Herefordshire HR9 6EU* Tel (01989) 770487

BREWIN, Karan Rosemary. b 42. CA Tr Coll 77 Glas NSM Course 80. **dss** 84 **d** 85. Clarkston *Glas* 84-89; Hon C 86-89 and from 91; OHP from 89. *85 Mearns Road, Clarkston, Glasgow G76 7LF* Tel 0141-620 3203

BREWIN, Wilfred Michael. b 45. Nottm Univ BA69. Cuddesdon Coll 69. **d** 70 **p** 71. C Walker *Newc* 70-73; C Alnwick St Paul 73-74; C Alnwick w Edlingham and Bolton Chpl 74-77; Fell Sheff Univ 77-79; C Greenhill *Sheff* 79; P-in-c Eggleston *Dur* 79-81; V Norton St Mich 81-87; V Headington *Ox* from 87. *The Vicarage, 33 St Andrew's Road, Oxford OX3 9DL* Tel (01865) 761094

BREWSTER, David Pearson. b 30. Clare Coll Cam BA54 MA58 Lon Univ BA65 Or Coll Ox MA66 DPhil76. Ridley Hall Cam. **d** 58 **p** 59. C Southampton St Mary w H Trin *Win* 58-61; C N Audley Street St Mark *Lon* 61-62 and 63-65; Tunisia 62-63; Home Sec JEM 65-66; C Ox St Mary V w St Cross and St Pet *Ox* 66-68; Lect Lady Spencer-Churchill Coll Ox 68-71; New Zealand 71-78; V Brockenhurst *Win* 78-95; rtd 95. *4 Saxonford Road, Christchurch, Dorset BH23 4ES* Tel (01425) 277860

BREWSTER, Jonathan David. b 67. **d** 94 **p** 95. C Gt Horton *Bradf* from 94. *18 Windermere Road, Great Horton, Bradford BD7 4RQ* Tel (01274) 573261

BREWSTER (née BEATTIE), Margaret. b 43. S'wark Ord Course 90. **d** 93 **p** 94. NSM S'wark H Trin w St Matt *S'wark* 93-97; NSM Newington St Paul from 97. *1 Charlston Street, London SE17 1NG* Tel 0171-701 4010

BREWSTER, Noel Theodore. b 16. CCC Cam BA38 MA42. Qu Coll Birm 38. **d** 39 **p** 40. C Portswood Ch Ch *Win* 39-42; C Pokesdown All SS 42-46; C Portsea N End St Mark *Portsm* 46-49; Canada 49-52; V St Mary Bourne w Litchfield *Win* 52-60; R Fawley 61-69; R Chilcomb w Win All SS and Chesil 69-70; V Grantchester *Ely* 71-86; rtd 86; Perm to Offic *Ely* 86-90; Chapl St Cross Win 86-90. *5 Carthagena, Sutton Scotney, Winchester, Hants SO21 3LJ* Tel (01962) 760667

BREWSTER, Mrs Susan Jacqueline (Sue). b 48. SEITE 94. **d** 97. NSM Goodmayes St Paul *Chelmsf* from 97. *12 Avery Gardens, Gants Hill, Ilford, Essex IG2 6UJ* Tel 0181-550 0333 Fax 550 7766

BREWSTER, William Taylor. b 26. Bps' Coll Cheshunt 58. **d** 59 **p** 60. C Bideford *Ex* 59-61; R Woolfardisworthy w Kennerleigh 61-71; R Washford Pyne w Puddington 61-71; P-in-c Cruwys Morchard 68-71; RD Cadbury 68-71; P-in-c Poughill w Stockleigh English 71; Asst Chapl HM Pris Man 71; Chapl HM Pris Maidstone 72-77; Chapl HM Pris Blundeston 77-84; Chapl HM Pris Featherstone 84-89; rtd 89; Perm to Offic *Lich* from 89. *4 Pinfold Road, Lichfield, Staffs WS13 7BX* Tel (01543) 254983

BRIAN, Brother. *See* HARLEY, Brother Brian Mortimer

BRIAN, Stephen Frederick. b 54. Brighton Coll of Educn CertEd76 Sussex Univ BEd77 Birm Univ DipTh84 Open Univ MA90. Qu Coll Birm 82. **d** 85 **p** 86. C Scotforth *Blackb* 85-88; V Freckleton from 88. *Holy Trinity Vicarage, 3 Sunnyside Close, Freckleton, Preston PR4 1YJ* Tel (01772) 632209

BRICE, Christopher John. b 48. St Edm Ho Cam MA80. Wycliffe Hall Ox 82. **d** 82 **p** 83. C N Hinksey *Ox* 82-86; Chapl Nuff Coll Ox 84-86; V S Hackney St Mich w Haggerston St Paul *Lon* 86-93; Dir Dioc Bd for Soc Resp from 93. *141 Culford Road, London N1 4HX* Tel 0171-249 6290

BRICE, Jonathan Andrew William. b 61. **d** 92 **p** 93. C Buckhurst Hill *Chelmsf* 92-96; C Victoria Docks Ascension 96; P-in-c from 96. *5 Broadgate Road, London E16 3TL* Tel 0171-476 6887

BRICE, Neil Alan. b 59. Man Univ BA81 Hughes Hall Cam CertEd87. Westcott Ho Cam 82. **d** 84 **p** 85. C Longton *Lich* 84-86; Hd of Relig Studies Coleridge Community Coll Cam 87-89; NSM Cherry Hinton St Andr *Ely* 88-89; C Fulbourn 89-92; C Gt Wilbraham 89-92; C Lt Wilbraham 89-92; V Arrington from 92; R Orwell from 92; R Wimpole from 92; R Croydon w Clopton from 92. *The Rectory, Fishers Lane, Orwell, Royston, Herts SG8 5QX* Tel (01223) 208653 Fax as telephone

BRICE, Paul Earl Philip. b 54. Bath Univ BSc77. Wycliffe Hall Ox 83. **d** 86 **p** 87. C Gt Baddow *Chelmsf* 86-89; Chapl Imp Coll *Lon* 89-95; St Mary's Hosp Med Sch 89-95; Chapl RCA 90-95; Sec HE/Chapl Gen Syn Bd of Educn from 95; Hon C S Kensington St Jude *Lon* from 95. *18 Collingham Road, London SW5 0LX* Tel 0171-259 2301

BRIDCUT, William John. b 38. CITC 67. **d** 70 **p** 71. C Lisburn Ch Ch Cathl *Conn* 71-74; Dublin Irish Ch Miss *D & G* from 74; Chapl Arbour Hill Pris 88-90; Chapl Mountjoy Pris 88-90; Asst Chapl Arbour Hill Pris from 90. *Irish Church Missions, 28 Bachelor's Walk, Dublin 1, Irish Republic* Tel Dublin (1) 873 0829 or 821 2165 Fax 872 2669 E-mail icm@iol.ie

BRIDGE, The Very Revd Antony Cyprian. b 14. FSA. Linc Th Coll 53. **d** 55 **p** 56. C Hythe *Cant* 55-58; V Paddington Ch Ch *Lon* 58-68; Dean Guildf 68-86; rtd 86; Perm to Offic *Cant* from 86. *34 London Road, Deal, Kent CT14 9TE* Tel (01304) 366792

BRIDGE, Miss Helen Cecily. b 25. SRN47 SCM49 Open Univ BA80. Lambeth STh78 Dalton Ho Bris 70 Trin Coll Bris 70. **dss** 74 **d** 87 **p** 94. Tonbridge St Steph *Roch* 74-75; Countess of Ches Hosp 75-84; Plemstall w Guilden Sutton *Ches* 85-87; Hon Par Dn 87-88; NSM Stockport St Mary from 88. *25 Rectory Fields, Stockport, Cheshire SK1 4BX* Tel 0161-477 2154

BRIDGE, Martin. b 45. Lon Univ BA66 Linacre Coll Ox BA71 MA73. St Steph Ho Ox 69. **d** 72 **p** 73. C St Peter-in-Thanet *Cant* 72-77; New Zealand from 77. *PO Box 87 145, Meadowbank, Auckland, New Zealand* Tel Auckland (9) 521 0636 or 521 5013

BRIDGE-COLLYNS, Douglas Herbert. b 26. Nottm Univ BSc48 MPhil71. St Steph Ho Ox 51. **d** 53 **p** 54. C Leic St Pet *Leic* 53-57; S Rhodesia 58-65; C Nottingham St Pet and St Jas *S'well* 65-68; Lic to Offic *Derby* 68-85; Perm to Offic *S'well* 76-84; Chapl Abbots Bromley Sch 84-87; V Whatton w Aslockton, Hawksworth, Scarrington etc *S'well* from 87. *The Vicarage, Main Street, Aslockton, Nottingham NG13 9AL* Tel (01949) 51040

BRIDGEN, John William. b 40. K Coll Cam BA62 MA66. Ripon Hall Ox 66. **d** 70 **p** 72. C Headstone St Geo *Lon* 70-71; C Hanwell St Mary 71-75; C Tolladine *Worc* 75; TV Worc St Barn w Ch Ch 76; R Barrow *St E* 76-83; V Denham St Mary 76-83; Perm to Offic *Ely* 84-88 and from 91; rtd 88; Perm to Offic *Glas* 89-91. *57 St Philip's Road, Cambridge CB1 3DA* Tel (01223) 248096

BRIDGEN, Mark Stephen. b 63. K Coll Lon BD85. Cranmer Hall Dur 86. **d** 88 **p** 89. C Kidderminster St Jo *Worc* 88-90; C Kidderminster St Jo and H Innocents 90-92; C Nor St Pet Mancroft w St Jo Maddermarket *Nor* 92-94; V Longbridge *Birm* from 94. *St John's Vicarage, 220 Longbridge Lane, Birmingham B31 4JT* Tel 0121-475 3484

BRIDGER, Dr Francis William. b 51. Pemb Coll Ox BA73 MA78 Bris Univ DipTh75 PhD80. Trin Coll Bris 74. **d** 78 **p** 79. C Islington St Jude Mildmay Park *Lon* 78-82; C Mildmay Grove St Jude and St Paul 82; Lect St Jo Coll Nottm 82-90; Dir of Courses 88-89; Dir of Studies 89-90; Lic to Offic *S'well* 82-90; V Woodthorpe from 90. *St Mark's Vicarage, 37A Melbury Road, Nottingham NG5 4PG* Tel 0115-926 7859

BRIDGER, Canon Gordon Frederick. b 32. Selw Coll Cam BA53 MA58. Ridley Hall Cam 54. **d** 56 **p** 57. C Islington St Mary *Lon* 56-60; C Cambridge St Sepulchre *Ely* 60-62; V Fulham St Mary N End *Lon* 62-69; C Edin St Thos *Edin* 69-76; R Heigham H Trin *Nor* 76-87; RD Nor S 79-86; Hon Can Nor Cathl 84-87; Prin Oak Hill Th Coll 87-96; rtd 96; Perm to Offic *Nor* from 96. *The Elms, 4 Common Lane, Sheringham, Norfolk NR26 8PL* Tel (01263) 823522

BRIDGER, Malcolm John. b 36. AKC62. **d** 63 **p** 64. C Sheff St Cuth *Sheff* 63-66; C Wythenshawe Wm Temple Ch CD *Man* 66-67; C-in-c Lower Kersal CD 67-72; V Lower Kersal 72-74; C Ifield *Chich* 75-78; TV 78-84; P-in-c Brentford St Paul w St Lawr and St Geo *Lon* 84-87; P-in-c Gunnersbury St Jas 85-87; TR Brentford 87-94; R Tidworth, Ludgershall and Faberstown *Sarum* from 94; RD Avon from 95. *The Rectory, 10 St James' Street, Ludgershall, Andover, Hants SP11 9QF* Tel (01264) 790393

BRIDGER, Nigel Egerton. b 23. Dartmouth RN Coll 40. Wells Th Coll 59. **d** 61 **p** 62. C Neston *Ches* 61-64; S Africa from 64. *PO Box 119, Queenstown, 5320 South Africa* Tel Queenstown (451) 4377

BRIDGER, Mrs Renee Winifred. b 45. Lon Univ BD76. Trin Coll Bris. **dss** 80 **d** 87 **p** 94. Islington St Jude Mildmay Park *Lon* 80-82; Mildmay Grove St Jude and St Paul 82; St Jo Coll Nottm from 87; Hon Par Dn Chilwell *S'well* 87-88; C Woodthorpe 90-95; NSM from 95. *St Mark's Vicarage, 37A Melbury Road, Nottingham NG5 4PG* Tel 0115-926 7859

✠**BRIDGES, The Rt Revd Dewi Morris.** b 33. Univ of Wales (Lamp) BA54 CCC Cam BA56 MA60. Westcott Ho Cam 57. **d** 57 **p** 58 **c** 88. C Rhymney *Mon* 57-60; C Chepstow 60-63; V Tredegar St Jas 63-65; Lic to Offic *Worc* 65-69; V Kempsey 69-79; RD Upton 74-79; R Tenby and Gumfreston *St D* 79-85; RD Narberth 80-82; Adn St D 82-88; R Tenby 85-88; Bp S & B from 88. *Ely Tower, Brecon LD3 9DE* Tel (01874) 622008

BRIDGES, Mrs Gillian Mary (Gill). b 43. EAMTC 85. **d** 88 **p** 94. Hon C Hellesdon *Nor* 88-96; Hon C Lakenham St Jo from 96. *2 Vera Road, Norwich NR6 5HU* Tel (01603) 789634

BRIDGES, The Ven Peter Sydney Godfrey. b 25. ARIBA51 Birm Univ DipL&A67. Linc Th Coll 56. **d** 58 **p** 59. C Hemel Hempstead *St Alb* 58-64; Warden Angl Chapl Birm Univ 65-68; Perm to Offic *Birm* 65-72; Lect Aston Univ 68-72; Dir Dioc Research and Development Unit 72-77; Adn Southend *Chelmsf* 72-77; P-in-c Southend St Jo w St Mark, All SS w St Fran etc 72-77; Adn Cov 77-83; Can Th Cov Cathl 77-90; Adn Warwick 83-90; rtd 90; Dioc Adv for Chr Spirituality 90-93. *25 Rivermead Close, Romsey, Hants SO51 8HQ* Tel (01794) 512889

BRIDGEWATER, Guy Stevenson. b 60. Ch Ch Ox BA83. Trin Coll Bris BA87. **d** 87 **p** 88. C Radipole and Melcombe Regis *Sarum* 87-90; Chapl Lee Abbey 90-93; Lic to Offic *Ex* 90-93; V Cranbrook *Cant* from 93. *The Vicarage, Waterloo Road, Cranbrook, Kent TN17 3JQ* Tel (01580) 712150

BRIDGLAND, Cyril John Edwin. b 21. Trin Coll Bris 42. **d** 45 **p** 46. C Illogan *Truro* 45-47; C Northwood Em *Lon* 47-50; V Islington H Trin Cloudesley Square 50-58; V Redhill H Trin *S'wark* 58-87; rtd 87; Perm to Offic *Cant* from 89; Perm to Offic *Roch* from 89.

3 Barned Court, Barming, Maidstone, Kent ME16 9EL Tel (01622) 728451

BRIDGMAN, Canon Gerald Bernard. b 22. St Cath Coll Cam BA50 MA55. Wycliffe Hall Ox 50. **d** 51 **p** 52. C Broadwater St Mary *Chich* 51-54; C Ox St Aldate *Ox* 54-56; C-in-c Southgate CD *Chich* 56-59; V Southgate 59-67; V Kingston upon Hull H Trin *York* 67-87; Area Dean Cen and N Hull 81-86; Can and Preb York Minster 83-87; rtd 87; Perm to Offic *Chich* from 87. *129 The Welkin, Lindfield, Haywards Heath, W Sussex RH16 2PL* Tel (01444) 484563

BRIDGWATER, Edward Roden Gresham. b 98. Union Th Sem (NY) MDiv28 K Coll (NS) BA22 MA23. **d** 24 **p** 25. Canada 24-28 and 28-38; USA 28-38; C Kingsbury St Andr *Lon* 38-42; V Kensal Rise St Martin 42-51; V Hounslow St Steph 51-62; V Chilworth *Win* 62-72; rtd 72. *Flat 5, Capel Court, The Burgage, Prestbury, Cheltenham, Glos GL52 3EL* Tel (01242) 571812

BRIDGWATER, Philip Dudley. b 31. St Alb Minl Tr Scheme 88. **d** 91 **p** 92. NSM Buxton w Burbage and King Sterndale *Derby* 91-94; NSM Fairfield from 94. *Millstone, 9 College Road, Buxton, Derbyshire SK17 9DZ* Tel (01298) 72876

BRIDLE, Geoffrey Peter. b 52. CITC 87. **d** 87 **p** 88. C Lurgan Ch the Redeemer *D & D* 87-91; I Carnteel and Crilly *Arm* from 91. *St James' Rectory, 22 Carnteel Road, Aughnacloy, Co Tyrone BT69 6DU* Tel (01662) 557682 E-mail 100615,3340 @compuserve.com or geoffpbridle@psionworld.net

BRIDSON, Raymond Stephen. b 58. Southn Univ BTh82. Chich Th Coll. **d** 82 **p** 83. C St Luke in the City *Liv* 82-86; TV Ditton St Mich from 86. *All Saints' Vicarage, Hough Green Road, Widnes, Cheshire WA8 9SZ* Tel 0151-420 4963

BRIDSTRUP, Juergen Walter. b 44. St Alb Minl Tr Scheme 84. **d** 87 **p** 88. C Leagrave *St Alb* 87-90; V Goff's Oak St Jas from 90. *St James's Vicarage, St James's Road, Cheshunt, Waltham Cross, Herts EN7 6TP* Tel (01707) 872328 E-mail gw07@dial.pipex.com

BRIERLEY, Charles Ian. b 46. MIMI69 Plymouth Coll of Tech C&G65 C&G67. S Dios Minl Tr Scheme CECM93. **d** 93 **p** 94. NSM Wellington and Distr *B & W* from 93. *46 Oakfield Park, Wellington, Somerset TA21 8EY* Tel (01823) 666101

BRIERLEY, David James. b 53. Bris Univ BA75. Oak Hill Th Coll 75. **d** 77 **p** 78. C Balderstone *Man* 77-80; P-in-c Eccles St Andr 80-81; TV Eccles 81-85; Bp's Ecum Adv 81-88; V Harwood 85-95; Sec Bd Miss and Unity from 88; AD Walmsley from 95; V Walmsley from 95; P-in-c Belmont from 97. *Walmsley Vicarage, Egerton, Bolton BL7 9RZ* Tel (01204) 304283

BRIERLEY, Eric. b 21. St Aid Birkenhead 47. **d** 50 **p** 51. C Oldham St Paul *Man* 50-53; C Stand 53-54; R Moss Side St Jas 54-57; V Ramsbottom St Andr 57-66; V Horwich St Cath 66-74; V Irlam 74-81; V Farndon and Coddington *Ches* 81-86; rtd 86; Perm to Offic *Blackb* from 86. *6 Derbyshire Avenue, Garstang, Preston PR3 1DX* Tel (01995) 602047

BRIERLEY, John Michael. b 32. Lon Univ BD71. Lich Th Coll 57. **d** 60 **p** 61. C Lower Mitton *Worc* 60-62; C-in-c Dines Green St Mich CD 62-68; V Worc St Mich 69-71; R Eastham w Rochford 71-79; P-in-c Knighton-on-Teme 76-79; P-in-c Reddal Hill St Luke 79-81; V 81-92; rtd 92. *St Augustine's Vicarage, 1 Hallchurch Road, Dudley, W Midlands DY2 0TG* Tel (01886) 832759

BRIERLEY, Philip. b 49. CChem80 MRSC80 Salford Univ BSc74. LNSM course 89. **d** 92 **p** 93. NSM Stalybridge *Man* from 92. *Burnside, 30 Cranworth Street, Stalybridge, Cheshire SK15 2NW* Tel 0161-303 0809

BRIERLEY, Dr William David. b 64. Kent Univ BA87 New Coll Ox DPhil93. Ripon Coll Cuddesdon DipMin93. **d** 93 **p** 94. C Amersham *Ox* 93-97; TV Wheatley w Forest Hill and Stanton St John 97; TV Wheatley from 97. *The Vicarage, Cocks Lane, Stanton St John, Oxford OX33 1HW* Tel (01865) 351152

BRIERLEY, William Peter. b 13. Dur Univ BSc38. Cranmer Hall Dur 65. **d** 66 **p** 67. C Haltwhistle *Newc* 66-69; C Otterburn w Elsdon and Horsley w Byrness 69-75; V Greenhead 75-78; P-in-c Lambley w Knaresdale 77-78; rtd 78; Perm to Offic *Carl* 79-87. *7 Hitcombe Bottom Cottage, Horningsham, Warminster, Wilts BA12 7LA* Tel (01985) 844720

BRIERLY, Henry Barnard Lancelot. b 30. Or Coll Ox BA55 MA63. Clifton Th Coll 55. **d** 58 **p** 59. C Normanton *Derby* 58-61; C St Helens St Helen *Liv* 61-63; V Tebay *Carl* 63-69; R Ashwellthorpe w Wreningham *Nor* 69-74; P-in-c Fundenhall 70-74; P-in-c Tacolneston 70-74; TR Wreningham 74-86; R Tetsworth, Adwell w S Weston, Lewknor etc *Ox* 86-95; rtd 95. *85 Coombe Hill Crescent, Thame, Oxon OX9 2EQ* Tel (01844) 261871

BRIGGS, The Ven Archie. b 17. Dur Univ BA39 DipTh40 MA42. **d** 41 **p** 42. C Outwood *Wakef* 41-47; China 47-53; Australia 54-58; Perm to Offic *Ely* 58-59; Brunei 59-60; Br N Borneo 61-63; Malaysia 63-74; Hon Can and Adn Jesselton 63-68; Sabah 68-71; Dean Kota Kinabalu 70-74; Taiwan 75-85; rtd 85. *46 Kell Crescent, Sherburn Hill, Durham DH6 1PP* Tel 0191-372 2013

BRIGGS, Christopher Ronald (Chris). b 58. K Coll Lon BD79 AKC79 PGCE80. Sarum & Wells Th Coll 87. **d** 89 **p** 90. C Horsell *Guildf* 89-93; Hong Kong 93-97; V Norton *St Alb* from 97. *The Vicarage, 17 Norton Way North, Letchworth, Herts SG6 1BY* Tel (01462) 685059

BRIGGS, Derek. b 26. Lon Univ DipTh55. St Aid Birkenhead 52. **d** 55 **p** 56. C Brownhill *Wakef* 55-57; C Trowbridge St Jas *Sarum* 57-60; R Levenshulme St Pet *Man* 60-67; V Farsley *Bradf* 67-90; rtd 90; Perm to Offic *Bradf* from 90. *6 College Court, Bradley, Keighley, W Yorkshire BD20 9EA* Tel (01535) 630585

✠**BRIGGS, The Rt Revd George Cardell.** b 10. CMG80. SS Coll Cam BA33 MA37. Cuddesdon Coll 33. **d** 34 **p** 35 **c** 73. C Stockport St Alb Hall Street *Ches* 34-37; Tanzania 37-73; OGS from 39; Adn Newala 55-64; Can Zanzibar 64-65; Can Dar-es-Salaam 65-69; Can Masasi 69-73; Bp Seychelles 73-79; Asst Bp Derby 79-80; C Matlock and Tansley 79-80; rtd 80; Asst Bp Worc from 91. *1 Lygon Lodge, Beauchamp Community, The Quadrangle, Newland, Malvern, Worcester WR13 5AX* Tel (01684) 572941

BRIGGS, Canon John. b 39. Edin Univ MA61. Ridley Hall Cam 61. **d** 63 **p** 64. C Jesmond Clayton Memorial *Newc* 63-66; Schs Sec Scripture Union 66-79; Tutor St Jo Coll Dur 67-74; Lic to Offic *Dur* 67-74; Lic to Offic *Edin* 74-79; V Chadkirk *Ches* 79-88; RD Chadkirk 85-88; TR Macclesfield Team Par from 88; Hon Can Ches Cathl from 96; Chapl W Park Hosp Macclesfield from 90. *The Rectory, 85 Beech Lane, Macclesfield, Cheshire SK10 2DY* Tel (01625) 426110

BRIGGS, Michael Weston. b 40. Edin Th Coll 61. **d** 64 **p** 65. C Sneinton St Steph w St Alb *S'well* 64-67; C Beeston 67-70; P-in-c Kirkby Woodhouse 70-74; V Harworth 74-81; R Harby w Thorney and N and S Clifton 81-94; R N Wheatley, W Burton, Bole, Saundby, Sturton etc from 94. *The Rectory, Middlefield Road, North Wheatley, Retford, Notts DN22 9DA* Tel (01427) 880293

BRIGGS, The Ven Roger Edward. b 36. ALCD61. **d** 61 **p** 61. Canada 61-71; C Upper Armley *Ripon* 71-72; Canada from 72; Dean Arctic from 96. *Box 57, Iqaluit, Northern Territory, Canada X0A 0H0*

BRIGHAM, John Keith. b 48. FSAScot Man Univ CertEd70. St Steph Ho Ox 71. **d** 74 **p** 75. C Ches H Trin *Ches* 74-77; C Ealing Ch the Sav *Lon* 77-85; P-in-c Fulwell St Mich and St Geo 85-88; P-in-c Upper Teddington SS Pet and Paul 85-88; V Southport St Luke *Liv* 88-94; Dioc Chapl to the Deaf 88-94; V Lund *Blackb* from 94. *Lund Vicarage, Church Lane, Clifton, Preston PR4 0ZE* Tel (01772) 683617

BRIGHOUSE, George Alexander (Alex). b 46. N Ord Course 87. **d** 90 **p** 91. NSM Ingrow cum Hainworth *Bradf* 90-92; NSM Bradf St Wilfrid Lidget Green from 92. *38 Thirsk Grange, Clayton, Bradford, W Yorkshire BD14 6HS* Tel (01274) 816081

BRIGHT, George Frank. b 50. Peterho Cam BA71 MA75 Leeds Univ DipTh73 LSE MSc83. Coll of Resurr Mirfield 71. **d** 74 **p** 75. C Notting Hill *Lon* 74-77; Perm to Offic 77-84; P-in-c Kentish Town St Benet and All SS 84-89; P-in-c Kensington St Jo 89-93; V from 93. *The Vicarage, 176 Holland Road, London W14 8AH* Tel 0171-602 4655

BRIGHT, Patrick John Michael. b 36. Keble Coll Ox BA59 MA64. Chich Th Coll 59. **d** 61 **p** 62. C Bracknell *Ox* 61-68; V Hitchin H Sav *St Alb* 68-76; V Royston 76-90; RD Buntingford 88-96; R Ashwell 90-91; R Ashwell w Hinxworth and Newnham from 91. *The Rectory, Ashwell, Baldock, Herts SG7 6QG* Tel (01462) 742277

BRIGHT, Reginald. b 26. Tyndale Hall Bris 57. **d** 60 **p** 61. C Toxteth Park St Philemon w St Silas *Liv* 60-63; P-in-c Everton St Polycarp 63-65; R Orton St Giles *Carl* 65-72; V Holme 72-79; P-in-c W Newton 79-81; V Bromfield w Waverton 79-81; R Bowness 81-93; rtd 93; Perm to Offic *Carl* from 93. *Spinney House, Cannonfield, Roadhead, Carlisle CA6 6NB* Tel (016978) 645

BRIGHTMAN, Peter Arthur. b 30. Lon Coll of Div ALCD61 LTh74. **d** 64 **p** 65. C Westgate St Jas *Cant* 64-67; C Lydd 67-70; C Lt Coates *Linc* 70; C Heaton Ch Ch *Man* 71-72; V Bolton SS Simon and Jude 72-77; R Bath St Sav *B & W* 77-85; R Farmborough, Marksbury and Stanton Prior 85-90; C Coney Hill *Glouc* 90-93; C Hardwicke, Quedgeley and Elmore w Longney 93-95; rtd 95; Perm to Offic *B & W* from 95. *2 Westmead Cottages, Dean Hill Lane, Weston, Bath BA1 4DT* Tel (01225) 315076

BRIGHTON, Herbert Ernest. b 96. Bris Univ BA22. St Aid Birkenhead 23. **d** 24 **p** 25. C Bedminster St Aldhelm *Bris* 24-27; C Mitcham Ch Ch *S'wark* 27-30; V Baddesley Ensor *Birm* 30-39; R Barton Mills *St E* 39-47; R Burnsall *Bradf* 47-57; rtd 57. *46 Greensey, Appleshaw, Andover, Hants SP11 9HY* Tel (01264) 359248

BRIGHTON, Terrence William. b 43. SW Minl Tr Course 85. **d** 88 **p** 89. C Dawlish *Ex* 88-92; P-in-c Newton Poppleford w Harpford 92-94; V Newton Poppleford, Harpford and Colaton Raleigh from 94; RD Ottery from 96. *The Vicarage, Newton Poppleford, Sidmouth, Devon EX10 0HB* Tel (01395) 568390

BRIGNALL, Simon Francis Lyon. b 54. St Jo Coll Dur BA78. Wycliffe Hall Ox 80. **d** 83 **p** 84. C Colne St Bart *Blackb* 83-86; SAMS 86-96; Peru 86-96; P-in-c Tetsworth, Adwell w S Weston, Lewknor etc *Ox* from 96. *The Rectory, 46 High Street, Tetsworth, Oxford OX9 7AS* Tel (01844) 281267

BRIMICOMBE, Mark. b 44. Nottm Univ BA66 CertEd. SW Minl Tr Course 83. **d** 85 **p** 86. NSM Plympton St Mary *Ex* from 85. *4 David Close, Stoggy Lane, Plympton, Plymouth PL7 3BQ* Tel (01752) 338454

BRINDLE, John Harold. b 21. St Jo Coll Dur LTh42 BA43 MA46. St Aid Birkenhead 39. **d** 44 **p** 44. C Ashton-on-Ribble St Mich *Blackb* 44-47; C Sandylands 47-51; V Grimsargh 51-88; rtd 88; Perm to Offic *Blackb* from 88. *8 Sussex Drive, Garstang, Preston PR3 1ET* Tel (01995) 606588

BRINDLE, Peter John. b 47. MIStructE72. N Ord Course 78. **d** 81 **p** 82. NSM Bingley All SS *Bradf* 81-84; NSM Bingley H Trin 84-86; V Keighley All SS 86-91; V Kirkstall *Ripon* 91-96; V Beeston from 96. *Beeston Vicarage, 16 Town Street, Leeds LS11 8PN* Tel 0113-270 5529 or 277 1494

BRINDLEY, David Charles. b 53. K Coll Lon BD75 AKC75 MTh76 MPhil81. St Aug Coll Cant 75. **d** 76 **p** 77. C Epping St Jo *Chelmsf* 76-79; Lect Coll of SS Mary and Paul Cheltenham 79-82; Lic to Offic *Glouc* 79-82; Dioc Dir of Tr *Leic* 82-86; V Quorndon 82-86; Prin Glouc Sch for Min *Glouc* 87-92; Prin W of England Minl Tr Course 92-94; Dir of Minl Tr 87-94; Dioc Officer for NSM 88-94; Hon Can Glouc Cathl 92-94; TR Warwick *Cov* from 94. *St Mary's Vicarage, The Butts, Warwick CV34 4SS* Tel (01926) 492909

BRINDLEY, Canon Stuart Geoffrey Noel. b 30. St Jo Coll Dur BA53 DipTh55. **d** 55 **p** 56. C Newc St Anne *Newc* 55-58; C Tynemouth Cullercoats St Paul 58-60; C Killingworth 60-63; V Newsham 63-69; W Germany 69-76; Asst Master Wyvern Sch Weston-super-Mare 76-80; V Stocksbridge *Sheff* 80-88; RD Tankersley 85-88; V Rotherham 88-96; Hon Can Sheff Cathl 95-96; rtd 96. *Parasol, Back Crofts, Rothbury, Morpeth, Northd NE65 7XY* Tel (01669) 621472

BRINKWORTH, Christopher Michael Gibbs. b 41. Lanc Univ BA70. Kelham Th Coll 62. **d** 67 **p** 68. C Lancaster St Mary *Blackb* 67-70; C Milton *Portsm* 70-74; V Ault Hucknall *Derby* 74-84; V Derby St Anne and St Jo from 84. *The Vicarage, 25 Highfield Road, Derby DE22 1GX* Tel (01332) 32681

BRINSON, David Wayne Evans. b 32. Univ of Wales (Lamp) BA53 LTh55. **d** 55 **p** 56. C Tylorstown *Llan* 55-58; C Skewen 58-63; P-in-c Swansea St Jo *S & B* 63-82; V Llanrhidian w Llanmadoc and Cheriton 82-90; rtd 90. *Rosenberg, 157 Terrace Road, Mount Pleasant, Swansea SA1 6HU* Tel (01792) 474069

BRION, Martin Philip. b 33. Ex Univ BA55. Ridley Hall Cam 57. **d** 59 **p** 60. C Balderstone *Man* 59-62; C Morden *S'wark* 62-66; V Low Elswick *Newc* 66-73; P-in-c Giggleswick *Bradf* 73-77; V 77-80; V Camerton H Trin W Seaton *Carl* 80-86; V Dearham 86-95; rtd 95; Perm to Offic *Carl* from 95. *7 Falcon Place, Moresby Parks, Whitehaven, Cumbria CA28 8YF* Tel (01946) 691912

BRISCOE, Allen. b 42. Liv Univ BSc64 CertEd65. Coll of Resurr Mirfield 90. **d** 92 **p** 93. C Shiremoor *Newc* 92-95; V Barnsley St Pet and St Jo *Wakef* from 95. *The Vicarage, 1 Osborne Mews, Barnsley, S Yorkshire S70 1UU* Tel (01226) 282220

BRISCOE, Canon Frances Amelia. b 35. Univ of Wales CertEd55 Leeds Univ DipRE62 Man Univ BA71 MA74. Gilmore Course 74. **dss** 77 **d** 87 **p** 94. Gt Crosby St Luke *Liv* 77-81; Dioc Lay Min Adv 81-87; Chapl Liv Cathl 81-89; Dir Diaconal Mins 87-89; Lect St Deiniol's Minl Tr Scheme from 88; Hon Can Liv Cathl *Liv* from 88; AD Sefton from 89; Dir of Reader Studies from 89; D-in-c Hightown 92-94; P-in-c from 94. *St Stephen's Vicarage, St Stephen's Road, Liverpool L38 0BL* Tel 0151-926 2469

BRISCOE, Gordon Michael. b 24. Leeds Univ CertEd50. Ely Th Coll 51. **d** 53 **p** 54. C Isleworth St Fran *Lon* 53-54; Hon C 66-67; C Ealing Ch the Sav 54-57; W Germany 57-62; C Twickenham St Mary *Lon* 62-65; Chapl Fortescue Ho Sch Twickenham 62-65; Hon C Brookfield St Anne, Highgate Rise *Lon* 67-77; Hon C Paddington St Steph w St Luke 77-80; Hon C St Marylebone Annunciation Bryanston Street 80-83; Chapl Bedford Modern Sch 83-84; Hon Chapl 84-94; R Dunton w Wrestlingworth and Eyeworth *St Alb* 84-94; rtd 94. *59 Furland Road, Crewkerne, Somerset TA18 8DD* Tel (01460) 78812

BRISON, The Ven William Stanly (Bill). b 29. Alfred Univ NY BSc51 Connecticut Univ MDiv57 STM71. Berkeley Div Sch. **d** 57 **p** 57. USA 57-72; V Davyhulme Ch Ch *Man* 72-81; R Newton Heath All SS 81-85; AD N Man 81-85; Hon Can Man Cathl 82-85; Adn Bolton 85-92; TV E Farnworth and Kearsley 85-89; C Bolton St Thos 89-92; CMS 92-94; Nigeria 92-94; P-in-c Pendleton St Thos w Charlestown *Man* 94-95; TR Pendleton from 95. *Pendleton Rectory, 14 Eccles Old Road, Salford M6 7AF* Tel 0161-737 2107

BRISTOL, Archdeacon of. *See* BANFIELD, The Ven David John

BRISTOL, Bishop of. *See* ROGERSON, The Rt Revd Barry

BRISTOL, Dean of. *See* GRIMLEY, Robert William

BRISTOW, Arthur George Raymond. b 09. Lich Th Coll 32. **d** 35 **p** 36. C Longton St Mary and St Chad *Lich* 35-38; Perm to Offic *Roch* 38; Perm to Offic *Ox* 38-39 and 41; Perm to Offic *Lich* 39-40; C Sheff St Matt *Sheff* 41-43; V Saltley *Birm* 43-52; R Wednesbury St Jo *Lich* 52-57; V Willenhall St Steph 57-75; rtd 75; C Emscote *Cov* from 75; Perm to Offic *Lich* from 85. *41 Badgers Way, Heath Hayes, Cannock, Staffs WS12 5XQ* Tel (01543) 275530

BRISTOW, Keith Raymond Martin. b 56. Ex Univ BA78. Chich Th Coll 87. **d** 89 **p** 90. C Kirkby *Liv* 89-93; C Portsea St Mary *Portsm* from 93. *166 Shearer Road, Portsmouth PO1 5LS* Tel (01705) 820486

BRISTOW, Peter. b 49. Pontificium Institutum Internationale Angelicum Rome JCL77 St Jos Coll Upholland 67. **d** 72 **p** 73. In RC Ch 72-87; C Poplar *Lon* 89-92; Lay Tr Officer 89-90; TV Droitwich Spa *Worc* 92-94; TR from 94. *The Rectory, 29 Old Coach Road, Droitwich, Worcs WR9 8BB* Tel (01905) 772841

BRISTOW, Roger. b 60. Aston Tr Scheme 81 Ridley Hall Cam 83. **d** 86 **p** 87. C Leyton St Mary w St Edw *Chelmsf* 86-90; TV Kings Norton *Birm* from 90. *Immanuel Vicarage, 53 Wychall Park Grove, Birmingham B38 8AG* Tel 0121-458 1836 or 458 3289 Fax 486 2825

BRITT, Eric Stanley. b 47. St Jo Coll Nottm LTh74 BTh75. **d** 74 **p** 75. C Chorleywood Ch Ch *St Alb* 74-78; C Frimley *Guildf* 78-80; P-in-c Alresford *Chelmsf* 80-88; R Takeley w Lt Canfield 88-93; Asst Chapl R Free Hosp Lon 93-96; Chapl Mid Essex Hosp Services NHS Trust from 96. *The Chaplain's Office, Broomfield Hospital, Chelmsford CM1 5ET* Tel (01245) 514069

BRITTAIN, John. b 23. St Aug Coll Cant 59. **d** 60 **p** 61. C Heref St Martin *Heref* 60-62; V Highley 62-88; rtd 88. *Fosbrooke House, 8 Clifton Drive, Lytham, Lancs FY8 5RE*

BRITTON, John Anthony. b 39. Dur Univ BA60. Wycliffe Hall Ox 61. **d** 63 **p** 64. C Sheff St Swithun *Sheff* 63-64; C Sheff St Aid w St Luke 64-66; C Doncaster St Geo 66-68; C Grantham St Wulfram *Linc* 68-72; V Surfleet 72-76; V Bolsover *Derby* 76-86; V Harworth *S'well* from 86; RD Bawtry from 96. *The Vicarage, Tickhill Road, Harworth, Doncaster, S Yorkshire DN11 8PD* Tel (01302) 744157

BRITTON, John Timothy Hugh. b 50. Dundee Univ BSc73. Trin Coll Bris 73. **d** 76 **p** 77. C Cromer *Nor* 76-79; P-in-c Freethorpe w Wickhampton 79-82; P-in-c Beighton and Moulton 79-82; P-in-c Halvergate w Tunstall 79-82; CMS 82-89; Uganda 83-89; R Allesley *Cov* from 89. *The Rectory, Allesley, Coventry CV5 9EQ* Tel (01203) 402006

BRITTON, Canon Paul Anthony. b 29. SS Coll Cam BA52 MA57. Linc Th Coll 52. **d** 54 **p** 55. C Upper Norwood St Jo *Cant* 54-57; C Wantage *Ox* 57-61; V Stanmore *Win* 61-70; V Bitterne Park 70-80; Can Res Win Cathl 80-94; Lib 81-85; Treas 85-94; rtd 94. *Pemberton, High Street, Hindon, Salisbury SP3 6DR* Tel (01747) 820406

BRITTON, Robert. b 40. Univ of Wales DipTh64. St Mich Coll Llan 61. **d** 64 **p** 65. C Aberdare St Jo *Llan* 64-67; C Coity w Nolton 67-71; V Abercynon 71-75; V Tycoch *S & B* from 75; RD Clyne from 97. *The Vicarage, 26 Hendrefoilan Road, Swansea SA2 9LS* Tel (01792) 204476

BRITTON, Robert (Bob). b 37. Oak Hill Th Coll 78. **d** 79 **p** 80. C St Helens St Helen *Liv* 79-83; V Lowton St Mary from 83; AD Winwick from 89. *The Vicarage, 1 Barford Drive, St Mary's Park, Lowton, Warrington WA3 1DD* Tel (01942) 607705

BRITTON, Ronald George Adrian Michael (Robert). b 24. St D Coll Lamp 63 Lambeth STh82. **d** 82 **p** 82. Arabia 82-85; Chapl Alassio *Eur* 85-90 and 92-93; Chapl San Remo 86; Hon C Southbourne St Kath *Win* 90-92; rtd 96; Perm to Offic *Bris* from 97. *2 Cherry Tree Road, Bristol BS16 4EY* Tel 0117-965 5734

BRIXTON, Miss Corinne Jayne. b 63. Ex Univ BSc84. Wycliffe Hall Ox BTh95. **d** 95. C Leytonstone St Jo *Chelmsf* from 95. *86 Mornington Road, London E11 3DX* Tel 0181-539 3935

BRIXWORTH, Suffragan Bishop of. *See* BARBER, The Rt Revd Paul Everard

BROAD, David. b 59. Man Univ BA. Edin Th Coll. **d** 87 **p** 88. C Fulham All SS *Lon* 87-90; TV Clare w Poslingford, Cavendish etc *St E* 90-93; TV Totton *Win* from 93. *Eling Vicarage, Eling Hill, Totton, Southampton SO40 9HF* Tel (01703) 866426

BROAD, Hugh Duncan. b 37. Lich Th Coll 64. **d** 67 **p** 68. C Heref H Trin *Heref* 67-72; Asst Master Bp's Sch Heref 72-73; C Fareham SS Pet and Paul *Portsm* 74-76; V Heref All SS *Heref* 76-90; R Matson *Glouc* 90-97; V Glouc St Geo w Whaddon from 97. *St George's Vicarage, Grange Road, Tuffley, Gloucester GL4 0PE* Tel (01452) 520851 or 0831-808349 (Mobile)

BROAD, Hugh Robert. b 49. St Mich Coll Llan 67. **d** 72 **p** 73. C Tenby w Gumfreston *St D* 72-75; C Caerau w Ely *Llan* 75-79; V Llanharan w Peterston-super-Montem 79-89; RD Bridgend 88-89; Ex-Paroch Officer 90; V Whatborough Gp of Par *Leic* from 90. *The Vicarage, Oakham Road, Tilton on the Hill, Leicester LE7 9LB* Tel 0116-259 7244

BROAD, William Ernest Lionel. b 40. Ridley Hall Cam 64. **d** 66 **p** 67. C Ecclesfield *Sheff* 66-69; Chapl HM Pris Wormwood Scrubs 69; Chapl HM Pris Albany 70-74; Chapl HM Rem Cen Risley 74-76; V Ditton St Mich *Liv* 76-81; TR 82-83; P-in-c Mayland *Chelmsf* 83-91; P-in-c Steeple 83-91; V Blackhall *Dur* from 91. *The Vicarage, Blackhall, Hartlepool, Cleveland TS27 4LE* Tel 0191-586 4202

BROADBENT, Mrs Doreen. b 36. Local Minl Tr Course 91. **d** 94 **p** 95. NSM Stalybridge *Man* from 94. *Lynford Cottage, Chamberlain Road, Heyrod, Stalybridge, Cheshire SK15 3BS* Tel 0161-303 0501

BROADBENT, Edward Ronald. b 23. Man Univ BSc44. Westcott Ho Cam 53. **d** 55 **p** 56. C Runcorn St Mich *Ches* 55-59; C Ches St Pet 59-62; Youth Chapl 59-62; V Bredbury St Mark 62; SPCK

Staff 63-87; Hon C Wilton w Netherhampton and Fugglestone *Sarum* 78-80; P-in-c S Newton 80-83; Hon C Chalke Valley W 84-91; rtd 88; Perm to Offic *Sarum* from 92. *2 Marlborough Road, Salisbury SP1 3TH* Tel (01722) 326809

BROADBENT, Hugh Patrick Colin. b 53. Selw Coll Cam BA75 MA. Wycliffe Hall Ox DipTh78. **d** 78 **p** 79. C Chatham St Steph *Roch* 78-82; C Shortlands 82-84; C Edenbridge 84-87; C Crockham Hill H Trin 84-87; V Bromley H Trin from 87; Chapl St Olave's Gr Sch Orpington from 95. *Holy Trinity Vicarage, Church Lane, Bromley BR2 8LB* Tel 0181-462 1280

BROADBENT, Neil Seton. b 53. Qu Coll Birm DipTh80. **d** 81 **p** 82. C Knaresborough *Ripon* 81-84; C Leeds Gipton Epiphany 84-87; Lic to Offic 87-89; Chapl Minstead Community *Derby* 89; Perm to Offic from 89; Dir Sozein from 93. *The Old Vicarage, Church Lane, Horsley Woodhouse, Ilkeston, Derbyshire DE7 6BB* Tel (01332) 780598

BROADBENT, Paul John. b 41. Oak Hill Th Coll DipTh83. **d** 85 **p** 86. C Duston *Pet* 85-88; TV Ross w Brampton Abbotts, Bridstow and Peterstow *Heref* 88-91; R Pattishall w Cold Higham and Gayton w Tiffield *Pet* from 91. *The Vicarage, Pattishall, Towcester, Northants NN12 8NB* Tel (01327) 830043

BROADBENT, The Ven Peter Alan (Pete). b 52. Jes Coll Cam BA74 MA78. St Jo Coll Nottm DipTh75. **d** 77 **p** 78. C Dur St Nic *Dur* 77-80; C Holloway Em w Hornsey Road St Barn *Lon* 80-83; Chapl N Lon Poly 83-89; Hon C Islington St Mary 83-89; V Harrow Trin St Mich 89-94; AD Harrow 94; Adn Northolt from 95. *247 Kenton Road, Harrow, Middx HA3 0HQ* Tel 0181-907 5941 Fax 909 2368

BROADBENT, Ralph Andrew. b 55. K Coll Lon BD76 AKC76. Chich Th Coll 77. **d** 78 **p** 79. C Prestwich St Mary *Man* 78-82; R Man Miles Platting 82-84; CF 84-87; TV Wordsley *Lich* 88-93; Chapl Wordsley and Ridge Hill Hosps 88-93; V Wollescote *Worc* from 93. *The Vicarage, Oakfield Road, Stourbridge, W Midlands DY9 9DG* Tel (01384) 422695

BROADBENT, Thomas William. b 45. Chu Coll Cam BA66 MA70 PhD70. Ridley Hall Cam 75. **d** 78 **p** 79. C Allington and Maidstone St Pet *Cant* 78-82; Chapl Mid Kent Coll of H&FE 80-82; C Kings Heath *Birm* 82-84; Hon C Pendleton St Thos *Man* 84-89; TV Pendleton St Thos w Charlestown 89-92; Chapl Salford Univ 84-92; Chmn Man Coun of Chr and Jews 89-92; R Claydon and Barham *St E* from 92; Chapl Suffolk Coll of HE from 92. *The Rectory, 7 Back Lane, Claydon, Ipswich IP6 0EB* Tel (01473) 830362

BROADBERRY, Canon Richard St Lawrence. b 31. TCD BA53 BD59 MLitt66. **d** 54 **p** 55. C Dublin St Thos *D & G* 54-56; C Dublin Grangegorman 56-62; Min Can St Patr Cathl Dublin 58-62; Hon Clerical V Ch Ch Cathl Dublin *D & G* 62-64; C Dublin Clontarf 62-64; C Thornton Heath St Jude *Cant* 64-66; V Norwood All SS 66-82; RD Croydon N 81-84; Hon Can Cant Cathl 82-84; V Upper Norwood All SS w St Marg 82-84; Hon Can S'wark Cathl *S'wark* from 85; RD Croydon N 85; V Merton St Mary 85-92; V Riddlesdown from 92. *St James's Vicarage, 1B St James's Road, Purley, Surrey CR8 2DL* Tel 0181-660 5436

BROADHEAD, Dr Alan John. b 38. Lon Univ MD62. Cuddesdon Coll 65. **d** 66 **p** 67. C Willenhall H Trin *Lich* 66-68; USA from 71. *517 Third Avenue SE, Jamestown, North Dakota, 58401, USA*

✠**BROADHURST, The Rt Revd John Charles.** b 42. AKC65. Lambeth STh82. **d** 66 **p** 67. C Southgate St Mich *Lon* 66-70; C Wembley Park St Aug 70-73; P-in-c 73-75; V 75-85; AD Brent 82-85; TR Wood Green St Mich w Bounds Green St Gabr etc 85-96; AD E Haringey 85-91; Suff Bp Fulham from 96. *26 Canonbury Park South, London N1 2FN* Tel 0171-354 2334 Fax 354 2335

BROADHURST, John James. b 08. Birm Univ BA31. **d** 32 **p** 33. C Heckmondwike *Wakef* 32-37; V Shelley 37-42; V Newton in Makerfield St Pet *Liv* 42-59; Chapl Red Bank Schs 43-59; R S Hill w Callington *Truro* 59-73; rtd 73. *18 Monmouth Gardens, Beaminster, Dorset DT8 3BT* Tel (01308) 862509

BROADHURST, Jonathan Robin. b 58. Univ Coll Ox BA81 MA86. Wycliffe Hall Ox 85. **d** 88 **p** 89. C Hull Newland St Jo *York* 88-91; P-in-c Burton Fleming w Fordon, Grindale etc 91-92; V from 92. *The Vicarage, Back Street, Burton Fleming, Driffield, N Humberside YO25 0RD* Tel (01262) 470668

BROADHURST, Kenneth. b 33. Lon Coll of Div 56. **d** 59 **p** 60. C Bucknall and Bagnall *Lich* 59-63; R Rodington 63-67; V Longdon-upon-Tern 63-67; R Clitheroe St Jas *Blackb* 67-82; V Leyland St Andr 82-88; rtd 89; Perm to Offic *Blackb* from 89. *Paris House, 12 Ramsgreave Road, Ramsgreave, Blackburn BB1 9BH* Tel (01254) 240924

BROADLEY, Michael John. b 66. Roehampton Inst BA87. Trin Coll Bris 93. **d** 96 **p** 97. C Egham *Guildf* from 96. *33 Grange Road, Egham, Surrey TW20 9QP* Tel (01784) 434137

BROCK, Michael John. b 52. Birm Univ BSc74 Nottm Univ BA77. St Jo Coll Nottm 75. **d** 78 **p** 79. C Stapleford *S'well* 78-82; C Bestwood St Matt 82-86; TV Bestwood 86-90; R Epperstone from 90; R Gonalston from 90; V Oxton from 90; RD S'well 93-96; Dioc Adv in Rural Affairs from 97. *The Rectory, Main Street, Epperstone, Notts NG14 6AG* Tel 0115-966 4220

BROCK, Preb Patrick Laurence. b 18. MBE45. Trin Coll Ox BA46 MA48. Ripon Hall Ox 55. **d** 57 **p** 58. C Gt Malvern St Mary *Worc* 57-59; C St Martin-in-the-Fields *Lon* 59-62; V Belsize Park 62-72; R Finchley St Mary 72-89; Preb St Paul's Cathl 80-89; AD Cen Barnet 80-85; rtd 89; Perm to Offic *Lon* from 89. *10 Albert Street, London NW1 7NZ* Tel 0171-383 0198

BROCKBANK, Arthur Ross. b 51. Wigan Coll of Tech BTEC ND85. N Ord Course 87. **d** 90 **p** 91. C Haughton St Mary *Man* 90-93; V Bircle from 93; Chapl Fairfield Gen Hosp Bury from 93. *The Vicarage, 33 Castle Hill Road, Bury, Lancs BL9 7RW* Tel 0161-764 3853

BROCKBANK, Donald Philip. b 56. Univ of Wales (Ban) BD78. Sarum & Wells Th Coll 79. **d** 81 **p** 82. C Prenton *Ches* 81-85; TV Birkenhead Priory 85-91; V Altrincham St Jo 91-96; Urban Officer 91-96; Dioc Ecum Officer *Lich* from 96; C Lich St Mary w St Mich 96; C Lich St Mich w St Mary and Wall from 96. *66 Heritage Court, Lichfield, Staffs WS14 9ST*

BROCKBANK, John Keith. b 44. Dur Univ BA65. Wells Th Coll 66. **d** 68 **p** 69. C Preston St Matt *Blackb* 68-71; C Lancaster St Mary 71-73; V Habergham All SS 73-83; P-in-c Gannow 81-83; V W Burnley 83-86; Dioc Stewardship Adv 86-92; P-in-c Shireshead 86-92; V Kirkham from 92. *The Vicarage, Kirkham, Preston PR4 2SE* Tel (01772) 683644

BROCKBANK, Leslie David. b 35. St Aid Birkenhead 60. **d** 63 **p** 64. C Corby SS Pet and Andr *Pet* 63-66; C Darley w S Darley *Derby* 66-72; New Zealand from 72. *RD 1, Maungaturoto, New Zealand* Tel Auckland (9) 431 8855

BROCKHOUSE, Grant Lindley. b 47. Adelaide Univ BA71 Ex Univ MA81. St Barn Coll Adelaide 70 ACT ThL72. **d** 73 **p** 74. Australia 73-78; C Ex St Jas *Ex* 78-80; Asst Chapl Ex Univ 80-83; Dep PV Ex Cathl from 81; V Marldon from 83. *The Vicarage, 1 Love Lane Close, Marldon, Paignton, Devon TQ3 1TH* Tel (01803) 557294

BROCKIE, William James Thomson. b 36. Pemb Coll Ox BA58 MA62. Linc Th Coll 58. **d** 60 **p** 61. C Lin St Jo Bapt CD *Linc* 60-63; V Gt Staughton *Ely* 63-68; Chapl HM Youth Cust Cen Gaynes Hall 63-68; TV Edin St Jo *Edin* 68-76; Chapl Edin Univ 71-76; USA 76; R Edin St Martin *Edin* from 76; P-in-c Edin St Luke 79-90. *15 Ardmillan Terrace, Edinburgh EH11 2JW* Tel 0131-337 5493 or 337 9714

BROCKLEBANK, John. b 32. N Ord Course 83. **d** 86 **p** 87. NSM Warrington St Barn *Liv* 86-93; NSM Orford St Marg from 93. *55 St Mary's Road, Penketh, Warrington WA5 2DT* Tel (01925) 722398

BROCKLEHURST, John Richard. b 51. Univ Coll Ox BA72 Lon Univ CertEd74. Oak Hill Th Coll BA81. **d** 81 **p** 82. C Harwood *Man* 81-85; V Hopwood 85-97; P-in-c Friarmere from 97. *The Vicarage, 1 Cobler's Hill, Delph, Oldham OL3 5HT* Tel (01457) 874209

BROCKLEHURST, Simon. b 63. Cranmer Hall Dur 86. **d** 89 **p** 90. C Clifton *S'well* 89-93; TV 93-96; P-in-c Mabe *Truro* from 96; Miss to Seamen from 96. *The Vicarage, Church Road, Mabe, Penryn, Cornwall TR10 9HN* Tel (01326) 373201

BRODDLE, Christopher Stephen Thomas. b 57. **d** 87 **p** 88. C Lisburn St Paul *Conn* 87-90; CF from 90. *MOD Chaplains (Army), Trenchard Lines, Upavon, Pewsey, Wilts SN9 6BE* Tel (01980) 615804 Fax 615800

BRODIE, Frederick. b 40. Leic Teacher Tr Coll TCert61. St Jo Coll Nottm DCM92. **d** 92 **p** 93. C Lutterworth w Cotesbach *Leic* 92-95; P-in-c Mountsorrel Ch Ch and St Pet 95-97; V from 97. *Christ Church Vicarage, 4 Rothley Road, Loughborough, Leics LE12 7JU* Tel 0116-230 2235

BRODY, Paul. b 40. N Ord Course 85. **d** 88 **p** 89. C Leigh St Mary *Man* 88-90; C Peel 90-91; TR from 91. *The Rectory, 122 Peel Lane, Worsley, Manchester M28 6FL* Tel 0161-790 4202

BROGGIO, Canon Bernice Muriel Croager. b 35. Bedf Coll Lon BA57 K Coll Lon BD66 IDC66 Glas Univ DSocStuds71 DASS72. K Coll Lon 63. **dss** 84 **d** 87 **p** 94. Bris St Paul w St Barn *Bris* 84-87; Hon Par Dn Bris St Paul's 87-88; C Charlton St Luke w H Trin *S'wark* 88-95; Hon Can S'wark Cathl from 95; V Upper Tooting H Trin from 95; RD Tooting from 96. *Holy Trinity Vicarage, 14 Upper Tooting Park, London SW17 7SW* Tel 0181-672 4790

BROMAGE, Kenneth Charles. b 51. EAMTC. **d** 90 **p** 91. NSM Woolpit w Drinkstone *St E* 90-92; Chapl RN from 92. *Royal Naval Chaplaincy Service, Room 203, Victory Building, HM Naval Base, Portsmouth PO1 3LS* Tel (01705) 727903 Fax 727112

BROMFIELD, Michael. b 32. Kelham Th Coll 54 Lich Th Coll 59. **d** 62 **p** 63. C Sedgley All SS *Lich* 62-64; C Tunstall Ch Ch 64-67; P-in-c Grindon 67-70; R 70-80; P-in-c Butterton 67-70; V 70-80; R Hope Bowdler w Eaton-under-Heywood *Heref* from 80; R Rushbury from 80; V Cardington from 80. *The Rectory, Hope Bowdler, Church Stretton, Shropshire SY6 7DD* Tel (01694) 722918

BROMFIELD, Richard Allan. b 47. Chich Th Coll 86. **d** 88 **p** 89. C Durrington *Chich* 88-95; V Woodingdean from 95. *The Vicarage, 2 Downsway, Brighton BN2 6BD* Tel (01273) 681582

BROMIDGE, Robert Harold. b 28. K Coll Lon BD52 AKC52. **d** 53 **p** 54. C Sheff St Cuth *Sheff* 53-56; C Mexborough 56-59; V Dalton 59-61; Min Arbourthorne CD 61-70; Lic to Offic from 71; rtd 88. *4 Barnfield Close, Sheffield S10 5TF* Tel 0114-230 7889

BROMILEY, Paul Nigel. b 49. Univ of Wales (Cardiff) BSc71. Oak Hill Th Coll 88. **d** 90 **p** 91. C Gee Cross *Ches* 90-94; P-in-c

Millbrook from 94. *St James's Vicarage, 28 Buckton Vale Road, Stalybridge, Cheshire SK15 3LW* Tel (01457) 833295

BROMLEY, Mrs Janet Catherine Gay. b 45. Surrey Univ BSc68 Bradf Univ MSc72 Brunel Tech Coll Bris FETC86. S Dios Minl Tr Scheme 91. **d** 94 **p** 96. C Westbury-on-Trym H Trin *Bris* 94-96; C Wroughton from 96. *21 Anthony Road, Wroughton, Swindon SN4 9HN* Tel (01793) 813929

BROMLEY, William James. b 44. Edin Univ BD74. Edin Th Coll 70. **d** 74 **p** 75. C Glas St Mary *Glas* 74-77; Bangladesh 77-80; R Glas H Cross *Glas* 80-89; R Stottesdon w Farlow, Cleeton and Silvington *Heref* from 89. *The Rectory, Stottesdon, Kidderminster, Worcs DY14 8UE* Tel (0174632) 297

BROMLEY, Archdeacon of. *See* NORMAN, The Ven Garth

BROMWICH, Edmund Eustace. b 15. Bris Univ BA35 St Cath Soc Ox BA39 MA43 TCD MA50. Ripon Hall Ox 37. **d** 40 **p** 41. C Barnehurst *Roch* 40-41; C Bexleyheath Ch Ch 41-43; Lic Preacher *Ox* 43-45; Perm to Offic *Bris* 43-45; Argentina 45-49; Asst Master Wanstrow w Cloford *B & W* 49-57; Tutor Brighton Coll 57-61; Lic to Offic *Chich* 57-61; Lic to Offic *Ex* 61-64; Chapl and Asst Master Chilton Cantelo Ho 64-67; Asst Master St Hilary Sch Alderley 67-80; Lic to Offic *Ches* from 68; rtd 80. *5B London Road, Alderley Edge, Cheshire SK9 7JT* Tel (01625) 585366

BRONNERT, Preb David Llewellyn Edward. b 36. Ch Coll Cam BA57 MA61 PhD61 Lon Univ BD62. Tyndale Hall Bris 60. **d** 63 **p** 64. C Cheadle Hulme St Andr *Ches* 63-67; C Islington St Mary *Lon* 67-69; Chapl N Lon Poly 69-75; V Southall Green St Jo from 75; Preb St Paul's Cathl from 89; P-in-c Southall St Geo from 92; AD Ealing W 84-90. *St John's Vicarage, Church Avenue, Southall, Middx UB2 4DH* Tel 0181-574 2055

BRONNERT, John. b 33. FCA57 Lon Univ DipTh68 Man Univ MA(Theol)84. Tyndale Hall Bris 65. **d** 68 **p** 69. C Hoole *Ches* 68-71; P-in-c Parr *Liv* 71-73; TV 73-85; V Runcorn St Jo Weston *Ches* from 85; Perm to Offic *Liv* from 85. *The Vicarage, 225 Heath Road South, Weston, Runcorn, Cheshire WA7 4LY* Tel (01928) 573798

BROOK, Kathleen Marjorie. b 23. IDC. Lightfoot Ho Dur 57. **dss** 66 **d** 87 **p** 94. Linthorpe *York* 66-75; Ormesby 75-83; rtd 83. *6 Station Square, Saltburn-by-the-Sea, Cleveland TS12 1AG* Tel (01287) 624006

BROOK, Peter Geoffrey (Brother Simon). b 47. N Ord Course 91. **d** 94 **p** 95. CGA from 71; NSM Heywood and Middleton Deanery 94-96. *The Priory, Lamacraft Farm, Start Point, Chivelstone, Kingsbridge, Devon TQ7 2NG* Tel (01548) 511474

BROOK, Stephen Edward. b 44. Univ of Wales (Abth) BSc65 DipEd66 Lisbon Univ 89. Wycliffe Hall Ox 71 All Nations Chr Coll 85. **d** 74 **p** 75. C Heworth *York* 74-77; C Linthorpe 77-80; TV Deane *Man* 80-85; BCMS 86-93; Crosslinks 93-96; Portugal 88-96; P-in-c Bacup St Sav *Man* from 96. *St Saviour's Vicarage, 10 Park Crescent, Bacup, Lancs OL13 9RL* Tel (01706) 873362

BROOK, William Neville. b 31. S'wark Ord Course 66. **d** 69 **p** 70. C Maidstone St Martin *Cant* 69-75; V Hartlip w Stockbury 75-80; R Willesborough w Hinxhill 80-86; R Willesborough 87-89; V Gt Staughton *Ely* 89-96; V Hail Weston 89-96; rtd 96; Perm to Offic *Chich* from 96. *27 Middleton Drive, Eastbourne, E Sussex BN23 6HD* Tel (01323) 731243

BROOKE, Miss Bridget Cecilia. b 31. DBO51. Coll of Resurr Mirfield 88. **d** 89 **p** 94. Hon Par Dn Ranmoor *Sheff* 89-94; Hon C from 94; Bp's Officer for NSMs from 94. *166 Tom Lane, Sheffield S10 3PG* Tel 0114-230 2147

BROOKE, Michael Zachery. b 21. G&C Coll Cam BA43 MA46. Cuddesdon Coll 46. **d** 48 **p** 49. C Attercliffe w Carbrook *Sheff* 48-51; Ind Chapl 51-57; R Old Trafford St Cuth *Man* 57-63; rtd 86. *21 Barnfield, Urmston, Manchester M31 1EW* Tel 0161-746 8140

BROOKE, Robert. b 44. Birm Univ DPS77. Qu Coll Birm 70. **d** 73 **p** 74. C Man Resurr *Man* 73-76; C Bournville *Birm* 76-77; Chapl Qu Eliz Coll *Lon* 77-82; C Bramley *Ripon* 82-85; TV 85-86; V Hunslet Moor St Pet and St Cuth 86-93; Community Chapl for Mental Handicap 86-93; C Seacroft from 93; Chapl People w Learning Disabilities from 93. *51 St James's Approach, Leeds LS14 6JJ* Tel 0113-273 1396

BROOKE, Rosemary Jane. b 53. Cam Univ BEd75 Open Univ BA83. N Ord Course 86. **d** 89 **p** 94. NSM Poynton *Ches* from 89. *45 Brookfield Avenue, Poynton, Stockport, Cheshire SK12 1JE* Tel (01625) 872822

BROOKE, Timothy Cyril. b 38. Jes Coll Cam BA60 MA70 Middx Poly CQSW76. Ripon Coll Cuddesdon 84. **d** 86 **p** 87. C Hillmorton *Cov* 86-90; V Earlsdon from 90. *St Barbara's Vicarage, 24 Rochester Road, Coventry CV5 6AG* Tel (01203) 674057

BROOKE, Vernon. b 41. St Aid Birkenhead 62. **d** 65 **p** 66. C Crofton Park St Hilda w St Cypr *S'wark* 65-68; C Eccleshill *Bradf* 68-70; Ind Chapl *Linc* 70-84; Ind Chapl *Derby* 84-97; Ind Chapl *Chich* from 97. *52 Brangwyn Drive, Patcham, Brighton BN1 8XD* Tel (01273) 540316

BROOKE, Canon William Edward. b 13. Birm Univ BA34 MA35. Westcott Ho Cam 35. **d** 37 **p** 38. C Wylde Green *Birm* 37-40; C Sparkbrook St Agatha 40-44; P-in-c Birm St Jude 44-50; V 50-60; R Castle Bromwich SS Mary and Marg 60-78; Hon Can Birm Cathl 61-78; rtd 78; Perm to Offic *Heref* from 78. *Ivy Cottage, Tarrington, Hereford HR1 4HZ* Tel (01432) 890357

BROOKER, Mrs Wendy Ann. b 41. St Alb Minl Tr Scheme 82. **dss** 85 **d** 87 **p** 94. Pinner *Lon* 85-87; Greenhill St Jo 87; Par Dn 87-88; Ind Chapl 89-94; NSM Hayes St Edm 94; C from 95. *19 Wimborne Avenue, Hayes, Middx UB4 0HG* Tel 0181-561 6933

BROOKES, Arthur George. b 21. ACIB52. Worc Ord Coll 64. **d** 66 **p** 67. C Lower Mitton *Worc* 66-67; C Fladbury w Throckmorton, Wyre Piddle and Moor 67-70; C Abberton w Bishampton 67-70; R 70-73; V Cradley 73-78; P-in-c Castle Morton 78-79; P-in-c Holly Bush w Birtsmorton 78-79; P-in-c Castlemorton, Hollybush and Birtsmorton 79-80; P-in-c Norton w Whittington 80-81; TV Worc St Martin w St Pet, St Mark etc 81-86; rtd 86; Perm to Offic *Worc* from 86; Perm to Offic *Glouc* from 96. *9 Bredon Lodge, Main Road, Bredon, Tewkesbury, Glos GL20 7LT* Tel (01684) 772338

BROOKES, David Charles. b 45. St Mich Coll Llan 84. **d** 86 **p** 87. C Llanishen and Lisvane *Llan* 86-88; TV Brighouse St Martin *Wakef* 89-92; TV Brighouse and Clifton 92-94; V Hollingbourne and Hucking w Leeds and Broomfield *Cant* from 94. *The Vicarage, Hollingbourne, Maidstone, Kent ME17 1UJ* Tel (01622) 880243

BROOKES, Derrick Meridyth. b 17. Trin Hall Cam BA38 MA42. Westcott Ho Cam 39. **d** 40 **p** 41. C Macclesfield St Mich *Ches* 40-44; Chapl RAFVR 44-46; C Wilmslow *Ches* 47-49; V Chipping Sodbury and Old Sodbury *Glouc* 49-53; Youth Chapl 51-53; Chapl RAF 53-71. *Woodpeckers, Pilcorn Street, Wedmore, Somerset BS28 4AW* Tel (01934) 712352

BROOKES, Geoffrey John Denis. b 24. CMS Tr Coll Crowther Hall 78 Ridley Hall Cam 84. **d** 85 **p** 86. Bahrain 85-88; Project Officer Ch Action w the Unemployed 88-91; Hon C Hastings All So *Chich* 88-91; Asst Chapl Milan w Genoa and Varese *Eur* 91-94; Canada from 94. *c/o Bertling, 226 Jane Street, PO Box 390, Rodney, Ontario, Canada, N0L 2C0* Tel Ontario (519) 785 2329

BROOKES, Keith Roy. b 37. St Aid Birkenhead 64. **d** 80 **p** 81. Hon C Stockport St Thos *Ches* 80-86; Hon C Stockport St Thos w St Pet 86-91; C from 91. *42 Derby Road, Stockport, Cheshire SK4 4NE* Tel 0161-442 0307

BROOKES, Robin Keenan. b 47. Trin Coll Bris 72. **d** 75 **p** 76. C Livesey *Blackb* 75-78; C Burnley St Pet 78-80; P-in-c Bawdeswell w Foxley *Nor* 80-83; I Donagh w Tyholland and Errigal Truagh *Clogh* 83-91; RD Monaghan 86-91; Dioc Info Officer 90-91; I Dublin Drumcondra w N Strand *D & G* from 91. *74 Grace Park Road, Drumcondra, Dublin 9, Irish Republic* Tel Dublin (1) 837 2505 Mobile 088-642973 Fax 837 0204 E-mail rbrookes @connect.ie

BROOKES, Steven David. b 60. Lanc Univ BA81. Ripon Coll Cuddesdon 82. **d** 85 **p** 86. C Stanley *Liv* 85-88; C W Derby St Mary 88-90; Chapl RN 90-94; R Weybridge *Guildf* from 94. *The Rectory, 3 Churchfields Avenue, Weybridge, Surrey KT13 9YA* Tel (01932) 842566

BROOKFIELD, Patricia Anne. b 50. St Mary's Coll Dur BA72. Cranmer Hall Dur DipTh73 MA74. **dss** 84 **d** 87 **p** 94. Kingston upon Hull St Nic *York* 84-86; Acomb St Steph 86-87; Par Dn 87-94; C 94-96; TV Preston Risen Lord *Blackb* from 96. *St Mary's Vicarage, St Mary's Close, Preston PR1 4XN* Tel (01772) 794222

BROOKHOUSE, Leslie. b 28. Ridley Hall Cam 69 St Aid Birkenhead 68. **d** 70 **p** 71. C Tonge *Man* 70-72; C Didsbury Ch Ch 72-74; V Newall Green 74-80; V High Crompton 80-86; R Ashwater, Halwill, Beaworthy, Clawton etc *Ex* from 86; RD Holsworthy from 94. *The Rectory, Ashwater, Beaworthy, Devon EX21 5EZ* Tel (01409) 211205

BROOKS, Andrew Richard. b 44. Leeds Univ BA Birm Poly PGCE DipInstAM. Qu Coll Birm 83. **d** 86 **p** 87. C Olton *Birm* 86-87; C Sheldon 87-89; V Erdington St Chad from 89. *St Chad's Vicarage, 10 Shepherd's Green Road, Birmingham B24 8EX* Tel 0121-373 3915 or 373 8984

BROOKS, Mrs Christine Ellen. b 43. Sheff Univ BA65 Lon Univ BD81. Lambeth STh81 EAMTC 86. **d** 88 **p** 94. NSM Palgrave w Wortham and Burgate *St E* 88-89; Par Dn Thorndon w Rishangles, Stoke Ash, Thwaite etc 89-94; P-in-c Aldringham w Thorpe, Knodishall w Buxlow etc from 94. *The Rectory, Friston, Saxmundham, Suffolk IP17 1NP* Tel (01728) 688972

BROOKS, Edward Charles. b 18. Leeds Univ PhD71. Coll of Resurr Mirfield 42. **d** 44 **p** 45. C Bushey *St Alb* 44-46; C Hove St Barn *Chich* 46-48; C Epsom St Barn *Guildf* 48-52; R Elsing w Bylaugh *Nor* 52-57; V Thetford St Cuth w H Trin 57-69; RD Thetford 58-68; P-in-c Herringfleet 69-83; R Somerleyton w Ashby 69-83; rtd 83; Perm to Offic *St E* from 83. *Wheelwrights, Thorpe Morieux, Bury St Edmunds, Suffolk IP30 0NR* Tel (01284) 828353

BROOKS, Canon Francis Leslie. b 35. Kelham Th Coll 55. **d** 59 **p** 60. C Woodlands *Sheff* 59-61; Ind Missr S Yorkshire Coalfields 61-66; V Moorends 66-72; Chapl HM Borstal Hatf 67-72; Chapl HM Pris Acklington 72-75; Chapl HM Borstal Wellingborough 75-79; Chapl HM Pris Wakef 79-83; Area Sec (Dios Wakef and Bradf) USPG 83-88; V Carleton *Wakef* 88-96; V E Hardwick 88-96; Can Mara (Tanzania) from 88; rtd 96. *6 Long Meadows,*

Stainland Road, Barkisland, Halifax, W Yorkshire HX4 0AR Tel (01422) 822339

BROOKS, Henry Craven. b 12. CITC 62. **d** 64 **p** 65. C Dublin St Michan w St Paul and St Mary *D & G* 64-67; I Dunlavin w Ballymore Eustace and Hollywood 67-85; rtd 85; Lic to Offic *D & G* from 87. *9 Orwell Court, Braemor Road, Churchtown, Dublin 14, Irish Republic* Tel Dublin (1) 298 5659

BROOKS, Ian George. b 47. Selw Coll Cam BA68 MA72. Chich Th Coll 68. **d** 70 **p** 71. C Stoke Newington St Mary *Lon* 70-74; C Hoxton St Anne w St Sav and St Andr 74-75; C Hoxton St Anne w St Columba 75-80; P-in-c Croxteth St Paul CD *Liv* 80-81; V Croxteth from 81. *St Paul's Vicarage, Delabole Road, Liverpool L11 6LG* Tel 0151-548 9009

BROOKS, Jeremy. **d** 97. C Highgate St Mich *Lon* from 97. *17 Bisham Gardens, London N6 6DJ* Tel 0181-340 7676

BROOKS, John Cowell. b 09. St Jo Coll Cam BA31 MA35. Coll of Resurr Mirfield 46. **d** 47 **p** 48. C Northolt Park St Barn *Lon* 47-54; Vice-Prin Cuddesdon Coll 54-61; N Rhodesia 61-64; Zambia 64-71; Lic to Offic *Cant* 71-74; Chapl Dover Coll 71-74; R Northbourne, Tilmanstone w Betteshanger and Ham *Cant* 74-86; rtd 86; Perm to Offic *Cant* from 86. *3 Mill Road, Deal, Kent CT14 9AB* Tel (01304) 367961

BROOKS, Jonathan Thorburn. b 53. Solicitor 76 G&C Coll Cam BA75 DipHE. Trin Coll Bris 84. **d** 86 **p** 87. C Dagenham *Chelmsf* 86-88. *12 Hyde Avenue, Thornbury, Bristol BS12 1JA* Tel (01454) 411853

BROOKS, Canon Joseph (Joe). b 27. Univ Coll Dur BA53. St Aid Birkenhead 52. **d** 54 **p** 55. C Birch St Agnes *Man* 54-56; C Davyhulme St Mary 57-59; R Oldham St Andr 59-65; V Ipswich St Fran *St E* 65-75; R Freston w Woolverstone 75-76; P-in-c Holbrook and Stutton 75-76; R Holbrook w Freston and Woolverstone 76-82; R Horringer cum Ickworth 82-88; Chapl Ipswich Hosp 88-92; Hon Can St E Cathl *St E* 90-92; rtd 92. *289 Henley Road, Ipswich IP1 6TB* Tel (01473) 748245

BROOKS, Malcolm David. b 45. Univ of Wales (Lamp) DipTh71. **d** 71 **p** 72. C Pontlottyn w Fochriw *Llan* 71-72; C Caerphilly 72-78; V Ferndale w Maerdy 78-81; C Port Talbot St Theodore 82-84; V Ystrad Mynach 84-85; V Ystrad Mynach w Llanbradach from 85. *The Vicarage, Nelson Road, Ystrad Mynach, Hengoed CF82 7EG* Tel (01443) 813246

BROOKS, Neville Charles Wood. b 16. Bps' Coll Cheshunt 50. **d** 53 **p** 54. C Whitburn *Dur* 53-56; C-in-c Kimblesworth 56-61; V Rastrick St Jo *Wakef* 61-63; C S Kirkby 63-66; R Gilmorton w Peatling Parva *Leic* 66-86; R Gilmorton w Peatling Parva and Kimcote etc 86; rtd 86. *1 Cherry Tree Walk, Southam, Leamington Spa, Warks CV33 0EF*

BROOKS, Patrick John. b 27. Man Univ BA49 DipEd. Oak Hill Th Coll 78. **d** 77 **p** 79. Burundi 77-80; Perm to Offic *Ex* 80-83; P-in-c Phillack w Gwithian and Gwinear *Truro* 83-88; R 88-93; rtd 93; Perm to Offic *Chich* from 93. *Abbots, Claigmar Road, Rustington, Littlehampton, W Sussex BN16 2NL*

BROOKS, Paul John. b 59. Loughb Univ BSc81 DTS89 DPS90. St Jo Coll Nottm 87. **d** 90 **p** 91. C Long Eaton St Jo *Derby* 90-94; Min Jersey St Paul Prop Chpl *Win* from 94. *5 Claremont Avenue, St Saviour, Jersey, Channel Islands JE2 7SF* Tel (01534) 880393

BROOKS, Peter Joseph. b 54. **d** 83 **p** 84. C Portslade St Nic and St Andr *Chich* 83-86; C Kingstanding St Luke *Birm* 86-91; V Nork *Guildf* from 91. *The Vicarage, Warren Road, Banstead, Surrey SM7 1LG* Tel (01737) 353849

BROOKS, Philip David. b 52. MA Cam Univ MTh. St Jo Coll Nottm 80. **d** 83 **p** 84. C Ipsley *Worc* 83-87; V Fulford w Hilderstone *Lich* 87-95; Chapl Stallington Hosp 87-95; P-in-c Crich *Derby* from 95. *The Vicarage, 21 Coasthill, Crich, Matlock, Derbyshire DE4 5DS* Tel (01773) 852449

BROOKS, Raymond Samuel. b 11. ARIBA39. Clifton Th Coll 63. **d** 65 **p** 66. C Worthing St Geo *Chich* 65-69; P-in-c Hastings Em and St Mary in the Castle 69-71; V 71-82; rtd 82; Perm to Offic *Chich* from 82. *Brighnorton, Eight Acre Lane, Three Oaks, Hastings, E Sussex TN25 4NL* Tel (01424) 754432

BROOKS, Mrs Susan Vera. b 51. N Ord Course 87. **d** 90 **p** 94. Par Dn Carleton *Wakef* 90-93; Par Dn E Hardwick 90-93; TV Almondbury w Farnley Tyas from 93. *150 Fleminghouse Lane, Huddersfield HD5 8UD* Tel (01484) 545085

BROOKS, Mrs Vivien June. b 47. Univ of Wales (Ban) BA68 Southn Univ MA70. Ridley Hall Cam 87. **d** 89 **p** 95. C Exning St Martin w Landwade *St E* 89-92; Par Dn Hermitage and Hampstead Norreys, Cold Ash etc *Ox* 92-94; C 94-95; P-in-c Cox Green from 95. *The Vicarage, Warwick Close, Maidenhead, Berks SL6 3AL* Tel (01628) 22139

BROOKS, Vivienne Christine. *See* ARMSTRONG-MacDONNELL, Mrs Vivienne Christine

BROOKSBANK, Alan Watson. b 43. Univ of Wales (Lamp) BA64 Edin Univ MEd76. Edin Th Coll 64. **d** 66 **p** 67. C Cleator Moor w Cleator *Carl* 66-70; V Dalston 70-80; P-in-c Greystoke, Matterdale and Mungrisdale 80-81; R 81-83; R Watermillock 81-83; R Hagley *Worc* 83-95; Bp's Officer for NSM 88-95; V Claines St Jo from 95. *The Vicarage, Claines Lane, Worcester WR3 7RN* Tel (01905) 51251

BROOKSTEIN, Canon Royston. b 29. Qu Coll Birm 60. **d** 62 **p** 63. C Rubery *Birm* 62-66; V Cotteridge 66-75; V Hall Green St Pet 75-94; Hon Can Birm Cathl 84-94; rtd 94. *257 Wake Green Road, Birmingham B13 9XH* Tel 0121-777 7989

BROOM, Andrew Clifford. b 65. Keele Univ BSocSc86. Trin Coll Bris BA92. **d** 92 **p** 93. C Wellington, All SS w Eyton *Lich* 92-96; C Brampton St Thos *Derby* from 96. *2 Stanford Way, Walton, Chesterfield, Derbyshire SH42 7NH* Tel (01246) 568342

BROOM, Bernard William. b 21. Roch Th Coll 64. **d** 66 **p** 67. C Diss *Nor* 66-67; C Witton w Brundall and Braydeston 67-69; R Alderford w Attlebridge and Swannington 69-75; RD Sparham 73-75; R Drayton 75-80; P-in-c Felthorpe w Haveringland 77-80; R Drayton w Felthorpe 80-81; TV Eckington w Handley and Ridgeway *Derby* 84-88; rtd 88; Perm to Offic *Nor* 88-96. *119A High Street, Blakeney, Holt, Norfolk NR25 7NU* Tel (01263) 740001

BROOM, Donald Rees. b 14. St Cath Soc Ox BA38 MA42. St D Coll Lamp BA36 BD45 Wycliffe Hall Ox 36. **d** 38 **p** 39. C Heworth H Trin *York* 38-41; C York St Mary Castlegate w St Mich Spurriergate 38-41; C Whitby 41-42; Chapl RAF 42-46; V Kingston upon Hull St Steph *York* 47-52; V Hunslet Moor St Pet *Ripon* 52-56; V Hunslet Moor St Pet and St Cuth 56-62; V Middleton Tyas and Barton 62-75; V Barton and Manfield w Cleasby 75-82; rtd 82. *47 Linden Avenue, Darlington, Co Durham DL3 8PS* Tel (01325) 284216

BROOM, Jacqueline Anne. b 52. R Holloway Coll Lon BSc73. Trin Coll Bris DipHE81. **dss** 82 **d** 95 **p** 95. Easton H Trin w St Gabr and St Lawr and St Jude *Bris* 82-86; OMF Internat from 87; Hong Kong 87-95; Macao from 96. *St Mark's Church, 53 Rua Pedro Rolasco da Silva, Macao*

BROOME, David Curtis. b 36. Leeds Univ BA63. Coll of Resurr Mirfield. **d** 65 **p** 66. C Winshill *Derby* 65-69; C Leigh-on-Sea St Marg *Chelmsf* 69-74; V Leeds St Marg *Ripon* 74-81; V Stoke H Cross w Dunston *Nor* 81-93; P-in-c Caistor w Markshall 92-93; P-in-c Arminghall 92-93; R Stoke H Cross w Dunston, Arminghall etc from 93. *The Vicarage, Stoke Holy Cross, Norwich NR14 8AB* Tel (01508) 492305

BROOME, William Harold. b 09. Man Egerton Hall 32. **d** 34 **p** 35. C Coseley Ch Ch *Lich* 34-37; C Tynemouth Ch Ch *Newc* 38-41; V Newc St Hilda 41-48; R Fort William *Arg* 48-50; V Holy Is *Newc* 50-53; V Hanley St Jude *Lich* 53-55; R Forres *Mor* 55-61; V Lode and Longmeadow *Ely* 61-64; R Nairn *Mor* 64-73; Can St Andr Cathl Inverness 66-73; R Selkirk *Edin* 73-75; rtd 75; Lic to Offic *Newc* 75-77; Hon C Morpeth 77-80; Hon C St Andrews St Andr *St And* 80-87. *122 North Street, St Andrews, Fife KY16 9AF* Tel (01334) 473204

BROOMFIELD, David John. b 37. Reading Univ BA59. Oak Hill Th Coll 64. **d** 66 **p** 67. C Gresley *Derby* 66-71; C Rainham *Chelmsf* 71-77; R High Ongar w Norton Mandeville 77-88; RD Ongar 83-88; P-in-c Stanford Rivers 84-86; P-in-c Loughton St Mary and St Mich 88-95; P-in-c Loughton St Mary 95-97; R from 97. *St Mary's Rectory, High Road, Loughton, Essex IG10 1BB* Tel 0181-508 3643

BROOMFIELD, Iain Jonathan. b 57. Univ Coll Ox MA. Wycliffe Hall Ox 80. **d** 83 **p** 84. C Beckenham Ch Ch *Roch* 83-87; Schs Worker Scripture Union Independent Schs from 87; Perm to Offic *Ox* 87-89. *91 Walton Street, Oxford OX2 6EB* Tel (01865) 59006 or 0171-782 0013 Fax 0171-782 0014

BROSNAN, Mark. b 61. St Martin's Coll Lanc BA83 RMN88 Otley Agric Coll. EAMTC 92. **d** 95 **p** 96. C Rushmere *St E* from 95. *5 The Limes, Rushmere, Ipswich IP5 7EA* Tel (01473) 713690

BROSTER, Godfrey David. b 52. Ealing Tech Coll BA75. Ripon Coll Cuddesdon 78. **d** 81 **p** 82. C Crayford *Roch* 81-82; C Brighton Resurr *Chich* 82-86; C-in-c The Hydneye CD 86-91; R Plumpton w E Chiltington 91-93; R Plumpton w E Chiltington cum Novington from 93. *The Rectory, Station Road, Plumpton, Lewes, E Sussex BN7 3BU* Tel (01273) 890570

BROTHERSTON, Miss Isabel Mary. b 42. Cranmer Hall Dur 81. **dss** 83 **d** 87 **p** 94. Coleshill *Birm* 83-87; Par Dn Duddeston w Nechells 87-92; Par Dn Harlescott *Lich* 92-94; C from 94. *14 Maple Drive, Harlescott, Shrewsbury SY1 3SE* Tel (01743) 350907

BROTHERTON, The Ven John Michael. b 35. St Jo Coll Cam BA59 MA63. Cuddesdon Coll 59. **d** 61 **p** 62. C Chiswick St Nic w St Mary *Lon* 61-65; Trinidad and Tobago 65-75; V Cowley St Jo *Ox* 76-81; Chapl St Hilda's Coll Ox 76-81; RD Cowley *Ox* 78-81; V Portsea St Mary *Portsm* 81-91; Hon Can Kobe Japan from 86; Adn Chich from 91. *4 Canon Lane, Chichester, W Sussex PO19 1PX* Tel (01243) 779134 Fax 536452

BROTHERTON, Leslie Charles. b 22. OStJ FSCA MInstAM. St Steph Ho Ox 68. **d** 68 **p** 69. C Fenny Stratford *Ox* 68-70; C Solihull *Birm* 71-76; C 91-92; V Moseley St Anne 76-91; rtd 93; Perm to Offic *Birm* from 93. *3 St Alphege Close, Solihull, W Midlands B91 3RQ* Tel 0121-705 7038

BROTHERTON, Michael. b 56. MBE93. Univ of Wales (Abth) BD80. Wycliffe Hall Ox 80. **d** 81 **p** 82. Hon Chapl Miss to Seamen 81-84; C Pembroke Dock *St D* 81-84; Chapl RN from 84. *Royal Naval Chaplaincy Service, Room 203, Victory Building, HM Naval Base, Portsmouth PO1 3LS* Tel (01705) 727903 Fax 727112

BROTHERWOOD, Nicholas Peter. b 50. Oak Hill Th Coll BA83. **d** 83 **p** 84. C Nottingham St Nic *S'well* 83-86; Canada from 86.

3498 Harvard Avenue, Montreal, Quebec, Canada, H4A 2W3 Tel Montreal (514) 489-4158

BROTHWELL, Canon Paul David. b 37. Lich Th Coll 62. **d** 65 **p** 66. C Honley *Wakef* 65-68; Min Can Wakef Cathl 68-71; V Whittington St Giles *Lich* 71-83; P-in-c Weeford 78-83; V Whittington w Weeford 83-92; Chapl Kidderminster Gen Hosp 92-94; Chapl Kidderminster Health Care NHS Trust from 94. *Kidderminster General Hospital, Bewdley Road, Kidderminster, Worcs DY11 6RJ* Tel (01562) 823424/861951 Fax 67412

BROTHWOOD, Ian Sidney. b 56. K Coll Lon BD84. Linc Th Coll 87. **d** 89 **p** 90. C Selsdon St Jo w St Fran *S'wark* 89-93; P-in-c S Norwood St Alb from 93. *The Vicarage, 6 Dagmar Road, London SE25 6HZ* Tel 0181-653 6092

BROTHWOOD, Dr John. b 31. Peterho Cam MA55 MB, ChB55. S'wark Ord Course 89. **d** 91 **p** 92. NSM Dulwich St Barn *S'wark* from 91. *81 Calton Avenue, London SE21 7DF* Tel 0181-693 8273

BROUGH, Gerald William. b 32. Trin Coll Cam BA55 MA59. Ridley Hall Cam 55. **d** 57 **p** 58. C Westgate St Jas *Cant* 57-60; C New Addington 60-62; V Mancetter *Cov* 62-73; P-in-c Bourton w Frankton and Stretton on Dunsmore etc 73-74; R 74-93; rtd 93. *17 Brookhurst Court, Beverley Road, Leamington Spa, Warks CV32 6PB* Tel (01926) 430759

BROUGHALL, Rodney John. b 32. LNSM course 95. **d** 96. NSM Watton w Carbrooke and Ovington *Nor* from 96. *15 Garden Close, Watton, Thetford, Norfolk IP25 6DP* Tel (01953) 881989

BROUGHTON, Canon Harry. b 09. Dur Univ LTh32. Lich Th Coll 29. **d** 32 **p** 33. C Haxby *York* 32-35; C Helmsley 35-37; V Bransdale cum Farndale 37-43; V Thirsk 43-48; V Thirsk w S Kilvington 48-56; RD Thirsk 44-56; V Coxwold w Yearsley 56-60; V Coxwold 60-69; RD Easingwold 62-69; Can and Preb York Minster 66-94; rtd 70; RD Helmsley *York* 74-75. *Charters Garth, Hutton-le-Hole, York YO6 6UD* Tel (01751) 417288

BROUGHTON, James Roger. b 48. Leeds Univ BA71 Nottm Univ CertEd72. Wycliffe Hall Ox 87. **d** 89 **p** 90. C Stoneycroft All SS *Liv* 89-92; P-in-c Carr Mill 92-94; V 94-96; Chapl Duke of York's R Mil Sch Dover from 96. *Kent House, Duke of York's Royal Military School, Guston, Dover, Kent CT15 5DR* Tel (01304) 202437

BROUGHTON, Stuart Roger. b 36. Univ of Wales DipTh65. St Mich Coll Llan 61 Wilson Carlile Coll 59. **d** 64 **p** 65. C Bromley Ch Ch *Roch* 64-67; SAMS 67-79; V Stoke sub Hamdon *B & W* 79-83; Hon CF 82-86; V Blackb Ch Ch w St Matt *Blackb* 83-86; Portugal 86-91; 97; Brazil 91-96; rtd 96; Chapl Agia Napa Cyprus 96-97; Falkland Is from 97. *PO Box 160, Stanley, Falkland Islands* Tel Cascais (1) 487-1209

BROUN, Canon Claud Michael. b 30. BNC Ox BA55. Edin Th Coll 56. **d** 58 **p** 59. Chapl St Mary's Cathl *Edin* 58-62; Can St Mary's Cathl *Glas* 84-95; P-in-c Cambuslang 62-70; R 70-75; R Hamilton 75-88; R Gatehouse of Fleet 88-95; R Kircudbright 88-95; rtd 95; Hon Can St Mary's Cathl *Glas* from 95. *Martin Lodge, Ardross Place, Alness, Ross-shire IV17 0PX* Tel (01349) 882442

BROWN, Canon Alan. b 37. Tyndale Hall Bris 59. **d** 63 **p** 64. C Braintree *Chelmsf* 63-66; C Tooting Graveney St Nic *S'wark* 66-68; C Chesham St Mary *Ox* 68-70; V Hornsey Rise St Mary *Lon* 70-75; V Sidcup Ch Ch *Roch* 75-88; V Newport St Jo *Portsm* from 88; RD W Wight 91-96; Hon Can Portsm Cathl from 95; P-in-c Newport St Thos from 96. *St John's Vicarage, 3 Cypress Road, Newport, Isle of Wight PO30 1EY* Tel (01983) 522148 Fax as telephone

BROWN, Alan George. b 51. Bradf Univ BSc84 Leeds Univ CertEd81 MBA92 SRN72 RMN75 RNT81. N Ord Course 92. **d** 95 **p** 96. NSM Ilkley St Marg *Bradf* from 95. *Waverley, Wheatley Road, Ilkley, W Yorkshire LS29 8TS* Tel (01943) 601115 Fax as telephone

BROWN, Alan Michael Ernest. b 52. St Chad's Coll Dur BA74. St Jo Coll Nottm 81. **d** 83 **p** 84. C Bridlington Priory *York* 83-86; V Morton St Luke *Bradf* from 86. *The Vicarage, Morton, Keighley, W Yorkshire BD20 5RS* Tel (01274) 563829

BROWN, Albert Harry Alfred Victor. b 12. **d** 81 **p** 83. Hon C Kennington Park St Agnes *S'wark* 81-92; Perm to Offic from 92. *61 Brittany Point, Lollard Street, London SE11 6PX* Tel 0171-274 5982

BROWN, Alec Charles. b 33. AKC58. **d** 59 **p** 60. C S Mimms St Mary and Potters Bar *Lon* 59-63; C S Ashford Ch Ch *Cant* 63-66; New Zealand from 66. *151 Tasman Street, Nelson, New Zealand* Tel Christchurch (3) 548 3644

BROWN, Alec George. b 53. Univ of Zimbabwe DipSocWork80 Univ of Wales (Cardiff) MSc(Econ)87. St Deiniol's Hawarden 88 N Ord Course 90. **d** 93 **p** 94. C Stockton Heath *Ches* 93-96; C Weaverham 96; C Thelwall 96-97; V from 97. *The Vicarage, Bell Lane, Thelwall, Warrington WA4 2SX* Tel (01925) 661166

BROWN, Alexander Peter-Aidan (Alex). b 48. Sarum & Wells Th Coll. **d** 82 **p** 83. C Ifield *Chich* 82-86; TV 86-91; V St Leonards SS Pet and Paul from 91. *The Vicarage, 10 Bloomfield Road, St Leonards-on-Sea, E Sussex TN37 6HH* Tel (01424) 445606

BROWN, Allan James. b 47. K Coll Lon BD69 AKC69 MTh70. St Aug Coll Cant 69. **d** 73 **p** 74. Jerusalem 73-75; C Clifton *S'well* 75-77; CF from 77. *MOD Chaplains (Army), Trenchard Lines, Upavon, Pewsey, Wilts SN9 6BE* Tel (01980) 615804 Fax 615800

BROWN, Andrew. b 55. St Pet Hall Ox BA80 MA82. Ridley Hall Cam 79. **d** 80 **p** 81. C Burnley St Pet *Blackb* 80-82; C Elton All SS *Man* 82-86; P-in-c Ashton St Pet 86-93; V 94-96; V Halliwell St Luke from 96. *St Luke's Vicarage, Chorley Old Road, Bolton BL1 3BE* Tel (01204) 843060

BROWN, Andrew. b 65. LNSM course 92. **d** 95 **p** 96. NSM Heywood St Marg *Man* from 95. *24 Honiton Close, Heywood, Lancs OL20 3PF* Tel (01706) 623091

BROWN, Anthony Frank Palmer (Tony). b 31. Fitzw Ho Cam BA56 Fitzw Coll Cam MA84. Cuddesdon Coll 56. **d** 58 **p** 59. C Aldershot St Mich *Guildf* 58-61; C Chiswick St Nic w St Mary *Lon* 61-66; Asst Chapl Lon Univ 65-70; Lic to Offic 70-72; C-in-c Hammersmith SS Mich and Geo White City Estate CD 72-74; P-in-c Upper Sunbury St Sav 74-80; V from 80. *St Saviour's Vicarage, 205 Vicarage Road, Sunbury-on-Thames, Middx TW16 7TP* Tel (01932) 782800

BROWN, Anthony Paul. b 55. ARICS87 Reading Univ BSc75. Qu Coll Birm 77. **d** 80 **p** 81. C Pelsall *Lich* 80-83; C Leighton Buzzard w Eggington, Hockliffe etc *St Alb* 83-87; TV Langley Marish *Ox* 87-93; V Pet St Mary Boongate *Pet* from 93. *St Mary's Vicarage, 214 Eastfield Road, Peterborough PE1 4BD* Tel (01733) 343418

BROWN, Antony William Keith. b 26. RN Coll Dartmouth 43. Trin Coll Bris 86. **d** 87 **p** 88. NSM Lawrence Weston *Bris* 87-89; Chapl Casablanca *Eur* 89-93; Asst Chapl Paris St Mich from 94. *25 Hameau de Bois Fountaine, 78170 La Celle St Cloud, France* Tel France (33) 30 78 01 58 Fax as telephone

BROWN, Arthur Basil Etheredge. b 17. Reading Univ BA39. Wycliffe Hall Ox 46. **d** 47 **p** 48. C Camborne *Truro* 47-50; Org Sec (Midl) CPAS 50-53; PC Scarborough H Trin *York* 53-58; V Heworth H Trin 58-66; R Camborne *Truro* 66-82; rtd 82; Perm to Offic from 82. *14 Tregenna Fields, Camborne, Cornwall TR14 7QS* Tel (01209) 716196

BROWN, Arthur William Stawell. b 26. St Jo Coll Ox BA50 MA51. Cuddesdon Coll 63. **d** 65 **p** 66. C Edin St Jo *Edin* 65-66; C Petersfield w Sheet *Portsm* 67-75; V Portsea St Alb 75-79; R Smithfield St Bart Gt *Lon* 79-91; R St Sepulchre w Ch Ch Greyfriars etc 81-91; Chapl Madeira *Eur* 90-93; rtd 91; Perm to Offic *Ex* from 93. *9 Little Silver, Exeter EX4 4HU* Tel (01392) 217630

BROWN, Barry Ronald. b 48. Ridley Coll Melbourne ThL72. **d** 73 **p** 74. Australia 73-77 and 82-95; C Richmond St Mary *S'wark* 78-79; C Richmond St Mary w St Matthias and St Jo 79; C Edin Old St Paul *Edin* 79-80; Chapl Belgrade w Zagreb *Eur* 81-82; Canada from 95. *401/360 Bloor Street, Toronto, Ontario, Canada MW4 3M3*

BROWN, Canon Bernard Herbert Vincent. b 26. Mert Coll Ox BA50 MA52. Westcott Ho Cam 50. **d** 52 **p** 53. C Rugby St Andr *Cov* 52-56; C Stoke Bishop *Bris* 56-59; Youth Chapl 56-62; Ind Chapl *Roch* 62-73; Bp's Dom Chapl 66-73; R Crawley *Chich* 73-79; TR 79-83; Ind Chapl *Bris* 83-92; Bp's Soc and Ind Adv 84-92; Hon Can Bris Cathl 85-92; RD Bris City 85-91; rtd 92. *33B London Road, Dorchester, Dorset DT1 1NF* Tel (01305) 260806

BROWN, Bernard Maurice Newall. b 26. Oak Hill Th Coll 47. **d** 51 **p** 52. C Penn Fields *Lich* 51-53; S Area Sec BCMS 53-55; Kenya 55-62; R Hartshorne *Derby* 62-68; V Stapenhill w Cauldwell 68-72; C Weston-super-Mare Ch Ch *B & W* 72-74; R Spaxton w Charlynch 74-80; rtd 80. *12 Ewart Road, Weston-super-Mare, Avon BS22 8NU* Tel (01934) 412170

BROWN, Bill Charles Balfour. b 44. Linc Th Coll 87. **d** 89 **p** 90. C Moulsham St Luke *Chelmsf* 89-91; C Prittlewell 91-94; V Worksop St Paul *S'well* from 95. *St Paul's Vicarage, Cavendish Road, Worksop, Notts S80 2ST* Tel (01909) 473289

BROWN, Brian Ernest. b 36. ALA64. Oak Hill NSM Course 82. **d** 85 **p** 86. NSM Wallington H Trin *S'wark* 85-91; C from 91. *St Patrick's House, 47 Park Hill Road, Wallington, Surrey SM6 0RU* Tel 0181-647 5882

BROWN, Charles Hubert. b 21. S'wark Ord Course 82. **d** 84 **p** 85. NSM Shortlands *Roch* 84-86; P-in-c Seal St Lawr 86-90; P-in-c Underriver 86-90; rtd 90; Perm to Offic *Roch* from 90. *Barton Croft, 11 St Mary's Close, Sevenoaks, Kent TN15 8NH* Tel (01732) 882893

BROWN, Christopher. b 38. AKC62. **d** 63 **p** 64. C Crofton Park St Hilda w St Cypr *S'wark* 63-64; C S Beddington St Mich 64-67; C Herne Hill St Paul 67-68; Lic to Offic 68-72; Lic to Offic *Lich* 72-76; Lic to Offic *Worc* 77-79; Lic to Offic *Ox* 79-86; Lic to Offic *Chelmsf* from 86; Dir NSPCC from 89. *7 Baronia Croft, Highwoods, Colchester CO4 4EE* Tel (01206) 844705

BROWN, Christopher. b 43. Linc Th Coll 79. **d** 81 **p** 82. C Stafford St Jo *Lich* 81-85; C Stafford St Jo and Tixall w Ingestre 85; V Alton w Bradley-le-Moors and Oakamoor w Cotton 85-94; Chapl Asst Nottm City Hosp NHS Trust from 94. *The Chaplain's Office, Nottingham City Hospital, Hucknall Road, Nottingham NG5 1BP* Tel 0115-969 1169 or 962 7616

BROWN, Christopher Charles. b 58. Solicitor 82 Univ of Wales (Cardiff) LLB79. Westcott Ho Cam 87. **d** 90 **p** 91. C Taunton St Mary *B & W* 90-94; R Timsbury and Priston from 94. *The Rectory, Timsbury, Bath BA3 1HY* Tel (01761) 470153

BROWN, Christopher David. b 49. Birm Univ CertEd71 BEd72 Univ of Wales (Cardiff) DipPTh94. St Mich Coll Llan 93. **d** 94

p 95. C Swansea St Thos and Kilvey *S & B* 94-96; C Swansea St Jas from 96. *21 Ffynone Drive, Swansea SA1 6DB* Tel (01792) 470248

BROWN, Christopher Edgar Newall. b 31. Oak Hill Th Coll 51. **d** 55 **p** 56. C Surbiton Hill Ch Ch *S'wark* 55-57; C Gipsy Hill Ch Ch 57-61; V Plumstead All SS 61-70; V Sissinghurst *Cant* 70-73; P-in-c Frittenden 72-73; V Sissinghurst w Frittenden 73-76; Perm to Offic *S & M* 84-91 and from 96; Bp's Dom Chapl 91-95; rtd 96. *21 College Green, Castletown, Isle of Man IM9 1BE* Tel (01624) 822364

BROWN, Christopher Francis. b 44. Sarum Th Coll 68. **d** 71 **p** 72. C High Wycombe *Ox* 71-74; C Sherborne w Castleton and Lillington *Sarum* 74-77; P-in-c Wylye, Fisherton Delamere and the Langfords 77-79; R Yarnbury 79-82; R Portland All SS w St Pet 82-88; RD Weymouth 85-88; R Trowbridge St Jas from 88; Chapl Trowbridge & Distr Hosp from 88; RD Bradford from 94. *The Rectory, Union Street, Trowbridge, Wilts BA14 8RU* Tel (01225) 755121

BROWN, Christopher James (Chris). b 50. Open Univ BA92. Trin Coll Bris DipHE93. **d** 93 **p** 94. C Skelmersdale St Paul *Liv* 93-97; Asst Chapl Salford R Hosps NHS Trust from 97. *Staff Residentiary, Stott Lane, Salford, Manchester M6 8HD*

BROWN, Clive Lindsey. b 33. Southn Univ BA55. Oak Hill Th Coll 57. **d** 59 **p** 60. C Becontree St Mary *Chelmsf* 59-62; Australia from 62. *30 William Street, Roseville, NSW, Australia 2069* Tel Sydney (2) 417 2377 Fax 417 5746

BROWN, Prof Colin. b 32. Liv Univ BA53 Lon Univ BD58 Nottm Univ MA61 Bris Univ PhD70. Tyndale Hall Bris 55. **d** 58 **p** 59. C Chilwell *S'well* 58-61; Lect Tyndale Hall Bris 61-78; Vice Prin 67-70; Dean Studies 70-71; USA from 78; Prof Systematic Th Fuller Th Sem California from 78; Assoc Dean Adv Th Studies from 88. *1024 Beverly Way, Altadena, California 91001, USA* Tel Pasadena (818) 584-5239

BROWN, David Charles Girdlestone. b 42. Solicitor 67. S'wark Ord Course 87. **d** 90 **p** 91. NSM Milford *Guildf* 90-92; Hon C Haslemere from 92. *Boundary House, Highercombe Road, Haslemere, Surrey GU27 2LQ* Tel (01428) 651889

BROWN, David Frederick. b 38. Illinois Univ BA60. Seabury-Western Th Sem MDiv67. **d** 67 **p** 67. USA 67-78; Hon C Battersea Ch Ch and St Steph *S'wark* 78-83; Chapl R Marsden Hosp Lon and Surrey 83-94; Sen Chapl R Marsden NHS Trust Lon and Surrey from 94; Perm to Offic *S'wark* from 83. *The Royal Marsden Hospital NHS Trust, Fulham Road, London SW3 6JJ* Tel 0171-352 8171 or 351 6082 Fax 351 2191

BROWN, David Lloyd. b 44. DipTh80 TCD BTh90. **d** 86 **p** 87. C Cregagh *D & D* 86-91; Bp's C Knocknagoney from 91. *19 Old Holywood Road, Belfast BT4 2HJ* Tel (01232) 763343

BROWN, David Victor Arthur. b 44. Em Coll Cam BA66 MA70 CertEd. Linc Th Coll 72. **d** 74 **p** 75. C Bourne *Linc* 74-77; Chapl St Steph Coll Broadstairs 77-79; TV Grantham *Linc* 79-81; Chapl Asst N Gen Hosp Sheff 81-84; C Sheff St Cuth *Sheff* 81-84; Chapl Ridge Lea Hosp Lanc from 84; Chapl Lanc Moor Hosp from 84; Chapl Lanc R Infirmary from 87. *Chaplain's Office, Royal Lancaster Infirmary, Ashton Road, Lancaster LA1 4PR* Tel (01524) 586436 or 65994

BROWN, Prof David William. b 48. Edin Univ MA70 Or Coll Ox BA72 Clare Coll Cam PhD76. Westcott Ho Cam 75. **d** 76 **p** 77. Chapl, Fell and Tutor Or Coll Ox 76-90; Van Mildert Prof Div Dur Univ from 90; Can Res Dur Cathl *Dur* from 90. *14 The College, Durham DH1 3EQ* Tel 0191-386 4657

BROWN, Dennis Cockburn. b 27. Hatf Coll Dur BSc48 K Coll Dur PhD54. WMMTC 79. **d** 82 **p** 83. C Bilton *Cov* 82-84; V Wolford w Burmington 84-96; R Cherington w Stourton 84-96; R Barcheston 84-96; rtd 96. *13 Cleveland Court, 41 Kenilworth Road, Leamington Spa, Warks CV32 6JA* Tel (01926) 423771

BROWN, Canon Derek Frederick. b 27. St Fran Coll Brisbane ThL52. **d** 52 **p** 54. Australia 52-58; C Merstham and Gatton *S'wark* 59-61; R Deptford St Paul 61-69; Chapl RNR from 62; R Havant *Portsm* from 69. *St Faith's Rectory, Emsworth Road, Havant, Hants PO9 2FR* Tel (01705) 483485

BROWN, Derek Henry Pridgeon. b 46. Cam Coll of Art and Tech BA67 Leeds Univ PGCE71. St Steph Ho Ox 90. **d** 92 **p** 93. C Finchley St Mary *Lon* 92-95; C W Hampstead St Jas from 95. *42A Birchington Road, London NW6 4LJ* Tel 0171-372 1050

BROWN, Donald Evans. b 10. Ch Coll Cam BA34 MA38. Lon Coll of Div 34. **d** 37 **p** 38. C Luton Ch Ch *Roch* 37-39; C Mile Cross *Nor* 39-41; V Earlham St Anne 41-48; R Wells next the Sea 48-55; V Hemingford Grey *Ely* 55-77; rtd 77. *29 King George VI Drive, Hove, E Sussex BN3 6XF*

BROWN, Canon Donald Fryer. b 31. St Jo Coll Dur BA56 DipTh61. Cranmer Hall Dur 60. **d** 61 **p** 62. Min Can Bradf Cathl *Bradf* 61-64; C Bingley All SS 64-66; V Low Moor H Trin 66-97; Hon Can Bradf Cathl 85-97; RD Bowling and Horton 87-95; rtd 97. *3 Northfield Gardens, Wibsey, Bradford, W Yorkshire BD6 1LQ* Tel (01274) 678859

BROWN, Mrs Doreen Marion. b 39. Cam Univ CertEd67 DCouns85. N Ord Course 85. **d** 88 **p** 94. Par Dn Axminster, Chardstock, Combe Pyne and Rousdon *Ex* 88-92; Ind Chapl *Linc* from 92. *23 Montaigne Crescent, Glebe Park, Lincoln LN2 4QN*

BROWN, Douglas Adrian Spencer. Univ of W Aus BA50. St Mich Th Coll Crafers ThL50. **d** 53 **p** 54. SSM from 54; Australia 53-60 and 67-90; Lic to Offic *S'wark* 60-67; Tutor and Chapl Kelham Th Coll 60-67; Chapl Bucharest w Sofia *Eur* 90-91; Dir Angl Cen Rome 91-95; Chapl Palermo w Taormina *Eur* 95-96; Papua New Guinea from 97. *Newton Theological College, Popondetta, Papua New Guinea*

BROWN, Miss Elizabeth Charlotte (Beth). b 54. Bris Univ BSc76 PGCE77. Trin Coll Bris DipHE95. **d** 95 **p** 96. C Taunton Lyngford *B & W* from 95. *1 Kirke Grove, Taunton, Somerset TA2 8FB* Tel (01823) 321801

BROWN, Eric. b 28. NW Ord Course 73. **d** 76 **p** 77. NSM S Kirkby *Wakef* 76-83; NSM Knottingley 83-94; NSM Kellington w Whitley 89-94; Sub Chapl HM Pris Lindholme 90-94; Perm to Offic from 94. *Wynberg, Barnsley Road, South Kirby, Pontefract, W Yorkshire WF9 3BG* Tel (01977) 643683

BROWN, Canon Ernest George. b 23. Em Coll Cam BA51 MA56. Oak Hill Th Coll 52. **d** 53 **p** 54. C Darfield *Sheff* 53-56; V Ardsley 56-66; V Thurnby w Stoughton *Leic* 67-90; RD Gartree II 78-90; Hon Can Leic Cathl 82-90; rtd 90; Perm to Offic *Leic* from 90. *16 Holbeck Drive, Broughton Astley, Leics LE9 6UR* Tel (01455) 285458

BROWN, Ernest Harry. b 32. St Mich Coll Llan. **d** 59 **p** 60. C Swansea St Pet *S & B* 59-62; CF (TA) 62-68; C Gowerton w Waunarlwydd *S & B* 62-68; Chapl to the Deaf from 68. *Montreaux, 30 Lon Cedwyn, Sketty, Swansea SA2 0TH* Tel (01792) 207628

BROWN, Frank Seymour. b 10. S'wark Ord Course 62 St Aug Coll Cant 65. **d** 65 **p** 66. C Bexleyheath Ch Ch *Roch* 65-70; R Cratfield w Heveningham and Ubbeston *St E* 70-76; rtd 76; Perm to Offic *St E* 76-86; P-in-c Ixworth and Ixworth Thorpe 78; P-in-c Euston w Barnham and Fakenham 80; Perm to Offic *St Alb* from 86. *3 Windsor Gardens, Kimbolton Road, Bedford MK40 3BU* Tel (01234) 210999

BROWN, Geoffrey Gilbert. b 38. FBIS Dur Univ BA62 DipEd63 Fitzw Coll Cam BA69 MA73. Westcott Ho Cam 67. **d** 70 **p** 71. C Gosforth All SS *Newc* 70-73; Chapl Dauntsey's Sch Devizes 73-76; New Zealand 76-78 and 86-90; V Barrow St Aid *Carl* 79-86; C Digswell and Panshanger *St Alb* 91-93; NSM from 93; Chapl E Herts Hospice Care from 94. *Isabel Wing, Douglas Tilbe House, Hall Grove, Welwyn Garden City, Herts AL7 4PH* Tel (01707) 330686 Fax 393132

BROWN, Canon Geoffrey Harold. b 30. Trin Hall Cam BA54 MA58. Cuddesdon Coll 54. **d** 56 **p** 57. C Plaistow St Andr *Chelmsf* 56-60; C Birm St Pet *Birm* 60-63; R Birm St Geo 63-73; TR Gt Grimsby St Mary and St Jas *Linc* 73-85; Can and Preb Linc Cathl 79-85; V St Martin-in-the-Fields *Lon* 85-95; rtd 95. *32 Church Street, Hagley, Stourbridge, W Midlands DY9 0NA* Tel (01562) 883609

BROWN, Canon Gerald Arthur Charles. b 35. CCC Cam BA56 MA60 CCC Ox BA58 DipTh59. St Steph Ho Ox 58. **d** 60 **p** 61. C Wolverhampton St Pet *Lich* 60-66; V Trent Vale 66-74; V Wolverhampton St Andr 74-82; Chapl Milan w Cadenabbia and Varese *Eur* 82-90; Adn Scandinavia 90-95; Can Brussels Cathl 90-95; Chapl Oslo w Bergen, Trondheim, Stavanger etc 90-92; Chapl Stockholm w Gavle and Vasteras 92-95; Chapl Riga, Latvia 94-95; rtd 95. *20 Gardnor Mansions, Church Row, London NW3 6UR*

BROWN, Graeme Eric. b 37. St Jo Coll Auckland 58. **d** 62 **p** 63. New Zealand 62-74 and from 75; C Nor Heartsease St Fran *Nor* 74-75. *104 Masters Avenue, Hamilton, New Zealand* Tel Hamilton (7) 843 7024 or 839 8726 ext 8167 Fax 839 8799

BROWN, Graham Stanley. b 51. Sarum & Wells Th Coll 82. **d** 84 **p** 85. C Crediton and Shobrooke *Ex* 84-87; Chapl RAF 87-93; R Elgin w Lossiemouth *Mor* from 93. *The Rectory, 8 Gordon Street, Elgin, Morayshire IV30 1JQ* Tel (01343) 547505

BROWN, Harold. b 53. SEN74 SRN77 RMN82 RCN CCT84. Edin Th Coll 86. **d** 88 **p** 89. C Upperby St Jo *Carl* 88-90; C Carl H Trin and St Barn 90-91; C Workington St Mich 91-93; TV 93-95; P-in-c Crosscrake and Preston Patrick from 95. *The Vicarage, Shyreakes Lane, Crosscrake, Kendal, Cumbria LA8 0AB* Tel (015395) 60333

BROWN, Mrs Harriet Nina. b 37. Open Univ BA77 Lon Univ CertEd57. Gilmore Course 80 Oak Hill Th Coll 83. **dss** 83 **d** 87 **p** 94. Greenstead juxta Colchester *Chelmsf* 83-90; Par Dn 87-90; Asst Chapl R Hosp Sch Holbrook 90-93; Perm to Offic *Chelmsf* from 93; Perm to Offic *St E* 93-96; P-in-c Gt and Lt Blakenham w Baylham and Nettlestead from 96. *The Rectory, 74 Stowmarket Road, Great Blakenham, Ipswich IP6 0LS* Tel (01473) 832068 Minicom 01743-833201

BROWN, Henry. b 27. Lon Univ BSc51 BSc52. NW Ord Course 72. **d** 75 **p** 76. NSM Padiham *Blackb* 75-80; V Warton St Paul 80-90; rtd 90; Perm to Offic *Blackb* from 90. *18 Windsor Gardens, Garstang, Preston PR3 1EG* Tel (01995) 606592

BROWN, Ian. b 48. N Ord Course 89. **d** 91 **p** 92. C Burnage St Marg *Man* 91-94; P-in-c Halliwell St Paul from 94; Chapl Bolton Hosps NHS Trust from 94. *St Paul's Vicarage, Halliwell Road, Bolton BL1 8BP* Tel (01204) 495038

BROWN, Ian Barry. b 53. Ruskin Coll Ox 75 St Cuth Soc Dur BA80 PGCE81. Westmr Past Foundn CCouns90 Sarum & Wells Th Coll 84. **d** 86 **p** 87. C Winchmore Hill St Paul *Lon* 86-89; Hon

Chapl Chase Farm Hosp Enfield 86-88; Hon Chapl Harley Street Area Hosps 88-90; Hon Chapl RAM 89; C St Marylebone w H Trin 89-94; rtd 94. *139 Whitfield Street, London W1P 5RY* Tel 0171-387 1017

BROWN, Ian David. b 53. UEA BA76. Wycliffe Hall Ox BA80. **d** 81 **p** 82. C Southsea St Jude *Portsm* 81-84; Chapl Coll of SS Mary and Paul Cheltenham 84-89; V Lt Heath *St Alb* from 89. *The Vicarage, Thornton Road, Potters Bar, Herts EN6 1JJ* Tel (01707) 654414

BROWN, Ivan James. b 24. Cant Sch of Min 84. **d** 86 **p** 87. NSM St Nicholas at Wade w Sarre and Chislet w Hoath *Cant* 86-94; rtd 94; Perm to Offic *Cant* from 94. *Hurst Cottage, Millbank, Hoath, Canterbury, Kent CT3 4LP* Tel (01227) 860210

BROWN, Jack Robin. b 44. Linc Th Coll 67. **d** 69 **p** 70. C Canning Town St Cedd *Chelmsf* 69-72; C Dunstable *St Alb* 72-78; V Luton St Andr 78-85; V Kempston Transfiguration from 85; RD Bedford from 92. *The Transfiguration Vicarage, Cleveland Street, Kempston, Bedford MK42 8DW* Tel (01234) 854788

BROWN, James Douglas. b 52. S'wark Ord Course 93. **d** 96. NSM Shooters Hill Ch Ch *S'wark* from 96. *42 Ashridge Crescent, London SE18 3EB* Tel 0181-855 8140

BROWN, James Michael. b 49. St Jo Coll Morpeth 74. **d** 77 **p** 78. Australia 77-81; C Eyres Monsell *Leic* 81-83; Australia from 83. *The Rectory, 19 Tank Street, Morpeth, NSW, Australia 2321* Tel Cessnock (49) 336218

BROWN, Canon James Philip. b 30. Ex Coll Ox BA54 MA55. Westcott Ho Cam 54. **d** 56 **p** 57. C Hemel Hempstead *St Alb* 56-63; V Hellesdon *Nor* 63-71; P-in-c Kirkley w Lowestoft St Jo 71-79; TV Lowestoft St Marg 76-78; TV Lowestoft and Kirkley 79-81; P-in-c Northleach w Hampnett and Farmington *Glouc* 81-95; RD Northleach 83-92; P-in-c Cold Aston w Notgrove and Turkdean 86-95; Hon Can Glouc Cathl 91-95; rtd 95; Perm to Offic *Ex* from 95. *The Priest's House, 1 St Scholactica's Abbey, Teignmouth, Devon TQ14 8FF* Tel (01626) 773623

BROWN, The Ven James Russell. b 19. Qu Coll Ox BA52 MA56 Nashotah Ho Wisconsin DD70 Winnipeg Univ LLD77 LTh DD. Kelham Th Coll 37. **d** 43 **p** 44. C Bris St Jude w St Matthias *Bris* 43-45; C Portishead *B & W* 47-49; USA 52-55; C Brighton Gd Shep Preston *Chich* 55-47; C Abbots Langley *St Alb* 55-56; Canada from 56; Prof Nashotah Ho Wisconsin 61-70; Warden and Vice-Chan St Jo Coll Winnipeg 70-80; Can St Jo Cathl Winnipeg 70-80; Hon Can from 80; Lect Manitoba Univ from 80. *96 Kingsway Avenue, Winnipeg, Manitoba, Canada, R3M 0G9*

BROWN, Jane Madeline. d 97. C Aylestone St Andr w St Jas *Leic* from 97. *58 Belvoir Drive, Aylestone, Leicester LE2 8PA* Tel 0116-283 2003

BROWN, Mrs Joan Leslie. b 31. SS Hild & Bede Coll Dur CertEd55. Oak Hill Th Coll BA85. **dss** 85 **d** 87 **p** 94. Fulwood *Sheff* 85-87; Par Dn 87-88; TD Netherthorpe 88-93; rtd 93; NSM Ellesmere St Pet *Sheff* from 93. *2 Kingston Street, Sheffield S4 7SU* Tel 0114-243 3534

BROWN, John. b 21. **d** 50 **p** 51. C Tydavnet *Clogh* 50-51; P-in-c Drum 51-58; I Clontibret w Tullycorbet 58-62; I Clabby 62-75; V Dunham w Darlton and Ragnall *S'well* 75-87; R Fledborough 76-87; rtd 87; Perm to Offic *Heref* from 87. *The Groton, Norbury, Bishops Castle, Shropshire SY9 5DX* Tel (01588) 61272

BROWN, John. b 64. Kent Univ BA86. Westcott Ho Cam 87. **d** 90 **p** 91. C Lt Ilford St Mich *Chelmsf* 90-94; C E Ham w Upton Park St Alb 94; TV from 94. *147 Katherine Road, London E6 1ES* Tel 0181-472 1067

BROWN, John Bruce. b 42. Nottm Univ BA64 MA68. Cuddesdon Coll 64. **d** 66 **p** 67. C Warwick St Nic *Cov* 66-71; C Hatfield *St Alb* 71-78; V Watford St Mich from 78; RD Watford from 94. *St Michael's Vicarage, 5 Mildred Avenue, Watford WD1 7DY* Tel (01923) 232460

BROWN, Canon John Derek. b 41. Linc Th Coll 71. **d** 73 **p** 74. C Rotherham *Sheff* 73-76; P-in-c W Pinchbeck *Linc* 76-78; V Surfleet 76-82; R Boultham 83-94; RD Christianity 85-92; Can and Preb Linc Cathl from 88; P-in-c Epworth and Wroot from 94; RD Is of Axholme from 96. *St Andrew's Rectory, Belton Road, Epworth, Doncaster, S Yorkshire DN9 1JL* Tel (01427) 872471

BROWN, John Dixon. b 28. Pemb Coll Cam BA52. Oak Hill Th Coll 52. **d** 54 **p** 55. C Worthing St Geo *Chich* 54-57; C S w N Bersted 57-63; V W Hampnett 63-91; rtd 91; Perm to Offic *Chich* from 91. *3 Manor Way, Elmer Sands, Bognor Regis, W Sussex PO22 6LA* Tel (01243) 583449

BROWN, Canon John Duncan. b 43. St Pet Coll Ox BA64 BA66 MA68 Lon Univ BSc. Wycliffe Hall Ox 65. **d** 67 **p** 68. C Kingston upon Hull H Trin *York* 67-69; C St Leonards St Leon *Chich* 69-72; Hon C Norbiton *S'wark* 72-75; C Kirkcaldy *St And* 75-78; Prec and Chapl Chelmsf Cathl *Chelmsf* 78-86; P-in-c Kelvedon Hatch 86-92; P-in-c Navestock 86-92; P-in-c Fryerning w Margaretting from 92; Bp's ACORA Officer from 92; Hon Can Chelmsf Cathl from 93. *The Vicarage, Pennys Lane, Margaretting, Ingatestone, Essex CM4 0HA* Tel (01277) 355692

✠**BROWN, The Rt Revd John Edward.** b 30. Lon Univ BD68. Kelham Th Coll 50. **d** 55 **p** 56 **c** 87. Jerusalem 55-57; C Reading St Mary V *Ox* 57-60; Sudan 60-64; V Stewkley *Ox* 64-69; V Maidenhead St Luke 69-73; V Bracknell 73-77; RD Sonning 73-77; Adn Berks 78-87; Warden Ascot Priory 80-87; Bp Cyprus and the Gulf 87-95; rtd 95; Asst Bp Linc from 95. *130 Oxford Street, Cleethorpes, S Humberside DN35 0BP* Tel (01472) 698840

BROWN, Canon John Roger. b 37. AKC60. **d** 61 **p** 62. C New Eltham All SS *S'wark* 61-64; C Bexhill St Pet *Chich* 64-68; V Eastbourne St Elisabeth 68-75; V E Grinstead St Swithun from 75; Chapl Qu Victoria's Hosp E Grinstead from 75; RD E Grinstead *Chich* 82-93; Can and Preb Chich Cathl from 89. *St Swithun's Vicarage, Church Lane, East Grinstead, W Sussex RH19 3BB* Tel (01342) 323307

BROWN, John William Etheridge. b 13. St Pet Hall Ox BA35 MA39. Wycliffe Hall Ox 35. **d** 37 **p** 38. C Stratford New Town St Paul *Chelmsf* 37-40; C Rawtenstall St Mary *Man* 40-42; C Thame *Ox* 42-45; OCF 43-45; V St Keverne *Truro* 45-51; V Hoo All Hallows w Stoke *Roch* 51-55; V Crich *Derby* 55-61; V Leusden *Ex* 61-79; V Widecombe in the Moor 61-79; P-in-c Holne 70-74; P-in-c Princetown 74-79; RD Moreton 74-80; Asst Chapl HM Pris Dartmoor 75-82; V Widecombe, Leusden and Princetown etc *Ex* 79-82; rtd 82; Lic to Offic *Ex* from 82. *8 Emmetts Park, Ashburton, Newton Abbot, Devon TQ13 7DB* Tel (01364) 653072

BROWN, Jonathan. b 60. Univ Coll Dur BA83 MA85 Ex Univ CertEd86. Ripon Coll Cuddesdon 86 Ch Div Sch of the Pacific (USA) 88. **d** 89 **p** 90. C Esher *Guildf* 89-97; TV Crawley *Chich* from 97. *St Richard's Vicarage, 1 Crossways, Crawley, W Sussex RH10 1QF* Tel (01293) 533727

BROWN, Kenneth Arthur Charles. b 27. ACP65. LNSM course 85. **d** 84 **p** 85. NSM Ingoldsby *Linc* from 84. *11 Ingoldsby Road, Lenton, Grantham, Lincs NG33 4HB* Tel (01476) 85763

BROWN, Canon Kenneth Edward. b 22. Qu Coll Cam BA43 MA47. Ridley Hall Cam 46. **d** 47 **p** 48. C Farlington *Portsm* 47-51; C Attercliffe w Carbrook *Sheff* 51-52; V Rounds Green *Birm* 52-58; S Africa 58-63; V Seend *Sarum* 63-69; V Southbroom 69-83; RD Devizes 77-83; Can and Preb Sarum Cathl 77-87; TV Tisbury 83-87; rtd 87. *24 Broadleas Road, Devizes, Wilts SN10 5DG* Tel (01380) 728254

BROWN, Kenneth Roger. b 48. Dur Univ BA69 St Chad's Coll Dur DipTh72. Liturg Inst Trier DipLit73. **d** 73 **p** 74. C Patchway *Bris* 73-77; C Fishponds St Jo 77-79; Chapl RAF 79-95; Chapl HM Pris Pentonville 95-96; Chapl HM Pris Wellingborough from 96. *Chaplaincy, HM Prison, Millers Park, Doddington Road, Wellingborough, Northants NN8 2NH* Tel (01933) 224151 Fax 273903

BROWN, Dr Leslie Maurice. b 04. Bris Univ BSc24 MSc25 St Andr Univ PhD38 FRSE47. Edin Th Coll 74. **d** 74 **p** 74. Hon C Edin St Jo *Edin* 74-89; rtd 89. *51 Muirfield, Braids Hill Nursing Home, Liberton Drive, Edinburgh EH16 6NS* Tel 0131-672 1084

✠**BROWN, The Rt Revd Leslie Wilfrid.** b 12. CBE65. Lon Univ BD36 MTh44 DD57 Cam Univ Hon MA53. Trin Coll Toronto Hon DD63 ALCD35. **d** 35 **p** 36 **c** 53. C Milton *Portsm* 35-38; India 38-43 and 44-50; Chapl Down Coll Cam 43-44; C Cambridge H Trin *Ely* 43-44; Chapl Jes Coll Cam 50-51; Bp Uganda 53-60; Abp Uganda, Rwanda and Burundi 60-65; Bp Namirembe 60-65; Bp St E 66-78; ChStJ from 68; rtd 78. *Manormead Nursing Home, Tilford Road, Hindhead, Surrey GU26 6RA* Tel (01428) 604780

BROWN, Miss Louise Margaret. b 53. Trin Coll Bris DipHE82. **dss** 83 **d** 87 **p** 94. Woodley St Jo the Ev *Ox* 84-87; Par Dn Woodley 87-92; Asst Chapl Reading Hosps 92-94; C Shinfield 93-94; P-in-c Dedworth from 94. *The Vicarage, 3 Pierson Road, Windsor, Berks SL4 5RJ* Tel (01753) 864591

BROWN, Malcolm Arthur. b 54. Or Coll Ox BA76 MA82. Westcott Ho Cam 77. **d** 79 **p** 80. C Riverhead w Dunton Green *Roch* 79-83; TV Southampton (City Cen) *Win* 83-91; Assoc Dir Wm Temple Foundn from 91; Exec Sec from 93; Lic to Offic *Man* from 91; Hon C Heaton Moor from 95. *The William Temple Foundation, Manchester Business School, Manchester M15 6PB* Tel 0161-275 6534 Fax 272 8663

BROWN (née PATTERSON), Mrs Marjorie Jean. b 54. Wooster Coll USA BA76 St Andr Univ 77. S Dios Minl Tr Scheme 92. **d** 95 **p** 96. C Poplar *Lon* from 95. *St Michael's Vicarage, St Leonard's Road, London E14 6PW* Tel 0171-987 1795

BROWN, Mark Edward. b 61. Southn Univ BSc83 Cam Univ PGCE84. Trin Coll Bris DipHE87 BA88. **d** 88 **p** 89. C Egham *Guildf* 88-92; C Northwood Em *Lon* from 92; AV and Bp's Officer for Evang from 96. *14 Greenheys Close, Northwood, Middx HA6 2FR* Tel (01923) 825505

BROWN, The Ven Michael Rene Warneford. b 15. St Pet Coll Ox BA37 MA41. St Steph Ho Ox 38. **d** 41 **p** 42. C W Grinstead *Chich* 41-43; Chapl RNVR 43-46; Chapl St Pet Hall Ox 46; C Ox St Mary V *Ox* 46; RN Coll Greenwich 46-47; Fell St Aug Coll Cant 48-52; Lib 48-50; P-in-c Bekesbourne *Cant* 49-50; Asst Sec CACTM 50-60; Chapl Ch Ho Westmr 55-60; Adn Nottingham *S'well* 60-77; Perm to Offic *Cant* from 77; rtd 80; Hon OCF R Marines Sch of Music Deal from 85. *Faygate, 72 Liverpool Road, Deal, Kent CT14 7LR* Tel (01304) 361326

BROWN, Nicholas Francis Palgrave. b 23. Fitzw Ho Cam BA51 MA54. **d** 53 **p** 54. C Warwick St Nic *Cov* 53-55; C Birm St Paul *Birm* 55-60; V Temple Balsall 60-66; Gen Sec Ind Chr Fellowship 66-76; V St Kath Cree *Lon* 66-71; Chapl and Dir of Studies

Holland Ho Cropthorne 76-80; P-in-c Cropthorne w Charlton *Worc* 76-88; Adult Educn Officer 80-85; rtd 88. *Bredon View, Rear of 40 Bridge Street, Pershore, Worcs WR10 1AT* Tel (01386) 556816

BROWN, Canon Norman Charles Harry. b 27. Univ of Wales BSc46. St Mich Coll Llan 48. **d** 50 **p** 51. C Canton St Jo *Llan* 50-57; C Llanishen and Lisvane 58-63; V Miskin from 63; RD Aberdare 82-97; Can Llan Cathl from 86. *The Vicarage, Miskin, Mountain Ash CF45 3NE* Tel (01443) 473247

BROWN, Norman John. b 34. Thames Poly MA90. Ripon Hall Ox 72. **d** 74 **p** 75. C High Wycombe *Ox* 74-78; V Tilehurst St Cath 78-82; V Boyne Hill from 82; Chapl Windsor and Maidenhead Coll 87-89. *All Saints' Vicarage, Westmorland Road, Maidenhead, Berks SL6 4HB* Tel (01628) 26921

BROWN, Paul David Christopher. b 50. Lon Univ LLB71. EMMTC 81. **d** 84 **p** 85. NSM Wollaton *S'well* from 84. *32 Benington Drive, Wollaton, Nottingham NG8 2TF* Tel 0115-928 4493

BROWN, Penelope Jane (Penny). b 57. St Steph Ho Ox DipMin94. **d** 96 **p** 97. C Croydon St Jo *S'wark* from 96. *8 The Ridgeway, Croydon CR0 4AB* Tel 0181-686 3706 E-mail ibrown @worldscope.net

BROWN, Peter. b 38. Leeds Univ BSc62 PhD65. Nashotah Ho 85. **d** 87 **p** 88. USA 87-89; C Sprowston *Nor* 89-90; C Sprowston w Beeston 90-92; P-in-c W Winch w Setchey and N Runcton from 92; P-in-c Middleton w E Winch from 96. *The Rectory, West Winch, King's Lynn, Norfolk PE33 0NR* Tel (01553) 840835

BROWN, Peter. b 47. RMN69. Kelham Th Coll 69. **d** 74 **p** 75. C Hendon *Dur* 74-80; C Byker St Ant *Newc* 80-90; C Brandon *Dur* from 90. *The Clergy House, Sawmill Lane, Brandon, Durham DH7 8NS* Tel 0191-378 0845

BROWN, Peter. b 53. St Chad's Coll Dur BA75. Sarum & Wells Th Coll 75. **d** 77 **p** 78. C Tunstall Ch Ch *Lich* 77-79; C Tunstall 79-80; C Willenhall H Trin 80-83; V Weston Rhyn 83-88; Australia 88-90; R Hubbertson *St D* from 90. *The Rectory, 35 Westaway Drive, Hubberston, Milford Haven SA73 3EQ* Tel (01646) 692251

BROWN, Peter Russell. b 43. Oak Hill Th Coll. **d** 71 **p** 72. C Gt Faringdon w Lt Coxwell *Ox* 71-73; C Reading Greyfriars 73-74; V Forty Hill Jes Ch *Lon* 74-81; V Laleham from 81. *The Vicarage, Laleham, Staines, Middx TW18 1SB* Tel (01784) 457330

BROWN, Philip Anthony. b 54. Oak Hill Th Coll BA91. **d** 91 **p** 92. C Rock Ferry *Ches* 91-95; V Hattersley from 95. *St Barnabas's Vicarage, Hattersley Road East, Hyde, Cheshire SK14 3EQ* Tel 0161-368 2795

BROWN, Philip Roy. b 41. St Steph Ho Ox 78. **d** 80 **p** 81. C Highters Heath *Birm* 80-83; P-in-c Washwood Heath 83-87; V Tysoe w Oxhill and Whatcote *Cov* 87-93; R Harbury and Ladbroke from 93; RD Southam 95-97. *The Rectory, 2 Vicarage Lane, Harbury, Leamington Spa, Warks CV33 9HA* Tel (01926) 612377

BROWN, Phillip Murray. b 59. Keele Univ BSc80. Trin Coll Bris DipTh86 ADPS87. **d** 87 **p** 88. C Greasbrough *Sheff* 87-91; Ind Chapl from 87; V Thorne from 91. *The Vicarage, 2 Brooke Street, Thorne, Doncaster, S Yorkshire DN8 4AZ* Tel (01405) 814055

BROWN, Raymond Isaac Harry. b 14. Kelham Th Coll 36. **d** 42 **p** 43. C Romford St Andr *Chelmsf* 42-48; Metrop Area Sec UMCA 48-52; V Wellingborough St Mary *Pet* 52-66; V Tintinhull *B & W* 66-74; RD Martock 70-75; Lesotho from 76; rtd 79. *Community of the Holy Name, PO Box 43, Leribe 300, Lesotho, South Africa* Tel Lesotho (266) 400249

BROWN, Raymond John. b 49. Ox Univ BEd71. Wycliffe Hall Ox 72. **d** 75 **p** 76. C Barking St Marg w St Patr *Chelmsf* 75-78; C Walton H Trin *Ox* 78-82; V Enfield St Mich *Lon* 82-91; Chapl St Mich Hosp Enfield 82-91; R Springfield All SS *Chelmsf* from 91. *The Rectory, 9 Mulberry Way, Chelmsford CM1 7SN* Tel (01245) 356720

BROWN, Richard George. b 38. Dur Univ BSc63. Wells Th Coll 63. **d** 65 **p** 66. C Norton St Mary *Dur* 65-69; C N Gosforth *Newc* 69-71; Chapl Wells Cathl Sch 71-81; P-in-c Dulverton and Brushford *B & W* 81-83; R 83-86; Chapl Millfield Jun Sch Somerset 86-89; Chapl Brighton Coll 89-92; Chapl Benenden Sch Kent 92-94; Perm to Offic *Chich* from 94. *26A Eaton Place, Brighton BN2 1EG* Tel (01273) 621840

BROWN, Richard Lessey. b 27. Keble Coll Ox BA51 MA55. Qu Coll Birm 51. **d** 53 **p** 54. C York St Lawr w St Nic *York* 53-55; C Fulford 55-57; V Fridaythorpe w Fimber and Thixendale 57-61; V York St Luke 61-75; V Barlby 75-92; rtd 92; Perm to Offic *York* from 92. *1 Kings Court, King Street, Cottingham, N Humberside HU16 5RW* Tel (01482) 845299

BROWN, The Ven Robert Saville. b 14. Selw Coll Cam BA39 MA43. Linc Th Coll 39. **d** 40 **p** 41. C Gt Berkhamsted *St Alb* 40-44; C Hitchin St Mary 44-47; V Wonersh *Guildf* 47-53; R Gt Berkhamsted *St Alb* 53-69; P-in-c Bourne End 56-65; RD Berkhamsted 60-67; Hon Can St Alb 65-74; V Bedford St Paul 69-74; Chapl HM Pris Bedf 69-74; Adn Bedford *St Alb* 74-79; P-in-c Old Warden 74-79; rtd 79; Perm to Offic *Ox* 79-87. *The Rowans, 29 The Rise, Amersham, Bucks HP7 9AG* Tel (01494) 728376

BROWN, Robin. b 38. Leeds Univ BA60 MPhil69. Qu Coll Birm 89. **d** 91 **p** 92. C Far Headingley St Chad *Ripon* 91-94; V Hawksworth Wood from 94. *St Mary's Vicarage, Cragside Walk, Leeds LS5 3QE* Tel 0113-258 2923

BROWN, Capt Roger George. b 37. **d** 95 **p** 96. C Maidstone St Martin *Cant* from 95. *1 Fordcombe Close, Senacre Wood, Maidstone, Kent ME15 8SU* Tel (01622) 750016

BROWN, Roger Lee. b 42. Univ of Wales (Lamp) BA63 Univ Coll Lon MA73. Wycliffe Hall Ox 66. **d** 68 **p** 69. C Dinas w Penygraig *Llan* 68-70; C Bargoed and Deri w Brithdir 70-72; TV Glyncorrwg w Afan Vale and Cymmer Afan 72-74; R 74-79; V Tongwynlais 79-93; R Welshpool w Castle Caereinion *St As* from 93. *The Vicarage, Church Street, Welshpool SY21 7DP* Tel (01938) 553164

✠**BROWN, The Rt Revd Ronald.** b 26. St Jo Coll Dur BA50 DipTh52. **d** 52 **p** 53 **c** 74. C Chorley St Laur *Blackb* 52-56; V Whittle-le-Woods 56-61; V Halliwell St Thos *Man* 61-69; R Ashton St Mich 69-74; RD Ashton-under-Lyne 69-74; Suff Bp Birkenhead *Ches* 74-92; rtd 92; Perm to Offic *Ches* from 92. *Hurst Cottage, Moss Lane, Burscough, Ormskirk, Lancs L40 4BA* Tel (01704) 897314

BROWN, Ronald Glyn. b 34. Lich Th Coll 70. **d** 73 **p** 74. C Weymouth St Paul *Sarum* 73-78; C Swanage 78-79; P-in-c Bromham 79-80; P-in-c Chittoe 79-80; R Bromham, Chittoe and Sandy Lane from 80. *The Rectory, Bromham, Chippenham, Wilts SN15 2HA* Tel (01380) 850322

BROWN, Simon John. b 66. Birm Univ BSc87 PGCE88 Nottm Univ MA93. St Jo Coll Nottm DTS92. **d** 93 **p** 94. C Holbrooks *Cov* 93-97; C Leamington Priors All SS from 97; C Leamington Spa and Old Milverton from 97. *27 Leam Terrace, Leamington Spa, Warks CV31 1BQ* Tel (01926) 425083

BROWN, Canon Simon Nicolas Danton. b 37. Clare Coll Cam BA61 MA65. S'wark Ord Course 61 Linc Th Coll 63. **d** 64 **p** 65. C Lambeth St Mary the Less *S'wark* 64-66; Chapl and Warden LMH Settlement 66-72; P-in-c Southampton St Mary w H Trin *Win* 72-73; TV Southampton (City Cen) 73-79; R Gt Brickhill w Bow Brickhill and Lt Brickhill *Ox* 79-84; TR Burnham w Dropmore, Hitcham and Taplow from 84; RD Burnham and Slough from 87; Hon Can Ch Ch from 94. *The Rectory, The Precincts, Burnham, Slough SL1 7HU* Tel (01628) 604173

BROWN, Stanley George. b 19. Bps' Coll Cheshunt 66. **d** 67 **p** 68. C Shrub End *Chelmsf* 67-71; R Dengie w Asheldham 71-89; V Tillingham 71-89; RD Maldon and Dengie 82-89; rtd 89; Perm to Offic *Ely* from 90. *134 Lynn Road, Ely, Cambs CB6 1DE* Tel (01353) 662888

BROWN, Stephen Charles. b 60. Leeds Univ BA83 BA89 Reading Univ PGCE89. Coll of Resurr Mirfield 87. **d** 90 **p** 91. C Whitkirk *Ripon* 90-93; Asst Youth Chapl 92-95; C Chapel Allerton 93-95; R Stanningley St Thos from 95. *The Rectory, Stanningley Road, Stanningley, Pudsey, W Yorkshire LS28 6NB* Tel 0113-257 3460 or 255 3830

BROWN, Stephen James. b 44. Bradf Univ BSc69. Westcott Ho Cam 71. **d** 72 **p** 73. C Seaton Hirst *Newc* 72-75; C Marton-in-Cleveland *York* 75-77; Dioc Youth Adv *Dur* 77-82; V Thorner *Ripon* 82-92; Dioc Officer for Local Min from 90; P-in-c Ripley from 92; Chapl Leeds Coll of Building from 92. *The Rectory, Ripley, Harrogate, N Yorkshire HG3 3AY* Tel (01423) 770147

BROWN, Mrs Verity Joy. b 68. Qu Mary Coll Lon BA89. Ripon Coll Cuddesdon BTh93. **d** 93 **p** 94. C Barnard Castle w Whorlton *Dur* 93-95; C Bensham 95-97. *75 Eamont Gardens, Hartlepool, Cleveland TS26 9JE* Tel (01429) 423186

BROWN, Victor Charles. b 31. S'wark Ord Course 67. **d** 71 **p** 72. C Pinhoe *Ex* 71-73; C Egg Buckland 73-74; C Oakdale St Geo *Sarum* 74-77; R Old Trafford St Hilda *Man* 77-83; R Chigwell Row *Chelmsf* 83-92; R Fenny Bentley, Kniveton, Thorpe and Tissington *Derby* 92-96; rtd 96. *377 Sopwith Crescent, Wimborne, Dorset BH21 1XJ* Tel (01202) 841274

BROWN, Wallace. b 44. Oak Hill Th Coll 77. **d** 79 **p** 80. C Oadby *Leic* 79-85; V Quinton Road W St Boniface *Birm* from 85. *St Boniface Vicarage, Quinton Road West, Birmingham B32 2QD* Tel 0121-427 1939

BROWN, Walter Bertram John. b 09. K Coll Lon 43. **d** 43 **p** 44. C Glouc St Mark *Glouc* 43-47; Chapl Glouc Dioc Assn for Deaf and Dumb 43-47; Sussex Assn 47-50; RADD Chapl (N Lon) 50-53; Ex and Devon Miss to Adult Deaf & Dumb 53-73; Chapl to the Deaf *Chich* 73-75; rtd 75; Perm to Offic *Chich* 80-91. *7 Cowslip Meadow, Woodmancote, Cheltenham, Glos GL52 4TT* Tel (01242) 673648

BROWN, William Martyn. b 14. Pemb Coll Cam BA36 MA47. Nor Ord Course 76. **d** 76 **p** 77. NSM Thornage w Brinton w Hunworth and Stody *Nor* 76-77; NSM Field Dalling w Saxlingham 77-84; RD Holt 84-88; NSM Gunthorpe w Bale w Field Dalling, Saxlingham etc 84-88; Perm to Offic from 88. *Lodge Cottage, Field Dalling, Holt, Norfolk NR25 7AS* Tel (01328) 830403

BROWNBRIDGE, Bernard Alan. b 19. NW Ord Course 74. **d** 77 **p** 78. NSM Huntington *York* 77-80; V Sand Hutton 80-86; rtd 87; Hon C Birdsall w Langton *York* 87-92; Perm to Offic from 92. *2 Duncombe Close, Malton, N Yorkshire YO17 0YY* Tel (01653) 697626

BROWNBRIDGE, Peter John. b 31. BD. **d** 81 **p** 82. NSM Wingham w Elmstone and Preston w Stourmouth *Cant* 81-87; V from 87. *St Mary's House, 5 St Mary's Meadow, Wingham, Canterbury, Kent CT3 1DF* Tel (01227) 721530

BROWNE, Anthony Douglas. b 40. BD69 Aston Univ MSc74. Oak Hill NSM Course 88. **d** 91 **p** 92. NSM Woodford St Mary w St Phil and St Jas *Chelmsf* 91-93; Perm to Offic 93-94. *1 Broadfield Way, Buckhurst Hill, Essex IG9 5AG* Tel 0181-504 9540

BROWNE, Dr Arnold Samuel. b 52. MBPsS92 St Jo Coll Ox BA73 MA77 SS Coll Cam PhD87 Surrey Univ MSc89. Westcott Ho Cam 76. **d** 78 **p** 79. C Esher *Guildf* 78-81; C Worplesdon 81-86; Chapl R Holloway and Bedf New Coll 86-92; Fell and Dean of Chpl Trin Coll Cam from 92. *Trinity College, Cambridge CB2 1TQ* Tel (01223) 338400 Fax 338564

BROWNE, Arthur Donal. b 11. MC44. St Edm Hall Ox BA34 MA54. Wycliffe Hall Ox DipTh35. **d** 35 **p** 36. C St Marylebone Annunciation Bryanston Street *Lon* 35-39; V 46-62; CF (EC) 39-45; V S Kensington St Jude *Lon* 62-78; rtd 78; P-in-c Lydgate w Ousden and Cowlinge *St E* 80-82; P-in-c Glenurquhart *Mor* 84-89; Perm to Offic from 89. *Ham Farm, Dunnet, Thurso, Caithness KW14 8XP* Tel (01847) 851232

BROWNE, Aubrey Robert Caulfeild. b 31. Moore Th Coll Sydney 54. **d** 55 **p** 56. Australia 55-71; Producer of Relig Radio Progr USPG 72-84; Hon C S Kensington St Steph *Lon* 78-88; Hd of Area Sec Dept USPG 84-87; P-in-c Nunhead St Antony *S'wark* 88-90; V Nunhead St Antony w St Silas 90-96; rtd 97; Australia from 97. *14 Appian Way, Burwood, NSW 2134, Australia*

BROWNE, Miss Christine Mary. b 53. Nottm Univ BEd75. EMMTC 87. **d** 90 **p** 94. Par Dn Bulwell St Mary *S'well* 90-94; C 94-95; TV Hucknall Torkard from 95. *The Vicarage, Ruff's Drive, Hucknall, Nottingham NG15 6JG* Tel 0115-963 3640

BROWNE, Herman Beseah. b 65. K Coll Lon BD90 AKC90 Heythrop Coll Lon DPhil94. Cuttington Univ Coll BTh86. **d** 87 **p** 97. C N Lambeth *S'wark* 90-91; Tutor Simon of Cyrene Th Inst 90-96; Abp's Asst Sec for Ecum and Anglican Affairs *Cant* from 96; Perm to Offic *S'wark* from 96. *Lambeth Palace, London SE1 7JU* Tel 0171-928 8282

BROWNE, Ian Cameron. b 51. St Cath Coll Ox BA74 MA78 Fitzw Coll Cam BA76 MA80. Ridley Hall Cam 74. **d** 77 **p** 78. C Cheltenham Ch Ch *Glouc* 77-80; Hon C Shrewsbury St Chad *Lich* 80-83; Asst Chapl Shrewsbury Sch 80-83; Chapl Bedford Sch 83-96; Sen Chapl Oundle Sch from 97. *The School, Oundle, Peterborough PE8 4EN* Tel (01832) 273372

BROWNE, John Burnell. b 15. MC45. Qu Coll Cam BA36 MA40. Westcott Ho Cam 46. **d** 47 **p** 48. C Leeds St Pet *Ripon* 47-52; V Wortley de Leeds 52-59; V Barnard Castle *Dur* 59-71; RD Barnard Castle 59-71; V Billingham St Cuth 71-80; rtd 80; Perm to Offic *Wakef* 80-86. *40 Slack Top, Heptonstall, Hebden Bridge, W Yorkshire HX7 7HA* Tel (01422) 843099

BROWNE, Leonard Joseph. b 58. St Cath Coll Cam BA81 MA84. Trin Coll Bris 87. **d** 89 **p** 90. C Reading Greyfriars *Ox* 89-92; V Cambridge St Barn *Ely* from 92. *The Vicarage, St Barnabas Road, Cambridge CB1 2BX* Tel (01223) 352924 or 316228

BROWNE, Norman Desmond. b 21. TCD BA42 BD46 MA61. CITC 43. **d** 44 **p** 45. C Dublin Grangegorman *D & G* 44-47; C Dublin Ch Ch Leeson Park 47-59; P-in-c Upton cum Chalvey *Ox* 59-61; R Hedgerley 61-80; rtd 80. *8 Brett House Close, West Hill, London SW15 3JD* Tel 0181-788 1365

BROWNE, Peter Clifford. b 59. SRN82 Bris Univ BA80. Ripon Coll Cuddesdon 88. **d** 90 **p** 91. C Southgate Ch Ch *Lon* 90-92; NSM Kemp Town St Mary *Chich* 93-95; Chapl United Bris Healthcare NHS Trust from 96. *Bristol Royal Infirmary, Marlborough Street, Bristol BS2 8HW* Tel 0117-928 2136

BROWNING, Edward Barrington Lee (Barry). b 42. St Pet Coll Saltley TCert65. Ripon Coll Cuddesdon 90. **d** 92 **p** 93. C Falmouth K Chas *Truro* 92-96; R Roche and Withiel from 96. *The Rectory, Fore Street, Roche, St Austell, Cornwall PL26 8EP* Tel (01726) 890301

BROWNING, Mrs Jacqueline Ann. b 44. Sarum Th Coll 93. **d** 96 **p** 97. NSM New Alresford w Ovington and Itchen Stoke *Win* from 96. *1 Paddock Way, Alresford, Hants SO24 9PN* Tel (01962) 734372

BROWNING, Canon John William. b 36. Keele Univ BA61. Ripon Hall Ox 61. **d** 63 **p** 64. C Baswich *Lich* 63-66; Chapl Monyhull Hosp Birm 67-71; Chapl Wharncliffe Hosp Sheff 71-78; Chapl Middlewood Hosp Sheff 71-94; Hon Can Sheff Cathl *Sheff* from 84; Chapl Sheff Mental Health Unit 85-94; Chapl Community Health Sheff NHS Trust from 94; Chapl Sheff (South) Mental Health Centres from 94. *131 Low Road, Stannington, Sheffield S6 5FZ* Tel 0114-271 6518 or 271 6310

BROWNING, Julian. b 51. St Jo Coll Cam BA72 MA76. Ripon Coll Cuddesdon 77. **d** 80 **p** 81. C Notting Hill *Lon* 80-81; C W Brompton St Mary w St Pet 81-84; Perm to Offic 84-91. *82 Ashworth Mansions, Grantully Road, London W9 1LN* Tel 0171-286 6034

BROWNING, Canon Richard Geoffrey Claude. b 25. Selw Coll Cam BA50 MA55. Lon Coll of Div BD53 ALCD53. **d** 53 **p** 54. C Walthamstow St Mary *Chelmsf* 53-56; V E Ham St Paul 56-65; V Old Hill H Trin *Worc* 65-91; Hon Can Worc Cathl 77-91; rtd 91; Perm to Offic *Ban* from 91. *Llwyn Rhug, Ffordd Dewi Sant, Nefyn, Pwllheli LL53 6EG* Tel (01758) 720834

BROWNING, Robert Frank. b 11. K Coll Lon 56. **d** 57 **p** 58. C Headley All SS *Guildf* 57-59; C-in-c Lightwater CD 59-63; V Lightwater 63-76; rtd 76; Perm to Offic *Guildf* from 76. *Braeholme, Rectory Lane, Windlesham, Surrey GU20 6BW* Tel (01276) 474813

BROWNING, Thomas Clive (Tom). b 35. Lon Univ DipTh65 BD67. Wycliffe Hall Ox 63. **d** 67 **p** 68. C Ipswich St Jo *St E* 67-69; Chapl Scargill Ho 69-70; C Downend *Bris* 70-73; C Hagley *Worc* 73-76; Asst Master Bay Ho Sch Gosport from 77; Perm to Offic *Portsm* from 82. *71 Western Way, Alverstoke, Gosport, Hants PO12 2RD* Tel (01705) 584738

BROWNING, Canon Wilfrid Robert Francis. b 18. Ch Ch Ox BA40 MA44 BD49. Cuddesdon Coll 40. **d** 41 **p** 42. C Towcester w Easton Neston *Pet* 41-44; C Woburn Square Ch Ch *Lon* 44-46; Chapl St Deiniol's Lib Hawarden 46-48; Chapl Heswall Nautical Sch 46-48; C-in-c Hove St Rich CD *Chich* 48-51; Lect Cuddesdon Coll 51-59; R Gt Haseley *Ox* 51-59; Ed Bulletin Angl 55-60; Warden Whalley Abbey 59-63; Can Res Blackb Cathl *Blackb* 59-65; Dir of Post-Ord Tr 62-65; Lect Cuddesdon Coll 65-70; Can Res Ch Ch *Ox* 65-87; Hon Can 87-89; Dir of Post-Ord Tr 65-85; Dir of Ords 65-85; Lect Wycliffe Hall Ox 67-69; Dir Ox NSM Course 72-89; rtd 87. *42 Alexandra Road, Oxford OX2 0DB* Tel (01865) 723464

BROWNLESS, Brian Paish. b 25. TD72. Keble Coll Ox BA50 MA50. Wells Th Coll 50. **d** 52 **p** 53. C Man St Aid *Man* 52-54; C Chorlton-cum-Hardy St Clem 54-56; C Swinton St Pet 56-58; V Elton St Steph 58-66; CF (TA) 60-66; Area Sec (Dio Lich) USPG 66-77; Lic to Offic *Lich* 66-77; CF (TA - R of O) 66-72; R Yoxall *Lich* 77-82; V S Ramsey St Paul *S & M* 82-87; rtd 87; Perm to Offic *Heref* from 87. *10 Caple Avenue, Kings Caple, Hereford HR1 4TX* Tel (01432) 840246

BROWNLESS, Philip Paul Stanley. b 19. Selw Coll Cam BA41 MA45. Ridley Hall Cam 46. **d** 47 **p** 48. C Prittlewell St Mary *Chelmsf* 47-50; Min Prittlewell St Mary CD 50-54; Chapl & Hd Master Lambrook Sch Bracknell 54-71; V Heckfield cum Mattingley *Win* 71-74; V Heckfield w Mattingley and Rotherwick 74-84; RD Odiham 83-84; rtd 85; Perm to Offic *Chich* from 85. *The Hornpipe, Oakmeadow, Birdham, Chichester, W Sussex PO20 7BH* Tel (01243) 512177

BROWNLIE, Miss Caroline Heddon. b 47. Suffolk Poly CQSW75. St Jo Coll Nottm DPS80 Qu Coll Birm IDC81. **d** 87 **p** 94. Asst Chapl Fairfield Hosp Hitchin 87-91; NSM Ashwell w Hinxworth and Newnham *St Alb* from 92. *16 Kingland Way, Ashwell, Baldock, Herts SG7 5PZ* Tel (01462) 743296

BROWNRIDGE, Allan John Michael. b 32. Chan Sch Truro 80. **d** 82 **p** 83. C St Keverne *Truro* 82-86; P-in-c Werrington, St Giles in the Heath and Virginstow 86-92; R Boyton, N Tamerton, Werrington etc from 92; RD Trigg Major from 94. *The Rectory, Werrington, Launceston, Cornwall PL15 8TP* Tel (01566) 773932

BROWNRIGG, Canon Ronald Allen. b 19. Em Coll Cam BA47 MA50 FRSA91. Westcott Ho Cam 47. **d** 49 **p** 50. C Beverley Minster *York* 49-51; Dean Jerusalem 51-54; C Stanmore *Win* 54-60; R Bletchingley *S'wark* 60-74; V Petersham 74-85; Hon Can S'wark Cathl 78-85; Consultant Inter-Ch Travel from 83; rtd 85. *6 Stoneleigh Lodge, Branston Road, Kew, Richmond, Surrey TW9 3LD* Tel 0181-940 3506

BROWNSELL, Preb John Kenneth. b 48. Hertf Coll Ox BA69 BA72 MA89. Cuddesdon Coll 70. **d** 73 **p** 74. C Notting Hill All SS w St Columb *Lon* 73-74; C Notting Hill 74-76; TV 76-82; V Notting Hill All SS w St Columb from 82; AD Kensington 84-92; Preb St Paul's Cathl from 92. *All Saints' Vicarage, Powis Gardens, London W11 1JG* Tel 0171-727 5919

BROXTON, Alan. b 40. UMIST BSc72 CEng MICE79 MISE77. LNSM course 93. **d** 96 **p** 97. NSM Rhodes *Man* from 96. *241 Heywood Old Road, Middleton, Manchester M24 4QR* Tel 0161-643 6319 Fax as telephone

BRUCE, David Ian. b 47. Univ of Wales (Cardiff) DipTh73. St Mich Coll Llan 70. **d** 73 **p** 74. C Bordesley St Benedict *Birm* 73-74; C Llanishen and Lisvane *Llan* 74-81; V Canley *Cov* 81-90; V Longford from 90. *St Thomas's Vicarage, Hurst Road, Coventry CV6 6EL* Tel (01203) 364078

BRUCE, Francis Bernard. b 30. Trin Coll Ox BA52 MA56. Westcott Ho Cam 52. **d** 54 **p** 55. C Bury St Mary *Man* 54-59; C Sherborne w Castleton and Lillington *Sarum* 59-61; R Croston *Blackb* 61-86; V Bibury w Winson and Barnsley *Glouc* 86-95; rtd 95; Perm to Offic *Glouc* from 95. *6 Gloucester Street, Cirencester, Glos GL7 2DJ* Tel (01285) 641954

BRUCE, James Hamilton. b 57. Newc Univ MSc79 Dur Univ BSc78. Trin Coll Bris DipTh84. **d** 84 **p** 85. C Walmley *Birm* 84-86; Perm to Offic *Carl* 87-95; W Cumbria Sch Worker N Schs Chr Union 87-93; Nat Development Officer Wales Scripture Union 93; Kenya 95-96; NSM St Andrews St Andr *St And* from 96. *19 Scooniehill Road, St Andrews, Fife KY16 8HA* Tel (01334) 464735 E-mail jhb@st.and.co.uk

BRUCE, John. b 26. **d** 50 **p** 51. Canada 50-62; V Broughton Moor *Carl* 63-66; V Carl St Herbert w St Steph 66-74; P-in-c Kendal St Geo 74-76; V 76-83; V Coundon *Dur* 83-86; rtd 86; Perm to Offic *Carl* 86-93. *9 Penton Close, Carlisle CA3 0PX*

BRUCE, Dr Leslie Barton. b 23. Liv Univ MB, ChB48. **d** 71 **p** 72. NSM Wavertree H Trin *Liv* from 71. *3 Childwall Park Avenue, Liverpool L16 0JE* Tel 0151-722 7664

BRUECK, Ms Jutta. b 61. LSE MSc89 Heythrop Coll Lon MA92 Fitzw Coll Cam BA96. Westcott Ho Cam 94. **d** 97. C Is of Dogs Ch Ch and St Jo w St Luke *Lon* from 97. *Flat 2, St Mildred's House, Roserton Street, London E14 3PG* Tel 0171-538 9697

BRUEK, Ms Jutta. d 97. C Is of Dogs Ch Ch and St Jo w St Luke *Lon* from 97. *Flat 2, St Mildred's House, Roserton Street, London E14 3PG* Tel 0171-515 7975

BRUMPTON, Canon John Charles Kenyon. b 16. Selw Coll Cam BA38 MA42. Linc Th Coll 38. **d** 40 **p** 41. C Grimsby All SS *Linc* 40-44; C Rashcliffe *Wakef* 44-47; V Hepworth 47-52; V Cudworth 52-65; Chapl Asst Barnsley Gen Hosp 65-88; RD Barnsley *Wakef* 65-88; R Barnsley St Mary 66-88; Hon Can Wakef Cathl 67-88; rtd 88; Perm to Offic *Linc* from 88. *Greenside, 199 Legsby Avenue, Grimsby, S Humberside DN32 0AD* Tel (01472) 753258

BRUMWELL, Francis John Thomas. b 33. Lich Th Coll 57. **d** 61 **p** 62. C Birm St Geo *Birm* 61-63; C Gorton St Mark *Man* 63-64; V Calderbrook 65-73; V Bradley St Martin *Lich* 73-89; P-in-c Bilston St Mary 75-78; R Gorton St Phil *Man* 89-95; rtd 95. *53 Audmore Road, Gnosall, Stafford ST20 0HE* Tel (01785) 822808

BRUNDLE, Michael Roy. b 52. Qu Coll Birm. **d** 84 **p** 85. C Swindon New Town *Bris* 84-88; TV Halifax *Wakef* 88-92; Chapl HM Young Offender Inst Feltham 92-94; C Notting Dale St Clem w St Mark and St Jas *Lon* 94-95; V Swanley St Mary *Roch* from 95. *St Mary's Vicarage, London Road, Swanley, Kent BR8 7AQ* Tel (01322) 662201 Fax as telephone

BRUNING, Arthur Frederick. b 17. ALCD54. **d** 54 **p** 55. C Ingrow cum Hainworth *Bradf* 54-57; C Lambeth St Andr w St Thos *S'wark* 57-59; C Hatcham St Jas 59-62; V Chalk *Roch* 62-66; V Deptford St Luke *S'wark* 66-72; V Sporle w Gt and Lt Palgrave *Nor* 72-81; rtd 81; Perm to Offic *Nor* from 81. *3 Adams Road, Norwich NR7 8QT* Tel (01603) 400457

BRUNNING, Canon David George. b 32. St D Coll Lamp BA53. St Mich Coll Llan 53. **d** 55 **p** 56. C Llantwit Major and St Donat's *Llan* 55-59; C Usk and Monkswood w Glascoed Chpl and Gwehelog *Mon* 59-62; V Abercarn 62-71; V Pontnewydd 71-89; RD Pontypool from 89; R Panteg from 90; Can St Woolos Cathl from 94. *Panteg Rectory, The Highway, New Inn, Pontypool NP4 0PH* Tel (01495) 763724

BRUNNING, Neil. b 29. NW Ord Course 73. **d** 76 **p** 77. C Cheadle Hulme All SS *Ches* 76-79; V 79-88; V Glentworth *Linc* 88-93; P-in-c Hemswell w Harpswell 88-93; V Glentworth Gp 93-94; rtd 94; Perm to Offic *Linc* from 94. *11 Drovers Court, Lea Road, Gainsborough, Lincs DN21 1AN* Tel (01427) 617938

BRUNNING, Sidney John George. b 13. Ely Th Coll 46. **d** 49 **p** 50. C Aldershot St Mich *Guildf* 49-51; C Clacton St Jas *Chelmsf* 51-55; R Sunningwell *Ox* 55-81; rtd 81; Perm to Offic *Nor* 81-95. *c/o 47 Church Lane, Little Abington, Cambridge CB1 6BQ* Tel (01223) 891960

BRUNO, Canon Allan David. b 34. AKC59. St Boniface Warminster 59. **d** 60 **p** 61. C Darlington H Trin *Dur* 60-64; S Africa 64-65 and 76-80; Rhodesia 65-70; Overseas Chapl Scottish Episc Ch 70-75; C Edin Old St Paul *Edin* 75-76; Namibia 80-86; Dean Windhoek 81-86; R Falkirk *Edin* 86-95; Hon Can Kinkizi from 95; Bp's Dom Chapl *Bradf* from 96. *Bishopscroft, Ashwell Road, Heaton, Bradford, W Yorkshire BD9 4AU, or 48 Toller Grove, Heaton, Bradford, W Yorkshire BD9 5NP* Tel Bradford (01274) 545414 or 482059 Fax 544831

BRUNSDON, Canon Thomas Kenneth. b 08. Univ of Wales BA33. St Mich Coll Llan 33. **d** 34 **p** 35. C Knighton *S & B* 34-40; V Llandegley 40-47; V Builth w Alltmawr and Llanynys 47-61; RD Builth 55-61; V Newton St Pet 61-76; Can Brecon Cathl 58-72; Treas 72-76; rtd 76. *121 Homegower House, St Helen's Road, Swansea SA1 4DW* Tel (01792) 463473

BRUNSKILL, Mrs Sheila Kathryn. *See* BANYARD, Ms Sheila Kathryn

BRUNSWICK, Canon Robert John. b 38. TD86. St Aid Birkenhead 60. **d** 63 **p** 64. C Neston *Ches* 63-66; CF (TA - R of O) from 65; C Warrington St Paul *Liv* 66-68; V Liv St Paul Stoneycroft 68-78; V Southport St Luke 78-87; R Croston *Blackb* from 87; Chapl Bp Rawstorne Sch Preston from 88; Hon Can Koforidua from 94. *St Michael's Rectory, 19 Westhead Road, Croston, Preston PR5 7RQ* Tel (01772) 600877

BRUNT, Prof Peter William. OBE. Liv Univ MB59 MD67 Lon Univ FRCP74. Ab Dioc Tr Course. **d** 96 **p** 97. NSM Bieldside *Ab* from 96. *17 Kingshill Road, Aberdeen AB15 5JY* Tel (01224) 314204 or 681818 Ext 52287 Fax 840711

BRUNYEE, Miss Hilary. b 46. Linc Th Coll 76. **dss** 81 **d** 87 **p** 94. Longsight St Jo w St Cypr *Man* 81-87; Par Dn Peel 87-94; TV from 94. *7 Trent Drive, Worsley, Manchester M28 5TF* Tel 0161-790 7761

BRUSH, Sally. b 47. Lon Univ BD. Trin Coll Bris 73. **dss** 76 **d** 80 **p** 97. Flint *St As* 76-80; C 80-83; C Cefn 83-87; Chapl St As Cathl 83-87; C St As and Tremeirchion 83-87; D-in-c Cerrigydrudion w Llanfihangel etc 87-97; R from 97. *The Rectory, Cerrigydrudion, Corwen LL21 0RU* Tel (01490) 82313

BRUTON, Keith Leslie. b 39. S Dios Minl Tr Scheme 91. **d** 94 **p** 96. NSM Camelot Par *B & W* from 94. *Castle View House, Sparkford, Yeovil, Somerset BA22 7LH* Tel (01935) 440859 Fax as telephone

BRUTTON, Robert Springett. b 14. Trin Coll Cam BA34 MA55. Cuddesdon Coll 54. **d** 55 **p** 56. C Wendover *Ox* 55-57; V Radley 57-65; V Sonning 65-74; rtd 74; Perm to Offic *Sarum* from 75. *7 North Street, Langton Matravers, Swanage, Dorset BH19 3HL* Tel (01929) 425681

BRYAN, Cecil William. b 43. TCD BA66 MA73. CITC 66. **d** 68 **p** 69. C Dublin Zion Ch *D & G* 68-72; Chapl RAF 72-75; Dioc Info Officer *D & G* 75-90; I Castleknock w Mulhuddart, Clonsilla etc 75-89; Chapl K Hosp Sch Dub from 89. *The King's Hospital, Palmerstown, Dublin 20, Irish Republic* Tel Dublin (1) 626 5933 or 626 5959

BRYAN, Dr David John. b 56. Liv Univ BSc77 Hull Univ BTh85 Qu Coll Ox DPhil89. Ox Min Course 89. **d** 90 **p** 91. C Abingdon *Ox* 90-93; Tutor Qu Coll Birm from 93; Lic to Offic *Birm* from 93. *The Queen's College, Somerset Road, Birmingham B15 2QH* Tel 0121-454 7506 or 454 8189

BRYAN, Dr Judith Claire. b 57. Aston Univ BSc79 PhD82 Trent Poly PGCE83. St Jo Coll Nottm BTh94 LTh95. **d** 95 **p** 96. C Wolverhampton St Matt *Lich* from 95. *29 Denmore Gardens, Wolverhampton WV1 2BN* Tel (01902) 453031

BRYAN, Leslie Harold. b 48. Div Hostel Dub 70. **d** 73 **p** 74. C Cork St Fin Barre's Cathl *C, C & R* 73-75; I Templebreedy w Tracton and Nohoval 75-79; CF from 79. *MOD Chaplains (Army), Trenchard Lines, Upavon, Pewsey, Wilts SN9 6BE* Tel (01980) 615804 Fax 615800

BRYAN, Michael John Christopher. b 35. MSBiblLit MCBiblAA Wadh Coll Ox BA58 BTh59 MA63 Ex Univ PhD83. Ripon Hall Ox 59. **d** 60 **p** 61. C Reigate St Mark *S'wark* 60-64; Tutor Sarum & Wells Th Coll 64-69; Vice-Prin 69-71; USA 71-74 and from 83; Sen Officer Educn and Community Dept *Lon* 74-79; Chapl Ex Univ *Ex* 79-83; rtd 95; Perm to Offic *Ex* from 95. *148 Proctors Hall Road, Sewanee, Tennessee 37383-1000, USA*

BRYAN, Nigel Arthur. b 39. Univ of Wales (Lamp) BA61. Burgess Hall Lamp 61. **d** 63 **p** 64. C Llanstadwel *St D* 63-69; Chapl RAF 69-94; R Gt w Lt Milton and Gt Haseley *Ox* from 94. *The Rectory, Great Milton, Oxford OX44 7PN* Tel (01844) 279498

BRYAN, Patrick Joseph. b 41. St Jo Coll Cam BA63 MA67. St Steph Ho Ox 73. **d** 75 **p** 76. C Rushall *Lich* 75-78; C Brierley Hill 78-80; P-in-c Walsall St Mary and All SS Palfrey 80-87. *49 Hawthorn Road, Shelfield, Walsall WS5 4NB* Tel (01922) 963234

BRYAN, Canon Percival John Milward. b 19. St Pet Coll Ox BA40 MA46 BTh47. Wycliffe Hall Ox 46. **d** 48 **p** 49. C Belvedere All SS *Roch* 48-51; Australia 51-52; C Blindley Heath *S'wark* 53-54; R Warkton and Weekley *Pet* 54-56; R Kings Cliffe 56-85; Can Pet Cathl 73-86; rtd 86; Perm to Offic *Pet* from 86; Perm to Offic *Linc* from 91. *3 Saxon Road, Barnack, Stamford, Lincs PE9 3EQ* Tel (01780) 740906

BRYAN, Canon Philip Richard. b 40. Dur Univ BA61. Wycliffe Hall Ox 72. **d** 74 **p** 75. C Macclesfield St Mich *Ches* 74-77; V St Bees *Carl* from 77; Chapl St Bees Sch Cumbria from 77; RD Calder *Carl* 88-96; Hon Can Carl Cathl from 91. *The Priory, St Bees, Cumbria CA27 0DR* Tel (01946) 822279

BRYAN, Mrs Sherry Lee. b 49. WMMTC 88. **d** 91 **p** 94. Par Dn St Columb Minor and St Colan *Truro* 91-94; C 94-96; P-in-c St Teath from 96. *The Vicarage, Whitewell Lane, St Teath, Bodmin, Cornwall PL30 3LH* Tel (01208) 850292

BRYAN, Timothy Andrew. b 56. St Edm Hall Ox MA80. S'wark Ord Course 93. **d** 96. NSM Morden *S'wark* from 96. *39 Highfield Road, Sutton, Surrey SM1 4JY* Tel 0181-642 0576

BRYAN, Timothy James Bryan. b 23. Chich Th Coll 53. **d** 54 **p** 55. C Weybridge *Guildf* 54-57; Lebanon from 65. *PO Box 4008, Beirut, Lebanon*

BRYAN, William Terence. b 38. Chich Th Coll 73. **d** 75 **p** 76. C Shrewsbury St Giles *Lich* 75-79; V Churchstoke w Hyssington and Sarn *Heref* from 79. *The Vicarage, Church Stoke, Montgomery SY15 6AF* Tel (01588) 620228

BRYANS, Joseph. b 15. TCD BA39 MA43. CITC 40. **d** 42 **p** 43. C Kirby Moorside w Gillamoor *York* 42-45; C Thornaby on Tees St Luke 45-47; C Seapatrick *D & D* 47-54; I Gleneely w Culdaff *D & R* 54-60; I Tamlaghtard w Aghanloo 60-90; rtd 90. *1 Eventide Gardens, Limavady, Co Londonderry BT49 0AX* Tel (01504) 762768

BRYANT, Andrew Watts. b 57. MA. Qu Coll Birm. **d** 83 **p** 84. C Pelsall *Lich* 83-87; NSM 92-96; Perm to Offic 87-92; NSM Beckbury, Badger, Kemberton, Ryton, Stockton etc from 96. *Kaleidoscope Theatre, 19 Mellish Road, Walsall WS4 2DQ* Tel (01922) 642751

BRYANT, Canon Christopher. b 32. AKC60. **d** 61 **p** 62. C Fareham H Trin *Portsm* 61-65; C Yatton Keynell *Bris* 65-71; V Chirton, Marden and Patney *Sarum* 71-76; V Chirton, Marden, Patney, Charlton and Wilsford 76-78; P-in-c Devizes St Jo w St Mary 78-79; R 79-97; RD Devizes 83-92; Can and Preb Sarum Cathl from 87; Master St Nic Hosp Salisbury from 97. *The Master's House, St Nicholas Hospital, St Nicholas Road, Salisbury SP1 2SW* Tel (01722) 336874

BRYANT, David Charles. b 48. St Andr Univ BSc71. St Mich Coll Llan 71. **d** 74 **p** 75. C Llanilid w Pencoed *Llan* 74-78; C Caerphilly 78-79; V Crynant 79-84; V Llanegryn and Llanfihangel-y-Pennant etc *Ban* 84-93; V Llandwrog and Llanwnda from 93. *The Vicarage, Groeslon, Caernarfon LL54 7DL* Tel (01286) 830584 Fax 830614

BRYANT, David Henderson. b 37. K Coll Lon BD60 AKC60. **d** 61 **p** 62. C Trowbridge H Trin *Sarum* 61-63; C Ewell *Guildf* 63-67; V Leiston *St E* 67-73; Chapl RN 73; C Northam *Ex* 74-75; P-in-c Clavering w Langley *Chelmsf* 76-77; Teacher Mountview High Sch Harrow 77-85; P-in-c Boosbeck w Moorsholm *York* 85-89; V 89-90; V Sowerby 90-95; P-in-c Sessay 90-95; V Lastingham w Appleton-le-Moors, Rosedale etc from 95. *The Vicarage, Lastingham, York YO6 6TN* Tel (01751) 417344

✠**BRYANT, The Rt Revd Denis William.** b 18. DFC42. Qu Coll Birm 56. **d** 58 **p** 59 **c** 67. C Bourne *Guildf* 58-60; C Cuddington 60-61; Australia from 61; Adn Goldfields 66-67; Bp Kalgoorlie 67-72; Adn Northam 72-75; Asst Bp Perth 74-75; rtd 94. *Unit 3, Dorothy Genders Village, 99 McCabe Street, Mosman Park, W Australia 6012* Tel Perth (9) 385 4515

BRYANT, Donald Thomas. b 29. FSS59 SE Essex Coll BSc56 Birkb Coll Lon BSc58. S'wark Ord Course 85. **d** 88 **p** 89. NSM Redhill St Matt *S'wark* from 88. *21 Windermere Way, Reigate, Surrey RH2 0LW* Tel (01737) 762382

BRYANT, Canon Douglas William. b 17. St Boniface Warminster. **d** 41 **p** 42. C Two Mile Hill St Mich *Bris* 41-44; C Branksome St Aldhelm *Sarum* 44-45; C Salisbury St Mark 45-50; V Devizes St Pet 50-57; V Burpham *Guildf* 57-70; V Egham Hythe 70-75; Hon Can Guildf Cathl 70-83; R Fetcham 75-83; rtd 83; Perm to Offic *Guildf* from 83. *4 Clandon Road, Guildford, Surrey GU1 2DR* Tel (01483) 572682

BRYANT, Edgar James. b 28. Univ of Wales (Swansea) BA49. St Mich Coll Llan 49. **d** 51 **p** 52. C Brynmawr *S & B* 51-55; C Llandrindod w Cefnllys 55-59; V Bettws Disserth w Llansantffraed in Elwell 59-69; V Disserth 59-69; V Llanelwedd w Llanfaredd w Llansantffraed etc 69-72; C Aymestrey and Leinthall Earles w Wigmore etc *Heref* 72-86 and 86-92; NSM Fownhope w Mordiford, Brockhampton etc 93-94; C Stoke Lacy, Moreton Jeffries w Much Cowarne etc from 95. *20 Bridgeford Close, Kings Acre, Hereford HR4 0QX* Tel (01432) 265021

BRYANT, Edward Francis Paterson. b 43. S'wark Ord Course 75. **d** 78 **p** 79. NSM Hadlow *Roch* 78-84; C Dartford St Alb 84-87; R Hollington St Leon *Chich* 87-93; V Bexhill St Aug from 93. *St Augustine's Vicarage, St Augustine's Close, Bexhill-on-Sea, E Sussex TN39 3AZ* Tel (01424) 210785 Fax as telephone

BRYANT, Graham Trevor. b 41. Keble Coll Ox BA63 DipTh64 MA67. Chich Th Coll 64. **d** 66 **p** 67. C Leeds St Wilfrid *Ripon* 66-69; C Haywards Heath St Wilfrid *Chich* 69-74; V Crawley Down All SS 74-79; V Bexhill St Aug 79-85; V Charlton Kings St Mary *Glouc* from 85. *St Mary's Vicarage, 63 Church Street, Charlton Kings, Cheltenham, Glos GL53 8AT* Tel (01242) 253402

BRYANT, Canon Mark Watts. b 49. St Jo Coll Dur BA72. Cuddesdon Coll 72. **d** 75 **p** 76. C Addlestone *Guildf* 75-79; C Studley *Sarum* 79-83; V 83-88; Chapl Trowbridge Coll 79-83; Voc Development Adv *Cov* 88-96; Dioc Dir of Ords 88-96; Hon Can Cov Cathl from 93; TR Coventry Caludon from 96. *Stoke Rectory, 365A Walsgrave Road, Coventry CV2 4BG* Tel (01203) 635731 or 443691

BRYANT, Patricia Ann. b 46. Lon Univ BA. **d** 91 **p** 97. NSM Llanbadoc *Mon* 91-93; NSM Llangybi and Coedypaen w Llanbadoc from 93; Chapl FE from 95. *Ty'r Ynys Fach, The Rhadyr, Llanbadoc, Usk NP5 1PY* Tel (01291) 672082

BRYANT, Peter James. b 35. Jes Coll Cam BA58 MA64 UWIST FInstM. St Deiniol's Hawarden 85 St Mich Coll Llan 96. **d** 97. NSM Raglan-Usk *Mon* from 97. *Ty'r Ynys Fach, The Rhadyr, Llanbadoc, Usk NP5 1PY* Tel (01291) 672082 Mobile 0378-806046 Fax as telephone

BRYANT, Canon Richard Kirk. b 47. Ch Coll Cam BA68 MA72 Nottm Univ DipTh70. Cuddesdon Coll 70. **d** 72 **p** 73. C Newc St Gabr *Newc* 72-75; C Morpeth 75-78; C Benwell St Jas 78-82; V Earsdon and Backworth 82-93; V Wylam 93-97; Hon Can Newc Cathl from 97; Tr Dir for Local Min from 97; Dir of Reader Tr from 97. *2 Burlington Court, Hadrian Park, Wallsend, Tyne & Wear NE28 9YH* Tel 0191-263 7922

BRYANT, Richard Maurice. b 46. MAAIS80. W of England Minl Tr Course 90. **d** 93 **p** 94. NSM The Stanleys *Glouc* from 93. *6 Church Street, Kings Stanley, Stonehouse, Glos GL10 3HW* Tel (01453) 823172

BRYANT, Royston George. b 09. St Aid Birkenhead 54. **d** 56 **p** 57. C Clifton Ch Ch *Bris* 56-59; C Swindon Ch Ch 59-61; V Stratton St Margaret 61-69; V Fishponds All SS 69-76; rtd 76; Perm to Offic *Bris* 76-93. *c/o M G Bryant Esq, 18 Beechwood Drive, Scawby, Brigg, S Humberside DN20 9AR*

BRYANT, Sidney John. b 29. Linc Coll Ox BA52 MA56. St Steph Ho Ox 52. **d** 54 **p** 55. C Southgate St Andr *Lon* 54-58; C Tottenham Ch Ch W Green 58-60; V New Southgate St Paul 60-71; R Gt Leighs *Chelmsf* 71-92; P-in-c Lt Leighs 71-92; rtd 92. *16 Rydal Avenue, Felixstowe, Suffolk IP11 9SE* Tel (01394) 275822

BRYANT, William George. b 22. Selw Coll Cam MA48. St Alb Minl Tr Scheme 78. **d** 81 **p** 82. NSM Welwyn w Ayot St Peter *St Alb* 81-82; NSM Balsall Heath St Paul *Birm* 82-85; P-in-c Teme Valley S *Worc* 85-89; rtd 89. *28 De Havilland Way, Christchurch, Dorset BH23 3JE* Tel (01202) 499231

BRYARS, Peter John. b 54. BA MEd PhD. St Jo Coll Nottm. **d** 84 **p** 85. C Kingston upon Hull St Martin *York* 84; C Hull St Martin w Transfiguration 84-87; TV Drypool 87-90; TV Glendale Gp *Newc* 90-94; P-in-c Heddon-on-the-Wall from 94; Adult Educn Adv from 94. *St Andrew's Vicarage, Towne Gate, Heddon-on-the-Wall, Newcastle upon Tyne NE15 0DT* Tel (01661) 853142

BRYCE, Michael Adrian Gilpin. b 47. TCD BA. CITC 74. **d** 77 **p** 78. C Dublin Ch Ch Cathl Gp *D & G* 77-79; Chapl Univ Coll Dub 79-82; I Ardamine w Kiltennel, Glascarrig etc *C & O* 82-84; CF from 84. *MOD Chaplains (Army), Trenchard Lines, Upavon, Pewsey, Wilts SN9 6BE* Tel (01980) 615804 Fax 615800

BRYER, Anthony Colin (Tony). b 51. Lon Univ BSc72 Bris Univ DipTh75. Trin Coll Bris 72. **d** 75 **p** 76. C Preston St Cuth *Blackb* 75-78; C Becontree St Mary *Chelmsf* 78-81; TV Loughton St Mary and St Mich 81-88; C Clifton St Paul *Bris* 88-91; P-in-c 91-94; R Bris St Mich and St Paul 94-96; Dir of Outreach Edin SS Andr and Geo (C of S) from 96; Lic to Offic *Edin* from 96. *St Andrew and St George Church, George Street, Edinburgh EH2 2PA* Tel 0131-225 3847

BRYER, Paul Donald. b 58. Sussex Univ BEd80. St Jo Coll Nottm DipTh90. **d** 90 **p** 91. C Tonbridge St Steph *Roch* 90-94; TV Camberley St Paul *Guildf* from 94. *St Mary's House, 37 Park Road, Camberley, Surrey GU15 2SP* Tel (01276) 22085

BUBBERS, David Bramwell. b 23. Lambeth MA84 Oak Hill Th Coll 51. **d** 54 **p** 55. C Beckenham St Jo *Roch* 54-58; V Wandsworth St Mich *S'wark* 58-65; V Northwood Em *Lon* 65-74; Perm to Offic *St Alb* 74-93; Lic to Offic *Lon* 74-88; Gen Sec CPAS 74-88; rtd 88; Perm to Offic *Chich* from 88. *2 Earlsmead Court, 15 Granville Road, Eastbourne, E Sussex BN20 7HE* Tel (01323) 737077

BUBBINGS, Charles Gardam. b 26. Qu Coll Birm 68. **d** 69 **p** 70. C Scarborough St Mary w Ch Ch, St Paul and St Thos *York* 69-72; C Fulford 72-74; V Middlesbrough St Oswald 74-81; V Ringley *Man* 81-88; rtd 88; Perm to Offic *Man* from 88. *4 Hilton Grove, Little Hulton, Manchester M38 0RY* Tel 0161-702 9402

BUCHAN, The Ven Eric Ancrum. b 07. St Chad's Coll Dur BA32. **d** 33 **p** 34. C Knowle H Nativity *Bris* 33-40; Chapl RAFVR 40-45; V Cov St Mark *Cov* 45-59; V Cov St Barn 45-59; Chapl Cov and Warks Hosp 46-59; Hon Can Cov Cathl *Cov* 53-65; RD Coventry 54-63; Dioc Dir Chr Stewardship 59-77; Bp's Dom Chapl 61-65; R Baginton 63-69; Adn Cov 65-77; rtd 77; Perm to Offic *Glouc* from 78. *The College of St Barnabas, Blackberry Lane, Lingfield, Surrey RH7 6NJ* Tel (01342) 870573

BUCHAN, Geoffrey Herbert. b 38. CEng MIMechE. Nor Ord Course 91. **d** 94 **p** 95. NSM Barnton *Ches* from 94. *12 Hough Lane, Anderton, Northwich, Cheshire CW9 6AB* Tel (01606) 74512

✠**BUCHANAN, The Rt Revd Colin Ogilvie.** b 34. Linc Coll Ox MA. Lambeth Hon DD93 Tyndale Hall Bris 59. **d** 61 **p** 62 **c** 85. C Cheadle *Ches* 61-64; Tutor St Jo Coll Nottm 64-85; Lib 64-69; Registrar 69-74; Dir of Studies 74-75; Vice-Prin 75-78; Prin 79-85; Hon Can S'well Minster *S'well* 81-85; Suff Bp Aston *Birm* 85-89; Asst Bp Roch 89-96; V Gillingham St Mark 91-96; Asst Bp S'wark 90-91; Area Bp Woolwich from 96. *37 South Road, London SE23 2UH*

BUCHANAN, Canon Eric. b 32. Leeds Univ BA54. Coll of Resurr Mirfield 54. **d** 56 **p** 57. C Cov St Mark *Cov* 56-59; Asst Chapl Lon Univ *Lon* 59-64; C Bloomsbury St Geo w St Jo 59-64; V Duston *Pet* 64-79; RD Wootton 75-79; Can Pet Cathl 77-97; V Wellingborough All Hallows 79-90; V Higham Ferrers w Chelveston 90-97; Chapl to The Queen 92-97; rtd 97. *8 College Street, Higham Ferrers, Wellingborough, Northants NN10 8DZ* Tel (01933) 411232

BUCHANAN, George Rowland. b 15. St Aug Coll Cant. **d** 59 **p** 60. C Sherborne w Castleton and Lillington *Sarum* 59-63; V Bradford Abbas w Clifton Maybank 63-67; R Gt Wishford 67-73; R Lt Langford 67-73; RD Wylye and Wilton 69-73; Org Sec (Dios Ex and B & W) CECS 73-77; rtd 77; Perm to Offic *Sarum* from 77. *Cobblers, Greenhill, Sherborne, Dorset DT9 4EP* Tel (01935) 812263

BUCHANAN, John Fraser Walter. b 32. Em Coll Cam BA55. LNSM course 91. **d** 93 **p** 94. NSM Wainford *St E* from 93. *The Hermitage, Bridge Street, Beccles, Suffolk NR34 9BA* Tel (01502) 712154

BUCK, Eric Joseph. b 14. Lon Univ BA35 DipEd54. Ridley Hall Cam 60. **d** 61 **p** 62. C Wymondham *Nor* 61-62; V Wicklewood and Crownthorpe 62-79; P-in-c Deopham w Hackford 75-79; rtd 79; Perm to Offic *Nor* 80-95. *10 Robins Close, Great Bentley, Colchester CO7 8QH* Tel (01206) 250623

BUCK, Nicholas John. b 57. BScEng. Ridley Hall Cam 81. **d** 84 **p** 85. C Oakwood St Thos *Lon* 84-87; C Attercliffe *Sheff* 87-90; C Darnall H Trin 87-90; V Kimberworth 90-96; Scargill Ho from 96; Perm to Offic *Bradf* from 96. *Scargill House, Kettlewell, Skipton, N Yorkshire BD23 5HU* Tel (01756) 760234

BUCK, Canon Richard Peter Holdron. b 37. AKC64. Lambeth Hon MA93. **d** 65 **p** 66. C Mill Hill Jo Keble Ch *Lon* 65-68; C

St Marylebone All SS 68-74; Can Res and Treas Truro Cathl *Truro* 74-76; V Primrose Hill St Mary w Avenue Road St Paul *Lon* 76-84; Bp's Ecum Adv *S'wark* 84-91; P-in-c Dulwich Common St Pet 84-86; Hon Can S'wark Cathl from 90; C Rotherhithe St Kath w St Barn 91-92; C Bermondsey St Kath w St Bart 92-94; C Greenwich St Alfege w St Pet and St Paul from 94. *88 Ashburnham Grove, London SE10 8UJ* Tel 0181-691 9916

BUCK, William Ashley. b 61. Man Univ BA82 Ox Univ BA86. Ripon Coll Cuddesdon 84. **d** 87 **p** 88. C Addington *S'wark* 87-91; C Pimlico St Pet w Westmr Ch Ch *Lon* 91-94; TV Wenlock *Heref* from 94. *The Vicarage, Harley Road, Cressage, Shrewsbury SY5 6DF* Tel (01952) 510355

BUCKBY, Gary. b 69. Leeds Univ BA90. Coll of Resurr Mirfield 93. **d** 95 **p** 96. C Wolverhampton St Steph *Lich* from 95. *St Stephen's Vicarage, Hilton Street, Wolverhampton WV10 0LF* Tel (01902) 454662

BUCKETT, Canon James Frederick. b 27. MBE97. ACP. Roch Th Coll 60. **d** 62 **p** 63. C Rowner *Portsm* 62-64; Lic to Offic 64-66; Chapl Highbury Tech Coll Portsm 64-66; V St Helens *Portsm* 66-72; CF (TA) 72-95; V Newport St Thos *Portsm* 72-95; Hon Can Portsm Cathl 81-95; rtd 95. *The Coach House, 140A Staplers Road, Newport, Isle of Wight PO30 2DJ* Tel (01983) 521847

BUCKINGHAM, The Ven Hugh Fletcher. b 32. Hertf Coll Ox BA57 MA60. Westcott Ho Cam 55. **d** 57 **p** 58. C Halliwell St Thos *Man* 57-60; C Sheff Gillcar St Silas *Sheff* 60-65; V Hindolveston *Nor* 65-70; V Guestwick 65-70; R Fakenham w Alethorpe 70-88; Chmn Dioc Bd Soc Resp 81-88; RD Burnham and Walsingham 81-87; Hon Can Nor Cathl 85-88; Adn E Riding *York* from 88; Can and Preb York Minster from 88. *Brimley Lodge, 27 Molescroft Road, Beverley, N Humberside HU17 7DX* Tel (01482) 881659

BUCKINGHAM, Richard Arthur John. b 49. Univ of Wales (Cardiff) BA71 PGCE72. Chich Th Coll 73. **d** 76 **p** 77. C Llantwit Major *Llan* 76-80; C Leigh-on-Sea St Marg *Chelmsf* 80-84; C Westmr St Matt *Lon* 84-87; R Stock Harvard *Chelmsf* from 87. *The Rectory, 61 High Street, Stock, Ingatestone, Essex CM4 9BN* Tel (01277) 840453

BUCKINGHAM, Archdeacon of. *See* MORRISON, The Ven John Anthony

BUCKINGHAM, Area Bishop of. *See* BENNETTS, The Rt Revd Colin James

BUCKLE, Graham Martin. b 62. Southn Univ BTh89. Sarum & Wells Th Coll 85. **d** 89 **p** 90. C Paddington St Jas *Lon* 89-94; P-in-c Paddington St Pet from 94. *St Peter's Vicarage, 59 Elgin Avenue, London W9 2DB* Tel 0171-289 2011

BUCKLER, Andrew Jonathan Heslington. b 68. Trin Coll Ox BA89 MA96. Wycliffe Hall Ox BTh93. **d** 96 **p** 97. C Ox St Aldate *Ox* from 96. *9 Pembroke Street, Oxford OX1 1BP* Tel (01865) 244713

BUCKLER, George Anthony (Tony). b 35. Open Univ BA74. Lich Th Coll 58. **d** 61 **p** 62. C Old Swinford *Worc* 61-65; C Droitwich St Nic w St Pet 65-67; C Droitwich St Andr w St Mary 65-67; Chapl Claybury Hosp Woodford Bridge 67-78; Chapl St Geo and Co Hosps Linc 78-87; Chapl Lawn Hosp Linc 78-81; Chapl Wexham Park Hosp Slough 87-90; Chapl Mapperley Hosp Nottm 90-94; Chapl Nottm Mental Illness and Psychiatric Unit 90-96; Chapl Wells Rd Cen Nottm 94-96; Chapl Qu Medical Cen Nottm 94-96; Chapl Highbury Hosp Nottm 94-96; rtd 96. *73 Westfield Drive, Lincoln LN2 4RE*

BUCKLER, Guy Ernest Warr. b 46. ACA69 FCA79. Linc Th Coll 71. **d** 74 **p** 75. C Dunstable *St Alb* 74-77; C Houghton Regis 77-86; TV Willington Team *Newc* 86-88; TR 88-95; Chapl N Tyneside Coll of FE 88-95; R Bedford St Pet w St Cuth *St Alb* from 95. *St Peter's Rectory, 36 De Parys Avenue, Bedford MK40 2TP* Tel (01234) 354543

BUCKLER, Canon Peter. b 17. OBE79. Lon Univ BSc38. Linc Th Coll. **d** 66 **p** 67. C Baddesley Ensor *Birm* 66-67; C Grendon 67-68; R 68-71; P-in-c Burton Dassett *Cov* 71-74; Hon Can Cov Cathl 76-83; P-in-c Baxterley w Hurley and Wood End and Merevale etc *Birm* 80-83; rtd 83; Perm to Offic *Cov* from 83; Perm to Offic *Birm* from 83; Perm to Offic *Leic* from 91. *9 St Michael's Close, Atherstone, Warks CV9 1LU* Tel (01827) 720133

BUCKLER, Philip John Warr. b 49. St Pet Coll Ox BA70 MA74. Cuddesdon Coll 70. **d** 72 **p** 73. C Bushey Heath *St Alb* 72-75; Chapl Trin Coll Cam 75-81; Min Can and Sacr St Paul's Cathl *Lon* 81-87; V Hampstead St Jo from 87; AD N Camden (Hampstead) from 93. *The Vicarage, 14 Church Row, London NW3 6UU* Tel 0171-435 0553 or 794 5808

BUCKLEY, Alan. b 40. Tyndale Hall Bris. **d** 67 **p** 68. C Owlerton *Sheff* 67-70; C Mansfield St Pet *S'well* 70-73; C Charlesworth *Derby* 73-75; P-in-c Whitfield 76-84; V Moldgreen *Wakef* 84-90; V Hadfield *Derby* from 90. *St Andrew's Vicarage, 122 Hadfield Road, Hadfield, Hyde, Cheshire SK14 8DR* Tel (01457) 852431

BUCKLEY, Alexander Christopher Nolan. b 67. Univ of Wales (Abth) BD89. St Mich Coll Llan DPS91. **d** 91 **p** 94. C Llandudno *Ban* 91-92; C Ynyscynhaearn w Penmorfa and Porthmadog 92-93 and 94-96; Jesuit Volunteer Community Manchester 93-94; C Caerau w Ely *Llan* from 96; Chapl ATC from 96. *92 Bishopston Road, Caerau, Cardiff CF5 5DZ* Tel (01222) 566297

BUCKLEY, Christopher Ivor. b 48. Chich Th Coll. **d** 86 **p** 87. C Felpham w Middleton *Chich* 86-89; C Jersey St Brelade *Win* 89-93; Chapl HM Pris Jersey from 90; V Jersey St Mark *Win* from 93. *St Mark's Vicarage, Springfield Road, St Helier, Jersey, Channel Islands JE2 4LE* Tel (01534) 20595

BUCKLEY, David Rex. b 47. Ripon Coll Cuddesdon 75. **d** 77 **p** 78. C Witton *Ches* 77-81; V Backford 81-85; Youth Chapl from 81; V Barnton 85-93; P-in-c Harthill and Burwardsley from 93; P-in-c Bickerton w Bickley from 93. *The Vicarage, Harthill Road, Tattenhall, Chester CH3 9NU* Tel (01829) 70067

BUCKLEY, Canon Derek Haslam. b 17. Bps' Coll Cheshunt 52. **d** 54 **p** 55. C Chapelthorpe *Wakef* 54-57; C Bakewell *Derby* 57-59; R Fenny Bentley, Thorpe and Tissington 59-67; V Scropton 67-73; R Boylestone 67-73; HM Det Cen Foston Hall 67-73; RD Longford *Derby* 71-81; P-in-c Ch Broughton w Boylestone amd Sutton on the Hill 73-76; V 76-83; P-in-c Trusley 77-83; Hon Can Derby Cathl 79-83; rtd 83; Perm to Offic *Derby* from 83. *St Oswald's House, 52 Belle Vue Road, Ashbourne, Derbyshire DE6 1AT* Tel (01335) 345155

BUCKLEY, Ernest Fairbank. b 25. Jes Coll Cam BA49 MA50 Jes Coll Ox BLitt53. Westcott Ho Cam 55. **d** 55 **p** 56. C Rochdale *Man* 55-58; V Hey 58-64; V Baguley 64-79; V Clun w Chapel Lawn, Bettws-y-Crwyn and Newcastle *Heref* 79-87; RD Clun Forest 82-87; rtd 88. *Hawthorn Bank, Clunton, Craven Arms, Shropshire SY7 0HP* Tel (01588) 660281

BUCKLEY, John. b 42. **d** 95 **p** 96. C Macclesfield Team Par *Ches* from 95. *4 Harvest Road, Macclesfield, Cheshire SK10 2LH*

BUCKLEY, Michael. b 49. St Jo Coll Dur Cranmer Hall Dur 77. **d** 79 **p** 80. C Birkdale St Jo *Liv* 79-82; TV Maghull 82-88; V Earlestown from 88. *The Vicarage, 63 Market Street, Newton-le-Willows, Merseyside WA12 9BS* Tel (01925) 224771

BUCKLEY, Canon Michael Richard. b 20. Lon Univ BD42 AKC42. Cuddesdon Coll 42. **d** 43 **p** 44. C Whitton St Aug *Lon* 43-45; C Hatfield *St Alb* 45-48; C Leatherhead *Guildf* 48-52; V Stoneleigh 52-67; R Weybridge 67-85; Hon Can Guildf Cathl 76-85; rtd 85; Perm to Offic *Chelmsf* from 85; Perm to Offic *Ely* from 86. *Bourn Cottage, High Street, Great Chesterford, Saffron Walden, Essex CB10 1PL* Tel (01799) 530398

BUCKLEY, Richard Francis. b 44. Ripon Hall Ox 69. **d** 72 **p** 73. C Portsea St Cuth *Portsm* 72-75; C Portsea All SS w St Jo Rudmore 75-79; Chapl RN from 79. *Royal Naval Chaplaincy Service, Room 203, Victory Building, HM Naval Base, Portsmouth PO1 3LS* Tel (01705) 727903 Fax 727112

BUCKLEY, Dr Richard John. b 43. Hull Univ BSc64 PhD87 Strathclyde Univ MSc69. Sarum Th Coll 64. **d** 66 **p** 67. C Huddersfield St Jo *Wakef* 66-68; C Sutton St Jas *York* 69-71; TV Sutton St Jas and Wawne 71-75; V Handsworth Woodhouse *Sheff* 75-85; R Adwick-le-Street 85-91; V Wentworth from 91. *The Vicarage, Church Drive, Wentworth, Rotherham, S Yorkshire S62 7TW* Tel (01226) 742274

BUCKLEY, Dr Robert William. b 50. Grey Coll Dur BSc70 PhD73 DipEd73 MInstP75 CPhys75 MInstE91 FCollP92 FRSA94. N Ord Course 85. **d** 87 **p** 88. NSM N Greenford All Hallows *Lon* 87-91; P-in-c 91-94; NSM W Acton St Martin 94-95; NSM Ealing All SS 94-95; C from 95. *All Saints Vicarage, Elm Grove Road, London W5 3JH* Tel 0181-567 8166 Fax 840 7261

BUCKLEY, Stephen Richard. b 45. Cranmer Hall Dur 82. **d** 84 **p** 85. C Iffley *Ox* 84-88; TV Halesowen *Worc* from 88. *St Margaret's Vicarage, 55 Quarry Lane, Halesowen, W Midlands B63 4PD* Tel 0121-550 8744

BUCKLEY, Timothy Denys. b 57. BA. St Jo Coll Nottm DipTh. **d** 83 **p** 84. C S Westoe *Dur* 83-85; C Paddington Em Harrow Road *Lon* 85-88; C Binley *Cov* from 88; Min Binley Woods LEP from 88. *20 Daneswood Road, Coventry CV3 2BJ* Tel (01203) 543003

BUCKMAN, Rossly David. b 36. TCD BA64 MA67 St Pet Coll Ox BA65. Moore Th Coll Sydney ACT ThL59. **d** 59 **p** 60. Australia 59-61 and 76-80 and from 89; C Dublin Harold's Cross *D & G* 61-64; C Ox St Mich *Ox* 64-65; Lect Th Bris Univ 65-69; Lic to Offic *Bris* 65-69; CF 69-76; P-in-c Mid Marsh Gp *Linc* 81-82; R 82-89. *St Martin's Rectory, 9 Centre Street, Blakehurst, Sydney, NSW, Australia 2221* Tel Sydney (2) 546 8022 Fax 546 8096

BUCKMASTER, Charles. b 20. St Jo Coll Dur BA50. Wells Th Coll 50. **d** 51 **p** 52. C Battersea St Luke *S'wark* 51-53; Lic to Offic *Derby* 60-68; Prin St Pet Coll Birm 68-78; Cyprus 78-82; P-in-c Viney Hill *Glouc* 82-89; rtd 89; Perm to Offic *Glouc* from 89. *Hazledene, Johnsons Way, Yorkley, Lydney, Glos GL15 4RZ* Tel (01594) 564167

BUCKNALL, Ms Alison Mary. b 55. Leeds Univ BA76 Trin Coll Bris MA94. Qu Coll Birm 94. **d** 96. C The Quinton *Birm* from 96. *111 Glyn Farm Road, Quinton, Birmingham B32 1NJ*

BUCKNALL, Allan. b 35. ALCD62. Lon Coll of Div 62. **d** 62 **p** 63. C Harlow New Town w Lt Parndon *Chelmsf* 62-69; Chapl W Somerset Miss to Deaf 69-71; Perm to Offic *Bris* 71-77; P-in-c Wisborough Green *Chich* 77-79; R Tillington 78-86; R Duncton 82-86; R Up Waltham 82-86; C Henfield w Shermanbury and Woodmancote 86-89; Asst Chapl Princess Marg Hosp Swindon 89-96; Angl Chapl Swindon and Marlborough NHS Trust from 96. *Princesss Margaret Hospital, Okus Road, Swindon SN1 4JU, or, 5 The Willows, Swindon SN6 7PG* Tel (01793) 426263 or 762721

BUCKNALL, Miss Ann Gordon. b 32. K Coll Lon BSc53 Hughes Hall Cam DipEd54. Qu Coll Birm 80. **dss** 81 **d** 87 **p** 94. Birm St Aid Small Heath *Birm* 81-85; Balsall Heath St Paul 85-92; Par Dn 87-92; C Handsworth St Jas 92-95; rtd 95; Perm to Offic *Lich* from 95. *20 St Margaret's Road, Lichfield, Staffs WS13 7RA* Tel (01543) 257382

BUCKNALL, William John. b 44. Lon Univ DipTh67. Kelham Th Coll 63. **d** 68 **p** 69. C Carl H Trin *Carl* 68-71; C Baswich *Lich* 71-73; P-in-c Ilam w Blore Ray and Okeover 73-76; V Wednesbury St Paul Wood Green 76-84; RD Wednesbury 78-84; TR Wordsley 84-90. *198 The Broadway, Dudley, W Midlands DY1 3DR* Tel (01384) 214047

BUDD, John Christopher. b 51. DLIS QUB BA73 TCD DipTh82. **d** 82 **p** 83. C Ballymena *Conn* 82-85; C Jordanstown w Monkstown 85-88; I Craigs w Dunaghy and Killagan 88-96; RD Ballymena 89-97; Dioc Info Officer 89-97; Bp's Dom Chapl from 94; I Derriaghy w Colin from 97. *Derriaghy Vicarage, 20 Derriaghy Road, Magheralave, Lisburn, Co Antrim BT28 3SH* Tel (01232) 610859

BUDD, John Victor. b 31. CCC Ox BA55 MA58. Bps' Coll Cheshunt 57. **d** 59 **p** 60. C Friern Barnet St Jas *Lon* 59-64; C Harrow Weald All SS 64-70; Lic to Offic *St Alb* 70-73; V Lt Amwell 73-96; RD Hertford 83-88; rtd 96. *37 Wykewane, Malvern, Worcs WR14 2XD* Tel (01684) 566174

BUDD, Philip John. b 40. St Jo Coll Dur BA63 DipTh65 MLitt71 Bris Univ PhD78. Cranmer Hall Dur. **d** 66 **p** 67. C Attenborough w Chilwell *S'well* 66-69; Lect Clifton Th Coll 69-71; Lect Trin Coll Bris 72-80; Tutor Ripon Coll Cuddesdon 80-88; Tutor Westmr Coll Ox from 80; Asst Chapl and Lect 88-90; Chapl from 90. *Westminster College, Harcourt Hill, Oxford OX2 9AT* Tel (01865) 242788

BUDDEN, Clive John. b 39. Chich Th Coll. **d** 84 **p** 86. C Gaywood, Bawsey and Mintlyn *Nor* 84-87; TV Brixham w Churston Ferrers and Kingswear *Ex* 87-90; R Exton and Winsford and Cutcombe w Luxborough *B & W* from 90. *The Rectory, Winsford, Minehead, Somerset TA24 7JE* Tel (0164385) 301

BUDGE, Leonard Percival. b 11. Dur Univ LTh40. St Aug Coll Cant 37. **d** 40 **p** 41. C Easington w Skeffling and Kilnsea *York* 40-43; C Hertford St Andr *St Alb* 43-45; Tanganyika 45-48; C Stourbridge St Thos *Worc* 48-51; V Castle Morton 51-58; V Amblecote 58-64; V Frithelstock *Ex* 64-76; V Monkleigh 64-76; P-in-c Littleham 64-70; V 70-76; rtd 76; Perm to Offic *Ex* from 76. *2 Chestnut Close, Braunton, Devon EX33 2EH* Tel (01271) 814313

BUDGELL, Peter Charles. b 50. Lon Univ BD. **d** 83 **p** 84. C Goodmayes All SS *Chelmsf* 83-86; C Chipping Barnet w Arkley *St Alb* 86-88; V Luton St Anne from 88. *The Vicarage, 7 Blaydon Road, Luton LU2 0RP* Tel (01582) 20052

BUDGELL, Rosemary Anne. b 51. Lon Bible Coll BD73 CertEd76. **dss** 83 **d** 87 **p** 94. Goodmayes All SS *Chelmsf* 83-86; Chipping Barnet w Arkley *St Alb* 86-88; Hon Par Dn 87-88; Hon Par Dn Luton St Anne 88-94; Hon C from 94. *The Vicarage, 7 Blaydon Road, Luton LU2 0RP* Tel (01582) 20052

BUDGETT, Preb Anthony Thomas. b 26. TD60. Or Coll Ox BA50 MA57. Wells Th Coll 57. **d** 59 **p** 60. C Hendford *B & W* 59-63; PC Lopen 63-68; R Seavington St Mich w St Mary 63-68; V Somerton 68-80; RD Ilchester 72-81; P-in-c Compton Dundon 76-80; R Somerton w Compton Dundon 80-81; R Somerton w Compton Dundon, the Charltons etc 81-84; Preb Wells Cathl 83-90; P-in-c Bruton w Lamyatt, Wyke and Redlynch 84-85; P-in-c Batcombe w Upton Noble 84-85; P-in-c S w N Brewham 84-85; TR Bruton and Distr 85-90; rtd 90; Perm to Offic *Ex* from 90; Perm to Offic *B & W* from 94. *Cornerways, White Ball, Wellington, Somerset TA21 0LS* Tel (01823) 672321

BUFFEE, Canon Leslie John. b 30. AKC53 Open Univ BA88. **d** 54 **p** 55. C Lewisham St Swithun *S'wark* 54-57; Australia 57-62; C Cheam *S'wark* 63-65; P-in-c Becontree St Pet *Chelmsf* 65-67; V 67-72; Min Parkeston CD 72-83; TV Dovercourt and Parkeston 83-89; Miss to Seamen 83-89; C Southend St Sav Westcliff *Chelmsf* 89-95; rtd 95; Perm to Offic *Chelmsf* from 95. *46 Stonebridge Way, Faversham, Kent ME13 7SB* Tel (01795) 535970

BUFFETT, Frederick. b 11. Keble Coll Ox BA34 MA39. St Steph Ho Ox 34. **d** 35 **p** 36. C Chesterfield St Mary and All SS *Derby* 35-37; Canada 38-42; CF (EC) 42-46; C Cowley St Jo *Ox* 46-47; V Whitworth *Man* 47-53; V Kirton in Holland *Linc* 53-64; V Ipplepen w Torbryan *Ex* 64-82; rtd 82; Perm to Offic *Ex* from 82. *Bramble Down Nursing Home, Woodland Road, Denbury, Newton Abbot, Devon TQ12 6DY* Tel (01803) 812844

BUFFREY, Canon Samuel John Thomas. b 28. Keble Coll Ox BA52 MA57. Cuddesdon Coll 52. **d** 54 **p** 55. C Lower Tuffley St Geo CD *Glouc* 54-56; C Branksome St Aldhelm *Sarum* 56-61; R Gussage St Michael and Gussage All Saints 61-69; V Amesbury 69-80; RD Avon 77-80; P-in-c Broadstone 80-82; V 82-93; Can and Preb Sarum Cathl 87-93; rtd 93. *34 Woolslope Road, West Moors, Ferndown, Dorset BH22 0PD* Tel (01202) 875522

BUGBY, Timothy. b 53. AKC75. Chich Th Coll 76. **d** 77 **p** 78. C Hockerill *St Alb* 77-81; C Pimlico St Mary Graham Terrace *Lon* 81-87; V Highgate St Aug from 87. *St Augustine's Vicarage, Langdon Park Road, London N6 5BH* Tel 0181-340 3567

BUGDEN, Ernest William. b 16. Lich Th Coll 56. **d** 58 **p** 59. C Esher *Guildf* 58-68; Hon C 68-81; rtd 81; Perm to Offic *Ely* from 91. *32 French's Road, Cambridge CB4 3LA* Tel (01223) 311306

BUGG, Canon Peter Richard. b 33. Univ of BC BA62. Wells Th Coll 63. **d** 64 **p** 64. C Whitley Ch Ch *Ox* 64-67; C Ludlow *Heref* 67-69; Zambia 69-72; P-in-c Brill w Boarstall *Ox* 72-78; P-in-c Chilton w Dorton 77-78; V Brill, Boarstall, Chilton and Dorton from 78; Hon Can Ch Ch from 92. *The Vicarage, Brill, Aylesbury, Bucks HP18 9ST* Tel (01844) 238325

BUGLER, Canon Derek Leslie. b 25. QUB. Gen Th Sem NY LTh64. **d** 64 **p** 64. USA from 64; rtd 90; Lic to Offic *Win* from 90. *Wintney House, London Road, Hartley Wintney, Basingstoke, Hants RG27 8RN* Tel (01252) 344239

BUIK, Allan David. b 39. St Andr Univ BSc61. Coll of Resurr Mirfield 66. **d** 68 **p** 69. Perm to Offic *Win* 68-69; C Eastleigh 69-72; C Brighton St Bart *Chich* 72-74; C Lavender Hill Ascension *S'wark* 74-78; V Kingstanding St Mark *Birm* 78-86; Guyana 86-91; V Tunstall *Lich* from 91. *Christchurch Vicarage, 26 Stanley Street, Tunstall, Stoke-on-Trent ST6 6BW* Tel (01782) 838288

BUIKE, Desmond Mainwaring. b 32. Ex Coll Ox BA55 MA69 Leeds Univ CertEd72. Qu Coll Birm DipTh57. **d** 57 **p** 58. C Man St Aid *Man* 57-60; C Ox SS Phil and Jas *Ox* 60-63; V Queensbury *Bradf* 63-71; Perm to Offic 71-85; V Glaisdale *York* 85-93; rtd 93; Perm to Offic *York* from 93. *Wayside, 3 White Bridge Road, Whitby, N Yorkshire YO21 1BJ* Tel (01947) 821440

BULL, Mrs Christine. b 45. Bedf Coll Lon BA67. N Ord Course 91. **d** 94 **p** 95. NSM High Lane *Ches* from 94. *Walk Mill Cottage, Hayfield, Stockport SK12 5ER* Tel (01663) 744606

BULL, Christopher Bertram. b 45. Lon Bible Coll BA87. Wycliffe Hall Ox 88. **d** 90 **p** 91. C Leominster *Heref* 90-95; P-in-c Westbury from 95; P-in-c Yockleton from 95; P-in-c Gt Wollaston from 95. *The Rectory, Westbury, Shrewsbury SY5 9QX* Tel (01743) 884216

BULL, Christopher David (Chris). b 59. St Jo Coll Nottm 89. **d** 91 **p** 92. C Bowbrook S *Worc* 91-95; P-in-c Flackwell Heath *Ox* from 95; RD Wycombe from 97. *The Vicarage, 9 Chapel Road, Flackwell Heath, High Wycombe, Bucks HP10 9AA* Tel (01628) 522795

BULL, Malcolm George. b 35. Portsm Dioc Tr Course 87. **d** 87. NSM Farlington *Portsm* 87-90; NSM Widley w Wymering 92-93; NSM S Hayling 93-97; NSM Hayling Is St Andr from 97. *20 Charleston Close, Hayling Island, Hants PO11 0JY* Tel (01705) 462025

BULL, Malcolm Harold. b 44. BDS. St Alb Minl Tr Scheme. **d** 83 **p** 84. NSM Bedford St Paul *St Alb* from 83. *27 Cardington Road, Bedford MK42 0BN* Tel (01234) 368163

BULL, Martin Wells. b 37. Worc Coll Ox BA61 MA68. Ripon Hall Ox 61. **d** 63 **p** 64. C Blackley St Andr *Man* 63-67; C Horton *Bradf* 67-68; V Ingrow cum Hainworth 68-78; RD S Craven 74-77; V Bingley All SS 78-80; TR 80-92; P-in-c Gargrave from 92. *The Vicarage, Gargrave, Skipton, N Yorkshire BD23 3NQ* Tel (01756) 749392

BULL, Michael John. b 35. Roch Th Coll 65. **d** 67 **p** 68. C N Wingfield *Derby* 67-69; C Skegness *Linc* 69-72; R Ingoldmells w Addlethorpe 72-79; Area Sec (Dio S'wark) USPG 79-85; Area Org RNLI (Lon) 86-88; C Croydon St Jo *S'wark* 89-93; P-in-c Mitcham Ch Ch 93-97; V from 97. *Christ Church Vicarage, Christchurch Road, London SW19 2NY* Tel 0181-542 5125

BULL, Dr Norman John. b 16. Trin Coll Ox BTh38 BA39 MA48 Reading Univ PhD67. Linc Th Coll 38. **d** 39 **p** 40. C Colchester St Botolph w H Trin and St Giles *Chelmsf* 39-41; C Loughton St Mary 41-43; P-in-c Petersfield w Sheet *Portsm* 44-45; C Croydon *Cant* 45-46; Dioc Youth Chapl 46-48; Chapl St Luke's Coll Ex 49-60; Lect 49-75. *21 Wonford Road, Exeter EX4 2LH* Tel (01392) 55806

BULL, Robert David. b 51. Man Univ DSPT86. Ripon Coll Cuddesdon 74. **d** 77 **p** 78. C Worsley *Man* 77-80; C Peel 80-81; TV 81-86; P-in-c Wisbech St Aug *Ely* 86-88; V from 88; RD Wisbech from 92. *St Augustine's Vicarage, Lynn Road, Wisbech, Cambs PE13 3DL* Tel (01945) 583724

BULL, Stephen Andrew (Steve). b 58. St Jo Coll Nottm DCM93. **d** 93 **p** 94. C Wroughton *Bris* 93-96; P-in-c Eyemouth *Edin* from 96. *The Parsonage, Beach Avenue, Eyemouth, Berwickshire TD14 5AB* Tel (01890) 750000

BULL, William George. b 28. Sarum Th Coll 65. **d** 66 **p** 67. C Salisbury St Mich *Sarum* 66-69; V Swallowcliffe w Ansty 69-75; Dioc Youth Officer 69-71; P-in-c Laverstock 75-81; V 81-93; rtd 94. *Bungalow 1, Boreham Field, Warminster, Wilts BA12 9EB* Tel (01985) 847830

BULLAMORE, John Richard. b 41. Linc Coll Ox BA64 MA. Wycliffe Hall Ox 74. **d** 95 **p** 95. Hon C Eorrapaidh *Arg* from 95. *White Rose House, 26 Sheshader, Isle of Lewis HS2 0EW* Tel (01851) 870743

BULLEN, Richard David Guy. b 43. Brasted Place Coll 71. Ripon Hall Ox 73. **d** 75 **p** 76. C Pocklington w Yapham-cum-Meltonby, Owsthorpe etc *York* 75-78; TV Thornaby on Tees 78-84; V New Marske 84-90; P-in-c Wilton 84-90; Ind Chapl 90-95. *26 Chestnut Close, Saltburn-by-the-Sea, Cleveland TS12 1PE* Tel (01287) 623287

BULLEY, Roger Charles. b 12. Lon Univ BCom34 BA37. Wells Th Coll 38. **d** 40 **p** 41. C Stepney St Matt *Lon* 40-42; C Lon Docks St Pet w Wapping St Jo 42-48; Perm to Offic *Ox* 48-50; C Clifton All SS *Bris* 50-53; V Penton Street St Silas w All SS *Lon* 53-58; V Winterbourne Down *Bris* 58-71; Chapl Frenchay Hosp Bris 65-70; Chapl Community St Jo Bapt Clewer 71-79; rtd 78; Chapl Convent of Sisters of Charity Knowle 79-88. *c/o Mr and Mrs J Hunt, Heath Farm, Homersfield, Harleston, Norfolk IP20 0EX*

BULLEY, William Joseph. b 28. Chich Th Coll 65. **d** 67 **p** 68. C Littleham w Exmouth *Ex* 67-72; V Harberton w Harbertonford 72-77; R Chagford 77-79; R Chagford w Gidleigh and Throwleigh 79-84; V Widecombe, Leusden and Princetown etc 84-85; TR Widecombe-in-the-Moor, Leusdon, Princetown etc 85-88; P-in-c Inverness St Jo *Mor* 88-93; Chapl Raigmore Hosp Inverness 88-93; rtd 93. *Dalcharn, Barevan, Cawdor, Nairn IV12 5XU* Tel (01667) 493215

BULLIMORE, Christine. BA PGCE Cert Counselling. **d** 96 **p** 97. NSM S Ossett *Wakef* from 96. *137 Edge Lane, Thornhill, Dewsbury, W Yorkshire WF12 0HB* Tel (01924) 463911

BULLIVANT, Ronald. b 32. CertEd DCouns. St Mich Coll Llan. **d** 59 **p** 60. C Roath St German *Llan* 59-61; P-in-c Bradf H Trin *Bradf* 61-66; V Horbury *Wakef* 66-69; Lic to Offic *Ripon* 70-78; Perm to Offic *Nor* 78-81; Lic to Offic from 81; rtd 94. *22 Cleaves Drive, Walsingham, Norfolk NR22 6EQ* Tel (01328) 820526

BULLOCK, Andrew Belfrage. b 50. Univ of Wales (Ban) BSc73 MEd81 Westmr Coll Ox PGCE79. Wycliffe Hall Ox DipMin94. **d** 97. C Sandhurst *Ox* from 97. *78 Branksome Hill Road, Sandhurst, Berks GU47 0QT* Tel 0958-654331 (Mobile)

BULLOCK, Andrew Timothy. b 56. Southn Univ BTh91. Sarum & Wells Th Coll 89. **d** 91 **p** 92. C Erdington St Barn *Birm* 91-94; TV Solihull from 94. *St Francis House, Redlands Close, Solihull, W Midlands B91 2LZ* Tel 0121-705 3234

BULLOCK, Canon John Raymond. b 16. Ch Ch Ox BA37 MA46. Westcott Ho Cam 46. **d** 48 **p** 49. C S Westoe *Dur* 48-50; C St Martin-in-the-Fields *Lon* 50-54; V Easington Colliery *Dur* 54-62; RD Easington 58-62; RD Hartlepool 62-78; V Hartlepool St Paul 62-86; P-in-c Hartlepool Ch Ch 65-73; Hon Can Dur Cathl 71-86; rtd 86. *4 The Green, Greatham, Hartlepool, Cleveland TS25 2HG* Tel (01429) 870600

BULLOCK, Kenneth Poyser. b 27. Down Coll Cam BA50 MA55. Ridley Hall Cam 50. **d** 52 **p** 53. C Aston SS Pet and Paul *Birm* 52-56; R Openshaw *Man* 56-63; V Ainsworth 63-91; rtd 91. *26 Plas Penrhyn, Penrhyn Bay, Llandudno LL30 3EU* Tel (01492) 543343

BULLOCK, Michael. b 49. Hatf Coll Dur BA71 Leeds Univ DipTh74. Coll of Resurr Mirfield 72. **d** 75 **p** 76. C Pet St Jo *Pet* 75-79; Zambia 79-86; V Longthorpe *Pet* 86-91; Chapl Naples w Sorrento, Largo Patria and Bari *Eur* 91-93; Chapl Naples w Sorrento, Capri and Bari from 93. *via S Pasquala a Chiaia 15B, 80121 Naples, Italy* Tel Naples (81) 411842

BULLOCK, Miss Rosemary Joy. b 59. Portsm Poly BA81 Southn Univ BTh94. Sarum & Wells Th Coll 89. **d** 91 **p** 94. Par Dn Warblington and Emsworth *Portsm* 91-94; C 94-95; C Gt Parndon *Chelmsf* from 95. *29 Woodhill, Harlow, Essex CM18 7JS* Tel (01279) 417644

BULLOCK (née WHEALE), Mrs Sarah Ruth. b 64. Surrey Univ BA86 St Jo Coll Dur BA93. Cranmer Hall Dur 90. **d** 93 **p** 94. C Kersal Moor *Man* from 93. *6 Woodward Road, Prestwich, Manchester M25 8TU* Tel 0161-773 1109

BULLOCK, Dr Stephanie Clair. b 46. St Mary's Hosp Medical Sch Lon MB, BS70. Ripon Coll Cuddesdon 90. **d** 92 **p** 94. Par Dn Cuddesdon *Ox* 92-94; Tutor Ripon Coll Cuddesdon 92-94; Asst Chapl Ox Radcliffe Hosp NHS Trust 94-97; Chapl from 97. *10 St Andrew's Road, Oxford OX3 9DL, or The Churchill, Old Road, Oxford OX3 7LJ* Tel (01865) 63226 or 741841

BULLOCK, Father Victor James Allen. b 67. Southn Univ BTh90 St Mary's Coll Twickenham PGCE91. St Steph Ho Ox DipMin94. **d** 94 **p** 95. C Cowley St Jas *Ox* 94-95; C Reading St Giles from 95. *St Saviour's House, 31 Holybrook Road, Reading RG1 6DG* Tel 0118-959 5280

BULLOCK-FLINT, Peter. b 22. Kelham Th Coll 39. **d** 45 **p** 46. C Deptford St Paul *S'wark* 45-48; C Streatham Ch Ch 48-50; C Boyne Hill *Ox* 50-56; C-in-c Tilehurst St Mary CD 56-72; V Hughenden 72-83; V Ivinghoe w Pitstone and Slapton 83-91; RD Mursley 86-91; rtd 91. *1 Wellow Cottage, Salisbury Road, Pimperne, Blandford Forum, Dorset DT11 8UW* Tel (01258) 450142

BULLOUGH, Canon Walter Herbert. b 15. AKC39. **d** 39 **p** 40. C Widnes St Mary *Liv* 39-41; Hon C Much Woolton 41-44; V Highfield 44-59; RD Wigan 58-59; R Halsall 59-91; RD Ormskirk 69-78; Hon Can Liv Cathl 71-91; rtd 91; Perm to Offic *Liv* from 91. *49 Moss Lane, Southport, Merseyside PR9 7QS*

BULMAN, Mrs Madeline Judith. b 61. K Coll Lon BD AKC. **dss** 86 **d** 87 **p** 94. Shepperton *Lon* 86-87; Par Dn 87-88; Par Dn Brentford 88-94; C 94-96; V Cobbold Road St Sav w St Mary from 96. *St Saviour's Vicarage, Cobbold Road, London W12 9LQ* Tel 0181-743 4769

BULMAN, Michael Thomas Andrew. b 34. Jes Coll Cam BA59 MA61. Ridley Hall Cam 58. **d** 60 **p** 61. C Blackpool St Mark *Blackb* 60-63; C Branksome St Clem *Sarum* 63-67; V York St Barn *York* 67-84; CMJ 84-93; Israel 85-93; Can Jerusalem 87-93; R Maresfield *Chich* from 94; V Nutley from 94. *The Vicarage, Nutley, Uckfield, E Sussex TN22 2NH* Tel (01825) 712692

BULMAN, William Mark. b 61. K Coll Lon BD84. Sarum & Wells Th Coll 84. **d** 86 **p** 87. C Shepperton *Lon* 86-87; NSM Wootton w Glympton and Kiddington *Ox* 91-93; C Carterton 93-94; TV Halesworth w Linstead, Chediston, Holton etc *St E* from 94. *The Vicarage, Holton St Peter, Halesworth, Suffolk IP19 8NG* Tel (01986) 874548

BUNCE, Raymond Frederick. b 28. Lon Univ DipSocSc53. Ely Th Coll 54. **d** 57 **p** 58. C Hillingdon St Andr *Lon* 57-62; C Greenford H Cross 62-67; V Ealing All SS 67-89; rtd 89; Chapl Ascot Priory 89-90; Perm to Offic *Portsm* from 91. *Dwarf Croft, Steephill Road, Ventnor, Isle of Wight PO38 1UF* Tel (01983) 855145

BUNCH, Andrew William Havard. b 53. Selw Coll Cam BA74 MA78 PhD79. Ox NSM Course 84. **d** 87 **p** 88. NSM Wantage *Ox* 87-91; C New Windsor 91-93; TV from 93. *The Vicarage, Hermitage Lane, Windsor, Berks SL4 4AZ* Tel (01753) 858720

BUNDAY, Canon Paul. b 30. Wadh Coll Ox BA54 MA58. ALCD56. **d** 56 **p** 57. C Woking St Jo *Guildf* 56-60; Chapl Reed's Sch Cobham 60-66; R Landford w Plaitford *Sarum* 66-77; RD Alderbury 73-77; TR Radipole and Melcombe Regis 77-86; RD Weymouth 82-85; Can and Preb Sarum Cathl 83-95; TV Whitton 86-91; TR 91-95; Chapl Duchess of Somerset Hosp Froxfield 86-94; rtd 95. *16 St John's Close, Tisbury, Salisbury SP3 6PN* Tel (01747) 871530

BUNDOCK, Anthony Francis. b 49. Qu Coll Birm 81. **d** 83 **p** 84. C Stansted Mountfitchet *Chelmsf* 83-86; TV Borehamwood *St Alb* 86-94; TR Seacroft *Ripon* from 94. *The Rectory, 47 St James Approach, Leeds LS14 6JJ* Tel 0113-273 2390

BUNDOCK, Dr Edward Leigh. b 52. Keble Coll Ox BA73 Open Univ PhD94. St Steph Ho Ox 74. **d** 76 **p** 77. C Malvern Link w Cowleigh *Worc* 76-80; C-in-c Portslade Gd Shep CD *Chich* 80-88; V Wisborough Green 88-94; Perm to Offic *Guildf* from 96. *Oak Cottage, Kirdford, Billingshurst, W Sussex RH14 0LX* Tel (01403) 820481

BUNDOCK, John Nicholas Edward. b 45. Wells Th Coll 66. **d** 70 **p** 71. C Chingford SS Pet and Paul *Chelmsf* 70-74; P-in-c Gt Grimsby St Matt Fairfield CD *Linc* 74-81; V Hindhead *Guildf* from 81; RD Farnham 91-96. *The Vicarage, Wood Road, Hindhead, Surrey GU26 6PX* Tel (01428) 605305

BUNDOCK, Ronald Michael (Ron). b 44. Leeds Univ BSc65. Ox NSM Course 87. **d** 90 **p** 91. NSM Buckingham *Ox* from 90. *1 Holton Road, Buckingham MK18 1PQ* Tel (01280) 813887

BUNKER, Harry. b 28. Oak Hill Th Coll. **d** 59 **p** 60. C Longfleet *Sarum* 59-63; R Blisworth *Pet* 63-97; rtd 97. *14 Wardlow Close, West Hunsbury, Northampton NN4 9YQ*

BUNKER, John Herbert George. b 31. AKC56. **d** 57 **p** 58. C Newc St Jo *Newc* 57-60; C Cullercoats St Geo 61-65; V Byker St Mich 65-74; V Ashington 74-84; V Halifax St Aug *Wakef* 84-93; rtd 93; Perm to Offic *Wakef* from 93. *1 Hebble Dean, Hebble Lane, Halifax, W Yorkshire HX3 5JL*

BUNKER, The Very Revd Michael. b 37. Oak Hill Th Coll 59. **d** 63 **p** 64. C Alperton *Lon* 63-66; C St Helens St Helen *Liv* 66-70; V Muswell Hill St Matt *Lon* 70-79; V Muswell Hill St Jas 78-79; V Muswell Hill St Jas w St Matt 79-92; AD W Haringey 85-90; Preb St Paul's Cathl 90-92; Dean Pet from 92. *The Deanery, Minster Precincts, Peterborough PE1 1XS* Tel (01733) 62780 Fax 897874

BUNKER, Neil John. b 59. K Coll Lon BD77 AKC77. Ripon Coll Cuddesdon 82. **d** 83 **p** 84. C Bromley St Andr *Roch* 83-87; Chapl Farnborough Psychiatric Unit 85-87; Chapl Farnborough and Orpington Hosps from 87; Distr Chapl Bromley HA 89-95; Chapl Thameslink NHS Trust from 91; Chapl Dartford and Gravesham NHS Trust from 91; Chapl Oxleas NHS Trust from 93; Chapl Ravensbourne NHS Trust from 95; Chapl Cane Hill Secure Unit from 95. *191 London Road, Stone, Dartford DA2 6BL* Tel (01322) 221032 or (01689) 853339

BUNN, Mrs Rosemary Joan (Rosie). b 60. EAMTC 94. **d** 97. NSM Sprowston w Beeston *Nor* from 97. *11 Chamberlin Close, Norwich NR3 3LP* Tel (01603) 290280 Fax 298888

BUNNELL, Adrian. b 49. Univ of Wales (Abth) BSc72. St Mich Coll Llan 74. **d** 75 **p** 76. C Wrexham *St As* 75-78; C Rhyl w St Ann 78-79; CF 79-95; R Aberfoyle *St And* from 95; R Callander from 95. *St Mary's Rectory, Aberfoyle, Stirling FK8 3UJ* Tel (01877) 382887

BUNT, Brian William. b 34. Bris Univ BA63 Lon Univ BD67. Tyndale Hall Bris. **d** 68 **p** 69. C Chich St Pancras and St Jo *Chich* 68-72; C Camborne *Truro* 72-75; P-in-c Kenwyn St Jo 75-93; P-in-c Penzance St Jo 93-94; rtd 94. *28 Trewidden Close, Truro, Cornwall TR1 1LN* Tel (01872) 77753

BUNTING, Canon Ian David. b 33. Ex Coll Ox BA58 MA61. Tyndale Hall Bris 57 Princeton Th Sem ThM60. **d** 60 **p** 61. C Bootle St Leon *Liv* 60-63; V Waterloo St Jo 64-71; Dir Past Studies St Jo Coll Dur 71-78; R Chester le Street *Dur* 78-87; RD Chester-le-Street 79-84; Kingham Hill Fellow 87-89; Dioc Dir of Ords *S'well* from 90; C Lenton 90-97; Hon Can S'well Minster from 93; Bp's Research Officer from 97. *8 Crafts Way, Southwell, Notts NG25 0BL* Tel (01636) 831868

BUNTING, Jeremy John. b 34. St Cath Coll Cam BA56 MA60 Worc Coll Ox BA58 MA60. St Steph Ho Ox 57. **d** 59 **p** 60. C Bickley *Roch* 59-62; C Cambridge St Mary Less *Ely* 62-66; USA 66-68; R Stock Harvard *Chelmsf* 68-87; RD Wickford 73-79; V Hampstead Garden Suburb *Lon* 87-94. *Fairview, 82 New Road, Haslingfield, Cambridge CB3 7LP* Tel (01223) 871602

BUNYAN, David Richard. b 48. Edin Th Coll 93. **d** 96 **p** 97. NSM Musselburgh *Edin* from 96; NSM Prestonpans from 96. *14 Clerwood Bank, Edinburgh EH12 8PZ* Tel 0131-334 6586 or 668 5724 E-mail bunyand@ptsehl.agw.bt.co.uk

BUNYAN, Richard Charles. b 43. Oak Hill Th Coll 63 Ridley Hall Cam 69. **d** 71 **p** 72. C Luton Ch Ch *Roch* 71-74; C Bexleyheath Ch Ch 74-76; C Bexley St Jo 76-79; TV Northampton Em *Pet* 79-81; V Erith St Jo *Roch* 81-86; V S Woodham Ferrers *Chelmsf* 86-89; Chapl Scargill Ho 89-91; Sub-Chapl HM Pris Swaleside 91-94; Dep Chapl HM Pris Belmarsh 94-96; Chapl HM Pris Littlehey from 96. *HM Prison Littlehey, Perry, Huntingdon, Cambs PE18 0SR* Tel (01480) 812202 Fax 81251

BURBERY, Ian Edward. b 37. Univ of Wales (Lamp) BA59. Coll of Resurr Mirfield 59. **d** 61 **p** 62. C Penarth w Lavernock *Llan* 61-68; V Porth 68-77; V Cainscross w Selsley *Glouc* 77-89; P-in-c Cheltenham Em 89-95; V Cheltenham Em w St Steph from 95. *Emmanuel Vicarage, 115 Old Bath Road, Cheltenham, Glos GL53 7DE* Tel (01242) 525059

BURBRIDGE, The Very Revd John Paul. b 32. FSA89 K Coll Cam BA54 MA58 New Coll Ox BA54 MA58. Wells Th Coll 58. **d** 59 **p** 60. C Eastbourne St Mary *Chich* 59-62; V Choral York Minster *York* 62-66; Can Res and Prec 66-76; Adn Richmond *Ripon* 76-83; Can Res Ripon Cathl 76-83; Dean Nor 83-95; rtd 95. *The School House, High Fremington, Richmond, N Yorkshire DL11 6AS*

BURBRIDGE, Richard James. b 47. Univ of Wales (Ban) BSc68. Oak Hill Th Coll 68. **d** 72 **p** 73. C Rodbourne Cheney *Bris* 72-75; C Downend 75-78; P-in-c Bris H Cross Inns Court 78-83; P-in-c Fishponds All SS 83-86; V from 86; RD Stapleton 89-95. *All Saints' Vicarage, Grove Road, Fishponds, Bristol BS16 2BW* Tel 0117-965 4143

BURCH, Cyril John. b 18. AKC49. **d** 49 **p** 50. C Milton next Sittingbourne *Cant* 49-51; C Croydon St Mich 51-52; PV Wells Cathl *B & W* 52-57; Chapl Prestfelde Sch Shrewsbury 57-58; Chapl Llan Cathl Sch 58-63; V Stoke Mandeville *Ox* 63-86; rtd 86. *4 Gange Mews, Middle Row, Faversham, Kent ME13 7ED* Tel (01795) 538166

BURCH, Canon John Christopher (Chris). b 50. Trin Coll Cam BA71 MA76 Leeds Univ MPhil95. St Jo Coll Nottm 73. **d** 76 **p** 77. C Sheff St Jo *Sheff* 76-79; C Holbeck *Ripon* 79-82; V Burmantofts St Steph and St Agnes 82-95; Can Res and Prec Cov Cathl *Cov* from 95. *35 Asthill Grove, Coventry CV3 6HN* Tel (01203) 505426 or 227597

BURCH, Canon Peter John. b 36. ACA60 FCA71. Ripon Hall Ox 62. **d** 64 **p** 65. C Brixton St Matt *S'wark* 64-67; Sierra Leone 67-72; P-in-c Chich St Pet *Chich* 72-76; V Broadwater Down 76-85; V Steyning 85-94; R Ashurst 85-94; Hon Can Bauchi from 93; V Broadway *Worc* 94-96; V Broadway w Wickhamford from 96. *The Vicarage, 4 Lifford Gardens, Broadway, Worcs WR12 7DA* Tel (01386) 852352

BURCH, Stephen Roy. b 59. St Jo Coll Nottm LTh82. **d** 85 **p** 86. C Ipswich St Aug *St E* 85-89; P-in-c Kinwarton w Gt Alne and Haselor *Cov* from 89; Youth Chapl 89-94. *The Rectory, Great Alne, Alcester, Warks B49 6HY* Tel (01789) 488344

BURCH, Victor Ernest Charles. b 18. Nor Ord Course 73. **d** 76 **p** 77. NSM Heigham St Barn w St Bart *Nor* 76-80; NSM Lakenham St Jo 80-88; Perm to Offic from 88. *35 Oaklands, Framingham Earl, Norwich NR14 7QS* Tel (01508) 492790

BURCHILL, Dr Jane. b 31. Dalhousie Univ Canada BSc54 Aber Univ PhD81. Moray Ho Edin CertEd56 St Jo Coll Nottm 85. **d** 88 **p** 94. NSM Inverurie *Ab* from 88; NSM Auchindoir from 88; NSM Alford from 88; NSM Kemnay from 88. *5 Hopetoun Avenue, Bucksburn, Aberdeen AB2 9QU* Tel (01224) 712931

BURDEN, Miss Anne Margaret. b 47. Ex Univ BSc69 LSE DSA70 DipSocWork72 CQSW72. Linc Th Coll 89. **d** 91 **p** 94. Par Dn Mill Hill Jo Keble Ch *Lon* 91-94; C 94; TV Basingstoke *Win* from 94. *219 Paddock Road, Basingstoke, Hants RG22 6QP* Tel (01256) 464393

BURDEN, Arthur Theodore. b 11. St Pet Hall Ox BA35 MA42. Wycliffe Hall Ox 35. **d** 37 **p** 38. C Forest Gate Em *Chelmsf* 37-38; C Dagenham 38-41; C Sidbury *Ex* 41-42; Chapl RAFVR 42-46; V Finchley St Paul Long Lane *Lon* 46-63; V Dorking St Paul *Guildf* 63-73; V Defford w Besford *Worc* 73-78; V Eckington 73-78; rtd 78; Perm to Offic *Glouc* from 78; Perm to Offic *Worc* from 78; P-in-c Ripple, Earls Croome w Hill Croome and Strensham 87. *Wellspring, 7 Golden Valley, Castlemorton, Malvern, Worcs WR13 6AA* Tel (01684) 833341

BURDEN, Derek. b 29. St Edm Hall Ox BA52 MA56. Wells Th Coll 56. **d** 58 **p** 59. C Mitcham St Mark *S'wark* 58-61; V Coombe Bissett w Homington *Sarum* 61-69; V N Bradley 69-79; V Steeple Ashton w Semington 79-84; V Keevil 79-84; V Steeple Ashton w Semington and Keevil 84-89; rtd 89. *9 Farleigh Avenue, Trowbridge, Wilts BA14 9DS* Tel (01225) 754759

BURDEN, Derek Ronald. b 37. Sarum Th Coll 59. **d** 62 **p** 63. C Cuddington *Guildf* 62-64; C Leamington Priors All SS *Cov* 64-66; C Stamford All SS w St Pet *Linc* 66-74; C-in-c Stamford Ch Ch CD 71-74; P-in-c Ashbury w Compton Beauchamp *Ox* 74-77; V 77-81; V Ashbury, Compton Beauchamp and Longcot w Fernham 81-84; V Wokingham St Sebastian 84-97; P-in-c Wooburn from 97. *Wooburn Vicarage, Winsdor Hill, Wooburn Green, High Wycombe, Bucks HP10 0EH* Tel (01628) 520030

BURDEN, Michael Henry. b 36. Selw Coll Cam BA59 MA63 Hull Univ MEd81. Ridley Hall Cam 60. **d** 62 **p** 63. C Ashton on Mersey St Mary *Ches* 62-65; Chapl St Pet Sch York 65-70; Asst Master Beverley Gr Sch 70-74; R Walkington *York* 74-77; Chapl Asst Berwick R Infirmary 82-94; P-in-c Berwick H Trin *Newc* 82-87; V 87-89; P-in-c Berwick St Mary 82-87; V Berwick H Trin and St Mary 89-94; P-in-c Skirwith, Ousby and Melmerby w Kirkland *Carl* from 94; Sec Guild of St Raphael from 94. *The Vicarage, Skirwith, Penrith, Cumbria CA10 1RQ* Tel (01768) 88663

BURDEN, Paul. b 62. AMIMechE87 Rob Coll Cam BA84 MA88. Wycliffe Hall Ox BA91. **d** 92 **p** 93. C Clevedon St Andr and Ch Ch *B & W* 92-96; R Bathampton w Claverton from 96. *The Vicarage, Bathampton Lane, Bath BA2 6SW* Tel (01225) 463570

BURDETT, John Fergusson. b 25. Pemb Coll Cam BA47 MA79. **d** 79 **p** 80. C Edin St Jo *Edin* 79-87 and 90-95; Cyprus 87-90; rtd 95. *80/1 Barnton Park View, Edinburgh EH4 6HJ* Tel 0131-339 7226

BURDETT, Stephen Martin. b 49. AKC72. St Aug Coll Cant 73. **d** 74 **p** 75. C Walworth St Pet *S'wark* 74-75; C Walworth 75-77; C Benhilton 77-80; P-in-c Earlsfield St Jo 80-83; V 83-89; V N Dulwich St Faith from 89; Ldr Post Ord Tr Woolwich Episc Area from 96. *St Faith's Vicarage, Red Post Hill, London SE24 9JQ* Tel 0171-274 1338 or 274 3924

BURDITT, Jeffrey Edward (Jeff). b 46. Ex Univ BA67 CertEd68 Lon Univ MPhil79. Westcott Ho Cam 86. **d** 88 **p** 89. C Saffron Walden w Wendens Ambo and Littlebury *Chelmsf* 88-92; V Hatfield Peverel w Ulting 92-95. *26 Mill Road, Burnham-on-Crouch, Essex CM0 8PZ* Tel (01621) 786154

BURDON, Anthony James (Tony). b 46. Ex Univ LLB67 Lon Univ BD73. Oak Hill Th Coll 71. **d** 73 **p** 74. C Ox St Ebbe w St Pet *Ox* 73-76; C Church Stretton *Heref* 76-78; Cand Sec CPAS 78-81; Hon C Bromley Ch Ch *Roch* 78-81; V Filkins w Broadwell, Broughton, Kelmscot etc *Ox* 81-84; R Broughton Poggs w Filkins, Broadwell etc 84-85; V Reading St Jo 85-96; P-in-c California from 96. *California Vicarage, Vicarage Close, Finchampstead, Berks RG11 4JW* Tel 0118-973 0030

BURDON, Christopher John. b 48. Jes Coll Cam BA70 MA74 Leeds Univ DipTh73. Coll of Resurr Mirfield 71. **d** 74 **p** 75. C Chelmsf All SS *Chelmsf* 74-78; TV High Wycombe *Ox* 78-84; P-in-c Olney w Emberton 84-90; R 90-92; Lic to Offic *Glas* 92-94; Lay Tr Officer *Chelmsf* from 94. *9 Boswells Drive, Chelmsford CM2 6LD* Tel (01245) 283235

BURDON, Edward Arthur. b 11. Linc Th Coll 44. **d** 46 **p** 47. C Taunton H Trin *B & W* 46-48; C Mayfield *Chich* 48-54; V Gosfield *Chelmsf* 54-72; V Coggeshall w Markshall 72-80; rtd 80; Perm to Offic *St E* from 81. *The Nutshell, 20 Naverne Meadows, Woodbridge, Suffolk IP12 1HU* Tel (01394) 384787

BURDON, Mrs Pamela Muriel (Pam). b 46. Ex Univ BA68 Reading Univ DipEd69. Wycliffe Hall Ox 88. **d** 90 **p** 94. Par Dn Reading St Jo *Ox* 90-94; C 94-96; P-in-c California from 96. *California Vicarage, Vicarage Close, Finchampstead, Wokingham, Berks RG11 4JW* Tel (0118) 973 0030

BURDON, William. b 23. Leeds Univ BA51. Coll of Resurr Mirfield 51. **d** 53 **p** 54. C Derby St Anne *Derby* 53-57; C Weston-super-Mare All SS *B & W* 57-62; C Clifton All SS *Bris* 63-64; V Skirwith *Carl* 64-73; V Skirwith w Ousby and Melmerby 73-84; R Maidwell w Draughton, Scaldwell, Lamport etc *Pet* 84-88; rtd 88. *Flat 29, Stuart Court, High Street, Kibworth, Leicester LE8 0LE*

BURFITT, Edward Ronald (Eddy). b 42. MIMA64 Liv Univ CSocSc67 Newc Univ DASS68. Cranmer Hall Dur CTMin93. **d** 93 **p** 94. C Monkseaton St Mary *Newc* 93-97; rtd 97. *11 St Nicholas Road, Hexham, Northd NE46 2EZ* Tel (01434) 600744

BURGE, Edward Charles Richard. b 70. Liv Univ BA92. Ridley Hall Cam CTM93. **d** 96 **p** 97. C Cayton w Eastfield *York* from 96. *4 Hawson Close, Osgodby, Scarborough, N Yorkshire YO11 3QW* Tel (01723) 583282

BURGER, David Joseph Cave. b 31. Selw Coll Cam BA58 MA62 Leic Univ 68. Coll of Resurr Mirfield 58. **d** 60 **p** 61. C Chiswick St Paul Grove Park *Lon* 60-63; C Charlton St Luke w H Trin *S'wark* 63-65; Warden St Luke Tr Ho Charlton 63-65; Chapl Moor Park Coll Farnham 66; Teacher Ysgol y Gader Dolgellau Gwynedd 68-85; Resettlement Officer Ches Aid to the Homeless 88-93; rtd 92. *Pwllygele Mawr, Llanfachreth, Dolgellau LL40 2DP* Tel (01341) 450350

BURGESS, Alan James. b 51. Ridley Hall Cam 87. **d** 89 **p** 90. C Glenfield *Leic* 89-92; V Donisthorpe and Moira w Stretton-en-le-Field from 92. *St John's Vicarage, Donisthorpe, Swadlincote, Derbyshire DE12 7PX* Tel (01530) 271456

BURGESS, Alfred George. b 18. Univ of Wales BA39. St Mich Coll Llan 39. **d** 41 **p** 42. C Swansea Ch Ch *S & B* 41-44; C Llandrindod w Cefnllys 44-47; C Stratford-on-Avon *Cov* 47-49; V Longford 49-58; V Alveston 58-81; RD Stratford-on-Avon

69-73; R Ilmington w Stretton on Fosse and Ditchford 81-84; rtd 84; Perm to Offic *Cov* from 84; Perm to Offic *Glouc* from 84. *139 Evesham Road, Stratford-upon-Avon, Warks CV37 9BP* Tel (01789) 293321

BURGESS, David James. b 58. Southn Univ BSc80. St Jo Coll Nottm LTh89 DPS89. **d** 89 **p** 90. C S Mimms Ch Ch *Lon* 89-93; C Hanwell St Mary w St Chris from 93. *The Vicarage, Bordars Road, London W7 1AG* Tel 0181-578 2796

BURGESS, David John. b 39. Trin Hall Cam BA62 MA66 Univ Coll Ox MA66 FRSA91. Cuddesdon Coll 62. **d** 65 **p** 66. C Maidstone All SS w St Phil *Cant* 65; Asst Chapl Univ Coll Ox 66-70; Chapl 70-78; Can and Treas Windsor 78-87; Chapl to The Queen from 87; V St Lawr Jewry *Lon* from 87. *St Lawrence Jewry Vicarage, Next Guildhall, London EC2V 5AA* Tel 0171-600 9478

BURGESS, Derek Mark. b 31. Brasted Place Coll 61. St Mich Coll Llan 61. **d** 89 **p** 90. Australia 89-92; P-in-c Knowbury *Heref* from 93; P-in-c Coreley w Doddington from 93. *Knowbury Vicarage, Clee Hill, Ludlow, Shropshire SY8 3JG* Tel (01584) 890129

BURGESS, Edwin Michael. b 47. Ch Coll Cam BA69 MA73. Coll of Resurr Mirfield 70. **d** 72 **p** 73. C Beamish *Dur* 72-77; C Par *Truro* 77-80; P-in-c Duloe w Herodsfoot 80-83; R 83-86; Jt Dir SW Min Tr Course *Ex* 80-86; Subwarden St Deiniol's Lib Hawarden 86-91; R Oughtrington *Ches* from 91; P-in-c Warburton from 93. *The Rectory, Oughtrington, Lymm, Cheshire WA13 9JB* Tel (01925) 752388

BURGESS, Canon Henry James. b 08. Lon Univ BA31 MA49 PhD54. Wycliffe Hall Ox 35. **d** 36 **p** 37. Can Res Sheff Cathl *Sheff* 70-75; C Bath St Paul *B & W* 36-38; C Tunbridge Wells St Jo *Roch* 38-39; Chapl Weymouth Coll 39-40; V Poughill *Truro* 40-44; V Sidcup Ch Ch *Roch* 44-50; V Cudham 50-61; Dioc Schs Adv 55-61; V Lucton w Eyton *Heref* 61-66; R Hooton Roberts *Sheff* 66-70; Hon Can Sheff Cathl 66-70; Can Res 70-75; Dioc Dir of Educn 70-75; rtd 75; Perm to Offic *Truro* 75-85; Perm to Offic *Roch* 85-95. *Flat 21, Bromley College, London Road, Bromley BR1 1PE* Tel 0181-290 1362

BURGESS, Canon Henry Percival. b 21. Leeds Univ BA48. Coll of Resurr Mirfield 48. **d** 50 **p** 51. C Northfield *Birm* 50-54; V Shaw Hill 54-62; V Wylde Green 62-89; Hon Can Birm Cathl 75-90; RD Sutton Coldfield 76-88; rtd 90. *39 Chestnut Drive, Birmingham B36 9BH* Tel 0121-747 9926

BURGESS, The Ven John Edward. b 30. Lon Univ BD57. ALCD56. **d** 57 **p** 58. C Bermondsey St Mary w St Olave and St Jo *S'wark* 57-60; C Southampton St Mary w H Trin *Win* 60-62; V Dunston w Coppenhall *Lich* 62-67; Chapl Stafford Coll of Tech 63-67; V Keynsham w Queen Charlton *B & W* 67-75; R Burnett 67-75; RD Keynsham 72-75; Adn Bath and Preb Wells Cathl 75-95; rtd 96; Perm to Offic *B & W* from 96. *12 Berryfield Road, Bradford-on-Avon, Wilts BA15 1SX* Tel (01225) 868905

BURGESS, John Henry William. b 35. Westhill Coll Birm CYCW72. Wells Th Coll 65. **d** 67 **p** 68. C Teddington St Alb *Lon* 67-72; C Northolt W End St Jos 72-74; Perm to Offic *B & W* from 93; rtd 95. *10 Pendragon Park, Glastonbury, Somerset BA6 9PQ* Tel (01458) 833287

BURGESS, John Michael. b 36. ALCD61. **d** 61 **p** 62. C Eccleston St Luke *Liv* 61-64; S Rhodesia 64-65; Rhodesia 65-74; V Nottingham St Andr *S'well* 74-79; Bp's Adv on Community Relns 77-79; V Earlestown *Liv* 79-87; RD Warrington 82-87; TR Halewood 87-94; V Southport St Phil and St Paul from 94; AD N Meols from 95. *St Philip's Vicarage, Scarisbrick New Road, Southport, Merseyside PR8 6QF* Tel (01704) 532886

BURGESS, John Mulholland. b 32. Cranmer Hall Dur 58. **d** 61 **p** 62. C Frimley *Guildf* 61-67; C Cheltenham St Luke and St Jo *Glouc* 67-69; P-in-c Withington w Compton Abdale 69-74; R Woolstone w Gotherington and Oxenton 74-75; Chapl Rotterdam w Schiedam etc *Eur* 75-78; Sliema 78-80; C Nottingham All SS *S'well* 80; C Rolleston w Morton 80-83; C Rolleston w Fiskerton, Morton and Upton 83-84; V Mansfield St Aug from 84; Asst RD Mansf 88-92; RD Mansfield from 92. *St Augustine's Vicarage, 46 Abbott Road, Mansfield, Notts NG19 6DD* Tel (01623) 21247

BURGESS (née BOND), Mrs Kim Mary. b 58. SRN79. Trin Coll Bris BA87. **d** 87 **p** 94. Par Dn Cullompton *Ex* 87-91; Asst Chapl N Staffs R Infirmary Stoke-on-Trent 91-95; NSM Audley *Lich* from 95. *6 Quarry Cottages, Nantwich Road, Audley, Stoke-on-Trent ST7 8DW* Tel (01782) 722961

BURGESS, Michael Anglin. b 34. St Deiniol's Hawarden 81. **d** 83 **p** 84. C Habergham Eaves St Matt *Blackb* 83-85; C Burnley (Habergham Eaves) St Matt w H Trin 85-86; V Preston St Matt 86-93; V Nelson St Bede from 93. *St Bede's Vicarage, Railway Street, Nelson, Lancs BB9 0LT* Tel (01282) 614197 E-mail maburgess@internexus.co.uk

BURGESS, Michael James. b 42. Coll of Resurr Mirfield 74. **d** 76 **p** 77. C Leigh-on-Sea St Marg *Chelmsf* 76-79; C St Peter-in-Thanet *Cant* 79-82; Canada from 82. *66 Spencer Avenue, Toronto, Ontario, Canada, M6K 2J6* Tel Toronto (416) 531-4037

BURGESS, Michael Walter. Bps' Coll Cheshunt 66. **d** 68 **p** 70. C Hammersmith St Matt *Lon* 68-70; C Boreham Wood All SS *St Alb* 70-73; V Flamstead 74-77; V St Marylebone Annunciation Bryanston Street *Lon* from 77. *4 Wyndham Place, London W1H 1AP* Tel 0171-262 4329

BURGESS, Neil. b 53. Univ of Wales (Lamp) BA75 Nottm Univ MTh87 PhD93. St Mich Coll Llan 75. **d** 77 **p** 78. C Cheadle *Lich* 77-79; C Longton 79-82; TV Hanley H Ev 82-86; C Uttoxeter w Bramshall 86-87; Lect Linc Th Coll 87-95; Hon C Linc Minster Gp *Linc* 88-95; Dioc Dir of Clergy Tr *S'well* from 95; C Newark from 97. *Dunham House, Westgate, Southwell, Notts NG25 0JH* Tel Newark (01636) 814331 Fax 815084

BURGESS, Sister Patricia Jean. b 16. Edin Univ BSc38. **dss** 69 **d** 86. NSM Roslin (Rosslyn Chpl) *Edin* 69-73; Community of the Transfiguration Midlothian from 72. *House of the Transfiguration, 70E Clerk Street, Loanhead, Midlothian EH20 9RG*

BURGESS, Paul Christopher James. b 41. Qu Coll Cam BA63 MA67. Lon Coll of Div 66. **d** 68 **p** 69. C Islington St Mary *Lon* 68-72; C Church Stretton *Heref* 73-74; Pakistan 74-83; Warden Carberry Tower (Ch of Scotland) 84-86; Progr Co-ord 86-88; TV Livingston LEP *Edin* from 88. *124 Mowbray Rise, Livingston, West Lothian EH54 6JP* Tel (01506) 417158

BURGESS, Roy. b 32. S Dios Minl Tr Scheme 80. **d** 83 **p** 84. NSM Bentworth and Shalden and Lasham *Win* 83-89; R Ingoldsby *Linc* from 89; RD Beltisloe 93-97. *The Rectory, Back Lane, Ingoldsby, Grantham, Lincs NG33 4EW* Tel (01476) 585746

BURGESS, Roy Graham. b 47. Birm Univ CertCYW72 Bulmershe Coll of HE DMS81. Ox Min Course CBTS94. **d** 94 **p** 95. C Easthampstead *Ox* from 94. *St Michael's House, Crowthorne Road, Bracknell, Berkshire RG12 4ER* Tel (01344) 429397

BURGHALL, Kenneth Miles. b 34. Selw Coll Cam BA57 MA61. Qu Coll Birm 57. **d** 59 **p** 60. C Macclesfield St Mich *Ches* 59-63; CF 63-66; P-in-c Birkenhead Priory *Ches* 67-71; V Macclesfield St Paul 71-87; V Nether Peover from 87; P-in-c Over Peover from 92. *The Vicarage, Lower Peover, Knutsford, Cheshire WA16 9PZ* Tel (01565) 722304

BURGIN, Henry Kenneth. b 36. FRSA95. S'wark Ord Course 70. **d** 71 **p** 72. C Caterham Valley *S'wark* 71-73; C Benhilton 73-77; V Cheam Common St Phil 77-82; P-in-c Blackheath All SS 82-89; V from 89. *All Saints' Vicarage, 10 Duke Humphrey Road, London SE3 0TY* Tel 0181-852 4280

BURGON, Canon George Irvine. b 41. Edin Th Coll. **d** 65 **p** 66. C Dundee St Mary Magd *Bre* 65-68; C Wellingborough All Hallows *Pet* 68-71; P-in-c Norton 71-73; TV Daventry w Norton 73-75; V Northampton St Mary from 75; Can Pet Cathl from 95. *St Mary's Vicarage, Towcester Road, Northampton NN4 9EZ* Tel (01604) 761104

BURGOYNE, Percy John (Jack). b 19. OBE74. Univ of Wales (Cardiff) BSc41. St Mich Coll Llan. **d** 43 **p** 44. C Cardiff St Mary and St Steph w St Dyfrig etc *Llan* 43-47; C Roath St Marg 47-52; Chapl RN 52-78; QHC 72-75; P-in-c Kelsale w Carlton *St E* 78-85; R Kelsale-cum-Carlton, Middleton-cum-Fordley etc 85-90; rtd 90; Perm to Offic *St E* from 90. *St Dyfrig, Woods Lane, Melton, Woodbridge, Suffolk IP12 1JF* Tel (01394) 384884

BURKE, Charles Michael. b 28. Keble Coll Ox BA51 MA54 Ox Univ DipEd52. Glouc Th Course. **d** 84 **p** 85. C Colwall w Upper Colwall and Coddington *Heref* 84-88; V Canon Pyon w Kings Pyon and Birley from 88; P-in-c Wellington w Pipe-cum-Lyde and Moreton-on-Lugg from 96. *The Vicarage, Brookside, Canon Pyon, Hereford HR4 8NY* Tel (01432) 830802

BURKE, Christopher Mark (Chris). b 65. Cov Poly LLB87. Ripon Coll Cuddesdon 89. **d** 92 **p** 93. C Nunthorpe *York* 92-96; V S Bank from 96. *The Vicarage, 259 Normanby Road, Middlesbrough, Cleveland TS6 6TB* Tel (01642) 453679 Fax as telephone

BURKE, Colin Douglas. b 41. Bp Otter Coll CertEd64 LNSM course. **d** 92 **p** 93. NSM Fressingfield, Mendham, Metfield, Weybread etc *St E* from 92. *St Andrews, Weybread, Diss, Norfolk IP21 5TU* Tel (01379) 852063

BURKE, Eric John. b 44. Llan Dioc Tr Scheme 81. **d** 85 **p** 86. NSM Cardiff St Jo *Llan* 85-95; Chapl Asst Univ Hosp of Wales Cardiff from 95; Chapl Asst Cardiff Royal Infirmary from 95. *University Hospital of Wales, Heath Park, Cardiff CF4 4XW, or 81 Ty-mawr Road, Rumney, Cardiff CF3 8BS* Tel (01222) 743230 or 798147

BURKE, Jonathan. b 53. Lon Univ BEd. Westcott Ho Cam 79. **d** 82 **p** 83. C Weymouth H Trin *Sarum* 82-85; R Bere Regis and Affpuddle w Turnerspuddle 85-92. *Address temp unknown*

BURKE, Michael Robert. b 61. Leeds Univ BA83. Trin Coll Bris BA89. **d** 89 **p** 90. C Anston *Sheff* 89-92; V Crosspool from 92. *The Vicarage, 1 Barnfield Road, Sheffield S10 5TD* Tel 0114-230 2531

BURKE, William Spencer Dwerryhouse. b 46. Ripon Coll Cuddesdon 90. **d** 92 **p** 93. C Watford St Mich *St Alb* 92-95; R Castor w Sutton and Upton w Marholm *Pet* from 95. *The Rectory, 5 Church Hill, Castor, Peterborough PE5 7AU* Tel (01733) 380244

BURKETT, Christopher Paul. b 52. Warw Univ BA75 Birm Univ DipTh77 Westmr Coll Ox DipApTh92 Ox Univ MTh93. Qu Coll Birm 75. **d** 78 **p** 79. C Streetly *Lich* 78-81; C Harlescott 81-83; TV Leek and Meerbrook 83-89; Chapl Leek Moorlands Hosp 83-89; Area Sec (Dio Ches) USPG 89-92; Lic to Offic *Ches* 89-92; V Whitegate w Lt Budworth from 92. *The New Vicarage, Cinder*

Hill, Whitegate, Northwich, Cheshire CW8 2BH Tel (01606) 882151

BURKILL, Mark Edward. b 56. MA PhD. Trin Coll Bris. **d** 84 **p** 85. C Cheadle *Ches* 84-88; C Harold Wood *Chelmsf* 88-91; V Leyton Ch Ch from 91. *The Vicarage, 52 Elm Road, London E11 4DN* Tel 0181-539 4980

BURKITT, Paul Adrian. b 49. RMN75 SRN77 Coll of Ripon & York St Jo CCouns89. St Steph Ho Ox 84. **d** 86 **p** 87. C Whitby *York* 86-90; V Egton w Grosmont 90-93; V Newington w Dairycoates 93-96; P-in-c Kingston upon Hull St Mary from 96. *223 Cottingham Road, Hull HU5 4AU*

BURKITT, Richard Francis. b 49. Leeds Univ BA71 CertEd72. Sarum & Wells Th Coll 82. **d** 90 **p** 90. R Fraserburgh w New Pitsligo *Ab* 90-95; R Fortrose *Mor* from 95; R Cromarty from 95; R Arpafeelie from 95. *St Andrew's Rectory, 1 Deans Road, Fortrose, Ross-shire IV10 8TJ* Tel (01381) 620255

BURLAND, Clive Beresford. b 37. Sarum & Wells Th Coll 81. **d** 85 **p** 86. C Warblington and Emsworth *Portsm* 85-87; C Cowes St Mary 87-92; R Gurnard from 92; R Northwood from 93. *The Rectory, Chawton Lane, Cowes, Isle of Wight PO31 8PR* Tel (01983) 292050

BURLEIGH, David John. b 42. FCII69. St Deiniol's Hawarden 84. **d** 87 **p** 88. NSM Lache cum Saltney *Ches* 87-88; NSM Eastham 89-92; C Birkenhead Priory 92-95; P-in-c Duloe w Herodsfoot *Truro* from 95; TV Liskeard, St Keyne, St Pinnock, Morval etc from 95. *The Rectory, Duloe, Liskeard, Cornwall PL14 4PW* Tel (01503) 263974

BURLEIGH, Walter Coleridge. b 41. WMMTC 89. **d** 89 **p** 90. NSM N Evington *Leic* from 90. *90 Farrier Lane, Leicester LE4 0WA* Tel 0116-235 9663

BURLES, Robert John. b 54. Bris Univ BSc75. St Jo Coll Nottm LTh86. **d** 88 **p** 89. C Mansfield St Pet *S'well* 88-91; C The Lydiards *Bris* 91-92; TV W Swindon and the Lydiards from 92. *1 Brandon Close, Swindon SN5 6AA* Tel (01793) 870244

BURLEY, Canon John Anderson. b 11. Selw Coll Cam BA33 MA37. Ely Th Coll 33. **d** 34 **p** 35. C Buckhurst Hill *Chelmsf* 34-39; V Walthamstow St Pet 39-59; CF 40-46; V Clacton St Jas *Chelmsf* 59-70; Hon Can Utrecht Old Cathl Ch *Eur* from 69; R Gt and Lt Braxted *Chelmsf* 70-83; rtd 83; Perm to Offic *Cant* from 83. *Braxted, Church Road, Lyminge, Kent CT18 8JA* Tel (01303) 862610

BURLEY, John Roland James. b 46. St Jo Coll Cam BA67 MA70 Ball Coll Ox DipGeochem68. Trin Episc Sch for Min Ambridge Penn MDiv88. **d** 81 **p** 82. SAMS 81-90; Chile 81-90; TV Southgate *Chich* from 90. *Holy Trinity Vicarage, Titmus Drive, Crawley, W Sussex RH10 5EU* Tel (01293) 525809

BURLEY, Michael. b 58. Ridley Hall Cam 86. **d** 89 **p** 90. C Scarborough St Mary w Ch Ch and H Apostles *York* 89-92; C Drypool 93; TV 93-97; V Sutton St Mich from 97. *St Michael's Vicarage, 751 Marfleet Lane, Hull HU9 4TJ* Tel (01482) 374509

BURLTON, Aelred Harry. b 49. Sarum & Wells Th Coll 75. **d** 78 **p** 79. C Feltham *Lon* 78-82; Chapl Heathrow Airport 83-94; P-in-c Harmondsworth 92-94; R St Buryan, St Levan and Sennen *Truro* from 94. *The Rectory, St Buryan, Penzance, Cornwall TR19 6BB* Tel (01736) 810216

BURLTON, Robert Michael. b 18. Nashdom Abbey 34 Ely Th Coll 40 Chich Th Coll 41. **d** 42 **p** 43. C W Bromwich St Fran *Lich* 42-45; C Godalming *Guildf* 45-47; C Southbourne St Kath *Win* 47-48; C St Teath w Michaelstow *Truro* 48-50; V St Gennys 50-52; V Penponds 52-63; R Lound *Nor* 65-76; P-in-c Fritton St Edm 65-83; R Blundeston w Flixton and Lound 76-83; rtd 83. *Heatherley, 3 Furze Park, Trelights, Port Isaac, Cornwall PL29 3TG*

BURLTON, William Frank. b 12. K Coll Lon. **d** 43 **p** 44. C Glouc St Mark *Glouc* 43-46; C Northleach and Hampnett w Stowell and Yanworth 46-48; C St Briavels 48-51; R Cromhall 51-78; Chapl HM Pris Leyhill 54-89; R Cromhall w Tortworth *Glouc* 78-82; rtd 82; Perm to Offic *Glouc* 82-89; Perm to Offic *Truro* from 89. *24 Godolphin Terrace, Marazion, Penzance, Cornwall TR17 0EX* Tel (01736) 710699

BURMAN, Philip Harvey. b 47. Kelham Th Coll 66. **d** 70 **p** 71. C Huyton St Mich *Liv* 70-75; C Farnworth 75-77; TV Kirkby 77-83; V Hindley All SS 83-93; V Middlesbrough St Martin *York* from 93. *St Martin's Vicarage, Whinney Banks, Middlesbrough, Cleveland TS5 4LA* Tel (01642) 819634

BURMAN, Thomas George (Tom). b 41. S'wark Ord Course 86. **d** 89 **p** 90. NSM Forest Hill *S'wark* from 89. *131 Como Road, London SE23 2JN* Tel 0181-699 8929

BURMAN, William Guest. b 26. St Cath Coll Cam MA55 Worc Coll Ox MA63. St Steph Ho Ox 81. **d** 83 **p** 84. C Weymouth H Trin *Sarum* 83-86; R Exton and Winsford and Cutcombe w Luxborough *B & W* 86-89; TV Langport Area Chs 89-91; rtd 91; Perm to Offic *B & W* from 91; Chapl Bath St Mary Magd Holloway from 94. *8 Stoneleigh Court, Lansdown Road, Bath BA1 5TL* Tel (01225) 312140

BURN, Canon Alan Edward. b 24. St Chad's Coll Dur BA49 DipTh51. **d** 51 **p** 52. C Hartlepool St Jas *Dur* 51-53; C Donnington Wood *Lich* 53-55; P-in-c Darlington St Mark CD *Dur* 55-58; V Darlington St Mark 58-61; Malaya 61-63; Malaysia 63-67; Dean Kota Kinabalu 64-67; V Binley *Cov* 67-73; R Allesley 73-89; RD Cov E 71-73; RD Cov N 79-87; Hon Can Cov Cathl 87-89; rtd 89. *8 Purleigh Avenue, Worcester WR4 0DX* Tel (01905) 25575

BURN, Dr Geoffrey Livingston. b 60. Sydney Univ BSc83 Imp Coll Lon PhD87. St Jo Coll Dur BA93 Cranmer Hall Dur DipMin95. **d** 96 **p** 97. C St Austell *Truro* from 96. *10 Glenview, St Austell, Cornwall PL25 5HR* Tel (01726) 63028

BURN, Ms Kathleen Doreen. b 48. Bp Grosseteste Coll CertEd69. NY Th Sem MDiv82. **d** 82 **p** 83. USA 82-93 and from 95; TV Dunstable *St Alb* 94-95. *address temp unknown*

BURN, Leonard Louis. b 44. K Coll Lon BD67 AKC67. **d** 68 **p** 69. C Kingswinford St Mary *Lich* 68-70; C S Ascot *Ox* 70-72; C Caversham 72-76; Chapl Selly Oak Hosp Birm 76-81; Bris City Hosp 81-82; P-in-c Bris St Mich *Bris* 81-83; R Peopleton and White Ladies Aston etc *Worc* 83-88; V Bengeworth 88-97; Chapl St Richard's Hospice Worc 88-97; Chapl Evesham Coll 90-97; rtd 97. *The Vicarage, 1 Broadway Road, Bengeworth, Evesham, Worcs WR11 6BB* Tel (01386) 446164

BURN, Richard James Southerden. b 34. Pemb Coll Cam BA56. Wells Th Coll 56. **d** 58 **p** 59. C Cheshunt *St Alb* 58-62; C Leighton Buzzard 65-66; C Glastonbury St Jo *B & W* 66-68; P-in-c Prestonpans *Edin* 68-71; P-in-c Stokesay *Heref* 71-75; P-in-c Dorrington 75-81; P-in-c Stapleton 75-81; P-in-c Leebotwood w Longnor 75-81; P-in-c Smethcott w Woolstaston 81; TR Melbury *Sarum* 81-87; P-in-c Quendon w Rickling and Wicken Bonhunt *Chelmsf* 87-92; R Quendon w Rickling and Wicken Bonhunt etc 92-95; rtd 95; NSM Isleworth St Fran *Lon* from 95. *St Francis Vicarage, 865 Great West Road, Isleworth, Middx TW7 5PD* Tel 0181-568 9098

BURN, Dr Robert Pemberton. b 34. Peterho Cam BA56 MA60 Lon Univ PhD68. CMS Tr Coll Chislehurst 60. **d** 63 **p** 81. India 63-71; Perm to Offic *Ely* 71-81; P-in-c Foxton 81-88; Perm to Offic *Ex* from 89. *Flat 4, 9 Lansdowne Terrace, Exeter EX2 4JJ* Tel (01392) 430028

BURN-MURDOCH, Aidan Michael. b 35. Trin Coll Cam BA60 MA63. Ridley Hall Cam. **d** 61 **p** 62. C Bishopwearmouth St Gabr *Dur* 61-63; Tutor Ridley Hall Cam 63-67; CMS Miss 67-70; India 68-70; R Hawick *Edin* 70-77; Bp's Co-ord of Evang *S & B* 77-81; R Reynoldston w Penrice and Llangennith 77-83; V Port Eynon w Rhosili and Llanddewi and Knelston 83-89; R Uddingston *Glas* from 89; R Cambuslang from 89. *5 Brownside Road, Cambuslang, Glasgow G72 8NL* Tel 0141-641 1173

BURNE, Christopher John Sambrooke. b 16. DSO45. Linc Th Coll 58. **d** 59 **p** 60. C S w N Hayling *Portsm* 59-63; V N Leigh *Ox* 63-81; rtd 81; Perm to Offic *Win* from 81. *Beam Ends, Middle Road, Tiptoe, Lymington, Hants SO41 6FX* Tel (01590) 682898

BURNET, Norman Andrew Gray. b 32. Aber Univ BEd77. Edin Th Coll 53. **d** 55 **p** 56. C Ayr *Glas* 55-58; S Africa 58-69; R Leven *St And* 69-72; Perm to Offic *Ab* 73-81; Perm to Offic *Bre* 73-81; Perm to Offic *Ely* 73-81; P-in-c Brinkley, Burrough Green and Carlton 82-83; P-in-c Westley Waterless 82-83; Australia 83-84; R Fraserburgh w New Pitsligo *Ab* 85-89; P-in-c Bicker *Linc* 89; V Bicker and Wigtoft 89-97; Perm to Offic *Nor* from 97; rtd 97. *Sunny Corner, 10 The Londs, Overstrand, Cromer, Norfolk NR27 0PW* Tel (01263) 579274

BURNETT, Canon John Capenhurst. b 19. AKC49. **d** 49 **p** 50. C Shirehampton *Bris* 49-53; C Stoke Bishop 53-56; R Wroughton 56-76; RD Cricklade 70-76; Hon Can Bris Cathl 74-85; V Bris St Andr w St Bart 76-85; rtd 85; Perm to Offic *Bris* from 85. *7 Queen Victoria Road, Bristol BS6 7PD* Tel 0117-973 8856

BURNETT, Mrs Patricia Kay. **d** 97. NSM Jarvis Brook *Chich* from 97. *20 St Richards Road, Crowborough, E Sussex TN6 3AT* Tel (01892) 655668

BURNETT, Susan Mary. b 50. Lon Univ BEd73 St Jo Coll Dur DipTh76. **dss** 78 **d** 87 **p** 94. Welling *S'wark* 78-83; E Greenwich Ch Ch w St Andr and St Mich 83-91; Par Dn 87-91; Par Dn Sydenham All SS 91-94; C 94-95; C Lower Sydenham St Mich 91-95; V from 95. *St Michael's Vicarage, Champion Crescent, London SE26 4HH* Tel 0181-778 7196

BURNETT-HALL, Mrs Karen. b 46. Bp Grosseteste Coll CertEd68 Lon Univ BD82. Oak Hill Th Coll 86. **d** 89 **p** 94. NSM Norbury *Ches* 89-90; Par Dn 90-92; NSM York St Paul *York* 93-95; NSM York St Barn from 95. *12 Kyme Street, York YO1 1HG* Tel (01904) 638935

BURNHAM, Andrew. b 48. ARCO New Coll Ox BA69 BA71 Westmr Coll Ox CertEd72. St Steph Ho Ox 81. **d** 83 **p** 84. Hon C Clifton *S'well* 83-85; C Beeston 85-87; V Carrington 87-94; Vice-Prin St Steph Ho Ox from 95. *St Stephen's House, 16 Marston Street, Oxford OX4 1JX* Tel (01865) 247874

BURNHAM, Cecil Champneys. b 14. AKC39. **d** 39 **p** 40. C Sidcup St Jo *Roch* 39-41; Hon C Lamorbey H Trin 41-43; C Pembury 43-45; C Gt and Lt Driffield *York* 45-47; V Watton w Beswick and Kilnwick 47-49; V Anlaby St Pet 50-55; C Heathfield *Chich* 55-58; R Hastings All SS 58-66; V Westham 66-74; R Harting 74-79; rtd 79; Perm to Offic *Chich* from 87. *25 Sovereign Court, Campbell Road, Bognor Regis, W Sussex PO21 1AH* Tel (01243) 822119

BURNHAM, Frank Leslie. b 23. Edin Th Coll 52. **d** 55 **p** 56. C York St Mary Bishophill Senior *York* 55-58; C Marfleet 58-62; V 62-72; TR 72-74; V Acomb St Steph 74-85; C Fulford 85-88; rtd 88; Perm to Offic *York* from 88. *Dulverton Hall, St Martin's*

Square, Scarborough, N Yorkshire YO11 2DB Tel (01723) 373082

BURNINGHAM, Frederick George. b 34. ALCD60. **d** 60 **p** 61. C New Beckenham St Paul *Roch* 60-63; Canada 63-68 and 89-95; C Wisley w Pyrford *Guildf* 68-69; P-in-c Sydenham H Trin *S'wark* 69-71; C Broadwater St Mary *Chich* 72-77; R Sotterley, Willingham, Shadingfield, Ellough etc *St E* 77-82; R Ipswich St Clem w H Trin 82-89; P-in-c Thorndon w Rishangles, Stoke Ash, Thwaite etc from 95. *The Rectory, Standwell Green, Thorndon, Eye, Suffolk IP23 7JL* Tel (01379) 678603

BURNINGHAM, Richard Anthony. b 47. Keele Univ BA70 Aber Univ CQSW77 Roehampton Inst PGCE85. All Nations Chr Coll 82 Oak Hill Th Coll 94. **d** 96 **p** 97. C Reigate St Mary *S'wark* from 96. *3 St Clair Close, Reigate, Surrey RH2 0QB* Tel (01737) 242391

BURNISTON, Aubrey John. b 53. St Jo Coll Dur BA. Cranmer Hall Dur. **d** 83 **p** 84. C Owton Manor *Dur* 83-86; TV Rugby St Andr *Cov* 86-93; V Heaton St Martin *Bradf* from 93. *St Martin's Vicarage, Haworth Road, Bradford, W Yorkshire BD9 6LL* Tel (01274) 543004

BURNLEY, William Francis Edward. b 06. Lon Univ BD40. Sarum Th Coll 32. **d** 35 **p** 36. C Shirehampton *Bris* 35-38; C Stapleton 38-40; CF (EC) 40-45; Hon CF from 45; I Bowden Hill *Bris* 45-54; V Corston w Rodbourne 54-62; R Foxley w Bremilham 54-62; V Highworth w Sevenhampton and Inglesham etc 62-68; P-in-c Hannington 62-68; V Westwood *Sarum* 68-74; rtd 74. *Sunnyhill, 2A Perry's Lane, Seend, Melksham, Wilts SN12 6QA* Tel (01380) 828510

BURNLEY, Suffragan Bishop of. *See* JARRETT, The Rt Revd Martyn William

BURNS, Dane. b 51. DipTh. **d** 85 **p** 86. C Enniskillen *Clogh* 85-87; I Augher w Newtownsaville and Eskrahoole 87-92; Dioc Info Officer 91-92; I Camus-juxta-Bann *D & R* 92-96. *Plas Loyd, 35 Sea Road, Castlerock, Co Londonderry*

BURNS, Douglas Thomas. b 32. **d** 85 **p** 86. NSM Dublin Crumlin *D & G* 85-91; NSM Dublin Crumlin w Chapelizod 91; NSM Leighlin w Grange Sylvae, Shankill etc *C & O* 91-96; Vice-Pres Nat Bible Soc of Ireland from 93. *100 Cherryfield Road, Dublin 12, Irish Republic* Tel Dublin (1) 460 0526

BURNS, Canon Edward Joseph. b 38. Liv Univ BSc58 St Cath Soc Ox BA61 MA64. Wycliffe Hall Ox 58. **d** 61 **p** 62. C Leyland St Andr *Blackb* 61-64; C Burnley St Pet 64-67; V Chorley St Jas 67-75; V Fulwood Ch Ch from 75; RD Preston 79-86; Chapl Sharoe Green Hosp Preston 81-94; Hon Can Blackb Cathl *Blackb* from 86; Bp's Adv on Hosp Chapls 89-94. *Christ Church Vicarage, 19 Vicarage Close, Fulwood, Preston PR2 8EG* Tel (01772) 719210

BURNS, James Denis. b 43. Lich Th Coll 69. **d** 72 **p** 73. C Gt Wyrley *Lich* 72-75; C Atherton *Man* 75-76; Asst Chapl Sheff Ind Miss *Sheff* 76-79; C-in-c Masborough St Paul w St Jo 76-78; C-in-c Northfield St Mich 76-78; V Rotherham Ferham Park 78-79; V Lancaster Ch Ch *Blackb* 79-81; V Lancaster Ch Ch w St Jo and St Anne 81-86; V Chorley St Pet 86-96; R Rufford from 96; Warden Past Aux from 96. *St Mary's Rectory, 17 Church Road, Rufford, Ormskirk, Lancs L40 1TA* Tel (01704) 821261

BURNS, John Macdonald. *See* ODA-BURNS, John Macdonald

BURNS, Michael John. b 53. AKC76. Chich Th Coll 76. **d** 77 **p** 78. C Broseley w Benthall *Heref* 77-81; C Stevenage All SS Pin Green *St Alb* 81-84; V Tattenham Corner and Burgh Heath *Guildf* 84-92; C and Chapl Younger People Milton Keynes *Ox* from 92. *2 Symington Court, Shenley Lodge, Milton Keynes MK5 7AN* Tel (01908) 235265 or 237777

BURNS, Robert Joseph. b 34. Wycliffe Hall Ox 67. **d** 71 **p** 72. C Portswood Ch Ch *Win* 71-73; C Woking St Jo *Guildf* 73-77; C Glas St Mary *Glas* 77; Bp's Dom Chapl 77-78; R Glas Gd Shep and Ascension 78-92; rtd 92. *85/8 Lancefield Quay, Glasgow G3 8HA*

BURNS, Stephen. b 70. Grey Coll Dur BA92 MA94. Ridley Hall Cam 93. **d** 96 **p** 97. C Houghton le Spring *Dur* from 96. *Kepier Flat, Church Street, Houghton-le-Spring, Tyne & Wear DH4 4DN* Tel 0191-584 8970

BURNS, Brother Stuart Maitland. b 46. Leeds Univ BA67. Coll of Resurr Mirfield 67. **d** 69 **p** 70. C Wyther Ven Bede *Ripon* 69-73; Asst Chapl Leeds Univ 73-77; Asst Chapl Leeds Poly 73-77; P-in-c Thornthwaite w Thruscross and Darley 77-84; V Leeds Gipton Epiphany 84-89; OSB from 89; Priory of Our Lady Burford from 89; Lic to Offic *Ox* from 89. *Burford Priory, Priory Lane, Burford, Oxford OX18 4SQ* Tel (01993) 823605

BURR, Mrs Ann Pamela. b 39. S Dios Minl Tr Scheme 83. **dss** 86 **d** 87 **p** 94. Fareham H Trin *Portsm* 86-87; Hon C from 87; Hon Asst Chapl Knowle Hosp Fareham 86-90; Asst Chapl Qu Alexandra Hosp Portsm 90-92; Chapl Portsm Hosps NHS Trust from 92. *3 Bruce Close, Fareham, Hants PO16 7QJ* Tel (01329) 281375

BURR, Brian Gilbert. b 23. AKC49. St Boniface Warminster 50. **d** 50 **p** 51. C Babbacombe *Ex* 50-52; C Brixham 52-55; Lic to Offic 55; V Tideford *Truro* 56-58; V Kingswear *Ex* 58-63; V Churston Ferrers w Goodrington 63-76; RD Ipplepen 69-77; V Brixham 76-77; V Brixham w Churston Ferrers 77; R Cen Torquay 77-81; TR Torre 81-87; rtd 87; Perm to Offic *Ex* 89-91; Chapl Beauchamp Community 91-96. *5 St Barnabas, Beauchamp Community, The Quadrangle, Newland, Malvern, Worcs WR13 5AX* Tel (01684) 561044

BURR, Raymond Leslie. b 43. NE Ord Course 82 Edin Th Coll 84. **d** 85 **p** 86. C Hartlepool St Paul *Dur* 85-87; C Sherburn w Pittington 87-89; R Lyons 89-95; RD Houghton 94-96; V S Shields St Hilda w St Thos from 95. *St Hilda's Vicarage, 40 Lawe Road, South Shields, Tyne & Wear NE33 2EU* Tel 0191-454 1414

BURRELL, David Philip. b 56. Southn Univ BTh90. Sarum & Wells Th Coll 85. **d** 88 **p** 89. C Ixworth and Bardwell *St E* 88-91; P-in-c Haughley w Wetherden 91-96; P-in-c Culford, W Stow and Wordwell w Flempton etc from 96. *The Rectory, West Stow, Bury St Edmunds, Suffolk IP28 6ET* Tel (01284) 728556

BURRELL, Godfrey John. b 49. Reading Univ BSc70 Qu Coll Ox CertEd71. Wycliffe Hall Ox 84. **d** 86 **p** 87. C Didcot All SS *Ox* 86-89; S Africa from 90. *St Alban's College, Private Bag 1, Alkantrant, Pretoria, 0005 South Africa* Tel Pretoria (12) 476147 or 475451

BURRELL, Martin John. b 51. ARCM71. Trin Coll Bris BA95. **d** 95 **p** 96. C Cant St Mary Bredin *Cant* from 95. *38 Nunnery Road, Canterbury, Kent CT1 3LS* Tel (01227) 455723

BURRELL, Canon Maurice Claude. b 30. Bris Univ BA54 MA63 Lanc Univ PhD78. Tyndale Hall Bris. **d** 55 **p** 56. C Wandsworth St Steph *S'wark* 55-57; C Whitehall Park St Andr Hornsey Lane *Lon* 57-59; R Kirby Cane *Nor* 59-63; R Ellingham 61-63; Chapl K Sch Gutersloh, W Germany 63-67; R Widford *Chelmsf* 67-71; Chapl and Lect St Mary's Coll Cheltenham 71-75; Dir of Educn *Nor* 75-86; Hon Can Nor Cathl 77-95; Dioc Dir of Tr 87-95; rtd 95; Perm to Offic *Nor* from 95. *37 Ireton Close, Thorpe St Andrew, Norwich NR7 0TW* Tel (01603) 702510

BURRIDGE, Richard Alan. b 55. Univ Coll Ox BA77 MA81 Nottm Univ CertEd78 DipTh83 PhD89. St Jo Coll Nottm 82. **d** 85 **p** 86. C Bromley SS Pet and Paul *Roch* 85-87; Chapl Ex Univ *Ex* 87-94; Dean K Coll Lon from 94. *King's College, Strand, London WC2R 2LS* Tel 0171-873 2333 E-mail r.a.burridge@kcl.ac.uk

BURRIDGE-BUTLER, Paul David. *See* BUTLER, Paul David

✠**BURROUGH, The Rt Revd John Paul.** b 16. MBE46. St Edm Hall Ox BA37 DipTh38 MA45. Ely Th Coll 45. **d** 46 **p** 47 **c** 68. C Aldershot St Mich *Guildf* 46-51; Korea 51-59; Chapl to Overseas Peoples *Birm* 59-67; Hon Can Birm Cathl 65-67; Can Res 67-68; Bp Mashonaland 68-81; R Empingham *Pet* 81-85; Asst Bp Pet 81-85; RD Rutland 82-85; rtd 85; Perm to Offic *Ox* from 85. *6 Mill Green Close, Bampton, Oxon OX8 2HF* Tel (01993) 850952

BURROUGHS, Edward Graham. b 36. K Coll Lon BD AKC. **d** 60 **p** 61. C Walton St Mary *Liv* 60-63; S Rhodesia 63-65; Rhodesia 65-80; Zimbabwe from 80. *Box 8045, Belmont, Bulawayo, Zimbabwe* Tel Bulawayo (9) 78711

BURROW, Miss Alison Sarah. b 59. Homerton Coll Cam BEd82. Westcott Ho Cam 84. **d** 87. Par Dn Hebden Bridge *Wakef* 87-88; Par Dn Prestwood and Gt Hampden *Ox* 88-90; Par Dn Olney w Emberton 90-92; rtd 92. *13 Willoughby Close, Great Barford, Bedford MK44 3LD*

BURROW, Ronald. b 31. Univ Coll Dur BA55. St Steph Ho Ox 83. **d** 85 **p** 86. C Dawlish *Ex* 85-87; TV Ottery St Mary, Alfington, W Hill, Tipton etc 87-91; P-in-c Pyworthy, Pancrasweek and Bridgerule 91-95; rtd 95; Perm to Offic *Ex* from 95. *3 Riverside, Dolphin Street, Colyton, Devon EX13 6LU* Tel (01297) 553882

BURROWES, Thomas Cecil. b 13. TCD BA36 MA43. TCD Div Sch Div Test36. **d** 37 **p** 38. C Whitehouse *Conn* 37-41; C Belfast All SS 41-44; P-in-c Killough *D & D* 44-50; I Killinchy 50-78; RD Killinchy 71-78; rtd 78. *1 Kilmood Church Road, Kilmood, Killinchy, Newtownards, Co Down BT23 6SA* Tel (01238) 541942

BURROWS, Canon Brian Albert. b 34. Lon Univ DipTh59. St Aid Birkenhead. **d** 59 **p** 60. C Sutton St Geo *Ches* 59-62; Canada 62-69 and from 74; V Stratton St Margaret *Bris* 70-74; Hon Can Frobisher Bay 78-80. *705 Main Street East, Hamilton, Ontario, Canada, L8M 1K8*

BURROWS, Prof Clifford Robert. b 37. MIMechE68 Univ of Wales BSc62 Lon Univ PhD69. Chich Th Coll 75. **d** 76 **p** 77. NSM Brighton St Pet *Chich* 76-78; NSM Brighton St Pet w Chpl Royal 78-80; NSM Brighton St Pet w Chpl Royal and St Jo 80-82; Perm to Offic *Glas* 82-85 and 86-89; NSM Clarkston 85-86; NSM Bath Ch Ch Prop Chpl *B & W* from 90. *Stonecroft, Entry Hill Drive, Bath BA2 5NL* Tel (01225) 334743

BURROWS, David. b 62. Leeds Univ BA85. Linc Th Coll 86. **d** 88 **p** 89. C Kippax w Allerton Bywater *Ripon* 88-91; C Manston 91-95; V Halifax St Anne Southowram *Wakef* from 95. *St Anne's Vicarage, Church Lane, Southowram, Halifax, W Yorkshire HX3 9TD* Tel (01422) 365229

BURROWS, David MacPherson. b 43. N Ord Course. **d** 82 **p** 83. NSM Newburgh *Liv* 82-93; NSM Newburgh w Westhead from 93. *34 Woodrow Drive, Newburgh, Wigan, Lancs WN8 7LB* Tel (01257) 462948

BURROWS, Canon George Henry Jerram. b 10. TCD BA31 MA37. TCD Div Sch 31. **d** 33 **p** 38. Dioc C (Leigh) and Hd Master D'Israeli Sch 33-34; Hd Master Villiers Endowed Sch Limerick 34-47; Dioc C 41-47; Hd Master Gr High Sch Cork

47-71; Min Can Cork Cathl *C, C & R* 67-69; Can Cork and Ross Cathls 69-71; P-in-c Dublin St Luke *D & G* 71-78; Succ St Patr Cathl Dublin 71-77; Chan V 77-81; rtd 78; Clerical V Ch Ch Cathl Dublin *D & G* 81-90. *22 Longwood Avenue, Dublin 8, Irish Republic* Tel Dublin (1) 454 3629

BURROWS, Graham Charles. b 47. Leeds Univ CertEd69 Open Univ BA81. N Ord Course 87. **d** 90 **p** 91. C Chorlton-cum-Hardy St Clem *Man* 90-93; TV Horwich 93; TV Horwich and Rivington 93-94. *101 Bramhall Avenue, Bolton BL2 4EX6* Tel (01204) 525188

BURROWS, Miss Jean. b 54. CertEd75. Trin Coll Bris 89. **d** 91 **p** 94. C Allesley *Cov* 91-95; C Thorley *St Alb* from 95. *18 Broadleaf Avenue, Thorley Park, Bishop's Stortford, Herts CM23 4JY* Tel (01279) 504574

BURROWS, John Edward. b 36. Leeds Univ BA60 PGCE63. Coll of Resurr Mirfield. **d** 63 **p** 65. C Much Hadham *St Alb* 63-65; Hon C Haggerston St Mary w St Chad *Lon* 65-73; P-in-c Finsbury St Clem w St Barn and St Matt 73-76; Chapl Woodbridge Sch 76-83; Lic to Offic *St E* 76-83; V Ipswich St Bart from 83. *St Bartholomew's Vicarage, Newton Road, Ipswich IP3 8HQ* Tel (01473) 727441

BURROWS, Joseph Atkinson (Joe). b 32. St Aid Birkenhead 58. **d** 61 **p** 62. C Hoole *Ches* 61-67; Jamaica 67-68; C Ayr *Glas* 68-74; R Prestwick 74-78; Hon Chapl RAF 74-78; Hon Chapl RN 74-78; Australia from 78; rtd 97. *3B Cowan Road, St Ives, Sydney NSW, Australia 2075* Tel Sydney (2) 9488 9393

BURROWS, Canon Michael Andrew James. b 61. TCD BA82 MA85 MLitt86 DipTh87. **d** 87 **p** 88. C Douglas Union w Frankfield *C, C & R* 87-91; Dean of Res TCD 91-94; Lic to Offic *D & G* 91-94; Min Can St Patr Cathl Dublin from 91; I Bandon Union *C, C & R* from 94; Can Cork and Cloyne Cathls from 96. *The Rectory, Bandon, Co Cork, Irish Republic* Tel Bandon (23) 41259 Fax as telephone

BURROWS, Paul Anthony. b 55. Nottm Univ BA77. Gen Th Sem (NY) STM88 St Steph Ho Ox 77. **d** 79 **p** 80. C Camberwell St Giles *S'wark* 79-81; C St Helier 81-83; C Fareham SS Pet and Paul *Portsm* 83-85; USA from 85. *800 52nd Court, West Des Moines, IA 50265, USA*

BURROWS, Peter. b 55. BTh. Sarum & Wells Th Coll 80. **d** 83 **p** 84. C Baildon *Bradf* 83-87; R Broughton Astley *Leic* 87-95; TR Broughton Astley and Croft w Stoney Stanton from 95; RD Guthlaxton I from 94; Dir of Ords from 97. *St Mary's Rectory, St Mary's Close, Broughton Astley, Leicester LE9 6PF* Tel (01455) 282261

BURROWS, Philip Geoffrey. b 59. Birm Univ BSc80. Oak Hill Th Coll DipHE92. **d** 92 **p** 93. C Poynton *Ches* 92-96; Min Cheadle Hulme Em CD from 96. *198 Bruntwood Lane, Cheadle Hulme, Cheshire SK8 6BE* Tel 0161-485 1154

BURROWS, Samuel Reginald (Sam). b 30. AKC57. **d** 58 **p** 59. C Shildon *Dur* 58-62; C Heworth St Mary 62-67; C-in-c Leam Lane CD 67-72; C-in-c Bishopwearmouth St Mary V w St Pet CD 72-77; R Bewcastle and Stapleton *Carl* 77-82; R Harrington 82-90; P-in-c Millom 90; V 90-95; rtd 95. *1 Nettleham Close, Lincoln LN2 1SJ* Tel (01522) 576441

✠**BURROWS, The Rt Revd Simon Hedley.** b 28. K Coll Cam BA52 MA56. Westcott Ho Cam 52. **d** 54 **p** 55 **c** 74. C St Jo Wood *Lon* 54-57; Chapl Jes Coll Cam 57-60; V Wyken *Cov* 60-67; V Fareham H Trin *Portsm* 67-71; TR 71-74; Suff Bp Buckingham *Ox* 74-87; Area Bp Buckingham 87-94; rtd 94. *8 Quarry Road, Winchester, Hants SO23 0JF* Tel (01962) 853332

BURSELL, Chan Rupert David Hingston. b 42. QC. Ex Univ LLB63 St Edm Hall Ox BA67 MA72 DPhil72. St Steph Ho Ox 67. **d** 68 **p** 69. NSM St Marylebone w H Trin *Lon* 68-69; NSM Almondsbury *Bris* 69-71; NSM Bedminster St Fran 71-75; NSM Bedminster 75-82; NSM Bris Ch Ch w St Ewen and All SS 83-88; NSM City of Bris 83-88; Lic to Offic 88-95; Lic to Offic *B & W* 72-92; Chan from 92; NSM Cheddar from 93. *Brookside, 74 Church Road, Winscombe, Avon BS25 1BP*

BURSLEM, Christopher David Jeremy Grant. b 35. AKC85. **d** 59 **p** 60. C Bocking St Mary *Chelmsf* 59-63; C Glouc All SS *Glouc* 64-67; R Amberley 67-87; P-in-c Withington and Compton Abdale w Haselton from 87. *The Rectory, Withington, Cheltenham, Glos GL54 4BG* Tel (01242) 890242

BURSON-THOMAS, Michael Edwin. b 52. Sarum & Wells Th Coll 84. **d** 86 **p** 87. C Bitterne Park *Win* 86-89; V Lockerley and E Dean w E and W Tytherley 89-95; P-in-c Fotherby *Linc* from 95; Asst Local Min Officer from 95. *The Vicarage, Peppin Lane, Fotherby, Louth, Lincs LN11 0UG* Tel (01507) 606403

BURSTON, Richard John. b 46. ARICS70 MRTPI73. S Dios Minl Tr Scheme 89. **d** 93 **p** 94. Hon C Stratton St Margaret w S Marston etc *Bris* from 93. *17 Crawley Avenue, Swindon SN3 4LB* Tel (01793) 822403

BURSTON, Canon Robert Benjamin Stuart. b 45. St Chad's Coll Dur BA68 DipTh70. **d** 70 **p** 71. C Whorlton *Newc* 70-77; V Alwinton w Holystone and Alnham 77-83; TR Glendale Gp from 83; Hon Can Newc Cathl from 95. *The Rectory, 5 Fenton Drive, Wooler, Northd NE71 6DT* Tel (01668) 281551

BURT, Leslie Reginald. b 22. ACIS49. St Aug Coll Cant 65. **d** 66 **p** 67. C Petersfield w Sheet *Portsm* 66-70; Perm to Offic from 82. *44B Victoria Road South, Southsea, Hants PO5 2BT* Tel (01705) 730989

BURT, Noel Bryce. b 21. Clare Coll Cam BA49 MA53. Cuddesdon Coll 49. **d** 51 **p** 52. C York St Olave w St Giles *York* 51-54; C Scarborough St Martin 54-56; V Scarborough St Sav 56-61; V Sledmere 61-67; R Cowlam 61-67; R Invergowrie *Bre* 67-76; R Glencarse 71-76; V Denton and Ingleton *Dur* 76-88; rtd 88. *49 Balmer Hill, Gainford, Darlington, Co Durham DL2 3EL* Tel (01325) 730075

BURT, Paul Andrew. b 52. Leeds Univ BA74. Ridley Hall Cam 82. **d** 84 **p** 85. C Edin St Thos *Edin* 84-88; CMS 88-90; Bahrain 88-90; R Melrose *Edin* from 91; Chapl Borders Gen Hosp from 93. *The Rectory, 20 High Cross Avenue, Melrose, Roxburghshire TD6 9SU* Tel (01896) 822626

BURT, Robert. b 08. Lich Th Coll 31. **d** 34 **p** 35. C Ferryhill *Dur* 34-40; C W Hartlepool Ch Ch 40-45; V Newbottle 45-61; V Darlington St Matt 61-77; rtd 77; Perm to Offic *Dur* from 77. *Dulverton Hall, St Martin's Square, Scarborough YO11 2DB* Tel (01723) 373082

BURT, Roger Malcolm. b 45. St Jo Coll Auckland LTh74 SSC. **d** 73 **p** 74. New Zealand 73-80; P-in-c Colton *Nor* 80; P-in-c Easton 80; V Easton w Colton and Marlingford 80-88; CF from 88. *MOD Chaplains (Army), Trenchard Lines, Upavon, Pewsey, Wilts SN9 6BE* Tel (01980) 615804 Fax 615800

BURTON, Andrew John. b 63. St Kath Coll Liv BA84 CertDiv84. Cranmer Hall Dur 86. **d** 88 **p** 89. C Harlescott *Lich* 88-91; C Ches H Trin *Ches* 91-94; P-in-c Congleton St Jas from 94. *St James's Vicarage, 116 Holmes Chapel Road, Congleton, Cheshire CW12 4NX* Tel (01260) 273722

BURTON, Antony William James. b 29. Ch Coll Cam BA52 MA56. Cuddesdon Coll 52. **d** 54 **p** 55. C Linc St Nic w St Jo Newport *Linc* 54-57; C Croydon *Cant* 57-62; V Winterton *Linc* 62-82; V Roxby w Risby 70-82; RD Manlake 76-82; V Nettleham 82-94; rtd 94; Perm to Offic *Linc* from 94. *28 Eastfield Road, Messingham, Scunthorpe, S Humberside DN17 3PG* Tel (01724) 763916

BURTON, Christopher Paul (Chris). b 38. FCA75. Clifton Th Coll 67. **d** 69 **p** 70. C Wandsworth All SS *S'wark* 69-72; C York St Paul *York* 72-75; V Castle Vale *Birm* 75-82; R Gt Parndon *Chelmsf* from 82. *Great Parndon Rectory, Perry Road, Harlow, Essex CM18 7NP* Tel (01279) 432626

BURTON, Daniel John Ashworth. b 63. Regent's Park Coll Ox BA88 MA93 Heythrop Coll Lon MTh93. St Mich Coll Llan 93. **d** 94 **p** 95. C Mountain Ash *Llan* 94-97; R St Brides Minor w Bettws from 97. *St Bride's Rectory, Heol Persondy, Sarn, Bridgend CF32 9RH* Tel (01656) 720274

BURTON, David Alan. b 53. St Jo Coll Dur BA. Westcott Ho Cam 81. **d** 84 **p** 85. C Bedford St Andr *St Alb* 84-87; C Leighton Buzzard w Eggington, Hockliffe etc 87-91; V Kingsbury Episcopi w E Lambrook *B & W* 91-94; V Kingsbury Episcopi w E Lambrook, Hambridge etc 94-95; R Bishops Lydeard w Bagborough and Cothelstone from 95. *The Rectory, Bishops Lydeard, Taunton, Somerset TA4 3AT* Tel (01823) 432414

BURTON, Desmond Jack. b 49. Sarum & Wells Th Coll 70. **d** 73 **p** 74. C Lakenham St Jo *Nor* 73-77; C Gt Yarmouth 77-80; R Tidworth *Sarum* 80-83; Chapl HM Pris Pentonville 83-84; Chapl HM Pris Standford Hill 84-88; Chapl HM Pris Swaleside 88-93; Chapl HM Pris Roch from 93. *HM Prison, 1 Fort Road, Rochester, Kent ME1 3QS* Tel (01634) 838100 Fax 826712

BURTON, Edward Arthur. b 15. Tyndale Hall Bris 39. **d** 42 **p** 43. C Tipton St Martin *Lich* 42-45; P-in-c W Derby St Nath Windsor *Liv* 45-46; C Morden *S'wark* 46-49; V Birm Bp Ryder *Birm* 49-51; V Tipton St Paul *Lich* 51-55; V Tibshelf *Derby* 55-63; V Beckford w Ashton under Hill *Glouc* 63-78; rtd 78; Perm to Offic *Chich* from 83. *B5 Hatfield Court, Salisbury Road, Hove, E Sussex BN3 3AA* Tel (01273) 727560

BURTON, Frank Victor. b 10. Linc Th Coll 76. **d** 76 **p** 77. Hon C Folkingham w Laughton *Linc* 76-77; Hon C S Lafford 77-79; Hon C Helpringham 79; Hon C New Sleaford 79-80; Perm to Offic from 80. *Address temp unknown*

BURTON, Graham John. b 45. Bris Univ BA69. Tyndale Hall Bris 69. **d** 71 **p** 72. C Leic St Chris *Leic* 71-75; C Southall Green St Jo *Lon* 75-79; CMS 80-92; Pakistan 80-92; P-in-c Basford w Hyson Green *S'well* from 92. *18 Russell Road, Nottingham NG7 6HB* Tel 0115-978 7473

BURTON, Hugh Anthony. b 56. Edin Univ BD79. Cranmer Hall Dur 81. **d** 83 **p** 84. C Coalville and Bardon Hill *Leic* 83-87; P-in-c Packington w Normanton-le-Heath 87-92; V 92-96; TV Kidderminster St Geo *Worc* from 96. *38 Comberton Avenue, Kidderminster, Worcs DY10 3EG* Tel (01562) 824490

BURTON, John Richard. b 22. Em Coll Cam BA47 MA51. Wycliffe Hall Ox 49. **d** 50 **p** 51. C Reading St Jo *Ox* 50-52; C Plymouth St Andr *Ex* 52-56; V Plymouth Ch Ch 56-59; V Ellacombe 59-74; TV Cen Torquay 74-76; Warden Maillard Ho of Healing 76-87; Hon C Torre 76-82; rtd 87; Perm to Offic *Ex* 87-94. *6 Princess Cottages, Coffinswell, Newton Abbot, Devon TQ12 4SR* Tel (01803) 873758

BURTON, Leslie Samuel Bertram. b 23. **d** 91 **p** 92. NSM St Cleer *Truro* 91-93; Perm to Offic from 93. *41 Park View, Liskeard, Cornwall PL14 3EF* Tel (01579) 344891

BURTON, Michael John. b 55. Leeds Univ BSc76 Leeds Poly BSc80. St Jo Coll Nottm LTh88. **d** 88 **p** 89. C Charles w Plymouth St Matthias *Ex* 88-92; V Paignton St Paul Preston from 92. *St Paul's Vicarage, Locarno Avenue, Preston, Paignton, Devon TQ3 2DH* Tel (01803) 522872

BURTON, Nicholas John. b 52. St Steph Ho Ox 77. **d** 80 **p** 81. C Leic St Matt and St Geo *Leic* 80-82; C Leic Resurr 82-83; TV 83-88; C Narborough and Huncote 88-90; R from 90. *All Saints' Rectory, 15 Church View, Narborough, Leicester LE9 5GY* Tel 0116-275 0388

BURTON, Norman George. b 30. N Ord Course. **d** 83 **p** 84. C Rothwell w Lofthouse *Ripon* 83-86; C Rothwell 86-87; V Lofthouse 87-96; rtd 96. *28 Temple Row Close, Colton, Leeds LS15 9HR* Tel 0113-260 1129

BURTON, Richard Peter. b 56. Nottm Univ BA80. Cranmer Hall Dur 80. **d** 82 **p** 83. C Linthorpe *York* 82-85; R Bishop Burton w Walkington 85-91; V Tadcaster w Newton Kyme from 91. *The Vicarage, 78 Station Road, Tadcaster, N Yorkshire LS24 9JR* Tel (01937) 833394

BURTON EVANS, David. *See* EVANS, David Burton

BURTON-JONES, Simon David. b 62. Em Coll Cam BA84 MA88 Nottm Univ BTh92 MA93. St Jo Coll Nottm 90. **d** 93 **p** 94. C Darwen St Pet w Hoddlesden *Blackb* 93-96; C Biggin Hill *Roch* from 96. *22 Foxearth Close, Biggin Hill, Westerham, Kent TN16 3HQ* Tel (01959) 575900

BURTT, Andrew Keith. b 50. Massey Univ (NZ) BA72 MA74 DipEd76. St Jo Coll (NZ) LTh82. **d** 81 **p** 82. New Zealand 81-83; CF 84-92; Sen Chapl Brighton Coll from 93. *Brighton College, Eastern Road, Brighton BN2 2AL, or 8 Walpole Road, Brighton BN2 2EA* Tel Brighton (01273) 606524

BURTWELL, Stanley Peter. b 32. Leeds Univ BA55. Coll of Resurr Mirfield 55. **d** 57 **p** 58. C Leeds St Hilda *Ripon* 57-61; S Africa 61-72; P-in-c Gt Hanwood *Heref* 72-78; R 78-83; RD Pontesbury 80-83; V Upper Norwood St Jo *Cant* 83-84; V Upper Norwood St Jo *S'wark* 85-90; RD Croydon N 85-90; TR Bourne Valley *Sarum* from 90. *The Rectory, Newton Toney Road, Allington, Salisbury SP4 0BZ* Tel (01980) 610663

BURY, Herbert John Malcolm. b 28. Linc Coll Ox BA52 MA56. Roch Th Coll 68. **d** 69 **p** 70. C Bexleyheath Ch Ch *Roch* 69-72; V Ryarsh w Birling 72-83; P-in-c Addington w Trottiscliffe 76-83; R Knockholt w Halstead 83-93; rtd 93; Perm to Offic *Chich* from 93. *Star Cottage, High Street, Burwash, Etchingham, E Sussex TN19 7HA* Tel (01435) 882326

BURY, The Very Revd Nicholas Ayles Stillingfleet (Nick). b 43. Qu Coll Cam BA65 MA69 Ch Ch Ox MA71. Cuddesdon Coll. **d** 68 **p** 69. C Liv Our Lady and St Nic *Liv* 68-71; Chapl Ch Ch *Ox* 71-75; V Stevenage St Mary Shephall *St Alb* 75-84; V St Peter-in-Thanet *Cant* 84-97; RD Thanet 93-97; Hon Can Cant Cathl 94-97; Dean Glouc from 97. *The Deanery, 1 Millers Green, Gloucester GL1 1BP* Tel (01452) 524167

BUSBY, Ian Frederick Newman. b 32. Roch Th Coll 61. **d** 64 **p** 65. C Bedale *Ripon* 64-67; C Stevenage St Geo *St Alb* 67-71; V Stevenage St Mary Shephall 71-75; V Kildwick *Bradf* 75-92; rtd 93; Perm to Offic *Bradf* from 93. *65 Main Street, Farnhill, Keighley, W Yorkshire BD20 9BJ* Tel (01535) 633001

BUSBY, Jack Wright. b 12. Leeds Univ BA35. Coll of Resurr Mirfield 35. **d** 37 **p** 38. C Sneinton St Steph *S'well* 37-41; C Hucknall Torkard 41-47; Chapl Newstead Abbey and Colliery 47-56; V Blidworth 56-66; V Goxhill *Linc* 66-70; R Barkestone cum Plungar and Redmile *Leic* 70-77; rtd 77; Perm to Offic *Linc* from 77. *43 Chestnut Avenue, Waltham, Grimsby, S Humberside DN37 0DF* Tel (01472) 823208

BUSBY, John. b 38. CEng St Cath Coll Cam MA60. Local Minl Tr Course. **d** 93 **p** 94. NSM Worplesdon *Guildf* from 93. *Iona, Fox Corner, Worplesdon, Guildford, Surrey GU3 3PP* Tel (01483) 234562

BUSH, Alfred Edward Leonard. b 09. ALCD39. **d** 39 **p** 40. C Becontree St Mary *Chelmsf* 39-42; P-in-c Becontree St Alb 42-43; V Kentish Town *Lon* 43-58; V Oakwood St Thos 58-75; rtd 75; Perm to Offic *Chich* 75-78; Perm to Offic *St E* 78-86; Perm to Offic *Ox* 86-97; Perm to Offic *Nor* from 97. *Oakwood, Back Street, Reepham, Norwich NR10 4JW* Tel (01603) 872749

BUSH, Mrs Ann Kathleen. b 47. MATCA65. Marlow Past Foundn DCouns90 Ox Min Course 90. **d** 93 **p** 94. NSM Warfield *Ox* 93-96; Dep Chapl HM Pris Wormwood Scrubs 96-97; Chapl HM Pris Reading from 97. *The Chaplain's Office, HM Prison Reading, Forbury Road, Reading RG1 3HY* Tel (01734) 587031 Fax 591058

BUSH, David. b 25. FRIBA47 Liv Univ BArch47. S'wark Ord Course 73. **d** 77 **p** 77. C Douglas St Geo and St Barn *S & M* 77-80; Chapl Ballamona Hosp and Cronk Grianagh 80-86; V Marown 80-87; R The Rissingtons *Glouc* 87-92; rtd 92; Perm to Offic *Glouc* 92-97; Perm to Offic *S & M* from 97. *Colby Mill, Glen Road, Colby, Isle of Man IM9 4NY* Tel (01624) 833522

BUSH, George Raymond. b 57. St Jo Coll Cam BA81 MA84 Univ of Wales LLM95. Ripon Coll Cuddesdon BA84 MA88. **d** 85 **p** 86. C Leeds St Aid *Ripon* 85-89; Chapl St Jo Coll Cam 89-94; V Hoxton St Anne w St Columba *Lon* from 94. *St Anne's Vicarage, 37 Hemsworth Street, London N1 5LF* Tel 0171-729 1243

BUSH, Mrs Glenda. b 41. **d** 95 **p** 96. NSM Bolton St Phil *Man* from 95. *46 Mary Street West, Horwich, Bolton BL6 7JU* Tel (01204) 691539

BUSH, Roger Charles. b 56. K Coll Lon BA78 Leeds Univ BA85. Coll of Resurr Mirfield 83. **d** 86 **p** 87. C Newbold w Dunston *Derby* 86-90; TV Leic Resurr *Leic* 90-94; TR Redruth w Lanner and Treleigh *Truro* from 94; RD Carnmarth N from 96. *The Rectory, 53 Clinton Road, Redruth, Cornwall TR15 2LP* Tel (01209) 215258

BUSHAU, Reginald Francis. b 49. St Steph Ho Ox BA73. **d** 74 **p** 75. C Deptford St Paul *S'wark* 74-77; C Willesden St Andr *Lon* 77; C Gladstone Park St Fran 77-82; P-in-c Brondesbury St Anne w Kilburn H Trin 83-88; V Paddington St Mary Magd 88-97; AD Westmr Paddington 92-97; P-in-c S Kensington St Steph from 97. *9 Eldon Road, London W8 5PU* Tel 0171-937 5083

BUSHELL, Anthony Colin. b 59. Pemb Coll Ox MA82 Barrister 83. S'wark Ord Course 93. **d** 96. NSM Felsted *Chelmsf* 96; NSM Felsted and Lt Dunmow from 96. *Pump Hall, Middle Green, Wakes Colne, Colchester CO6 2BS* Tel (01787) 222487 Fax 222361

BUSHELL, Roy. b 32. NW Ord Course 75. **d** 79 **p** 80. NSM Croft w Southworth *Liv* 79-87; C Netherton 87-89; R Newton in Makerfield Em 89-97. *98 New Village, Ingleton, Carnforth, Lancs LA6 3DQ*

BUSHELL, Stephen Lionel. b 60. K Coll Lon BA84. Ripon Coll Cuddesdon 92. **d** 94 **p** 95. C Exhall *Cov* from 94. *222 Coventry Road, Exhall, Coventry CV7 9BH* Tel (01203) 313975

BUSK, David Westly. b 60. Magd Coll Cam BA. Cranmer Hall Dur. **d** 89 **p** 90. C Old Swinford Stourbridge *Worc* 89-93; USPG from 93. *8 Bedcote Place, Stourbridge, W Midlands DY8 1LD* Tel (01384) 390367

BUSK, Horace. b 34. Clifton Th Coll 56. **d** 60 **p** 61. C Burton All SS *Lich* 60-63; Paraguay 63-66; C Silverhill St Matt *Chich* 66-67; Lic to Offic *Sarum* 67-69; C W Kilburn St Luke w St Simon and St Jude *Lon* 69-74; TV Ashwellthorpe w Wreningham *Nor* 74-81; TV Wreningham 81; P-in-c Meysey Hampton w Marston Meysey and Castle Eaton *Glouc* 81-82; R from 82. *The Rectory, Church Street, Meysey Hampton, Cirencester, Glos GL7 5JX* Tel (01285) 851249

BUSS, Gerald Vere Austen. b 36. CCC Cam PhD87. St Steph Ho Ox 59. **d** 63 **p** 64. C Petersham *S'wark* 63-66; C Brompton H Trin *Lon* 66-69; Asst Chapl Hurstpierpoint Coll Hassocks 70-73; Chapl 74-90; Ho Master 90-94; History teacher 94-96; rtd 96. *Souches, The Street, Albourne, Hassocks, W Sussex BN6 9DJ* Tel (01273) 832465 Fax as telephone

BUSS, Philip Hodnett. b 37. Ch Coll Cam BA59 MA63. Tyndale Hall Bris 61. **d** 63 **p** 64. Tutor Lon Coll of Div 62-66; Chapl 66-69; Hon C Northwood Em *Lon* 63-70; V Handsworth Woodhouse *Sheff* 70-74; V Fulham Ch Ch *Lon* 74-82; V Woking St Pet *Guildf* 82-88; Hon C Ham St Rich *S'wark* from 94. *80 Woodville Road, Ham, Richmond, Surrey TW10 7QN* Tel 0181-940 3703

BUSSELL, Ronald William. b 34. CA Tr Coll 57 St Deiniol's Hawarden 81. **d** 83 **p** 84. C Claughton cum Grange *Ches* 83-85; P-in-c Preston St Oswald *Blackb* 85-87; V Fleetwood St Nic 87-93; Dioc Chapl MU 91-95; R Tarleton 93-95; rtd 95; Perm to Offic *Blackb* from 95. *4 Willoughby Avenue, Thornton-Cleveleys, Blackpool FY5 2BW*

BUSSEY, Norman. b 22. Clifton Th Coll 63. **d** 65 **p** 66. C Upton (Overchurch) *Ches* 65-69; V Bradley *Wakef* 69-88; rtd 88; Perm to Offic *Glouc* from 88. *43 Crispin Road, Winchcombe, Cheltenham, Glos GL54 5JX* Tel (01242) 602754

BUSTARD, Guy Nicholas. b 51. K Coll Lon BD77 AKC77. St Steph Ho Ox 77. **d** 78 **p** 79. C Hythe *Cant* 78-81; Chapl RN 81-85; V Haddenham *Ely* 85-89; V Wilburton 85-89; Chapl Qu Eliz Hosp Welwyn Garden City from 89. *The Chaplain's Office, Queen Elizabeth II Hospital, Welwyn Garden City, Herts AL7 4HQ* Tel (01707) 328111

BUSTIN, Canon Peter Ernest. b 32. Qu Coll Cam BA56 MA60. Tyndale Hall Bris 56. **d** 57 **p** 58. C Welling *Roch* 57-60; C Farnborough *Guildf* 60-62; V Hornsey Rise St Mary *Lon* 62-70; R Barnwell *Pet* 70-78; RD Oundle 76-84; P-in-c Luddington w Hemington and Thurning 77-78; R Barnwell w Thurning and Luddington 78-84; V Southwold *St E* 84-97; RD Halesworth 90-95; Hon Can St E Cathl 91-97; rtd 97. *55 College Street, Bury St Edmunds, Suffolk IP33 1NH* Tel (01284) 767708

BUSTIN, Peter Laurence. b 54. St Steph Ho Ox. **d** 83 **p** 84. C Northolt St Mary *Lon* 83-86; C Pimlico St Pet w Westmr Ch Ch 86-88; C Heston 88-91; P-in-c Twickenham All SS from 91. *All Saints' Vicarage, 18 Belmont Road, Twickenham TW2 2DA* Tel 0181-894 3580

BUTCHER, Andrew John. b 43. Trin Coll Cam BA66 MA69. Cuddesdon Coll 66. **d** 68 **p** 69. C Sheff St Mark Broomhall *Sheff* 68-70; P-in-c Louth H Trin *Linc* 70-72; Chapl RAF 72-87; Lic to Offic *Ox* 85-87; TR Cove St Jo *Guildf* 87-91; V Egham Hythe from 91. *St Paul's Vicarage, 214 Wendover Road, Staines, Middx TW18 3DF* Tel (01784) 453625

BUTCHER, Canon Douglas Claude. b 08. Ch Coll Cam BA29 MA44. Oak Hill Th Coll 50. **d** 51 **p** 52. Egypt 33-56 and 60-72; Prin English Miss Coll Cairo 46-56; Hon Can All SS Cathl Cairo from 55; Tunisia 57; P-in-c Hampstead St Jo *Lon* 57-60; CMJ 57-60; Chapl Alexandria St Mark and All SS 60-72; Acting Provost Cairo Cathl 67-72; C Swanage *Sarum* 72-78; rtd 78. *7 Brookside, Shreen Way, Gillingham, Dorset SP8 4HR* Tel (01747) 823865

BUTCHER, Edwin William (Eddie). b 39. Portsm Dioc Tr Course 91. **d** 92. NSM Ryde All SS *Portsm* from 92. *23 Quarry Road, Ryde, Isle of Wight PO33 2TX* Tel (01983) 616889

BUTCHER, Dr Hubert Maxwell. b 24. Ch Coll Cam BA48 MA53. Trin Coll Toronto BD68 San Francisco Th Sem DMin78 Wycliffe Hall Ox 49. **d** 51 **p** 52. C Tunbridge Wells St Jo *Roch* 51-53; India 54-58; P-in-c Bradf St Jo *Bradf* 58-62; Canada from 63; rtd 88. *Box 129, Sorrento, British Columbia, Canada, V0E 2W0* Tel Sorrento (604) 675 2783

BUTCHER, Ivan. b 50. Oak Hill Th Coll DipHE92. **d** 92 **p** 93. C Gtr Corsham *Bris* 92-96; V Overbury w Teddington, Alstone etc *Worc* from 96. *The Vicarage, Station Road, Beckford, Tewkesbury, Glos GL20 7AD* Tel (01386) 881380

BUTCHER, Philip Warren. b 46. Trin Coll Cam BA68 MA70. Cuddesdon Coll 68. **d** 70 **p** 71. C Bris St Mary Redcliffe w Temple etc *Bris* 70-73; Hon C W Wickham St Fran *Cant* 73-78; Chapl Abingdon Sch 78-85; Chapl K Edw VI Sch Nor from 85. *17 Welsford Road, Eaton Rise, Norwich NR4 6QA* Tel (01603) 664042

BUTCHER, Richard Peter. b 50. St Chad's Coll Dur BA71. Chich Th Coll 73. **d** 74 **p** 75. C Yeovil St Mich *B & W* 74-77; Chapl Wellingborough Sch 77-83; R Gt w Lt Billing *Pet* 83-88; Chapl Bp Stopford Sch Kettering 88-90; Perm to Offic *Pet* from 90. *55 Field Street, Kettering, Northants NN16 8EN*

BUTCHERS, Mark Andrew. b 59. Trin Coll Cam BA81 Southn Univ BTh87 K Coll Lon MTh90. Chich Th Coll 84. **d** 87 **p** 88. C Chelsea St Luke *Lon* 87; C Chelsea St Luke and Ch Ch 87-90; C Mitcham SS Pet and Paul *S'wark* 90-93; R N Tawton, Bondleigh, Sampford Courtenay etc *Ex* from 93. *The Rectory, Essington, North Tawton, Devon EX20 2EX* Tel (01837) 82645

BUTLAND, Cameron James. b 58. BA. Ripon Coll Cuddesdon 81. **d** 84 **p** 85. C Tettenhall Regis *Lich* 84-88; V Bodicote *Ox* 88-95; TR Witney from 95; RD Witney from 97. *The Rectory, 13 Station Lane, Witney, Oxon OX8 6BH* Tel (01993) 702517

BUTLAND, Godfrey John. b 51. Grey Coll Dur BA72. Wycliffe Hall Ox 73. **d** 75 **p** 76. C Much Woolton *Liv* 75-78; Bp's Dom Chapl 78-81; V Everton St Geo 81-94; AD Liv N from 89; V Allerton from 94. *Allerton Vicarage, Harthill Road, Liverpool L18 3HU* Tel 0151-724 1561

BUTLAND, William Edwin (Joe). b 09. St Andr Pampisford 48 Lon Coll of Div 49. **d** 51 **p** 52. C Kentish Town *Lon* 51-54; C Chorleywood Ch Ch *St Alb* 54-58; P-in-c Colney Heath St Mark 58-59; V 59-80; rtd 80; Perm to Offic *St Alb* from 80. *9 Studley Road, Wootton, Bedford MK43 9DL* Tel (01234) 767620

BUTLER, Alan. b 53. Carl Dioc Tr Inst 89. **d** 89 **p** 90. NSM Flookburgh *Carl* 89-93; C Maryport 93-96; C Flimby 93-96; P-in-c from 96. *The Vicarage, Church Road, Flimby, Maryport, Cumbria CA15 8TJ* Tel (01900) 812386 Fax as telephone

BUTLER, Alan. b 57. Leic Univ BA78. Coll of Resurr Mirfield 80. **d** 83 **p** 84. C Skerton St Luke *Blackb* 83-87; C Birch w Fallowfield *Man* 87-90; V Claremont H Angels 90-95; Chapl Pendleton Coll from 95; TV Pendleton *Man* from 95. *The Vicarage, Moorfield Road, Salford M6 7EY* Tel 0161-736 3064

BUTLER, Canon Alan John. b 30. Kelham Th Coll 51. **d** 56 **p** 57. S Africa 56-65 and 79-95; Bechuanaland 65-66; Botswana 66-70; V Fletchamstead *Cov* 71-79; Adn Griqualand W 79-85; Adn Kuruman 79-85; Dir Moffat Miss, Kuruman 81-95; TV Hanley H Ev *Lich* 95; rtd 95. *4 Osborne Road, Wimborne, Dorset BH21 1BL* Tel (01202) 848859

BUTLER, Ms Angela Elizabeth. b 31. Studley Coll DipHort53. Gilmore Ho 60 DipTh64 Lambeth STh64. **dss** 81 **d** 87 **p** 94. Cookham *Ox* 81-86; Wheatley w Forest Hill and Stanton St John 86-87; Hon Par Dn 87-89; NSM 93-97; NSM Wheatley from 97; rtd 91. *10 River Gardens, Purley-on-Thames, Reading RG8 8BX* Tel 0118-942 2055

BUTLER, Angela Madeline. b 47. Oak Hill NSM Course 87. **d** 90 **p** 94. Hon Par Dn Chipperfield St Paul *St Alb* 90-93; D-in-c 93-94; P-in-c from 94; Staff Oak Hill Th Coll from 93. *The Vicarage, Chipperfield, Kings Langley, Herts WD4 9BJ* Tel (01923) 263054 Fax 0181-441 5996

BUTLER, Betty. b 47. **d** 96. NSM Sully *Llan* from 96. *10 Nurston Close, Rhoose, Barry CF62 3EF*

BUTLER, Christopher John. b 25. Leeds Univ BA50. Chich Th Coll 50. **d** 52 **p** 53. C Kensington St Mary Abbots w St Geo *Lon* 52-57; Australia 57-59; V Blackmoor *Portsm* 60-70; V Wellingborough St Andr *Pet* 70-79; P-in-c Garsington *Ox* 79-83; R Garsington and Horspath 83-95; rtd 95; Perm to Offic *Portsm* from 95; Perm to Offic *Chich* from 95; Perm to Offic *Guildf* from 95. *33 Oak Tree Road, Whitehill, Bordon, Hants GU35 9DF* Tel (01420) 475311

BUTLER, Colin Sydney. b 59. Bradf Univ BSc81. Wycliffe Hall Ox 81. **d** 84 **p** 85. C Farsley *Bradf* 84-87; C Bradf St Aug Undercliffe 87-89; P-in-c Darlaston All SS *Lich* 89-95; Ind Missr 89-95; TR Chell from 95. *The Rectory, 203 St Michael's Road, Stoke-on-Trent ST6 6JT* Tel (01782) 838708

BUTLER, The Ven Cuthbert Hilary. b 13. St Jo Coll Cam BA35 MA39. Westcott Ho Cam. **d** 40 **p** 41. C Preston *Chich* 40-42; Chapl RNVR 42-46; P-in-c Brighton St Matthias *Chich* 46-47; V 47-51; R Crawley 51-58; Canada 58-84; Adn Colombia 77-78; rtd 78; Perm to Offic *Ex* from 85. *Four Chimneys, Bratton Clovelly, Okehampton, Devon EX20 4JS* Tel (01837) 87409

BUTLER, David Edwin. b 56. ACA83 Jes Coll Ox BA79 BA86. St Steph Ho Ox MA87. **d** 87 **p** 88. C Hulme Ascension *Man* 87-90; V Patricroft 90-94. *77A Mountside Crescent, Prestwich, Manchester M25 3JH*

BUTLER, Derek John. b 53. Aston Univ BSc74 St Jo Coll York PGCE75. St Jo Coll Dur 79. **d** 82 **p** 83. C Bramcote *S'well* 82-86; Perm to Offic *Roch* 86-88; Perm to Offic *Portsm* 86-92; Lon and SE Co-ord CPAS 86-88; NSM Bromley Ch Ch *Roch* 88-91; NSM Chesham Bois *Ox* from 92. *121 Woodside Road, Amersham, Bucks HP6 6AL* Tel (01494) 724577

BUTLER, Donald Arthur. b 31. **d** 79 **p** 80. Hon C Apsley End *St Alb* 79-80; Hon C Chambersbury (Hemel Hempstead) from 80. *143 Belswains Lane, Hemel Hempstead, Herts HP3 9UZ*

BUTLER, Edward Daniel. b 42. Rhodes Univ BA65 MA70. Qu Coll Birm. **d** 68 **p** 69. C Edgbaston St Bart *Birm* 68-72; Perm to Offic 72-73; Perm to Offic *Chich* from 74. *43 Princes Terrace, Brighton BN2 5JS*

BUTLER, Frederick Walter (Fred). b 28. Chich Th Coll 67. **d** 69 **p** 70. C Seaford w Sutton *Chich* 69-73; V Peacehaven 73-75; P-in-c Copthorne 75-81; V 81-83; TR Moulsecoomb 83-86; R Etchingham 86-94; V Hurst Green 86-94; rtd 94; Perm to Offic *Chich* from 94. *5 Robin Close, Eastbourne, E Sussex BN23 7RJ* Tel (01323) 765717

BUTLER, George James. b 53. AKC74 Kent Univ MA95. St Aug Coll Cant 75. **d** 76 **p** 77. C Ellesmere Port *Ches* 76-79; C Eastham 79-81; Chapl RAF 81-83; C W Kirby St Bridget *Ches* 83-84; V Newton 84-86; CF 86-91; V Folkestone St Sav *Cant* from 91. *St Saviour's Vicarage, 134 Canterbury Road, Folkestone, Kent CT19 5PH* Tel (01303) 254686

BUTLER, George William. DipTh. **d** 90 **p** 91. C Drung w Castleterra, Larah and Lavey etc *K, E & A* 90-93; I 93-95; I Castlemacadam w Ballinaclash, Aughrim etc *D & G* from 95. *The Vicarage, Castlemacadam, Avoca, Co Wicklow, Irish Republic* Tel Avoca (402) 35127

BUTLER, Henry. b 25. Ridley Hall Cam 73. **d** 75 **p** 76. C Cambridge St Paul *Ely* 75-77; P-in-c Stilton w Denton and Caldecote 77-83; P-in-c Folksworth w Morborne 77-83; V Histon 83-90; P-in-c Impington 84-90; rtd 90; Perm to Offic *Ely* from 90. *85 High Street, Cherry Hinton, Cambridge CB1 4LU*

BUTLER, Huw. b 63. Univ of Wales (Ban) BSc84. St Mich Coll Llan DipTh94 BTh95. **d** 95 **p** 96. C Llantwit Fadre *Llan* from 95. *63 St Anne's Drive, Llantwit Fardre, Pontypridd CF38 2PB* Tel (01443) 206857

BUTLER, Ian Malcolm. b 39. Bris Univ BA67 BA69. Clifton Th Coll 67. **d** 69 **p** 70. C Clapham Common St Barn *S'wark* 69-73; C Reigate St Mary 73-78; V Sissinghurst w Frittenden *Cant* 78-91; rtd 92; Perm to Offic *Cant* from 91. *High Cedars, Theobalds, Hawkhurst, Cranbrook, Kent TN18 4AJ* Tel (01580) 752366

BUTLER, Ivor John. b 36. Dur Univ BA58. Ely Th Coll 58. **d** 60 **p** 60. C W Bromwich All SS *Lich* 60-64; V Upper Gornal 64-72; V Tividale 72-79; Hon Chapl RN from 79; V Dartmouth *Ex* 79-95; RD Totnes 90-95; P-in-c Mullion *Truro* from 95. *The Vicarage, Nansmellyon Road, Mullion, Helston, Cornwall TR12 7DH* Tel (01326) 240325

BUTLER, John. b 38. Univ of Wales DipTh67 DPS68 Gwent Coll Newport CertEd77. St Mich Coll Llan. **d** 68 **p** 69. C Ebbw Vale *Mon* 68-70; TV 70-75; Perm to Offic 76-77 and 79-88; P-in-c Crumlin 77-78; R Gt and Lt Casterton w Pickworth and Tickencote *Pet* 88-91; R Woolstone w Gotherington and Oxenton etc *Glouc* from 91. *The Rectory, Malleson Road, Woolstone, Cheltenham, Glos GL52 4EX* Tel (01242) 672921

BUTLER, John Philip. b 47. Leeds Univ BA70. Coll of Resurr Mirfield 70. **d** 72 **p** 73. C Elton All SS *Man* 72-75; C Bolton St Pet 75-78; Chapl Bolton Colls of FE 75-78; Hon C Clifton St Paul *Bris* 78-81; Asst Chapl Bris Univ 78-81; V Llansawel w Briton Ferry *Llan* 81-84; Warden Bp Mascall Cen *Heref* 84-88; Vice-Prin Glouc Sch for Min 85-88; Chapl Univ of Wales (Ban) *Ban* from 88. *Anglican Chaplaincy Centre, Prince's Road, Bangor LL57 2BD* Tel (01248) 370566 Fax 354472

BUTLER, Linda Jane. b 56. SRN77. St Jo Coll Nottm 85. **d** 88 **p** 94. Par Dn Burbage w Aston Flamville *Leic* 88-90; Chapl Asst Leic R Infirmary 91-93; Chapl Asst Leics Mental Health Service Unit 92-97; Chapl from 97; Chapl Asst Towers Hosp Humberstone from 93. *Mental Health Services Unit, Towers Hospital, Gypsy Lane, Leicester LE5 0TD* Tel 0116-246 0460

BUTLER, Malcolm. b 40. Linc Th Coll 76. **d** 78 **p** 79. C Whickham *Dur* 78-82; V Leam Lane 82-87; R Penshaw 87-90; rtd 90. *2 Lapwing Court, Barcus Close Lane, Burnopfield, Newcastle upon Tyne NE16 4DZ* Tel (01207) 71559

BUTLER, Michael. b 41. Univ of Wales (Ban) DipTh62. St Mich Coll Llan 62 St Deiniol's Hawarden 63. **d** 64 **p** 65. C Welshpool *St As* 64; C Welshpool w Castle Caereinion 65-73; TV Aberystwyth *St D* 73-80; Chapl Univ of Wales (Abth) 73-80; V St Issell's and Amroth from 80; RD Narberth from 94. *St Issell's Vicarage, Saundersfoot SA69 9BD* Tel (01834) 812375

BUTLER, Canon Michael John. b 32. Keble Coll Ox BA58 MSW. Coll of Resurr Mirfield. **d** 59 **p** 60. C Poplar All SS w St Frideswide *Lon* 59-68; Hon C St Steph Walbrook and St Swithun etc 68-73; C Godalming *Guildf* 73-76; P-in-c Brighton St Anne *Chich* 77-79; Dioc Communications Officer and Dir Soc Resp 77-83; Dir Dioc Bd of Soc Resp 83-94; Soc

Resp Adv from 94; Can and Preb Chich Cathl from 85. *30 Bigwood Avenue, Hove, E Sussex BN3 6FD* Tel (01273) 725811

BUTLER, Canon Michael Weeden. b 38. Clare Coll Cam BA60 MA65. Westcott Ho Cam 63. **d** 65 **p** 66. C Bermondsey St Mary w St Olave, St Jo etc *S'wark* 65-68; Ind Chapl 68-72; Sierra Leone 73-77; Ind Chapl *Cant* 77-86; R Gt Chart 77-86; RD E Charing 81-86; V Glouc St Jas and All SS *Glouc* from 86; RD Glouc City from 94; Hon Can Glouc Cathl from 96. *The Vicarage, 1 The Conifers, Upton Street, Gloucester GL1 4LP* Tel (01452) 422349 E-mail 101542.607@compuserve.com

BUTLER, Ms Pamela. b 53. Nottm Univ BTh86. Linc Th Coll 83. **dss** 86 **d** 87 **p** 94. Rotherhithe H Trin *S'wark* 86-87; Par Dn 87-88; Par Dn Old Trafford St Jo *Man* 88-89; Par Dn Claremont H Angels 90-94; C 94-95; C Pendleton from 95; Perm to Offic from 95; Chapl Asst S Man Univ Hosps NHS Trust from 96. *The Vicarage, Moorfield Road, Salford M6 7EY* Tel 0161-736 3064

BUTLER, Paul David. b 67. Sheff Univ BA88. Linc Th Coll CMM92. **d** 92 **p** 93. C Handsworth Woodhouse *Sheff* 92-96; V Bellingham St Dunstan *S'wark* from 96. *St Dunstan's Vicarage, 32 Bellingham Green, London SE6 3JB* Tel 0181-698 3291

BUTLER, Paul Roger. b 55. Nottm Univ BA77 St Mary's Coll Dur BD91. Wycliffe Hall Ox BA82. **d** 83 **p** 84. C Wandsworth All SS *S'wark* 83-87; Inner Lon Ev Scripture Union 87-92; Dep Hd of Miss 92-94; NSM E Ham St Paul *Chelmsf* 87-94; P-in-c Walthamstow St Mary w St Steph 94-97; P-in-c Walthamstow St Luke 94-97; P-in-c Walthamstow St Gabr 97; TR Walthamstow from 97. *St Mary's Rectory, 117 Church Hill, London E17 3BD* Tel 0181-520 4281 Fax as telephone

BUTLER, Dr Perry Andrew. b 49. FRHistS York Univ BA70 Jes Coll Ox DPhil78 Nottm Univ DipTh79. Linc Th Coll 78. **d** 80 **p** 81. C Chiswick St Nic w St Mary *Lon* 80-83; C S Kensington St Steph 83-87; V Bedford Park 87-95; Angl Adv Lon Weekend TV from 87; P-in-c Bloomsbury St Geo w Woburn Square Ch Ch *Lon* from 95. *6 Gower Street, London WC1E 6DP* Tel 0171-584 4010

BUTLER, Richard Charles Burr. b 34. St Pet Hall Ox BA59 MA62. Linc Th Coll 58. **d** 60 **p** 61. C St Jo Wood *Lon* 60-63; V Kingstanding St Luke *Birm* 63-75; R Lee St Marg *S'wark* from 75. *St Margaret's Rectory, Brandram Road, London SE13 5EA* Tel 0181-852 0633

BUTLER, Robert Clifford. b 25. AKC54. **d** 55 **p** 56. C Gt Berkhamsted *St Alb* 55-59; C Dunstable 59-63; V Stanbridge w Tilsworth 63-73; R Maulden 73-80; R Oldbury *Sarum* 80-93; rtd 93. *3 Mithras Close, Dorchester, Dorset DT1 2RF* Tel (01305) 264817

BUTLER, Canon Robert Edwin (Bob). b 37. Ely Th Coll 60. **d** 62 **p** 63. C Lewisham St Jo Southend *S'wark* 62-65; C Eastbourne St Elisabeth *Chich* 65-69; V Langney 69-96; Can and Preb Chich Cathl from 94; rtd 96; Perm to Offic *Chich* from 97. *10 Langdale Close, Langney, Eastbourne, E Sussex BN23 8HS* Tel (01323) 461135

BUTLER (née McVEIGH), Mrs Sandra (Sandie). b 58. Reading Univ BA80. Cranmer Hall Dur CTMin95. **d** 95 **p** 96. C Stranton *Dur* from 95. *41 Arncliffe Gardens, Hartlepool, Cleveland TS26 9JG* Tel (01429) 277591

BUTLER, Simon. b 64. UEA BSc86 RN Coll Greenwich. St Jo Coll Nottm DTS91 MA92. **d** 92 **p** 93. C Chandler's Ford *Win* 92-94; C Northolt W End St Jos *Lon* 94-97; V Streatham Immanuel and St Andr *S'wark* from 97. *Immanuel Vicarage, 19 Streatham Common South, London SW16 3BU* Tel 0181-764 5103

✠**BUTLER, The Rt Revd Thomas Frederick.** b 40. Leeds Univ BSc61 MSc62 PhD72. Coll of Resurr Mirfield 62. **d** 64 **p** 65 **c** 85. C Wisbech St Aug *Ely* 64-66; C Folkestone St Sav *Cant* 66-67; Zambia 68-73; Chapl Kent Univ *Cant* 73-80; Six Preacher Cant Cathl 79-84; Adn Northolt *Lon* 80-85; Area Bp Willesden 85-91; Bp Leic from 91. *Bishop's Lodge, 10 Springfield Road, Leicester LE2 3BD* Tel 0116-270 8985 Fax 270 3288

BUTLER-SMITH, Basil George (Bob). b 30. Bps' Coll Cheshunt 66. **d** 67 **p** 68. C Bray and Braywood *Ox* 67-71; R Norton *St E* 71-74; P-in-c Tostock 71-74; R Rotherfield Peppard *Ox* from 76; P-in-c Rotherfield Greys 79-80; R from 80. *The Rectory, Rotherfield Peppard, Henley-on-Thames, Oxon RG9 5JN* Tel (01491) 628603

BUTLIN, David Francis Grenville. b 55. Bris Univ BA77 Ox Univ CertEd78. Sarum & Wells Th Coll 85. **d** 87 **p** 88. C Bedford St Andr *St Alb* 87-90; C Milton *Portsm* 90-92; V Hurst Green *S'wark* from 92. *The Vicarage, 14 Oast Road, Oxted, Surrey RH8 9DU* Tel (01883) 712674

BUTLIN, Timothy Greer. b 53. St Jo Coll Dur BA75 Ox Univ CertEd76. Wycliffe Hall Ox 85. **d** 87 **p** 88. C Eynsham and Cassington *Ox* 87-91; V Loudwater from 91. *The Vicarage, Loudwater, High Wycombe, Bucks HP10 9QL* Tel (01628) 526087

BUTT, Adrian. b 37. **d** 71 **p** 72. S Africa 71-76; C Ilkeston St Mary *Derby* 76-79; P-in-c Sturton w Littleborough *S'well* 79-84; P-in-c Bole w Saundby 79-84; R N and S Wheatley w W Burton 79-84; R N Wheatley, W Burton, Bole, Saundby, Sturton etc 84-85; R Kirkby in Ashfield from 85. *The Rectory, 12 Church Street, Kirkby-in-Ashfield, Nottingham NG17 8LE* Tel (01623) 753790

BUTT, Christopher Martin. b 52. St Pet Coll Ox BA74 Fitzw Coll Cam BA77. Ridley Hall Cam 75. **d** 79 **p** 80. C Cambridge St Barn *Ely* 79-82; Hong Kong 82-89; P-in-c Windermere *Carl* from 89. *The Rectory, Longlands, Windermere, Cumbria LA23 3AS* Tel (015394) 43063

BUTT, Edward. b 46. Huddersfield Poly DipSocWork80 CQSW80. Trin Coll Bris DipHE88. **d** 88 **p** 89. C Erith St Paul *Roch* 88-92; C Shirley *Win* from 92. *16 Radway Road, Southampton SO15 7PW* Tel (01703) 779605

BUTT, Martin James. b 52. Sheff Univ LLB75. Trin Coll Bris 75. **d** 78 **p** 79. C Aldridge *Lich* 78-84; C Walsall 84-87; TV 87-94; P-in-c Farewell from 94; P-in-c Gentleshaw from 94; C Hammerwich from 96. *The Vicarage, Budds Road, Rugeley, Staffs WS15 4NB* Tel (01543) 684329

BUTT, William Arthur. b 44. Kelham Th Coll 70 Linc Th Coll 71. **d** 71 **p** 72. C Mackworth St Fran *Derby* 71-75; C Aston cum Aughton *Sheff* 76-79; V Dalton 79-88; TR Staveley and Barrow Hill *Derby* from 88. *The Rectory, Staveley, Chesterfield, Derbyshire S43 3XZ* Tel (01246) 472270

BUTTANSHAW, Graham Charles. b 59. TCD BA(Econ)80 BA85. St Jo Coll Nottm 88. **d** 91 **p** 92. C Toxteth St Cypr w Ch Ch *Liv* 91-94; CMS from 94; Uganda from 95. *c/o The Rt Rev Seme Solomona, Diocese of Yei, PO Box 370, Arua, Uganda*

BUTTERFIELD, David John. b 52. Lon Univ BMus73. St Jo Coll Nottm DipTh75. **d** 77 **p** 78. C Southport Ch Ch *Liv* 77-81; Min Aldridge St Thos CD *Lich* 81-91; V Lilleshall and Sheriffhales from 91; RD Edgmond from 97. *The Vicarage, 25 Church Road, Lilleshall, Newport, Shropshire TF10 9HE* Tel (01952) 604281 Fax as telephone

BUTTERFIELD, John Kenneth. b 52. Nottm Univ BCombStuds. Linc Th Coll 79. **d** 82 **p** 83. C Cantley *Sheff* 82-84; C Doncaster St Leon and St Jude 84-86; TV Ilfracombe, Lee, Woolacombe, Bittadon etc *Ex* 86-88; V Thurcroft *Sheff* 88-96; Chapl Chesterfield and N Derbyshire NHS Trust from 96. *Chesterfield and North Derbyshire Royal Hospital, Chesterfield, Derbyshire S44 5BL* Tel (01246) 277271

BUTTERWORTH, Antony James. b 51. Hull Univ BSc73 Bris Univ DipTh76. Trin Coll Bris 73. **d** 76 **p** 77. C Halliwell St Pet *Man* 76-81; V Werneth 81-90; V Tonge Fold from 90. *St Chad's Vicarage, 9 Tonge Fold Road, Bolton BL2 6AW* Tel (01204) 525809

BUTTERWORTH, Derek. b 27. Wells Th Coll 63. **d** 65 **p** 65. C Bottesford *Linc* 65-73; TV Bottesford w Ashby 73-83; Chapl St Hilda's Sch Whitby 83-85; V Derringham Bank *York* 85-90; rtd 90. *26 St Mary's Gate, Ripon, N Yorkshire HG4 1LX*

BUTTERWORTH, Elsie. b 27. Linc Th Coll 81. **dss** 83 **d** 87 **p** 94. OHP 83-85; Derringham Bank *York* 85-87; Par Dn 87-88; Par Dn Filey 88-94; C 94-97; rtd 93. *3 Brooklands Close, Filey, N Yorkshire YO14 9BJ* Tel (01723) 515781

BUTTERWORTH, George John. b 58. Liv Univ BA85. Chich Th Coll CMT92. **d** 92 **p** 93. C Mayfield *Chich* 92-93; C Hastings St Clem and All SS 93-96; TV Brighton Resurr from 96. *St Alban's Vicarage, 10 Natal Road, Brighton BN2 4BN* Tel (01273) 602357

BUTTERWORTH, Dr George Michael. b 41. Man Univ BSc63 Lon Univ BD67 PhD89 Nottm Univ MPhil71. Tyndale Hall Bris. **d** 67 **p** 68. C S Normanton *Derby* 67-71; India 72-79; Lect Oak Hill Th Coll 80-96; Perm to Offic *St Alb* from 80; Prin St Alb and Ox Min Course *Ox* from 97. *9 Fulmar Court, Bicester, Oxon OX6 7FG* Tel (01869) 240932 or 790084 Mobile 0976-910161

BUTTERWORTH, Ian Eric. b 44. Aber Univ MA67 MTh79. Edin Th Coll 67. **d** 69 **p** 70. C Langley All SS and Martyrs *Man* 69-71; Prec St Andr Cathl *Ab* 71-75; V Bolton St Matt w St Barn *Man* 75-85; C-in-c Lostock CD 85-92; Perm to Offic from 92. *21 Polperro Close, Heyside, Royton, Oldham OL2 6LA*

BUTTERWORTH, Canon James Frederick. b 49. St Chad's Coll Dur BA70. Cuddesdon Coll 70. **d** 72 **p** 73. C Kidderminster St Mary *Worc* 72-76; P-in-c Dudley St Barn 76-79; V 79-82; Prec and Min Can Worc Cathl 82-88; TR Bridgnorth, Tasley, Astley Abbotts, Oldbury etc *Heref* 88-94; Can Res and Treas Heref Cathl from 94. *7 College Cloisters, Cathedral Close, Hereford HR1 2NG* Tel (01432) 341432

BUTTERWORTH, James Kent. b 49. Southn Univ BTh79. Chich Th Coll 75. **d** 79 **p** 80. C Heckmondwike *Wakef* 79-83; V Wrenthorpe 83-95; V Staincross from 95. *St John's Vicarage, 48 Greenside, Mapplewell, Barnsley, S Yorkshire S75 6AY* Tel (01226) 382261

BUTTERWORTH, John Walton. b 49. St Jo Coll Dur BSc70 DipTh73. **d** 74 **p** 75. C Todmorden *Wakef* 74-77; Chapl Wakef Cathl 77-78; C Wakef Cathl 77-78; V Outwood from 78. *Outwood Vicarage, 424 Leeds Road, Wakefield, W Yorkshire WF1 2JB* Tel (01924) 823150

BUTTERWORTH, Canon Julia Kay. b 42. Edin Univ MA64 Bris Univ CertEd66 Nottm Univ DipTh75. Linc Th Coll 73. **dss** 77 **d** 87 **p** 94. Cov E *Cov* 77-79; Cant Cathl *Cant* 79-84; Dioc Adv in Women's Min from 82; Faversham 84-87; Par Dn 87-92; TD Whitstable 92-94; TV 94-97; Hon Can Cant Cathl from 96; P-in-c Tenterden St Mich from 97. *The Vicarage, Ashford Road, St Michaels, Tenterden, Kent TN30 6PY* Tel (01580) 764670

BUTTERWORTH, Roy. b 31. Selw Coll Cam BA55 MA59. Wells Th Coll 55. **d** 57 **p** 58. C Bathwick w Woolley *B & W* 57-61; Prec

St Paul's Cathl Dundee *Bre* 61-63; V Dearnley *Man* 63-81; V Tyldesley w Shakerley 81-83; V Healey 83-94; rtd 94. *102 Greenbank Road, Rochdale, Lancs OL12 0EN* Tel (01706) 350808

BUTTERY, Graeme. b 62. York Univ BA84. St Steph Ho Ox 85. **d** 88 **p** 89. C Peterlee *Dur* 88-91; C Sunderland 91-92; TV 92-94; V Horsley Hill S Shields from 94. *St Lawrence House, 84 Centenary Avenue, South Shields, Tyne & Wear NE34 6SF* Tel 0191-456 1747

BUTTIMORE, Canon John Charles. b 27. St Mich Coll Llan 55. **d** 57 **p** 58. C Treherbert w Tynewydd and Ynsfeio *Llan* 57-60; C Aberdare St Fagan 60-64; V Williamstown 64-71; Chapl Ely Hosp Cardiff from 71; V Caerau w Ely *Llan* from 71; RD Cardiff 83-89; Can Llan Cathl from 87. *The Vicarage, Cowbridge Road West, Cardiff CF5 5BQ* Tel (01222) 563254

BUTTLE, Leslie Albert. b 32. Open Univ BA89. Edin Th Coll 61. **d** 64 **p** 65. C Sowerby Bridge w Norland *Wakef* 64-66; C Plymstock *Ex* 66-69; C Ilfracombe H Trin 69-71; V Woolfardisworthy and Buck Mills 71-76; C Sticklepath 76-77; Asst Chapl HM Pris Leeds 77-80; Lic to Offic *Ripon* 77-80; Chapl HM Youth Cust Cen Hindley 80-84; Perm to Offic *Ex* 86-93; Hon C Braunton from 93; rtd 97. *Church House, Saunton, Braunton, Devon EX33 1LG* Tel (01271) 817022

BUTTLE, Leslie Ronald Frank. b 07. Lon Univ BA28. **d** 34 **p** 35. C Wanstead St Mary *Chelmsf* 34-36; Asst Master R Wanstead Sch 31-36; Asst Chapl 34-36; Chapl K Coll Otahuhu 36-38; R Water Stratford *Ox* 38-39; Asst Chapl Felsted Sch Essex 40; Chapl RNVR 41-47; R Goldhanger w Lt Totham *Chelmsf* 47-50; R Purleigh 50-55; V Gt w Lt Packington *Cov* 55-58; V Maxstoke *Birm* 55-58; R Fordham *Chelmsf* 58-63; V Hatfield Broad Oak 63-66; V Bush End 63-66; R Lowick w Sudborough and Slipton *Pet* 67-73; rtd 73; Perm to Offic *Truro* from 73. *5 Castle Street, Launceston, Cornwall PL15 8BA* Tel (01566) 772052

BUTTON, David Frederick. b 27. St Chad's Coll Dur BA53 DipTh54. **d** 54 **p** 55. C Jarrow Docks *Dur* 54-58; C Seacroft *Ripon* 58-60; V Holland Fen *Linc* 60-64; V Surfleet 64-71; R Belton SS Pet and Paul 71-78; V Barkston w Syston 72-78; V Honington 73-78; R Gunhouse w Burringham 78-82; P-in-c Gt w Lt Hockham w Wretham w Illington *Nor* 82-84; P-in-c Shropham w Larling and Snetterton 82-84; V Hockham w Shropham Gp of Par 84-91; rtd 91; Perm to Offic *Nor* 91-96. *6 Vallibus Close, Oulton, Lowestoft, Suffolk NR32 3DS* Tel (01502) 585670

BUXTON, Canon Derek Major. b 31. Lon Univ BD63. Ripon Hall Ox 58. **d** 60 **p** 61. C Leic St Nic *Leic* 60-64; Chapl Leic Univ 60-64; Chapl Leic Coll of Art and Tech 61-65; Min Can Leic Cathl 64-69; Prec 67; R Ibstock 69-76; R Ibstock w Heather 76-87; Chapl ATC from 78; OCF and Cen and E Regional Chapl from 87; RD Akeley S *Leic* 84-87; P-in-c Woodhouse Eaves 87-91; V Woodhouse and Woodhouse Eaves from 91; Chapl Roecliffe Manor Cheshire Home from 87; Chapl Coun OStJ from 87; Hon Can Leic Cathl *Leic* from 88. *The Vicarage, 32 Church Hill, Woodhouse Eaves, Loughborough, Leics LE12 8RI* Tel (01509) 890226

BUXTON, Canon Digby Hugh. b 16. Trin Coll Cam BA38 MA41. Wycliffe Hall Ox 39. **d** 41 **p** 42. C Stoke next Guildf St Jo *Guildf* 41-43; C Bethnal Green St Jas Less *Lon* 43-46; C Queensbury All SS 46-50; Canada 50-77; Can Quebec 76-77; C Gt Burstead *Chelmsf* 77-78; C Sandhurst *Ox* 78-81; rtd 81; Hon C Barkway, Reed and Buckland w Barley *St Alb* 81-87. *Rosemary Holt, Edward Road, St Cross, Winchester, Hants SO23 9RB* Tel (01962) 860877

BUXTON, Edmund Francis. b 42. Trin Coll Cam BA65 MA68 DPS74. Linc Th Coll 65. **d** 67 **p** 68. C Wanstead St Mary *Chelmsf* 67-70; C Cambridge Gt St Mary w St Mich *Ely* 70-73; C Barking St Marg w St Patr *Chelmsf* 74-75; India 75-79; Chapl Bath Univ *B & W* 79-89; TR Willenhall H Trin *Lich* 89-96; Manager Univ Hosp Birm NHS Trust from 96. *The Chaplaincy Office, Queen Elizabeth Hospital, Edgbaston, Birmingham B15 2TH* Tel 0121-472 1311 or 459 9527

BUXTON, Preb Edmund Digby. b 08. Trin Coll Cam BA29 MA33. Ridley Hall Cam 29. **d** 33 **p** 34. C St Helens St Helen *Liv* 33-37; C E Twickenham St Steph *Lon* 37-39; V Peckham St Mary *S'wark* 39-44; V Wembley St Jo *Lon* 44-54; V Milborne Port w Goathill *B & W* 54-74; RD Merston 57-68; Preb Wells Cathl 64-74; rtd 74; Perm to Offic *Win* 74-75 and 78-95; Tristan da Cunha 75-78. *10 Pound Hill, Alresford, Hants SO24 9BW* Tel (01962) 732353

BUXTON, Edward Brian. b 41. AKC65 BEd79. **d** 66 **p** 67. C Laindon w Basildon *Chelmsf* 66-73; P-in-c Grays All SS 73-76; Perm to Offic 76-85. *Address temp unknown*

BUXTON, Graham. b 45. BA MSc. St Jo Coll Nottm 83. **d** 83 **p** 84. C Ealing Dean St Jo *Lon* 83-84; C W Ealing St Jo w St Jas 84-86; C S Harrow St Paul 86-89; P-in-c 89-91; Australia from 91. *5 Heron Place, Flagstaff Hill, S Australia 5159* Tel Adelaide (8) 370 6038

BUXTON, James Andrew Denis. b 64. Newc Univ BA86. Westcott Ho Cam 96. **d** 97. C Portsea St Mary *Portsm* from 97. *1 Glebe Flats, Nutfield Place, Portsmouth PO1 4JF* Tel (01705) 830154

BUXTON, Dr Richard Fowler. b 40. Lon Univ BSc62 Linacre Coll Ox BA67 MA71 Ex Univ PhD73. St Steph Ho Ox 65. **d** 68 **p** 69. C Whitley Ch Ch *Ox* 68-70; C Pinhoe *Ex* 70-71; Asst Chapl Ex Univ 71-73; Tutor Sarum & Wells Th Coll 73-77; Vice-Prin 77; Perm to Offic *Ches* from 77; Lect Liturgy Man Univ 80-94; Perm to Offic *Man* 81-94; Subwarden St Deiniol's Lib Hawarden 94-97; Lic to Offic *St As* 94-97; Perm to Offic *Ban* from 96; Perm to Offic *St As* from 97. *Golygfa'r Orsaf, 6 Rhesdai Garth, Porthmadog LL49 9BE* Tel (01766) 514782

BUXTON, Trevor George. b 57. Ex Univ BEd78. Chich Th Coll 81. **d** 83 **p** 84. C Hove All SS *Chich* 83-87; C Burgess Hill St Jo 87-91; V Brighton St Aug and St Sav from 91. *St Augustine's House, 24 Stanford Avenue, Brighton BN1 6EA* Tel (01273) 561755 Mobile 0585-942901 Fax (01273) 562094

BUXTON, William Arnold Greaves (Paddy). b 33. FBIM78 FInstD78 FInstM79. Sarum & Wells Th Coll 80. **d** 82 **p** 83. C Durrington *Chich* 82-85; R Kingston Buci 85-89; TR Rye 89-94; rtd 94; Perm to Offic *Cant* from 95; Perm to Offic *Chich* from 95. *The Old House, 45 The Mint, Rye, E Sussex TN31 7EN* Tel (01797) 223191

BYE, Dennis Robert. b 20. **d** 86 **p** 87. NSM Bishop's Cleeve *Glouc* 86-90; rtd 90; Perm to Offic *Glouc* from 90. *Cotswold, 26 Priory Lane, Bishops Cleeve, Cheltenham, Glos GL52 4JL* Tel (01242) 673587

BYE, Peter John. b 39. Lon Univ BD65. Clifton Th Coll 62. **d** 67 **p** 68. C Hyson Green *S'well* 67-70; C Dur St Nic *Dur* 70-73; V Lowestoft Ch Ch *Nor* 73-80; V Carl St Jo *Carl* from 80; Chapl Carl Gen Hosp from 80. *St John's Vicarage, London Road, Carlisle CA1 2QQ* Tel (01228) 21601 or 595792

BYERS, Canon Christopher Martin. b 33. Jes Coll Ox BA59 MA62. Wycliffe Hall Ox 59. **d** 60 **p** 61. C Bermondsey St Mary w St Olave, St Jo etc *S'wark* 60-66; R Mottingham St Andr 66-86; TR Thamesmead from 86; Hon Can S'wark Cathl from 96. *Thamesmead Rectory, 22 Manor Close, London SE28 8EY* Tel 0181-311 7278 or 310 6814

BYFORD, Canon David Charles. b 30. Bps' Coll Cheshunt 58. **d** 61 **p** 62. C Short Heath *Birm* 61-63; C Londonderry 63-65; Chapl Selly Oak Hosp Birm 65-70; V Rowley Regis *Birm* 70-78; V Polesworth 78-95; RD Polesworth 84-91; Hon Can Birm Cathl 87-95; rtd 95. *Rose Cottage, Stratford sub Castle, Salisbury SP1 3LB* Tel (01722) 322569

BYFORD, The Ven Edwin Charles. b 47. Aus Nat Univ BSc70 MA Melbourne Univ BD73. Trin Coll Melbourne 70. **d** 73 **p** 73. Hon C Chorlton-cum-Hardy St Werburgh *Man* 77-79; Hon C Holbrook w Freston and Woolverstone *St E* 79-80; Australia from 80; Adn The Darling from 95. *PO Box 185, Broken Hill, NSW, Australia 2880* Tel Broken Hill (80) 873221

BYLES, Canon Raymond Vincent. b 30. Univ of Wales (Lamp) BA52. St Mich Coll Llan 52. **d** 54 **p** 55. C Llanfairisgaer *Ban* 54-57; C Llandudno 57-59; V Carno 59-64; V Trefeglwys 63; V Newmarket and Gwaenysgor *St As* 64-72; R Llysfaen 72-80; V Bodelwyddan and St George 80-85; V Bodelwyddan 85-95; Hon Can St As Cathl from 89; rtd 95. *20 Lon Dderwen, Tan-y-Goppa Park, Abergele LL22 7DW* Tel (01745) 833604

BYLLAM-BARNES, Paul William Marshall. b 38. Birm Univ BCom Lon Univ MSc. Sarum & Wells Th Coll. **d** 84 **p** 85. C Gt Bookham *Guildf* 84-87; R Cusop w Clifford, Hardwicke, Bredwardine etc *Heref* from 87; RD Abbeydore from 96. *The Vicarage, Cusop, Hay-on-Wye, Hereford HR3 5RF* Tel (01497) 820634

BYNON, William. b 43. St Aid Birkenhead 63. **d** 66 **p** 67. C Huyton St Mich *Liv* 66-69; C Maghull 69-72; TV 72-75; V Highfield 75-82; V Southport All SS 82-88; P-in-c Southport All So 86-88; V Newton in Makerfield St Pet 88-94; V Caerhun w Llangelynin w Llanbedr-y-Cennin *Ban* from 94. *Caerhun Vicarage, Tyn-y-Groes, Conwy LL32 8UG* Tel (01492) 650250

BYRNE, David Patrick. b 48. St Jo Coll Nottm 74. **d** 77 **p** 78. C Bordesley Green *Birm* 77-79; C Weoley Castle 79-82; TV Kings Norton 82-92; TV Hodge Hill 92-94; Perm to Offic from 94; Chapl Asst Birmingham Heartlands and Solihull NHS Trust from 96. *Birmingham Heartlands Hospital, Bordesley Green East, Birmingham B9 5SS* Tel 0121-766 6611 Fax 773 6897

BYRNE, David Rodney. b 47. St Jo Coll Cam BA70 MA73. Cranmer Hall Dur 71. **d** 73 **p** 74. C Maidstone St Luke *Cant* 73-77; C Patcham *Chich* 77-83; TV Stantonbury *Ox* 83-87; TV Stantonbury and Willen 87-92; TV Woodley from 92. *Airfield Church Centre, 171 Hurricane Way, Woodley, Reading RG5 4UH* Tel 0118-969 2981

BYRNE, Canon John Victor. b 47. FCA. St Jo Coll Nottm LTh73. **d** 73 **p** 74. C Gillingham St Mark *Roch* 73-76; C Cranham Park *Chelmsf* 76-80; V Balderstone *Man* 80-87; V Southsea St Jude *Portsm* from 87; P-in-c Southsea St Pet from 95; Hon Can Portsm Cathl from 97. *St Jude's Vicarage, 7 Hereford Road, Southsea, Hants PO5 2DH* Tel (01705) 821071

BYRNE, The Very Revd Matthew. b 27. Man Univ MA69 TCD HDipEd81. Tyndale Hall Bris 47. **d** 51 **p** 52. C Rawtenstall St Mary *Man* 51-54; OCF 54-57; R Moss Side St Jas *Man* 57-62; R Whalley Range St Marg 62-80; P-in-c Chapelizod *D & G* 80-83; Chapl K Hosp Sch Dub 83-89; Dean Kildare *M & K* 89-93; I Kildare w Kilmeague and Curragh 89-93; Producer Relig Dept RTE 83-92; Chapl Defence Forces 89-92; rtd 92. *5 Fairfield Park, Greystones, Co Wicklow, Irish Republic* Tel Dublin (1) 287 3622 Fax as telephone

BYRNE, Miriam Alexandra Frances. b 46. Westcott Ho Cam. **d** 87 **p** 94. Par Dn Beoley *Worc* 87-90; C Ayr *Glas* 90-92; D-in-c pt Dumbarton 92-94; P-in-c from 94. *45 St Andrew's Crescent, Dumbarton G82 3ES* Tel (01389) 764590 or 734514

BYRNE, Robert James Matthew (Bob). b 64. Oak Hill Th Coll BA95. **d** 95 **p** 96. C Tonbridge St Steph *Roch* from 95. *20 Woodfield Road, Tonbridge, Kent TN9 2LQ* Tel (01732) 770944

BYRNE, Rodney Edmund. b 18. **d** 84 **p** 84. Hon C Leckhampton SS Phil and Jas w Cheltenham St Jas *Glouc* 84-88; rtd 88; Perm to Offic *Glouc* from 88. *39 Collum End Rise, Cheltenham, Glos GL53 0PA* Tel (01242) 526428

BYRNE, Ronald Brendan Anthony (Bryn). b 31. Reading Univ BA72. Westcott Ho Cam 86. **d** 64 **p** 65. Chapl Cov Cathl *Cov* 87-91; Chapl Lanchester Poly 87-91; Lic to Offic 91-94; Chapl Limerick Univ *L & K* from 94; Lic to Offic from 94; Chapl Villier's Sch Limerick from 95; rtd 96. *Modreeny Rectory, Cloughjordan, Co Tipperary, Irish Republic* Tel 00 353 505 42183

BYROM, Canon John Kenneth. b 20. Selw Coll Cam BA41 MA45. Westcott Ho Cam 41. **d** 43 **p** 44. C Neston *Ches* 43-48; C Stockport St Matt 48-50; V Cheadle Hulme All SS 50-63; Warden Brasted Place Coll Westerham 64-74; V Swaffham Prior *Ely* 74-88; Dir of Ords 75-87; Dir of Post-Ord Tr 75-87; Hon Can Ely Cathl 78-88; RD Fordham 78-83; rtd 88. *62 Cambridge Road, Great Shelford, Cambridge CB2 5JS* Tel (01223) 844015

BYROM, Canon Malcolm Senior. b 37. Edin Th Coll 65. **d** 67 **p** 68. C Allerton *Bradf* 67-69; C Padstow *Truro* 69-72; V Hessenford 72-77; P-in-c St Martin by Looe 72-77; V Kenwyn 77-91; R Kenwyn w St Allen from 91; Sub-Warden Community of the Epiphany Truro from 85; RD Powder *Truro* 88-90; Hon Can Truro Cathl from 92. *The Vicarage, Kenwyn Close, Truro, Cornwall TR1 3DX* Tel (01872) 72664

BYRON, Frederick. b 14. Dur Univ BA38. St Jo Coll Dur 38. **d** 39 **p** 40. C Openshaw *Man* 39-43; C Oldham St Paul 43-46; C Moston St Mary 46-50; R Old Trafford St Cuth 50-56; V Bolton St Barn 56-68; V Out Rawcliffe *Blackb* 68-78; C Standish 78-79; rtd 79. *18 Scott Avenue, Hindley, Wigan, Lancs WN2 4DG* Tel (01942) 53807

BYRON, Terence Sherwood. b 26. Keble Coll Ox BA50 MA54. Linc Th Coll 50. **d** 52 **p** 53. C Melton Mowbray w Burton Lazars, Freeby etc *Leic* 52-55; C Whitwick St Jo the Bapt 55-60; India 60-76; C-in-c Beaumont Leys (Ex-paroch Distr) *Leic* 76-85; V Beaumont Leys 85-86; RD Christianity N 86-92; P-in-c Leic St Phil 86-88; V 88-92; rtd 93; Perm to Offic *Leic* from 93. *84 Flax Road, Leicester LE4 6QD* Tel 0116-266 1922

BYRON-DAVIES, Peter. b 49. K Coll Lon BD75 AKC75 Nottm Univ MTh85. St Aug Coll Cant 75. **d** 76 **p** 77. C Wootton Bassett *Sarum* 76-79; Chapl Charterhouse Godalming 79-80; R Bassingham *Linc* 80-85; V Aubourn w Haddington 80-85; V Carlton-le-Moorland w Stapleford 80-85; R Thurlby w Norton Disney 80-85; Canada 85-88; R Chalke Valley E *Sarum* 88-96; Perm to Offic from 96; Perm to Offic *B & W* from 96. *22 Broomground, Winsley, Bradford-on-Avon, Wilts BA15 2JT*

BYSOUTH, Paul Graham. b 55. Oak Hill Th Coll. **d** 84 **p** 85. C Gorleston St Andr *Nor* 84-87; C Ripley *Derby* 87-91; TV N Wingfield, Clay Cross and Pilsley from 91. *Pilsley Vicarage, Chesterfield, Derbyshire S45 8EF* Tel (01773) 590529

BYWATER, Hector William Robinson. b 10. ALCD32. **d** 33 **p** 34. C Darlaston All SS *Lich* 33-36; C Brierley Hill 36-40; V Derby St Alkmund *Derby* 40-84; rtd 84; Perm to Offic *Derby* from 84. *Grasmere, 2 Linden Drive, Prestatyn LL19 9EH*

BYWORTH, Christopher Henry Briault (Chris). b 39. Or Coll Ox BA61 MA65 Bris Univ BA63. Lon Coll of Div 64. **d** 65 **p** 66. C Low Leyton *Chelmsf* 65-68; C Rusholme H Trin *Man* 68-70; Lic to Offic *Lon* 71-75; TR Thetford *Nor* 75-79; Warden Cranmer Hall Dur 79-83; TR Fazakerley Em *Liv* 83-90; P-in-c St Helens St Helen 90-94; TR from 94; AD St Helens from 90. *The Vicarage, 51A Rainford Road, St Helens, Merseyside WA10 6BZ* Tel (01744) 22067

BYWORTH, Mrs Ruth Angela. b 49. Cranmer Hall Dur BA82. **dss** 83 **d** 92 **p** 94. Kirkby *Liv* 83-89; Aintree St Pet 89-92; D-in-c 92-94; P-in-c from 94. *The Vicarage, 51A Rainford Road, St Helens, Merseyside WA10 6BZ* Tel (01744) 22067

C

CABLE, Patrick John. b 50. AKC72. **d** 74 **p** 75. C Herne *Cant* 74-78; CF from 78; Lic to Offic *Cant* from 78. *MOD Chaplains (Army), Trenchard Lines, Upavon, Pewsey, Wilts SN9 6BE* Tel (01980) 615804 Fax 615800

CADDELL, Richard Allen. b 54. Auburn Univ Alabama BIE77. Trin Coll Bris BA88. **d** 88 **p** 89. C Uphill *B & W* 88-94; Perm to Offic 94-96; TV Beaconsfield *Ox* from 96. *St Thomas's House, Mayflower Way, Beaconsfield, Bucks HP9 1UF* Tel (01494) 672750

CADDEN, Brian Stuart. b 58. BSc BTh TCD. **d** 89 **p** 90. C Lecale Gp *D & D* 89-92; C Killowen *D & R* 92-95; I Muckamore *Conn* from 95. *The Rectory, 5 Ballycraigy Road, Muckamore, Antrim BT41 1QP* Tel (01849) 462073

CADDEN, Terence John. b 60. TCD BTh89. CITC 86. **d** 89 **p** 90. C Coleraine *Conn* 89-92; C Lurgan Ch the Redeemer *D & D* from 92. *14 Sandhill Park, Lurgan, Craigavon, Co Armagh BT66 7AX* Tel (01762) 326040

CADDICK, Jeremy Lloyd. b 60. St Jo Coll Cam BA82 MA86 K Coll Lon MA93. Ripon Coll Cuddesdon BA86 MA91. **d** 87 **p** 88. C Kennington St Jo w St Jas *S'wark* 87-90; Chapl Lon Univ *Lon* 90-94; Chapl R Free Medical Sch 90-94; Chapl R Veterinary Coll Lon 90-94; PV Westmr Abbey 92-94; Dean Em Coll Cam from 94. *Emmanuel College, Cambridge CB2 3AP* Tel (01223) 334264 Fax 334426 E-mail jlc24@cam.ac.uk

CADDICK, Canon Lloyd Reginald. b 31. Bris Univ BA56 St Cath Coll Ox BA58 MA62 Nottm Univ MPhil73 K Coll Lon PhD78 Open Univ Hon MA79. St Steph Ho Ox 56. **d** 59 **p** 59. C N Lynn w St Marg and St Nic *Nor* 59-62; Chapl Oakham Sch 62-66; P-in-c Bulwick, Harringworth w Blatherwycke and Laxton *Pet* 66-67; R Bulwick, Blatherwycke w Harringworth and Laxton 67-77; V Oundle 77-96; Can Pet Cathl 94-96; rtd 96. *18A Glapthorn Road, Oundle, Peterborough PE8 4JQ* Tel (01832) 273616

CADDY, Dennis Gordon James. b 27. Bps' Coll Cheshunt 62. **d** 64 **p** 65. C Greenhill St Jo *Lon* 64-67; C Harlington 67-69; C-in-c Harlington Ch Ch CD 69-72; V N Harrow St Alb 72-83; R Corsley *Sarum* 83-92; rtd 92. *2 Ivy Cottage, Marcombelake, Bridport, Dorset DT6 6EE* Tel (01297) 489120

CADDY, Michael George Bruce Courtenay. b 45. K Coll Lon. **d** 71 **p** 72. C Walton St Mary *Liv* 71-76; C Solihull *Birm* 76-79; TV 79-81; V Shard End 81-87; TV Shirley 87; TR from 87; P-in-c Tanworth St Patr Salter Street from 97; RD Shirley from 97. *The Vicarage, 2 Bishopton Close, Shirley, Solihull, W Midlands B90 4AH* Tel 0121-744 3123

CADE, Simon Peter Vincent. b 69. Univ of Wales BA90. Westcott Ho Cam CTM94. **d** 94 **p** 95. C Calne and Blackland *Sarum* from 94; Chapl St Mary's Sch Calne from 94. *5 Tyning Park, Calne, Wilts SN11 0QE* Tel (01249) 814860

CADMAN, Kenneth Claude. b 14. St Jo Coll Dur BA40. **d** 40 **p** 41. C Harpurhey Ch Ch *Man* 40-44; C Rochdale 44-45; C Worsley 45-47; R Heaton Norris All SS 47-52; CF (TA) 49-52; CF (TA - R of O) 52-69; V Rainow w Saltersford and Forest *Ches* 52-54; R Higher Broughton *Man* 54-59; R Guernsey St Michel du Valle *Win* 59-65; V Alderney 65-69; R Guernsey St Pierre du Bois 69-81; R Guernsey St Philippe de Torteval 80-81; Vice Dean Guernsey 70-81; rtd 81; Perm to Offic *Win* from 82. *Marske, Rue de St Apolline, St Saviour's, Guernsey, Channel Islands GU7 9QJ* Tel (01481) 63720

CADMAN, Robert Hugh. b 49. Nottm Univ DipTh76. St Jo Coll Nottm 77. **d** 78 **p** 79. C Ecclesall *Sheff* 78-82; C Worting *Win* 82-84; C-in-c Winklebury CD 84-87; R Widford *Chelmsf* 87-94; Chapl Anglia Poly Univ 94-95. *64 Anne of Cleves Road, Dartford DA1 2BQ*

CADMORE, Albert Thomas. b 47. Open Univ BA81 NE Lon Poly Nor City Coll DMS84 SS Mark & Jo Coll Plymouth Lon Inst of Educn CertEd68. EAMTC 85. **d** 88 **p** 89. NSM Gorleston St Andr *Nor* from 88; NSM Winterton w E and W Somerton and Horsey from 94. *10 Upper Cliff Road, Gorleston, Great Yarmouth, Norfolk NR31 6AL* Tel (01493) 668762

CADOGAN, Paul Anthony Cleveland. b 47. AKC74. **d** 75 **p** 76. C Fishponds St Jo *Bris* 75-79; C Swindon New Town 79-81; P-in-c Swindon All SS 81-82; V 82-90; R Lower Windrush *Ox* 90-94. *2 Malthouse Close, Ashbury, Oxon SN6 8PB* Tel (01793) 710488

CAESAR, Canon Anthony Douglass. b 24. LVO87. CVO91. FRCO47 Magd Coll Cam BA47 MusB47 MA49. St Steph Ho Ox 59. **d** 61 **p** 62. C Kensington St Mary Abbots w St Geo *Lon* 61-65; Chapl RSCM Addington 65-70; Asst Sec CACTM 65-66; ACCM 65-70; Dep P in O 67-68; P-in-O 68-70; C Bournemouth St Pet *Win* 70-73; Prec and Sacr Win Cathl 74-79; Hon Can 75-76 and 79-91; Can Res 76-79; Dom Chapl to The Queen 79-91; Extra Chapl to The Queen from 91; Sub Almoner and Dep Clerk of the Closet 79-91; Sub Dean of HM Chpls Royal 79-91; rtd 91; Chapl St Cross Hosp Win 91-93. *Flat 2, Old Kiln, Brading, Sandown, Isle of Wight PO36 0BP* Tel (01983) 406435

CAFFYN, Douglas John Morris. b 36. ACIS77 Peterho Cam MA60 Nairobi Univ MSc69 Westmr Coll Ox DipEd61. S Dios Minl Tr Scheme 87. **d** 90 **p** 91. NSM Hampden Park *Chich* 90-94; Chapl among Deaf People 94-97; Jt Sec Cttee for Min among Deaf People 95-97; Asst Sec from 97. *255 King's Drive, Eastbourne, E Sussex BN21 2UR* Tel (01323) 500977

CAHILL, Nigel. b 59. St Mich Coll Llan DipTh80 DPS82. **d** 82 **p** 83. C Whitchurch *Llan* 82-86; V Tonypandy w Clydach Vale 86-96; RD Rhondda 93-96; V Fairwater from 96. *St Peter's Vicarage, 21 St Fagan's Road, Fairwater, Cardiff CF5 3DW* Tel (01222) 562551

CAIGER, Canon Douglas George Colley. b 23. Kelham Th Coll 39. **d** 46 **p** 48. C Coulsdon St Andr *S'wark* 46-48; C Kingswood

48-49; C Havant *Portsm* 49-54; V St Helens 54-58; Dioc Insp of Schs 55-69; R Warblington and Emsworth 58-69; R Lowestoft St Marg *Nor* 69-78; Hon Can Nor Cathl 73-78; TR Shaston *Sarum* 78-86; rtd 86; Perm to Offic *Portsm* from 86; Perm to Offic *Chich* from 86. *11 Record Road, Emsworth, Hants PO10 7NS* Tel (01243) 376058

CAIN, Andrew David. b 63. Aber Univ BSc86. Ripon Coll Cuddesdon BA89. **d** 90 **p** 91. C Walworth St Jo *S'wark* 90-94; Bp's Dom Chapl *Ox* from 94. *55 Marsh Lane, Marston, Oxford OX3 0NQ* Tel (01865) 67946

CAIN, Frank Robert. b 56. Oak Hill Th Coll BA88. **d** 88 **p** 89. C Aughton Ch Ch *Liv* 88-91; P-in-c Toxteth Park St Clem from 91. *The Vicarage, 76 Beaumont Street, Liverpool L8 0XA* Tel 0151-709 9880

CAIN, Michael Christopher. b 68. St Jo Coll Dur BA90 K Coll Lon MA92. Ridley Hall Cam BA95. **d** 95 **p** 96. C Wimbledon Em Ridgway Prop Chpl *S'wark* from 95. *4 Sheep Walk Mews, London SW19 4QL* Tel 0181-946 1145

CAIN, Michael John Patrick. b 62. Chich Th Coll 88. **d** 91 **p** 92. C Cainscross w Selsley *Glouc* 91-94; C Mackworth St Fran *Derby* 94-97; V Derby St Luke from 97. *St Luke's Vicarage, 48 Peet Street, Derby DE22 3RF* Tel (01332) 345720 Fax 203233

CAINK, Richard David Somerville. b 37. Lich Th Coll 68. **d** 71 **p** 72. C Prittlewell St Mary *Chelmsf* 71-74; C Gt Yarmouth *Nor* 74-76; P-in-c Blickling w Ingworth 76-80; P-in-c Saxthorpe and Corpusty 76-80; P-in-c Oulton SS Pet and Paul 76-80; R Cheddington w Mentmore and Marsworth *Ox* 80-87; P-in-c Wooburn 87-90; V 90-96; P-in-c Lacey Green from 96. *The Vicarage, Church Lane, Lacey Green, Princes Risborough, Aylesbury, Bucks HP27 0PL* Tel (01844) 347741

✠**CAIRD, The Rt Revd Donald Arthur Richard.** b 25. TCD BA49 MA55 BD55 HDipEd59 Hon DD88 Hon LLD93. TCD Div Sch 49. **d** 50 **p** 51 **c** 70. C Dundela *D & D* 50-53; Chapl and Asst Master Portora R Sch Enniskillen 53-57; Lect St D Coll Lamp 57-60; I Rathmichael *D & G* 60-69; Asst Master St Columba's Coll Dub 60-62; Lect TCD 62-64; Lect in Philosophy of Relig Div Hostel Dub 64-69; Dean Ossory *C & O* 69-70; Preb Leighlin Cathl 69-70; I Kilkenny 69-70; Bp Limerick, Ardfert and Aghadoe *L & K* 70-76; Bp M & K 76-85; Abp Dublin *D & G* 85-96; Preb Cualaun St Patr Cathl Dublin 85-96; rtd 96. *3 Crofton Avenue, Dun Laoghaire, Co Dublin, Irish Republic* Tel Dublin (1) 280 7869

CAIRNS, Henry Alfred. Melbourne Univ BA49 Ridley Coll Melbourne. ACT ThL43. **d** 42 **p** 43. Australia 42-81; Can Gippsland 59-60; Perm to Offic *Cant* 81-83; Perm to Offic *St Alb* 81-83 and from 85; Hon C Radlett 83-85. *47 Westminster Court, St Stephen's Hill, St Albans, Herts AL1 2DX* Tel (01727) 850949

CAIRNS, Robert Hill. b 21. Aber Univ MA50. St Deiniol's Hawarden. **d** 83 **p** 83. Lic to Offic *Ab* 83-86; Portsoy 86-88; Perm to Offic from 88. *Flat 3, South College House, Elgin, Morayshire IV30 1EP* Tel (01343) 541190

CALAMINUS, Peter Andrew Franz. b 14. Lon Univ BA44. Cuddesdon Coll 69. **d** 71 **p** 71. C Westbury *Sarum* 71-73; P-in-c Pitcombe w Shepton Montague and Bratton St Maur *B & W* 73-76; V 76-78; rtd 79. *9 St Matthew's Cottages, Macalister Street, Rockhampton, Queensland, Australia 4701* Tel Rockhampton (79) 225386

CALCOTT-JAMES, Colin Wilfrid. b 25. Bris Univ BSc48. S'wark Ord Course 77. **d** 80 **p** 81. NSM Barnes H Trin *S'wark* 80-85; C Hykeham *Linc* 85-88; R Barrowby 88-92; rtd 92; Perm to Offic *Lon* from 93; Perm to Offic *S'wark* from 93. *23 Gwendolen Avenue, London SW15 6ET* Tel 0181-788 6591

CALDER, David Ainsley. b 60. NE Lon Poly BSc86 Dur Univ BA93. St Jo Coll Dur DMS95. **d** 96. C Ireland Wood *Ripon* from 96. *6 Holt Park Gardens, Leeds LS16 7RB* Tel 0113-281 7854

CALDER, Ian Fraser. b 47. York Univ BA68 CertEd69. Glouc Sch of Min 84. **d** 87 **p** 88. NSM Lydney w Aylburton *Glouc* 87-91; C Cirencester 91-95; V Coney Hill from 95. *St Oswald's Vicarage, Coney Hill, Gloucester GL4 4LX* Tel (01452) 523618

CALDER, Roger Paul. b 53. Hatf Coll Dur BA75. Chich Th Coll 76. **d** 79 **p** 80. C Addlestone *Guildf* 79-82; C Grangetown *Dur* 82-84; TV Brighton Resurr *Chich* 84-87; CF 87-92; P-in-c Cocking, Bepton and W Lavington *Chich* 92-95; P-in-c Bognor from 95. *The Vicarage, 17 Victoria Drive, Bognor Regis, W Sussex PO21 2RH* Tel (01243) 821965

CALDICOTT, Anthony. b 31. ARCO52 FRCO62 ADCM66 St Jo Coll Dur BA53. Ripon Hall Ox 55. **d** 57 **p** 58. C Finham *Cov* 57-61; C Bedford St Andr *St Alb* 61-64; Chapl Lindisfarne Coll 64-67; C W Bromwich All SS *Lich* 67-69; Lic to Offic *Cov* 69-75; Hon C Twickenham St Mary *Lon* 75-89; Perm to Offic from 91; rtd 96. *38 Lyndhurst Avenue, Twickenham TW2 6BX* Tel 0181-894 6859

CALDICOTT, Canon John Michael Parlane. b 46. Selw Coll Cam BA69. St Steph Ho Ox 69. **d** 71 **p** 72. C Mayfield *Chich* 71-74; Hon C Deptford St Paul *S'wark* 74-76; P-in-c Sydenham St Phil 76-83; P-in-c Forest Hill Ch Ch 83-91; P-in-c Forest Hill St Paul 84-91; RD W Lewisham 87; V Hove All SS *Chich* 91-93; P-in-c Hove St Jo 91-93; TR Hove from 93; Chapl Catisfield Hosp from 91; RD Hove *Chich* from 92; Can and Preb Chich Cathl from 92. *The Vicarage, Wilbury Road, Hove, E Sussex BN3 3PB* Tel (01273) 733331

CALDWELL, Alan. b 29. Oak Hill Th Coll 65. **d** 67 **p** 68. C Aldershot H Trin *Guildf* 67-69; C New Malden and Coombe *S'wark* 69-73; C Edgware St Andr CD *Lon* 73-78; P-in-c Pettaugh and Winston *St E* 78; R Helmingham w Framsden and Pettaugh w Winston 78-87; R Cowden w Hammerwood *Chich* 87-94; rtd 94; Perm to Offic *Ban* from 94. *Ael-y-Bryn, Druid Road, Menai Bridge LL59 5BY* Tel (01248) 713550

CALDWELL, David Denzil. b 24. TD70. Bps' Coll Cheshunt 53. **d** 55 **p** 56. C Carnmoney *Conn* 55-59; CF (TA) 57-67; C Antrim All SS w Muckamore *Conn* 59-61; I Kilwaughter w Cairncastle 61-90; CF (TAVR) 67-90; RD Carrickfergus *Conn* 70-90; CF (R of O) 70-80; Asst ChStJ from 80; rtd 90. *30 Shandon Park, Ballymena, Co Antrim BT42 2ED* Tel (01266) 42650

CALDWELL, Ian Charles Reynolds. b 43. St Mich Coll Llan 68. **d** 70 **p** 71. C Oakham w Hambleton and Egleton *Pet* 70-74; C Swindon New Town *Bris* 74-78; P-in-c Honicknowle *Ex* 78-80; V 80-88; V Norton St Mich *Dur* 88-94. *Address excluded by request*

CALDWELL, Mrs Jill. b 47. Lon Univ BPharm69 MRPharmS70. S Dios Minl Tr Scheme 89. **d** 92 **p** 94. NSM Yiewsley *Lon* 92-97; NSM St Marylebone w H Trin from 97; Chapl Lon Univ from 97; Chapl St Marylebone Girl's Sch Lon from 97; Chapl R Academy of Music from 97; Chapl Lon Sch of Pharmacy from 97. *40 Clarence Gate Gardens, London NW1 6BA* Tel 0171-723 2077

CALDWELL, Canon John Donaldson. b 19. TCD BA41. **d** 42 **p** 43. C Belfast St Aid *Conn* 42-47; C Magheralin *D & D* 47-50; I Drumgath 50-55; I Kilmegan w Maghera 55-89; RD Kilmegan 62-89; Can Dromore Cathl 85-89; rtd 89; Lic to Offic *D & D* from 90. *66 Castlewellan Road, Newcastle, Co Down BT33 0JP* Tel (01396) 724874

CALDWELL, Robert McKinley. b 20. Pittsburgh Univ BSc42. Nashotah Ho MDiv64. **d** 64 **p** 64. USA 64-85 and from 97; P-in-c Kenmare w Sneem, Waterville etc *L & K* 87-96; rtd 97. *Address temp unknown*

CALDWELL, Roger Fripp. b 31. Cranmer Hall Dur. **d** 64 **p** 65. C Gosforth St Nic *Newc* 64-67; C Sugley 67-74; R Helmdon w Stuchbury and Radstone *Pet* 74-91; R Greatworth 74-91; rtd 91. *Quiet Waters, Station Road, Heyford, Oxford OX5 3PD*

CALE, Clifford Roy Fenton. b 38. St Mich Coll Llan 65. **d** 67 **p** 68. C Griffithstown *Mon* 67-72; V Cwm 72-73; V Abersychan 73-79; V Abersychan and Garndiffaith 79-82; R Goetre w Llanover and Llanfair Kilgeddin 82-85; R Goetre w Llanover from 85; RD Raglan-Usk from 90. *The Rectory, Nantyderry, Abergavenny NP7 9DW* Tel (01873) 880378

CALE, Nicholas. b 66. St Mich Coll Llan DipTh92. **d** 92 **p** 93. C Tenby *St D* 92-95; R Begelly w Ludchurch and Crunwere from 95. *The Rectory, Begelly, Kilgetty SA68 0YG* Tel (01834) 812348

CALEY, Charles Joseph. b 16. AKC47. Bp Wilson Coll 35. **d** 39 **p** 40. C Becontree St Alb *Chelmsf* 39-42; CF 42-46; Hon CF 47; C Paddington St Pet *Lon* 46-47; C Stoke Poges *Ox* 47-54; P-in-c 58-62; V Sturminster Marshall *Sarum* 54-58; V E Farleigh and Coxheath *Roch* 62-82; Chapl Linton Hosp Maidstone 65-82; rtd 82; Perm to Offic *Roch* from 82; Perm to Offic *Cant* from 83. *1 Bakery Cottages, Oakvale, Chatham Road, Sandling, Maidstone, Kent ME14 3BE* Tel (01622) 673397

CALLADINE, Matthew Robert Michael. b 65. St Jo Coll Dur BSc87 Reading Univ MSc89. Cranmer Hall Dur BA93 DMS93. **d** 96 **p** 97. C Blurton *Lich* from 96. *St Alban's House, 51 Ripon Road, Blurton, Stoke-on-Trent ST3 3BS* Tel (01782) 315029

CALLAGHAN, Canon Harry. b 34. AKC59 Open Univ BA83. **d** 60 **p** 61. C Sheff Parson Cross St Cecilia *Sheff* 60-63; Br Guiana 63-66; Guyana 66-70; Barbados 70-74; Lic to Offic *Man* 74-84; Miss to Seamen 74-76; Area Sec (Dios Blackb, Man and S & M) USPG 76-84; P-in-c Wythenshawe St Martin *Man* 84-85; V 85-91; V Bolton St Jo from 91; Hon Can Mass from 92. *St John's Vicarage, 7 Alford Close, Bolton BL2 6NR* Tel (01204) 418233

CALLAGHAN, Martin Peter. b 57. Edin Th Coll 91. **d** 93 **p** 94. C Ayr *Glas* 93-96; P-in-c Gretna from 96; P-in-c Eastriggs from 96. *4 Kingfisher Lane, Gretna, Dumfriesshire DG16 5JS* Tel (01461) 338176 or 338773

CALLAGHAN, Robert Paul. b 59. K Coll Lon BD81. Linc Th Coll 81. **d** 83 **p** 85. C Winchmore Hill St Paul *Lon* 83-85; C Paddington St Jo w St Mich 85-91; V Dartford St Edm *Roch* from 91. *The Vicarage, St Edmund's Road, Temple Hill, Dartford DA1 5ND* Tel (01322) 225335

CALLAN, Canon Terence Frederick. b 26. CITC 55. **d** 57 **p** 58. C Monaghan *Clogh* 57-58; I Clogh 58-64; C Derriaghy *Conn* 64-66; P-in-c Ballymacash 67-70; I Belfast St Aid 70-79; I Agherton 79-94; Can Conn Cathl from 86; Treas from 90; rtd 94. *18 Central Avenue, Portstewart, Co Londonderry BT55 7BS* Tel (01265) 832704

CALLAN-TRAVIS, Anthony. b 46. N Ord Course 90. **d** 93 **p** 94. C Tong *Bradf* 93-97; C Harrogate St Wilfrid *Ripon* from 97. *7 Lindrick Way, Harrogate, N Yorkshire HG3 2SU* Tel (01423) 508128

CALLARD, Canon David Kingsley. b 37. St Pet Coll Ox BA61 MA65. Westcott Ho Cam 61. **d** 63 **p** 64. C Leamington Priors H Trin *Cov* 63-66; C Wyken 66-68; C Hatfield *St Alb* 68-73; R Bilton *Cov* 73-83; TR Swanage and Studland *Sarum* 83-93; TR

Oakdale from 93; Can and Preb Sarum Cathl from 95. *The Rectory, 99 Darby's Lane, Poole, Dorset BH15 3EU* Tel (01202) 675419

CALLENDER, Thomas Henry. b 13. SS Coll Cam BA35 MA39. Sarum Th Coll 35. **d** 37 **p** 38. C Kidderminster St Jo *Worc* 37-41; C Pershore w Wick 41-46; V Powyke 46-51; V Tuffley *Glouc* 51-55; V S Kensington St Pet *Lon* 55-57; R Lt Stanmore St Lawr 57-66; V Carbrooke *Nor* 66-76; R Ovington 66-76; V Carbrooke w Ovington, Woodrising and Scoulton 76-78; rtd 78; Perm to Offic *Nor* from 78. *5 Paddock Gardens, Attleborough, Norfolk NR17 2EW* Tel (01953) 454727

CALLER, Laurence Edward Harrison. b 19. Lon Univ BMus77 MA82. Lich Th Coll 39. **d** 42 **p** 43. C Ipswich St Matt *St E* 42-45; C Walsall St Pet *Lich* 45-46; C Hednesford 46-48; R Stafford St Mary 48-55; Subchanter Lich Cathl 55-57; V Shrewsbury St Alkmund 57-63; V Harlescott 63-67; rtd 84. *103 Fronks Road, Dovercourt, Harwich, Essex CO12 4EG* Tel (01255) 504501

CALLON, Andrew McMillan. b 56. Chich Th Coll 77. **d** 80 **p** 81. C Wigan All SS *Liv* 80-85; V Abram 85-90; V Bickershaw 89-90; Chapl RN from 90. *Royal Naval Chaplaincy Service, Room 203, Victory Building, HM Naval Base, Portsmouth PO1 3LS* Tel (01705) 727903 Fax 727112

CALTHROP-OWEN, William Gordon. b 35. Chich Th Coll 62. **d** 63 **p** 64. C Egremont St Jo *Ches* 63-68; C Bawtry w Austerfield *S'well* 68-69; P-in-c Radford All So w Ch Ch 69-73; P-in-c Radford St Mich 69-73; R Bilsthorpe 73-90; R Eakring 73-90; P-in-c Winkburn 77-90; P-in-c Maplebeck 77-90; V Woodborough from 90; Chapl HM Young Offender Inst Lowdham Grange 90-91; RD Gedling *S'well* from 96. *The Vicarage, Lingwood Lane, Woodborough, Nottingham NG14 6DX* Tel 0115-965 2250

CALVER, Mrs Gillian Margaret. b 47. Qu Eliz Coll Lon BSc68. Cant Sch of Min 89. **d** 92 **p** 94. NSM Folkestone H Trin w Ch Ch *Cant* 92-95; P-in-c Alkham w Capel le Ferne and Hougham from 95; Chapl Dover Coll from 95. *The Vicarage, 20 Alexandra Road, Capel-le-Ferne, Folkestone, Kent CT18 7LD* Tel (01303) 244119

CALVER, Nicholas James. b 58. Nottm Univ BTh83 Dur Univ MA90. Cranmer Hall Dur 86. **d** 88 **p** 89. C Forest Hill Ch Ch *S'wark* 88-91; C Forest Hill 91-92; P-in-c Mottingham St Edw 92-95; V from 95; Voc Adv Lewisham Adnry from 94. *St Edward's Vicarage, St Keverne Road, London SE9 4AQ* Tel 0181-857 6278

CALVER, Sydney Bertram. b 10. Keble Coll Ox BA33. Chich Th Coll 33. **d** 35 **p** 36. C Thatcham *Ox* 35-38; C Walworth St Pet *S'wark* 38-42; Chapl RAFVR 42-46; Toc H 46-49; Asst Educn Officer Ch Assembly Adult Educn Coun 49-56; R Stonesfield *Ox* 56-75; rtd 75; Perm to Offic *Ox* 75-77; Perm to Offic *B & W* 77-93. *8 Parkfield Drive, Taunton, Somerset TA1 5BT* Tel (01823) 272535

CALVERT, Dr Geoffrey Richard. b 58. Edin Univ BSc79 PhD84 Leeds Univ BA86. Coll of Resurr Mirfield 84. **d** 87 **p** 88. C Curdworth w Castle Vale *Birm* 87-90; C Barnsley St Mary *Wakef* 90-92; TV Halifax 92-94; V Halifax H Trin from 95. *Holy Trinity Vicarage, 9 Love Lane, Halifax, W Yorkshire HX1 2BQ* Tel (01422) 352446

CALVERT, Canon Jean. b 34. Lightfoot Ho Dur IDC. **dss** 78 **d** 87 **p** 94. S Bank *York* 78-84; Chapl Asst Rampton Hosp Retford from 84; D-in-c Dunham w Darlton and Ragnall *S'well* 88-89; D-in-c E Drayton w Stokeham 88-89; D-in-c Fledborough 88-89; D-in-c Dunham-on-Trent w Darlton, Ragnall etc 89-94; P-in-c from 94; Hon Can S'well Minster from 93. *The Vicarage, Dunham-on-Trent, Newark, Notts NG22 0UL* Tel (01777) 228707

CALVERT, John Raymond. b 42. Lon Coll of Div 64. **d** 67 **p** 68. C Kennington St Mark *S'wark* 67-70; C Southborough St Pet *Roch* 70-72; C Barton Seagrave *Pet* 72-75; Asst Master Shaftesbury High Sch 78-79; Dioc Children's Officer *Glouc* 79-87; P-in-c S Cerney w Cerney Wick and Down Ampney 87-89; V from 89. *The Vicarage, Silver Street, South Cerney, Cirencester, Glos GL7 5TP* Tel (01285) 860221

CALVERT, John Stephen. b 27. Lon Univ BSc53. Wycliffe Coll Toronto BTh61. **d** 61 **p** 62. Canada 61-63; C Preston St Jo *Blackb* 63-70; rtd 92; Perm to Offic *Blackb* from 92. *17 Leyster Street, Morecambe, Lancs LA4 5NE* Tel (01524) 424491

CALVERT, Canon Peter Noel. b 41. Ch Coll Cam BA63 MA67. Cuddesdon Coll 64. **d** 66 **p** 67. C Brighouse *Wakef* 66-71; V Heptonstall 71-82; V Todmorden from 82; P-in-c Cross Stone 83-93; RD Calder Valley from 84; Hon Can Wakef Cathl from 92. *The Vicarage, Todmorden, Lancs OL14 7BS* Tel (01706) 813180

CALVIN-THOMAS, David Nigel. b 43. Univ of Wales (Cardiff) BSc64 Lon Univ BD77 Leeds Univ DipC&G88. St Mich Coll Llan 77. **d** 78 **p** 79. C Pontypridd St Cath *Llan* 78-80; Malawi 81-84; V Rastrick St Matt *Wakef* 84-88; V Birchencliffe 88-93; Chapl Huddersfield R Infirmary 88-93; R Aberdeen St Pet *Ab* from 93; P-in-c Cove Bay from 93. *123 Walker Road, Aberdeen AB1 3DH* Tel (01224) 248193

CALWAY, Geoffrey. b 45. Bris Sch of Min. **d** 87 **p** 88. NSM Cotham St Sav w St Mary *Bris* 87-94; NSM Horfield H Trin 94-97; P-in-c Publow w Pensford, Compton Dando and Chelwood *B & W* from 97. *The Rectory, High Barn, Old Road, Pensford, Bristol BS18 4BB* Tel (01761) 490221

CAM, Julian Howard. b 48. York Univ BA69 Birm Univ DipTh74. Qu Coll Birm 73. **d** 75 **p** 76. C St Ives *Truro* 75-80; C Lelant 78-80; V Flookburgh *Carl* 80-82; V St Stephen by Saltash *Truro* 82-83; V Low Marple *Ches* from 83. *St Martin's Vicarage, 15 Brabyns Brow, Marple Bridge, Stockport, Cheshire SK6 5DT* Tel 0161-427 2736

CAMENISCH, Richard Frank. b 12. Univ Coll Dur BA34. Wells Th Coll 34. **d** 35 **p** 36. C Sheff St Cuth *Sheff* 35-37; C Burghwallis w Skelbrooke 39-41; C Staveley *Derby* 47-50; R Treswell and Cottam *S'well* 50-59; V Laxton 59-68; V Egmanton 59-68; V Bicker *Linc* 68-77; rtd 77; Perm to Offic *S'well* from 77; Perm to Offic *Sheff* from 86. *The Whipping Post, Norwell Lane, Newark, Notts NG23 6JQ* Tel (01636) 821423

✠**CAMERON, The Rt Revd Andrew Bruce.** b 41. New Coll Edin CPS72. Sheff Urban Th Unit 82 Edin Th Coll 61. **d** 64 **p** 65 **c** 92. C Helensburgh *Glas* 64-67; C Edin H Cross *Edin* 67-71; Prov and Dioc Youth Chapl 69-75; Chapl St Mary's Cathl 71-75; R Dalmahoy 75-82; Chapl Heriot-Watt Univ 75-82; TV Livingston LEP 82-88; R Perth St Jo *St And* 88-92; Convener Prov Miss Bd 88-92; Bp Ab from 92. *Bishop's House, Ashley House, Ashley Gardens, Aberdeen AB10 6RQ* Tel (01224) 208142 or 636653 Fax 208142 or 636186

CAMERON, David Alan. b 59. Glas Univ MA81 DipEd82 PGCE82. Ripon Coll Cuddesdon 88. **d** 91 **p** 92. C Farncombe *Guildf* 91-93; C Guildf H Trin w St Mary 93-96; V Fenton *Lich* from 96. *The Vicarage, 65 Glebedale Road, Stoke-on-Trent ST4 3AQ* Tel (01782) 412417

CAMERON, David Alexander. b 42. MRTPI Reading Univ BA63 Leeds Art Coll DipTP69. St And Dioc Tr Course 80. **d** 90 **p** 93. NSM Blairgowrie *St And* from 90; NSM Coupar Angus from 90; NSM Alyth from 90. *Firgrove, Golf Course Road, Blairgowrie, Perthshire PH10 6LF* Tel (01250) 873272 or 874583

CAMERON, Donald Eric Nelson. b 29. St Jo Coll Dur 68. **d** 70 **p** 71. C Kingston upon Hull H Trin *York* 70-73; V Eston 73-82; R Balerno *Edin* 82-87; rtd 94. *The Granary, Crauchie, East Linton, East Lothian EH40 3EB* Tel (01620) 860067

✠**CAMERON, The Rt Revd Douglas MacLean.** b 35. Univ of S Tennessee 61. Edin Th Coll 59. **d** 62 **p** 63 **c** 93. C Falkirk *Edin* 62-65; Papua New Guinea 66-74; Adn New Guinea Mainland 72-74; P-in-c Edin St Fillan *Edin* 74-78; R 78-88; R Edin St Hilda 77-88; R Dalkeith 88-92; R Lasswade 88-92; Can St Mary's Cathl 90-91; Syn Clerk 90-91; Dean Edin 91-92; Bp Arg from 93. *Bishop's Office, The Pines, Ardconnel Road, Oban, Argyll PA34 5DR* Tel (01631) 566912 Fax as telephone

CAMERON, Gregory Kenneth. b 59. Linc Coll Ox BA80 MA84 Down Coll Cam BA82 MA85 Univ of Wales (Cardiff) DPS83 MPhil92. St Mich Coll Llan 82. **d** 83 **p** 84. C Newport St Paul *Mon* 83-86; Tutor St Mich Coll Llan 86-89; C Llanmartin *Mon* 86-87; TV 87-88; Chapl Wycliffe Coll Glos 88-94; Dir Bloxham Project from 94. *St Thomas's House, 12 St Thomas's Square, Monmouth NP5 3ES* Tel (01600) 716912 Fax as telephone

CAMERON, Mrs Janis Irene. b 43. Reading Univ BA. St And Dioc Tr Course 87. **d** 96 **p** 96. C Blairgowrie *St And* from 96; C Coupar Angus from 96; C Alyth from 96. *Firgrove, Golf Course Road, Blairgowrie, Perthshire PH10 6LF* Tel (01250) 873272

CAMERON, Mrs Margaret Mary. b 48. Qu Mary Coll Lon BA69 Liv Univ DAA70 Ex Univ MA95. SW Minl Tr Course 87. **d** 90 **p** 94. NSM Budleigh Salterton *Ex* 90-95; C Whipton 95-97; R Hemyock w Culm Davy, Clayhidon and Culmstock from 97. *The Rectory, Hemyock, Cullompton, Devon EX15 3RQ* Tel (01823) 681189

CAMERON, Michael John. b 41. Sheff Tech Coll HNC63 DipM66 Nottm Univ CTPS90. Linc Th Coll 91. **d** 92 **p** 93. C Dinnington *Sheff* 92-96; V Beighton from 96. *The Vicarage, 27 Tynker Avenue, Beighton, Sheffield S19 6DX* Tel 0114-248 7635

CAMERON, Peter Samuel Griswold. b 30. TD76. New Coll Ox BA53 MA56. Wells Th Coll 53. **d** 55 **p** 56. C Westbury-on-Trym St Alb *Bris* 55-58; C Henbury 58-60; CF (TA) 59-70, 72-78 and 80-87; Chapl K Coll Cam 60-63; C-in-c Davyhulme CD *Man* 63-69; V Davyhulme Ch Ch 69-72; V Worsley 72-79; V Waterbeach *Ely* 79-83; R Landbeach 79-83; RD Quy 81-83; V Chesterton Gd Shep 83-93; P-in-c Fenstanton 93-94; V from 94; P-in-c Hilton 93-94; V from 94. *The Vicarage, 16 Church Street, Fenstanton, Huntingdon, Cambs PE18 9JL* Tel (01480) 463334

CAMERON, William Hugh Macpherson. b 59. Edin Univ LLB82 BD86. Edin Th Coll 83. **d** 86 **p** 87. C Cheadle Hulme All SS *Ches* 86-89; Asst Chapl and Hd Relig Studies Wellington Coll 89-93; Chapl K Sch Bruton from 93. *King's School, Bruton, Somerset BA10 0ED* Tel (01749) 813326

CAMERON, William James. b 35. St Aid Birkenhead 60. **d** 64 **p** 65. C Halewood *Liv* 64-66; C-in-c Halewood St Mary CD 66-68; Asst Chapl Leeds Univ *Ripon* 68-71; Ind Chapl *Liv* 71-77; Tr Officer Gen Syn Bd of Educn 77-84; V Hickling and Waxham w Sea Palling *Nor* 89-95; RD Waxham 93-96; P-in-c Ludham w Potter Heigham 94-95; V Ludham, Potter Heigham and Hickling from 95. *The Vicarage, Norwich Road, Ludham, Great Yarmouth, Norfolk NR29 5QA* Tel (01692) 678282

CAMIER, Canon James. b 12. TCD BA33 MA67 Div Test. **d** 35 **p** 36. I Borrisokane w Ardcroney, Aglishclohane etc *L & K* 61-86;

RD Ely O'Carroll 62-86; Can Killaloe Cathl from 65; Prec 72-86; rtd 86. *Ferndale, Shillelagh, Co Wicklow, Irish Republic* Tel Shillelagh (55) 29227

CAMMELL, William John. b 36. Glouc Sch of Min 89. **d** 92 **p** 93. NSM Ruardean *Glouc* from 92. *The Beeches, High Beech, The Pludds, Ruardean, Glos GL17 9UD* Tel (01594) 860603

CAMP, Brian Arthur Leslie. b 50. St Jo Coll Nottm. **d** 83 **p** 84. C Blackheath *Birm* 83-86; TV Halesowen *Worc* 86-96; P-in-c Sheldon *Birm* 96-97; R from 97. *The Rectory, 165 Church Road, Sheldon, Birmingham B26 3TT* Tel 0121-743 2033

CAMP, Frederick Walter. b 19. Sarum Th Coll 47. **d** 49 **p** 50. C Brookfield St Mary *Lon* 49-54; CF 54-58; V Brigham *Carl* 58-80; V Whittingham *Newc* 80-84; V Whittingham and Edlingham w Bolton Chapel 84-85; rtd 85; Perm to Offic *Carl* from 85. *2 Ellen Court, Church Terrace, Ellenborough, Maryport, Cumbria CA15 7PR* Tel (01900) 817936

CAMP, John Edward. b 44. Barrister 69 Jes Coll Ox MA68 Brunel Univ MTech69. Ripon Coll Cuddesdon DipTh88. **d** 88 **p** 89. NSM High Wycombe *Ox* 88-89; Chapl St Andr Hosp Northn from 89; Chapl Three Shires Hosp Northn from 89; Lic to Offic *Pet* from 89. *St Andrew's Hospital, Billing Road, Northampton NN1 5DG, or 4 Elwes Way, Great Billing, Northampton NN3 9EA* Tel (01604) 29696 or 785130 Fax 232325 E-mail camp@bigfoot.com

CAMP, Michael Maurice. b 52. BTh CertEd. Sarum & Wells Th Coll 78. **d** 81 **p** 82. C Loughton St Jo *Chelmsf* 81-84; C Chingford SS Pet and Paul 84-87; V Northfleet *Roch* 87-94; V Hadlow from 94. *The Vicarage, Maidstone Road, Hadlow, Tonbridge, Kent TN11 0DJ* Tel (01732) 850238 Fax as telephone

CAMPBELL, Allan. b 14. Selw Coll Cam BA36 MA40. Westcott Ho Cam 36. **d** 38 **p** 39. C Crosthwaite Keswick *Carl* 38-39; Chapl RNVR 39-46; R Bletchley *Ox* 46-63; RD Bletchley 56-63; R Amersham 63-86; Chapl Amersham Gen Hosp 63-86; rtd 86; Perm to Offic *Carl* from 86. *Bridge House, Cockermouth, Cumbria CA13 0HF* Tel (01900) 826748

CAMPBELL, Andrew Victor. b 20. St Chad's Coll Dur 39. Linc Th Coll 46. **d** 49 **p** 50. C Poplar All SS w St Frideswide *Lon* 49-52; S Africa 52-72; Adn N Transvaal 67-72; V Hunstanton St Edm *Nor* 72-74; Chapl Coll of the Ascension Selly Oak 74-75; TV Devonport St Aubyn *Ex* 75-76; P-in-c Whitleigh 76-80; V 80-83; RD Plymouth 79-82; P-in-c Harberton w Harbertonford 83-85; rtd 85; Perm to Offic *Ex* 85-92. *Little Clevedale, 24 Christchurch Road, Winchester, Hants SO23 9SS* Tel (01962) 864317

CAMPBELL, Miss Brenda. b 47. St Jo Coll Nottm DipTh94. **d** 94 **p** 95. C Rothley *Leic* 94-97; C Market Bosworth, Cadeby w Sutton Cheney etc from 97. *4 Springfield Avenue, Market Bosworth, Nuneaton, Warks CV13 0NS* Tel (01455) 292157

CAMPBELL, David. b 70. St Andr Univ MTheol92 New Coll Edin MTh94. Edin Th Coll CECM94. **d** 94 **p** 95. C Perth St Jo *St And* 94-96; P-in-c Newport-on-Tay from 96; P-in-c Tayport from 96. *St Mary's Rectory, Newport-on-Tay, Fife DD6 8DA* Tel (01382) 543311 Fax as telephone

CAMPBELL, Frederick David Gordon. b 15. Ex Coll Ox BA39. Wells Th Coll 39. **d** 40 **p** 41. C Portsea St Mary *Portsm* 40-45; Chapl RNVR 45-48; C Fareham SS Pet and Paul *Portsm* 48-49; Bp's Press Sec *Lon* 49-51; V Isleworth St Mary 51-54; SSJE from 57; Superior Gen SSJE 76-91; Lic to Offic *Lon* from 69; rtd 85. *St Edward's House, 22 Great College Street, London SW1P 3QA* Tel 0171-222 9234

CAMPBELL, George St Clair. b 32. Lon Univ BSc53. Clifton Th Coll 58. **d** 60 **p** 61. C Tunbridge Wells St Pet *Roch* 60-64; C Clitheroe St Jas *Blackb* 64-70; V Tibshelf *Derby* 70-86; V W Bromwich H Trin *Lich* 86-97; Chapl Heath Lane Hosp 87-97; rtd 97. *2 Doreen Close, Farnborough, Hants GU14 9HB*

CAMPBELL, Canon Ian David. b 33. AKC57. **d** 58 **p** 59. C Liv Our Lady and St Nic w St Anne *Liv* 58-62; V Edge Hill St Dunstan 62-70; TR Loughborough Em *Leic* 70-80; V Leamington Priors All SS *Cov* 80-91; Hon Can Cov Cathl 87-91; RD Warwick and Leamington 87-91; Can Emer Cov Cathl from 91; TR Brixham w Churston Ferrers and Kingswear *Ex* 91-97; rtd 97. *The Rectory, 6 Durleigh Road, Brixham, Devon TQ5 9JJ* Tel (01803) 854924

CAMPBELL, Ian Hartley. b 39. RAF Coll Cranwell 62 Cranfield Inst of Tech MSc81 CEng FIMgt MRAeS. EAMTC 96 ADipR93. **d** 97. NSM Felixstowe St Jo *St E* from 97. *Drenagh, 7 Victoria Road, Felixstowe, Suffolk IP11 7PT* Tel (01394) 275631 Fax as telephone

CAMPBELL, James Duncan. b 55. Qu Eliz Coll Lon BSc77. St Jo Coll Dur 85. **d** 87 **p** 88. C Hendon St Paul Mill Hill *Lon* 87-92; V Stevenage St Hugh and St Jo *St Alb* from 92. *St Hugh's House, 4 Mobbsbury Way, Chells, Stevenage, Herts SG2 0HL* Tel (01438) 354307

CAMPBELL, James Larry. b 46. Indiana Univ BSc69 E Kentucky Univ MA73 Hull Univ MA91. Linc Th Coll 86. **d** 88 **p** 89. C N Hull St Mich *York* 88-92; C Hessle 92-95; V Burton Pidsea and Humbleton w Elsternwick from 95. *The New Vicarage, Back Lane, Burton Pidsea, Hull HU12 9AN* Tel (01964) 671074

CAMPBELL, James Malcolm. b 55. ARICS81 R Agric Coll Cirencester DipREM77. Wycliffe Hall Ox 89. **d** 91 **p** 92. C Scole, Brockdish, Billingford, Thorpe Abbots etc *Nor* 91-95; R Bentley and Binsted *Win* from 95. *Holy Cross Vicarage, Binsted, Alton, Hants GU34 4NX* Tel (01420) 22174

CAMPBELL, James Norman Thompson. b 49. BTh. **d** 86 **p** 87. C Arm St Mark w Aghavilly *Arm* 86-89; I Belfast H Trin and Ardoyne *Conn* 89-95; I Dundela *D & D* from 95. *St Mark's Rectory, 4 Sydenham Avenue, Belfast BT4 2DR* Tel (01232) 659047

CAMPBELL, John Frederick Stuart. b 25. Open Univ BA80. ACT ThL50 Oak Hill Th Coll 51. **d** 52 **p** 53. C Northwood Em *Lon* 52-55; Chapl RAF 56-59; Australia 59-61; V Camelsdale *Chich* 62-64; Australia 65-74; V Bath Weston St Jo *B & W* 74-80; R Bath Weston St Jo w Kelston 81-90; rtd 90; Chapl Shepton Mallet Community Hosp 91-96; Perm to Offic *B & W* from 91. *3 Lewmond Avenue, Wells, Somerset BA5 2TS* Tel (01749) 675016

CAMPBELL, Canon John Norman. b 16. Ch Coll Cam BA38 MA42. Ridley Hall Cam 38. **d** 40 **p** 41. C Tonbridge SS Pet and Paul *Roch* 40-43; C Hornsey Ch Ch *Lon* 43-45; Lon Dioc Home Missr Edmonton St Alphege 45-49; Uganda 49-70; R Stapleton *Bris* 70-85; rtd 85; Perm to Offic *Bris* 85-95. *71 Gloucester Road, Malmesbury, Wilts SN16 0AJ* Tel (01666) 822730

CAMPBELL, Kenneth Scott. b 47. BA82. Oak Hill Th Coll. **d** 82 **p** 83. C Aughton St Mich *Liv* 82-85; V Brough w Stainmore *Carl* 85-90; R Brough w Stainmore, Musgrave and Warcop 90-92; rtd 92. *4 Quarry Close, Kirkby Stephen, Cumbria CA17 4SS* Tel (017683) 72390

CAMPBELL, Lawrence Henry. b 41. TCD BA63 MA66. **d** 63 **p** 65. C Larne and Inver *Conn* 63-66; C Finaghy 66-67; Chapl RN 67-83; R Brancaster w Burnham Deepdale and Titchwell *Nor* 83-95; P-in-c Hunstanton St Mary w Ringstead Parva, Holme etc 94-95; R Hunstanton St Mary w Ringstead Parva etc from 95. *St Mary's Rectory, Hunstanton, Norfolk PE36 6JS* Tel (01485) 532169

CAMPBELL, Patrick Alistair. b 36. Qu Coll Birm 64. **d** 67 **p** 68. C Paston *Pet* 67-71; C Stockton Heath *Ches* 71-73; V Egremont St Jo 73-78; V Bredbury St Mark 78-85; R Astbury and Smallwood 85-91; V Wybunbury w Doddington 91-97; rtd 97. *9 Pinewood Court, Wistaston, Crewe CW2 6XS* Tel (01270) 669158

CAMPBELL, Robin William. b 41. TCD BA63 MA67. Ridley Hall Cam 63. **d** 65 **p** 66. C Netherton *Liv* 65-68; C Liv Our Lady and St Nic w St Anne 68-70; V Hooton *Ches* from 70. *Hooton Vicarage, Chester Road, Wirral, Merseyside L66 1QH* Tel 0151-339 2020

CAMPBELL, Roger Stewart. b 40. Birm Univ BSc61 PhD65 St Jo Coll Dur BA71. Cranmer Hall Dur 68. **d** 71 **p** 72. C Jesmond Clayton Memorial *Newc* 71-77; Singapore 78-85; C Nottingham St Nic *S'well* 86-90; V Holloway St Mark w Em *Lon* 90-92; TR Tollington from 92. *St Mark's Vicarage, 1 Moray Road, London N4 3LD* Tel 0171-272 5376

CAMPBELL, Stephen James. b 60. **d** 91 **p** 92. C Lisburn Ch Ch *Conn* 91-95; I Kilcronaghan w Draperstown and Sixtowns *D & R* from 95. *The Rectory, 12 Rectory Road, Tobermore, Magherafelt, Co Londonderry BT45 5QP* Tel (01648) 28823

CAMPBELL-SMITH, Canon Robert Campbell (Bob). b 38. CCC Cam BA61 MA66 Ibadan Univ Nigeria 62. Linc Th Coll 61. **d** 63 **p** 64. C Norbury St Steph *Cant* 63-66; C W Wickham St Mary 66-71; V Croydon St Aug 71-81; V Goudhurst 81-87; RD W Charing 82-89; P-in-c Kilndown 83-87; V Goudhurst w Kilndown from 87; Hon Can Cant Cathl from 94. *The Vicarage, Goudhurst, Cranbrook, Kent TN17 1AN* Tel (01580) 211332

CAMPBELL-TAYLOR, William Goodacre. b 65. **d** 94 **p** 95. C Chingford SS Pet and Paul *Chelmsf* from 94. *2 Sunnyside Drive, London E4 7DZ*

CAMPBELL-WILSON, Allan. b 43. Dur Univ BEd74. NE Ord Course 79. **d** 82 **p** 83. NSM Boosbeck w Moorsholm *York* 82-85; R Easington w Skeffling, Kilnsea and Holmpton 85-87; P-in-c Middlesbrough St Jo the Ev 89-95; V from 95. *St John's Vicarage, 45 Lothian Road, Middlesbrough, Cleveland TS4 2HS* Tel (01642) 242926

CAMPEN, William Geoffrey. b 50. Liv Univ CertEd71 Southn Univ BTh81. Sarum & Wells Th Coll 76. **d** 79 **p** 80. C Peckham St Jo w St Andr *S'wark* 79-83; P-in-c Mottingham St Edw 83-92; R Charlwood from 92; R Sidlow Bridge from 92. *The Rectory, The Street, Charlwood, Horley, Surrey RH6 0EE* Tel (01293) 862343

CAMPION, Keith Donald. b 52. S Dios Minl Tr Scheme. **d** 84 **p** 87. NSM Is of Scilly *Truro* from 84. *20 Launceston Close, St Mary's, Isles of Scilly TR21 0LN* Tel (01720) 22606

CAMPION (née HOUSEMAN), Ms Patricia Adele. b 39. St D Coll Lamp DipTh90 St Mich Coll Llan DipPTh93. **d** 93 **p** 97. C St Issell's and Amroth *St D* 93-95; C Llanegryn w Aberdyfi w Tywyn *Ban* 95-97. *3 Mariner's Reach, The Strand, Saundersfoot SA69 9EX* Tel (01834) 811047

CAMPION, Peter Robert. b 64. Bp's Univ Canada BA87 TCD BTh90 PGCE MA. **d** 90 **p** 91. C Belfast H Trin and Ardoyne *Conn* 90-93; Canada 93-94; C Taney *D & G* from 94; Dean's V St Patr Cathl Dublin from 96. *The Garden Flat, Upper Kevin Street, Dublin 8, Irish Republic* Tel Dublin (1) 473 4416

CAMPLING, The Very Revd Christopher Russell. b 25. St Edm Hall Ox BA50 MA54. Cuddesdon Coll 50. **d** 51 **p** 52. C Basingstoke *Win* 51-55; Min Can Ely Cathl *Ely* 55-60; Chapl K Sch Ely 55-60; Chapl Lancing Coll 60-68; P-in-c Birlingham w

Nafford *Worc* 68-75; V Pershore w Wick 68-75; RD Pershore 70-76; Hon Can Worc Cathl 74-84; V Pershore w Pinvin, Wick and Birlingham 75-76; Dioc Dir of Educn 76-84; Adn Dudley 76-84; P-in-c Dodderhill 76-84; Dean Ripon 84-95; Chmn CCC 88-94; rtd 95; Perm to Offic *Chich* from 95. *Pebble Ridge, Aglaia Road, Worthing, W Sussex BN11 5SW* Tel (01903) 246598

CAMPLING, Michael. b 27. Trin Coll Cam BA50 MA61. Wells Th Coll 51. **d** 53 **p** 54. C Calne *Sarum* 53-57; C Roehampton H Trin *S'wark* 57-61; V Crowthorne *Ox* 61-75; P-in-c Foleshill St Laur *Cov* 75-81; V 81-83; R Old Alresford and Bighton *Win* 83-92; rtd 92; Chapl St Marg Convent E Grinstead from 92. *The Chaplain's Cottage, St Margaret's Convent, East Grinstead, W Sussex RH19 3LE* Tel (01342) 323497

CANDLER, David Cecil. b 24. Cape Town Univ BSc47 Keble Coll Ox BA50 MA55. St Paul's Grahamstown 56. **d** 56 **p** 57. S Rhodesia 57-65; Rhodesia 65-80; Zimbabwe 80-85; R Barningham w Matlaske w Baconsthorpe etc *Nor* 85-94; Perm to Offic from 94; rtd 94. *Millstone, Mill Lane, Aldborough, Norwich NR11 7NS* Tel (01263) 577420

CANE, Anthony William Nicholas Strephon. b 61. Cape Town Univ BA81 Birm Univ MPhil93. Westcott Ho Cam 87. **d** 90 **p** 91. C Kings Heath *Birm* 90-93; Chapl Brighton Univ *Chich* from 93. *3 Great Wilkins, Brighton BN1 9QW* Tel (01273) 643592

CANEY, Canon Robert Swinbank. b 37. St Jo Coll Cam 57. Lich Th Coll 58. **d** 61 **p** 62. C Kingswinford H Trin *Lich* 61-64; C Castle Church 64-67; V Bradwell *Derby* 67-73; V Fairfield 73-84; RD Buxton 78-84; P-in-c Peak Forest and Wormhill 79-83; R Wirksworth w Alderwasley, Carsington etc 84-92; TR Wirksworth from 92; Hon Can Derby Cathl from 93. *The Rectory, Wirksworth, Matlock, Derbyshire DE4 4FB* Tel (01629) 824707

CANHAM, John Graham. b 33. Univ of Wales (Lamp) BA55. Chich Th Coll 55. **d** 57 **p** 58. C Hawarden *St As* 57-64; Asst Chapl Ellesmere Coll Shropshire 64-66; Chapl Ches Cathl Choir Sch 66-73; Chapl Choral Ches Cathl *Ches* 66-73; Asst Chapl Rossall Sch Fleetwood 73-76 and 83-93; Chapl 76-83; V Minera *St As* from 93. *The Vicarage, Church Road, Minera, Wrexham LL11 3DA* Tel (01978) 755679

CANHAM, Philip Edward. b 15. St Aid Birkenhead 46. **d** 46 **p** 47. C Bury St Paul *Man* 46-49; India 49-52; P-in-c Carl St Herbert w St Steph *Carl* 52-56; R Clayhidon *Ex* 56-58; P-in-c Inverkeithing *St And* 58-60; P-in-c Rosyth 58-60; R Aikton *Carl* 60-65; V Dalston 65-70; V Irthington 70-76; P-in-c Addingham 76-79; P-in-c Edenhall w Langwathby and Culgaith 76-79; P-in-c Greenhead *Newc* 79-80; P-in-c Lambley w Knaresdale 79-80; rtd 80. *6 Eden Park Crescent, Carlisle CA1 2UF* Tel (01228) 47236

CANHAM, Robert Edwin Francis. b 24. FRCO59 ARCM. **d** 74 **p** 75. NSM Newlyn St Pet *Truro* 74-75; C Phillack w Gwithian 75-79; P-in-c Phillack w Gwithian and Gwinear 79-83; V Greenham *Ox* 83-93; rtd 93; Perm to Offic *Chich* from 93. *Cross Way, 1A Torton Hill Road, Arundel, W Sussex BN18 9HF* Tel (01903) 883614

CANHAM, William Alexander. b 26. Clare Coll Cam BA47 MA56. Roch Th Coll 65. **d** 67 **p** 68. C Orpington St Andr *Roch* 67-70; C Guernsey St Steph *Win* 70-75; Chapl Eliz Coll Guernsey 72-75; R Tadley St Pet *Win* 75-83; V Bournemouth St Luke 83-91; R Guernsey St Marguerite de la Foret 91-96; rtd 96. *56 The Causeway, Petersfield, Hants GU31 4JS*

CANN, Christopher James. b 64. St Andr Univ BA MA. St Steph Ho Ox. **d** 91 **p** 92. C Newport St Julian *Mon* 91-93; Chapl Smallwood Manor Sch Uttoxeter from 93. *Smallwood Manor School, Uttoxeter, Staffs ST14 8NS* Tel (01889) 562083

CANN, Stanley George. b 16. St Boniface Warminster 40 Linc Th Coll. **d** 43 **p** 44. C Cov St Alb *Cov* 43-45; Tanganyika 45-62; Area Sec UMCA/USPG 63-66; V Sidley *Chich* 66-84; P-in-c 84; RD Battle and Bexhill 77-84 and 85-86; rtd 84; Perm to Offic *Chich* from 86. *45 First Avenue, Bexhill-on-Sea, E Sussex TN40 2PL* Tel (01424) 211867

CANNAM, Martin Stafford John. b 68. Jes Coll Ox BA90 MA95. Wycliffe Hall Ox 93. **d** 96 **p** 97. C Childwall All SS *Liv* from 96. *80 Green Lane North, Childwall, Liverpool L16 8NL* Tel 0151-737 2214

CANNER, Canon Peter George. b 24. St Chad's Coll Dur BA49 DipTh51 MA55. **d** 51 **p** 52. C Stoke *Cov* 51-53; S Africa 53-63; V Tynemouth Ch Ch *Newc* 63-77; V Ponteland 77-89; Hon Can Newc Cathl 80-89; rtd 89. *The Rigg, 4 Back Croft, Rothbury, Morpeth, Northd NE65 7YB* Tel (01669) 21319

CANNING, Arthur Brian. b 12. St Jo Coll Dur BA37 MA40. **d** 37 **p** 38. C Darlington St Cuth *Dur* 37-42; V Sellack and King's Caple *Heref* 42-50; V Lugwardine w Bartestree 50-66; Bp's Dom Chapl 54-65; V New Romney w Hope and St Mary's Bay etc *Cant* 66-71; V Boughton Monchelsea 71-79; rtd 79; Perm to Offic *Heref* 81-96. *Harp Cottage, Old Radnor, Presteigne LD8 2RH* Tel (01544) 350212

CANNING, Arthur James. b 45. St Jo Coll Dur BA66 Linacre Coll Ox BA70 MA74 Lambeth STh90. Ripon Hall Ox 67. **d** 71 **p** 72. C Coleshill *Birm* 71-74; C Frome St Jo *B & W* 75-76; V Frizington and Arlecdon *Carl* 76-80; P-in-c Foleshill St Paul *Cov* 80-81; V from 81. *St Paul's Vicarage, 13 St Paul's Road, Coventry CV6 5DE* Tel (01203) 688283

CANNING, Graham Gordon Blakeman. b 33. S'wark Ord Course 73. **d** 76 **p** 77. NSM Mill Hill Jo Keble Ch *Lon* 76-78; TV Dorchester *Ox* 78-85; V Shipton-under-Wychwood w Milton-under-Wychwood from 85; RD Chipping Norton from 95. *The Vicarage, Shipton-under-Wychwood, Chipping Norton, Oxon OX7 6BP* Tel (01993) 830257

CANNING, John Graham. b 21. Edin Th Coll 47. **d** 49 **p** 50. C Penton Street St Silas w All SS *Lon* 49-54; C Poplar 54-55; N Rhodesia 55-62; V Hammersmith St Jo *Lon* 62-90; rtd 90; Perm to Offic *B & W* from 90. *11 Circus Field Road, Glastonbury, Somerset BA6 9PE* Tel (01458) 833708

CANNING, Peter Christopher. b 52. Birm Poly DipSocWork78 CQSW. St Jo Coll Nottm 87. **d** 89 **p** 90. C Cov St Mary *Cov* 89-93; V Hartshill 93-96; rtd 96. *11 Thackeray Close, Galley Common, Nuneaton, Warks CV10 9RT* Tel (01203) 398828

CANNON, Alan George. b 35. FRSA MBIM Lon Univ BA57 MA63 PhD71 AKC. Sarum & Wells Th Coll 76. **d** 80 **p** 81. Hon C Whipton *Ex* 80-89; Perm to Offic from 89. *6 Devonshire Place, Exeter EX4 6JA* Tel (01392) 55944

CANNON, Elizabeth Mary (Liz). b 50. EAMTC 94. **d** 97. NSM New Catton Ch Ch *Nor* from 97. *88 Colney Lane, Cringleford, Norwich NR4 7RG* Tel (01603) 506445

CANNON, Mark Harrison. b 60. Keble Coll Ox BA82. Cranmer Hall Dur 83. **d** 85 **p** 86. C Skipton Ch Ch *Bradf* 85-88; Dioc Youth Officer 88-92; C Baildon 88-92; P-in-c Church Coniston *Carl* from 92; P-in-c Torver from 92. *St Andrew's Vicarage, Yewdale Road, Coniston, Cumbria LA21 8DB* Tel (015394) 41262

CANNON, Tony Arthur. b 57. Oak Hill Th Coll 94. **d** 96 **p** 97. C Church Stretton *Heref* from 96. *The Old School House, 23 Church Street, Church Stretton, Shropshire SY6 6DQ* Tel (01694) 723215

CANSDALE, George Graham. b 38. Mert Coll Ox BA60 MA64 DipEd61. Clifton Th Coll 62. **d** 64 **p** 65. C Heatherlands St Jo *Sarum* 64-67; Kenya 68-76; P-in-c Clapham *St Alb* 76-80; V 80-89; Bedford Sch 89-93; Lic to Offic *St Alb* from 93. *40 Bridle Drive, Clapham, Bedford MK41 6BE* Tel (01234) 328184

CANSDALE, Simon James Lee. b 68. Keble Coll Ox BA90. Wycliffe Hall Ox 93. **d** 95 **p** 96. C Bletchley *Ox* from 95. *65 Bushey Close, Bletchley, Milton Keynes MK3 6PX* Tel (01908) 643902

CANT, Christopher Somerset Travers. b 51. Keble Coll Ox BA72 MA76 Ex Univ PGCE77. All Nations Chr Coll 80 Wycliffe Hall Ox 93. **d** 87 **p** 90. Pakistan 87-92; Lic to Offic *Cov* 92-93; Warden St Clem Family Cen Ox 93-95; C Gt Ilford St Andr *Chelmsf* from 95. *49 St Andrew's Road, Ilford, Essex IG1 3PE* Tel 0181-554 7423

CANT, David Edward. b 49. Sheff Univ LLB70. Oak Hill Th Coll DipTh89. **d** 89 **p** 90. C Newburn *Newc* 89-92; C N Shields 92-93; TV from 93; Chapl Tynemouth Coll from 94. *The Vicarage, 51 Drummond Terrace, North Shields, Tyne & Wear NE30 2AW* Tel 0191-258 3083

CANTERBURY, Archbishop of. *See* CAREY, The Most Revd and Rt Hon George Leonard

CANTERBURY, Archdeacon of. *See* PRITCHARD, The Ven John Lawrence

CANTERBURY, Dean of. *See* SIMPSON, The Very Revd John Arthur

CANTI, Mrs Christine. b 24. St Alb Minl Tr Scheme 82. **dss** 85 **d** 87 **p** 94. Radlett *St Alb* 85-86; Hon C Pitminster w Corfe *B & W* 87-90; Perm to Offic from 90. *Brook Farm House, Corfe, Taunton, Somerset TA3 7BU* Tel (01823) 421623

CANTRELL, David Grindon. b 59. Bris Univ BSc80 Nottm Univ PhD83 Pemb Coll Cam BA88. Ridley Hall Cam 86. **d** 89 **p** 90. C Low Harrogate St Mary *Ripon* 89-90; C Horsforth 90-94; Chapl Nottm Trent Univ *S'well* from 94. *2 College Drive, Clifton, Nottingham NG11 8NS* Tel 0115-921 4560

CAPE TOWN, Archbishop of. *See* NDUNGANE, The Most Revd Winston Hugh Njongonkulu

CAPE TOWN, Dean of. *See* SMITH, The Very Revd Rowan Quentin

CAPEL-EDWARDS, Dr Maureen. b 36. Southn Univ BSc60 Reading Univ PhD69. St Alb Minl Tr Scheme 84. **d** 87 **p** 94. NSM Ware St Mary *St Alb* 87-90; Chapl Ware Coll 87-90; NSM Hertford All SS 90-94; NSM Aspenden and Layston w Buntingford 94-95; NSM Aspenden, Buntingford and Westmill from 95. *5 Pearman Drive, Dane End, Ware, Herts SG12 0LW* Tel (01920) 438365

CAPENER, Herbert Francis. b 30. Jes Coll Ox BA53 MA58. Cuddesdon Coll 53. **d** 55 **p** 56. C Highgate St Aug *Lon* 55-60; C Ashford *Cant* 60-63; V Shirley St Geo 63-70; V Folkestone St Pet 70-89; rtd 90; Perm to Offic *Cant* from 89. *1 Baldric Road, Folkestone, Kent CT20 2NR* Tel (01303) 254579

CAPERON, John Philip. b 44. Bris Univ BA66 Open Univ MPhil80 Ox Univ MSc83. Ox NSM Course 80. **d** 83 **p** 84. NSM Hook Norton w Gt Rollright, Swerford etc *Ox* 83-86; NSM Knaresborough *Ripon* 86-93; Dep Hd St Aid Sch Harrogate 86-93; Chapl Bennett Memorial Sch Tunbridge Wells from 93. *Bennett Memorial School, Culverden Down, Tunbridge Wells, Kent TN4 9SH* Tel (01892) 521595 Fax 514424

CAPES, Arthur Geoffrey. b 33. Bps' Coll Cheshunt 58. **d** 61 **p** 62. C Seacroft *Ripon* 61-66; Guyana 66-80; V Claremont H Angels

Man 80-85; V Blyton w Pilham *Linc* 85-90; V E Stockwith 86-90; V Laughton w Wildsworth 86-90; R Broad Town, Clyffe Pypard and Tockenham *Sarum* 90-94; R Broad Town, Clyffe Pypard, Hilmarton etc from 94. *The Rectory, Wood Lane, Clyffe Pypard, Swindon SN4 7PY* Tel (01793) 731623

CAPES, Dennis Robert. b 34. Linc Th Coll 65 Handsworth Coll Birm DipTh58. **d** 64 **p** 65. In Meth Ch (Sarawak) 59-63; C Lt Coates *Linc* 64-66; Malaysia 66-69; V Gosberton Clough *Linc* 69-71; V Kirton in Holland 71-80; Area Sec (Dios Cov, Heref and Worc) USPG 80-87; Chapl Copenhagen w Aarhus *Eur* 87-93; TV Liv Our Lady and St Nic w St Anne *Liv* from 93. *29 Moel Famau View, Priory Park, Riverside Drive, Liverpool L17 5AX* Tel 0151-727 0576 or 236 5287

CAPIE, Fergus Bernard. b 47. Auckland Univ BA68 MA71. Wycliffe Hall Ox BA77. **d** 77 **p** 78. C Ox St Mich w St Martin and All SS *Ox* 77-80; Chapl Summer Fields Sch Ox 80-91; Hon C Wolvercote w Summertown *Ox* 87-91; Perm to Offic *St E* 91; TV E Ham w Upton Park St Alb *Chelmsf* 91-95; P-in-c Brondesbury St Anne w Kilburn H Trin *Lon* from 95; Chapl NW Lon Coll from 95. *49 Keslake Road, London NW6 6DH* Tel 0181-968 3898

CAPITANCHIK, Mrs Sophie Rebecca. b 72. Leeds Univ BA93. Wycliffe Hall Ox MPhil94. **d** 97. C Shipley St Pet *Bradf* from 97. *43 George Street, Shipley, W Yorkshire BD18 4PT* Tel (01274) 583457 E-mail cscapi@globalnet.co.uk

CAPLE, Stephen Malcolm. b 55. Chich Th Coll 86. **d** 88 **p** 89. C Newington St Mary *S'wark* 88-92; V Eltham St Sav from 92. *St Saviour's Vicarage, 98 Middle Park Avenue, London SE9 5JH* Tel 0181-850 6829

CAPON, Canon Anthony Charles. b 26. Trin Coll Cam BA51 MA55. Wycliffe Coll Toronto BD65 DD82 Oak Hill Th Coll 51. **d** 53 **p** 54. C Portman Square St Paul *Lon* 53-56; Canada from 56; Hon Can Montreal from 78; Prin Montreal Dioc Th Coll 78-91. *5 Loradean Crescent, Kingston, Ontario, Canada, K7K 6X9*

CAPON, Canon Martin Gedge. b 09. Magd Coll Cam BA31 MA36. Wycliffe Hall Ox 34. **d** 35 **p** 36. C St Leonard *Ex* 35-36; Kenya 36-68; Can Mombasa 49-64; C Sparkhill St Jo *Birm* 68-70; V Breage w Germoe *Truro* 70-74; rtd 74; Perm to Offic *Ex* from 74. *Flat 2, 26 Alexandra Terrace, Exmouth, Devon EX8 1BB* Tel (01395) 265128

✠**CAPPER, The Rt Revd Edmund Michael Hubert.** b 08. OBE61. Dur Univ LTh32. St Aug Coll Cant 28. **d** 32 **p** 33 **c** 67. C Strood St Mary *Roch* 32-36; Tanganyika 36-62; Adn Lindi 48-54; Adn Dar-es-Salaam 54-57; Provost 57-62; Chapl Palma *Eur* 62-67; Bp St Helena 67-73; Asst Bp Eur from 73; Chapl Malaga 73-76; Asst Bp S'wark from 81; rtd 86. *Flat 8, Morden College, London SE3 0PW* Tel 0181-858 9169

CAPPER, Mrs Elizabeth Margaret. b 31. St Chris Coll Blackheath 52. **dss** 79 **d** 87 **p** 94. The Dorothy Kerin Trust Burrswood 79-91; Whitstable *Cant* 80-96; Hon Par Dn 87-94; Hon C 94-96; rtd 91. *11 North Road, Loughor, Swansea SA4 6QE* Tel (01792) 892834

CAPPER, Canon James Frank. b 18. Qu Coll Ox BA40 MA44. Westcott Ho Cam 48. **d** 48 **p** 49. C Selly Oak St Mary *Birm* 48-52; C Keighley *Bradf* 52-54; P-in-c Sutton Coldfield St Columba *Birm* 54-64; V Erdington St Barn 64-75; V Coleshill 75-82; V Maxstoke 75-82; RD Coleshill 77-82; Hon Can Birm Cathl 80-82; Perm to Offic *Ex* from 82; rtd 83. *Martlets, Harpford, Sidmouth, Devon EX10 0NQ* Tel (01395) 68198

CAPPER, John Raymond. b 29. Liv Univ BA53. Coll of Resurr Mirfield 53. **d** 55 **p** 56. C Birm St Aid Small Heath *Birm* 55-58; C Widley w Wymering *Portsm* 60-63; C Portsea St Sav 63-68; V Gosport H Trin from 68. *Holy Trinity Vicarage, Trinity Green, Gosport, Hants PO12 1HL* Tel (01705) 580173

CAPPER, Canon Richard. b 49. Leeds Univ BSc70 Fitzw Coll Cam BA72 MA79. Westcott Ho Cam 70. **d** 73 **p** 74. C Wavertree H Trin *Liv* 73-76; P-in-c Ince St Mary 76-79; V 79-83; V Gt Crosby St Faith 83-97; AD Bootle 89-97; Can Res Wakef Cathl *Wakef* from 97. *3 Cathedral Close, Wakefield, W Yorkshire WF1 2DP* Tel (01924) 210007

CAPPER, Robert Melville (Bob). b 52. Chu Coll Cam BA74 MA. Wycliffe Hall Ox 74. **d** 77 **p** 78. C Maindee *Mon* 77-81; Chapl Univ of Wales (Abth) *St D* 81-87; TV Aberystwyth 81-87; V Malpas *Mon* from 87. *The Vicarage, Malpas Road, Newport NP9 6GQ* Tel (01633) 852047

CAPPER, William Alan. QUB BTh. **d** 88 **p** 89. C Dundonald *D & D* 88-91; C Lisburn Ch Ch *Conn* 91-94; I Tamlaght O'Crilly Upper w Lower *D & R* 94-96. *Address temp unknown*

CAPRON, David Cooper. b 45. Open Univ BA80. Sarum & Wells Th Coll 71. **d** 75 **p** 76. C Cov St Mary *Cov* 75-79; V Shottery St Andr 79-86; TV Stratford-on-Avon w Bishopton 79-86; V Shottery St Andr 86; V Newton Aycliffe *Dur* 86-89; TR 89-90; P-in-c Alcester and Arrow w Oversley and Weethley *Cov* 90-95; R from 95; Chapl Warks Fire and Rescue Service from 93. *St Nicholas' Rectory, Old Rectory Garden, Alcester, Warks B49 5DB* Tel (01789) 764261 Fax as telephone Mobile (0585) 308414

CAPRON, Ronald Beresford. b 35. Clifton Th Coll. **d** 62 **p** 63. Canada 62-65; C Evington *Leic* 65-67; R Gaddesby w S Croxton 67-71; R Beeby 67-71; Chapl RAF 71-83; rtd 95. *12 Mountbatten Road, Oakham, Leics LE15 6LS* Tel (01572) 756219

CAPSTICK, John Nowell. b 30. AKC54. **d** 55 **p** 56. C Skipton Ch Ch *Bradf* 55-57; C Buxton *Derby* 57-61; V Codnor and Loscoe 61-63; C-in-c Rawthorpe CD *Wakef* 63-64; V Rawthorpe 64-70; V Netherthong 70-89; TV Upper Holme Valley 89-95; rtd 95. *8 Town End Avenue, Holmfirth, Huddersfield HD7 1YW* Tel (01484) 688708

CAPSTICK, William Richard Dacre. b 32. Pemb Coll Ox. Chich Th Coll 61. **d** 64 **p** 65. C Hunslet St Mary and Stourton St Andr *Ripon* 64-67; C Knaresborough H Trin 67-71; V Stratfield Mortimer *Ox* 71-76; P-in-c St Marylebone Ch Ch w St Paul *Lon* 76-78; TV St Marylebone Ch Ch 78-79; TR Newbury *Ox* 79-89; TV Brighton St Pet and St Nic w Chpl Royal *Chich* from 89. *28 Bloomsbury Street, Brighton BN2 1HQ* Tel (01273) 681171

CARBERRY, Leon Carter. b 54. Pennsylvania Univ BSc76. St Steph Ho Ox 81. **d** 84 **p** 85. C Peterlee *Dur* 84-87; C Newton Aycliffe 87-89; V Choral York Minster *York* 89-94; Chapl St Pet Sch York 94-95; V Fylingdales and Hawsker cum Stainsacre from 95. *The Vicarage, Mount Pleasant South, Robin Hood's Bay, Whitby, N Yorkshire YO22 4RQ* Tel (01947) 880232

CARBY, Stuart Graeme. b 51. CBiol77 MIBiol77 LRSC78 Man Univ BSc73 Leeds Univ PGCE74. St Jo Coll Nottm DTS92. **d** 92 **p** 93. C Magor w Redwick and Undy *Mon* 92-96; TV Cyncoed from 96. *100 Hill Rise, Cardiff CF2 6UL* Tel (01222) 733915

CARD, Terence Leslie. b 37. K Coll Lon BD68 AKC68 Heythrop Coll Lon MTh84. **d** 69 **p** 70. C Thundersley *Chelmsf* 69-72; Lic to Offic *Bradf* 72-75; V Chingford St Anne *Chelmsf* 75-81; RD Waltham Forest 78-81; R Springfield All SS 81-83; C Becontree St Jo 85-87; rtd 87. *11 Harvey Goodwin Gardens, Cambridge CB4 3EZ* Tel (01223) 367715

CARD, Thomas Ian. b 36. RD76. Master Mariner 61. Portsm Dioc Tr Course 88. **d** 89. NSM Binstead *Portsm* 89-95; Miss to Seamen from 89; NSM Swanmore St Mich w Havenstreet *Portsm* 89-92; NSM Havenstreet St Pet 92-95; NSM Ryde All SS from 95. *Dolphins, 49 Mayfield Road, Ryde, Isle of Wight PO33 3PR* Tel (01983) 564749

CARDALE, Charles Anthony. b 21. St D Coll Lamp BA47 Lich Th Coll 55. **d** 56 **p** 57. C Honicknowle CD *Ex* 56-58; C Bideford 58-60; R Wembworthy w Eggesford 60-69; V Brushford 63-69; V Staverton w Landscove 69-87; R Broadhempston, Woodland, Staverton etc 88-89; Perm to Offic from 89; rtd 90. *Keyberry, 13 Woodland Close, Staverton, Totnes, Devon TQ9 6PQ* Tel (0180426) 277

CARDALE, Edward Charles. b 50. CCC Ox BA72. Cuddesdon Coll 72 Union Th Sem (NY) STM74. **d** 74 **p** 75. C E Dulwich St Jo *S'wark* 74-77; USA 77-80; V Ponders End St Matt *Lon* 80-84; V Lytchett Minster *Sarum* from 84. *The Vicarage, New Road, Lytchett Minster, Poole, Dorset BH16 6JQ* Tel (01202) 622253

CARDELL-OLIVER, John Anthony. b 43. Em Coll Cam BA67 MA72 Univ of W Aus BEd75 MEd85. Westcott Ho Cam 86. **d** 86 **p** 88. Australia 86-88; Perm to Offic *Ely* 88-89; C Stansted Mountfitchet *Chelmsf* 89-92; R Boxted w Langham from 92. *The Rectory, Wick Road, Langham, Colchester CO4 5PG* Tel (01206) 230666

CARDEN, Edwin William Eddie. b 54. Cranmer Hall Dur 85. **d** 87 **p** 88. C Thundersley *Chelmsf* 87-91; CUF 91-93; NSM Poplar *Lon* 91-93; Chapl Wandsworth HA Mental Health Unit from 93; Chapl Springfield Hosp Lon from 93. *The Chaplaincy, Springfield Hospital, 61 Glenburnie Road, London SW17 7DJ* Tel 0181-672 9911

CARDEN, John Brumfitt. b 24. Lon Coll of Div 48. **d** 52 **p** 53. Pakistan 52-55 and 57-60 and 65-69; C Leeds Halton St Wilfrid *Ripon* 56-57; Lit Sec CMS 60-65; Asia Sec CMS 70-76; Hon C Croydon St Sav *Cant* 75-76; C-in-c Bath St Steph *B & W* 76-82; V 82-84; CMS 84-89; Jerusalem 84-87; Exec Asst WCC Geneva 87-89; rtd 89; Miss Partner CMS from 89. *81 The Village, Haxby, York YO3 3JE* Tel (01904) 750035

CARDIGAN, Archdeacon of. *See* JONES, The Ven Benjamin Jenkin Hywel

CARDINAL, Ian Ralph. b 57. Qu Coll Birm 81. **d** 84 **p** 85. C Whitkirk *Ripon* 84-87; C Knaresborough 87-89; P-in-c Wilsford *Linc* 89; P-in-c Ancaster 89; R Ancaster Wilsford Gp 89-94; P-in-c Wigginton *Lich* from 94; Warden of Readers from 96. *The Vicarage, Wigginton, Tamworth, Staffs B79 9DN* Tel (01827) 64537

CARDWELL, Edward Anthony Colin. b 42. Trin Coll Cam BA63 MA68. St Jo Coll Nottm 73. **d** 75 **p** 76. C Stapenhill w Cauldwell *Derby* 75-78; C Bramcote *S'well* 78-81; V S'well H Trin 81-92; R Eastwood from 92. *The Rectory, 5A Woodland Way, Eastwood, Nottingham NG16 3BU* Tel (01773) 712395

CARDWELL, Joseph Robin. b 47. Qu Coll Cam BA68 MA77. Trin Coll Bris 73. **d** 76 **p** 77. C Bromley Ch Ch *Roch* 76-79; C Shirley *Win* 79-82; V Somborne w Ashley 82-90; V Derry Hill *Sarum* 90-94; V Derry Hill w Bremhill and Foxham from 94; Community Affairs Chapl from 90. *The Vicarage, Derry Hill, Calne, Wilts SN11 9NN* Tel (01249) 812172

CARE, Canon Charles Richard. b 21. Univ of Wales (Lamp) BA42. St Mich Coll Llan 42. **d** 44 **p** 45. C Grangetown *Llan* 44-57; R St Brides Minor 57-88; RD Bridgend 75-88; Can Llan Cathl 83-88; Prec 87-88; rtd 88; Perm to Offic *Llan* from 88.

31 Laburnum Drive, Danygraig, Porthcawl CF36 5UA Tel (01656) 715446

CAREW, Bryan Andrew. b 38. AIB63 ACIB87. St D Coll Lamp DipTh69. **d** 67 **p** 68. C Pembroke Dock *St D* 67-70; CF 70-74; P-in-c Gt and Lt Henny w Middleton *Chelmsf* 74-76; P-in-c Wickham St Paul w Twinstead 75-76; R Gt and Lt Henny w Middleton, Wickham St Paul etc from 76. *The Rectory, Great Henny, Sudbury, Suffolk CO10 7NW* Tel (01787) 269336

CAREY, Alan Lawrence. b 29. K Coll Lon AKC53. **d** 54 **p** 55. C Radford *Cov* 54-57; C Burnham *Ox* 57-65; C-in-c Cippenham CD 65-77; rtd 94. *12 Ormsby Street, Reading RG1 7YR* Tel 0118-961 2309

CAREY, Charles John. b 29. K Coll Lon BD53 AKC53. St Aug Coll Cant 71. **d** 72 **p** 73. C Spring Park *Cant* 72-74; C Ifield *Chich* 74-78; C Burgess Hill St Jo 78-80; Chapl Rush Green Hosp Romford 80-94; Chapl Oldchurch Hosp Romford 80-94; rtd 94. *Address excluded by request*

CAREY, Christopher Lawrence John (Chris). b 38. St Andr Univ BSc61 Lon Univ BD64. Clifton Th Coll 61. **d** 64 **p** 65. C Battersea Park St Sav *S'wark* 64-67; Kenya 68-79; Overseas Regional Sec for E Africa CMS from 79; Perm to Offic *Roch* from 81. *5 Downs Avenue, Chislehurst, Kent BR7 6HG* Tel 0181-325 1943 or 0171-928 8681 Fax 0171-401 3215

✠**CAREY, The Most Revd and Rt Hon George Leonard.** b 35. PC91. Lon Univ BD62 MTh65 PhD71 Dur Univ Hon DD93 Open Univ Hon DD95 FKC93 FRSA91. ALCD61. **d** 62 **p** 63 **c** 87. C Islington St Mary *Lon* 62-66; Lect Oak Hill Th Coll 66-70; Lect St Jo Coll Nottm 70-75; V Dur St Nic *Dur* 75-82; Chapl HM Rem Cen Low Newton 77-81; Prin Trin Coll Bris 82-87; Hon Can Bris Cathl *Bris* 84-87; Bp B & W 87-91; Abp Cant from 91. *Lambeth Palace, London SE1 7JU, or The Old Palace, Canterbury, Kent CT1 2EE* Tel 0171-928 8282 or (01227) 459401 Fax 0171-261 9836

CAREY, Graham Charles. b 33. Kelham Th Coll 53. **d** 57 **p** 58. C Millfield St Mary *Dur* 57-66; V Northfield St Mich *Sheff* 66-76; P-in-c Jarrow St Mark *Dur* 76-77; TV Jarrow 77-84; P-in-c Southwick St Pet *Chich* from 84; Miss to Seamen from 84. *St Peter's Vicarage, Gardner Road, Southwick, Brighton BN41 1PN* Tel (01273) 592474

CAREY, The Very Revd James Maurice George. b 26. TCD BA49 MA52 BD52. CITC 51. **d** 52 **p** 53. C Larne and Inver *Conn* 52-55; USA 55-56; C Dublin St Ann *D & G* 57-58; Hon Clerical V Ch Ch Cathl Dublin 58; Dean of Res QUB 58-64; I Dublin St Bart *D & G* 64-71; Dean Cork *C, C & R* 71-93; I Cork St Nic w H Trin 71-75; I Cork St Fin Barre's Cathl 71-87; I Cork St Fin Barre's Union 87-93; Radio Officer (Cork) 90-93; P-in-c Dublin Sandymount *D & G* from 93. *91 Clonkeen Road, Blackrock, Co Dublin, Irish Republic* Tel Dublin (1) 289 5121

CAREY, Mark Jonathan. b 65. St Jo Coll Nottm BTh94. **d** 94 **p** 95. C S Ossett *Wakef* from 94. *40 Broomcroft Road, Ossett, W Yorkshire WF5 8LH* Tel (01924) 263320

CAREY, Canon Ronald Clive Adrian. b 21. K Coll Cam BA46 MA48. Chich Th Coll 47. **d** 48 **p** 49. C Harborne St Pet *Birm* 48-50; Bp's Dom Chapl *Chich* 50-52; C Keighley *Bradf* 52-55; V Illingworth *Wakef* 55-59; Perm to Offic *S'wark* 59-68; Asst in Relig Broadcasting BBC 59-68; V Claygate *Guildf* 68-78; RD Emly 72-77; Hon Can Guildf Cathl 78-86; R Guildf H Trin w St Mary 78-86; RD Guildf 84-86; rtd 86; Perm to Offic *Roch* from 86. *4 Chart View, Kemsing, Sevenoaks, Kent TN15 6PP* Tel (01732) 762629

CAREY, Mrs Wendy Marion. b 45. Bris Univ BA66 Lon Inst of Educn CertEd67. WMMTC 90. **d** 93 **p** 94. NSM Milton Keynes *Ox* 93-96; Sub Chapl HM Pris Woodhill 93-96; Chapl HM Pris Bullingdon from 96. *HM Prison Bullingdon, PO Box 50, Bicester, Oxon OX6 0PR* Tel (01869) 322111

CARHART, John Richards. b 29. Bris Univ BA50 Salford Univ MSc77. St Deiniol's Hawarden 63. **d** 65 **p** 66. C Ches St Oswald w Lt St Jo *Ches* 65-72; Lect Ches Coll of HE 65-72; Prin Lect from 72; Dean Academic Studies from 88; C Ches 72; Lic to Offic 73-85; Hon C Ches St Mary from 85. *29 Abbot's Grange, Chester CH2 1AJ* Tel (01244) 380923

CARLESS, Canon Frank. b 22. Lon Univ BD56. St Aid Birkenhead 53. **d** 56 **p** 57. C Normanton *Wakef* 56-59; V Rashcliffe 59-64; V Warley 64-87; RD Halifax 82-86; Hon Can Wakef Cathl 86-87; rtd 87; Perm to Offic *Wakef* from 87. *130 Savile Park Road, Halifax, W Yorkshire HX1 2EX* Tel (01422) 348379

CARLILL, Adam Jonathan. b 66. Keble Coll Ox BA88. Linc Th Coll 88. **d** 90 **p** 91. C Romford St Edw *Chelmsf* 90-94; C Uckfield *Chich* from 94. *School House, Belmont Road, Uckfield, E Sussex TN22 1BP* Tel (01825) 761373

CARLILL, Richard Edward. b 38. Westcott Ho Cam 77. **d** 79 **p** 80. C Prittlewell *Chelmsf* 79-83; TV Saffron Walden w Wendens Ambo and Littlebury 83-89; V Langtoft w Foxholes, Butterwick, Cottam etc *York* 89-94; V Gt and Lt Driffield from 94. *The Vicarage, Downe Street, Driffield, N Humberside YO25 7DX* Tel (01377) 253394

CARLIN, William Patrick Bruce. b 53. St Steph Ho Ox 75. **d** 78 **p** 79. C Penistone *Wakef* 78-81; C Barnsley St Mary 81-83; V Stockton St Chad *Dur* 83-93; V Hedworth from 93. *St Nicholas Vicarage, Hedworth Lane, Boldon Colliery, Tyne & Wear NE35 9JA* Tel 0191-536 7552

CARLING, Mrs Bronwen Noel. b 43. SRN65 SCM73. Linc Th Coll 89. **d** 91 **p** 94. C Blakeney w Cley, Wiveton, Glandford etc *Nor* 91-94; C Trunch 94-96; TV from 96. *The Rectory, Clipped Hedge Lane, Southrepps, Norwich NR11 8NS* Tel (01263) 833404

CARLISLE, Christopher John. b 39. Sheff Univ BEng62. NW Ord Course 72. **d** 75 **p** 76. C Bury St Paul *Man* 75-80; C Walkden Moor 80-82; V Lytham St Jo *Blackb* from 82. *The Vicarage, East Beach, Lytham, Lytham St Annes, Lancs FY8 5EX* Tel (01253) 734396

CARLISLE, John Patrick. b 66. St Andr Univ MTh89 Hughes Hall Cam PGCE90. St Steph Ho Ox 93. **d** 95 **p** 96. C Hendon St Alphage *Lon* from 95. *18 Montrose Avenue, Edgware, Middx HA8 0DW* Tel 0181-952 1635

CARLISLE, Archdeacon of. *See* TURNBULL, The Ven David Charles

CARLISLE, Bishop of. *See* HARLAND, The Rt Revd Ian

CARLISLE, Dean of. *See* STAPLETON, The Very Revd Henry Edward Champneys

CARLOS, Francis John. b 29. Jes Coll Cam BA54 MA57. Wells Th Coll 52. **d** 55 **p** 56. C Canning Town St Matthias *Chelmsf* 55-57; C-in-c Thundersley CD *St E* 57-64; V New Thundersley *Chelmsf* 64-65; R Wentnor and Ratlinghope w Myndtown and Norbury *Heref* 65-89; P-in-c More w Lydham 82-89; P-in-c Snead 85-89; R Wentnor w Ratlinghope, Myndtown, Norbury etc 89-94; rtd 94; Perm to Offic *Heref* from 94. *16 Springfield Park, Clee Hill, Ludlow, Shropshire SY8 3QY* Tel (01584) 891253

CARLSSON, Miss Siw. b 43. **d** 92 **p** 94. Par Dn Barnes St Mary *S'wark* 92-93; C Mitcham SS Pet and Paul from 93. *32 Lewis Road, Mitcham, Surrey CR4 3DE* Tel 0181-646 2268

CARLTON, Roger John. b 51. **d** 80 **p** 81. NSM Downend *Bris* 80-83; NSM Heavitree w Ex St Paul *Ex* 83-87; Chapl St Marg Sch Ex 83-87; Chapl Ex Sch 83-87; TV Bickleigh (Plymouth) *Ex* 87-91; TR 91-93; TR Bickleigh (Roborough) and Shaugh Prior from 94; RD Ivybridge from 93. *The Vicarage, 2 Blackeven Close, Roborough, Plymouth PL6 7AX* Tel (01752) 702119

CARLYON (née ENGLAND), Mrs Jessie Marguerite Tarie. b 44. Westf Coll Lon BA66 K Coll Lon PGCE67. WMMTC 92. **d** 95 **p** 97. C Pontypool *Mon* from 95. *St Matthew's House, Victoria Road, Pontypool NP4 5JU* Tel (01495) 758676

CARMARTHEN, Archdeacon of. *See* JOHN, The Ven Islwyn David

CARMICHAEL, Elizabeth Dorothea Harriet (Liz). b 46. MBE95. LMH Ox MA73 BM73 BCh73 Worc Coll Ox BA83 Ox Univ DPhil91. **d** 91 **p** 92. S Africa 91-96; Chapl and Tutor St Jo Coll Ox from 96. *St John's College, Oxford OX1 3JP* Tel (01865) 277300 Fax 277435

CARMICHAEL, Peter Iain. b 28. Chich Th Coll 75. **d** 75 **p** 76. C Rye w Rye Harbour and Playden *Chich* 75-79; C Rye, Rye Harbour and Playden and Iden 79-80; R Earnley and E Wittering 80-94; rtd 94; Perm to Offic *Chich* from 94. *20 East Street, Selsey, Chichester, W Sussex PO20 0BJ* Tel (01243) 606197

CARMODY, Preb Dermot Patrick Roy. b 41. CITC 77. **d** 77 **p** 78. C Dublin Zion Ch *D & G* 77-79; I Dunganstown w Redcross 79-84; TV Dublin Ch Ch Cathl Gp 84-93; Can Ch Ch Cathl Dublin 84-92; Preb Ch Ch Cathl Dublin 92-93; I Mullingar, Portnashangan, Moyliscar, Kilbixy etc *M & K* from 93; Dir of Ords (Meath) from 97. *All Saints' Rectory, Mullingar, Co Westmeath, Irish Republic* Tel Mullingar (44) 48376 Fax as telephone

CARMYLLIE, Robert Jonathan. b 63. Cov Poly BSc85. St Jo Coll Dur 85. **d** 88 **p** 89. C Horwich *Man* 88-92; P-in-c Edgeside from 92. *St Anne's Vicarage, Ashworth Road, Edgeside, Waterfoot, Rossendale, Lancs BB4 9JE* Tel (01706) 221889

CARNE, Canon Brian George. b 29. FSA Liv Univ BCom50. Qu Coll Birm 53. **d** 55 **p** 56. C Swindon St Aug *Bris* 55-58; C Bris St Andr w St Bart 58-60; R Lydiard Millicent w Lydiard Tregoz 60-68; V Bris St Andr Hartcliffe 68-74; V Almondsbury 74-91; RD Westbury and Severnside 80-86; Hon Can Bris Cathl 82-91; P-in-c Littleton on Severn w Elberton 83-91; P-in-c Olveston 83-91; rtd 91; Perm to Offic *Bris* from 92; Perm to Offic *Glouc* from 92. *Whitehouse Farm, English Bicknor, Coleford, Glos GL16 9PA* Tel (01594) 860200

CARNE, Norman David John. b 27. Roch Th Coll 59. **d** 62 **p** 63. C Roch St Justus *Roch* 62-66; C Strood St Mary 66-68; R Westcote Barton and Steeple Barton *Ox* 68-74; P-in-c Enstone and Heythrop 74-82; V 82-92; rtd 92; Perm to Offic *Leic* from 93. *45 Beckingthorpe Drive, Bottesford, Nottingham NG13 0DN* Tel (01949) 843890

CARNE-ROSS, Stewart Pattison. b 24. Wycliffe Hall Ox 58. **d** 59 **p** 60. C Brockley Hill St Sav *S'wark* 59-62; C Dulwich St Barn 62-64; V Champion Hill St Sav 64-70; P-in-c Stanton Lacy *Heref* 70-72; V 72-77; V Bromfield 70-77; R Culmington w Onibury 70-77; V Hambledon *Portsm* 77-79; Chapl HM Pris Kingston (Portsm) 79-90; C Portsea St Mary *Portsm* 86-90; rtd 90. *7 Hanover Court, Highbury Street, Portsmouth PO1 2BN* Tel (01705) 752698

CARNELL, Canon Geoffrey Gordon. b 18. St Jo Coll Cam BA40 MA44. Cuddesdon Coll 40. **d** 42 **p** 43. C Abington *Pet* 42-49; Chapl St Gabr Coll Camberwell 49-53; Lect 49-53; R Isham *Pet*

53-71; V Gt w Lt Harrowden 53-71; Dir of Ords 62-85; Can Pet Cathl 65-85; R Boughton 71-85; Chapl to The Queen 81-88; rtd 85; Perm to Offic *Pet* from 86. *52 Walsingham Avenue, Kettering, Northants NN15 5ER* Tel (01536) 511415

CARNELLEY, The Ven Desmond. b 29. Open Univ BA77 Leeds Univ CertEd Ex Univ CertRE. Ripon Hall Ox 59. **d** 60 **p** 61. C Aston cum Aughton *Sheff* 60-63; C-in-c Ecclesfield St Paul CD 63-67; V Balby w Hexthorpe 67-73; P-in-c Mosborough 73-74; V 74-85; RD Attercliffe 79-84; Adn Doncaster 85-94; Dioc Dir of Educn 91-94; rtd 94; Perm to Offic *Sheff* from 94; Perm to Offic *Derby* from 94. *7 Errwood Avenue, Buxton, Derbyshire SK17 9BD* Tel (01298) 71460

CARNELLEY, Ms Elizabeth Amy. b 64. St Aid Coll Dur BA85 Selw Coll Cam MPhil87. Ripon Coll Cuddesdon 88. **d** 90 **p** 94. Par Dn Sheff Sharrow *Sheff* 90-93; Par Dn Is of Dogs Ch Ch and St Jo w St Luke *Lon* 93-94; C 94-95; P-in-c Woolfold *Man* from 95. *St James's Vicarage, 280 Walshaw Road, Bury, Lancs BL8 1PY* Tel 0161-764 6217

CARNEY, David Anthony. b 42. Salford Univ BSc77. Linc Th Coll 77. **d** 79 **p** 80. C Wythenshawe St Martin *Man* 79-81; CF 81-84; Canada 84-91; P-in-c Whaplode *Linc* 91-97; V from 97; P-in-c Holbeach Fen 91-97; V from 97. *St Mary's Vicarage, Whaplode, Spalding, Lincs PE12 6TD* Tel (01406) 370318

CARNEY, Mrs Mary Patricia. b 42. Univ of Wales (Ban) BSc62 DipEd63. Wycliffe Hall Ox. **d** 90 **p** 94. Par Dn Carterton *Ox* 90-93; Par Dn Harwell w Chilton 93-94; C from 94. *31 Crafts End, Chilton, Didcot, Oxon OX11 0SA* Tel (01235) 832366

CARNEY, Richard Wayne. b 52. Lon Teachers Coll Ontario TCert73 Toronto Univ BA79. Trin Coll Toronto MDiv84. **d** 84 **p** 85. Canada 84-95; Bp's C Clonfert Gp of Par *L & K* from 95. *The Rectory, Banagher, Birr, Co Offaly, Irish Republic* Tel Birr (509) 51269 Fax as telephone

CARNLEY, Ronald Birch. b 18. Pemb Coll Ox BA47 MA47. Cuddesdon Coll 47. **d** 49 **p** 50. C Kidderminster St Mary *Worc* 49-52; C Halesowen 52-56; R Lydiard Millicent w Lydiard Tregoz *Bris* 56-59; V Matfield *Roch* 59-78; Perm to Offic *Chich* from 79; Perm to Offic *Roch* 79-93; rtd 83. *5 Cleeve Avenue, Hawkenbury, Tunbridge Wells, Kent TN2 4TY* Tel (01892) 530045

CARPENTER, Bruce Leonard Henry. b 32. Lon Univ BA54 St Chad's Coll Dur DipTh59. **d** 59 **p** 60. C Portsea N End St Mark *Portsm* 59-63; C Fareham SS Pet and Paul 63-67; V Locks Heath 67-74; TR Fareham H Trin 74-84; RD Alverstoke 71-76; Hon Can Portsm Cathl 79-84; V Richmond St Mary w St Matthias and St Jo *S'wark* 84-91; Chapl Ch Ch Sch Ashford Kent 91-93; P-in-c S Ashford Ch Ch *Cant* 94-97; Chapl Huggens' Coll Northfleet from 97. *The Chaplain's House, Huggens College, Northfleet, Kent DA11 9DL* Tel (01474) 352428

CARPENTER, David James. b 52. St Steph Ho Ox 74. **d** 76 **p** 77. C Newport St Julian *Mon* 76-77; C Pontypool 77-79; C Ebbw Vale 79-81; TV 81-85; V Pontnewynydd 85-88; V Bedwellty from 88; Chapl Aberbargoed Hosp from 88. *The Rectory, Bedwellty, Blackwood NP2 0BE* Tel (01443) 831078

CARPENTER, Canon Derek George Edwin. b 40. K Coll Lon BD62 AKC62. **d** 63 **p** 64. C Friern Barnet All SS *Lon* 63-66; C Chingford SS Pet and Paul *Chelmsf* 66-70; V Dartford St Alb *Roch* 70-79; R Crayford 79-90; RD Erith 82-90; R Beckenham St Geo from 90; Hon Can Roch Cathl from 97. *The Rectory, 14 The Knoll, Beckenham, Kent BR3 5JW* Tel 0181-650 0983

CARPENTER, Donald Arthur. b 35. Roch Th Coll 65. **d** 67 **p** 68. C Thornton Heath St Jude *Cant* 67-73; V Earby *Bradf* 73-78; V Skipton Ch Ch 78-88; V Baildon 88-91; P-in-c Perivale *Lon* 91-96; rtd 96. *9 Drew Gardens, Greenford, Middlesex UB6 7QF* Tel 0181-903 9697

CARPENTER, The Very Revd Dr Edward Frederick. b 10. K Coll Lon BA32 MA34 BD35 AKC35 PhD43. Lambeth DD79. **d** 35 **p** 36. C St Marylebone H Trin *Lon* 35-41; C Harrow St Mary 41-45; R Gt Stanmore 45-51; Can Westmr Abbey 51-74; Treas 59-74; Adn Westmr 63-74; Dean Westmr 74-85; rtd 85. *6 Selwyn Avenue, Richmond, Surrey TW9 2HA* Tel 0181-940 3896

CARPENTER, The Ven Frederick Charles. b 20. SS Coll Cam BA47 MA49 St Cath Soc Ox DipTh48 Ex Univ MPhil93. Wycliffe Hall Ox 47. **d** 49 **p** 50. C Woodford St Mary *Chelmsf* 49-51; Asst Chapl Sherborne Sch 51-58; Chapl 58-62; V Moseley St Mary *Birm* 62-68; Can Res Portsm Cathl *Portsm* 68-77; Dir RE 68-75; Adn Is of Wight 77-86; P-in-c Binstead 77-86; rtd 86; Perm to Offic *Portsm* from 86; Perm to Offic *Sarum* from 86; Chapl Godolphin Sch Salisbury from 89. *Gilston, Mount Pleasant, Stoford, Salisbury SP2 0PP* Tel (01722) 790335

CARPENTER, Gilbert Lant. b 10. Down Coll Cam BA34 MA38. Ely Th Coll 34. **d** 35 **p** 36. C Mansfield St Mark *S'well* 35-39; C E Finchley All SS *Lon* 39-41; V Tottenham St Phil 51-57; C Willesden St Andr 41-51; V 57-76; rtd 76. *2 Rushbury Court, Station Road, Hampton, Middx TW12 2DD* Tel 0181-941 1449

CARPENTER, Mrs Judith Margaret. b 47. Bris Univ BA68 CertEd69. Trin Coll Bris BA95. **d** 95 **p** 96. C Warmley, Syston and Bitton *Bris* from 95. *Beaufort House, 52 Park Road, Bristol BS16 1AU* Tel 0117-965 4191

CARPENTER, Leonard Richard. b 32. EMMTC. **d** 85 **p** 86. NSM Leic H Apostles *Leic* 85-90; P-in-c Barlestone from 90. *The New Vicarage, 22 Bosworth Road, Barlestone, Nuneaton, Warks CV13 0EL* Tel (01455) 290249

CARPENTER, William Brodie (Bill). b 35. St Alb Minl Tr Scheme 76. **d** 79 **p** 80. NSM Hemel Hempstead *St Alb* 79-85; C Hatfield 85-88; C Caversham and Mapledurham *Ox* 88-89; R Caversham St Andr from 89. *St Andrew's Vicarage, Harrogate Road, Reading RG4 7PW* Tel 0118-947 2788

CARR, Alan Cobban. b 49. Nottm Univ BTh88. Linc Th Coll 85. **d** 88 **p** 89. C Rustington *Chich* 88-92; V Highbrook and W Hoathly from 92. *The Vicarage, West Hoathly, East Grinstead, W Sussex RH19 4QF* Tel (01342) 810494

CARR, Anthony Howard. b 62. Ex Univ BA. **d** 92 **p** 93. C Taverham w Ringland *Nor* 92-97; P-in-c S Darley, Elton and Winster *Derby* from 97. *The Vicarage, Winster, Matlock, Derbyshire DE4 2DH* Tel (01629) 650256

CARR, The Very Revd Arthur Wesley. b 41. Jes Coll Ox BA64 MA67 Jes Coll Cam BA66 MA70 Sheff Univ PhD75. Ridley Hall Cam 65. **d** 67 **p** 68. C Luton w E Hyde *St Alb* 67-71; Tutor Ridley Hall Cam 70-71; Chapl 71-72; Hon C Ranmoor *Sheff* 72-74; Chapl Chelmsf Cathl *Chelmsf* 74-78; Can Res Chelmsf Cathl 78-87; Dep Dir Cathl Cen for Research and Tr 74-82; Dioc Dir of Tr 76-84; Dean Bris 87-97; Dean Westmr from 97. *The Deanery, Westminster Abbey, London SW1P 3PA* Tel 0171-222 2953 Fax 233 2072

CARR, Douglas Nicholson. b 20. Jes Coll Cam BA47 MA50. Cranmer Hall Dur. **d** 65 **p** 66. C Reigate St Mary *S'wark* 65-69; Home Dir OMF 69-85; Lic to Offic *S'wark* 77-86; rtd 85; Perm to Offic *Glouc* from 85. *Willow Cottage, 435 Paiswick Road, Gloucester GL4 9BY* Tel (01452) 507455

CARR, Miss Eveline. b 45. St Jo Coll Dur 91. **d** 93 **p** 95. NSM Eighton Banks *Dur* from 93. *10 Lanchester Avenue, Gateshead, Tyne & Wear NE9 7AJ* Tel 0191-482 1157

CARR, Geoffrey. b 09. Ch Coll Cam BA33. Ridley Hall Cam 34. **d** 35 **p** 36. C W Hampstead St Luke *Lon* 35-37; Chapl Corfu *Eur* 37-38; C Southport Ch Ch *Liv* 38-41; V Castle Town *Lich* 41-44; V Wellington w Eyton 44-49; R Bradfield *Ox* 49-63; P-in-c Stanford Dingley 54-56; RD Bradfield 60-63; R Arborfield 63-76; rtd 76; Chapl St Luke's Hosp Guildf 77-78; Hon Chapl from 78; Perm to Offic *Guildf* from 78. *9 Denehyrst Court, York Road, Guildford, Surrey GU1 4EA* Tel (01483) 502923

CARR, Preb James Arthur. b 28. St Aid Birkenhead 62. **d** 64 **p** 65. C Cannock *Lich* 64-68; V Edensor 68-72; V Caverswall 72-85; P-in-c Dilhorne 83-85; P-in-c St Martin's 85-86; V 86-94; RD Oswestry 87-92; Preb Lich Cathl 89-94; rtd 94. *7 Mickleby Way, Meir Park, Stoke-on-Trent, Staffs ST3 7RU* Tel (01782) 399547

CARR, John Robert. b 40. ACII62. Oak Hill Th Coll 63. **d** 66 **p** 67. C Tonbridge St Steph *Roch* 66-70; C Cheadle Hulme St Andr *Ches* 70-79; R Widford *Chelmsf* 79-87; TV Becontree W 87-93; V Basildon St Andr w H Cross from 93. *St Andrew's Vicarage, 3 The Fremnells, Basildon, Essex SS14 2QX* Tel (01268) 520516

CARR, Miss Joy Vera. b 32. DipEd52. Dalton Ho Bris 56. **dss** 80 **d** 87 **p** 94. Scarborough St Jas and H Trin *York* 80-82; Kingston upon Hull St Matt w St Barn 82-87; Par Dn 87-89; Par Dn Elloughton and Brough w Brantingham 89-92; rtd 92; Perm to Offic *York* from 92. *15 Sea View Gardens, Scarborough, N Yorkshire YO11 3JD* Tel (01723) 376986

CARR, Paul Anthony. b 62. Oak Hill Th Coll DipHE95 Aston Tr Scheme 93. **d** 97. C Handforth *Ches* from 97. *61 Pickmere Road, Handforth, Wilmslow, Cheshire SK9 3TB* Tel (01625) 529570

CARRE, Canon John Trenchard. b 23. Lich Th Coll 42 Linc Th Coll 45. **d** 46 **p** 47. C Gt Bookham *Guildf* 46-48; C Hodnet w Weston under Redcastle *Lich* 48-50; C Cannock 50-53; V Bodicote *Ox* 53-60; V Steeple Morden *Ely* 60-74; V Guilden Morden 60-74; RD Shingay 67-74; V Wendy w Shingay 69-74; R Croydon w Clopton 69-74; R Hatley 69-74; V Litlington w Abington Pigotts 69-74; V Tadlow w E Hatley 69-74; V Chesterton St Andr 74-88; Hon Can Ely Cathl 79-88; rtd 88. *North Barn, 17 Cromwell Road, Ely, Cambs CB6 1AS* Tel (01353) 662471

CARRICK, Canon Ian Ross. b 13. Clare Coll Cam BA35 MA39. Chich Th Coll 35. **d** 37 **p** 38. C Sculcoates St Paul *York* 37-39; C Staveley *Derby* 39-43; Min St Barn CD Northolt 43-54; V Northolt Park St Barn *Lon* 54-58; S Africa from 58. *65 First Crescent, Fish Hoek, 7975 South Africa* Tel Cape Town (21) 825586

CARRINGTON, Mrs Elizabeth Ashby (Liz). b 46. EMMTC 86. **d** 90 **p** 94. NSM Nottingham St Ann w Em *S'well* 90-91; C Basford w Hyson Green from 92. *The Vicarage, 152 Perry Road, Nottingham NG5 1GL* Tel 0115-960 5602

CARRINGTON, Philip John. b 48. MIEE MBIM Leeds Poly CEng. Chich Th Coll 83. **d** 85 **p** 86. C W Acklam *York* 85-88; V Middlesbrough St Agnes 88-92; Chapl Middlesb Gen Hosp 92-93; Chapl S Cleveland Hosp from 93. *South Cleveland Hospital, Marton Road, Middlesbrough, Cleveland TS4 3BW* Tel (01642) 850850 or 854802

CARRIVICK, Derek Roy. b 45. Birm Univ BSc66. Ripon Hall Ox 71. **d** 74 **p** 75. C Enfield St Jas *Lon* 74-78; C-in-c Woodgate Valley CD *Birm* 78-83; TR Chelmsley Wood 83-92; Dioc Ecum Officer 86-96; R Baxterley w Hurley and Wood End and Merevale etc from 92; RD Polesworth from 96. *The Rectory, Dexter Lane, Hurley, Atherstone, Warks CV9 2JQ* Tel (01827) 874252

CARROLL, The Ven Charles William Desmond. b 19. TCD BA43 MA46. St Chad's Coll Dur. **d** 48 **p** 49. C Stanwix *Carl* 48-50; V 50-59; Hon Can Blackb Cathl *Blackb* 59-64; Dir RE 59-73; Can Res Blackb Cathl 64-75; Adn Blackb 73-86; V Balderstone 73-86; rtd 86; Lic to Offic *Blackb* from 86. *11 Assheton Road, Blackburn BB2 6SF* Tel (01254) 251915

CARROLL, Frederick Albert. b 16. Worc Coll Ox BA51 MA55. Ripon Hall Ox 46. **d** 51 **p** 52. C Oldbury *Birm* 51-56; V Cotteridge 56-65; C-in-c Castle Vale CD 65-68; V Castle Vale 68-74; V Coughton *Cov* 74-87; R Spernall, Morton Bagot and Oldberrow 74-87; RD Alcester 84-87; rtd 87. *8 Gracey Court, Woodland Road, Broadclyst, Exeter EX5 3LP* Tel (01392) 460788

CARROLL, James Thomas. b 41. Pittsburgh Univ MA85. St Deiniol's Hawarden 89 Oblate Fathers Sem Dub 59. **d** 63 **p** 64. C Dublin St Patr Cathl Gp *D & G* 89-92; Min Can St Patr Cathl Dublin 90-96; I Raheny w Coolock *D & G* from 92; Chan V St Patr Cathl Dublin from 96. *403 Howth Road, Raheny, Dublin 5, Irish Republic* Tel Dublin (1) 831 3929

CARROLL, John Hugh. b 31. Bris Univ BA57. Tyndale Hall Bris 54. **d** 58 **p** 59. C Slough *Ox* 58-61; V S Lambeth St Steph *S'wark* 61-72; V Norwood St Luke 72-81; P-in-c Purley Ch Ch 81-85; V 85-93; rtd 93; Perm to Offic *S'wark* from 93. *75 Court Avenue, Coulsdon, Surrey CR5 1HJ* Tel (01737) 552464

CARROLL, Miss Joy Ann. b 59. SS Mark & Jo Coll Plymouth BEd82. Cranmer Hall Dur 85. **d** 88 **p** 94. Par Dn Hatcham St Jas *S'wark* 88-93; Par Dn Streatham Immanuel and St Andr 93-94; C from 94. *98 Ellison Road, London SW16 5DD* Tel 0181-679 4301

CARROLL, Laurence William (Laurie). b 44. Birm Univ CertEd66 Open Univ BA73 Leic Univ BEd74 FRHS66 ACP67 LCP68. LNSM course 92. **d** 95 **p** 96. NSM Mid Marsh Gp *Linc* from 95. *Old Rectory Cottage, Church Lane, Manby, Louth, Lincs LN11 8HL* Tel (01507) 327630

CARRUTHERS, Alan. b 15. **d** 60 **p** 61. C Walton St Luke *Liv* 60-62; C Wigan St Jas 62-65; V 65-70; P-in-c Wigan St Thos 65-70; V Wigan St Jas w St Thos 70-87; rtd 87; Perm to Offic *Carl* from 87. *Low Meadow, Cat Tree Road, Grange-over-Sands, Cumbria LA11 7ED* Tel (015395) 33037

CARRUTHERS, Arthur Christopher (Kester). b 35. Lon Coll of Div ALCD60 LTh73. **d** 60 **p** 61. C Addiscombe St Mary *Cant* 60-62; Prec Bradf Cathl *Bradf* 62-64; CF 64-92; R W Tanfield and Well w Snape and N Stainley *Ripon* from 92. *The Rectory, Main Street, West Tanfield, Ripon, N Yorkshire HG4 5JJ* Tel (01677) 470321

CARRY, Canon Edward Austin. b 18. TCD BA41 MA47. **d** 42 **p** 43. I Killiney H Trin *D & G* 56-86; Preb St Patr Cathl Dublin 83-86; rtd 86. *2 Roxboro Close, Ballinclea Road, Killiney, Co Dublin, Irish Republic* Tel Dublin (1) 285 8847

CARSON, Christopher John. b 69. QUB BA91 TCD BTh94. **d** 94 **p** 95. C Bangor St Comgall *D & D* 94-97; Bp's C Kilmegan w Maghera from 97. *50 Main Street, Dundrum, Newcastle, Co Down BT33 0LY* Tel (01396) 751225

CARSON, Ernest. b 17. S'wark Ord Course 68. **d** 71 **p** 72. C Baldock w Bygrave and Clothall *St Alb* 71-75; R Hertingfordbury 75-86; rtd 86; Perm to Offic *Worc* from 86. *16 Woodward Close, Pershore, Worcs WR10 1LP* Tel (01386) 553511

CARSON, Gerald James Alexander. b 24. TCD BA49 MA52. **d** 49 **p** 50. C Belfast St Phil *Conn* 49-51; C Derry Cathl *D & R* 51-54; I Kilteevogue 54-57; I Dunfanaghy 57-68; RD Kilmacrenan W 60-85; Can Raphoe Cathl 67-81; I Urney w Sion Mills 68-85; Can Derry Cathl 81-85; I Clonallon w Warrenpoint *D & D* 85-90; rtd 90. *84 Avonbrook Gardens, Mountsandel, Coleraine, Co Derry BT52 1SS* Tel (01265) 56047

CARSON, Herbert Moore. b 22. TCD BA43 BD45. **d** 45 **p** 46. V Blackheath Park St Mich *S'wark* 53-58; V Cambridge St Paul *Ely* 58-65; rtd 87. *19 Hillcrest Road, Leicester LE2 6HG* Tel 0116-288 2720

CARSON, James Irvine. b 59. TCD BA DipTh84 MTh. **d** 84 **p** 85. C Willowfield *D & D* 84-87; C Lecale Gp 87-89; I Devenish w Boho *Clogh* 89-95; Dioc Youth Adv 91-95; Dioc Info Officer 93-95; I Belfast Upper Malone (Epiphany) *Conn* from 95. *The Rectory, 74 Locksley Park, Upper Lisburn Road, Belfast BT10 0AS* Tel (01232) 601588

CARSON-FEATHAM, Lawrence William. b 53. AKC DipTh74. **d** 78 **p** 79. SSM from 77; C Walton St Mary *Liv* 78-82; Chapl Bolton Colls of FE 82-87; C Bolton St Pet *Man* 82-87; TV Oldham 87-92; V Ashton St Jas 92-95. *Ground Floor Flat, 29 Queens Road, Southport, Merseyside PR9 9HN*

CARTER, Andrew Graham. b 65. UEA BSc86. St Jo Coll Nottm DTS90 DPS91. **d** 91 **p** 92. C Biggleswade *St Alb* 91-95; C Leavesden All SS from 95. *24 Kimpton Place, Garston, Watford WD2 6RD* Tel (01923) 670318

CARTER, Anthony James. b 24. Sarum Th Coll 54. **d** 56 **p** 57. C Farncombe *Guildf* 56-60; C Tattenham Corner and Burgh Heath 60-62; V Chessington 62-68; V Walton-on-Thames 68-78; P-in-c Lytchett Minster *Sarum* 78-81; V 81-83; V Teddington St Mark *Lon* 83-88; V Teddington St Mark and Hampton Wick St Jo 88-89; rtd 89. *3 Westport Cottages, West Street, Wareham, Dorset BH20 4LF* Tel (01929) 554255

CARTER, Arthur. b 32. **d** 97. C Clonmel w Innislounagh, Tullaghmelan etc *C & O* from 97. *Suirvilla, Barnora, Cahir, Co Tipperary, Irish Republic* Tel Tipperary (52) 41524

CARTER, Barry Graham. b 54. K Coll Lon BD76 AKC76. St Steph Ho Ox 76. **d** 77 **p** 78. C Evesham *Worc* 77-81; C Amblecote 81-84; TV Ovingdean w Rottingdean and Woodingdean *Chich* 84-85; V Woodingdean 85-95; V Lancing St Mich from 95. *The Vicarage, 117 Penhill Road, Lancing, W Sussex BN15 8HD* Tel (01903) 753653

CARTER, Celia. b 38. JP74. Glouc Sch of Min 86. **d** 89 **p** 94. NSM Avening w Cherington *Glouc* from 89; Asst Chapl Stoud Gen Hosp from 89. *Avening Park, Avening, Tetbury, Glos GL8 8NE* Tel (01453) 832716

CARTER, Canon Charles Trevelyan Aubrey. b 14. TCD BA36 MA46. TCD Div Sch Div Test37. **d** 37 **p** 38. C Dublin Sandford *D & G* 37-43; Chapl Female Orphanage Ho Dublin 43-55; I Dublin St Steph 52-59; I Dublin Crumlin 59-67; I Dublin Sandford 67-82; I Dublin Sandford w Milltown 82-85; Can Ch Ch Cathl Dublin 71-85; rtd 85. *7 South Hill, Dartry, Dublin 6, Irish Republic* Tel Dublin (1) 497 1171

CARTER (née SMITH), Mrs Christine Lydia. b 43. Lon Hosp SRN64 Bristol Hosp SCM67 Bris Poly DipNursing76 Wolv Poly CertFE84. Trin Coll Bris DipHE91. **d** 91 **p** 94. Par Dn Penkridge Team *Lich* 91-94; C 94-96; Perm to Offic *Blackb* 96-97; NSM Blackb Sav from 97; Chapl Asst St Helen's and Knowsley Hosps Trust from 97. *The Vicarage, Onchan Road, Blackburn BB2 3NT* Tel (01254) 255344

CARTER, Christopher Franklin. b 37. Wadh Coll Ox BA59 MA63. Wycliffe Hall Ox 60. **d** 64 **p** 65. C Clifton St Jas *Sheff* 64-67; C Handsworth 67-70; C Clun w Chapel Lawn *Heref* 70-74; Lic to Offic 74-76; P-in-c Ironbridge 76-78; C Coalbrookdale, Iron-Bridge and Lt Wenlock 78-80; V Llansilin w Llangadwaladr and Llangedwyn *St As* from 80; RD Llanfyllin from 88. *The Vicarage, Llansilin, Oswestry, Shropshire SY10 7PX* Tel (01691) 70209

CARTER, Dr Colin John. b 56. FRCS86 Fitzw Coll Cam BA77 MA81 Cam Univ MB80 BChir80. Trin Coll Bris BA93. **d** 93 **p** 94. C Ripley *Derby* 93-97; TV Horsham *Chich* from 97. *St John's House, Church Road, Broadbridge Heath, Horsham, W Sussex RH12 3ND* Tel (01403) 265238

CARTER, David John. b 37. Chich Th Coll 64. **d** 67 **p** 68. C Plaistow St Andr *Chelmsf* 67-70; C Wickford 70-73; Chapl Asst Runwell Hosp Essex 71-73; Chapl Basingstoke Distr Hosp 73-80; R E Woodhay and Woolton Hill *Win* from 80. *The Rectory, The Mount, Woolton Hill, Newbury, Berks RG15 9QZ* Tel (01635) 253323

CARTER, Dudley Herbert. b 25. Peterho Cam BA49 MA51. Ridley Hall Cam 49. **d** 51 **p** 52. C Longfleet *Sarum* 51-53; C Rainham *Chelmsf* 54-56; R Tollard Royal w Farnham *Sarum* 60-64; Chapl Colston's Sch Bris 65-67; Lic to Offic *B & W* 67-85; Perm to Offic from 85; rtd 90. *24 Caernarvon Way, Burnham-on-Sea, Somerset TA8 2DQ* Tel (01278) 789572

CARTER, Duncan Robert Bruton. b 58. Univ of Wales (Cardiff) BA79 Cam Univ BA83 MA89. Ridley Hall Cam 81. **d** 84 **p** 85. C Harold Wood *Chelmsf* 84-88; C S Kensington St Luke *Lon* 88-90; V Rotherfield Greys H Trin *Ox* from 90. *Holy Trinity Vicarage, Church Street, Henley-on-Thames, Oxon RG9 1SE* Tel (01491) 574822

CARTER, Edward John. b 67. Ex Univ BA88. Ripon Coll Cuddesdon BA94. **d** 97. C Thorpe St Matt *Nor* from 97. *15 Stanley Road, Norwich NR7 0BE*

CARTER, Eric. b 17. **d** 58 **p** 59. C S Shore H Trin *Blackb* 58-62; V Preesall 62-69; RD Garstang 68-69; V Adlington 69-75; V Garstang St Thos 75-84; rtd 84. *1 Arncliffe Road, Harrogate, N Yorkshire HG2 8NQ* Tel (01423) 884867

CARTER, Frank Howard James. b 23. Chich Th Coll 58. **d** 59 **p** 60. C Bethnal Green St Matt *Lon* 59-64; V Ipstones *Lich* 64-65; V Haggerston All SS *Lon* 65-75; V Alexandra Park St Andr 75-88; rtd 88. *53 Naylor Road, London N20 0HE* Tel 0181-445 0982

CARTER, Dr Grayson Leigh. b 53. Univ of S California BSc76 Ch Ch Ox DPhil90. Fuller Th Sem California MA84 Wycliffe Hall Ox 89. **d** 90 **p** 91. C Bungay H Trin w St Mary *St E* 90-92; Chapl BNC Ox 92-96; Hon C Ox St Mary V w St Cross and St Pet *Ox* 93-96; USA from 96. *508 Westmont Drive, Fayetteville, N Carolina, 28305 USA*

CARTER, Hazel June. b 48. Doncaster Coll of Educn CertEd72. Carl Dioc Tr Inst 89. **d** 92 **p** 94. C Wreay *Carl* from 92; C Dalston from 92; C Raughton Head w Gatesgill from 92. *The Vicarage, Wreay, Carlisle CA4 0RL* Tel (016974) 73463

CARTER, Ian Sutherland. b 51. Trin Coll Ox BA73 MA77 DPhil77 Leeds Univ BA80. Coll of Resurr Mirfield 78. **d** 81 **p** 82. C Shildon *Dur* 81-84; C Darlington H Trin 84-87; Chapl Liv Univ *Liv* 87-93; V Hindley St Pet from 93. *St Peter's Vicarage, Wigan Road, Hindley, Wigan, Lancs WN2 3DF* Tel (01942) 55505

CARTER (née O'NEILL), Mrs Irene. b 44. Worc Coll of Educn CertEd65. EMMTC CTPS92. **d** 93. NSM N and S Leverton *S'well* from 93. *25 Mill Close, North Leverton, Retford, Notts DN22 0AT* Tel (01427) 880451

CARTER, John Henry. b 24. Oak Hill Th Coll 66. **d** 68 **p** 69. C Halliwell St Paul *Man* 68-71; V Bolton St Phil 71-76; Chapl to the Deaf (Dios Man and Blackb) 76-82; V Childs Ercall *Lich*

82-87; R Stoke upon Tern 82-87; rtd 87. *3 Chestnut Drive, Hemingbrough, Selby, N Yorkshire YO8 7UE* Tel (01757) 638197

CARTER, John Howard Gregory. b 55. York Univ BA76. St Jo Coll Nottm LTh87. **d** 87 **p** 88. C Nailsea H Trin *B & W* 87-91; TV Camberley St Paul *Guildf* from 91; Chapl Elmhurst Ballet Sch Camberley from 91. *61 Goldney Road, Camberley, Surrey GU15 1DW* Tel (01276) 20897

✠**CARTER, The Rt Revd John Stanley.** b 21. Lon Univ BA47. Oak Hill Th Coll 46 Wycliffe Hall Ox 48. **d** 49 **p** 50 **c** 68. C Walthamstow St Mary *Chelmsf* 49-52; C Streatham Immanuel w St Anselm *S'wark* 52-53; S Africa from 53; Suff Bp Johannesburg 68-77. *The Rectory, 43 Pypies Plein, Devil's Peak, Cape Town, 8001 South Africa* Tel Cape Town (21) 461-5350

CARTER, Leslie Alfred Arthur. b 27. K Coll Lon 50 St Boniface Warminster 53. **d** 54 **p** 55. C Northolt Park St Barn *Lon* 54-56; S Africa 57-62; C Wimbledon *S'wark* 63-68; Chapl Quainton Hall Sch Harrow 68-77; TV Brighton Resurr *Chich* 77-81; TV Southend St Jo w St Mark, All SS w St Fran etc *Chelmsf* 81-82; TV Southend 82-88; V Gt Waltham w Ford End 88-93; rtd 94. *52 Masefield Road, Warminster, Wilts BA12 8HY* Tel (01985) 215268

CARTER, Ms Marian. b 40. Whitelands Coll Lon TCert61 Lon Univ DipTh62 BD67 Reading Univ DASE73 Nottm Univ MPhil79. Nor Bapt Coll MA84. **d** 92 **p** 94. Par Dn Kempshott *Win* 92-93; Tutor SW Minl Tr Course 92-96; Tutor Coll of SS Mark and Jo Plymouth from 93; NSM Plymstock and Hooe *Ex* from 94. *Shalom, 20 St Mark's Road, Plymouth PL6 8BS* Tel (01752) 709321

CARTER, Canon Michael John. b 32. St Alb Minl Tr Scheme 81. **d** 84 **p** 85. NSM Radlett *St Alb* 84-88; Chapl SW Herts HA 88-94; Chapl Watford Gen Hosp 88-94; Chapl Mt Vernon and Watford Hosps NHS Trust from 94; Hon Can St Alb *St Alb* from 96. *Watford General Hospital, Vicarage Road, Watford WD1 8HB* Tel (01923) 244366 or 856009

CARTER, Nicholas Adrian. b 47. Ripon Hall Ox 71. **d** 74 **p** 75. C Sowerby *Wakef* 74-79; V Hanging Heaton 79-83; CF 83-86; V Elton All SS *Man* 86-90; C Milton *Win* 90-94; P-in-c Boscombe St Andr 94; V from 94. *St Andrew's Vicarage, 3 Wilfred Road, Bournemouth BH5 1NB* Tel (01202) 394575

CARTER, Nigel John. b 53. N Staffs Poly C&G80 Bolton Inst of Educn CertEd89. Sarum & Wells Th Coll DCM93. **d** 93 **p** 94. C Burntwood *Lich* 93-96; V Bentley from 96. *The Vicarage, Cairn Drive, Bentley, Walsall WS2 0HP* Tel (01922) 242000

CARTER, Noel William. b 53. Birm Univ BSc75 Bris Univ CertEd76 Nottm Univ BSc83. Linc Th Coll. **d** 83 **p** 84. C Penrith w Newton Reigny and Plumpton Wall *Carl* 83-86; TR 91-97; C Barrow St Matt 86-87; V Netherton 87-91; P-in-c Jersey St Brelade *Win* from 97. *The Rectory, La Marquanderie, St Brelade, Jersey JE3 8EP* Tel (01534) 42302

CARTER, Canon Norman. b 23. Leeds Univ BSc48. Coll of Resurr Mirfield 48. **d** 50 **p** 51. C Liv Our Lady and St Nic w St Anne *Liv* 50-54; C Orford St Marg 54-56; V 56-71; PC Knotty Ash H Spirit 71-74; V Dovecot 74-83; RD W Derby 78-83; Hon Can Liv Cathl 82-88; V Formby St Pet 83-88; rtd 88; Perm to Offic *Liv* from 88. *34 Granby Close, Southport, Merseyside PR9 9QG* Tel (01704) 232821

CARTER, Canon Paul Brian. b 22. AKC49. **d** 50 **p** 51. C Scarborough St Columba *York* 50-53; C Pocklington w Yapham-cum-Meltonby, Owsthorpe etc 53-55; V Kingston upon Hull St Jo Newington 55-60; R Ainderby Steeple and Scruton *Ripon* 60-79; P-in-c Danby Wiske w Yafforth and Hutton Bonville 76-79; R Ainderby Steeple w Yafforth and Scruton 79-87; Hon Can Ripon Cathl 86-87; rtd 87. *Cliffe Cottage, West Tanfield, Ripon, N Yorkshire HG4 5JR* Tel (01677) 470203

CARTER, Paul Joseph. b 67. St Chad's Coll Dur BA88. St Steph Ho Ox 89. **d** 91 **p** 92. C Ipswich All Hallows *St E* 91; C Newmarket St Mary w Exning St Agnes 91-94; V Thorpe-le-Soken *Chelmsf* from 94. *The Vicarage, Mill Lane, Thorpe-le-Soken, Clacton-on-Sea, Essex CO16 0ED* Tel (01255) 861234

CARTER, Paul Mark. b 56. BA78 MA90. Ridley Hall Cam 79. **d** 81 **p** 82. C Kidsgrove *Lich* 81-84; CF from 84. *MOD Chaplains (Army), Trenchard Lines, Upavon, Pewsey, Wilts SN9 6BE* Tel (01980) 615804 Fax 615800

CARTER, Paul Rowley. b 45. Lon Univ BD69 Lon Bible Coll ALBC69 Southn Univ PGCE70. Trin Coll Bris. **d** 91 **p** 92. C Penkridge Team *Lich* 91-96; V Blackb Sav *Blackb* from 96. *The Vicarage, Onchan Road, Blackburn BB2 3NT* Tel (01254) 255344

CARTER, Raymond Timothy. b 27. Qu Coll Birm 57. **d** 59 **p** 60. C Wembley St Jo *Lon* 59-62; C Hatch End St Anselm 62-67; V Harrow Weald St Mich 67-79; V Teddington St Mary w St Alb 79-92; rtd 92. *21 Manor Road, Teddington, Middx TW11 8AA* Tel 0181-943 9489

CARTER, Robert Desmond (Bob). b 35. Cranmer Hall Dur 62. **d** 65 **p** 66. C Otley *Bradf* 65-69; C Keighley 69-73; V Cowling from 73. *The Vicarage, Gill Lane, Cowling, Keighley, W Yorkshire BD22 0DD* Tel (01535) 632050

CARTER, Robert Edward. b 44. Univ of Wales (Ban) BSc66. St Jo Coll Nottm 79. **d** 81 **p** 82. C Caverswall *Lich* 81-86; V Biddulph 86-94; V Wolverhampton St Jude from 94. *St Jude's Vicarage, St Jude's Road, Wolverhampton WV6 0EB* Tel (01902) 753360

CARTER, Robin. b 46. Chich Th Coll 71. **d** 74 **p** 75. C Wortley de Leeds *Ripon* 74-76; C Hutton *Chelmsf* 76-78; C Wickford 78-81; TV Wickford and Runwell 81-83; Chapl HM Pris Leeds 83-85; Chapl HM Pris Reading 85-89; Chapl HM Young Offender Inst Huntercombe and Finnamore 85-89; Chapl HM Young Offender Inst Finnamore Wood Camp 86-89; Lic to Offic *Ox* 85-89; Gov HM Pris Channings Wood from 89; Perm to Offic *Ex* from 90. *HM Prison Channings Wood, Denbury, Newton Abbot, Devon TQ12 6DW* Tel (01803) 812361 Fax 813175

CARTER, Ronald George. b 31. Leeds Univ BA58. Coll of Resurr Mirfield 58. **d** 60 **p** 61. C Wigan St Anne *Liv* 60-63; Prec Wakef Cathl *Wakef* 63-66; V Woodhall *Bradf* 66-77; Chapl Qu Marg Sch Escrick Park 77-83; Min Can, Prec and Sacr Pet Cathl *Pet* 83-88; R Upper St Leonards St Jo *Chich* 88-94; rtd 94; Perm to Offic *York* from 95. *5 Greenwich Close, York YO3 6WN* Tel (01904) 610237

CARTER, Ronald William. b 01. ATCL25 ALCD31. **d** 31 **p** 32. C Isleworth St Mary *Lon* 31-32; CMS 32-39; C Staines St Pet *Lon* 39-41; V 41-78; RD Staines 68-73; rtd 78; Perm to Offic *Win* 78-95. *24 Vespasian Way, Eastleigh, Hants SO53 2DF* Tel (01703) 269520

CARTER, Russell James Wigney. b 29. Chich Th Coll 80. **d** 82 **p** 83. C Aldwick *Chich* 82-86; R Buxted and Hadlow Down 86-90; rtd 90; Perm to Offic *Chich* from 90. *6 Lucerne Court, Aldwick, Bognor Regis, W Sussex PO21 4XL* Tel (01243) 862858

CARTER, Samuel. b 49. St Jo Coll Dur BA71 DipTh72. Cranmer Hall Dur 73. **d** 74 **p** 75. C Kingswinford St Mary *Lich* 74-77; C Shrewsbury H Cross 77-84; V Normacot 84-94. *Address excluded by request*

CARTER, Stanley Reginald. b 24. St Jo Coll Dur BA49 DipTh50. **d** 50 **p** 51. C Stoughton *Guildf* 50-53; C Bucknall and Bagnall *Lich* 53-56; R Salford St Matthias w St Simon *Man* 56-62; V Highbury New Park St Aug *Lon* 62-69; V Sneinton St Chris w St Phil *S'well* 69-89; rtd 89; Perm to Offic *S'well* from 89. *31 Pateley Road, Nottingham NG3 5QF* Tel 0115-926 4054

CARTER, Stephen. b 56. Univ of Wales (Lamp) BA77 Southn Univ BTh81. Sarum & Wells Th Coll 78. **d** 81 **p** 82. C Halstead St Andr w H Trin and Greenstead Green *Chelmsf* 81-84; C Loughton St Jo 84-89; V N Shoebury 89-95; R Lexden from 95. *The Rectory, 2 Wroxham Close, Colchester CO3 3RQ* Tel (01206) 575966

CARTER, Stephen Howard. b 47. City Univ BSc72. St Jo Coll Nottm LTh85. **d** 85 **p** 86. C Hellesdon *Nor* 85-88; Chapl Asst Birm Children's Hosp 88-91; Chapl Asst Birm Maternity Hosp 88-91; Lic to Offic *Birm* 88-91; TV Tettenhall Wood *Lich* from 91; Chapl Compton Hall Hospice Wolv from 91. *The Vicarage, 12 Windmill Lane, Wolverhampton WV3 8HJ* Tel (01902) 761170

CARTER, Stuart Conway. b 58. Lon Bible Coll DipRS83 St Jo Coll Nottm DipMM92. **d** 92 **p** 93. C Birm St Luke *Birm* 92-96; C The Quinton from 96. *95 Oak Road, Quinton, Birmingham B68 0BH* Tel 0121-422 3621

CARTER, Terence John (Terry). b 31. K Coll Lon BD57 AKC57 Lon Univ BA68 PGCE69. **d** 58 **p** 59. C Winchmore Hill H Trin *Lon* 58-60; PV S'wark Cathl *S'wark* 60-63; Sacr S'wark Cathl 60-61; Succ S'wark Cathl 61-63; R Ockham w Hatchford *Guildf* 63-69; Lic to Offic *S'wark* 69-78; Lic to Offic *Portsm* 78-82; Perm to Offic from 82; rtd 91. *15 Balliol Road, Portsmouth PO2 7PP* Tel (01705) 699167

CARTLEDGE, Mark John. b 62. Lon Bible Coll BA85. Oak Hill Th Coll MPhil89. **d** 88 **p** 89. C Formby H Trin *Liv* 88-91; Miss Partner CMS 91-93; Nigeria 91-93; Chapl Liv Univ *Liv* from 93. *The Beeches, 71 Woodlands Road, Liverpool L17 0AL* Tel 0151-727 6291 or 794 3302/3 Fax 708 6502 E-mail mjc@liv.ac.uk

CARTMAN, James. b 10. OBE55. Man Univ BA37 MA50 Lon Univ BD44 MTh48. Westcott Ho Cam 51. **d** 51 **p** 51. C Hayes *Roch* 51-53; C Bromley Common St Luke 54-57; Educn Officer Ceylon Students in UK 50-57; Hon Chapl to Ceylon Forces in UK 55-57; Portugal 57-59; V Winchcombe w Gretton and Sudeley Manor *Glouc* 59-62; RD Winchcombe 62; Sen Div Master Pate's Gr Sch Cheltenham 62-66; P-in-c Farmington 65-69; Prin Lect Relig Studies Heref Coll of Educn 69-78; rtd 78; Perm to Offic *Win* 78-95; Perm to Offic *Guildf* 79-92. *9 Handcroft Close, Crondall, Farnham, Surrey GU10 5RY* Tel (01252) 850234

CARTMELL, Richard Peter. b 43. Cranmer Hall Dur 77. **d** 79 **p** 80. C Whittle-le-Woods *Blackb* 79-85; V Lower Darwen St Jas from 85; RD Darwen from 91. *The Vicarage, Stopes Brow, Lower Darwen, Darwen, Lancs BB3 0QP* Tel (01254) 253898

CARTMILL, Canon Ralph Arthur. b 40. St Jo Coll Dur BA62 Em Coll Cam MA64. Ridley Hall Cam 63. **d** 65 **p** 66. C Dukinfield St Jo *Ches* 65-68; C Wilmslow 68-69; Warden Walton Youth Cen Liv 69-70; Asst Master Aylesbury Gr Sch 70-74; Perm to Offic *Ox* 72-74; V Terriers 74-85; P-in-c Chinnor w Emmington and Sydenham 85-86; R Chinnor w Emmington and Sydenham etc from 86; Hon Can Ch Ch from 97. *The Rectory, Chinnor, Oxon OX9 4DH* Tel (01844) 351309

CARTWRIGHT, Cyril Hicks. b 13. Selw Coll Cam BA35 MA44. Linc Th Coll 36. **d** 38 **p** 39. C Wadhurst *Chich* 38-41; C Rye 41-43; C Barcombe 43-45; C Haywards Heath St Wilfrid 45-49; C Nuthurst 49-50; C Gillingham St Mary *Roch* 51-52; C Pembury 53-54; C Belvedere All SS 54-56; C Southwick *Chich* 56-62; C Forest Row 62-70; V Whitehawk 70-75; C Hove All SS 76-80; rtd 80; Perm to Offic *Chich* from 80. *Barford Court, 157 Kingsway, Hove, E Sussex BN3 4GL* Tel (01273) 737814

CARTWRIGHT, Preb Hugh Bent. b 07. St Steph Ho Ox 30. **d** 32 **p** 33. C Friern Barnet All SS *Lon* 32-36; C Hendon All SS Childs Hill 37-40; P-in-c Colindale St Matthias 40-46; V Alexandra Park St Andr 46-73; Preb St Paul's Cathl 69-73; rtd 73; Perm to Offic *Heref* from 73. *21 Queens Court, Ledbury, Herefordshire HR8 2AL* Tel (01531) 633123

CARTWRIGHT, John Walter Deryk. b 25. Lon Univ BSc. Ox NSM Course. **d** 82 **p** 83. NSM Welford w Wickham and Gt Shefford *Ox* 82-85; TV Newbury 85-93; rtd 93. *St Mary's Vicarage, 14 Strawberry Hill, Newbury, Berks RG13 1XJ* Tel (01635) 40889

CARTWRIGHT, Michael John. b 42. Birm Univ DipL&A70. Qu Coll Birm 67. **d** 70 **p** 71. C Astwood Bank w Crabbs Cross *Worc* 70-75; P-in-c Worc St Mich 75-77; V Stockton St Paul *Dur* 77-87; V Market Rasen *Linc* from 87; R Linwood from 87; V Legsby from 87; RD W Wold from 89; R Wickenby Gp from 95. *The Vicarage, 13 Lady Frances Drive, Market Rasen, Lincs LN8 3JJ* Tel (01673) 843424

✠**CARTWRIGHT, The Rt Revd Richard Fox.** b 13. Pemb Coll Cam BA35 MA39 Univ of the South (USA) Hon DD69. Cuddesdon Coll 35. **d** 36 **p** 37 **c** 72. C Kennington Cross St Anselm *S'wark* 36-40; C Kingswood 40-45; V Surbiton St Andr 45-52; V Bris St Mary Redcliffe w Temple etc *Bris* 52-72; Hon Can Bris Cathl 60-72; Suff Bp Plymouth *Ex* 72-81; rtd 82; Asst Bp Truro from 82; Asst Bp Ex from 88. *5 Old Vicarage Close, Ide, Exeter EX2 9RT* Tel (01392) 211270

CARTWRIGHT, Roy Arthur. b 29. CCC Cam BA52 MA56. Wycliffe Hall Ox. **d** 54 **p** 55. C Hornchurch St Andr *Chelmsf* 54-56; C Gt Clacton 56-60; C-in-c Prittlewell St Steph CD 60-69; V Prittlewell St Steph 69-72; rtd 72; Hon C S Shoebury *Chelmsf* 77-94; Perm to Offic *Glouc* from 94. *21 Winfield, Newent, Glos GL18 1QB* Tel (01531) 821335

CARTWRIGHT, Samuel. b 27. Cuddesdon Coll 71. **d** 72 **p** 72. C Rochdale *Man* 72-76; V Roundthorn 76-83; V Ashton Ch Ch 83-93; rtd 93; Perm to Offic *Derby* from 93. *8 Wentworth Avenue, Walton, Chesterfield, Derbyshire S40 3JB* Tel (01246) 232252

CARTWRIGHT, Sidney Victor. b 22. Launde Abbey 73. **d** 74 **p** 75. C Braunstone *Leic* 74-78; P-in-c Arnesby w Shearsby 78-86; R Arnesby w Shearsby and Bruntingthorpe 86-87; rtd 87; Perm to Offic *Leic* from 87; Perm to Offic *Pet* from 87. *32 Northleigh Grove, Market Harborough, Leics LE16 9QX* Tel (01858) 463915

CARTWRIGHT, William Michael. b 44. Birm Univ CertEd67. Coll of Resurr Mirfield 83. **d** 83 **p** 84. Hd Master Chacombe Sch 83-85; Hon C Middleton Cheney w Chacombe *Pet* 83-85; Hd Master Chacombe Sch Banbury 83-85; C Kettering SS Pet and Paul *Pet* 85-86; Perm to Offic 86-88; Chapl Northaw Prep Sch Win 89-92; P-in-c Altarnon w Bolventor, Laneast and St Clether *Truro* 92-97; V Treverbyn from 97. *The Vicarage, Treverbyn Road, Stenalees, St Austell, Cornwall PL26 8TL* Tel (01726) 850335

CARUANA, Mrs Rosemary Anne. b 38. St Alb Minl Tr Scheme 81. **dss** 84 **d** 87 **p** 94. Hertford St Andr *St Alb* 84-87; Par Dn Hertingfordbury 87-94; C 94; C from 94. *36 Holly Croft, Sele Farm Estate, Hertford SG14 2DR* Tel (01992) 587625

CARVER, Arthur Tregarthen. b 15. Lon Univ 37. Tyndale Hall Bris 37. **d** 41 **p** 42. C Southport Ch Ch *Liv* 41-43; P-in-c 43-44; P-in-c St Helens St Matt Thatto Heath 44-48; V St Helens St Mark 48-53; V Marple All SS *Ches* 53-69; R Uphill *B & W* 69-80; rtd 80; Perm to Offic *Ches* from 80. *Copinsay, 20 Hayton Street, Knutsford, Cheshire WA16 0DR* Tel (01565) 651622

CARVOSSO, John Charles. b 45. ACA71 FCA79. Oak Hill Th Coll 75. **d** 78 **p** 79. C Chelsea St Jo w St Andr *Lon* 78-81; Chapl RAF 81-84; P-in-c Tawstock *Ex* 84-85; TV Newport, Bishops Tawton and Tawstock 85-96; TV Newton Tracey, Horwood, Alverdiscott etc from 96. *The Rectory, Tawstock, Barnstaple, Devon EX31 3HZ* Tel (01271) 74963

CASE, Catherine Margaret. b 44. Ripon Coll Cuddesdon 86. **d** 88 **p** 94. C Blurton *Lich* 88-92; Min to Hanley Care Agencies from 92; TD Hanley H Ev 92-94; P-in-c Wrockwardine Wood from 95. *The Rectory, Church Road, Wrockwardine Wood, Telford, Shropshire TF2 7AH* Tel (01952) 613865

CASE, Philip Thomas Charles. b 17. Lon Univ BSc(Econ)51. Sarum Th Coll 51. **d** 53 **p** 54. C Westmr St Steph w St Jo *Lon* 53-56; C Ashford St Matt 56-58; C-in-c Ashford St Hilda CD 58-61; V St Helier *S'wark* 61-66; V Witley *Guildf* 66-84; RD Godalming 79-84; rtd 84; Perm to Offic *Ex* from 85. *15 Lawpool Court, Wells, Somerset BA5 2AN* Tel (01749) 670859

CASEBOW, Ronald Philip. b 31. Roch Th Coll 59. **d** 61 **p** 62. C Southgate Ch Ch *Lon* 61-64; C Oseney Crescent St Luke w Camden Square St Paul 64-70; Warden St Paul's Ho Student Hostel 64-70; V Colchester St Steph *Chelmsf* 70-74; V Burnham 74-89; rtd 89; Perm to Offic *Nor* from 95. *The Priory, Priory Road, Palgrave, Diss, Norfolk IP22 1AJ* Tel (01379) 651804 Fax as telephone

CASEY, Ernest George. b 14. St Chad's Coll Dur BA36 DipTh. **d** 37 **p** 38. C Benfieldside *Dur* 37-40; C Winlaton 40-44; P-in-c Cassop cum Quarrington 44-45; V Chilton Moor 45-59; V Dur St Giles 59-79; rtd 79. *7 Hampshire Road, Belmont, Durham DH1 2DJ* Tel 0191-384 9228

CASHEL, Dean of. *See* KNOWLES, The Very Revd Philip John

CASHEL, WATERFORD AND LISMORE, Archdeacon of. *See* MURRAY, The Ven John Grainger

CASHEL, WATERFORD, LISMORE, OSSORY, FERNS AND LEIGHLIN, Bishop of. *See* NEILL, The Rt Revd John Robert Winder

CASIOT, David John. b 39. St Pet Coll Ox BA63 MA67. Clifton Th Coll 63. **d** 65 **p** 66. C Drypool St Columba w St Andr and St Pet *York* 65-67; C Barking St Marg *Chelmsf* 67-71; R Whalley Range St Edm *Man* 71-84; V Wandsworth St Mich *S'wark* from 84. *St Michael's Vicarage, 73 Wimbledon Park Road, London SW18 5TT* Tel 0181-874 7682

CASON, Preb Ronald Arthur. b 28. Kelham Th Coll 48. **d** 53 **p** 54. C Fenton *Lich* 53-56; V Brereton 56-63; V Hugglescote w Donington *Leic* 63-67; R Blakenall Heath *Lich* 67-74; R Stoke upon Trent 74-80; Preb Lich Cathl 75-93; RD Stoke 78-88; TR Stoke-upon-Trent 80-91; Lect Tettenhall Par 91-93; rtd 93; Perm to Offic *Lich* from 93. *130 Main Road, Brereton, Rugeley, Staffs WS15 1EB* Tel (01889) 582267

CASSAM, Victor Reginald. b 33. Chich Th Coll 59. **d** 62 **p** 63. C Portsea St Jo Rudmore *Portsm* 62-64; C W Leigh CD 64-66; C Torquay St Martin Barton *Ex* 66-69; C Stanmer w Falmer and Moulsecoomb *Chich* 69-73; P-in-c Catsfield 73-76; R Catsfield and Crowhurst 76-81; R Selsey from 81; RD Chich from 96. *The Rectory, St Peter's Crescent, Selsey, Chichester, W Sussex PO20 0NA* Tel (01243) 602363

CASSELTON, John Charles. b 43. Univ of Wales (Swansea) MA95. Oak Hill Th Coll DipTh67. **d** 68 **p** 69. C Upton *Ex* 68-73; C Braintree *Chelmsf* 73-80; V Ipswich St Jo *St E* 80-92; RD Ipswich 86-92; Chapl St Clem Hosp and St Eliz Hospice Ipswich from 92. *331 Woodbridge Road, Ipswich IP4 4AX, or St Clement's Hospital, Foxhall Road, Ipswich IP3 8LS* Tel (01473) 273665 or 715111

CASSIDY, Brian Ross. b 31. Cape Town Univ. St Bede's Coll Umtata 88. **d** 89 **p** 91. S Africa 89-92; C Lymington *Win* 92-93; P-in-c Hyde Common 93-96; P-in-c Ellingham and Harbridge and Ibsley 95-96; V Ellingham and Harbridge and Hyde w Ibsley from 96. *The Vicarage, Hyde, Fordingbridge, Hants SP6 2QJ* Tel (01425) 653216

CASSIDY, The Ven George Henry. b 42. QUB BSc65 Lon Univ MPhil67. Oak Hill Th Coll 70. **d** 72 **p** 73. C Clifton Ch Ch w Em *Bris* 72-75; V Sea Mills 75-82; V Portman Square St Paul *Lon* 82-87; Adn Lon and Can Res St Paul's Cathl from 87; P-in-c St Ethelburga Bishopgate 89-91. *2 Amen Court, Warwick Lane, London EC4M 7BU* Tel 0171-248 3312 Fax 489 8579

CASSIDY, The Very Revd Herbert. b 35. TCD BA57 MA65. CITC 58. **d** 58 **p** 59. C Belfast H Trin *Conn* 58-60; C Londonderry Ch Ch *D & R* 60-62; I Aghavilly w Derrynoose *Arm* 62-65; Hon V Choral Arm Cathl 63-85; C Portadown St Columba 65-67; I 67-85; Dean Kilmore *K, E & A* 85-89; I Kilmore w Ballintemple 85-86; I Kilmore w Ballintemple, Kildallon etc 86-89; Dir of Ords 89; Dean Arm and Keeper of Public Lib *Arm* from 89; I Arm St Patr from 89; Hon Sec Gen Syn from 90. *The Library, Abbey Street, Armagh BT61 7DY* Tel (01861) 523142 Fax 524177

CASSIDY, Ian. **d** 97. NSM Everton St Geo *Liv* from 97. *79 Gilroy Road, Liverpool L6 6BG* Tel 0151-263 9751

CASSIDY, Joseph Patrick. b 54. Loyola Univ 80 Toronto Univ STB86 MDiv86 Ottawa Univ PhD95 St Paul Univ Ottawa LTh89 DTh95 Detroit Univ MA80 Concordia Univ Montreal BA76. **d** 85 **p** 86. Canada 85-96; NSM Laverstock *Sarum* 96-97; NSM Salisbury St Martin 96-97; Prin St Chad's Coll Dur from 97. *St Chad's College, University of Durham, 18 North Bailey, Durham DH1 3RH* Tel 0191-374 3370 Fax 386 3422 E-mail jcassidy@internexus.co.uk

CASSIDY, Patrick Nigel. b 40. TCD BA63 MA66. Sarum Th Coll 64. **d** 66 **p** 67. C Heaton St Barn *Bradf* 66-68; Asst Chapl Brussels *Eur* 68-70; Chapl SW France 70-72; V Oseney Crescent St Luke w Camden Square St Paul *Lon* 72-83; Chapl Strasbourg w Stuttgart and Heidelberg *Eur* 83-84; Perm to Offic *Chich* 86-90; Chapl Marseille w Aix-en-Provence *Eur* from 90; Hon Chapl Miss to Seamen from 90. *18 rue du Jeune Anacharsis, 13001 Marseille, France* Tel France (33) 4 91 55 57 38

CASSIDY, Ronald. b 43. Lon Univ BD66 Man Univ MPhil85. Tyndale Hall Bris 63. **d** 68 **p** 69. C Kirkdale St Lawr *Liv* 68-70; C Bolton Em *Man* 70-74; V Roughtown 74-89; R Denton St Lawr from 89; AD Ashton-under-Lyne from 97. *St Lawrence's Rectory, 131 Town Lane, Denton, Manchester M34 2DJ* Tel 0161-320 4895

CASSON, David Christopher. b 41. Qu Coll Cam BA64 MA68. Ridley Hall Cam 65. **d** 67 **p** 68. C Birm St Martin *Birm* 67-72; C Luton St Mary *St Alb* 72-77; P-in-c 77; V Luton St Fran 77-84; V Richmond H Trin and Ch Ch *S'wark* from 84. *Holy Trinity*

Vicarage, Sheen Park, Richmond, Surrey TW9 1UP Tel 0181-940 3995

CASSON, Canon James Stuart. b 32. Liv Univ BA54 Nottm Univ MPhil70. Ridley Hall Cam. **d** 61 **p** 62. C Eccleston Ch Ch *Liv* 61-64; C Littleover *Derby* 64-67; V Dearham *Carl* 67-76; V Holme Eden from 76; RD Brampton 91-96; Hon Can Carl Cathl from 93; P-in-c Croglin from 93. *St Paul's Vicarage, Warwick Bridge, Carlisle CA4 8RF* Tel (01228) 560332

CASSWELL, David Oriel. b 52. Loughb Coll of Educn CertEd74 Leeds Univ CQSW79. Oak Hill Th Coll DipHE87. **d** 87 **p** 88. C Acomb St Steph *York* 87-91; Dep Chapl HM Pris Leeds 91-92; Chapl HM Pris Everthorpe 92; Chapl HM Wolds Rem Cen from 92. *The Chaplain's Office, HM Wolds Remand Centre, Everthorpe, Brough, N Humberside HU15 7JZ* Tel (01430) 421588 Fax 421589

CASSWELL, Canon Peter Joyce. b 22. Trin Coll Cam BA48 MA50. Ridley Hall Cam 48. **d** 50 **p** 51. C Addiscombe St Mildred *Cant* 50-53; C-in-c New Addington CD 53-55; V New Addington 55-64; Chapl Forest Gate Hosp Lon 64-78; R Buckhurst Hill *Chelmsf* 64-78; Hon Can Chelmsf Cathl 75-78; R Lutterworth w Cotesbach *Leic* 78-90; RD Guthlaxton II 89-90; rtd 90; Perm to Offic *Leic* from 90. *74 Coventry Road, Broughton Astley, Leics LE9 6QA* Tel (01455) 282630

CASTLE, Dr Brian Colin. b 49. Lon Univ BA72 Ox Univ BA77 MA80 Birm Univ PhD89. Cuddesdon Coll 74. **d** 77 **p** 78. C Sutton St Nic *S'wark* 77; C Limpsfield and Titsey 77-81; USPG 81-84; Zambia 81-84; Lect Ecum Inst WCC Geneva 84-85; V N Petherton w Northmoor Green *B & W* 85-92; Dir of Studies & Vice-Prin Ripon Coll Cuddesdon from 92; Lic to Offic *Ox* from 92. *3 College Fields, Cuddesdon, Oxford OX44 9HL* Tel (01865) 874974

CASTLE, Brian Stanley. b 47. Oak Hill Th Coll 70. **d** 73 **p** 74. C Barnsbury St Andr w St Thos and St Matthias *Lon* 73-76; C Lower Homerton St Paul 76-79; P-in-c Bethnal Green St Jas Less from 79. *St James the Less Vicarage, St James's Avenue, London E2 9JD* Tel 0181-980 1612

CASTLE, Daphne Susan (Dee). b 39. Lon Inst of Educn TCert60 Open Univ BA88. Ox Min Course CBTS93. **d** 93 **p** 94. NSM Newbury *Ox* from 93; Chapl Clere Sch Newbury from 93. *20 Falkland Garth, Newbury, Berks RG14 6PB*

CASTLE, John Arthur. b 61. G&C Coll Cam BA83 S Bank Univ DMS88. Aston Tr Scheme 90 Cranmer Hall Dur BA95. **d** 95 **p** 96. C Southborough St Pet w Ch Ch and St Matt *Roch* from 95. *54 Holden Park Road, Southborough, Tunbridge Wells, Kent TN4 0EP* Tel (01892) 529153

CASTLE, Michael David. b 38. Wells Th Coll 69. **d** 71 **p** 72. C Acocks Green *Birm* 71-75; C Weoley Castle 76-78; V from 78. *St Gabriel's Vicarage, 83 Marston Road, Birmingham B29 5LS* Tel 0121-475 1194

CASTLE, Phillip Stanley. b 43. LNSM course 94. **d** 97. NSM E Farnworth and Kearsley *Man* from 97. *73 Bradford Street, Farnworth, Bolton, Lancs BL4 9JY* Tel (01204) 571439

CASTLE, Roger James. b 39. St Jo Coll Cam BA62 MA66. Clifton Th Coll 63. **d** 65 **p** 66. C Rushden w Newton Bromswold *Pet* 65-68; C Stapenhill w Cauldwell *Derby* 68-72; V Hayfield 72-89; R Coxheath w E Farleigh, Hunton and Linton *Roch* from 89. *The Rectory, 19 Westerhill Road, Coxheath, Maidstone, Kent ME17 4DQ* Tel (01622) 747570

CASTLE, Vincent Clifton. b 15. ALCD37 St Jo Coll Dur LTh38 BA39. **d** 39 **p** 40. C Moulsham St Jo *Chelmsf* 39-42; CF (EC) 42-47 and 54-58; C-in-c Oakdale St Geo CD *Sarum* 47-50; P-in-c Coalpit Heath *Bris* 50-54; V Avonmouth St Andr 58-63; Miss to Seamen 63-71; V Creeksea w Althorne *Chelmsf* 71-79; RD Dengie 74-82; V Creeksea w Althorne, Latchingdon and N Fambridge 80-82; rtd 82; Perm to Offic *Chelmsf* from 82. *49 Winstree Road, Burnham-on-Crouch, Essex CM0 8ET* Tel (01621) 782807

CASTLE, Wilfrid Thomas Froggatt. b 11. Qu Coll Cam BA33 MA37. Wycliffe Hall Ox 33. **d** 35 **p** 36. C Leyton Ch Ch *Chelmsf* 35-38; C Dover St Mary *Cant* 38-39; C Skipton H Trin *Bradf* 39-42; V Cowling 42-45; Cyprus 45-54; Chapl Cannes *Eur* 54-63; Chapl Istanbul 63-65; V Bocking St Pet *Chelmsf* 65-72; R Paisley St Barn *Glas* 72-77; P-in-c 77-79; rtd 77. *5 Freemen's Court, Water Lane, Clifton, York YO3 6PR* Tel (01904) 640185

CASTLETON, David Miles. b 39. Oak Hill Th Coll 69. **d** 72 **p** 73. C Canonbury St Steph *Lon* 72-76; C Stoke next Guildf St Jo *Guildf* 76; C Guildf St Sav w Stoke-next-Guildford 76-89. *26 Keswick Road, Great Bookham, Leatherhead, Surrey KT23 4BH* Tel (01372) 454990

CASWELL, Roger John. b 47. St Chad's Coll Dur BA70. St Steph Ho Ox 75. **d** 77 **p** 78. C Brighton Resurr *Chich* 77-83; TV Crawley 83-90; TR Littlehampton and Wick from 90; Chapl Littlehampton Hosp from 90. *34 Fitzalan Road, Littlehampton, W Sussex BN17 5ET* Tel (01903) 724410

CASWELL, Thomas Hubert (Tom). b 55. Aston Tr Scheme 90 Coll of Resurr Mirfield 92. **d** 94 **p** 95. C Sheff Norwood St Leon *Sheff* 94-97; P-in-c Sheff Parson Cross St Cecilia from 97. *St Cecilia's Priory, 98 Chaucer Close, Sheffield S5 9QE* Tel (0114) 232 1084

CATCHPOLE, Geoffrey Alan (Geoff). b 53. AKC. Westcott Ho Cam 76. **d** 77 **p** 78. C Camberwell St Luke *S'wark* 77-80; C Dulwich St Barn 80-82; TV Canvey Is *Chelmsf* 82-87; Ind Chapl from 83; P-in-c Bradwell on Sea 87-92; V Holland-on-Sea from 92. *The Vicarage, 297 Frinton Road, Clacton-on-Sea, Essex CO15 5SP* Tel (01255) 812420

CATCHPOLE, Guy St George. b 30. **d** 82 **p** 83. Kenya 82-89; C Woodford Wells *Chelmsf* 89-95; rtd 95. *137 Chatham Road, Maidstone, Kent ME14 2NB* Tel (01622) 201582

CATCHPOLE, Canon Keith William. b 30. AKC56. St Boniface Warminster 54. **d** 57 **p** 58. C Woodchurch *Ches* 57-61; C W Kirby St Bridget 61-64; C-in-c Upton Priory CD 64-72; R Lavant *Chich* 72-82; RD Chich 80-96; Can and Preb Chich Cathl from 82; V Chich St Paul and St Pet 82-95; P-in-c W Hampnett 91-95; TR Chichester from 95. *The Rectory, Tower Close, Chichester, W Sussex PO19 1QN* Tel (01243) 531624

CATCHPOLE, Richard James Swinburne. b 65. St Steph Ho Ox 92. **d** 95 **p** 96. C Eastbourne St Andr *Chich* from 95. *75 Churchdale Road, Eastbourne, E Sussex BN22 8RX* Tel (01323) 736312

CATCHPOLE, Roy. b 46. St Jo Coll Nottm LTh74 MMin MTheol. **d** 74 **p** 75. C Rainham *Chelmsf* 74-76; C Hyson Green *S'well* 76-79; V Broxtowe 79-86; V Calverton 86-94. *Society of St Francis, The Friary, Hilfield, Dorchester, Dorset DT2 7BE* Tel (01300) 341181

CATCHPOOL, Terence David Housden (Terry). b 34. MIBiol Hatf Coll Dur BSc56. Trin Coll Bris 85. **d** 86 **p** 87. NSM Bath Odd Down w Combe Hay *B & W* from 86. *119 Rush Hill, Bath BA2 2QT* Tel (01225) 424828

CATER, Henry Derek. b 17. Chich Th Coll 49. **d** 51 **p** 52. C Beeston Hill St Luke *Ripon* 51-55; C Knottingley *Wakef* 55-62; V Barnsley St Edw 62-65; Lic to Offic *Eur* 65-66; Can Paroch *Wakef* 66-69; rtd 69; Lic to Offic *Eur* 69-84. *5 Furniss Court, Cranleigh, Surrey GU6 8TN* Tel (01483) 275941

CATER, Lois May. b 37. S Dios Minl Tr Scheme 81. **dss** 84 **d** 87 **p** 94. Calne and Blackland *Sarum* 84-89; Hon Par Dn 87-89; Hon Par Dn Devizes St Jo w St Mary 89-94; Hon C 94-96; Hon TV Alderbury Team from 96. *Hope Cottage, The Street, Farley, Salisbury SP5 1AA* Tel (01722) 712743 Fax as telephone

CATERER, James Albert Leslie Blower. b 44. New Coll Ox BA67 MA81. Sarum & Wells Th Coll 79. **d** 81 **p** 82. C Cheltenham St Luke and St Jo *Glouc* 81-85; V Standish w Haresfield and Moreton Valence etc 85-96; P-in-c Glouc St Steph from 96. *St Stephen's Vicarage, 84 Frampton Road, Gloucester GL1 5QB* Tel (01452) 524694 E-mail jcaterer@atlas.co.uk

CATES, Canon Geoffrey Charles. b 18. Leeds Univ BA42. Coll of Resurr Mirfield 42. **d** 44 **p** 45. C Whitworth w Spennymoor *Dur* 44-46; C Brandon 46-47; C Ushaw Moor 48-49; Chapl Butlin's Clacton-on-Sea 49-52; C Clacton St Jas *Chelmsf* 49-51; Ghana 52-61; Br Guiana 61-66; Guyana 66-71; Dean Georgetown 61-71; R Salford Sacred Trin *Man* 71-82; RD Salford 71-82; Hon Can Man Cathl 80-82; Soc Resp Adv *St E* 82-88; Hon Can St E Cathl 85-88; rtd 88. *55 Berners Street, Ipswich IP1 3LN* Tel (01473) 216629

CATHCART, Adrian James. b 51. N Ord Course. **d** 87 **p** 88. C Blackley St Andr *Man* 87-90. *54 Tweedhill Road, Manchester M9 3LG* Tel 0161-740 6774

CATHERALL, Mark Leslie. b 64. Chich Th Coll BTh93. **d** 93 **p** 94. C Lancing w Coombes *Chich* 93-95; C Selsey from 95. *18 Glen Crescent, Selsey, Chichester, W Sussex PO20 0QT* Tel (01243) 605948

CATHIE, Sean Bewley. b 43. Dur Univ BA67. Cuddesdon Coll 67. **d** 69 **p** 70. C Kensal Rise St Martin *Lon* 69-73; C Paddington H Trin w St Paul 73-75; P-in-c Bridstow w Peterstow *Heref* 76-79; Hon C Westmr St Jas *Lon* from 85. *23 Brookfield Mansions, Highgate West Hill, London N6 6AS* Tel 0181-340 6603

CATLEY, John Howard. b 37. AKC60. **d** 61 **p** 62. C Sowerby Bridge w Norland *Wakef* 61-64; C Almondbury 64-67; V Earl's Heaton 67-75; V Brownhill 75-86; V Morley St Pet w Churwell 86-92; V St Annes St Marg *Blackb* from 92; RD Kirkham from 94. *St Margaret's Vicarage, 13 Rowsley Road, Lytham St Annes, Lancs FY8 2NS* Tel (01253) 722648

CATLING, Michael David. b 56. Golds Coll Lon CertEd77 DipEd84 Whitelands Coll Lon DipC&S88. Cranmer Hall Dur 88. **d** 90 **p** 91. C Cullercoats St Geo *Newc* 90-94; TV Glendale Gp from 94. *Eglingham Vicarage, Alnwick, Northd NE66 2TX* Tel (0166578) 250

CATLING, Canon Robert Mason. b 19. St Jo Coll Ox BA41 MA44. St Steph Ho Ox 41. **d** 43 **p** 44. C Falmouth All SS *Truro* 43-57; Lib Pusey Ho 57-61; Asst Chapl Univ Coll Ox 57-61; C Falmouth All SS *Truro* 61-64; V Beckenham St Barn *Roch* 64-72; V Devoran *Truro* 72-87; Hon Can Truro Cathl 77-87; rtd 87; Perm to Offic *Ex* and *Truro* from 87. *Ground Floor Flat, 31 Cranford Avenue, Exmouth, Devon EX8 2QA* Tel (01395) 267896

CATO (formerly LEGGETT), Ms Vanessa Gisela. b 51. St Osyth Coll of Educn TCert75. Westcott Ho Cam CTMin93. **d** 93 **p** 94. C Southchurch H Trin *Chelmsf* 93-97; R Orsett and Bulphan and Horndon on the Hill from 97. *The Rectory, Orsett, Grays, Essex RM16 3JT* Tel (01375) 891254

CATON, David Arthur. b 25. Trin Coll Ox BA50 MA50. St Steph Ho Ox 49. **d** 51 **p** 52. C Seaton Hirst *Newc* 51-55; S Africa 55-61; V Stapleford *Ely* 61-69; V Hurst *Man* 69-75; V Hanwell St Thos *Lon* 75-84; AD Ealing W 82-84; V Staincross *Wakef* 84-95; rtd 95. *72 Drayton Bridge Road, London W7 1EP* Tel 0181-567 3587

CATON, Philip Cooper. b 47. Oak Hill Th Coll 79. **d** 81 **p** 82. C Much Woolton *Liv* 81-85; TV Parr from 85. *St Paul's Vicarage, 75 Chain Lane, St Helens, Merseyside WA11 9QF* Tel (01744) 34335

CATT, Albert Henry. b 08. St Steph Ho Ox 34. **d** 37 **p** 38. C Somers Town St Mary *Lon* 37-40; CF (EC) 40-46; Hon CF from 46; C Harrow St Pet *Lon* 46-48; V Hornsey St Geo 49-74; rtd 74; Perm to Offic *Ely* 75-88. *48 Green Park, Chatteris, Cambs PE16 6DL* Tel (01354) 693102

CATT, Douglas Gordon. b 23. MCSP49 SRP67. Roch Th Coll 61. **d** 63 **p** 64. C Cant St Martin w St Paul *Cant* 63-66; R Croughton *Pet* 66-75; R Hinton in the Hedges w Steane 66-75; V Evenley 72-75; Chapl St Andr Hosp Northn 75-89; Lic to Offic *Pet* from 75; rtd 88. *195 Billing Road, Northampton NN1 5RS* Tel (01604) 27710

CATTANACH, Alexander Hamilton Avery. b 16. Univ of Wales BA37. St Mich Coll Llan 38. **d** 39 **p** 40. C St Brides and Marloes *St D* 39-43; C Pembroke Dock 43-46; C Accrington St Jas *Blackb* 46-51; C-in-c Lostock Hall CD 51-54; C-in-c Lt Thornton CD 54-61; V Lt Thornton 61-81; rtd 81; Lic to Offic *Blackb* from 81. *4 Dawson Road, St Annes, Lytham St Annes, Lancs FY8 3AJ* Tel (01253) 727099

CATTELL, The Ven Jack. b 15. Univ Coll Dur BA37 DipTh38 MA40 Lon Univ BD53. Sarum & Wells Th Coll 38. **d** 39 **p** 40. C Royston *Wakef* 39-41; Perm to Offic *Sarum* 41-42; CF (EC) 42-46; Lic to Offic *Ripon* 46-49; Chapl R Wanstead Sch 49-53; Bermuda 53-82; Adn Bermuda 61-82; Perm to Offic *Mon* from 82. *39A Risca Road, Newport NP9 4HX* Tel (01633) 54529

CATTELL, John Eugene Brownlow. b 11. TD62. Selw Coll Cam BA34 MA44. Wells Th Coll 35. **d** 36 **p** 37. C S w N Bersted *Chich* 36-38; C Soham *Ely* 38-40; CF (EC) 40-45; CF (TA) 50-67; R St Just in Roseland *Truro* 45-49; R Snailwell *Ely* 49-65; V Chippenham 49-65; RD Fordham 53-65; V Piddletrenthide w Alton Pancras and Plush *Sarum* 65-74; R Piddlehinton 73-74; P-in-c Kington Magna and Buckhorn Weston 74-77; rtd 77; Perm to Offic *Truro* from 77. *Tredinnock, Bishops Hill Road, New Polzeath, Wadebridge, Cornwall PL27 6UF* Tel (01208) 862388

CATTERALL, David Arnold. b 53. ARCS Lon Univ BSc74. Cranmer Hall Dur DipTh78. **d** 78 **p** 79. C Swinton St Pet *Man* 78-81; C Wythenshawe St Martin 81-83; R Heaton Norris Ch w All SS 83-88; I Fanlobbus Union *C, C & R* 88-95; RD Mid W Cork 90-95; Can Cork and Ross Cathls 93-95; Warden Ch's Min of Healing in Ireland from 95. *Drung Vicarage, Drung, Co Cavan, Irish Republic* Tel Cavan (49) 38204 or Dublin (1) 872 7876 Fax Cavan (49) 38204

CATTERALL, Mrs Janet Margaret. b 53. Univ of Wales (Ban) BA74. Cranmer Hall Dur DipTh77. **dss** 81 **d** 87 **p** 90. Wythenshawe St Martin *Man* 81-83; Heaton Norris Ch w All SS 83-87; Par Dn 87-88; C Bandon Union *C, C & R* 88-89; Dioc Youth Adv (Cork) 89-94; Dioc Youth Chapl 94-95; I Drung w Castleterra, Larah and Lavey etc *K, E & A* from 95. *Drung Vicarage, Drung, Co Cavan, Irish Republic* Tel Cavan (49) 38204 Fax as telephone

CATTERICK, Matthew John. b 68. W Sussex Inst of HE BA92. St Steph Ho Ox BTh95. **d** 95 **p** 96. C Colchester St Jas, All SS, St Nic and St Runwald *Chelmsf* from 95. *Benson House, 13 Roman Road, Colchester CO1 1UR* Tel (01206) 573038

CATTLE, Richard John. b 40. WMMTC 88. **d** 90 **p** 91. NSM Brixworth Deanery *Pet* 90-91; NSM Welford w Sibbertoft and Marston Trussell 91-92; V from 92. *The Vicarage, 35 The Leys, Welford, Northampton NN6 7HS* Tel (01858) 575252

CATTLEY, Richard Melville. b 49. Trin Coll Bris DipTh73. **d** 73 **p** 74. C Kendal St Thos *Carl* 73-77; Nat Sec Pathfinders CPAS 77-82; Exec Sec 82-85; V Dalton-in-Furness *Carl* 85-90; V Dulwich St Barn *S'wark* from 90; Chapl Alleyn's Foundn Dulwich from 90. *St Barnabas's Vicarage, 38 Calton Avenue, London SE21 7DG* Tel 0181-693 2936

CATTON, Canon Cedric Trevor. b 36. JP. DipRJ. Lambeth STh94 Wells Th Coll 70. **d** 72 **p** 73. C Solihull *Birm* 72-74; R Whepstead w Brockley *St E* 74-75; R Hawstead and Nowton w Stanningfield etc 74-79; Dioc Stewardship Adv 77-83; R Cockfield 79-83; V Exning St Martin w Landwade from 83; Chapl Newmarket Gen Hosp from 85; Hon Can St E Cathl *St E* from 90; Chapl Dio Mothers Union from 94. *The Vicarage, New River Green, Exning, Newmarket, Suffolk CB8 7HS* Tel (01638) 577413

CAUNT, Mrs Margaret. b 55. Coll of Ripon & York St Jo MTh97. N Ord Course 93. **d** 97. NSM Brightside w Wincobank *Sheff* from 97. *12 Barkby Road, Wincobank, Sheffield S9 1JX* Tel 0114-249 2757

CAVAGAN, Dr Raymond. b 35. Hull Univ MA86 PhD87. Oak Hill Th Coll DipTh62. **d** 63 **p** 64. C Upper Holloway St Pet *Lon* 63-66; C Hurworth *Dur* 66-68; V New Shildon 68-76; P-in-c Toxteth Park St Andr Aigburth Road *Liv* 76-77; V Toxteth Park St Mich 76-77; V Toxteth Park St Mich w St Andr 78-88; V Stamfordham w Matfen *Newc* from 88; Hon CF from 90. *The Vicarage, Stamfordham, Newcastle upon Tyne NE18 0QQ* Tel (01661) 886456 Fax as telephone

CAVAGHAN, Dennis Edgar. b 45. St Jo Coll Nottm BTh72. **d** 72 **p** 73. C Hartford *Ches* 72-76; C Plymouth St Andr w St Paul and St Geo *Ex* 76-80; V Cofton w Starcross 80-88; P-in-c W Exe 88-93; Perm to Offic *B & W* from 93. *The Manor House, Thurloxton, Taunton, Somerset TA2 8RH* Tel (01823) 413777

CAVAN, Lawrence Noel. b 38. Trin Coll Bris 72. **d** 75 **p** 76. C Lurgan Ch Ch *D & D* 75-78; C Chorleywood Ch Ch *St Alb* 78-82; I Durrus *C, C & R* 82-85; I Portarlington w Cloneyhurke and Lea *M & K* 85-90; TV Eston w Normanby *York* from 90. *The Vicarage, 73A High Street, Eston, Middlesbrough, Cleveland TS6 9EH* Tel (01642) 456755

CAVANAGH, Capt Kenneth Joseph. b 41. CA Tr Coll 60. **d** 77 **p** 77. CA from 64; Paraguay 70-83; P-in-c Gt w Lt Snoring *Nor* 83-85; R Gt w Lt Snoring w Kettlestone and Pensthorpe 85-88; R Glencarse *Bre* 88-94; CA Co-ord (Scotland/Ireland) & Regional Voc Adv from 90; R Dundee St Luke from 95. *The Rectory, 4 St Luke's Road, Downfield, Dundee DD3 0LD* Tel (01382) 825165

CAVANAGH, Michael Richard. b 49. MIDPM78. N Ord Course 89. **d** 92 **p** 93. NSM Stalybridge H Trin and Ch Ch *Ches* from 92. *139 Mottram Road, Stalybridge, Cheshire SK15 2QU* Tel 0161-303 1314 Fax 304 9997

CAVANAGH, Peter Bernard. b 49. Sarum & Wells Th Coll 71. **d** 73 **p** 74. C Gt Crosby St Faith *Liv* 73-76; C Stanley 76-79; V Anfield St Columba from 79. *St Columba's Vicarage, Pinehurst Avenue, Liverpool L4 2TZ* Tel 0151-474 7231

CAVE, Canon Alan John. b 17. IPFA52 Lon Univ DipTh65. Cuddesdon Coll 64. **d** 65 **p** 66. C St Annes *Blackb* 65-68; C Ribbleton 68-72; V Burnley St Cath 72-78; P-in-c Burnley St Alb w St Paul 77-78; R Ribchester w Stidd 78-85; Hon Can Blackb Cathl 81-85; rtd 85; Perm to Offic *Guildf* from 86. *Mellstock, 23 Portmore Park Road, Weybridge, Surrey KT13 8ET* Tel (01932) 851635

CAVE, Anthony Sidney. b 32. EMMTC. **d** 84 **p** 85. C Immingham *Linc* 84-88; V Keelby 88-89; V Riby 88-89; V Keelby w Riby and Aylesby from 89. *The Vicarage, Keelby, Grimsby, S Humberside DN37 8EH* Tel (01469) 560251

CAVE, Bill. *See* CAVE-BROWNE-CAVE, Bernard James William

CAVE, Brian Malcolm. b 37. St Cath Soc Ox BA60 MA64. Oak Hill Th Coll. **d** 63 **p** 64. C Streatham Park St Alb *S'wark* 63-66; C Ruskin Park St Sav and St Matt 66-68; C Tunbridge Wells St Jas *Roch* 68-71; V Bootle St Leon *Liv* 71-75; Min St Mary w St John Bootle 73-75; Area Sec Leprosy Miss 75-81; V Hurst Green *Bradf* 81-82; P-in-c Mitton 81-82; V Hurst Green and Mitton 82-91; rtd 91. *63 Westway, Nailsea, Avon BS19 1EF* Tel (01275) 654892

CAVE, Cyril Hayward. b 20. Nottm Univ MA60 BD63. AKC49. **d** 50 **p** 51. C Upholland *Liv* 50-53; P-in-c Darley w S Darley *Derby* 53-56; V Ticknall 56-65; Lic to Offic *Ex* from 65; Lect Th Ex Univ 65-80; Sen Lect 80-85; rtd 85. *Berry House, Cheriton Fitzpaine, Crediton, Devon EX17 4HZ* Tel (01363) 866548

CAVE, Douglas Lionel. b 26. Lon Bible Coll 50 Lon Coll of Div 64. **d** 66 **p** 67. C Upper Holloway St Jo *Lon* 66-69; C Barking St Marg *Chelmsf* 69-73; V Blackb St Barn *Blackb* 73-81; Ind Chapl *Lon* 81-91; rtd 91. *8 Wood Rise, Pinner, Middx HA5 2JD* Tel (01895) 677426

CAVE, The Ven Guy Newell. b 19. TCD BA41 MA58. CITC 41. **d** 42 **p** 43. C Knockbreda *D & D* 42-45; P-in-c Kildrumferton w Ballymachugh *K, E & A* 45-73; Preb St Patr Cathl Dublin 65-72; Adn Kilmore *K, E & A* 72-87; P-in-c Ballymachugh w Kildrumferton and Ballyjamesduff 73-87; rtd 87. *5 Yew Point, Hodson's Bay, Athlone, Co Westmeath, Irish Republic* Tel Athlone (902) 92718

CAVE, John Edwin Dawson. b 43. Cranmer Hall Dur 71. **d** 74 **p** 75. C Gt Ayton w Easby and Newton in Cleveland *York* 74-77; C Redcar w Kirkleatham 77-78; C Redcar 78-80; P-in-c Aislaby and Ruswarp 80-81; V 81-87; V Dormanstown 87-97; V Marton-in-Cleveland from 97. *The Vicarage, Stokesley Road, Marton-in-Cleveland, Middlesbrough, Cleveland TS7 8JU* Tel (01642) 316201

CAVE, Robert Philip. b 23. Roch Th Coll 64. **d** 67 **p** 68. C York Town St Mich *Guildf* 67-71; C Yaxley *Ely* 71-75; R Cottenham 75-88; rtd 88; Perm to Offic *Pet* from 89. *14 St Mary's Way, Roade, Northampton NN7 2PQ* Tel (01604) 864420

CAVE BERGQUIST, Julie Anastasia. b 59. St Jo Coll Dur BA80 Franciscan Univ Rome STL87. St Steph Ho Ox 85. **d** 87. Par Dn Kennington *Cant* 87-89; Chapl Trin Coll Cam 89-94; Chapl Westcott Ho Cam 94-97. *7 Corder Close, St Albans, Herts AL3 4NH* Tel (01727) 841116

CAVE-BROWNE-CAVE, Bernard James William (Bill). b 54. Trin Hall Cam BA76 MA80 Bradf Univ MA90. Westcott Ho Cam 77. **d** 79 **p** 80. C Chesterton Gd Shep *Ely* 79-83; Chapl Lanc Univ *Blackb* 83-95; Chapl HM Pris Service from 95. *HM Prison Service Chaplaincy, Abell House, John Islip Street, London SW1P 4LH* Tel 0171-217 5685 Fax 217 5090

✠**CAVELL, The Rt Revd John Kingsmill.** b 16. Qu Coll Cam BA39 MA44. Wycliffe Hall Ox 39. **d** 40 **p** 41 **c** 72. C Folkestone H Trin *Cant* 40; C Addington 40-44; Lic to Offic *Ox* 45-52; Area Sec (Dio Ox) CMS 44-52; Dio Pet 44-49; Tr Officer 49-52; V Cheltenham Ch Ch *Glouc* 52-62; V Plymouth St Andr *Ex* 62-72; RD Plymouth 67-72; Preb Ex Cathl 67-72; V E Stonehouse 68-72; Suff Bp Southampton *Win* 72-84; Hon Can Win Cathl 72-84; rtd 84; Perm to Offic *Win* from 84; Asst Bp Sarum from 88; Can and

Preb Sarum Cathl from 88. *5 Constable Way, West Harnham, Salisbury SP2 8LN* Tel (01722) 334782 Fax 413112

CAVELL-NORTHAM, Canon Cavell Herbert James. b 32. St Steph Ho Ox 53. **d** 56 **p** 57. C W Wycombe *Ox* 56-61; CF (TA) 60-63; V Lane End *Ox* 61-68; V Stony Stratford from 68; P-in-c Calverton 69-72; R from 72; Hon Can Ch Ch from 91. *The Vicarage, London Road, Stony Stratford, Milton Keynes MK11 1JA* Tel (01908) 562148

CAW, Alison Mary. b 40. Natal Univ BA62 Ox Univ PGCE64. Ox Min Course CBTS93. **d** 93 **p** 94. NSM Beaconsfield *Ox* from 93. *1 Westway, Beaconsfield, Bucks HP9 1DQ* Tel (01494) 674524

CAW, Miss Hannah Mary. b 69. Birm Univ BMus91. St Jo Coll Nottm DTS94 MA95 LTh95. **d** 95 **p** 96. C Northampton St Giles *Pet* from 95. *18 The Avenue, Cliftonville, Northampton NN1 5BT* Tel (01604) 24797

CAWDELL, Mrs Sarah Helen Louise. b 65. St Hugh's Coll Ox MA91 Trin Coll Cam BA94. Ridley Hall Cam BA94 CTM95. **d** 95 **p** 96. C Belmont *S'wark* from 95. *75 Brinkley Road, Worcester Park, Surrey KT4 8JE* Tel 0181-330 7210

CAWDELL, Simon Howard. b 65. Univ Coll Dur BA86. Ridley Hall Cam CTM94. **d** 94 **p** 95. C Cheam Common St Phil *S'wark* from 94. *75 Brinkley Road, Worcester Park, Surrey KT4 8JE* Tel 0181-330 7210

CAWLEY, David Lewis. b 44. FSA81. AKC71 St Aug Coll Cant 71. **d** 72 **p** 73. C Sprowston *Nor* 72-75; Chapl HM Pris Nor 74-75; C Wymondham *Nor* 75-77; C Buckland in Dover w Buckland Valley *Cant* 77-83; V Eastville St Anne w St Mark and St Thos *Bris* 83-95; V Leic St Mary *Leic* from 95; TV Leic H Spirit from 97; Chapl Trin Hosp Leic from 96. *The Vicarage, 15 Castle Street, Leicester LE1 5WN* Tel 0116-262 8727

CAWLEY, Stephen. b 42. RMCM GRSM63. St Deiniol's Hawarden 81. **d** 84 **p** 85. C Tranmere St Paul w St Luke *Ches* 84-88; TV Hawarden *St As* 88-93; V Gwernaffield and Llanferres from 93. *The Vicarage, Cilcain Road, Gwernaffield, Mold CH7 5DQ* Tel (01352) 740205

CAWRSE, Christopher William. b 60. Univ of Wales (Cardiff) DipTh. Westcott Ho Cam. **d** 84 **p** 85. C Stoke Newington St Mary *Lon* 84-86; Chapl St Mark's Hosp Lon 86-90; C Islington St Jas w St Phil *Lon* 86-87; C Islington St Jas w St Pet 87-90; Chapl Asst Charing Cross Hosp Lon 90-93; rtd 93; C Isleworth All SS *Lon* 93. *179 Grange Hill Road, London SE9 1SR*

CAWTE, Canon David John. b 30. St Mich Coll Llan. **d** 65 **p** 66. C Chorley St Laur *Blackb* 65-67; C Boyne Hill *Ox* 67-74; C-in-c Cox Green CD 75-78; V Cox Green 78-94; Hon Can Ch Ch 88-94; rtd 94. *6 Broadfields Close, Milford on Sea, Lymington, Hants SO41 0SE* Tel (01590) 642793

CAWTHORNE, Jack. b 22. ATD50 Lon Univ DipTh71. Cuddesdon Coll 69. **d** 71 **p** 72. NSM Newchurch *Man* 71-86; NSM Garforth *Ripon* 87-88; Perm to Offic from 88. *15 Arran Drive, Garforth, Leeds LS25 2BU* Tel 0113-286 9527

CAYTON, John. b 32. Bps' Coll Cheshunt 54. **d** 57 **p** 58. C Hindley All SS *Liv* 57-59; C Littleham w Exmouth *Ex* 59-63; V Burnley St Cath *Blackb* 63-72; V Marton 72-87; V Fleetwood 87-97; Miss to Seamen from 87; rtd 97. *19 Parkstone Avenue, Thornton-Cleveleys, Lancs FY5 5AE* Tel (01253) 854088

CECIL, Kevin Vincent. b 54. BA PGCE. St Mich Coll Llan DipTh82. **d** 82 **p** 83. C Llanilid w Pencoed *Llan* 82-85; C Coity w Nolton 85-88; Area Sec (Dios St D, Llan, Mon and S & B) CMS from 88. *Gronw House, Llanharry, Pontyclun CF72 9LH* Tel (01443) 225035 Fax 0171-401 3215

CEELY, Ms Sandra Elizabeth. b 44. N Ord Course 94. **d** 97. C Gt and Lt Driffield *York* from 97. *15 Riverside View, Malton, N Yorkshire YO17 0PB* Tel (01653) 690131

CERRATTI, Christa Elisabeth. b 54. Ox Coll FE NNEB93. Wycliffe Hall Ox DipMin94. **d** 97. C Chipping Norton *Ox* from 97. *137 Cornish Road, Chipping Norton, Oxon OX7 5LA* Tel (01608) 641005

CHADD, Jeremy Denis. b 55. Jes Coll Cam BA77 MA81. Coll of Resurr Mirfield 78. **d** 81 **p** 82. C Seaton Hirst *Newc* 81-84; C N Gosforth 84-88; V Sunderland St Chad *Dur* from 88. *St Chad's Vicarage, Charter Drive, Sunderland SR3 3PG* Tel 0191-528 2397

CHADD, Canon Leslie Frank. b 19. Leeds Univ BSc41. Coll of Resurr Mirfield 41. **d** 43 **p** 44. C Portsea All SS w St Jo Rudmore *Portsm* 43-46; Chapl RNVR 46-48; C Greenford H Cross *Lon* 48-54; C Littlehampton St Mary *Chich* 54-58; V Hanworth All SS *Lon* 58-65; V Fareham SS Pet and Paul *Portsm* 65-92; Relig Adv STV 72-81; Hon Can Portsm Cathl 81-92; rtd 92. *Tree Tops, Hoads Hill, Wickham, Fareham, Hants PO17 5BX* Tel (01329) 834397

CHADWICK, Charles John Peter. b 59. Birm Univ BA81 Slough Coll DMS84 Southn Univ BTh90. Sarum & Wells Th Coll 85. **d** 88 **p** 89. C Chalfont St Peter *Ox* 88-91; C Gt Marlow 91-93; TV Gt Marlow w Marlow Bottom, Lt Marlow and Bisham 93-95; P-in-c Stokenchurch and Ibstone from 95; Asst Dir Chiltern Ch Tr Course from 95. *The Vicarage, Wycombe Road, Stokenchurch, High Wycombe, Bucks HP14 3RG* Tel (01494) 483384

CHADWICK, David Guy Evelyn St Just. b 36. Bps' Coll Cheshunt 61. **d** 68 **p** 69. C Edmonton All SS *Lon* 68-71; C Edmonton St Mary w St Jo 71-72; C Greenhill St Jo 72-74; Bp's Dom Chapl *Truro* 74-79; Chapl Community of the Epiphany Truro 77-78; P-in-c Crantock *Truro* 79-83; R Clydebank *Glas* 83-87; R Renfrew 87-94; rtd 94. *La Verna, 1 Nithsdale Crescent, Bearsden, Glasgow G61 4DF*

CHADWICK, Francis Arnold Edwin. b 30. AKC54. **d** 55 **p** 56. C Chapel Allerton *Ripon* 55-58; C Hayes *Roch* 58-61; V Arreton *Portsm* 61-67; V Newchurch 61-67; V Kingshurst *Birm* 67-73; V York Town St Mich *Guildf* 73-83; P-in-c Long Sutton w Long Load *B & W* 83-87; R Stockbridge and Longstock and Leckford *Win* 87-93; rtd 93; Chapl Helsinki w Tallinn *Eur* from 95. *Mannerheimintie 19 A7, 00250 Helsinki, Finland* Tel Helsinki (0) 490424 Fax 447987

CHADWICK, Canon George Bancroft. b 12. Linc Th Coll 40. **d** 42 **p** 43. C S Shore H Trin *Blackb* 42-45; C Hexham *Newc* 45-48; C Gosforth All SS 48-50; P-in-c Newsham 50-55; V Cullercoats St Geo 55-70; RD Tynemouth 67-70; V Corbridge w Halton 70-81; Hon Can Newc Cathl 74-82; P-in-c Newton Hall 79-81; V Corbridge w Halton and Newton Hall 82; rtd 82. *14 Alexandra Terrace, Hexham, Northd NE46 3JH* Tel (01434) 602092

✠**CHADWICK, The Rt Revd Graham Charles.** b 23. Keble Coll Ox BA49 MA53. St Mich Coll Llan 49. **d** 50 **p** 51 **c** 76. C Oystermouth *S & B* 50-53; Basutoland 53-63; Chapl Univ of Wales (Swansea) *S & B* 63-68; Sen Bursar Qu Coll Birm 68-69; Lic to Offic *S'wark* 69-70; Lesotho 70-76; S Africa 76-82; Bp Kimberley and Kuruman 76-82; Dioc Adv on Spirituality *St As* 83-90; Chapl St As Cathl 83-90; rtd 90; Asst Bp Liv 90-95. *66 Hulse Road, Salisbury SP1 3LY* Tel (01722) 416287

CHADWICK, Helen Jane. *See* MARSHALL, Mrs Helen Jane

CHADWICK, Canon Prof Henry. b 20. KBE89 OM(Ger)93. FBA60 MRIA Magd Coll Cam BA41 MusBac41 MA45 DD57 Glas Univ Hon DD57 Uppsala Univ Hon DD67 Yale Univ Hon DD70 Man Univ Hon DD75 Leeds Univ Hon DD80. Ridley Hall Cam 42. **d** 43 **p** 44. C S Croydon Em *Cant* 43-45; Asst Chapl Wellington Coll Berks 45-46; Chapl Qu Coll Cam 46-50; Dean 50-55; Can Ch Ch *Ox* 59-69; Regius Prof Div Ox Univ 59-69; Vice-Pres Br Academy 68-69; Dean Ch Ch *Ox* 69-79; Regius Prof Div Cam Univ 79-82; Hon Can Ely Cathl *Ely* 79-83; Lic to Offic from 83; Master Peterho Cam 87-93. *46 St John Street, Oxford OX1 2LH* Tel (01865) 512814

CHADWICK, Canon Martin James. b 27. Trin Hall Cam BA51 MA54. Cuddesdon Coll 52. **d** 54 **p** 55. C Earl's Court St Cuth w St Matthias *Lon* 54-58; Chapl Trin Hall Cam 58-63; Chapl Ch Ch Ox 63-67; V Market Lavington and Easterton *Sarum* 67-79; V Charlbury w Shorthampton *Ox* 79-96; RD Chipping Norton 79-95; Hon Can Ch Ch 91-96; rtd 96. *6 Crecy Walk, Woodstock, Oxford OX20 1US*

CHADWICK, Peter MacKenzie. b 21. Lich Th Coll 63. **d** 65 **p** 66. C Buckhurst Hill *Chelmsf* 65-66; Jt Hd Master Forres Sch Swanage 56-81; Chapl 66-85; NSM Kingston, Langton Matravers and Worth Matravers *Sarum* 85-92; rtd 89; Perm to Offic *Sarum* from 92. *Cull's, Langton Matravers, Swanage, Dorset BH19 3HJ* Tel (01929) 422258

CHADWICK, Roger Vernon. b 39. Dur Univ BA60. Cranmer Hall Dur DipTh62. **d** 62 **p** 63. C Swinton St Pet *Man* 62-65; C Heworth St Mary *Dur* 65-68; Hon C 68-74; V Hartlepool St Aid 75-84; R Egglescliffe from 84. *The Rectory, 10 Butts Lane, Egglescliffe, Stockton-on-Tees, Co Durham TS16 9BT* Tel (01642) 780185

CHADWICK, Prof William Owen. b 16. OM83 KBE82. FBA62 St Jo Coll Cam BA39 MA42 BD51 DD55 St Andr Univ Hon DD60 Ox Univ Hon DD73. Cuddesdon Coll 39. **d** 40 **p** 41. C Huddersfield St Jo *Wakef* 40-42; Chapl Wellington Coll Berks 42-46; Lic to Offic *Ely* from 47; Fell Trin Hall Cam 47-56; Dean 49-56; Master Selw Coll Cam 56-83; Dixie Prof Ecclesiastical Hist 58-68; Regius Prof Modern Hist 68-83; Pres Br Academy 81-85; Chan UEA from 85. *67 Grantchester Street, Cambridge CB7 9HZ* Tel (01223) 314000

CHAFFEY, Jane Frances. b 59. Somerville Coll Ox BA80 MA84 St Jo Coll Dur BA86. Cranmer Hall Dur 84. **d** 88 **p** 94. Par Dn Roby *Liv* 88-90; NSM Finningley w Auckley *S'well* 95-96; Perm to Offic *Pet* from 96. *8 Boxer Road, Wittering, Peterborough PE8 6AE* Tel (01780) 784431

CHAFFEY, Jonathan Paul Michael. b 62. St Chad's Coll Dur BA83. Cranmer Hall Dur 84. **d** 87 **p** 88. C Gateacre *Liv* 87-90; Chapl RAF from 90. *Chaplaincy Services (RAF), HQ, Personnel and Training Command, RAF Innsworth, Gloucester GL3 1EZ* Tel (01452) 712612 Ext 5164 Fax 510828

CHAFFEY, Michael Prosser. b 30. Lon Univ BA51. St Steph Ho Ox 53. **d** 55 **p** 56. C Victoria Docks Ascension *Chelmsf* 55-59; C Leytonstone H Trin Harrow Green 59-62; V Walthamstow St Mich 62-69; R Cov St Jo *Cov* 69-85; P-in-c Cov St Thos 69-75; Hon C Bideford *Ex* 85; P-in-c Charlestown *Man* 85-88; V Sutton St Mich *York* 88-96; rtd 96. *1 School Lane, Burton Fleming, Driffield, N Humberside YO25 0PX* Tel (01262) 470439

CHALCRAFT, Christopher Warine Terrell (Kit). b 37. Oak Hill Th Coll. **d** 67 **p** 68. C Egham *Guildf* 67-70; P-in-c Slough *Ox* 70-73; TV Bramerton w Surlingham *Nor* 73-87; P-in-c Cockley Cley w Gooderstone 87-95; P-in-c Gt and Lt Cressingham w Threxton 87-95; P-in-c Didlington 87-95; P-in-c Hilborough w Bodney 87-95; P-in-c Oxborough w Foulden and Caldecote 87-95. *Address temp unknown*

CHALK, Francis Harold. b 25. Lich Th Coll 61. **d** 62 **p** 63. C Linc St Nic w St Jo Newport *Linc* 62-64; R Kirkby Laythorpe w Asgarby 64-69; V Ewerby w Evedon 65-69; R Gt Gonerby 69-89; rtd 89; Perm to Offic *Truro* from 90. *Chalkleigh, 3 Church Street, St Just, Penzance, Cornwall TR19 7HA* Tel (01736) 787925

CHALK, John Edward. b 33. St D Coll Lamp BA57. **d** 58 **p** 59. C Connah's Quay *St As* 58-61; C Abergele 61-65; V Cyfarthfa *Llan* 65-72; V Pyle w Kenfig 72-77; Lect in FE 84-92; NSM Mansfield Woodhouse *S'well* 92; Perm to Offic *Lich* 92-94; NSM Salt and Sandon w Burston 94-96. *The Old School House, Sunny Bank, Ashbourne, Derbyshire DE6 2LB* Tel (01335) 346487

CHALK, Norman Albert. b 25. S'wark Ord Course 69. **d** 71 **p** 72. C Northwood Hills St Edm *Lon* 71-76; R Cowley 76-90; rtd 91. *23 Rushmoor Avenue, Hazelmere, High Wycombe, Bucks HP15 7NT* Tel (01494) 813438

CHALK, Miss Susan Christine (Sue). b 50. Warw Univ BSc71 Man Univ CertEdD72. S Dios Minl Tr Scheme 90. **d** 93 **p** 94. NSM Bradford Peverell, Stratton, Frampton etc *Sarum* from 93. *2 Dorchester Road, Stratton, Dorchester, Dorset DT2 9RT* Tel (01305) 268464

CHALKLEY, Andrew William Guy. b 64. Aston Tr Scheme 90 St Jo Coll Nottm BTh92. **d** 95 **p** 96. C Liskeard, St Keyne, St Pinnock, Morval etc *Truro* from 95. *1 Maddever Crescent, Liskeard, Cornwall PL14 3PT* Tel (01579) 342136

CHALKLEY, Henry Roy. b 23. St Aid Birkenhead 58. **d** 59 **p** 60. C Bromborough *Ches* 59-63; Miss to Seamen 63-88; rtd 88. *32 Spriteshall Lane, Felixstowe, Suffolk IP11 9QY* Tel (01394) 277600

CHALLEN, Canon Peter Bernard. b 31. Clare Coll Cam BA56 MA60 FRSA94. Westcott Ho Cam 56. **d** 58 **p** 59. C Goole *Sheff* 58-61; V Dalton 61-67; Sen Ind Chapl *S'wark* 67-96; R S'wark Ch Ch 67-96; Hon Can S'wark Cathl 74-96; rtd 96; Perm to Offic *S'wark* from 96. *21 Bousfield Road, London SE14 5TP* Tel 0171-207 0509

CHALLEN, Victor Stanley. b 14. Bede Coll Dur BSc39. **d** 41 **p** 43. C Vauxhall St Pet *S'wark* 41-44; C Cheshunt *St Alb* 44-50; N of England Area Sec UMCA 51; V Bedford St Martin *St Alb* 52-83; rtd 83; Perm to Offic *St Alb* 83-93; Perm to Offic *Nor* from 93. *57 Hunstanton Road, Dersingham, King's Lynn, Norfolk PE31 6ND* Tel (01485) 540964

CHALLENDER, Canon Clifford. b 32. CITC 67. **d** 67 **p** 68. C Belfast St Luke *Conn* 67-70; C Kilkenny w Aghour and Odagh *C & O* 70-71; Bp's V and Lib Kilkenny Cathl 70-71; Dioc Registrar (Ossory, Ferns and Leighlin) 70-71; I Fenagh w Myshall and Kiltennel 71-76; I Fenagh w Myshall, Aghade and Ardoyne 76-79; I Crosspatrick Gp 79-95; Preb Ferns Cathl 85-88; Dioc Glebes Sec (Ferns) 86-91; Treas Ferns Cathl 88-91; Chan from 91; I Killeshin w Cloydagh and Killabban from 95; RD Wexford from 89. *The Rectory, Ballickmoyler, Carlow, Irish Republic* Tel Carlow (507) 25321 Mobile 087-433 678 Fax as telephone

CHALLENGER, Peter Nelson. b 33. St Jo Coll Cam BA57 MA61. Ripon Hall Ox 57. **d** 59 **p** 60. C Bushbury *Lich* 59-62; V Horsley Woodhouse *Derby* 62-67; V Derby St Barn 67-75; Brazil 75-80; TV New Windsor *Ox* 80-89; V Wootton (Boars Hill) from 89. *Wootton Vicarage, Boars Hill, Oxford OX1 5JL* Tel (01865) 735661

CHALLENGER, Miss Susanne Christine. b 41. Bp Grosseteste Coll TCert64 Leeds Poly DipSocSc68 Teesside Poly DMS86. NE Ord Course 88. **d** 91 **p** 94. NSM Middlesbrough St Cuth *York* from 91. *Hundlebrook, 11 Garbutts Lane, Hutton Rudby, Yarm, Cleveland TS15 0UN* Tel (01642) 700391

CHALLICE, John Richard. b 34. ACP65. Sarum & Wells Th Coll 73. **d** 75 **p** 76. C Warminster St Denys *Sarum* 75-78; R Longfield *Roch* from 78. *The Rectory, 67 Main Road, Longfield, Kent DA3 7PQ* Tel (01474) 702201

CHALLIS, Ian. b 46. St Jo Coll Nottm 82. **d** 84 **p** 85. C Heatherlands St Jo *Sarum* 84-86; C Lytchett Minster 86-88; Perm to Offic from 88; NSM Canford Magna from 95. *9 Haven Road, Corfe Mullen, Wimborne, Dorset BH21 3SY* Tel (01202) 691300

CHALLIS, Terence Peter. b 40. St Aid Birkenhead 65. **d** 68 **p** 69. C Billericay St Mary *Chelmsf* 68-71; Kenya 72-75; P-in-c Sparkbrook Ch Ch *Birm* 76-80; V Enfield St Jas *Lon* 80-89; V Astley Bridge *Man* from 89. *St Paul's Vicarage, Sweetloves Lane, Bolton BL1 7ET* Tel (01204) 304119

CHALLIS, William George. b 52. Keble Coll Ox BA73 K Coll Lon MTh75. Oak Hill Th Coll 73. **d** 75 **p** 76. C Islington St Mary *Lon* 75-79; Lect Trin Coll Bris 79-81; C Stoke Bishop *Bris* 79-81; Lect Oak Hill Th Coll 82; Burundi 82-85; P-in-c Bishopston *Bris* 86-89; TR 89-92; Vice-Prin Wycliffe Hall Ox from 93. *Wycliffe Hall, 54 Banbury Road, Oxford OX2 6PW* Tel (01865) 274200/5 Fax 274215 E-mail wycliffe@sable.ox.ac.uk

CHALMERS, Canon Brian. b 42. Or Coll Ox BA64 MA68 DPhil70 BA71. Wycliffe Hall Ox 71. **d** 72 **p** 73. C Luton St Mary *St Alb* 72-76; Chapl Cranfield Inst of Tech 76-81; Chapl Kent Univ *Cant* 81-89; Six Preacher Cant Cathl from 85; V Charing w Charing Heath and Lt Chart from 89; Hon Can Cant Cathl from 97. *The Vicarage, Pett Lane, Charing, Ashford, Kent TN27 0DL* Tel (01233) 712598

CHALMERS, Robert Alan. b 66. LLCM QUB LLB88 TCD BTh91. **d** 91 **p** 92. C Lurgan etc w Ballymachugh, Kildrumferton etc *K, E & A* 91-94; Dioc Registrar (Kilmore) 92-94; I Kildrumferton w Ballymachugh and Ballyjamesduff 94-96; Bp's C Boyle and Elphin w Aghanagh, Kilbryan etc 96-97. *Address temp unknown*

CHALONER, Stephen Mason. b 34. Dur Univ BA57. Ridley Hall Cam 57. **d** 59 **p** 60. C Aspley *S'well* 59-62; Chapl RNR from 61; P-in-c Eakring *S'well* 62-65; R 65-69; R Bilsthorpe 62-69; Chapl Saxondale Hosp Radcliffe-on-Trent 69-73; P-in-c Holme Pierrepont w Adbolton *S'well* 69-73; V Shelford 69-73; V Radcliffe-on-Trent 69-73; C Rowner *Portsm* 73-74; Hon C 74-81; Miss to Seamen 81-86; P-in-c Binstead *Portsm* 86-92; R from 92; P-in-c Swanmore St Mich w Havenstreet 86-92; V Havenstreet St Pet from 92; RD E Wight 88-94. *The Rectory, Pitts Lane, Ryde, Isle of Wight PO33 3SU* Tel (01983) 562890

CHAMBERLAIN, Allen Charles William. b 29. Lon Univ CertEd52 Birkb Coll Lon BSc56. LNSM course 95. **d** 96. NSM Gunton St Pet *Nor* from 96. *28 Yarmouth Road, Lowestoft, Suffolk MR32 4AG* Tel (01502) 573637

CHAMBERLAIN, David (Bernard). b 28. Fitzw Ho Cam BA51. Linc Th Coll 52. **d** 54 **p** 55. C Brighouse *Wakef* 54-57; C Sheff Parson Cross St Cecilia *Sheff* 57-61; CR 63-85; S Africa 68-70; Bp's Adv on Community Relns *Wakef* 71-85; Bp's Adv Community Relns & Inter-Faith Dialogue *Bris* 86-93; V Easton All Hallows 86-93; rtd 93; Perm to Offic *B & W* 94-96. *43 Bath Road, Wells, Somerset BA5 3HR* Tel (01749) 679369

CHAMBERLAIN, David Murray. b 22. Cuddesdon Coll 55. **d** 57 **p** 58. C Barkingside H Trin *Chelmsf* 57-60; Japan 60-71 and 76-81; V Edgbaston St Germain *Birm* 71-76; Miss to Seamen N Australia 81-88; rtd 88; Perm to Offic *Truro* from 88. *42 Tresawls Road, Truro, Cornwall TR1 3LE* Tel (01872) 72270

CHAMBERLAIN, Eric Edward. b 34. Lon Univ DipTh64. Tyndale Hall Bris 62. **d** 65 **p** 66. C Chell *Lich* 65-73; P-in-c Preston St Mary *Blackb* 73-76; V 76-89; P-in-c Preston St Luke 81-83; R S Normanton *Derby* from 89. *The Rectory, Church Street, South Normanton, Alfreton, Derbyshire DE55 2BT* Tel (01773) 811273

CHAMBERLAIN, Frederick George. b 19. Univ of Wales (Lamp) BA50. Chich Th Coll 50. **d** 52 **p** 53. C Weybridge *Guildf* 52-54; C Bourne 54-57; V Blindley Heath *S'wark* 57-63; V Tilshead *Sarum* 63-71; R The Orchestons 66-71; V Chitterne 69-71; R Tilshead, Orcheston and Chitterne 71-80; P-in-c Handley w Gussage St Andrew and Pentridge 80-82; R 82-84; rtd 84. *Mill Cottage, High Street, Codford St Mary, Warminster, Wilts BA12 0ND* Tel (01985) 850519

CHAMBERLAIN, Malcolm Leslie. b 69. York Univ BA92. Wycliffe Hall Ox 93. **d** 96 **p** 97. C Walsall Pleck and Bescot *Lich* from 96. *16 Bescot Drive, Walsall WS2 9DF* Tel (01922) 613927

✠**CHAMBERLAIN, The Right Revd Neville.** b 39. Nottm Univ BA61 MA73 CQSW73. Ripon Hall Ox 61. **d** 63 **p** 64 **c** 97. C Balsall Heath St Paul *Birm* 63-64; C Hall Green Ascension 64-66; C-in-c Gospel Lane CD 66-69; V Gospel Lane St Mich 69-72; Lic to Offic *Linc* 73-74; Soc Resp Sec 74-82; Can and Preb Linc Cathl from 79; R Edin St Jo *Edin* 82-97; Bp Bre from 97. *St Paul's Cathedral, 1 High Street, Dundee DD1 1TD* Tel (01382) 29230 or 24486

CHAMBERLAIN, Dr Nicholas Alan. b 63. St Chad's Coll Dur BA85 PhD91 New Coll Edin BD91. **d** 91 **p** 92. C Cockerton *Dur* 91-94; C Newton Aycliffe 94-95; TV 95-96; TV Gt Aycliffe from 96. *St Francis's Vicarage, Burnhope, Newton Aycliffe, Co Durham DL5 7ER* Tel (01325) 321533

CHAMBERLAIN, Roger Edward. b 53. BEd76 BA87. Trin Coll Bris 84. **d** 87 **p** 88. C Plymouth Em w Efford *Ex* 87-90; C Selly Park St Steph and St Wulstan *Birm* 90-94; V Yardley St Cypr Hay Mill 94-96; Perm to Offic from 96. *22 Hanbury Croft, Acocks Green, Birmingham B27 6RX*

CHAMBERLAIN, Roy Herbert. b 44. Oak Hill Th Coll 91 N Ord Course 95. **d** 96 **p** 97. C Gee Cross *Ches* from 96. *36 Baron Road, Hyde, Cheshire SK14 5RW* Tel 0161-368 3037

CHAMBERLAIN, Russell Charles. b 51. Oak Hill Th Coll 75. **d** 78 **p** 79. C Harold Hill St Geo *Chelmsf* 78-80; C Uckfield *Chich* 80-83; R Balcombe 83-90; V Okehampton w Inwardleigh *Ex* 90-94; TR Okehampton w Inwardleigh, Bratton Clovelly etc from 94; RD Okehampton from 93. *The Vicarage, 1 Church Path, Okehampton, Devon EX20 1LW* Tel (01837) 52731

CHAMBERLIN, David John. b 56. St Jo Coll Nottm DipThMin94. **d** 94 **p** 95. C Chatham St Phil and St Jas *Roch* 94-97; R Swardeston w E Carleton, Intwood, Keswick etc *Nor* from 97. *The Vicarage, The Common, Swardeston, Norwich NR14 8EB* Tel (01508) 570550 E-mail vicar@swardeston.demon.co.uk

CHAMBERLIN, John Malcolm. b 38. Carl Dioc Tr Course 84. **d** 87 **p** 88. NSM Cockermouth w Embleton and Wythop *Carl* from 87. *45 Dale View, Cockermouth, Cumbria CA13 9EW* Tel (01900) 822849

CHAMBERS, Anthony Frederick John. b 40. Sarum Th Coll 69. **d** 71 **p** 72. C Hall Green St Pet *Birm* 71-74; C Holdenhurst *Win* 74-77; P-in-c Ropley w W Tisted 77-79; P-in-c Bishop's Sutton 79; R Bishop's Sutton and Ropley and W Tisted 79-83; V

Pokesdown St Jas from 83; RD Bournemouth from 95. *St James's Vicarage, 12 Harewood Avenue, Bournemouth BH7 6NQ* Tel (01202) 425918

CHAMBERS, Mrs Barbara Mary Sinnott. b 43. SRN65 RM67 Birm Poly HVCert75 TCert77. WMMTC 87. **d** 93 **p** 94. Par Dn Blurton *Lich* 93-94; C 94-96; Chapl Asst Qu Medical Cen Nottm Univ Hosp NHS Trust from 96. *University Hospital, Queen's Medical Centre, Nottingham NG7 2UH* Tel 0115-942 9924

CHAMBERS, George William. b 24. TCD BA46 MA57. CITC 47. **d** 47 **p** 48. C Conwall *D & R* 47-50; Chapl Portora R Sch Enniskillen 50-51; I Tullyaughnish w Milford *D & R* 51-61; I Adare *L & K* 61-81; Dioc Registrar (Limerick etc) 62-81; Adn Limerick 69-81; Dean Limerick 81-86; I Killeshin w Cloydagh and Killabban *C & O* 86-95; Preb Ossory and Leighlin Cathls 90-92; Treas Ossory and Leighlin Cathls 92-95; rtd 95. *12 Rathdown Court, Greystones, Co Wicklow, Irish Republic* Tel Dublin (1) 287 1140

CHAMBERS, Canon Peter Lewis. b 43. Imp Coll Lon BScEng64. St Steph Ho Ox 64. **d** 66 **p** 67. C Llan w Capel Llanilltern *Llan* 66-70; Chapl Ch in Wales Youth Coun 70-73; Youth Chapl *Bris* 73-78; V Bedminster St Mich 78-84; RD Bedminster 81-84; Adv Ho of Bps Marriage Educn Panel Gen Syn 84-88; Dir Dioc Coun for Soc Resp *Guildf* 88-94; Hon Can Guildf Cathl 89-94; Dir Tr *Sheff* from 95; Hon Can Sheff Cathl from 96. *27 Common Road, Thorpe Salvin, Worksop, Notts S80 3JJ* Tel (01909) 770260

CHAMP, Darren David. b 60. Kent Univ BA93. Linc Th Coll DipMM94. **d** 95 **p** 96. C Ashford *Cant* 95-97. *c/o The Dean of Chapel's Bungalow, North Holmes Road, Canterbury, Kent CT1 1QU*

CHAMPION, Canon John Oswald Cecil. b 27. St Chad's Coll Dur BA49 DipTh51. **d** 51 **p** 52. C Worc St Martin *Worc* 51-53; Chapl RN 53-57; C Cant St Martin w St Paul *Cant* 57-60; C-in-c Stourbridge St Mich Norton CD *Worc* 60-64; V Astwood Bank w Crabbs Cross 64-68; V Redditch St Steph 68-75; R Fladbury, Wyre Piddle and Moor 75-93; RD Pershore 79-85; Hon Can Worc Cathl 81-93; rtd 93. *Black Horse Cottage, 3 Church Row, Pershore, Worcs WR10 1BL* Tel (01386) 552403

CHAMPNEYS, Michael Harold. b 46. LRAM66 GRSM67 ARCO67. Linc Th Coll 69. **d** 72 **p** 73. C Poplar *Lon* 72-73; C Bow w Bromley St Leon 73-75; P-in-c Bethnal Green St Barn 75-76; C Tewkesbury w Walton Cardiff *Glouc* 76-78; V Bedford Park *Lon* 78-83; V Shepshed *Leic* 84-87; Community Educn Tutor Bolsover 88-93; Perm to Offic *Derby* 90-92; NSM Bolsover 92-93; V Potterspury, Furtho, Yardley Gobion and Cosgrove *Pet* from 93; RD Towcester from 94. *The Vicarage, 11 Church Lane, Potterspury, Towcester, Northants NN12 7PU* Tel (01908) 542428

CHANCE, David Newton. b 44. Univ of Wales (Lamp) BA68. St Steph Ho Ox 68. **d** 70 **p** 71. C Selsdon St Jo w St Fran *Cant* 70-73; C Plymstock *Ex* 73-77; P-in-c Northam 77-79; TR Northam w Westward Ho! and Appledore 79-93; V Banstead *Guildf* from 93. *The Vicarage, Court Road, Banstead, Surrey SM7 2NQ* Tel (01737) 351134

CHAND, Wazir. b 29. Punjab Univ BA56 BT59. Ox NSM Course. **d** 90 **p** 91. NSM Cowley St Jas *Ox* from 90. *7 Frederick Road, Oxford OX4 3HL* Tel (01865) 714160

CHANDA, Daniel Khazan. b 28. Punjab Univ BA57 MA62 Saharanputh Coll. **d** 70 **p** 70. Hon C Handsworth St Jas *Birm* 70-83; Hon C Perry Barr 83-89; C Small Heath St Greg 89-92; C Small Heath from 92. *22 Tennyson Road, Birmingham B10 0HB* Tel 0121-766 5659

CHANDLER, Anthony. b 43. Lon Inst of Educn CertEd65. EAMTC CertHE94. **d** 97. NSM March St Mary *Ely* from 97; NSM March St Pet from 97. *Greenwood House, 17 St Peter's Road, March, Cambs PE15 9NA* Tel (01354) 652894 Mobile 0410-498778 Fax as telephone

CHANDLER, Derek Edward. b 67. Southn Univ BTh91 Nottm Univ MDiv93. Linc Th Coll 91. **d** 93 **p** 94. C Bitterne Park *Win* 93-97; C Sholing from 97. *St Francis House, 75 Montague Avenue, Southampton SO19 0QQ* Tel (01703) 443773

CHANDLER, Ian Nigel. b 65. K Coll Lon BD89 AKC89. Chich Th Coll CMT92. **d** 92 **p** 93. C Hove All SS *Chich* 92-93; C Hove 93-96; Bp's Dom Chapl from 96. *Monk's Cottage, Palace Yard, Canon Lane, Chichester, W Sussex PO19 3DH* Tel (01243) 780982

CHANDLER, John Charles. b 46. Solicitor. Oak Hill Th Coll 91. **d** 94 **p** 95. C Tonbridge St Steph *Roch* from 94. *35 Waterloo Road, Tonbridge, Kent TN9 2SW* Tel (01732) 351906

CHANDLER, John Edmond Owen. b 18. St Cath Soc Ox BA48 MA48. Cuddesdon Coll 68. **d** 68 **p** 69. Hon C Quarndon *Derby* 68-72; Lic to Offic *S'well* 73-78; P-in-c Oxton 79-85; R Epperstone 79-85; R Gonalston 79-85; rtd 85; Perm to Offic *S'well* from 85. *18 Thoresby Dale, Hucknall, Nottingham NG15 7UG* Tel 0115-963 5945

CHANDLER, Canon Michael John. b 45. Lon Univ DipTh75 K Coll Lon PhD87. Lambeth STh80 Linc Th Coll 70. **d** 72 **p** 73. C Cant St Dunstan w H Cross *Cant* 72-75; C Margate St Jo 75-78; V Newington w Bobbing and Iwade 78-83; P-in-c Hartlip w Stockbury 80-83; V Newington w Hartlip and Stockbury 83-88; RD Sittingbourne 84-88; R Hackington 88-95; RD Cant 94-95; Can Res Cant Cathl from 95. *15 The Precincts, Canterbury, Kent CT1 2EL* Tel (01227) 463056

CHANDLER, Quentin David. b 62. Aston Tr Scheme 87 Trin Coll Bris DipHE91 BA92. **d** 92 **p** 93. C Goldington *St Alb* 92-96; TV Rushden w Newton Bromswold *Pet* from 96. *45 Pytchley Road, Rushden, Northants NN10 9XB* Tel (01933) 56398

CHANDRA, Kevin Douglas Naresh. b 65. Qu Coll Birm 94 Lon Bible Coll BA88. **d** 96 **p** 97. C Walmley *Birm* from 96. *90 Walmley Ash Road, Walmley, Sutton Coldfield, W Midlands B76 1JB* Tel 0121-351 1245

CHANNER, Christopher Kendall. b 42. K Coll Lon BD64 AKC64. **d** 65 **p** 66. C Norbury St Steph *Cant* 65-68; C S Elmsall *Wakef* 68-70; V Dartford St Edm *Roch* 70-75; Chapl Joyce Green Hosp Dartford 73-75; V Bromley St Andr *Roch* 75-81; V Langton Green 81-94; Chapl Holmewood Ho Sch Tunbridge Wells from 94; Perm to Offic *Chich* from 94. *The Little House, Holmewood House Sch, Langton Green, Tunbridge Wells, Kent TN3 0EB* Tel (01892) 861285

CHANT, Edwin John. b 14. Lon Univ BA62. K Coll Lon 39 Clifton Th Coll 46. **d** 47 **p** 48. C Erith St Paul *Roch* 47-49; C Darfield *Sheff* 49-51; C Conisbrough 51-53; C Cliftonville *Cant* 53-56; V Gentleshaw *Lich* 56-80; V Farewell 56-80; rtd 80; Perm to Offic *Lich* from 80. *31 Huntsmans Gate, Burntwood, Staffs WS7 9LL*

CHANT, Harry. b 40. Oak Hill Th Coll DipHE78. **d** 78 **p** 79. C Heatherlands St Jo *Sarum* 78-81; P-in-c Bramshaw 81-83; P-in-c Landford w Plaitford 81-83; R Bramshaw and Landford w Plaitford 83-87; V Fareham St Jo *Portsm* from 87. *St John's Vicarage, 3A St Michael's Grove, Fareham, Hants PO14 1DN* Tel (01329) 280762

CHANT, Kenneth William. b 37. St Deiniol's Hawarden 67. **d** 70 **p** 71. C Ynyshir *Llan* 70-74; C Bargoed and Deri w Brithdir 74; P-in-c Aberpergwm and Blaengwrach 74-77; V 77-81; V Cwmavon from 81. *The Vicarage, Coed Parc, Cwmavon, Port Talbot SA12 9BN* Tel (01639) 896254

CHANT, Maurice Ronald. b 26. Chich Th Coll 51. **d** 54 **p** 55. C Mitcham St Mark *S'wark* 54-57; C Surbiton St Matt 57-60; P-in-c Cookridge CD Ripon 60-64; V Cookridge H Trin 64-67; Chapl Miss to Seamen Tilbury 67-71; Gt Yarmouth 71-77; Australia 77-84 and from 85; Singapore 84-85; rtd 91. *Unit 2, 95 Charlotte Street, Wynnum, Queensland, Australia 4178*

CHANTER, Canon Anthony Roy. b 37. ACP60 Open Univ BA72 Lon Univ MA75. Sarum Th Coll 64. **d** 66 **p** 67. C W Tarring *Chich* 66-69; Chapl St Andr Sch Worthing 69-70; Hd Master Bp King Sch Linc 70-73; Hon PV Linc Cathl *Linc* 70-73; Hd Master Grey Court Comp Sch Richmond 73-76; Hon C Kingston All SS *S'wark* 73-76; Hd Master Bp Reindorp Sch Guildf 77-84; Hon Can Guildf Cathl *Guildf* from 84; Dir of Educn from 84. *Grasshoppers, Woodland Avenue, Cranleigh, Surrey GU6 7HU* Tel (01483) 273833 or 571826

CHANTREY, Dr David Frank. b 48. K Coll Cam BA70 PhD73 MA74. Westcott Ho Cam 83. **d** 86 **p** 87. C Wordsley *Lich* 86-89; C Beckbury 89-90; P-in-c 90-93; C Badger 89-90; P-in-c 90-93; C Kemberton, Sutton Maddock and Stockton 89-90; P-in-c 90-93; C Ryton 89-90; P-in-c 90-93; R Beckbury, Badger, Kemberton, Ryton, Stockton etc from 93. *The Rectory, Beckbury, Shifnal, Shropshire TF11 9DG* Tel (0195287) 474

CHANTRY, Ms Helen Fiona. b 59. Bradf Univ BSc82 Leeds Univ CertEd83. Trin Coll Bris BA89. **d** 89 **p** 94. NSM Hyde St Geo *Ches* 89-92; Dioc Youth Officer from 92; NSM Barrow from 94. *The Rectory, Mill Lane, Great Barrow, Chester CH3 7JF* Tel (01829) 740263 Fax as telephone

CHANTRY, Peter Thomas. b 62. Bradf Univ BSc83. Trin Coll Bris BA89. **d** 89 **p** 90. C Hyde St Geo *Ches* 89-92; Dioc Youth Officer 91-94; P-in-c Barrow from 94. *The Rectory, Mill Lane, Great Barrow, Chester CH3 7JF* Tel (01829) 740263 Fax as telephone

CHANTRY, Richard Michael. b 31. Hertf Coll Ox BA55 MA57. Ridley Hall Cam 55. **d** 57 **p** 57. C Boulton *Derby* 57-59; C Ox St Aldate w H Trin *Ox* 59-68; P-in-c 74-75; Chapl Hertf Coll Ox from 61; Chapl Ox United Football Club from 65; Chapl Somerville Coll Ox from 95; rtd 96. *11 Talbot Road, Oxford OX2 8LL* Tel (01865) 58286 or 279400

CHANTRY, Mrs Sandra Mary. b 41. Cam Inst of Educn CertEd63. EMMTC 83. **dss** 86 **d** 87 **p** 94. Loughb Gd Shep *Leic* 86-87; Par Dn 87-89; Par Dn Belton and Osgathorpe 89-90; Par Dn Hathern, Long Whatton and Diseworth w Belton etc 90-94; C from 94. *The Rectory, Presents Lane, Belton, Loughborough, Leics LE12 9UN* Tel (01530) 222554

CHAPLIN, Colin. b 33. Edin Dioc NSM Course 74. **d** 76 **p** 77. NSM Penicuik *Edin* 76-91; P-in-c Peebles 89-90; NSM Bathgate 91-95; rtd 95. *26 Broomhill Road, Penicuik, Midlothian EH26 9EE* Tel (01968) 672050

CHAPLIN, Douglas Archibald. b 59. Em Coll Cam BA81. St Jo Coll Nottm DipTh84. **d** 86 **p** 87. C Glouc St Geo w Whaddon *Glouc* 86-89; C Lydney w Aylburton 89-93; R Worc St Clem *Worc* from 93. *St Clement's Rectory, 124 Laugherne Road, Worcester WR2 5LT* Tel (01905) 422675 E-mail doug.c @virgin.net

CHAPLIN, Frederick David. b 20. CCC Ox BA49 MA54. Cuddesdon Coll 49. **d** 51 **p** 52. C Glastonbury St Jo *B & W* 51-55; Chapl Wells Th Coll 55-57; Vice-Prin 57-61; Trinidad and Tobago 61-72; Asst to Gen Sec ACC 72-78; Sec C of E

Partnership for World Miss 79-85; Perm to Offic *Ox* from 83; rtd 86. *19 Granville Court, Cheney Lane, Oxford OX3 0HS* Tel (01865) 240489

CHAPLIN, Paul. b 57. Hull Univ BA80 CertEd81 K Coll Lon MA89. St Steph Ho Ox 85. **d** 87 **p** 88. C Ex St Jas *Ex* 87-90; C Wokingham St Paul *Ox* from 90. *St Nicholas House, 13 Brook Close, Wokingham, Berks RG41 1ND* Tel (0118) 978 0034

CHAPMAN, Canon Albert Aidan. b 09. TD. Em Coll Cam BA35 MA39. Lon Coll of Div. **d** 37 **p** 38. C Beckenham St Jo *Roch* 37-39; CF (TA) 39-55; V Erith St Paul *Roch* 46-50; R Farnborough 50-64; Chapl Orpington Hosp 52-59; Chapl Farnborough Hosp 59-64; RD Orpington *Roch* 55-64; V Westerham 64-76; RD Sevenoaks 64-74; Hon Can Roch Cathl 64-76; rtd 76; Perm to Offic *St E* from 76. *4 Lorenden Park, Hawkhurst, Cranbrook, Kent TN18 4LF* Tel (01580) 754434

CHAPMAN, Ms Ann Beatrice. b 53. Hull Coll of Educn BEd77 Leeds Univ BA87. St Jo Coll Nottm MA95. **d** 95 **p** 96. C Burley *Ripon* from 95. *2 Woodside View, Leeds LS4 2SR* Tel 0113-274 4073

CHAPMAN, Barry Frank. b 48. Trin Coll Bris. **d** 82 **p** 83. NSM Bradford-on-Avon Ch Ch *Sarum* from 82; Assoc Chapl Bath Univ *B & W* from 83. *16 Church Acre, Bradford-on-Avon, Wilts BA15 1RL* Tel (01225) 866861 or 826826 Ext 5714 Fax 826110 E-mail b.f.chapman@bath.ac.uk

CHAPMAN, Mrs Celia. b 32. Whitelands Coll Lon TCert53 Open Univ BA82. WMMTC 84. **d** 87 **p** 94. NSM Bilston *Lich* 87-93; Ind Chapl Black Country Urban Ind Miss from 93; Chapl St Pet Colleg Sch Wolv from 93. *St Leonard's Vicarage, Dover Street, Bilston, W Midlands WV14 6AW* Tel (01902) 491560

CHAPMAN, Canon Christopher Robin. b 37. Nottm Univ DipAdEd71 Cam Univ DipRK74. Ripon Hall Ox 72. **d** 73 **p** 74. C Kidbrooke St Jas *S'wark* 73-77; V Corton *Nor* 77-80; V Hopton 77-80; RD Lothingland 80-86; V Hopton w Corton 80-92; P-in-c Loddon w Sisland 92-93; P-in-c Loddon, Sisland w Hales and Heckingham from 93; RD Loddon from 95; Hon Can Nor Cathl from 96; P-in-c Chedgrave w Hardley and Langley from 97. *The Vicarage, 4 Market Place, Loddon, Norwich NR14 6EY* Tel (01508) 20251

CHAPMAN, Colin. b 38. St Andr Univ MA60 Lon Univ BD62. Ridley Hall Cam. **d** 64 **p** 65. C Edin St Jas *Edin* 64-67; Egypt 68-74; Perm to Offic *Birm* 74-77; Lebanon 77-83; Lect Trin Coll Bris 83-90; Prin Crowther Hall CMS Tr Coll Selly Oak from 90. *Crowther Hall, Weoley Park Road, Birmingham B29 6QT* Tel 0121-472 4228

CHAPMAN, David John. b 28. Jes Coll Ox BA52 MA56. Wells Th Coll 52. **d** 54 **p** 55. C Sedgley All SS *Lich* 54-57; C Cannock 57-60; V Tipton St Matt 60-69; R Sawley *Derby* 69-79; P-in-c Holkham w Egmere and Waterden *Nor* 79-83; P-in-c Warham w Wighton 79-83; R Wells next the Sea 79-83; R Holkham w Egmere w Warham, Wells and Wighton 83; V Feltham *Lon* 83-93; rtd 93. *12 Little Penny Rope, Pershore, Worcestershire WR10 1QN* Tel (01386) 561558

CHAPMAN, Canon Derek. b 22. Westcott Ho Cam 52. **d** 53 **p** 54. C Earlsdon *Cov* 53-56; C Rugby St Andr 56-58; V E Malling *Roch* 58-79; CF (TA) 60-67; R Hever w Mark Beech *Roch* 79-89; P-in-c Four Elms 80-89; Hon Can Roch Cathl 84-89; rtd 89; Perm to Offic *Roch* from 89; Perm to Offic *Chich* from 89. *1 Moat Lane, Sedlescombe, Battle, E Sussex TN33 0RZ* Tel (01424) 754455

CHAPMAN, Mrs Dorothy. b 38. Nottm Univ CTPS. EMMTC. **d** 89 **p** 94. Par Dn Bingham *S'well* 89-92; Sub-Chapl HM Pris Whatton 89-92; C Lenton from 92. *86 Kenrick Road, Nottingham NG3 6FB* Tel 0115-950 3088

CHAPMAN, Drummond John. b 36. Cant Sch of Min 80. **d** 83 **p** 86. C Kington w Huntington, Old Radnor, Kinnerton etc *Heref* 83-84; C Llanidloes w Llangurig *Ban* 86-90; V Llanwnnog and Caersws w Carno from 90. *The Vicarage, Llanwnnog, Caersws SY17 5JG* Tel (01686) 688318

CHAPMAN, Edwin Thomas. b 32. Man Univ BA60. St Mich Coll Llan 62. **d** 63 **p** 64. C Cleveleys *Blackb* 63-65; C Ox St Mary V w St Cross and St Pet *Ox* 65-67; Chapl LMH Ox 67-68; Asst Dir of Educn *York* 68-75; R E Gilling 68-76; P-in-c Hockley *Chelmsf* 76-77; V 77-82; P-in-c Gosberton Clough and Quadring *Linc* 82-83; Chapl St Cath Sch Bramley 83-86; R Bulmer w Dalby, Terrington and Welburn *York* from 86; RD Bulmer and Malton from 91. *The Rectory, Terrington, York YO6 4PU* Tel (01653) 648226

CHAPMAN, Canon Eric Ronald. b 19. Man Univ BA41 BD59. Bps' Coll Cheshunt 41. **d** 43 **p** 44. C Chorley St Pet *Blackb* 43-46; C Skerton St Luke 46-51; V Bolton St Mark *Man* 51-58; V Kells *Carl* 58-66; RD Whitehaven 66-70; R Egremont 66-81; Hon Can Carl Cathl 79-85; TR Egremont and Haile 81-85; rtd 85; Perm to Offic *Carl* from 86. *Bernaville, Highfield Road, Grange-over-Sands, Cumbria LA11 7JA* Tel (015395) 34351

CHAPMAN, Gorran. b 55. Dur Univ BA. Westcott Ho Cam 78. **d** 80 **p** 81. C Par *Truro* 80-82; C Kenwyn 82-84; P-in-c Penwerris 84-89; V 89-92; V Torquay St Martin Barton *Ex* from 92; Perm to Offic *Truro* from 92. *St Martin's Vicarage, Beechfield Avenue, Barton, Torquay TQ2 8HU* Tel (01803) 327223

CHAPMAN, Guy Godfrey. b 33. Southn Univ BSc57. Clifton Th Coll 60. **d** 62 **p** 63. C Chadderton Ch Ch *Man* 62-67; V Edgeside 67-70; P-in-c Shipton Bellinger *Win* 70-72; V 72-83; RD Andover 75-85; Hon Can Win Cathl 79-91; R Over Wallop w Nether Wallop 83-91; V Ambrosden w Mert and Piddington *Ox* from 91; RD Bicester and Islip from 95. *The Vicarage, Ambrosden, Bicester, Oxon OX6 0UJ* Tel (01869) 247813

CHAPMAN, Henry Davison (Harry). b 31. Bris Univ BA55. Tyndale Hall Bris 52. **d** 56 **p** 57. C St Helens St Mark *Liv* 56-60; R Clitheroe St Jas *Blackb* 60-67; V Tipton St Martin *Lich* 67-68; SW Area Sec CPAS 68-72; V Eccleston St Luke *Liv* 72-78; P-in-c Ringshall w Battisford, Barking w Darmsden etc *St E* 78-80; R 80-93; RD Bosmere 87-91; rtd 93. *Daracombe, The Clays, Market Lavington, Devizes, Wilts SN10 4AY* Tel (01380) 813774

CHAPMAN, Ian Martin. b 47. Oak Hill Th Coll BA94. **d** 94 **p** 95. C S Mimms Ch Ch *Lon* from 94. *8 Wentworth Road, Barnet, Herts EN5 4NT* Tel 0181-441 0645

CHAPMAN (née CRAVEN), Mrs Janet Elizabeth. b 58. St Jo Coll Dur BSc80 Dur Univ MA92. Cranmer Hall Dur 84. **d** 87 **p** 95. Par Dn Darlington St Cuth *Dur* 87-92; NSM Edin Gd Shep *Edin* 93-95; NSM Rufforth w Moor Monkton and Hessay *York* from 95; NSM Long Marston from 95. *Milestone House, Wetherby Road, Rufforth, York YO2 3QF* Tel (01904) 738328

CHAPMAN, John. b 24. St Cuth Soc Dur BA51 St Chad's Coll Dur DipTh53. **d** 53 **p** 54. C Billingham St Cuth *Dur* 53-55; C Harton 55-57; PC Hedgefield 57-63; PC Annfield Plain 63-78; V Bolton All So w St Jas *Man* 78-85; V Baddesley Ensor w Grendon *Birm* 85-91; rtd 91; Perm to Offic *Birm* from 91. *The Angelus, 49 Alfriston Road, Coventry CV3 6FG* Tel (01203) 413758

CHAPMAN (née WHITFIELD), Mrs Joy Verity. b 46. SRN67 SCM71 MTD80. Trin Coll Bris BA88. **d** 88 **p** 94. C Littleover *Derby* 88-92; Par Dn Bucknall and Bagnall *Lich* 92-94; C 94; TV 94-97; Chapl LOROS Hospice from 97. *58 Swanmore Road, Littleover, Derby DE23 7SY* Tel (01332) 519498

CHAPMAN, Mrs Margaret. b 34. Univ Coll Lon BA72 Qu Mary Coll Lon MA74. EAMTC 94. **d** 95 **p** 96. NSM Theydon Bois *Chelmsf* from 95. *25 Woburn Avenue, Theydon Bois, Epping, Essex CM16 7JR* Tel (01992) 814659

CHAPMAN, Dr Mark David. b 60. Trin Coll Ox MA83 DipTh84 DPhil89. Ox Min Course 93. **d** 94 **p** 95. Lect Ripon Coll Cuddesdon from 92; NSM Dorchester *Ox* from 94. *Ripon College, Cuddesdon, Oxford OX44 9EX* Tel (01865) 874310

CHAPMAN, Mary Elizabeth. NE Ord Course. **dss** 84 **d** 87 **p** 94. Newc St Gabr *Newc* 84-87; Hon C 87-95. *9 Sefton Avenue, Newcastle upon Tyne NE6 5QR* Tel 0191-265 9931

CHAPMAN, The Ven Michael Robin. b 39. Leeds Univ BA61. Coll of Resurr Mirfield 61. **d** 63 **p** 64. C Southwick St Columba *Dur* 63-68; Chapl RN 68-84; V Hale *Guildf* 84-91; RD Farnham 88-91; Adn Northn *Pet* from 91. *Westbrook, 11 The Drive, Northampton NN1 4RZ* Tel (01604) 714015 Fax 792016

CHAPMAN, Miss Patricia Ann. b 42. **dss** 84 **d** 87 **p** 94. Rainworth *S'well* 84-87; Par Dn 87-94; C 94-96; P-in-c Mansfield Oak Tree Lane from 96. *8 Hartington Court, Mansfield, Notts NG18 3QJ* Tel (01623) 645030

CHAPMAN, Canon Percy Frank. b 06. Bris Univ BSc27 MA31. **d** 36 **p** 37. C Barnwood *Glouc* 36-41; Asst Chapl Marlborough Coll 41-65; V Aldbourne and Baydon *Sarum* 65-72; R Whitton 65-72; V Coombe Bissett w Homington 72-81; P-in-c Bishopstone w Stratford Tony 80-81; R Chalke Valley E 81-88; Can and Preb Sarum Cathl 83-88; rtd 88; Perm to Offic *Chich* from 92. *College of St Barnabas, Blackberry Lane, Lingfield, Surrey RH7 6NJ* Tel (01342) 870762

CHAPMAN, Peter Harold White. b 40. AKC64. **d** 65 **p** 66. C Havant *Portsm* 65-69; C Stanmer w Falmer and Moulsecoomb *Chich* 69-73; Chapl RN 73-86; Chapl Chigwell Sch Essex 86-90; P-in-c Stapleford Tawney w Theydon Mt *Chelmsf* from 87. *The Rectory, Theydon Mount, Epping, Essex CM16 7PW* Tel (01992) 578723

CHAPMAN, Peter John. b 33. Dur Univ BA56. Cranmer Hall Dur DipTh59. **d** 59 **p** 60. C Boulton *Derby* 59-62; Uganda 63-70; P-in-c Southampton St Matt *Win* 71-73; TV Southampton (City Cen) 73-78; V Bilston St Leon *Lich* 78-79; P-in-c Bilston St Mary 78-79; TR Bilston from 80; RD Wolverhampton from 89. *St Leonard's Vicarage, Dover Street, Bilston, W Midlands WV14 6AW* Tel (01902) 491560

CHAPMAN, Raymond. b 24. FRSA90 Jes Coll Ox BA45 MA59 Lon Univ MA47 BD75 PhD78. S'wark Ord Course 72. **d** 74 **p** 75. NSM St Mary le Strand w St Clem Danes *Lon* 74-82; NSM Barnes St Mary *S'wark* 82-94; Perm to Offic from 94; Perm to Offic *Lon* 82-91. *6 Kitson Road, London SW13 9HJ* Tel 0181-748 9901

CHAPMAN, Raymond. b 41. Linc Th Coll 68. **d** 71 **p** 72. C Dronfield *Derby* 71-74; C Delaval *Newc* 75-76; TV Whorlton 76-79; V Newc St Hilda 79-83; V Blyth St Cuth 83-89; Hon C Fareham SS Pet and Paul *Portsm* from 95. *170 White Hart Lane, Fareham, Hants PO16 9AX* Tel (01705) 324537

CHAPMAN, Canon Rex Anthony. b 38. Univ Coll Lon BA62 St Edm Hall Ox BA64 MA68 Birm Univ DPS67. Wells Th Coll 64. **d** 65 **p** 66. C Stourbridge St Thos *Worc* 65-68; Chapl Aber Univ *Ab* 68-78; Can St Andr Cathl 76-78; Bp's Adv for Educn *Carl* 78-85; Dir of Educn from 85; Can Res Carl Cathl from 78; Chapl to The Queen from 97. *1 The Abbey, Carlisle CA3 8TZ* Tel (01228) 597614 or 38086 Fax 598220

CHAPMAN, Rodney Andrew. b 53. AKC75. St Aug Coll Cant 75. **d** 76 **p** 77. C Hartlepool St Aid *Dur* 76-81; Lic to Offic 81-83; C Owton Manor 83-87; P-in-c Kelloe 87-92; V Sharlston *Wakef* from 92. *St Luke's Vicarage, 45 West Lane, Sharlston Common, Wakefield, W Yorkshire WF4 1EP* Tel (01924) 862414

CHAPMAN, Roger John. b 34. AKC58. **d** 59 **p** 60. C Guildf Ch Ch *Guildf* 59-61; Kenya 61-67; R S Milford *York* 68-77; RD Selby 72-77; V Beverley St Mary 77-88; RD Beverley 85-88; V Desborough *Pet* 88-95; R Brampton Ash w Dingley and Braybrooke 88-95; rtd 95; Perm to Offic *York* from 95. *14 Scrubwood Lane, Beverley, N Humberside HU17 7BE* Tel (01482) 881267

CHAPMAN, Mrs Sally Anne. b 55. Lanchester Poly BSc76 Univ of Wales (Swansea) PGCE77. WMMTC 87. **d** 90 **p** 94. Par Dn Stoneydelph St Martin CD *Lich* 90; Par Dn Glascote and Stonydelph 90-93; Par Dn Willenhall H Trin 93-94; C 94-96; TV from 96. *18 Heather Grove, Willenhall, W Midlands WV12 4BT* Tel (01902) 631498

CHAPMAN, Mrs Sarah Jean. b 55. Lon Univ DipCOT77. Sarum & Wells Th Coll 86. **d** 89 **p** 94. NSM Rogate w Terwick and Trotton w Chithurst *Chich* 89-94; NSM Easebourne 94-96; Perm to Offic *Portsm* 96-97; V Sheet from 97. *Sheet Vicarage, 2 Pulens Lane, Petersfield, Hants GU31 4DB* Tel (01730) 263673 Fax as telephone

CHAPMAN, Sydney William. b 12. Didsbury Meth Coll 32 Sarum Th Coll 55. **d** 56 **p** 57. C Ringwood *Win* 56-60; In Meth Ch 32-55; V Walberton w Binsted *Chich* 60-81; rtd 81; Perm to Offic *Win* 82-91. *16 Walberton Park, Walberton, Arundel, W Sussex BN18 0PJ* Tel (01243) 551777

CHAPMAN, Thomas Graham (Tom). b 33. Trin Coll Bris 73. **d** 75 **p** 76. C Branksome St Clem *Sarum* 75-81; V Quarry Bank *Lich* 81-93; V Quarry Bank *Worc* from 93. *The Vicarage, Maughan Street, Brierley Hill, W Midlands DY5 2DN* Tel (01384) 565480

CHAPMAN, William Henry Stanley (Peter). b 08. OBE58. St Chad's Coll Dur BA31. **d** 32 **p** 33. C Monkwearmouth St Pet *Dur* 32-35; Chapl RN 35-63; V W Dean *Chich* 63-73; rtd 73; Perm to Offic *Chich* from 73. *Moons, Green Lane, Crowborough, E Sussex TN6 2DE* Tel (01892) 661568

CHAPMAN, William Howard Dale. b 11. Edin Th Coll 33. **d** 38 **p** 39. C Ayr *Glas* 38-41; R Brechin *Bre* 41-47; P-in-c Girvan *Glas* 47; P-in-c Stranraer 47; P-in-c Portpatrick 47; C Ayr 47-49; V Coverham w Horsehouse *Ripon* 49-53; V Askrigg w Stallingbusk 53-60; V Kemble w Poole Keynes *Glouc* 60-71; R Brookthorpe w Whaddon and Harescombe 71-76; rtd 76; Perm to Offic *Glouc* 85-91. *c/o Mr R Anderton, 4 Alderwood Avenue, Chandler's Ford, Eastleigh, Hants SO53 4TH* Tel (01703) 251367

CHAPMAN, Miss Yvonne Hazel. b 35. Brighton Coll of Educn CertEd55. Coll of Ascension 60 Serampore Th Coll BRE63 EAMTC 95. **d** 96 **p** 97. NSM Duston Team *Pet* from 96. *18 Sundew Court, Northampton NN4 9XH* Tel (01604) 762091

CHAPPELL, Allan. b 27. Selw Coll Cam BA51 MA56. Coll of Resurr Mirfield 51. **d** 53 **p** 54. C Knowle *Bris* 53-57; Zanzibar 57-63; C Long Eaton St Laur *Derby* 64-67; C-in-c Broxtowe CD *S'well* 67-73; P-in-c Flintham 73-82; R Car Colston w Screveton 73-82; V Mansfield St Lawr 82-92; rtd 93; Perm to Offic *S'well* from 93. *43 Hillsway Crescent, Mansfield, Notts NG18 5DR* Tel (01623) 654155

CHAPPELL, Edward Michael. b 32. Glouc Sch of Min 84. **d** 87 **p** 88. NSM Wotton-under-Edge w Ozleworth and N Nibley *Glouc* from 87. *20 Old Town, Wotton-under-Edge, Glos GL12 7DH* Tel (01453) 844250

CHAPPELL, Eric Richardson. b 08. Keble Coll Ox BA30 MA34. Cuddesdon Coll 30. **d** 31 **p** 32. C Teddington St Mark *Lon* 31-35; C Hillingdon St Andr 35-43; Chapl RAFVR 43-47; Chapl RAF 47-63; V Goodnestone H Cross w Chillenden and Knowlton *Cant* 64-78; P-in-c Adisham 75-78; rtd 78; Perm to Offic *Cant* from 78. *33 Sandgate Hill, Folkestone, Kent CT20 3AX* Tel (01303) 248141

CHAPPELL, Frank Arnold. b 37. Dur Univ BA58. Bps' Coll Cheshunt. **d** 60 **p** 61. C Headingley *Ripon* 60-65; V Beeston Hill St Luke 65-73; R Garforth 73-91; V Dacre w Hartwith and Darley w Thornthwaite from 91. *The Vicarage, Dacre Banks, Harrogate, N Yorkshire HG3 4ED* Tel (01423) 780262

CHAPPELL, Preb George Thomas. b 04. St Jo Coll Dur LTh28 BA29 MA32. Lon Coll of Div 24. **d** 28 **p** 29. C Birkenhead St Mary w St Paul *Ches* 28-31; C Cliftonville *Cant* 31-34; Org Sec (Dios Ox and Cov) CMS 34-41; (Dio Pet) 35-41; P-in-c Paddington St Jas *Lon* 41-43; V 43-71; Chapl St Mary's Hosp Paddington 44-54; RD Paddington 56-67; RD Westmr Paddington 67-69; Preb St Paul's Cathl 63-71; rtd 71; C S Kensington H Trin w All SS *Lon* 71-74; P-in-c 74-75; Perm to Offic 75-85. *Flat 3, 19 Burton Road, Poole, Dorset BH13 6DT* Tel (01202) 764665

CHAPPELL, Michael Paul. b 35. Selw Coll Cam BA57 MA61 ACertCM65. Cuddesdon Coll 60. **d** 62 **p** 63. C Pershore w Pinvin, Wick and Birlingham *Worc* 62-65; Malaysia 65-67; V Choral and Chapl Heref Cathl *Heref* 67-71; Min Can Dur Cathl *Dur* 71-76; Prec 72-76; Chapl H Trin Sch Stockton 76-87; C-in-c Stockton Green Vale H Trin CD *Dur* 82-87; V Scarborough St Luke *York* from 87; Chapl Scarborough Gen Hosp from 87. *The Vicarage, 37 Woodland Ravine, Scarborough, N Yorkshire YO12 6TA* Tel (01723) 372831

CHARD, Canon Francis Eric. b 24. Dur Univ BA53 MLitt81. St Jo Coll Dur DipTh55. **d** 55 **p** 56. C Cleveleys *Blackb* 55-57; C Preston St Jo 57-60; V Ewood 60-72; V Downham 72-88; RD Whalley 83-89; Hon Can Blackb Cathl 86-93; Co Ecum Officer 88-93; rtd 93; Perm to Offic *Blackb* from 93. *21 Moorland Crescent, Clitheroe, Lancs BB7 4PY* Tel (01200) 27480

CHARD, Reginald Jeffrey. b 40. Univ of Wales (Lamp) BA62 Birm Poly CQSW75. Coll of Resurr Mirfield 62. **d** 64 **p** 65. C Ystrad Mynach *Llan* 64-67; C Aberdare St Fagan 67-71; V Hirwaun 71-74; Hon C Stechford *Birm* 74-78; TV Banbury *Ox* 78-86; Ind Chapl from 86; P-in-c Claydon w Mollington 86-96; R Ironstone from 96. *The Rectory, Church Street, Wroxton, Banbury, Oxon OX15 6QE* Tel (01295) 730344

CHARE, Frederic Keith. b 16. Hatf Coll Dur LTh38 BA39. Edin Th Coll 35. **d** 39 **p** 40. C Greenock *Glas* 39-43; C Dumfries 43-46; C Forton *Portsm* 46-52; V Camberwell St Phil *S'wark* 52-57; Min Barming Heath CD *Cant* 57-69; V Barming Heath 69-73; V Upchurch 74-75; V Upchurch w Lower Halstow 75-82; rtd 82; Perm to Offic *Cant* from 82. *71 Douglas Road, Maidstone, Kent ME16 8ER* Tel (01622) 761370

CHARING CROSS, Archdeacon of. *See* JACOB, The Ven William Mungo

CHARKHAM, Rupert Anthony. b 59. Ex Univ BA81. Wycliffe Hall Ox 83. **d** 89 **p** 89. C Ox St Aldate w St Matt *Ox* 89-92; P-in-c Fisherton Anger *Sarum* from 92. *St Paul's Rectory, Salisbury SP2 7QW* Tel (01722) 334005

CHARLES, Jonathan. b 42. St Luke's Coll Ex CertEd64. Ripon Hall Ox 72 Ripon Coll Cuddesdon 78. **d** 79 **p** 80. C Leagrave *St Alb* 79-82; Chapl Denstone Coll Uttoxeter 82-86; Chapl Malvern Girls' Coll 86-89; Chapl K Sch Worc 89-95; Min Can Worc Cathl *Worc* 89-95; P-in-c Burnham Gp of Par *Nor* from 95. *The Rectory, The Pound, Church Walk, Burnham Market, King's Lynn, Norfolk PE31 8DH* Tel (01328) 738317

CHARLES, Martin. b 40. **d** 90 **p** 91. C Market Harborough *Leic* 90-91; P-in-c Higham-on-the-Hill w Fenny Drayton and Witherley from 91. *The Rectory, Old Forge Road, Fenny Drayton, Nuneaton, Warks CV13 6BD* Tel (01827) 715460

CHARLES, Mary Cecilia. b 49. Univ of Wales BEd. Trin Coll Carmarthen. **d** 96 **p** 97. NSM Letterston w Llanfair Nant-y-Gof etc *St D* from 96. *Hen Eglwys Farm, St David's Road, Letterston, Haverfordwest SA62 5SR*

CHARLES, Meedperdas Edward. b 28. Fitzw Ho Cam BA60 MA64. Bangalore Th Coll BD54. **d** 54 **p** 55. Malaya 54-55; Singapore 55-58 and 64-66; Perm to Offic *Ely* 58-60; V Sheff St Bart Langsett Road *Sheff* 60-64; V Gravelly Hill *Birm* 66-78; V Endcliffe *Sheff* 79-90; rtd 91; Perm to Offic *Sheff* from 91. *60 Ringinglow Road, Sheffield S11 7PQ* Tel 0114-266 4980

CHARLES, Robert Sidney James. b 40. Lon Univ CertEd77 Open Univ BA79 Univ of Wales LLM97. St Mich Coll Llan DipTh65. **d** 65 **p** 66. C Merthyr Tydfil *Llan* 65-68; C Shotton *St As* 68-70; R Stock and Lydlinch *Sarum* 70-74; R Hubberston *St D* 74-76; Perm to Offic *Chelmsf* 81-83; V Crossens *Liv* 83-97; V Budleigh Salterton *Ex* from 97. *St Peter's Vicarage, 4A West Hill Lane, Budleigh, Devon EX9 6AA* Tel (01395) 443195

CHARLES, Robin. b 50. N Staffs Poly HND72. Sarum & Wells Th Coll. **d** 86 **p** 87. C Chesterton *Lich* 86-89; C Rugeley 89-90; TV 90-97; TV E Scarsdale *Derby* from 97. *Langwith Bassett Rectory, Upper Langwith, Mansfield, Notts NG20 9RE* Tel (01623) 742413

CHARLES, Theodore Arthur Barker. b 24. K Coll Cam BA45 MA48 Lon Univ DipRS71. S'wark Ord Course 68. **d** 71 **p** 72. C Cuckfield *Chich* 71-77; V Rudgwick 77-89; rtd 89; Perm to Offic *Ox* from 89. *1 Herringcote, Dorchester-on-Thames, Wallingford, Oxon OX10 7RD* Tel (01865) 341321

CHARLES-EDWARDS, David Mervyn. b 38. Trin Coll Cam BA61. Linc Th Coll 62. **d** 64 **p** 89. C Putney St Mary *S'wark* 64-65; Chief Exec Officer Br Assn for Counselling 82-87; Gen Manager Lon Lighthouse AIDS Project 87-88; Consultant and Counsellor on Human Development from 88; NSM Rugby St Andr *Cov* from 89. *236 Hillmorton Road, Rugby, Warks CV22 5BG* Tel (01788) 569212

CHARLESWORTH, Eric Charlesworth. b 29. Kelham Th Coll 49. **d** 54 **p** 56. C Woodbridge St Mary *St E* 54-57; Asst Chapl Oslo St Edm *Eur* 57-59; Canada 60-66; R Huntingfield w Cookley *St E* 66-70; R Slimbridge *Glouc* 70-96; rtd 96. *Gardener's Cottage, Fairford Park, Fairford, Glos GL7 4JQ* Tel (01285) 712411

CHARLESWORTH, Ian Peter. b 65. Lanc Univ BA87. St Mich Coll Llan DipTh93. **d** 93 **p** 94. C Caereithin *S & B* 93-95; C Oystermouth 95-97; R Llandefalle and Llyswen w Boughrood etc from 97. *The Rectory, Church Lane, Llyswen, Brecon LD3 0UU* Tel (01874) 85255

CHARLEY, Canon Julian Whittard. b 30. New Coll Ox BA55 MA58. Ridley Hall Cam 55. **d** 57 **p** 58. C St Marylebone All So w SS Pet and Jo *Lon* 57-64; Lect Lon Coll of Div 64-70; Vice-Prin St Jo Coll Nottm 70-74; Warden Shrewsbury Ho 74-87; TR Everton St Pet *Liv* 74-87; P-in-c Gt Malvern St Mary *Worc* 87-97; Hon Can Worc Cathl 91-97; rtd 97. *155A Old Hollow, Malvern, Worcs WR14 4NN* Tel (01684) 596801

CHARLTON, Canon Arthur David. b 23. Open Univ BA73 BPhil83. Chich Th Coll. **d** 66 **p** 67. C Rotherfield *Chich* 66-70; C Uckfield 70-72; C Isfield 70-72; C Lt Horsted 70-72; R Cocking w Bepton 72-79; P-in-c W Lavington 78-79; R Cocking, Bepton and W Lavington 79-90; Can and Preb Chich Cathl 88-90; rtd 90; Perm to Offic *Chich* from 91; Perm to Offic *Roch* from 91. *33 High Cross Field, Crowborough, E Sussex TN6 2SN* Tel (01892) 661351

CHARMAN, Ms Jane Ellen Elizabeth. b 60. St Jo Coll Dur BA81 Selw Coll Cam BA84 MA88. Westcott Ho Cam 82. **d** 87 **p** 94. C Glouc St Geo w Whaddon *Glouc* 87-90; Chapl and Fell Clare Coll Cam 90-95; R Duxford *Ely* from 95; V Hinxton from 95; V Ickleton from 95. *The Rectory, 13 St John's Street, Duxford, Cambridge CB2 4RA* Tel (01223) 832137 Fax 511944

CHARNOCK, Deryck Ian. b 47. Oak Hill Th Coll 78. **d** 80 **p** 81. C Rowner *Portsm* 80-84; TV Southgate *Chich* 84-90; V Penge St Paul *Roch* from 90. *St Paul's Vicarage, Hamlet Road, London SE19 2AW* Tel 0181-653 0978

CHARNOCK, Ernest Burrell. b 14. ACIS42 AACCA50 Lon Univ DipTh60. **d** 61 **p** 62. C Bowdon *Ches* 61-64; V Buglawton 64-70; R Tattenhall 70-77; P-in-c Handley 72-77; R Tattenhall and Handley 77-80; rtd 80; Perm to Offic *Ches* 85-87; Perm to Offic *Glouc* from 87. *26 Pegasus Court, St Stephen's Road, Cheltenham, Glos GL51 5AB* Tel (01242) 578651

CHARRETT, Geoffrey Barton. b 36. ALCM Nottm Univ BSc57. Ridley Hall Cam 65. **d** 67 **p** 68. C Clifton *York* 67-68; Lic to Offic *Blackb* 69-80; C Walthamstow St Mary w St Steph *Chelmsf* 81-82; TV 82-87; Chapl Gordon's Sch Woking 87-94; P-in-c Hambledon *Guildf* 94-97; rtd 97. *2 Station Road, Sutton-on-Sea, Mablethorpe, Lincs LN12 2HN* Tel (01507) 443525

CHARRINGTON, Nicholas John. b 36. MA. Cuddesdon Coll 60. **d** 62 **p** 63. C Shrewsbury St Chad *Lich* 62-65; C Gt Grimsby St Mary and St Jas *Linc* 65-72; P-in-c Wellington Ch Ch *Lich* 72-78; R Edgmond 78-89; R Edgmond w Kynnersley and Preston Wealdmoors 89-91; C Plymstock *Ex* 91-94; Chapl St Luke's Hospice Plymouth 91-94; P-in-c Longden and Annscroft w Pulverbatch *Heref* from 94. *The Rectory, Longden, Shrewsbury SY5 8ET* Tel (01743) 861003

CHARTERIS, Hugo Arundale. b 64. Witwatersrand Univ BA88. Cranmer Hall Dur 90. **d** 93 **p** 94. C Byker St Mark and Walkergate St Oswald *Newc* from 93. *258 Westbourne Avenue, Newcastle-upon-Tyne NE6 4XU* Tel 0191-262 4875

CHARTERS, Alan Charles. b 35. Trin Hall Cam BA60 MA63. Linc Th Coll 60. **d** 62 **p** 63. C Gt Grimsby St Mary and St Jas *Linc* 62-65; Chapl Eliz Coll Guernsey 65-70; Dep Hd Master Park Sch Swindon 70-74; Chapl St Jo Sch Leatherhead 74-77; Dep Hd Master 77-83; Master K Sch Glouc 83-92; V Aberedw w Llandeilo Graban and Llanbadarn etc *S & B* from 92. *The Vicarage, Aberedw, Builth Wells LD2 3UW* Tel (01982) 560359

CHARTERS, John Nicholson. b 27. Trin Hall Cam BA51 MA55. Westcott Ho Cam 51. **d** 53 **p** 54. C Selby Abbey *York* 53-55; C Hornsea and Goxhill 55-57; C Milton *Portsm* 57-60; Chapl RN 60-64; R Thorndon w Rishangles *St E* 64-68; Hon C Beeford w Lissett *York* 68-77; Hon C Beeford w Frodingham and Foston 77-89; R 90-93; rtd 93; Perm to Offic *York* from 93. *2 Alton Park, Beeford, Driffield, N Humberside YO25 8BZ* Tel (01262) 488485

✠**CHARTRES, The Rt Revd and Rt Hon Richard John Carew.** b 47. PC96. Trin Coll Cam BA68 MA73 BD83. Cuddesdon Coll 69 Linc Th Coll 72. **d** 73 **p** 74 **c** 92. C Bedford St Andr *St Alb* 73-75; Bp's Dom Chapl 75-80; Abp's Chapl *Cant* 80-84; P-in-c Westmr St Steph w St Jo *Lon* 84-85; V 86-92; Dir of Ords 85-92; Prof Div Gresham Coll 86-92; Six Preacher Cant Cathl *Cant* 91-97; Area Bp Stepney *Lon* 92-95; Bp Lon from 95; Dean of HM Chpls Royal and Prelate of OBE from 95. *The Bishop's House, The Old Deanery, Dean's Court, London EC4V 5AA* Tel 0171-248 6233

CHASE, Lt Col Frederick Jack. b 14. Westcott Ho Cam 61. **d** 62 **p** 63. C Newquay *Truro* 62-64; R St Dennis 64-69; Rhodesia 69-70; V St Columb Minor *Truro* 71-73; V St Columb Minor and St Colan 73-76; P-in-c Arreton *Portsm* 76-82; rtd 82; Perm to Offic *Cant* 82-93. *St Luke's Nursing Home, Latimer Road, Headington, Oxford OX3 7PF* Tel (01865) 750220

CHATER, John Leathley. b 29. Qu Coll Cam BA54 MA58. Ridley Hall Cam 54. **d** 56 **p** 57. C Bath Abbey w St Jas *B & W* 56-60; V Bermondsey St Anne *S'wark* 60-64; Ind Chapl 60-64; V Heslington *York* 64-69; Chapl York Univ 64-69; V Lawrence Weston *Bris* 69-73; Perm to Offic 74-80; P-in-c Wraxall *B & W* 80-82; R 82-84; V Battle *Chich* 84-90; Dean Battle 84-90; RD Battle and Bexhill 86-90; R St Marylebone w H Trin *Lon* 90-96; rtd 96; Perm to Offic *Chich* from 96. *75 Braemore Road, Hove, E Sussex BN3 4HA* Tel (01273) 748402

CHATFIELD, Adrian Francis. b 49. Leeds Univ BA71 MA72 MPhil89. Coll of Resurr Mirfield 71. **d** 72 **p** 73. Trinidad and Tobago 72-83; TV Barnstaple, Goodleigh and Landkey *Ex* 83-84; TV Barnstaple 85; TR 85-88; Lect St Jo Coll Nottm from 88; Perm to Offic *Derby* from 88. *5 Peatfield Road, Stapleford, Nottingham NG9 8GN* Tel 0115-939 1287 or 925 1114 Fax 922 0134 or 943 6438

CHATFIELD, Preb Frederick Roy. b 06. **d** 32 **p** 33. C Ex St Thos *Ex* 32-36; C Budleigh Salterton 36-40; V Thorverton 40-47; V Cockington 47-72; RD Ipplepen 66-69; Preb Ex Cathl 71-82; rtd 72; Lic to Offic *Ex* 73-95; Perm to Offic from 95. *Aspreys Nursing Home, 1 Kents Road, Torquay TQ1 2NL* Tel (01803) 201500

CHATFIELD, Mrs Gillian (Jill). b 50. Leeds Univ BA71 PGCE72. St Jo Coll Nottm MA94. **d** 94 **p** 95. C Greasley *S'well* from 94. *2 Grantham Close, Giltbrook, Nottingham NG16 2WB* Tel 0115-938 4960

CHATFIELD, Neil Patrick. b 66. Nottm Univ BTh95. Linc Th Coll 93 Westcott Ho Cam 95. **d** 96 **p** 97. C Bexhill St Pet *Chich* from 96. *14 Barrack Road, Bexhill-on-Sea, E Sussex TN40 2AT* Tel (01424) 212453

CHATFIELD, Canon Norman. b 37. Fitzw Ho Cam BA59 MA68. Ripon Hall Ox 60. **d** 62 **p** 63. C Burgess Hill St Jo *Chich* 62-65; C Uckfield 65-69; V Lower Sandown St Jo *Portsm* 69-76; V Locks Heath 76-83; Bp's Chapl for Post Ord Tr 78-85; R Alverstoke 83-91; Chapl HM Pris Haslar 83-90; Chapl Gosport War Memorial Hosp 83-91; Hon Can Portsm Cathl *Portsm* 85-91; Can Res Glouc Cathl *Glouc* from 91. *6 College Green, Gloucester GL1 2LX* Tel (01452) 521954

CHATFIELD, Thomas William. b 19. Lon Univ. Chich Th Coll 44. **d** 46 **p** 47. C Hanworth All SS *Lon* 46-49; C Woolwich St Mich *S'wark* 49-51; C Eastbourne St Andr *Chich* 51-55; V Hastings St Clem 55-68; P-in-c Hastings St Mary Magd 68-71; R 71-78; P-in-c Bishopstone 78-84; rtd 84; Perm to Offic *Chich* from 84. *5 Leeds Close, Victoria Avenue, Ore Village, Hastings, E Sussex TN35 5BX* Tel (01424) 437413

CHATFIELD-JUDE, Canon Henry. b 09. OBE76. AKC32. **d** 32 **p** 33. C N Acton St Gabr *Lon* 32-34; Hon C Uckfield *Chich* 34-35; C Tormohun *Ex* 35-37; India 37-45; Hon CF 46; Australia 48-50; Chapl RAF 50-57; R Michelmersh w Eldon w Timsbury *Win* 57-62; Chapl Madeira *Eur* 62-66; Chapl Lisbon 66-76; Hon Can Gib Cathl from 71; rtd 76; Perm to Offic *Win* 76-94; Perm to Offic *Chich* from 94. *Flat 1, Manormead, Tilford Road, Hindhead, Surrey GU26 6RA* Tel (01428) 605843

CHATHAM, Richard Henry. b 28. Launde Abbey 71. **d** 71 **p** 72. C Aylestone *Leic* 71-76; R Hoby cum Rotherby 76-77; P-in-c Brooksby 76-77; R Hoby cum Rotherby w Brooksby, Ragdale & Thru'ton 77-85; R Overstrand *Nor* 85-93; rtd 93; Perm to Offic *Nor* from 93. *Sandyside, Sandy Lane, Cromer, Norfolk NR27 9JT* Tel (01263) 513456

CHATTERJI DE MASSEY, Robert Arthur Sovan Lal. b 15. Chich Th Coll 54. **d** 56 **p** 57. C Romford St Edw *Chelmsf* 56-60; R Abberton w Langenhoe 60-90; rtd 90. *Clare House, 82 Main Street, Witchford, Ely, Cambs CB6 2HQ*

CHATWIN, Barbara. b 07. MCSP33. Selly Oak Coll 62. **dss** 65 **d** 87. Birm St Dav *Birm* 63-67; Londonderry 67-69; Pershore w Pinvin, Wick and Birlingham *Worc* 69-87; Hon C from 87; Perm to Offic from 90. *Myrtle Cottage, Broad Street, Pershore, Worcs WR10 1BB* Tel (01386) 552080

CHATWIN, Ronald Ernest. b 34. St Aid Birkenhead 58. **d** 60 **p** 61. C Selsdon *Cant* 60-64; C Crawley *Chich* 64-68; V Coldwaltham 68-74; TV Ovingdean w Rottingdean and Woodingdean 74-83; V Saltdean 83-91; V Hellingly and Upper Dicker from 91. *The Vicarage, Hellingly, Hailsham, E Sussex BN27 4EY* Tel (01323) 843346

CHAVE, Brian Philip. b 51. Open Univ BA. Trin Coll Bris. **d** 84 **p** 85. C Cullompton *Ex* 84-87; TV Bishopsnympton, Rose Ash, Mariansleigh etc 87-93; Chapl for Agric *Heref* 93-96; Communications Adv and Bp's Staff Officer from 97; Bp's Dom Chapl from 97. *Church Gate, Almeley, Hereford HR3 6LB* Tel (01544) 328497

CHAVE-COX, Guy. b 56. St Andr Univ BSc79. Wycliffe Hall Ox 83. **d** 86 **p** 87. C Wigmore Abbey *Heref* 86-88; C Bideford *Ex* 88-91; TV Barnstaple from 91. *St Paul's Vicarage, Old Sticklepath Hill, Barnstaple, Devon EX31 2BG* Tel (01271) 44400

CHAVNER, Robert. b 59. ALCM82 AGSM85 Guildhall Sch of Music and Drama PdipEM86. Linc Th Coll 90. **d** 92 **p** 93. C Beckenham St Geo *Roch* 92-96; Min Sevenoaks St Luke CD 96; V Sevenoaks St Luke from 96. *St Luke's House, 30 Eardley Road, Sevenoaks, Kent TN13 1XT* Tel (01732) 452462

CHEADLE, Preb Robert. b 24. MBE71 TD66. Leeds Univ BA49. Coll of Resurr Mirfield 49. **d** 51 **p** 52. C Newbury St Jo *Ox* 51-55; C Tunstall Ch Ch *Lich* 55-57; TR Hanley H Ev 57-60; V Bloxwich 60-72; V Penkridge w Stretton 72-89; Preb Lich Cathl 79-89; P-in-c Dunston w Coppenhall 79-82; V 82-89; P-in-c Acton Trussell w Bednall 80-82; V 82-89; rtd 89; Perm to Offic *Lich* from 89. *26 Audley Place, Newcastle, Staffs ST5 3RS* Tel (01782) 618685

CHEALL, Henry Frederick Knowles. b 34. Ex Coll Ox BA56 MA60. Ripon Hall Ox 58. **d** 60 **p** 61. C Sutton *Liv* 60-63; C Blundellsands St Mich 63-66; Nigeria 66-68; R Crumpsall St Matt *Man* 68-76; R Crumpsall 76-84; V Chipping and Whitewell *Blackb* 84-96; R Wensley *Ripon* from 96; V W Witton from 96. *The Rectory, Wensley, Leyburn, N Yorkshire DL8 4HS* Tel (01969) 623736

CHEATLE, Adele Patricia. b 46. York Univ BA73. Trin Coll Bris 76. **d** 87. Par Dn Harborne Heath *Birm* 87; NSM 92-93; Perm to Offic *Heref* from 96. *The Mews House, Mordiford, Hereford HR1 4LN* Tel (01432) 870440

CHEATLE, Christopher Robert David. b 41. Leeds Univ BA63. Coll of Resurr Mirfield. **d** 65 **p** 66. C Hangleton *Chich* 65-66; C

Corringham *Chelmsf* 66-70; Bp's Adv on Child Protection from 95; NSM Southend from 96. *28 Park Road, Leigh-on-Sea, Essex SS9 2PE* Tel (01702) 79043

CHEDZEY, Derek Christopher. b 67. Trin Coll Bris BA93. **d** 93 **p** 94. C Bedgrove *Ox* 93-95; C Haddenham w Cuddington, Kingsey etc from 95. *1 Dadbrook Farm Cottages, Cuddington, Aylesbury, Bucks HP18 0AG* Tel (01844) 291484

CHEEK, Richard Alexander. b 35. Lon Univ LDS60. Ox NSM Course 72. **d** 75 **p** 76. NSM Maidenhead St Luke *Ox* 75-94; Asst Chapl Heatherwood and Wexham Park Hosp NHS Trust from 94. *Windrush, Sheephouse Road, Maidenhead, Berks SL6 8EX* Tel (01628) 28484

CHEESEMAN, Colin Henry. b 47. Reading Univ BA. Sarum & Wells Th Coll 82. **d** 84 **p** 85. C Cranleigh *Guildf* 84-87; C Godalming 87-89; V Cuddington 89-96; Chapl HM Pris Wealstun 96-97; Chapl HM Pris Leeds from 97. *HM Prison, Armley, Leeds LS12 2TJ* Tel 0113-263 6411 Fax 279 0151

CHEESEMAN, John Anthony. b 50. Or Coll Ox BA73 MA75. Trin Coll Bris DipTh76. **d** 76 **p** 77. C Sevenoaks St Nic *Roch* 76-79; C Egham *Guildf* 79-82; V Leyton Ch Ch *Chelmsf* 82-90; V Westgate St Jas *Cant* from 90. *St James's Vicarage, Orchard Gardens, Westgate-on-Sea, Kent CT9 5JT* Tel (01843) 832073

CHEESEMAN, Kenneth Raymond (Ken). b 29. Roch Th Coll 63. **d** 66 **p** 67. C Crayford *Roch* 66-69; C Beckenham St Jas 69-75; V Belvedere St Aug 75-83; V Thorley *Portsm* 83-94; R Yarmouth 83-94; rtd 94; Perm to Offic *Portsm* from 94. *10 St Catherine's View, Godshill, Ventnor, Isle of Wight PO38 3JJ* Tel (01983) 840700

CHEESEMAN, Dr Trevor Percival. b 38. Auckland Univ PhD64. **d** 68 **p** 69. C Warmsworth *Sheff* 68-71; New Zealand from 71. *Kings College, PO Box 22 012, Otahuhu, South Auckland 1006, New Zealand* Tel Auckland (9) 276 7989 or 276 0673 Fax 276 0670 E-mail t.cheeseman@kings.ak.school.nz

CHEESMAN, Ashley Frederick Bruce. b 53. Oak Hill Th Coll. **d** 83 **p** 84. C Tranmere St Cath *Ches* 83-88; R Gaulby *Leic* from 88. *The Rectory, Gaulby, Leicester LE7 9BB* Tel 0116-259 6228

CHEESMAN, Peter. b 43. ACA65 FCA76 MIMgt. Ridley Hall Cam 66. **d** 69 **p** 70. C Herne Bay Ch Ch *Cant* 69-74; TV Lowestoft St Marg *Nor* 75-78; TV Lowestoft and Kirkley 79-81; Ind Chapl *Glouc* 81-84; P-in-c Saul w Fretherne and Framilode 84-85; V Frampton on Severn, Arlingham, Saul etc from 85. *The Vicarage, The Street, Frampton on Severn, Gloucester GL2 7ED* Tel (01452) 740966

CHEETHAM, Richard Ian. b 55. CCC Ox BA77 CertEd78 MA82. Ripon Coll Cuddesdon 85. **d** 87 **p** 88. C Newc H Cross *Newc* 87-90; V Luton St Aug Limbury *St Alb* from 90; RD Luton from 94. *The Vicarage, 215 Icknield Way, Luton LU3 2JR* Tel (01582) 572415

CHEEVERS, George Alexander. b 42. CITC 70. **d** 73 **p** 74. C Carrickfergus *Conn* 73-81; C Kilroot 78-81; I Kilmakee 82-91; I Magheragall from 91. *Magheragall Rectory, 70 Ballinderry Road, Lisburn, Co Antrim BT28 2QS* Tel (01846) 621273

CHELMSFORD, Bishop of. *See* PERRY, The Rt Revd John Freeman

CHELMSFORD, Provost of. *See* JUDD, The Very Revd Peter Somerset Margesson

CHELTENHAM, Archdeacon of. *See* LEWIS, The Ven John Arthur

CHENNELL, Capt Arthur John. b 28. St Deiniol's Hawarden 77. **d** 77 **p** 78. CA from 58; C Prenton *Ches* 77-79; V Liscard St Thos 79-82; V Lt Thornton *Blackb* 82-94; rtd 94; Perm to Offic *Ches* from 94. *79 Cobham Road, Moreton, Wirral, Merseyside L46 0RA* Tel 0151-678 5708

CHERRILL, John Oliver. b 33. Bath Univ MArch75 DipArch61. Sarum & Wells Th Coll 76. **d** 79 **p** 80. NSM Blackmoor *Portsm* 79-83; NSM Headley All SS *Guildf* 83-85; C 86-90; Perm to Offic *Portsm* from 94. *7 Oaktree Road, Whitehill, Bordon, Hants GU35 9DF* Tel (01420) 473193

CHERRIMAN, Colin Wilfred (Brother Colin Wilfred). b 37. Leeds Univ BA63. Coll of Resurr Mirfield 63. **d** 65 **p** 66. C Bournemouth St Fran *Win* 65-69; SSF from 69; Lic to Offic *Chelmsf* 73-75; Lic to Offic *Cant* 75-77; Lic to Offic *Edin* 77-79; Lic to Offic *Sarum* 79-82; Lic to Offic *Newc* 82-88; Perm to Offic *Lon* 88-91; Adv HIV/AIDS Unit 91-92; HIV Support Worker Aldgate St Botolph Lon from 92. *St Botolph's Church, Aldgate, London EC3N 1AB* Tel 0171-283 1670

CHERRY, David. b 30. Roch Th Coll 59. **d** 61 **p** 62. C Seacroft *Ripon* 61-67; R Bamford *Derby* 67-75; Chapl Malaga w Almunecar and Nerja *Eur* 83-91; rtd 91; NSM Waltham *Ox* from 97. *The Parsonage, School Road, Waltham St Lawrence, Reading RG10 0NU* Tel 0118-934 5082

CHERRY, David Warwick. b 61. Cape Town Univ BMus86 Leeds Univ BA91. Coll of Resurr Mirfield CPT92. **d** 92 **p** 93. C Hammersmith SS Mich and Geo White City Estate CD *Lon* from 92. *St Luke's Vicarage, 450 Uxbridge Road, London W12 0NS* Tel 0181-749 7523

CHERRY, Malcolm Stephen. b 28. Open Univ BA81. Sarum Th Coll 51. **d** 54 **p** 55. C Mill Hill Jo Keble Ch *Lon* 54-57; C Hendon All SS Childs Hill 57-59; V Colchester St Anne *Chelmsf* 59-68; V Horndon on the Hill 68-79; Ind Chapl 69-79; Voc Officer Southend Adnry 74-79; R Lochgilphead *Arg* 79-82; V Mill End and Heronsgate w W Hyde *St Alb* 82-90; TV Chipping Barnet w Arkley 90-94; rtd 94. *Nether Hankleys, Barrow Road, Higham, Bury St Edmunds, Suffolk IP28 6NN* Tel (01284) 810269

CHERRY, Stephen Arthur. b 58. St Chad's Coll Dur BSc79 Fitzw Coll Cam BA85. Westcott Ho Cam 83. **d** 86 **p** 87. C Baguley *Man* 86-89; Chapl K Coll Cam 89-94; R Loughborough All SS w H Trin *Leic* from 94; RD Akeley E from 96. *The Rectory, Steeple Row, Loughborough, Leics LE11 1UX* Tel (01509) 212780

CHESHAM, William Gerald. b 23. MIMechE55 Birm Univ DPS66. Wells Th Coll 61. **d** 63 **p** 64. C Ashford *Cant* 63-66; C Edgbaston St Bart *Birm* 66-68; V Smethwick 68-72; Lic to Offic *Heref* 72-78; TV Glendale Gp *Newc* 78-84; rtd 84; Hon Asst Chapl Algarve *Eur* 84-97. *1 St Georges Close, Lower Street, West Harnham, Salisbury SP2 8HA* Tel (01722) 323484

CHESSUN, Christopher Thomas James. b 56. Univ Coll Ox BA78 MA82 Trin Hall Cam BA82. Westcott Ho Cam. **d** 83 **p** 84. C Sandhurst *Ox* 83-87; C Portsea St Mary *Portsm* 87-89; Min Can and Chapl St Paul's Cathl *Lon* 89-93; Voc Adv from 90; R Stepney St Dunstan and All SS from 93; AD Tower Hamlets from 97. *The Rectory, Rectory Square, London E1 3NG* Tel 0171-791 3545

CHESTER, Dr David Kenneth. b 50. Dur Univ BA73 Aber Univ PhD78. Nor Ord Course 93. **d** 96 **p** 97. Hon C Hoylake *Ches* from 96. *Yenda, Grange Road, West Kirby, Wirral, Merseyside L48 4ET* Tel 0151-625 8004

CHESTER, Mark. b 55. Lanc Univ BA79. Wycliffe Hall Ox 86. **d** 88 **p** 89. C Plymouth St Andr w St Paul and St Geo *Ex* 88-94; V Burney Lane *Birm* from 94. *Christ Church Vicarage, Burney Lane, Birmingham B8 2AS* Tel 0121-783 7455

CHESTER, Maureen Olga. b 47. Univ of Wales (Swansea) BA70. NE Ord Course DipHE94. **d** 97. NSM Morpeth *Newc* from 97. *10 Leland Place, Morpeth, Northd NE61 2AN* Tel (01670) 514569

CHESTER, Philip Anthony Edwin. b 55. Birm Univ LLB76. St Jo Coll Dur DipTh80. **d** 80 **p** 81. C Shrewsbury St Chad *Lich* 80-85; C St Martin-in-the-Fields *Lon* 85-88; Chapl K Coll Lon 88-95; PV Westmr Abbey from 90; P-in-c Westmr St Matt *Lon* from 95. *St Matthew's Clergy House, 20 Great Peter Street, London SW1P 2BU* Tel 0171-222 3704

CHESTER, Archdeacon of. *See* HEWETSON, The Ven Christopher

CHESTER, Bishop of. *See* FORSTER, The Rt Revd Peter Robert

CHESTER, Dean of. *See* SMALLEY, The Very Revd Stephen Stewart

CHESTERFIELD, Archdeacon of. *See* GARNETT, David Christopher

CHESTERMAN, Canon George Anthony (Tony). b 38. Man Univ BSc62 DipAdEd Nottm Univ PhD89. Coll of Resurr Mirfield 62. **d** 64 **p** 65. C Newbold w Dunston *Derby* 64-68; C Derby St Thos 68-70; Adult Educn Officer 70-79; R Mugginton and Kedleston 70-89; Vice-Prin EMMTC 79-86; Can Res Derby Cathl *Derby* from 89; Dioc Clergy In-Service Tr Adv from 89. *13 Newbridge Road, Ambergate, Belper, Derbyshire DE56 2GR* Tel (01773) 852236

CHESTERMAN, Lawrence James. b 16. AKC91. K Coll Lon 48 St Boniface Warminster. **d** 49 **p** 50. C Braunstone *Leic* 49-52; C S w N Hayling *Portsm* 52-55; V Whitwick St Andr *Leic* 55-60; R Thornford w Beer Hackett *Sarum* 60-69; P-in-c Bradford Abbas w Clifton Maybank 61-63; V Idmiston 69-73; TR Bourne Valley 73-81; rtd 81; Perm to Offic *Sarum* from 81; Offg Chapl RAF 88. *2 Beacon Close, Amesbury, Salisbury SP4 7EG* Tel (01980) 622205

✠**CHESTERS, The Rt Revd Alan David.** b 37. St Chad's Coll Dur BA59 St Cath Soc Ox BA61 MA65. St Steph Ho Ox 59. **d** 62 **p** 63 **c** 89. C Wandsworth St Anne *S'wark* 62-66; Hon C 66-68; Chapl Tiffin Sch Kingston 66-72; Hon C Ham St Rich *S'wark* 68-72; Dioc Dir of Educn *Dur* 72-85; R Brancepeth 72-85; Hon Can Dur Cathl 75-85; Adn Halifax *Wakef* 85-89; Bp Blackb from 89. *Bishop's House, Ribchester Road, Blackburn BB1 9EF* Tel (01254) 248234 Fax 246668 E-mail bishop@blackburn.anglican.org.uk.

CHESTERS, Peter Durrant. b 17. ACII52. K Coll Lon 54. **d** 56 **p** 57. C Crofton Park St Hilda *S'wark* 56-58; C Camberwell St Geo 58-60; R Durweston *Sarum* 60-66; V Stourpaine 60-66; R Ludgershall and Faberstown 66-82; rtd 82; Perm to Offic *Heref* 82-93; Perm to Offic *Ex* from 95. *18 Gracey Court, Woodland Road, Broadclyst, Exeter EX5 3LP* Tel (01392) 462574

CHESTERS, Simon. b 66. Rob Coll Cam BA87 MA91. Wycliffe Hall Ox BA94 DipMin95. **d** 95 **p** 96. C Bidston *Ches* from 95. *55 Bridle Close, Birkenhead, Merseyside L43 9UU* Tel 0151-677 8700

CHESTERTON, Robert Eric. b 31. St Aid Birkenhead 63. **d** 65 **p** 66. C Kirby Muxloe *Leic* 65-67; Canada 67-68 and 75-78; C St Annes *Blackb* 68-69; V Southminster *Chelmsf* 69-75; V Wythenshawe Wm Temple Ch *Man* 78-82; TV Marfleet *York* 82-85; V Marshchapel *Linc* 85-88; R N Coates 85-88; V Grainthorpe w Conisholme 85-88; V Langtoft Gp 88-91; V Kingsbury *Birm* 91-94; rtd 94; Perm to Offic *Pet* from 95; Perm to Offic *Leic* from 96. *46 Tyne Road, Oakham, Leics LE15 6SJ* Tel (01572) 757262

CHETWOOD, Noah. b 14. St Jo Coll Dur BA38 DipTh39 MA41 Nottm Univ MEd58. **d** 39 **p** 40. C Ludlow *Heref* 39-45; Lic to Offic *Derby* 45-54; Lic to Offic *Ox* from 54. *Evergreens, 10 Longfield Drive, Amersham, Bucks HP6 5HD* Tel (01494) 725259

CHETWYND, Edward Ivor. b 45. Leeds Univ DipTh68. Coll of Resurr Mirfield 68. **d** 70 **p** 71. C Westgate Common *Wakef* 70-74; C Penistone w Midhope 74-75; V Smawthorpe St Mich from 75. *St Michael's Vicarage, St Michael's Close, Castleford, W Yorkshire WF10 4ER* Tel (01977) 557079

CHEVALIER, Harry Ensor Estienne. b 23. Mert Coll Ox BA49 MA56. Ely Th Coll 49. **d** 51 **p** 52. C Weymouth St Paul *Sarum* 51-53; C Broadstairs *Cant* 53-55; C Paignton St Jo *Ex* 55-63; V Taddington and Chelmorton *Derby* 63; C Reading St Mary V *Ox* 63-66; V Bradninch *Ex* 66-71; Perm to Offic 71-74; Hon C Christchurch *Win* 74-75; rtd 75; Perm to Offic *Win* 75-95. *18 Trent Drive, Wareham, Dorset BH20 4DF*

CHEVERTON, Miss Jill. b 48. RGN71 RHV77 Leeds Poly DSocStuds73. Cranmer Hall Dur CTMin93. **d** 93 **p** 94. Par Dn Bilton *Ripon* 93-94; C 94-96; TV Burmantofts St Steph and St Agnes 96; V from 96. *St Agnes Vicarage, 21 Shakespeare Close, Leeds LS9 7UQ* Tel 0113-248 2648

CHICHESTER, Archdeacon of. *See* BROTHERTON, The Ven John Michael

CHICHESTER, Bishop of. *See* KEMP, The Rt Revd Eric Waldram

CHICHESTER, Dean of. *See* TREADGOLD, The Very Revd John David

CHICKEN, Peter Lindsay. b 46. St Andr Univ BSc71. Chich Th Coll 77. **d** 79 **p** 80. C High Wycombe *Ox* 79-83; V The Stanleys *Glouc* 83-96; Bp's Adv for Continued Minl Educn from 92; V Leckhampton SS Phil and Jas w Cheltenham St Jas from 96. *The Vicarage, 80 Painswick Road, Cheltenham, Glos GL50 2EU* Tel (01242) 525460

CHIDLAW, Richard Paul. b 49. St Cath Coll Cam BA71 MA. Ripon Hall Ox 72. **d** 74 **p** 81. C Ribbesford w Bewdley and Dowles *Worc* 74-76; NSM Coaley *Glouc* 81-83; NSM Frampton on Severn 81-83; NSM Arlingham 81-83; NSM Saul w Fretherne and Framilode 83-84; NSM Cam w Stinchcombe 85-90; Perm to Offic 90-91; NSM Berkeley w Wick, Breadstone and Newport from 91. *38 May Lane, Dursley, Glos GL11 4HU* Tel (01453) 547838

CHIDWICK, Alan Robert. b 49. MIL MA. Oak Hill NSM Course. **d** 84 **p** 85. NSM Pimlico St Pet w Westmr Ch Ch *Lon* from 84. *119 Eaton Square, London SW1W 9AL* Tel 0171-235 4242

CHILCOTT, Dr Mark David. b 62. Ch Coll Cam BA83 MA87 PhD88. Ripon Coll Cuddesdon BA92. **d** 93 **p** 94. C Warrington St Elphin *Liv* from 93. *Church House, 133 Church Street, Warrington WA1 2TL* Tel (01925) 633940

CHILD, Margaret Mary. *See* MASLEN, Mrs Margaret Mary

CHILD, Canon Rupert Henry. b 29. St Jo Coll Dur 50 K Coll Lon DipTh56 St Boniface Warminster 57. **d** 58 **p** 59. C Tavistock and Gulworthy *Ex* 58-61; C Dunstable *St Alb* 61-65; V Luton St Chris Round Green 65-74; V Sawbridgeworth 74-95; Hon Can St Alb 86-95; rtd 95. *6 Lakes Close, Langford, Biggleswade, Beds SG18 9SJ* Tel (01462) 700303

CHILD, Theodore Hilary. b 09. MA. **d** 33 **p** 34. C Southampton St Mary Extra *Win* 33-36; C Sheringham *Nor* 36-38; P-in-c Leic St Chad *Leic* 38-40; R W Lynn *Nor* 40-47; CF 43-46; R E w W Harling *Nor* 47-59; R Bridgham and Roudham 50-59; V Southwold *St E* 59-74; rtd 74; P-in-c Starston *Nor* 75-87; Perm to Offic from 87; Perm to Offic *St E* from 87. *41 Deans Mill Court, The Causeway, Canterbury, Kent CT1 2BF* Tel (01227) 785920

CHILDS, Ernest Edmund. b 23. Lich Th Coll 63. **d** 65 **p** 66. C Billesley Common *Birm* 65-68; C Elland *Wakef* 68-69; Clerical Org Sec CECS (Dios Pet, Leic and Ely) 69-72; V Staverton w Helidon and Catesby *Pet* 72-76; rtd 77; Perm to Offic *Nor* 77-91; Hon C W Lynn *Ely* 92-94; P-in-c 94-95; Perm to Offic from 95; Perm to Offic *Nor* from 96. *4 Fieldview Court, The Paddocks, Fakenham, Norfolk NR21 8PB* Tel (01328) 856595

CHILDS, Leonard Neil. b 43. Leeds Univ BA65. Wells Th Coll 66. **d** 68 **p** 69. C Matlock and Tansley *Derby* 68-72; C Chesterfield St Mary and All SS 72-74; P-in-c Stonebroom 74-81; P-in-c Morton 78-81; R Morton and Stonebroom 81-84; TV Buxton w Burbage and King Sterndale 84-92; V Derby St Mark from 92. *St Mark's Vicarage, 119 Francis Street, Derby DE21 6DE* Tel (01332) 340183

CHILDS, Theodore John. b 12. St Edm Hall Ox BA34 MA47 BLitt47. Ripon Hall Ox 37. **d** 40 **p** 41. C Yeovil St Jo w Preston Plucknett *B & W* 40-48; V Winsham w Cricket St Thomas 48-61; R Chelvey w Brockley 61-70; R Ballaugh *S & M* 70-77; rtd 77; Perm to Offic *S & M* from 77. *9 Ballagorry Drive, Glen Mona, Ramsey, Isle of Man IM7 1HE* Tel (01624) 861993

CHILLINGWORTH, The Very Revd David Robert. b 51. TCD BA73 Or Coll Ox BA75 MA81. Ripon Coll Cuddesdon 75. **d** 76 **p** 77. C Belfast H Trin *Conn* 76-79; Ch of Ireland Youth Officer 79-83; C Bangor Abbey *D & D* 83-86; I Seagoe from 86; Dean Dromore from 95. *8 Upper Church Lane, Portadown, Craigavon, Co Armagh BT63 5JE* Tel (01762) 332538 or 350583 Mobile 0410-451619 Fax 350583 E-mail chillingworth@seagoe.source.co.uk

CHILLMAN, David James. b 59. Southn Univ BA82. Trin Coll Bris ADMT95. **d** 95 **p** 96. C Yateley *Win* from 95. *37 Walnut Close, Yateley, Camberley, Surrey GU17 7DA* Tel (01252) 875798

CHILTON, Kenneth Chapman. b 20. St Cuth Soc Dur BA49 DipTh51. **d** 51 **p** 52. C Billingham St Cuth *Dur* 51-53; C Eaton *Nor* 53-57; V Thorpe St Matt 57-85; rtd 85; Perm to Offic *Nor* from 85. *3 Hillcrest Road, Norwich NR7 0JZ* Tel (01603) 36948

CHIN, Michael Shoon Chion. b 41. Lon Univ BD71 Melbourne Univ BA76 DipEd79. Moore Th Coll Sydney 60 Trin Th Coll Singapore BTh64 Ridley Coll Melbourne 68 Melbourne Coll of Div DipRE74. **d** 64 **p** 65. Malaysia 64-68; Australia 69-80 and 87-91; Miss to Seamen from 72; USA 81-82; Perm to Offic *Win* from 93; Gen Sec Internat Chr Maritime Assn from 93. *International Christian Maritime Ass, 2/3 Orchard Place, Southampton SO14 3BR* Tel (01703) 336111 Fax 333567

CHING, Derek. b 37. MA. Qu Coll Birm. **d** 83 **p** 84. C Finham *Cov* 83-87; V Butlers Marston and the Pillertons w Ettington 87-96. *25 Kirkby Road, Ripon, N Yorkshire HG4 2EY* Tel (01765) 609419

CHIPLIN, Christopher Gerald. b 53. Lon Univ BSc75. St Steph Ho Ox BA77 MA81. **d** 78 **p** 79. C Chesterfield St Mary and All SS *Derby* 78-80; C Thorpe *Nor* 80-84; V Highbridge *B & W* 84-94; V Midsomer Norton w Clandown from 94. *The Vicarage, 42 Priory Close, Midsomer Norton, Bath BA3 2HZ* Tel (01761) 412118

CHIPLIN, Gareth Huw. b 50. Worc Coll Ox BA71 MA. Edin Th Coll 71. **d** 73 **p** 74. C Friern Barnet St Jas *Lon* 73-75; C Eastcote St Lawr 76-79; C Notting Hill St Mich and Ch Ch 79-84; V Hammersmith St Matt from 84. *St Matthew's Vicarage, 1 Fielding Road, London W14 0LL* Tel 0171-603 9769

CHIPLIN, Howard Alan. b 43. Sarum & Wells Th Coll 84. **d** 86 **p** 87. C Caerleon *Mon* 86-89; V Ferndale w Maerdy *Llan* 89-91; V Ysbyty Cynfyn w Llantrisant and Eglwys Newydd *St D* 91-95; R Narberth w Mounton w Robeston Wathen and Crinow from 95. *The Rectory, Adams Drive, Narberth SA67 7AE* Tel (01834) 860370

CHIPLIN, Malcolm Leonard. b 42. Llan Dioc Tr Scheme 86. **d** 88 **p** 89. C Newton Nottage *Llan* 88-91; V Pwllgwaun w Llanddewi Rhondda from 91. *The Vicarage, Lanelay Crescent, Maesycoed, Pontypridd CF37 1JB* Tel (01443) 402417

CHIPPENDALE, Peter David. b 34. Dur Univ BA55. Linc Th Coll 57. **d** 59 **p** 60. C Claines St Jo *Worc* 59-63; V Defford w Besford 63-73; P-in-c Eckington 66-69; V 69-73; V Kidderminster St Geo 73-76; V The Lickey *Birm* 76-96; rtd 96. *1 The Fairways, Pershore, Worcs WR10 1HA* Tel (01386) 553478

CHIPPENDALE, Robert William. b 42. DipTh68 BA79 DipT84. **d** 67 **p** 68. Australia 67-72 and from 79; V Shaw *Man* 72-78. *4 Violet Way, Gaven, Australia 4211* Tel Brisbane (7) 5596 2247 or 5532 4922

CHISHOLM, David Whitridge. b 23. Keble Coll Ox BA48 MA48. Linc Th Coll 48. **d** 50 **p** 51. C Sudbury St Andr *Lon* 50-53; C Enfield Jes Chpl 53-57; V Edmonton St Aldhelm 57-66; V N Harrow St Alb 66-72; V Paddington St Jas 72-78; RD Westmr Paddington 74-79; C Paddington St Jas 78-79; V Hurley *Ox* 79-90; rtd 90. *32 Herons Place, Marlow, Bucks SL7 3HP* Tel (01628) 483243

CHISHOLM, Ian Keith. b 36. AKC62. **d** 63 **p** 64. C Lich St Chad *Lich* 63-66; C Sedgley All SS 66-69; V Rough Hills 69-77; V Harrow Weald All SS *Lon* 77-88; V W Moors *Sarum* from 88. *The Vicarage, 57 Glenwood Road, West Moors, Wimborne, Dorset BH22 0EN* Tel (01202) 893197

CHISHOLM, Ian Stuart. b 37. ALCD63. **d** 63 **p** 64. C Worksop St Jo *S'well* 63-66; Succ Sheff Cathl *Sheff* 66-68; Bp's Chapl for Soc Resp 68-72; C Ox St Andr *Ox* 72-76; Tutor Wycliffe Hall Ox 72-76; V Conisbrough *Sheff* 76-94; Chapl Conisbrough Hosp 76-94; RD W Doncaster 82-87 and 93-94; V Chilwell *S'well* from 94. *Christ Church Vicarage, 8 College Road, Beeston, Nottingham NG9 4AS* Tel 0115-922 2809

CHISHOLM, Canon Reginald Joseph. b 13. TCD BA40 MA51. CITC 42. **d** 42 **p** 43. C Belfast St Donard *D & D* 42-45; C Bangor Abbey 45-48; I Ardglass w Dunsford 48-51; I Newtownards 51-82; Min Can Belf Cathl 52-62; Treas Down Cathl *D & D* 80-82; rtd 82. *20 Glendun Park, Bangor, Co Down BT20 4UX* Tel (01247) 450100

CHISHOLM, Samuel James. b 20. Edin Th Coll 74 St Jo Coll Nottm 86. **d** 86 **p** 87. NSM Eastriggs *Glas* 87-92; NSM Gretna 90-91; rtd 92; Perm to Offic *Chich* from 95. *1 Elm Tree House, 5 Hastings Road, Bexhill-on-Sea, E Sussex TN40 2HJ* Tel (01424) 219294

CHITHAM, Ernest John. b 57. LSE BSc79 PGCE80 Dur Univ MA84. **d** 91 **p** 92. C Swanborough *Sarum* 91-94; CMS from 94; Lebanon from 95. *All Saints Church, PO Box 11-2211, Beirut, Lebanon* Tel Grand Beirut (1) 803630

CHITTENDEN, John Bertram d'Encer. b 24. ASCA. Lon Coll of Div 56. **d** 58 **p** 59. C St Mary-at-Lambeth *S'wark* 58-64; R Acrise *Cant* 64-82; R Hawkinge 64-82; R Hawkinge w Acrise and Swingfield 82-90; rtd 91; Perm to Offic *Cant* from 91. *19 Hasborough Road, Folkestone, Kent CT19 6BQ* Tel (01303) 241773

CHITTENDEN, Nils Philip d'Encer. b 69. St Chad's Coll Dur BA91. Westcott Ho Cam CTM95. **d** 95. C Benfieldside *Dur* 95-97; Urban Regeneration Chapl Gateshead from 97. *St Ninian's House, Ivy Lane, Low Fell, Gateshead, Tyne & Wear NE9 6QD* Tel 0191-491 0917 Mobile 0585-306119 Fax as telephone

CHITTLEBOROUGH, Canon Gordon Arthur. b 16. Adelaide Univ 38 K Coll Lon BD62. Moore Th Coll Sydney 37. **d** 63 **p** 63. Tanzania 63-78; Can Tanganyika 63-66; Kenya 78-84; Perm to Offic *S'wark* from 94. *2 Brooklands Park, London SE3 9BL* Tel 0181-852 0205

CHITTY, Philip Crofts. b 27. Roch Th Coll 61. **d** 63 **p** 64. C Holbrooks *Cov* 63-68; V Long Itchington 68-77; R Ufton 69-77; P-in-c Cov St Marg 77-84; rtd 84. *17 Rotherham Road, Coventry CV6 4FF* Tel (01203) 685398

✠**CHIU, The Rt Revd Joshua Ban It.** b 18. Barrister-at-Law (Inner Temple) 41 K Coll Lon AKC41 LLB41. Westcott Ho Cam 43. **d** 45 **p** 46 **c** 66. C Bournville *Birm* 45-47; Malaya 47-50; Singapore 50-59 and 66-82; Hon Can St Andr Cathl Singapore 56-59; Australia 59-62; Service Laymen Abroad WCC Geneva 62-65; Fell St Aug Coll Cant 65-66; Bp Singapore and Malaya 66-70; Bp Singapore 70-82; Member Cen Cttee WCC 68-75; Member ACC 75-79; rtd 82; Perm to Offic *Sarum* from 82. *12 Dewlands Road, Verwood, Dorset BH31 6PL* Tel (01202) 822307

CHIVERS, Christopher Mark (Chris). b 67. Magd Coll Ox BA88 MA92 Selw Coll Cam BTh96. Westcott Ho Cam 94. **d** 97. C Friern Barnet St Jas *Lon* from 97. *2 Hatley Close, London N11 3LN* Tel 0181-361 9228

CHIVERS, Ernest Alfred John. b 34. Bris & Glouc Tr Course. **d** 83 **p** 84. NSM Bedminster *Bris* 83-87; NSM Whitchurch from 87. *40 Calcott Road, Bristol BS4 2HD* Tel 0117-977 7867

CHIVERS, Ronald. b 27. Dur Univ BA52. Oak Hill Th Coll 52. **d** 53 **p** 54. C Blackpool All SS *Blackb* 53-57; V W Derby St Nath Windsor *Liv* 57-60; PC Samlesbury *Blackb* 60-61; N Sec CCCS 61-71; Lic to Offic *Ripon* 61-65; Lic to Offic *Blackb* 66-71; V Woodside *Ripon* 71-91; rtd 91; Perm to Offic *York* from 91; Perm to Offic *Bradf* from 91. *18 Spen Road, West Park, Leeds LS16 5BT* Tel 0113-274 7709

CHIVERS, Royston George (Roy). b 34. Glouc Th Course. **d** 83 **p** 84. NSM Gorsley w Cliffords Mesne *Glouc* 83-85; NSM Newent and Gorsley w Cliffords Mesne from 85. *Mayfield, Gorsley, Ross-on-Wye, Herefordshire HR9 7SJ* Tel (01989) 720492

CHIVERS, Canon William Herbert. b 20. Univ of Wales (Cardiff) BA42. Coll of Resurr Mirfield 42. **d** 44 **p** 45. C Roath St Sav *Llan* 44-48; C Pontlottyn 50-51; C Peterston-super-Ely 51-53; C Bushey *St Alb* 53-58; V Bollington St Jo *Ches* 58-60; R Bushey *St Alb* 60-81; Australia 81-83; R Llandogo and Tintern *Mon* 83-86; rtd 86; Asst Chapl Athens w Kifissia, Patras, Thessaloniki & Voula *Eur* 86-91. *3 Downing Court, Grenville Street, London WC1N 1LX* Tel 0171-713 7847

CHIVERTON, Dennis Lionel Dunbar. b 26. St D Coll Lamp BA51. **d** 53 **p** 54. C Cardiff St Mary *Llan* 53-54; C Dowlais 54-57; C Bargoed w Brithdir 57-61; P-in-c Cymmer and Abercregan 61-67; R Llanfabon 67-91; rtd 91; Perm to Offic *Llan* from 91. *3 Park Terrace, Trelewis, Treharris CF46 6BT* Tel (01443) 411237

CHORLTON, John Samuel Woodard. b 45. Newc Univ BSc67. Wycliffe Hall Ox 89. **d** 89 **p** 91. Jerusalem 82-92; C Ox St Aldate w St Matt *Ox* 92-94; C Ox St Aldate from 95. *2 Shirelake Close, Oxford OX1 1SN* Tel (01865) 721150

CHOW, Ting Suie Roy. b 46. Brasted Th Coll 68 Sarum & Wells Th Coll 70. **d** 72 **p** 73. C Weaste *Man* 72-74; C Swinton St Pet 74-78; R Blackley St Paul 78-85; Sec SPCK (Dio Man) from 80; R Burnage St Nic *Man* 85-95; P-in-c Man Gd Shep 95-97; P-in-c Openshaw 95-97; R Manchester Gd Shep and St Barn from 97. *All Soul's Rectory, Every Street, Ancoats, Manchester M4 7DQ* Tel 0161-273 6582

CHOWN, Ernest John Richard. b 17. St Steph Ho Ox 48. **d** 51 **p** 52. C Ox St Paul *Ox* 51-53; C Brighton St Paul *Chich* 53-65; V Swanley St Mary *Roch* 65-72; V Worthing St Andr *Chich* from 72. *St Andrew's Vicarage, 21 Victoria Road, Worthing, W Sussex BN11 1XB* Tel (01903) 233442

CHOWN, William Richard Bartlett. b 27. AKC54. **d** 55 **p** 56. C Egremont *Carl* 55-58; C Upminster *Chelmsf* 58-61; R Romford St Andr 61-78; R Newton Longville w Stoke Hammond, Whaddon etc *Ox* 78-83; P-in-c Kidmore End 83-85; V 85-90; rtd 90; NSM Harpsden w Bolney *Ox* 93-94; Perm to Offic from 94. *26 Lovell Close, Henley-on-Thames, Oxon RG9 1PX* Tel (01491) 575735

CHRICH-SMITH, Andrew James. b 70. Girton Coll Cam BA92 MA96. Cranmer Hall Dur BA93. **d** 96 **p** 97. C Gerrards Cross and Fulmer *Ox* from 96. *7 Gaviots Close, Gerrards Cross, Bucks SL9 7EJ* Tel (01753) 892562

CHRICH-SMITH, Mrs Joanne Elizabeth. b 71. Qu Coll Cam BA93 MA96. Cranmer Hall Dur BA94 Ripon Coll Cuddesdon 96. **d** 97. C Amersham on the Hill *Ox* from 97. *7 Gaviots Close, Gerrards Cross, Bucks SL9 7EJ* Tel (01753) 892562

CHRISMAN, John Aubrey. b 33. US Naval Academy BS58. Westcott Ho Cam 86. **d** 88 **p** 89. NSM Orwell *Ely* 88-89; NSM Wimpole 88-89; NSM Arrington 88-89; NSM Croydon w Clopton 88-89; Asst Chapl Oslo St Edm *Eur* 89-91; USA from 91. *St George's Episcopal Church, 14 Rhode Island Avenue, Newport, Rhode Island 02840, USA*

CHRISTENSEN, Canon Norman Peter. b 37. St D Coll Lamp BA63. Ridley Hall Cam 63. **d** 65 **p** 66. C Barnston *Ches* 65-70; V Over St Jo 70-77; R Bromborough 77-92; RD Wirral S 86-92; Hon Can Ches Cathl from 90; Chapl Arrowe Park Hosp Wirral 92-96; V Higher Bebington *Ches* from 96. *The Vicarage, Higher Bebington, Wirral, Merseyside L63 8LX* Tel 0151-608 4429

CHRISTIAN, Mrs Alison Jean. b 51. Cen Sch Speech & Drama DipAct72. S Dios Minl Tr Scheme 88. **d** 91 **p** 94. Par Dn Uxbridge *Lon* 91-94; C 94-95; Chapl Uxbridge Coll 91-95; V Sudbury St Andr *Lon* from 95. *St Andrew's Vicarage, 956 Harrow Road, Wembley, Middx HA0 2QA* Tel 0181-904 4016

CHRISTIAN, Anthony Clive Hammond. b 46. Kent Univ BA74. K Coll Lon 74 St Aug Coll Cant 74. **d** 76 **p** 77. C Faversham *Cant* 76-79; C St Laurence in the Isle of Thanet 79-81; P-in-c 81-84; R Gt Mongeham w Ripple and Sutton by Dover 84-88; V Pevensey *Chich* 88-94; P-in-c from 94. *Marsh Hall, Church Lane, Pevensey, E Sussex BN24 5LD* Tel (01323) 762247

CHRISTIAN, Brother. *See* PEARSON, Christian David John

CHRISTIAN, Gerald. b 29. MBIM SSC FCP. Qu Coll Birm 74. **d** 77 **p** 77. NSM Stirchley *Birm* 77-82; S Africa from 82. *PO Box 905-1397, Garsfontein, Pretoria, 0042 South Africa* Tel Pretoria (12) 348-9094

CHRISTIAN, Mark Robert. b 58. Linc Th Coll CMinlStuds95. **d** 95 **p** 96. C Stockport SW *Ches* from 95. *40 Beechfield Road, Stockport, Cheshire SK3 8SF* Tel 0161-483 3350

CHRISTIAN, Paul. b 49. Cant Sch of Min 84. **d** 87 **p** 88. C Folkestone St Sav *Cant* 87-91; R Temple Ewell w Lydden from 91. *The Rectory, Green Lane, Temple Ewell, Dover, Kent CT16 3AS* Tel (01304) 822865

CHRISTIAN, Richard. b 37. Nottm Univ DipEd74 Ox Univ MA81. AKC62. **d** 63 **p** 65. C Camberwell St Mich w All So w Em *S'wark* 63-66; C Woolwich St Mary w H Trin 66-70; Chapl and Lect Bp Lonsdale Coll Derby 70-74; P-in-c Hurley *Ox* 76-79; Chapl Lancing Coll 79-81; Chapl Harrow Sch 82-89; Chapl R W Sussex Hosp Chich 89-91; P-in-c Cowley *Lon* 91-95; Chapl Hillingdon Hosp Uxbridge from 91. *Chaplain's Office, Hillingdon Hospital, Uxbridge, Middx UB8 3NN* Tel (01895) 279433

CHRISTIAN, Canon Ronald George. b 20. AKC48. **d** 49 **p** 50. C Mansfield Woodhouse *S'well* 49-52; C Margate St Jo *Cant* 52-56; V Bramford w Burstall *St E* 56-62; V Bramford 62-91; Dioc Ecum Officer 66-88; Hon Can St E Cathl 75-91; Bruges Link Dioc Co-ord from 88; rtd 91; Perm to Offic *St E* from 91. *54 Pine View Road, Ipswich IP1 4HR* Tel (01473) 463031

CHRISTIAN-EDWARDS, Canon Michael Thomas. b 36. Down Coll Cam BA60 MA64. Clifton Th Coll 60. **d** 62 **p** 63. C Ex St Leon w H Trin *Ex* 62-67; V Trowbridge St Thos *Sarum* 67-75; R Wingfield w Rowley 67-75; P-in-c Fisherton Anger 75-81; R 81-92; Ind Chapl 85-92; RD Salisbury 85-90; Can and Preb Sarum Cathl 87-92; V Crofton *Portsm* from 92. *The Vicarage, 40 Vicarage Lane, Stubbington, Fareham, Hants PO14 2JX* Tel (01329) 661154 or 662007

CHRISTIANSON, Canon Rodney John (Bill). b 47. St Paul's Grahamstown DipTh72. **d** 72 **p** 73. S Africa 72-76 and 82-91; C St Sav Cathl Pietermaritzburg 72-76; Miss to Seamen from 76; Min Sec from 93; Hon C Milton next Gravesend Ch Ch *Roch* 78-82; Chapl Miss to Seamen and R St Andr Richard's Bay 82-91; Chapl Hull Miss to Seamen 91-93; Hon Can Bloemfontein Cathl from 93; Lic to Offic *Lon* from 94. *Missions to Seamen, St Michael Paternoster Royal, College Hill, London EC4R 2RL* Tel 0171-248 5202 Fax 248 4761

CHRISTIE, Alexander Robert (Sandy). b 58. Qu Coll Cam BA79 LLM80. Oak Hill Th Coll DipHE94. **d** 94 **p** 95. C W Norwood St Luke *S'wark* from 94. *12 Chestnut Road, London SE27 9LF* Tel 0181-670 2400

CHRISTIE, David James. b 58. York Univ BA80 MA83 PGCE81 Leeds Univ MPhil88. Cranmer Hall Dur 89. **d** 91 **p** 92. C Drypool *York* 91-95; V Patrick Brompton and Hunton *Ripon* from 95. *The Vicarage, Patrick Brompton, Bedale, N Yorkshire DL8 1JN* Tel (01677) 450439

CHRISTIE, Canon Graham. b 08. Leeds Univ BA31. Coll of Resurr Mirfield 31. **d** 33 **p** 34. C Swinton St Pet *Man* 33-36; C Ex St Jas *Ex* 36-37; C Hollinwood *Man* 37-38; V Winton 38-45; R Roos w Tunstall *York* 46-60; P-in-c Garton w Grimston and Hilston 48-58; Lect in Drama (LEA) 49-58; V Garton w Grimston and Hilston 58-60; Tutor Hull Univ 55-80; RD S Holderness 58-60; V Millington w Gt Givendale 60-81; V Pocklington w Yapham-cum-Meltonby, Owsthorpe etc 60-81; RD Pocklington 60-75; Can and Preb York Minster 62-81; rtd 81; Perm to Offic *York* from 81; Asst Chapl York Distr Hosp 81-95. *Pax Intranti, 66 Wold Road, Pocklington, York YO4 2QG* Tel (01759) 304200

CHRISTIE, Canon Thomas Richard. b 31. CCC Cam BA53 MA57. Linc Th Coll 55. **d** 57 **p** 58. C Portsea N End St Mark *Portsm* 57-60; C Cherry Hinton St Andr *Ely* 60-62; C-in-c Cherry Hinton St Jas CD 62-66; V Wisbech St Aug 66-73; V Whitstable All SS *Cant* 73-75; V Whitstable All SS w St Pet 75-80; Can Res and Treas Pet Cathl *Pet* from 80; RD Pet 87-96. *Prebendal House, Minster Precincts, Peterborough PE1 1XX* Tel (01733) 69441

CHRISTOPHER, Richard. b 53. NTMTC 94 Birm Bible Inst 80. **d** 97. C Southall Green St Jo *Lon* from 97. *22 Witley Gardens, Southall, Middx UB2 4ES* Tel 0181-574 0253

CHRISTOU, Sotirios. b 51. Avery Hill Coll DipHE80. St Jo Coll Nottm 84. **d** 88 **p** 92. C Berechurch St Marg w St Mich *Chelmsf* 88-89; C Goodmayes All SS 89-90; NSM Harston w Hauxton *Ely* 92-94; Lic to Offic 94-95; C Burgess Hill St Andr *Chich* from 95. *9 Pendean, Burgess Hill, W Sussex RH15 0DW* Tel (01444) 247179

CHUBB, John Nicholas. b 33. St Cath Soc Ox BA55 MA58. Qu Coll Birm 57. **d** 59 **p** 60. C Kirby Moorside w Gillamoor *York* 59-62; C Scarborough St Mary 62-64; V Potterspury w Furtho and Yardley Gobion *Pet* 64-69; V Brixworth 69-74; P-in-c Holcot 73-74; V Brixworth w Holcot 74-81; V Hampton Hill *Lon* 81-88; Chapl Pet Distr Hosp 88-97; Chapl Edith Cavell Hosp 88-97; Perm to Offic *Linc* from 88; Perm to Offic *Nor* 88-96; Perm to Offic *Ely* from 95; rtd 97. *8 Sebrights Way, South Bretton, Peterborough PE3 9BT*

CHUBB, Richard Henry. b 45. Univ of Wales (Cardiff) BMus67 Bris Univ PGCE76 DipChD92. Linc Th Coll 67. **d** 70 **p** 71. C Chippenham St Andr w Tytherton Lucas *Bris* 71-72; C-in-c Stockwood CD 72-73; C Bris Ch the Servant Stockwood 73-76; Perm to Offic 76-79; Min Can and Succ Bris Cathl 79-88; Chapl to the Deaf from 83; Chapl Qu Eliz Hosp Sch Bris 87-92. *55 Pembroke Road, Bristol BS8 3BE* Tel 0117-973 7658

CHUDLEY, Cyril Raymond. b 29. Lon Univ BA53 DipEd. Wells Th Coll 70. **d** 72 **p** 73. C Newark St Mary *S'well* 72-75; C Egg Buckland *Ex* 75-77; P-in-c Plymouth St Aug 77-80; V 80-83; V Milton Abbot, Dunterton, Lamerton etc 83-91; TV Wickford and Runwell *Chelmsf* 91-95; rtd 95; Perm to Offic *Truro* from 95. *Ten Acres, Cox Park, Gunnislake, Cornwall PL18 9AZ* Tel (01822) 832345

CHURCH, Mrs Linda Ann. b 51. MCSP73. EMMTC 88. **d** 91 **p** 94. NSM Kirkby in Ashfield St Thos *S'well* 91-95; NSM Skegby from 95. *246 Diamond Avenue, Kirkby-in-Ashfield, Notts NG17 7NA* Tel (01623) 758966

CHURCHILL, Canon Aubrey Gilbert Roy. b 12. Southn Univ 36. Sarum Th Coll 37. **d** 39 **p** 40. C Fareham SS Pet and Paul *Portsm* 39-42; C Horfield H Trin *Bris* 42-45; C Banbury *Ox* 45-47; C Cov St Jo *Cov* 47-51; V Wilmcote 51-55; R Wilmcote w Billesley 55-76; RD Alcester 59-69; Hon Can Cov Cathl 72-76; rtd 76; Perm to Offic *Cov* from 76. *9 Farley Avenue, Harbury, Leamington Spa, Warks CV33 9LX* Tel (01926) 613309

CHURCHMAN, David Ernest Donald (Don). b 21. Clifton Th Coll 45. **d** 48 **p** 49. C Preston All SS *Blackb* 48-49; C Braintree *Chelmsf* 50-52; V Harold Wood 52-59; V Southsea St Jude *Portsm* 59-74; V Enfield Ch Ch Trent Park *Lon* 74-86; RD Enfield 75-82; rtd 86. *Heronsbrook, 158 Havant Road, Hayling Island, Hants PO11 0LJ* Tel (01705) 463216

CHURCHUS, Eric Richard Ivor. b 28. Lon Univ BSc MSc56. **d** 78 **p** 79. Hon C Withington w Westhide *Heref* 78-82; C Heref St Martin 82-85; P-in-c Woolhope 85-93; rtd 93; Perm to Offic *Heref* from 93. *27 Aconbury Avenue, Hereford HR2 6HR* Tel (01432) 267022

CHYNCHEN, John Howard. b 38. FRICS72. Sarum & Wells Th Coll 88. **d** 89 **p** 90. Bp's Dom Chapl *Sarum* from 89; Hong Kong from 90. *18 The Circus, Bath BA1 2ET, or B2, On Lee, 2 Mount Davis Road, Hong Kong* Tel (01225) 316269 or Hong Kong (852) 28550005 Fax 28550420

CIANCHI, Dalbert Peter. b 28. Lon Univ BSc57. Westcott Ho Cam 69. **d** 70 **p** 71. C Harpenden St Nic *St Alb* 70-74; TV Woughton *Ox* 74-80; P-in-c Wavendon w Walton 74-80; P-in-c Lavendon w Cold Brayfield 80-84; R Lavendon w Cold Brayfield, Clifton Reynes etc 84-94; rtd 94. *20 Springfield Drive, Bromham, Bedford MK43 8LE*

CIECHANOWICZ, Edward Leigh Bundock. *See* BUNDOCK, Dr Edward Leigh

CIRCUS, Robert William. b 19. Lon Univ BSc(Econ)90. Wycliffe Hall Ox 52. **d** 54 **p** 55. C Rayleigh *Chelmsf* 54-56; V Northampton St Andr *Pet* 56-60; V Werrington 60-70; R The Quinton *Birm* 70-76; P-in-c Wolverley *Worc* 76-82; V Wolverley and Cookley 82-84; rtd 84; Perm to Offic *Worc* from 84. *5 Berrow Hill Road, Franche, Kidderminster, Worcs DY11 5LH* Tel (01562) 637949

CLABON, Harold William George. b 31. **d** 85 **p** 86. NSM Newport St Julian *Mon* 85-91; rtd 91. *38 St Julian's Avenue, Newport NP9 7JU* Tel (01633) 215419

CLACEY, Derek Phillip. b 48. LTh. St Jo Coll Nottm 76. **d** 79 **p** 80. C Gt Parndon *Chelmsf* 79-82; C Walton H Trin *Ox* 82-88; R Bramshaw and Landford w Plaitford *Sarum* from 88. *The Rectory, Wych Green, Bramshaw, Lyndhurst, Hants SO4 7JF* Tel (01794) 390256

CLACK, Robert John Edmund. b 63. Lanc Univ BA85. Coll of Resurr Mirfield 89. **d** 92 **p** 93. C Bury St Pet *Man* 92-95; Chapl Bury Colls of FE 93-95; TV New Bury 95-97; R Ashton upon Mersey St Martin *Ches* from 97. *St Martin's Rectory, 367 Glebelands Road, Sale, Cheshire M33 5GG* Tel 0161-973 4204

CLACKER, Martin Alexander. b 56. Trin Coll Bris DipHE95. **d** 95 **p** 96. C Yate New Town *Bris* from 95. *67 Mountbatten Close, Yate, Bristol BS17 5TE* Tel (01454) 316920

CLANCEY, Ms Blanche Elizabeth Fisher. b 28. SRN50 Lon Univ CertEd71. Gilmore Ho 64. **dss** 78 **d** 87 **p** 94. Bromley Common St Aug *Roch* 78-83; Hanley H Ev *Lich* 83-87; D-in-c 87-89; rtd 89; NSM Gamston and Bridgford *S'well* 91-97; NSM Cropwell Bishop w Colston Bassett, Granby etc from 97. *4 Granby Hill, Granby, Notts NG13 9PQ* Tel (01949) 851679

CLANCY, Michael. b 24. Kensington Univ (USA) BA82. Glas NSM Course 76. **d** 79 **p** 80. Hon C Glas St Silas *Glas* 79-96; Perm to Offic from 96. *33 Highfield Drive, Clarkston, Glasgow G76 7SW* Tel 0141-638 4469

CLAPHAM, John. b 47. Open Univ BA76. Sarum & Wells Th Coll 77. **d** 80 **p** 81. Dep PV Ex Cathl *Ex* from 80; C Lympstone 85-87; P-in-c from 87; RD Aylesbeare from 96. *The Rectory, Lympstone, Exmouth, Devon EX8 5HP* Tel (01395) 273343

CLAPHAM, Kenneth. b 47. Trin Coll Bris 76. **d** 78 **p** 79. C Pemberton St Mark Newtown *Liv* 78-81; C Darfield *Sheff* 81-83; P-in-c Over Kellet *Blackb* 83-88; V from 88. *The Vicarage, 3 Kirklands Road, Over Kellet, Carnforth, Lancs LA6 1DJ* Tel (01524) 734189

CLAPP, Nicholas Michel Edward. b 48. Univ of Wales (Cardiff) DipTh74. St Mich Coll Llan 71. **d** 74 **p** 75. C Walsall St Gabr Fulbrook *Lich* 74-77; C Burnley St Cath *Blackb* 77-80; R Blackley H Trin *Man* 80-87; V Carl St Aid and Ch Ch *Carl* from 87. *St Aidan's Vicarage, 6 Lismore Place, Carlisle CA1 1LX* Tel (01228) 22942

CLAPSON, Clive Henry. b 55. Leeds Univ BA76. Trin Coll Toronto MDiv79. **d** 79 **p** 80. Canada 79-83; USA 83-88; C Hawley H Trin *Guildf* 88-90; Miss to Seamen from 90; R Invergordon St Ninian *Mor* from 90; Prin Ord and Lay Tr Course from 90. *St Ninian's Rectory, 132 High Street, Invergordon, Ross-shire IV18 0AE* Tel (01349) 852392

CLARE, Christopher. b 52. Sheff Univ BSc73 Nottm Univ PGCE74. Ox Min Course 89. **d** 92 **p** 93. NSM Chesham Bois *Ox* from 92. *3 The Gowers, Chestnut Lane, Amersham, Bucks HP6 5ER* Tel (01494) 722748

CLARE, Lionel Philip. b 19. St Aid Birkenhead 46. **d** 49 **p** 50. C Far Headingley St Chad *Ripon* 49-52; C Low Harrogate St Mary 52-54; R Addingham *Bradf* 54-66; V Sunnyside w Bourne End *St Alb* 66-74; V Kirkbymoorside w Gillamoor, Farndale etc *York* 74-84; rtd 84; Perm to Offic *Bradf* from 84. *Flat 1, Regent Court, 20 Regent Road, Ilkley, W Yorkshire LS29 9EA* Tel (01943) 609330

CLARE, Sister. *See* LOCKHART, Clare Patricia Anne

CLARIDGE, Antony Arthur John. b 37. LRAM Hull Univ MA. Bris & Glouc Tr Course. **d** 84 **p** 85. NSM Keynsham *B & W* from 84; Bp's Officer for NSMs from 90. *62 Cranwells Park, Weston, Bath BA1 2YE* Tel (01225) 427462

CLARIDGE, Michael John. b 61. MIEH Matt Bourton Tech Coll Birm DipEH82. Qu Coll Birm 89 Bossey Ecum Inst Geneva CES92. **d** 92 **p** 93. C Harlescott *Lich* 92-95; P-in-c Wellington Ch Ch 95-97; V from 97. *Christ Church Vicarage, 1 Church Walk, Wellington, Telford, Shropshire TF1 1RW* Tel (01952) 223185

CLARINGBULL, Canon Denis Leslie. b 33. MIPM85 K Coll Lon BD57 AKC57. **d** 58 **p** 59. C Croydon St Aug *Cant* 58-62; Ind Chapl to Bp Croydon 62-71; Ind Chapl *Cov* 71-75; Chapl Cov Cathl 71-75; Succ 72-75; V Norbury St Phil *Cant* 75-80; Sen Ind Chapl *Birm* from 80; P-in-c Birm St Paul 85-88; V from 88; Hon Can Birm Cathl from 87. *197 Russell Road, Birmingham B13 8RR* Tel 0121-449 1435 or 449 1435

CLARINGBULL (née DAVID), Mrs Faith Caroline. b 55. St Aid Coll Dur BA77 Univ of Wales (Abth) DipLib80. Ripon Coll Cuddesdon 87. **d** 89 **p** 94. Par Dn Is of Dogs Ch Ch and St Jo w St Luke *Lon* 89-93; Chapl Asst R Lon Hosp (Whitechapel) 93-94; Chapl Asst R Lon Hosp (Mile End) 93-94; Asst Chapl R Lon Hosps NHS Trust from 94. *Royal London Hospital, London E1 1BB, or 138D Brooke Road, London N16 7RR* Tel 0171-377 7385 or 0181-806 1337

CLARK, Albert Percival (Peter). b 17. Hatf Coll Dur LTh39 BA39. St Boniface Warminster 36. **d** 40 **p** 41. C Wildmore *Linc* 40-42; C New Cleethorpes 42-44; C Linc St Botolph by Bargate 44-46; R Strubby w Woodthorpe and Maltby-le-Marsh 46-50; S Africa 50-61 and 77-80; R The Quinton *Birm* 61-70; V Werrington *Pet* 70-77; R Chipping Warden w Edgcote and Aston le Walls 80-83; rtd 83; Perm to Offic *S'wark* from 83; Perm to Offic *Guildf* from 86. *3 Falconhurst, The Crescent, Surbiton, Surrey KT6 4BP* Tel 0181-399 2032

CLARK, Alexander Rees. b 19. Univ of Wales (Lamp) BA48 Hull Univ CertEd50. St D Coll Lamp 50. **d** 51 **p** 52. C Ysbyty Ystwyth w Ystradmeurig *St D* 51-53; C Eglwysnewydd 53-55; V 84-90; V Gwynfe and Llanddeusant 55-61; V Pontyates 61-74; V Ysbyty Cynfyn w Llantrisant 74-90; rtd 90. *Llety'r Dryw, 1 Lon Tyllwyd, Llanfarian, Aberystwyth SY23 4UH* Tel (01970) 612736

CLARK, Andrew James. b 50. ACIB72 ACIS76. EMMTC DipPThS94. **d** 94 **p** 95. NSM Allestree *Derby* from 94. *44 Crabtree Close, Allestree, Derby DE22 2SW* Tel (01332) 552492

CLARK, Antony (Tony). b 61. York Univ BA83. Wycliffe Hall Ox 84. **d** 88 **p** 89. C Ashton on Mersey St Mary *Ches* 88-92; Chapl

Lee Abbey 92-95; Lic to Offic *Ex* 92-95; Chapl Univ Westmr *Lon* from 95. *4A Luxborough Street, London W1M 3LG* Tel 0171-911 5822

CLARK, Arthur. b 30. MIBiol FRSC Sheff Univ BSc MCB. St D Dioc Tr Course. **d** 88 **p** 89. NSM Haverfordwest St Mary and St Thos w Haroldston *St D* 88-91; C 91-92; V Llawhaden w Bletherston and Llanycefn 92-96; rtd 96. *84 Portfield, Haverfordwest SA61 1BT* Tel (01437) 762694

CLARK, Arthur Towers. b 08. OBE45. AKC36. **d** 36 **p** 37. C Guiseley *Bradf* 36-40; V Esholt 40-48; C Leeds St Pet *Ripon* 51-56; V Roberttown *Wakef* 56-58; Perm to Offic from 73; rtd 86. *32 Broomcroft Road, Ossett, W Yorkshire WF5 8LH* Tel (01924) 261139

CLARK, Bernard Charles. b 34. Open Univ BA81. S'wark Ord Course 65. **d** 68 **p** 69. C Pemberton St Jo *Liv* 68-71; C Winwick 71-73; P-in-c Warrington St Barn 74-76; V 76-78; V Hindley All SS 78-83; Perm to Offic 86-94; P-in-c Hollinfare 94; C Newchurch and Glazebury 94; R Glazebury w Hollinfare from 94. *The Vicarage, 11 Meadow Bank Gardens, Glazebury, Warrington WA3 5LX* Tel (01925) 767946

CLARK, David. b 30. Nottm Univ BSc51 Lon Univ DipTh57. St Aid Birkenhead 55. **d** 57 **p** 58. C Tyldesley w Shakerley *Man* 57-60; V Ashton St Jas 60-64; rtd 93. *Roz an Avalou, 22340 Mael-Carhaix, France* Tel France (33) 96 24 65 04

CLARK, Canon David George Neville. b 25. Linc Coll Ox BA49 MA59. Wells Th Coll 49. **d** 51 **p** 52. C Sanderstead All SS *S'wark* 51-54; C Lewisham St Jo Southend 54-59; V Sutton New Town St Barn 59-72; R Charlwood 72-90; P-in-c Sidlow Bridge 76-77; R 77-90; P-in-c Buckland 85-87; P-in-c Leigh 87-90; Hon Can S'wark Cathl 88-90; rtd 90. *12 Marlborough Road, Coventry CV2 4EP* Tel (01203) 442400

CLARK, David Gordon. b 29. Clare Coll Cam BA52 MA57. Ridley Hall Cam 52. **d** 54 **p** 55. C Walthamstow St Jo *Chelmsf* 54-57; V 60-69; C Gt Ilford St Andr 57-60; R Stansted *Roch* 69-82; R Stansted w Fairseat and Vigo 82-94; rtd 94. *1 Coastguard Cottages, Wareham, Dorset BH20 5PF* Tel (01929) 480753

CLARK, David Humphrey. b 39. G&C Coll Cam BA60. Wells Th Coll 62. **d** 64 **p** 65. C Leigh St Mary *Man* 64-68; Min Can and Prec Man Cathl 68-70; Ind Chapl *Nor* 70-85; P-in-c Nor St Clem and St Geo 70-76; P-in-c Nor St Sav w St Paul 70-76; V Norwich-over-the-Water Colegate St Geo 76-79; Hon AP Nor St Pet Mancroft 79-85; R Oadby *Leic* from 85. *St Peter's Rectory, 1 Leicester Road, Oadby, Leicester LE2 5BD* Tel 0116-271 2135

CLARK, David John. b 40. CEng MIStructE Surrey Univ MPhil75. Ridley Hall Cam 81. **d** 83 **p** 84. C Combe Down w Monkton Combe and S Stoke *B & W* 83-89; Voc Adv Bath Adnry from 89; R Freshford, Limpley Stoke and Hinton Charterhouse from 89. *The Rectory, Crowe Lane, Freshford, Bath BA3 6EB* Tel (01225) 723135

CLARK, Dennis Henry Graham. b 26. St Steph Ho Ox 52. **d** 55 **p** 56. C Southall St Geo *Lon* 55-58; C Barbourne *Worc* 58-61; Chapl RAF 61-78; Asst Chapl-in-Chief RAF 78-82; Chapl St Clem Danes (RAF Ch) 79-82; V Godmanchester *Ely* 82-91; rtd 91; Perm to Offic *Ely* from 91. *8 Arran Way, St Ives, Huntingdon, Cambs PE17 6DT* Tel (01480) 301951

CLARK, Edward Robert. b 39. Ex Coll Ox BA61 MA65 Bris Univ DSA68 CASS69. St Steph Ho Ox 61. **d** 63 **p** 64. C Solihull *Birm* 63-67; Perm to Offic *Bris* 67-69; Perm to Offic *Leic* 69-71; Perm to Offic *Ox* 71-80; Perm to Offic *St Alb* 80-84; Perm to Offic *Cant* from 84. *41 The Street, Kingston, Canterbury, Kent CT4 6JQ* Tel (01227) 830074

CLARK, Ellen Jane. *See* CLARK-KING, Mrs Ellen Jane

CLARK, Eric Douglas Colbatch. b 08. OBE66 MBE62. St Jo Coll Ox BA29. Wycliffe Hall Ox 39. **d** 40 **p** 41. Nigeria 37-67; Sierra Leone 67-70; Dir Overseas Students Commendation Cen Lon 70-71; Warden Student Res Cen Wimbledon 72-83; rtd 83; Perm to Offic *S'wark* from 82. *11 Rosemary Cottages, The Drive, London SW20 8TQ* Tel 0181-879 0344

CLARK, Frederick Albert George. b 15. MBE68. ACP66. **d** 67 **p** 68. Hon C Stroud *Glouc* 67-84; Hon C Stroud and Uplands w Slad 84-85; Perm to Offic from 85. *2 Terrace Cottages, Thrupp, Stroud, Glos GL5 2BN* Tel (01453) 882060

CLARK, Henry. b 23. AKC52. **d** 53 **p** 54. C Tuffley *Glouc* 53-56; C High Wycombe All SS *Ox* 56-63; V Middlesbrough St Chad *York* 63-91; rtd 91; Perm to Offic *Chelmsf* from 91. *Broadview, Ferry Road, Fingringhoe, Colchester CO5 7BY* Tel (01206) 729248

CLARK, Ian. b 31. Lich Th Coll 63. **d** 65 **p** 66. C Droylsden St Mary *Man* 65-68; C Bedford Leigh 68-70; V Broughton Moor *Carl* 70-80; R Kirton *S'well* 80-94; V Walesby 80-94; P-in-c Egmanton 80-81; V 81-94; rtd 96. *27 Barripper Road, Camborne, Cornwall TR14 7QW* Tel (01209) 716084

CLARK, Dr Ian Duncan Lindsay. b 35. K Coll Cam BA59 MA63 PhD64 Ox Univ DipTh63. Ripon Hall Ox 62. **d** 64 **p** 65. C Willington *Newc* 64-66; India 66-76; Chapl St Cath Coll Cam 76; Tutor 78-85; Dean of Chpl 80-85. *4 Yewtree Lane, Yetholm, Kelso, Roxburghshire TD5 8RZ* Tel (01573) 420323

CLARK, Miss Janet Elizabeth. b 44. Derby Coll of Educn CertEd65 Open Univ BA75. All Nations Chr Coll CertRS84 Oak Hill Th Coll DipHE91 BA92. **d** 92 **p** 94. Par Dn Edmonton All SS w St Mich *Lon* 92-94; C 94-96; V Ealing St Steph Castle Hill from 96. *St Stephen's Vicarage, Sherbourne Gardens, London W13 8AT* Tel 0181-998 3863

CLARK, Mrs Jean Robinson. b 32. K Coll Lon AKC BD79. St Chris Coll Blackheath CertRK53. **dss** 85 **d** 87 **p** 94. Cov E *Cov* 85-87; C 87-88; NSM Upper Mole Valley Gp *S'wark* 89-90; Hon Par Dn Charlwood 89-90; Lic to Offic *Cov* from 90; rtd 92. *12 Marlborough Road, Coventry CV2 4EP* Tel (01203) 442400

CLARK, Jeremy James. b 66. Cant Univ (NZ) BA88. BTh92. **d** 94 **p** 95. New Zealand 94-97; C Upton (Overchurch) *Ches* from 97. *65 Devonshire Road, Upton, Wirral, Merseyside L49 6NN* Tel 0151-606 9995 Fax 606 1935

CLARK, John David Stanley. b 36. Dur Univ BA64. Ridley Hall Cam 64. **d** 66 **p** 67. C Benchill *Man* 66-69; C Beverley Minster *York* 69-74; Perm to Offic *S'well* 74-76; Lic to Offic 76-77; Lic to Offic *Chelmsf* 77-80; Miss to Seamen 77-80; Perm to Offic *York* 80-83; V Egton w Grosmont 83-89; R Thornton Dale w Ellerburne and Wilton from 89. *Thornton Dale Rectory, Pickering, N Yorkshire YO18 7QH* Tel (01751) 474244

CLARK, John Edward Goodband. b 49. Chich Th Coll 70. **d** 73 **p** 74. C Thorpe *Nor* 73-76; C Earlham St Anne 76-78; Chapl RN 78-82; P-in-c Tittleshall w Godwick, Wellingham and Weasenham *Nor* 82-85; P-in-c Helhoughton w Raynham 82-85; R South Raynham, E w W Raynham, Helhoughton, etc 85-90; R Taverham w Ringland 90-96; R Middleton-in-Teesdale w Forest and Frith *Dur* from 96; V Eggleston from 96. *The Rectory, 1 The Hude, Middleton-in-Teesdale, Barnard Castle, Co Durham DL12 0QW* Tel (01833) 40267

CLARK, John Michael. b 35. DSMS63 DipYW65 Leic Poly DCEd80. EMMTC 87. **d** 90 **p** 91. Chapl to the Deaf *Linc* from 86; NSM Bracebridge Heath from 90. *3 Hawthorn Road, Cherry Willingham, Lincoln LN3 4JU* Tel (01522) 751759

CLARK, Dr John Patrick Hedley. b 37. St Cath Coll Cam BA61 MA65 Worc Coll Ox BA63 MA72 BD74 Lambeth Hon DD89. St Steph Ho Ox 61. **d** 64 **p** 65. C Highters Heath *Birm* 64-67; C Eglingham *Newc* 67-72; P-in-c Newc St Anne 72-77; V Longframlington w Brinkburn 77-95; V Chevington from 95. *The Vicarage, 98 The Farnes, South Broomhill, Morpeth, Northd NE65 9SE* Tel (01670) 760273

CLARK, John Ronald Lyons. b 47. TCD BA69 MA72. Div Hostel Dub 67. **d** 70 **p** 71. C Dundela *D & D* 70-72; CF 72-75; C Belfast St Aid *Conn* 75-76; I Stranorlar w Meenglas and Kilteevogue *D & R* 76-81; Chapl Wythenshawe Hosp Man 81-95; I Kilgariffe Union *C, C & R* 95-96; Chapl Blackb, Hyndburn and Ribble Valley NHS Trust from 96. *10 Dale View, Blackburn BB2 4LE, or Queen's Park Hospital, Haslingden Road, Blackburn BB2 3HH* Tel (01254) 708364, 263555 or 294807 Pager 01893-964731

CLARK, Jonathan Dunnett. b 61. Ex Univ BA83 DipHE86 Bris Univ MLitt90 Southn Univ MA96. Trin Coll Bris 84. **d** 88 **p** 89. C Stanwix *Carl* 88-92; Chapl Bris Univ *Bris* 92-93; Dir of Studies S Dios Minl Tr Scheme 94-97; Chapl N Lon Univ *Lon* from 97. *123 Calabria Road, London N5 1HS* Tel 0171-704 9914 Fax as telephone E-mail jd.clark@unl.ac.uk

CLARK, Jonathan Jackson. b 57. Linc Coll Ox 79 Down Coll Cam 83. Ridley Hall Cam 81. **d** 84 **p** 85. C W Derby St Luke *Liv* 84-87; C Gt Clacton *Chelmsf* 87-93; V Hammersmith St Simon *Lon* from 93; AD Hammersmith from 96. *153 Blyth Road, London W14 0HL* Tel 0171-602 1043 or 603 4879

CLARK, Kathleen Christine. *See* LEFROY, Mrs Kathleen Christine

CLARK, The Ven Kenneth James. b 22. DSC44. St Cath Soc Ox BA48 MA52. Cuddesdon Coll 52. **d** 52 **p** 53. C Brinkworth *Bris* 52-53; C Cricklade w Latton 53-56; C-in-c Filwood Park CD 56-59; V Bris H Cross Inns Court 59-61; V Westbury-on-Trym H Trin 61-72; V Bris St Mary Redcliffe w Temple etc 72-82; P-in-c Bedminster St Mich 73-78; RD Bedminster 73-79; Hon Can Bris Cathl 74-92; Adn Swindon 82-92; rtd 92. *6 Saxon Road, Harnham, Salisbury SP2 8JZ* Tel (01722) 421410

CLARK, Lance Edgar Dennis. b 52. MBE93. Linc Th Coll 74. **d** 77 **p** 78. C Arnold *S'well* 77-82; V Brinsley w Underwood 82-87; Chapl RAF from 87. *Chaplaincy Services (RAF), HQ, Personnel and Training Command, RAF Innsworth, Gloucester GL3 1EZ* Tel (01452) 712612 ext 5164 Fax 510828

CLARK, Canon Malcolm Aiken. b 05. Lich Th Coll 32. **d** 34 **p** 35. C Greenock *Glas* 34-38; R Lockerbie 38-49; R Langholm 39-42; Chapl RAFVR 42-46; P-in-c Dalkeith *Edin* 49-56; R Edin Gd Shep 56-77; rtd 77; Chapl Edin St Vin *Edin* from 77; Dean Edin 82-85; Can St Mary's Cathl 82-85; Hon Can St Mary's Cathl from 85. *12 St Vincent Street, Edinburgh EH3 6SH* Tel 0131-557 3662

CLARK, Martin Hudson. b 46. K Coll Lon BD68 AKC68 MTh91 Birm Univ PGCE89. **d** 71 **p** 72. C S'wark H Trin *S'wark* 71-74; C Parkstone St Pet w Branksea and St Osmund *Sarum* 74-77; V E Wickham *S'wark* 77-86; V Wandsworth St Anne from 86; RD Wandsworth 90-95. *St Anne's Vicarage, 182 St Ann's Hill, London SW18 2RS* Tel 0181-874 2809

CLARK, Michael Arthur. b 46. S Dios Minl Tr Scheme. **d** 83 **p** 84. NSM Monkton Farleigh, S Wraxall and Winsley *Sarum* from 83. *62 Tyning Road, Winsley, Bradford-on-Avon, Wilts BA15 2JW* Tel (01225) 866652

CLARK, Michael David. b 45. Ox Univ MA68. Trin Coll Bris DipTh72. **d** 72 **p** 73. C Cheadle *Ches* 72-76; Brazil 77-86; Bolivia 86-88; C Wilton *B & W* 89-90; TV from 90. *St Michael's House, 1 Comeytrowe Lane, Taunton, Somerset TA1 5PA* Tel (01823) 337458

CLARK, Michael Wilford. b 23. OBE91 JP75. Loughb Univ TCert49. **d** 87 **p** 88. In Meth Ch 57-87; Chapl Asst Nightingale MacMillan Hospice Derby 87-89; Hon C Marston on Dove w Scropton *Derby* 87-89; P-in-c Longford, Long Lane, Dalbury and Radbourne 89-95; rtd 95; Perm to Offic *Derby* from 95. *Ashcroft, Etwall Road, Mickleover, Derby DE3 5DN* Tel (01332) 516968

CLARK, Miss Patricia Mary (Pat). b 36. Liv Univ BSc. **d** 88 **p** 94. Par Dn Leasowe *Ches* 88-92; Bp's Officer for Women in Min 89-97; Par Dn Davenham 92-94; C 94-97; rtd 97. *3 Sylvan Close, Firdale Park, Northwich, Cheshire CW8 4AU* Tel (01606) 350458

CLARK, Canon Peter. b 39. Ch Coll Cam BA61 MA65. Chich Th Coll 61. **d** 63 **p** 64. C Huddersfield St Pet and St Paul *Wakef* 63-67; C Notting Hill St Jo *Lon* 67-74; Grenada 75-79; C Hove All SS *Chich* 79; P-in-c Hove St Patr 79-82; V Hove St Patr w Ch Ch and St Andr 82-83; V Battersea Ch Ch and St Steph *S'wark* from 83; RD Battersea from 90; Hon Can S'wark Cathl from 96. *Christ Church Vicarage, Candahar Road, London SW11 2PU* Tel 0171-228 1225

CLARK, Peter. b 45. Sarum & Wells Th Coll 87. **d** 89 **p** 90. C Portsea St Cuth *Portsm* 89-92; TV Rye *Chich* 92-96; P-in-c Chiddingly w E Hoathly from 96. *The Rectory, East Hoathly, Lewes, E Sussex BN8 6EG* Tel (01825) 840270

CLARK, Peter Norman. b 53. Qu Coll Cam BA79. Westcott Ho Cam 78. **d** 80 **p** 81. C Bris St Mary Redcliffe w Temple etc *Bris* 80-83; C Potternewton *Ripon* 83-86; R Longsight St Luke *Man* from 86. *St Luke's Rectory, Stockport Road, Longsight, Manchester M13 9AB* Tel 0161-273 6662

CLARK, Mrs Prudence Anne. b 44. Man Coll of Educn CertEd78. N Ord Course 89. **d** 92 **p** 94. NSM Royton St Anne *Man* 92-94; Hon C 94-95; NSM Haughton St Anne from 95. *1 Hereford Way, Stalybridge, Cheshire SK15 2TD* Tel 0161-338 5275

CLARK, Reginald Isaac. b 16. AKC47. **d** 47 **p** 48. C Somersham w Pidley and Oldhurst *Ely* 47-49; C Luton St Mary *St Alb* 49-53; C-in-c Luton St Chris Round Green CD 53-59; V Luton St Chris Round Green 59-64; Chapl Shenley Hosp Radlett Herts 65-84; rtd 84; Perm to Offic *Linc* from 84. *1 Monks Walk, Spalding, Lincs PE11 3LG* Tel (01775) 768304

CLARK, Richard Martin. b 60. Ch Coll Cam MA81. Trin Coll Bris BA86. **d** 86 **p** 87. C Orpington Ch Ch *Roch* 86-89; C Marple All SS *Ches* 89-92; V Nottingham St Andr *S'well* from 92. *St Andrew's Vicarage, Chestnut Grove, Nottingham NG3 5AD* Tel 0115-960 4961

CLARK, Robert Henry. b 32. Oak Hill Th Coll 61. **d** 64 **p** 65. C Haydock St Mark *Liv* 64-67; C Tranmere St Cath *Ches* 67-75; V Platt Bridge *Liv* 75-84; V Litherland St Paul Hatton Hill 84-94; rtd 94; Perm to Offic *Liv* from 94. *9 Lime Vale, Spring Gardens, Wigan, Lancs WN3 4PE* Tel (01942) 861751

CLARK, Canon Robert James Vodden. b 07. Edin Th Coll 40. **d** 41 **p** 42. C Edin St Paul and St Geo *Edin* 41-44; R Fort William *Arg* 44-48; Warden Scottish Cen of Outdoor Tr 48-49; P-in-c Rothiemurchus *Mor* 48-49; C-in-c Edin St Dav *Edin* 49-54; CF (TA) 50-60; R Falkirk *Edin* 54-69; Can St Mary's Cathl 62-76; Hon Can from 76; Dean Edin 67-76; R Lasswade 69-79; rtd 79. *15 North Street, St Andrews, Fife KY16 9PW* Tel (01334) 76237

CLARK, Canon Robin. b 27. Lon Univ BA49 BD69 MPhil77 St Jo Coll Dur DipTh54. **d** 54 **p** 55. C Newton Heath All SS *Man* 54-58; Asst Master Woodhouse Gr Sch Sheff 58-61; R Brant Broughton w Stragglethorpe *Linc* 61-90; P-in-c Welbourn 65-66; RD Loveden 72-93; Can and Preb Linc Cathl from 84; R Brant Broughton and Beckingham 90-93; rtd 93; Perm to Offic *Linc* from 93. *Ravenshurst Cottage, 23 The Green, Ingham, Lincoln LN1 2XT*

CLARK, Preb Roland Mark Allison. b 21. St Cath Coll Cam BA48 MA53. Wells Th Coll 48. **d** 50 **p** 51. C Battersea St Paul *S'wark* 50-52; C Greenwich St Alfege w St Pet 52-56; Chapl RNVR 53-56; V Wilton *B & W* 56-79; RD Taunton S 60-65; Preb Wells Cathl from 63; R Backwell 79-88; RD Portishead 82-86; rtd 88; Perm to Offic *Chich* from 88; Perm to Offic *Bris* from 95; Perm to Offic *B & W* from 88. *21 The Chimes, Nailsea, Bristol BS19 2NH* Tel (01275) 852670

CLARK, Roy. b 21. MBE64. Roch Th Coll 65. **d** 67 **p** 68. C New Sleaford *Linc* 67-70; R Stickney 70-72; rtd 87. *33 Fydell Crescent, Boston, Lincs P21 8SS* Tel (01205) 361017

CLARK, Russell John. b 15. LSE BSc(Econ)38. LNSM course. **d** 93 **p** 93. NSM Hoxne w Denham, Syleham and Wingfield *St E* from 93. *Old School, Wingfield, Diss, Norfolk IP21 5RG* Tel (01379) 384537

CLARK, Stephen Kenneth. b 52. Bris Univ BEd74. Wycliffe Hall Ox 80. **d** 83 **p** 84. C Pitsea *Chelmsf* 83-86; Chapl Scargill Ho 86-89; R Elmley Castle w Bricklehampton and Combertons *Worc* 89-96; Chapl Burrswood Chr Cen *Roch* from 96. *Swedish Log House, Burrswood, Groombridge, Tunbridge Wells, Kent TN3 9PU* Tel (01892) 863637 Fax 862597

CLARK, Trevor Bartholomew. b 44. Qu Coll Birm 68. **d** 71 **p** 72. C Maltby *Sheff* 71-75; V New Rossington 75-80; V Campsall 80-95; rtd 96. *44 Elmdale Drive, Edenthorpe, Doncaster, S Yorkshire DN3 2LE*

CLARK-KING (née CLARK), Mrs Ellen Jane. b 62. Newnham Coll Cam BA85 MA89 Reading Univ PCVG86. Ripon Coll Cuddesdon 89. **d** 92 **p** 94. C Colwall w Upper Colwall and Coddington *Heref* 92-95; Chapl SS Coll Cam from 95. *Sidney Sussex College, Cambridge CB2 3HU* Tel (01223) 338870 or 316653 Fax 338884

CLARK-KING (formerly KING), Jeremy Norman. b 66. K Coll Lon BD88 AKC88. Ripon Coll Cuddesdon 88. **d** 90 **p** 91. C Ashby-de-la-Zouch St Helen w Coleorton *Leic* 90-93; C Ledbury w Eastnor *Heref* 93-96; C Cambridge Gt St Mary w St Mich *Ely* from 96; Chapl Girton Coll Cam from 96. *79 Alpha Road, Cambridge CB4 3DQ* Tel (01223) 316653 or 338900 Fax 338896 E-mail jc223@cam.ac.uk

CLARKE, Alan John. b 55. St Jo Coll Dur BA77 MA85. Westcott Ho Cam 78. **d** 80 **p** 81. C Heworth St Mary *Dur* 80-83; C Darlington St Jo 83-87; Asst Chapl Bryanston Sch Dorset 87-91; Chapl St Pet High Sch Ex from 93. *41 Stuart Road, Exeter EX1 2SZ* Tel (01392) 213596 or 74383

CLARKE, Alan Keith. b 38. Leic Coll of Educn DipYL64 Newc Univ DipAdEdStud73 MA89. SW Minl Tr Course. **d** 87 **p** 88. NSM Wolborough w Newton Abbot *Ex* from 87. *School House, 20 Coach Place, Newton Abbot, Devon TQ12 1ES* Tel (01626) 63515

CLARKE, Alfred Charles Reginald. b 19. ACII. Qu Coll Birm 71. **d** 74 **p** 74. Hon C Yardley St Cypr Hay Mill *Birm* 74-80; Hon C Packwood w Hockley Heath 80-89; rtd 89; Lic to Offic *Birm* from 89. *15 Newton Road, Knowle, Solihull, W Midlands B93 9HL* Tel (01564) 773861

CLARKE, Miss Alison Clare. b 33. MCST54 Open Univ BA85. EAMTC 90. **d** 93 **p** 94. NSM Lt Ilford St Mich *Chelmsf* from 93. *29 Glengall Road, Woodford Green, Essex IG8 0DN* Tel 0181-504 5106

CLARKE, Andrew John. b 58. New Coll Edin BD82 Graduate Soc Dur PGCE89. Linc Th Coll 84. **d** 86 **p** 87. C High Harrogate Ch Ch *Ripon* 86-88; RE Teacher Royds Hall High Sch Huddersfield 89-91; C Thornbury *Bradf* 91-93; P-in-c Bingley H Trin from 93. *Holy Trinity Vicarage, Oak Avenue, Bingley, W Yorkshire BD16 1ES* Tel (01274) 563909

CLARKE, Arthur. b 34. Lon Univ BD66 Nottm Univ MPhil75 DipEd. Sarum & Wells Th Coll 75. **d** 76 **p** 77. C Wollaton *S'well* 76-79; P-in-c Normanton on Soar 79-91; R Sutton Bonington 79-91; R Sutton Bonington w Normanton-on-Soar 91-93; P-in-c Arnold 93-94; V from 94. *St Mary's Vicarage, Church Lane, Arnold, Nottingham NG5 8HJ* Tel 0115-926 2946

CLARKE, Miss Audrey May. b 35. Gilmore Ho 65. **dss** 75 **d** 87 **p** 94. Crofton Park St Hilda w St Cypr *S'wark* 75-79; Chapl Asst Middx Hosp Lon 80-84; Mottingham St Andr *S'wark* 84-87; Par Dn 87-89; C Westborough *Guildf* 89-95; rtd 95; Hon C St Mary's Bay w St Mary-in-the-Marsh etc *Cant* from 95; Hon C New Romney w Old Romney and Midley from 95. *The Vicarage, Jefferstone Lane, St Mary's Bay, Romney Marsh, Kent TN29 0SW* Tel (01303) 874188

CLARKE, Benjamin Blanchard. b 08. Birm Univ BSc31 MSc34 St Cath Soc Ox BA33 MA37. Ripon Hall Ox 31. **d** 33 **p** 34. C Edgbaston St Germain *Birm* 33-37; C Erdington St Barn 37-40; V Birm St Matthias 40-46; R Byford w Mansel Gamage *Heref* 46-55; P-in-c Preston-on-Wye 46-55; V Padstow *Truro* 55-73; RD Pydar 58-61; rtd 73; Perm to Offic *Truro* from 73. *4 Athelstan Park, Bodmin, Cornwall PL31 1DS* Tel (01208) 73989

CLARKE, Bernard Ronald. b 53. FRGS. Ridley Hall Cam 74. **d** 77 **p** 78. C Leigh Park *Portsm* 77-78; C Petersfield w Sheet 78-81; Chapl RN from 81; Dir of Ords RN from 93. *Royal Naval Chaplaincy Service, Room 205, Victory Building, HM Naval Base, Portsmouth PO1 3LS* Tel (01705) 727900 Fax 727112

CLARKE, Charles David. b 37. LCP77 Univ of Wales BA76 DPS90 Cam Univ DipEd77. St Mich Coll Llan 88. **d** 90 **p** 91. C Whitchurch *Llan* 90-93; V Graig 93-96; P-in-c Cilfynydd 93-96; TV Cyncoed *Mon* from 96. *62 Hollybush Road, Cyncoed, Cardiff CF2 6TA* Tel (01222) 755306

CLARKE, Miss Christine Vera. b 45. Lon Univ CertEd66. Qu Coll Birm 79. **dss** 81 **d** 87 **p** 94. Bris St Mary Redcliffe w Temple etc *Bris* 81-86; Ind Chapl 86-95; NSM Westbury-on-Trym St Alb 94-95; P-in-c Wraxall *B & W* from 95. *The Rectory, Wraxall, Bristol BS19 1NA* Tel (01275) 857086

CLARKE, Canon Christopher George (Chris). b 43. Sarum Th Coll 67. **d** 68 **p** 69. C Sprowston *Nor* 68-72; V Hemsby 72-77; V Sutton Courtenay w Appleford *Ox* 77-84; TR Bracknell 84-97; RD Bracknell 90-96; Hon Can Ch Ch from 95; P-in-c Sonning from 97. *The Vicarage, Thames Street, Sonning, Reading RG4 0UR* Tel 0118-969 3298

CLARKE, Colin David Emrys. b 42. Leeds Univ DipAdEd82 MEd84. Wells Th Coll 67. **d** 68 **p** 69. C Plumstead St Nic *S'wark* 68-71; C N Lynn w St Marg and St Nic *Nor* 71-75; Miss to Seamen 71-75; Asst Chapl HM Pris Wakef 75-77; V Birkenshaw w Hunsworth *Wakef* 77-87; V Illingworth 87-92; R Burnsall w Rylstone *Bradf* 92-96; V Menston w Woodhead from 96. *The*

Vicarage, 12 Fairfax Gardens, Menston, Ilkley, W Yorkshire LS29 6ET Tel (01943) 872818

CLARKE, Daniel (Dan). b 17. TCD BA39 MA44 BD66. **d** 41 **p** 42. C Dublin St Bart *D & G* 41-44; Dioc C Killaloe *L & K* 44-46; Chapl Roscrea Hosp Inst 46-48; C-in-c Corbally 46-48; I Borrisokane 48-59; RD Upper Ormond 55-57; RD Ely O'Carroll 58-59; Asst Master Robert Bloomfield Sch Shefford 59-62; Hd Relig Studies Reigate Gr Sch 62-82; Chapl 75-84; Chapl St Mary's Sch Reigate 85-92; Hon Chapl 92-97; rtd 97; Perm to Offic *S'wark* from 85. *4 Orchard Way, Reigate, Surrey RH2 8DT* Tel (01737) 246169

CLARKE, Canon David George Alexander. b 23. TCD BA47 MA51 BD55 PhD57. **d** 48 **p** 49. C Dromore *Clogh* 48-49; P-in-c Drum 49-50; I Clonbroney w Killoe *K, E & A* 50-51; I Clogh 52-54; C Abbeystrewry *C, C & R* 55-57; TR Usworth *Dur* 57-61; I Kilrossanty *C & O* 61-73; Preb Newcastle St Patr Cathl Dublin 65-89; RD Dungarvan, Waterford and Lismore *C & O* 65-67; Prec Waterford and Lismore 67-73; Dean Cashel 73-83; I Cashel St Jo 73-83; I Ballymascanlan w Creggan, Forkhill etc *Arm* 83-89; rtd 89; Lic to Offic *Arm* from 90; Lic to Offic *D & D* from 90. *2 Ashley Court, Warrenpoint, Newry, Co Down BT34 3RN* Tel (01693) 772416

CLARKE, Dr David James. b 55. Univ of Wales (Abth) BSc(Econ)77 Keele Univ MA78 PhD83. Trin Coll Bris DipTh84. **d** 84 **p** 85. C Cardigan and Mwnt and Y Ferwig *St D* 84-87; P-in-c Llansantffraed and Llanbadarn Trefeglwys etc 87-88; V 88-91; Chapl Coll of St Mark and St Jo Plymouth *Ex* 91-96; V Lindfield *Chich* from 96. *The Vicarage, High Street, Lindfield, Haywards Heath, W Sussex RH16 2HR* Tel (01444) 482386

CLARKE, Denis John. b 23. LNSM course. **d** 87 **p** 88. NSM Brothertoft Gp *Linc* from 87. *49 Punchbowl Lane, Boston, Lincs PE21 8HU* Tel (01205) 363512

CLARKE, Douglas Charles. b 33. Bps' Coll Cheshunt 65. **d** 66 **p** 67. C Chingford SS Pet and Paul *Chelmsf* 66-72; V Romford Ascension Collier Row 72-79; V Bembridge *Portsm* 79-83; V Bournemouth St Mary *Win* 83-87; R High Wych and Gilston w Eastwick *St Alb* from 87. *The Rectory, High Wych, Sawbridgeworth, Herts CM21 0HX* Tel (01279) 723346

CLARKE, Dudley Barrington. b 22. OBE. Em Coll Cam BA46 MA48 PhD. Ridley Hall Cam 46. **d** 48 **p** 49. C Aldershot H Trin *Guildf* 48-50; Chapl Monkton Combe Sch Bath 50-58; Australia from 59; rtd 87. *60 Duke Street, Sandy Bay, Tasmania, Australia 7005* Tel Hobart (02) 240784

CLARKE, Duncan James Edward. b 54. Wycliffe Hall Ox 75. **d** 78 **p** 79. C Newport St Andr *Mon* 78-80; C Griffithstown 80-82; Trinidad and Tobago 82-84; NSM Fleckney and Kilby *Leic* 92-95; USPG from 95; Trinidad and Tobago from 95. *St Mary's Rectory, Eastern Main Road, Tacarigua, Trinidad, W Indies* Tel Trinidad and Tobago 6405163

CLARKE, Edward. b 02. Dur Univ LTh28 St Jo Coll Dur BA30 MA32. St Aid Birkenhead 25. **d** 29 **p** 30. C Huddersfield St Pet *Wakef* 29-34; V Newsome 34-46; V Golcar 46-51; V Lupset 51-64; V Kirkburton 64-70; RD Kirkburton 68-70; rtd 70; Perm to Offic *Wakef* from 70. *Timinetes, Northgate Road, Honley, Huddersfield HD7 2QL*

CLARKE, Edwin Joseph Alfred. b 18. Ripon Hall Ox 64. **d** 66 **p** 67. C Yardley St Edburgha *Birm* 66-70; R Nether Whitacre 70-88; rtd 89; Perm to Offic *Lich* from 90. *114 Main Street, Clifton Campville, Tamworth, Staffs B79 0AP* Tel (0182786) 587

CLARKE, Eric Samuel. b 26. Nottm Univ BSc51 St Cath Coll Ox BA69 MA69. Wycliffe Hall Ox 51. **d** 54 **p** 55. C Gedling *S'well* 54-57; C Nottingham St Pet and St Jas 57-69; Perm to Offic *Derby* from 63. *16 Menin Road, Allestree, Derby DE22 2NL*

CLARKE, Frank. b 21. St Jo Coll Nottm. **d** 85 **p** 87. NSM Farnsfield *S'well* from 85. *Belvedere, Tippings Lane, Farnsfield, Newark, Notts NG22 8EP* Tel (01623) 882528

CLARKE, Capt Geoffrey. b 53. CA Tr Coll DipEvang84 Trin Coll Bris DipHE94. **d** 97. C Belmont *Lon* from 97. *116 Uppingham Avenue, Stanmore, Middx HA7 2JU* Tel 0181-907 8573

CLARKE, Geraldine Ann. b 46. Hockerill Coll of Educn CertEd68 Coll of Preceptors ACP81. Oak Hill Th Coll 93. **d** 96 **p** 97. NSM Aldersbrook *Chelmsf* from 96. *78 Wanstead Park Avenue, London E12 5EN* Tel 0181-530 3425

CLARKE, Canon Harold George. b 29. St D Coll Lamp 58. **d** 61 **p** 62. C Ebbw Vale Ch Ch *Mon* 61-64; C Roath St German *Llan* 64-73; Chapl Wales Poly 73-74; V Glyntaff 73-84; V Roath St Martin from 84; RD Cardiff from 89; Can Llan Cathl from 91. *St Martin's Vicarage, Strathnairn Street, Roath, Cardiff CF2 3JL* Tel (01222) 482295

CLARKE, Harold Godfrey Codrington. *See* CODRINGTON CLARKE, Harold Godfrey

CLARKE, The Ven Herbert Lewis. b 20. Jes Coll Ox BA43 MA46. Union Th Sem (NY) STM50 Linc Th Coll 44. **d** 45 **p** 46. C Llanelli *St D* 45-48; PV Wells Cathl *B & W* 48-49; Lect Wells Th Coll 48-49; Lect St D Coll Lamp 50-52; Canada 52-57; C-in-c Barry Is CD *Llan* 57-59; Sub-Warden St Mich Coll Llan 59-67; R Caerphilly *Llan* 67-77; Can Llan Cathl 75-77; Adn Llan 77-88; R St Fagans w Michaelston-super-Ely 77-90; rtd 90; Perm to Offic *Llan* from 90. *First Floor Flat, St Andrew, High Street, Llandaff, Cardiff CF5 2DX* Tel (01222) 578581

CLARKE, Canon Hilary James. b 41. JP. Univ of Wales (Lamp) BA64 Ox Univ DipEd65. St Steph Ho Ox 64. **d** 66 **p** 67. C Kibworth Beauchamp *Leic* 66-68; Chapl to the Deaf 68-71; Prin Officer Ch Miss for Deaf Walsall 71-73; Prin Officer & Sec Leic and Co Miss for the Deaf 73-89; Hon C Leic St Anne *Leic* from 73; TV Leic H Spirit 82-89; Hon Can Leic Cathl from 88; Sec Gen Syn Coun for the Deaf from 88; Bp's Press Relns and Dio Communications Officer *Leic* 95-96. *158 Westcotes Drive, Leicester LE3 0SP* Tel 0116-255 7283 Fax 233 0839

CLARKE, Jason Scott. b 65. Leeds Univ BA87. Coll of Resurr Mirfield 89. **d** 91 **p** 92. C Hendon St Mary *Lon* 91-95; V Enfield St Geo from 95. *St George's Vicarage, 706 Hertford Road, Enfield, Middx EN3 6NR* Tel (01992) 762581

CLARKE, John Charles. b 31. St Jo Coll Nottm 91. **d** 92 **p** 93. NSM Winshill *Derby* 92-95; P-in-c Stanley from 95. *The Vicarage, Station Road, Stanley, Derby DE7 6FB* Tel 0115-932 2942

CLARKE, John David Maurice. b 60. **d** 89 **p** 90. C Dublin Whitechurch *D & G* 89-92; Asst Chapl St Vin Hosp Donnybrook 89-92; I Navan w Kentstown, Tara, Slane, Painestown etc *M & K* from 92. *The Rectory, Boyne Road, Navan, Co Meath, Irish Republic* Tel Navan (46) 21172

CLARKE, John Martin. b 52. Hertf Coll Ox BA89 MA89 Edin Univ BD76. Edin Th Coll 73. **d** 76 **p** 77. C Kenton Ascension *Newc* 76-79; Prec St Ninian's Cathl Perth *St And* 79-82; Info Officer to Scottish Episc Gen Syn 82-87; Greece 87-88; V Battersea St Mary *S'wark* 89-96; Prin Ripon Coll Cuddesdon from 97. *Ripon College, Cuddesdon, Oxford OX44 9HP* Tel (01865) 874404

CLARKE, John Patrick Hatherley. b 46. Pemb Coll Ox BA68 Man Univ MBA73. St Jo Coll Nottm DipTh83. **d** 83 **p** 84. C Leic H Trin w St Jo *Leic* 83-87; C Selly Park St Steph and St Wulstan *Birm* 87-92; Hon C Woking St Mary *Guildf* 92-94; V Greenham *Ox* from 94. *The Vicarage, New Road, Greenham, Newbury, Berks RG14 7RZ* Tel (01635) 41075

CLARKE, John Percival. b 44. TCD BA67. **d** 69 **p** 70. C Belfast St Simon *Conn* 69-72; C Monkstown *D & G* 72-76; Asst Chapl TCD 76-78; I Durrus *C, C & R* 79-82; I Carrigrohane Union 82-89; Tanzania 89-92; I Wicklow w Killiskey *D & G* from 92; Abp's Dom Chapl from 95. *The Rectory, Wicklow, Irish Republic* Tel Wicklow (404) 67132

CLARKE, John Philip. b 31. Trin Hall Cam BA54 MA62. Linc Th Coll. **d** 57 **p** 58. C Walworth Lady Marg w St Mary *S'wark* 57-59; C Warlingham w Chelsham and Farleigh 59-62; C Mottingham St Andr 62-67; C Eltham Park St Luke 67-72; Chapl Leeds Gen Infirmary 72-91; C Far Headingley St Chad *Ripon* 91-96; Bp's Adv on Chr Healing 91-96; rtd 96. *75 Weetwood Lane, Leeds LS16 5NU* Tel 0113-275 9526

CLARKE, Miss Joyce Nancy. b 32. CertEd58. N Ord Course 82. **dss** 85 **d** 87 **p** 94. Prestbury *Ches* 85-87; Par Dn 87-94; C from 94. *2 Peterborough Close, Macclesfield, Cheshire SK10 3DT* Tel (01625) 611809

CLARKE, Mrs Joyce Willoughby Price. b 36. Gilmore Course 78. **dss** 81 **d** 87 **p** 94. Heston *Lon* 81-87; Par Dn 87-89; Deanery Youth Chapl *Sarum* 90-96; rtd 96. *Weir Bridge, Duck Street, Wool, Wareham, Dorset BH20 6DE* Tel (01929) 554115

CLARKE, Canon Kenneth Herbert (Ken). b 49. TCD BA71. **d** 72 **p** 73. C Magheralin *D & D* 72-75; C Dundonald 75-78; Chile 78-82; I Crinken *D & G* 82-86; I Coleraine *Conn* from 86; Chmn SAMS (Ireland) from 94; Preb Conn Cathl from 96. *St Patrick's Rectory, Mountsandel Road, Coleraine, Co Londonderry BT52 1JE* Tel (01265) 43429 or 44213

CLARKE, Canon Malcolm Methuen. b 08. K Coll Cam BA36 MA40. Cuddesdon Coll 37. **d** 38 **p** 39. C Northampton St Matt *Pet* 38-49; V Wellingborough All Hallows 49-78; rtd 78; Hon C Northampton St Matt *Pet* from 78. *11A Kingsley Road, Northampton NN2 7BN* Tel (01604) 713695

CLARKE, Canon Margaret Geraldine. b 33. Dalton Ho Bris 62. **dss** 68 **d** 87 **p** 94. Wells St Thos w Horrington *B & W* 68-74; Easthampstead *Ox* 74-87; Par Dn 87-94; C 94; Hon Can Ch Ch 90-94; rtd 94. *Hermon, London Road, Bracknell, Berks RG12 2XH* Tel (01344) 427451

CLARKE, Martin Geoffrey. b 45. Dur Univ BA66. Wells Th Coll 67. **d** 69 **p** 70. C Atherstone *Cov* 69-72; C Keresley and Coundon 72-75; R Scorborough w Leconfield *York* 75-79; P-in-c Lockington w Lund 78-79; R Lockington and Lund and Scorborough w Leconfield 79-81; R Romsley *Worc* 81-96; Chapl Halesowen Coll 81-96; P-in-c Walsham le Willows and Finningham w Westhorpe *St E* from 96; P-in-c Badwell Ash w Gt Ashfield, Stowlangtoft etc from 96. *The Rectory, The Causeway, Walsham-le-Willows, Bury St Edmunds, Suffolk IP31 3AB* Tel (01359) 259310

CLARKE, Martin Howard. b 47. AKC70. St Aug Coll Cant 70. **d** 71 **p** 72. C Saffron Walden w Wendens Ambo *Chelmsf* 71-74; C Ely 74-78; V Messing w Inworth *Chelmsf* 78-90; V Layer-de-la-Haye from 90. *45 Malting Green Road, Layer-de-la-Haye, Colchester CO2 0JJ* Tel (01206) 734243

CLARKE, Ms Mary Margaret. b 65. K Coll Lon BD86 AKC86. Linc Th Coll CMM89. **d** 89 **p** 94. Par Dn Northampton St Jas *Pet* 89-93; Chapl Nene Coll of HE Northn 92-93; TD Coventry Caludon *Cov* 93-94; TV from 94. *St Catherine's House, 7 St Catherine's Close, Coventry CV3 1EH* Tel (01203) 635737

CLARKE, Maurice Fulford Lovell. b 12. Clare Coll Cam BA34 MA38. Wells Th Coll 35. **d** 36 **p** 37. C Benwell St Jas *Newc* 36-46; CF (EC) 40-46; CF (TA) 48-54; Vice-Prin Sarum Th Coll 46-53; V Lewisham St Swithun *S'wark* 54-65; Chapl Hither Green Hosp 54-65; R Ashley *Lich* 65-77; P-in-c Hales 65-73; rtd 77; Perm to Offic *Heref* from 77. *Flat 5, Ellesborough Manor, Butlers Cross, Aylesbury, Bucks HP17 0XF*

CLARKE, Maurice Gordon. b 29. Lon Univ BSc52 MSc79. Westcott Ho Cam 52. **d** 54 **p** 55. C Hitchin St Mary *St Alb* 54-58; C Chipping Barnet 58-62; Dir Past Counselling and Public Preacher *S'wark* 64-69; rtd 91. *Bancroft Cottage, Mill Green, Burston, Diss, Norfolk IP22 3TJ* Tel (01379) 741296

CLARKE, Maurice Harold. b 30. K Alfred's Coll Win CertEd56 Sussex Univ MA79 LCP69. Cuddesdon Coll 65. **d** 67 **p** 68. Hd Master Co Sec Sch Cowplain (Lower Sch) 67-72; Hon C Waterlooville *Portsm* 67-70; Hon C Fareham SS Pet and Paul 70-72; Hon C Higham and Merston *Roch* 72-83; Dep Hd Master Thamesview High Sch 72-80; Hd Master Eltham Green Comp Sch 80-83; V Hamble le Rice *Win* 83-90; rtd 91; Perm to Offic *Chich* from 92. *10 Worcester Road, Chichester, W Sussex PO19 4DJ* Tel (01243) 775646

CLARKE, Michael. b 39. Ely Th Coll 60. **d** 62 **p** 63. C S Stoneham *Win* 62-64; C Greenford H Cross *Lon* 64-69; Hon C Milton *Portsm* 69-74; Chapl St Jas Hosp Portsm 69-91; Chapl Hurstpierpoint Coll Hassocks 91-92; R Highnam, Lassington, Rudford, Tibberton etc *Glouc* from 92. *The Rectory, Maidenhall, Highnam, Gloucester GL2 8DL* Tel (01452) 525567

CLARKE, Neil Malcolm. b 53. Solicitor 79 MLawSoc80. WMMTC 89. **d** 92 **p** 93. NSM Desborough *Pet* from 92; NSM Brampton Ash w Dingley and Braybrooke from 92. *53 Breakleys Road, Desborough, Kettering, Northants NN14 2PT* Tel (01536) 760667

CLARKE, Norman. b 28. Keble Coll Ox BA52 MA58. St Steph Ho Ox 52. **d** 54 **p** 55. C Ellesmere Port *Ches* 54-57; C Kettering St Mary *Pet* 57-60; Ghana 60-62; C Friern Barnet All SS *Lon* 62-63; Lic to Offic *Leic* 63-74; C Knighton St Mary Magd 74-81; Dioc Communications Officer 81-88; P-in-c Sproughton w Burstall *St E* 81-88; P-in-c Dunsford and Doddiscombsleigh *Ex* 88-95; P-in-c Cheriton Bishop 88-95; rtd 95; Perm to Offic *Ex* from 95. *78 Malden Road, Sidmouth, Devon EX10 9NA* Tel (01395) 515849

CLARKE, Oswald Reeman. b 12. Liv Univ BA35 St Cath Soc Ox BA37 MA40. Ripon Hall Ox 34. **d** 36 **p** 37. C Whitehaven Ch Ch w H Trin *Carl* 36-37; C Addingham 37-38; Hon C Carl H Trin 38-39; C Wavertree St Mary *Liv* 39-43; P-in-c Widnes St Mary 43-44; V Liv St Sav 44-53; V Tulse Hill H Trin *S'wark* 53-58; V Upper Chelsea St Simon *Lon* 58-85; rtd 85; Perm to Offic *Lon* 85-90; P-in-c St Mary Abchurch from 90. *13 Down Quadrangle, Morden College, 19 St Germans Place, London SE3 0PW* Tel 0181-293 1181

CLARKE, Canon Peter. b 25. Lon Univ BSc49 St Chad's Coll Dur DipTh51. **d** 51 **p** 52. C Linc St Giles *Linc* 51-53; C Gt Grimsby St Mary and St Jas 53-60; V Linc All SS 60-68; V Bardney 68-75; V Apley w Stainfield 68-75; V Linc St Nic w St Jo Newport 75-88; RD Christianity 78-85; Can and Preb Linc Cathl from 79; rtd 88; Perm to Offic *Linc* from 88. *46 Swallow Avenue, Skellingthorpe, Lincoln LN6 5XW* Tel (01522) 684261

CLARKE, Peter Gerald. b 38. Cuddesdon Coll 74. **d** 76 **p** 77. Hon C Marston Magna w Rimpton *B & W* 76-79; Hon C Queen Camel, Marston Magna, W Camel, Rimpton etc 79-87; Hon C Chilton Cantelo, Ashington, Mudford, Rimpton etc 87-88; R Tintinhull w Chilthorne Domer, Yeovil Marsh etc 88-94; TV Weston-super-Mare Cen Par 94-95; V Weston super Mare All SS and St Sav from 96. *The Vicarage, 46 Manor Road, Weston-super-Mare, Avon BS23 2SU* Tel (01934) 623230

CLARKE, Peter John. b 36. Qu Coll Ox BA60 MA64 Lon Univ BD79. Clifton Th Coll 62. **d** 62 **p** 63. C Upper Tulse Hill St Matthias *S'wark* 62-64; CMJ 64-96; Dir for S America 88-96; rtd 97. *Pedro Moran 4414, 1419 Buenos Aires, Argentina* Tel Buenos Aires (1) 4629 Fax as telephone

CLARKE, Philip John. b 44. Bris Univ BA65 Univ of Wales (Abth) DipEd66. N Ord Course 84. **d** 87 **p** 88. NSM Crewe Ch Ch and St Pet *Ches* 87-88; NSM Coppenhall 88-90; Lic to Offic 90-91; C Altrincham St Geo 91-95; C Odd Rode from 95. *53 Heath Avenue, Rode Heath, Stoke-on-Trent ST7 3RY* Tel (01270) 877762

CLARKE, Richard Leon. b 37. Sarum Th Coll 62. **d** 65 **p** 66. C Fordington *Sarum* 65-68; C Haywards Heath St Rich *Chich* 68-72; C Goring-by-Sea 72-76; P-in-c Portslade St Andr 76-77; P-in-c Southwick St Pet 76-77; V Portslade St Pet and St Andr 77-79; R Clayton w Keymer from 79; RD Hurst from 90. *The Rectory, Keymer, Hassocks, W Sussex BN6 8RB* Tel (01273) 843570

✠**CLARKE, The Most Revd Richard Lionel.** b 49. TCD BA71 MA79 PhD90 K Coll Lon BD75 AKC75. **d** 75 **p** 76. C Holywood *D & D* 75-77; C Dublin St Bart w Leeson Park *D & G* 77-79; Dean of Residence TCD 79-84; I Bandon Union *C, C & R* 84-93; Dir of Ords 85-93; Cen Dir of Ords 82-93; Can Cork and Ross Cathls 91-93; Dean Cork 93-96; I Cork St Fin Barre's Union 93-96; Chapl Univ Coll Cork 95-96; Bp M & K from 96. *Bishop's House, Moyglare, Maynooth, Co Kildare, Irish Republic* Tel Dublin (1) 628 9354 Fax 628 9696

CLARKE, Dr Robert George. b 36. Natal Univ PhD83. Cranmer Hall Dur BA65 DipTh67. **d** 67 **p** 68. C Basingstoke *Win* 67-70; S Africa from 71. *26 Somerset Street, Grahamstown, 6140 South Africa* Tel Grahamstown (461) 27803 or 311100

CLARKE, Robert Graham (Bob). b 28. S Dios Minl Tr Scheme 78. **d** 81 **p** 82. NSM Woolston *Win* 81-89; NSM Portswood St Denys 89-93; Chapl Torrevieja *Eur* 93-95; Perm to Offic *Win* from 95; Perm to Offic *Eur* from 95. *10 River Green, Hamble, Southampton SO31 4JA* Tel (01703) 454230

CLARKE, Robert James. b 22. ACP58 DTh. CITC 67. **d** 69 **p** 70. C Belfast St Mary *Conn* 69-70; C and Min Can Limerick Cathl *L & K* 70-72; Asst Chapl Wilson's Hosp Sch Multyfarnham 72-85; Chapl 85-87; Lic to Offic *M & K* from 87. *Strangriff House Nursing Home, Stranorlar, Ballybofey, Co Donegal, Irish Republic* Tel Letterkenny (74) 31024

CLARKE, Robert Michael (Bob). b 45. Oak Hill Th Coll BD71 Sarum & Wells Th Coll 78. **d** 78 **p** 79. Hon C Glastonbury St Jo w Godney *B & W* 78-81; Asst Hd Master Edington Sch 78-81; Chapl Felsted Sch Essex 81-84; Asst Chapl and Ho Master 85-92; Lic to Offic *Chelmsf* 85-92; Hd Master Brocksford Hall from 92; Lic to Offic *Derby* from 92. *Brocksford Hall, Doveridge, Ashbourne, Derbyshire DE6 5PA* Tel (01889) 562809 Fax 567972

CLARKE, Robert Sydney. b 35. AKC64 K Coll Lon MA65. **d** 65 **p** 66. C Hendon St Mary *Lon* 65-69; C Langley Marish *Ox* 69-70; Chapl New Cross Hosp Wolv 70-74; Chapl Dorchester Hosps 74-79; Sen Chapl Westmr Hosp Lon 80-85; Sen Chapl Win Hosps 88-94; Chapl to The Queen from 87; Sec and Dir Tr Gen Syn Hosp Chapl Coun from 94; Perm to Offic *S'wark* from 95; Perm to Offic *Lon* from 95. *Hospital Chaplaincies Council, Fielden House, Little College Street, London SW1P 3SH* Tel 0171-222 5090 Fax 222 5156

CLARKE, Robert William. b 56. TCD DipTh83. **d** 83 **p** 84. C Cloughfern *Conn* 83-85; C Drumragh w Mountfield *D & R* 85-87; I Edenderry w Clanabogan from 87. *Edenderry Rectory, 91 Crevenagh Road, Omagh, Co Tyrone BT79 0EZ* Tel (01662) 245525

CLARKE, Roger David. b 58. Man Univ BA Ox Univ MA. Ripon Coll Cuddesdon 80. **d** 83 **p** 84. C Frodsham *Ches* 83-86; C Wilmslow 86-88; V High Lane 88-93; V Heald Green St Cath from 93. *The Vicarage, 217 Outwood Road, Cheadle, Cheshire SK8 3JS* Tel 0161-437 4614

CLARKE, Ronald George (Ron). b 31. Oak Hill Th Coll. **d** 64 **p** 65. C Carlton-in-the-Willows *S'well* 64-68; V Bestwood St Matt 68-76; V Barnsbury St Andr w St Thos and St Matthias *Lon* 76-77; V Barnsbury St Andr 77-78; V Barnsbury St Andr w H Trin 79-80; P-in-c Battle Bridge All SS w Pentonville St Jas 79-80; V Barnsbury St Andr and H Trin w All SS 81-86; TR Bath Twerton-on-Avon *B & W* 86-94; rtd 94; P-in-c Churchstanton, Buckland St Mary and Otterford *B & W* 94-97. *Myrtle Cottage, 35 High Street, Chard, Somerset TA20 1QL* Tel (01460) 65495

CLARKE, Steven Peter. b 61. Oak Hill Th Coll DipHE95. **d** 97. C Frinton *Chelmsf* from 97. *38 St Mary's Road, Frinton-on-Sea, Essex CO13 9LY*

CLARKE, Thomas Percival. b 15. Univ of Wales BA39. Lich Th Coll 39. **d** 41 **p** 42. C Cardiff St Mary *Llan* 41-45; C Walcot *B & W* 45-48; C Bathwick w Woolley 48-49; V Hendford 49-52; Area Sec (E Counties) UMCA 52-56; Metrop Area Sec UMCA 56-59; C S Kensington St Steph *Lon* 56-59; V Blackheath All SS *S'wark* 59-72; Chapl Leighton Hosp Crewe 72-73; Chapl Charing Cross Hosp Lon 73-82; rtd 82. *1 Trenos Gardens, Bryncae, Pontyclun CF72 9SZ* Tel (01443) 227662

CLARKE, Ms Valerie Diane. b 45. N Ord Course 91. **d** 95 **p** 96. C Sherburn in Elmet w Saxton *York* from 95. *23A Springfield Road, Sherburn in Elmet, Leeds LS25 6BU* Tel (01977) 684774

CLARKE, Vernon Douglas. b 18. Jes Coll Cam BA48 MA50. Bps' Coll Cheshunt 47. **d** 49 **p** 50. C Bulwell St Mary *S'well* 49-51; C Ambleside w Rydal *Carl* 51-54; V Aspatria 54-63; V Millom H Trin 63-71; V Cockermouth All SS w Ch Ch 71-74; P-in-c Kirkland 75-83; P-in-c Gt Salkeld 79-80; C Gt Salkeld w Lazonby 80-83; rtd 83; Perm to Offic *Carl* 84-93. *Birchfield, Great Salkeld, Penrith, Cumbria CA11 9LW* Tel (01768) 898380

CLARKE, Mrs Yvonne Veronica. b 58. CA Tr Coll. **dss** 86 **d** 87 **p** 94. Nunhead St Silas *S'wark* 86-87; Par Dn 87-90; Par Dn Nunhead St Antony w St Silas 90-91; Par Dn Mottingham St Andr 91-94; C from 94. *St Alban's Parsonage, 132 William Barefoot Drive, London SE9 3BP* Tel 0181-857 7702

CLARKSON, The Ven Alan Geoffrey. b 34. Ch Coll Cam BA57 MA61. Wycliffe Hall Ox 57. **d** 59 **p** 60. C Penn *Lich* 59-60; C Oswestry St Oswald 60-63; C Wrington *B & W* 63-65; V Chewton Mendip w Emborough 65-74; Dioc Ecum Officer 65-75; V Glastonbury St Jo w Godney 74-84; P-in-c W Pennard 80-84; P-in-c Meare 81-84; P-in-c Glastonbury St Benedict 82-84; V Glastonbury w Meare, W Pennard and Godney 84; Hon Can Win Cathl *Win* from 84; Adn Win from 84; V Burley Ville from 84. *The Vicarage, Church Corner, Burley, Ringwood, Hants BH24 4AP* Tel (01425) 402303 Fax 403753

CLARKSON, David James. b 42. St Andr Univ BSc66. N Ord Course 85. **d** 88 **p** 89. NSM Slaithwaite w E Scammonden *Wakef*

88-89; C Morley St Pet w Churwell 89-91; R Cumberworth w Denby Dale 91-93; P-in-c Denby 91-93; R Cumberworth, Denby and Denby Dale from 93. *The Rectory, 43 Hollybank Avenue, Upper Cumberworth, Huddersfield HD8 8NY* Tel (01484) 606225

CLARKSON, Eric George. b 22. St Jo Coll Dur BA48 DipTh50. **d** 50 **p** 51. C Birkdale St Jo *Liv* 50-52; C Grassendale 52-54; PC W Derby St Luke 54-66; V Blackb St Mich *Blackb* 66-75; V Blackb St Mich w St Jo 75; V Chapeltown *Sheff* 75-86; C Ranmoor 86-87; V Crosspool 87-92; rtd 92; Perm to Offic *York* from 92. *2 Harewood Drive, Filey, N Yorkshire YO14 0DE* Tel (01723) 513957

CLARKSON, Geoffrey. b 35. AKC61. **d** 62 **p** 63. C Shildon *Dur* 62-65; Asst Chapl HM Pris Liv 65-66; Chapl HM Borstal Feltham 66-71; Hon C Hampton St Mary *Lon* 71-90; Chapl HM Rem Cen Ashford 88-90; Chapl HM Pris Coldingley from 90; Chapl HM Pris Send 92-94. *HM Prison Coldingley, Bisley, Woking, Surrey GU24 9EX* Tel (01483) 476721 Fax 488586

CLARKSON, Canon John Thomas. b 30. AKC54. St Boniface Warminster 55. **d** 54 **p** 55. C Luton St Sav *St Alb* 54-59; Australia 59-73 and from 77; V Dallington *Pet* 73-77; Hon Can Bathurst Cathl from 95; rtd 96. *134 Mitre Street, Bathurst, NSW, Australia 2795*

CLARKSON, Michael Livingston. b 48. California Univ BA70 Loyola Univ JD73. Wycliffe Hall Ox 87. **d** 89 **p** 90. C Kensington St Barn *Lon* 89-93; Min Oaktree Angl Fellowship from 93. *41 South Parade, London W4 1JS* Tel 0181-743 2784

CLARKSON, Richard. b 33. Man Univ BSc54 Ball Coll Ox DPhil57. Oak Hill Th Coll 89. **d** 91 **p** 92. NSM Sunnyside w Bourne End *St Alb* from 91. *Kingsmead, Gravel Path, Berkhamsted, Herts HP4 2PH* Tel (01442) 873014

CLARKSON, Richard Michael. b 38. St Jo Coll Dur BA60 Lanc Univ PGCE68. Cranmer Hall Dur DipTh62. **d** 62 **p** 63. C St Annes *Blackb* 62-66; C Lancaster St Mary 66-68; Asst Master Kirkham Gr Sch 68-90; Asst Master Hurstpierpoint Coll Hassocks 90-91; Asst Master St Mary's Hall Brighton from 92; rtd 93; Perm to Offic *Chich* from 93. *121 College Lane, Hurstpierpoint, Hassocks, W Sussex BN6 9AF* Tel (01273) 834117

CLARKSON, Robert Christopher. b 32. Dur Univ BA53 DipEd54. S Dios Minl Tr Scheme 85. **d** 87 **p** 88. NSM Wonston and Stoke Charity w Hunton *Win* from 87. *27 Wrights Way, South Wonston, Winchester, Hants SO21 3HE* Tel (01962) 881692

CLARRIDGE, Donald Michael. b 41. DipOT86. Oak Hill Th Coll 63. **d** 66 **p** 67. C Newc St Barn and St Jude *Newc* 66-70; C Pennycross *Ex* 70-76; R Clayhanger 76-83; R Petton 76-83; R Huntsham 76-83; V Bampton 76-83. *5 Surrey Close, Tunbridge Wells, Kent TN2 5RF* Tel (01892) 533796

CLASBY, Michael Francis Theodore. b 37. Lon Univ BA59. Chich Th Coll 59. **d** 61 **p** 62. C Leigh-on-Sea St Marg *Chelmsf* 61-64; C Forest Gate St Edm 64-69; V Walthamstow St Mich 69-70; Chapl Community of Sisters of the Love of God 87-89; Perm to Offic *St Alb* 87-89; NSM Hemel Hempstead 90-93; Perm to Offic from 93. *47 Wrensfield, Hemel Hempstead, Herts HP1 1RP* Tel (01442) 254400

CLASPER, John. b 42. AKC67. **d** 68 **p** 69. C Leeds All Hallows w St Simon *Ripon* 68-71; C Hawksworth Wood 72-74; Ind Chapl *Dur* from 74; TV Jarrow St Paul 75-77; TV Jarrow 77-91; Dioc Urban Development Officer 90-91; TR E Darlington from 91. *East Darlington House, 30 Smithfield Road, Darlington, Co Durham DL1 4DD* Tel (01325) 369523

CLASSON, Michael Campbell. b 32. TCD BA52 HDipEd54 MA55. CITC 87. **d** 89 **p** 91. NSM Conwal Union w Gartan *D & R* 89-90; NSM Ardara w Glencolumbkille, Inniskeel etc from 90. *Summy, Portnoo, Co Donegal, Irish Republic* Tel Portnoo (75) 45242

CLATWORTHY, Jonathan Richard. b 48. Univ of Wales BA70. Sarum & Wells Th Coll 71. **d** 76 **p** 77. C Man Resurr *Man* 76-78; C Bolton St Pet 78-81; V Ashton St Pet 81-85; Chapl Sheff Univ *Sheff* 85-91; V Denstone w Ellastone and Stanton *Lich* from 91. *The Vicarage, Denstone, Uttoxeter, Staffs ST14 5HF* Tel (01889) 590263

CLAUSEN, John Frederick. b 37. Sarum Th Coll 65. **d** 68 **p** 69. C Kentish Town St Jo *Lon* 68-71; C Rainham *Roch* 71-77; R Stone 77-89; Lic to Dartford RD from 89. *14 Watling Street, Dartford DA1 1RF* Tel (01322) 279570

CLAWSON, Derek George. b 35. AMCST62. Qu Coll Birm 63. **d** 66 **p** 67. C Ditton St Mich *Liv* 66-70; C Speke All SS 70-72; V Hindley Green 72-85; V Wigan St Mich from 85. *St Michael's Vicarage, Duke Street, Wigan, Lancs WN1 2DN* Tel (01942) 42381

CLAXTON, Leslie Edward Mitchell. b 10. MC46. ARCM61 Peterho Cam BA33 MA48. Cuddesdon Coll 34. **d** 35 **p** 36. C Hounslow H Trin *Lon* 35-38; C Dartford H Trin *Roch* 38-39; CF 39-58; Dep Asst Chapl Gen 58-64; Asst Chapl Gen 64-68; QHC 67-68; R St Olave Hart Street w All Hallows Staining etc *Lon* 68-85; rtd 85. *Flat 5, 83 St George's Drive, London SW1V 4DB* Tel 0171-834 9407

CLAY, Canon Colin Peter. b 32. Ch Coll Cam BA55 MA59. Em Coll Saskatoon Hon DD91 Wells Th Coll 55. **d** 57 **p** 58. C Malden St Jas *S'wark* 57-59; Canada from 59; Asst Prof Relig Studies Laurentian Univ 69-72; Hon Can Saskatoon from 97. *College of Emmanuel and St Chad, 1337 College Drive, Saskatoon, Saskatchewan, Canada, S7N 0W6* Tel Saskatoon (306) 966-8500 Fax 966 8670 E-mail clay@skyfox.usask.ca

CLAY, Elizabeth Jane. b 50. Ridley Hall Cam. **dss** 86 **d** 87 **p** 94. Birstall *Wakef* 86-87; Hon Par Dn Lupset 87-90; Par Dn 90-94; C 94-96; Chapl HM Pris New Hall from 96. *The Vicarage, Broadway, Lupset, Wakefield, W Yorkshire WF2 8AA* Tel (01924) 373088

CLAY, Geoffrey. b 51. CertEd. Ridley Hall Cam. **d** 86 **p** 87. C Birstall *Wakef* 86-90; V Lupset from 90. *The Vicarage, Broadway, Lupset, Wakefield, W Yorkshire WF2 8AA* Tel (01924) 373088

CLAY, Peter Herbert. b 31. Lich Th Coll 62. **d** 64 **p** 65. C Ross *Heref* 64-67; C Leamington Priors All SS *Cov* 67-70; P-in-c Temple Grafton w Binton 70-73; V 73-75; P-in-c Exhall w Wixford 70-73; V 73-75; TV Cen Telford *Lich* 75-86; USPG 86-90; V Loughb Gd Shep *Leic* 90-96; rtd 96; Perm to Offic *Leic* from 96. *78 Eastlands Road, Rugby, Warks CV21 3RR* Tel (01788) 569138

CLAY, Timothy Francis (Tim). b 61. St Mark & St Jo Coll Lon BA85 Ealing Coll of Educn 89. Linc Th Coll CMinlStuds95. **d** 95 **p** 96. C Wickford and Runwell *Chelmsf* from 95. *8 Honington Close, Wickford, Essex SS11 8XB* Tel (01268) 561044

CLAYDEN, David Edward. b 42. Oak Hill Th Coll 74. **d** 76 **p** 77. C Worksop St Jo *S'well* 76-79; V Clarborough w Hayton 79-84; C Bloxwich *Lich* 87-90; TV 90-93; TV Tollington *Lon* from 93. *Emmanuel Vicarage, 145 Hornsey Road, London N7 6DU* Tel 0171-700 7110

CLAYDON, Preb Graham Leonard. b 43. K Coll Lon BA65. Clifton Th Coll 66. **d** 68 **p** 69. C Walthamstow St Mary w St Steph *Chelmsf* 68-73; Hon C St Marylebone All So w SS Pet and Jo *Lon* 73-81; V Islington St Mary from 81; Preb St Paul's Cathl from 92. *St Mary's Vicarage, Upper Street, London N1 2TX* Tel 0171-226 3400 or 354 3427

CLAYDON, John Richard. b 38. St Jo Coll Cam BA61 MA65. Trin Coll Bris DipTh72. **d** 73 **p** 74. C Finchley Ch Ch *Lon* 73-76; Asst Chapl K Edw Sch Witley 76-77; C Macclesfield St Mich *Ches* 77-81; V Marple All SS 81-91; CMJ from 91; Israel from 91. *Immanuel House, PO Box 2773, Tel Aviv 61027, Israel* Tel Tel Aviv (3) 821459

CLAYPOLE WHITE, Douglas Eric. b 29. FCA ATII. St Alb Minl Tr Scheme 77. **d** 80 **p** 81. NSM Sharnbrook and Knotting w Souldrop *St Alb* 80-82; NSM Felmersham 82-87; P-in-c from 87. *Homelands, High Street, Turvey, Bedford MK43 8DB* Tel (01234) 881661

CLAYTON, Canon Anthony Edwin Hay. b 36. Sarum Th Coll 61. **d** 63 **p** 64. C Tooting All SS *S'wark* 63-68; Perm to Offic *Leic* 69-74; Perm to Offic *S'well* 73-80; Hon C Lockington w Hemington *Leic* 74-80; P-in-c Eastwell 80-83; P-in-c Eaton 80-83; P-in-c Croxton Kerrial, Knipton, Harston, Branston etc 83-84; R 84-93; R High Framland Parishes 93-96; Chapl Belvoir Castle 85-96; RD Framland 90-94; Hon Can Leic Cathl 92-96; rtd 97. *18 Commerce Square, Nottingham NG1 1HS* Tel 0115-988 1920

CLAYTON, Geoffrey Buckroyd. b 26. Newc Univ BA67. Roch Th Coll 62. **d** 64 **p** 65. C Newc St Geo *Newc* 64-67; C Byker St Ant 67-68; C Cheddleton *Lich* 69-72; V Arbory *S & M* from 72; RD Castletown 82-97; V Santan from 88. *Arbory Vicarage, Ballabeg, Castletown, Isle of Man IM9 4LG* Tel (01624) 823595

CLAYTON, George Hamilton. b 42. Strathclyde Univ BSc65. S'wark Ord Course 90. **d** 93 **p** 94. NSM Send *Guildf* from 93. *137 Knightswood, Woking, Surrey GU21 3PX* Tel (01483) 720698

CLAYTON, Canon Giles. b 21. Keble Coll Ox BA42 MA47. St Steph Ho Ox 42. **d** 44 **p** 45. C Riddlesdown *S'wark* 44-46; C Plymstock *Ex* 46-49; C Littleham w Exmouth 49-52; R Durrington *Sarum* 52-70; RD Avon 67-70; R Salisbury St Martin 70-86; RD Salisbury 72-77; Can and Preb Sarum Cathl 73-92; rtd 86; Master St Nic Hosp Salisbury from 86. *9 Fisherton Island, Salisbury SP2 7TG* Tel (01722) 320177

CLAYTON, Canon John. b 11. Leeds Univ BA33 MA43. Wells Th Coll 34. **d** 35 **p** 36. C Dewsbury Moor *Wakef* 35-38; C Halifax St Jo Bapt 38-41; Lect 40-41; V Lupset 41-51; Chapl Snapethorpe Hosp 49-51; V Bolton St Jas *Bradf* 51-65; RD Calverley 56-65; V Otley 65-76; RD Otley 68-73; Hon Can Bradf Cathl 63-76; rtd 76; Perm to Offic *Bradf* from 76. *10 Sandy Walk, Bramhope, Leeds LS16 9DW* Tel 0113-261 1388

CLAYTON, Dr Melanie Yvonne. b 62. St Aid Coll Dur BA84 Victoria Univ (BC) MA85 Hertf Coll Ox DPhil89. WMMTC 91. **d** 94 **p** 95. C Penn *Lich* from 94. *105 Brenton Road, Penn, Wolverhampton WV4 5NS* Tel (01902) 335439

CLAYTON, Norman James. b 24. AKC52. **d** 53 **p** 54. C Long Benton St Mary *Newc* 53-55; N Rhodesia 55-60; S Africa 60-78; Dioc Communications Officer *Derby* 78-88; P-in-c Risley 78-87; R 87-89; rtd 89; Perm to Offic *Derby* from 89. *6 Allendale Avenue, Beeston, Nottingham NG9 6AN* Tel 0115-925 0060

CLAYTON, Sydney Cecil Leigh. b 38. Pemb Coll Ox BA62 MA65 Lon Univ BD65. Linc Th Coll. **d** 65 **p** 66. C Birch St Jas *Man* 65-68; Lect Bolton Par Ch 68-77; V Denshaw from 77. *The Vicarage, Huddersfield Road, Denshaw, Oldham OL3 5SB* Tel (01457) 874575

CLAYTON, William Alan. b 32. Liv Univ BSc54 Lon Univ BD60. **d** 63 **p** 64. C Wallasey St Hilary *Ches* 63-67; R Burton Agnes w Harpham *York* 67-69; V Batley St Thos *Wakef* 69-72; Lic to Offic *Ripon* 73-85; Hon C Grinton 75-85; R Barningham w Hutton Magna and Wycliffe from 85. *The Rectory, Barningham, Richmond, N Yorkshire DL11 7DW* Tel (01833) 621217

CLAYTON-JONES, Roger Francis. b 39. AKC64. **d** 66 **p** 67. C Oxton *Ches* 66-69; Asst Chapl R Hosp Sch Holbrook 69-71; Jamaica 71-73; CF 73-93; Chapl St Mary's Sch Wantage from 93. *Alma House, 35 Newbury Street, Wantage, Oxon OX12 8DJ* Tel (01235) 763617

CLEAR, Peter Basil. b 13. New Coll Ox BA35 MA40. Chich Th Coll 35. **d** 36 **p** 37. C Pimlico St Mary Graham Terrace *Lon* 36-39 and 46-48; Chapl RNVR 39-46; Chapl Convent of Reparation Woking 49-50; P-in-c Haselbury Plucknett w N Perrott *B & W* 50-52; R Pen Selwood 52-68; rtd 69. *21 Portland Court, Lyme Regis, Dorset DT7 3ND* Tel (01297) 442273

CLEASBY, The Very Revd Thomas Wood Ingram. b 20. Magd Coll Ox BA47 MA47. Cuddesdon Coll 47. **d** 49 **p** 50. C Huddersfield St Pet *Wakef* 49-52; Abp's Dom Chapl *York* 52-56; C Nottingham St Mary *S'well* 56-63; Chapl Nottm Univ 56-63; V Chesterfield St Mary and All SS *Derby* 63-70; Hon Can Derby Cathl 63-78; Adn Chesterfield 63-78; R Morton 70-78; Dean Ches 78-86; rtd 86; Perm to Offic *Carl* from 86; Perm to Offic *Bradf* from 87. *Low Barth, Dent, Sedbergh, Cumbria LA10 5SZ* Tel (015396) 25476

CLEATON, John. b 39. Open Univ BA86. S Dios Minl Tr Scheme 89. **d** 92 **p** 93. NSM Wareham *Sarum* from 92. *1 Avon Drive, Wareham, Dorset BH20 4EL* Tel (01929) 553149

CLEAVER, Gerald. b 20. Lon Univ BSc52. St Jo Coll Nottm 85. **d** 86 **p** 87. NSM W Bridgford *S'well* 86-96; NSM Clifton from 96. *62 South Road, Nottingham NG2 7AH* Tel 0115-981 0196

CLEAVER, Gordon Philip. b 29. SW Minl Tr Course. **d** 78 **p** 79. NSM St Ruan w St Grade *Truro* 78-86; Perm to Offic from 86. *Bryn-Mor, Cadgwith, Ruan Minor, Helston, Cornwall TR12 7JZ* Tel (01326) 290328

CLEAVER, John Martin. b 42. K Coll Lon BD64 AKC64. St Boniface Warminster 61. **d** 65 **p** 66. C Bexley St Mary *Roch* 65-69; C Ealing St Steph Castle Hill *Lon* 69-71; P-in-c Bostall Heath *Roch* 71-76; V Green Street Green 76-85; Primary Adv Lon Dioc Bd for Schs *Lon* 85-92; V Teddington St Mary w St Alb from 92. *The Vicarage, 11 Twickenham Road, Teddington, Middx TW11 8AQ* Tel 0181-977 2767

CLEAVER, Stuart Douglas. b 46. ACIS. Oak Hill Th Coll. **d** 83 **p** 84. C Portsdown *Portsm* 83-86; C Blendworth w Chalton w Idsworth etc 86-88; P-in-c Whippingham w E Cowes from 88. *The Rectory, 73 Cambridge Road, East Cowes, Isle of Wight PO32 6AH* Tel (01983) 292130

CLEEVE, Admire William. b 43. ACIS78 MBIM81 CPPS83 Ox Univ MTh96. Sierra Leone Th Hall 78. **d** 82 **p** 83. Sierra Leone 82-86; NSM Douglas St Geo and St Barn *S & M* 87-91; TV Langley Marish *Ox* from 91. *Christ the Worker Vicarage, Parlaunt Road, Slough SL3 8BB* Tel (01753) 545167 Fax as telephone

CLEEVE, Martin. b 43. ACP67 Open Univ BA80. Bp Otter Coll TCert65 Oak Hill Th Coll 69. **d** 72 **p** 73. C Margate H Trin *Cant* 72-76; V Southminster *Chelmsf* 76-86; Perm to Offic from 86; Teacher Castle View Sch Canvey Is 86-91; Hd RE Bromfords Sch Wickford from 91. *44 Ditton Court Road, Westcliffe-on-Sea, Essex SS0 7HF*

CLEEVES, David John. b 56. Univ of Wales (Lamp) BA Fitzw Coll Cam MA85. Westcott Ho Cam. **d** 82 **p** 83. C Cuddington *Guildf* 82-85; C Dorking w Ranmore 85-87; V Ewell St Fran 87-94; P-in-c Rotherfield w Mark Cross *Chich* from 94. *The Rectory, Rotherfield, Crowborough, E Sussex TN6 3LU* Tel (0189285) 2536

CLEGG, David Kneeshaw. b 46. N Ord Course 77. **d** 80 **p** 81. C Briercliffe *Blackb* 80-83; Chapl Lancs (Preston) Poly 83-89; rtd 89; Perm to Offic *Dur* from 89. *Field House, Albert Street, Durham DH1 4RL* Tel 0191-386 5806

CLEGG, Herbert. b 24. Fitzw Ho Cam BA59 MA63 Bris Univ MA65. Sarum Th Coll 52. **d** 54 **p** 55. C Street *B & W* 54-56; Perm to Offic *Ely* 56-59; Jamaica 59-61; R Newington Bagpath w Kingscote and Ozleworth *Glouc* 61-65; Uganda 65-69; P-in-c Aldsworth *Glouc* 70-75; P-in-c Sherborne w Windrush 70-75; V Marcham w Garford *Ox* 75-83; R Chipping Warden w Edgcote and Aston le Walls *Pet* 83-89; rtd 89; C Ox St Giles and SS Phil and Jas w St Marg *Ox* 90-94. *6 Floreys Close, Hailey, Witney, Oxford OX8 5UG* Tel (01993) 700281

CLEGG, Jeffrey Thomas. b 50. Padgate Coll of Educn BEd79 DAES85. N Ord Course 87. **d** 90 **p** 91. C Gateacre *Liv* 90-93; V W Derby Gd Shep 93-94; V Wigan St Cath from 94. *St Catharine's Vicarage, St Catharine Terrace, Wigan, Lancs WN1 3JW* Tel (01942) 820668

CLEGG, John Anthony Holroyd. b 44. Kelham Th Coll 65. **d** 70 **p** 71. C St Annes *Blackb* 70-74; C Lancaster St Mary 74-76; V Lower Darwen St Jas 76-80; TV Shaston *Sarum* 80-86; Chapl HM Youth Cust Cen Guys Marsh 80-86; R Poulton-le-Sands w Morecambe St Laur *Blackb* 86-97; RD Lancaster 89-94; P-in-c Grange-over-Sands *Carl* from 97. *The Vicarage, Hampsfell Road, Grange-over-Sands, Cumbria LA11 6BE* Tel (015395) 32757

CLEGG, John Lovell. b 48. Qu Coll Ox BA70 MA74. Trin Coll Bris DipTh75. **d** 75 **p** 76. C Barrow St Mark *Carl* 75-79; R S Levenshulme *Man* from 79. *St Andrew's Rectory, 27 Errwood Road, Levenshulme, Manchester M19 2PN* Tel 0161-224 5877

CLEGG, Peter Douglas. b 49. Sarum & Wells Th Coll 83. **d** 85 **p** 86. C Hangleton *Chich* 85-88; C-in-c Portslade Gd Shep CD 88-94; V Portslade Gd Shep from 94. *35 Stanley Avenue, Portslade, Brighton, E Sussex BN41 2WH* Tel (01273) 419518

CLEGG, Roger Alan. b 46. St Jo Coll Dur BA68 Nottm Univ CertEd69 DipTh76. St Jo Coll Nottm 75. **d** 78 **p** 79. C Harwood *Man* 78-81; TV Sutton St Jas and Wawne *York* 81-87; V Kirk Fenton w Kirkby Wharfe and Ulleskelfe from 87; OCF from 87; Chapl HM Pris Askham Grange from 95. *The Vicarage, Church Street, Church Fenton, Tadcaster, N Yorkshire LS24 9RD* Tel (01937) 557387

CLELAND, Richard. b 26. Belf Coll of Tech MPS47. St Aid Birkenhead 58. **d** 60 **p** 61. C Lisburn Ch Ch *Conn* 60-63; C Ballynafeigh St Jude *D & D* 63-66; C Portman Square St Paul *Lon* 66-67; V Ilkley All SS *Bradf* 67-83; Master Wyggeston's Hosp Leic 83-97; rtd 97. *1 Palmer Road, Retford, Notts DN22 6SR* Tel (01777) 704886

CLELAND, Trevor. b 66. Belf Coll of Tech ONC91 QUB BTh94 TCD MPhil97. CITC 94. **d** 96 **p** 97. C Lisburn Ch Ch *Conn* from 96. *74 Woodland Park, Lisburn, Co Antrim BT28 1LD* Tel (01846) 601618

CLEMAS, Nigel Antony. b 53. Wycliffe Hall Ox. **d** 83 **p** 84. C Bootle St Mary w St Paul *Liv* 83-87; V Kirkdale St Mary and St Athanasius 87-91; TV Netherthorpe *Sheff* 91-93; V Netherthorpe St Steph from 93. *The Rectory, 115 Upperthorpe Road, Sheffield S6 3EA* Tel 0114-276 7130

CLEMENCE, Paul Robert Fraser. b 50. MRTPI82 Man Univ DipTP74 St Edm Hall Ox MA90. Wycliffe Hall Ox 88. **d** 90 **p** 91. C Lancaster St Mary *Blackb* 90-94; Chapl HM Pris Lanc Castle 90-94; V Lt Thornton *Blackb* from 94. *St John's Vicarage, 35 Station Road, Thornton-Cleveleys, Blackpool FY5 5HY* Tel (01253) 825107

CLEMENT, Miss Barbara Winifred. b 20. Gilmore Ho 49. **dss** 56 **d** 87. Frimley Green *Guildf* 53-66; Hd Dss 66-74; Dioc Adv Lay Min 74-82; Frimley 74-82; Frimley Hosp 74-87; rtd 82; Perm to Offic *Guildf* 82-96. *9 Merlin Court, The Cloisters, Frimley, Camberley, Surrey GU16 5JN* Tel (01276) 22527

CLEMENT, Peter James. b 64. UMIST BSc88. Qu Coll Birm 89. **d** 92 **p** 93. C Grange St Andr *Ches* 92-95; C Man Apostles w Miles Platting *Man* from 95. *116A Victoria Square, Manchester M4 5EA* Tel 0161-237 1955

CLEMENT, Thomas Gwyn. b 51. Lon Univ BMus73 Golds Coll Lon PGCE74. St Steph Ho Ox DipMin93. **d** 93 **p** 94. C Friern Barnet St Jas *Lon* 93-96; V Edmonton St Alphege from 96. *St Alphege's Vicarage, Rossdale Drive, London N9 7LG* Tel 0181-245 3588

CLEMENT, Timothy Gordon (Tim). b 54. Usk Coll of Agric NCA75 OND76. Trin Coll Bris 92. **d** 94 **p** 95. C Chepstow *Mon* 94-97; R Bettws Newydd w Trostrey etc from 97. *The Rectory, Bettws Newydd, Usk NP5 1JN* Tel (01873) 880258

CLEMENTS, Alan Austin. b 39. ACIB66 Newc Univ MA93. Linc Th Coll 74. **d** 76 **p** 77. C Woodley St Jo the Ev *Ox* 76-79; C Wokingham All SS 79-83; V Felton *Newc* 83-95; P-in-c Wallsend St Pet from 95. *St Peter's Rectory, Wallsend, Tyne & Wear NE28 6PY* Tel 0191-262 3852

CLEMENTS, Andrew. b 48. K Coll Lon BD72 AKC72. St Aug Coll Cant 72. **d** 73 **p** 74. C Langley All SS and Martyrs *Man* 73-76; C Westhoughton 76-81; R Thornton Dale w Ellerburne and Wilton *York* 81-89; Prec Leic Cathl *Leic* 89-91; V Market Weighton *York* from 91; R Goodmanham from 91. *The Vicarage, 38 Cliffe Road, Market Weighton, York YO4 3BN* Tel (01430) 873230

CLEMENTS, Doris Thomasina Sara. b 46. TCD BA MA. **d** 95 **p** 96. NSM Killala w Dunfeeny, Crossmolina, Kilmoremoy etc *T, K & A* from 95. *Doobeg House, Bunnadadden, Ballymote, Co Sligo, Irish Republic* Tel Sligo (71) 85425

CLEMENTS, Edwin George. b 41. Chich Th Coll 77. **d** 79 **p** 80. C Didcot St Pet *Ox* 79-83; C Brixham w Churston Ferrers *Ex* 83; TV 84-86; TV Brixham w Churston Ferrers and Kingswear 86-88; P-in-c Hagbourne *Ox* 88; V 88-90; P-in-c Blewbury 89-90; P-in-c Upton 89-90; R Blewbury, Hagbourne and Upton from 90. *The Rectory, Blewbury, Didcot, Oxon OX11 9QH* Tel (01235) 850267 Fax 850267

CLEMENTS, John Derek Howard. b 65. Man Univ BA88. St Steph Ho Ox 88. **d** 90 **p** 91. C Ex St Jas *Ex* 90-93; TV Withycombe Raleigh from 93. *All Saints Vicarage, Church Road, Exmouth, Devon EX8 1RZ* Tel (01395) 263572

CLEMENTS, Miss Mary Holmes. b 43. Bedf Coll Lon BA64 Lon Bible Coll DipTh66 Lon Univ CertEd69. Ox Min Course DipMin94. **d** 94 **p** 95. NSM High Wycombe *Ox* from 94. *2 Firs Close, Hazlemere, High Wycombe, Bucks HP15 7TF* Tel (01494) 814707

CLEMENTS, Philip Christian. b 38. K Coll Lon BD64 AKC64. **d** 65 **p** 66. C S Norwood St Mark *Cant* 65-68; Chapl R Russell Sch Croydon 68-75; Asst Chapl Denstone Coll Uttoxeter 75-76; Chapl 76-81; Chapl Lancing Coll 82-90; R Ninfield *Chich* from

90; V Hooe from 90. *The Rectory, Church Lane, Ninfield, Battle, E Sussex TN33 9JW* Tel (01424) 892308

CLEMENTS, Philip John Charles. b 42. Nottm Univ CertEd64. Ridley Hall Cam. **d** 85 **p** 86. C Aylestone St Andr w St Jas *Leic* 85-87; P-in-c Swinford w Catthorpe, Shawell and Stanford 87-91; V from 91; RD Guthlaxton II from 94; P-in-c N w S Kilworth and Misterton from 96. *The Vicarage, Kilworth Road, Swinford, Lutterworth, Leics LE17 6BQ* Tel (01788) 860221

CLEMENTS, Canon Roy Adrian. b 44. Dur Univ BA68 DipTh69 MA. St Chad's Coll Dur 65. **d** 69 **p** 70. C Royston *Wakef* 69-73; V Clifton 73-77; V Rastrick St Matt 77-84; V Horbury Junction 84-92; Dioc Communications Officer from 84; Bp's Chapl from 92; Hon Can Wakef Cathl from 94. *Bishop's Lodge, Woodthorpe Lane, Wakefield, W Yorkshire WF2 6JJ* Tel (01924) 255349 Fax 250202 E-mail 100612,1514@compuserve.com

CLEMETSON, Thomas Henry. b 22. **d** 62 **p** 63. C Timperley *Ches* 62-65; V Hurdsfield 65-76; V Stockport St Sav 76-88; rtd 88; Perm to Offic *Ches* from 88. *23 Old Field Crescent, Lache Lane, Chester CH4 7PD* Tel (01244) 676492

CLEMETT, Peter Thomas. b 33. Univ of Wales (Lamp) BA60. Sarum Th Coll 59. **d** 61 **p** 62. C Tredegar St Geo *Mon* 61-63; Chapl St Woolos Cathl 63-66; CF from 66; Chapl R Memorial Chpl Sandhurst 84-88; rtd 88. *MOD Chaplains (Army), Trenchard Lines, Upavon, Pewsey, Wilts SN9 6BE* Tel (01980) 615804 Fax 615800

CLENCH, Brian Henry Ross. b 31. Ripon Coll Cuddesdon. **d** 82 **p** 83. C Fulham All SS *Lon* 82-85; Ind Chapl *Truro* 85-92; P-in-c St Mewan 85-92; rtd 92. *Briar Cottage, Uploders, Bridport, Dorset DT6 4PG*

CLENDON, David Arthur. b 33. Em Coll Cam BA56 MA61. Wells Th Coll 56. **d** 58 **p** 59. C Hockerill *St Alb* 58-62; C Digswell 62-63; C Luton Ch Ch 63-65; P-in-c 71-76; V Caddington 65-71; P-in-c Pirton 75-85; V 85-91; P-in-c Offley w Lilley 85-88; rtd 91. *1 Docklands, Pirton, Hitchin, Herts SG5 3QF* Tel (01462) 712741

CLEPHANE, Alexander Honeyman (Alex). b 48. LNSM course 94. **d** 97. NSM Flixton St Mich *Man* from 97. *306 Church Road, Urmston, Manchester M41 6JJ* Tel 0161-747 8816 Mobile 0468-035444

CLEVELAND, Michael Robin. b 52. Warw Univ BA73. St Jo Coll Nottm 86 Serampore Th Coll BD88. **d** 88 **p** 89. C Bushbury *Lich* 88-92; V Foleshill St Laur *Cov* from 92. *St Laurence's Vicarage, 142 Old Church Road, Coventry CV6 7ED* Tel (01203) 688271

CLEVELAND, Archdeacon of. *See* HAWTHORN, The Ven Christopher John

CLEVERLEY, Michael Frank. b 36. Man Univ BScTech57. Wells Th Coll 61. **d** 63 **p** 64. C Halifax St Aug *Wakef* 63; C Huddersfield St Jo 63-66; C Brighouse 66-69; V Gomersal 69-83; P-in-c Clayton W w High Hoyland 83-89; P-in-c Scissett St Aug 83-89; R High Hoyland, Scissett and Clayton W 89-96; rtd 96; NSM Leathley w Farnley, Fewston and Blubberhouses *Bradf* from 96. *The Rectory, Stainburn Lane, Leathley, Otley, W Yorkshire LS21 2LF* Tel 0113-284 3744

CLEVERLY, Charles St George (Charlie). b 51. Ox Univ MA. Trin Coll Bris. **d** 82 **p** 83. C Cranham Park *Chelmsf* 82-89; V 89-92; BCMS 92-93; Crosslinks from 93; Perm to Offic *Chelmsf* from 92. *c/o Crosslinks, 251 Lewisham Way, London SE4 1XF* Tel 0181-691 6111 Fax 694 8023

CLEWS, Nicholas. b 57. CIPFA85 SS Coll Cam BA80 MA84 Leeds Univ BA87. Coll of Resurr Mirfield 85. **d** 88 **p** 89. C S Elmsall *Wakef* 88-91; V Featherstone from 91. *All Saints' Vicarage, Featherstone, Pontefract, W Yorkshire WF7 6AH* Tel (01977) 792280

CLIFF, Frank Graham. b 38. Lon Univ DipTh66. Clifton Th Coll. **d** 66 **p** 67. C Park Estate St Chris CD *Leic* 66-69; C Whitton and Thurleston w Akenham *St E* 69-71; USA from 71. *210 Spring Hill Road, Honesdale, Pennsylvania 18431, USA*

CLIFF, Philip Basil. b 15. Lon Univ BSc61 Birm Univ PhD. Independent Coll Bradf. **d** 77 **p** 77. Hon C Northfield *Birm* 77-91; Perm to Offic from 91. *4 Fox Hill Close, Birmingham B29 4AH* Tel 0121-472 1556

CLIFFE, Christopher George. b 47. CITC 94. **d** 97. C Waterford *C & O* from 97; C Fiddown w Clonegam, Guilcagh and Kilmeaden from 97. *The Rectory, Piltown, Co Kilkenny, Irish Republic* Tel Waterford (51) 643275 Mobile 087-236 8682

CLIFFORD, Douglas Newson. b 16. St And Dioc Tr Course 81. **d** 83 **p** 84. NSM Strontian *Arg* from 83; NSM Fort William from 83; NSM Kinlochmoidart from 83; Bp's Dom Chapl from 83. *Bellsgrove Lodge, Strontian, Acharacle, Argyll PH36 4JB* Tel (01967) 402152

CLIFFORD, Raymond Augustine. b 45. Birkb Coll Lon CertRS91. Coll of Resurr Mirfield 91. **d** 93 **p** 94. C Saltdean *Chich* 93-96. *124 Arnold Estate, Druid Street, London SE1 2DT*

CLIFT, Norman Charles. b 21. Kelham Th Coll 40. **d** 45 **p** 46. C Leytonstone St Marg w St Columba *Chelmsf* 45-54; V 61-75; C-in-c Gt Ilford St Alb CD 54-58; V Gt Ilford St Alb 58-61; V Gt and Lt Bardfield 75-91; rtd 91; Perm to Offic *Chelmsf* from 91. *Squirrels, High Street, Great Chesterford, Saffron Walden, Essex CB10 1TL* Tel (01799) 531319

CLIFTON, Robert Walter. b 39. Solicitor. Westcott Ho Cam 82. **d** 84 **p** 85. C Bury St Edmunds St Geo *St E* 84-87; P-in-c Culford, W Stow and Wordwell 87-88; R Culford, W Stow and Wordwell w Flempton etc 88-95; P-in-c Fornham All SS and Fornham St Martin w Timworth 93-95; RD Thingoe 93-95; P-in-c Orford w Sudbourne, Chillesford, Butley and Iken from 95; RD Woodbridge from 96. *The Rectory, Orford, Woodbridge, Suffolk IP12 2NN* Tel (01394) 450336

CLIFTON, Canon Roger Gerald. b 45. ACA70 FCA. Sarum & Wells Th Coll 70. **d** 73 **p** 74. C Winterbourne *Bris* 73-76; P-in-c Brislington St Cuth 76-83; P-in-c Colerne w N Wraxall 83-95; RD Chippenham 88-94; Hon Can Bris Cathl from 94; TR Gtr Corsham from 95. *The Rectory, Newlands Road, Corsham, Wilts SN13 0BS* Tel (01249) 713232

CLIFTON-SMITH, Gregory James. b 52. GGSM73 Lon Univ TCert74 Golds Coll Lon BMus82. Sarum & Wells Th Coll 87. **d** 89 **p** 90. C Welling *S'wark* 89-93; V Tattenham Corner and Burgh Heath *Guildf* from 93. *St Mark's Vicarage, St Mark's Road, Epsom, Surrey KT18 5RD* Tel (01737) 353011

CLINCH, Christopher James. b 60. Nottm Univ BEd82 BTh89. Linc Th Coll 86. **d** 89 **p** 90. C Newc St Geo *Newc* 89-92; C Seaton Hirst 92-94; TV Ch the King in the Dio of Newc from 94. *The Vicarage, 2 East Acres, Dinnington, Newcastle upon Tyne NE13 7NA* Tel (01661) 871377

CLINCH, Kenneth Wilfred. b 22. Bps' Coll Cheshunt 62. **d** 64 **p** 65. C Old Shoreham *Chich* 64-67; C Lancing St Mich 67-73; R Upper St Leonards St Jo 73-88; rtd 88; Perm to Offic *Chich* from 88. *Brae Cottage, 193 Hastings Road, Battle, E Sussex TN33 0TP* Tel (01424) 774130

CLINES, Emma Christine. **d** 97. C Birm St Martin w Bordesley St Andr *Birm* from 97. *175 St Andrews Road, Bordesley, Birmingham B9 4NB* Tel 0121-771 0237

CLINES, Jeremy Mark Sebastian. **d** 97. C Birm St Martin w Bordesley St Andr *Birm* from 97. *175 St Andrews Road, Bordesley, Birmingham B9 4NB* Tel 0121-771 0237

CLITHEROW, Andrew. b 50. St Chad's Coll Dur BA72 Ex Univ MPhil87. Sarum & Wells Th Coll 78. **d** 79 **p** 80. Hon C Bedford Ch Ch *St Alb* 79-84; Asst Chapl Bedford Sch 79-84; Chapl Caldicott Sch Farnham Royal 84-85; C Penkridge w Stretton *Lich* 85-88; Min Acton Trussell w Bednall 85-88; Chapl Rossall Sch Fleetwood 89-94; V Scotforth *Blackb* from 94. *St Paul's Vicarage, 24 Scotforth Road, Lancaster LA1 4ST* Tel (01524) 32106

CLOCKSIN (née HOYLE), Mrs Pamela Margaret. b 61. Nottm Univ BA82. St Jo Coll Nottm 84. **d** 87 **p** 94. Par Dn Bulwell St Jo *S'well* 87-91; Cam Pastorate Chapl 91-95; Par Dn Cambridge H Trin w St Andr Gt *Ely* 91-92; C Cambridge H Trin 92-95; Perm to Offic from 95. *The Beeches, Manor Farm Court, Lower End, Swaffham Prior, Cambridge CB5 0LJ* Tel (01638) 743698

CLOCKSIN, Dr William Frederick. b 55. BA76 St Cross Coll Ox MA81 Trin Hall Cam MA87 PhD93. EAMTC 91. **d** 94 **p** 95. Asst Chapl Trin Hall Cam from 94. *Trinity Hall, Cambridge CB2 1TJ* Tel (01223) 332543 Fax 334678 E-mail wfc@cl.cam.ac.uk

CLODE, Arthur Raymond Thomas. b 35. Roch Th Coll 67. **d** 69 **p** 70. C Blackheath *Birm* 69-72; V Londonderry 73-75; R Bride *S & M* 75-79; UAE 80-83; Min Stewartly LEP 86-90; C Wootton *St Alb* 86-90; C St Alb St Paul 90-94; rtd 94. *Little Waggoners, The Spinney, Grayshott, Hindhead, Surrey GU26 6DY* Tel (01428) 605219

CLOETE, Richard James. b 47. AKC71. St Aug Coll Cant 72. **d** 72 **p** 73. C Redhill St Matt *S'wark* 72-76; V Streatham St Paul 76-84; P-in-c W Coker *B & W* 84-88; P-in-c Hardington Mandeville w E Chinnock and Pendomer 84-88; R W Coker w Hardington Mandeville, E Chinnock etc 88; R Wincanton 88-97; R Pen Selwood 88-97; Sec and Treas Dioc Hosp Chapl Fellowship 91-97. *25 Carlisle Mansions, Carlisle Place, London SW1P 1EZ* Tel 0171-834 1325

CLOGHER, Archdeacon of. *See* PRINGLE, The Ven Cecil Thomas

CLOGHER, Bishop of. *See* HANNON, The Rt Revd Brian Desmond Anthony

CLOGHER, Dean of. *See* MOORE, The Very Revd Thomas Robert

CLONMACNOISE, Dean of. *See* FURLONG, The Very Revd Andrew William Ussher

CLOSE, Brian Eric. b 49. St Chad's Coll Dur BA74 MA76. Ridley Hall Cam 74. **d** 76 **p** 77. C Far Headingley St Chad *Ripon* 76-79; C Harrogate St Wilfrid 79-80; C Harrogate St Wilfrid and St Luke 80-82; P-in-c Alconbury w Alconbury Weston *Ely* 82-83; V 83-86; P-in-c Buckworth 82-83; R 83-86; P-in-c Upton and Copmanford 82-83; Chapl Reed's Sch Cobham 86-96; Chapl Malvern Coll from 96. *The Chaplain's House, College Road, Malvern, Worcs WR14 3DD* Tel (01684) 892694 Fax 572398

CLOSS-PARRY, The Ven Selwyn. b 25. Univ of Wales (Lamp) BA50. St Mich Coll Llan 50. **d** 52 **p** 53. C Dwygyfylchi *Ban* 52-58; V Tryddyn *St As* 58-66; R Llangystennin 66-71; V Holywell 71-77; Can St As Cathl 76-82; Prec 82-84; Preb 82-90; V Colwyn 77-84; Adn St As 84-90; R Trefnant 84-90; rtd 91. *3 Llys Brompton, Brompton Avenue, Rhos-on-Sea LL28 4TB* Tel (01492) 545801

CLOTHIER, Gerald Harry. b 34. Oak Hill Th Coll 75. **d** 78 **p** 79. Hon C Highwood *Chelmsf* 78-79; Hon C Writtle w Highwood 79-83; P-in-c Westhall w Brampton and Stoven *St E* 83-86; TV

Beccles St Mich 86-93; R Rougham, Beyton w Hessett and Rushbrooke from 93. *The Rectory, Rougham, Bury St Edmunds, Suffolk IP30 9JJ* Tel (01359) 70250

CLOVER, Brendan David. b 58. LTCL74 G&C Coll Cam BA79 MA83. Ripon Coll Cuddesdon 79. **d** 82 **p** 83. C Friern Barnet St Jas *Lon* 82-85; C W Hampstead St Jas 85-87; Chapl Em Coll Cam 87-92; Dean Em Coll Cam 92-94; P-in-c St Pancras w St Jas and Ch Ch *Lon* from 94; P-in-c St Pancras H Cross w St Jude and St Pet from 96. *6 Sandwich Street, London WC1H 9EL* Tel 0171-388 1630

CLOWES, John. b 45. AKC67. **d** 68 **p** 69. C Corby St Columba *Pet* 68-71; R Itchenstoke w Ovington and Abbotstone *Win* 71-74; V Acton w Gt and Lt Waldingfield *St E* 74-80; Asst Dioc Chr Stewardship Adv 75-80; TV Southend St Jo w St Mark, All SS w St Fran etc *Chelmsf* 80-82; TV Southend 82-85; Ind Chapl 80-85; R Ashwick w Oakhill and Binegar *B & W* 85-91; P-in-c Brompton Regis w Upton and Skilgate from 91. *The Vicarage, Brompton Regis, Dulverton, Somerset TA22 9NN* Tel (013987) 239

CLOYNE, Dean of. *See* HILLIARD, The Very Revd George Percival St John

CLUCAS, Robert David (Bob). b 55. Cranmer Hall Dur. **d** 82 **p** 83. C Gateacre *Liv* 82-86; P-in-c Bishop's Itchington *Cov* 86-93; CPAS Staff from 93. *CPAS, Athena Drive, Tachbrook Park, Warwick CV34 6NG* Tel (01926) 334242 Fax 337613

CLUER, Donald Gordon. b 21. S'wark Ord Course 61. **d** 64 **p** 65. C Malden St Jas *S'wark* 64-68; C Bexhill St Pet *Chich* 68-73; V Shoreham Beach 73-77; V Heathfield St Rich 77-86; C Eastbourne St Mary 86-90; rtd 90; Perm to Offic *Ox* from 90. *10 Windsor Street, Oxford OX3 7AP* Tel (01865) 67270

CLUES, David Charles. b 66. K Coll Lon BD87. St Steph Ho Ox 88. **d** 90 **p** 91. C Notting Hill All SS w St Columb *Lon* 90-94; NSM from 94. *28 Barlby Road, London W10 6AR*

CLUETT, Michael Charles. b 53. Kingston Poly BSc78. St Steph Ho Ox 84. **d** 86 **p** 87. C Pontesbury I and II *Heref* 86-90; TV Wenlock from 90. *14 Stretton Road, Much Wenlock, Shropshire TF13 6AS* Tel (01952) 728211

CLULEE, Miss Elsie Ethel. b 18. St Andr Ho Portsm 46. **dss** 56 **d** 87. Stirchley *Birm* 66-87; Hon Par Dn 87-90; Perm to Offic from 90. *42 Woodbrooke Road, Birmingham B30 1UD* Tel 0121-472 2662

CLUNIE, Grace. b 60. Ulster Univ BA82 MA91 QUB DipLib85. CITC BTh95. **d** 95 **p** 96. C Newtownards *D & D* from 95. *10 Londonderry Road, Newtownards, Co Down BT23 3AY* Tel (01247) 814750

CLUTTERBUCK, Herbert Ivan. b 16. Ch Coll Cam BA38 MA42. Chich Th Coll 38. **d** 39 **p** 40. C Lamorbey H Trin *Roch* 39-41; Hon CF 41-44; Chapl and Sen Classics Master Wellingborough Sch 44-47; Chapl RN 47-62; V Lanteglos by Fowey *Truro* 62-66; Org Sec Ch Union 66-74; Chapl Qu Marg Sch Escrick Park 74-76; Chapl and Dir Relig Studies Roedean Sch Brighton 76-81; rtd 82; Master St Jo Hosp Lich 82-91. *7 Springfield Road, St Martin Field, East Looe, Cornwall PL13 1HB* Tel (01503) 263509

CLUTTERBUCK, Miss Marion Isobel. b 56. All Nations Chr Coll DipRS87 Oak Hill Th Coll BA91. **d** 92 **p** 94. C Lindfield *Chich* 92-96; TV Alderbury Team *Sarum* from 96. *The Vicarage, Common Road, Whiteparish, Salisbury SP5 2SU* Tel (01794) 884315

CLYDE, John. b 39. CITC BTh70. **d** 71 **p** 72. C Belfast St Aid *Conn* 71-74; I Belfast St Barn 74-80; I Belfast H Trin 80-89; Bp's C Acton w Drumbanagher *Arm* 89-94; I Desertlyn w Ballyeglish from 94. *24 Cookstown Road, Moneymore, Magherafelt, Co Londonderry BT45 7QF* Tel (01648) 748200

CLYNES, William. b 33. Sarum & Wells Th Coll 78. **d** 79 **p** 80. C Winterbourne *Bris* 79-83; TV Swindon St Jo and St Andr 83-91; rtd 91. *185A Claverham Road, Claverham, Bristol BS19 4LE*

COATES, Alan Thomas. b 55. St Jo Coll Nottm 87. **d** 89 **p** 90. C Heeley *Sheff* 89-90; C Bramley and Ravenfield 90-92; V Askern 92-96; Chapl RAF from 96. *Chaplaincy Services (RAF), HQ, Personnel and Training Command, RAF Innsworth, Gloucester GL3 1EZ* Tel (01452) 712612 ext 5164 Fax 510828

COATES, Christopher Ian. b 59. Qu Coll Birm 81. **d** 84 **p** 85. C Cottingham *York* 84-87; TV Howden TM 87-91; V Sherburn in Elmet 91-94; V Sherburn in Elmet w Saxton from 94. *The Vicarage, 2 Sir John's Lane, Sherburn-in-Elmet, Leeds LS25 6BJ* Tel (01977) 682122

COATES, Canon Francis Gustav. b 10. OBE63. G&C Coll Cam BA32 MA36. Ridley Hall Cam 32. **d** 52 **p** 54. Uganda 52-65; C Worthing St Paul *Chich* 65-68; P-in-c Wickmere w Wolterton and Lt Barningham *Nor* 68-71; R Heydon w Irmingland 68-82; P-in-c Booton w Brandiston 71-82; Hon Can Busoga from 81; rtd 82; Perm to Offic *Nor* 82-96. *13 Stuart Court, Recorder Road, Norwich NR1 1NP* Tel (01603) 664910

COATES, Ms Jean Margaret. b 47. Sussex Univ BSc68 Reading Univ PhD77 MIBiol CBiol. St Alb and Ox Min Course 93. **d** 96. C Wallingford w Crowmarsh Gifford etc *Ox* from 96. *23 Charter Way, Wallingford, Oxon OX10 0TD* Tel (01491) 836353

COATES, John David Spencer. b 41. Dur Univ BA64 DipTh66. Cranmer Hall Dur 64. **d** 66 **p** 67. C Chipping Campden w Ebrington *Glouc* 66-69; CF 69-96; rtd 96; Perm to Offic *B & W* from 96. *c/o Lloyds Bank PLC, 19 The Parade, Minehead, Somerset TA24 5LU*

COATES, Canon Kenneth Will. b 17. St Jo Coll Dur LTh45 BA46. Tyndale Hall Bris 39. **d** 42 **p** 43. C Daubhill *Man* 42-44; Perm to Offic *Bris* 44-47; C Cheadle *Ches* 47-49; V Preston All SS *Blackb* 49-60; TR St Helens St Helen *Liv* 60-88; Hon Can Liv Cathl 71-88; rtd 88; Perm to Offic *Liv* from 88. *122 Broadway, Eccleston, St Helens WA10 5DH* Tel (01744) 29629

COATES, Maxwell Gordon (Max). b 49. Lon Univ CertEd70 Open Univ BA83 ADEd87 UEA MA86. Trin Coll Bris DipTh77. **d** 77 **p** 78. C Blackheath Park St Mich *S'wark* 77-79; Chapl Greenwich Distr Hosp Lon 77-79; Asst Teacher Saintbridge Sch Glouc 79-81; Teacher Gaywood Park High Sch King's Lynn 81-85; NSM Lynn St Jo *Nor* 81-85; Dep Hd Teacher Winton Comp Sch Bournemouth 85-90; Hd Teacher St Mark's Comp Sch Bath from 90; NSM Canford Magna *Sarum* 85-86; NSM Stoke Gifford *Bris* 93-97; Perm to Offic *B & W* from 97. *3 Oakley Road, Wimborne, Dorset BH21 1QJ* Tel (01202) 883162

COATES, Nigel John. b 51. Reading Univ BSc MA. Trin Coll Bris. **d** 83 **p** 84. C Epsom St Martin *Guildf* 83-86; C Portswood Ch Ch *Win* 86-88; Chapl Southn Univ 89-97; Chapl Southn Inst of HE 89-95; P-in-c Freemantle from 97. *The Rectory, 129 Paynes Road, Southampton SO15 3BW* Tel (01703) 221804

COATES, Peter Frederick. b 50. K Coll Lon BD79 AKC79. St Steph Ho Ox 79. **d** 80 **p** 81. C Woodford St Barn *Chelmsf* 80-83; C E and W Keal *Linc* 83-86; R The Wainfleets and Croft 86-94; R The Wainfleet Gp from 94; RD Calcewaithe and Candleshoe from 92. *The Rectory, Vicarage Lane, Wainfleet St Mary, Skegness, Lincs PE24 4JJ* Tel (01754) 880401

COATES, Robert. b 63. Aston Tr Scheme 87 St Steph Ho Ox 89. **d** 92 **p** 93. C Heavitree w Ex St Paul *Ex* 92-95; Chapl RN from 95. *Royal Naval Chaplaincy Service, Room 203, Victory Building, HM Naval Base, Portsmouth PO1 3LS* Tel (01705) 727903 Fax 727112

COATES, Robert Charles (Bob). b 44. Open Univ BA76. Cant Sch of Min 83. **d** 86 **p** 87. C Deal St Leon and St Rich and Sholden *Cant* 86-89; V Loose from 89. *The Vicarage, 17 Linton Road, Loose, Maidstone, Kent ME15 0AG* Tel (01622) 743513

COATES, Stuart Murray. b 49. Lon Univ BA70 Edin Univ MTh91. Wycliffe Hall Ox 72. **d** 75 **p** 76. C Rainford *Liv* 75-78; C Orrell 78-79; V 79-86; Chapl Strathcarron Hospice Denny from 86; Hon C Stirling *Edin* 86-90; NSM Doune *St And* from 89; NSM Aberfoyle from 89. *Westwood Smithy, Chalmerston Road, Stirling FK9 4AG* Tel (01786) 860531

COATSWORTH, Nigel George. b 39. Trin Hall Cam BA61 MA. Cuddesdon Coll 61. **d** 63 **p** 64. C Hellesdon *Nor* 63-66; Ewell Monastery 66-80; TV Folkestone H Trin and St Geo w Ch Ch *Cant* 83-85; C Milton next Sittingbourne 85-86; P-in-c Selattyn *Lich* 86-91; P-in-c Weston Rhyn 88-91; R Weston Rhyn and Selattyn from 91. *The Rectory, Selattyn, Oswestry, Shropshire SY10 7DH* Tel (01691) 659755

COBB, Douglas Arthur. b 25. Kelham Th Coll 49. **d** 54 **p** 55. C Notting Hill St Mich and Ch Ch *Lon* 54-57; C Ruislip St Mary 57-63; V Kentish Town St Silas 63-87; P-in-c Kentish Town St Martin w St Andr 81-85; Chapl Convent of St Mary at the Cross Edgware 87-92; rtd 92. *Padre Pio House, 10 Buckingham Gardens, Edgware, Middx HA8 6NB* Tel 0181-951 1231

COBB, George Reginald. b 50. Oak Hill Th Coll BA81. **d** 81 **p** 82. C Ware Ch Ch *St Alb* 81-84; C Uphill *B & W* 84-89; R Alresford *Chelmsf* from 89. *The Rectory, St Andrew's Close, Alresford, Colchester CO7 8BL* Tel (01206) 822088

COBB, John Philip Andrew. b 43. Man Univ BSc65 New Coll Ox BA67 MA71. Wycliffe Hall Ox 66. **d** 68 **p** 69. Par Dn Reading St Jo *Ox* 68-71; Par Dn Romford Gd Shep Collier Row *Chelmsf* 71-73; SAMS from 74; Chile from 74. *Iglesia Anglicana del Chile, Casilla 50675, Correo Central, Santiago, Chile* Tel Santiago (2) 227-5713

COBB, Miss Marjorie Alice. b 24. St Chris Coll Blackheath IDC52. **dss** 61 **d** 87. CSA 56-85; rtd 85; Perm to Offic *Cant* from 87; Chapl Jes Hosp Cant from 90. *2 John Boys Wing, Jesus Hospital, Sturry Road, Canterbury, Kent CT1 1BS* Tel (01227) 472615

COBB, Mark Robert. b 64. Lanc Univ BSc86. Ripon Coll Cuddesdon 88. **d** 91 **p** 92. C Hampstead St Jo *Lon* 91-94; Asst Chapl Derbyshire R Infirmary NHS Trust 94-96; Chapl Palliative Care and Health Care Derbyshire R Infirmary NHS Trust from 96. *Chaplaincy Services, Derbyshire Royal Infirmary NHS Trust, London Road, Derby DE1 2QY* Tel (01332) 347141 Fax 295652

COBB, Canon Peter George. b 37. Ch Ch Ox BA59 MA63. St Steph Ho Ox 64. **d** 65 **p** 66. C Solihull *Birm* 65-69; Lib Pusey Ho 69-71; Sen Tutor St Steph Ho Ox 71-76; Cust Lib Pusey Ho 76-78; V Clandown *B & W* 78-83; V Midsomer Norton 78-83; V Midsomer Norton w Clandown 83-84; RD Midsomer Norton 83-84; V Clifton All SS w St Jo *Bris* from 84; Hon Can Bris Cathl from 92. *All Saints' Vicarage, 68 Pembroke Road, Bristol BS8 3ED* Tel 0117-974 1355

COBB, Peter Graham. b 27. St Jo Coll Cam BA48 MA52. Ridley Hall Cam 66. **d** 68 **p** 69. C Porthkerry *Llan* 68-71; P-in-c Penmark 71-72; V Penmark w Porthkerry 72-81; V Magor w Redwick and

Undy *Mon* 82-95; rtd 95. *2 Talycoed Court, Talycoed, Monmouth NP5 4HR* Tel (01600) 780309

COBERN, Canon Charles John Julian. b 14. Keble Coll Ox BA36 MA62. Cuddesdon Coll 36. **d** 37 **p** 38. C Apsley End *St Alb* 37-41; C Noel Park St Mark *Lon* 41-49; V Hitchin H Sav *St Alb* 49-68; RD Hitchin 62-68; V Woburn Sands 68-79; Hon Can St Alb 64-79; rtd 79; Perm to Offic *Chich* from 89. *Miles Court, Hereford Street, Brighton BN2 1JT* Tel (01273) 696017

COCHLIN, Maurice Reginald. b 19. ACP60 FFChM Sussex Univ CertEd70. Lambeth STh74 Chich Th Coll 70. **d** 70 **p** 71. C Rowlands Castle *Portsm* 70-72; Chapl Paulsgrove Sch Cosham 71; C Warblington and Emsworth *Portsm* 72-75; C S w N Bersted *Chich* 76-78; Hd Littlemead Upper Sch Chich 78-79; C Saltdean *Chich* 79-83; V Kirdford 83-88; rtd 88; Perm to Offic *Chich* from 88. *56 Farnhurst Road, Barnham, Bognor Regis, W Sussex PO22 0JW* Tel (01243) 553584

COCHRANE, Alan George. b 28. S'wark Ord Course. **d** 82 **p** 83. NSM Clapham Old Town *S'wark* 82-85; C Spalding St Jo w Deeping St Nicholas *Linc* 85-87; R Southery *Ely* from 87; V Fordham St Mary 87-91; R Hilgay from 87. *The Rectory, Hilgay, Downham Market, Norfolk PE38 0JL* Tel (01366) 384418

COCHRANE, Canon Kenneth Wilbur. b 27. TCD BA58 MA61 Trin Coll Newburgh PhD88. **d** 58 **p** 59. C Belfast St Aid *Conn* 58-61; C Belfast St Nic 61-62; C Lisburn Ch Ch 62-63; P-in-c Lisburn St Paul 63-65; I from 65; Can Belf Cathl from 86; Preb Clonmethan St Patr Cathl Dublin from 90. *St Paul's Rectory, 3 Ballinderry Road, Lisburn, Co Antrim BT28 1UD* Tel (01846) 663520

COCHRANE, Norman John Michael Antony Ferguson. b 24. QUB BA46. Linc Th Coll 49. **d** 51 **p** 52. C Headstone St Geo *Lon* 51-56; C Horsham *Chich* 56-76; V Aldwick 76-90; rtd 90; Perm to Offic *Guildf* from 93. *41 Grindstone Crescent, Knaphill, Woking, Surrey GU21 2RZ* Tel (01483) 487981

COCHRANE, Canon Roy Alan. b 25. AKC53. **d** 54 **p** 55. C Linc St Faith *Linc* 54-56; C Skegness 56-59; R Thurlby w Norton Disney 59-65; V Swinderby 59-65; Chapl HM Borstal Morton Hall 59-65; R N Coates *Linc* 65-69; Chapl RAF 65-69; V Marshchapel *Linc* 65-69; V Grainthorpe w Conisholme 65-69; V Glanford Bridge 69-89; Chapl Glanford Hosp 69-89; RD Yarborough 76-81; Can and Preb Linc Cathl from 77; Chapl and Warden St Anne's Bedehouses 89-93; rtd 90. *5 Chippendale Close, Doddington Park, Lincoln LN6 3PR*

COCKAYNE, Gordon. b 34. RMN73. **d** 92 **p** 93. NSM Owlerton *Sheff* from 92. *6 Austin Close, Loxley, Sheffield S6 6QD* Tel 0114-233 3057

COCKAYNE, Mark Gary. b 61. UEA LLB82. St Jo Coll Nottm BTh92 MA93. **d** 93 **p** 94. C Armthorpe *Sheff* 93-96; V Malin Bridge from 96. *St Polycarp's Vicarage, 33 Wisewood Lane, Sheffield S6 4WA* Tel 0114-234 3450

COCKBILL, Douglas John. b 53. Chicago Univ BA75. Gen Th Sem (NY) MDiv78. **d** 78 **p** 79. Virgin Is 79-80; Bahamas 80-83; USA 84-90; P-in-c Roxbourne St Andr *Lon* 90-92; V from 92. *St Andrew's Vicarage, Malvern Avenue, Harrow, Middx HA2 9ER* Tel 0181-422 3633

COCKBURN, Sidney. b 14. Leeds Univ BA36. Coll of Resurr Mirfield 36. **d** 38 **p** 40. C Hartlepool St Jas *Dur* 38-39; Hon C Roath St German *Llan* 39-40; C Gateshead St Cuth w St Paul *Dur* 40-42; C Newc St Mary *Newc* 42-43; RAFVR 43-47; C Heanor *Derby* 47-51; C-in-c Marlpool 47-51; V Long Eaton St Jo 51-85; rtd 85; Perm to Offic *Derby* from 85. *10 Poplar Road, Breaston, Derby DE7 3BH* Tel (01332) 872363

COCKCROFT, Basil Stanley. b 26. CEng MICE Leeds Univ BSc49. Wells Th Coll 64. **d** 66 **p** 67. C Featherstone *Wakef* 66-69; C Norton St Mary *Dur* 69-71; P-in-c Eldon 71-75; NSM Elland *Wakef* 75-92; rtd 91. *9 Dene Close, South Parade, Elland, W Yorkshire HX5 0NS* Tel (01422) 374465

COCKE, James Edmund. b 26. Wadh Coll Ox BA50 MA55. Wells Th Coll 50. **d** 52 **p** 53. C Christchurch *Win* 52-57; V Highfield *Ox* from 57; Chapl Wingfield-Morris Hosp Ox 57-90; Chapl Nuff Orthopaedic Cen Ox from 90. *All Saints' Vicarage, 85 Old Road, Oxford OX3 7LB* Tel (01865) 62536

COCKELL, Ms Helen Frances. b 69. Trin Hall Cam BA90 MA94. Qu Coll Birm BD94. **d** 95. C Bracknell *Ox* from 95. *15 Oakwood Road, Bracknell, Berks RG12 2SP* Tel (01344) 51952

COCKELL, Timothy David (Tim). b 66. Qu Coll Birm BTh95. **d** 95 **p** 96. C Bracknell *Ox* from 95. *15 Oakwood Road, Bracknell, Berks RG12 2SP* Tel (01344) 51952

COCKER, Frances Rymer (Mother Frances Anne). **d** 95. *St Denys Convent, Vicarage Street, Warminster, Wilts BA12 8JD* Tel (01985) 213020

COCKERELL, David John. b 47. Univ of Wales (Cardiff) BA71 Univ of Wales (Swansea) MA74 Qu Coll Cam BA75. Westcott Ho Cam 73. **d** 76 **p** 77. C Chapel Allerton *Ripon* 76-79; C Farnley 79-81; TV Hitchin *St Alb* 81-89; TV Dorchester *Ox* 89-92; Adult Educn and Tr Officer *Ely* from 92. *1 Granta Close, Witchford, Ely, Cambs CB6 2HR* Tel (01353) 669460

COCKERTON, Canon John Clifford Penn. b 27. Liv Univ BA48 St Cath Soc Ox BA54 MA58. Wycliffe Hall Ox 51. **d** 54 **p** 55. C St Helens St Helen *Liv* 54-58; Tutor Cranmer Hall Dur 58-60; Chapl 60-63; Warden 68-70; Vice-Prin St Jo Coll Dur 63-70; Prin 70-78; R Wheldrake *York* 78-84; R Wheldrake w Thorganby 84-92; Can and Preb York Minster 87-92; rtd 92. *50 Allerton Drive, Nether Poppleton, York YO2 6NW* Tel (01904) 789287

COCKERTON, Thomas Charles (Tom). b 24. **d** 88 **p** 90. NSM Bermondsey St Mary w St Olave, St Jo etc *S'wark* 88-94; Perm to Offic from 94. *30 Carrick Court, Kennington Park Road, London SE11 4EE* Tel 0171-735 6966

COCKETT, Elwin Wesley. b 59. Aston Tr Scheme 86 Oak Hill Th Coll DipHE90 BA91. **d** 91 **p** 92. C Chadwell Heath *Chelmsf* 91-94; Chapl W Ham United Football Club from 92; C Harold Hill St Paul 94-95; P-in-c 95-97; V from 97. *St Paul's Vicarage, Redcar Road, Romford RM3 9PT* Tel (014023) 41225

COCKING, Martyn Royston. b 53. Trin Coll Bris 83. **d** 85 **p** 86. C Weston-super-Mare Cen Par *B & W* 85-88; C Kingswood *Bris* 88-89; TV 89-93; V Pill w Easton in Gordano and Portbury *B & W* 93-96. *68 Friary Grange Park, Winterbourne, Bristol BS17 1NB* Tel (01454) 886771

COCKMAN, David Willis. b 32. Ex & Truro NSM Scheme. **d** 82 **p** 83. Warden Mercer Ho 82-97; NSM Exwick *Ex* 82-86; Lic to Offic 86-97; rtd 97. *4 The Fairway, Pennsylvania, Exeter EX4 5ZW*

✠**COCKS, The Rt Revd Francis William.** b 13. CB59. St Cath Coll Cam BA35 MA43. Westcott Ho Cam 35. **d** 37 **p** 37 **c** 70. C Portswood Ch Ch *Win* 37-39; Chapl RAFVR 39-45; Chapl RAF 45-50; Asst Chapl-in-Chief RAF 50-59; Chapl-in-Chief RAF 59-65; QHC 59-65; Can and Preb Linc Cathl *Linc* 59-65; R Wolverhampton St Pet *Lich* 65-70; RD Wolverhampton 65-70; P-in-c Wolverhampton All SS 66-70; P-in-c Wolverhampton St Geo 67-70; Preb Lich Cathl 68-70; Suff Bp Shrewsbury 70-80; rtd 80; Perm to Offic *St E* from 80. *41 Beatrice Avenue, Felixstowe, Suffolk IP11 9HB* Tel (01394) 283574

COCKS, Howard Alan Stewart. b 46. St Barn Coll Adelaide 78 ACT ThD. **d** 80 **p** 81. Australia 80-82; C Prestbury *Glouc* 82-87; P-in-c Stratton w Baunton 87-94; P-in-c N Cerney w Bagendon 91-94; R Stratton, N Cerney, Baunton and Bagendon from 95. *The Rectory, 94 Gloucester Road, Cirencester, Glos GL7 2LJ* Tel (01285) 653359

COCKS, Canon John Cramer. b 14. Lon Univ BD50. ALCD50. **d** 50 **p** 51. C Iver *Ox* 50-53; CMJ 53-56; V Woodford Halse *Pet* 56-62; V Rothwell w Orton 62-83; rtd 83; Perm to Offic *Pet* 85-94. *30 Playford Close, Rothwell, Kettering, Northants NN14 6TU* Tel (01536) 418319

COCKS, Michael Dearden Somers. b 28. Univ of NZ MA50 St Cath Coll Ox BA53 MA57. **d** 53 **p** 54. New Zealand 53-93; Chapl Gothenburg w Halmstad, Jonkoping etc *Eur* from 93. *Norra Liden 15, 411-18 Gothenburg, Sweden* Tel Gothenburg (31) 711-1915

COCKSEDGE, Hugh Francis. b 26. Magd Coll Cam BA50 MA52. **d** 88 **p** 89. NSM Alton All SS *Win* 88-89; Lic to Offic 89-91; Chapl Ankara *Eur* 91-96; rtd 96. *Stancomb, Stancomb Lane, Medstead, Alton, Hants GU34 5QB* Tel (01420) 563624

COCKSWORTH, Dr Christopher John. b 59. Man Univ BA80 PGCE81 PhD89. St Jo Coll Nottm 84. **d** 88 **p** 89. C Epsom Common Ch Ch *Guildf* 88-92; Chapl R Holloway and Bedf New Coll 92-97; Dir S Th Educn and Tr Scheme from 97. *19 The Close, Salisbury SP1 2EE, or 10 Marlborough Road, Sailsbury SP1 3JH* Tel (01722) 412996 or 329880 Fax 338508

CODLING, Timothy Michael (Tim). b 62. Trin Coll Ox BA84 MA91. St Steph Ho Ox 89. **d** 91 **p** 92. C N Shoebury *Chelmsf* 91-97; V Tilbury Docks from 97. *St John's Vicarage, Dock Road, Tilbury, Essex RM18 7PP* Tel (01375) 842417

CODRINGTON, Canon George Herbert. b 13. ALCD34 St Jo Coll Dur BA36 LTh36 MA39. **d** 36 **p** 37. C Finchley H Trin *Lon* 36-40; C Belmont 40; Chapl RNVR 40-46; Chapl RN 46-48; C Birm St Martin *Birm* 48-52; Australia 52-65; Adn Kew 60-62; Adn Brighton 62-65; V Melton Mowbray w Thorpe Arnold *Leic* 65-80; RD Framland II 65-79; Hon Can Leic Cathl 70-80; rtd 81; C Welsh Newton w Llanrothal *Heref* 81-85; C St Weonards w Orcop, Garway, Tretire etc 85-87. *Glebe Cottage, Staunton-on-Arrow, Leominster, Herefordshire HR6 9HR* Tel (01544) 388378

CODRINGTON CLARKE, Harold Godfrey. b 26. S'wark Ord Course 71. **d** 74 **p** 75. C Redhill St Jo *S'wark* 74-79; P-in-c Blindley Heath 79-96; rtd 96. *The Vicarage, Blindley Heath, Lingfield, Surrey RH7 6JR* Tel (01342) 832337

COE, Andrew Derek John. b 58. Nottm Univ BTh86. St Jo Coll Nottm 83. **d** 86 **p** 87. C Pype Hayes *Birm* 86-88; C Erdington St Barn 88-91; C Birm St Martin w Bordesley St Andr 91-96; P-in-c Hamstead St Bernard 96; V from 96. *The Vicarage, 147 Hamstead Road, Great Barr, Birmingham B43 5BB* Tel 0121-358 1286

COE, David. b 45. **d** 69 **p** 70. C Belfast St Matt *Conn* 69-72; C Belfast St Donard *D & D* 72-75; I Tullylish 75-81; I Lurgan St Jo 81-89; I Ballymacarrett St Patr from 89. *St Patrick's Vicarage, 155 Upper Newtownards Road, Belfast BT4 3HX* Tel (01232) 657180

COE, John Norris. b 31. Oak Hill Th Coll 57. **d** 59 **p** 60. C Stoughton *Guildf* 59-61; C Guernsey St Michel du Valle *Win* 61-63; C Norbiton *S'wark* 63-67; V Bath Widcombe *B & W* 67-84; R Publow w Pensford, Compton Dando and Chelwood 84-96; rtd 96; Perm to Offic *B & W* from 96. *11 Porlock Road, Bath BA2 5PG* Tel (01225) 840248

COE, Stephen David. b 49. Ch Coll Cam MA72. Ox Min Course CBTS93. **d** 93 **p** 94. NSM Abingdon *Ox* 93-97; Assoc Min Ox St Andr from 97. *9 Apppleford Drive, Abingdon, Oxon OX14 2DB* Tel (01235) 523228

COEKIN, Philip James. b 64. Wye Coll Lon BScAgr87. Oak Hill Th Coll BA93. **d** 96 **p** 97. C Eastbourne All SS *Chich* from 96. *1F Grassington Road, Eastbourne, E Sussex BN20 7BP* Tel (01323) 721231

COEKIN, Richard John. b 61. Solicitor 86 Jes Coll Cam BA83 MA87. Wycliffe Hall Ox 89. **d** 91 **p** 92. C Cheadle *Ches* 91-95; Hon C Wimbledon Em Ridgway Prop Chpl *S'wark* from 95. *107 Merton Hall Road, London SW19 3PY* Tel 0181-542 8739

COFFEY, Hubert William (Bill). b 15. MBE46. TCD BA37 MA40. TCD Div Sch Div Test38. **d** 38 **p** 39. C Errigle Keerogue w Ballygawley and Killeshil *Arm* 38-41; Chapl RN 41-47; I Milltown *Arm* 47-52; Australia from 53; rtd 80. *23 Hawthorn Avenue, Caulfield North, Victoria, Australia 3161* Tel Melbourne (3) 9527 7875

COFFIN, Stephen. b 52. Pemb Coll Ox BA74 MA79. Trin Coll Bris 74. **d** 77 **p** 78. C Illogan *Truro* 77-80; C Liskeard w St Keyne and St Pinnock 80-82; C Liskeard w St Keyne, St Pinnock and Morval 82; CMS 82-86; Burundi 82-86; V St Germans *Truro* from 86. *The Vicarage, Quay Road, St Germans, Saltash, Cornwall PL12 5LY* Tel (01503) 30275

✠**COGGAN of Canterbury and Sissinghurst, The Most Revd and Rt Hon Lord (Frederick Donald).** b 09. PC61. St Jo Coll Cam BA31 MA35 Leeds Univ Hon DD58 Cam Univ Hon DD62 Aber Univ Hon DD63 Tokyo Univ Hon DD63 Lanc Univ Hon DLitt67 Liv Univ Hon LLD72 Man Univ Hon DD72 Kent Univ Hon DCL75 York Univ DUniv75. Wycliffe Coll Toronto BD41 Hon DD44 Lambeth DD57 Gen Th Sem (NY) Hon STD67 Wycliffe Hall Ox 34. **d** 34 **p** 35 **c** 56. C Islington St Mary *Lon* 34-37; Canada 37-44; Prin Lon Coll of Div 44-56; Bp Bradf 56-61; Abp York 61-74; Abp Cant 74-80; FKC from 75; rtd 80; Asst Bp Cant 80-88. *28 Lions Hall, St Swithun Street, Winchester SO23 9HW* Tel (01962) 864289

COGGINS, Edwin Stanley Claude. b 14. Bris Univ BSc36 DipEd37. Leic Dioc Th Course 63. **d** 64 **p** 65. Hon C Knighton St Mary Magd *Leic* 64-72; V Barlestone 72-77; P-in-c E w W Beckham *Nor* 78-84; rtd 84; Perm to Offic *Nor* 84-96. *21 Caxton Park, Beeston Regis, Sheringham, Norfolk NR26 8ST* Tel (01263) 824119

COGGINS, Glenn. b 60. Warw Univ BA81. St Jo Coll Dur CTM95. **d** 95 **p** 96. C Cley Hill Warminster *Sarum* from 95. *39 Manor Gardens, Warminster, Wilts BA12 8PN* Tel (01985) 214953

COGGINS, Richard James. b 29. Ex Coll Ox BA50 MA54 DipTh53 BD75. St Steph Ho Ox 52. **d** 54 **p** 55. C Withycombe Raleigh *Ex* 54-57; Tutor St Steph Ho Ox 57-60; Chapl 60-62; Asst Chapl Ex Coll Ox 57-62; Chapl Magd Coll Ox 60-62; Lic to Offic *Lon* 64-94; Sub-Warden K Coll Lon 62-67; Lect 62-81; Sen Lect 81-94; rtd 94. *3 de Mowbray Way, Lymington, Hants SO41 3PD* Tel (01590) 673626

COGHLAN, Patrick John. b 47. Down Coll Cam BA(Econ)69 Nottm Univ MA73. St Jo Coll Nottm LTh72. **d** 73 **p** 74. C Crookes St Thos *Sheff* 73-78; Brazil 78-92; V Anston *Sheff* from 92. *The Vicarage, 17 Rackford Road, Anston, Sheffield S31 7DE* Tel (01909) 563447

COGMAN, Canon Frederick Walter. b 13. Lon Univ BD38 AKC38. **d** 38 **p** 39. C Upton cum Chalvey *Ox* 38-42; Chapl St Geo Sch Harpenden 42-48; R Guernsey St Martin *Win* 48-76; Dean Guernsey 67-78; Hon Can Win Cathl 67-79; R Guernsey St Peter Port 76-78; rtd 78; Perm to Offic *Win* from 78. *Oriana Lodge, Les Fontenelles, Forest, Guernsey GY8 0BL* Tel (01481) 64940

COHEN, Canon Clive Ronald Franklin. b 46. ACIB71. Sarum & Wells Th Coll 79. **d** 81 **p** 82. C Esher *Guildf* 81-85; R Winterslow *Sarum* from 85; RD Alderbury 89-93; Can and Preb Sarum Cathl from 92. *The Rectory, Winterslow, Salisbury SP5 1RE* Tel (01980) 862231

COHEN, David Mervyn Stuart. b 42. Sydney Univ BA63 MA78. **d** 67 **p** 68. Mauritius 67-69; New Zealand 70-72; Regional Sec (Africa) Bible Soc 73-75; Australia 75-85; Gen Dir Scripture Union (England and Wales) 86-93; Perm to Offic *Lon* 92-94. *75 The Heights, London SE7 8JQ* Tel 0181-853 2257

COHEN, Ian Geoffrey Holland. b 51. Nottm Univ BA74. Ripon Coll Cuddesdon 77. **d** 79 **p** 80. C Sprowston *Nor* 79-83; TV Wallingford w Crowmarsh Gifford etc *Ox* 83-88; V Chalgrove w Berrick Salome from 88. *The Vicarage, 58 Brinkinfield Road, Chalgrove, Oxford OX44 7QX* Tel (01865) 890392

COHEN, Malcolm Arthur. b 38. Canberra Coll of Min DipTh79. **d** 78 **p** 79. Australia 79-84; Chapl Asst Thurrock Hosp 84-86; Hon Chapl ATC from 86; R Stifford *Chelmsf* 84-92; P-in-c Mayland 92-95; P-in-c Steeple 92-95; C Prittlewell from 95. *St Stephen's Vicarage, 213 Manners Way, Southend-on-Sea SS2 6QS* Tel (01702) 341402

COKE, William Robert Francis. b 46. St Edm Hall Ox BA68 MA79 Lon Univ BD78. Trin Coll Bris 75. **d** 79 **p** 80. C Blackb Sav *Blackb* 79-83; V Fence in Pendle 83-84; P-in-c Newchurch-in-Pendle 83-84; V Fence and Newchurch-in-Pendle 84-89; Switzerland 89-95; Chapl Ardingly Coll Haywards Heath 95-96; V Ambleside w Brathay *Carl* from 96. *The Vicarage, Millans Park, Ambleside, Cumbria LA22 9AD* Tel (01539) 433205

COKER, Alexander Bryan (Alex). b 48. MCollP84 K Coll Lon BD75 AKC76 MTh76 ThD81 MA84 MEd87. St Aug Coll Cant 75. **d** 86 **p** 87. Overstone Coll Northn 82-87; NSM Belsize Park *Lon* 86-90; Thames Educn Inst 87-90; C Croydon Woodside *S'wark* 90-93; C Cheam Common St Phil 93-94. *Address temp unknown*

COKER, Barry Charles Ellis. b 46. K Coll Lon BD69 AKC69. **d** 70 **p** 71. C Newton Aycliffe *Dur* 70-74; Trinidad and Tobago 74-78; R Matson *Glouc* 78-90; V Stroud and Uplands w Slad from 90; RD Bisley from 94. *The Vicarage, Church Street, Stroud, Glos GL5 1JL* Tel (01453) 764555

COLBOURN, John Martin Claris. b 30. Selw Coll Cam BA52 MA56. Ridley Hall Cam 52. **d** 54 **p** 55. C Cheadle *Ches* 54-58; V Trowbridge St Thos *Sarum* 59-65; V Fareham St Jo *Portsm* 65-87; V Crich *Derby* 87-95; RD Alfreton 88-95; rtd 95; Perm to Offic *Derby* from 95. *Stanton View Cottage, Dale Road North, Darley Dale, Matlock, Derbyshire DE4 2HX* Tel (01629) 733284

COLBY, David Allan. b 33. Ox NSM Course 78. **d** 81 **p** 82. NSM Gt Faringdon w Lt Coxwell *Ox* 81-83; TV Ewyas Harold w Dulas, Kenderchurch etc *Heref* 83-84; TV Ewyas Harold w Dulas, Kenderchurch etc 84-91; V Westbury-on-Severn w Flaxley and Blaisdon *Glouc* from 91. *The Vicarage, Westbury-on-Severn, Glos GL14 1LW* Tel (01452) 760592

COLBY, Preb Robert James. b 31. Roch Th Coll 62. **d** 64 **p** 65. C Luton Ch Ch *St Alb* 64-68; C Chirbury *Heref* 68-70; P-in-c 70-78; V 78-79; P-in-c Trelystan 70-78; V 78-79; P-in-c Marton 70-78; V 78-79; P-in-c Whitbourne 79-82; P-in-c Tedstone Delamere and Edvin Loach etc 80-82; P-in-c Upper Sapey w Wolferlow 80-82; R Edvin Loach w Tedstone Delamere etc 82-96; Preb Heref Cathl 94-96; rtd 96. *20 Colsons Way, Olney, Bucks MK46 5EQ* Tel (01234) 713593

COLCHESTER, Archdeacon of. *See* WALLACE, The Ven Martin William

COLCHESTER, Area Bishop of. *See* HOLLAND, The Rt Revd Edward

✠**COLCLOUGH, The Rt Revd Michael John.** b 44. Leeds Univ BA69. Cuddesdon Coll 69. **d** 71 **p** 72. C Burslem St Werburgh *Lich* 71-75; C Ruislip St Mary *Lon* 75-79; P-in-c Hayes St Anselm 79-85; V 85-86; AD Hillingdon 85-92; P-in-c Uxbridge St Marg 86-88; P-in-c Uxbridge St Andr w St Jo 86-88; TR Uxbridge 88-92; Adn Northolt 92-94; P-in-c St Vedast w St Mich-le-Querne etc 94-96; Bp's Sen Chapl 94-96; Dean of Univ Chapls from 94; Dep P in O from 95; Area Bp Kensington *Lon* from 96. *19 Campden Hill Square, London W8 8JY* Tel 0171-727 9818 Fax 229 3651

COLDERWOOD, Alfred Victor. b 26. Bps' Coll Cheshunt 58. **d** 60 **p** 61. C Oakwood St Thos *Lon* 60-63; C Enfield St Jas 63-66; V Edmonton St Aldhelm 66-91; rtd 91; Perm to Offic *Cant* from 91. *11 Mill Row, Birchington, Kent CT7 9TT* Tel (01843) 41544

COLDHAM, Miss Geraldine Elizabeth. b 35. FLA66 Trevelyan Coll Dur BA80. Cranmer Hall Dur 82. **dss** 83 **d** 87 **p** 94. S Normanton *Derby* 83-87; Par Dn 87; Par Dn Barking St Marg w St Patr *Chelmsf* 87-90; Par Dn Stifford 90-94; C 94-95; rtd 95. *6 Metcalfe Close, Abingdon, Oxon OX14 5TH* Tel (01235) 536194

COLDWELLS, Canon Alan Alfred. b 30. Univ Coll Ox BA55 MA57. Wells Th Coll 53. **d** 55 **p** 56. C Rugby St Andr *Cov* 55-62; V Sprowston *Nor* 62-73; R Beeston St Andr 62-73; RD Nor N 70-72; R Rugby St Andr *Cov* 73-82; TR 83-87; RD Rugby 73-78; Hon Can Cov Cathl 83-87; Can and Treas Windsor 87-95; rtd 95. *26 King Edward Street, Slough SL1 2QS* Tel (01753) 538589

COLE, Adrian Peter. *See* ROBBINS-COLE, Adrian Peter

COLE, Canon Alan John. b 35. Cam Univ CCouns90. Bps' Coll Cheshunt 63. **d** 66 **p** 67. C Boreham Wood All SS *St Alb* 66-69; C St Alb St Mich 69-72; V Redbourn 72-80; R Thorley w Bishop's Stortford H Trin 80-87; Chapl St Edw K and Martyr Cam *Ely* 87-94; Chapl Arthur Rank Hospice Cam 87-94; SSF from 88; P-in-c Gamlingay w Hatley St Geo and E Hatley *Ely* from 94; Hon Can Ely Cathl from 96. *The Rectory, Stocks Lane, Gamlingay, Sandy, Beds SG19 3JP* Tel (01767) 651204

COLE, Alan Michael. b 40. Melbourne Univ DipEd74 BA74. ACT DipTh67. **d** 66 **p** 67. Australia 66-75 and from 90; Chapl Bp Otter Coll Chich 76-77; Chapl Ardingly Coll Haywards Heath 77-82; Chapl Bonn w Cologne *Eur* 82-86; Chapl Helsinki w Moscow 86-90. *St Peter's Rectory, PO Box 67, Dimboola, Victoria, Australia 3414* Tel Ballarat (53) 891850

COLE, Brian Robert Arthur. b 35. Nottm Univ BA57. Ridley Hall Cam 59. **d** 61 **p** 62. C Tye Green w Netteswell *Chelmsf* 61-64; C Keighley *Bradf* 64-67; Chapl Halifax Gen Hosp 67-73; V Copley *Wakef* 67-73; R Gt w Lt Dunham *Nor* 73-82; R Gt w Lt Fransham 74-82; P-in-c Sporle w Gt and Lt Palgrave 81-82; R Gt and Lt Dunham w Gt and Lt Fransham and Sporle from 83; RD Brisley and Elmham from 93. *The Rectory, Great Dunham, King's Lynn, Norfolk PE32 2LQ* Tel (01328) 701466

COLE, Charles Vincent. b 26. Kelham Th Coll 47. **d** 51 **p** 52. C Harton *Dur* 51-54; C Gateshead St Jas 54-56; V Blackhall 56-91; rtd 91; Perm to Offic *Wakef* from 91. *66 Scott Green Crescent, Gildersome, Leeds LS27 7DF* Tel 0113-253 0021

COLE, Canon David. b 40. Qu Coll Birm 66. **d** 66 **p** 67. C Kensington St Helen w H Trin *Lon* 66-69; C Altham w Clayton le Moors *Blackb* 69-72; P-in-c Preston St Luke 72-75; V Inskip 75-80; C-in-c Chelmsley Wood St Aug CD *Birm* 80-87; C Cannock *Lich* 87-93; I Kinneigh Union *C, C & R* from 93; Preb Cork Cathl from 96; Preb Ross Cathl from 96. *The Rectory, Ballineen, Co Cork, Irish Republic* Tel Clonakilty (23) 47047

COLE, David Henry. b 30. San Francisco Th Sem DMin87 ALCD56. **d** 56 **p** 57. C Ashtead *Guildf* 56-59; C Farnham 59-60; Canada from 60. *10922 79A Avenue, Delta, British Columbia, Canada, V4C 1T4* Tel New Westminster (604) 596-4987 Fax Toronto (416) 340-9755

COLE, Canon Donald Robertson. b 24. Edin Th Coll 57. **d** 59 **p** 60. C Edin Ch Ch *Edin* 59-62; R Lasswade 62-69; R Edin St Cuth 69-94; Hon Can St Mary's Cathl from 91; rtd 94. *92 Spottiswoode Street, Edinburgh EH9 1DJ* Tel 0131-447 9230

COLE, Guy Spenser. b 63. Univ of Wales (Ban) BA84 Jes Coll Cam BA88. Westcott Ho Cam 85. **d** 88 **p** 89. C Eastville St Anne w St Mark and St Thos *Bris* 88-92; P-in-c Penhill 92-95; V from 95. *The Vicarage, Bremhill Close, Penhill, Swindon SN2 5LJ* Tel (01793) 721921

COLE, Henry Frederick Charles. b 23. ALCD52. **d** 52 **p** 53. C Bexleyheath Ch Ch *Roch* 52-55; C-in-c Wigmore w Hempstead CD 55-59; V Lawkholme *Bradf* 59-67; Ind Chapl *Sheff* 67-72; V Wadsley 72-88; RD Hallam 83-87; rtd 88; Perm to Offic *Sheff* from 88. *Julians, 217 Tullibardine Road, Sheffield S11 7GQ* Tel 0114-268 4719

COLE, John Charles. b 22. CQSW70. EMMTC CPTS82. **d** 82 **p** 83. NSM Skirbeck H Trin *Linc* from 82. *27 Blackthorn Lane, Boston, Lincs PE21 9BG* Tel (01205) 366255

COLE, John Gordon. b 43. Magd Coll Cam BA65 MA69. Cuddesdon Coll 66. **d** 68 **p** 69. C Leeds St Pet *Ripon* 68-71; C Moor Allerton 71-75; P-in-c Pendleton *Blackb* 75-86; Dioc Communications Officer 75-86; Dioc Missr *Linc* from 86. *Pelham House, Little Lane, Wrawby, Brigg, S Humberside DN20 8RW* Tel (01652) 657484

COLE, John Spensley. b 39. FCA65 Clare Coll Cam BA62 MA66 Nottm Univ DipTh79. Linc Th Coll 78. **d** 80 **p** 81. C Cowes St Mary *Portsm* 80-83; C Portchester 83-87; V Modbury *Ex* 87-95; R Aveton Gifford 87-95; TR Modbury, Bigbury, Ringmore w Kingston etc from 95. *The Vicarage, Modbury, Ivybridge, Devon PL21 0TA* Tel (01548) 830260

COLE, Lawrence Howard. b 09. ALCD39 Dur Univ BA47. **d** 39 **p** 40. C Bermondsey St Mary w St Olave and St Jo *S'wark* 39-42; C Watford *St Alb* 42-43; CF (EC) 43-46; C Dur St Nic *Dur* 46-47; R Hawkwell *Chelmsf* 47-51; V Bethnal Green St Jas Less *Lon* 51-60; Chapl Lon Chest Hosp 51-60; V Cogges *Ox* 60-77; rtd 77; Perm to Offic *Worc* from 77. *Perrins House, Moorlands Road, Malvern, Worcs WR14 2TZ* Tel (01684) 563732

COLE, Michael Berkeley. b 44. **d** 72 **p** 73. C Shepshed *Leic* 72-76; V Leic St Chad 76-79; NSM Painswick w Sheepscombe *Glouc* 94-97; NSM Painswick w Sheepscombe and Cranham from 97. *The Barn, Well Farm, Wick Street, Painswick, Glos GL6 7QR* Tel (01452) 812824

COLE, Dr Michael George. b 35. CD75. Wesley Th Sem Washington DMin88 Kelham Th Coll 56 Lich Th Coll 57. **d** 60 **p** 61. C Doncaster Ch Ch *Sheff* 60-63; Chapl RAF 63-68; Canada 68-82; USA from 82. *484 Mountain Road, Halifax, Virginia 24558-2171, USA* Tel Norfolk (804) 476-6473 E-mail ugthorpe@halifax.com

COLE, Canon Michael John. b 34. St Pet Hall Ox BA56 MA60. Ridley Hall Cam 56. **d** 58 **p** 59. C Finchley Ch Ch *Lon* 58; C Leeds St Geo *Ripon* 58-61; Travelling Sec IVF 61-64; V Crookes St Thos *Sheff* 64-71; R Rusholme H Trin *Man* 71-75; V Woodford Wells *Chelmsf* from 75; Chapl Leytonstone Ho Hosp from 85; Hon Can Chelmsf Cathl *Chelmsf* from 89. *All Saints' Vicarage, 4 Inmans Row, Woodford Green, Essex IG8 0NH* Tel 0181-504 0266

COLE, Mrs Norma Joan. b 46. EAMTC 93. **d** 96 **p** 97. C Ipswich St Mary at Stoke w St Pet *St E* from 96. *4 The Chestnuts, Ipswich IP2 9TB* Tel (01473) 687259

COLE, Canon Peter George Lamont. b 27. Pemb Coll Cam BA49 MA52. Cuddesdon Coll 50. **d** 52 **p** 53. C Aldershot St Mich *Guildf* 52-55; S Rhodesia 55-65; V Bromley St Andr *Roch* 65-72; V Folkestone St Mary and St Eanswythe *Cant* 72-87; Hon Can Cant Cathl 80-87; V E and W Worldham, Hartley Mauditt w Kingsley etc *Win* 87-92; RD Alton 89-92; rtd 92; RD Petworth *Chich* 94-95; Perm to Offic from 95. *Marula Cottage, Lower Street, Fittleworth, Pulborough, W Sussex RH20 1JE* Tel (01798) 865540

COLE, Richard Leslie. b 08. Ball Coll Ox BA31 MA35. St Steph Ho Ox DipTh32. **d** 32 **p** 33. C Portsea N End St Mark *Portsm* 32-34; C Gillingham St Mary *Roch* 35-44; Chapl RNVR 44-46; Vice-Prin Chich Th Coll 46-48; Lic to Offic *Chich* 46-48; Perm to Offic *Llan* 48-50; Lect St Mich Coll Llan 49-56; C Llanblethian w Cowbridge *Llan* 50-56; C Wilmington *York* 56-61; Guyana 61-84; rtd 84; Perm to Offic *Llan* 84-93. *Ellesborough Manor, Butlers Cross, Aylesbury, Bucks HP17 0XF* Tel (01296) 696817

COLE, Canon Robert Alan. b 23. TCD BA44 MA46 PhD48 Lon Univ BD49 MTh51. Oak Hill Th Coll 46. **d** 50 **p** 51. C Deptford St Luke *S'wark* 50-51; CMS 51-61; Australia 61-62 and 69-88 and from 94; Hon Can Sydney 79-94; Singapore 62-68 and 88-94; rtd 94. *1/20 Musgrave Street, Mosman, NSW, Australia 2088* Tel Sydney (2) 9960 3161

COLE, Timothy Alexander Robertson. b 60. Aber Univ MA83 Edin Univ BD86. Edin Th Coll 83. **d** 86 **p** 87. C Dunfermline *St And* 86-89; Vice-Provost St Andr Cathl Inverness *Mor* 89-90; R Inverness St Andr 89-90; R Edin St Mich and All SS *Edin* 90-95; CF from 95. *MOD Chaplains (Army), Trenchard Lines, Upavon, Pewsey, Wilts SN9 6BE* Tel (01980) 615804 Fax 615800

COLE, Walter John Henden. b 04. Bps' Coll Cheshunt 25. **d** 27 **p** 28. C Frindsbury *Roch* 27-31; C Tottenham St Benet Fink *Lon* 31-33; C Regent's Park St Mark 33-41; V St Marylebone St Mark w St Luke 41-52; V Stone w Ebony *Cant* 52-55; V W Hampstead St Jas *Lon* 55-76; rtd 76. *87 College Road, Isleworth, Middx TW7 5DP* Tel 0181-568 2708

COLE, William Pritchard. b 09. OBE51. St D Coll Lamp BA32. **d** 33 **p** 35. C Swansea St Matt w Greenhill *S & B* 33-35; C Swansea St Thos 35-36; C New Windsor H Trin *Ox* 36-39; RAChD 39-59; Chapl Upper Chine Sch Shanklin 65-76; rtd 76. *27 Burton Road, Bridport, Dorset DT6 4JD* Tel (01308) 56289

COLE-KING, Canon Susan Mary. b 34. Lon Univ MB, BS62 DTPH71. Gen Th Sem (NY) 84. **d** 86 **p** 87. USA 86-88; Par Dn Dorchester *Ox* 89-92; D-in-c Drayton St Pet (Berks) 92-94; P-in-c 94-97; Hon Can Ch Ch from 95; rtd 97. *2 Godley Road, Harnham, Salisbury SP2 8EQ*

COLEBROOK, Canon Christopher John. b 36. Qu Mary Coll Lon BA60 BD69. St D Coll Lamp DipTh62. **d** 62 **p** 63. C Llandeilo Tal-y-bont *S & B* 62-66; C Llansamlet 66-71; V Nantmel w St Harmon's and Llanwrthwl 71-76; V Glantawe 76-85; V Gowerton from 85; RD Llwchwr from 93; Hon Can Brecon Cathl from 97. *The Vicarage, Church Street, Gowerton, Swansea SA4 3EA* Tel (01792) 872266

COLEBROOK, Peter Acland. b 29. Coates Hall Edin 52. **d** 55 **p** 56. C Northfield *Birm* 58-62; C Bideford *Ex* 62-66; rtd 89. *Vale Cottage, Ham Lane, Marnhull, Sturminster Newton, Dorset DT10 1JN* Tel (01258) 820246

COLEBROOKE, Andrew. b 50. Imp Coll Lon BSc71 MSc72 PhD75. Ridley Hall Cam 92. **d** 94 **p** 95. C Shrub End *Chelmsf* from 94. *St Cedd's House, Eldred Avenue, Colchester CO2 9AR* Tel (01206) 572017

COLEBY, Andrew Mark. b 59. FRHistS88 Linc Coll Ox MA85 DPhil85 Dur Univ BA90. Cranmer Hall Dur 88. **d** 91 **p** 92. C Heeley *Sheff* 91-94; TV Gleadless 94-97; Chapl Ox Brookes Univ *Ox* from 97. *46 Lower Road, Chinnor, Oxon OX9 4DU* Tel (01844) 354052

COLEMAN, Mrs Ann Valerie. b 51. K Coll Lon BD72. St Aug Coll Cant. **dss** 80 **d** 87 **p** 94. Hampstead Garden Suburb *Lon* 80-84; Golders Green 85-87; Selection Sec and Voc Adv ACCM 87-91; ABM 91; Teacher Bp Stoppard Sch 92-93; Perm to Offic *Lon* 92-93; C Eastcote St Lawr from 93; Chapl Bp Ramsey Sch from 93. *St Lawrence's Vicarage, 2 Bridle Road, Pinner, Middx HA5 2SJ* Tel 0181-866 1263

COLEMAN, Beverley Warren. b 20. Leeds Univ BA41. Coll of Resurr Mirfield 41. **d** 43 **p** 44. C Greenford H Cross *Lon* 43-46; C Stepney St Dunstan and All SS 46-47; CF 47-52; CF (TA) 52-87; PC Barrow Gurney *B & W* 52-54; Malaya 54-56; Indonesia 56-63; P-in-c Albrighton *Lich* 63-64; V 64-71; R Jersey St Sav *Win* 71-84; rtd 87. *44 Walnut Crescent, Fruit Lands, Malvern Wells, Worcs WR14 4AX* Tel (01684) 563535

COLEMAN, Brian James. b 36. K Coll Cam BA58 MA61. Ripon Hall Ox 58. **d** 60 **p** 61. C Allestree *Derby* 60-65; V Allestree St Nic 65-69; Chapl and Lect St Mich Coll Sarum 69-77; P-in-c Matlock Bank 77-86; R Frimley *Guildf* 86-92; V Guildf All SS from 92. *All Saints' Vicarage, 18 Vicarage Gate, Guildford, Surrey GU2 5QJ* Tel (01483) 572006

COLEMAN, Charles Romaine Boldero. b 10. Clifton Th Coll 46. **d** 39 **p** 40. C Downend *Bris* 39-41; C Keynsham *B & W* 41-43; R Felthorpe w Haveringland *Nor* 43-49; V Waxham w Sea Palling 49-55; R Horsey 52-55; R Buckenham w Hassingham and Strumpshaw 55-61; R Sampford Brett *B & W* 61-77; rtd 78; Perm to Offic *Nor* from 81. *1 The Firs, Redgate Hill, Hunstanton, Norfolk TE36 6LQ* Tel (01485) 532946

COLEMAN, David. b 49. K Coll Lon BD72 AKC72. St Aug Coll Cant 72. **d** 73 **p** 74. C Is of Dogs Ch Ch and St Jo w St Luke *Lon* 73-77; C Greenford H Cross 77-80; V Cricklewood St Pet 80-85; V Golders Green 85-90; V Eastcote St Lawr from 90. *St Lawrence's Vicarage, 2 Bridle Road, Pinner, Middx HA5 2SJ* Tel 0181-866 1263

COLEMAN, Dr Frank. b 58. Hull Univ BA Ox Univ BA83 MA87 PhD88. St Steph Ho Ox 80. **d** 83 **p** 84. C Brandon *Dur* 83-85; C Newton Aycliffe 85-88; V Denford w Ringstead *Pet* from 88; P-in-c Islip from 95. *The Vicarage, 11 Mountbatten Drive, Ringstead, Kettering, Northants NN14 4TX* Tel (01933) 624627

COLEMAN, Frederick Philip. b 11. Lon Univ BSc(Econ)33. St Steph Ho Ox 38. **d** 40 **p** 41. C S'wark St Alphege *S'wark* 40-42; C Lewisham St Steph 42-48; V Nunhead St Antony 48-52; V Ellesmere Port *Ches* 52-55; Hon C S'wark St Alphege *S'wark* 55-64; Gen Sec Ch Union 55-68; Hon C St Andr-by-the-Wardrobe w St Ann, Blackfriars *Lon* 64-68; R 71-84; Warden Community of St Jo Bapt Clewer 68-79; P-in-c St Nic Cole Abbey 78-82; AD The City 79-82; rtd 84; Hon C St Botolph

Aldgate w H Trin Minories *Lon* from 85. *Charterhouse, Charterhouse Square, London EC1M 6AN* Tel 0171-608 1077

COLEMAN, John Edward Noel. b 15. St Chad's Coll Dur BA37 DipTh39 MA49. **d** 39 **p** 40. C Latchford St Jas *Ches* 39-48; V Allithwaite *Carl* 48-55; V Silverdale *Blackb* 55-82; rtd 82; Perm to Offic *Blackb* from 82; Perm to Offic *Carl* 83-92. *25 Coach Road, Warton, Carnforth, Lancs LA5 9PR* Tel (01524) 732368

COLEMAN, John Harold. b 38. Cant Sch of Min 83. **d** 86 **p** 87. NSM Dover St Martin *Cant* 86-92; V St Mary's Bay w St Mary-in-the-Marsh etc from 92; P-in-c New Romney w Old Romney and Midley from 95. *The Vicarage, North Street, New Romney, Kent TN28 8DC* Tel (01679) 362308

COLEMAN, John Wycliffe. b 24. Ch Coll Cam MA43 St Thos Hosp Lon MB, BCh46 FRCS69. **d** 77 **p** 78. Iran 79-81; Egypt 84-91. *25 Southborough Road, London E9 7EF* Tel 0181-981 7525 Fax 981 3966 E-mail 100530,620@compuserve.com

COLEMAN, Miss Mary Eileen. b 30. **dss** 84 **d** 87 **p** 94. Harlesden All So *Lon* 84-87; Par Dn 87-89; Par Dn Brondesbury St Anne w Kilburn H Trin 89-90; rtd 90; NSM Langley Marish *Ox* from 94. *37 Willoughby Road, Langley, Slough SL3 8JH* Tel (01753) 581940

COLEMAN, Michael M. b 28.. **d** 95. NSM E Kilbride *Glas* from 95. *51 Lammermoor, Calderwood, East Kilbride G74 3SE* Tel (01355) 243745

COLEMAN, Patrick Francis. b 58. Ven English Coll and Pontifical Gregorian Univ Rome 77. **d** 82 **p** 83. In RC Ch 82-96; NSM Abergavenny St Mary w Llanwenarth Citra *Mon* from 96. *22 Twmpath Road, Pontypool NP4 6AG* Tel (01495) 764944 Fax as telephone E-mail patrick.coleman@virgin.net

✠**COLEMAN, The Rt Revd Peter Everard.** b 28. Barrister 65 Lon Univ LLB53 AKC53 Bris Univ MLitt76. Westcott Ho Cam 53. **d** 55 **p** 56 **c** 84. C Bedminster St Fran *Bris* 55-58; C St Helen Bishopsgate w St Martin Outwich *Lon* 58-60; Asst Sec SCM 58-60; Chapl and Lect K Coll Lon 60-66; V Clifton St Paul *Bris* 66-71; Chapl Bris Univ 66-71; Can Res Bris Cathl 71-81; Dir Ord Tr 71-81; Dir Bris & Glouc Tr Course 77-81; Adn Worc and Can Res Worc Cathl *Worc* 81-84; Suff Bp Crediton *Ex* 84-96; rtd 96; Asst Bp B & W from 96. *Boxenwood Cottage, Westwood, Bishop's Lydeard, Taunton, Somerset TA4 3HQ* Tel (01984) 618607 Fax 618352

COLEMAN, Peter Nicholas. b 42. St Mich Coll Llan 83. **d** 85 **p** 86. C Skewen *Llan* 85-88; V Ystradyfodwg from 88; RD Rhondda from 96. *The Vicarage, St David's Close, Pentre CF41 7AX* Tel (01443) 434201

COLEMAN, Robert William Alfred. b 16. Ch Coll Cam BA39 MA42. Bible Churchmen's Coll 39. **d** 40 **p** 41. C Broadwater St Mary *Chich* 40-42; CF 42-46; V Tiverton St Geo *Ex* 46-50; V Ealing Dean St Jo *Lon* 50-60; Chapl Seaford Coll E Sussex 60-81; rtd 81; Perm to Offic *Chich* from 83. *Villa Florence, 24 West Drive, Bognor Regis, W Sussex PO22 7TS* Tel (01243) 583410

COLEMAN, Sybil Jean. b 30. St Deiniol's Hawarden 83. **d** 85 **p** 97. NSM Manselton *S & B* 85-90; C Swansea St Mark and St Jo 90-94; P-in-c from 94. *The Parsonage, 27 Bowen Road, Swansea SA1 2NA* Tel (01792) 465074

COLEMAN, Terence Norman. b 37. St Mich Coll Llan 83. **d** 85 **p** 86. C Machen *Mon* 85-87; C Penmaen and Crumlin 87-89; V 89-93; V Newbridge from 93. *St Paul's Vicarage, High Street, Newbridge, Newport NP1 4FW* Tel (01495) 243975

COLEMAN, Timothy (Tim). b 57. CEng86 MIChemE86 Southn Univ BSc79. Ridley Hall Cam 87. **d** 89 **p** 90. C Bisley and W End *Guildf* 89-93; C Hollington St Jo *Chich* 93-97; V Aldborough Hatch *Chelmsf* from 97. *The Vicarage, St Peter's Close, Oaks Lane, Ilford, Essex IG2 7QN* Tel 0181-599 0524

COLES, Alasdair Charles. b 67. St Andr Univ BSc90 Homerton Coll Cam PGCE91. Cuddesdon Coll 93. **d** 96 **p** 97. C Wymondham *Nor* from 96. *76A Norwich Road, Wymondham, Norfolk NR18 0SZ* Tel (01953) 604342 Fax as telephone

COLES, Miss Alison Elizabeth. b 60. St Mary's Coll Dur BA81. Ripon Coll Cuddesdon 95. **d** 97. C Leckhampton SS Phil and Jas w Cheltenham St Jas *Glouc* from 97. *32 Gratton Road, Leckhampton, Cheltenham, Glos GL50 2BU* Tel (01242) 516362

COLES, The Rt Revd David John. b 43. **d** 68 **p** 69. Hon C Fallowfield *Man* 72-74; New Zealand from 74; Bp Christchurch from 90. *Bishop's Lodge, 12 Idris Road, Christchurch 8005, New Zealand* Tel Christchurch (3) 351 7711 or 343 0519 Fax 348 3827

COLES, Francis Herbert. b 35. Selw Coll Cam BA59 MA63. Coll of Resurr Mirfield 59. **d** 61 **p** 62. C Wolvercote *Ox* 61-65; C Farnham Royal 65-69; V Lynton and Brendon *Ex* 69-73; V Countisbury 70-73; TR Lynton, Brendon, Countisbury, Lynmouth etc 73-76; P-in-c Iffley *Ox* 76-88; V Ivybridge w Harford *Ex* from 88. *The Vicarage, Blachford Road, Ivybridge, Devon PL21 0AD* Tel (01752) 690193

COLES, Geoffrey Herbert. b 38. Nottm Univ CertEd59 TCert60 Loughb Coll of Educn DLC60. N Ord Course 77. **d** 80 **p** 81. NSM Shelf *Bradf* 80-85; C Manningham 85-86; TV 86-92; P-in-c Wyke from 92. *St Mary's Vicarage, 6 Vicarage Close, Wyke, Bradford, W Yorkshire BD12 8QW* Tel (01274) 678216

COLES, John Spencer Halstaff. b 50. Hertf Coll Ox BA72 MA76. Wycliffe Hall Ox 72. **d** 75 **p** 76. C Reading Greyfriars *Ox* 75-79; C Clifton Ch Ch w Em *Bris* 79-82; V Woodside Park St Barn *Lon* from 82. *St Barnabas' Vicarage, 68 Westbury Road, London N12 7PD* Tel 0181-445 3598 or 446 7506

COLES, Robert Charles. b 41. Bps' Coll Cheshunt 66. **d** 68 **p** 69. C Northampton St Alb *Pet* 68-72; C Durrington *Chich* 72-74; C Portslade St Nic 74-78; C Horsham 78-82; C-in-c Parklands St Wilfrid CD 82-87; V Eastbourne St Phil from 87. *The Vicarage, 1 St Philip's Avenue, Eastbourne, E Sussex BN22 8LU* Tel (01323) 732381

COLES, Robert Reginald (Bob). b 47. Surrey Univ BSc69. Cant Sch of Min 82. **d** 85 **p** 86. NSM Sittingbourne St Mich *Cant* 85-87; C St Laur in Thanet 87-93; P-in-c St Nicholas at Wade w Sarre and Chislet w Hoath from 93; P-in-c Minster w Monkton from 96. *The Vicarage, The Length, St Nicholas-at-Wade, Birchington, Kent CT7 0PW* Tel (01843) 47200

COLES, Stephen Richard. b 49. Univ Coll Ox BA70 MA74 Leeds Univ BA80. Coll of Resurr Mirfield 78. **d** 81 **p** 82. C Stoke Newington St Mary *Lon* 81-84; Chapl K Coll Cam 84-89; V Finsbury Park St Thos *Lon* from 89. *25 Romilly Road, London N4 2QY* Tel 0171-359 5741

COLEY, Frederick Albert. b 13. Lich Th Coll 65. **d** 66 **p** 67. C Headless Cross *Worc* 66-68; C Tardebigge 68-72; P-in-c Stoke Bliss w Kyre Wyard 72-73; P-in-c Hanley William w Hanley Child 72-73; P-in-c Stoke Bliss w Kyre Wyard, Hanley William etc 73-78; rtd 78; Perm to Offic *Worc* from 78; Perm to Offic *Heref* from 90. *Greenfields, Kyre Wood, Tenbury Wells, Worcs WR15 8SQ* Tel (01584) 810961

COLEY, Peter Leonard. b 45. CEng MIMechE Bath Univ BSc67 City Univ MSc84. Oak Hill Th Coll 85. **d** 87 **p** 88. C Mile Cross *Nor* 87-92; R Stratton St Mary w Stratton St Michael etc from 92. *The Rectory, Flowerpot Lane, Long Stratton, Norwich NR15 2TS* Tel (01508) 30238

COLIN WILFRED, Brother. *See* CHERRIMAN, Colin Wilfred

COLLARD, Fred. b 25. Lon Bible Coll 51 Wycliffe Hall Ox 61. **d** 61 **p** 63. OMF 61-81; Malaya 61-63; Malaysia 63-75; Perm to Offic *Ox* 71-81; TV Cheltenham St Mary, St Matt, St Paul and H Trin *Glouc* 81-92; rtd 92. *17 Dubrae Close, St Albans, Herts AL3 4JT* Tel (01727) 869138

COLLARD, Canon Harold. b 27. Wycliffe Hall Ox 51. **d** 53 **p** 54. C Rainham *Chelmsf* 53-56; C Kingston upon Hull H Trin *York* 56-59; V Upper Armley *Ripon* 59-68; R Chesterfield H Trin *Derby* 68-77; P-in-c Matlock Bath 77-83; V 83-92; Hon Can Derby Cathl 87-92; RD Wirksworth 88-92; rtd 92. *10 Kirkby Avenue, Ripon, N Yorkshire HG4 2DR* Tel (01765) 606306

COLLARD, John Cedric. b 30. Pemb Coll Cam BA53 MA76. St Alb Minl Tr Scheme 77. **d** 80 **p** 81. NSM Roxton w Gt Barford *St Alb* 80-84; C Liskeard w St Keyne, St Pinnock and Morval *Truro* 84-87; TV Liskeard, St Keyne, St Pinnock, Morval etc 87-93; rtd 93; Perm to Offic *Truro* from 93. *Curlew Cottage, Bohetherick, Saltash, Cornwall PL12 6SZ* Tel (01579) 350560

COLLARD, Norton Harvey. b 22. Open Univ BA80. Roch Th Coll 63. **d** 65 **p** 66. C Swanley St Mary *Roch* 65-67; C Dartford H Trin 67-70; V Grantham St Anne *Linc* 70-87; rtd 87; Perm to Offic *Linc* from 87. *1 Kenwick Drive, Grantham, Lincs NG31 9DP* Tel (01476) 577345

COLLAS, Canon Victor John. b 23. Pemb Coll Ox BA44 MA48. Wycliffe Hall Ox 49. **d** 51 **p** 52. R Guernsey St Andr *Win* 58-81; Perm to Offic from 81; rtd 88. *Paradis, La Rue du Paradis, Vale, Guernsey, Channel Islands GY3 5BL* Tel (01481) 44450

COLLEDGE, Christopher Richard (Chris). b 58. Chich Th Coll. **d** 82 **p** 83. C Deal St Leon *Cant* 82-83; C Deal St Leon and St Rich and Sholden 83-85; Bermuda 85-88; TV Wickford and Runwell *Chelmsf* 88-90; Chapl Runwell Hosp Essex 88-90; Chapl RAD from 90; Perm to Offic *Chelmsf* from 90. *St Saviour's Centre, 1 Armstrong Road, London W3 7JL* Tel 0181-743 2209

COLLESS, Mrs Salma. b 55. SRN77 RM80. EAMTC 89. **d** 92 **p** 94. NSM Chesterton St Andr *Ely* 92-93; Australia from 93. *3 Cooba Place, Rivett, ACT, Australia 2611* Tel Canberra (6) 288 7835

COLLETT, Albert Ernest Jack. b 15. S'wark Ord Course 62. **d** 65 **p** 66. C Lewisham St Jo Southend *S'wark* 65-73; C-in-c Reigate St Phil CD 73-82; rtd 83; Perm to Offic *S'wark* from 83. *42 Wimborne Avenue, Redhill RH1 5AG* Tel (01737) 763218

COLLETT-WHITE, Thomas Charles. b 36. Trin Coll Cam BA61 MA86. Ridley Hall Cam 60. **d** 62 **p** 63. C Gillingham St Mark *Roch* 62-66; V 79-90; C Normanton *Wakef* 66-69; V Highbury New Park St Aug *Lon* 69-76; Canada 76-79; Chapl Medway Hosp Gillingham 79-85; P-in-c Clerkenwell St Jas and St Jo w St Pet *Lon* 90-96. *53 Pathfield Road, London SW16 5NZ* Tel 0181-769 0035

COLLIE, Canon Bertie Harold Guy. b 28. Glas Univ MB, ChB56. Glas NSM Course 75. **d** 76 **p** 77. NSM Ayr *Glas* 76-84; NSM Maybole from 76; NSM Girvan from 76; NSM Pinmore from 76; Dioc Supernumerary from 91; Can St Mary's Cathl from 96. *Hillside, Cargill Road, Maybole, Ayrshire KA19 8AF* Tel (01655) 883564

COLLIE, Canon John Norman. b 25. Em Coll Cam BA51 MA56. Ridley Hall Cam 52. **d** 54 **p** 55. C Leic H Apostles *Leic* 54-57; C Melton Mowbray w Thorpe Arnold 57-59; Chapl Lee Abbey 59-62; V Streatham Immanuel w St Anselm *S'wark* 62-68; V Ecclesall *Sheff* 68-90; Hon Can Sheff Cathl 83-90; RD Ecclesall

85-89; rtd 90; Perm to Offic *Sheff* from 90. *46 Sunnyvale Road, Totley, Sheffield S17 4FB* Tel 0114-235 2249

COLLIER, Anthony Charles. b 45. Peterho Cam BA68 MA72 Or Coll Ox DipTh70 Whitelands Coll Lon CertEd76. Cuddesdon Coll 68. **d** 71 **p** 72. C N Holmwood *Guildf* 71-75; Perm to Offic *S'wark* 75-79; Chapl Colfe's Sch Lon 80-84; Hon C Shirley St Jo *Cant* 80-84; Hon C Shirley St Jo *S'wark* from 85. *56 Bennetts Way, Croydon CR0 8AB* Tel 0181-777 5719

COLLIER, Michael Francis. b 29. Wycliffe Hall Ox 71. **d** 73 **p** 74. C Hamstead St Paul *Birm* 73-75; P-in-c Castleton *Derby* 75-80; P-in-c Hope 78-80; V Hope and Castleton from 80; RD Bakewell and Eyam 90-95. *The Vicarage, Hope, Sheffield S30 2RN* Tel (01433) 620534

COLLIER, Paul Clive. b 53. Trin Coll Bris 80. **d** 82 **p** 83. C Hazlemere *Ox* 82-90; V from 90. *The New Vicarage, 260 Amersham Road, High Wycombe, Bucks HP15 7PZ* Tel (01494) 439404

COLLIER, Paul Edward (Edge). b 63. Solicitor 93 Mert Coll Ox BA85 Lon Univ PGCE87. S'wark Ord Course 91. **d** 94 **p** 95. C E Dulwich St Jo *S'wark* from 94. *11 Hinckley Road, London SE15 4HZ* Tel 0171-732 8983

COLLIER, Richard John Millard. b 45. FRSA92. EAMTC 78. **d** 81 **p** 82. NSM Nor St Pet Mancroft *Nor* 81-82; NSM Nor St Pet Mancroft w St Jo Maddermarket from 82. *11 The Close, Norwich NR1 4DH* Tel (01603) 624204

COLLIER, Stephen John. b 46. St Pet Coll Ox MA68 Univ of Wales (Cardiff) DipSocWork74. Qu Coll Birm DipTh94. **d** 94 **p** 95. C Thorpe *Nor* from 94. *24 Naseby Way, Norwich NR7 0TP* Tel (01603) 31868

COLLIN, David John. b 36. Lon Univ BSc60 Westmr Coll Ox BTh94. St Alb and Ox Min Course 94. **d** 96. NSM Antwerp St Boniface *Eur* from 96. *Jan van Rijswicklaan 166A, B2020 Antwerp, Belgium* Tel Antwerp (3) 257 08 41

COLLIN, Terry. b 39. St Aid Birkenhead 65. **d** 67 **p** 68. C Bolton St Jas w St Chrys *Bradf* 67-71; C Keighley 71-74; V Greengates from 74. *The Vicarage, 138 New Line, Greengates, Bradford, W Yorkshire BD10 0BX* Tel (01274) 613111

COLLING, Canon James Oliver (Joc). b 30. MBE95. Man Univ BA50. Cuddesdon Coll 52. **d** 54 **p** 55. C Wigan All SS *Liv* 54-59; V Padgate Ch Ch 59-71; R Padgate 71-73; RD Warrington 70-82 and 87-89; AD from 89; R Warrington St Elphin from 73; Hon Can Liv Cathl from 76; Chapl to The Queen from 90. *The Rectory, Warrington WA1 2TL* Tel (01925) 635020

COLLING, Terence John. b 47. Linc Th Coll 84. **d** 86 **p** 87. C Wood End *Cov* 86-90; V Willenhall from 90. *The Vicarage, Robin Hood Road, Coventry CV3 3AY* Tel (01203) 303266

COLLINGS, Canon Neil. b 46. K Coll Lon BD69 AKC69. **d** 70 **p** 71. C Littleham w Exmouth *Ex* 70-72; TV 72-74; Chapl Westmr Abbey 74-79; Preb Heref Cathl *Heref* 79-86; Dir of Ords and Post Ord Tr 79-86; R Heref St Nic 79-86; Bp's Dom Chapl 82-86; R Harpenden St Nic *St Alb* from 86; Hon Can St Alb from 96. *The Rectory, 9 Rothamsted Avenue, Harpenden, Herts AL5 2DD* Tel (01582) 712202

COLLINGS, Robert Frank. b 26. Lon Univ BD53. ALCD52. **d** 52 **p** 53. C Bayswater *Lon* 52-55; Australia from 55; rtd 87. *Unit 5/2 Wattle Street, Bunbury, W Australia 6230* Tel Dardanup (97) 281264

COLLINGWOOD, Canon Christopher Paul. b 54. MA BMus. Ripon Coll Cuddesdon. **d** 83 **p** 84. C Tupsley *Heref* 83-86; Prec St Alb Abbey *St Alb* 86-90; V Bedford St Paul 90-97; Can Res and Prec Guildf Cathl *Guildf* from 97. *3 Cathedral Close, Guildford, Surrey GU2 5TL* Tel (01483) 569682

COLLINGWOOD, Deryck Laurence. b 50. St Jo Coll Cam BA72. Edin Th Coll BD85. **d** 85 **p** 85. Chapl Napier Poly *Edin* 85-88; Chapl Napier Univ from 95; C Edin Ch Ch 85-88; TV from 88; Tutor Edin Th Coll from 89; Asst P Edin St Hilda *Edin* from 94; Asst P Edin St Fillan from 94. *St Hilda's House, 1A Oxgangs Avenue, Edinburgh EH13 9JA* Tel 0131-441 1235 or 455 4694 Fax 455 4695 E-mail d.collingwood@napier.ac.uk

COLLINGWOOD, Graham Lewis. b 63. Open Univ BA92. St Steph Ho Ox DipMin95. **d** 95 **p** 96. C Heavitree w Ex St Paul *Ex* 95-97; CF from 97. *MOD Chaplains (Army), Trenchard Lines, Upavon, Pewsey, Wilts SN9 6BE* Tel (01980) 615804 Fax 615800

COLLINGWOOD, John Jeremy Raynham. b 37. Barrister 64 CCC Cam BA60 MA68 Lon Univ BD78. Trin Coll Bris 75. **d** 78 **p** 79. C Henleaze *Bris* 78-80; P-in-c Clifton H Trin, St Andr and St Pet 80-81; V 81-91; RD Clifton 84-87; Bp's Officer for Miss and Evang 87-91; V Guildf Ch Ch *Guildf* from 91; RD Guildf from 95. *Christ Church Vicarage, 25 Waterden Road, Guildford, Surrey GU1 2AZ* Tel (01483) 68886

COLLINS, Adelbert Andrew. b 15. Lich Th Coll. **d** 61 **p** 62. C Sedgley All SS *Lich* 61-77; P-in-c Enville 77-81 and 86-88; R 81-86; C Kinver and Enville 88-90; rtd 90; Perm to Offic *Lich* from 90. *West Cottage, Bridgnorth Road, Enville, Stourbridge, W Midlands DY7 5JA* Tel (01384) 873733

COLLINS, Barry Douglas. b 47. Kelham Th Coll 66. **d** 70 **p** 71. C Peel Green *Man* 70-73; C Salford St Phil w St Steph 73-75; R Blackley H Trin 75-79; Perm to Offic *Ripon* 80-83; Perm to Offic *Pet* 83-85; Perm to Offic *Cov* from 85. *c/o 10 Onley Park, Willoughby, Rugby, Warks CV23 8AN* Tel (01788) 817579

COLLINS, Bruce Churton. b 47. BSc. Oak Hill Th Coll. **d** 83 **p** 84. C Notting Hill St Jo *Lon* 83-87; C Notting Hill St Jo and St Pet 87-90; V Roxeth Ch Ch and Harrow St Pet 90-93; P-in-c S Harrow St Paul 91-93; TR Roxeth from 93. *48 Whitmore Road, Harrow, Middx HA1 4AD*

COLLINS, Ms Cheryl Anne. b 62. MCA90 Rob Coll Cam BA85 MA89. Ripon Coll Cuddesdon 91. **d** 93 **p** 94. C Sheff Sharrow *Sheff* 93-95; Chapl Sheff Univ from 95; Hon C Endcliffe from 96. *119 Ashdell Road, Sheffield S10 3DB* Tel 0114-266 9243 or 282 4956 E-mail c.a.collins@sheffield.ac.uk

COLLINS, Christopher. b 46. K Coll Lon BSc67 AKC67 Pemb Coll Ox BA70. St Steph Ho Ox 68. **d** 71 **p** 72. C Pennywell St Thos and Grindon St Oswald CD *Dur* 71-74; C Pallion 74-76; C Millfield St Mary 74-76; C Bishopwearmouth Gd Shep 74-76; C Harton Colliery 76-78; TV Winlaton 78-85; V Grangetown from 85. *St Aidan's Vicarage, Grangetown, Sunderland SR2 9RS* Tel 0191-514 3485

COLLINS, Christopher David. b 43. Sheff Univ BA(Econ)64. Tyndale Hall Bris 65. **d** 68 **p** 69. C Rusholme H Trin *Man* 68-71; C Bushbury *Lich* 71-74; V Fairfield *Liv* 74-81; V Tunbridge Wells St Jo *Roch* 81-92; R Luton Ch Ch from 92; RD Roch from 94. *Luton Rectory, Capstone Road, Chatham, Kent ME5 7PN* Tel (01634) 843780

COLLINS, Donard Michael. b 55. TCD BA. Oak Hill Th Coll. **d** 83 **p** 84. C Lurgan Ch the Redeemer *D & D* 83-87; I Ardmore w Craigavon from 87. *Ardmore Rectory, Derryadd, Lurgan, Craigavon, Co Armagh BT66 6QR* Tel (01762) 340357

COLLINS, Frank. b 56. Oak Hill Th Coll BA92. **d** 92 **p** 93. C Heref St Pet w St Owen and St Jas *Heref* 92-95; CF from 95. *MOD Chaplains (Army), Trenchard Lines, Upavon, Pewsey, Wilts SN9 6BE* Tel (01980) 615804 Fax 615800

COLLINS, Canon Frederick Spencer (Fred). b 36. FACCA Birm Univ DipTh67. Ripon Hall Ox. **d** 67 **p** 68. C Evington *Leic* 67-71; C Hall Green Ascension *Birm* 71-73; V Burney Lane 73-79; Dioc Stewardship Adv 79-84; V Yardley St Edburgha 84-96; RD Yardley 86-92; Hon Can Birm Cathl from 89; rtd 96; Perm to Offic *Birm* from 96. *237 Old Birmingham Road, Marlbrook, Bromsgrove, Worcs B60 1HQ* Tel 0121-447 7687

COLLINS, Gavin Andrew. b 66. Trin Hall Cam BA89 MA93. Trin Coll Bris BA94 MA94. **d** 97. C Cambridge St Barn *Ely* from 97. *80 St Barnabas Road, Cambridge CB1 2DE* Tel (01223) 367578

COLLINS, George Martyn. b 36. Bris Univ BA58. Coll of Resurr Mirfield. **d** 62 **p** 63. C Widley w Wymering *Portsm* 62-64; C Kingstanding St Mark CD *Birm* 64-69; V Weoley Castle 69-78; R Curdworth 78-83; TR Curdworth w Castle Vale 83-88; V Westbury-on-Trym H Trin *Bris* from 88. *Holy Trinity Vicarage, 44 Eastfield Road, Westbury-on-Trym, Bristol BS9 4AG* Tel 0117-962 1536 or 950 8644

COLLINS, Canon Ian Geoffrey. b 37. Hull Univ BA60 CertEd. Sarum Th Coll 60. **d** 62 **p** 63. C Gainsborough All SS *Linc* 62-65; Min Can Windsor 65-81; Succ Windsor 67-81; R Kirkby in Ashfield *S'well* 81-85; Can Res S'well Minster from 85; P-in-c Edingley w Halam from 91. *5 Vicar's Court, Southwell, Notts NG25 0HP* Tel (01636) 815056

COLLINS, James Frederick. b 10. St Jo Coll Cam BA34 MA38. Westcott Ho Cam 34. **d** 35 **p** 36. C Benwell St Jas *Newc* 35-38; Chapl Miss to Seamen Port Sudan 38-41; Chapl RNVR 36-46; C Milford *Win* 46-47; V Rothwell w Orton *Pet* 47-51; R Bromham *Sarum* 51-62; V Chisledon and Draycot Foliatt 62-68; Dir of Ords 68-73; Hon C Devizes St Jo w St Mary 68-75; rtd 75; Perm to Offic *St Alb* 81-96. *3 Parkinson Close, Marford Road, Wheathampstead, St Albans, Herts AL4 8DP* Tel (01582) 833944

COLLINS, Miss Janet May. b 55. Qu Mary Coll Lon BA78 St Jo Coll Dur BA84. Cranmer Hall Dur 82. **dss** 85 **d** 87 **p** 94. Willington Team *Newc* 85-88; C 87-88; Par Dn Stevenage St Hugh Chells *St Alb* 88-90; Par Dn Goldington 90-93; TD Witney *Ox* 93-94; TV 94-96; Tutor St Alb and Ox Min Course from 96. *The Vicarage, St Margaret's Road, Oxford OX2 6RX* Tel (01865) 514958

COLLINS, John Gilbert. b 32. S'wark Ord Course 67. **d** 71 **p** 72. C Coulsdon St Jo *S'wark* 71-75; Chapl St Fran Hosp Haywards Heath 75-84; Chapl Hurstwood Park Hosp Haywards Heath 75-84; R Stedham w Iping, Elsted and Treyford-cum-Didling *Chich* 84-92; rtd 92; Perm to Offic *Chich* from 94. *12 Exeter Road, Broyle, Chichester, W Sussex PO19 4EF* Tel (01243) 536861

COLLINS, Preb John Theodore Cameron Bucke. b 25. Clare Coll Cam BA49 MA52. Ridley Hall Cam 49. **d** 51 **p** 52. C St Marylebone All So w SS Pet and Jo *Lon* 51-57; V Gillingham St Mark *Roch* 57-71; Chapl Medway Hosp Gillingham 70-71; V Canford Magna *Sarum* 71-80; RD Wimborne 79-80; V Brompton H Trin w Onslow Square St Paul *Lon* 80-85; C 85-89; AD Chelsea 84-88; Preb St Paul's Cathl 85-89; rtd 89; Perm to Offic *Lon* 89-90; Perm to Offic *Win* 89-97. *27 Woodstock Close, Oxford OX2 8DB* Tel (01865) 556228

COLLINS, Ms Kathryne Broncy. b 51. Portland State Univ BSc75 Lon Univ MSc76. Linc Th Coll 92. **d** 94 **p** 95. C Bishop's Castle w Mainstone *Heref* from 94. *7 Lavender Bank, Bishops Castle, Shropshire SY9 5BD* Tel (01588) 638024

COLLINS, Mrs Lindsay Rosemary Faith. b 70. K Coll Lon BD91 AKC91 PGCE92. Ripon Coll Cuddesdon MTh95. **d** 97. C Witney *Ox* from 97. *The Vicarage, New Yatt Road, North Leigh, Witney, Oxon OX8 6TT* Tel (01993) 881136 Fax as telephone

COLLINS, Maurice Arthur Reily. b 19. Clare Coll Cam BA41 MA45. Westcott Ho Cam 45. **d** 47 **p** 48. C Bishop's Stortford St Mich *St Alb* 47-50; C Rugby St Andr *Cov* 50-51; Perm to Offic *Guildf* 52-53; R Ockley 53-82; R Ockley, Okewood and Forest Green 82-85; rtd 85; Perm to Offic *Portsm* from 86. *Old Wheatsheaf, Privett, Alton, Hants GU34 3NX* Tel (01730) 828287

COLLINS, Canon Norman Hilary. b 33. Mert Coll Ox BA55 MA58. Wells Th Coll 58. **d** 60 **p** 61. C Ystrad Mynach *Llan* 60-62; C Gelligaer 62-67; V Maerdy 67-77; R Penarth w Lavernock from 77; RD Penarth and Barry from 87; Can Llan Cathl from 92. *The Rectory, 13 Hickman Road, Penarth CF64 2AJ* Tel (01222) 709463

COLLINS, Paul David Arthur. b 50. Lanc Univ MSc91. K Coll Lon BD72 AKC72 St Aug Coll Cant 73. **d** 73 **p** 74. C Rotherhithe St Mary w All SS *S'wark* 73-76; C Stocking Farm *Leic* 76-78; V 78-83; R Husbands Bosworth w Mowsley and Knaptoft etc 83-87; Soc Resp Officer *Blackb* 87-94; R Worc City St Paul and Old St Martin etc *Worc* from 94; Chapl Worc Tech Coll from 94; Min Can Worc Cathl *Worc* from 95. *The Rectory, 7 Aldersey Close, Worcester WR5 3EH* Tel (01905) 767912

COLLINS, Paul Myring. b 53. St Jo Coll Dur BA75. St Steph Ho Ox BA78 MA83. **d** 79 **p** 80. C Meir *Lich* 79-82; C Fenton 82-83; TV Leek and Meerbrook 83-87; Tutor in Th and Liturgy Chich Th Coll 87-94; Dir of Studies 90-94; V Brighton Gd Shep Preston *Chich* 94-96; Tutor Qu Coll Birm from 96. *2 Tutor Houses, Queen's College, Somerset Road, Birmingham B15 2QH* Tel 0121-452 2606

COLLINS, Canon Peter Churton. b 13. Lon Univ BD35. Ely Th Coll 35. **d** 36 **p** 37. C Crayford *Roch* 36-42; V Dartford St Alb 42-60; R Crayford 60-78; Hon Can Roch Cathl 63-78; RD Erith 65-78; rtd 79; Chapl Huggens Coll Northfleet 79-87; Perm to Offic *Roch* from 92. *College of St Barnabas, Blackberry Lane, Lingfield, Surrey RH7 6NJ* Tel (01342) 870697 Fax as telephone

COLLINS, Peter John. b 33. Open Univ BA. Oak Hill Th Coll 64. **d** 66 **p** 67. C Low Leyton *Chelmsf* 66-69; C Portsdown *Portsm* 69-72; V Gatten St Paul 72-79; C-in-c Ingrave St Steph CD *Chelmsf* 79-85; V Roydon from 85. *St Peter's Vicarage, Church Mead, Roydon, Harlow, Essex CM19 5EY* Tel (01279) 792103

COLLINS, Philip Howard Norton. b 50. AKC73. St Aug Coll Cant 73. **d** 74 **p** 75. C Stamford Hill St Thos *Lon* 74-78; C Upwood w Gt and Lt Raveley *Ely* 78-81; C Ramsey 78-81; R Leverington 81-92; P-in-c Wisbech St Mary 89-92; RD Wisbech 90-92; TR Whittlesey and Pondersbridge 92-95; TR Whittlesey, Pondersbridge and Coates from 95. *8 The Grove, Whittlesey, Peterborough PE7 2RF* Tel (01733) 202563

COLLINS, Richard Andrew. b 65. K Coll Lon BD92 AKC92. St Steph Ho Ox 92. **d** 94 **p** 95. C Whickham *Dur* 94-97; TV Bensham from 97. *12 Red Admiral Court, Gateshead, Tyne & Wear NE11 9TW* Tel 0191-488 3015 Fax as telephone

COLLINS, Rodney Harry. b 20. SSC Open Univ BA74. S'wark Ord Course 75. **d** 78 **p** 79. NSM Swanley St Mary *Roch* 78-94. *16 Stanhope Road, Sidcup, Kent DA15 7AA* Tel 0181-302 0867

COLLINS, Roger Richardson. b 48. Birm Univ BPhil88. WMMTC 78. **d** 81 **p** 82. NSM Cotteridge *Birm* from 81. *6 Chesterfield Court, Middleton Hall Road, Birmingham B30 1AF* Tel 0121-459 4009

COLLINS, Ross Nicoll Ferguson. b 64. Ripon Coll Cuddesdon. **d** 92 **p** 93. C Goring w S Stoke *Ox* 92-96; P-in-c N Leigh from 96. *The Vicarage, New Yatt Road, North Leigh, Witney, Oxon OX8 6TT* Tel (01993) 881136

COLLINS, Canon Stella Vivian. b 32. S Dios Minl Tr Scheme 74. **dss** 77 **d** 87 **p** 94. Harnham *Sarum* 77-88; Hon Par Dn 87-88; Dioc Lay Min Adv 82-97; Adv for Women's Min 82-97; Hon Par Dn Wilton w Netherhampton and Fugglestone 88-94; Hon C 94-97; RD Wylye and Wilton 89-94; Can and Preb Sarum Cathl 93-97; rtd 97. *Shawmeare, Coombe Road, Salisbury SP2 8BT* Tel (01722) 336420

COLLINS, William Arthur Donovan. b 21. AKC49. **d** 50 **p** 51. C Huddersfield St Jo *Wakef* 50-52; S Africa 52-61; C Friern Barnet All SS *Lon* 61-62; V Kellington w Whitley *Wakef* 62-66; S Africa 66-80; Adn Cape Town 75-80; V Birchington w Acol and Minnis Bay *Cant* 80-85; Warden Coll of St Barn Lingfield 85-88; rtd 88. *26 Weavers Court, Sudbury, Suffolk CO10 6HY* Tel (01787) 373359

COLLINS, William Carpenter. b 35. BA55 MA57 MDiv65. Ch Div Sch of the Pacific (USA) 63. **d** 66 **p** 67. USA 66-71; Hon C Newlyn St Pet *Truro* 82-93; Perm to Offic from 93. *Cape House, Cape Cornwall, St Just, Penzance, Cornwall TR19 7NN* Tel (01736) 787112

COLLINS, William Francis Martin. b 43. St Cath Coll Cam BA66 MA70. Cuddesdon Coll 68. **d** 70 **p** 71. C Man Victoria Park *Man* 70-73; P-in-c Ancoats 73-78; Chapl Abraham Moss Cen 78-91; Hon C Cheetham Hill 81-84; Chs' FE Officer for Gtr Man 84-91; V Norbury *Ches* from 91. *Norbury Vicarage, 75 Chester Road, Hazel Grove, Stockport, Cheshire SK7 5PE* Tel 0161-483 8640

COLLINS, Winfield St Clair. b 41. Univ of W Indies BA83 Man Univ BA88 MEd91. Codrington Coll Barbados LTh77. **d** 76 **p** 76. Asst Chapl HM Pris Wakef 76; Barbados 76-84; Asst Chapl HM Pris Wandsworth 85; Chapl HM Young Offender Inst Thorn Cross 85-91; Chapl HM Pris Pentonville from 91. *HM Prison Pentonville, Caledonian Road, London N7 8TT* Tel 0171-607 5353 Fax 700 0244

COLLINSON, Ernest John. b 12. ALCD36. **d** 36 **p** 37. C Southall Green St Jo *Lon* 36-38; Sudan 38-46; R Graveley w Chivesfield *St Alb* 46-48; V Laleham *Lon* 48-52; Africa Inland Miss 52-54; V Penge St Jo *Roch* 54-63; Rwanda Miss 63-66; V Tiverton St Geo *Ex* 66-73; Perm to Offic from 74; rtd 77. *Flat 4, Lion House, 2 Carlton Hill, Exmouth, Devon EX8 2ST* Tel (01395) 265202

COLLINSON, Canon Joan Irene. b 31. ALA55 Westf Coll Lon BA52. **dss** 63 **d** 87 **p** 94. Westmr St Steph w St Jo *Lon* 65-68; R Foundn of St Kath 68-73; Qu Mary Coll 68-73; Notting Hill St Jo 73-74; Kent Univ *Cant* 74-82; Dean of Women's Min *S'wark* 82-89; Hon Can S'wark Cathl 88-89; TD Newc Epiphany *Newc* 89-94; TV 94-96; Hon Can Newc Cathl 89-96; Adv for Accredited Lay Min 89-94; Asst Dio Dir of Ords 94-96; rtd 96; Perm to Offic *S'wark* from 96. *4 The Park, Carshalton, Surrey SM5 3BY* Tel 0181-647 3318

COLLINSON, Leslie Roland (Les). b 47. St Jo Coll Nottm DCM92. **d** 92 **p** 93. C Gorleston St Andr *Nor* 92-96; TV Banbury *Ox* from 96. *St Francis House, Highlands, Banbury, Oxon OX16 7FA* Tel (01295) 275449

COLLINSON, Roger Alfred. b 36. St Jo Coll Dur BA58 Cranmer Hall Dur 60. **d** 63. C Liv St Mich *Liv* 63-64; NSM Ormside *Carl* from 97; NSM Appleby from 97. *1 Caesar's View, Appleby-in-Westmorland, Cumbria CA16 6SH* Tel (01768) 352886

COLLIS, Michael Alan. b 35. K Coll Lon BD60 AKC60. **d** 61 **p** 62. C Worc St Martin *Worc* 61-63; C Dudley St Thos 63-66; C St Peter-in-Thanet *Cant* 66-70; V Croydon H Trin 70-77; P-in-c Norbury St Steph 77-81; V 81-82; V Sutton Valence w E Sutton and Chart Sutton 82-89; R New Fishbourne *Chich* from 89; P-in-c Appledram from 89. *The Rectory, 12 Fishbourne Road, Chichester, W Sussex PO19 3HX* Tel (01243) 783364

COLLIS, Stephen Thomas. b 47. MHCIMA94. Cranmer Hall Dur 80. **d** 82 **p** 83. C Crewe All SS and St Paul *Ches* 82-84; C Wilmslow 84-86 and from 95; Chapl RAF 86-95. *25 Stanneylands Road, Wilmslow, Cheshire SK9 4EJ* Tel (01625) 533397

COLLIS SMITH, Charles Philip. b 39. St Cath Coll Cam BA61. Lich Th Coll 61. **d** 63 **p** 64. C Wednesfield St Thos *Lich* 63-66; C Hednesford 66-71; V High Offley 71-80; R Myddle 80-92; V Broughton 80-92; rtd 92; Perm to Offic *Lich* from 92. *Trenance, 19 Wellgate, Wem, Shrewsbury SY4 5ES* Tel (01939) 235013

COLLISON, Christopher John. b 48. Oak Hill Th Coll 68. **d** 72 **p** 73. C Cromer *Nor* 72-75; C Costessey 76-78; V 87-95; C Heckmondwike *Wakef* 78-79; P-in-c Shepley 79-83; Dioc Communications Officer 79-83; Chapl Flushing Miss to Seamen *Eur* 83-85; Asst Min Sec Miss to Seamen 85-87; C St Mich Paternoster Royal *Lon* 85-87; P-in-c Swainsthorpe w Newton Flotman *Nor* from 95; Dioc Evang Officer from 95. *The Rectory, Church Road, Newton Flotman, Norwich NR15 1QB* Tel (01508) 470762

COLLISON, Ms Elizabeth. b 38. Man Univ CertEd58. N Ord Course 85. **d** 88 **p** 94. C Huyton St Mich *Liv* 88-94; C Rainhill from 94. *26 Calder Drive, Prescot, Merseyside L35 0NW* Tel 0151-426 3853

COLLYER, Canon David John. b 38. JP. Keble Coll Ox BA61 Ox Univ MA86. Westcott Ho Cam 61. **d** 63 **p** 64. C Perry Beeches *Birm* 63-65; Bp's Chapl for Special Youth Work 65-70; P-in-c Deritend 66-70; Bp's Youth Chapl and Dioc Youth Officer 70-73; R Northfield 73-78; Hon Chapl Birm Cathl 78-81; Hon C Birm St Geo 81-86; V Handsworth St Andr 86-97; Hon Can Birm Cathl from 95; Dioc Development Officer from 97. *27 Sundbury Rise, Northfield, Birmingham B31 2EZ* Tel 0121-428 1114

COLMAN, Cyril Vickers. b 14. ALCD40. **d** 40 **p** 41. C Barrow St Mark *Carl* 40-45; C Deal St Leon *Cant* 45-48; R Bromsberrow *Glouc* 48-53; V Boughton under Blean *Cant* 53-55; R Blaisdon w Flaxley *Glouc* 55-58; R Orlestone w Ruckinge *Cant* 58-70; V Lower Halstow 70-72; V Guernsey St Matt *Win* 72-84; rtd 84; Perm to Offic *Win* 84-95. *12 Freeman's Walk, Upper Lamphey Road, Pembroke SA71 4AS* Tel (01646) 686354

COLMAN, Geoffrey Hugh. b 29. Univ Coll Ox BA53 MA68. Wells Th Coll 67. **d** 68 **p** 69. C Wanstead St Mary *Chelmsf* 68-72; V Barking St Erkenwald 72-77; Youth Chapl 78-81; C Maidstone All SS and St Phil w Tovil *Cant* 85-88; P-in-c Norton 88-93; R 93-96; P-in-c Teynham 88-93; P-in-c Lynsted w Kingsdown 88-93; V Teynham w Lynsted and Kingsdown 93-96; rtd 96. *Ikeja Lodge, Clovelly Drive, Minster, Sheppey, Kent ME12 2SF* Tel (01795) 522510

COLMER, Andrew John. b 68. De Montfort Univ Leic BSc90. St Jo Coll Nottm MA96 LTh97. **d** 97. C Roby *Liv* from 97. *42 Buttermere Road, Liverpool L16 2NN* Tel 0151-489 5910

COLMER, Malcolm John. b 45. Sussex Univ MSc67 Nottm Univ BA73. St Jo Coll Nottm 71. **d** 73 **p** 74. C Egham *Guildf* 73-76; C Chadwell *Chelmsf* 76-79; V S Malling *Chich* 79-85; V Hornsey Rise St Mary w St Steph *Lon* 85-87; TR Hornsey Rise Whitehall

Park Team 87-96; AD Islington 90-94; Adn Middx from 96. *59 Sutton Lane South, London W4 3ZR* Tel 0181-994 8148 Fax 995 5374

COLSON, Major Alexander Francis Lionel. b 21. MBE45. St Jo Coll Cam BA43 MA61. Tyndale Hall Bris 60. **d** 62 **p** 63. C Slough *Ox* 62-65; R Elmswell *St E* 65-73; V W Kilburn St Luke w St Simon and St Jude *Lon* 73-82; R Thrandeston, Stuston and Brome w Oakley *St E* 82-86; rtd 86; Perm to Offic *Nor* from 86. *10 Soanes Court, Lyng, Norwich NR9 5RE* Tel (01603) 872812

COLSON, Ian Richard. b 65. Wolv Poly BSc86 Nottm Univ BTh89. Linc Th Coll 86. **d** 89 **p** 90. C Nunthorpe *York* 89-92; C Thornaby on Tees 92-93; Chapl RAF from 93. *Chaplaincy Services (RAF), HQ, Personnel and Training Command, RAF Innsworth, Gloucester GL3 1EZ* Tel (01452) 712612 ext 5164 Fax 510828

COLSTON, John Edward. b 43. Open Univ BA91 Leeds Univ MA94. Lich Th Coll 65. **d** 68 **p** 69. C Bromsgrove All SS *Worc* 68-71; C Tettenhall Wood *Lich* 71-74; V Alrewas 74-88; V Wychnor 74-88; R Ainderby Steeple w Yafforth and Kirby Wiske etc *Ripon* 88-95; Warden of Readers 90-96; V High Harrogate Ch Ch from 95. *Christ Church Vicarage, 11 St Hilda's Road, Harrogate, N Yorkshire HG2 8JX* Tel (01423) 883390

COLTHURST, The Ven Reginald William Richard. b 22. TCD BA44. CITC 45. **d** 45 **p** 46. C Portadown St Mark *Arm* 45-48; C Belfast All SS *Conn* 48-55; I Ardtrea w Desertcreat *Arm* 55-66; I Richhill 66-94; RD Kilmore 79-94; Adn Arm 85-92; rtd 94. *14 Cabin Hill Gardens, Belfast BT75 7AP* Tel (01232) 472288

COLTON, Leonard Henry. b 35. All Nations Chr Coll 59 Bris & Glouc Tr Course 81. **d** 84 **p** 85. NSM Swindon Ch Ch *Bris* 84-90; NSM Lyddington w Wanborough 90-91; NSM Bishopstone w Hinton Parva 90-91; C Shepton Mallet w Doulting *B & W* 91-94; Chapl HM Pris Shepton Mallet 92-94; TV Wellington and Distr *B & W* from 94. *The Vicarage, Ashbrittle, Wellington, Somerset TA21 0LF* Tel (01823) 672495

COLTON, William Paul. b 60. NUI BCL81 TCD DipTh84 MPhil87. **d** 84 **p** 85. C Lisburn St Paul *Conn* 84-87; Bp's Dom Chapl 85-90; V Choral Belf Cathl 87-90; Min Can Belf Cathl 89-90; PV, Registrar and Chapter Clerk Ch Ch Cathl Dub *D & G* 90-95; I Castleknock and Mulhuddart, w Clonsilla from 90; Co-ord Protestant Relig Progr RTE from 93; RD St Mary from 94; Hon Chapl Actors' Ch Union 94-96; Area Chapl (Ireland) Actors' Ch Union 96-97. *Castleknock Rectory, 12 Hawthorn Lawn, Castleknock, Dublin 15, Irish Republic* Tel Dublin (1) 821 3083 Fax as telephone E-mail wpcolton@iol.ie.

COLVER, Canon John Lawrence. b 14. Keble Coll Ox BA36 MA40. Cuddesdon Coll 36. **d** 37 **p** 38. C Linc St Nic w St Jo Newport *Linc* 37-40; C E Dulwich St Jo *S'wark* 40-42; C Plumstead St Nic 42-45; R Lt Coates *Linc* 45-52; V Caistor w Holton le Moor and Clixby 52-63; P-in-c Easington Colliery *Dur* 63-65; V Bembridge *Portsm* 65-79; rtd 79; Perm to Offic *Portsm* from 81. *Lynton, 10 Yelfs Road, Ryde, Isle of Wight PO33 2LY* Tel (01983) 566498

COLVILLE, Gary Stanley. b 59. QPFF83. Sarum & Wells Th Coll 90. **d** 92 **p** 93. C Plaistow St Mary *Roch* 92-94; P-in-c Foots Cray 94-96; R from 96. *The Rectory, Rectory Lane, Sidcup, Kent DA14 5BP*

COLWILL, James Patrick (Jay). b 68. Man Poly BA91. St Jo Coll Nottm BTh93 MA94. **d** 94 **p** 95. C Reading St Agnes w St Paul *Ox* from 94. *St Paul's House, 3 Whitley Wood Lane, Reading RG2 8PN* Tel 0118-986 2513

COLWILL, Raymond William (Ray). b 06. Ripon Hall Ox. **d** 71 **p** 71. Hon C Wilton *B & W* from 71. *Hamara, Comeytrowe Lane, Taunton, Somerset TA1 5JB* Tel (01823) 331833

COMBE, Edward Charles. b 40. N Ord Course. **d** 89 **p** 90. NSM Broadheath *Ches* 89-94; USA from 94. *Address temp unknown*

COMBE, The Very Revd John Charles. b 33. TCD BA53 MA56 BD57 MLitt65 PhD70. **d** 56 **p** 57. C Cork St Luke w St Ann *C, C & R* 56-58; C Ballynafeigh St Jude *D & D* 58-61; I Crinken *D & G* 61-66; Hon Clerical V Ch Ch Cathl Dublin 63-66; C Belfast St Bart *Conn* 66-70; I Belfast St Barn 70-74; I Portadown St Mark *Arm* 74-84; I Arm St Mark w Aghavilly 84-90; Can Arm Cathl 85-90; Dean Kilmore *K, E & A* 90-96; I Kilmore w Ballintemple, Kildallon etc 90-96; rtd 96. *2 Hampton Court, Croft Road, Holywood, Co Down BT18 0HU* Tel (01232) 427656

COMBER, Mrs Alison. LNSM course. **d** 94 **p** 95. C New Bury *Man* from 94. *12 Seymour Grove, Farnworth, Bolton BL4 0HF* Tel (01204) 397745

COMBER, The Ven Anthony James. b 27. Leeds Univ BSc49 MSc52. St Chad's Coll Dur 53. **d** 56 **p** 57. C Manston *Ripon* 56-60; V Oulton 60-69; V Hunslet St Mary 69-77; RD Armley 72-75 and 79-81; R Farnley 77-82; Hon Can Ripon Cathl 80-92; Adn Leeds 82-92; rtd 92; Perm to Offic *Bradf* from 93. *24 Stanks Cross, Leeds LS14 5PS* Tel 0113-228 4825

COMBER, Keith Charles. b 15. Wycliffe Hall Ox 71. **d** 73 **p** 74. C Walmley *Birm* 73-76; V Barston 76-79; rtd 80; Perm to Offic *Ely* 80-86; Perm to Offic *Nor* 80-86; Lic to Offic *Chich* 86-88; Perm to Offic from 88. *2 Boscobel Court, 42 West Hill Road, St Leonards-on-Sea, E Sussex TN38 0ND* Tel (01424) 720334

COMBER, Michael. b 35. **d** 72 **p** 72. CA 59-72; C Carl H Trin and St Barn *Carl* 72-73; C Upperby St Jo 73-76; V Dearham 76-81; V Harraby 81-84; R Orton and Tebay w Ravenstonedale etc 84-90; I Clonfert Gp of Par *L & K* 90-94; I Convoy w Monellan and Donaghmore *D & R* from 94. *Convoy Rectory, Convoy, Lifford, Co Donegal, Irish Republic* Tel Convoy (74) 47164

COMBES, Roger Matthew. b 47. K Coll Lon LLB69. Ridley Hall Cam 72. **d** 74 **p** 75. C Onslow Square St Paul *Lon* 74-77; C Brompton H Trin 76-77; C Cambridge H Sepulchre w All SS *Ely* 77-86; R Silverhill St Matt *Chich* from 86. *The Rectory, St Matthew's Road, St Leonards-on-Sea, E Sussex TN38 0TN* Tel (01424) 423790

COMER, Michael John. b 30. St Mich Coll Llan 79. **d** 81 **p** 82. C Bistre *St As* 81-84; R Llanfyllin and Bwlchycibau 84-91; C Hattersley *Ches* 91; V 91-94; rtd 94. *134 Sycamore Drive, Newtown SY16 2QE* Tel (01686) 624557

COMFORT, Alan. b 64. Ridley Hall Cam CTM94. **d** 94 **p** 95. C Chadwell Heath *Chelmsf* 94-97; C Buckhurst Hill from 97. *The Vicarage, 10 Albert Road, Buckhurst Hill, Essex IG9 6BH* Tel 0181-504 1931

COMLEY, Thomas Hedges. b 36. Leeds Univ BA62 Birm Univ DipSocWork78. Coll of Resurr Mirfield 62. **d** 64 **p** 65. C Leadgate *Dur* 64-67; C Shirley *Birm* 67-71; V Smethwick St Alb 71-76; Perm to Offic 76-82; V N Wembley St Cuth *Lon* 82-92; V Taddington, Chelmorton and Flagg, and Monyash *Derby* from 92. *The Vicarage, Monyash, Bakewell, Derbyshire DE45 1JH* Tel (01629) 812234

COMMANDER, Reginald Arthur. b 20. RGN Aston Univ DHSA BA. Qu Coll Birm 75. **d** 78 **p** 79. NSM Wolverhampton *Lich* 78-92; Perm to Offic from 92; Perm to Offic *Heref* from 95. *15 Coulter Grove, Perton, Wolverhampton WV6 7UA* Tel (01902) 744276

COMPTON, Barry Charles Chittenden. b 33. Linc Th Coll 60. **d** 62 **p** 63. C Beddington *S'wark* 62-65; C Limpsfield and Titsey 66-68; Hon C 71-94; R Ridley *Roch* 69-70; R Ash 69-70; Perm to Offic *S'wark* from 70; rtd 94. *14 Hallsland Way, Oxted, Surrey RH8 9AL* Tel (01883) 714896 Fax 722842

COMYNS, Clifford John. b 28. TCD BA50 HDipEd53 MA53 BD67. **d** 51 **p** 52. C Chapelizod *D & G* 51-55; CF 55-75; Asst Master Eastbourne Coll from 75; Asst Chapl from 85; Perm to Offic *Chich* from 75. *Eastbourne College, Eastbourne, E Sussex BN21 4JY* Tel (01323) 737411

CONANT, Fane Charles. b 44. Oak Hill Th Coll 83. **d** 85 **p** 86. C Hoole *Ches* 85-89; V Kelsall from 89. *St Philip's Vicarage, Chester Road, Kelsall, Tarporley, Cheshire CW6 0SA* Tel (01829) 51472

CONAWAY, Barry Raymond. b 41. CertEd69 Nottm Univ BEd70. Sarum & Wells Th Coll 86. **d** 88 **p** 89. C Ross w Brampton Abbotts, Bridstow and Peterstow *Heref* 88-91; R Bishop's Frome w Castle Frome and Fromes Hill 91-96; P-in-c Acton Beauchamp and Evesbatch 91-96; P-in-c Charminster and Stinsford *Sarum* from 96. *The Vicarage, Mill Lane, Charminster, Dorchester, Dorset DT2 9QP* Tel (01305) 262477

CONDELL, Canon Joseph Alfred Ambrose. b 48. CITC 70. **d** 73 **p** 74. C Donaghcloney *D & D* 73-76; I Achonry w Tubbercurry and Killoran *T, K & A* 76-79; I Roscrea w Kyle, Bourney and Corbally *L & K* from 79; Can Killaloe Cathl 83-89; RD Killaloe and Roscrea 89-95; Prec Limerick and Killaloe Cathls from 89; Sec Dioc Bd of Educn from 91. *St Conan's Rectory, Roscrea, Co Tipperary, Irish Republic* Tel Roscrea (505) 21725 Fax 21993

CONDER, Paul Collingwood Nelson. b 33. St Jo Coll Cam BA56 MA60. Ridley Hall Cam 56. **d** 58 **p** 59. C Grassendale *Liv* 58-61; Tutor St Jo Coll Dur 61-67; R Sutton *Liv* 67-74; TR 74-75; V Thames Ditton *Guildf* 75-86; RD Emly 82-86; V Blundellsands St Mich *Liv* from 86. *St Michael's Vicarage, 41 Dowhills Road, Liverpool L23 8SJ* Tel 0151-924 3424

CONDRY, Edward Francis. b 53. UEA BA74 Ex Coll Ox DipSocAnth75 BLitt77 DPhil80 Nottm Univ DipTh81. Linc Th Coll 80. **d** 82 **p** 83. C Weston Favell *Pet* 82-85; V Bloxham w Milcombe and S Newington *Ox* 85-93; TR Rugby St Andr *Cov* from 93. *The Rectory, Church Street, Rugby, Warks CV21 3QH* Tel (01788) 565609

CONEY, Joanna Margery. b 39. Culham Coll of Educn CertEd75 Open Univ BA83. Ox Min Course CBTS93. **d** 93 **p** 94. Par Dn Wolvercote w Summertown *Ox* 93-94; C 94-97; LNSM Tr Officer (Ox Adnry) from 97. *13 Sparey Place, Oxford OX2 8NL*

CONEY, Miss Mary Margaret. b 37. K Coll Lon BD58 CertEd59 DipAdEd78 Ex Univ MA87. **d** 87 **p** 94. NSM Penzance St Mary w St Paul *Truro* 87-90; Public Preacher from 90. *The Old Chapel, Lady Downs, Newmill, Penzance, Cornwall TR20 8UZ* Tel (01736) 797164

CONEY, Preb Peter Norman Harvey. b 28. Keble Coll Ox BA51 MA55. Cuddesdon Coll 51. **d** 53 **p** 54. C Northallerton w Deighton and Romanby *York* 53-56; C Wakef Cathl *Wakef* 56-59; V Milverton *B & W* 59-65; Chapl K Coll Taunton 65-70; V Martock *B & W* 70-72; V Martock w Ash 72-92; RD Martock 80-90; Dioc Press Officer 83-88; Preb Wells Cathl 85-92; rtd 93. *Les Aubepines, Le Causse, 46500 Mayrinhac-Lentour, France* Tel France (33) 65 38 22 19

CONEYS, Stephen John. b 61. Sheff Univ LLB82. St Jo Coll Nottm 87. **d** 90 **p** 91. C Plymouth Em w Efford *Ex* 90-92; C Plymouth Em, Efford and Laira 93-94; TV Whitstable *Cant* from 94. *11 Kimberley Grove, Seasalter, Whitstable, Kent CT5 4AY* Tel (01227) 276795

CONGDON, John Jameson. b 30. St Edm Hall Ox BA53 MA57. Wycliffe Hall Ox 53. **d** 55 **p** 56. C Aspley *S'well* 55-58; C-in-c Woodthorpe CD 58-63; V Woodthorpe 63-69; V Spring Grove St Mary *Lon* 70-84; V Woodley St Jo the Ev *Ox* 84-89; Chapl W Middx Univ Hosp Isleworth 89-95; rtd 95. *95 Harewood Road, Isleworth, Middlesex TW7 5HN* Tel 0181-568 6504

CONLEY, James Alan. b 29. Dur Univ BSc51. St Jo Coll Nottm. **d** 87 **p** 88. NSM Cropwell Bishop w Colston Bassett, Granby etc *S'well* from 87. *8 Willow Lane, Langar, Nottingham NG13 9HL* Tel (01949) 60820

CONLON, Shaun. b 69. Birm Univ BA90. Ripon Coll Cuddesdon DipMin93. **d** 93 **p** 94. C Castle Bromwich SS Mary and Marg *Birm* 93-97; C Hockerill *St Alb* from 97. *17 Legions Way, Bishop's Stortford, Herts CM23 2AU* Tel (01279) 657261

CONN, Alistair Aberdein. b 37. Down Coll Cam BA60 MA64. Linc Th Coll 60. **d** 62 **p** 63. C W Hartlepool St Paul *Dur* 62-65; Uganda 65-66; Chapl Shrewsbury Sch 66-73; R Coupar Angus *St And* 73-78; V Ravenshead *S'well* 78-93; RD Newstead 90-93; R Collingham w S Scarle and Besthorpe and Girton from 93; RD Newark from 95. *The Rectory, 1 Vicarage Close, Collingham, Newark, Notts NG23 7PQ* Tel (01636) 892317

CONN, Robert Edwin. b 14. TCD BA38 MA44. **d** 39 **p** 40. C Belfast Trin Coll Miss *Conn* 39-42; C Marlyn *L & K* 42-45; P-in-c Kilwarlin Upper *D & D* 45-53; I 53-63; P-in-c Killyleagh 63-65; I 65-88; rtd 88. *9 Drumkeen Court, Belfast BT8 4FY* Tel (01232) 644305

CONNELL, Miss Heather Josephine. b 38. SRN60 SCM61 Open Univ BA86. S'wark Ord Course 77. **dss** 79 **d** 87 **p** 94. Heston *Lon* 79-84; Gillingham St Barn *Roch* 84-96; Par Dn 87-90; NSM 91-96; Chapl Medway Hosp Gillingham 91-96; NSM Gillingham H Trin *Roch* from 96. *31 Brenchley Road, Gillingham, Kent ME8 6HD* Tel (01634) 230289

CONNELL, John Richard. b 63. K Coll Lon BD84. St Mich Coll Llan DPT94. **d** 94 **p** 96. C Caldicot *Mon* 94-97; C Risca from 97. *18 Commercial Street, Risca, Newport NP1 6AY*

CONNER, Mrs Cathryn. b 42. Birm Univ BSc64. NE Ord Course 91. **d** 94 **p** 95. NSM Bainton w N Dalton, Middleton-on-the-Wolds etc *York* from 94. *Centre House, North Dalton, Driffield, N Humberside YO25 9XA* Tel (01377) 217265

CONNER, Charles Borthwick. b 20. Keble Coll Ox BA43 MA49. St Steph Ho Ox 48. **d** 50 **p** 51. C Saltburn-by-the-Sea *York* 50-52; Chapl Ely Th Coll 52-53; CF 53-70; Perm to Offic *Sarum* from 80. *Angel Cottage, West Knighton, Dorchester, Dorset DT2 8PE* Tel (01305) 852465

✠**CONNER, The Rt Revd David John.** b 47. Ex Coll Ox BA69 MA77. St Steph Ho Ox 69. **d** 71 **p** 72 **c** 94. Hon C Summertown *Ox* 71-76; Asst Chapl St Edw Sch Ox 71-73; Chapl 73-80; TV Wolvercote w Summertown *Ox* 76-80; Chapl Win Coll 80-87; V Cambridge Gt St Mary w St Mich *Ely* 87-94; RD Cambridge 89-94; Suff Bp Lynn *Nor* from 94. *The Old Vicarage, Castle Acre, King's Lynn, Norfolk PE32 2AA* Tel (01760) 755553 Fax 755085

CONNOLL, Miss Helen Dorothy. b 45. Oak Hill Th Coll BA86. **dss** 86 **d** 87 **p** 94. Leytonstone St Jo *Chelmsf* 86-87; Par Dn 87-90; Asst Chapl Grimsby Distr Gen Hosp 90-93; Chapl Kent and Cant Hosp 93-94; Chapl Kent and Cant Hosps NHS Trust from 94. *Kent and Canterbury Hospital, Ethelbert Road, Canterbury, Kent CT1 3NG* Tel (01227) 766877

CONNOLLY, Daniel (Dan). b 51. BEng. St Jo Coll Nottm DPS84. **d** 84 **p** 85. C Bedgrove *Ox* 84-87; C-in-c Crookhorn Ch Cen CD *Portsm* 87-88; V Crookhorn 88-97; R Sutton Coldfield H Trin *Birm* from 97. *The Rectory, 16 Coleshill Street, Sutton Coldfield, W Midlands B72 1SH* Tel 0121-354 3607 Fax 269708

CONNOLLY, Miss Lynne. b 53. Aston Tr Scheme 88 Linc Th Coll CMinlStuds92. **d** 92 **p** 94. Par Dn Hurst *Man* 92-94; C 94-96; R Burnage St Nic from 96. *296 Wilbraham Road, Manchester M21 1UU* Tel 0161-860 4521

CONNOLLY, Sydney Herbert. b 40. Leeds Univ BA66. Coll of Resurr Mirfield 66. **d** 68 **p** 69. C W Derby St Mary *Liv* 68-71; C Prescot 71-74; V Burtonwood 74-80; V Walker *Newc* 80-89; TR Whorlton 89-96; V Chapel House from 96. *The Vicarage, 44 Queensbury Drive, North Walbottle, Newcastle upon Tyne NE15 9SF* Tel 0191-267 4069

CONNOR, Dennis George Austin. b 16. K Coll Lon BD40 AKC40. **d** 40 **p** 41. C Shoreditch St Leon *Lon* 40-42; C Mill Hill Jo Keble Ch 42-47; C Enfield St Andr 47-52; V Harefield 52-94; Chapl Harefield Hosp Middx 52-94; RD Hillingdon *Lon* 70-75; rtd 94. *2 Springwell Lane, Harefield, Middx UB9 6PG* Tel (01895) 824915

CONNOR, Ellis Jones. b 16. Univ of Wales BA38. St Mich Coll Llan 38. **d** 39 **p** 41. C Broughton *St As* 39-43; C Llandegfan and Beaumaris *Ban* 43-48; V Liv St Chris Norris Green *Liv* 48-55; R Desford *Leic* 55-73; R N Hill *Truro* 73-75; V Lewannick 73-75; R Llanddewi Skirrid w Llanvetherine etc *Mon* 75-78; C Spalding St Jo *Linc* 79-82; rtd 82; Perm to Offic *Leic* from 82. *35 Sycamore Street, Blaby, Leicester LE8 4FL* Tel 0116-277 7725

CONNOR, Geoffrey. b 46. K Coll Lon BD73 AKC73. St Aug Coll Cant. **d** 74 **p** 75. C Cockerton *Dur* 74-79; Dioc Recruitment Officer 79-87; Chapl St Chad's Coll 84-87; Vice-Provost St Mary's Cathl *Edin* 87-90; R Edin St Mary 87-90; Dioc Dir of Ords (Dios Edin and Arg) 87-90; V Whitechapel w Admarsh-in-Bleasdale *Blackb* from 90; Dir of Ords from 90. *The Vicarage, Church Lane, Whitechapel, Preston PR3 2EP* Tel (01995) 640282

CONNOR, Patrick Francis Latham. b 25. Ex Coll Ox BA47 MA52. Gen Th Sem (NY) STB53. **d** 53 **p** 53. USA 53-55 and 59-62; R N Tamerton *Truro* 55-59; R St Ive 62-64; R Sparkford w Weston Bampfylde *B & W* 64-85; P-in-c Sutton Montis 70-85; R Mawnan *Truro* 85-89; rtd 89; Perm to Offic *Truro* from 89. *Trelatham, Boyton, Launceston, Cornwall PL15 9RJ* Tel (01566) 776078

CONNOR, Stephen John. b 58. MA. Ridley Hall Cam. **d** 84 **p** 85. C Beamish *Dur* 84-86; C Wordsley *Lich* 86-90; TV Langport Area Chs *B & W* from 90. *The Vicarage, 2 Mill Road, High Ham, Langport, Somerset TA10 9DJ* Tel (01458) 253038

CONNOR, Archdeacon of. *See* HARPER, The Ven Alan Edwin Thomas

CONNOR, Bishop of. *See* MOORE, The Rt Revd James Edward

CONNOR, Dean of. *See* RUSK, Canon Frederick John

CONRAD, Paul Derick. b 54. Worc Coll Ox BA76 MA82. St Steph Ho Ox 78. **d** 80 **p** 81. C Wanstead St Mary *Chelmsf* 80-83; C Somers Town St Mary *Lon* 83-85; P-in-c Kentish Town St Martin w St Andr 85-91; V 91-95; P-in-c Hampstead Ch Ch from 95. *Christ Church Vicarage, 10 Cannon Place, London NW3 1EJ* Tel 0171-435 6784

CONSTABLE, Douglas Brian. b 40. Lon Univ BA62. Linc Th Coll 63. **d** 65 **p** 66. C Stockwood CD *Bris* 65-70; Hon C Clifton St Paul 70-72; Asst Chapl Bris Univ 70-72; Chapl Lee Abbey 72-77; V Derby St Thos *Derby* 77-85; TV Southampton (City Cen) *Win* 85-92; rtd 92. *9 Ordnance Road, Southampton SO15 2AZ* Tel (01703) 228953

CONSTANT, Arden. b 09. K Coll Cam BA32 MA36. Cuddesdon Coll. **d** 34 **p** 35. C King Cross *Wakef* 34-39; C Lowestoft St Marg *Nor* 39-43; Chapl RNVR 41-46; Ceylon 47-59; V Heaton St Barn *Bradf* 59-66; V Kirkby Malham 66-73; rtd 72. *38 Bushwood Road, Kew, Richmond, Surrey TW9 3BQ* Tel 0181-940 3156

CONSTANTINE, Miss Elaine Muriel. b 50. Univ of Wales (Swansea) BSc72 CertEd73 DipEd75 Lon Univ MEd78. St Alb Minl Tr Scheme. **dss** 86 **d** 87 **p** 94. Bedford St Martin *St Alb* 86-87; Par Dn 87-88; Par Dn Leighton Buzzard w Eggington, Hockliffe etc 88-94; C from 94. *Emmaus House, 63 Jupiter Drive, Leighton Buzzard, Beds LU7 8XA* Tel (01525) 373167

CONSTANTINE, Leonard. b 30. AKC57. **d** 58 **p** 59. C W Hartlepool St Aid *Dur* 58-61; C Sheff St Geo and St Steph *Sheff* 61-62; Nyasaland 62-64; Malawi 64-69; V W Pelton *Dur* 69-73; V Shotton 73-78; V Stillington 78-80; V Grindon and Stillington 80-82; V Corbridge w Halton and Newton Hall *Newc* 82-95; Chapl Charlotte Straker Hosp 82-95; rtd 95; Perm to Offic *Wakef* from 95. *28 Tenterfield Road, Ossett, W Yorkshire WF5 0RU* Tel (01924) 276180

CONVERY, Arthur Malcolm. b 42. Sheff Univ BSc63 DipEd64. N Ord Course 79. **d** 82 **p** 83. NSM Parr *Liv* 82-87; V Marown *S & M* from 87. *The Vicarage, Marown, Crosby, Isle of Man IM4 4BH* Tel (01624) 851378

CONWAY, Alfred Sydney. b 22. Kelham Th Coll 40. **d** 45 **p** 46. C Fulham St Oswald w St Aug *Lon* 45-49; V Allenton and Shelton Lock *Derby* 49-55; P-in-c Chaddesden St Phil 55-63; V Croxley Green All SS *St Alb* 63-81; V Walton St Jo *Liv* 81-89; rtd 89; Perm to Offic *Ex* from 89. *14 Mount Close, Honiton, Devon EX14 8QZ* Tel (01404) 46052

CONWAY, Glyn Haydn. b 38. St Mich Coll Llan DipTh65. **d** 65 **p** 66. C Wrexham *St As* 65-71; TV 71-77; V Holywell 77-83; V Upton Ascension *Ches* from 83. *The Vicarage, Demage Lane, Chester CH2 1EL* Tel (01244) 383518

CONWAY, John Arthur. b 67. Leeds Univ BEng90 DipTh93 Edin Univ BD97. **d** 97. C Edin St Mary *Edin* from 97. *Flat 2FR, 2 St Peter's Place, Edinburgh EH3 9PJ* Tel 0131-229 9955 Fax as telephone

CONWAY, Kevin Sean. b 66. Leeds Univ BSc88 Dur Univ PGCE91. Cranmer Hall Dur BA93. **d** 96 **p** 97. C Peterlee *Dur* from 96. *1 Orwell Close, Peterlee, Co Durham SR8 1HL* Tel 0191-586 1018

CONWAY, Canon Owen Arnott. b 35. Dur Univ BA58. St Steph Ho Ox 58. **d** 60 **p** 61. C Manston *Ripon* 60-64; V Osmondthorpe St Phil 64-70; Warden Dioc Ho Barrowby 70-73; V Armley w New Wortley 73-81; V Headingley 81-91; RD Headingley 87-91; Hon Can Ripon Cathl 87-91; Can Res Ches Cathl *Ches* from 91. *9 Abbey Street, Chester CH1 2JF* Tel (01244) 316144

CONWAY, Philip James. b 66. Liv Inst of Educn BA91. St Steph Ho Ox DipMin95. **d** 95 **p** 96. C High Harrogate Ch Ch *Ripon* from 95. *7 Kingsway Drive, Harrogate, N Yorkshire HG1 5NJ* Tel (01432) 526846

CONWAY, Mrs Sandra Coralie (Sandy). b 45. Bris Univ BA66. S'wark Ord Course DipRS92. **d** 92. Hon C Kenley *S'wark* from 92. *28 Russell Hill, Purley, Surrey CR8 2JA* Tel 0181-668 2890

CONWAY, Stephen David. b 57. Keble Coll Ox BA80 MA84 CertEd81 Selw Coll Cam BA85. Westcott Ho Cam 83. **d** 86 **p** 87. C Heworth St Mary *Dur* 86-89; C Bishopwearmouth St Mich w St Hilda 89-90; Hon C Dur St Marg 90-94; Dir of Ords 90-94; P-in-c Cockerton 94-96; V from 96. *St Mary's Vicarage, Cockerton, Darlington, Co Durham DL3 9EX* Tel (01325) 367092

CONWAY, Thomas Robertson. b 36. DipTh. **d** 86 **p** 87. C Bangor Abbey *D & D* 86-95; I Dungiven w Bovevagh *D & R* 89-95; I Carrowdore w Millisle *D & D* from 95. *The Rectory, 40 Woburn Road, Millisle, Newtownards, Co Down BT22 2HY* Tel (01247) 861226

CONWAY-LEE, Stanley. b 17. Linc Th Coll 68. **d** 70 **p** 71. C Dedham *Chelmsf* 70-72; C Lt Ilford St Mich 72-74; V Tollesbury 74-75; V Tollesbury w Salcot Virley 75-79; V Bocking St Pet 79-85; rtd 85; Perm to Offic *Chelmsf* from 85. *10 Northumberland Close, Braintree, Essex CM7 6NLL* Tel (01376) 550117

COOGAN, The Ven Robert Arthur William. b 29. Univ of Tasmania BA51 St Jo Coll Dur DipTh53. **d** 53 **p** 54. C Plaistow St Andr *Chelmsf* 53-56; Australia 56-62; V N Woolwich *Chelmsf* 62-73; P-in-c W Silvertown St Barn 62-73; V Hampstead St Steph *Lon* 73-77; P-in-c N St Pancras All Hallows 74-77; RD S Camden (Holborn and St Pancras) 75-81; P-in-c Old St Pancras w Bedford New Town St Matt 76-80; V Hampstead St Steph w All Hallows 77-85; P-in-c Kentish Town St Martin w St Andr 78-81; AD N Camden (Hampstead) 78-83; Preb St Paul's Cathl 82-85; Adn Hampstead 85-94; rtd 94; Perm to Offic *Chich* from 94. *30 Marchwood Gate, Marchwood, Chichester, W Sussex PO19 4HA* Tel (01243) 528828

COOK, Alan. b 27. St Deiniol's Hawarden 79. **d** 80 **p** 81. Hon C Gatley *Ches* 80-83; Chapl Man R Eye Hosp 83-86; Chapl Asst Man R Infirmary 80-83 and 86-88; V Congleton St Jas *Ches* 89-93; rtd 93; Perm to Offic *Ches* from 93. *15 Buttermere Road, Gatley, Cheadle, Cheshire SK8 4RQ* Tel 0161-428 4350

COOK, Canon Brian Edwin. b 36. Sarum & Wells Th Coll 78. **d** 80 **p** 81. C E Wickham *S'wark* 80-83; C Petersfield w Sheet *Portsm* 83-86; R Liss from 86; RD Petersfield 91-96; Hon Can Portsm Cathl from 96. *The Rectory, Station Road, Liss, Hants GU33 7AQ* Tel (01730) 893175

COOK, Brian Robert. b 43. Chich Th Coll 83. **d** 85 **p** 86. C Whyke w Rumboldswhyke and Portfield *Chich* 85-87; C Worth 87-90; TV 90-94; P-in-c Chidham from 94. *The Vicarage, Chidham, Chichester, W Sussex PO18 8TA* Tel (01243) 573147

COOK, Canon Charles Peter. b 32. St Jo Coll Dur BA54 DipTh58. **d** 58 **p** 59. C Kingston upon Hull H Trin *York* 58-64; V High Elswick St Paul *Newc* 64-74; V Cheadle Hulme St Andr *Ches* from 74; Hon Can Ches Cathl from 91. *St Andrew's Priory, Cheadle Road, Cheadle Hulme, Cheadle, Cheshire SK8 5EU* Tel 0161-485 1112 or 485 2648

COOK, Christopher. b 44. Qu Coll Birm 68. **d** 69 **p** 70. C Gt Ilford St Mary *Chelmsf* 69-72; C Corringham 72-77; R E Donyland 77-84; R Pentlow, Foxearth, Liston and Borley 84-88; Chapl RAD Essex Area 88-89; rtd 89; Perm to Offic *Chelmsf* from 89. *Oak Mill, Field View Lane, Little Totham, Maldon, Essex CM9 8ND* Tel (01621) 893280

COOK, The Ven Christopher Arthur. Edin Th Coll 53. **d** 56 **p** 58. C Motherwell *Glas* 56-59; S Africa 61-64 and from 70; Adn Grahamstown from 80; USPG 65-70. *PO St Matthews 5680, 5680 South Africa* Tel St Matthews (12) 40242

COOK, David. b 46. Hertf Coll Ox BA MA72. Wycliffe Hall Ox 69. **d** 73 **p** 74. C Hartlepool All SS Stranton *Dur* 74-75; Lect Qu Coll Birm 75-81; Chapl Cranbrook Sch Kent from 81. *33 Oatfield Drive, Cranbrook, Kent TN17 3LA* Tel (01580) 713310

COOK, David Arthur. b 50. St Jo Coll Dur BA74. St Steph Ho Ox 86. **d** 88 **p** 89. C S Bank *York* 88-91; C Up Hatherley *Glouc* 91-93; P-in-c Cumbernauld *Glas* from 93. *The Rectory, Fleming Road, Cumbernauld, Glasgow G67 1LJ* Tel (01236) 721599

COOK, David Charles Murray. b 41. MA. Wycliffe Hall Ox 65. **d** 67 **p** 68. C Chatham St Phil and St Jas *Roch* 67-71; S Africa 71-89; TR Newbury *Ox* from 89. *The Rectory, 64 North Croft Lane, Newbury, Berks RG13 1BN* Tel (01635) 40326

COOK, Canon David Reginald Edmund. b 25. Wells Th Coll 65. **d** 67 **p** 68. C Gt Ilford St Clem *Chelmsf* 67-71; P-in-c Langdon Hills 71-75; R 75-79; RD Basildon 76-79; P-in-c W Bergholt 79-80; R 80-90; Hon Can Chelmsf Cathl 86-90; rtd 90; Perm to Offic *Chelmsf* from 90. *177 Straight Road, Lexden, Colchester CO3 5DG* Tel (01206) 573231

COOK, David Smith. b 47. Hull Univ BTh88 MA93. Lich Th Coll 68. **d** 71 **p** 72. C Tudhoe Grange *Dur* 71-75; C Bishopwearmouth St Mary V w St Pet CD 75-77; V Copley *Wakef* 77-80; V Birstall 80-83; V Holme-on-Spalding Moor *York* from 83; RD S Wold from 96. *The Vicarage, Holme-on-Spalding Moor, York YO4 4AG* Tel (01430) 860248

COOK, Canon Derek Edward. b 23. AKC51. **d** 52 **p** 53. C Radlett *St Alb* 52-56; C Hatfield Hyde 56-64; V Luton St Paul 64-78; P-in-c Stanbridge w Tilsworth 78-80; V Totternhoe, Stanbridge and Tilsworth 80-88; Hon Can St Alb 85-88; rtd 88; Perm to Offic *Ely* from 93. *8 Ridgeway, Eynesbury, St Neots, Huntingdon, Cambs PE19 2QY* Tel (01480) 475141

COOK, Canon Edward Rouse. b 28. Linc Coll Ox BA51 MA55. Linc Th Coll 51. **d** 53 **p** 54. C Louth H Trin *Linc* 53-56; C Crosby 56-57; Lect Boston 58-60; R Lt Coates 60-67; V Saxilby 67-90; R Broxholme 69-90; P-in-c Burton by Linc 78-94; Can and Preb Linc Cathl 79-94; Chmn Dioc Readers 86-94; RD Corringham 87-93; R Saxilby w Ingleby and Broxholme 90-94; rtd 94; Perm to Offic *Linc* from 94. *80 Lincoln Road, Dunholme, Lincoln LN2 3QY* Tel (01673) 861534

COOK, Dr Elspeth Jean. b 34. Edin Univ BSc56 PhD66. S Dios Minl Tr Scheme 85. **d** 88 **p** 94. C Yateley *Win* 88-91; Assoc Chapl Ld Mayor Treloar Hosp Alton 91-93; NSM Dunfermline *St And* from 93; P-in-c Aberdour from 96. *12 River View, Dalgety Bay, Dunfermline, Fife KY11 5YE* Tel (01383) 825222

COOK, Geoffrey John Anderson. b 64. DipBS84. St Steph Ho Ox 95. **d** 97. C St Leonards Ch Ch and St Mary *Chich* from 97. *31 Alfred Street, St Leonard's-on-Sea, E Sussex TN38 0HD* Tel (01424) 443956

COOK, George Basil Frederick. b 21. K Coll Lon BA42 St Cath Soc Ox BA48 MA52. Ripon Hall Ox 46. **d** 49 **p** 50. C Maidenhead St Luke *Ox* 49-52; C Camberley St Paul *Guildf* 52-53; C Upton cum Chalvey *Ox* 53-55; V Mitcham St Barn *S'wark* 55-91; rtd 91; Perm to Offic *S'wark* from 91. *6 Cranmer Road, Mitcham, Surrey CR4 4LD* Tel 0181-648 1980

COOK, Helen. b 50. New Coll Edin BD74. **d** 96. C Rothiemurchus *Mor* from 96. *Dukesville, Duke Street, Kingussie, Inverness-shire PH21 1JG* Tel (01540) 661724

COOK, Ian Bell. b 38. NW Ord Course 70. **d** 73 **p** 74. C Oldham St Paul *Man* 73-75; Ind Chapl 76-79; P-in-c Newton Heath St Wilfrid and St Anne 76-79; V Middleton Junction from 79. *The Vicarage, Greenhill Road, Middleton Junction, Manchester M24 2BD* Tel 0161-643 5064

COOK, Preb Ian Brian. b 38. MBIM73 Aston Univ MSc72 Birm Univ MA76. Kelham Th Coll 58. **d** 63 **p** 64. C Langley Marish *Ox* 63-66; C Stokenchurch and Cadmore End 66-68; V Lane End 68-72; P-in-c Ibstone w Fingest 68-72; Tutor W Bromwich Coll of Comm and Tech 72-74; Sen Tutor 74-80; Perm to Offic *Lich* 75-77; NSM W Bromwich St Pet 77-80; P-in-c Wednesbury St Jo 80; P-in-c Wednesbury St Jas and St Jo 80; R from 80; Dir St Jas Tr Inst from 81; RD Wednesbury from 88; Preb Lich Cathl from 94. *The Rectory, 1 Hollies Drive, Wednesbury, W Midlands WS10 9EQ* Tel 0121-505 1188 or 505 1568

COOK, James Christopher Donald. b 49. Ch Ch Ox BA70 MA74. St Steph Ho Ox 79. **d** 80 **p** 81. C Witney *Ox* 80-83; CF from 83. *MOD Chaplains (Army), Trenchard Lines, Upavon, Pewsey, Wilts SN9 6BE* Tel (01980) 615804 Fax 615800

COOK, Mrs Joan Lindsay. b 46. SRN70. St Jo Coll Dur 86. **d** 88 **p** 94. Par Dn Hartlepool St Hilda *Dur* 88-93; D-in-c 93-94; P-in-c 94-96; rtd 96. *10 Peakston Close, Hartlepool, Cleveland TS26 0PN* Tel (01429) 231778

COOK, John. b 32. Linc Th Coll 87. **d** 89 **p** 90. C Bourne *Linc* 89-92; R Colsterworth Gp from 92. *The Rectory, Church Street, Skillington, Grantham, Lincs NG33 5HQ* Tel (01476) 861443

COOK, John Edward. b 35. AKC61. **d** 62 **p** 63. C York Town St Mich *Guildf* 62-67; Singapore 67-77; P-in-c Beoley *Worc* 78-83; V 83-89; V Bromsgrove All SS from 89. *All Saints' Vicarage, 20 Burcot Lane, Bromsgrove, Worcs B60 1AE* Tel (01527) 579849 Fax as telephone

COOK, John Henry. b 11. Mert Coll Ox BA34 BSc35 MA39 MSc81. Clifton Th Coll 36. **d** 38 **p** 39. C Gt Faringdon w Lt Coxwell *Ox* 38-42; C Newbury St Nic 42-45; V Winkfield 45-52; V Furze Platt 52-68; R Witney 68-78; rtd 79; Hon C Witney *Ox* from 79. *9 Church View Road, Witney, Oxon OX8 7HT* Tel (01993) 704609

COOK, John Michael. b 48. Coll of Resurr Mirfield 72. **d** 74 **p** 75. C Weymouth H Trin *Sarum* 74-76; C Felixstowe St Jo *St E* 76-79; P-in-c Gt and Lt Whelnetham 79-84; P-in-c Cockfield 84-85; P-in-c Bradfield St George w Bradfield St Clare etc 84-85; R Cockfield w Bradfield St Clare, Felsham etc 85-87; V Workington St Jo *Carl* from 87. *St John's Vicarage, 59 Thorncroft Gardens, Workington, Cumbria CA14 4DP* Tel (01900) 602383

COOK, John Richard Millward. b 61. St Jo Coll Dur BA. Wycliffe Hall Ox 83. **d** 85 **p** 86. C Brampton St Thos *Derby* 85-89; C Farnborough *Guildf* 89-92; C Langham Place All So *Lon* from 92. *12 De Walden Street, London W1M 7PH* Tel 0171-935 9811 or 580 3522 Fax 436 3019

COOK, Kenneth George Thomas. b 36. ACA59 AHA69 FCA70 Man Univ DSA65. Coll of Resurr Mirfield 86. **d** 88 **p** 89. C Stocking Farm *Leic* 88-91; Chapl Leics Hospice 91-96; Chapl Hinchingbrooke Healthcare NHS Trust from 96. *Hinchingbrooke Hospital, Huntingdon, Cambs PE18 8NT* Tel (01480) 416416

COOK, Canon Kenneth Hugh. b 30. ALAM. AKC55. **d** 56 **p** 57. C Netherfield *S'well* 56-59; C Newark w Coddington 59-61; V Basford St Aid 61-67; V Gargrave *Bradf* 67-77; Dir of Ords 77-89; Can Res Bradf Cathl 77-95; rtd 95. *25 Hollins Close, Hampsthwaite, Harrogate, N Yorkshire HG3 2EH*

COOK, Kenneth Robert. b 42. Huddersfield Poly BA86. Chich Th Coll 66. **d** 68 **p** 69. C Upton *Ox* 68-72; C Duston *Pet* 72-76; V Halifax St Hilda *Wakef* 76-79; Chapl Huddersfield Poly 79-90; V Linc St Mary-le-Wigford w St Benedict etc *Linc* from 90. *220 Boultham Park Road, Lincoln LN6 7SU* Tel (01522) 540549

COOK, Marcus John Wyeth. b 41. Chich Th Coll 67. **d** 70 **p** 71. C Friern Barnet St Jas *Lon* 70-73; Hon C St Geo-in-the-East w St Paul from 73. *St George-in-the-East Church, Cannon Street Road, London E1 0BH* Tel 0171-481 1345

COOK, Nicholas Leonard. b 59. Nottm Univ BCombStuds84. Linc Th Coll 81. **d** 84 **p** 85. C Leic St Pet *Leic* 84-85; C Knighton St Mich 85-86; Chapl Asst Towers Hosp Humberstone 86-89;

Chapl Leics Mental Health Service Unit 89-91; Chapl Quainton Hall Sch Harrow 91-94; CF(V) 88-94; CF from 94. *MOD Chaplains (Army), Trenchard Lines, Upavon, Pewsey, Wilts SN9 6BE* Tel (01980) 615804 Fax 615800

COOK, Peter John. b 57. Ridley Hall Cam CTM95. **d** 95 **p** 96. C Romford Gd Shep Collier Row *Chelmsf* from 95. *470 Mawney Road, Romford RM7 8QB* Tel (01708) 728720

COOK, Peter John Arthur. b 42. Reading Univ BA64 Brandeis Univ (USA) MA65 QUB PhD81. Tyndale Hall Bris 68. **d** 71 **p** 72. C Everton St Chrys *Liv* 71-74; Chapl Stranmillis Coll of Educn Belf 74-87; Hon C Belfast All SS *Conn* 81-87; USA from 87. *123 West Sale Road, Lake Charles, Louisiana 70605, USA*

COOK, Richard John Noel. b 49. Univ Coll Ox BA70 MA74 PGCE72. Wycliffe Hall Ox MA77. **d** 78 **p** 79. C Fulwood *Sheff* 78-80; C Bolton St Paul w Em *Man* 81-86; TV 86-93; V Goldsworth Park *Guildf* from 93. *St Andrew's Vicarage, 8 Cardingham, Woking, Surrey GU21 3LN* Tel (01483) 764523

COOK, Canon Robert Bond. b 28. Dur Univ BSc54. Ripon Hall Ox 54. **d** 56 **p** 57. C Benwell St Jas *Newc* 56-60; C Sugley 60-64; V Denton 64-75; V Haltwhistle 75-88; P-in-c Greenhead 84-88; V Haltwhistle and Greenhead 88-93; RD Hexham 88-93; Hon Can Newc Cathl 92-93; rtd 93. *Ashcroft, Heath Road, Woolpit, Bury St Edmunds, Suffolk IP30 9RN* Tel (01359) 240670

COOK, Ronald Thomas (<u>Ron</u>). b 50. St Steph Ho Ox BA79 MA83. **d** 80 **p** 81. C Willesden St Andr *Lon* 80-83; USA 83-87; C Northolt Park St Barn *Lon* 87-90; Chapl HM Pris Blundeston 90-96; V Kettering All SS *Pet* from 96. *All Saints' Vicarage, 80 Pollard Street, Kettering, Northants NN16 9RP* Tel (01536) 513376

COOK, Stephen. b 62. Brunel Univ BSc(Econ)84 Birkb Coll Lon CertRS91 DipRS92. S'wark Ord Course 89. **d** 92 **p** 93. Hon C Forest Hill St Aug *S'wark* from 92. *20 Goodrich Road, London SE22 9EQ* Tel 0181-693 7703

COOK, Stephen William. b 57. BA DipHE. Lambeth STh87 Trin Coll Bris. **d** 85 **p** 86. C Heref St Pet w St Owen and St Jas *Heref* 85-89; TV Keynsham *B & W* 89-95; V Hanham *Bris* from 95. *Christchurch Vicarage, Church Road, Bristol BS15 3AF* Tel 0117-967 3580

COOK, Timothy John. b 62. Cranmer Hall Dur CTMin95. **d** 95 **p** 96. C Dorchester *Sarum* from 95. *10 Treves Road, Dorchester, Dorset DT1 2HD* Tel (01305) 260552

COOK, Trevor Vivian. b 43. Sarum Th Coll 67. **d** 69 **p** 70. C Lambeth St Phil *S'wark* 69-73; C St Buryan, St Levan and Sennen *Truro* 73-75; V The Ilketshalls *St E* 75-79; P-in-c Rumburgh w S Elmham 75-79; R Rumburgh w S Elmham w the Ilketshalls 79-84; TR Langport Area Chs *B & W* 84-96; P-in-c Rode Major from 96. *The Rectory, Church Lane, Rode, Bath BA3 6PN* Tel (01373) 831234

COOK, Canon William George. b 14. St Jo Coll Dur LTh36 BA37. St Aid Birkenhead 33. **d** 37 **p** 38. C Elmton *Derby* 37-40; CF (EC) 40-46; R Bonsall *Derby* 46-51; V Stanley 51-56; R Aston-on-Trent and Weston-on-Trent 56-68; RD Melbourne 66-68; V Allestree 68-79; Hon Can Derby Cathl 78-79; rtd 79; Perm to Offic *St E* from 79; Perm to Offic *Pet* 85-94; P-in-c Starston *Nor* 85; Perm to Offic from 85. *1 Orchard Grove, Diss, Norfolk IP22 3LX* Tel (01379) 642058

COOKE, Alan. b 50. Nottm Univ BTh74 Lanc Univ PGCE75. Kelham Th Coll 69. **d** 75 **p** 76. C Tyldesley w Shakerley *Man* 75-78; C Salford Ordsall St Clem 78; C Langley All SS and Martyrs 80-82; TV Langley and Parkfield 82-83; P-in-c Chadderton St Mark 83-85; V from 85. *St Mark's Vicarage, Milne Street, Chadderton, Oldham OL9 0HR* Tel 0161-624 2005

COOKE, Angela Elizabeth. b 42. SRN65 SCM67 MTD72. St Jo Coll Nottm 85. **d** 87 **p** 94. Par Dn Walton H Trin *Ox* 87-92; Par Dn Bexleyheath Ch Ch *Roch* 92-94; C 94-97; V St Mary Cray and St Paul's Cray from 97. *The Vicarage, Main Road, Orpington, Kent BR5 3EN* Tel (01689) 827697

COOKE, Arthur Lewis. b 16. Keble Coll Ox BA38 MA43 Univ of Wales BD48. St Mich Coll Llan 39. **d** 39 **p** 41. C Llandysilio (or Menai Bridge) *Ban* 39-41; C Ffestiniog w Blaenau Ffestiniog 41-43; C Maentwrog w Trawsfynydd 41-43; C Ban St Jas 43-50; V Llanidan w Llanddaniel-fab w Llanedwen 50-59; R Hope *St As* 59-82; rtd 82. *144 Gresford Road, Llay, Wrexham LL12 0NW* Tel (01978) 853644

COOKE, Mrs Beatrice Lilian. b 21. Gilmore Ho 67 Linc Th Coll. **dss** 77 **d** 87. Northaw *St Alb* 77-87; Hon Par Dn from 87. *30 St Michael's Gardens, South Petherton, Somerset TA13 5BD* Tel (01460) 241195

COOKE, Charles James. b 31. TCD BA54 MA61 HDipEd59. **d** 56 **p** 57. C Ballymena *Conn* 56-58; Clerical V Ch Ch Cathl Dublin *D & G* 58-63; Perm to Offic *Derby* 65-94. *Address temp unknown*

COOKE, Christopher Stephen. b 54. Lon Univ BA76 MA77 Ox Univ BA81 MA88. Ripon Coll Cuddesdon 79. **d** 82 **p** 83. C Cen Telford *Lich* 82-86; R Uffington, Upton Magna and Withington 86-95; RD Wrockwardine from 92; TR Wrockwardine Deanery from 95. *The Rectory, Wrockwardine, Wellington, Shropshire TF6 5DD* Tel (01952) 240969

COOKE, David John. b 31. Linc Th Coll 60. **d** 62 **p** 63. C Brighton Gd Shep Preston *Chich* 62-65; C Clayton w Keymer 65-70; R Stone w Hartwell w Bishopstone *Ox* 70-77; R Stone w Dinton and Hartwell from 77. *The Rectory, Stone, Aylesbury, Bucks HP17 8RZ* Tel (01296) 748215

COOKE, Edward Alan. b 18. St D Coll Lamp BA41. **d** 46 **p** 47. C Blaenavon w Capel Newydd *Mon* 46-48; C Trevethin 48-50; CF 50-73; R Ightfield w Calverhall *Lich* 73-83; P-in-c Ash 78-83; rtd 83. *Guadalest, Hollins Lane, Tilstock, Whitchurch, Shropshire SY13 3NT* Tel (01948) 880421

COOKE, Frederic Ronald. b 35. Selw Coll Cam BA58 MA61. Ridley Hall Cam 59. **d** 61 **p** 62. C Flixton St Mich *Man* 61-64; C-in-c Flixton St Jo CD 64-67; V Flixton St Jo 68-74; R Ashton St Mich 74-77; Jerusalem 77-80; V Walmsley *Man* 80-85; AD Walmsley 81-85; Malaysia 85-90; Prin Ho of Epiphany Th Coll Borneo 85-90; P-in-c Accrington *Blackb* 90-91; TR 91-96; P-in-c Ringley w Prestolee *Man* from 96. *The Vicarage, 9 Stoneleigh Drive, Radcliffe, Manchester M26 1FZ* Tel (01204) 573742

COOKE, Geoffrey. b 38. Sarum Th Coll 61. **d** 64 **p** 65. C Eastover *B & W* 64-67; Chapl RAF 67-71; C Bridgwater St Jo *B & W* 71-76; R N Newton w St Michaelchurch and Thurloxton 76-78; R N Newton w St Michaelchurch, Thurloxton etc 78-83; TV Yeovil 83-88; V Yeovil H Trin 88-89; R Staple Fitzpaine, Orchard Portman, Thurlbear etc 89-96; rtd 96; Perm to Offic *B & W* from 96. *34 Bluebell Close, Taunton, Somerset TA1 1XQ* Tel (01823) 324235

COOKE (married name SHEARD), Ms Gillian Freda. b 39. Lon Univ DipTh70 BD73 Leeds Univ MA87. Linc Th Coll IDC75. **dss** 78 **d** 87 **p** 94. Cricklewood St Pet CD *Lon* 78-80; Chapl Middx Poly 78-80; Chapl Leeds Poly *Ripon* 80-87; N Humberside Ind Chapl *York* 87-90; Asst Chapl HM Pris Hull 90-94; Chapl Keele Univ *Lich* 94-97; Assoc Min Betley and Keele 94-97; Chapl Rampton Hosp Retford from 97. *4 Galen Avenue, Woodbeck, Retford, Notts DN22 0JJ* Tel (01777) 248003 or 247523 Fax 248442

COOKE, Harry Burford. b 18. **d** 64 **p** 65. C Slad *Glouc* 64-68; Chapl Marling Sch Stroud 68-78; Hon C Bisley, Oakridge, Miserden and Edgeworth *Glouc* 83-88; Perm to Offic from 88. *Norman Cottage, Miserden, Stroud, Glos GL6 7JA* Tel (01285) 821672

COOKE, Canon Hereward Roger Gresham. b 39. ACA64 K Coll Lon BD69 AKC70. **d** 70 **p** 71. C Rugby St Andr *Cov* 70-76; P-in-c St Kath Cree *Lon* 76-82; P-in-c St Botolph without Aldersgate 82-89; AD The City 82-85; P-in-c St Edm the King and St Mary Woolnoth etc 82-89; TV Nor St Pet Parmentergate w St Jo *Nor* 89-93; Ind Miss 89-93; Sen Ind Chapl from 93; RD Nor E from 93; Hon C Nor St Pet Mancroft w St Jo Maddermarket from 93; Hon Can Nor Cathl from 97. *St John's Vicarage, 31 Bracondale, Norwich NR1 2AT* Tel (01603) 624827

COOKE, James Percy. b 13. St D Coll Lamp BA51. **d** 52 **p** 54. C Prestatyn *St As* 52-57; R Derwen and Llanelidan 57-83; rtd 83. *28 Maes Cantaba, Ruthin LL15 1YP* Tel (01824) 704905

COOKE, John Stephen. b 35. K Coll Lon BD58 AKC58. **d** 59 **p** 60. C W Bromwich St Fran *Lich* 59-62; C Chalfont St Peter *Ox* 62-66; V Cross Heath *Lich* 66-72; R Haughton 72-86; P-in-c Ellenhall w Ranton 72-80; V Eccleshall from 86; Sub-Chapl HM Pris Drake Hall from 86. *The Vicarage, Church Street, Eccleshall, Stafford ST21 6BY* Tel (01785) 850351

COOKE, Canon Kenneth <u>John</u>. b 29. Linc Coll Ox BA53 MA57. Ely Th Coll 53. **d** 55 **p** 56. C Nuneaton St Mary *Cov* 55-58; C Cov St Thos 58-61; V Willenhall 61-66; V Meriden 66-76; V Cov St Geo 76-84; V Leamington Spa and Old Milverton 84-94; Hon Can Cov Cathl 92-94; rtd 94. *47 Brook End Drive, Henley-in-Arden, Solihull, W Midlands B95 5JD* Tel (01564) 792281

COOKE, Dr Michael David. b 46. New Coll Ox BA68 MA71 DPhil71. Ox NSM Course 75. **d** 78 **p** 79. NSM Newport Pagnell *Ox* 78-85; NSM Newport Pagnell w Lathbury and Moulsoe 85-88; NSM Beckenham Ch Ch *Roch* 90-96; P-in-c Seal St Lawr from 96; P-in-c Underriver from 96. *St Lawrence Vicarage, Stone Street, Sevenoaks, Kent TN15 0LQ* Tel (01732) 761766

COOKE, Michael John. b 39. Ab Dioc Tr Course 78. **d** 80 **p** 81. NSM St Andr Cathl *Ab* 80-81; Chapl Miss to Seamen 81-88; Hon C Immingham *Linc* 81-88; Miss to Seamen Tilbury 88-91; Ind Chapl Teesside *Dur* 91-97; V Kelloe and Coxhoe from 97. *8 Mulbery, Coxhoe, Durham DH6 4SN* Tel 0191-377 3722

COOKE, Miss Priscilla Garland Hamel. b 24. Gilmore Ho 69. **dss** 80 **d** 87 **p** 94. Bromsgrove St Jo *Worc* 80-82; Lee Abbey 82-85; Torquay St Matthias, St Mark and H Trin *Ex* 86-87; NSM 87-92 and from 94; Perm to Offic 92-94. *St Nicholas, Woodend Road, Torquay, Devon TQ1 2PZ* Tel (01803) 297366

COOKE, Raymond. b 34. Liv Univ BSc56. Wells Th Coll 58. **d** 60 **p** 61. C Newton Heath All SS *Man* 60-64; C-in-c Failsworth H Family CD 64-75; R Failsworth H Family 75-83; P-in-c Man Gd Shep 83-88; V Westleigh St Pet from 88. *St Peter's Vicarage, 6 Malham Close, Leigh, Lancs WN7 4SD* Tel (01942) 673626

COOKE, Richard James. b 60. Pemb Coll Ox BA82 MA88. Trin Coll Bris 85. **d** 88 **p** 89. C Rugby St Matt *Cov* 88-92; V Fletchamstead from 92. *St James's Vicarage, 395 Tile Hill Lane, Coventry CV4 9DP* Tel (01203) 466262

COOKMAN, Alan George. b 26. Keble Coll Ox BA50 MA56. St Steph Ho Ox 50. **d** 52 **p** 53. C Plymouth St Pet *Ex* 52-60; C Richmond St Jo *S'wark* 60-61; R Lower Broughton Ascension *Man* 61-65; V Lavender Hill Ascension *S'wark* 65-72; R Lympstone *Ex* 72-81; V Laira 81-88; Chapl Convent of Sisters of Charity Knowle 88-91; rtd 91. *Little Orchard, Priestlands, Sherborne, Dorset DT9 4HW* Tel (01935) 813467

COOKSON, Miss Diane Veronica. b 51. N Ord Course 81. **dss** 84 **d** 87 **p** 94. Gt Sutton *Ches* 84-86; Neston 86-87; Par Dn 87-94; C 94-96; V Stockport St Sav from 96. *St Saviour's Vicarage, 22 St Saviour's Road, Great Moor, Stockport, Cheshire SK2 7QE* Tel 0161-483 2633

COOKSON, Graham Leslie. b 37. Sarum Th Coll 64. **d** 67 **p** 68. C Upton Ascension *Ches* 67-69; C Timperley 69-75; V Godley cum Newton Green 75-83; R Tarporley from 83. *The Rectory, Tarporley, Cheshire CW6 0AG* Tel (01829) 732491

COOLING, Derrick William. b 35. AKC58 Heref Coll of Educn TCert68 Lon Univ BD69 DipEd71 Univ of Wales (Cardiff) MEd81. St Boniface Warminster 58. **d** 59 **p** 60. C Haydock St Jas *Liv* 59-61; C Hove St Barn *Chich* 61-63; V Llangattock w St Maughan's etc *Mon* 63-68; R Blaina 68-70; Perm to Offic *Sarum* 70-74; Chapl Windsor Girls' Sch Hamm 74-75; Asst Master Croesyceiliog Sch Cwmbran 75-81; Perm to Offic *Mon* 79-81; Chapl Epsom Coll 81-84; V Bettws *Mon* 84-95; P-in-c Purleigh, Cold Norton and Stow Maries *Chelmsf* from 95. *All Saints Rectory, The Street, Purleigh, Chelmsford CM3 6QH* Tel (01621) 828743 Fax as telephone

COOLING, Mrs Margaret Dorothy. b 37. K Coll Lon BA59 AKC Lon Univ BD69 DipEd71 Univ of Wales (Cardiff) MEd81. St Deiniol's Hawarden. **d** 90 **p** 95. NSM Bettws *Mon* 90-95; NSM Purleigh, Cold Norton and Stow Maries *Chelmsf* from 95. *All Saints Rectory, The Street, Purleigh, Chelmsford CM3 6QH* Tel (01621) 828743 Fax as telephone

COOMBE, James Anthony. b 31. Em Coll Cam BA53 MA57 Lon Univ BD60. Tyndale Hall Bris 57. **d** 60 **p** 61. C Chadderton Ch Ch *Man* 60-63; C Worthing St Geo *Chich* 63-65; V Wandsworth St Mich *S'wark* 65-74; P-in-c Warboys *Ely* 74-76; R 76-87; RD St Ives 83-87; P-in-c Broughton 84-87; P-in-c Wistow 84-87; V Alconbury w Alconbury Weston 87-96; R Buckworth 87-96; rtd 96. *12 Nursery Fields, Hythe, Kent CT21 4DL* Tel (01303) 262151

COOMBE, John Morrell (Brother Martin). b 25. Chich Th Coll 56. **d** 57 **p** 58. SSF from 49; Lic to Offic *Sarum* 57-59; C-in-c Hillfield and Hermitage 59-66; Asst Chapl Ellesmere Coll Shropshire 66-69; Chapl Ranby Ho Sch Retford 69-71; V Cambridge St Benedict *Ely* 71-85; Perm to Offic Jerusalem 85-86; Lic to Offic *Linc* 86-95; Prov Sec SSF from 86; rtd 95; Perm to Offic *Ely* from 96. *St Francis House, 14/15 Botolph Lane, Cambridge CB2 3RD* Tel (01223) 321576 Fax as telephone

COOMBE, Kenneth Harry Southcott. b 24. Clifton Th Coll 61. **d** 63 **p** 64. C Cullompton *Ex* 63-66; C-in-c Elburton CD 66-73; V Elburton from 73. *St Matthew's Vicarage, 3 Sherford Road, Plymouth PL9 8DQ* Tel (01752) 402771

COOMBE, Michael Thomas. b 31. Lon Univ BA64. Ox NSM Course 73. **d** 75 **p** 76. Chapl St Piran's Sch Maidenhead 75-81; NSM Furze Platt *Ox* 75-81; C 86-88; Asst Chapl Oslo St Edm *Eur* 81-84; Chapl Belgrade w Zagreb 84-86; Chapl Marseille w St Raphael, Aix-en-Provence etc 88-89; Chapl Reading Gp of Hosps 89-91; C Old Windsor *Ox* 91; P-in-c Clewer St Andr 91-92; C New Windsor 92-93; C Reading St Mark 93-95; C Reading H Trin 93-95; Prec Gib Cathl and Port Chapl *Eur* 95-97; rtd 96. *Flying Angel Club, North Mole, Gibraltar* Tel Gibraltar 41799

COOMBER, Ian Gladstone. b 47. Ch Ch Coll Cant CertEd68 Southn Univ BTh79. Sarum & Wells Th Coll 73. **d** 76 **p** 77. C Weeke *Win* 76-79; TV Saffron Walden w Wendens Ambo and Littlebury *Chelmsf* 79-82; V Weston *Win* 82-90; R Bedhampton *Portsm* 90-96; R Botley from 96. *All Saints' Rectory, Brook Lane, Botley, Southampton SO3 2ER* Tel (01489) 781534

COOMBES, Derek Fennessey. b 42. Nottm Univ Cert Counselling 95. Edin Th Coll 61. **d** 65 **p** 66. Prec St Andr Cathl Inverness *Mor* 65-68; Bp's Chapl 65-68; Perm to Offic *Nor* 76-79; V Happisburgh w Walcot 79-83; C Tewkesbury Abbey 84-85; Ind Chapl *S'wark* 85-89; R Asterby Gp *Linc* 89-95; Mental Health Chapl Louth 91-95; Perm to Offic *Lich* from 95. *23 The Carousels, Victoria Mews, Victoria Crescent, Burton-on-Trent, Staffs DE14 2QA* Tel (01283) 539225

COOMBES, Edward David. b 39. Dur Univ BA61. Qu Coll Birm DipTh63. **d** 63 **p** 64. C Claines St Jo *Worc* 63-65; C Halesowen 65-69; V Beoley 69-77; V Edgbaston St Bart *Birm* from 77; Chapl Birm Univ from 77. *Edgbaston Vicarage, 1B Arthur Road, Birmingham B15 2UW* Tel 0121-454 0070

COOMBES, Frederick Brian John. b 34. FRTPI63 Nottm Univ BA56 Univ Coll Lon DipTP63 Plymouth Poly MPhil73. SW Minl Tr Course 85. **d** 88 **p** 89. NSM Bodmin w Lanhydrock and Lanivet *Truro* from 88. *5 Valley View, Bodmin, Cornwall PL31 1BE* Tel (01208) 73036

COOMBS, Edward Neve. b 66. Bris Univ BSc88. Cranmer Hall Dur BA93 DMS94. **d** 94 **p** 95. C Edin St Thos *Edin* 94-96; C Dagenham *Chelmsf* from 97. *8 Church Lane, Dagenham, Essex RM10 9UL* Tel 0181-517 2664

COOMBS, John Allen. b 46. Portsm Poly BSc70. Oak Hill Th Coll DipHE88 Sarum & Wells Th Coll 89. **d** 89 **p** 90. C Leverington *Ely* 89-93; C Wisbech St Mary 89-93; P-in-c Emneth 93-96; V Emneth and Marshland St James from 96. *The Vicarage, Church Road, Emneth, Wisbech, Cambs PE14 8AF* Tel (01945) 583089

COOMBS, John Kendall. b 47. Culham Coll Ox BEd73. Sarum & Wells Th Coll 75. **d** 77 **p** 78. C Fareham H Trin *Portsm* 77-80; C Petersfield w Sheet 80-83; TV Beaminster Area *Sarum* 83-87; TR Preston w Sutton Poyntz and Osmington w Poxwell 87-97; TR Hermitage and Hampstead Norreys, Cold Ash etc *Ox* from 97. *The Rectory, High Street, Hermitage, Thatcham, Berks RG18 9ST* Tel (01635) 202967

COOMBS, Patrick Michael Joseph. b 65. St Steph Ho Ox BTh94. **d** 94 **p** 95. C Torquay St Martin Barton *Ex* 94-95; C Goodrington from 95. *Curates Egg, 40 Steed Close, Paignton, Devon TQ4 7SN* Tel (01803) 844999

COOMBS, The Ven Peter Bertram. b 28. Bris Univ BA58 MA61. Clifton Th Coll 55. **d** 60 **p** 61. C Beckenham Ch Ch *Roch* 60-63; R Nottingham St Nic *S'well* 63-68; V New Malden and Coombe *S'wark* 68-75; RD Kingston 71-75; Adn Wandsworth 75-88; Adn Reigate 88-95; rtd 95. *92 Locks Heath Park Road, Locks Heath, Southampton SO31 6LZ* Tel (01489) 577288

COOMBS, Richard Murray. b 63. St Chad's Coll Dur BSc85 Rob Coll Cam BA89 MA90. Ridley Hall Cam 87. **d** 90. C Enfield Ch Ch Trent Park *Lon* 90-94; C St Helen Bishopsgate w St Andr Undershaft etc from 94; P-in-c St Pet Cornhill from 95. *12 Merrick Square, London SE1 4JB* Tel 0171-378 0229

COOMBS, Stephen John. b 54. Open Univ BA86. Trin Coll Bris 85. **d** 87 **p** 88. C Norton Canes *Lich* 87-90; Chapl Trowbridge Coll *Sarum* 90-94; C Studley 90-94. *48 Whitstone Rise, Shepton Mallet, Somerset BA4 5QB* Tel (01749) 343750

COOMBS, Canon Walter James Martin. b 33. Keble Coll Ox BA57 MA61. Cuddesdon Coll 59. **d** 61 **p** 62. C Kennington St Jo *S'wark* 61-64; Chapl Em Coll Cam 64-68; Bp's Dom Chapl *S'wark* 68-70; V E Dulwich St Jo 70-77; V Pershore w Pinvin, Wick and Birlingham *Worc* 77-92; Hon Can Worc Cathl from 84; RD Pershore 85-91; TV Dorchester *Ox* from 92. *The Vicarage, The Green North, Warborough, Oxford OX10 7DW* Tel (0186732) 8381

COONEY, Michael Patrick. b 55. City of Lon Poly BA77. Ripon Coll Cuddesdon 77. **d** 80 **p** 81. C Cov E *Cov* 80-83; C Old Brumby *Linc* 83-85; V Linc St Jo 85-90; V Frodingham from 90. *The Vicarage, Vicarage Gardens, Scunthorpe, S Humberside DN15 7AZ* Tel (01724) 842726

COONEY, William Barry. b 47. K Coll Lon 69. **d** 70 **p** 71. C W Bromwich All SS *Lich* 70-73; C Wolverhampton St Pet 73-75; C Rugeley 75-78; V Sneyd Green 78-87; R Sandiacre *Derby* from 87. *St Giles's Rectory, Church Drive, Sandiacre, Nottingham NG10 5EE* Tel 0115-939 7163

COOPER, Alfred Philip. b 50. Bris Univ BA71. All Nations Chr Coll 72. **d** 77 **p** 78. Chile from 75; SAMS from 77. *Inglesia Anglicana del Chile, Casilla 50675, Correo Central, Santiago, Chile* Tel Santiago (2) 226-8794

COOPER, Andrew John. b 62. W Sussex Inst of HE BA87. St Steph Ho Ox 88. **d** 91 **p** 92. C Rawmarsh w Parkgate *Sheff* 91-93; C Mosborough 93-95; P-in-c Donnington Wood *Lich* 95-96; CF from 96. *MOD Chaplains (Army), Trenchard Lines, Upavon, Pewsey, Wilts SN9 6BE* Tel (01980) 615804 Fax 615800

COOPER, Andrew John Gearing. b 48. Sir John Cass Coll Lon BSc70. Ripon Coll Cuddesdon 73. **d** 76 **p** 77. C Potternewton *Ripon* 76-79; Antigua 79-81; Anguilla 81-87; V W Bromwich St Andr w Ch Ch *Lich* 88-92. *50 Hunter Avenue, Burntwood, Walsall, W Midlands WS7 9AQ* Tel (01543) 677817

COOPER, Mrs Annette Joy. b 53. Open Univ BA80 Lon Univ DipSocWork84 CQSW84. S'wark Ord Course DipRS88. **d** 88 **p** 94. NSM Pembury *Roch* 88; Chapl Asst Tunbridge Wells Hosps 88-91; Chapl Asst Kent and Sussex Hosp Tunbridge Wells 88-91; Chapl Asst Leybourne Grange Hosp W Malling 88-91; Chapl Bassetlaw Hosp and Community Services NHS Trust 91-96; P-in-c Edwinstowe w Carburton *S'well* from 96; Chapl Center Parcs Holiday Village from 96. *The Vicarage, 5 West Lane, Edwinstowe, Mansfield, Notts NG21 9QT* Tel (01623) 822430

COOPER, Barrie Keith. b 56. Oak Hill Th Coll. **d** 85 **p** 86. C Partington and Carrington *Ches* 85-89; V Stockport St Mark 89-93; Chapl HM Young Offender Inst Stoke Heath from 93; Perm to Offic *Heref* from 93. *HM Young Offender Institution, Stoke Heath, Market Drayton, Shropshire TF9 2LJ* Tel (01630) 654231 Fax 838875

COOPER, Barry Jack. Sarum Th Coll 59. **d** 61 **p** 62. C Norbury St Oswald *Cant* 61-64; C Crook *Dur* 64-68; R Cheriton *Cant* 68-84; V Cant All SS from 84. *All Saints' Vicarage, Military Road, Canterbury, Kent CT1 1PA* Tel (01227) 463505

COOPER, Canon Bede Robert. b 42. Ex Univ BA69. Coll of Resurr Mirfield 69. **d** 71 **p** 72. C Weymouth H Trin *Sarum* 71-74; P-in-c Broad Town 74-79; V Wootton Bassett 74-86; R Wilton w Netherhampton and Fugglestone from 86; Can and Preb Sarum Cathl from 88. *The Rectory, 27A West Street, Wilton, Salisbury SP2 0DL* Tel (01722) 743159

COOPER, Brian Hamilton. b 35. Keble Coll Ox BA58 MA67. Ripon Hall Ox 58. **d** 60 **p** 61. C Woolwich St Mary w H Trin *S'wark* 60-64; Canada 64-66; Vice-Prin Westcott Ho Cam 66-71; R Downham Market w Bexwell *Ely* 71-82; RD Fincham 80-82; V Chesterfield St Mary and All SS *Derby* 82-91; V Herringthorpe *Sheff* from 91; RD Rotherham from 93. *493 Herringthorpe*

Valley Road, Rotherham, S Yorkshire S60 4LB Tel (01709) 836052

COOPER, Carl Norman. b 60. Univ of Wales (Lamp) BA82. Wycliffe Hall Ox 82. **d** 85 **p** 86. C Llanelli *St D* 85-87; P-in-c Llanerch Aeron w Ciliau Aeron and Dihewyd etc 87-88; R 88-93; R Dolgellau w Llanfachreth and Brithdir etc *Ban* from 93. *The Rectory, Dolgellau LL40 3YW* Tel (01341) 422225

COOPER, Cecil Clive. b 26. TD75. AKC52. **d** 53 **p** 54. C Chipping Campden *Glouc* 53-55; C Cheltenham St Mary 55-60; V Stroud 60-65; CF (TA) 63-75; R Woodmansterne *S'wark* 65-91; RD Sutton 80-90; rtd 91; Perm to Offic *Pet* from 91; Perm to Offic *Cov* from 91. *10 Mill Close, Braunston, Daventry, Northants NN11 7HY* Tel (01788) 890596

COOPER, Chan Cecil William Marcus. b 32. TCD BA58 MA66. CITC 57. **d** 59 **p** 60. C Cork St Fin Barre and St Nic *C, C & R* 59-62; Bp's V, Lib and Registrar Kilkenny Cathl *C & O* 62-64; C Knockbreda *D & D* 65-67; Asst Ed Ch of Ireland Gazette 66-82; Ed from 82; I Magheradroll 67-82; Dioc Registrar 81-90; I Drumbeg from 82; Can Down Cathl from 86; Prec Down Cathl 90-91; Chan Down Cathl from 91. *The Rectory, Drumbeg Road, Dunmurry, Belfast BT17 9LE* Tel (01232) 613265 Fax (01846) 675743

COOPER, Clive Anthony Charles. b 38. Lon Univ BEd74. ALCD62. **d** 62 **p** 63. C Morden *S'wark* 62-65; Argentina 65-71; Hon C Cranleigh *Guildf* 78-79; Hon C Ewhurst 80-82; Hon Chapl Duke of Kent Sch 83-92; Chapl Felixstowe Coll 92-93; Perm to Offic *Ex* 94-95; Chapl Puerto Pollensa *Eur* from 95. *Lista de Correos Apt 78, Pollensa, Mallorca, Spain*

COOPER, Colin. b 55. Open Univ BA. St Jo Coll Nottm 83. **d** 86 **p** 87. C Cheadle Hulme St Andr *Ches* 86-89; C Tunbridge Wells St Jo *Roch* 89-93; V Whitfield *Derby* from 93. *The Vicarage, 116 Charlestown Road, Glossop, Derbyshire SK13 8LB* Tel (01457) 864938

COOPER, Colin Charles. b 40. Oak Hill Th Coll 62. **d** 66 **p** 67. C Islington St Andr w St Thos and St Matthias *Lon* 66-69; Bermuda 69-76; V Gorleston St Andr *Nor* 77-94; USA from 94. *111 Battery Avenue, Emporia VA, 23847 USA*

COOPER, David. b 44. AKC69. **d** 69 **p** 70. C Wortley de Leeds *Ripon* 69-73; CF 73-83; Lic to Offic *Ox* from 84; Chapl Eton Coll from 85. *Eton College, Windsor, Berks SL4 6DW* Tel (01753) 864587

COOPER, David Jonathan. b 44. Sarum & Wells Th Coll 70. **d** 74 **p** 75. C Charlton-in-Dover *Cant* 74-79; TV Wednesfield *Lich* 79-83; SSF 83-85; V Grimsby St Aug *Linc* 85-89; TV Trowbridge H Trin *Sarum* from 89. *Nyewood House, 67A Drynham Road, Trowbridge, Wilts BA14 0PF* Tel (01225) 751275

COOPER, David Philip. b 65. York Univ BA86. Qu Coll Birm BTh94. **d** 94 **p** 95. C Burslem *Lich* from 94. *3 Ullswater Avenue, Burslem, Stoke-on-Trent ST6 4JW* Tel (01782) 827715

COOPER, Dennis Bradley. b 29. New Coll Ox BA52 MA57. Cuddesdon Coll 52. **d** 54 **p** 55. C Bedford St Mary *St Alb* 54-56; C Hackney Wick St Mary of Eton w St Aug *Lon* 56-59; V York St Chad *York* 59-67; V Middlesbrough St Martin 67-74; V Norton juxta Malton 74-92; RD Buckrose 85-90; rtd 93; Perm to Offic *York* from 93. *156 Long Street, Easingwold, York YO6 3JA* Tel (01347) 822953

COOPER, Derek Edward. b 30. Bps' Coll Cheshunt 61. **d** 62 **p** 63. C Bishop's Stortford St Mich *St Alb* 62-66; V Westcliff St Cedd *Chelmsf* 66-89; R Camerton w Dunkerton, Foxcote and Shoscombe *B & W* 89-95; rtd 95. *6 Caerleon Drive, Andover, Hants SP10 4DE* Tel (01264) 362807

COOPER, Donald Martin. b 12. K Coll Lon BD35 AKC35 MTh40 PhD44. **d** 35 **p** 36. C Barnstaple St Pet *Ex* 35-38; C Brampford Speke 38-41; C Landkey 41-44; PC Stanford Bp Heref 44-51; Chapl Tooting Bec Hosp Lon 51-77; rtd 77; Perm to Offic *Guildf* 82-91. *17 Killasser Court, Station Approach, Tadworth, Surrey KT20 5AN* Tel (01737) 812954

COOPER, Eric John. b 22. Cam Univ MA47. Chich Th Coll 52. **d** 53 **p** 54. V Bedminster Down *Bris* 66-72; rtd 87. *6 Deveron Grove, Keynsham, Bristol BS18 1UJ* Tel 0117-986 7339

COOPER, Frederick. b 30. Cranmer Hall Dur 68. **d** 70 **p** 71. C Preston All SS *Blackb* 70-72; C Preston St Jo 72-76; TV 76-78; V Higher Walton 78-91; P-in-c Preston All SS 91-95; rtd 95; Perm to Offic *Blackb* from 95. *31 Churchfields, Fulwood, Preston PR2 8GT* Tel (01772) 713808

COOPER, Ms Gillian Anne. b 55. LMH Ox BA76 CertEd77 MA80. St Jo Coll Nottm 84. **dss** 86 **d** 87 **p** 94. Tutor EMMTC from 86; Beeston *S'well* 86-87; Lect St Jo Coll Nottm from 87. *24 Chapel Street, Beeston, Nottingham NG9 3HB* Tel 0115-925 3573 or 925 1114 Fax 922 0134 or 943 6438

COOPER, Gordon William. b 54. Aston Tr Scheme 93 Ripon Coll Cuddesdon DipMin95. **d** 97. C Kippax w Allerton Bywater *Ripon* from 97. *55 Goodwood Avenue, Kippax, Leeds LS25 7HS* Tel 0113-286 1111

COOPER, Graham Denbigh. b 48. Nottm Univ BTh75. St Jo Coll Nottm LTh75. **d** 75 **p** 76. C Collyhurst *Man* 75-78; C Stambermill *Worc* 78-80; V The Lye and Stambermill 80-90; P-in-c Frome H Trin *B & W* 90; V 91-95; Appeals Organiser Children's Soc from 95. *Flat 3, 3 St Leonard's Road, Surbiton, Surrey KT6 4DE* Tel 0181-390 9763

COOPER, Herbert William (Bert). b 29. Chich Th Coll 77. **d** 79 **p** 80. C Leigh Park *Portsm* 79-82; C-in-c Hayling St Pet CD 82-85; V Whitwell 85-94; R St Lawrence 85-94; P-in-c Niton 89-94; rtd 94. *10 Henley Orchards, Ludlow, Shropshire SY8 1TN* Tel (01584) 874985

COOPER, Ian Clive. b 48. FCA Ex Univ BA76 K Coll Lon MTh94. Linc Th Coll 76. **d** 78 **p** 79. C Sunbury *Lon* 78-81; P-in-c Astwood Bank *Worc* 81-85; P-in-c Feckenham w Bradley 82-85; TV Hemel Hempstead *St Alb* 85-95; R Bushey from 95. *The Rectory, High Street, Bushey, Watford WD2 1BD* Tel 0181-950 6408 or 950 1546

COOPER, Jack. b 44. St Jo Coll Nottm 76. **d** 78 **p** 79. C Roundhay St Edm *Ripon* 78-80; C Ripley *Derby* 81-82; V Willington 82-88; V Findern 82-88; P-in-c Parwich w Alsop en le Dale 88-94. *Park View, 14 Chubb Hill Road, Whitby, N Yorkshire YO21 1JU* Tel (01947) 604213

COOPER, James Peter. b 61. Westf Coll Lon BSc82. Sarum & Wells Th Coll 82. **d** 85 **p** 86. C Durrington *Chich* 85-88; C Clayton w Keymer 88-95; TV Chichester from 95; Chapl Chich Coll of Tech from 95. *Rowmar Cottage, Maudlin Lane, Westhampnett, Chichester, W Sussex PO18*

COOPER, Jeremy John. b 45. Kelham Th Coll 65 Linc Th Coll 71. **d** 71 **p** 72. C Derby St Luke *Derby* 71-76; TV Malvern Link w Cowleigh *Worc* 76-79; P-in-c Claypole *Linc* 79-80; P-in-c Westborough w Dry Doddington and Stubton 79-80; C Eye w Braiseworth and Yaxley *St E* 80-82; P-in-c Hundon w Barnardiston 82-83; R from 83. *The Vicarage, 5 Armstrong Close, Hundon, Sudbury, Suffolk CO10 8HD* Tel (01440) 786617

COOPER, John. b 34. BEd. N Ord Course. **d** 83 **p** 84. C Tong *Bradf* 83-87; V Bingley H Trin 87-92; V Silsden from 92. *The Vicarage, Briggate, Silsden, Keighley, W Yorkshire BD20 9JS* Tel (01535) 652670

COOPER, John. b 47. Sarum & Wells Th Coll 71. **d** 74 **p** 75. C Spring Grove St Mary *Lon* 74-77; C Shepherd's Bush St Steph w St Thos 77-82; V Paddington St Pet 82-89; V Darwen St Cuth w Tockholes St Steph *Blackb* 89-96; V Northampton St Mich w St Edm *Pet* from 96. *St Michael's Vicarage, 19 St Michael's Avenue, Northampton NN1 4JQ* Tel (01604) 37928

COOPER, John Edward. b 40. K Coll Lon BD63 AKC63. **d** 64 **p** 65. C Prittlewell St Mary *Chelmsf* 64-67; C Up Hatherley *Glouc* 67-69; C-in-c Dorridge CD *Birm* 69-71; P-in-c Alkmonton w Yeaveley *Derby* 71-76; V Longford 71-76; TV Canvey Is *Chelmsf* 76-82; R Spixworth w Crostwick *Nor* 82-91; R Frettenham w Stanninghall 82-91; V Gt w Lt Harrowden and Orlingbury *Pet* from 91. *The Vicarage, 18 Kings Lane, Little Harrowden, Wellingborough, Northants NN9 5BL* Tel (01933) 678225

COOPER, Canon John Leslie. b 33. Lon Univ BD65 MPhil78. Chich Th Coll 59. **d** 62 **p** 63. C Kings Heath *Birm* 62-65; Asst Chapl HM Pris Wandsworth 65-66; Chapl HM Borstal Portland 66-68; Chapl HM Pris Bris 68-72; P-in-c Balsall Heath St Paul *Birm* 73-81; V 81-82; Adn Aston and Can Res Birm Cathl 82-90; Adn Coleshill 90-93; C Sutton Coldfield H Trin 93-97; Hon Can Birm Cathl 93-97; rtd 97. *4 Ireton Court, Kirk Ireton, Ashbourne, Derby DE6 3JP*

COOPER, John Northcott. b 44. MIIM81. Ox Min Course DipRS92. **d** 92 **p** 93. NSM Burghfield *Ox* from 92. *Westmore, Palmers Lane, Burghfield Common, Reading RG7 3DU* Tel 0118-983 2754

COOPER, Jonathan Mark Eric. b 62. Man Univ BSc83 Edin Univ BD88. Edin Th Coll 85. **d** 88 **p** 89. C Stainton-in-Cleveland *York* 88-91; C W Bromwich All SS *Lich* 91-93; C-in-c Ingleby Barwick CD *York* from 93. *4 Barwick Close, Ingleby Barwick, Stockton-on-Tees, Cleveland TS17 0SY* Tel (01642) 766033

COOPER, Joseph Trevor. b 32. Linc Th Coll 65. **d** 67 **p** 68. C Fletchamstead *Cov* 67-69; Ind Chapl 69-90; rtd 92. *16 Trevor Close, Tile Hill, Coventry CV4 9HP* Tel (01203) 462341 or 27597

COOPER, Kenneth Cantlay. b 17. Qu Coll Cam BA39 MA43. Ridley Hall Cam 39. **d** 41 **p** 42. C Radipole and Melcombe Regis *Sarum* 41-46; C Broadwater St Mary *Chich* 46-50; V Cumnor *Ox* 50-65; R Fisherton Anger *Sarum* 65-74; P-in-c Fovant w Compton Chamberlayne etc 74-79; R Fovant, Sutton Mandeville and Teffont Evias etc 79-82; rtd 82; Perm to Offic *B & W* from 83. *8 Helena Road, East Coker, Yeovil, Somerset BA20 2HQ* Tel (01935) 862291

COOPER, Ms Louise Helena. b 68. Leeds Univ BA90. Qu Coll Birm DipTh93. **d** 93 **p** 94. Par Dn Dovecot *Liv* 93-94; C 94-96; Chapl HM Young Offender Inst Glen Parva from 96. *HM Young Offender Institution, Glen Parva, Tiger's Road, Wigston, Leics LE18 2TN* Tel 0116-277 2022 Fax 247 7679

COOPER, Malcolm Tydeman. b 37. Pemb Coll Ox BA61 MA64. Linc Th Coll 63. **d** 63 **p** 64. C Spennithorne *Ripon* 63-66; C Caversham *Ox* 66-71; Hon C Blackbird Leys CD 71-75; Lic to Offic *Sarum* 75-78; Lic to Offic *B & W* 78-82; NSM Sutton *Ely* from 82; NSM Witcham w Mepal from 82; rtd 97. *91 The Row, Sutton, Ely, Cambs CB6 2PB* Tel (01353) 777310 Fax 777422

COOPER, Marc Ashley. b 62. Leeds Univ BA85. Linc Th Coll CMM92. **d** 92 **p** 93. C Bolton St Jas w St Chrys *Bradf* 92-96; P-in-c Fishtoft *Linc* 96-97; R from 97. *The Rectory, Rectory Close, Fishtoft, Boston, Lincs PE21 0RZ* Tel (01205) 363216

COOPER, Sister Margery. b 26. Cam Inst of Educn CertRK52. CA Tr Coll 49. **dss** 79 **d** 87 **p** 94. Evang Family Miss (Dios Dur,

Newc and York) 79-86; rtd 86; Perm to Offic *York* 86-91; NSM Fulford from 91. *7 Grange Street, Fulford Road, York YO1 4BH* Tel (01904) 633990

COOPER, Mark Richard. b 69. St Jo Coll Morpeth DipTh95. **d** 95 **p** 95. Australia 95-96; C Rainham *Roch* from 96. *70 Elmstone Road, Rainham, Gillingham, Kent ME8 9BE* Tel (01634) 233786

COOPER, Maxwell Edgar. b 11. CD63. Jes Coll Cam BA37 MA41. Wycliffe Hall Ox 37. **d** 39 **p** 40. C Meole Brace *Lich* 39-41; CF (EC) 41-46; CF 46-54; Canada 55-91; Perm to Offic *Win* from 96. *St Cross Grange, 140 St Cross Road, Winchester, Hants SO23 9RJ* Tel (01962) 852547

COOPER, Canon Michael Leonard. b 30. St Jo Coll Cam BA53 MA58. Cuddesdon Coll 53. **d** 55 **p** 56. C Croydon *Cant* 55-61; V Spring Park 61-71; V Boxley 71-82; RD Sutton 74-80; Hon Can Cant Cathl 76-97; V Cranbrook 82-92; Hon Chapl to Suff Bp Dover 93-97; Asst Chapl Kent and Cant Hosps NHS Trust 94-97; Perm to Offic *Roch* from 97. *The Rectory, Plaxtol, Sevenoaks, Kent TN15 0QG* Tel (01732) 810319

COOPER, Michael Sydney. b 41. Univ of Wales (Lamp) BA63. Westcott Ho Cam 63. **d** 65 **p** 66. C Farlington *Portsm* 65-69; Pakistan 70-71; Mauritius 71-73; C-in-c Hayling St Pet CD *Portsm* 74-81; V Carisbrooke St Mary 81-92; V Carisbrooke St Nic 81-92; P-in-c Gatcombe 85-86; V Hartplain from 92. *The Vicarage, 61 Hartplain Avenue, Waterlooville, Hants PO8 8RG* Tel (01705) 264551

COOPER, Nigel Scott. b 53. CBiol MIBiol Ox Univ MA Cam Univ MA PGCE. Ripon Coll Cuddesdon. **d** 83 **p** 84. C Moulsham St Jo *Chelmsf* 83-88; R Rivenhall from 88. *The Rectory, 40 Church Road, Rivenhall, Witham, Essex CM8 3PQ* Tel (01376) 511161

COOPER, Noel. b 49. Oak Hill Th Coll. **d** 88 **p** 89. C Plymouth St Jude *Ex* 88-92; V Clapham Park All SS *S'wark* from 92. *All Saints' Vicarage, 250 Lyham Road, London SW2 5NP* Tel 0181-678 6020 or 674 4994

COOPER, Peter David. b 48. Sarum & Wells Th Coll 70. **d** 73 **p** 74. C Yateley *Win* 73-78; C Christchurch 78-81; P-in-c Southampton St Mark 81-83; V from 83. *St Mark's Vicarage, 54 Archers Road, Southampton SO15 2LU* Tel (01703) 636425

COOPER, Richard Thomas. b 46. Leeds Univ BA69. Coll of Resurr Mirfield 69. **d** 71 **p** 72. C Rothwell *Ripon* 71-75; C Adel 75-78; C Knaresborough 78-81; P-in-c Croft 81-90; P-in-c Eryholme 81-90; P-in-c Middleton Tyas and Melsonby 81-90; RD Richmond 86-90; V Aldborough w Boroughbridge and Roecliffe from 90; RD Ripon 93-96. *The Vicarage, Church Lane, Boroughbridge, York YO5 9BA* Tel (01423) 322433

COOPER, Robert Gerard (Bob). b 68. Univ of Wales (Abth) BD91. Linc Th Coll CMM93. **d** 93 **p** 94. C Whitkirk *Ripon* 93-96; C Leeds Richmond Hill from 96. *St Hilda's Clergy House, 70 Cross Green Lane, Leeds LS9 0DG* Tel 0113-248 1145

COOPER, Robert James. b 52. Bris Univ BA75. Ridley Hall Cam 76. **d** 78 **p** 79. C Street w Walton *B & W* 78-82; C Batheaston w St Cath 82-86; Asst Chapl to Arts and Recreation from 86; P-in-c Sadberge *Dur* from 86. *The Rectory, Middleton Road, Sadberge, Darlington, Co Durham DL2 1RP* Tel (01325) 333771

COOPER, Roger Charles. b 48. GRSM ARMCM69 PGCE70. Coll of Resurr Mirfield 79. **d** 81 **p** 82. C Monkseaton St Mary *Newc* 81-83; C Morpeth 83-87; Min Can and Prec Man Cathl *Man* 87-90; V Blackrod from 90. *St Katharine's Vicarage, Blackhorse Street, Blackrod, Bolton BL6 5EN* Tel (01204) 68150

COOPER, Seth William. b 62. Westcott Ho Cam 94. **d** 96 **p** 97. C Golders Green *Lon* from 96. *1 St Albans Close, London NW11 7RA* Tel 0181-458 5846

COOPER, Stephen. b 54. Bernard Gilpin Soc Dur 73 Chich Th Coll 74. **d** 77 **p** 78. C Horbury *Wakef* 77-78; C Horbury w Horbury Bridge 78-81; C Barnsley St Mary 81-84; TV Elland 84-91; Hon C Huddersfield St Thos 93-94; P-in-c Middlesbrough St Columba w St Paul *York* from 94; Chapl Middlesb Gen Hosp from 94. *St Columba's Vicarage, 115 Cambridge Road, Middlesbrough, Cleveland TS5 5HF* Tel (01642) 824779

COOPER, Stephen Paul Crossley (Steve). b 58. Aston Tr Scheme 89 Trin Coll Bris DipTh93. **d** 93 **p** 94. C Blackb Redeemer *Blackb* 93-95; C Altham w Clayton le Moors from 95. *1 Oakfield Avenue, Clayton le Moors, Accrington, Lancs BB5 5XG* Tel (01254) 231227

COOPER, Susan Mira. *See* RAMSARAN, Dr Susan Mira

COOPER, Sydney Bernard Nikon. b 27. K Coll Lon BD49 AKC49. **d** 51 **p** 52. C St Marylebone Ch Ch w St Barn *Lon* 51-54; C Palmers Green St Jo 54-58; P-in-c Staines Ch Ch 58-66; V Stoke Newington St Olave 66-76; R Chigwell Row *Chelmsf* 76-83; P-in-c Easton on the Hill, Collyweston w Duddington etc *Pet* 83; R 84-88; rtd 88. *Chase View, Church Road, Walpole St Peter, Wisbech, Cambs PE14 7NU* Tel (01945) 780473

COOPER, Thomas. b 20. Man Univ BA42. Edin Th Coll 42. **d** 44 **p** 45. C Sandylands *Blackb* 44-46; C Burnley St Pet 46-49; C Chorley St Geo 49-51; V Chorley St Jas 51-57; PC Blackb St Jas 57-63; CF (TA) 59-67; V Bolton le Sands *Blackb* 63-85; rtd 85; Perm to Offic *Blackb* from 85. *Hillcrest, 21 Hazelmount Drive, Warton, Carnforth, Lancs LA5 9HR* Tel (01524) 732507

COOPER, Dr Thomas Joseph Gerard Strickland. b 46. Lanc Univ PhD85. Ven English Coll and Pontifical Gregorian Univ Rome PhL67 STL71. **d** 70 **p** 70. In RC Ch 70-92; Chapl St Woolos Cathl *Mon* 93-95; V Llandaff N *Llan* from 95. *All Saint's Vicarage, 59 Station Road, Llandaff, Cardiff CF4 2FB* Tel (01222) 564096

COOPER, Trevor John. b 51. Ex Univ MA95. Wycliffe Hall Ox 75. **d** 79 **p** 95. C Southsea St Pet *Portsm* 79-80; NSM Heavitree w Ex St Paul *Ex* 93-96; C Standish *Blackb* from 96. *St Wilfrid's House, 7 Rectory Lane, Standish, Wigan, Lancs WN6 0XA* Tel (01257) 425806

COOPER, Wallace Peter. b 24. Kelham Th Coll 47. **d** 51 **p** 52. C Watford St Mich *St Alb* 51-52; C Ealing St Barn *Lon* 52-54; C New Brompton St Luke *Roch* 54-56; Perm to Offic *Ox* 62-81; Hon C Earley St Pet 81-83; Hon C Earley St Nic from 83; rtd 90. *10 Morton Court, Christchurch Road, Reading RG2 7BB* Tel 0118-986 0528

COOPER, William Douglas. b 42. ARCST65 Dur Univ CertEd69 Open Univ BA83 Nottm Univ DipMM94. St Jo Coll Nottm CTPS92 Qu Coll Birm 93. **d** 94 **p** 95. NSM Melbourne *Derby* 94-97; C Penwortham St Mary *Blackb* from 97. *15 Corn Croft, Penwortham, Preston PR1 9YP* Tel (01772) 740211

COOPER, The Very Revd William Hugh Alan. b 09. Ch Coll Cam BA31 MA35. Lon Coll of Div 31. **d** 32 **p** 33. C Lee St Marg *S'wark* 32-36; C Cambridge H Trin *Ely* 36-38; Nigeria 38-41; C Farnham *Guildf* 41-42; R Ashtead 42-51; V Plymouth St Andr *Ex* 51-62; P-in-c Plymouth Ch Ch 61-62; Preb Ex Cathl 58-62; Provost Bradf 62-77; rtd 77; Pakistan 77-81; P-in-c Chrishall *Chelmsf* 81-88. *4 Eastgate Gardens, Guildford, Surrey GU1 4AZ* Tel (01483) 567128

COOPER-SMITH, Alfred Riddington. b 13. TD63. St Deiniol's Hawarden 74. **d** 74 **p** 75. Hon C Smeeton Westerby w Saddington *Leic* 74-80; Perm to Offic from 80; Perm to Offic *Pet* from 80. *8 Poplar Close, Uppingham, Leics LE15 9RQ* Tel (01572) 822412

COOTE, Anthony John. b 54. Qu Coll Birm 95. **d** 97. C Malvern H Trin and St Jas *Worc* from 97. *30 Layton Avenue, Malvern, Worcs WR14 2ND*

COOTE, Bernard Albert Ernest. b 28. Lon Univ BD53. Chich Th Coll 54. **d** 55 **p** 56. C Addiscombe St Mary *Cant* 55-57; C Hawkhurst 57-59; C Sanderstead All SS *S'wark* 59-63; Chapl HM Borstal E Sutton Park 63-74; V Sutton Valence w E Sutton *Cant* 63-76; P-in-c Chart next Sutton Valence 71-76; Chapl and Dir R Sch for the Blind Leatherhead 76-91; rtd 91; Perm to Offic *Chich* from 91; Perm to Offic *Guildf* from 91. *6 Coxham Lane, Steyning, W Sussex BN44 3JG* Tel (01903) 813762

✠**COOTE, The Rt Revd Roderic Norman.** b 15. TCD BA37 MA41 DD54. TCD Div Sch. **d** 38 **p** 39 **c** 51. C Dublin St Bart *D & G* 38-41; Gambia 41-57; Bp Gambia and Rio Pongas 51-57; Suff Bp Fulham *Lon* 57-66; Suff Bp Colchester *Chelmsf* 66-84; Area Bp Colchester 84-87; Adn Colchester 69-72; rtd 87; Perm to Offic *Guildf* from 94. *Friday Woods, Stoke Road, Cobham, Surrey KT11 3AS* Tel (01932) 867306

COPE, James Brian Andrew. b 58. Chich Th Coll 80. **d** 83 **p** 84. C Poulton-le-Fylde *Blackb* 83-86; C Fleetwood 86-87; V Fleetwood St Dav 87-94; P-in-c Somercotes *Derby* from 94. *The Vicarage, Nottingham Road, Somercotes, Alfreton, Derbyshire DE55 4LY* Tel (01773) 602840

COPE, Mrs Melia Lambrianos. b 53. Cape Town Univ BSocSc73 Worc Coll of Tech CertMS84. St Jo Coll Nottm 80 WMMTC 83. **dss** 86 **d** 93 **p** 94. W Bromwich All SS *Lich* 86-93; NSM 93-94; NSM W Bromwich St Mary Magd CD 93-94; Ecum Youth Chapl from 94; TV Cen Telford from 94; Chapl HM Pris Shrewsbury from 95. *Church House, 50 Deepdale, Hollinswood, Telford, Shropshire TF3 2EJ* Tel (01952) 200546

COPE, Miss Olive Rosemary. b 29. Birm Univ DPS73. Gilmore Ho 63. **dss** 69 **d** 87 **p** 94. Kentish Town St Martin w St Andr *Lon* 69-72; Enfield St Andr 73-87; Par Dn 87-89; Hon Par Dn 89-94; Hon C from 94; rtd 89. *7 Calder Close, Enfield, Middx EN1 3TS* Tel 0181-363 8221

COPE, Dr Peter John. b 42. Mert Coll Ox BA64 MA68 Lon Univ MSc74 Man Univ PhD91. Cuddesdon Coll 64. **d** 66 **p** 67. C Chapel Allerton *Ripon* 66-69; Ind Chapl *Lon* 69-76; Min Can Worc Cathl *Worc* 76-85; Ind Chapl 76-85; P-in-c Worc St Mark 76-81; Min W Bromwich St Mary Magd CD *Lich* 85-94; Ind Chapl 85-94; Town Cen Chapl from 94; W Midl FE Field Officer from 94; Perm to Offic *Heref* from 96. *Church House, 50 Deepdale, Hollinswood, Telford, Shropshire TF3 2EJ* Tel (01952) 200546

COPE, Stephen Victor. b 60. St Jo Coll Ox BA81 DipTh84 MA87. Chich Th Coll 86. **d** 89 **p** 90. C Newmarket St Mary w Exning St Agnes *St E* 89-92; C Northampton St Matt *Pet* 92-94; V Rudston w Boynton and Kilham *York* from 94. *The Vicarage, Rudston, Driffield, N Humberside YO25 0XA* Tel (01262) 420313

COPELAND, Christopher Paul. b 38. AKC64. **d** 65 **p** 66. C Luton St Andr *St Alb* 65-67; C Droitwich St Nic w St Pet *Worc* 67-71; C Kings Norton *Birm* 71-72; TV 73-78; V Tyseley 78-88; P-in-c Grimley w Holt *Worc* 88-96; Dioc Stewardship Missr 88-96; P-in-c Forest of Dean Ch Ch w English Bicknor *Glouc* from 96. *Christ Church Vicarage, Ross Road, Coleford, Glos GL16 7NS* Tel (01594) 832855

COPELAND, Derek Norman. b 38. Worc Coll Ox BA62 MA68. Westcott Ho Cam 63. **d** 64 **p** 65. C Portsea St Mary *Portsm* 64-71; P-in-c Avonmouth St Andr *Bris* 71-77; P-in-c Chippenham St Paul w Langley Burrell 78-79; Ind Chapl from 78; TR Chippenham St Paul w Hardenhuish etc 79-89; V Kington 79-89; Perm to Offic *B & W* from 90. *51B Lowden, Chippenham, Wilts SN15 2BG* Tel (01249) 443879

COPESTAKE, Leslie. b 13. ALCD39. **d** 39 **p** 40. C Macclesfield Ch Ch *Ches* 39-42; C Mottram in Longdendale w Woodhead 42-45; C Stockport St Geo 45-47; V Hurdsfield 47-51; Area Sec CMS 51-55; V Liv St Chris Norris Green *Liv* 55-61; V Beckermet St Jo *Carl* 61-71; V Egton w Newland 71-78; rtd 78; Perm to Offic *Carl* 78-93. *Fosbrooke House, 8 Clifton Drive, Lytham, Lytham St Annes, Lancs FY8 5RE* Tel (01253) 735904

COPINGER, Stephen Hubert Augustine (Brother Hubert). b 18. Lon Univ BA48. Ely Th Coll 60. **d** 62 **p** 63. SSF from 61; C Cambridge St Benedict *Ely* 62-64; Hooke Sch Sarum 64-68; P-in-c Hillfield and Hermitage *Sarum* 68-76; Lic to Offic *Conn* 76-83; Lic to Offic *M & K* 78-80; Chapl R Victoria Hosp Belf 83-86; rtd 86. *The Society of St Francis, The Friary, Hilfield, Dorchester, Dorset DT2 7BE* Tel (01300) 341345

COPLAND, Carole Jean. b 37. Man Univ BA60. Wm Temple Coll Rugby DipRK67. **d** 87 **p** 94. NSM Northallerton w Kirby Sigston *York* 87-90; Dioc Adv in Children's Work 81-90; Par Dn Dunnington 90-94; Faith in the City Link Officer 90-96; C Dunnington 94-96; V Ledsham w Fairburn from 96. *The Vicarage, 11 Main Street, Ledston, Castleford, W Yorkshire WF10 2AA* Tel (01977) 556946

COPLAND, Canon Charles McAlester. b 10. CCC Cam BA33 MA36. Cuddesdon Coll 33. **d** 34 **p** 35. C Pet St Jo *Pet* 34-38; India 38-52; R Arbroath *Bre* 53-59; R Oban St Jo *Arg* 59-79; Provost St Jo Cathl Oban 59-79; Dean Arg 77-79; rtd 79; Hon Can St Jo Cathl Oban *Arg* from 79. *3 West Hill Road, Kirriemuir DD8 4PR* Tel (01575) 575415

COPLEY, Dr Colin. b 30. FRSA85 Nor City Coll HNC49. Kelham Th Coll 51. **d** 55 **p** 56. C Linc St Swithin *Linc* 55-58; C Bottesford 58-60; Chapl HM Borstal Hollesley 60-66; Chapl HM Pris Liv 66-70; Chapl HM Pris Styal 70-73; N Regional Chapl HM Pris and Borstals 70-73; Midl Region 73-75; Chapl HM Pris Drake Hall 73-75; Asst Chapl Gen of Pris (Midl) 75-90; Chapl HM Open Pris Sudbury 90-95; Chapl HM Pris Foston Hall 90-95; Perm to Offic *Lich* from 90; rtd 95. *67 Porlock Avenue, Stafford ST17 0HT* Tel (01785) 663162

COPLEY, David Judd. b 15. Linc Coll Ox BA48 MA53. Wycliffe Hall Ox 48. **d** 50 **p** 51. C Old Swinford *Worc* 50-53; Chapl to Bp Worc 52-55; Min Stourbridge St Mich Norton CD 53-56; R Romsley 56-67; Chapl Romsley Hosp 56-67; V Tardebigge 67-81; rtd 81; Perm to Offic *Worc* from 82. *220 Bromsgrove Road, Hunnington, Halesowen, W Midlands B62 0JS* Tel (01562) 710247

COPLEY, Edmund Miles. b 27. Lon Univ BScEng50 Birm Univ DipTh57. Qu Coll Birm 55. **d** 57 **p** 58. C Allestree *Derby* 57-61; R Banff *Ab* 61-65; R Portsoy 61-65; R Uggeshall w Sotherton, Wangford and Henham *St E* 65-94; rtd 94. *Bullions, Uggeshall, Beccles, Suffolk NR34 8BB* Tel (0150278) 235

COPPEN, Colin William. b 53. BCombStuds85. Linc Th Coll. **d** 85 **p** 86. C Tokyngton St Mich *Lon* 85-88; C Somers Town St Mary 88-90; P-in-c Edmonton St Alphege 90-92; V 92-95; P-in-c W Hampstead St Jas 95-97; P-in-c Kilburn St Mary w All So 95-97; TR Wood Green St Mich w Bounds Green St Gabr etc from 97. *St Michael's Rectory, 39 Bounds Green Road, London N22 4HE* Tel 0181-888 1968 or 881 0202

COPPEN, Martin Alan. b 48. Ex Univ BA69 Nottm Univ DipTh84. St Jo Coll Nottm 83. **d** 85 **p** 86. C Bitterne *Win* 85-88; V St Mary Bourne and Woodcott from 88. *The Vicarage, St Mary Bourne, Andover, Hants SP11 6AY* Tel (01264) 738308

COPPEN, Peter Euan. b 39. Ripon Coll Cuddesdon 79. **d** 81 **p** 82. C New Sleaford *Linc* 81-86; V Scawby and Redbourne 86-89; V Scawby, Redbourne and Hibaldstow 89-95; rtd 95; Perm to Offic *Pet* from 95. *Fleet House, Church Street, Greatworth, Banbury, Oxon OX17 2DU*

COPPEN, Robert George. b 39. Cape Town Univ BA66. St Jo Coll Dur 79. **d** 81 **p** 82. C Douglas St Geo and St Barn *S & M* 81-84; TV Kidlington w Hampton Poyle *Ox* from 84; Chapl HM Young Offender Inst Campsfield Ho 84-91. *St John's Vicarage, The Broadway, Kidlington, Oxon OX5 1EF* Tel (01865) 375611

COPPIN, Canon Ronald Leonard. b 30. Birm Univ BA52. Ridley Hall Cam 54. **d** 56 **p** 57. C Harrow Weald All SS *Lon* 56-59; Bp's Dom Chapl *Man* 59-63; Chapl St Aid Birkenhead 63-65; Vice-Prin 65-68; Selection Sec ACCM 68-71; Selection Sec and Sec Cttee for Th Educn ACCM 71-74; Lib Dur Cathl from 74; Dir of Clergy Tr *Dur* 74-96; Can Res Dur Cathl from 74; Warden NE Ord Course 76-84; Dir Post-Ord Tr from 86. *3 The College, Durham DH1 3EQ* Tel 0191-384 2415

COPPING, John Frank Walter Victor. b 34. K Coll Lon BD58 AKC58. **d** 59 **p** 60. C Hampstead St Jo *Lon* 59-62; C Bray and Braywood *Ox* 62-65; V Langley Mill *Derby* 65-71; V Cookham Dean *Ox* from 71; RD Maidenhead 87-94. *The Vicarage, Cookham Dean, Maidenhead, Berks SL6 9PN* Tel (01628) 483342

COPPING, Raymond. b 36. Wycliffe Hall Ox 72. **d** 74 **p** 75. C High Wycombe *Ox* 74-77; TV 77-87; TV Digswell and Panshanger *St Alb* 87-95; P-in-c Charlton Kings H Apostles *Glouc* from 95. *The Vicarage, Langton Grove Road, Charlton Kings, Cheltenham, Glos GL52 6JA* Tel (01242) 512254

COPSEY, Canon Harry Charles Frederick. b 05. Linc Th Coll 31. **d** 34 **p** 35. C Loughborough Em *Leic* 34-36; C Bognor St Jo *Chich* 36-38; V Lower Beeding 39-43; V Willingdon 43-54; V E Grinstead St Swithun 54-75; Chapl Qu Victoria's Hosp E Grinstead 55-75; Chapl Sackville Coll E Grinstead 56-75; Can and Preb Chich Cathl *Chich* 70-85; rtd 75; Perm to Offic *Chich* from 75. *Flat 22, Old Parsonage Court, Otterbourne, Winchester, Hants PO21 2EP* Tel (01962) 715425

COPSEY, Nigel John. b 52. K Coll Lon BD75 AKC75 Surrey Univ MSc. St Aug Coll Cant 72. **d** 76 **p** 77. C Barkingside St Fran *Chelmsf* 76-78; C Canning Town St Cedd 78-80; P-in-c Victoria Docks Ascension 80-87; Chapl Cane Hill Hosp Coulsdon 87-90; Chapl Netherne Hosp Coulsdon 87-90; Chapl E Surrey Mental Health Unit 90-94; Chapl E Surrey Learning Disability NHS Trust from 94. *Chaplain's Office, Royal Earlswood, Brighton Road, Redhill RH1 6JL* Tel (01737) 763591

COPUS, Brian George. b 36. AKC59. **d** 60 **p** 61. C Croydon St Mich *Cant* 60-63; C Swindon New Town *Bris* 63-69; V Colebrooke *Ex* 69-73; P-in-c Hittisleigh 69-73; R Perivale *Lon* 73-82; V Ruislip St Mary from 82. *St Mary's Vicarage, 9 The Fairway, South Ruislip, Middx HA4 0SP* Tel 0181-845 3485

COPUS, James Lambert. b 19. Edin Th Coll 47. **d** 50 **p** 51. C Fairfield *Derby* 50-52; C Edin St Ninian *Edin* 52-55; C Sutton Ch Ch *S'wark* 55-57; C Norwood St Luke 57-58; V S Lambeth All SS and St Barn 58-77; TV Eling, Testwood and Marchwood *Win* 77-78; TV Totton 78-79; rtd 80. *94 Moorfield, Harlow, Essex CM18 7QG* Tel (01279) 417666

COPUS, John Cecil. b 38. TCert64 Maria Grey Coll Lon DipEd71 Open Univ BA78. Cant Sch of Min. **d** 83 **p** 84. Hon C Folkestone H Trin and St Geo w Ch Ch *Cant* 83-85; Hon C Midsomer Norton w Clandown *B & W* 85-91; Dioc Adv for Children's Work *Ex* from 91; Hon C Aylesbeare, Rockbeare, Farringdon etc from 95. *The Vicarage, Rockbeare, Exeter EX5 2EG* Tel (01404) 822569

COPUS, Jonathan Hugh Lambert. b 44. LGSM66 BNC Ox BA66 MA71. S'wark Ord Course 68. **d** 71 **p** 72. C Horsell *Guildf* 71-73; Producer Relig Progr BBC Radio Solent 73-87; Lic to Offic *Win* from 74. *55 Lower Ashley Road, New Milton, Hants BH25 5QF* Tel (01425) 619400

CORBET-MILWARD, Canon Richard George Corbet. b 12. K Coll Cam BA36 MA40. Cuddesdon Coll 37. **d** 38 **p** 39. C S'wark St Sav w All Hallows *S'wark* 38-41; PV and Sacr S'wark Cathl 39-41; C Heref All SS *Heref* 41-43; C Romsey *Win* 43-48; V Portsea St Alb *Portsm* 48-74; RD Portsm 65-70; Hon Can Portsm Cathl 68-79; V Ryde H Trin 74-79; RD E Wight 75-78; rtd 80; Perm to Offic *Portsm* from 82; Perm to Offic *Chich* from 96. *College of St Barnabas, Blackberry Lane, Lingfield, Surrey RH7 6NJ* Tel (01342) 870717

CORBETT, Canon Charles Eric. b 17. Jes Coll Ox BA39 MA43. Wycliffe Hall Ox 39. **d** 40 **p** 41. C Gresford *St As* 40-44; CF (EC) 44-47; C Llanrhos *St As* 47-49; R Harpurhey Ch Ch *Man* 49-54; V Wigan St Cath *Liv* 54-61; V Farnworth 61-71; RD Farnworth 64-71; Adn Liv 71-79; Can Res Liv Cathl 71-83; Treas 79-83; rtd 83; Perm to Offic *Liv* from 83; Perm to Offic *Ches* from 85. *80 Latham Avenue, Helsby, Cheshire WA6 0EB* Tel (01928) 724184

CORBETT, George. b 18. Bible Churchmen's Coll 47. **d** 50 **p** 51. C Wednesfield Heath *Lich* 50-52; R Salford St Matthias w St Simon *Man* 52-55; N Area Sec BCMS 55-58; V S Lambeth St Steph *S'wark* 58-61; Assoc Home Sec BCMS 61-63; V Hatherleigh *Ex* 63-78; P-in-c Ringmore and Kingston 78-84; R Bigbury, Ringmore and Kingston 84-86; rtd 86; Perm to Offic *Heref* from 87. *2 Quantock Close, Hereford HR4 0TD* Tel (01432) 269211

CORBETT, Henry. b 53. CCC Cam BA75. Wycliffe Hall Ox DipTh78. **d** 78 **p** 79. C Everton St Pet *Liv* 78-84; TV 84-87; TR from 87. *Shrewsbury House, Langrove Street, Liverpool L5 3LT* Tel 0151-207 1948

CORBETT, The Very Revd Ian Deighton. b 42. St Cath Coll Cam BA64 MA68 Salford Univ MSc83. Westcott Ho Cam 67. **d** 69 **p** 70. C New Bury *Man* 69-72; C Bolton St Pet 72-75; Chapl Bolton Colls of FE 72-75; Dioc FE Officer 74-83; R Man Victoria Park *Man* 75-80; Chapl Salford Univ 80-83; Hon Can Man Cathl 83-87; P-in-c Salford Sacred Trin 83-87; Dir of In-Service Tr 83-87; Lesotho 87-96; Dean Tuam *T, K & A* from 97; I Tuam w Cong and Aasleagh from 97. *The Rectory, Deanery Place, Cong, C Mayo, Irish Republic* Tel Cong (92) 46017 Fax as telephone

CORBETT, John David. b 32. Or Coll Ox BA55 MA59. St Steph Ho Ox 55. **d** 57 **p** 58. C Plymouth St Pet *Ex* 57-64; V Marldon 64-74; TV Bournemouth St Pet w St Swithun, H Trin etc *Win* 74-83; V Beckenham St Barn *Roch* 83-88; V King's Sutton and Newbottle and Charlton *Pet* from 88. *The Vicarage, Church Avenue, Kings Sutton, Banbury, Oxon OX17 3RJ* Tel (01295) 811364

CORBETT, Miss Phyllis. b 34. Cranmer Hall Dur 76. **dss** 80 **d** 87 **p** 94. Walsall Wood *Lich* 80-87; Par Dn Baswich 87-94; C 94-95;

rtd 95; Perm to Offic *Lich* from 95. *9 Redhill Gorse, Crab Lane, Trinity Fields, Stafford ST16 1SW*

CORBETT, Stephen Paul. b 57. BA80. St Jo Coll Nottm 83. **d** 85 **p** 86. C Tollington Park St Mark w St Anne *Lon* 85-86; C Holloway St Mark w Em 86-91; V Chitts Hill St Cuth 91-93; V Springfield *Birm* from 93. *The Vicarage, 172 Woodlands Road, Birmingham B11 4ET* Tel 0121-777 4908

CORBIN, Frederick Athelston. b 42. S Dios Minl Tr Scheme 80. **d** 83 **p** 85. NSM Basingstoke *Win* 83-84; C Hulme Ascension *Man* 84-86; Lic to Hulme Deanery 86-87; C E Crompton 87-89; V Oldham St Barn from 89. *St Barnabas' Vicarage, 1 Arundel Street, Oldham OL4 1NL* Tel 0161-624 7708

CORBYN, John. b 58. Man Univ BA79 Ven English Coll and Pontifical Gregorian Univ Rome 83. Wycliffe Hall Ox BA83 MA87. **d** 84 **p** 85. C Deane *Man* 84-87; C Lancaster St Mary *Blackb* 87-90; Chapl HM Pris Lanc 89-90; V Blackb St Gabr *Blackb* from 90. *St Gabriel's Vicarage, 284 Pleckgate Road, Blackburn BB1 8QU* Tel (01254) 248430

CORBYN, John Robert. b 54. Qu Coll Birm. **d** 82 **p** 83. C Northolt W End St Jos *Lon* 82-86; Urban Miss Priest *York* 86-88; C Sutton St Mich 86-88; V Dalton *Sheff* 88-96; R Cressing *Chelmsf* from 96. *The Rectory, 18 Wright's Avenue, Tye Green, Braintree, Essex CM7 8JG* Tel (01376) 343740

CORDELL, Derek Harold. b 34. Chich Th Coll 57. **d** 60 **p** 61. C Whitstable All SS *Cant* 60-63; C Moulsecoomb *Chich* 63-69; Chapl Bucharest *Eur* 69-71; V Brighton St Wilfrid *Chich* 71-74; Chapl HM Borstal Roch 74-80; Asst Chapl HM Pris Man 80-81; Chapl HM Pris The Verne 81-89; Chapl HM Pris Channings Wood 89-90; Chapl Milan w Genoa and Varese *Eur* 90-91; Chapl Mojacar 91-94. *9 Elwell Street, Weymouth, Dorset DT3 5QF*

CORDINER, Alan Dobson. b 61. W Cumbria Coll of Science and Tech HTC83 Westmr Coll Ox BA87. **d** 92 **p** 93. C Upperby St Jo *Carl* from 92. *49 Carliol Drive, Harraby, Carlisle CA1 2RF* Tel (01228) 34457

CORDINGLEY, Canon Brian Lambert. b 30. St Aid Birkenhead 55. **d** 57 **p** 58. Ind Chapl *Sheff* 57-63; C Clifton St Jas 57-61; C Rotherham 61-63; Ind Chapl *Man* 63-92; R Old Trafford St Cuth 63-81; V Hamer 81-92; Hon Can Man Cathl 87-92; rtd 92. *Wellsprings, 27 Fernthorpe Avenue, Uppermill, Oldham OL3 6EA* Tel (01457) 820130

CORE, Edward. b 54. BTh. Sarum & Wells Th Coll. **d** 82 **p** 83. C Newbold w Dunston *Derby* 82-86; Chapl RAF from 86. *Chaplaincy Services (RAF), HQ, Personnel and Training Command, RAF Innsworth, Gloucester GL3 1EZ* Tel (01452) 712612 ext 5164 Fax 510828

CORFE, David Robert. b 35. Pemb Coll Cam BA58 MA62. Lambeth DipTh70 Cuddesdon Coll 58. **d** 60 **p** 61. C Wigan All SS *Liv* 60-63; India 63-68 and 70-75; C Northwood Em *Lon* 75; V Westwell *Cant* 75-80; R Eastwell w Boughton Aluph 75-80; V Hildenborough *Roch* 80-91; Lic to Offic *Man* from 91; Lic Preacher Stretford St Bride from 91; Miss Partner CMS from 91. *3 Blair Street, Old Trafford, Manchester M16 9AZ* Tel 0161-232 9388 or 860 4224

CORFIELD, John Bernard. b 24. Jes Coll Cam BA49 MA51. Ridley Hall Cam 64. **d** 66 **p** 67. C Cherry Hinton St Jo *Ely* 66-69; P-in-c Bledlow Ridge *Ox* 69-75; P-in-c Bradenham 71-75; R Sherington w Chicheley, N Crawley, Astwood etc 75-82; V Terrington St Clement *Ely* 82-90; rtd 90; Perm to Offic *Ox* from 90. *13 Sturt Road, Charlbury, Chipping Norton, Oxon OX7 3SX* Tel (01608) 811464

CORK, Ronald Edward. b 43. Plymouth Poly CQSW72. N Ord Course 89. **d** 92 **p** 93. Hon C Altrincham St Geo *Ches* 92-96; P-in-c Altrincham St Jo from 96. *St John's Vicarage, 52 Ashley Road, Altrincham, Cheshire WA14 2LY* Tel 0161-928 3236

CORK, CLOYNE AND ROSS, Archdeacon of. *See* WHITE, The Ven Robin Edward Bantry

CORK, CLOYNE AND ROSS, Bishop of. *See* WARKE, The Rt Revd Robert Alexander

CORK, Dean of. *See* JACKSON, The Very Revd Michael Geoffrey St Aubyn

CORKE, Bryan Raymond. b 49. Westmr Coll Lon 81 FBIST77 BAPO95. LNSM course 92. **d** 95 **p** 96. NSM Flixton St Jo *Man* from 95. *40 Daresbury Avenue, Manchester M41 8GL* Tel 0161-748 1827

CORKE, Colin John. b 59. St Pet Coll Ox BA81. Cranmer Hall Dur 83. **d** 85 **p** 86. C Chapel Allerton *Ripon* 85-88; C Burmantofts St Steph and St Agnes 88-91; P-in-c Tatsfield *S'wark* from 91; Reigate Adnry Ecum Officer from 92. *The Rectory, Ricketts Hill Road, Tatsfield, Westerham, Kent TN16 2NA* Tel (01959) 577289

CORKE, John Harry. b 29. AKC55. **d** 56 **p** 57. C Stockingford *Cov* 56-58; C Nuneaton St Nic 58-60; V Hartshill 60-80; R Hampton Lucy w Charlecote and Loxley 80-94; rtd 94; Perm to Offic *Linc* from 95. *18 Haven Close, Fleet, Spalding, Lincs PE12 8NS* Tel (01406) 426038

CORKE, Louise. **d** 97. C Ipsley *Worc* from 97. *77 Edgmond Close, Redditch, Worcs B98 0JQ*

CORKE, Roderick Geoffrey (Rod). b 58. UEA BEd79. St Jo Coll Nottm DTS92. **d** 92 **p** 93. C Trimley *St E* 92-95; C Walton from 95. *1 Parsonage Close, Felixstowe, Suffolk IP11 8QR* Tel (01394) 284803

CORKER, John Anthony. b 37. TD93. ACIB75 AKC63. **d** 64 **p** 65. C Lindley *Wakef* 64-68; V Brotherton 68-72; Perm to Offic 72-82; CF (TA) 80-93; Hon C Askham Bryan *York* 82-91; Asst P York All SS Pavement w St Crux and St Martin etc 91-96; C Amblecote *Worc* from 96. *2 Lakeside Court, Lakeside, Brierley Hill, W Midlands DY5 3RQ* Tel (01384) 892118

CORKER, Canon Ronald. b 30. Ely Th Coll 51. **d** 54 **p** 55. C Whitworth w Spennymoor *Dur* 54-58; Min Dunstan St Nic ED 58-65; Chapl Dunston Hill Hosp Gateshead 58-68; V Dunston St Nic *Dur* 65-68; R Willington 68-75; P-in-c Sunnybrow 73-75; R Willington and Sunnybrow 75-80; V Billingham St Cuth 80-85; RD Stockton 83-85; TR Jarrow 85-95; Hon Can Dur Cathl from 90; rtd 95. *195 Beaconsides, Cleadon Manor, South Shields, Tyne & Wear NE34 7PT* Tel 0191-454 2987

CORKETT, Canon Cecil Harry. b 10. Dur Univ LTh41. Sarum Th Coll 32. **d** 35 **p** 36. C Morley St Pet w Churwell *Wakef* 35-38; C Felkirk w Brierley 38-43; V Whitechapel 43-80; Hon Can Wakef Cathl 71-80; rtd 80; Perm to Offic *Wakef* 80-92. *4 Woodland View, Southwell, Notts NG25 0AG*

CORLESS, Canon Keith Ronald. b 37. Edin Th Coll 58. **d** 61 **p** 62. C Cheltenham All SS *Glouc* 61-64; C Leckhampton SS Phil and Jas 66-69; R Ashchurch 69-96; Hon Can Glouc Cathl from 95; V Staverton w Boddington and Tredington etc from 96. *The Vicarage, Staverton, Cheltenham, Glos GL51 0TW* Tel (01242) 680307

CORLETT, Ewan Christian Brew. b 23. OBE85. FEng74 FRSA FIMarE FRIN FRINA Qu Coll Ox MA47 K Coll Dur PhD50. Is of Man Tr Inst 88. **d** 91 **p** 92. NSM Maughold *S & M* from 91. *Cottimans, Port-e-Vullen, Ramsey, Isle of Man IM7 1AP* Tel (01624) 814009

CORNE, Ronald Andrew. b 51. Sarum & Wells Th Coll 87. **d** 89 **p** 90. Par Dn Bitterne Park *Win* 89-92; C 92-93; R King's Worthy from 93. *The Rectory, Campion Way, King's Worthy, Winchester, Hants SO23 7QP* Tel (01962) 882166

CORNECK, Canon Warrington Graham. b 35. FCA62 ACA60. Clifton Th Coll. **d** 65 **p** 66. C Islington St Jude Mildmay Park *Lon* 65-67; C Southgate *Chich* 67-73; P-in-c Deptford St Nic w Ch Ch *S'wark* 73-76; P-in-c Deptford St Luke 73-76; V Deptford St Nic and St Luke from 76; RD Deptford from 85; Hon Can S'wark Cathl from 91. *St Nicholas' Vicarage, 41 Creek Road, London SE8 3BU* Tel 0181-692 2749

CORNELIUS, Donald Eric. b 31. K Coll Lon BD AKC. **d** 84 **p** 85. Hon C Crowle *Linc* from 84; Hon C Flixborogh w Burton upon Stather from 91. *4 Mulberry Drive, Crowle, Scunthorpe, S Humberside DN17 4JF* Tel (01724) 710279

CORNELL, Miss Jean Cranston. b 36. Man Univ CertEd59 BA64 York Univ BPhil71. Ripon Coll Cuddesdon 87. **d** 89 **p** 94. C Matson *Glouc* 89-92; C Bishop's Cleeve 92-96; rtd 96; NSM Winchcombe, Gretton, Sudeley Manor etc *Glouc* from 96. *5 Stancombe View, Winchcombe, Cheltenham, Glos GL54 5LE* Tel (01242) 602193

CORNELL, John Lister. b 12. St Pet Hall Ox BA34 MA39. Wycliffe Hall Ox 35. **d** 35 **p** 36. C Bermondsey St Anne *S'wark* 35-40; C Putney St Mary 40-44; R Spexhall w Wissett *St E* 44-53; R Mickleham *Guildf* 53-78; rtd 78. *Staddles, Windmill Hill, Ashill, Ilminster, Somerset TA19 9NT* Tel (01823) 480012

CORNELL, Michael Neil. b 45. Ripon Coll Cuddesdon 79. **d** 81 **p** 82. C Gt Bookham *Guildf* 81-84; C York Town St Mich 84-93; V Camberley St Martin Old Dean 93-95; Regional Adv (SE) CMJ from 96. *20 College Road, College Town, Camberley, Surrey GU15 4QU* Tel (01276) 600218

CORNES, Andrew Charles Julian. b 49. CCC Ox BA70 MA73 St Jo Coll Dur DipTh73. Wycliffe Hall Ox 70 Cranmer Hall Dur 72. **d** 73 **p** 74. C York St Mich-le-Belfrey *York* 73-76; C St Marylebone All So w SS Pet and Jo *Lon* 76-85; USA 85-88; V Crowborough *Chich* from 89; RD Rotherfield from 97. *All Saints' Vicarage, Chapel Green, Crowborough, E Sussex TN6 1ED* Tel (01892) 667384

CORNFIELD, Richard James. b 67. St Jo Coll Nottm BA96. **d** 96 **p** 97. C Cheltenham Ch Ch *Glouc* from 96. *1 Kensington Avenue, Cheltenham, Glos GL50 2NQ* Tel (01242) 515915

CORNISH, Anthony. b 30. Roch Th Coll 64. **d** 67 **p** 68. C Goodmayes All SS *Chelmsf* 67-71; C Buckhurst Hill 71-73; V Westcliff St Andr 73-83; R Rawreth w Rettendon 83-96; rtd 96. *12 Fleetwood Avenue, Clacton-on-Sea, Essex CO15 5SE*

CORNISH, Dennis Henry Ronald. b 31. FCIB72 FCIS81. S'wark Ord Course 83. **d** 86 **p** 87. NSM Uxbridge *Lon* 86-89; R Lurgashall, Lodsworth and Selham *Chich* 89-96; rtd 96; Perm to Offic *Chich* from 96. *Stocks Cottage, 55 Stocks Lane, East Wittering, Chichester, W Sussex PO20 8NH* Tel (01243) 672481

CORNISH, Canon Edward Maurice John. b 14. TD51. Qu Coll Birm 48. **d** 48 **p** 49. C Hatfield *St Alb* 48-50; R Docking w the Birchams *Nor* 50-56; V Chorley St Geo *Blackb* 56-70; Bp's Dom Chapl 70-78; R Ribchester w Stidd 70-78; Hon Can Blackb Cathl 74-78; rtd 78; C Fairhaven *Blackb* 78-87; Perm to Offic from 87. *16 Ripon Road, Ansdell, Lytham St Annes, Lancs FY8 4DS* Tel (01253) 739845

CORNISH, Francis John. b 14. Hertf Coll Ox BA36 MA42. Wycliffe Hall Ox 37. **d** 38 **p** 39. C Shirley St Jo *Cant* 38-40; C Phillack w Gwithian *Truro* 40-42; C Plymouth St Andr *Ex* 42-46; V Buckland Monachorum 46-57; R Poynings *Chich* 57-79; R

Edburton 57-79; rtd 79; Perm to Offic *Chich* from 79. *Four Winds, The Street, Clapham, Worthing, W Sussex BN13 3UU* Tel (01903) 871359

CORNISH, Gillian Lesley. b 45. ACIB77. St Jo Coll Nottm 90 LNSM course 93. **d** 96 **p** 97. NSM Moston St Mary *Man* from 96. *11 Rishworth Drive, New Moston, Manchester M40 3PS* Tel 0161-681 2839

CORNISH, Graham Peter. b 42. Dur Univ BA67. NE Ord Course 82. **d** 84 **p** 85. NSM Harrogate St Wilfrid *Ripon* from 84. *33 Mayfield Grove, Harrogate, N Yorkshire HG1 5HD* Tel (01423) 562747

CORNISH, Ivor. b 40. Reading Univ BSc61 DipEd62 ADipR79. Ox Min Course 86. **d** 89 **p** 90. NSM Aston Clinton w Buckland and Drayton Beauchamp *Ox* from 89. *79 Weston Road, Aston Clinton, Aylesbury, Bucks HP22 5EP* Tel (01296) 630345

CORNISH, John Douglas. b 42. Lich Th Coll 67. **d** 70 **p** 71. C Lt Stanmore St Lawr *Lon* 70-73; C Harefield 73-96. *46 Arnos Grove, London N14 7AR*

CORNISH, Peter Andrew. b 55. Ch Ch Ox BA77 MA80 Ex Univ CertEd78. St Jo Coll Nottm 84. **d** 87 **p** 88. C Sanderstead All SS *S'wark* 87-92; TV Cen Telford *Lich* from 92. *20 Burlington Close, Dawley, Telford, Shropshire TF4 3TD* Tel (01952) 595915

CORNISH, Philip Gordon Pym. b 01. K Coll Lon AKC25 BD28. **d** 26 **p** 27. C Roehampton H Trin *S'wark* 26-29; Canada 29-33; C Upper St Leonards St Jo *Chich* 33-37; V Hastings St Clem 37-44; V Danehill 44-59; RD Uckfield 56-59; R Lt Waltham *Chelmsf* 59-67; rtd 67. *Penn Haven, 13 Penn Hill Avenue, Poole, Dorset BH14 9LU* Tel (01202) 747085

CORNWALL-JONES, Canon Guy Rupert. b 30. Jes Coll Cam BA54 MA59. Westcott Ho Cam 55. **d** 57 **p** 58. C Longton St Jas *Lich* 57-60; C Wood End *Cov* 60-64; R Caldecote 64-84; R Weddington 64-84; RD Nuneaton 79-84; Hon Can Cov Cathl from 80; R Bilton 84-91; P-in-c Leek Wootton from 91. *The Vicarage, Leek Wootton, Warwick CV35 7QL* Tel (01926) 54832

CORNWALL, Archdeacon of. *See* McCABE, The Ven John Trevor

CORNWELL, Christopher Richard. b 43. Dur Univ BA67. Cuddesdon Coll 67. **d** 69 **p** 70. C Cannock *Lich* 69-75; P-in-c Hadley 75-80; V 80-81; Bp's Dom Chapl 81-86; Subchanter Lich Cathl 81-86; V Ellesmere 86-89; V Welsh Frankton 86-89; V Ellesmere and Welsh Frankton 89-92; TV Leeds City *Ripon* from 92; RD Allerton from 94. *St Peter's Vicarage, 15 Parkside Green, Leeds LS6 4NY* Tel 0113-278 7449

CORNWELL, Gertrude Florence. b 21. CertEd48 Nottm Univ DipEd72. Gilmore Ho 56 Lambeth STh60. **dss** 62 **d** 87. Sen Lect Bp Grosseteste Coll Linc 64-81; rtd 81; Perm to Offic *Linc* from 91. *Flat 2A, 14 Minster Yard, Lincoln LN2 1PW* Tel (01522) 527249

CORRADINE, John. b 29. St Aid Birkenhead. **d** 58 **p** 59. C Tarporley *Ches* 58-61; C Wilmslow 61-64; V Moulton 64-95; rtd 95. *6 Beach Road, Hoylake, Wirral, Merseyside L47 1HT* Tel 0151-632 3042

CORRAN, Dr Henry Stanley. b 15. Trin Coll Cam BA36 PhD41. CITC 76. **d** 77 **p** 78. NSM Bray Ch Ch *D & G* 77-85; rtd 85. *71 Alderley Road, Hoylake, Wirral, Merseyside L47 2AU* Tel 0151-632 2750

CORRIE, John. b 48. Imp Coll Lon BScEng69 MSc70 DIC70 PhD73 Lon Univ DipTh77 Nottm Univ MTh86. Trin Coll Bris 74. **d** 77 **p** 78. C Kendal St Thos *Carl* 77-80; C Attenborough *S'well* 80-86; Chapl Intercon Ch Soc 86-91; Peru 86-91; Tutor and Lect All Nations Chr Coll Ware from 91. *10 Peters Wood Hill, Ware, Herts SG12 9NR* Tel (01920) 462676

CORRIE, Paul Allen. b 43. St Jo Coll Nottm 77. **d** 79 **p** 80. C Beverley Minster *York* 79-82; V Derby St Werburgh *Derby* 82-84; V Derby St Alkmund and St Werburgh 84-95; Singapore from 95. *7 Deal Road, Medway Park, Singapore 0513* Tel Singapore (650) 776-1891 Fax as telephone

CORRIGAN, The Ven Thomas George. b 28. TCD BTh91. CITC 56. **d** 58 **p** 59. C Cavan and Drung *K, E & A* 58-60; I Drung 60-67; I Belfast St Mich *Conn* 67-70; I Kingscourt w Drumconrath, Syddan and Moybologue *M & K* 70-96; Adn Meath 81-96; Dioc Registrar (Meath) 87-90; rtd 96. *The Beeches, Turner's Hill, Kingscourt, Co Cavan, Irish Republic* Tel Dundalk (42) 68348

CORRY, Caroline Anne. b 58. St Hilda's Coll Ox BA79 Ox Univ MA97. S Tr Scheme 94. **d** 97. C Weston *Guildf* from 97. *27 Blair Avenue, Esher, Surrey KT10 8BQ*

CORSIE, Andrew Russell. b 57. Trin Coll Bris DipHE93. **d** 93 **p** 94. C Northolt Park St Barn *Lon* 93-97; C Perivale from 97. *Perivale Rectory, Federal Road, Greenford, Middx UB6 7AP* Tel 0181-997 1948

CORSTORPHINE, Miss Margaret. b 34. SRN57 SCM59. Cranmer Hall Dur 70. **dss** 84 **d** 87 **p** 94. Colchester St Jo *Chelmsf* 84-87; Par Dn 87-94; C 94; rtd 94; Perm to Offic *Portsm* from 94. *12 Oakmeadow Close, Emsworth, Hants PO10 7RL*

CORTEEN, Robert. b 18. ACII. Coll of Resurr Mirfield 77. **d** 79 **p** 80. NSM Chorlton-cum-Hardy St Clem *Man* 79-88; Perm to Offic from 88. *23 Meadow Bank, Manchester M21 2EF* Tel 0161-881 1118

CORWIN, Nigel Trevor. b 47. EAMTC 95. **d** 97. NSM Bury St Edmunds Ch Ch *St E* from 97. *121 Raedwald Drive, Bury St Edmunds, Suffolk IP32 7DG* Tel (01284) 725284

CORY, Ms Valerie Ann (Val). b 44. CertEd65 Nottm Univ BEd85. EMMTC 85. **d** 88 **p** 94. Area Sec (Dios Linc and Pet) CMS 87-91; NSM Grantham *Linc* 88-91; Par Dn Ealing St Mary *Lon* 91-94; Chapl NW Lon Poly 91-92; Chapl Thames Valley Univ 92-96; C Ealing St Mary 94-96; Chapl Birm Cathl *Birm* from 96. *Birmingham Cathedral Office, Colmore Row, Birmingham B3 2QB* Tel 0121-236 4333 or 6323 Fax 212 0868

COSBY, Ingrid St Clair. b 34. ALCM LLCM DipEd Lon Univ DipTh. **dss** 71 **d** 86 **p** 96. Cumbernauld *Glas* 71-73; Asst CF 73-78; Stromness *Ab* 83-86; NSM from 86. *Quarrybrae, Hillside Road, Stromness, Orkney KW16 3HR* Tel (01856) 850832 Fax as telephone

COSENS, William Edward Hyde (Ted). b 38. Lich Th Coll 61. **d** 64 **p** 65. C W Drayton *Lon* 64-68; C Roehampton H Trin *S'wark* 68-70; ILEA Youth Ldr 69-70; Miss to Seamen 70-94; Chapl Rotterdam Miss to Seamen *Eur* 70-72; Tilbury 72-76; Australia 76-81; New Zealand 81-89; Chapl Immingham Seafarers' Cen 89-94; Hon C Immingham *Linc* 89-94; Perm to Offic *Chelmsf* 94-97; Chapl Avonmouth Miss to Seamen from 97. *4 Penlea Court, Shirehampton, Bristol BS11 0BY* Tel 0117-982 6107 or 982 2335

COSH, Roderick John. b 56. Lon Univ BSc78. St Steph Ho Ox 78. **d** 81 **p** 82. C Swindon New Town *Bris* 81-86; Chapl Asst R Marsden Hosp Lon and Surrey 86-91; V Whitton St Aug *Lon* from 91. *St Augustine's Vicarage, Hospital Bridge Road, Whitton, Middx TW2 6DE* Tel 0181-894 3764 Fax 894 4543 E-mail stang@respite.demon.co.uk

COSLETT, Anthony Allan. b 49. Cuddesdon Coll. **d** 84 **p** 85. C Notting Hill St Clem and St Mark *Lon* 84-85; C Brentford 85-87; C-in-c Hounslow Gd Shep Beavers Lane CD 87-90; V Hounslow W Gd Shep 90-92; CF from 92. *MOD Chaplains (Army), Trenchard Lines, Upavon, Pewsey, Wilts SN9 6BE* Tel (01980) 615804 Fax 615800

COSSAR, David Vyvyan. b 34. Lon Univ BA63. Chich Th Coll 63. **d** 65 **p** 66. C Upper Clapton St Matt *Lon* 65-68; C Withycombe Raleigh *Ex* 68-72; V Honicknowle 72-78; V Brixham w Churston Ferrers 78-86; P-in-c Kingswear 85-86; TR Brixham w Churston Ferrers and Kingswear 86-90; V Lamorbey H Trin *Roch* from 90. *Holy Trinity Vicarage, 1 Hurst Road, Sidcup, Kent DA15 9AE* Tel 0181-300 8231

COSSAR, Miss Heather Jillian Mackenzie. b 27. **dss** 83 **d** 91 **p** 94. Miss Partner CMS 83-90; Kenya 83-90; Slindon, Eartham and Madehurst *Chich* 90-91; NSM from 91. *Gwitu, 38 Spinney Walk, Barnham, Bognor Regis, W Sussex PO22 0HT* Tel (01243) 552718

COSSINS, John Charles. b 43. Hull Univ BSc65. Oak Hill Th Coll 65. **d** 67 **p** 68. C Kenilworth St Jo *Cov* 67-70; C Huyton St Geo *Liv* 70-73; TV Maghull 73-79; Chapl Oakwood Hosp Maidstone 79-85; Maidstone Hosp 85-88; Chapl Park Lane Hosp Liv from 88; Chapl Moss Side Hosp Liv from 88; Chapl Ashworth Hosp from 88. *9 Longton Drive, Liverpool L37 7ET, or Ashworth Hospital, Parkbourn, Maghull, Liverpool L31 1HW* Tel (01704) 833136/0151-471 2608

COSSINS, Roger Stanton. b 40. K Coll Lon BD67 AKC67. **d** 68 **p** 69. C Bramley *Ripon* 68-71; C W End *Win* 71-76; V Bramley 76-91; P-in-c Bournemouth H Epiphany 91-94; V from 94. *The Vicarage, 81 Castle Lane West, Bournemouth BH9 3LH* Tel (01202) 512481

COSSLETT, Dominic Simon. b 72. **d** 96 **p** 97. C Newton St Pet *S & B* from 96. *29 Summerland Lane, Newton, Swansea SA3 4UJ*

COSSLETT, Ronald James. b 38. St D Coll Lamp DipTh70. **d** 70 **p** 71. C Newport St Teilo *Mon* 70-74; C Epsom St Barn *Guildf* 74-78; C Shrewsbury St Mary w All SS and St Mich *Lich* 78-80; V Smallthorne 80-91; V Landore *S & B* from 91. *The Vicarage, 16 Trewyddfa Terrace, Plasmarl, Swansea SA6 8BP* Tel (01792) 773680

COSTERTON, Alan Stewart. b 40. Bris Univ BA67. Clifton Th Coll 67. **d** 69 **p** 70. C Peckham St Mary Magd *S'wark* 69-73; C Forest Gate St Sav w W Ham St Matt *Chelmsf* 73-76; TV 76-79; V Thornton cum Bagworth *Leic* 79-85; V Thornton, Bagworth and Stanton 85-95; TR Sileby, Cossington and Seagrave from 95. *The Rectory, 11 Mountsorrel Lane, Sileby, Loughborough, Leics LE12 7NE* Tel (01509) 813455

COTGROVE, Alan Edward. b 26. AKC51 Westmr Coll Ox TCert71. **d** 52 **p** 53. C Earl's Court St Cuth w St Matthias *Lon* 52-55; Perm to Offic *Ox* 56-58; Lic to Offic 58-62 and 65-76; SSJE from 58; India 62-65; Lic to Offic *Lon* from 76; rtd 96. *32A Marston Street, Oxford OX4 1JU*

COTGROVE, Canon Edwin John. b 23. Kelham Th Coll 42. **d** 47 **p** 48. C Bris St Jude w St Matthias *Bris* 47-50; C Southall St Geo *Lon* 50-52; S Africa 52-56; Swaziland 56-57; V Bromley St Mich *Lon* 57-64; V Hampton All SS 64-82; RD Hampton 72-82; R Bartlow *Ely* 82-91; V Linton 82-91; P-in-c Shudy Camps 85-91; P-in-c Castle Camps 85-91; RD Linton 88-93; Hon Can Ely Cathl from 89; rtd 91; Perm to Offic *Ely* from 91. *96 The High Street, Great Abington, Cambridge CB1 6AE* Tel (01223) 893735

COTMAN, John Sell Granville (Jan). b 44. St Jo Coll Dur BA69 Bris Univ DSA72. Wells Th Coll 70. **d** 73 **p** 74. C Leigh St Mary

Man 73-76; P-in-c Coldhurst 76-78; TV Oldham 78-82; TV E Ham w Upton Park St Alb *Chelmsf* 82-85; C Hove All SS *Chich* 88-93; TV Hove from 93. *25 Connaught Road, Hove, E Sussex BN3 3WB* Tel (01273) 721176

COTTAM, Kenneth Michael David. b 46. FTC70 Leic Univ NDA70 Brooksby Agric Coll NDFOM70. St Mich Coll Llan DMinlStuds93. **d** 93 **p** 94. Lic to Offic Llangadog and Llandeilo Deanery *St D* 93-96; V Llangadog and Gwynfe w Llanddeusant from 96. *The Vicarage, Walters Road, Llanadog SA19 9AE* Tel (01550) 777604

COTTEE, Christopher Paul. b 54. Newc Univ BSc75. Wycliffe Hall Ox 77. **d** 80 **p** 81. C Much Woolton *Liv* 80-84; C Prescot 84-88; NSM Parr 89-91; V Watford St Pet *St Alb* from 91. *St Peter's Vicarage, 61 Westfield Avenue, Watford WD2 4HT* Tel (01923) 226717

COTTEE, Mary Jane. b 43. CertEd64 Open Univ BA81. Oak Hill Th Coll 87. **d** 90 **p** 94. NSM Gt Baddow *Chelmsf* 90-95; NSM Woodham Ferrers and Bicknacre from 95. *19 Avenue Road, Great Baddow, Chelmsford CM2 9TY* Tel (01245) 266225

COTTELL, Avril Jane. *See* GAUNT, Mrs Avril Jane

COTTER, Graham Michael. b 50. Univ of Wales (Ban) BA72. Ridley Hall Cam 75. **d** 78 **p** 79. C Headley All SS *Guildf* 78-81; C Plymouth St Andr w St Paul and St Geo *Ex* 81-84; V Buckland Monachorum from 84; RD Tavistock from 93. *The Vicarage, Buckland Monachorum, Yelverton, Devon PL20 7LQ* Tel (01822) 852227

COTTER, James England. b 42. G&C Coll Cam BA64 MA67. Linc Th Coll 65. **d** 67 **p** 68. C Stretford St Matt *Man* 67-70; Lect Linc Th Coll 70-73; Lic to Offic *Lon* 73-74; Chapl G&C Coll Cam 74-77; C Leavesden All SS *St Alb* 77-83; Asst Prin St Alb Minl Tr Scheme 77-83; Course Dir 83-86; Perm to Offic *Ex* 86-88; Perm to Offic *Sheff* 88-89; Lic to Offic from 89. *47 Firth Park Avenue, Sheffield S5 6HF* Tel 0114-243 1182

COTTER, Canon John Beresford Dolmage. b 20. TCD BA47 BD55. **d** 47 **p** 48. C Glencraig *D & D* 47-49; Chile and Bolivia 49-53; Peru 53; I Tempo *Clogh* 54-55; I Garrison 55-60; I Donagh 60-67; Dir of Ords 62-69; Can Clogh Cathl 62-69; I Dromore 67-69; Preb Donaghmore St Patr Cathl Dublin 69; Bahrain 69-75; V Towednack *Truro* 76-89; V Zennor 76-89; Past Tr Chapl 82-89; rtd 89; Perm to Offic *B & W* from 89. *Thimble Cottage, 64 Mount Road, Bath BA2 1LH* Tel (01225) 337414

COTTERELL, Michael Clifford. b 54. Oak Hill Th Coll 81. **d** 84 **p** 85. C Lutterworth w Cotesbach *Leic* 84-87; C Belper *Derby* 87-91; V Locking *B & W* from 91. *The Vicarage, The Green, Locking, Weston-super-Mare, Avon BS24 8DA* Tel (01934) 823556

COTTERILL, Joseph Charles (Joe). b 17. AMCT38 Lon Univ DipTh BD California Coll Peking MA46. Ox Min Course 92. **d** 93 **p** 94. NSM Marcham w Garford *Ox* from 93. *8 Draycott Road, Southmoor, Abingdon, Oxon OX13 5BY* Tel (01865) 820436

COTTINGHAM, Peter John Garnet. b 24. Wadh Coll Ox BA48 MA50. Ridley Hall Cam 48. **d** 50 **p** 51. C Cheadle *Ches* 50-55; R Ox St Clem *Ox* 55-68; V S Mimms Ch Ch *Lon* 68-81; V Derby St Pet and Ch Ch w H Trin *Derby* 81-89; rtd 89; Perm to Offic *Ban* from 89. *5 Broadway, Rhos-on-Sea, Colwyn Bay LL28 4AR* Tel (01492) 548840

COTTON, Charles Anthony. b 50. Linc Coll Ox BA72 MA77 PGCE73. Ridley Hall Cam 89. **d** 91 **p** 92. C Hendon St Paul Mill Hill *Lon* 91-96; C Wandsworth All SS *S'wark* from 96. *56 Lebanon Gardens, London SW18 1RH* Tel 0181-874 3438

COTTON, Canon John Alan. b 24. Qu Coll Ox BA48 MA52. Chich Th Coll 50. **d** 51 **p** 52. C Doncaster St Geo *Sheff* 51-54; C Ifield *Chich* 54-56; P-in-c Jevington 56-57; R 57-60; Chief Org Sec SPCK 60-63; Chapl Sussex Univ 63-69; V Fairwarp 69-82; Dir of Educn 72-78; Can and Preb Chich Cathl 72-89; Bp's Adv on Min 79-89; Dir of Ords 79-89; rtd 89; Perm to Offic *Carl* from 91. *1 Westhaven, Thursby, Carlisle CA5 6PH* Tel (01228) 711506

COTTON, John Horace Brazel. b 28. MIMechE St Jo Coll Cam BA50 MA76. St Alb Minl Tr Scheme 78. **d** 81 **p** 82. NSM Lt Berkhamsted and Bayford, Essendon etc *St Alb* 81-87; P-in-c 87-96; rtd 96. *49 Sherrardspark Road, Welwyn Garden City, Herts AL8 7LD* Tel (01707) 321815

COTTON, John Kenneth. b 25. Westcott Ho Cam 57. **d** 58 **p** 59. C S Ormsby w Ketsby, Calceby and Driby *Linc* 58-61; R Wrentham w Benacre, Covehithe and Henstead *St E* 61-68; R Sotterley w Willingham 63-68; R Shadingfield 63-68; Canada 68-71; TV Sandringham w W Newton *Nor* 71-76; P-in-c Assington *St E* 80-86; P-in-c Lt Cornard 80-86; P-in-c Newton 80-86; P-in-c Eyke w Bromeswell, Rendlesham, Tunstall etc 87-92; P-in-c Alderton w Ramsholt and Bawdsey 89-92; rtd 92. *8 Chillesford Lodge Bungalows, Sudbourne, Woodbridge, Suffolk IP12 2AN* Tel (01394) 450740

COTTON, Canon John Wallis. b 31. Wells Th Coll 57. **d** 59 **p** 60. C Stepney St Dunstan and All SS *Lon* 59-64; C Hanworth All SS 64-67; V Hammersmith St Sav 67-74; R Lancing w Coombes *Chich* 75-86; RD Worthing 83-85; R Bexhill St Pet 86-90; TR from 90; RD Battle and Bexhill from 92; Can and Preb Chich Cathl from 96. *The Rectory, Old Town, Bexhill-on-Sea, E Sussex TN40 2HE* Tel (01424) 211115

COTTON, John William. b 53. Basford Coll Nottm DipInstBM74. Oak Hill Th Coll DipHE86. **d** 86 **p** 87. C New Clee *Linc* 86-89; Chapl St Andr Hospice Grimsby 88-89; R Middle Rasen Gp 89-95; P-in-c Broughton 95-97; R from 97. *The Rectory, 22 Scawby Road, Broughton, Brigg, S Humberside DN20 0AF* Tel (01652) 652506

COTTON, Mrs Margaret Elizabeth. b 30. JP79. Newnham Coll Cam BA53 MA66. St Alb Minl Tr Scheme 78. **dss** 82 **d** 87 **p** 94. Lt Berkhamsted and Bayford, Essendon etc *St Alb* 82-87; Hon Par Dn 87-94; Hon C 94-96; rtd 96. *49 Sherrardspark Road, Welwyn Garden City, Herts AL8 7LD* Tel (01707) 321815

COTTON, Norman Joseph. b 39. Kelham Th Coll 59. **d** 64 **p** 65. C Auckland St Helen *Dur* 64-67; C Withington St Chris *Man* 67-68; C Hucknall Torkard *S'well* 69-71; TV 71-73; TV Fenny Stratford *Ox* 73-75; TV Fenny Stratford and Water Eaton 75-82; P-in-c Broughton and Milton Keynes 82; P-in-c Wavendon w Walton 82; R Walton 82-90; TR Walton Milton Keynes 90-92; V Stewkley w Soulbury and Drayton Parslow from 92; RD Mursley from 94. *The Vicarage, Stewkley, Leighton Buzzard, Beds LU7 0OH* Tel (01525) 240287

COTTON, Miss Patricia Constance. b 32. Gilmore Ho 54. **dss** 60 **d** 87 **p** 94. Forest Gate St Edm *Chelmsf* 60-64; Reading St Giles *Ox* 64-65; Basildon St Martin w H Cross and Laindon *Chelmsf* 65-79; Gt Burstead 79-87; Par Dn Maldon All SS w St Pet 87-91; rtd 92; NSM Holland-on-Sea *Chelmsf* 94-96; Perm to Offic from 96. *21 Stallards Crescent, Kirby Cross, Frinton-on-Sea, Essex CO13 0TN* Tel (01255) 672711

COTTON, Patrick Arthur William. b 46. Essex Univ BA67 Cam Univ MA73. Linc Th Coll 68. **d** 71 **p** 72. C Earlham St Anne *Nor* 71-73; Chapl Down Coll Cam 73-78; V Eaton Socon *St Alb* 78-84; TR Newc Epiphany *Newc* 84-90; V Tunstall w Melling and Leck *Blackb* 90-95; rtd 95. *Address temp unknown*

COTTON, Canon Peter John. b 45. BNC Ox BA66 Bris Univ CQSW76. Cuddesdon Coll 67. **d** 69 **p** 70. C Salford St Phil w St Steph *Man* 69-73; Asst Educn Officer *St Alb* 73-75; C Bris St Geo *Bris* 75-76; C-in-c Portsea St Geo CD *Portsm* 76-80; Soc Resp Adv 78-88; Can Res Portsm Cathl 84-88; V St Laurence in the Isle of Thanet *Cant* 88-93; TR St Laur in Thanet 93-97; Hon Min Can Cant Cathl 93-97; TR Hemel Hempstead *St Alb* from 97. *The Rectory, 40 High Street, Hemel Hempstead, Herts HP1 3AE* Tel (01442) 233401 or 213838 Fax 213838

COTTON, Richard William (Dick). b 35. Hertf Coll Ox BA58 MA62. Clifton Th Coll 58. **d** 60 **p** 61. C Harold Wood *Chelmsf* 60-64; C Higher Openshaw *Man* 64-67; Lic to Offic 67-71; Ch Youth Fellowships Assn & Pathfinders 67-71; Nat Sec Pathfinders CPAS 71-76; Lic to Offic *St Alb* 73-76; V Chislehurst Ch Ch *Roch* 76-92; V Herne Bay Ch Ch *Cant* from 92; RD Reculver from 93. *Christ Church Vicarage, 38 Beltinge Road, Herne Bay, Kent CT6 5BP* Tel (01227) 374906 or 366640

COTTON, Robert Lloyd. b 58. Mert Coll Ox MA79 Louvain Univ Belgium DipTh81. Westcott Ho Cam 81. **d** 83 **p** 84. C Plaistow St Mary *Roch* 83-86; C Bisley and W End *Guildf* 87-89; P-in-c E Molesey St Paul 89-96; Dir of Reader Tr from 90; R Guildf H Trin w St Mary from 96. *Holy Trinity Rectory, 9 Eastgate Gardens, Guildford, Surrey GU1 4AZ* Tel (01483) 575489

COTTON, Roy William. b 29. Jes Coll Ox BA53 MA61. Chich Th Coll 66. **d** 66 **p** 67. C Eastney *Portsm* 66-71; R Harting *Chich* 71-74; P-in-c Eastbourne St Andr 74-76; V 76-84; R Brede w Udimore from 84. *The Rectory, Brede, Rye, E Sussex TN31 6DX* Tel (01424) 882457

COTTRELL, Bertram Lionel. b 23. Lich Th Coll 51. **d** 54 **p** 56. C Lynworth *Glouc* 54-56; C Glouc St Aldate 56-57; C Gt Yarmouth *Nor* 57-58; C Hendon St Paul Mill Hill *Lon* 58-61; C Christchurch *Win* 61-63; V Isleworth St Jo *Lon* 63-83; rtd 83; Perm to Offic *Lon* from 83. *13 Sutton Square, Heston, Middx TW5 0JB* Tel 0181-572 5034

COTTRELL, Stephen Geoffrey. b 58. Poly Cen Lon BA79. St Steph Ho Ox 81. **d** 84 **p** 85. C Forest Hill Ch Ch *S'wark* 84-88; C-in-c Parklands St Wilfrid CD *Chich* 88-93; Asst Dir of Past Studies Chich Th Coll 88-93; Dioc Missr *Wakef* from 93; Bp's Chapl for Evang from 93. *22 Grimescar Meadows, Huddersfield HD2 2DZ* Tel (01484) 542163

COTTRILL, Derek John. b 43. MA. Qu Coll Birm. **d** 82 **p** 83. C Southampton Maybush St Pet *Win* 82-85; V Barton Stacey and Bullington etc 85-92; R Bishopstoke from 92. *The Rectory, 10 Stoke Park Road, Eastleigh, Hants SO50 6DA* Tel (01703) 612192

COUCH, Andrew Nigel. b 48. K Coll Lon BD70 AKC70 Ex Coll Ox PGCE72. St Aug Coll Cant 70. **d** 71 **p** 72. C St Ives *Truro* 71-74; C St Martin-in-the-Fields *Lon* 74-78; USPG 78-91; Uruguay 79-84; Argentina 85-91; Chapl Qu Mary Coll *Lon* 91-94; V St Ives *Truro* from 94. *The Parsonage, St Andrew's Street, St Ives, Cornwall TR26 1AH* Tel (01736) 796404

COUCHMAN, Anthony Denis. b 37. Sarum Th Coll 66. **d** 69 **p** 70. C Barkingside St Fran *Chelmsf* 69-71; C Chingford SS Pet and Paul 71-76; P-in-c Walthamstow St Barn and St Jas Gt 76-80; V from 80. *St Barnabas' Vicarage, St Barnabas Road, London E17 8JZ* Tel 0181-520 5323

COUGHTREY, Miss Sheila Frances. b 48. RSCN73 SRN73 S Bank Poly BSc79. Qu Coll Birm 79. **dss** 81 **d** 87 **p** 94. Sydenham St Bart *S'wark* 81-85; Roehampton H Trin 85-87;

Par Dn 87-91; Par Dn Brixton Hill St Sav 91-94; Min K Acre LEP from 91; C Brixton Hill St Sav 94; P-in-c from 94. *6 Blenheim Gardens, London SW2 5ET* Tel 0181-674 6914

COULDRIDGE, Janice Evelyn. *See* FOX, Mrs Janice Evelyn

COULING, David Charles. b 36. Open Univ BA89. Qu Coll Birm 61. **d** 63 **p** 64. C Harborne St Faith and St Laur *Birm* 63-66; C E Grinstead St Mary *Chich* 66-70; V Copthorne 70-75; V Eastbourne St Mich 75-82; V Brighton St Matthias 82-83; C-in-c Harton St Lawr CD *Dur* 84-90; V Horsley Hill S Shields 91-94; P-in-c Greatham 94-97; V from 97; Master Greatham Hosp from 94; RD Hartlepool from 95. *Greatham Hall, Greatham, Hartlepool, Cleveland TS25 2HS* Tel (01429) 871148

COULSON, Stephen Hugh. b 60. St Edm Hall Ox BA82 MA88 Lon Univ CertEd83. Wycliffe Hall Ox 85. **d** 88 **p** 89. C Summerfield *Birm* 88-91; Perm to Offic 91-92; CMS from 92; Uganda from 92. *PO Box 5627, Kampala, Uganda*

COULSON, Canon Thomas Stanley. b 32. TCD BA54 MA68. TCD Div Sch 55. **d** 55 **p** 56. C Maghera *D & R* 55-62; I Aghalurcher and Tattykeeran *Clogh* 62-63; I Woodschapel w Gracefield *Arm* 63-96; Preb Arm Cathl from 88; RD Tullyhogue from 90; Treas Arm Cathl 94-96; Chan Arm Cathl from 96. *140 Ballyronan Road, Magherafelt, Co Derry BT45 6HT* Tel (01648) 418230

COULSON, Tony Erik Frank. b 32. St Edm Hall Ox BA55 DipTh56 MA59. Wycliffe Hall Ox 55. **d** 57 **p** 58. C Walthamstow St Mary *Chelmsf* 57-60; C Reading St Jo *Ox* 60-63; V Iver 63-86; R White Waltham w Shottesbrooke from 86. *The Vicarage, White Waltham, Maidenhead, Berks SL6 3JD* Tel (01628) 822000

COULTER, Edmond James. b 60. QUB BSc82 TCD DipTh87. **d** 87 **p** 88. C Ballymena w Ballyclug *Conn* 87-90; C Knockbreda *D & D* 90-92; I Belfast Upper Falls *Conn* 92-97; I Milltown *Arm* from 97. *10 Derrylileagh Road, Birches, Portadown, Craigavon, Co Armagh BT62 1TQ* Tel (01762) 851246

COULTER, Richard Samuel Scott. b 09. Dur Univ LTh39. Clifton Th Coll 35. **d** 38 **p** 39. C Parr Mt *Liv* 38-40; CF 40-46; C Huyton St Mich *Liv* 46-50; Chapl Whiston Hosp 47-50; V Wavertree St Bridget *Liv* 50-61; Hon CF from 46; V Upton Snodsbury w Broughton Hackett etc *Worc* 61-77; rtd 77. *29 Greenheart Way, Southmoor, Abingdon, Oxon OX13 5DF* Tel (01865) 820912

COULTHARD, Miss Nina Marion. b 50. CertEd71 Bp Lonsdale Coll BEd72. Trin Coll Bris DipHE91. **d** 91 **p** 94. Par Dn Cant St Mary Bredin *Cant* 91-94; C 94-95; C Bath Abbey w St Jas *B & W* from 95. *7 Holloway, Bath BA2 4PS* Tel (01225) 484469

COULTHURST, Jeffrey Evans. b 38. Man Univ BA. LNSM course 85. **d** 84 **p** 85. NSM Ancaster *Linc* 84-89; NSM Ancaster Wilsford Gp from 89. *5 North Drive, Ancaster, Grantham, Lincs NG32 3RB* Tel (01400) 30280

COULTON, David Stephen. b 41. Sarum Th Coll 64. **d** 67 **p** 68. C Guildf H Trin w St Mary *Guildf* 67-70; Asst Chapl Radley Coll Oxon 70-83; Chapl from 83. *Radley College, Abingdon, Oxon OX14 2HR* Tel (01235) 534651

COULTON, The Very Revd Nicholas Guy. b 40. Lon Univ BD72. Cuddesdon Coll 65. **d** 67 **p** 68. C Pershore w Wick *Worc* 67-70; Bp's Dom Chapl *St Alb* 71-75; P-in-c Bedford St Paul 75-79; V 79-90; Hon Can St Alb 89-90; Provost Newc from 90. *The Cathedral Vicarage, 26 Mitchell Avenue, Jesmond, Newcastle upon Tyne NE2 3LA* Tel 0191-281 6554 or 232 1939

COULTON, Philip Ernest. b 31. St Cath Coll Cam BA54 MA58 TCD BD68 Open Univ BA84. Ely Th Coll 55. **d** 57 **p** 58. C Newark w Coddington *S'well* 57-61; Min Can and Sacr Cant Cathl *Cant* 61-63; Min Can Ripon Cathl *Ripon* 63-68; Hd of RE Ashton-under-Lyne Gr Sch 69-84; Perm to Offic *Ches* 70-71; Lic to Offic 71-84; V Ulceby Gp *Linc* 85-89; P-in-c Ingatestone w Buttsbury *Chelmsf* from 89; P-in-c Fryerning w Margaretting 89-92. *1 Rectory Close, Ingatestone, Essex CM4 0DB* Tel (01277) 353768

COUNSELL, Edwin Charles Robert. b 63. Univ of Wales (Cardiff) BA84. St Steph Ho Ox 85. **d** 88 **p** 89. C Cardiff St Mary and St Steph w St Dyfrig etc *Llan* 88-94; Sub-Chapl HM Pris Cardiff 90-94; V Pendoylan and Welsh St Donats from 94. *The Vicarage, 9 Heol St Cattwg, Pendoylan, Cowbridge CF71 7UJ* Tel (01446) 760210

COUNSELL, Michael John Radford. b 35. Pemb Coll Cam BA59 MA63. Ripon Hall Ox 59. **d** 61 **p** 62. C Handsworth St Mary *Birm* 61-63; Singapore 64-68; Vietnam and Cambodia 68-71; Seychelles 72-76; Dean Mahe 73-76; V Harborne St Pet *Birm* 76-89; Relig Consultant to Inter-Ch Travel Ltd 89-90; V Forest Hill St Aug *S'wark* from 90; Perm to Offic *Cant* from 91. *St Augustine's Vicarage, 8 Hengrave Road, London SE23 3NW* Tel 0181-699 1535

COUPAR, Thomas. b 50. BA71. Edin Dioc NSM Course 77. **d** 80 **p** 81. NSM Dunbar *Edin* 80-86; NSM Haddington 80-86; Hd Master Pencaitland Primary Sch E Lothian 80-81; Hd Master K Meadow Sch E Lothian 81-87; Asst Dioc Supernumerary *Edin* from 87; Primary Educn Adv Fife from 88; Dioc Supernumerary Chapl from 90. *8A Garscube Terrace, Edinburgh EH12 6BU*

COUPER, Jeanette Emily (Jean). b 40. S'wark Ord Course 85. **d** 88. Par Dn Mitcham SS Pet and Paul *S'wark* 88-93; Perm to Offic from 93; Chapl Asst Guy's Hosp Lon 93-94. *Ivy Lodge, Morden Hall Road, Morden, Surrey SM4 5JD* Tel 0181-640 8137

COUPER, Jonathan George. b 51. St Jo Coll Dur BA73. Wycliffe Hall Ox 73. **d** 75 **p** 76. C Clifton *York* 75-78; C Darfield *Sheff* 78-81; V Bridlington Quay Ch Ch *York* from 81. *21 Kingston Road, Bridlington, N Humberside YO15 3NF* Tel (01262) 673538

COUPLAND, Dr Simon Charles. b 59. St Jo Coll Cam BA82 PGCE83 MA85 PhD87. Ridley Hall Cam 88. **d** 91 **p** 92. C Bath St Luke *B & W* 91-95; TV Broadwater St Mary *Chich* from 95. *67 Normandy Road, Broadwater, Worthing, W Sussex BN14 7EA* Tel (01903) 203201

COURAGE, Roy Kenneth. b 25. ACCS63 ACIS70. St D Coll Lamp 67. **d** 69 **p** 70. C Blaenavon w Capel Newydd *Mon* 69-71; R Blaina 71-78; V Blackwood 78-89; rtd 89. *Ysgubor Wen, Tylsaf Farm, Llechryd, Rhymney NP2 5QU* Tel (01685) 841260

COURT, David Eric. b 58. Southn Univ BSc80 PhD83 PGCE84. Oak Hill Th Coll BA91. **d** 91 **p** 92. C Barton Seagrave w Warkton *Pet* 91-94; C Kinson *Sarum* 94-97; P-in-c Mile Cross *Nor* from 97. *St Catherine's Vicarage, Aylsham Road, Mile Cross, Norwich NR3 2RJ* Tel (01603) 426767

COURT, Canon Kenneth Reginald. b 36. AKC60. **d** 61 **p** 62. C Garforth *Ripon* 61-63; C Harrogate St Wilfrid 63-65; V Thornbury *Bradf* 65-73; Prec Leic Cathl *Leic* 73-76; V Douglas St Matt *S & M* 76-84; V Syston *Leic* 84-93; TR Syston TM from 93; RD Goscote 90-95; Hon Can Leic Cathl from 92. *The Vicarage, Upper Church Street, Syston, Leicester LE7 1HR* Tel 0116-260 8276

COURT, Martin Jeremy. b 61. GRNCM84 Nottm Univ BTh89. Linc Th Coll 86. **d** 89 **p** 90. C Thurmaston *Leic* 89-92; C Leic St Jas 92-93; TV Leic Resurr from 93. *St Gabriel's House, 20 Kerrysdale Avenue, Leicester LE4 7GH* Tel 0116-266 1452

COURT, Nicholas James Keble. b 56. SSC. Chich Th Coll 86. **d** 88 **p** 89. C Golders Green *Lon* 88-91; C Westbury-on-Trym H Trin *Bris* 91-94; PV Llan Cathl *Llan* 94-96; V Graig from 96; P-in-c Cilfynydd from 96. *St John's Vicarage, 28 Llantrisant Road, The Graig, Pontypridd CF37 1LW* Tel (01443) 402436

COURT, Richard Leonard. b 54. UEA CertHE96. EAMTC 94. **d** 97. NSM Framlingham w Saxtead *St E* from 97. *9 Howard Close, Framlingham, Woodbridge, Suffolk IP13 9SH* Tel (01728) 724230

COURTAULD, Augustine Christopher Caradoc. b 34. Trin Coll Cam BA58. Westcott Ho Cam 58. **d** 60 **p** 61. C Oldham St Mary *Man* 60-63; Chapl Trin Coll Cam 63-68; Chapl The Lon Hosp (Whitechapel) 68-78; V Wilton Place St Paul *Lon* from 78; AD Westmr St Marg from 92. *St Paul's Vicarage, 32 Wilton Place, London SW1X 8SH* Tel 0171-235 1810 or 235 3460

COURTIE, Dr John Malcolm. b 42. BNC Ox BA65 DPhil72 St Jo Coll Dur BA76 DipTh77. Cranmer Hall Dur 74. **d** 77 **p** 78. C Mossley Hill St Matt and St Jas *Liv* 77-80; V Litherland St Paul Hatton Hill 80-84; Wellingborough Sch 84-89; Hon C Wollaston and Strixton *Pet* 84-89; V Woodford Halse w Eydon from 89. *The New Vicarage, Parsons Street, Woodford Halse, Daventry, Northants NN11 3RE* Tel (01327) 261477 Fax as telephone Mobile 0589-319801

COURTNEY, Canon Brian Joseph. b 44. BD92. CITC 70. **d** 73 **p** 74. C Willowfield *D & D* 73-78; I Aghavea *Clogh* 78-83; I Carrickfergus *Conn* 83-95; I Enniskillen *Clogh* from 95; Prec Clogh Cathl from 95. *St Macartin's Rectory, 13 Church Street, Enniskillen, Co Fermanagh BT74 7DW* Tel (01365) 322465 or 322917

COURTNEY, Michael Monlas. b 19. Coll of Resurr Mirfield 58. **d** 60 **p** 61. C Shrewsbury St Chad *Lich* 60-63; P-in-c N Keyham *Ex* 63-68; V 68-73; TV Sidmouth, Woolbrook and Salcombe Regis 73-79; TV Sidmouth, Woolbrook, Salcombe Regis etc 79-84; rtd 84; Perm to Offic *Ex* from 86. *Furzehill Farm House, Sidbury, Sidmouth, Devon EX10 0RE* Tel (01395) 597440

COUSINS, Christopher William. b 44. Oak Hill Th Coll DipHE87. **d** 87 **p** 88. C Wallasey St Hilary *Ches* 87-90; R Rollesby w Burgh w Billockby w Ashby w Oby etc *Nor* 90-94; P-in-c Ormesby w Scratby 92-94; V Ormesby St Marg w Scratby, Ormesby St Mich etc from 94; RD Gt Yarmouth from 94. *The Vicarage, Ormesby, Great Yarmouth, Norfolk NR29 3PZ* Tel (01493) 730234

COUSINS, Graham John. b 55. Oak Hill Th Coll BA91. **d** 91 **p** 92. C Birkenhead St Jas w St Bede *Ches* 91-95; C Bebington from 95. *48 Acreville Road, Bebington, Wirral, Merseyside L63 2HY* Tel 0151-645 9584

COUSINS, Herbert Ralph. b 13. Bps' Coll Cheshunt 52. **d** 54 **p** 55. C Leagrave *St Alb* 54-58; R Maulden 58-63; RD Ampthill 62-63; C-in-c Luton St Hugh Lewsey CD 63-65; Min 65-67; V 67-70; V Southill 70-71; R Clophill 71-78; rtd 78; Perm to Offic *B & W* from 78. *Evensong, Sand Road, Weston-super-Mare, Avon BS22 9UF* Tel (01934) 413260

COUSINS, Peter Gareth. b 37. **d** 95 **p** 96. NSM Cwmparc *Llan* from 95. *15 Conway Road, Cwmparc, Treorchy CF42 6UW* Tel (01443) 773669

COUSINS, Canon Philip John. b 35. K Coll Cam BA58 MA62. Cuddesdon Coll 59. **d** 61 **p** 62. C Marton *Blackb* 61-63; PV Truro Cathl *Truro* 63-67; Ethiopia 67-75; V Henleaze *Bris* 75-84; RD Clifton 79-84; Provost All SS Cathl Cairo 84-89; Chan Malta Cathl *Eur* 89-95; Valletta w Gozo 89-95; R Llandudno *Ban* from

95. *The Rectory, Church Walks, Llandudno LL30 2HL* Tel (01492) 876624

COUSLAND, Andrew Oliver. b 41. Golds Coll Lon MA92. Edin Th Coll 62. **d** 65 **p** 66. C Broughty Ferry *Bre* 65-68; C Ayr *Glas* 68-70; R Renfrew 70-75; Perm to Offic *St E* 75-79; CF (TAVR) 76-82; Perm to Offic *Bre* 79-84; Perm to Offic *S'wark* 89-94; R Fraserburgh w New Pitsligo *Ab* from 94. *St Peter's Rectory, 6 Crimond Court, Fraserburgh AB43 5QW* Tel (01346) 518158 E-mail jl95@dial.pipex.com

COUSSENS, Mervyn Haigh Wingfield. b 47. St Jo Coll Nottm BTh74. **d** 74 **p** 75. C Clifton Ch Ch w Em *Bris* 74-77; C Morden *S'wark* 77-83; V Patchway *Bris* 83-91; R Lutterworth w Cotesbach *Leic* from 91; P-in-c Bitteswell from 95. *The Rectory, Coventry Road, Lutterworth, Leics LE17 4SH* Tel (01455) 552669

COUSSMAKER, Canon Colin Richard Chad. b 34. Worc Coll Ox BA57 BSc58 MA63 MSc85. Chich Th Coll 59. **d** 60 **p** 61. C Newtown St Luke *Win* 60-64; C Whitley Ch Ch *Ox* 64-67; Chapl Istanbul *Eur* 67-72; Chapl Sliema 72-77; Chapl Antwerp St Boniface 77-93; Can Brussels Cathl from 81; Chapl Moscow from 93. *Moscow, c/o FCO, King Charles Street, London SW1A 2AH* Tel Moscow (095) 245-3837 or 266-0907 Fax 956-7480

COUTTS, Ian Alexander. b 56. Warw Univ BA77 Jes Coll Ox MSc80 CQSW80. St Jo Coll Nottm DipTh89. **d** 89 **p** 90. C Hamstead St Bernard *Birm* 89-92; C Warlingham w Chelsham and Farleigh *S'wark* 92-97; TV from 97. *St Christopher's Vicarage, Chelsham Road, Warlingham, Surrey CR6 9EQ* Tel (01883) 624494

COUTTS, James Allan. b 58. Fitzw Coll Cam MA. St Jo Coll Nottm MTh84. **d** 84 **p** 85. C Thorpe Acre w Dishley *Leic* 84-88; TV Kirby Muxloe from 88. *106 Hinckley Road, Leicester Forest East, Leicester LE3 3JS* Tel 0116-238 6344 or 238 6811

COUTTS, Canon James Walter Cargill. b 35. Univ of Wales (Lamp) BA57 CCC Cam BA59. St Mich Coll Llan 59. **d** 60 **p** 61. C Cardiff St Mary *Llan* 60-63; C Greenford H Cross *Lon* 63-67; C Swansea St Gabr *S & B* 67-71; V Llanwrtyd w Llanddulas in Tir Abad etc 71-78; V Brecon St Dav 78-80; V Brecon St David w Llanspyddid and Llanilltyd 80-84; V Monmouth *Mon* from 84; Can St Woolos Cathl from 94. *The Vicarage, The Parade, Monmouth NP5 3PA* Tel (01600) 713141

COUTTS, Robin Iain Philip. b 52. Sarum & Wells Th Coll. **d** 83 **p** 84. C Alverstoke *Portsm* 83-86; Min Leigh Park St Clare CD 86-89; V Warren Park St Clare 89-91; V Purbrook from 91. *The Vicarage, London Road, Purbrook, Waterlooville, Hants PO7 5RS* Tel (01705) 262307

COVE, Kenneth John. b 34. Lich Th Coll 58. **d** 60 **p** 61. C Crosland Moor *Wakef* 60-63; C Halifax St Jo Bapt 63-65; V Wakef St Jo 65-73; V Appleby *Carl* 73-78; RD Appleby 74-78; V Ambleside w Brathay 78-87; V Thames Ditton *Guildf* 87-94; P-in-c Morland, Thrimby and Gt Strickland *Carl* 94-96; V Morland, Thrimby, Gt Strickland and Cliburn from 96. *The Vicarage, Morland, Penrith, Cumbria CA10 3AX* Tel (01931) 714620

COVENTRY, Archdeacon of. *See* RUSSELL, The Ven Harold Ian Lyle

COVENTRY, Bishop of. *Vacant*

COVENTRY, Provost of. *See* PETTY, The Very Revd John Fitzmaurice

COVINGTON, Canon Michael William Rock. b 38. Open Univ BA78. Sarum Th Coll 60. **d** 63 **p** 64. C Daventry *Pet* 63-66; C Woolwich St Mary w H Trin *S'wark* 66-68; C Northampton All SS w St Kath *Pet* 68-71; V Longthorpe 71-86; Hon Min Can Pet Cathl 75-86; Can Pet Cathl from 86; V Warmington, Tansor, Cotterstock and Fotheringhay 86-95; Warden Dioc Assn of Readers from 87; RD Oundle 89-95; V Oakham, Hambleton, Egleton, Braunston and Brooke from 95. *The Vicarage, Oakham, Leics LE15 6EG* Tel (01572) 722108

COWARD, Colin Charles Malcolm. b 45. Westcott Ho Cam 75. **d** 78 **p** 79. C Camberwell St Geo *S'wark* 78-82; P-in-c Wandsworth St Faith 82-90; V 90-96; Chapl Richmond, Twickenham and Roehampton NHS Trust from 96. *11 Murfett Close, London SW19 6QB* Tel 0181-788 1384

COWARD, Raymond. b 41. NW Ord Course 79. **d** 82 **p** 83. C Turton *Man* 82-84; C Heaton Ch Ch 84-86; V Rochdale St Geo w St Alb 86-92; V Daisy Hill from 92. *The Vicarage, Lower Leigh Road, Daisy Hill, Westhoughton, Bolton BL5 2EH* Tel (01942) 813155

COWBURN, John Charles. b 48. Sarum & Wells Th Coll 88. **d** 90 **p** 91. C Andover w Foxcott *Win* 90-94; C Christchurch 94-96; Chapl to the Deaf *Lich* from 96. *The Vicarage, Upper Belgrave Road, Stoke-on-Trent ST3 4QJ* Tel (01782) 319695

COWDREY, Herbert Edward John. b 26. Trin Coll Ox BA49 MA51. St Steph Ho Ox 50. **d** 52 **p** 53. Tutor St Steph Ho Ox 52-56; Chapl 54-56; Asst Chapl Ex Coll Ox 52-56; Lic to Offic *Ox* from 52; Fell St Edm Hall Ox from 56; Chapl 56-78; rtd 91. *30 Oxford Road, Old Marston, Oxford OX3 0PQ* Tel (01865) 279015

COWDRY, Gilbert. b 26. Wells Th Coll 70. **d** 72 **p** 73. C Bath Twerton-on-Avon *B & W* 72-76; V Long Sutton w Long Load 76-82; TV S Molton w Nymet St George, High Bray etc *Ex* 82-96; RD S Molton 87-93; rtd 96. *17 Hillcrest Park, Exeter EX4 4SH*

COWELL, Arthur John. b 10. Wycliffe Hall Ox 40. **d** 41 **p** 42. C Horley *S'wark* 41-43; C Cheam 43-48; V Camberwell St Jas 48-51; V Kingston St Jo 51-54; CF (TA) 53-65; Org Sec Miss to Seamen (SW England) 54-60; V Prittlewell St Pet *Chelmsf* 60-80; Chapl Southend Gen Hosp 68-80; rtd 80; Perm to Offic *Chelmsf* from 80. *Nazareth House, London Road, Southend-on-Sea SS1 1PP* Tel (01702) 345627

COWELL, Mrs Irene Christine. b 58. RGN80. Ridley Hall Cam CTM94. **d** 94 **p** 95. C Litherland St Phil *Liv* from 94. *3 Harrington Road, Litherland, Liverpool L21 7NA* Tel 0151-928 7879

COWELL, Peter James. b 58. Peterho Cam BA80 MA84. Coll of Resurr Mirfield 80. **d** 82 **p** 83. C Folkestone St Sav *Cant* 82-86; Chapl Asst St Thos Hosp Lon 86-90; Chapl R Lon Hosp (Mile End) 90-94; Chapl R Lon Hosp (Whitechapel) 90-94; Chapl R Lon Hosps NHS Trust from 94; PV Westmr Abbey from 94. *The Chaplain's Office, The Royal London Hospital, London E1 1BB* Tel 0171-377 7000 or 377 7385

COWEN, Brian. b 45. Nottm Univ BTh77. Linc Th Coll 73. **d** 77 **p** 78. C Hexham *Newc* 77-80; C Eastnor *Heref* 80-81; C Ledbury 80-81; C Ledbury w Eastnor 81; TV Glendale Gp *Newc* 81-90; V Lesbury w Alnmouth from 90; RD Alnwick from 93. *The Vicarage, Lesbury, Alnwick, Northd NE66 3AU* Tel (01665) 830281

COWEN, Richard James. b 48. St Jo Coll Nottm. **d** 83 **p** 84. C Kenilworth St Jo *Cov* 83-87; TV Becontree W *Chelmsf* 87-96; P-in-c Reading St Agnes w St Paul *Ox* from 96. *The Vicarage, 290 Northumberland Avenue, Reading RG2 8DE* Tel 0118-987 4448

COWGILL, Michael. b 48. Linc Th Coll 84. **d** 86 **p** 87. C Bolton St Jas w St Chrys *Bradf* 86-89; V Buttershaw St Paul 89-93; P-in-c Cullingworth from 93; Dir Dioc Foundn Course from 93. *The Vicarage, Halifax Road, Cullingworth, Bradford, W Yorkshire BD13 5DE* Tel (01535) 272434

COWHAM, Hugh Nicholas Gerard. b 26. MACE81 Selw Coll Cam BA51 MA78 Aber Univ CertEd73. LNSM course 75. **d** 78 **p** 79. Hon C Elgin w Lossiemouth *Mor* 78-81; Asst Chapl Gordonstoun Sch 78-81; Australia from 81. *25 Equinox Court, Mudgeeraba, Queensland, Australia 4123* Tel Gold Coast (75) 5530 2378

COWIE, Derek Edward. b 33. S'wark Ord Course 70. **d** 73 **p** 74. C Maldon All SS w St Pet *Chelmsf* 73-76; R Bowers Gifford w N Benfleet 76-79; V Chelmsf Ascension 79-84; V Shrub End 84-95; P-in-c Gosfield from 95. *The Vicarage, Church Road, Halstead, Essex CO9 1UD* Tel (01787) 473857

COWIE, John William Stephen. Wycliffe Hall Ox BTh97. **d** 97. C Shoreditch St Leon and Hoxton St Jo *Lon* from 97. *48 Hemsworth Court, Hemsworth Road, London N1 5LD* Tel 0171-739 5616 Fax as telephone E-mail stephen.cowie @dlondon.org.uk

COWIE, Leonard Wallace. b 19. Pemb Coll Ox BA41 DipTh43 MA46 Lon Univ PhD54. Ripon Hall Ox 42. **d** 43 **p** 44. C High Wycombe All SS *Ox* 43-45; Tutor Coll SS Mark and Jo Chelsea 45-68; Chapl 45-47; Tutor Whitelands Coll Putney 68-82; Lic to Offic *S'wark* from 68. *38 Stratton Road, London SW19 3JG* Tel 0181-542 5036

COWLAN, William Thomas. b 12. OBE. Leeds Univ BD. **d** 79 **p** 79. NSM Kenton w Mamhead and Powderham *Ex* 79-82; Perm to Offic from 82. *4 Court Hall, Kenton, Exeter EX6 8NA* Tel (01626) 890210

COWLES, Richard Martin. b 53. Birm Univ BSc74 DipTh76. Ripon Coll Cuddesdon DipMin93. **d** 93 **p** 94. C Iffley *Ox* 93-96; TV Wheatley w Forest Hill and Stanton St John 96-97; TV Wheatley from 97. *The Rectory, 17 South End, Garsington, Oxford OX44 9HD* Tel (01865) 361381

COWLEY, Charles Frederick. *See* HOWARD-COWLEY, Joseph Charles

COWLEY, Mrs Elizabeth Mary (Liz). b 47. Bris Univ PQCSW84. WMMTC 89. **d** 92 **p** 94. NSM Wolston and Church Lawford *Cov* from 92; Soc Resp Officer from 97. *14 Sycamore Grove, Rugby, Warks CV21 2QY* Tel (01788) 576723

COWLEY, Geoffrey Willis. b 17. FICE50 FRTPI54. St Alb Minl Tr Scheme 77. **d** 80 **p** 81. NSM Stevington *St Alb* 80-87; rtd 87; Lic to Offic *St Alb* 87-97. *7 Windmill Field, Windlesham, Surrey GU20 6QD* Tel (01276) 479287

COWLEY, Herbert Kenneth. b 20. Glouc Sch of Min 75. **d** 79 **p** 80. Hon C Lydney w Aylburton *Glouc* 79-89; rtd 89; Perm to Offic *B & W* from 89. *19 Beechwood Road, Nailsea, Bristol BS19 2AF* Tel (01275) 856198

COWLEY, Ian Michael. b 51. Natal Univ BCom72 BA75 Sheff Univ MA83. Wycliffe Hall Ox 75. **d** 78 **p** 79. S Africa 78-81 and 83-94; C Norton Woodseats St Chad *Sheff* 81-83; R Milton *Ely* from 94. *The Rectory, Church Lane, Milton, Cambridge CB4 4AB* Tel (01223) 861511

COWLEY (née BLACK), Mrs Jean Louie Cameron. b 39. CertEd59. St Alb and Ox Min Course 94. **d** 96. Hon C Chorleywood Ch Ch *St Alb* from 96. *Little Croft, 59 Lower Road, Chorleywood, Rickmansworth, Herts WD3 5LA* Tel (01923) 283816

COWLEY, Leslie. b 22. St Jo Coll Nottm 70. **d** 71 **p** 72. C Worksop St Jo *S'well* 71-73; P-in-c Awsworth w Cossall 74-77; V Basford St Leodegarius 77-88; rtd 88; Perm to Offic *Linc* from 88. *12 Ridgeway, Nettleham, Lincoln LN2 2TL* Tel (01522) 752447

COWLEY, Samuel Henry (Sam). b 44. St Jo Coll Nottm 85. **d** 87 **p** 88. C Hadleigh w Layham and Shelley *St E* 87-91; P-in-c Ipswich St Mich from 91. *22 Tuddenham Road, Ipswich IP4 2SG* Tel (01473) 252939

COWLING, Canon Douglas Anderson. b 19. Leeds Univ BA40. Coll of Resurr Mirfield 40. **d** 42 **p** 43. C Linc St Andr *Linc* 42-45; R Candlesby w Scremby 47-53; R Carlton Scroop w Normanton 53-61; V Spalding St Paul 61-84; Can and Preb Linc Cathl 77-93; rtd 84; Perm to Offic *Linc* from 84. *24 Campbell's Close, Spalding, Lincs PE11 2UH* Tel (01775) 767044

COWLING, John Francis. b 32. K Coll Cam BA56. Linc Th Coll 56. **d** 58 **p** 59. C Leigh St Mary *Man* 58-61; Sec SCM in Schs Liv and Ches 61-65; V Bolton St Matt 65-71; V Bolton St Matt w St Barn 71-75; V Southport H Trin *Liv* 75-91; R St Olave Hart Street w All Hallows Staining etc *Lon* from 91; Dir of Ords from 92. *St Olave's Rectory, 8 Hart Street, London EC3R 7NB* Tel 0171-488 4318 Fax 702 0811

COWLING, Simon Charles. b 59. G&C Coll Cam BA80 MA88 K Coll Lon PGCE82. Linc Th Coll BTh91. **d** 91 **p** 92. C Potternewton *Ripon* 91-94; C Far Headingley St Chad 94-96; V Roundhay St Edm from 96. *St Edmund's Vicarage, 5A North Park Avenue, Leeds LS8 1DN* Tel 0113-266 2550

COWLING, Wilfred Edmund. b 14. Dur Univ BA38 MA42. St Aid Birkenhead 38. **d** 40 **p** 41. C Benwell St Aid *Newc* 40-43; Chapl Miss to Seamen 43-45; C Leeds St Geo *Ripon* 45-47; P-in-c Scarborough St Thos *York* 47-57; V Kirkburn 57-83; V Garton on the Wolds 57-83; RD Harthill 63-73 and 78-80; rtd 83; Perm to Offic *York* from 83. *14 Ashleigh Drive, Beeford, Driffield, N Humberside YO25 8AU* Tel (01262) 488277

COWMEADOW, Derek Lowe. b 28. Wells Th Coll 68. **d** 70 **p** 71. C Ledbury *Heref* 70-72; C Llanrhos *St As* 72-74; V Bringhurst w Gt Easton *Leic* 74-77; P-in-c Coln St Aldwyn w Hatherop and Quenington *Glouc* 77-82; V Coln St Aldwyns, Hatherop, Quenington etc 82-93; rtd 93; Perm to Offic *Glouc* from 93. *2 Hampton Grove, Meysey Hampton, Cirencester, Glos GL7 5JN* Tel (01285) 851645

COWPER, Christopher Herbert. b 44. AKC67 Open Univ BA76. **d** 68 **p** 69. C Pitsmoor *Sheff* 68-71; C Ulverston St Mary w H Trin *Carl* 71-74; R Kirklinton w Hethersgill and Scaleby 74-83; V Bridekirk 83-94; Chapl Dovenby Hall Hosp Cockermouth 83-94; P-in-c Wetheral w Warw *Carl* from 94. *The Rectory, Plains Road, Wetheral, Carlisle CA4 8LE* Tel (01228) 560216

COWPER, Peter James. b 67. Wadh Coll Ox BA89. Edin Th Coll BD94. **d** 94 **p** 95. C Kippax w Allerton Bywater *Ripon* 94-97; C Stanningley St Thos from 97. *50 Lane End, Pudsey, Leeds LS28 9AD* Tel 0113-256 6535 Fax 264 5530

COX, Alan. b 44. **d** 68 **p** 69. C N Reddish *Man* 68; C Birch St Agnes 69-71; C Withington St Crispin 71-74; R Ardwick St Thos 74-78; Lic Preacher from 78. *31 St John's Road, Longsight, Manchester M13 0NE* Tel 0161-225 4062

COX, Alan John. b 34. Lon Coll of Div ALCD65 LTh. **d** 65 **p** 66. C Kirkheaton *Wakef* 65-67; C Keynsham w Queen Charlton *B & W* 67-71; R Chipstable w Huish Champflower and Clatworthy 71-76; TV Strood *Roch* 76-80; V Strood St Fran 80-83; R Keston 83-95; rtd 95. *12 Beech Court, 46 Copers Cope Road, Beckenham, Kent BR3 1LD*

COX, Alexander James. b 12. Pemb Coll Ox BA34 MA43. Westcott Ho Cam 34. **d** 36 **p** 37. C Liversedge *Wakef* 36-39; C Handsworth St Andr *Birm* 39-41; C Acocks Green 41-45; C Weoley Castle 45-50; Min Bartley Green St Mich CD 50-52; Chapl United Birm Hosps 52-56; Br Guiana 56-60; CR from 63; Barbados 64-75; rtd 82. *House of the Resurrection, Mirfield, W Yorkshire WF14 0BN* Tel (01924) 494318

COX, Canon Anthony James Stuart (Tony). b 46. BNC Ox BA68 MA74. Qu Coll Birm DipTh70 DPS71. **d** 71 **p** 72. C Smethwick St Matt w St Chad *Birm* 71-74; Chapl Liv Univ *Liv* 74; Malawi 75-87; Hon Can S Malawi from 80; Chapl Loughborough Gr Sch from 87. *Loughborough Grammar School, Denton House, 7 Burton Walks, Loughborough, Leics LE11 2DU* Tel (01509) 267225

COX, Brian Leslie. b 49. S Dios Minl Tr Scheme 91. **d** 94 **p** 95. C Southampton Maybush St Pet *Win* from 94. *St Peter's House, Lockersley Crescent, Southampton SO16 4BP* Tel (01703) 775014

COX, Bryan Leslie. b 41. Qu Coll Birm 77. **d** 79 **p** 80. C Stantonbury *Ox* 79-82; TV Fenny Stratford and Water Eaton 82-89; P-in-c Elford *Lich* 89-97; Dioc Past Counsellor 89-97; rtd 97. *18 The Charters, Lichfield, Staffs WS13 7LX*

COX, Canon Christopher George Stuart. b 17. St Jo Coll Dur BA38 DipTh39 MA41. **d** 40 **p** 41. C Deptford St Luke *S'wark* 40-42; CMS 43-54; R Kirby Muxloe *Leic* 55-69; RD Sparkenhoe III 64-69; Hon Can Leic Cathl 65-83; V Knighton St Jo 69-77; R Appleby 77-81; R Appleby Magna and Swepstone w Snarestone 81-83; rtd 83; Perm to Offic *Leic* from 83. *Stuart Court, High Street, Kibworth, Leicester LE8 0LE*

COX, David. b 20. SS Coll Cam BA46 MA48 BD57. Qu Coll Birm 47. **d** 48 **p** 49. C Warsop *S'well* 48-51; C Loughton St Mary *Chelmsf* 52-53; C Chislehurst St Nic *Roch* 53-55; V Chatham All SS 55-75; V Southborough St Thos 75-87; rtd 87; Perm to Offic *Cant* from 88. *9 Hollicondane Road, Ramsgate, Kent CT11 7JP* Tel (01843) 585775

COX, David John. b 51. S Bank Poly HNC76. Qu Coll Birm 76. **d** 79 **p** 80. C Brampton Bierlow *Sheff* 79-82; Miss Partner CMS 82-88; Malaysia 83-88; V Friarmere *Man* 88-96; P-in-c Denton Ch Ch from 96. *Christ Church Rectory, 1 Windmill Lane, Denton, Manchester M34 3RN* Tel 0161-336 2126

COX, Canon Eric William. b 30. Dur Univ BA54. Wells Th Coll 54. **d** 56 **p** 57. C Sutton in Ashfield St Mary *S'well* 56-59; Asst Chapl Brussels *Eur* 59-62; V Winnington *Ches* 62-71; V Middlewich 71-76; Chapl Leighton Hosp Crewe 73-95; P-in-c Biley *Ches* 73-76; V Middlewich w Byley 76-95; RD Middlewich 80-94; Hon Can Ches Cathl 84-95; rtd 95; Perm to Offic *Ches* from 95; Perm to Offic *Lich* from 96. *Lovel Hollow, Church Road, Baschurch, Shrewsbury SY4 2EE* Tel (01939) 261258

COX, Geoffrey Sidney Randel. b 33. Mert Coll Ox BA56 MA60. Tyndale Hall Bris. **d** 58 **p** 59. C St Paul's Cray St Barn CD *Roch* 58-61; C Bromley Ch Ch 61-64; V Gorsley w Cliffords Mesne *Glouc* 64-79; V Hucclecote 79-89; V Wollaston and Strixton *Pet* 89-96; rtd 96. *32 Murvagh Close, Cheltenham, Glos GL53 7QY*

COX, George William. b 25. St Steph Ho Ox 83. **d** 86 **p** 87. NSM Abingdon *Ox* 86-95; rtd 92. *103 Bath Street, Abingdon, Oxon OX14 1EG* Tel (01235) 521375

COX, James David Robert. b 65. Lanc Univ BA88. Qu Coll Birm BD92. **d** 93 **p** 94. C Harborne St Pet *Birm* 93-96; C Chelmsley Wood from 96. *The Apple Cart, Birmingham Road, Bacons End, Birmingham B37 6RB*

COX, James Edward Thomas. b 20. Sheff Univ BA47. Cuddesdon Coll 47. **d** 49 **p** 50. C Boxley *Cant* 49-52; C-in-c Buckland Valley CD 52-59; R Hawkinge 59-64; R Acrise 59-64; Chapl RAF 59-62; Chapl Abbey Sch Malvern 64-79; V Lt Malvern *Worc* 65-85; P-in-c 85-90; rtd 85; Perm to Offic *Heref* from 93. *4 Lucerne Avenue, Malvern, Worcs WR14 3QA* Tel (01684) 564392

COX, John Anthony. b 45. Hull Univ BA67 Birm Univ DipTh72. Qu Coll Birm 71. **d** 73 **p** 74. C Buckingham *Ox* 73-76; C Whitley Ch Ch 76-81; V Reading St Agnes w St Paul 81-83; V Chaddesley Corbett and Stone *Worc* from 83. *The Vicarage, Butts Lane, Stone, Kidderminster, Worcs DY10 4BH* Tel (01562) 69438

COX, John Edgar. b 26. CEng MIEE56 Lon Univ BSc50 MSc69. Bps' Coll Cheshunt 67. **d** 68 **p** 69. NSM Harlow St Mary Magd *Chelmsf* 68-76; C S Petherwin w Trewen *Truro* 77-79; P-in-c 79-82; P-in-c Lawhitton 81-82; P-in-c Lezant 81-82; R Lezant w Lawhitton and S Petherwin w Trewen 82-83; V Breage w Germoe 83-91; rtd 91. *Manderley, 8 Trewartha Road, Praa Sands, Penzance, Cornwall TR20 9ST* Tel (01736) 762582

COX, John Hamilton. b 23. Univ of Wales (Cardiff) BA48. St Mich Coll Llan 49. **d** 51 **p** 52. C Merthyr Tydfil *Llan* 51-56; C Skewen 56-61; V Tylorstown 61-85; V Llansawel w Briton Ferry 85-89; rtd 89; Perm to Offic *Llan* from 89. *59 Cwrt Sart, Briton Ferry, Neath SA11 2SR* Tel (01639) 820515

COX, The Ven John Stuart. b 40. Fitzw Ho Cam BA62 MA66 Linacre Coll Ox BA67 Birm Univ DPS68. Wycliffe Hall Ox 64. **d** 68 **p** 69. C Prescot *Liv* 68-71; C Birm St Geo *Birm* 71-73; R 73-78; Selection Sec ACCM 78-83; Hon C Orpington All SS *Roch* 78-83; Dioc Dir of Ords *S'wark* 83-91; Can Res and Treas S'wark Cathl 83-91; V Roehampton H Trin 91-95; Adn Sudbury *St E* from 95. *Archdeacon's House, 84 Southgate Street, Bury St Edmunds, Suffolk IP33 2BJ* Tel (01284) 766796 Fax 768655

COX, Leonard James William. b 27. Sarum & Wells Th Coll 79. **d** 81 **p** 82. C Hythe *Cant* 81-84; V Thanington 84-92; rtd 92; Perm to Offic *Cant* from 92. *3 Nursery Walk, Forty Acres Road, Canterbury, Kent CT2 7TF*

COX, Martin Lloyd. b 57. Wilson Carlile Coll and Sarum & Wells Th Coll. **d** 88 **p** 89. C Risca *Mon* 88-91; TV Pontypool 91-96; V Monkton *St D* from 96. *Priory Vicarage, Church Terrace, Monkton, Pembroke SA71 4LW* Tel (01646) 682723

COX, Paul Graham. b 40. Keele Univ BA62 DipEd62 Ibadan Univ Nigeria 63. Westcott Ho Cam 77. **d** 78 **p** 79. NSM Kemsing w Woodlands *Roch* 78-80; Hd Master and Chapl St Mich Sch Otford 81-90; C Petham and Waltham w Lower Hardres etc *Cant* 90-95; P-in-c from 95; C Elmsted w Hastingleigh 90-95; P-in-c from 95; Bp's Officer for NSM from 91. *The Vicarage, Elmsted, Hastingleigh, Ashford, Kent TN25 5HP* Tel (01233) 750414

COX, Peter Allard. b 55. Univ of Wales (Lamp) BA76. Wycliffe Hall Ox 77. **d** 79 **p** 80. C Penarth All SS *Llan* 79-82; V Aberpergwm and Blaengwrach 82-86; V Bargoed and Deri w Brithdir 86-97; V Penarth All SS from 97. *All Saints Vicarage, 2 Lower Cwrtyvil Road, Penarth CF64 3HQ* Tel (01222) 708952

COX, Mrs Sheila Stuart. b 41. Robert Gordon Inst of Tech Aber TDDSc62 Aber Coll of Educn CertEd63. Edin Dioc NSM Course 85. **d** 88 **p** 94. NSM Livingston LEP *Edin* 88-93; Asst Chapl St Jo and Bangour Hosps W Lothian 89-93; NSM Edin St Mark 93-95; Missr Edin St Andr and St Aid 95-96. *6 Pentland Park, Livingston, West Lothian EH54 5NR* Tel (01506) 434874

COX, Dr Simon John. b 53. MIBiol79 CBiol79 Qu Mary Coll Lon BSc74 Liv Univ PhD81 Selw Coll Cam BA81 MA85 Lanc Univ MA87. Ridley Hall Cam 79. **d** 82 **p** 83. C Livesey *Blackb* 82-85; C Cheadle Hulme St Andr *Ches* 85-89; V Disley 89-94; R Bispham

Blackb from 94. *The Rectory, All Hallows Road, Blackpool FY2 0AY* Tel (01253) 351886

COX, Stephen. b 38. Open Univ BA80. Bps' Coll Cheshunt 65. **d** 68 **p** 69. C Gaywood, Bawsey and Mintlyn *Nor* 68-72; Youth Chapl 72-82; C N Lynn w St Marg and St Nic 73-82; Chapl Guildf Coll of Tech 82-87; Chapl Surrey Univ *Guildf* 82-91; Jas Paget Hosp Gorleston 91-94; Jas Paget Hosp NHS Trust Gorleston from 94. *James Paget Hospital, Gorleston, Great Yarmouth, Norfolk NR31 6LA* Tel (01493) 452019

COX, Stephen John Wormleighton. b 54. New Coll Ox MA79 Fitzw Coll Cam BA79. Ridley Hall Cam 77. **d** 80 **p** 81. C Clapton Park All So *Lon* 80-85; TV Hackney Marsh 85-87; V Holloway St Mary w St Jas 87-88; P-in-c Barnsbury St Dav w St Clem 87-88; V Holloway St Mary Magd from 88; AD Islington from 95. *St Mary Magdalene Vicarage, 28 Witherington Road, London N5 1PP* Tel 0171-607 3919

COX, William John Francis. b 24. SW Minl Tr Course. **d** 77 **p** 78. NSM Liskeard w St Keyne and St Pinnock *Truro* 77-82; NSM Liskeard w St Keyne, St Pinnock and Morval 82-86; NSM N Hill w Altarnon, Bolventor and Lewannick 86-87; TV Bolventor 87-92; P-in-c North Hill and Lewannick 92-94; rtd 94; Perm to Offic *Truro* from 94. *9 Trelawney Rise, Callington, Cornwall PL17 7PT* Tel (01579) 384347

COXHEAD, Mrs Margaret. b 40. S Dios Minl Tr Scheme 91. **d** 94 **p** 95. NSM High Hurstwood *Chich* from 94. *Rock Hall, Chillies Lane, High Hurstwood, Uckfield, E Sussex TN22 4AD* Tel (01825) 733833

COYNE, John Edward. b 55. Oak Hill Th Coll BA79. **d** 79 **p** 80. C Cheadle Hulme St Andr *Ches* 79-81; C Macclesfield St Mich 81-83; V Stalybridge H Trin and Ch Ch 83-88; Chapl RAF from 88. *Chaplaincy Services (RAF), HQ, Personnel and Training Command, RAF Innsworth, Gloucester GL3 1EZ* Tel (01452) 712612 ext 5164 Fax 510828

COYNE, Terence Roland Harry. b 39. Chich Th Coll 64. **d** 66 **p** 67. C Meir *Lich* 66-69; C Horninglow 69-72; V Walsall St Gabr Fulbrook from 72. *St Gabriel's Vicarage, Walstead Road, Walsall WS5 4LZ* Tel (01922) 22583

COZENS, Mrs Audrey Lilian. b 35. St Hugh's Coll Ox BA56 MA84. Gilmore Course 79. **dss** 82 **d** 87 **p** 94. Shenfield *Chelmsf* 82-87; Par Dn 87-89; Par Dn Westcliff St Andr 89-94; C 94-95; P-in-c Chelmsf St Andr from 95; P-in-c The Chignals w Mashbury from 95. *The Vicarage, 88 Chignal Road, Chelmsford CM1 2JB* Tel (01245) 496722

COZENS, Daniel Harry. b 44. Oak Hill Th Coll DipTh70. **d** 71 **p** 72. C St Paul's Cray St Barn *Roch* 71-74; C Deptford St Nic w Ch Ch *S'wark* 74-76; C Deptford St Nic and St Luke 76-78; Dioc Missr *Ely* from 78; Six Preacher Cant Cathl *Cant* from 94. *The Rectory, 73 High Street, Coton, Cambridge CB3 7PL* Tel (01954) 210239

COZENS, Michael Graeme. b 59. Chich Th Coll 91. **d** 93 **p** 94. C Emscote *Cov* 93-96; C Prestbury *Glouc* from 96. *8 Boulton Road, Cheltenham, Glos GL50 4RZ* Tel (01242) 523177

CRABB, Paul Anthony. b 58. St Chad's Coll Dur BSc79 Leeds Univ PGCE80. Qu Coll Birm 90. **d** 91 **p** 92. C Gomersal *Wakef* 91-95; V Drighlington from 95. *The Vicarage, Drighlington, Bradford, W Yorkshire BD11 1LS* Tel 0113-285 2402

CRABTREE, Derek. b 32. Leic Univ BSc(Econ)53. Cant Sch of Min 91. **d** 94 **p** 95. C Hackington *Cant* from 94; Asst Chapl Kent Univ from 94. *53 Hackington Road, Tyler Hill, Canterbury, Kent CT2 9HE* Tel (01227) 471503

CRABTREE, Stephen. *See* JONES-CRABTREE, Stephen

CRABTREE, Stephen John. b 62. Roehampton Inst BEd85 Surrey Univ MA93. SEITE 93. **d** 96 **p** 97. NSM N Farnborough *Guildf* from 96. *42 Avenue Road, Farnborough, Hants GU14 7BL* Tel (01252) 541873

CRABTREE, Victor. b 18. Kelham Th Coll 36. **d** 43 **p** 44. C Shirebrook *Derby* 43-46; C Burton St Paul *Lich* 46-50; P-in-c Shirebrook *Derby* 50-56; P-in-c Bradwell 56-66; R Shirland 66-84; P-in-c Brackenfield w Wessington 77-79; rtd 84; Perm to Offic *York* from 90. *31 Pinelands, Briergate, Haxby, York YO3 3YT* Tel (01904) 761941

CRACE, John Allan. b 21. DSC43. Master Mariner 62. Wells Th Coll 62. **d** 64 **p** 65. C Westbury *Sarum* 64-67; V Milton Lilbourne w Easton Royal 67-86; R Wootton Rivers 71-86; RD Pewsey 79-84; rtd 86; Perm to Offic *Portsm* from 86; Perm to Offic *Win* 86-95; Perm to Offic *Chich* from 86. *72 Grenehurst Way, Petersfield, Hants GU31 4AZ* Tel (01730) 263553

CRADDOCK, Brian Arthur. b 40. Chich Th Coll 67. **d** 70 **p** 71. C Stoke-upon-Trent *Lich* 70-74; Bermuda 75-89; P-in-c Bury and Houghton *Chich* 89-95; Chapl St Mich Sch Burton Park 89-95; Chapl Mojacar *Eur* from 95. *Apartment 617, Mojacar Playa, Almeria 04638, Spain* Tel Almeria (50) 478066

CRADDOCK, Jeremy Graham. b 37. Lon Univ BSc64 Nottm Univ MPhil72. EAMTC 93. **d** 94 **p** 95. NSM Godmanchester *Ely* from 94. *8 Hall Close, Hartford, Huntingdon, Cambs PE18 7XJ* Tel (01480) 458011

CRADDUCK, Martin Charles. b 50. Hull Univ BSc71. St Jo Coll Nottm DipTh77. **d** 79 **p** 80. C W Kilburn St Luke w St Simon and St Jude *Lon* 79-83; C Oxhey All SS *St Alb* 83-86; Asst Chapl HM Pris Man 86-87; Dep Chapl HM Young Offender Inst Glen Parva 87-89; Chapl HM Pris Stocken 89-95. *35 Worcester Road, Grantham, Lincs NG31 8SF* Tel (01476) 71351

CRAFT, William Newham. b 46. MIPM70 Lon Univ BSc68. Oak Hill Th Coll 87. **d** 89 **p** 90. C Werrington *Pet* 90-93; C-in-c Norfolk Park St Leonard CD *Sheff* from 93. *19 Norfolk Park Avenue, Sheffield S2 2RA* Tel 0114-272 7423

✠**CRAGG, The Rt Revd Albert Kenneth.** b 13. Jes Coll Ox BA34 MA38 DPhil50 Huron Coll Hon DD63 Leeds Univ Hon DD93. Virginia Th Sem Hon DD85 Tyndale Hall Bris 34. **d** 36 **p** 37 **c** 70. C Tranmere St Cath *Ches* 36-39; Lebanon 39-47; R Longworth *Ox* 47-51; USA 51-56; Can Res Jerusalem 56-59; St Aug Coll Cant 59-60; Sub-Warden 60-61; Warden 61-67; Hon Can Cant Cathl *Cant* 61-80; Hon Can Jerusalem 65-73; Asst Bp Jerusalem 70-73; Bye-Fellow G&C Coll Cam 69-70; Asst Bp Chich 73-78; Asst Bp Wakef 78-81; V Helme 78-81; rtd 81; Asst Bp Ox from 82. *3 Goring Lodge, White House Road, Oxford OX1 4QE* Tel (01865) 249895

CRAGG, Canon Leonard Albert. b 28. TCD BA53 MA56. Cuddesdon Coll 54. **d** 55 **p** 56. C Morecambe St Barn *Blackb* 55-57; C Skerton St Luke 57-60; V Brierfield 60-63; Chapl Whittingham Hosp Preston 63-69; V Padiham *Blackb* 69-80; V Lytham St Cuth 80-93; Hon Can Blackb Cathl 84-93; RD Fylde 85-88; rtd 93; Perm to Offic *Blackb* from 93. *18 Old Well Hall, Dournham, Clitheroe, Lancs BB7 4BW* Tel (01200) 441804

CRAGGS, Colin Frederick. b 41. Open Univ BA80. Sarum & Wells Th Coll 85. **d** 88 **p** 89. NSM Wilton *B & W* 88-90; NSM Taunton St Andr from 90. *89 Galmington Road, Taunton, Somerset TA1 5NW* Tel (01823) 271989

CRAGGS, Michael Alfred. b 43. Open Univ BA79. St Mich Coll Llan 66. **d** 69 **p** 70. C Clee *Linc* 69-72; C Old Brumby 72-76; TV Kingsthorpe w Northn St Dav *Pet* 76-83; P-in-c Gt w Lt Addington 83-89; RD Higham 88-89; TR Corby SS Pet and Andr w Gt and Lt Oakley from 89; RD Corby 90-95. *The Rectory, 40 Beanfield Avenue, Corby, Northants NN18 0EH* Tel (01536) 267620 or 402442

CRAGO, Geoffrey Norman. b 44. Linc Th Coll 67. **d** 70 **p** 71. C Matson *Glouc* 70-75; V Dean Forest H Trin 75-80; Relig Progr Producer Radio Severn Sound 80-85; P-in-c Huntley 80-82; Perm to Offic 82-90; Dioc Communications Officer 84; Gen Syn Broadcasting Dept 85-88; Hon C Highnam, Lassington, Rudford, Tibberton etc from 90; Acting Dioc Communications Officer from 97. *Milestones, 2 Two Mile Lane, Highnam, Gloucester GL2 8DW* Tel (01452) 750575 or 410022

CRAIG, Canon Alan Stuart. b 38. Leeds Univ BA59. Cranmer Hall Dur DipTh61. **d** 61 **p** 62. C Newcastle w Butterton *Lich* 61-65; C Scarborough St Mary w Ch Ch, St Paul and St Thos *York* 65-67; V Werrington *Lich* 67-72; Asst Chapl HM Pris Man 72-73; Chapl HM Borstal Hindley 73-78; Chapl HM Pris Acklington 78-84; V Longhirst *Newc* 84-90; RD Morpeth 84-95; R Morpeth from 90; Chapl St Geo and Cottage Hosp Morpeth from 90; Hon Can Newc Cathl *Newc* from 90. *The Rectory, Cottingwood Lane, Morpeth, Northd NE61 1ED* Tel (01670) 513517

CRAIG, David Paul. b 46. Hon DD94. Aus Coll of Th ThDip. **d** 84 **p** 85. Australia 84-89; Canada 89-94; Miss to Seamen 89-94; Chapl Immingham Seafarers' Cen from 94; Gen Preacher *Linc* from 97. *The Seafarers' Centre, Lockside Road, Immingham, Grimsby, S Humberside DN40 2NN* Tel (01469) 574195 Fax 574740

CRAIG, Eric. b 39. Birm Univ BA62 DipTh63. Qu Coll Birm 62. **d** 64 **p** 65. C Todmorden *Wakef* 64-68; C Hurstpierpoint *Chich* 68-70; C Cobham *Guildf* 70-73; V Dawley St Jerome *Lon* 73-76; V Stainland *Wakef* 76-87; R Yarnton w Begbroke and Shipton on Cherwell *Ox* from 87. *The Rectory, 26 Church Lane, Yarnton, Kidlington, Oxon OX5 1PY* Tel (01865) 375749

CRAIG, Gillean Weston. b 49. York Univ BA72 Qu Coll Cam BA76 MA80. Westcott Ho Cam 76. **d** 77 **p** 78. C St Marylebone Ch Ch *Lon* 77-82; C Ealing St Barn 82-88; P-in-c St Geo-in-the-East w St Paul 88-89; R from 89. *St George's Rectory Flat, Cannon Street Road, London E1 0BH* Tel 0171-481 1345

CRAIG, Canon John Newcome. b 39. Selw Coll Cam BA63 MA67. Linc Th Coll 63. **d** 65 **p** 66. C Cannock *Lich* 65-71; V Gt Wyrley 71-79; TR Wednesfield 79-91; Prec Leic Cathl *Leic* from 91; Hon Can Leic Cathl from 93. *154 Barclay Street, Leicester LE3 0JB* Tel 0116-255 7327

CRAIG, Julie Elizabeth. *See* LEAVES, Julie Elizabeth

CRAIG, Julie Elizabeth. *See* EATON, Mrs Julie Elizabeth

CRAIG, Patrick Thomas (Paddy). b 36. BA. St D Coll Lamp 59 Bps' Coll Cheshunt 59. **d** 61 **p** 62. C Belfast St Mary *Conn* 61-65; C Belfast St Pet 65-69; CF 69-88; R Hartfield w Coleman's Hatch *Chich* from 88. *The Rectory, Hartfield, E Sussex TN7 4AG* Tel (01892) 770850

CRAIG, Richard Harvey. b 31. Em Coll Cam BA58. Linc Th Coll. **d** 60 **p** 61. C Bottesford *Linc* 60-65; Bp's Ind Chapl 65-69; Dioc Adv on Laity Tr *Bris* 69-74; V Whitchurch 74-86; TV N Lambeth *S'wark* 86-96; Bp's Ecum Adv 88-96; Ecum Officer 90-96; rtd 96. *73 Dudley Street, Bedford MK40 3TA* Tel (01234) 357360

CRAIG, Robert Joseph. b 43. TCD BA65 Div Test66 Birm Univ CertEd70. **d** 66 **p** 67. C Carrickfergus *Conn* 66-69; Chapl Ld Wandsworth Coll Hants 75-85; Chapl K Sch Macclesfield from 85; Lic to Offic *Ches* from 85. *5 Lincoln Close, Rainow, Macclesfield, Cheshire SK10 5UH* Tel (01625) 573720 or 422505

CRAIG-WILD, Ms Dorothy Elsie. b 54. Birm Univ BA77. Qu Coll Birm 79. **dss** 81 **d** 87 **p** 94. Middleton St Mary *Ripon* 81-87; Par Dn Chapeltown *Sheff* 88-94; C 94-96; P-in-c Bruntcliffe *Wakef* from 96. *The Vicarage, Vicarage Meadow, Mirfield, W Yorkshire WF14 9JL* Tel (01924) 492188

CRAIG-WILD, Peter John. b 55. Leeds Univ BA77. Qu Coll Birm 77. **d** 80 **p** 81. C Rothwell w Lofthouse *Ripon* 80-83; C Beeston 83-87; V Chapeltown *Sheff* 87-96; RD Tankersley 93-96; V Mirfield *Wakef* from 96. *The Vicarage, Vicarage Meadow, Mirfield, W Yorkshire WF14 9JL* Tel (01924) 492188

CRAM, Mrs Ruth Frances Isobel. b 52. Kingston Poly BA87 Poly Cen Lon MA92. N Ord Course 94. **d** 97. C E Crompton *Man* from 97. *9 Scarr Lane, Shaw, Oldham OL2 8HQ* Tel (01706) 299472

CRAMERI, Mrs Mary Barbara. b 44. K Coll Lon BD65 AKC91 Lon Inst of Educn PGCE66. S Dios Minl Tr Scheme 86. **d** 88 **p** 94. C Whitton SS Phil and Jas *Lon* 88-91; Staff Member S Dios Minl Tr Scheme 91-97; Minl Development Officer S Th Educn and Tr Scheme from 97; Vice-Prin Sarum & Wells Th Coll from 93; Par Dn Bemerton *Sarum* 91-92. *2 Richard's Way, Harnham, Salisbury SP2 8NT* Tel (01722) 338673

CRAMPTON, Canon John Leslie. b 41. CITC 64. **d** 67 **p** 68. C Lurgan Ch Ch *D & D* 67-71; C Dundela 71-73; Rhodesia 73-80; Zimbabwe 80-82; I Killanne w Killegney, Rossdroit and Templeshanbo *C & O* 82-88; Preb Ferns Cathl 85-88; Chapl Wilson's Hosp Sch Multyfarnham *M & K* 88-91; C Mullingar, Portnashangan, Moyliscar, Kilbixy etc 89-91; I Athy w Kilberry, Fontstown and Kilkea *D & G* from 91; Can Ch Ch Cathl Dublin from 95. *The Rectory, Church Road, Athy, Co Kildare, Irish Republic* Tel Athy (507) 31446

CRAN, Preb Alexander Strachan. b 09. St Jo Coll Dur BA31 MA43. St Aid Birkenhead 31. **d** 32 **p** 33. C Ashton-on-Ribble St Andr *Blackb* 32-36; C Blackb St Silas 36-38; V Preston Ch Ch 38-48; V Congresbury *B & W* 48-73; RD Locking 59-72; Preb Wells Cathl 61-95; P-in-c Puxton w Hewish St Ann and Wick St Lawrence 71-73; rtd 73. *Rowan Wick, Wolvershill Road, Banwell, Weston-super-Mare, Avon BS24 6DR* Tel (01934) 823209

CRANCH, Peter Kenneth. b 47. St Chad's Coll Dur BA70 DipTh71 PGCE72. **d** 73 **p** 74. C Tavistock and Gulworthy *Ex* 73-78; TV Cen Torquay 78-80; C Heavitree w Ex St Paul 80-84; TV Withycombe Raleigh 84-93; C Ex St Sidwell and St Matt 93-96; C Ex St Mark, St Sidwell and St Matt from 96. *10 Victoria Park Road, Exeter EX2 4NT* Tel (01392) 277685

CRANE, John Walter. b 32. Chich Th Coll. **d** 58 **p** 59. C Forest Town *S'well* 58-60; C Primrose Hill St Mary w Avenue Road St Paul *Lon* 60-64; R Greenford H Cross 64-67; Min Can and Chapl Windsor 67-79; Chapl St Geo Sch Ascot 67-79; Warden Dioc Retreat Ho (Holland Ho) Cropthorne *Worc* 79-83; P-in-c Harvington and Norton and Lenchwick 84-87; rtd 87. *16 Allesborough Drive, Pershore, Worcs WR10 1JH* Tel (01386) 556444

CRANE, Mrs Judith. b 53. Matlock Coll of Educn BCombStuds81. Cranmer Hall Dur 94. **d** 96 **p** 97. C Tadcaster w Newton Kyme *York* from 96. *11 Wharfe Bank Terrace, Tadcaster, N Yorkshire LS24 9BA* Tel (01937) 832249

CRANE, Ronald Edward. b 48. SSC. Wilson Carlile Coll 73 St Steph Ho Ox 83. **d** 85 **p** 86. C Bicester w Bucknell, Caversfield and Launton *Ox* 85-88; P-in-c Washwood Heath *Birm* 88-92; V from 92. *St Mark's Vicarage, 266 Washwood Heath Road, Birmingham B8 2XS* Tel 0121-327 1461 Fax as telephone

CRANE, Vincent James. b 10. St Aid Birkenhead 62. **d** 64 **p** 65. C Penn *Lich* 64-70; R Himley 70-78; V Swindon 70-78; rtd 78. *14 Holcroft Road, Wall Heath, Kingswinford, W Midlands DY6 0HP* Tel (01384) 292208

CRANFIELD, Dr Nicholas William Stewart. b 56. Mert Coll Ox BA77 MA81 DPhil88 Leeds Univ BA81 Cam Univ PhD95. Coll of Resurr Mirfield 79 Union Th Sem (NY) STM84. **d** 86 **p** 87. C Ascot Heath *Ox* 86-89; Prin Berks Chr Tr Scheme 89-92; Hon C Reading St Mary w St Laur 89-92; Chapl and Fell Selw Coll Cam from 92; Dean Chapel from 94; Chapl Newnham Coll Cam from 92. *Selwyn College, Cambridge CB3 9DQ* Tel (01223) 335875 Fax 335837 E-mail nwsc100@hermes.cam.ac.uk

CRANIDGE, Mrs Wendy Ann. b 31. Sheff Univ CertEd52. Cant Sch of Min 81. **dss** 84 **d** 87 **p** 94. Roch 84-87; Hon Par Dn 87-88; Soc Resp Adv (Dios Cant and Roch) 86-88; Hon C Washingborough w Heighington and Canwick *Linc* 88-92; Perm to Offic 92-93; Perm to Offic *Roch* 93-94; C Farnborough 94-96; rtd 96; Perm to Offic *Roch* from 96. *8 Russett Close, Aylesford, Kent ME20 7PL* Tel (01622) 790969

CRANKSHAW, Ronald. b 41. Coll of Resurr Mirfield 74. **d** 76 **p** 77. C Orford St Andr *Liv* 76; C N Meols 76-79; V Abram 79-85; V Wigan St Anne from 85; AD Wigan W from 94. *St Anne's Vicarage, 154 Beech Hill Avenue, Wigan, Lancs WN6 7TA* Tel (01942) 41930

CRANWELL, Brian Robert. b 32. Sheff Poly MSc. Cranmer Hall Dur. **d** 84 **p** 85. C Ecclesfield *Sheff* 84-86; V Handsworth Woodhouse from 86. *St James's Vicarage, Tithe Barn Lane, Woodhouse, Sheffield S13 7LL* Tel 0114-269 4146

CRAPNELL, Graham Nicholas (Nick). b 31. Lon Univ BSc55. St Alb Minl Tr Scheme 89. **d** 92 **p** 93. NSM Woodside w E Hyde *St Alb* from 92. *25 Wardown Crescent, Luton LU2 7JS* Tel (01582) 21840

CRASKE, Leslie Gordon Hamilton. b 29. AKC54 Lambeth STh80. **d** 55 **p** 56. C Malden St Jo *S'wark* 55-58; C Streatham St Leon 58-60; S Rhodesia 60-65; Rhodesia 65-66; V Upper Norwood St Jo *Cant* 67-83; R Guernsey St Sav *Win* 83-97. *La Gruterie, 3 Mount Row, St Peter Port, Guernsey GY1 1NS* Tel (01481) 716027

CRASTON (née FULLALOVE), Mrs Brenda Hurst. b 33. Open Univ BA75 Man Univ MPhil86. St Mich Ho Ox 58. **dss** 80 **d** 87 **p** 94. Bolton St Paul w Em *Man* 80-87; Par Dn 87-93; rtd 93; Hon C Horwich and Rivington *Man* from 94; Perm to Offic from 94. *12 Lever Park Avenue, Horwich, Bolton BL6 7LE* Tel (01204) 699972

CRASTON, Canon Richard Colin. b 22. Bris Univ BA49 Lon Univ BD51 Lambeth DD92. Tyndale Hall Bris 46. **d** 51 **p** 52. C Dur St Nic *Dur* 51-54; V Bolton St Paul *Man* 54-76; P-in-c Bolton Em 64-66; V 66-76; Hon Can Man Cathl 68-93; RD Bolton 72-93; V Bolton St Paul w Em 77-86; TR 86-93; Chapl to The Queen 85-93; rtd 93; Perm to Offic *Man* from 93. *12 Lever Park Avenue, Horwich, Bolton BL6 7LE1* Tel (01204) 842303

CRATE, Canon George Frederick Jackson. b 28. Lon Univ BD56. ALCD55. **d** 56 **p** 57. C Penge St Jo *Roch* 56-58; C Tonbridge St Steph 58-60; R Knossington and Cold Overton *Leic* 60-64; V Owston and Withcote 60-64; V Mountsorrel Ch Ch 64-83; RD Akeley E 75-92; Hon Can Leic Cathl 80-94; V Mountsorrel Ch Ch and St Pet 83-94; rtd 94; Perm to Offic *Leic* from 94. *115 Nanpantan Road, Loughborough, Leics LE11 3YB* Tel (01509) 269505

CRAVEN, Alan. b 32. N Ord Course. **d** 87. NSM Hessle *York* 87-91; NSM Newington w Dairycoates from 91. *28 Weelsby Way, Boothferry Road, Hessle, N Humberside HU13 0JW* Tel (01482) 643214

CRAVEN, Canon Allan. b 35. LTCL77 Univ of Wales (Lamp) BA57 Lon Univ BD72. Chich Th Coll 57. **d** 59 **p** 60. C Blaenau Ffestiniog *Ban* 59-61; C Milford Haven *St D* 61-65; V Llwynhendy 65-68; R Nolton w Roch from 68; RD Roose from 85; Can St D Cathl from 91. *The Rectory, Nolton, Haverfordwest SA62 3NW* Tel (01437) 710213

CRAVEN, Colin Peter. b 48. Dartmouth RN Coll. St Steph Ho Ox 83. **d** 85 **p** 86. C Holbeach *Linc* 85-88; Chapl Fleet Hosp 86-97; TV Grantham *Linc* 88-97; OCF from 88; P-in-c Fairfield *Derby* from 97. *The Vicarage, Fairfield, Buxton, Derbyshire SK17 7EB* Tel (01298) 23629

CRAVEN, Gordon Forster. b 26. Qu Coll Cam BA50 MA55. Wells Th Coll 51. **d** 53 **p** 54. C Castleford All SS *Wakef* 53-57; V King Sterndale *Derby* 57-72; V Fairfield 57-72; Perm to Offic *B & W* from 81; rtd 91. *Kingfisher Cottage, 41 Southover, Wells, Somerset BA5 1UH* Tel (01749) 672282

CRAVEN, Janet Elizabeth. *See* CHAPMAN, Mrs Janet Elizabeth

CRAVEN, Archdeacon of. *See* GRUNDY, The Ven Malcolm Leslie

CRAWFORD, Albert Edward. b 13. TCD BA37 MA43. **d** 37 **p** 38. C Southport St Andr *Liv* 37-42; I Camlough *Arm* 65-78; rtd 78. *Shalom, 54 Edenvale Avenue, Banbridge, Co Down BT32 3RH* Tel (018206) 22924

CRAWFORD, Duncan Alexander. b 59. Newc Univ BA81 MA83 K Coll Lon CertEd83. St Jo Coll Nottm 86. **d** 89 **p** 90. C Hatcham St Jas *S'wark* 89-92; Perm to Offic from 93. *26 Millmark Grove, London SE14 6QR* Tel 0181-692 4645

CRAWFORD, Miss Ivy Elizabeth. b 50. Trin Coll Bris DipTh85. **dss** 85 **d** 87 **p** 94. Collier Row St Jas *Chelmsf* 85; Collier Row St Jas and Havering-atte-Bower 86-87; Par Dn 87-89; Par Dn Harlow New Town w Lt Parndon 89-94; C Harlow Town Cen w Lt Parndon 94-95; V Blackmore and Stondon Massey from 95. *The Vicarage, Church Street, Blackmore, Ingatestone, Essex CM4 0RN* Tel (01277) 821464

CRAWFORD, John. b 22. TCD BA50. **d** 51 **p** 53. C Dunmurry *Conn* 51-58; C Monaghan *Clogh* 58-60; C S Kensington St Luke *Lon* 60-63; C Stoke Newington St Mary 63-65; C Wickford *Chelmsf* 65-67; C Lt Marlow *Ox* 67-83; rtd 83. *33 Wenlock Edge, Charvil, Reading RG10 9QG* Tel 0118-934 1848

CRAWFORD, Canon John William Rowland. b 53. AKC75 Open Univ BA81 NUI MA95. CITC 75. **d** 76 **p** 77. C Dundela *D & D* 76-79; C Taney Ch Ch *D & G* 79-84; V Dublin St Patr Cathl Gp from 84; Preb Tipperkevin St Patr Cathl Dublin from 84. *248 South Circular Road, Dolphin's Barn, Dublin 8, Irish Republic* Tel Dublin (1) 454 2274

CRAWFORD, Kenneth Ian. b 48. Melbourne Univ BMus77 Columbia Univ MA79 MEd80 MACE84. Trin Coll Melbourne BD86. **d** 87 **p** 87. Australia 87-97; P-in-c Warndon St Nic *Worc* from 97. *The Vicarage, 4 Daty Croft, Home Meadow, Worcester WR4 0JB* Tel (01905) 616109

CRAWFORD, Peter. b 22. Trin Coll Cam BA49 MA54. Wycliffe Hall Ox 49. **d** 51 **p** 52. C Ashton St Mich *Man* 51-54; V Pendlebury St Jo 54-60; Chapl R Man Children's Hosp 54-60; V Masham *Ripon* 60-75; RD Ripon 70-75; V Masham and Healey 75-79; R E Bergholt *St E* 79-87; RD Samford 82-86; rtd 87; Perm to Offic *St E* from 87. *3 Burl's Yard, Crown Street, Needham Market, Ipswich IP6 8AJ* Tel (01449) 722343

CRAWFORD, Philip Hugh Southern. b 16. Lon Univ BA40. Chich Th Coll 41. **d** 42 **p** 43. C W Wycombe *Ox* 42-46; Australia 46-52; V Lane End *Ox* 52-60; V Healaugh w Wighill and Bilbrough *York* 60-78; P-in-c Slingsby 78-86; P-in-c Hovingham 78-86; V 86; RD Bulmer and Malton 80-85; rtd 86; C Hovingham *York* 86-88; Perm to Offic from 88. *44 Bootham Crescent, York YO3 7AH* Tel (01904) 630386

CRAWFORD, Robin. b 33. Pemb Coll Cam BA57 MA61. Roch Th Coll. **d** 67 **p** 80. Ghana 67-69; Dep Sec Chrs Abroad 69-73; Dep Hd Priory Sch Lewes 74-76; Nigeria 77-79; Dep Sec Buttle Trust 79-86; Sec 86-90; Dir 90-92; Hon C Win H Trin *Win* 80-82; Hon C Notting Hill All SS w St Columb *Lon* 82-87; Hon C Westmr St Matt from 87; rtd 96. *52 Dean Abbott House, 70 Vincent Street, London SW1P 4BS* Tel 0171-931 8013 Fax as telephone

CRAWLEY, David. b 47. TD. St Steph Ho Ox 75. **d** 78 **p** 79. C Solihull *Birm* 78-81; TV Newbury *Ox* 81-84; Lic to Offic 84-95; Chapl Stoke Mandeville Hosp Aylesbury 84-95; Distr Chapl 88-95; Hd Chapl Services W Suffolk Hosps NHS Trust from 95. *West Suffolk Hospital, Hardwick Lane, Bury St Edmunds, Suffolk IP33 2QZ, or 22 Westbury Avenue, Bury St Edmunds, Suffolk IP33 3QE* Tel (01284) 713486 or 750526

CRAWLEY, John Lloyd Rochfort. b 22. Selw Coll Cam BA47 MA52. Cuddesdon Coll 47. **d** 49 **p** 50. C Newc H Cross *Newc* 49-52; V Byker St Ant 52-59; V Longhoughton w Howick 59-69; Chapl Newc Univ 69-74; Master Newc St Thos Prop Chpl 69-74; P-in-c Cockermouth All SS w Ch Ch *Carl* 74-77; TR Cockermouth w Embleton and Wythop 77-86; Perm to Offic *Arg* from 86; rtd 87. *Croft House, Cove Road, Tarbert, Argyll PA29 6TX* Tel (01880) 820842

CRAWLEY, Nicholas Simon (Nick). b 58. ACIB82 AIIM85 Southn Univ BSc79. Wycliffe Hall Ox 85. **d** 88 **p** 89. C E Twickenham St Steph *Lon* 88-93; Zimbabwe 93-96; Perm to Offic *Ex* from 96. *Craddock Lodge, Cullompton, Devon EX15 3LL* Tel (01884) 841837

CRAWLEY, Simon Ewen. b 31. Em Coll Cam BA57 MA60. Ridley Hall Cam 56. **d** 58 **p** 59. C Denton Holme *Carl* 58-61; P-in-c Cinderford St Steph w Littledean *Glouc* 61-67; V Margate H Trin *Cant* 67-74; V Folkestone H Trin w Ch Ch 74-81; R Patterdale *Carl* 81-87; RD Penrith 83-86; R Culworth w Sulgrave and Thorpe Mandeville etc *Pet* 87-95; RD Brackley 89-95; rtd 95. *Craddock Lodge, Craddock, Cullompton, Devon EX15 3LL* Tel (01884) 841837

CRAWLEY-BOEVEY, Robert Arthur. b 12. Hertf Coll Ox BA34 MA38. Cuddesdon Coll 35. **d** 37 **p** 38. C Farnham Royal *Ox* 37-43; Chapl RNVR 43-46; R Waltham on the Wolds and Stonesby *Leic* 47-51; V Cuddington w Dinton *Ox* 51-59; V Seer Green 59-78; rtd 78. *3 St Michael's Close, Urchfont, Devizes, Wilts SN10 4QJ* Tel (01380) 840635

CRAWSHAW, Henry Michael Aitken. b 15. Em Coll Cam BA37 MA43. Westcott Ho Cam 39. **d** 40 **p** 41. Asst Chapl Gresham's Sch Holt 40-43; Chapl Uppingham Sch Leics 43-48; V Stourport *Worc* 48-51; R Knebworth *St Alb* 51-57; R Chedgrave w Hardley and Langley *Nor* 57-64; RD Loddon 61-64; R Barnham Broom w Kimberley, Bixton etc 64-70; R Brandon Parva 64-70; R Wramplingham w Barford 64-70; R Coston w Runhall 64-70; R Hardingham 64-70; R Garveston w Thuxton 64-70; R Burnham Deepdale 71-80; R Brancaster 70-80; R Brancaster w Burnham Deepdale and Titchwell 80-83; rtd 83; Perm to Offic *Nor* 83-92. *c/o M Crawshaw Esq, 7 Gresham Close, King's Lynn, Norfolk PE30 3EJ*

CRAWTE, William Richard. b 30. TCD BA54. **d** 55 **p** 56. C Belfast St Aid *Conn* 55-57; C Newcastle *D & D* 57-59; CF 59-79. *23 Gotsfield Close, Acton, Sudbury, Suffolk CO10 0AS* Tel (01787) 377356

CRAY, Graham Alan. b 47. Leeds Univ BA68. St Jo Coll Nottm 69. **d** 71 **p** 72. C Gillingham St Mark *Roch* 71-75; N Area Co-ord CPAS Youth Dept 75-78; C York St Mich-le-Belfrey *York* 78-82; V 82-92; Prin Ridley Hall Cam from 92; Six Preacher Cant Cathl *Cant* from 97. *Ridley Hall, Cambridge CB3 9HG* Tel (01223) 353040 Fax 301287

CREAN, Patrick John Eugene. b 38. TCD BA81 MA84. Edin Th Coll 82. **d** 84 **p** 85. C Perth St Jo *St And* 84-86; P-in-c Liv St Phil w St Dav *Liv* 86-87; V 87-90; R Cupar *St And* 90-92; R Ladybank 90-92; P-in-c Sefton *Liv* from 92; Dioc Children's Officer from 92. *The Rectory, Glebe End, Liverpool L29 6YB* Tel 0151-531 7021

CREASER, Canon David Edward. b 35. St Cath Coll Cam BA58 MA62. Clifton Th Coll 59. **d** 61 **p** 62. C Cheadle *Ches* 61-67; V Weston *Bradf* 67-69; P-in-c Denton 67-69; V Weston w Denton 69-74 and from 82; Dir Educn 73-96; V Frizinghall 74-82; Hon Can Bradf Cathl from 80; P-in-c Leathley w Farnley, Fewston and Blubberhouses from 96. *The Vicarage, Askwith, Otley, W Yorkshire LS21 2HX* Tel (01943) 461139

CREASEY, Graham. b 51. Trent Poly BA. Cranmer Hall Dur 80. **d** 83 **p** 84. C Birstall and Wanlip *Leic* 83-87; C-in-c Wheatley Park St Paul CD *Sheff* 87-92; V Wheatley Park 92-95; P-in-c Gleadless Valley from 95. *Holy Cross Vicarage, Spotswood Mount, Sheffield S14 1LG* Tel 0114-239 8852

CREBER, Arthur Frederick. b 45. Lon Univ DipTh67. N Ord Course 84. **d** 87 **p** 88. C Rickerscote *Lich* 87-91; V Gt Wyrley from 91; RD Rugeley from 94. *St Mark's Vicarage, 1 Cleves Crescent, Cheslyn Hay, Walsall WS6 7LR* Tel (01922) 414309

CREDITON, Suffragan Bishop of. *See* HAWKINS, The Rt Revd Richard Stephen

CREE, John Richard. b 44. Open Univ BA74. Coll of Resurr Mirfield. **d** 83 **p** 84. C Blackb St Jas *Blackb* 83-86; V Feniscowles from 86; Chapl Blackb Coll from 86. *The Vicarage, 732 Preston Old Road, Feniscowles, Blackburn BB2 5EN* Tel (01254) 201236

CREER, Irene. *See* SHAW, Mrs Irene

CREERY-HILL, Anthony Thomas. b 23. BNC Ox BA49 MA54. Ridley Hall Cam 49. **d** 51 **p** 52. C Highbury Ch Ch *Lon* 51-53; Travelling Sec CSSM 53-58; Chapl Dean Close Sch Cheltenham 59-74; Dep Hd Master Larchfield Sch Helensburgh 75-77; Kenya 77-83; Chapl Chantilly *Eur* 83-86; rtd 87; Perm to Offic *Heref* from 87. *Under Down, Ledbury, Herefordshire HR8 2JE* Tel (01531) 635608

CREES, Geoffrey William. b 35. ONC Open Univ BA85. Cranmer Hall Dur 65. **d** 67 **p** 68. C Hoddesdon *St Alb* 67-70; C Harwell *Ox* 70-73; C Chilton All SS 70-73; V Greenham 73-82; AD E Hull Deanery 82-88; TR Marfleet *York* 82-88; TR Rodbourne Cheney *Bris* from 88. *St Mary's Rectory, 298 Cheney Manor Road, Swindon SN2 2PF* Tel (01793) 522379

CREGAN, Mark. b 59. Lon Bible Coll BA91. Wycliffe Hall Ox 95. **d** 97. C Chippenham St Pet *Bris* from 97. *11 Aintree Drive, Cepen Park, Chippenham, Wilts SN14 0FA* Tel (01249) 654835

CREIGHTON, Frederick David. b 50. ACII74 TCD BTh88. **d** 88 **p** 89. C Lisburn Ch Ch *Conn* 88-91; I Drumclamph w Lower and Upper Langfield *D & R* from 91. *The Rectory, 70 Greenville Road, Castlederg, Co Tyrone BT81 7NU* Tel (01662) 671433

CREIGHTON, Mrs Judith. b 36. Reading Univ BSc57. Trin Coll Bris 80 Edin Th Coll 81. **dss** 83 **d** 87 **p** 94. Greenock *Glas* 83-85; Lawrence Weston *Bris* 85-87; Par Dn Kingswood 87-90; Chapl Stoke Park and Purdown Hosps Stapleton 90-93; Hon C Marshfield w Cold Ashton and Tormarton etc *Bris* 93-97; rtd 96; Perm to Offic *Bris* from 97. *Home Farm Cottage, West Littleton, Marshfield, Chippenham, Wilts SN14 8JE* Tel (01225) 891021

CREIGHTON, Ms Rachel Margaret Maxwell. b 64. Br Is Nazarene Coll BTh86 BD87. Cranmer Hall Dur DMinlStuds94 Lon Bible Coll MA89. **d** 94 **p** 95. C Basford w Hyson Green *S'well* 94-96; C Nottingham All SS from 96. *8 Austen Avenue, Nottingham NG7 6PE* Tel 0115-978 5541

CRELLIN, Howard Joseph. b 30. Magd Coll Cam BA52 MA56 Magd Coll Ox BA54 DipTh55 MA56. Wycliffe Hall Ox 53. **d** 55 **p** 56. C Dovercourt *Chelmsf* 55-58; R Theydon Garnon 58-70; Select Preacher Ox Univ 68; Perm to Offic *Ox* 70-82; Hon C High Wycombe 72-77; Master K Chas I Sch Kidderminster 74-80; rtd 77; Perm to Offic *Chelmsf* 82-91; Master Caldicott Sch Farnham 80-82; Fryerns Sch Basildon 82-88; St Anselm's Sch Basildon 88-91; P-in-c Whatfield w Semer, Nedging and Naughton *St E* from 91. *The Rectory, Whatfield, Ipswich IP7 6QU* Tel (01473) 822100

CRESSALL, Paul Richard. b 51. UEA BA74. Ripon Coll Cuddesdon 86. **d** 88 **p** 89. C Stevenage H Trin *St Alb* 88-91; V Caldecote All SS 91-95; V Old Warden 91-95; V Rothwell *Ripon* from 95. *The Vicarage, Beech Grove, Rothwell, Leeds LS26 0EL* Tel 0113-282 2369

CRESSEY, Roger Wilson. b 35. Chich Th Coll 72. **d** 74 **p** 75. C Pontefract St Giles *Wakef* 74-77; Hon C Dewsbury All SS 77-80; Chapl Pinderfields Gen Hosp Wakef 80-94; Chapl Carr Gate Hosp Wakef 80-94; Chapl Fieldhead Hosp Wakef 80-94; Chapl Pinderfields Hosps NHS Trust from 94. *Pinderfields General Hospital, Aberford Road, Wakefield, W Yorkshire WF1 4DG* Tel (01924) 201688

CRESSWELL, Howard Rex. b 31. Ely Th Coll 56. **d** 59 **p** 60. C Dovercourt *Chelmsf* 59-61; C Victoria Docks Ascension 61-64; V 64-71; R E w W Harling *Nor* 71-72; TV Quidenham w Eccles and Snetterton 72-75; V Arminghall 75-82; R Caistor w Markshall 75-82; V Trowse 75-82; V Heigham St Barn w St Bart 82-91; Perm to Offic from 91; rtd 91. *3 Cranleigh Rise, Eaton, Norwich NR4 6PQ* Tel (01603) 484889

CRESSWELL, Canon Jack Joseph. b 11. Qu Coll Cam BA39 MA43. Wycliffe Hall Ox 39. **d** 40 **p** 41. C St Helens St Helen *Liv* 40-46; V Iver *Ox* 46-56; R Windlesham *Guildf* 56-62; V Horsell 62-70; Hon Can Guildf Cathl 69-78; R Busbridge 70-78; Perm to Offic *Glouc* from 75; rtd 78; C Broughton Poggs w Filkins, Broadwell etc *Ox* 88-93. *12 Eastleach, Cirencester, Glos GL7 3NQ* Tel (01367) 850261

CRESSWELL, Jeremy Peter. b 49. St Jo Coll Ox BA72 MA78. Ridley Hall Cam 73. **d** 75 **p** 76. C Wisley w Pyrford *Guildf* 75-78; C Weybridge 78-82; P-in-c E Clandon 82-83; P-in-c W Clandon 82-83; R E and W Clandon 83-90; V Oxshott from 90. *The Vicarage, Steel's Lane, Oxshott, Leatherhead, Surrey KT22 0QH* Tel (01372) 842071

CRESSWELL, Preb Kenneth Benjamin. b 17. St D Coll Lamp BA50. **d** 51 **p** 52. C Porthill *Lich* 51-55; R Longton St Jo 55-67; V Horninglow 67-81; Preb Lich Cathl 80-83; TV Stoke-upon-Trent 81-83; rtd 83; Perm to Offic *Lich* 83-95. *1 Chartwell Close, Woodsetton, Dudley, W Midlands DY1 4LY* Tel (01902) 663354

CRETNEY, Mrs Antonia Lois. b 48. York Univ BA69 Bris Univ BA87 PGCE89. S Dios Minl Tr Scheme 92. **d** 94 **p** 95. NSM

Bedminster *Bris* 94-96; C 96-97; P-in-c Beedon and Peasemore w W Ilsley and Farnborough *Ox* from 97. *The Vicarage, 3 Drakes Farm, Peasemore, Newbury, Berks RG20 7DF*

CRIBB, Robert John. b 22. Spurgeon's Coll 45. **d** 85 **p** 86. NSM Curry Rivel w Fivehead and Swell *B & W* 85-89; rtd 89; Perm to Offic *B & W* 89-94. *4 Heale Lane, Curry Rivel, Langport, Somerset TA10 0PG* Tel (01458) 252333

CRICHTON, James Kenneth. b 35. Glouc Sch of Min 78. **d** 80 **p** 80. NSM Minchinhampton *Glouc* 80-83; NSM Nailsworth 83-86; Dep Chapl HM Pris Pentonville 86-87; Chapl HM Pris The Mount 87-97; rtd 97. *Pennant, Horeb, Llandysul SA44 4JG* Tel (01559) 362448

CRICK, Canon Peter. b 39. Lon Univ BD68 NY Univ DMin84. Wells Th Coll 66. **d** 67 **p** 68. C Horsham *Chich* 67-71; Asst Dioc Youth Officer *Ox* 71-75; R Denham 75-88; Bp's Adv for Continuing Minl Educn *Dur* from 88; P-in-c Coniscliffe from 88; Hon Can Dur Cathl from 93. *76 Merrybent Village, Darlington, Co Durham DL2 2LE* Tel (01325) 374510

CRICK, Philip Benjamin Denton (Ben). b 33. Bris Univ BA63. Clifton Th Coll 60. **d** 64 **p** 65. C Clerkenwell St Jas and St Jo w St Pet *Lon* 64-67; CF 67-72; C Southall Green St Jo *Lon* 72-75; P-in-c Southall H Trin 75-83; P-in-c Kidbrooke St Jas *S'wark* 83-85; TV Kidbrooke 85-92; C E Acton St Dunstan w St Thos *Lon* 92-95; Sub-Chapl HM Pris Wormwood Scrubs 92-95; rtd 95; Perm to Offic *Cant* from 95. *232 Canterbury Road, Birchington, Kent CT7 9TD* Tel (01843) 845712

CRINKS, Kevin David. b 63. Aston Tr Scheme 86 Sarum & Wells Th Coll BTh91. **d** 93 **p** 94. C Aylesford *Roch* 93-96; C Hessle *York* 96-97; TV Upholland *Liv* from 97. *158 Birleywood, Skelmersdale, Lancs WN8 9BX*

CRIPPS, Harold Ernest. b 04. AKC47. **d** 47 **p** 48. C Warrington St Elphin *Liv* 47-52; P-in-c New Springs 52-53; V 53-59; V Burtonwood 59-74; rtd 74; Perm to Offic *Chich* 77-92. *15 Hillyard Court, Mill Lane, Wareham, Dorset BN20 4QX* Tel (01929) 550926

CRIPPS, Keith Richard John. b 21. Trin Coll Cam BA43 MA47 Newc Univ PhD80. Ridley Hall Cam 43. **d** 45 **p** 47. Inter-Colleg Sec SCM (Man) 45-47; C Man Victoria Park *Man* 45-47; C Aston SS Pet and Paul *Birm* 47-50; R Chorlton upon Medlock *Man* 50-60; Chapl Man Univ 51-60; Chapl and Lect Ripon Tr Coll 60-65; Lic to Offic *Ripon* 60-65; Lic to Offic *Newc* 65-84; Lic to Offic *Ely* 84-86; Lect Newc Poly 74-79; Chapl Jes Coll Cam 84; rtd 86; Perm to Offic *Ely* from 86. *9 Pentlands Court, Pentlands Close, Cambridge CB4 1JN* Tel (01223) 354216

CRIPPS, Martyn Cyril Rowland. b 46. Solicitor 71 Birm Univ LLB68. Wycliffe Hall Ox 80. **d** 82 **p** 83. C Canford Magna *Sarum* 82-86; V Preston St Cuth *Blackb* 87-94; Guernsey St Andr *Win* 94; Warden Les Cotils 94-96; V Gipsy Hill Ch Ch *S'wark* from 96. *Christ Church Vicarage, 1 Highland Road, London SE19 1DP* Tel 0181-670 0385

CRIPPS, Michael Frank Douglas. b 28. Ch Ch Ox BA50 MA53. Ridley Hall Cam 58. **d** 59 **p** 60. C Cambridge Gt St Mary w St Mich *Ely* 59-62; Ceylon 62-66; C-in-c Swindon Covingham CD *Bris* 66-72; V Swindon St Paul 72-73; P-in-c Aldbourne and Baydon *Sarum* 73; TV Whitton 73-81; C Marlborough 81-94; rtd 94; Chapl Pau *Eur* 94-96. *9 Silverless Street, Marlborough, Wilts SN8 1JQ*

CRIPPS, Thomas Royle. b 12. St Jo Coll Lusaka 64. **d** 68 **p** 68. S Africa 68-88; rtd 88; Perm to Offic *S'wark* 88-91; Perm to Offic *Chich* from 91. *College of St Barnabas, Blackberry Lane, Lingfield, Surrey RH7 6NJ* Tel (01342) 870760

CRISALL, Christopher James Philip. b 34. St Deiniol's Hawarden 87. **d** 89 **p** 90. NSM Low Marple *Ches* 89-90; C Woodchurch 90-92; V Latchford Ch Ch from 92; P-in-c Weaverham 96-97. *Christchurch Vicarage, Wash Lane, Warrington WA4 1HT* Tel (01925) 630846

CRITCHLEY, Colin. b 41. Dur Univ BA63 Liv Univ MA69. NW Ord Course 75. **d** 78 **p** 79. NSM Halewood *Liv* from 78; Dioc Child Protection Adv from 96. *53 Elwyn Drive, Halewood, Liverpool L26 0UX* Tel 0151-487 5710

CRITCHLOW, Trevor Francis. b 61. Lanc Univ BA83 K Coll Lon MA96. Westcott Ho Cam 88. **d** 90 **p** 91. C Croydon St Jo *S'wark* 90-92; C Lewisham St Mary 92-94; Development Dir Westmr St Matt from 95; Perm to Offic *Lon* from 97. *28 Broad Street, Cambridge CB1 2NJ, or 20 Great Peter Street, London SW1P 2BU* Tel (01223) 501010 or 0171-222 5522 Fax (01223) 501010 or 0171-233 0255 E-mail trevor501@aol.com

CRITTALL, Richard Simon. b 47. Sussex Univ BA69 Linacre Coll Ox BA71. St Steph Ho Ox 69. **d** 72 **p** 73. C Oswestry H Trin *Lich* 72-75; C E Grinstead St Mary *Chich* 75-78; TV Brighton Resurr 78-83; R E Blatchington 83-95; V Heathfield St Rich from 95. *St Richard's Vicarage, Hailsham Road, Heathfield, E Sussex TN21 8AF* Tel (01435) 862744

CROAD, Arthur Robert. b 35. Down Coll Cam BA58 MA61. Clifton Th Coll 58. **d** 61 **p** 62. C Sneinton St Chris w St Phil *S'well* 61-64; C Kinson *Sarum* 64-72; R Sherfield English *Win* 72-74; R Awbridge w Sherfield English 74-92; P-in-c Hinton Ampner w Bramdean and Kilmeston from 92. *The Rectory, Bramdean, Alresford, Hants SO24 0JN* Tel (01962) 771223

CROAD, David Richard. b 31. Reading Univ BSc55. Clifton Th Coll. **d** 57 **p** 58. C Iver *Ox* 57-60; C Rushden *Pet* 60-63; V Loudwater *Ox* 63-72; SW Area Sec CPAS 72-78; V Bovingdon *St Alb* 78-91; Min Hampstead St Jo Downshire Hill Prop Chpl *Lon* 91-94; rtd 94. *The Old Parsonage, Bentley, Farnham, Surrey GU10 5JN* Tel (01420) 23227

CROCKER, Jeremy Robert. b 67. South Bank Univ MCIM92 MA94. Westcott Ho Cam CTM94. **d** 97. C Stevenage H Trin *St Alb* from 97. *14 Church Lane, Stevenage, Herts SG1 3QR* Tel (01438) 312982

CROCKER, Keith Gwillam. b 49. Lanchester Poly BSc70 DipTh78. Oak Hill Th Coll 74. **d** 77 **p** 78. C Whitnash *Cov* 77-80; C Gt Horton *Bradf* 80-83; C Grays SS Pet and Paul, S Stifford and W Thurrock *Chelmsf* 83-84; TV Grays Thurrock 84-88; TR Wreningham *Nor* 88-95; P-in-c New Catton Ch Ch from 95. *Christ Church Vicarage, 65 Elm Grove Lane, Norwich NR3 3LF* Tel (01603) 408332

CROCKER, Peter David. b 56. **d** 96 **p** 97. NSM Bassaleg *Mon* from 96. *4 Marigold Close, Foxgloves, Rogerstone, Newport NP1 9AZ*

CROCKER, Richard Campbell. b 54. BSc Nottm Univ MA. Wycliffe Hall Ox. **d** 82 **p** 83. C Summerfield *Birm* 82-84; Chapl K Edw Sch Birm 84-91; USA from 91. *821 Ironwood Court, Council Bluffs, Iowa 51503, USA*

CROCKETT, Peter James Sinclair. b 44. Sarum & Wells Th Coll 74. **d** 77 **p** 78. C Heavitree *Ex* 77; C Heavitree w Ex St Paul 78-80; TV Ex St Thos and Em 80-87; V Countess Wear from 87. *The Vicarage, 375 Topsham Road, Exeter EX2 6HB* Tel (01392) 873263

CROCKETT, Phillip Anthony. b 45. K Coll Lon BA67 BD70 AKC70 Univ of Wales MA91. St Mich Coll Llan DPS71. **d** 71 **p** 72. C Aberdare St Jo *Llan* 71-74; C Whitchurch 74-78; V Llanfihangel-y-Creuddyn, Llanafan w Llanwnnws *St D* 78-86; Sec Prov Selection Panel 83-87; V Ysbyty Ystwyth 84-86; R Dowlais *Llan* 86-91; Exec Sec for Min from 91. *3 Cosmeston Drive, Penarth CF64 5FA, or 39 Cathedral Close, Cardiff CF1 9XF* Tel (01222) 705015 or 231638

CROFT, Bernard Theodore. b 10. Kelham Th Coll 30. **d** 35 **p** 36. C Conisbrough *Sheff* 35-37; C Glas St Mary *Glas* 37-39; C Cowley St Jas *Ox* 39-42; Chapl RAFVR 42-46; Chapl Radley Coll Oxon 47-48; Lic to Offic *Ox* 48-49; R Saxby All Saints *Linc* 49-51; V Horkstow 49-51; Chapl RAF 51-54; Chapl Woolpit Sch Ewhurst 54-60; V Birm St Jude *Birm* 60-68; V Reighton w Speeton *York* 68-75; rtd 75; Perm to Offic *York* from 75. *4 Freemens Court, Water Lane, York YO3 6PR* Tel (01904) 656611

CROFT, James Stuart. b 57. K Coll Lon BD80 Leeds Univ MA95. Ripon Coll Cuddesdon 83. **d** 85 **p** 86. C Friern Barnet St Jas *Lon* 85-88; R Lea *Linc* 88-93; V Knaith 88-93; V Upton 88-93; R Gate Burton 88-93; Chapl N Lincs Coll 90-93; R Lea Gp *Linc* 93-97; V Froyle and Holybourne *Win* from 97. *The Vicarage, Church Lane, Holybourne, Alton, Hants GU34 4HD* Tel (01420) 83240

CROFT, John Armentieres. b 15. MC44. Sarum Th Coll 56. **d** 57 **p** 58. C Madron w Morvah *Truro* 57-60; V Gwinear 60-70; rtd 70; Perm to Offic *Truro* from 70; Perm to Offic *Sarum* from 70; Perm to Offic *B & W* from 70. *Vine House, Common Road, Wincanton, Somerset BA9 9RB* Tel (01963) 32253

CROFT, Michael Peter. b 60. GradIPM. Trin Coll Bris BA88. **d** 88 **p** 89. C Drypool *York* 88-91; P-in-c Sandal St Cath *Wakef* 91-95; V from 95; Chapl Manygates Maternity Hosp Wakef from 91. *The Vicarage, 157 Agbrigg Road, Wakefield, W Yorkshire WF1 4AU* Tel (01924) 254176

CROFT, Canon Peter Gardom. b 25. St Jo Coll Cam BA48 MA50. Wells Th Coll 50. **d** 52 **p** 53. C Rugby St Andr *Cov* 52-58; V Stockingford 58-65; R Washington *Dur* 65-78; Dioc Info Officer *Sheff* 78-83; Can Res and Sub-Dean Guildf Cathl *Guildf* 83-94; rtd 94; Perm to Offic *Ely* from 94. *45 Gough Way, Cambridge CB3 9LN* Tel (01223) 355026

CROFT, Ronald. b 30. St Aid Birkenhead 61. **d** 63 **p** 64. C Lawton Moor *Man* 63-65; C Withington St Crispin 65-66; R 74-86; C Prestwich St Marg 66-67; V Oldham St Ambrose 67-71; P-in-c Oldham St Jas 67-68; V 68-71; V Prestwich St Hilda 71-74; R Heaton Norris St Thos 86-96; P-in-c Prestwich St Hilda from 96. *St Hilda's Vicarage, 55 Whittaker Lane, Prestwich, Manchester M25 5ET* Tel 0161-773 1642

CROFT, Simon. b 51. St Steph Ho Ox 75. **d** 78 **p** 79. C Heavitree w Ex St Paul *Ex* 78-83; V Seaton 83-93; P-in-c Ex St Mark 93-96; P-in-c Ex St Sidwell and St Matt 96; R Ex St Mark, St Sidwell and St Matt from 96. *St Mark's Rectory, 8 Lamacraft Drive, Honeylands, Exeter EX4 8QS* Tel (01392) 421050

CROFT, Steven John Lindsey. b 57. MA PhD. Cranmer Hall Dur 80. **d** 83 **p** 84. C Enfield St Andr *Lon* 83-87; V Ovenden *Wakef* 87-96; Dioc Miss Consultant 94-96; Warden Cranmer Hall Dur from 96. *16 Briardene, Durham DH1 4QU, or St John's College, 3 South Bailey, Durham DH1 3RJ* Tel 0191-374 3500 Fax 374 3573

CROFT, Canon Warren David. b 36. ACT ThL. **d** 61 **p** 62. Australia 61-77 and from 79; C Mottingham St Andr *S'wark* 77-78. *57 Princes Highway, Kogarah, NSW, Australia 2217* Tel Sydney (2) 587 5951

CROFT, William Alan. b 15. Lich Th Coll 55. **d** 57 **p** 58. C Ex St Thos *Ex* 57-59; R Ashprington 59-73; V Cornworthy 59-73; R Cheriton Fitzpaine, Woolfardisworthy etc 73-74; TR Cheriton Fitzpaine, Woolfardisworthy etc 74-76; TR N Creedy 76-80; rtd

80. *The Old Estate House, The Square, North Molton, South Molton, Devon EX36 3HT* Tel (01598) 740573

CROFT, William Stuart (Bill). b 53. Trin Hall Cam BA76 MA79 MTh88. Ripon Coll Cuddesdon BA80. **d** 80 **p** 81. C Friern Barnet St Jas *Lon* 80-83; Tutor Chich Th Coll 83-92; Vice-Prin 88-92; V Fernhurst *Chich* from 92. *The Vicarage, Fernhurst, Haslemere, Surrey GU27 3EA* Tel (01428) 652229

CROFTON, Edwin Alan. b 46. Univ Coll Ox BA68 MA72. Cranmer Hall Dur DipTh72. **d** 73 **p** 74. C Hull Newland St Jo *York* 73-77; C Worksop St Jo *S'well* 77-81; Chapl Kilton Hosp Worksop 80-81; V Scarborough St Mary w Ch Ch and H Apostles *York* 81-91; Miss to Seamen 81-91; Chapl St Mary's Hosp Scarborough 82-91; V Cheltenham Ch Ch *Glouc* from 91; RD Cheltenham from 95. *Christ Church Vicarage, Malvern Road, Cheltenham, Glos GL50 2NU* Tel (01242) 515983

CROFTS, Charles Arthur. b 14. Ball Coll Ox BA38 MA48. Lich Th Coll 38. **d** 39 **p** 40. C Shrewsbury St Chad *Lich* 39-41; C Tettenhall Regis 42-48; Min Can Worc Cathl *Worc* 48-50; Asst Master K Sch Worc 48-50; V Ox St Cross *Ox* 51-62; CF (TA) 54-64; V Crowhurst *S'wark* 62-68; Sen Insp of Schools 62-68; V Hexton *St Alb* 69-77; Hon Can St Alb 69-76; Dir RE 69-71; Teacher Herts and Beds Secondary Schools 71-76; N Herts FE Coll 76; Chapl St Bede's Ecum Sch Reigate 77-80; C Merstham and Gatton *S'wark* 77-80; rtd 80; Perm to Offic *Chich* from 80. *5 Manaton Close, Haywards Heath, W Sussex RH16 3HS* Tel (01444) 457190

CROFTS, Ian Hamilton. b 55. BSc. St Jo Coll Nottm 79. **d** 82 **p** 83. C Leamington Priors St Paul *Cov* 82-86; C Oadby *Leic* 86; TV 86-91; V Maidstone St Faith *Cant* from 91. *St Faith's Vicarage, Moncktons Lane, Maidstone, Kent ME14 2PY* Tel (01622) 201164

CROMBIE, William Ian. b 52. Ex Coll Ox BA76 MA79. Ripon Coll Cuddesdon 76. **d** 78 **p** 79. C Broadstone *Sarum* 78; C Warminster St Denys 78-81; C Fleetwood *Blackb* 81-85; Tanzania from 85. *PO Box 2184, Dar es Salaam, Tanzania*

CROMPTON, Roger Martyn Francis. b 47. Sheff Univ BA69 PGCE73. St Jo Coll Dur Cranmer Hall Dur BA84. **d** 85 **p** 86. C Woodford Wells *Chelmsf* 85-89; V Golcar *Wakef* from 89. *The Vicarage, Church Street, Golcar, Huddersfield HD7 4PX* Tel (01484) 654647

CRONK, Simon Nicholas. b 59. CQSW85 Wales Poly BA82. Wycliffe Hall Ox 89. **d** 92 **p** 93. C Cheltenham Ch Ch *Glouc* 92-96; V Cinderford St Steph w Littledean from 96. *The Vicarage, St Annal's Road, Cinderford, Glos GL14 2AS* Tel (01594) 822286

CROOK, Colin. b 44. JP. Brighton Poly ALA67 DMS81 Lon Univ BSc(Econ)74. S'wark Ord Course 87. **d** 90 **p** 91. NSM Dartford Ch Ch *Roch* from 90. *Walliscote, 4 Swaisland Road, Dartford DA1 3DA* Tel (01322) 272957

CROOK, David Creighton. b 37. Trin Coll Cam BA61 MA68. Cuddesdon Coll 61. **d** 63 **p** 64. C Workington St Mich *Carl* 63-66; C Penrith St Andr 66-70; V Barrow St Jas 70-78; V Maryport 78-81; TV Greystoke, Matterdale and Mungrisdale 81-87; TV Watermillock 84-87; V Hesket-in-the-Forest and Armathwaite from 87. *The Vicarage, High Hesket, Carlisle CA4 0HU* Tel (016974) 73320

CROOK, Frederick Herbert. b 17. Oak Hill Th Coll. **d** 52 **p** 53. C Bournemouth St Jo *Win* 52-55; V Margate H Trin *Cant* 55-66; Gen Sec Commonwealth and Continental Ch Soc 66-71; Canada 71-89; Perm to Offic *Ches* from 89. *4 Heathfield Road, Bebington, Wirral, Merseyside L63 3BS* Tel 0151-645 2664

CROOK, George Brian. b 56. Univ of Ottawa BAdmin78. Wycliffe Hall Ox. **d** 86 **p** 87. C Chaddesden St Mary *Derby* 86-89; Chapl Asst Gt Ormond Street Hosp for Sick Children Lon 89-91; Perm to Offic *Roch* 89-91; Perm to Offic Edmonton Episc Area *Lon* 89-91; Asst Chapl Vevey w Chateau d'Oex and Villars *Eur* 91-94; Hong Kong from 94. *Jian Hua Foundation, PO Box 71675, Kowloon CPO, Hong Kong* Tel Hong Kong (852) 336-5312 Fax 337-2965

CROOK, Graham Leslie. b 49. Chich Th Coll 74. **d** 76 **p** 77. C Withington St Crispin *Man* 76-79; C Prestwich St Marg 79-82; V Nelson St Bede *Blackb* 82-92; Chapl Southend Health Care NHS Trust from 92. *Southend Hospital, Prittlewell Chase, Westcliff-on-Sea, Essex SS0 0RY* Tel (01702) 435555

CROOK, Canon John Michael. b 40. Univ of Wales (Lamp) BA62. Coll of Resurr Mirfield 62. **d** 64 **p** 65. C Horninglow *Lich* 64-66; C Bloxwich 66-70; R Inverness St Mich *Mor* 70-78; R Inverness St Jo 74-78; Dioc Youth Chapl *St And* 78-86; R Aberfoyle 78-87; R Doune 78-87; R Callander 78-87; Can St Ninian's Cathl Perth from 85; R Bridge of Allan from 87; Syn Clerk from 97. *21 Fountain Road, Bridge of Allan, Stirling FK9 4AT* Tel (01786) 832368

CROOK, Malcolm Geoffrey. b 53. St Steph Ho Ox 88. **d** 90 **p** 91. C Pet St Jude *Pet* 90-93; C Barrow St Matt *Carl* 93-96; TV Langley and Parkfield *Man* from 96. *The Vicarage, 316 Windermere Road, Middleton, Manchester M24 4LA* Tel 0161-654 8562

CROOK, Rowland William. b 39. Lon Univ DipTh63. Tyndale Hall Bris 61. **d** 64 **p** 65. C Penn Fields *Lich* 64-68; C Lower Broughton St Clem w St Matthias *Man* 68-70; C Bucknall and Bagnall *Lich* 70-76; V New Shildon *Dur* 76-86; V Northwich St Luke and H Trin *Ches* from 86. *St Luke's Vicarage, Dyar Terrace, Northwich, Cheshire CW8 4DL* Tel (01606) 74632

CROOKS, Christopher John (Kip). b 53. St Bede's Coll Dur CertEd75. Trin Coll Bris BA90. **d** 90 **p** 91. C The Quinton *Birm* 90-93; V Ince Ch Ch *Liv* from 93. *The Vicarage, 70 Belle Green Lane, Ince, Wigan, Lancs WN2 2EP* Tel (01942) 495831

CROOKS, Canon David William Talbot. b 52. TCD BA75 MA78 BD83. **d** 77 **p** 78. C Glendermott *D & R* 77-81; C Edin Old St Paul *Edin* 81-84; I Taughboyne, Craigadooish, Newtowncunningham etc *D & R* from 84; Bp's Dom Chapl from 88; Can Raphoe Cathl from 91. *Taughboyne Rectory, Churchtown, Carrigans, Lifford, Co Donegal, Irish Republic* Tel Letterkenny (74) 40135

CROOKS, Eric. b 34. Oak Hill Th Coll 68. **d** 70 **p** 71. C Chadderton Ch Ch *Man* 70-73; C Bolton St Paul 73-75; C Lurgan Ch Ch *D & D* 75-77; I Aghaderg w Donaghmore 77-80; I Dundonald from 80. *St Elizabeth's Rectory, 26A Ballyregan Road, Dundonald, Belfast BT16 0HY* Tel (01232) 483153

CROOKS, Frederick Walter (Mike). b 18. TCD BA41 MA45. TCD Div Sch Div Test41. **d** 41 **p** 42. C Kilkenny *C & O* 41-43; Dean's V St Canice's Cathl 41-43; Chapl RNVR 43-46; C High Wycombe All SS *Ox* 46-48; V Whitechapel St Paul w St Mark *Lon* 48-52; V Cobham *Guildf* 52-62; R Haslemere 62-69; RD Godalming 67-69; V Epsom St Martin 69-74; Hon Can Guildf Cathl 69-74; V Shalfleet *Portsm* 74-80; V Thorley 75-80; Perm to Offic from 80; rtd 83; Perm to Offic *Chich* from 83. *Flat 23, Carlton Court, 24/25 South Parade, Southsea, Hants PO5 2JF* Tel (01705) 870470

CROOKS, Henry Cecil. b 15. Edin Th Coll 71. **d** 72 **p** 72. P-in-c Kinross *St And* 72-75; R 75-81; P-in-c Dollar 76-81; rtd 81; Perm to Offic *Bris* 81-86; Perm to Offic *Chich* from 87. *Terry's Cross, Bungalow 8, Brighton Road, Henfield, W Sussex BN5 9SX* Tel (01273) 493802

CROOKS, Kenneth Robert. b 36. CEng FBIM FIEE. S'wark Ord Course 80. **d** 83 **p** 84. NSM Wisley w Pyrford *Guildf* from 83. *Combley Wood, Hurst Way, Woking, Surrey GU22 8PH* Tel (01932) 336600

CROOKS, Peter James. b 50. St Jo Coll Cam BA72. Cranmer Hall Dur DipTh76. **d** 76 **p** 77. C Onslow Square St Paul *Lon* 76-77; C Brompton H Trin w Onslow Square St Paul 77-79; C Wembley St Jo 79-82; CMS 82-92; Lebanon 83-89; Syria 85-89; Dean Jerusalem 89-92; P-in-c Hunningham *Cov* from 92; P-in-c Wappenbury w Weston under Wetherley from 92; P-in-c Offchurch from 96; V Long Itchington and Marton from 96. *The Vicarage, Leamington Road, Long Itchington, Rugby, Warks CV23 8PL* Tel (01926) 812518

CROOKSHANK, Stephen Graham. b 08. Lon Univ BA37. Westcott Ho Cam 39. **d** 40 **p** 41. C Dulwich St Barn *S'wark* 40-43; C Kingswood 43-47; Min Tadworth CD 47-50; R Mottingham St Andr 50-58; V Gillingham H Trin *Roch* 58-66; V Seal St Pet 66-73; rtd 73; Lic to Offic *Roch* 73-92. *Manormead Residential Home, Tilford Road, Hindhead, Surrey GU26 6RA* Tel (01428) 607930

CROSBY, Bernard Edward. b 47. Oak Hill Th Coll 86. **d** 88 **p** 89. C Springfield H Trin *Chelmsf* 88-91; C Penn Fields *Lich* 91-94; V St Leonards St Ethelburga *Chich* from 94. *St Ethelburga's Vicarage, 4 Gretham Way, St Leonards-on-Sea, E Sussex TN38 0UE* Tel (01424) 421488

CROSFIELD, Canon George Philip Chorley. b 24. OBE90. Selw Coll Cam BA50 MA55. Edin Th Coll 46. **d** 51 **p** 52. C Edin St Dav *Edin* 51-53; C St Andrews St Andr *St And* 53-55; R Hawick *Edin* 55-60; Chapl Gordonstoun Sch 60-67; Can St Mary's Cathl 68-91; Vice-Provost 68-70; Provost 70-90; R Edin St Mary 70-90; rtd 90; Hon Can St Mary's Cathl *Edin* from 91. *21 Biggar Road, Silverburn, Penicuik, Midlothian EH26 9LQ* Tel (01968) 676607

CROSS, Canon Alan. b 43. Chich Th Coll 68. **d** 70 **p** 71. C Bordesley St Oswald *Birm* 70; C S Yardley St Mich 70-73; C Colchester St Jas, All SS, St Nic and St Runwald *Chelmsf* 73-77; V Leigh-on-Sea St Jas 77-89; V Woodford St Barn from 89; Hon Can Chelmsf Cathl from 97. *127 Snakes Lane East, Woodford Green, Essex IG8 7HX* Tel 0181-504 4687

CROSS, Preb Elizabeth Mary (Liz). b 46. Leeds Univ BA69 CertEd70. Sarum Th Coll 80. **dss** 83 **d** 87 **p** 94. Wootton Bassett *Sarum* 83-86; Westbury 86-87; Par Dn 87-89; C Glastonbury w Meare, W Pennard and Godney *B & W* 89-95; Asst Dir of Ords 89-95; Preb Wells Cathl from 93; V Wedmore w Theale and Blackford from 95. *The Vicarage, Manor Lane, Wedmore, Somerset BS28 4EL* Tel (01934) 713566

CROSS, Greville Shelly. b 49. Birm Univ DPS80. Sarum & Wells Th Coll 73. **d** 76 **p** 77. C Kidderminster St Mary *Worc* 76-80; P-in-c Worc St Mark 80-81; TV Worc St Martin w St Pet, St Mark etc 81-85; R Inkberrow w Cookhill and Kington w Dormston from 85; RD Evesham from 93. *The Vicarage, High Street, Inkberrow, Worcester WR7 4DU* Tel (01386) 792222

CROSS, James Stuart (Jim). b 36. Magd Coll Ox BA65 MA71. Ripon Hall Ox 62. **d** 65 **p** 66. C Leckhampton SS Phil and Jas *Glouc* 65-66; CF 66-92; QHC 89-92; R Stretford St Pet *Man* from 92. *The Rectory, 24 Canute Road, Stretford, Manchester M32 0RJ* Tel 0161-865 1802

CROSS, Jeremy Burkitt. b 45. St Pet Coll Ox BA68 MA71. Wycliffe Hall Ox 67. **d** 69 **p** 70. C Mildenhall *St E* 69-72; C Lindfield *Chich* 72-77; V Framfield 77-89; R St Leonards St Leon from 89. *81A Filsham Road, St Leonards-on-Sea, E Sussex TN38 0PE* Tel (01424) 422199

CROSS, John Henry Laidlaw. b 30. Peterho Cam BA53 MA57. Ridley Hall Cam 53. **d** 55 **p** 56. C Ealing Dean St Jo *Lon* 55-58; C Gt Baddow *Chelmsf* 58-60; V Maidenhead St Andr and St Mary *Ox* 60-68; News Ed C of E Newspaper 68-71; Assoc Ed 71-72; Ed 72-75; Hon C St Pet Cornhill *Lon* 68-87; P-in-c 87-95; Hon C Chelsea All SS 76-93; rtd 95. *4 Coombe Hill Glade, Kingston-upon-Thames, Surrey KT2 7EF* Tel 0181-942 7563

CROSS, Michael Anthony. b 45. Leeds Univ BA67 BA69. Coll of Resurr Mirfield 68. **d** 70 **p** 71. S Africa 70-73; C Adel *Ripon* 74-76; Chapl Birm Univ *Birm* 76-81; V Chapel Allerton *Ripon* 81-92; V Headingley from 92; RD Headingley from 96. *Headingley Vicarage, 16 Shire Oak Road, Leeds LS6 2DE* Tel 0113-275 1526

CROSS, Canon Michael Harry. b 28. Liv Univ BVSc50. Cuddesdon Coll 74. **d** 76 **p** 77. C Ledbury *Heref* 76-79; P-in-c Bosbury 79-82; P-in-c Coddington 79-82; P-in-c Wellington Heath 79-82; V Bosbury w Wellington Heath etc 82-83; V Bishop's Castle w Mainstone 83-84; P-in-c Snead 83-84; V Morland, Thrimby and Gt Strickland *Carl* 84-93; RD Appleby 91-93; Hon Can Carl Cathl 92-93; rtd 93; Perm to Offic *Carl* from 93. *Hollin Knowle, Kilmidyke Road, Grange-over-Sands, Cumbria LA11 7AQ* Tel (015395) 35908

CROSSE, Canon Michael Selby. b 09. Linc Th Coll 29. **d** 33 **p** 34. C Derby St Jo *Derby* 33-36; C Grantham *Linc* 36-38; Chapl Derby Cathl *Derby* 38-41; P-in-c Riddings 39-41; Chapl RAFVR 41-46; Bp's Dom Chapl *Linc* 46-47; V Lenton w Ingoldsby 47-51; V Linc St Faith 51-57; Bp's Dom Chapl *Dur* 57-64; V Taddington and Chelmorton *Derby* 64-68; V Hazelwood 68-74; rtd 74; Perm to Offic *Glouc* from 74. *Astell, Overton Park Road, Cheltenham, Glos GL50 3BT* Tel (01242) 517823

CROSSEY, Nigel Nicholas. b 59. Cam Univ BA TCD DipTh84. **d** 84 **p** 85. C Drumglass w Moygashel *Arm* 84-87; I Magheraculmoney *Clogh* 87-93; CF from 93. *MOD Chaplains (Army), Trenchard Lines, Upavon, Pewsey, Wilts SN9 6BE* Tel (01980) 615804 Fax 615800

CROSSLAND, Felix Parnell. b 20. CEng MIMechE57 Univ of Wales (Swansea) BSc49. St Deiniol's Hawarden 73. **d** 75 **p** 76. Hon C Skewen *Llan* 75-78; Hon C Neath w Llantwit 78-85; rtd 85; Perm to Offic *Llan* from 85. *21 Cimla Road, Neath SA11 3PR* Tel (01639) 643560

CROSSLAND, Sister Joyce. b 19. Gilmore Ho IDC48. **dss** 54 **d** 87. CSA 49-78; St Etheldreda's Children's Home Bedf 62-90; Hon Par Dn Bedford St Paul *St Alb* 87-91; rtd 91; Perm to Offic *St Alb* 91-94; Perm to Offic *Ox* from 94. *6 Linford Lane, Willen, Milton Keynes MK15 9DL* Tel (01908) 661554

CROSSLAND, Richard Henry. b 49. Ex Univ BA72. S'wark Ord Course 91. **d** 94 **p** 96. NSM Surbiton St Andr and St Mark *S'wark* 94-95; NSM Linc Cathl *Linc* from 95. *3 Vicars' Court, Minster Yard, Lincoln LN2 1PT* Tel (01522) 535225

CROSSLEY, David. b 50. FISMM94. Coll of Resurr Mirfield 80. **d** 82 **p** 83. C Barton w Peel Green *Man* 82-85; TV Swinton St Pet 85-87; Perm to Offic from 89. *106 Buckstones Road, Shaw, Oldham OL2 8DN* Tel (01706) 882171

CROSSLEY, Dennis Thomas. b 23. AKC52 St Boniface Warminster. **d** 53 **p** 54. C Crofton Park St Hilda *S'wark* 53-56; C Beddington 56-59; C Talbot Village *Sarum* 59-62; R Finchampstead *Ox* 62-97; rtd 97. *1 Larkswood Close, Sandhurst, Camberley, Surrey GU47 8QJ*

CROSSLEY, George Alan. b 34. St Jo Coll Dur BA56. Cranmer Hall Dur DipTh60. **d** 60 **p** 61. C Blackb St Steph *Blackb* 60-63; C Ashton-on-Ribble St Andr 63-65; V Oswaldtwistle St Paul 65-72; R Dufton *Carl* 72-73; P-in-c Milburn w Newbiggin 72-73; R Long Marton w Dufton and w Milburn 73-76; P-in-c Beckermet St Jo 76-78; V Beckermet St Jo and St Bridget w Ponsonby 78-84; Chapl Furness Gen Hosp 84-89; TV Newbarns w Hawcoat *Carl* 84-89; Chapl Princess R Hosp Telford 89-97; rtd 95; P-in-c Bilsborrow *Blackb* from 97. *The Vicarage, Church Lane, Bilsborrow, Preston PR3 0RL* Tel (01995) 640269

CROSSLEY, Dr George John. b 57. Bradf Univ BA81 PhD84. N Ord Course 91. **d** 94 **p** 95. C Balderstone *Man* from 94. *2 Buersil Avenue, Rochdale, Lancs OL16 4TP* Tel (01706) 357633 E-mail 101457.3005@compuserve.com

CROSSLEY, Hugh Vaughan. b 20. AKC42. Bps' Coll Cheshunt. **d** 47 **p** 48. C Loughton St Jo *Chelmsf* 47-49; S Africa 49-52; Portuguese E Africa 52-57; Org Sec Miss to Seamen E Distr 57-58; V Shalford *Chelmsf* 58-60; S Africa 60-73; Adn Mafeking 66-70; R Orsett *Chelmsf* 73-85; P-in-c Bulphan 77-85; rtd 85; Perm to Offic *Nor* 86-96. *Flat 2, 7 Chatsworth Gardens, Eastbourne, E Sussex BN20 7JP*

CROSSLEY, James Salter Baron. b 39. Linc Th Coll 70. **d** 72 **p** 74. C Chesterfield St Mary and All SS *Derby* 72-75; Chapl Doncaster R Infirmary 75-92; Chapl Doncaster R Infirmary & Montague Hosp NHS Trust 92-95; Chapl Asst Tickhill Road and St Cath Hosps 75-92; Hon C Doncaster Intake *Sheff* 78-95; rtd 95; Perm to Offic *Sheff* from 95. *143 Thorne Road, Doncaster, S Yorkshire DN2 5BH* Tel (01302) 326306

CROSSLEY, John Eric. b 51. St Martin's Coll Lanc BA92. Carl Dioc Tr Inst 92. **d** 94 **p** 95. C Westf St Mary *Carl* from 94. *34 Ashfield Road, Workington, Cumbria CA14 3JT* Tel (01900) 603158

CROSSLEY, Canon Dr Robert Scott. b 36. Lon Univ BSc61 BD68 PhD75. ALCD64. **d** 64 **p** 65. C Beckenham St Jo *Roch* 64-68; C Morden *S'wark* 68-72; Chapl Ridley Hall Cam 72-75; V Camberley St Paul *Guildf* 75-83; TR from 83; RD Surrey Heath 81-84; Hon Can Guildf Cathl from 89. *St Paul's Rectory, Crawley Ridge, Camberley, Surrey GU15 2AD* Tel (01276) 22773

CROSSLEY, William Jeremy Hugh. b 55. St Jo Coll Dur BA76. Cranmer Hall Dur 81. **d** 84 **p** 85. C Gillingham St Mark *Roch* 84-87; C Ches Square St Mich w St Phil *Lon* 87-94; V Westminster St Jas the Less from 94. *13 Churton Place, London SW1V 2LN* Tel 0171-630 6282

CROSSMAN, Mrs Charmian Jeanette. b 27. Lon Univ BA48 Lanc Univ MA81 Edin Univ DipMin84. **d** 91 **p** 94. NSM Carl St Jo *Carl* 91-94; RD Carl 94-95; P-in-c Thursby 95-97. *12 Ashfurlong Road, Sheffield S17 3NL* Tel 0114-236 0731

CROSSMAN, Miss Sharon Margaret Joan. b 65. St Loyes Sch of Occupational Therapy DipCOT87. Linc Th Coll BTh93. **d** 93 **p** 94. Par Dn Chippenham St Andr w Tytherton Lucas *Bris* 93-94; C 94-96; Chapl Univ of the W of England from 96; Hon C Almondsbury from 97. *1 Saxon Way, Bradley Stoke North, Bristol BS12 9AR* Tel (01454) 202480 or 0117-965 6261 Fax 0117-976 3964

CROSTHWAITE, George Roger. b 38. Dur Univ BSc62. Ridley Hall Cam 62 Fuller Th Sem California DMin83. **d** 65 **p** 66. C Bradf Cathl Par *Bradf* 65-67; C Ox St Aldate w H Trin *Ox* 67-70; Youth Adv CMS 70-73; P-in-c Derby St Werburgh *Derby* 73-78; V 78-82; USA 77-78; V Anston *Sheff* 82-83; C St Giles-in-the-Fields *Lon* 83-86; V Barnes St Mich *S'wark* 86-88; Perm to Offic *Guildf* 88-93; Dir Cen Essential Psychology from 92. *Dial Cottage, 23 High Street, Tarring, Worthing, W Sussex BN14 7NN* Tel (01903) 529478

CROUCH, Keith Matheson. b 45. AKC70 Whitelands Coll Lon CertEd71. **d** 72 **p** 73. C Hill *Birm* 72-75; P-in-c Woodgate Valley CD 75-77; V Bishop's Castle w Mainstone *Heref* from 91. *The Vicarage, Church Lane, Bishops Castle, Shropshire SY9 5AF* Tel (01588) 638445

CROUCH, Raymond. b 21. Cuddesdon Coll 66. **d** 68 **p** 69. C Bracknell *Ox* 68-71; P-in-c Littlemore 71-78; C Boxgrove *Chich* 78-81; C Tangmere 78-81; P-in-c Oving w Merston 78-81; V Winkfield *Ox* 81-84; P-in-c Cranbourne 81-84; C Thame w Towersey 84-86; rtd 86; Perm to Offic *Ox* from 86. *9 Orchard Close, Chalgrove, Oxford OX44 7RA* Tel (01865) 890653

CROUCHMAN, Eric Richard. b 30. Bps' Coll Cheshunt 64. **d** 66 **p** 67. C Ipswich H Trin *St E* 66-69; C Ipswich All Hallows 69-72; R Crowfield w Stonham Aspal and Mickfield 72-81; R Combs 81-90; RD Stowmarket 84-90; P-in-c Lydgate w Ousden and Cowlinge 90-95; R Wickhambrook w Lydgate, Ousden and Cowlinge 95-96; rtd 96. *6 Mitre Close, Woolpit, Bury St Edmunds, Suffolk IP30 9SJ*

CROW, Arthur. b 26. St Chad's Coll Dur BA51 DipTh52. **d** 52 **p** 53. C Thornhill *Wakef* 52-54; C Holmfirth 54-57; V Shelley 57-63; V Flockton cum Denby Grange 63-91; rtd 91; Perm to Offic *York* from 91. *2 Thatchers Croft, Copmanthorpe, York YO2 3YD* Tel (01904) 709861

CROW, Michael John. b 35. AKC63. **d** 64 **p** 65. C Welwyn Garden City *St Alb* 64-67; C Sawbridgeworth 67-69; C Biscot 69-71; V Luton St Aug Limbury 71-79; TR Borehamwood 79-87; V Markyate Street from 87. *The Vicarage, High Street, Markyate, St Albans, Herts AL3 8PD* Tel (01582) 841701

CROWDER, The Ven Norman Harry. b 26. St Jo Coll Cam BA48 MA52. Westcott Ho Cam 50. **d** 52 **p** 53. C Radcliffe-on-Trent *S'well* 52-55; Bp's Res Chapl *Portsm* 55-59; Asst Chapl Canford Sch Wimborne 59-64; Chapl 64-72; V Oakfield St Jo *Portsm* 72-75; Can Res Portsm Cathl 75-85; Dir RE 75-85; Adn Portsm 85-93; rtd 93; Perm to Offic *Portsm* from 92. *37 Rectory Road, Salisbury SP2 7SD* Tel (01722) 320052

CROWE, Anthony Murray (Tony). b 34. St Edm Hall Ox BA58 MA61. Westcott Ho Cam 57. **d** 59 **p** 60. C Stockingford *Cov* 59-62; C New Eltham All SS *S'wark* 62-66; V Clapham St Jo 66-73; R Charlton St Luke w H Trin 73-94; rtd 94; Sub-Chapl HM Pris Swaleside from 94; Sub-Chapl HM Pris Elmley from 94; Perm to Offic *Cant* from 94. *9 Park Avenue, Whitstable, Kent CT5 2DD* Tel (01227) 273046

CROWE, Eric Anthony. b 29. St Jo Coll Dur BA53. Cuddesdon Coll 53. **d** 55 **p** 56. C Huddersfield St Jo *Wakef* 55-58; C Barnsley St Pet 58-60; R High Hoyland w Clayton W 60-68; V Battyeford 68-74; P-in-c Pitminster w Corfe *B & W* 75-76; V 76-90; rtd 90; Perm to Offic *Ex* from 90. *5 Oak Tree Close, Upottery, Honiton, Devon EX14 9QG* Tel (01404) 861639

CROWE, Canon John Yeomans. b 39. Keble Coll Ox BA62 MA66. Linc Th Coll 62. **d** 64 **p** 65. C Tettenhall Regis *Lich* 64-67; C Caversham *Ox* 67-71; V Hampton *Worc* 72-76; P-in-c Leek St Edw *Lich* 76-79; TR Leek 79-83; TR Leek and Meerbrook 83-87; RD Leek 82-87; TR Dorchester *Ox* from 87; RD Aston and Cuddesdon from 93; Hon Can Ch Ch from 94. *The Rectory,*

Dorchester-on-Thames, Wallingford, Oxon OX10 7HZ Tel (01865) 340007

CROWE, Leonard Charles (Len). b 25. S Dios Minl Tr Scheme 80. **d** 82 **p** 83. NSM Buxted and Hadlow Down *Chich* 82-84; NSM Fairlight 84-86; P-in-c 86-89; V 89-92; rtd 92; RD Rye *Chich* 93-95; Perm to Offic from 95. *Deforal, Sea Road, Fairlight, Hastings, E Sussex TN55 4AX*

CROWE, Canon Norman Charles. b 23. ADipR62. Launde Abbey. **d** 63 **p** 64. C Leic Martyrs *Leic* 63-66; C-in-c Leic St Chad CD 66-68; V Leic St Chad 68-73; V Market Harborough 73-88; RD Gartree I 76-81; Hon Can Leic Cathl 80-88; rtd 88; Perm to Offic *Leic* from 88; Perm to Offic *Pet* from 88. *8 Wilton Close, Desborough, Kettering, Northants NN14 2QJ* Tel (01536) 760820

CROWE, Canon Philip Anthony. b 36. Selw Coll Cam BA60 MA64. Ridley Hall Cam 60. **d** 62 **p** 63. Tutor Oak Hill Th Coll 62-67; C Enfield Ch Ch Trent Park *Lon* 62-65; Ed C of E Newspaper 67-71; Lect Birm St Martin 71-76; R Breadsall *Derby* 77-88; Prin and Tutor Sarum & Wells Th Coll 88-95; Can and Preb Sarum Cathl *Sarum* 91-95; R Overton and Erbistock and Penley *St As* from 95. *The Rectory, 4 Sundorne, Overton, Wrexham LL13 0EB* Tel (01978) 710229

CROWE, Canon Sydney Ralph. b 32. Edin Th Coll 61. **d** 63 **p** 64. C Bingley H Trin *Bradf* 63-66; C Bierley 66-69; V Toller Lane St Chad from 69; Hon Can Bradf Cathl from 85; RD Airedale from 95. *The Vicarage, St Chad's Road, Toller Lane, Bradford, W Yorkshire BD8 9DE* Tel (01274) 543957

CROWHURST, David Brian. b 40. Qu Coll Birm 77. **d** 80 **p** 81. NSM Ribbesford w Bewdley and Dowles *Worc* 80-82; Hon Chapl Birm Cathl *Birm* 81-82; C Kidderminster St Jo *Worc* 82-83; C-in-c Wribbenhall 83-84; P-in-c 84-87; V Oswestry St Oswald *Lich* 87-94; P-in-c Oswestry H Trin 93-94; P-in-c Rhydycroesau 90-91; R from 91; V Oswestry from 94; RD Oswestry from 95. *The Vicarage, Penylan Lane, Oswestry, Shropshire SY11 2AN* Tel (01691) 653467 or 652861

CROWIE, Hermon John. b 41. Kelham Th Coll 61. **d** 69 **p** 73. C Sneinton St Cypr *S'well* 69; C Balderton 72-75; V Basford St Aid 75-78; R Everton and Mattersey w Clayworth 78-84; St Helena 84-89; Chapl HM Pris Nor 89-91; Chapl HM Pris Cant from 91. *The Chaplain's Office, HM Prison, 46 Longport, Canterbury, Kent CT1 1PJ* Tel (01227) 762244 Fax 450203

CROWLEY, Brian Golland. b 01. Keble Coll Ox BA23 MA28. Westcott Ho Cam 26. **d** 27 **p** 28. C Liv St Phil *Liv* 27-29; India 29-45; V Shedfield *Portsm* 45-54; V Clifton Hampden *Ox* 54-69; rtd 69. *c/o B N Crowley Esq, 25 Linkway, Crowthorne, Berkshire RG45 6ES*

CROWLEY, Michael Patrick Sainsbury. b 51. Newc Univ BA74 PGCE75. Lon Bible Coll BA78 MA84. **d** 87 **p** 87. Chile from 87. *Casilla 87, Valdivia, Chile, or Casilla 50675, Santiago, Chile* Tel Santiago (2) 683009 Fax 639-4581

CROWSON, Richard Charles Marriott. b 39. Down Coll Cam BA62 MA66. Lich Th Coll 62. **d** 64 **p** 65. C Smethwick *Birm* 64-67; V Nottingham St Andr *S'well* 67-74; Chapl Community Relns *Pet* 74-80; Perm to Offic *Lon* 80-92; Asst Sec for Race and Community Relns Gen Syn 92-97; Public Preacher *Lon* from 93; rtd 97. *11 Ellington Street, London N7 8PP* Tel 0171-609 1984

✠**CROWTHER, The Rt Revd Clarence Edward.** b 29. Leeds Univ BA50 LLB52 LLM53 California Univ PhD75. Cuddesdon Coll 55. **d** 56 **p** 57 **c** 65. C Ox SS Phil and Jas *Ox* 56-59; USA 59-64 and from 67; S Africa 64-67; Bp Kimberley and Kuruman 65-67; Asst Bp California from 73. *PO Box 1559, Summerland, California 93067, USA*

CROWTHER, Donald James. b 23. Oak Hill NSM Course. **d** 82 **p** 83. NSM Seal St Lawr *Roch* 82-85; NSM Sevenoaks St Nic 85-87; P-in-c Sevenoaks Weald 87-90; Perm to Offic from 90. *Midhope, Pilgrims Way, Kemsing, Sevenoaks, Kent TN15 6LS* Tel (01732) 761035

CROWTHER, Frank. b 28. Qu Coll Birm 68. **d** 69 **p** 70. C Bulwell St Mary *S'well* 69-72; TV Clifton 72-77; V Kirkby in Ashfield St Thos 77-85; rtd 86; Perm to Offic *S'well* from 86; Perm to Offic *Derby* from 86. *30 Bramley Court, Sutton-in-Ashfield, Notts NG17 4AT* Tel (01623) 443251

CROWTHER, Ronald. b 22. Sarum Th Coll. **d** 53 **p** 54. C Hawley H Trin *Guildf* 53-55; Chapl RAF 55-58; Canada 58-63; R Fugglestone w Bemerton *Sarum* 63-67; V Tooting All SS *S'wark* 67-73; R Brinkley, Burrough Green and Carlton *Ely* 73-80; P-in-c Westley Waterless 78-80; R Brandon and Santon Downham *St E* 80-87; rtd 87. *54 Castle Street, Thetford, Norfolk IP24 2DP* Tel (01842) 765653

CROWTHER, Stephen Alfred. b 59. TCD DipTh87. **d** 87 **p** 88. C Willowfield *D & D* 87-89; I Belfast St Chris 89-92; I Kiltegan w Hacketstown, Clonmore and Moyne *C & O* from 93. *The Rectory, Kiltegan, Baltinglass, Co Wicklow, Irish Republic* Tel Kiltegan (508) 73368 Fax 73414

CROWTHER-ALWYN, Benedict Mark. b 53. Kent Univ BA74. Qu Coll Birm 74. **d** 77 **p** 78. C Fenny Stratford and Water Eaton *Ox* 77-80; C Moulsecoomb *Chich* 80-81; TV 81-83; R Glas St Serf *Glas* 83-87; R Baillieston 83-87; R Bassingham *Linc* 87-90; V Aubourn w Haddington 87-90; V Carlton-le-Moorland w Stapleford 87-90; R Thurlby w Norton Disney 87-90; V Elmton *Derby* from 90. *The Vicarage, Creswell, Worksop, Notts S80 4HD* Tel (01909) 721264

CROWTHER-GREEN, Canon John Patrick Victor. b 18. Hatf Coll Dur LTh41 BA42. St Boniface Warminster 39. **d** 42 **p** 44. C Croydon H Trin *Cant* 42-44; C New Windsor H Trin *Ox* 44-49; V Shackerstone and Congerstone *Leic* 49-53; R Willoughby Waterleys, Peatling Magna etc 53-58; V Leic St Sav 58-73; V Blaby 73-87; RD Guthlaxton I 81-87; Hon Can Leic Cathl 82-87; rtd 87; Perm to Offic *Leic* from 87. *40 Craighill Road, Knighton, Leicester LE2 3FB* Tel 0116-270 7615

CROWTHER-GREEN, Michael Leonard. b 36. K Coll Lon 56. **d** 60 **p** 61. C Caterham *S'wark* 60-64; C Lewisham St Jo Southend 64-69; Chr Aid Area Sec (Berks, Oxon and Bucks) 69-78; Lic to Offic *Ox* 78-83; Dioc Stewardship Adv 83-92; rtd 92. *8 Egerton Road, Reading RG2 8HQ* Tel (01734) 872502

CROYDON, Archdeacon of. *See* DAVIES, The Ven Vincent Anthony

CROYDON, Area Bishop of. *See* WOOD, The Rt Revd Wilfred Denniston

CRUICKSHANK, Jonathan Graham. b 52. K Coll Lon BD74 AKC74 Ox Univ PGCE75. St Aug Coll Cant 75. **d** 76 **p** 77. C Stantonbury *Ox* 76-79; C Burnham 79-82; Chapl RNR 80-83; C Burnham w Dropmore, Hitcham and Taplow *Ox* 82-83; Chapl RN 83-89; TV New Windsor *Ox* from 89. *Holy Trinity Rectory, 73 Alma Road, Windsor, Berks SL4 3HD* Tel (01753) 853585 Fax as telephone

CRUISE, Brian John Alexander. Bris Univ BA TCD BTh. **d** 88 **p** 89. C Lurgan Ch the Redeemer *D & D* 88-92; I Kildress w Altedesert *Arm* from 92. *Kildress Rectory, 6 Rectory Road, Cookstown, Co Tyrone BT80 9RX* Tel (01648) 51215

CRUMP, John. b 27. AKC54. **d** 55 **p** 56. C Wanstead H Trin Hermon Hill *Chelmsf* 55-58; C-in-c Harold Hill St Geo CD 58-65; V Highams Park All SS 65-78; RD Waltham Forest 75-78; R Lambourne w Abridge and Stapleford Abbotts 78-83; V Walton le Soken 83-90; rtd 90; Perm to Offic *Chelmsf* from 90. *14 Kenilworth Road, Holland-on-Sea, Clacton-on-Sea, Essex CO15 5NX* Tel (01255) 814511

CRUMPTON, Colin. b 38. AKC61. **d** 64 **p** 65. C Billingham St Cuth *Dur* 64-66; C Shirley *Birm* 66-69; V Mossley *Ches* 69-75; Miss to Seamen 75-77; V Burslem St Paul *Lich* 77-82; V Edensor from 82. *The Vicarage, 131 Longton Hall Road, Stoke-on-Trent ST3 2EL* Tel (01782) 319210

CRUSE, Jack. b 35. ARIBA67. Sarum & Wells Th Coll 76. **d** 79 **p** 80. NSM W Teignmouth *Ex* 79-85; NSM Ideford, Luton and Ashcombe 85-87; C 87-89; NSM Bishopsteignton 85-87; C 87-89; C Teignmouth, Ideford w Luton, Ashcombe etc 90; R Broadhempston, Woodland, Staverton etc from 90; RD Totnes from 94. *The Rectory, Broadhempston, Totnes, Devon TQ9 6AU* Tel (01803) 813646

CRUSE, John Jeremy. b 58. Univ of Wales (Lamp) BA79 Hughes Hall Cam CertEd87. Sarum & Wells Th Coll 81. **d** 82 **p** 83. C Newton St Pet *S & B* 82-84; P-in-c Newbridge-on-Wye and Llanfihangel Brynpabuan 84-86; Perm to Offic *Heref* 88-89; C Waltham H Cross *Chelmsf* 89-91; TV Yatton Moor *B & W* from 91. *The Vicarage, North End Road, Yatton, Bristol BS19 4AS* Tel (01934) 832776

CRUTTENDEN, Leslie Roy. b 39. Cant Sch of Min. **d** 84 **p** 85. NSM Maidstone St Luke *Cant* 84-86; NSM Charlton-in-Dover 86-90; NSM River from 90. *6 Citadel Heights, Dover, Kent CT17 9DS* Tel (01304) 205281

CRYER, Gordon David. b 34. St D Coll Lamp BA63 DipTh64. **d** 64 **p** 65. C Mortlake w E Sheen *S'wark* 64-67; C Godstone 67-70; Chapl St Dunstan's Abbey Sch Plymouth from 71; R Stoke Damerel *Ex* from 71; P-in-c Devonport St Aubyn from 88. *The Rectory, 6 Underhill Road, Plymouth PL3 4BP* Tel (01752) 562348

CRYER, Neville Barker. b 24. Hertf Coll Ox BA48 MA52. Ridley Hall Cam. **d** 50 **p** 51. C Derby St Werburgh *Derby* 50-53; C Ilkeston St Mary 53-54; R Blackley St Pet *Man* 55-59; V Addiscombe St Mary *Cant* 59-67; Sec Conf Br Miss Socs 67-70; Gen Sec BFBS 70-86; rtd 86; Perm to Offic *York* from 90. *14 Carmires Road, Haxby, York YO3 3NN* Tel (01904) 763371

CUBITT, Paul. b 64. Sheff Univ BA86. Cranmer Hall Dur 95. **d** 97. C Bromyard *Heref* from 97. *12 Lower Thorn, Bromyard, Herefordshire HR7 4AZ* Tel (01885) 482620

CUFF, Gregor John. b 61. Keele Univ BSc82. Ridley Hall Cam CTMin95. **d** 95 **p** 96. C Stanley *Liv* from 95. *Vicarage Flat, 8 Derwent Square, Liverpool L13 6QT* Tel 0151-252 1522

CUFF, Mrs Pamela (Pam). b 47. MCSP68. S Dios Minl Tr Scheme 89. **d** 92 **p** 94. NSM Nether Stowey w Over Stowey *B & W* 92-93; NSM Quantoxhead from 93; Asst Chapl Taunton Hosps 93-94; Asst Chapl Taunton and Somerset NHS Trust from 94. *Millands, Kilve, Bridgwater, Somerset TA5 1EA* Tel (01278) 741229

CULBERTSON, Eric Malcolm. b 54. Ch Ch Ox BA76 MA80 K Coll Lon PhD91. Edin Th Coll 78. **d** 80 **p** 81. C Edin St Thos *Edin* 80-83; C Ealing St Mary *Lon* 83-87; R Clarkston *Glas* 87-89; Area Sec BCMS 89-93; Area Sec Crosslinks 93-94; Hon C Halliwell St Luke *Man* 90-94; I Tullaniskin w Clonoe *Arm* from 94; Perm to Offic *Man* from 94. *215 Brackaville Road, Newmills, Dungannon, Co Tyrone BT71 4EJ* Tel (01868) 747154

CULL, Ernest Geoffrey. b 20. Coll of Resurr Mirfield 57. **d** 57 **p** 58. C Heref H Trin *Heref* 57-61; PC Barrowhill *Derby* 61-70; V Derby St Paul 71-80; V Mackworth St Fran 80-90; rtd 90; Perm to Offic *Derby* from 90. *15 Lodge Lane, Spondon, Derby DE21 7GD* Tel (01332) 674562

CULL, Canon Francis Cyril Duncan. b 15. Natal Univ BA63 York Univ MPhil73 Univ of S Africa DLitt79. Clifton Th Coll 35. **d** 38 **p** 39. C Waltham Abbey *Chelmsf* 38-40; C Streatham St Paul *S'wark* 40-42; C Newington St Mary 42-45; Min St Mary's CD Welling 46-52; V Battersea St Steph 52-57; S Africa from 58; Lect Rhodes Univ 65-73; Lect Witwatersrand Univ 74-78; Prov Can from 88. *Bishopscourt, Bishopscourt Drive, Claremont, South Africa* Tel Cape Town (21) 797-6451

CULL, John. b 31. Oak Hill Th Coll 56. **d** 59 **p** 60. C Radipole *Sarum* 59-66; Chapl Mariners' Ch Glouc 66-70; R Woodchester *Glouc* 70-90; RD Stonehouse 85-89; V Walton *St E* 90-94; rtd 94; Perm to Offic *Glouc* from 94. *Hillgrove Stables, Bear Hill, Woodchester, Stroud, Glos GL5 5DH* Tel (01453) 872145

CULLEN, Canon John Austin. b 43. FRSA89 Auckland Univ BA67 Otago Univ BD76 Keble Coll Ox DPhil86 St Jo Coll Auckland 66. **d** 69 **p** 70. New Zealand 69-78; Asst Chapl Keble Coll Ox 79-82; Perm to Offic *Lon* 82-84; Chapl and Lect Worc Coll Ox 84-86; C St Botolph Aldgate w H Trin Minories *Lon* 86-87; Hon C St Marylebone All SS 87-91; Dir Inst of Chr Studies 87-91; Dir of Tr *Win* from 91; Hon Can Win Cathl from 96. *Church House, 9 The Close, Winchester SO23 9LS* Tel Winchester (01962) 844644 Fax 841815

CULLIFORD, Michael. b 26. Qu Coll Birm 56. **d** 58 **p** 59. C Birkenhead St Jas *Ches* 58-60; C Bollington St Jo 60-62; V Heald Green St Cath 62-80; Perm to Offic *Man* from 89; rtd 91. *23 Field Vale Drive, Stockport, Cheshire SK5 6XZ* Tel 0161-432 1706

CULLING, Dr Elizabeth Ann. b 58. St Mary's Coll Dur BA76 St Jo Coll Dur PhD86 Rob Coll Cam BA88 PGCE80. Ridley Hall Cam 86. **d** 89 **p** 94. Par Dn S Cave and Ellerker w Broomfleet *York* 89-92; Tutor Cranmer Hall Dur 93-95; Perm to Offic *Dur* 93-95; P-in-c Cherry Burton *York* from 95; Abp's Sen Adv on Rural Affairs from 95; Chapl Bp Burton Coll York from 95. *The Rectory, Main Street, Cherry Burton, Beverley, N Humberside HU17 7RF* Tel (01964) 550293

CULLINGWORTH, Anthony Robert. b 42. BSc. Ox NSM Course. **d** 83 **p** 84. NSM Slough *Ox* from 83. *375 Goodman Park, Slough SL2 5NW* Tel (01753) 536274

CULLIS, Andrew Stanley Weldon. b 48. Hertf Coll Ox BA69 LTh. St Jo Coll Nottm 70. **d** 73 **p** 74. C Reigate St Mary *S'wark* 73-78; C Yateley *Win* 78-82; V Dorking St Paul *Guildf* from 82; RD Dorking from 94. *St Paul's Vicarage, South Terrace, Dorking, Surrey RH4 2AB* Tel (01306) 883023

CULLWICK, Christopher John. b 53. Hull Univ BA75 Reading Univ Ox Univ BA80 MA85. Wycliffe Hall Ox 78. **d** 81 **p** 82. C Nottingham St Jude *S'well* 81-84; C York St Mich-le-Belfrey *York* 84-87; TV Huntington from 87. *The Vicarage, 64 Strensall Road, Huntington, York YO3 9SH* Tel (01904) 764608

CULLY, Miss Elizabeth Faith. b 46. SRN67 SCM69 RGN72. Trin Coll Bris BA88. **d** 88 **p** 94. Par Dn Filton *Bris* 88-92; Par Dn Fishponds St Jo 92-94; C 94-95; P-in-c Brinsley w Underwood *S'well* from 95. *The Vicarage, 102A Church Lane, Brinsley, Nottingham NG16 5AB* Tel (01773) 713978

CULPIN, Albert. b 16. Open Univ BA75. St Deiniol's Hawarden 76. **d** 77 **p** 78. NSM Bidston *Ches* 77-87; Perm to Offic from 87. *27 Derwent Road, Meols, Wirral, Merseyside L47 8XY* Tel 0151-632 3542

CULROSS, James Fred. b 17. Lon Univ BD51. Bps' Coll Cheshunt 47. **d** 50 **p** 51. C Pateley Bridge *Ripon* 50-54; C Romaldkirk 54-55; V Middleton St Cross 55-62; R Glas St Jas *Glas* 62-65; C Bramley *Guildf* 65-67; Chapl R Wanstead Sch 67-71; Chapl Sir Roger Manwood's Sch Sandwich 71-79; R Barrowden and Wakerley w S Luffenham *Pet* 79-82; rtd 82; Perm to Offic *B & W* from 82. *34 Heritage Court, Magdalene Street, Glastonbury, Somerset BA6 9ER* Tel (01458) 834179

CULVERWELL, Martin Phillip. b 48. Sarum & Wells Th Coll 72. **d** 75 **p** 76. C Ashford St Hilda *Lon* 75-78; C Chelsea St Luke 78-80; Chapl RN 80-83; TV Yeovil *B & W* 83-87; P-in-c Sarratt *St Alb* 87-90; NSM Bradford w Oake, Hillfarrance and Heathfield *B & W* 90-92; R Rode Major 92-96. *Habersfield, High Street, Rode, Bath BA3 6NZ* Tel (01373) 830476 E-mail revmpcul@aol.com

CUMBERLAND, The Very Revd Barry John. b 44. Birm Univ BA67 Worc Coll Ox DipEd68 Trin Coll Singapore MDiv88. **d** 88 **p** 89. NSM Westmr St Matt *Lon* 88-90; Perm to Offic from 90; The Philippines 90-96; Dean Manila 92-96; Chapl Stockholm w Gavle and Vasteras *Eur* from 96. *Styrmansgatan 1, 11454 Stockholm, Sweden* Tel Stockholm (8) 663-8248 Fax 663-8911

CUMBERLAND, Leslie Hodgson. b 15. Leeds Univ BA37. Coll of Resurr Mirfield 37. **d** 39 **p** 40. C Birtley *Dur* 39-44; C Medomsley 44-49; Min Kimblesworth 49-55; V Bradf St Columba *Bradf* 55-64; Lic to Offic 64-85; rtd 80; Perm to Offic *Bradf* from 85. *29 Union Road, Low Moor, Bradford, W Yorkshire BD12 0DW* Tel (01274) 676138

CUMBERLEGE, Francis Richard. b 41. AKC65. **d** 66 **p** 67. C Leigh Park St Fran CD *Portsm* 66-71; Papua New Guinea 71-81; Adn N Papua 74-81; C Portsea St Mary *Portsm* 81; R Hastings St Clem and All SS *Chich* 81-86; V Broadwater Down 86-91; V Tunbridge Wells St Mark *Roch* from 91; RD Tunbridge Wells from 96. *The Vicarage, 1 St Mark's Road, Tunbridge Wells, Kent TN2 5LT* Tel (01892) 526069

CUMBERLIDGE, Anthony Wynne. b 49. ACIB75. Sarum & Wells Th Coll 79. **d** 82 **p** 83. C Llanrhos *St As* 82-85; R Llanfair Talhaearn and Llansannan etc 85-87; CF from 87. *MOD Chaplains (Army), Trenchard Lines, Upavon, Pewsey, Wilts SN9 6BE* Tel (01980) 615804 Fax 615800

CUMBRAE, Provost of. *Vacant*

CUMING, Mark Alexander. b 53. AKC75. Westcott Ho Cam 76. **d** 77 **p** 78. C Newc H Cross *Newc* 77-80; Perm to Offic *Birm* 87-93; Perm to Offic *Newc* 93-95; R Blanchland w Hunstanworth and Edmundbyers etc from 95. *The Vicarage, Blanchland, Consett, Co Durham DH8 9ST* Tel (01434) 675207

CUMINGS, Llewellyn Frank Beadnell. b 29. Natal Univ BA50 St Cath Coll Cam CertEd53. Ridley Hall Cam 65. **d** 67 **p** 68. C Leamington Priors St Mary *Cov* 67-70; V Lobley Hill *Dur* 70-74; R Denver *Ely* 74-82; V Ryston w Roxham 74-82; R St Leonards St Leon *Chich* 82-88; V Billinghay *Linc* 88-93; rtd 93. *Y Bwthyn, Coedllan, Llanfyllin SY22 5BP* Tel (01691) 648013

CUMMING, Nigel Patrick. b 42. St Jo Coll Nottm 73. **d** 75 **p** 76. C Castle Hall *Ches* 75-77; C Stalybridge H Trin and Ch Ch 77-78; C Tadley St Pet *Win* 78-82; R Overton w Laverstoke and Freefolk from 82; RD Whitchurch from 89. *The Rectory, 54 Lordsfield Gardens, Overton, Basingstoke, Hants RG25 3EW* Tel (01256) 770207

CUMMING, Ms Susan Margaret. b 47. Man Univ BSc68 Makerere Univ Kampala DipEd69. EMMTC CTPS82. **dss** 82 **d** 87 **p** 95. Cinderhill *S'well* 82-85; Dioc Adv in Adult Educn 85-92; Par Dn Nottingham St Mary and St Cath 93-95; Lect 95-97; Asst Chapl Qu Medical Cen Nottm Univ Hosp NHS Trust from 97. *The Rectory, 569 Farnborough Road, Clifton, Nottingham NG11 9DG* Tel 0115-941 7156

CUMMINGS, Elizabeth. b 45. St Jo Coll Dur BA84. NE Ord Course. **d** 87 **p** 94. NSM Dur St Giles *Dur* 87-89; Chapl HM Pris Dur 89-90; Chapl HM Rem Cen Low Newton 90-95; Chapl HM Pris Stocken 95-96; Chapl HM Pris Frankland from 96. *HM Prison Frankland, Finchdale Avenue, Durham DH1 5YD* Tel 0191-384 5544 Fax 384 9203

CUMMINGS, Richard Vivian Payn. b 21. Lon Univ BSc41. Chich Th Coll 51. **d** 53 **p** 54. C Pet All SS *Pet* 53-55; C Wellingborough All SS 55-60; V Wollaston and Strixton 60-69; V Wellingborough St Barn 69-73; RD Wellingborough 70-73; P-in-c Milton Malsor 73-80; R Collingtree w Courteenhall 73-80; R Collingtree w Courteenhall and Milton Malsor 80-90; rtd 90; Perm to Offic *Pet* from 90. *55 Watersmeet, Northampton NN1 5SQ* Tel (01604) 37027

CUMMINGS, The Very Revd William Alexander Vickery. b 38. Ch Ch Ox BA62 MA64. Wycliffe Hall Ox 61. **d** 64 **p** 65. C Leytonstone St Jo *Chelmsf* 64-67; C Writtle 67-71; R Stratton St Mary w Stratton St Michael *Nor* 71-73; R Wacton Magna w Parva 71-73; R Stratton St Mary w Stratton St Michael etc 73-91; RD Depwade 81-91; Hon Can Nor Cathl 90-91; V Battle *Chich* from 91; Dean Battle from 91. *The Deanery, Mount Street, Battle, E Sussex TN33 0JY* Tel (01424) 772693

CUMMINS, Ashley Wighton. b 56. St Andr Univ BD83. Coates Hall Edin DipMin84. **d** 84 **p** 85. C Broughty Ferry *Bre* 84-87; P-in-c Dundee St Ninian 87-92; P-in-c Invergowrie from 92; Chapl Angl Students Dundee Univ from 92. *27 Errol Road, Invergowrie, Dundee DD2 5AG* Tel (01382) 562525

CUMMINS, James Ernest. b 32. Westcott Ho Cam 57. **d** 60 **p** 61. C Baswich *Lich* 60-64; V Hales w Heckingham *Nor* 64-70; V Raveningham 70-76; Perm to Offic *Heref* from 76. *Skyborry, Knighton LD7 1TW* Tel (01547) 528369

CUMMINS, Julian Peter Francis. b 55. TD91. K Coll Cam BA77 MA80 Bradf Univ MBA91 MCIM84. N Ord Course 94. **d** 97. NSM Kirkby Overblow *Ripon* from 97. *31 St Helen's Lane, Adel, Leeds LS16 8BR* Tel 0113-259 1000 or 267 3006 Fax 259 1102 or 267 3588

CUMMINS, The Very Revd Nicholas Marshall. b 36. CITC. **d** 67 **p** 68. C Ballymena *Conn* 67-70; C Belfast St Nic 70-73; I Buttevant Union *C, C & R* 73-78; I Mallow Union 78-83; I Kilmoe Union 83-96; Preb Cork Cathl 90-96; Treas Cork Cathl 95-96; Preb Tymothan St Patr Cathl Dublin from 95; Dean Killaloe, Kilfenora and Clonfert *L & K* from 95; Dean Kilmacduagh from 96; I Killaloe w Stradbally from 96. *The Deanery, Killaloe, Co Clare, Irish Republic* Tel Killaloe (61) 376687 Fax as telephone

CUMMINS, William Frederick. b 17. St Pet Hall Ox BA39 DipTh40 MA44. Wycliffe Hall Ox 39. **d** 41 **p** 42. C Stretford St Matt *Man* 41-43; C Kersal Moor 43-46; V Pendleton St Barn 46-49; V Blackb St Jude *Blackb* 49-52; V Preston St Paul 52-60; V Pendleton 60-67; Dioc Youth Chapl 60-67; Chapl R Gr Sch Worc 67-75; P-in-c Peopleton *Worc* 70-75; R 75-78; P-in-c White Ladies Aston w Spetchley and Churchill 76-78; R Peopleton and White Ladies Aston etc 78-83; rtd 83; Perm to Offic *Birm* from 84; Perm to Offic *Cov* from 86. *27 The Birches, Bulkington, Nuneaton, Warks CV12 9PW* Tel (01203) 317830

CUMPSTY, Prof John Sutherland. b 31. K Coll Dur BSc54 PhD56 Barrister-at-Law (Middle Temple) 56 Carnegie-Mellon Univ MS58 St Jo Coll Dur DipTh60. Cranmer Hall Dur 58. **d** 60 **p** 61. C Normanton *Wakef* 60-62; Tutor St Jo Coll Dur 62-66; Lect Glas Univ 66-69; S Africa from 70; Prof Relig Studies Cape Town Univ from 70; rtd 96. *University of Cape Town, Dept of Religious Studies, Rondebosch, 7700 South Africa* Tel Cape Town (21) 650-3454 Fax 650-3761

CUNDIFF, Mrs Margaret Joan. b 32. Man Univ DMS60. St Mich Ho Ox 51. **dss** 77 **d** 87 **p** 94. Broadcasting Officer *York* from 75; Angl Adv Yorkshire TV 79-90; Selby St Jas *York* 77-87; Par Dn 87-94; C from 94; NSM Wistow from 87. *37 Oaklands, Camblesforth, Selby, N Yorkshire YO8 8HH* Tel (01757) 618148

✠**CUNDY, The Rt Revd Ian Patrick Martyn.** b 45. Trin Coll Cam BA67 MA71. Tyndale Hall Bris 67. **d** 69 **p** 70 **c** 92. C New Malden and Coombe *S'wark* 69-73; Lect Oak Hill Th Coll 73-77; TR Mortlake w E Sheen *S'wark* 78-83; Warden Cranmer Hall Dur 83-92; Area Bp Lewes *Chich* 92-96; Bp Pet from 96. *The Palace, Peterborough PE1 1YA* Tel (01733) 62492 Fax 890077

CUNLIFFE, Christopher John. b 55. Ch Ch Ox BA77 MA81 DPhil81 Trin Coll Cam BA82 MA86 ARHistS94. Westcott Ho Cam 80. **d** 83 **p** 84. C Chesterfield St Mary and All SS *Derby* 83-85; Chapl Linc Coll Ox 85-89; Chapl Guildhall Sch of Music & Drama 89-91; Chapl City Univ *Lon* 89-91; Voc Officer and Selection Sec ABM 91-97; Perm to Offic *S'wark* from 91; Dir Professional Min *Lon* from 97; Lic to Offic from 97. *London Diocesan House, 36 Causton Street, London SW1P 4AU* Tel 0171-932 1100 Fax 932 1112

CUNLIFFE, Gerald Thomas. b 35. Linc Th Coll 74. **d** 76 **p** 77. C Sidcup St Jo *Roch* 76-80; C Pembury 80-82; V Lamorbey H Redeemer 82-89; V Riverhead w Dunton Green from 89. *The Vicarage, Riverhead, Sevenoaks, Kent TN13 3BS* Tel (01732) 455736

CUNLIFFE, Harold. b 28. St Aid Birkenhead 57. **d** 60 **p** 61. C Hindley All SS *Liv* 60-64; V Everton St Chad w Ch Ch 64-69; R Golborne 70-93; rtd 93; Perm to Offic *Liv* from 93. *51 Greenfields Crescent, Ashton-in-Makerfield, Wigan, Lancs WN4 8QY* Tel (01942) 274021

CUNLIFFE, Canon Helen Margaret. b 54. St Hilda's Coll Ox BA77 MA78. Westcott Ho Cam 81. **dss** 83 **d** 87 **p** 94. Chesterfield St Mary and All SS *Derby* 83-85; Ox St Mary V w St Cross and St Pet *Ox* 86-89; Par Dn 87-89; Chapl Nuff Coll Ox 86-89; TD Clapham TM *S'wark* 89-94; TV 94-96; Can Res S'wark Cathl from 96; Chapl Welcare from 96. *35 Oswin Street, London SE11 4TF*

CUNLIFFE, Peter Henry. b 54. SRN77 RSCN79 RCN83 Univ of Wales MA93 Lon Univ DN84. Trin Coll Bris DipHE94. **d** 94 **p** 95. C Carshalton Beeches *S'wark* 94-95; C Reigate St Mary from 95. *3 Ringwood Avenue, Redhill, Surrey RH1 2DY* Tel (01737) 762593

CUNNINGHAM, Dr Arthur. b 48. Man Univ PhD95. Inst of Chr Tr Dallas DipMin79 Oak Hill Th Coll DipHE87 BA88 Lon Bible Coll MA89 N Ord Course 92. **d** 93 **p** 94. C Walkden Moor *Man* 93; C Walkden Moor w Lt Hulton 93-96; Chapl Salford Coll 93-96; C Camelot Par *B & W* 96; Chapl Yeovil College from 96; C Camelot Par from 96. *6 The Close, North Cadbury, Yeovil, Somerset BA22 7DX* Tel (01963) 440469 E-mail arthur.cunningham@ukonline.co.uk

CUNNINGHAM, Brian James. b 65. York Univ BA88. Ripon Coll Cuddesdon BA91. **d** 92 **p** 93. C Merrow *Guildf* 92-96; C Kennington St Jo w St Jas *S'wark* from 96. *96 Vassall Road, London SW9 6JA* Tel 0171-582 2162

CUNNINGHAM, Philip John. b 52. St Jo Coll Dur BA74 PGCE75 MA85. N Ord Course 93. **d** 95 **p** 96. NSM York St Luke *York* 95-97; NSM York St Olave w St Giles from 97. *9 Upper Newborough Street, York YO3 7AR* Tel (01904) 647657

CUNNINGHAM, Robert Stewart. b 16. **d** 59 **p** 60. C Belfast St Mary *Conn* 59-62; C Belfast All SS 62-63; I Portglenone 63-74; I Belfast Whiterock 74-83; I Sallaghy *Clogh* 83-86; I Monaghan w Tydavnet and Kilmore 86-91; Can Clogh Cathl 88-89; Preb Clogh Cathl 89-91; rtd 91. *19 Edenaveys Crescent, Newry Road, Armagh BT60 1NT* Tel (01861) 527868

CUNNINGTON, Andrew Thomas. b 56. Southn Univ BTh86. Sarum & Wells Th Coll 82. **d** 85 **p** 86. C Ifield *Chich* 85-89; TV Haywards Heath St Wilfrid 89-94; V Midhurst from 94; R Woolbeding from 94. *The Vicarage, June Lane, Midhurst, W Sussex GU29 9EW* Tel (01730) 813339

CUNNINGTON, Miss Averil. b 41. St Mary's Coll Cheltenham CertEd61 Man Univ BA68 MEd73. N Ord Course 93. **d** 95 **p** 96. NSM Milnrow *Man* from 95. *Alston Londes, 629 Huddersfield Road, Lees, Oldham OL4 3PY* Tel 0161-624 9614

CUNNINGTON, Edgar Alan. b 37. Oak Hill Th Coll 68. **d** 70 **p** 71. C Highbury Ch Ch *Lon* 70-73; P-in-c W Holloway St Dav 73-76; V Martham *Nor* 76-83; V W Somerton 76-83; V Martham w Repps w Bastwick 83-89; RD Flegg (Gt Yarmouth) 84-87; TV Trunch 89-96; P-in-c Lyng, Sparham, Elsing and Bylaugh 96-97; P-in-c Bawdeswell w Foxley 96-97; R Lyng, Sparham, Elsing, Bylaugh, Bawdeswell etc from 97. *The Rectory, Rectory Road, Lyng, Norwich NR9 5RA* Tel (01603) 872381

CUNNINGTON, Howard James. b 56. Southn Univ BA77 St Jo Coll Dur PGCE78. Trin Coll Bris ADMT92. **d** 92 **p** 93. C Ex St Leon w H Trin *Ex* 92-96; V Sandown Ch Ch *Portsm* from 96. *The Vicarage, 26 Nunwell Street, Sandown, Isle of Wight PO36 9DE* Tel (01983) 402548

CUPITT, Don. b 34. Trin Hall Cam BA55 MA58 Bris Univ Hon DLitt84. Westcott Ho Cam 57. **d** 59 **p** 60. C Salford St Phil w St Steph *Man* 59-62; Vice-Prin Westcott Ho Cam 62-66; Lic to Offic *Ely* 63-94; Dean Em Coll Cam 66-91; Asst Lect Div Cam Univ 68-73; Lect 73-96; rtd 96. *Emmanuel College, Cambridge CB2 3AP*

CURD, Christine Veronica Letsom. b 51. Bris Univ BA. Oak Hill Th Coll 84 WMMTC 88. **d** 89 **p** 94. NSM Widecombe-in-the-Moor, Leusdon, Princetown etc *Ex* 89-93; Asst Chapl HM Pris Channings Wood from 92; NSM Bovey Tracey SS Pet, Paul and Thos w Hennock *Ex* from 94. *The Vicarage, Ilsington, Newton Abbot, Devon TQ13 9RW* Tel (01364) 661245 Fax (01803) 813175

CURD, Clifford John Letsom. b 45. RNT Qu Eliz Coll Lon SRN. Oak Hill Th Coll 84. **d** 86 **p** 87. C Stone Ch Ch *Lich* 86-89; C Stone Ch Ch and Oulton 89; TV Widecombe-in-the-Moor, Leusdon, Princetown etc *Ex* 89-93; P-in-c Ilsington from 93. *The Vicarage, Ilsington, Newton Abbot, Devon TQ13 9RW* Tel (01364) 661245

CURGENVEN, Peter. b 10. MBE45. CCC Cam BA33 MA36. Cuddesdon Coll 48. **d** 49 **p** 50. C Goring-by-Sea *Chich* 49-51; Chapl Cuddesdon Coll 51-53; Recruitment Sec CACTM 53-54; Gen Sec 54-59; V Goring-by-Sea *Chich* 59-70; R Rotherfield 70-79; RD E Grinstead 75-77; rtd 79; Perm to Offic *Sarum* from 79; Perm to Offic *B & W* 81-93. *Tretawn, 2 Church Hill, Marnhull, Sturminster Newton, Dorset DT10 1PU* Tel (01258) 820802

CURL, Roger William. b 50. BA BD DPhil. Oak Hill Th Coll. **d** 82 **p** 83. C Cromer *Nor* 82-86; C Sevenoaks St Nic *Roch* 86-88; V Fulham St Mary N End *Lon* from 88. *St Mary's Vicarage, 2 Edith Road, London W14 9BA* Tel 0171-602 1996

CURNEW, Dr Brian Leslie. b 48. Qu Coll Ox BA69 DPhil77 MA77 DipTh78. Ripon Coll Cuddesdon 77. **d** 79 **p** 80. C Sandhurst *Ox* 79-82; Tutor St Steph Ho Ox 82-87; V Fishponds St Mary *Bris* 87-94; TR Ludlow, Ludford, Ashford Carbonell etc *Heref* from 94. *The Rectory, 4 College Street, Ludlow, Shropshire SY8 1AN* Tel (01584) 874988

CURNOCK, Mrs Karen Susan. b 50.. Linc Th Coll BTh74. **d** 95 **p** 97. NSM Graffoe Gp *Linc* 95-96; Sec DBF *Sarum* from 96; NSM Chalke Valley W from 96. *Ashlands, Newtown, Broad Chalke, Salisbury SP5 5DS* Tel (01722) 411922

CURNOW, Terence Peter. b 37. Univ of Wales (Lamp) BA62 DipTh63. **d** 63 **p** 64. C Llanishen and Lisvane *Llan* 63-71; Youth Chapl 67-71; Asst Chapl K Coll Taunton 71-74; Chapl Taunton Sch 74-84; Ho Master from 84; Perm to Offic *B & W* from 84. *Fairwater, Taunton School, Taunton, Somerset TA2 6AD* Tel (01823) 275988

CURRAH, Michael Ewart. b 31. Down Coll Cam BA54 MA58. Sarum Th Coll 54. **d** 56 **p** 57. C Calne *Sarum* 56-60; V Southbroom 60-69; Perm to Offic 70-88; Asst Master Woodroffe Sch Lyme Regis 71-85; Hon C Taunton H Trin *B & W* 88-96; rtd 96; Perm to Offic *B & W* from 96. *123 South Road, Taunton, Somerset TA1 3ED* Tel (01823) 284057

CURRAN, Patrick Martin Stanley. b 56. Southn Univ BTh84. K Coll (NS) BA80 Chich Th Coll 80. **d** 84 **p** 85. C Heavitree w Ex St Paul *Ex* 84-87; Bp's Chapl to Students *Bradf* 87-93; Chapl Bonn w Cologne *Eur* from 93. *c/o The British Embassy, Friedrich-Ebert Allee 77, 53113 Bonn, Germany* Tel Bonn (228) 234061 or 384925

CURRAN, Thomas Heinrich. b 49. Toronto Univ BA72 Dalhousie Univ Canada MA75 Hatf Coll Dur PhD91. Atlantic Sch of Th MTS80. **d** 78 **p** 79. Canada 77-81 and from 92; Chapl Hatf Coll Dur 88-92. *Tacoma RPO, Box 28010, Dartmouth, Nova Scotia, Canada, B2W 6E2*

CURRELL, Miss Linda Anne. b 62. K Alfred's Coll Win BEd84. Trin Coll Bris BA92. **d** 92 **p** 94. Par Dn Tunbridge Wells St Mark *Roch* 92-94; C 94-97; TV Walthamstow St Mary w St Steph *Chelmsf* 97; TV Walthamstow from 97. *St Stephen's Vicarage, 41 Fraser Road, London E17 9DD* Tel 0181-521 1361

CURRIE, Piers William Edward. b 13. MC44. BNC Ox BA35 MA62. EAMTC 79. **d** 80 **p** 81. Hon C Holt *Nor* 80-82; P-in-c Baconsthorpe and Hempstead 84-85; Perm to Offic 85-86; Hon C Blakeney w Cley, Wiveton, Glandford etc 86-89; Hon C Nor St Mary in the Marsh 90-96; Hon PV Nor Cathl 94-96; Hon C Glaven Gp from 97. *10 Meadow Close, Holt, Norwich NR25 6JP* Tel (01263) 713266

CURRIE, Stuart William. b 53. Hertf Coll Ox MA79 Fitzw Coll Cam BA85 CertEd. Westcott Ho Cam 82. **d** 85 **p** 86. C Whitley Ch Ch *Ox* 85-89; TV Banbury 89-94; V Barbourne *Worc* from 94. *St Stephen's Vicarage, 1 Beech Avenue, Worcester WR3 8PZ* Tel (01905) 452169

CURRIE, Walter. b 39. Lon Univ DipTh66. Tyndale Hall Bris 64. **d** 67 **p** 68. C Cromer *Nor* 67-70; C Macclesfield St Mich *Ches* 70-74; R Postwick *Nor* 74-87; Chapl Jas Paget Hosp Gorleston 87-94; Chapl Jas Paget Hosp NHS Trust Gorleston from 94. *11 Langham Green, Blofield, Norwich NR13 4LD* Tel (01603) 713484

CURRIE, William George. b 08. Clifton Th Coll 38. **d** 41 **p** 42. C Chadwell Heath *Chelmsf* 41-44; P-in-c Becontree St Alb 44-45; R

Holton w Bratton St Maur *B & W* 45-51; R Abbas Combe 51-60; V Kingston Lacy and Shapwick *Sarum* 60-65; V Lt Bedwyn 65-81; V Gt Bedwyn 65-81; V Savernake Forest 65-81; rtd 81. *The Old School House, Savernake, Marlborough, Wilts SN8 3BG* Tel (01672) 870267

CURRIN, John. b 56. Keele Univ CertEd78 Birm Poly DipMathEd87. St Jo Coll Nottm DTS92 MA93. **d** 93 **p** 94. C Eastwood *S'well* from 93. *26 Coppice Drive, Eastwood, Nottingham NG16 3PL* Tel (01773) 712395

CURRY, Anthony Bruce. b 31. ARCO49 St Edm Hall Ox BA53 MA56. Wells Th Coll 53. **d** 55 **p** 56. C Northfleet *Roch* 55-56; Chapl K Sch Cant 56-61; R Penshurst *Roch* 61-75; Dir Music Kelly Coll Tavistock 75-85; Hon C Calstock *Truro* 75-85; R Brasted *Roch* 85-93; rtd 93. *L'Ecurie, Montceau-Echarnant, 21360 Bligny-Sur-Ouche, France* Tel France (33) 80 20 25 12

CURRY, Bruce. b 39. Dur Univ BA61. Wells Th Coll 61. **d** 63 **p** 64. C Shepton Mallet *B & W* 63-67; C Cheam *S'wark* 67-71; R W Walton *Ely* 71-78; V St Neots 78-94; RD St Neots from 90; P-in-c Everton w Tetworth from 94; P-in-c Abbotsley from 94; P-in-c Waresley from 94. *The Vicarage, Everton, Sandy, Beds SG19 3JY* Tel (01767) 691827

CURRY, David John. b 24. St Cath Coll Cam BA48 MA58 DipTh. Oak Hill Th Coll 73. **d** 74 **p** 75. C Watford *St Alb* 74-77; V Whitehall Park St Andr Hornsey Lane *Lon* 77-82; P-in-c Heydon w Lt Chishall *Chelmsf* 82; R Heydon w Gt and Lt Chishill 82-88; rtd 89; Perm to Offic *Chich* from 89. *3 St Mary's Cottages, Rectory Lane, Pulborough, W Sussex RH20 2AD* Tel (01798) 873409

CURRY, Canon George Christopher. b 14. TCD BA42 MA55 Div Test. **d** 44 **p** 45. I Edenderry *D & R* 57-64; I Edenderry w Clanabogan 64-86; RD Newtownstewart and Omagh 60; Can Derry Cathl 79-86; rtd 86. *8 Rutherglen Park, Bangor, Co Down BT19 1DX* Tel (01247) 455970

CURRY, George Robert. b 51. JP90. Bede Coll Dur BA72. Cranmer Hall Dur DipTh74 Oak Hill Th Coll DPS76. **d** 76 **p** 77. C Denton Holme *Carl* 76-81; V Low Elswick *Newc* from 81; P-in-c High Elswick St Paul from 97. *St Stephen's Vicarage, Clumber Street, Newcastle upon Tyne NE4 7ST* Tel 0191-273 4680

CURRY, James Sebastian. b 63. Hatf Coll Dur BA84. Ripon Coll Cuddesdon BTh93. **d** 93 **p** 94. C Four Oaks *Birm* 93-96; C Erdington St Barn from 96. *62 Dunvegan Road, Birmingham B24 9HH* Tel 0121-382 6169

CURRY, Thomas Christopher (Tom). b 47. Sarum & Wells Th Coll 71. **d** 74 **p** 75. C Bradford-on-Avon *Sarum* 74-78; Asst Chapl Hurstpierpoint Coll Hassocks 78-82; P-in-c The Donheads *Sarum* from 82; RD Chalke 87-92. *The Rectory, Donhead St Andrew, Shaftesbury, Dorset SP7 9DZ* Tel (01747) 828370

CURSON, James Desmond. b 30. Keble Coll Ox BA54 MA60. St Steph Ho Ox 54. **d** 56 **p** 57. C Teddington St Alb *Lon* 56-58; C Ruislip St Martin 58-62; V Tottenham St Paul 62-67; V Hockley *Chelmsf* 67-75; Chapl HM Borstal Bullwood Hall 68-75; V Treverbyn *Truro* 75-79; P-in-c Marazion 79-85; P-in-c St Hilary w Perranuthnoe 81-83; R 83-93; rtd 93; Perm to Offic *Nor* from 93. *Roslyn, 3 Kenwyn Close, Holt, Norfolk NR25 6RS* Tel (01263) 712976

CURTIS, Bert. b 20. Lon Univ BCom42 BA46. Ripon Hall Ox. **d** 46 **p** 47. Perm to Offic *Carl* from 74. *Greystones, Embleton, Cockermouth, Cumbria CA13 9YP* Tel (017687) 76503

CURTIS, Clement Ernest. b 09. Ch Coll Cam BA32 MA36. Ely Th Coll 32. **d** 33 **p** 35. C Plumstead Ascension *S'wark* 33-37; C Poplar *Lon* 37-38; C Stepney St Aug w St Phil 38-46; V Wrawby *Linc* 46-61; V Gateshead St Chad Bensham *Dur* 61-74; rtd 74. *Park View Cottage, King's Arms Lane, Alston, Cumbria CA9 3JF* Tel (01434) 381693

CURTIS, Colin. b 47. ALA69 Open Univ BA80. LNSM course 80 St Jo Coll Nottm CertCS91. **d** 93 **p** 94. Hon C Clarkston *Glas* from 93. *78 Auldhouse Road, Glasgow G43 1UR* Tel 0141-569 4206

✠**CURTIS, The Most Revd Ernest Edwin.** b 06. CBE76. ARCS27 Lon Univ BSc27. Wells Th Coll 32. **d** 33 **p** 34 **c** 66. C Waltham Cross *St Alb* 33-36; Mauritius 37-44; C Portsea St Mary *Portsm* 44-47; V Portsea All SS 47-55; Chapl Portsm R Hosp 47-55; C-in-c Portsea St Agatha 54-55; V Locks Heath *Portsm* 55-66; RD Alverstoke 64-66; Bp Mauritius 66-76; Abp Indian Ocean 72-76; rtd 76; Asst Bp Portsm from 76. *5 Elizabeth Gardens, Havenstreet, Ryde, Isle of Wight PO33 4DU* Tel (01983) 883049

CURTIS, Frederick John. b 36. SS Coll Cam MA64. Ridley Hall Cam 77. **d** 79 **p** 80. C Chilvers Coton w Astley *Cov* 79-82; V Claverdon w Preston Bagot 82-87; V Allesley Park and Whoberley from 87. *St Christopher's Vicarage, 99 Buckingham Rise, Coventry CV5 9HF* Tel (01203) 672879

CURTIS, Canon Geoffrey John. b 35. Dur Univ BA57. Ripon Hall Ox 59. **d** 61 **p** 62. C Gosport Ch Ch *Portsm* 61-65; C Bedhampton 65-68; Producer Schs Broadcasting Dept BBC Lon 68-75; Dioc Communications Adv *Guildf* from 75; P-in-c Grayswood 75-91; Dir Grayswood Studio from 84; Hon Can Guildf Cathl from 87. *The Vicarage, Clammer Hill Road, Grayswood, Haslemere, Surrey GU27 2DZ* Tel (01428) 644208

CURTIS, Gerald Arthur. b 46. Lon Univ BA69. Sarum & Wells Th Coll 85. **d** 87 **p** 88. C Allington and Maidstone St Pet *Cant* 87-90; TV Gt Grimsby St Mary and St Jas *Linc* 90-95; P-in-c Morton w Hacconby 95-96; R Ringstone in Aveland Gp from 96. *Rippingale Rectory, Rippingale, Bourne, Lincs PE10 0SR* Tel (01778) 440380

CURTIS, Miss Jacqueline Elaine. b 60. Sarum & Wells Th Coll 87. **d** 90 **p** 94. Par Dn Bridport *Sarum* 90-94; C 94-95; TV Melbury from 95. *The Vicarage, Maiden Newton, Dorchester, Dorset DT2 0AT* Tel (01300) 320284

CURTIS, Mrs Jane Darwent. b 64. Leic Univ BA86. Linc Th Coll BTh93. **d** 93 **p** 94. Par Dn Oadby *Leic* 93-94; C 94-96; Chapl De Montfort Univ from 96; C Leic H Spirit from 96. *St Philip's House, 2A Stoughton Drive North, Leicester LE5 5UB* Tel 0116-273 6204

CURTIS, John Durston. b 43. Lich Th Coll 65. **d** 68 **p** 69. C Coseley Ch Ch *Lich* 68-71; C Sedgley All SS 71-74; CF 74-79; P-in-c Newton Valence *Win* 79-82; P-in-c Selborne 79-82; R Newton Valence, Selborne and E Tisted w Colemore 82-87; R Marchwood from 87. *St John's Vicarage, Vicarage Road, Marchwood, Southampton SO40 4UZ* Tel (01703) 861496

CURTIS, Layton Richard. b 61. Leic Univ BSc84 PGCE85. Linc Th Coll BTh93. **d** 93 **p** 94. C Knighton St Mary Magd *Leic* 93-96; C Leic St Phil from 96. *St Philip's House, 2A Stoughton Drive North, Leicester LE5 5UB* Tel 0116-273 6204

CURTIS, Peter Bernard. b 35. St Pet Hall Ox BA60 MA64. Westcott Ho Cam 60. **d** 62 **p** 63. C Warsop *S'well* 62-65; Chapl Dur Univ *Dur* 65-69; V Worle *B & W* 69-78; R Crewkerne w Wayford from 78. *The Rectory, Gouldsbrook Terrace, Crewkerne, Somerset TA18 7JA* Tel (01460) 72047

CURTIS, Thomas John (Tom). b 32. Pemb Coll Ox BA55 MA59 Lon Univ BD58. Clifton Th Coll 55. **d** 58 **p** 59. C Wandsworth All SS *S'wark* 58-61; Chile 61-71; R Saxmundham *St E* 71-77; V Cheltenham St Mark *Glouc* 77-84; TR 84-86; V Chipping Norton *Ox* 86-95; rtd 95. *Touchwood Cottage, Chapel Road, Saxstead, Woodbridge, Suffolk IP13 9QZ* Tel (01728) 685719

CURTIS, The Very Revd Wilfred Frank. b 23. AKC51. **d** 52 **p** 53. C High Wycombe All SS *Ox* 52-55; Area Sec (Dios Ex and Truro) CMS 55-65; Lic to Offic *Ex* 55-74; SW Sec CMS 62-65; Home Sec CMS 65-74; Provost Sheff 74-88; Hon Can N Maseno from 82; rtd 88; Perm to Offic *Ex* from 88; RD Okehampton 89-92. *Ashplant's Fingle Cottage, Church Gate, Drewsteignton, Exeter EX6 6QX* Tel (01647) 281253

CURTIS, Wilfrid Fitz-Harold. b 23. St Aug Coll Cant 47 Linc Th Coll 49. **d** 51 **p** 52. C New Sleaford *Linc* 51-53; Chapl Butlin's Skegness 53 and 60-62; Chapl Actor's Ch Union 53; C Skegness 53-57; Chapl Butlin's Filey 54-55; V Westcliff St Paul *Chelmsf* 57-60; CF (TA) 58-90; R Ingoldmells w Addlethorpe *Linc* 60-67; V Filey *York* 67-90; rtd 90; P-in-c Hackness w Harwood Dale *York* from 91; Chapl St Catherine's Hospice Scarborough from 91. *23 Scholes Park Road, Scarborough, N Yorkshire YO12 6RE* Tel (01723) 366410

CURWEN, David. b 38. St Cath Coll Cam BA62. Cuddesdon Coll 62. **d** 64 **p** 65. C Orford St Andr *Liv* 64-67; Ind Chapl *Cant* 67-77 and 83-84; C S'wark Ch Ch *S'wark* 78-83; Ind Chapl 78-83 and 85-88; Dioc Soc Resp Adv *St E* 88-93; Dioc Adv for Continuing Minl Educn from 93. *41 Cuckfield Avenue, Ipswich IP3 8SA* Tel (01473) 727632

CURZEN, Prof Peter. b 31. MRCOG62 FRCOG70 Lon Univ BSc52 MB, BS55 MD66. Sarum & Wells Th Coll 93. **d** 94 **p** 95. NSM Bemerton *Sarum* from 94. *2 Bishop's Drive, Harnham Wood, Salisbury SP2 8NZ* Tel (01722) 412713

CUTCLIFFE, Neil Robert. b 50. NUU BA72 TCD BA72. **d** 75 **p** 76. C Belfast St Mary *Conn* 75-78; C Lurgan Ch the Redeemer *D & D* 78-80; I Garrison w Slavin and Belleek *Clogh* 80-86; I Mossley *Conn* from 86. *558 Doagh Road, Mossley, Newtownabbey, Co Antrim BT36 6TA* Tel (01232) 832726

CUTHBERT, Frederick Norton. b 07. Worc Ord Coll 67. **d** 68 **p** 69. C Cov St Marg *Cov* 68-73; C Coventry Caludon 73-79; rtd 79; Perm to Offic *Cov* from 79. *2 Harefield Road, Coventry CV2 4DF* Tel (01203) 452248

CUTHBERT, Dr John. b 52. Edin Univ BSc76 PhD80. Coates Hall Edin BD92. **d** 92 **p** 93. Chapl St Mary's Cathl *Edin* from 92; C Edin St Mary from 92. *33 Manor Place, Edinburgh EH3 7EB* Tel 0131-226 3389

CUTHBERT, John Hamilton. b 34. Univ of Wales (Lamp) BA59. Coll of Resurr Mirfield 59. **d** 61 **p** 62. C Cov St Pet *Cov* 61-64; Australia 64-69; C Willesden St Andr *Lon* 69-72; C Sheff Parson Cross St Cecilia *Sheff* 72-74; V Lavender Hill Ascension *S'wark* 74-97; rtd 97. *29 The Cloisters, Welwyn Garden City, Herts AL8 6DU* Tel (01707) 376748

CUTHBERTSON, Christopher Martin (Chris). b 48. K Coll Lon BD74 AKC74 CertEd75 MTh80. St Aug Coll Cant 75. **d** 76 **p** 77. C Whitstable All SS w St Pet *Cant* 76-79; Chapl Princess Marg R Free Sch Windsor 79-84; Perm to Offic *Win* from 84; Chapl Bp Wordsworth Sch Salisbury from 84. *14 Stephen Martin Gardens, Parsonage Park, Fordingbridge, Hants SP6 1RF* Tel (01425) 655865

CUTHBERTSON, John Dickon. b 19. Lon Univ BSc49. Oak Hill Th Coll 51. **d** 53 **p** 54. C Penn Fields *Lich* 53-56; R High Halstow w All Hallows and Hoo St Mary *Roch* 56-62; V W Hampstead St Cuth *Lon* 62-69; V Upper Holloway St Jo 69-77; R Stanstead w Shimplingthorne and Alpheton *St E* 77-84; P-in-c Lawshall

80-84; rtd 84; Perm to Offic *Ox* from 84. *86 Evans Road, Eynsham, Witney, Oxon OX8 1QS* Tel (01865) 880904

CUTHBERTSON, Raymond. b 52. AKC75. Coll of Resurr Mirfield 76. **d** 77 **p** 78. C Darlington St Mark w St Paul *Dur* 77-81; C Usworth 81-83; C Darlington St Cuth 83-86; V Shildon w Eldon from 86; RD Auckland 94-96. *St John's Vicarage, Central Parade, Shildon, Co Durham DL4 1DW* Tel (01388) 772122

CUTLER, Nicholas (Nick). b 59. St Jo Coll Cam MA84. St Jo Coll Nottm DTS94. **d** 94 **p** 95. C Cambridge St Phil *Ely* from 94. *99 Brooks Road, Cambridge CB1 3HP* Tel (01233) 412749

CUTLER, Robert Francis. b 37. Lon Univ BSc57. Clifton Th Coll 62. **d** 64 **p** 65. C Peckham St Mary Magd *S'wark* 64-68; C Redhill H Trin 68-70; Travel Sec Inter-Coll Chr Fellowship of IVF 70-74; Hon C Selly Hill St Steph *Birm* 70-74; Partner Interserve Internat 74-93; Bangladesh 74-93; Internat Fellowship Evangelical Students 74-85; Bible Students Fellowship of Bangladesh 85-93; V Rochdale Deeplish St Luke *Man* from 94. *St Luke's Vicarage, 9 Deeplish Road, Rochdale, Lancs OL11 1NY* Tel (01706) 354628

CUTLER, Roger Charles. b 49. MInstPkg76. Coll of Resurr Mirfield 86. **d** 88 **p** 89. C Walney Is *Carl* 88-91; Chapl RN from 91; Perm to Offic *Glas* from 91; Hon C Challoch w Newton Stewart from 95. *Royal Naval Chaplaincy Service, Room 203, Victory Building, HM Naval Base, Portsmouth PO1 3LS* Tel (01705) 727903 Fax 727112

CUTT, Canon Samuel Robert. b 25. Selw Coll Cam BA50 MA54. Cuddesdon Coll 51. **d** 53 **p** 54. C W Hartlepool St Aid *Dur* 53-56; Tutor St Boniface Coll Warminster 56-59; Sub Warden St Boniface Coll Warminster 59-65; Tutor Chich Th Coll 65-71; PV Chich Cathl *Chich* 66-71; Min Can St Paul's Cathl *Lon* 71-79; Lect K Coll Lon 73-79; P in O 75-79; Can Res Wells Cathl *B & W* 79-93; Chan 79-85; Treas 85-93; Dir of Ords 79-86; Warden Community of St Denys Warminster 87-93; rtd 93; Perm to Offic *Pet* from 94. *9 Eastfield Grove, Peterborough PE1 4BB* Tel (01733) 345197

CUTTELL, Jeffrey Charles. b 59. Birm Univ BSc80 PhD83 Sheff Univ MA92. Trin Coll Bris DipHE86. **d** 87 **p** 88. C Normanton *Wakef* 87-91; V 91-95; Producer Relig Progr BBC Radio Stoke from 95; Perm to Offic *Ches* from 95; Perm to Offic *Lich* from 95. *15 Henshall Drive, Sandbach, Cheshire CW11 1YN* Tel (01270) 766918

CUTTER, John Douglas. b 31. Lon Univ BD61. Chich Th Coll 56. **d** 59 **p** 60. C Blyth St Mary *Newc* 59-62; C Rugeley *Lich* 62-65; V Rocester 65-73; V Shrewsbury St Giles 73-83; R Yoxall 83-91; Dean's V Lich Cathl 83-91; rtd 91. *Little Wykeham, 111 Teg Down Meads, Winchester SO22 5NN* Tel (01962) 852203

CUTTING, Alastair Murray. b 60. Westhill Coll Birm BEd83. St Jo Coll Nottm LTh86 DPS87. **d** 87 **p** 88. C Woodlands *Sheff* 87-88; C Wadsley 89-91; C Uxbridge *Lon* 91-96; Chapl to the Nave and Uxbridge Town Cen 91-96; V Copthorne *Chich* from 96. *St John's Vicarage, Copthorne, Crawley, W Sussex RH10 3RD* Tel (01342) 712063 E-mail alastair@cutting.sonnet.co.uk

CUTTS, David. b 52. Van Mildert Coll Dur BSc73 Nottm Univ BA79. St Jo Coll Nottm BA77. **d** 80 **p** 81. C Ipswich St Matt *St E* 80-82; Bp's Dom Chapl 82-85; R Coddenham w Gosbeck and Hemingstone w Henley 85-94; RD Bosmere 92-94; V Ipswich St Marg from 94; RD Ipswich from 96. *St Margaret's Vicarage, 32 Constable Road, Ipswich IP4 2UW* Tel (01473) 253906

CUTTS, Elizabeth Joan Gabrielle. *See* STRICKLAND, Mrs Elizabeth Joan Gabrielle

CUTTS, Nigel Leonard. b 57. Sheff Univ BA86 BTh. Linc Th Coll 83. **d** 87 **p** 88. C Old Brampton and Loundsley Green *Derby* 87-89; C Chesterfield St Mary and All SS 89-91; V Morecambe St Barn *Blackb* from 91. *St Barnabas' Vicarage, 101 Regent Road, Morecambe, Lancs LA3 1AG* Tel (01524) 411283

CYSTER, Canon Raymond Frederick. b 13. CCC Ox BA35 MA40. Wycliffe Hall Ox 40. **d** 42 **p** 43. C Ipswich St Jo *St E* 42-45; Chapl Norwich Tr Coll 45-64; R Fenny Compton and Wormleighton *Cov* 64-76; Hon Can Cov Cathl 74-80; P-in-c Hampton Lucy w Charlecote 76-79; R Hampton Lucy w Charlecote and Loxley 79-80; rtd 80; Perm to Offic *Cov* from 80. *47 Cherry Orchard, Stratford-upon-Avon, Warks CV37 9AP* Tel (01789) 295012

CZERNIAWSKA EDGECUMBE, Mrs Irena Christine. b 59. Trin Coll Ox BA82. Oak Hill Th Coll 93. **d** 95 **p** 96. NSM De Beauvoir Town St Pet *Lon* from 95. *24 Calabria Road, London N5 1JA* Tel 0171-359 7526

D

DABBS, Roger Stevens. b 09. Bp Wilson Coll 29. **d** 32 **p** 33. C Birm St Thos *Birm* 32-35; Toc H Padre (E Midl) 35-38; V Cosby *Leic* 38-47; V Ashby-de-la-Zouch H Trin 47-53; RD Akeley W 48-53; R Jersey Grouville *Win* 53-74; rtd 74; Perm to Offic *Ex* from 74. *Flat 21, Bedford Park, Pearn Road, Plymouth PL3 5JF* Tel (01752) 774677

DABORN, Robert Francis. b 53. Keble Coll Ox BA74 MA78 Fitzw Coll Cam BA77. Ridley Hall Cam 75. **d** 78 **p** 79. C Mortlake w E Sheen *S'wark* 78-81; Chapl Collingwood and Grey Coll *Dur* 82-86; V Lapley w Wheaton Aston *Lich* 86-91; P-in-c Blymhill w Weston-under-Lizard 89-91; P-in-c Tibberton w Bolas Magna and Waters Upton from 91; Shropshire Local Min Adv from 91; P-in-c Childs Ercall 92-95; P-in-c Stoke upon Tern 92-95. *The Rectory, Tibberton, Newport, Shropshire TF10 8NN* Tel (01952) 550409

DACK, Miss Margaret Patricia. b 39. Offley Teacher Tr Coll TCert61. All Nations Chr Coll CDRS82 Oak Hill NSM Course 91. **d** 93 **p** 94. NSM Letchworth St Paul w Willian *St Alb* from 93. *91 Penn Way, Letchworth, Herts SG6 2SH* Tel (01462) 685168

DACK, Paul Marven. K Coll Lon AKC51 BD51. St Boniface Warminster. **d** 52 **p** 53. C Leckhampton St Pet *Glouc* 52-55; R Bourton on the Hill 55-61; R Quedgeley 61-82; P-in-c Hasfield w Tirley and Ashleworth 82-90; rtd 90; Perm to Offic *Glouc* from 90. *19 Arle Gardens, Cheltenham, Glos GL51 8HP* Tel (01242) 261627

DACRE, Roy Aubrey. b 17. AKC41 Lon Univ BD41. Linc Th Coll 41. **d** 41 **p** 42. C Basingstoke *Win* 41-47; CF 47-51; Hon CF 51; R Newnham, Nately Scures and Mapledurwell etc *Win* 51-59; V Alton St Lawr 59-66; Chapl Alton Gen Hosp 59-66; RD Alton 63-66; Hd Relig and Soc Studies Wombwell High Sch 66-82; rtd 82; Perm to Offic *Chich* from 83. *27 The Lawns, Sompting, Lancing, W Sussex BN15 0DT* Tel (01903) 754840

DADD, Alan Edward. b 50. St Jo Coll Nottm 77. **d** 78 **p** 79. C Bishopsworth *Bris* 78-81; V Springfield *Birm* 81-85; Chapl Poly Cen Lon 85-86; V Hanger Lane St Ann 86-93; rtd 93. *124 Chelsfield Lane, Orpington, Kent BR5 4PZ*

DADD, Canon Peter Wallace. b 38. Sheff Univ BA59. Qu Coll Birm 59. **d** 61 **p** 62. C Grays Thurrock *Chelmsf* 61-65; C Grantham St Wulfram *Linc* 65-70; C Grantham w Manthorpe 70-72; TV 72-73; V Haxey 73-90; RD Is of Axholme 82-90; V Gainsborough All SS from 90; Can and Preb Linc Cathl from 91. *All Saints' Vicarage, 32 Morton Terrace, Gainsborough, Lincs DN21 2RQ* Tel (01427) 612965

DADSON, Lawrence Michael (Mike). b 29. G&C Coll Cam MA56 Lon Univ BSc(Econ)64. St Deiniol's Hawarden 80. **d** 92 **p** 92. NSM Bramhall *Ches* from 92. *14 Yew Tree Park Road, Cheadle Hulme, Cheadle, Cheshire SK8 7EP* Tel 0161-485 2482

DADSON, Stephen Michael. b 57. BA. Cuddesdon Coll. **d** 84 **p** 85. C Wednesfield *Lich* 84-87; Lic to Offic *Ox* 88-91; Chapl Asst John Radcliffe Hosp Ox 88-91; Chapl Asst Radcliffe Infirmary Ox 88-91. *Laurel Cottage, Wareham, Dorset BH20 7AB* Tel (01929) 556786

DADSWELL, David Ian. b 58. New Coll Ox BA80 MA83. Westcott Ho Cam 80. **d** 83 **p** 84. C W Derby St Mary *Liv* 83-87; Chapl Brunel Univ *Lon* 87-96. *243 St Leonards Road, Windsor, Berks SL4 3DR* Tel (01753) 864827 E-mail se@cielo.demon.co.uk

DAFFERN, Adrian Mark. b 68. St Jo Coll Dur BA89. St Steph Ho Ox 90. **d** 92 **p** 93. C Lich St Chad *Lich* 92-95; TV Stafford from 95; Treas V Lich Cathl from 97. *St Bertelin's Vicarage, Holmcroft Road, Stafford ST16 1JG* Tel (01785) 252874

DAFFURN, Lionel William. b 19. DFC43. AKC49. **d** 50 **p** 51. C Rugby St Andr *Cov* 50-53; V Cov St Thos 53-57; R Brampton St Thos *Derby* 57-74; P-in-c Hindon w Chicklade w Pertwood *Sarum* 74-76; R E Knoyle, Hindon w Chicklade and Pertwood 76-84; rtd 84; Perm to Offic *Cov* from 84. *Bankside, Quineys Road, Stratford-upon-Avon, Warks CV37 9BW* Tel (01789) 292703

DAGGER, John Henry Kynaston. b 07. Selw Coll Cam BA31 MA35. Cuddesdon Coll. **d** 32 **p** 34. C Wolverhampton St Pet *Lich* 32-37; C W Bromwich All SS 37-40; Chapl RAFVR 40-46; Chapl RAF 46-61; R Sutton w Bignor *Chich* 61-77; R Barlavington 62-77; rtd 77; Perm to Offic *Win* from 78. *Greenways, Copthorne Lane, Fawley, Southampton SO45 1DP* Tel (01703) 891582

DAGGER, Kenneth (Ken). b 46. Bernard Gilpin Soc Dur 72 Cranmer Hall Dur 73. **d** 76 **p** 77. C Blackb St Jas *Blackb* 76-79; C Colne St Bart 79-81; R Hesketh w Becconsall 81-85; Deputation Appeals Org Children's Soc 85-89; C Lowton St Mary *Liv* 89-91; C Rainhill 91-94; TV Maghull from 94. *St James Vicarage, 23 Green Link, Maghull, Liverpool L31 8DW* Tel 0151-526 6626

DAGGETT, Michael Wayne. b 47. Portland State Univ BSc72. Ridley Hall Cam 84. **d** 86 **p** 87. C Tyldesley w Shakerley *Man* 86-90; V Swinton H Rood from 90. *Holy Rood Vicarage, 33 Moorside Road, Swinton, Manchester M27 3EL* Tel 0161-794 2464

DAGLEISH, John. b 38. ACIB74 BAC Acc85 Lon Univ DipRS78 UKRC Reg Ind Counsellor 96. S'wark Ord Course 75. **d** 78 **p** 79. NSM Riddlesdown *S'wark* from 78; NSM All Hallows by the Tower etc *Lon* 79-89; Chapl Asst Guy's Hosp Lon 87-89. *42 Brancaster Lane, Purley, Surrey CR8 1HF* Tel 0181-660 6060

DAGLISH, John Davis. b 44. RMCS BSc70. Cranmer Hall Dur 76. **d** 77 **p** 78. C Ormesby *York* 77-79; C Kirk Ella 79-82; V Hull St Cuth from 82. *St Cuthbert's Vicarage, 112 Marlborough Avenue, Hull HU5 3JX* Tel (01482) 42848

DAGNALL, Bernard. b 44. CChem MRSC K Coll Lon BSc65 AKC65 Ox Univ BA75 MA78. St Steph Ho Ox 72. **d** 75 **p** 76. C Stanningley St Thos *Ripon* 75-76; C Lightbowne *Man* 76-78; C-in-c Grahame Park St Aug CD *Lon* 78-84; V Earley St Nic *Ox* 84-91; Ind Chapl 85-91; TR N Huddersfield *Wakef* 91-93; TV Newbury *Ox* from 93. *The Vicarage, 1 Chesterfield Road, Newbury, Berks RG14 7QA* Tel (01635) 40387

DAILEY, Arthur John Hugh. b 25. Lon Univ BScEng45. Clifton Th Coll 63. **d** 65 **p** 66. C Wandsworth All SS *S'wark* 65-70; V Frogmore *St Alb* 70-81; RD Aldenham 75-79; C St Alb St Paul 82-90; rtd 90; Perm to Offic *St Alb* from 90. *24 Clifton Street, St Albans, Herts AL1 3RY* Tel (01727) 850639

DAILEY, Douglas Grant. b 56. Nottm Univ BTh88. Linc Th Coll 85. **d** 88 **p** 89. C Leominster *Heref* 88-91; USA from 91. *PO Box 1103, Statesville, NC, 28677 USA*

DAIMOND, John Ellerbeck. b 39. Dur Univ BA61. Ripon Hall Ox 61. **d** 63 **p** 64. C Caverswall *Lich* 63-66; Chapl RAF 66-85; Asst Chapl-in-Chief RAF 85-91; QHC 89-91; V Shawbury *Lich* 91-95; V Stanton on Hine Heath 91-95; R Moreton Corbet 91-95.

✠**DAIN, The Rt Revd Arthur John.** b 12. OBE79. Ridley Hall Cam 59. **d** 59 **p** 59 **c** 65. Australia 59-82; Asst Bp Sydney 65-82; rtd 82; Perm to Offic *Chich* 87-90. *14 Kipling Court, Winnals Park, Haywards Heath, W Sussex RH16 1EX* Tel (01444) 453091

DAIN, Frederick Ronald. OBE80. Jes Coll Ox BA31 MA43. St Aug Coll Cant 61. **d** 62 **p** 64. Kenya 62-80; Perm to Offic *St Alb* 80-92. *Pax Hill Residential Home, Bentley, Farnham, Surrey GU34 5SJ* Tel (01420) 22251

DAINTREE, Geoffrey Thomas. b 54. Bris Univ BSc77. Trin Coll Bris 78. **d** 81 **p** 82. C Old Hill H Trin *Worc* 81-85; C Tunbridge Wells St Jo *Roch* 85-89; V Framfield *Chich* from 89; RD Uckfield from 96. *The Vicarage, Framfield, Uckfield, E Sussex TN22 5NH* Tel (01825) 890365

DAINTY, James Ernest (Jim). b 46. Open Univ BA86 Lon Bible Coll DipTh68 ALBC68 AMIC. Cranmer Hall Dur 71. **d** 73 **p** 74. C Normanton *Wakef* 73-76; C Gillingham St Mark *Roch* 76-78; V Barnsley St Geo *Wakef* 78-88; Chapl Barnsley Distr Gen Hosp 78-88; Chapl Seacroft Hosp Leeds 88-94; Chapl Killingbeck and Meanwood Park Hosps Leeds 88-94; P-in-c Turnham Green Ch Ch *Lon* from 94. *The Vicarage, 2 Wellesley Road, London W4 4BL* Tel 0181-994 1617 E-mail jimdainty@aol.com

DAKIN (née HOLLETT), Mrs Catherine Elaine (Cathy). b 53. Qu Eliz Coll Lon BSc74 DipTh90. St Jo Coll Nottm 88. **d** 90. Par Dn Horley *S'wark* 90-93; NSM Heydon, Gt and Lt Chishill, Chrishall etc *Chelmsf* 93-97; NSM Gt and Lt Maplestead w Gestingthorpe from 97. *The Vicarage, Church Street, Great Maplestead, Halstead, Essex CO9 2RG* Tel (01787) 60294

DAKIN, Canon John Edward Clifford. b 10. AKC40. **d** 40 **p** 41. C E Retford *S'well* 40-42; CF (EC) 42-46; C-in-c Bircotes CD *S'well* 46-50; V Colston Bassett 50-57; R Langar 50-57; R Thrapston *Pet* 57-78; RD Thrapston 59-70; Can Pet Cathl 71-78; rtd 78; Lic to Offic *Pet* 78-85; Perm to Offic from 85. *8 Derling Drive, Raunds, Wellingborough, Northants NN9 6LF* Tel (01933) 623069

DAKIN, Peter David. b 57. Wye Coll Lon BSc79. St Jo Coll Nottm DTS91. **d** 91 **p** 92. NSM Southgate *Chich* 91-93; C Heydon, Gt and Lt Chishill, Chrishall etc *Chelmsf* 93-97; P-in-c Gt and Lt Maplestead w Gestingthorpe from 97. *The Vicarage, Church Street, Great Maplestead, Halstead, Essex CO9 2RG* Tel (01787) 60294

DAKIN, Reginald James Blanchard. b 25. S'wark Ord Course 66. **d** 70 **p** 71. C Preston Ascension *Lon* 70-74; C Greenhill St Jo 74-76; P-in-c Littleton 76-80; R 80-95; CF (ACF) 78-95; Warden for Readers (Kensington Episc Area) 88-95; rtd 95; Perm to Offic *Nor* from 95. *22 Heywood Avenue, Diss, Norfolk IP22 3DN* Tel (01379) 641167

DAKIN, Canon Stanley Frederick. b 30. Roch Th Coll 63. **d** 65 **p** 66. C Meole Brace *Lich* 65-68; V 68-72; R Sutton 68-72; Kenya 72-75; P-in-c Nettlebed *Ox* 75-81; P-in-c Bix w Pishill 77-81; P-in-c Highmore 78-81; R Nettlebed w Bix and Highmore 81; V Ealing Dean St Jo *Lon* 81-84; P-in-c Ealing St Jas 81-84; V W Ealing St Jo w St Jas 84-92; Hon Can Mombasa from 89; CA from 92. *c/o Church Army, Independents Road, London SE3 9LG* Tel 0181-318 1226

DALAIS, Duncan John. b 56. St Paul's Grahamstown. **d** 83 **p** 84. S Africa 83-87; C Chingford SS Pet and Paul *Chelmsf* 87-92; V Aldersbrook from 92. *St Gabriel's Vicarage, 12 Aldersbrook Road, London E12 5HH* Tel 0181-989 0315

DALBY, John. b 43. Cuddesdon Coll 72. **d** 74 **p** 75. C Baildon *Bradf* 74-78; P-in-c Austwick 78-85; P-in-c Clapham 84-85; V Clapham-with-Keasden and Austwick from 85. *The Vicarage, Austwick, Lancaster LA2 8BE* Tel (015242) 51313

DALBY, The Ven Dr John Mark Meredith. b 38. Ex Coll Ox BA61 MA65 Nottm Univ PhD77. Ripon Hall Ox 61. **d** 63 **p** 64. C Hambleden *Ox* 63-68; C Medmenham 66-68; V Birm St Pet *Birm* 68-75; RD Birm City 73-75; Hon C Tottenham All Hallows *Lon* 75-80; Selection Sec and Sec Cttee for Th Educn ACCM 75-80; V Worsley *Man* 80-84; TR 84-91; AD Eccles 87-91; Adn Rochdale from 91. *21 Belmont Way, Rochdale, Lancs OL12 6HR* Tel (01706) 48640 Fax as telephone

DALE, Miss Barbara. b 48. Cranmer Hall Dur 78. **dss** 81 **d** 87 **p** 94. N Wingfield, Pilsley and Tupton *Derby* 81-87; Par Dn 87-90; Par Dn N Wingfield, Clay Cross and Pilsley 90-94; TD 94; TV from 94. *The Vicarage, Ankerbold Road, Tupton, Chesterfield, Derbyshire S42 6BX* Tel (01246) 864524

DALE, Ms Christine. b 62. Ox Poly DipCart82. Trin Coll Bris BA94. **d** 94 **p** 95. C Thatcham *Ox* from 94. *28 Masefield Road, Newbury, Berks RG13 4AS* Tel (01635) 872004

DALE, David William. b 35. Open Univ BA74 MPhil87 Heref Coll of FE CertEd78. Wells Th Coll 61. **d** 63 **p** 64. C Weybridge *Guildf* 63-66; C Farnham 67-69; P-in-c Downton w Burrington and Aston and Elton *Heref* 69-76; P-in-c Brampton Bryan w Lingen 69-76; V Leintwardine 69-76; P-in-c Wigmore w Leinthall Starkes 72-76; V Heref H Trin 76-81; Chapl Shiplake Coll Henley 81-91; Lic to Offic *Ox* 85-92; Chapl Reading Sch 91-92; P-in-c Ryde All SS *Portsm* 92; V from 92. *3 Coniston Drive, Ryde, Isle of Wight PO33 3AE* Tel (01983) 611749

DALE, Eric Stephen. b 24. Roch Th Coll 63. **d** 65 **p** 66. C Kippax *Ripon* 65-67; C Fulford *York* 67-69; V Askham Bryan 69-70; V Askham Richard 69-70; V Askham Bryan w Askham Richard 70-78; Chapl HM Pris Askham Grange 69-78; Chapl HM Pris Wakef 78-79; Chapl HM Pris Gartree 79-82; Chapl HM Pris Leeds 82-89; rtd 89. *31 Kirkwood Lane, Leeds LS16 7EN* Tel 0113-230 0766

DALE, Miss Olive Sylvia. b 44. Stockwell Coll of Educn TCert66. Faculte de Theologie Evangelique Vaux-sur-Seine France MScRel76 W of England Minl Tr Course 91. **d** 94 **p** 97. C Highley *Heref* 94-96; C Leominster from 96. *The Vicarage, 1A School Road, Leominster, Hereford HR6 8NJ* Tel (01568) 612124

DALES, Douglas John. b 52. FRHistS90 Ch Ch Ox BA74 MA78 BD89. Cuddesdon Coll 74. **d** 77 **p** 78. C Shepperton *Lon* 77-81; C Ely 81-83; Chapl Marlborough Coll from 84; Hd of RE from 84. *Hillside, Bath Road, Marlborough, Wilts SN8 1NN* Tel (01672) 514557 or 515511

DALEY, David Michael. b 50. Oak Hill Th Coll BA90. **d** 92 **p** 92. C Enfield Ch Ch Trent Park *Lon* 92-94; V Chitts Hill St Cuth from 94. *St Cuthbert's Vicarage, 85 Wolves Lane, London N22 5JD* Tel 0181-888 6178

DALEY, Preb Victor Leonard. b 38. Chich Th Coll 76. **d** 78 **p** 79. C Durrington *Chich* 78-81; C Somerton w Compton Dundon, the Charltons etc *B & W* 81-87; P-in-c Cheddar 87-88; V from 88; RD Axbridge from 91; Preb Wells Cathl from 97. *The Vicarage, Church Street, Cheddar, Somerset BS27 3RF* Tel (01934) 742535

DALL, Kathleen Ria Agnes. b 32. St Andr Univ MA54 Edin Univ DipEd57 HDipRE57. **dss** 82 **d** 86 **p** 94. NSM Dundee St Paul *Bre* 82-89; D-in-c Muchalls 89-94; P-in-c from 94. *St Ternan's Rectory, Muchalls, Stonehaven, Kincardineshire AB3 3PP* Tel (01569) 730625

DALLAWAY, Philip Alan. b 48. Chich Th Coll 80. **d** 81 **p** 82. C Newbury *Ox* 81-83; C Newport Pagnell w Lathbury 83-85; C Newport Pagnell w Lathbury and Moulsoe 85; V Stewkley w Soulbury and Drayton Parslow 85-92; P-in-c Didcot All SS from 92. *The Rectory, 140 Lydalls Road, Didcot, Oxon OX11 7EA* Tel (01235) 813244

DALLING, Roger Charles. b 26. Lon Univ BSc53 DChemEng55. S Dios Minl Tr Scheme 79. **d** 83 **p** 84. NSM Lewes St Jo sub Castro *Chich* 83-84; NSM Uckfield from 84; NSM Isfield from 84; NSM Lt Horsted from 84. *The Parsonage, Isfield, Uckfield, E Sussex TN22 5TX* Tel (01825) 750439

DALLISTON, Christopher Charles. b 56. Ox Univ BA Cam Univ MA. St Steph Ho Ox 81. **d** 84 **p** 85. C Halstead St Andr w H Trin and Greenstead Green *Chelmsf* 84-87; Bp's Dom Chapl 87-91; V Forest Gate St Edm 91-95; P-in-c Boston *Linc* 95-97; V from 97. *The Vicarage, Wormgate, Boston, Lincs PE21 6NP* Tel (01205) 362864

DALLOW, Gillian Margaret. b 45. Univ of Wales BA86 DipEd67 Bris Univ MEd88. Oak Hill Th Coll CertEd94. **d** 96 **p** 97. NSM W Ealing St Jo w St Jas *Lon* from 96. *57 High Street, Northwood, Middx HA6 1EB* Tel (01923) 827149

DALLY, Keith Richard. b 47. FCCA77. St Jo Coll Nottm 80. **d** 82 **p** 83. C Southend St Sav Westcliff *Chelmsf* 82-85; Ind Chapl 85-93; C Southend 85-86; TV 86-92; C Harold Hill St Geo 92-93; Hon C Cen Co-ord Langham Place All So Clubhouse *Lon* from 97. *33 Yorke Road, Croxley Green, Rickmansworth, Herts WD3 3DW* Tel (01923) 770690

DALRIADA, Archdeacon of. *See* ROONEY, The Ven James

DALTON, Anthony Isaac. b 57. Em Coll Cam BA78 MA82 Leeds Univ BA82. Coll of Resurr Mirfield. **d** 82 **p** 83. C Carl St Aid and Ch Ch *Carl* 82-86; C Caversham and Mapledurham *Ox* 86-88; P-in-c Accrington St Mary *Blackb* 88-91; V 91-92; Chapl Victoria Hosp Accrington 88-92; V Sheff Parson Cross St Cecilia *Sheff* 92-96; P-in-c Burnley St Cath w St Alb and

St Paul *Blackb* from 96. *The Vicarage, 156 Todmorden Road, Burnley, Lancs BB11 3ER* Tel (01282) 423351

DALTON, Canon Arthur Benjamin. b 07. Univ Coll Lon BA27 Ox Univ BA30 MA35. Ripon Hall Ox 27. **d** 30 **p** 31. C Caversham *Ox* 30-34; C Wandsworth All SS *S'wark* 34-42; V S Lambeth All SS and St Barn 42-49; V Forest Hill St Aug 49-75; Hon Can S'wark Cathl 71-75; rtd 75. *c/o Bickley Court, 36 Chislehurst Road, Bromley BR1 2NW* Tel 0181-467 3918

DALTON, Bertram Jeremy (Tod). b 32. AIB64. Sarum & Wells Th Coll 81. **d** 83 **p** 84. C Ringwood *Win* 83-86; R Norton sub Hamdon, W Chinnock, Chiselborough etc *B & W* from 86. *The Rectory, Cat Street, Chiselborough, Stoke-sub-Hamdon, Somerset TA14 6TT* Tel (01935) 881202

DALTON, Derek. b 40. N Ord Course. **d** 84 **p** 85. NSM Pool w Arthington *Ripon* 84-87; P-in-c Thornton Watlass w Thornton Steward 87-90; C Bedale 87-90; R Wensley 90-95; V W Witton 90-95; R Romaldkirk w Laithkirk 95-97; rtd 97. *North Wing, Thornton Watlass Hall, Ripon, N Yorkshire HG4 4AS*

DALTON, Kevin. b 32. TCD BA65. Ch Div Sch of the Pacific (USA) BD67 CITC 66. **d** 66 **p** 67. C Stillorgan *D & G* 66-72; I Dublin Drumcondra w N Strand 72-79; I Monkstown from 79. *62 Monkstown Road, Monkstown, Blackrock, Co Dublin, Irish Republic* Tel Dublin (1) 280 6596

DALTON, Ronald. b 20. St Deiniol's Hawarden 60. **d** 61 **p** 62. C N Ferriby *York* 61-64; V Rillington 64-73; V Scampston 64-73; rtd 73. *15 Ambrey Close, Hunmanby, Filey, N Yorkshire YO14 0LZ* Tel (01723) 890037

DALTRY, Paul Richard. b 56. Tottenham Coll of Tech DipEH79. St Jo Coll Nottm DCM92. **d** 92 **p** 93. C Ipswich St Matt *St E* 92-96; P-in-c Needham Market w Badley from 96. *The Vicarage, 3 Stowmarket Road, Needham Market, Ipswich IP6 8DR* Tel (01449) 720316

DALY, Ms Bernadette. b 45. TCD BTh94. **d** 97. C Taney *D & G* from 97. *Church Cottage, 19 Taney Road, Dundrum, Dublin 14* Tel Dublin (1) 295 1895

DALY, Jeffrey. b 50. Bris Univ BA73 Jes Coll Cam PGCE74 Fitzw Coll Cam BA82 MA86. Ridley Hall Cam 80. **d** 83 **p** 84. C Tilehurst St Mich *Ox* 83-89; P-in-c Steventon w Milton 89-92; Asst Chapl Sherborne Sch 92-96; Chapl St Pet Sch York from 96. *St Peter's School, York YO3 6AB* Tel (01904) 623213

DAMIAN, Brother. *See* KIRKPATRICK, Roger James

DAMMERS, The Very Revd Alfred Hounsell. b 21. Pemb Coll Cam BA45 MA47. Westcott Ho Cam 46. **d** 48 **p** 49. C Adlington *Blackb* 48-50; Lect Qu Coll Birm 50-53; C Edgbaston St Bart *Birm* 50-53; India 53-57; V Millhouses H Trin *Sheff* 57-65; Can Res Cov Cathl *Cov* 65-73; Dean Bris 73-87; rtd 87; Perm to Offic *Bris* from 87. *4 Bradley Avenue, Bristol BS11 9SL* Tel 0117-982 9121

DAMPIER, Robert Cecil Walter. b 19. Pemb Coll Cam BA40 MA47. Ely Th Coll 46. **d** 48 **p** 49. C Camberwell St Giles *S'wark* 48-52; C-in-c Welling St Mary CD 52-55; V Welling 55-60; V Lewisham St Steph 60-67; V Tettenhall Wood *Lich* 67-82; V Coven 82-90; rtd 90; Hon C Lapley w Wheaton Aston *Lich* from 90; Hon C Blymhill w Weston-under-Lizard from 90. *Blymhill Rectory, Shifnal, Shropshire TF11 8LL* Tel (0195276) 273

DANA, Canon Edmund Francis Kinnaird (Eddie). b 15. ALCD40. **d** 40 **p** 41. C Cheltenham St Paul *Glouc* 40-45; P-in-c Petersfield w Sheet *Portsm* 45-49; R Shanklin St Blasius 49-62; V Crofton 62-63; R Northwood 63-80; RD W Wight 73-77; P-in-c W Cowes H Trin 77-78; V 78-80; Hon Can Portsm Cathl 77-80; rtd 80; Perm to Offic *Portsm* from 82. *15 Littlestairs Road, Shanklin, Isle of Wight PO37 6HR* Tel (01983) 864153

DANCE, Peter Patrick. b 31. Em Coll Saskatoon 66. **d** 69 **p** 69. Canada 69-71; C Hednesford *Lich* 71-75; P-in-c Westcote Barton and Steeple Barton *Ox* 76-77; P-in-c Sandford St Martin 76-77; R Westcote Barton w Steeple Barton, Duns Tew etc 77-89; R Castle Douglas *Glas* 89-97; rtd 97. *Mannville, High Street, Adderbury, Banbury, Oxon OX17 3NA* Tel (01295) 811989

DAND, Robert William Scrymgour. b 17. Pemb Coll Ox BA MA45. Cuddesdon Coll. **d** 47 **p** 48. C Portsea St Mary *Portsm* 47-50; V Finchingfield *Chelmsf* 50-59; R Woodbridge St Mary *St E* 59-60; Portugal 60-67; V Bracknell *Ox* 68-72; C Upton cum Chalvey 73-82; rtd 82; Perm to Offic *Cov* from 82. *11 Foxes Way, Warwick CV34 6AX* Tel (01926) 490864

DANDO, Stephen. b 49. Golds Coll Lon TCert70. Coll of Resurr Mirfield 81. **d** 83 **p** 84. C Wandsworth St Anne *S'wark* 83-87; V Stainland *Wakef* from 87. *The Vicarage, 295 Stainland Road, Holywell Green, Halifax, W Yorkshire HX4 9EH* Tel (01422) 374767

DANES, Charles William. b 28. Chich Th Coll 54. **d** 56 **p** 57. C N Greenford All Hallows *Lon* 56-59; C Caversham *Ox* 59-63; V Walsgrave on Sowe *Cov* 63-65; P-in-c Hanworth All SS *Lon* 65-67; V 68-76; P-in-c Wick *Chich* 76-78; V Littlehampton St Jas 76-78; P-in-c Littlehampton St Mary 76-78; V W Worthing St Jo 78-87; Chapl Monte Carlo *Eur* 87-93; rtd 93; Perm to Offic *Chelmsf* from 93. *31 Oakley Road, Braintree, Essex CM7 5QS* Tel (01376) 324586

DANGERFIELD, Andrew Keith. b 63. Univ of Wales (Ban) BD87. St Steph Ho Ox 87. **d** 89 **p** 90. C St Marychurch *Ex* 89-93; C-in-c Grahame Park St Aug CD *Lon* 93-96; V Tottenham St Paul from 96. *St Paul's Vicarage, 60 Park Lane, London N17 0JR* Tel 0181-808 7297

DANIEL, Alan Noel. b 09. AKC35. Ripon Hall Ox 35. **d** 36 **p** 37. C Kingston St Jo *S'wark* 36-39; V Upper Tooting H Trin 39-47; V Brockley Hill St Sav 47-58; V Dormansland 58-76; rtd 76; Perm to Offic *Chich* from 76. *31 Large Acres, Selsey, Chichester, W Sussex PO20 9BA* Tel (01243) 604566

DANIEL, Arthur Guy St John. b 12. K Coll Cam BA33 MA37. Cuddesdon Coll 34. **d** 35 **p** 36. C Blandford Forum *Sarum* 35-38; C Reading St Giles *Ox* 38-40; C Gt Marlow 40-46; V Colnbrook 46-78; TV Riverside 78-80; rtd 80; Perm to Offic *Ox* 80-87. *2 Gervis Court, Penwerris Avenue, Osterley, Middx TW7 4QU* Tel 0181-572 1848

DANIEL, Herrick Haynes. b 38. Open Univ BA81. Trin Coll Bris 73. **d** 75 **p** 76. C Harlesden St Mark *Lon* 75-78; C Livesey *Blackb* 78-81; V Blackb St Barn from 81. *St Barnabas' Vicarage, 20 Buncer Lane, Blackburn BB2 6SE* Tel (01254) 56587

DANIEL, Mrs Joy. b 44. Gilmore Course 81 Oak Hill Th Coll 82. **dss** 84 **d** 87 **p** 94. Luton St Fran *St Alb* 84-87; Par Dn 87-94; C from 94. *22 Rowelfield, Luton LU2 9HN* Tel (01582) 35237

DANIEL, Michael George. b 23. Magd Coll Cam BA49 MA52 Lon Univ BSc64 MPhil67. Linc Th Coll 49. **d** 51 **p** 52. C Welwyn Garden City *St Alb* 51-56; V Warnham *Chich* 57-61; C Ches Square St Mich w St Phil *Lon* 61-64; Adv R Foundn of St Kath Stepney 64-66; rtd 66. *84 North Lane, Rustington, Littlehampton, W Sussex BN16 3PW* Tel (01903) 773837

DANIEL, Philip Sharman. b 62. Man Univ BA83 Rob Coll Cam CertEd84. Wycliffe Hall Ox 84. **d** 86 **p** 87. C Macclesfield Team Par *Ches* 86-89; C Cheadle 89-94; V Disley from 94. *Disley Vicarage, Red Lane, Disley, Stockport, Cheshire SK12 2NP* Tel (01663) 762068

DANIEL, Rajinder Kumar. b 34. St Steph Coll Delhi 55 Westcott Ho Cam 61. **d** 63 **p** 64. C Purley St Barn *S'wark* 63-66; C Battersea St Pet 66-67; C N Harrow St Alb *Lon* 67-72; TV Beaconsfield *Ox* 72-75; V Smethwick St Matt w St Chad *Birm* 75-87; Dioc Adv on Black Min 87-92; Chapl Birm Gen Hosp 91-92; TR Braunstone *Leic* from 92. *The Rectory, Main Street, Braunstone, Leicester LE3 3AL* Tel 0116-289 3377

DANIELL, Robert. b 37. **d** 87 **p** 88. C Camberwell St Giles w St Matt *S'wark* 90-92; V Lewisham St Swithun from 92. *St Swithun's Vicarage, 191 Hither Green Lane, London SE13 6QE* Tel 0181-852 5088

DANIELS, Alan Henry. b 14. Keble Coll Ox BA35 BSc39 MA39. Wycliffe Hall Ox 63. **d** 64 **p** 65. C Rowner *Portsm* 64-67; R Yarmouth 67-82; rtd 82; Perm to Offic *Portsm* from 82. *11 Queens Close, Freshwater, Isle of Wight PO40 9EU* Tel (01983) 752681

DANIELS, Geoffrey Gregory. b 23. St Pet Coll Ox BA48 MA53. Lambeth STh60 Linc Th Coll 73. **d** 73 **p** 75. NSM Diss *Nor* 73-74; NSM Bexhill St Pet *Chich* 74-83; C Eastbourne St Andr 83-84; V Horam 84-88; rtd 88; Chapl Convent of Dudwell St Mary from 88; NSM Bexhill St Andr CD *Chich* 90-95; Perm to Offic from 95. *20 Richmond Grove, Bexhill-on-Sea, E Sussex TN39 3EQ* Tel (01424) 211719

DANIELS, Dr John Wyn. b 60. Southn Univ BSc82 PhD87 Bris Univ MA92. Trin Coll Bris DipHE91. **d** 92 **p** 93. C Roundhay St Edm *Ripon* 92-95; India 96; C Ambleside w Brathay *Carl* from 97; Chapl St Martin's Coll Lanc from 97. *Hazeldene, Hook Lane, Ambleside, Cumbria LA22 9BJ* Tel (015394) 30303 or 30268

DANIELS, Kenneth Percival Thomas. b 17. AKC50. St Boniface Warminster 50. **d** 51 **p** 52. C Eltham Park St Luke *S'wark* 51-54; C St Helier 54-58; V Lamorbey H Redeemer *Roch* 58-75; V Kemsing w Woodlands 75-82; rtd 82; Perm to Offic *Roch* from 83. *Shepherd's Hey, 21 Priestley Drive, Tonbridge, Kent TN10 4RS* Tel (01732) 352677

DANIELS, Norman. b 38. Leeds Univ BA60. St Mich Coll Llan 71. **d** 73 **p** 74. C Pontnewynydd *Mon* 73-76; W Germany 76-82; Chapl Giggleswick Sch 82-93; P-in-c Keighley All SS *Bradf* from 93. *All Saints Vicarage, 21 View Road, Keighley, W Yorkshire BD20 6JN* Tel (01535) 607002

DANKS, Alan Adam. b 41. Edin Th Coll 61. **d** 64 **p** 65. C Dumfries *Glas* 64-67; C Earl's Court St Cuth w St Matthias *Lon* 68-71; C St Steph Walbrook and St Swithun etc 71-74; C Brookfield St Mary 75-76; C Hendon St Mary 76-85. *33 Park Road, London W4 3EY* Tel 0181-994 3131

DANSIE, Bruce John. b 40. CEng72 Woolwich Poly BSc67 Univ Coll Lon MSc71. Linc Th Coll CMinlStuds92. **d** 92 **p** 93. C Ivybridge w Harford *Ex* 92-96; P-in-c Charleton w Buckland Tout Saints etc from 96. *The Rectory, West Charleton, Kingsbridge, Devon TQ7 2AJ* Tel (01548) 531211

DANSKIN, William Campbell. b 35. Edin Th Coll 78. **d** 80 **p** 81. C Largs *Glas* 80-81; C Gourock 80-81; P-in-c 81-84; P-in-c Pinmore 84-87; R Girvan 84-87; R Maybole 84-87; R Challoch w Newton Stewart 87-95. *Address temp unknown*

DANSON, Mrs Mary Agatha. MPS48 Strathclyde Univ PhC48. St Jo Coll Nottm 82. **d** 88 **p** 94. NSM Uddingston *Glas* from 88; NSM Cambuslang from 88. *3 Golf Road, Rutherglen, Glasgow G73 4JW* Tel 0141-634 4330

DAPLYN, Timothy James (Tim). b 52. Ripon Coll Cuddesdon DipMin94. **d** 94 **p** 95. C Southmead *Bris* 94-97; P-in-c Abbots

Leigh w Leigh Woods from 97. *The Vicarage, Church Road, Abbots Leigh, Bristol BS8 3QU* Tel (01275) 373996

DARBY, Anthony Ernest. b 26. Linc Th Coll 74. **d** 76 **p** 77. C Chilvers Coton w Astley *Cov* 76-79; P-in-c Longford 79-81; V 81-84; V Cov St Mary 84-91; RD Cov S 88-91; rtd 91; Chapl Cov Cathl *Cov* from 91. *53 Ivybridge Road, Styvechale, Coventry CV3 5PF* Tel (01203) 414174

DARBY, Michael Barwick. b 34. St D Coll Lamp BA61 Tyndale Hall Bris 61. **d** 63 **p** 64. C Islington St Andr w St Thos and St Matthias *Lon* 63-66; C Ealing Dean St Jo 66-68; V Broomfleet *York* 68-73; Area Sec (Dios York and Sheff) CCCS 68-73; V Paddington Em Harrow Road *Lon* 73-78; Iran 78-79; Brazil 80-83; Perm to Offic *Cant* 80-84; V Maidstone St Faith 84-90; UAE 90-92; V Platt Bridge *Liv* from 93. *The Vicarage, Ridyard Street, Platt Bridge, Wigan, Lancs WN2 3TD* Tel (01942) 866269

DARBY, Nicholas Peter. b 50. Kent Univ BA82. Sarum & Wells Th Coll 71. **d** 74 **p** 75. C Walton-on-Thames *Guildf* 74-78; C Horsell 78-80; USA 82-84; Chapl Lon Univ *Lon* 84-89; Chapl R Lon Hosp (Whitechapel) 90-91; Perm to Offic *S'wark* 90-91; Perm to Offic *Lon* 90-91; V Kew St Phil and All SS w St Luke *S'wark* from 91. *St Philip's Vicarage, 70 Marksbury Avenue, Richmond, Surrey TW9 4JF* Tel 0181-392 1425

DARBY, Philip William. b 44. Bede Coll Dur TCert66. Qu Coll Birm DipTh70. **d** 70 **p** 71. C Kidderminster St Geo *Worc* 70-74; P-in-c Dudley St Jo 74-79; V 79-80; P-in-c Catshill 80-82; V Catshill and Dodford 82-88; V Ipplepen w Torbryan *Ex* from 88; RD Ipplepen from 93. *The Vicarage, Paternoster Lane, Ipplepen, Newton Abbot, Devon TQ12 5RY* Tel (01803) 812215

DARBYSHIRE, Brian. b 48. Kent Univ DipTh81 BA83. Oak Hill Th Coll. **d** 83 **p** 84. C Enfield St Jas *Lon* 83-86; R Slaidburn *Bradf* 86-92; V Gt Harwood St Jo *Blackb* from 92. *St John's Vicarage, 29 Kingsway, Great Harwood, Blackburn BB6 7AX* Tel (01254) 886309

DARCH, John Henry. b 52. Univ of Wales (Lamp) BA73 PhD97 Lon Univ PGCE74 MA77 DipHE82. Trin Coll Bris 80. **d** 82 **p** 83. C Meole Brace *Lich* 82-85; C Hoole *Ches* 85-88; V Hyde St Geo from 88; P-in-c Godley cum Newton Green 89-93; RD Mottram from 91. *The Vicarage, 85 Edna Street, Hyde, Cheshire SK14 1DR* Tel 0161-367 8787 E-mail john.darch@ichthus.dircon.co.uk

DARK, Ronald Henry Richard (Ron). b 31. Oak Hill Th Coll. **d** 85 **p** 86. NSM Fyfield *Chelmsf* 85-89; NSM Fyfield and Moreton w Bobbingworth 90-93; NSM Fyfield, Moreton w Bobbingworth etc 93-94; Perm to Offic from 94. *74 Warescot Road, Brentwood, Essex CM15 9HE* Tel (01277) 214797

DARLEY, Canon Shaun Arthur Neilson. b 36. Dur Univ BA61 DipTh63 Reading Univ MSc75. Cranmer Hall Dur 61. **d** 63 **p** 64. C Luton w E Hyde *St Alb* 63-67; Chapl Bris Tech Coll 67-69; Chapl Bris Poly *Bris* 69-92; Chapl Univ of the W of England from 92; Lect 69-75; Sen Lect from 75; Lic to Offic 67-69; Bp's Cathl Chapl from 69; Hon Can Bris Cathl from 89. *24 Downs Park East, Bristol BS6 7QD, or The Octagon, UWE, Coldharbour Lane, Bristol BS16 1QY* Tel 0117-962 9219 or 965 6261 Fax 976 3964

DARLING, David (Brother David Francis). **d** 96 **p** 97. SSF from 96; NSM Edin St Ninian *Edin* from 96. *Society of St Francis, Little Portion, 111/2 Lothian Road, Edinburgh EH3 9AN* Tel 0131-228 3077

✠**DARLING, The Rt Revd Edward Flewett.** b 33. TCD BA55 MA58. **d** 56 **p** 57 **c** 85. C Belfast St Luke *Conn* 56-59; C Orangefield *D & D* 59-62; C-in-c Carnalea 62-72; Chapl Ban Hosp 63-72; I Belfast Malone St Jo *Conn* 72-85; Min Can Belf Cathl 78-85; Chapl Ulster Independent Clinic 81-85; Bp L & K from 85. *Bishop's House, North Circular Road, Limerick, Irish Republic* Tel Limerick (61) 451532 Mobile 087-627160 Fax 451100

DARLING, John. b 47. CMBHI. Sarum & Wells Th Coll 76. **d** 79 **p** 80. NSM Trowbridge St Thos *Sarum* 79-82; NSM Trowbridge St Thos and W Ashton from 82. *24 Eastbourne Road, Trowbridge, Wilts BA14 7HN* Tel (01225) 762864

DARLISON, Geoffrey Stuart. b 49. MRTPI80 Liv Poly DipTP74. St Jo Coll Nottm DCM91. **d** 91 **p** 92. C Horncastle w Low Toynton *Linc* 91-95; P-in-c Welton and Dunholme w Scothern 95-97; V from 97. *The Vicarage, Holmes Lane, Dunholme, Lincoln LN2 3QT* Tel (01673) 860132

DARMODY, Richard Arthur (Aidan). b 52. Lon Univ DipTh77 BD90. Linc Th Coll MDiv94. **d** 94 **p** 95. C Cherry Hinton St Jo *Ely* from 94. *46 Holbrook Road, Cambridge CB1 4ST* Tel (01223) 246469

DARRALL, Charles Geoffrey. b 32. Nottm Univ BA55 MA57. Qu Coll Birm 56. **d** 57 **p** 58. C Cockermouth All SS w Ch Ch *Carl* 57-63; Chapl Dioc Youth Cen 63-95; V St Johns-in-the-Vale w Wythburn 63-95; P-in-c Threlkeld 85-95; rtd 96. *Piper House, Naddle, Keswick, Cumbria CA12 4TF* Tel (017687) 74500

DARRALL, John Norman. b 34. Nottm Univ BA57. Ripon Hall Ox 57. **d** 60 **p** 61. C Nottingham St Mary *S'well* 60-65; Chapl Nottm Children's Hosp 64-65; V Bole w Saundby *S'well* 65-66; V Sturton w Littleborough 65-66; Chapl Oakham Sch from 84; Lic to Offic *Pet* from 84. *Choir Close, 3 Church Passage, Oakham, Leics LE15 6DR* Tel (01572) 723136

DARROCH, Ronald Humphrey. b 45. Trin Coll Cam BA67 MA71 Ch Ch Ox BA67 MA71. Ripon Hall Ox 67. **d** 70 **p** 71. C Kingston upon Hull St Nic *York* 70-73; Hon C 73-74; Hon C Perth St Jo *St And* from 74; Chapl Stancliffe Hall Derby 84-87; Perm to Offic *Worc* from 87; Chapl Old Swinford Hosp Sch Worc from 89. *17 Viewlands Terrace, Perth PH1 1BN, or Old Swinford Hospital, Stourbridge, W Midlands DY8 1QX* Tel (01738) 628880 or (01384) 396541

DART, John Peter. b 40. St Jo Coll Ox BA63. Cuddesdon Coll 62. **d** 64 **p** 65. C W Hartlepool St Aid *Dur* 64-67; C Alverthorpe *Wakef* 67-70; Lic to Offic 70-84. *3 Springhill Avenue, Crofton, Wakefield, W Yorkshire WF4 1HA* Tel (01924) 863782

DARVILL, Christopher Mark. b 61. Ox Univ BA83. St Steph Ho Ox 84. **d** 86 **p** 87. C Tottenham St Paul *Lon* 86-88; C Oystermouth *S & B* 88-90; Chapl Univ of Wales (Swansea) 90-94; Asst Dioc Warden of Ords from 92; V Llansamlet from 94. *The Vicarage, 61 Church Road, Llansamlet, Swansea SA7 9RL* Tel (01792) 771420

DARVILL, Geoffrey. b 43. Aston Univ DipHE81. Oak Hill Th Coll 79. **d** 81 **p** 82. C Barking St Marg w St Patr *Chelmsf* 81-84; C Widford 84-86; P-in-c Ramsden Crays w Ramsden Bellhouse 86-90; Dep Chapl HM Pris Pentonville 90-91; Chapl HM Young Offender Inst Onley from 91. *HM Young Offender Institution, Onley, Willoughby, Rugby, Warks CV23 8AP* Tel (01788) 522022 Fax 522260

DARVILL, Canon George Collins. b 36. Kelham Th Coll 56. **d** 61 **p** 62. C Middlesbrough St Chad *York* 61-64; C Manston *Ripon* 64-66; V Kippax 66-79; V Catterick 79-88; RD Richmond 80-86; P-in-c Adel 88-89; R from 89; RD Headingley 91-96; Hon Can Ripon Cathl from 91. *The Rectory, 25 Church Lane, Adel, Leeds LS16 8DQ* Tel 0113-267 3676

✠**DARWENT, The Rt Revd Frederick Charles.** b 27. JP87. ACIB. Wells Th Coll 61. **d** 63 **p** 64 **c** 78. C Pemberton St Jo *Liv* 63-65; R Strichen *Ab* 65-71; R New Pitsligo 65-71; R Fraserburgh w New Pitsligo 71-78; Can St Andr Cathl 71-78; Dean Ab 73-78; Bp Ab 78-92; rtd 92; Lic to Offic *Ab* from 92. *107 Osborne Place, Aberdeen AB25 2DD* Tel (01224) 646497

DASH, Mrs Janet Eleanor Gillian (Jan). b 47. SRN69. Cant Sch of Min 89. **d** 93 **p** 94. C Morden *S'wark* 93-96; C S Croydon Em from 96. *12 Hurst View Road, Croydon CR2 7AG* Tel 0181-688 5861

DATSON, Sheila Mary. CertEd67. S'wark Ord Course 76. **dss** 78 **d** 87 **p** 94. Bexleyheath Ch Ch *Roch* 78-87; Hon Par Dn 87-94; NSM Stourport and Wilden *Worc* from 94. *17 Moorhall Lane, Stourport-on-Severn, Worcs DY13 8RB* Tel (01299) 823044

DAUBNEY, Howard. b 49. Woolwich Poly BA70. S'wark Ord Course 86. **d** 89 **p** 90. NSM Roch from 89. *Trehaun, 20 City Way, Rochester, Kent ME1 2AB* Tel (01634) 401691

DAUBUZ, Michael Claude. b 19. Trin Coll Cam BA40 MA53. Wells Th Coll 40. **d** 42 **p** 43. C Fareham SS Pet and Paul *Portsm* 42-47; Hon C Blandford Forum *Sarum* 47-50; C Gillingham 50-53; R Brading w Yaverland *Portsm* 53-59; Perm to Offic *Win* 62-64; C Twyford 64-70; V Colden 70-84; rtd 84. *31 St Osmund Close, Yetminster, Sherborne, Dorset DT9 6LU* Tel (01935) 872584

DAUGHTERY, Stephen John. b 61. Kent Univ BSc82. Trin Coll Bris BA94. **d** 96 **p** 97. C Guildf Ch Ch *Guildf* from 96. *23A Waterden Road, Guildford, Surrey GU1 2AZ* Tel (01483) 502902

DAULMAN, John Henry. b 33. Lich Th Coll 60. **d** 62 **p** 63. C Monkseaton St Mary *Newc* 62-65; Min Can Newc Cathl 65-67; Chapl Crumpsall & Springfield Hosp 67-73; V Tyldesley w Shakerley *Man* 73-81; V Turton from 81. *St Anne's Vicarage, High Street, Turton, Bolton BL7 0EH* Tel (01204) 852222

DAUNTON-FEAR, Andrew. b 45. Univ of Tasmania BSc64 Qu Coll Cam BA67 MA72 Lon Univ DipLib74 St Andr Univ BPhil76. Ridley Hall Cam 67 ACT ThL68. **d** 68 **p** 70. Australia 68-71; P-in-c Islington H Trin Cloudesley Square *Lon* 71-75; Hon C Islington St Mary 71-75; C Stoke Bishop *Bris* 76-79; R Thrapston *Pet* 79-89; R Barming *Roch* from 89. *The Rectory, Church Lane, Barming, Maidstone, Kent ME16 9HA* Tel (01622) 726263

DAVAGE, William Ernest Peter. b 50. BA80 PGCE81 MPhil. St Steph Ho Ox 89. **d** 91 **p** 92. C Eyres Monsell *Leic* 91-94; Priest Lib Pusey House Ox from 94. *Pusey House, Oxford OX1 3LZ* Tel (01865) 278415

DAVENPORT (née HILL), Ms Elizabeth Jayne Louise. b 55. St Hugh's Coll Ox BA77 MA81. Fuller Th Sem California ThM89 N Ord Course 79. **dss** 82 **d** 87 **p** 91. Halliwell St Pet *Man* 82-83; Paris St Mich *Eur* 83-85; Lic to Offic *St Alb* 85-87; Hon Par Dn Chorleywood St Andr 87-89; USA from 89. *University of Southern California, Student Union 202, Los Angeles, California 90089-0890, USA*

DAVENPORT, Ian Arthan. b 54. Linc Th Coll 85. **d** 87 **p** 88. C Ches H Trin *Ches* 87-91; V Newton 91-97; V Oxton from 97. *Oxton Vicarage, 8 Wexford Road, Birkenhead, Merseyside L43 9TB* Tel 0151-652 1194

DAVENPORT, Michael Arthur. b 38. Kelham Th Coll 58 Lich Th Coll 60. **d** 62 **p** 63. C Bilborough w Strelley *S'well* 62-66; C Kettering St Mary *Pet* 66-69; V Tottenham St Benet Fink *Lon* from 69. *St Benet's Vicarage, Walpole Road, London N17 6BH* Tel 0181-888 4541

DAVENPORT, Miss Sybil Ann. b 36. Nottm Univ DipTh88. EMMTC 85. **d** 89 **p** 94. NSM Thurgarton w Hoveringham and Bleasby etc *S'well* 89-94; NSM Collingham w S Scarle and Besthorpe and Girton from 94. *Holmedale, North Muskham, Newark, Notts NG23 6HQ* Tel (01636) 701552

DAVEY, Andrew John. b 53. Univ of Wales (Cardiff) DPS77. St Mich Coll Llan DipTh76. **d** 77 **p** 78. C Gt Stanmore *Lon* 77-79; C Potters Bar *St Alb* 92-95; P-in-c Clenchwarton *Ely* 95-96; P-in-c W Lynn 95-96; R Clenchwarton and W Lynn from 96. *The Rectory, Clenchwarton, King's Lynn, Norfolk PE34 4DT* Tel (01553) 772089

DAVEY, Andrew John. b 57. Magd Coll Ox BA78 MA83. Wycliffe Hall Ox 80. **d** 83 **p** 84. C Bermondsey St Jas w Ch Ch *S'wark* 83-87; Chapl Trin Coll Cam 87-92; Pilsdon Community from 94. *Pilsdon Manor, Pilsdon, Bridport, Dorset DT6 5NZ* Tel (01308) 868308

DAVEY, Andrew Paul. b 61. Southn Univ BA82. Westcott Ho Cam 85. **d** 87 **p** 88. C S'wark H Trin w St Matt *S'wark* 87-91; V Camberwell St Luke 91-96; Min Development Officer Woolwich Area Miss Team from 96. *7 Bousfield Road, London SE14 5TP* Tel 0171-277 9688

DAVEY, Christopher Mark. b 64. EN(G)84 RGN89. St Steph Ho Ox DipMin95. **d** 95 **p** 96. C Leeds Belle Is St Jo and St Barn *Ripon* from 95. *St Barnabas House, Low Grange View, Leeds LS10 3DR* Tel 0113-271 1457

DAVEY, Canon Clive Herbert George. b 09. St Jo Coll Dur BA31 MA34. Wycliffe Hall Ox 31. **d** 32 **p** 33. C Dur St Mary le Bow w St Mary the Less *Dur* 32-36; Chapl St Jo Coll Dur 32-36; C Middleton *Man* 36-41; R Moston St Jo 41-46; V Maidstone St Faith *Cant* 46-54; Asst Chapl HM Pris Maidstone 47-54; V Gt Faringdon w Lt Coxwell *Ox* 54-63; RD Vale of White Horse 61-63; V Guildf Ch Ch *Guildf* 63-78; RD Guildf 73-78; Hon Can Guildf Cathl 76-78; rtd 78; Perm to Offic *Ex* 78-87; Perm to Offic *B & W* from 87. *24 Preywater Road, Wookey, Wells, Somerset BA5 1LE* Tel (01749) 677865

DAVEY, Dr Colin Hugh Lancaster. b 34. Em Coll Cam BA56 MA60 PhD89. Cuddesdon Coll 59. **d** 61 **p** 62. C Moseley St Agnes *Birm* 61-64; Lic to Offic *Eur* 64-65; Sub Warden St Boniface Coll Warminster 66-69; C Bath Weston St Jo *B & W* 69-70; Asst Gen Sec C of E Coun on Foreign Relns 70-74; Hon C St Dunstan in the West *Lon* 71-73; Hon C Kennington St Jo *S'wark* 73-74; V S Harrow St Paul *Lon* 74-80; V Paddington St Jas 80-83; Lic to Offic from 83; Asst Gen Sec BCC 83-90; Ch Life Sec CCBI from 90; Perm to Offic *S'wark* from 90. *30 Westwick Gardens, London W14 0BU* Tel 0171-602 6860 or 620 4444

DAVEY, Eric Victor. b 28. Wycliffe Hall Ox 53 Ridley Hall Cam. **d** 56 **p** 57. C Stockton St Thos *Dur* 56-59; C Stretford St Matt *Man* 59-61; V Slaithwaite w E Scammonden *Wakef* 61-68; V Pontefract St Giles 68-83; V Wakef St Jo 83-93; rtd 93; Perm to Offic *Wakef* from 93. *15B St John's Croft, Wakefield, W Yorkshire WF1 2RQ*

DAVEY, Canon Frederick Hutley David. b 14. Cranmer Hall Dur 58. **d** 60 **p** 62. C Bishopwearmouth St Nic *Dur* 60-62; C Dur St Giles 62-64; India 64-69; E Pakistan 69-71; Bangladesh 71-76; Chapl De Beer Miss to Seamen *Eur* 77-82; rtd 82; Perm to Offic *B & W* 82-95. *126 Ashtree Road, Frome, Somerset BA11 2SF* Tel (01373) 467545

DAVEY, James Garland. b 21. **d** 75 **p** 76. C Liskeard w St Keyne and St Pinnock *Truro* 75-77; Perm to Offic *B & W* 77-80; TV S Molton w Nymet St George, High Bray etc *Ex* 80-86; rtd 86; Perm to Offic *B & W* from 86. *25 Homeville, Hendford, Yeovil, Somerset BA20 1UZ* Tel (01935) 76118

DAVEY, Dr John. b 35. FRSH89 CPsychol92 AFBPsS92 Birkb Coll Lon BSc84 MPhil87 PhD91. Chich Th Coll 67. **d** 69 **p** 70. C Eastbourne St Elisabeth *Chich* 69-72; C Eastbourne St Mary 72-74; V W Wittering 74-77; Min Can and Chapl Windsor 77-81; R The Rissingtons *Glouc* 81-85; R Alfriston w Lullington, Litlington and W Dean *Chich* 85-92; Chapl Bramshill Police Coll *Win* 92-96; rtd 97. *Bewick, 13 Fairfield Close, Old Bosham, Chichester, W Sussex PO18 8JQ* Tel (01243) 573447

DAVEY, John Michael. b 31. St Chad's Coll Dur BA54 Sunderland Poly DMS76. St Chad's Coll Dur DipTh56. **d** 56 **p** 61. C Southwick H Trin *Dur* 56-57; C Harton 60-64; C Bawtry w Austerfield *S'well* 64-67; V Stillington *Dur* 67-70; Lic to Offic 70-78; Perm to Offic *Sheff* 78-93; rtd 96. *11 Darfield Close, Owlthorpe, Sheffield S19 6SW* Tel 0114-248 0917

DAVEY, Julian Metherall. b 40. Jes Coll Ox BA62 MA65. Wells Th Coll 62. **d** 64 **p** 65. C Weston-super-Mare St Jo *B & W* 64-66; Perm to Offic *St Alb* 66-68; Chapl St Alb Sch 68-73; Chapl Merchant Taylors' Sch Crosby 73-82; Perm to Offic *Truro* 82-83; P-in-c Meavy w Sheepstor *Ex* 83-85; P-in-c Walkhampton 83-85; R Meavy, Sheepstor and Walkhampton 85; Chapl Warw Sch 86-89; P-in-c The Winterbournes and Compton Valence *Sarum* 89-94; TV Marshwood Vale TM from 96. *The Vicarage, Hawkchurch, Axminster, Devon EX13 5XD* Tel (01297) 678225

DAVEY, Dr Julian Warwick. b 45. LRCPI DCH DRCOG. Qu Coll Birm 78. **d** 81 **p** 82. NSM Ipsley *Worc* from 81. *The Field House, Allimore Lane, Alcester, Warks B49 5PR* Tel (01789) 764640

DAVEY, Kenneth William. b 41. Lanc Coll HNC. Qu Coll Birm 84. **d** 86 **p** 87. C Baswich *Lich* 86-90; V Lostock Gralam *Ches* 90-96; P-in-c Thornton le Moors w Ince and Elton from 96. *The Vicarage, Ince Lane, Elton, Chester CH2 4QB* Tel (01928) 724028

DAVEY, Preb Norman John. b 23. Bps' Coll Cheshunt 51. **d** 53 **p** 54. C Highweek *Ex* 53-57; R Ashreigney 57-62; V Burrington 57-62; RD Chulmleigh 60-62; R Stockleigh Pomeroy 62-66; R Shobrooke 62-66; C Ex St Martin, St Steph, St Laur etc 67-70; R Ex St Mary Arches 70-73; TR Cen Ex 74-77; P-in-c Ide 75-77; Dioc Dir of Educn 77-88; Preb Ex Cathl 77-88; V Holcombe Burnell 77-88; rtd 88; Perm to Offic *Ex* from 88. *2 The Poplars, Park Lane, Pinhoe, Exeter EX6 9HH*

DAVEY, Peter Francis. b 40. Trin Coll Cam BA63 MA68. Cuddesdon Coll 63. **d** 65 **p** 66. C Atherton *Man* 65-69; C Leesfield 69-72; V High Crompton 72-79; V Blackrod 79-89; P-in-c Ringley 89-91; V Ringley w Prestolee 91-95; P-in-c Dearnley from 95. *The Vicarage, Arm Road, Littleborough, Lancs OL15 8NJ* Tel (01706) 78466

DAVEY, Peter William. b 44. Culham Coll of Educn TCert65. Linc Th Coll CMinlStuds93. **d** 93 **p** 94. C Cheadle w Freehay *Lich* 93-96; P-in-c Calton, Cauldon, Grindon and Waterfall from 96. *The Vicarage, Waterfall Lane, Waterhouses, Stoke-on-Trent ST10 3HT* Tel (01538) 308506

DAVEY, Piers Damer. b 57. Dur Univ BSc. Coll of Resurr Mirfield 80. **d** 83 **p** 84. C Heworth St Mary *Dur* 83-86; C Barnard Castle w Whorlton 86-89; V Aycliffe 89-95; V Chilton Moor from 95. *St Andrew's Vicarage, Chilton Moor, Houghton le Spring, Tyne & Wear DH4 6LU* Tel 0191-385 8747

DAVEY, Richard Henry. b 66. Man Univ BA88. Linc Th Coll BTh93. **d** 93 **p** 94. C Parkstone St Pet w Branksea and St Osmund *Sarum* 93-96; Min Can St E Cathl *St E* from 96; Chapl St E Cathl from 96. *Clopton Cottage, The Churchyard, Bury St Edmunds, Suffolk IP33 1RS*

DAVID, Brother. *See* JARDINE, David John

DAVID, Evan David Owen Jenkin. b 10. St D Coll Lamp BA34. **d** 34 **p** 35. C Machynlleth and Llanwrin *Ban* 34-41; R Llwydiarth and Llanfihangel yng Nghwynfa *St As* 41-53; R Llandyrnog and Llangwyfan 53-77; rtd 77; Perm to Offic *Ches* from 90. *Flat 29, Cromer Court, 81 Alderley Road, Hoylake, Wirral, Merseyside L47 2AU* Tel 0151-632 6474

DAVID, Faith Caroline. *See* CLARINGBULL, Mrs Faith Caroline

DAVID, Canon Kenith Andrew. b 39. Natal Univ BA(Theol)64. Coll of Resurr Mirfield 64. **d** 66 **p** 67. C Harpenden St Nic *St Alb* 66-69; S Africa 69-71; P-in-c Southwick *Chich* 71-72; Th Educn Sec Chr Aid 72-75; Project Officer India and Bangladesh 76-81; Hon C Kingston All SS *S'wark* 72-76; Hon C Kingston All SS w St Jo 76-81; Botswana 81-83; Hon C Geneva *Eur* 83-95; Co-ord Urban Rural Miss WCC 83-94; Can Dio Lundi Zimbabwe from 93; V Hessle *York* from 95. *The Vicarage, 4 Chestnut Avenue, Hessle, N Humberside HU13 0RH* Tel (01482) 648555 Fax as telephone

DAVID, Michael Anthony Louis. b 29. AKC58. **d** 59 **p** 60. C Greenhill St Jo *Lon* 59-63; V Gravesend St Mary *Roch* 63-78; V Foremark *Derby* 78-81; V Repton 78-81; TV Buxton w Burbage and King Sterndale 81-85; R Warlingham w Chelsham and Farleigh *S'wark* 85-90; rtd 91. *95 Lulworth Avenue, Hamworthy, Poole, Dorset BH15 4DH* Tel (01202) 684475

DAVID, Philip Evan Nicholl. b 31. Jes Coll Ox BA53 MA57 Univ of Wales BA61 Nottm Univ MPhil86 Leic Univ MEd88. St Mich Coll Llan 56. **d** 57 **p** 58. C Llanblethian w Cowbridge *Llan* 57-60; C Cardiff St Jo 60-64; Chapl Ch Coll Brecon 64-75; P-in-c Aberyscir and Llanfihangel Nantbran *S & B* 70-75; Chapl Loretto Sch Musselburgh 75-82; Lic to Offic *Derby* 80-91; Chapl Trent Coll Nottm 83-91; R Llanfyllin and Bwlchycibau *St As* 91-96; P-in-c Llangynog 95-96; rtd 96. *Woodside, The Bron, Cross Gates, Llandrindod Wells LD1 6RS*

DAVID COLUMBA, Brother. *See* HARE, David

DAVID FRANCIS, Brother. *See* DARLING, David

DAVID STEPHEN, Brother. *See* STEVENS, Canon David Johnson

DAVIDSON, Canon Charles Hilary. b 29. St Edm Hall Ox BA52 MA56 Leic Univ MPhil89. Lich Th Coll 52. **d** 54 **p** 55. C Abington *Pet* 54-59; C Pet St Jo 59-60; R Sywell w Overstone 60-66; P-in-c Lamport w Faxton 66-76; R Maidwell w Draughton and Scaldwell 67-76; R Maidwell w Draughton, Scaldwell, Lamport etc 77-80; RD Brixworth 77-79; Can Pet Cathl 79-94; V Roade 80-87; V Roade and Ashton w Hartwell 87-94; RD Towcester 91-94; rtd 94; Perm to Offic *Pet* from 94. *Croftside, Butlins Lane, Roade, Northampton NN7 2PU* Tel (01604) 863016

DAVIDSON, Christopher John. b 45. EAMTC. **d** 91 **p** 92. NSM Taverham w Ringland *Nor* 91-93; Dir of Educn 91-93; V Whixley w Green Hammerton *Ripon* 93-96; RE Adv 93-96; Dioc Dir of Educn *Ex* from 97. *14 Pridham Way, Exminster, Exeter EX6 8TA* Tel (01392) 824709 Fax 824710

DAVIDSON, Ian George. b 32. Lon Univ BSc53. Linc Th Coll 55. **d** 58 **p** 59. C Waltham Cross *St Alb* 58-60; C St Alb Abbey 61-63; Hon PV S'wark Cathl *S'wark* 63-67; V Gt Cornard *St E* 67-72; R Lt Cornard 67-70; Lic to Offic 72-79; Student Counsellor Suffolk

Coll 72-79; P-in-c Witnesham w Swilland and Ashbocking 79-83; Warden Scargill Ho 83-88; Chapl Chr Fellowship of Healing (Scotland) from 88. *28 Fox Spring Crescent, Edinburgh EH10 6NQ* Tel 0131-445 3381

DAVIDSON, John. b 34. Edin Th Coll. **d** 66 **p** 67. C Helensburgh *Glas* 66-69; C Kirkby *Liv* 69-70; TV 70-74. *Flat 19, 153-155 Seymour Place, London W1H 5TQ* Tel 0171-723 4262

DAVIDSON, John Lindsay. b 27. LRCP51 St Cath Soc Ox DipTh57. St Steph Ho Ox. **d** 58 **p** 59. C Croydon St Mich *Cant* 58-61; P-in-c H Cross Miss 62-66; V Lewisham St Steph *S'wark* 67-70; V Croydon St Mich *Cant* 70-80; V Croydon St Mich w St Jas 80-81; TR N Creedy *Ex* 81-92; RD Cadbury 86-90; rtd 92; Perm to Offic *Ex* from 92. *12 Highfield, Lapford, Crediton, Devon EX17 6PY* Tel (01363) 83764

DAVIDSON, Canon John Noble. b 15. Edin Th Coll 52. **d** 54 **p** 55. C Carl H Trin *Carl* 54-57; V Netherton 57-63; V Walney Is 63-69; V Southport H Trin *Liv* 69-75; V Rockcliffe and Blackford *Carl* 75-78; rtd 78; Perm to Offic *Carl* 78-81; Hon Can Malta Cathl *Eur* 81-84. *6 Netherend Road, Penrith, Cumbria CA11 8PF* Tel (01768) 863274

DAVIDSON, Air Vice-Marshal Sinclair Melville. b 22. CBE68. CEng FRAeS FIEE. Chich Th Coll 79. **d** 81 **p** 81. Hon C High Hurstwood *Chich* 81-82; P-in-c 83-88; Perm to Offic from 88. *Trinity Cottage, Chilles Lane, High Hurstwood, Uckfield, E Sussex TN22 4AA* Tel (01825) 732151

DAVIDSON, Trevor John. b 49. CertEd DipHE. Oak Hill Th Coll 80. **d** 85 **p** 86. C Drypool *York* 85-88; V Bessingby from 88; V Carnaby from 88; Chapl Bridlington and Distr Gen Hosp from 88. *The Vicarage, Kent Road, Bessingby, Bridlington, N Humberside YO16 4RU* Tel (01262) 670399

DAVIDSON, William Watkins. b 20. Wadh Coll Ox BA48 MA53. Westcott Ho Cam 49. **d** 50 **p** 51. C Radcliffe-on-Trent *S'well* 50-53; Chapl RN 53-57; R Esher *Guildf* 57-65; V Westmr St Steph w St Jo *Lon* 65-83; rtd 85. *32 Hamilton Avenue, Woking, Surrey GU22 8RS* Tel (01932) 342711

DAVIE (née JONES), Mrs Alyson Elizabeth. b 58. Ex Univ BA86. Wycliffe Hall Ox 86. **d** 88 **p** 94. Par Dn Ipswich St Fran *St E* 88-92; Perm to Offic *Ox* 92-93; Perm to Offic *St Alb* 93-94; NSM E Barnet 94-97; Asst Chapl Oak Hill Th Coll 94-97; P-in-c The Mundens w Sacombe *St Alb* from 97. *2 Forge Cottages, Munden Road, Dane End, Ware, Herts SG12 0LP*

DAVIE, Peter Edward Sidney. b 36. Lon Univ BSc57 MPhil78 Birm Univ MA73 Kent Univ PhD91. Coll of Resurr Mirfield 57. **d** 60 **p** 61. C De Beauvoir Town St Pet *Lon* 60-63; C-in-c Godshill CD *Portsm* 63-67; R Upton St Leonards *Glouc* 67-73; Sen Lect Ch Ch Coll Cant from 73. *8 Brockenhurst Close, Canterbury, Kent CT2 7RX* Tel (01227) 451572

DAVIE, Stephen Peter (Steve). b 52. MRTPI77 S Bank Poly BA75 Cam Univ DipRS90. Oak Hill Th Coll BA93. **d** 93 **p** 94. C Luton Ch Ch *Roch* 93-97; R Cobham w Luddesdowne and Dode from 97. *The Vicarage, Battle Street, Cobham, Gravesend, Kent DA12 3DB* Tel (01474) 814332 Fax as telephone

DAVIES, Adrian Paul. b 43. K Coll Lon. **d** 69 **p** 70. C Nottingham St Mary *S'well* 69-74; C Gt w Lt Billing *Pet* 74-75; P-in-c Marholm 75-82; R Castor 75; R Castor w Sutton and Upton 76-82; V Byker St Mich w St Lawr *Newc* 82-94; rtd 95. *9 Arrow Lane, Halton, Lancaster LA2 6QS*

DAVIES, Alan Arthur. b 35. Sarum & Wells Th Coll 83. **d** 85 **p** 86. C Eastleigh *Win* 85-88; C Portsea N End St Mark *Portsm* 88-90; V Lydiate *Liv* from 90. *The Vicarage, Lydiate, Liverpool L31 4HL* Tel 0151-526 0512

DAVIES, Alastair John. b 56. Nottm Univ BA MTh. Westcott Ho Cam. **d** 84 **p** 85. C Eltham St Jo *S'wark* 84-87; C Dulwich St Barn 87-89; Chapl RAF from 89. *Chaplaincy Services (RAF), HQ, Personnel and Training Command, RAF Innsworth, Gloucester GL3 1EZ* Tel (01452) 712612 ext 5032 Fax 712612 5987

DAVIES, Alcwyn Ivor. b 09. Univ of Wales BA32 DipEd33. St D Coll Lamp 36. **d** 38 **p** 39. C Llanddewi Rhondda w Bryn Eirw *Llan* 38-41; C Wisbech SS Pet and Paul *Ely* 41-44; R Hamerton 44-48; V Winwick 44-48; V Friday Bridge 48-53; V Coldham 48-53; R Fowlmere 53-76; V Thriplow 53-76; RD Barton 62-67; rtd 76; Perm to Offic *Ely* from 76. *17 Station Road, Lode, Cambridge CB5 9HB* Tel (01223) 811867

DAVIES, Aldwyn Ivan. b 09. St D Coll Lamp BA31. St Mich Coll Llan. **d** 32 **p** 33. C Swansea Ch Ch *S & B* 32-36; C Milford Haven *St D* 36-39; V New Radnor and Llanfihangel Nantmelan etc *S & B* 43-46; V Bradf St Wilfrid Lidget Green *Bradf* 54-56; R Halwill w Beaworthy *Ex* 57-63; Miss to Seamen 39-43, 46-54, 56-57 and 63-78; V Port Eynon w Rhosili and Llanddewi and Knelston *S & B* 69-74; V Llangennith 75-77; rtd 77. *Sea Beach Nursing Home, Horton, Swansea SA3 1LB* Tel (01792) 390252

DAVIES, Alexander Richard. b 12. St Deiniol's Hawarden 63. **d** 64 **p** 65. C Llangollen *St As* 64-69; V Llanfihangel Crucorney w Oldcastle etc *Mon* 69-77; rtd 77; Perm to Offic *St As* from 77; Perm to Offic *Ches* 83-89; Perm to Offic *Ban* from 90; Perm to Offic *Llan* from 95. *2 Station Avenue, Chirk, Wrexham LL14 5LU*

DAVIES, Canon Alfred Joseph. b 23. St D Coll Lamp BA49. **d** 50 **p** 51. C Llanegwad *St D* 50-53; C Llanelli Ch Ch 53-54; V Llangeler 54-74; RD Emlyn 70-73; Chapl Cardigan Hosp 74-88; V Cardigan and Mwnt and Y Ferwig *St D* 74-88; Can St D Cathl 79-88; rtd 88; Hon Can St D Cathl *St D* from 88. *19 Penbryn Avenue, Carmarthen SA31 3DH* Tel (01267) 234045

DAVIES, Alun Edwards. b 13. Univ of Wales BA40. St D Coll Lamp 45. **d** 46 **p** 47. C Treharris *Llan* 46-48; C Cardigan *St D* 48-50; CF 50-56; Hon CF 56; R Byford w Mansel Gamage *Heref* 56-58; P-in-c Preston-on-Wye w Blakemere 56-58; V Birch St Mary *Man* 58-62; R Lower Crumpsall 62-84; rtd 84; Perm to Offic *Man* from 84. *48 Ashtree Road, Crumpsall, Manchester M8 5AT* Tel 0161-720 8345

DAVIES, The Very Revd Alun Radcliffe. b 23. Univ of Wales BA45 Keble Coll Ox BA47 MA51. St Mich Coll Llan 47. **d** 48 **p** 49. C Roath St Marg *Llan* 48-49; Lect St Mich Coll Llan 49-53; Warden of Ords *Llan* 50-71; Dom Chapl to Abp Wales 52-57; Chapl RNVR 53-58; Dom Chapl Bp Llan 57-59; Chapl RNR 58-60; V Ystrad Mynach *Llan* 59-75; Chan Llan Cathl 69-71; Adn Llan 71-77; Can Res Llan Cathl 75-77; Dean Llan 77-93; V Llan w Capel Llanilltern 77-93; rtd 93. *15 Sinclair Drive, Penylan, Cardiff CF3 7AH* Tel (01222) 456149

DAVIES, Canon Arthur Cadwaladr. b 19. Univ of Wales BA41. Wells Th Coll 41. **d** 43 **p** 44. C Broughton *St As* 43-48; C Llanrhos 48-52; V Spalding St Paul *Linc* 52-57; V Ches Ch Ch *Ches* 57-64; V Stockton Heath 64-85; RD Gt Budworth 81-85; rtd 85; Perm to Offic *Ban* from 85. *Highfield, Treforris Road, Penmaenmawr LL34 6RH* Tel (01492) 623739

DAVIES, Arthur Gerald Miles. b 29. Univ of Wales (Ban) BA51. St Mich Coll Llan. **d** 53 **p** 54. C Shotton *St As* 53-60; R Nannerch 60-63; V Llansilin and Llangadwaladr 63-68; V Llansilin w Llangadwaladr and Llangedwyn 68-71; V Llanfair Caereinion w Llanllugan 71-75; TV Wrexham 75-83; V Hanmer, Bronington, Bettisfield, Tallarn Green 83-94; rtd 94. *Elland, School Lane, Bronington, Whitchurch, Shropshire SY13 3HN* Tel (01948) 73296

DAVIES, Arthur Lloyd. *See* LLOYD-DAVIES, Arthur

DAVIES, Basil Tudor. b 18. Keble Coll Ox BA40 MA48. Westcott Ho Cam 40. **d** 42 **p** 43. C Charlton St Luke w St Paul *S'wark* 42-44; C Stockwell Green St Andr 44-49; India 49-53; C Wantage *Ox* 53-57; V Wigston Magna *Leic* 57-73; R Upwell St Pet *Ely* 73-77; P-in-c Nordelph 75-77; Chapl Community of St Mary V Wantage 77-88; Lic to Offic *Ox* 77-88 and from 89; rtd 88; P-in-c Steventon w Milton *Ox* 88-89. *St Katharine's House, Garden Flat B, Ormond Road, Wantage, Oxon OX12 8EA* Tel (01235) 760883

DAVIES, Benjamin John. b 27. Glouc Sch of Min 80 Trin Coll Bris 87. **d** 88 **p** 89. NSM Cinderford St Steph w Littledean *Glouc* from 88. *Mannings Well, The Ruffit, Littledean, Cinderford, Glos GL14 3LA* Tel (01594) 822352

DAVIES, Bernard. b 24. St D Coll Lamp BA49. **d** 51 **p** 52. C New Tredegar *Mon* 51-53; C Gelligaer *Llan* 53-54; V Deeping Fen *Linc* 56-58; R Beswick *Man* 58-63; V Stand Lane St Jo 63-66; rtd 84. *7 Maritoba Close, Lakeside, Cardiff CF2 6HD*

DAVIES, Canon Bernard. b 34. Lon Univ BD63. Oak Hill Th Coll 59. **d** 63 **p** 64. C Rawtenstall St Mary *Man* 63-69; Sec Rwanda Miss 69-71; R Widford *Chelmsf* 71-78; V Braintree from 78; RD Braintree 87-95; Hon Can Chelmsf Cathl from 92. *St Michael's Vicarage, 10A Marshalls Road, Braintree, Essex CM7 7LL* Tel (01376) 322840

DAVIES, Bruce Edmund. b 22. Univ of Wales BA44. St Mich Coll Llan 44. **d** 46 **p** 47. C Canton St Luke *Llan* 46-48; C Roath St Marg 48-56; P-in-c Cardiff St Dyfrig 56-66; Chapl Univ of Wales (Cardiff) 56-78; R Peterston-super-Ely w St Brides-super-Ely 78-87; rtd 87; Perm to Offic *Llan* from 87. *7 St Paul's Court, Heol Fair, Llandaff, Cardiff CF5 2ES* Tel (01222) 553144

DAVIES, Cadoc Trevor. b 28. Keble Coll Ox BA52 MA57. Cuddesdon Coll 57. **d** 57 **p** 58. C Cheltenham St Steph *Glouc* 57-60; C Shalford *Guildf* 60-64; V Water Orton *Birm* 64-83; R Kislingbury w Rothersthorpe *Pet* 83-92; rtd 92; C Ridgeway *Ox* 92-94. *15 Union Street, Oxford OX4 1JP* Tel (01865) 727823

DAVIES, Carol Ann. d 96. NSM Oakfield St Jo *Portsm* from 96. *79 George Street, Ryde, Isle of Wight PO33 2JF*

DAVIES, Catharine Mary. *See* FURLONG, Mrs Catharine Mary

DAVIES, Charles William Keith. b 48. MIOT71. Linc Th Coll. **d** 83 **p** 84. C Hythe *Cant* 83-86; Chapl RAF from 86; Perm to Offic *Linc* 93-96. *Chaplaincy Services (RAF), HQ, Personnel and Training Command, RAF Innsworth, Gloucester GL3 1EZ* Tel (01452) 712612 ext 5164 Fax 510828

DAVIES, Christopher John. b 55. St Alb Minl Tr Scheme 83. **d** 86 **p** 87. C Tooting All SS *S'wark* 86-90; V Malden St Jas 90-96; RD Kingston 92-96; TR Wimbledon from 96. *St Mary's Rectory, 14 Arthur Road, London SW19 7DZ* Tel 0181-946 2605

DAVIES, Clifford Morgan. b 19. Univ of Wales BA41. St Mich Coll Llan 41. **d** 43 **p** 44. C Gabalfa *Llan* 43-46; C Pontypridd St Cath 46-51; C Pokesdown All SS *Win* 51-56; V Shipton Bellinger w S Tidworth 56-61; Chapl Duke of York's R Mil Sch Dover 61-77; rtd 84. *37 Applegarth Avenue, Guildford, Surrey GU2 6LX* Tel (01483) 579415

DAVIES, Clifford O'Connor. b 17. Lon Univ BCom37. St Aug Coll Cant 42. **d** 44 **p** 45. C Lamorbey H Trin *Roch* 44-46; S Africa from 46. *64 Schuller Street, Forest Hill, 2091 South Africa* Tel Johannesburg (11) 683-3680

DAVIES, Clifford Thomas. b 41. Glouc Th Course. **d** 83 **p** 84. NSM Dean Forest H Trin *Glouc* 83-87; C Huntley and Longhope 87; R

Ruardean from 87. *The Rectory, High Street, Ruardean, Glos GL17 9US* Tel (01594) 542214

DAVIES, David Anthony (Tony). b 57. ARICS84 Thames Poly BSc81. Coll of Resurr Mirfield 85. **d** 88 **p** 89. C Stalybridge *Man* 88-91; C Swinton and Pendlebury 91-92; TV from 92. *All Saint's Vicarage, 4 Banbury Mews, Wardley, Swinton, Manchester M27 3QZ* Tel 0161-794 5934

DAVIES, David Arthur Guy Hampton. b 27. St Jo Coll Ox BA50 DipTh51 MA55. Ely Th Coll 51. **d** 53 **p** 54. C Somers Town St Mary *Lon* 53-55; C Cranford 55-60; C Shrewsbury H Cross *Lich* 60-62; R Stamford St Mary and St Mich *Linc* 62-90; rtd 90; Perm to Offic *Lich* from 97. *8 Holywell Terrace, Shrewsbury SY2 5DF* Tel (01743) 245086

DAVIES, David Barry Grenville. b 38. St Jo Coll Dur BA60 MA77. Sarum Th Coll 61. **d** 63 **p** 64. C Aberystwyth St Mich *St D* 63-66; Min Can St D Cathl 66-72; R Stackpole Elidor w St Petrox 72-83; V Laugharne w Llansadwrnen and Llandawke from 83. *The Vicarage, King Street, Laugharne SA33 4QE* Tel (01994) 427218

DAVIES, David Berwyn. b 42. Univ of Wales DPT66. St Mich Coll Llan 95. **d** 96 **p** 97. C Llanelli *St D* from 96. *4 Hedley Terrace, Llanelli SA15 3RE* Tel (01554) 750355

DAVIES, David Christopher (Chris). b 52. Lon Univ BSc73 Leeds Univ DipTh75. Coll of Resurr Mirfield 73. **d** 76 **p** 77. C Bethnal Green St Jo w St Simon *Lon* 76-78; C Bethnal Green St Jo w St Bart 78-80; C-in-c Portsea St Geo CD *Portsm* 80-81; Relig Affairs Producer Radio Victory 81-86; V Portsea St Geo 81-87; Chapl Ham Green Hosp Bris 87-94; Chapl Southmead Hosp Bris 87-94; Chapl Southmead Health Services NHS Trust Bris from 94; Perm to Offic *B & W* from 94. *Southmead Hospital, Westbury-on-Trym, Bristol BS10 5NB, or 28 Hortham Lane, Almondsbury, Bristol BS12 4JL* Tel 0117-950 5050 or 959 5447

DAVIES, David Geoffrey George. b 24. Univ of Wales (Ban) BA49 Lon Univ BD55 Chorley Coll of Educn PGCE75. St Mich Coll Llan 49. **d** 51 **p** 52. C Brecon St Mary w Battle and Llanhamlach *S & B* 51-55; Min Can Brecon Cathl 53-55; C Oystermouth 55-59; V Cwm *St As* 59-63; Warden of Ords 62-70; V Ruabon 63-70; Hon Can St As Cathl 66-69; Cursal Can 69-70; NSM W Derby (or Tuebrook) St Jo *Liv* 70-81; Chapl to Welsh Speaking Angl in Liv 74-81; TV Bourne Valley *Sarum* 81-87; TR 87-89; Bp's Chapl to Schs 83-89; RD Alderbury 86-89; rtd 89; Hon Chapl Liv Cathl *Liv* from 89; Sub-Chapl HM Pris Risley 90-96. *55 Hattons Lane, Liverpool L16 7QR* Tel 0151-722 1415

DAVIES, David Hywel. b 13. Univ of Wales BA40. St Mich Coll Llan 41. **d** 42 **p** 43. C Tonypandy w Clydach Vale *Llan* 42-47; C St Andrews Major and Dinas Powys 47-53; V Pembroke St Mary and St Mich *St D* 53-67; V Carmarthen St Pet 67-83; Can St D Cathl 72-82; Chan 82-83; rtd 83. *The Vicarage, Llanfihangel Abercywyn, St Clears SA33 4ND* Tel (01994) 231019

DAVIES, Canon David Ioan Gwyn. b 19. Univ of Wales BA41 MA54. Lich Th Coll 41. **d** 43 **p** 44. C Llandeilo Tal-y-bont *S & B* 43-47; C Llansamlet 47-49; C Blackpool St Jo *Blackb* 49-53; V Blackb St Mich 53-56; V Preston St Jude 56-59; V Blackpool St Paul 59-86; RD Blackpool 73-84; Hon Can Blackb Cathl 77-86; rtd 86. *37 Oakfield Street, Pontardulais, Swansea SA4 1LN* Tel (01792) 883947

DAVIES, David Islwyn. b 42. St Deiniol's Hawarden 83. **d** 85 **p** 86. C Llangiwg *S & B* 85-87; C Swansea St Pet 87-89; Miss to Seamen 89-94; The Netherlands *Eur* 89-92; Chapl Schiedam Miss to Seamen 89-92; Chapl Milford Haven Miss to Seamen 92-94; V Pontyates and Llangyndeyrn *St D* from 94. *The Vicarage, 1 Heol Mansant, Pontiets, Llanelli SA15 5SB* Tel (01269) 860451

DAVIES, Canon David Jeremy Christopher. b 46. CCC Cam BA68 MA72. Westcott Ho Cam 68. **d** 71 **p** 72. C Stepney St Dunstan and All SS *Lon* 71-74; Chapl Qu Mary Coll 74-78; Chapl Univ of Wales (Cardiff) *Llan* 78-85; Can Res Sarum Cathl *Sarum* from 85. *Hungerford Chantry, 54 The Close, Salisbury SP1 2EL* Tel (01722) 330914 E-mail djcdavies@aol.com

DAVIES, David John. b 36. St Cath Soc Ox BA58 MA62. St D Coll Lamp 58. **d** 60 **p** 61. C Rhosddu *St As* 60-68; Chr Aid Area Sec (Glos, Herefordshire and Worcs) 68-85; Midl Regional Co-ord 78-85; Area Co-ord (Devon and Cornwall) from 86; Perm to Offic *Ex* from 94. *Poldhu, 8 Carne Road, Newlyn, Penzance, Cornwall TR18 5QA* Tel (01736) 60401

DAVIES, David Leslie Augustus. b 25. St D Coll Lamp BA50. **d** 51 **p** 52. C Aberystwyth *St D* 51-55; C Llanelli St Paul 55-56; V Castlemartin and Warren 56-61; R Eglwysilan *Llan* 61-65; Chapl Mayday, Qu and St Mary's Hosps Croydon 65-71; V Penrhyncoch and Elerch *St D* 71-74; Chapl R Berks and Reading Distr Hosps 74-89; rtd 90; Perm to Offic *Win* from 90. *Basset Down, 31 Three Acre Drive, New Milton, Hants BH25 7LG* Tel (01425) 610376

DAVIES, David Michael Cole. b 44. St D Coll Lamp DipTh69. **d** 68 **p** 69. C Carmarthen St Pet *St D* 68-72; R Dinas 72-77; V Ty-Croes w Saron 77-80; V Llanedi w Tycroes and Saron 80-90; RD Dyffryn Aman 85-90; V Dafen and Llwynhendy 90-94; V Dafen from 94. *The Vicarage, Bryngwyn Road, Dafen, Llanelli SA14 8LW* Tel (01554) 774730

DAVIES, Prof David Protheroe. b 39. CCC Cam BA62 MA66 CCC Ox MA69 BD69. Ripon Hall Ox 62. **d** 64 **p** 65. C Swansea St Mary w H Trin *S & B* 64-67; Lect Th Univ of Wales (Lamp) 67-75; Sen Lect 75-86; Dean Faculty of Th 75-77 and from 81; Hd Th and Relig Studies from 84; Prof Th Univ of Wales (Lamp) from 86; Bp's Chapl for Th Educn *S & B* from 79. *St David's College, Lampeter SA48 7ED* Tel (01570) 422351

DAVIES, Dr David Vernon. b 14. AFBPsS68 Univ of Wales (Swansea) BA35 BD38 St Cath Coll Ox MA40 K Coll Lon PhD56. St D Coll Lamp 41. **d** 41 **p** 42. C Llanelli Ch Ch *St D* 41-46; Bahamas 46-50; Chapl Cane Hill Hosp Coulsdon 50-61; Lic to Offic *S'wark* 50-61; Lect St Luke's Coll Ex 61-65; Lic to Offic *Ex* 61-68; Sen Lect St Luke's Coll Ex 65-68; Lic to Offic *Llan* 68-94; Prin Lect Llan Coll of Educn 68-77; Sen Lect Univ of Wales (Cardiff) 77-79; rtd 79; Perm to Offic *Llan* from 94. *41 Cefn Coed Avenue, Cyncoed, Cardiff CF2 6HF* Tel (01222) 757635

DAVIES, David William. b 64. **d** 90 **p** 91. C Newton St Pet *S & B* 90-93; V Llywel and Traean-glas w Llanulid 93-97; CF from 97. *MOD Chaplains (Army), Trenchard Lines, Upavon, Pewsey, Wilts SN9 6BE* Tel (01980) 615804 Fax 615800

DAVIES, Dennis William. b 24. Leeds Univ BA46 K Coll Lon AKC54 BD65. **d** 54 **p** 55. C Aylesbury *Ox* 54-58; Lic to Offic from 60; rtd 90-96. *45 Green End Street, Aston Clinton, Aylesbury, Bucks HP22 5JE* Tel (01296) 630989

DAVIES, Dewi Caradog. b 14. St D Coll Lamp BA35. **d** 38 **p** 39. C Abercynon *Llan* 38-44; C Cilybebyll 44-49; C-in-c Crynant 49-54; V Tonypandy w Clydach Vale 54-66; R Canton St Jo 66-79; rtd 79. *10 Insole Gardens, Llandaff, Cardiff CF5 2HW* Tel (01222) 563743

DAVIES, Dillwyn. b 30. St Mich Coll Llan 52. **d** 54 **p** 55. C Laugharne w Llansadwrnen and Llandawke *St D* 54-57; Lic to Offic *Dur* 57-58; Miss to Seamen 57-58; Ceylon 58-62; R Winthorpe *S'well* 62-71; V Langford w Holme 62-71; V Mansfield Woodhouse 71-85; R Gedling 85-92; RD Gedling 85-90; Hon Can S'well Minster 90-92; rtd 92. *7 Norbury Drive, Mansfield, Notts NG18 4HT*

DAVIES, Canon Dilwyn Morgan. b 10. Univ of Wales BA32 DipEd33. St Mich Coll Llan 32. **d** 34 **p** 35. C Dinas w Penygraig *Llan* 34-36; C Bassaleg *Mon* 36-40; CF (EC) 40-46; V Finham *Cov* 46-54; R Stoke 54-61; R Rugby St Andr 61-72; Hon Can Cov Cathl 65-80; P-in-c Ilmington w Stretton on Fosse and Ditchford 72-76; R 77-80; rtd 80; Perm to Offic *Cov* from 80. *6 Manor Barns, Ilmington, Shipston-on-Stour, Warks CV36 4LS* Tel (01608) 682568

DAVIES, Dorrien Paul. b 64. Univ of Wales (Ban) DipTh86. Llan Dioc Tr Scheme. **d** 88 **p** 89. C Llanelli *St D* 88-91; V Llanfihangel Ystrad and Cilcennin w Trefilan etc from 91. *Ystrad Vicarage, Felinfach, Lampeter, Dyfed SA48 8AE* Tel (01570) 471073

DAVIES, Prof Douglas James. b 47. St Jo Coll Dur BA69 St Pet Coll Ox MLitt72 Nottm Univ PhD80. Cranmer Hall Dur 71. **d** 75 **p** 76. Lect Nottm Univ 75-97; Sen Lect 90-97; Hon C Wollaton *S'well* 75-83; Hon C Attenborough 83-85; Hon C E Leake 85-91; Hon C Daybrook 91-97; Prof Relig Studies Nottm Univ 93-97; Prin SS Hild and Bede Coll Dur from 97; Prof Th Dur Univ from 97. *College of St Hild and St Bede, St Hild Lane, Durham DH1 1SZ* Tel 0191-374 3069

DAVIES, Canon Douglas Tudor. b 20. Univ of Wales (Ban) BA44. Coll of Resurr Mirfield 44. **d** 46 **p** 47. C Swansea Ch Ch *S & B* 46-52; C Oystermouth 52-57; R Llangynllo and Bleddfa 57-63; C-in-c Treboeth CD 63-65; V Treboeth 65-90; RD Penderi 78-90; Hon Can Brecon Cathl 82-83; Can from 83; rtd 90. *245A Swansea Road, Waunarlwydd, Swansea SA5 4SN* Tel (01792) 879587

DAVIES, Edna Nansi Margaret. b 37. **d** 97. NSM Netherwent *Mon* from 97. *Junipers, Court House Road, LLanfair Discoed, Chepstow NP6 6LW* Tel (01633) 400519

DAVIES, Edward Earl. b 40. Llan Dioc Tr Scheme 88. **d** 90 **p** 91. C Pontypridd St Cath w St Matt *Llan* 90-93; V Ferndale w Maerdy from 93. *The Vicarage, Woodville Place, Maerdy, Ferndale CF43 4LS* Tel (01443) 756322

DAVIES, Edward Trevor. b 37. LRSC62 MInstE74 CEng78. N Ord Course 92. **d** 95 **p** 96. NSM Waverton *Ches* from 95; Asst Chapl (NSM) Countess of Chester Hosp NHS Trust from 95. *Athergreen, 5 Allansford Avenue, Waverton, Chester CH3 7QH* Tel (01244) 332106 Fax as telephone

DAVIES, Edward William Llewellyn. b 51. Nottm Univ BTh77. St Jo Coll Nottm 73. **d** 78 **p** 79. C Southsea St Jude *Portsm* 78-81; C Alverstoke 81-84; R Abbas and Templecombe w Horsington *B & W* 84-89; Perm to Offic *Ches* from 89. *2 Cranford Avenue, Macclesfield, Cheshire SK10 7DJ* Tel (01625) 500544

DAVIES, Dr Elizabeth Jean. b 39. MRCS LRCP65 Lon Univ MB, BS63. S Dios Minl Tr Scheme 86 Chich Th Coll 86. **d** 89 **p** 95. Par Dn Southwick *Chich* 89-91; Par Dn Littlehampton and Wick 91-95; C Seaford w Sutton from 95. *51 Chyngton Gardens, Seaford, E Sussex BN25 3RS* Tel (01323) 893876

DAVIES, Eric Brian. b 36. St Jo Coll Nottm. **d** 87 **p** 89. NSM Castle Donington and Lockington cum Hemington *Leic* 87-88; Hon C Hathern, Long Whatton and Diseworth 89-90; Hon C Hathern, Long Whatton and Diseworth w Belton etc 90-93; C Minster in Sheppey *Cant* from 93. *St Peter's House, Halfway, Sheerness, Kent ME12 3DD* Tel (01795) 662399

DAVIES, Evan Wallis. b 08. Bps' Coll Cheshunt. **d** 42 **p** 43. C Biggleswade *St Alb* 42-45; C Lougher *S & B* 45-46; C Northaw

St Alb 46-48; V Pirton 48-52; Lic to Offic 52-65; rtd 71. *7 Treetops, Swiss Valley Park, Llanelli SA14 8DW* Tel (01554) 752316

DAVIES, Evelyn Dorothy. d 96 **p** 97. NSM Llangynog *St As* from 96. *Iscoed, Pennant Melangell, Llangynog, Oswestry, Shropshire SY10 0HQ*

DAVIES, Frances Elizabeth. b 38. BA CertEd Napier Poly Edin DipC&G. Moray Ord Course. **d** 95. Hon C Thurso *Mor* from 95; Hon C Wick from 95. *22 Granville Crescent, Thurso, Caithness KW14 7NP* Tel (01847) 892386

DAVIES, The Ven Francis James Saunders. b 37. Univ of Wales (Ban) BA60 Selw Coll Cam BA62 MA66 Bonn Univ 63. St Mich Coll Llan 62. **d** 63 **p** 64. C Holyhead w Rhoscolyn *Ban* 63-67; Chapl Ban Cathl 67-69; R Llanllyfni 69-75; Can Missr Ban Cathl 75-78; V Gorseinon *S & B* 78-86; RD Llwchwr 83-86; V Cardiff Dewi Sant *Llan* 86-93; Adn Meirionnydd *Ban* from 93; R Criccieth w Treflys from 93. *The Rectory, Criccieth LL52 0AG* Tel (01766) 523222

DAVIES, Frank Ernest. b 13. Dur Univ LTh43. Clifton Th Coll 39. **d** 43 **p** 44. C Walton St Luke *Liv* 43-45; C Ravenhead 45-48; C Didsbury Ch Ch *Man* 48-50; R Ardwick St Thos 50-56; V Plymouth St Aug *Ex* 56-60; R Bigbury 60-84; rtd 84; Perm to Offic *Ches* from 84. *93 Heywood Boulevard, Thingwall, Wirral, Merseyside L61 3XE* Tel 0151-648 3561

DAVIES, Gareth Rhys. b 51. DipHE. Oak Hill Th Coll. **d** 83 **p** 84. C Gt Warley Ch Ch *Chelmsf* 83-86; C Oxhey All SS *St Alb* 86-90; C Aldridge *Lich* from 90. *227 Walsall Road, Aldridge, Walsall WS9 0QA* Tel (01922) 57732

DAVIES, Gary. b 37. AKC62. **d** 63 **p** 64. C Dovercourt *Chelmsf* 63-65; C Lambeth St Phil *S'wark* 65-68; P-in-c 68-70; V W Brompton St Mary *Lon* 70-72; V W Brompton St Mary w St Pet 73-83; RD Chelsea 76-80; Dir Post-Ord Tr 78-81; Perm to Offic from 83. *21 Margravine Gardens, London W6 8RL* Tel 0181-741 9315

DAVIES, Canon Geoffrey Lovat. b 30. St Aid Birkenhead. **d** 62 **p** 63. C Davenham *Ches* 62-65; C Higher Bebington 65-67; V Witton 67-80; R Lymm 80-96; Dioc Clergy Widows and Retirement Officer 87-91; Hon Can Ches Cathl 88-96; RD Gt Budworth 91-96; P-in-c Weaverham 96; rtd 96; Perm to Offic *Liv* from 96. *21 Howbeck Close, Birkenhead, Merseyside L43 6TH* Tel 0151-653 2441

DAVIES, Geoffrey Michael. b 43. St D Coll Lamp DipTh70. **d** 70 **p** 71. C Brynmawr *S & B* 70-73; Coll of the Ascension Selly Oak 73-74; S Africa 74-91; C Roath St Marg *Llan* 91-95; V Llanishen w Trellech Grange and Llanfihangel etc *Mon* from 95. *The Vicarage, Llanishen, Chepstow NP6 6QL* Tel (01600) 860845

DAVIES, George Vivian. b 21. CCC Cam BA47 MA49. Ely Th Coll. **d** 49 **p** 50. C Maidstone St Martin *Cant* 49-51; C Folkestone St Mary and St Eanswythe 51-56; V Leysdown w Harty 56-59; R Warehorne w Kenardington 59-74; R Rounton w Welbury *York* 74-86; rtd 86; Perm to Offic *Derby* from 86. *12 Rectory Drive, Wingerworth, Chesterfield, Derbyshire S42 6RT* Tel (01246) 279222

DAVIES, George William. b 51. MIPD MIMgt MBTI Open Univ BA74 MPhil89 Liv Univ DMS76 CPsychol96 Ox Univ DPhil97. Sarum & Wells Th Coll 83. **d** 85 **p** 86. C Mansfield St Pet *S'well* 85-89; Chapl Cen Notts HA 86-89; P-in-c Fobbing *Chelmsf* 89-96; Ind Chapl 89-96; Chapl ATC 92-95; Chapl Thurrock Lakeside Shopping Cen *Chelmsf* 93-96; CF (TA) from 94; R Mottingham St Andr *S'wark* from 96. *The Rectory, 233 Court Road, London SE9 4TQ* Tel 0181-857 1691 or 851 1909

DAVIES, Glanmor Adrian. b 51. St D Coll Lamp DipTh73. **d** 73 **p** 75. C Llanstadwel *St D* 73-78; R Dinas w Llanllawer and Pontfaen w Morfil etc 78-84; V Lamphey w Hodgeston 84-85; V Lamphey w Hodgeston and Carew from 85. *The Vicarage, Lamphey, Pembroke SA71 5NR* Tel (01646) 672407

DAVIES, Glenn Naunton. b 50. Sydney Univ BSc72 BD78 ThM79. **d** 81 **p** 81. Australia 81-85 and from 87; Hon C Fulwood *Sheff* 85-87. *The Rectory, 12 Ascot Place, PO Box 26, Miranda, NSW, Australia 2228* Tel Sydney (2) 540 4558 or 525 4310 Fax 525 8655

DAVIES, Glyn Richards. b 28. Solicitor 52. **d** 79 **p** 80. NSM Michaelston-y-Fedw and Rudry *Mon* 79-88; NSM St Mellons and Michaelston-y-Fedw 88-96; NSM St Mellons from 96. *Ty Golau, 8 Tyr Winch Road, St Mellons, Cardiff CF3 9UX* Tel (01222) 792813

DAVIES, Glyndwr George. b 36. Glouc Sch of Min 88. **d** 91 **p** 92. NSM Clodock and Longtown w Craswall, Llanveynoe etc *Heref* from 91. *White House Farm, Llanfihangel Crucorney, Abergavenny NP7 8HW* Tel (01873) 890251

DAVIES, The Ven Graham James. b 35. Univ of Wales BD72 St D Coll Lamp BA56. St Mich Coll Llan 56 Episc Th Sch Cam Mass 58. **d** 59 **p** 60. C Johnston w Steynton *St D* 59-62; C Llangathen w Llanfihangel Cilfargen 62-64; Min Can St D Cathl 64-66; R Burton 66-71; R Hubberston 71-74; Hon C Lenham w Boughton Malherbe *Cant* 74-80; V Cwmddauddwr w St Harmon's and Llanwrthwl *S & B* 80-86; V Cydweli and Llandyfaelog *St D* 86-97; Can St D Cathl from 92; Adn St D from 96; V Steynton from 97. *The New Vicarage, Steynton, Milford Haven SA73 1AW*

DAVIES, Harry Bertram. b 11. Chich Th Coll 70. **d** 70 **p** 71. C Fareham H Trin *Portsm* 70-74; R Lowick w Sudborough and Slipton *Pet* 74-81; P-in-c Islip 78-81; rtd 81; Perm to Offic *Lich* 81-93. *22 Beachwood Avenue, Wall Heath, Kingswinford, W Midlands DY6 0HL* Tel (01384) 292000

DAVIES, Hedleigh Llewelyn. b 17. Worc Coll Ox BA40 MA44. Westcott Ho Cam 40. **d** 41 **p** 42. C Beaufort *Mon* 41-43; RAChD 43-48; C Norwood St Luke *S'wark* 48-49; V Mitcham St Barn 49-54; R Motcombe *Sarum* 54-59; V Catton *Nor* 59-66; Hon Min Can Nor Cathl 60-66; Sacr Nor Cathl 66-71; V Nor St Andr 66-72; P-in-c Nor St Mich at Plea and St Pet Hungate 66-72; V Nor St Mary in the Marsh 67-72; R Brooke w Kirstead 72-82; Hon Min Can Nor Cathl from 78; rtd 82; Perm to Offic *Nor* from 91. *April Rise, Rectory Road, East Carleton, Norwich NR14 8HT* Tel (01508) 70420

DAVIES, Henry Joseph. b 38. Univ of Wales (Cardiff) BSc61. St Mich Coll Llan 75. **d** 76 **p** 77. C Griffithstown *Mon* 76-79; TV Cwmbran 79-85; V Newport St Andr from 85. *The Vicarage, 1 Brookfield Close, Liswerry, Newport NP9 0LA* Tel (01633) 271904

DAVIES, Canon Henry Lewis. b 20. St Jo Coll Dur BA42 DipTh43 MA45. **d** 43 **p** 44. C Upton-upon-Severn *Worc* 43-47; C Dudley St Jo 47-49; C Halesowen 49-52; V Cradley 52-65; R Old Swinford 65-78; R Old Swinford Stourbridge 78-85; rtd 85; Perm to Offic *Worc* from 87. *15 Bramley Road, Bewdley, Worcs DY12 2BU* Tel (01299) 402713

DAVIES, Herbert John. b 30. Glouc Sch of Min 84. **d** 87 **p** 88. NSM Cheltenham St Mark *Glouc* from 87. *45 Farmington Road, Benhall, Cheltenham, Glos GL51 6AG* Tel (01242) 515996

DAVIES, Herbert Lewis Owen. b 08. CBE. Ox Univ BA31 MA36. St Steph Ho Ox 31. **d** 32 **p** 33. C Newport St Paul *Mon* 32-35; CF 35-61; QHC 59-61; R Newent *Glouc* 61-68; R Bourton on the Hill 68-75; rtd 75. *Conway, Croft Drive West, Caldy, Wirral, Merseyside L48 2JQ* Tel 0151-625 1860

✠**DAVIES, The Rt Revd Howell Haydn.** b 27. ARIBA55 DipArch54. Tyndale Hall Bris 56. **d** 59 **p** 60 **c** 81. C Heref St Pet w St Owen *Heref* 59-61; Kenya 61-79; Adn N Maseno 71-74; Provost Nairobi 74-79; V Woking St Pet *Guildf* 79-81; Uganda 81-87; Bp Karamoja 81-87; V Wolverhampton St Jude *Lich* 87-93; rtd 93; Perm to Offic *Heref* from 93. *3 Gilberts Wood, Ewyas Harold, Hereford HR2 0JL* Tel (01981) 240984

DAVIES, Hugh Middlecott. b 19. Worc Ord Coll 58. **d** 59 **p** 60. C Whitchurch *Lich* 59-61; R Scarning w Wendling *Nor* 61-66; R Ightfield w Calverhall *Lich* 66-72; Chapl HM Borstal Stoke Heath 70-72; R Catfield *Nor* 72-74; Chapl Nor Hosp 74-75; Asst Chapl HM Pris Nor 74-77; R Bunwell w Carleton Rode 75-77; Master Charterhouse Hull 77-80; rtd 80; Chapl Addenbrooke's Hosp Cam 80-81; Perm to Offic *Nor* 81-94. *Flat 5, Manormead, Tilford Road, Hindhead, Surrey GU26 6RA* Tel (01428) 608904

DAVIES, Hywel John. b 45. Univ of Wales (Abth) BA67 Univ of Wales (Ban) DipEd68 Univ of Wales (Cardiff) MA. Qu Coll Birm DipTh96. **d** 97. Min Can Ban Cathl *Ban* from 97. *Caplandy, Glanrafon, Bangor LL57 2LH* Tel (01248) 352466

DAVIES, Ian. b 45. Man Coll of Educn TCert74 Open Univ BA79. Carl Dioc Tr Inst 88. **d** 91 **p** 92. NSM Harraby *Carl* 91-95; C Barrow St Jo 95-96; P-in-c from 96. *St John's Vicarage, James Watt Terrace, Barrow-in-Furness, Cumbria LA14 2TS* Tel (01229) 821101

DAVIES, Ian Charles. b 51. Sarum & Wells Th Coll 78. **d** 81 **p** 82. C E Bedfont *Lon* 81-84; C Cheam *S'wark* 84-87; V Merton St Jas 87-96; RD Merton 91-96; Chapl Tiffin Sch Kingston from 96; P-in-c Kingston St Luke *S'wark* from 96. *The Vicarage, 4 Burton Road, Kingston upon Thames, Surrey KT2 5TE* Tel 0181-546 4064

DAVIES, Father Ian Elliott. b 64. Univ of Wales (Ban) BD85. Ridley Hall Cam 86. **d** 88 **p** 89. C Baglan *Llan* 88-90; C Skewen 90-96; C St Marylebone All SS *Lon* from 96. *6 Margaret Street, London W1N 7LG* Tel 0171-636 1788 or 636 9961 Fax 436 4470

DAVIES, Canon Ivor Llewellyn. b 35. Univ of Wales BA56 St Cath Soc Ox BA58 MA63. Wycliffe Hall Ox 56. **d** 62 **p** 63. C Wrexham *St As* 62-64; India 65-71; V Connah's Quay *St As* 71-79; P-in-c Gorsley w Cliffords Mesne *Glouc* 79-84; P-in-c Hempsted 84-90; Dir of Ords 84-90; Hon Can Glouc Cathl from 89; V Dean Forest St Paul from 90; P-in-c Viney Hill from 97. *The Vicarage, Parkend, Lydney, Glos GL15 4HL* Tel (01594) 562284

DAVIES, Canon Ivor Llewelyn. b 23. Univ of Wales (Swansea) BA49 St Cath Soc Ox DipTh52 Fitzw Coll Cam BA56 MA60. Wycliffe Hall Ox 49. **d** 51 **p** 52. C Knighton and Heyope *S & B* 51-54; Hon C Cambridge St Andr Gt *Ely* 54-56; C-in-c Llanwrthwl *S & B* 56-59; R Llanfeugan w Llanddetty and Glyncollwg 59-70; P-in-c Llansantffraed-juxta-Usk 67-70; V Hay 70-72; RD Hay 73-82; V Hay w Llanigon and Capel-y-Ffin 72-87; Hon Can Brecon Cathl 76-79; Can Brecon Cathl 79-89; RD Hay 85-87; V Knighton and Norton 87-89; Treas Brecon Cathl 88-89; rtd 89. *Bracken Lea, Hazler Road, Church Stretton, Shropshire SY6 7AQ* Tel (01694) 724459

DAVIES, James Alan. b 38. St Jo Coll Nottm Lambeth STh95. **d** 83 **p** 84. C Fletchamstead *Cov* 83-87; P-in-c Hartshill 87-89; V 89-93; Asst RD Nuneaton 90-93; V E Green from 93. *St Andrew's Vicarage, Church Lane, Eastern Green, Coventry CV5 7BX* Tel (01203) 466215

DAVIES, James Owen. b 26. St Aid Birkenhead 60. **d** 61 **p** 62. C Drayton in Hales *Lich* 61-65; V Tipton St Jo 65-69; P-in-c Lt

Drayton 70-73; V from 73. *The Vicarage, Little Drayton, Market Drayton, Shropshire TF9 1DY* Tel (01630) 652801

DAVIES, Canon James Trevor Eiddig. b 17. St D Coll Lamp BA39 AKC41. **d** 41 **p** 42. C Rhymney *Mon* 41-44; C Newport St Andr 44-47; P-in-c 47-51; P-in-c Nash 50-51; R Bettws Newydd w Trostrey and Kemeys Commander 51-58; V Blaenavon w Capel Newydd 58-68; V Llantarnam 68-71; R Cwmbran 71-86; Hon Can St Woolos Cathl 83-86; rtd 86. *34 Rockfield Road, Monmouth NP5 3BA* Tel (01600) 716649

DAVIES, James William. b 51. Trin Hall Cam BA72 MA76 St Jo Coll Dur BA79. **d** 80 **p** 81. C Croydon Ch Ch Broad Green *Cant* 80-83; CMS 83-86; Chapl Bethany Sch Goudhurst 86-90; P-in-c Parkstone St Luke *Sarum* from 90. *The Vicarage, 2 Birchwood Road, Parkstone, Poole, Dorset BH14 9NP* Tel (01202) 741030

DAVIES, Mrs Jane Ann. b 58. Heref Coll of FE ONC77 Coll of Ripon & York St Jo MA97. N Ord Course 94 Aston Tr Scheme 91 W of England Minl Tr Course 93. **d** 96 **p** 97. NSM Heref S Wye *Heref* 96-97; C from 97. *89 Belmont Road, Hereford HR2 7JN* Tel (01432) 271137 Fax 275034

DAVIES, Sister Joan Margaret. b 06. Bedf Coll Lon BA28 Maria Grey Coll Lon DipEd29. **dss** 37 **d** 87. CSA from 34; Notting Hill St Clem *Lon* 37-43; Paddington St Steph w St Luke 48-69; Shadwell St Paul w Ratcliffe St Jas 69-73; R Foundn of St Kath in Ratcliffe 69-73; Abbey Ho Malmesbury 76-79; Lic to Offic *Bris* 76-79. *St Andrew's House, 2 Tavistock Road, London W11 1BA* Tel 0171-229 2662

DAVIES, John Atcherley. b 27. St Jo Coll Dur BA55. Wycliffe Hall Ox 55. **d** 57 **p** 58. C Eastbourne St Jo *Chich* 57-61; Chapl RN 61-82; V Hyde Common *Win* 82-92; rtd 92. *6 Durlston Crescent, St Catherine's Hill, Christchurch, Dorset BH23 2ST* Tel (01202) 484398

DAVIES, John Barden. b 47. Univ of Wales (Ban) DipTh70. St D Coll Lamp 70. **d** 71 **p** 72. C Rhosllannerchrugog *St As* 71-75; R Llanbedr-y-Cennin *Ban* 75-86; Adult Educn Officer 86-93; V Betws-y-Coed and Capel Curig w Penmachno etc 86-93; R Llanfwrog and Clocaenog and Gyffylliog *St As* from 93; RD Dyffryn Clwyd from 95. *The Rectory, Mwrog Street, Ruthin LL15 1LE* Tel (01824) 24866 E-mail jbarden@dial.pipex.com

DAVIES, Preb John Conway de la Tour. b 16. Jes Coll Cam BA38 MA42. Ripon Hall Ox 39. **d** 40 **p** 41. C Chipping Norton *Ox* 40-44; CF 44-52; V Highters Heath *Birm* 52-57; V Peterchurch *Heref* 57-83; V Vowchurch and Turnastone 57-83; P-in-c Bredwardine w Brobury 77-83; R Peterchurch w Vowchurch, Turnastone and Dorstone 83-92; RD Abbeydore 78-84; Preb Heref Cathl 79-92; rtd 92; Perm to Offic *Heref* from 92. *The Palace, Peterchurch, Hereford HR2 0RY* Tel (01981) 550445

DAVIES, John David Edward. b 53. Southn Univ LLB74 Univ of Wales (Cardiff) DipTh84. St Mich Coll Llan 82. **d** 84 **p** 85. C Chepstow *Mon* 84-86; C Michaelston-y-Fedw and Rudry 86-89; R Bedwas and Rudry 89-95; V Maindee from 95. *St John's Vicarage, 25 St John's Road, Maindee, Newport NP9 8GR* Tel (01633) 277009

✠**DAVIES, The Rt Revd John Dudley.** b 27. Trin Coll Cam BA51 MA63. Linc Th Coll 52. **d** 53 **p** 54 **c** 87. C Leeds Halton St Wilfrid *Ripon* 53-56; S Africa 57-71; Sec Chapls in HE Gen Syn Bd of Educn 71-74; P-in-c Keele *Lich* 74-76; Chapl Keele Univ 74-76; Lic to Offic *Birm* 76-81; Prin USPG Coll of the Ascension Selly Oak 76-81; Preb Lich Cathl *Lich* 76-87; Can Res, Preb and Sacr St As Cathl *St As* 82-85; Dioc Missr 82-87; V Llanrhaeadr-ym-Mochnant, Llanarmon, Pennant etc 85-87; Suff Bp Shrewsbury *Lich* 87-92; Area Bp Shrewsbury 92-94; rtd 94. *Angorfa, 3 Canal Terrace, Canalside, Froncysyllte, Llangollen LL20 7RB*

DAVIES, John Edwards Gurnos. b 18. Ch Coll Cam BA41 MA45. Westcott Ho Cam 40. **d** 42 **p** 43. C Portwood St Paul *Ches* 42-44; CF (EC) 44-46; CF 46-73; Asst Chapl Gen 70; Hon Chapl to The Queen 72; R Monk Sherborne and Pamber *Win* 73-76; P-in-c Sherborne 76; R The Sherbornes w Pamber 76-83; rtd 83. *3 Parsonage Lane, Edington, Westbury, Wilts BA13 4QS* Tel (01380) 830479

DAVIES, John Gwylim. b 27. Ripon Hall Ox 67. **d** 70 **p** 71. C Ox St Mich *Ox* 70-71; C Ox St Mich w St Martin and All SS 71-72; TV New Windsor 73-77; R Hagley *Worc* 77-83; TV Littleham w Exmouth *Ex* 83-92; Asst Dioc Stewardship Adv 83-92; rtd 92; Perm to Offic *Ex* from 92. *5 The Retreat, The Retreat Drive, Topsham, Exeter EX3 0LS* Tel (01392) 876995

DAVIES, John Gwyn. b 12. St Cath Coll Cam BA36 MA40. Ely Th Coll 36. **d** 37 **p** 38. C Fleetwood *Blackb* 37-39; C Wyken *Cov* 39-44; P-in-c 44-45; V 45-54; V Rowington 54-77; rtd 78; Perm to Offic *Cov* from 78. *Lapwater, Pinley, Claverdon, Warwick CV35 8NA* Tel (01926) 842597

DAVIES, John Harverd. b 57. Keble Coll Ox BA80 MA84 CCC Cam MPhil82. Westcott Ho Cam 82. **d** 84 **p** 85. C Liv Our Lady and St Nic w St Anne *Liv* 84-87; C Pet St Jo *Pet* 87-90; Min Can Pet Cathl 88-90; V Anfield St Marg *Liv* 90-94; Chapl Fell and Lect Keble Coll Ox from 94. *Keble College, Oxford OX1 3PG* Tel (01865) 272787 or 272727

DAVIES, Canon John Howard. b 29. St Jo Coll Cam BA50 MA54 Nottm Univ BD62. Westcott Ho Cam 54. **d** 55 **p** 56. Succ Derby Cathl *Derby* 55-58; Chapl Westcott Ho Cam 58-63; Lect Th Southn Univ 63-81; Lic to Offic *Win* 63-81; Sen Lect 74-81; Dir Th and Relig Studies Southn Univ 81-94; Can Th Win Cathl *Win* 81-91; Hon C Southampton St Alb 88-91; Hon C Swaythling 91-94; rtd 94. *13 Glen Eyre Road, Southampton SO16 3GA* Tel (01703) 679359

DAVIES, Canon John Howard. b 35. Ely Th Coll 62. **d** 64 **p** 65. C Bromsgrove All SS *Worc* 64-67; C Astwood Bank w Crabbs Cross 67-70; R Worc St Martin 70-74; P-in-c Worc St Pet 72-74; R Worc St Martin w St Pet 74-79; RD Worc E 77-79; TR Malvern Link w Cowleigh 79-93; Hon Can Worc Cathl from 81; RD Malvern 83-92; V Bromsgrove St Jo from 93. *The Vicarage, 12 Kidderminster Road, Bromsgrove, Worcs B61 7JW* Tel (01527) 876517

DAVIES, John Hugh Conwy. b 42. CEng MICE72 Bris Univ BSc64 PhD67. Linc Th Coll 84. **d** 86 **p** 87. C Limber Magna w Brocklesby *Linc* 86-89; R Wickenby Gp 89-94; R Denbigh and Nantglyn *St As* from 94. *The Rectory, St David's Lane, Denbigh LL16 3EP* Tel (01745) 812970

DAVIES, John Hywel Morgan. b 45. St D Coll Lamp BA71 LTh73. **d** 73 **p** 74. C Milford Haven *St D* 73-77; V from 89; R Castlemartin w Warren and Angle etc 77-82; R Walton W w Talbenny and Haroldston W 82-89. *St Katharine's Vicarage, 1 Sandhurst Road, Milford Haven SA73 3JU* Tel (01646) 693314

DAVIES, John Ifor. b 20. ACP DipEd. **d** 80 **p** 81. Hon C Allerton *Liv* 80-84; Hon C Ffynnongroyw *St As* 84-87; Hon C Whitford 87-88. *Hafan Deg, Ffordd-y-Graig, Lixwm, Holywell CH8 8LY* Tel (01352) 781151

DAVIES, John Keith. b 33. St Mich Coll Llan 80. **d** 82 **p** 83. C Llanbadarn Fawr w Capel Bangor and Goginan *St D* 82-84; V Llandygwydd and Cenarth w Cilrhedyn etc 84-89; V Abergwili w Llanfihangel-uwch-Gwili etc from 89; RD Carmarthen from 93. *The Vicarage, Wellfield Road, Abergwili, Carmarthen SA31 2JQ* Tel (01267) 234189

DAVIES, John Melvyn George. b 37. Wycliffe Hall Ox 68. **d** 71 **p** 72. C Norbury *Ches* 71-75; C Heswall 76-78; V Claughton cum Grange 78-83; R Waverton from 83; RD Malpas from 90. *The Vicarage, Waverton, Chester CH3 7QN* Tel (01244) 335581

DAVIES, John Neville Milwyn. b 15. MBE45. Univ of Wales BA37. St Steph Ho Ox 37. **d** 38 **p** 39. C Monmouth *Mon* 38-40; C Roath St Marg *Llan* 40-41; Perm to Offic *St D* 41-42; CF 42-73; QHC 69-73; V Clapham H Spirit *S'wark* 73-80; rtd 80; Perm to Offic *B & W* 91-94. *Brooklands, Durcott Lane, Camerton, Bath BA3 1QE* Tel (01225) 471361

DAVIES, Canon John Oswell. b 27. St D Coll Lamp 74. **d** 75 **p** 76. C Henfynyw w Aberaeron and Llanddewi Aberarth *St D* 75-76; P-in-c Eglwysnewydd w Ysbyty Ystwyth 76-77; V 77-83; R Maenordeifi and Capel Colman w Llanfihangel etc 83-93; RD Cemais and Sub-Aeron 87-93; Hon Can St D Cathl 92-93; rtd 93. *Hafod, Carregwen, Llechryd, Cardigan SA43 2PJ* Tel (01239) 682568

DAVIES, The Ven John Stewart. b 43. MSOTS Univ of Wales BA72 Qu Coll Cam MLitt74. Westcott Ho Cam 72. **d** 74 **p** 75. C Hawarden *St As* 74-78; Tutor St Deiniol's Lib Hawarden 76-83; V Rhosymedre *St As* 78-87; Dir Dioc Minl Tr Course from 83; Warden of Ords 83-91; Hon Can St As Cathl from 86; V Mold 87-92; Adn St As from 91; R Llandyrnog and Llangwyfan from 92. *The Rectory, Fford Las, Llandyrnog, Denbigh LL16 4LT* Tel (01824) 790777

DAVIES, Canon John Treharne. b 14. St D Coll Lamp BA36. **d** 38 **p** 39. C Swansea St Matt w Greenhill *S & B* 38-42; C Calne *Sarum* 42-52; V Bradpole 52-59; V Potterne 59-73; V Worton 67-73; RD Devizes 65-73; Can and Preb Sarum Cathl 72-82; P-in-c Ramsbury 73-74; R Whitton 74-76; TR Whitton 76-81; rtd 81; Perm to Offic *Heref* from 82. *16 Lambourne Close, Ledbury, Herefordshire HR8 2HW* Tel (01531) 634629

DAVIES, John Vernon. b 16. Or Coll Ox BA40 MA43. Cuddesdon Coll 40. **d** 41 **p** 42. C Llantwit Fadre *Llan* 41-44; C Roath St Martin 44-45; C Peterston-super-Ely 47-51; P-in-c Flemingston and Gileston 51-54; R 54-56; Org Sec SPCK (Dio Llan) 55-64; V Cardiff St Andr and St Teilo 56-69; R Radyr 69-83; rtd 83; Perm to Offic *Llan* from 83. *8 Insole Gardens, Llandaff, Cardiff CF5 2HW* Tel (01222) 562130

DAVIES, John Vernon. b 20. Clifton Th Coll 66. **d** 68 **p** 69. C Surbiton Hill Ch Ch *S'wark* 68-70; C Heatherlands St Jo *Sarum* 70-75; V Wandsworth St Mich *S'wark* 75-83; rtd 83; Perm to Offic *Llan* from 83. *11 Pearson Avenue, Parkstone, Poole, Dorset BH14 0DT* Tel (01202) 731591

DAVIES, Johnston ap Llynfi (Ion). b 28. St D Coll Lamp BA51 St Mich Coll Llan 51. **d** 53 **p** 54. C Swansea Ch Ch *S & B* 53-55; C Sketty 55-57; Nigeria 57-61; R Whittington *Derby* 61-64; Chapl Broadmoor Hosp Crowthorne 64-66; Perm to Offic *Ox* 67-72; Perm to Offic *York* 72-86; V Creeksea w Althorne, Latchingdon and N Fambridge *Chelmsf* 86-88; rtd 88; Asst Chapl Costa Blanca *Eur* 89-92; Chapl Costa Blanca 92-93; Lic to Offic 93-95. *55 Castle Acre, Swansea SA3 5TH*

DAVIES, Jonathan Byron. b 69. Univ of Wales DipTh94 BTh95. St Mich Coll Llan BTh94. **d** 96 **p** 97. C Betws w Ammanford *St D* from 96. *44 Maes-y-Coed, Ammanford SA18 2JB* Tel (01269) 591035

DAVIES, Dr Julian Edward. b 60. Jes Coll Ox BA82 MA86 DPhil87 Selw Coll Cam BA92. Ridley Hall Cam 90. **d** 94 **p** 95. C Hucknall Torkard *S'well* 94-96; C Eglwysilan *Llan* from 96.

1 Caerphilly Road, Senghenydd, Caerphilly CF83 4FR Tel (01222) 830392

DAVIES, Kenneth John. b 42. Ripon Coll Cuddesdon 79. **d** 80 **p** 81. C Buckingham *Ox* 80-83; V Birstall *Wakef* 83-91; TV Crookes St Thos *Sheff* 91-94; TR Huntington *York* from 94. *The Rectory, New Lane, Huntington, York YO3 9NU* Tel (01904) 768160

DAVIES, Kevin Godfrey (Kev). b 62. Univ Coll Ox BA84 MA87. Trin Coll Bris BA93. **d** 93 **p** 94. C Otley *Bradf* 93-97; P-in-c Scotby *Carl* from 97. *The Vicarage, Lambley Bank, Scotby, Carlisle CA4 8BX* Tel (01228) 513205

DAVIES, Laurence Gordon. b 28. Down Coll Cam BA52 MA56. Linc Th Coll 52. **d** 54 **p** 55. C E Dulwich St Jo *S'wark* 54-57; C Boyne Hill *Ox* 57-61; V Brigstock w Stanion *Pet* 61-69; R Gt w Lt Billing 69-83; V Welton w Ashby St Ledgers 83-88; rtd 88; Perm to Offic *Ox* from 89. *Cherry Pie, 56 Couching Street, Watlington, Oxon OX9 5PU* Tel (01491) 612446

DAVIES, Lawrence. b 14. Univ of Wales (Lamp) BA36. Chich Th Coll 36. **d** 38 **p** 39. C Ruabon *St As* 38-45; Chapl RNVR 45-48; Chapl RN 48-53; V Longdon *Worc* 54-78; V Queenhill w Holdfast 54-78; V Longdon, Bushley and Queenhill w Holdfast 78-86; RD Upton 80-86; rtd 86; Perm to Offic *Worc* from 86. *Theocsbury, Bushley, Tewkesbury, Glos GL20 6HX* Tel (01684) 294220

DAVIES, Lawrence. b 20. BEM45. Tyndale Hall Bris 46. **d** 49 **p** 50. C Cambridge St Paul *Ely* 49-54; V Nottingham St Ann *S'well* 54-61; V Preston All SS *Blackb* 61-73; V St Michaels on Wyre 73-85; rtd 85; Perm to Offic *Blackb* from 85; Perm to Offic *Carl* from 85. *23 Inglemere Gardens, Arnside, Carnforth, Lancs LA5 0BX* Tel (01524) 762141

DAVIES, Lawrence Vercoe. b 40. Lich Th Coll 67. **d** 70 **p** 71. C Glan Ely *Llan* 70-77; V Grangetown from 77. *St Paul's Vicarage, Llanmaes Street, Cardiff CF1 7LR* Tel (01222) 228707

DAVIES, The Ven Lorys Martin. b 36. JP. ALCM52 Univ of Wales (Lamp) BA57. Wells Th Coll 57. **d** 59 **p** 60. C Tenby w Gumfreston *St D* 59-62; Brentwood Sch Essex 62-66; Chapl Solihull Sch 66-68; V Moseley St Mary *Birm* 68-81; Can Res Birm Cathl 81-92; Dioc Dir of Ords 82-90; Adn Bolton *Man* from 92; Bp's Adv Hosp Chaplaincies from 92; Warden of Readers from 92. *45 Rudgwick Drive, Brandlesholme, Bury, Lancs BL8 1YA* Tel 0161-761 6117 Fax as telephone

DAVIES, Malcolm. b 35. St Mich Coll Llan 82. **d** 84 **p** 85. C Roath St Marg *Llan* 84-88; C Pentre 88-94; V Llancarfan w Llantrithyd from 94. *The Vicarage, Llancarfan, Barry CF62 3AD* Tel (01446) 750241

DAVIES, Malcolm Thomas. b 36. Open Univ BA81. St Mich Coll Llan 71. **d** 73 **p** 74. C Betws w Ammanford *St D* 73-76; V Cil-y-Cwm and Ystrad-ffin w Rhandir-mwyn etc 76-80; V Llangyfelach *S & B* 80-85; V Lougher 85-94; V Llanelli St Paul *St D* from 94. *St Peter's Vicarage, St Peter's Terrace, Llanelli SA15 2RT* Tel (01554) 752378

DAVIES, Mrs Margaret Adelaide. b 45. Weymouth Coll of Educn CertEd67. S Dios Minl Tr Scheme 92. **d** 95 **p** 96. NSM Westbury *Sarum* from 95. *60 Newtown, Westbury, Wilts BA13 3EF* Tel (01373) 823735

DAVIES, Mark. b 62. BA85. Coll of Resurr Mirfield 86. **d** 89 **p** 90. C Barnsley St Mary *Wakef* 89-95; R Hemsworth from 95. *The Rectory, 3 Church Close, Hemsworth, Pontefract, W Yorkshire WF9 4SJ* Tel (01977) 610507

DAVIES, Martyn John. b 60. Chich Th Coll 82. **d** 85 **p** 86. C Llantrisant *Llan* 85-87; C Whitchurch 87-90; V Porth w Trealaw from 90. *St Paul's Vicarage, Birchgrove Street, Porth CF39 9UU* Tel (01443) 682401

DAVIES, Mervyn Morgan. b 25. Univ of Wales BA49. Coll of Resurr Mirfield 49. **d** 51 **p** 52. C Penarth w Lavernock *Llan* 51-58; Lic to Offic *Wakef* 58-60; C Port Talbot St Theodore *Llan* 60-63; V Pontycymer and Blaengarw 63-69; V Fairwater 69-95; RD Llan 81-95; Ed Welsh Churchman from 82; Can Llan Cathl 84-89; Prec 89-95; rtd 95. *20 Palace Avenue, Llandaff, Cardiff CF5 2DU* Tel (01222) 575327

DAVIES, Meurig Ceredig. b 21. Univ of Wales (Abth) BA43. St Mich Coll Llan 43. **d** 45 **p** 46. C Llangeler *St D* 45-47; C Llanfihangel Geneu'r Glyn 47-49; C Pen-bre 49-51; V Gwynfe and Llanddeusant 51-55; CF 56-59; V Clydach *S & B* 59-60; Perm to Offic *Pet* 64-74; V St Dogmael's w Moylgrove and Monington *St D* 74-86; rtd 86. *Geinfe, Gelliwen, Llechryd, Cardigan SA43 2PQ* Tel (01239) 682550

DAVIES, Miss Moira Kathleen. b 41. Cant Sch of Min. **d** 88 **p** 94. Par Dn Walmer *Cant* 88-94; C 94-96; P-in-c Somercotes and Grainthorpe w Conisholme *Linc* from 96. *The Rectory, Keeling Street, North Somercotes, Louth, Lincs LN11 7QU* Tel (01507) 358829

DAVIES, Canon Mostyn David. b 37. AKC64. **d** 65 **p** 66. C Corby St Columba *Pet* 65-69; Ind Chapl from 69; P-in-c Pet St Barn from 80; Can Pet Cathl from 95. *16 Swanspool, Peterborough PE3 7LS* Tel (01733) 262034

DAVIES, Myles Cooper. b 50. Sarum & Wells Th Coll 71. **d** 74 **p** 75. C W Derby St Mary *Liv* 74-77; C Seaforth 77-80; V 80-84; Chapl Rathbone Hosp Liv from 84; V Stanley *Liv* from 84; Dir of Ords from 94. *St Anne's Vicarage, 8 Derwent Square, Liverpool L13 6QT* Tel 0151-228 5252

DAVIES, Neil Anthony Bowen. b 52. Ex Univ BSc74. Westcott Ho Cam 75. **d** 78 **p** 79. C Llanblethian w Cowbridge and Llandough etc *Llan* 78-80; C Aberdare St Jo 80-82; V Troedyrhiw w Merthyr Vale 82-88; Min Lower Earley LEP *Ox* 88-92; V Earley Trinity 92-95; P-in-c Reading St Luke w St Bart from 95. *St Luke's Vicarage, 14 Erleigh Road, Reading RG1 5LH* Tel 0118-926 2372

DAVIES, Nigel Lawrence. b 55. Lanc Univ BEd77. Sarum & Wells Th Coll 84. **d** 87 **p** 88. C Heywood St Luke w All So *Man* 87-91; V Burneside *Carl* from 91. *St Oswald's Vicarage, Burneside, Kendal, Cumbria LA9 6QJ* Tel (01539) 722015

DAVIES, Noel Paul. b 47. Chich Th Coll 83. **d** 85 **p** 86. C Milford Haven *St D* 85-89; R Jeffreyston w Reynoldston and E Williamston etc from 89. *The Rectory, Jeffreyston, Kilgetty SA68 0SG* Tel (01646) 651269

DAVIES, Norman Edward. b 37. Worc Coll Ox BA62. Cuddesdon Coll 62. **d** 64 **p** 65. C Mottingham St Andr *S'wark* 64-67; Hon C 67-75 and 83-87; Hd Master W Hatch Sch Chigwell 76-82; Hd Master Sedghill Sch Lon 82-87; Hon C Eltham H Trin *S'wark* 77-82; V Plumstead St Mark and St Marg 87-96; rtd 96; Perm to Offic *S'wark* from 96; Perm to Offic *Chich* from 96. *Little Mow Bungalow, Guist Bottom Road, Fakenham, Norfolk NR21 0AG*

DAVIES, Miss Patricia Elizabeth. b 36. Westf Coll Lon BA58 Hughes Hall Cam CertEd59 Leeds Univ MA74. NE Ord Course 83. **dss** 86 **d** 87 **p** 94. Killingworth *Newc* 86-87; Hon C 87-90; Hon C Newc H Cross 91-96; NSM Newc Epiphany from 96. *The Vicarage, Wansbeck Road, Newcastle upon Tyne NE3 2LR* Tel 0191-285 8792

DAVIES, Paul Lloyd. b 46. Solicitor 71 Bris Univ LLB68 Trin Coll Carmarthen 84. **d** 87 **p** 88. NSM Newport w Cilgwyn and Dinas w Llanllawer *St D* from 87. *Priorswood, The Paddock, Fishguard SA65 9NU* Tel (01348) 873306

DAVIES, Paul Martin. b 35. Lon Univ BD75. Sarum & Wells Th Coll 75. **d** 75 **p** 76. C Walthamstow St Mary w St Steph *Chelmsf* 75-79; Kenya 79-86; R Leven w Catwick *York* 86-95; RD N Holderness 90-95; rtd 95; Perm to Offic *York* from 95. *54 The Meadows, Cherry Burton, Beverley, N Humberside HU17 7SD* Tel (01964) 551739

DAVIES, Paul Scott. b 59. Cranmer Hall Dur 85. **d** 88 **p** 89. C New Addington *S'wark* 88-91; C Croydon H Sav 91-94; P-in-c Norton in the Moors *Lich* from 94. *The New Rectory, Norton Lane, Stoke-on-Trent ST6 8BY* Tel (01782) 534622

DAVIES, Percy Sharples. b 10. Univ of Wales BA32. St Steph Ho Ox 32. **d** 34 **p** 35. C Hanmer *St As* 34-40; C Perry Hill St Geo *S'wark* 40-44; P-in-c Forest Hill St Paul 44-51; V Plumstead St Mark 51-68; V Plumstead St Mark and St Marg 68-77; rtd 77; Perm to Offic *Cant* from 77. *The Sharples, West Lane, Felton, Bristol BS18 7UF*

DAVIES, Peter Huw. b 57. Crewe & Alsager Coll BEd79. Wycliffe Hall Ox 87. **d** 89 **p** 90. C Moreton *Ches* 89-93; V Weston-super-Mare St Paul *B & W* from 93. *St Paul's Vicarage, 33 Clarence Road North, Weston-super-Mare, Avon BS23 4AW* Tel (01934) 412687

DAVIES, Peter Richard. b 32. St Jo Coll Ox BA55 MA58. Westcott Ho Cam 56. **d** 58 **p** 59. C Cannock *Lich* 58-62; Kenya 63-76; Chapl Bedford Sch 76-85; V Dale and St Brides w Marloes *St D* 85-92; rtd 92. *Canthill Cottage, Dale, Haverfordwest SA62 3QZ* Tel (01646) 636535

DAVIES, Peter Timothy William. b 50. Leeds Univ BSc74. Oak Hill Th Coll 75. **d** 78 **p** 79. C Kingston Hill St Paul *S'wark* 78-81; C Hove Bp Hannington Memorial Ch *Chich* 81-88; V Audley *Lich* from 88. *The Vicarage, Wilbraham Walk, Audley, Stoke-on-Trent ST7 8HL* Tel (01782) 720392

DAVIES, The Ven Philip Bertram. b 33. Cuddesdon Coll 61. **d** 63 **p** 64. C Atherton *Man* 63-66; V Winton 66-71; R Salford St Phil w St Steph 71-76; V Radlett *St Alb* 76-87; RD Aldenham 79-87; Adn St Alb from 87. *6 Sopwell Lane, St Albans, Herts AL1 1RR* Tel (01727) 857973

DAVIES, Philip James. b 58. UEA BA79 Keswick Hall Coll PGCE80. Ridley Hall Cam 86. **d** 89 **p** 90. C Rainham *Roch* 89-90; C Gravesend St Geo 90-95; V Rosherville from 95. *St Mark's Vicarage, 123 London Road, Gravesend, Kent DA11 9NH* Tel (01474) 534430

DAVIES, Philip Simon. b 65. Trin Coll Ox BA87 MA91. Aston Tr Scheme 93 Ridley Hall Cam 95. **d** 97. C Burntwood *Lich* from 97. *9 Derwent Close, Burntwood, Lichfield, Staffs WS7 9JN*

DAVIES, Philip Wyn. b 50. Univ of Wales BA72 MA82 DAA82. St D Dioc Tr Course 93 St Mich Coll Llan BD96. **d** 96 **p** 97. C Llandysul *St D* from 96. *Glenview, Church Street, Llandyssul SA44 4QS* Tel (01559) 362404

DAVIES, Raymond Emlyn Peter. b 25. St Mich Coll Llan 51. **d** 53 **p** 54. C Llangeinor *Llan* 53-58; C Llanishen and Lisvane 58-62 and 65-68; R Glyncorrwg w Afan Vale and Cymmer Afan 62-65; V Penrhiwceiber w Matthewstown and Ynysboeth 68-72; C Whitchurch 72-73; V Childs Ercall *Lich* 73-81; R Stoke upon Tern 73-81; P-in-c Hamstall Ridware w Pipe Ridware 81-82; P-in-c Kings Bromley 81-82; P-in-c Mavesyn Ridware 81-82; R The Ridwares and Kings Bromley 83-90; rtd 90; Perm to Offic *B & W* from 95. *22 Drake Road, Wells, Somerset BA5 3JX* Tel (01749) 679155

DAVIES, Reginald Charles. b 33. Tyndale Hall Bris 58. **d** 64 **p** 65. C Heywood St Jas *Man* 64-66; C Drypool St Columba w St Andr and St Pet *York* 66-69; V Denaby Main *Sheff* from 69. *The Vicarage, Church Road, Denaby Main, Doncaster, S Yorkshire DN12 4AD* Tel (01709) 862297

DAVIES, Rendle Leslie. b 29. St Chad's Coll Dur BA52 DipTh54. **d** 54 **p** 55. C Monmouth *Mon* 54-58; V Llangwm Uchaf w Llangwm Isaf w Gwernesney etc 58-63; V Usk and Monkswood w Glascoed Chpl and Gwehelog from 63; Chapl HM Young Offender Inst Usk and Prescoed 63-95. *The Vicarage, Castle Parade, Usk NP5 1AA* Tel (01291) 672653 Fax 673800

DAVIES, Richard Henry. b 44. Mansf Coll Ox BA72 MA78. St Steph Ho Ox 68. **d** 72 **p** 73. C Higham Ferrers w Chelveston *Pet* 72-80; C Cantley *Sheff* 80-82; V Leic St Aid *Leic* 82-85; C Tonge Moor *Man* 85-94. *46 Ashford Road, Withington, Manchester M20 3EH* Tel 0161-445 2987

DAVIES, Richard James. b 42. Peterho Cam BA64 MA68. St Steph Ho Ox 67. **d** 69 **p** 70. Rhodesia 69-72 and 75-80; Zimbabwe from 80; C Southwick *Chich* 72-74; P-in-c Malmesbury w Westport *Bris* 75. *James's Mission, PO Box 23, Nyamandlovu, Zimbabwe*

DAVIES, Richard Paul. b 48. Wycliffe Hall Ox 72. **d** 75 **p** 76. C Everton St Sav w St Cuth *Liv* 75-78; Chapl Asst Basingstoke Distr Hosp 78-80; TV Basingstoke *Win* 80-85; V Southampton Thornhill St Chris 85-94; V Eastleigh from 94. *The Vicarage, 1 Cedar Road, Eastleigh, Hants SO50 9DB* Tel (01703) 612073

DAVIES, Richard Paul. b 73. Univ of Wales (Lamp) BA94. Ripon Coll Cuddesdon 94. **d** 97. Min Can St D Cathl *St D* from 97. *Pembroke Cottage, Glasfryn Lane, St Davids, Haverfordwest SA62 6ST* Tel (01437) 720252

DAVIES, Robert Emlyn. b 56. N Staffs Poly BA79. Coll of Resurr Mirfield 83. **d** 86 **p** 87. C Cardiff St Jo *Llan* 86-90; V Cwmparc 90-97; V Aberdare St Jo from 97. *The Vicarage, 26 Abernant Road, Aberdare CF44 0PY* Tel (01685) 884769

DAVIES, Roger Charles. b 46. Univ of Wales BD73. St Mich Coll Llan 69. **d** 73 **p** 74. C Llanfabon *Llan* 73-76; CF (TAVR) 75-94; C Llanblethian w Cowbridge and Llandough etc *Llan* 76-78; CF 78-84; TV Halesworth w Linstead, Chediston, Holton etc *St E* 84-87; R Claydon and Barham 87-91; R Lavant *Chich* 91-94; Chapl Lavant Ho Sch W Sussex 91-94. *Address excluded by request*

DAVIES, Ross Owen. b 55. Melbourne Univ BA77 LLB79. ACT ThL81. **d** 81 **p** 82. Australia 81-91; P-in-c Mundford w Lynford *Nor* 91-94; P-in-c Ickburgh w Langford 91-94; P-in-c Cranwich 91-94; C Somerton w Compton Dundon, the Charltons etc *B & W* from 94. *The Parsonage, Charlton Adam, Somerton, Somerset TA11 7AS* Tel (01458) 223061

DAVIES, Preb Roy Basil. b 34. Bris Univ BA55. Westcott Ho Cam 57. **d** 59 **p** 60. C Ipswich St Mary le Tower *St E* 59-63; C Clun w Chapel Lawn *Heref* 63-70; V Bishop's Castle w Mainstone 70-83; RD Clun Forest 72-83; Preb Heref Cathl from 82; P-in-c Billingsley w Sidbury 83-86; P-in-c Chelmarsh 83-86; P-in-c Chetton w Deuxhill and Glazeley 83-86; P-in-c Middleton Scriven 83-86; R Billingsley w Sidbury, Middleton Scriven etc 86-89; RD Bridgnorth 87-89; TR Wenlock from 89. *The Rectory, Much Wenlock, Shropshire TF13 6BN* Tel (01952) 727396

DAVIES, Roy Gabe. b 38. Univ of Wales DipTh64. St Mich Coll Llan 61. **d** 64 **p** 65. C St Issells *St D* 64-65; C Milford Haven 65-67; C Codsall *Lich* 67-70; V Wolverhampton St Steph 70-79; V Newport St Julian *Mon* 79-89; V Lakenheath *St E* 89-94; R Llanllwchaearn and Llanina *St D* 94-96; V W Bromwich St Fran *Lich* from 96. *Friar Park Vicarage, 1 Freeman Road, Wednesbury, W Midlands WS10 0HJ* Tel 0121-556 5823

✠**DAVIES, The Rt Revd Roy Thomas.** b 34. St D Coll Lamp BA55 Jes Coll Ox DipTh58 BLitt59. St Steph Ho Ox 57. **d** 59 **p** 60 **c** 85. C Llanelli St Paul *St D* 59-64; V Llanafan y Trawscoed and Llanwnnws 64-67; Chapl Univ of Wales (Abth) 67-73; C Aberystwyth 67-69; TV 70-73; Sec Ch in Wales Prov Coun for Miss and Unity 73-79; V Carmarthen St Dav *St D* 79-83; Adn Carmarthen 82-85; V Llanegwad w Llanfynydd 83-85; Bp Llan from 85. *Llys Esgob, The Cathedral Green, Llandaff, Cardiff CF5 2YE* Tel (01222) 562400

DAVIES, Miss Sally Jane. b 63. Linc Coll Ox BA86. Trin Coll Bris BA92. **d** 92 **p** 94. C E Molesey St Paul *Guildf* 92-96; C Chalfont St Peter *Ox* from 96. *All Saints' Parsonage, Oval Way, Chalfont St Peter, Bucks SL9 8PZ* Tel (01753) 883839

DAVIES, Sarah Isabella. b 39. Llan Dioc Tr Scheme 87. **d** 91 **p** 97. NSM Pontypridd St Cath w St Matt *Llan* 91-93; NSM Ferndale w Maerdy 93-97; C from 97. *The Vicarage, Woodville Place, Maerdy, Ferndale CF43 4LS* Tel (01443) 756322

DAVIES, Sidney. b 16. St D Coll Lamp BA40. **d** 41 **p** 42. C Llandysul *St D* 41-44; C Llanfihangel-ar-arth 44-53; V Llanerch Aeron w Ciliau Aeron 53-69; R Llanerch Aeron w Ciliau Aeron and Dihewyd 69-82; rtd 82. *12 Pontfaen, Porthyrhyd, Carmarthen SA32 8PE* Tel (01267) 275525

DAVIES, Stanley James. b 18. MBE54. St Chad's Coll Dur BA40 DipTh41 MA44. **d** 41 **p** 42. C Walton St Marg Belmont Road *Liv* 41-42; C Wigan All SS 42-45; CF 45-68; Asst Chapl Gen Lon 68-70; BAOR 70-73; Hon Chapl to The Queen from 72; R Uley w Owlpen and Nympsfield *Glouc* 73-84; rtd 84; Perm to Offic *Ex* from 86. *Peverell Cottage, Doddiscombsleigh, Exeter EX6 7PR* Tel (01647) 252616

DAVIES, Stephen John (Steve). b 65. Nottm Univ BA86 Reading Univ MPhil88 ARICS90. Wycliffe Hall Ox BTh94. **d** 97. C Barton Seagrave w Warkton *Pet* from 97. *Rectory Cottage, St Botolph's Road, Barton Seagrave, Kettering, Northants NN15 6SR* Tel (01536) 517760

DAVIES, Stephen Walter. b 26. AKC54. **d** 55 **p** 56. C Plympton St Mary *Ex* 55-58; C Ex St Mark 58-61; Chapl RAF 61-77; R Feltwell *Ely* 78-84; R N Newton w St Michaelchurch, Thurloxton etc *B & W* 84-91; rtd 91. *5 Manchester Road, Exmouth, Devon EX8 1DE*

DAVIES, Stuart Simeon. b 13. St Chad's Coll Dur BA41 DipTh42 MA44. Knutsford Test Sch 37. **d** 42 **p** 43. C Anfield St Columba *Liv* 42-44; C Epsom St Barn *Guildf* 44-47; C Chieveley w Winterbourne and Oare *Ox* 47-52; V Kennington 52-65; R Fifield w Idbury 65-74; rtd 74. *Wing 3, Home of St Monica, Cote Lane, Bristol BS9 3UN* Tel 0117-962 9281

DAVIES, Preb Thomas Derwent. b 16. St D Coll Lamp BA38 St Mich Coll Llan 39. **d** 39 **p** 41. C Pontypridd St Cath *Llan* 39-45; C Bideford *Ex* 45-48; Lic to Offic 48-51; Asst Sec DBF 48-51; V Devonport St Mark Ford 51-58; R Bideford 58-74; Preb Ex Cathl 69-97; V Cadbury 74-81; V Thorverton 74-81; rtd 82; Perm to Offic *Ex* from 82. *12 Blagdon Rise, Crediton, Devon EX17 1EN* Tel (01363) 773856

DAVIES, Canon Thomas Philip. b 27. Univ of Wales (Ban) BEd73. St Mich Coll Llan 55. **d** 56 **p** 57. C Ruabon *St As* 56-59; C Prestatyn 59-62; V Penley 62-69; V Bettisfield 66-69; V Holt and Isycoed 69-77; Dioc Dir of Educn 76-92; Dioc RE Adv 76-92; RD Wrexham 76-77; R Hawarden 77-92; Can St As Cathl 79-92; rtd 93. *11 Rosewood Grove, Buckley CH7 3JT*

DAVIES, Thomas Stanley. b 10. Nashdom Abbey 33. **d** 37 **p** 38. C St Cath Coleman *Lon* 37-40; C Shoreditch St Mich 40-41; C Isleworth St Fran 41-45; C Burton St Paul *Lich* 45-47; R Sutton *Chelmsf* 47-55; V Shopland 47-55; V Leigh-on-Sea St Jas 55-71; V Stansted Mountfitchet 71-78; rtd 78; Perm to Offic *Chelmsf* from 78. *54 Newbiggen Street, Thaxted, Essex CM6 2QT* Tel (01371) 830110

DAVIES, Timothy Robert (Tim). b 64. Bradf Univ BSc87. Wycliffe Hall Ox BTh93. **d** 93 **p** 94. C Eynsham and Cassington *Ox* from 93. *44 Shakespeare Road, Eynsham, Witney, Oxon OX8 1PY* Tel (01865) 881669

DAVIES, Canon Trevor Gwesyn. b 28. Univ of Wales (Ban) BEd73. St Mich Coll Llan 55. **d** 56 **p** 57. C Holywell *St As* 56-63; V Cwm 63-74; V Colwyn Bay 74-95; Can St As Cathl from 79; rtd 95. *Dalkeith, 37 Brompton Avenue, Rhos on Sea, Colwyn Bay LL28 4TF* Tel (01492) 548044

DAVIES, The Ven Vincent Anthony (Tony). b 46. Brasted Th Coll 69 St Mich Coll Llan 71. **d** 73 **p** 74. C Owton Manor CD *Dur* 73-76; C Wandsworth St Faith *S'wark* 76-78; P-in-c 78-81; V Walworth St Jo 81-94; RD S'wark and Newington 88-93; Adn Croydon from 94. *246 Pampisford Road, South Croydon, Surrey CR2 6DD* Tel 0181-688 2943

DAVIES, Walter Hugh. b 28. St Deiniol's Hawarden 64. **d** 66 **p** 67. C Ban St Mary *Ban* 66-69; P-in-c Rhosybol and Llandyfrydog 70; TV Amlwch, Rhosybol and Llandyfrydog 71-74; R Llanfaethlu w Llanfwrog and Llanrhuddlad etc 74-93; RD Llifon and Talybolion 85-93; rtd 93; Lic to Offic *Ban* from 93. *14 Y Fron, Cemaes Bay LL67 0HU* Tel (01407) 710333

DAVIES, Canon William David. b 19. Bris Univ BA41. St Mich Coll Llan 48. **d** 43 **p** 44. C Ebbw Vale Ch Ch *Mon* 43-46; C Buckley *St As* 46-48; Chapl Llan Cathl *Llan* 48-50; C-in-c Fairwater CD 50-67; V Fairwater 67-68; R Porthkerry 68-72; R Barry All SS 72-85; RD Penarth and Barry 75-85; Can Llan Cathl 82-85; rtd 85; Perm to Offic *Llan* from 85. *3 Brookfield Park Road, Cowbridge CF7 7HS* Tel (01446) 775259

DAVIES, Canon William John Morgan. b 10. St D Coll Lamp BA32. **d** 36 **p** 37. C Lougher *S & B* 36-41; C Ystradgynlais 41-47; V Crickadarn and Gwenddwr 47-54; V Defynnog w Rhydybriw and Llandeilo'r Fan 54-84; RD Builth 54-55; RD Brecon II 76-80; Can Brecon Cathl 78-84; rtd 84. *Bronwysg, Sennybridge, Brecon LD3 8PG* Tel (01874) 636226

DAVIES, William Martin. b 56. Univ of Wales (Cardiff) BSc78. Wycliffe Hall Ox 78. **d** 81 **p** 82. C Gabalfa *Llan* 81-84; P-in-c Beguildy and Heyope *S & B* 84-85; V 85-87; V Swansea St Thos and Kilvey 87-93; Asst Chapl Miss to Seamen from 89; V Belmont *Lon* from 93. *St Anselm's Vicarage, Ventnor Avenue, Stanmore, Middx HA7 2HU* Tel 0181-907 3186

DAVIES, William Morris. b 19. LCP56 Univ of Wales (Lamp) BA41 Jes Coll Ox BA43 MA47 Man Univ DipEd61 Liv Univ MEd68. St Mich Coll Llan 43. **d** 44 **p** 45. C Ysbyty Ystwyth w Ystradmeurig *St D* 44-49; V 49-57; Chapl Sandbach Sch 57-65; Lect Div Crewe Coll Educn 65-68; Sen Lect 68-71; Hd Div Dept 71-75; Tutor Th and Educn Crewe and Alsager Coll of HE 75-79; Tutor Open Univ 78-81; V Norley *Ches* 79-85; Tutor St Deiniol's Lib Hawarden 83-85; rtd 85; Sub-Chapl HM Young Offender Inst Thorn Cross 85-89; Lic to Offic *Ches* from 85. *Eastwood, Willington, Tarporley, Cheshire CW6 0NE* Tel (01829) 52181

DAVIES, William Morris. b 23. St Mich Coll Llan 66. **d** 68 **p** 68. C Llangiwg *S & B* 68-72; V Bryngwyn and Newchurch and

Llanbedr etc 72-77; R Bedwas *Mon* 77-88; rtd 88. *31 Landore Avenue, Killay, Swansea SA2 7BP* Tel (01792) 206704

DAVIES-COLE, Charles Sylester. b 38. New Coll Dur BA BD. Edin Th Coll 66. **d** 66. Hon C Edin Old St Paul *Edin* from 66. *121 Mayburn Avenue, Loanhead, Midlothian EH20 9ER* Tel 0131-440 4190

DAVILL, Robin William. b 51. CertEd73 SS Paul & Mary Coll Cheltenham BEd74 Leic Univ MA79. Westcott Ho Cam 86. **d** 88 **p** 89. C Broughton *Blackb* 88-91; C Howden TM *York* 91-93; NSM Crayke w Brandsby and Yearsley from 93. *Leyland House, 44 Uppleby, Easingwold, York YO6 3BB* Tel (01347) 823472

DAVINA, Sister. *See* WILBY, Mrs Jean

DAVIS, Alan. b 34. Birm Univ BSc56. Ox NSM Course. **d** 75 **p** 76. NSM Chesham St Mary *Ox* 75-80; NSM Gt Chesham from 80. *18 Cheyne Walk, Chesham, Bucks HP5 1AY* Tel (01494) 782124

DAVIS, Alan John. b 33. St Alb Minl Tr Scheme 77. **d** 80 **p** 81. NSM Goldington *St Alb* 80-84; C Benchill *Man* 84-86; R Gt Chart *Cant* from 86. *The Rectory, Great Chart, Ashford, Kent TN23 3AY* Tel (01233) 620371

DAVIS, The Ven Alan Norman. b 38. Open Univ BA75. Lich Th Coll 63. **d** 65 **p** 66. C Kingstanding St Luke *Birm* 65-68; C-in-c Ecclesfield St Paul CD *Sheff* 68-73; V Sheff St Paul Wordsworth Avenue 73-75; V Shiregreen St Jas and St Chris 75-80; R Maltby 80-81; TR 81-89; Abp's Officer for UPA 90-92; Lic to Offic *St Alb* 90-92; P-in-c Carl St Cuth w St Mary *Carl* 92-96; Dioc Communications Officer from 92; Adn W Cumberland from 96; Hon Can Carl Cathl from 96. *50 Stainburn Road, Workington, Cumbria CA14 1SN* Tel (01900) 66190 Fax 873021

DAVIS, Andrew Fisher. b 46. St Chad's Coll Dur BA67. St Steph Ho Ox 68. **d** 70 **p** 71. C Beckenham St Jas *Roch* 70-74; C Kensington St Mary Abbots w St Geo *Lon* 74-80; V Sudbury St Andr 80-90; AD Brent 85-90; V Ealing Ch the Sav from 90. *The Clergy House, The Grove, London W5 5DX* Tel 0181-567 1288

DAVIS, Andrew George (Andy). b 63. Bath Univ BSc Edin Univ BD. Edin Th Coll. **d** 89 **p** 90. C Alverstoke *Portsm* 89-92; C Portsea N End St Mark 92-96; Bp's Dom Chapl from 96. *46 Blackbrook Park Avenue, Fareham, Hants PO15 5JL* Tel (01329) 221326

DAVIS, Arthur Vivian. b 24. Clifton Th Coll 60. **d** 62 **p** 63. C Derby St Chad *Derby* 62-65; C Cambridge St Andr Less *Ely* 65-68; V 68-75; V Kirtling 75-86; V Wood Ditton w Saxon Street 75-86; P-in-c Cheveley 83-86; P-in-c Ashley w Silverley 83-86; rtd 86; Perm to Offic *Ely* from 86. *408 Studland Park, Newmarket, Suffolk CB8 7BB* Tel (01638) 661709

DAVIS, Canon Bernard Rex. b 33. FRSA87 Sydney Univ BA55 Newc Univ MA67. Gen Th Sem (NY) MDiv60 Coll of Resurr Mirfield. **d** 57 **p** 58. C Guildf St Nic *Guildf* 57-59; USA 59-61; Australia 62-68; Exec Sec Unit 3 WCC Geneva 68-77; Warden Edw K Ho from 77; Can Res and Sub Dean Linc Cathl *Linc* from 77; Treas from 85. *The Subdeanery, 18 Minster Yard, Lincoln LN2 1PX* Tel (01522) 521932

DAVIS, Canon Brian. b 40. AKC69 BD69. St Aug Coll Cant 69. **d** 70 **p** 71. C Humberstone *Leic* 70-73; C Kirby Muxloe 73-74; V Countesthorpe w Foston 74-91; RD Guthlaxton I 90-91; V Hinckley St Mary from 91; RD Sparkenhoe W from 92; Hon Can Leic Cathl from 94. *St Mary's Vicarage, Hinckley, Leics LE10 1EQ* Tel (01455) 234241

DAVIS, Christopher Eliot. b 28. Pemb Coll Cam BA50 MA55. Wells Th Coll 52. **d** 54 **p** 55. C Dudley St Aug Holly Hall *Worc* 54-56; C Bromyard *Heref* 57; Min Can Carl Cathl *Carl* 57-59; Prec Worc Cathl *Worc* 60-62; Perm to Offic *Lich* 62-95; P-in-c Lich St Mary 65-66; PV Lich Cathl 65-67; Chapl Magd Coll Ox 71-74; rtd 93. *28 Newbridge Crescent, Wolverhampton WV6 0LH* Tel (01902) 759220

DAVIS, Christopher James. b 63. Worc Coll Ox BA85. Cranmer Hall Dur 88. **d** 91 **p** 92. C Margate H Trin *Cant* 91-94; C Cambridge H Sepulchre *Ely* from 94. *9 Victoria Street, Cambridge CB1 1JP* Tel (01223) 359314

DAVIS, Clinton Ernest Newman. b 46. Solicitor 71. Wycliffe Hall Ox 78. **d** 80 **p** 81. C Margate H Trin *Cant* 80-84; C St Laurence in the Isle of Thanet 84-87; V Sandgate St Paul 87-92; P-in-c Folkestone St Geo 92; R Sandgate St Paul w Folkestone St Geo 92-97; Chapl HM Pris Standford Hill from 97. *HM Prison Standford Hill, Church Road, Eastchurch, Sheerness, Kent ME12 4AA* Tel (01795) 880441 Fax 880267

DAVIS, Donald Cyril (Don). b 26. Open Univ BA79. NTMTC 94. **d** 96 **p** 97. NSM N Greenford All Hallows *Lon* from 96. *33 Sherwood Avenue, Greenford, Middx UB6 0PG* Tel 0181-864 1060

DAVIS, Donald Richard. b 59. Oak Hill Th Coll DipHE94. **d** 94 **p** 95. C Plymouth St Jude *Ex* from 94. *120 Salisbury Road, Plymouth PL4 8TB* Tel (01752) 224877

DAVIS, Edwin John Charles. b 36. Dur Univ BA60 St Cath Soc Ox BA62 MA66. Ripon Hall Ox 60. **d** 62 **p** 63. C Kington w Huntington *Heref* 62-65; Lect Lich Th Coll 65-66; Chapl Edin Th Coll 66-70; Hon Chapl St Mary's Cathl *Edin* 66-70; P-in-c Hope w Shelve *Heref* 70-78; R 78-81; P-in-c Middleton 70-78; V 78-81; P-in-c Worthen 75-78; R 78-81; V S Hinksey *Ox* from 81; Dep Dir Tr Scheme for NSM from 84. *New Hinksey Vicarage, Vicarage Road, Oxford OX1 4RD* Tel (01865) 245879

DAVIS, Mrs Elizabeth Jane. b 42. S'wark Ord Course 91. **d** 94 **p** 95. NSM Plaistow St Mary *Roch* from 94. *3 Kinnaird Avenue, Bromley BR1 4HG* Tel 0181-460 4672

DAVIS, Canon Herbert Roger. b 36. Kelham Th Coll 60. **d** 65 **p** 66. C Barkingside St Fran *Chelmsf* 65-69; C Harpenden St Nic *St Alb* 69-73; P-in-c Eaton Bray 73-75; V Eaton Bray w Edlesborough 75-81; RD Dunstable 77-81; R Gt Berkhamsted 81-95; Hon Can St Alb 93-95. *6 St Thomas Terrace, St Thomas Street, Wells, Somerset BA5 2XG* Tel (01749) 677195

DAVIS, Ian Andrew. b 58. MIBiol85 CBiol85 Sheff Univ BSc79 PGCE80. St Jo Coll Nottm LTh89 DPS90. **d** 90 **p** 91. C Hatfield *Sheff* 90-92; C Beighton 92-95; R Thurnscoe St Helen from 95. *The Rectory, 4 High Street, Thurnscoe, Rotherham, S Yorkshire S63 0SU* Tel (01709) 893186

DAVIS, Jack. b 35. LRSC63 CChem80 MRSC80 Sheff City Poly HNC59 Sheff Univ MSc88. Oak Hill Th Coll DipHE88. **d** 88 **p** 89. C Owlerton *Sheff* 88-91; V Manea *Ely* 91-93; R Wimblington 91-93; P-in-c Walsoken 93-94; R from 94. *The Rectory, Walsoken, Wisbech, Cambs PE13 3RA* Tel (01945) 583740

DAVIS, John Basil. b 20. Lon Univ BA69. Bps' Coll Cheshunt 46. **d** 49 **p** 50. V Bacton w Edingthorpe *Nor* 61-66; Perm to Offic *S'well* 71-86; rtd 85; Hon C Bingham *S'well* from 86. *1 Banks Crescent, Bingham, Nottingham NG13 8BP* Tel (01949) 837721

DAVIS, John Brian. b 33. Linc Th Coll 72. **d** 75 **p** 76. Hon C Bungay H Trin w St Mary *St E* 75-84; P-in-c Barrow 84-85; P-in-c Denham St Mary 84-85; R Barrow w Denham St Mary and Higham Green from 85. *The Rectory, Barrow, Bury St Edmunds, Suffolk IP29 5AA* Tel (01284) 810279

DAVIS, John George. b 65. **d** 96 **p** 97. C Newton Nottage *Llan* from 96. *5B Belle Vue Court, West End Avenue, Nottage, Porthcawl CF36 3NE*

DAVIS, John Harold. b 54. St Jo Coll Dur BSc76 DipTh78 MA86. Cranmer Hall Dur 76. **d** 79 **p** 80. C Marske in Cleveland *York* 79-82; C Pocklington w Yapham-cum-Meltonby, Owsthorpe etc 82-83; TV Pocklington Team 84-86; V Carlton and Drax 86-95; Ind Chapl from 88; V Sowerby from 95; P-in-c Sessay from 95. *The Vicarage, The Close, Sowerby, Thirsk, N Yorkshire YO7 1JA* Tel (01845) 523546

DAVIS, John Stephen. b 51. N Staffs Poly BSc75. Wycliffe Hall Ox 75. **d** 78 **p** 79. C Meole Brace *Lich* 78-81; C Bloxwich 81-85; V Walsall St Paul 85-96; Development Officer Prince's Trust from 96. *15 Heygate Way, Aldridge, Walsall WS9 8SD* Tel (01922) 58510

DAVIS, Preb Kenneth William (Ken). b 25. Ripon Hall Ox 60. **d** 62 **p** 63. C Lyngford *B & W* 62-65; R Axbridge 65-72; V Wells St Cuth 72-73; V Wells St Cuth w Wookey Hole 73-92; RD Shepton Mallet 79-86; Preb Wells Cathl 83-92; rtd 92; Perm to Offic *B & W* from 92. *Ramel, Green Lane, Street, Somerset BA16 0QL* Tel (01458) 841673

DAVIS, Michael James Burrows. b 36. ED JP87. St Deiniol's Hawarden Ridley Hall Cam. **d** 72 **p** 72. Bermuda from 72. *PO Box SN 74, Southampton SN BX, Bermuda* Tel Bermuda (1-441) 238-0236 Fax 238-3767

DAVIS, Nicholas Anthony Wylie. b 56. BA. Chich Th Coll. **d** 84 **p** 85. C N Lambeth *S'wark* 84-88; TV Catford (Southend) and Downham 88-94; V Camberwell St Phil and St Mark from 94. *St Philip's Vicarage, Avondale Square, London SE1 5PD* Tel 0171-237 3239

DAVIS, Norman. b 38. FCII66. Oak Hill Th Coll 77. **d** 79 **p** 80. C Walton *St E* 79-82; P-in-c Bredfield w Boulge 86-91; P-in-c Grundisburgh w Burgh 82-91; RD Woodbridge 90-96; R Boulge w Burgh and Grundisburgh from 91. *The Rectory, Grundisburgh, Woodbridge, Suffolk IP13 6UF* Tel (01473) 735749

DAVIS, Norman John. b 41. Oak Hill Th Coll 63. **d** 66 **p** 67. C Wellington w Eyton *Lich* 66-70; C Higher Openshaw *Man* 70-72; R S Levenshulme 72-79; P-in-c Berrow w Pendock and Eldersfield *Worc* 79-81; R 81-87; R Churchill-in-Halfshire w Blakedown and Broome from 87. *The Rectory, 5 Mill Lane, Blakedown, Kidderminster, Worcs DY10 3ND* Tel (01562) 700293

DAVIS, Paul Montague. b 29. St Jo Coll Dur BA52. Ely Th Coll 52. **d** 54 **p** 55. C Malden St Jas *S'wark* 54-56; C Boreham Wood All SS *St Alb* 56-57; C Colchester St Jas, All SS, St Nic and St Runwald *Chelmsf* 57-61; Hon C 72-81; CF 61-63; C Leigh St Clem *Chelmsf* 63-67; C Hockley 67-70; V Lt Horkesley 81-85; R The Bromleys 85-94; rtd 94; Perm to Offic *Chelmsf* from 94. *5 Coltsfoot Court, Colchester CO4 5UD* Tel (01206) 852474

DAVIS, Ronald Frank. b 26. Oak Hill Th Coll 62. **d** 64 **p** 65. C Bilton *Ripon* 64-67; V N and S Otterington *York* 67-77; C Rainham *Chelmsf* 77-82; V Hainault 82-88; rtd 88; Perm to Offic *Bradf* from 90. *Home View, Westview Grove, Keighley, W Yorkshire BD20 6JJ* Tel (01535) 681294

DAVIS, Ronald Geoffrey. b 47. St Jo Coll Nottm 79. **d** 81 **p** 81. C Maidstone St Luke *Cant* 81-84; P-in-c Lostwithiel *Truro* 84-86; P-in-c Lanhydrock 84-86; Asst Dioc Youth Officer 84-86; P-in-c Boughton Monchelsea *Cant* 86-88; V from 88; Six Preacher Cant Cathl from 94; C-in-c Parkwood CD from 95. *The Vicarage,*

Church Hill, Boughton Monchelsea, Maidstone, Kent ME17 4BU Tel (01622) 743321

DAVIS, Royston Grandfield. b 33. Sarum & Wells Th Coll 86. **d** 88 **p** 89. C Cainscross w Selsley *Glouc* 88-90; TV Hugglescote w Donington, Ellistown and Snibston *Leic* 90-93; P-in-c Gilmorton w Peatling Parva and Kimcote etc 93-95; R Ogwell and Denbury *Ex* from 95. *The Rectory, 1 St Bartholomew Way, Ogwell, Newton Abbot, Devon TQ12 6YW* Tel (01626) 54330

DAVIS, Russell Earls. b 14. Sydney Univ LLB50. Moore Th Coll Sydney ThL52. **d** 52 **p** 53. Australia 52-76; Can Perth 54-60; Australia from 77; P-in-c Brislington St Luke *Bris* 76-77; rtd 88. *51 Cromarty Road, Floreat Park, W Australia 6014* Tel Perth (9) 387 5629

DAVIS, Sidney Charles. b 31. DMA61 ACIS61 FCIS73. S Dios Minl Tr Scheme 80. **d** 83 **p** 84. NSM Amesbury *Sarum* 83-93; Nat Chapl Ex-Prisoners of War Assn from 90. *4 Stonehenge Road, Amesbury, Salisbury SP4 7BA* Tel (01980) 623248

DAVIS, Simon Charles. b 63. Plymouth Poly BSc86. Trin Coll Bris BA92. **d** 92 **p** 93. C Bollington St Jo *Ches* 92-96; P-in-c Abbots Bromley w Blithfield *Lich* from 96. *The Vicarage, Market Place, Abbots Bromley, Rugeley, Staffs WS15 3BP* Tel (01283) 840242

DAVIS, Stephen Charles. b 19. AKC48 St Cath Soc Ox BA50 MA54. Wycliffe Hall Ox 48. **d** 50 **p** 51. C Slough *Ox* 50-52; S Africa 52-57; V Leic H Trin *Leic* 58-64; Chapl HM Pris Leic 58-64; R Dur St Marg *Dur* 64-87; rtd 87. *6 Juniper Way, Malvern, Worcs WR14 4XG* Tel (01684) 561039

DAVIS, Thomas Edward. b 20. **d** 83 **p** 84. NSM Cen Telford *Lich* 83-91; Perm to Offic from 91. *14 Bembridge, Telford, Shropshire TF3 1NA* Tel (01952) 592352

DAVIS, Timothy Charles (Tim). b 59. Reading Univ BA81 Homerton Coll Cam PGCE82. Trin Coll Bris DipHE91. **d** 91 **p** 92. C Normanton *Wakef* 91-95; C Fisherton Anger *Sarum* from 95. *7 Empire Road, Salisbury SP2 9DE* Tel (01772) 335155

DAVIS, Trevor Lorenzo. b 45. Simon of Cyrene Th Inst 92. **d** 94 **p** 95. NSM Upper Norwood St Jo *S'wark* from 94. *31B Thornlaw Road, London SE27 0SH* Tel 0181-766 6238

DAVIS, William Henry (Bill). b 17. Open Univ BA84. Bps' Coll Cheshunt. **d** 67 **p** 68. C Sudbury St Andr *Lon* 67-70; V Wickhambrook *St E* 70-72; V Wickhambrook w Stradishall and Denston 72-91; V Wickhambrook 91-95; P-in-c Stansfield 76-78; rtd 95. *Folly Barn, 10 Bellevue Road, Weymouth, Dorset DT4 8RX* Tel (01305) 784853

DAVIS, Mrs Yvonne Annie. b 30. LNSM course 93. **d** 96. Hon C Purley St Barn *S'wark* from 96. *1 Hurnford Close, Sanderstead, Surrey CR2 0AN* Tel 0181-657 2097

DAVIS-JONES, Noel Jenkin. b 10. St D Coll Lamp BA32. **d** 33 **p** 34. C Llansantffraed-juxta-Usk w Llanddetty etc *S & B* 33-40; Chapl RAFVR 40-46; R Ludford Magna w Ludford Parva *Linc* 46-51; V Kelstern, Calcethorpe and E Wykeham 46-51; Chapl RAF 51-54; Venezuela 54-60; Bermuda 60-65; R Amcotts w Luddington and Garthorpe *Linc* 65-76; RD Is of Axholme 69-76; P-in-c Althorpe 70-76; rtd 76; P-in-c Llanddewi Ystradenni and Abbey Cwmhir *S & B* 76-84; P-in-c Llanddewi Ystradenni 84-94; P-in-c Llanbister and Llanbadarn Fynydd w Llananno 84-87. *Llandewi Vicarage, Llandrindod Wells LD1 6SE* Tel (01597) 851424

DAVISON, Miss Beryl. b 37. Lightfoot Ho Dur 62. **d** 87 **p** 94. Par Dn Consett *Dur* 87-92; D-in-c Holmside 92-94; P-in-c from 94. *Holmside Vicarage, Burnhope, Durham DH7 0DP* Tel (01207) 529274

DAVISON, George Thomas William. b 65. St Andr Univ BD88. Oak Hill Th Coll 88 CITC BTh92. **d** 92 **p** 93. C Portadown St Mark *Arm* 92-95; I Kinawley w H Trin *K, E & A* from 95; Dir of Ords from 97. *The Rectory, Cloghan, Derrylin, Enniskillen, Co Fermanagh BT92 9LD* Tel (01365) 748994 Fax as telephone

DAVISON, Ralph Guild. b 13. Ely Th Coll 33. **d** 36 **p** 37. C Bishops Hull St Jo *B & W* 36-40; CF (EC) 40-45; V Taunton H Trin *B & W* 45-47; Chapl Taunton and Somerset Hosp 46-47; V Bury H Trin *Man* 47-53; R Mamhead *Ex* 53-62; R Ashcombe 53-62; R Bagborough *B & W* 63-78; rtd 78; Chapl Franciscans Posbury from 78; Lic to Offic *Ex* from 78. *St Mary of the Angels, Posbury, Crediton, Devon EX17 3QF* Tel (01363) 773280

DAVISON, Richard Ireland. b 42. St Chad's Coll Dur BSc63. Linc Th Coll 64. **d** 66 **p** 67. C Cockerton *Dur* 66-70; C Houghton le Spring 70-73; V Heworth St Alb 73-80; Ascension Is 80-82; V Dunston *Dur* 82-85; V Bishopwearmouth Ch Ch from 85; RD Wearmouth from 94. *Christ Church Vicarage, 7 St Bede's Park, Sunderland SR2 7DZ* Tel 0191-565 8077

DAVISON, Richard John. b 32. St Andr Univ MA56. Linc Th Coll 56. **d** 58 **p** 59. C S Shields St Hilda *Dur* 58-61; C Dur St Cuth 61-63; R Wyberton *Linc* 63-86; RD Holland W 84-86; TR Swan *Ox* 86-91; V Streatley w Moulsford 91-96; rtd 97. *37 Stirling Road, Stamford, Lincs PE9 2XF*

DAVISON, Canon Roger William. b 20. Kelham Th Coll 46. **d** 51 **p** 52. C Tonge Moor *Man* 51-55; V 55-65; Hon Can Man Cathl 63-65; V Higham Ferrers w Chelveston *Pet* 65-88; rtd 88; Perm to Offic *Roch* from 88. *17 Hermitage Road, Higham, Rochester, Kent ME3 7DB* Tel (01474) 823824

DAVISON, Thomas Alfred. b 28. St Aug Coll Cant 48 St Chad's Coll Dur 52. **d** 60 **p** 61. C Tetbury w Beverston *Glouc* 60-62; C Malvern Link St Matthias *Worc* 62-65; R Coates *Glouc* 65-76; R Coates, Rodmarton and Sapperton etc 76-78; Chapl R Agric Coll Cirencester 67-78; P-in-c Bleadon *B & W* 78-81; Chapl HM Pris Leeds 81-84; Chapl HM Pris Channings Wood 84-89; P-in-c Pyworthy, Pancrasweek and Bridgerule *Ex* 89-91; P-in-c Otterton and Colaton Raleigh 91-94; rtd 94; Perm to Offic *Ex* from 94. *6 Grosvenor Terrace, Ferndale Road, Teignmouth, Devon TQ14 8NE* Tel (01626) 779202

DAVISON, William. b 18. St D Coll Lamp 58. **d** 60 **p** 61. C Horsington w Stixwould *Linc* 60-62; R Welby 62-65; V Heydour and Culverthorpe 62-65; R Offord D'Arcy w Offord Cluny *Ely* 65-66; R Mareham le Fen *Linc* 66-76; Lic to Offic 77-78; R Barkestone cum Plungar and Redmile *Leic* 78-81; rtd 82; Perm to Offic *Linc* from 82. *28 Stoney Way, Tetney, Grimsby, S Humberside DN36 5PG* Tel (01472) 814252

DAVOLL, Ivan John (Snowy). b 33. DipYW67. LNSM course 87. **d** 88 **p** 90. NSM Bermondsey St Jas w Ch Ch *S'wark* 88-93; C from 93. *2 Thurland Road, London SE16 4AA* Tel 0171-237 8741

DAVY, Peter Geoffrey. b 31. **d** 94. NSM St Columb Minor and St Colan *Truro* from 94. *9 Tredour Road, Newquay, Cornwall TR7 2EY* Tel (01637) 872241

DAW, Geoffrey Martin (Geoff). b 57. Oak Hill Th Coll 81. **d** 84 **p** 85. C Hollington St Leon *Chich* 84-87; C Seaford w Sutton 87-90; V Iford w Kingston and Rodmell from 90. *The Rectory, 14 Lockitt Way, Kingston, Lewes, E Sussex BN7 3LG* Tel (01273) 473665

DAWE, David Fife Purchas. b 20. Keble Coll Ox BA41 MA45. Wells Th Coll 41. **d** 43 **p** 44. C Wolstanton *Lich* 43-46; C Meole Brace 46-47; C Leek All SS 47-50; C Tardebigge *Worc* 50-52; R Stoke Bliss w Kyre Wyard 52-54; R Jackfield *Heref* 54-61; V Criftins *Lich* 61-77; V Dudleston 63-77; P-in-c Alkmonton w Yeaveley *Derby* 77-81; P-in-c Cubley w Marston Montgomery 77-81; V Alkmonton, Cubley, Marston, Montgomery etc 81-85; rtd 85; Perm to Offic *Derby* 85-94; Perm to Offic *Lich* 85-94; Perm to Offic *Pet* from 94. *11 Coaching Walk, Northampton NN3 3EU* Tel (01604) 414083

DAWES, Dori Katherine. b 37. ARCM. Oak Hill NSM Course 85. **d** 88 **p** 94. Par Dn Watford St Luke *St Alb* 88-90; Par Dn Watford 90-94; C 94-96; P-in-c Dunton w Wrestlingworth and Eyeworth from 96. *The Rectory, 7 Braggs Lane, Wrestlingworth, Sandy, Beds SG19 2ER* Tel (01767) 631596

DAWES, Hugh William. b 48. Univ Coll Ox BA71 MA76. Cuddesdon Coll 71. **d** 74 **p** 75. C Purley St Mark Woodcote *S'wark* 74-77; Chapl G&C Coll Cam 77-82; Lic to Offic *Ely* 78-87; Chapl Em Coll Cam 82-87; V Cambridge St Jas *Ely* from 87. *St James's Vicarage, 110 Wulfstan Way, Cambridge CB1 4QJ* Tel (01223) 246419

DAWES, Julian Edward. b 27. RAF Coll Cranwell 49. Bps' Coll Cheshunt 58. **d** 59 **p** 60. C Whitton St Aug *Lon* 59-62; Chapl RAF 62-65; V Overbury w Alstone, Teddington and Lt Washbourne *Worc* 65-70; V Cropthorne w Charlton 70-76; Chapl Dioc Conf Cen 70-76; Chapl Exe Vale Hosp Gp 76-84; Chapl Bromsgrove and Redditch Distr Gen Hosp 84-86; rtd 91; Perm to Offic *Ex* from 91. *41 Thornton Hill, Exeter EX4 4NR* Tel (01392) 277928

DAWES, Peter Martin. b 24. Westmr Coll Cam 52. **d** 81 **p** 81. C Dunscroft Ch Ch *Sheff* 81-83; V 83-89; rtd 89; Perm to Offic *Bris* from 89. *2 Holway Cottages, The Mall, Swindon SN1 4JB* Tel (01793) 615878

✠**DAWES, The Rt Revd Peter Spencer.** b 28. Hatf Coll Dur BA52. Tyndale Hall Bris 53. **d** 54 **p** 55 **c** 88. C Whitehall Park St Andr Hornsey Lane *Lon* 54-57; C Ox St Ebbe *Ox* 57-60; Tutor Clifton Th Coll 60-65; V Romford Gd Shep Collier Row *Chelmsf* 65-80; Hon Can Chelmsf Cathl 78-80; Adn W Ham 80-88; Dioc Dir of Ords 80-86; Bp Derby 88-95; rtd 95. *45 Arundell, Ely, Cambs CB6 1BQ* Tel (01353) 661241

DAWES, Victor. b 18. Wycliffe Hall Ox 63. **d** 64 **p** 65. V Andreas St Jude *S & M* 67-73; V Jurby 67-73; Warden Baycliff Healing Cen 73-83; Perm to Offic from 85; rtd 89. *48 Ballakane Close, Port Erin, Isle of Man IM9 6EH* Tel (01624) 832921

DAWKES, Peter. b 31. Roch Th Coll 64. **d** 66 **p** 67. C Newbold w Dunston *Derby* 66-69; C Buxton 69-72; V Somercotes 72-93; rtd 93; Hon C Kenton, Mamhead, Powderham, Cofton and Starcross *Ex* from 93. *All Saints House, Kenton, Exeter EX6 8NG* Tel (01626) 890214

DAWKIN, Peter William. b 60. Nottm Univ BTh88 Open Univ BA91. St Jo Coll Nottm 85. **d** 88 **p** 89. C Birkdale St Jo *Liv* 88-91; C Netherton 91-93; V Liv Ch Ch Norris Green from 93. *Christ Church Vicarage, Sedgemoor Road, Liverpool L11 3BR* Tel 0151-226 1774

DAWKINS, Canon Alan Arthur Windsor. b 26. Lon Univ DipTh54. St Aid Birkenhead 53. **d** 55 **p** 56. C Preston Em *Blackb* 55-57; C S Shore H Trin 57-59; V Slade Green *Roch* 59-61; V St Mary Cray and St Paul's Cray 61-63; V White Colne *Chelmsf* 63-66; R Pebmarsh 63-66; P-in-c Mt Bures 65-66; V Westgate St Jas *Cant* 66-74; V Herne Bay Ch Ch 74-83; Hon Can Cant Cathl 79-91; P-in-c Chilham 83-85; Adv for Miss and Unity 85-91; rtd 91; Chapl St Jo Hosp Cant from 96. *St John's House, 40 Northgate, Canterbury, Kent CT1 1BE* Tel (01227) 764935

DAWKINS, Anthony Norman. b 32. HNC55. NW Ord Course 70. **d** 73 **p** 74. C Man Clayton St Cross w St Paul *Man* 73-74; C

Chorlton-cum-Hardy St Werburgh 74-77; C Scarborough St Martin *York* 77-78; P-in-c Kexby w Wilberfoss 78-84; R Dodleston *Ches* 84-88; V Felkirk w Brierley *Wakef* from 88. *The Vicarage, George Street, South Hiendley, Barnsley, S Yorkshire S72 9BX* Tel (01226) 715315

DAWKINS, Michael Howard. b 44. BTh Man Univ MA96. Tyndale Hall Bris 67. **d** 69 **p** 69. C Drypool St Columba w St Andr and St Pet *York* 69-73; CF 74-80; P-in-c Bulford *Sarum* 80-81; P-in-c Figheldean w Milston 80-81; R Meriden *Cov* from 85. *The Rectory, The Green, Meriden, Coventry CV7 7LN* Tel (01676) 22719

DAWSON, Alan. b 28. St Jo Coll Dur BA54 Liv Univ MA67. Clifton Th Coll 54. **d** 56 **p** 57. C Bowling St Steph *Bradf* 56-59; C Attenborough w Bramcote *S'well* 59-62; V Everton St Jo *Liv* 62-69; V Birkdale St Pet 69-91; rtd 91. *8 Dunbar Avenue, Kirkcudbright DG6 4HD* Tel (01557) 30017

DAWSON, Arthur Roger. b 38. Sarum Th Coll 64. **d** 66 **p** 66. C Addiscombe St Mildred *Cant* 66-67; C Cove St Jo *Guildf* 67-69; C-in-c Newton-in-Makerfield Em CD *Liv* 75-77; R Newton in Makerfield Em 77-83; BCC 83-87; Hon C Dulwich St Barn *S'wark* 84-92; R Hockering, Honingham, E and N Tuddenham *Nor* from 92. *The Rectory, Hockering, Dereham, Norfolk NR20 3HP* Tel (01603) 880121

DAWSON, Barry. b 38. Lon Univ DipTh65. Oak Hill Th Coll 63. **d** 66 **p** 67. C Fulham St Mary N End *Lon* 66-69; C St Marylebone All So w SS Pet and Jo 69-73; Bp's Chapl *Nor* 73-76; Gen Sec CEMS 76-81; V Rye Park St Cuth *St Alb* 81-89; V Attenborough *S'well* from 89. *The Vicarage, 6 St Mary's Close, Attenborough, Notts NG9 6AT* Tel 0115-925 9602

DAWSON, Canon Brian. b 33. Leeds Univ BA54 Lon Univ DipTh57 Man Univ MA84. Coll of Resurr Mirfield 56. **d** 58 **p** 59. C Hollinwood *Man* 58-62; C Rawmarsh w Parkgate *Sheff* 62-63; V Royton St Anne *Man* 63-75; V Urswick *Carl* 75-86; V Bardsea 75-86; R Skelton and Hutton-in-the-Forest w Ivegill from 86; RD Penrith 91-96; Hon Can Carl Cathl from 94. *The Rectory, Skelton, Penrith, Cumbria CA11 9SE* Tel (017684) 84295

DAWSON, Christopher John Rowland. b 26. OBE QPM. Lon Univ DipTh86. S'wark Ord Course 82. **d** 86 **p** 87. NSM Sevenoaks St Jo *Roch* from 86. *Craggan House, 58 Oak Hill Road, Sevenoaks, Kent TN13 1NT* Tel (01732) 458037

DAWSON, Clifford Mildmay Asquith. b 22. Wycliffe Hall Ox. **d** 58 **p** 59. C Sutton *Liv* 58-60; R Laceby *Linc* 60-68; V Irby on Humber 64-68; R Bradfield *Sheff* 68-77; V Brodsworth 77; V Brodsworth w Hooton Pagnell, Frickley etc 77-80; V Wentworth 80-87; rtd 87; Perm to Offic *Linc* from 87. *2A Trinity Lane, Louth, Lincs LN11 8DL* Tel (01507) 603167

DAWSON, Canon Cyril. b 34. St Chad's Coll Dur BA58 DipTh59. **d** 59 **p** 60. C Honicknowle *Ex* 59-63; C Paignton St Jo 63-66; V Heptonstall *Wakef* 66-71; V Todmorden 71-82; RD Calder Valley 75-82; Can Res Wakef Cathl 82-92; Vice-Provost 86-92; Hon Can from 92; V Darrington w Wentbridge from 92. *The Vicarage, Darrington, Pontefract, W Yorkshire WF8 3AB* Tel (01977) 704744

DAWSON, Edward. **d** 81 **p** 83. Hon C Newington St Paul *S'wark* 81-85; Hon C Walworth St Jo from 85; Chapl Asst Maudsley Hosp Lon from 87. *3 Ethel Street, London SE17 1NH* Tel 0171-701 8923

DAWSON, Francis Andrew Oliver Duff. b 48. Keble Coll Ox BA70 MA74. St Jo Coll Nottm 74. **d** 76 **p** 77. C Billericay St Mary *Chelmsf* 76-77; C Billericay and Lt Burstead 77-80; C Childwall All SS *Liv* 80-84; Chapl St Kath Coll 80-84; V Shevington *Blackb* from 84. *St Anne's Vicarage, Gathurst Lane, Shevington, Wigan, Lancs WN6 8HW* Tel (01257) 252136

DAWSON, Frederick William (Fred). b 44. St Chad's Coll Dur BA66 Nottm Univ MTh74. Linc Th Coll 67. **d** 69 **p** 70. C Caversham *Ox* 69-72; C Ranmoor *Sheff* 72-79; R Kibworth Beauchamp *Leic* 79-82; R Kibworth and Smeeton Westerby and Saddington 82-94; R Tilehurst St Mich *Ox* from 94. *Tilehurst Rectory, Routh Lane, Reading RG3 4JY* Tel (0118) 941 1127 or 942 7331

DAWSON, Ian Douglas. b 52. Liv Univ BSc73. N Ord Course 83. **d** 86 **p** 87. NSM Southport SS Simon and Jude *Liv* 86-93; NSM Birkdale St Jas from 93. *15 Melling Road, Southport, Merseyside PR9 9DY* Tel (01704) 533172

DAWSON, John William Arthur. b 43. EMMTC DipTh95. **d** 95 **p** 96. NSM Breedon cum Isley Walton and Worthington *Leic* from 95. *Orchard House, Manor Drive, Worthington, Ashby-de-la-Zouch, Leics LE65 1RN* Tel (01530) 222673

DAWSON, Miss Mary. b 51. Loughb Coll of Educn ALA73. EMMTC 85. **d** 90 **p** 94. Par Dn Braunstone *Leic* 90-92; Par Dn Shrewsbury H Cross *Lich* 92-94; C 94-95; P-in-c Glentworth Gp *Linc* from 95. *The Vicarage, 1 Stone Lane, Glentworth, Gainsborough, Lincs DN21 5DF* Tel (01427) 668203

DAWSON, Neil. b 49. Ripon Hall Ox 71. **d** 74 **p** 75. C Putney St Mary *S'wark* 74-78; C Camberwell St Giles 78-80; TV N Lambeth 84-86; V E Dulwich St Clem 86; V Dulwich St Clem w St Pet 86-89; NSM Wilton Place St Paul *Lon* from 92. *5 Clitheroe Road, London SW9 9DY* Tel 0171-326 4682

DAWSON, Nicholas Anthony. b 52. St Jo Coll Nottm 88. **d** 90 **p** 91. C Mortomley St Sav High Green *Sheff* 90-95; V Owlerton from 95. *The Vicarage, Forbes Road, Sheffield S6 2NW* Tel 0114-234 3560

DAWSON, Norman William. b 41. K Coll Lon BD63 AKC63. **d** 65 **p** 66. C Salford St Phil w St Steph *Man* 65-68; C Heaton Ch Ch 68-70; R Longsight St Jo 70-75; R Longsight St Jo w St Cypr 75-82; R Withington St Paul from 82; AD Withington from 91. *The Rectory, 491 Wilmslow Road, Manchester M20 4AW* Tel 0161-445 3781

DAWSON, Paul Christopher Owen. b 61. Leeds Univ BA82. Ripon Coll Cuddesdon 83. **d** 85 **p** 86. C Dovecot *Liv* 85-89; V Westbrook St Phil 89-94; Bp's Dom Chapl from 94. *48 Babbacombe Road, Liverpool L16 9JW* Tel 0151-722 7543 or 709 9722

DAWSON, The Ven Peter. b 29. Keble Coll Ox BA52 MA56. Ridley Hall Cam 52. **d** 54 **p** 55. C Morden *S'wark* 54-59; R 68-77; V Barston *Birm* 59-63; R Higher Openshaw *Man* 63-68; RD Merton *S'wark* 75-77; Adn Norfolk *Nor* 77-93; rtd 93; Perm to Offic *Nor* from 93. *Elm Cottage, The Drift, Church Road, Tostock, Bury St Edmunds, Suffolk IP30 9PD* Tel (01359) 70005

DAWSON, Peter. b 34. EMMTC 73. **d** 76 **p** 77. NSM Blyton w Pilham *Linc* 76-80; NSM Laughton w Wildsworth 76-80; C E Stockwith 77-80; C Blyth St Mary *Newc* 80-84; P-in-c Lowick and Kyloe w Ancroft 84-89; P-in-c Ford 87-89; P-in-c Sleekburn from 89. *St John's Vicarage, North View, Bedlington, Northd NE22 7ED* Tel (01670) 822309

DAWSON, Ronald Eric John. b 27. St Mark & St Jo Coll Lon TCert54 Lon Univ BD64. Bps' Coll Cheshunt 62. **d** 62 **p** 63. C Dartford H Trin *Roch* 62-66; C Fulham St Etheldreda *Lon* 66-74; V Brentford St Faith 74-80; rtd 92. *13 Birkbeck Road, London W5 4ES* Tel 0181-560 3564

DAWSON, Thomas Douglas. b 52. Newc Univ BA. St Steph Ho Ox. **d** 80 **p** 82. C N Gosforth *Newc* 80-81; C Leic St Chad *Leic* 82-85; TV Catford (Southend) and Downham *S'wark* 85-88; V Chevington *Newc* 88-94; V Cowgate 94-96; P-in-c Cresswell and Lynemouth from 96. *The Vicarage, 33 Till Grove, Ellington, Morpeth, Northd NE61 5ER* Tel (01670) 860242

DAWSON, William James Andrew. b 48. TCD MA72. CITC 88. **d** 88 **p** 89. NSM Killyman *Arm* 88-91; NSM Pomeroy from 91. *Tamlaght, Coagh, Cookstown, Co Tyrone BT80 0AB* Tel (01648) 737151

DAWSON, William John. b 26. ACP68 TEng74 MIEE74. CITC 77. **d** 80 **p** 81. NSM Lisburn St Paul *Conn* 80-85; Dioc C from 85. *55 Thornleigh Drive, Lisburn, Co Antrim BT28 2DA* Tel (01846) 670252

DAWSWELL, Jonathan Andrew. b 65. Jes Coll Cam BA86. Wycliffe Hall Ox BA91. **d** 92 **p** 93. C Childwall All SS *Liv* 92-96; C Leyland St Andr *Blackb* from 96. *3 Beech Avenue, Leyland, Preston PR5 2AL* Tel (01772) 622446

DAWTRY, Dr Anne Frances. b 57. Westf Coll Lon BA79 PhD85. Ripon Coll Cuddesdon DipMin93. **d** 93 **p** 94. C Corfe Mullen *Sarum* 93-96; C Parkstone St Pet w Branksea and St Osmund 96-97; Chapl Bournemouth and Poole Coll of FE from 97. *21B Laidlaw Close, Talbot Village, Dorset BH14 5EW* Tel (01202) 743016

DAXTER, Gregory. b 42. Lon Univ DipTh66. Oak Hill Th Coll 64. **d** 68 **p** 69. C Paignton St Paul Preston *Ex* 68-72; C Woodford Wells *Chelmsf* 72-75; Hon C Harold Hill St Paul 75-77; Hon C Wilmington *Roch* 77-87; Chapl Ex Cathl Sch from 87; PV Ex Cathl *Ex* from 87. *6A The Close, Exeter EX1 1EZ* Tel (01392) 58892

DAY, Audrey. b 30. CA Tr Coll IDC57. **d** 88 **p** 94. Par Dn Mildenhall *St E* 88-91; Dioc Officer for the Care of the Elderly 91-95; NSM Blackbourne from 94; rtd 95; Perm to Offic *St E* from 95. *Peace Haven, Duke Street, Stanton, Bury St Edmunds, Suffolk IP33 2AB* Tel (01359) 250742

DAY, Charles George. b 28. Keble Coll Ox BA51 MA63. Cuddesdon Coll 51. **d** 53 **p** 54. C Hythe *Cant* 53-56; C S Norwood St Alb 56-59; R Stisted *Chelmsf* 59-65; V Brenchley *Roch* 65-75; rtd 93. *Sparks Hall, Forsham Lane, Sutton Valence, Maidstone, Kent ME17 3EW* Tel (01622) 843248 Fax 844298

DAY, Charles Ian. b 48. Univ of Wales (Ban) BA72. St Mich Coll Llan 73. **d** 75 **p** 76. C Llanrhos *St As* 75-79; V Mochdre 79-83; CF 83; V Minera *St As* 83-92; Dioc Soc Resp Officer from 89; V Mold from 92. *The Vicarage, Church Lane, Mold CH7 1BW* Tel (01352) 752960

DAY, Canon Colin Michael. b 40. Lon Univ BSc62 AKC62 Em Coll Cam BA66 MA71. Ridley Hall Cam 65. **d** 67 **p** 68. C Heworth w Peasholme St Cuth *York* 67-70; C Ox St Clem *Ox* 70-76; V Kidsgrove *Lich* 76-86; Exec Officer Angl Evang Assembly & C of E Coun 86-90; Adv on Miss and Evang *Sarum* 90-95; Can and Preb Sarum Cathl from 94; P-in-c Branksome Park All SS from 95; Dioc Tr in Evang from 95. *The Vicarage, 28 Western Road, Poole, Dorset BH13 7BP* Tel (01202) 708202

DAY, David John. b 44. CEng72 MICE72. Trin Coll Bris DipHE. **d** 90 **p** 91. C Stratton St Margaret w S Marston etc *Bris* 90-94; Perm to Offic from 94. *56 Beechcroft Road, Swindon SN2 6PX* Tel (01793) 725721

DAY, David William. b 37. St Andr Univ MA58 BD61 CertEd73. St And Dioc Tr Course 74. **d** 76 **p** 77. C St Andrews All SS *St And* 76-77; P-in-c Dundee St Ninian *Bre* 77-84; Itinerant Priest *Arg* from 84; R Duror from 91; P-in-c Gruline from 91;

P-in-c Kentallen from 91; P-in-c Kinlochleven from 91; P-in-c Kinlochmoidart from 91; P-in-c Lochbuie from 91; P-in-c Portnacrois from 91; P-in-c Strontian from 91. *St Adamnan's Rectory, Duror of Appin, Argyll PA38 4BS* Tel (01631) 740218

DAY, Frank Henry. b 18. Clifton Th Coll 40 St Aid Birkenhead 41 LTh. **d** 43 **p** 44. C Bris St Ambrose Whitehall *Bris* 43-46; C Chippenham St Paul 46-50; C Brinkworth 50-52; R Stanton St Quintin 52-59; P-in-c Seagry 53-54; V 54-59; R Grittleton w Leigh Delamere 59-68; P-in-c Kington 64-65; P-in-c Stanton St Quintin w Grittleton etc 65-68; R 68-76; P-in-c Hullavington 73-76; P-in-c Norton Coleparle 73-76; R Stanton St Quintin, Hullavington, Grittleton etc 76-81; Chapl RAF Hullavington 71-83; rtd 81; Perm to Offic *Bris* from 81. *17 Avon Mead, Chippenham, Wilts SN15 3PP* Tel (01249) 660966

DAY, George Chester. b 45. Ex Univ BA66 Lon Univ BD70. Clifton Th Coll 67. **d** 71 **p** 72. C Reading St Jo *Ox* 71-75; C Morden *S'wark* 75-81; Sec for Voc and Min CPAS 81-86; Hon C Bromley Ch Ch *Roch* 83-86; V St Paul's Cray St Barn from 86. *The Vicarage, Rushet Road, Orpington, Kent BR5 2PU* Tel (01689) 821353

DAY, Hilary Paul Wilfrid. b 13. Qu Coll Birm 47. **d** 48 **p** 49. C Cannock *Lich* 48-52; V Stubbins *Man* 52-55; R Moston St Chad 55-62; V Slade Green *Roch* 62-71; R Milton next Gravesend w Denton 71-87; rtd 87. *1 Killick Road, Hoo St Werburgh, Rochester, Kent ME3 9EP* Tel (01634) 252960

DAY, Canon James Alfred. b 23. DFC44. AKC49. **d** 50 **p** 51. C Wembley Park St Aug *Lon* 50-52; Mauritius 52-57; V E and W Ravendale w Hatcliffe *Linc* 57-60; R Beelsby 57-60; PC Gt Grimsby St Paul 60-66; V Tattershall 66-80; R Coningsby 66-80; RD Horncastle 73-80; Can and Preb Linc Cathl from 77; V Heckington 80-89; rtd 89. *22 Ancaster Drive, Sleaford, Lincs NG34 7LY* Tel (01529) 305318

DAY, Jennifer Ann. *See* BRADSHAW, Mrs Jennifer Ann

DAY, John. b 44. Oak Hill NSM Course 87. **d** 90 **p** 91. NSM Bexleyheath St Pet *Roch* 90-93; C Erith Ch Ch 93-95; C Erith St Jo 93-95; P-in-c 95-97; V from 97. *St John's Church House, 100 Park Crescent, Erith, Kent DA8 3DZ* Tel (01322) 432555

DAY, Canon John Alfred. b 25. TCD BA51. **d** 51 **p** 52. C Enniskillen and Trory *Clogh* 51-54; I Clontibret w Tullycorbet 54-58; I Drumkeeran 58-67; I Maguiresbridge w Derrybrusk 67-91; Can Clogh Cathl from 78; rtd 91. *Killeenifinane Cottage, 40 Ballylucas Road, Tamlaght, Enniskillen, Co Fermanagh BT74 4HD* Tel (01365) 387835

DAY, John Cuthbert. b 36. Sarum Th Coll 66. **d** 68 **p** 69. C Bedhampton *Portsm* 68-72; V Froxfield 72-73; V Froxfield w Privett 73-77; V Warminster Ch Ch *Sarum* 77-81; R Pewsey 81-90; Chapl Pewsey Hosp Wilts 81-90; P-in-c Sturminster Newton and Hinton St Mary *Sarum* from 90; P-in-c Stock and Lydlinch from 90. *The Vicarage, Sturminster Newton, Dorset DT10 1DB* Tel (01258) 472531

DAY, John Kenneth. b 58. Hull Univ BA85. Cranmer Hall Dur 85. **d** 87 **p** 88. C Thornbury *Bradf* 87-90; V 90-96; V Whitkirk *Ripon* from 96. *Whitkirk Vicarage, 386 Selby Road, Leeds LS15 0AA* Tel 0113-264 5790

DAY, John Nathaniel. b 36. Kelham Th Coll 59. **d** 64 **p** 65. C Mansfield St Mark *S'well* 64-69; C W Wycombe *Ox* 69-75; TV High Wycombe 75-77; C-in-c Britwell St Geo CD 77-78; TV W Slough 78-87; TV Langley Marish 87-96; Warden St Columba's Retreat and Conf Cen 96-97; Chapl Community of St Pet Woking 96-97; TV Chipping Barnet w Arkley *St Alb* from 97. *St Peter's Vicarage, Barnet Road, Arkley, Herts EN5 3JF* Tel 0181-440 2046

DAY, Miss Mary Elizabeth. b 57. Leic Poly BEd79. St Jo Coll Nottm DTS93. **d** 93 **p** 94. C Newbarns w Hawcoat *Carl* from 93. *50 Furness Park Road, Barrow-in-Furness, Cumbria LA14 5PS* Tel (01229) 836953

DAY, Michael. b 37. AKC61 RCA(Lon) MA75. **d** 62 **p** 63. C Hulme St Phil *Man* 62-65; Asst Chapl Newc Univ *Newc* 65-70; Chapl Chelsea Coll *Lon* 70-85; Chapl R Coll of Art 70-90; Chapl Cen, Chelsea and St Martin's Schs of Art *Lon* 85-90; P-in-c Bloomsbury St Geo w Woburn Square Ch Ch 91-95; C St Pancras w St Jas and Ch Ch from 95. *40 Thistlewaite Road, London E5 0QQ* Tel 0181-985 8568

DAY, Paul Geoffrey. b 51. Dur Univ BEd75. Trin Coll Bris 76. **d** 78 **p** 79. C Roxeth Ch Ch *Lon* 78-82; C Roxeth Ch Ch and Harrow St Pet 82; TV Barking St Marg w St Patr *Chelmsf* 82-87; V Barrow St Mark *Carl* from 87. *St Mark's Vicarage, Rawlinson Street, Barrow-in-Furness LA14 1BX* Tel (01229) 820405

DAY, Paul Geoffrey. b 56. St Pet Coll Ox BA77. St Jo Coll Nottm 87. **d** 89 **p** 90. C Mildmay Grove St Jude and St Paul *Lon* 89-92; C Loughborough Em *Leic* 92-95; TV Loughborough Em and St Mary in Charnwood from 95. *134 Valley Road, Loughborough, Leics LE11 3QA* Tel (01509) 234472

DAY, Peter. b 50. BPharm71. Coll of Resurr Mirfield 85. **d** 87 **p** 88. C Eastcote St Lawr *Lon* 87-91; C Wembley Park St Aug 91-94; V Glen Parva and S Wigston *Leic* from 94. *The Vicarage, 1 St Thomas's Road, Wigston, Leics LE18 4TA* Tel 0116-278 2830

DAY, Robert Clifford. b 08. **d** 70 **p** 71. C Lt Stanmore St Lawr *Lon* 70-75; Perm to Offic *Worc* from 75. *10 Forge Lane, Blakedown, Kidderminster, Worcs DY10 3JF* Tel (01562) 700205

DAY, Robert Murray. b 63. St Jo Coll Dur BA87. Trin Coll Bris BA95. **d** 97. C Beckenham St Geo *Roch* from 97. *37 Rectory Road, Beckenham, Kent BR3 1HL* Tel 0181-658 7005

DAY, Roy Frederick. b 24. S'wark Ord Course 63. **d** 67 **p** 68. C Newington St Paul *S'wark* 67-70; C Radlett *St Alb* 70-72; P-in-c Ponsbourne 72-76; R Campton 76-82; V Shefford 76-82; R Shenley 82-89; rtd 89. *11 Hill End Lane, St Albans, Herts AL4 0TX* Tel (01727) 845782

DAY, Canon Samuel Richard. b 14. Reading Univ BSc36 Ch Ch Ox BA48 MA52 DPhil56. St D Coll Lamp 37. **d** 38 **p** 39. C Birkdale St Jo *Liv* 38-40; CF (EC) 40-46; C Ox St Mich *Ox* 46-49; R Chinnor 49-66; R Emmington 50-66; P-in-c Sydenham 51-66; Lect Ripon Hall Ox 57-62; V Gt Marlow 66-89; RD Wycombe 68-74; Hon Can Ch Ch 70-89; rtd 89. *3 Leighton House, Glade Road, Marlow, Bucks SL7 1EA* Tel (01628) 484922

DAY, Terence Patrick. b 30. Lon Univ BD60 K Coll Lon MTh63 PhD66. Lon Coll of Div ALCD59. **d** 60 **p** 61. C Polegate *Chich* 60-63; India 63-71; CMS 66-71; Kenya 71-73; Canada from 73; Prof Religions Univ of Manitoba 74-95; rtd 95. *7 Hazel Park Drive, Winnipeg, Manitoba, Canada, R3T 5H5*

DAY, William Charles (Bill). b 47. Portsm Poly BEd86. Ripon Coll Cuddesdon 88. **d** 90 **p** 91. C Bishops Waltham *Portsm* 90-93; P-in-c Greatham w Empshott and Hawkley w Prior's Dean 93-95; R from 95. *The Vicarage, Hawkley, Liss, Hants GU33 6NF* Tel (01730) 827459

DAYKIN, Timothy Elwin (Tim). b 54. Lon Univ BSc75 Dur Univ DipTh77 MA81 K Coll Lon MPhil93 MEHS. Cranmer Hall Dur 75. **d** 78 **p** 79. C Bourne *Guildf* 78-81; Chapl K Alfred Coll *Win* 82-87; C-in-c Valley Park CD 87-91; V Valley Park 91-92; P-in-c Fordingbridge from 92; P-in-c Hale w S Charford from 94. *The Vicarage, Church Street, Fordingbridge, Hants SP6 1BB* Tel (01425) 653163 Fax 656709

DAYNES, Andrew John. b 47. Jes Coll Cam BA69 MA73. Westcott Ho Cam 69. **d** 72 **p** 73. C Radlett *St Alb* 72-76; Chapl St Alb Abbey 76-80; Chapl Bryanston Sch Dorset from 80. *Bryanston School, Blandford Forum, Dorset DT11 0PX* Tel (01258) 456863 or 452411

DAZELEY, Mrs Lorna. b 31. CertEd53 New Hall Cam BA82 MA86. EAMTC 82. **dss** 84 **d** 87 **p** 94. Chesterton St Andr *Ely* 84-87; C from 87. *Chesterton House, Church Street, Chesterton, Cambridge CB4 1DT* Tel (01223) 356243

de BERRY, Andrew Piers. b 44. St Jo Coll Dur BA66. Ripon Hall Ox 70. **d** 74 **p** 75. C Aylesbury *Ox* 74-77; USA 78; TV Clyst St George, Aylesbeare, Clyst Honiton etc *Ex* 78-80; Asst Chapl HM Pris Wormwood Scrubs 80-82; Chapl HM Pris Sudbury 82-84; V Blackwell *Derby* 84-91; V Thurgarton w Hoveringham and Bleasby etc *S'well* from 91. *The Vicarage, 208 Southwell Road, Thurgarton, Nottingham NG14 7QP* Tel (01636) 830234

de BERRY, Robert Delatour. b 42. Qu Coll Cam BA64 MA68. Ridley Hall Cam 65. **d** 67 **p** 68. Min Can Bradf Cathl *Bradf* 67-70; Uganda 71-75; V Attercliffe *Sheff* 75-83; V W Kilburn St Luke w St Simon and St Jude *Lon* from 83; Chapl City of Westmr Coll from 84. *The Vicarage, 19 Macroom Road, London W9 3HY* Tel 0181-969 0876

de BOWEN, Alfred William. b 24. KStJ KLJ. Leeds Univ DipHort. St Paul's Grahamstown 76. **d** 78 **p** 86. S Africa 78-86; NSM Cil-y-Cwm and Ystrad-ffin w Rhandir-mwyn etc *St D* 86-88; Lic to Offic *Linc* 88-92; rtd 90. *Sunhaven, 11 Sea Way, Middleton-on-Sea, Bognor Regis, W Sussex PO22 7RZ* Tel (01243) 587352

de BRETT, Rodney John Harry. b 13. Open Univ BA89. Wells Th Coll 63. **d** 64 **p** 65. C Wells St Cuth *B & W* 64-66; V Stoke St Gregory 66-75; V Stoke St Gregory w Burrowbridge 75-78; V Stoke St Gregory w Burrowbridge and Lyng 78-81; RD Taunton N 80-81; rtd 81; Perm to Offic *Ex* 81-95. *106 Whipton Lane, Exeter EX1 3DJ* Tel (01392) 55940

de BURGH-THOMAS, George Albert. b 30. Univ of Wales (Ban) BA50. St Mich Coll Llan 51. **d** 53 **p** 54. C Hawarden *St As* 53-56 and 60-63; C Roath St Martin *Llan* 56-58; C Llangeinor 58-60; V Bampton and Mardale *Carl* 63-70; V Fritwell *Ox* 70-83; R Souldern 70-83; R Fritwell w Souldern and Ardley w Fewcott 83-87; R Hawridge w Cholesbury and St Leonard 87-96; V Lee 87-96; rtd 96. *6 Priory Orchard, Wantage, Oxon OX12 9EL* Tel (01235) 767780

de CHAZAL, John Robert. b 16. Bris Univ. Wycliffe Hall Ox 53. **d** 55 **p** 56. C Redland *Bris* 55-57; C Brislington St Anne 57; C Boxwell w Leighterton *Glouc* 58-60; C Newington Bagpath w Kingscote and Ozleworth 58-60; P-in-c 60; Iraq 61-64; R Caldecote *Cov* 64-71; R Bradford Peverell w Stratton *Sarum* 72-77; P-in-c Sydling St Nic 77; P-in-c Frampton 77; R Bradford Peverell, Stratton, Frampton etc 77-80; rtd 81. *Lavender Cottage, East Street, Sydling St Nicholas, Dorchester, Dorset DT2 9NX* Tel (01300) 341693

de CHAZAL, Mrs Nancy Elizabeth. b 28. Bedf Coll Lon BA52 Lambeth STh90. Sarum & Wells Th Coll 81. **dss** 84 **d** 87 **p** 94. NSM Melbury *Sarum* from 84. *Lavender Cottage, East Street, Sydling St Nicholas, Dorchester, Dorset DT2 9NX* Tel (01300) 341693

de GARIS, Jean Helier Thomson. b 60. K Alfred's Coll Win BA82 PGCE83. Sarum & Wells Th Coll BTh93. **d** 93 **p** 94. C Chandler's Ford *Win* from 93. *St Martin's House, 50 Randall Road, Eastleigh, Hants SO53 1AL* Tel (01703) 254469

de GREY-WARTER, Philip. b 67. Leeds Univ BEng89. Ridley Hall Cam BA94 CTM94. **d** 94 **p** 95. C Bromley Ch Ch *Roch* 94-97; C Sevenoaks St Nic from 97. *c/o The Parish Office, The Rectory, Rectory Lane, Sevenoaks, Kent TN13 1JA* Tel (01732) 740340 Fax 742810

DE GRUYTHER, Albert Alfred. b 14. Magd Coll Ox BA48 MA60. Ridley Hall Cam. **d** 50 **p** 51. C St Helens St Helen *Liv* 50-53; P-in-c Eccleston Park 53-59; R Ulverston H Trin *Carl* 59-67; R Ulverston St Mary w H Trin 67-73; R Gt Salkeld 73-79; rtd 79; Perm to Offic *Carl* from 82. *Ainby House, Lindale, Grange-over-Sands, Cumbria LA11 6LF* Tel (01539) 532968

DE HOOP, Brother Thomas Anthony. b 38. Bp's Univ Lennox BA63 LTh63. **d** 68 **p** 69. Canada 68-79; SSF from 79; P-in-c Cambridge St Benedict *Ely* 85-88; V 88-92; Perm to Offic from 92. *42 Balaam Street, London E13 8AQ* Tel 0171-476 5189

DE KEYSER, Nicholas David Llewellyn (Nick). b 49. Nottm Univ BTh75 MTh86. St Jo Coll Nottm 71. **d** 75 **p** 76. C Portswood Ch Ch *Win* 75-77; C Yateley 77-81; TV Grantham *Linc* 81-86; V Heyside *Man* 86-91; R Charlton-in-Dover *Cant* from 91. *The Rectory, St Alphege Road, Dover, Kent CT17 2PU* Tel (01304) 201143 E-mail 106352.3331@compuserve.com

de la BAT SMIT, Reynaud. b 50. St Edm Hall Ox BA80 MA86 Dur Univ PhD94 FRSA94. Ripon Coll Cuddesdon. **d** 82 **p** 83. C Headington *Ox* 82-85; Chapl St Hild and St Bede Coll *Dur* 85-96; Chapl Cheltenham Coll from 96. *Cheltenham College, Bath Road, Cheltenham, Glos GL53 7LD* Tel (01242) 513540

de la HOYDE, Canon Denys Ralph Hart. b 33. G&C Coll Cam BA57 MA61. Westcott Ho Cam 57. **d** 59 **p** 60. C Moss Side Ch Ch *Man* 59-60; Chapl G&C Coll Cam 60-64; India 64-68; C Eltham H Trin *S'wark* 68-69; Chapl Bromsgrove Sch 69-71; Lic to Offic *Ripon* 71-78; V Pool w Arthington from 86; Dioc Dir of Ords from 86; Hon Can Ripon Cathl from 92. *The Vicarage, Old Pool Bank, Pool in Wharfedale, Otley, W Yorkshire LS21 1LH* Tel 0113-284 3706

de la MARE, Benedick James Hobart. b 38. Trin Coll Ox BA63 MA67. Cuddesdon Coll 63. **d** 65 **p** 66. C Gosforth All SS *Newc* 65-68; Chapl Trin Coll Cam 68-73; V Newc St Gabr *Newc* 73-81; V Dur St Oswald *Dur* from 81; Chapl Collingwood Coll from 95. *St Oswald's Vicarage, Church Street, Durham DH1 3DG* Tel 0191-386 4313

de la MOUETTE, Norman Harry. b 39. Southn Univ BEd73. Sarum & Wells Th Coll 76. **d** 79 **p** 80. NSM Win St Lawr and St Maurice w St Swithun *Win* from 79; Deputation Appeals Org (Win and Portsm) CECS 83-96; Chapl St Jo Win Charity from 96. *146 Greenhill Road, Winchester, Hants SO22 5DR* Tel (01962) 853191

DE LACEY, Thomas. b 46. HNC68. Carl Dioc Tr Inst 88. **d** 91 **p** 92. NSM Ingol *Blackb* 91-93; NSM Ribbleton from 93. *5 Fulwood Hall Lane, Fulwood, Preston PR2 8DA* Tel (01772) 700923

DE MEL, Basil William. b 18. Keble Coll Ox BA41 MA47 BLitt47. Westcott Ho Cam 41. **d** 43 **p** 44. C Tottenham All Hallows *Lon* 43-46; C Cowley St Jas *Ox* 47-48; C Headington Quarry 48-50; C Iffley 50-53; Chapl Manor Hosp Epsom 53-83; rtd 83; Perm to Offic *Guildf* from 85. *83 Manor Green Road, Epsom, Surrey KT19 8LW* Tel (01372) 722134

de MELLO, Gualter Rose. b 34. Ridley Hall Cam 63. **d** 64 **p** 65. C S Hackney St Jo w Ch Ch *Lon* 64-66; Toc H Chapl (Hackney) 66-72; Dir Friends Anonymous Service from 73; Hon C All Hallows by the Tower etc *Lon* from 73; Dir Community of Reconciliation & Fellowship from 88. *Prideaux House, 10 Church Crescent, London E9 7DL* Tel 0181-986 2233

DE MURALT, Dr Robert Willem Gaston. b 25. Utrecht Univ LLM48 DLSc54. Chich Th Coll 90. **d** 90 **p** 91. Hon Asst Chapl The Hague *Eur* from 90. *Zuidwerflaan 5, 2594 CW The Hague, The Netherlands* Tel The Hague (70) 383-8520

✠**de PINA CABRAL, The Rt Revd Daniel Pereira dos Santos.** b 24. Lisbon Univ LLB47. Lon Coll of Div. **d** 47 **p** 49 **c** 67. Portugal 47-67; Portuguese E Africa 67-75; Mozambique 75-76; Asst Bp Lebombo 67-68; Bp Lebombo 68-76; Asst Bp Eur from 76; Hon Can Gib Cathl 79-87; Adn Gib 87-93; rtd 89. *Rua Henrique Lopes de Mendonça 253-42, 4150 Oporto, Portugal* Tel Oporto (2) 617-7772

DE POE SILK, Ronald Charles. b 32. Lich Th Coll 65. **d** 67 **p** 68. C Tottenham St Phil *Lon* 67-68; C Edmonton St Mary w St Jo 68-70; V Stamford Hill St Bart 70-74; rtd 97. *122 Kings Hedges Road, Cambridge CB4 2PB* Tel (01223) 424190

de POMERAI, David Ian Morcamp. b 50. Edin Univ BSc72 Univ Coll Lon PhD75. EMMTC 90. **d** 93 **p** 94. NSM Sutton in Ashfield St Mary *S'well* 93-96; NSM Clifton from 96. *St Francis Vicarage, Southchurch Drive, Clifton, Nottingham NG11 8AQ* Tel 0115-974 7138

de POMERAI, Mrs Lesley Anne. b 60. AIPM82. St Jo Coll Nottm BTh90. **d** 92 **p** 94. Par Dn Sutton in Ashfield St Mary *S'well* 92-94; C 94-96; TV Clifton from 96. *St Francis Vicarage, Southchurch Drive, Clifton, Nottingham NG11 8AQ* Tel 0115-974 7138

DE PURY, Andrew Robert. b 28. K Coll Lon BD57 AKC57. **d** 58 **p** 59. C Epping St Jo *Chelmsf* 58-60; C Loughton St Jo 60-65; V Harold Hill St Geo 65-72; Missr Swan Par Gp *Ox* 72-76; TR Swan 76-85; R Worminghall w Ickford, Oakley and Shabbington 85-95; rtd 95; Perm to Offic *B & W* from 95. *8 Russell Pope Avenue, Chard, Somerset TA20 2JN* Tel (01460) 66714

DE SAUSMAREZ, Canon John Havilland Russell. b 26. Lambeth MA81 Wells Th Coll 54. **d** 56 **p** 57. C N Lynn w St Marg and St Nic *Nor* 56-58; C Hythe *Cant* 58-61; V Maidstone St Martin 61-68; V St Peter-in-Thanet 68-81; RD Thanet 74-81; Hon Can Cant Cathl 78-81; Can Res Cant Cathl 81-94; rtd 94; Perm to Offic *Cant* from 94. *9 St Peter's Court, Broadstairs, Kent CT10 2UU* Tel (01843) 867050

DE SILVA, David Ebenezer Sunil. b 48. Sri Lanka Nat Sem DipTh. **d** 72 **p** 73. Sri Lanka 72-84; C Elm Park St Nic Hornchurch *Chelmsf* 84-87; R Mistley w Manningtree and Bradfield 87-90; TR Stanground and Farcet *Ely* from 90. *The Rectory, 9 Mace Road, Stanground, Peterborough PE2 8RQ* Tel (01733) 890552

DE SMET, Andrew Charles. b 58. Ex Univ BSc79 Southn Univ BTh88. Sarum & Wells Th Coll 85. **d** 88 **p** 89. C Portsea St Mary *Portsm* 88-93; R Shipston-on-Stour w Honington and Idlicote *Cov* from 93. *Shipston Rectory, 8 Glen Close, Shipston-on-Stour, Warks CV36 4ED* Tel (01608) 662661

DE VERNY, David Dietrich. b 55. Trier Univ MTh81 DTh89. **d** 83 **p** 83. Asst Chapl Bonn *Eur* 83; C Henfield w Shermanbury and Woodmancote *Chich* 84-86; C Westmr St Sav and St Jas Less *Lon* 86-88; P-in-c Cheddington w Mentmore and Marsworth *Ox* 88-90; Gen Sec Fellowship of St Alb and St Sergius 90-92. *147 Friern Barnet Lane, London N20 0NP* Tel 0181-445 7844

de VIAL, Raymond Michael. b 39. Oak Hill Th Coll 77. **d** 80 **p** 81. NSM Beckenham St Jo *Roch* 80-84; C Morden *S'wark* 84-88; TV 88-94; V Kingston Hill St Paul from 94. *The Vicarage, 33 Queen's Road, Kingston upon Thames, Surrey KT2 7SF* Tel 0181-549 8597

de VOIL, Paul Walter. b 29. FTII64 Solicitor 67 Hertf Coll Ox BA50 MA87. LNSM course. **d** 92 **p** 93. NSM Denston w Stradishall and Stansfield *St E* from 92. *Water Lane Barn, Denston, Newmarket, Suffolk CB8 8PP* Tel (01440) 820181 Fax as telephone

✠**de WAAL, The Rt Revd Hugo Ferdinand.** b 35. Pemb Coll Cam BA58 MA63. Ridley Hall Cam 59. **d** 60 **p** 61 **c** 92. C Birm St Martin *Birm* 60-64; Chapl Pemb Coll Cam 64-68; P-in-c Dry Drayton *Ely* 64-68; R 68-74; Min Bar Hill LEP 68-74; V Blackpool St Jo *Blackb* 74-78; Prin Ridley Hall Cam 78-92; Lic to Offic *Ely* 78-86; Hon Can Ely Cathl 86-92; Suff Bp Thetford *Nor* from 92. *Rectory Meadow, Bramerton, Norwich NR14 7OW* Tel (01508) 538251 Fax 538371

de WAAL, Dr Victor Alexander. b 29. Pemb Coll Cam BA49 MA53 Nottm Univ Hon DD83. Ely Th Coll 50. **d** 52 **p** 53. C Isleworth St Mary *Lon* 52-56; Lic to Offic *Ely* 56-59; Chapl Ely Th Coll 56-59; Chapl K Coll Cam 59-63; Hon C Nottingham St Mary *S'well* 63-69; Chapl Nottm Univ 63-69; Can Res and Chan Linc Cathl *Linc* 69-76; Dean Cant 76-86; Perm to Offic *Heref* from 88; rtd 90; Chapl Soc of Sacred Cross Tymawr from 90; Lic to Offic *Mon* from 90. *Cwm Cottage, Rowlestone, Hereford HR2 0DP* Tel (01981) 240391

DE WIT, John. b 47. Or Coll Ox BA69 MA73 Clare Coll Cam BA78 MA84. Westcott Ho Cam 75. **d** 78 **p** 79. C The Quinton *Birm* 78-81; TV Solihull 81-85; V Kings Heath 85-94; RD Moseley 91-94; P-in-c Hampton in Arden from 94. *The Vicarage, Hampton in Arden, Solihull, W Midlands B92 0AE* Tel (01675) 442604

DEACON, Charles Edward. b 57. Westf Coll Lon BSc78. Ridley Hall Cam CTM94. **d** 94 **p** 95. C Ex St Jas *Ex* from 94. *103 Old Tiverton Road, Exeter EX4 6LD* Tel (01392) 412575

DEACON, Donald (Brother Angelo). Chich Th Coll 66. **d** 68 **p** 69. SSF from 63; Lic to Offic *Man* 69-70; USA 70-72; C Kennington St Jo *S'wark* 72-74; C Wilton Place St Paul *Lon* 74-75; Angl-Franciscan Rep Ecum Cen Assisi *Eur* 75; Franciscanum Sem 76-78; Perm to Offic *Sarum* 78-82; Lic to Offic *Chelmsf* 82-90; Lic to Offic *Birm* 90-93; Lic to Offic *Linc* 94-96; Lic to Offic *Lon* from 97. *110 Ellesmere Road, London NW10 1JS* Tel 0181-452 7285 Fax as telephone

DEACON, Frederick George Raymond. b 15. Tyndale Hall Bris 63. **d** 65 **p** 66. C Kingswood *Bris* 65-69; C Leckhampton SS Phil and Jas *Glouc* 69-71; V Longcot *Ox* 71-72; V Longcot w Fernham and Bourton 72-77; Zambia 77-80; P-in-c Cressage w Sheinton *Heref* 80-81; P-in-c Harley w Kenley 80-81; TV Wenlock 81-85; rtd 85; Perm to Offic *Heref* 85-90. *29 Robinson Meadow, Ledbury, Herefordshire HR8 1SU* Tel (01531) 634500

DEACON, John. b 37. Arm Aux Min Course 87. **d** 90 **p** 91. NSM Enniscorthy w Clone, Clonmore, Monart etc *C & O* from 90. *The Rectory, Creagh, Gorey, Co Wexford, Irish Republic* Tel Gorey (55) 20354

DEACON, Canon Peter Olford. b 26. MBIM84 MInstAM84. K Coll Lon 48. **d** 52 **p** 53. C Lewisham St Mary *S'wark* 52-58; C Whippingham w E Cowes *Portsm* 58-61; Chapl City of Lon Freeman's Sch Ashtead Park 61-62; C-in-c Gurnard All SS CD *Portsm* 62-68; Chapl RN 68-85; V Gen to Bp Eur 85-92; Can Gib Cathl 86-92; rtd 92. *46 Valiant House, Vicarage Crescent, London SW11 3LU* Tel 0171-2233 6559

DEACON, Timothy Randall. b 55. Ex Univ BA78. Chich Th Coll 79. **d** 80 **p** 81. C Whitleigh *Ex* 80-83; P-in-c Devonport St Aubyn 83-88; P-in-c Newton Ferrers w Revelstoke 88-94; R from 94;

P-in-c Holbeton from 93. *The Rectory, Court Road, Newton Ferrers, Plymouth PL8 1DL* Tel (01752) 872530

DEADMAN, Richard George Spencer. b 63. Ex Univ BA85. Coll of Resurr Mirfield 86. **d** 88 **p** 89. C Grangetown *York* 88-91; P-in-c 91-93; V 93-96; V Wallsend St Luke *Newc* from 96. *St Luke's Vicarage, 148 Park Road, Wallsend, Tyne & Wear NE28 7QS* Tel 0191-262 3723

DEAKIN, Preb John Hartley. b 27. K Coll Cam BA50 MA63. Cranmer Hall Dur DipTh65. **d** 65 **p** 66. C Newcastle St Geo *Lich* 65-70; V Cotes Heath 70-84; RD Eccleshall 82-92; R Standon and Cotes Heath 84-95; Preb Lich Cathl from 88; Sub-Chapl HM Pris Drake Hall 89-95; rtd 95; Hon C Kinver and Enville *Lich* from 95. *The Vicarage, The Close, Enville, Stourbridge, W Midlands DY7 5HX*

DEAN, The Ven Alan. b 38. Hull Univ BA61. Qu Coll Birm DipTh63. **d** 63 **p** 64. C Clitheroe St Mary *Blackb* 63-67; C Burnley St Pet 67-68; CF 68-93; Dep Chapl Gen 93-95; Adn for the Army 93-95; QHC from 93; rtd 95. *1 Midway Avenue, Nether Poppleton, York YO2 6NT* Tel (01904) 785305

DEAN, Andrew Duncan. b 40. Sarum Th Coll 62. **d** 64 **p** 65. C Stockton Heath *Ches* 64-68; C Mottram in Longdendale w Woodhead 68-71; P-in-c Over Tabley 71-73; V Over Tabley and High Legh 73-79; R Astbury and Smallwood 79-85; R Woodchurch from 85. *The Rectory, Church Lane, Upton, Wirral, Merseyside L49 7LS* Tel 0151-677 5352

DEAN, Andrew James. b 40. FCII ACIArb. W of England Minl Tr Course 92. **d** 95 **p** 96. NSM Rodbourne Cheney *Bris* from 95. *Koinonia, 2 Wicks Close, Haydon Wick, Swindon SN2 3QH* Tel (01793) 725526

DEAN, Archibald Charles. b 13. Wycliffe Hall Ox 52. **d** 54 **p** 55. C Yeovil St Jo w Preston Plucknett *B & W* 54-61; R Odcombe 61-91; R Brympton 61-91; R Lufton 61-91; P-in-c Montacute 78-86; rtd 91; Perm to Offic *B & W* from 91. *3 Chur Lane, West Coker, Yeovil, Somerset BA22 9BH* Tel (01935) 862224

DEAN, Arthur. b 32. Southn Univ CQSW80. S Dios Minl Tr Scheme 89 Wesley Coll Leeds 55. **d** 90 **p** 90. NSM Eastney *Portsm* 90-96; P-in-c Portsea St Alb from 96. *9 Kingsley Road, Southsea, Hants PO4 8HJ* Tel (01705) 735773

DEAN, Canon Desmond Keable. b 06. ALCD30 St Jo Coll Dur LTh30 BA31 MA37 BD41. **d** 30 **p** 31. C Islington H Trin Cloudesley Square *Lon* 30-32; Tutor Tyndale Hall Bris 32-35; C Bris St Bart *Bris* 33-35; V Upper Holloway St Pet *Lon* 35-41; Chapl RAFVR 41-45; R Higher Openshaw *Man* 45-51; R Tooting Graveney St Nic *S'wark* 51-76; Chapl Fountain Hosp 51-61; Grove Hosp 54-58; Hon Can S'wark Cathl 63-76; RD Tooting 65-75; rtd 76; Perm to Offic *Chich* from 76. *68 Milland Road, Harmers Hay, Hailsham, E Sussex BN27 1TY* Tel (01323) 843910

DEAN, Francis John Michael. b 15. Univ Coll Ox BA38 MA42. Cuddesdon Coll 38. **d** 39 **p** 40. C Clifton All SS *Bris* 39-46; Hd Master All SS Sch Clifton 43-46; Chapl Ch Ch *Ox* 46-52; Priest Lib Pusey House Ox 46-52; V Bournemouth St Steph *Win* 52-57; R Cranford *Lon* 57-64; V Regent's Park St Mark 64-81; rtd 81. *74 Temple Fortune Lane, London NW11 7TT* Tel 0181-455 6309

DEAN, John Milner. b 27. S'wark Ord Course 69. **d** 72 **p** 73. C Lewisham St Mary *S'wark* 72-75; C Merton St Mary 75-77; V S Beddington St Mich 77-97; rtd 97. *69 Groveside Close, Carshalton, Surrey SM5 2ER*

DEAN, Malcolm. b 34. Tyndale Hall Bris 67. **d** 69 **p** 70. C Daubhill *Man* 69-73; P-in-c Constable Lee 73-74; V 74-79; P-in-c Everton St Sav w St Cuth *Liv* 79-86; P-in-c Anfield SS Simon and Jude 81-86; V Walton Breck Ch Ch 86-89; rtd 89; Perm to Offic *Man* from 89. *6 Sunny Lea Street, Rawtenstall, Rossendale, Lancs BB4 8JE* Tel (01706) 215953

DEAN, Preb Raymond Charles. b 27. Bris Univ BA51. Wycliffe Hall Ox 51. **d** 53 **p** 54. C Weston-super-Mare St Jo *B & W* 53-59; V Lyngford 59-70; V Burnham 70-93; Preb Wells Cathl 73-93; RD Burnham 82-91; RD Axbridge 87-91; rtd 93; Perm to Offic *B & W* from 93. *258 Berrow Road, Berrow, Burnham-on-Sea, Somerset TA8 2JH* Tel (01278) 780979

DEAN, Simon Timothy Michael Rex. b 62. Liv Univ BEng83. Ridley Hall Cam 86. **d** 89 **p** 90. C St German's Cathl *S & M* 89-92; V Castletown from 92. *The Vicarage, Arbory Road, Castletown, Isle of Man IM9 1ND* Tel (01624) 823509

DEANE, Gilbert Ernest. b 06. Lon Univ BD38. Lon Coll of Div 34. **d** 38 **p** 39. C Dawlish *Ex* 38-40; C Budleigh Salterton 40-47; V Countess Wear 47-55; Chapl RAF 43-46 and 55-61; Teacher Bexleyheath Sch 61-64; Teacher Forest Sch Horsham 64-74; rtd 74. *1 Barnfield Close, Lower Park Road, Braunton, Devon EX33 2HL* Tel (01271) 812949

DEANE, Nicholas Talbot Bryan. b 46. Bris Univ BA69. Clifton Th Coll 70. **d** 72 **p** 73. C Accrington Ch Ch *Blackb* 72-75; OMF 75-89; Korea 75-89; P-in-c Newburgh *Liv* 90-93; P-in-c Westhead 90-93; V Newburgh w Westhead 93-97; R Chadwell *Chelmsf* from 97. *The Rectory, Rigby Gardens, Grays, Essex RM16 4JJ* Tel (01375) 842176

DEANE, Robert William. b 52. DipTh85. CITC 85. **d** 85 **p** 86. C Raheny w Coolock *D & G* 85-88; I Clonsast w Rathangan, Thomastown etc *M & K* from 88; Dioc Youth Officer (Kildare) from 90; Can Kildare Cathl from 97. *The Rectory, Edenderry, Co Offaly, Irish Republic* Tel Edenderry (405) 31585 Fax same as telephone

DEANE, Stuart William. b 45. Sarum & Wells Th Coll 86. **d** 88 **p** 89. C Bromyard *Heref* 88-92; V Astley, Clive, Grinshill and Hadnall *Lich* from 92. *The Vicarage, Hadnall, Shrewsbury SY4 4AQ* Tel (01939) 210241

DEANE-HALL, Henry Michael. b 21. Leeds Univ BA46. Coll of Resurr Mirfield 47. **d** 49 **p** 50. C Poplar St Sav w St Gabr and St Steph *Lon* 49-51; C Kirkley *Nor* 51-53; C Reading St Mary V *Ox* 53-56; Chapl St Gabr Convent Sch Newbury 56-62; V Hermitage *Ox* 58-65; V Kirk Patrick 65-67; R Boughton *Pet* 67-71; R Duloe w Herodsfoot *Truro* 71-79; V Morval 71-79; P-in-c Donhead St Mary *Sarum* 79-80; R The Donheads 80-82; rtd 82; Perm to Offic *Ex* 82-95; Warden CJGS 82-95. *Flat 10, Westfield House, Cote Lane, Westbury-on-Trym, Bristol BS9 3UN* Tel (0117) 949 4810

DEAR, Graham Frederick. b 44. St Luke's Coll Ex CertEd66. Wycliffe Hall Ox 67. **d** 70 **p** 71. C Chigwell *Chelmsf* 70-73; C Chingford SS Pet and Paul 73-75; V Southchurch Ch Ch 75-82; CF 82-89; P-in-c The Cowtons *Ripon* 89-94; RE Adv 89-94; V Startforth and Bowes and Rokeby w Brignall from 94. *The Vicarage, High Startforth, Barnard Castle, Co Durham DL12 9AF* Tel (01833) 637371

DEAR, Neil Douglas Gauntlett. b 35. Linc Th Coll 87. **d** 89 **p** 90. C Framlingham w Saxtead *St E* 89-92; P-in-c Eyke w Bromeswell, Rendlesham, Tunstall etc from 92. *The Rectory, Eyke, Woodbridge, Suffolk IP12 2QW* Tel (01394) 460289

DEARDEN, James Varley. b 22. Wycliffe Hall Ox 61. **d** 62 **p** 63. C Drypool St Columba w St Andr and St Pet *York* 62-66; V Newington Transfiguration 66-75; V Huddersfield H Trin *Wakef* 75-87; rtd 87; Perm to Offic *Wakef* from 87. *26 Sycamore Avenue, Meltham, Huddersfield HD7 3EE* Tel (01484) 852519

DEARDEN, Canon Philip Harold. b 43. AKC65. **d** 66 **p** 67. C Haslingden w Haslingden Grane *Blackb* 66-69; C Burnley St Pet 69-71; V Langho Billington 71-78; TR Darwen St Pet w Hoddlesden 78-91; RD Darwen 86-91; V Altham w Clayton le Moors from 91; RD Accrington from 95; Hon Can Blackb Cathl from 96. *The Vicarage, Church Street, Clayton le Moors, Accrington, Lancs BB5 5HT* Tel (01254) 384321 E-mail 100537.2123@compuserve.com

DEARING, Henry Ernest. b 26. Lon Univ BD53. St Deiniol's Hawarden 55. **d** 55 **p** 56. C Skerton St Chad *Blackb* 55-57; V Huncoat 57-60; rtd 95. *7 Troon Way, Abergele LL22 7TT* Tel (01745) 826714

DEARING, Trevor. b 33. Lon Univ BD58. Qu Coll Birm MA63. **d** 61 **p** 62. C Todmorden *Wakef* 61-63; V Silkstone 63-66; V Northowram 66-68; C Harlow New Town w Lt Parndon *Chelmsf* 68-70; V Hainault 70-75; Dir Healing Miss 75-79; Hon C Gt Ilford St Andr 75-79; Perm to Offic *Linc* 80-81; USA 81-83; rtd 83. *4 Rock House Gardens, Radcliffe Road, Stamford, Lincs PE9 1AS* Tel (01780) 51680

DEARNLEY, Mark Christopher. b 59. Cranmer Hall Dur 84. **d** 87 **p** 88. C Purley Ch Ch *S'wark* 87-91; C Addiscombe St Mary 91-93; C Addiscombe St Mary Magd w St Martin 93-94; V Hook from 94. *The Vicarage, 278 Hook Road, Chessington, Surrey KT9 1PF* Tel 0181-397 3521

DEARNLEY, Preb Patrick Walter. b 34. Nottm Univ BA55 LTh75. ALCD64. **d** 64 **p** 65. C New Malden and Coombe *S'wark* 64-68; C Portswood Ch Ch *Win* 68-71; C Leeds St Geo *Ripon* 71-74; Hon C Nottingham St Nic *S'well* 74-77; P-in-c Holloway Em w Hornsey Road St Barn *Lon* 77-85; AD Islington 80-85; Abp's Officer for UPA 85-90; Preb St Paul's Cathl *Lon* 86-91; P-in-c Waterloo St Jo *Liv* from 91. *St John's Vicarage, 16 Adelaide Terrace, Waterloo, Liverpool L22 8QD* Tel 0151-928 3793

DEAS, Leonard Stephen. b 52. New Coll Ox BA75 CertEd76 MA78. St Mich Coll Llan 81. **d** 82 **p** 83. C Dowlais *Llan* 82-84; Chapl St Mich Coll Llan 84-85; Chapl Univ of Wales (Cardiff) *Llan* 85-86; V Newbridge *Mon* 86-93; Can Res St Woolos Cathl 92-96; Master of the Charterhouse Kingston upon Hull from 96. *The Charterhouse, Charterhouse Lane, Hull HU2 8AF* Tel (01482) 329307

DEAVE, Mrs Gillian Mary. b 31. EMMTC 79. **dss** 82 **d** 87 **p** 94. Nottingham St Pet and St Jas *S'well* 82-87; Par Dn 87-91; rtd 91; Perm to Offic *S'well* from 91; Perm to Offic *Leic* from 91. *Greensmith Cottage, Stathern, Melton Mowbray, Leics LE14 4HE* Tel (01949) 60340

DEBENHAM, Mrs Joan Winifred. b 26. LRAM57 Lon Univ BA47 Cam Univ DipEd48. SW Minl Tr Course. **dss** 82 **d** 87 **p** 94. Plymouth St Jas Ham *Ex* 82-86; Asst Chapl Coll of SS Mark and Jo Plymouth 87-89; Par Dn Teignmouth, Ideford w Luton, Ashcombe etc *Ex* from 89. *The Vicarage, Upottery, Honiton, Devon EX14 9RW* Tel (01404) 861630

DEBNEY, Canon Wilfred Murray. b 26. ACA48 FCA60. Wycliffe Hall Ox 58. **d** 60 **p** 61. C Leic H Apostles *Leic* 60-65; V Thorpe Edge *Bradf* 65-69; TV Wendy w Shingay *Ely* 69-75; R Brampton 75-94; Offg Chapl RAF 75-94; RD Huntingdon *Ely* 81-94; Hon Can Ely Cathl 85-94; rtd 94; Perm to Offic *Ely* from 94. *3 Hoo Close, Buckden, St Neots, Huntingdon, Cambs PE18 9TX* Tel (01480) 810652

DEBOO, Alan John. b 45. Qu Coll Cam BA73 MA77. Westcott Ho Cam 72. **d** 74 **p** 75. C Brackley St Pet w St Jas *Pet* 74-77; Perm to Offic *Sarum* 85-94; NSM Wexcombe from 94. *Mayzells Cottage, Collingbourne Kingston, Marlborough, Wilts SN8 3SD* Tel (01264) 850683

DEBOYS, David Gordon. b 54. QUB BD76 Wolfs Coll Ox MLitt. Ridley Hall Cam 90. **d** 92 **p** 93. C Ipswich St Aug *St E* 92-93; C Whitton and Thurleston w Akenham 93-95; R Hardwick *Ely* from 95; R Toft w Caldecote and Childerley from 95. *The Rectory, 50 Main Street, Hardwick, Cambridge CB3 7QS* Tel (01954) 210695

DEDMAN, Roger James. b 45. Oak Hill Th Coll 68. **d** 71 **p** 72. C Gresley *Derby* 71-74; C Ipswich St Fran *St E* 74-79; P-in-c Bildeston w Wattisham 79-92; P-in-c Bramford from 92; P-in-c Somersham w Flowton and Offton w Willisham from 94; RD Bosmere from 96. *The Vicarage, Vicarage Lane, Bramford, Ipswich IP8 4AE* Tel (01473) 741105

DEE, Clive Hayden. b 61. Ripon Coll Cuddesdon 86. **d** 89 **p** 90. C Bridgnorth, Tasley, Astley Abbotts, Oldbury etc *Heref* 89-93; P-in-c Wellington w Pipe-cum-Lyde and Moreton-on-Lugg 93-96. *Ross Cottage, Crumpton Hill Road, Storridge, Malvern, Worcs WR13 5HE*

DEEDES, Canon Arthur Colin Bouverie. b 27. Bede Coll Dur BA51. Wells Th Coll 51. **d** 53 **p** 54. C Milton *Portsm* 53-58; C Worplesdon *Guildf* 58-60; V Weston 60-66; V Fleet 66-73; RD Aldershot 69-73; TR Bournemouth St Pet w St Swithun, H Trin etc *Win* 73-80; RD Bournemouth 74-80; Hon Can Win Cathl 78-92; Master Win St Cross w St Faith 80-92; rtd 92. *Dolphins, 17 Chesil Street, Winchester, Hants SO23 0HU* Tel (01962) 861617

DEEDES, Ms Rosie Anne. b 66. Birm Univ BA87 City Univ 90. Westcott Ho Cam 94. **d** 96 **p** 97. C St Botolph Aldgate w H Trin Minories *Lon* from 96. *37 Lawrence Close, London E3 2AS* Tel 0181-983 3716

DEEGAN, Arthur Charles. b 49. CertEd71 Birm Univ BEd86. Qu Coll Birm 86. **d** 88 **p** 89. C Leic St Jas *Leic* 88-91; C Melton Gt Framland 91-92; TV 92-93; TV Melton Mowbray 93-96; R Barwell w Potters Marston and Stapleton from 96. *The Rectory, 14 Church Lane, Barwell, Leicester LE9 8DG* Tel (01455) 843866

DEEMING, Paul Leyland. b 44. CA Tr Coll 65 CMS Tr Coll Selly Oak 70. **d** 80 **p** 80. CMS 71-82; Pakistan 71-82; R E and W Horndon w Lt Warley *Chelmsf* 83-89; V Gt Ilford St Andr from 89. *The Vicarage, St Andrew's Road, Ilford, Essex IG1 3PE* Tel 0181-554 3858

DEES, Miss Marilyn Monica Mandy. b 34. Nottm Univ BSc55 PGCE56. W of England Minl Tr Course 94. **d** 96 **p** 97. NSM Fownhope w Mordiford, Brockhampton etc *Heref* from 96. *Hazelbank, 24 Nover Wood Drive, Fownhope, Hereford HR1 4PN* Tel (01432) 860369

DEETH, William Stanley. b 38. St Pet Coll Ox BA59 MA67. St Steph Ho Ox 66. **d** 68 **p** 69. C Eastbourne St Mary *Chich* 68-71; C Benwell St Jas *Newc* 71-75; C-in-c Byker St Martin CD 75-76; P-in-c Byker St Martin 76; V 76-89; P-in-c Bothal 89-91; R Bothal and Pegswood w Longhirst 91-94; rtd 94. *17 Osborne Gardens, North Sunderland, Seahouses, Northd NE68 7UF* Tel (01665) 720067

DEFTY, Henry Gordon. b 14. St Chad's Coll Dur BA38 MA41 DipTh41. **d** 39 **p** 40. C Cockerton *Dur* 39-43; C Ferryhill 43-48; PC Hedgefield 48-51; V Hartlepool St Aid 51-73; Can Res Ches Cathl *Ches* 73-74; V Gainford *Dur* 74-80; P-in-c Winston 74-76; R 76-80; rtd 80; Perm to Offic *Dur* from 80. *39 Crossgate, Durham DH1 4PS* Tel 0191-384 4334

DEGG, Ralph William. b 26. Lon Univ BSc57. Wells Th Coll 61. **d** 63 **p** 64. C Sutton Coldfield H Trin *Birm* 63-66; C The Lickey 66-71; R Grendon 71-78; V Tanworth St Patr Salter Street 78-86; rtd 89; Perm to Offic *Birm* from 89. *23 Wayfield Road, Shirley, Solihull, W Midlands B90 3HF* Tel 0121-744 3564

DeGROOSE, Leslie John. b 28. Oak Hill Th Coll 62. **d** 64 **p** 65. C Gunton St Pet *Nor* 64-67; Chapl RN 67-83; P-in-c Gt Oakley *Chelmsf* 83-85; R Gt Oakley w Wix 85-92; rtd 92. *1 Queensberry Mews, Newmarket, Suffolk CB8 9AE* Tel (01638) 660599

✠**DEHQANI-TAFTI, The Rt Revd Hassan Barnaba.** b 20. Tehran Univ BA43. Virginia Th Sem DD81 Ridley Hall Cam 47. **d** 49 **p** 50 **c** 61. Iran 49-61; Bp Iran 61-90; Pres Bp Episc Ch Jerusalem and Middle E 76-86; Asst Bp Win from 82; rtd 90. *Sohrab House, 1 Camberry Close, Basingstoke, Hants RG21 3AG* Tel (01256) 27457

DEIGHTON, Ian Armstrong. b 19. Glas Univ MA40. Edin Th Coll 40. **d** 43 **p** 44. C Paisley H Trin *Glas* 43-45; Bp's Dom Chapl *Arg* 45-47; P-in-c Nether Lochaber 45-47; P-in-c Kinlochleven 45-47; R Clydebank *Glas* 52-57; R Musselburgh *Edin* 57-84; P-in-c Prestonpans 76-84; rtd 84. *6 Duddingston Park South, Edinburgh EH15 3PA* Tel 0131-669 5108

DEIGHTON, William John. b 44. K Coll Lon AKC68 Plymouth Poly CQSW74. St Boniface Warminster 68. **d** 69 **p** 70. C Kenwyn *Truro* 69-72; Hon C Winterbourne *Bris* from 90. *22 Salem Road, Winterbourne, Bristol BS17 1QF* Tel (01454) 778847

DEIMEL, Mrs Margaret Mary. b 49. WMMTC 91. **d** 94 **p** 95. NSM Bidford-on-Avon *Cov* 94-97; NSM Studley from 97. *3 Manor Mews, Manor Road, Studley, Warks B80 7NA* Tel (01527) 852830

DEIMEL, Richard Witold. b 49. Lon Univ BA84. Cranmer Hall Dur 86. **d** 88 **p** 89. C Bilton *Cov* 88-93; P-in-c Studley 93-97; V from 97. *3 Manor Mews, Manor Road, Studley, Warks B80 7NA* Tel (01527) 852830

DELACOUR, Arthur Winter. b 14. Lon Univ BSc52. Sarum & Wells Th Coll 79. **d** 80 **p** 81. NSM Gtr Corsham *Bris* 80-83; Perm to Offic *Win* 83-86; Chapl St Jo Win Charity 86-89; Perm to Offic *Cov* from 89. *3 Margetts Close, Kenilworth, Warks CV8 1EN* Tel (01926) 55667

DELAMERE, Allen Stephen. BTh. **d** 90 **p** 91. C Bangor Abbey *D & D* 90-93; I Saintfield from 93. *The Vicarage, 11 Lisburn Road, Saintfield, Ballynahinch, Co Down BT24 7AZ* Tel (01238) 510286

DELANEY, Anthony. b 65. Man Poly HNC91. St Jo Coll Bramcote BTh95. **d** 95 **p** 96. C Cullompton *Ex* from 95. *27 Forcefield Road, Cullompton, Devon EX15 1QB* Tel (01884) 32509

DELANEY, Canon Peter Anthony. b 37. AKC65. **d** 66 **p** 67. C St Marylebone w H Trin *Lon* 66-70; Chapl Nat Heart Hosp Lon 66-70; Res Chapl Univ Ch Ch the K 70-73; Can Res and Prec S'wark Cathl *S'wark* 73-77; V All Hallows by the Tower etc *Lon* from 77; Can Cyprus and the Gulf from 88; Preb St Paul's Cathl *Lon* from 95. *All Hallows by the Tower, Byward Street, London EC3R 5BJ* Tel 0171-488 4772 or 481 2928 Fax 488 3333

DELANY, Michael Edward. b 34. Lon Univ BSc55 PhD58. S'wark Ord Course 80. **d** 83 **p** 84. NSM Hampton St Mary *Lon* 83-87; R Copythorne and Minstead *Win* 87-94; rtd 94. *Littlecott, Tytherley Road, Winterslow, Salisbury SP5 1PZ* Tel (01980) 862183

DELFGOU, John. b 35. Oak Hill Th Coll 81. **d** 84 **p** 85. NSM Loughton St Mary and St Mich *Chelmsf* 84-90; NSM Loughton St Jo 90-93; C 93-94; TV from 94. *20 Carroll Hill, Loughton, Essex IG10 1NN* Tel 0181-508 6333

DELFGOU, Jonathan Hawke. b 63. Aston Tr Scheme 89 Linc Th Coll BTh94. **d** 94 **p** 95. C Greenstead juxta Colchester *Chelmsf* from 94. *1 Stour Walk, Colchester CO4 3UX* Tel (01206) 871757

DELIGHT, The Ven John David. b 25. Liv Univ CSocSc48 Open Univ BA75. Oak Hill Th Coll 49. **d** 52 **p** 53. C Tooting Graveney St Nic *S'wark* 52-55; C Wallington H Trin 55-58; Lic to Offic *Man* 58-61; Travelling Sec IVF 58-61; C-in-c Leic St Chris CD *Leic* 61-68; Chapl HM Pris Leic 64-67; V Leic St Chris *Leic* 68-69; R Aldridge *Lich* 69-82; Preb Lich Cathl 80-90; RD Walsall 81-82; Adn Stoke 82-90; rtd 90; Perm to Offic *Lich* from 90. *42 Little Tixall Lane, Great Haywood, Stafford ST18 0SE* Tel (01889) 881684

DELL, Dr Murray John. b 31. Cape Town Univ BA51 BSc54 Edin Univ MB, ChB59. Westcott Ho Cam 63. **d** 65 **p** 65. S Africa 65-70; Dean Windhoek 71-80; V Lyme Regis *Sarum* 80-96; Chapl Lyme Regis Hosp 80-96; rtd 96. *3 Empsons Close, Dawlish, Devon EX7 9BG* Tel (01626) 866193

DELL, The Ven Robert Sydney. b 22. Em Coll Cam BA46 MA50. Ridley Hall Cam 46. **d** 48 **p** 49. C Islington St Mary *Lon* 48-50; C Cambridge H Trin *Ely* 50-53; Lic to Offic *Lich* 53-55; Asst Chapl Wrekin Coll Shropshire 53-55; R Mildenhall *St E* 55-57; Vice-Prin Ridley Hall Cam 57-65; V Chesterton St Andr *Ely* 66-73; Adn Derby 73-92; Hon Can Derby Cathl 73-81; Can Res 81-92; rtd 92; Perm to Offic *Derby* from 92. *Pinehurst Lodge, 35 Range Road, Cambridge CB3 9AU* Tel (01223) 365466

DELVE, Albert William John. b 15. Leeds Univ BA38. Coll of Resurr Mirfield 38. **d** 40 **p** 41. C Brixham *Ex* 40-43; C Tavistock and Gulworthy 43-47; C-in-c Burnt Ho Lane CD 47-55; V Dawlish 55-69; RD Kenn 68-69; R Thurlestone 69-83; R Thurlestone w S Milton 83-85; rtd 85; Perm to Offic *Ex* from 85. *Jalmar, Littlemead Lane, Exmouth, Devon EX8 3BU* Tel (01395) 278373

DELVE, Eric David. b 42. Trin Coll Bris. **d** 89 **p** 90. NSM Bris St Matt and St Nath *Bris* 89-92; P-in-c Kirkdale St Lawr *Liv* 93-96; V Maidstone St Luke *Cant* from 96. *The Vicarage, 24 Park Avenue, Maidstone, Kent ME14 5HN* Tel (01622) 754856

DELVES, Anthony James. b 47. Birm Univ BSocSc70 Hull Univ PhD94. St Steph Ho Ox 83. **d** 85 **p** 86. C Cantley *Sheff* 85-90; V Goldthorpe w Hickleton from 90. *Goldthorpe Presbytery, Lockwood Road, Goldthorpe, Rotherham, S Yorkshire S63 9JY* Tel (01709) 898426

DELVES BROUGHTON, Simon Brian Hugo. b 33. Ex Coll Ox BA56 MA64. Kelham Th Coll 56. **d** 59 **p** 60. Ox Miss to Calcutta 60-64; C Skirbeck St Nic *Linc* 64-67; E Pakistan/Bangladesh 67-74; Chapl Chittagong 67-69; V St Thos Cathl Dhaka 69-74; V Northampton Ch Ch *Pet* 74-95; Chapl Northn Gen Hosp 77-87; rtd 95. *71A Observatory Street, Oxford OX2 6EP* Tel (01865) 515463

DENBY, Canon Paul. b 47. NW Ord Course 73. **d** 76 **p** 77. C Stretford All SS *Man* 76-80; V Stalybridge 80-87; Chapl Tameside Distr Gen Hosp Ashton-under-Lyne 82-87; Dir of Ords *Man* 87-95; Hon Can Man Cathl 92-95; Can Admin and Prec Man Cathl from 95; Lic Preacher from 95. *1 Barn Hill Road, Manchester M25 9WH* Tel 0161-773 3171

DENCH, Christopher David. b 62. RGN83. Aston Tr Scheme 86 Sarum & Wells Th Coll 88. **d** 91 **p** 92. C Crayford *Roch* 91-94; P-in-c Leybourne from 94. *The Rectory, 73 Rectory Lane, Leybourne, Maidstone, Kent ME19 5HD* Tel (01732) 842187

DENERLEY, John Keith Christopher. b 34. Qu Coll Ox BA58 MA61. St Steph Ho Ox 58. **d** 61 **p** 62. C Airedale w Fryston *Wakef* 61-64; Chapl Sarum Th Coll 64-68; Min Can Cov Cathl *Cov* 68-76; Chapl Lanchester Poly 70-76; Chapl The Dorothy Kerin Trust Burrswood 76-85; V Trellech and Cwmcarvan *Mon* 85-87; V Penallt 85-87; V Penallt and Trellech from 87; Chapl Ty Mawr Convent (Wales) from 85; RD Mon from 93. *The Vicarage, Penallt, Monmouth NP5 4SE* Tel (01600) 716622

DENFORD, Keith Wilkie. b 35. AKC62. **d** 63 **p** 64. C Gunnersbury St Jas *Lon* 63-66; C Brighton St Pet *Chich* 66-71; Min Can Cant Cathl *Cant* 71-75; R W Tarring *Chich* 75-85; V Burgess Hill St Jo 85-90; R Pulborough 90-96; rtd 96; Perm to Offic *Chich* from 96. *31 John Street, Shoreham-by-Sea, W Sussex BN43 5DL* Tel (01273) 464251

DENGATE, Richard Henry (Dick). b 39. Cant Sch of Min 82. **d** 85 **p** 86. NSM Wittersham w Stone-in-Oxney and Ebony *Cant* 85; R Sandhurst w Newenden from 90. *The Rectory, Bodium Road, Sandhurst, Hawkhurst, Kent TN18 5LE* Tel (01580) 850213

DENHAM, Anthony Christopher (Chris). b 43. Keble Coll Ox BA65 MA70. Oak Hill Th Coll DipHE93. **d** 93 **p** 94. C Hythe *Cant* 93-97; V Haddenham w Cuddington, Kingsey etc *Ox* from 97. *The Vicarage, 27A The Gables, Haddenham, Aylesbury, Bucks HP17 8AD* Tel (01844) 291244

DENHAM, Nicholas Philip. b 50. Salford Univ BSc72 Birm Univ CertEd74. Wycliffe Hall Ox 87. **d** 89 **p** 90. C Bishopwearmouth St Gabr *Dur* 89-90; C Chester le Street 90-92; TV Rushden w Newton Bromswold *Pet* 92-95; R Teigh w Whissendine and Market Overton from 95. *The Vicarage, 3 Paddock Close, Whissendine, Oakham, Leics LE15 7HW* Tel (01664) 474333

DENHAM, Thomas William. b 17. Wycliffe Hall Ox 58. **d** 59 **p** 60. C Bexley St Jo *Roch* 59-62; Area Sec CMS 62-82; Perm to Offic *Liv* 62-73; P-in-c Bishopwearmouth St Gabr *Dur* 73-82; rtd 82. *Forresters Cottage, Nether Ervie, Parton, Castle Douglas, Kirkcudbrightshire DG7 3NG* Tel (016447) 215

DENHOLM, Canon Robert Jack. b 31. Edin Th Coll 53. **d** 56 **p** 57. C Dundee St Mary Magd *Bre* 56-59; C Edin St Pet *Edin* 59-61; R Bridge of Allan *St And* 61-69; Chapl Stirling Univ 67-69; R N Berwick *Edin* 69-80; R Gullane 76-80; R Edin St Mark 80-90; Can St Mary's Cathl from 88; rtd 90. *39 South Street, St Andrews, Fife KY16 9QR* Tel (01334) 75971

DENING, John Cranmer. b 21. Clare Coll Cam BA48 MA52. Qu Coll Birm 50. **d** 52 **p** 53. C Allerton *Liv* 52-55; C Bournemouth St Andr *Win* 55-58; C Lillington *Cov* 59-60; C Yeovil St Jo w Preston Plucknett *B & W* 61-67; C Moulsham St Jo *Chelmsf* 69-70; C W Teignmouth *Ex* 70-73; C N Stoneham *Win* 73-80; C Sholing 80-85; rtd 86. *27 The Paddocks, Brandon, Suffolk IP27 0DX*

DENISON, Canon Keith Malcolm. b 45. Down Coll Cam BA67 MA71 PhD70. Westcott Ho Cam 70. **d** 71 **p** 72. C Chepstow *Mon* 71-72; C Bassaleg 72-75; Post-Ord Tr Officer 75-85; V Mathern and Mounton 75-80; V Mathern and Mounton w St Pierre 80-85; RD Chepstow 82-85; V Risca 85-91; V Goldcliffe and Whiston and Nash 91-96; Dir of Educn from 91; Hon Can St Woolos Cathl 91-94; Can from 94; Can Res from 96. *16 Stow Park Crescent, Newport NP9 4HD*

DENISON, Philip. b 55. York Univ BA77 CertEd. St Jo Coll Nottm 83. **d** 86 **p** 87. C Barnoldswick w Bracewell *Bradf* 86-88; P-in-c Basford St Leodegarius *S'well* 88-91; C Basford w Hyson Green 91-94; V Nether Stowey w Over Stowey *B & W* from 94. *St Mary's Vicarage, 25 St Mary Street, Nether Stowey, Bridgwater, Somerset TA5 1LJ* Tel (01278) 732247

DENMAN, Frederick George. b 46. Chich Th Coll 67. **d** 70 **p** 71. C Stafford St Mary *Lich* 70-72; C Ascot Heath *Ox* 72-75; P-in-c Culham 75-77; P-in-c Sutton Courtenay w Appleford 75-77; P-in-c Clifton Hampden 77; TV Dorchester 78-81; C Ox St Mich w St Martin and All SS 80; Chapl Henley Memorial Hosp 81-82; P-in-c W Hill *Ex* 82; TV Ottery St Mary, Alfington and W Hill 82-87; V Sparkwell from 87; V Shaugh Prior 87-93. *The Vicarage, Sparkwell, Plymouth PL7 5DB* Tel (01752) 837218

DENMAN, Preb Ronald. b 19. St Chad's Coll Dur LTh44 BA46. St Aug Coll Cant 40. **d** 44 **p** 45. C Gillingham St Aug *Roch* 44-47; C Clevedon St Andr *B & W* 47-51; R N w S Barrow 51-57; P-in-c Lovington 51-57; V Cheddar 57-86; Preb Wells Cathl 77-86; rtd 86; Perm to Offic *B & W* from 86. *3 Gardenhurst Close, Burnham-on-Sea, Somerset TA8 2EQ* Tel (01278) 781386

DENNEN, Lyle. b 42. Harvard Univ LLB67 Trin Coll Cam BA70 MA75. Cuddesdon Coll 72. **d** 72 **p** 73. C S Lambeth St Ann *S'wark* 72-75; C Richmond St Mary 75-78; P-in-c Kennington St Jo 78-79; V Kennington St Jo w St Jas from 79; P-in-c Brixton Road Ch Ch 81-89; RD Brixton from 90. *The Vicarage, 92 Vassall Road, London SW9 6IA* Tel 0171-735 9340

DENNESS, Mrs Linda Christine. b 51. Portsm Dioc Tr Course. **d** 89. NSM Milton *Portsm* 89-93; NSM Portsea St Mary 93-96; Lic to Offic from 96. *24 Donaldson Road, Cosham, Portsmouth PO6 2SZ* Tel (01705) 781381

DENNETT, John Edward. b 36. Tyndale Hall Bris 66. **d** 68 **p** 69. C Chell *Lich* 68-71; C Bispham *Blackb* 71-73; C Cheltenham Ch Ch *Glouc* 73-75; V Coppull *Blackb* 75-79; P-in-c Parkham, Alwington and Buckland Brewer *Ex* 79-80; R 80-84; V Blackpool St Thos *Blackb* 84-92; rtd 92; Perm to Offic *Blackb* from 92. *37 Village Way, Bispham, Blackpool FY2 0AH* Tel (01253) 58039

DENNIS, Mrs Barbara Christine. b 56. NTMTC 94. **d** 97. NSM Romford St Edw *Chelmsf* from 97. *4 Oaklands Avenue, Romford RM1 4DB* Tel (01708) 724977

DENNIS, Drucilla Lyn. S Tr Scheme. **d** 95 **p** 96. NSM Cowes H Trin and St Mary *Portsm* from 95. *40 Park Road, Cowes, Isle of Wight PO31 7LT* Tel (01983) 297002

✠**DENNIS, The Rt Revd John.** b 31. St Cath Coll Cam BA54 MA59. Cuddesdon Coll 54. **d** 56 **p** 57 **c** 79. C Armley St Bart *Ripon* 56-60; C Kettering SS Pet and Paul *Pet* 60-62; V Is of Dogs Ch Ch and St Jo w St Luke *Lon* 62-71; V Mill Hill Jo Keble Ch 71-79; RD W Barnet 73-79; Preb St Paul's Cathl 77-79; Suff Bp Knaresborough *Ripon* 79-86; Dioc Dir of Ords 80-86; Bp St E 86-96; rtd 96. *15 Mackenzie Road, Cambridge CB1 2AN*

DENNIS, Canon John Daniel. b 20. LLCM. St D Coll Lamp BA41 LTh43. **d** 43 **p** 44. C Haverfordwest St Mary w St Thos *St D* 43-48; C Newport St Mark *Mon* 48-54; V New Tredegar 54-62; R Worthenbury w Tallarn Green *St As* 62-71; V Chirk 71-86; RD Llangollen 74-86; Hon Can St As Cathl 83-86; rtd 86; Perm to Offic *St As* from 86. *Mount Cottage, Chirk, Wrexham LL14 5HD* Tel (01691) 773382

DENNIS, John William. b 13. St Pet Hall Ox BA38 MA45. Linc Th Coll 38. **d** 39 **p** 40. C Hebburn St Cuth *Dur* 39-45; C Linc St Nic w St Jo Newport *Linc* 45-49; PC Gt Grimsby St Paul 49-60; V Linc St Andr 60-68; V Linc St Swithin 60-82; rtd 83; Perm to Offic *Linc* from 83. *17 Eastbrook Road, Swallowbeck, Lincoln LN6 7ER* Tel (01522) 680373

DENNIS, Keith Aubrey Lawrence. b 55. City of Lon Poly BA79. Cranmer Hall Dur 88. **d** 90 **p** 91. C Bushbury *Lich* 90-94; P-in-c Newcastle St Geo from 94. *St George's Vicarage, 28 Hempstalls Lane, Newcastle, Staffs ST5 0SS* Tel (01782) 710056

DENNIS, Patrick John. b 44. Linc Th Coll 67. **d** 70 **p** 71. C Eccleshill *Bradf* 70-72; C Ponteland *Newc* 73-75; Chr Aid Org Leic and Linc 75-78; TV Cullercoats St Geo *Newc* 78-82; Dioc Ecum Officer 79-82; R Bradfield *Sheff* 82-91; Dioc Ecum Adv 82-93; Sec & Ecum Officer S Yorkshire Ecum Coun 91-93; R Braithwell w Bramley 91-93. *Address excluded by request*

DENNIS, Canon Dr Trevor John. b 45. St Jo Coll Cam BA68 MA71 PhD74. Westcott Ho Cam 71. **d** 72 **p** 73. C Newport Pagnell *Ox* 72-74; Chapl Eton Coll 75-82; Tutor Sarum & Wells Th Coll 82-94; Vice-Prin and Admissions Tutor 89-94; Can Res Ches Cathl *Ches* from 94. *13 Abbey Street, Chester CH1 2JF* Tel (01244) 314408 Fax 313155

DENNISON, Philip Ian. b 52. Nottm Univ BTh81. St Jo Coll Nottm 77. **d** 81 **p** 82. C Stalybridge H Trin and Ch Ch *Ches* 81-84; C Heswall 84-91; TV Bushbury *Lich* from 91. *131 Taunton Avenue, Wolverhampton WV10 6PN* Tel (01902) 781944

DENNISTON, James Keith Stuart. b 49. Barrister-at-Law 70 Down Coll Cam MA70. Oak Hill Th Coll DipEd92. **d** 93 **p** 94. C Harborne Heath *Birm* 93-97; Chapl Lee Abbey from 97. *Lee Abbey Community, Lynton, Devon EX35 6JJ* Tel (01598) 752621

DENNISTON, Robin Alastair. b 26. Ch Ch Ox MA48. **d** 78 **p** 79. NSM Clifton upon Teme *Worc* 78-81; NSM Clifton-on-Teme, Lower Sapey and the Shelsleys 81-85; NSM S Hinksey *Ox* 85-87; NSM Gt w Lt Tew 87-90; NSM Aberdour *St And* 90-94; NSM W Fife Team Min 90-94; Hon C St Marylebone St Mark Hamilton Terrace *Lon* 94-95; P-in-c Gt w Lt Tew *Ox* from 95; P-in-c Over w Nether Worton from 95. *The Vicarage, Great Tew, Oxford OX7 4AG* Tel (01608) 83293

DENNO, Basil. b 52. Dundee Univ BSc74. Oak Hill Th Coll BA81. **d** 81 **p** 83. C Chaddesden St Mary *Derby* 81-83; Hon C 83-84. *21 Parkside Road, Chaddesden, Derby DE21 6QR* Tel (01332) 672687

DENNY, John Peter Sekeford. b 43. RIBA69 Portsm Sch of Architecture DipArch67. Chich Th Coll 90. **d** 91 **p** 92. C Aylmerton w Runton *Nor* 91-95; P-in-c Barney, Fulmodeston w Croxton, Hindringham etc 95-96; R Barney, Fulmodeston w Croxton, Hindringham etc from 96. *The Vicarage, The Street, Hindringham, Fakenham, Norfolk NR21 0AA* Tel (01328) 878338

DENNY, Laurence Eric. b 29. Oak Hill Th Coll 54. **d** 57 **p** 58. C Wallington H Trin *S'wark* 57-61; V Leyton St Edw *Chelmsf* 61-64; P-in-c 65-69; V Low Leyton 64-69; V Leyton St Mary w St Edw 64-72; V Pennycross *Ex* 73-93; rtd 93; Perm to Offic *Ex* from 94. *5 Treloweth Close, Manadon, Plymouth PL2 3SL* Tel (01752) 781405

DENNY, Michael Thomas. b 47. Kelham Th Coll 68 St Jo Coll Nottm 71. **d** 73 **p** 74. C Gospel Lane St Mich *Birm* 73-77; P-in-c Frankley 77-82; R from 82. *The Rectory, Frankley Green, Birmingham B32 4AS* Tel 0121-475 3724

DENNY, Peter Bond. b 17. Lon Univ BA41. Bps' Coll Cheshunt 41. **d** 43 **p** 44. C Bushey Heath *St Alb* 43-45; C Calstock *Truro* 52-56; V Newlyn St Newlyn 56-83; RD Pydar 61-64 and 74-81; rtd 83; Perm to Offic *Truro* from 83. *Tralee, The Crescent, Truro, Cornwall TR1 3ES* Tel (01872) 74492

DENT, Christopher Mattinson. b 46. K Coll Lon BA68 AKC68 MTh69 Jes Coll Cam BA72 MA76 New Coll Ox MA76 DPhil80.

Westcott Ho Cam 70. **d** 72 **p** 73. C Chelsea St Luke *Lon* 72-76; Asst Chapl New Coll Ox 76-79; Fell Chapl and Dean Div 79-84; V Hollingbourne and Hucking w Leeds and Broomfield *Cant* 84-93; V Bedford St Andr *St Alb* from 93. *St Andrew's Vicarage, 1 St Edmond Road, Bedford MK40 2NQ* Tel (01234) 354234 or 216881

DENT, Michael Leslie. b 54. Leeds Univ BEd76. St Steph Ho Ox DipMin95. **d** 95 **p** 96. C Cockerton *Dur* from 95. *213 Brinkburn Road, Darlington, Co Durham DL3 9LE* Tel (01352) 603944

DENT, Nigel Clive. b 56. K Coll Lon BD77 Keble Coll Ox DPhil85. St Steph Ho Ox 83. **d** 85 **p** 86. C High Wycombe *Ox* 85-89; Dep Chapl HM Pris Wormwood Scrubs 89-90; Chapl HM Young Offender Inst Wellingborough 90-95; TR Duston Team *Pet* from 96. *The Vicarage, 3 Main Road, Duston, Northampton NN5 6JB* Tel (01604) 752591

DENT, Raymond William. b 47. Birm Coll of Educn CertEd68 Open Univ BA84. Ridley Hall Cam 70. **d** 73 **p** 74. C Hyde St Geo *Ches* 73-76; C Eastham 76-79; TV E Runcorn w Halton 79-80; V Hallwood 80-83; V New Brighton Em 83-94; V Willaston from 94. *The Vicarage, 13 Hooton Road, Willaston, South Wirral L64 1SE* Tel 0151-327 4737

DENT, Richard William. b 32. Down Coll Cam BA56 MA LLB59. Bris Sch of Min 73. **d** 77 **p** 78. NSM Southmead *Bris* 77-81; NSM Henleaze 81-85; V Highworth w Sevenhampton and Inglesham etc 85-88; TV Oldland 88-91; V Longwell Green 91-93; C Bedminster St Mich 93-94; C 94-97; Chapl Asst Frenchay Healthcare NHS Trust Bris 94-97; rtd 97. *1 Addison Road, Bristol BS3 4QH* Tel 0117-966 0278

DENTON, Kenneth Percival. b 14. Clifton Th Coll 54. **d** 55 **p** 56. C Buttershaw St Paul *Bradf* 55-57; C Otley 57-59; C Morpeth *Newc* 59-62; R Winteringham *Linc* 62-69; V Middlesbrough St Thos *York* 69-73; C Rufforth w Moor Monkton and Hessay 73-76; P-in-c Escrick 76-80; rtd 80; Perm to Offic *B & W* from 81. *46 Pedlars Grove, Packsaddle Way, Frome, Somerset BA11 2SX* Tel (01373) 463875

DENTON, Peter Brian. b 37. Kelham Th Coll 57. **d** 62 **p** 63. C Ellesmere Port *Ches* 62-66; Chapl HM Borstal Hollesley 66-69; CF 69-90; Warden Bridge Cen from 90; C Hounslow H Trin w St Paul *Lon* 90-92; V Northolt Park St Barn from 92; P-in-c Southall Green St Jo from 97. *The Vicarage, Raglan Way, Northolt, Middx UB5 4SX* Tel 0181-422 3775

DENTON, Peter Charles. St Jo Coll Dur BA52. Oak Hill Th Coll 49. **d** 52 **p** 53. C Ushaw Moor *Dur* 52-54; C-in-c Throckley St Mary CD *Newc* 54-58; V Long Horsley 58-67; Lect City of Newc Coll of Educn 67-75; Sen Lect Newc Poly 75-90; rtd 90. *10 Whitesmocks Avenue, Durham DH1 4HP* Tel 0191-384 3247

DENYER, Alan Frederick. b 31. Wycliffe Hall Ox 80. **d** 82 **p** 83. C Rodbourne Cheney *Bris* 82-84; P-in-c Garsdon w Lea and Cleverton 84-87; R Garsdon, Lea and Cleverton and Charlton 87-91; R Lydbury N w Hopesay and Edgton *Heref* from 91; Asst Dioc Soc Resp Officer from 91. *The Vicarage, Lydbury North, Shropshire SY7 8AU* Tel (01588) 680609

DENYER, Paul Hugh. b 46. Lon Univ BA68. Ripon Coll Cuddesdon 74. **d** 77 **p** 78. C Horfield H Trin *Bris* 77-82; TV Yate New Town 82-88; V Bris Lockleaze St Mary Magd w St Fran 88-95; Dioc Dir of Ords from 95. *The Vicarage, Kington Langley, Chippenham, Wilts SN15 5NJ* Tel (01249) 750231

DENZIL, Sister. *See* ONSLOW, Sister Denzil Octavia

DEO, Paul. b 60. Coll of Ripon & York St Jo CertEd81. St Jo Coll Nottm 95. **d** 97. C Tong *Bradf* from 97. *207 Broadstone Way, Holme Wood, Bradford, W Yorkshire BD4 9BT* Tel (01274) 685256

DEPPEN, Jay Ralph Keim. b 18. Gen Th Sem (NY) MDiv44 STD67. **d** 43 **p** 44. USA 43-75 and from 78; P-in-c Battlesden and Pottesgrove *St Alb* 75-78; P-in-c Flamstead 75-78; rtd 84. *870 Morningside Drive, GS 328, Fullerton, CA 92835, USA* Tel Fullerton (714) 256 8273

DERBRIDGE, Roger. b 39. Clifton Th Coll 63. **d** 66 **p** 69. C Surbiton Hill Ch Ch *S'wark* 66-67; C Richmond Ch Ch 67-70; C Toxteth Park St Philemon *Liv* 70-75; TV Toxteth St Philemon w St Gabr 75-84; V Woking St Mary *Guildf* from 84. *St Mary of Bethany Vicarage, West Hill Road, Woking, Surrey GU22 7UJ* Tel (01483) 761269

DERBY, Archdeacon of. *See* GATFORD, The Ven Ian

DERBY, Bishop of. *See* BAILEY, The Rt Revd Jonathan Sansbury

DERBY, Provost of. *See* LEWERS, The Very Revd Benjamin Hugh

DERBYSHIRE, Alan George. b 16. Lon Univ BA41. Linc Th Coll 41. **d** 43 **p** 44. C Dunstable *St Alb* 43-47; CF 47-67; R Merrow *Guildf* 67-81; rtd 81; Perm to Offic *Heref* 81-94. *1 Abbey Cottages, Abbey Precinct, Tewkesbury, Glos GL20 5SR* Tel (01684) 295743

DERBYSHIRE, Mrs Anne Margaret. b 31. Lon Univ CertEd75 Open Univ BA87. SW Minl Tr Course. **dss** 84 **d** 87. NSM Tiverton St Pet *Ex* 87-90; Perm to Offic from 90. *38 Greenway Gardens, King Street, Tiverton, Devon EX16 5JL* Tel (01884) 255966

DERBYSHIRE, Douglas James. b 26. **d** 81 **p** 82. Hon C Heald Green St Cath *Ches* 81-86; Hon C Stockport St Geo 86-89; C 89-91; rtd 91; Perm to Offic *Man* from 92; Perm to Offic *Ches* from 92. *91 East Avenue, Heald Green, Cheadle, Cheshire SK8 3BR* Tel 0161-437 3748

DERBYSHIRE, Philip Damien. b 50. Sarum & Wells Th Coll 80. **d** 82 **p** 83. C Chatham St Wm *Roch* 82-86; Zimbabwe 86-88; TV Burnham w Dropmore, Hitcham and Taplow *Ox* 88-92; Chapl HM Pris Reading 92-97; Chapl HM Pris Holloway from 97. *The Chaplain's Office, HM Prison, Parkhurst Road, London N7 0NU* Tel 0171-607 6747 Fax 700 0296

DERHAM, Miss Hilary Kathlyn. b 50. MRPharmS Nottm Univ BPharm71. Chich Th Coll 89. **d** 91 **p** 95. Par Dn Stevenage H Trin *St Alb* 91-94; C from 94. *413 Scarborough Avenue, Stevenage, Herts SG1 2QA* Tel (01438) 361179

DERISLEY, Canon Albert Donald. b 20. Ely Th Coll 60. **d** 62 **p** 63. C Gt Yarmouth *Nor* 62-66; V Gt w Lt Plumstead 66-72; V N Elmham w Billingford 72-85; RD Brisley and Elmham 77-85; Hon Can Nor Cathl 78-85; rtd 85; Perm to Offic *Nor* from 85. *22 Stuart Road, Aylsham, Norwich NR11 6HN* Tel (01263) 734579

DERMOTT, David John. b 34. Hull Univ BA60. Cuddesdon Coll 67. **d** 68 **p** 69. C Howden *York* 68-71; C W Acklam 71-74; TV Thornaby on Tees 74-79; R Hinderwell w Roxby from 79. *The Rectory, Hinderwell, Saltburn, Cleveland TS13 5JH* Tel (01947) 840249

DEROY-JONES, Philip Antony (Tony). b 49. St Mich Coll Llan DMinlStuds92. **d** 92 **p** 93. C Neath w Llantwit *Llan* 92-95; V Caerau St Cynfelin from 95. *The Vicarage, Cymmer Road, Caerau, Maesteg CF34 0YR* Tel (01656) 736500

DERRETT, Canon Leslie John. b 14. St Jo Coll Dur BA41 MA45. **d** 41 **p** 42. C Grays Thurrock *Chelmsf* 41-43; C Walthamstow St Mary 43-44; Chapl Ellesmere Coll Shropshire 44-45; Chapl Dur Sch 45-48; V Whitehaven St Nic *Carl* 48-54; V Hedworth *Dur* 54-58; V E Ham St Mary *Chelmsf* 58-68; TR Witham 68-76; Hon Can Chelmsf Cathl 76-80; V Thorpe-le-Soken 76-80; rtd 80; Perm to Offic *Chelmsf* from 80. *27 Bromley College, London Road, Bromley BR1 1PE* Tel 0181-460 0291

DERRICK, David John. b 46. S'wark Ord Course. **d** 84 **p** 85. NSM Angell Town St Jo *S'wark* from 84; NSM St Mary le Strand w St Clem Danes *Lon* 86-93. *Weavers Cottage, 8 Bellvue Place, London E1 4UG* Tel 0171-791 2943

DERRICK, Mrs Dorothy Margaret. b 41. St Mary's Coll Cheltenham CertEd63 RTC63. Ox Min Course CBTS92. **d** 92 **p** 94. NSM Gt Missenden w Ballinger and Lt Hampden *Ox* from 92. *14 Elmtree Green, Great Missenden, Bucks HP16 9AF* Tel (01494) 866610

DERRIMAN, Graham Scott. b 39. Bps' Coll Cheshunt 63. **d** 66 **p** 67. C Wandsworth St Mich *S'wark* 66-70; C Merton St Mary 70-74; P-in-c Earlsfield St Andr 75-81; V Camberwell St Luke 81-90; V Croydon St Aug from 90; Voc Adv Croydon Adnry from 93; RD Croydon Cen from 95. *The Vicarage, 23A St Augustine's Avenue, Croydon CR2 6JN* Tel 0181-688 2663

DERRY, Eric Leonard Stobart. b 15. Worc Ord Coll 62. **d** 64 **p** 65. C Mirfield *Wakef* 64-67; C Almondbury 67-68; V Luddenden 68-73; V Dodworth 73-83; rtd 84; Perm to Offic *Wakef* from 84. *29 Barnsley Road, Cawthorne, Barnsley, S Yorkshire S75 4HW* Tel (01226) 790697

DERRY, Hugh Graham. b 10. Or Coll Ox BA35 MA50. Ely Th Coll 46. **d** 48 **p** 49. C Plymouth St Pet *Ex* 48-50; C Summertown *Ox* 50-51; Chapl Radcliffe Infirmary Ox 51-56; Lic to Offic *Ox* 52-58; S Africa 58-72; rtd 72; Perm to Offic *Ex* from 74. *Beech Tree Cottage, Cheriton Fitzpaine, Crediton, Devon EX17 4JJ* Tel (01363) 866438

DERRY AND RAPHOE, Bishop of. *See* MEHAFFEY, The Rt Revd Dr James

DERRY, Archdeacon of. *See* McLEAN, The Ven Donald Stewart

DERRY, Dean of. *Vacant*

DESBRULAIS, Mrs Patricia Mary. b 27. Qu Coll Birm 77. **dss** 79 **d** 87. Gt Bowden w Welham *Leic* 79-83; Market Harborough 83-87; Hon Par Dn 87-89; rtd 89; Perm to Offic *Leic* from 89. *78 Rainsborough Gardens, Market Harborough, Leics LE16 9LW* Tel (01858) 466766

DESERT, Thomas Denis. b 31. Bps' Coll Cheshunt 54. **d** 56 **p** 57. C Goldington *St Alb* 56-60; C-in-c Luton St Hugh Lewsey CD 60-63; C St Alb St Sav 63-65; C Cheshunt 65-68; V Bedford All SS 68-89; R Northill w Moggerhanger 89-96; rtd 96. *2 Phillpotts Avenue, Bedford MK40 3UJ* Tel (01234) 211413

DESHPANDE, Miss Lakshmi Anant. b 64. Liv Univ BSc86 Ex Univ PGCE87. Wycliffe Hall Ox BTh94. **d** 94 **p** 95. C Long Eaton St Jo *Derby* from 94. *66 Curzon Street, Long Eaton, Nottingham NG10 4FT* Tel 0115-946 0557

DESMOND, Mrs Elspeth Margaret. b 49. Trin Coll Bris CPS90 S Dios Minl Tr Scheme 90. **d** 93 **p** 95. NSM Filton *Bris* from 93. *14 Kenmore Crescent, Bristol BS7 0TH* Tel 0117-976 3390

DESON, Rolston Claudius. b 39. Qu Coll Birm 85. **d** 84 **p** 85. NSM Saltley *Birm* 84-86; C Edgbaston SS Mary and Ambrose 86-90; V W Bromwich St Phil *Lich* from 90. *The Vicarage, 33 Reform Street, West Bromwich, W Midlands B70 7PF* Tel 0121-525 1985

DESPARD, Canon Eric Herbert. b 17. TCD BA40 BD48. CITC 41. **d** 41 **p** 42. C Roscommon *K, E & A* 41-43; C Dublin St Pet *D & G* 43-51; I Blessington w Kilbride 51-65; RD Rathdrum 63-77; I Lucan w Leixlip 65-92; Can Ch Ch Cathl Dublin 73-92; RD Ballymore 77-85; RD Omorthy 86-92; rtd 92. *59 Sweetmount*

Park, Dundrum, Dublin 14, Irish Republic Tel Dublin (1) 298 2489

DESROSIERS, Jacques Thomas Maurice. b 55. Qu Univ Kingston Ontario BCom77. S'wark Ord Course 91. **d** 94 **p** 95. NSM Benenden *Cant* from 94. *2 Twysden Cottage, Bodiam Road, Sandhurst, Kent TN18 5LF* Tel (01580) 850592

DETTMER, Douglas James. b 64. Univ of Kansas BA86 Yale Univ MDiv90. Berkeley Div Sch 90. **d** 90 **p** 91. C Ilfracombe, Lee, Woolacombe, Bittadon etc *Ex* 90-94; Bp's Dom Chapl from 94. *2 Palace Cottages, Palace Gate, Exeter EX1 1HY* Tel (01392) 213960

DEUCHAR, Canon Andrew Gilchrist. b 55. Southn Univ BTh86. Sarum & Wells Th Coll 81. **d** 84 **p** 85. C Alnwick St Mich and St Paul *Newc* 84-88; TV Heref St Martin w St Fran (S Wye TM) *Heref* 88-90; Adv to Coun for Soc Resp (Dios Cant and Roch) *Cant* 90-94; Sec for Angl Communion Affairs from 94; Hon Can Cant Cathl from 95; Perm to Offic *Roch* from 95. *73 St Luke's Road, Maidstone, Kent ME14 5AS* Tel (01622) 765010

DEUCHAR, John. b 24. Or Coll Ox BA49 MA50. Westcott Ho Cam 49. **d** 51 **p** 52. C Rugby St Andr *Cov* 51-55; V Bournemouth St Andr *Win* 55-61; V Eastleigh 61-68; R Woolwich St Mary w H Trin *S'wark* 68-72; V Whitley Ch Ch *Ox* 72-84; Chapl and Tutor Whittington Coll Felbridge 84-89; rtd 89; Perm to Offic *Sarum* from 89; Perm to Offic *Win* from 89. *2 The Leys, 63 Church Street, Fordingbridge, Hants SP6 1BB* Tel (01425) 655407

DEVAMANIKKAM, Trevor. b 47. Ripon Hall Ox 74. **d** 76 **p** 77. C Manston *Ripon* 76-79; P-in-c Moor Allerton 79-81; P-in-c Harrogate St Wilfrid and St Luke 81-84; V Buttershaw St Aid *Bradf* 84-85; Succ St D Cathl *St D* 85-87; V Llanwnda, Goodwick, w Manorowen and Llanstinan 87-90; Chapl RN 90-94; Chapl Fuengirola St Andr *Eur* 94-96; rtd 96. *6 Wetherby Road, Harrogate, N Yorkshire HG2 7SA* Tel (01423) 889732

DEVENNEY, Raymond Robert Wilmont. b 47. TCD BA69 MA73. CITC 70. **d** 70 **p** 71. C Ballymena *Conn* 70-75; C Ballyholme *D & D* 75-81; I Killinchy w Kilmood and Tullynakill from 81. *The Rectory, 11 Whiterock Road, Killinchy, Newtownards, Co Down BT23 6PR* Tel (01238) 541249

✠**DEVENPORT, The Rt Revd Eric Nash.** b 26. Open Univ BA74. Kelham Th Coll 46. **d** 51 **p** 52 **c** 80. C Leic St Mark *Leic* 51-54; C Barrow St Matt *Carl* 54-56; Succ Leic Cathl *Leic* 56-59; V Shepshed 59-64; R Oadby 64-73; Hon Can Leic Cathl 73-80; Dioc Missr 73-80; Suff Bp Dunwich *St E* 80-92; rtd 92; Adn Italy *Eur* 92-97; Chapl Florence w Siena 92-97; Asst Bp Eur 93-97. *32 Bishopgate, Norwich NR1 4AA* Tel (01603) 664121

DEVERELL, William Robert Henry. b 61. CITC 88 St Jo Coll Nottm CertCS92. **d** 92 **p** 93. C Agherton *Conn* 92-95; I Sixmilecross w Termonmaguirke *Arm* from 95. *104 Cooley Road, Sixmilecross, Co Tyrone BT79 9DH* Tel (01662) 758218

DEVEREUX, Canon John Swinnerton. b 32. Lon Univ BSc53. Wells Th Coll. **d** 58 **p** 59. C Wigan St Mich *Liv* 58-60; C Goring-by-Sea *Chich* 60-69; Ind Chapl 69-97; Can and Preb Chich Cathl 90-97; rtd 97; Perm to Offic *Chich* from 97. *40 Hillside Avenue, Worthing, W Sussex BN14 9QT* Tel (01903) 234044

DEVERILL, Jennifer (Jenny). b 40. Auckland Medical Sch MSR62. LNSM course 93. **d** 96. NSM Battersea St Luke *S'wark* from 96. *48 Gayville Road, London SW11 6JP* Tel 0171-228 7674

DEVONISH, Clive Wayne. b 51. Ridley Hall Cam. **d** 96 **p** 97. C Meole Brace *Lich* from 96. *19 High Ridge Way, Radbrook Green, Shrewsbury SY3 6DJ* Tel (01743) 367707

DEVONSHIRE, Roger George. b 40. AKC62. **d** 63 **p** 64. C Rotherhithe St Mary w All SS *S'wark* 63-67; C Kingston Hill St Paul 67-71; Chapl RN 71-95; Hon Chapl to The Queen 92-95; R Pitlochry *St And* from 95; R Kilmaveonaig from 95. *The Rectory, Lettoch Terrace, Pitlochry, Perthshire PH16 5BA* Tel (01796) 472539

DEW, Glyn. Worc Coll of Educn BEd90. St Jo Coll Nottm MA97. **d** 97. C Beoley *Worc* from 97. *4 Marshfield Close, Church Hill North, Redditch, Worcs B98 8RW*

DEW, Lindsay Charles. b 52. Cranmer Hall Dur 85. **d** 86 **p** 86. C Knottingley *Wakef* 86-89; V Batley St Thos 89-97; RD Dewsbury from 96; R Thornhill and Whitley Lower from 97. *The Rectory, 51 Frank Lane, Dewsbury, W Yorkshire WF12 0JW* Tel (01924) 465064

DEW, Robert David John (Bob). b 42. St Pet Coll Ox BA63. St Steph Ho Ox 63. **d** 65 **p** 66. C Abington *Pet* 65-69; Chapl Tiffield Sch Northants 69-71; Ind Chapl *Pet* 71-79; Ind Chapl *Liv* 79-87; Sen Ind Missr 88-91; V Skelsmergh w Selside and Longsleddale *Carl* from 91; Bp's Research Officer 91-95; CME Adv from 95. *The Vicarage, Skelsmergh, Kendal, Cumbria LA9 6NU* Tel (01539) 724498

DEWAR, Francis John Lindsay. b 33. Keble Coll Ox BA56 MA59. Cuddesdon Coll 58. **d** 60 **p** 61. C Hessle *York* 60-63; C Stockton St Chad *Dur* 63-66; V Sunderland St Chad 66-81; Org Journey Inward, Journey Outward Project from 82; rtd 97. *Wellspring, Church Road, Wookey, Wells, Somerset BA5 1JX* Tel (01749) 675365

DEWAR, Ian John James. b 61. Kingston Poly BA83. Cranmer Hall Dur 89. **d** 92 **p** 93. C Blackb St Gabr *Blackb* 92-95; C Darwen St Cuth w Tockholes St Steph 95-97; V Appley Bridge from 97. *The Vicarage, Finch Lane, Appley Bridge, Wigan, Lancs WN6 9DT* Tel (01257) 252875 E-mail dewarijj@mail.warp.co.uk

DEWAR, John. b 32. Chich Th Coll 58. **d** 61 **p** 62. C Leeds St Hilda *Ripon* 61-65; C Cullercoats St Geo *Newc* 65-69; V Newsham 69-76; V Kenton Ascension 76-86; R Wallsend St Pet 86-92; V Longhorsley and Hebron 92-96; rtd 96. *51 Bonner Lane, Calverton, Nottingham NG14 6FU* Tel (0115) 965 2599

DEWES, Ms Deborah Mary. b 59. **d** 92 **p** 94. C Stockton St Pet *Dur* 92-96; C Knowle *Birm* from 96. *St Anne's Cottage, 1713 High Street, Knowle, Solihull, W Midlands B93 0LN* Tel (01564) 775672

DEWEY, David Malcolm. b 43. Lon Univ BA72 LSE MSc(Econ)87 Fitzw Coll Cam MPhil94. Westcott Ho Cam 76. **d** 78 **p** 79. Sen Lect Middx Poly 72-92; Sen Lect Middx Univ from 92; Hon C Enfield St Mich *Lon* 78-79; Hon C Bush Hill Park St Steph 79-84; Hon C Palmers Green St Jo 84-90; Perm to Offic 90-95; Perm to Offic *St Alb* from 95. *44 The Elms, Hertford SG13 7UX* Tel (01992) 501214

DEWEY, Peter Lewis. b 38. Wycliffe Hall Ox 69. **d** 71 **p** 72. C Hammersmith St Sav *Lon* 71-73; Chapl to Bp Kensington 73-75; C Isleworth All SS 75-81; TV Dorchester *Ox* 81-91; CF (TA) 86-91; Chapl Gordonstoun Sch 92-97; TR St Laur in Thanet *Cant* from 97. *St Laurence Rectory, Newington Road, Ramsgate, Kent CT11 0QT* Tel (01843) 592478

DEWEY, Sanford Dayton. b 44. Syracuse Univ AB67 MA72. Gen Th Sem (NY) MDiv79. **d** 79 **p** 80. USA 79-87; C St Mary le Bow w St Pancras Soper Lane etc *Lon* 87-92; C Hampstead St Steph w All Hallows 92-94; NSM from 94. *43 Shirlock Road, London NW3 2HR* Tel 0171-482 1527

DEWHURST, Gabriel George. b 30. **d** 59 **p** 60. In RC Ch 60-69; C Darlington St Jo *Dur* 70; C Bishopwearmouth St Nic 71-73; C-in-c Stockton St Mark CD 73-81; V Harton 81-86; R Castle Eden w Monkhesleden 86-97; rtd 97. *9 Knott Lane, Easingwold, York YO6 3LX* Tel (01904) 613604

DEWHURST, George. b 34. TD76. AKC58. **d** 59 **p** 60. C Chorley St Pet *Blackb* 59-61; C-in-c Oswaldtwistle All SS CD 61-65; CF (TA) 63-67; V Shevington *Blackb* 65-83; CF (TAVR) 67-83; CF (TA - R of O) 83-88; V Horsley and Newington Bagpath w Kingscote *Glouc* 83-96; rtd 96; Perm to Offic *Glouc* from 96. *St Nicholas House, Cherington, Tetbury, Glos GL8 8SN* Tel (01285) 841367

DEWIS, Harry Kenneth. b 19. NW Ord Course 75. **d** 78 **p** 79. NSM Bedale *Ripon* 78-89; Perm to Offic from 89. *11 Masham Road, Bedale, N Yorkshire DL8 2AF* Tel (01677) 423588

DEWSBURY, Michael Owen. b 31. St Aid Birkenhead 54 St Jo Coll Dur 53. **d** 57 **p** 58. C Hellesdon *Nor* 57-60; C Speke All SS *Liv* 60-62; R Gt and Lt Glemham *St E* 62-67; R W Lynn *Nor* 67-68; Australia from 68; rtd 96. *6B Livingstone Street, Beaconsfield, W Australia 6162* Tel Perth (9) 335 6852

DEXTER, Canon Frank Robert. b 40. Cuddesdon Coll 66. **d** 68 **p** 69. C Newc H Cross *Newc* 68-71; C Whorlton 71-73; V Pet Ch Carpenter *Pet* 73-80; V High Elswick St Phil *Newc* 80-85; RD Newc W 81-85; V Newc St Geo from 85; Hon Can Newc Cathl from 94; P-in-c Newc St Hilda from 95. *St George's Vicarage, St George's Close, Jesmond, Newcastle upon Tyne NE2 2TF* Tel 0191-281 1628

DEY, Charles Gordon Norman. b 46. Lon Coll of Div DipTh70. **d** 71 **p** 72. C Almondbury *Wakef* 71-76; V Mixenden 76-85; TR Tong *Bradf* from 85. *The Rectory, Holmewood Road, Tong, Bradford, W Yorkshire BD4 9EJ* Tel (01274) 682100

DEY, John Alfred. b 33. ALCD57 ALCM57. **d** 57 **p** 58. C Man Albert Memorial Ch *Man* 57-60; C Pennington 60-62; V Mosley Common 62-69; V Chadderton Em 69-79; V Flixton St Jo 79-96; rtd 96. *8 Woodlands Avenue, Urmston, Manchester M41 6NE*

DI CASTIGLIONE, Nigel Austin. b 57. St Jo Coll Dur BA78. St Jo Coll Nottm MA94. **d** 94 **p** 95. C Tamworth *Lich* from 94. *19 Perrycrofts Crescent, Tamworth, Staffs B79 8UA* Tel (01827) 69021

DIAMOND, Canon Michael Lawrence. b 37. St Jo Coll Dur BA60 MA74 Sussex Univ DPhil84. Lon Coll of Div ALCD62 LTh74. **d** 62 **p** 63. C Wandsworth St Mich *S'wark* 62-64; C Patcham *Chich* 64-69; R Hamsey 70-75; P-in-c Cambridge St Andr Less *Ely* 75-86; V from 86; Hon Can Ely Cathl from 94; RD Cambridge from 97. *The Vicarage, Parsonage Street, Cambridge CB5 8DN* Tel (01223) 353794

DIAMOND, Capt Richard Geoffrey Colin. b 49. CA Tr Coll DipEvang89. **d** 93 **p** 93. Miss to Seamen from 90; Kenya from 90. *The Missions to Seamen, PO Box 80424, Mombasa, Kenya* Tel Mombasa (11) 312817 or 316502 Fax 316391

DIAPER, James Robert (Bob). b 30. Portsm Dioc Tr Course 84. **d** 85. NSM Portsea St Sav *Portsm* 85-89 and 91-95; NSM Milton 89-91; rtd 95; Perm to Offic *Portsm* from 95. *48 Wallington Road, Portsmouth PO2 0HB* Tel (01705) 691372

DIAPER, Trevor Charles. b 51. ALA79. Coll of Resurr Mirfield 88. **d** 90 **p** 91. C N Walsham w Antingham *Nor* 90-94; P-in-c Ardleigh *Chelmsf* 94-95; P-in-c The Bromleys 94-95; R Ardleigh and The Bromleys 95-97; V Bocking St Pet from 97. *The Vicarage, 6 St Peter's in the Fields, Bocking, Braintree, Essex CM7 9AR* Tel (01376) 322698

DIBB SMITH, John. b 29. Ex & Truro NSM Scheme 78. **d** 81 **p** 82. NSM Carbis Bay *Truro* 81-82; NSM Carbis Bay w Lelant 82-84;

Warden Trelowarren Fellowship Helston 84-91; Chapl 89-91; NSM Halsetown *Truro* from 91. *St John in the Fields Vicarage, St Ives, Cornwall TR26 2HG* Tel (01736) 796035

DIBBENS, Hugh Richard. b 39. Lon Univ BA63 MTh67 St Pet Coll Ox BA65 MA74. Oak Hill Th Coll 60. **d** 67 **p** 68. C Holborn St Geo w H Trin and St Bart *Lon* 67-72; CMS 73-74; Japan 74-77; TR Chigwell *Chelmsf* 78-92; V Hornchurch St Andr from 92. *222 High Street, Hornchurch, Essex RM12 6QP* Tel (01708) 441571

DIBBS, Canon Geoffrey. b 24. Man Univ BA51 ThD69. Wycliffe Hall Ox 51. **d** 53 **p** 54. C Droylsden St Mary *Man* 53-56; V Chadderton St Luke 56-59; R Burton Agnes w Harpham *York* 59-66; Canada from 66; rtd 88. *13414 Desert Glen Drive, Sun City West, Az 85375, USA*

DIBDEN, Alan Cyril. b 49. Hull Univ LLB70 Fitzw Coll Cam BA72 MA76. Westcott Ho Cam 70. **d** 73 **p** 74. C Camberwell St Luke *S'wark* 73-77; TV Walworth 77-79; TV Langley Marish *Ox* 79-84; C Chalfont St Peter 84-90; TV Burnham w Dropmore, Hitcham and Taplow from 90. *Taplow Rectory, Maidenhead, Berks SL6 0ET* Tel (01628) 661182

DIBDIN, Ronald Frank. b 20. Glouc Sch of Min 84 Trin Coll Bris 84. **d** 84 **p** 84. NSM Newent *Glouc* 84-85; NSM Newent and Gorsley w Cliffords Mesne 85-90; rtd 90; Perm to Offic *Glouc* from 90. *The Retreat, High Street, Newent, Glos GL18 1AS* Tel (01531) 822090

DICK, Alexander Walter Henry. b 20. Lon Univ BSc49 BSc(Econ)56. Sarum & Wells Th Coll 73. **d** 74 **p** 75. C Totnes *Ex* 74-77; Min Estover LEP 77-80; V Estover 80-81; P-in-c Broadwoodwidger 81-83; V 83-86; P-in-c Kelly w Bradstone 81-83; R 83-86; P-in-c Lifton 81-83; R 83-86; rtd 86; Perm to Offic *Ex* 86-95; Perm to Offic *Lon* 86-94. *Flat 1, Fairfield, Huxtable Hill, Torquay TQ2 6RN* Tel (01803) 605126

DICK, Miss Angela. b 62. Sheff Univ BA92. St Jo Coll Nottm MA94. **d** 96 **p** 97. C Mixenden *Wakef* 96-97; C Mount Pellon from 97. *Woodburn Cottage, Albert Road, Pellon, Halifax, W Yorkshire HX2 0BY* Tel (01422) 369982

DICK, Mrs Caroline Ann. b 61. Nottm Univ BTh88. Linc Th Coll 85. **d** 88 **p** 94. Par Dn Houghton le Spring *Dur* 88-93; Par Dn Hetton le Hole 93-94; C 94-96; Asst Chapl Sunderland Univ from 94; C Harton from 96. *182 Sunderland Road, South Shields, Tyne & Wear NE34 6AD* Tel 0191-456 1855

DICK, Cecil Bates. b 42. TD97. Selw Coll Cam BA68 MA72. EMMTC 73. **d** 76 **p** 78. NSM Cinderhill *S'well* 76-79; Chapl Dame Allan's Schs Newc 79-85; CF (TA) from 84; C Gosforth All SS *Newc* 85-87; Chapl HM Pris Dur 88-89; Chapl HM Pris Hull from 89. *The Chaplain's Office, HM Prison Hull, Hedon Road, Hull HU9 5LS* Tel (01482) 320673 Ext 325 Fax 229018

DICK, Norman MacDonald. b 32. ACIB. Ox NSM Course 87. **d** 90 **p** 91. NSM Bedgrove *Ox* 90-95; NSM Ellesborough, The Kimbles and Stoke Mandeville from 95. *21 Camborne Avenue, Aylesbury, Bucks HP21 7UH* Tel (01296) 85530

DICK, Raymond Owen. b 53. Edin Univ BD77. Edin Th Coll 73. **d** 77 **p** 78. C Glas St Mary *Glas* 77-84; Perm to Offic *St Alb* 84-85; P-in-c Edin St Paul and St Geo *Edin* 85; P-in-c Edin SS Phil and Jas 85-86; P-in-c Edin St Marg 85-87; TV Edin Old St Paul 87-88; R Hetton le Hole *Dur* 88-96; V Harton from 96. *182 Sunderland Road, South Shields, Tyne & Wear NE34 6AD* Tel 0191-456 1855

DICKEN, Dr Eric William Trueman. b 19. Ex Coll Ox BA39 MA46 DD64. Cuddesdon Coll 49. **d** 49 **p** 50. C Hucknall Torkard *S'well* 49-54; V Caunton 54-65; V Maplebeck 54-65; Warden Lenton Hall Nottm Univ 65-80; R Maidwell w Draughton, Scaldwell, Lamport etc *Pet* 80-84; rtd 84. *Forsythia Cottage, Victoria Street, Bourton-on-the-Water, Cheltenham, Glos GL54 2BX* Tel (01451) 821867

DICKENS, Adam Paul. b 65. Man Univ BA89 Nottm Univ MDiv93. Linc Th Coll 91. **d** 93 **p** 94. C Pershore w Pinvin, Wick and Birlingham *Worc* from 93. *10 Redlands, Pershore, Worcs WR10 1EJ* Tel (01386) 553294

DICKENS, Philip Henry Charles (Harry). b 28. S'wark Ord Course 76. **d** 79 **p** 80. NSM Headley All SS *Guildf* 79-81; C 81-84; V Wrecclesham 84-96; rtd 96; Perm to Offic *Guildf* from 96. *Stephen's Orchard, Headley Road, Grayshott, Hindhead, Surrey GU26 6DL* Tel (01428) 605729

DICKENS, Timothy Richard John. b 45. Leeds Univ BSc68. Westcott Ho Cam 68. **d** 71 **p** 72. C Meole Brace *Lich* 71-74; C-in-c Stamford Ch Ch CD *Linc* 74-80; V Anlaby St Pet *York* 80-91; V Egg Buckland *Ex* from 91. *The Vicarage, 100 Church Hill, Plymouth PL6 5RD* Tel (01752) 701399

DICKENSON, Charles Gordon. b 29. Bps' Coll Cheshunt 53. **d** 56 **p** 57. C Ellesmere Port *Ches* 56-61; R Egremont St Columba 61-68; V Latchford Ch Ch 68-74; P-in-c Hargrave 74-79; V Birkenhead St Jas w St Bede 79-83; R Tilston and Shocklach 83-94; rtd 94; Perm to Offic *Ches* from 94. *58 Kingsway, Crewe CW2 7ND* Tel (01270) 60722

DICKENSON, Geoffrey. b 20. Kelham Th Coll 38. **d** 44 **p** 45. C Averham w Kelham *S'well* 44-47; C Sedgley All SS *Lich* 47-49; C Fenton 49-53; S Africa 53-57; C Greenford H Cross *Lon* 57-59; R Sandiacre *Derby* 59-67; PC Frecheville 67-70; RD Staveley 68-70; V Scarcliffe 70-75; R Walton on Trent w Croxall 75-83; Perm to Offic *Heref* from 83; rtd 85. *26 Churchill Road, Church Stretton, Shropshire SY6 6AE* Tel (01694) 723015

DICKENSON, Robin Christopher Wildish (Rob). b 44. Ex Univ BPhil Lon Univ CertEd. SW Minl Tr Course. **d** 97. NSM Week St Mary w Poundstock and Whitstone *Truro* from 97. *Penlea, Crackington Haven, Bude, Cornwall EX23 0JQ* Tel (01840) 230311

DICKER, Canon David. b 31. St Pet Hall Ox BA57 MA58. Linc Th Coll 55. **d** 57 **p** 58. C Wootton Bassett *Sarum* 57-60; C Broad Town 57-60; C Weymouth H Trin 60-63; Antigua 63-64; R Tisbury *Sarum* 64-71; Argentina 71-77; Miss to Seamen 77-81; Chapl Dunkerque w Lille Arras etc Miss to Seamen *Eur* 81-86; TR Shaston *Sarum* 86-96; RD Blackmore Vale 90-95; Can and Preb Sarum Cathl 95-96; rtd 96. *25 Dunholme Road, Welton, Lincoln LN2 3RS* Tel (01673) 863233

DICKER, Ms Jane Elizabeth. b 64. Whitelands Coll Lon BA87. Linc Th Coll 87. **d** 89 **p** 94. Par Dn Merton St Jas *S'wark* 89-93; C Littleham w Exmouth *Ex* from 93; Chapl Plymouth Univ from 93. *The Vicarage, 96 Littleham Road, Littleham, Exmouth, Devon EX8 2QX* Tel (01395) 272061

DICKER, Miss Mary Elizabeth. b 45. Girton Coll Cam BA66 MA70 Sheff Univ MSc78. Cranmer Hall Dur 83. **dss** 85 **d** 87 **p** 94. Mortlake w E Sheen *S'wark* 85-87; Par Dn 87-88; Par Dn Irlam *Man* 88-92; Par Dn Ashton Ch Ch 92-94; C from 94. *33 Taunton Road, Ashton-under-Lyne, Lancs OL7 9DP* Tel 0161-339 6128

DICKIE, James Graham Wallace. b 50. Worc Coll Ox BA72 MA BLitt77. Westcott Ho Cam 78. **d** 81 **p** 82. C Bracknell *Ox* 81-84; Lic to Offic *Ely* 84-89; Chapl Trin Coll Cam 84-89; Chapl Clifton Coll Bris 89-96; Sen Chapl Marlborough Coll from 96. *The Old Rectory, High Street, Marlborough, Wilts SN8 1PA* Tel (01672) 512648

DICKINSON, Anthony William (Tony). b 48. New Coll Ox BA71 MA74 Nottm Univ DipHE82. Linc Th Coll 80. **d** 82 **p** 83. C Leavesden All SS *St Alb* 82-86; TV Upton cum Chalvey *Ox* 86-94; P-in-c Terriers from 94. *St Francis's Vicarage, Terriers, High Wycombe, Bucks HP13 5AB* Tel (01494) 520676

DICKINSON, The Very Revd the Hon Hugh Geoffrey. b 29. Trin Coll Ox BA53 DipTh54 MA56. Cuddesdon Coll 54. **d** 56 **p** 57. C Melksham *Sarum* 56-58; Chapl Trin Coll Cam 58-63; Chapl Win Coll 63-69; P-in-c Milverton *Cov* 69-77; V St Alb St Mich *St Alb* 77-86; Dean Sarum 86-96; rtd 96. *22 St Peter's Road, Cirencester, Glos GL7 1RG* Tel (01285) 657710

DICKINSON, Robert Edward. b 47. Nottm Univ BTh74. St Jo Coll Nottm 70. **d** 74 **p** 75. C Birm St Martin *Birm* 74-78; P-in-c Liv St Bride w St Sav *Liv* 78-81; TV St Luke in the City 81-86; Chapl Liv Poly 86-92; Chapl Liv Jo Moores Univ from 92. *45 Queen's Drive, Liverpool L18 2DT* Tel 0151-722 1625 or 231 2121

DICKINSON, Stephen Paul. b 54. SRN75. N Ord Course 85. **d** 88 **p** 89. Hon C Purston cum S Featherstone *Wakef* 88-91; C Goldthorpe w Hickleton *Sheff* 91-94; V New Bentley from 94. *The Vicarage, Victoria Road, Bentley, Doncaster, S Yorkshire DN5 0EZ* Tel (01302) 875266

DICKINSON, Victor Tester. b 48. Univ of Wales (Cardiff) BSc70. St Steph Ho Ox 70. **d** 73 **p** 74. C Neath w Llantwit *Llan* 73-76; Asst Chapl Univ of Wales (Cardiff) 76-79; TV Willington Team *Newc* 79-86; V Kenton Ascension 86-97; V Lowick and Kyloe w Ancroft from 97; R Ford and Etal from 97. *The Vicarage, 1 Main Street, Lowick, Berwick-upon-Tweed TD15 2UD* Tel (01289) 388229

DICKINSON, Wilfrid Edgar. b 21. AKC42 Lon Univ BD42. Linc Th Coll. **d** 44 **p** 45. C Prittlewell St Mary *Chelmsf* 44-47; C Chingford SS Pet and Paul 47-49; C Saffron Walden 49-51; V Gt Wakering 51-54; V Chigwell 54-74; TR 74-78; V Hatfield Heath 78-86; rtd 86; Perm to Offic *Heref* from 86. *4 Bearcroft, Weobley, Hereford HR4 8TA* Tel (01544) 318641

DICKSON, Anthony Edward. b 59. Nottm Univ BTh88. Linc Th Coll 85. **d** 88 **p** 89. C Portsea St Alb *Portsm* 88-91; C Cleobury Mortimer w Hopton Wafers *Heref* 91-94; R Fownhope w Mordiford, Brockhampton etc from 94. *The Vicarage, Fownhope, Hereford HR1 4PS* Tel (01432) 860365

DICKSON, Brian John. b 19. Reading Univ BSc41 Birm Univ DipTh51. Qu Coll Birm 49. **d** 51 **p** 52. C S Wimbledon H Trin *S'wark* 51-53; C Golders Green St Alb *Lon* 53-55; Sec SCM Th Colls Dept 53-55; Chapl Hulme Gr Sch Oldham 55-59; Min Can Worc Cathl *Worc* 60-67; Chapl K Sch Worc 60-67; Lic to Offic *Bris* 67-74; Chapl Colston's Sch Bris 67-74; V Bishopston *Bris* 74-85; RD Horfield 80-85; rtd 85; Perm to Offic *Worc* from 85. *One Acre Cottage, Abberley, Worcester WR6 6BS* Tel (01299) 896442

DICKSON, Colin Patrick Gavin. b 56. **d** 96 **p** 97. C Grays Thurrock *Chelmsf* from 96. *48 Parker Road, Grays, Essex RM17 5YN* Tel (01375) 379309

DICKSON, Richard Arthur. b 67. LSE BSc(Econ)88. Ripon Coll Cuddesdon BA92. **d** 93 **p** 94. C Sale St Anne *Ches* 93-96; Sweden from 96. *Snapphanev 92, 175 34 Jarfalla, Sweden* Tel Stockholm (8) 580-386-92

DICKSON, Canon Samuel Mervyn James. b 41. CITC. **d** 66 **p** 67. C Ballyholme *D & D* 66-70; C Knockbreda 70-75; I Clonallon w Warrenpoint 75-84; RD Kilbroney 82-95; I Down H Trin w Hollymount from 84; RD Lecale from 85; Can Down Cathl from

91. *12 The Meadows, Strangford Road, Downpatrick, Co Down BT30 6LN* Tel (01396) 612286

DILL, Peter Winston. b 41. ACP66 K Coll Lon BD72 AKC72. **d** 73 **p** 74. C Warsop *S'well* 73-75; C Rhyl w St Ann *St As* 75-77; C Oxton *Ches* 77-78; V Newton in Mottram 78-82; P-in-c Oxon and Shelton *Lich* 82-84; V 84-87; Chapl Clifton Coll Bris from 87. *85 Pembroke Road, Clifton, Bristol BS8 3EB* Tel 0117-973 9769

DILNOT, Canon John William. b 36. Selw Coll Cam BA60 MA64. Cuddesdon Coll 60. **d** 62 **p** 63. C Stafford St Mary *Lich* 62-66; C Stoke upon Trent 66-67; V Leek All SS 67-74; V Leeds w Broomfield *Cant* 74-79; P-in-c Aldington 79-81; P-in-c Bonnington w Bilsington 79-81; P-in-c Fawkenhurst 79-81; R Aldington w Bonnington and Bilsington 81-87; RD N Lympne 82-87; Hon Can Cant Cathl from 85; V Folkestone St Mary and St Eanswythe from 87. *The Vicarage, Priory Gardens, Folkestone, Kent CT20 1SW* Tel (01303) 252947

DILWORTH, Anthony. b 41. St Deiniol's Hawarden 87. **d** 90 **p** 91. NSM Gt Saughall *Ches* 90-93; P-in-c Cwmcarn *Mon* 93-95; V from 95. *The Vicarage, Park Street, Cwmcarn, Cross Keys, Newport NP1 7EL* Tel (01495) 270479

DIMMER, Harry James. b 12. Chich Th Coll 73. **d** 73 **p** 73. NSM Fareham H Trin *Portsm* 73-82; rtd 82; Perm to Offic *Portsm* 82-90. *9 Bradley Road, Fareham, Hants PO15 5BW* Tel (01329) 847131

DIMOLINE, Keith Frederick. b 22. Clifton Th Coll 48. **d** 51 **p** 52. C Watford Ch Ch *St Alb* 51-54; C Corsham *Bris* 54-59; C-in-c Swindon St Jo Park CD 59-62; V Swindon St Jo 62-65; V Coalpit Heath 65-74; V Hanham 74-83; C Cudworth w Chillington *B & W* 83-84; P-in-c Dowlishwake w Chaffcombe, Knowle St Giles etc 83-84; R Dowlishwake w Chaffcombe, Knowle St Giles etc 84-88; rtd 88; Perm to Offic *B & W* from 88. *16 Exeter Road, Weston-super-Mare, Avon BS23 4DB* Tel (01934) 635006

DINES, Anthony Bernard. b 25. Clifton Th Coll 57. **d** 60 **p** 61. C Highbury Ch Ch *Lon* 60-63; C Weymouth St Jo *Sarum* 63-67; R Glas St Silas *Glas* 67-78; R Gunton St Pet *Nor* 78-90; rtd 90; NSM Flixton w Homersfield and S Elmham *St E* 90-92; NSM S Elmham and Ilketshall 92-93; Perm to Offic *Glouc* from 93. *215 Prestbury Road, Cheltenham, Glos GL52 3ES* Tel (01242) 525840

DINES, Philip Joseph (Griff). b 59. BSc PhD MA. Westcott Ho Cam 83. **d** 86 **p** 87. C Northolt St Mary *Lon* 86-89; C Withington St Paul *Man* 89-91; V Wythenshawe St Martin from 91; P-in-c Newall Green from 95. *St Martin's Vicarage, 2 Blackcarr Road, Manchester M23 1LX* Tel 0161-998 3408

DINNEN, The Very Revd John Frederick. b 42. TCD BA65 BD72 QUB MTh91. **d** 66 **p** 67. C Belfast All SS *Conn* 66-68; ICM Dub 69-71; C Carnmoney 71-73; Asst Dean of Residences QUB 73-74; Dean 74-84; I Hillsborough *D & D* from 84; Preb Down Cathl from 93; Dir of Ords from 96; Dean Down from 96. *17 Dromore Road, Hillsborough, Co Down BT26 6HS* Tel (01846) 682366 Fax as telephone

DINSMORE, Stephen Ralph. b 56. Wye Coll Lon BSc78. Cranmer Hall Dur 82. **d** 85 **p** 86. C Haughton le Skerne *Dur* 85-88; C Edgware *Lon* 88-93; V Plymouth St Jude *Ex* from 93; RD Plymouth Sutton from 96. *St Jude's Vicarage, Knighton Road, Plymouth PL4 9BU* Tel (01752) 661232

DISNEY, Peter James. b 13. Univ of BC BA36. Angl Th Coll (BC) LTh37. **d** 37 **p** 38. Canada 37-46; C Wandsworth Common St Mary *S'wark* 46-47; C Dufton *Carl* 47-48; V Godmanchester *Ely* 48-57; V Ipswich All SS *St E* 57-63; Distr Sec (Essex and Herts) BFBS 63-69; (Surrey) 65-69; V Halstead H Trin *Chelmsf* 69-78; rtd 78; Perm to Offic *St E* from 78. *Flat 10, Baker's Mill, Lavenham, Sudbury, Suffolk CO10 9RD* Tel (01787) 247500

DISS, Canon Ronald George. b 31. Sarum Th Coll 58. **d** 61 **p** 62. C Greenwich St Alfege w St Pet *S'wark* 61-65; Lic to Offic 65-80; Lic to Offic *Lon* 68-77; Chapl Lon Univ 68-71; Bp's Dom Chapl *Win* 78-80; V Southampton Maybush St Pet 80-91; Hon Can Win Cathl 85-96; R Freemantle 91-96; rtd 96; Hon Chapl to Suff Bp Dover *Cant* from 97. *35 Castle Row, Canterbury, Kent CT1 2QY* Tel (01227) 462410

DITCH, David John. b 45. St Cath Coll Cam BA67 MA70 Leeds Univ PGCE68. WMMTC 88. **d** 91 **p** 92. C Biddulph *Lich* 91-94; V Hednesford from 94. *The Vicarage, Church Hill, Hednesford, Cannock, Staffs WS12 5BD* Tel (01543) 422635

DITCHBURN, Canon Hazel. b 44. NE Ord Course 82. **dss** 84 **d** 87 **p** 94. Scotswood *Newc* 84-86; Ind Chapl *Dur* 86-95; RD Gateshead from 92; Hon Can Dur Cathl from 94; TV Gateshead from 95. *3 Wordsworth Street, Gateshead, Tyne & Wear NE8 3HE* Tel 0191-478 2730

DITCHFIELD, Timothy Frederick. b 61. CCC Cam BA83. Cranmer Hall Dur 85. **d** 88 **p** 89. C Accrington St Jo *Blackb* 88-89; C Accrington St Jo w Huncoat 89-91; C Whittle-le-Woods 91-95; Chapl K Coll Lon from 95. *19 Maunsel Street, London SW1P 2QN, or King's College, Strand, London WC2R 2LS* Tel 0171-828 1772 or 873 2373 Fax 873 2344 E-mail tim.ditchfield @kc.ac.uk

DITTMER, Canon Michael William. b 17. St Edm Hall Ox BA39 MA43. Sarum Th Coll 40. **d** 41 **p** 42. C Bromley St Andr *Roch* 41-43; C Horfield H Trin *Bris* 43-49; C-in-c Lockleaze St Fran CD 49-52; V Yatton Keynell 52-88; R Biddestone w Slaughterford 53-88; R Castle Combe 53-88; RD Chippenham 66-76; R W Kington 75-88; Hon Can Bris Cathl 84-88; P-in-c Nettleton w Littleton Drew 85-88; rtd 88; Perm to Offic *B & W* from 88. *Greenacres, Summerhedge Lane, Othery, Bridgwater, Somerset TA7 0JD* Tel (01823) 698288

DIVALL, David Robert. b 40. New Coll Ox BA64 Sussex Univ DPhil74. Sarum & Wells Th Coll 75. **d** 77 **p** 78. Hon C Catherington and Clanfield *Portsm* 77-92; Hon C Rowlands Castle 92-93. *17 Pipers Mead, Clanfield, Waterlooville, Hants PO8 0ST* Tel (01705) 594845

DIXON, Miss Anne Nicholson. b 28. Lightfoot Ho Dur 54. **dss** 60 **d** 87 **p** 94. Chapl Asst WRAF 60-62; Dioc RE Adv *Dur* 62-83; RE Consultant Gateshead 83-89; rtd 89. *12 Wellbank Road, Washington, Tyne & Wear NE37 1NH* Tel 0191-416 1130

DIXON, Bruce Richard. b 42. Lon Univ BScEng63. Sarum Th Coll 66. **d** 68 **p** 69. C Walton St Mary *Liv* 68-70; C Harnham *Sarum* 70-73; C Streatham St Leon *S'wark* 73-77; R Thurcaston *Leic* 77-83; R Cranborne w Boveridge, Edmondsham etc *Sarum* from 83. *The Rectory, Grugs Lane, Cranborne, Wimborne, Dorset BH21 5PX* Tel (01725) 517232

DIXON, Bryan Stanley. b 61. St Jo Coll Nottm BTh93. **d** 93 **p** 94. C Beverley Minster *York* 93-96; C Kingston upon Hull St Aid Southcoates from 96. *57 Telford Street, Hull HU9 3DX*

DIXON, Charles William. b 41. NW Ord Course 78. **d** 81 **p** 82. C Almondbury *Wakef* 81-82; C Almondbury w Farnley Tyas 82-84; P-in-c Shepley 84-88; P-in-c Shelley 84-88; V Shelley and Shepley 88-89; V Ripponden 89-94; V Barkisland w W Scammonden 89-94; P-in-c Thornes St Jas w Ch Ch from 94. *The Vicarage, St James Court, Park Avenue, Wakefield, W Yorkshire WF2 8DW* Tel (01924) 290501

DIXON, Canon David. b 19. Lich Th Coll 57. **d** 58 **p** 59. C Barrow St Luke *Carl* 58-61; V Westf St Mary 61-68; Warden Rydal Hall 68-84; P-in-c Rydal 78-84; rtd 84; Perm to Offic *Carl* from 84; Hon Can Carl Cathl 84-85. *Rheda, The Green, Millom, Cumbria LA18 5JA* Tel (01229) 774300

DIXON, David Hugh. b 40. Chich Th Coll 90. **d** 92 **p** 93. C Launceston *Truro* 92-95; TV Probus, Ladock and Grampound w Creed and St Erme from 95. *The Rectory, Ladock, Truro, Cornwall TR2 4PL* Tel (01726) 882554

DIXON, Edward Ashby. b 15. AKC40 BD45. **d** 40 **p** 41. C Bordesley St Benedict *Birm* 40-46; C Clewer St Andr *Ox* 46-49; C Malvern Link St Matthias *Worc* 49-53; R Coates, Rodmarton and Sapperton etc *Glouc* 53-59; Chapl R Agric Coll Cirencester 53-59; V Glouc All SS *Glouc* 59-66; V Frampton on Severn 66-75; V Frampton on Severn w Whitminster 75-80; P-in-c Arlingham 66-80; RD Glouc S 67-79; rtd 80; Perm to Offic *Glouc* 80-96. *3 Grange Close, Minchinhampton, Stroud, Glos GL6 9DF* Tel (01453) 882560

DIXON, Edward Michael (Mike). b 42. St Chad's Coll Dur BA64 DipTh66 Newc Univ MA93. **d** 66 **p** 67. C Hartlepool H Trin *Dur* 66-70; C Howden *York* 70-73; Chapl HM Pris Liv 73; Chapl HM Pris Onley 74-82; Chapl HM Pris Frankland 82-87; Chapl HM Pris Dur 87-97; Chapl HM Pris Acklington from 97. *HM Prison Acklington, Morpeth, Northd NE65 9XF* Tel (01670) 760411 or (01665) 575800 Fax 761362

DIXON, Eric. b 31. MPS. EMMTC 78. **d** 81 **p** 82. NSM Kirk Langley *Derby* 81-96; NSM Mackworth All SS 81-96. *Silverdale, Lower Road, Mackworth, Derby DE22 4NG* Tel (01332) 824543

DIXON, Mrs Francesca Dorothy. b 52. Cam Univ MA73 Birm Univ DipTh83. **dss** 84 **d** 87 **p** 94. W Bromwich All SS *Lich* 84-94; Par Dn 87-94; C 94; Chapl Burrswood Chr Cen *Roch* 95. *46 Arun Vale, Cold Waltham, Pulborough, W Sussex RH20 1LP* Tel (01798) 872177

DIXON, John Kenneth (Ken). b 40. Linc Th Coll 79. **d** 81 **p** 82. C Goldington *St Alb* 81-85; V Cardington 85-94; RD Elstow 89-94; R Clifton 94-95; P-in-c Southill 94-95; R Clifton and Southill from 95; RD Shefford from 95. *The Rectory, 8 Rectory Close, Clifton, Shefford, Beds SG17 5EL* Tel (01462) 812295

DIXON, John Martin. b 42. DMS96 MIMgt96. Kelham Th Coll Lich Th Coll. **d** 72 **p** 73. C Ellesmere Port *Ches* 72-74; C Bredbury St Barn 74-75; P-in-c Greenlands *Blackb* 75-78; Chapl Victoria Hosp Blackpool 75-78; Chapl RAF 78-81; Asst Chapl HM Pris Featherstone 81-85; Dep Chapl HM Pris Wormwood Scrubs 85-87; Chapl HM Pris Rudgate and Thorp Arch 87-89; Chapl HM Pris Leeds 89-93; Chapl HM Pris Stafford from 93. *HM Prison, 54 Gaol Road, Stafford ST16 3AW* Tel (01782) 254421 Fax 249591

DIXON, Canon John Wickham. b 18. St Jo Coll Dur BA43 MA46. St Aid Birkenhead LTh41. **d** 43 **p** 44. C Ashton-on-Ribble St Andr *Blackb* 43-46; Tutor St Aid Birkenhead 46-50; Chapl Wycliffe Hall Ox 51-54; V Blackb St Steph *Blackb* 54-85; Can Res Blackb Cathl 65-73; Hon Can 74-85; rtd 86; Perm to Offic *Blackb* from 86. *11A Sunnyside Avenue, Wilpshire, Blackburn BB1 9LW* Tel (01254) 246145

DIXON, Nicholas Scarth. b 30. G&C Coll Cam BA54 MA63. Westcott Ho Cam 54. **d** 56 **p** 57. C Walney Is *Carl* 56-59; CF 59-62; V Whitehaven Ch Ch w H Trin *Carl* 62-70; R Blofield w Hemblington *Nor* 70-77; P-in-c Bowness *Carl* 77-79; R 79-81; V Frizington and Arlecdon 81-87; V Barton, Pooley Bridge and Martindale 87-95; rtd 95; Perm to Offic *Carl* from 95.

7 Mayburgh Avenue, Penrith, Cumbria CA11 8PA Tel (01768) 892864

DIXON, Dr Peter. b 36. Qu Coll Ox BA58 MA62. Qu Coll Birm DipTh60 BD65 PhD75. **d** 60 **p** 61. C Mountain Ash *Llan* 60-63; C Penrhiwceiber w Matthewstown and Ynysboeth 63-68; P-in-c 68-70; V Bronllys and Llanfilo w Llandefaelog Tre'graig *S & B* from 70; Bp's Chapl for Readers from 80; Bp's Chapl for Th Educn from 83; RD Hay from 90. *The Vicarage, Bronllys, Brecon LD3 0HS* Tel (01874) 711200

DIXON, Peter David. b 48. Edin Univ BSc71. **d** 79 **p** 80. NSM Prestonpans *Edin* 79-91; NSM Musselburgh 79-91; P-in-c Edin St Barn from 91. *8 Oswald Terrace, Prestonpans, East Lothian EH32 9EG* Tel (01875) 812985

DIXON, Philip. b 48. Leeds Univ BSc69. St Jo Coll Nottm 77. **d** 80 **p** 81. C Soundwell *Bris* 80-82; C Stoke Bishop 82-84; TV Hemel Hempstead *St Alb* 84-85; Chapl Westonbirt Sch from 85; Perm to Offic *Bris* from 86. *East Lodge, Westonbirt School, Tetbury, Glos GL8 8QG* Tel (01666) 880333

DIXON, Philip Roger. b 54. CCC Ox BA77 MA80. Oak Hill Th Coll BA80. **d** 80 **p** 81. C Droylsden St Mary *Man* 80-84; TV Rochdale 84-91; V Audenshaw St Steph from 91. *St Stephen's Vicarage, 176 Stamford Road, Audenshaw, Manchester M34 5WW* Tel 0161-370 1863

DIXON, Richard Russell. b 32. Dur Univ BA60. Chich Th Coll 60. **d** 62 **p** 70. C Scarborough St Martin *York* 62-63; C Thirsk w S Kilvington 69-73; P-in-c Swine 73-81; Youth Officer 73-78; V Beverley St Nic 81-91; rtd 91; Perm to Offic *York* from 91. *7 Mallard Avenue, Leven, Hull HU17 5NA* Tel (01903) 544989

DIXON, Robert. b 50. Univ of Wales (Lamp) BA80. Chich Th Coll 80. **d** 81 **p** 82. C Maidstone St Martin *Cant* 81-84; Chapl HM Youth Cust Cen Dover 84-88; C All Hallows by the Tower etc *Lon* 88-90; P-in-c Southwick H Trin *Dur* 90-97; R from 97. *The Rectory, Church Bank, Southwick, Sunderland SR5 2DU* Tel 0191-548 1349

DIXON, Roger John. b 33. Magd Coll Cam BA58 MA61. EAMTC 78. **d** 79 **p** 80. NSM Fakenham w Alethorpe *Nor* 79-82; C Brandeston w Kettleburgh *St E* 82-84; P-in-c from 84; Asst Chapl Framlingham Coll Suffolk from 82; RD Loes *St E* from 97. *The Rectory, Kettleburgh, Woodbridge, Suffolk IP13 7JP* Tel (01728) 723080

DIXON, Ms Sheila. b 46. Open Univ BA78 Trent Poly CertEd79. St Jo Coll Nottm DTS93. **d** 93 **p** 94. Par Dn Ordsall *S'well* 93-94; C 94-97; P-in-c Sutton w Carlton and Normanton upon Trent etc from 97. *The Vicarage, Old North Road, Sutton-on-Trent, Newark, Notts NG23 6PL* Tel (01636) 821797

DIZERENS, Charles Robert (Frère François). b 18. Lausanne Univ. **d** 97. Asst Chapl Montreux *Eur* from 97. *Avenue de Valmont 16, Lausanne 1010, Switzerland* Tel Lausanne (21) 653 1090 or 963 43654 Fax 963 4391

D'MORIAS, Sydney James. b 07. Madras Univ BA29 Serampore Coll BD32. Bp's Coll Calcutta 30. **d** 32 **p** 33. India 32-55 and 56-61; C Southfields St Barn *S'wark* 55; C Hornsey St Mary *Lon* 61-67; V Finsbury Park St Thos 68-78; rtd 78; Hon C Wood Green St Mich w Bounds Green St Gabr etc *Lon* 83-86; Perm to Offic from 89. *Ground Floor Flat, 21 Albert Road, London N22 4AA* Tel 0181-888 6427

DOAN, Charles Bryce. b 24. AS48 Univ of Michigan AB50 MA52 Nashotah Ho Wisconsin MDiv65 STM79. **d** 65 **p** 65. USA 65-87 and from 91; Warden Spennithorne Hall *Ripon* 87-91; rtd 92. *3007 9th Avenue, South Milwaukee, Wisconsin 53172, USA*

DOBB, Canon Arthur Joseph. b 31. ARIBA54 Man Coll of Art DA52 ACertCM80. Oak Hill Th Coll 56. **d** 58 **p** 59. C Bolton St Paul *Man* 58-60; C Rawtenstall St Mary 60-62; V Bircle 62-72; V Harwood 72-84; Hon Can Man Cathl 81-96; V Wingates 84-96; rtd 96. *97 Turton Heights, Bromley Cross, Bolton BL2 3DU* Tel (01204) 308419

DOBB, Christopher. b 46. Dur Univ BA68. Cuddesdon Coll 68. **d** 70 **p** 71. C Portsea St Mary *Portsm* 70-73; Lic to Offic *S'wark* 73-77; Perm to Offic *Bris* 77-79; Lic to Offic 79-81; V Swindon St Aug from 81. *St Augustine's Vicarage, Morris Street, Swindon SN2 2HT* Tel (01793) 522741 Fax 611998

DOBBIE, Charles William Granville. b 49. OBE92. Wycliffe Hall Ox 94. **d** 96 **p** 97. C Morriston *S & B* from 96; Asst Chapl Morriston Hosp Swansea from 97. *Wern House, Old Wern Road, Ystalyfera, Swansea SA9 2LL* Tel (01639) 844285 Fax as telephone

DOBBIE, Gary. b 51. FSA St Andr Univ MA75 BD77 Magd Coll Cam CertEd80. **d** 83 **p** 83. Kimbolton Sch Cambs 83-84; Hon C Kimbolton *Ely* 83-84; Chapl Ch Hosp Horsham from 84. *Middleton A, Christ's Hospital, Horsham, W Sussex RH13 7LP* Tel (01403) 266305

DOBBIN, Canon Charles Philip. b 51. Jes Coll Cam BA73 MA77 Or Coll Ox BA75 MA88. St Steph Ho Ox 74. **d** 76 **p** 77. C New Addington *Cant* 76-79; C Melton Mowbray w Thorpe Arnold *Leic* 79-83; V Loughb Gd Shep 83-89; V Ashby-de-la-Zouch St Helen w Coleorton from 89; RD Akeley W from 93; Hon Can Leic Cathl from 94. *The Rectory, Prior Park, Ashby-de-la-Zouch, Leics LE65 1BH* Tel (01530) 412180

DOBBIN, Harold John. b 47. Liv Univ BSc69. St Steph Ho Ox 70. **d** 73 **p** 74. C Newbold w Dunston *Derby* 73-77; C Leckhampton SS Phil and Jas w Cheltenham St Jas *Glouc* 77-80; V Hebburn St Cuth *Dur* 80-86; R Barlborough *Derby* 86-95; P-in-c Alfreton from 95. *The Vicarage, 13 Church Street, Alfreton, Derbyshire DE55 7AH* Tel (01773) 833280

DOBBS, George Christopher. b 43. Linc Th Coll 66. **d** 68 **p** 69. C Hykeham *Linc* 68-71; Asst Master Heneage Sch Grimsby 71-78; Perm to Offic *S'well* 78-80; TV Chelmsley Wood *Birm* 80-84; TV Rochdale *Man* from 84. *St Aidan's Vicarage, 498 Manchester Road, Rochdale, Lancs OL11 3HE* Tel (01706) 31812 E-mail g3rjv@gqpr.demon.co.uk

DOBBS, Michael John. b 48. Linc Th Coll 74. **d** 77 **p** 78. C Warsop *S'well* 77-82; V Worksop St Paul 82-89; P-in-c Mansfield St Mark from 89. *St Mark's Vicarage, Nottingham Road, Mansfield, Notts NG18 1BP* Tel (01623) 655548

DOBBYN, Dr Michael Newham. b 27. St Edm Hall Ox BA50 MA52 Columbia Univ EdD62. Cuddesdon Coll 50. **d** 52 **p** 53. C Petworth *Chich* 52-55; Asst Chapl Eliz Coll Guernsey 55-57; rtd 92. *Mathurst Barn, Goudhurst Road, Staplehurst, Tonbridge, Kent TN12 0HQ*

DOBLE, Mrs Maureen Mary Thompson. b 44. RGN65. S Dios Minl Tr Scheme CECM93. **d** 93 **p** 94. NSM Kingston St Mary w Broomfield etc *B & W* from 93. *Davestones, Mill Cross, Kingston St Mary, Taunton, Somerset TA2 8HH* Tel (01823) 451209

DOBLE, Dr Peter. b 29. Univ of Wales (Cardiff) BA51 Fitzw Coll Cam BA54 MA58 St Edm Hall Ox MA68 Leeds Univ PhD92. Wesley Ho Cam 52. **d** 55 **p** 58. In Ch of S India 55-60; In Meth Ch 60-64; Hd of RE Qu Mary Sch Lytham St Annes *Blackb* 64-67; Lect Relig Studies Culham Coll Abingdon *Ox* 67-69; Sen Lect 69-74; Prin Lect and Hd Relig Studies 74-80; Perm to Offic *York* from 80; Dir York RE Cen from 80. *The York Religious Education Centre, College of Ripon and York St John, Lord Mayor's Walk, York YO3 7EX* Tel (01904) 656771 Fax 612512

DOBSON, Christopher John. b 62. Univ of Wales (Abth) BA84 Ox Univ BA88. Wycliffe Hall Ox 86. **d** 89 **p** 90. C Biggin Hill *Roch* 89-92; C Tunbridge Wells St Jas w St Phil 92-95; USPG from 95; Zimbabwe from 95. *College of the Ascension, Weoley Park Road, Selly Oak, Birmingham B29 6RD* Tel 0121-472 1667

DOBSON, Geoffrey Norman. b 46. ACP70. MCCEd71 Leeds Univ CertEd68 BA77 Open Univ BA73. Wells Th Coll 71. **d** 74 **p** 75. C S Woodford H Trin CD *Chelmsf* 74-76; Colchester Adnry Youth Chapl 76-78; C Halstead St Andr w H Trin and Greenstead Green 76-78; Asst Dir Educn (Youth) *Carl* 78-82; P-in-c Kirkandrews-on-Eden w Beaumont and Grinsdale 78-82; V Illingworth *Wakef* 82-86; V Roxton w Gt Barford *St Alb* 86-93; P-in-c Newton Heath St Wilfrid and St Anne *Man* from 93; Chapl N Man Healthcare NHS Trust from 93. *St Wilfrid's Rectory, 929 Oldham Road, Manchester M40 2EB* Tel 0161-205 1235

DOBSON, Canon John Francis Alban. b 12. **d** 38 **p** 45. V New Groombridge *Chich* 57-58; Canada from 58. *10 Kensington Road, Suite 1509, Bramalea, Ontario, Canada, L6T 3V4*

DOBSON, John Haselden. b 29. Mert Coll Ox BA52 MA55 Lon Univ BD58. Oak Hill Th Coll 54. **d** 56 **p** 57. C Rugby St Matt *Cov* 56-59; C W Hampstead St Luke *Lon* 59-60; Uganda 60-72; C Gorleston St Andr *Nor* 73-77; R Saxlingham Nethergate w Saxlingham Thorpe 77-90; V Shotesham 77-90; R Saxlingham Nethergate and Shotesham 90-93; rtd 94; Perm to Offic *Nor* from 94. *Karanga, The Street, Hardwick, Norwich NR15 2AB* Tel (01508) 30611

DOBSON, John Richard. b 64. Van Mildert Coll Dur BA87. Ripon Coll Cuddesdon 87. **d** 89 **p** 90. C Benfieldside *Dur* 89-92; C Darlington St Cuth 92-96; C-in-c Blackwell All SS and Salutation CD from 96. *65 Carmel Road South, Darlington, Co Durham DL3 8DS* Tel (01325) 354503

DOBSON, Kenneth Shuard. b 26. Oak Hill Th Coll 53. **d** 56 **p** 57. C Hatcham St Jas *S'wark* 56-59; C Wimbledon 59-62; R W Lynn *Nor* 62-66; Lic to Offic 66-68; P-in-c Deopham w Hackford 68-74; Chapl Eccles Hall Sch Quidenham 74-78; R Elvedon *St E* 78-84; R Eriswell 78-84; R Icklingham 78-84; RD Mildenhall 80-81; RD Newmarket 80-81; rtd 84; Chapl Wayland Hosp Norfolk 84-87; Lic to Offic *Nor* 84-97. *St Joseph's, 14 Salthouse Close, Crofty, Swansea SA4 3SN* Tel (01792) 851652

DOBSON, Philip Albert. b 52. Lanc Univ BA73 CertEd74. Trin Coll Bris DipHE89. **d** 89 **p** 90. C Grenoside *Sheff* 89-92; C Cove St Jo *Guildf* 92-93; TV 93-96; V Camberley St Martin Old Dean from 96. *St Martin's Vicarage,, 2A Hampshire Road, Camberley, Surrey GU15 4DW* Tel (01276) 23958

DOBSON, Stuart Joseph. b 51. Westmr Coll Ox BA85. Chich Th Coll 86. **d** 88 **p** 89. C Costessey *Nor* 88-90; C Chaddesden St Phil *Derby* 90-92; C Friern Barnet St Jas *Lon* 92-93; TV Plymouth Em, Efford and Laira *Ex* 93-96; P-in-c Laira 96; R Withington St Crispin *Man* from 96. *St Crispin's Rectory, 2 Hart Road, Manchester M14 7LE* Tel 0161-224 3452

✠**DOCKER, The Rt Revd Ivor Colin.** b 25. Birm Univ BA46 St Cath Soc Ox BA49 MA52. Wycliffe Hall Ox 46. **d** 49 **p** 50 **c** 75. C Normanton *Wakef* 49-52; C Halifax St Jo Bapt 52-54; Area Sec (Dios Derby Linc and S'well) CMS 54-58; Metrop Sec (S) 58-59; V Midhurst *Chich* 59-64; RD Midhurst 61-64; R Woolbeding 61-64; V Seaford w Sutton 64-71; RD Seaford 64-71; Can and Preb Chich Cathl 66-91; V Eastbourne St Mary 71-75; RD Eastbourne 71-75; Suff Bp Horsham 75-84; Area Bp Horsham 84-91; rtd 91; Asst Bp Ex from 91. *Braemar, Bradley*

Road, Bovey Tracey, Newton Abbot, Devon TQ13 9EU Tel (01626) 832468

DODD, Alan Henry. b 42. Man Univ BA70 MA79. Chich Th Coll 82. **d** 82 **p** 83. C Fareham H Trin *Portsm* 82-84; TV 84-89; V Osmotherley w Harlsey and Ingleby Arncliffe *York* from 89. *The Vicarage, Osmotherley, Northallerton, N Yorkshire DL6 3BB* Tel (01609) 883282

DODD, Charles Nathanael. b 30. Westcott Ho Cam. **d** 57 **p** 58. C Milton *Portsm* 57-62; Australia 62-91; P-in-c Bretby w Newton Solney *Derby* 91-96; Bp's Ind Adv from 91. *The Vicarage, Twyford Road, Barrow-on-Trent, Derby DE73 1HA* Tel (01332) 701027

DODD, Cyril. b 20. SS Hild & Bede Coll Dur MA48 DipEd. Coll of Resurr Mirfield 80. **d** 81 **p** 82. Hon C Guiseley *Bradf* 81-83; Hon C Guiseley w Esholt 83-90; rtd 90; Perm to Offic *Bradf* from 90. *Brierley, 37 Croft Park, Menston, Ilkley, W Yorkshire LS29 6LY* Tel (01943) 872132

DODD, Graham Michael. b 30. St Jo Coll York CertEd61 Hull Coll of Educn DipEd67. Nor Ord Course 93. **d** 96 **p** 97. NSM Golcar *Wakef* from 96. *9 Broom Bank, Huddersfield, W Yorkshire HD2 2DJ* Tel (01484) 539832

DODD, Ian Neville. b 16. ACA39 FCA52. LTh. **d** 67 **p** 68. Canada 67-74; C Kingstanding St Mark *Birm* 74-75; P-in-c Smallburgh w Dilham w Honing and Crostwight *Nor* 75-81; rtd 81; Perm to Offic *Chich* from 81. *Flat 2, High Trees, Carew Road, Eastbourne, E Sussex BN21 2JB* Tel (01323) 644809

DODD, James Henry Birchenough. b 25. CPsychol AFBPsS Ox Univ MA. Westcott Ho Cam 85. **d** 85 **p** 86. NSM Epping Upland *Chelmsf* 85-95; NSM Epping Distr 95-96; Perm to Offic from 96. *The Chequers, Epping, Essex CM16 6PH* Tel (01992) 572561

DODD, John Dudley. b 15. Liv Univ BA36 Lon Univ BD51 DipEd54. Westcott Ho Cam 54. **d** 54 **p** 55. C Jersey St Helier *Win* 54-78; rtd 78; P-in-c Jersey Gouray St Martin *Win* 78-93; NSM Jersey St Luke from 94. *10 Clos de Gouray, Gorey Village, Jersey, Channel Islands JE3 9EN* Tel (01534) 854713

DODD, John Stanley. b 24. Huron Coll Ontario 46. **d** 50 **p** 51. Canada 50-52; Leeds St Jo Ev *Ripon* 52-54; C High Harrogate Ch Ch 54-58; V Stainburn 58-65; V Weeton 58-64; V Meanwood 65-89; rtd 89. *3 Shawdene, Burton Crescent, Leeds LS6 4DN* Tel 0113-278 9069

DODD, Lawrence Walter. b 04. Wells Th Coll 45. **d** 47 **p** 47. C Prestbury *Glouc* 47-49; PC Capesthorne w Siddington *Ches* 49-55; RD Macclesfield 52-55; V Stratton *Truro* 55-69; RD Stratton 63-66; rtd 69. *Little Thrift, Sycamore Close, Splatt, St Minver, Wadebridge, Cornwall PL27 6PR*

DODD, Malcolm Ogilvie. b 46. Dur Univ BSc67 Loughb Univ MSc90. Edin Th Coll 67. **d** 70 **p** 71. C Hove All SS *Chich* 70-73; C Crawley 73-78; P-in-c Rusper 79-83; Chapl Brighton Coll Jun Sch 83; Perm to Offic *Derby* from 84; Chapl Stancliffe Hall Sch from 84. *40 Jackson Road, Matlock, Derbyshire DE4 3JQ* Tel (01629) 582800

DODD, Michael Christopher. b 33. Ch Coll Cam BA55 MA59. Ridley Hall Cam 57. **d** 59 **p** 60. C Stechford *Birm* 59-62; V Quinton Road W St Boniface 62-72; TV Paston *Pet* 72-77; TR Hodge Hill *Birm* 77-89; rtd 90; Perm to Offic *Birm* from 90. *39 Regency Gardens, Birmingham B14 4JS* Tel 0121-474 6945

DODD, Canon Peter Curwen. b 33. St Jo Coll Cam BA57 FRSA93. Linc Th Coll 58 Wm Temple Coll Rugby 59. **d** 60 **p** 61. C Eastwood *Sheff* 60-63; Ind Chapl 63-67; Ind Chapl *Newc* from 67; RD Newc E 78-83 and 92-95; Hon Can Newc Cathl from 82. *Glenesk, 26 The Oval, Benton, Newcastle upon Tyne NE12 9PP* Tel 0191-266 1293

DODD, Peter Lawrence. b 38. MBE. Leeds Univ BA61. Qu Coll Birm DipTh62. **d** 63 **p** 64. C Marske in Cleveland *York* 63-67; Malaysia 67-69; CF 70-89; V Selby Abbey *York* 90-93; Chapl Castle Hill Hosp 93-94; Chapl E Yorkshire Hosps NHS Trust from 94. *Castle Hill Hospital, Castle Road, Cottingham, N Humberside HU16 5JQ* Tel (01482) 875875

DODD, William Samuel (Bill). b 31. RMN80. Oak Hill Th Coll 64. **d** 66 **p** 67. C Dagenham *Chelmsf* 66-67; C Stratford St Jo and Ch Ch w Forest Gate St Jas 67-70; C Woodford Wells 70-72; V E Ham St Paul 72-77; Perm to Offic 77-82; V Harwich 82-89; Chapl Jes Hosp Bray 89-90; Perm to Offic *Ox* from 90; rtd 91. *37 Brunel Road, Maidenhead, Berks SL6 2RP* Tel (01628) 76876

DODDS, Alan Richard. b 46. **d** 95 **p** 96. C Deal St Geo *Cant* from 95. *39 St Andrew's Road, Deal, Kent CT14 6AT* Tel (01304) 361866

DODDS, Canon Arthur Whitfield. b 20. FRMetS Qu Coll Ox BA48 MA53. Wells Th Coll 49. **d** 50 **p** 51. C Horley *S'wark* 50-53; R Honiley *Cov* 53-58; V Atherstone 58-64; V Chedworth w Yanworth and Stowell *Glouc* 64-75; RD Northleach 73-83; V Chedworth, Yanworth and Stowell, Coln Rogers etc 75-85; Hon Can Glouc Cathl 78-90; rtd 86; Perm to Offic *Glouc* from 90. *Church Lane Cottage, Harnhill, Cirencester, Glos GL7 5PT* Tel (01285) 851288

DODDS, Brian Martin. b 37. AKC62. **d** 63 **p** 64. C Morpeth *Newc* 63-67; Guyana 67-71; V Willington *Newc* 71-74; TV Brayton *York* 75-79; V Gravelly Hill *Birm* 79-83; V Winterton *Linc* 83-85; V Winterton Gp 85-90; V Gainsborough St Jo 90-96; V Morton 95-96; R Walesby from 96. *The Rectory, Walesby, Market Rasen, Lincs LN8 3UT* Tel (01673) 838513

DODDS, Graham Michael. b 58. GTCL80. Trin Coll Bris. **d** 84 **p** 85. C Reigate St Mary *S'wark* 84-91; P-in-c Bath Walcot *B & W* 91-93; R 93-96; Lay Tr Adv from 96; Dir Reader Studies from 96. *25 Wood Close, Wells, Somerset BA5 2GA* Tel (01749) 677531

DODDS, Canon Neil Sutherland. b 35. ARCO59 Keble Coll Ox BA59 DipTh61 MA63. Linc Th Coll 60. **d** 62 **p** 63. C Handsworth St Jas *Birm* 62-65; V Highters Heath 65-75; V Olton from 75; RD Solihull 79-89; Hon Can Birm Cathl from 82. *St Margaret's Vicarage, 5 Old Warwick Road, Solihull, W Midlands B92 7JU* Tel 0121-706 2318

DODDS, Norman Barry. b 43. Open Univ BA. CITC 73. **d** 76 **p** 77. C Ballynafeigh St Jude *D & D* 76-80; I Belfast St Mich *Conn* from 80; Chapl HM Pris Belf from 84; RD M Belfast *Conn* from 93. *5 Sunningdale Park, Belfast BT14 6RU* Tel (01232) 715463

DODDS, Peter. b 35. WMMTC 88 Qu Coll Birm 88. **d** 91 **p** 92. NSM Hartshill *Cov* from 91. *Wem House, 51 Magyar Crescent, Nuneaton, Warks CV11 4SQ* Tel (01203) 384061

DODGSON, Ronald. b 27. Sarum & Wells Th Coll 72. **d** 74 **p** 75. Sub Warden Barn Fellowship Blandford Forum 74-85; Hon C Canford Magna *Sarum* 78-85; C Hartley Wintney, Elvetham, Winchfield etc *Win* 85-92; rtd 92. *84 Tavistock Road, Fleet, Aldershot, Hants GU13 8EZ* Tel (01252) 624991

DODHIA, Hitesh Kishorilal. b 57. Cranmer Hall Dur 85. **d** 88 **p** 89. C Leamington Priors All SS *Cov* 88-91; Chapl HM Young Offender Inst Glen Parva 91-92; Asst Chapl from 94; Chapl HM Pris Roch 92-94. *HM Young Offender Institution, Glen Parva, Tiger's Road, Wigston, Leics LE18 2TN* Tel 0116-277 2022 Fax 247 7679

DODSON, Canon Gordon. b 31. Barrister 56 Em Coll Cam BA54 LLB55 MA58. Ridley Hall Cam 57. **d** 59 **p** 60. C Belhus Park *Chelmsf* 59-60; C Barking St Marg 60-63; CMS 63-67; C New Malden and Coombe *S'wark* 67-69; V Snettisham *Nor* 69-81; RD Heacham and Rising 76-81; P-in-c Reepham and Hackford w Whitwell and Kerdiston 81-83; P-in-c Salle 81-83; P-in-c Thurning w Wood Dalling 81-83; R Reepham, Hackford w Whitwell, Kerdiston etc 83-94; Hon Can Nor Cathl 85-94; rtd 94; Perm to Offic *Nor* from 94. *Poppygate, 2 The Loke, Cromer, Norfolk NR27 9DH* Tel (01263) 511811

DODSON, James Peter. b 32. DipMin88. Lich Th Coll 58. **d** 61 **p** 62. C Chasetown *Lich* 61-63; C Hednesford 63-68; V Halifax St Hilda *Wakef* 68-76; V Upperthong 76-85; TV York All SS Pavement w St Crux and St Martin etc *York* 85-90; rtd 92. *5B Mawson Lane, Ripon, N Yorkshire HG4 1PW* Tel (01756) 602030

DODSWORTH, George Brian Knowles. b 34. Univ of Wales DipTh62 Birm Univ DPS66 Open Univ AdvDipCrim92 BSc94. St Mich Coll Llan 59. **d** 62 **p** 63. C Kidderminster St Mary *Worc* 62-67; Asst Chapl HM Pris Man 67-68; Chapl HM Pris Eastchurch 68-70; Chapl HM Pris Wakef 70-74; Chapl HM Pris Wormwood Scrubs 74-83; Asst Chapl Gen of Pris (SE) 83-90; Asst Chapl Gen of Pris (HQ) 90-94; Chapl HM Pris Brixton 94-95; Lic to Offic *Lon* from 83; Lic to Offic *S'wark* from 94. *1C Underhill Road, London SE22 0AH* Tel 0181-693 9976 Fax as telephone

DOE, Canon Francis Harold. b 22. S'wark Ord Course 68. **d** 71 **p** 72. C Sompting *Chich* 71-74; C Stopham 74-78; C Hardham 74-78; P-in-c Sutton w Bignor 79-81; P-in-c Barlavington 79-81; V Warnham 81-87; R Stopham and Fittleworth 87-92; RD Petworth 88-92; Can and Preb Chich Cathl 89-92; rtd 92; Hon C Stansted *Chich* 92-94; Perm to Offic from 94. *30 School Hill, Warnham, Horsham, W Sussex RH12 3QN* Tel (01403) 218291

DOE, Martin Charles. b 54. Lon Univ BSc(Econ)75 PGCE87 MA95. St Steph Ho Ox 89. **d** 91 **p** 92. C Portsea St Mary *Portsm* 91-94; Chapl Abbey Grange High Sch Leeds from 94. *Abbey Grange CE High School, Butcher Hill, Leeds LS16 5EA, or St Andrew's House, Butcher Hill, Leeds LS16 5BG* Tel 0113-275 7877 or 278 4560

✠**DOE, The Rt Revd Michael David.** b 47. St Jo Coll Dur BA69. Ripon Hall Ox 69. **d** 72 **p** 73 **c** 94. C St Helier *S'wark* 72-76; Youth Sec BCC 76-81; C-in-c Blackbird Leys CD *Ox* 81-88; V Blackbird Leys 88-89; RD Cowley 86-89; Soc Resp Adv *Portsm* 89-94; Can Res Portsm Cathl 89-94; Suff Bp Swindon *Bris* from 94. *Mark House, Field Rise, Old Town, Swindon SN1 4HP* Tel (01793) 538654 Fax as telephone E-mail 106064.431 @compuserve.com

DOHERTY, Deana Rosina Mercy. b 21. St Aid Coll Dur BA55. **dss** 82 **d** 87 **p** 94. Sutton St Jas and Wawne *York* 82-87; Par Dn 87-94; C 94-95; Perm to Offic from 95. *Sutton-on-Hull Rectory, Hull HU7 4TL* Tel (01482) 782154

DOHERTY, Terence William. b 30. Shoreditch Coll Lon TCert St Jo Coll Dur BA56. Ripon Hall Ox 56. **d** 58 **p** 59. C Church Stretton *Heref* 58-60; C Halesowen *Worc* 60-62; Lic to Offic 62-64 and 69-78; R Hagley 64-69; Warden Dioc Conf Cen *Ches* 69-78; Lic to Offic *B & W* 70-78; TR Sutton St Jas and Wawne *York* from 78. *Sutton-on-Hull Rectory, Hull HU7 4TL* Tel (01482) 782154

DOHERTY, Thomas Alexander. b 48. Chich Th Coll 73. **d** 76 **p** 77. V Choral Derry Cathl *D & R* 76-79; C Llan w Capel Llanilltern *Llan* 79-80; PV Llan Cathl 80-84; V Penmark w Porthkerry 84-90;

R Merthyr Dyfan from 90. *Merthyr Dyfan Rectory, 10 Buttrills Road, Barry CF62 8EF* Tel (01446) 735943

DOIDGE, Dr Charles William. b 44. RIBA ARCUK Univ Coll Lon BSc65 MSc67 PhD72. EMMTC CTPS93. **d** 93 **p** 94. NSM Blaby *Leic* 93-96; P-in-c Willoughby Waterleys, Peatling Magna etc from 96. *32 Peveril Road, Ashby Magna, Lutterworth, Leics LE17 5NQ* Tel (01455) 209800

DOIG, Dr Allan George. b 51. Univ of BC BA69 K Coll Cam BA73 MA80 PhD82. Ripon Coll Cuddesdon 86. **d** 88 **p** 89. C Abingdon *Ox* 88-91; Chapl LMH Ox from 91. *Liddell Building, 60 Iffley Road, Oxford OX4 1EQ or, Lady Margaret Hall, Oxford OX2 6QA* Tel (01865) 242715 or 274386 Fax 511069

DOLAN, Miss Louise. b 68. St Paul's Cheltenham BA89 Reading Univ PGCE90. Aston Tr Scheme 92 Linc Th Coll 94 Westcott Ho Cam MA95. **d** 96 **p** 97. C N Stoneham *Win* from 96. *All Saints Lodge, Point Out Road, Bassett, Southampton SO16 7DL* Tel (01703) 791090

DOLL, Dr Peter Michael. b 62. Yale Univ BA84 Ch Ch Ox DPhil89. Cuddesdon Coll BA94 DipMin95. **d** 95 **p** 96. C Cowley St Jo *Ox* from 95. *129 Magdalen Road, Oxford OX4 1RJ* Tel (01865) 241804

DOLMAN, Derek Alfred George Gerrit. b 40. ALCD64. **d** 64 **p** 65. C St Alb St Paul *St Alb* 65-68; C Bishopwearmouth St Gabr *Dur* 68-72; R Jarrow Grange 72-80; V New Catton St Luke *Nor* from 80. *St Luke's Vicarage, Aylsham Road, Norwich NR3 2HF* Tel (01603) 425959

DOMINIC MARK, Brother. *See* IND, Dominic Mark

DOMINY, Canon Peter John. b 36. Qu Coll Ox BA60 MA64 Aber Univ MLitt83. Oak Hill Th Coll 60. **d** 62 **p** 63. C Bedworth *Cov* 62-66; Nigeria 67-84; R Broadwater St Mary *Chich* 84-92; TR from 92; Can and Preb Chich Cathl from 93. *Broadwater Rectory, 8 Sompting Avenue, Worthing, W Sussex BN14 8HT* Tel (01903) 823916

DOMMETT, Canon Richard Radmore. b 19. St Jo Coll Ox BA41 MA45. Wells Th Coll 41. **d** 43 **p** 44. C E Dulwich St Jo *S'wark* 43-48; C Peckham St Jo 48-52; V Clapham St Pet 52-60; R Caister *Nor* 60-81; Hon Can Nor Cathl 77-85; P-in-c Saxthorpe and Corpusty 81-85; P-in-c Oulton SS Pet and Paul 81-85; P-in-c Blickling w Ingworth 81-85; P-in-c Heydon w Irmingland 82-85; rtd 85; Perm to Offic *St E* from 85; Perm to Offic *Nor* from 85. *14 Norwich Road, Halesworth, Suffolk IP19 8HN* Tel (01986) 873778

DONALD, Andrew William. b 19. St Jo Coll Morpeth 47 ACT ThL50. **d** 49 **p** 50. Australia 49-57; C St Pet Park Road Lon 57-58; Gothenburg *Eur* 58-65; Chapl Lausanne 65-68; Australia from 68; rtd 84. *Eriswell, 18A Cobham Way, Westfield Park, Kelmscott, W Australia 6111* Tel Perth (8) 9390 8425

DONALD, Brother. *See* GREEN, Donald Pentney

DONALD, Dennis Curzon. b 38. Oak Hill Th Coll 68. **d** 70 **p** 71. C Carl St Jo *Carl* 70-73; Lic to Offic 73-77; Warden Blaithwaite Ho Chr Conf Cen Wigton from 73; Perm to Offic *Carl* from 77; Chapl Eden Valley Hospice Carl from 92. *Windyfell, Raughton Head, Carlisle CA5 7DG* Tel (016974) 76246

DONALD, Robert Francis. b 49. St Jo Coll Nottm BTh75 LTh. **d** 75 **p** 76. C New Barnet St Jas *St Alb* 75-79; C St Alb St Paul 79-86; C St Alb St Mary Marshalswick 86-87; Lic to Offic from 87; Dir Chr Alliance Housing Assn Ltd from 87. *85A Abbots Park, St Albans, Herts AL1 1TN, or Exton Street, London SE1 8UE* Tel (01727) 841647 or 0171-620 1455

DONALD, Steven. b 55. CertEd76. Oak Hill Th Coll BA88. **d** 88 **p** 89. C Cheadle All Hallows *Ches* 88-91; C Ardsley *Sheff* 91; V Kendray from 92. *St Andrew's Vicarage, 84 Hunningley Lane, Barnsley, S Yorkshire S70 3DT* Tel (01226) 203906

DONALD, William. b 30. Lon Univ DipTh61. Tyndale Hall Bris 58. **d** 61 **p** 62. C Stapenhill w Cauldwell *Derby* 61-63; Perm to Offic *Ox* 63-66; Lic to Offic *Bris* 66-70; C Cheltenham St Mark *Glouc* 70-77; C Glouc St Jas 77-82; Lic to Offic from 82; rtd 95. *82 Forest View Road, Gloucester GL4 0BY* Tel (01452) 506993

DONALDSON, Christopher William. b 17. Lon Univ BD49. Kelham Th Coll. **d** 42 **p** 43. C Norbury St Steph *Cant* 42-46; C Buckland in Dover 47-51; R St Mary in the Marsh 51-55; R Newchurch 51-55; V Birchington w Acol 55-63; R Cant St Martin and St Paul 63-76; Six Preacher Cant Cathl 72-78; rtd 82; Perm to Offic *B & W* 82-94. *The Cottage, 13 Beadon Lane, Merriott, Crewkerne, Somerset TA16 5QT* Tel (01460) 72593

DONALDSON, Miss Elizabeth Anne. b 55. Univ of Wales (Ban) BSc76 Surrey Univ MSc80 Nottm Univ BA82. St Jo Coll Nottm DPS83. **dss** 83 **d** 87 **p** 94. Guildf Ch Ch *Guildf* 83-86; Cuddington 86-87; C 87-90; C Keresley and Coundon *Cov* from 90. *32 Parkfield Road, Keresley, Coventry CV7 8LR* Tel (01203) 333694

DONALDSON, Malcolm Alexander. b 48. Cranmer Hall Dur 84. **d** 86 **p** 87. C Heworth *York* 86-89; Chapl York Distr Hosp 86-89; C Marfleet *York* 89-90; TV 90-96; R Collyhurst *Man* from 96. *The Rectory, Eggington Street, Collyhurst, Manchester M40 7RN* Tel 0161-205 2808

DONALDSON, Maurice Coburne. b 19. Univ of Wales BA40 Lon Univ BD47. St Mich Coll Llan 41. **d** 42 **p** 43. C Blaenau Ffestiniog *Ban* 42-44; C Conwy w Gyffin 44-47; C Llandysilio (or Menai Bridge) 47-49; P-in-c Llanfachraeth 49-53; V Ynyscynhaearn w Penmorfa 53-57; V Ysbyty Ystwyth w Ystradmeurig *St D* 57-70; V Ruabon *St As* 70-77; V Abergele 77-84; rtd 84; Perm to Offic *St As* from 84; Perm to Offic *Ban* from 84. *7 Llys Mair, Bryn Eithinog, Bangor LL57 2LA* Tel (01248) 354589

DONALDSON, Roger Francis. b 50. Jes Coll Ox BA71 MA75. Westcott Ho Cam 72. **d** 74 **p** 75. C Mold *St As* 74-78; V Denio w Abererch *Ban* 78-95; R Llanbeblig w Caernarfon and Betws Garmon etc from 95. *The Rectory, 4 Ffordd Menai, Caernarfon LL55 1LF* Tel (01286) 673750

DONALDSON, William Richard. b 56. St Cath Coll Cam BA78 MA81. Ridley Hall Cam 79. **d** 82 **p** 83. C Everton St Sav w St Cuth *Liv* 82-85; C Reigate St Mary *S'wark* 85-89; V Easton H Trin w St Gabr and St Lawr and St Jude *Bris* from 89. *The Vicarage, 69 Stapleton Road, Easton, Bristol BS5 0PQ* Tel 0117-955 4255

DONCASTER, Reginald Arthur. b 23. Leeds Univ BA48. Coll of Resurr Mirfield. **d** 50 **p** 51. C Chesterfield St Mary and All SS *Derby* 50-54; R Pleasley 54-73; V Ardleigh *Chelmsf* 73-91; rtd 91. *Manormead, Tilford Road, Hindhead, Surrey GU26 6RA* Tel Hindhead (01428) 604780

DONCASTER, Archdeacon of. *See* HOLDRIDGE, Bernard Lee

DONCASTER, Suffragan Bishop of. *See* GEAR, The Rt Revd Michael Frederick

DONE, Mrs Margaret. b 43. LNSM course 84 Linc Th Coll 91. **d** 92 **p** 94. NSM Coningsby w Tattershall *Linc* from 92. *43 Park Lane, Coningsby, Lincoln LN4 4SW* Tel (01526) 343013

DONELLA, Mother. *See* MATHIE, Patricia Jean

DONKIN, Robert. b 50. Univ of Wales (Cardiff) DipTh74. St Mich Coll Llan 71. **d** 74 **p** 75. C Mountain Ash *Llan* 74-77; C Coity w Nolton 77-79; V Oakwood 79-84; V Aberaman and Abercwmboi 84-91; V Aberaman and Abercwmboi w Cwmaman from 91. *St Margaret's Vicarage, Gladstone Street, Aberaman, Aberdare CF44 6SA* Tel (01685) 872871

DONNELLY, Trevor. b 71. K Coll Lon BA93 AKC93. Cuddesdon Coll 94. **d** 97. C Southgate Ch Ch *Lon* from 97. *62 Oakfield Road, London N14 6LX* Tel 0181-886 3346

DONOHOE, Olive. MA. BTh. **d** 95 **p** 96. C Bandon Union *C, C & R* from 95. *3 The Pines, Kilbrittain Road, Bandon, Co Cork, Irish Republic* Tel Bandon (23) 41053

DONSON, Miss Helen Cripps. b 32. Somerville Coll Ox DipEd55 MA58. Dalton Ho Bris 58 Gilmore Ho 69. **dss** 79 **d** 87. Staines St Pet *Lon* 80-83; Staines St Mary and St Pet 83-90; Par Dn 87-90; Par Dn Herne Bay Ch Ch *Cant* 90-92; rtd 93; Hon Par Dn Bexhill St Aug *Chich* 93-94. *2 St Augustine's Close, Cooden Drive, Bexhill-on-Sea, E Sussex TN39 3AZ* Tel (01424) 734640

DOOGAN, Simon Edward. b 70. Univ of Wales (Abth) LLB92. CITC BTh94. **d** 97. C Cregagh *D & D* from 97. *St Finnian's Curatage, 54 Rochester Avenue, Belfast BT6 9JW* Tel (01232) 796193

DOOLAN, Leonard Wallace. b 57. St Andr Univ MA79 Ox Univ BA82 MA88. Ripon Coll Cuddesdon 80. **d** 83 **p** 84. C High Wycombe *Ox* 83-85; C Bladon w Woodstock 85-88; C Wootton by Woodstock 85-88; P-in-c 88-90; C Kiddington w Asterleigh 85-88; P-in-c 88-90; P-in-c Glympton 88-90; R Wootton w Glympton and Kiddington 90-91; TR Halesworth w Linstead, Chediston, Holton etc *St E* from 91; RD Halesworth from 95. *The Rectory, Highfield Road, Halesworth, Suffolk IP19 8LP* Tel (01986) 872602

DOORES, Peter George Herbert. b 46. DipYESTB71 Hull Univ BSc67 Birm Univ PGCE68. Linc Th Coll CMinlStuds92. **d** 92 **p** 93. C N Stoneham *Win* 92-96; V St Leonards and St Ives from 96. *The Vicarage, 30 Pine Drive, St Leonards, Ringwood, Hants BH24 2LN* Tel (01425) 473406

DORAN, Edward Roy. b 47. St Jo Coll Nottm. **d** 85 **p** 86. C Roby *Liv* 85-88; V Ravenhead from 88. *St John's Vicarage, Crossley Road, Ravenhead, St Helens, Merseyside WA10 3ND* Tel (01744) 23601

DORAN, Sidney William. b 12. AKC40. **d** 40 **p** 41. C Lower Edmonton *Lon* 40-43; C Caversham *Ox* 43-51; V Uffington w Woolstone and Baulking 51-58; V Bray 58-60; V Bray and Braywood 61-77; RD Maidenhead 74-77; rtd 77; Perm to Offic *Truro* 77-85; Hon C Boscastle w Davidstow from 85; Perm to Offic *Ex* 80-94. *St Michael's, Combe Lane, Widemouth Bay, Bude, Cornwall EX23 0AA* Tel (01288) 361386

DORBER, Adrian John. b 52. St Jo Coll Dur BA74 K Coll Lon MTh91. Westcott Ho Cam 76. **d** 79 **p** 80. C Easthampstead *Ox* 79-85; P-in-c Emmer Green 85-88; Chapl Portsm Poly *Portsm* 88-92; Chapl Portsm Univ 92-97; Lect 91-97; Public Orator 92-97; Hon Chapl Portsm Cathl 92-97; P-in-c Brancepeth *Dur* from 97; Dir Min and Tr from 97. *The Rectory, Brancepeth, Durham DH7 8EL* Tel 0191-378 0503 or 374 4407

DORCHESTER, Area Bishop of. *See* RUSSELL, The Rt Revd Anthony John

DORE, Eric George. b 47. S Dios Minl Tr Scheme 87. **d** 90 **p** 91. NSM Hove Bp Hannington Memorial Ch *Chich* 90-92; C Burgess Hill St Andr 92-95; R Frant w Eridge from 95. *The Rectory, Frant, Tunbridge Wells, Kent TN3 9DX* Tel (01892) 750638

DORE, Robert Edward Frederick. b 28. Birm Univ BCom51. Wycliffe Hall Ox. **d** 58 **p** 59. C Cheltenham Ch Ch *Glouc* 58-62; C Bridgnorth St Mary *Heref* 62-67; R Billingsley w Sidbury 67-82;

R Chetton w Deuxhill and Glazeley 67-82; R Middleton Scriven 67-82; RD Bridgnorth 71-78; Preb Heref Cathl 75-82; P-in-c Chelmarsh 80-82; V 82; P-in-c Carhampton *B & W* 82-84; P-in-c Dunster 82-84; R Dunster, Carhampton and Withycombe w Rodhuish 84-93; rtd 93. *26 Church Hill Meadow, Ledbury, Herefordshire HR8 2DG*

DOREY, Trevor Eric. b 30. ACIS53. S Dios Minl Tr Scheme 87. **d** 90 **p** 91. NSM E Woodhay and Woolton Hill *Win* 90-96; P-in-c Manaccan w St Anthony-in-Meneage and St Martin *Truro* from 96. *The Vicarage, Manaccan, Helston, Cornwall TR12 6HA* Tel (01326) 231261

DORGU, Dr Woyin Karowei. b 58. MB, BS85. Lon Bible Coll BA93 Oak Hill Th Coll DipHE95. **d** 95 **p** 96. C Tollington *Lon* from 95. *St Mark's Church, 68 Tollington park, London N4 3RA* Tel 0171-263 5384

DORKING, Archdeacon of. *See* WILSON, The Ven Mark John Crichton

DORKING, Suffragan Bishop of. *See* BRACKLEY, The Rt Revd Ian James

DORMAN, John Richard. b 16. MBE97. Keble Coll Ox BA38 MA55. Ely Th Coll 38. **d** 39 **p** 40. C Dalston *Carl* 39-42; C Maryport 42-44; P-in-c Threlkeld 44-46; R 46-57; Br Guiana 57-66; Guyana 66-95; rtd 85. *1 Bishop Street, London N1 8PH*

DORMANDY, Richard Paul. b 59. Univ Coll Lon BA81 St Edm Ho Cam BA88. Ridley Hall Cam 86. **d** 89 **p** 90. C Sydenham H Trin *S'wark* 89-93; V from 93. *Holy Trinity Vicarage, 1 Sydenham Park Road, London SE26 4DY* Tel 0181-699 5303

DORMER, Canon Christopher Robert. b 39. Bris Univ BA61. Lich Th Coll 61. **d** 63 **p** 64. C Sheff Parson Cross St Cecilia *Sheff* 63-67; C Greenford H Cross *Lon* 67-69; Australia 69-74; Sec (Ireland) USPG 74-75; R Catton *York* 75-78; R Stamford Bridge Gp of Par 78-81; RD Pocklington 80-81; Itinerant Priest *Mor* from 81; P-in-c Lochalsh from 81; P-in-c Poolewe from 81; P-in-c Ullapool from 81; P-in-c Kishorn from 81; Miss to Seamen from 81; Can St Andr Cathl Inverness *Mor* from 94. *The Rectory, 25 Market Street, Ullapool, Ross-shire IV26 2XE* Tel (01854) 612143

DORMOR, Duncan James. b 67. Magd Coll Ox BA88 Lon Univ MSc89. Ripon Coll Cuddesdon BA94 DipMin95. **d** 95 **p** 96. C Wolverhampton *Lich* from 95. *7 Merridale Avenue, Wolverhampton WV3 9RE* Tel (01902) 22048

DORMOR, Duncan Stephen. b 36. St Edm Hall Ox BA60. Cuddesdon Coll 60. **d** 62 **p** 63. C Headington *Ox* 62-66; USA 66-72; R Hertford St Andr *St Alb* 72-88; RD Hertford 77-83; R Burford I *Heref* from 88; TR Tenbury from 88; R Burford II w Greete and Hope Bagot from 88; R Burford III w Lt Heref from 88; V Tenbury St Mich from 94; RD Ludlow from 96. *The Vicarage, Tenbury Wells, Worcs WR15 8BP* Tel (01584) 810702

DORRINGTON, Brian Goodwin. b 32. Leeds Univ CertEd55. St Deiniol's Hawarden 65. **d** 66 **p** 67. C Poynton *Ches* 66-71; Perm to Offic *Truro* 71-78; Hd Master Veryan Sch Truro 71-84; Hon C Veryan *Truro* 78-84; C N Petherwin 84-87; C Boyton w N Tamerton 84-87; TV Bolventor 87-90; R Kilkhampton w Morwenstow from 90; RD Stratton from 92. *The Rectory, East Road, Kilkhampton, Bude, Cornwall EX23 9QS* Tel (01288) 321314

DORRINGTON, Richard Bryan. b 48. Linc Th Coll 79. **d** 81 **p** 82. C Streetly *Lich* 81-84; C Badger 84-85; R 85-88; C Ryton 84-85; R 85-88; C Beckbury 84-85; R 85-88; V Geddington w Weekley *Pet* from 88. *The Vicarage, West Street, Geddington, Kettering, Northants NN14 1BD* Tel (01536) 742200

DORSET, Archdeacon of. *See* WALTON, The Ven Geoffrey Elmer

DORSETT, Dr Mark Richard. b 63. Univ of Wales (Lamp) BA84 MTh86 Birm Univ PhD90. Ripon Coll Cuddesdon 91. **d** 93 **p** 94. C Yardley St Edburgha *Birm* 93-96; Chapl K Edw Sixth Form Coll Worc from 96; Min Can Worc Cathl *Worc* from 96. *12A College Green, Worcester WR1 2LH*

DOSSETOR, Robert Francis. b 14. St Pet Hall Ox BA37 MA62 Lon Univ BA63 MA67. Ripon Hall Ox 37. **d** 37 **p** 38. C Surbiton St Matt *S'wark* 37-39; C Putney St Mary 39-41; R Black Torrington *Ex* 41-48; R Stone w Hartwell w Bishopstone *Ox* 48-53 and 54-59; CF (EC) 43-46; Chapl Stone Co Mental Hosp 48-54; Chapl Windsor Sch 53-54; Chapl City of Lon Freeman's Sch Ashtead Park 59-61; V Lower Streatham St Andr *S'wark* 61-80; rtd 80; P-in-c Tilshead, Orcheston and Chitterne *Sarum* 80-85. *42 Fowlers Road, Salisbury SP1 2PU* Tel (01722) 320725

DOSSOR, John Haley. b 41. Leeds Univ BA62. EAMTC 87. **d** 90 **p** 91. NSM Hadleigh *St E* from 90. *Butterfly Hall, Hadleigh, Ipswich IP7 5JZ* Tel (01473) 823338

DOTCHIN, Mrs Joan Marie. b 47. NE Ord Course 84. **d** 87 **p** 94. C Newc St Gabr *Newc* 87-92; TD Willington Team 92-94; TV 94-95; TR from 95. *St Mary's Vicarage, 67 Churchill Street, Wallsend, Tyne & Wear NE28 7TE* Tel 0191-262 8208

DOTY, Joseph Bonn. b 27. Woodstock Coll PhL51 STL58 Fordham Univ MA63. **d** 57 **p** 57. In RC Ch 57-70; USA 57-85; Prec St Ninian's Cathl Perth *St And* 85-88; R Church Brampton, Chapel Brampton, Harleston etc *Pet* 88-93; rtd 93. *Sun Cottage, Broad Chalke, Salisbury SP5 5EN* Tel (01722) 780008

DOUBLE, Canon Richard Sydney (Brother Samuel). b 47. K Coll Lon BD69 AKC69. St Aug Coll Cant 69. **d** 70 **p** 71. C Walton St Mary *Liv* 70-74; SSF from 75; Lic to Offic *Liv* 88-94; Guardian Hilfield Friary Dorchester from 94; Can and Preb Sarum Cathl *Sarum* from 95. *The Friary, Hilfield, Dorchester, Dorset DT2 7BE* Tel (01300) 341345

DOUBTFIRE, Miss Barbara. b 39. LMH Ox BA61 MA65. **d** 91 **p** 94. Par Development Adv *Ox* from 88; NSM Kidlington w Hampton Poyle from 91. *6 Meadow Walk, Woodstock, Oxon OX20 1NR* Tel (01993) 812095

DOUBTFIRE, Samuel. b 33. Edin Th Coll 63. **d** 66 **p** 66. C Knottingley *Wakef* 66-68; V Ripponden 68-76; V Crosthwaite Keswick *Carl* 76-81; V Barrow St Matt 81-87; R N Reddish *Man* 87-92; rtd 92; Perm to Offic *Bradf* from 92. *Greenacre, Station Road, Threshfield, Skipton, N Yorkshire BD23 5EP* Tel (01756) 752260

DOUGALL, David Brian. b 23. CBE. Oak Hill Th Coll. **d** 81 **p** 82. C Sandringham w W Newton *Nor* 81-83; P-in-c Fritton St Edm 83-84; R Somerleyton w Ashby 83-84; R Somerleyton w Ashby, Fritton and Herringfleet 84-92; rtd 92; Perm to Offic *Bris* from 92. *Somerley, The Green, Dauntsey, Chippenham, Wilts SN15 4HY* Tel (01666) 510759

DOUGHTY, Andrew William. b 56. K Coll Lon BD AKC. Westcott Ho Cam. **d** 82 **p** 83. C Alton St Lawr *Win* 82-85; TV Basingstoke 85-91; V Chilworth w N Baddesley 91-95; Bermuda from 95. *PO Box WK 530, Warwick WK BX, Bermuda* Tel Bermuda (1-441) 236-5744 Fax 236-3667

DOUGLAS, Canon Alexander Joseph. b 18. TCD BA45 MA61. CITC 45. **d** 45 **p** 46. I Orangefield w Moneyreagh *D & D* 63-86; rtd 86. *6 Rannoch Road, Holywood, Co Down BT18 0NA* Tel (01232) 423661

DOUGLAS, Ann Patricia. b 49. Lon Univ CertEd71. Oak Hill NSM Course 85. **d** 88 **p** 94. Par Dn Chorleywood Ch Ch *St Alb* 88-94; V Oxhey All SS from 94. *All Saints' Vicarage, Gosforth Lane, Watford WD1 6AX* Tel 0181-428 3696

DOUGLAS, Anthony Victor. b 51. St Jo Coll Nottm 74. **d** 76 **p** 77. C Gt Crosby St Luke *Liv* 76-79; TV Fazakerley Em 79-84; TR Speke St Aid 84-90; TR Gt and Lt Coates w Bradley *Linc* from 90. *St Michael's Rectory, 28 Great Coates Road, Grimsby, S Humberside DN34 4NE* Tel (01472) 844570

DOUGLAS, Canon Archibald Sholto. b 14. TD50. Selw Coll Cam BA37 MA46. Wells Th Coll 38. **d** 47 **p** 48. C Macclesfield St Mich *Ches* 47-51; CF (TA) 49-64; C Ashton on Mersey St Mary *Ches* 51-52; V Wharton 52-55; V Capesthorne w Siddington 55-69; P-in-c Marton 65-69; V Capesthorne w Siddington and Marton 69-82; Hon Can Ches Cathl 78-82; rtd 82; Perm to Offic *Ches* from 82. *Monks Heath Hall Farm, Chelford, Macclesfield, Cheshire SK10 4SY* Tel (01625) 861154

DOUGLAS, Charles David. b 29. Leeds Univ BSc50. Linc Th Coll 68. **d** 70 **p** 71. C Royton St Anne *Man* 70-73; V Edenfield 73-83; V Spotland 83-88; P-in-c Calderbrook 88-95; P-in-c Shore 92-95; rtd 95; Perm to Offic *Man* from 95. *11 Harrison Crescent, Blackrod, Bolton BL6 5EX* Tel (01204) 667595

DOUGLAS, George Gawain. b 35. Qu Coll Birm 59. **d** 61 **p** 62. C Workington St Jo *Carl* 61-64; C Upperby St Jo 64-67; C-in-c Carl St Luke Morton CD 67-68; V Carl St Luke Morton 68-72; V Aspatria w Hayton 72-92; P-in-c Leven Valley from 92. *The Vicarage, Haverthwaite, Ulverston, Cumbria LA12 8AJ* Tel (015395) 31476

DOUGLAS, Ian Alexander. b 11. St Aug Coll Cant 71. **d** 71 **p** 72. C Palmers Green St Jo *Lon* 71-81; rtd 81; Perm to Offic *Lon* from 82. *105 The Chine, London N21 2EG* Tel 0181-360 3472

DOUGLAS, Miss Janet Elizabeth. b 60. SS Paul & Mary Coll Cheltenham BEd83. Cranmer Hall Dur 88. **d** 90 **p** 94. Par Dn Yardley St Edburgha *Birm* 90-93; Par Dn Hamstead St Paul 93-94; C from 94. *14 Yateley Avenue, Birmingham B42 1JN* Tel 0121-358 0351

DOUGLAS, John Beresford. b 36. Sarum & Wells Th Coll 78. **d** 81 **p** 82. NSM Bath Bathwick *B & W* 81-94. *241 Bailbrook Lane, Bath BA1 7AA* Tel (01225) 858936

DOUGLAS, John Howard Barclay. b 23. St Jo Coll Dur BA48. Bps' Coll Cheshunt 48. **d** 50 **p** 51. C Hartlepool St Hilda *Dur* 50-53; C Woodhouse *Wakef* 53-55; PC Gateshead St Edm *Dur* 55-60; V Thirkleby w Kilburn and Bagby *York* 60-88; rtd 88; Perm to Offic *York* from 88. *6 St Giles Close, York Road, Thirsk, N Yorkshire YO7 3BU* Tel (01845) 524573

DOUGLAS, Martyn Graham. b 59. St Steph Ho Ox 85. **d** 88 **p** 89. C Stanmore *Win* 88-91; TV Basingstoke 91-94; USA from 94. *2509 Reabok Circle, Huntsville, Alabama 35803, USA* Tel Mobile (205) 881-7041 or 534-7733 Fax 534-7733

DOUGLAS (née MAGGS), Mrs Pamela Jean. b 47. Girton Coll Cam MA76 K Coll Lon BD79 AKC79. Qu Coll Birm 79. **dss** 80 **d** 87. Tottenham H Trin *Lon* 80-84; Asst Chapl Bryanston Sch Dorset 84-87; Perm to Offic *Chich* 87-94. *40 Maidenhead Lane, Borrowdale, Harare, Zimbabwe*

DOUGLAS, Peter. b 47. **d** 96 **p** 97. Hon C Prestwick *Glas* from 96. *Whinneyknowe, Newmilns, Ayrshire KA16 9LR* Tel (01560) 320007

DOUGLAS-JONES, Ian Elliot. b 14. Trin Hall Cam BA35 MA39. Wycliffe Hall Ox 35. **d** 37 **p** 38. C Highbury Ch Ch *Lon* 37-40; C Tunbridge Wells H Trin *Roch* 40-41; Chapl RAFVR 41-46; V Penge St Jo *Roch* 46-54; R Rushden *Pet* 54-63; P-in-c Newton Bromswold 60-63; V Fulwood *Sheff* 63-68; V Mayfield *Lich*

68-79; rtd 79; Perm to Offic *Worc* 79-92; Perm to Offic *Ox* from 92. *48 Webbs Close, Wolvercote, Oxford OX2 8PX* Tel (01865) 52444

DOUGLAS LANE, Charles Simon Pellew. b 47. BNC Ox MA71 Brooklands Tech Coll MIPM79. Oak Hill Th Coll 91. **d** 94 **p** 95. C Whitton St Aug *Lon* 94-97; P-in-c Hounslow W Gd Shep from 97. *Good Shepherd House, 360 Beavers Lane, Hounslow TW4 6HJ* Tel 0181-570 4035

DOUGLASS, Philip. b 48. Open Univ BA88. St Steph Ho Ox 87. **d** 89 **p** 90. C Peterlee *Dur* 89-92; V Crowan w Godolphin *Truro* from 92. *Crowan Vicarage, 37 Trethannas Gardens, Praze, Camborne, Cornwall TR14 9NB* Tel (01209) 831009

DOULL, Iain Sinclair. b 43. Univ of Wales (Cardiff) DPS88. **d** 88 **p** 89. C Malpas *Mon* 88-91; P-in-c Newport All SS from 91. *The Vicarage, Brynglas Road, Newport NP9 5QY* Tel (01633) 854657

DOULTON, Dick (Dic). b 32. St Cath Coll Cam BA60 MA64. Ridley Hall Cam 61. **d** 63 **p** 64. C Gedling *S'well* 63-65; C Danbury *Chelmsf* 65; Lic to Offic *Ox* 88-90; Lic to Offic *L & K* from 90. *Ballygriffin, Kenmare, Killarney, Co Kerry, Irish Republic* Tel Killarney (64) 41743

DOULTON, Roderick John (Rod). b 55. Oak Hill Th Coll DipHE93. **d** 93 **p** 94. C Hoddesdon *St Alb* 93-96; P-in-c Caldecote All SS from 96; P-in-c Old Warden from 97. *The Vicarage, 2A Biggleswade Road, Upper Caldecote, Biggleswade, Beds SG18 9BL* Tel (01767) 315578

DOVE, Canon Reginald George James Thomas. b 16. Leeds Univ BA38. Coll of Resurr Mirfield 38. **d** 40 **p** 41. C Blyth St Mary *Newc* 40-43; S Africa from 43; rtd 88. *PO Box 2263, Edenvale, 1610 South Africa* Tel Johannesburg (11) 609-4257

DOVER, Canon Oswald Leslie Simpson. b 18. Edin Th Coll 46. **d** 47 **p** 48. C Stirling *Edin* 47-50; P-in-c Bo'ness 50-51; C Harrogate St Wilfrid *Ripon* 52-53; R Galashiels *Edin* 53-59; R Melrose 59-85; Hon Can St Mary's Cathl from 77; rtd 85; Hon C Galashiels *Edin* from 88. *12 Shielswood Court, Tweedbank, Galashiels, Selkirkshire TD1 3RH* Tel (01896) 756946

DOVER, Suffragan Bishop of. *See* LLEWELLIN, The Rt Revd John Richard Allan

DOW, Andrew John Morrison. b 46. Univ Coll Ox BA67 MA71. Oak Hill Th Coll 69. **d** 71 **p** 72. C Watford St Luke *St Alb* 71-74; C Chadderton Ch Ch *Man* 75-78; V Leamington Priors St Paul *Cov* 78-88; V Knowle *Birm* from 88; RD Solihull from 95. *The Vicarage, 1811 Warwick Road, Knowle, Solihull, W Midlands B93 0DS* Tel (01564) 773666

✠**DOW, The Rt Revd Geoffrey Graham.** b 42. Qu Coll Ox BA63 BSc65 MA68 Birm Univ DipTh74 Ox Univ MSc Nottm Univ MPhil82. Clifton Th Coll 66. **d** 67 **p** 68 **c** 92. C Tonbridge SS Pet and Paul *Roch* 67-72; Chapl St Jo Coll Ox 72-75; Lect St Jo Coll Nottm 75-81; V Cov H Trin *Cov* 81-92; Can Th Cov Cathl 88-92; Area Bp Willesden *Lon* from 92. *173 Willesden Lane, London NW6 7YN* Tel 0181-451 0189 Fax 451 4606

DOWD, Canon Garfield George. b 60. QUB BSc TCD DipTh83. **d** 86 **p** 87. C Monkstown *D & G* 86-90; I Carlow w Urglin and Staplestown *C & O* from 90; Preb Ossory Cathl from 96. *The Rectory, Green Road, Carlow, Irish Republic* Tel Carlow (503) 32565

DOWDEN, Gordon Frederick. b 25. Selw Coll Cam BA51 MA55. Chich Th Coll 51. **d** 53 **p** 54. C Salisbury St Mich *Sarum* 53-56; C St Neots *Ely* 56-58; C Gt w Lt Paxton and Toseland 56-58; R Hulme St Phil *Man* 58-70; R Hulme Ascension 70-78; RD Hulme 73-78; P-in-c Holybourne cum Neatham *Win* 78-82; RD Alton 79-82; C Man Resurr *Man* 82; AD Ardwick 82-90; C Man Gd Shep 82-91; Chapl Ancoats Hosp Man 85-90; rtd 91; Perm to Offic *Man* from 91. *41 Rozel Square, Manchester M3 4FQ* Tel 0161-832 5592

DOWDING, Edward Brinley. b 47. St Mich Coll Llan 70 St D Coll Lamp BA71. **d** 72 **p** 73. C Canton St Cath *Llan* 72-75; C Aberdare St Jo 75-78; V Aberavon H Trin 78-85; R Sully from 85. *The Rectory, 26 South Road, Sully, Penarth CF64 5TG* Tel (01222) 530221

DOWDING, Jeremy Charles. b 51. RMN72. St Steph Ho Ox 89. **d** 91 **p** 92. C Newport St Steph and H Trin *Mon* 91-94; C Risca 94-96; P-in-c Whitleigh *Ex* from 96. *The Vicarage, 17 Whitleigh Green, Plymouth PL5 4DD* Tel (01752) 773547

DOWDING, Stanley Frederick. b 10. ALCD32 St Jo Coll Dur BA33 LTh33. **d** 34 **p** 35. C Bris St Silas *Bris* 34-37; C Downend 37-39; C Portland All SS w St Pet *Sarum* 39-42; OCF 39-42; P-in-c Weston Mill *Ex* 42-46; V Preston St Luke *Blackb* 46-55; Chapl HM Pris Preston 51-52; V Nelson in Lt Marsden *Blackb* 55-75; Chapl Reedyford Hosp 64; RD Burnley 68-70; RD Pendle 70-75; rtd 75; Lic to Offic *Blackb* 76-93; Perm to Offic from 93. *4 Hillside Avenue, Reedley, Burnley, Lancs BB10 2NF* Tel (01282) 693030

DOWDLE, Miss Cynthia. b 48. Cranmer Hall Dur 88. **d** 90 **p** 94. C Allerton *Liv* 90-94; TR Halewood from 94. *22 Kenton Road, Halewood, Liverpool L26 9LA* Tel 0151-486 3180

DOWDY, Simon Mark Christopher. b 67. Trin Hall Cam BA89 MA93. Wycliffe Hall Ox 93. **d** 96 **p** 97. C Beckenham Ch Ch *Roch* from 96. *78 The Drive, Beckenham, Kent BR3 1EG* Tel 0181-650 7669

DOWELL, Graham Moffat. b 26. Magd Coll Cam BA48 MA53. Ely Th Coll 51. **d** 53 **p** 54. C Derby Cathl *Derby* 53-56; Chapl Derby Cathl 53-56; Cyprus 56-59; C Sheff St Geo and St Steph *Sheff* 59-63; Chapl Sheff Univ 59-63; Ethiopia 64-67; Zambia 68-70; Chapl LSE *Lon* 70-74; V Hampstead St Jo 74-86; Perm to Offic *Heref* from 87; rtd 91. *8 Bridge Street, Clun, Craven Arms, Shropshire SY7 8JP* Tel (01588) 640521

DOWIE, Miss Winifred Brenda McIntosh. b 57. Callendar Park Coll of Educn Falkirk DipEd78. Trin Coll Bris BA91. **d** 92 **p** 94. Par Dn Downend *Bris* 92-94; C 94-95; Chapl Asst Southmead Health Services NHS Trust Bris from 95. *Southmead Hospital, Southmead Road, Westbury-on-Trym, Bristol BS10 5NB* Tel 0117-950 5050 or 959 5447

DOWLAND, Martin John. b 48. Lon Univ BD70 Southn Univ PGCE71. Wycliffe Hall Ox 75. **d** 77 **p** 78. C Jesmond Clayton Memorial *Newc* 77-80; C Chadderton Ch Ch *Man* 80-85; R Haughton St Mary from 85. *Haughton Green Rectory, Meadow Lane, Denton, Manchester M34 1GD* Tel 0161-336 4529

DOWLEN, Edward Mark. b 25. DLC47 Cranfield Inst of Tech MSc49. St Jo Coll Dur 79. **d** 79 **p** 80. C Rhyl w St Ann *St As* 79-82; C Warton St Paul *Blackb* 83-90; rtd 90; Lic to Offic *Sarum* from 90; Lic to Offic *Mor* from 93. *33 Hythe Road, Poole, Dorset BH15 3NN* Tel (01202) 737699 or 770636

DOWLER, Robert Edward Mackenzie. b 67. Ch Ch Ox BA89 Selw Coll Cam BA93. Westcott Ho Cam 91. **d** 94 **p** 95. C Southgate Ch Ch *Lon* 94-97; C Somers Town St Mary from 97. *St Marys Church House, Eversholt Street, London NW1 1BN* Tel 0171-387 7301

DOWLING, Donald Edward. b 43. St Jo Coll Dur DipTh74 St Andr Univ MA66. **d** 74 **p** 75. C Thame w Towersey *Ox* 74-77; C Norton *St Alb* 77-80; V Wilbury from 81. *Church House, 103 Bedford Road, Letchworth, Herts SG6 4DU* Tel (01462) 679236

DOWLING, Kingsley Avery Paul. b 60. Leeds Univ DipM91 MCIM. Aston Tr Scheme 93 Ripon Coll Cuddesdon DipMin95. **d** 97. C Headingley *Ripon* from 97. *5 Derwentwater Grove, Headingley, Leeds LS6 3EN* Tel 0113-275 8937 E-mail 100756.2502@compuserve.com

DOWLING, Paul Martin. b 55. ACA G&C Coll Cam MA79. Cranmer Hall Dur 88. **d** 90 **p** 91. C Redhill St Jo *S'wark* 90-94; V Wakef St Jo *Wakef* from 94. *St John's Vicarage, 65 Bradford Road, Wakefield, W Yorkshire WF1 2AA* Tel (01924) 371029

DOWMAN, Peter Robert. b 52. City Univ BSc. Wycliffe Hall Ox 82. **d** 84 **p** 85. C Cheltenham Ch Ch *Glouc* 84-87; C Danbury *Chelmsf* 87-90; R Woodham Ferrers and Bicknacre 90-95; Regional Consultant E England CPAS from 95; Perm to Offic *Chelmsf* from 95. *33 Nightingale Avenue, Cambridge CB1 4SG* Tel (01223) 244331

DOWN, Martin John. b 40. Jes Coll Cam BA62 MA68. Westcott Ho Cam 63. **d** 65 **p** 66. C Bury St Mary *Man* 65-68; C Leigh St Mary 68-70; R Fiskerton *Linc* 70-75; V Irnham w Corby 75-79; RD Beltisloe 76-84; P-in-c Creeton w Swinstead 78-79; P-in-c Swayfield 78-79; V Corby Glen 79-84; Good News Trust 84-88; Perm to Offic 84-88; Perm to Offic *Pet* 86-88; P-in-c Ashill w Saham Toney *Nor* 88-94; R from 94. *The Rectory, Ashill, Thetford, Norfolk IP25 7BT* Tel (01760) 440247

DOWN, Peter Michael. b 54. K Coll Lon BD78 AKC. Coll of Resurr Mirfield 78. **d** 79 **p** 80. C Swindon Ch Ch *Bris* 79-82; C Southmead 82-84; TV Cannock *Lich* 84-92; V Coleford w Holcombe *B & W* from 92. *The Vicarage, Church Street, Coleford, Bath BA3 5NG* Tel (01373) 813382

DOWN, Philip Roy. b 53. R Melbourne Inst of Tech DipApSc76 Hull Univ MA93. Melbourne Coll of Div BTh82 MTh88. **d** 89 **p** 89. C Gt Grimsby St Mary and St Jas *Linc* 89-91; TV 91-95; R Hackington *Cant* from 95. *St Stephen's Rectory, St Stephen's Green, Canterbury, Kent CT2 7JU* Tel (01227) 765391

✠**DOWN, The Rt Revd William John Denbigh (Bill).** b 34. St Jo Coll Cam BA57 MA61 FNI91. Ridley Hall Cam 57. **d** 59 **p** 60 **c** 90. C Fisherton Anger *Sarum* 59-63; Miss to Seamen 63-90; Australia 71-74; Dep Gen Sec Miss to Seamen 75; Gen Sec 76-90; Hon C Gt Stanmore *Lon* 75-90; Chapl St Mich Paternoster Royal 76-90; Perm to Offic *St Alb* 78-90; Hon Can Gib Cathl *Eur* 85-90; Hon Can Kobe Japan from 87; Bp Bermuda 90-95; P-in-c Humberstone *Leic* from 95; Asst Bp Leic from 95. *St Mary's Vicarage, 56 Vicarage Lane, Humberstone, Leicester LE5 1EE* Tel 0116-276 7281 Fax 276 4504

DOWN AND DROMORE, Bishop of. *See* MILLER, The Rt Revd Harold Creeth

DOWN, Archdeacon of. *See* McCAMLEY, The Ven Gregor Alexander

DOWN, Dean of. *See* DINNEN, The Very Revd John Frederick

DOWNER, Cuthbert John. b 18. S'wark Ord Course 60. **d** 74 **p** 75. Hon C Kirdford *Chich* 74-76; C Halesworth w Linstead and Chediston *St E* 76-79; P-in-c Knodishall w Buxlow 79-80; P-in-c Friston 79-80; R Bacton w Wyverstone 80-83; P-in-c Cotton and Wickham Skeith 80-83; R Bacton w Wyverstone and Cotton 83-84; rtd 84; Perm to Offic *St E* 84-87; Perm to Offic *B & W* 88-95. *4 Finch Close, Shepton Mallet, Somerset BA4 5GA*

DOWNES, Gregory Charles (Rory). b 69. Roehampton Inst BSc91 Hughes Hall Cam PGCE92. Wycliffe Hall Ox BA95 DipMin93. **d** 96 **p** 97. C Hazlemere *Ox* from 96. *101 Rose Avenue,*

Hazlemere, High Wycombe, Bucks HP15 7UP Tel (01494) 815561

DOWNES, Richard John. b 63. Cranmer Hall Dur CTM94. **d** 94 **p** 95. C Bishopwearmouth St Gabr *Dur* 94-97; CF from 97. *MOD Chaplains (Army), Trenchard Lines, Upavon, Pewsey, Wilts SN9 6BE* Tel (01980) 615804 Fax 615800

DOWNEY, Canon John Stewart. b 38. QUB CertEd60 Open Univ BA76. Oak Hill Th Coll 63. **d** 66 **p** 67. C Londonderry St Aug *D & R* 66-71; I Dungiven w Bovevagh 71-82; Bp's Dom Chapl 75-82; V Bishopwearmouth St Gabr *Dur* 82-91; V New Malden and Coombe *S'wark* from 91; Hon Can S'wark Cathl from 97. *The Vicarage, 93 Coombe Road, New Malden, Surrey KT3 4RE* Tel 0181-942 0915

DOWNHAM, Canon Peter Norwell. b 31. Man Univ BA52. Ridley Hall Cam 54. **d** 56 **p** 57. C Cheadle *Ches* 56-62; V Rawtenstall St Mary *Man* 62-68; Chapl Rossendale Gen Hosp 62-68; V Denton Holme *Carl* 68-79; V Reading Greyfriars *Ox* 79-95; Hon Can Ch Ch 90-95; rtd 95; Hon C Cotehill and Cumwhinton *Carl* from 95. *The Vicarage, Cotehill, Carlisle CA4 0DY* Tel (01228) 560323

DOWNHAM, Simon Garrod. b 61. Solicitor 87 K Coll Lon LLB84. Wycliffe Hall Ox BA93 DipMin94. **d** 94 **p** 95. C Brompton H Trin w Onslow Square St Paul *Lon* from 94. *3 Holy Trinity Church House, Brompton Road, London SW7 2RW* Tel 0171-589 3589 Fax 589 3390

DOWNIE, James Hubert. b 23. DL. Barrister 58 FRSA70. **d** 92 **p** 93. NSM Stornoway *Arg* 92-94; C Leverburgh 92-94; P-in-c from 94. *Dunarin, Strond, Leverburgh, Isle of Harris HS5 3UD* Tel (01859) 520247

DOWNING, Francis Gerald. b 35. Qu Coll Ox BA56 MA60. Linc Th Coll. **d** 58 **p** 59. C Filwood Park CD *Bris* 58-60; Tutor Linc Th Coll 60-64; V Unsworth *Man* 64-80; Tutor N Ord Course 80-82; Vice-Prin 82-90; Lic to Offic *Man* 80-90; V Bolton SS Simon and Jude from 90. *The Vicarage, 15 Lowick Avenue, Bolton BL3 2DS* Tel (01204) 523919

DOWNS, Miss Geinor. b 47. UEA BA72 Southn Univ BTh89. Chich Th Coll 85. **d** 87 **p** 94. Par Dn Wellingborough All SS *Pet* 87-89; Development Officer Chich Th Coll 89-92; C Durrington *Chich* 92-95; Chapl City Hosp NHS Trust Birm from 95. *Chaplaincy Department, City Hospital NHS Trust, Dudley Road, Birmingham B18 7QH* Tel 0121-554 3801 Fax 523 0951

DOWNS, Ivan Frederick. b 26. Chich Th Coll 65. **d** 66 **p** 67. C Corbridge w Halton *Newc* 66-70; C Tynemouth Ch Ch 70-74; V Walker 74-79; V Dudley 79-89; V Weetslade 90-91; rtd 91. *East Cottage, Stannersburn, Hexham, Northd NE48 1DD* Tel (01434) 240471

DOWNS, John Alfred. b 58. MIBiol80 CBiol80 Leic Univ BSc79 PGCE80. EMMTC 90. **d** 93 **p** 94. NSM Barlestone *Leic* 93-96; NSM Thornton, Bagworth and Stanton from 96; NSM Markfield from 96. *29 Meadow Road, Barlestone, Nuneaton, Warks CV13 0JG* Tel (01455) 290195

DOWSE, Edgar. b 10. Dur Univ LTh35 Lon Univ BD37 Fitzw Coll Cam BA72 MA74 Lon Univ MPhil90. Clifton Th Coll 32. **d** 35 **p** 36. Asst Chapl and Tutor Clifton Th Coll 35-36; C Chippenham St Andr w Tytherton Lucas *Bris* 36-40; Tutor St Andr Th Coll Whittlesford 40-42; C Bournemouth St Mich *Win* 42-45; P-in-c Bournemouth H Epiphany 45-51; R Freemantle 51-57; V Bethnal Green St Bart *Lon* 57-70; Lect Lon Bible Coll 60-61; Lect St Mich Cornhill 60-63; St Steph Walbrook 65-68; St Dunstan-in-the-Wall 70-71; P-in-c Acton Green St Alb *Lon* 71-72; V 72-75; rtd 75. *87 College Road, Isleworth, Middx TW7 5DP* Tel 0181-568 2548

DOWSE, Ivor Roy. b 35. ARHistS MRSL. St Deiniol's Hawarden 66. **d** 68 **p** 70. C Harrow St Pet *Lon* 68-69; C Sudbury St Andr 69-71; C Weeke *Win* 71-73; Min Can Ban Cathl *Ban* 73-78; V Hollym w Welwick and Holmpton *York* 78-81; R Bearwood *Ox* 81-82; P-in-c Rothesay *Arg* 83-86; C Boxmoor St Jo *St Alb* 86-92; rtd 92; Hon C Cowes H Trin and St Mary *Portsm* 92-94; Perm to Offic from 94. *14 Charles Road, Cowes, Isle of Wight PO31 8HG* Tel (01983) 294782

DOWSETT, Alan Charles. b 27. Selw Coll Cam BA51 MA55 Bris Poly CQSW76. Cuddesdon Coll 51. **d** 53 **p** 54. C Portsea St Mary *Portsm* 53-57; C Wokingham All SS *Ox* 57-60; V Water Orton *Birm* 60-64; Chapl Colston's Sch Bris 64-65; C Stoke Bishop *Bris* 65-68; Lic to Offic 69-89; rtd 89. *23 Upper Cranbrook Road, Bristol BS6 7UW* Tel 0117-924 3227

DOWSETT, Marian Ivy Rose. b 40. **d** 88 **p** 97. NSM Rumney *Mon* 88-94; C St Mellons and Michaelston-y-Fedw 94-96; C St Mellons from 96. *114 Ridgeway Road, Cardiff CF3 9AB* Tel (01222) 792635

DOWSON, Roger Christopher. b 32. Clifton Th Coll 60. **d** 63 **p** 64. C Virginia Water *Guildf* 63-66; C Darfield *Sheff* 66-68; V Thorpe Edge *Bradf* 68-80; V Wyke 80-91; rtd 91; Hon C Coley *Wakef* from 91; Perm to Offic *Bradf* from 93. *1 Windsor Villas, Norwood Green, Halifax, W Yorkshire HX3 8QS* Tel (01274) 674557

DOWSON, Simon Paul. b 63. Bris Univ BSc85 Cam Univ PGCE89. Cranmer Hall Dur 95. **d** 97. C Bradf St Aug Undercliffe *Bradf* from 97. *96 Sydenham Place, Otley Road, Bradford, W Yorkshire BD3 0DA* Tel (01274) 229887

DOXSEY, Roy Desmond. b 41. St D Coll Lamp 64. **d** 67 **p** 68. C Pembroke St Mary and St Mich *St D* 67-70; C Milford Haven 70-73; C Loughton *Ox* 73-75; Chapl Llandovery Coll 75-81 and 92-96; Zambia 81-86; Chapl Epsom Coll 86-92; V Roath St German *Llan* from 96. *St Germans Vicarage, Metal Street, Roath, Cardiff CF2 1LA* Tel (01222) 494488

DOYE, Andrew Peter Charles. b 64. BNC Ox BA85. Trin Coll Bris BA93. **d** 93 **p** 94. C Surbiton St Matt *S'wark* 93-96; C Bourne *Guildf* from 96. *Heavitree, 5 Dene Lane, Lower Bourne, Farnham, Surrey GU10 3AW* Tel (01252) 725879

DOYLE, Canon Alan Holland. b 22. JP. Lon Univ BD55 Birm Univ MA86 Buckm Univ DPhil93. Wycliffe Hall Ox 52. **d** 52 **p** 53. C Braddan *S & M* 52-54; C Douglas St Geo 54-55; R Oldham St Andr *Man* 55-59; S Rhodesia 59-62; V Chaddesley Corbett *Worc* 62-66; CF (TA) 63-67; V Kidderminster St Jo *Worc* 66-67; R Salwarpe 67-74; RD Droitwich 69-78; P-in-c Himbleton w Huddington 74-78; Hon Can Worc Cathl 74-87; P-in-c Ombersley w Doverdale 78-83; R 83-87; rtd 87. *3 Graham Court, Graham Road, Malvern, Worcs WR14 2HX* Tel (01684) 892133

DOYLE, Andrew Michael. b 63. K Coll Lon BD85 AKC85. Ripon Coll Cuddesdon 86. **d** 88 **p** 89. C Lytchett Minster *Sarum* 88-92; TV Kirkby *Liv* from 92. *The Vicarage, 9 Redwood Way, Tower Hill, Liverpool L32 4DU* Tel 0151-548 7969

DOYLE, Brian William. b 31. Sarum Th Coll 87. **d** 87 **p** 88. NSM Heene *Chich* 87-91; Chapl Qu Alexandra's Hosp Worthing 89-91; C W Tarring *Chich* 91-93; C Hangleton 93-95; rtd 95; Perm to Offic *Chich* from 96. *56A Langdale Gardens, Hove, E Sussex BN3 4HH* Tel (01273) 727910

DOYLE, Edward Michael. b 70. Univ of Wales (Cardiff) DipTh91. St Mich Coll Llan BTh93. **d** 94 **p** 95. C Sketty *S & B* 94-96; C Llwynderw from 96. *23 Mayals Avenue, Blackpill, Swansea SA3 5DE*

DOYLE, Graham Thomas. b 48. Worc Coll Ox BA85 MA90. St Barn Coll Adelaide ThL73 ThSchol77. **d** 73 **p** 74. Australia 73-83; Perm to Offic *Ox* 83-85; C Cobbold Road St Sav w St Mary *Lon* 86; P-in-c Bradf St Oswald Chapel Green *Bradf* 86-91; Chapl Belgrade w Zagreb *Eur* 91-93; Chapl Belgrade 93-97; Taiwan from 97. *Chaplain's Flat, 1 Branks Djonovica, 11000 Belgrade, Serbia* Tel Belgrade (11) 660186 Fax 659651 E-mail gdoyle@eunet.yu

DOYLE, Robin Alfred. b 43. Dur Univ BA65. Westcott Ho Cam 66. **d** 68 **p** 69. C Edgbaston St Geo *Birm* 68-70; C Erdington St Barn 70-73; P-in-c Oldbury 73-81; V Maker w Rame *Truro* from 81. *The Vicarage, Fore Street, Torpoint, Cornwall PL10 1NB* Tel (01752) 822302

DRACKLEY, John Oldham. b 36. Em Coll Cam BA57 MA61. Wells Th Coll 57. **d** 59 **p** 60. C Eckington *Derby* 59-62; C Lee Gd Shep w St Pet *S'wark* 62-63; C Derby St Thos *Derby* 63-67; C Matlock and Tansley 67-77; P-in-c Radbourne 77-82; P-in-c Dalbury, Long Lane and Trusley 77-82; P-in-c Longford 77-82; Sec Dioc Cttee for Care of Chs from 82; rtd 95. *26 Highfield Drive, Matlock, Derbyshire DE4 3FZ* Tel (01629) 55902

DRAFFAN, Prof Ian William. b 42. FBCS77 CEng88 Aston Univ BSc65 MSc66. N Ord Course 83. **d** 86 **p** 87. NSM Millhouses H Trin *Sheff* from 86. *8 Silverdale Crescent, Sheffield S11 9JH* Tel 0114-236 4523

DRAIN, Walter. b 39. ACP66 Open Univ BA76. NW Ord Course 76. **d** 79 **p** 80. NSM Cheadle *Ches* 79-81; C 81-84; V Chatburn *Blackb* from 84; Asst Chapl HM Pris Preston from 94. *The Vicarage, Chatburn, Clitheroe, Lancs BB7 4AA* Tel (01200) 441317

DRAKE, Miss Frances. b 43. Brentwood Coll of Educn TCert67 Sussex Univ BEd74. S'wark Ord Course 90. **d** 93 **p** 94. NSM Fryerning w Margaretting *Chelmsf* from 93. *Little Pump House, Ongar Road, Kelvedon Hatch, Brentwood, Essex CM15 0LA* Tel (01277) 364383

DRAKE, Graham. b 46. Linc Th Coll 81. **d** 83 **p** 85. C Alford w Rigsby *Linc* 83-84; Perm to Offic *Wakef* 84-85; Hon C Purston cum S Featherstone 85-89; NSM Castleford All SS 89-92; C Cudworth 92-95. *Flat 3, Woodland House, 5 Mill Hill, Pontefract, W Yorkshire WF8 4HR* Tel (01977) 708713

DRAKE, Graham Rae. b 45. Fitzw Coll Cam BA68 MA72. Qu Coll Birm 70. **d** 73 **p** 74. C New Windsor *Ox* 73-77; TV 77-78; P-in-c Bath Ascension *B & W* 78-81; TV Bath Twerton-on-Avon 81-86; P-in-c Buxton w Oxnead *Nor* 86-90; P-in-c Lammas w Lt Hautbois 86-90; RD Ingworth 88-94; R Buxton w Oxnead, Lammas and Brampton 90-95; P-in-c Cockley Cley w Gooderstone from 95; P-in-c Gt and Lt Cressingham w Threxton from 95; P-in-c Didlington from 95; P-in-c Hilborough w Bodney from 95; P-in-c Oxborough w Foulden and Caldecote from 95. *The Rectory, Gooderstone, Kings Lynn, Norfolk PE33 9DF* Tel (01366) 328425

DRAKE, John Paul. b 19. Qu Coll Ox BA41 MA44. Cuddesdon Coll 46. **d** 47 **p** 48. C Stepney St Dunstan and All SS *Lon* 47-54; V Brighton All So *Chich* 54-59; Chapl St Edw Sch Ox 59-69; V Stewkley *Ox* 69-75; V Stewkley w Soulbury and Drayton Parslow 75-85; RD Mursley 77-83; rtd 85; Perm to Offic *St Alb* from 85. *3 The Cloisters, Welwyn Garden City, Herts AL8 6DU* Tel (01707) 325379

DRAKE, Leslie Sargent. b 47. Boston Univ BA69 MTh72 Hull Univ BPhil74. Coll of Resurr Mirfield 78. **d** 78 **p** 79. C Oldham *Man* 78-81; TV Rochdale 81-83; V Palmers Green St Jo *Lon*

83-89; Chapl St Mary's Sch Cheshunt from 89. *29 Arundel Gardens, London N21 3AG* Tel 0181-886 9104

DRAKELEY, Stephen Richard Francis. b 51. Aston Univ BSc73. Chich Th Coll 76. **d** 76 **p** 77. C Yardley Wood *Birm* 76-79; V Rednal 79-89; TV Bodmin w Lanhydrock and Lanivet *Truro* from 89. *The Vicarage, Rectory Road, Lanivet, Bodmin, Cornwall PL30 5HG* Tel (01208) 831743

DRAPER, The Ven Alfred James. b 23. Natal Univ BA50. St Aug Coll Cant DipTh59 St Paul's Grahamstown LTh54. **d** 54 **p** 54. S Africa 54-63 and 75-87; V Tile Cross *Birm* 63-72; V Olton 72-75; Adn Durban 79-87; R S Ferriby *Linc* 87-93; V Horkstow 87-93; R Saxby All Saints 87-93; rtd 93; Perm to Offic *Ches* from 93. *4 Rugby Close, Macclesfield, Cheshire SK10 2HW* Tel (01625) 619033

DRAPER, Charles. b 59. Dur Univ BSc80 Cam Univ BA86. Ridley Hall Cam 84. **d** 87 **p** 88. C Wareham *Sarum* 87-90; C Maltby *Sheff* 90-93; R The Claydons *Ox* from 93. *The Rectory, Queen Catherine Road, Steeple Claydon, Buckingham MK18 2PY* Tel (01296) 738055

DRAPER, Derek Vincent. b 38. Linc Th Coll 65. **d** 68 **p** 69. C Orpington All SS *Roch* 68-72; C Bramley *Guildf* 72-74; P-in-c Kempston *St Alb* 74-76; Min Kempston Transfiguration CD 77-79; V Kempston Transfiguration 79-84; RD Bedford 79-84; V Bromham w Oakley 84-88; P-in-c Stagsden 84-88; V Bromham w Oakley and Stagsden from 88; Chapl Bromham Hosp from 84. *The Vicarage, 47 Stagsden Road, Bromham, Bedford MK43 8PY* Tel (01234) 823268

DRAPER, Elizabeth Ann. *See* BRADLEY, Mrs Elizabeth Ann

DRAPER, Dr Ivan Thomas. b 32. FRCP FRCPGlas Aber Univ MB, ChB56. St Jo Coll Nottm 87. **d** 90 **p** 91. NSM Glas St Bride *Glas* 90-96; P-in-c from 96. *13/1 Whistlefield Court, 2 Canniesburn Road, Bearsden, Glasgow G61 1PX* Tel 0141-943 0954

DRAPER, Jack William. b 18. Oak Hill Th Coll 51. **d** 53 **p** 54. C New Catton St Luke *Nor* 53-54; R Colney w Earlham 54-57; V W Ashton *Sarum* 57-62; P-in-c Heywood 60-62; R Bramerton w Surlingham *Nor* 62-75; R Ashby w Thurton, Claxton and Carleton 70-75; R Rockland St Mary w Hellington 70-75; R Framingham Pigot 70-75; R Bergh Apton w Yelverton 70-75; RD Loddon 71-75; P-in-c Hoxne w Denham St Jo *St E* 75-79; P-in-c Hoxne w Denham St Jo and Syleham 79-80; V 80-84; rtd 84; Lic to Offic *St E* 84-85 and from 92; Hon C Yoxford 85-91; Hon C Yoxford and Peasenhall w Sibton 91-92; Lic to Offic *Nor* from 92. *18 Eastgate House, Eastgate Street, Bury St Edmunds, Suffolk IP33 1YP* Tel (01284) 755125

DRAPER, Jean Margaret. b 31. **d** 80 **p** 97. NSM Pontnewydd *Mon* 80-83; BRF from 82; NSM Llantillio Pertholey w Bettws Chpl etc *Mon* 83-96; NSM Newport St Andr from 96. *Govilon House, Merthyr Road, Govilon, Abergavenny NP7 9PT* Tel (01873) 830380

DRAPER, John William. b 54. Aston Tr Scheme 86 Qu Coll Birm 88. **d** 90 **p** 91. C Stepney St Dunstan and All SS *Lon* 90-94; C Leigh Park *Portsm* 94-96; C Warren Park St Clare 94-96; R Rowner from 96. *The Rectory, 174 Rowner Lane, Gosport, Hants PO13 9SU* Tel (01705) 581834

DRAPER, Dr Jonathan Lee. b 52. Gordon Coll Mass BA76 St Jo Coll Dur BA78 PhD84. Ripon Coll Cuddesdon 83. **d** 83 **p** 84. C Baguley *Man* 83-85; Dir Academic Studies Ripon Coll Cuddesdon 85-92; V Putney St Mary *S'wark* from 92. *The Vicarage, 45 St John's Avenue, London SW15 6AL* Tel 0181-788 4575

DRAPER, The Ven Martin Paul. b 50. Birm Univ BA72 Southn Univ BTh79. Chich Th Coll 72. **d** 75 **p** 76. C Primrose Hill St Mary w Avenue Road St Paul *Lon* 75-78; C Westmr St Matt 79-84; Chapl Paris St Geo *Eur* from 84; Adn France from 94; Can Gib Cathl from 94. *7 rue Auguste-Vacquerie, 75116 Paris, France* Tel Paris (331) 47 20 22 51

DRAPER, Patrick Hugh. b 43. S Dios Minl Tr Scheme 91. **d** 94 **p** 95. NSM Boscombe St Jo *Win* from 94. *82 Tuckton Road, Bournemouth BH6 3HT* Tel (01202) 424100

DRAPER, Paul Richard. b 64. Glas Univ MA87 TCD BTh90. **d** 90 **p** 91. C Drumragh w Mountfield *D & R* 90-94; I Ballydehob w Aghadown *C, C & R* from 94. *The Rectory, Ballydehob, Co Cork, Irish Republic* Tel Ballydehob (28) 37117

DRAPER, Raymond James. b 48. Ex Coll Ox BA70 MA75 Em Coll Cam BA73 MA78. Ridley Hall Cam 71. **d** 74 **p** 75. C Sheff Manor *Sheff* 74-78; Ind Chapl 78-82; R Wickersley from 82. *The Rectory, Church Lane, Wickersley, Rotherham, S Yorkshire S66 0ES* Tel (01709) 543111

DRAPER, Mrs Sylvia Edith. b 39. ARCM60. N Ord Course 86. **d** 89 **p** 94. C Aughton St Mich *Liv* 89-92; Par Dn Wigan St Jas w St Thos 92-94; Asst Chapl Billinge Hosp Wigan from 92; C Wigan St Jas w St Thos *Liv* from 94. *16 Mervyn Place, Wigan WN3 5JS* Tel (01942) 496922

DRAX, Elizabeth Margaret. *See* ANSON, Mrs Elizabeth Margaret

DRAY, John. b 66. St Chad's Coll Dur BSc87. St Steph Ho Ox BTh95. **d** 95 **p** 96. C Byker St Ant *Newc* from 95. *87 St Anthony's House, Caldbeck Avenue, Newcastle upon Tyne NE6 3SH* Tel 0191-265 4101 E-mail drayjohn@msn.com

DRAYCOTT, John. b 53. Sheff Univ BA84 DCEd82. Br Isles Nazarene Coll DipTh77 Linc Th Coll 85. **d** 85 **p** 86. In Wesleyan Reform Union 77-82; C Wombwell *Sheff* 85-87; V W Bessacarr 87-92; V Erith Ch Ch *Roch* from 92; P-in-c Erith St Jo 92-95. *Christ Church Vicarage, Victoria Road, Erith, Kent DA8 3AN* Tel (01322) 334729

DRAYCOTT, Philip John. b 27. Sarum & Wells Th Coll. **d** 83 **p** 84. C Bishop's Cleeve *Glouc* 83-86; V Chedworth, Yanworth and Stowell, Coln Rogers etc 86-93; rtd 94; Perm to Offic *B & W* from 94. *April Cottage, Newton Road, North Petherton, Bridgwater, Somerset TA6 6NA* Tel (01278) 662487

DRAYSON, Nicholas James Quested. b 53. Keble Coll Ox BA75 MA83. Wycliffe Hall Ox DipTh83. **d** 79 **p** 79. SAMS from 79; Argentina 79-82 and from 93; Spain 83-92; Adn Andalucia 88-90; C Kirkheaton *Wakef* 85. *Iglesia Anglicana, Casilla 30, 4560 Tartagal, Salta, Argentina* Tel Salta (87) 311718

DRAYTON, James Edward. b 30. St Deiniol's Hawarden 81. **d** 84 **p** 86. Hon C Heald Green St Cath *Ches* 84-88; C Bollington St Jo 88-92; P-in-c Lt Leigh and Lower Whitley 92-96; P-in-c Aston by Sutton 92-96; P-in-c Antrobus 92-96; rtd 96. *87 Wharfedale, Filey, N Yorkshire YO14 0DP*

DREDGE, David John. b 32. Cranmer Hall Dur 69. **d** 71 **p** 72. C Goole *Sheff* 71-74; P-in-c Eastoft 74-77; V Whitgift w Adlingfleet 74-77; V Whitgift w Adlingfleet and Eastoft 77-78; V Walkley 78-81; TV Bicester w Bucknell, Caversfield and Launton *Ox* 81-86; V N Brickhill and Putnoe *St Alb* 86-90; P-in-c Sarratt 90-95; rtd 95; Perm to Offic *Lich* from 95. *19 Waterdale, Wombourne, Wolverhampton WV5 0DH* Tel (01902) 897467

DREDGE, David Julian. b 36. ALA74 Sheff Univ BA59. Cranmer Hall Dur 61 Ban Ord Course 85. **d** 87 **p** 88. NSM Dwygyfylchi *Ban* 87-92; R Llanllechid from 92. *The Rectory, Llanllechid, Bangor LL57 3SD* Tel (01248) 602779

DREW, Gerald Arthur. b 36. Bps' Coll Cheshunt 59. **d** 61 **p** 62. C Lyonsdown H Trin *St Alb* 61-67; C Tring 67-71; R Bramfield w Stapleford and Waterford 71-78; V Langleybury St Paul 78-90; P-in-c Hormead, Wyddial, Anstey, Brent Pelham etc 90-95; V from 95. *The Vicarage, Great Hormead, Buntingford, Herts SG9 0NT* Tel (01763) 289258

DREW, Joseph Harold. b 09. St D Coll Lamp BA30. St Mich Coll Llan 30. **d** 32 **p** 33. C Blaenavon w Capel Newydd *Mon* 32-35; C Roath St Sav *Llan* 35-38; C Newport St Jo Bapt *Mon* 38-39; V 39-50; Chapl HM Borstal Feltham 50-55; Chapl HM Pris Man 55-58; Chapl HM Pris Pentonville 58-64; Chapl and Sec Pris Chapl Coun 64-74; Asst Chapl Gen of Pris 64-74; rtd 74; Perm to Offic *S'wark* from 82. *50 Kingsley Court, Pincott Road, Bexleyheath, Kent DA6 7LA* Tel 0181-298 1216

DREW, Michael Edgar Cecil. b 31. Or Coll Ox BA55 MA59. St Steph Ho Ox 55. **d** 57 **p** 58. C Plymouth St Pet *Ex* 57-63; Missr Pemb Coll Cam Miss Walworth 63-67; Asst Chapl All Hallows Sch Rousdon 67-75; Chapl 80-81; Lic to Offic *Ex* 76-83; Chapl Ex Sch 81-83; V Hungarton *Leic* 83-87; V Scraptoft 83-97; P-in-c Leic St Eliz Nether Hall 87-97; V Scraptoft 97; rtd 97. *The Vicarage, Church Hill, Scraptoft, Leicester LE7 9ST* Tel 0116-241 2318

DREW, Mrs Rosemary. b 43. SRN64. EAMTC 90. **d** 93 **p** 94. NSM Gt Dunmow *Chelmsf* 93-96; NSM Gt Dunmow and Barnston from 96. *Stocks Farm, Rayne, Braintree, Essex CM7 8SY* Tel (01376) 343257

DREWERY, Dr Graeme Robert. b 66. FRCO89 St Jo Coll Cam BA88 MA92 PhD94. Linc Th Coll MDiv94. **d** 94 **p** 95. C Paston *Pet* 94-97; C Cottingham *York* from 97. *10 Kingtree Avenue, Cottingham, N Humberside HU16 4DS*

DREWETT, Canon Mervyn Henry. b 27. Wadh Coll Ox BA50 MA53. Linc Th Coll 52. **d** 54 **p** 55. C Filwood Park CD *Bris* 54-58; C Bishopston 58-61; V Brislington St Chris 61-67; V Henbury 67-80; RD Westbury and Severnside 79-80; Hon Can Bris Cathl 80-94; TR Gtr Corsham 80-94; RD Chippenham 82-88; rtd 94; Perm to Offic *Bris* from 94. *14 The Beeches, Shaw, Melksham, Wilts SN12 8EP* Tel (01225) 702726

DREYER, The Ven Rodney Granville. b 55. **d** 81 **p** 82. NSM Northolt St Mary *Lon* 86-87; C Portsea St Mary *Portsm* 87-90; V Sudbury St Andr *Lon* 90-94; S Africa from 94; Adn W and S Free State, S Africa from 94. *5 Anjon Street, Bayswater, Bloemfontein, South Africa 9301*

DRINKWATER, Frank. b 10. K Coll Lon BSc32 AKC34. **d** 34 **p** 35. C Hunslet Moor St Pet *Ripon* 34-36; Nigeria 37-55; Prin St Paul's Coll Awka 46-54; Hon Can Niger 52-54; Lect St Mary's Coll Cheltenham 55-61; Asst Chapl Cheltenham Tr Colls 55-61; V Mansfield St Lawr *S'well* 61-67; Chapl Bp King Secondary Sch Linc 67-69; C Earley St Pet *Ox* 69-72; V Coley *Wakef* 72-77; RD Brighouse and Elland 74-77; rtd 77; Perm to Offic *Glouc* 78-94; Perm to Offic *Chelmsf* from 94. *The Springs Annexe, Lower Pond Street, Duddenhoe End, Saffron Walden, Essex CB11 4UP* Tel (01763) 837114

DRISCOLL, David. b 42. Lon Univ BSc64 Nottm Univ DipTh69. Linc Th Coll 68. **d** 71 **p** 72. C Walthamstow St Jo *Chelmsf* 71-76; Chapl NE Lon Poly 71-79; C-in-c Plaistow St Mary 76-79; P-in-c Stratford St Jo and Ch Ch w Forest Gate St Jas 79-89; V Theydon Bois from 89; RD Epping Forest from 92. *The Vicarage, 2 Piercing Hill, Theydon Bois, Epping, Essex CM16 7JN* Tel (01992) 814725

DRISCOLL, Edward Llewellyn. b 09. Kelham Th Coll 33. **d** 38 **p** 39. C Warminster St Denys *Sarum* 38-42; V Longbridge

Deverill w Hill Deverill 42-45; Chapl RNVR 45-46; V Burnley St Jas *Blackb* 46-56; V Ribbleton 56-67; V Fairhaven 67-74; rtd 75; Lic to Offic *Blackb* from 75. *32 Ashley Road, Lytham St Annes, Lancs FY8 3AS* Tel (01253) 727026

DRIVER, Anthony. b 28. Chich Th Coll 76. **d** 76 **p** 77. Prec Gib Cathl *Eur* 76-78; C Harton *Dur* 78-82; V Tow Law 82-91; rtd 91; Perm to Offic *York* from 93. *34 Minster Avenue, Beverley, N Humberside HU17 0NL* Tel (01482) 864448

DRIVER, Arthur John Roberts. b 44. FCIPA73 SS Coll Cam MA70 Nottm Univ DipTh75. Linc Th Coll 73. **d** 76 **p** 77. C S'wark H Trin w St Matt *S'wark* 76-80; TV N Lambeth 80-85; CMS 85-92; Sri Lanka 86-92; V Putney St Marg *S'wark* 92-97; V Streatham St Paul from 97. *St Paul's Vicarage, 63 Chillerton Road, London SW17 9BL* Tel 0181-672 5536

DRIVER, Bruce Leslie. b 42. Lon Univ LLB73 Nottm Univ DipTh77. Linc Th Coll 76. **d** 78 **p** 79. C Dunstable *St Alb* 78-81; TV 81-86; V Rickmansworth from 86; RD Rickmansworth from 91. *The Vicarage, Bury Lane, Rickmansworth, Herts WD3 1ED* Tel (01923) 772627

DRIVER, Geoffrey. b 41. Chich Th Coll 86. **d** 88 **p** 89. C Pontefract St Giles *Wakef* 88-91; V Glasshoughton 91-97; Chapl Pontefract Hosps NHS Trust from 97. *Pontefract General Infirmary, Friarwood Lane, Pontefract, W Yorkshire WF8 1PL* Tel (01977) 600600

DRIVER, Geoffrey Lester. b 59. Liv Poly BA83. Chich Th Coll 86. **d** 89 **p** 90. C Walton St Mary *Liv* 89-92; C Walton-on-the-Hill 92; C Selsey *Chich* 92-95; V Cowfold from 95. *The Vicarage, Cowfold, Horsham, W Sussex RH13 8AH* Tel (01403) 864296

DRIVER, Gordon Geoffrey. b 32. Garnett Coll Lon DipT59. Trin Coll Bris. **d** 95 **p** 96. NSM Radipole and Melcombe Regis *Sarum* from 95. *11 Greenway Close, Weymouth, Dorset DT3 5BQ* Tel (01305) 812784

DRIVER (née FRENCH), Janet Mary. b 43. Leeds Univ BA65 PGDE66. Linc Th Coll 73. **dss** 78 **d** 92 **p** 94. St Paul's Cathl *Lon* 79-80; Miss Partner CMS 86-92; Sri Lanka 86-92; NSM Putney St Marg *S'wark* 92-97; Hon C Streatham St Paul from 97. *St Paul's Vicarage, 63 Chillerton Road, London SW17 9BL* Tel 0181-672 5536

DRIVER, Miss Penelope May. b 52. N Ord Course. **d** 87 **p** 94. Dioc Youth Adv *Newc* 86-88; C Cullercoats St Geo 87-88; Youth Chapl *Ripon* 88-96; Dioc Adv Women's Min from 91; Asst Dir of Ords from 96; C Min Can Ripon Cathl from 96. *The School House, Berrygate Lane, Sharow, Ripon, N Yorkshire HG4 5BJ* Tel (01765) 607017

DRIVER, Roger John. b 64. Trin Coll Bris BA88. **d** 90 **p** 91. C Much Woolton *Liv* 90-93; C Fazakerley Em 93-94; TV from 94. *St Paul's Vicarage, Formosa Drive, Liverpool L10 7LB* Tel 0151-521 3344

DRIVER, Canon Stuart Clare. b 15. Ch Coll Cam BA37 MA41. Ridley Hall Cam 37. **d** 38 **p** 39. C Weaste *Man* 38-45; V Werneth 45-80; Hon Can Man Cathl 76-80; RD Oldham 76-80; rtd 80; Perm to Offic *Ches* from 80; Perm to Offic *Man* from 80. *9 Brookside Lane, High Lane, Stockport, Cheshire SK6 8HL* Tel (01663) 762263

DROMORE, Archdeacon of. *See* NEILL, The Ven William Barnet

DROMORE, Dean of. *See* CHILLINGWORTH, The Very Revd David Robert

DROWLEY, Arthur. b 28. Oak Hill Th Coll 54. **d** 56 **p** 57. C Longfleet *Sarum* 56-59; C Wallington H Trin *S'wark* 59-62; V Taunton St Jas *B & W* 62-73; RD Taunton N 72-73; V Rodbourne Cheney *Bris* 73-87; R Bigbury, Ringmore and Kingston *Ex* 87-94; rtd 94; NSM Bigbury, Ringmore and Kingston *Ex* 94-95; NSM Modbury, Bigbury, Ringmore w Kingston etc from 95. *29 Summerhill Crescent, Liverton, Newton Abbot, Devon TQ12 6HG* Tel (01626) 824809

DROWN, Richard. b 19. BNC Ox BA41 MA43. Wycliffe Hall Ox 41. **d** 42 **p** 43. C St Helens St Helen *Liv* 42-45; Chapl K Coll Budo Uganda 46-65; Hd Master St Andr Sch Turi Kenya 65-73; Hd Master Edin Ho Sch New Milton 73-84; rtd 84; Hon C Brockenhurst *Win* from 85. *3 Waters Green Court, Brockenhurst, Hants SO42 7QR* Tel (01590) 624038

DRUCE, Brian Lemuel. b 31. ARICS55. Bps' Coll Cheshunt 58. **d** 60 **p** 61. C Whitton St Aug *Lon* 60-63; C Minehead *B & W* 63-66; R Birch St Agnes *Man* 66-70; V Overbury w Alstone, Teddington and Lt Washbourne *Worc* 70-81; Ind Chapl 81-91; rtd 91. *Park Cottage, Elmley Castle, Pershore, Worcs WR10 3HU* Tel (01386) 710577

DRUCE, John Perry. b 34. ALCM86 Em Coll Cam BA57 MA61 Lambeth STh97. Wycliffe Hall Ox 57. **d** 59 **p** 60. C Wednesbury St Bart *Lich* 59-62; C Bushbury 62-64; V Walsall Wood 64-74; R Farnborough *Roch* 74-87; R E Bergholt *St E* from 87; P-in-c Bentley w Tattingstone from 95. *The Rectory, White Horse Road, Colchester CO7 6TR* Tel (01206) 298076

DRUMMOND, Canon Christopher John Vaughan. b 26. Magd Coll Ox MA51 Magd Coll Cam MA56. Ridley Hall Cam 51. **d** 53 **p** 54. C Barking St Marg *Chelmsf* 53-56; Tutor Ridley Hall Cam 56-59; Lic to Offic *Ely* 57-62; Chapl Clare Coll Cam 59-62; Nigeria 63-69; V Walthamstow St Jo *Chelmsf* 69-74; P-in-c Stantonbury *Ox* 74-75; R 75-84; P-in-c Ducklington 84-88; Dioc Ecum Officer 84-88; Can Ibadan from 87; Home Sec Gen Syn Bd for Miss and Unity 88-91; rtd 91; P-in-c Colton *Lich* 91-94; Perm to Offic from 94. *Church Cottage, Slitting Mill, Rugeley, Staffs WS15 2TG* Tel (01889) 570172

DRUMMOND, John Malcolm. b 44. Nottm Univ CertEd65. Edin Th Coll 68. **d** 71 **p** 72. C Kirkholt *Man* 71-74; C Westleigh St Pet 74-76; Hd of RE Leigh High Sch from 76; Lic Preacher from 76; Hon C Leigh St Jo 84-90; Hon C Tonge Moor from 90. *14 Bull's Head Cottages, Turton, Bolton BL7 0HS* Tel (01204) 852232

DRUMMOND, Josceline Maurice Vaughan (Jos). b 29. Lon Univ DipTh59 BD70. Wycliffe Hall Ox 55. **d** 58 **p** 59. C Tunbridge Wells St Jo *Roch* 58-60; C Walthamstow St Mary *Chelmsf* 60-62; V Oulton *Lich* 62-68; V Leyton St Cath *Chelmsf* 71-85; Gen Dir CMJ 85-94; Public Preacher *St Alb* 88-94; rtd 94. *3 Fryth Mead, St Albans, Herts AL3 4TN* Tel (01727) 857620

DRURY, Esmond Peter. b 24. Sheff Univ BSc43 Newc Univ DipEd64. Coll of Resurr Mirfield 47. **d** 49 **p** 50. C Alfreton *Derby* 49-53; C Long Eaton St Laur 53-55; C Beighton 55-57; Min Hackenthorpe Ch Ch CD 57-60; rtd 89. *74 Beach Road, North Shields, Tyne & Wear NE30 2QW* Tel 0191-257 4350

DRURY, The Very Revd John Henry. b 36. Trin Hall Cam MA66. Westcott Ho Cam 61. **d** 63 **p** 64. C St Jo Wood *Lon* 63-66; Chapl Down Coll Cam 66-69; Chapl Ex Coll Ox 69-73; Can Res Nor Cathl *Nor* 73-79; Vice-Dean 78-79; Lect Sussex Univ 79-81; Dean and Chapl K Coll Cam 81-91; Dean Ch Ch *Ox* from 91. *The Deanery, Christ Church, Oxford OX1 1DP* Tel (01865) 276162

DRURY, Michael Dru. b 31. Trin Coll Ox BA55 MA59. Wycliffe Hall Ox DipTh57. **d** 58 **p** 59. C Fulham St Mary N End *Lon* 58-62; C Blackheath St Jo *S'wark* 62-64; Chapl and Asst Master Canford Sch Wimborne 64-80; Chapl and Teacher Fernhill Manor Sch New Milton 80-81; P-in-c Stowe *Ox* 82-92; Asst Master Stowe Sch Bucks 82-92; R Rampton w Laneham, Treswell, Cottam and Stokeham *S'well* 92-96; rtd 96. *Tanfield, Giddy Lane, Wimborne, Dorset BH21 2QT* Tel (01202) 881246

DRURY, Valerie Doreen. b 40. MBATOD80 Univ of Wales (Cardiff) BA62 K Coll Lon PGCE63 Lon Inst of Educn ADEDC80. Oak Hill Th Coll 85. **d** 87 **p** 94. NSM Becontree St Alb *Chelmsf* 87-89; NSM Becontree S from 89. *63 Tilney Road, Dagenham, Essex RM9 6HL* Tel 0181-592 7285

DRURY, William. b 30. Qu Coll Cam BA53 MA56. Trin Coll Toronto STB61. **d** 61 **p** 61. Canada 61-66; C Ashford *Cant* 66-70; V Milton next Sittingbourne 70-96; rtd 96. *Whitefriars Cottage, 9 Langdon Street, Tring, Herts HP23 6AZ* Tel (01442) 891979

DRYDEN, Canon Leonard. b 29. MIEE59 MIMechE59 Lon Univ BD64 Bath Univ MSc73. Ridley Hall Cam. **d** 61 **p** 62. C Luton w E Hyde *St Alb* 61-65; C-in-c Bedminster *Bris* 65-74; Bp's Soc and Ind Adv 65-74; Chapl Bris Cathl 66-70; Hon Can Bris Cathl 70-74; Dir CORAT 74-76; Sec from 76; Team Ldr and Convener Lon Ind Chapl *Lon* 77-85; V Frindsbury w Upnor *Roch* 85-91; rtd 91; P-in-c Sevenoaks Weald *Roch* 91-95. *1 King Alfred Terrace, Winchester SO23 7DE* Tel (01962) 852170

DRYE, Douglas John. b 37. Man Univ BSc61. Clifton Th Coll. **d** 63 **p** 64. C Whalley Range St Edm *Man* 63-66; C Drypool St Columba w St Andr and St Pet *York* 66-68; V Worsbrough Common *Sheff* 68-86; R Armthorpe 86-92; rtd 92; Perm to Offic *Pet* from 92. *25 Willow Crescent, Oakham, Leics LE15 6EQ* Tel (01572) 770429

DUBLIN (Christ Church), Dean of. *See* PATERSON, The Very Revd John Thomas Farquhar

DUBLIN (St Patrick's), Dean of. *See* STEWART, The Very Revd Maurice Evan

DUBLIN and Bishop of Glendalough, Archbishop of. *See* EMPEY, The Most Revd Walton Newcome Francis

DUBLIN, Archdeacon of. *See* LINNEY, The Ven Gordon Charles Scott

DUCE, Alan Richard. b 41. St Pet Coll Ox BA65 MA68. Cuddesdon Coll 65. **d** 67 **p** 68. C Boston *Linc* 67-71; Chapl St Geo Hosp Lon 71-75; Chapl HM Pris Pentonville 75-76; Chapl HM Pris The Verne 76-81; Chapl HM Pris Linc from 81; Gen Preacher *Linc* from 81. *The Chaplain's Office, HM Prison, Greetwell Road, Lincoln LN2 4BD* Tel (01522) 533633 Fax 532116

DUCKETT, Brian John. b 45. ALCD70. **d** 70 **p** 71. C S Lambeth St Steph *S'wark* 70-73; C Norwood St Luke 73-75; C Bushbury *Lich* 75-77; TV 77-79; V Dover St Martin *Cant* 79-92; TR Swindon Dorcan *Bris* from 92; RD Highworth from 95. *The Vicarage, St Paul's Drive, Swindon SN3 5BY* Tel (01793) 525130

DUCKETT, Edward. b 36. Keble Coll Ox BA59 MA61 Portsm Poly CQSW72. Cuddesdon Coll 59. **d** 61 **p** 62. C Portsea St Cuth *Portsm* 61-65; C Rotherham *Sheff* 65-68; Lic to Offic *Portsm* 68-69; Hon Chapl Portsm Cathl 69-75; Perm to Offic *Ely* 75-82; R Rampton 82-89; R Willingham 82-89; RD N Stowe 83-89; P-in-c Ramsey 89-90; P-in-c Upwood w Gt and Lt Raveley 89-90; TR The Ramseys and Upwood 90-92; RD St Ives 89-92; P-in-c Bassingbourn 93-95; V 95-96; P-in-c Whaddon 93-95; V 95-96; rtd 96. *77 Lower Chestnut Street, Worcester WR1 1PD* Tel (01905) 21862

DUCKETT, John Dollings. b 41. Nottm Univ BA62 BTh81. Linc Th Coll 79. **d** 81 **p** 82. C Boston *Linc* 81-84; V Baston 84-86; V Langtoft Gp 86-88; V Sutterton and Wigtoft 88-89; R Sutterton w Fosdyke and Algarkirk 89-92; P-in-c Chapel St Leonards w Hogsthorpe 92-97; V from 97. *The Vicarage, Church Lane,*

Chapel St Leonards, Skegness, Lincs PE24 5UJ Tel (01754) 872666

DUCKWORTH, Capt Brian George. b 47. CA79. Edin Th Coll 85. **d** 87 **p** 88. C Sutton in Ashfield St Mary *S'well* 87-95; C Sutton in Ashfield St Mich 89-95; P-in-c from 95. *The Vicarage, 11A Deepdale Gardens, Sutton-in-Ashfield, Notts NG17 4ER* Tel (01623) 555031

DUCKWORTH, Derek. b 29. Fitzw Ho Cam BA52 MA58 Lon Univ PGCE66 Lanc Univ PhD72. Oak Hill Th Coll 52. **d** 54 **p** 55. C Preston All SS *Blackb* 54-57; C Sutton *Liv* 57-58; Hon C Wakef St Jo *Wakef* 58-60; Public Preacher *Blackb* 60-64; C Whalley 64-73; Hon C Newbury *Ox* 73-80; Perm to Offic 80-81; Perm to Offic *Cant* 81-84 and 85-86; P-in-c Dymchurch w Burmarsh and Newchurch 84-85; Chapl Leybourne Grange Hosp W Malling 85-86; P-in-c Rampton w Laneham, Treswell, Cottam and Stokeham *S'well* 86-89; R 89-91; rtd 91; Perm to Offic *Cant* from 91. *Glebe Cottage, 11 Church Walk, Headcorn, Ashford, Kent TN27 9ND* Tel (01622) 890143

DUDDING, Edward Leslie (Father Gregory). b 30. Auckland Univ MSc52 St Jo Coll Auckland LTh56. **d** 57 **p** 57. New Zealand 57-60; Lic to Offic *Chich* from 62; CSWG from 62; Father Superior from 73. *Monastery of The Holy Trinity, Crawley Down, Crawley, W Sussex RH10 4LH* Tel (01342) 712074

DUDLEY, Harold George. b 14. St Mich Coll Llan 68. **d** 70 **p** 70. C Fleur-de-Lis *Mon* 70-73; V Goldcliffe and Whiston and Nash 73-83; rtd 83; Lic to Offic *Mon* from 83. *3 St John's Court, Oakfield Road, Newport NP6 4LNJ* Tel (01633) 253610

DUDLEY, Mrs Janet Carr. b 36. EMMTC 86. **d** 89 **p** 94. Hon C Countesthorpe w Foston *Leic* 89-94; Hon C Arnesby w Shearsby and Bruntingthorpe from 94. *The Vicarage, Fenny Lane, Shearsby, Lutterworth, Leics LE17 6PL* Tel 0116-247 8371

DUDLEY, John Donald Swanborough. b 34. Edin Univ DipAgr53 Ox Univ BTh95. St Alb and Ox Min Course 96. **d** 97. NSM Emmer Green *Ox* from 97. *26 Russet Glade, Caversham, Reading RG4 8UJ* Tel 0118-947 0265

DUDLEY, John Rea. b 31. Pemb Coll Cam BA54 MA58. St Steph Ho Ox. **d** 57 **p** 58. C Kennington St Jo *S'wark* 57-61; C Merstham and Gatton 61-68; V N Gosforth *Newc* 68-79; RD Newc Cen 77-82; V Newc St Jo 79-91; V Sunbury *Lon* from 91. *The Vicarage, Thames Street, Sunbury-on-Thames, Middx TW16 6AA* Tel (01932) 785448

DUDLEY, Dr Martin Raymond. b 53. K Coll Lon BD77 AKC77 MTh78 PhD94 DPS79 FRHistS95. St Mich Coll Llan 78. **d** 79 **p** 80. C Whitchurch *Llan* 79-83; V Weston *St Alb* 83-88; P-in-c Ardeley 87-88; V Owlsmoor *Ox* 88-95; Lect Simon of Cyrene Th Inst 92-95; R Smithfield St Bart Gt *Lon* from 95. *The Watch House, Giltspur Street, London EC1A 9DE* Tel 0171-606 5171 or 248 3110 Fax 600 6909

DUDLEY, Miss Wendy Elizabeth. b 46. City of Sheff Coll CertEd68. Cranmer Hall Dur 79. **dss** 81 **d** 87 **p** 94. Cumnor *Ox* 81-87; Par Dn 87-89; Par Dn Hodge Hill *Birm* 89-94; C 94-95; TV from 95. *95 Hodge Hill Road, Birmingham B34 6DX* Tel 0121-783 0140

DUDLEY-SMITH, James. b 66. Fitzw Coll Cam BA89 MA92. Wycliffe Hall Ox BTh94. **d** 97. C New Borough and Leigh *Sarum* from 97. *7 Ethelbert Road, Wimborne, Dorset BH21 1BH* Tel (01202) 889405

✠**DUDLEY-SMITH, The Rt Revd Timothy.** b 26. Pemb Coll Cam BA47 MA51. Lambeth MLitt91 Ridley Hall Cam 48. **d** 50 **p** 51 **c** 81. C Erith St Paul *Roch* 50-53; Lic to Offic *S'wark* 53-62; Hd of Cam Univ Miss Bermondsey 53-55; Chapl 55-60; Ed Sec Evang Alliance and Ed Crusade 55-59; Asst Sec CPAS 59-65; Gen Sec 65-73; Adn Nor 73-81; Suff Bp Thetford 81-91; rtd 92. *9 Ashlands, Ford, Salisbury SP4 6DY* Tel (01722) 326417

DUDLEY, Archdeacon of. *See* GATHERCOLE, The Ven John Robert

DUDLEY, Area Bishop of. *See* HOARE, The Rt Revd Rupert William Noel

DUERDEN, Martin James. b 55. Liv Poly BA77. Oak Hill Th Coll 86. **d** 88 **p** 89. C Tunbridge Wells St Jas *Roch* 88-92; V Southport SS Simon and Jude *Liv* from 92. *The Vicarage, 128 Roe Lane, Southport, Merseyside PR9 7PJ* Tel (01704) 27095

DUFF, Adam Alexander Howard. b 16. Linc Coll Ox BA38 DipTh43 MA46. Wycliffe Hall Ox 42. **d** 43 **p** 44. C Langley St Jo *Birm* 43-45; C Enfield St Andr *Lon* 45-47; Asst Master Ch Ch Cathl Sch Ox 47-49; Lic to Offic *Ox* 48-54; Org Dir W Midl Area ICF 49-51; Asst Dir Lon and SE England 54-59; Lic to Offic *Ripon* 51-54; C Kensington St Mary Abbots w St Geo *Lon* 59-62; V Paddington H Trin w St Paul 62-79; C Kilburn St Aug w St Jo 79-81; rtd 81. *Cedar Cottage, Water Eaton Road, Oxford OX2 7QQ* Tel (01865) 58621

DUFF, Mrs Alison. b 59. SEN79. Sarum & Wells Th Coll CMinlStuds92. **d** 92 **p** 94. Par Dn Banbury *Ox* 92-94; C 94-95; C Wokingham All SS from 95. *43A Eastheath Avenue, Wokingham, Berks RG41 2PP* Tel 0118-979 1152

DUFF, Andrew John. b 57. MIOT. Sarum & Wells Th Coll CMinlStuds92. **d** 92 **p** 93. C Banbury *Ox* 92-95; C Bracknell 95-96; TV from 96. *St Andrew's Vicarage, Stoney Road, Bracknell, Berks RG42 1XY* Tel 01344 425229

DUFF, Garden Ian. b 34. ACGI56 Imp Coll Lon BScEng56. Sarum & Wells Th Coll 92. **d** 93 **p** 94. NSM Ashton Gifford *Sarum* from 93. *West Farm, Knook, Warminster, Wilts BA12 0JF* Tel (01985) 850291

DUFF, John Alexander. b 57. York Univ BA78. EMMTC DTPS94. **d** 94 **p** 95. NSM Linc St Geo Swallowbeck *Linc* from 94. *34 Swallowbeck Avenue, Lincoln LN6 7HA* Tel (01522) 683475

DUFF, Timothy Cameron. b 40. Solicitor 65 G&C Coll Cam BA62 LLM63 MA66. NE Ord Course 90. **d** 93 **p** 94. NSM Tynemouth Priory *Newc* 93-96; NSM N Shields from 96. *26 The Drive, North Shields, Tyne & Wear NE30 4JW* Tel 0191-257 1463 Fax 296 1904

DUFFETT, Canon Paul Stanton. b 33. Keble Coll Ox BA55 MA59. Ripon Hall Ox DipTh58. **d** 59 **p** 60. C Portsea St Cuth *Portsm* 59-63; S Africa 63-80; P-in-c Greatham w Empshott *Portsm* 80-85; R 85-88; Hon Can Zululand from 87; R Papworth Everard *Ely* from 88; Chapl Papworth Hosps from 88. *The Rectory, Papworth Everard, Cambridge CB3 8QJ* Tel (01480) 830061

DUFFETT-SMITH (née RUSHTON), Ms Patricia Mary (Trisha). b 54. Lon Univ BPharm76 MRPharmS77. EAMTC 94. **d** 97. NSM Haddenham *Ely* from 97. *41 Denmark Road, Cottenham, Cambridge CB4 4QS* Tel (01954) 201276 E-mail pmd23.cam.ac.uk

DUFFIELD, Dr Ian Keith. b 47. K Coll Lon BD71 AKC71 MTh73. NY Th Sem DMin84. **d** 73 **p** 74. C Broxbourne *St Alb* 73-77; C Harpenden St Nic 77-81; TV Sheff Manor *Sheff* 81-87; V Walkley from 87. *St Mary's Vicarage, 150 Walkley Road, Sheffield S6 2XQ* Tel 0114-234 5029

DUFFIELD, John Ernest. b 55. BA86. Oak Hill Th Coll 83. **d** 86 **p** 87. C Walton Breck Ch Ch *Liv* 86-89; TV Fazakerley Em from 89. *St George's Vicarage, 72 Stopgate Lane, Liverpool L9 6AR* Tel 0151-523 1536

DUFFIELD, Ronald Bertram Charles (Ron). b 26. Hull Univ Coll BA49 TCert50. Sarum & Wells Th Coll 91. **d** 92 **p** 93. NSM E Knoyle, Semley and Sedgehill *Sarum* 92-95; rtd 95. *Address temp unknown*

DUFTON, Francis Trevor. b 29. Trin Coll Cam BA51 MA55. Ridley Hall Cam 51. **d** 53 **p** 54. C Ware Ch Ch *St Alb* 53-56; V Bengeo Ch Ch 56-67; R Elmdon and Wendon Lofts *Chelmsf* 67-80; R Strethall 67-80; P-in-c Bottisham *Ely* 80-85; P-in-c Swaffham Bulbeck 80-85; rtd 85; Perm to Offic *Ely* 85-91. *23 Hyde Road, Eastbourne, E Sussex BN21 4SX* Tel (01323) 416659

✠**DUGGAN, The Rt Revd John Coote.** b 18. TCD BA40 BD47. CITC 41. **d** 41 **p** 42 **c** 70. C Cork St Luke *C, C & R* 41-43; C Taney Ch Ch *D & G* 43-48; R Portarlington *M & K* 48-55; I Glenageary *D & G* 55-69; I Aughaval *T, K & A* 69-70; Adn Tuam 69-70; Bp T, K & A 70-85; rtd 85; Chapl Malaga *Eur* 93-94. *22 Pennington Park, Cairnshill Road, Belfast BT8 4GJ*

DUGUID, Reginald Erskine. b 29. S'wark Ord Course. **d** 88 **p** 89. NSM Notting Hill All SS w St Columb *Lon* from 88. *53 Sandbourne, Dartmouth Close, London W11 1DA* Tel 0171-221 4436

DUKE, Alan Arthur. b 38. Tyndale Hall Bris 59. **d** 64 **p** 65. C Whalley Range St Marg *Man* 64-67; C Folkestone H Trin w Ch Ch *Cant* 67-71; V Queenborough 71-76; V Bearsted w Thurnham 76-86; P-in-c Thurnham w Detling 77-82; P-in-c Torquay St Luke *Ex* 86-91; R Barham w Bishopsbourne and Kingston *Cant* from 91; Dioc Communications Officer 91-95. *The Rectory, The Street, Barham, Canterbury, Kent CT4 6PA* Tel (01227) 831340 Fax as telephone

DUKE, Brian Peter. b 33. Pemb Coll Cam BA55 MA59. Ely Th Coll 55. **d** 57 **p** 58. C Blyth St Mary *Newc* 57-61; C Newc St Andr 61-63; Perm to Offic *Guildf* from 64. *24 Regent Close, Fleet, Aldershot, Hants GU13 9NS* Tel (01252) 614548

DULFER, John Guidi. b 37. Lich Th Coll 62. **d** 64 **p** 65. C Fenny Stratford and Water Eaton *Ox* 64-67; C Cheshunt *St Alb* 67-68; C Kennington Cross St Anselm *S'wark* 68-74; C N Lambeth 74-76; P-in-c Kensington St Phil Earl's Court *Lon* 76-79; V 79-84; Chapl Odstock Hosp Salisbury 84; USA from 84. *135 West 22 Street, New York, NY 10011, USA*

DULLEY, Arthur John Franklyn. b 32. Mert Coll Ox BA54 MA57. St Jo Coll Nottm 69. **d** 71 **p** 72. Lect St Jo Coll Nottm 71-96; Hon C Attenborough w Chilwell *S'well* 71-73; C Penn Fields *Lich* 73-74; Chapl Aldenham Sch Herts 74-79; Chapl HM Pris Ashwell 79-87; V Langham *Pet* 79-96; rtd 96. *8 Prickwillow Road, Ely, Cambs CB7 4QP* Tel (01353) 664381

DUMAT, Mrs Jennifer (Jenny). b 42. ARCM62. Qu Coll Birm 80 EMMTC 82. **dss** 83 **d** 87 **p** 94. Chapl Asst Pilgrim Hosp Boston 83-94; P-in-c Friskney *Linc* from 94. *The Vicarage, Yawling Road, Friskney, Boston, Lincs PE22 8NA* Tel (01754) 820418

✠**DUMPER, The Rt Revd Anthony Charles (Tony).** b 23. Ch Coll Cam BA45 MA48. Westcott Ho Cam. **d** 47 **p** 48 **c** 77. C E Greenwich Ch Ch w St Andr and St Mich *S'wark* 47-49; Malaya 49-63; Malaysia 63-64; Dean Singapore 64-70; V Stockton St Pet *Dur* 70-77; P-in-c Stockton H Trin 76-77; RD Stockton 70-77; Suff Bp Dudley *Worc* 77-93; rtd 93; Asst Bp Birm from 93. *117 Burberry Close, Birmingham B30 1TB* Tel 0121-458 3011

DUNBAR, George Alban Charles. b 08. AKC40. **d** 40 **p** 41. C Teddington St Mark *Lon* 40-44; Chapl RAFVR 44-47; V Is of Dogs Ch Ch and St Jo w St Luke *Lon* 47-53; V Kentish Town St Barn 53-56; V Whetstone St Jo 56-81; rtd 81; Perm to Offic

Linc from 82. *63 Harrowby Road, Grantham, Lincs NG31 9ED* Tel (01476) 562935

DUNBAR, Peter Lamb. b 46. Bede Coll Dur DipEd68. Lambeth STh77 N Ord Course 78. **d** 81 **p** 82. NSM Knaresborough *Ripon* 81-82; C Knaresborough 82-84; R Farnham w Scotton, Staveley, Copgrove etc 84-92; V Upper Nidderdale from 92; Chapl St Aid Sch Harrogate 86-94. *The Vicarage, Pateley Bridge, Harrogate, N Yorkshire HG3 5LQ* Tel (01423) 711414

DUNCAN, Canon Anthony Douglas. b 30. Chich Th Coll 60. **d** 62 **p** 63. C Tewkesbury w Walton Cardiff *Glouc* 62-65; V Dean Forest St Paul 65-69; R Highnam w Lassington and Rudford 69-73; V Newc St Jo *Newc* 73-79; V Warkworth and Acklington 79-87; Hon Can Newc Cathl 84-95; V Whitley 87-95; Chapl Hexham Gen and War Memorial Hosps 87-95; rtd 95. *7 Aydon Drive, Corbridge, Northd NE45 5DE* Tel (01434) 633149

DUNCAN, Canon Bruce. b 38. MBE93. FRSA Leeds Univ BA60. Cuddesdon Coll 65. **d** 67 **p** 68. C Armley St Bart *Ripon* 67-69; Lic to Offic *Ely* 69-70; Chapl Vienna w Budapest and Prague *Eur* 71-75; V Crediton *Ex* 75-82; R Crediton and Shobrooke 82-86; RD Cadbury 76-81 and 84-86; Can Res Man Cathl *Man* 86-95; Prin Sarum & Wells Th Coll from 95; Can and Preb Sarum Cathl *Sarum* from 95. *Sarum and Wells Theological College, 19 The Close, Salisbury SP1 2EE* Tel (01722) 332235

DUNCAN, Charles Patrick Maxwell. b 37. Ch Ch Ox MA62. St Jo Coll Dur 78. **d** 81 **p** 82. C York St Mich-le-Belfrey *York* 81-84; Perm to Offic 84-86; Asst Chapl Ch Hosp Horsham from 86. *Christ's Hospital, Horsham, W Sussex RH13 7LS* Tel (01403) 258195

DUNCAN, Christopher Robin (Chris). b 41. AKC71. **d** 72 **p** 73. C Allington *Cant* 72-77; P-in-c Wittersham 77-82; R Wittersham w Stone-in-Oxney and Ebony 82-85; P-in-c Chilham 85-86; V 86-92; P-in-c Challock w Molash 87-92; RD W Bridge 92-95; V Chilham w Challock and Molash from 92. *The Vicarage, 3 Hambrook Close, Chilham, Canterbury, Kent CT4 8EJ* Tel (01227) 730235

DUNCAN, Colin Richard. b 34. SS Coll Cam BA58 MA60. Ripon Coll Cuddesdon 83. **d** 85 **p** 86. C Stafford *Lich* 85-89; C Wednesfield 89-90; TV from 90. *St Alban's House, Griffiths Drive, Wolverhampton WV11 2LJ* Tel (01902) 732317

DUNCAN, The Very Rev Gregor Duthie. b 50. Glas Univ MA72 Clare Coll Cam PhD77 Or Coll Ox BA83. Ripon Coll Cuddesdon 81. **d** 83 **p** 84. C Oakham, Hambleton, Egleton, Braunston and Brooke *Pet* 83-86; Edin Th Coll 87-89; R Largs *Glas* from 89; Dean Glas from 96. *St Columba's Rectory, Aubery Crescent, Largs, Ayrshire KA30 8PR* Tel (01475) 673143 Fax 67020

DUNCAN, James Montgomerie. b 29. Edin Th Coll 53. **d** 56 **p** 57. C Edin St Pet *Edin* 56-59; C Edin Old St Paul 59-60; S Africa 60-65; Prov Youth Org Scotland 65-69; R Edin St Salvador *Edin* 69-86; Chapl HM Pris Saughton 69-86; R Aberlour *Mor* from 86; R Fochabers from 86. *Gordon Chapel House, Castle Street, Fochabers, Morayshire IV32 7DW* Tel (01343) 820337

DUNCAN, John. b 22. Open Univ BA. Roch Th Coll 64. **d** 66 **p** 67. C Gainsborough All SS *Linc* 66-68; C Boultham 68-71; V W Pinchbeck 72-76; Canada 76-81; R Ridgewell w Ashen, Birdbrook and Sturmer *Chelmsf* 81-88; rtd 88; Perm to Offic *Pet* from 91. *20 Westcott Way, Northampton NN3 3BE* Tel (01604) 30797

DUNCAN, The Ven John Finch. b 33. Univ Coll Ox BA57 MA63. Cuddesdon Coll 57. **d** 59 **p** 60. C S Bank *York* 59-61; SSF 61-62; C Birm St Pet *Birm* 62-65; Chapl Birm Univ 65-76; V Kings Heath 76-85; Hon Can Birm Cathl 83-85; Adn Birm from 85. *122 Westfield Road, Birmingham B15 3JQ* Tel 0121-454 3402 Fax 455 6178

DUNCAN, Peter Harold Furlong. b 25. AKC52 Lon Univ BA68 Golds Coll Lon BA71 MPhil79. **d** 53 **p** 54. C Sheff St Geo and St Steph *Sheff* 53-56; C Wealdstone H Trin *Lon* 56-57; V Battersea St Pet *S'wark* 57-64; Nigeria 64-66; Hon C All Hallows by the Tower etc *Lon* 67-73; Ind Chapl Lon Docks 67-73; Sen Lect in Sociology City of Lon Poly 73-87; Hon C Gt Ilford St Andr *Chelmsf* 73-80; P-in-c Gt Canfield 80-87; P-in-c N Woolwich w Silvertown 87-93; rtd 93; Perm to Offic *York* from 93. *179 Windsor Drive, Haxby, York YO3 3YD* Tel (01904) 769888

DUNCAN, Tom. **d** 97. NSM Poplar *Lon* from 97. *1 Chardwell Close, London E6 4RR*

DUNCAN, Mrs Virginia Elinor. b 39. DNEd. WMMTC 86 Qu Coll Birm 86. **d** 89 **p** 94. Par Dn Wednesfield *Lich* 89-94; C from 94. *St Alban's House, Griffiths Drive, Wolverhampton WV11 2LJ* Tel (01902) 732317

DUNCAN, The Ven William Albert. b 30. TCD BA53 MA61 BD66. CITC 54. **d** 54 **p** 55. C Bangor Abbey *D & D* 54-57; C Larne and Inver *Conn* 57-61; Hd of Trin Coll Miss Belf 61-66; I Rasharkin w Finvoy 66-78; I Ramoan w Ballycastle and Culfeightrin 78-96; Adn Dalriada 93-96; rtd 96. *8 Beech Hill, Ballymoney, Co Antrim BT53 6DB* Tel (01265) 664285

DUNCAN-JONES, Andrew Roby. b 14. St Edm Hall Ox BA38 MA41. Linc Th Coll 39. **d** 40 **p** 41. C Bolsover *Derby* 40-42; Chapl St Mary's Cathl *Edin* 42-45; Hd Master Prebendal Sch Chich 45-51; PV Chich Cathl *Chich* 45-51; India 51-53; V Amport w Monxton *Win* 53-56; Hd St Chad's Cathl Sch Lich 57-70; Preb Lich Cathl *Lich* 67-68; R Lochgilphead *Arg* 70-79; rtd 79; Perm to Offic *Arg* from 79. *Barrachourin, Kilmartin, Lochgilphead, Argyll PA31 8QP* Tel (01546) 510204

DUNCANSON, Derek James. b 47. TD93. AKC69 Open Univ BA80 Lon Univ MA(Ed)93 FCollP94. St Aug Coll Cant 69. **d** 70 **p** 71. C Norbury St Oswald *Cant* 70-72; CF (TAVR) from 71; C Woodham *Guildf* 72-76; CF 76-79; V Burneside *Carl* 79-84; R Coppull St Jo *Blackb* 84-86; Chapl Bloxham Sch from 86. *Courtington House, Courtington Lane, Bloxham, Banbury, Oxon OX15 4PQ* Tel (01295) 720626

DUNDAS, Edward Paul. b 67. NUU BSc88. TCD Div Sch BTh91. **d** 91 **p** 92. C Portadown St Mark *Arm* 91-95; I Ardtrea w Desertcreat from 95. *Tullyhogue Rectory, 50 Lower Grange Road, Cookstown, Co Tyrone BT80 8SL* Tel (01648) 761163

DUNDAS, Edward Thompson. b 36. TCD BA63. **d** 64 **p** 65. C Conwall *D & R* 64-67; I Kilbarron 67-78; I Donagheady 78-84; I Kilmore St Aid w St Sav *Arm* from 84. *38 Vicarage Road, Portadown, Craigavon, Co Armagh BT62 4HF* Tel (01762) 332664

DUNDEE, Provost of. *Vacant*

DUNFORD, Malcolm. b 34. FCA74. EMMTC 73. **d** 76 **p** 77. NSM Frodingham *Linc* from 76. *57 Rowland Road, Scunthorpe, S Humberside DN16 1SP* Tel (01724) 840879

DUNFORD, Reginald John. b 15. Worc Ord Coll. **d** 60 **p** 61. C Selston *S'well* 60-61; V Bestwood St Matt 61-68; V Lenton 68-80; rtd 80; Perm to Offic *S'well* from 80. *Mosley, 33 Cow Lane, Bramcote, Nottingham NG9 3DJ* Tel 0115-925 6841

DUNHILL, Robin Arnold. b 15. BNC Ox BA38 MA46. Cuddesdon Coll. **d** 46 **p** 47. C Pet All SS *Pet* 46-53; V Wellingborough All SS 53-63; V Hampstead Garden Suburb *Lon* 63-73; RD W Barnet 70-73; Perm to Offic *Pet* from 74; rtd 80. *Manor Cottage, Newton, Kettering, Northants NN14 1BW* Tel (01536) 460659

DUNK, Michael Robin. b 43. Oak Hill Th Coll BA82. **d** 82 **p** 83. C Northampton All SS w St Kath *Pet* 82-86; Ind Chapl *Birm* 86-96; P-in-c Warley Woods 96; V from 96. *St Hilda's Vicarage, Abbey Road, Smethwick, Warley, W Midlands B67 5NQ* Tel 0121-429 1384

DUNK, Peter Norman. b 43. Sarum Th Coll 67. **d** 69 **p** 70. C Sheff St Mary w St Simon w St Matthias *Sheff* 69-71; C Margate St Jo *Cant* 71-74; Dioc Youth Officer *Birm* 74-78; R Hulme Ascension *Man* 78-83; V E Farleigh and Coxheath *Roch* 83; P-in-c Linton w Hunton 83; R Coxheath w E Farleigh, Hunton and Linton 83-88; Australia from 88. *105 Shenton Road, Swanbourne, W Australia 6010* Tel Perth (9) 384 2958 or 385 2236

DUNKERLEY, James Hobson. b 39. Seabury-Western Th Sem BD69 STh70. **d** 64 **p** 65. C Stirchley *Birm* 64-66; C Perry Barr 66-70; USA from 70. *621 Belmont Avenue, Chicago, Illinois 60657, USA*

DUNKLEY, Christopher. b 52. Edin Univ MA74 Ox Univ BA77 MA81. St Steph Ho Ox 75. **d** 78 **p** 79. C Newbold w Dunston *Derby* 78-82; C Chesterfield St Mary and All SS 82; Chapl Leic Univ *Leic* 82-85; P-in-c Leic St Aid 85; TV Leic Ascension 85-92; V Leic St Aid 92-97; V Holbrooks *Cov* from 97. *St Luke's Vicarage, Rotherham Road, Coventry CV7 4FE* Tel (01203) 688604

DUNKLEY, Reginald Alfred Lorenz. b 13. Clifton Th Coll 56. **d** 58 **p** 59. C Meopham *Roch* 59-60; C Belvedere All SS 60-64; R Longfield 64-78; rtd 78. *33 Sheriff Drive, Chatham, Kent ME5 9PU* Tel (01634) 862143

DUNLOP, Canon Arthur John. b 27. AKC52. **d** 53 **p** 54. C Loughton St Jo *Chelmsf* 53-57; C-in-c Chelmsf All SS CD 57-65; R Laindon w Basildon 65-72; RD Basildon 65-72; V Maldon All SS w St Pet 72-92; RD Maldon 73-82; Hon Can Chelmsf Cathl 80-92; RD Maldon and Dengie 89-92; rtd 92; Perm to Offic *Chelmsf* from 92. *Maeldune, 64 Highfield Road, Sudbury, Suffolk CO10 6QJ* Tel (01787) 881699

DUNLOP, Canon Ian Geoffrey David. b 25. FSA New Coll Ox BA48 MA56. Linc Th Coll 54. **d** 56 **p** 57. C Hatfield *St Alb* 56-60; Chapl Westmr Sch 60-62; C Bures *St E* 62-72; Can Res and Chan Sarum Cathl *Sarum* 72-92; Dir Post-Ord Tr 72-92; Dir of Ords 73-92; Lect Sarum & Wells Th Coll 76-92; rtd 92. *Gowanbrae, The Glebe, Selkirk TD7 5AB* Tel (01750) 20706

DUNLOP, Peter John. b 44. TCD BA68 MA72 Dur Univ DipTh70 CertEd71. Cranmer Hall Dur. **d** 71 **p** 72. C Barking St Marg w St Patr *Chelmsf* 71-75; C Gt Malvern Ch Ch *Worc* 75-78; Chapl K Sch Tynemouth 78-89; V Monkseaton St Pet *Newc* 90-96; rtd 96. *19 Cliftonville Gardens, Whitley Bay, Tyne & Wear NE26 1QJ* Tel 0191-251 0983

DUNLOP, Terence Andrew. b 66. QUB BA89. CITC BTh97. **d** 97. C Belfast H Trin and Ardoyne *Conn* from 97. *27 Wheatfield Gardens, Belfast BT14 7HU* Tel (01232) 715478

DUNN, Alastair Matthew Crusoe. b 40. Lon Univ LLB64 AKC64. Wycliffe Hall Ox 78. **d** 80 **p** 81. C Yardley St Edburgha *Birm* 80-83; R Bishop's Sutton and Ropley and W Tisted *Win* 83-90; V Milford from 90. *The Vicarage, Lymington Road, Milford on Sea, Lymington, Hants SO41 0QN* Tel (01590) 643289

DUNN, Mrs Barbara Anne. b 42. Man Univ BA72 Sheff Univ CQSW76. N Ord Course 92. **d** 95 **p** 96. NSM Stretford St Matt *Man* from 95. *71 Manley Road, Whalley Range, Manchester M16 8WF* Tel 0161-881 6929

DUNN, Brian. b 40. St Aid Birkenhead 66. **d** 69 **p** 70. C Over Darwen H Trin *Blackb* 69-71; C Burnley St Pet 71-74; V Darwen St Barn 74-84; V S Shore H Trin from 84; Chapl Arnold Sch Blackpool from 84. *Holy Trinity Vicarage, 1 Windermere Road, Blackpool FY4 2BX* Tel (01253) 42362

DUNN, Christopher George Hunter. b 28. Pemb Coll Cam BA49 MA53. Oak Hill Th Coll 51. **d** 53 **p** 54. C Tunbridge Wells H Trin *Roch* 53-54; C Broadwater St Mary *Chich* 54-58; R Garsdon w Lea and Cleverton *Bris* 58-74; V Tiverton St Geo *Ex* from 74; Chapl Marie Curie Foundn (Tidcombe Hall) from 74; RD Tiverton *Ex* 84-91. *St George's Vicarage, St Andrew Street, Tiverton, Devon EX16 6PH* Tel (01884) 252184 or 243281

DUNN, David. b 42. Univ of Wales DipTh65. St Mich Coll Llan 62. **d** 66 **p** 67. C Brighton St Wilfrid *Chich* 66-69; C Tunbridge Wells St Barn *Roch* 69-74; TV Brighton Resurr *Chich* 74-77; V Southsea H Spirit *Portsm* 77-88; P-in-c Bournemouth St Mary *Win* 88-95; Chapl Southn Gen Hosp 95; C Andover w Foxcott *Win* from 95. *4 Winterdyne Mews, Andover, Hants SP10 3AG* Tel (01264) 354451

DUNN, David James. b 47. CertEd79 BA82 DipHE90. Trin Coll Bris 88. **d** 90 **p** 91. C Magor w Redwick and Undy *Mon* 90-92; C St Mellons and Michaelston-y-Fedw 92-93; V Pontnewydd from 93. *The Vicarage, 44 Church Road, Pontnewydd, Cwmbran NP44 1AT* Tel (01633) 482300

DUNN, David Michael. b 47. AKC70. St Aug Coll Cant 70. **d** 71 **p** 72. C Padgate *Liv* 71-74; C Halliwell St Marg *Man* 74-76; V Lever Bridge 76-84; V Bradshaw from 84. *The New Vicarage, Bolton Road, Bolton BL2 3EU* Tel (01204) 304240

DUNN, David Whitelaw Thomas. b 34. Trin Coll Carmarthen CertEd54. St Mich Coll Llan 87 St Deiniol's Hawarden 83. **d** 83 **p** 85. NSM Brecon St Mary and Battle w Llanddew *S & B* 83-87; Min Can Brecon Cathl 87-88; V Llanfihangel Crucorney w Oldcastle etc *Mon* from 88. *The Vicarage, Llanfihangel Crucorney, Abergavenny NP7 8DH* Tel (01873) 890349

DUNN, Derek William Robert. b 48. AMusTCL74 LTCL75 Stranmillis Coll CertEd70 Open Univ BA81 QUB DASE86. **d** 85 **p** 87. NSM Carnalea *D & D* 85-91; Lic to Offic from 91. *13 Wandsworth Park, Carnalea, Bangor, Co Down BT19 1BD* Tel (01247) 456898

DUNN, John Frederick. b 44. Trin Coll Bris 71. **d** 74 **p** 75. C Carl St Jo *Carl* 74-77; C Tooting Graveney St Nic *S'wark* 77-82; V Attleborough *Cov* 85; Perm to Offic *Cant* from 86. *73 St Luke's Avenue, Ramsgate, Kent CT11 7JY* Tel (01843) 581632

DUNN, Julian. b 46. Open Univ BA84 Kingston Univ DipSocWork93. K Coll Lon 67 St Aug Coll Cant 70. **d** 71 **p** 72. C Hanworth All SS *Lon* 71-74; C Kidlington *Ox* 74-76; C-in-c Cleethorpes St Fran CD *Linc* 76-77; TV Cleethorpes 77-85; Chapl Friarage and Distr Hosp Northallerton 85-88; Chapl Broadmoor Hosp Crowthorne 88; Ind Chapl *York* 88-89; P-in-c Micklefield 88-89; Perm to Offic *Ox* from 91. *1 Lewington Close, Great Haseley, Oxford OX44 7LS* Tel (01844) 279687

DUNN, Kevin Lancelot. b 62. Newc Univ BSc83. St Steph Ho Ox 89. **d** 92 **p** 93. C Tynemouth Cullercoats St Paul *Newc* 92-95; C Newc St Matt w St Mary from 95. *St Matthews Vicarage, 10 Winchester Terrace, Newcastle upon Tyne NE4 6EY* Tel 0191-232 2866

DUNN, Michael Henry James. b 34. Em Coll Cam BA56 MA62. Cuddesdon Coll 57 and 62. **d** 62 **p** 63. C Chatham St Steph *Roch* 62-66; C Bromley SS Pet and Paul 66-70; V Roch St Justus 70-83; P-in-c Malvern Wells and Wyche *Worc* 83-85; P-in-c Lt Malvern, Malvern Wells and Wyche 85-97; rtd 97. *253 Oldbury Road, Worcester WR2 6JT* Tel (01905) 429938

DUNN, Paul James Hugh. b 55. Dur Univ PhD93. Ripon Coll Cuddesdon. **d** 83 **p** 84. C Wandsworth St Paul *S'wark* 83-87; C Richmond St Mary w St Matthias and St Jo 88-92; TV Wimbledon from 92. *St Matthew's House, 61 Melbury Gardens, London SW20 0DL* Tel 0181-946 0092

DUNN, Reginald Hallan. b 31. Oak Hill NSM Course. **d** 82 **p** 83. NSM Enfield St Andr *Lon* 82-93; NSM Enfield Chase St Mary from 93. *3 Conway Gardens, Enfield, Middx EN2 9AD* Tel 0181-366 3982

DUNN, Struan Huthwaite. b 43. Ch Coll Hobart 66 Moore Th Coll Sydney ThL68 Clifton Th Coll 68. **d** 70 **p** 71. C Orpington Ch Ch *Roch* 70-74; C Cheltenham St Mary *Glouc* 74-76; C Cheltenham St Mary, St Matt, St Paul and H Trin 76; C Welling *Roch* 76-79; Chapl Barcelona w Casteldefels *Eur* 79-83; R Addington w Trottiscliffe *Roch* 83-89; P-in-c Ryarsh w Birling 83-89; P-in-c S Gillingham 89-90; TR 90-96; RD Gillingham 91-96; R Meopham w Nurstead from 96. *The Rectory, Shipley Hills Road, Meopham, Gravesend, Kent DA13 0AD* Tel (01474) 815259

DUNNAN, Donald Stuart. b 59. Harvard Univ AB80 AM81 Ch Ch Ox BA85 MA90. Gen Th Sem (NY). **d** 86 **p** 87. USA 86-87 and from 92; Lib Pusey Ho 87-89; Lic to Offic *Ox* 87-92; Perm to Offic *Cant* 87-92; Chapl Linc Coll Ox 90-92. *St James School, St James, MD 21781, USA*

DUNNE, Kevin Headley. b 43. Cranmer Hall Dur 85. **d** 87 **p** 88. C Chester le Street *Dur* 87-90; V S Hetton w Haswell 90-94; P-in-c Oxclose from 94. *37 Brancepeth Road, Washington, Tyne & Wear NE38 0LA* Tel 0191-416 2561

DUNNE, Nigel Kenneth. BA BTh. **d** 90 **p** 91. C Dublin St Bart w Leeson Park *D & G* 90-93; C Taney 93-95; I Blessington w Kilbride, Ballymore Eustace etc from 95. *The Rectory, Blessington, Co Wicklow, Irish Republic* Tel Naas (45) 865178

DUNNETT, John Frederick. b 58. CQSW82 SS Coll Cam MA84 Worc Coll Ox MSc83. Trin Coll Bris BA87. **d** 88 **p** 89. C Kirkheaton *Wakef* 88-93; V Cranham Park *Chelmsf* from 93. *St Luke's Vicarage, 201 Front Lane, Upminster, Essex RM14 1LD* Tel (01708) 225262

DUNNETT, Robert Curtis. b 31. SS Coll Cam BA54 MA58. Oak Hill Th Coll 56. **d** 58 **p** 59. C Markfield *Leic* 58-60; C Bucknall and Bagnall *Lich* 60-73; Perm to Offic *Birm* from 72; Chapl and Tutor Birm Bible Inst 72-79; Vice-Prin 84-92; Hon Vice-Prin from 92; rtd 96. *30 Station Road, Harborne, Birmingham B17 9LY* Tel 0121-428 3945 Fax 428 3370

DUNNILL, Dr John David Stewart. b 50. UEA BA72 Birm Univ DipTh82 PhD88. Ripon Coll Cuddesdon 86. **d** 88 **p** 89. C Tupsley *Heref* 88-92; Australia from 92. *Anglican Institute of Theology, Mount Claremont, Perth, W Australia 6010* Tel Perth (9) 386 8326 or 383 4403 Fax 386 8327

DUNNING, David John. b 52. Liv Univ BA Ox Univ CertEd. Ripon Coll Cuddesdon 79. **d** 82 **p** 84. C N Gosforth *Newc* 82-83; C Willington Team 83-85; C Bellingham/Otterburn Gp 85-86; Chapl Magd Coll Sch Ox 86-94; Chapl Sherborne Sch from 94. *Sherborne School, Abbey Road, Sherborne, Dorset DT9 3AP* Tel (01935) 812249

DUNNING, John Stanley. b 19. Lon Univ BSc41. EMMTC 78. **d** 81 **p** 82. NSM Nottingham St Pet and St Jas *S'well* 81-85; rtd 85; Perm to Offic *S'well* from 85. *12 Brookhill Drive, Wollaton, Nottingham NG8 2PS* Tel 0115-928 3357

DUNNING, Martyn Philip. b 51. MRTPI77 Reading Univ MSc79 Dur Univ MA95. St Jo Coll Dur 89. **d** 92 **p** 93. C Beverley Minster *York* 92-96; P-in-c Leven w Catwick 96-97; P-in-c Brandesburton 96-97; R Brandesburton and Leven w Catwick from 97. *The Rectory, West Street, Leven, Beverley, N Humberside HU17 5LR* Tel (01964) 543793

DUNNINGS, Reuben Edward. b 36. Clifton Th Coll 62. **d** 66 **p** 67. C Longfleet *Sarum* 66-70; C Melksham 70-73; TV 73-78; R Broughton Gifford w Gt Chalfield 78-84; V Holt St Kath 78-84; R Broughton Gifford, Gt Chalfield and Holt 85-86; V Salisbury St Fran from 86. *The Vicarage, 52 Park Lane, Salisbury SP1 3NP* Tel (01722) 333762

DUNSETH, George William. b 52. Multnomah Sch of the Bible Oregon BRE79. Oak Hill Th Coll BA85. **d** 85 **p** 86. C Cheadle All Hallows *Ches* 85-88; C New Borough and Leigh *Sarum* 88-91; V Thurnby w Stoughton *Leic* from 91. *The Vicarage, Thurnby, Leicester LE7 9PN* Tel 0116-241 2263

DUNSTAN, Canon Alan Leonard. b 28. Wadh Coll Ox BA49 MA52. Ripon Hall Ox 50. **d** 52 **p** 53. C Barford *Cov* 52-55; C Brompton H Trin *Lon* 55-57; V Gravesend St Mary *Roch* 57-63; Chapl Wycliffe Hall Ox 63-66; Vice-Prin 66-70; Hon C Ox St Mary V w St Cross and St Pet *Ox* 70-78; Chapl Keble Coll Ox 70-71; Vice-Prin Ripon Hall Ox 71-74; Acting Prin 74-75; Vice-Prin Ripon Coll Cuddesdon 75-78; Can Res Glouc Cathl *Glouc* 78-93; rtd 93; Perm to Offic *Truro* from 93. *7 The Crescent, Truro, Cornwall TR1 3ES* Tel (01872) 79604

DUNSTAN, Prof Gordon Reginald. b 17. CBE89. Leeds Univ BA38 MA39 Ex Univ Hon DD73 Leic Univ Hon LLD86 Hon MRCP87 FRCOG90 Hon FRCGP93 Hon FRCP95. Coll of Resurr Mirfield 39. **d** 41 **p** 42. C King Cross *Wakef* 41-45; C Huddersfield St Pet 45-46; Subwarden St Deiniol's Lib Hawarden 46-49; Lect Wm Temple Coll 46-49; V Sutton Courtenay w Appleford *Ox* 49-55; Lect Ripon Hall Ox 53-55; Clerical Sec C of E Coun for Soc Work 55-63; Sec Ch Assembly Jt Bd of Studies 63-66; Ed *Theology* 65-75; Min Can Windsor 55-59; Min Can Westmr Abbey 59-67; Dep P in O 59-64; P in O 64-76; Select Preacher Cam Univ 60 and 77; Can Th Leic Cathl *Leic* 66-82; Prof Moral and Soc Th K Coll Lon 67-82; Chapl to The Queen 76-87; rtd 82; Perm to Offic *Ex* from 82. *9 Maryfield Avenue, Exeter EX4 6JN* Tel (01392) 214691

DUNSTAN, Gregory John Orchard. b 50. Cam Univ MA75 TCD BTh90. **d** 90 **p** 91. C Ballymena w Ballyclug *Conn* 90-93; I Belfast St Matt from 93. *Shankill Rectory, 51 Ballygomartin Road, Belfast BT13 3LA* Tel (01232) 714325

DUNSTAN, Kenneth Ian (Ken). b 40. ACP Golds Coll Lon BEd71. Oak Hill NSM Course 86. **d** 88 **p** 89. NSM Creeksea w Althorne, Latchingdon and N Fambridge *Chelmsf* 88-94; P-in-c Woodham Mortimer w Hazeleigh from 94. *35 Ely Close, Southminster, Essex CM0 7AQ* Tel (01621) 772199

DUNSTAN-MEADOWS, Victor Richard. b 63. Chich Th Coll BTh90. **d** 90 **p** 91. C Clacton St Jas *Chelmsf* 90-93; C Stansted Mountfitchet 93-95; CF from 95. *MOD Chaplains (Army), Trenchard Lines, Upavon, Pewsey, Wilts SN9 6BE* Tel (01980) 615804 Fax 615800

DUNTHORNE, Paul. b 63. K Coll Lon LLB85 Paris Sorbonne 85 St Jo Coll Dur BA90. Cranmer Hall Dur 88. **d** 91 **p** 92. C Heacham and Sedgeford *Nor* 91-95; C Heacham 95; C Eastbourne H Trin *Chich* from 95. *20 Chamberlain Road, Eastbourne, E Sussex BN21 1RU*

DUNWICH, Suffragan Bishop of. *See* STEVENS, The Rt Revd Timothy John

DUNWOODY, Stephen John Herbert. b 71. Univ of Wales BA91. St Steph Ho Ox BTh93. **d** 96 **p** 97. C Skewen *Llan* from 96.

Manod, Drummau Road, Neath Abbey SA10 6NT Tel (01792) 321324

DUNWOODY, Canon Thomas Herbert Williamson. b 35. TCD BA58 MA64. TCD Div Sch Div Test59. **d** 59 **p** 60. C Newcastle *D & D* 59-61; C Ballymacarrett St Martin 61-63; C Lurgan Ch Ch 63-66; I Ardglass w Dunsford 66-74; V Urmston *Man* 74-85; Miss to Seamen from 85; I Wexford w Ardcolm and Killurin *C & O* 85-93; Can Ferns Cathl 88-93; RD Wexford 92-93; I Newry St Mary and St Patr *D & D* from 93. *Glebe House, Windsor Avenue, Newry, Co Down BT34 1EQ* Tel (01693) 62621

DUPLOCK, Canon Peter Montgomery. b 16. OBE76. Qu Coll Cam BA38 MA42. Ridley Hall Cam 38. **d** 40 **p** 41. C Morden *S'wark* 40-43; CF (EC) 43-47; R Nottingham St Nic *S'well* 47-52; R Loddington w Harrington *Pet* 52-55; V Kettering St Andr 55-64; Chapl Geneva *Eur* 64-71; Chapl Brussels w Charleroi, Liege and Waterloo 71-81; Chan Brussels Cathl 81; Adn NW Eur 81; rtd 81; Hon Can Brussels Cathl *Eur* from 81; R Breamore *Win* 81-86; Perm to Offic 86-95. *14 Broomfield Drive, Alderholt, Fordingbridge, Hants SP6 3HY* Tel (01425) 656000

DUPREE, Hugh Douglas. b 50. Univ of the South (USA) BA72 Ch Ch Ox MA86 Ball Coll Ox DPhil88. Virginia Th Sem MDiv75. **d** 75 **p** 76. USA 75-80; Hon C Ox St Mich w St Martin and All SS *Ox* 80-87; Asst Chapl Ball Coll Ox 84-87; Chapl from 87; Chapl HM Pris Ox from 88. *Balliol College, Oxford OX1 3BJ* Tel (01865) 277777 or 721261 Fax 723453

DURAND, Noel Douglas. b 33. Jes Coll Cam BA57 MA61 BD76. Westcott Ho Cam 72. **d** 74 **p** 75. C Eaton *Nor* 74-78; V Cumnor *Ox* from 78. *The Vicarage, 1 Abingdon Road, Cumnor, Oxford OX2 9QN* Tel (01865) 862198

DURANT, Robert-Ashton. b 23. OSB Univ of Wales (Lamp) BA47. Bp Burgess Hall Lamp. **d** 48 **p** 49. C Brynmawr *S & B* 48-49; C Fleur-de-Lis *Mon* 49-51; C Bassaleg 51-56; CF (TA) 53-55; V Trellech and Cwmcarvan *Mon* 56-69; Priest Tymawr Convent 56-69; V Slapton *Ex* 69-81; V Strete 69-81; R E Allington, Slapton and Strete 81-92; rtd 92; Perm to Offic *Ex* from 92. *18 Grosvenor Avenue, Torquay TQ2 7LA* Tel (01803) 613710

DURANT, Stanton Vincent. b 42. S'wark Ord Course 69. **d** 72 **p** 73. C Ickenham *Lon* 72-76; C Paddington Em Harrow Road 76-78; V 78-87; AD Westmr Paddington 84-87; TR Hackney Marsh 87-91; Adn Liv 91-93; V Stoneycroft All SS 91-93; Hon Can Liv Cathl 91-93. *Address temp unknown*

DURANT, William John Nicholls. b 55. K Coll Lon BA76 DipTh DPS. St Jo Coll Nottm 77. **d** 80 **p** 81. C Norwood St Luke *S'wark* 80-83; C Morden 83-88; TV 88-92; V Frindsbury w Upnor *Roch* from 92. *All Saints' Vicarage, 4 Parsonage Lane, Frindsbury, Rochester, Kent ME2 4UR* Tel (01634) 717580

DURBIN, Roger. b 41. Bris Sch of Min 83. **d** 85 **p** 86. NSM Bedminster *Bris* 85-91; NSM Henbury 91-94; NSM Clifton All SS w St Jo from 94. *13 Charbury Walk, Bristol BS11 9UU* Tel 0117-982 7858

DURELL, Miss Jane Vavasor. b 32. Bedf Coll Lon BSc55. Gilmore Ho 61 Lambeth STh64. **dss** 86 **d** 87 **p** 94. Banbury *Ox* 86-87; Par Dn 87-92; rtd 92; Perm to Offic *Nor* from 92. *51 Branford Road, Norwich NR3 4QD2* Tel (01603) 486084

DURHAM, Archdeacon of. *See* WILLMOTT, The Ven Trevor

DURHAM, Bishop of. *See* TURNBULL, The Rt Revd Anthony Michael Arnold

DURHAM, Dean of. *See* ARNOLD, The Very Revd John Robert

DURKIN, Anthony Michael (Tony). b 45. Sarum & Wells Th Coll 87. **d** 89 **p** 90. C Faversham *Cant* 89-92; V St Margarets-at-Cliffe w Westcliffe etc from 92. *The Vicarage, Sea Street, St Margarets-at-Cliffe, Dover, Kent CT15 6AR* Tel (01304) 852179

DURNDELL, Miss Irene Frances. b 43. Nottm Univ DipRE78. Trin Coll Bris DipHE86. **dss** 86 **d** 87 **p** 94. Erith Ch Ch *Roch* 86-87; Par Dn 87-93; Par Dn Erith St Paul 93-94; C from 94; Asst Dir of Tr from 93. *113 Belmont Road, Erith, Kent DA8 1LF* Tel (01322) 334762

DURNELL, John. b 32. St Aid Birkenhead 64. **d** 66 **p** 67. C Newport w Longford *Lich* 66-69; P-in-c Church Aston 69-72; R 72-77; V Weston Rhyn 77-82; P-in-c Petton w Cockshutt and Weston Lullingfield etc 82-83; R Petton w Cockshutt, Welshampton and Lyneal etc 83-97; rtd 97. *Fron Lwyd, Hirnant, Penybontfawr, Oswestry, Shropshire SY10 0HP*

DURNFORD, Miss Catherine Margaret. b 36. St Mary's Coll Dur BA57 DipEd58. Gilmore Course 78 NW Ord Course 77. **d** 87 **p** 94. Area Sec (Dios York and Ripon) USPG 82-89; Par Dn Whitby *York* 89-92; Par Dn Redcar 92-94; C 94; C Selby Abbey 94-97; V New Marske from 97; P-in-c Wilton 97. *The Vicarage, 10 Allendale Tee, New Marske, Redcar, Cleveland TS11 8HN* Tel (01642) 484833

DURNFORD, John Edward. b 30. CCC Cam BA53 MA61. Linc Th Coll 53. **d** 55 **p** 56. C Selby Abbey *York* 55-58; C Newland St Jo 58-62; S Rhodesia 62-65; Rhodesia 65-76; V Hebden Bridge *Wakef* 76-84; RD Calder Valley 82-84; P-in-c Blanchland w Hunstanworth *Newc* 84-90; P-in-c Edmundbyers w Muggleswick *Dur* 84-90; RD Corbridge *Newc* 88-93; R Blanchland w Hunstanworth and Edmundbyers etc 90-94; rtd 94. *7 Islestone Drive, Seahouses, Nothd NE68 7XB* Tel (01665) 721032

DURNFORD, Comdr Peter Jeffrey. b 20. Bps' Coll Cheshunt 63. **d** 65 **p** 66. C Edmonton St Alphege *Lon* 65-67; Chapl Bonn w Cologne *Eur* 67-69; R St Just in Roseland *Truro* 70-82; P-in-c Ruan Lanihorne w Philleigh 70-82; P-in-c St Mewan 82-85; Chapl Mount Edgcumbe Hospice 82-88; rtd 85; Perm to Offic *Truro* from 85. *8 Tredenham Road, St Mawes, Truro, Cornwall TR2 5AN* Tel (01326) 270793

DURRAN, Ms Margaret (Maggie). b 47. Lady Spencer Chu Coll of Educn CertEd70. S'wark Ord Course 88. **d** 91 **p** 94. Par Dn Brixton St Matt *S'wark* 91-94; C 94; C Streatham St Leon 94-95; V Walworth St Chris from 95. *76 Tatum Street, London SE17 1QR* Tel 0171-701 4162

DURRANS, Canon Anthony. b 37. Leeds Univ BA59. Linc Th Coll 60. **d** 62 **p** 63. C Stanningley St Thos *Ripon* 62-64; C Chorlton upon Medlock *Man* 64-69; SCM Field Sec Man 64-66; NW Sec 66-68; Asst Gen Sec 68-69; R Old Trafford St Jo *Man* 69-80; V Langley All SS and Martyrs 80-82; TR Langley and Parkfield 82-85; R Man Miles Platting 85-87; P-in-c Man Apostles 85-87; R Man Apostles w Miles Platting 87-97; Hon Can Man Cathl from 86; AD Ardwick 91-96; P-in-c Stretford All SS from 97. *The Rectory, 233 Barton Road, Stretford, Manchester M32 9RB* Tel 0161-865 1350

DURRANT, Reginald Patrick Bickersteth. b 37. AKC64. **d** 65 **p** 66. C Summertown *Ox* 65-68; C Ascot Heath 68-71; C Heene *Chich* 71-76; R Burwash 76-94; rtd 94. *17 Glebeland Close, West Stafford, Dorchester, Dorset DT2 8AE*

DURSTON, Canon David Michael Karl. b 36. Em Coll Cam BA60 MA64. Clifton Th Coll 61. **d** 63 **p** 64. C Wednesfield Heath *Lich* 63-66; Project Officer Grubb Inst 67-78; Ind Chapl *Lich* 78-84; P-in-c W Bromwich St Paul Golds Hill 78-82; V 82-84; Adult Educn Officer 84-92; Preb Lich Cathl 89-92; Can Res and Chan Sarum Cathl *Sarum* from 92. *24 The Close, Salisbury SP1 2EH* Tel (01722) 336809

DUSSEK, Jeremy Neil James Christopher. b 70. St Jo Coll Dur BA92. Westcott Ho Cam 96. **d** 97. C Whickham *Dur* from 97. *St Mary's House, 7A Coalway Drive, Whickham, Newcastle upon Tyne NE16 4BT* Tel 0191-488 3015 Fax as telephone

DUST, Simon Philip. b 63. Oak Hill Th Coll BA95. **d** 95 **p** 96. C Chesham Bois *Ox* from 95. *67A Woodley Hill, Chesham, Bucks HP5 1SP* Tel (01494) 774868

DUTFIELD, Canon Alan. b 20. Linc Th Coll 54. **d** 55 **p** 56. C Kimberworth *Sheff* 55-60; V New Rossington 60-71; R Old Brumby *Linc* 71-77; TR 77-86; Can and Preb Linc Cathl 81-86; RD Manlake 82-86; rtd 86; Perm to Offic *Linc* 89-94. *30 Barnes Green, Scotter, Gainsborough, Lincs DN21 3RW* Tel (01724) 764220

DUTHIE, Elliot Malcolm. b 31. Clifton Th Coll 63. **d** 66 **p** 67. C Eccleston St Luke *Liv* 66-69; Malaysia 70-75; P-in-c Bootle St Leon *Liv* 76-78; V 78-81; V Charlton Kings H Apostles *Glouc* 81-94; rtd 94; Perm to Offic *Glouc* from 94. *71 North Upton Lane, Barnwood, Gloucester GL4 7XW*

DUTTON, Leonard Arthur (Len). b 35. Bps' Coll Cheshunt 63. **d** 66 **p** 67. C Knighton St Jo *Leic* 66-70; C Chilvers Coton w Astley *Cov* 70-73; R Hathern *Leic* 73-79; V Ashby-de-la-Zouch H Trin from 79. *Holy Trinity Vicarage, 1 Trinity Close, Ashby-de-la-Zouch, Leics LE65 2GQ* Tel (01530) 412339

DUVAL, Canon David. b 14. Ch Ch Ox BA36 MA41. Wells Th Coll 36. **d** 38 **p** 39. C Wanstead St Mary *Chelmsf* 38-41; C Hurstpierpoint *Chich* 41-42; C Cuckfield 42-45; C Heathfield 45-47; V Lyminster 47-49; V Gt Barton *St E* 49-59; RD Thingoe 54-62; R Fornham All SS 59-62; Dean Bocking *Chelmsf* 62-63; R Hadleigh w Layham and Shelley *St E* 62-73; RD Hadleigh *Chelmsf* 67-71; Hon Can St E Cathl *St E* 62-83; R Withersfield 73-79; P-in-c 79-82; rtd 79; TV Haverhill w Withersfield, the Wrattings etc *St E* 82-83; Perm to Offic from 83. *The Cromwell House Nursing Home, 82 The High Street, Huntingdon, Cambs PE16 6DP*

DUVAL, Canon Philip Ernest. b 18. MBE45. Mert Coll Ox BA45 MA45. Westcott Ho Cam 47. **d** 47 **p** 48. C Tooting All SS *S'wark* 47-51; C Raynes Park St Sav 51-55; V Balham St Mary 55-66; R Merstham and Gatton 66-86; Hon Can S'wark Cathl 78-86; rtd 86; Perm to Offic *Cant* from 88. *2 The Holt, Frogs Hill, Newenden, Hawkhurst, Kent TN18 5PX* Tel (01797) 252578

DUVALL, Michael James. b 31. **d** 79 **p** 80. Hon C Kings Langley *St Alb* 79-89; Hon C Selworthy and Timberscombe and Wootton Courtenay *B & W* 89-95; Hon C Luccombe 89-95; Hon C Selworthy, Timberscombe, Wootton Courtenay etc from 95. *The Parsonage, Luccombe, Minehead, Somerset TA24 8TE* Tel (01643) 862834

DUXBURY, Clive Robert. b 49. St Jo Coll Nottm DCM92. **d** 92 **p** 93. C Horwich *Man* 92-93; C Horwich and Rivington 93-96; P-in-c Bury St Paul from 96. *St Paul's Vicarage, Fir Street, Bury, Lancs BL9 7QG* Tel 0161-761 6991

DUXBURY, Canon James Campbell. b 33. Tyndale Hall Bris 58. **d** 61 **p** 62. C Southport SS Simon and Jude *Liv* 61-65; V Tittensor *Lich* 65-70; V W Bromwich Gd Shep w St Jo 70-75; P-in-c Wellington w Eyton 75-80; V 80-85; V Padiham *Blackb* from 85; Hon Can Blackb Cathl from 97. *The Vicarage, 1 Arbory Drive, Padiham, Burnley, Lancs BB12 8JS* Tel (01282) 772442

DUXBURY, Miss Margaret Joan. b 30. JP81. DipEd52. St Jo Coll Nottm 83. **dss** 84 **d** 87 **p** 94. Thornthwaite w Thruscross and Darley *Ripon* 84-86; Middleton St Cross 86-87; C 87-90; Par Dn Dacre w Hartwith and Darley w Thornthwaite 90-94; C 94-96;

rtd 97. *Scot Beck House, Darley, Harrogate, N Yorkshire HG3 2QN* Tel (01423) 780451

DYALL, Henry. b 19. ARICS51 Lon Univ BSc51 LLB58. S'wark Ord Course 81. **d** 82 **p** 83. Hon C St Mary Cray and St Paul's Cray *Roch* 82-84; Perm to Offic 84-86; Hon C Sidcup Ch Ch from 86. *8 Saxville Road, Orpington, Kent BR5 3AW* Tel (01689) 872598

DYAS, Stuart Edwin. b 46. Lon Univ BSc67. Ridley Hall Cam 78. **d** 80 **p** 81. C Bath Weston St Jo *B & W* 80; C Bath Weston St Jo w Kelston 81-83; C Tunbridge Wells St Jas *Roch* 83-90; V Nottingham St Jude *S'well* from 90; AD Nottingham Cen from 93. *St Jude's Vicarage, Woodborough Road, Mapperley, Nottingham NG3 5HE* Tel 0115-960 4102

DYER, Mrs Anne Catherine. b 57. St Anne's Coll Ox MA80 Lon Univ MTh89. Wycliffe Hall Ox 84. **d** 87 **p** 94. NSM Beckenham St Jo *Roch* 87-88; NSM Beckenham St Geo 88-89; Hon Par Dn Luton Ch Ch 89-94; Chapl for Evang from 93; NSM Istead Rise from 94. *The Vicarage, Upper Avenue, Gravesend, Kent DA13 9DA* Tel (01474) 832403

DYER, Ms Catherine Jane. b 46. Westf Coll Lon BA68. Ox NSM Course 85. **d** 88 **p** 94. Hon C Wokingham All SS *Ox* 88-90; C 90-95; TV W Slough from 95. *Saint Andrew's House, Washington Drive, Slough SL1 5RE* Tel (01628) 661994

DYER, Mrs Christine Anne. b 53. Nottm Univ BEd75. EMMTC 81. **dss** 84 **d** 87 **p** 94. Mickleover St Jo *Derby* 85-87; Par Dn 87-90; Dioc Voc Adv 86-90; Par Educn Adv from 90; Dioc Youth Officer from 91. *4 Chain Lane, Mickleover, Derby DE3 5AJ* Tel (01332) 514390

DYER, Mrs Gillian Marie. b 50. Sheff Univ BA71 Leic Univ CertEd72. S Dios Minl Tr Scheme 81. **dss** 84 **d** 87 **p** 94. Witney *Ox* 84-85; Carl St Cuth w St Mary *Carl* 86-87; Par Dn 87-89; Dioc Communications Officer 86-89; Par Dn Kirkbride w Newton Arlosh 89-91; Par Dn Carl H Trin and St Barn 91-94; TV from 94. *Holy Trinity Vicarage, 25 Wigton Road, Carlisle CA2 7BB* Tel (01228) 26284

DYER, Canon James Henry. b 14. ALCD39. **d** 39 **p** 40. C S Hackney St Jo w Ch Ch *Lon* 39-43; C New Malden and Coombe *S'wark* 43-50; New Zealand from 50; Hon Can Nelson Cathl 85; Can Emer from 85. *41 Oxford Street, Richmond, Nelson, New Zealand* Tel Christchurch (3) 544 7440

DYER, Janet. b 35. LNSM course 77. **dss** 85 **d** 86 **p** 94. Balerno *Edin* 85-86; NSM 86-93; Chapl Edin R Infirmary 88-93; D-in-c Roslin (Rosslyn Chpl) *Edin* 93-94; P-in-c 94-97. *499 Lanark Road West, Balerno, Midlothian EH14 7AL* Tel 0131-449 3767

DYER, John Alan. b 31. Linc Coll Ox BA53 MA57 Lon Univ BD58. Tyndale Hall Bris 53. **d** 56 **p** 57. C Weston-super-Mare Ch Ch *B & W* 56-60; V Battersea St Geo w St Andr *S'wark* 60-69; Australia from 69; C-in-c Narraweena 69-74; R 74-96; AD Warringah 85-92; rtd 96. *5 Crisallen Street, Port Macquarie, NSW, Australia 2444* Tel Port Macquarie (65) 842868

DYER, Ronald Whitfield. b 29. Solicitor 51. Guildf Dioc Min Course 91. **d** 95 **p** 96. NSM Fleet *Guildf* from 95. *7 Dukes Mead, Fleet, Hants GU13 8HA* Tel (01252) 621457

DYER, Stephen Roger. b 57. Brunel Univ BSc. Wycliffe Hall Ox 83. **d** 86 **p** 87. C Beckenham St Jo *Roch* 86-89; C Luton Ch Ch 89-94; V Istead Rise from 94. *The Vicarage, Upper Avenue, Gravesend, Kent DA13 9DA* Tel (01474) 832403

DYER, Sydney Charles George. b 03. ALCD33 St Jo Coll Dur LTh33 BA34 MA38. **d** 34 **p** 35. C Malden St Jas *S'wark* 34-36; C Raynes Park St Sav 36-40; V Clapham St Jo 40-45; V Herne Hill St Paul 45-55; V Redhill St Jo 55-69; rtd 69; Hon C Tenerife *Eur* 72-75. *85 Old Fort Road, Shoreham-by-Sea, W Sussex BN43 5HA* Tel (01273) 454422

DYER, Sylvia Mary. b 30. Westf Coll Lon BA66. Ab Dioc Tr Course 66. **d** 95. NSM Turriff *Ab* from 95. *The Sheiling, Westfield Road, Turriff, Aberdeenshire AB53 7AF* Tel (01888) 562530

DYER, Terence Neville. b 50. Sheff Univ BEng71 Leic Univ PGCE72. Carl Dioc Tr Course 86. **d** 89 **p** 90. NSM Kirkbride w Newton Arlosh *Carl* 89-91; NSM Carl H Trin and St Barn from 91. *Holy Trinity Vicarage, 25 Wigton Road, Carlisle CA2 7BB* Tel (01228) 26284

DYKE, Mrs Elizabeth Muriel. b 55. St Mary's Coll Dur BSc77 St Martin's Coll Lanc PGCE78. Oak Hill Th Coll 92. **d** 94 **p** 95. C High Wycombe *Ox* 94-95; C W Wycombe w Bledlow Ridge, Bradenham and Radnage from 95. *283 Deeds Grove, High Wycombe, Bucks HP12 3PF* Tel (01494) 533622

DYKE, George Edward. b 22. TCD BA65 BCom65 MA80. CITC. **d** 79 **p** 80. NSM Dublin St Geo *D & G* 79-82; NSM Tallaght 83-89; NSM Killiney Ballybrack 89-90; Bp's C Dublin St Geo and St Thos and Finglas 90-95; Bp's C Dublin St Geo and St Thos 95-96; Chapl Mountjoy Pris 90-96; Chapl Arbour Hill Pris 90-96; rtd 96. *45 Thornhill Road, Mount Merrion, Co Dublin, Irish Republic* Tel Dublin (1) 288 9376

DYKE, Kenneth Aubrey. b 30. Sarum Th Coll 61. **d** 63 **p** 64. C Bournville *Birm* 63-66; Chapl RAF 66-82; R Bottesford and Muston *Leic* 82-92; rtd 92. *18 Nursery Road, Bingham, Nottingham NG13 8EH* Tel (01949) 837052

DYKES, John Edward. b 33. DipHE84. Trin Coll Bris 82. **d** 84 **p** 85. C Rushden w Newton Bromswold *Pet* 84-87; R Heanton Punchardon w Marwood *Ex* from 87. *The Rectory, Heanton, Barnstaple, Devon EX31 4DG* Tel (01271) 812249

DYKES, Michael David Allan. b 42. Chich Th Coll 68. **d** 71 **p** 72. C Pocklington w Yapham-cum-Meltonby, Owsthorpe etc *York* 72-75; C Howden 75-77; V Eskdaleside w Ugglebarnby and Sneaton 77-85; R Stokesley from 85; P-in-c Hilton in Cleveland 85-95; P-in-c Seamer in Cleveland from 85. *The Rectory, Leven Close, Stokesley, Middlesbrough, Cleveland TS9 5AP* Tel (01642) 710405

DYKES, Philip John. b 61. Loughb Univ BSc83 DIS83. Trin Coll Bris DTS90 ADPS91. **d** 91 **p** 92. C Morden *S'wark* 91-95; C St Helier from 95. *Bishop Andrews House, Wigmore Road, Carshalton, Surrey SM4 1RG* Tel 0181-644 9203

DYSON, Prof Anthony Oakley. b 35. Em Coll Cam BA59 MA63 Ex Coll Ox BD64 DPhil68. Ripon Hall Ox 59. **d** 61 **p** 62. C Putney St Mary *S'wark* 61-63; Chapl Ripon Hall Ox 63-68; Prin 69-74; Can Windsor 74-77; Lect Kent Univ 77-80; Perm to Offic *Man* from 80; Prof of Soc and Past Th Man Univ from 80. *33 Danesmoor Road, Manchester M20 9JT* Tel 0161-434 5410

DYSON, Frank. b 28. Open Univ BA. Oak Hill Th Coll 60. **d** 62 **p** 63. C Parr *Liv* 62-65; V Newchapel *Lich* 65-77; R Bunwell w Carleton Rode *Nor* 77-79; P-in-c Tibenham 78-80; R Bunwell w Carleton Rode and Tibenham 80-81; R Pakefield 81-93; Perm to Offic from 93; rtd 93. *12 Viburnum Green, Lowestoft, Suffolk NR32 2SN* Tel (01502) 574898

DYSON, Peter Whiteley. b 51. Man Univ BA73 LLB75. Qu Coll Birm DipTh80. **d** 81 **p** 82. C Swindon Ch Ch *Bris* 81-84; P-in-c Brislington St Luke 84-91; V Bourne *Guildf* 91-92. *28 Wellesley Avenue, Iver, Bucks SL0 9BN* Tel (01753) 653980

DYSON, The Ven Thomas. b 17. OBE91. Man Univ BA38 Lon Univ BD44 St Edm Hall Ox DipEd47 BA50 MA53. Ely Th Coll 38. **d** 40 **p** 41. C Kennington Cross St Anselm *S'wark* 40-43; Chapl RNVR 43-47; V Ox St Pet in the E w St Jo *Ox* 47-54; Chapl St Edm Hall Ox 47-54; Chapl and Asst Master Windsor Sch Hamm (BAOR) 54-55; V Colne Ch Ch *Blackb* 55-57; Bermuda from 57; Miss to Seamen from 57; Hon Can Bermuda Cathl from 73; Adn Bermuda 82-94; rtd 94. *The Rectory, 15 Longford Road, PO Box 248 WK, Warwick WK 06, Bermuda* Tel Bermuda (1-441) 236-5744

E

EADE, John Christopher. b 45. Ch Coll Cam BA68 MA72. Linc Th Coll 68. **d** 70 **p** 71. C Portsea N End St Mark *Portsm* 70-73; C Henleaze *Bris* 73-77; V Slad *Glouc* 77-82; V N Bradley, Southwick and Heywood *Sarum* 82-91; R Fovant, Sutton Mandeville and Teffont Evias etc from 91. *The Rectory, Brookwood House, Fovant, Salisbury SP3 5JA* Tel (01722) 714826

EADES, Jonathan Peter. b 51. Dundee Univ MA74 Edin Univ BD77. Coates Hall Edin 74. **d** 77 **p** 78. Chapl St Paul's Cathl Dundee *Bre* 77-88; Chapl Dundee Univ 79-88; TV Leek and Meerbrook *Lich* 88-96; RD Leek 93-96; TR Wolstanton from 96. *Wolstanton Rectory, Knutton Road, Newcastle, Staffs ST5 0HU* Tel (01782) 717561

EADY, David Robert. b 43. Salford Univ BSc Birm Univ DSocStuds. Glouc Th Course 82. **d** 85 **p** 86. NSM Highnam, Lassington, Rudford, Tibberton etc *Glouc* 85-95; NSM Stratton, N Cerney, Baunton and Bagendon from 95. *Little Gables, Hayes Lane, Woodmancote, Cirencester, Glos GL7 7EE* Tel (01285) 813725

EADY, Timothy William (Tim). b 57. Open Univ BA. Cranmer Hall Dur 82. **d** 85 **p** 86. C Boulton *Derby* 85-88; C Portchester *Portsm* 88-92; Relig Progr Adv Ocean Sound Radio from 88; R Brighstone and Brooke w Mottistone *Portsm* from 92. *The Rectory, Rectory Lane, Brightstone, Newport, Isle of Wight PO30 4AQ* Tel (01983) 740267

EAGER, Ms Rosemary Anne McDowall. b 65. St Andr Univ MA87 Strathclyde Univ 88. Ridley Hall Cam CTM95. **d** 95 **p** 96. C Walthamstow St Mary w St Steph *Chelmsf* from 95. *9 Church End, London E17 9RJ* Tel 0181-509 3746 Fax 520 4281

EAGGER, Mrs Christine Mary. b 32. **d** 94 **p** 95. NSM Arlesey w Astwick *St Alb* from 94; NSM Upper w Lower Gravenhurst from 94. *43 Cainhoe Road, Clophill, Bedford MK43 4AQ* Tel (01525) 860973

EAGLE, John Frederick Laurence. b 16. St Chad's Coll Dur BA39 DipTh40 MA42. **d** 41 **p** 41. C Greasley *S'well* 41-43; C Bestwood Park 43-47; C Malden St Jo *S'wark* 47-53; C Mortlake w E Sheen 53-58; R Stanwick *Pet* 58-72; P-in-c Hargrave 59-72; R Stanwick w Hargrave 72-87; rtd 87; Perm to Offic *Pet* from 87. *Mandell House, Minster Precincts, Peterborough PE1 1XX* Tel (01733) 61807

EAGLE, Canon Julian Charles. b 32. Qu Coll Cam BA56 MA60. Westcott Ho Cam. **d** 58 **p** 59. C Billingham St Aid *Dur* 58-61; C Eastleigh *Win* 61-65; Ind Chapl from 65; Hon Can Win Cathl from 83. *24 Butterfield Road, Southampton SO16 7EE* Tel (01703) 791097

EAGLES, Peter Andrew. b 59. K Coll Lon BA82 AKC82 Ox Univ BA88. St Steph Ho Ox 86. **d** 89 **p** 90. C Ruislip St Martin *Lon* 89-92; CF from 92. *MOD Chaplains (Army), Trenchard Lines, Upavon, Pewsey, Wilts SN9 6BE* Tel (01980) 615804 Fax 615800

EALES, Geoffrey Pellew (Geoff). b 50. Trin Coll Bris 95. **d** 97. C Uphill *B & W* from 97. *6 Ellesmere Road, Weston-super-Mare, Avon BS23 4UT* Tel (01934) 415802

EALES, Howard Bernard. b 46. Sarum & Wells Th Coll 73. **d** 76 **p** 77. C Timperley *Ches* 76-78; C Stockport St Thos 78-82; V Wythenshawe Wm Temple Ch *Man* 82-95; V Cheadle Hulme All SS *Ches* from 95. *All Saints' Vicarage, 27 Church Road, Cheadle Hulme, Cheadle, Cheshire SK8 7JL* Tel 0161-485 3455

EALES WHITE, Donald James. b 16. MC45. St Jo Coll Ox BA44 MA44. St Deiniol's Hawarden 60. **d** 61 **p** 62. C Strichen *Ab* 61-62; R 62-64; R New Pitsligo 62-64; R Ballachulish *Arg* 64-66; R Glencoe 65-66; R Bardwell *St E* 68-69; Lic to Offic *Arg* 69-71; V Mendham *St E* 71-72; P-in-c Metfield w Withersdale 71-72; Perm to Offic 73-74; P-in-c Eorrapaidh *Arg* 74-77 and 79-81; R Dalbeattie *Glas* 77-79; P-in-c Dornoch *Mor* 81-82; P-in-c Brora 81-82; rtd 82; Perm to Offic *Arg* from 82. *Dell Cottage, South Dell, Isle of Lewis HS2 0SP* Tel (01851) 810726

EAMAN, Michael Leslie. b 47. Ridley Hall Cam 87. **d** 89 **p** 90. C Wharton *Ches* 89-93; V Buglawton from 93. *St John's Vicarage, Buxton Road, Congleton, Cheshire CW12 2DT* Tel (01260) 273294

✠**EAMES, The Most Revd Robert Henry Alexander.** b 37. QUB LLB60 PhD63 Hon LLD89 TCD Hon LLD92 Cam Univ Hon DD94 Lanc Univ Hon LLD94 Aber Univ Hon LLD97. TCD Div Sch Div Test 60. **d** 63 **p** 64 **c** 75. C Bangor St Comgall *D & D* 63-66; I Gilnahirk 66-74; Bp's Dom Chapl 70-72; I Dundela 74-75; Bp D & R 75-80; Bp D & D 80-86; Abp Arm from 86. *The See House, Cathedral Close, Armagh BT61 7EE* Tel (01861) 522851 or 527144 Fax 527823

EARDLEY, John. b 38. Ch Coll Cam BA61. Ridley Hall Cam 60. **d** 62 **p** 63. C Barnston *Ches* 62-65; C Wilmslow 65-67; V Hollingworth 67-75; V Leasowe 75-91; RD Wallasey 86-91; V Church Hulme from 91; Chapl Cranage Hall Hosp from 91. *The Vicarage, Holmes Chapel, Crewe CW4 7BD* Tel (01477) 533124

EARDLEY, Canon John Barry. b 35. MBE97. MEd87. AKC62. **d** 63 **p** 64. C Merton St Jas *S'wark* 63-66; C St Helier 66-69; C Bilton *Cov* 69-70; C Canley CD 70-74; P-in-c Church Lawford w Newnham Regis 74-80; P-in-c Leamington Hastings and Birdingbury 82-88; Dioc Educn Officer from 82; Hon Can Cov Cathl from 87. *The Rectory, Bubbenhall, Coventry CV8 3BD* Tel (01203) 302345 or 674328

EARDLEY, Paul Wycliffe. b 19. ALCD42. **d** 42 **p** 43. C Brierfield *Blackb* 42-44; C Somers Town St Mary *Lon* 46-48; Chapl Guy's Hosp Lon 48-49; Warden Stanford Priory 49-50; Warden Edw Wilson Ho 50-55; C St Ethelburga Bishopgate 55-57; Lic to Offic *Chich* 57-62; R Ripe w Chalvington 62-71; V Kemp Town St Mark and St Matt 71-84; rtd 84; Perm to Offic *Chich* from 84. *Saxons, 2 Falmer Road, Rottingdean, Brighton BN2 7DA* Tel (01273) 302255

EARDLEY, Robert Bradford. b 44. St Alb Minl Tr Scheme 90. **d** 93 **p** 94. NSM Digswell and Panshanger *St Alb* 93-96; NSM Wheathampstead from 96. *16 Coneydale, Welwyn Garden City, Herts AL8 7RZ* Tel (01707) 332609

EARDLEY, William Robert. b 56. Oak Hill Th Coll DipHE96. **d** 96 **p** 97. C Whitfield *Derby* from 96. *1 Cedar Close, Glossop, Derbyshire SK13 9BP* Tel (01457) 855896

EAREY, Mark Robert. b 65. Loughb Univ BSc87. Cranmer Hall Dur BA91. **d** 91 **p** 92. C Glen Parva and S Wigston *Leic* 91-94; C Luton Ch Ch *Roch* 94-97. *19 Estcourt Road, Salisbury SP1 3AP* Tel (01722) 330616

EARIS, Stanley Derek. b 50. Univ Coll Dur BA71 BCL80. Ripon Hall Ox BA73 MA80. **d** 74 **p** 75. C Sutton St Jas and Wawne *York* 74-77; C Acomb St Steph 77-81; V Skelmanthorpe *Wakef* 81-87; R Market Deeping *Linc* from 87. *The Rectory, Church Street, Market Deeping, Peterborough PE6 8DA* Tel (01778) 342237

EARL, David Arthur. b 34. Hartley Victoria Coll 63 Coll of Resurr Mirfield. **d** 83 **p** 83. In Meth Ch 67-83; P-in-c Paddock *Wakef* 83-84; C Huddersfield St Pet and All SS from 84. *All Saints Vicarage, 17 Cross Church Street, Huddersfield HD1 4SN* Tel (01484) 530814

EARL, The Very Revd David Kaye Lee. b 28. TCD BA54. **d** 55 **p** 56. C Chapelizod *D & G* 55-58; I Rathkeale *L & K* 58-65; I Killarney 65-79; RD Tralee 71-77; Prec Limerick Cathl 77-79; Dean Ferns *C & O* 79-94; I Ferns w Kilbride, Toombe, Kilcormack etc 79-94; rtd 94. *Random, Seafield, Tramore, Co Waterford, Irish Republic* Tel Waterford (51) 390503

EARL, Simon Robert. b 50. Culham Coll of Educn CertEd71 Open Univ BA82. Linc Th Coll DMS94. **d** 96 **p** 97. C Bexhill St Aug *Chich* from 96. *18 Woodville Road, Bexhill-on-Sea, E Sussex TN39 3EU* Tel (01424) 215460

EARL, Stephen Geoffrey Franklyn. b 53. Univ Coll Lon BA76 Golds Coll Lon PGCE77. Ridley Hall Cam 91. **d** 93 **p** 94. C Sawston *Ely* 93-96; V Burwell from 96. *The Vicarage, High Street, Burwell, Cambridge CB5 0HB* Tel (01638) 741262

EARL, Victor Charles. b 22. Bede Coll Dur BA49. ALCD51. **d** 51 **p** 52. C Stechford *Birm* 51-54; C Newbarns w Hawcoat *Carl* 54-57; R Plumbland and Gilcrux 57-61; R Man St Phil w St Mark *Man* 61-67; Lic to Offic 67-82; R Gorton St Phil 82-88; rtd 88; Perm to Offic *Derby* from 88. *4 Burdekin Close, Chapel-en-le-Frith, Stockport, Cheshire SK12 6QA* Tel (01298) 815312

EARLE, Charles Walter. b 08. Keble Coll Ox BA31 MA35. Linc Th Coll 31. **d** 32 **p** 33. C Sutton in Ashfield St Mich *S'well* 32-35; C Nottingham St Pet and St Jas 35-37; C-in-C Bircotes CD 37-42; Chapl RNVR 42-46; V Worksop St Anne *S'well* 46-56; C-in-c Scofton w Osberton 51-56; R Chipping Barnet *St Alb* 56-69; RD Barnet 59-66; Hon Can St Alb 68-69; R Newent *Glouc* 69-76; rtd 76. *39 Kingsfield Road, Dane End, Ware, Herts SG12 0LZ* Tel (01920) 438514

EARLE, Canon George Halden. b 14. St Chad's Coll Dur LTh39 BA40 MA44. Qu Coll Newfoundland 35. **d** 38 **p** 39. Canada 38-40; from 57; C Monkseaton St Pet *Newc* 40-45; R Falstone 45-52; V Choppington 52-57; Can St Jo Cathl Newfoundland from 72; rtd 79. *5 Howlett Avenue, St John's, Newfoundland, Canada, A1B 1K8*

EARLEY, Stephen John. b 48. Trin Coll Bris DipHE93. **d** 93 **p** 94. C Stroud H Trin *Glouc* from 93. *Waldringfield, London Road, Stroud, Glos GL5 2AJ* Tel (01453) 758618

EARNEY, Graham Howard. b 45. AKC67. **d** 68 **p** 69. C Auckland St Helen *Dur* 68-72; C Corsenside *Newc* 72-76; P-in-c 76-79; TV Willington Team 79-83; TR 83-87; Dioc Soc Resp Officer *B & W* 87-95; Dir Bp Mascall Cen *Heref* from 95; Hon TV Ludlow, Ludford, Ashford Carbonell etc from 95; Dioc Development Rep from 96. *Bishop Mascall Centre, Lower Galdeford, Ludlow, Shropshire SY8 1RZ* Tel (01584) 873882 Fax 877945

EARNSHAW, Alan Mark. b 36. CQSW81. Lon Coll of Div LTh60. **d** 60 **p** 61. C Fazakerley Em *Liv* 60-65; V Ovenden *Wakef* 65-79; NSM Halifax St Jude 79-90; V Coley from 90. *The Vicarage, 41 Ing Head Terrace, Shelf, Halifax, W Yorkshire HX3 7LB* Tel (01422) 202292

EARNSHAW, Robert Richard (Rob). b 42. N Ord Course 78. **d** 81 **p** 82. NW Area Sec Bible Soc 78-85; NSM Liv All So Springwood *Liv* 81-85; R Hinton Ampner w Bramdean and Kilmeston *Win* 85-87; Chapl HM Young Offender Inst Huntercombe and Finnamore 87-92; Chapl HM Young Offender Inst Finnamore Wood Camp 87-92; R Spaxton w Charlynch, Goathurst, Enmore etc *B & W* from 92. *The Rectory, Church Road, Spaxton, Bridgwater, Somerset TA5 1DA* Tel (01278) 671265

EARP, John William. b 19. Jes Coll Cam BA42 MA45. Ridley Hall Cam 42. **d** 43 **p** 44. C Portman Square St Paul *Lon* 43-46; Tutor Ridley Hall Cam 46-48; Chapl 48-51; Vice-Prin 51-56; Chapl Eton Coll 56-62; V Hartley Wintney and Elvetham *Win* 62-77; RD Odiham 76-83; V Hartley Wintney, Elvetham, Winchfield etc 77-88; rtd 88; Perm to Offic *Nor* from 89. *3 The Driftway, Sheringham, Norfolk NR26 8LD* Tel (01263) 825487

EARWAKER, John Clifford. b 36. Keble Coll Ox BA59 MA63 Man Univ MEd71. Linc Th Coll 59. **d** 61 **p** 62. C Ecclesall *Sheff* 61-64; Succ St Mary's Cathl *Edin* 64-65; Lic to Offic *Man* 65-69; Lic to Offic *Sheff* from 69; Chapl and Lect Sheff Poly 81-92; Chapl and Lect Sheff Hallam Univ 92-93; rtd 93. *89 Dransfield Road, Sheffield S10 5RP* Tel 0114-230 3487

EASON, Canon Cyril Edward. b 21. Leeds Univ BA43 MA67. Coll of Resurr Mirfield 43. **d** 45 **p** 46. C Tonge Moor *Man* 45-51; C Blackpool H Cross *Blackb* 51-53; V Lever Bridge *Man* 53-65; Area Sec (Dio B & W) USPG 65-86; Area Sec (Dios Ex and Truro) USPG 75-86; Perm to Offic *Truro* 75-86; Hon Can Mufulira from 85; rtd 86; P-in-c Tilshead, Orcheston and Chitterne *Sarum* 86-92; Perm to Offic *Truro* from 92. *11 Bishop's Court, Williamson Drive, Ripon, N Yorkshire HG4 1AY* Tel (01765) 608300

EAST, Bryan Victor. b 46. Oak Hill Th Coll DipHE93. **d** 93 **p** 94. C Waltham Cross *St Alb* 93-96; C Wotton St Mary *Glouc* from 96. *30 Simon Road, Longlevens, Gloucester GL2 0TP* Tel (01452) 523803

EAST, Mark Richard. b 57. Trin Coll Bris BA89. **d** 89 **p** 90. C Dalton-in-Furness *Carl* 89-93; TV Bucknall and Bagnall *Lich* from 93. *St John's Parsonage, 28 Greasley Road, Stoke-on-Trent ST2 8JE* Tel (01782) 542861

EAST, Peter Alan. b 61. ACIB89 Southn Univ LLB82. Cranmer Hall Dur 90. **d** 93 **p** 94. C Combe Down w Monkton Combe and S Stoke *B & W* 93-97; R Wiveliscombe w Chipstable, Huish Champflower etc from 97. *The Vicarage, South Street, Wiveliscombe, Taunton, Somerset TA4 2LZ* Tel (01984) 623309

EAST, Reginald Walter. b 16. St Jo Coll Dur BA49 DipTh50. **d** 50 **p** 51. C Loughton St Mary *Chelmsf* 50-52; Youth Chapl 52-57; V W Mersea 57-71; R E Mersea 57-71; C Winterborne Whitechurch w Clenston *Sarum* 71-75; Warden Barn Fellowship Whatcombe Ho 75-80; Lic to Offic 80-85; rtd 85. *Shepherds Cottage, Winterborne Whitechurch, Blandford Forum, Dorset DT11 0NZ* Tel (01258) 880190

EAST, Richard Kenneth. b 47. Oak Hill Th Coll 86. **d** 88 **p** 89. C Necton w Holme Hale *Nor* 88-92; R Garsdon, Lea and Cleverton and Charlton *Bris* from 92; RD Malmesbury from 93. *The Rectory, Lea, Malmesbury, Wilts SN16 9PG* Tel (01666) 823861

EAST, Stuart Michael. b 50. Chich Th Coll 86. **d** 88 **p** 89. C Middlesbrough St Martin *York* 88-92; R Upper Ryedale 92-97; V Macclesfield St Paul *Ches* from 97. *St Paul's Vicarage, Swallow Close, Lark Hall Road, Macclesfield, Cheshire SK10 1QN* Tel (01625) 422910 or 501773 Fax 422910

EAST RIDING, Archdeacon of. *See* BUCKINGHAM, The Ven Hugh Fletcher

EASTER, Sister Ann Rosemarie. SRN68 DipRS78. Qu Coll Birm. **dss** 80 **d** 87 **p** 94. Chapl Asst Newham Gen Hosp 80-89; Stratford St Jo and Ch Ch w Forest Gate St Jas *Chelmsf* 80-87; Par Dn 87-89; NSM Forest Gate Em w Upton Cross from 89; AD Newham from 97. *St Luke's House, 36 Stratford Street, London E14 8LT* Tel 0171-538 9316

EASTER, Dr Brian James Bert. b 33. Lon Univ DipTh55 Birm Univ DPS75 PhD83. Tyndale Hall Bris 53 St Aug Coll Cant 56. **d** 57 **p** 58. C Tipton St Martin *Lich* 57-59; Midl Area Sec BCMS 59-64; V Barston *Birm* 64-72; Chapl Mentally Handicapped S Birm HA 72-94; Chapl Monyhull Hosp Birm 72-94; Lect Birm Univ from 86; Chapl S Birm Mental Health NHS Trust from 94. *995 Yardley Wood Road, Birmingham B14 4BS* Tel 0121-474 2622 or 627 1627

EASTER, Stephen Talbot. b 22. St Cath Coll Cam BA47 MA53. Ely Th Coll. **d** 50 **p** 51. C Whitstable All SS *Cant* 50-53; S Rhodesia 53-56; V Womenswold *Cant* 56-61; C-in-c Aylesham CD 56-61; V St Margarets-at-Cliffe w Westcliffe etc 61-85; rtd 85; Perm to Offic *Cant* from 85. *9/11 Blenheim Road, Deal, Kent CT14 7AJ* Tel (01304) 368021

EASTERN ARCHDEACONRY, Archdeacon of. *See* PEAKE, The Ven Simon Jeremy Brinsley

EASTGATE, Canon John. b 30. Kelham Th Coll 47. **d** 54 **p** 55. C Ealing St Pet Mt Park *Lon* 54-58; C-in-c Leic St Gabr CD *Leic* 58-64; V Leic St Gabr 64-69; Asst RD Christianity 64-69; V Glen Parva and S Wigston 69-74; V Woodley St Jo the Ev *Ox* 74-83; V Hughenden 83-94; RD Wycombe 87-90; Hon Can Ch Ch 90-94; rtd 94. *11 Orchard Park, Holmer Green, High Wycombe, Bucks HP15 6QY* Tel (01494) 713761

EASTOE, Robin Howard Spenser. b 53. Lon Univ BD75 AKC75. Coll of Resurr Mirfield 77. **d** 78 **p** 79. C Gt Ilford St Mary *Chelmsf* 78-81; C Walthamstow St Sav 81-84; V Barkingside St Fran 84-92; V Leigh-on-Sea St Marg from 92. *St Margaret's Vicarage, 1465 London Road, Leigh-on-Sea, Essex SS9 2SB* Tel (01702) 471773

EASTON, Christopher Richard Alexander. b 60. TCD BA DipTh. **d** 84 **p** 85. C Belfast St Donard *D & D* 84-89; I Inishmacsaint *Clogh* 89-95; I Magheralin w Dollingstown *D & D* from 95. *The Rectory, 12 New Forge Road, Magheralin, Craigavon, Co Armagh BT67 0QJ* Tel (01848) 611273 Fax 619569

EASTON, Dr Donald Fyfe. b 48. St Edm Hall Ox BA69 MA85 Nottm Univ CertEd70 Univ Coll Lon MA76 PhD90 Clare Hall Cam MA85. Westcott Ho Cam 89. **d** 90 **p** 91. NSM Fulham St Andr Fulham Fields *Lon* 90-94; Perm to Offic from 94. *12 Weltje Road, London W6 9TG* Tel 0181-741 0233

EASTON, John. b 34. St Cath Soc Ox BA59 MA63. Chich Th Coll 59. **d** 61 **p** 62. C Rugeley *Lich* 61-64; TR 72-87; C Shrewsbury All SS 64-66; Ind Chapl *Sheff* 66-72; V Bolsover *Derby* from 87; RD Bolsover and Staveley from 93. *The Vicarage, Bolsover, Chesterfield, Derbyshire S44 6BG* Tel (01246) 824888

EASTON, Richard Huntingford. b 26. Or Coll Ox BA51 MA51. Westcott Ho Cam 53. **d** 54 **p** 55. C Bris St Ambrose Whitehall *Bris* 54-57; New Zealand from 57. *271 Muriwai Road, RD1, Waimauku, Auckland 1250, New Zealand* Tel Auckland (9) 411 8320

EASTWOOD, Arthur Christopher John. b 17. St Edm Hall Ox BA45 MA45. Westcott Ho Cam 45. **d** 47 **p** 48. C Gt Ilford St Clem *Chelmsf* 47-50; C Portsea St Mary *Portsm* 50-54; C-in-c Cowplain St Wilfrid CD 54-62; V Cowplain 62-86; rtd 86; Perm to Offic *Bris* from 87. *40 Templar Road, Yate, Bristol BS17 5TG* Tel (01454) 322405

EASTWOOD, Colin Foster. b 34. Leeds Univ BA56 MA66. Linc Th Coll 65. **d** 67 **p** 68. C Cottingham *York* 67-70; C Darlington St Cuth *Dur* 70-75; V Eighton Banks 75-81; V Sutton St Jas *Ches* from 81. *St James's Vicarage, Sutton, Macclesfield, Cheshire SK11 0DS* Tel (01260) 252228

EASTWOOD, Harry. b 26. Man Univ BSc48. Ridley Hall Cam 81. **d** 82 **p** 83. NSM Barton Seagrave w Warkton *Pet* from 82. *22 Poplars Farm Road, Kettering, Northants NN15 5AF* Tel (01536) 513271

EASTWOOD, Miss Janet. b 54. Wycliffe Hall Ox 83. **dss** 86 **d** 87 **p** 94. Ainsdale *Liv* 86-87; Par Dn 87-90; TD Kirkby Lonsdale *Carl* 90-94; TV 94-95; Dioc Youth Officer 90-94; R Wavertree H Trin *Liv* from 95; P-in-c Wavertree St Thos 95-97. *Wavertree Rectory, Hunters Lane, Liverpool L15 8HL* Tel 0151-733 2172

EATOCK, John. b 45. Lanc Univ MA82. Lich Th Coll 67. **d** 70 **p** 71. C Crumpsall St Mary *Man* 70-73; C Atherton 73-74; C Ribbleton *Blackb* 74-77; V Ingol 77-83; V Laneside 83-92; RD Accrington 90-92; Perm to Offic from 92. *57 Heys Avenue, Haslingden, Rossendale, Lancs BB4 5DU* Tel (01706) 222531

EATON, Barry Anthony. b 50. Wilson Carlile Coll DipEvang79 Carl and Blackb Tr Inst 94. **d** 97. C W Burnley *Blackb* from 97. *23 Brantfell Drive, Burnley, Lancs BB12 8AW* Tel (01282) 455170

EATON, David Andrew. b 58. ACA83 Man Univ BSc79. Trin Coll Bris BA89. **d** 89 **p** 90. C Barking St Marg w St Patr *Chelmsf* 89-92; C Billericay and Lt Burstead 92-95; P-in-c Vange from 95. *Vange Rectory, 782 Clay Hill Road, Basildon, Essex SS16 4NG* Tel (01268) 581574 Fax as telephone

EATON, David John. b 45. Nottm Univ LTh BTh74. St Jo Coll Nottm 70. **d** 74 **p** 75. C Headley All SS *Guildf* 74-77; Ind Chapl *Worc* 77-82; TV Halesowen 80-82; V Rowledge *Guildf* 82-89; V Leatherhead from 89; RD Leatherhead from 93. *The Vicarage, 3 St Mary's Road, Leatherhead, Surrey KT22 8EZ* Tel (01372) 372313

✠EATON, The Rt Revd Derek Lionel. b 41. QSM85. DMSchM68 Neuchatel Univ Switz Cert Français 69 Internat Inst Chr Communication Nairobi 74 Univ of Tunis CertFAI70 Univ of Missouri MA78. Trin Coll Bris DipTh66 WEC Miss Tr Coll DipTh66. **d** 71 **p** 71 **c** 90. C Brislington St Luke *Bris* 71-72; Chapl Br Emb Tunisia 72-78; Provost All SS Cathl Cairo and Chapl Br Emb 78-83; Hon Can from 85; New Zealand from 84; Bp Nelson from 90. *Bishopdale, PO Box 100, 218 Trafalgar Street, Nelson, New Zealand* Tel Christchurch (3) 548 8991 or 548 3124 Fax 548 2125 E-mail +derek@nn.ang.org.nz

EATON (née CRAIG), Mrs Julie Elizabeth. b 57. SEN81. Trin Coll Bris DipHE89. **d** 89 **p** 94. Par Dn Gt Ilford St Andr *Chelmsf* 89-92; NSM Billericay and Lt Burstead 92-95; C 95-96; TV from 96; Chapl St Andr Hosp Billericay from 92. *Vange Rectory, 782 Clay Hill Road, Basildon, Essex SS16 4NG* Tel (01268) 581574 Fax as telephone

EATON, Mrs Margaret Anne. b 44. Ab Dioc Tr Course 82. **dss** 84 **d** 86 **p** 94. NSM Ellon *Ab* 84-95; NSM Cruden Bay 84-95; NSM Bridge of Don from 95. *84 Woodcroft Avenue, Bridge of Don, Aberdeen AB22 8DW* Tel (01224) 705091

EATON, Canon Oscar Benjamin (Ben). b 37. Puerto Rico Th Coll STB66. **d** 66 **p** 67. Ecuador 66-69; C Wandsworth St Anne *S'wark* 69-71; C Aldrington *Chich* 71-73; TV Littleham w Exmouth *Ex* 74-79; R Alphington 79-84; Chapl Barcelona w Casteldefels *Eur* 84-88; Chapl Maisons-Laffitte from 88; Can Malta Cathl from 96. *15 avenue Carnot, 78600 Maisons-Laffitte, France* Tel France (331) 39 62 34 97

EATON, Canon Peter David. b 58. K Coll Lon BA82 AKC82 Qu Coll Cam BA85 MA89 Magd Coll Ox MA90. Westcott Ho Cam 83. **d** 86 **p** 87. C Maidstone All SS and St Phil w Tovil *Cant* 86-89; Fells' Chapl Magd Coll Ox 89-91; Lic to Offic *Ox* from 89; USA from 91; Assoc R Salt Lake City St Paul 91-95; Hon Can Th Dio Utah from 91; R Lancaster St Jas from 95. *119 N Duke Street, Lancaster, Pennsylvania 17602-2815, USA* Tel (717) 397-4858 or 291-6408 Fax 397-7548

EATON, Miss Phyllis Mary. b 42. SRD Qu Eliz Coll Lon BSc63 Univ of S Africa BA79. WMMTC 87. **d** 90 **p** 94. NSM Washwood Heath *Birm* 90-91; NSM Edgbaston SS Mary and Ambrose 91-95; Perm to Offic from 95. *Flat 14, Mark House, 14 Wake Green Road, Birmingham B13 9HA* Tel 0121-449 2431

EAVES, Alan Charles. b 37. Lon Univ DipTh64. Tyndale Hall Bris 62. **d** 65 **p** 66. C Southport SS Simon and Jude *Liv* 65-66; C Eccleston Ch Ch 66-70; V Earlestown 70-79; V Orpington Ch Ch *Roch* from 79. *Christ Church Vicarage, 165 Charterhouse Road, Orpington, Kent BR6 9EP* Tel (01689) 870923

EAVES, Brian Maxwell. b 40. Tyndale Hall Bris 66. **d** 69 **p** 70. C Wolverhampton St Jude *Lich* 69-72; C Fazeley 72-75; TV Ipsley *Worc* 75-79; Chapl Amsterdam *Eur* 79-86; Chapl Bordeaux w Riberac, Cahors, Duras etc 86-91; Monaco 91-93; TV Buckhurst Hill *Chelmsf* 93-96; R Culworth w Sulgrave and Thorpe Mandeville etc *Pet* from 96. *The Rectory, Culworth, Banbury, Oxon OX17 2AT* Tel (01295) 760383

EBBITT, Francis Simon (Frank). b 20. TCD BA42 MA49 BD56. TCD Div Sch 40. **d** 43 **p** 44. C Belfast St Mary Magd *Conn* 43-46; C Lurgan Ch Ch *D & D* 46-48; C Bangor St Comgall 48-50; I Ballee 50-53; I Aghalee 53-59; V Stanwix *Carl* 59-65; V Rainhill *Liv* 65-74; V Stanford in the Vale w Goosey and Hatford *Ox* 74-80; RD Vale of White Horse 75-80; V Furze Platt 80-87; Chapl St Mark's and Clarefield Hosps Ox 80-87; rtd 87; Asst Chapl Malaga *Eur* 87-90. *229A Courthouse Road, Maidenhead, Berks SL6 6HF* Tel (01628) 22418

EBBITT, Robert David. b 22. TCD BA44 MA56. TCD Div Sch 44. **d** 45 **p** 46. C Belfast St Nic *Conn* 45-47; CF 47-65; Dep Asst Chapl Gen 65-72; Asst Chapl Gen 72-78; Perm to Offic *D & D* from 94. *13 The Meadow, Groomsport, Co Down BT19 6JH* Tel (01247) 464443

EBBSFLEET, Suffragan Bishop of (Provincial Episcopal Visitor). *See* RICHARDS, The Rt Revd John

EBELING, Mrs Barbara. b 44. **d** 94 **p** 95. C Stevenage St Hugh and St Jo *St Alb* from 94. *156 Durham Road, Stevenage, Herts SG1 4HZ* Tel (01438) 740621

ECCLES, Ernest Pattison. b 23. Kelham Th Coll 46. **d** 50 **p** 51. C Sheff Norwood St Leon *Sheff* 50-54; P-in-c Elsecar 54; P-in-c Thorpe Salvin 55-56; R Braithwell w Bramley 56-88; P-in-c Hooton Roberts w Ravenfield 62-75; rtd 88; Perm to Offic *Sheff* from 88. *Stonegates, Back Lane, Clifton, Maltby, Rotherham, S Yorkshire S66 7RA* Tel (01709) 867910

ECCLES, James Henry. b 30. DLC64 Lon Univ CertPsych70 DipEd. Wycliffe Hall Ox 86. **d** 87 **p** 88. NSM Llandudno *Ban*

87-91; rtd 91; NSM Llanrhos *St As* from 94. *Lowlands, 7 St Seiriol's Road, Llandudno LL30 2YY* Tel (01492) 878524

ECCLES, Mrs Vivien Madeline. LNSM course. **d** 92 **p** 94. NSM Stretford St Bride *Man* from 92. *479 Barton Road, Stretford, Manchester M32 9TA* Tel 0161-748 9795

ECKERSLEY, Mrs Nancy Elizabeth. b 50. York Univ BA72 Leeds Univ CertEd73. NE Ord Course 86. **d** 89 **p** 94. C Clifton *York* from 89; Chapl York Distr Hosp 90-93; Lay Tr Officer *York* from 93. *30 Howard Drive, Rawcliffe, York YO3 6XB* Tel (01904) 658905

ECKERSLEY, Canon Richard Hugh. b 25. Trin Coll Cam BA48 MA50. Chich Th Coll 49. **d** 51 **p** 52. C Portsea St Jo Rudmore *Portsm* 51-57; C Portsea N End St Mark 57-62; V Paulsgrove 62-73; V Brighton St Nic *Chich* 73-84; Can Res Portsm Cathl *Portsm* 84-92; rtd 92. *136 Kensington Road, Portsmouth PO2 0QY* Tel (01705) 653512

EDDERSHAW, Lionel Francis Trevor. b 34. Down Coll Cam BA58 MA62. Linc Th Coll 58. **d** 60 **p** 61. C Wallsend St Luke *Newc* 60-63; C Balkwell CD 63-68; R Falstone 68-75; R St John Lee 75-84; R Rothbury from 84; Chapl Coquetdale Cottage Hosp from 84. *The Rectory, Rothbury, Morpeth, Northd NE65 7TL* Tel (01669) 20482

EDDISON, Frederick Donald Buchanan. b 19. Trin Coll Cam BA41 MA46. Ridley Hall Cam 47. **d** 48 **p** 49. C Fulham St Matt *Lon* 48-51; C St Marylebone All So w SS Pet and Jo 51-53; Asst Chapl and Asst Master Forres Sch Swanage 53-56; Chapl CSSM 56-65; V Tunbridge Wells St Jo *Roch* 65-80; rtd 80; Perm to Offic *Roch* from 81; Perm to Offic *Chich* from 81. *43 East Cliff Road, Tunbridge Wells, Kent TN4 9AG* Tel (01892) 520991

EDDISON, Robert John Buchanan. b 16. Trin Coll Cam BA38 MA42. Ridley Hall Cam 38. **d** 39 **p** 40. C Tunbridge Wells St Jo *Roch* 39-43; Travelling Sec Scripture Union 42-80; rtd 81; Perm to Offic *Chich* from 81. *Durham Lodge, Crowborough, E Sussex TN6 1EW* Tel (01892) 652606

EDE, The Ven Dennis. b 31. Nottm Univ BA55 Birm Univ MSocSc73. Ripon Hall Ox 55. **d** 57 **p** 58. C Sheldon *Birm* 57-60; C Castle Bromwich SS Mary and Marg 60-64; Chapl E Birm Hosp 60-76; C-in-c Hodge Hill CD *Birm* 64-70; V Hodge Hill 70-72; TR 72-76; Chapl Sandwell Distr Gen Hosp 76-90; V W Bromwich All SS *Lich* 76-90; P-in-c W Bromwich Ch Ch 76-79; RD W Bromwich 76-90; Preb Lich Cathl 83-90; Adn Stoke 90-97; rtd 97; P-in-c Tilford *Guildf* from 97. *All Saints Vicarage, Tilford, Farnham, Surrey GU10 2DA* Tel (01252) 792333

EDE, Preb Oswald George. b 16. Lich Th Coll 37. **d** 39 **p** 40. C Cheadle *Lich* 39-46; V Marchington w Marchington Woodlands 46-82; RD Uttoxeter 66-76; Preb Lich Cathl 73-82; rtd 82; Perm to Offic *Lich* from 82. *19 St Mary's Crescent, Uttoxeter, Staffs ST14 7BH* Tel (01889) 566106

EDEN, Grenville Mervyn. b 37. Bris Univ BA58 Lon Univ MPhil78. Ox Min Course 88. **d** 95 **p** 96. NSM Burnham w Dropmore, Hitcham and Taplow *Ox* from 95. *Langdale, Grays Park Road, Stoke Poges, Slough SL2 4JG* Tel (01753) 525962

EDEN, Henry. b 36. G&C Coll Cam BA59 MA64. Ox NSM Course. **d** 87 **p** 88. NSM Abingdon w Shippon *Ox* 87-88; Chapl Brentwood Sch Essex 88-95; TV Beaconsfield *Ox* from 95. *St Michael's Parsonage, St Michael's Green, Beaconsfield, Bucks HP9 2BN* Tel (01494) 673464

EDEN, Mrs Lesley Patricia. b 54. Nor Ord Course 93. **d** 96 **p** 97. C Wallasey St Hilary *Ches* from 96. *18 Broadway Avenue, Wallasey, Wirral, Merseyside L45 6TA* Tel 0151-346 9553

EDEN, Leslie Thomas Ernest. b 19. ACII55. S'wark Ord Course. **d** 69 **p** 70. NSM Kidbrooke *S'wark* 69-94; rtd 94; Perm to Offic *S'wark* from 94. *47 Begbie Road, London SE3 8DA* Tel 0181-856 3088

EDEN, Michael William. b 57. Nottm Univ BTh86. Linc Th Coll 83. **d** 86 **p** 87. C Daventry *Pet* 86-89; TV Northampton Em 89-92; V Corby St Columba from 92. *St Columba's Vicarage, 157 Studfall Avenue, Corby, Northants NN17 1LG* Tel (01536) 204158 or 261436

EDGAR, David. b 59. Newc Univ BA81. Linc Th Coll BTh86. **d** 86 **p** 87. C Wednesbury St Paul Wood Green *Lich* 86-91; V Winterton Gp *Linc* from 91. *The Vicarage, High Street, Winterton, Scunthorpe, S Humberside DN15 9PU* Tel (01724) 732262

EDGAR, Canon Granville George. b 25. St Pet Hall Ox BA46 MA50. St Mich Coll Llan 46. **d** 48 **p** 49. C Monmouth *Mon* 48-50; Chapl St Woolos Cathl 50-59; V Ebbw Vale St Jo 59-65; V Newport St Paul 65-69; V Llantilio Crossenny and Llanfihangel Ystern etc 69-73; Dioc Dir RE 73-86; R Llangybi 73-91; Can St Woolos Cathl 75-91; rtd 91. *28 Manor Court, Baron Street, Usk NP5 1DQ* Tel (01291) 673451

EDGE, Canon John Francis. b 32. Ex Coll Ox BA54 MA56. St Steph Ho Ox 54. **d** 58 **p** 59. C Oswestry H Trin *Lich* 58-62; V 64-79; Tutor Lich Th Coll 62-64; Malaysia 79-87; Hon Can Kuching from 88; TV Wolverhampton *Lich* 88-91; Chapl R Hosp Wolv 88-91; Subwarden St Deiniol's Lib Hawarden 91-93; C Briercliffe *Blackb* 93-96; C W Felton *Lich* 96-97; Res Min from 97; rtd 97. *St Michael's Rectory, West Felton, Oswestry, Shropshire SY11 4LE* Tel (01691) 610228

EDGE, Michael MacLeod. b 45. St Andr Univ BSc68 Qu Coll Cam BA70 MA74. Westcott Ho Cam 68. **d** 72 **p** 73. C Allerton *Liv* 72-76; R Bretherton *Blackb* 76-82; P-in-c Kilpeck *Heref* 82-84; P-in-c St Devereux w Wormbridge 82-84; TR Ewyas Harold w Dulas, Kenderchurch etc 82-93; RD Abbeydore 84-90; V Enfield St Andr *Lon* from 93. *The Vicarage, Silver Street, Enfield, Middx EN1 3EG* Tel 0181-363 8676

EDGE, Philip John. b 54. Ripon Coll Cuddesdon 77. **d** 80 **p** 81. C N Harrow St Alb *Lon* 80-83; C St Giles Cripplegate w St Bart Moor Lane etc 83-86; P-in-c Belmont 86-88; V 88-92; V Ellesmere and Welsh Frankton *Lich* 92-97; V Ellesmere from 97. *The Vicarage, Church Hill, Ellesmere, Shropshire SY12 0HB* Tel (01691) 622571

EDGE, Miss Renate Erika. b 50. Bonn Chamber of Commerce TransDip75 DIL77. Cranmer Hall Dur 86. **d** 88. Par Dn Leic H Spirit *Leic* 88-89; Asst Chapl Leic and Co Miss for the Deaf 88-89; Par Dn Leic H Apostles *Leic* 89-94. *3 Whitfield Cross, Glossop, Derbyshire SK13 8NW* Tel (01457) 855777

EDGE, Timothy Peter. b 55. CEng85 MIEE85 FRAS80 Brighton Poly BSc80. Westcott Ho Cam 85. **d** 88 **p** 89. C Norton *Ches* 88-91; C Bedworth *Cov* 91-96; TV Witney *Ox* from 96. *4 Maidley Close, Witney, Oxon OX8 6ER* Tel (01993) 773438

EDGECUMBE, Irena Christine. *See* CZERNIAWSKA EDGECUMBE, Mrs Irena Christine

EDGELL, Hugh Anthony Richard. b 31. ARHistS84. AKC57. **d** 58 **p** 59. C N Lynn w St Marg and St Nic *Nor* 58-64; R S Walsham 64-74; V Upton w Fishley 64-74; R Hingham 74-81; R Hingham w Woodrising w Scoulton 81-85; OStJ 79-88; SBStJ from 88; V Horning *Nor* 85-89; P-in-c Beeston St Laurence w Ashmanhaugh 85-89; R Horning w Beeston St Laurence and Ashmanhaugh 89-95; Prior St Benet's Abbey Horning 87-95; rtd 95; Perm to Offic *Nor* from 95. *Brambles, Brimbelow Road, Hoveton, Norwich NR12 8UJ* Tel (01604) 782206

EDGELL, William John Raymond. b 15. St Aid Birkenhead 63. **d** 65 **p** 66. C Sutton *Liv* 65-68; V Bury St Paul *Man* 68-77; rtd 80; Perm to Offic *Man* from 80. *99 Turton Road, Tottington, Bury, Lancs BL8 4AQ* Tel (01204) 885246

EDGERTON, Ms Hilary Ann. b 66. R Holloway and Bedf New Coll Lon BSc88. Wycliffe Hall Ox BTh93. **d** 93 **p** 94. Par Dn S Cave and Ellerker w Broomfleet *York* 93-94; C from 94. *11 St Katherine's Road, South Cave, Brough, N Humberside HU15 2JB* Tel (01430) 421014

EDINBOROUGH, David. b 36. BA MEd. EMMTC. **d** 82 **p** 83. NSM Bramcote *S'well* from 82; P-in-c from 94; Dioc Officer for NSMs 89-94. *105A Derby Road, Beeston, Nottingham NG9 3GZ* Tel 0115-925 1066

EDINBURGH, Bishop of. *See* HOLLOWAY, The Most Revd Richard Frederick

EDINBURGH, Dean of. *See* MORRIS, The Very Revd Timothy David

EDINBURGH, Provost of. *See* FORBES, The Very Revd Graham John Thompson

EDIS, John Oram. b 26. ACIS50 ACP52 FCP89 CDipAF78 Open Univ BA81. Ox NSM Course 85. **d** 88 **p** 89. Hon Warden and Chapl E Ivor Hughes Educn Foundn from 88; NSM Gt Chesham *Ox* from 88. *21 Greenway, Chesham, Bucks HP5 2BW* Tel (01494) 785815

EDMEADS, Andrew. b 53. Linc Th Coll 84. **d** 86 **p** 87. C Sholing *Win* 86-89; R Knights Enham 89-97; rtd 97. *10 Altona Gardens, Andover, Hants SP10 4LG* Tel (01264) 391464

EDMONDS, Bernard Bruce. b 10. Ch Coll Cam BA32 MA36. St Steph Ho Ox 36. **d** 37 **p** 38. C Kenton *Lon* 37-48; V Oxhey St Matt *St Alb* 48-61; P-in-c Watford St Jas 54-60; V Caxton *Ely* 61-72; rtd 73; Perm to Offic *St Alb* from 74. *26 Bosmere Court, The Causeway, Needham Market, Ipswich IP6 8BQ* Tel (01449) 720238

EDMONDS (née HARRIS), Mrs Catherine Elizabeth. b 52. Leic Coll of Educn CertEd73 ACP79 K Alfred's Coll Win 86 Basingstoke Coll of Tech 87. S Dios Minl Tr Scheme 91. **d** 95 **p** 96. NSM Basing *Win* from 95. *Woodside, Elms Road, Hook, Hants RG27 9DP* Tel (01256) 764486

EDMONDS, Clive. b 42. ACII. S'wark Ord Course 78. **d** 81 **p** 82. C Horsell *Guildf* 81-85; R Bisley and W End 85-92; RD Surrey Heath 90-92; R Haslemere from 92. *The Rectory, 7 Derby Road, Haslemere, Surrey GU27 2PA* Tel (01428) 644578

EDMONDS, Canon Joseph William. b 12. Bps' Coll Cheshunt 46. **d** 49 **p** 50. C Tottenham St Paul *Lon* 49-54; V Edmonton St Alphege 54-66; R Dickleburgh *Nor* 66-69; P-in-c Thelveton w Frenze 66-69; R Dickleburgh w Thelveton and Frenze 69-80; R Dickleburgh w Thelveton w Frenze and Shimpling 80-81; RD Redenhall 73-88; rtd 81; Perm to Offic *Nor* from 81; Hon Can Nor Cathl 84-89. *Cliff House, 114 Beach Road, Scratby, Great Yarmouth, Norfolk NR29 3PG* Tel (01493) 720578

EDMONDS, Sidney. b 20. Oak Hill Th Coll. **d** 58 **p** 59. C Holborn St Geo w H Trin and St Bart *Lon* 58-61; Chapl HM Pris Liv 61-63; Dur 63-69; Parkhurst 69-74; Chapl HM Pris Reading 74-85; V Aldworth and Ashampstead *Ox* 74-85; rtd 85. *22 Sandlea Park, Wirral, Merseyside L48 0QF* Tel 0151-625 6147

EDMONDS-SEAL, Dr John. b 34. FFARCS63 Lon Univ MB, BS58. Ox NSM Course DipTh90. **d** 90 **p** 91. NSM Ox St Aldate w St Matt *Ox* 90-94; NSM Ox St Aldate from 95. *Otway, Woodperry Road, Oxford OX3 9UY* Tel (01865) 351582

EDMONDSON, Christopher Paul (Chris). b 50. Dur Univ BA71 MA81 St Jo Coll Dur DipTh72. **d** 73 **p** 74. C Kirkheaton *Wakef* 73-79; V Ovenden 79-86; Bp's Adv on Evang 81-86; P-in-c Bampton w Mardale *Carl* 86-92; Dioc Officer for Evang 86-92; V Shipley St Pet *Bradf* from 92. *The Vicarage, 2 Glenhurst Road, Shipley, W Yorkshire BD18 4DZ* Tel (01274) 584488 or 583381

EDMONDSON, John James William. b 55. St Jo Coll Dur BA83 MA91. Cranmer Hall Dur 80. **d** 83 **p** 84. C Gee Cross *Ches* 83-86; C Camberley St Paul *Guildf* 86-88; TV 88-90; V Foxton w Gumley and Laughton and Lubenham *Leic* 90-94; R Bexhill St Mark *Chich* from 94. *St Mark's Rectory, 11 Coverdale Avenue, Bexhill-on-Sea, E Sussex TN39 4TY* Tel (01424) 843733

EDMONDSON, Canon Norman Ross. b 16. St Jo Coll Dur BA39. **d** 39 **p** 40. C Annfield Plain *Dur* 39-43; Chapl RAFVR 43-47; V Chilton *Dur* 48-55; R Crook 55-72; RD Stanhope 61-72; Hon Can Dur Cathl 66-91; R Sedgefield 72-84; RD Sedgefield 78-84; rtd 84. *2 Spring Lane, Sedgefield, Stockton-on-Tees, Cleveland TS21 2DG* Tel (01740) 620629

EDMONTON, Area Bishop of. *See* MASTERS, The Rt Revd Brian John

EDMUND, Brother. *See* BLACKIE, Richard Footner

EDMUNDS, Andrew Charles. b 57. Whitelands Coll Lon BEd80 Croydon Coll DASS83 CQSW83. Oak Hill NSM Course 87. **d** 89 **p** 90. NSM Hawkwell *Chelmsf* 89-95; C Torquay St Matthias, St Mark and H Trin *Ex* from 95. *St Martin, 9 Lower Warberry Road, Torquay, Devon TQ1 1QP* Tel (01803) 212872

EDMUNDS, Eric John. b 39. Univ of Wales TCert60. WMMTC 87. **d** 90 **p** 91. NSM Brewood *Lich* 90-93; Chapl R Wolv Sch 91-92; R Llanerch Aeron w Ciliau Aeron and Dihewyd etc *St D* 93-97; V Aberporth w Tremain w Blaenporth and Betws Ifan from 97. *The Rectory, Aberporth, Cardigan SA43 2BX* Tel (01239) 810556

EDMUNDS, Gerald. b 12. ACIB. Glouc Th Course 72. **d** 72 **p** 73. NSM Tewkesbury w Walton Cardiff *Glouc* 72-82; Perm to Offic from 82. *29 Manor Park, Tewkesbury, Glos GL20 8BQ* Tel (01684) 294150

EDMUNDSON, Thomas. b 09. Oak Hill Th Coll 58. **d** 59 **p** 60. C Hyson Green *S'well* 59-61; V Halliwell St Paul *Man* 61-75; rtd 75; Lic to Offic *Blackb* from 76. *10 The Hayels, Blackburn BB1 9HZ* Tel (01254) 246408

EDNEY, William Henry. b 13. Birm Univ BA34. Qu Coll Birm 77. **d** 78 **p** 79. Hon C Cov St Geo *Cov* 78-85; Perm to Offic from 85. *20 Loudon Avenue, Coventry CV6 1JH* Tel (01203) 592168

EDSON, The Ven Michael (Mike). b 42. Birm Univ BSc64 Leeds Univ BA71. Coll of Resurr Mirfield 69. **d** 72 **p** 73. C Barnstaple St Pet w H Trin *Ex* 72-77; TV Barnstaple and Goodleigh 77-79; TV Barnstaple, Goodleigh and Landkey 79-82; V Roxbourne St Andr *Lon* 82-89; AD Harrow 85-89; P-in-c S Harrow St Paul 86-89; Warden Lee Abbey 89-94; Lic to Offic *Ex* 89-94; Adn Leic from 94. *13 Stoneygate Avenue, Leicester LE2 3HE* Tel 0116-270 4441 Fax 270 1091

EDWARD, Brother. *See* LEES-SMITH, Christopher John

EDWARDS, Preb Albert. b 20. Univ of Wales (Lamp) BA48. St Mich Coll Llan 48. **d** 50 **p** 51. C Welshpool *St As* 50-54; V Stanton on Hine Heath *Lich* 54-58; R Hanley w Hope 58-64; RD Stoke N 63-64; V Tamworth 65-86; RD Tamworth 69-81; Preb Lich Cathl 73-86; rtd 86; Perm to Offic *Lich* from 86; Perm to Offic *Heref* from 89. *Broom Cottage, Mount Street, Welshpool SY21 7LW* Tel (01938) 554008

EDWARDS, Aled. b 55. Univ of Wales (Lamp) BA77. Trin Coll Bris 77. **d** 79 **p** 80. C Glanogwen *Ban* 79-82; V Llandinorwig w Penisa'r-waen 82-85; R Mellteyrn w Botwnnog and Llandygwnnin etc 85-93; V Cardiff Dewi Sant *Llan* from 93. *Hafod-Lon, 51 Heath Park Avenue, Cardiff CF4 3RF* Tel (01222) 751418

EDWARDS, Andrew Colin. b 55. ACA81 Pemb Coll Cam BA77 MA80. St Mich Coll Llan BD89. **d** 89 **p** 90. C Newport St Paul *Mon* 89-91; C Newport St Woolos 91-93; Min Can St Woolos Cathl 91-93; P-in-c Ynysddu 93-95; TV Mynyddislwyn from 95. *The Vicarage, Commercial Road, Cwmfelinfach, Newport NP1 7HW* Tel (01495) 200257

EDWARDS, Andrew David. b 42. Tyndale Hall Bris 67. **d** 70 **p** 71. C Blackpool Ch Ch *Blackb* 70-73; C W Teignmouth *Ex* 73-76; P-in-c Ilfracombe SS Phil and Jas 76-85; C-in-c Lundy Is 79-89; V Ilfracombe SS Phil and Jas w W Down 85-89; TV Canford Magna *Sarum* from 89. *The Vicarage, 11 Plantagenet Crescent, Bournemouth BH11 9PL* Tel (01202) 573872

EDWARDS, Andrew James. b 54. York Univ BA76. Wycliffe Hall Ox 77. **d** 80 **p** 81. C Beckenham St Jo *Roch* 80-83; C Luton Ch Ch 83-87; V Skelmersdale Ch at Cen *Liv* 87-95; V Netherton from 95. *The Vicarage, 183 St Oswald's Lane, Bootle, Merseyside L30 5SR* Tel 0151-525 1882

EDWARDS, Andrew Jonathan Hugo. b 56. Ex Univ BA78. Sarum & Wells Th Coll BTh93. **d** 93 **p** 94. C Honiton, Gittisham, Combe Raleigh, Monkton etc *Ex* 93-97; P-in-c Queen Thorne *Sarum* from 97. *The Rectory, Trent, Sherborne, Dorset DT9 4SL* Tel (01935) 851049

EDWARDS, Canon Arthur John. b 42. Qu Mary Coll Lon BA64 MPhil66. St Mich Coll Llan 66. **d** 68 **p** 69. C Newport St Woolos *Mon* 68-71; V Llantarnam 71-74; Chapl The Bp of Llan High Sch 74-78; V Griffithstown *Mon* 78-86; Dioc Dir RE from 86; R Cwmbran 86-95; Hon Can St Woolos Cathl 88-91; Can from 91; V Caerleon from 95. *The Vicarage, Caerleon, Newport NP6 1AZ* Tel (01633) 420248

EDWARDS, Canon Carol Rosemary. b 46. Lon Univ DipTh76. Trin Coll Bris 74. **dss** 81 **d** 87 **p** 94. Hengrove *Bris* 81-82; Filton 82-85; Brislington St Chris 85-87; D-in-c 87-94; P-in-c from 94; Hon Can Bris Cathl from 93. *The Vicarage, 24 Hampstead Road, Bristol BS4 3HJ* Tel 0117-977 3670

EDWARDS, Charles Grayson. b 37. Macalester Coll (USA) BSc59. Ripon Hall Ox 64. **d** 66 **p** 67. C Bletchley *Ox* 66-68; C Ware St Mary *St Alb* 68-73; TV Basingstoke *Win* 73-80; P-in-c Sandford w Upton Hellions *Ex* 80-82; R 82-94; Perm to Offic from 95. *The Peak, Crediton, Devon EX17 2EU* Tel (01363) 772530

EDWARDS, Cyril Arthur. b 28. St Jo Coll York TCert47. Ripon Hall Ox 54. **d** 56 **p** 57. C Rotherham *Sheff* 56-61; Lic to Offic *Bris* 61-92; Hd RE Cotham Gr Sch 61-65; Chapl and Hd RE St Mary Redcliffe and Temple Sch 65-86; Sen Master 65-86; rtd 92. *Bungalow 4, Connaught Court, St Oswald's Road, York YO1 4QA* Tel (01904) 620679

EDWARDS, David Arthur. b 26. Wadh Coll Ox BA50 MA51. Wycliffe Hall Ox 50. **d** 52 **p** 53. C Didsbury St Jas and Em *Man* 52-55; Liv Sec SCM 55-58; Chapl Liv Univ *Liv* 55-58; R Burnage St Nic *Man* 58-65; V Yardley St Edburgha *Birm* 65-73; Org Sec (Dios Blackb, Carl and Man) CECS 73-78; R Man Resurr *Man* 78-81; V Lorton and Loweswater w Buttermere *Carl* 81-87; USPG 87-92; Malaysia 87-92; rtd 92. *Glentarkie, Lochmaben, Lockerbie, Dumfriesshire DG11 1SB* Tel (01387) 86231

EDWARDS, David Henry Oswald. b 16. St D Coll Lamp BA38. **d** 41 **p** 42. C Letterston *St D* 41-44; Chapl RN 44-71; C Fishguard w Llanychar *St D* 71-81; rtd 81. *Walmer House, West Street, Fishguard SA65 9DF* Tel (01348) 873329

EDWARDS, David John. b 60. Loughb Univ BA81 Homerton Coll Cam PGCE82. CA Tr Coll 86. **d** 95 **p** 96. C High Ongar w Norton Mandeville *Chelmsf* from 95. *101 Longfields, Ongar, Essex CM5 9DE* Tel (01277) 362500

EDWARDS, The Very Revd David Lawrence. b 29. OBE95. Magd Coll Ox BA52 MA56 Lambeth Hon DD90. Westcott Ho Cam 53. **d** 54 **p** 55. Fell All So Coll Ox 52-59; Tutor Westcott Ho Cam 54-55; SCM Sec 55-58; C Hampstead St Jo *Lon* 55-58; C St Martin-in-the-Fields 58-66; Ed SCM Press 59-66; Gen Sec SCM 65-66; Dean K Coll Cam 66-70; Six Preacher Cant Cathl *Cant* 69-76; Can Westmr Abbey 70-78; R Westmr St Marg 70-78; Chapl to Speaker of Ho of Commons 72-78; Sub-Dean Westmr 74-78; Chmn Chr Aid 71-78; Dean Nor 78-83; Provost S'wark 83-94; rtd 94. *19 Crispstead Lane, Winchester SO23 9SF* Tel (01962) 862597

EDWARDS, Ms Diana Clare. b 56. SRN77 RSCN81 Nottm Univ BTh86. Linc Th Coll 83. **dss** 86 **d** 87 **p** 94. S Wimbledon H Trin and St Pet *S'wark* 86-87; Par Dn 87-90; Par Dn Lingfield and Crowhurst 90-94; C 94-95; Chapl St Piers Hosp Sch Lingfield 90-95; R Bletchingley *S'wark* from 95. *The Rectory, Out Wood Lane, Bletchingley, Redhill RH1 4LR* Tel (01883) 743252

EDWARDS, Dudley James Milne. b 15. AKC38. **d** 38 **p** 39. C Beeston *S'well* 38-42; C N Hinksey *Ox* 42-44; C Maidenhead St Luke 44-46; S Africa 46-49; V Wigan St Andr *Liv* 49-51; S Rhodesia 51-63; R Barlborough *Derby* 63-68; V Mackworth St Fran 68-75; R Ashwick w Oakhill and Binegar *B & W* 75-80; rtd 80; Perm to Offic *B & W* from 81. *Trefechan, The Street, Draycott, Cheddar, Somerset BS27 3TH* Tel (01934) 743573

EDWARDS, Canon Emrys Llewelyn. b 14. St D Coll Lamp BA37. **d** 39 **p** 41. C Wrexham *St As* 39-44; C Lampeter Pont Steffan *St D* 44-47; V Betws Leiki and Gartheli 47-60; RD Ultra Aeron 58-60; V Llanelli Ch Ch 60-72; RD Cydweli 65-79; R Llanbadarn Fawr 72-79; Can St D Cathl 72-79; rtd 79. *Llys-y-Coed, New Road, New Quay SA45 9SB* Tel (01545) 560143

EDWARDS, Frances Mary. b 39. RSCN61 SRN64. St Mich Ho Ox CertRK68 Cranmer Hall Dur IDC71. **d** 92 **p** 94. NSM Skerton St Chad *Blackb* 92-97; Asst Chapl R Albert Hosp Lanc 92-94; Chapl 94-96; Regional Co-ord (NW) Ch Action on Disability from 96. *17 Church Brow, Bolton le Sands, Carnforth, Lancs LA5 8DY* Tel (01524) 822229

EDWARDS, Canon Geoffrey Lewis. b 14. Lon Univ BD39 AKC39. **d** 39 **p** 40. C Twickenham All Hallows *Lon* 39-44; C Bushey *St Alb* 44-47; V Mill End 47-72; V W Hyde St Thos 47-72; RD Watford 68-70; RD Rickmansworth 70-72; V Hockerill 72-84; RD Bishop's Stortford 74-84; Hon Can St Alb 76-84; rtd 84; Perm to Offic *Heref* from 84; Perm to Offic *Ox* from 89. *91 Early Road, Witney, Oxon OX8 6ET* Tel (01993) 704342

EDWARDS, Canon Geraint Wyn. b 47. Univ of Wales (Ban) BTh93. St D Coll Lamp DipTh70. **d** 71 **p** 72. C Llandudno *Ban* 71-73; C Ban St Mary 73-74; V Penisarwaen and Llanddeiniolen 74-77; V Llandinorwig w Penisarwaun and Llanddeiniolen 77-78; R Llanfechell w Bodewryd w Rhosbeirio etc from 78; RD Twrcelyn from 94; Hon Can Ban Cathl from 97. *The Rectory, Penbodeistedd Estate, Llanfechell, Amlwch LL68 0RE* Tel (01407) 710356

EDWARDS, Canon Gerald Lalande. b 30. Bris Univ MEd72. Glouc Th Course 75. **d** 76 **p** 76. NSM Cheltenham All SS *Glouc* 76-79; NSM Cheltenham St Mich 79-96; Hon Can Glouc Cathl

91-96; rtd 96; Perm to Offic *Glouc* from 96. *26 Monica Drive, Cheltenham, Glos GL50 4NQ* Tel (01242) 516863

EDWARDS, Dr Gordon Henry. b 33. FRICS60 FCILA67 FCIArb72 Reading Univ PhD87. Ripon Coll Cuddesdon 89. **d** 90 **p** 91. Hon C Sherston Magna, Easton Grey, Luckington etc *Bris* 90-92; Hon C Yatton Keynell 92-96; Hon C Chippenham St Paul w Hardenhuish etc from 96; Hon C Kington from 96. *The Old Vicarage, Sherston, Malmesbury, Wilts SN16 0LR* Tel (01666) 840405

EDWARDS, Canon Graham Arthur. b 32. St D Coll Lamp 56. **d** 61 **p** 62. C Betws w Ammanford *St D* 61-65; V Castlemartin and Warren 65-69; R Castlemartin w Warren and Angle etc 69-77; V St Clears w Llangynin and Llanddowror 77-83; CF (TAVR) 78-94; V St Clears w Llangynin and Llanddowror etc *St D* 83-94; Can St D Cathl 90-94; rtd 94. *Caswell, Station Road, St Clears, Carmarthen SA33 4BX* Tel (01994) 230342

EDWARDS, Graham Charles. b 40. Qu Coll Birm 80. **d** 82 **p** 83. C Baswich *Lich* 82-86; C Tamworth 86-88; R Hertford St Andr *St Alb* from 88. *St Andrew's Rectory, 43 North Road, Hertford SG14 1LZ* Tel (01992) 582726

EDWARDS, Harold James. b 50. Lon Univ CertEd72. Ridley Hall Cam 84 Qu Coll Birm 78. **d** 81 **p** 82. NSM The Quinton *Birm* 81-84; C Highters Heath 84-85; V Llanwddyn and Llanfihangel and Llwydiarth *St As* 85-88; V Ford *Heref* 88-97; V Alberbury w Cardeston 88-97; Chapl Shropshire and Mid-Wales Hospice from 96. *Shropshire and Mid-Wales Hospice, Bicton Heath, Shrewsbury SY3 8HS* Tel (01743) 236565

EDWARDS, Harry Steadman. b 37. St Aid Birkenhead 64. **d** 66 **p** 67. Hon C Handsworth St Jas *Birm* 66-83; Hon C Curdworth w Castle Vale 83-85; P-in-c Small Heath St Greg 85-88; V High Crompton *Man* from 88. *St Mary's Vicarage, 18 Rushcroft Road, Shaw, Oldham OL2 7AA* Tel (01706) 847455

EDWARDS, Ms Helen. b 55. Natal Univ BSW75. St Steph Ho Ox DipMin94. **d** 96 **p** 97. C Gravelly Hill *Birm* from 96. *107 Mere Road, Erdington, Birmingham B23 7LN* Tel 0121-373 6702

EDWARDS, Helen Glynne. *See* WEBB, Mrs Helen Glynne

EDWARDS, The Ven Henry St John. b 30. Southn Univ DipEd. Ripon Hall Ox. **d** 59 **p** 60. C Wickford *Chelmsf* 59-62; Australia from 62; Dean Grafton 69-78; Adn Moreton 85-89; W Moreton 91-93; Gold Coast 93-95; rtd 95. *PO Box 416, Dorrigo, Queensland, Australia 2453* Tel Dorrigo (66) 574018

EDWARDS, Henry Victor (Harry). b 48. AKC71 Open Univ BA85. St Aug Coll Cant 72. **d** 73 **p** 74. C W Leigh CD *Portsm* 73-77; V Cosham 77-84; V Reydon *St E* 84-86; V Blythburgh w Reydon 86-96; Chapl St Felix Sch Southwold 86-96; Chapl Blythburgh Hosp 86-96; P-in-c Campsea Ashe w Marlesford, Parham and Hacheston *St E* from 96; Dioc Adv for Counselling and Past Care from 96. *The Rectory, Marlesford, Woodbridge, Suffolk IP13 0AT* Tel (01728) 746747

EDWARDS, Herbert Joseph. b 29. Nottm Univ BA51. Wells Th Coll 54. **d** 56 **p** 57. C Leic St Pet *Leic* 56-61; C-in-c Broom Leys CD 61-65; V Broom Leys 65-68; Lect Lich Th Coll 68-71; Rhodesia 71-79; Botswana 74-75; V Bloxwich *Lich* 80-84; R Asfordby *Leic* 84-92; R N w S Kilworth and Misterton 92-96; rtd 96. *St John's Hospital, St John Street, Lichfield, Staffs WS13 6PB* Tel (01543) 416620

EDWARDS, Canon James Frederick. b 36. ALCD62. **d** 62 **p** 63. C Kenwyn *Truro* 62-68; V Tuckingmill 68-76; V St Columb Minor and St Colan from 76; RD Pydar 84-93; Hon Can Truro Cathl from 92. *The Vicarage, Parkenbutts, St Columb Minor, Newquay, Cornwall TR7 3HE* Tel (01637) 873496

EDWARDS, Mrs Jill Kathleen. b 48. Man Univ BA69 Golds Coll Lon CQSW72 Lon Univ DipRS85. S'wark Ord Course 90. **d** 93 **p** 95. NSM Grays Thurrock *Chelmsf* from 93. *The Old Tennis Court, Allenby Crescent, Grays, Essex RM17 6DH* Tel (01375) 372887

EDWARDS, John Gregory. b 29. Univ of Wales BA49 MA53. St Steph Ho Ox 64. **d** 66 **p** 67. C Ealing Ch the Sav *Lon* 66-70; C Greenford H Cross 70-75; P-in-c Poundstock *Truro* 75-82; R Week St Mary w Poundstock and Whitstone 82-94; rtd 94. *8 Vestry Drive, Exeter EX2 8FG* Tel (01392) 432603

EDWARDS, Jonathan Guy. b 63. Bris Univ BA85. Ridley Hall Cam BA93. **d** 94 **p** 95. C Preston Plucknett *B & W* from 94. *5 Lime Kilns, Yeovil, Somerset BA21 3RW* Tel (01935) 22553

EDWARDS, Kenneth Barnsley. b 19. Birm Univ BSc48. Wells Th Coll 70. **d** 72 **p** 73. C Furze Platt *Ox* 72-74; C Henley 74-77; P-in-c Hatch Beauchamp w Beercrocombe *B & W* 77-80; P-in-c W Hatch 77-80; P-in-c Curry Mallet 79-80; C Ex St Thos and Em *Ex* 81; Perm to Offic *B & W* 82-87; R Tollard Royal w Farnham, Gussage St Michael etc *Sarum* 87-89; rtd 89. *3 St George's Close, West Harnham, Salisbury SP2 8HA* Tel (01722) 338409

EDWARDS, Leigh Cameron. b 17. St Cath Soc Ox BA38 MA42. St Steph Ho Ox 38. **d** 40 **p** 41. C Roath St Marg *Llan* 40-43; P-in-c Llangeview *Mon* 43-46; P-in-c Gwernesney 43-46; C Bournemouth St Mary *Win* 46-49; V Southampton St Jas 49-54; C Win St Jo cum Winnall 54-58; R Carshalton *S'wark* from 58. *The Rectory, 2 Talbot Road, Carshalton, Surrey SM5 3BS* Tel 0181-647 2366

EDWARDS, Leslie. b 27. Univ of Wales (Ban) DipTh54. St D Coll Lamp 54. **d** 55 **p** 56. C Rhyl w St Ann *St As* 55-59; V Llawrybettws and Bettws Gwerfyl Goch 59-62; V Caerfallwch 62-66; R Halkyn and Caerfallwch 66-92; P-in-c Rhesycae 74-92; rtd 92. *23 Troed-y-Fenlli, Llanbedr Dyffryn Clwyd, Ruthin LL15 1BQ* Tel (01824) 703922

EDWARDS, Malcolm Ralph. b 27. Man Univ 49. Cranmer Hall Dur 57. **d** 59 **p** 60. C Withington St Paul *Man* 59-62; C Chadderton Em 62-64; R Longsight St Jo 64-70; V Halliwell St Thos 70-81; V Milnrow 81-92; rtd 92; Perm to Offic *Man* from 92. *20 Upper Lees Drive, Westhoughton, Bolton BL5 3UE* Tel (01942) 813279

EDWARDS, Mark Anthony. b 61. Moorlands Bible Coll DipThMin86 St Jo Coll Dur CTMin95. **d** 95. C Ulverston St Mary w H Trin *Carl* 95-97; C Barrow St Jo from 97. *11 Park Drive, Barrow-in-Furness, Cumbria LA13 9BA* Tel (01229) 839686

EDWARDS, Mrs Mary. **d** 96. NSM Avon Valley *Sarum* from 96. *5 Hampshire Cross, Tidworth, Hants SP9 7SG* Tel (01980) 847520

EDWARDS, Michael Norman William. b 34. St Paul's Grahamstown 62. **d** 63 **p** 65. S Africa 63-81; Tristan da Cunha 81-83; R Aston-on-Trent and Weston-on-Trent *Derby* 84-87; V Derby St Thos 87-95; P-in-c Blackwell from 95. *The Vicarage, Church Hill, Blackwell, Alfreton, Derbyshire DE55 5HN* Tel (01773) 863242

EDWARDS, Nicholas John. b 53. UEA BA75 Fitzw Coll Cam BA77 MA80. Westcott Ho Cam 75. **d** 78 **p** 79. C Kirkby *Liv* 78-81; V Cantril Farm 81-87; V Hale 87-94; R Chingford SS Pet and Paul *Chelmsf* from 94; Asst RD Waltham Forest from 94. *The Rectory, 2 The Green Walk, London E4 7ER* Tel 0181-529 1291

EDWARDS, Mrs Nita Mary. b 50. Univ of Wales (Ban) BD72 Nottm Univ PGCE73. Cranmer Hall Dur DMinlStuds93. **d** 93 **p** 94. C Ormesby *York* 93-95; C Billingham St Aid *Dur* from 95. *1 Lanchester Avenue, Billingham, Cleveland TS23 2TD* Tel (01642) 562566

EDWARDS, Mrs Patricia Anne. b 52. EMMTC 76. **dss** 79 **d** 87 **p** 94. Hon Par Dn Clifton *S'well* 87-91; NSM Edwalton from 91. *148 Wilford Road, Ruddington, Nottingham NG11 6FB* Tel 0115-984 3402

EDWARDS, Peter Clive. b 50. Lon Univ BA72. St Steph Ho Ox 83. **d** 85 **p** 86. C Lee St Aug *S'wark* 85-90; V Salfords 90-97; R Newington St Mary from 97. *The Rectory, 57 Kennington Park Road, London SE11 4JQ* Tel 0171-735 1894

EDWARDS, Canon Peter John Smallman. b 48. Univ of Wales (Ban) BD72 MTh75. Linc Th Coll 72. **d** 73 **p** 74. C Llanelli *St D* 73-76; Prec St Andr Cathl Inverness *Mor* 76-77; R Walton W w Talbenny and Haroldston W *St D* 77-81; P-in-c Invergordon St Ninian *Mor* 81-86; I 86-89; Prin Moray Dioc Ord Course 81-88; Can St Andr Cathl Inverness 81-89; Offg Chapl RAF 82-88; Syn Clerk *Mor* 85-89; Hon Can St Andr Cathl Inverness from 90; V Caldicot *Mon* from 89; Hon Can Mahajanga from 95. *The Vicarage, 39 Church Road, Caldicot, Newport NP6 4HT* Tel (01291) 420221

EDWARDS, Canon Philip John. b 28. Lon Univ MRCS51 LRCP51. Chich Th Coll 58. **d** 60 **p** 61. C Orpington St Andr *Roch* 60-67; C Mayfield *Chich* 67-71; V Haywards Heath St Rich 71-91; Can and Preb Chich Cathl 84-91; rtd 91; Perm to Offic *Chich* from 91. *21 Haywards Road, Haywards Heath, W Sussex RH16 4HX* Tel (01444) 457880

EDWARDS, Philip Osbert Clifford. b 11. St Jo Coll Ox BA33 MA47. Wycliffe Hall Ox 35. **d** 35 **p** 36. C Bayswater *Lon* 35-38; C Chelsea St Luke 38-39; C Woburn Square Ch Ch 39-41; Chapl RAFVR 41-47; New Zealand 47-54; Chapl Oundle Sch 54-69; P-in-c Stoke Doyle *Pet* 60-63; Chapl St Chris Hospice Sydenham 69-74; Chapl Algarve *Eur* 74-77; rtd 77; Perm to Offic *Heref* 86-92. *8 The Old Orchard, Nash Meadows, South Warnborough, Hants RG25 1RJ* Tel (01256) 862960

EDWARDS, Phillip Gregory. b 52. MSOSc90 Lon Univ BSc73 Imp Coll Lon ARCS73. Qu Coll Birm DipTh80. **d** 81 **p** 82. C Lillington *Cov* 81-85; P-in-c Cov St Alb 85-86; TV Cov E from 86. *St Alban's Vicarage, Mercer Avenue, Coventry CV2 4PQ* Tel (01203) 452493 E-mail edwards_family@msn.com

EDWARDS, Raymond Lewis. Keble Coll Ox BA46 MA47. St Deiniol's Hawarden 69. **d** 70 **p** 71. Prin Educn Cen Penmaenmawr 56-81; Hon C Dwygyfylchi *Ban* 70-81; P-in-c Llandwrog 81-82; V 82-90; Dioc Dir of Educn from 84; rtd 90; Lic to Offic *Ban* from 90. *Dulyn View, 23 Rhiwlas Road, Talysarn, Penygroes LL54 6HU* Tel (01286) 881090

EDWARDS, Rhys Meurig. b 16. St D Coll Lamp BA37. **d** 39 **p** 41. C Garw Valley *Llan* 39-41; C Harrow Weald St Mich *Lon* 41-44; C Norwood St Luke *S'wark* 44-48; Australia 48-55; R Wongan Hills 48-51; R Mundaring 52-55; V Kenley *S'wark* 55-74; V Kingston Vale St Jo 74-84; rtd 84; Perm to Offic *Chich* from 84. *5 Paddock Close, Fernhurst, Haslemere, Surrey GU27 3JZ* Tel (01428) 656695

EDWARDS, Richard John. b 47. Queensland Univ BA85. St Fran Coll Brisbane 83 McAuley Coll Brisbane DipRE85. **d** 85 **p** 85. Australia 85-87 and 88-96; C Olveston *Bris* 87-88; R Kingston St Mary w Broomfield etc *B & W* from 96. *The Vicarage, Kingston St Mary, Taunton, Somerset TA2 8HW* Tel (01823) 451257

EDWARDS, Roger Brian. b 41. Sarum & Wells Th Coll 87. **d** 89 **p** 90. C Wellington and Distr *B & W* 89-92; V Hursley and Ampfield *Win* from 92. *The Vicarage, Knapp Lane, Ampfield, Romsey, Hants SO5 9BT* Tel (01794) 368291

EDWARDS, Canon Ronald William. b 20. Kelham Th Coll 37. **d** 43 **p** 44. C Perry Street *Roch* 43-46; S Africa 46-57; V Godmanchester *Ely* 57-62; Australia from 62; Adn of the Coast 71-74; Dean Bathurst 74-77; Can Perth 79-88; rtd 88. *2/31 Park Street, Como, W Australia 6152* Tel Perth (9) 450 6272

EDWARDS, Rowland Thomas. b 62. **d** 88 **p** 89. C Llangiwg *S & B* 88-90; C Morriston 90-91; V Llangorse, Cathedine, Llanfihangel Talyllyn etc from 91. *Llangorse Vicarage, Brecon LD3 7UG* Tel (01874) 84298

EDWARDS, Rupert Quintin. b 67. Bris Univ LLB89. Wycliffe Hall Ox BTh94. **d** 97. C Bromley Ch Ch *Roch* from 97. *4 Meadow Road, Shortlands, Bromley, Kent BR2 0DX* Tel 0181-290 4506

EDWARDS, Dr Ruth Blanche. b 39. Girton Coll Cam BA61 MA65 PhD68 Aber Coll of Educn CertEd75. Ab Dioc Tr Course 77. **d** 87 **p** 94. Lect Aber Univ *Ab* 77-90; Sen Lect 90-96; NSM Aberdeen St Jas 87-88; NSM Aberdeen St Jo 88-96; Lect Ripon Coll Cuddesdon from 96; Lic to Offic *Ox* from 96. *Flat 11, Runcie Building, Ripon College Cuddesdon, Oxford OX44 9EY* Tel (01865) 875546 or 874595

EDWARDS, Stephen. b 44. S'wark Ord Course. **d** 82 **p** 83. C Benhilton *S'wark* 82-86; P-in-c Clapham Ch Ch and St Jo 86-87; TV Clapham TM 87-94; Chapl HM Pris Wormwood Scrubs 94-96; Chapl HM Pris Maidstone from 96. *The Chaplain's Office, HM Prison, County Road, Maidstone, Kent ME14 1UZ* Tel (01622) 755611 Fax 688038

EDWARDS, Stephen Michael. b 72. **d** 96 **p** 97. C Colwyn Bay *St As* from 96. *29 Bryn Rhyg, Colwyn Heights, Colwyn Bay LL29 6DP*

EDWARDS, Dr Steven Charles. b 58. Sheff Poly HND80 Lanc Univ BSc82 PhD86. Linc Th Coll CMinlStuds94. **d** 94 **p** 95. C Bradshaw *Man* from 94. *5 Hilmarton Close, Bolton BL2 3HJ* Tel (01204) 305442 Fax as telephone E-mail steveedwar@aol.com

EDWARDS, Stuart. b 46. Lon Univ DipTh70 Lanc Univ BA73. Kelham Th Coll 66. **d** 71 **p** 72. C Skerton St Luke *Blackb* 71-76; C Ribbleton 76-80; TV 80-82; V Blackb St Mich w St Jo and H Trin 82-91; V Blackpool H Cross from 91; RD Blackpool 93-94. *Holy Cross Vicarage, Central Drive, Blackpool FY1 6LA* Tel (01253) 341263

EDWARDS, Mrs Susan. b 54. R Holloway Coll Lon BSc75 SS Hild & Bede Coll Dur PGCE76. Qu Coll Birm 78. **dss** 81 **d** 87 **p** 94. Lillington *Cov* 81-85; Cov E 85-87; Par Dn 87-94; C from 94. *St Alban's Vicarage, Mercer Avenue, Coventry CV2 4PQ* Tel (01203) 452493 E-mail edwards_family@msn.com

EDWARDS, Mrs Susan Diane. b 48. St Alb Minl Tr Scheme 86 Cranmer Hall Dur 91. **d** 92 **p** 94. Par Dn Borehamwood *St Alb* 92-94; C 94-96; V Arlesey w Astwick from 96. *The Vicarage, 77 Church Lane, Arlesey, Beds SG15 6UX* Tel (01462) 731227

EDWARDS, The Very Revd Thomas Erwyd Pryse. b 33. Univ of Wales (Lamp) BA56. St Mich Coll Llan 56. **d** 58 **p** 59. C Llanbeblig w Caernarfon *Ban* 58-63; Chapl Asst St Geo Hosp Lon 63-66; Lic to Offic *S'wark* 63-72; Chapl K Coll Hosp Lon 66-72; R Penmon and Llangoed w Llanfihangel Dinsylwy *Ban* 72-75; V Llandysilio and Llandegfan 75-81; V Glanadda 81-85; Chapl St D Hosp Ban 81-84; Chapl Gwynedd Hosp Ban 84-86; V Caerhun w Llangelynin w Llanbedr-y-Cennin *Ban* 86-88; Dean Ban from 88; Hon Can Ban Cathl from 88; R Ban 88-93. *The Deanery, Cathedral Close, Bangor LL57 1LH* Tel (01248) 370693 or 353983 Fax 353882

EDWARDS, Thomas Harold David. b 16. Jes Coll Ox BA38 MA46. Westmr Coll Cam 38 St Aug Coll Cant 58. **d** 58 **p** 59. C Southbroom *Sarum* 58-61; V Upper Tooting H Trin *S'wark* 61-64; V Bledlow *Ox* 64-73; RD Aylesbury 72-77; R Bledlow w Saunderton and Horsenden 73-89; rtd 89; Perm to Offic *Heref* 89-95. *22 St Anne's Grove, Knowle, Solihull, W Midlands B93 9JB* Tel (01564) 772593

EDWARDS, Thomas Victor. b 22. Univ of Wales (Lamp) BA52 LTh54 Birm Univ MA57. **d** 54 **p** 55. C Griffithstown *Mon* 54-56; Special Service Clergyman *Lich* 56-57; C Kingswinford St Mary 57-59; V Tipton St Jo 59-65; V Oxley 65-71; R Kingsley 71-90; rtd 90; Perm to Offic *Lich* from 90. *14 Pastoral Close, Madeley, Crewe CW3 9PU* Tel (01782) 751502

EDWARDSON, David Roger Hately. b 54. Stirling Univ BSc79 DipEd79 Edin Univ BD91. Edin Th Coll 88. **d** 91 **p** 92. C Edin St Jo *Edin* 91-93; R Kelso from 93. *The Rectory, Forestfield, Kelso, Roxburghshire TD5 7BX* Tel (01573) 224163

EDWARDSON, Joseph Philip. b 28. Dur Univ BA52 Leeds Univ PGCE53. Wells Th Coll 61. **d** 63 **p** 64. C Macclesfield St Mich *Ches* 63-66; V Egremont St Jo 66-72; V Eastham 72-81; V Poulton 81-94; rtd 94; Perm to Offic *Ches* from 94. *Keppler, 38 Hazel Grove, Irby, Wirral, Merseyside L61 4UZ*

EDY, Robert James (Bob). b 48. Southn Univ BA70 CertEd71. Ox Min Course CBTS93. **d** 93 **p** 94. Dep Hd Master Henry Box Sch Witney from 90; NSM Ducklington *Ox* from 93. *4 Elm Close, Witney, Oxon OX8 5BT* Tel (01993) 705376

EDYE, Ian Murray. b 21. K Coll Lon BD AKC. S'wark Ord Course 66. **d** 69 **p** 70. NSM E Grinstead St Swithun *Chich* from 69. *Thrush Field, Coombe Hill Road, East Grinstead, W Sussex RH19 4LY* Tel (01342) 323157

EFEMEY, Raymond Frederick. b 28. Ball Coll Ox BA51 MA64. Cuddesdon Coll 51. **d** 53 **p** 54. C Croydon St Mich *Cant* 53-57; C Hendford *B & W* 57-60; V Upper Arley *Worc* 60-66; Ind Chapl 60-66; P-in-c Dudley St Jas 66-69; V Dudley St Thos 66-69; V Dudley St Thos and St Luke 69-75; Hon C Stretford All SS *Man* 76-82; SSF from 81; P-in-c Weaste *Man* 82-87; V 87-93; rtd 93. *20 Groby Road, Chorlton-cum-Hardy, Manchester M21 1DD* Tel 0161-860 5416

EGERTON, George. b 28. S'wark Ord Course 70. **d** 73 **p** 74. NSM Shere *Guildf* 73-94; Perm to Offic from 94. *6 Heathrow, Gomshall, Guildford, Surrey GU5 9QD* Tel (01483) 202549

EGERTON, Ronald. b 14. St D Coll Lamp BA37 St Mich Coll Llan 37. **d** 38 **p** 39. C Newtown *St As* 38-42; C Hanmer 42-47; V Welshampton *Lich* 47-54; V Lineal cum Colemere 52-54; V Silverdale 54-63; R Rhydycroesau 63-77; R Selattyn 63-77; RD Oswestry 76-77; R Chewton Mendip w Ston Easton, Litton etc *B & W* 77-80; rtd 80; Perm to Offic *Lich* from 80. *10 Rosehill Close, Whittington, Oswestry, Shropshire SY11 4DY* Tel (01691) 662453

EGGERT, Max Alexander. b 43. AKC67 Birkb Coll Lon BSc74 Poly Cen Lon MA87 CPsychol90. **d** 67 **p** 68. C Whitton St Aug *Lon* 67-69; Hon C Hackney 72-74; Hon C Llantwit Major *Llan* 74-76; NSM Haywards Heath St Rich *Chich* 78-93; Lic to Offic from 93. *94 High Street, Lindfield, Haywards Heath, W Sussex RH16 2HP* Tel (01444) 483057

EGGINGTON, William Charles. b 10. Lon Univ BSc31. Coll of Resurr Mirfield 32. **d** 34 **p** 35. C Leic St Matt *Leic* 34-39; C Aldenham *St Alb* 39-40; CF (EC) 40-46; V Abbots Langley *St Alb* 46-50; C Hitchin St Mary 50-60; V Barnet Vale St Mark 60-80; rtd 80; Perm to Offic *St Alb* from 80. *The Rectory, Pirton Road, Holwell, Hitchin, Herts SG5 3SS* Tel (01462) 712307

EGLIN, Ian. b 55. St Jo Coll Dur BA76. Coll of Resurr Mirfield 77. **d** 79 **p** 80. C Cov St Mary *Cov* 79-83; TV Kingsthorpe w Northn St Dav *Pet* 83-87; Chapl RN from 87. *Royal Naval Chaplaincy Service, Room 203, Victory Building, HM Naval Base, Portsmouth PO1 3LS* Tel (01705) 727903 Fax 727112

EICHELMAN, Canon George Charles. b 14. Roch Univ NY BA37. **d** 40 **p** 40. USA 40-78; rtd 79; Hon C Costa Blanca *Eur* 83-86; Hon Can Gib Cathl 85-86. *6C Marisol Park, Calpe, Alicante, Spain*

EKE, Canon Robert Foord Stansfield. b 17. K Coll Lon BD39 AKC39. Ely Th Coll 40. **d** 40 **p** 41. C Carl St Aid and Ch Ch *Carl* 40-43; C Bournemouth St Clem *Win* 43-46; C Wimbledon *S'wark* 46-54; V Clapham Ch Ch 54-62; St Kitts-Nevis 62-72; V Alton St Lawr *Win* 72-89; Bp's Ecum Officer 80-82; Hon Can Win Cathl 82-89; RD Alton 82-89; rtd 89; Perm to Offic *Chich* from 89; Hon Can Antigua from 95. *77 Hangleton Way, Hove, E Sussex BN3 8AF* Tel (01273) 421443

EKIN, Tom Croker. b 29. Linc Th Coll 59. **d** 60 **p** 61. C Leamington Priors All SS *Cov* 60-63; R Ilmington w Stretton-on-Fosse 63-72; S Africa 72-77; R Moreton-in-Marsh w Batsford *Glouc* 77-83; R Moreton-in-Marsh w Batsford, Todenham etc 83-94; rtd 95. *St Mark's House, Englefield, Reading RG7 5EN* Tel 0118-930 2227

ELBOURNE, Keith Marshall. b 46. Nottm Univ BTh74 Lon Univ BD76. Westmr Past Foundn DAPC89 St Jo Coll Nottm 70. **d** 74 **p** 75. C Romford Gd Shep Collier Row *Chelmsf* 74-78; C Victoria Docks St Luke 78-81; P-in-c 81-92; V Walthamstow St Pet from 92. *121 Forest Rise, London E17 3PW* Tel 0181-520 3854

ELBOURNE, Raymond Nigel Wilson. b 43. Dur Univ BA66. Linc Th Coll 67. **d** 69 **p** 70. C Liscard St Mary *Ches* 69-72; V Hattersley 72-77; R Odd Rode from 77; RD Congleton from 97. *Odd Rode Rectory, Church Lane, Scholar Green, Cheshire ST7 3QN* Tel (01270) 882195

ELBOURNE, Timothy (Tim). b 60. Selw Coll Cam BA81 PGCE82 MA85. Westcott Ho Cam 84. **d** 86 **p** 87. C Tottenham H Trin *Lon* 86-88; Chapl York Univ *York* 88-94; P-in-c Thorp Arch w Walton from 94. *The Vicarage, Church Causeway, Thorp Arch, Wetherby, W Yorkshire LS23 7AE* Tel (01937) 842430

ELCOAT, Canon George Alastair. b 22. Qu Coll Birm. **d** 51 **p** 52. C Corbridge w Halton *Newc* 51-55; V Spittal 55-62; V Chatton w Chillingham 62-70; V Sugley 70-81; RD Newc W 77-81; Hon Can Newc Cathl 79-91; P-in-c Tweedmouth 81-87; V 87-91; RD Norham 82-91; Miss to Seamen 81-91; Chapl to The Queen 82-93; rtd 91. *42 Windsor Crescent, Berwick-upon-Tweed, Northd TD15 1NT* Tel (01289) 331936

ELDER, Andrew John. b 49. Sunderland Poly BSc72 MSc76. NE Ord Course 91. **d** 94 **p** 95. NSM Wallsend St Luke *Newc* from 94. *51 Rowantree Road, Newcastle upon Tyne NE6 4TE* Tel 0191-262 8795

ELDER, David. b 28. Brechin NSM Ord Course 75. **d** 79 **p** 80. NSM Dundee St Salvador *Bre* 79-93; rtd 93; P-in-c Dundee St Martin *Bre* from 93. *Thistlemount, 21 Law Road, Dundee DD3 6PZ* Tel (01382) 827844

ELDER, Nicholas John. b 51. Hatf Poly BA73. Cuddesdon Coll 73. **d** 76 **p** 77. C Mill End *St Alb* 76-77; C Mill End and Heronsgate w W Hyde 77-79; TV Borehamwood 79-85; V Bedford St Mich 85-90; V Bedford All SS from 90. *All Saints' Vicarage, 1 Cutliffe Place, Bedford MK40 4DF* Tel (01234) 266945

ELDRID, John Gisborne Charteris. b 25. OBE97. AKC52. **d** 53 **p** 54. C St Geo-in-the-East w Ch Ch w St Jo *Lon* 53-56; C E Grinstead St Mary *Chich* 56-58; C St Steph Walbrook and St Swithun etc *Lon* 58-64 and 72-81; V Portsea All SS *Portsm* 64-71; P-in-c Portsea St Jo Rudmore 69-71; V Portsea All SS w St Jo Rudmore 71-72; Gen Consultant Cen Lon Samaritans 72-74; Dir The Samaritans 74-87; Gen Consultant-Dir from 87; Lic to Offic *Lon* from 82; rtd 90. *46 Marshall Street, London W1V 1LR* Tel 0171-439 1406

ELDRIDGE, John Frederick. b 48. Loughb Univ BSc70 Golden Gate Sem (USA) MDiv83 Fuller Th Sem California DMin96. Oak Hill Th Coll 90. **d** 92 **p** 93. C Maidstone St Luke *Cant* 92-97; C-in-c Prince's Park CD *Roch* from 97. *6 Thrush Close, Chatham, Kent ME5 7TG* Tel (01634) 685828

ELDRIDGE, John Kenneth Tristan. b 59. St Steph Ho Ox 90. **d** 92 **p** 93. C Brighton Resurr *Chich* 92-96; C Hangleton from 96. *St Richard's House, 139 Godwin Road, Hove, E Sussex BN3 7FS* Tel (01273) 422810

ELDRIDGE, Canon Richard Henry. b 21. Lon Univ BSc48 MSc50 BD61. Ridley Hall Cam 56. **d** 58 **p** 59. C Knotty Ash St Jo *Liv* 58-61; V Luton St Matt High Town *St Alb* 61-67; V Lt Heath 67-76; P-in-c Belper *Derby* 76-88; RD Duffield 81-87; Hon Can Derby Cathl 83-88; rtd 88; Perm to Offic *Pet* from 89. *16 Polwell Lane, Kettering, Northants NN15 6UA* Tel (01536) 83138

ELDRIDGE, Stephen William. b 50. Chich Th Coll 87. **d** 89 **p** 90. C Stroud and Uplands w Slad *Glouc* 89-92; C Glouc St Mary de Crypt w St Jo and Ch Ch 92-95; Bp's Chapl 92-93; P-in-c Kingswood w Alderley and Hillesley from 95. *The Rectory, High Street, Kingswood, Wotton-under-Edge, Glos GL12 8RS* Tel (01453) 843361

ELEY, John Edward. b 49. Sarum & Wells Th Coll 74. **d** 77 **p** 78. C Sherborne w Castleton and Lillington *Sarum* 77-80; Min Can Carl Cathl *Carl* 80-84; V Bromsgrove All SS *Worc* 84-88; Perm to Offic *St E* from 90. *Topos, Lackford, Bury St Edmunds IP28 6HR* Tel (01284) 728511

ELFORD, Keith Anthony. b 59. Em Coll Cam BA80 MA84. Wycliffe Hall Ox 87. **d** 90 **p** 91. C Chertsey *Guildf* 90-94; P-in-c Ockham w Hatchford from 94; Bp's Chapl from 94. *The Rectory, Ockham Lane, Ockham, Woking, Surrey GU23 6NP* Tel (01483) 225358

ELFORD, Canon Robert John. b 39. Man Univ MA71 Ex Univ PhD74. Brasted Th Coll 64 Ridley Hall Cam 66. **d** 68 **p** 69. C Denton St Lawr *Man* 68-71; P-in-c Gwinear *Truro* 71-74; R Phillack w Gwithian and Gwinear 74-78; Lect Man Univ 78-87; Hon C Withington St Paul *Man* 79-83; Warden St Anselm Hall 82-87; Lic to Offic 84-87; Hd and Pro-R Liv Inst of HE from 88; Lic to Offic *Liv* from 88; Can Th Liv Cathl from 92. *St Katharine's College, Stand Park Road, PO Box 6, Liverpool L16 9JD* Tel 0151-722 2361

ELFRED, Michael William. b 48. BA76 MPhil. Linc Th Coll 77. **d** 79 **p** 80. C Boultham *Linc* 79-82; C Croydon H Sav *Cant* 82-84; C Upper Norwood All SS w St Marg 84; C Upper Norwood All SS *S'wark* 85-88; V Sanderstead St Mary from 88. *The Vicarage, 85 Purley Oaks Road, South Croydon, Surrey CR2 0NY* Tel 0181-657 1725

ELGAR, Frederick Stanton. b 20. AKC56. **d** 56 **p** 57. C Mansfield St Pet *S'well* 56-60; C-in-c Pound Hill CD *Chich* 60-80; rtd 85. *31 Byrefield Road, Guildford, Surrey GU2 6UB* Tel (01483) 37587

ELGAR, Dr Richard John. b 50. MRCGP80 Charing Cross Hosp Medical Sch MB, BS73 LRCP73 MRCS73. St Jo Coll Nottm DTS92. **d** 92 **p** 93. NSM Derby St Alkmund and St Werburgh *Derby* 92-96; P-in-c Derby St Barn from 96. *St Barnabas' Vicarage, 122 Radbourne Street, Derby DE22 3BU* Tel (01332) 342553

ELIOT, Whately Ian. b 12. **d** 39 **p** 40. C Wolborough w Newton Abbot *Ex* 39-48; V Thorverton 48-55; C-in-c Burnt Ho Lane CD 55-64; Min 64-69; R Ex St Paul 69-77; RD Christianity 68-70; rtd 77; Perm to Offic *Ex* from 77. *21 Rydon Lane, Exeter EX2 7AN* Tel (01392) 873034

ELIZABETH, Sister. *See* WEBB, Marjorie Valentine

ELIZABETH MARY, Sister. *See* NOLLER, Hilda Elizabeth Mary

ELKINGTON, Mrs Audrey Anne. b 57. St Cath Coll Ox BA80 UEA PhD83 Nottm Univ DipTh86. St Jo Coll Nottm 85 EAMTC 86. **dss** 88 **d** 92 **p** 94. Monkseaton St Mary *Newc* 88-91; Ponteland 91-92; Par Dn 92-93; C Prudhoe from 93. *The Vicarage, 5 Kepwell Court, Prudhoe, Northd NE42 5PE* Tel (01661) 836059

ELKINGTON, David John. b 51. Nottm Univ BTh76 Leic Univ MEd81. St Jo Coll Nottm 73. **d** 76 **p** 77. C Leic Martyrs *Leic* 76-78; C Kirby Muxloe 78-80; Asst Chapl Leic Univ 80-82; Hon C Leic H Spirit 82; Chapl UEA *Nor* 82-88; TV Newc Epiphany *Newc* 88-91; TR 91-93; P-in-c Prudhoe from 93. *The Vicarage, 5 Kepwell Court, Prudhoe, Northd NE42 5PE* Tel (01661) 836059

ELKINS, Alan Bernard. b 47. Sarum & Wells Th Coll 70. **d** 73 **p** 74. C Wareham *Sarum* 73-77; P-in-c Codford, Upton Lovell and Stockton 77-79; P-in-c Boyton w Sherrington 77-79; C Ashton Gifford 79; R Bishopstrow and Boreham 79-92; R Corfe Mullen from 92. *The Rectory, Wareham Road, Corfe Mullen, Wimborne, Dorset BH21 3LE* Tel (01202) 692129

ELKINS, Mrs Joy Kathleen. b 45. Sarum Th Coll 93. **d** 96. NSM Corfe Mullen *Sarum* from 96. *The Rectory, Wareham Road, Corfe Mullen, Wimborne, Dorset BH21 3LE* Tel (01202) 692129

ELKINS, Canon Patrick Charles. b 34. St Chad's Coll Dur BA57 DipTh60 DipEd. **d** 60 **p** 61. C Moordown *Win* 60-63; C Basingstoke 64-67; V Bransgore from 67; Hon Can Win Cathl from 89. *The Vicarage, Ringwood Road, Bransgore, Christchurch, Dorset BH23 8JH* Tel (01425) 672327 Fax 674190

ELKS, Roger Mark. b 60. ACGI83 Imp Coll Lon BSc83. Wycliffe Hall Ox 89. **d** 92 **p** 93. C St Austell *Truro* 92-95; V Carbis Bay w Lelant from 95. *The Vicarage, Porthrepta Road, Carbis Bay, St Ives, Cornwall TR26 2LD* Tel (01736) 796206

ELLA, David John. b 51. Trin Coll Bris DipTh83. **d** 85 **p** 86. C Canford Magna *Sarum* 85-89; TV Southend *Chelmsf* 89-93; Youth Development Officer from 89; TR Canvey Is from 93. *St Nicholas House, 210 Long Road, Canvey Island, Essex SS8 0JR* Tel (01268) 511098

ELLAM, Stuart William. b 53. Westcott Ho Cam. **d** 85 **p** 86. C Ditton St Mich *Liv* 85-88; C Greenford H Cross *Lon* 88-91; Perm to Offic 91-94. *26 Church Road, Cowley, Uxbridge, Middx UB8 3NA* Tel (01895) 238815

ELLEANOR, David John. b 48. Leic Univ LLB70 St Jo Coll Dur BA88. Cranmer Hall Dur 85. **d** 88 **p** 89. C Consett *Dur* 88-90; P-in-c Ingleton from 96. *Ingleton Vicarage, Darlington, Co Durham DL2 3HS* Tel (01325) 730928

ELLEL, Thomas Fielding. b 20. Cranmer Hall Dur. **d** 63 **p** 64. C Colne St Bart *Blackb* 63-66; C-in-c Hapton St Marg CD 66-67; V Huncoat 67-74; V Worsthorne 74-88; rtd 88. *12 Trevethan Court, Mitchell Road, Falmouth, Cornwall TR11 2UQ*

ELLEM, Peter Keith. b 58. CQSW. St Jo Coll Nottm BTh90. **d** 90 **p** 91. C Islington St Mary *Lon* 90-94; C Leeds St Geo *Ripon* from 94. *22 Hanover Square, Leeds LS3 1AP* Tel 0113-244 0604 or 243 8498

ELLENS (or STEWART ELLENS), Dr Gordon Frederick Stewart. b 26. FRAS Columbia Univ (NY) MPhil62 PhD68. K Coll Lon BD52 AKC52 St Boniface Warminster 52. **d** 53 **p** 54. C Old Street St Luke w St Mary Charterhouse etc *Lon* 53-55; C Chiswick St Mich 55-57; Canada 57-60; USA 62-66 and from 88; Japan 70-88; Asst Prof Relig St Sophia Univ Tokyo 70-75; Rikkyo Women's Univ 75-84; Prof Humanities Ueno Gakueu 84-88; rtd 92. *PO Box 1578, Santa Monica, California 90406, USA* Tel Santa Monica (310) 396-2062 Fax 396-5543

ELLERTON, Mrs Mary Diane. b 45. RGN67 RHV68 Huddersfield Poly CertHE89. N Ord Course 90. **d** 93 **p** 94. NSM Upper Holme Valley *Wakef* from 93. *16 Binns Lane, Holmfirth, Huddersfield HD7 1BL* Tel (01484) 684207 Fax 545411

ELLERY, Arthur James Gabriel. b 28. St Jo Coll Dur BSc49. Linc Th Coll 51. **d** 53 **p** 54. C Milton next Sittingbourne *Cant* 53-56; C St Laurence in the Isle of Thanet 56-58; C Darlington St Cuth *Dur* 58-62; V Tanfield 62-70; Chapl St Olave's Sch York 70-78; V Gt Ayton w Easby and Newton in Cleveland *York* 78-81; Chapl Bancroft's Sch Woodford Green 81-86; V Chipperfield St Paul *St Alb* 86-93; rtd 93; Perm to Offic *Ely* from 93; Perm to Offic *Pet* from 93. *7 Church Drive, Orton Waterville, Peterborough PE2 5EX* Tel (01733) 231800

ELLERY, Ian Martyn William. b 56. K Coll Lon BD AKC. Chich Th Coll. **d** 82 **p** 83. C Hornsey St Mary w St Geo *Lon* 82-85; V Choral York Minster *York* 85-89; Subchanter York Minster 86-89; R Patrington w Hollym, Welwick and Winestead 89-97; TR Howden TM from 97. *The Minster Rectory, Howden, Goole, N Humberside DN14 7BL* Tel (01430) 430332

ELLINGTON, David John. b 39. Or Coll Ox BA63 MA. Cuddesdon Coll 63. **d** 65 **p** 66. C Sheff St Mark Broomhall *Sheff* 65-68; C Timperley *Ches* 68-72; P-in-c Altrincham St Jo 72-74; V 74-80; P-in-c Ashley 82-86; rtd 86; Perm to Offic *Ches* from 87. *6 Hough Green, Ashley, Altrincham, Cheshire WA15 0QS* Tel (01705) 828972

ELLIOT, Hugh Riversdale. b 25. Bps' Coll Cheshunt. **d** 62 **p** 65. C Swaffham *Nor* 62-64; C Kessingland 64-67; C Mutford w Rushmere 65-67; P-in-c 67-68; P-in-c Gisleham 67-68; P-in-c Welborne 68-72; P-in-c Yaxham 68-80; P-in-c N Tuddenham 72-80; R E w W Harling 80-90; R Bridgham and Roudham 81-90; R E w W Harling and Bridgham w Roudham 90-92; rtd 92; Perm to Offic *Nor* from 93. *Berryfields, 27 The Street, Alburgh, Harleston, Norfolk IP20 0DJ* Tel (01986) 86498

ELLIOT, Neil Robert Minto. b 63. Hatfield Poly BEng87 Herts Univ CertEd93. St Jo Coll Nottm 94. **d** 96 **p** 97. C Walbrook Epiphany *Derby* from 96. *70 Violet Street, Derby DE23 8SQ* Tel (01332) 762821

ELLIOT, William (Bill). b 33. Glouc Sch of Min 84. **d** 87 **p** 88. C Kington w Huntington, Old Radnor, Kinnerton etc *Heref* 87-90; C Heref H Trin 90-92; Chapl Corfu *Eur* from 92. *The Chaplaincy Flat, 21 L Mavili Street, Corfu, Greece 491 00* Tel Corfu (661) 31467

ELLIOT, William Brunton. b 41. Edin Th Coll 90 Edin Dioc NSM Course 81. **d** 84 **p** 85. NSM Lasswade *Edin* 84-92; NSM Dalkeith 84-92; NSM Edin St Pet 92-94; R Selkirk from 94. *St John's Rectory, 23 Viewfield Park, Selkirk TD7 4LH* Tel (01750) 21364

ELLIOT-NEWMAN, Christopher Guy. b 43. Bede Coll Dur TCert67 Hull Univ BTh83 MEd87. Westcott Ho Cam 67. **d** 70 **p** 71. C Ditton St Mich *Liv* 70-73; C Hazlemere *Ox* 73-77; R Stockton-on-the-Forest w Holtby and Warthill *York* 77-87; Dir of Educn *Cant* 87-94. *12 Priestlands Road, Hexham, Northd NE46 4AJ* Tel (01434) 607853

ELLIOTT, Brian. b 49. Dur Univ BA73. Coll of Resurr Mirfield 73. **d** 75 **p** 76. C Nunthorpe *York* 75-77; CF from 77; Perm to Offic *Bris* from 94. *MOD Chaplains (Army), Trenchard Lines, Upavon, Pewsey, Wilts SN9 6BE* Tel (01980) 615804 Fax 615800

ELLIOTT, Charles. b 15. Lon Univ BA55. St Steph Ho Ox 51. **d** 53 **p** 54. C Shrewsbury St Chad *Lich* 53-56; Min Birches Head CD 56-61; V Lower Gornal 61-80; rtd 80; Lic to Offic *Lich* from 80; Lic to Offic *Worc* 81-83; Perm to Offic from 83. *1 The Village, Kingswinford, W Midlands DY6 8AY* Tel (01384) 279360

ELLIOTT, Charles Middleton. b 39. Linc Coll Ox BA60 Nuff Coll Ox DPhil62. Linc Th Coll 62. **d** 64 **p** 65. Lect Nottm Univ 63-65; C Wilford *S'well* 64-65; Zambia 65-69; Chapl Lusaka Cath 65-69; Asst Gen Sec Jt Cttee WCC 69-72; Asst Gen Sec Pontifical Commn Justice and Peace 69-72; Sen Lect UEA 72-77; Hon Min Can Nor Cathl *Nor* 73-77; Prof Development Studies Univ of Wales (Swansea) 77-82; Dir Chr Aid 82-84; Asst Gen Sec BCC 82-84; Prof Bris Univ 85-87; Australia 87-88; Visiting Prof K Coll Lon 88-89; Preb Lich Cathl *Lich* 88-97; Dean and Chapl Trin Hall Cam from 90. *Trinity Hall, Cambridge CB2 1TJ* Tel (01223) 332525 or 69233 Fax 332537

ELLIOTT, Christopher John. b 44. Sarum Th Coll 66. **d** 69 **p** 70. C Walthamstow St Pet *Chelmsf* 69-71; C Witham 71-74; P-in-c Gt and Lt Bentley 74-80; R Colchester Ch Ch w St Mary V 80-85; R Sible Hedingham 85-93; V Leigh-on-Sea St Aid from 93. *St Aidan's Vicarage, Moor Park Gardens, Leigh-on-Sea, Essex SS9 4PY* Tel (01702) 525338

ELLIOTT, Christopher John. b 67. Southn Univ 93. Chich Th Coll CMT94. **d** 94 **p** 95. C Alton St Lawr *Win* 94-97. *72 Woodlands, Fleet, Hants GU13 8NU*

ELLIOTT, Canon Colin. b 23. St Pet Coll Ox BA48 DipTh49 MA52. Wycliffe Hall Ox 48. **d** 49 **p** 50. C Wigan St Cath *Liv* 49-52; C Blundellsands St Nic 52-55; V Southport St Paul 55-59; Chapl and Lect St Kath Coll Liv 57-59; R Windermere St Martin *Carl* 59-88; RD Windermere 79-84; Hon Can Carl Cathl 81-88; rtd 88; Perm to Offic *Carl* from 88. *Fairbank View, Brow Lane, Staveley, Kendal, Cumbria LA8 9PJ* Tel (01539) 821758

ELLIOTT, Colin David. b 32. AKC55. **d** 56 **p** 57. C W Wickham St Jo *Cant* 56-59; C Dover St Mary 59-64; V Linton 64-66; V Gillingham H Trin *Roch* 66-81; V Belvedere All SS 81-88; V Bromley St Jo from 88. *St John's Vicarage, 9 Orchard Road, Bromley BR1 2PR* Tel 0181-460 1844

ELLIOTT, The Very Revd David. b 31. Bps' Coll Cheshunt 60. **d** 63 **p** 64. C Chingford St Anne *Chelmsf* 63-64; C Woodford St Mary 64-66; Trucial States 67-69; Prec St Alb Abbey *St Alb* 69-72; Zambia 72-75; Dean Ndola 72-75; Can Ndola (Zambia) from 75; TR Borehamwood *St Alb* 75-79; Dean Jerusalem 79-86; OStJ 80-82; CStJ from 82; R Covent Garden St Paul *Lon* from 86. *21A Down Street, London W1Y 7DN* Tel 0171-499 5290

ELLIOTT, David Reed. b 62. Lon Bible Coll BA91. Oak Hill Th Coll 91. **d** 93 **p** 94. C Luton Lewsey St Hugh *St Alb* from 93. *247 Leagrave High Street, Luton LU4 0NA*

ELLIOTT, Derek John. b 26. Pemb Coll Cam BA50 MA55. Oak Hill Th Coll 48. **d** 51 **p** 53. C Ealing Dean St Jo *Lon* 51-53; C New Milverton *Cov* 53-55; C Boscombe St Jo *Win* 55-57; V Biddulph *Lich* 57-63; R Rushden w Newton Bromswold *Pet* 63-68; RD Higham 66-68; Chapl Bedford Modern Sch 68-83; V Potten End w Nettleden *St Alb* 83-91; rtd 91; Hon C Twickenham St Mary *Lon* from 91. *23 Bonser Road, Twickenham TW1 4RQ* Tel 0181-744 2761

ELLIOTT, Miss Eveline Mary. b 39. ALA63 Bedf Coll Lon BA60. EAMTC 92. **d** 95 **p** 96. NSM Bury St Edmunds St Mary *St E* 95-97; NSM Culford, W Stow and Wordwell w Flempton etc from 97; NSM Fornham All SS and Fornham St Martin w Timworth from 97. *4 St Michael's Close, Northgate Street, Bury St Edmunds, Suffolk IP33 1HT* Tel (01284) 753592

ELLIOTT, George Evan. b 17. Sarum Th Coll. **d** 58 **p** 59. C Padiham *Blackb* 58-61; C Cleveleys 61-63; V Kimblesworth *Dur* 63-71; V Sutton St James *Linc* 71-77; V Sutton St Edmund 71-77; P-in-c Bishop Norton 77-80; R Wadingham w Snitterby 77-80; R Bishop Norton, Wadingham and Snitterby 80-82; rtd 82; Perm to Offic *Nor* from 82. *10 Dugard Avenue, Norwich NR1 4NQ* Tel (01603) 435806

ELLIOTT, Gordon. b 25. St Aid Birkenhead 63. **d** 65 **p** 66. C Latchford St Jas *Ches* 65-68; C Bollington St Jo 68-70; V Dukingfield St Mark 70-73; TV Tenbury *Heref* 74-78; V Bromfield 78-82; R Culmington w Onibury 78-82; V Stanton Lacy 78-82; P-in-c Withybrook w Copston Magna *Cov* 82-83; P-in-c Wolvey, Burton Hastings and Stretton Baskerville 82-83; V Wolvey w Burton Hastings, Copston Magna etc 83-90; rtd 90. *12 Handbury Road, Malvern, Worcs WR14 1NN* Tel (01684) 569388

ELLIOTT, Ian David. b 40. Qu Coll Cam BA61 MA65. Tyndale Hall Bris 64. **d** 66 **p** 67. C Halewood *Liv* 66-71; C Gt Crosby St Luke 71-74; C-in-c Dallam CD 74-80; V Dallam 80-83; TV Fazakerley Em 83-92; V Warrington H Trin from 92. *Holy Trinity Vicarage, 6 Palmyra Square North, Warrington WA1 1JQ* Tel (01925) 630057

ELLIOTT, John George. b 15. Qu Coll Ox BA37 MA46. Westcott Ho Cam 46. **d** 47 **p** 48. C Oxton *Ches* 47-51; Ceylon 51-61; Chapl Loughborough Gr Sch 61-80; rtd 80; Perm to Offic *Leic* from 80. *14 Victoria Street, Loughborough, Leics LE11 2EN* Tel (01509) 263365

ELLIOTT, John Philip. b 37. MIChemE61 MBIM Salford Univ CEng. Glouc Th Course 79. **d** 80 **p** 80. NSM Brimscombe *Glouc* 80-86; C Caverswall *Lich* 86-91; R Tredington and Darlingscott w Newbold on Stour *Cov* 91-97; rtd 97. *Pipers Barn, 69 Bownham Park, Stroud, Glos GL5 5BZ*

ELLIOTT, Joseph William. b 37. Chich Th Coll. **d** 66 **p** 67. C Whickham *Dur* 66-72; V Lamesley 72-78; TR Usworth 78-93; P-in-c Belmont 93-95; V from 95. *Belmont Vicarage, Broomside Lane, Durham DH1 2QW* Tel 0191-386 1545

ELLIOTT, Capt Keith Alcock. b 51. St Jo Coll Dur 95 CA Tr Coll 83. **d** 95 **p** 96. C Chulmleigh *Ex* 95-96; C Chawleigh w Cheldon 95-96; C Wembworthy w Eggesford 95-96; C Chulmleigh, Chawleigh w Cheldon, Wembworthy etc from 96. *The Rectory, Chawleigh, Chulmleigh, Devon EX18 7HJ* Tel (01769) 581163

ELLIOTT (née JUTSUM), Mrs Linda Mary. b 56. St Pet Coll Birm CertEd77. WMMTC 92. **d** 95 **p** 96. NSM Longthorpe *Pet* from 95. *68 Bradwell Road, Peterborough PE3 9PZ* Tel (01733) 262593

ELLIOTT, Maurice John. b 65. St Andr Univ MA87 TCD BTh92 MPhil93. CITC 89. **d** 93 **p** 94. C Coleraine *Conn* from 93. *42 Kenuarra Park, Coleraine, Co Londonderry BT52 1RT* Tel (01265) 57828

ELLIOTT, Michael Cowan. b 38. Auckland Univ BA63 Episc Th Sch Mass BD66 Massey Univ (NZ) MPhil82. St Jo Coll (NZ) LTh61. **d** 61 **p** 62. New Zealand 61-65; USA 65-66; Warden Pemb Coll Miss Walworth *S'wark* 66-70; Jerusalem 70-74; BCC 74-75; C Amersham *Ox* 74-75; Ecum Secretariat on Development NZ 76-84; Dir Chr Action NZ 84-87; Chapl City of Lon Poly *Lon* 87-89; Dir Inner City Aid from 89; Tutor Westmr Coll Ox from 91. *Westminster College, Harcourt Hill, Oxford OX2 9AT* Tel (01865) 253335

ELLIOTT, Michael James. b 58. LTh. St Jo Coll Nottm 80. **d** 83 **p** 84. C Pontypridd St Cath *Llan* 83-86; C Leamington Priors St Paul *Cov* 86-89; Chapl RAF from 89. *Chaplaincy Services (RAF), HQ, Personnel and Training Command, RAF Innsworth, Gloucester GL3 1EZ* Tel (01452) 712612 ext 5164 Fax 510828

ELLIOTT, Nigel Harvey. b 55. St Jo Coll Nottm DCM92. **d** 92 **p** 93. C Radcliffe *Man* 92-95; V Kilnhurst *Sheff* from 95. *The Vicarage, Highthorne Road, Kilnhurst, Rotherham, S Yorkshire S62 5TX* Tel (01709) 589674

ELLIOTT, The Ven Peter. b 41. Hertf Coll Ox BA63 MA68. Linc Th Coll 63. **d** 65 **p** 66. C Gosforth All SS *Newc* 65-68; C Balkwell 68-72; V High Elswick St Phil 72-80; V N Gosforth 80-87; V Embleton w Rennington and Rock 87-93; RD Alnwick 89-93; Hon Can Newc Cathl 90-93; Adn Northd and Can Res Newc Cathl from 93. *80 Moorside North, Newcastle upon Tyne NE4 9DU* Tel 0191-273 8245

ELLIOTT, Peter Wolstenholme. b 31. CChem MRSC. NE Ord Course 78. **d** 81 **p** 82. NSM Yarm *York* from 81. *48 Butterfield Drive, Eaglescliffe, Stockton-on-Tees, Cleveland TS16 0EZ* Tel (01642) 782788

ELLIOTT, Simon Richard James. b 66. Lon Univ BSc88. Cranmer Hall Dur BA95. **d** 95 **p** 96. C Hendon St Paul Mill Hill *Lon* from 95. *46 Shakespeare Road, London NW7 4BE* Tel 0181-959 8461

ELLIOTT, Stanley Griffin. b 19. Lon Univ BA50. Ridley Hall Cam 50. **d** 52 **p** 53. C Astley Bridge *Man* 52-54; C Bedford Leigh 54-56; R Salford St Clem Ordsall 56-59; R Ashton upon Mersey St Martin *Ches* 59-80; V Tile Hill *Cov* 80-85; rtd 85; Perm to Offic *Win* from 85. *Flat 3 Chartwell, 8 The Avenue, Branksome Park, Poole, Dorset BH13 6AG* Tel (01202) 766080

ELLIOTT, William (Bill). b 20. Lon Univ BA56. Ripon Hall Ox 60. **d** 61 **p** 62. C Kidderminster St Mary *Worc* 61-70; V Bewdley Far Forest 70-78; V Rock w Heightington w Far Forest 78-82; V Mamble w Bayton, Rock w Heightington etc 82-85; rtd 85; Perm to Offic *Heref* from 85; Perm to Offic *Worc* from 85. *8 Lea View, Cleobury Mortimer, Kidderminster DY14 8EE* Tel (01299) 270993

ELLIOTT, William Henry Venn (Ben). b 34. K Coll Cam BA55 MA59. Wells Th Coll 59. **d** 61 **p** 62. C Almondbury *Wakef* 61-66; V Bramshaw *Sarum* 66-81; P-in-c Landford w Plaitford 77-81; V Mere w W Knoyle and Maiden Bradley from 81. *The Vicarage, Angel Lane, Mere, Warminster, Wilts BA12 6DH* Tel (01747) 860292

ELLIOTT, Dr William James. b 38. Jes Coll Cam BA62 MA66 Birm Univ MA69 PhD74. Qu Coll Birm 62. **d** 64 **p** 65. C Hendon St Paul Mill Hill *Lon* 64-67; C St Pancras w St Jas and Ch Ch 67-69; P-in-c Preston St Paul *Blackb* 69-74; R Elstree *St Alb* from 74. *The Rectory, St Nicholas' Close, Elstree, Borehamwood, Herts WD6 3EW* Tel 0181-953 1411

ELLIOTT, William Norman. b 20. Kelham Th Coll 37. **d** 43 **p** 44. C Tividale *Lich* 43-50; C Barnsley St Mary *Wakef* 50-55; V Smawthorpe St Mich 55-63; V S Crosland 64-85; rtd 85; Chapl

Community of St Pet Horbury from 85. *18 Woodlands, Horbury, Wakefield, W Yorkshire WF4 5HH* Tel (01924) 265547

ELLIOTT SMITH, Mark Charles. b 59. LRAM85 GRSM86 DipRAM87 ARCO88. St Steph Ho Ox 92. **d** 94. C W Hampstead St Jas *Lon* 94-95; C Tottenham St Paul from 96. *St Paul's Vicarage Flat, 60 Park Lane, London N17 0JW* Tel 0181-885 1395

ELLIS, Anthony Colin. b 56. Keble Coll Ox BA77 Man Univ PhD80. Linc Th Coll 80. **d** 81 **p** 82. C Mill Hill Jo Keble Ch *Lon* 81-83; Staff Tutor in Relig Studies Man Univ from 83; C Stretford St Pet *Man* 83-87; NSM Shore 87-89; Lic Preacher from 89. *2 Crowther Terrace, Blackshaw, Hebden Bridge, W Yorkshire HX7 6DE* Tel (01422) 844242 or 0161-275 3302

ELLIS, Canon Bryan Stuart. b 31. Qu Coll Cam BA54 MA58. Ridley Hall Cam 55. **d** 57 **p** 58. C Ramsgate St Luke *Cant* 57-59; C Herne Bay Ch Ch 59-62; V Burmantofts St Steph and St Agnes *Ripon* 62-81; RD Wakef from 81; V Wakef St Andr and St Mary from 81; Hon Can Wakef Cathl from 89. *2 Kilnsey Road, Wakefield, W Yorkshire WF1 4RW* Tel (01924) 372105

ELLIS, Charles Harold. b 50. N Ord Course 78. **d** 81 **p** 82. C Davyhulme St Mary *Man* 81-85; V Tonge w Alkrington 85-91; P-in-c Radcliffe St Thos and St Jo 91; P-in-c Radcliffe St Mary 91; TR Radcliffe from 91; AD Radcliffe and Prestwich from 96. *The Vicarage, Heber Street, Radcliffe, Manchester M26 2TG* Tel 0161-723 2123

ELLIS, Christopher Charles. b 55. Societas Oecumenica 90 Edin Univ BD78 Hull Univ MA80. Edin Th Coll 76 Irish Sch of Ecum 78. **d** 79 **p** 80. C Selby Abbey *York* 79-82; C Fulford 82-85; Dioc Ecum Officer from 81; Dioc Ecum Adv from 90; Lect Ecum Th Hull Univ from 84; P-in-c Kexby w Wilberfoss *York* 85-90; Ecum Officer S Cleveland and N Yorkshire Ecum Coun from 88. *21 Sandstock Road, Pocklington, York YO4 2HN* Tel (01759) 305881

ELLIS, Canon David Craven. b 34. Man Univ BA56 MA57. St Aid Birkenhead 59. **d** 61 **p** 62. C Gt Crosby St Luke *Liv* 61-65; Hong Kong 65-69; P-in-c Sawrey *Carl* 69-74; Dioc Youth Officer 69-74; V Halifax St Aug *Wakef* 74-84; R Greystoke, Matterdale and Mungrisdale *Carl* 84-87; R Watermillock 84-87; TR Greystoke, Matterdale, Mungrisdale etc 88-91; RD Penrith 87-91; TR Carl H Trin and St Barn 91-96; Hon Can Carl Cathl 91-96; rtd 96; Perm to Offic *Carl* from 97. *Calderstones, 5 Fellside, Allithwaite, Grange-over-Sands, Cumbria LA11 7RN*

ELLIS, Gay. d 96 **p** 97. NSM Nazeing *Chelmsf* from 96. *97 Herons Wood, Harlow, Essex CM20 1RT* Tel (01279) 432908

ELLIS, Hugh William. b 54. Sussex Univ BSc76. Ridley Hall Cam 88. **d** 90 **p** 91. C Reading St Jo *Ox* 90-93; P-in-c Bradfield and Stanford Dingley from 93. *The Rectory, Southend Road, Bradfield, Reading RG7 6EU* Tel (0118) 974 4333

ELLIS, Dr Ian Morton. b 52. QUB BD75 MTh82 TCD PhD89. CITC. **d** 77 **p** 78. C Portadown St Columba *Arm* 77-79; C Arm St Mark 79-85; Chapl Arm R Sch 79-85; Hon V Choral Arm Cathl 82-93; I Mullavilly 85-93; Dom Chapl to Abp Arm 86-93; Tutor for Aux Min (Arm) 90-93; Dioc Adv on Ecum 92-93; I Newcastle *D & D* from 93. *The Rectory, 1 King Street, Newcastle, Co Down BT33 0HD* Tel (01396) 22439

ELLIS, Ian William. b 57. QUB BSc78 CertEd79 TCD BTh89. CITC 86. **d** 89 **p** 90. C Arm St Mark w Aghavilly *Arm* 89-91; I Loughgall w Grange from 91. *2 Main Street, Loughgall, Armagh BT61 8HZ* Tel (01762) 891587

ELLIS, Jean Miriam. b 35. St Mich Coll Llan DipMin92. **d** 95 **p** 97. NSM Llanelli *S & B* from 95. *Llanelli Rectory, Abergavenny Road, Gilwern, Abergavenny NP7 0AD* Tel (01873) 830280

ELLIS, John. b 27. Glouc Th Course 82. **d** 85 **p** 86. NSM Dowdeswell and Andoversford w the Shiptons etc *Glouc* 85-94; rtd 94; Perm to Offic *Glouc* from 94. *18 Hunter's Way, Andoversford, Cheltenham, Glos GL54 4JW* Tel (01242) 820746

ELLIS, John Anthony (Tony). b 47. Univ of Wales (Lamp) DipTh70 Open Univ BA80. Coll of Resurr Mirfield 70. **d** 72 **p** 73. C Sketty *S & B* 72-75; C Duston *Pet* 75-80; R Lichborough w Maidford and Farthingstone 80-85; V Stratfield Mortimer *Ox* from 85; P-in-c Mortimer W End w Padworth from 85. *The Vicarage, 10 The Avenue, Mortimer Common, Reading RG7 3QU* Tel (0118) 933 2404

ELLIS, John Beaumont. b 45. Univ of Wales (Lamp) BA67 LTh69. Bp Burgess Hall Lamp. **d** 69 **p** 70. C Abergavenny St Mary w Llanwenarth Citra *Mon* 69-72; C Swansea St Gabr *S & B* 72-75; V Llanbister and Llanbadarn Fynydd w Llananno 75-77; V Newport St Andr *Mon* 77-80; V Risca 80-84; V Cheadle Heath *Ches* 84-94. *12 Upper Hibbert Lane, Marple, Stockport, Cheshire SK6 7HX* Tel 0161-427 1963

ELLIS, John Franklyn. b 34. Leeds Univ BA58. Linc Th Coll 58. **d** 60 **p** 61. C Ladybarn *Man* 60-63; C Stockport St Geo *Ches* 63-66; V High Lane 66-81; V Chelford w Lower Withington from 81. *The Vicarage, Chelford, Macclesfield, Cheshire SK11 9AH* Tel (01625) 861231

ELLIS, John Frederick Alexander. b 23. Sarum Th Coll 50. **d** 52 **p** 53. C Fishponds St Mary *Bris* 52-55; SSF 55-57; C Bris St Mary Redcliffe w Temple *Bris* 57-62; V S Leamington St Jo *Cov* 62-65; V Harnham *Sarum* 65-80; RD Salisbury 77-80; Can and Preb Sarum Cathl 77-80; P-in-c Belstone *Ex* 80-81; P-in-c S Tawton 80-81; R S Tawton and Belstone 81-87; RD Okehampton 82-87; TR Yelverton, Meavy, Sheepstor and Walkhampton 87-89; rtd 89. *55 Church Street, Tisbury, Salisbury SP3 6NH* Tel (01747) 871447

ELLIS, John Raymond. b 63. St Steph Ho Ox 95. **d** 97. C Clare w Poslingford, Cavendish etc *St E* from 97. *20 March Place, Clare, Suffolk CO10 8RH* Tel (01787) 277552

ELLIS, John Roland. b 32. Wells Th Coll 67. **d** 69 **p** 70. C Kettering SS Pet and Paul *Pet* 69-71; C Kingsthorpe 71-73; TV 73-74; TV Ebbw Vale *Mon* 74-76; V Llanddewi Rhydderch w Llanvapley etc 76-83; Miss to Seamen from 79; V New Tredegar *Mon* 83-86; V Llanelli *S & B* from 86; RD Crickhowell from 91. *Llanelli Rectory, Abergavenny Road, Gilwern, Abergavenny NP7 0AD* Tel (01873) 830280

ELLIS, John Wadsworth. b 42. TCD BA64. **d** 66 **p** 67. C Lisburn Ch Ch Cathl *Conn* 66-69; C Norbiton *S'wark* 69-72; C New Clee *Linc* 72-85; V from 85; RD Grimsby and Cleethorpes from 94. *120 Queen Mary Avenue, Cleethorpes, S Humberside DN35 7SZ* Tel (01472) 696521

ELLIS, Joseph Walter. b 08. St D Coll Lamp BA32. **d** 32 **p** 33. C Droylsden St Mary *Man* 32-36; C Oldham 36-40; V Oldham St Steph and All Martyrs 40-50; V Royton St Paul 50-64; V Gt w Lt Chesterford *Chelmsf* 64-77; rtd 77; Perm to Offic *Chelmsf* from 77. *5 Southfield, Back Lane, Ickleton, Saffron Walden, Essex CB10 1TE* Tel (01799) 530334

ELLIS, Keith. b 39. Univ of Wales (Swansea) BSc60 Birm Poly BSc(Econ)74 Liv Univ CertEd61. St Jo Coll Nottm 95. **d** 96 **p** 97. NSM Marple All SS *Ches* from 96. *4 Compton Close, Marple, Stockport, Cheshire SK6 6PU* Tel 0161-449 8646

ELLIS, Sister Lillian. b 44. Keswick Hall Coll TCert66. Wilson Carlile Coll DipEvang90 Oak Hill Th Coll 95. **d** 96 **p** 97. C Vange *Chelmsf* from 96. *26 Rivertons, Vange, Basildon, Essex SS16 4UY* Tel (01268) 559764

ELLIS, Malcolm Railton. b 35. LTCL71 Univ of Wales (Lamp) BA56. Sarum Th Coll 56. **d** 58 **p** 59. C Llangynwyd w Maesteg *Llan* 58-61; C Llantrisant 61-67; V Troedrhiwgarth 67-70; PV Truro Cathl *Truro* 70-73; V Egloshayle 73-81; V Margam *Llan* 81-87; V Cardiff St Jo from 87; Offic Chapl Priory for Wales OStJ from 87; Prec Llan Cathl from 96. *The Vicarage, 16 Queen Anne Square, Cathays Park, Cardiff CF1 3ED* Tel (01222) 220375

ELLIS, Preb Mark Durant. b 39. Ex Univ BA62. Cuddesdon Coll 62. **d** 64 **p** 65. C Lyngford *B & W* 64-67; V Weston-super-Mare St Andr Bournville 67-76; TV Yeovil 76-88; V Yeovil St Mich from 88; Preb Wells Cathl from 90; RD Merston from 94. *St Michael's Vicarage, Yeovil, Somerset BA21 4LH* Tel (01935) 75752

ELLIS, Paul. b 56. Man Poly HNC79. Aston Tr Scheme 88 Trin Coll Bris DipHE92. **d** 92 **p** 93. C Pennington *Man* 92-96; TV Deane from 96. *St Andrew's Vicarage, Over Hulton, Bolton BL5 1EN* Tel (01204) 651851

ELLIS, Peter Andrew. b 46. St D Coll Lamp 65. **d** 69 **p** 70. C Milford Haven *St D* 69-71; R Walwyn's Castle w Robeston W 71-74; Miss to Seamen from 74; Hong Kong 74-75 and from 92; Singapore 75-82; The Tees and Hartlepool 82-92. *The Mariner's Club, 11 Middle Road, Kowloon, Hong Kong* Tel Hong Kong (852) 368-8261 Fax 366-0928

ELLIS, Robert Albert. b 48. K Coll Lon BD70 AKC70. St Aug Coll Cant 70. **d** 72 **p** 73. C Liv Our Lady and St Nic w St Anne *Liv* 72-76; P-in-c Meerbrook *Lich* 76-80; Producer Relig Progr BBC Radio Stoke 76-80; V Highgate All SS *Lon* 80-81; Dioc Communications Officer *Lich* from 81; P-in-c Longdon 81-87. *The Pump House, Jacks Lane, Marchington, Uttoxeter, Staffs ST14 8LW* Tel (01283) 820732

ELLIS, The Ven Robin Gareth. b 35. Pemb Coll Ox BA57 BCL58 MA62. Chich Th Coll 58. **d** 60 **p** 61. C Swinton St Pet *Man* 60-63; Asst Chapl Worksop Coll Notts 63-66; V Swaffham Prior *Ely* 66-74; Asst Dir Educn 66-74; V Wisbech St Aug 74-82; V Yelverton *Ex* 82-86; Adn Plymouth from 82. *33 Leat Walk, Roborough, Plymouth PL6 7AT* Tel (01752) 793397 Fax 774618

ELLIS, Roger Henry. b 40. Natal Univ BA61 Selw Coll Cam BA64 MA68 Linacre Coll Ox BLitt69. **d** 66 **p** 67. C Ox St Mich *Ox* 66-68; S Africa 68-76; P-in-c Wortham *St E* 77; V Wheatley Hills *Sheff* 77-84; Chapl St Edm Sch Cant from 84. *1 The Close, Canterbury, Kent CT2 8HU* Tel (01227) 450218 or 454575

ELLIS, Miss Sheila. b 39. Lon Univ CertRK. St Mich Ho Ox 67 Dalton Ho Bris 68. **dss** 80 **d** 87 **p** 94. Kirkdale St Mary and St Athanasius *Liv* 80-86; Earlestown 86-87; Par Dn 87-91; C W Derby St Luke 91-96; V Everton St Chrys from 96. *The Vicarage, 43 St Chrysostom's Way, Liverpool L6 2NQ* Tel 0151-263 3755

ELLIS, Simon David. b 68. Univ of Wales (Cardiff) BSc89 Bris Univ PGCE90. St Steph Ho Ox BTh94. **d** 97. C Knowle H Nativity *Bris* from 97. *12 Woodbridge Road, Knowle, Bristol BS4 2EU* Tel 0117-977 2918

ELLIS, Susannah Margaret (Suzie). b 44. Open Univ BA82. EAMTC 93. **d** 96 **p** 97. NSM S Elmham and Ilketshall *St E* from 96; Warden Quiet Waters Chr Retreat Ho from 96. *Quiet Waters, Flixton Road, Bungay, Suffolk NR35 1PD* Tel (01986) 893201

ELLIS, Timothy William. b 53. AKC75. St Aug Coll Cant 75. **d** 76 **p** 77. C Old Trafford St Jo *Man* 76-80; V Pendleton St Thos 80-87; Chapl Salford Coll of Tech 80-87; V Sheff Norwood St Leon *Sheff* from 87; P-in-c Shiregreen St Hilda from 94; RD Ecclesfield from 94. *St Leonard's Vicarage, Everingham Road, Sheffield S5 7LE* Tel 0114-243 6689 Fax as telephone

ELLIS, Canon Vorley Michael Spencer. b 15. St Edm Hall Ox BA38 MA41. St Steph Ho Ox 37. **d** 39 **p** 40. C Llanrhos *St As* 39-42; CF (EC) 42-47; Lic to Offic *St As* 47-48; C Hawarden 48-49; V Keswick St Jo *Carl* 50-83; Hon Can Carl Cathl 78-83; P-in-c Threlkeld 80-83; rtd 83; Perm to Offic *Leic* from 83. *12 Brookfield Way, Kibworth, Leicester LE8 0SA* Tel 0116-279 3138

ELLIS JONES, Betty Mary. CertEd41. Bps' Coll Cheshunt. **dss** 62 **d** 87 **p** 94. Perm to Offic *St E* from 62. *St Martin's Cottage, 8 Old Kirton Road, Trimley, Ipswich IP10 0QH* Tel (01394) 275233

✠**ELLISON, The Rt Revd John Alexander.** b 40. ALCD67. **d** 67 **p** 68 **c** 88. C Woking St Paul *Guildf* 67-74; SAMS from 80; Argentina 80-83; R Aldridge *Lich* 83-88; Bp Paraguay from 88. *Iglesia Anglicana Paraguaya, Casilla 1124, Asunción, Paraguay*

ELLISTON, John Ernest Nicholas. b 37. ALCD61. **d** 61 **p** 62. C Gipsy Hill Ch Ch *S'wark* 61-64; C Whitton and Thurleston w Akenham *St E* 64-68; P-in-c New Clee *Linc* 68-71; V New Clee 75-76; V Grimsby St Steph 71-75; P-in-c Mildenhall *St E* 77-79; RD Mildenhall 81-84; R Barton Mills, Beck Row w Kenny Hill etc 80-84; V Ipswich St Aug 84-96; R Guernsey St Peter Port *Win* from 96. *The Rectory, Cornet Street, St Peter Port, Guernsey, Channel Islands GY1 1BZ* Tel (01481) 720036

ELLMORE, Geoffrey Richard. b 36. CEng68 MIMechE68 Leic Coll of Art & Tech BScEng57. S'wark Ord Course 86. **d** 87 **p** 88. NSM Coxheath w E Farleigh, Hunton and Linton *Roch* from 87. *31 Parkway, Coxheath, Maidstone, Kent ME17 4HH* Tel (01622) 744737

ELLMORE, Peter Robert. b 44. HNC70. Sarum & Wells Th Coll 84. **d** 86 **p** 87. C Bridgemary *Portsm* 86-89; C Portsea N End St Mark 89-91; Asst Chapl St Mary's Hosp Portsm 91-92; Chapl Qu Alexandra Hosp Portsm 91-93; Chapl Portsm Hosps NHS Trust 93-97; P-in-c Cosham *Portsm* from 97. *St Philip's Vicarage, 269 Hawthorn Crescent, Cosham, Portsmouth PO6 2DY* Tel (01705) 326179

ELLOR, Michael Keith (Mick). b 52. St Jo Coll Nottm 92. **d** 94 **p** 95. C Stafford St Jo and Tixall w Ingestre *Lich* 94-97; TV Bucknall and Bagnall from 97. *12 Tansey Close, Bucknall, Stoke on Trent ST2 9QX*

ELLSLEY, Howard. b 23. Roch Th Coll 65. **d** 67 **p** 68. C Glas St Marg *Glas* 67-71; R Dalbeattie 71-77; TV Melton Mowbray w Thorpe Arnold *Leic* 77-78; R Balcombe *Chich* 78-83; R Airdrie *Glas* 83-88; R Gartcosh 83-88; rtd 88. *Auchencraig, Lower Barcaple, Ringford, Castle Douglas, Kirkcudbrightshire DG7 2AP* Tel (01557) 820228

ELLSON, Montague Edward. b 33. Birm Univ BA56 Cam Univ ACertEd67. EAMTC 84. **d** 87 **p** 88. Hon C Freethorpe w Wickhampton, Halvergate etc *Nor* 87-90; C Gaywood, Bawsey and Mintlyn 90-92; Miss to Seamen from 90; R Pulham *Nor* 92-94; P-in-c Starston 93-94; Dioc NSM Officer 94-97; R Pulham Market, Pulham St Mary and Starston 94-97; RD Redenhall 95-97; rtd 97. *Barn Cottage, Neatishead Road, Horning, Norfolk NR12 8LB*

ELLSWORTH, Dr Lida Elizabeth. b 48. Columbia Univ (NY) BA70 Girton Coll Cam PhD76. EMMTC. **d** 88 **p** 94. NSM Bakewell *Derby* from 88. *Apple Croft, Granby Gardens, Bakewell, Derbyshire DE45 1ET* Tel (01629) 814255

ELLWOOD, Keith Brian. b 36. AIGCM58 FRSA65 DipRIPH&H65 ACP66 FCollP83 Curwen Coll Lon BA58 MMus65 Bede Coll Dur CertEd59. Bps' Coll Cheshunt 64. **d** 64 **p** 65. Chapl R Wanstead Sch 64-66; C Wanstead St Mary *Chelmsf* 64-66; CF 66-70; OCF 70-71 and 76-79; Hong Kong 70-71; P-in-c Bicknoller *B & W* 71-73; Chapl Roedean Sch Brighton 73-76; Perm to Offic *B & W* 74-79; W Germany 76-79; Chapl Trin Coll Glenalmond 79-81; Hd Master St Chris Sch Burnham-on-Sea 82-86; Hon C Burnham *B & W* 82-86; R Staple Fitzpaine, Orchard Portman, Thurlbear etc 86-89; P-in-c Hugill *Carl* 89-93; Educn Adv 89-93; P-in-c Coldwaltham and Hardham *Chich* 93-95; rtd 96; Perm to Offic *Chich* from 96. *11 Oak Tree Lane, Woodgate, Chichester, W Sussex PO20 6GU* Tel (01243) 544559

ELMES, Sister Evelyn Sandra. b 61. **d** 97. C Southchurch H Trin *Chelmsf* from 97. *254 Woodgrange Drive, Southend-on-Sea, Essex SS1 2SH* Tel (01702) 616192

ELMORE, Graeme Martin. b 47. Sarum & Wells Th Coll 71. **d** 74 **p** 75. C Norbury St Oswald *Cant* 74-77; P-in-c St Allen *Truro* 77-79; P-in-c St Erme 77-79; V Newlyn St Pet 79-85; CF (TA) 80-86; R Redruth w Lanner *Truro* 85-86; Chapl RN from 86. *Royal Naval Chaplaincy Service, Room 203, Victory Building, HM Naval Base, Portsmouth PO1 3LS* Tel (01705) 727903 Fax 727112

ELPHICK, Robin Howard. b 37. ALCD63. **d** 64 **p** 65. C Clapham Common St Barn *S'wark* 64-67; C Woking St Pet *Guildf* 67-71; R Rollesby w Burgh w Billockby *Nor* 71-80; P-in-c Ashby w Oby, Thurne and Clippesby 79-80; R Rollesby w Burgh w Billockby w Ashby w Oby etc 80-84; R Frinton *Chelmsf* 84-94; P-in-c W w E Mersea from 94; P-in-c Peldon w Gt and Lt Wigborough from 94. *The Rectory, 93 Kingsland Road, West Mersea, Colchester CO5 8AG* Tel (01206) 385635

ELPHICK, Miss Vivien Margaret. b 53. Solicitor 77 Kent Univ BA74. Trin Coll Bris BA90. **d** 90 **p** 94. C Oulton Broad *Nor* 90-94; P-in-c Burlingham St Edmund w Lingwood, Strumpshaw etc from 94. *The Rectory, Barn Close, Lingwood, Norwich NR13 4TS* Tel (01603) 713880

ELPHIN AND ARDAGH, Archdeacon of. *See* JOHNSON, The Ven Stanley

ELPHIN AND ARDAGH, Dean of. *See* McGEE, The Very Revd Stuart Irwin

ELSDON, Bernard Robert. b 29. Roch Th Coll 65. **d** 67 **p** 68. C Wallasey St Hilary *Ches* 67-71; C Liv Our Lady and St Nic w St Anne *Liv* 71-72; V Anfield St Marg 73-89; Dioc Exec Dir for Chr Resp 80-83; rtd 89; Perm to Offic *Man* from 89; Perm to Offic *Ches* from 89. *31 Douglas Road, Hazel Grove, Stockport, Cheshire SK7 4JE* Tel 0161-456 6824

ELSDON, Janice Margaret. b 49. **d** 95 **p** 96. NSM Cloughfern *Conn* from 95. *128 Station Road, Greenisland, Carrickfergus, Co Antrim BT38 8UW* Tel (01232) 869123

ELSEY, Cyril. b 08. Ridley Hall Cam 65. **d** 66 **p** 67. C Rolleston *Lich* 66-69; C Anslow 66-69; R Petton w Cockshutt 69-75; rtd 75; Perm to Offic *Ex* from 82. *9 Raleigh Court, Raleigh Road, Budleigh Salterton, Devon EX9 6HR* Tel (01395) 445504

ELSMORE, Guy Charles. b 66. Edin Univ BSc88. Ridley Hall Cam CTMin93. **d** 93 **p** 94. C Huyton St Mich *Liv* from 93. *1 The Cross, Stanley Road, Huyton, Liverpool L36 9XL* Tel 0151-449 3800

ELSON, Christopher John. b 52. K Coll Lon BD75 AKC75. St Aug Coll Cant. **d** 76 **p** 77. C New Haw *Guildf* 76-79; C Guildf H Trin w St Mary 79-82; C Hale 85-87; V Ripley from 87; Sub-Chapl HM Pris Send from 88. *The Vicarage, High Street, Ripley, Woking, Surrey GU23 6AE*

ELSON, John Frederick. Roch Th Coll 62. **d** 64 **p** 65. C Tenterden St Mildred w Smallhythe *Cant* 64-68; P-in-c Chart next Sutton Valence 68-71; V Fletching *Chich* 71-93; Chapl Wivelsfield Green Hospice 91-93; rtd 93; Perm to Offic *Chich* from 93. *Fernbank, 36 Olive Meadow, Uckfield, E Sussex TN22 1QY* Tel (01825) 760663

ELSTOB, Stephen William. b 57. Sarum & Wells Th Coll. **d** 86 **p** 87. C Sunderland Springwell w Thorney Close *Dur* 86-88; C Upholland *Liv* 88-89; TV 89-96; V Cinnamon Brow from 96. *The Vicarage, 1 Briers Close, Fearnhead, Warrington WA2 0DN* Tel (01925) 823108

ELSTON, Philip Herbert. b 35. RD80 and Bar 90 KCT95. Leeds Univ MA76. AKC63. **d** 64 **p** 65. C Thurnby Lodge *Leic* 64-66; Hon C 66-67; Chapl RNR 67-90; Malawi 68-75; Hon C Far Headingley St Chad *Ripon* 75-79; V Knowl Hill w Littlewick *Ox* 79-84; Chapl RN Sch Haslemere 85-89; C Felpham w Middleton *Chich* 89-90; Asst S Regional Dir Miss to Seamen 91-93; Dep S Regional Dir from 93; Corps Chapl Sea Cadet Corps 83-95; Perm to Offic *Win* from 93; Perm to Offic *Cant* from 94. *The Missions to Seamen, Flying Angel House, 3 Arundel Road, Littlehampton, W Sussex BN17 5BY* Tel (01903) 726969 Fax 734455

ELTON, Clarence Edward. b 09. ALCD36. **d** 36 **p** 37. C Fulwood *Sheff* 36-38; C Ramsgate Ch Ch *Cant* 38-39; Org Sec (Midl Area) CCCS 39-43; Lic to Offic *Worc* 42; V Boulton *Derby* 43-47; Chapl Amsterdam *Eur* 47-49; RD The Netherlands 48-49; Sec CPAS Metrop Area 49-51; Lic to Offic *S'wark* 49-51; V Belper *Derby* 51-53; Asst Sec CCCS 53-57; R Hambledon *Guildf* 57-74; rtd 74; Perm to Offic *Guildf* from 74; Perm to Offic *Chich* from 83. *76 Church Road, Milford, Godalming, Surrey GU8 5JD* Tel (01483) 417959

ELTON, Canon Derek Hurley. b 31. Lon Univ BSc52. Wycliffe Hall Ox 53. **d** 55 **p** 56. C Ashton-on-Ribble St Andr *Blackb* 55-57; India 58-70; R Wickmere w Lt Barningham and Itteringham *Nor* 71-79; R Lt w Gt Ellingham 79-83; P-in-c Rockland All SS and St Andr w St Pet 81-83; R Lt w Gt Ellingham w Rockland 83-88; Chapl Wayland Hosp Norfolk 84-88; Miss to Seamen from 89; Algeria 89-94; Eritrea from 94; rtd 96. *98 Emperor Johannes Avenue, PO Box 4151, Asmara, Eritrea* Tel Asmara (1) 127208

ELTRINGHAM, Mrs Fiona Ann. b 48. CertEd69. NE Ord Course 86. **d** 89 **p** 94. Par Dn Willington Team *Newc* 89-92; Chapl HM Young Offender Inst Castington 92-97; Chapl HM Pris Dur from 97. *HM Prison Durham, Old Elvet, Durham DH1 3HU* Tel 0191-386 2621 Fax 386 2524

ELVERSON, Ronald Peter Charles. b 50. St Edm Hall Ox BA73 MA86. St Jo Coll Nottm 84. **d** 86 **p** 87. C Whitnash *Cov* 86-90; V Dunchurch from 90. *The Vicarage, 11 Critchley Drive, Dunchurch, Rugby, Warks CV22 6PJ* Tel (01788) 810274

ELVEY, Ms Charlotte Evanthia. b 44. St Anne's Coll Ox BA66 Bris Univ CertEd67 Open Univ DipReadDev86. S'wark Ord Course 91. **d** 94 **p** 95. NSM Sydenham St Bart *S'wark* 94-95; C from 95. *30 Overhill Road, London SE22 0PH* Tel 0181-693 1735

ELVIN, Jonathan Paul Alistair. b 65. Bris Univ BSc90 Fitzw Coll Cam BA94. Ridley Hall Cam CTM95. **d** 95 **p** 96. C Gravesend St Geo *Roch* from 95. *105 Wrotham Road, Gravesend, Kent DA11 0QP* Tel (01474) 320886

ELVIN, Keith Vernon. b 24. Bris Univ BSc52. **d** 65 **p** 65. C St Clement *Truro* 65-66 and 67-75 and 76-79; Chapl Truro Cathl Sch 66-67; C St John w Millbrook *Truro* 75-76; Hon C Truro St Paul and St Clem 79-80; Vice-Prin Chan Sch and SW Minl Tr Sch Truro 80-82; Lic to Offic 80-84; Perm to Offic 84-90. *26 Westfield House, Cote Lane, Bristol BS9 3UN* Tel 0117-962 8328

ELVY, Canon Peter David. b 38. Lon Univ BA62 Fitzw Ho Cam BA64 MA68 Edin Univ PhD95. Ridley Hall Cam. **d** 65 **p** 66. C Herne *Cant* 65-66; C New Addington 66-68; C Addiscombe St Mildred 69-71; Youth Chapl *Chelmsf* 71-80; V Gt Burstead 75-92; Can Chelmsf Cathl 80-92; V Chelsea All SS *Lon* from 92. *4 Old Church Street, London SW3 5DQ* Tel 0171-352 5627 Fax 352 5467

ELWIN, Ernest John. b 31. Selw Coll Cam BA54 MA58. Ridley Hall Cam 54. **d** 56 **p** 57. C Wandsworth All SS *S'wark* 56-59; C Harlow New Town w Lt Parndon *Chelmsf* 59-61; Asst Teacher Tidworth Down Sch Dorset 61-63; V Soundwell *Bris* 63-66; Asst Teacher Seldown Sch Dorset 66-68; Wareham Modern Sch 68-69; Perm to Offic *Sarum* from 67; Lect S Dorset Tech Coll Weymouth 70-85; Weymouth Coll 85-88; Sub Chapl HM Youth Cust Cen Portland 93-96; rtd 96. *4 Portesham Hill, Portesham, Weymouth, Dorset DT3 4EU* Tel (01305) 871358

ELWIS, Malcolm John. b 42. Melbourne Univ DipEd84. St Jo Coll Morpeth 69 ACT LTh84. **d** 70 **p** 72. Australia 70-80; Perm to Offic *Chich* from 80; Chapl Hellingly and Amberstone Hosps from 88; Sub Chapl HM Prison Lewes from 92. *Meads Place, Meads, Eastbourne, E Sussex BN20 7QH* Tel (01323) 722464

ELWOOD, Alan Roy. b 54. Sarum & Wells Th Coll 90. **d** 92 **p** 93. C Street w Walton *B & W* 92-96; V Kingsbury Episcopi w E Lambrook, Hambridge etc from 96. *The Vicarage, Folly Road, Kingsbury Episcopi, Martock, Somerset TA12 6BH* Tel (01935) 824605

ELY, Nigel Patrick. b 62. Thames Poly BA83 Southn Univ BTh92. Chich Th Coll 89. **d** 92 **p** 93. C Rustington *Chich* 92-93; C Bexhill St Pet 93-96; Chapl Post 16 Cen *Birm* from 96. *4 Inverclyde Road, Handsworth Wood, Birmingham B20 2LJ*

ELY, Archdeacon of. *See* WATSON, The Ven Jeffrey John Seagrief

ELY, Bishop of. *See* SYKES, The Rt Revd Stephen Whitefield

ELY, Dean of. *See* HIGGINS, The Very Revd Michael John

EMBERTON, John Nicholas. b 45. FCA69. Oak Hill NSM Course 85. **d** 88 **p** 89. NSM Purley Ch Ch *S'wark* 88-94; Vineyard Min Internat (UK) from 96. *49 Oakwood Avenue, Purley, Surrey CR8 1AR* Tel 0181-668 2684

EMBLETON, Harold. b 21. Ch Coll Cam BA47 MA52. Qu Coll Birm 47. **d** 49 **p** 50. C Kidderminster St Mary *Worc* 49-52; CF (TA) 50-52; C Wimbledon *S'wark* 52-53; Chapl RN 53-76; QHC 74-76; V Bognor *Chich* 76-84; RD Arundel and Bognor 77-82; V Skirwith, Ousby and Melmerby w Kirkland *Carl* 84-87; rtd 87; Perm to Offic *Carl* 87-93; Perm to Offic *Chich* from 93. *Flat 3, 7 Chatsworth Gardens, Eastbourne, E Sussex BN20 7JP* Tel (01323) 411426

EMBLIN, Richard John. b 48. BEd71 MA81. S Dios Minl Tr Scheme 83. **d** 86 **p** 87. C S w N Hayling *Portsm* 86-89; P-in-c Wootton 89-95; V Cowes H Trin and St Mary from 95. *The Vicarage, Church Road, Cowes, Isle of Wight PO31 8HA* Tel (01983) 292509

EMBRY, Miss Eileen Margaret. b 38. Westf Coll Lon BA60 Lon Univ BD71. **dss** 81 **d** 87 **p** 94. Lect Trin Coll Bris 81-83; Bishopsworth *Bris* 83-87; Par Dn 87-89; rtd 89; Perm to Offic *Bris* from 89; Tutor Trin Coll Bris from 92. *2 Bishop's Cove, Bristol BS13 8HH* Tel 0117-964 2588

EMERSON, Arthur Edward Richard. b 24. Lich Th Coll 69. **d** 72 **p** 73. C Barton upon Humber *Linc* 72-74; V Chapel St Leonards 75-88; P-in-c Hogsthorpe 77-88; V Chapel St Leonards w Hogsthorpe 88-91; rtd 91; Perm to Offic *Linc* from 91. *47 Highfields, Nettleham, Lincoln LN2 2SZ* Tel (01522) 754175

EMERSON, David. b 43. BNC Ox BA66 MA70 DPhil70. Edin Dioc NSM Course 83. **d** 86 **p** 87. NSM Edin St Hilda *Edin* from 86; NSM Edin St Fillan from 86. *25 Little Road, Edinburgh EH16 6SH* Tel 0131-664 3035

EMERSON, Mrs Jan Vivien. b 44. S Dios Minl Tr Scheme 89. **d** 92 **p** 95. NSM Chich St Paul and St Pet *Chich* 92-94; NSM Bosham from 94. *23 Lavant Road, Chichester, W Sussex PO19 4RA* Tel (01243) 527214

EMERTON, Canon John Adney. b 28. FBA79 CCC Ox BA50 MA54 CCC Cam BD60 DD73 Edin Univ Hon DD77. Wycliffe Hall Ox 50. **d** 52 **p** 53. C Birm Cathl *Birm* 52-53; Asst Lect Th Birm Univ 52-53; Lect Hebrew Dur Univ 53-55; Lect Div Cam Univ 55-62; Reader in Semitic Philology Ox Univ 62-68; Lic to Offic *Ely* from 68; Regius Prof Hebrew Cam Univ from 68; Fell St Jo Coll Cam from 70; Hon Can Jerusalem from 84. *34 Gough Way, Cambridge CB3 9LN* Tel (01223) 63219

EMERY, Ms Karen Maureen. b 53. R Holloway Coll Lon BA74. St Alb Minl Tr Scheme 88. **d** 92 **p** 94. Par Dn Royston *St Alb* 92-94; C 94-96; TV Chipping Barnet w Arkley from 96. *St Stephen's Vicarage, 1 Spring Close, Barnet, Herts EN5 2UR* Tel 0181-449 7758

EMES, Leonard Bingham. b 10. Wycliffe Hall Ox 69. **d** 70 **p** 70. C Thame *Ox* 70-73; P-in-c Tetsworth 73-77; P-in-c Adwell w S Weston 73-77; rtd 77; Perm to Offic *St E* 77-83; Perm to Offic *Cant* 83-93. *47 Summerlands Lodge, Wellbrook Road, Farnborough, Kent BR6 8ME* Tel (01689) 851076

EMM, Robert Kenneth. b 46. K Coll Lon BD68 AKC68. **d** 69 **p** 70. C Hammersmith SS Mich and Geo White City Estate CD *Lon* 69-72; C Keynsham *B & W* 72-75; C Yeovil 75-80; TV Gt Grimsby St Mary and St Jas *Linc* 80-85; R N Thoresby 85-94; R Grainsby 85-94; V Waithe 85-94; R The North-Chapel Parishes from 94. *The Rectory, North Thoresby, Grimsby, S Humberside DN36 5QG* Tel (01472) 840029 E-mail bob@bobemm.demon.co.uk

EMMEL, Canon Malcolm David. b 32. Qu Coll Birm DipTh58. **d** 58 **p** 59. C Hessle *York* 58-62; Canada 62-66; V Catterick *Ripon* 66-73; V Pateley Bridge and Greenhow Hill 73-77; P-in-c Middlesmoor w Ramsgill 76-77; V Upper Nidderdale 77-88; RD Ripon 79-86; Hon Can Ripon Cathl from 84; R Bedale from 88; P-in-c Leeming from 88. *The Rectory, Bedale, N Yorkshire DL8 1AB* Tel (01677) 422103

EMMERSON, Peter Barrett. b 29. Fitzw Ho Cam BA54 MA58. Tyndale Hall Bris 50. **d** 54 **p** 57. Canada 54-58; V Fazakerley St Nath *Liv* 59-64; Distr Sec BFBS (Northd and Dur) 64-70; Distr Sec BFBS (Warks, Staffs and Birm) 70-74; W Midl Regional Sec BFBS 72-74; Hon C Boldmere *Birm* 71-74; C-in-c Crown E CD *Worc* 74-77; P-in-c Crown E and Rushwick 77-81; R Stoke Prior, Wychbold and Upton Warren 81-93; rtd 93; Perm to Offic *Worc* from 93. *Fir Tree Cottage, Ivy Lane, Fernhill Heath, Worcester WR3 8RW* Tel (01905) 456416

✠EMMERSON, The Rt Revd Ralph. b 13. AKC38 Lon Univ BD38. Westcott Ho Cam 38. **d** 38 **p** 39 **c** 72. C Leeds St Geo *Ripon* 38-41; C-in-c Seacroft CD 41-48; C Methley 48-49; P-in-c 49-52; R 52-56; P-in-c Mickletown 49-52; R 52-56; V Headingley 56-66; Hon Can Ripon Cathl 64-66; Can Res Ripon Cathl 66-72; Suff Bp Knaresborough 72-79; rtd 79; Asst Bp Ripon from 86. *Flat 1, 15 High St Agnes Gate, Ripon, N Yorkshire HG4 1QR* Tel (01765) 701626

EMMET, Herbert Gerald. b 18. Trin Coll Cam BA40. Linc Th Coll 40. **d** 42 **p** 43. C Leic St Pet *Leic* 42-44; C Melksham *Sarum* 44-48; C St Alb St Sav *St Alb* 48-51; V Leic St Nic *Leic* 51-56; Ind Chapl 51-53; V Hatfield Hyde *St Alb* 56-64; V Harpenden St Jo 64-73; V Kings Langley 73-80; RD Wheathampstead 70-72; rtd 80; Perm to Offic *St Alb* from 80. *39 Linwood Grove, Leighton Buzzard, Beds LU7 8RP* Tel (01525) 377360

EMMETT, Kerry Charles. b 46. St Jo Coll Dur BA68. St Jo Coll Nottm 71. **d** 73 **p** 74. C Attenborough w Chilwell *S'well* 73-75; C Chilwell 75-76; C Wembley St Jo *Lon* 76-79; V Hanworth St Rich 79-89; R Ravenstone and Swannington *Leic* from 89; RD Akeley S from 97. *The Rectory, 9 Orchard Close, The Limes, Ravenstone, Coalville, Leics LE67 2JW* Tel (01530) 839802

EMMETT, Thomas. b 40. Chich Th Coll 67. **d** 70 **p** 71. C Shiremoor *Newc* 70-73; C Haltwhistle 73-75; V Newc Ch Ch 75-80; P-in-c Newc St Anne 77-80; V Newc Ch Ch w St Ann 81-87; V Bywell St Pet from 87; P-in-c Mickley from 97. *St Peter's Vicarage, Meadowfield Road, Bywell, Stocksfield, Northd NE43 7PY* Tel (01661) 842272

EMMOTT, David Eugene. b 41. St Chad's Coll Dur BA63 DipTh66. **d** 66 **p** 67. C Bingley H Trin *Bradf* 66-69; C Anfield St Marg *Liv* 69-70; C Kirkby 70-75; Chapl Newc Poly *Newc* 75-78; Hon C Toxteth Park St Marg *Liv* 78-80; TV Upholland 80-88; V Southfields St Barn *S'wark* from 88. *St Barnabas's Vicarage, 430 Merton Road, London SW18 5AE* Tel 0181-874 7768

EMMOTT, Douglas Brenton. b 45. K Coll Lon BD78 AKC78. Linc Th Coll 79. **d** 80 **p** 81. C Kingston upon Hull St Alb *York* 80-83; V Scarborough St Sav w All SS 83-91; V York St Chad from 91. *St Chad's Vicarage, Campleshon Road, York YO2 1EY* Tel (01904) 654707

EMMOTT, John Charles Lionel. **d** 96. Hon C Tenterden St Mich *Cant* from 96. *58 Grange Crescent, Tenterden, Kent TN30 6DZ* Tel (01580) 762092

EMPEY, Canon Clement Adrian. b 42. TCD BA64 MA68 PhD71. CITC. **d** 74 **p** 75. Hon Chapl Miss to Seamen from 75; C Dublin St Ann *D & G* 75-76; I Kells-Inistioge Gp *C & O* 76-84; Preb Tassagard St Patr Cathl Dublin from 82; I Clane w Donadea and Coolcarrigan *M & K* 84-88; I Dublin St Ann and St Steph *D & G* from 88; Treas St Patr Cathl Dublin 89-91; Chan 91-96; Prec from 96. *St Ann's Vicarage, 88 Mount Anville Wood, Lower Kilmacud Road, Dublin 14, Irish Republic* Tel Dublin (1) 288 0663 E-mail adrianemp@conect.ie

✠EMPEY, The Most Revd Walton Newcome Francis. b 34. TCD BA57. K Coll (NS) BD68. **d** 58 **p** 59 **c** 81. C Glenageary *D & G* 58-60; Canada 60-66; I Stradbally *C & O* 66-71; I Limerick St Mich *L & K* 71-81; Dean Limerick 71-81; Preb Taney St Patr Cathl Dublin 73-81; Bp L & K 81-85; Bp M & K 85-96; Abp Dublin *D & G* from 96; Preb Cualaun St Patr Cathl Dublin from 96. *The See House, 17 Temple Road, Milltown, Dublin 6, Irish Republic* Tel Dublin (1) 497 7849 Fax 497 6355

EMSLEY, John Stobart. b 13. Qu Coll Birm 39. **d** 41 **p** 41. C Norwood St Luke *S'wark* 41-44; C Charlton St Luke w St Paul 44-46; C Ilkley St Marg *Bradf* 46-51; V Bradf St Oswald Chapel Green 51-71; V Yeadon St Andr 71-79; rtd 79. *11 Bishop Garth, Pateley Bridge, Harrogate, N Yorkshire HG3 5LL* Tel (01423) 711835

EMSON, Stanley George. b 26. Glouc Sch of Min. **d** 89 **p** 90. NSM Cirencester *Glouc* 89-92; NSM Coates, Rodmarton and Sapperton etc from 92. *Flat 1, Rodmarton Manor, Rodmarton, Cirencester, Glos GL7 6PF* Tel (01285) 841362

EMTAGE, Miss Susan Raymond. b 34. St Mich Ho Ox 63. **dss** 79 **d** 87 **p** 94. SW Area Sec CPAS Women's Action 75-82; Leic St Chris *Leic* 82-86; Bramerton w Surlingham *Nor* 86-87; C 87-88; C Rockland St Mary w Hellington, Bramerton etc 88-89; Par Dn W Bromwich St Jas *Lich* 89-94; C 94; Par Dn W Bromwich St Paul Golds Hill 89-94; C 94; rtd 94; Hon C Stapleton *Bris* from 96. *55 Sheldrake Drive, Bristol BS16 1UE* Tel 0117-965 7188

ENDALL, Peter John. b 38. Linc Th Coll 83. **d** 85 **p** 86. C Burley in Wharfedale *Bradf* 85-88; V Thwaites Brow from 88; RD S Craven from 96. *The Vicarage, Spring Avenue, Thwaites Brow, Keighley, W Yorkshire BD21 4TA* Tel (01535) 602830

ENDEAN, Michael George Devereux. b 33. Ox NSM Course. **d** 84 **p** 85. NSM Wantage Downs *Ox* from 84. *2 Mount Pleasant, East Hendred, Wantage, Oxon OX12 8LA* Tel (01235) 833497

ENDICOTT, Michael. **d** 97. NSM Pontnewydd *Mon* from 97. *Forge House, Clomendy Road, Cwmbran NP44 3LS* Tel (01633) 868685

ENEVER, John William. b 44. MBE92. NTMTC 94. **d** 97. NSM Waltham H Cross *Chelmsf* from 97. *St Lawrence House, 46 Mallion Court, Waltham Abbey, Essex EN9 3EQ* Tel (01992) 767916

ENEVER, Mrs Rosemary Alice Delande. b 45. Oak Hill Th Coll 86. **d** 88 **p** 94. NSM Gt Ilford St Jo *Chelmsf* 88-94; TV Waltham H Cross from 94. *St Lawrence House, 46 Mallion Court, Ninefields, Waltham Abbey, Essex EN9 3EQ* Tel (01992) 767916

ENEVER, Mrs Susan Elizabeth. b 33. WMMTC 87. **d** 92 **p** 94. NSM Rugby St Andr *Cov* from 92. *7 Rocheberie Way, Rugby, Warks CV22 6EG* Tel (01788) 813135

ENEVER, Vivian John. b 61. Collingwood Coll Dur BA82 Cam Univ PGCE85. Westcott Ho Cam 88. **d** 91 **p** 92. C Gt Crosby St Faith *Liv* 91-95; C Cantril Farm 95-97; TV Halesowen *Worc* from 97. *The Rectory, St Kenelms Road, Romsley, Halesowen, W Midlands B62 0PH*

ENGEL, Jeffrey Davis. b 38. Man Univ BA59 Liv Univ PGCE60 Keele Univ ADC69 Aston Univ MSc82 FCP83. St Deiniol's Hawarden 86. **d** 89 **p** 90. NSM Formby St Pet *Liv* 89-92; C Prescot 92-94; Dioc Adv for Past Care and Counselling from 94; P-in-c Hale from 94. *The Vicarage, Hale, Liverpool L24 4AX* Tel 0151-425 3195

ENGELSEN, Christopher James. b 57. Nottm Univ BTh86. Linc Th Coll 83. **d** 86 **p** 87. C Sprowston *Nor* 86-89; C High Harrogate Ch Ch *Ripon* 89-92; TV Seacroft 92-95; P-in-c Foulsham w Hindolveston and Guestwick *Nor* from 95. *The Rectory, Guist Road, Foulsham, Dereham, Norfolk NR20 5RZ* Tel (01362) 683275

ENGH, Timm Gray. b 38. Univ of the South (USA) 79 Arizona Univ BSc66 Michigan State Univ MSc69. **d** 81 **p** 82. USA 81-86; R Melrose *Edin* 86-90; R Edin St Mark from 90; R Edin St Andr and St Aid from 90. *27 Argyle Crescent, Edinburgh EH15 2QE* Tel 0131-669 3452 E-mail 106043.71@compuserve.com

ENGLAND, Jessie Margaret Tarie. *See* CARLYON, Mrs Jessie Marguerite Tarie

ENGLAND, Robert Gordon. b 39. TCD BA62 QUB MTh76. TCD Div Sch Div Test65. **d** 66 **p** 67. C Raheny w Coolock *D & G* 66-69; C Lisburn Ch Ch *Conn* 72-73; Lic to Offic *D & D* from 74; Hd RE Regent Ho Sch Newtownards from 74. *20 Loury Court, 27 Hampton Park, Belfast BT7 3JY*

ENGLER, Mrs Margaret Dorothy. b 44. Lon Univ TCert77. S'wark Ord Course 90. **d** 93 **p** 94. NSM Harlesden All So *Lon* from 93. *22A Langton Road, London NW2 6QA* Tel 0181-450 2395

ENGLISH, Peter Gordon. b 31. Edin Univ MA55. Ripon Hall Ox 59. **d** 61 **p** 62. C Bingley All SS *Bradf* 61-64; V Cottingley 64-66; Uganda 66-72; rtd 86. *9 Carlton Row, Trowbridge, Wilts B14 0RJ* Tel (01225) 752243

ENGLISH, Peter Redford. b 26. Ridley Hall Cam 70. **d** 72 **p** 73. C Tyldesley w Shakerley *Man* 72-74; C Worsley 74-76; R Levenshulme St Mark 76-81; R Heytesbury and Sutton Veny *Sarum* 81-91; rtd 91. *The Old Rectory, Bromsberrow, Ledbury, Herefordshire HT8 1RU* Tel (01531) 650362

ENNION, Peter. b 56. Aston Tr Scheme 85 Coll of Resurr Mirfield 87. **d** 89 **p** 90. C Middlewich w Byley *Ches* 89-91; C Aylestone St Andr w St Jas *Leic* 91-92; C Coppenhall *Ches* 92-94; P-in-c Newton in Mottram from 94. *St Mary's Vicarage, 39 Bradley Green Road, Hyde, Cheshire SK14 4NA* Tel 0161-368 1489

ENNIS, Martin Michael. b 58. MCollP84 Man Univ BSc80. Sarum & Wells Th Coll 87. **d** 89 **p** 90. C Newquay *Truro* 89-92; C Tewkesbury w Walton Cardiff *Glouc* 92-95; P-in-c Brockworth 95-96; V from 96. *The Vicarage, 42 Court Road, Gloucester GL3 4ET* Tel (01452) 862725 E-mail 100576.3126 @compuserve.com

ENOCH, David John. b 34. Univ of Wales (Ban) BA55 Univ of Wales (Abth) MA69. United Th Coll Abth 55 Glouc Sch of Min 89. **d** 91 **p** 92. NSM Much Birch w Lt Birch, Much Dewchurch etc *Heref* 91-94; P-in-c How Caple w Sollarshope, Sellack etc 94; P-in-c from 95. *The Rectory, Kings Caple, Hereford HR1 4TX* Tel (01432) 840485

ENOCH, William Frederick Palmer. b 30. EMMTC 76. **d** 79 **p** 80. NSM Ilkeston St Mary *Derby* 79-85; P-in-c Ilkeston H Trin 85-95; rtd 95; Perm to Offic *Derby* from 95. *9 Henley Way, West Hallam, Derbyshire DE7 6LU* Tel 0115-944 3003

ENRIGHT, Canon James Leslie. b 06. **d** 66 **p** 66. C Dromod *L & K* 66-67; I 67-76; Can Limerick Cathl 72-76; Prec Limerick Cathl 72-76; rtd 76. *8 Seafield, Newtown Hill, Tramore, Co Waterford, Irish Republic* Tel Tramore (51) 381855

ENSOR, David Alec. b 25. Cape Town Univ BA67. Cuddesdon Coll 48. **d** 50 **p** 51. S Africa 50-60; Br Guiana 60-64; V Warrington St Barn *Liv* 64-68; V Quadring *Linc* 68-73; V Gt Grimsby St Andr and St Luke 73-74; V Grimsby St Aug 73-84; R Claypole 84-86; V Whaplode Drove 86-91; V Gedney Hill 86-91; rtd 91; Perm to Offic *Linc* from 91. *2 Curtois Close, Branston, Lincoln LN4 1LJ* Tel (01522) 794265

ENSOR, Keith Victor. b 08. Dur Univ LTh32. Lon Coll of Div 27. **d** 31 **p** 32. C Holloway St Jas *Lon* 31-34; Org Sec (N Prov) BCMS 34-38; Algeria 38-39; Chapl RAFVR 39-47; V Wolvey, Burton Hastings and Stretton Baskerville *Cov* 47-50; Chapl RAF 50-63; R Horton and Lt Sodbury *Glouc* from 64. *The Rectory, Horton, Chipping Sodbury, Bristol BS17 6QP* Tel (01454) 313256

ENSOR, Paul George. b 56. Ripon Coll Cuddesdon. **d** 82 **p** 83. C Newington St Mary *S'wark* 82-87; TV Croydon St Jo 87-91; P-in-c Brandon and Santon Downham *St E* 91-92; R Brandon and Santon Downham w Elveden 92-95; V Mitcham St Olave *S'wark* from 95. *St Olave's Vicarage, 22 Church Walk, London SW16 5JH* Tel 0181-764 2048

ENSOR, Stephen Herbert Paulett. b 07. ALCD31 St Jo Coll Dur LTh31 BA32. **d** 32 **p** 33. C Leyland St Andr *Blackb* 32-35; C Bris St Bart *Bris* 35-36; Tutor BCMS and Bris Th Coll 35-40; Org Sec (SW and Midl) BCMS 36-40; V Patcham *Chich* 40-48; R Bispham *Blackb* 48-69; TR Bedworth *Cov* 70-81; RD Bedworth 71-76; rtd 81; Perm to Offic *B & W* from 82. *Hillside Cottage, South Street, Castle Cary, Somerset BA7 7ES* Tel (01963) 351003

ENSOR, Terrence Bryon. b 45. K Coll Lon BD78 AKC78. Westcott Ho Cam 78. **d** 79 **p** 80. C S'wark St Sav w All Hallows *S'wark* 79-82; Seychelles 82-85; V Northampton St Benedict *Pet* 85-90; Uruguay 90-93; USPG Fieldworker (Blackb, Bradf, Carl and Wakef) 93-96; V Blackb St Jas *Blackb* from 96. *St James's Vicarage, Cromer Place, Blackburn BB1 8EL* Tel (01254) 256465

ENTWISTLE, Alan. b 41. Nottm Univ CertEd67 ACP69 Open Univ BA80 Man Univ MEd85 FRSA96. NW Ord Course 72. **d** 75 **p** 76. C Bury H Trin *Man* 75-78; Hd Master Hazlehurst Sch Bury 78-95; RE Adv Bury LEA from 96; Lic to Offic *Man* from 78. *1 Alderwood Grove, Edenfield, Bury, Lancs BL0 0HQ* Tel (01706) 824221

ENTWISTLE, Christopher John. b 47. N Ord Course 79. **d** 82 **p** 83. NSM Colne H Trin *Blackb* 82-84; C Poulton-le-Fylde 84-87; V Blackpool St Paul 87-96; RD Blackpool 94-96; P-in-c Overton from 96. *St Helen's Vicarage, Chapel Lane, Overton, Morecambe, Lancs LA3 3HU* Tel (01524) 858234

ENTWISTLE, Frank Roland. b 37. Dur Univ BA59 DipTh60. Cranmer Hall Dur 59. **d** 61 **p** 62. C Harborne Heath *Birm* 61-65; S Area Sec BCMS 65-66; Educn Sec 66-73; Hon C Wallington H Trin *S'wark* 68-73; UCCF from 73; Hon C Ware Ch Ch *St Alb* 73-76; Hon C Leic H Trin w St Jo *Leic* from 76. *157 Shanklin Drive, Leicester LE2 3QG* Tel 0116-270 0759 or 255 1700 Fax 255 5316

ENTWISTLE, Harry. b 40. St Chad's Coll Dur BSc61 DipTh63. **d** 63 **p** 64. C Fleetwood *Blackb* 63-69; P-in-c Aston Abbots w Cublington *Ox* 69-74; P-in-c Hardwick St Mary 69-74; Chapl HM Pris Aylesbury 69-74; Chapl HM Pris Lewes 74-77; Chapl HM Rem Cen Risley 77-81; Chapl HM Pris Wandsworth 81-88; Australia from 88; Adn Northam from 92. *48 Chidlow Street, Northam, W Australia 6401* Tel Northam (96) 221016 Fax 225 889

ENTWISTLE, Howard Rodney. b 36. Ball Coll Ox BA61. Linc Th Coll 61. **d** 63 **p** 64. C Langley St Aid CD *Man* 63-64; C Langley All SS and Martyrs 64-66; V Wythenshawe St Martin 66-73; R Stretford St Matt from 73. *St Matthew's Rectory, 39 Sandy Lane, Stretford, Manchester M32 9DB* Tel 0161-865 2535

EPERSON, Canon Donald Birkby. b 04. Ch Ch Ox BA27 MA30. Ripon Hall Ox 30. **d** 30 **p** 31. Asst Chapl Sherborne Sch 30-38; V Charminster *Sarum* 38-53; Chapl Dorset Co Mental Hosp 38-53; Can and Preb Sarum Cathl 51-53; Chapl and Lect Bp Otter Coll Chich 53-64; Hon PV Chich Cathl 54-64; Sen Lect Ch Ch Coll Cant 64-69; Perm to Offic *Cant* from 64; Hon Min Can Cant Cathl 67-72; rtd 71. *Old Rectory, Ickham, Canterbury, Kent CT3 1QN*

EPPS, Christopher Derek (Chris). b 54. ACII79. Linc Th Coll CMinlStuds95. **d** 95 **p** 96. C Clevedon St Jo *B & W* from 95. *53 Woodington Road, Clevedon, Avon BS21 5LB* Tel (01275) 879832

EPPS, Gerald Ralph. b 31. Open Univ BA79. Oak Hill Th Coll 52 K Coll Lon 54. **d** 57 **p** 58. C Slade Green *Roch* 57-60; V Freethorpe w Wickhampton *Nor* 60-70; P-in-c Halvergate w Tunstall 62-67; V 67-70; R Pulham St Mary Magd 70-80; P-in-c Alburgh 76-77; P-in-c Denton 76-77; P-in-c Pulham St Mary V

76-80; R Pulham 80-91; rtd 91; Perm to Offic *Nor* from 91. *10 Lime Close, Harleston, Norfolk IP20 9DG* Tel (01379) 854532

EQUEALL, David Edward Royston. b 41. Open Univ BA. St Mich Coll Llan 68. **d** 71 **p** 72. C Mountain Ash *Llan* 71-74; C Gabalfa 74-77; Chapl Asst Univ Hosp of Wales Cardiff 74-77; Chapl 77-79; Chapl N Gen Hosp Sheff 79-94; Chapl N Gen Hosp NHS Trust Sheff from 94. *Northern General Hospital, Herries Road, Sheffield S5 7AU, or 2 Longley Lane, Sheffield S5 7JD* Tel 0114-271 5056 or 243 4343

ERDAL, Miss Ayshe Anne. b 61. Nottm Univ BA84. Ripon Coll Cuddesdon 88. **d** 90. C Daventry *Pet* 90-91; C Corby SS Pet and Andr w Gt and Lt Oakley 91-92; C Chellaston *Derby* from 97. *30 Woodgate Drive, Chellaston, Derby DE73 1UX* Tel (01332) 701236

ERRIDGE, David John. b 45. Lon Univ DipTh68. Tyndale Hall Bris 66. **d** 69 **p** 70. C Bootle St Matt *Liv* 69-72; C Horwich H Trin *Man* 72-77; R Blackley St Andr from 77; AD N Man 85-94. *The Vicarage, Churchdale Road, Higher Blackley, Manchester M9 3ND* Tel 0161-740 2961

ERSKINE, Canon Samuel Thomas. b 19. TCD BA42 MA46. **d** 43 **p** 44. C Romford Gd Shep Collier Row *Chelmsf* 43-44; C Barking St Marg 45-47; Youth Chapl 47-52; V Gt Ilford St Andr 52-60; R Mortlake w E Sheen *S'wark* 60-68; RD Canewdon and Southend *Chelmsf* 68-84; V Prittlewell St Mary 68-77; V Prittlewell 77-84; rtd 84; Perm to Offic *Chelmsf* from 84; Perm to Offic *St E* from 85. *11 Kembold Close, Moreton Rise, Bury St Edmunds, Suffolk IP32 7EF* Tel (01284) 706337

ESAU, John Owen. b 39. St Mich Coll Llan DipPTh95. **d** 95 **p** 96. Min Can St D Cathl *St D* 95-97; V Llanpumsaint w Llanllawddog from 97. *The Vicarage, Llanpumsaint, Carmarthen SA33 6BZ* Tel (01267) 253205

ESCOLME, Miss Doreen. b 29. St Jo Coll Nottm 82. **dss** 83 **d** 87 **p** 94. Hunslet Moor St Pet and St Cuth *Ripon* 83-87; C 87-88; Par Dn Wyther Ven Bede 88-94; C 94; rtd 94; Perm to Offic *Ripon* from 94. *6 Heather Gardens, Leeds LS13 4LF* Tel 0113-257 9055

ESCRITT, Canon Margaret Ruth. b 37. Selly Oak Coll IDC62. **d** 87 **p** 94. Dioc Adv for Diaconal Mins *York* 85-91; Chapl HM Pris Full Sutton 92-94; C Kexby w Wilberfoss *York* 93-94; Chapl HM Pris Everthorpe from 95; Can and Preb York Minster *York* from 95. *HM Young Offender Institution, Everthorpe, Brough, N Humberside HU15 1RB* Tel (01430) 422471 Fax 421351

ESCRITT, Michael William. b 35. Birm Univ DipTh67. Qu Coll Birm 64. **d** 67 **p** 68. C Huntington *York* 67-69; Abp's Dom Chapl 69-72; V Bishopthorpe 72-83; V Acaster Malbis 73-83; V Selby Abbey 83-90; TR Haxby w Wigginton from 90. *The Rectory, 3 Westfield Close, Haxby, York YO3 3JG* Tel (01904) 760455

ESDAILE, Canon Adrian George Kennedy. b 35. Mert Coll Ox BA57 MA61. Wells Th Coll 59. **d** 61 **p** 62. C St Helier *S'wark* 61-64; C Wimbledon 64-68; V Hackbridge and N Beddington 68-80; RD Sutton 76-80; TR Chipping Barnet w Arkley *St Alb* from 80; RD Barnet 89-94; Hon Can St Alb from 94. *The Rectory, 38 Manor Road, Barnet, Herts EN5 2JJ* Tel 0181-449 3894

ESPIN-BRADLEY, Richard John. b 61. Lanc Univ BSc84. Oak Hill Th Coll DipHE95. **d** 95 **p** 96. C Brundall w Braydeston and Postwick *Nor* from 95. *8 Greenacre Close, Brundall, Norwich NR13 5QF* Tel (01603) 714570

ESSER, Lindsay Percy David. b 53. BA. Oak Hill Th Coll. **d** 84 **p** 85. C Barnsbury St Andr and H Trin w All SS *Lon* 84-87; Chapl Paris St Mich *Eur* 87-90; C Spring Grove St Mary *Lon* 90-95; Mauritius from 95. *The Rectory, St Barnabas Church, Royal Road, Pamplemousses, Mauritius*

ESSERY, Canon Eric Albert. b 28. TD ED78. Univ of Wales (Lamp) BA53 Reading Univ CertEd76. St Mich Coll Llan 53. **d** 55 **p** 56. C Skewen *Llan* 55-57; C Oakwood 57-59; C Sunbury *Lon* 59-63; Ind Chapl *Chich* 63-64; P-in-c Crawley 63-64; V Hammersmith St Paul *Lon* 64-74; CF (TAVR) from 65; V Shinfield *Ox* 74-84; V Whitley Ch Ch from 84; RD Reading 85-95; Hon Can Ch Ch from 88. *Christ Church Vicarage, 4 Vicarage Road, Reading RG2 7AJ* Tel 0118-987 1250

ESTDALE, Canon Francis Albert. b 26. ALCD53. **d** 53 **p** 54. C Penn *Lich* 53-56; C Watford Ch Ch *St Alb* 56-61; V Stopsley 61-94; Hon Can St Alb Abbey 90-94; rtd 94; Perm to Offic *Ely* from 94; Perm to Offic *Pet* from 94. *4 Peacock Way, South Bretton, Peterborough PE3 9AA* Tel (01733) 261048

ETCHELLS, Peter. b 26. Kelham Th Coll 48. **d** 52 **p** 53. C Chesterton St Geo *Ely* 52-55; C Leic St Marg *Leic* 55-58; R Willoughby Waterleys, Peatling Magna etc 58-96; rtd 96. *29 Upperfield Drive, Felixstowe, Suffolk IP11 9LS*

ETCHES, Haigh David. b 45. St Jo Coll Dur BA71 DipTh72. **d** 73 **p** 74. C Whitnash *Cov* 73-77; C Wallingford *Ox* 77-79; C Wallingford w Crowmarsh Gifford etc 79-83; P-in-c Bearwood 83-86; R from 86. *The Rectory, 6 St Catherine's Close, Wokingham, Berks RG11 5BZ* Tel (0118) 979 4364

ETHERIDGE, Mrs Marjorie. b 18. Univ of Wales (Ban) BA38 Open Univ BA84. St Alb Minl Tr Scheme 80. **dss** 83 **d** 87 **p** 94. Hitchin *St Alb* 83-94; Hon Par Dn 87-94; Lic to Offic from 94. *23 Stormont Road, Hitchin, Herts SG5 1SH* Tel (01462) 450496

ETHERIDGE, Canon Richard Thomas. b 32. Lon Univ BD62. ALCD61. **d** 62 **p** 63. C Wilmington *Roch* 62-65; C Rainham 65-69; V Langley St Jo *Birm* from 69; P-in-c Oldbury from 83; P-in-c Langley St Mich from 95; Hon Can Birm Cathl from 97. *The Vicarage, St John's Road, Oldbury, Warley, W Midlands B68 9RF* Tel 0121-552 5005

ETHERIDGE, Terry. b 44. Wells Th Coll 68. **d** 70 **p** 71. C Barrow St Jo *Carl* 70-73; C Wilmslow *Ches* 73-76; V Knutsford St Cross 76-85; R Malpas and Threapwood from 85. *The Rectory, Malpas, Cheshire SY14 8PP* Tel (01948) 860209

ETHERINGTON, Ernest Hugh. b 12. CCC Cam BA34 MA39. Linc Th Coll 34. **d** 35 **p** 36. C Iford *Win* 35-39; C Bromborough *Ches* 39-41; CF (EC) 41-48; Chr Reconstruction in Eur 48-50; C Haywards Heath St Wilfrid *Chich* 50-53; R Southwick 53-58; Asst Master Wakef Tutorial Sch 58-61; Asst Master Horbury Sec Sch 61-77; Perm to Offic *Wakef* 72-94; rtd 77. *Fosbrooke House, Clifton Drive, Lytham, Lytham St Annes, Lancs FY8 5RE* Tel (01253) 795399

ETHERINGTON, Mrs Ferial Mary Gould. b 44. FILEx83. St Alb Minl Tr Scheme 86. **d** 93 **p** 94. NSM Luton St Chris Round Green *St Alb* from 93. *St Christopher's Vicarage, 33 Felix Avenue, Luton LU2 7LE* Tel (01582) 24754 Fax 718581

ETHERINGTON, Robert Barry. b 37. Man Univ BA62. Linc Th Coll 62. **d** 64 **p** 65. C Linc St Jo *Linc* 64-67; C Frodingham 67-69; V Reepham 69-78; Ind Chapl 70-78; Ind Chapl *St Alb* 78-88; V Luton St Chris Round Green from 88. *St Christopher's Vicarage, 33 Felix Avenue, Luton LU2 7LE* Tel (01582) 24754 Fax 718581

ETTERLEY, Peter Anthony Gordon. b 39. Kelham Th Coll 63 Wells Th Coll 66. **d** 68 **p** 69. C Gillingham St Aug *Roch* 68-71; Papua New Guinea 71-80; V Cleeve w Chelvey and Brockley *B & W* 80-84; V Seaton Hirst *Newc* 84-86; TR 86-96; P-in-c Felton from 96; P-in-c Longframlington w Brinkburn from 96. *The Vicarage, 1 Benlaw Grove, Felton, Morpeth, Northd NE65 9NG* Tel (01670) 787263

ETTLINGER, Max Brian. b 28. Sarum & Wells Th Coll 70. **d** 72 **p** 73. C Mill Hill Jo Keble Ch *Lon* 72-74; Min Cricklewood St Pet CD 74-78; R Monken Hadley 78-88; Bp's Dom Chapl *St E* 88-91; Dioc Communications Officer 88-91; P-in-c Stratford St Mary 91-93; P-in-c Raydon 91-93; P-in-c Holton St Mary w Gt Wenham 91-93; P-in-c Higham 92-93; rtd 93. *11 Bowthorpe Close, Ipswich IP1 3PZ* Tel (01473) 214362

ETTRICK, Peter Alured. b 14. OBE67 TD56 and Bars. Ch Coll Cam BA36 MA41. Qu Coll Birm 36. **d** 37 **p** 38. C Werneth *Man* 37-39; P-in-c Blackley St Pet 39-40; P-in-c Ashton Ch Ch 40-42; CF (EC) 42-47; R Heaton Norris Ch w All SS *Man* 47-52; Sen CF (TA) 48-62; Dep Asst Chapl Gen 62-66; R Flixton St Mich *Man* 52-61; V Gaydon w Chadshunt *Cov* 61-65; Asst Dir RE 61-65; V Radford 65-70; V Bisley *Glouc* 70-79; rtd 79; Perm to Offic *Glouc* from 80. *Meiktila, The Ridge, Bussage, Stroud, Glos GL6 8BB* Tel (01453) 883272

EUROPE, Archdeacon in. *See* REID, The Ven William Gordon

EUROPE, Bishop of Gibraltar in. *See* HIND, The Rt Revd John William

EUROPE, Suffragan Bishop in. *See* SCRIVEN, The Rt Revd Henry William

EUSTICE, Peter Lafevre. b 32. AKC56. **d** 57 **p** 58. C Finsbury Park St Thos *Lon* 57-60; C Redruth *Truro* 60-63; V Treslothan 63-71; V Falmouth All SS 71-76; R St Stephen in Brannel 76-97; rtd 97. *21 Gloucester Avenue, Carlyon Bay, St Austell, Cornwall PL25 3PT* Tel (01726) 817343

EVA, Canon Owen Vyvyan. b 17. MBE83. Selw Coll Cam BA39 MA43. Ridley Hall Cam 46. **d** 47 **p** 48. C Garston *Liv* 47-51; V Edge Hill St Cath 51-57; Hong Kong 57-61; P-in-c Warrington H Trin *Liv* 61-62; R Halewood 62-83; TR 83-86; RD Farnworth 71-81; Hon Can Liv Cathl 74-86; rtd 86; Perm to Offic *Ches* from 87; Perm to Offic *Liv* from 87. *10 Saddlers Rise, Norton, Runcorn, Cheshire WA7 6PG* Tel (01928) 717119

EVANS, Alan David Carter. b 35. Clifton Th Coll 62. **d** 65 **p** 66. C Gt Baddow *Chelmsf* 65-68; C Walthamstow St Mary 68-72; V Forest Gate St Mark 72-77; V Chadwell Heath 77-86; V Squirrels Heath 86-96; Chapl Havering Coll of F&HE 88-94. *15 Benleaze Way, Swanage, Dorset BH19 2ST* Tel (01929) 423648

EVANS, Alun Wyn. b 47. Down Coll Cam BA70 MA73. Cuddesdon Coll 70. **d** 72 **p** 73. C Bargoed w Brithdir *Llan* 72-74; C Bargoed and Deri w Brithdir 74-75; C Coity w Nolton 75-77; V Cwmavon 77-81; Warden of Ords 80-81; V Llangynwyd w Maesteg 81-86; Prov Officer for Soc Resp 86-93; V Llanishen Ch Ch from 93. *Christ Church Vicarage, 25 Mountbatten Close, Cardiff CF2 5QG* Tel (01222) 757190

EVANS, Mrs Amanda Jane. **d** 97. C Faversham *Cant* from 97. *78 Cyprus Road, Faversham, Kent ME13 8HD* Tel (01795) 538334

EVANS, Andrew. b 57. Southn Univ BEd80. S Dios Minl Tr Scheme 88. **d** 91 **p** 92. NSM Cricklade w Latton *Bris* from 91. *35 Pittsfield, Cricklade, Wilts SN6 6AW* Tel (01793) 751688

EVANS, Anthony Nigel. b 53. Nottm Univ BA74 Fitzw Coll Cam BA76. Westcott Ho Cam 74. **d** 77 **p** 78. C Sneinton St Cypr *S'well* 77-80; C Worksop Priory 80-83; V Nottingham St Geo w St Jo 83-88; R Ordsall 88-95; P-in-c Sutton in Ashfield St Mary from 95. *St Mary's Vicarage, Church Avenue, Sutton-in-Ashfield, Notts NG17 2GR* Tel (01623) 554509

EVANS, Benjamin John. b 13. JP. St Mich Coll Llan 75. **d** 76 **p** 77. NSM Barry All SS *Llan* 76-83; rtd 83; Perm to Offic *Llan* from 83. *167 Pontypridd Road, Barry CF6 8LW* Tel (01446) 734742

EVANS, Brian. b 34. Univ of Wales (Cardiff) DipTh58 Open Univ BA86. St Deiniol's Hawarden 70. **d** 71 **p** 72. C Porthkerry *Llan* 71-72; C Barry All SS 72-75; V Abercynon 75-82; V Pendoylan and Welsh St Donats 82-87; R Maentwrog w Trawsfynydd *Ban* from 87. *The Rectory, Trawsfynydd, Blaenau Ffestiniog LL41 4RY* Tel (01766) 540482

EVANS, Caroline Mary. b 46. CertEd69. St Jo Coll Nottm DipTh86. **d** 86 **p** 97. C Llanbeblig w Caernarfon and Betws Garmon etc *Ban* 86-88; D-in-c Bodedern w Llechgynfarwy and Llechylched etc from 88; RD Llifon and Talybolion from 96. *The Vicarage, Bodedern, Holyhead LL65 3SU* Tel (01407) 740340

EVANS, Charles Wyndham. b 28. Univ of Wales (Ban) BA49 St Cath Soc Ox BA51 MA55. St Steph Ho Ox 49. **d** 52 **p** 53. C Denbigh *St As* 52-56; Lic to Offic *St D* 56-79; Chapl Llandovery Coll 56-67; Chapl and Sen Lect Trin Coll Carmarthen 67-79; V Llanrhaeadr-yng-Nghinmeirch and Prion *St As* from 79; Dioc RE Adv from 82; Tutor St Deiniol's Lib Hawarden from 84; Chapl Ruthin Sch from 84; RD Denbigh *St As* from 84. *The Vicarage, Llanrhaeadr, Denbigh LL16 4NN* Tel (01745) 78250

EVANS, Prof Christopher Francis. b 09. CCC Cam BA32 MA38 Ox Univ MA48 Southn Univ Hon DLitt77 Glas Univ Hon DD85 FBA91 FKC70. Linc Th Coll 33. **d** 34 **p** 35. C Southampton St Barn *Win* 34-38; Tutor Linc Th Coll 38-44; Chapl and Lect Linc Dioc Tr Coll 44-48; Chapl and Fell CCC Ox 48-58; Select Preacher Ox Univ 55-57; Select Preacher Cam Univ 59-60; Lightfoot Prof Div Dur Univ 58-62; Can Res Dur Cathl *Dur* 58-62; Prof NT Studies K Coll Lon 62-77; rtd 77. *4 Church Close, Cuddesdon, Oxford OX44 9EX* Tel (01865) 874406

EVANS, Christopher Idris. b 51. Chich Th Coll 74. **d** 77 **p** 78. C Gelligaer *Llan* 77-80; C St Andrew's Major and Michaelston-le-Pit 80-81; V Llangeinor 81-87; V Watlington w Pyrton and Shirburn *Ox* 87-97; R Icknield from 97. *The Vicarage, Hill Road, Watlington, Oxon OX9 5AD* Tel (01491) 612494

EVANS, Christopher Jonathan. b 43. AKC67 AKC88. **d** 68 **p** 69. C Wednesfield St Thos *Lich* 68-71; C Dorridge *Birm* 71-74; V Marston Green 74-81; V Acocks Green 81-86; RD Yardley 84-86; V Hill 86-88; Area Officer COPEC Housing Trust 88-91; V Harborne St Pet from 91. *The Vicarage, Old Church Road, Birmingham B17 0BB* Tel 0121-427 1949

EVANS, Clive Roger. b 59. Worc Coll Ox BA80 MA84. St Jo Coll Nottm DTS94. **d** 94 **p** 95. C Barton Seagrave w Warkton *Pet* 94-97; V Long Buckby w Watford from 97. *The Vicarage, 10 Hall Drive, Long Buckby, Northampton NN6 7QU* Tel (01327) 842909

EVANS, Canon Colin Rex. b 24. Reading Univ BA49. Linc Th Coll. **d** 57 **p** 58. C Boultham *Linc* 57-59; C Linc St Nic w St Jo Newport 59-62; V Linc St Mary-le-Wigford w St Martin 62-66; P-in-c Linc St Faith 63-66; R Bassingham 66-74; V Aubourn w Haddington 66-74; V Carlton-le-Moorland w Stapleford 66-74; R Skinnand 66-74; R Thurlby w Norton Disney 66-74; RD Graffoe 69-74; RD Elloe E 74-89; Can and Preb Linc Cathl 74-89; V Holbeach 74-89; rtd 90; Hon C Dawlish *Ex* from 90; RD Kenn from 95. *87 West Cliff Park Drive, Dawlish, Devon EX7 9EL* Tel (01626) 862860

EVANS, Miss Daphne Gillian. b 41. Bible Tr Inst Glas 67 Trin Coll Bris IDC75. **dss** 83 **d** 87. Wenlock *Heref* 83-88; TD 87-88; rtd 88. *12 Greenmeadow Grove, Endon, Stoke-on-Trent ST9 9EU* Tel (01782) 504686

EVANS, David. b 37. Keble Coll Ox BA60 MA65 Lon Univ BD64. Wells Th Coll 62. **d** 64 **p** 65. Min Can Brecon Cathl *S & B* 64-68; C Brecon w Battle 64-68; C Swansea St Mary and H Trin 68-71; Chapl Univ of Wales (Swansea) 68-71; Bp's Chapl for Samaritan and Soc Work *Birm* 71-75; Jt Gen Sec Samaritans 75-84; Gen Sec 84-89; Lic to Offic *Ox* 75-89; R Heyford w Stowe Nine Churches *Pet* 89-96; Chapl Northants Police from 89; RD Daventry from 96; R Heyford w Stowe Nine Churches and Flore 96; R Heyford w Stowe Nine Churches and Flore etc from 97. *The Rectory, Church Lane, Nether Heyford, Northampton NN7 3LQ* Tel (01327) 340487

EVANS, David. b 37. Open Univ BA73 FRSA95. St Mich Coll Llan 65. **d** 67 **p** 68. C Swansea St Pet *S & B* 67-70; C St Austell *Truro* 70-75; R Purley *Ox* 75-90; RD Bradfield 85-90; R Bryanston Square St Mary w St Marylebone St Mark *Lon* from 90; P-in-c St Marylebone Ch Ch 90-91. *73 Gloucester Place, London W1H 3PF* Tel 0171-935 2200

EVANS, David Alexander Noble. b 13. Pemb Coll Ox BA36 MA41. Wells Th Coll 38. **d** 40 **p** 41. C Leeds St Pet *Ripon* 40-44; CF (EC) 44-47; Univ Coll Sch Frognal 47-50; V Eton w Boveney *Ox* 50-67; V Sunningdale 67-80; rtd 80; Perm to Offic *Ex* from 80. *High Bank, Chapel Lane, Manaton, Newton Abbot, Devon TQ13 9UA* Tel (01647) 221336

EVANS, David Aylmer. b 28. Lon Univ CertEd62 Reading Univ DipC&G73. St D Coll Lamp BA49 LTh51. **d** 51 **p** 52. C Brecon St David w Llanspyddid and Llanilltyd *S & B* 51-53; C Colwyn Bay *St As* 53-54; C Macclesfield St Mich *Ches* 54-56; V Lostock Gralam 56-59; Perm to Offic *Chelmsf* 58-65; Perm to Offic *Ox* 65-73; Chapl Endsleigh Sch 59-65; Wokingham Gr Sch 65-72; Counsellor S Molton Sch and Community Coll 73-87; V Middlezoy and Othery and Moorlinch *B & W* 87-93; rtd 93; Perm to Offic *Ex* from 94; Perm to Offic *B & W* from 94. *2 Higher Mead, Hemyock, Cullompton, Devon EX15 3QH* Tel (01823) 680974

EVANS (or BURTON EVANS), David Burton. b 35. Open Univ BA87 Golds Coll Lon BMus93. K Coll Lon 58 Edin Th Coll 60. **d** 62 **p** 63. C Leeds St Hilda *Ripon* 62-63; C Cross Green St Sav and St Hilda 63-67; Min Can Dur Cathl *Dur* 67-71; Chapl Prebendal Sch Chich 71-74; PV Chich Cathl *Chich* 71-74; V Lynch w Iping Marsh 74-79; Chapl K Edw VII Hosp Midhurst 77-86; V Easebourne *Chich* 79-86; R St Mich Cornhill w St Pet le Poer etc *Lon* 86-96; rtd 96; Chapl Pau *Eur* from 96. *43 rue Montpensier, 64000 Pau, France* Tel France (33) 59 62 56 45

EVANS, Canon David Conrad. b 16. St D Coll Lamp BA40. **d** 42 **p** 43. C Llandeilo Tal-y-bont *S & B* 42-45; CF (EC) 45-48; C Gorseinon *S & B* 48-50; C Aberystwyth St Mich *St D* 50-53; V Beddgelert *Ban* 53-56; R Llangelynin 56-59; R Llanllyfni 59-63; V Llanfihangel Abercywyn *St D* 63-83; RD St Clears 77-83; Hon Can St D Cathl 79-83; rtd 83. *17 Penbryn Avenue, Carmarthen SA31 3DH* Tel (01267) 234333

EVANS, David Elwyn. b 43. St Mich Coll Llan 71. **d** 73 **p** 74. C Llandybie *St D* 73-75; C Llanelli 75-78; V Tre-lech a'r Betws w Abernant and Llanwinio from 78. *Tre-Lech Vicarage, Pen-y-Bont, Carmarthen SA33 6PJ* Tel (01994) 484335

EVANS, David Frederick Francis. b 35. Univ of Wales BSc59. Wells Th Coll 59. **d** 61 **p** 62. C Eltham St Jo *S'wark* 61-64; C Banbury *Ox* 64-69; V Brize Norton and Carterton 69-73; V Tilehurst St Geo 73-84; V Lydney w Aylburton *Glouc* 84-95; V Lydney from 95; RD Forest S 90-95. *The Vicarage, Church Road, Lydney, Glos GL15 5EG* Tel (01594) 842321

EVANS, Canon David Geraint. b 24. Univ of Wales BA47. St D Coll Lamp 49. **d** 49 **p** 50. C St Ishmael's w Llan-saint and Ferryside *St D* 49-54; C Llandeilo Fawr and Llandefeisant 54-58; V Strata Florida 58-68; R Ystradgynlais *S & B* 68-91; Hon Can Brecon Cathl 86-91; rtd 91; Perm to Offic *St D* from 91. *Tan-ur-Allt, 117 Heol Cae Gurwen, Gwaun Cae Gurwen, Ammanford SA18 1PD* Tel (01269) 842719

EVANS, David John. b 49. Univ of Wales (Ban) BSc72 Bath Univ CertEd73 Leeds Univ DipTh77. Coll of Resurr Mirfield 75. **d** 78 **p** 79. C Wandsworth St Anne *S'wark* 78-81; C Angell Town St Jo 81-82; TV Catford (Southend) and Downham 82-90; P-in-c Somersham w Pidley and Oldhurst *Ely* 90-91; P-in-c Broughton 90-91; R Somersham w Pidley and Oldhurst from 91. *The Rectory, Rectory Lane, Somersham, Huntingdon, Cambs PE17 3EL* Tel (01487) 840676

EVANS, David Leslie Bowen. b 28. Univ of Wales (Lamp) BA52 LTh54. **d** 54 **p** 55. C Cardigan *St D* 54-57; C Llangathen w Llanfihangel Cilfargen 57-58; C Betws w Ammanford 58-60; V Betws Ifan 60-64; V Burry Port and Pwll 64-76; V Cardiff Dewi Sant *Llan* 76-86; Asst Chapl HM Pris Cardiff 76-86; V Llan-llwch w Llangain and Llangynog *St D* 86-95; Can St D Cathl 89-90; rtd 95. *35 Ger y Capel, Llangain, Carmarthen SA33 5AQ* Tel (01267) 241916

EVANS, David Richard. b 47. St Steph Ho Ox 68. **d** 72 **p** 73. C Cardiff St Jo *Llan* 72-76; PV Llan Cathl 76-80; V Cleeve Prior and The Littletons *Worc* from 80. *The Vicarage, South Littleton, Evesham, Worcs WR11 5TJ* Tel (01386) 830397

✠**EVANS, The Rt Revd David Richard John.** b 38. G&C Coll Cam BA63 MA66. Clifton Th Coll 63. **d** 65 **p** 66 **c** 78. C Enfield Ch Ch Trent Park *Lon* 65-68; Argentina 69-77; Peru 77-88; Bp Peru 78-88; Bp Bolivia 82-88; Asst Bp Bradf 88-93; Gen Sec SAMS from 93; Asst Bp Roch from 95; Lic to Offic *Cant* from 95. *c/o SAMS, Allen Gardiner House, Pembury Road, Tunbridge Wells, Kent TN2 3QU, or The Rectory, Maresfield, Uckfield, E Sussex TN22 2HB* Tel (01892) 538647/8 Fax (01892) 525797 or (01825) 763817

EVANS, David Russell. Liv Univ BA57. Ripon Hall Ox 59. **d** 61 **p** 62. C Netherton CD *Liv* 61-65; Asst Chapl Canon Slade Sch Bolton from 65; Lic Preacher *Man* from 66; Perm to Offic *Liv* from 76. *2 Rushford Grove, Bolton BL1 8TD* Tel (01204) 592981

EVANS, David Victor (formerly David John Parker Smith). b 47. S'wark Ord Course 83. **d** 86 **p** 95. SSF 71-94; Hon C Stepney St Dunstan and All SS *Lon* 86-89; Educn Development Officer 86-89; Guardian Hilfield Friary Dorchester 89-91; Novice Guardian Liv 91-93; Birm 93-94; Lic to Offic Sarum 89-91; Liv 91-93; Birm 93-94; NSM Southmead *Bris* from 94; Par Co-ord Southmead St Steph from 94. *The Garden Flat, 9 Cotham Gardens, Bristol BS6 6HD* Tel 0117-959 3290

EVANS, Derek. b 38. St As Minl Tr Course 93. **d** 97. NSM Llangollen w Trevor and Llantysilio *St As* from 97. *Fern Mount, 68 Berwyn Street, Llangollen LL20 8NA* Tel (01978) 861893

EVANS, Derek. b 45. St D Coll Lamp DipTh68. **d** 68 **p** 69. C Pembroke Dock *St D* 68-74; V Ambleston, St Dogwells, Walton E and Llysyfran 74-78; V Wiston w Ambleston, St Dogwells and Walton E 78-81; V Wiston w Ambleston, St Dogwells, Walton E etc 81-85; R Haverfordwest St Mary and St Thos w Haroldston from 85. *The Rectory, Scarrowscant Lane, Haverfordwest SA61 1EP* Tel (01437) 763170

EVANS, Preb Derek Courtenay. b 29. Down Coll Cam BA52 MA56. St Aid Birkenhead 55. **d** 57 **p** 58. C Taunton St Mary *B & W* 57-61; V Trull 61-77; RD Taunton S 72-77; P-in-c Walton

77; R Street 77; Preb Wells Cathl 77-94; R Street w Walton 78-94; RD Glastonbury 79-82; R Greinton 81-93; rtd 94; Perm to Offic *B & W* from 94. *41 Moorham Road, Winscombe, Avon BS25 1HS* Tel (01934) 843150

EVANS, Desmond. b 26. Univ of Wales (Lamp) BA48 St Cath Soc Ox BA50 MA54. St Steph Ho Ox 48. **d** 51 **p** 52. C Clydach *S & B* 51-54; V 82-87; Chapl Cranleigh Sch Surrey 54-59; Lic to Offic *Ban* 59-78; V Llanwrtyd w Llanddulas in Tir Abad etc *S & B* 78-82; RD Builth 79-82; V Abercraf and Callwen 87-95; rtd 95. *26 Palleg Road, Lower Cwmtwrch, Swansea SA9 2QE*

EVANS, Donald Henry. b 13. St D Coll Lamp BA35. **d** 36 **p** 37. C Wrexham *St As* 36-48; R Worthenbury w Tallarn Green 48-61; V Towyn 61-64; V Seighford, Derrington and Cresswell *Lich* 64-78; rtd 78; Perm to Offic *Ches* from 80. *3 Highfield Avenue, Audlem, Crewe CW3 0HW* Tel (01270) 811165

EVANS, Edward John. b 47. Univ of Wales (Cardiff) DipTh71. St Mich Coll Llan 67. **d** 71 **p** 72. C Llantwit Fadre *Llan* 71-77; R Eglwysilan 77-88; V Laleston w Tythegston and Merthyr Mawr from 88; RD Bridgend from 94. *The Vicarage, Rogers Lane, Laleston, Bridgend CF32 0LB* Tel (01656) 654254

EVANS, Elwyn David. b 36. Keble Coll Ox BA58 MA62. St Mich Coll Llan 60. **d** 61 **p** 62. C Aberystwyth H Trin *St D* 61-63; C Llanelli St Paul 63-66; C Roath St German *Llan* 66-69; V Crynant 69-78; R Llanilid w Pencoed 79-95; rtd 95. *23 Christopher Rise, Pontlliw, Swansea SA4 1EN* Tel (01792) 891961

EVANS, Emrys. b 17. St D Coll Lamp BA41. **d** 42 **p** 43. C Tidenham w Beachley and Lancaut *Glouc* 42-46; C Charlton Kings St Mary 46-50; V Viney Hill 50-55; V Glouc All SS 55-59; V Twickenham All SS *Lon* 60-81; rtd 81; Perm to Offic *Chich* from 81. *5 Rowan Drive, Billingshurst, W Sussex RH14 9NE* Tel (01403) 784312

EVANS, Ernest Maurice. b 28. MIMechE66. St As Minl Tr Course 84. **d** 86 **p** 87. NSM Hope *St As* 86-89; P-in-c Corwen and Llangar 89-90; R Corwen and Llangar w Gwyddelwern and Llawrybetws 90-95; rtd 95. *43 Cil-y-Graig, Llanfairpwllgwyngyll LL61 5NZ* Tel (01248) 714447

EVANS, Evan Walter. b 16. MBE66. St D Coll Lamp BA36. **d** 39 **p** 40. C Narberth *St D* 39-40; C Cardigan 40-42; CF (EC) 42-47; R Didmarton w Oldbury-on-the-Hill and Sopworth *Glouc* 47-52; CF 52-72; Chapl R Hosp Chelsea 72-81; Perm to Offic *St D* from 85. *3 Cilgwyn Row, Llandysul SA44 4BD* Tel (01559) 362275

EVANS, Frank Owen. b 23. Univ of Wales BA44. St D Coll Lamp 44. **d** 46 **p** 63. C Hubberston *St D* 46; C Llanelli 63-81; Hd Master Coleshill Secondary Sch Dyfed 74-82; Hon C Cydweli and Llandyfaelog *St D* 81-82; V Martletwy w Lawrenny and Minwear and Yerbeston 82-87; rtd 87. *35 Stradey Park Avenue, Llanelli SA15 3EG* Tel (01554) 777149

EVANS, Frederick Albert (Fred). b 29. **d** 83 **p** 84. NSM Maisemore *Glouc* 83-94; NSM Glouc St Geo w Whaddon 86-94; Perm to Offic from 94. *10 Hillborough Road, Gloucester GL4 0JQ* Tel (01452) 526034

EVANS, Frederick James Stephens. b 21. Qu Coll Cam BA42 MA46. St D Coll Lamp LTh44. **d** 44 **p** 45. C Shirley *Birm* 44-47; R Scotter w E Ferry *Linc* 47-65; CF (TA) 48-51; R Chalfont St Peter *Ox* 65-78; V Rustington *Chich* 78-86; rtd 86; Perm to Offic *Chich* from 86. *45 Falmer Avenue, Goring-by-Sea, Worthing, W Sussex BN12 4SY* Tel (01903) 503905

EVANS, Canon Frederick John Margam. b 31. Magd Coll Ox BA53 MA57. St Mich Coll Llan 53. **d** 54 **p** 55. C New Tredegar *Mon* 54-58; C Chepstow 58-60; Asst Chapl United Sheff Hosps 60-62; Chapl Brookwood Hosp Woking 62-70; V Crookham *Guildf* from 70; RD Aldershot 78-83; Hon Can Guildf Cathl from 89. *14 Gally Hill Road, Church Crookham, Fleet, Hants GU13 0LH* Tel (01252) 617130

EVANS, Gareth Clive. b 68. Univ of Wales (Cardiff) DipTh91. Ripon Coll Cuddesdon BTh96. **d** 96 **p** 97. C Gosforth All SS *Newc* from 96. *1 Northfield Road, Gosforth, Newcastle upon Tyne NE3 3UL* Tel 0191-284 8568

EVANS, Gareth Milton. b 39. Bris Univ LLB60 St Cath Coll Ox BA62 MA66. Ripon Hall Ox 60. **d** 63 **p** 64. C Hengrove *Bris* 63-65; Min Can Bris Cathl 65-68; C Bishopston 68-71; C Notting Hill *Lon* 71-83; V Bayswater from 83. *St Matthew's Vicarage, 27 St Petersburgh Place, London W2 4LA* Tel 0171-229 2192

EVANS, The Ven Geoffrey Bainbridge. b 34. St Mich Coll Llan 56 Lambeth MA94. **d** 58 **p** 59. C Llan All SS CD *Llan* 58-60; C Llandaff N 60-67; Guyana 67-73; Chapl Izmir (Smyrna) w Bornova *Eur* 73-94; Adn Aegean 78-94; Chapl Ankara 85-91; Chapl Istanbul 87-89; Chapl Rome from 94. *All Saints, via del Babuino 153, 00187 Rome, Italy* Tel Rome (6) 36002171 or 36001881

EVANS, Geoffrey David. b 44. Ex Univ PGCE74. K Coll Lon BD69 AKC69 St Aug Coll Cant 69. **d** 70 **p** 71. C Lawrence Weston *Bris* 70-73; Chapl Grenville Coll Bideford 74-79; Chapl Eastbourne Coll 79-82; Chapl Taunton and Somerset Hosp 83-91; Chapl Musgrove Park Hosp 83-91; Chapl Taunton Sch from 92. *Hele Manor, Bradford on Tone, Taunton, Somerset TA4 1AH* Tel (01823) 461561

EVANS, Gerald Arthur. b 35. Univ of Wales (Swansea) BA57 Lon Univ DipRS77. S'wark Ord Course 74. **d** 77 **p** 78. NSM Balcombe *Chich* 77-81; NSM Cuckfield 81-87; R Tillington 87-93; R Duncton 87-93; R Up Waltham 87-93; R W Chiltington from 93; Dioc Ecum Officer from 93; RD Storrington from 93. *The Rectory, West Chiltington, Pulborough, W Sussex RH20 2JY* Tel (01798) 813117

EVANS, Mrs Gillian (Jill). b 39. Imp Coll Lon BSc61 Univ of Wales (Cardiff) DPS88. Mon Dioc Tr Scheme 84. **d** 88 **p** 94. NSM Penallt and Trellech *Mon* 88-89; NSM Overmonnow w Wonastow and Michel Troy 89-92; C Ludlow *Heref* 92-93; C Ludlow, Ludford, Ashford Carbonell etc 93-95; Dioc Ecum Officer 92-95; Pakistan from 96. *Upper Grove, Newcastle, Monmouth NP5 4NT* Tel (01600) 750241

EVANS, Canon Glyn. b 10. Univ of Wales BA33. St Steph Ho Ox 33. **d** 34 **p** 35. C Dolgellau *Ban* 34-39; C Llanfairfechan 39-43; R Llanallgo w Llaneugrad 43-55; V St Issells *St D* 55-80; RD Narberth 65-80; Can St D Cathl 69-80; Treas 77-80; rtd 80. *3 Flemish Close, St Florence, Tenby SA70 8LT* Tel (01834) 871434

EVANS, Glyn. b 59. Nene Coll Northampton BA80 Leic Univ BA80 Ch Ch Coll Cant CertEd82 Kent Univ PGCE82 Birm Univ DipTh87. Qu Coll Birm 85. **d** 88 **p** 89. C Denton *Newc* 88-92; V Choppington 92-97; P-in-c Longhorsley and Hebron from 97; Chapl HM Pris Acklington from 97. *The Vicarage, Longhorsley, Morpeth, Northd NE65 8UU* Tel (01670) 788218

EVANS, Glyn Peter. b 54. Leeds Univ BA75. Ripon Coll Cuddesdon 76. **d** 77 **p** 78. C Binley *Cov* 77-80; C Clifton upon Dunsmore w Brownsover 80-84; P-in-c Lacock w Bowden Hill *Bris* 84-89; P-in-c Lt Compton w Chastleton, Cornwell etc *Ox* from 89; Agric Chapl from 89. *The Rectory, Little Compton, Moreton-in-Marsh, Glos GL56 0SE* Tel (01608) 674313

EVANS, Guy Maxwell Lyon. b 23. Univ of Wales (Cardiff) BA50 BA51. Llan Dioc Tr Scheme 81. **d** 82 **p** 83. NSM Cardiff Dewi Sant *Llan* 82-84; P-in-c Llanfihangel-ar-arth *St D* 84-85; V 85-91; rtd 91; Perm to Offic *Llan* from 91. *86 Redlands Road, Penarth CF64 2WL* Tel (01222) 701963

EVANS, Canon Gwyneth Mary. b 43. Gilmore Ho Linc Th Coll 69. **dss** 74 **d** 87 **p** 94. Stamford Hill St Thos *Lon* 72-79; Chapl Asst R Free Hosp Lon 79-89; Chapl Odstock Hosp Salisbury 89-94; Chapl Salisbury Healthcare NHS Trust from 89; Can and Preb Sarum Cathl *Sarum* from 96. *Salisbury District Hospital, Salisbury SP2 8BJ* Tel (01722) 336262

EVANS, Canon Henry Thomas Platt. b 28. Selw Coll Cam BA51 MA55. Linc Th Coll 51. **d** 53 **p** 54. C Lt Ilford St Barn *Chelmsf* 53-56; C-in-c Stocking Farm CD *Leic* 56-58; V Stocking Farm 58-67; R Stretford St Matt *Man* 67-73; V Knighton St Mary Magd *Leic* 73-83; Hon Can Leic Cathl 76-93; RD Christianity S 81-83; Warden Launde Abbey 83-93; P-in-c Loddington *Leic* 83-92; rtd 93; Perm to Offic *Leic* from 93. *16 Central Avenue, Leicester LE2 1TB* Tel 0116-270 2169

EVANS, Hilary Margaret. b 49. Chester Coll 92. N Ord Course BTh94. **d** 97. NSM Heald Green St Cath *Ches* from 97. *103 Baslow Drive, Heald Green, Cheadle, Cheshire SK8 3HW* Tel 0161-437 2395

EVANS, Mrs Jennifer (Jennie). b 41. Sarum Th Coll. **d** 88. C Bramshott *Portsm* 88-91; C Bramshott and Liphook 91-92; Par Dn Whippingham w E Cowes 92-95. *Erron, 1A Addison Road, Sarisbury Green, Southampton SO31 7ER* Tel (01489) 572129

EVANS, Jill. *See* EVANS, Mrs Gillian

EVANS, John Andrew. b 53. Hull Univ BSc74 Univ of Wales MSc75. Trin Coll Bris 94. **d** 96 **p** 97. C Walton H Trin *Ox* from 96. *5 Bateman Drive, Aylesbury, Bucks HP21 8AF* Tel (01296) 82096

EVANS, The Ven John Barrie. b 23. Univ of Wales (Lamp) BA47 St Edm Hall Ox BA49 MA54. St Mich Coll Llan 50. **d** 51 **p** 52. C Trevethin *Mon* 51-57; V Caerwent w Dinham and Llanfair Discoed 57-64; V Chepstow 64-79; Can St Woolos Cathl 71-77; Adn Mon 77-86; R Llanmartin w Wilcrick and Langstone 79-83; R Llanmartin 83-86; Adn Newport 86-93; rtd 93; Perm to Offic *Glouc* from 93. *Rockfield, Coleford Road, Tutshill, Chepstow NP6 7BU* Tel (01291) 626147

EVANS, John David Vincent. b 41. CQSW78. Lich Th Coll 66. **d** 68 **p** 70. C Kingsthorpe *Pet* 68-69; C Corby Epiphany w St Jo 69-72; Bp's Adv in Children's Work 72-74; Perm to Offic 88-90; R Green's Norton w Bradden 90-91; R Greens Norton w Bradden and Lichborough 91-96; V Northampton Ch Ch from 96. *Christ Church Vicarage, 3 Christ Church Road, Northampton NN1 5LL* Tel (01604) 33254

EVANS, John Eric. b 14. St D Coll Lamp BA38. **d** 38 **p** 39. C Wolverhampton St Andr *Lich* 38-41; C Ogley Hay 41-42; C Hednesford 42-46; V Bayston Hill 46-53; V St Martin's 53-64; V Churchstoke w Hyssington *Heref* 64-77; V Churchstoke w Hyssington and Sarn 77-79; rtd 79. *The Willows, 15 Rhoslan, Guilsfield, Welshpool SY21 9NR*

EVANS, Canon John Griffiths. b 37. Glouc Th Course 76. **d** 77 **p** 77. Hd Master Corse Sch Glos from 70; C Hartpury w Corse and Staunton *Glouc* 77-79; P-in-c from 79; Hon Can Glouc Cathl from 96. *Gadfield Elm House, Staunton, Gloucester GL19 3PA* Tel (01452) 840302

EVANS, Canon John Hopkin. b 17. St D Coll Lamp BA41. **d** 42 **p** 44. C Llanycil w Bala *St As* 42-51; V Llanwddyn 51-60; R Llanfechain 60-82; V Bwlch-y-Cibau 67-80; RD Llanfyllin 73-82;

Hon Can St As Cathl 76-82; rtd 82. *Church View, Llanfechain SY22 6UL* Tel (01691) 828446

EVANS, John Laurie. b 34. Pretoria Univ BSc54 Imp Coll Lon BSc55 Rhodes Univ BA59. Ripon Coll Cuddesdon 84. **d** 86 **p** 87. C Bruton and Distr *B & W* 86-89; P-in-c Ambrosden w Mert and Piddington *Ox* 89-91; C Pet St Mary Boongate *Pet* 91-93; V Michael *S & M* 93-96; R Ballaugh 93-96; rtd 96; Chapl Goring Heath Almshouses from 96. *The Chaplaincy, Allnutt's Hospital, Goring Heath, Oxon RG8 7RR* Tel (01491) 680261 Fax as telephone

EVANS, John Miles. b 39. Yale Univ BA61 JD67 St Cath Coll Cam BA64 MA68. NY Th Sem MDiv93. **d** 95 **p** 95. Chapl St Jo Cathl Oban *Arg* from 95. *Bon Accord, Glenmore Road, Oban, Argyll PA34 4ND* Tel (01631) 562451 Fax as telephone

EVANS, John Morgan. b 14. MBE87. St D Coll Lamp BA37. **d** 37 **p** 38. C Brynmawr *S & B* 37-46; CF (EC) 46-48; V Glascwm and Rhulen *S & B* 48-55; V Llangenny 55-79; OCF from 55; CF (TA) 61-87; rtd 79; Lic to Offic *S & B* from 79. *Milfraen, 1 St John's Road, Brecon LD3 9DS* Tel (01874) 624054

EVANS, John Rhys. b 45. Hull Univ BSc66. Sarum & Wells Th Coll 77. **d** 79 **p** 80. C Alton St Lawr *Win* 79-82; C Tadley St Pet 82-85; V Colden 85-91; V Bitterne Park from 91. *Bitterne Park Vicarage, 7 Thorold Road, Southampton SO18 1HZ* Tel (01703) 555814

EVANS, John Ronald. b 16. Univ of Wales BA40. St Mich Coll Llan 41. **d** 42 **p** 44. C Rhosllannerchrugog *St As* 42-45; C Holywell 45-54; V Glyndyfrdwy 54-81; RD Edeyrnion 64-81; Dioc Sec SPCK 66-81; rtd 81. *21 Bryn Hyfryd, Johnstown, Wrexham LL14 1PR* Tel (01978) 842300

EVANS, Canon John Thomas. b 43. Univ of Wales DipTh66 DPS67. St Mich Coll Llan 66. **d** 67 **p** 68. C Connah's Quay *St As* 67-71; C Llanrhos 71-74; Chapl Rainhill Hosp Liv 74-78; TV Wrexham *St As* 78-83; V Holywell 83-96; RD Holywell 95-96; V Colwyn Bay from 96; Can Cursal St As Cathl from 96. *The Vicarage, 1 Woodland Road East, Colwyn Bay LL29 7DT* Tel (01492) 532403

EVANS, The Very Revd John Wyn. b 46. FSA88 Univ of Wales (Cardiff) BA68 BD71. St Mich Coll Llan 68. **d** 71 **p** 72. C St D Cathl *St D* 71-72; Min Can St D Cathl 72-75; Perm to Offic *Ox* 75-76; Dioc Archivist *St D* 76-82; R Llanfallteg w Clunderwen and Castell Dwyran etc 77-82; Warden of Ords 78-83; Dioc Dir of Educn 82-94; Chapl Trin Coll Carmarthen 82-94; Dean of Chpl 90-94; Hon Can St D Cathl *St D* 88-90; Can St D Cathl 90-94; Dean St D from 94; V St D Cathl from 94. *The Deanery, St Davids, Haverfordwest SA62 6RH* Tel (01437) 720202 Fax 721885

EVANS, Jonathan Alan. b 53. Fitzw Coll Cam BA75 PGCE77 MA79. St Jo Coll Nottm MA95. **d** 95 **p** 96. C Drypool *York* from 95. *2 Pavilion Close, Chamberlain Road, Hull HU8 8EA* Tel (01482) 712597

EVANS, Joseph Henry Godfrey. b 31. Univ of Wales (Lamp) BA50 St Mary's Coll Cheltenham CertEd75 Kingston Poly 89. Qu Coll Birm 53. **d** 55 **p** 56. C Hackney St Jo *Lon* 55-58; C Stonehouse *Glouc* 58-60; V Selsley 60-65; V Cheltenham St Pet 65-74; R Willersey w Saintbury 74-77; Chapl Tiffin Sch Kingston 77-94; rtd 95. *300 Raeburn Avenue, Surbiton, Surrey KT5 9EF* Tel 0181-390 0936

EVANS, Keith. b 57. Trin Coll Carmarthen CertEd81 BEd82. St D Coll Lamp BA84 Sarum & Wells Th Coll 84. **d** 85 **p** 86. C Swansea St Thos and Kilvey *S & B* 85-87; C Gorseinon 87-89; V Oxwich w Penmaen and Nicholaston 89-94; Dir of Post-Ord Tr from 93; R Ystradgynlais from 94. *The Rectory, 2 Heol yr Eglwys, Ystradgynlais, Swansea SA9 1EY* Tel (01639) 843200

EVANS, Kenneth. b 50. Bp Burgess Hall Lamp DipTh74. **d** 74 **p** 75. C Llanaber w Caerdeon *Ban* 74-79; C Upper Clapton St Matt *Lon* 79-82; P-in-c Tottenham St Phil from 82. *St Philip's Vicarage, 226 Philip Lane, London N15 4HH* Tel 0181-808 4235

✠**EVANS, The Rt Revd Kenneth Dawson.** b 15. Clare Coll Cam BA37 MA41. Ripon Hall Ox 37. **d** 38 **p** 39 **c** 68. C Northampton St Mary *Pet* 38-41; C Northampton All SS w St Kath 41-45; R Ockley *Guildf* 45-49; V Ranmore 49-57; V Dorking 49-57; V Dorking w Ranmore 57-63; RD Dorking 57-63; Hon Can Guildf Cathl 55-63 and 79-85; Can Res Guildf Cathl 63-68; Adn Dorking 63-68; Suff Bp Dorking 68-85; rtd 85. *3 New Inn Lane, Guildford, Surrey GU4 7HN* Tel (01483) 67978

EVANS, Kenneth Roy. b 47. Lon Univ BSc. Ridley Hall Cam 79. **d** 81 **p** 81. C Stratford-on-Avon w Bishopton *Cov* 81-82; C Trunch *Nor* 82-85; Chapl Mapperley Hosp Nottm 85-89; Chapl Nottm Mental Illness and Psychiatric Unit from 85; Lic to Offic *S'well* from 85; Dir Sherwood Psychotherapy Tr Inst from 87. *31 Foxhill Road, Burton Joyce, Nottingham NG14 5DR* Tel 0115-931 4081

EVANS, Kevin Stuart. b 56. Bris Poly CQSW80. Qu Coll Birm DipTh95. **d** 95 **p** 96. C Madeley *Heref* from 95. *7 Mellor Close, Madeley, Telford, Shropshire TF7 5SS* Tel (01952) 588332

EVANS, Lewys Thomas Gareth. b 29. St Mich Coll Llan. **d** 58 **p** 59. C Clydach *S & B* 58-65; R Vaynor and Capel Taffechan 65-80; V Defynnog w Rhydybriw, Llandeilo'r Fan etc 80-83; V Defynnog w Rhydybriw and Llandilo'r-fan 83-87; V Ystalyfera 87-95; rtd 95. *15 Beech Grove, Brecon LD3 9ET* Tel (01874) 622480

EVANS, Ms Linda Mary. b 49. Univ of Wales (Cardiff) BA71 K Coll Lon BD74 AKC74. Yale Div Sch STM76. **dss** 76 **d** 80. Llanishen and Lisvane *Llan* 76-78; Wrexham *St As* 78-80; C 80-82; Chapl Maudsley Hosp Lon 82-84; Bethlem R Hosp Beckenham 82-84; Chapl Lon Univ *Lon* 84-87. *2 Rhes Eldon, Allt Glanrafon, Bangor LL57 2RA* Tel (01248) 370561

EVANS, Miss Madeleine Thelma Bodenham. b 30. K Coll Lon BD76 AKC76. Gilmore Course 80. **dss** 85 **d** 87 **p** 94. Chapl Pipers Corner Sch 85-91; Par Dn Calne and Blackland *Sarum* 91-94; C from 94; Chapl St Mary's Sch Calne from 91. *62 Braemor Road, Calne, Wilts SN11 9DU* Tel (01249) 814245

EVANS, Ms Margaret Elizabeth. b 48. Leeds Univ BA69 Lon Inst of Educn CertEd70. Oak Hill Th Coll 91. **d** 94 **p** 95. NSM Canonbury St Steph *Lon* from 94. *5 Canonbury Place, London N1 2NQ* Tel 0171-359 4343

EVANS, Martin Lonsdale. b 69. Man Univ BA91. Ripon Coll Cuddesdon DipMin95. **d** 95 **p** 96. C Morpeth *Newc* from 95. *42 Grange Road, Stobhill, Morpeth, Northd NE61 2UF* Tel (01670) 513413

EVANS, Michael. b 49. St Jo Coll Nottm 88. **d** 90 **p** 91. C Beeston *S'well* 90-93; P-in-c Kirkby in Ashfield St Thos 93-97; V from 97. *The Vicarage, 109 Diamond Avenue, Kirkby-in-Ashfield, Nottingham NG17 7LX* Tel (01623) 755131

EVANS, Neil Glynne. b 55. Lon Univ DipTh78 Leeds Univ BA81. Trin Coll Bris DPS82. **d** 82 **p** 83. C Llandybie *St D* 82-86; NSM 87-89; V Gwaun-cae-Gurwen 90-92; Tutor St Jo Coll Dur 92-94; Chapl from 94. *St John's College, South Bailey, Durham DH1 3RJ* Tel 0191-374 3593

EVANS, Neil Robert. b 54. Lon Univ MA93. Coll of Resurr Mirfield. **d** 84 **p** 85. C Bethnal Green St Jo w St Bart *Lon* 84-86; C St Jo on Bethnal Green 87-88; P-in-c Stoke Newington Common St Mich 88-95; V from 95. *St Michael's Vicarage, 55 Fountayne Road, London N16 7ED* Tel 0181-806 4225 Fax as telephone

EVANS, Nicholas Anthony Paul. b 60. Sheff Univ BA81 Liv Univ PGCE86. Qu Coll Birm 81. **d** 84 **p** 87. C Ludlow *Heref* 84-85; C Sunbury *Lon* 86-92; Head RE Guilford County Sch from 93; NSM Crookham *Guildf* 94-96; Perm to Offic from 96. *93 Cambridge Road, Aldershot, Hants GU11 3LD* Tel (01252) 343890

EVANS, Norman Cassienet. b 30. Keble Coll Ox MA54. Guildf Dioc Min Course 91. **d** 95 **p** 96. NSM Seale, Puttenham and Wanborough *Guildf* from 95. *Tree Tops, Seale Lane, Puttenham, Guildford, Surrey GU3 1AX* Tel (01483) 810677

EVANS, The Ven Patrick Alexander Sidney. b 43. Linc Th Coll 70. **d** 73 **p** 74. C Lyonsdown H Trin *St Alb* 73-76; C Royston 76-78; V Gt Gaddesden 78-82; V Tenterden St Mildred w Smallhythe *Cant* 82-89; Adn Maidstone from 89; Hon Can Cant Cathl from 89; Dir of Ords 89-93. *The Archdeacon's House, Charing, Ashford, Kent TN27 0LU* Tel (01233) 712294 Fax 713651

EVANS, Peter. b 35. St Aid Birkenhead 57. **d** 60 **p** 61. C Higher Bebington *Ches* 60-63; C W Kirby St Bridget 63-66; P-in-c Lower Tranmere 66-68; V Flimby *Carl* 68-74; V Kirkby Ireleth 74-79; P-in-c Kirkbride w Newton Arlosh 79-80; R 80-85; V Beckermet St Jo and St Bridget w Ponsonby from 85. *St John's Vicarage, 11 Lowrey Close, Beckermet, Cumbria CA21 2YX* Tel (01946) 841327

EVANS, Peter. b 40. S'wark Ord Course 75. **d** 75 **p** 76. C Welling *S'wark* 75-78; C Sutton New Town St Barn 78-81; C Kingston All SS w St Jo 81-87; V Croydon Woodside from 87. *St Luke's Vicarage, Portland Road, London SE25 4RB* Tel 0181-654 1225

EVANS, Peter Anthony. b 36. Lon Univ BScEng Ox Univ DipTh59. St Steph Ho Ox 58. **d** 60 **p** 61. C Surbiton St Mark *S'wark* 60-63; Asst Chapl Lon Univ *Lon* 63-64; C S Kensington St Luke 64-68; C Surbiton St Andr and St Mark *S'wark* 68-69; C Loughton St Jo *Chelmsf* 69-74; P-in-c Becontree St Geo 74-82; NSM Romford St Alb 89-93; NSM Coopersale 93-95; NSM Epping Distr from 95. *6 Woodhall Crescent, Hornchurch, Essex RM11 3NN* Tel (01708) 474995

EVANS, Peter Gerald. b 41. Man Univ BA71. AKC65. **d** 65 **p** 66. C Kidbrooke St Jas *S'wark* 65-68; C Fallowfield *Man* 68-71; C Brockley Hill St Sav *S'wark* 71-73; P-in-c Colchester St Botolph w H Trin and St Giles *Chelmsf* 74-79; V 79-92; Perm to Offic from 93. *97 Northgate Street, Colchester CO1 1EY* Tel (01206) 43297

EVANS, Peter Kenneth Dunlop. b 38. Ch Coll Cam BA60. St D Coll Lamp 72. **d** 74 **p** 75. C Roath St Marg *Llan* 74-77; V Buttington and Pool Quay *St As* 77-87; V Llanfair Caereinion w Llanllugan from 87. *The Vicarage, Llanfair Caereinion, Welshpool SY21 0RR* Tel (01938) 810146

EVANS, Philip Ronald. b 55. Qu Coll Cam BA77 MA81 Dur Univ CCouns90. Cranmer Hall Dur 88. **d** 90 **p** 91. C Devonport St Budeaux *Ex* 90-92; C Torquay St Matthias, St Mark and H Trin 92-94; Chapl St Jas Univ Hosp NHS Trust Leeds from 94. *The Chaplain's Office, St James's University Hospital, Leeds LS9 7TF* Tel 0113-243 3144

EVANS, Reginald Arthur. b 07. Bris Univ BA38. Sarum Th Coll 38 Wells Th Coll 39. **d** 40 **p** 41. C Bedminster St Aldhelm *Bris* 40-43; C Guildf H Trin w St Mary *Guildf* 43-45; V Stoke Newington St Andr *Lon* 45-49; V Batheaston w St Cath *B & W* 49-77; RD Keynsham 59-71; Preb Wells Cathl 63-77; rtd 77; Perm to Offic *Bris* 81-95. *The White Horse Residential Home, Station Road, Minety, Malmesbury, Wilts SN16 9QT*

EVANS, Richard Edward Hughes. b 14. Univ of Wales BA44. St Mich Coll Llan. **d** 45 **p** 46. C Nantymoel *Llan* 45-48; C Pontyberem *St D* 48-50; C Llandeilo Fawr 50-53; V Ysbyty Cynfyn 53-64; V Llanybydder and Llanwenog w Llanwnnen 64-72; V Llanychaiarn 72-79; rtd 79. *23 Gwarfelin, Llanilar, Aberystwyth SY23 4PE* Tel (01974) 241357

EVANS, Richard Edward Victor. b 21. Linc Th Coll 66. **d** 68 **p** 69. C Aston cum Aughton *Sheff* 68-71; C Prestwich St Mary *Man* 71-74; R Moston St Jo 74-83; R Failsworth H Family 83-91; rtd 91; Perm to Offic *Man* from 91. *508 Edge Lane, Droylesden, Manchester M35 6JW* Tel 0161-370 1947

EVANS, Richard Gregory. b 50. Univ of Wales (Cardiff) DipTh72. St Mich Coll Llan 69. **d** 73 **p** 74. C Oystermouth *S & B* 73-76; C Clydach 76-79; CF 78-81; V Llanddew and Talachddu *S & B* 79-83; Youth Chapl 79-83; Hon Min Can Brecon Cathl 79-83; New Zealand from 83. *97 Liverpool Street, Wanganui, New Zealand* Tel Wanganui (6) 345 0587 or 345 1112 ext 730 Fax 345 9706 E-mail rgevans@whanganui.ac.nz

EVANS, Richard Neville. b 15. Qu Coll Cam BA36 MA44. Ripon Hall Ox 36. **d** 38 **p** 39. C E Wickham *S'wark* 38-43; Chapl RNVR 43-46; C Surbiton St Andr *S'wark* 46-47; R Southacre *Nor* 47-55; V Westacre 47-55; V Castle Acre w Newton 49-55; Chapl R Free Hosp Lon 55-60; V Cambridge St Andr Gt *Ely* 60-72; V Waterbeach 72-74; Perm to Offic 75-86; rtd 84; Perm to Offic *Truro* 86-95. *2 Hounster Drive, Millbrook, Torpoint, Cornwall PL10 1BZ* Tel (01752) 822811

EVANS, Richard Trevor. b 33. Jes Coll Ox MA58 DipEd58. St And Dioc Tr Course 73. **d** 76 **p** 76. NSM Leven *St And* 76-95; NSM St Andrews St Andr from 95. *33 Huntingtower Park, Whinnyknowe, Glenrothes, Fife KY6 3QF* Tel (01592) 741670

EVANS, Canon Robert Arthur. b 24. Univ of Wales (Cardiff) BA48. St Mich Coll Llan 48. **d** 50 **p** 51. C Aberdare St Fagan *Llan* 50-52; C Roath St Marg 52-57; C Llan w Capel Llanilltern 57-61; Asst Chapl Mersey Miss to Seamen 61-62; Chapl Supt Mersey Miss to Seamen 62-74 and 79-89; Chapl RNR 67-89; V Rainhill *Liv* 74-79; Perm to Offic *Ches* 79-91; Hon Can Liv Cathl *Liv* 88-89; rtd 89; Perm to Offic *Liv* from 89. *1 Floral Wood, Riverside Gardens, Liverpool L17 7HR* Tel 0151-727 3608

EVANS, Robert Charles. b 55. K Coll Lon BA77 AKC77 MA78 MTh89 Qu Coll Cam BA80 MA83 CertEd85. Westcott Ho Cam 79. **d** 81 **p** 87. C St Breoke *Truro* 81-83; C St Columb Minor and St Colan 83-84; Chapl Rob Coll Cam 87-92; Lect Ches Coll *Ches* from 92. *Chester College, Cheyney Road, Chester CH1 4BJ* Tel (01244) 375444

EVANS, Robert George Roger. b 49. Cam Univ MA. Trin Coll Bris 74. **d** 77 **p** 78. C Bispham *Blackb* 77-80; C Chadwell *Chelmsf* 80-84; V Ardsley *Sheff* from 84. *The Vicarage, Doncaster Road, Barnsley, S Yorkshire S71 5EF* Tel (01226) 203784

EVANS, Robert Stanley. b 51. Univ of Wales (Lamp) BA72 Univ of Wales (Cardiff) PGCE73. St Mich Coll Llan DPS92. **d** 92 **p** 93. C Penarth All SS *Llan* 92-95; R Gelligaer from 95. *The Rectory, Church Road, Gelligaer, Hengoed CF82 8FW* Tel (01443) 830303

EVANS, Ronald. b 47. Univ of Wales (Cardiff) DipTh87. St Mich Coll Llan 85. **d** 87 **p** 88. C Flint *St As* 87-91; TV Wrexham 91-97; V Rhosymedre from 97. *The Vicarage, Church Street, Rhosymedre, Wrexham LL14 3EA* Tel (01978) 822125

EVANS, Simon. b 55. Newc Univ BA77. St Steph Ho Ox 78. **d** 80 **p** 81. C Pet St Jude *Pet* 80-84; C Wantage *Ox* 84-87; V W Leigh *Portsm* 87-96; V Ruislip St Martin *Lon* from 96. *The Vicarage, 13 Eastcote Road, Ruislip, Middx HA4 8BE* Tel (01895) 633040

EVANS, Simon Andrew. b 59. Sarum & Wells Th Coll 81. **d** 84 **p** 85. C Norbury St Steph and Thornton Heath *Cant* 84; C Norbury St Steph and Thornton Heath *S'wark* 85-88; C Putney St Mary 88-92; P-in-c Telford Park St Thos 92-94; V from 94. *St Thomas's Vicarage, 39 Telford Avenue, London SW2 4XL* Tel 0181-674 4343

EVANS, Stanley Munro. b 30. AKC53. **d** 54 **p** 55. C Norbury St Oswald *Cant* 54-57; C St Laurence in the Isle of Thanet 57-63; V Bredgar 63-71; V Bredgar w Bicknor and Huckinge 71-72; V Westgate St Sav from 72. *St Saviour's Vicarage, Thanet Road, Westgate-on-Sea, Kent CT8 8PB* Tel (01843) 831869

EVANS, Stephen John. b 60. Dartmouth RN Coll 81 Ox Univ BA85 MA89. St Steph Ho Ox 83. **d** 86 **p** 87. Prec St Andr Cathl Inverness *Mor* 86-89; R Montrose *Bre* 89-91; P-in-c Inverbervie 89-91; Miss to Seamen 89-91; V Northampton St Paul *Pet* from 91. *St Paul's Vicarage, 104 Semilong Road, Northampton NN2 6EX* Tel (01604) 712688

EVANS, Ms Susan Mary. b 55. St Jo Coll Dur BA76 CertEd77 Nottm Univ BCombStuds84. Linc Th Coll 81. **dss** 84 **d** 87 **p** 94. Weaste *Man* 84-87; Par Dn 87-88; Par Dn Longsight St Luke 88-92; Par Dn Claydon and Barham *St E* 92-94; C from 94. *The Rectory, 7 Back Lane, Claydon, Ipswich IP6 0EB* Tel (01473) 830362

EVANS, Terence. b 35. St Mich Coll Llan 67. **d** 69 **p** 70. C Lougher *S & B* 69-73; C Gowerton w Waunarlwydd 73-77; V Llanbister and Llanbadarn Fynydd w Llananno 77-82; V Llanyrnewydd from 82. *The Vicarage, Crofty, Penclawdd, Swansea SA4 3RP* Tel (01792) 850285

EVANS, Terence Robert (Terry). b 45. N Ord Course 82. **d** 85 **p** 86. C Warrington St Elphin *Liv* 85-88; V Cantril Farm 88-94; V Rainhill from 94. *St Ann's Vicarage, View Road, Prescot, Merseyside L35 0LE* Tel 0151-426 4666

EVANS, Thomas Howell. b 13. St Cath Soc Ox BA37 MA40. Ripon Hall Ox 36. **d** 37 **p** 38. C Loughborough All SS *Leic* 37-40; V Prestwold w Hoton 40-49; R Hoby cum Rotherby 49-58; V Anstey *St Alb* 58-74; V Brent Pelham w Meesden 58-74; P-in-c Albury 74-79; rtd 79; Perm to Offic *Chelmsf* 79-93; Perm to Offic *St Alb* 79-93. *Farm Cottage, 1 Coxford Abbey, Coxford, King's Lynn, Norfolk PE31 6TB* Tel (01485) 528042

EVANS, Canon Thomas Norman. b 30. K Coll Lon BA51 BD53 AKC56. **d** 56 **p** 57. C Handsworth *Sheff* 56-59; C Mexborough 59-61; V Denaby Main 61-65; V Wythenshawe Wm Temple Ch *Man* 65-78; RD Withington 72-78; R Prestwich St Mary 78-85; AD Radcliffe and Prestwich 78-85; Hon Can Man Cathl 79-85; R Skelton w Upleatham *York* from 87; RD Guisborough from 91. *The Rectory, North Terrace, Skelton-in-Cleveland, Cleveland TS12 2ES* Tel (01287) 650329

EVANS, Timothy Simon. b 57. York Univ BA79 Sussex Univ MA81 Fitzw Coll Cam BA85 MA88. Ridley Hall Cam 83. **d** 87 **p** 88. C Whitton St Aug *Lon* 87-90; C Ealing St Steph Castle Hill 90-93; P-in-c Shireshead *Blackb* 93-97; Asst Chapl Lanc Univ 93-97; P-in-c Natland *Carl* from 97; Dep Prin Carl and Blackb Dioc Tr Inst from 97. *The Vicarage, Natland, Kendal, Cumbria LA9 7QQ* Tel (015395) 60355

EVANS, Trefor Rhys. b 06. Univ of Wales BA32. St Mich Coll Llan 33. **d** 33 **p** 34. C Llantrisant *Llan* 33-35; Chapl St D Cathl *St D* 35-38; R Llangeitho 38-43; V Llandysul 43-56; V Lampeter Pont Steffan 56-74; rtd 74. *60 Penbryn, Lampeter SA48 7EU* Tel (01570) 422060

EVANS, Canon Trevor Owen. b 37. Univ of Wales BSc59. Coll of Resurr Mirfield 59. **d** 61 **p** 62. C Llanaber w Caerdeon *Ban* 61-64; C Llandudno 64-70; TV 70-75; V Llanidloes w Llangurig 75-89; RD Arwystli 75-89; Can and Preb Ban Cathl from 82; Dioc Adv on Spirituality from 84; R Trefdraeth 89-90; Dir of Min from 89; R Llanfairpwll w Penmynydd from 90. *The Rectory, Holyhead Road, Llanfairpwll LL61 5SX* Tel (01248) 716472

EVANS, Walter James. b 29. Huron Coll Ontario LTh58. **d** 58 **p** 59. Canada 58-63; C Wolborough w Newton Abbot *Ex* 63-65; R Chilthorne Domer, Yeovil Marsh and Thorne Coffin *B & W* 65-70; V Chalford *Glouc* 70-91; rtd 91; Perm to Offic *Glouc* from 91. *67 Mandara Grove, Gloucester GL4 9XT* Tel (01452) 385157

EVANS, Walter Tenniel. b 26. Ox NSM Course. **d** 84 **p** 85. NSM Beaconsfield *Ox* from 84. *Candlemas, Jordans, Beaconsfield, Bucks HP9 2ST* Tel (01494) 873165

EVANS, Canon William Brewster. b 15. TCD BA37 MA43. CITC 37. **d** 38 **p** 39. C Londonderry Ch Ch *D & R* 38-44; I Cumber Upper w Learmount 44-60; I Castlerock Union 60-82; Can Derry Cathl 72-82; rtd 82. *4 Bells Hill, Limavady, Co Londonderry BT49 0DQ* Tel (01504) 764349

EVANS, William James Lynn. b 30. St D Coll Lamp 73. **d** 75 **p** 76. P-in-c Penbryn and Blaenporth *St D* 75-77; V Penbryn and Betws Ifan w Bryngwyn 77-79; V Penrhyncoch and Elerch 79-83; V Cynwil Elfed and Newchurch 83-87; V Llandybie 87-95; rtd 95. *5 Dolau Tywi, Manordeilo, Llandeilo SA19 7BL* Tel (01550) 777944

EVANS-PUGHE, Thomas Goronwy. b 29. TCD. Wycliffe Hall Ox 59. **d** 61 **p** 62. C Grassendale *Liv* 61-63; P-in-c Mossley Hill St Matt and St Jas 63-64; C 64-65; Prec Chelmsf Cathl *Chelmsf* 65-69; R Birchanger 69-94; rtd 94; Perm to Offic *Glouc* from 94. *Bath Orchard, Blockley, Moreton-in-Marsh, Glos GL56 9HU* Tel (01386) 701223

EVASON, Stuart Anthony. b 44. Salford Univ BSc. Chich Th Coll 79. **d** 81 **p** 82. C Heref St Martin *Heref* 81-85; TV Cleethorpes *Linc* 85-87; TV Howden TM *York* 87-92; V Heywood St Jas *Man* from 92. *St James's Vicarage, 46 Bury Old Road, Heywood, Lancs OL10 3JD* Tel (01706) 369745

EVE, Cedric Robert Sutcliff. b 18. Lon Coll of Div 63. **d** 65 **p** 66. C Plumstead St Jas w St Jo *S'wark* 65-68; C Plumstead St Jo w St Jas and St Paul 68-69; C Ipsley *Worc* 69-73; TV 73-78; P-in-c Norton and Lenchwick 78; P-in-c Harvington 78; P-in-c Harvington and Norton and Lenchwick 78-84; rtd 84; Perm to Offic *Chich* from 85; Perm to Offic *Guildf* from 93. *Flat 2, Woodfold, Fernhurst, Haslemere, Surrey GU27 3ET* Tel (01428) 654085

EVE, David Charles Leonard. b 45. AKC74 St Aug Coll Cant 74. **d** 75 **p** 76. C Hall Green Ascension *Birm* 75-79; TV Kings Norton 79-84; V Rowley Regis 84-93; Perm to Offic *Heref* from 94. *Cleanlyseat Farm, Neen Savage, Cleobury Mortimer, Kidderminster, Worcs DY14 8EN* Tel (01299) 270510

EVE, Hilary Anne. b 57. Lon Univ BEd80. Ripon Coll Cuddesdon 89. **d** 91 **p** 94. Par Dn Coulsdon St Andr *S'wark* 91-94; C 94-95; Chapl Croydon Coll 92-94; Asst Chapl Mayday Healthcare NHS Trust Thornton Heath from 94; Chapl Harestone Marie Curie Cen Caterham from 94. *23 Rickman Hill, Coulsdon, Surrey CR5 3DS* Tel (01737) 557732

EVELEIGH, Raymond. b 36. Univ of Wales (Cardiff) BSc58. NW Ord Course 73. **d** 76 **p** 77. NSM S Cave and Ellerker w Broomfleet *York* 76-79; P-in-c Kingston upon Hull St Mary 79-82; Chapl Hull Coll of FE from 79; V Anlaby Common St Mark *York* 82-94; V Langtoft w Foxholes, Butterwick,

Cottam etc from 94. *The Vicarage, Langtoft, Driffield, N Humberside YO25 0TN* Tel (01377) 87226

EVENS, Philip Alistair. b 36. Leic Univ BA61. Trin Coll Bris 84. **d** 86 **p** 87. C Aston SS Pet and Paul *Birm* 86-89; V Tyseley from 89. *St Edmund's Vicarage, 277 Reddings Lane, Tyseley, Birmingham B11 3DD* Tel 0121-777 2433

EVENS, The Ven Robert John Scott (Bob). b 47. ACIB74 DipTh. Trin Coll Bris 74. **d** 77 **p** 78. C Southsea St Simon *Portsm* 77-79; C Portchester 79-83; V Locks Heath 83-96; RD Fareham 93-96; Adn Bath and Preb Wells Cathl *B & W* from 96. *56 Grange Road, Saltford, Bristol BS18 3AG* Tel (01225) 873609

EVEREST, Harold William. b 26. Lon Univ BD54. Tyndale Hall Bris 51. **d** 54 **p** 55. C Crookes St Thos *Sheff* 54-57; C Leyland St Andr *Blackb* 57-59; V Darwen St Barn 59-67; V Sheff St Jo *Sheff* 67-78; V Tinsley 78-91; Ind Chapl 78-91; rtd 91. *34 Oakdale Road, Bakersfield, Nottingham NG3 7EE* Tel 0115-987 6155

EVEREST, Canon John Cleland. b 45. Sarum Th Coll 66. **d** 68 **p** 69. C Moulsecoomb *Chich* 68-71; C Easthampstead *Ox* 71-74; C Southwick *Chich* 74-77; Dioc Soc Services Adv *Worc* 77-84; Ind Chapl from 84; R Worc City St Paul and Old St Martin etc 84-93; RD Worc E 89-93; Hon Can Worc Cathl from 90; TR Halesowen from 93; RD Dudley from 95. *The Rectory, Bundle Hill, Halesowen, W Midlands B63 4AR* Tel 0121-550 1158

EVERETT, Alan Neil. b 57. St Cath Coll Ox BA79 DPhil96 SS Coll Cam BA84. Westcott Ho Cam 82. **d** 85 **p** 86. C Hindley All SS *Liv* 85-88; Chapl Qu Mary Coll *Lon* 88-91; V S Hackney St Mich w Haggerston St Paul from 94. *97 Lavender Grove, London E8 3LR* Tel 0171-249 4440

EVERETT, Anthony William. b 60. S Bank Poly BA82. Oak Hill Th Coll BA89. **d** 89 **p** 90. C Hailsham *Chich* 89-92; C New Malden and Coombe *S'wark* 92-97; V Streatham Park St Alb from 97. *St Alban's Vicarage, 5 Fayland Avenue, London SW16 1SR* Tel 0181-677 4521 or 769 5415

EVERETT, Bryan John. b 25. ALCD54. **d** 54 **p** 55. C Penge Lane H Trin *Roch* 54-56; C Gorleston St Andr *Nor* 56-59; V E w W Beckham 59-62; R Bodham 59-62; Area Sec (Dios Derby and Lich) CMS 62-69; V Lullington *Derby* 69-80; R Nether and Over Seale 69-80; P-in-c Longstone 80-90; rtd 90; Perm to Offic *Derby* from 90. *2 Lime Grove, Ashbourne, Derbyshire DE6 1HP* Tel (01335) 300303

EVERETT, Mrs Christine Mary. b 46. St Osyth Coll of Educn CertEd67. Westcott Ho Cam 90. **d** 92 **p** 94. Par Dn Ipswich St Fran *St E* 92-94; C 94-95; C Gt and Lt Bealings w Playford and Culpho 96; P-in-c from 96. *190 Hawthorne Drive, Ipswich, Suffolk IP2 0QQ* Tel (01473) 688339

EVERETT, Colin Gerald Grant. b 44. Open Univ BA77 Keswick Hall Coll CertEd. Ripon Coll Cuddesdon 79. **d** 81 **p** 82. C Aston cum Aughton *Sheff* 81-84; R Fornham All SS and Fornham St Martin w Timworth *St E* 84-92; P-in-c Old Newton w Stowupland 92-94; C Ipswich All Hallows 94-95; TV Ipswich St Fran from 95. *190 Hawthorne Drive, Ipswich, Suffolk IP2 0QQ* Tel (01473) 688339

EVERETT, David Gordon. b 45. Pemb Coll Ox BA67 MA. Lon Coll of Div LTh68. **d** 70 **p** 71. C Hatcham St Jas *S'wark* 70-73; C Reading St Jo *Ox* 73-77; TV Fenny Stratford and Water Eaton 77-82; Hon C Bletchley 82-87; C Loughton 84-85; NSM Stantonbury and Willen 87-92; Chapl Ox Brookes Univ 92-96; NSM Iffley 93-96; C Treslothan *Truro* from 96. *Church House, 4 Treslothan Road, Troon, Camborne, Cornwall TR14 9EJ* Tel (01209) 718859 Fax as telephone

EVERETT, Canon John Wilfred. b 37. Qu Coll Cam BA61 MA65. Cuddesdon Coll 64. **d** 66 **p** 67. C St Helier *S'wark* 66-69; C Yeovil St Jo w Preston Plucknett *B & W* 69-73; R Wincanton 73-82; R Pen Selwood 80-82; V Ashford *Cant* from 82; Hon Can Cant Cathl from 90; Chapl S Kent Hosps NHS Trust from 94. *The College, Church Yard, Ashford, Kent TN23 1QG* Tel (01233) 620672

EVERETT, Robert Henry. b 60. Em Coll Cam BA82 BA85 MA86. St Steph Ho Ox 83. **d** 86 **p** 87. C Ex St Thos and Em *Ex* 86-88; C Plymstock 88-91; R St Dominic, Landulph and St Mellion w Pillaton *Truro* 91-96; V Reading All SS *Ox* from 96. *All Saints' Vicarage, 14 Downshire Square, Reading RG1 6NH* Tel 0118-957 2000

EVERETT, Robin Nigel. b 34. Dur Univ BA55 DipTh59. Cranmer Hall Dur 57. **d** 59 **p** 60. C New Humberstone *Leic* 59-62; C Humberstone 62-66; V Quorndon 66-74; V Castle Donington 74-82; P-in-c Lockington w Hemington 81-82; V Castle Donington and Lockington cum Hemington 82-86; Antigua 86-87; R Ibstock w Heather *Leic* from 87. *The Rectory, Ibstock, Leics LE67 6JQ* Tel (01530) 260246

EVERETT, Simon Francis. b 58. Oak Hill Th Coll BA89. **d** 89 **p** 90. C Wroughton *Bris* 89-93; TV Wexcombe *Sarum* from 93. *The Vicarage, Collingbourne Ducis, Marlborough, Wilts SN8 3EL* Tel (01264) 850279

EVERETT-ALLEN, Clive. b 47. AKC70. St Aug Coll Cant 69. **d** 70 **p** 71. C Minera *St As* 70-72; C Hatcham St Cath *S'wark* 72-75; C Beaconsfield *Ox* 75; TV 75-83; R Southwick *Chich* from 83. *The Rectory, 22 Church Lane, Southwick, Brighton BN42 4GB* Tel (01273) 592389

EVERITT, Mark. b 34. Linc Coll Ox BA58 MA62. Wells Th Coll. **d** 60 **p** 61. C Hangleton *Chich* 60-63; Chapl Mert Coll Ox from 63. *Merton College, Oxford OX1 4JD* Tel (01865) 276365

EVERITT, Michael John. b 68. K Coll Lon BD90 AKC90. Qu Coll Birm 90 English Coll Rome 91. **d** 92 **p** 93. C Cleveleys *Blackb* 92-95; S Africa from 95. *Cathedral Church of St Andrew, PO Box 1523, Bloemfontein 9300, South Africa* Tel Bloemfontein (51) 474266 Fax 483078

EVERITT, William Frank James. b 38. FCA63 Dur Univ BA68 DipTh69. Cranmer Hall Dur 65. **d** 69 **p** 70. C Leic St Phil *Leic* 69-73; P-in-c Prestwold w Hoton 73-77; R Settrington w N Grimston and Wharram *York* 77-84; RD Buckrose 80-84; V Cheltenham St Pet *Glouc* from 84. *St Peter's Vicarage, 375 Swindon Road, Cheltenham, Glos GL51 9LB* Tel (01242) 524369

EVERS, Dr Timothy Michael. b 48. Birm Univ BA70 Witwatersrand Univ MA75 PhD89 UNISA BTh93. LNSM course 79. **d** 82 **p** 84. S Africa 82-88; Australia from 88. *PO Box 34, 49 Berkeley Crescent, Floreat Park, W Australia 6014* Tel Perth (9) 387 1304 Fax 387 8997

EVERSON, Canon Owen Neville. b 32. St Jo Coll Cam BA56 MA61. Wycliffe Hall Ox 56. **d** 58 **p** 59. C Edgbaston St Aug *Birm* 58-63; Tutor Wycliffe Hall Ox 63-66; Chapl 66-67; V Lee Gd Shep w St Pet *S'wark* 67-85; Hon Can S'wark Cathl from 83; V W Wickham St Fran from 85. *St Francis's Vicarage, 2 The Grove, West Wickham, Kent BR4 9JS* Tel 0181-777 6010

EVERSON, Simon Charles. b 58. Leeds Univ BA80. Ripon Coll Cuddesdon 80. **d** 83 **p** 84. C Rotherhithe St Mary w All SS *S'wark* 83-87; P-in-c Kennington Park St Agnes 87-94; V 94-96; Chapl Hurstpierpoint Coll Hassocks from 96. *Ruckford One, Malthouse Lane, Hurstpierpoint, Hassocks, W Sussex BN6 9LX* Tel (01273) 835581

EVERY, Canon Edward. b 09. Mert Coll Ox BA30 MA46. Linc Th Coll 36. **d** 36 **p** 37. C Caistor w Holton le Moor and Clixby *Linc* 36-38; C Burnley St Pet *Blackb* 38-40; C Glouc St Paul *Glouc* 40-41; Chapl RAFVR 41-46; Field Officer Chr Reconstruction in Eur Greece 46-47; C St Helier *S'wark* 48-49; Jerusalem 50-79; Can Res 52-79; Acting Dean 78-79; rtd 79; Perm to Offic *Lon* 82-86; Perm to Offic *S'wark* 86-91. *College of St Barnabas, Blackberry Lane, Lingfield, Surrey RH7 6NJ* Tel (01342) 870806

EVES, Barry. b 51. Sunderland Poly DipHums86. Cranmer Hall Dur 86. **d** 88 **p** 89. C Tadcaster w Newton Kyme *York* 88-91; C York St Paul 91-93; V Bubwith w Skipwith from 93. *The Vicarage, North Duffield, Selby, N Yorkshire YO8 7RR* Tel (01757) 288613

EWBANK, The Very Revd Robert Arthur Benson. b 22. Ox Univ MA48. Cuddesdon Coll 46. **d** 48 **p** 49. C Boston *Linc* 48-52; Chapl Uppingham Sch Pet 52-56; S Rhodesia 57-65; Rhodesia 65-80; Zimbabwe from 80; Dean Bulawayo 82-90. *45A Leander Avenue, Bulawayo, Zimbabwe*

EWBANK, Canon Robin Alan. b 42. Ex Coll Ox BA64 MA88 Lon Univ BD68. Clifton Th Coll 66. **d** 69 **p** 70. C Woodford Wells *Chelmsf* 69-72; Warden Cam Univ Miss Bermondsey 72-76; TV Sutton St Jas and Wawne *York* 76-82; R Bramshott *Portsm* 82-91; R Bramshott and Liphook from 91; Chmn IDWAL (Dios Chich, Guildf and Portsm) from 90; Hon Can Koforidua from 96. *The Rectory, 6 Portsmouth Road, Bramshott, Liphook, Hants GU30 7AA* Tel (01428) 723119 or 725390 Fax 724505

EWBANK, The Ven Walter Frederick. b 18. Ball Coll Ox BA45 MA45 BD52. Bps' Coll Cheshunt. **d** 46 **p** 47. C Windermere St Martin *Carl* 46-49; V Hugill 49-52; V Casterton H Trin 52-62; V Raughton Head w Gatesgill 62-66; Hon Can Carl Cathl 66-78 and 83-84; V Carl St Cuth 66-71; Adn Westmorland and Furness 71-77; V Winster 71-78; Adn Carl 78-84; Can Res Carl Cathl 78-82; rtd 84; Perm to Offic *Carl* from 84. *7 Castle Court, Castle Street, Carlisle CA3 8TP* Tel (01228) 810293

EWEN, Keith John McGregor. b 43. Sarum & Wells Th Coll 77. **d** 79 **p** 80. C Kington w Huntington *Heref* 79-82; C Kington w Huntington, Old Radnor, Kinnerton etc 82-83; P-in-c Culmington w Onibury 83-89; P-in-c Bromfield 83-89; P-in-c Stanton Lacy 83-89; R Culmington w Onibury, Bromfield etc from 90. *The Vicarage, Bromfield, Ludlow, Shropshire SY8 2JP* Tel (01584) 77234

EWER, Edward Sydney John (Jonathan). b 36. Univ of New England BA69. ACT ThL63. **d** 62 **p** 63. Australia 62-83; SSM from 68; Perm to Offic *Blackb* 83-84; Lic to Offic *Dur* from 84; Prior SSM Priory Dur from 85; Dir of Ords from 94. *St Antony's Priory, Claypath, Durham DH1 1QT* Tel 0191-384 3747

EWINGTON, John. b 43. ARICS65. Chich Th Coll 74. **d** 78 **p** 79. C Walthamstow St Jo *Chelmsf* 78-81; Papua New Guinea 81-87; V Southend St Sav Westcliff *Chelmsf* 87-96; TV Northam w Westward Ho! and Appledore *Ex* 96; TV Bideford, Northam, Westward Ho!, Appledore etc from 96. *The Vicarage, Meeting Street, Appledore, Bideford, Devon EX39 1RJ* Tel (01237) 470469

EXALL, John Aubrey. b 20. Univ Coll Lon BSc41. Cuddesdon Coll 46. **d** 48 **p** 49. C Bitterne Park *Win* 48-53; C Romsey 53-56; P-in-c Southampton St Barn 56-57; V 57-85; rtd 86; Perm to Offic *Win* from 86. *Delve Cottage, 36 Church Lane, Romsey, Hants SO51 8EP* Tel (01794) 522928

EXCELL, Robin Stanley. b 41. AKC64. St Boniface Warminster 64. **d** 65 **p** 66. C Ipswich St Mary Stoke *St E* 65-68; C Melton

Mowbray w Thorpe Arnold *Leic* 68-70; TV 70-71; R Gt and Lt Blakenham w Baylham *St E* 71-76; R Gt and Lt Blakenham w Baylham and Nettlestead 76-86; RD Bosmere 84-86; NSM Sproughton w Burstall 91-94; R Rattlesden w Thorpe Morieux and Brettenham from 94; P-in-c Hitcham w Lt Finborough from 95. *The Rectory, High Street, Rattlesden, Bury St Edmunds, Suffolk IP30 0RA* Tel (01449) 737993

EXELL, Ernest William Carter. b 28. Qu Coll Cam BA52 MA53. Tyndale Hall Bris 49. **d** 52 **p** 53. C Sydenham H Trin *S'wark* 52-54; C E Ham St Paul *Chelmsf* 54-57; Uganda 57-65; Tanzania 66-70; R Abbess and Beauchamp Roding *Chelmsf* 70-71; P-in-c White Roding w Morrell Roding 70-71; R Abbess Roding, Beauchamp Roding and White Roding 71-94; RD Roding 75-79; rtd 94. *8 Ickworth Drive, Bury St Edmunds, Suffolk IP33 3PX* Tel (01284) 724726

EXELL, Michael Andrew John (Mike). b 45. MRIPHH67 MICA70. Sarum & Wells Th Coll 87. **d** 89 **p** 90. C Ryde H Trin *Portsm* 89-93; C Swanmore St Mich w Havenstreet 89-92; C Swanmore St Mich and All Angels 92-93; P-in-c Carisbrooke St Mary from 93. *The Vicarage, 1 Clatterford Road, Newport, Isle of Wight PO30 1PA* Tel (01983) 522095

EXETER, Archdeacon of. *See* TREMLETT, The Ven Anthony Frank

EXETER, Bishop of. *See* THOMPSON, The Rt Revd Geoffrey Hewlett

EXETER, Dean of. *See* JONES, The Very Revd Keith Brynmor

EXLEY, Malcolm. b 33. Cranmer Hall Dur. **d** 67 **p** 68. C Sutton St Jas *York* 67-73; V Mappleton w Goxhill 73-77; V Market Weighton 77-90; P-in-c Goodmanham 77-78; R 78-90; V Bridlington Em from 90. *Emmanuel Vicarage, 72 Cardigan Road, Bridlington, York YO15 3JT* Tel (01262) 604948

EXLEY-STEIGLER, Canon George Ebdon. b 16. Syracuse Univ BS. Berkeley Div Sch STM. **d** 53 **p** 54. USA 53-79 and from 89; rtd 79; Hon C Knowsley *Liv* 80-81; Hon C Upholland 81-89. *1471 Long Pond Road 247, Rochester, NY 14626, USA*

EYDEN, Christopher David. b 59. DipRSAMDA81. St Steph Ho Ox 88. **d** 91 **p** 92. C Tottenham St Paul *Lon* 91-93; C Ealing St Pet Mt Park 93-96; TV Wimbledon *S'wark* from 96. *55 Alwyne Road, London SW19 7AE* Tel 0181-946 4175

EYDEN, Canon Eric Westley. b 09. Lon Univ BA31 AKC33 BD34. **d** 33 **p** 34. C Newington St Matt *S'wark* 33-36; C Kingston All SS 37-39; Bp's Chapl for Youth 37-39; V Battersea St Steph 39-44; V Raynes Park St Sav 44-54; RD Wimbledon 53-54; R Shepton Mallet *B & W* 54-64; RD Shepton Mallet 57-64; Can Res and Prec Heref Cathl *Heref* 64-75; rtd 75; Perm to Offic *B & W* from 75. *Little Croft, 5 The Grange, Chilton Polden, Bridgwater, Somerset TA7 9DW* Tel (01278) 722622

EYLES, Anthony John. b 34. Bris Univ BSc57. Sarum Th Coll 61. **d** 63 **p** 64. C Wellington w W Buckland *B & W* 63-67; C Wilton 67-74; Ind Chapl *Dur* 74-85; Ind Chapl *Worc* 85-90; P-in-c Bickenhill w Elmdon *Birm* 90; P-in-c Bickenhill St Pet from 90; Chapl Birm Airport from 90. *The Vicarage, Barndale House, Church Lane, Solihull, W Midlands B92 0DT* Tel (01675) 442215

EYLES, David William. b 45. Sarum & Wells Th Coll 75. **d** 77 **p** 78. C Knaresborough *Ripon* 77-80; C Chapel Allerton 80-82; P-in-c W Tanfield and Well w Snape and N Stainley 82-83; R 83-91; P-in-c Middleham w Coverdale and E Witton 93-94; R from 94; P-in-c Thornton Watlass w Thornton Steward from 94. *The Rectory, The Springs, Middleham, Leyburn, N Yorkshire DL8 4RB* Tel (01969) 622276

EYNON, John Kenneth. b 56. Nottm Univ BA77 BArch80. LNSM course 93. **d** 96. Hon C Croydon Ch Ch *S'wark* from 96. *33 Fairlands Avenue, Thornton Heath, Surrey CR7 6HD* Tel 0181-684 9866

EYRE, John Trevor. b 42. BA88. Oak Hill Th Coll 86. **d** 89 **p** 90. C Watton w Carbrooke and Ovington *Nor* 89-94; P-in-c Kirkley St Pet and St Jo 94-95; R from 95. *3 Aldwyck Way, Lowestoft, Suffolk NR33 9JQ* Tel (01502) 508289

EYRE, The Very Revd Richard Montague Stephens. b 29. Or Coll Ox BA53 MA56. St Steph Ho Ox 53. **d** 56 **p** 57. C Portsea N End St Mark *Portsm* 56-59; Tutor Chich Th Coll 59-61; Chapl 61-62; Chapl Eastbourne Coll 62-65; V Arundel w Tortington and S Stoke *Chich* 65-73; V Brighton Gd Shep Preston 73-75; Dir of Ords 75-79; Adn Chich 75-81; Can Res and Treas Chich Cathl 78-81; Dean Ex 81-95; rtd 95; Perm to Offic *B & W* from 95. *Hathersage, Enmore Road, Enmore, Bridgwater, Somerset TA5 2DP* Tel (01278) 671790

EYRE, Richard Stuart. b 48. Nottm Univ MTh86 Bris Univ BEd81. Linc Th Coll 74. **d** 77 **p** 78. C Henbury *Bris* 77-81; C Bedminster 81-82; TV 82-84; Chapl Bp Grosseteste Coll Linc 84-95; Sen Tutor 89-95; Chapl Riseholme Coll of Agric 84-95; P-in-c Long Bennington w Foston *Linc* 95; P-in-c Saxonwell 95-97; R from 97; RD Grantham from 96. *Saxonwell Vicarage, Church Street, Long Bennington, Newark, Notts NG23 5ES* Tel (01400) 282545

EYRE-WALKER, John Benson. b 15. St Pet Hall Ox BA40 DipTh41 MA44. Wycliffe Hall Ox. **d** 42 **p** 43. C Beckenham Ch Ch *Roch* 42-44; C Hove Bp Hannington Memorial Ch *Chich* 44-48; V Leigh *Roch* 48-57; V Burton *Ches* 57-80; rtd 80; Perm to Offic *Carl* 81-93. *Sunrise Cottage, Kilmidyke Road, Grange-over-Sands, Cumbria LA11 7AQ* Tel (01539) 532647

F

FACER, Miss Rosemary Jane. b 44. LTCL72 Hull Univ BA65 Reading Univ CertEd66. Trin Coll Bris DipHE80. **dss** 80 **d** 87. St Paul's Cray St Barn *Roch* 80-87; Par Dn 87-88; C Cheltenham St Mark *Glouc* from 88. *33 Campden Road, Cheltenham, Glos GL51 6AA* Tel (01242) 239477

FACEY, Andrew John. b 57. Barrister 80 Trin Coll Cam MA83. Trin Coll Bris BA92. **d** 92 **p** 93. C Egham *Guildf* 92-96; P-in-c E Molesey St Paul from 96. *St Paul's Vicarage, 101 Palace Road, East Molesey, Surrey KT8 9DU* Tel 0181-979 1580

FAGAN, John Raymond. b 32. Lon Univ BD69. Ripon Hall Ox 71. **d** 72 **p** 73. C Stalybridge *Man* 72-74; C Madeley *Heref* 74-79; V Amington *Birm* 79-91; P-in-c Stonnall *Lich* from 91; Chapl HM Young Offender Inst Swinfen Hall from 91. *2 St Peter's Close, Stonnall, Walsall WS9 9EN* Tel (01543) 373088 Fax 480138

FAGAN, Thomas. b 27. MCIOB67 Man Univ CertEd70. NW Ord Course 78. **d** 81 **p** 82. NSM Rainhill *Liv* 81-90; NSM Prescot 90-97; rtd 97. *4 Wensleydale Avenue, Prescot, Merseyside L35 4NR* Tel 0151-426 4788

FAGBEMI, Olubunmi Ayobami (Bunmi). b 57. Lagos Univ LLB78 LSE LLM81 Qu Mary Coll Lon PhD91 Solicitor 79. Ripon Coll Cuddesdon 95. **d** 97. C Enfield St Andr *Lon* from 97. *159 Parsonages Lane, Enfield, Middx EN1 3UJ* Tel 0181-364 6628

FAGERSON, Joseph Leonard Ladd. b 35. Harvard Univ BA57 Lon Univ DipTh62. Ridley Hall Cam 61. **d** 63 **p** 64. C Tonbridge SS Pet and Paul *Roch* 63-67; Afghanistan 67-74; P-in-c Marbury *Ches* 74-75; P-in-c Kinloch Rannoch *St And* from 75; Chapl Rannoch Sch Perthshire from 75. *The Chaplain's House, Rannoch School, Rannoch Station, Perthshire PH17 2QQ* Tel (01882) 632235

FAGG, Alan Gordon. b 06. K Coll Lon 54. **d** 55 **p** 56. C Camberwell St Geo *S'wark* 55-58; Chapl HM Pris Maidstone 58-63; V Forest Row *Chich* 63-70; Perm to Offic from 70; rtd 78. *11 Davis Court, Marlborough Road, St Albans, Herts AL1 3XU* Tel (01727) 847146

FAHIE, Mrs Stephanie Bridget. b 48. St Jo Coll Nottm 85. **d** 87 **p** 94. Par Dn Leic St Chris *Leic* 87-90; Chapl Scargill Ho 90-95; P-in-c Hickling w Kinoulton and Broughton Sulney *S'well* from 95. *The Rectory, 41 Main Street, Kinoulton, Nottingham NG12 3EA* Tel (01949) 81657

FAINT, Paul Edward. b 38. Qu Coll Birm 85. **d** 87 **p** 88. C Cradley *Worc* 87-90; V Hanley Castle, Hanley Swan and Welland 90-94; V Northwood H Trin *Lon* from 94. *Holy Trinity Vicarage, Gateway Close, Northwood, Middx HA6 2RW* Tel (01923) 825732

FAIRALL, Michael John. b 45. SW Minl Tr Course 88. **d** 90 **p** 91. NSM Southway *Ex* from 90. *132 Lakeview Close, Tamerton Foliot, Plymouth PL5 4LX* Tel (01752) 707694

FAIRBAIRN, John Alan. b 46. Trin Coll Cam BA67 MA72. Wycliffe Hall Ox 84. **d** 86 **p** 87. C Boscombe St Jo *Win* 86-89; C Edgware *Lon* 89-95; R Gunton St Pet *Nor* from 95. *The Rectory, 36 Gunton Church Lane, Lowestoft, Suffolk NR32 4LF* Tel (01502) 572600

FAIRBAIRN, Stella Rosamund. **d** 87 **p** 94. NSM Banbury *Ox* from 87; Perm to Offic *Pet* 88-94. *Hillside, Overthorpe, Banbury, Oxon OX17 2AF* Tel (01295) 710648

FAIRBANK, Brian Douglas Seeley. b 53. AKC75. St Steph Ho Ox 77. **d** 78 **p** 79. C Newton Aycliffe *Dur* 78-81; C Stocking Farm *Leic* 81-84; TV Ratby w Groby 84-91; Chapl RN from 91. *Royal Naval Chaplaincy Service, Room 203, Victory Building, HM Naval Base, Portsmouth PO1 3LS* Tel (01705) 727903 Fax 727112

FAIRBROTHER, Robin Harry. b 44. Univ of Wales DipTh68. Ho of Resurr Mirfield 64 Wells Th Coll 68. **d** 69 **p** 70. C Wrexham *St As* 69-74; C Welshpool w Castle Caereinion 74-77; V Bettws Cedewain and Tregynon 77-80; V Betws Cedewain and Tregynon and Llanwyddelan 80-92; TR Marshwood Vale TM *Sarum* from 92. *The Rectory, Whitchurch Canonicorum, Bridport, Dorset DT6 6RQ* Tel (01297) 489223

FAIRBROTHER, Ronald Peter. b 20. St Steph Ho Ox 59. **d** 61 **p** 62. C Dawlish *Ex* 61-69; R Newton Ferrers w Revelstoke 69-83; V Abbotskerswell 83-89; rtd 90. *3 Chestnut Court, Alphington, Exeter EX2 8XY*

FAIRBURN, Peter. b 16. Linc Th Coll 42. **d** 42 **p** 43. C Linc St Faith and St Mary-le-Wigford etc *Linc* 42-46; C Harrogate St Wilfrid *Ripon* 46-51; V Downholme 51-54; P-in-c Hudswell 51-53; V 53-54; V Arkendale 54-82; R Goldsborough 54-82; rtd 82. *c/o Mrs T Mundy, 82 Lyndon Avenue, Garforth, Leeds LS25 1DZ* Tel 0113-286 0231

FAIRCLOUGH, John Frederick. b 40. DMS78 MBIM St Jo Coll Dur BA63 MA68. Coll of Resurr Mirfield 81. **d** 83 **p** 84. C Horninglow *Lich* 83-87; V Skerton St Luke *Blackb* 87-94; V Thornton-le-Fylde from 94. *The Vicarage, Meadows Avenue, Thornton Cleveleys, Lancs FY5 2TW* Tel (01253) 855099

FAIRHURST, Canon Alan Marshall. b 30. Clare Coll Cam BA52 MA56 Lon Univ BD56. Tyndale Hall Bris 53 Hask's Th

Academy Istanbul 54 Wycliffe Hall Ox 55. **d** 56 **p** 57. Tutor St Jo Coll Dur 56-60; C Stockport St Geo *Ches* 60-62; Ceylon 62-66; R Ashley w Silverley *Ely* 67-71; R Stockport St Mary *Ches* 71-95; Chapl Stepping Hill Hosp Stockport 76-95; Hon Can Ches Cathl *Ches* 81-95; RD Stockport 86-95; rtd 95; Perm to Offic *Ches* from 95. *50 Ridge Park, Bramhall, Stockport, Cheshire SK7 2BL* Tel 0161-439 3126

FAIRHURST, John Graham. b 39. Linc Th Coll 86. **d** 88 **p** 89. C Whiston *Sheff* 88-91; V Elsecar from 91. *The Vicarage, Wath Road, Elsecar, Barnsley, S Yorkshire S74 8HJ* Tel (01226) 742149

FAIRHURST, Ms Rosemary Anne (Rosy). b 63. Newnham Coll Cam BA85 MA85 Lon Inst of Educn PGCE86. Wycliffe Hall Ox BA92. **d** 93 **p** 94. C Hackney Marsh *Lon* from 93. *84 Roding Road, London E5 0DS* Tel 0181-533 4034

FAIRLAMB, Neil. b 49. Univ of Wales (Ban) BA71 Jes Coll Ox BPhil73 Pemb Coll Cam CertEd74. S'wark Ord Course 90. **d** 93 **p** 94. Hon C Dulwich St Barn *S'wark* 93-95; P-in-c Elerch w Penrhyncoch w Capel Bangor and Goginan *St D* 95-96; V from 96. *The Vicarage, 78 Geryllan, Penrhyncoch, Aberystwyth SY23 3HQ* Tel (01970) 828746

FAIRWEATHER, David James. b 35. Keele Univ BEd79. Wycliffe Hall Ox 70. **d** 72 **p** 73. C Trentham *Lich* 72-76; C Cheddleton 76; C Hanley H Ev 77-79; C Rugeley 79-86; V Brown Edge from 86. *St Anne's Vicarage, Church Road, Brown Edge, Stoke-on-Trent ST6 8TD* Tel (01782) 502134

FAIRWEATHER, John. b 39. K Coll Lon AKC66 BD72. **d** 67 **p** 68. C Plymouth St Jas Ham *Ex* 67-69; C Townstal w St Sav and St Petrox w St Barn 69-73; R Corringham w Springthorpe *Linc* 73-78; P-in-c Blyborough 76-78; P-in-c Heapham 76-78; P-in-c Willoughton 76-78; V Pinchbeck 78-82; V Exwick *Ex* from 82. *Exwick Vicarage, Exwick Road, Exeter EX4 2AT* Tel (01392) 55500

FAIRWEATHER, Miss Sally Helen. b 69. St Hilda's Coll Ox BA91. Cranmer Hall Dur 94. **d** 97. C Illingworth *Wakef* from 97. *77 Whitehill Road, Illingworth, Halifax, W Yorkshire HX2 9EU*

FALCONER, Ian Geoffrey. b 40. BNC Ox BA62. Cuddesdon Coll 62. **d** 64 **p** 65. C Chiswick St Nic w St Mary *Lon* 64-68; C-in-c Hounslow Gd Shep Beavers Lane CD 68-76; P-in-c Hammersmith St Matt 76-84; P-in-c Byker St Silas *Newc* 84-93; V 93-95; P-in-c Newc St Phil and St Aug from 95; P-in-c Newc St Matt w St Mary from 95. *The Vicarage, St Philip's Close, Newcastle upon Tyne NE4 5JE* Tel 0191-273 7407

FALCONER, John Geikie. b 13. Selw Coll Cam BA33 MA37. Lon Coll of Div 33. **d** 36 **p** 37. C Silloth *Carl* 36-37; C Lowther w Askham 37-39; Chapl RN 39-60; Perm to Offic *D & G* 61-62; Deputation Sec Leprosy Miss 62-70; Perm to Offic *Lon* from 71; rtd 78. *10 Hounslow Avenue, Hounslow TW3 2DX* Tel 0181-898 1122

FALKNER, Jonathan Michael Shepherd. b 47. Open Univ BA74 St Jo Coll Dur DipTh78. **d** 79 **p** 80. C Penrith *Carl* 79; C Penrith w Newton Reigny 79-81; C Penrith w Newton Reigny and Plumpton Wall 81-82; C Dalton-in-Furness 82-84; V Clifton 84-90; P-in-c Dean 85-89; R 89-90; P-in-c Rumburgh w S Elmham w the Ilketshalls *St E* 90-92; R S Elmham and Ilketshall from 92; RD Beccles and S Elmham from 94. *Church House, Ilkestall St Margaret, Bungay, Suffolk NR35 1QZ* Tel (01986) 781345

FALL, Harry. b 17. Leeds Univ BA40 BD51 Dur Univ BA42 MA48. **d** 42 **p** 43. C Eccles St Mary *Man* 42-44; C Heaton Norris Ch Ch 44-45; C Linthorpe *York* 45-49; V Danby 49-54; V Harden *Bradf* 54-57; R Scrayingham *York* 57-71; R York H Trin w St Jo Micklegate and St Martin 71-84; rtd 84; Perm to Offic *York* from 84. *20 Weaponness Valley Road, Scarborough, N Yorkshire YO11 2JF* Tel (01723) 361822

FALL, John David McPherson. b 29. St Paul's Grahamstown LTh64. **d** 64 **p** 65. S Rhodesia 64-65; Rhodesia 65-80; Zimbabwe 80-82; P-in-c Dorrington *Heref* 82-92; P-in-c Leebotwood w Longnor 82-92; P-in-c Stapleton 82-92; P-in-c Smethcott w Woolstaston 82-92; rtd 92. *69 Raymead Close, West Mersea, Colchester CO5 8DN* Tel (01206) 385277

FALLA, Miles. b 43. DipM74 MCIM. EAMTC 93. **d** 96 **p** 97. Hon C Buckden *Ely* from 96. *Bowlings, Silver Street, Buckden, St Neots, Huntingdon, Cambs PE18 9TS* Tel (01480) 810879

FALLONE, Christopher (Chris). b 55. Aston Tr Scheme 85 Oak Hill Th Coll 87. **d** 90 **p** 91. C Rochdale *Man* 90-93; P-in-c Thornham w Gravel Hole 93-94; TV Middleton w Thornham from 94. *St John's Vicarage, 1177 Manchester Road, Rochdale, Lancs OL11 2XZ* Tel (01706) 31825

FALLOWS, Stuart Adrian. b 50. Moray Ho Edin 75. **d** 78 **p** 79. Hon C Forres *Mor* 78-81; Hon C Elgin w Lossiemouth 81-86; C Brighton St Geo w St Anne and St Mark *Chich* 86-89; V Wivelsfield from 89. *New Vicarage, Church Lane, Wivelsfield, Haywards Heath, W Sussex RH17 7RD* Tel (01444) 471783

FALSHAW, Simon Meriadoc. b 60. Leeds Univ BSc82. Oak Hill Th Coll BA93. **d** 93 **p** 94. C Stapleford *S'well* from 93. *3 Ash Grove, Stapleford, Nottingham NG9 7GL* Tel 0115-939 2643

FANE, Clifford Charles. b 39. Kelham Th Coll 62. **d** 67 **p** 68. C Heston *Lon* 67-73; C Bedminster St Mich *Bris* 73-76; P-in-c 76-77; C Gaywood, Bawsey and Mintlyn *Nor* 77-81; V Bolton St Jo *Man* 81-90; rtd 90. *10 Booth Road, Little Lever, Bolton BL3 1JY* Tel (01204) 709420

FANTHORPE, Robert Lionel. b 35. FBIM81 FCP90 CertEd63 Open Univ BA80. Llan Dioc Tr Scheme. **d** 87 **p** 88. NSM Roath St German *Llan* from 87. *Rivendell, 48 Claude Road, Roath, Cardiff CF2 3QA* Tel (01222) 498368

FARADAY, John. b 49. Leeds Univ BSc71 MICE78. Oak Hill Th Coll 81. **d** 83 **p** 84. C Sutton *Liv* 83-86; C Rainhill 86-89; Chapl Whiston Hosp 86-89; V Over Darwen St Jas *Blackb* from 89. *St James's Vicarage, Winterton Road, Darwen, Lancs BB3 0ER* Tel (01254) 702364

FARAH, Mones Anton. b 64. Trin Coll Bris BA88. **d** 88 **p** 89. C Aberystwyth *St D* 88-91; Chapl St D Coll Lamp from 91. *Gelli Aur, Bryn Road, Lampeter SA48 7EE* Tel (01570) 422984

FARAH, The Ven Rafiq Amin. b 21. Beirut Univ BA45. Near E Sch of Th 45. **d** 46 **p** 48. Jerusalem 46-86; Adn and Can Res 74-86; Min to Arab Angl and Evang in Lon 86-92; Hon C Herne Hill *S'wark* 86-92; Canada 92-95. *27 Fordington House, Sydenham Hill, London SE26 6TX* Tel 0181-291 0696

FARBRIDGE, Nicholas Brisco. b 33. FCA. Sarum & Wells Th Coll 75. **d** 77 **p** 78. C Gt Bookham *Guildf* 77-80; C Ewell 80-83; V Addlestone 83-89; R Shere 89-95; rtd 96; Perm to Offic *Guildf* from 96. *55 Curling Vale, Guildford, Surrey GU2 5PH* Tel (01483) 31140

FARDON, Jean Audrey May. b 24. Westf Coll Lon BA45 Lon Inst of Educn DipEd46. Gilmore Ho DipTh69. **dss** 79 **d** 87 **p** 94. St Alb St Pet *St Alb* 79-92; Hon Par Dn 87-92; NSM Powyke *Worc* 92-94; Perm to Offic from 94. *35 King's End Road, Powick, Worcester WR2 4RB* Tel (01905) 830472

FARDON, Raymond George Warren. b 30. St Pet Hall Ox BA52 MA56. Ridley Hall Cam 54. **d** 59 **p** 60. C High Wycombe All SS *Ox* 59-63; Chapl Bedford Secondary Modern Sch 63-68; Hd Master K Sch Grantham 72-82; Travelling Ev 82-95; Hon C Longfleet *Sarum* 82-83; Perm to Offic from 83; rtd 95. *26 Kingland Road, Poole, Dorset BH15 1TP* Tel (01202) 675609

FAREY, David Mark. b 56. St Jo Coll Dur BA85. Cranmer Hall Dur 82. **d** 86 **p** 87. C Brackley St Pet w St Jas *Pet* 86-89; TV Kingsthorpe w Northn St Dav 89-96; R Laughton w Ripe and Chalvington *Chich* from 96; Chapl to Area Bp Lewes from 96. *The Rectory, Church Lane, Laughton, Lewes, E Sussex BN8 6AH* Tel (01323) 811642

FARGUS, Gavin James Frederick. b 30. AKC54. **d** 55 **p** 57. C Salisbury St Mark *Sarum* 55-57; C Wareham w Arne 57-60; C Marlborough 60-63; P-in-c Davidstow w Otterham *Truro* 63-65; R Nether Lochaber *Arg* 65-81; R Kinlochleven 65-81; rtd 81; Lic to Offic *Arg* from 82. *61 East Lavoch, Ballachulish, Argyll PA39 4JB* Tel (01855) 811851

FARGUS, Maxwell Stuart. b 34. Linc Coll Ox BA57 MA61 Leeds Univ DipAdEd79. Cuddesdon Coll 57. **d** 59 **p** 60. C Newc St Fran *Newc* 59-62; C Rothbury 62-64; Dioc Youth Officer *Ripon* 64-76; R Kirkby Wiske 64-76; Community Educn Officer Barnsley MBC 76-88; Perm to Offic *Sheff* 77-88; Perm to Offic *Wakef* 77-88; Perm to Offic *York* 77-88; V Rudston w Boynton and Kilham 88-93; rtd 93; Perm to Offic *York* from 93. *56 Fir Tree Drive, Filey, N Yorkshire YO14 9NR*

FARISH, Alan John. b 58. Lanc Univ BA. St Jo Coll Nottm LTh86 DPS86. **d** 86 **p** 87. C Bishopwearmouth St Gabr *Dur* 86-89; C Fatfield from 89. *17 Whittonstall, Washington, Tyne & Wear NE38 8PH* Tel 0191-415 5424

FARLEY, David Stuart. b 53. Univ Coll Dur BA75 Nottm Univ DipTh82. St Jo Coll Nottm. **d** 84 **p** 85. C Bath Weston All SS w N Stoke *B & W* 84-87; Chapl Scargill Ho 87-90; Min Hedge End N CD *Win* 90-94; V Hedge End St Luke from 94. *16 Elliot Rise, Hedge End, Southampton SO30 2RU* Tel (01489) 786717

FARLEY, Edward Albert (Ted). b 36. Lon Univ BSc59 ARCS59 Em Coll Cam BA61. Ridley Hall Cam 60. **d** 62 **p** 63. C Bitterne *Win* 62-65; C Swindon Ch Ch *Bris* 65-68; V Dunston w Coppenhall *Lich* 68-71; V Blurton 71-82; V Cheddleton 82-92; Chapl St Edward's Hosp Cheddleton 82-92; RD Leek *Lich* 87-92; P-in-c Bourton-on-the-Water w Clapton *Glouc* 92-97; rtd 97. *95 Dartmouth Avenue, Newcastle, Staffs ST5 3NS* Tel (01782) 615915

FARLEY, Dr Ian David. b 56. Linc Coll Ox BA78 MA87 Dur Univ PhD88. Cranmer Hall Dur 84. **d** 87 **p** 88. C Thorpe Acre w Dishley *Leic* 87-92; V S Lambeth St Steph *S'wark* from 92. *The Vicarage, St Stephen's Terrace, London SW8 1DH* Tel 0171-735 8461

FARLEY, James Trevor. b 37. IEng MIEE FRSA. EMMTC 80. **d** 82 **p** 83. NSM Grantham *Linc* from 82. *Highfield Cottage, Station Road, Bottesford, Nottingham NG13 0EN* Tel (01949) 43646

FARLEY, Lionel George Herbert. b 10. Chich Th Coll 32. **d** 35 **p** 36. C Parkstone St Osmund *Sarum* 35-39; C Bournemouth St Fran *Win* 39-46; C St Austell *Truro* 46-48; V Lewannick 48-51; V Marazion 51-78; rtd 78. *Karenza, 22 Chestnut Way, Gillingham, Dorset SP8 4RT* Tel (01747) 823530

FARLEY, Ronald Alexander. b 30. Oak Hill NSM Course. **d** 79 **p** 80. NSM Stoke Newington St Faith, St Matthias and All SS *Lon* from 79. *20 Chaucer Court, Howard Road, London N16 8TS* Tel 0171-249 4349

FARLIE, Canon Hugh. b 29. Lon Univ BSc53. Linc Th Coll 53. **d** 55 **p** 56. C Bilston St Leon *Lich* 55-58; C Stoke Newington St Olave *Lon* 58-63; Asst Chapl Bris Univ *Bris* 63-65; Chapl Bris Coll of Science and Tech 63-65; Chapl Bath Univ *B & W* 65-73; P-in-c Knowle St Barn *Bris* 73-85; V 85-94; Hon Can Bris Cathl 89-94; rtd 94; Perm to Offic *Chich* from 94. *16 Croft Road, Hastings, E Sussex TN34 3HJ*

FARMAN, Robert Joseph. b 54. Ridley Hall Cam 86. **d** 88 **p** 89. C Sutton St Nic *S'wark* 88-90; C Cheam Common St Phil 90-92; R Wootton w Glympton and Kiddington *Ox* from 92. *The Vicarage, Castle Road, Wooton, Oxon OX20 1EG* Tel (01993) 812543

FARMAN, Mrs Roberta. b 48. Aber Univ MA70 Cam Univ CertEd72. Qu Coll Birm 78. **dss** 82 **d** 87. Ovenden *Wakef* 80-82; Scargill Ho 83-84; Coulsdon St Jo *S'wark* 85-86; Hon Par Dn Cambridge St Mark *Ely* 86-88; Hon Par Dn Sutton St Nic *S'wark* 88-92; Hon Par Dn Wootton w Glympton and Kiddington *Ox* from 92. *The Vicarage, Castle Road, Wooton, Oxon OX20 1EG* Tel (01993) 812543

FARMBOROUGH, James Laird McLelland. b 22. MBE90. Magd Coll Cam BA49 MA54. Tyndale Hall Bris. **d** 52 **p** 53. C Wolverhampton St Luke *Lich* 52-55; C Holloway St Mary w St Jas *Lon* 55-56; C Broadwater St Mary *Chich* 56-58; Brazil 58-64; Org Sec SAMS 65-70; V Marple All SS *Ches* 70-80; Chile 80-92; Miss to Seamen 80-92; rtd 88. *Heatherlea Grange, Wolsingham, Bishop Auckland, Co Durham DL13 3LZ* Tel (01388) 528784

✠**FARMBROUGH, The Rt Revd David John.** b 29. Linc Coll Ox BA51 MA53. Westcott Ho Cam 51. **d** 53 **p** 54 **c** 81. C Hatfield *St Alb* 53-57; P-in-c 57-63; V Bishop's Stortford St Mich 63-74; RD Bishop's Stortford 73-74; Adn St Alb 74-81; Suff Bp Bedford 81-93; rtd 94. *St Michael Mead, 110 Village Road, Bromham, Bedford MK43 8HU* Tel (01234) 825042

FARMER, George Wilson. b 37. Lich Th Coll 61. **d** 65 **p** 66. C Kingston All SS *S'wark* 65-69; C Heston *Lon* 69-74; C Southmead *Bris* 74-75; C Bedminster 75-80; TV Langley Marish *Ox* 80-86; R Wexham from 86. *The Rectory, 7 Grangewood, Wexham, Slough SL3 6LP* Tel (01753) 523852

FARMER, Robert John. b 62. Kent Univ BA84 SSC. St Steph Ho Ox 91. **d** 93 **p** 94. C Leigh St Clem *Chelmsf* 93-96; P-in-c Wellingborough St Mary *Pet* from 96. *St Mary's Vicarage, 193 Midland Road, Wellingborough, Northants NN8 1NG* Tel (01933) 225626 E-mail rjfarmer@wildnet.co.uk

FARMER, Simon John. b 60. Birm Univ BSc82. St Jo Coll Nottm. **d** 89 **p** 90. C Ulverston St Mary w H Trin *Carl* 89-92; CF 92-97; rtd 97. *MOD Chaplains (Army), Trenchard Lines, Upavon, Pewsey, Wilts SN9 6BE* Tel (01980) 615804 Fax 615800

FARMER, Canon William John Cotton. b 19. St Jo Coll Dur LTh42 BA43. St Aid Birkenhead. **d** 43 **p** 44. C Ipswich St Aug *St E* 43-45; C Warwick St Mary *Cov* 45-49; C Solihull *Birm* 49-54; V Blackheath 54-64; V Packwood w Hockley Heath 64-81; Hon Can Birm Cathl 80-81; rtd 84. *Flat 12, Bowling Green Court, Moreton-in-Marsh, Glos GL56 0BX* Tel (01608) 51082

FARMILOE, Trevor James. b 42. Sarum & Wells Th Coll. **d** 82 **p** 82. C S Petherton w the Seavingtons *B & W* 82-85; R Norton St Philip w Hemington, Hardington etc 85-93; Chapl Rural Affairs Wells Adnry 87-92; RD Frome 89-93; V Martock w Ash from 93; RD Ivelchester from 95. *The Vicarage, 10 Water Street, Martock, Somerset TA12 6JN* Tel (01935) 822579

FARNHAM, Douglas John (Doug). b 30. SS Mark & Jo Coll Plymouth TCert52 Ex Univ ADEd66 MEd75. S Dios Minl Tr Scheme 80. **d** 83 **p** 84. Lect Bp Otter Coll Chich 70-78; Sen Lect W Sussex Inst of HE 78-92; NSM Barnham and Eastergate *Chich* 83-85; NSM Aldingbourne, Barnham and Eastergate 85-92; R 92-96; rtd 96; Perm to Offic *Chich* from 96. *16 Henty Close, Walberton, Arundel, W Sussex BN18 0PW* Tel (01243) 555992

FARNWORTH, Michael Godfrey Frankland. b 18. Selw Coll Cam BA40 MA46. Westcott Ho Cam 40. **d** 42 **p** 43. C Horsham *Chich* 42-47; C Storrington 47-50; CF 50-72; P-in-c Hindringham and Binham *Nor* 72-77; R 77-84; rtd 84; Perm to Offic *Nor* from 85. *15 Sheldrake Close, Fakenham, Norfolk NR21 8ND* Tel (01328) 855211

FARNWORTH, Russell. b 60. Lon Bible Coll BA82 Nottm Univ MTh85. St Jo Coll Nottm DPS84. **d** 84 **p** 85. C Blackpool St Jo *Blackb* 84-87; TV Darwen St Pet w Hoddlesden 87-91; V Kidsgrove *Lich* from 91. *St Thomas's Vicarage, The Avenue, Kidsgrove, Stoke-on-Trent ST7 1AG* Tel (01782) 771367

FARQUHAR, Miss Patricia Ann. b 42. **dss** 78 **d** 87 **p** 94. S Hackney St Jo w Ch Ch *Lon* 80-87; Par Dn 87-94; C from 94. *19 Valentine Road, London E9 7AD* Tel 0181-986 6273

FARQUHARSON, Hunter Buchanan. b 58. ALAM LLAM. Edin Th Coll 85. **d** 88 **p** 89. C Dunfermline *St And* 88-91; R Glenrothes 91-97; R Leven 95-97; R Dunfermline from 97. *The Rectory, 17 Ardeer Place, Dunfermline, Fife KY11 4YX* Tel (01383) 723901 E-mail 100736.1422@compuserve

FARQUHARSON-ROBERTS, Donald Arthur (Don). b 21. Bps' Coll Cheshunt 64. **d** 65 **p** 66. C Preston *Sarum* 65-68; R Pimperne 68-89; P-in-c Stourpaine, Durweston and Bryanston 77-89; rtd 90. *30 East House Avenue, Fareham, Hants PO14 2RE* Tel (01329) 667333

FARR, Arthur Ronald. b 24. JP77. Llan Dioc Tr Scheme 77. **d** 80 **p** 81. NSM Penarth All SS *Llan* 80-90; rtd 90; Perm to Offic *Llan* from 90. *3 Cymric Close, Ely, Cardiff CF5 4GR* Tel (01222) 561765

FARR, Mark Julian Richard. b 60. **d** 87 **p** 88. C Clapham TM *S'wark* 87-91; TV Wimbledon 91-95; USA from 96. *Sojourners, 2401 15th Street NW, Washington DC, 20009, USA*

FARR, Richard William. b 55. Ridley Hall Cam. **d** 83 **p** 84. C Enfield Ch Ch Trent Park *Lon* 83-87; C Eastbourne H Trin *Chich* 87-90; P-in-c Henham and Elsenham w Ugley *Chelmsf* from 90. *The Vicarage, Carters Lane, Henham, Bishop's Stortford, Herts CM22 6AQ* Tel (01279) 850281

FARRAN, Canon George Orman. b 35. Worc Coll Ox BA58 MA62. Wycliffe Hall Ox 58. **d** 60 **p** 61. C Tyldesley w Shakerley *Man* 60-62; Tutor Wycliffe Hall Ox 62-64; V Netherton *Liv* 64-73; R Sefton 69-73; R Credenhill w Brinsop, Mansel Lacey, Yazor etc *Heref* 73-83; RD Heref Rural 81-83; R Ditcheat w E Pennard and Pylle *B & W* 83-94; Dir of Ords 86-89; Can and Chan Wells Cathl 85-97; rtd 97. *Bethany, Ashton Hill, Corston, Bath BA2 9EY* Tel (01225) 872348

FARRANCE, William Kenneth. b 22. Univ of Wales (Ban) 46. Bps' Coll Cheshunt 49. **d** 52 **p** 53. C Newc St Gabr *Newc* 52-58; V Newsham 58-63; V Heddon-on-the-Wall 63-78; Chapl Tynemouth Hosps 79-82; AP Tynemouth Ch Ch 79-82; rtd 82; Perm to Offic *Newc* from 82. *5 Prestwick Terrace, Prestwick, Ponteland, Newcastle upon Tyne NE20 9BZ* Tel (01661) 825163

FARRANT, David Stuart. b 38. Ripon Coll Cuddesdon 82. **d** 84 **p** 85. C Woodford St Mary w St Phil and St Jas *Chelmsf* 84-87; P-in-c Clymping *Chich* 87; V Clymping and Yapton w Ford 87-92; Lic to Offic from 92; Dioc Schs Admin Officer from 92; Chapl Qu Alexandra's Hosp Home Worthing from 95. *101 Nutley Crescent, Goring-by-Sea, Worthing, W Sussex BN12 4LB* Tel (01903) 507458

FARRANT, Canon John Frederick Ames. b 30. Aber Univ MA51 BD58 MTh80. Edin Th Coll 51. **d** 53 **p** 54. C Dundee St Mary Magd *Bre* 53-58; R Clydebank *Glas* 58-65; R Motherwell 65-70; Papua New Guinea 70-73 and 81-84; R Glas St Bride *Glas* 73-81; Can St Mary's Cathl 77-81; Provost Rabaul 81-84; R Penicuik *Edin* 85-96; R W Linton 85-96; Can St Mary's Cathl 92-96; Chapl Madeira *Eur* from 96. *The Parsonage, rua do Quebra Costas 20, 9000 Funchal, Madeira, Portugal* Tel Madeira (91) 220674

FARRANT, Jonathan. b 44. St Mark's Dar-es-Salaam 72. **d** 73 **p** 74. Tanzania 73-78; SSF 74-78; Lic to Offic *Heref* 78-80. *Address temp unknown*

FARRANT, Canon Martyn John. b 38. AKC61. **d** 62 **p** 63. C Hampton St Mary *Lon* 62-65; C Shere *Guildf* 65-67; V Stoneleigh 67-75; V Addlestone 75-83; V Dorking w Ranmore from 83; RD Dorking 89-94; Hon Can Guildf Cathl from 96. *St Martin's Vicarage, Westcott Road, Dorking, Surrey RH4 3DP* Tel (01306) 882875

FARRAR, Canon James Albert. b 27. TCD BA55 MA57. CITC 56. **d** 56 **p** 57. C Dublin Drumcondra w N Strand *D & G* 56-59; C Dublin Rathmines 59-61; I Ballinaclash 61-72; I Dunganstown w Redcross 72-79; Warden Ch Min of Healing 79-95; Hon Clerical V Ch Ch Cathl Dublin 79-92; Can Ch Ch Cathl Dublin from 92; rtd 95. *15 Hillside, Greystones, Co Wicklow, Irish Republic* Tel Dublin (1) 287 2706

FARRELL, Peter Godfrey Paul. b 39. Sarum & Wells Th Coll 72. **d** 74 **p** 75. C St Just in Roseland *Truro* 74-77; C Kenwyn 77-80; V Knighton St Jo *Leic* 80-86; TR Clarendon Park St Jo w Knighton St Mich 86-89; V Woodham *Guildf* from 89. *The Vicarage, 25 Woodham Waye, Woodham, Woking, Surrey GU21 5SW* Tel (01483) 762857

FARRELL, Robert Edward. b 54. Univ of Wales (Abth) BA74 Jes Coll Ox BA77 MA81. Qu Coll Birm 85. **d** 86 **p** 87. C Llanrhos *St As* 86-88; C Prestwich St Marg *Man* 89-91; V Moulsham St Luke *Chelmsf* from 91. *St Luke's House, 26 Lewis Drive, Chelmsford CM2 9EF* Tel (01245) 354479

FARRELL, Ronald Anthony. b 57. Edin Univ BD84 Birm Univ MA86. Qu Coll Birm 84. **d** 86 **p** 87. C Shard End *Birm* 86-87; C Shirley 87-89; Bp's Officer for Schs and Young People 89-93; V Kingstanding St Mark from 93. *St Mark's Clergy House, Bandywood Crescent, Birmingham B44 9JX* Tel 0121-360 7288

FARRELL, Thomas Stanley. b 32. Lon Univ BD71. Ridley Hall Cam 69. **d** 71 **p** 72. C Much Woolton *Liv* 71-73; C Gt Sankey 73-74; Asst Chapl Dulwich Coll 74-76; Chapl 76-81; P-in-c Wonersh *Guildf* 81-86; V 86-90; RD Cranleigh 87-90; R St Marg Lothbury and St Steph Coleman Street etc *Lon* from 90; P-in-c St Botolph without Aldersgate 90-97. *The Rectory, 1 St Olave's Court, London EC2V 8EX* Tel 0171-600 2379 or 606 0684

FARRER, Miss Carol Elizabeth. b 47. Open Univ BA88. Cranmer Hall Dur 81. **dss** 83 **d** 87 **p** 94. Newbarns w Hawcoat *Carl* 83-86; Egremont and Haile 86-87; Par Dn 87-91; Dioc Lay Min Adv 87-88; Assoc Dir of Ords from 88; TD Penrith w Newton Reigny and Plumpton Wall 91-94; TV from 94. *4 Barco Terrace, Penrith, Cumbria CA11 8NB* Tel (01768) 899540 or 62867

FARRER, Canon Michael Robert Wedlake. b 22. St Pet Hall Ox BA52 MA57. Tyndale Hall Bris 47. **d** 52 **p** 53. C Ox St Ebbe *Ox* 52-56; Tutor Clifton Th Coll 56-65; R Barton Seagrave *Pet* 65-73; R Barton Seagrave w Warkton 73-78; V Cambridge St Paul *Ely* 78-92; RD Cambridge 84-89; Hon Can Ely Cathl 88-92; rtd 92;

Bp's Sen Chapl *Ely* 92-95. *2 Houghton Gardens, Ely, Cambs CB7 4JN* Tel (01353) 665654

FARRER, Simon James Anthony. b 52. St Cath Coll Cam MA77 BD78. AKC78 Coll of Resurr Mirfield 78. **d** 79 **p** 80. C St Jo Wood *Lon* 79-84; C N Harrow St Alb 84-87; P-in-c Hammersmith St Luke 87-93; USPG from 93; Zambia from 94. *St George's Church, PO Box 90189, Luanshya, Zambia*

FARRINGTON, Canon Christine Marion. b 42. Birkb Coll Lon BA65 Nottm Univ DASS66 Middx Poly MA75. St Alb Minl Tr Scheme 79. **dss** 82 **d** 87 **p** 94. Redbourn *St Alb* 82-87; Dir Past Studies Linc Th Coll 86-87; HM Pris Linc 86-87; Dir Sarum Chr Cen 87-93; Dn Sarum Cathl *Sarum* 87-93; Co-Dir Ords and Dir Women's Min *Ely* from 93; Hon Can Ely Cathl from 93; C Cambridge Gt St Mary w St Mich 93-96; V Cambridge St Mark from 96; Chapl Wolfs Coll Cam from 97. *St Mark's Vicarage, Barton Road, Cambridge CB3 9JZ* Tel (01223) 63339

FARROW, Edward. b 38. Sarum Th Coll 69. **d** 71 **p** 72. C Parkstone St Pet w Branksea *Sarum* 71-74; R Tidworth 74-79; P-in-c W and E Lulworth 79-80; P-in-c Winfrith Newburgh w Chaldon Herring 79-80; R The Lulworths, Winfrith Newburgh and Chaldon 80-83; V Ensbury Park from 83; Chapl Talbot Heath Sch Bournemouth 83-97. *The Vicarage, 42 Coombe Avenue, Bournemouth BH10 5AE* Tel (01202) 514286

FARROW, Elizabeth Maura. b 43. Edin Th Coll. **d** 91 **p** 96. NSM Knightswood H Cross Miss *Glas* 91-96; TV Bearsden from 96. *5 Campsie Road, Strathblane G63 9AB* Tel (01360) 770936

FARROW, Ian Edmund Dennett. b 38. S'wark Ord Course 70. **d** 72 **p** 73. C Tunbridge Wells St Jo *Roch* 72-78; Chapl N Cambs Gen Hosp Gp 78-92; P-in-c Walsoken *Ely* 78-80; R 80-92; V Bisley, Oakridge, Miserden and Edgeworth *Glouc* from 92. *The Vicarage, Monor Street, Bisley, Stroud, Glos GL6 7BJ* Tel (01452) 770056

FARROW, Peter Maurice. b 44. St Chad's Coll Dur BSc65 DipTh68. **d** 68 **p** 69. C Gt Yarmouth *Nor* 68-71; C N Lynn w St Marg and St Nic 71-75; P-in-c Sculthorpe w Dunton and Doughton 75-77; Perm to Offic 78-89; TV Lowestoft and Kirkley 89-94; Ind Miss 89-94; Sen Ind Chapl from 94; Asst RD Lothingland 94-95; TV Gaywood St Faith from 95. *The Church Bungalow, Gayton Road, King's Lynn, Norfolk PE30 4DZ* Tel (01553) 766552

FARROW, Robin Thomas Adrian. b 72. K Coll Lon BA93 AKC93. St Steph Ho Ox 94. **d** 96 **p** 97. C Lancing w Coombes *Chich* from 96. *30 Greenoaks, Lancing, W Sussex BN15 0HE* Tel (01903) 767077

FARTHING, Michael Thomas. b 28. St Cuth Soc Dur 48. Lambeth STh81 St Steph Ho Ox. **d** 58 **p** 59. C St Marylebone St Mark w St Luke *Lon* 58-63; C Newport Pagnell *Ox* 63-69; R Standlake 69-76; R Yelford 69-76; R Lower Windrush 76-82; V Wheatley w Forest Hill and Stanton St John 82-95; rtd 95. *32 Falstaff Close, Eynsham, Oxford OX8 1QA* Tel (01865) 883805

FARTHING, Ronald Edward. b 27. Oak Hill Th Coll. **d** 58 **p** 59. C Tollington Park St Anne *Lon* 58-61; C Tollington Park St Mark 58-61; V Clodock and Longtown w Craswell and Llanveyno *Heref* 61-67; R Langley *Cant* 67-72; V Bapchild w Tonge and Rodmersham 72-80; TV Widecombe, Leusden and Princetown etc *Ex* 80-84; P-in-c Riddlesworth w Gasthorpe and Knettishall *Nor* 84-87; P-in-c Garboldisham w Blo' Norton 84-87; P-in-c Brettenham w Rushford 84-87; R Garboldisham w Blo' Norton, Riddlesworth etc 88-92; rtd 92; Perm to Offic *Nor* from 92. *Fairways, New Street, Stradbroke, Eye, Suffolk IP21 5JJ* Tel (01379) 388189

FASHOLE-LUKE, Edward William. b 34. Dur Univ BA63. Cranmer Hall Dur 61. **d** 62 **p** 63. C Dur St Cuth *Dur* 62-64; Sierra Leone from 64. *Fourah Bay College, Freetown, Sierra Leone*

FASS, Michael John. b 44. Trin Coll Cam MA75. Edin Dioc NSM Course 89. **d** 95 **p** 95. NSM Penicuik *Edin* 95-97; NSM W Linton 95-97; NSM Roslin (Rosslyn Chpl) from 97. *60 Braid Road, Edinburgh EH10 6AL* Tel 0131-446 9356

FATHERS, Canon Derek Esmond. b 27. Magd Coll Ox MA50 DipEd52. St Aid Birkenhead DipTh56. **d** 56 **p** 57. Tutor St Aid Birkenhead 56-59; C W Kirby St Bridget *Ches* 59-63; V Thornton Hough 63-86; RD Wirral S 78-86; Hon Can Ches Cathl 82-92; C Woodchurch 86-89; Chapl Arrowe Park Hosp Wirral 86-92; rtd 92; Perm to Offic *Ches* from 92. *6 Ashton Drive, West Kirby, Wirral, Merseyside L48 0RQ* Tel 0151-625 1181

FATHERS, Jeremy Mark. b 54. WMMTC. **d** 96. NSM Baxterley w Hurley and Wood End and Merevale etc *Birm* from 96. *1 Colebridge Crescent, Coleshill, Birmingham B46 1HF* Tel (01675) 464047

FAULDS, John Parker. b 33. Edin Th Coll 55. **d** 57 **p** 58. C Edin St Dav *Edin* 57-58; C Edin St Jo 58-60; Chapl Dundee Hosps 60-63; Chapl Qu Coll Dundee 60-63; Dioc Supernumerary *Bre* 60-63; Lic to Offic *Birm* 65-66 and from 87; P-in-c Aston Brook 66-69; V Handsworth St Pet 69-87. *6 Little Heath Close, Audlem, Crewe CW3 0HX*

FAULKES, Edmund Marquis. b 62. Hatf Coll Dur BA. Ridley Hall Cam 87 Coates Hall Edin 90. **d** 91 **p** 92. C Broughty Ferry *Bre* 91-93; P-in-c Dundee St Ninian from 93. *St Ninian's Church House, Kingsway East, Dundee DD4 7RW* Tel (01382) 459626

FAULKNER, Brian Thomas. b 48. S Dios Minl Tr Scheme. **d** 84 **p** 85. C W Leigh *Portsm* 84-88; R Foulsham w Hindolveston and Guestwick *Nor* 88-93; P-in-c Erpingham w Calthorpe, Ingworth, Aldborough etc 93-94; R from 94. *The Rectory, Erpingham, Norwich NR11 7QX* Tel (01263) 768073

FAULKNER, David Ernest. b 43. Univ of Wales (Lamp) DipTh65. St Mich Coll Llan 65. **d** 66 **p** 67. C Aberystwyth St Mich *St D* 66-68; C Tenby and Gumfreston 68-69; C Burry Port and Pwll 69-73; R Jeffreyston w Reynalton and E Williamston 73-79; R Jeffreyston w Reynoldston and E Williamston etc 79-89; V Whitland and Kiffig 89-90; V Whitland w Cyffig and Henllan Amgoed etc 90-96; V Llawhaden w Bletherston and Llanycefn from 96. *The Vicarage, Rock Road, Llawhaden, Narberth SA67 8DS* Tel (01437) 541225

FAULKNER, Henry Odin. b 35. G&C Coll Cam BA56 MA60. St Jo Coll Nottm DipTh73. **d** 74 **p** 75. C Heigham H Trin *Nor* 74-76; C Heeley *Sheff* 76-80; TV Netherthorpe 80-84; Perm to Offic *St Alb* from 84. *69 Holywell Hill, St Albans, Herts AL1 1HF* Tel (01727) 854177

FAULKNER, Peter Charles. b 37. Chich Th Coll 72. **d** 74 **p** 75. C Armley w New Wortley *Ripon* 74-76; C Tilehurst St Mich *Ox* 76-80; V Calcot 80-82; V Hagbourne 82-88; TV W Slough 88-95; TV Aylesbury w Bierton and Hulcott from 95. *The Vicarage, St James Way, Bierton, Aylesbury, Bucks HP22 5ED* Tel (01296) 23920

FAULKNER, Peter Graham. b 47. Lon Univ CertEd69. Oak Hill Th Coll BA87. **d** 82 **p** 83. C Crofton *Portsm* 87-89; R Mid Marsh Gp *Linc* from 89. *The Rectory, 37 Tinkle Street, Grimoldby, Louth, Lincs LN11 8SW* Tel (01507) 327429

FAULKNER, Robert Henry. b 20. St Edm Hall Ox BA48 MA53. Wycliffe Hall Ox 48. **d** 50 **p** 51. V Thame w Towersey *Ox* 60-85; R Aston Sandford 73-85; rtd 85; Perm to Offic *Ox* from 85. *5 Mavor Close, Old Woodstock, Oxon OX20 1YL* Tel (01993) 812059

FAULKNER, Canon Roger Kearton. b 36. AKC62. **d** 63 **p** 64. C Oxton *Ches* 63-67; C Ellesmere Port 67-69; V Runcorn H Trin 69-73; TV E Runcorn w Halton 73-76; V Altrincham St Geo 76-90; Chapl Altrincham Gen Hosp 80-96; Hon Can Ches Cathl *Ches* 88-96; V Higher Bebington 90-96; rtd 96; Perm to Offic *Ches* from 96. *58 Albermarle Road, Wallasey, Wirral, Merseyside L44 6LX*

FAULKS, David William. b 45. EMMTC 82. **d** 86 **p** 87. C Market Harborough *Leic* 86-88; C Wootton Bassett *Sarum* 88-90; R Clipston w Naseby and Haselbech w Kelmarsh *Pet* from 90. *The Rectory, 18 Church Lane, Clipston, Market Harborough, Leics LE16 9RW* Tel (01858) 525342

FAULL, The Very Revd Cecil Albert. b 30. TCD BA52. **d** 54 **p** 55. C Dublin Zion Ch *D & G* 54-57; C Dublin St Geo 57-59; Hon Clerical V Ch Ch Cathl Dublin 58-63; C Dun Laoghaire 59-63; I Portarlington w Cloneyhurke and Lea *M & K* 63-71; I Dublin St Geo and St Thos *D & G* 71-80; I Clondalkin w Rathcoole 81-91; Can Ch Ch Cathl Dublin 90-91; I Dunleckney w Nurney, Lorum and Kiltennel *C & O* 91-96; Dean Leighlin from 91; P-in-c Leighlin w Grange Sylvae, Shankill etc from 91. *136 Beech Park, Lucan, Co Dublin, Irish Republic* Tel Dublin (1) 628 0593

FAULL, Canon Vivienne Frances. b 55. St Hilda's Coll Ox BA77 MA82 Clare Coll Cam MA90. St Jo Coll Nottm BA81 DPS82. **dss** 82 **d** 87 **p** 94. Mossley Hill St Matt and St Jas *Liv* 82-85; Chapl Clare Coll Cam 85-90; Chapl Glouc Cathl *Glouc* 90-94; Can Res Cov Cathl *Cov* from 94; Vice-Provost from 95. *35 Morningside, Coventry CV5 6PD* Tel (01203) 675446 or 227597 Fax 631448

FAULL, William Baines. b 29. FRCVS Lon Univ BSc51. NW Ord Course 77. **d** 79 **p** 80. NSM Willaston *Ches* 79-80; NSM Neston 80-82; P-in-c Harthill and Burwardsley 82-86; Perm to Offic 87-91; Sen Fell Liv Univ from 89; V Ashton Hayes *Ches* 91-96; rtd 96. *Tioman, Briardale Road, Willaston, South Wirral L64 1TD* Tel 0151-327 4424

FAVELL, Brian Jeffrey. b 23. Cuddesdon Coll 64. **d** 66 **p** 67. C Rubery *Birm* 66-69; Lic to Offic 70-76; V Cwmtillery *Mon* 76-86; P-in-c Six Bells 77-86; RD Blaenau Gwent 83-86; V Cwmcarn 86-88; rtd 88. *3 Church Street, Fladbury, Pershore, Worcs WR10 2QB* Tel (01386) 860585

FAWCETT, Canon Frederick William. TCD BA49 MA52. CITC 50. **d** 50 **p** 51. C Belfast St Aid *Conn* 50-52; C-in-c Draperstown *D & R* 52-59; I 59-60; I Cumber Upper w Learmount 60-87; Can Derry Cathl from 86; I Camus-juxta-Mourne from 87. *The Rectory, Newtown Street, Strabane, Co Tyrone BT82 8DW* Tel (01504) 882314

FAWCETT, Canon Pamela Margaret. b 29. Univ Coll Lon BA52 DipEd75. EAMTC 83. **dss** 86 **d** 87 **p** 94. Stiffkey w Morston, Langham Episcopi etc *Nor* 86-87; Hon C Stiffkey and Cockthorpe w Morston, Langham etc 87-90; Hon Asst Min Repps Deanery 91-93; Hon C Trunch from 93; Asst Dioc Dir of Ords from 93; Bp's Consultant for Women's Min from 93; Hon Can Nor Cathl from 94. *Seekings, 47A High Street, Mundesley, Norwich NR11 8JL* Tel (01263) 721752

FAWCETT, Timothy John. b 44. K Coll Lon BD66 AKC67 PhD71. **d** 67 **p** 68. C Blackpool St Steph *Blackb* 67-70; Hon C St Marylebone All SS *Lon* 68-70; C Southgate St Mich 70-72; Sacr Dur Cathl *Dur* 72-75; V Wheatley Hill 75-79; V Torrisholme

Blackb 79-84; V Thaxted *Chelmsf* 84-89; Perm to Offic *Nor* 89-94; NSM Holt Deanery from 94. *Dowitchers, 14 The Cornfield, Langham, Holt, Norfolk NR25 7DQ* Tel (01328) 830415

FAYERS, Robert Stanley. b 48. DipFD. St Steph Ho Ox 82. **d** 84 **p** 85. C Deptford St Paul *S'wark* 84-88; V Beckenham St Mich w St Aug *Roch* from 88. *St Michael's Vicarage, 120 Birkbeck Road, Beckenham, Kent BR3 4SS* Tel 0181-778 6569

FAYLE, David Charles Wilfred. b 51. Sarum & Wells Th Coll. **d** 83 **p** 84. C Parkstone St Pet w Branksea and St Osmund *Sarum* 83-87; TV Dorchester 87-96; P-in-c Taunton All SS *B & W* from 96. *All Saints' Vicarage, Roman Road, Taunton, Somerset TA1 2DE* Tel (01823) 324730

FAZZANI, Keith. b 47. Portsm Poly BSc70. Cant Sch of Min 93. **d** 96. NSM Appledore w Brookland, Fairfield, Brenzett etc *Cant* from 96. *Oakhouse Farm, Appledore, Ashford, Kent TN26 2BB* Tel (01233) 758322

FEAK, Christopher Martin (Chris). b 52. Keele Univ BA75 Trent Poly DCG76. Trin Coll Bris DipHE94. **d** 94 **p** 95. C Handsworth St Mary *Birm* from 94. *43 St Christophers, Birmingham B20 1BP* Tel 0121-554 7749

FEARN, Anthony John. b 34. Lich Th Coll 58. **d** 61 **p** 62. C Redditch St Steph *Worc* 61-64; C Bladon w Woodstock *Ox* 64-66; V Ruscombe and Twyford 67-85; P-in-c Westmill w Gt Munden *St Alb* 85-87; Asst Dioc Stewardship Adv 85-87; Chr Giving Adv *Heref* from 87. *Crozen Cottage, Felton, Hereford HR1 3PW* Tel (01432) 820161 Fax as telephone

FEARN, Michael Wilfrid (Mike). b 47. MBIM MIHT Plymouth Poly 70. Sarum & Wells Th Coll DipTh94. **d** 94 **p** 95. C Blandford Forum and Langton Long *Sarum* from 94. *50 East Leaze Road, Blandford Forum, Dorset DT11 7UN* Tel (01258) 480445

FEARN, Robert Benjamin. b 27. Bps' Coll Cheshunt 62. **d** 64 **p** 65. C Newark St Mary *S'well* 64-68; V Basford St Aid 68-74; V Beckingham w Walkeringham 74-83; V N and S Muskham 83-94; R Averham w Kelham 83-94; rtd 94. *Brentwood, Low Street, Elston, Newark, Notts NG23 5PA* Tel (01636) 525138

FEARNLEY, Jeffrey Malcolm. b 46. Newc Univ BSc69. St Jo Coll Nottm DCM92. **d** 92 **p** 93. C Bispham *Blackb* 92-95; C Bolton w Ireby and Uldale *Carl* from 95. *The Rectory, Ireby, Carlisle CA5 1EX* Tel (01697) 371307

FEARON, Mrs Doris Ethel Elizabeth. b 26. Gilmore Ho 66. **dss** 72 **d** 87. Lingfield *S'wark* 68-75; Farnborough *Roch* 75-77; Bitterne *Win* 78-86; rtd 86; Bexhill St Pet *Chich* 86-87; Hon Par Dn 87-89; Perm to Offic 89-95. *4 Huapai Street, Onehunga, Auckland 6, New Zealand*

FEAST, Robert Butler. b 08. Trin Hall Cam BA30 MA36. Cuddesdon Coll 30. **d** 31 **p** 32. C Guisborough *York* 31-35; V Thetford St Mary *Nor* 36-42; Chapl RN 39-46; R Somerleyton w Ashby *Nor* 46-53; R Litcham w Kempston 53-56; R Swainsthorpe w Newton Flotman 56-69; R Northlew w Ashbury *Ex* 69-73; rtd 73. *Rose Cottage, Boddington Lane, Northleigh, Witney, Oxon OX8 6PU* Tel (01993) 881396

FEATHERSTONE, Andrew. b 53. St Chad's Coll Dur BA74. Sarum & Wells Th Coll 78. **d** 80 **p** 81. C Newc H Cross *Newc* 80-83; C Seaton Hirst 83-86; TV 86-87; R Crook *Dur* from 87; V Stanley from 87; RD Stanhope from 94. *The Rectory, 14 Hartside Close, Crook, Co Durham DL15 9NH* Tel (01388) 764024 E-mail andrew@andf.demon.co.uk

FEATHERSTONE, Gray. b 42. Stellenbosch Univ BA62 LLB64. Cuddesdon Coll. **d** 67 **p** 68. S Africa 67-70; Swaziland 70-72; Portuguese E Africa 73-75; Mozambique 75-76; Miss to Seamen 76-80; V Upper Clapton St Matt *Lon* 80-83; V Stamford Hill St Thos 80-89; Chr Aid Area Sec (NW Lon) from 89. *1 Oak Lane, London N2 8LP* Tel 0181-349 1838 or 0171-620 4444 Fax 0171-620 0719

FEATHERSTONE, John. b 23. Kelham Th Coll 40. **d** 46 **p** 47. C Swinton St Pet *Man* 46-51; V Glodwick Ch Ch 51-55; V Dormanstown *York* 55-61; R Roos w Tunstall 61-66; V Garton w Grimston and Hilston 61-66; V Longford *Derby* 66-70; V Alkmonton w Yeaveley 66-70; V Chaddesden St Phil 70-72; V Denby 72-77; R Whitwell 77-84; RD Bolsover and Staveley 78-81; P-in-c Gt Barlow 84-88; rtd 88; Perm to Offic *Derby* from 88. *16 Fern Close, Eckington, Sheffield S31 9HE* Tel (01246) 432440

FEATHERSTONE, John. b 32. Man Univ BA53 St Cath Soc Ox MTh59 Dur Univ DipEd66. Wycliffe Hall Ox 57. **d** 60 **p** 61. C Newland St Aug *York* 60-62; C Kidderminster St Jo and H Innocents *Worc* 62-65; Hd RE Co Gr Sch Pet 66-70; Hd RE Qu Anne Gr Sch York 70-85; Chapl Tangier *Eur* 86-87 and 90-93; Chapl Pau w Biarritz 87-88; C Mexborough *Sheff* 88-90; rtd 93; Perm to Offic *York* from 93. *39 Cambridge Avenue, Marton-in-Cleveland, Middlesbrough, Cleveland TS7 8EH* Tel (01642) 318181

FEATHERSTONE, Robert Leslie. b 54. LLCM74 Lon Univ CertEd75. Chich Th Coll 84. **d** 86 **p** 87. C Crayford *Roch* 86-89; V Belvedere St Aug 89-94; V Withyham St Jo *Chich* from 94. *St John's Vicarage, St John's Road, Crowborough, E Sussex TN6 1RZ* Tel (01892) 654660

✠**FEAVER, The Rt Revd Douglas Russell.** b 14. Keble Coll Ox BA35 MA39. Wells Th Coll 37. **d** 38 **p** 39 **c** 72. C St Alb Abbey *St Alb* 38-42; Chapl RAFVR 42-46; Can Res and Sub-Dean St Alb *St Alb* 46-58; V Nottingham St Mary *S'well* 58-72; RD Nottingham 58-72; Hon Can S'well Minster 58-72; Bp Pet 72-84; rtd 84; Perm to Offic *Ely* from 85; Perm to Offic *B & W* 85-95. *6 Mill Lane, Bruton, Somerset BA10 0AT* Tel (01749) 813485

FEENEY, Damian Prescott Anthony. b 62. ALCM81 Grey Coll Dur BA83 PGCE84. Chich Th Coll BTh94. **d** 94 **p** 95. C Harrogate St Wilfrid *Ripon* 94-96; C Preston St Jo and St Geo *Blackb* from 96. *Glebe House, 33 Bairstow Street, Preston PR1 3TN* Tel (01772) 884921

FEHRENBACH, Donald Joseph. b 17. Selw Coll Cam BA49 MA53. Qu Coll Birm 49. **d** 51 **p** 52. C Beverley Minster *York* 51-54; Min Can Sarum Cathl *Sarum* 54-59; Min Can Windsor 59-65; V Sandford-on-Thames *Ox* 65-84; rtd 84; Perm to Offic *Ox* from 84. *2 Walbury, Bracknell, Berks RG12 9JB* Tel (01344) 640062

FEIST, Nicholas James. b 45. Solicitor 70. St Jo Coll Nottm LTh76. **d** 76 **p** 77. C Didsbury St Jas *Man* 76-80; TV Didsbury St Jas and Em 80; V Friarmere 80-88; R Middleton 88-94; TR Middleton w Thornham from 94. *St Leonard's Rectory, Mellalieu Street, Middleton, Manchester M24 3DN* Tel 0161-643 2693

FEIT, Michael John. b 24. FICE68 FIStructE68. S'wark Ord Course. **d** 69 **p** 71. C Feltham *Lon* 69-76; C Ashford St Matt 76-78; C Hykeham *Linc* 78-81; V Cranwell 81-85; R Leasingham 81-85; R Bishop Norton, Wadingham and Snitterby 85-90; rtd 90. *14717-109A Avenue, Surrey, British Columbia, Canada, V3R 1Y7*

FELCE, Brian George. b 30. Jes Coll Ox BA54 MA57. Oak Hill Th Coll. **d** 58 **p** 59. C E Twickenham St Steph *Lon* 58-60; C Ramsgate St Luke *Cant* 60-64; R Bedingfield w Southolt *St E* 64-73; V Preston All SS *Blackb* 73-86; rtd 86. *11 St Barnabas Road, Sutton, Surrey SM1 4NL* Tel 0181-642 7885

FELIX, David Rhys. b 55. Solicitor 81 Univ of Wales (Cardiff) LLB76. Ripon Coll Cuddesdon 83. **d** 86 **p** 87. C Bromborough *Ches* 86-89; V Grange St Andr from 89; Chapl Halton Gen Hosp from 95; P-in-c Runcorn H Trin *Ches* from 96. *37 Lime Grove, Runcorn, Cheshire WA7 5JZ* Tel (01928) 574411

FELIX, Donald Cameron. b 24. St Aid Birkenhead 64. **d** 65 **p** 66. C Walsall *Lich* 65-68; V Pype Hayes *Birm* 68-73; V Burslem St Paul *Lich* 73-76; V Bloxwich 76-79; P-in-c Seighford, Derrington and Cresswell 79-81; V 81-86; V Hanbury w Newborough 86-94; rtd 94; NSM Hanbury w Newborough *Lich* 94-97; NSM Hanbury w Newborough and Rangemore from 97. *The New Vicarage, Hanbury, Burton-on-Trent, Staffs DE13 8TF* Tel (01283) 813357

FELL, Canon Alan William. b 46. Ball Coll Ox BA69 Leeds Univ DipTh70. Coll of Resurr Mirfield 68. **d** 71 **p** 72. C Woodchurch *Ches* 71-74; C Man Clayton St Cross w St Paul *Man* 74-75; C Prestwich St Marg 75-77; V Hyde St Thos *Ches* 77-80; R Tattenhall and Handley 80-86; V Sedbergh, Cautley and Garsdale *Bradf* from 86; Hon C Firbank, Howgill and Killington from 86; Hon Can Bradf Cathl from 96. *The Vicarage, Loftus Hill, Sedbergh, Cumbria LA10 5SQ* Tel (015396) 20283

FELL, Stephen. b 18. St Jo Coll Dur LTh41 BA42. Oak Hill Th Coll 38. **d** 42 **p** 43. C Preston Em *Blackb* 42-45; C Tottenham All Hallows *Lon* 45-49; C Luton St Mary *St Alb* 49-52; R Toddington 52-58; R Castleford All SS *Wakef* 58-83; rtd 83. *255 Lower Mickletown, Methley, Leeds LS26 9AN* Tel (01977) 515530

FELL, Willis Marshall. b 29. NW Ord Course 73. **d** 75 **p** 76. C Bolsover *Derby* 75-78; C Clay Cross 78-80; V Brampton St Mark 80-94; rtd 95; Perm to Offic *Derby* from 95. *The Willows, 12 Brandene Close, Calow, Chesterfield, Derbyshire S44 5TS* Tel (01246) 270824

FELLINGHAM, John. b 25. RMC 44. Lon Coll of Div 52. **d** 55 **p** 56. C Pakefield *Nor* 55-59; R Coltishall w Gt Hautbois 59-70; P-in-c Horstead 62-65; Chapl RAF 63-65; RD Ingworth *Nor* 65-70; Chapl HM Pris Nor 69-73; P-in-c Nor St Helen *Nor* 70-73; Perm to Offic from 73; rtd 90; Asst Chapl HM Pris Wayland 90-96. *Fielding Cottage, Anchor Corner, Attleborough, Norfolk NR17 1JX* Tel (01953) 455185

FELLOWS, Grant. b 56. K Coll Lon BD77 AKC77. Coll of Resurr Mirfield 79. **d** 80 **p** 81. C Addington *Cant* 80-84; C S Gillingham *Roch* 84-86; V Heath and Reach *St Alb* 86-94; V Radlett from 94. *The Vicarage, Church Field, Christchurch Crescent, Radlett, Herts WD7 8EE* Tel (01923) 856606

FELLOWS, John Lambert. b 35. LTCL67 SS Mark & Jo Coll Chelsea CertEd58. Portsm Dioc Tr Course 86. **d** 88. NSM Portsea St Cuth *Portsm* 88-94; NSM Farlington from 94. *7 Court Lane, Portsmouth PO6 2LG* Tel (01705) 377270

FELLOWS, John Michael. b 46. Or Coll Ox MA77. Coll of Resurr Mirfield 74. **d** 77 **p** 78. C Kings Heath *Birm* 77-80; TV E Ham w Upton Park St Alb *Chelmsf* 80-85; P-in-c Wormingford 85-90; P-in-c Mt Bures 85-90; P-in-c Lt Horkesley 85-90; V Wormingford, Mt Bures and Lt Horkesley 90; R Compton w Shackleford and Peper Harow *Guildf* from 90. *The Rectory, The Street, Compton, Guildford, Surrey GU3 1ED* Tel (01483) 810328

FELLOWS, Peter William. b 48. CertEd70 DipEd79. Chich Th Coll 86. **d** 88 **p** 89. C Westmr St Steph w St Jo *Lon* 88-93; R

Deptford St Paul *S'wark* from 93. *St Paul's Rectory, 35 Albury Street, London SE8 3PT* Tel 0181-692 0989

FELTHAM, Keith. b 40. Lon Univ DipTh66. **d** 75 **p** 76. In Bapt Ch 66-75; C Plympton St Mary *Ex* 75-79; TV Northam w Westward Ho! and Appledore 79-82; TR Lynton, Brendon, Countisbury, Lynmouth etc 82-85; P-in-c Bickleigh (Plymouth) 85-86; TR 86-91; Chapl R Bournemouth Gen Hosp 91-95; P-in-c Whimple, Talaton and Clyst St Lawr *Ex* from 95. *The Rectory, Grove Road, Whimple, Exeter EX5 2TP* Tel (01404) 822521

FENN, Norman Alexander. b 20. Kelham Th Coll 37. **d** 43 **p** 44. C Tunstall Ch Ch *Lich* 43-47; C Leek St Edw 47-51; V Tilstock 51-55; V Milton 55-61; V Ellesmere 61-85; V Welsh Frankton 62-85; RD Ellesmere 70-85; rtd 85; Perm to Offic *Lich* from 85. *1 Larkhill Road, Oswestry, Shropshire SY11 4AW* Tel (01691) 659411

FENN, Dr Roy William Dearnley. b 33. FRHistS70 FCP86 FSA88 Jes Coll Ox BA54 MA59 BD68. St Mich Coll Llan 54. **d** 56 **p** 57. C Swansea St Mary and H Trin *S & B* 57-59; C Cardiff St Jo *Llan* 59-60; C Coity w Nolton 60-63; V Glascombe w Rhulen and Gregrina *S & B* 63-68; V Glascwm and Rhulen 68-74; P-in-c Letton w Staunton, Byford, Mansel Gamage etc *Heref* 75-79; Perm to Offic *S & B* 80-85; Perm to Offic *Heref* 85-95. *9 Victoria Road, Kington, Herefordshire HR5 3BX* Tel (01544) 230018

FENNELL, Canon Alfred Charles Dennis. b 15. Bp's Coll Calcutta 35. **d** 38 **p** 39. India 38-48; C Kensington St Helen w H Trin *Lon* 48-50; Min Queensbury All SS 50-54; V 54-62; Prec Birm Cathl *Birm* 62-65; V Yardley St Cypr Hay Mill 65-80; Hon Can Birm Cathl 78-80; rtd 80; Perm to Offic *Birm* from 80. *27 Madresfield Road, Malvern, Worcs WR14 2AS* Tel (01684) 560613

FENNELL, Anthony Frederick Rivers. b 26. Pemb Coll Cam BA50 MA55 York Univ BPhil76. Ab Dioc Tr Course 90. **d** 90 **p** 91. NSM Braemar *Ab* from 90; NSM Ballater from 90; NSM Aboyne from 90. *19 Craigendarroch Circle, Ballater, Aberdeenshire AB35 5ZA* Tel (01339) 755048

FENNEMORE, Nicholas Paul. b 53. Wycliffe Hall Ox 76. **d** 79 **p** 80. C N Mymms *St Alb* 79-82; C Chipping Barnet w Arkley 82-83; TV 83-84; TV Preston w Sutton Poyntz and Osmington w Poxwell *Sarum* 84-86; Chapl St Helier Hosp Carshalton 86-90; Chapl Jo Radcliffe Hosp Ox 90-94; Chapl Ox Radcliffe Hosp NHS Trust 94-96; Sen Chapl from 96. *John Radcliffe Hospital, Oxford OX3 9DU* Tel (01865) 741166 or 221732

FENNING, John Edward. b 32. CITC 86. **d** 88 **p** 89. NSM Douglas Union w Frankfield *C, C & R* 88-89; Chapl Ashton Sch Cork 88-96; NSM Moviddy Union *C, C & R* from 89. *Moviddy Rectory, Aherla, Co Cork, Irish Republic* Tel Cork (21) 331511 or 966044 Fax 966321

FENSOME, Anthony David (Tony). b 49. DipYL74 Open Univ BA89. Sarum & Wells Th Coll 82. **d** 84 **p** 85. C Gtr Corsham *Bris* 84-88; P-in-c Lyddington w Wanborough 88-91; P-in-c Bishopstone w Hinton Parva 88-91; R Lyddington and Wanborough and Bishopstone etc 91-93; V Chippenham St Pet from 93; RD Chippenham from 94. *St Peter's Vicarage, Lords Mead, Chippenham, Wilts SN14 0LL* Tel (01249) 654835

FENTIMAN, David Frank. b 43. RIBA74 Poly Cen Lon DipArch72. S Dios Minl Tr Scheme 90. **d** 93 **p** 94. NSM Hastings St Clem and All SS *Chich* from 93. *4 Barnfield Close, Hastings, E Sussex TN34 1TS* Tel (01424) 432854

FENTON, Barry Dominic. b 59. Leeds Univ BA85. Coll of Resurr Mirfield 85. **d** 87 **p** 88. C Leigh Park *Portsm* 87-90; Chapl and Prec Portsm Cathl 90-95; Prec Westmr Abbey from 95. *7 Little Cloister, London SW1P 3PL* Tel 0171-222 6428 or 222 4023 Fax 233 2072

FENTON, Christopher Miles Tempest. b 28. MInstPC75 Qu Coll Cam BA50 LLB51 MA55. Ridley Hall Cam 52. **d** 54 **p** 55. C Welling *Roch* 54-57; Lic to Offic *Bradf* 57-63; Chapl Malsis Prep Sch Keighley 57-63; C Hove Bp Hannington Memorial Ch *Chich* 63-65; V Ramsgate Ch Ch *Cant* 65-71; Hd Dept of Gp Studies Westmr Past Foundn 71-83; P-in-c Mottingham St Andr *S'wark* 71-73; Sen Tutor Cambs Consultancy in Counselling 73-85; Perm to Offic *Ely* 73-85; Co-ord of Tr St Alb Past Foundn 80-88; Perm to Offic *St Alb* 80-88; Dir St Anne's Trust for Psychotherapy Ledbury from 85; Perm to Offic *Heref* from 85; rtd 93. *The Leys, Aston, Kingsland, Leominster, Herefordshire HR6 9PU* Tel (01568) 708632

FENTON, Heather. b 48. Trin Coll Bris CertEd78. **d** 87 **p** 97. C Corwen and Llangar *St As* 87-89; C Corwen and Llangar w Gwyddelwern and Llawrybetws from 89; Dioc Rural Min Co-ord from 87. *Coleg y Groes, The College, Corwen LL21 0AU* Tel (01490) 412169

FENTON, Ian Christopher Stuart. b 40. AKC62. **d** 63 **p** 64. C Banstead *Guildf* 63-67; V N Holmwood 67-84; RD Dorking 80-84; V Witley from 84. *The Vicarage, Petworth Road, Witley, Godalming, Surrey GU8 5LT* Tel (01428) 682886

FENTON, Canon John Charles. b 21. Qu Coll Ox BA43 MA47 BD53. Linc Th Coll 43. **d** 44 **p** 45. C Hindley All SS *Liv* 44-47; Chapl Linc Th Coll 47-51; Sub-Warden 51-54; V Wentworth *Sheff* 54-58; Prin Lich Th Coll 58-65; Prin St Chad's Coll Dur 65-78; Can Res Ch Ch *Ox* 78-91; rtd 91; Hon Can Ch Ch *Ox* 91-92. *8 Rowland Close, Oxford OX2 8PW* Tel (01865) 554099

FENTON, Michael John. b 42. Linc Th Coll 67. **d** 69 **p** 70. C Guiseley *Bradf* 69-72; C Heswall *Ches* 72-75; TV Birkenhead Priory 75-81; V Alvanley 81-91; Chapl Crossley Hosp Cheshire 82-91; V Holbrook and Lt Eaton *Derby* from 91. *The Vicarage, 30 Moorside Lane, Holbrook, Belper, Derbyshire DE56 0TW* Tel (01332) 880254

FENTON, Miss Penelope Ann (Penny). b 41. Leic Univ BSc64. Cant Sch of Min 92. **d** 95 **p** 96. NSM Eastling w Ospringe and Stalisfield w Otterden *Cant* from 95. *9 Brogdale Road, Faversham, Kent ME13 8SX* Tel (01795) 536366

FENTON, Vincent Thompson. b 52. 94. **d** 96 **p** 97. C Heworth St Mary *Dur* from 96. *24 Hopedene, Leam Lane, Gateshead, Tyne & Wear NE10 8JB* Tel 0191-442 2860

FENTON, Canon Wallace. b 32. TCD. **d** 64 **p** 65. C Glenavy *Conn* 64-67; I Tullaniskin w Clonoe *Arm* 67-87; Bp's C Sallaghy *Clogh* 87-96; Warden of Readers 91-96; RD Clones 93-96; Preb Clogh Cathl 95-96; I Kilwarlin Upper w Kilwarlin Lower *D & D* from 96. *Kilwarlin Rectory, 9 St John's Road, Hillsborough, Co Down BT26 6ED* Tel (01846) 683299

FENWICK, Edward Hartwig. b 05. Fitzw Coll Cam BA33 MA43. Westcott Ho Cam 32. **d** 33 **p** 34. C Benwell St Aid *Newc* 33-35; C Monkwearmouth St Andr *Dur* 35-38; V Benfieldside 38-60; Chapl Shotley Bridge Gen Hosp 40-60; India 46-47; R Lapworth *Birm* 60-76; R Baddesley Clinton 60-76; rtd 76; C Solihull *Birm* 76-90. *1 St Alphege Close, Church Hill Road, Solihull, W Midlands B91 3RQ* Tel 0121-704 4736

FENWICK, Canon Jeffrey Robert. b 30. Pemb Coll Cam BA53 MA57. Linc Th Coll 53. **d** 55 **p** 56. C Upholland *Liv* 55-58; S Rhodesia 58-64; Area Sec (Dio Ox) USPG 64-65; Rhodesia 65-78; Adn Charter 73-75; Dean Bulawayo 75-78; Adn Bulawayo 75-78; Can Res Worc Cathl *Worc* 78-89; R Guernsey St Peter Port *Win* 89-95; Dean Guernsey 89-95; Hon Can Win Cathl 89-95; Pres Guernsey Miss to Seamen 89-95; rtd 95; Zimbabwe from 95. *4 Moffat Avenue, Hillside, Bulawayo, Zimbabwe*

FENWICK, Dr John Robert Kipling. b 51. Van Mildert Coll Dur BSc72 Nottm Univ BA74 MTh78 K Coll Lon PhD85. Lambeth STh84 St Jo Coll Nottm 72. **d** 77 **p** 78. C Dalton-in-Furness *Carl* 77-80; Lect Trin Coll Bris 80-88; Chapl 80-87; Lic to Offic *Bris* 81-88; Abp Cant's Asst Sec for Ecum Affairs 88-92; NSM Purley Ch Ch *S'wark* 88-92; Asst ChStJ from 89; R Chorley St Laur *Blackb* from 92. *The Rectory, Rectory Close, Chorley, Lancs PR7 1QW* Tel (01257) 263114

FENWICK, Canon Malcolm Frank. b 38. Cranmer Hall Dur 62. **d** 65 **p** 66. C Tynemouth Cullercoats St Paul *Newc* 65-68; C Bywell St Pet 68-73; V Alnmouth 73-75; CF (TAVR) 75-83; V Lesbury w Alnmouth *Newc* 75-80; V Delaval 80-91; RD Bedlington 83-88; V Riding Mill from 91; P-in-c Whittonstall from 91; Chapl Shepherd's Dene Retreat Ho from 91; RD Corbridge from 93; Hon Can Newc Cathl from 97. *The Vicarage, Oaklands, Riding Mill, Northd NE44 6AS* Tel (01434) 682811

FENWICK, The Very Revd Richard David. b 43. FLCM68 FTCL76 Univ of Wales (Lamp) BA66 MA86 TCD MusB79 MA92 Univ of Wales (Lamp) PhD95. Ridley Hall Cam 66. **d** 68 **p** 69. C Skewen *Llan* 68-72; C Penarth w Lavernock 72-74; PV, Succ and Sacr Roch Cathl *Roch* 74-78; Min Can St Paul's Cathl *Lon* 78-79; Min Can and Succ 79-83; Warden Coll Min Cans 81-83; PV Westmr Abbey 83-90; V Ruislip St Martin *Lon* 83-90; Can Res and Prec Guildf Cathl *Guildf* 90-97; Sub-Dean 96-97; Dean Mon from 97; V Newport St Woolos from 97. *The Deanery, Stow Hill, Newport NP9 4ED* Tel (01633) 263338

FEREDAY, Adrian Paul. b 57. Huddersfield Poly CQSW88 DipSocWork88. Coll of Resurr Mirfield 92. **d** 94 **p** 95. C Gleadless *Sheff* 94-96; TV Aston cum Aughton w Swallownest, Todwick etc from 96. *The Vicarage, 27 Skipton Road, Swallownest, Sheffield S31 0NQ* Tel 0114-287 9271

FEREDAY, Harold James Rodney (Rod). b 46. Sheff Univ CEIR76. St Jo Coll Nottm 87. **d** 89 **p** 90. C Rastrick St Matt *Wakef* 89-92; V Siddal from 92. *St Mark's Vicarage, 15 Whitegate Road, Siddal, Halifax, W Yorkshire HX3 9AD* Tel (01422) 369558

FERGUSON, Aean Michael O'Shaun. b 39. CITC 87. **d** 90 **p** 91. NSM Kilmallock w Kilflynn, Kilfinane, Knockaney etc *L & K* 90-91; NSM Killaloe w Stradbally 91-94; NSM Adare w Kilpeacon and Croom 94-97; C Killala w Dunfeeny, Crossmolina, Kilmoremoy etc *T, K & A* from 97. *The Rectory, Crossmolina, Ballina, Co Mayo, Irish Republic* Tel Mayo (96) 31384 Mobile 086-812 1020

FERGUSON, Dr Alastair Stuart. b 45. MRCS69 LRCP69 Ball Coll Ox BA78 MA82 Lon Univ MB, BS69. St Steph Ho Ox. **d** 82 **p** 83. NSM Dengie w Asheldham *Chelmsf* 82-86; NSM Mayland 86-89; NSM Steeple 86-89; Perm to Offic 89-91; Zimbabwe from 91. *St Andrew's Rectory, PO Box 21, Mvurwi, Zimbabwe* Tel Mvurwi (77) 2401

FERGUSON, Anthony David Norman. b 51. Wycliffe Hall Ox 75. **d** 78 **p** 79. C Tipton St Matt *Lich* 78-79; USA from 79. *5042 Timuquana Road, Jacksonville, Florida 32210, USA*

FERGUSON, Ian John. b 51. Aber Univ BD77. Trin Coll Bris 77. **d** 78 **p** 79. C Foord St Jo *Cant* 78-82; C Bieldside *Ab* 82-86; Dioc Youth Chapl 82-86; P-in-c Westhill 86-96; R from 96. *1 Westwood Drive, Westhill, Skeene, Aberdeenshire AB32 6WW* Tel (01224) 740007

FERGUSON, John Aitken. b 40. ARCST64 Glas Univ BSc64 Strathclyde Univ PhD74 CEng MICE. Linc Th Coll 79. **d** 81 **p** 82.

C Morpeth *Newc* 81-85; V Whittingham and Edlingham w Bolton Chapel 85-96. *Cold Harbour Cottage, Cold Harbour, Berwick-upon-Tweed TD15 2TQ*

FERGUSON, John Richard Preston. b 34. CITC 63. **d** 65 **p** 66. C Dundela *D & D* 65-70; I Annahilt 70-76; I Belfast St Brendan 76-94; rtd 94. *49 Kinedale Park, Ballynahinch, Co Down BT24 8YS* Tel (01238) 562599

FERGUSON, Mrs Kathleen (Kathy). b 46. ALA76 LMH Ox BA68 MA72. **d** 88 **p** 97. NSM Llanidloes w Llangurig *Ban* from 88. *Oerle, Trefeglwys, Caersws SY17 5QX* Tel (01686) 430626

FERGUSON, Michelle. Ottawa Univ BA. Cranmer Hall Dur. **d** 95 **p** 96. NSM Gt Aycliffe *Dur* from 95; Chapl Asst HM Pris Holme Ho from 97. *4 Highside Road, Heighington Village, Newton Aycliffe, Co Durham DL5 6PG* Tel (01325) 320860

FERGUSON, Canon Paul John. b 55. FRCO75 New Coll Ox BA76 MA80 K Coll Cam BA84 MA88. Westcott Ho Cam 82. **d** 85 **p** 86. C Ches St Mary *Ches* 85-88; Sacr and Chapl Westmr Abbey 88-92; Prec 92-95; Can Res and Prec York Minster *York* from 95. *2 Minster Court, York YO1 2JJ* Tel (01904) 624965 or 642526 Fax 654604

FERGUSON, Richard Archie. b 39. Dur Univ BA62. Linc Th Coll 62. **d** 64 **p** 65. C Stretford St Matt *Man* 64-68; Bp's Dom Chapl *Dur* 68-69; C Newc St Geo *Newc* 69-71; V Glodwick *Man* 71-77; V Tynemouth Ch Ch *Newc* 77-82; P-in-c Tynemouth St Aug 82-87; V Tynemouth Ch Ch w H Trin 82-87; TR N Shields 87-90; TR Upton cum Chalvey *Ox* 90-95; V Kirkwhelpington, Kirkharle, Kirkheaton and Cambo *Newc* from 95; RD Morpeth from 95. *The Vicarage, Kirkwhelpington, Newcastle upon Tyne NE19 2RT* Tel (01830) 540260

FERGUSON, Robert Garnett Allen. b 48. Leeds Univ LLB70 Clare Coll Cam. Cuddesdon Coll 71. **d** 73 **p** 74. C Wakef Cathl *Wakef* 73-76; V Lupset 76-83; Chapl Cheltenham Coll 83-87; Sen Chapl Win Coll from 87. *Winchester College, Winchester, Hants SO23 9NA* Tel (01962) 884056

FERGUSON, Robin Sinclair. b 31. Worc Coll Ox BA53 MA57 Lon Univ CertEd63. ALCD55 Wycliffe Coll Toronto 55. **d** 57 **p** 58. C Brompton H Trin *Lon* 57-60; C Brixton St Matt *S'wark* 60-63; Hon C Framlingham w Saxtead *St E* 63-65; Hon C Haverhill 65-67; Chapl St Mary's Sch Richmond 67-75; C Richmond St Mary *S'wark* 68-76; P-in-c Shilling Okeford *Sarum* 76-87; Chapl Croft Ho Sch Shillingstone 76-87; R Milton Abbas, Hilton w Cheselbourne etc *Sarum* 87-96; rtd 96. *11 Stowell Crescent, Wareham, Dorset BH20 4PT* Tel (01929) 551340

FERGUSON, Ronald Leslie. b 36. Open Univ BA86 BA89 Newc Poly CertFT90. Chich Th Coll 65. **d** 68 **p** 69. C Toxteth Park St Marg *Liv* 68-72; C Oakham w Hambleton and Egleton *Pet* 72-74; Asst Chapl The Dorothy Kerin Trust Burrswood 74-76; V Castleside *Dur* 76-96; C Washington from 96; Chapl Gateshead Hosps NHS Trust from 96. *33 Woburn, Biddick, Washington, Co Durham NE38 7JX* Tel 0191-416 2895

FERGUSON, Wallace Raymond. b 47. Qu Coll Birm BTh CITC 76. **d** 78 **p** 79. C Lurgan Ch Ch *D & D* 78-80; I Newtownards w Movilla Abbey 80-84; I Mullabrack w Markethill and Kilcluney *Arm* from 84; Hon V Choral Arm Cathl from 86; Dioc Chapl to Rtd Clergy from 92. *Mullabrack Rectory, Mullurg Road, Markethill, Armagh BT60 1QN* Tel (01861) 551092

FERGUSSON, Miss Catherine Margaret (Kate). b 28. MIPM Birm Univ CSocStuds50. Linc Th Coll 77. **dss** 79 **d** 87 **p** 94. Watford St Pet *St Alb* 79-82; Prestwood *Ox* 82-86; Gt Horwood 86-87; Par Dn 87-89; Dir Cottesloe Chr Tr Progr 86-89; rtd 89. *Checkmate, Middle Ground, Fovant, Salisbury SP3 5LP* Tel (01722) 720314

FERMER, Michael Thorpe. b 30. Lon Univ BSc52 ARCS52 St Cath Soc Ox BA54. Wycliffe Hall Ox 52. **d** 54 **p** 55. C Upper Holloway All SS *Lon* 54-57; C Plymouth St Andr *Ex* 57-59; V Tamerton Foliot 59-63; Asst Chapl United Sheff Hosps 63-64; Chapl 64-66; Lic to Offic *Sheff* 66-73; V Holmesfield *Derby* 73-79; TR Old Brampton and Loundsley Green 79-83; V Brightside St Thos and St Marg *Sheff* 83; V Brightside w Wincobank 83-89; V Loscoe *Derby* 89-94; rtd 94; Perm to Offic *Derby* from 94. *123 Bacons Lane, Chesterfield, Derbyshire S40 2TN* Tel (01246) 555793

FERN, John. b 36. Nottm Univ BA57 DipRE64 MA88. Coll of Resurr Mirfield 57. **d** 59 **p** 60. C Carlton *S'well* 59-61; C Hucknall Torkard 61-68; V Rainworth 68-97; rtd 97. *17 Wharfdale Gardens, Mansfield, Notts NG18 3GZ*

FERNANDO, Percy Sriyananda. b 49. Dundee Coll DCEd81. St And Dioc Tr Course 85. **d** 88 **p** 89. NSM Blairgowrie *St And* from 88; NSM Coupar Angus from 89; NSM Alyth from 89. *Gowrie Cottage, Perth Road, Blairgowrie, Perthshire PH10 6QB*

FERNS, Stephen Antony Dunbar. b 61. St Chad's Coll Dur BA84 Ox Univ BA87. Ripon Coll Cuddesdon 85. **d** 88 **p** 89. C Billingham St Cuth *Dur* 88-90; Chapl Dur Univ 91; Chapl Van Mildert and Trevelyan Coll 91-95; V Norton St Mary from 95. *Norton Vicarage, 71 The Glebe, Stockton-on-Tees, Cleveland TS20 1EL* Tel (01642) 558888

FERNS, Archdeacon of. *See* WILKINSON, The Ven Kenneth Samuel

FERNS, Dean of. *See* FORREST, The Very Revd Leslie David Arthur

FERNYHOUGH, The Ven Bernard. b 32. St D Coll Lamp BA53. **d** 55 **p** 56. Trinidad and Tobago 55-61; R Stoke Bruerne w Grafton Regis and Alderton *Pet* 61-67; RD Preston 65-67; V E Haddon 67-69; V Ravensthorpe 67-69; R Holdenby 67-69; RD Haddon 68-71; V Ravensthorpe w E Haddon and Holdenby 69-77; RD Brixworth 71-77; Can Pet Cathl 74-77 and from 89; Can Res Pet Cathl 77-89; Adn Oakham from 77; P-in-c Empingham and Exton w Horn w Whitwell from 95. *The Rectory, 5 Nook Lane, Empingham, Oakham, Leics LE15 8PT* Tel (01780) 86215

FERNYHOUGH, Timothy John Edward. b 60. Leeds Univ BA81. Linc Th Coll 81. **d** 83 **p** 84. C Daventry *Pet* 83-86; Chapl Tonbridge Sch 86-92; Chapl Dur Sch from 92. *7 Pimlico, Durham DH1 4QW* Tel 0191-384 3664 or 384 7977

FERRIDAY, Donald Martin. b 30. Univ of Wales (Lamp) BA55. Qu Coll Birm 55. **d** 57 **p** 58. C Stockport St Sav *Ches* 57-59; C Heswall 59-64; V Cheadle Hulme All SS 64-72; V Ches 72-76; TR Ches Team 76-77; R W Kirby St Bridget from 77. *The Rectory, West Kirby, Wirral, Merseyside L48 7HL* Tel 0151-625 5229

FERRIER, Malcolm. b 38. St Mich Coll Llan 67. **d** 69 **p** 70. C Solihull *Birm* 69-73; C E Grinstead St Swithun *Chich* 73-75; V Saltley *Birm* 75-82; V Waterlooville *Portsm* from 82. *The Vicarage, 62 Stakes Hill Road, Waterlooville, Hants PO7 7LB* Tel (01705) 262145

FERRY, David Henry John. b 53. TCD BTh88. **d** 88 **p** 89. C Enniskillen *Clogh* 88-90; I Leckpatrick w Dunnalong *D & R* from 90; Bp's Dom Chapl from 96. *1 Lowertown Road, Ballymagorry, Strabane, Co Tyrone BT82 0LE* Tel (01504) 883545

FERRY, Malcolm Ronald Keith. b 66. QUB BEd88. CITC BTh93. **d** 96 **p** 97. C Agherton *Conn* from 96. *35 Dunsuivnish Avenue, Portstewart, Co Londonderry BT55 7EP* Tel (01265) 834150

FESSEY, Mrs Annis Irene. b 40. St Mary's Coll Cheltenham CertEd60. Ripon Coll Cuddesdon 88. **d** 90 **p** 94. Par Dn Bris St Andr Hartcliffe *Bris* 90-94; C The Lydiards 94-95; C Penhill from 95. *The Vicarage, 4 Church Street, Purton, Swindon SN5 9DS* Tel (01793) 771886

FESSEY, Brian Alan. b 39. Bris Univ CertEd61 Leeds Univ DipEd71. Ripon Coll Cuddesdon 88. **d** 90 **p** 91. Hon C Bishopsworth *Bris* 90; C Withywood CD 91-94; V Purton from 94. *The Vicarage, 4 Church Street, Purton, Swindon SN5 9DS* Tel (01793) 770210

FETHNEY, John Garside. b 27. Linc Coll Ox BA52 NE Lon Poly DCS72. Linc Th Coll 51. **d** 53 **p** 54. C W Hackney St Barn *Lon* 53-55; P-in-c 56; Pakistan 57-68; Area Sec (Dio York) USPG 68-70; (Dio Lon) 70-73; (Dios Chich and Guildf) 86-92; Deputation and Th Colls Sec 73-83; Adult and HE Officer 83-86; Hon C St Botolph without Bishopgate *Lon* 73-86; rtd 92; Perm to Offic *Chich* from 92; Perm to Offic *Guildf* from 92. *21 Plover Close, East Wittering, Chichester, W Sussex PO20 8PW* Tel (01243) 670145 or 670000

FEWKES, Jeffrey Preston. b 47. Wycliffe Hall Ox 72. **d** 75 **p** 76. C Chester le Street *Dur* 75-78; C Kennington St Mark *S'wark* 78-81; V Bulwell St Jo *S'well* from 81. *St John's Vicarage, Snape Wood Road, Bulwell, Nottingham NG6 7GH* Tel 0115-927 8025

FICKE, Michael John. b 46. LNSM course 96. **d** 97. NSM Marnhull *Sarum* from 97. *13 Plowman Close, Marnhull, Sturminster Newton, Dorset DT10 1LB* Tel (01258) 820509

FIDDAMAN, Ernest Robert. b 13. **d** 78 **p** 78. Hon C Preston *Chich* 78-83; Chapl Wokingham Hosp 83-95; Hon C Wokingham All SS *Ox* 83-95; rtd 96. *2 Beckett Close, Wokingham, Berks RG40 1YZ* Tel (0118) 979 1451

FIDDYMENT, Alan John. b 40. Cant Sch of Min 91. **d** 94 **p** 95. NSM Chatham St Wm *Roch* 94-96; NSM Spalding *Linc* from 96. *18 Maple Grove, Spalding, Lincs PE11 2LE* Tel (01775) 712851

FIDLER, John Harvey. b 49. Hatf Poly BSc72. St Alb Minl Tr Scheme 84. **d** 87 **p** 88. NSM Royston *St Alb* from 87. *8 Stamford Avenue, Royston, Herts SG8 7DD* Tel (01763) 241886

FIELD, David Hibberd. b 36. K Coll Cam BA58. Oak Hill Th Coll 58. **d** 60 **p** 61. C Aldershot H Trin *Guildf* 60-63; C Margate H Trin *Cant* 63-66; Sec Th Students Fellowship 66-68; Tutor Oak Hill Th Coll 68-93; Vice Prin 79-93; Dean Minl Tr Course 88-93; Dir Professional Min Div CPAS from 94; Patr Sec CPAS from 94. *CPAS, Athena Drive, Tachbrook Park, Warwick CV43 6NG* Tel (01926) 334242 Fax 337613

FIELD, Donald Charles. b 21. Lon Univ BSc50. Glouc Th Course 65. **d** 66 **p** 67. C Stonehouse *Glouc* 66-69; C Tewkesbury w Walton Cardiff 69-72; V Standish w Hardwicke and Haresfield 72-74; V Standish w Haresfield and Moreton Valence 74-80; V Deerhurst, Apperley w Forthampton and Chaceley 80-86; rtd 86; Perm to Offic *St D* from 87. *27 Highfield Road, Ammanford SA18 1JL* Tel (01269) 822716

FIELD, Geoffrey Alder. b 13. Ely Th Coll. **d** 47 **p** 48. C King Cross *Wakef* 47-50; C Ely 50-54; V Whittlesey St Andr 54-75; V Foxton 75-80; rtd 81; Perm to Offic *Ely* from 81. *14 Poplar Close, Great Shelford, Cambridge CB21 5LX* Tel (01223) 842099

FIELD, Gerald Gordon. b 54. K Coll Lon BD75 AKC75. Coll of Resurr Mirfield 76. **d** 77 **p** 78. C Broughton *Blackb* 77-79; C Blackpool St Steph 79-82; V Skerton St Luke 82-86; NSM Westleigh St Pet *Man* 92-93; V Shap w Swindale and Bampton w Mardale *Carl* from 93. *The Vicarage, Shap, Penrith, Cumbria CA10 3LB* Tel (01931) 716232

FIELD, Leonard Frederick. b 34. Man Univ BSc56 Lon Univ CertEd57. EMMTC 85. **d** 88 **p** 89. NSM Holton-le-Clay *Linc* 88-94. *35 Bedford Road, Humberston, Grimsby, S Humberside DN35 0PZ* Tel (01472) 812489

FIELD, Martin Richard. b 55. Keswick Hall Coll CertEd76 Leic Univ MA87. St Jo Coll Nottm BTh82 LTh. **d** 82 **p** 83. C Gaywood, Bawsey and Mintlyn *Nor* 82-85; Perm to Offic *Leic* 85-87; Hon C S'well Minster *S'well* 87-88; Hon C Stand *Man* 88-89; Dioc Press and Communications Officer 88-91. *2 Hamilton Road, Prestwich, Manchester M25 8GG* Tel 0161-773 5963

FIELD, Miss Olwen Joyce. b 53. St Jo Coll Nottm 86. **d** 88 **p** 94. Par Dn Kensal Rise St Mark and St Martin *Lon* 88-91; Par Dn Northwood H Trin 91-94; C 94-95; Chapl Mount Vernon Hosp from 91. *81 Myrtleside Close, Northwood, Middx HA6 2XQ* Tel (01923) 823221

FIELD, Richard Colin (Dick). b 33. St Cath Soc Ox BA54 MA63. Clifton Th Coll 63. **d** 65 **p** 66. C Highbury Ch Ch *Lon* 65-70; V Hanger Lane St Ann 70-85; V Leytonstone St Jo *Chelmsf* from 85. *St John's Vicarage, 44 Hartley Road, London E11 3BL* Tel 0181-989 5447

FIELD, Miss Susan Elizabeth (Sue). b 59. York Univ BA80 Birm Univ CertEd81. Qu Coll Birm 84. **d** 87 **p** 94. C Coleshill *Birm* 87-90; Chapl Loughb Univ *Leic* from 91; Dir Post Ord Tr from 95; Bp's Adv for Women's Min from 97. *13 Spinney Hill Drive, Loughborough, Leics LE11 3LB* Tel (01509) 268203 or 263171 Fax 223902 E-mail s.field@lboro.ac.uk

FIELD, William Jenkin. b 25. St Deiniol's Hawarden. **d** 66 **p** 67. C Cardiff St Jo *Llan* 66-72; V Llancarfan w Llantrithyd 72-94; rtd 94; Perm to Offic *Llan* from 94. *20 Whitmore Park Drive, Barry CF62 8JL* Tel (01446) 701027

FIELDEN, Hugh. b 66. BNC Ox BA88 Birm Univ PGCE90. Qu Coll Birm 91. **d** 93 **p** 94. C Sholing *Win* 93-97; TV Bramley *Ripon* from 97. *27 Hough End Lane, Bramley, Leeds LS13 4EY* Tel 0113-257 6202

FIELDEN, Robert. b 32. Linc Th Coll 65. **d** 67 **p** 68. C Bassingham *Linc* 67-72; R Anderby w Cumberworth 72-88; P-in-c Huttoft 72-88; P-in-c Mumby 77-88; R Fiskerton w Reepham 88-90; rtd 90; Perm to Offic *Linc* from 91; Perm to Offic *Carl* from 91. *Valley Howe, Allithwaite Road, Cartmel, Grange-over-Sands, Cumbria LA11 7SB* Tel (015395) 36159

FIELDER, Canon Arthur John. b 14. Lon Univ DipTh48. Bps' Coll Cheshunt 46. **d** 47 **p** 50. C Luton All SS *St Alb* 47-48; C Taunton St Mary *B & W* 48-50; C Bexhill St Pet *Chich* 50-56; V Luton All SS *St Alb* 56-61; Youth Chapl *Leic* 61-67; Hon Can Leic Cathl 67-77; Dioc Dir of Educn 67-77; Master Wyggeston's Hosp Leic 68-78; rtd 78; Perm to Offic *St Alb* 78-93; Perm to Offic *Chich* from 92. *3 Morley House, College of St Barnabas, Lingfield, Surrey RH7 6NJ* Tel (01342) 870407

FIELDER, Joseph Neil (Joe). b 67. Univ of Wales BSc89. Wycliffe Hall Ox 93. **d** 96 **p** 97. C Cheadle All Hallows *Ches* from 96. *26 Kelsall Road, Cheadle, Cheshire SK8 2NE* Tel 0161-491 2204

FIELDGATE, John William Sheridan. b 44. St Jo Coll Dur BA68. Ox NSM Course 75. **d** 79 **p** 80. NSM Haddenham w Cuddington, Kingsey etc *Ox* 79-90; C Northleach w Hampnett and Farmington *Glouc* 90-92; C Cold Aston w Notgrove and Turkdean 90-92; P-in-c Upper and Lower Slaughter w Eyford and Naunton from 92. *The Rectory, Copse Hill Road, Lower Slaughter, Cheltenham, Glos GL54 2HY* Tel (01451) 810812

FIELDING, John Joseph. b 29. TCD BA53 MA65. **d** 54 **p** 55. C Belfast St Luke *Conn* 54-57; C Belfast St Mary Magd 57-60; W Germany 61-69; Chapl St Edw Sch Ox 69-73; V Highgate St Mich *Lon* 73-95; rtd 95; Perm to Offic *Guildf* from 95. *30 Sackville Mews, Sackville Road, Sutton, Surrey SM2 6HS*

FIELDING, Canon Ronald Jeffrey. b 17. Lon Univ BSc38. Qu Coll Birm 40. **d** 42 **p** 43. C Selly Oak St Mary *Birm* 42-46; S Africa from 46; Hon Can Grahamstown Cathl from 86. *40 Kennington Road, Nahoon, East London, 5241 South Africa* Tel East London (431) 353735

FIELDING, Stephen Aubrey. b 67. Ulster Univ BSc89 TCD BTh93. CITC 90. **d** 93 **p** 94. C Bangor Abbey *D & D* 93-97; I Templepatrick w Donegore *Conn* from 97. *926 Antrim Road, Templepatrick, Ballyclare, Co Antrim BT39 0AT* Tel (01849) 432300 E-mail stejul@bander.dnet.co.uk

FIELDING, Canon William (Bill). b 35. St Jo Coll Dur BA60. Ridley Hall Cam. **d** 62 **p** 63. C Ashton-on-Ribble St Mich *Blackb* 62-64; C Broughton 64-67; V Knuzden 67-75; V Darwen St Cuth 75-85; RD Darwen 77-87; P-in-c Tockholes 79-83; V Darwen St Cuth w Tockholes St Steph 85-87; V St Annes 87-95; RD Kirkham 91-94; Hon Can Blackb Cathl 93-95; rtd 95; Perm to Offic *Sheff* from 95. *10 Bullivant Road, Hatfield, Doncaster, S Yorkshire DN7 6QH* Tel (01302) 841961

FIELDSEND, John Henry. b 31. Nottm Univ BSc54 Lon Univ BD61. Lon Coll of Div ALCD59 BD61. **d** 61 **p** 62. C Pennington *Man* 61-64; C Didsbury Ch Ch 64-66; P-in-c Bayston Hill *Lich* 66-67; V 67-88; UK Dir CMJ 89-91; Min at Large CMJ 91-96; rtd 96; Perm to Offic *St Alb* from 96. *27 Charmouth Road, St Albans, Herts AL1 4RS* Tel (01727) 869537

FIELDSON, Robert Steven. b 56. Qu Coll Cam BA78 MA81 Wye Coll Lon MSc79 Nottm Univ BA86. St Jo Coll Nottm 84. **d** 87 **p** 88. C Walmley *Birm* 87-90; Oman 90-95; P-in-c Cofton Hackett w Barnt Green *Birm* from 95. *The Vicarage, 8 Cofton Church Lane, Barnt Green, Birmingham B45 8PT* Tel 0121-445 1269

FIENNES, The Very Revd the Hon Oliver William. b 26. New Coll Ox BA54 MA55. Cuddesdon Coll 52. **d** 54 **p** 55. C Milton *Win* 54-58; Chapl Clifton Coll Bris 58-63; R St Mary-at-Lambeth *S'wark* 63-68; RD Lambeth 68; Can and Preb Linc Cathl *Linc* from 69; Dean Linc 69-89; rtd 89; Perm to Offic *Pet* from 89. *Home Farm House, Colsterworth, Grantham, Lincs NG33 5NE* Tel (01476) 860811

FIFE, Miss Janet Heather. b 53. Sussex Univ BA77. Wycliffe Hall Ox 84. **d** 87 **p** 94. Chapl Bradf Cathl *Bradf* 87-89; Par Dn York St Mich-le-Belfrey *York* 89-92; Chapl Salford Univ *Man* from 92; Hon C Pendleton St Thos w Charlestown 92-95; Hon C Pendleton 95-96. *2 Hilton Drive, Prestwich, Manchester M25 8NN* Tel 0161-773 9408 or 745 5000

FIGG, Robin Arthur Rex. b 62. RN Eng Coll Plymouth BScEng84. Westcott Ho Cam CTM94. **d** 94 **p** 95. C Old Cleeve, Leighland and Treborough *B & W* 94-97; C Gt Berkhamsted *St Alb* from 97. *All Saints House, Shrublands Road, Berkhamstead, Herts HP4 3HY*

FILBERT-ULLMANN, Mrs Clair. b 51. Louvain Univ Belgium BTh94. Virginia Th Sem. **d** 94 **p** 96. USA 94-95; Asst Chapl Charleroi *Eur* from 95. *avenue des Pelerins 16, B1380 Lasne, Belgium* Tel Brussels (2) 633-5043

FILBY, John Michael (Jack). b 34. Oak Hill Th Coll 56. **d** 60 **p** 61. C Penge St Jo *Roch* 60-64; C Foord St Jo *Cant* 64-66; Dioc Ev (Dios Roch, Guildf and Chelmsf) 66-75; Perm to Offic *Roch* 66-68; Perm to Offic *Guildf* 68-71; Perm to Offic *Chelmsf* 71-75; V Broxted w Chickney and Tilty and Lt Easton 75-85; P-in-c Gt Easton 83-85; R Broxted w Chickney and Tilty etc from 85. *The Rectory, Park Road, Little Easton, Dunmow, Essex CM6 2JJ* Tel (01371) 872509

FILBY, The Ven William Charles Leonard. b 33. Lon Univ BA58. Oak Hill Th Coll 53. **d** 59 **p** 60. C Eastbourne All SS *Chich* 59-62; C Woking St Jo *Guildf* 62-65; V Richmond H Trin *S'wark* 65-71; V Hove Bp Hannington Memorial Ch *Chich* 71-79; R Broadwater St Mary 79-83; RD Worthing 80-83; Can and Preb Chich Cathl 81-83; Adn Horsham from 83. *The Archdeaconry, Itchingfield, Horsham, W Sussex RH13 7NX* Tel (01403) 790315 Fax 791153

FILE, Canon Roy Stephen. b 23. Leeds Univ BA50. Coll of Resurr Mirfield 50. **d** 53 **p** 54. C Liv Our Lady and St Nic *Liv* 53-55; C Pemberton St Jo 55-57; V Mitcham St Olave *S'wark* 57-66; S Africa 66-80; V Ilkley St Marg *Bradf* 80-88; rtd 88; Perm to Offic *Bradf* from 88; Hon Can Cape Town from 90. *4 Bowling View, Skipton, N Yorkshire BD23 1SR* Tel (01756) 795599

FILER, Victor John. b 43. Sarum Th Coll 66. **d** 69 **p** 70. C Mortlake w E Sheen *S'wark* 69-74; SSF 75-82; P-in-c Plaistow SS Phil and Jas w St Andr *Chelmsf* 80-83; Chapl Plaistow Hosp 81-83; TV Plaistow 83; TV Beaconsfield *Ox* 84-90; TR Maltby *Sheff* from 90. *The Rectory, 69 Blyth Road, Maltby, Rotherham, S Yorkshire S66 7LF* Tel (01709) 812684

FILES, Ian James. b 54. Loughb Univ BSc76. Chich Th Coll 85. **d** 87 **p** 88. C Prestwich St Mary *Man* 87-89; C Man Clayton St Cross w St Paul 89-91. *12 Freestone Close, Woodhill, Bury BL8 1US* Tel 0161-763 3447

FILLERY, William Robert. b 42. Univ of Wales BA65 Surrey Univ MA96. St D Coll Lamp CPS68 BD69. **d** 68 **p** 69. C Llangyfelach and Morriston *S & B* 68-71; C Morriston 71-72; Lic to Offic *Ox* 73-76; W Germany 76-81; Chapl Reed's Sch Cobham 81-86; V Oxshott *Guildf* 86-89; P-in-c Seale 89-91; P-in-c Puttenham and Wanborough 89-91; Hd of RE Streatham Hill & Clapham Sch for Girls from 91. *20 Moor Park Lane, Farnham, Surrey GU9 9JB* Tel (01252) 734790

FILMER, Paul James. b 58. Open Univ BA88. Aston Tr Scheme 95 Oak Hill Th Coll DipHE95. **d** 97. C Petham and Waltham w Lower Hardres etc *Cant* from 97. *The Rectory, Curtis Lane, Stelling Minnis, Canterbury, Kent CT4 6BT* Tel (01227) 709318

FINCH, Christopher. b 41. Lon Univ BA63 AKC63 BD69. Sarum Th Coll 63. **d** 65 **p** 66. C High Wycombe *Ox* 65-69; Prec Leic Cathl *Leic* 69-73; R Lt Bowden St Nic 73-81; V Evington from 81; P-in-c Leic St Phil from 95. *The Vicarage, Stoughton Lane, Evington, Leicester LE2 2FH* Tel 0116-271 2032

FINCH, David Walter. b 40. FIBMS69 Cam Univ MA74. Ridley Hall Cam. **d** 91 **p** 92. C Ixworth and Bardwell *St E* 91-92; C Blackbourne 92-94; P-in-c Stoke by Nayland w Leavenheath from 94; P-in-c Polstead from 95. *The Vicarage, Church Street, Stoke by Nayland, Colchester CO6 4QH* Tel (01206) 262248

FINCH, Canon Edward Alfred. b 23. Lon Univ BSc50. Sarum Th Coll 50. **d** 52 **p** 53. C Wealdstone H Trin *Lon* 52-55; C E Grinstead St Swithun *Chich* 55-59; V Walthamstow St Pet *Chelmsf* 59-70; Can Res Chelmsf Cathl 70-85; Dir Interface Assn 85-90; rtd 90; Perm to Offic *St E* from 91; Perm to Offic *Chelmsf* from 90. *St Clare, The Street, Pakenham, Bury St Edmunds, Suffolk IP31 2LG* Tel (01359) 323885

FINCH, Frank. b 33. Qu Coll Birm 72. **d** 74 **p** 75. C Bilston St Leon *Lich* 74-78; R Sudbury and Somersal Herbert *Derby* 78-87; Chapl HM Pris Sudbury 78-87; HM Det Cen Foston Hall 80-87; V Lilleshall and Sheriffhales *Lich* 87-90; R The Ridwares and Kings Bromley from 90. *The Rectory, Alrewas Road, Kings Bromley, Burton-on-Trent, Staffs DE13 7HP* Tel (01543) 472932

FINCH, Frederick. b 22. Lon Coll of Div 59. **d** 60 **p** 61. C Halliwell St Pet *Man* 60-63; V Tonge Fold 63-68; Area Sec (W Midl) CPAS 68-71; V Blackpool Ch Ch *Blackb* 71-77; Canada from 78; rtd 90. *327 Gage Street, Niagara on the Lake, Ontario LO5 1JO, Canada* Tel Toronto (905) 468 8271

FINCH, Jeffrey Walter. b 45. Man Univ BA(Econ)66 Liv Univ DASE80. Linc Th Coll 82. **d** 84 **p** 85. C Briercliffe *Blackb* 84-87; P-in-c Brindle 87-93; Asst Dir of Educn 87-93; V Laneside from 93. *St Peter's Vicarage, Laneside, Haslingden, Rossendale, Lancs BB4 4BG* Tel (01706) 213838

FINCH, John. b 20. Bps' Coll Cheshunt 59. **d** 61 **p** 62. C Middlesbrough St Paul *York* 61-64; V Easington w Skeffling and Kilnsea 64-68; V Habergham Eaves St Matt *Blackb* 68-75; V Garstang St Helen Churchtown 75-86; rtd 86; Perm to Offic *Blackb* from 86. *55 Worcester Avenue, Garstang, Preston PR3 1FJ* Tel (01995) 602386

FINCH, Paul William. b 50. Oak Hill Th Coll DipTh73 Lon Bible Coll. **d** 75 **p** 76. C Hoole *Ches* 75-78; C Charlesworth *Derby* 78-87; C Charlesworth and Dinting Vale 87-88; TV Radipole and Melcombe Regis *Sarum* from 88. *The Vicarage, 74 Field Barn Drive, Weymouth, Dorset DT4 0EF* Tel (01305) 778995

FINCH, Richard William. b 62. Westcott Ho Cam 95. **d** 97. C Saffron Walden w Wendens Ambo and Littlebury *Chelmsf* from 97. *17 Saxon Way, Saffron Walden, Essex CB11 4BQ* Tel (01799) 500194

FINCH, Ronald. b 15. Qu Coll Birm 79. **d** 80 **p** 80. Hon C Welford w Weston and Clifford Chambers *Glouc* 80-85; Perm to Offic *Ches* from 85. *Cornerstone, 1 Penrhyd Road, Irby, Wirral L61 2XJ* Tel 0151-648 1559

FINCH, Miss Rosemary Ann. b 39. Leeds Univ CertEd60. LNSM course 91. **d** 93 **p** 94. NSM S Elmham and Ilketshall *St E* from 93. *St John's Lodge Barn, Ilketshall St John, Beccles, Suffolk NR34 8JH* Tel (01986) 781533

FINCH, Canon Stanley James. b 31. Mert Coll Ox BA55 MA58. Wells Th Coll 55. **d** 57 **p** 58. C Lancaster St Mary *Blackb* 57-61; C Leeds St Pet *Ripon* 61-65; V Habergham All SS *Blackb* 65-73; V S Shore H Trin 73-84; V Broughton from 84; RD Preston 86-92; Hon Can Blackb Cathl from 91. *The Vicarage, 410 Garstang Road, Broughton, Preston PR3 5JB* Tel (01772) 862330

FINCH, Thomas. b 20. Lon Univ BD57. Edin Th Coll 48. **d** 51 **p** 51. Chapl St Andr Cathl *Ab* 51-55; C St Marylebone St Cypr *Lon* 55-58; V Warmington *Pet* 58-67; RD Oundle 62-67; V Wellingborough St Mary 67-88; rtd 88; Perm to Offic *Blackb* from 88. *18 Royal Avenue, Leyland, Preston PR5 1BQ* Tel (01772) 433780

FINCHAM, Nicholas Charles. b 56. St Jo Coll Dur BA78 MA80. Westcott Ho Cam 80 Bossey Ecum Inst Geneva 81. **d** 82 **p** 83. C Seaham w Seaham Harbour *Dur* 82-85; C Lydney w Aylburton *Glouc* 85-87; C Isleworth All SS *Lon* 87-95; P-in-c Chiswick St Mich from 95. *St Michael's Vicarage, 69 Sutton Lane South, London W4 3JT* Tel 0181-994 3173

FINDLAY, Brian James. b 42. Wellington Univ (NZ) BA62 MA63 BMus66 Magd Coll Ox MA75. Qu Coll Birm DipTh71. **d** 72 **p** 73. C Deptford St Paul *S'wark* 72-75; Chapl and Dean of Div Magd Coll Ox 75-84; V Tonge Moor *Man* from 84. *St Augustine's Vicarage, Ainsworth Lane, Bolton BL2 2QW* Tel (01204) 523899

FINDLAYSON, Roy. b 44. Man Univ CQSW69 MA89. Sarum & Wells Th Coll 80. **d** 82 **p** 83. C Benwell St Jas *Newc* 82-83; Hon C 83-85; C Morpeth 85-88; C N Gosforth 88; TV Ch the King in the Dio of Newc 88-94; V Newc St Fran from 94. *St Francis's Vicarage, Cleveland Gardens, Newcastle upon Tyne NE7 7RE* Tel 0191-266 1071

FINDLEY, Peter. b 55. Barrister-at-Law (Gray's Inn) 78 Trin Coll Ox MA77. Trin Coll Bris DipHE92. **d** 92 **p** 93. C Yateley *Win* 92-97; V Westwood *Cov* from 97. *Westwood Vicarage, Westwood Heath Road, Coventry CV4 7DD* Tel (01203) 695026

FINDON, Dr John Charles. b 50. Keble Coll Ox BA71 MA75 DPhil79. Ripon Coll Cuddesdon DipTh76. **d** 77 **p** 78. C Middleton *Man* 77-80; Lect Bolton St Pet 80-83; V Astley 83-91; V Baguley from 91. *St John's Vicarage, 186 Brooklands Road, Sale, Cheshire M33 3PB* Tel 0161-973 5947

FINKENSTAEDT, Harry Seymour. b 23. Yale Univ BA49 Mass Univ MA68. Episc Th Sch Cam Mass BD50. **d** 53 **p** 54. USA 53-71; C Hazlemere *Ox* 71-73; C Huntingdon St Mary w St Benedict *Ely* 73-75; R Castle Camps 75-84; R Shudy Camps 75-84; P-in-c W Wickham 79-84; P-in-c Horseheath 79-81; P-in-c Gt w Lt Stukeley 84-88; rtd 88; Perm to Offic *Ely* from 88. *4 The Fairway, Bar Hill, Cambridge CB3 8SR* Tel (01954) 782224

FINLAY, Hueston Edward. b 64. TCD BA85 BAI85 BTh89 MA92. CITC 86. **d** 89 **p** 90. C Kilkenny w Aghour and Kilmanagh *C & O* 89-92; Bp Ossory Dom Chapl 89-92; Lib and Registrar Kilkenny Cathl 89-92; Bp's V Ossory Cathl 90-92; Chapl Girton Coll Cam 92-95; C Cambridge Gt St Mary w St Mich *Ely* 92-95; Chapl Magd Coll Cam from 95. *9 Hertford Street, Cambridge CB4 3AE, or Magdalene College, Cambridge CB3 0AG* Tel (01223) 332129

FINLAY, Michael Stanley. b 45. N Ord Course 78. **d** 81 **p** 82. C Padgate *Liv* 81-85; V Newton-le-Willows 85-90; V Orford St Marg from 90. *St Margaret's Vicarage, St Margaret's Avenue, Orford, Warrington WA2 8DT* Tel (01925) 631937

FINLAYSON, Duncan. b 24. LNSM course 73. **d** 76 **p** 76. NSM Bridge of Allan *St And* from 76; NSM Alloa from 77; NSM Dollar from 77; Hon AP Hillfoots Team 80-87. *29 Cawdor Road, Bridge of Allan, Stirling FK9 4JJ* Tel (01786) 833074

FINLAYSON, Capt Grantley Adrian. b 55. Wilson Carlile Coll 74 Chich Th Coll 87. **d** 89 **p** 90. C Watford St Mich *St Alb* 89-92; TV W Slough *Ox* from 92. *St Michael's House, Whitby Road, Slough, Berks SL1 3DW* Tel (01753) 521785

FINLINSON, Paul. b 58. St Chad's Coll Dur BA79 St Martin's Coll Lanc PGCE81. Carl Dioc Tr Course 86. **d** 89 **p** 90. NSM Kirkby Lonsdale *Carl* from 89; Perm to Offic *Blackb* from 95. *6 Sandown Road, Lancaster LA1 4LN* Tel (01524) 69652

FINN, Gordon Frederick. b 33. Dur Univ BA60. Ely Th Coll 60. **d** 62 **p** 63. C Kingswinford St Mary *Lich* 62-65; C Northampton St Mary *Pet* 65-67; Chapl Barnsley Hall Hosp Bromsgrove 67-71; Chapl Lea Hosp Bromsgrove 67-71; C Swanage *Sarum* 71-73; P-in-c Ford End *Chelmsf* 73-79; V S Shields St Oswin *Dur* from 79. *The Vicarage, St Oswin's Street, South Shields, Tyne & Wear NE33 4SE* Tel 0191-455 3072

FINN, Ian Michael. b 58. AKC. Chich Th Coll 81. **d** 82 **p** 83. C Habergham All SS *Blackb* 82-83; C W Burnley 83-85; C Torrisholme 85-87; V Lancaster Ch Ch w St Jo and St Anne 87-91; P-in-c Tillingham *Chelmsf* from 91; P-in-c Dengie w Asheldham from 91. *Tillingham Vicarage, 6 Bakery Close, Southminster, Essex CM0 7TW* Tel (01621) 778017 E-mail 101742.2416@compuserve.com

FINN, Miss Sheila. b 30. LMH Ox BA68 MA69. Gilmore Ho 68. **dss** 78 **d** 87 **p** 94. Tettenhall Wood *Lich* 78-86; Dioc Ecum Officer 86-95; The Ridwares and Kings Bromley 86-87; Par Dn 87-94; C 94-95; rtd 95. *15 Leacroft Road, Penkridge, Stafford ST19 5BU* Tel (01785) 716018

FINNEMORE, Ernest Harold. b 28. Keble Coll Ox BA49 MA53. St Steph Ho Ox 51. **d** 53 **p** 54. C Almondbury *Wakef* 53-55; C Talke *Lich* 55-57; V Longnor 57-64; V Hanford 64-90; rtd 90; Perm to Offic *Lich* from 90. *24 Belgrave Road, Newcastle-under-Lyme, Staffs ST5 1LR* Tel (01782) 638179

FINNEMORE, James Christopher. b 59. Pemb Coll Cam BA81 MA85. Coll of Resurr Mirfield. **d** 85 **p** 86. C Manston *Ripon* 85-88; C Hessle *York* 88-92; R Bishop Wilton w Full Sutton, Kirby Underdale etc from 92. *The Rectory, Bishop Wilton, York YO4 1RZ* Tel (01759) 368230

FINNEY, David. b 41. St Mich Coll Llan 68. **d** 70 **p** 71. C Wythenshawe Wm Temple Ch *Man* 70-73; C Bedford Leigh 73-75; V Royton St Anne 75-81; V Dearnley 81-94; TV Rochdale from 94. *The Vicarage, Clement Royds Street, Rochdale, Lancs OL12 6PL* Tel (01706) 46272

FINNEY, Canon Fred. b 17. Bris Univ BA38 DipEd39. Wycliffe Hall Ox 61. **d** 62 **p** 63. C Gt Crosby St Luke *Liv* 62-66; V Ashton-in-Makerfield St Thos 66-86; Hon Can Liv Cathl 83-86; rtd 86; Perm to Offic *Blackb* from 86; Perm to Offic *Liv* from 86. *1 Howard Drive, Tarleton, Preston PR4 6DA* Tel (01772) 812598

FINNEY, Canon John Thomas. b 27. Sheff Univ BA51 DipEd52. Ripon Hall Ox 60. **d** 62 **p** 63. C Leigh St Mary *Man* 62-65; V 83-97; V Peel 65-69; Chapl Hockerill Coll Bishop's Stortford 69-74; V Astley *Man* 74-83; AD Leigh 85-93; Hon Can Man Cathl 87-97; rtd 97. *36 Station Road, Blackrod, Bolton BL6 5BW* Tel (01204) 698010

✠**FINNEY, The Rt Revd John Thornley.** b 32. Hertf Coll Ox BA55. Wycliffe Hall Ox DipTh58. **d** 58 **p** 59 **c** 93. C Highfield *Ox* 58-61; C Weston Turville 61-65; R Tollerton *S'well* 65-71; V Aspley 71-80; Bp's Adv on Evang 80-89; Bp's Research Officer 88-89; Hon Can S'well Minster 84-89; Officer for Decade of Evang in C of E 90-93; Suff Bp Pontefract *Wakef* from 93. *181A Manygates Lane, Wakefield, W Yorkshire WF2 7DR* Tel (01924) 250781 Fax 240490

FINNEY, Ms Melva Kathleen. b 24. LTh76. St Jo Coll Auckland 47 Gilmore Ho 56. **dss** 57 **d** 78. E Dulwich St Jo *S'wark* 57-59; Community of Sisters of the Love of God Ox 59-61; New Zealand from 61; rtd 86. *22 Gunns Crescent, Cashmere, Christchurch, New Zealand 8002* Tel Christchurch (3) 332 7100

FINNIE, Robert. b 20. **d** 84 **p** 84. NSM Aberdeen St Andr *Ab* from 84; NSM Aberdeen St Ninian from 84. *10 Cairngorm Crescent, Aberdeen AB1 5BL* Tel (01224) 874669

FINNIMORE, Keith Anthony. b 36. AKC59. **d** 60 **p** 61. C Wanstead H Trin Hermon Hill *Chelmsf* 60-63; C Kingswood *S'wark* 63-65; V Bolney *Chich* 65-67; V Elmstead *Chelmsf* 67-73; R Pentlow, Foxearth, Liston and Borley 73-77; NSM Cockfield w Bradfield St Clare, Felsham etc *St E* 89-91; R Hawstead and Nowton w Stanningfield etc 91-96; rtd 96; P-in-c Hawstead and Nowton w Stanningfield etc *St E* from 96. *Larkhill, Rede Road, Whepstead, Bury St Edmunds, Suffolk IP29 4SS* Tel (01284) 735291

FIRMIN, Mrs Dorrie Eleanor Frances. b 19. LNSM course. **d** 88 **p** 94. NSM Ellon *Ab* from 88; NSM Cruden Bay from 88. *Minas Tirith, 7 Slains Avenue, Ellon, Aberdeenshire AB41 9ZA* Tel (01358) 721623

FIRMIN, Paul Gregory. b 57. ACIB80. Trin Coll Bris BA87. **d** 87 **p** 88. C Swindon Ch Ch *Bris* 87-91; V Shrewsbury H Trin w St Julian *Lich* from 91. *Holy Trinity Vicarage, Greyfriars Road, Shrewsbury SY3 7EP* Tel (01743) 232158

FIRMSTONE, Ian Harry. b 44. Qu Coll Birm. **d** 82 **p** 83. C Warminster St Denys *Sarum* 82-84; C N Stoneham *Win* 84-88; R Freemantle 88-90; V Littleport *Ely* 90-91; TV Stanground and Farcet from 91; P-in-c Holme w Conington 95-96. *The Vicarage, Main Street, Farcet, Peterborough PE7 3AX* Tel (01733) 240286

FIRTH, Barry. b 37. ACA60 FCA71. NW Ord Course 74. **d** 77 **p** 78. NSM Brighouse *Wakef* 77-81; P-in-c Batley St Thos 81-85; V 85-88; V Rastrick St Matt 88-95; RD Brighouse and Elland 92-96; TV Brighouse and Clifton 95-97; rtd 97. *51 Bolehill Park, Hove Edge, Brighouse, W Yorkshire HD6 2RS* Tel (01484) 710227

FIRTH, Christopher John Kingsley. b 37. St Mich Coll Llan DipTh66. **d** 66 **p** 67. C Sutton in Ashfield St Mary *S'well* 66-70; V Langold 70-74; C Falmouth K Chas *Truro* 74-77; P-in-c Mabe 77-81; V 81-95; RD Carnmarth S 90-94. *19 Olivey Place, Bells Hill, Mylor Bridge, Falmouth, Cornwall TR11 5RX*

FIRTH, Cyril Bruce. b 05. Fitzw Ho Cam BA28 MA32. Cheshunt Coll Cam 25. **d** 65 **p** 66. Asia Sec Conf of Miss Socs of GB & Ireland 65-74; Hon C Wellow *Win* 65-88; rtd 88. *Steplake Cottage, Sherfield English, Romsey, Hants SO51 6EP* Tel (01794) 22563

FIRTH, George Cuthbert. b 19. Keble Coll Ox BA41 MA45. Lich Th Coll 41. **d** 43 **p** 44. C Shelton *Lich* 43-46; Chapl to the Deaf *Ox* 46-49; Chapl to the Deaf *Man* 49-52; Chapl to the Deaf *Sarum* 52-58; R Steeple Langford 58-64; Chapl to the Deaf *Truro* 64-66; Chapl to the Deaf *Lich* 66-71; P-in-c Patshull 71-73; Lic to Offic *Ex* 74-84; Chapl to the Deaf 74-84; rtd 84. *18 Sydney Road, Exeter EX2 9AH* Tel (01392) 275568

FIRTH, Graham Alfred. b 38. Man Univ BA60. Ripon Hall Ox. **d** 62 **p** 63. C Norton Woodseats St Paul *Sheff* 62-65; C-in-c Kimberworth Park CD 65-69; V Kimberworth Park 69-71; P-in-c Egmanton *S'well* 71-77; P-in-c Laxton 71-77; V Sibthorpe from 77; R Elston w Elston Chapelry from 77; R E Stoke w Syerston from 77; R Shelton from 91. *The Rectory, Top Street, Elston, Newark, Notts NG23 5PC* Tel (01636) 525383

✠**FIRTH, The Rt Revd Peter James.** b 29. Em Coll Cam BA52 MA63. St Steph Ho Ox 53. **d** 55 **p** 56 **c** 83. C Barbourne *Worc* 55-58; C Malvern Link St Matthias 58-62; R Abbey Hey *Man* 62-66; Asst Network Relig Broadcasting BBC Man 66-67; Sen Producer/Org Relig Progr TV & Radio BBC Bris 67-83; Hon Can Bris Cathl *Bris* 74-83; Suff Bp Malmesbury 83-94; Angl Adv HTV W 84-94; rtd 94. *7 Ivywell Road, Bristol BS9 1NX* Tel 0117-968 5931

FIRTH, Ronald Mahlon. b 22. Linc Th Coll 60. **d** 61 **p** 62. C Marske in Cleveland *York* 61-64; C Thornaby on Tees St Paul 64-66; V York St Thos w St Maurice 66-73; V Marton-in-Cleveland 73-87; rtd 87; Perm to Offic *York* from 87. *24 Whenby Grove, Huntington, York YO3 9DS* Tel (01904) 634531

FISH, Winthrop. b 40. Dalhousie Univ Canada BA63 BEd Birm Univ BPhil76 MEd78. K Coll (NS) 62. **d** 64 **p** 65. Canada 64-74; Perm to Offic *Birm* 74-77; Asst Chapl Solihull Sch 77-79; Chapl Wroxall Abbey Sch 79-82; C Newquay *Truro* 82-84; V Highertown and Baldhu 84-89; P-in-c Newlyn St Newlyn from 89; Dioc Children's Adv from 89; Dioc Adv in RE from 95. *The Vicarage, Newlyn East, Newquay, Cornwall TR8 5LJ* Tel (01872) 510383

FISHER, Adrian Charles Proctor. b 24. TCD BA48 MA62. TCD Div Sch Div Test47. **d** 49 **p** 50. C Carlow *C & O* 49-52; C Tintern 49-52; C Killesk 49-52; CF 52-57 and 62-69; I Fethard w Killesk, Tintern and Templetown *C & O* 57-62; P-in-c N Stoke w Mongewell and Ipsden *Ox* 70-83; V 83-92; Chapl Oratory Prep Sch 73-80; rtd 92. *Aldermaston Soke, Silchester, Reading RG7 2PB* Tel (0118) 970 0246

FISHER, Mrs Diana Margaret. b 44. EMMTC DipTh94. **d** 94 **p** 95. NSM E and W Leake, Stanford-on-Soar, Rempstone etc *S'well* 94-97; NSM W Bridgford from 97. *The Thatch, 6 Main Street, Rempstone, Loughborough, Leics LE12 6RH* Tel (01509) 881512

FISHER, Eric Henry George. b 48. NTMTC 94. **d** 97. NSM Heydon, Gt and Lt Chishill, Chrishall etc *Chelmsf* from 97. *5 Elm Court, Elmdon, Saffron Walden, Essex CB11 4NP* Tel (01763) 838716

FISHER, Eric William. b 30. Birm Univ BA53. Coll of Resurr Mirfield 70. **d** 72 **p** 73. C Styvechale *Cov* 72-75; C Chesterfield St Mary and All SS *Derby* 75-78; Chapl Buxton Hosps 78-84; TV Buxton w Burbage and King Sterndale *Derby* 78-84; R Shirland 84-89; V Sheff St Matt *Sheff* 89-95; rtd 95; Perm to Offic *Lich* from 95. *25 Robertville Road, Stoke-on-Trent ST2 9HD* Tel (01782) 215571

FISHER, George Arnold. b 54. Lon Univ BD75. N Ord Course 81. **d** 84 **p** 85. C Conisbrough *Sheff* 84-92; V Blackpool St Thos *Blackb* from 92. *St Thomas's Vicarage, 80 Devonshire Road, Blackpool FY3 8AE* Tel (01253) 392544

FISHER, Gordon. b 44. NW Ord Course 74. **d** 77 **p** 78. NSM Airedale w Fryston *Wakef* 77-81; C Barkisland w W Scammonden 81-84; C Ripponden 81-84; V Sutton St Mich *York* 84-87; V Marton-in-Cleveland 87-96; R Kettering SS Pet and Paul *Pet* from 96. *The Rectory, 8 Southlands, Kettering, Northants NN15 7QG* Tel (01536) 513385

FISHER, Henry John. b 25. Lich Th Coll 64. **d** 66 **p** 67. C Kings Norton *Birm* 66-70; C Weston-super-Mare St Jo *B & W* 70-75; C Weston-super-Mare H Trin 72-75; P-in-c Leigh upon Mendip 75-78; P-in-c Stoke St Michael 75-78; P-in-c Leigh upon Mendip w Stoke St Michael 78-80; C Wilton 80-88; C Street w Walton 88-90; rtd 90. *18 Hawker's Lane, Wells, Somerset BA5 3JL* Tel (01458) 42044

FISHER, Humphrey John. b 33. **d** 91 **p** 92. NSM Bryngwyn and Newchurch and Llanbedr etc *S & B* from 91. *Rose Cottage, Newchurch, Kington, Hereford HR5 3QF* Tel (01544) 22632

FISHER, Dr Ian St John. b 59. Down Coll Cam BA80 MA84 Leic Univ PhD84. St Steph Ho Ox BA88. **d** 88 **p** 89. C Colwall w Upper Colwall and Coddington *Heref* 88-91; Chapl Surrey Univ *Guildf* 92-97; V Hurst *Man* from 97. *St John's Vicarage, 155 Kings Road, Ashton-under-Lyne, Lancs OL6 8EZ* Tel 0161-330 1935

FISHER, James Atherton. b 09. SS Coll Cam BA32 MA45. Cuddesdon Coll 32. **d** 33 **p** 34. C Oxhey St Matt *St Alb* 33-36; C Dunstable 36-39; Chapl Bedford Sch 39-43; V Pet St Paul *Pet* 43-53; Asst in Relig Broadcasting BBC 53-58; Can and Treas Windsor 58-78; rtd 78. *1 Thames Close, Charfield, Wotton-under-Edge, Glos GL12 8UA* Tel (01454) 260144

FISHER, John Andrew. b 63. Bath Univ BSc85. Wycliffe Hall Ox BA93 DipMin94. **d** 94 **p** 95. C Rayleigh *Chelmsf* from 94. *86 Lower Lambricks, Rayleigh, Essex SS6 8DB* Tel (01268) 777430

FISHER, John Victor. b 33. Brasted Th Coll 64 Coll of Resurr Mirfield 66. **d** 68 **p** 69. C Stepney St Dunstan and All SS *Lon* 68-71; C E Ham w Upton Park *Chelmsf* 71-73; P-in-c Becontree St Pet 73-82; V Barkingside St Geo from 82. *St George's Vicarage, Woodford Avenue, Ilford, Essex IG2 6XQ* Tel 0181-550 4149

FISHER, Kenneth Francis McConnell (Frank). b 36. K Coll Lon 57. **d** 61 **p** 62. C Sheff St Geo and St Steph *Sheff* 61-63; Chapl Sheff Univ 64-69; Chapl Lon Univ *Lon* 69-75; P-in-c Dean *Carl* 75-80; Soc Resp Officer 75-80; TR Melksham *Sarum* 80-90; P-in-c Stapleford *Ely* from 90; Dioc Ecum Officer from 90; RD Shelford from 94. *Stapleford Vicarage, Cambridge CB2 5BG* Tel (01223) 842150

FISHER, Canon Michael Harry. b 39. Ex Univ BA61. St Steph Ho Ox 61. **d** 63 **p** 64. C Wolverhampton St Pet *Lich* 63-67; C Newquay *Truro* 67-70; V Newlyn St Pet 70-75; P-in-c Launceston St Steph w St Thos 75-82; V Carbis Bay w Lelant 82-95; Hon Can Truro Cathl from 85; RD Penwith from 88; V Newquay from 95. *The Vicarage, 41 Trebarwith Crescent, Newquay, Cornwall TR7 1DX* Tel (01637) 872724

FISHER, Michael John. b 43. Leic Univ BA64 Keele Univ MA67. Qu Coll Birm 75. **d** 78 **p** 79. NSM Stafford St Mary and St Chad *Lich* 78-79; NSM Stafford from 79. *35 Newland Avenue, Stafford ST16 1NL* Tel (01785) 45069

FISHER, Paul Vincent. b 43. ARCM73 Worc Coll Ox BA66 MA70. Qu Coll Birm DipTh68. **d** 70 **p** 71. C Redditch St Steph *Worc* 70-73; C Chorlton upon Medlock *Man* 73-79; Chapl Man Univ 73-79; Exec Sec Community Affairs Division BCC 79-81; Asst Dir of Tr and Dir of Lay Tr *Carl* 81-86; P-in-c Raughton Head w Gatesgill 81-85; Lay Tr Officer *S'wark* 86-90; Dir of Tr 90-94; V Kingswood from 94. *The Vicarage, Woodland Way, Tadworth, Surrey KT20 6NW* Tel (01737) 832164

FISHER, Peter Francis Templar. b 36. CCC Cam BA60 MA. Wells Th Coll 62. **d** 63 **p** 64. C Gt Ilford St Mary *Chelmsf* 63-67; C Colchester St Mary V 67-70; C-in-c Basildon St Andr CD 70-72; P-in-c Edstaston *Lich* 83-87; P-in-c Whixall 83-87; P-in-c Tilstock 84-87; V Oxon and Shelton from 87. *The Vicarage, Shelton Gardens, Bicton, Shrewsbury SY3 8DJ* Tel (01743) 232774

FISHER, Peter Timothy. b 44. Dur Univ BA68 MA75. Cuddesdon Coll 68. **d** 70 **p** 71. C Bedford St Andr *St Alb* 70-74; Chapl Surrey Univ *Guildf* 74-78; Sub-Warden Linc Th Coll 78-83; R Houghton le Spring *Dur* 83-94; RD Houghton 87-92; Prin Qu Coll Birm from 94. *71 Farquhar Road, Birmingham B15 2QP, or Queen's College, Somerset Road, Birmingham B15 2QH* Tel 0121-455 7577 or 454 1527

✠**FISHER, The Rt Revd Reginald Lindsay (Brother Michael).** b 18. Lambeth MA78 Westcott Ho Cam 51. **d** 53 **p** 54 **c** 79. SSF from 42; Lic to Offic *Ely* 53-62; Lic to Offic *Newc* 62-67; Lic to Offic *Sarum* 67-79; Suff Bp St Germans *Truro* 79-85; Bp HM Pris 85; Min Gen SSF 85-91; rtd 85; Asst Bp Ely from 85. *15 Botolph Lane, Cambridge CB2 3RD* Tel (01223) 353903

FISHER, Richard John. b 60. K Coll Lon BA82 AKC82 Selw Coll Cam BA87 Cam Univ MA95. Ridley Hall Cam 85. **d** 88 **p** 89. C Woodley St Jo the Ev *Ox* 88-91; C Acomb St Steph *York* 91-95. *15 Corse Wynd, Kingswells, Aberdeen AB15 8TP* Tel (01224) 743955 Fax as telephone

FISHER, Roy Percy. b 22. Linc Th Coll 51. **d** 53 **p** 54. C Lewisham St Jo Southend *S'wark* 53-56; Clare Coll Miss Rotherhithe 56-59; V Boughton under Blean *Cant* 59-66; V Westgate St Sav 66-71; R Staplegrove *B & W* 71-79; TR Eckington w Handley and Ridgeway *Derby* 79-87; rtd 87; Perm to Offic *Llan* from 87. *258 New Road, Porthcawl CF36 5BA* Tel (01656) 718682

FISHER, Stephen Newson. b 46. CEng82 MIEE82 Univ of Wales (Swansea) BSc67. Linc Th Coll 84. **d** 86 **p** 87. C Nunthorpe *York* 86-89; P-in-c Middlesbrough St Oswald 89-90; V 90-94; V Redcar from 94. *St Peter's Vicarage, 66 Aske Road, Redcar, Cleveland TS10 2BP* Tel (01642) 490700

FISHER, Thomas Andrew (Tom). b 35. Sarum & Wells Th Coll 84. **d** 86 **p** 87. C Win Ch Ch *Win* 86-89; Chapl Salisbury Coll of Tech *Sarum* 89-94; Chapl Salisbury Coll of FE 89-94. *Mombasa, Manor Farm Road, Salisbury SP1 2RR* Tel (01722) 335155

FISHER, Thomas Ruggles. b 20. Cranmer Hall Dur 58. **d** 60 **p** 61. C Melton Mowbray w Thorpe Arnold *Leic* 60-63; R Husbands Bosworth 63-74; R Husbands Bosworth w Mowsley and Knaptoft 74-79; R Husbands Bosworth w Mowsley and Knaptoft etc 79-82; Perm to Offic 82-96; Perm to Offic *Pet* from 83; rtd 85. *12 The Dell, Oakham, Leics LE15 6JG* Tel (01572) 757630

FISHER-BAILEY, Mrs Carol. b 56. **d** 96 **p** 97. C Eccleshill *Bradf* from 96. *3 Hall Road, Eccleshill, Bradford BD2 2DP* Tel (01274) 640286

FISHWICK, Alan. b 48. Chich Th Coll 87. **d** 89 **p** 90. C Laneside *Blackb* 89-92; C Accrington 92-93; TV 93-96; V Blackb St Aid from 96. *St Aidan's Vicarage, St Aidan's Avenue, Blackburn BB2 4EA* Tel (01254) 253519

FISHWICK, Ian Norman. b 54. Lanc Univ BEd. St Jo Coll Nottm DipTh. **d** 82 **p** 83. C High Wycombe *Ox* 82-87; V Walshaw Ch Ch *Man* 87-93; Area Voc Adv 88-93; V W Ealing St Jo w St Jas *Lon* from 93; Dioc Dir Ords Willesden from 94. *St John's Vicarage, 23 Culmington Road, London W13 9NJ* Tel 0181-566 3462 or 566 3507

FISK, Paul. b 35. St Jo Coll Cam BA60 MA64. Wells Th Coll 60. **d** 62 **p** 63. C Ipswich H Trin *St E* 62-65; C Wrentham w Benacre, Covehithe and Henstead 65-67; R Copdock w Washbrook and Belstead 67-73; R Brantham 73-75; RD Samford 73-75; TV Old Brumby *Linc* 85-88; W Germany 88-90; Germany from 90. *Selma-Lagerloef-Strasse 3, D-63454 Hanau, Germany*

FISKE, Dr Paul Francis Brading. b 45. St Jo Coll Dur BA68 PhD72. Wycliffe Hall Ox DipTh72. **d** 73 **p** 74. C Sutton *Liv* 73-76; TV Cheltenham St Mary, St Matt, St Paul and H Trin *Glouc* 76-80; C-in-c Hartplain CD *Portsm* 80-84; Hd of Miss UK CMJ 84-86; Hon C Edgware *Lon* 84-86; R Broughton Gifford, Gt Chalfield and Holt *Sarum* 86-95; TV Bourne Valley 95-97; Adv Chr Action from 95; P-in-c Princes Risborough w Ilmer *Ox* from 97. *The Rectory, 54 Manor Park Avenue, Princes Risborough, Bucks HP27 9AR* Tel (01844) 344784 Fax as telephone

FISON, Geoffrey Robert Martius. b 34. Dur Univ BA59. Ely Th Coll 59. **d** 61 **p** 62. C Heavitree *Ex* 61-64; Australia 64-69; BSB 64-69; C Southampton Maybush St Pet *Win* 70-73; TV Strood *Roch* 73-79; TV Swindon Dorcan *Bris* 79-83; P-in-c Brislington St Cuth from 83. *St Cuthbert's Vicarage, 35 Wick Crescent, Bristol BS4 4HG* Tel 0117-977 6351

FITCH, Alan John. b 45. Open Univ BA82 Warw Univ MA84. Wilson Carlile Coll 64 Qu Coll Birm 92. **d** 92 **p** 93. CA from 66; C Glouc St Jas and All SS *Glouc* 92-97; NSM Wotton St Mary 93-97; V Douglas St Thos *S & M* from 97. *St Thomas's Vicarage, Marathon Avenue, Douglas, Isle of Man IM2 4JA* Tel (01624) 611503

FITCH, Canon John Ambrose. b 22. CCC Cam BA44 MA48. Wells Th Coll 45. **d** 47 **p** 48. C Newmarket All SS *St E* 47-50; Chapl St Felix Sch Southwold 51-69; V Reydon *St E* 51-70; R Brandon and Santon Downham 70-80; Hon Can St E Cathl 75-87; RD Mildenhall 78-80; R Monks Eleigh w Chelsworth and Brent Eleigh etc 80-87; rtd 87; Perm to Offic *St E* from 87; Perm to Offic *Chelmsf* from 87. *The Oak House, High Street, Great Yeldham, Halstead, Essex CO9 4EX* Tel (01787) 237058

FITZ, Lionel Alfred. b 24. **d** 87 **p** 88. NSM Cheltenham St Mary, St Matt, St Paul and H Trin *Glouc* 87-94; Perm to Offic from 94. *9 Foxgrove Drive, Cheltenham, Glos GL52 6TQ* Tel (01242) 243405

FITZGERALD, Gerald. b 26. **d** 54 **p** 55. C Salford St Phil *Man* 54-57; New Zealand from 57. *8 Searidge Lane, Scarborough, Christchurch, New Zealand* Tel Christchurch (3) 326 6112 Fax 326 6186

FITZGERALD, John Edward. b 44. Oak Hill Th Coll 74. **d** 76 **p** 77. C Rainham *Chelmsf* 76-79; C Cambridge St Andr Less *Ely* 79-86; V Holmesfield *Derby* 86-88; Chapl HM Pris Wakef 88-90; Chapl HM Pris Nottm from 90; Chapl HM Pris Whatton 90-93. *The Chaplaincy Office, HM Prison Nottingham, Perry Road, Sherwood, Nottingham NG5 3AG* Tel 0115-962 5022 Fax 960 3605

FITZGIBBON, Kevin Peter. b 49. St Jo Coll Nottm BTh81. **d** 81 **p** 82. C Corby St Columba *Pet* 81-85; V Newborough from 85. *The Vicarage, Newborough, Peterborough PE6 7QZ* Tel (01733) 810682

FITZHARRIS, Barry. b 47. Lon Univ BA69 W Ontario Univ MA70 K Coll Lon BD72 AKC72. St Aug Coll Cant 72. **d** 73 **p** 74. C Whitstable All SS *Cant* 73-75; C Whitstable All SS w St Pet 75-76; Hon C Clapham Old Town *S'wark* 77-79; Asst Chapl Abp Tenison's Gr Sch Kennington 78-84; Hd of Relig Studies 87-90; Hon C Streatham Ch Ch *S'wark* 80-84; R Radwinter w Hempstead *Chelmsf* 84-87. *Poste Restante, Batsi, Andros 84503, Greece*

FITZHARRIS, Robert Aidan. b 46. Sheff Univ BDS71. Linc Th Coll 87. **d** 89 **p** 90. C Dinnington *Sheff* 89-92; V Bentley from 92; RD Adwick from 95. *The Vicarage, 3A High Street, Bentley, Doncaster, S Yorkshire DN5 0AA* Tel (01302) 876272 Fax as telephone

FITZSIMONS, Mrs Kathryn Anne. b 57. Bedf Coll of Educn CertEd78. NE Ord Course 87. **d** 90 **p** 94. NSM Bilton *Ripon* from 90. *17 Strawberry Dale Avenue, Harrogate, N Yorkshire HG1 5EA* Tel (01423) 563074

FITZWILLIAMS, Canon Mark Morshead. b 36. Trin Coll Cam BA59 MA64. Westcott Ho Cam 59. **d** 61 **p** 62. C St Jo Wood *Lon* 61-64; C Hempnall *Nor* 64-70; R Lathbury *Ox* 70-78; R Newport Pagnell 70-78; RD Newport 73-78; TR Beaconsfield 78-94; RD Amersham 82-86; Hon Can Ch Ch from 88; P-in-c Hambleden Valley from 94. *The Rectory, Hambleden, Henley-on-Thames, Oxon RG9 6RP* Tel (01491) 571231

FLACH, Deborah Mary Rollins (Debbie). b 54. Trin Coll Bris DipHE81 Sarum & Wells Th Coll 88. **d** 94 **p** 97. C Chantilly *Eur* 94-96; C Maisons-Laffitte from 96. *63 rue des Boissy, 60340 St Leu d'Esserent, France* Tel France (33) 44 56 76 08

FLACK, Miss Heather Margaret. b 47. **d** 95 **p** 96. C Shenley Green *Birm* from 95. *57 Radford Road, Selly Oak, Birmingham B29 4RB* Tel 0121-476 4052

✠**FLACK, The Rt Revd John Robert.** b 42. Leeds Univ BA64. Coll of Resurr Mirfield 64. **d** 66 **p** 67. C Armley St Bart *Ripon* 66-69; C Northampton St Mary *Pet* 69-72; V Chapelthorpe *Wakef* 72-81; V Ripponden 81-85; V Barkisland w W Scammonden 81-85; V Brighouse 85-88; TR Brighouse St Martin 88-92; RD Brighouse and Elland 86-92; Hon Can Wakef Cathl 89-92; Adn Pontefract 92-97; Suff Bp Huntingdon *Ely* from 97. *14 Lynn Road, Ely, Cambs CB6 1DA* Tel (01353) 662137 Fax 669357

FLAGG, David Michael. b 50. CCC Cam BA71 MA75. St Jo Coll Nottm BA76 DipPs77 DipPC94. **d** 77 **p** 78. C Hollington St Leon *Chich* 77-80; C Woodley St Jo the Ev *Ox* 80-86; Chapl The Dorothy Kerin Trust Burrswood 86-94; R Knockholt w Halstead *Roch* from 94. *The Rectory, Church Road, Halstead, Sevenoaks, Kent TN14 7HQ* Tel (01959) 532133

✠**FLAGG, The Rt Revd John William Hawkins (Bill).** b 29. **d** 59 **p** 61 **c** 69. Paraguay 59-63; Argentina 64-73; Adn N Argentina 65-69; Bp Paraguay and N Argentina 69-73; Asst Bp Chile 73-77; Bp Peru 73-77; Asst Bp Liv 78-86; V Toxteth St Cypr w Ch Ch 78-85; P-in-c Litherland Ch Ch 85-86; Gen Sec SAMS 86-93; Asst Bp Roch 87-92; Asst Bp S'well 92-96; Dioc Stewardship Adv 93-96; Dioc Adv in Rural Affairs 93-96; Dioc Adv for Overseas Affairs 94-96; rtd 97; Hon Asst Bp S'well from 97. *8 Ransome Close, Newark, Notts NG24 2LQ* Tel (01636) 74889

FLAHERTY, Alan Thomas. b 45. N Ord Course 85. **d** 88 **p** 89. NSM Howe Bridge *Man* 88-90; C 90-92; V Ainsworth from 92. *The Vicarage, Ainsworth Hall Road, Ainsworth, Bolton BL2 5RY* Tel (01204) 398567

FLAHERTY, Jane Venitia. *See* ANDERSON, Mrs Jane Venitia

FLATHER, Peter George. b 29. Sarum Th Coll. **d** 59 **p** 60. C Fordingbridge w Ibsley *Win* 59-63; C Lyndhurst 63-65; R E w W Bradenham *Nor* 65-72; P-in-c Speke All SS *Liv* 72-73; P-in-c Sharrington *Nor* 73-87; R Gunthorpe w Bale 73-87; P-in-c Gt w Lt Snoring 77-83; R Gunthorpe w Bale w Field Dalling, Saxlingham etc 87-89; rtd 89; Perm to Offic *Nor* from 89. *29 Jannys Close, Aylsham, Norwich NR11 6DL* Tel (01263) 733548

FLATT, Donald Clifford. b 15. Worc Ord Coll 63. **d** 65 **p** 66. C Tring *St Alb* 65-67; V Wigginton 67-75; Chapl HM Pris Bedf 75-80; V Biddenham *St Alb* 75-82; rtd 83; P-in-c Oare w Culbone *B & W* 83-86; Perm to Offic from 86. *The Stables Cottage, Lamb Court, Dulverton, Somerset TA22 9HB* Tel (01398) 323088

FLATT, Roy Francis Ferguson. b 47. Edin Th Coll 78. **d** 80 **p** 81. C St Andrews St Andr *St And* 80-82; C Elie and Earlsferry 80-82; C Pittenweem 80-82; Dioc Supernumerary 82-83; R Kilmartin *Arg* from 83; R Lochgilphead from 83; Dioc Sec 83-87; Dioc Youth Chapl from 83; R Inveraray 83-90. *Bishopton, Bishopton Road, Lochgilphead, Argyll PA31 8PY* Tel (01546) 602315

FLATT, Stephen Joseph. b 57. Sarum & Wells Th Coll CMinlStuds92. **d** 92 **p** 93. C Limpsfield and Titsey *S'wark* 92-96; TV Pewsey TM *Sarum* from 96. *The Vicarage, Crossways, Easton Royal, Pewsey, Wilts SN9 5LS* Tel (01672) 810970

FLATTERS, Clive Andrew. b 56. Sarum & Wells Th Coll 83. **d** 86 **p** 88. C Weston Favell *Pet* 86-87; C Old Brumby *Linc* 88-91; C Syston *Leic* 91-93; TV Syston TM from 93. *The Vicarage, 20 Hoby Road, Thrussington, Leicester LE7 4TH* Tel (01664) 424962

FLAVELL, Paul William Deran. b 44. Univ of Wales (Ban) DipTh66. St Mich Coll Llan DPS68. **d** 68 **p** 69. Australia 68-71; C Blaenavon w Capel Newydd *Mon* 71-74; V Ynysddu 74-84; R Llanaber w Caerdeon *Ban* from 84. *The Rectory, Mynach Road, Barmouth LL42 1RL* Tel (01341) 280516

FLEET, Daniel James Russell. b 60. Wye Coll Lon BSc84. St Jo Coll Nottm LTh88 DPS89. **d** 89 **p** 90. C Boldmere *Birm* 89-92; C Caverswall and Weston Coyney w Dilhorne *Lich* 92-95; V Alton w Bradley-le-Moors and Oakamoor w Cotton from 95. *The New Vicarage, Limekiln Lane, Alton, Stoke-on-Trent ST10 4AR* Tel (01538) 702469

FLEETWOOD, John Arnold. b 10. K Coll Lon BD39 AKC39. **d** 39 **p** 40. C Leyton All SS *Chelmsf* 39-42; C Barking St Marg w St Patr 42-45; V Leytonstone St Andr 45-57; V Canvey Is 57-73; R Kelvedon Hatch 73-78; V Navestock 73-78; rtd 78; Perm to

Offic *Chelmsf* from 78. *15 Orchard Piece, Blackmore, Ingatestone, Essex CM4 0RX* Tel (01277) 822683

FLEMING, The Ven David. b 37. Kelham Th Coll 58. **d** 63 **p** 64. C Walton St Marg Belmont Road *Liv* 63-67; Chapl HM Borstal Gaynes Hall 68-76; V Gt Staughton *Ely* 68-76; RD St Neots 72-76; V Whittlesey 76-85; RD March 77-82; Hon Can Ely Cathl 82-93; P-in-c Ponds Bridge 83-85; Adn Wisbech 84-93; V Wisbech St Mary 85-89; Chapl Gen of Pris from 93. *123 Wisbech Road, Littleport, Ely, Cambs CB6 1JJ, or Cleland House, Page Street, London SW1P 4LN* Tel (01353) 862498 or 0171-217 6266 Fax 0171-217 6635

FLEMING, George. b 39. IDC. CITC. **d** 78 **p** 79. C Donaghcloney w Waringstown *D & D* 78-80; C Newtownards 80; I Movilla 80; C Heref St Pet w St Owen and St Jas *Heref* 80-85; V Holmer w Huntington 85-96; P-in-c Worfield from 96. *The Vicarage, Worfield, Bridgnorth, Shropshire WV15 5JZ* Tel (01746) 716698

FLEMING, Mrs Penelope Rawling. b 43. Glas Univ MA63. Westcott Ho Cam 87. **d** 89 **p** 94. C Bourne *Guildf* 89-94; R Wotton and Holmbury St Mary from 94; Dioc Voc Adv from 94. *The Rectory, Holmbury St Mary, Dorking, Surrey RH5 6NL* Tel (01306) 730285

FLEMING, Ronald Thorpe. b 29. Codrington Coll Barbados 52. **d** 56 **p** 57. Barbados 56-61; C Delaval *Newc* 61-64; V Cambois 64-69; V Ancroft w Scremerston 69-81; V Longhirst 81-84; Lic to Offic from 84; Chapl Preston Hosp N Shields 84-94; Chapl N Tyneside Hosps 84-94; rtd 94. *18 Holly Avenue, Whitley Bay, Tyne & Wear NE26 1ED* Tel 0191-252 7414

FLEMING, William Edward Charlton. b 29. TCD BA51 MA65. CITC 52. **d** 52 **p** 53. C Dublin Santry *D & G* 52-56; C Arm St Mark *Arm* 56-61; I Tartaraghan 61-80; Prov Registrar 79-96; I Tartaraghan w Diamond 80-96; Can Arm Cathl 86-96; Treas Arm Cathl 88-92; Chan Arm Cathl 92-96; rtd 96. *65 Annareagh Road, Drumorgan, Richhill, Co Armagh BT61 9JT* Tel (01762) 879612

FLENLEY, Benjamin Robert Glanville (Ben). b 50. Sarum & Wells Th Coll 86. **d** 88 **p** 89. C Eastleigh *Win* 88-92; V Micheldever and E Stratton, Woodmancote etc from 92. *The Vicarage, Micheldever, Winchester, Hants SO21 3DA* Tel (01962) 774233

FLENLEY, Kenneth Bernard Akin. *See* AKIN-FLENLEY, Kenneth Bernard

FLETCHER, Anthony Peter Reeves. b 46. Bede Coll Dur CertEd Nottm Univ BTh78. Kelham Th Coll 63 Ridley Hall Cam DPT. **d** 74 **p** 75. C Luton St Mary *St Alb* 74-78; Chapl RAF from 78. *Chaplaincy Services (RAF), HQ, Personnel and Training Command, RAF Innsworth, Gloucester GL3 1EZ* Tel (01452) 712612 ext 5164 Fax 510828

FLETCHER, Arthur William George. b 24. Leeds Univ BA50. Coll of Resurr Mirfield 50. **d** 52 **p** 53. C Bush Hill Park St Mark *Lon* 52-55; Chapl RAF 55-58 and 61-72; V Topcliffe *York* 58-61; R Challoch w Newton Stewart *Glas* 73-75; R Kilmacolm 75-82; R Bridge of Weir 75-82; R Largs 82-89; rtd 89; Perm to Offic *Glas* from 89. *Westhaven, Main Road, Inverkip, Greenock, Renfrewshire PA16 0EA* Tel (01475) 521611

FLETCHER, Miss Barbara. b 41. ALAM79. WMMTC 93. **d** 96 **p** 97. NSM Smethwick *Birm* 96-97; C from 97. *231 Abbey Road, Smethwick, Warley, W Midlands B67 5NN* Tel 0121-429 9354

FLETCHER, Dr Christopher Ian. b 43. BSc PhD. Glouc Sch of Min. **d** 89 **p** 90. C Tenbury *Heref* 89-93; R Bredenbury w Grendon Bishop and Wacton etc from 93. *The Rectory, Bredenbury, Bromyard, Herefordshire HR7 4TF* Tel (01885) 482236

FLETCHER, Colin John. b 46. Chich Th Coll. **d** 83 **p** 84. C Lt Ilford St Mich *Chelmsf* 83-86; C Hockerill *St Alb* 86-89; V New Cantley *Sheff* 89-95; C Kenton *Lon* from 95. *St Leonard's House, 3 Abercorn Gardens, Harrow, Middx HA3 0PB* Tel 0181-907 4905

FLETCHER, Canon Colin William. b 50. Trin Coll Ox BA72 MA76. Wycliffe Hall Ox 72. **d** 75 **p** 76. C Shipley St Pet *Bradf* 75-79; Tutor Wycliffe Hall Ox 79-84; Hon C Ox St Andr *Ox* 79-84; V Margate H Trin *Cant* 84-93; RD Thanet 88-93; Abp's Chapl from 93; Hon Can Dallas from 93. *7 The Cottages, Lambeth Palace, London SE1 7JU* Tel 0171-928 8282

FLETCHER, David Clare Molyneux. b 32. Worc Coll Ox BA55 MA59 DipTh56. Wycliffe Hall Ox 56. **d** 58 **p** 59. C Islington St Mary *Lon* 58-62; Hon C 62-83; Field Worker Scripture Union 62-86; Lic to Offic *St Alb* 83-86; R Ox St Ebbe w H Trin and St Pet *Ox* from 86. *St Ebbe's Rectory, 2 Roger Bacon Lane, Oxford OX1 1QE* Tel (01865) 248154

FLETCHER, David Mark. b 56. Chich Th Coll 84. **d** 87 **p** 88. C Taunton St Andr *B & W* 87-91; P-in-c Chard Furnham w Chaffcombe, Knowle St Giles etc 91-95; P-in-c Tiverton St Andr *Ex* from 95. *St Andrew's Vicarage, Blackmore Road, Tiverton, Devon EX16 4AR* Tel (01884) 257865

FLETCHER, Douglas. b 40. Coll of Resurr Mirfield 67. **d** 68 **p** 69. C Notting Hill St Jo *Lon* 68-73; C Cambridge St Mary Less *Ely* 73-74; C Fulham St Jo Walham Green *Lon* 74-76; C Walham Green St Jo w St Jas 76-84; P-in-c Kensal Town St Thos w St Andr and St Phil 84-92; V from 92. *St Thomas's Vicarage, 231 Kensal Road, London W10 5DB* Tel 0181-960 3703

FLETCHER, Francis Cecil. b 12. Clifton Th Coll 33. **d** 36 **p** 38. C Burton Ch Ch *Lich* 36-39; C Chasetown 39-44; C Gresley *Derby* 44-46; V Shrewsbury St Julian *Lich* 46-49; V Darlaston All SS 49-54; V Hammerwich 54-66; V Weston upon Trent 66-75; rtd 77. *243 Congleton Road, Biddulph, Stoke-on-Trent ST8 7RQ*

FLETCHER, Capt Frank. b 40. Wilson Carlile Coll 71 EAMTC 94. **d** 96 **p** 96. Asst Chapl HM Pris Highpoint 90-97; Chapl HM Pris Wealstun from 97. *The Chaplain's Office, HM Prison Wealstun, Wetherby, W Yorkshire L23 7AY* Tel (01937) 844844

FLETCHER, George Henry Yorke. b 11. Wycliffe Hall Ox 58. **d** 59 **p** 60. C Yardley Wood *Birm* 59-62; V Hursley *Win* 62-67; V Hall Green St Pet *Birm* 67-75; V Clive w Grinshill *Lich* 75-80; rtd 80; Perm to Offic *Lich* from 80. *4 Croft Close, Bomere Heath, Shrewsbury SY4 3PZ* Tel (01939) 290337

FLETCHER, Gordon Wolfe. b 31. Edin Th Coll. **d** 62 **p** 63. C Eston *York* 62-65; C Harton Colliery *Dur* 65-68; V Pelton 68-81; V Ryhope 81-96; rtd 96. *23 Swinburne Road, Darlington, Co Durham DL3 7TD* Tel (01325) 282633

FLETCHER, James Anthony. b 36. St Edm Hall Ox BA60 DipTh61 MA66. St Steph Ho Ox 60. **d** 62 **p** 63. C Streatham St Pet *S'wark* 62-65; C Hobs Moat CD *Birm* 65-68; C Cowley St Jo *Ox* 68-77; V Hanworth All SS *Lon* from 77; P-in-c Hanworth St Geo 89-91. *All Saints' Vicarage, Uxbridge Road, Feltham, Middx TW13 5EE* Tel 0181-894 9330

FLETCHER, Jeremy James. b 60. Dur Univ BA81. St Jo Coll Nottm DipTh86. **d** 88 **p** 89. C Stranton *Dur* 88-91; C Nottingham St Nic *S'well* 91-94; P-in-c Skegby from 94; P-in-c Teversal from 96. *The Vicarage, Mansfield Road, Skegby, Sutton-in-Ashfield, Notts NG17 3ED* Tel (01623) 558800

FLETCHER, John Alan Alfred. b 33. Oak Hill Th Coll 58. **d** 61 **p** 62. C Erith St Paul *Roch* 61-64; C Rushden *Pet* 64-67; R Hollington St Leon *Chich* 67-86; V Chadwell Heath *Chelmsf* from 86; Chapl Chadwell Heath Hosp from 86; RD Barking and Dagenham *Chelmsf* from 91. *The Vicarage, 10 St Chad's Road, Romford RM6 6JB* Tel 0181-590 2054

FLETCHER, Jonathan James Molyneux. b 42. Hertf Coll Ox BA66 MA68. Wycliffe Hall Ox 66. **d** 68 **p** 69. C Enfield Ch Ch Trent Park *Lon* 68-72; C Cambridge St Sepulchre *Ely* 72-76; C St Helen Bishopsgate w St Martin Outwich *Lon* 76-81; Min Wimbledon Em Ridgway Prop Chpl *S'wark* from 82. *Emmanuel Parsonage, 8 Sheep Walk Mews, London SW19 4QL* Tel 0181-946 4728

FLETCHER, Keith. b 47. Man Univ DipTh72. Chich Th Coll 79. **d** 80 **p** 81. C Hartlepool St Paul *Dur* 80-82; V Eighton Banks 82-85; V Haydon Bridge *Newc* 85-96; RD Hexham 93-96; P-in-c Beltingham w Henshaw 93-96; R Horning w Beeston St Laurence and Ashmanhaugh *Nor* from 96. *The Vicarage, Church Road, Horning, Norwich NR12 8PZ* Tel (01692) 630216

FLETCHER, Miss Linden Elisabeth. b 50. Lon Univ BEd73 MA80. St Jo Coll Nottm 87. **d** 89 **p** 94. C Fakenham w Alethorpe *Nor* 89-93; C Cumnor *Ox* from 93. *2 Ashcroft Close, Oxford OX2 9SE* Tel (01865) 863224

FLETCHER, Mrs Patricia (Pat). b 34. K Alfred's Coll Win CertEd74. Chich Th Coll DCS94. **d** 94. NSM Droxford *Portsm* from 94; NSM Meonstoke w Corhampton cum Exton from 94. *The Yarn Market, Waltham Chase, Southampton SO32 2LX* Tel (01489) 892037

FLETCHER, Paul Gordon MacGregor. b 61. St Andr Univ MTh84. Edin Th Coll 84. **d** 86 **p** 87. C Cumbernauld *Glas* 86-89; C-in-c Glas H Cross 89-93; P-in-c Milngavie from 93. *73 Finlay Rise, Milngavie, Glasgow G62 6QL* Tel 0141-956 2363

FLETCHER, Ralph Henry Maurice. b 43. St Steph Ho Ox 71. **d** 74 **p** 75. C Chislehurst Annunciation *Roch* 74-77; Chapl Quainton Hall Sch Harrow 77-87 and from 94; Hon C Hillingdon All SS *Lon* 87-94. *8 Radnor Road, Harrow, Middx HA1 1RY* Tel 0181-723 0548 or 427 1304

FLETCHER, Robert Alexander. b 52. Ridley Hall Cam. **d** 84 **p** 85. C Chalfont St Peter *Ox* 84-88; C Bushey *St Alb* 88-93; TV 93; TV Digswell and Panshanger from 93. *71 Haldens, Welwyn Garden City, Herts AL7 1DH* Tel (01707) 335537

FLETCHER, Canon Robin Geoffrey. b 32. Nottm Univ BA57. Ridley Hall Cam 57. **d** 59 **p** 60. C S Mimms Ch Ch *Lon* 59-64; V Wollaton Park *S'well* 64-71; V Clifton *York* from 71; Chapl Clifton Hosp York 71-88; RD City of York 86-97; Can and Preb York Minster from 89. *The Vicarage, Clifton, York YO6 6BH1* Tel (01904) 655071

FLETCHER, Mrs Sheila Elizabeth. b 35. Nottm Univ BA57 CertEd58. NE Ord Course 84. **d** 87 **p** 94. NSM Dringhouses *York* 87-90; Par Dn 90-94; C 94-97; P-in-c Sutton on the Forest from 97. *The Vicarage, Sutton on the Forest, York YO6 1DW* Tel (01347) 810251

FLETCHER, Stanley Philip. b 27. St Jo Coll Dur BA52 MA73. **d** 54 **p** 55. C Knighton St Jo *Leic* 54-58; V Fleckney w Saddington 58-61; Nigeria 61-66; V Bishopton w Gt Stainton *Dur* 66-76; V Cornforth 76-82; R Hartlepool St Hilda 82-92; RD Hartlepool 86-91; rtd 92. *8 Serpentine Gardens, Hartlepool, Cleveland TS26 0HQ* Tel (01429) 223154

FLETCHER, Stephen. b 57. Man Univ BA79 MA84. St Jo Coll Nottm 82. **d** 84 **p** 85. C Didsbury St Jas and Em *Man* 84-88; R Kersal Moor from 88. *St Paul's Rectory, 1 Moorside Road, Kersal, Salford M7 3PJ* Tel 0161-792 5362

FLETCHER, Stephen William. b 62. Wolv Poly BA84 Birm Univ DipTh87. Qu Coll Birm 85. **d** 88 **p** 89. C Rainham *Roch* 88-91; C

Shottery St Andr *Cov* 91-97; Min Bishopton St Pet 91-97; V Llanrumney *Mon* from 97. *The Vicarage, Countisbury Avenue, Cardiff CF3 9RN* Tel (01222) 792761

FLETCHER, Steven John Carylon. b 60. NCTJ83. Aston Tr Scheme 89 Ripon Coll Cuddesdon 89. **d** 92. C Newquay *Truro* 92-93. *10 Boswedden Terrace, St Just, Penzance, Cornwall TR19 7NF* Tel (01736) 788994

FLETCHER-CAMPBELL, Walter John Fletcher. b 12. Magd Coll Ox BA33 BSc38 MA44. Wells Th Coll 37. **d** 38 **p** 39. C Portsea St Mary *Portsm* 38-45; V Sarisbury 45-47; V Milton 47-60; RD Portsm 55-60; Metrop Sec USPG (Lon and Chelmsf) 60-66; Promotion and Tr Sec 66-68; Dep Home Sec 68-70; V Stanton Harcourt w Northmoor *Ox* 70-75; RD Witney 71-76; P-in-c Bampton Aston w Shifford 75-76; P-in-c Bampton Proper w Bampton Lew 75-76; rtd 77; RD Abingdon *Ox* 80-87; C Radley and Sunningwell 89-93. *153 Upper Road, Kennington, Oxford OX1 5LR* Tel (01865) 730467

FLEWKER, David William. b 53. Birm Univ BA75. Wycliffe Hall Ox 76. **d** 78 **p** 79. C Netherton *Liv* 78-82; C Prescot 82-84; V Seaforth 84-88; TV Whitstable *Cant* 88-96; Miss to Seamen 88-96; V Bethersden w High Halden *Cant* from 96. *The Vicarage, Bull Lane, Bethersden, Ashford, Kent TN26 3HA* Tel (01233) 820266

FLIGHT, Michael John. b 41. Sarum Th Coll 68. **d** 71 **p** 72. C Wimborne Minster *Sarum* 71-75; R Tarrant Gunville, Tarrant Hinton etc 75-78; P-in-c Tarrant Rushton, Tarrant Rawston etc 77-78; R Tarrant Valley 78-80; V Westbury from 80; RD Heytesbury 83-87 and from 96. *The Vicarage, Bitham Lane, Westbury, Wilts BA13 3BU* Tel (01373) 822209

FLINDALL, Roy Philip. b 39. Lon Univ BD64 MPhil71 Keswick Hall Coll PGCE71. St Boniface Warminster 58 K Coll Lon AKC61. **d** 63 **p** 64. C Gt Yarmouth *Nor* 63-68; V Nor St Sav w St Paul 68-70; C-in-c Nor St Clem and St Geo 68-70; Lic to Offic *Ely* 90-92; Teacher Bluecoat Sch Lon 92-95; Lic to Offic *S'wark* 92-95; Chapl Pet High Sch from 95. *Peterborough High School, Westwood House, Thorpe Road, Peterborough PE3 6JF* Tel (01733) 68879

FLINN, Canon John Robert Patrick. b 30. **d** 65 **p** 66. C Dublin Rathfarnham *D & G* 65-67; I Baltinglass w Ballynure etc *C & O* 67-76; I Castlepollard and Oldcastle w Loughcrew etc *M & K* 76-84; rtd 84; Treas Ossory and Leighlin Caths *C & O* 90-92; Chan Ossory and Leighlin Cathls from 92. *The Old School House, Kells, Kilkenny, Irish Republic* Tel Kilkenny (56) 28297

FLINT, Howard Michael. b 59. Edge Hill Coll of HE BEd81. Cranmer Hall Dur 95. **d** 97. C Chipping Campden w Ebrington *Glouc* from 97. *Millbank, Blind Lane, Chipping Campden, Glos GL55 6ED* Tel (01386) 840730

FLINT, John Hedley. b 32. Edin Th Coll 55. **d** 57 **p** 58. C Glas Ch Ch *Glas* 57-60; C Motherwell 60-62; P-in-c Glas St Gabr 62-65; C-in-c Harlow Green CD *Dur* 65-73; V Gannow *Blackb* 74-76; Chapl RADD S Lon 76-79; P-in-c Idridgehay *Derby* 79-84; P-in-c Kirk Ireton 79-84; Chapl to the Deaf 84-87; C Derby St Luke from 87. *75 Otter Street, Derby DE1 3FD* Tel (01332) 345251

FLINT, Nicholas Angus. b 60. Chich Th Coll 84. **d** 87 **p** 88. C Aldwick *Chich* 87-91; Bp's Asst Chapl for the Homeless *Lon* 91-92; TV Ifield *Chich* 92-96; R Rusper w Colgate from 96. *The Rectory, High Street, Rusper, Horsham, W Sussex RH12 4PX* Tel (01293) 871251

FLOATE, Herbert Frederick Giraud. b 25. Keble Coll Ox BA50 MA54. Qu Coll Birm 50. **d** 61 **p** 62. Seychelles 61; Hon C Quarrington w Old Sleaford *Linc* 63-65; P-in-c Mareham le Fen 65-66; Australia 66-72; R Stroxton *Linc* 72-74; R Harlaxton w Wyville and Hungerton 72-74; Lect Shenston New Coll Worcs 74-78; P-in-c Redditch St Geo *Worc* 78-79; Lic to Offic 80-84; R Upton Snodsbury and Broughton Hackett etc 84-89; Chapl Mojacar *Eur* 89-91; rtd 91. *15 Progress Close, Ledbury, Hereford HR8 2QZ* Tel (01531) 635509

FLOOD, Nicholas Roger. b 42. FCA. Ripon Hall Ox 71. **d** 92 **p** 93. NSM Romsey *Win* 92-95; Chapl Win and Eastleigh Healthcare NHS Trust from 95. *Royal Hampshire County Hospital, Romsey Road, Winchester, Hants SO22 5DG* Tel (01962) 824906 or 863535

FLORANCE, James Andrew Vernon. b 44. MCIOB. Linc Th Coll 84. **d** 86 **p** 87. C Lt Ilford St Mich *Chelmsf* 86-90; TV Becontree S 90-93; P-in-c Orsett and Bulphan 93; P-in-c Horndon on the Hill 93; R Orsett and Bulphan and Horndon on the Hill 93-97; P-in-c Liscard St Mary w St Columba *Ches* from 97. *St Mary's Vicarage, 107 Manor Road, Wallasey, Merseyside L45 7LU* Tel 0151-639 1553

FLORY, John Richard. b 35. Clare Coll Cam BA59 MA63. Westcott Ho Cam 69. **d** 71 **p** 72. C Shirehampton *Bris* 71-74; V Patchway 74-82; R Lydiard Millicent w Lydiard Tregoz 82-86; TR The Lydiards 86-93; R Box w Hazlebury and Ditteridge from 93. *The Vicarage, Church Lane, Box, Corsham, Wilts SN13 8NR* Tel (01225) 744458

FLOWER, David. b 48. IPFA75. EMMTC DTPS95. **d** 95 **p** 96. NSM Ashby-de-la-Zouch H Trin *Leic* from 95. *29 Money Hill, Ashby-de-la-Zouch, Leics LE65 1JA* Tel (01530) 414939

FLOWER, Roger Edward. b 45. AKC68. **d** 69 **p** 70. C Gt Stanmore *Lon* 69-72; C Wells St Cuth w Coxley and Wookey Hole *B & W* 72-77; V Tatworth 77-82; P-in-c Taunton St Andr 82-84; V 84-96; RD Taunton 90-96; Preb Wells Cathl 92-96; V Dartmouth *Ex* from 96. *The Vicarage, Northford Road, Dartmouth, Devon TQ6 9EP* Tel (01803) 832415

FLOWERDAY, Andrew Leslie. b 53. Imp Coll Lon BSc75. St Jo Coll Nottm DipTh. **d** 90 **p** 91. C Farnborough *Guildf* 90-95; TV Morden *S'wark* from 95. *140 Stonecot Hill, Sutton, Surrey SM3 9HQ* Tel 0181-330 6566 or 337 6421

FLOWERDEW, Martin James. b 56. Herts Coll CertEd78 Pemb Coll Cam BEd79 UEA CertCS82. Sarum & Wells Th Coll 89. **d** 91 **p** 92. C Leagrave *St Alb* 91-95; C Radlett from 95. *46 Elm Walk, Radlett, Herts WD7 8DP*

FLOWERS, John Henry. b 33. Qu Coll Birm 63. **d** 65 **p** 66. C Aberdare St Fagan *Llan* 65-68; C Llantrisant 68-72; V Nantymoel w Wyndham 72-76; Asst Chapl HM Pris Wormwood Scrubs 76-78; Chapl HM Pris Birm 78-80; Chapl HM Pris Albany 80-93; rtd 93; Perm to Offic *Portsm* from 93. *1 Ulster Crescent, Newport, Isle of Wight PO30 5RU* Tel (01983) 525493

FLUCK, Canon Peter Ernest. b 29. Linc Th Coll. **d** 61 **p** 62. C Maidstone All SS w St Phil *Cant* 61-64; R Uffington *Linc* 64-70; V Tallington 64-70; P-in-c Barholm w Stowe 65-66; V 66-70; V Linc St Nic w St Jo Newport 70-75; P-in-c Haugh 75-84; P-in-c Harrington w Brinkhill 75-84; P-in-c Oxcombe 75-84; P-in-c Ruckland w Farforth and Maidenwell 75-84; P-in-c Somersby w Bag Enderby 75-84; P-in-c Tetford and Salmonby 75-84; R S Ormsby w Ketsby, Calceby and Driby 75-84; V Boston 84-94; Miss to Seamen 84-94; Can and Preb Linc Cathl *Linc* 87-94; rtd 94. *Glebe House, Moorby, Revesby, Boston, Lincs PE22 7PL* Tel (01507) 568769

FLUX, Brian George. b 39. Oak Hill Th Coll 68. **d** 71 **p** 72. C Chadderton Ch Ch *Man* 71-74; C Preston All SS *Blackb* 74-76; Min Preston St Luke 76-81; CF (TA) from 78; R Higher Openshaw *Man* 81-88; Chapl HM Pris Haverigg 88-92; rtd 92. *Greenbank, Silecroft, Millom, Cumbria LA18 5LS* Tel (01229) 775224

FLYNN, Alexander Victor George. b 45. DTh. **d** 90 **p** 91. C Kilsaran w Drumcar, Dunleer and Dunany *Arm* 90-91; P-in-c 91-94; I from 94. *Dromena House, Dromiskin Road, Castlebellingham, Co Louth, Irish Republic* Tel Castlebellingham (42) 72699

FLYNN, Peter Murray. b 35. Oak Hill Th Coll 76. **d** 79 **p** 80. Hon C Finchley St Mary *Lon* 79-83; Hon C Mill Hill Jo Keble Ch 84-86; C Mill End and Heronsgate w W Hyde *St Alb* 86-92; V Chessington *Guildf* from 92. *The Vicarage, Garrison Lane, Chessington, Surrey KT9 2LB* Tel 0181-397 3016

FODEN, Eric. Local Minl Tr Course. **d** 93 **p** 94. NSM New Bury *Man* 93-96. *45 Stetchworth Drive, Worsley, Manchester M28 1FU* Tel 0161-790 4627

FOGDEN, Canon Elizabeth Sally. b 40. MCSP61 DipRS77. Qu Coll Birm 76. **dss** 78 **d** 87 **p** 94. Chevington w Hargrave and Whepstead w Brockley *St E* 78-84; Honington w Sapiston and Troston 84-87; Par Dn 87-92; Par Dn Euston w Barnham, Elvedon and Fakenham Magna 90-92; TD Blackbourne 92-94; Chapl Center Parc Elvedon from 90; Dioc Adv Women's Min from 90; Hon Can St E Cathl from 92; TV Blackbourne from 94. *The Rectory, Honington, Bury St Edmunds, Suffolk IP31 1RG* Tel (01359) 269265

FOIZEY, Michael John. b 24. Trin Coll Cam BA45 MA65. Westcott Ho Cam 45. **d** 47 **p** 48. C Munster Square St Mary Magd *Lon* 47-53; V Willesden St Matt 53-60; R Lon Docks St Pet w Wapping St Jo 60-82; V Ealing Ch the Sav 82-89; Preb St Paul's Cathl 83-89; rtd 89. *157 Birmingham Road, Kidderminster, Worcs DY10 2SL* Tel (01562) 823277

FOLEY, Geoffrey Evan. b 30. **d** 53 **p** 54. Australia 53-90 and from 91; Perm to Offic *S'wark* 90-91; C Stoke-upon-Trent *Lich* 91; rtd 93. *198 Dawson Street, Lismore, NSW, Australia 2480* Tel Lismore (66) 214684 Fax 218133

✠**FOLEY, The Rt Revd Ronald Graham Gregory.** b 23. St Jo Coll Dur BA49 DipTh50. **d** 50 **p** 51 **c** 82. C S Shore H Trin *Blackb* 50-54; V Blackb St Luke 54-60; Dir RE *Dur* 60-71; R Brancepeth 60-71; Hon Can Dur Cathl 65-71; Hon Can Ripon Cathl *Ripon* 71-82; V Leeds St Pet 71-82; Chapl to The Queen 77-82; Suff Bp Reading *Ox* 82-87; Area Bp Reading 87-89; rtd 89; Asst Bp York from 95. *3 Poplar Avenue, Kirkbymoorside, York YO6 6ES* Tel (01751) 303943

FOLKARD, Oliver Goring. b 41. Nottm Univ BA63. Lich Th Coll 64. **d** 66 **p** 67. C Carlton *S'well* 66-67; C Worksop Priory 67-68; C Brewood *Lich* 68-71; C Folkingham w Laughton *Linc* 72-75; P-in-c Gedney Hill 76-77; V 77-84; V Whaplode Drove 76-84; V Sutton St Mary 84-94; RD Elloe E 89-94; P-in-c Scotter w E Ferry from 94. *The Rectory, Church Lane, Scotter, Gainsborough, Lincs DN21 3RZ* Tel (01724) 762662

FOLKS, Andrew John. b 42. St Jo Coll Dur BA65 DipTh69. **d** 69 **p** 70. C Stranton *Dur* 69-72; Chapl Sandbach Sch 73-80; Lic to Offic *Carl* 80-85; Chapl Casterton Sch Lancs 80-85; Hd Master Fernhill Manor Sch New Milton from 85; Perm to Offic *Win* from 85. *Fernhill Manor School, New Milton, Hants BH25 5JL* Tel (01425) 611090

FOLKS, Peter William John. b 30. FRCO56 ARCM. Launde Abbey 72. **d** 72 **p** 73. C Leic St Aid *Leic* 72-76; V Newfoundpool 76-84; V Whetstone 84-94; rtd 94; Perm to Offic *Leic* from 94.

34 Triumph Road, Glenfield, Leicester LE3 8FR Tel 0116-287 3177

FOLLAND, Mark Wilkins. b 59. Univ of Wales (Cardiff) DipTh86 Southn Univ BTh88. Sarum & Wells Th Coll 86. **d** 88. C Kirkby *Liv* 88-91; Asst Chapl Man R Infirmary 91-93; Chapl Cen Man Healthcare NHS Trust from 93; Lic Preacher *Man* from 91. *Chaplain's Department, Central Manchester Healthcare Trust, Oxford Road, Manchester M13 9WL* Tel 0161-276 4582 or 276 1234

FOLLETT, Jeremy Mark. b 60. Jes Coll Cam BA82. St Jo Coll Nottm DTS90. **d** 91 **p** 92. C Newark *S'well* 91-95; C Hellesdon *Nor* from 95. *50 Wensum Valley Close, Norwich NR6 5DJ* Tel (01603) 483790

FOLLETT, Neil Robert Thomas. b 50. RMCS BSc75 Open Univ BA85. EAMTC 86. **d** 89 **p** 90. C Godmanchester *Ely* 89-92; V from 92. *The Vicarage, 59 Post Street, Godmanchester, Huntingdon, Cambs PE18 8AQ* Tel (01480) 453354

FOLLIS, Raymond George Carlile. b 23. DFC45. Lich Th Coll 63. **d** 65 **p** 66. C Walsall Wood *Lich* 65-69; R New Fishbourne *Chich* 69-88; P-in-c Appledram 84-88; rtd 88; Perm to Offic *Chich* from 88. *8 Old Rectory Gardens, Felpham, Bognor Regis, W Sussex PO22 7EP* Tel (01243) 825388

FOOD, Frank Herbert. b 02. Wycliffe Hall Ox 37. **d** 38 **p** 39. C Islington St Mary *Lon* 38-41; V Cambridge St Matt *Ely* 41-45; V Heworth H Trin *York* 45-52; V Leyton St Mary w St Edw *Chelmsf* 52-58; Perm to Offic *Leic* 61; R Markfield 61-71; rtd 71; Chapl Torbay Hosp Torquay 71-77; Perm to Offic *Ex* from 77. *Gracey Court, Woodland Road, Broadclyst, Exeter EX5 3LP*

FOOKES, Roger Mortimer. b 24. VRD63 and Bars 73. Ch Ch Ox BA49 MA53. Wells Th Coll 48. **d** 50 **p** 51. C Westbury-on-Trym H Trin *Bris* 50-53; Chapl RNVR 51-58; C Frome St Jo *B & W* 53-55; R Barwick 55-62; R Closworth 55-62; Chapl RNR 58-74; V Midsomer Norton *B & W* 62-78; RD Midsomer Norton 72-78; P-in-c Stratton on the Fosse 74-78; P-in-c Clandown 75-78; V Wotton-under-Edge w Ozleworth and N Nibley *Glouc* 78-89; RD Dursley 85-89; rtd 89; Perm to Offic *Ex* from 90; Perm to Offic *B & W* from 90. *Feniton Cottage, Feniton, Honiton, Devon EX14 0BE* Tel (01404) 850300

FOOKS, George Edwin. b 25. Trin Hall Cam BA49 MA52 Reading Univ ADEd70. Linc Th Coll 49. **d** 51 **p** 52. C Portsea St Cuth *Portsm* 51-53; C Fareham SS Pet and Paul 53-55; Chapl Earnseat Sch Carl 55-59; V Sheff St Cuth *Sheff* 59-64; Hd Careers Fairfax Gr Sch Bradf 64-66; Hd RE/Careers Buttershaw Comp Sch Bradf 66-70; Counsellor Ifield Sch Crawley 70-73; Hd Guidance Hengrove Sch Bris 73-78; Counsellor w Hearing Impaired Children (Avon) 78-89; Perm to Offic *Bris* from 83; Chapl Southmead Hosp Bris 89-90; Chapl Qu Eliz Hosp Bris 90-96; Chapl Thornbury Hosp from 90; rtd 90. *26 Rudgeway Park, Rudgeway, Bristol BS12 2RU* Tel (01454) 614072

FOORD, Claude Victor. b 07. Worc Ord Coll. **d** 56 **p** 57. C Worc St Clem *Worc* 56-58; R 60-64; C Old Swinford 58-60; V Cleeve Prior 64-72; rtd 72. *9 Lincoln Green, Worcester WR5 1QU* Tel (01905) 359322

FOOT, Adam Julian David. b 58. Garnett Coll Lon CertEd87 Thames Poly BSc80. Trin Coll Bris DipHE95. **d** 97. C Luton Ch Ch *Roch* from 97. *11 Fallowfield, Chatham, Kent ME5 0DU* Tel (01634) 302349

FOOT, Daniel Henry Paris. b 46. Peterho Cam BA67 MA74 Didsbury Coll of Educn CertEd68 Selw Coll Cam 76. Ridley Hall Cam 77. **d** 79 **p** 80. C Werrington *Pet* 79-82; P-in-c Cranford w Grafton Underwood 82; R Cranford w Grafton Underwood and Twywell from 83. *The Rectory, Cranford, Kettering, Northants NN14 4AH* Tel (01536) 78231

FOOT, Leslie Frank. b 07. Dur Univ 30. St Boniface Warminster 27. **d** 32 **p** 33. C Dundee St Jo *Bre* 32-35; Australia 35-38; Ceylon 38-40; CF (EC) 40-46; Hon CF 46; R E Stoke and E Holme *Sarum* 46-47; CF 47-50; Chapl RAF 50-63; R Eastergate *Chich* 63-75; rtd 75; Perm to Offic *Chich* from 75. *120 Little Breach, Chichester, W Sussex PO19 4TZ* Tel (01243) 789640

FOOT, Leslie Robert James. b 33. Bris Univ BSc54. Wells Th Coll 67. **d** 69 **p** 70. Hon C Yeovil *B & W* 69-76; Lic to Offic 76-95. *45 The Roman Way, Glastonbury, Somerset BA6 8AB* Tel (01458) 832247

FOOT, Paul. b 41. Lon Univ BA64. Chich Th Coll 65. **d** 67 **p** 68. C Portsea N End St Mark *Portsm* 67-72; C Grimsbury *Ox* 72-74; V Cury w Gunwalloe *Truro* 74-80; P-in-c Port Isaac 80-83; P-in-c St Kew 80-83; V St Day 83-91; rtd 95. *Aeaea, 39 New Road, Llandovery SA20 0EA* Tel (01550) 720140

FOOTE, Desmond. b 46. S Dios Minl Tr Scheme. **d** 82 **p** 83. NSM Furze Platt *Ox* 82-88; NSM Ruscombe and Twyford from 88. *52 Broadwater Road, Twyford, Reading RG10 0KU* Tel 0118-934 2603

FOOTE, Dr John Bruce. b 18. FRCPath G&C Coll Cam BA39 MA43 MD51. St Jo Coll Nottm 78. **d** 79 **p** 80. NSM Crookes St Thos *Sheff* 79-88; Perm to Offic *Derby* from 79; rtd 88; Perm to Offic *Sheff* from 88. *67 St Thomas Road, Sheffield S10 1UW* Tel 0114-266 5021

FOOTTIT, The Ven Anthony Charles. b 35. K Coll Cam BA57 MA70. Cuddesdon Coll 59. **d** 61 **p** 62. C Wymondham *Nor* 61-64; C Blakeney w Lt Langham 64-67; P-in-c Hindringham w Binham and Cockthorpe 67-71; P-in-c Yarlington *B & W* 71-76; R N Cadbury 71-75; P-in-c S Cadbury w Sutton Montis 75-76; TR Camelot Par 76-81; RD Cary 79-81; Dioc Missr *Linc* 81-87; Can and Preb Linc Cathl 86-87; Dioc Rural Officer *Nor* 87; Adn Lynn from 87; P-in-c Cockley Cley w Gooderstone 95; P-in-c Gt and Lt Cressingham w Threxton 95; P-in-c Didlington 95; P-in-c Hilborough w Bodney 95; P-in-c Oxborough w Foulden and Caldecote 95. *Ivy House, Whitwell Street, Reepham, Norwich NR10 4RA* Tel (01603) 870340 Fax as telephone

FORAN, Andrew John. b 55. Aston Tr Scheme 84 Linc Th Coll 86. **d** 88 **p** 89. C Epping St Jo *Chelmsf* 88-92; TV Canvey Is 92-97; C Dorking w Ranmore *Guildf* from 97; Chapl HM Pris Send from 97. *79 Ashcombe Road, Dorking, Surrey RH4 1LX* Tel (01306) 882065

FORBES, Mrs Angela Laura. b 47. Ox Min Course 91. **d** 94 **p** 96. NSM Cowley St Jo *Ox* from 94. *80 Southfield Road, Oxford OX4 1PA* Tel (01865) 242697

FORBES, The Very Revd Graham John Thompson. b 51. Aber Univ MA73 Edin Univ BD76. Edin Th Coll 73. **d** 76 **p** 77. C Edin Old St Paul *Edin* 76-82; Can St Ninian's Cathl Perth *St And* 82-90; R Stanley 82-88; Provost St Ninian's Cathl Perth 82-90; R Perth St Ninian 82-90; Provost St Mary's Cathl *Edin* from 90; R Edin St Mary from 90. *8 Landsdowne Crescent, Edinburgh EH12 5EQ* Tel 0131-225 2978 or 225 6293 Fax 225 3181

FORBES, Iain William. b 56. Ex Univ BA81. Chich Th Coll 83. **d** 85 **p** 86. C Upper Norwood St Jo *S'wark* 85-88; C Lewisham St Mary 88-90; Chapl St Martin's Coll of Educn *Blackb* 90-94; P-in-c Woodplumpton from 94; Dio Voc Adv from 94. *The Vicarage, Sandy Lane, Woodplumpton, Preston PR4 0RX* Tel (01772) 690355

FORBES, James Paterson. b 32. Brechin NSM Ord Course 85. **d** 88 **p** 90. NSM Dundee St Jo *Bre* 88-90; Hon C from 90. *12 Balmore Street, Dundee DD4 6SY* Tel (01382) 461640

FORBES, John Francis. b 29. CITC 85. **d** 88 **p** 90. C Ferns w Kilbride, Toombe, Kilcormack etc *C & O* 88-90; NSM Gorey w Kilnahue, Leskinfere and Ballycanew from 90. *Ballinabarna House, Enniscorthy, Co Wexford, Irish Republic* Tel Enniscorthy (54) 33353

FORBES, The Very Revd John Franey. b 33. AKC57. **d** 58 **p** 59. C Darlington H Trin *Dur* 58-62; S Africa from 62; Dean Pietermaritzburg from 76. *Deanery, PO Box 1639, Pietermaritzburg, 3200 South Africa* Tel Pietermaritzburg (331) 425848

FORBES, Patrick. b 38. Lon Univ DipSoc74 Open Univ BA82. Linc Th Coll 64. **d** 66 **p** 67. C Yeovil *B & W* 66-69; C Plumstead Wm Temple Ch Abbey Wood CD *S'wark* 69-70; Thamesmead Ecum Gp 70-73; TV Thamesmead 73-78; Dioc Communications Officer *St Alb* 78-90; P-in-c Offley w Lilley 78-82; Lic to Offic 91-95; Info Officer Communications Dept Ch Ho Lon 91-95; Press Officer Miss to Seamen from 95. *Missions to Seamen, St Michael Paternoster Royal, College Hill, London EC4R 2RL* Tel 0171-248 5202 Fax 248 4761

FORBES, Raymond John. b 34. ALCD58. **d** 58 **p** 59. C Wandsworth St Steph *S'wark* 58-61; C Kewstoke *B & W* 61-63; V Fordcombe *Roch* 63-73; R Ashurst 64-73; P-in-c Morden w Almer and Charborough *Sarum* 73-76; P-in-c Bloxworth 73-76; V Red Post 76-84; P-in-c Hamworthy 84-92; P-in-c Symondsbury and Chideock 92-96; rtd 96. *65A Millhams Road, Bournemouth BH10 7LJ*

FORBES, Stuart. b 33. Lon Univ BD59. Oak Hill Th Coll 56. **d** 61 **p** 62. C Halliwell St Pet *Man* 61-64; P-in-c Wicker w Neepsend *Sheff* 64-69; V Stainforth 69-77; V Salterhebble All SS *Wakef* 77-89; V Toxteth Park St Mich w St Andr *Liv* from 89. *St Michael's Vicarage, 6 St Michael's Church Road, Liverpool L17 7BD* Tel 0151-727 2601

FORBES ADAM, Stephen Timothy Beilby. b 23. Ball Coll Ox. Chich Th Coll 59. **d** 61 **p** 62. C Guisborough *York* 61-64; R Barton in Fabis *S'well* 64-70; V Thrumpton 65-70; P-in-c S Stoke *B & W* 74-81; C Combe Down w Monkton Combe and S Stoke 81-83; Perm to Offic 83-86; Perm to Offic *Ox* 86-87; NSM Epwell w Sibford, Swalcliffe and Tadmarton 87-92; rtd 88. *Woodhouse Farm, Escrick, York YO4 6HT* Tel (01904) 878827

FORCE-JONES, Graham Roland John. b 41. Sarum Th Coll 65. **d** 68 **p** 69. C Calne and Blackland *Sarum* 68-73; TV Oldbury 73-78; R 78-80; TR Upper Kennet 80-94; RD Marlborough 90-94; P-in-c Atworth w Shaw and Whitley from 94. *The Vicarage, Corsham Road, Shaw, Melksham, Wilts SN12 8EH* Tel (01706) 703335

FORD, Adam. b 40. Lanc Univ MA72 K Coll Lon BD63 AKC63. **d** 65 **p** 65. C Cirencester *Glouc* 65-70; V Hebden Bridge *Wakef* 70-76; Chapl St Paul's Girls' Sch Hammersmith from 77; Lic to Offic *Lon* from 77; P in O 84-91. *55 Bolingbroke Road, London W14 0AH* Tel 0171-602 5902

FORD, Mrs Avril Celia. b 43. St Mary's Coll Dur BSc64 Chelsea Coll Lon PGCE65. LNSM course 85. **d** 92 **p** 94. NSM Horncastle w Low Toynton *Linc* from 92; NSM High Toynton from 92. *Frolic, Reindeer Close, Horncastle, Lincs LN9 5AA* Tel (01507) 526234

FORD, Benjamin Pierson. b 22. Princeton Univ AB48. Gen Th Sem (NY) MDiv51. **d** 51 **p** 52. USA 51-85 and from 87; C Gt Grimsby St Mary and St Jas *Linc* 85-87. *1544 Union Road, Waldoboro, Maine 04572, USA*

FORD (née HARRISON-WATSON), Mrs Carole. b 44. Reading Univ BSc66 St Martin's Coll Lanc PGCE79. Carl Dioc Tr Inst 92. **d** 95 **p** 96. NSM Windermere *Carl* from 95. *Acre Lodge, Bridge Lane, Troutbeck, Windermere, Cumbria LA23 1LA* Tel (01539) 442670

FORD, Dr Christopher Simon. b 51. AKC74 Leeds Univ MPhil86 PhD91. **d** 75 **p** 76. C Wythenshawe Wm Temple Ch *Man* 75-77; C New Bury 77-80; R Old Trafford St Jo 80-94; Bp's Adv on Archives from 93; R Moston St Jo from 94; AD N Man from 94. *St John's Rectory, Railton Terrace, Manchester M9 1WW* Tel 0161-205 4967

FORD, Canon Colin David. b 28. MIMechE59. Oak Hill Th Coll 60. **d** 62 **p** 63. C Dover St Martin *Cant* 62-67; V Goodnestone St Bart and Graveney 67-71; V Croydon Ch Ch Broad Green 71-84; V Croydon Ch Ch *S'wark* 85-93; Hon Can S'wark Cathl 93; rtd 93; Perm to Offic *Chich* from 93. *11 Boston Close, Eastbourne, E Sussex BN23 6RA* Tel (01323) 470164

FORD, David George. b 37. Lon Coll of Div ALCD61 LTh74. **d** 61 **p** 62. C Walthamstow St Barn and St Jas Gt *Chelmsf* 61-64; C Wisbech SS Pet and Paul *Ely* 64-66; C-in-c Cherry Hinton St Jas CD 66-73; V Cambridge St Jas 73-80; Can Res Ripon Cathl *Ripon* 80-95; rtd 97. *Green Row, Whitegate, East Keswick, Leeds LS17 9HB* Tel (01937) 573057

FORD, David John. b 38. Lon Coll of Div BD68. **d** 69 **p** 70. C Blackheath St Jo *S'wark* 69-71; C Westlands St Andr *Lich* 71-75; V Sheff St Steph w St Phil and St Ann *Sheff* 75-77; R Netherthorpe 77-80; TR 80-84; R Thrybergh 82-84; R Thrybergh w Hooton Roberts 84-94; Ind Chapl 86-87; TV Parkham, Alwington, Buckland Brewer etc *Ex* from 94. *The Vicarage, Hartland, Bideford, North Devon EX39 6BP* Tel (01237) 441240

FORD, Derek Ernest. b 32. St Mich Coll Llan 56. **d** 58 **p** 59. C Roath St Martin *Llan* 58-61; C Newton Nottage 61-67; V Abercanaid 67-70; Perm to Offic *Win* 70-80; SSF from 72; Lic to Offic *Sarum* 73-80; Lic to Offic *Newc* 75-80; USA from 80. *Little Portion Friary, PO Box 399, Mount Sinai, New York 11766, USA* Tel Mount Sinai (516) 473-0553

FORD, Eric Charles. b 31. Ely Th Coll 56. **d** 59 **p** 60. C Kettering St Mary *Pet* 59-65; R Bowers Gifford *Chelmsf* 65-69; V Walthamstow St Barn and St Jas Gt 69-76; V Chingford St Edm from 76. *St Edmund's Vicarage, Larkswood Road, London E4 9DS* Tel 0181-529 5226

FORD, Eric Copeland. b 20. Linc Th Coll 68. **d** 70 **p** 71. C Lupset *Wakef* 70-73; V Cornholme 73-78; V Sharlston 78; V Wragby w Sharlston 78-85; P-in-c Hightown 85-87; V 87-88; V Hartshead and Hightown 88-90; rtd 90; P-in-c Halifax St Jo *Wakef* 90-91; Chapl Las Palmas *Eur* 91-97. *Calle Montevideo 2, 35007 Las Palmas, Canary Islands* Tel Las Palmas (28) 267202

FORD, Canon Henry Malcolm. b 33. Em Coll Cam BA54 MA58. Ely Th Coll 58. **d** 59 **p** 69. C Ipswich St Matt *St E* 59-61; Hon C Bury St Edmunds St Jo 66-76; Hon C Hawstead and Nowton w Stanningfield etc 76-89; Hon Can St E Cathl from 86; NSM Cockfield w Bradfield St Clare, Felsham etc from 89. *Cross Green, Cockfield, Bury St Edmunds, Suffolk IP30 0LG* Tel (01284) 828479

FORD, Hubert. b 14. Kelham Th Coll 30. **d** 38 **p** 39. C Stepney St Dunstan and All SS *Lon* 38-42; C St Helier *S'wark* 42-46; Chapl Miss to Seamen 46-52; V Bishopwearmouth Ch Ch *Dur* 52-63; Chapl Sunderland Eye Infirmary 52-63; C-in-c Hurst Green CD *S'wark* 63-64; V Hurst Green 64-79; rtd 79; Perm to Offic *Chich* from 79. *88 Barrington Road, Worthing, W Sussex BN12 4RS* Tel (01903) 244428

FORD, John. b 31. Sarum Th Coll 58. **d** 61 **p** 62. C Saffron Walden *Chelmsf* 61-64; C Chingford SS Pet and Paul 64-67; V Choral S'well Minster *S'well* 67-72; R N and S Wheatley w W Burton 72-78; P-in-c Sturton w Littleborough 72-78; P-in-c Bole w Saundby 72-78; V Edwinstowe w Carburton 78-95; rtd 95. *Sidings, 21 The Lawns, Collingham, Newark, Notts NG23 7NT* Tel (01636) 892588

FORD, Canon John Albert. b 13. TCD BA35 MA38. CITC 36. **d** 36 **p** 37. C Derryloran *Arm* 36-39; C Arm St Mark 39-44; I Portadown St Sav 44-61; I Drumcree 61-83; Can Arm Cathl 75-83; rtd 83. *84 Bleary Road, Portadown, Co Armagh BT63 5NF* Tel (01762) 345484

FORD, John Frank. b 52. Chich Th Coll 76. **d** 79 **p** 80. C Forest Hill Ch Ch *S'wark* 79-82; V Lee St Aug 82-91; V Lower Beeding *Chich* 91-94; Dom Chapl to Area Bp Horsham 91-94; Dioc Missr from 94. *27 Gatesmead, Haywards Heath, W Sussex RH16 1SN* Tel (01444) 414658 Fax as telephone

FORD, Jonathan Laurence. *See* ALDERTON-FORD, Jonathan Laurence

FORD, Leslie Charles. b 08. S'wark Ord Course 65. **d** 68 **p** 69. C Norwood St Luke *S'wark* 68-76; rtd 76. *Capel Court, The Burgage, Prestbury, Cheltenham, Glos GL52 3EL* Tel (01242) 579410

FORD, Lionel Peter. b 32. St Mich Coll Llan 57. **d** 60 **p** 61. C Ribbesford w Bewdley and Dowles *Worc* 60-63; C St Mary in the Marsh *Cant* 63-67; P-in-c 76-78; V Elmsted w Hastingleigh 67-71; V New Romney w Hope 71-78; RD S Lympne 75-81; V New Romney w Hope and St Mary's Bay etc 78-82; Hon Can Cant Cathl 82-94; V New Romney w Old Romney and Midley 82-94; Asst Chapl Oslo w Bergen, Trondheim, Stavanger etc *Eur* 94-97; rtd 97; Perm to Offic *Heref* from 97. *9 Mayfields, Fishmore, Ludlow, Shropshire SY8 2QB* Tel (01584) 876832 Fax as telephone

FORD, Peter. b 46. Bede Coll Dur TCert72 ACP75 York Univ MA96. Linc Th Coll 76. **d** 78 **p** 79. OGS from 72; C Hartlepool H Trin *Dur* 78-81; Dioc Youth Officer *Wakef* 81-84; C Mirfield Eastthorpe St Paul 82-84; C Upper Hopton 82-84; V Dodworth 84-88; Chapl and Hd Relig Studies Rishworth Sch W Yorks 88-97; Ho Master 94-97; P-in-c Accrington St Mary *Blackb* from 97. *St Mary Magdalen's Vicarage, 5 Queens Road, Accrington, Lancs BB5 6AR* Tel (01254) 233763 Fax 823231

FORD, Peter Collins. b 23. Roch Th Coll 60. **d** 62 **p** 63. C Keighley *Bradf* 62-64; V Buttershaw St Aid 65-67; V Milton next Gravesend Ch Ch *Roch* 69-72; V Gosfield *Chelmsf* 72-84; RD Colne 79-81; RD Halstead and Coggeshall 81-84; rtd 88; Perm to Offic *Chelmsf* from 88. *Little Winster, 12 Upper Fourth Avenue, Frinton-on-Sea, Essex CO13 9JS* Tel (01255) 677151

FORD, Richard Graham. b 39. AKC65 Open Univ BA96. **d** 66 **p** 67. C Morpeth *Newc* 66-71; C Fordingbridge w Ibsley *Win* 71-73; TV Whorlton *Newc* 73-80; Chapl RNR 75-92; V Choppington *Newc* 80-92; V Tynemouth Priory from 92. *Holy Saviour Vicarage, 1 Crossway, North Shields, Tyne & Wear NE30 2LB* Tel 0191-257 1636

FORD, Roger James. b 33. Sarum & Wells Th Coll 81. **d** 83 **p** 84. C Sidcup St Jo *Roch* 83-86; V Darenth from 86. *Darenth Vicarage, Lane End, Dartford DA2 7JR* Tel (01322) 227153

FORD, Roger Lindsay. b 47. Ex Univ LLB68. Llan Dioc Tr Scheme 87. **d** 91 **p** 92. NSM Fairwater *Llan* 91-96; NSM Llan w Capel Llanilltern from 96. *46 St Michael's Road, Llandaff, Cardiff CF5 2AP* Tel (01222) 565716

FORD, Mrs Shirley Elsworth. b 40. Open Univ BA88. Sarum & Wells Th Coll 89. **d** 91 **p** 94. C Farnham *Guildf* 91-96; V Wrecclesham from 96. *The Vicarage, 2 King's Lane, Wrecclesham, Farnham, Surrey GU10 4QB* Tel (01252) 716431

FORD, William John. b 50. Linc Th Coll 89. **d** 91 **p** 92. C Marton-in-Cleveland *York* 91-94; V Whorlton w Carlton and Faceby from 94. *The Vicarage, 18 Church Lane, Swainby, Northallerton, N Yorkshire DL6 3EA* Tel (01642) 700321

FORDE, Stephen Bernard. b 61. Edin Univ BSc TCD DipTh. **d** 86 **p** 87. C Belfast St Mary *Conn* 86-89; Chapl QUB 89-95; Min Can Belf Cathl 89-91; Bp's Dom Chapl *Conn* 90-95; I Dublin Booterstown *D & G* from 95; Dean of Res UCD from 95. *The Rectory, Cross Avenue, Blackrock, Co Dublin, Irish Republic* Tel Dublin (1) 288 7118

FORDER, The Ven Charles Robert. b 07. Ch Coll Cam BA28 MA32. Ridley Hall Cam 28. **d** 30 **p** 31. C Hunslet Moor St Pet *Ripon* 30-33; C Burley 33-34; V Wibsey *Bradf* 34-40; V Bradf St Clem 40-47; V Drypool St Andr and St Pet *York* 47-55; Chapl HM Pris Hull 49-51; Chapl HM Borstal Hull 51-52; R Routh *York* 55-57; V Wawne 55-57; Adn York 57-72; Can and Preb York Minster 57-76; R Sutton upon Derwent 57-63; R York H Trin w St Jo Micklegate and St Martin 63-66; rtd 72; Perm to Offic *York* from 76. *Dulverton Hall, St Martin's Square, Scarborough, N Yorkshire YO11 2DB* Tel (01723) 379534

FORDHAM, Mrs June Erica. b 28. DCR52. Oak Hill Th Coll 83. **dss** 86 **d** 87 **p** 94. Digswell and Panshanger *St Alb* 86-87; Par Dn 87-90; TD 91-93; rtd 93; NSM Lemsford *St Alb* from 93. *22 Crossway, Welwyn Garden City, Herts AL8 7EE* Tel (01707) 326997

FORDHAM, Philip Arthur Sidney. b 51. Avery Hill Coll DipEd. St Steph Ho Ox. **d** 81 **p** 82. C Wanstead St Mary *Chelmsf* 81-82; C Romford St Edw 82-83; C Shrub End 83-86; TV Brighton St Pet and St Nic w Chpl Royal *Chich* 86-88; V Eastbourne Ch Ch from 88. *18 Addingham Road, Eastbourne, E Sussex BN22 7DY* Tel (01323) 721952

FORDHAM, Richard George. b 34. AIMarE60 LicIM&C67 TEng71 FBIM74 SBStJ84 ONC62. **d** 91 **p** 92. NSM Cookham *Ox* 91-94; NSM Hedsor and Bourne End from 94. *Warrington, Hedsor Road, Bourne End, Bucks SL8 5DH* Tel (01628) 523134

FOREMAN, Joseph Arthur (Joe). **d** 86 **p** 87. NSM Win St Bart *Win* from 86. *4 Denham Close, Winchester, Hants SO23 7BL* Tel (01962) 852138

FOREMAN, Patrick Brian. b 41. CertEd. St Jo Coll Nottm 77. **d** 79 **p** 80. C Gainsborough All SS *Linc* 79-83; V Thornton St Jas *Bradf* 83-91; R Hevingham w Hainford and Stratton Strawless *Nor* from 91; RD Ingworth from 94. *The Rectory, Westgate Green, Hevingham, Norfolk NR10 5NH* Tel (01603) 754643

FOREMAN, Roy Geoffrey Victor. b 31. Oak Hill Th Coll 62. **d** 64 **p** 65. C Chitts Hill St Cuth *Lon* 64-67; C Rodbourne Cheney *Bris* 67-70; C Walthamstow St Mary w St Steph *Chelmsf* 71-92; TV 92-96; rtd 96. *1 Vicarage Road, Croydon CR0 4JS* Tel 0181-681 3303

FORGAN, Eleanor. b 44. St Andr Univ MA66 Aber Univ DipEd67. St And Dioc Tr Course. **d** 89 **p** 95. NSM Alloa *St And* from 89. *8 Crophill, Sauchie, Alloa, Clackmannanshire FK10 3EZ* Tel (01259) 212836

FORMAN, Alastair Gordon. b 48. St Jo Coll Nottm 78. **d** 80 **p** 81. C Pennycross *Ex* 80-83; C Woking St Jo *Guildf* 83-88; V Luton Lewsey St Hugh *St Alb* 88-95; P-in-c Jersey Millbrook St Matt

Win from 95. *St Matthew's Vicarage, Millbrook, Jersey, Channel Islands JE3 1LN* Tel (01534) 20934

FORMAN, Diana Blanche Grant. b 19. DCR51. Edin Dioc NSM Course 79. **dss** 83 **d** 86 **p** 94. Edin St Jo *Edin* 83-86; NSM 86-91; rtd 91. *7/3 Myreside Court, Edinburgh EH10 5LX* Tel 0131-447 4463

FORRER, Michael Dennett Cuthbert. b 34. St Pet Hall Ox BA59 MA63. Wycliffe Hall Ox 59. **d** 60 **p** 61. C Westwood *Cov* 60-63; Ind Chapl 63-69; C Cov Cathl 63-71; Sen Ind Chapl 69-71; Hon C All Hallows by the Tower etc *Lon* from 76. *117 London Road, Marlborough, Wilts SN8 1LH* Tel (01672) 55275

FORREST, John Sagar. b 15. Ridley Hall Cam 65. **d** 66 **p** 67. C New Bury *Man* 66-69; R Man St Pet Oldham Road w St Jas 69-75; R Man St Paul New Cross 72-75; Chapl Wythenshawe and Christie Hosps Man 75-80; rtd 80; Perm to Offic *Man* from 80. *8 Merton Street, Bury, Lancs BL8 1AW*

FORREST, Canon Kenneth Malcolm. b 38. Linc Coll Ox BA61 MA65. Wells Th Coll 60. **d** 62 **p** 63. C Walton St Mary *Liv* 62-65; Asst Chapl Liv Univ 65-67; Chapl Blue Coat Sch Liv 67-75; R Wavertree H Trin 67-75; R Wigan All SS from 75; Hon Can Liv Cathl from 87; AD Wigan E from 89. *The Hall, Wigan, Lancs WN1 1HN* Tel (01942) 44459

FORREST, The Very Revd Leslie David Arthur. b 46. TCD BA68 MA86. CITC 70. **d** 70 **p** 71. C Conwall *D & R* 70-73; I Tullyaughnish 73-80; I Athenry w Monivea *T, K & A* 80-82; I Galway w Kilcummin 80-95; RD Tuam 82-91; Dir of Ords 84-95; Can Tuam Cathl 86-95; Provost Tuam 91-95; Preb Tassagard St Patr Cathl Dublin 91-95; Dean Ferns *C & O* from 95; I Ferns w Kilbride, Toombe, Kilcormack etc from 95. *The Deanery, Ferns, Co Wexford, Irish Republic* Tel Wexford (54) 66124

FORREST, Michael Barry Eric. b 38. Lon Univ BA87 MA89. NZ Bd of Th Studies LTh62 Chich Th Coll 64. **d** 66 **p** 67. C Beckenham St Jas *Roch* 66-70; Papua New Guinea 70-76; C Altarnon and Bolventor *Truro* 76-78; TV N Hill w Altarnon, Bolventor and Lewannick 78-79; R St Martin w E and W Looe 79-84; V Kensington St Phil Earl's Court *Lon* from 84. *St Philip's Vicarage, 46 Pembroke Road, London W8 6NU* Tel 0171-602 5025 or 373 4847

FORREST, The Very Revd Robin Whyte. b 33. Edin Th Coll 58. **d** 61 **p** 62. C Glas St Mary *Glas* 61-66; R Renfrew 66-70; R Motherwell 70-79; R Wishaw 75-79; R Forres *Mor* from 79; R Nairn 79-92; Can St Andr Cathl Inverness from 88; Syn Clerk 91-92; Dean Mor from 92. *St John's Rectory, Victoria Road, Forres, Morayshire IV36 0BN* Tel (01309) 672856

FORRESTER, Edward. b 27. MIEH76 MIHE79 MIOSH80 R Tech Coll Salford DipEH51. St Aid Birkenhead 58. **d** 60 **p** 61. C Birch St Agnes *Man* 60-62; R Salford St Clem w St Cypr Ordsall 62-71; V Bury St Pet 71-73; rtd 93; Hon C Salford Ordsall St Clem *Man* 93-96; P-in-c from 96; Perm to Offic from 93. *62 Affleck Avenue, Radcliffe, Manchester M26 9HN* Tel (01204) 578216

FORRESTER, Herbert Howarth. b 19. Liv Univ LLB46. Wycliffe Hall Ox 65. **d** 67 **p** 68. C Blundellsands St Nic *Liv* 67-70; V Liv St Phil 70-76; V Liv St Phil w St Dav 76-85; rtd 85; Perm to Offic *Liv* from 85. *5 Kenilworth Road, Liverpool L16 7PS* Tel 0151-722 1365

FORRESTER, Ian Michael. b 56. Chich Th Coll. **d** 82 **p** 83. C Leigh-on-Sea St Marg *Chelmsf* 82-84; Min Can, Succ and Dean's V Windsor 84-86; Perm to Offic *Ox* 84-86; Chapl Distinguished Conduct Medal League 86-95; Chapl Gallantry Medallists' League from 95; Prec and Chapl Chelmsf Cathl *Chelmsf* 86-91; Perm to Offic from 91; Chapl Lancing Coll from 91. *Lancing College, Lancing, W Sussex BN15 0RW, or Ladywell House, Lancing, W Sussex BN15 0RN* Tel (01273) 452213 or 454624

FORRESTER, James Oliphant. b 50. SS Coll Cam BA72 MA76. Wycliffe Hall Ox 73. **d** 76 **p** 77. C Hull Newland St Jo *York* 76-80; C Fulwood *Sheff* 80-87; V Lodge Moor St Luke 87-90; V Ecclesfield from 90. *The Vicarage, 230 The Wheel, Ecclesfield, Sheffield S30 3ZB* Tel 0114-257 0002

FORRESTER, Mrs Joyce. b 33. Thornbridge Hall Coll of Educn TCert53 ACP84 Crewe & Alsager Coll MSc88. St Jo Coll Nottm 94. **d** 94 **p** 95. NSM Endon w Stanley *Lich* from 94. *Sprinks Farm, The Hollands, Biddulph Moor, Stoke-on-Trent ST8 7LE* Tel (01782) 513626

FORRESTER, Kenneth Norman. b 22. Ely Th Coll 46. **d** 49 **p** 50. C Ely 49-51; C Wymondham *Nor* 51-53; V Shotesham 53-56; R Inverness St Jo *Mor* 56-60; Itinerant Priest 60-61; P-in-c Thurso 61; V Tilney All Saints w Tilney St Lawrence *Ely* 61-68; C Brighton St Bart *Chich* 68-71; Chapl Montreux *Eur* 71-79; Chapl Malaga w Almunecar and Nerja 79-81; Chapl Pau w Biarritz 81-86; rtd 87. *27 rue Duboue, 6400 Pau, France* Tel France (33) 59 98 68 15

FORRESTER, Matthew Agnew. b 31. Univ of Wales (Cardiff) BA64 Lon Univ DipTh72. Trin Coll Bris 70. **d** 72 **p** 73. C Tonbridge SS Pet and Paul *Roch* 72-77; Chapl Elstree Sch Woolhampton 77-78; Chapl Duke of York's R Mil Sch Dover 78-96; rtd 96; Perm to Offic *Cant* from 96. *4 Abbots Place, Canterbury, Kent CT1 2AM* Tel (01304) 823758

FORRYAN, Canon John Edward. b 31. Wells Th Coll 58. **d** 60 **p** 61. C Leckhampton SS Phil and Jas *Glouc* 60-63; C Cirencester 63-68; V Glouc St Paul 68-78; R Rodborough 78-91; P-in-c Deerhurst, Apperley w Forthampton and Chaceley 91-95; V from 95; Hon Can Glouc Cathl from 94. *The Vicarage, 1 The Green, Apperley, Gloucester GL19 4EB* Tel (01452) 780880

FORRYAN, Thomas Quested (Tom). b 64. Pemb Coll Cam BA85 DipTh86. Wycliffe Hall Ox 87. **d** 90 **p** 91. C Cheadle Hulme St Andr *Ches* 90-93; C Aberavon *Llan* 93-94; UCCF from 94. *c/o UCCF, 38 De Montfort Street, Leicester LE7 7GP* Tel 0116-255 1700

FORSE, Reginald Austin (Reg). b 43. Oak Hill Th Coll 77. **d** 79 **p** 80. C Crofton *Portsm* 79-84; NSM Gosport Ch Ch 91-96; NSM Alverstoke from 96. *40 Osprey Gardens, Lee-on-the-Solent, Hants PO13 8LJ* Tel (01705) 553395

FORSHAW, David Oliver. b 27. Trin Coll Cam BA50 MA52. Qu Coll Birm. **d** 53 **p** 54. C Glen Parva and S Wigston *Leic* 53-55; Singapore 55-59; V Heptonstall *Wakef* 59-66; V Whitehaven St Nic *Carl* 66-76; P-in-c Whitehaven Ch Ch w H Trin 73-76; V Benchill *Man* 76-89; C Elton All SS 89-92; rtd 92; Perm to Offic *Carl* from 92. *Tynashee, Church Street, Broughton-in-Furness, Cumbria LA20 6HJ* Tel (01229) 716068

FORSHAW, Canon Eric Paul. b 42. Lon Univ BSc63 Birm Univ MA78 Zurich Univ ThD90. Ridley Hall Cam 67 Gossner Inst Mainz 73. **d** 70 **p** 71. C Yardley St Edburgha *Birm* 70-72; Ind Chapl 72-78; Hon C Edgbaston St Geo 72-78; Bp's Adv on Ind Soc *S'well* 78-90; Perm to Offic 78-82; Assoc Min Nottm St Pet and St Jas 82-94; Hon Can S'well Minster from 86; Bp's Research Officer 90-92; Progr Dir Nottm Common Purpose 92-94; TR Clifton from 94. *The Rectory, 569 Farnborough Road, Clifton, Nottingham NG11 9DG* Tel 0115-974 9388 Fax as telephone

FORSTER, Andrew James. b 67. QUB BA89. CITC BTh92. **d** 92 **p** 93. C Willowfield *D & D* 92-95; Dean of Res QUB from 95; C of I Adv Downtown Radio Newtownards from 96. *20 Elmwood Avenue, Belfast BT9 6AY* Tel (01232) 667754 Fax 661640

FORSTER, Bennet Fermor. b 21. BNC Ox BA48 MA53. Cuddesdon Coll. **d** 51 **p** 52. C Stepney St Dunstan and All SS *Lon* 51-53; C Petersfield w Sheet *Portsm* 53-57; V Portsea St Cuth 57-65; Chapl Bedford Sch 65-72; C Bedford St Pet *St Alb* 72-73; Lic to Offic 73-78; P-in-c Froxfield w Privett *Portsm* 78-81; V 81-88; P-in-c Hawkley w Prior's Dean 78-81; V 81-88; rtd 88. *39 Parkview, Abbey Road, Malvern, Worcs WR14 3HG* Tel (01684) 567915

FORSTER, Charles Clifford. b 34. AKC59. **d** 60 **p** 61. C Marske in Cleveland *York* 60-63; C Auckland St Andr and St Anne *Dur* 63-65; V Brafferton w Pilmoor and Myton on Swale *York* 65-72; V Derringham Bank 72-81; V Brompton w Snainton 81-83; V Brompton-by-Sawdon w Snainton, Ebberston etc 83-92; rtd 92; Perm to Offic *York* from 92. *33 Marshall Drive, Pickering, N Yorkshire YO18 7JT* Tel (01751) 473655

FORSTER, Eric Lindsay. b 11. Worc Coll Ox BA33 MA38. Wycliffe Hall Ox 34. **d** 39 **p** 40. C Bolton Sav *Man* 39-41; C Mottram in Longdendale w Woodhead *Ches* 41-42; C Skipton Ch Ch *Bradf* 42-44; C Redditch St Geo *Worc* 44-47; V Bacup St Jo *Man* 47-52; V Nelson St Bede *Blackb* 52-57; V Spaldwick w Barham *Ely* 57-65; P-in-c Woolley 57-65; R Spaldwick w Barham and Woolley 65-75; P-in-c Easton 57-58; V 58-75; rtd 75; Perm to Offic *Ely* from 75. *32 Tudor Road, Godmanchester, Huntingdon, Cambs PE18 8DP* Tel (01480) 433183

FORSTER, Gregory Stuart. b 47. Worc Coll Ox BA69 MA73 DipSocAnth70. Wycliffe Hall Ox 69. **d** 72 **p** 73. C Bath Walcot *B & W* 72-74; C Bolton Em *Man* 74-76; C Bolton St Paul w Em 77-79; R Northenden from 79. *The Rectory, Ford Lane, Northenden, Manchester M22 4NQ* Tel 0161-998 2615

FORSTER, Ian Duncan. b 51. St Mich Coll Llan 95. **d** 97. C Lampeter Pont Steffan w Silian *St D* from 97. *Talavera, Cambrian Road, Lampeter SA48 7DP* Tel (01570) 422777

FORSTER, Ian Robson. b 33. AKC59. **d** 60 **p** 61. C Leigh St Mary *Man* 60-62; C Chorlton-cum-Hardy St Werburgh 62-64; Grenada 64-66; St Lucia 66-69; P-in-c Alberbury w Cardeston *Heref* 69-76; V Ford 69-76; P-in-c Wolverhampton St Chad *Lich* 76-78; TV Wolverhampton 78-86; V Battersea St Phil w St Bart *S'wark* from 86. *St Philip's Vicarage, Queenstown Road, London SW8 3RT* Tel 0171-622 1929

FORSTER, Dr Kenneth. b 27. St Jo Coll Cam BA50 MA52 Salford Univ MSc77 PhD80. NE Ord Course 83. **d** 86 **p** 87. NSM Hessle *York* 86-92; Chapl Humberside Poly 87-91; Chapl Humberside Univ 92; rtd 92; NSM Hull St Mary Sculcoates *York* 92-95. *Birchwood, 12 Tower View, Anlaby, Hull HU10 7EG* Tel (01482) 657931

✠**FORSTER, The Rt Revd Peter Robert.** b 50. Mert Coll Ox MA73 Edin Univ BD77 PhD85. Edin Th Coll 78. **d** 80 **p** 81. C Mossley Hill St Matt and St Jas *Liv* 80-82; Sen Tutor St Jo Coll Dur 83-91; V Beverley Minster *York* 91-96; C Routh 91-96; Bp Ches from 96. *Bishop's House, Abbey Square, Chester CH1 2JD* Tel (01244) 350864 Fax 314187

FORSTER, Thomas Shane. b 72. QUB BA93. CITC BTh93. **d** 96 **p** 97. C Drumglass w Moygashel *Arm* from 96; Hon V Choral Arm Cathl from 97. *Kinore, 84 Killyman Road, Dungannon, Co Tyrone BT71 6QD* Tel (01868) 727131

FORSTER, The Ven Victor Henry. b 17. TCD BA45 MA49. **d** 45 **p** 46. C Magheralin *D & D* 45-47; C-in-c Garrison w Slavin *Clogh* 47-51; Bp's C Ballybay 51-52; I Killeevan 52-59; I Rathgraffe

M & K 59-67; I Aghalurcher w Tattykeeran, Cooneen etc *Clogh* 67-89; RD Clogh 73-89; Preb Clogh Cathl 80-83; Adn Clogh 83-89; rtd 89; Lic to Offic *D & D* from 90. *4 Ard-Na-Ree, Groomsport, Bangor, Co Down BT19 2JL* Tel (01247) 464548

FORSTER, William (Bill). b 50. Liv Poly HNC71. N Ord Course 92. **d** 95 **p** 96. C Ashton-in-Makerfield St Thos *Liv* from 95. *79 Greenfields Crescent, Ashton-in-Makerfield, Wigan, Lancs WN4 8QY* Tel (01942) 273611

FORSYTH, Jeanette Mary Shaw. b 48. Moray Ho Edin 67 St Jo Coll Nottm 85. **d** 89. NSM Old Deer *Ab* 89-92; NSM Longside 89-92; NSM Strichen 89-92; NSM Fraserburgh 92-94. *Moss-side of Strichen, Bogensourie, Strichen, Fraserburgh, Aberdeenshire AB43 4TU* Tel (01771) 637230

FORSYTH, William. b 10. Lich Th Coll 55. **d** 56 **p** 57. C Fenham St Jas and St Basil *Newc* 56-59; V Cleator *Carl* 59-65; V Netherton 65-70; V Levens 70-77; rtd 77; Perm to Offic *Carl* from 77. *2 Vicarage Road, Levens, Kendal, Cumbria LA8 8PY* Tel (015395) 60926

FORSYTHE, John Leslie. b 27. CITC. **d** 65 **p** 66. C Cloughfern *Conn* 65-67; C Carnmoney 67-71; I Mossley 71-80; I Antrim All SS 80-95; Preb Conn Cathl 94-95; rtd 95. *96 Hopefield Road, Portrush, Co Antrim BT56 8HF* Tel (01265) 822623

FORTNUM, Brian Charles Henry. b 48. Hertf Coll Ox MA Imp Coll Lon MSc. Wycliffe Hall Ox 82. **d** 84 **p** 85. C Tonbridge St Steph *Roch* 84-87; V Shorne 87-94; P-in-c Speldhurst w Groombridge and Ashurst from 94. *The Rectory, Southfield Road, Speldhurst, Tunbridge Wells, Kent TN3 0PD* Tel (01892) 862821

FORTUNE-WOOD, Dr Janet. b 61. Selw Coll Cam BA82 MA88 CertEd83. Trin Coll Bris 86. **d** 88 **p** 94. Par Dn Rotherhithe H Trin *S'wark* 88-92; TD Swindon St Jo and St Andr *Bris* 92-94; TV 94-95; P-in-c Kingshurst *Birm* from 95. *St Barnabas' Vicarage, 51 Overgreen Drive, Birmingham B37 6EY* Tel 0121-770 3972

FORWARD, Eric Toby. b 50. Nottm Univ BEd72 Hull Univ MA93. Cuddesdon Coll 74. **d** 77 **p** 78. C Forest Hill Ch Ch *S'wark* 77-80; Chapl Golds Coll Lon 80-84; Chapl Westwood Ho Sch Pet 84-86; V Brighton St Aug and St Sav *Chich* 86-90; Perm to Offic *York* 90-95; V Kingston upon Hull St Alb from 95. *St Alban's Vicarage, 62 Hall Road, Hull HU6 8SA* Tel (01482) 446639 Fax as telephone

FORWARD, Canon Ronald George. b 25. Selw Coll Cam BA50 MA54. Ridley Hall Cam 50. **d** 52 **p** 53. C Denton Holme *Carl* 52-55; C-in-c Mirehouse St Andr CD 55-61; V Mirehouse 61-66; V Kendal St Thos 66-90; V Crook 78-90; Hon Can Carl Cathl 79-90; rtd 90; Perm to Offic *Carl* from 90. *51 Mayo Park, Cockermouth, Cumbria CA13 0BJ* Tel (01900) 824359

FOSBUARY, David Frank. b 32. Leeds Univ BA63. Coll of Resurr Mirfield 63. **d** 65 **p** 66. C Fleetwood *Blackb* 65-68; Lesotho 69-76; C Dovercourt *Chelmsf* 76-78; TV 78-79; TV Basildon St Martin w H Cross and Laindon etc 79-82; R Colsterworth *Linc* 82-84; R Colsterworth Gp 84-90; RD Beltisloe 89-90; R Lawshall w Shimplingthorne and Alpheton *St E* 90-96; rtd 96. *56 Lindisfarne Road, Bury St Edmunds, Suffolk IP33 2EH* Tel (01284) 767687

FOSDIKE, Lewis Bertram. b 23. Keble Coll Ox BA52 MA56. Wells Th Coll 52. **d** 54 **p** 55. C Westbury-on-Trym H Trin *Bris* 54-58; V Bedminster St Fran 58-64; V Summertown *Ox* 64-76; TR Wolvercote w Summertown 76-89; rtd 89; Chapl St Hugh's Coll Ox 89-97. *18 Osberton Road, Oxford OX2 7NU* Tel (01865) 515817

FOSKETT, Eric William. b 29. Qu Coll Birm 75. **d** 78 **p** 79. NSM Billesley Common *Birm* 78-82; V Allens Cross 82-95; Chapl Hollymoor Hosp Birm 90-95; rtd 95; Perm to Offic *Birm* from 95. *1 Warmington Road, Hollywood, Birmingham B47 5PE* Tel (01564) 526181

FOSKETT, Canon John Herbert. b 39. St Cath Coll Cam BA62. Chich Th Coll 62. **d** 64 **p** 65. C Malden St Jo *S'wark* 64-70; P-in-c Kingston St Jo 70-76; Chapl Maudsley Hosp Lon 76-94; Chapl Bethlem R Hosp Beckenham 76-94; Hon Can S'wark Cathl *S'wark* 88-94; rtd 94; Perm to Offic *B & W* from 95. *Cob Cottage, Duck Lane, Limington, Yeovil, Somerset BA22 8EL* Tel (01935) 840941

FOSS, David Blair. b 44. Bris Univ BA65 Dur Univ MA66 Fitzw Coll Cam BA68 MA72 K Coll Lon PhD86. St Chad's Coll Dur 68. **d** 69 **p** 70. C Barnard Castle *Dur* 69-72; Sierra Leone 72-74; Chapl St Jo Coll York 74-75; Chapl Ch Ch Coll Cant 75-80; Chapl Elmslie Girls' Sch Blackpool 80-83; Tutor Coll of Resurr Mirfield 83-88; V Battyeford *Wakef* from 88. *The Vicarage, 109 Stocksbank Road, Mirfield, W Yorkshire WF14 9QT* Tel (01924) 493277

FOSS, William Cecil Winn. b 40. Man Univ BA68 MA87 Lon Univ DipTh66 CertEd72 BD76. Ely Th Coll 64. **d** 68 **p** 69. C S'wark St Geo *S'wark* 68-73; Perm to Offic *Ches* 73-79; V Crewe Ch Ch 79-83; V Crewe Ch Ch and St Pet from 83. *Christ Church Vicarage, 3 Heathfield Avenue, Crewe CW1 3BA* Tel (01270) 213148

FOSSETT, Michael Charles Sinclair. b 30. CEng MIMechE59 Dur Univ BSc54. NE Ord Course 82. **d** 90 **p** 91. Hon C Nether w Upper Poppleton *York* from 90. *20 Fairway Drive, Upper Poppleton, York YO2 6HE* Tel (01904) 794712

FOSTEKEW, Dean James Benedict. b 63. Bulmershe Coll of HE BEd86. Chich Th Coll 89. **d** 92 **p** 93. C Boyne Hill *Ox* 92-95; P-in-c Lockerbie *Glas* from 95; P-in-c Annan from 95. *All Saints Rectory, Ashgrove Terrace, Lockerbie, Dumfriesshire DG11 2BQ* Tel (01576) 202484 Fax as telephone

FOSTER, Preb Albert Edward John. b 29. Lich Th Coll 52. **d** 55 **p** 56. C Is of Dogs Ch Ch and St Jo w St Luke *Lon* 55-58; C Notting Hill St Mich and Ch Ch 58-60; C Bethnal Green St Matt 60-62; P-in-c Bethnal Green St Jas the Gt w St Jude 62-69; V Paddington St Mary 69-94; Preb St Paul's Cathl 86-94; AD Westmr Paddington 87-92; rtd 94. *18 Trafalgar Road, Weston, Bath BA1 4EW* Tel (01225) 447117

FOSTER, Antony John. b 39. Down Coll Cam BA61 MA65. Ridley Hall Cam 65. **d** 66 **p** 67. C Sandal St Helen *Wakef* 66-69; Uganda 69-74; V Mount Pellon *Wakef* 74-92; rtd 92; Perm to Offic *Wakef* from 92. *32 Savile Drive, Halifax, W Yorkshire HX1 2EU* Tel (01422) 344152

FOSTER, Canon Christopher Richard James. b 53. Univ Coll Dur BA75 Man Univ MA77 Trin Hall Cam BA79 MA83 Wadh Coll Ox MA83. Westcott Ho Cam 78. **d** 80 **p** 81. C Tettenhall Regis *Lich* 80-82; Chapl Wadh Coll Ox 82-86; C Ox St Mary V w St Cross and St Pet *Ox* 82-86; V Southgate Ch Ch *Lon* 86-94; Continuing Minl Educn Officer 88-94; Can Res St Alb from 94. *The Old Rectory, Sumpter Yard, St Albans AL1 1BY* Tel (01727) 854827 or 860780

FOSTER, David Brereton. b 55. Selw Coll Cam BA77 MA81 Ox Univ BA80. Wycliffe Hall Ox 78. **d** 81 **p** 82. C Luton St Mary *St Alb* 81-84; C Douglas St Geo and St Barn *S & M* 84-87; V S Ramsey St Paul 87-91; Dir Dioc Tr Inst 88-91; Asst Dir Buckm Adnry Chr Tr Scheme *Ox* 91-95; Dir Buckm Adnry Chr Tr Sch 95-97; C W Wycombe w Bledlow Ridge, Bradenham and Radnage 91-97; TV High Wycombe from 97. *15 The Brackens, High Wycombe, Bucks HP11 1EB* Tel (01494) 531628

FOSTER, Donald Wolfe. b 24. St Cath Coll Cam BA48 MA50 TCD BD56. **d** 50 **p** 51. Ireland 50-52; C Coseley Ch Ch *Lich* 52-54; C Newland St Aug *York* 54-58; Chapl HM Borstal Hull 58-62; V Kingston upon Hull St Mary *York* 58-62; V Osbaldwick w Murton 62-67; Asst Chapl Loughborough Gr Sch 67-80; Chapl 80-87; Perm to Offic *Leic* from 81; rtd 87. *90 Brook Street, Wymeswold, Loughborough, Leics LE12 6TU* Tel (01509) 880029

FOSTER, Edward James Graham. b 12. St Jo Coll Cam BA34 MusBac35 MA38. Wells Th Coll 35. **d** 37 **p** 38. C Kidderminster St Mary *Worc* 37-43; C Feckenham w Astwood Bank 43-45; Chapl and Lect Dioc Tr Coll Chester 45-51; V Balby w Hexthorpe *Sheff* 51-67; V Ashford w Sheldon *Derby* 67-78; rtd 78; Perm to Offic *Derby* from 78. *Montrose, Ashford Road, Bakewell, Derbyshire DE45 1GL* Tel (01629) 813718

FOSTER, Edward Philip John. b 49. Trin Hall Cam BA70 MA74. Ridley Hall Cam 76. **d** 79 **p** 80. C Finchley Ch Ch *Lon* 79-82; C Marple All SS *Ches* 82-86; P-in-c Cambridge St Matt *Ely* 86-90; V from 90. *St Matthew's Vicarage, 24 Geldart Street, Cambridge CB1 2LX* Tel (01223) 63545 Fax 512304 E-mail aak66@dial.pipex.com

FOSTER, Frances Elizabeth. *See* TYLER, Mrs Frances Elizabeth

FOSTER, Francis Desmond. b 11. ALCD33. **d** 34 **p** 35. C Norbury St Phil *S'wark* 34-39; C Faversham *Cant* 39-48; V Throwley 48-75; P-in-c Stalisfield w Otterden 73-75; V Throwley w Stalisfield and Otterden 75-77; rtd 77; Perm to Offic *Chich* from 78. *43 Milton Road, Eastbourne, E Sussex BN21 1SH* Tel (01323) 639430

FOSTER, Gareth Glynne. b 44. Open Univ BA. Chich Th Coll 66. **d** 69 **p** 70. C Fairwater *Llan* 69-71; C Merthyr Tydfil 71-72; C Merthyr Tydfil and Cyfarthfa 72-76; TV 76-87; Dioc Soc Resp Officer from 87; P-in-c Abercanaid from 87. *19 The Walk, Merthyr Tydfil CF47 8RU, or Diocesan Office, Heol Fair, Llandaff, Cardiff CF5 2EE* Tel (01685) 722375 or (01222) 578899

FOSTER, James. b 29. Man Univ BA52 MA55 Lon Univ CertEd53 Leeds Univ MEd74. NE Ord Course 82. **d** 85 **p** 86. NSM Aldborough w Boroughbridge and Roecliffe *Ripon* 85-91; P-in-c Kirby-on-the-Moor, Cundall w Norton-le-Clay etc 91; P-in-c 91-97; rtd 97. *Ford House, Farnham, Knaresborough, N Yorkshire HG5 9JD* Tel (01423) 340200

FOSTER, John Francis. b 13. Chich Th Coll 47. **d** 49 **p** 50. C Atherton *Man* 49-52; C Halliwell St Marg 52-53; V Briercliffe *Blackb* 53-59; V Michael *S & M* 59-64; V S Ramsey St Paul 64-79; rtd 79; P-in-c Leck *Blackb* 79-83; Perm to Offic from 84; Perm to Offic *Carl* from 85; Perm to Offic *Bradf* from 87. *49 Fairgarth Drive, Kirkby Lonsdale, Carnforth, Lancs LA6 2DT* Tel (015242) 71753

FOSTER, The Very Revd John William. b 21. BEM. St Aid Birkenhead 51. **d** 54 **p** 55. C Loughborough All SS *Leic* 54-57; Hong Kong 57-73; Dean Hong Kong 64-73; Hon Can Hong Kong from 73; V Lythe *York* 73-78; Angl Adv Channel TV 78-88; Hon Can Win Cathl *Win* 78-88; R Guernsey St Peter Port 78-88; Dean Guernsey 78-88; rtd 88; Perm to Offic *York* from 90. *14 Lightfoots Avenue, Scarborough, N Yorkshire YO12 5NS* Tel (01723) 379012

FOSTER, Jonathan Guy Vere. b 56. Golds Coll Lon BA78. Wycliffe Hall Ox 83. **d** 86 **p** 87. C Hampreston *Sarum* 86-90;

Chapl Chantilly *Eur* 90-97; V Branksome St Clem *Sarum* from 97. *The Vicarage, 7 Parkstone Heights, Branksome, Poole, Dorset BH14 0QE* Tel (01202) 748058

FOSTER, Joseph James Frederick (Joe). b 22. SS Paul & Mary Coll Cheltenham CertEd42 Birm Univ DipEd59. **d** 88 **p** 88. NSM Elstead *Guildf* 88-94; Perm to Offic from 94. *Wodenscroft, Thursley Road, Elstead, Godalming, Surrey GU8 6DH* Tel (01252) 703198

FOSTER, Leslie (Les). b 49. Linc Th Coll 89. **d** 91 **p** 92. C Coseley Ch Ch *Lich* 91-93; C Coseley *Worc* 93-95; V Firbank, Howgill and Killington *Bradf* from 95. *5 Highfield Road, Sedbergh, Cumbria LA10 5DH* Tel (015396) 20670

FOSTER, Michael John. b 52. St Steph Ho Ox 76. **d** 79 **p** 80. C Wood Green St Mich *Lon* 79-82; C Wood Green St Mich w Bounds Green St Gabr etc 82; TV Clifton *S'well* 82-85; P-in-c Aylesbury *Ox* 85-87; Dep Warden Durning Hall Chr Community Cen 87-89; V Lydbrook *Glouc* from 89. *The Vicarage, Church Hill, Lydbrook, Glos GL17 9SW* Tel (01594) 860225

FOSTER, Neville Colin. b 34. Aston Univ BSc67. WMMTC 78. **d** 81 **p** 82. C Castle Bromwich St Clem *Birm* 81-84; V Tile Cross 84-97; rtd 97. *Collybrook Cottage, Knowbury, Ludlow, Shropshire S78 3LP*

FOSTER, Paul. b 60. MAAT80. Oak Hill Th Coll DipHE93. **d** 93 **p** 94. C New Clee *Linc* 93-96; P-in-c Aldington w Bonnington and Bilsington *Cant* from 96; Chapl HM Pris Aldington from 96. *The Rectory, Aldington, Ashford, Kent TN25 7ES* Tel (01233) 720898

FOSTER, Robin. b 46. ACP70 Bede Coll Dur CertEd67 Nottm Univ BTh75 Lanc Univ MA87 Open Univ BA88. Linc Th Coll 71. **d** 75 **p** 76. C Briercliffe *Blackb* 75-77; Asst Dir RE 77-79; P-in-c Tockholes 77-79; Lic to Offic 80-83; Hon C Walmsley *Man* 83-88; Lic to Offic *Dur* 88-94; NSM Bolton le Sands *Blackb* from 94. *3 Tarnbrook Close, Crag Bank, Carnforth, Lancs LA5 9UL* Tel (01524) 734395

FOSTER, Ronald George. b 25. Bris Univ BSc51 AKC51. **d** 52 **p** 53. C Lydney w Aylburton *Glouc* 52-54; C Leighton Buzzard *St Alb* 54-60; Chapl Bearwood Coll Wokingham 60-83; R Wantage Downs *Ox* 83-91; rtd 91; RD Wantage *Ox* 92-95. *Ascension Cottage, Horn Lane, East Hendred, Wantage, Oxon OX12 8LD* Tel (01235) 820790

FOSTER, Simon Cuthbert. b 63. Kent Univ BA88. Chich Th Coll 89. **d** 92 **p** 93. C Sunderland Pennywell St Thos *Dur* 92-94; C Consett 94-97; P-in-c Darlington St Hilda and St Columba from 97. *239 Parkside, Darlington, Co Durham DL1 5TG* Tel (01325) 486712

FOSTER, Simon John Darby. b 57. Qu Mary Coll Lon BSc78. Wycliffe Hall Ox 85. **d** 88 **p** 89. C Bedgrove *Ox* 88-92; C Glyncorrwg w Afan Vale and Cymmer Afan *Llan* 92-94; R Breedon cum Isley Walton and Worthington *Leic* from 94. *The Rectory, Rectory Close, Breedon-on-the-Hill, Derby DE73 1AT* Tel (01332) 864056

FOSTER, Stephen. b 47. Leeds Univ CertEd69. NE Ord Course 83. **d** 86 **p** 87. NSM Kingston upon Hull St Nic *York* 86-89; NSM Aldbrough, Mappleton w Goxhill and Withernwick from 89. *1 Westbourne Road, Hornsea, N Humberside HU18 1PQ* Tel (01964) 533679

FOSTER, Stephen Arthur. b 54. Coll of Resurr Mirfield 75. **d** 78 **p** 79. C Ches H Trin *Ches* 78-82; C Tranmere St Paul w St Luke 82-83; V Grange St Andr 83-88; V Cheadle Hulme All SS 88-94; P-in-c Stockport St Matt from 94; Asst Dir of Ords from 96. *St Matthew's Vicarage, 99 Chatham Street, Stockport, Cheshire SK3 9EG* Tel 0161-480 5515

FOSTER, Steven. b 52. Wadh Coll Ox BA75 MA80. Ridley Hall Cam 76. **d** 79 **p** 80. C Ipsley *Worc* 79-83; TV Woughton *Ox* 83-94; V Walshaw Ch Ch *Man* from 94. *Christ Church Vicarage, 37 Gisburn Drive, Walshaw, Bury, Lancs BL8 8DH* Tel 0161-763 1193

FOSTER, Steven Francis. b 55. FRSA90 Lon Univ BD76 AKC76 Open Univ BA91. Coll of Resurr Mirfield 77. **d** 78 **p** 79. C Romford St Edw *Chelmsf* 78-80; C Leigh St Clem 80-83; Ed Mayhew McCrimmon Publishers 84-86; Lic to Offic 84; Hon C Southend 85-86; P-in-c Sandon 86-90; R 90-91; R Wanstead St Mary 91-93; R Wanstead St Mary w Ch Ch from 93. *The Rectory, 37 Wanstead Place, London E11 2SW* Tel 0181-989 9101

FOSTER, Stuart Jack. b 47. DipHE79 BA80. Lambeth STh86 Oak Hill Th Coll 77. **d** 80 **p** 81. C Worting *Win* 80-84; C-in-c Kempshott CD 84-88; R Hook 88-95; Chapl Bp Grosseteste Coll Linc from 95. *Bishop Grosseteste College, Newport, Lincoln LN1 3DY* Tel (01522) 527347

FOSTER, Thomas Arthur. b 23. Univ of Wales (Lamp) BA47. Cuddesdon Coll 47. **d** 49 **p** 50. C Risca *Mon* 49-52; C Win H Trin *Win* 52-55; C Rhymney *Mon* 55-56; V Cwmtillery 56-59; R Llanfoist and Llanellen 59-92; rtd 92. *The Bungalow, 5 The Bryn, Llangattock-juxta-Usk, Abergavenny NP7 9AG* Tel (01873) 840516

FOSTER, William Basil. b 23. Worc Ord Coll 65. **d** 67 **p** 68. C Folkingham w Laughton *Linc* 67-71; P-in-c Gedney Hill 71-75; V Whaplode Drove 71-75; R Heydour w Culverthorpe, Welby and Londonthorpe 75-77; P-in-c Ropsley 75-79; R 79-93; R Sapperton w Braceby 79-93; R Old Somerby 82-93; rtd 93. *31 Hedgefield Road, Barrowby, Grantham, Lincs NG32 1TA* Tel (01476) 575925

FOTHERGILL, Anthony Page. b 36. Dur Univ BA60. Cranmer Hall Dur DipTh62. **d** 62 **p** 63. C Wolverhampton St Mark *Lich* 62-66; C Chasetown 66-69; V Wellington St Luke 69-77; TV Hanley H Ev 77-78; V Rocester 78-87; P-in-c Croxden 85-87; RD Uttoxeter 87; rtd 87. *Bowerleigh, 24 Purley Rise, Purley-on-Thames, Reading RG8 8AE* Tel 0118-984 2984

FOTHERGILL, Guy Sherbrooke. Lon Coll of Div. **d** 47 **p** 48. C Sevenoaks St Nic *Roch* 47-50; C Edgware *Lon* 50-52; V Kirkdale St Lawr *Liv* 52-57; V Slough *Ox* 57-65; V Drax *Sheff* 65-72; V Eldersfield *Worc* 72-77; rtd 77; Perm to Offic *Glouc* from 77. *96 Colesbourne Road, Cheltenham, Glos GL51 6DN* Tel (01242) 527884

FOTHERGILL, Richard Patrick. b 61. Newc Univ BA83. Trin Coll Bris DipHE93. **d** 95 **p** 96. C E Twickenham St Steph *Lon* from 95. *29 St Margaret's Road, Twickenham, Middx TW1 2LN* Tel 0181-892 6809

FOULDS, John Stuart. b 64. Lanc Univ BA87 Southn Univ BTh91. Chich Th Coll 88. **d** 91 **p** 92. C Eastcote St Lawr *Lon* 91-95; C Wembley Park St Aug from 95. *194 Windermere Avenue, Wembley, Middx HA9 8QT* Tel 0181-908 2252

FOULGER, Bernard Darwin. b 28. Cant Sch of Min 86. **d** 89 **p** 90. NSM Sittingbourne H Trin w Bobbing *Cant* from 89. *30 Frederick Street, Sittingbourne, Kent ME10 1AU* Tel (01795) 422724

FOULIS BROWN, Graham Douglas. b 50. JP. St Steph Ho Ox 80. **d** 82 **p** 83. C Hungerford and Denford *Ox* 82-84; C Bicester w Bucknell, Caversfield and Launton 84-85; TV 85-90; V Kidmore End from 90. *The Vicarage, Kidmore End, Reading RG4 9AY* Tel (0118) 972 3987

FOULKES, Chan Meurig. b 21. St D Coll Lamp BA46. St Mich Coll Llan 46. **d** 47 **p** 48. C Llanbeblig w Caernarfon *Ban* 47-55; Bp's Private Chapl 55-58; V Harlech and Llanfair juxta Harlech 58-66; RD Ardudwy 64-76; R Llanaber w Caerdeon 66-76; Can Ban Cathl 71-89; Treas 74-83; Chan 83-89; R Llandegfan and Beaumaris w Llanfaes w Penmon etc 76-89; rtd 90; Lic to Offic *Ban* from 90. *Llanaber, 11 Gogarth Avenue, Penmaenmawr LL34 6PY* Tel (01492) 623011

FOULKES, Simon. b 58. Ox Poly BA81. Oak Hill Th Coll BA89. **d** 89 **p** 90. C St Austell *Truro* 89-92; C Boscombe St Jo *Win* 92-94; P-in-c Portswood St Denys from 94. *St Denys Vicarage, 54 Whitworth Crescent, Southampton SO18 1GD* Tel (01703) 672108

FOUNTAIN, David Roy (Brother Malcolm). b 48. Qu Coll Birm 85. **d** 87 **p** 88. SSF from 72; NSM Handsworth St Mich *Birm* 87-92. *Monastery of St Mary at the Cross, Glasshampton, Shrawley, Worcester WR6 6TQ* Tel (01299) 896345

FOUNTAIN, John Stephen. b 43. RAF Coll Cranwell 65 Solicitor 80. LNSM course 91. **d** 93 **p** 94. NSM Nacton and Levington w Bucklesham and Foxhall *St E* from 93. *High Trees, Bridge Road, Levington, Ipswich IP10 0LZ* Tel (01473) 659908

FOUTS, Arthur Guy. b 44. Washington Univ BA72. Ridley Hall Cam 78. **d** 81 **p** 82. C Alperton *Lon* 81-84; R Pinxton *Derby* 84-87; USA from 88. *9601 Lorain Avenue, Silver Spring, Maryland 20901, USA*

FOWELL, Graham Charles. b 48. Southn Univ BTh85. Chich Th Coll. **d** 82 **p** 83. C Clayton *Lich* 82-86; C Uttoxeter w Bramshall 86-90; V Oxley 90-95; P-in-c Shifnal from 95. *St Andrew's Vicarage, Manor Close, Shifnal, Shropshire TF11 9AJ* Tel (01952) 463694

FOWKE, Lt Comdr Thomas Randall. b 07. Master Mariner 33. Chich Th Coll 52. **d** 54 **p** 55. C Haywards Heath St Wilfrid *Chich* 54-57; V Fletching 57-63; V Brighton St Aug 63-76; rtd 76. *6 Lower Road, Pontesbury, Shrewsbury SY5 0YH* Tel (01743) 790450

FOWLER, Anthony Lewis (Tony). b 57. Oak Hill Th Coll BA93. **d** 93 **p** 94. C Walton *St E* 93-96; P-in-c Combs from 96. *The Rectory, 135 Poplar Hill, Combs, Stowmarket, Suffolk IP14 2AY* Tel (01449) 612076

FOWLER, Colin. b 40. DCMus83. Linc Th Coll 80. **d** 82 **p** 83. C Barbourne *Worc* 82-85; TV Worc St Martin w St Pet, St Mark etc 85-86; TV Worc SE 86-92; P-in-c Moulton *Linc* 92-95; Chapl Puerto de la Cruz Tenerife *Eur* from 95. *Apartado 68, Taora Park, 38400 Puerto de la Cruz, Tenerife, Canary Islands* Tel Tenerife (22) 384038

FOWLER, David Mallory. b 51. Lancs Coll of Agric OND72. Trin Coll Bris 75. **d** 78 **p** 79. C Rainhill *Liv* 78-81; C Houghton *Carl* 81-84; P-in-c Grayrigg 84-89; P-in-c Old Hutton w New Hutton 84-89; V Kirkoswald, Renwick and Ainstable from 89. *The Vicarage, Kirkoswald, Penrith, Cumbria CA10 1DQ* Tel (01768) 898176

FOWLER, Mrs Janice Karen Brenda (Jan). b 56. Oak Hill Th Coll DipHE93. **d** 93 **p** 94. NSM Walton *St E* from 93. *The Rectory, 135 Poplar Hill, Combs, Stowmarket, Suffolk IP14 2AY* Tel (01449) 612076

FOWLER, John Douglass. b 22. Worc Ord Coll 61. **d** 63 **p** 64. C Portishead *B & W* 63-67; P-in-c Huish Champflower w Clatworthy 67-71; P-in-c Chipstable w Raddington 67-71; R Chelvey w Brockley 71-73; Asst Chapl Scilly Is *Truro* 73; TV Is of

Scilly 74-78; P-in-c Ashbrittle w Bathealton, Stawley and Kittisford *B & W* 78-81; TV Wellington and Distr 81-86; Perm to Offic *Ex* from 86; rtd 87. *Rosedene, 1 Venn Lane, Stoke Fleming, Dartmouth, Devon TQ6 0QH* Tel (01803) 770362

FOWLER, John Ronald. b 30. Ely Th Coll 55. **d** 58 **p** 59. C Surbiton St Andr *S'wark* 58-61; Guyana 61-70 and 83-89; V Sydenham All SS *S'wark* 70-81; V Wood End *Cov* 81-83; Can St Geo Cathl 86-89; Adn Demerara 86-89; V Bedford St Mich *St Alb* 90-95; rtd 95. *21 Painters Lane, Sutton, Ely, Cambs CB6 2NS* Tel (01353) 776268

FOWLER, Canon John Sims. b 25. Trin Coll Cam BA46 MA50 Lon Univ BD52. Clifton Th Coll 48. **d** 52 **p** 53. C Rodbourne Cheney *Bris* 52-55; Nigeria 56-60 and 61-72; Acting Tutor CMS Tr Coll Chislehurst 60-61; Hon Can Ibadan from 71; Hon Can Lagos from 72; R Crieff *St And* 73-78; R Muthill 74-78; R Comrie 77-78; Warden Leasow Ho Selly Oak 78-84; V Fulham St Dionis Parson's Green *Lon* 84-90; rtd 90; Perm to Offic *Worc* from 90. *5 Mason Close, Malvern Link, Worcs WR14 2NF* Tel (01684) 574463

FOWLER, Miss Morag Margaret. b 45. CertEd67 DipRE67 DipLib76 St Andr Univ MA66. St Jo Coll Nottm 84. **dss** 85 **d** 87 **p** 94. Skipton H Trin *Bradf* 85-87; Par Dn 87-89; Par Dn Market Bosworth, Cadeby w Sutton Cheney etc *Leic* 90-94; C 94; TV 94-96; rtd 96. *25 Springfield Avenue, Market Bosworth, Nuneaton, Warks CV13 0NS* Tel (01455) 292157

FOWLES, Canon Christopher John. b 31. Lich Th Coll 54. **d** 58 **p** 59. C Englefield Green *Guildf* 58-63; C Worplesdon 63-69; V Chessington 69-77; V Horsell 77-95; RD Woking 92-94; Hon Can Guildf Cathl 94-95; rtd 95; Perm to Offic *Guildf* from 95. *78 St Jude's Road, Egham, Surrey TW20 0DF* Tel (01784) 439457

FOX, Albert. b 06. MBE. **d** 73 **p** 74. C Bris St Ambrose Whitehall *Bris* 73-75; Hon C E Bris 75-79; rtd 79. *20 New Brunswick Avenue, Bristol BS5 8PW* Tel 0117-967 2632

FOX, Canon Bernard John Gurney. b 07. Hertf Coll Ox BA28 MA35. Cuddesdon Coll 31. **d** 32 **p** 33. C Millfield St Mary *Dur* 32-35; India 35-41; C S Bank *York* 41-44; V Grangetown *Dur* 44-49; Singapore 49-54; C-in-c Thorney Close CD *Dur* 54-58; R Winlaton 58-67; V Warkworth and Acklington *Newc* 68-73; rtd 74; Perm to Offic *Newc* 74-93; Hon Can Kuala Lumpur from 87. *59 West Avenue, Filey, N Yorkshire YO14 9AX* Tel (01723) 513289

FOX, Cecil George. b 15. TCD BA47 MA64. **d** 48 **p** 49. C Thurles *C & O* 48-50; I Newport w Killoscully and Abington *L & K* 50-54; I Killarney 54-64; Can Limerick Cathl 63-64; Chapl HM Pris Man 64-66; Chapl HM Pris Lewes 66-70; V Charsfield *St E* 70-77; R Monewden and Hoo 70-77; V Charsfield w Debach and Monewden w Hoo 77-82; rtd 82; Perm to Offic *St E* from 82. *1 Ivy Cottages, Walberswick, Southwold, Suffolk IP18 6UX* Tel (01502) 724263

FOX, Canon Charles Alfred. b 08. St Aid Birkenhead 31. **d** 33 **p** 34. C Bradf Cathl Par *Bradf* 33; C Gt Horton 33-35; C Stratford St Jo *Chelmsf* 35-37; V Leyton Em 37-58; CF (TA) 37-78; CF (R of O) 39-45; P-in-c Stratford Ch Ch *Chelmsf* 58-62; V Stratford St Jo and Ch Ch w Forest Gate St Jas 62-78; Hon Can Chelmsf Cathl 63-78; rtd 78; Perm to Offic *Lich* from 78. *5 Limewood Close, Blythe Bridge, Stafford ST11 9NZ* Tel (01782) 395164

FOX, Charles Edward. b 36. Lich Th Coll 62. **d** 66 **p** 67. C S Bank *York* 66-69; C Stokesley 69-72; P-in-c Ugthorpe 72-82; V Egton w Grosmont 72-82; P-in-c Newbold Verdon *Leic* 82-83; R Newbold de Verdun and Kirkby Mallory from 84. *The Rectory, Main Street, Newbold Verdon, Leicester LE9 9NN* Tel (01455) 822528

FOX, Colin George. b 46. TD. Southn Univ DipTh75. Sarum & Wells Th Coll 73. **d** 75 **p** 76. C N Hammersmith St Kath *Lon* 75-79; CF (TA) 76-90; C Heston *Lon* 79-81; TV Marlborough *Sarum* 81-90; P-in-c Pewsey 90-91; TR Pewsey TM from 91; Chapl Pewsey Hosp Wilts 90-95. *The Rectory, Church Street, Pewsey, Wilts SN9 5DL* Tel (01672) 63203

FOX, Harvey Harold. b 27. Lich Th Coll 58. **d** 60 **p** 61. C Birchfield *Birm* 60-62; C Boldmere 62-65; V Sparkbrook Em 65-71; V Dordon 71-77; V Four Oaks 77-82; V Packwood w Hockley Heath 82-90; rtd 90. *3 St James' Close, Kissing Tree Lane, Alveston, Stratford-upon-Avon, Warks CV37 7RH* Tel (01789) 268263

FOX, Canon Herbert Frederick. b 26. Leeds Univ BA50. Coll of Resurr Mirfield 50. **d** 52 **p** 53. C Bury St Thos *Man* 52-55; V Unsworth 55-61; V Turton 61-72; V Farnworth and Kearsley 72-78; RD Farnworth 77-84; TR E Farnworth and Kearsley 78-84; Hon Can Man Cathl 81-84; V Ashford Hill w Headley *Win* 84-91; rtd 91; Perm to Offic *Man* from 91. *9 Highfield Road, Blackrod, Bolton BL6 5BP* Tel (01204) 698368

FOX, Canon Ian James. b 44. Selw Coll Cam BA66 MA70. Linc Th Coll 66. **d** 68 **p** 69. C Salford St Phil w St Steph *Man* 68-71; C Kirkleatham *York* 71-73; TV Redcar w Kirkleatham 73-77; V Bury St Pet *Man* 77-85; V Northallerton w Kirby Sigston *York* from 85; RD Northallerton 85-91; Chapl Friarage and Distr Hosp Northallerton from 88; Can and Preb York Minster *York* from 95. *The Vicarage, Northallerton, N Yorkshire DL7 8DJ* Tel (01609) 780825

FOX, Miss Jacqueline Frederica. b 43. Ripon Coll of Educn CertEd66 Leeds Univ BEd74 MEd84 Hon RCM85. S Dios Minl Tr Scheme 83. **dss** 85 **d** 87 **p** 94. RCM *Lon* 85-86; Dioc FE Officer 87-96; Hon C Acton St Mary 87-96; R from 96; Dean of Women's Min from 96. *The Rectory, 14 Cumberland Park, London W3 6SX* Tel 0181-992 8876

FOX, Mrs Jane. b 47. ALA70 Bp Otter Coll Chich CertEd75 Open Univ BA91. S Dios Minl Tr Scheme 92. **d** 95 **p** 96. NSM W Blatchington *Chich* from 95. *68 Poplar Avenue, Hove, E Sussex BN3 8PS* Tel (01273) 726955

FOX (née COULDRIDGE), Mrs Janice Evelyn. b 49. Bognor Regis Coll of Educn CertEd71. Glouc Sch of Min 89. **d** 92 **p** 94. C Tupsley w Hampton Bishop *Heref* 92-96; P-in-c Orleton w Brimfield from 96; Dioc Ecum Officer from 96. *The Vicarage, Orleton, Ludlow, Shropshire SY8 4HW* Tel (01568) 780324

FOX, Jeremy Robin. b 68. St Chad's Coll Dur BA89 MA92 Leeds Univ BA94. Coll of Resurr Mirfield 92. **d** 95 **p** 96. C S Shields All SS *Dur* from 95. *4 Mitford Road, South Shields, Tyne & Wear NE34 0EQ* Tel 0191-456 1300

FOX, John Brian. b 38. **d** 94 **p** 95. NSM Phillack w Gwithian and Gwinear *Truro* 94-96; NSM Godrevy from 96. *Abbeydale, 26 Tresdale Parc, Connor Downs, Hayle, Cornwall TR27 5DX* Tel (01736) 753935

FOX, Jonathan Alexander. b 56.. St Jo Coll Nottm LTh77 BTh78. **d** 81 **p** 82. C Chasetown *Lich* 81-85; TV Fazakerley Em *Liv* 85-89; TV Madeley *Heref* from 97. *The Vicarage, Park Lane, Woodside, Telford, Shropshire TF7 5HN* Tel (01952) 588958

FOX, Leonard (Len). b 41. AKC66. **d** 67 **p** 68. C Salford Stowell Memorial *Man* 67-68; C Hulme St Phil 68-72; C Portsea All SS w St Jo Rudmore *Portsm* 72-75; V Oakfield St Jo 75-92; P-in-c Portsea All SS from 92; Dir All SS Urban Miss Cen from 92. *All Saints' Vicarage, 51 Staunton Street, Portsmouth PO1 2EJ* Tel (01705) 872815

FOX, Mrs Lynn. b 51. EMMTC CTPS92. **d** 92 **p** 94. Assoc Priest Clifton *S'well* 92-96 and from 96. *St Mary's Rectory, 58 Village Road, Nottingham NG11 0NE* Tel 0115-921 1856

FOX, Maurice Henry George. b 24. Lon Univ BD58. St Aid Birkenhead 47. **d** 49 **p** 50. C Eccleshill *Bradf* 49-52; C Bingley All SS 52-56; V Cross Roads cum Lees 56-62; V Sutton 62-79; V Grange-over-Sands *Carl* 79-88; rtd 89. *7 Manor Close, Topcliffe, Thirsk, N Yorkshire YO7 3RH* Tel (01845) 578322

FOX, The Ven Michael John. b 49. Hull Univ BSc63. Coll of Resurr Mirfield 64. **d** 66 **p** 67. C Becontree St Elisabeth *Chelmsf* 66-70; C Wanstead H Trin Hermon Hill 70-72; V Victoria Docks Ascension 72-76; V Chelmsf All SS 76-88; P-in-c Chelmsf Ascension 85-88; RD Chelmsf 86-88; R Colchester St Jas, All SS, St Nic and St Runwald 88-93; Hon Can Chelmsf Cathl 91-93; Adn Harlow 93-95; Adn W Ham from 95. *86 Aldersbrook Road, London E12 5DH* Tel 0181-989 8557

FOX, Michael John Holland. b 41. Lon Univ BD68. Oak Hill Th Coll 64. **d** 69 **p** 70. C Reigate St Mary *S'wark* 69-73; Hon C from 76; C Guildf St Sav *Guildf* 73-76; C Guildf St Sav w Stoke-next-Guildford 76; Asst Chapl Reigate Gr Sch 76-81; Chapl from 81. *71 Blackborough Road, Reigate, Surrey RH2 7BU* Tel (01737) 249017 E-mail 101707.23.22@compuserve.com

FOX, Nigel Stephen. b 35. Sarum Th Coll 59. **d** 62 **p** 63. C Rainbow Hill St Barn *Worc* 62-65; C Kidderminster St Geo 65-67; C-in-c Warndon CD 67-69; V Warndon 69-74; R S Hill w Callington *Truro* 74-85; RD E Wivelshire 78-81; R St Martin w E and W Looe 85-95; rtd 95; Perm to Offic *Truro* from 95. *Newlair, 4 Bindown Court, Nomansland, Looe, Cornwall PL13 1PX* Tel (01503) 263070

FOX, Norman Stanley. b 39. Univ of Wales DipTh64. St Mich Coll Llan 61. **d** 64 **p** 65. C Brierley Hill *Lich* 64-67; C Tettenhall Regis 67-70; V Cradley *Worc* 70-73; Asst Chapl HM Pris Wakef 73-74; Chapl HM Pris The Verne 74-76; R Clayton W w High Hoyland *Wakef* 76-81; R Cumberworth 81-84; C Tettenhall Wood *Lich* 85-89; TV 89-91; V Pensnett 91-93. *Address temp unknown*

FOX, Peter John. b 52. AKC74. St Aug Coll Cant 74. **d** 75 **p** 76. C Wymondham *Nor* 75-79; Papua New Guinea 79-85; P-in-c Tattersett *Nor* 85-88; P-in-c Houghton 85-88; P-in-c Syderstone w Barmer and Bagthorpe 85-88; P-in-c Tatterford 85-88; P-in-c E w W Rudham 85-88; R Coxford Gp 88-89; TR Lynton, Brendon, Countisbury, Lynmouth etc *Ex* 89-95; RD Shirwell 93-95; P-in-c Harpsden w Bolney *Ox* from 95; Gen Sec Melanesian Miss from 95. *The Rectory, 2 Harpsden Way, Henley-on-Thames, Oxon RG9 1NL* Tel (01491) 573401

FOX, Raymond. b 46. QUB BSc69. CITC 71. **d** 71 **p** 72. C Holywood *D & D* 71-75; C Min Can Down Cathl 75-78; I Killinchy w Kilmood and Tullynakill 78-81; I Belfast St Mary *Conn* 81-88; I Killaney w Carryduff *D & D* from 88; RD Killinchy from 93. *700 Saintfield Road, Carryduff, Belfast BT8 8BU* Tel (01232) 812342 Fax as telephone

FOX, Robert. b 54. Man Univ BEd76. N Ord Course 89. **d** 91 **p** 92. NSM Stalybridge *Man* 91; NSM Ashton St Mich 91-96; NSM Stalybridge from 96. *36 Norman Road, Stalybridge, Cheshire SK15 1LY* Tel 0161-338 8481

FOX, Dr Sidney. b 47. Nottm Univ BTh79 PhD93. Linc Th Coll 75. **d** 79 **p** 80. C Middlesbrough St Oswald *York* 79-81; P-in-c 81-86; V 86-87; V Newby 87-92; R Auchmithie *Bre* from 92; R Brechin from 92; R Tarfside from 92. *39 Church Street, Brechin, Angus DD9 6HB* Tel (01356) 622708

FOX, Timothy William Bertram. b 37. CCC Cam BA61. Qu Coll Birm 66. **d** 68 **p** 69. C Cannock *Lich* 68-72; C Bilston St Leon 72-75; V Essington 75-81; R Buildwas and Leighton w Eaton Constantine etc 81-92; RD Wrockwardine 88-92; P-in-c Moreton and Church Eaton 92; P-in-c Bradeley St Mary and All SS 92; R Bradeley, Church Eaton and Moreton from 92. *The Rectory, Church Eaton, Stafford ST20 0AG* Tel (01785) 823091

FOX-WILSON, Francis James (Frank). b 46. Nottm Univ BTh73. Linc Th Coll 69. **d** 73 **p** 74. C Eastbourne St Elisabeth *Chich* 73-76; C Seaford w Sutton 76-78; P-in-c Hellingly 78-79; P-in-c Upper Dicker 78-79; V Hellingly and Upper Dicker 79-85; V Goring-by-Sea 85-93; R Alfriston w Lullington, Litlington and W Dean from 93. *The Rectory, Sloe Lane, Alfriston, Polegate, E Sussex BN26 5UY* Tel (01323) 870376

FOXWELL, Rupert Edward Theodore. b 54. Solicitor 79 Magd Coll Cam BA76 MA80. Wycliffe Hall Ox 91. **d** 93 **p** 94. C Tonbridge SS Pet and Paul *Roch* from 93. *14 Salisbury Road, Tonbridge, Kent TN10 4PB* Tel (01732) 355200

FOY, Malcolm Stuart. b 48. ACP80 FCollP FRSA Univ of Wales (Lamp) BA71 Magd Coll Cam CertEd72 K Coll Lon MA89. Ox NSM Course 84. **d** 87 **p** 88. NSM Tilehurst St Mich *Ox* 87-90; C Ireland Wood *Ripon* 90-96; Adv RE Leeds Adnry 90-96; Dir Educn *Bradf* from 96. *1 Westview Way, Keighley, W Yorkshire BD20 6JA* Tel (01535) 665112

FRAIS, Jonathan Jeremy. b 65. Kingston Poly LLB87. Oak Hill Th Coll BA92. **d** 92 **p** 93. C Orpington Ch Ch *Roch* 92-96; Chapl Moscow *Eur* from 96. *Poste Restante, British Embassy, Nab Sofiyskaya 14, Moscow, Russia, or Pinafore, 11 Nineveh Shipyard, 93 River Road, Arundel, W Sussex BN18 9SU* Tel (01903) 885356

FRAMPTON, Miss Marcia Ellen. b 36. SRN65 SCM66. Ripon Coll Cuddesdon 86. **d** 88 **p** 95. Par Dn Paston *Pet* 88-89; Par Dn Burford w Fulbrook and Taynton *Ox* 90-92; Par Dn Witney 92-93; NSM Heref St Martin w St Fran (S Wye TM) *Heref* 94-95; NSM Heref S Wye 95-96; rtd 96. *27 Webb Tree Avenue, Hereford HR2 6HG* Tel (01432) 269606

FRAMPTON-MORGAN, Anthony Paul George. b 57. Sarum & Wells Th Coll 89. **d** 91 **p** 92. C Plymstock *Ex* 91-95; P-in-c Wolborough w Newton Abbot from 95. *5 Coach Place, Newton Abbot, Devon TQ12 1ES* Tel (01626) 52088

FRANCE, Archdeacon of. *See* DRAPER, The Ven Martin Paul

FRANCE, Evan Norman Lougher. b 52. Jes Coll Cam BA74 MA78. Wycliffe Hall Ox 76. **d** 79 **p** 80. C Hall Green Ascension *Birm* 79-82; CMS 82-84; C Bexhill St Pet *Chich* 84-87; V Westf from 87. *The Vicarage, Westfield, Hastings, E Sussex TN35 4SD* Tel (01424) 751029

FRANCE, Geoffrey. b 37. S Dios Minl Tr Scheme 87. **d** 90 **p** 91. NSM Uckfield *Chich* 90-92; C 92-94; R Warbleton and Bodle Street Green from 94. *Warbleton Rectory, Rushlake Green, Heathfield, E Sussex TN21 9QJ* Tel (01435) 830421

FRANCE, Canon Geoffrey Charles. b 23. Ripon Hall Ox 57. **d** 59 **p** 60. C Mansfield St Mark *S'well* 59-61; V Rainworth 61-68; V Sneinton St Cypr 68-90; Hon Can S'well Minster 87-90; rtd 90; Perm to Offic *Nor* from 90. *11 Elsden Close, Holt, Norfolk NR25 6JW* Tel (01263) 711210

FRANCE, Dr Malcolm Norris. b 28. Ch Ch Ox BA53 MA57 Essex Univ PhD75. Westcott Ho Cam 53. **d** 55 **p** 56. C Ipswich St Mary le Tower *St E* 55-58; V Esholt *Bradf* 58-64; Chapl Essex Univ *Chelmsf* 64-73; Perm to Offic *Chich* 77-87; P-in-c Starston *Nor* 87-93; rtd 93; Perm to Offic *Nor* from 93. *The Old Rectory, Starston, Harleston, Norfolk IP20 9NG* Tel (01379) 854326

FRANCE, Canon Dr Richard Thomas (Dick). b 38. Ball Coll Ox BA60 MA63 Lon Univ BD62 Bris Univ PhD67. Tyndale Hall Bris 60. **d** 66 **p** 67. C Cambridge St Matt *Ely* 66-69; Nigeria 69-73 and 76-77; Hon Can Ibadan from 94; Lib Tyndale Ho Cam 73-76; Warden 78-81; Vice-Prin Lon Bible Coll 81-88; Prin Wycliffe Hall Ox 89-95; R Wentnor w Ratlinghope, Myndtown, Norbury etc *Heref* from 95. *The Rectory, Wentnor, Bishops Castle, Shropshire SY9 5EE* Tel (01588) 650244 Fax 650244

FRANCE, Robert Alistair. b 71. Ox Poly BA92. Oak Hill Th Coll BA94. **d** 97. C Hartford *Ches* from 97. *71 School Lane, Hartford, Northwich, Cheshire CW8 1PF* Tel (01606) 784755

FRANCE, William Michael. b 43. Sydney Univ BA68 Lon Univ BD72. Moore Th Coll Sydney LTh70. **d** 73 **p** 73. Australia 73-76 and from 78; C Barton Seagrave w Warkton *Pet* 76-78. *19 Cobran Road, Cheltenham, NSW, Australia 2119* Tel Sydney (2) 868 2276 or 9909 3133 Fax 9909 3228

FRANCES, Nicholas Francis. b 61. Nor Ord Course. **d** 95 **p** 96. NSM Anfield St Columba *Liv* from 95. *12 Prince Alfred Road, Liverpool L15 5BG* Tel 0151-733 3128

FRANCES ANNE, Mother. *See* COCKER, Frances Rymer

FRANCIS, Miss Annette. b 44. DCR66. Trin Coll Bris DipHE93. **d** 93 **p** 94. NSM Belmont *Lon* 93; C 94-97; C Swansea St Pet *S & B* from 97. *St Illtyd's Parsonage, 18 Ystrad Road, Fforestfach, Swansea SA5 4BT* Tel (01792) 586437

FRANCIS, Brother. *See* TYNDALE-BISCOE, William Francis

FRANCIS, Claude Vernon Eastwood. b 15. Univ of Wales BA38. Ripon Hall Ox 38. **d** 40 **p** 41. C Cilybebyll *Llan* 40-44; C Treorchy 44-46; C Whitchurch 46-49; C Winscombe *B & W* 49-55; R E Pennard w Pylle 55-75; R Ditcheat w E Pennard and Pylle 75-81; rtd 81; Perm to Offic *B & W* from 81. *Millbank, Mill Lane, Alhampton, Shepton Mallet, Somerset BA4 6PX* Tel (01749) 860225

FRANCIS, David Carpenter. b 45. Southn Univ BSc66 Loughb Univ MSc71 Sussex Univ MA83. Westcott Ho Cam 85. **d** 87 **p** 88. C Ealing St Mary *Lon* 87-90; Chapl Ealing Coll of HE 87-90; Chapl Clayponds Hosp Ealing 88-90; P-in-c Wembley St Jo *Lon* 90-93; Chapl Wembley Hosp 90-93; V Platt *Roch* from 93; Post Ord Tr Officer from 93. *The Vicarage, Comp Lane, Platt, Sevenoaks, Kent TN15 8NR* Tel (01732) 885482

FRANCIS, David Everton Baxter. b 45. St Deiniol's Hawarden 76. **d** 77 **p** 78. C Llangyfelach *S & B* 77-78; C Llansamlet 78-80; V Llanrhaeadr-ym-Mochnant, Llanarmon, Pennant etc *St As* 80-85; V Penrhyncoch and Elerch *St D* 85-93; V Borth and Eglwys-fach w Llangynfelyn from 93. *The Vicarage, Swn y Mor, The Cliff, Borth SY24 5NG* Tel (01970) 871594

FRANCIS, Donald. b 31. Bris Univ BA52. St Mich Coll Llan 52. **d** 54 **p** 55. C Newport St Julian *Mon* 54-59; C Pokesdown St Jas *Win* 59-61; R Wolvesnewton w Kilgwrrwg and Devauden *Mon* 61-74; V Llantilio Pertholey w Bettws Chpl 74-83; V Llantillio Pertholey w Bettws Chpl etc 83-93; RD Abergavenny 87-93; rtd 93; Perm to Offic *Heref* from 93. *114 Park Street, Hereford HR1 2RE* Tel (01432) 269674

FRANCIS, The Ven Edward Reginald (Ted). b 29. Roch Th Coll 59. **d** 61 **p** 62. Chapl TS Arethusa 61-64; C Frindsbury *Roch* 61-64; C-in-c Chatham St Wm CD 64-71; V Chatham St Wm 71-73; RD Roch 73-78; V Roch 73-78; Hon Can Roch Cathl 79-94; Ind Chapl 79-89; Dir Continuing Minl Educn 89-94; Adn Bromley 79-94; rtd 94; Perm to Offic *Roch* from 94. *71 Ash Tree Drive, West Kingsdown, Sevenoaks, Kent TN15 6LW*

FRANCIS, Canon Ernest Walter. b 08. MBE45. Bible Churchmen's Coll 29. **d** 36 **p** 37. BCMS Burma 32-67; CF 43-46; Area Sec BCMS 67-76; rtd 76; Hon Can Sittwe Burma from 82. *7 Margetts Close, Kenilworth, Warks CV8 1EN* Tel (01926) 852560

FRANCIS, Miss Gillian Cartwright. b 40. CertEd61. Dalton Ho Bris Trin Coll Bris DipTh71. **dss** 85 **d** 87 **p** 94. Blackheath *Birm* 86-87; Par Dn 87-94; C 94; P-in-c Stechford from 94. *The Vicarage, Albert Road, Birmingham B33 8UA* Tel 0121-783 2463

FRANCIS, Graham John. b 45. Univ of Wales (Cardiff) DipTh70. St Mich Coll Llan 66. **d** 70 **p** 71. C Llanblethian w Cowbridge and Llandough etc *Llan* 70-76; V Penrhiwceiber w Matthewstown and Ynysboeth from 76. *The Vicarage, Penrhiwceiber, Mountain Ash CF45 3YF* Tel (01443) 473716

FRANCIS, Hilton Barrington. b 23. Selw Coll Cam BA46 MA48. Ridley Hall Cam 61. **d** 62 **p** 63. C Eaton *Nor* 62-67; V Trowse 67-69; V Arminghall 67-69; Lect Nor City Coll 69-75; Tutor Adult Educn 75-81; P-in-c Gt w Lt Plumstead 81-87; rtd 88; Perm to Offic *Ely* from 88. *190 Church End, Cherry Hinton, Cambridge CB1 3LB* Tel (01223) 212081

FRANCIS, James More MacLeod. b 44. Edin Univ MA65 BD68 PhD74. Yale Div Sch STM69. **d** 87 **p** 87. NSM Sunderland St Chad *Dur* 87-97; NSM Sunderland from 97. *73 Hillcrest, Sunderland SR3 3NN* Tel 0191-528 1326

FRANCIS, Canon James Woodcock. b 28. OBE97. Wilberforce Univ Ohio AB57 Payne Th Sem Ohio BD58. Bexley Hall Div Sch Ohio 59. **d** 59 **p** 60. USA 59-84; Can Res Bermuda Cathl from 85. *PO Box HM 627, Hamilton HM CX, Bermuda* Tel Bermuda (1-809) 295-1125 Fax 292-5421

FRANCIS, Jeffrey Merrick. b 46. Bris Univ BSc69. Qu Coll Birm 72. **d** 76 **p** 77. C Bris Ch the Servant Stockwood *Bris* 76-79; C Bishopston 79-82; V Bris St Andr Hartcliffe 82-93; TV Bris St Paul's from 93. *St Werburgh's Vicarage, 15 St Werburgh's Park, Bristol BS2 9XD* Tel 0117-955 8863

FRANCIS, Jeremy Montgomery. b 31. BNC Ox BA53 MA. Glouc Sch of Min 84. **d** 87 **p** 88. NSM Chedworth, Yanworth and Stowell, Coln Rogers etc *Glouc* 87-90; NSM Coates, Rodmarton and Sapperton etc from 90; NSM Daglingworth w the Duntisbournes and Winstone 95-97; NSM Brimpsfield w Birdlip, Syde, Daglingworth, etc from 97. *Old Barnfield, Duntisbourne Leer, Cirencester, Glos GL7 7AS* Tel (01285) 821370

FRANCIS, John Sims. b 25. Fitzw Ho Cam BA54 MA58. St D Coll Lamp BA47 LTh49. **d** 49 **p** 50. C Swansea St Barn *S & B* 49-52; C Chesterton St Andr *Ely* 52-54; C Swansea St Mary and H Trin *S & B* 54-58; V Newbridge-on-Wye and Llanfihangel Brynpabuan 58-65; R Willingham *Ely* 65-82; RD N Stowe 78-82; R Rampton 82; P-in-c Buckden 82-91; rtd 91; Perm to Offic *Linc* from 92; Perm to Offic *Ely* from 92. *3 The Brambles, Bourne, Lincs PE10 9TF* Tel (01778) 426396

FRANCIS, Julian Montgomery. b 60. Selw Coll Cam MA83. S'wark Ord Course 88. **d** 91 **p** 92. C S Wimbledon H Trin and St Pet *S'wark* 91-95; V Cottingley *Bradf* from 95. *St Michael's Vicarage, Littlelands, Cottingley, Bingley, W Yorkshire BD16 1RR* Tel (01274) 562278

FRANCIS, Kenneth. b 30. Em Coll Cam BA56 MA60. Coll of Resurr Mirfield. **d** 58 **p** 59. C De Beauvoir Town St Pet *Lon* 58-61; N Rhodesia 62-64; Zambia 64-70; V Harlow St Mary Magd *Chelmsf* 70-76; V Felixstowe St Jo *St E* from 76. *St John's*

Vicarage, Princes Road, Felixstowe, Suffolk IP11 7PL Tel (01394) 284226

FRANCIS, Kenneth Charles. b 22. Oak Hill Th Coll 46. **d** 50 **p** 51. C Wandsworth All SS *S'wark* 50-53; V Deptford St Nic w Ch Ch 53-61; V Summerstown 61-77; R Cratfield w Heveningham and Ubbeston etc *St E* 77-87; rtd 87. *Wheal Alfred, Chapel Hill, Bolingey, Perranporth, Cornwall TR6 0DQ* Tel (01872) 571317

FRANCIS (or ROOSE FRANCIS), Leslie. b 18. Magd Coll Ox BA48 MA52. Westcott Ho Cam 48. **d** 49 **p** 50. C Rochdale *Man* 49-52; C Odiham w S Warnborough *Win* 52-54; V Awbridge w Mottisfont 54-60; V Bournemouth H Epiphany 60-68; R Compton Bassett *Sarum* 68; V Hilmarton and Highway 68-78; rtd 78. *2 Glebelands, Pig Leg Lane, Okehampton, Devon EX20 4ER* Tel (01837) 861493

FRANCIS, Prof Leslie John. b 47. Qu Coll Cam ScD97 FBPsS88 FCP94 Pemb Coll Ox BA70 MA74 BD90 Qu Coll Cam PhD76 Lon Univ MSc77 Nottm Univ MTh76. Westcott Ho Cam 70. **d** 73 **p** 74. C Haverhill *St E* 73-77; P-in-c Gt Bradley 78-82; P-in-c Lt Wratting 79-82; P-in-c N Cerney w Bagendon *Glouc* 82-85; Research Officer Culham Coll Inst 82-88; Perm to Offic from 85; Fell Trin Coll Carmarthen from 89; Dean of Chpl from 95; Prof Th Univ of Wales (Lamp) from 92. *Trinity College, Carmarthen SA31 3EP* Tel (01267) 676806 Fax 676766

FRANCIS, Martin Rufus. b 37. Pemb Coll Ox BA60 MA64. Linc Th Coll 60. **d** 63 **p** 64. C W Hartlepool St Paul *Dur* 63-67; C Yeovil St Jo w Preston Plucknett *B & W* 67-69; Chapl Tonbridge Sch 69-83; Chapl and Dep Hd St Jo Sch Leatherhead 83-94; R Herstmonceux and Wartling *Chich* from 94. *The Rectory, Herstmonceux, Hailsham, E Sussex BN27 4NY* Tel (01323) 833124

FRANCIS, Noel Charles. b 14. St Andr Univ. St D Coll Lamp BA36. **d** 38 **p** 39. C Llanegwad *St D* 38-40; C Carmarthen St Dav 40-42; C Penistone w Midhope *Wakef* 42-51; S Africa 51-65; I Muckross w Templecarne *Clogh* 65-68; Perm to Offic *St And* 68-69; V Manningham St Paul and St Jude *Bradf* 69-81; I Aughaval w Burrishoole, Knappagh and Louisburgh *T, K & A* 81-85; rtd 85; Perm to Offic *York* from 87. *5 Foxcroft, Haxby, York YO3 3GY* Tel (01904) 769160

FRANCIS, Paul Edward. b 52. Southn Univ BTh84. Sarum & Wells Th Coll 78. **d** 81 **p** 82. C Biggin Hill *Roch* 81-85; R Fawkham and Hartley 85-90; V Aylesford from 90. *The Vicarage, Vicarage Close, Aylesford, Kent ME20 7BB* Tel (01622) 717434

FRANCIS, The Very Revd Peter Brereton. b 53. St Andr Univ MTh77. Qu Coll Birm 77. **d** 78 **p** 79. C Hagley *Worc* 78-81; Chapl Qu Mary Coll *Lon* 81-87; R Ayr *Glas* 87-92; Miss to Seamen 87-92; Provost St Mary's Cathl *Glas* 92-96; R Glas St Mary 92-96; Warden and Lib St Deiniol's Lib Hawarden from 97. *St Deiniol's Library, Hawarden, Deeside CH5 3DF* Tel (01244) 532350

FRANCIS, Peter Philip. b 48. St Jo Coll Dur BA73. Wycliffe Hall Ox 73. **d** 75 **p** 76. C Foord St Jo *Cant* 75-78; C Morden *S'wark* 78-83; P-in-c Barford St Martin, Dinton, Baverstock etc *Sarum* 83-88; P-in-c Fovant, Sutton Mandeville and Teffont Evias etc 83-86; R Newick *Chich* from 88. *The Rectory, Church Road, Newick, Lewes, E Sussex BN8 4JX* Tel (01825) 722692

FRANCIS, Philip Thomas. b 58. St D Coll Lamp BA81. Chich Th Coll 81. **d** 82 **p** 83. C Llanelli St Paul *St D* 82-84; C Barnsley St Mary *Wakef* 84-87; V Burton Dassett *Cov* from 87; V Gaydon w Chadshunt from 87. *Burton Dassett Vicarage, Northend, Leamington Spa, Warks CV33 0TH* Tel (01295) 770400

FRANCIS-DEHQANI, Lee Thomas. b 67. Nottm Univ BA89. Sarum & Wells Th Coll 92 Trin Coll Bris BA95. **d** 95 **p** 96. C Putney St Mary *S'wark* from 95. *8 Deodar Road, London SW15 2NN* Tel 0181-785 3821 Fax 788 4414

FRANK, Derek John. b 49. ACGI70 Imp Coll Lon BScEng70 Warw Univ MSc71. Cranmer Hall Dur 83. **d** 85 **p** 86. C Clay Cross *Derby* 85-87; C Crookes St Thos *Sheff* 87-90; TV 90-93; Chapl Vevey w Chateau d'Oex and Villars *Eur* from 93. *The Parsonage, Chemin de Champsavaux 1, 1807 Blonday, Switzerland* Tel Lausanne (21) 943-2239

FRANK, Canon Richard Patrick Harry. b 40. St Chad's Coll Dur BA66 DipTh68. **d** 68 **p** 69. C Darlington H Trin *Dur* 68-72; C Monkwearmouth St Andr 72-74; C-in-c Harlow Green CD 74-79; R Skelton and Hutton-in-the-Forest w Ivegill *Carl* 79-86; V Carl St Luke Morton 86-92; RD Carl 88-89; P-in-c Thursby 89-90; P-in-c Kirkbride w Newton Arlosh 89-92; TR Greystoke, Matterdale, Mungrisdale etc from 92; P-in-c Patterdale from 95; RD Penrith from 96; Hon Can Carl Cathl from 97. *The Rectory, Greystoke, Penrith, Cumbria CA11 0TJ* Tel (017684) 83293

FRANKLIN, Archibald William. b 01. Lon Univ BD32 AKC32. **d** 32 **p** 33. C Portsea St Mary *Portsm* 32-40; V Hawksworth Wood *Ripon* 40-61; V York Town St Mich *Guildf* 61-66; V Pool *Ripon* 66-74; V Pool w Arthington 74-77; rtd 77. *Terry's Cross House, Woodmancote, Henfield, W Sussex BN5 9SX* Tel (01273) 495421

FRANKLIN, Eric Edward Joseph. b 29. St Pet Hall Ox BA53 MA58. Qu Coll Birm DipTh55. **d** 55 **p** 56. C Knighton St Mary Magd *Leic* 55-60; Chapl Brasted Place Coll Westerham 60-66; Tutor St Chad's Coll Dur 66-72; Tutor Chich Th Coll 72-74; C Margate St Jo *Cant* 74-83; Vice-Prin St Steph Ho Ox 83-90; Dir of Studies St Steph Ho Ox 91-94; rtd 94; Perm to Offic *Cant* from 94. *St Stephen's House, 16 Marston Street, Oxford OX4 1JX* Tel (01865) 247874 or 243427

FRANKLIN, Hector Aloysius. b 32. Sheff Univ DipTech79. N Ord Course 94. **d** 97. NSM Chapeltown *Sheff* from 97. *13 Staindrop View, Chapeltown, Sheffield S30 4YS* Tel 0114-246 9650

FRANKLIN, Joan Mary. b 20. St Andr Ho Portsm 47. **dss** 61 **d** 87. Scunthorpe St Jo *Linc* 66-70; Gt Grimsby St Mary and St Jas 70-86; rtd 86. *56 Vicarage Gardens, Grimsby, S Humberside DN34 4PZ* Tel (01472) 242341

FRANKLIN, Richard Charles Henry. b 48. Ch Ch Coll Cant CertEd70. Sarum & Wells Th Coll 75. **d** 78 **p** 79. C Pershore w Pinvin, Wick and Birlingham *Worc* 78-80; Educn Chapl 80-85; V Wollescote 85-92; V Fareham SS Pet and Paul *Portsm* from 92. *St Peter and St Paul's Vicarage, 22 Harrison Road, Fareham, Hants PO16 7EJ* Tel (01329) 280256 or 236003

FRANKLIN, Richard Heighway. b 54. Southn Univ BA75 MPhil83. Sarum & Wells Th Coll 75. **d** 78 **p** 79. C Thame w Towersey *Ox* 78-81; Asst Chapl Southn Univ *Win* 81-83; Dir of Studies Chich Th Coll 83-89; P-in-c Stalbridge *Sarum* 89-94; V Weymouth H Trin from 94. *Holy Trinity Vicarage, 7 Glebe Close, Weymouth, Dorset DT4 9RL* Tel (01305) 760354

FRANKLIN, Simon George. b 54. Bris Univ BA75. Ridley Hall Cam 77. **d** 79 **p** 80. C Woodmansterne *S'wark* 79-83; C St Peter-in-Thanet *Cant* 83-86; R Woodchurch 86-96; P-in-c Ottery St Mary, Alfington, W Hill, Tipton etc *Ex* from 96. *The Vicar's House, 7 College Road, Ottery St Mary, Devon EX11 1DQ* Tel (01404) 812062

FRANKLIN, Stephen Alaric (Steve). b 58. Lon Univ BD87. Sarum & Wells Th Coll 87. **d** 89 **p** 90. C Chenies and Lt Chalfont, Latimer and Flaunden *Ox* 89-93; CF from 93. *MOD Chaplains (Army), Trenchard Lines, Upavon, Pewsey, Wilts SN9 6BE* Tel (01980) 615804 Fax 615800

✠**FRANKLIN, The Rt Revd William Alfred.** b 16. OBE64. Kelham Th Coll 33. **d** 40 **p** 41 **c** 72. C Bethnal Green St Jo *Lon* 40-42; C Palmers Green St Jo 43-45; Argentina 45-58; Chile 58-65; Colombia 65-78; Adn 66-71; Bp 72-78; Asst Bp Pet 78-86; rtd 86; Asst Bp Cant 86-92; Perm to Offic from 93. *Flat C, 26 The Beach, Walmer, Deal, Kent CT14 7HJ* Tel (01304) 361807

FRANKLIN, William Henry. b 50. Macquarie Univ (NSW) BA78 Birkb Coll Lon MA82. Moore Th Coll Sydney 76 Melbourne Coll of Div 83 Chich Th Coll 85. **d** 86 **p** 87. C S Leamington St Jo *Cov* 86-89; Chapl RN from 89. *Royal Naval Chaplaincy Service, Room 203, Victory Building, HM Naval Base, Portsmouth PO1 3LS* Tel (01705) 727903 Fax 727112

FRANKS, John Edward. b 29. **d** 61 **p** 62. C Plymouth St Matthias *Ex* 61-66; V Upton Grey w Weston Patrick and Tunworth *Win* 66-77; V Upton Grey, Weston Patrick, Tunworth etc 77-79; P-in-c Wolverton cum Ewhurst and Hannington 79-80; R Baughurst, Ramsdell, Wolverton w Ewhurst etc 81-94; rtd 94. *Victoria, 26 Triq Santa Lucia, Naxxar, NXR 02, Malta*

FRANZ, The Very Revd Kevin Gerhard. b 53. Edin Univ MA74 BD79. Edin Th Coll 76. **d** 79 **p** 80. C Edin St Martin *Edin* 79-83; R Selkirk 83-90; Provost St Ninian's Cathl Perth *St And* from 90; R Perth St Ninian from 90. *St Ninian's House, 40 Hay Street, Perth PH1 5HS* Tel (01738) 626874

FRASER, Alister Douglas. b 26. Qu Coll Cam BA49 MA55. Tyndale Hall Bris 50. **d** 68 **p** 69. C Weymouth St Jo *Sarum* 68-72; R Kingswood *Glouc* 72-80; V Woodside St Steph 80-84; RD Forest S 84-88; V Cinderford St Steph w Littledean 84-90; rtd 90; Perm to Offic *Ex* from 91. *4 Stevens Cross Close, Sidmouth, Devon EX10 9QJ* Tel (01395) 579568

FRASER, Andrew Thomas. b 52. Newc Univ Aus BA81. St Jo Coll (NSW) ThL79. **d** 81 **p** 82. Australia 81-87; C Prestbury *Glouc* 87-91; C Wotton St Mary 91-92. *79 Victoria Street, Gloucester GL1 4EP* Tel (01452) 381082

FRASER, David Ian. b 32. Em Coll Cam BA54 MA58. Oak Hill Th Coll 56. **d** 58 **p** 59. C Bedford St Jo *St Alb* 58-61; C Cheadle Hulme St Andr *Ches* 61-64; R Fringford w Hethe and Newton Purcell *Ox* 64-67; V Preston St Luke *Blackb* 67-71; V Surbiton Hill Ch Ch *S'wark* 71-91; rtd 91. *7 Godwyn Close, Abingdon, Oxon OX14 1BU* Tel (01235) 532049

FRASER, Ernest William Emerson. b 04. AKC27. Westcott Ho Cam 28. **d** 28 **p** 29. C Tunbridge Wells Ch Ch *Roch* 28-31; C Gt Malvern St Mary *Worc* 32-37; Perm to Offic *Roch* 38-39; V Hildenborough 39-51; V Downe 51-57; Perm to Offic *Chich* from 57; rtd 69. *The Goodalls, Ellerslie Lane, Bexhill-on-Sea, E Sussex TN39 4LJ* Tel (01424) 211141

FRASER, Geoffrey Michael. b 29. Sarum Th Coll. **d** 59 **p** 60. C Thames Ditton *Guildf* 59-63; C Shere 63-65; C Dunsford and Doddiscombsleigh *Ex* 65-70; V Uffculme 70-92; rtd 92. *46 Priory Road, Great Malvern, Worcs WR14 3DB* Tel (01684) 576302

FRASER, Giles. b 64. Ripon Coll Cuddesdon. **d** 93 **p** 94. C Streetly *Lich* from 93. *Christ Church Rectory, Blakenall Heath, Walsall, W Midlands WS3 1HT*

FRASER, Air Marshal Sir Henry Paterson. b 07. KBE61 CB53 AFC37. CEng FRAeS Pemb Coll Cam BA29 MA73. **d** 77 **p** 78. APM Ramsey Deanery *S & M* from 77; Perm to Offic from 94. *803 King's Court, Ramsey, Isle of Man IM8 1LP* Tel (01624) 813069

FRASER, Jane Alicia. b 44. Man Univ BA. Glouc Sch of Min. **d** 89 **p** 94. NSM Upton-upon-Severn *Worc* from 89. *Sunnybank House, Holly Green, Upton-on-Severn, Worcester WR8 0PG* Tel (01684) 594715

FRASER, Canon John Sheean. b 23. TCD BA47 MA52. **d** 47 **p** 50. C Dublin St Geo *D & G* 47-48; C Dublin St Steph 50-52; I Leney and Kilbixy *M & K* 52-59; I Killucan Union 59-65; I Limerick St Mary *L & K* 65-67; Can Res and Preb Limerick Cathl 67-76; Sub-Dean 74-76; Lic to Offic from 82. *5 Ashbrook, Ennis Road, Limerick, Irish Republic* Tel Limerick (61) 453502

FRASER, Lesley. b 34. ALCD62. **d** 62 **p** 63. C St Helens St Matt Thatto Heath *Liv* 62-64; C Fazakerley Em 64-67; R Collyhurst St Oswald and St Cath *Man* 67-72; P-in-c Collyhurst St Jas 67-72; R Collyhurst 72-74; RNLI 75-92; rtd 95; Hon C Bispham *Blackb* from 95. *Ingol, 9 Hodgson Road, Blackpool FY1 2LZ* Tel (01253) 592538

FRASER, Ross Dominic. b 24. St Jo Coll Morpeth. **d** 47 **p** 48. Chapl All SS Coll Bathurst 47-51; Australia 51-59; C Auckland St Helen *Dur* 59-60; V Witton Park 60-61; V Ryhope 61-74; P-in-c Elton 74-75; P-in-c Medomsley 75-76; V 76-84; rtd 84. *19 Laburnum Gardens, Low Fell, Gateshead, Tyne & Wear NE9 5TN*

FRASER-SMITH, Keith Montague. b 48. St Jo Coll Dur BA70. Trin Coll Bris DipTh72. **d** 73 **p** 74. C Bishopsworth *Bris* 73-75; CMS 76-84; Egypt 76-80; Jerusalem 80-84; Asst Chapl Marseille w St Raphael, Aix-en-Provence etc *Eur* 84-90; Media Dir Arab World Min 84-94; NSM Worthing Ch the King *Chich* 90-94; Cyprus from 94. *52 Ben Nevis Road, Tranmere, Birkenhead, Merseyside L42 6QY*

FRAY, Roger William. b 43. Philippa Fawcett Coll TCert69 Reading Univ BEd76. St Jo Coll Nottm MA95. **d** 95 **p** 96. C Grove *Ox* from 95. *21 Albermarle Drive, Grove, Wantage, Oxon OX12 0NB* Tel (01235) 769722

FRAY, Vernon Francis. b 41. Southn Coll of Tech HNC62 FCIOB79. S'wark Ord Course 91. **d** 94 **p** 95. NSM Heston *Lon* 94-96; NSM Twickenham All Hallows from 96. *75 Central Avenue, Hounslow, Middx TW3 2QW* Tel 0181-894 5774

FRAY, Mrs Vivienne Jane. b 49. Liv Univ CertEd71 BEd72. W of England Minl Tr Course 91. **d** 94 **p** 95. NSM Glouc St Jas and All SS *Glouc* from 94. *56 Stonechat Avenue, Abbeydale, Gloucester GL4 9XE* Tel (01452) 301075

FRAYLING, Canon Nicholas Arthur. b 44. Ex Univ BA69. Cuddesdon Coll 69. **d** 71 **p** 72. C Peckham St Jo *S'wark* 71-74; V Tooting All SS 74-83; Can Res and Prec Liv Cathl *Liv* 83-87; R Liv Our Lady and St Nic w St Anne 87-90; TR from 90; Hon Can Liv Cathl from 89. *25 Princes Park Mansions, Sefton Park Road, Liverpool L8 3SA* Tel 0151-727 4692 or 236 5287

FRAYNE, The Very Revd David. b 34. St Edm Hall Ox BA58 MA62 Birm Univ DipTh60. Qu Coll Birm 58. **d** 60 **p** 61. C E Wickham *S'wark* 60-63; C Lewisham St Jo Southend 63-67; V N Sheen St Phil and All SS 67-73; R Caterham 73-83; RD Caterham 80-83; Hon Can S'wark Cathl 82-83; V Bris St Mary Redcliffe w Temple etc *Bris* 83-92; RD Bedminster 86-92; Hon Can Bris Cathl 91-92; Provost Blackb from 92. *The Provost's House, Preston New Road, Blackburn BB2 6PS* Tel (01254) 252502 E-mail provost@blackburn.anglican.org.uk

FRAZER, The Ven Albert Henry Victor. b 14. TCD BA38 MA62. CITC 38. **d** 38 **p** 39. C Belfast St Steph *Conn* 38-43; I Donoughmore w Donard *D & G* 43-66; I Rathdrum w Glenealy, Derralossary and Laragh 66-84; Can Ch Ch Cathl Dublin 59-70; Adn Glendalough 70-84; rtd 83; Chapl Kingston Coll Co Cork from 84. *17 Kingston College, Michelstown, Co Cork, Irish Republic* Tel Fermoy (25) 24429

FRAZER, David. b 60. QUB BSSc TCD DipTh84. TCD Div Sch. **d** 84 **p** 85. C Taney *D & G* 84-87; C Dublin Ch Ch Cathl Gp 87-88; I Clane w Donadea and Coolcarrigan *M & K* from 88. *St Michael's Vicarage, Sallins, Naas, Co Kildare, Irish Republic* Tel Kildare (45) 868276

FRAZER, Ian Martin. b 44. QUB DipTh MTh. **d** 91 **p** 93. Lic to Offic *D & D* from 91. *The Stacks, Deramore Park South, Belfast BT9 5JY* Tel (01232) 667100

FRAZER, Chan James Stewart. b 27. TCD. **d** 57 **p** 58. C Belfast Whiterock *Conn* 57-59; C Belfast St Matt 59-61; I Lack *Clogh* 61-64; I Mullaglass *Arm* 64-65; I Milltown 65-70; Australia 70-74; I Dromore *Clogh* 74-82; RD Kesh 78-82; Bp Dom Chapl 82; I Derryvullen S w Garvary 82-90; Can Clogh Cathl 83-85; Preb 85-94; RD Enniskillen 89-90; I Clogh w Errigal Portclare 90-94; Glebes Sec 91-94; Chan Clogh Cathl 93-94; rtd 94. *34 Clonlee Drive, Belfast BT4 3DA* Tel (01232) 659593

FRAZER, Milburn Ronald. b 18. Worc Ord Coll 63. **d** 65 **p** 66. C Rainbow Hill St Barn *Worc* 65-67; C Bexhill St Pet *Chich* 67-71; R Tillington 71-78; Chapl Upper Chine Sch Shanklin 78-84; rtd 85; Chapl Shoreham Coll 86-90; Perm to Offic *Chich* from 92. *34 Overmead, Shoreham-by-Sea, W Sussex BN43 5NS* Tel (01273) 455023

FREAR, Philip Scott. b 45. Univ of Wales (Lamp) BA66. **d** 80 **p** 81. Hon C Purton *Bris* 80-81; C Rodbourne Cheney 81-85; V Hengrove 85-95; V Braddan *S & M* from 95; Perm to Offic *B & W* from 95. *The Vicarage, Saddle Road, Bradden, Douglas, Isle of Man IM4 4LB* Tel (01624) 675523

FREARSON, Andrew Richard. b 57. BA. Wycliffe Hall Ox. **d** 83 **p** 84. C Acocks Green *Birm* 83-86; C Moseley St Mary 86-89; P-in-c Holme-in-Cliviger *Blackb* 89-96; USA from 96. *Christ Church, 16 West Peach Tree Street, Norcross, GA 30071, USA* Tel (404) 448-1166

FREATHY, Nigel Howard. b 46. Lon Univ BA68 CertEd. Sarum & Wells Th Coll 79. **d** 81 **p** 82. C Crediton *Ex* 81-82; C Crediton and Shobrooke 82-84; TV Ex St Thos and Em 84-86; V Beer and Branscombe from 86; RD Honiton from 96. *The Vicarage, Mare Lane, Beer, Seaton, Devon EX12 3NB* Tel (01297) 20996

FREDERICK, Dr John Bassett Moore. b 30. Princeton Univ BA51 Birm Univ PhD73. Gen Th Sem (NY) MDiv54. **d** 54 **p** 55. USA 54-56 and 61-71; C All Hallows Barking *Lon* 56-58; C Ox SS Phil and Jas *Ox* 58-60; R Bletchingley *S'wark* 74-95; Reigate Adnry Ecum Officer 90-95; RD Godstone 92-95; rtd 95. *32 Chestnut Street, Princeton, New Jersey 08542, USA* Tel Princeton (609) 924 7590

FREDERICK, Warren Charles. b 47. Qu Coll Birm 86. **d** 88 **p** 89. C W Leigh *Portsm* 88-91; V N Holmwood *Guildf* from 91. *The Vicarage, Willow Green, North Holmwood, Dorking, Surrey RH5 4JB* Tel (01306) 882135

FREDRIKSEN, Martin. b 47. St Chad's Coll Dur BA69 DipTh70. **d** 70 **p** 71. C Bideford *Ex* 70-73; C Guildf St Nic *Guildf* 73-76; R Cossington *B & W* 76-82; V Woolavington 76-82; Asst Chapl K Coll Taunton 82-84; C Hatfield *St Alb* 84-94; P-in-c Broadstone *Sarum* 94; V from 94. *St John's Vicarage, Macaulay Road, Broadstone, Dorset BH18 8AR* Tel (01202) 694109

FREE, Canon James Michael. b 25. K Coll Lon BD50 AKC50. **d** 51 **p** 52. C Corsham *Bris* 51-54; Trinidad and Tobago 54-62; PC Knowle St Barn *Bris* 62-67; V Pilning 67-75; P-in-c Lydiard Millicent w Lydiard Tregoz 75-82; Hon Can Bris Cathl 76-82; Can Res, Prec and Sacr Bris Cathl 82-83; Can Treas 83-90; Bp's Adv for Miss 82-87; Bp's Officer for Miss and Evang 87-89; rtd 90; Perm to Offic *Bris* from 90; Perm to Offic *B & W* from 90. *23 Manor Drive, Merriott, Somerset TA16 5PB* Tel (01460) 76053

FREEBAIRN-SMITH, Mrs Jane. b 36. K Coll Lon DipTh59. St Chris Coll Blackheath IDC60. **d** 88 **p** 94. NSM Uddingston *Glas* 88-91; NSM Cambuslang 88-91; Dioc Missr 88-92; Dioc Past Counsellor 92-95; NSM Baillieston 91-92; C St Mary's Cathl 92-95; TV Hykeham *Linc* from 95. *23 Baildon Crescent, North Hykeham, Lincoln LN6 8HS* Tel (01522) 690885

FREEBORN, John Charles Kingon. b 30. G&C Coll Cam BA52 MA56. Ridley Hall Cam 53. **d** 55 **p** 56. C Doncaster St Geo *Sheff* 55-57; Tutor Wycliffe Hall Ox 57-61; R Flixton St Mich *Man* 61-72; C Leic H Apostles *Leic* 72-73; Teacher Greenacres Sch Oldham 73-75; C E Crompton *Man* 73-74; Hon C Ashton St Mich 74-76; Teacher St Jo Sch Ellesmere 75-79; Perm to Offic 77-80; Hd Master H Trin Sch Halifax 80-88; Teacher St Chad's Sch Hove Edge Wakef 88-91; Lic to Offic *Wakef* 80-83; Hon C Sowerby 83-94; NSM Salterhebble All SS from 94; rtd 95. *27 Crossley Hill, Halifax, W Yorkshire HX3 0PL* Tel (01422) 342489

FREEMAN, Canon Alan John Samuel. b 27. SS Coll Cam BA48 MA52. Sarum Th Coll 50. **d** 52 **p** 53. C Tottenham Ch Ch W Green *Lon* 52-55; C Harpenden St Nic *St Alb* 55-60; R Aspley Guise 60-75; RD Fleete 67-70; RD Ampthill 70-75; Hon Can St Alb 74-92; V Boxmoor St Jo 75-92; Chapl Hemel Hempstead Gen Hosp (W Herts Wing) 75-92; RD Berkhamsted *St Alb* 85-92; rtd 92. *3A Queen Street, Leighton Buzzard, Beds LU7 7BZ* Tel (01525) 384799

FREEMAN, Anthony John Curtis. b 46. Ex Coll Ox BA68 MA72. Cuddesdon Coll 70. **d** 72 **p** 73. C Worc St Martin *Worc* 72-74; C Worc St Martin w St Pet 74-75; Bp's Dom Chapl *Chich* 75-78; C-in-c Parklands St Wilfrid CD 78-82; V Durrington 82-89; P-in-c Staplefield Common 89-94; Bp's Adv Continuing Minl Educn 89-93; Asst Dir of Ords 89-93. *4 Godolphin Close, Newton St Cyres, Exeter EX5 5BZ* Tel (01392) 851453 Fax as telephone E-mail anthony@imprint.co.uk

FREEMAN, Douglas James. b 20. Ox NSM Course 80. **d** 83 **p** 84. NSM Ellesborough *Ox* 83-91; NSM Wendover Deanery from 87; NSM Ellesborough, The Kimbles and Stoke Mandeville from 91. *Chadley, Butlers Cross, Aylesbury, Bucks HP17 0TS* Tel (01296) 623240

FREEMAN, Gordon Bertie. b 37. CITC BTh95. **d** 95 **p** 96. C Lecale Gp *D & D* from 95. *St Nicholas' Rectory, 48 High Street, Ardglass, Downpatrick, Co Down BT30 7TU* Tel (01396) 841311

FREEMAN, James Henry. b 14. **d** 79 **p** 80. Hon C Wandsworth St Steph *S'wark* from 79. *43 Oakhill Road, London SW15 2QJ* Tel 0181-874 1501

FREEMAN, Karl Fredrick. b 57. St Luke's Coll Ex BEd80. **d** 90 **p** 91. C Plymouth St Andr w St Paul and St Geo *Ex* 90-95; TV Plymouth St Andr and St Paul Stonehouse 95-96; Chapl Coll of St Mark and St Jo Plymouth from 90. *College of St Mark and St John, Staff House 4, Derriford Road, Plymouth PL6 8BH* Tel (01752) 789910

FREEMAN, Malcolm Robin. b 48. St And NSM Tr Scheme 85. **d** 88 **p** 89. NSM Kirkcaldy *St And* 88-94; NSM Kinghorn 91-94. *26 Fairdown Avenue, Westbury, Wilts BA13 3HS* Tel (01373) 858083

FREEMAN (née ADAMS), Mrs Margaret Anne. b 27. AKC48. Gilmore Ho. **dss** 82 **d** 87 **p** 94. Gt Yarmouth *Nor* 80-87; rtd 87; Hon Par Dn Malborough w S Huish, W Alvington and Churchstow *Ex* 87-94; Hon C 94-96. *9 Barton Way, Ormesby, Great Yarmouth, Norfolk NR29 5SD* Tel (01493) 730101

FREEMAN, Michael Charles. b 36. Magd Coll Cam BA61 MA68 Lon Univ BD69. Clifton Th Coll 67. **d** 69 **p** 70. C Bedworth *Cov* 69-72; C Morden *S'wark* 72-77; P-in-c Westcombe Park St Geo 77-85; V Kingston Vale St Jo 85-94. *Flat 3, 2 Westbourne Park Road, Bournemouth NH4 8HG* Tel (01202) 752113

FREEMAN, Michael Curtis. b 51. Lanc Univ BA72. Cuddesdon Coll 72. **d** 75 **p** 76. C Walton St Mary *Liv* 75-78; C Hednesford *Lich* 78-81; TV Solihull *Birm* 81-86; V Yardley Wood 86-90; V Farnworth *Liv* from 90. *The Vicarage, Coroners Lane, Farnworth, Widnes, Cheshire WA8 9HY* Tel 0151-424 2735

FREEMAN, Michael Raymond. b 58. Chu Coll Cam BA80 MA84 Ox Univ BA87. St Steph Ho Ox 85. **d** 88 **p** 89. C Clifton All SS w St Jo *Bris* 88-92; TV Elland *Wakef* from 92. *All Saints Vicarage, Charles Street, Elland, W Yorkshire HX5 0JF* Tel (01422) 373184

FREEMAN, Mrs Pamela Mary. b 45. WMMTC 83. **dss** 86 **d** 87 **p** 94. Cannock *Lich* 86-88; Par Dn 87-88; Min for Deaf (Salop Adnry) 88-95; Par Dn Oxon and Shelton 88-94; C 94-95; TV Stafford from 95. *The Vicarage, Victoria Terrace, Stafford ST16 3HA* Tel (01785) 52523

FREEMAN, Philip Martin. b 54. Westcott Ho Cam 76. **d** 79 **p** 80. C Stanley *Liv* 79-82; C Bromborough *Ches* 82-84; Chapl Halton Gen Hosp 84-91; V Runcorn H Trin *Ches* 84-91; R Ashton upon Mersey St Martin 91-96; SSF from 96. *The Friary, Hilfield, Dorchester, Dorset DT2 7BE* Tel (01300) 341345

FREEMAN, Philip Michael. b 25. Jes Coll Cam BA50 MA54. Qu Coll Birm 50. **d** 52 **p** 53. C Gainsborough All SS *Linc* 52-58; V Messingham 58-65; V Goxhill 65-66; P-in-c Bottesford w Ashby 66-73; TR 73-75; P-in-c Warwick St Nic *Cov* 75-76; TV Warwick 77-87; P-in-c Claverdon w Preston Bagot 87-90; rtd 90; Perm to Offic *Cov* from 90. *38 Cocksparrow Street, Warwick CV34 4ED* Tel (01926) 411431

FREEMAN, Richard Alan. b 52. Ripon Coll Cuddesdon. **d** 83 **p** 84. C Crayford *Roch* 83-86; V Slade Green 86-94; R Eynsford w Farningham and Lullingstone from 94. *The Rectory, Pollyhaugh, Eynsford, Dartford DA4 0HE* Tel (01322) 863050

FREEMAN, Canon Robert John. b 52. St Jo Coll Dur BSc74 Fitzw Coll Cam BA76 MA. Ridley Hall Cam 74. **d** 77 **p** 78. C Blackpool St Jo *Blackb* 77-81; TV Chigwell *Chelmsf* 81-85; V Leic Martyrs *Leic* from 85; Hon Can Leic Cathl from 94; RD Christianity S from 95. *The Vicarage, 17 Westcotes Drive, Leicester LE3 0QT* Tel 0116-254 6162

FREEMAN, Rodney. **d** 95 **p** 96. NSM Chelmondiston and Erwarton w Harkstead *St E* from 95. *Lavender Cottage, Harkstead, Ipswich IP9 1BN* Tel (01473) 328381

FREEMAN, Ronald Mercer. b 24. Trin Coll Cam BA45 MA50. Wycliffe Hall Ox 47. **d** 49 **p** 50. C Worsley *Man* 49-52; Nigeria 52-62; V Pendleton St Barn *Man* 62-67; R Kersal Moor 67-78; V Walmersley 78-90; rtd 90; Perm to Offic *Man* from 90. *3 High Avenue, Bolton BL2 5AZ* Tel (01204) 385341

FREEMAN, Shirley Beckett. b 14. Ch Coll Cam BA36 MA40. Ridley Hall Cam 36. **d** 38 **p** 39. C Cheltenham St Mary *Glouc* 38-39; R Bromsberrow 40-47; V Gt and Lt Dalby *Leic* 47-52; R Landford w Plaitford *Sarum* 52-65; R Compton Valence 65-75; R Long Bredy w Lt Bredy and Kingston Russell 65-75; rtd 74. *Eckling Grange, Norwich Road, Dereham, Norfolk NR20 3BB* Tel (01362) 691189

FREEMAN, Terence. b 40. Wells Th Coll 67. **d** 70 **p** 71. C Hanham *Bris* 70-75; C Cockington *Ex* 75-77; R Sampford Spiney w Horrabridge 77-89; V Wembury from 89; Hon Chapl RN from 89. *The Vicarage, 63 Church Road, Wembury, Plymouth PL9 0JJ* Tel (01752) 862319

FREER, Andrew Selwyn Bruce. b 26. Wells Th Coll 55. **d** 57 **p** 58. C Yardley St Edburgha *Birm* 57-62; R Byfield *Pet* 62-71; V Brackley St Pet w St Jas 71-81; R Bincombe w Broadwey, Upwey and Buckland Ripers *Sarum* 81-91; rtd 91. *1 Grove Cottages, Mill Lane, Chetnole, Sherborne, Dorset DT9 6PB* Tel (01935) 873468

FREER, Bernard. b 22. St Aid Birkenhead 60. **d** 62 **p** 63. C Boulton *Derby* 62-65; V Stanley 65-73; P-in-c Scropton 73; P-in-c Marston on Dove 73; V Marston on Dove w Scropton 74-92; RD Longford 81-86; rtd 92; Perm to Offic *Derby* from 92. *95 Scropton Road, Hatton, Derby DE65 5GJ* Tel (01283) 812681

FREETH, Barry James. b 35. Birm Univ BA60. Tyndale Hall Bris 60. **d** 62 **p** 64. C Selly Hill St Steph *Birm* 62-63; C Birm St Jo Ladywood 63-71; Chapl RAF 71-75; P-in-c Crudwell w Ashley *Bris* 75-81; P-in-c Lanreath *Truro* 81-84; R 84-87; P-in-c Pelynt 81-84; V 84-87; R Harvington and Norton and Lenchwick *Worc* 87-93; V Ramsden, Finstock and Fawler, Leafield etc *Ox* from 93. *The Vicarage, Mount Skippett, Ramsden, Chipping Norton, Oxon OX7 3AP* Tel (01993) 868687

FREETH, The Ven John Stanton. b 40. Selw Coll Cam BA62 MA66. Ridley Hall Cam 64. **d** 66 **p** 67. C Gillingham St Mark *Roch* 66-72; TV Heslington *York* 72-80; Chapl York Univ 72-80; S Africa from 80; Adn Athlone from 88. *18 St John's Road, Wynberg, 7800 South Africa*

FREETH, Patricia. Wycliffe Hall Ox BTh95. **d** 95 **p** 96. NSM Ramsden, Finstock and Fawler, Leafield etc *Ox* from 95. *The Vicarage, Mount Skippett, Ramsden, Chipping Norton, Oxon OX7 3AP* Tel (01993) 868687

FREETH, Richard Hudson de Wear. b 13. Worc Ord Coll. **d** 64 **p** 65. C Southend St Jo *Chelmsf* 64-67; V Mayland 67-76; V Steeple 67-76; rtd 76. *Manormead Residential Home, Tilford Road, Hindhead, Surrey GU26 6RA*

FRENCH, Basil Charles Elwell. b 19. Edin Th Coll LTh44. **d** 45 **p** 46. C Falkirk *Edin* 45-46; C Bris St Aid *Bris* 46-49; C Hendford *B & W* 49-51; V Ash 51-58; P-in-c Long Load 57-58; S Rhodesia 59-65; Rhodesia 65-80; Zimbabwe 80-85; rtd 85; Hon C Wrington w Butcombe *B & W* 85-88; Perm to Offic 88-92; Perm to Offic *Ex* from 92. *9 Elmbridge Gardens, Exeter EX4 4AE* Tel (01392) 215933

FRENCH, Clive Anthony. b 43. AKC70. St Aug Coll Cant 70. **d** 71 **p** 72. C Monkseaton St Mary *Newc* 71-73; Dioc Youth Adv 73-76; Chapl RN 76-97; Chapl RN Coll Greenwich 75-97; Dir of Ords RN 85-90; R Cheam *S'wark* from 97. *14 Darby Road, Cheam, Sutton, Surrey SM1 2BL* Tel 0181-643 4253

FRENCH, Canon Dendle Charles. b 29. Lon Univ BD56. ALCD55. **d** 56 **p** 57. C Gt Yarmouth *Nor* 56-63; Jamaica 63-66; V Sedgeford w Southmere *Nor* 66-71; P-in-c Gt Ringstead 66-67; R 67-71; TV Thetford 71-74; Chapl Hockerill Coll Bishop's Stortford 74-78; P-in-c St Paul's Walden *St Alb* 78-85; V 85-94; RD Hitchin 84-89; Hon Can St Alb 91-94; rtd 94; Chapl Glamis Castle from 94. *Woodfaulds, Glamis, Forfar, Angus DD8 1RW* Tel (01307) 840485

FRENCH, Derek John. b 47. Ripon Coll Cuddesdon DipMin95. **d** 95 **p** 96. C Stand *Man* from 95. *67 Bury Old Road, Whitefield, Manchester M45 6TB* Tel 0161-798 9261

FRENCH, George Leslie. b 47. AIFST NE Lon Poly BSc70. S'wark Ord Course 86. **d** 89 **p** 90. NSM Reading St Barn *Ox* from 89. *Hawthorne House, 2 Cutbush Close, Lower Earley, Reading RG6 4XA* Tel 0118-986 1886

FRENCH, Janet Mary. *See* DRIVER, Janet Mary

FRENCH, Jonathan David Seabrook. b 60. Westcott Ho Cam 84. **d** 87 **p** 88. C Loughton St Jo *Chelmsf* 87-90; Chapl St Bede's Ch for the Deaf Clapham 90-92; C Richmond St Mary w St Matthias and St Jo *S'wark* 92-95; TV from 96; Chapl amongst the Deaf from 92. *19 Old Deer Park Gardens, Richmond, Surrey TW9 2TN* Tel 0181-940 8359

FRENCH, Ms Judith Karen. b 60. St D Coll Lamp BA89. St Steph Ho Ox 89. **d** 91 **p** 94. Par Dn Botley *Portsm* 91-94; C Bilton *Cov* 94-97; V Charlbury w Shorthampton *Ox* from 97. *The Vicarage, Charlbury, Chipping Norton, Oxon OX7 3PX* Tel (01608) 810286

FRENCH, Michael Anders. b 61. Ch Coll Cam BA83 MA87. Ridley Hall Cam BA91. **d** 92 **p** 93. C Norbury *Ches* 92-96; Chapl Ches Coll from 96. *85 Parkgate Road, Chester CH1 4AQ* Tel (01244) 375444

FRENCH, Michael John. b 37. W of England Minl Tr Course 92. **d** 95 **p** 96. NSM Cheltenham St Pet *Glouc* from 95. *8 Alexandria Walk, Cheltenham, Glos GL52 5LG* Tel (01242) 236661

FRENCH, Peter Robert. b 65. Man Univ BTh87. Qu Coll Birm 88. **d** 90 **p** 91. C Unsworth *Man* 90-93; C Bury Ch King w H Trin 93-95; V Bury Ch King from 95. *St Thomas's Vicarage, Pimhole Road, Bury, Lancs BL9 7EY* Tel 0161-764 1157

FRENCH, Philip Colin. b 50. Sarum & Wells Th Coll 81. **d** 83 **p** 84. C Llansamlet *S & B* 83-86; P-in-c Waunarllwydd 86-87; V 87-97; P-in-c Swansea St Barn from 97. *St Barnabas' Vicarage, 57 Sketty Road, Swansea SA2 0EN* Tel (01792) 298601

FRENCH, Richard John (Dick). b 34. Open Univ BA82. Tyndale Hall Bris 62. **d** 64 **p** 65. C Rustington *Chich* 64-68; C Walton H Trin *Ox* 68-72; V Grove from 72. *The Vicarage, Grove, Wantage, Oxon OX12 7LQ* Tel (01235) 766484

FRENCH, Stephen Robert James. b 52. St Jo Coll Nottm. **d** 87 **p** 88. C Chell *Lich* 87-91; TV 91-94; V Wednesfield Heath from 94. *Holy Trinity Vicarage, Bushbury Road, Heath Town, Wolverhampton WV10 0LY* Tel (01902) 738313

FREND, Prof William Hugh Clifford. b 16. TD59. FSA52 FRHistS54 FRSE79 FBA83 Keble Coll Ox BA37 DPhil40 MA51 DD66 Cam Univ BD64 Edin Univ Hon DD74. **d** 82 **p** 83. Prof Ecclesiastical Hist Glas Univ 69-84; NSM Aberfoyle *St And* 82-84; P-in-c Barnwell w Thurning and Luddington *Pet* 84-90; rtd 90; Perm to Offic *Ely* from 90. *The Clerk's Cottage, Little Wilbraham, Cambridge CB1 5CB* Tel (01223) 811731

FRERE, Christopher Michael Hanbury. b 21. Roch Th Coll 65. **d** 67 **p** 68. C Spilsby w Hundleby *Linc* 67-71; V N Kelsey 71-76; V Cadney 71-76; P-in-c Aisthorpe w W Thorpe and Scampton 75-79; P-in-c Brattleby 75-79; R Fillingham 76-78; V Ingham w Cammeringham 76-78; RD Lawres 78-84; V Ingham w Cammeringham w Fillingham 79-86; R Aisthorpe w Scampton w Thorpe le Fallows etc 79-86; rtd 86; Perm to Offic *Linc* from 86. *164 Newark Road, North Hykeham, Lincoln LN6 8LZ* Tel (01522) 689145

FRESTON, John Samuel Kern. b 28. Lich Th Coll 70. **d** 72 **p** 73. C Walsall *Lich* 72-75; TV Trunch w Swafield *Nor* 75-77; TV Trunch 77-82; R W Winch 82-91; Chapl St Jas Hosp King's Lynn 82-85; Qu Eliz Hosp King's Lynn 85-90; rtd 91; Perm to Offic *Nor* from

91; Perm to Offic *Ely* from 91. *71 The Howdale, Downham Market, Norfolk PE38 9AH* Tel (01366) 385936

FRETWELL, Brian George. b 34. TD. CEng MIMechE. Chich Th Coll 79. **d** 81 **p** 82. C Bude Haven *Truro* 81-82; C Saltash 82-85; C Walthamstow St Sav *Chelmsf* 85-87; V Doncaster Intake *Sheff* 87-97. *65 Little Breach, Chichester, W Sussex PO19 4TY*

FRETWELL, Cynthia Mary. b 37. EMMTC 90. **d** 91 **p** 94. Chapl Asst Doncaster R Infirmary 91-92; Chapl Asst Doncaster R Infirmary & Montague Hosp NHS Trust 92-95; Chapl 95-96; Chapl Asst Tickhill Road & St Cath Hosps 91-96; rtd 96. *65 Little Breach, Chichester, W Sussex PO19 4TY*

FREWIN, William Charles. b 46. Trin Coll Bris 84. **d** 86 **p** 87. C Southchurch H Trin *Chelmsf* 86-89; C Shrub End 89-91; R W Bergholt from 91. *The Rectory, 1 Church Close, West Bergholt, Colchester CO6 3JZ* Tel (01206) 240273

FREY, Christopher Ronald. b 44. AKC69 Uppsala Univ BD73 MTh77. St Aug Coll Cant 69. **d** 70 **p** 71. C Addington *Ox* 70-72; Lic to Offic *Eur* 73-78; Chapl Stockholm w Uppsala 78-85; Can Brussels Cathl 81-85; Lic to Offic *Carl* 85-89; Chapl Casterton Sch Lancs 85-89; Chapl Epsom Coll 89-91; Chapl Worksop Coll Notts 91-94; rtd 96. *Odengatan 2, 264 38 Klippan, Sweden* Tel Klippan (435) 14813

FRIARS, Ian Malcolm George. b 50. Sarum & Wells Th Coll 83. **d** 85 **p** 86. C Norton *St Alb* 85-88; C Ramsey *Ely* 88-90; TV The Ramseys and Upwood 90-93; P-in-c Cottenham 93-94; R from 94. *The Rectory, 6 High Street, Cottenham, Cambridge CB4 4SA* Tel (01954) 50454

FRIARS, Robert John. b 32. Trin Coll Cam BA55 MA59. Wells Th Coll 55. **d** 57 **p** 58. C Hackney St Jo *Lon* 57-62; Youth Tr Officer 62-65; C St Andr Holborn 62-70; Sen Youth Chapl 65-70; TV Hackney 70-79; V Sompting *Chich* 79-91; rtd 92. *47 Cowslip Close, Cansbrook Green, Gosport, Hants PO13 0BQ* Tel (01903) 234511

FRICKER, Canon David Duncan. b 27. Lon Univ BA53. Ridley Hall Cam 53. **d** 55 **p** 56. C Ecclesfield *Sheff* 55-58; C Luton St Mary *St Alb* 58-61; V Luton St Paul 61-64; R Bedford St Pet 64-75; RD Bedford 69-79; Hon Can St Alb 74-88; P-in-c Bedford St Paul 75-79; R Bedford St Pet w St Cuth 75-88; R Brightling, Dallington, Mountfield etc *Chich* 88-97; RD Dallington 88-95; rtd 97. *Merton, Langham Road, Robertsbridge, E Sussex TN32 5EP* Tel (01580) 880064

FRIEND, Frederick James. b 41. BA. Oak Hill NSM Course. **d** 82 **p** 83. NSM Hughenden *Ox* from 82. *The Chimes, Cryers Hill Road, High Wycombe, Bucks HP15 6JS* Tel (01494) 563168

FRIEND, Graham Arthur. b 39. Bernard Gilpin Soc Dur 59 Chich Th Coll 60. **d** 63 **p** 64. C Syston *Leic* 63-65; V 82-83; C Barnstaple St Pet w H Trin *Ex* 65-67; C Clewer St Andr *Ox* 67-74; R E and W Hendred 74-78; R Wantage Downs 78-82; P-in-c Mears Ashby and Hardwick and Sywell etc *Pet* 92-94; R 95-97; P-in-c Newbold w Dunston and Gt Barlow *Derby* from 97. *The Vicarage, Barlow, Sheffield S18 5TR* Tel 0114-289 0269

FRIENDSHIP, Roger Geoffrey (Brother John-Francis). b 46. ACII72. WMMTC 90. **d** 93 **p** 94. SSF from 76; NSM Harborne St Faith and St Laur *Birm* 93-94; Asst Novice Guardian Hilfield Friary from 94. *The Friary, Hilfield, Dorchester, Dorset DT2 7BE* Tel (01300) 341345

FRIESS, Herbert Friedrich. b 09. Leipzig Univ BD. **d** 41 **p** 42. C Attercliffe w Carbrook *Sheff* 42-48; V Elsecar 48-54; V Brighton St Luke *Chich* 54-59; R W Blatchington 59-64; I Killala w Dunfeeny, Crossmolina etc *T, K & A* 64-67; Dean Killala 67-73; I Achill w Dugort, Castlebar and Turlough 73-79; rtd 79. *Mulrany, Westport, Co Mayo, Irish Republic* Tel Westport (98) 36126

FRIGGENS, Canon Maurice Anthony. b 40. Sheff Univ BA65. Westcott Ho Cam 65. **d** 67 **p** 68. C Stocksbridge *Sheff* 67-70; C St Buryan, St Levan and Sennen *Truro* 70-72; R 72-84; RD Penwith 82-84; R St Columb Major w St Wenn 84-91; Hon Can Truro Cathl from 87; Dioc Dir of Ords from 87; V St Cleer from 91. *The Vicarage, St Cleer, Liskeard, Cornwall PL14 5DJ* Tel (01579) 343240

FRITH, Christopher John Cokayne. b 44. Ex Coll Ox BA65 MA69. Ridley Hall Cam 66. **d** 68 **p** 69. C Crookes St Thos *Sheff* 68-71; C Rusholme H Trin *Man* 71-74; R Haughton St Mary 74-85; R Brampton St Thos *Derby* from 85. *The Rectory, 481 Chatsworth Road, Chesterfield, Derbyshire S40 3AD* Tel (01246) 232717

FRITH, David William. b 65. K Coll Lon BD87 PGCE88. Westcott Ho Cam 88 Lambeth STh90. **d** 90 **p** 91. C St Jo Wood *Lon* 90-93; C Maidstone All SS and St Phil w Tovil *Cant* 93-95; V E Wickham *S'wark* from 96. *St Michael's Vicarage, Upper Wickham Lane, Welling, Kent DA16 3AP* Tel 0181-304 1214

FRITH, Canon Ivy Florence. b 24. CertEd56. Lambeth DipTh93 St Chris Coll Blackheath 48. **dss** 79 **d** 87 **p** 94. St Alb Abbey *St Alb* 79-82; Truro St Paul and St Clem *Truro* 82-84; C Truro St Mary from 85; Asst Dioc Dir of Ords from 85; Dioc Lay Min Adv from 85; Hon Cathl Dn Truro Cathl from 87; MU Chapl from 91; Hon Can Truro Cathl from 93; Hon C Feock from 94. *42 Tregolls Road, Truro, Cornwall TR1 1LA* Tel (01872) 79463

FRITH, Jonathan Paul (Jonty). b 72. Jes Coll Cam BA94 MA97. Wycliffe Hall Ox 95. **d** 97. C Houghton *Carl* from 97. *167 Kingstown Road, Carlisle CA3 0AX* Tel (01228) 591600

FRITH, The Ven Richard Michael Cokayne. b 49. Fitzw Coll Cam BA72 MA76. St Jo Coll Nottm 72. **d** 74 **p** 75. C Mortlake w E Sheen *S'wark* 74-78; TV Thamesmead 78-83; TR Keynsham *B & W* 83-92; Preb Wells Cathl from 91; Adn Taunton from 92. *4 Westerkirk Gate, Staplegrove, Taunton, Somerset TA2 6BQ* Tel (01823) 323838 Fax 325420

FRIZELLE, Thomas Herbert. b 07. TCD BA36 MA40. **d** 38 **p** 39. C Magheralin *D & D* 38-40; C Lisburn Ch Ch Cathl *Conn* 40-43; I Ballyhalbert w Ardkeen *D & D* 43-45; I Kilmore w Inch 45-51; I Dundonald 51-80; Treas Down Cathl 74-80; rtd 80. *Flat 10, Ashley Lodge, Sunnymede Park, Dunmurry, Belfast BT17 0AS* Tel (01232) 619542

FROGGATT, Jeffrey. b 27. Ch Coll Cam BA48 MA52. Ridley Hall Cam 49. **d** 51 **p** 52. C Scunthorpe St Jo *Linc* 51-53; C Doncaster St Jas *Sheff* 53-56; V New Edlington 56-62; V Malin Bridge 62-73; Ind Chapl 73-79; V Wortley 73-79; R Todwick 79-85; V Dore 85-92; rtd 92; Perm to Offic *Sheff* from 92; Perm to Offic *Derby* from 92. *20 Bocking Lane, Sheffield S8 7BH* Tel 0114-262 0914

FROGGATT, Peter Michael. b 65. St Hild Coll Dur BA86 PGCE88. Wycliffe Hall Ox BTh95. **d** 95 **p** 96. C Bebington *Ches* from 95. *8 Rolleston Drive, Bebington, Wirral, Merseyside L63 3DB* Tel 0151-645 6478

FROOM, Ian Leonard John. b 42. Sarum Th Coll 69. **d** 71 **p** 72. C Gillingham and Fifehead Magdalen *Sarum* 71-75; C Parkstone St Pet w Branksea and St Osmund 75-78; V Sedgley St Mary *Lich* 78-85; TV Weston-super-Mare Cen Par *B & W* 85-94; Perm to Offic 94-97; V Truro St Geo and St Jo *Truro* from 97. *St George's Vicarage, St George's Road, Truro, Cornwall TR1 3NW* Tel (01872) 272630

FROST, Alan Sydney. b 26. K Coll Lon BD50 AKC50. **d** 51 **p** 52. C Folkestone St Sav *Cant* 51-56; C Sneinton St Steph *S'well* 56-59; C Croydon Woodside *Cant* 60-63; Asst Chapl Mersey Miss to Seamen 63-66; rtd 91. *Address excluded by request*

FROST, David J. b 48. **d** 86 **p** 87. Hon C Upper Norwood All SS *S'wark* 86-89; C Battersea St Luke 90-94; V Shirley St Geo from 94. *St George's Vicarage, The Glade, Croydon CR0 7QJ* Tel 0181-654 8747

FROST, David Richard. b 54. Ridley Hall Cam 84. **d** 86 **p** 87. C Burgess Hill St Andr *Chich* 86-90; TV Rye 90-94; V Bexhill St Steph from 94. *The Vicarage, 67 Woodsgate Park, Bexhill-on-Sea, E Sussex TN39 4DL* Tel (01424) 211186

FROST, Derek Charles. b 47. Lich Th Coll 69. **d** 71 **p** 72. C Woodley St Jo the Ev *Ox* 71-76; V Bampton w Clanfield 76-81; V Minster Lovell and Brize Norton 81-88; TV Upper Kennet *Sarum* 88-92; P-in-c Seend and Bulkington from 92; Poulshot from 95. *The Vicarage, High Street, Seend, Melksham, Wilts SN12 6NR* Tel (01380) 828615

FROST, The Ven George. b 35. Dur Univ BA56 MA61. Linc Th Coll 57. **d** 60 **p** 61. C Barking St Marg *Chelmsf* 60-64; C-in-c Marks Gate CD 64-70; V Tipton St Matt *Lich* 70-77; V Penn 77-87; RD Trysull 84-87; Preb Lich Cathl 85-87; Adn Salop from 87; V Tong from 87; P-in-c Donington from 97. *Tong Vicarage, Shifnal, Shropshire TF11 8PW* Tel (01902) 372622 Fax 374021

FROST, James Michael. b 29. Liv Univ BA51 DipEd52 DUP54. NE Ord Course 81. **d** 84 **p** 85. NSM Huntington *York* 84-89; TV Heworth 89-95; rtd 95; Perm to Offic *York* from 95. *3 Elmpark Way, York YO3 0DY9* Tel (01904) 414667

FROST, Jonathan Hugh. b 64. Aber Univ BD88. Ridley Hall Cam CTMin93. **d** 93 **p** 94. C W Bridgford *S'well* 93-97; Police Chapl Trent Division 94-97; R Ash *Guildf* from 97. *The Rectory, Ash Church Road, Ash, Aldershot, Hants GU12 6LU* Tel (01252) 21517

FROST, Julian. b 36. Solicitor 57 Bris Univ BA61 MA65 Lon Univ CertEd70. Clifton Th Coll 64. **d** 65 **p** 66. C Welling *Roch* 65-69; Hon C 70-73; Dep Dir Schs Coun RE Project Lanc Univ 73-78; V New Beckenham St Paul from 78. *St Paul's Vicarage, Brackley Road, Beckenham, Kent BR3 1RB* Tel 0181-650 3400

FROST, Michael John (Mike). b 42. Westmr Coll Ox TCert64. LNSM course 92. **d** 95 **p** 96. NSM Harwood *Man* from 95. *62 Appledore Drive, Bolton BL2 4HH* Tel (01204) 535214

FROST, Ronald Andrew. b 48. Cam Univ DipRS77 Univ of S Carolina BTh81. Ridley Hall Cam 86. **d** 87 **p** 88. C Gt Wilbraham *Ely* 87-89; P-in-c Stow Longa 89-91; V from 91; P-in-c Kimbolton 89-91; V from 91. *The Vicarage, Kimbolton, Huntingdon, Cambs PE18 0HB* Tel (01480) 860279

FROST, Stanley. b 37. MIBiol FAEB Univ of Wales MSc Liv Univ PhD. N Ord Course 79. **d** 82 **p** 83. NSM Lower Kersal *Man* 82-87; NSM Patricroft 87-89; NSM Convenor (Dio Man) 87-95; Lic Preacher from 89. *5 Moorside Road, Kersal, Salford M7 0PJ* Tel 0161-792 3107

FROST, Preb William Selwyn. b 29. Wells Th Coll 61. **d** 62 **p** 63. C Cheddleton *Lich* 62-67; V Longdon-upon-Tern 67-81; R Rodington 67-81; RD Wrockwardine 77-84; Preb Lich Cathl 81-96; R Longdon-upon-Tern, Rodington, Uppington etc 81-84; R Whittington St Jo 84-86; C Trysull 86-89; TV Wombourne w Trysull and Bobbington 89-96; rtd 96; Perm to Offic *Heref* from 96. *Ty Ffos, Dilwyn, Hereford HR4 8HZ* Tel (01544) 318703

FROSTICK, Alan Norman. b 25. Ripon Hall Ox 74. **d** 75 **p** 76. C Crewkerne w Wayford *B & W* 75-78; P-in-c Brompton Regis w Upton and Skilgate 78-80; V Buttershaw St Aid *Bradf* 80-83; V

Aylesham *Cant* 83-85; P-in-c Adisham 84-85; R Aylesham w Adisham 85-90; rtd 90; Perm to Offic *Cant* from 90. *18 Hawthorn Close, St Marys Bay, Romney Marsh, Kent TN29 0SZ* Tel (01303) 875158

FROSTICK, Canon John George. b 23. Wells Th Coll 52. **d** 54 **p** 55. C Loughborough St Pet *Leic* 54-57; C Knighton St Mary Magd 57-58; V Frisby-on-the-Wreake w Kirby Bellars 58-71; V Shepshed 71-83; Hon Can Leic Cathl 80-83; R Kirton w Falkenham *St E* 83-90; rtd 90; Perm to Offic *Leic* from 91. *68 Melton Road, Barrow-upon-Soar, Loughborough, Leics LE12 8NX* Tel (01509) 620110

FROSTICK, Paul Andrew. b 52. CertEd. Ripon Hall Ox 74 Ripon Coll Cuddesdon 75. **d** 77 **p** 78. C Shepton Mallet *B & W* 77-80; TV Barton Mills, Beck Row w Kenny Hill etc *St E* 80-85; TV Mildenhall 85-86; TV Raveningham *Nor* 86-89; V Bottisham *Ely* 89-90; P-in-c Lode and Longmeadow 89-90; V Bottisham and Lode w Long Meadow 90-94. *Address temp unknown*

FROUD, Andrew William. b 65. Mansf Coll Ox BA87 St Cath Coll Cam MPhil92. Westcott Ho Cam 90. **d** 93 **p** 94. C Almondbury w Farnley Tyas *Wakef* 93-96; P-in-c Wootton *Portsm* from 96. *The Rectory, 32 Church Road, Wootton Bridge, Ryde, Isle of Wight PO33 4PX* Tel (01983) 882213

FROUD, James George (Jimmy). b 23. MBE89. **d** 54 **p** 55. Hong Kong 54-58; C All Hallows by the Tower etc *Lon* 58-61; Chapl Durning Hall Chr Community Cen Forest Gate 61-82; P-in-c Forest Gate St Jas *Chelmsf* 61-66; Chapl Forest Gate Hosp Lon 61-69; Chapl Aston Charities Trust from 82; NSM Barking St Marg w St Patr *Chelmsf* 91-94; Perm to Offic from 94. *37 The Drive, Loughton, Essex IG10 1HB* Tel 0181-508 6479

FROUDE (née WOOLCOCK), Mrs Christine Ann. b 47. ACIB73. S Dios Minl Tr Scheme 92. **d** 95 **p** 96. NSM Stoke Bishop *Bris* from 95. *2 Bramble Drive, Bristol BS9 1RE* Tel 0117-968 5449

FROWLEY, Peter Austin. b 32. CEng61 MIMechE61. WMMTC 82. **d** 84 **p** 85. NSM Tardebigge *Worc* 84-87; P-in-c 87-88; NSM Redditch St Steph 84-87; Hong Kong 88-92; V St Minver *Truro* 92-96; rtd 96; Perm to Offic *Ex* from 96. *Bramblecrest, Fortescue Road, Salcombe, Devon TQ8 8AP* Tel (01548) 842515

FRY, Dr Alison Jacquelyn. b 65. Newnham Coll Cam BA86 MA90 Hertf Coll Ox DPhil90. Cranmer Hall Dur BA93. **d** 96 **p** 97. C Milton *B & W* from 96. *475 Locking Road, Weston-super-Mare, Avon BS22 8QW*

FRY, Barry James. b 49. ACIB. Ripon Coll Cuddesdon 81. **d** 83 **p** 84. C Highcliffe w Hinton Admiral *Win* 83-87; V Southampton St Barn from 87. *St Barnabas' Vicarage, 12 Rose Road, Southampton SO14 6TE* Tel (01703) 223107

FRY, Mrs Florence Marion. b 24. WMMTC 87. **d** 88 **p** 94. Chapl and Welfare Officer to the Deaf 70-94; Chapl Cov Cathl *Cov* 88-94; Chmn Cov Coun of Chs 88-91; rtd 94. *37 Grace Gardens, Bishop's Stortford, Herts CM23 3EU* Tel (01279) 652315

FRY, Canon James Reinhold. b 30. St Cuth Soc Dur BSc53 MA70. Oak Hill Th Coll 55. **d** 57 **p** 58. C Bromley St Jo *Roch* 57-60; V Deptford St Luke *S'wark* 60-66; V Chalk *Roch* from 66; RD Gravesend 81-91; Hon Can Roch Cathl from 87. *The Vicarage, 2A Vicarage Lane, Gravesend, Kent DA12 4TF* Tel (01474) 567906 Fax as telephone

FRY, Miss Joan Aileen. b 29. Bedf Coll Lon BA50. Qu Coll Birm 79. **dss** 82 **d** 87 **p** 94. Colindale St Matthias *Lon* 82-87; Hendon St Mary 84-87; Hon Par Dn Swanage and Studland *Sarum* 87-95; Hon C Bridport from 95. *21 St James's Park, Bridport, Dorset DT6 3UR* Tel (01308) 458614

FRY, Michael John. b 59. Nottm Univ BA80 Sheff Univ CQSW83 Cam Univ BA85. Westcott Ho Cam 83. **d** 86 **p** 87. C Upholland *Liv* 86-89; C Dovecot 89-91; TV St Luke in the City from 91. *2 Minster Court, Crown Street, Liverpool L7 3QB* Tel 0151-709 9665

FRY, Nigel Edward. b 57. E Warks Coll DipGD78. St Jo Coll Nottm DCM93. **d** 93 **p** 94. C Wellingborough All Hallows *Pet* 93-96; R Peakirk w Glinton and Northborough from 96. *The Rectory, 11 Lincoln Road, Glinton, Peterborough PE6 7JR* Tel (01733) 252265

FRY, Roger Joseph Hamilton. b 29. Em Coll Cam BA52 MA56. Clifton Th Coll 52. **d** 54 **p** 55. C Walcot *B & W* 54-57; C Gresley *Derby* 57-61; P-in-c Bowling St Bart and St Luke *Bradf* 61-65; V Bowling St Jo 61-87; V Ingleton w Chapel le Dale 87-95; rtd 95; Perm to Offic *Bradf* from 95. *5 Margerison Crescent, Ilkley, W Yorkshire LS29 8QZ* Tel (01943) 608738

FRY, Roger Owen. b 30. Sarum Th Coll 58. **d** 60 **p** 61. C Yeovil St Mich *B & W* 60-63; P-in-c Weston-in-Gordano 64-70; R Clapton-in-Gordano 64-70; R Portishead 64-80; V Weston Zoyland w Chedzoy 80-94; rtd 94; Perm to Offic *B & W* from 95. *Two Jays, 37A Wellow Lane, Peasedown St John, Bath BA2 8HY*

FRY, Stephen. b 57. St Steph Ho Ox 83. **d** 86 **p** 87. C Wood Green St Mich w Bounds Green St Gabr etc *Lon* 86-89; C Kentish Town St Jo 89-93; C Kentish Town 93. *318 Fellows Court, Weymouth Terrace, London E2 8LA* Tel 0171-739 2662

FRYDAY, Mrs Barbara Yvonne. b 47. Ch of Ireland Tr Coll TCert67. CITC 90. **d** 92 **p** 93. Bp's VC Cashel Cathl and Educn Officer 92-96; NSM Cashel w Magorban, Tipperary, Clonbeg etc *C & O* 93-96; C Kilcooley w Littleon, Crohane and Fertagh from 96. *The Rectory, Grange Barna, Thurles, Co Tipperary, Irish Republic* Tel Kilkenny (56) 34147

FRYER, Anthony Charles. b 18. RMA. Wycliffe Hall Ox. **d** 60 **p** 60. C Furze Platt *Ox* 60-62; V Shinfield 62-73; Perm to Offic *Pet* 85-86 and from 91; P-in-c Charwelton w Fawsley and Preston Capes 86-91. *Byfield House, Byfield, Daventry, Northants NN11 6XN* Tel (01327) 60244

FRYER, Dr Charles Eric John. b 14. Lon Univ BA54 PhD84. Linc Th Coll 62. **d** 63 **p** 64. C Finham *Cov* 63-66; Perm to Offic *S'well* 66-75; Lic to Offic 75-79; R Killin *St And* 79-89; R Lochearnhead 79-89; Min Can Cork Cathl *C, C & R* from 97. *25 Vicar Street, Cork, Irish Republic* Tel Cork (21) 316397

FRYER, George. b 33. St Jo Coll Cam BA57 MA61. Ox NSM Course 73. **d** 76 **p** 77. NSM Wallingford *Ox* 76-79; C Wokingham St Paul 79-83; V Linc St Swithin *Linc* 83-88; P-in-c Walsden *Wakef* 88-97; P-in-c Cornholme 96-97; rtd 97. *The Rectory, Farthinghoe, Brackley, Northants NN13 5NY* Tel (01295) 710946

FRYER, Mrs Ida Doris. **d** 95 **p** 96. NSM Brantham w Stutton *St E* from 95. *The Grove, Stutton, Ipswich IP9 2SE* Tel (01473) 328230

FRYER, Mrs Jenifer Anne (Jeni). b 43. N Ord Course 89. **d** 92 **p** 94. Par Dn Ecclesfield *Sheff* 92-94; C 94-95; Chapl R Hallamshire Hosp Sheff 92-96; Chapl Asst N Gen Hosp NHS Trust Sheff from 96. *5 Nursery Drive, Ecclesfield, Sheffield S30 3XU* Tel 0114-246 1027

FRYER, Michael Andrew. b 56. St Jo Coll Nottm 88. **d** 90 **p** 91. C Hull St Martin w Transfiguration *York* 90-95; V Kingston upon Hull St Aid Southcoates from 95. *St Aidan's Vicarage, 139 Southcoates Avenue, Hull HU9 3HF* Tel (01482) 374403

FRYER, Preb Peter Hugh. b 25. Linc Th Coll 58. **d** 60 **p** 61. C Tavistock and Gulworthy *Ex* 60-64; R St Buryan *Truro* 64-72; R St Levan 66-72; R St Sennen 70-72; R Elgin w Lossiemouth *Mor* 72-76; Chapl RAF 72-76; P-in-c Lewannick *Truro* 76-78; P-in-c Altarnon and Bolventor 76-78; P-in-c N Hill 76-78; TR N Hill w Altarnon, Bolventor and Lewannick 78-84; P-in-c Laneast w St Clether and Tresmere 80-84; Preb St Endellion 84-90; R St Endellion w Port Isaac and St Kew 84-90; rtd 90; Perm to Offic *Truro* from 90. *Blythswood, Fore Street, Marazion, Cornwall TR17 0AS* Tel (01736) 711857

FUDGE, Prof Erik Charles. b 33. Ch Coll Cam BA55 MA59 Southn Univ CertEd58 Cam Univ PhD68. Ox Min Course 91. **d** 93 **p** 94. NSM Wokingham St Sebastian *Ox* from 93. *4 South Close, Wokingham, Berks RG11 2DJ* Tel (0118) 978 6081

FUDGER, David John. b 53. K Coll Lon 76 Sheff Univ MMin96. Coll of Resurr Mirfield 76. **d** 77 **p** 78. C Sutton in Ashfield St Mary *S'well* 77-80; P-in-c Duston *Pet* 80-82; V Radford All So w Ch Ch and St Mich *S'well* 82-91; Min Bermondsey St Hugh CD *S'wark* 91-97; P-in-c Blackheath Ascension from 97; Woolwich Area Miss Team from 97. *Ascension Vicarage, 40 Dartmouth Row, London SE10 8AP* Tel 0181-691 8884

FUDGER, Michael Lloyd. b 55. K Coll Lon BD77 AKC77. Coll of Resurr Mirfield 77. **d** 78 **p** 79. C Weston Favell *Pet* 78-82; C Pet H Spirit Bretton 82-84; V Irchester 84-90; TV Darnall-cum-Attercliffe *Sheff* 90-96; RD Attercliffe 91-96; TV Attercliffe, Darnall and Tinsley 96-97; TR from 97. *The Vicarage, 66 Mather Road, Sheffield S9 4GQ* Tel 0114-244 0167

FUGGLE, Francis Alfred. b 13. Selw Coll Cam BA34 MA38. Wells Th Coll 35. **d** 36 **p** 37. C Kingsbury St Andr *Lon* 36-38; S Africa from 38. *360A Florida Road, Durban, 4001 South Africa* Tel Durban (31) 238923

FULHAM, Suffragan Bishop of. *See* BROADHURST, The Rt Revd John Charles

FULLAGAR, Michael Nelson. b 35. SS Coll Cam BA57 MA61. Chich Th Coll 57. **d** 59 **p** 60. C Camberwell St Giles *S'wark* 59-61; C Northolt Park St Barn *Lon* 61-64; C Hythe *Cant* 64-66; Zambia 66-78; R Freemantle *Win* 78-87; P-in-c Westbury w Turweston, Shalstone and Biddlesden *Ox* 87-94; Chapl S Bucks NHS Trust 94-96; rtd 96. *Greensleeves, Bassetsbury Lane, High Wycombe, Bucks HP11 1RB* Tel (01494) 526255

FULLALOVE, Brenda Hurst. *See* CRASTON, Mrs Brenda Hurst

FULLARTON, Mrs Heather Mary. b 42. Whitelands Coll Lon TCert63. Qu Coll Birm 90. **d** 92 **p** 94. Par Dn Colwich w Gt Haywood *Lich* 92-94; C 94-97; C Wombourne w Trysull and Bobbington 97; P-in-c Swindon from 97; P-in-c Himley from 97. *The Vicarage, 12 St John's Close, Swindon, Dudley, W Midlands DY3 4PG* Tel (01384) 278532

FULLER, Alison Jane. b 61. St Andr Univ MTheol84. Edin Th Coll 85. **d** 87 **p** 94. C Selkirk *Edin* 87-89; C Melrose 87-89; C Galashiels 87-89; C Edin H Cross 89-92; D-in-c Edin St Columba 92-94; R from 94; Chapl Edin Univ from 96. *2/2 Boswell's Court, 352 Castlehill, Edinburgh EH1 2NF* Tel 0131-225 1634

FULLER, Alistair James. b 66. Univ of Wales (Lamp) BA87. Ripon Coll Cuddesdon 88. **d** 90 **p** 91. C Thornton-le-Fylde *Blackb* 90-95; V Skerton St Luke from 95. *St Luke's Vicarage, Slyne Road, Lancaster LA1 2HU* Tel (01524) 63249

FULLER, Christopher John. b 53. Chich Th Coll 85. **d** 87 **p** 88. C Swinton and Pendlebury *Man* 87-90; C Chiswick St Nic w St Mary *Lon* 90-92; V Hounslow W Gd Shep 92-96; V Stoke Newington St Faith, St Matthias and All SS from 96. *St Matthias Vicarage, Wordsworth Road, London N16 8DD* Tel 0171-254 5063

FULLER, Canon Frank William. b 22. Chich Th Coll 53. **d** 54 **p** 55. C Risby *St E* 54-55; P-in-c W Stow w Wordwell 55-57; P-in-c Lackford 55-59; R Culford, W Stow and Wordwell 58-61; R Cockfield 61-72; RD Lavenham 64-72; Hon Can St E Cathl 67-87; V Bungay H Trin w St Mary 73-87; RD Beccles and S Elmham 76-83; rtd 87; Perm to Offic *B & W* from 87. *23 Middle Street, Puriton, Bridgwater, Somerset TA7 8AU* Tel (01278) 684131

FULLER, Frederick Walter Tom. b 17. St Cath Coll Cam BA48 MA53 Bris Univ MLitt72 Ex Univ PhD74. Union Th Sem (NY) STM54 Cuddesdon Coll 49. **d** 51 **p** 52. C Helmsley *York* 51-53; Lect and Chapl St Luke's Coll Ex 59-78; Dep PV Ex Cathl *Ex* from 62; Hon C Swindon New Town *Bris* 79-82; rtd 82; Perm to Offic *Bris* from 89. *29 Oxford Road, Swindon SN3 4HP* Tel (01793) 824980

FULLER, Canon Graham Drowley. b 33. AKC58. **d** 59 **p** 60. C E Grinstead St Swithun *Chich* 59-62; C Coulsdon St Andr *S'wark* 62-64; Chapl RN 64-68; V Battersea St Luke *S'wark* 68-75; V S Stoneham *Win* 75-90; Bp's Ecum Officer 84-90; R Eversley 90-96; Hon Can Win Cathl 93-96; rtd 96. *Brookside Dairy, Nunnery Lane, Newport, Isle of Wight PO30 1YR* Tel (01983) 525976

FULLER, Canon John James. b 38. SS Coll Cam BA63 SS Coll Cam MA66. Chich Th Coll 63 Union Th Sem (NY) STM64. **d** 65 **p** 66. C Westmr St Steph w St Jo *Lon* 65-71; Tutor Cuddesdon Coll 71-75; Tutor Ripon Coll Cuddesdon 75-77; Prin S Dios Minl Tr Scheme 77-96; Can and Preb Sarum Cathl *Sarum* 83-97; V Wheatley w Forest Hill and Stanton St John *Ox* 96-97; TR Wheatley from 97. *The Vicarage, 18 London Road, Wheatley, Oxford OX33 1YA* Tel (01865) 872224

FULLER, Michael George. b 46. Chich Th Coll 90. **d** 92 **p** 93. C Fulham All SS *Lon* 92-94; C Kensington St Mary Abbots w St Geo from 94; Dir Post-Ord Tr Kensington Area from 94. *25 Campden Hill Square, London W8 7JY* Tel 0171-727 9486

FULLER, Dr Michael Jeremy. b 63. Worc Coll Ox BA85 MA89 DPhil89 Qu Coll Cam BA91. Westcott Ho Cam CTM92. **d** 92 **p** 93. C High Wycombe *Ox* 92-95; R Edin St Jo *Edin* from 95. *3 Randolph Place, Edinburgh EH3 7TQ* Tel 0131-226 5111

FULLER, Canon Reginald Horace. b 15. Cam Univ BA37 MA41. Qu Coll Birm 39. **d** 40 **p** 41. C Bakewell *Derby* 40-43; C Ashbourne w Mapleton 43-46; C Edgbaston St Bart *Birm* 46-50; Prof Th St D Coll Lamp 50-55; USA from 55; Lic to Offic *Derby* from 64; rtd 80; Hon Can St Paul's Cathl Burlington from 88. *Westminster-Canterbury House, Apt 320, 1600 Westbrook Avenue, Richmond, Virginia 23227, USA*

FULLER, Robert James. b 10. Lon Univ BD53. **d** 55 **p** 56. C Nottingham St Andr *S'well* 55; R Exford w Exmoor *B & W* 61-75; rtd 75. *Verna, Trefonen, Oswestry, Shropshire SY10 9DJ* Tel (01691) 653505

FULLER, Robert Peter. b 49. Bernard Gilpin Soc Dur 71 Trin Coll Bris 72. **d** 75 **p** 76. C Tonbridge SS Pet and Paul *Roch* 75-79; C Welling 79-83; V Nottingham St Sav *S'well* 83-89; V Ripley *Derby* from 89; Chapl Ripley and Distr Cottage Hosp from 89. *The Vicarage, 26 Mount Pleasant, Ripley, Derbyshire DE5 3DX* Tel (01773) 749641

FULLER, Canon Terence James. b 30. Bris Univ BA55. Clifton Th Coll 55. **d** 56 **p** 57. C Uphill *B & W* 56-60; V Islington St Jude Mildmay Park *Lon* 60-67; V Southgate *Chich* 67-80; R Stoke Climsland *Truro* 80-95; RD Trigg Major 85-91; P-in-c Lezant w Lawhitton and S Petherwin w Trewen 93-95; Hon Can Truro Cathl 94-96; rtd 96; Perm to Offic *Truro* from 96. *9 Westover Road, Callington, Cornwall PL17 7EW* Tel (01579) 370501

FULLERTON, Hamish John Neville. b 45. Ball Coll Ox BA68 MA73. S'wark Ord Course 76. **d** 79 **p** 80. NSM Clapham Old Town *S'wark* 79-82; Abp Tennison's Sch Kennington 79-88; Perm to Offic 82-89; Hon C Brixton Road Ch Ch 89-91; C Streatham Ch Ch 91-96; C Purley St Mark Woodcote from 96. *Flat 4, 21 Offerton Road, London SW4 0DJ* Tel 0171-622 7890

FULLJAMES, Mrs Janet Kathleen Doris. b 43. Open Univ BA79. Qu Coll Birm 85. **d** 87 **p** 94. Par Dn Harborne St Pet *Birm* 87-93; Par Dn Smethwick SS Steph and Mich 93-94; C 94-95; C Smethwick Resurr from 95. *99 Lewisham Road, Smethwick, Warley, W Midlands B66 2DD* Tel 0121-558 3583

FULLJAMES, Michael William. b 36. OBE94. AKC60. **d** 61 **p** 62. C Armley St Bart *Ripon* 61-64; C E Wells *B & W* 64-67; R Stanningley St Thos *Ripon* 67-73; Chapl St Aug Hosp Cant 73-88; St Martin's Hosp 82-88; RD W Bridge *Cant* 87-88; Chapl Rotterdam *Eur* 88-94; Sen Chapl Rotterdam Miss to Seamen 88-94; Sen Chapl Burrswood Chr Cen *Roch* from 94. *The Chaplain's House, Burrswood, Groombridge, Tunbridge Wells, Kent TN3 9PY* Tel (01892) 864459 Fax 862597

FULLJAMES, Peter Godfrey. b 38. BNC Ox BA60 MA64. Qu Coll Birm DipTh62. **d** 62 **p** 63. C Mexborough *Sheff* 62-65; India 65-69; Lic to Offic *Lich* 70-79; Moorside High Sch Werrington 71-79; Kenya 80-85; Research Fell Qu Coll Birm 85-87; Perm to Offic *Birm* 85-90; Tutor WMMTC 87-92; Lic to Offic *Birm* from 90; Tutor Crowther Hall CMS Tr Coll Selly Oak from 95. *99 Lewisham Road, Smethwick, Warley, W Midlands B66 2DD, or Crowther Hall, Selly Oak, Birmingham B29 6QT* Tel 0121-558 3583 or 472 4228

FULLWOOD, William. b 11. St Aid Birkenhead 45. **d** 48 **p** 49. C Horton *Bradf* 48-51; C Shipley St Pet 51-53; V Earby 53-64; V Blacktoft *York* 64-68; V Laxton 64-68; V Laxton w Blacktoft 68-74; V Rudston w Boynton 74-77; rtd 77; Perm to Offic *York* from 77. *11 Ambrey Close, Hunmanby, Filey, N Yorkshire YO14 0LZ* Tel (01723) 891027

FULTON, John William. b 49. Ex Coll Ox BA71 BPhil72 MA75 MPhil79. Wycliffe Hall Ox 72. **d** 76 **p** 77. C Bexleyheath Ch Ch *Roch* 76-79; C Ealing Dean St Jo *Lon* 79-83; V Aldborough Hatch *Chelmsf* 83-87; Chapl Chantilly *Eur* 87-90; R Hepworth, Hinderclay, Wattisfield and Thelnetham *St E* from 90. *The Rectory, Church Lane, Hepworth, Diss, Norfolk IP22 2PU* Tel (01359) 50285

FUNNELL, Norman Richard James. b 40. Univ of Wales (Lamp) BA64. Ripon Hall Ox 64. **d** 66 **p** 67. C Hackney *Lon* 66-70; Hon C 71-85; TV 85-93; R S Hackney St Jo w Ch Ch from 93. *The Rectory, Church Crescent, London E9 7DH* Tel 0181-985 5145

FURBER, Peter. b 43. Ex Univ BA. Sarum & Wells Th Coll 83. **d** 85 **p** 86. C Stanmore *Win* 85-88; TV Basingstoke 88-95; C Ringwood from 95. *15 Ashburn Garth, Hightown, Ringwood, Hants BH24 3DS* E-mail 100626.276@compuserve.com

FURLONG, The Very Revd Andrew William Ussher. b 47. TCD BA69 Jes Coll Cam BA71. Westcott Ho Cam 70 CITC 72. **d** 72 **p** 73. C Dundela *D & D* 72-76; C Dublin St Ann w St Mark and St Steph *D & G* 76-83; Zimbabwe 83-94; Adn W Harare 88-89; Can Harare 89-94; Asst Chapl United Leeds Teaching Hosps NHS Trust 94-97; Dean Clonmacnoise *M & K* from 97; I Trim and Athboy Gp from 97. *The Deanery, Lomar Street, Trim, Co Meath, Irish Republic* Tel Trim (46) 36698 Fax as telephone

FURLONG (née DAVIES), Mrs Catharine Mary. b 48. Philippa Fawcett Coll CertEd73. EMMTC 85. **d** 88 **p** 95. C Spalding *Linc* 88-92; Zimbabwe 92-94; C Gt w Lt Gidding and Steeple Gidding *Ely* 94-96; P-in-c from 96; P-in-c Brington w Molesworth and Old Weston from 96; P-in-c Leighton Bromswold from 96; P-in-c Winwick from 96. *The Rectory, 6 Luddington Road, Great Gidding, Huntingdon, Cambs PE17 5PA* Tel (01832) 293587

FURLONGER, Maurice Frank. b 25. AKC50. **d** 51 **p** 52. C Lewisham St Swithun *S'wark* 51-54; Chapl RAF 54-57; V Fillongley *Cov* 57-62; R St Levan *Truro* 62-65; R Gt Bookham *Guildf* 65-67; V St Minver *Truro* 67-70; V St Gluvias 70-74; TV Seacroft *Ripon* 74-77; V Hunslet St Mary 77-81; USA 81-88; C Dalton le Dale *Dur* 88-90; rtd 90; Hon C Diptford, N Huish, Harberton and Harbertonford *Ex* 91-94; Perm to Offic *Truro* from 94. *31 Penoweth, Mylor Bridge, Falmouth, Cornwall TR11 5NQ* Tel (01326) 374047

FURNELL, The Very Revd Raymond. b 35. Linc Th Coll 63. **d** 65 **p** 66. C Cannock *Lich* 65-69; V Clayton 69-75; RD Stoke N 75-81; R Shelton 75-77; TR Hanley H Ev 77-81; Provost St E 81-94; V St E Cathl Distr 81-94; Dean York from 94. *The Deanery, York YO1 2JD* Tel (01904) 623608

FURNESS, Colin. b 43. Lich Th Coll 65. **d** 68 **p** 69. C New Bentley *Sheff* 68; C Sheff Parson Cross St Cecilia 68-74; V Edlington 74-78; C Heavitree w Ex St Paul *Ex* 78-81; TV 81-89; R Sampford Spiney w Horrabridge from 89. *The Rectory, Tor View, Horrabridge, Yelverton, Devon PL20 7RE* Tel (01822) 855198

FURNESS, Dominic John. b 53. Bris Univ BA76. Ridley Hall Cam 82. **d** 84 **p** 85. C Downend *Bris* 84-88; V Stoke Hill *Guildf* from 88. *St Peter's House, 37 Hazel Avenue, Guildford, Surrey GU1 1NP* Tel (01483) 572078

FURNESS, Edward Joseph. b 42. S'wark Ord Course 74. **d** 77 **p** 78. NSM S Lambeth St Steph *S'wark* 77-81; Warden Mayflower Family Cen Canning Town *Chelmsf* 82-96; P-in-c Aston St Jas *Birm* from 96. *The Vicarage, 215 Albert Road, Aston, Birmingham B6 5NA* Tel 0121-327 3230

FURNESS, Edward Peter Alexander. b 29. St Edm Hall Ox BA52 MA56. St Aid Birkenhead 52. **d** 54 **p** 55. C Ashton-on-Ribble St Andr *Blackb* 54-57; C Storrington *Chich* 57-59; C Sullington 57-59; V Worsthorne *Blackb* 59-64 and 88-94; V Longridge 64-88; rtd 94; Perm to Offic *Blackb* from 94. *26 Severn Street, Longridge, Preston PR3 3ND* Tel (01772) 784092

FURNESS, John Alfred. b 31. Chich Th Coll 60. **d** 62 **p** 63. C Leeds St Aid *Ripon* 62-66; C Rickmansworth *St Alb* 66-73; R Wymington 73-75; P-in-c Podington w Farndish 74-75; R Wymington w Podington 75-79; V Waltham Cross 79-89; RD Cheshunt 84-89; R Swyncombe w Britwell Salome *Ox* 89-97; rtd 97. *5 Heathfield Court, Avenue Road, St Albans, Herts AL1 3QF* Tel (01727) 856836

FURST, John William. b 41. Ripon Coll Cuddesdon. **d** 84 **p** 85. C Bris Ch the Servant Stockwood *Bris* 84-88; V Hanham 88-94. *32 Riversdale, Llandaff, Cardiff CF5 2QL* Tel (01222) 567212

FUTCHER, Christopher David. b 58. Edin Univ BD80. Westcott Ho Cam 80. **d** 82 **p** 83. C Borehamwood *St Alb* 82-85; C Stevenage All SS Pin Green 85-88; V 88-96; V St Alb St Steph from 96. *St Stephen's Vicarage, 14 Watling Street, St Albans, Herts AL1 2PX* Tel (01727) 862598

FUTERS, Michael Roger. b 58. Trin & All SS Coll Leeds BEd80. St Jo Coll Nottm 82. **d** 85 **p** 86. C Narborough and Huncote *Leic* 85-87; C Spondon *Derby* 87-90; P-in-c Derby St Jas 90-95; TV

Walbrook Epiphany from 95. *St James's Vicarage, 224 Osmaston Road, Derby DE23 8JX* Tel (01332) 343911

FUTTER, Ivan Herbert. b 31. Roch Th Coll 62. **d** 64 **p** 65. C Buckhurst Hill *Chelmsf* 64-66; Canada from 66. *RR1, 3610 Fo'csle Road, Pender Island, British Columbia, Canada, V0N 2M0*

FYFE, Gordon Boyd. b 63. Aber Univ BD93 Edin Univ MTh95. **d** 96 **p** 97. C Ayr *Glas* from 96; C Maybole from 96; C Girvan from 96. *15C Mariner's Wharf, North Harbour Street, Ayr KA8 8AA* Tel (01292) 282084 Fax as telephone

FYFFE, Canon Robert Clark. b 56. Edin Univ BD78 Bris Poly DAVM87. Edin Th Coll 74. **d** 79 **p** 80. C Edin St Jo *Edin* 79-83; Youth Chapl *B & W* 83-87; Prov Youth Officer Scottish Episc Ch 87-92; Co-ord Internat Angl Youth Network from 88; R Perth St Jo *St And* from 93; Can St Ninian's Cathl Perth from 96. *23 Comley Bank, Perth PH2 7HU* Tel (01738) 625394 Fax 443053 E-mail bobfyffe@sol.co.uk

FYFFE, Timothy Bruce. b 25. New Coll Ox MA54. Westcott Ho Cam 54. **d** 56 **p** 57. C Lewisham St Mary *S'wark* 56-60; Nigeria 60-68; TV Lowestoft St Marg *Nor* 69-80; Chapl HM Pris Blundeston 70-78; TV Tettenhall Regis *Lich* 80-85; Chapl Compton Hall Hospice Wolv 85-87; NSM Wolverhampton St Andr *Lich* from 88; rtd 90. *21 Sandy Lane, Tettenhall, Wolverhampton WV6 9EB* Tel (01902) 752066

FYLES, Gordon. b 39. Trin Coll Bris 76. **d** 77 **p** 78. C Islington St Mary *Lon* 77-81; Ext Sec BCMS 81-88; Hon C Kingston Hill St Paul *S'wark* 82-88; C Wimbledon Em Ridgway Prop Chpl 88-97; I Crinken *D & G* from 97. *Crinken Parsonage, Bray, Co Wicklow, Irish Republic* Tel Dublin (1) 282 2048 E-mail gfyles@enterprise.net

FYSH, Leslie David. b 35. Glouc Sch of Min 88. **d** 91 **p** 92. NSM Stonehouse *Glouc* 91-95; Asst Chapl Wycliffe Coll Glos 91-95; NSM W Walton *Ely* from 95. *Cornerways, 53 School Road, West Walton, Wisbech, Cambs PE14 7ES* Tel (01945) 584631

G

GABB-JONES, Adrian William Douglas. b 43. ARICS. Ripon Coll Cuddesdon 79. **d** 81 **p** 82. C Northolt Park St Barn *Lon* 81-84; C Ruislip St Martin 84-89; V Minster Lovell and Brize Norton *Ox* from 89. *The Vicarage, Burford Road, Minster Lovell, Oxford OX8 5RA* Tel (01993) 776492

GABE, Dr Eric Sigurd. b 15. Lon Univ BA52 PhD94. St Aid Birkenhead 54. **d** 55 **p** 55. C W Kirby St Andr *Ches* 55-57; C Hoylake 57-60; V Cricklewood St Mich *Lon* 60-72; V Brondesbury St Anne w Kilburn H Trin 72-80; rtd 80; Perm to Offic *St Alb* from 80; Perm to Offic *Lon* from 81. *21 Cromer Road, Barnet, Herts EN5 5HT* Tel 0181-449 6779

GABLE, Michael David. b 70. Wales Poly BEng92. St Mich Coll Llan DipTh94 BTh95. **d** 95 **p** 96. C Newton Nottage *Llan* from 95. *79 Meadow Lane, Porthcawl CF36 5EY* Tel (01656) 788176

GABRIEL, Michael Hunt. b 29. BA. **d** 57 **p** 58. C Waterford Ch Ch *C & O* 57-60; C New Windsor H Trin *Ox* 60-62; C Albany Street Ch Ch *Lon* 62-63; R W and E Shefford *Ox* 63-67; C Hillingdon St Jo *Lon* 67-86; C Kingston Buci *Chich* 86-94; rtd 94. *Flat 1, 6 Dittons Road, Eastbourne, E Sussex BN21 1DN*

GADD, Dr Alan John. b 44. FRMetS67 Imp Coll Lon BSc65 PhD69. S'wark Ord Course 68. **d** 71 **p** 72. Asst Chapl Lon Univ *Lon* 71-72; Perm to Offic *S'wark* 73-91; C Battersea Park All SS 91-95; P-in-c 95-96; C Battersea Fields from 96. *100 Prince of Wales Drive, London SW11 4BD* Tel 0171-622 3809

GADD, Brian Hayward. b 33. Hatf Coll Dur BA54 DipEd55. Glouc Sch of Min 82. **d** 85 **p** 87. NSM Cleobury Mortimer w Hopton Wafers *Heref* 85-93; NSM Cleobury Mortimer w Hopton Wafers etc from 93. *34 Lower Street, Cleobury Mortimer, Kidderminster, Worcs DY14 8AB* Tel (01299) 270758

GADD, Bryan Stephen Andrew. b 56. Dur Univ BA Ox Univ CertEd. Chich Th Coll. **d** 81 **p** 82. C Newlyn St Pet *Truro* 81-86; R St Mawgan w St Ervan and St Eval 86-90; Chapl Summer Fields Sch Ox from 90; Perm to Offic *Truro* from 90. *Little Cottage, Summer Fields School, Oxford OX2 7EN* Tel (01865) 58729

GADEN, Timothy John. b 64. Melbourne Univ BA86 Monash Univ Aus PhD96. Melbourne Coll of Div BD90. **d** 91 **p** 91. Australia 91-96; C Battersea St Mary *S'wark* from 97. *35 Kerrison Road, London SW11 2QG* Tel 0171-223 6880

GAGE, Canon Robert Edward. b 47. Whitman Coll Washington BA69. Cuddesdon Coll BA75 MA81. **d** 76 **p** 77. C Cheshunt *St Alb* 76-79; C Harpenden St Nic 79-81; V S Mymms 81-82; P-in-c Ridge 81-82; V S Mymms and Ridge 82-97; Prec and Can Res Wakef Cathl *Wakef* from 97. *4 Cathedral Close, Margaret Street, Wakefield, W Yorkshire WF1 2DQ*

GAINER, Jeffrey. b 51. Jes Coll Ox BA73 MA77. Wycliffe Hall Ox 74. **d** 77 **p** 78. C Baglan *Llan* 77-81; V Cwmbach 81-85; V Tonyrefail w Gilfach Goch and Llandyfodwg 85-87; Dir NT Studies 87-92; Dir Past Studies St Mich Coll Llan 87-92; V Meidrim and Llanboidy and Merthyr *St D* from 92. *The Vicarage, Meidrim, Carmarthen SA33 5QF* Tel (01994) 231378

GAIR, Andrew Kennon. b 62. Westcott Ho Cam 88. **d** 91 **p** 92. C Clare w Poslingford, Cavendish etc *St E* 91-95; R Debden and Wimbish w Thunderley *Chelmsf* from 95. *The Rectory, Debden, Saffron Walden, Essex CB11 3LB* Tel (01799) 540285

✠**GAISFORD, The Rt Revd John Scott.** b 34. St Chad's Coll Dur BA59 DipTh60 MA76. **d** 60 **p** 61 **c** 94. C Audenshaw St Hilda *Man* 60-62; C Bramhall *Ches* 62-65; V Crewe St Andr 65-86; RD Nantwich 74-85; Hon Can Ches Cathl 80-86; Adn Macclesfield 86-94; Suff Bp Beverley (PEV) *York* from 94; Asst Bp Ripon from 96. *3 North Lane, Roundhay, Leeds LS8 2QJ* Tel 0113-273 2003 Mobile 0860-289550 Fax 0113-273 3002 E-mail 101740.2725@compuserve.com

GAIT, David James. b 48. BNC Ox BA71 BSc72 MA77 Ox Univ MSc83. Ridley Hall Cam 71. **d** 74 **p** 75. C Litherland St Paul Hatton Hill *Liv* 74-77; C Farnworth 77-80; V Widnes St Jo from 80; Chapl Widnes Maternity Hosp from 86. *St John's House, Greenway Road, Widnes, Cheshire WA8 6HA* Tel 0151-424 3134

GAKURU, Griphus Stephen. Makerere Univ Kampala BSc81 PGDE83 Selw Coll Cam MPhil92 PhD. Bp Tucker Coll Mukono BD88. **d** 88 **p** 91. Uganda 89-91; Hon C Cambridge H Trin w St Andr Gt *Ely* 91-92; Hon C Cambridge H Trin 92-95; Chapl Selw Coll Cam 91-95; C Small Heath *Birm* from 95. *St Oswalds Vicarage, 11 St Oswalds Road, Birmingham B10 9RB* Tel 0121-772 1682

GALBRAITH, Alexander Peter James. b 65. Qu Coll Ox BA86 MA90. Wycliffe Hall Ox 87. **d** 90 **p** 91. C Southport Em *Liv* 90-94; C Mossley Hill St Matt and St Jas 94-97; V Kew from 97; Chapl Southport and Formby NHS Trust from 97. *20 Markham Drive, Kew, Southport, Merseyside PR8 6XR* Tel (01704) 547758

GALBRAITH, Jane. **d** 95 **p** 96. NSM *M & K* from 95. *252 Beechdale, Dunboyne, Co Meath, Irish Republic* Tel Dublin (1) 825 1887

GALBRAITH, John Angus Frame. b 44. Sarum Th Coll 68. **d** 71 **p** 72. C Richmond St Mary *S'wark* 71-74; Chapl W Lon Colls 74-79; V S'wark H Trin w St Matt 79-95; V New Addington from 95. *St Edward's Vicarage, Cleves Crescent, Croydon CR0 0DL* Tel (01689) 845588

GALBRAITH, John Watson Joseph Denham. b 19. Glas Univ MA41. Bps' Coll Cheshunt 47. **d** 48 **p** 49. C Biggleswade *St Alb* 48-49; C Tring 49-51; C Challoch w Newton Stewart *Glas* 51-53; CF 53-67; Dep Asst Chapl Gen 67-72; R Hodnet w Weston under Redcastle *Lich* 72-77; V Deeping St James *Linc* 77-81; Chapl Oporto *Eur* 81-85; rtd 85; Perm to Offic *B & W* from 86. *64 High Street, Rode, Bath BA3 6PB* Tel (01373) 830077

GALBRAITH, Peter John. b 59. QUB BA MTh TCD DipTh. **d** 85 **p** 86. C Knockbreda *D & D* 85-88; C Ballynafeigh St Jude 88-91; I Broomhedge *Conn* from 91. *Broomhedge Rectory, 30 Lurganure Road, Broughmore, Lisburn, Co Antrim BT28 2TR* Tel (01846) 621229

GALE, Christopher. b 44. ALCD67. **d** 68 **p** 69. C Balderton *S'well* 68-72; C Bilborough St Jo 72-75; P-in-c Colwick 75-78; V Radford St Pet 78-84; V Sherwood from 84; AD Nottingham N from 90. *St Martin's Vicarage, Trevose Gardens, Sherwood, Nottingham NG5 3FU* Tel 0115-960 7547

GALE, Colin Edward. b 49. Lon Univ PGCE74. St Jo Coll Nottm LTh BTh73. **d** 79 **p** 80. C Hoole *Ches* 79-82; C Woodley St Jo the Ev *Ox* 82-87; V Clapham St Jas *S'wark* 87-96; V Sutton Ch Ch from 96. *Christ Church Vicarage, 14 Christchurch Park, Sutton, Surrey SM2 5TN* Tel 0181-642 2757

GALE, Douglas Norman. b 32. Birkb Coll Lon BA72. Franciscan Ho of Studies E Bergholt 53. **d** 61 **p** 61. Asst Master Judd Sch Tonbridge 72-74; K Sch Ches 74-80; C Ches Team *Ches* 79-83; TV 83-87; rtd 87; Perm to Offic *Ely* from 91. *6 Allen Court, Hauxton Road, Trumpington, Cambridge CB2 2LU* Tel (01223) 841197

GALE, The Ven John. b 34. Univ of Wales (Lamp) 67. **d** 69 **p** 70. C Aberdare St Jo *Llan* 69-71; C Merthyr Dyfan 71-74; S Africa from 74; R Knysna St Geo from 82; Adn Knysna from 93. *PO Box 67, Knysna, 6570 South Africa* Tel Knysna (445) 21239 Fax as telephone

GALE, Keith George. b 44. St Jo Coll Lusaka 68 Sarum Th Coll 69. **d** 70 **p** 71. C Sheff St Cuth *Sheff* 70-77; P-in-c Brightside All SS 72-77; C Birm St Martin *Birm* 77-81; USPG 81-94; Malawi 81-94; Adn Lilongwe Lake Malawi 89-92; TV Sampford Peverell, Uplowman, Holcombe Rogus etc *Ex* from 94. *The Vicarage, Lower Town, Halberton, Tiverton, Devon EX16 7AU* Tel (01884) 821149

GALE, Ms Lucille Catherine. b 67. Sarum & Wells Th Coll 92. **d** 94 **p** 95. C Welling *S'wark* from 94. *21 Hill View Drive, Welling, Kent DA16 3RS* Tel 0181-856 3500

GALE, Peter Simon. b 56. BD. St Mich Coll Llan. **d** 83 **p** 84. C Caerphilly *Llan* 83-89; Chapl RN 89-93; V Ystrad Rhondda w Ynyscynon *Llan* from 93. *St Stephen's Vicarage, Ystrad, Pentre CF41 7RR* Tel (01443) 434426

GALES, Alan. b 29. Sarum Th Coll 56. **d** 59 **p** 60. C Greenside *Dur* 59-60; C Peterlee 60-63; Ind Chapl 60-70; V Marley Hill 63-94; Asst Chapl HM Pris Dur 74-81; rtd 94. *46 Corsair, Whickham, Newcastle upon Tyne NE16 5YA* Tel 0191-488 7352

GALES, Bernard Henry. b 27. Lon Univ BSc(Econ)51. Wells Th Coll 62. **d** 64 **p** 65. C Sholing *Win* 64-67; C Fordingbridge w Ibsley 67-71; C S Molton w Nymet St George *Ex* 71-73; C Thelbridge 73-77; P-in-c 77-78; P-in-c Creacombe 77-78; P-in-c W w E Worlington 77-78; P-in-c Meshaw 77-78; P-in-c Witheridge 77-78; C Witheridge, Thelbridge, Creacombe, Meshaw etc 79-80; R Bow w Broad Nymet 80-93; V Colebrooke 80-93; R Zeal Monachorum 80-93; RD Cadbury 90-93; rtd 93; Perm to Offic *Ex* from 93. *8 Old Rectory Gardens, Morchard Bishop, Crediton, Devon EX17 6PF* Tel (01363) 877601

GALES, Simon Richard. b 59. CEng87 MICE87 Jes Coll Cam BA81 MA84. Wycliffe Hall Ox 91. **d** 93 **p** 94. C Houghton *Carl* 93-97; V Lindow *Ches* from 97. *St John's Vicarage, 137 Knutsford Road, Wilmslow, Cheshire SK9 6EL* Tel (01625) 583251

GALILEE, Canon George David Surtees. b 37. Or Coll Ox BA60 MA64. Westcott Ho Cam 61. **d** 62 **p** 63. C Knighton St Mary Magd *Leic* 62-67; V Stocking Farm 67-69; Tutor Westcott Ho Cam and Homerton Coll 69-71; V Sutton *Ely* 71-80; P-in-c Addiscombe St Mildred *Cant* 80-81; V 81-84; V Addiscombe St Mildred *S'wark* 85-95; Can Res and Chan Blackb Cathl *Blackb* from 95. *25 Ryburn Avenue, Blackburn BB2 7AU* Tel (01254) 671540

GALLAGHER, Adrian Ian. b 43. TCD Div Sch 89. **d** 92 **p** 93. C Drumachose *D & R* 92-96; I Camus-juxta-Bann from 96. *19 Dunderg Road, Macosquin, Coleraine, Co Londonderry BT51 4PN* Tel (01265) 43918

GALLAGHER, Hubert. b 31. Linc Th Coll 78. **d** 80 **p** 81. C Lupset *Wakef* 80-82; C Badsworth 82-86; V Kinsley 86-88; V Kinsley w Wragby 88-91; rtd 91; Perm to Offic *Wakef* from 91. *The Little House, Nostell Priory, Wakefield, W Yorkshire WF4 1QE* Tel (01924) 865498

GALLAGHER, Canon Ian. BTh. **d** 90 **p** 91. C Annagh w Drumgoon, Ashfield etc *K, E & A* 90-93; I Drumcliffe w Lissadell and Munninane from 93; Preb Elphin Cathl from 97; Dioc Sec (Elphin and Ardagh) from 97. *The Rectory, Drumcliffe, Co Sligo, Irish Republic* Tel Sligo (71) 63125 Fax as telephone

GALLAGHER, Michael Collins. b 48. Dur Univ BA. Sarum Th Coll. **d** 82 **p** 83. C Bridport *Sarum* 82-86; V Downton from 86; RD Alderbury from 93. *The Vicarage, Barford Lane, Downton, Salisbury SP5 3QA* Tel (01725) 510326

GALLAGHER, Neville Roy. b 45. Lon Univ CertEd66 AKC70 Lon Univ BD76. **d** 71 **p** 72. C Folkestone St Mary and St Eanswythe *Cant* 71-74; Hon C Sutton Valence w E Sutton and Chart Sutton 74-76; TV Cen Telford *Lich* 76-78; P-in-c Gt Mongeham *Cant* 78-80; P-in-c Ripple 78-80; R Gt Mongeham w Ripple and Sutton by Dover 80-83; V Kennington 83-88; Chapl Bedgebury Sch Kent from 88. *3 Beech Drive, Bedgebury Park, Goudhurst, Kent TN17 2SJ* Tel (01580) 211989 or 211221

GALLAGHER, Robert. b 43. St Chad's Coll Dur BSc65 DipTh67. **d** 67 **p** 68. C Crosland Moor *Wakef* 67-69; C Huddersfield St Pet and St Paul 69-71; Chapl Huddersfield Poly 72-79; Min Coulby Newham Ecum Project *York* 79-90; V Toxteth St Marg *Liv* from 90. *St Margaret's Vicarage, 3 Princes Road, Liverpool L8 1TG* Tel 0151-709 1526

GALLAGHER, Stephen. b 58. Southn Univ BTh89. Chich Th Coll 86. **d** 89 **p** 90. C S Shields All SS *Dur* 89-92; C Hartlepool St Paul 92-94; Chapl Hartlepool Gen Hosp 92-94; R Loftus and Carlin How w Skinningrove *York* 94-97; P-in-c Lower Beeding *Chich* from 97; Dioc Youth Officer from 97. *The Vicarage, Plummers Plain, Lower Beeding, Horsham, W Sussex RH13 6NU* Tel (01403) 891367

GALLETLY, Thomas. b 23. St Chad's Coll Dur BA50 DipTh52. **d** 52 **p** 53. C Woodhorn w Newbiggin *Newc* 52-55; Chapl Aycliffe Approved Sch Co Dur 56-57; Chapl Chailey Heritage Hosp and Sch Lewes 57-88; Lic to Offic *Chich* 59-88; rtd 88; Perm to Offic *Chich* from 88. *The Glen, Lewes Road, Scaynes Hill, Haywards Heath, W Sussex RH17 7PG* Tel (01444) 831510

GALLEY, Giles Christopher. b 32. Qu Coll Cam BA56 MA60. Linc Th Coll 56. **d** 58 **p** 59. C Gt Yarmouth *Nor* 58-62; C N Lynn w St Marg and St Nic 62-66; C Leeds St Pet *Ripon* 66-69; V N Hull St Mich *York* 70-79; V Strensall from 79; RD Easingwold from 82. *The Vicarage, 10 York Road, Strensall, York YO3 5UB* Tel (01904) 490683

GALLICHAN, Henry Ernest. b 45. Sarum Th Coll 70. **d** 72 **p** 73. C Kenton Ascension *Newc* 72-76; Tanzania 76-80; Lic to Offic *Truro* from 80. *Karibu, Trevelmond, Liskeard, Cornwall PL14 4LZ* Tel (01579) 20530

✠**GALLIFORD, The Rt Revd David George.** b 25. Clare Coll Cam BA49 MA51. Westcott Ho Cam. **d** 51 **p** 52 **c** 75. C Newland St Jo *York* 51-54; C Eton w Boveney *Ox* 54-56; Min Can Windsor 54-56; V Middlesbrough St Oswald *York* 56-61; R Bolton Percy 61-71; Dioc Adult Tr Officer 61-71; Can and Preb York Minster 69-70; Can Res and Treas 70-75; Suff Bp Hulme *Man* 75-84; Suff Bp Bolton 84-91; rtd 91; Asst Bp York from 95. *Bishopgarth, Maltongate, Thornton Dale, Pickering, N Yorkshire YO18 7SA* Tel (01751) 74605

GALLON, Edward George. b 16. St Steph Ho Ox 64. **d** 66 **p** 67. C Chelmsf All SS *Chelmsf* 66-69; C Hockley 69-74; R Takeley w Lt Canfield 74-83; rtd 83; Perm to Offic *S'wark* from 84. *42 Home Park, Oxted, Surrey RH8 0JU* Tel (01883) 714091

GALLOWAY, Charles Bertram. b 41. Lon Univ BA62 Birm Univ DipTh64. Qu Coll Birm 64. **d** 64 **p** 65. C Darlington H Trin *Dur* 64-68; Ind Chapl Teesside 68-77; Sen Ind Chapl *Liv* 77-87; Team Ldr and Convener Lon Ind Chapl *Lon* 87-93; P-in-c Gosforth w Nether Wasdale and Wasdale Head *Carl* from 93; Chapl Sellafield from 94. *The Rectory, Gosforth, Seascale, Cumbria CA20 1AZ* Tel (019467) 25251

GALLOWAY, Michael Edward. b 41. Chich Th Coll 72. **d** 74 **p** 75. C Aldwick *Chich* 74-77; C Bournemouth St Clem w St Mary *Win* 78-82; V S Benfleet *Chelmsf* from 83. *St Mary's Vicarage, 105 Vicarage Hill, Benfleet, Essex SS7 1PD* Tel (01268) 792294

GALLOWAY, Dr Peter John. b 54. OBE96 JP89. Golds Coll Lon BA76 K Coll Lon PhD87 FRSA88. St Steph Ho Ox 80. **d** 83 **p** 84. C St Jo Wood *Lon* 83-86; C St Giles-in-the-Fields 86-90; Warden of Readers (Lon Episc Area) 87-92; OStJ 86-92; ChStJ 92-97; KStJ from 97; P-in-c Hampstead Em W End *Lon* 90-95; V from 95. *Emmanuel Vicarage, Lyncroft Gardens, London NW6 1JU* Tel 0171-435 1911 Fax 431 5521

GALLUP, Peter Whitfield. b 06. Sarum Th Coll 51. **d** 53 **p** 54. C Portsea St Mary *Portsm* 53-61; R Buriton 61-74; rtd 74; Perm to Offic *Win* 74-95. *Brendon House, Park Road, Winchester SO23 7BE* Tel (01962) 854090

GALT, Ian Ross. b 34. Leeds Univ BSc56. **d** 76 **p** 77. NSM Newport St Julian *Mon* 76-87; NSM Newport St Teilo from 87. *47 Brynglas Avenue, Newport NP9 5LR* Tel (01633) 857134

GAMBLE, David Lawrence. b 34. AKC61. **d** 62 **p** 63. C-in-c Shrub End All SS CD *Chelmsf* 62-65; C Colchester St Jas, All SS, St Nic and St Runwald 65-69; V Chelmsf St Andr 69-73; P-in-c Hatfield Heath 69-73; C 74-77; TV Hemel Hempstead *St Alb* 77-82; P-in-c Renhold 82-90; Chapl HM Pris Bedf 82-90; P-in-c Petersham *S'wark* 90-96; Chapl HM Pris Latchmere Ho 90-96; P-in-c Portsea St Geo *Portsm* from 96. *The Vicarage, 8 Queen Street, Portsmouth PO1 3HL* Tel (01705) 812215

GAMBLE, Donald William. b 67. NUU BSc88. TCD Div Sch BTh91. **d** 91 **p** 92. C Belfast St Mich *Conn* 91-95; I Dromore *Clogh* from 95. *The Rectory, Galbally Road, Dromore, Omagh, Co Tyrone BT78 3EE* Tel (01662) 898300

GAMBLE, Ian Robert. b 66. Ulster Univ BA90 TCD BTh93. CITC 90. **d** 93 **p** 94. C Bangor St Comgall *D & D* 93-96; C Bangor Primacy 93-96; Bp's C Belfast Whiterock *Conn* from 96. *St James's Rectory, 33 Fortwilliam Park, Belfast BT15 4AP* Tel (01232) 779442

GAMBLE, Norman Edward Charles. b 50. TCD BA72 HDipEd73 PhD78. CITC 76. **d** 79 **p** 80. C Bangor St Comgall *D & D* 79-83; I Dunleckney w Nurney, Lorum and Kiltennel *C & O* 83-90; Warden of Readers 84-90; RD Aghade 85-90; P-in-c Leighlin w Grange Sylvae, Shankill etc 89-90; Preb Leighlin Cathl 89-90; Preb Ossory Cathl 89-90; I Malahide w Balgriffin *D & G* from 90; Abp's Dom Chapl from 95. *The Rectory, Church Road, Malahide, Co Dublin, Irish Republic* Tel Dublin (1) 845 4770

GAMBLE, Peter John. b 20. St Cath Soc Ox BA51 MA55 DipEd59. Ripon Hall Ox 48. **d** 52 **p** 53. C Erdington St Barn *Birm* 52-54; Chapl and Ho Master Milton Abbey Sch Dorset 55-59; Chapl and Tutor Millfield Sch Somerset 59-67; Prin Anglo-American Coll Faringdon 67-71; Chapl and Tutor Harrow Sch 72-82; rtd 82. *2 Lawn Road, Guildford, Surrey GU2 5DE* Tel (01483) 576902

GAMBLE, Robin Philip. b 53. Oak Hill Th Coll 74. **d** 77 **p** 78. C Kildwick *Bradf* 77-78; C Laisterdyke 78-80; C York St Paul *York* 80-82; V Bradf St Aug Undercliffe *Bradf* 82-95; Dioc Adv in Evang from 93. *6 Glenhurst Road, Shipley, W Yorkshire BD18 4DZ* Tel (01274) 586414

GAMBLE, Ronald George. b 41. Cant Sch of Min 92. **d** 95 **p** 96. NSM Loose *Cant* from 95. *18 Copper Tree Court, Maidstone, Kent ME19 9RW*

GAMBLES, Una Beryl. b 33. Man Univ BEd78. St Chris Coll Blackheath 59. **d** 87 **p** 94. NSM Upton Priory *Ches* from 87; Chapl Parkside Hosp Ches from 87. *23 Grangelands, Upton, Macclesfield, Cheshire SK10 4AB* Tel (01625) 421691

GAMESTER, Sidney Peter. b 27. SS Coll Cam BA51 MA55. Oak Hill Th Coll 56. **d** 58 **p** 59. C Surbiton Hill Ch Ch *S'wark* 58-61; C Worthing H Trin *Chich* 61-69; R Silverhill St Matt 69-86; R Bexhill St Mark 86-93; rtd 93; Perm to Offic *Chich* from 93. *18 Crofton Park Avenue, Bexhill-on-Sea, E Sussex TN39 3SE* Tel (01424) 842276

GAMMON, William Paul Lachlan (Bill). b 60. SS Hild & Bede Coll Dur BA82. St Steph Ho Ox 89. **d** 91 **p** 92. C Chalfont St Peter *Ox* 91-94; Lect Bolton St Pet *Man* from 94. *114 Bromwich Street, Bolton, Lancs BL2 1LL* Tel (01204) 393615

GANDIYA, Leonard Farirayi (Lee). b 64. Colorado Coll 87 Boston Univ 90 MA92. Ridley Hall Cam 92. **d** 94 **p** 95. NSM Camberwell St Luke *S'wark* 94-95; C Lowestoft St Marg *Nor* from 95; Dioc Rep for Black Anglican Concerns from 96. *5 Magdalen Close, Lowestoft, Suffolk NR32 4TP* Tel (01502) 517841

GANDON, Andrew James Robson. b 54. St Jo Coll Dur BA76. Ridley Hall Cam 76. **d** 78 **p** 79. C Aston SS Pet and Paul *Birm* 78-82; CMS 82-95; Zaire 82-88; Kenya 89-94; V Harefield *Lon* from 95. *9 Lewis Close, Harefield, Uxbridge, Middx UB9 6RD* Tel (01895) 825960

GANDON, James Philip. b 31. ALCD56. **d** 56 **p** 57. C Westcliff St Mich *Chelmsf* 56-58; Canada from 58; rtd 92. *185 Jones Street, Goderich, Ontario, Canada, N7A 3B5* Tel Goderich (519) 524-9718

GANDON, Percy James. b 22. ALCD53. **d** 53 **p** 54. C New Humberstone *Leic* 53-56; C Leic H Trin 56-57; Uganda 57-63; V Hoddesdon *St Alb* 63-83; RD Cheshunt 81-83; Perm to Offic *Nor* 83-85 and from 86; P-in-c Lyng w Sparham 85-86; rtd 87. *The Old Bakery, Hindolveston, Dereham, Norfolk NR20 5DF* Tel (01263) 861325

GANDY, Nicholas John. b 53. CBiol79 MIBiol Westf Coll Lon BSc75 Reading Univ MSc76 Ex Coll Ox CertEd78. St Steph Ho Ox 86. **d** 88 **p** 89. C Crowthorne *Ox* 88-89; C Tilehurst St Mary 89-93; P-in-c Didcot St Pet from 93. *St Peter's Vicarage, Didcot, Oxon OX11 8PN* Tel (01235) 812114

GANE, Canon Christopher Paul. b 33. Qu Coll Cam BA57 MA61. Ridley Hall Cam 57. **d** 59 **p** 60. C Rainham *Chelmsf* 59-62; C Farnborough *Guildf* 62-64; V Erith St Paul *Roch* 64-71; V Ipswich St Marg *St E* 71-88; Hon Can St E Cathl from 82; R Hopton, Market Weston, Barningham etc from 88. *The Rectory, Nethergate Street, Hopton, Diss, Norfolk IP22 2QZ* Tel (01953) 818239

GANE, Nicholas. b 57. St Jo Coll Nottm DipThMin95. **d** 95 **p** 96. C Keynsham *B & W* from 95. *88 Chandag Road, Keynsham, Bristol BS18 1QE* Tel 0117-986 1056

GANGA, Jeremy Franklin. b 62. Cape Town Univ BSocSc86 Lon Bible Coll BA92. St Jo Coll Nottm MA93 Ridley Hall Cam CTM95. **d** 95 **p** 96. C St Peter-in-Thanet *Cant* from 95. *64 High Street, St Peters, Broadstairs, Kent CT10 2TD*

GANJAVI, John Farhad. b 57. ACGI79 Imp Coll Lon BSc79. Ridley Hall Cam 79. **d** 82 **p** 83. C Yardley St Edburgha *Birm* 82-85; C Knowle 85-89; P-in-c Beaudesert and Henley-in-Arden w Ullenhall *Cov* 89-92; R from 92; RD Alcester from 92. *The Rectory, Beaudesert Lane, Henley-in-Arden, Solihull, W Midlands B95 5JY* Tel (01564) 792570

GANN, Canon Anthony Michael. b 37. TCD BA60 MA64 BD64. **d** 62 **p** 63. V Choral Derry Cathl *D & R* 62-66; Lesotho 66-74; Dioc Officer for Miss and Unity *Carl* 75-80; P-in-c Bampton and Mardale 75-80; TV Cen Telford *Lich* 80-89; TR Wolvercote w Summertown *Ox* from 89; RD Ox from 95. *The Rectory, Lonsdale Road, Oxford OX2 7ES* Tel (01865) 56079

GANN, John West. b 29. Ex Coll Ox BA55 MA59. Wells Th Coll 55. **d** 57 **p** 58. C Wendover *Ox* 57-59; C Walton St Mary *Liv* 59-62; R Didcot *Ox* 62-70; R Newbury St Nic 70-78; TR Newbury 73-78; V Twickenham St Mary *Lon* 78-87; Dir of Ords 81-87; TR Bridport *Sarum* 87-94; RD Lyme Bay 89-92; rtd 94; Perm to Offic *Bris* from 94. *Three Gables, Charlton Road, Tetbury, Glos GL6 8DX* Tel (01666) 503965

GANT, Canon Brian Leonard. b 45. K Coll Lon 72. **d** 73 **p** 74. C Hillmorton *Cov* 73-75; C Cov St Geo 76; P-in-c Maldon St Mary *Chelmsf* 76-79; R Muthill *St And* 79-81; R Crieff 79-81; R Comrie 79-81; V Walsall St Paul *Lich* 81-84; Min Can Worc Cathl *Worc* 84-89; Chapl K Sch Worc 84-89; V Tunbridge Wells K Chas *Roch* 89-95; Hon Can Kumasi from 94; V Wymondham *Nor* from 95. *The Vicarage, 5 Vicar Street, Wymondham, Norfolk NR18 0PL* Tel (01953) 602269

GANT, Peter Robert. b 38. BNC Ox BA60 MA64 G&C Coll Cam BA62 MA67. Ridley Hall Cam 61. **d** 63 **p** 64. C Portsea St Mary *Portsm* 63-67; V Blackheath *Birm* 67-73; Asst Master Harold Malley Gr Sch Solihull 73-75; Perm to Offic 73-75; Perm to Offic *Guildf* from 75; rtd 93. *8 Sandon Close, Esher, Surrey KT10 8JE* Tel 0181-398 5107

GANZ, Timothy Jon. b 36. ARCM63 Univ Coll Ox BA58 MA62. St Steph Ho Ox 58. **d** 61 **p** 62. C Shrewsbury H Cross *Lich* 61-65; Asst Chapl Hurstpierpoint Coll Hassocks 65-69; Chapl 69-73; Chapl Univ of Wales (Swansea) *S & B* 74-75; P-in-c Hanley All SS *Lich* 75-80; TV Stoke-upon-Trent 80-81; V Tutbury from 81. *The Vicarage, Tutbury, Burton-on-Trent, Staffs DE13 9JF* Tel (01283) 813127

GARBETT, Capt Phillip Ronald. b 52. CA Tr Coll CertRS80 EAMTC 95. **d** 97. C Ipswich St Fran *St E* from 97. *St Clare's House, 92 Belmont Road, Ipswich IP8 3RP* Tel (01473) 687847

GARBUTT, Gerald. b 41. St Aid Birkenhead 65. **d** 67 **p** 68. C Stretford All SS *Man* 67-70; Lic to Offic 70-72; R Salford St Bart 72-74; V Lower Kersal 74-79; V Bethnal Green St Jo w St Bart *Lon* 79-90; P-in-c Stepney St Pet w St Benet 85-87; Chapl Furness Gen Hosp 90-94; Chapl S Cumbria HA 90-94; Hosp Services Chapl Furness Hosps NHS Trust from 94; Chapl Westmorland Hosps NHS Trust from 94. *6 Dale Garth, Leece, Ulverston, Cumbria LA12 0QU* Tel (01229) 823852

GARDEN, Robert Andrew (Robin). b 26. MInstP58 FIMA72 Edin Univ BSc49 Kent Univ MA95. Cant Sch of Min 87. **d** 90 **p** 91. NSM Sandwich *Cant* 90-97; Chapl St Bart Hosp Sandwich from 97. *Naini, 164 St George's Road, Sandwich, Kent CT13 9LD* Tel (01304) 612116

GARDINER, Anthony Reade. b 35. Univ of NZ BA59. Cuddesdon Coll 60. **d** 62 **p** 63. C Gosforth All SS *Newc* 62-65; New Zealand 65-93; C Highcliffe w Hinton Admiral *Win* 93-94; TV N Creedy *Ex* from 94. *The Vicarage, Down St Mary, Crediton, Devon EX17 6EF* Tel (01363) 84835

GARDINER, James Carlisle. b 18. St Jo Coll Dur LTh48. Tyndale Hall Bris. **d** 49 **p** 50. C Blackpool Ch Ch *Blackb* 49-52; C Rushen *S & M* 52-56; R Ditton *Roch* 56-83; rtd 83; Perm to Offic *Roch* from 83. *5 Larch Crescent, Tonbridge, Kent TN10 3NN* Tel (01732) 362323

GARDINER, John. b 15. Clifton Th Coll 67. **d** 68 **p** 69. C Halliwell St Pet *Man* 68-71; V Monton 71-80; V Hoghton *Blackb* 80-84; rtd 84; Perm to Offic *Blackb* from 84. *18 Stuart Court, High Street, Kibworth, Leicester LE8 0LE* Tel 0116-279 6683

GARDINER, Canon Kenneth Ashton. b 27. S'wark Ord Course 60. **d** 63 **p** 64. C Sydenham H Trin *S'wark* 63-67; C Macclesfield St Mich *Ches* 67-70; V Chatham St Phil and St Jas *Roch* 70-93; RD Roch 88-93; Hon Can Roch Cathl 88-93; rtd 93; Perm to Offic *Roch* from 93. *44 Trevale Road, Rochester, Kent ME1 3PA* Tel (01634) 844524

GARDINER, Thomas Alfred (Tom). b 29. St Cuth Soc Dur BA52 MA56. Ridley Hall Cam 54. **d** 56 **p** 57. C Stockport St Geo *Ches* 56-60; Asst Chapl Brentwood Sch Essex 60-62; Chapl 62-88; R Greensted-juxta-Ongar w Stanford Rivers *Chelmsf* from 88. *The Rectory, Greensted, Ongar, Essex CM5 9LA* Tel (01277) 364694

GARDINER, William Gerald Henry. b 46. Lon Univ BD72. Oak Hill Th Coll 68. **d** 72 **p** 73. C Beckenham St Jo *Roch* 72-75; C Cheadle *Ches* 75-81; P-in-c Swynnerton *Lich* 81-83; P-in-c Tittensor 81-83; R Swynnerton and Tittensor 83-86; V Westlands St Andr from 86; RD Newcastle from 97. *St Andrew's Vicarage, 50 Kingsway West, Westlands, Newcastle, Staffs ST5 3PU* Tel (01782) 619594

GARDNER, Canon Anthony Brian. b 32. Lon Coll of Div 62. **d** 64 **p** 65. C Stoke *Cov* 64-68; R Whitnash from 68; RD Leamington 78-79; RD Warwick and Leamington 79-87; Hon Can Cov Cathl from 83. *St Margaret's Rectory, 2 Church Close, Whitnash, Leamington Spa, Warks CV31 2HJ* Tel (01926) 425070

GARDNER, Charles Graham. b 18. AKC49. **d** 50 **p** 51. C Clapham H Trin *S'wark* 50-54; S Africa from 54. *49 Dahlia Avenue, Virginia, 9430 South Africa* Tel Virginia (1722) 28187

GARDNER, The Ven Clifton Gordon. b 15. Toronto Univ BA36 Lon Univ BD39 AKC39. **d** 39 **p** 40. C Maidenhead St Luke *Ox* 39-41 and 46-47; Chapl RNVR 41-46; V Furze Platt *Ox* 47-52; Canada 52-76; Can St Paul's Cathl Lon Ontario 64-74; Adn Middx Ontario 74-76; Perm to Offic *Chelmsf* from 77. *1 Shepherd's Way, Saffron Walden, Essex CB10 2AH* Tel (01799) 527890

GARDNER, Clive Bruce. b 67. Selw Coll Cam BA89 Cam Univ MA92. Wycliffe Hall Ox BA93. **d** 96 **p** 97. C Beverley Minster *York* from 96. *23 Outer Trinities, Grovehill Road, Beverley, N Humberside HU17 0HN* Tel (01482) 888249 Fax as telephone

GARDNER, David. b 57. Oak Hill Th Coll BA87. **d** 87 **p** 88. C Ogley Hay *Lich* 87-91; TV Mildenhall *St E* from 91. *The Vicarage, 2 Oak Drive, Beck Row, Bury St Edmunds, Suffolk IP28 8UA* Tel (01638) 717331

GARDNER, David Edward. b 21. Oak Hill Th Coll 44. **d** 49 **p** 50. C Chitts Hill St Cuth *Lon* 49-52; C S Mimms Ch Ch 52-55; Chapl Dockland Settlement No 1 Canning Town *Chelmsf* 55-60; Nat Chapl and Evang to Boy's Covenanter Union from 60; rtd 90; Lic to Offic *Lon* from 90. *15 Churchmead Close, Barnet, Herts EN4 8UY* Tel 0181-449 4213

GARDNER, Geoffrey Maurice. b 28. K Coll Lon BA51 Lon Inst of Educn PGCE52 Bris Univ DipEd74. Cranmer Hall Dur DipTh59. **d** 59 **p** 60. C Bowling St Jo *Bradf* 59-62; Nigeria 62-72; Hon C Bath St Luke *B & W* 72-73; Perm to Offic 73-90; NSM Bath Widcombe 90-94; rtd 94; Perm to Offic *B & W* from 94. *4 St Winifred's Drive, Bath BA2 7HR* Tel (01225) 832953

GARDNER, Helen Jane. b 39. Man Univ BSc61 PGCE62. W of England Minl Tr Course 93. **d** 96. NSM Stow on the Wold *Glouc* from 96. *Melrose, Station Road, Blockley, Moreton-in-Marsh, Glos GL56 9DX* Tel (01386) 700684

GARDNER, Ian Douglas. b 34. St Pet Hall Ox BA58 MA62. Oak Hill Th Coll 58. **d** 60 **p** 61. C Biddulph *Lich* 60-63; C Weston St Jo *B & W* 64; Nigeria 65-76; P-in-c Hurstbourne Tarrant and Faccombe *Win* 77-79; V Hurstbourne Tarrant, Faccombe, Vernham Dean etc 79-85; R Nursling and Rownhams from 85. *The Vicarage, 27 Horns Drove, Rownhams, Southampton SO16 8AH* Tel (01703) 738293

GARDNER, Canon John Phillip Backhouse. b 21. St Aid Birkenhead 49. **d** 52 **p** 53. C Ashtead *Guildf* 52-55; C Bromley SS Pet and Paul *Roch* 55-57; V New Hythe 57-63; V Roch St Justus 63-69; R Wisley w Pyrford *Guildf* 70-87; RD Woking 82-87; Hon Can Guildf Cathl 86-87; rtd 87; Perm to Offic *Pet* from 87. *82 Water Lane, Wootton, Northampton NN4 0HG* Tel (01604) 760254

GARDNER, Leslie John Thomas. b 15. Wells Th Coll 68. **d** 69 **p** 70. C Tiverton St Pet *Ex* 69-70; C Thornton *Leic* 70-72; P-in-c Wilne and Draycott w Breaston *Derby* 72-74; C Fordingbridge w Ibsley *Win* 74-75; C Welwyn w Ayot St Peter *St Alb* 75-78; C Compton Gifford *Ex* 78-82; rtd 82; Perm to Offic *Ex* from 82.

93 Palmerston Park, Tiverton, Devon EX16 5PG Tel (01297) 21520

GARDNER, Mark Douglas. b 58. TCD BA80 MA83 DipTh83. **d** 83 **p** 84. C Ballymacarrett St Patr *D & D* 83-87; C Belfast St Steph w St Luke *Conn* 87-89; C Hendon and Sunderland *Dur* 89-90; TV Sunderland 90-95; I Dublin Santry w Glasnevin and Finglas *D & G* from 95; PV and Chapter Clerk Ch Ch Cathl Dublin from 96; Min Can St Patr Cathl Dublin from 96. *The Rectory, Church Street, Finglas, Dublin 11, Irish Republic* Tel Dublin (1) 834 1015 Fax 834 3462 E-mail mgardner@indigo.ie

GARDNER, Mary Christine. b 42. SRN65 Liv Univ HVCert71. St Jo Coll Nottm 80. **dss** 82 **d** 87 **p** 94. Ches St Paul *Ches* 82-84; Macclesfield St Mich 84-85; Macclesfield Team Par 85-87; Par Dn 87; Chapl Asst Nottm City Hosp 87-93; Chapl St Chris Hospice Lon from 93. *The Chaplain's Office, St Christopher's Hospice, Lawrie Park Road, London SE26 6DZ* Tel 0181-778 9252

GARDNER, Michael Ronald. b 53. Wilson Carlile Coll DipEvang86 Trin Coll Bris 95. **d** 97. C Stanmore *Win* from 97. *St Mark's House, Oliver's Battery Crescent, Winchester, Hants SO22 4EU* Tel (01962) 861970

GARDNER, Dr Paul Douglas. b 50. K Coll Lon BA72 AKC72 SS Coll Cam PhD89. Reformed Th Sem Mississippi MDiv79 Ridley Hall Cam 79. **d** 80 **p** 81. C Cambridge St Martin *Ely* 80-83; Lect Oak Hill Th Coll 83-90; V Hartford *Ches* from 90; RD Middlewich from 94. *St John's Vicarage, Hartford, Northwich, Cheshire CW8 1QA* Tel (01606) 77557

GARDNER, Richard Beverley Twynam. b 11. Chich Th Coll 33. **d** 36 **p** 37. C Gainsborough St Jo *Linc* 36-38; C Linc St Giles 38-39; C Horsell *Guildf* 39-42; Chapl RNVR 42-47; C York Town St Mich *Guildf* 47-48; V E Molesey St Paul 48-54; V Botleys and Lyne 54-71; V Long Cross 56-71; V Ewshott 71-76; rtd 76; Perm to Offic *Guildf* 81-93. *16 Palace Gate, Odiham, Hook, Hants RG29 1JZ* Tel (01256) 704563

GARDNER, Ronald Frederick. b 25. Dur Univ BA51 DipTh52 Birm Univ MA79. **d** 52 **p** 53. C Horsforth *Ripon* 52-56; C Whitchurch *Lich* 56-58; V Malins Lee 58-64; R Talke 64-69; V Forsbrook 69-83; V Mow Cop 83-89; rtd 89; Perm to Offic *Lich* from 89. *Rode Mill House, Church Lane, Scholar Green, Stoke-on-Trent ST7 3QR* Tel (01270) 872185

GARDOM, Francis Douglas. b 34. Trin Coll Ox BA55 MA59. Wells Th Coll 58. **d** 60 **p** 61. C Greenwich St Alfege w St Pet *S'wark* 60-68; C Lewisham St Steph and St Mark 68-76; Hon C from 76. *79 Maze Hill, London SE10 8XQ* Tel 0181-858 7052 or 825 1474 Fax 293 4407

GARDOM, James Theodore Douglas. b 61. St Anne's Coll Ox BA83 K Coll Lon PhD92. Ripon Coll Cuddesdon 87. **d** 90 **p** 91. C Witney *Ox* 90-92; USPG from 92; Zimbabwe from 92. *9 Thornburg Avenue, Mount Pleasant, Harare, Zimbabwe*

GARLAND, Dr Christopher John. b 47. Ex Univ BA69 PhD72. Qu Coll Birm 78. **d** 80 **p** 81. C Beckenham St Jas *Roch* 80-82; C Roch 82-84; Papua New Guinea 85-93; Australia 94-95; R Copford w Easthorpe and Messing w Inworth *Chelmsf* from 95. *The Vicarage, Kelvedon Road, Messing, Colchester CO5 9TN* Tel (01621) 815434

GARLAND, Michael. b 50. St D Coll Lamp DipTh72 Sarum & Wells Th Coll 72. **d** 73 **p** 74. C Swansea St Thos and Kilvey *S & B* 73-76; C Boldmere *Birm* 76-79; V Kingshurst 79-88; P-in-c Curdworth w Castle Vale 88-90; R Curdworth from 90. *The Rectory, Glebe Fields, Curdworth, Sutton Coldfield, W Midlands B76 9ES* Tel (01675) 470384

GARLAND, Peter Stephen John. b 52. N Lon Poly DipLib77 ALA79 Univ Coll Lon BA73 Univ of W Ontario MA74 Dur Univ PGCE75. Ripon Coll Cuddesdon 88. **d** 90 **p** 91. C Crookham *Guildf* 90-94; V Tongham from 94; Chapl Farnborough Coll of Tech from 94. *The Vicarage, Poyle Road, Tongham, Farnham, Surrey GU10 1DU* Tel (01252) 782224

GARLICK, Canon David. b 37. Nottm Univ BA62 Ox Univ DipPSA63. St Steph Ho Ox 62. **d** 64 **p** 65. C Kennington St Jo *S'wark* 64-66; Hon C Newington St Paul 66-68; P-in-c Vauxhall St Pet 68-79; V Lewisham St Mary from 79; RD E Lewisham from 92; Hon Can S'wark Cathl from 93. *Lewisham Vicarage, 48 Lewisham Park, London SE13 6QZ* Tel 0181-690 2682 or 690 1585

GARLICK, Dennis. b 26. ACIS. Qu Coll Birm. **d** 84 **p** 85. NSM Dronfield *Derby* 84-88; C 88-89; C-in-c Holmesfield 89-90; TV Dronfield w Holmesfield 90-93; rtd 93; Perm to Offic *Derby* from 93. *51 Holmesdale Road, Dronfield, Sheffield S18 6FA* Tel (01246) 418792

GARLICK, Mrs Kathleen Beatrice. b 49. Leeds Univ BA71 Birm Univ CertEd72. Glouc Sch of Min 87. **d** 90 **p** 94. Hon C Much Birch w Lt Birch, Much Dewchurch etc *Heref* from 90; Chapl Heref Sixth Form Coll from 96. *Birch Lodge, Much Birch, Hereford HR2 8HT* Tel (01981) 540666

GARLICK, Canon Peter. b 34. AKC57. **d** 58 **p** 59. C Swindon All SS *Bris* 58-63; St Kitts-Nevis 63-66; V Heyside *Man* 66-73; R Stretford All SS 73-79; RD Wootton *Pet* 79-88; V Duston 79-91; TR Duston Team 91-94; Can Pet Cathl 85-94; rtd 94; Perm to Offic *Pet* from 94. *120 Worcester Close, Northampton NN3 9GD* Tel (01604) 416511

GARMAN, Canon Bernard Wilfred. b 16. Edin Th Coll 47. **d** 49 **p** 50. C Grangemouth *Edin* 49-51; C Rothbury *Newc* 51-57; R Bellingham 57-66; V Bywell St Andr 66-73; V Riding Mill 66-77; Chapl Dioc Retreat Ho 69-77; Asst Dioc Tr Officer from 77; rtd 77; Hon Can Newc Cathl *Newc* 77-88. *Thropton Hill, Physic Lane, Thropton, Morpeth, Northd NE65 7HU* Tel (01669) 20840

GARNER, Alistair Ross. b 58. Pemb Coll Ox BA81 MA86. St Jo Coll Nottm DTS92. **d** 92 **p** 93. C Ashton on Mersey St Mary *Ches* 92-96; P-in-c Bredbury St Mark from 96. *St Mark's Vicarage, George Lane, Bredbury, Stockport, Cheshire SK6 1AT* Tel 0161-406 6552

GARNER, Canon Carl. b 42. Rhodes Univ BA62 Keble Coll Ox BA65 MA70. St Paul's Grahamstown 66. **d** 67 **p** 68. S Africa 67-84; Dioc Missr *St Alb* from 84; Can Res St Alb from 84. *Holywell Close, 43 Holywell Hill, St Albans, Herts AL1 1HE* Tel (01727) 854832

GARNER, David Henry. b 40. Trin Coll Bris 70. **d** 73 **p** 74. C Tunstead *Man* 73-75; C Fazeley *Lich* 76-78; V Sparkhill St Jo *Birm* 78-85; V Blackheath from 85. *St Paul's Vicarage, 83 Vicarage Road, Halesowen, W Midlands B62 8HX* Tel 0121-559 1000

GARNER, Geoffrey Walter. b 40. Ripon Hall Ox 69. **d** 71 **p** 72. C Stoke *Cov* 71-76; V Tile Hill 76-80; TV Hackney *Lon* 80-89; R Bow w Bromley St Leon from 89. *16 Tomlins Grove, London E3 4NX* Tel 0181-981 6710

GARNER, Martin Wyatt. b 39. Lon Coll of Div 60 Tyndale Hall Bris 63 Sarum Th Coll 66. **d** 66 **p** 67. C Coleraine *Conn* 66-70; C Cambridge St Martin *Ely* 70-72; V Edge Hill St Nath *Liv* 72-80; P-in-c Burton in Kendal *Carl* 80-87; R Burghclere w Newtown and Ecchinswell w Sydmonton *Win* 87-93; R Ewelme, Brightwell Baldwin, Cuxham w Easington *Ox* from 93. *The Rectory, Ewelme, Oxford OX10 6HP* Tel (01491) 837823

GARNER, Peter. b 35. Lon Univ BSc56 Leeds Univ MEd91. Wycliffe Hall Ox 56. **d** 58 **p** 59. C Walthamstow St Jo *Chelmsf* 58-61; V Hainault 61-70; R Theydon Garnon 70-73; P-in-c Kirby-le-Soken 73-74; V 74-82; P-in-c Fountains *Ripon* 82-88; P-in-c Kirkby Malzeard w Grewelthorpe and Mickley etc 82-88; Par Development Adv 88-93; P-in-c Birstwith 91-93; R Farnham w Scotton, Staveley, Copgrove etc from 93. *The Rectory, Staveley, Knaresborough, N Yorkshire HG5 9LD* Tel (01423) 340275

GARNER, Rodney George. b 48. MIPM75 Birm Univ DipTh77 Lon Univ BA87. Qu Coll Birm 75. **d** 78 **p** 79. C Tranmere St Paul w St Luke *Ches* 78-81; V Eccleston St Thos *Liv* 81-90; P-in-c Sculcoates St Paul w Ch Ch and St Silas *York* 90-95; Lay Tr Officer (E Riding Adnry) 90-95; P-in-c Southport H Trin *Liv* 95-96; V from 96. *24 Roe Lane, Southport, Merseyside PR9 9DX* Tel (01704) 538560

GARNER, Thomas Richard. b 43. K Coll Lon. **d** 69 **p** 70. C Tynemouth Ch Ch *Newc* 69-73; C Fenham St Jas and St Basil 73-76; V Hamstead St Bernard *Birm* 76-80; New Zealand from 80. *1/109 Hill Street, Thorndon, Wellington, New Zealand* Tel Wellington (4) 473 3511 or 472 0286

GARNETT, David Christopher. b 45. Nottm Univ BA67 Fitzw Coll Cam BA69 MA73. Westcott Ho Cam 67. **d** 69 **p** 70. C Cottingham *York* 69-72; Chapl Selw Coll Cam 72-77; P-in-c Patterdale *Carl* 77-80; Dir of Ords 78-80; V Heald Green St Cath *Ches* 80-87; R Christleton 87-92; TR Ellesmere Port 92-96; Adn Chesterfield *Derby* from 96; Hon Can Derby Cathl from 96. *The Old Parsonage, Taddington, Buxton, Derbyshire SK17 9TW* Tel (01298) 85607

GARNETT, James Arthur. b 42. N Ord Course 77. **d** 80 **p** 81. C Kirkby *Liv* 80-91; P-in-c Liv St Phil w St Dav from 91. *The Vicarage, 55 Sheil Road, Liverpool L6 3AD* Tel 0151-263 6202

GARNETT, Peter. b 17. Bps' Coll Cheshunt 49. **d** 51 **p** 52. C S Bank *York* 51-55; S Rhodesia 55-58 and 61-65; Rhodesia 69-71; C Bletchingley *S'wark* 59-61; P-in-c Burnley St Marg *Blackb* 66-67; C Wyken *Cov* 71-73; C Malden St Jo *S'wark* 73-77; C Headington Quarry *Ox* 77-82; rtd 82; Perm to Offic *York* from 94. *Dulverton Hall, St Martin's Square, Scarborough YO11 2DB* Tel (01723) 373082

GARNETT, Preb Ralph Henry. b 28. Cuddesdon Coll 58. **d** 60 **p** 61. C Broseley w Benthall *Heref* 60-64; V Leintwardine 64-69; P-in-c Downton w Burrington and Aston and Elton 66-69; RD Ludlow 72-75; R Burford II w Greete and Hope Bagot 69-87; R Burford III w Lt Heref 69-87; P-in-c Burford I 72-74; R 74-87; V Tenbury 69-74; TR 74-87; Preb Heref Cathl 82-93; P-in-c Fownhope 87-93; P-in-c Brockhampton w Fawley 87-93; RD Heref Rural 92-93; rtd 93; Perm to Offic *Heref* from 93. *5 Hampton Manor Close, Hereford HR1 1TG* Tel (01432) 880697

GARNETT, Roger James. b 58. Dur Univ BA79. Wycliffe Hall Ox 89. **d** 91 **p** 92. C Forest Gate St Sav w W Ham St Matt *Chelmsf* 91-94; C Collier Row St Jas and Havering-atte-Bower from 94. *St John's House, 428 Havering Road, Romford RM1 4DF* Tel (01708) 43330

GARNSEY, George Christopher. b 36. Qu Coll Ox BA63. **d** 60 **p** 60. Lic to Offic *Wakef* 78-79; C Lupset 80; Australia from 80. *The Rectory, Gresford, NSW, Australia 2311* Tel Newcastle (49) 389313

GARRARD, Mrs Christine Ann. b 51. LCST75 Open Univ BA86. EAMTC 87. **d** 90 **p** 94. Par Dn Kesgrave *St E* 90-94; C 94-96; V

Ipswich All Hallows from 96. *All Hallows' Vicarage, Reynolds Road, Ipswich IP3 0JH* Tel (01473) 727467

GARRARD, Dr James Richard. b 65. Dur Univ BA88 Ox Univ DipPhil92. Westcott Ho Cam CTM94. **d** 94 **p** 95. C Elland *Wakef* from 94. *41 West View, Paddock, Huddersfield HD1 4HX* Tel (01484) 312284

GARRARD, Nicholas James Havelock. b 62. Leeds Univ BA83. Westcott Ho Cam 86. **d** 88 **p** 89. C Scotforth *Blackb* 88-91; C Eaton *Nor* 91-95; V Heigham St Thos from 95. *St Thomas's Vicarage, Edinburgh Road, Norwich NR2 3RL* Tel (01603) 624390

✠**GARRARD, The Rt Revd Richard.** b 37. K Coll Lon BD60 AKC60. **d** 61 **p** 62 **c** 94. C Woolwich St Mary w H Trin *S'wark* 61-66; C Cambridge Gt St Mary w St Mich *Ely* 66-68; Chapl Keswick Hall Coll Nor 68-74; Prin CA Wilson Carlile Coll of Evang 74-79; Can Res and Chan S'wark Cathl *S'wark* 79-87; Dir of Tr 79-87; Can Res St E Cathl *St E* 87-94; Dioc Adv for Continuing Minl Educn 87-91; Adn Sudbury 91-94; Suff Bp Penrith *Carl* from 94. *Holm Croft, 13 Castle Road, Kendal, Cumbria LA9 7AU* Tel (01539) 727836 Fax 734380

GARRATT, Bernard John. b 43. Lon Univ BA65 Linacre Coll Ox BA67 MA71. St Steph Ho Ox 65. **d** 68 **p** 69. C Notting Hill St Jo *Lon* 68-71; C Fareham SS Pet and Paul *Portsm* 71-73; Chapl City of Lon Poly *Lon* 73-79; R Trowbridge H Trin *Sarum* 79-81; TR 81-87; V Wootton Bassett from 87; RD Calne 88-90. *The Vicarage, Glebe Road, Wootton Bassett, Swindon SN4 7DU* Tel (01793) 854302 or 853272

GARRATT, John William. b 11. **d** 78 **p** 78. Hon C Hounslow H Trin *Lon* 78-88; Hon C Hounslow H Trin w St Paul 88-94; Perm to Offic from 94. *Flat 25, Smoothfield, 130 Hibernia Road, Hounslow TW3 3RJ* Tel 0181-570 6009

GARRATT, Peter James. b 37. ALCD64. **d** 64 **p** 65. C Bingham *S'well* 64-67; C Mansfield St Pet 67-69; V Purlwell *Wakef* 69-73; R Kirk Sandall and Edenthorpe *Sheff* 73-82; R Whippingham w E Cowes *Portsm* 82-87; V Soberton w Newtown from 87. *The Vicarage, Soberton, Southampton SO3 1PF* Tel (01489) 877400

GARRATT, Roger Charles. b 50. St Jo Coll Dur BA72 DipTh73. Cranmer Hall Dur 73. **d** 74 **p** 75. C Leamington Priors St Paul *Cov* 74-77; Chapl Emscote Lawn Sch Warw from 77. *8 Wasdale Close, Leamington Spa, Warks CV32 6NF* Tel (01926) 335495 or 491961

GARRETT, Ms Celia Joy. b 60. RGN81 RM85. Cant Sch of Min 92. **d** 95. C S Ashford St Fran *Cant* from 95. *St Francis House, Cryol Road, Ashford, Kent TN23 5AS* Tel (01233) 625555

GARRETT, Christopher Hugh Ahlan. b 35. Sarum & Wells Th Coll 72. **d** 75 **p** 76. C Addiscombe St Mildred *Cant* 75-81; V Thornton Heath St Jude w St Aid *S'wark* from 81. *St Jude's Vicarage, 11 Dunheved Road North, Thornton Heath, Surrey CR7 6AH* Tel 0181-684 1630

GARRETT, Edgar Ashton. b 20. S'wark Ord Course 62. **d** 65 **p** 66. C Horsell *Guildf* 65-70; V Send 70-79; Perm to Offic *Chich* from 79; rtd 85. *14 Crosbie Close, Chichester, W Sussex PO19 2RZ* Tel (01243) 789770

GARRETT, Miss Elizabeth Clare. b 46. Trin Coll Bris. **d** 94 **p** 95. C Ewyas Harold w Dulas, Kenderchurch etc *Heref* 94-96; C Tupsley w Hampton Bishop from 96. *4 Kentchurch Close, Hereford HR1 1QS* Tel (01432) 267651

GARRETT, Canon Frederick Henry. b 18. TCD BA43. **d** 43 **p** 44. C Dromore Cathl *D & D* 43-45; C Rathkeale w Nantenan *L & K* 45-49; I Murragh w Killowen *C, C & R* 49-55; I Mallow 55-74; I Kilshannig 57-74; I Castlemagner 71-74; RD Midleton 65-75; I Glengarriff w Berehaven 74-87; Preb Ross Cathl 76-87; Preb Cork Cathl 76-87; rtd 87. *Meadow Cottage, Wood View, Mallow, Co Cork, Irish Republic* Tel Mallow (22) 21748

GARRETT, Geoffrey David. b 57. Oak Hill Th Coll 83. **d** 86 **p** 87. C Trentham *Lich* 86-90; V Rhodes *Man* from 90. *The Vicarage, Rhodes, Middleton, Manchester M24 4PU* Tel 0161-643 3224

GARRETT, Ian Lee. b 60. MCSP DipPh81. Sarum & Wells Th Coll 86. **d** 89 **p** 90. C Maidstone St Martin *Cant* 89-95; P-in-c S Ashford St Fran from 95. *St Francis House, Cryol Road, Ashford, Kent TN23 5AS* Tel (01233) 625555

GARRETT, John Watkins. b 09. St Chad's Coll Dur BA35 LTh36. **d** 36 **p** 37. C Leic St Mary *Leic* 36-38; C Win H Trin *Win* 38-42; C Staveley *Derby* 42-44; C Derby St Barn 44-48; R Aylestone Park *Leic* 48-59; Chapl Carlton Hayes Psychiatric Hosp Narborough 54-90; R Narborough 59-75; rtd 75; Lic to Offic *Leic* 75-81; Perm to Offic 81-95. *4 Walcot Lane, Folkingham, Sleaford, Lincs NG34 0TP* Tel (01529) 497385

GARRETT, Kevin George. b 48. Oak Hill Th Coll BA86. **d** 86 **p** 87. C Hoddesdon *St Alb* 86-89; C Loughton St Mary and St Mich *Chelmsf* 89-90; TV 90-95; P-in-c Loughton St Mich 95-96; Asst RD Redbridge 96; Public Preacher 97; V Dover St Martin *Cant* from 97. *St Martin's Vicarage, 339 Folkestone Road, Dover, Kent CT17 9JG* Tel (01304) 205391

GARROW, Alan John Philip. b 67. Lon Bible Coll BA90. Wycliffe Hall Ox MPhil94. **d** 93 **p** 94. C Waltham H Cross *Chelmsf* from 93. *Abbey Lodge, 5A Greenyard, Waltham Abbey, Essex EN9 1RD* Tel (01992) 763186 Fax as telephone

GARRUD, Christopher Charles. b 54. Cranmer Hall Dur DipTh84. **d** 85 **p** 86. C Watford *St Alb* 85-89; C Ireland Wood *Ripon* 89-95; Chapl Cookridge Hosp Leeds 93-95; R Farnley from 95. *The Rectory, 16 Cross Lane, Leeds LS12 5AA* Tel 0113-263 8064

GARSIDE, Canon Howard. b 24. Leeds Univ BA49. Coll of Resurr Mirfield 49. **d** 51 **p** 52. C Barnsley St Pet *Wakef* 51-53; C Linthorpe *York* 53-56; V Middlesbrough St Aid 56-64; V Manston *Ripon* 64-78; RD Whitkirk 70-78; Hon Can Ripon Cathl 78-89; V Harrogate St Wilfrid 78-80; P-in-c Harrogate St Luke 78-80; V Harrogate St Wilfrid and St Luke 80-89; RD Harrogate 83-88; rtd 89. *73 Kirkby Road, Ripon, N Yorkshire HG4 2HH* Tel (01765) 690625

GARSIDE, Melvin. b 42. N Ord Course 85. **d** 88 **p** 89. C Lindley *Wakef* 88-91; C Shelf *Bradf* 91-93; V Lundwood *Wakef* 93-97; V Hanging Heaton from 97. *The Vicarage, 150 High Street, Hanging Heaton, Batley, W Yorkshire WF17 6DW* Tel (01924) 461917

GARTLAND, Christopher Michael. b 49. Man Univ BA78. Coll of Resurr Mirfield 82. **d** 84 **p** 85. C Almondbury w Farnley Tyas *Wakef* 84-87; P-in-c Upperthong 87-89; TV Upper Holme Valley 89-91; Chapl Stanley Royd Hosp Wakef 91-94; Chapl Wakef HA (Mental Health Services) from 91; Chapl Wakef and Pontefract Community NHS Trust from 94. *Stanley Royd Hospital, Aberford Road, Wakefield, W Yorkshire WF1 2DQ* Tel (01924) 375217

GARTON, Derek John. b 33. ALCD59. **d** 59 **p** 60. C Bromley Common St Aug *Roch* 59-62; C Gravesend St Aid 62-66; Hon C Gravesend St Geo 66-73; Perm to Offic *Ex* 77-83; Australia from 83; rtd 94. *PO Box 12, Wonthaggi, Victoria, Australia 3995* Tel Launceston (03) 5672 1746

GARTON, Capt Jeremy. b 56. Wilson Carlile Coll 78 SEITE 94. **d** 96. C Clapham TM *S'wark* from 96. *23 Old Town, London SW4 0JT* Tel 0171-622 5733

✠**GARTON, The Rt Revd John Henry.** b 41. Worc Coll Ox BA67 MA DipTh67. Cuddesdon Coll 67. **d** 69 **p** 70 **c** 96. CF 69-73; Lect Linc Th Coll 73-78; TR Cov E *Cov* 78-86; Prin Ripon Coll Cuddesdon 86-96; V Cuddesdon *Ox* 86-96; Hon Can Worc Cathl *Worc* 87-96; Suff Bp Plymouth *Ex* from 96. *31 Riverside Walk, Tamerton Foliot, Plymouth PL5 4AQ* Tel (01752) 769818

GARTSIDE, Philip. b 60. Pemb Coll Ox BA82 MA86 Leeds Univ BA92. Coll of Resurr Mirfield CPT93. **d** 93 **p** 94. C Walton-on-the-Hill *Liv* from 93. *10 Lochinver Street, Walton, Liverpool L9 1ER* Tel 0151-523 6617

GARVIE, Anna-Lisa Karen. **d** 96. Hon C Caddington *St Alb* from 96. *2 Wensleydale, Luton LU2 7PN* Tel (01582) 617631

GARWOOD, Albert Wells. b 14. Ripon Hall Ox. **d** 59 **p** 60. C Dartford H Trin *Roch* 59-60; Canada from 60. *Apartment 515, 1186 Queen Street, Halifax, Nova Scotia, Canada, B3H 4K9*

GARWOOD, David John Shirley (Damian). b 31. Leeds Univ BA59. Coll of Resurr Mirfield. **d** 61 **p** 62. C Meir *Lich* 61-66; Lic to Offic *Wakef* 67-71 and from 74; CR from 68; S Africa 71-74. *House of the Resurrection, Mirfield, W Yorkshire WF14 0BN* Tel (01924) 494318

GASCOIGNE, Peter Francis. b 36. Linc Th Coll 85. **d** 87 **p** 88. C Wath-upon-Dearne w Adwick-upon-Dearne *Sheff* 87-90; R Thurnscoe St Helen 90-94; V New Rossington from 94. *St Luke's Vicarage, The Circle, New Rossington, Doncaster, S Yorkshire DN11 0QP* Tel (01302) 868288

GASCOIGNE, Philip. b 27. Oak Hill Th Coll. **d** 62 **p** 63. C Blackpool Ch Ch *Blackb* 62-65; V Bootle St Leon *Liv* 65-71; Staff Evang CPAS 71-74; V St Helens St Mark *Liv* 74-77; V Blackpool Ch Ch *Blackb* 77-81; V Blackpool Ch Ch w All SS from 81. *The Vicarage, 23A North Park Drive, Blackpool FY3 8LR* Tel (01253) 391235

GASH, Christopher Alan Ronald. b 39. St Andr Univ 57 Nottm Univ CPTS. EMMTC 83. **d** 86 **p** 87. C Thurmaston *Leic* 86-89; P-in-c Stoke Golding w Dadlington from 89. *The Vicarage, High Street, Stoke Golding, Nuneaton, Warks CV13 6HE* Tel (01455) 212317

GASH, Canon Wilfred John. b 31. Lon Univ DipTh62. St Aid Birkenhead 60. **d** 62 **p** 63. C St Mary Cray and St Paul's Cray *Roch* 62-65; C Bexley St Jo 65-67; R Levenshulme St Pet *Man* 67-72; V Clifton 72-94; AD Eccles 81-87; Hon Can Man Cathl from 86; P-in-c Pendlebury Ch Ch 86-87; P-in-c Pendlebury St Aug 86-87; Dioc Adv on Evang from 89; TR Bolton St Paul w Em 94-96; C Urmston from 96. *157 Stretford Road, Urmston, Manchester M41 9LZ* Tel 0161-748 8411

GASKELL, David. b 48. Lon Univ BD76. Trin Coll Bris 72. **d** 76 **p** 77. C Eccleston Ch Ch *Liv* 76-80; C Rainhill 80-83; V Over Darwen St Jas *Blackb* 83-88; V Livesey 88-95; V Preston St Cuth from 95. *St Cuthbert's Vicarage, 20 Black Bull Lane, Fulwood, Preston PR2 3PX* Tel (01772) 717346

GASKELL, Ian Michael. b 51. Nottm Univ BTh81. Linc Th Coll 77. **d** 81 **p** 82. C Wakef St Jo *Wakef* 81-83; Ind Chapl *Sheff* 83-86; V Cleckheaton St Luke and Whitechapel *Wakef* 86-93; V Birkenshaw w Hunsworth from 93; RD Birstall from 96. *St Paul's Vicarage, 6 Vicarage Gardens, Birkenshaw, Bradford, W Yorkshire BD11 2EF* Tel (01274) 683776

GASKELL, Preb John Bernard. b 28. Jes Coll Ox BA52 MA58. Chich Th Coll 59. **d** 60 **p** 61. C Beckenham St Jas *Roch* 60-64; C St Marylebone All SS *Lon* 64-68; C-in-c Grosvenor Chpl 68-79; Warden Liddon Ho Lon 68-79; V Holborn St Alb w Saffron Hill St Pet *Lon* 79-93; AD S Camden (Holborn and St Pancras)

81-86; Preb St Paul's Cathl 85-93; rtd 93. *8 Margaret Street, London W1N 7LG* Tel 0171-436 3287

GASKELL, Mary. b 50. Nottm Univ BTh81 Bradf and Ilkley Coll CertEd89. Linc Th Coll 77. **dss** 81 **d** 89 **p** 94. NSM Cleckheaton St Luke and Whitechapel *Wakef* 89-93; NSM Birkenshaw w Hunsworth 93-95; Asst Chapl St Jas Univ Hosp NHS Trust Leeds 95-97; Perm to Offic *Wakef* from 97. *St Paul's Vicarage, 6 Vicarage Gardens, Birkenshaw, Bradford, W Yorkshire BD11 2EF* Tel (01274) 683776

GASPER (née COHEN), Janet Elizabeth. b 47. Birm Univ CertEd70. W of England Minl Tr Course 93. **d** 96. NSM Leominster *Heref* from 96; Hon Chapl RAF from 97. *Deerfold, 3 Queenswood, Hope under Dinmore, Leominster, Herefordshire HR6 0PP* Tel (01568) 611760

GASTON, Raymond Gordon. b 62. Leeds Univ BA94. Linc Th Coll MTh94. **d** 96 **p** 97. C Leeds Gipton Epiphany *Ripon* from 96. *154 Amberton Road, Leeds LS9 6SP* Tel 0113-248 9924

GATENBY, Canon Denis William. b 31. Ex Coll Ox BA54 DipTh55 MA58 Man Univ DSPT82. Wycliffe Hall Ox 54. **d** 56 **p** 57. C Deane *Man* 56-60; C Bradf Cathl *Bradf* 60-63; V Bootle St Matt *Liv* 63-72; V Horwich H Trin *Man* 72-84; TR Horwich 84-93; TR Horwich and Rivington from 93; AD Deane from 87; Hon Can Man Cathl from 91. *The Rectory, Chorley Old Road, Horwich, Bolton BL6 6AX* Tel (01204) 68263

GATENBY, Paul Richard. b 32. Dur Univ BA55. Qu Coll Birm DipTh64. **d** 64 **p** 65. C Wellingborough St Barn *Pet* 64-68; V Braunston w Brooke 68-71; C Langley Marish *Ox* 71-72; TV Basildon St Martin w H Cross and Laindon *Chelmsf* 73-76; R Isham w Pytchley *Pet* from 77. *The Rectory, Kettering Road, Isham, Kettering, Northants NN14 1HQ* Tel (01536) 722371

GATENBY, Simon John Taylor. b 62. Nottm Univ BA83. St Jo Coll Nottm 84. **d** 87 **p** 88. C Haughton St Mary *Man* 87-90; C Newburn *Newc* 90-93; P-in-c Brunswick *Man* 93-96; R from 96. *The Rectory, Brunswick Street, Manchester M13 9TP* Tel 0161-273 2470

GATES, John Michael. b 35. Dur Univ BA56 DipTh60. Cranmer Hall Dur 58. **d** 60 **p** 61. C Felixstowe St Jo *St E* 60-67; R Boyton w Capel St Andrew and Hollesley from 67; P-in-c Shottisham w Sutton 87-92. *The Rectory, Hollesley, Woodbridge, Suffolk IP12 3RE* Tel (01394) 411252

GATES, John Richard. b 47. Oak Hill Th Coll DipTh73. **d** 73 **p** 74. C Iver *Ox* 73-76; C Broadwater St Mary *Chich* 76-79; Dioc Youth Officer *Nor* 79-82; V Cosby *Leic* 82-86. *Address temp unknown*

GATES, Richard James. b 46. BA85. Oak Hill Th Coll 82. **d** 85 **p** 86. C Heald Green St Cath *Ches* 85-89; V Norton from 89. *The Vicarage, Windmill Hill, Runcorn, Cheshire WA7 6QE* Tel (01928) 715225

GATES, Simon Philip. b 60. St Andr Univ MA82. Cranmer Hall Dur BA86. **d** 87 **p** 88. C Southall Green St Jo *Lon* 87-91; Hong Kong 91-95; V Clapham Park St Steph *S'wark* from 96. *The Vicarage, 2 Thornton Road, London SW12 0JU* Tel 0181-671 8276

GATFORD, The Ven Ian. b 40. AKC65. **d** 67 **p** 68. C Clifton w Glapton *S'well* 67-71; R 71-75; V Sherwood 75-84; Can Res Derby Cathl *Derby* from 84; Adn Derby from 93; Hon Can Derby Cathl from 93. *72 Pastures Hill, Littleover, Derby DE23 7BB* Tel (01332) 512700 Fax 292969

GATHERCOLE, The Ven John Robert. b 37. Fitzw Ho Cam BA59 MA63. Ridley Hall Cam 59. **d** 62 **p** 63. C Dur St Nic *Dur* 62-66; C Croxdale 66-69; Bp's Soc and Ind Adv 66-69; Ind Chapl *Worc* 69-87; RD Bromsgrove 77-85; Sen Chapl Worcs Ind Miss from 85; Hon Can Worc Cathl from 80; Adn Dudley from 87. *15 Worcester Road, Droitwich, Worcs WR9 8AA* Tel (01905) 773301 Fax as telephone

GATLIFFE, David Spenser. b 45. Keble Coll Ox BA67 Fitzw Coll Cam BA69. Westcott Ho Cam 67. **d** 69 **p** 70. C Oxted *S'wark* 69-72; C Roehampton H Trin 72-75; C S Beddington St Mich 76-77; TV Clapham Old Town 78-87; P-in-c Clapham Ch Ch and St Jo 81-87; TV Clapham TM 87-89; V S Wimbledon H Trin and St Pet from 89. *The Vicarage, 234 The Broadway, London SW19 1SB* Tel 0181-542 7098 or 542 1388

GATRILL, Adrian Colin. b 60. Southn Univ BTh82. Linc Th Coll 83. **d** 85 **p** 86. C W Bromwich St Andr *Lich* 85-88; C W Bromwich St Andr w Ch Ch 88-89; Chapl RAF from 89; Perm to Offic *St D* 90-95. *Chaplaincy Services (RAF), HQ, Personnel and Training Command, RAF Innsworth, Gloucester GL3 1EZ* Tel (01452) 712612 ext 5164 Fax 510828

GAUGE, Canon Barrie Victor. b 41. St D Coll Lamp BA62 Selw Coll Cam BA64 MA74 Liv Univ CQSW81. Bp Burgess Hall Lamp DPS65. **d** 65 **p** 66. C Newtown w Llanllwchaiarn w Aberhafesp *St As* 65-68; C Prestatyn 68-73; R Bodfari 73-76; Dioc RE Adv 73-76; Perm to Offic *Ches* 76-84; V Birkenhead St Jas w St Bede 84-90; Dir of Resources from 90; Hon Can Ches Cathl from 94; C Lache cum Saltney from 95. *103 Five Ashes Road, Chester CH4 7QA* Tel (01244) 680804 or 379222 Fax 680804

GAUNT, Arthur Raymond. b 15. St Aid Birkenhead 47. **d** 49 **p** 50. C Thornbury *Bradf* 49-51; C Skipton Ch Ch 51-52; C-in-c Pudsey St Jas CD 52-55; V Bingley H Trin 55-58; V Glaisdale *York* 58-63; V York H Trin Goodramgate w St Maurice 63-66; V Kexby w Wilberfoss 66-71; Dioc Rtd Clergy and Widows Officer 67-85; V Scarborough St Columba 71-78; rtd 78; Perm to Offic *Bradf* 80-84. *20 Grantley Drive, Harrogate, N Yorkshire HG3 2ST* Tel (01423) 504998

GAUNT (née COTTELL), Mrs Avril Jane. b 50. SRN72 SCM74 Lon Univ DipNursing81. S Dios Minl Tr Scheme 92. **d** 95 **p** 97. NSM Yatton Moor *B & W* 95-96; NSM Bourne *Guildf* from 96. *The Vicarage, 2 Middle Avenue, Farnham, Surrey GU9 8JL*

GAUNT, Eric Emmerson. b 33. Sarum Th Coll 65. **d** 67 **p** 68. C Hatch End St Anselm *Lon* 67-74; V Neasden cum Kingsbury St Cath 74-80; V Neasden St Cath w St Paul from 80. *The Vicarage, Tanfield Avenue, London NW2 7RX* Tel 0181-452 7322

GAUNT, Roger Cecil. b 30. K Coll Cam BA52. Westcott Ho Cam 53. **d** 55 **p** 56. C Barnard Castle *Dur* 55-58; C Newc St Jo *Newc* 58-61; V Coulsdon St Andr *S'wark* 61-66; V St Helier 66-68; R Limpsfield and Titsey 68-77; Dioc Dir of Educn *St Alb* 77-79; Can Res St Alb 77-79; Perm to Offic *Truro* 79-84; Perm to Offic *S'wark* 79-88; Lic to Offic 88-91; Hon C Charlwood from 91; Perm to Offic *Guildf* 84-86; rtd 95. *Apple Hill, Old Road, Buckland, Betchworth, Surrey RH3 7DU* Tel (01737) 843393

GAUSDEN, Canon Peter James. b 32. Qu Coll Birm 57. **d** 60 **p** 61. C Battersea St Pet *S'wark* 60-63; C St Peter-in-Thanet *Cant* 63-68; V Sturry 68-74; R Sturry w Fordwich and Westbere w Hersden from 74; Dioc Ecum Officer from 91; Hon Can Cant Cathl from 96. *The Rectory, 2 The Hamels, Church Lane, Sturry, Canterbury, Kent CT2 0BL* Tel (01227) 710320

GAVED, Kenneth John Drew. b 31. LNSM course 92. **d** 95 **p** 96. C W Wickham St Jo *S'wark* from 95. *42 Queensway, West Wickham, Kent BR4 9ER* Tel 0181-462 4326

GAVIGAN, Mrs Josephine Katherine. b 49. Sarum Th Coll 93. **d** 96. NSM Boxgrove *Chich* from 96. *25 Woodgate Park, Woodgate, Chichester, W Sussex PO20 6QP* Tel (01243) 543339 Fax as telephone

GAVIN, David Guy. b 63. Birm Univ BA85 Dur Univ BA90. Cranmer Hall Dur 88. **d** 91 **p** 92. C Parr *Liv* 91-95; TV Toxteth St Philemon w St Gabr and St Cleopas from 95. *St Cleopas Vicarage, Beresford Road, Liverpool L8 4SG* Tel 0151-727 0633

GAWITH, Canon Alan Ruthven. b 24. Man Univ SACert47. Lich Th Coll 54. **d** 56 **p** 57. C Appleby and Murton cum Hilton *Carl* 56-59; C Newton Aycliffe *Dur* 59-61; C-in-c Owton Manor CD 61-67; V Kendal St Geo *Carl* 67-74; Soc Resp Officer *Man* 74-89; Hon Can Man Cathl 82-89; Bp's Adv on AIDS 88-92; rtd 90; Perm to Offic *Man* from 90. *7 Redwaters, Leigh, Lancs WN7 1JD* Tel (01942) 676641

GAWNE-CAIN, John. b 38. CEng MICE G&C Coll Cam BA61 MA66. Cuddesdon Coll 74. **d** 76 **p** 77. C Cowley St Jas *Ox* 76-80; P-in-c Ox St Giles 80-85; V Ox St Giles and SS Phil and Jas w St Marg 85-92; P-in-c Uffington w Woolstone and Baulking 92-93; P-in-c Shellingford 92-93; R Uffington, Shellingford, Woolstone and Baulking from 93. *St Mary's Vicarage, Uffington, Faringdon, Oxon SN7 7RA* Tel (01367) 820633

GAWTHROP-DORAN, Mrs Sheila Mary. b 37. Birm Univ CertEd. Dalton Ho Bris 68. **dss** 79 **d** 87. Halliwell St Paul *Man* 79-82; New Bury 82-89; Par Dn 87-89; Par Dn Tonge w Alkrington 89-94; rtd 94; Perm to Offic *York* from 95. *8 The Vale, Skelton, York YO2 6YH* Tel (01904) 470218

GAY, Colin James. b 37. Univ of Wales (Lamp) BA63. Chich Th Coll 63. **d** 65 **p** 66. C W Hackney St Barn *Lon* 65-69; C Hitchin *St Alb* 69-74; P-in-c Apsley End 74-80; TV Chambersbury (Hemel Hempstead) 80-85; V Barnet Vale St Mark from 85. *St Mark's Vicarage, 56 Potters Road, Barnet, Herts EN5 5HN* Tel 0181-449 4265

GAY, David Charles. b 46. CCC Cam BA68 MA72 PhD71. Coll of Resurr Mirfield DipTh74. **d** 75 **p** 76. C Sheff St Mark Broomhall *Sheff* 75-78; Bp's Chapl for Graduates 78-80; Lib Pusey Ho 78-80; Lic to Offic *Sheff* 80-82; C Warmsworth 82-84; V Worsbrough St Thos and St Jas from 84. *The Vicarage, 13 Bank End Road, Worsbrough, Barnsley, S Yorkshire S70 4AF* Tel (01226) 203426

GAY, Dr John Dennis. b 43. St Pet Coll Ox BA64 DipTh65 MA68 DPhil69 MSc78. Ripon Hall Ox 64. **d** 67 **p** 68. C Paddington St Jas *Lon* 67-71; P-in-c 71-72; Lic to Offic *Ox* from 72; Chapl Culham Coll Abingdon 72-79; Lect Ox Univ 78-80; Dir Culham Coll Inst from 80; Perm to Offic *Chich* 87-89. *Culham College Institute, 60 East St Helen Street, Abingdon, Oxon OX14 5EB* Tel (01235) 520458 or 532992

GAY, Canon Perran Russell. b 59. St Cath Coll Cam BA81 MA85 Ex Univ CertEd82. Ripon Coll Cuddesdon BA86. **d** 87 **p** 88. C Bodmin w Lanhydrock and Lanivet *Truro* 87-90; Bp's Dom Chapl 90-94; Dioc Officer for Unity 90-94; Can Res and Chan Truro Cathl from 94; Dir of Tr from 94. *52 Daniell Road, Truro, Cornwall TR1 2DA* Tel (01872) 76491 or 76782 Fax 77788

GAYLER, Roger Kenneth. b 44. Lich Th Coll 68. **d** 70 **p** 71. C Chingford St Anne *Chelmsf* 70-75; P-in-c Marks Gate 75-81; V from 81. *The Vicarage, 187 Rose Lane, Romford RM6 5NR* Tel 0181-599 0415

GAZE, Canon Arthur Philip Atkinson. b 14. St Jo Coll Ox BA36 MA47 Otago Univ MLitt88. Linc Th Coll 39. **d** 41 **p** 42. C Romford St Edw *Chelmsf* 41-48; Master and Chapl Cumnor Sch 48-50; R Puttenham and Wanborough *Guildf* 50-57; Dioc Insp of

Schs 55-62; V Horsell 57-62; New Zealand from 62; Hon Can St Paul's Cathl 75-80. *18 Drivers Road, Maori Hill, Dunedin, New Zealand* Tel Christchurch (3) 467 5951

GAZE, George Henry. b 23. St Jo Coll Dur BA50 DipTh51 MA56. **d** 51 **p** 52. C Stapenhill w Cauldwell *Derby* 51-55; C Ramsgate St Luke *Cant* 55-56; R Slaidburn *Bradf* 56-85; rtd 85; Perm to Offic *Bradf* 86-90. *6 The Croft, Woods Lane, Stapenhill, Burton-on-Trent, Staffs DE15 9ED* Tel (01283) 536513

GAZE, Mrs Sally Ann. b 69. SS Coll Cam BA91 MA95 Birm Univ PGCE92. Qu Coll Birm 94. **d** 96 **p** 97. C Martley and Wichenford, Knightwick etc *Worc* from 96. *4 Taberners Close, Broadwas, Worcester WR6 5NF* Tel (01886) 821053

GAZZARD, Canon Richard George Edward. b 40. Lich Th Coll. **d** 67 **p** 68. C Lewisham St Mary *S'wark* 67-71; C Milton next Gravesend Ch Ch *Roch* 71-74; R Gravesend H Family w Ifield 74-81; V S Ashford Ch Ch *Cant* 81-93; RD E Charing 86-92; Hon Can Cant Cathl 90-93; rtd 96. *14 White Lands, Richmond, N Yorkshire DL10 7DR*

GEACH, Canon Michael Bernard. b 26. Qu Coll Cam BA51 MA56. Westcott Ho Cam 51. **d** 53 **p** 54. C Kenwyn *Truro* 53-56; C Bodmin 56-59; C Helland 56-59; R St Dominic 59-65; Chapl Cotehele Ho Chapl Cornwall 60-65; V Linkinhorne 65-84; R Veryan w Ruan Lanihorne 84-96; Hon Can Truro Cathl 92-96; rtd 96; Perm to Offic *Truro* from 96. *17 Paul's Row, Truro, Cornwall TR1 1HH*

GEAKE, Christopher Laidman. b 53. Univ of Wales (Cardiff) DipTh79. St Mich Coll Llan 75. **d** 79 **p** 80. C Coity w Nolton *Llan* 79-81; C Newton Nottage 81-82; Hon C St Marylebone All SS *Lon* 92-93; Perm to Offic *Chelmsf* from 96. *St Luke's Vicarage, 1A Baxter Road, Ilford, Essex IG1 2HN* Tel 0181-514 4458 Mobile 0802-156532

GEAKE, Peter Henry. b 17. Trin Hall Cam BA39 MA46. Cuddesdon Coll 45. **d** 47 **p** 48. C Portsea St Mary *Portsm* 47-50; C Southbroom *Sarum* 50-52; R Clovelly *Ex* 52-55; Chapl Canford Sch Wimborne 55-62; V Tattenham Corner and Burgh Heath *Guildf* 62-72; R Fulbeck *Linc* 72-82; P-in-c Carlton Scroop w Normanton 72-82; rtd 82; Perm to Offic *Ox* 94-95. *33 Abbey Mews, Amesbury, Salisbury SP4 7EX* Tel (01980) 624815

GEAR, John Arthur. b 37. St Aid Birkenhead 62. **d** 64 **p** 66. C Attleborough *Cov* 64-66; C Attercliffe *Sheff* 66-68; C Sheerness H Trin w St Paul *Cant* 68-73; Asst Youth Adv *S'wark* 73-78; Youth Chapl *Lich* 78-88; V Stafford St Jo and Tixall w Ingestre 88-92; Gen Sec NCEC 92-97; rtd 97. *Greenside, Lime Kiln Bank, Telford, Shropshire TF2 9NU* Tel (01952) 613487

✠**GEAR, The Rt Revd Michael Frederick.** b 34. Dur Univ BA59 DipTh61. Cranmer Hall Dur 59. **d** 61 **p** 62 **c** 93. C Bexleyheath Ch Ch *Roch* 61-64; C Ox St Aldate w H Trin *Ox* 64-67; V Clubmoor *Liv* 67-71; Rhodesia 71-76; Tutor Wycliffe Hall Ox 76-80; V Macclesfield St Mich *Ches* 80-85; RD Macclesfield 84-88; TR Macclesfield Team Par 85-88; Hon Can Ches Cathl 86-88; Adn Ches 88-93; Suff Bp Doncaster *Sheff* from 93. *Bishop's Lodge, Hooton Roberts, Rotherham, S Yorkshire S65 4PF* Tel (01709) 853370 Fax 852310

GEBAUER, George Gerhart. b 25. Sarum & Wells Th Coll 71. **d** 73 **p** 74. C Portsdown *Portsm* 73-78; V Purbrook 78-91; rtd 91; Perm to Offic *Portsm* from 91. *52 St John's Road, Locks Heath, Southampton SO31 6NF* Tel (01489) 575172

GEDDES, Gordon David. b 38. St Chad's Coll Dur BA59 DipTh60. **d** 61 **p** 62. C Bishopwearmouth St Mary V w St Pet CD *Dur* 61-65; P-in-c Jarrow 65-68; Teacher Crewe Boys' Gr Sch 68-71; Hd of Relig Studies 71-78; Hd of RE Ruskin Sch Crewe 78-90; Lic to Offic *Ches* 68-90; P-in-c Church Minshull w Leighton and Minshull Vernon 90-91; V Leighton-cum-Minshull Vernon from 91; Chapl Leighton Hosp Crewe from 91. *The Vicarage, Minshull Vernon, Crewe CW1 4RD* Tel (01270) 522213 Fax 522694

GEDDES, Peter Henry. b 51. DipHE86. Trin Coll Bris 84. **d** 86 **p** 87. C Blackpool St Mark *Blackb* 86-88; C Barnston *Ches* 88-92; V Haslington w Crewe Green from 92. *The Vicarage, 163 Crewe Road, Haslington, Crewe CW1 1RL* Tel (01270) 582388

GEDDES, Roderick Charles. b 47. Man Univ DipEd78 MPhil85. N Ord Course 88. **d** 91 **p** 93. C Alverthorpe *Wakef* 91-92; C S Ossett 92-94; V Jurby *S & M* from 94; R Andreas from 94; V Andreas St Jude from 94. *The Rectory, Village Road, Andreas, Ramsey, Isle of Man IM7 4HH* Tel (01624) 880419

GEDGE, Lloyd Victor. b 23. Cuddesdon Coll 54. **d** 57 **p** 58. C Headington *Ox* 57-60; Canada 60-63 and 66-82 and from 86; New Zealand 63-66; P-in-c N Creake *Nor* 82-83; P-in-c S Creake 82-83; R N and S Creake w Waterden 84-86; rtd 88. *PO Box 187, Holden, Alberta, Canada, T0B 2C0*

GEDGE, Simon John Francis. b 44. Keble Coll Ox BA67 MA73. Cuddesdon Coll 67. **d** 69 **p** 70. C Perry Barr *Birm* 69-73; C Handsworth St Andr 73-75; V Birm St Pet 75-81; Perm to Offic *Lon* 81-85; Hon C Croydon St Jo *S'wark* from 85. *121 Albany Road, London SE8 4EB* Tel 0181-692 7328

GEE, Mrs Dorothy Mary. b 33. St Jo Coll Nottm 88. **d** 89 **p** 94. Chapl Asst Univ Hosp Nottm 89-95; NSM Plumtree *S'well* 95-97; P-in-c from 97. *16 The Leys, Normanton-on-the-Wolds, Keyworth, Notts NG12 5NV* Tel 0115-937 4927

GEE, Canon Edward. b 28. St Deiniol's Hawarden 59. **d** 61 **p** 62. C Hanging Heaton *Wakef* 61-65; V Brownhill 65-75; V Alverthorpe 75-84; R Castleford All SS 84-92; Hon Can Wakef Cathl 87-92; rtd 92; Perm to Offic *Bradf* from 92; Perm to Offic *Wakef* from 92. *1 Holme Ghyll, Colne Road, Glusburn, Keighley, W Yorkshire BD20 8RG* Tel (01535) 630060

GEE, Michael Terence. b 29. Dur Univ BSc54. Tyndale Hall Bris 60. **d** 62 **p** 63. C Blackpool St Thos *Blackb* 62-64; C Selston *S'well* 64-68; V Brimscombe *Glouc* 68-80; V Tidenham w Beachley and Lancaut 80-91; P-in-c Sherborne, Windrush, the Barringtons etc 91-94; rtd 94; Perm to Offic *Glouc* from 94. *32 Homefield, Shortwood, Nailsworth, Stroud, Glos GL6 0SP* Tel (01453) 832742

GEE, Norman. b 11. Lon Univ BA33 St Cath Soc Ox BA35 MA42. Wycliffe Hall Ox 33. **d** 35 **p** 36. C Kilburn St Mary *Lon* 35-38; Youth Sec CMJ 38-41; P-in-c Woodside Park St Barn *Lon* 40-41; V 41-49; V Oakwood St Thos 49-58; V Bath St Bart *B & W* 58-73; V Curry Rivel 73-78; rtd 78; Perm to Offic *B & W* from 79. *5 Barn Close, Nether Stowey, Bridgwater, Somerset TA5 1PA* Tel (01278) 732317

GEEN, James William (Jim). b 50. Chich Th Coll 76. **d** 79 **p** 80. C Brandon *Dur* 79-84; C Sunderland Red Ho 84-86; P-in-c N Hylton St Marg Castletown 86-89; V 89-91; Dep Chapl HM Pris Dur 91-92; Chapl HM Young Offender Inst Lanc Farms 92-95; Chapl HM Pris Long Lartin from 95. *HM Prison Long Lartin, South Littleton, Evesham, Worcs WR11 5TZ* Tel (01386) 830101 Fax 832834

GEERING, Anthony Ernest. b 43. Lon Univ DipTh66 Columbia Pacific Univ BSc. Kelham Th Coll 62. **d** 68 **p** 69. C Cov St Mary *Cov* 68-71; New Zealand 71-75; P-in-c Brinklow *Cov* 75-77; R 77-81; V Monks Kirby w Pailton and Stretton-under-Fosse 77-81; R Harborough Magna 77-81; V Pilton w Ashford *Ex* 81-86; P-in-c Shirwell w Loxhore 83-86; R Crediton and Shobrooke from 86; RD Cadbury from 93. *The Vicarage, Crediton, Devon EX17 2AF* Tel (01363) 772669 or 773226

GEESON, Brian Alfred. b 30. Qu Coll Ox BA51 Trin & All SS Coll Leeds PGCE76. Qu Coll Birm 54. **d** 55 **p** 56. C Newbold w Dunston *Derby* 55-59; PC Calow 59-64; R Broughton *Bradf* 64-71; TV Seacroft *Ripon* 71-77; Hon C Hanging Heaton *Wakef* 77-87; Hon C Purlwell 87-94; rtd 94; Perm to Offic *Wakef* from 94. *30 Ullswater Avenue, Dewsbury, W Yorkshire WF12 7PL* Tel (01924) 465621

GEILINGER, John Edward. b 27. Lon Univ BSc53 BD58 BA76 MPhil79. Tyndale Hall Bris. **d** 59 **p** 60. C Plymouth St Jude *Ex* 59-61; Nigeria 63-77; Perm to Offic *Portsm* from 79; rtd 92. *Emmaus House, Colwell Road, Freshwater, Isle of Wight PO40 9LY* Tel (01983) 753030

GELDARD, Mark Dundas. b 50. Liv Univ BA71 Bris Univ MA75. Trin Coll Bris 73. **d** 75 **p** 76. C Aughton Ch Ch *Liv* 75-78; Tutor Trin Coll Bris 78-84; V Fairfield *Liv* 84-88; Dir of Ords *Lich* from 88; C Lich St Mary w St Mich 95-96; C Lich St Mich w St Mary and Wall from 96. *10 The Brambles, Lichfield, Staffs WS14 9SE* Tel (01543) 415318

GELLI, Frank Julian. b 43. Birkb Coll Lon BA78 K Coll Lon MTh82. Ripon Coll Cuddesdon 84. **d** 86 **p** 87. C Chiswick St Nic w St Mary *Lon* 86-89; Chapl Ankara *Eur* 89-91; C Kensington St Mary Abbots w St Geo *Lon* from 91. *1 Vicarage Cottage, Vicarage Gate, London W8 4HN* Tel 0171-937 2364

GELLING, Canon John Drury. b 22. Pemb Coll Ox BA44 DipTh45 MA48. Wycliffe Hall Ox 44. **d** 54 **p** 55. Hd Master Eccles High Sch 50-64; C Irlam *Man* 54-59; V Rushen *S & M* 64-77; RD Castletown 71-77; R Ballaugh 77-92; P-in-c Michael 77-78; V 78-92; Can St German's Cathl 80-92; rtd 92; Perm to Offic *S & M* from 93. *Uplands, Ballavitchell Road, Crosby, Douglas, Isle of Man IM4 2DN* Tel (01624) 851223

GELSTON, Dr Anthony. b 35. Keble Coll Ox BA57 MA60 DD85. Ridley Hall Cam 59. **d** 60 **p** 61. C Chipping Norton *Ox* 60-62; Lect Th Dur Univ *Dur* 62-76; Sen Lect 76-88; Reader 89-95; Dean Div Faculty 77-79; Lic to Offic from 62; rtd 95. *Lesbury, Hetton Road, Houghton le Spring, Tyne & Wear DH5 8JW* Tel 0191-584 2256

GEMMELL, Ian William Young. b 52. ALAM. St Jo Coll Nottm LTh77. **d** 77 **p** 78. C Old Hill H Trin *Worc* 77-81; C Selly Hill St Steph *Birm* 81; C Selly Park St Steph and St Wulstan 81-83; V Leic St Chris *Leic* 83-93; RD Christianity S 92-93; P-in-c Gt Bowden w Welham, Glooston and Cranoe from 93; P-in-c Church Langton w Tur Langton, Thorpe Langton etc from 93. *The Rectory, Dingley Road, Great Bowden, Market Harborough, Leics LE16 7ET* Tel (01858) 462032

GENDERS, Nigel Mark. b 65. Oak Hill Th Coll BA92. **d** 92 **p** 93. C New Malden and Coombe *S'wark* 92-96; C Enfield Ch Ch Trent Park *Lon* from 96. *2 Lakenheath, London N14 4RN* Tel 0181-886 5745

✠**GENDERS, The Rt Revd Roger Alban Marson (Anselm).** b 19. BNC Ox BA47 MA47. Coll of Resurr Mirfield 48. **d** 52 **p** 52 **c** 77. Lic to Offic *Wakef* 52-55; CR from 52; Barbados 55-65; Rhodesia 66-75; Adn E Distr 70-75; Bp Bermuda 77-82; Asst Bp Wakef from 83; rtd 84. *House of the Resurrection, Mirfield, W Yorkshire WF14 0BN* Tel (01924) 494318

GENEREUX, Patrick Edward. b 47. William Carey Coll BSc73 Univ of the South (USA) MDiv78. **d** 78 **p** 79. USA 78-81 and from 82; C Spalding *Linc* 81-82. *621 North 5th Street, Burlington, IA 52601-0608, USA*

GENT, Canon Comdr Anthony Leonard. b 20. CEng MIMechE. Sarum Th Coll 66. **d** 67 **p** 68. C Forrabury w Minster and Trevalga *Truro* 67-70; C Davidstow w Otterham 67-70; C Boscastle w Davidstow 67-70; V St Minver 70-91; RD Trigg Minor 73-84; P-in-c St Kew 77-78; Hon Can Truro Cathl 84-91; rtd 91. *15 Middleway, Taunton, Somerset TA1 3QH* Tel (01823) 323426

GENT, Mrs Miriam. b 29. Leeds Univ BA51. SW Minl Tr Course 84. **d** 87 **p** 94. NSM Pinhoe and Broadclyst *Ex* from 87. *Mosshaye Cottage, West Clyst, Exeter EX1 3TR* Tel (01392) 67288

GENT, Miss Susan Elizabeth (Sue). b 56. K Coll Lon LLB78 Brunel Univ BA95 SSC81. Wycliffe Hall Ox MPhil96. **d** 97. C Notting Hill St Jo and St Pet *Lon* from 97. *7 The Lodge, 23 Kensington Park Gardens, London W11 3AH* Tel 0171-792 8527 E-mail susangent@compuserve.com

GEOFFREY, Brother. *See* PEARSON, Harold

GEORGE, Canon Alec. b 29. Lich Th Coll 56. **d** 59 **p** 60. C Holbrooks *Cov* 59-65; R Lower Broughton Ascension *Man* 65-71; V Hollinwood 71-96; Hon Can Man Cathl 94-96; rtd 96. *107 Fairway, Fleetwood, Lancs FY7 8RA* Tel (01253) 771758

GEORGE, Alexander Robert. b 46. K Coll Lon BD69 AKC69. St Aug Coll Cant. **d** 70 **p** 71. C Newmarket St Mary w Exning St Agnes *St E* 70-74; C Swindon Ch Ch *Bris* 74-76; C Henbury 76-79; Lic to Offic 79-80; TV Oldland 80-88; C Ipswich St Aug *St E* 89; C Hadleigh w Layham and Shelley 89-90; P-in-c Assington 90-91; R Assington w Newton Green and Lt Cornard from 91; Dioc Moderator for Reader Tr from 95. *The Vicarage, Assington, Sudbury, Suffolk CO10 5LQ* Tel (01787) 210249

GEORGE, Charles Roy. b 32. St Edm Hall Ox BA55 MA59. Cuddesdon Coll 55. **d** 57 **p** 58. C Chorley St Laur *Blackb* 57-60; C Norton *Derby* 60-64; V Eltham St Barn *S'wark* 64-74; V Milton *Portsm* 74-90; R Rowner 90-96; rtd 96. *46 The Thicket, Fareham, Hants PO16 8PZ* Tel (01329) 288185

GEORGE, The Ven David Michael. b 45. Selw Coll Cam BA66 MA70. Chich Th Coll 70. **d** 73 **p** 74. C Chiswick St Nic w St Mary *Lon* 73-76; C Kensington St Mary Abbots w St Geo 76-78; C Northolt Park St Barn 78-81; Argentina from 81; Adn River Plate from 84. *San Lorenzo 2274, 1640 Martinez, Buenos Aires, Argentina* Tel Buenos Aires (1) 798-0078

GEORGE, Mrs Elizabeth Ann. b 33. Westf Coll Lon BA56. S Dios Minl Tr Scheme. **d** 87 **p** 94. NSM Basingstoke *Win* from 87. *71 Camrose Way, Basingstoke, Hants RG21 3AW* Tel (01256) 464763

GEORGE, Frederick. b 39. St Luke's Coll Ex CertEd61. Chich Th Coll 82. **d** 72 **p** 83. Australia 72-75; Brunei 75-80; Gambia 80-82 and 83-88; C Hellingly and Upper Dicker *Chich* 83; P-in-c Ringsfield w Redisham, Barsham, Shipmeadow etc *St E* 89-92; R Wainford from 92. *The Rectory, School Road, Ringsfield, Beccles, Suffolk NR34 8NZ* Tel (01502) 717862

GEORGE, Preb John Thomas. b 17. St D Coll Lamp BA42 Selw Coll Cam BA44 MA47. Westcott Ho Cam 44. **d** 45 **p** 46. C Llanstadwel *St D* 45-48; C Eastville St Thos *Bris* 48-50; C Wells St Cuth *B & W* 50-52; PV Wells Cathl 50-52; Teacher Wells Cathl Sch 50-52; V Cheddar 52-57; P-in-c Priddy 55-57; CF 57-60; V Thornton w Allerthorpe *York* 60-62; R Backwell *B & W* 62-72; RD Portishead 68-72; V Wellington w W Buckland and Nynehead 72-76; TR Wellington and Distr 76-82; Preb Wells Cathl 78-86; rtd 82; Hon C Diptford, N Huish, Harberton and Harbertonford *Ex* from 85. *12 Woolcombe Lane, Ivybridge, Devon PL21 0UA* Tel (01752) 698284

GEORGE, Martin Walter. b 31. TD85. Bris Univ BA58 BEd72. Sarum Th Coll. **d** 82 **p** 82. C Bruton w Lamyatt, Wyke and Redlynch *B & W* 82-85; V Middlezoy and Othery and Moorlinch 85-87; Perm to Offic from 87; rtd 96. *17 Lewis Crescent, Frome, Somerset BA11 2LF* Tel (01373) 462094

GEORGE, Nicholas Paul. b 58. St Steph Ho Ox 86. **d** 89 **p** 90. C Leeds St Aid *Ripon* 89-92; C Leeds Richmond Hill 92-96; Chapl Agnes Stewart C of E High Sch Leeds from 93; V Leeds Halton St Wilfrid *Ripon* from 96. *Halton Vicarage, Selby Road, Leeds LS15 7NP* Tel 0113-264 7000

✠**GEORGE, The Rt Revd Randolph Oswald.** b 24. Codrington Coll Barbados 46. **d** 50 **p** 51 **c** 76. Barbados 50-53; C Leigh *Lich* 53-55; C Ardwick St Benedict *Man* 55-57; C Bedford Park *Lon* 57-58; C Lavender Hill Ascension *S'wark* 58-60; Trinidad and Tobago 60-71; Hon Can Trinidad 68-71; Guyana from 71; Dean Georgetown 71-76; Suff Bp Stabroek 76-80; Bp Guyana 80-94; rtd 94. *Austin House, Kingston, Georgetown 1, Guyana*

GEORGE-JONES, Canon Gwilym Ifor. b 26. K Coll (NS) 56. **d** 57 **p** 57. Canada 57-61; V Kirton in Lindsey *Linc* 61-71; R Grayingham 61-71; R Manton 61-71; V Alford w Rigsby 71-92; R Maltby 71-92; R Well 71-92; V Bilsby w Farlesthorpe 71-92; R Hannah cum Hagnaby w Markby 71-92; R Saleby w Beesby 71-92; RD Calcewaithe and Candleshoe 77-85 and 87-89; Can and Preb Linc Cathl from 81; rtd 92. *42 Kelstern Road, Doddington Park, Lincoln LN6 3NJ* Tel (01522) 691896

GERARD, John William. b 23. BNC Ox BA47 MA52. **d** 51 **p** 51. Canada 51-61; Perm to Offic *Chelmsf* 74-89; rtd 81. *Oak Tree Cottage, 31 Wycke Lane, Tollesbury, Maldon, Essex CM9 8ST* Tel (01621) 869318

GERD, Sister. *See* SWENSSON, Sister Gerd Inger

GERRANS, Nigel Henry. b 31. Cam Univ MA54. St Steph Ho Ox 78. **d** 81 **p** 81. C Bicester w Bucknell, Caversfield and Launton *Ox* 81-84; Chapl Qu Alexandra Hosp Portsm 84-92; rtd 92; Perm to Offic *Chich* from 92. *56 Bishopsgate Walk, Chichester, W Sussex PO19 4FQ* Tel (01243) 539131

GERRARD, The Ven David Keith Robin. b 39. St Edm Hall Ox BA61. Linc Th Coll 61. **d** 63 **p** 64. C Stoke Newington St Olave *Lon* 63-66; C Primrose Hill St Mary w Avenue Road St Paul 66-69; V Newington St Paul *S'wark* 69-79; V Surbiton St Andr and St Mark 79-89; RD Kingston 84-88; Hon Can S'wark Cathl 85-89; Adn Wandsworth from 89. *68 North Side, London SW18 2QX* Tel 0181-874 5766 Fax 789 3985 E-mail davidgerrard@dswark.org.uk

GERRARD, Dr George Ernest. b 16. TEM. FCIS60 DD94. Ridley Hall Cam 66. **d** 68 **p** 69. OStJ from 65; C Hilborough w Bodney *Nor* 68-70; C Ramsey *Ely* 70-75; rtd 81; Perm to Offic *Nor* from 86. *1 Goodrick Place, Beech Close, Swaffham, Norfolk PE37 7RP* Tel (01760) 723311

GERRISH, David Victor. b 38. St Jo Coll Dur BSc61 MA65. Oak Hill Th Coll 61. **d** 64 **p** 65. C Fareham St Jo *Portsm* 64-66; Asst Chapl K Sch Roch 67-71; Asst Chapl Bryanston Sch Dorset 71-73; Chapl 73-77; Chapl Mon Sch 77-86; Chapl Warminster Sch 86-89; R Portland All SS w St Pet *Sarum* 89-96; Chapl Aquitaine *Eur* from 96. *The Presbytery, 1 Lotissement de la Caussade, 33270 Floirac, France*

GERRY, Brian John Rowland. b 38. Oak Hill Th Coll 69. **d** 71 **p** 72. C Hawkwell *Chelmsf* 71-74; C Battersea Park St Sav *S'wark* 74-77; C Battersea St Geo w St Andr 74-77; V Axmouth w Musbury *Ex* 77-86; R Upton from 86. *Upton Rectory, Furzehill Road, Torquay TQ1 3JG* Tel (01803) 211572

GERRY, Ulric James. **d** 97. C Hemel Hempstead *St Alb* from 97. *St Barnabas Vicarage, Everest Way, Hemel Hempstead, Herts HP2 4HY*

GHEST, Richard William Iliffe. b 31. Em Coll Cam BA53 MA57 Lon Univ BA66. Wells Th Coll 53. **d** 55 **p** 56. C Weston-super-Mare St Jo *B & W* 55-57; India 58-63; C Holborn St Geo w H Trin and St Bart *Lon* 63-67; Ceylon 67-68; C Combe Down *B & W* 68-73; C Combe Down w Monkton Combe 73-74; R Tickenham 74-96; rtd 96. *120 Cottrell Road, Roath, Cardiff CF2 3EX* Tel (01222) 481597

GHINN, Edward. b 45. Oak Hill Th Coll 71. **d** 74 **p** 75. C Purley Ch Ch *S'wark* 74-77; Chile 77-82; V Sevenoaks Weald *Roch* 82-86; Chapl HM Pris Hull 86-89; Chapl HM Pris Pentonville 89-91; Chapl HM Pris Maidstone 91-96; Brazil from 96. *Address temp unknown*

GHOSH, Dipen. b 43. St Jo Coll Nottm 71. **d** 74 **p** 75. C Bushbury *Lich* 74-77; Hon C 86-89; C Wednesfield Heath 89-91; TV Wolverhampton from 91. *St Marks Vicarage, 20 Tettenhall Road, Wolverhampton WV1 4SW* Tel (01902) 771375

GIBB, David Richard Albert. b 68. Cov Univ MPhil95. Lon Bible Coll BA90 Wycliffe Hall Ox DipMin95. **d** 95 **p** 96. C Ox St Ebbe w H Trin and St Pet *Ox* from 95. *Paravel, 25 Norreys Avenue, Oxford OX1 4ST* Tel (01865) 249828

GIBBARD, Roger. b 48. Southn Univ BA73. Cuddesdon Coll 73. **d** 75 **p** 76. C Portsea St Mary *Portsm* 75-79; P-in-c New Addington *Cant* 79-81; C Ditton St Mich *Liv* 81-82; TV 82-88; Asst Chapl HM Pris Liv 88-89; Chapl HM Young Offender Inst Hindley 89-92; Chapl HM Rem Cen Risley from 92. *HM Remand Centre, Warrington Road, Risley, Warrington WA3 6BP* Tel (01925) 763871 Fax 764103

GIBBINS, John Grenville. b 53. Aston Tr Scheme 89 Linc Th Coll 89. **d** 91 **p** 92. C Market Harborough *Leic* 91-95; P-in-c Blaby from 95. *The Rectory, Wigston Road, Blaby, Leicester LE8 3FU* Tel 0116-277 2588

GIBBON, Edward Herbert Morgan. b 15. St D Coll Lamp BA37 St Mich Coll Llan 38. **d** 40 **p** 41. C Canton St Luke *Llan* 40-42; C Ealing St Steph Castle Hill *Lon* 42-44; CF (EC) 44-47; R Pitsea *Chelmsf* 48-50; Chapl RAF 50-66; V Sunninghill *Ox* 66-79; rtd 79; Perm to Offic *Guildf* 82-96. *Starlings, Sandpit Hall Road, Chobham, Woking, Surrey GU24 8HA* Tel (01276) 856863

GIBBON, Gordon Percy. b 17. Oak Hill Th Coll 63. **d** 64 **p** 65. C Whitehall Park St Andr Hornsey Lane *Lon* 64-68; V Walthamstow St Gabr *Chelmsf* 68-82; rtd 82; Perm to Offic *Chich* from 82. *20 Black Path, Polegate, E Sussex BN26 5AP* Tel (01323) 486751

GIBBONS, David Austen. b 63. York Univ BSc84. Ch Div Sch of Pacific 93 Ripon Coll Cuddesdon BA94. **d** 94 **p** 95. C Ryde H Trin *Portsm* 94-97; C Swanmore St Mich and All Angels 94-97; C Gosport Ch Ch from 97. *6 Carlton Way, Gosport, Hants PO12 1LN* Tel (01705) 503921

GIBBONS, David Robin Christian. b 36. Chich Th Coll 82. **d** 84 **p** 85. C Seaford w Sutton *Chich* 84-87; R Harting 87-93; R Harting w Elsted and Treyford cum Didling from 93. *The Rectory, South Harting, Petersfield, Hants GU31 5QB* Tel (01730) 825234

GIBBONS, Eric. b 47. Sarum & Wells Th Coll 69. **d** 72 **p** 73. C New Haw *Guildf* 72-76; C Hawley H Trin 76-79; P-in-c Blackheath and Chilworth 79-90; V from 90. *The Vicarage, Brook Lane, Chilworth, Guildford, Surrey GU4 8ND* Tel (01483) 454070

GIBBONS, John. b 31. K Coll Lon 52. Oak Hill Th Coll 55. **d** 57 **p** 58. C Islington St Steph w St Bart and St Matt *Lon* 57-60; C

Rolleston *Lich* 60-63; C Anslow 60-63; V Bobbington 63-83; V N Axholme Gp *Linc* 83-96; RD Is of Axholme 91-96; rtd 96; Perm to Offic *Birm* from 96. *49 Meadow Drive, Hampton-in-Arden, Solihull, W Midlands B92 0BD* Tel (01675) 443024

GIBBONS, The Ven Kenneth Harry. b 31. Man Univ BSc52. Cuddesdon Coll 54. **d** 56 **p** 57. C Fleetwood *Blackb* 56-60; NE Sch Sec SCM 60-62; Hon C Leeds St Pet *Ripon* 60-62; C St Martin-in-the-Fields *Lon* 62-65; V New Addington *Cant* 65-70; V Portsea St Mary *Portsm* 70-81; RD Portsm 73-79; Hon Can Portsm Cathl 76-81; Dir of Post-Ord Tr *Blackb* 81-83; Acting Chapl HM Forces Weeton 81-85; Dir of Ords 82-90; Adn Lancaster 81-97; P-in-c Weeton 81-85; V St Michaels on Wyre 85-97; rtd 97. *112 Valley Road, Kenley, Surrey CR8 5BU* Tel 0181-660 7502

GIBBONS, Paul James. b 37. JP. Chich Th Coll 63. **d** 65 **p** 66. C Croydon St Mich *Cant* 65-72; V Maidstone St Mich from 72. *The Vicarage, 109 Tonbridge Road, Maidstone, Kent ME16 8JS* Tel (01622) 752710

GIBBONS, Mrs Susan Janet. b 51. St Mary's Coll Dur BA73 Birm Univ PGCE74. WMMTC 89. **d** 92 **p** 94. NSM Fladbury, Wyre Piddle and Moor *Worc* from 92. *The Old School, Bricklehampton, Pershore, Worcs WR10 3HJ* Tel (01386) 710475

GIBBONS, Thomas Patrick. b 59. St Jo Coll Dur BA82. St Steph Ho Ox 88. **d** 90 **p** 91. C Whorlton *Newc* 90-94; C Gosforth St Nic 94-96; R Radley and Sunningwell *Ox* from 96. *The Vicarage, Kennington Road, Radley, Abingdon, Oxon OX14 2JN* Tel (01235) 554739

GIBBONS, Canon William Simpson. b 32. TCD BA60 MA64. **d** 61 **p** 62. C Londonderry Ch Ch *D & R* 61-65; I Drumholm and Rossnowlagh 65-70; C Dublin St Ann w St Steph *D & G* 70-72; I Kill 72-95; Can Ch Ch Cathl Dublin 91-95; rtd 95. *Muthaiga, 8 Mount Bernard Drive, Castlederg, Co Tyrone BT81 7JA* Tel (01662) 670691

GIBBS, Colin Hugh. b 35. St Mich Coll Llan 82. **d** 84 **p** 85. C Bistre *St As* 84-87; V Penycae 87-92; rtd 92. *Asaph, 26 Cil y Coed, Ruabon, Wrexham LL14 6TA* Tel (01978) 823550

GIBBS, Colin Wilfred. b 39. Man Univ BA62 CertEd. St Jo Coll Nottm 71. **d** 73 **p** 74. C Crowborough *Chich* 73-76; C Rodbourne Cheney *Bris* 76-77; C Bickenhill w Elmdon *Birm* 77-80; CF 80-96; rtd 96. *132 Bay View Road, Bideford, Devon EX39 1BJ* Tel (01237) 425348 Fax as telephone E-mail colin@thenet.co.uk

GIBBS, Canon Derek Norman. b 38. Kelham Th Coll. **d** 62 **p** 63. C Newc Ch Ch w St Ann *Newc* 62-65; C Shiremoor 65-67; V New Bentley *Sheff* 67-68; V Sheff Parson Cross St Cecilia 68-80; RD Ecclesfield 75-80; V Cantley 80-92; RD Doncaster 82-92; Hon Can Sheff Cathl 88-92; P-in-c Doncaster Ch Ch 89-91; Cyprus from 93. *Margarita, Agios Demitrianos, Paphos, Cyprus* Tel Paphos (6) 732276

GIBBS, Prof Edmund. b 38. Lon Univ BD62. Fuller Th Sem California DMin81 Oak Hill Th Coll 58. **d** 63 **p** 64. C Wandsworth All SS *S'wark* 63-66; Chile 66-70; Sec SAMS 70-73; Educn Sec 73-77; Ch Progr Manager Bible Soc 77-84; USA from 84; Assoc Prof Evang and Ch Renewal Fuller Th Sem 84-94. *1244 West Michigan Avenue, Pasadena, CA, 91104 USA*

GIBBS, Mrs Fiorenza Silvia Elisabetta. b 49. SRN71 Surrey Univ DipHV72. St Alb Minl Tr Scheme 90. **d** 93. NSM Hitchin *St Alb* 93-96; NSM Pirton from 97. *41 West Lane, Pirton, Hitchin, Herts SG5 3QP* Tel (01462) 711846

GIBBS, Ian Edmund. b 47. Lon Univ BEd69. St Steph Ho Ox 72. **d** 75 **p** 76. C Stony Stratford *Ox* 75-79; V Forest Town *S'well* 79-83; R Diddlebury w Munslow, Holdgate and Tugford *Heref* from 83; R Abdon from 83. *The Rectory, Munslow, Craven Arms, Shropshire SY7 9ET* Tel (01584) 841688

GIBBS, Dr James Millard. b 28. Univ of Michigan BSE51 Nottm Univ PhD68. Seabury-Western Th Sem BD57. **d** 57 **p** 57. USA 57-60; Lic to Offic *S'well* 61-62 and 65-66; C Brandon *Dur* 62-64; Vice-Prin Lich Th Coll 66-71; Lic to Offic *Lich* 66-71; India 72-77; Tutor Qu Coll Birm 78-84; V Stechford *Birm* 84-93; rtd 93; Perm to Offic *Birm* from 93. *14 Metchley Court, Birmingham B17 0JP* Tel 0121-426 2108

✠**GIBBS, The Rt Revd John.** b 17. Bris Univ BA42 Lon Univ BD48. Linc Th Coll 55. **d** 55 **p** 56 **c** 73. C Brislington St Luke *Bris* 55-57; Chapl St Matthias's Coll Bris 57-64; Vice-Prin 61-64; Prin Keswick Hall Coll of Educn 64-73; Lic to Offic *Nor* 64-73; Hon Can Nor Cathl 68-73; Suff Bp Bradwell *Chelmsf* 73-76; Bp Cov 76-85; rtd 85; Asst Bp Bris from 85; Asst Bp Glouc from 85. *Farthingloe, Southfield, Minchinhampton, Stroud, Glos GL6 9DY* Tel (01453) 886211

GIBBS, Dr Jonathan Robert. b 61. Jes Coll Ox MA89 Jes Coll Cam PhD90. Ridley Hall Cam 84. **d** 89 **p** 90. C Stalybridge H Trin and Ch Ch *Ches* 89-92; Chapl Basle w Freiburg-im-Breisgau *Eur* from 92. *St Johanns-Ring 92, CH-4056, Basle, Switzerland* Tel Basle (61) 321-7477 Fax 321-7476

GIBBS, Mrs Patricia Louise. b 39. S'wark Ord Course 91. **d** 94 **p** 95. NSM Croydon H Sav *S'wark* from 94; Chapl Asst Mayday Healthcare NHS Trust Thornton Heath from 94. *41 Sandringham Road, Thornton Heath, Surrey CR7 7AX* Tel 0181-684 9720

GIBBS, Peter Winston. b 50. Ex Univ BA72 Leic Univ DipSocWork75 CQSW75. St Jo Coll Nottm DipTh. **d** 90 **p** 91. C Hampreston *Sarum* 90-94; P-in-c Ipswich St Matt *St E* from 94. *6 Collinsons, Hadleigh Road, Ipswich IP2 0DS* Tel (01473) 281364

GIBBS, Canon Philip Roscoe. b 33. Codrington Coll Barbados 57. **d** 60 **p** 61. Br Honduras 60-73; Belize 73-74; Hon Can Br Honduras 71-73; Hon Can Belize from 73; V Stoke Newington Common St Mich *Lon* 74-87; New Zealand from 87; rtd 93. *10 Gardener Street, Levin 5500, New Zealand* Tel Gisborne (6) 367 9884

GIBBS, Raymond George. b 55. NTMTC 94. **d** 97. NSM Becontree S *Chelmsf* from 97. *34 Maybank Avenue, Hornchurch, Essex RM12 5SB* Tel (01708) 452043

GIBBS, Canon Robert John. b 43. Dur Univ BA64. Westcott Ho Cam 66. **d** 68 **p** 69. C Costessey *Nor* 68-71; C Halesowen *Worc* 71-75; TV 75-76; P-in-c Dudley St Jas 77-79; V 79-82; Dioc Ecum Officer 82-89; R Ribbesford w Bewdley and Dowles 82-91; RD Kidderminster 83-89; Hon Can Worc Cathl 87-91; V Budleigh Salterton *Ex* 91-96; RD Aylesbeare 93-96. *12 Manorside, Badsey, Evesham, Worcs WR11 5EQ* Tel (01386) 833461

GIBBS, Canon William Gilbert. b 31. Bps' Coll Cheshunt 55. **d** 58 **p** 59. C Wellington w W Buckland *B & W* 58-61; C Kensington St Mary Abbots w St Geo *Lon* 61-68; V Guilsborough *Pet* 68; V Guilsborough w Hollowell 68-74; V Guilsborough w Hollowell and Cold Ashby from 74; Jt P-in-c Cottesbrooke w Gt Creaton and Thornby from 83; Can Pet Cathl from 88; Jt P-in-c Maidwell w Draughton, Lamport w Faxton from 88. *The Vicarage, Guilsborough, Northampton NN6 8PU* Tel (01604) 740297

GIBBY, Thomas Rees. b 12. St D Coll Lamp BA33 BD42. St Mich Coll Llan 33. **d** 35 **p** 36. C Llangeinor *Llan* 35-39; C Llantrisant 39-44; C Bideford *Ex* 44-45; R Langtree 45-58; P-in-c Lt Torrington 49-55; R 55-58; V Bradworthy 58-62; P-in-c W w E Putford 59-62; V Ivybridge 62-75; R Harford 63-75; RD Plympton 66-71; rtd 75; Perm to Offic *St D* from 75. *Penlon, Cwmann, Lampeter SA48 8DU* Tel (01570) 422100

GIBLIN, Brendan Anthony. b 64. K Coll Lon BD86 AKC93 Leeds Univ MA95. Wycliffe Hall Ox 90. **d** 92 **p** 93. C Tadcaster w Newton Kyme *York* 92-96; R Stockton-on-the-Forest w Holtby and Warthill from 96. *The Rectory, Sandy Lane, Stockton on the Forest, York YO3 9UU* Tel (01904) 400337

GIBLING, Derek Vivian. b 31. Wadh Coll Ox BA56 MA63. Wycliffe Hall Ox 70. **d** 72 **p** 73. C Fisherton Anger *Sarum* 72-74; C Yatton Keynell *Bris* 74-77; C Castle Combe 74-77; C Biddestone w Slaughterford 74-77; P-in-c Youlgreave *Derby* 77-82; P-in-c Stanton-in-Peak 77-82; V Youlgreave, Middleton, Stanton-in-Peak etc 82-88; P-in-c Hartington and Biggin 88-90; V Hartington, Biggin and Earl Sterndale 90-96; rtd 96; Perm to Offic *Linc* from 96. *The Hawthorns, Church Lane, West Keal, Spilsby, Lincs PE23 4BG*

GIBRALTAR AND IBERIA, Archdeacon of. *See* ROBINSON, The Ven John Kenneth

GIBRALTAR IN EUROPE, Bishop of. *See* HIND, The Rt Revd John William

GIBRALTAR, Dean of. *See* HORLOCK, The Very Revd Brian William

GIBSON, Alan. b 35. Birm Univ BSc56 Man Univ MSc72. NW Ord Course 71. **d** 74 **p** 75. C Sale St Anne *Ches* 74-77; V Runcorn St Mich 77-82; Educn Adv *Carl* 82-88; P-in-c Hugill 82-88; V Grange-over-Sands 88-97; rtd 97. *11 Ecclesbourne Drive, Buxton, Derbyshire SK17 9BX* Tel (01298) 22621

GIBSON, Alan Henry. b 11. MBE44. K Coll Lon BD37 AKC37 Ely Th Coll 37. **d** 37 **p** 38. C Balham Hill Ascension *S'wark* 37-40; C Battersea St Steph 40-42; CF 42-64; V Sandgate St Paul *Cant* 64-76; rtd 76; Lic to Offic *Cant* 76-87; Chapl St Mary's Hosp Etchinghill 80-87. *14 Orchard Walk, Stoney Lane, Weeke, Winchester, Hants SO22 6DL* Tel (01962) 883869

GIBSON, Alexander Douglas. b 21. Wycliffe Hall Ox 60. **d** 62 **p** 63. C St Helens St Helen *Liv* 62-65; V Gresley *Derby* 65-77; V Hartington 77-78; V Biggin 77-78; V Hartington and Biggin 78-88; rtd 88; Perm to Offic *Derby* from 88. *Westmead, Aldern Way, Baslow Road, Bakewell, Derbyshire DE45 1AJ* Tel (01629) 812723

GIBSON, Anthony Richard. b 43. Ridley Hall Cam 83. **d** 85 **p** 86. C Rushmere *St E* 85-88; P-in-c N Tawton and Bondleigh *Ex* 88; P-in-c Sampford Courtenay w Honeychurch 88; R N Tawton, Bondleigh, Sampford Courtenay etc 88-93; RD Okehampton 92-93; P-in-c Tiverton St Pet 93-95; P-in-c Tiverton St Pet and Chevithorne w Cove from 95. *St Peter's Rectory, 32 The Avenue, Tiverton, Devon EX16 4HW* Tel (01884) 254079

GIBSON, Catherine Snyder (Kate). b 39. Parson's Sch of Design (NY) 57. Ab Dioc Tr Course 82 Edin Th Coll 92. **d** 86 **p** 94. Colombia 86-87; NSM Aberdeen St Marg *Ab* 87-88; Dioc Hosp Chapl 89-92; C Aberdeen St Mary 93-94; Bp's Chapl for Tr and Educn 93-94; P-in-c Ballater 95-96; R from 96; P-in-c Aboyne 95-96; R from 96; P-in-c Braemar from 95. *The Rectory, 7 Invercauld Road, Ballater, Aberdeenshire AB35 5RP* Tel (01339) 755726 Fax as telephone E-mail k.gibson@btinternet.com

GIBSON, Colin Taylor. b 54. Trin Coll Cam BA77. Oak Hill Th Coll DipHE88. **d** 88 **p** 89. C Thrybergh w Hooton Roberts *Sheff* 88-91; P-in-c Tinsley 91-96; TV Attercliffe, Darnall and Tinsley from 96. *St Lawrence's Vicarage, 24 Highgate, Sheffield S9 1WL* Tel 0114-244 1740

GIBSON, Dr David Francis. b 36. Magd Coll Cam BA57 BChir60 MB61. SW Minl Tr Course 84. **d** 90 **p** 91. NSM Newport, Bishops Tawton and Tawstock *Ex* 90-95; Chapl N Devon Distr Hosp Barnstaple 95-96; Perm to Offic *Ex* from 96. *Little Beara, Marwood, Barnstaple, Devon EX31 4EH* Tel (01271) 814876

GIBSON, David Innes. b 31. NDD53. Oak Hill Th Coll 56. **d** 59 **p** 60. C S Croydon Em *Cant* 59-62; C Washfield *Ex* 62-63; Asst Master and Chapl Blundells Sch Tiverton 63-64; Chapl Sutton Valence Sch Maidstone 64-68; Chapl Dean Close Sch Cheltenham 68-75; Asst Chapl and Ho Master 75-85; Asst Master Brightlands Sch Newnham-on-Severn 85-90; C Cheltenham St Mary, St Matt, St Paul and H Trin *Glouc* 91-96; rtd 96; Perm to Offic *Glouc* from 96. *2 Withyholt Park, Charlton Kings, Cheltenham, Glos GL53 9BP* Tel (01242) 511612

GIBSON, Douglas Harold (Doug). b 20. Portsm Dioc Tr Course. **d** 87. NSM Portsea St Luke *Portsm* 87-92; Perm to Offic from 92. *83 Middle Street, Southsea, Hants PO5 4BW* Tel (01705) 829769

GIBSON, The Ven George Granville. b 36. Cuddesdon Coll 69. **d** 71 **p** 72. C Tynemouth Cullercoats St Paul *Newc* 71-73; TV Cramlington 73-77; V Newton Aycliffe *Dur* 77-85; R Bishopwearmouth St Mich w St Hilda 85-90; TR Sunderland 90-93; RD Wearmouth 85-93; Hon Can Dur Cathl from 88; Adn Auckland from 93. *Glebe House, Sunderland Bridge, Durham DH6 5HB* Tel 0191-378 0273 Fax 378 3885 E-mail veng@gibven.demon.co.uk

GIBSON, Henry Edward. b 15. Keble Coll Ox BA41 DipTh42 MA46. St Steph Ho Ox 41. **d** 43 **p** 44. C Summertown *Ox* 43-49; Warden Youth Ho and Youth Org Scottish Episc Ch 49-51; C Farlington *Portsm* 51-56; V Ryde H Trin 56-63; V Waterlooville 63-81; rtd 81; Perm to Offic *Portsm* 81-96; Perm to Offic *Chich* from 81. *8 Worcester Road, Chichester, W Sussex PO19 4DJ* Tel (01243) 779194

GIBSON, Ian. b 48. Open Univ BA85 MSc MIPD MIMgt. S Dios Minl Tr Scheme 82. **d** 85 **p** 86. NSM Uckfield *Chich* 85-88; NSM Lt Horsted 85-88; NSM Isfield 85-88; V Fairwarp 88-93; P-in-c from 94; V High Hurstwood 88-93; P-in-c from 94. *The Vicarage, Fairwarp, Uckfield, E Sussex TN29 3BL* Tel (01825) 712277 Fax 713557 E-mail ian_gibson@compuserve.com

GIBSON, John George. b 20. Chich Th Coll 47. **d** 50 **p** 51. C Notting Hill St Mich and Ch Ch *Lon* 50-53; C Kenton 53-58; V Gunnersbury St Jas 58-70; V Upper Teddington SS Pet and Paul 70-84; rtd 84; Perm to Offic *Chich* from 85. *College of St Barnabas, Blackberry Lane, Lingfield, Surrey RH7 6NJ* Tel (01342) 870703

GIBSON, John Murray Hope. b 35. Dur Univ BA58 DipTh60. Cranmer Hall Dur 58. **d** 60 **p** 61. C Chester le Street *Dur* 60-63; C Stockton 63-68; V Denton and Ingleton 68-75; V Swalwell from 75; Chapl Dunston Hill Hosp Dur from 80. *The Vicarage, Whickham Bank, Swalwell, Newcastle upon Tyne NE16 3JL* Tel 0191-488 7538

GIBSON, John Noel Keith. b 22. MBE89. Ch Coll Cam MA48 Lon Univ BD59. Coll of Resurr Mirfield 45. **d** 47 **p** 48. C S Elmsall *Wakef* 47-51; Antigua 51-56; Virgin Is from 56; rtd 87; Can All SS Cathl Virgin Is from 89. *PO Box 65, Valley, Virgin Gorda, British Virgin Islands* Tel Virgin Islands (180949) 55216

GIBSON, Kenneth George Goudie. b 54. Glas Univ MA83 Edin Univ BD87. Edin Th Coll 83. **d** 88 **p** 89. C Glas St Marg *Glas* 88-90; R E Kilbride from 90. *St Mark's Rectory, Telford Road, East Kilbride, Glasgow G75 0HN* Tel (01355) 225222

GIBSON, Mrs Laura Mary. b 50. N Ord Course 85. **d** 88 **p** 94. Par Dn Foley Park *Worc* 88-90; Par Dn Kidderminster St Jo and H Innocents 90-94; TV 94-96; P-in-c Mamble w Bayton, Rock w Heightington etc from 96. *The Vicarage, Far Forest, Kidderminster, Worcs DY14 9TT* Tel (01299) 266580

GIBSON, Mark. b 48. **d** 84 **p** 85. OSB from 67; Abbot of Alton 82-90; Perm to Offic *Win* 84-95; NSM Paddington St Sav *Lon* from 90; Acting Bp's Chapl 90-91; Perm to Offic from 91; NSM Paddington St Mary from 95. *6 Park Place Villas, London W2 1SP, or Alton Abbey, Alton, Hants GU34 4AP* Tel (01420) 562145 Fax 0171-724 5332

GIBSON, Nigel Stephen David. b 53. St Barn Coll Adelaide DipMin87. **d** 87 **p** 87. Australia 87-89; C Boston *Linc* 90-91; Lect 90-91; P-in-c Stamford St Mary and St Mich 91-92; P-in-c Stamford Baron 91-92; R Stamford St Mary and St Martin from 92. *The Rectory, Pinfold Lane, Stamford, Lincs PE9 2LS* Tel (01780) 51233

GIBSON, Paul Saison. b 33. BA LTh. **d** 56 **p** 57. C Bloomsbury St Geo w St Jo *Lon* 56-59; Canada from 60. *600 Jarvis Street, Toronto, Ontario, Canada, M4Y 2J6*

GIBSON, Philip Nigel Scott. b 53. St Jo Coll Dur BA78. Cranmer Hall Dur DipTh79. **d** 79 **p** 80. C Yardley St Edburgha *Birm* 79-82; C Stratford-on-Avon w Bishopton *Cov* 82-84; Chapl SW Hosp Lon 84-91; Chapl St Thos Hosp Lon 84-91; Assoc Priest Newington St Paul *S'wark* 91-92; Chapl Charing Cross Hosp Lon 92-93; Chapl R Lon Hosp (Whitechapel) 93-94; Chapl Bedford Hosp NHS Trust from 95. *Chaplain's Office, Bedford Hospital, South Wing, Kempston Road, Bedford MK42 9DJ* Tel (01234) 355122

GIBSON, Raymond. b 23. Ely Th Coll 60. **d** 62 **p** 63. C Leic St Jas *Leic* 62-67; Succ Leic Cathl 67-68; Chapl Leic R Infirmary 67-68; Chapl Nottm City Hosp 68-84; V Barlings *Linc* 84-88; rtd 88. *11 Cornell Drive, Nottingham NG5 8RF*

GIBSON, Raymond Frank. b 34. Toronto Bible Coll BTh61 Tyndale Hall Bris 62. **d** 64 **p** 65. C Gt Horton *Bradf* 64-67; C Otley 67-72; V Fairlight *Chich* 72-83; V Hallwood *Ches* 83-85; R Freethorpe w Wickhampton, Halvergate etc *Nor* from 85; P-in-c Reedham w Cantley w Limpenhoe and Southwood from 94. *The Vicarage, 60 Lower Green, Freethorpe, Norwich NR13 3AH* Tel (01493) 700322

GIBSON, Canon Robert Swinton. b 26. Wadh Coll Ox BA50 MA55. Wells Th Coll 50. **d** 53 **p** 54. C Greenwich St Alfege w St Pet *S'wark* 53-61; Ind Missr 55-62; Hon Chapl to Bp S'wark 56-67; Sen Chapl S Lon Ind Miss 62-67; Nigeria 67-69; R Guisborough *York* 69-83; RD Guisborough 73-83; TR Halifax *Wakef* 83-94; Hon Can Wakef Cathl 85-94; RD Halifax 86-92; rtd 94; Perm to Offic *Wakef* from 94. *The Cottage, Hutton Buscel, Scarborough, N Yorkshire YO13 9LL* Tel (01723) 862133

GIBSON, The Ven Terence Allen (Terry). b 37. Jes Coll Cam BA61 MA65. Cuddesdon Coll 61. **d** 63 **p** 64. C Kirkby *Liv* 63-66; TV 72-75; TR 75-84; Warden Cen 63 66-75; Youth Chapl 66-72; RD Walton 79-84; Adn Suffolk *St E* 84-87; Adn Ipswich from 87. *99 Valley Road, Ipswich IP1 4NF* Tel (01473) 250333 Fax 286877

GIBSON, Thomas Thomson. b 23. Sarum Th Coll 62. **d** 63 **p** 64. C E w W Harnham *Sarum* 63-66; V Rowde 66-74; R Poulshot 67-74; V Badminton w Acton Turville *Glouc* 74-84; P-in-c Hawkesbury 81-84; V Badminton w Lt Badminton, Acton Turville etc 84-93; rtd 93; Perm to Offic *Glouc* from 93; Perm to Offic *B & W* from 95. *9 Lansdown Place West, Bath BA1 5EZ* Tel (01225) 337903 Fax 483638

GIDDENS, Leslie Vernon. b 29. Bps' Coll Cheshunt 54. **d** 56 **p** 57. C Harrow St Pet *Lon* 56-58; C Tottenham St Benet Fink 58-63; C-in-c Hayes St Nic CD 63-94; rtd 94. *6 Ashdown Road, Uxbridge, Middlesex UB10 0HY* Tel (01895) 232406

GIDDEY, Canon William Denys. b 17. Leeds Univ BA39. Coll of Resurr Mirfield 39. **d** 41 **p** 42. C Weymouth St Paul *Sarum* 41-43; C St Geo-in-the-East St Mary *Lon* 43-48; R Binbrook *Linc* 48-61; R Swinhope w Thorganby 48-61; Chapl Eastbourne Hosp Gp 61-83; Can and Preb Chich Cathl *Chich* 78-90; rtd 82; Perm to Offic *Chich* from 90. *70 Sidley Road, Eastbourne, E Sussex BN22 7JP* Tel (01323) 722918

GIDDINGS, Mrs Jaqueline Mary (Jackie). b 44. St Aid Coll Dur BA67. SW Minl Tr Course 91. **d** 94 **p** 95. C Plympton St Mary *Ex* from 94. *Church House, 9 Horswell Close, Plympton, Plymouth PL7 3NG* Tel (01752) 346485

GIDDINGS, John Norton Cornock. b 22. **d** 86 **p** 87. NSM Cromhall w Tortworth and Tytherington *Glouc* 86-90; Hon C Stockland w Dalwood *Ex* 90-95; Hon C Stockland, Dalwood, Kilmington and Shute from 95. *The Vicarage, Stockland, Honiton, Devon EX14 9EF* Tel (01404) 88401

✠**GIGGALL, The Rt Revd George Kenneth.** b 14. OBE61. Man Univ BA37 St Chad's Coll Dur DipTh38. **d** 39 **p** 40 **c** 73. C Cheetwood St Alb *Man* 39-41; C Reddish 41-45; Chapl RN 45-69; QHC 67-69; Dean Gib *Eur* 69-73; Bp St Helena 73-79; Aux Bp Eur 79-81; Chapl San Remo w Bordighera 80-81; rtd 81; Asst Bp Blackb from 81. *Fosbrooke House, 8 Clifton Drive, Lytham St Annes, Lancs FY8 5RQ* Tel (01253) 735683

GILBERT, Anthony John David. b 54. LRSC83 Open Univ BA91. Ripon Coll Cuddesdon 83. **d** 86 **p** 87. C Exning St Martin w Landwade *St E* 86-89; Chapl RAF from 89. *Chaplaincy Services (RAF), HQ, Personnel and Training Command, RAF Innsworth, Gloucester GL3 1EZ* Tel (01452) 712612 ext 5164 Fax 510828

GILBERT, Arthur John. b 57. LTCL76 GBSM79 Reading Univ PGCE80. Coll of Resurr Mirfield 88. **d** 91 **p** 92. C Uppingham w Ayston and Wardley w Belton *Pet* 91-94; C Armley w New Wortley *Ripon* 94-96; V Doncaster St Jude *Sheff* from 96. *The Vicarage, 132 Shadyside, Doncaster, S Yorkshire DN4 0DG* Tel (01302) 852057

GILBERT, Barry. b 46. Leeds Univ BA67. Coll of Resurr Mirfield 67. **d** 69 **p** 70. C Malvern Link w Cowleigh *Worc* 69-73; P-in-c Bromsgrove All SS 73-81; V 81-83; P-in-c Lower Mitton 83-88; V 88-92; V Stourport and Wilden from 92; RD Stourport from 93. *The Vicarage, Church Avenue, Stourport-on-Severn, Worcs DY13 9DD* Tel (01299) 822041

GILBERT, Caroline Margaret. b 62. Nottm Univ BTh90. St Jo Coll Nottm 87. **d** 90. Hon C Aston SS Pet and Paul *Birm* 90-93. *St Luke's Vicarage, 18 Queen Street, Cannock, Staffs WS11 1AE* Tel (01543) 577392

GILBERT, Miss Christine Lesley. b 44. DipHE. Trin Coll Bris 79. **dss** 85 **d** 86 **p** 94. Par Dn Bilston *Lich* 87-94; TV Penkridge Team from 94. *The Vicarage, Top Road, Acton Trussell, Stafford ST17 0RQ* Tel (01785) 712408

GILBERT, Christopher Anthony. b 60. Aston Univ BSc82. St Jo Coll Nottm 86. **d** 89 **p** 90. C Aston SS Pet and Paul *Birm* 89-93; TV Parr *Liv* 93-97; TV Cannock *Lich* from 97. *St Luke's Vicarage, 18 Queen Street, Cannock, Staffs WS11 1AE* Tel (01543) 577392

GILBERT, Frederick Herbert. b 14. Worc Ord Coll 64. **d** 66 **p** 67. C Ex St Paul *Ex* 66-69; C Paignton Ch Ch 69-73; TV Offwell,

Widworthy, Cotleigh, Farway etc 73-79; rtd 80; Lic to Offic *Ex* from 80. *17 Hoskings Court, Strode Road, Buckfastleigh, Devon TQ11 0PE* Tel (01364) 43321

GILBERT, Frederick Joseph. b 29. Lich Th Coll 58. **d** 59 **p** 60. C Westhoughton *Man* 59-62; V Goodshaw 62-68; R Crumpsall St Matt 68-75; RD Cheetham 70-74; RD N Man 74-75; V Rochdale St Aid 75-78; TV Rochdale 78-80; V Westhoughton 80-84; TR 84-87; AD Deane 85-87; R W Bowbrook *Worc* 87-89; R Bowbrook N 89-93; rtd 93. *Freshways, Main Road, Peopleton, Pershore, Worcs WR10 2EG* Tel (01905) 841629

GILBERT, John Edwin. b 28. FCA62. Bps' Coll Cheshunt 54. **d** 57 **p** 58. C Luton Ch Ch *St Alb* 57-60; C Gt Berkhamsted 60-64; India 65-71; Perm to Offic *St Alb* 71-77; Lic to Offic 77-86; Hon C Sunnyside w Bourne End 86-89; TV Padgate *Liv* 89-94; rtd 94; Perm to Offic *Heref* from 94. *4 Westgate Drive, Bridgnorth, Shropshire WV16 4QF* Tel (01746) 762611

GILBERT, John Michael. b 06. St Boniface Warminster. **d** 31 **p** 32. C St Ives *Truro* 31-34; Solomon Is 34-35; C Shrewsbury All SS *Lich* 36-38; Namibia 38-49; P-in-c Tolpuddle *Sarum* 50-51; C St Austell *Truro* 51-52; S Africa 52-59; V Davidstow w Otterham *Truro* 59-63; V Porthleven 63-74; Lic to Offic 74-78; rtd 75; Chapl to Bp George 78-85. *229 Bishop's-Lea, Village, George, 6530 South Africa* Tel George (441) 741748

GILBERT, Joseph. b 12. Chich Th Coll 33. **d** 36 **p** 37. C Bolton St Mark *Man* 36-39; C Withington St Crispin 39-43; R Ardwick St Matt 43-49; V Heyside 49-65; V Lever Bridge 65-76; rtd 77; Perm to Offic *Man* from 77. *159 Bolton Road, Turton, Bolton BL7 0AF* Tel (01204) 852736

GILBERT, Mrs Margaret Ann. b 39. Dub Inst of Adult Educn DPastMin89 TCD DipTh91. CITC 89. **d** 92 **p** 93. NSM Dublin Clontarf *D & G* 92-96; NSM Dublin Santry w Glasnevin and Finglas from 96. *67 Grange Park Road, Raheny, Dublin 5, Irish Republic* Tel Dublin (1) 848 1340

GILBERT (formerly GRAFTON), Mrs Mary. b 63. **d** 97. C Walsall Wood *Lich* from 97. *40 Church Street, Clayhanger, Brownhills, Walsall WS8 7EG*

GILBERT, Michael Victor. b 61. Dur Univ BA84 Westhill Coll Birm CYCW86. Trin Coll Bris DipThe94. **d** 94 **p** 95. C Chapeltown *Sheff* 94-97; V Brightside w Wincobank from 97. *The Vicarage, 24 Beacon Road, Sheffield S9 1AD* Tel 0114-281 9360

GILBERT, Philip Mark. b 62. Liv Univ BA84. Coll of Resurr Mirfield 84. **d** 87 **p** 88. C Frodsham *Ches* 87-89; C Stockton Heath 89-92; R Tangmere and Oving *Chich* from 92. *St Andrew's Vicarage, 21 Gibson Road, Tangmere, Chichester, W Sussex PO20 6JA* Tel (01243) 785089

GILBERT, Raymond. b 34. AKC61. **d** 62 **p** 63. C Newbold w Dunston *Derby* 62-66; PV and Succ S'wark Cathl *S'wark* 66-68; P-in-c Stuntney *Ely* 68-74; Prec and Sacr Ely Cathl 68-74; Min Can Cant Cathl *Cant* 74-79; Hon Min Can from 79; P-in-c Patrixbourne w Bridge and Bekesbourne 79-81; V from 81; RD E Bridge from 92. *The Vicarage, 23 High Street, Bridge, Canterbury, Kent CT4 5JZ* Tel (01227) 830250

GILBERT, Raymond Frederick. b 44. LNSM course 91. **d** 93 **p** 94. NSM Stowmarket *St E* from 93. *3 Violet Hill Road, Stowmarket, Suffolk IP14 1NE* Tel (01449) 677700

GILBERT, Roger Charles. b 46. Ex Coll Ox BA69 MA74 Nottm Univ MEd81. St Steph Ho Ox 69. **d** 71 **p** 72. NSM Bridgwater St Mary w Chilton Trinity *B & W* 71-74; NSM Rugeley *Lich* 74-81; NSM Cannock 81-83; NSM Wednesbury St Jas and St Jo from 83. *41 Stafford Road, Cannock, Staffs WS11 2AF* Tel (01543) 570531

GILBERT, Canon Roger Geoffrey. b 37. K Coll Lon BD69 AKC69. **d** 70 **p** 71. C Walton-on-Thames *Guildf* 70-74; R St Mabyn *Truro* 74-81; P-in-c Helland 74-81; P-in-c Madron 81-86; R Falmouth K Chas from 86; Hon Can Truro Cathl from 94; RD Carnmarth S from 94; Chapl to The Queen from 96. *The Rectory, Albany Road, Falmouth, Cornwall TR11 3RP* Tel (01326) 314176

GILBERT, Roy Alan. b 48. Birm Univ BEd70 Lon Univ DipTh79. Ripon Coll Cuddesdon 74. **d** 76 **p** 77. C Moseley St Mary *Birm* 76-82; Australia from 82. *Guildford Grammar School, 11 Terrace Road, Guildford, W Australia 6055* Tel Perth (9) 279 1135 or 377 9222 Fax 378 2778

GILBERT, Sidney Horace. b 34. Dur Univ BA58 MA69 Univ of Wales BD62 CertEd83. St Mich Coll Llan 58. **d** 61 **p** 62. C Colwyn Bay *St As* 61-63; C Llanrhos 63-69; R Penley and Bettisfield 69-78; V Brymbo and Bwlchgwyn 78-82; Univ of Wales (Swansea) *S & B* 82-83; R Beeston Regis *Nor* from 84; Holiday Chapl 84-91; Sen Chapl from 91. *All Saints' Rectory, Cromer Road, Beeston Regis, Cromer, Norfolk NR27 9NG* Tel (01263) 822163

GILBERTSON, Michael Robert. b 61. New Coll Ox BA82 MA92. St Jo Coll Dur BA91. **d** 97. C Surbiton St Matt *S'wark* from 97. *172 Ellerton Road, Surbiton, Surrey KT6 7UD* Tel 0181-399 3636

GILCHRIST, David John. b 51. Mert Coll Ox BA75 MA79. St Jo Coll Nottm DPS79. **d** 79 **p** 80. C Gt Ilford St Andr *Chelmsf* 79-81; C Buckhurst Hill 81-84; Chapl Dover Coll 84-96; Chapl Brentwood Sch Essex from 96; Perm to Offic *Chelmsf* from 96. *Brentwood School, Brentwood, Essex CM15 8AS* Tel (01277) 214580

GILCHRIST, Gavin Frank. b 53. AKC74. Coll of Resurr Mirfield 76. **d** 77 **p** 78. C Newbold w Dunston *Derby* 77-80; C Addlestone *Guildf* 80-84; V Blackpool St Mary *Blackb* 84-92; P-in-c Carl St Herbert w St Steph *Carl* 92-97; V from 97. *St Herbert's Vicarage, Blackwell Road, Carlisle CA2 4RA* Tel (01228) 23375

GILCHRIST, Lawrence Edward. b 29. Liv Univ BSc52. NW Ord Course 74. **d** 76 **p** 77. NSM Buxton w Burbage and King Sterndale *Derby* 76-83; V Chinley w Buxworth 83-94; rtd 94. *18 Miles Hawk Way, Mildenhall, Bury St Edmunds, Suffolk IP28 7SE* Tel (01638) 711360

GILCHRIST, Spencer. b 66. QUB BA88. BTh. **d** 91 **p** 92. C Ballynafeigh St Jude *D & D* 91-97; I Connor w Antrim St Patr *Conn* from 97. *Connor Rectory, Church Road, Kells, Ballymena, Co Antrim BT42 3JU* Tel (01266) 891254

GILDING, James Peter. b 33. Leeds Univ BA64. Ely Th Coll 61. **d** 63 **p** 64. C Chorley St Geo *Blackb* 63-66; C Pemberton St Fran Kitt Green *Liv* 66-69; P-in-c Terrington St John *Ely* 69-73; P-in-c Walpole St Andrew 69-73; V Elm 74-81; TR Stanground and Farcet 81-89; V Haslingfield 89-95; R Harlton 89-95; R Haslingfield w Harlton and Gt and Lt Eversden 95-96; rtd 96. *Glenrosa, Barton-le-street, Malton, N Yorkshire YO17 0PL* Tel (01653) 628870

GILES, Canon Barry James. b 35. Kelham Th Coll 54. **d** 59 **p** 60. C Leytonstone St Marg w St Columba *Chelmsf* 59-62; Prec Gib Cathl *Eur* 62-66; V Darwen St Geo *Blackb* 66-69; V Forest Gate St Edm *Chelmsf* 69-73; R Jersey St Pet *Win* from 73; Vice-Dean Jersey from 84; Hon Can Win Cathl from 93. *St Peter's Rectory, Jersey, Channel Islands* Tel (01534) 481805

GILES, Brother. *See* HILL, The Rt Revd Michael John Giles

GILES, Brother. *See* SPRENT, Michael Francis

GILES, Edward Alban. b 34. Bps' Coll Cheshunt. **d** 58 **p** 59. C Colne St Bart *Blackb* 58-61; C Warrington St Paul *Liv* 61-63; S Africa 63-70; Chapl HM Pris Camp Hill 70-75; Chapl HM Pris Stafford 75-83; Chapl HM Young Offender Inst Hollesley Bay Colony 83-94; rtd 94; Sub-Chapl HM Pris Blundeston from 94. *The Hollies, Ferry Farm Drive, Sutton Hoo, Woodbridge, Suffolk IP12 3DR* Tel (01394) 387486 Fax 411071

GILES, Canon Eric Francis. b 34. Sarum Th Coll 61. **d** 63 **p** 64. C Plympton St Mary *Ex* 63-71; R Dumbleton w Wormington *Glouc* 71-77; P-in-c Toddington w Stanley Pontlarge 71-77; R Dumbleton w Wormington and Toddington 77-79; V Churchdown St Jo from 79; Hon Can Glouc Cathl from 95. *St John's Vicarage, St John's Avenue, Churchdown, Gloucester GL3 2DA* Tel (01452) 713421

GILES, Frank Edwin. b 22. St Aid Birkenhead 50. **d** 53 **p** 54. C Chester le Street *Dur* 53-56; V Sacriston 56-70; V Hook *S'wark* 70-81; V Langley St Mich *Birm* 81-88; rtd 88. *5 Victoria Terrace, Bourton-on-the-Water, Cheltenham, Glos GL52 6BN* Tel (01451) 820486

GILES, Gordon John. b 66. Lanc Univ BA88 Magd Coll Cam PhD95. Ridley Hall Cam BA95 CTM95. **d** 95 **p** 96. C Chesterton Gd Shep *Ely* from 95. *19 Hurrell Road, Cambridge CB4 3RQ* Tel (01223) 464348

GILES, Graeme John. b 56. Linc Th Coll 82. **d** 85 **p** 86. C Prestbury *Glouc* 85-88; C Paulsgrove *Portsm* 88-96; V Friern Barnet St Pet le Poer *Lon* from 96. *St Peter's Vicarage, 163 Colney Hatch Lane, London N10 1HA* Tel 0181-883 1526

GILES (née WILLIAMS), Mrs Gwenllian (Gwen). b 34. RSCN55 SRN58 SCM60. WMMTC 88. **d** 92 **p** 94. NSM Bromsgrove St Jo *Worc* from 92. *22 Hill Lane, Bromsgrove, Worcs B60 2BP* Tel (01527) 578313

GILES, Canon John Robert. b 36. Em Coll Cam BA60 MA65. Ripon Hall Ox 60. **d** 61 **p** 62. C Lowestoft St Marg *Nor* 61-65; Chapl UEA 65-72; R Kidbrooke St Jas *S'wark* 72-79; Sub-Dean Greenwich 74-79; V Sheff St Mark Broomhall *Sheff* 79-87; Ind Chapl 79-92; Can Res Sheff Cathl 87-92; V Lee Gd Shep w St Pet *S'wark* from 92. *The Vicarage, 47 Handen Road, London SE12 8NR* Tel 0181-852 5270

GILES, Maurice Alfred Douglas. b 15. Bps' Coll Cheshunt 66. **d** 66 **p** 67. C Finchley H Trin *Lon* 66-69; C Southgate St Andr 69-71; V New Southgate St Paul 71-75; C Friern Barnet St Jas 75-80; rtd 80; Perm to Offic *Lon* from 80. *66 Granville Road, London N12 0HT* Tel 0181-346 0214

GILES, Peter Michael Osmaston. b 40. Solicitor 65. S Dios Minl Tr Scheme 85. **d** 88 **p** 89. Hon C Wootton Bassett *Sarum* 88-90; Lic to RD Calne from 91. *The Old Vicarage, Honeyhill, Wootton Bassett, Swindon SN4 7AZ* Tel (01793) 852643

GILES, Canon Richard Stephen. b 40. MRTPI71 Newc Univ BA63 MLitt88. Cuddesdon Coll 64. **d** 65 **p** 66. C Higham Ferrers w Chelveston *Pet* 65-68; Perm to Offic *Ox* 69; C Oakengates *Lich* 70; C Stevenage St Geo *St Alb* 71-75; P-in-c Howdon Panns *Newc* 75-76; TV Willington Team 76-79; Bp's Adv for Planning *Pet* 79-87; V Pet St Jude 79-87; Par Development Officer *Wakef* from 87; P-in-c Huddersfield St Thos 87-94; Hon Can Wakef Cathl from 94; V Huddersfield St Thos from 94. *St Thomas's Vicarage, 78 Bankfield Road, Huddersfield HD1 3HR* Tel (01484) 420660

GILES, Robert Medwin (Bob). b 37. Man Univ BA(Econ)58 PGCE59. Ripon Hall Ox 64. **d** 66 **p** 67. C Peel *Man* 66-69; C

Alverstoke *Portsm* 69-71; P-in-c Edale *Derby* 71-79; Warden Champion Ho Youth Tr Cen 71-79; Sen Youth Officer *York* 79-86; P-in-c Shipley *Chich* 86-87; V 87-91; Area Sec (Dios Pet & St Alb) USPG 91-92; R Broughton w Loddington and Cransley etc *Pet* from 92. *The Rectory, Gate Lane, Broughton, Kettering, Northants NN14 1ND* Tel (01536) 791373

GILES, Susan Jane. b 58. BSc. **dss** 83 **d** 92 **p** 94. Balsall Heath St Paul *Birm* 83-85; Asst Chapl Southmead Hosp Bris 86-90; Asst Chapl HM Rem Cen Pucklechurch 90-96; Asst Chapl HM Pris Bris from 92. *HM Prison, Horfield, Bristol BS7 8PS* Tel 0117-942 6661

GILES, Timothy David. b 46. FCA69. Oak Hill Th Coll DipTh90. **d** 90 **p** 91. C Ipswich St Marg *St E* 90-94; C Reigate St Mary *S'wark* from 94. *63 Chart Lane, Reigate, Surrey RH2 7EA* Tel (01737) 243085

GILFORD, George. b 49. St Kath Coll Liv CertEd72 LTCL86. N Ord Course 88. **d** 91 **p** 92. NSM Gt Crosby St Faith *Liv* from 91. *Flat 2, 17 Alexandra Road, Waterloo, Liverpool L22 1RJ* Tel 0151-920 5744

GILKES, Donald Martin. b 47. St Jo Coll Nottm 78. **d** 80 **p** 81. C Conisbrough *Sheff* 80-84; P-in-c Balne 84-86; P-in-c Hensall 84-86; TV Gt Snaith 86-88; V Whittle-le-Woods *Blackb* from 88. *The Vicarage, Preston Road, Whittle-le-Woods, Chorley, Lancs PR6 7PS* Tel (01257) 263306

GILKS, Peter Martin. b 51. SRN77 Nottm Univ BMus72. Ripon Coll Cuddesdon 82. **d** 84 **p** 85. C Bitterne Park *Win* 84-87; TV Basingstoke 87-93; R Abbotts Ann and Upper and Goodworth Clatford from 93. *The Rectory, Upper Clatford, Andover, Hants SP11 7QP* Tel (01264) 352906

GILL, Alan Gordon. b 42. Sarum & Wells Th Coll 73. **d** 75 **p** 76. C Wimborne Minster *Sarum* 75-78; R Winterbourne Stickland and Turnworth etc 78-86; V Verwood from 86. *The Vicarage, Dewlands Way, Verwood, Dorset BH31 6JN* Tel (01202) 822298

GILL, Christopher John Sutherland. b 28. Selw Coll Cam BA52 MA70. Ely Th Coll 52. **d** 54 **p** 55. C Portslade St Nic *Chich* 54-58; C Goring-by-Sea 58-60; Chapl St Edm Sch Cant 60-76; Chapl Bennett Memorial Sch Tunbridge Wells from 76; Hon C Tunbridge Wells K Chas *Roch* 77-93; rtd 93; Perm to Offic *Roch* from 93. *Flat 1, Hurstleigh, Hurstwood Lane, Tunbridge Wells, Kent TN4 8YA* Tel (01892) 528409

GILL, David Brian Michael. b 55. Southn Univ BTh88. Sarum & Wells Th Coll 83. **d** 86 **p** 87. C Honiton, Gittisham, Combe Raleigh, Monkton etc *Ex* 86-89; C E Teignmouth 89; C W Teignmouth 89; C Teignmouth, Ideford w Luton, Ashcombe etc 90-91; TV Ex St Thos and Em from 91. *Emmanuel Vicarage, 49 Okehampton Road, Exeter EX4 1EL* Tel (01392) 435840

GILL, Donald Maule Harvell. b 08. Keble Coll Ox BA33 MA39. Wells Th Coll 34. **d** 35 **p** 36. C Bournemouth St Andr *Win* 35-38; C-in-c Bournemouth H Epiphany 38-45; V Micheldever 45-70; R Minstead 71-80; rtd 80; Perm to Offic *Win* 80-95. *4 Hereward Close, Romsey, Hants SO51 5RA* Tel (01794) 514591

GILL, Frank Emmanuel. b 34. Oak Hill Th Coll 73. **d** 75 **p** 76. Chapl Race Relns *Lon* 75-78; C Shepherd's Bush St Steph w St Thos 76-77; P-in-c Kensal Town St Thos w St Andr and St Phil 79-82; Barbados from 82; rtd 96. *Clifden, Jackmans, St Michael, Barbados* Tel Barbados 246

GILL, Mrs Gabrielle Mary (Gay). **d** 90 **p** 94. NSM Timperley *Ches* from 90. *The Croft, 3 Harrop Road, Hale, Altrincham, Cheshire WA15 9BU* Tel 0161-928 1800

GILL, Gary George. b 44. Culham Coll Ox CertEd70. Cant Sch of Min 85. **d** 87 **p** 88. C Addlestone *Guildf* 87-90; C Buckland in Dover w Buckland Valley *Cant* from 90; Chapl Buckland Hosp Dover from 90. *24 Dryden Road, Dover, Kent CT16 2BX* Tel (01304) 822004

GILL, Geoffrey Fitzell. b 17. Selw Coll Cam BA39 MA43. Linc Th Coll 39. **d** 41 **p** 42. C Wellingborough All SS *Pet* 41-46; C Knighton St Jo *Leic* 46-51; V Enderby 51-82; rtd 82. *The Poplars, Port Eynon, Gower, Swansea SA3 1NN* Tel (01792) 390206

GILL, James Joseph. b 45. Pontifical Univ Maynooth BD78. **d** 77 **p** 78. In RC Ch 77-82; C Howden TM *York* 82-83; TV 83-86; P-in-c Wragby w Sharlston *Wakef* 86-88; V Sharlston 88-91; V Tilehurst St Geo *Ox* from 91. *St George's Vicarage, 98 Grovelands Road, Reading RG3 2PD* Tel 0118-958 8354 or 950 9695

✠**GILL, The Rt Revd Kenneth Edward.** b 32. Hartley Victoria Coll. **d** 58 **p** 60 **c** 72. In Ch of S India 58-80; Bp Karnataka Cen 72-80; Asst Bp Newc from 80. *83 Kenton Road, Newcastle upon Tyne NE3 4NL* Tel 0191-285 2220 Fax 213 0728

GILL, Mrs Mary. b 20. Nottm Univ BA42. St Jo Coll Nottm CertCS43. **d** 88 **p** 96. NSM Alston Team *Newc* 88-90; rtd 90. *Old School, Garrigill, Alston, Cumbria CA9 3DP* Tel (01434) 381594

GILL, Michael John. b 59. K Coll Lon BA81 AKC81. St Mich Coll Llan BD85. **d** 85 **p** 86. Min Can St Woolos Cathl *Mon* 85-90; Chapl St Woolos Hosp Newport 87-90; Succ Heref Cathl *Heref* 90-93; C Heref St Jo 90-93; TV Ebbw Vale *Mon* 93-96; V Tonypandy w Clydach Vale *Llan* from 96. *The Vicarage, Richards Terrace, Tonypandy CF40 2LD* Tel (01443) 437759

GILL, Richard Ward. b 26. Lon Univ BD53. Oak Hill Th Coll 53. **d** 54 **p** 55. C Cambridge St Andr Less *Ely* 54-56; CMS 56-64; C Dagenham *Chelmsf* 64-65; V St Alb St Paul *St Alb* 65-91; rtd 91; Perm to Offic *Ex* from 92. *50 Woodbury Park, Axminster, Devon EX13 5QY*

GILL, Canon Robin Morton. b 44. K Coll Lon BD66 AKC66 Lon Univ PhD69 Birm Univ MSocSc72. **d** 68 **p** 69. C Rugby St Andr *Cov* 68-71; Papua New Guinea 71-72; Lect Th Edin Univ 72-86; Sen Lect 86-88; Assoc Dean Faculty of Div 85-88; P-in-c Edin SS Phil and Jas *Edin* 73-75; P-in-c Ford *Newc* 75-87; Perm to Offic 87-92; P-in-c Coldstream *Edin* 87-92; Wm Leech Prof Applied Th Newc Univ 88-92; Mich Ramsey Prof Modern Th Kent Univ from 92; Hon Can Cant Cathl *Cant* from 92. *Rutherford College, The University, Canterbury, Kent CT2 7NX* Tel (01227) 764000 or 781976 Fax 475473

GILL, Stanley. b 11. Clifton Th Coll 37. **d** 39 **p** 40. C Scotswood *Newc* 39-40; CF 40-46; Hon CF from 46; C Woodhorn w Newbiggin *Newc* 46-49; C Hornsea and Goxhill *York* 49-50; V Chatton w Chillingham *Newc* 50-60; V Alston cum Garrigill w Nenthead and Kirkhaugh 60-67; V Cornhill w Carham 67-74; V Branxton 71-74; rtd 76. *40 Prince of Wales Apartments, Esplanade, Scarborough, N Yorkshire YO11 2BB* Tel (01723) 507275

GILL, Stanley. b 34. Sarum Th Coll 66. **d** 68 **p** 69. C Ipswich St Mary at Stoke w St Pet & St Mary Quay *St E* 68-73 and 78-80; TV Ipswich St Mary at Stoke w St Pet & St Mary Quay 80-82; V Bury St Edmunds St Geo 73-78; P-in-c Childe Okeford, Manston, Hammoon and Hanford *Sarum* 82-89; R The Lulworths, Winfrith Newburgh and Chaldon 89-94; R Hazelbury Bryan and the Hillside Par from 94. *The Rectory, Hazelbury Bryan, Sturminster Newton, Dorset DT10 2ED* Tel (01258) 817251

GILL, Thomas. b 21. St Aid Birkenhead 62. **d** 63 **p** 64. C Newland St Aug *York* 63-67; V Burstwick w Thorngumbald 67-78; RD S Holderness 74-78; R Brandesburton 78-86; RD N Holderness 80-86; rtd 87; Perm to Offic *York* from 87. *Bellfield, Arnold Lane, Arnold, Hull HU11 5HP* Tel (01964) 562282

GILL, Timothy Charles (Tim). b 66. Newc Univ BA88. Westcott Ho Cam 89. **d** 92 **p** 93. C N Hull St Mich *York* 92-96; P-in-c Sculcoates St Paul w Ch Ch and St Silas from 96; P-in-c Hull St Mary Sculcoates from 96. *St Paul's Vicarage, Bridlington Avenue, Sculcoates, Hull HU2 0DU* Tel (01482) 224370

GILL, William. b 08. St Aid Birkenhead 59. **d** 60 **p** 61. C Menston w Woodhead *Bradf* 60-63; V Cowling 63-68; V Austwick 68-78; rtd 78; Perm to Offic *Bradf* 79-85; Perm to Offic *Linc* from 85. *14 Woodland Avenue, Skellingthorpe, Lincoln LN6 5TE* Tel (01522) 682529

GILLAN, Dr Ian Thomson. b 15. Aber Univ MA37 BD40 Edin Univ PhD43. **d** 52 **p** 53. In RC Ch 52-72; C Aberdeen St Andr *Ab* 73-74; P-in-c Fochabers *Mor* 74-75; P-in-c Aberlour 74-75; Provost St Andr Cathl Inverness 75; P-in-c Aberdeen St Clem *Ab* 76-78; rtd 79; Perm to Offic *Ab* from 79. *5 Park Crescent, Oldmeldrum, Aberdeen AB51 0DH* Tel (01651) 872308

GILLARD, Geoffrey Vernon (Geoff). b 48. Man Univ BA70 Nottm Univ MPhil80. Trin Coll Umuahia Nigeria 72 St Jo Coll Nottm 74. **d** 78 **p** 79. C Aughton Ch Ch *Liv* 78-81; Hong Kong 81-87; Dir of Studies St Alb Dio Minl Tr Scheme *St Alb* 87-92; Prin St Alb Dio Minl Tr Scheme from 92. *17 Eastmoor Park, Harpenden, Herts AL5 1BN* Tel (01582) 762005

GILLESPIE, George Henry. b 20. SS Coll Cam BA46 MA55. Cuddesdon Coll 46. **d** 48 **p** 49. C Wigan All SS *Liv* 48-53; C Ashbourne w Mapleton and Clifton *Derby* 53-55; V Allenton and Shelton Lock 56-71; Chapl Derby High Sch for Girls 58-71; V Bath Ascension *B & W* 71-78; P-in-c Norton St Philip w Hemington, Hardington etc 78-81; R 81-85; rtd 85; Perm to Offic *B & W* from 86. *18 South Lea Road, Bath BA1 3RW* Tel (01225) 339023

GILLESPIE, Michael David. b 41. EMMTC 86. **d** 89 **p** 90. NSM Countesthorpe w Foston *Leic* from 89. *3 Penfold Drive, Countesthorpe, Leicester LE8 3TP* Tel 0116-278 1130

GILLETT, Brian Alan Michael. b 42. ARICS73. Chich Th Coll. **d** 82 **p** 83. C Tupsley *Heref* 82-86; R Kingstone w Clehonger and Eaton Bishop 86-89; P-in-c Thruxton 89; P-in-c Allensmore 89; R Kingstone w Clehonger, Eaton Bishop etc from 89. *The Rectory, Kingstone, Hereford HR2 9EY* Tel (01981) 250350

GILLETT, Canon David Keith. b 45. Leeds Univ BA65 MPhil68. Oak Hill Th Coll 66. **d** 68 **p** 69. C Watford St Luke *St Alb* 68-71; Sec Pathfinders and CYFA N Area 71-74; Lect St Jo Coll Nottm 74-79; Ch of Ireland Renewal Cen 80-82; V Luton Lewsey St Hugh *St Alb* 82-88; Prin Trin Coll Bris from 88; Hon Can Bris Cathl *Bris* from 91. *16 Ormerod Road, Bristol BS9 1BB* Tel 0117-968 2646 or 968 2803 Fax 968 7470 E-mail david.gillett @bristol.ac.uk

GILLETT, Victor Henry John. b 31. Open Univ BA83 BTh87 Open Univ MTh94. Clifton Th Coll 59. **d** 62 **p** 63. C Walton Breck *Liv* 62-65; C Wednesfield Heath *Lich* 65-68; V Tipton St Paul 68-76; V Moulton *Pet* 76-92; TV Worthing Ch the King *Chich* from 92; Chapl Ramsay Hall from 92. *85 Heene Road, Worthing, W Sussex BN11 4PP* Tel (01903) 218026

GILLETT, Vincent. b 30. FCollP81 Lon Univ BSc55 UEA MSc72 DipSMan76. Chich Th Coll 59. **d** 61 **p** 62. C Blackpool St Mich *Blackb* 61-63; Ghana 63-72; Lic to Offic *Liv* 72-79; Lic to Offic *Ex* 79-84; Hd Master St Wilfrid's Sch Ex 79-84; R Atherington and High Bickington 84-94; V Burrington 84-94; rtd 95. *Birchy*

Barton Lodge, 2 Honiton Road, Heavitree, Exeter EX1 3EA Tel (01392) 436393

GILLETT, William Charles. b 05. Sarum Th Coll 28. **d** 31 **p** 32. C Southampton St Mary w H Trin *Win* 31-37; C Sunningdale *Ox* 37-40; C Tiverton St Andr *Ex* 40-44; R Sampford Peverell, Uplowman, Holcombe Rogus etc 44-49; R Kentisbeare w Blackborough 49-51; V Dunkeswell, Sheldon and Luppitt 49-51; R E w W Anstey 51-78; rtd 78; Perm to Offic *Ex* from 78; Perm to Offic *B & W* 81-93. *Sarum, East Anstey, Tiverton, Devon EX16 9JP* Tel (01398) 341284

GILLHAM, Martin John. b 45. Wilson Carlile Coll IDC66 Qu Coll Birm 72. **d** 75 **p** 76. C Whitley Ch Ch *Ox* 75-78; TV Crowmarsh Gifford w Newnham Murren 78-79; TV Wallingford w Crowmarsh Gifford etc 79-83; V Kintbury w Avington 83-94; Dioc Lay Min Adv and Warden of Readers 89-97; Thames Regional Guardian SSF 93-94; Prov Chapl Third Order SSF from 95; P-in-c W Wycombe w Bledlow Ridge, Bradenham and Radnage *Ox* from 94. *The Rectory, Church Lane, West Wycombe, High Wycombe, Bucks HP14 3AH* Tel (01494) 529988

GILLHAM, Mrs Patricia Anne. b 40. Wilson Carlile Coll IDC66 Ox Min Course CBTS93. **d** 93 **p** 94. Par Dn Kintbury w Avington *Ox* 93-94; C 94-95; C W Wycombe w Bledlow Ridge, Bradenham and Radnage from 95. *The Rectory, West Wycombe, High Wycombe, Bucks HP14 3AH* Tel (01494) 529988

GILLHESPEY, Canon Clive. b 28. Lon Univ DipTh66 BD73. Cranmer Hall Dur 63. **d** 65 **p** 66. C Barrow St Geo w St Luke *Carl* 65-69; V Flookburgh 69-74; R Barrow St Geo w St Luke 74-81; TR 81-92; Hon Can Carl Cathl 84-92; rtd 92; Perm to Offic *Carl* from 92. *Canon's Court, 43 Holyoake Avenue, Barrow-in-Furness, Cumbria LA13 9LH* Tel (01229) 839041

GILLIAN, Ronald Trevor. b 57. Ulster Univ DipMus77 MTD78 QUB BEd89 TCD BTh93. CITC 90. **d** 93 **p** 94. C Belfast St Donard *D & D* 93-96; I Aghalurcher w Tattykeeran, Cooneen etc *Clogh* from 96. *St Ronan's Rectory, Owenskerry Lane, Killarbran, Fivemiletown, Co Tyrone BT75 0SR* Tel (01365) 531822

GILLIAT, Canon Patrick Neville. b 10. G&C Coll Cam BA32 MA36. Tyndale Hall Bris 32. **d** 34 **p** 35. C Ox St Ebbe *Ox* 34-36; C S Harrow St Paul *Lon* 36-38; Lon Dioc Home Missr Oakwood St Thos 38-41; V 41-48; CF (EC) 44-46; V Brompton H Trin *Lon* 49-69; Chapl Chelsea Hosp for Women 50-54; Preb St Paul's Cathl 58-69; Can Res Sheff Cathl *Sheff* 69-76; RD Kensington *Lon* 60-65; Succ Sheff Cathl *Sheff* 69-76; rtd 76; Perm to Offic *B & W* 76-93. *Amberley, Sleepers Hill, Winchester SO22 4NB* Tel (01962) 865976

GILLIBRAND, John Nigel. b 60. Ox Univ BA82 MA86 Lon Univ PGCE83. **d** 88 **p** 89. C Dolgellau w Llanfachreth and Brithdir etc *Ban* 88-90; C Llanbeblig w Caernarfon and Betws Garmon etc 90-91; V Ffestiniog w Blaenau Ffestiniog 91-97; V Llandegfan w Llandysilio from 97. *6 Lon Ganol, Cae Tros Lon, Menai Bridge LL59 5LU* Tel (01248) 715598

GILLIES, Dr Robert Arthur (Bob). b 51. Edin Univ BD77 St Andr Univ PhD91. Edin Th Coll 73. **d** 77 **p** 78. C Falkirk *Edin* 77-80; C Edin Ch Ch 80-84; Chapl Napier Coll 80-84; Chapl Dundee Univ *Bre* 84-90; R St Andrews St Andr *St And* from 91; Dioc Dir of Ords from 96. *St Andrew's Rectory, Queen's Terrace, St Andrews, Fife KY16 9QF* Tel (01334) 473344

GILLIGAN, Harry. b 07. Dur Univ 56. **d** 58 **p** 59. C Southsea St Pet *Portsm* 58-66; V Everton St Polycarp *Liv* 66-68; Chapl to the Deaf (Southport) 71-79; rtd 74; Perm to Offic *Win* 82-95; Perm to Offic *Portsm* from 88. *4 Lampeter Avenue, Cosham, Portsmouth PO6 2AL* Tel (01705) 324710

GILLING, John Reginald. b 25. Cam Univ BA49 MA51 MLitt55. Cuddesdon Coll 53. **d** 55 **p** 56. C Romford St Alb *Chelmsf* 55-58; C Cambridge St Mary Less *Ely* 58-62; Chapl Ch Ch Ox 62-71; V Pimlico St Mary Graham Terrace *Lon* 71-90; AD Westmr St Marg 79-85; rtd 90; Perm to Offic *Chich* from 90. *49 Westgate, Chichester, W Sussex PO19 3EZ* Tel (01243) 775169

GILLINGHAM, John Bruce. b 48. Ch Ch Ox BA69 MA74. St Jo Coll Nottm BA73. **d** 73 **p** 74. C Plymouth St Andr w St Paul and St Geo *Ex* 73-77; C Ox St Aldate w H Trin *Ox* 78; Chapl Jes Coll Ox 78-88; Chapl Ox Pastorate 79-88; Dioc Missr *Birm* 88-92; R Ox St Clem *Ox* from 92. *St Clement's Rectory, 58 Rectory Road, Oxford OX4 1BW* Tel (01865) 248735

GILLINGHAM, Michael John. b 46. Univ of Wales (Swansea) DSCE80 Hull Univ MA90. Chich Th Coll 68. **d** 71 **p** 72. C Llanharan w Peterston-super-Montem *Llan* 71-73; C Skewen 73-76; Neath Deanery Youth Chapl 74-76; Perm to Offic 79-80; TV Kirkby *Liv* 76-77; Youth Chapl *Ches* 77-79; Perm to Offic *St Alb* 80-83; Sen Youth Worker 80-83; TV Sheff Manor *Sheff* 83-88; Chapl Sheff Sea Cadets from 87; R Frecheville from 88. *Frecheville Rectory, Brackenfield Grove, Sheffield S12 4XS* Tel 0114-239 9555

GILLINGS, The Ven Richard John. b 45. St Chad's Coll Dur BA67. Linc Th Coll 68. **d** 70 **p** 71. C Altrincham St Geo *Ches* 70-75; P-in-c Stockport St Thos 75-77; R 77-83; P-in-c Stockport St Pet 78-83; TR Birkenhead Priory 83-93; RD Birkenhead 85-93; Hon Can Ches Cathl from 92; V Bramhall 93-94; Adn Macclesfield from 94. *The Vicarage, Robin's Lane, Bramhall, Stockport, Cheshire SK7 2PE* Tel 0161-439 2254

GILLION, Canon Frederick Arthur. b 08. ALCD30 St Jo Coll Dur LTh30 BA31 MA34. **d** 31 **p** 32. C Gorleston St Andr *Nor* 31-34; C Tunbridge Wells St Jo *Roch* 34-35; V Mile Cross *Nor* 35-50; V Docking 50-54; V Sprowston 54-61; Hon Can Nor Cathl 59-75; Dir of RE 61-69; R Beeston Regis 69-75; rtd 75; Perm to Offic *Nor* from 75. *66 The Street, Ingworth, Norwich NR11 6AE* Tel (01263) 732583

GILLION, Robert Alan. b 51. LRAM. Sarum & Wells Th Coll 81. **d** 83 **p** 84. C E Dereham *Nor* 83-86; C Richmond St Mary w St Matthias and St Jo *S'wark* 86-90; Hong Kong from 90. *37A Seahorse Lane, Discovery Bay, Lantau Island, Hong Kong* Tel Hong Kong (852) 987-7106 Fax 987 8691

GILLIONS, Michael George. b 37. Ch Ch Ox MA65 Keele Univ PGCE74. W of England Minl Tr Course 93. **d** 96 **p** 97. NSM Dorrington w Leebotwood, Longnor, Stapleton etc *Heref* from 96. *The Maltsters, Dorrington, Shrewsbury SY5 7JD* Tel (01743) 718550

GILLMAN, Noel Francis. b 26. St D Dioc Tr Course St D Coll Lamp St Mich Coll Llan. **d** 79 **p** 80. NSM Llanelli *St D* 79-83; C 83-85; TV Tenby 85-91; rtd 91. *4 Oaklands, Swiss Valley, Llanelli SA14 8DA* Tel (01554) 772663

GILLMOR, Canon Samuel Frederick. b 29. St Aid Birkenhead. **d** 62 **p** 63. C Carlow Union *C & O* 62-64; I Fenagh Union 64-68; I Maryborough w Dysart Enos 68-79; Preb Ossory Cathl 78-79; Preb Leighlin Cathl 78-79; I Clane w Donadea *M & K* 79-84; I Mullingar, Portnashangan, Moyliscar, Kilbixy etc 84-93; Can Meath 92-93; I Achonry w Tubbercurry and Killoran *T, K & A* from 93; Can Achonry Cathl from 93. *Back Acre, Carrowdubh, Strandhill, Co Sligo, Irish Republic* Tel Sligo (71) 68571

GILLUM, Thomas Alan. b 55. Ex Univ BSc76. Cranmer Hall Dur 87. **d** 89 **p** 90. C Brompton H Trin w Onslow Square St Paul *Lon* 89-94; P-in-c Paddington St Steph w St Luke from 94. *St Stephen's Vicarage, 25 Talbot Road, London W2 5JF* Tel 0171-792 2283

GILMAN, Charles Philip. b 12. Tyndale Hall Bris 39. **d** 41 **p** 42. C Kirkdale St Mary *Liv* 41-43; C Wellington w Eyton *Lich* 43-46; Perm to Offic *Mon* 47-50; V Leyton St Cath *Chelmsf* 50-64; R Marks Tey 64-74; V Leigh *S'wark* 74-81; rtd 81; Perm to Offic *Win* 81-95. *36 Canon Street, Winchester, Hants SO23 9JJ* Tel (01962) 867980

GILMORE, Henry. b 51. Man Univ BA72 TCD BD82. CITC 75. **d** 75 **p** 76. C Arm St Mark w Aghavilly *Arm* 75-78; C Dublin St Patr Cathl Gp *D & G* 78-81; I Stranorlar w Meenglas and Kilteevogue *D & R* 81-84; I Achill w Dugort, Castlebar and Turlough *T, K & A* 84-91; I Moville w Greencastle, Donagh, Cloncha etc *D & R* from 91. *The Rectory, Castlebar, Moville, Co Donegal, Irish Republic* Tel Buncrana (77) 82572

GILMOUR, Ian Hedley. b 57. Ex Univ LLB Lon Univ BD. Wycliffe Hall Ox 80. **d** 83 **p** 84. C Harold Wood *Chelmsf* 83-86; C Thame w Towersey *Ox* 86-91; V Streatham Vale H Redeemer *S'wark* from 91. *The Vicarage, Churchmore Road, London SW16 5UZ* Tel 0181-764 5808

GILMOUR, John Logan. b 14. Cuddesdon Coll 46. **d** 48 **p** 49. C Reading St Mary V *Ox* 48-51; Min St Barn CD Reading 51-55; Thailand 55-58; V Ellel *Blackb* 58-60; S Africa from 60. *2 Russell Lodge, Main Road, Constantia, 7800 South Africa* Tel Cape Town (21) 794-1523

GILPIN, Jeremy David (Jerry). b 59. Pemb Coll Ox BA80 CertEd82. Trin Coll Bris BA88. **d** 88 **p** 89. C Southsea St Jude *Portsm* 88-92; R Itchingfield w Slinfold *Chich* 92-96; Chapl St Hugh's Coll Ox from 97. *12 Bay Tree Close, Iffley, Oxford OX4 4DT* Tel (01865) 770471 Fax as telephone E-mail gilpins@compuserve.com

GILPIN, Richard John. b 45. Lon Univ BSc66 Bris Univ DipTh69. Wells Th Coll 67. **d** 70 **p** 71. C Davyhulme Ch Ch *Man* 70-74; Pastor Gustav Adolf Berlin EKD 74-77; R Heaton Norris Ch w All SS 77-83; R Chorlton-cum-Hardy St Clem from 83; AD Hulme from 95. *The Rectory, 6 Edge Lane, Chorlton-cum-Hardy, Manchester M21 1JF* Tel 0161-881 3063

GILPIN, The Ven Richard Thomas. b 39. Lich Th Coll 60. **d** 63 **p** 64. C Whipton *Ex* 63-66; C Tavistock and Gulworthy 66-69; V 73-91; V Swimbridge 69-73; Preb Ex Cathl from 82; RD Tavistock 87-90; Dioc Dir of Ords 90-91; Adv for Voc and Dioc Dir of Ords 91-96; Sub-Dean Ex Cathl 92-96; Adn Totnes from 96. *Blue Hills, Bradley Road, Bovey Tracey, Newton Abbot, Devon TQ13 9EU* Tel (01626) 832064 Fax 834947

GIMSON, Francis Herbert. b 54. Reading Univ BSc79 LTh. St Jo Coll Nottm 83. **d** 86 **p** 87. C Menston w Woodhead *Bradf* 86-89; C Barnoldswick w Bracewell 89-91; V Langleybury St Paul *St Alb* from 91. *The Vicarage, Langleybury Lane, Kings Langley, Herts WD4 8QQ* Tel (01923) 270634

GINEVER, Preb John Haynes. b 20. St Jo Coll Dur. Westcott Ho Cam. **d** 43 **p** 44. C Preston Ascension *Lon* 43-46; C-in-c 46-50; R Greenford H Cross 50-63; V Mill Hill Jo Keble Ch 63-70; RD W Barnet 67-70; RD Wolverhampton *Lich* 70-89; P-in-c Wolverhampton St Geo 70-78; P-in-c Wolverhampton All SS 70-78; R Wolverhampton 73-78; Preb Lich Cathl 75-89; P-in-c Wolverhampton St Mark 76-78; P-in-c Wolverhampton St Chad 76-78; TR Wolverhampton 78-89; rtd 89. *Flat 4, 26 Branksome Wood Road, Bournemouth BH4 9JZ* Tel (01202) 763373

GINEVER, Paul Michael John. b 49. AKC71. **d** 72 **p** 73. C Davyhulme Ch Ch *Man* 72-75; Australia 76-77; C Tettenhall Wood *Lich* 77-80; C Halesowen *Worc* 80; TV 80-86; P-in-c Gt Malvern Ch Ch from 86. *The Vicarage, 8 Christchurch Road, Malvern, Worcs WR14 3BE* Tel (01684) 574106

GINGELL, John Lawrence. b 27. Lon Univ BD55. ALCD55. **d** 55 **p** 56. C Normanton *Derby* 55-58; C Ilkeston St Bart CD 58-61; Toc H Staff Padre 61-70; Asst Chapl S Lon Ind Miss 61-64; Lic to Offic *S'wark* 61-66; Lic to Offic *Liv* 67-70; V Somercotes *Derby* 70-72; Bp's Ind Adv 72-80; rtd 92. *18 Bournville Road, London SE6 4RN* Tel 0181-690 0148

GINN, Daniel Vivian. b 33. Univ of Wales (Cardiff) BSc55 DipEd56. Llan Dioc Tr Scheme 79. **d** 82 **p** 83. NSM Llantwit Major and St Donat's *Llan* 82-83; NSM Llantwit Major from 83; RD Llantwit Major and Cowbridge from 94. *Chenet, 24 Voss Park Drive, Llantwit Major CF61 1YE* Tel (01446) 792774

GINN, Richard John. b 51. ACIB Lon Univ BD77 Dur Univ DipTh78. Lambeth STh85 Cranmer Hall Dur 77. **d** 79 **p** 80. C Hornsey Ch Ch *Lon* 79-82; C Highgate St Mich 82-85; V Westleton w Dunwich *St E* from 85; V Darsham from 85. *The Vicarage, Westleton, Saxmundham, Suffolk IP17 3AQ* Tel (01728) 73271

GINNEVER, Canon John Buckley. b 20. Man Univ BA42. Ridley Hall Cam 46. **d** 48 **p** 49. C Tyldesley w Shakerley *Man* 48-51; C-in-c Oldham St Chad Limeside 51-57; R Levenshulme St Mark 57-76; V Chadderton St Matt 76-84; Hon Can Man Cathl 82-85; rtd 85; Perm to Offic *St As* from 85. *22 Glan Ffyddion, Waterfall Road, Dyserth, Rhyl LL18 6EG* Tel (01745) 570654

GINNO, Albert Charles. b 31. Lon Coll of Div 66. **d** 68 **p** 69. C Kemp Town St Mark and St Matt *Chich* 68-72; P-in-c E Hoathly 72-83; V Westham 83-96; rtd 96; Perm to Offic *Chich* from 96. *106 Sorrel Drive, Eastbourne, E Sussex BN23 8BJ* Tel (01323) 761479 Fax 768920

GIRARD, Canon William Nicholas Charles. b 35. Coll of Resurr Mirfield 65. **d** 67 **p** 68. C Yate *Glouc* 67-70; C Westbury-on-Trym St Alb *Bris* 70-73; Chapl K Sch Ely 73-76; V Fenstanton *Ely* 76-85; V Hilton 76-85; R Balsham from 85; P-in-c Horseheath 85-96; P-in-c W Wickham from 85; RD Linton 93-94 and from 96; Hon Can Ely Cathl from 97. *The Rectory, Balsham, Cambridge CB1 6DX* Tel (01223) 894010

GIRLING, Canon Andrew Martin. b 40. Em Coll Cam BA63 MA67. Wycliffe Hall Ox 63. **d** 65 **p** 66. C Luton w E Hyde *St Alb* 65-69; Chapl Hull Univ *York* 69-75; V Dringhouses from 75; Can and Preb York Minster from 97. *The Vicarage, Dringhouses, York YO2 2QG* Tel (01904) 706120

GIRLING, David Frederick Charles. b 33. Edin Th Coll 58. **d** 61 **p** 62. C Caister *Nor* 61-65; C Leigh St Clem *Chelmsf* 65-66; CF 66-83; V Prittlewell St Luke *Chelmsf* from 83. *The Vicarage, St Luke's Road, Southend-on-Sea SS2 4AB* Tel (01702) 467620

GIRLING, Francis Richard (Vincent). b 28. Worc Coll Ox BA52 MA56 Lon Univ BD65. Coll of Resurr Mirfield 55. **d** 57 **p** 59. CR from 57. *House of the Resurrection, Mirfield, W Yorkshire WF14 0BN* Tel (01924) 494318

GIRLING, Gordon Francis Hulbert. b 15. TD61. Univ Coll Ox BA37 MA41. Wells Th Coll 39. **d** 46 **p** 47. C Charlton St Luke w St Paul *S'wark* 46-49; C Finchley St Mary *Lon* 49-51; V Enfield St Geo 51-59; V Kingsbury H Innocents 59-79; rtd 79; Perm to Offic *Chich* from 80. *212 Coast Road, Pevensey Bay, Pevensey, E Sussex BN24 6NR* Tel (01323) 766359

GIRLING, Stephen Paul. b 61. Southn Univ BSc83. Trin Coll Bris BA91. **d** 91 **p** 92. C Ogley Hay *Lich* 91-95; TV S Molton w Nymet St George, High Bray etc *Ex* from 95. *The Vicarage, Chittlehampton, Umberleigh, Devon EX37 9QL* Tel (01769) 540654

GIRLING, Canon Timothy Havelock (Tim). b 43. St Aid Birkenhead 63. **d** 67 **p** 68. C Wickford *Chelmsf* 67-70; C Luton w E Hyde *St Alb* 70-74; Chapl Luton and Dunstable Hosp 74-80; C Luton All SS w St Pet *St Alb* 74-80; R Northill w Moggerhanger 80-89; Chapl Glenfield Hosp NHS Trust *Leic* from 89; Chapl Glenfrith Hosp 89-93; Hon Can Leic Cathl *Leic* from 97. *36 Winton Avenue, Leicester LE3 1DH, or Chaplain's Office, Glenfield Hospital, Groby Road, Leicester LE3 9QP* Tel 0116-291 3795 or 287 1471

GIRTCHEN, John Christopher. b 54. Linc Th Coll 94. **d** 96 **p** 97. C Bourne *Linc* from 96. *5 Hawthorn Road, Bourne, Lincs PE10 9SN* Tel (01778) 393789

GISBOURNE, Michael Andrew. b 65. Leeds Univ BA87. St Jo Coll Nottm BTh91 DipMM91. **d** 92 **p** 93. C Gateacre *Liv* 92-95; C Marton *Blackb* from 95. *74 Worcester Road, Blackpool FY3 9SZ* Tel (01253) 792118

GITTINGS, Graham. b 46. Qu Coll Birm 75. **d** 78 **p** 79. C Caverswall *Lich* 78-81; C Wolverhampton St Matt 81-82; C Walthamstow St Mary w St Steph *Chelmsf* 82-83; C Dagenham 83-89; V Earl Shilton w Elmesthorpe *Leic* from 89. *The Vicarage, Maughan Street, Earl Shilton, Leicester LE9 7BA* Tel (01455) 843961

GIVEN, Harold Richard. b 54. Oak Hill Th Coll 75. **d** 78 **p** 79. C Belfast St Clem *D & D* 78-80; C Belfast St Donard 80-83; I Tamlaght O'Crilly Upper w Lower *D & R* 83-92; I Tamlaghtfinlagan w Myroe from 92. *Finlagan Rectory, 77 Ballykelly Road, Limavady, Co Derry BT49 9DS* Tel (01504) 762743

GLADSTONE, Robert Michael (Rob). b 60. Ch Ch Ox BA82 MA86. Wycliffe Hall Ox DipMin94. **d** 94 **p** 95. C Trentham *Lich* from 94. *4 Oakshaw Grove, Stoke-on-Trent ST4 8UB* Tel (01782) 643457

✠**GLADWIN, The Rt Revd John Warren.** b 42. Chu Coll Cam BA65 MA68. Cranmer Hall Dur DipTh66. **d** 67 **p** 68 **c** 94. C Kirkheaton *Wakef* 67-71; Tutor St Jo Coll Dur 71-77; Dir Shaftesbury Project 77-82; Lic to Offic *S'well* 77-82; Sec Gen Syn Bd for Soc Resp 82-88; Preb St Paul's Cathl *Lon* 84-88; Provost Sheff 88-94; Angl Adv Yorkshire TV 88-94; Bp Guildf from 94. *Willow Grange, Woking Road, Guildford, Surrey GU4 7QS* Tel (01483) 590500 Fax 590501

GLADWIN, Thomas William. b 35. St Alb Minl Tr Scheme 78. **d** 81 **p** 82. NSM Hertford St Andr *St Alb* 81-82; NSM Digswell and Panshanger 82-86; C 86-96; rtd 96. *99 Warren Way, Welwyn, Herts AL6 0DL* Tel (01438) 714700

GLAISTER, James Richard. b 30. Oak Hill Th Coll 81. **d** 83 **p** 84. NSM Shrub End *Chelmsf* 83-85; NSM Lawshall w Shimplingthorne and Alpheton *St E* 85-87; NSM Lavenham 87-88; C Felixstowe St Jo 88-95; rtd 95. *Kipps, 9 High Street, Lavenham, Sudbury, Suffolk CO10 9BR* Tel (01787) 247384

GLAISYER, The Ven Hugh. b 30. Or Coll Ox BA51 MA55. St Steph Ho Ox 51. **d** 56 **p** 56. C Tonge Moor *Man* 56-62; C Sidcup St Jo *Roch* 62-64; V Milton next Gravesend Ch Ch 64-81; RD Gravesend 74-81; V Hove All SS *Chich* 81-91; Can and Preb Chich Cathl 82-91; RD Hove 82-91; P-in-c Hove St Jo 87-91; Adn Lewes and Hastings 91-97; rtd 97. *Florence Villa, Hangleton Lane, Ferring, Worthing, E Sussex BN12 6PP* Tel (01903) 244688 Mobile 0378-049822 Fax 476529

GLANVILLE-SMITH, Canon Michael Raymond. b 38. Leeds Univ MA95. AKC61. **d** 62 **p** 63. C St Marylebone St Mark w St Luke *Lon* 62-64; C Penzance St Mary *Truro* 64-68; R Worc St Andr and All SS w St Helen *Worc* 68-74; Dioc Youth Chapl 68-74; V Catshill 74-80; P-in-c Worc St Martin w St Pet 80-81; TR Worc St Martin w St Pet, St Mark etc 81-86; TR Worc SE 86-90; Hon Can Worc Cathl 83-90; Can Res Ripon Cathl *Ripon* from 90; RD Ripon 96-97. *St Wilfred's House, Minster Close, Ripon, N Yorkshire HG4 1QR* Tel (01765) 700211

GLARE, Michael Francis. b 28. Southn Univ BA54. St Steph Ho Ox 56. **d** 57 **p** 58. C Withycombe Raleigh *Ex* 57-62; C-in-c Goodrington CD 62-65; C Tamerton Foliot 65-70; R Weare Giffard w Landcross 70-76; RD Hartland 74-76; P-in-c Babbacombe 76-80; V 80-87; V Ilsington 87-93; rtd 93; Perm to Offic *Ex* from 94. *Poplar Lodge, 23 Albion Street, Shaldon, Teignmouth, Devon TQ14 0DF* Tel (01626) 872679

GLASBY, Alan Langland. b 46. Nottm Univ LTh77. Linc Th Coll DipMin89 St Jo Coll Nottm 74. **d** 77 **p** 78. C Erith St Paul *Roch* 77-80; C Moor Allerton *Ripon* 80-81; TV 81-87; V Middleton St Mary 87-92; V Bilton from 92. *Bilton Vicarage, Bilton Lane, Harrogate, N Yorkshire HG1 3DT* Tel (01423) 565129

GLASGOW AND GALLOWAY, Bishop of. *See* TAYLOR, The Rt Revd John Mitchell

GLASGOW AND GALLOWAY, Dean of. *See* DUNCAN, The Very Rev Gregor Duthie

GLASGOW, Provost of. *Vacant*

GLASS, Kenneth William. b 23. FRSA68. **d** 57 **p** 58. C Ipswich St Matt *St E* 57-59; R Glemsford 59-63; P-in-c Somerton 59-63; V Ipswich St Nic 63-73; P-in-c Ipswich St Helen 73; R Sproughton w Burstall 74-76; Perm to Offic from 76; rtd 83. *19 Chalkeith Road, Needham Market, Ipswich IP6 8HA* Tel (01449) 720393

GLASS, Mrs Yvonne Elizabeth. b 58. EMMTC 94. **d** 97. NSM Bingham *S'well* from 97. *30 Willoughby Road, West Bridgford, Nottingham NG2 6EZ* Tel 0115-923 5466

GLASSPOOL, John Martin. b 59. RGN87 Kent Univ BA83 Heythrop Coll Lon MTh95. Westcott Ho Cam 88. **d** 90 **p** 91. C Forest Gate Em w Upton Cross *Chelmsf* 90-93; P-in-c Theydon Garnon 93-95; Chapl St Marg Hosp Epping from 93; TV Epping Distr *Chelmsf* from 95. *The Rectory, Theydon Garnon, Epping, Essex CM16 7PQ* Tel (01992) 572608

GLAZEBROOK, Ronald Victor. b 19. FRHistS Keble Coll Ox BA41 MA48 DipEd53. St Steph Ho Ox 41. **d** 43 **p** 44. C Earl's Court St Cuth w St Matthias *Lon* 43-48; Chapl Ashford Res Sch 48-52; Australia 52-55; Nigeria 55-66; Chapl and Asst Master Greycoat Sch Lon 64-65; Perm to Offic *Cant* 64-65 and 70-77; C Upper Norwood St Jo *S'wark* 66-70; C Beckenham St Barn *Roch* 72-75; Warden St Marg Ho Bethnal Green 76-83; rtd 83; Perm to Offic *Chich* from 83. *Flat 1B, 11 Dane Road, St Leonards-on-Sea, E Sussex TN38 0RN*

GLAZEBROOK, William Leng (Bill). b 29. Edin Th Coll 76. **d** 76 **p** 77. C Dollar *St And* 76-82; Dioc Supernumerary 83; Chapl Trin Coll Glenalmond 84; P-in-c Glencarse *Bre* 84-87; Dioc Sec 84-87; Chapl HM Pris Perth 85-87; V Broughton Poggs w Filkins, Broadwell etc *Ox* 87-94; rtd 94; Perm to Offic *Bre* from 94. *10 Rose Terrace, Perth PH1 5HA* Tel (01738) 624913

GLEADALL, John Frederick. b 39. Ripon Hall Ox 66 Sarum Th Coll 69. **d** 70 **p** 71. C S Ashford Ch Ch *Cant* 70-76; P-in-c Hothfield 76-83; P-in-c Eastwell w Boughton Aluph 81-83; P-in-c Westwell 81-83; V Westwell, Hothfield, Eastwell and Boughton

Aluph from 84. *The Vicarage, Westwell, Ashford, Kent TN25 4LQ* Tel (01233) 712576

GLEDHILL, Alan. b 43. Lon Univ BSc(Econ). N Ord Course 81. **d** 84 **p** 85. C Knaresborough *Ripon* 84-87; P-in-c Easby 87-88; P-in-c Bolton on Swale 87-88; V Easby w Brompton on Swale and Bolton on Swale 88-96; Teacher St Fran Xavier Sch Richmond from 96. *St Francis Xavier School, Darlington Road, Richmond, N Yorkshire DL10 7DA, or 15 White Lands, Richmond, N Yorkshire DL10 7DR* Tel (01748) 823414

GLEDHILL, Canon James William. b 27. Dur Univ BA52. Westcott Ho Cam 52. **d** 56 **p** 57. C Mexborough *Sheff* 56-59; CF 59-61; C Bywell St Pet *Newc* 61-65; V Warden w Newbrough from 65; RD Hexham 78-88; Hon Can Newc Cathl from 88. *The Vicarage, Warden, Hexham, Northd NE46 4SL* Tel (01434) 603910

✠**GLEDHILL, The Rt Revd Jonathan Michael.** b 49. Keele Univ BA72 Bris Univ MA75. Trin Coll Bris 72. **d** 75 **p** 76. C Marple All SS *Ches* 75-78; C Folkestone H Trin w Ch Ch *Cant* 78-83; V Cant St Mary Bredin 83-96; Tutor Cant Sch of Min 83-96; RD Cant 88-94; Hon Can Cant Cathl 92-96; Suff Bp Southampton *Win* from 96. *Ham House, The Crescent, Romsey, Hants SO51 7NG* Tel (01794) 516005 Fax (01794) 830242

GLEDHILL, Peter. b 29. Ball Coll Ox BA53 MA54. Cuddesdon Coll 54. **d** 56 **p** 57. C Balham St Mary *S'wark* 56-58; C Loughton St Jo *Chelmsf* 58-63; Jamaica 63-66; Barbados 66-67; Asst Master Cheadle Gr Sch 68-70; Lic to Offic *Lich* 70-71; P-in-c Kingstone w Gratwich 71-83; P-in-c Llanyblodwel and Trefonen 83-84; R 84-89; C Menai and Malltraeth Deanery *Ban* 90-94; NSM from 95; rtd 94. *Yr Hen Felin, Pwllfanogl, Llanfairpwllgwyngyll, Ynys Mon LL61 6PD* Tel (01248) 714434

GLEESON, Robert Godfrey. b 49. Man Univ CQSW74. Qu Coll Birm 83. **d** 85 **p** 86. C Hall Green St Pet *Birm* 85-88; Asst Chapl Mental Health & Elderly Care Services Birm HA 88-90; Chapl 90-94; Chapl Moseley Hall Hosp Birm 90-94; Chapl S Birm Mental Health NHS Trust from 94. *180 Pineapple Road, Birmingham, B30 2TY, or Queen Elizabeth Hospital, Mindelsohn Way, Birmingham B15 2QZ* Tel 0121-444 2793 or 627 2885

GLEN, Robert Sawers. b 25. Qu Coll Cam BA49 MA56. Sarum & Wells Th Coll 79. **d** 81 **p** 82. Chapl Sherborne Sch 81-86; C Yetminster w Ryme Intrinseca and High Stoy *Sarum* 86-95; RD Sherborne 92-95; rtd 95. *Devan Haye, North Road, Sherborne, Dorset DT9 3BJ* Tel (01935) 812018

GLENDALOUGH, Archdeacon of. *See* SWANN, The Ven Edgar John

GLENDINING, Canon Alan. b 24. LVO79. Westcott Ho Cam 58. **d** 60 **p** 61. C S Ormsby w Ketsby, Calceby and Driby *Linc* 60-63; V Raveningham *Nor* 63-70; P-in-c Hales w Heckingham 63-70; R Thurlton w Thorpe next Haddiscoe 63-70; V Norton Subcourse 63-70; P-in-c Aldeby w Wheatacre w Burgh St Peter 66-70; P-in-c Haddiscoe w Toft Monks 68-70; Dom Chapl to The Queen 70-79; Chapl to The Queen from 79; R Sandringham w W Newton *Nor* 70-79; RD Heacham and Rising 72-76; Hon Can Nor Cathl 77-89; TR Lowestoft and Kirkley 79-85; Sen Chapl to Holidaymakers 85-89; V Ranworth w Panxworth and Woodbastwick 85-89; RD Blofield 87-89; rtd 90; Perm to Offic *Nor* from 90. *7 Bellfosters, Kings Staithe Lane, King's Lynn, Norfolk PE30 1LZ* Tel (01553) 760113

GLENFIELD, Samuel Ferran. b 54. QUB BA76 TCD MLitt90 BTh91. **d** 91 **p** 92. C Douglas Union w Frankfield *C, C & R* 91-94; I Rathcooney Union 94-96; I Kill *D & G* from 96. *The Rectory, Kill o' the Grange, Blackrock, Co Dublin, Irish Republic* Tel Dublin (1) 280 1721 or 289 6442 Fax 289 6442

GLENN, Michael David. b 37. Lich Th Coll 67. **d** 70 **p** 71. C Denton Ch Ch *Man* 70-74; Chapl Oldham Hosps 74-77; P-in-c Moss Side Ch Ch *Man* 77-78; Hon C Drayton Bassett *Lich* 78-82; Hon C Hints 78-82; Perm to Offic *Man* 82-90; TV Corby SS Pet and Andr w Gt and Lt Oakley *Pet* 90-97. *83A Main Road, Collyweston, Stamford, Lincs PE9 3PQ*

GLENNON, James Joseph. b 37. **d** 63 **p** 64. NSM Hadleigh w Layham and Shelley *St E* 88-95; C from 95; P-in-c Hintlesham w Chattisham from 95. *Orchard End, George Street, Hintlesham, Ipswich IP8 3NH* Tel (01473) 652100

GLEW, George William. b 24. Oak Hill Th Coll 64. **d** 66 **p** 67. C Cant St Mary Bredin *Cant* 66-69; C Willesborough w Hinxhill 69-73; R Burlingham St Edmund, St Andr, St Pet etc *Nor* 73-77; V Burlingham St Edmund w Lingwood 77-83; C Horsham *Chich* 83-85; P-in-c Worthing Ch Ch 85-89; rtd 89; Hon CF from 89; Lic to Offic *Cant* from 89. *17 Mead Way, Canterbury, Kent CT2 8BB* Tel (01227) 472639

GLOUCESTER, Archdeacon of. *See* WAGSTAFF, The Ven Christopher John Harold

GLOUCESTER, Bishop of. *See* BENTLEY, The Rt Revd David Edward

GLOUCESTER, Dean of. *See* BURY, The Very Revd Nicholas Ayles Stillingfleet

GLOVER, Canon Brian Reginald. b 38. St D Coll Lamp BA60 Sarum Th Coll 60. **d** 62 **p** 63. C Redditch St Steph *Worc* 62-68; V Redditch St Geo 68-74; V Ellistown *Leic* 74-77; V Leic St Aid 77-82; V Fleckney 82-84; V Fleckney and Kilby from 84; RD Gartree II 89-95; Hon Can Leic Cathl from 94. *The Vicarage, 12 Saddington Road, Fleckney, Leicester LE8 8AW* Tel 0116-240 2215

GLOVER, David Charles. b 66. St Jo Coll Dur BA87 St Jo Coll Cam MPhil91. Ridley Hall Cam 87. **d** 90 **p** 91. C Wath-upon-Dearne w Adwick-upon-Dearne *Sheff* 90-92; Chapl Hatf Coll Dur from 92; P-in-c Dur St Marg *Dur* from 95. *St Margaret's Rectory, South Street, Durham DH1 4QP* Tel 0191-384 3623

GLOVER, George Edward. b 58. Strathclyde Univ BSc80 Edin Univ BD83. Edin Th Coll 80. **d** 83 **p** 86. C Dunblane *St And* 83-84; C Southgate Ch Ch *Lon* 84-85; C Golders Green 85-88; Chapl Sunderland Mental Health Unit 88-90; C Sherburn w Pittington *Dur* 90-92; P-in-c Trimdon Station 92-95; C Stanley from 97. *St Stephen's House, Holly Hill Gardens East, South Stanley, Durham DH9 6NN*

GLOVER, Henry Arthur. b 32. Lon Univ BSc58. Wycliffe Hall Ox 59. **d** 61 **p** 62. C Fareham St Jo *Portsm* 61-63; C Liv Our Lady and St Nic *Liv* 63-64. *15 Thorncliffe Road, Wallasey, Merseyside L44 3AA* Tel 0151-638 6018

GLOVER, John. b 48. Kelham Th Coll 67. **d** 71 **p** 72. C Foley Park *Worc* 71-75; TV Sutton *Liv* 75-79; P-in-c Churchill w Blakedown *Worc* 79-84; R 84-87; R Belbroughton w Fairfield and Clent 87-91; Chapl Children's Family Trust from 91; NSM Flint *St As* 92-93; R Halkyn w Caerfallwch w Rhesycae 93-97; V Rhyl w St Ann from 97. *The Vicarage, 31 Bath Street, Rhyl LL18 3LU* Tel (01745) 353732

GLOVER, Mrs Judith Rosalind. b 53. NE Ord Course DipHE95. **d** 95 **p** 96. C Glendale Gp *Newc* from 95. *St Gregory's House, 20 Ryecroft Way, Wooler, Northd NE71 6BP* Tel (01668) 281495

GLOVER, Michael John Myers. b 28. CEng MICE MSAICE Bradf Tech Coll DipCivEng48 Lon Univ BSc48. Cuddesdon Coll 54. **d** 56 **p** 57. C Leic St Pet *Leic* 56-60; S Africa 60-73 and from 86; TR Northampton Em *Pet* 74-86; Bp's Chapl E Area Northn 73-74; rtd 93. *PO Box 447, Nongoma, 3950 South Africa* Tel (358) 310044

GLOVER, Richard John. b 47. Nottm Univ BTh77. Linc Th Coll 73. **d** 77 **p** 78. C Barrow St Geo w St Luke *Carl* 77-79; C Netherton 79-80; P-in-c Addingham 80-83; P-in-c Edenhall w Langwathby and Culgaith 80-83; V Addingham, Edenhall, Langwathby and Culgaith 83-84; V Bishops Hull *B & W* 84-89; V Shilbottle *Newc* 89-96; V Whittingham and Edlingham w Bolton Chapel from 96. *The Vicarage, Whittingham, Alnwick, Northd NE66 4UP* Tel (01665) 574224

GLYN-JONES, Alun. b 38. CCC Cam BA59 MA63. Bps' Coll Cheshunt 60. **d** 61 **p** 62. C Portsea St Mary *Portsm* 61-65; Chapl Hampton Sch Middx 65-76; Hd Master Abp Tenison Gr Sch Croydon 76-88; V Twickenham St Mary *Lon* from 88. *St Mary's Vicarage, Riverside, Twickenham TW1 3DT* Tel 0181-892 2318 or 744 2693

GOALBY, George Christian. b 55. Leeds Univ BA77. St Jo Coll Nottm DPS81. **d** 81 **p** 82. C Wakef St Andr and St Mary *Wakef* 81-84; Asst Chapl HM Pris Wakef 84-85; Chapl HM Youth Cust Cen Deerbolt 85-87; Chapl HM Pris Frankland 87-89; V Swinderby *Linc* from 89. *All Saints' Vicarage, Station Road, Swinderby, Lincoln LN6 6LY* Tel (01522) 586430

GOATCHER, Mrs Sara Jacoba Helena. b 46. LSE DSA68. Oak Hill NSM Course 86. **d** 89 **p** 94. NSM S Croydon Em *S'wark* 89-95; C 95-96; R Sutton St Nic from 96. *The Rectory, 34 Robin Hood Lane, Sutton, Surrey SM1 2RG* Tel 0181-642 3499

GOATER, Charles Frederick. b 16. **d** 82 **p** 82. NSM Fishponds St Mary *Bris* 82-89; Perm to Offic from 89. *72 Queensholme Crescent, Bristol BS16 6LH* Tel 0117-956 1147

GOATER, Michael Robert. b 46. York Univ BA MA. N Ord Course 89. **d** 92 **p** 93. C Norton *Sheff* 92-94; V Endcliffe from 94; Chapl Sheff Ind Miss 94-95; Assoc Chapl Sheff Hallam Univ from 95; Asst Post-Ord Tr Officer from 95; Dioc Voc Officer from 96. *St Augustine's Vicarage, 4 Clarke Drive, Sheffield S10 2NS* Tel 0114-266 1932

GOATER, William Arthur. b 12. Chich Th Coll 33. **d** 36 **p** 37. C Longton St Jas *Lich* 36-39; C Rotherhithe St Kath *S'wark* 39-46; V 46-53; V N Nibley *Glouc* 53-77; V Stinchcombe 55-77; rtd 77; Perm to Offic *Glouc* from 77. *2 Abbey Cottage, Abbey Precinct, Tewkesbury, Glos GL20 5SR* Tel (01684) 275411

GOBBETT, Michael George Timothy. b 64. St Chad's Coll Dur BSc86. St Steph Ho Ox BA89. **d** 90 **p** 91. C Hartlepool St Aid *Dur* 90-94; P-in-c Norton St Mich 94-95; V from 95. *The Vicarage, 13 Imperial Avenue, Norton, Stockton-on-Tees, Cleveland TS20 2EW* Tel (01642) 553984

GOBEY, Ian Clifford. b 48. W of England Minl Tr Course 94. **d** 96. NSM Whiteshill and Randwick *Glouc* from 96. *22 Borough Close, Kings Stanley, Stonehouse, Glos GL10 3LJ* Tel (01453) 828207

GOBLE, Clifford David. b 41. Oak Hill Th Coll 69. **d** 72 **p** 73. C Erith St Paul *Roch* 72-76; C Tunbridge Wells St Jas 76-79; R Southfleet from 79; RD Gravesend from 94. *The Rectory, Hook Green Road, Southfleet, Dartford DA13 9NQ* Tel (01474) 833252

GODBER, Francis Giles. b 48. Open Univ BA79. Ridley Hall Cam 72. **d** 75 **p** 76. C Blackheath *Birm* 75-78; C Wolverhampton St Matt *Lich* 78-80; TV Washfield, Stoodleigh, Withleigh etc *Ex* 80-85; R Shenley and Loughton *Ox* 85-88; TR Watling Valley

88-96; Chapl Heatherwood and Wexham Park Hosp NHS Trust from 96. *16 Buckland Avenue, Slough, Berks SL3 7PH* Tel (01753) 524293

GODDARD, Andrew John. b 67. St Jo Coll Ox BA88 MA93 DipTh89 DPhil96. Cranmer Hall Dur 94. **d** 96. C Cogges and S Leigh *Ox* from 96. *27 Newland Mill, Witney, Oxon OX8 6HH* Tel (01993) 775276 Fax as telephone

GODDARD, Charles Douglas James. b 47. CITC 67. **d** 70 **p** 71. C Orangefield *D & D* 70-73; C Stormont 73-75; Miss to Seamen from 75; Sen Chapl and Sec N Ireland from 77. *7 Abercorn Drive, Carnreagh Road, Hillsborough, Co Down BT26 6LB* Tel (01846) 683592

GODDARD, Christopher. b 45. Sarum & Wells Th Coll 79. **d** 81 **p** 82. C Whitehaven *Carl* 81-83; C Barrow St Geo w St Luke 83-85; P-in-c Hayton St Mary 85-90; V Brigham from 90; V Mosser from 90. *The Vicarage, 1 High Brigham, Cockermouth, Cumbria CA13 0TE* Tel (01900) 825383

GODDARD, Mrs Doris. b 48. St Mary's Coll Twickenham CertEd70 Open Univ BA80. S'wark Ord Course 93. **d** 96 **p** 97. NSM Addlestone *Guildf* from 96; Chapl John Nightingale Sch W Molesley from 96. *25 Albert Road, Addlestone, Surrey KT15 2PX* Tel (01932) 849505

GODDARD, Elisabeth Ann. b 64. St Hugh's Coll Ox BA89. Cranmer Hall Dur 94. **d** 96. C Cogges and S Leigh *Ox* from 96. *27 Newland Mill, Witney, Oxon OX8 6HH* Tel (01993) 775276 Fax as telephone

GODDARD, Canon Frederick Paul Preston. b 24. Jes Coll Cam BA49 MA51. Westcott Ho Cam 49. **d** 51 **p** 52. C Hatfield *St Alb* 51-57; New Zealand 57-61; V Abbots Langley *St Alb* 61-68; Chapl Yeatman and Coldharbour Hosp Dorset 69-87; V Sherborne w Castleton and Lillington *Sarum* 69-87; RD Sherborne 73-77; Can and Preb Sarum Cathl 75-87; rtd 87; Perm to Offic *Truro* from 92. *56 West Street, Polruan, Fowey, Cornwall PL23 1PL* Tel (01726) 870339

GODDARD, Giles William. b 62. Clare Coll Cam MA84. S'wark Ord Course 92. **d** 95 **p** 96. C N Dulwich St Faith *S'wark* from 95. *70 Frankfurt Road, London SE24 9NY* Tel 0171-274 3472

GODDARD, Harold Frederick. b 42. Keble Coll Ox BA63 DipTh65 MA69. Cuddesdon Coll 64. **d** 66 **p** 67. C Birm St Pet *Birm* 66-70; Chapl Dudley Road Hosp Birm 66-70; C Alverstoke *Portsm* 70-72; Chapl Gosport Cottage Hosp Portsm 70-72; P-in-c Portsea St Geo CD 72-76; Chapl Portsm Cathl 73-76; P-in-c Stoke Prior *Worc* 76-78; P-in-c Wychbold and Upton Warren 77-78; R Stoke Prior, Wychbold and Upton Warren 78-80; Chapl Forelands Orthopaedic Hosp Worc 77-80; Chapl R Marsden Hosp Lon and Surrey 80-83; R Martley and Wichenford *Worc* 83-88; P-in-c Knightwick w Doddenham, Broadwas and Cotheridge 85-88; R Martley and Wichenford, Knightwick etc 89-90; Bp's Adv on Min of Healing from 84; Chapl St Rich Hospice Worc 87-94; RD Martley and Worc W *Worc* 88-90; Chapl Kidderminster Gen Hosp 90-92; P-in-c Hallow *Worc* 91-92; P-in-c Sedgeberrow w Hinton-on-the-Green from 92; Chapl Evesham Community Hosp Worc from 93; Co-ord W Midl Healing Advisers from 94. *The Rectory, Sedgeberrow, Evesham, Worcs WR11 6UE* Tel (01386) 881291

GODDARD, Canon John William. b 47. St Chad's Coll Dur BA69 DipTh70. **d** 70 **p** 71. C S Bank *York* 70-74; C Cayton w Eastfield 74-75; V Middlesbrough Ascension 75-82; RD Middlesbrough 81-87; V Middlesbrough All SS 82-88; Can and Preb York Minster 87-88; Vice-Prin Edin Th Coll 88-92; TR Ribbleton *Blackb* from 92. *The Rectory, 238 Ribbleton Avenue, Ribbleton, Preston PR2 6QP* Tel (01772) 791747

GODDARD, Ms Marion. b 54. Sarum & Wells Th Coll 87. **d** 89 **p** 94. Par Dn Lewisham St Swithun *S'wark* 89-94; C 94-95; Chapl Brook Gen Hosp Lon 95-96; TV Thamesmead *S'wark* from 96. *5 Finchdale Road, London SE2 9PG* Tel 0181-310 5614

GODDARD, Matthew Francis. b 45. Lon Univ DipTh69. Kelham Th Coll 65. **d** 69 **p** 70. C Mansfield St Mark *S'well* 69-72; C Northolt Park St Barn *Lon* 72-78; P-in-c Acton Green St Pet 78-87; R Norwood St Mary 87-96; Perm to Offic from 97. *St Mary's Lodge, Church Street, Hampton, Middx TW12 2EB* Tel 0181-979 4102

GODDARD, Stuart David. b 53. Cen Sch of Art Lon BA76 Middx Poly PGCE82. Trin Coll Bris DipHE93. **d** 93 **p** 94. C Watling Valley *Ox* from 93. *2 Littlecote, Great Holm, Milton Keynes MK8 9EZ* Tel (01908) 560075

GODDARD, Canon Sydney Thomas. b 16. St Aid Birkenhead 46. **d** 49 **p** 50. C Ravenhead *Liv* 49-52; C St Helens St Helen 52-55; V Widnes St Ambrose 55-59; Warden World Friendship Ho 59-83; V Liv St Sav 59-71; Hon Can Liv Cathl 69-83; rtd 83; Perm to Offic *Ban* from 84. *Ynys Thomas, Bronaber, Trawsfynydd, Blaenau Ffestiniog LL41 4UR* Tel (01766) 540413

GODDARD, Canon William. b 09. Kelham Th Coll 29. **d** 34 **p** 35. C Wrangbrook w N Elmsall CD *Wakef* 34-37; C Small Heath St Greg *Birm* 37-39; C Bath Bathwick *B & W* 39-42; Chapl RAF 42-46; V Paulton *B & W* 46-50; V Swindon All SS *Bris* 50-52; V Bris St Agnes w St Simon 52-59; R Guildf St Nic *Guildf* 59-74; R Catworth Magna *Ely* 74-77; R Covington 75-77; R Tilbrook 75-77; rtd 77; Perm to Offic *Glouc* from 79. *c/o Mrs Davies, 52 Windsor Avenue, Cardiff CF4 8BY*

GODDARD, William Edwin George. b 14. Clifton Th Coll 66. **d** 68 **p** 69. C Rodbourne Cheney *Bris* 68-71; R Beaford and Roborough *Ex* 71-78; TV Newton Tracey 76-78; R Beaford, Roborough and St Giles in the Wood 78-79; rtd 79; Perm to Offic *Bris* 84-93; Perm to Offic *Leic* from 93. *26 Stuart Court, High Street, Kibworth, Leicester LE8 0LE* Tel 0116-279 6343

GODDEN, The Ven Max Leon. b 23. Worc Coll Ox BA50 MA54. Chich Th Coll 50. **d** 52 **p** 53. C Cuckfield *Chich* 52; C Brighton St Pet 53-57; PC Hangleton 57-62; V Glynde, W Firle and Beddingham 62-82; Adn Lewes 72-76; Adn Lewes and Hastings 76-88; rtd 88. *14 Oak Close, Chichester, W Sussex PO19 3AJ* Tel (01243) 531344

GODDEN, Peter David. b 47. ARCO70 Leeds Univ BA69. Linc Th Coll 85. **d** 87 **p** 88. C Bearsted w Thurnham *Cant* 87-90; C Hykeham *Linc* 90-91; TV 91-95; P-in-c Linc St Pet-at-Gowts and St Andr from 95. *St Peter-at-Gowts' Vicarage, Sibthorp Street, Lincoln LN5 7SP* Tel (01522) 530256

GODDEN, Timothy Richard James (Tim). b 62. Univ Coll Lon BA84. St Jo Coll Nottm DPS89. **d** 89 **p** 90. C Tulse Hill H Trin and St Matthias *S'wark* 89-93; TV Horsham *Chich* from 93. *St Mark's House, North Heath Lane, Horsham, W Sussex RH12 4PJ* Tel (01403) 254964

GODECK, John William George. b 30. Chich Th Coll 57. **d** 60 **p** 61. C Wadhurst *Chich* 60-62; C Tidebrook 60-62; C Eastbourne 62-63; R Bondleigh *Ex* 63-78; R Zeal Monachorum 63-78; P-in-c Broadwoodkelly 65-67; R 68-78; R Dunchideock and Shillingford St George w Ide 78-96; RD Kenn 83-89; rtd 96; Perm to Offic *Ex* from 96. *Boxgrove, 6 Barley Lane, Exeter EX4 1TE* Tel (01392) 424224

GODFREY, Ann Veronica. *See* MACKEITH, Mrs Ann Veronica

GODFREY, Dr Brian Ernest Searles. b 37. Lon Univ BSc60 MSc63 PhD72. S'wark Ord Course 78. **d** 81 **p** 82. NSM Hayes *Roch* 81-86; C 86-88; R Kingsdown 88-93; R Sundridge w Ide Hill from 93; RD Sevenoaks from 95. *The Rectory, Chevening Road, Sundridge, Sevenoaks, Kent TN14 6AB* Tel (01959) 563749 Fax as telephone

GODFREY, The Very Revd David Samuel George. b 35. CITC 64. **d** 66 **p** 67. C Londonderry Ch Ch *D & R* 66-68; I Tomregan w Drumlane *K, E & A* 68-71; I Cloonclare 71-79; I Templebreedy *C, C & R* 79-85; I Bray *D & G* 85-97; Can Ch Ch Cathl Dublin from 95; Dean Kilmore *K, E & A* from 97; I Kilmore w Ballintemple, Kildallon etc from 97. *The Deanery, Danesfort, Kilmore, Cavan, Irish Republic* Tel Cavan (45) 31918

GODFREY, Edward Colin. b 30. Wells Th Coll 63 ADipR62. **d** 65 **p** 66. C Lyndhurst and Emery Down *Win* 65-69; C Paignton Ch Ch *Ex* 69-73; V Stockland w Dalwood 73-77; Chapl HM Pris Man 77-78; Chapl HM Pris Cant 78-83; Chapl HM Pris Highpoint 83-85 and 90-95; Chapl HM Young Offender Inst Glen Parva 85-90; rtd 95. *11 De Burgh Place, Clare, Sudbury, Suffolk CO10 8QL*

✠**GODFREY, The Rt Revd Harold William.** b 48. AKC71. St Aug Coll Cant 71. **d** 72 **p** 73 **c** 87. C Warsop *S'well* 72-75; TV Hucknall Torkard 75-86; Dioc Ecum Officer 81-82; USPG from 86; Adn Montevideo and Can Buenos Aires 86-88; Asst Bp Argentina and Uruguay 87-88; Bp Uruguay from 88. *CC 6108, Montevideo 11.000, Uruguay* Tel (2) 959627 Fax 962519

GODFREY, John Frederick. b 31. Solicitor 57 Lon Univ LLB53 AKC54. Cuddesdon Coll 59. **d** 61 **p** 92. C Battersea St Luke *S'wark* 61-65; Min Reigate St Phil CD 65-72; Public Preacher *St Alb* from 73; rtd 96. *Thicketts, Theobald Street, Radlett, Herts WD7 7LS* Tel (01923) 855558

GODFREY, Joy. b 33. SW Minl Tr Course. **dss** 85 **d** 87 **p** 94. Devonport St Aubyn *Ex* 85-87; Hon Par Dn 87-94; Hon C from 94. *85 Browning Road, Plymouth PL2 3AW* Tel (01752) 564253

GODFREY, Michael. b 49. K Coll Lon BD70 AKC72. **d** 72 **p** 73. C Birtley *Dur* 72-75; Ind Chapl 76-79; Ind Chapl *Lich* 79-93; TV Bilston St Mary 79; TV Bilston 80-86; TV Wolverhampton 86-93; Preb Lich Cathl 87-93. *Address temp unknown*

GODFREY, Michael James. b 50. Sheff Univ BEd77. St Jo Coll Nottm DipTh79 CPS79. **d** 82 **p** 83. C Walton H Trin *Ox* 82-86; C Chadderton Ch Ch *Man* 86-91; V Woodlands *Sheff* from 91. *The Vicarage, 9 Great North Road, Woodlands, Doncaster, S Yorkshire DN6 7RB* Tel (01302) 723268

GODFREY, Nigel Philip. b 51. MRTPI76 Bris Poly DipTP73 Ox Univ BA78 MA84. Ripon Coll Cuddesdon 77. **d** 79 **p** 80. C Kennington St Jo w St Jas *S'wark* 79-89; Community of Ch the Servant 84-93; V Brixton Road Ch Ch *S'wark* from 89. *96 Brixton Road, London SW9 6BE* Tel 0171-793 9824 or 587 0375

GODFREY (née ROGERS), Mrs Pauline Ann. b 58. LMH Ox BA79 MA83 Ox Univ Inst of Educn PGCE80. S Dios Minl Tr Scheme 89. **d** 92 **p** 94. NSM Headley All SS *Guildf* 92-96; C from 96. *7 Windmill Drive, Headley, Bordon, Hants GU35 8AL* Tel (01428) 714565

GODFREY, Robert John. b 27. ACP St Jo Coll York CertEd48. Sarum Th Coll 52. **d** 54 **p** 55. C Roundhay St Edm *Ripon* 54-57; C Gt Marlow *Ox* 57-59; V Long Crendon 59-61; Chapl RAF 61-63; Chapl Crookham Court Sch Newbury 63-79; P-in-c Yattendon w Frilsham *Ox* 79-80; TV Hermitage and Hampstead Norreys, Cold Ash etc 80-88; Cyprus 88-92; rtd 92; C W Woodhay w Enborne, Hampstead Marshall etc *Ox* 92-96. *Apple Tree*

Cottage, 79 Monks Lane, Newbury, Berks RG14 7RJ Tel (01635) 551735

GODFREY, Rumley Myles. b 48. S'wark Ord Course. **d** 83 **p** 84. NSM Dorchester *Ox* from 83. *The Old Malthouse, Warborough, Oxon OX10 7DY* Tel (01867) 328627

GODFREY, Canon Rupert Christopher Race. b 12. Qu Coll Ox BA34 DipTh35 MA38. Ridley Hall Cam 35. **d** 36 **p** 37. C Ipswich St Helen *St E* 36-38; C Edgbaston St Geo *Birm* 38-46; CF 40-46; V Aldeburgh w Hazlewood *St E* 46-59; Hon Can St E Cathl 57-77; V Bury St Edmunds St Mary 59-77; rtd 77; Perm to Offic *St E* from 77. *Archway House, Pytches Road, Woodbridge, Suffolk IP12 1EY* Tel (01394) 382816

GODFREY, Simon Henry Martin. b 55. K Coll Lon BD AKC80. St Steph Ho Ox 80. **d** 81 **p** 82. C Kettering SS Pet and Paul *Pet* 81-84; R Crick and Yelvertoft w Clay Coton and Lilbourne 84-89; V Northampton All SS w St Kath from 89. *All Saints' Vicarage, 6 Albion Place, Northampton NN1 1UD* Tel (01604) 21854 or 32194

GODFREY, Stanley William (Stan). b 24. CEng MIEE67. Qu Coll Birm 71. **d** 74 **p** 74. C Sutton Coldfield St Chad *Birm* 74-78; Hon C Handsworth St Andr 78-86; Hon C Worc City St Paul and Old St Martin etc *Worc* 86-89; Hon C Droitwich Spa from 89. *2 The Pippins, Eckington, Pershore, Worcs WR10 3PY*

GODIN, Mrs Mary Louise. b 42. SRN64 QN66. Oak Hill NSM Course 89. **d** 92 **p** 94. NSM Surbiton Hill Ch Ch *S'wark* from 92. *58 Surbiton Hill Park, Surbiton, Surrey KT5 8ER* Tel 0181-339 5088 Fax as telephone

GODSALL, Andrew Paul. b 59. Birm Univ BA81. Ripon Coll Cuddesdon 86. **d** 88 **p** 89. C Gt Stanmore *Lon* 88-91; C Ealing All SS 91-94; V Hillingdon All SS from 94. *All Saints' Vicarage, Ryefield Avenue, Uxbridge, Middx UB10 9BT* Tel (01895) 233991

GODSALL, Ralph Charles. b 48. Qu Coll Cam BA71 MA75. Cuddesdon Coll 73. **d** 75 **p** 76. C Sprowston *Nor* 75-78; Chapl Trin Coll Cam 78-84; V Hebden Bridge *Wakef* 84-93; V Westmr St Steph w St Jo *Lon* from 93. *The Vicarage, 21 Vincent Square, London SW1P 2NA* Tel 0171-834 0950

GODSELL, Arthur Norman. b 22. St D Coll Lamp BA47. **d** 49 **p** 50. C Tenby and Gumfreston *St D* 49-62; V Heybridge w Langford *Chelmsf* 62-73; RD Maldon 70-73; R Rochford 73-91; RD Rochford 84-89; rtd 91; Perm to Offic *St D* from 91. *51 Westfa Felinfoel, Llanelli SA14 8DG* Tel (01554) 776561

GODSELL, David Brian. b 40. Lon Univ BA62. Coll of Resurr Mirfield 65. **d** 67 **p** 68. C Middlesbrough All SS *York* 67-73; C Stainton-in-Cleveland 73-75; V Byker St Ant *Newc* 75-90; P-in-c Brandon *Dur* 90-94; V from 94. *The Vicarage, Sawmill Lane, Brandon, Durham DH7 8NS* Tel 0191-378 0845

GODSELL, Kenneth James Rowland. b 22. Birm Univ DipTh50. Qu Coll Birm. **d** 76 **p** 77. Tutor Westhill Coll of HE Birm from 74; Hon C Selly Hill St Steph *Birm* 76-81; Hon C Selly Park St Steph and St Wulstan 81-94; Perm to Offic from 94. *7 Farquhar Road East, Birmingham B15 3RD* Tel 0121-454 3737 or 472 7245

GODSON, Alan. b 31. Ch Coll Cam BA61 MA65. Clifton Th Coll 61. **d** 63 **p** 64. C Preston All SS *Blackb* 63-66; Lic to Offic *Man* 66-69; Asst Chapl Emb Ch Paris 69; Dioc Ev *Liv* from 69; P-in-c Edge Hill St Mary 72-78; V from 78. *The Vicarage, Towerlands Street, Liverpool L7 8TT* Tel 0151-709 6710

GODSON, Mark Rowland. b 61. K Coll Lon BD83 AKC83 CertEd84. Linc Th Coll 84. **d** 86 **p** 87. C Hurst Green *S'wark* 86-88; C Fawley *Win* 88-90; TV Wimborne Minster and Holt *Sarum* 90-95; P-in-c Horton and Chalbury 90-95; P-in-c Stalbridge 95-96; Chapl Forest Healthcare NHS Trust Lon from 96. *Whipps Cross Hospital, Whipps Cross Road, London E11 1NR* Tel 0181-539 5522 Fax 558 8115

GODWIN, David Harold. b 45. Lon Univ DipTh71. Kelham Th Coll 67. **d** 71 **p** 72. C Camberwell St Phil and St Mark *S'wark* 71-75; Asst Chapl The Lon Hosp (Whitechapel) 75-79; Chapl R E Sussex Hosp Hastings 79-86; Chapl Glos R Hosp 86-94; Chapl Glos R Hosp NHS Trust from 94; Chapl Over Hosp Glouc 86-92. *Gloucestershire Royal Hospital, Great Western Road, Gloucester GL1 3NN* Tel (01452) 528555

GODWIN, Canon Michael Francis Harold. b 35. Nottm Univ BSc57. Ely Th Coll 59. **d** 61 **p** 62. C Farnborough *Guildf* 61-65; V Epsom St Barn 66-85; V Bramley and Grafham from 85; Hon Can Guildf Cathl from 89. *The Vicarage, Birtley Rise, Bramley, Guildford, Surrey GU5 0HZ* Tel (01483) 892109

GODWIN, Peter. b 19. MBE77. Malvern Coll. Ridley Hall Cam 76. **d** 77 **p** 78. C Headley All SS *Guildf* 77-78; Argentina from 78; rtd 88. *Avenida Belgrano 568, 1092 Buenos Aires, Argentina* Tel Buenos Aires (1) 302287

GOFTON, Canon William Alder. b 31. Dur Univ BA54. Coll of Resurr Mirfield 59. **d** 61 **p** 62. C Benwell St Aid *Newc* 61-64; C N Gosforth 64-69; V Seaton Hirst 69-77; V Newc H Cross 77-89; RD Newc W 85-89; Hon Can Newc Cathl 88-96; R Bolam w Whalton and Hartburn w Meldon 89-96; P-in-c Nether Witton 89-95; V 95-96; Chapl Kirkley Hall Coll 90-96; rtd 96. *4 Crossfell, Ponteland, Newcastle upon Tyne NE20 9EA* Tel (01661) 820344

GOLBOURNE, Winston George. b 30. Univ of W Indies BA53. Virginia Th Sem STM69 Sarum & Wells Th Coll 71. **d** 73 **p** 74. C Bitterne Park *Win* 73-76; Jamaica 76-79; C Handsworth St Andr *Birm* 79-83; V Perry Hill St Geo *S'wark* from 83. *St George's Vicarage, 2 Woolstone Road, London SE23 2SG* Tel 0181-699 2778

GOLD, Guy Alastair Whitmore. b 16. TD50. Trin Coll Cam BA38 MA48. Qu Coll Birm 55. **d** 55 **p** 56. C Prittlewell St Pet *Chelmsf* 55-57; Bp's Dom Chapl 58-61; R Wickham Bishops 62-69; R Hasketon *St E* 69-76; rtd 76; Perm to Offic *St E* 76-89. *Bridge House, Great Bealings, Woodbridge, Suffolk IP13 6NW* Tel (01473) 735518

GOLDEN, Stephen Gerard. b 61. Lon Univ BA84. St Steph Ho Ox 84. **d** 86 **p** 87. C Reading St Luke w St Bart *Ox* 86-90; CF 90-94. *Address temp unknown*

GOLDENBERG, Ralph Maurice. b 45. City Univ FBCO67 FBOA67. Trin Coll Bris DipHE90. **d** 90 **p** 91. C Kinson *Sarum* 90-93; C Edgware *Lon* 93-97; TV Roxeth from 97. *Christ Church Vicarage, Roxeth Hill, Harrow, Middx HA2 0JN* Tel 0181-422 3241

GOLDIE, Canon David. b 46. Glas Univ MA68 Fitzw Coll Cam BA70 MA74. Westcott Ho Cam 68. **d** 70 **p** 71. C Swindon Ch Ch *Bris* 70-73; C Troon *Glas* 73-75; R Ardrossan 75-82; Miss P Irvine 75-82; P Missr Milton Keynes *Ox* 82-86; V from 86; RD Milton Keynes 86-90; Borough Dean from 90; Hon Can Ch Ch from 90. *7 Alverton, Great Linford, Milton Keynes MK14 5EF* Tel (01908) 605150

GOLDIE, James Stuart. b 46. Edin Univ BTh73 BEd73. ALCD69. **d** 69 **p** 70. C Blackpool St Paul *Blackb* 69-70; C Gt Sankey *Liv* 70-73; Asst Chapl Greystone Heath Sch 70-73; Chapl Kilmarnock Academy 73-75; V Flixton St Jo *Man* 75-78; Chapl Friars Sch Man 75-78; V Skelmersdale St Paul *Liv* 78-80; Chapl Trin Sch Liv 78-80; Chapl Westbrook Hay Sch Hemel Hempstead 83-89; V Pennington w Lindal and Marton *Carl* 89-90; Chapl Bp Wand Sch *Lon* 90-95; Chapl Queenswood Sch Herts 96-97. *23 Ffordd Naddyn, Glan Conway, Colwyn Bay LL28 4NH*

GOLDING, Neil Christopher. b 47. Warw Univ BA69. S'wark Ord Course 92. **d** 95 **p** 96. C Mitcham Ascension *S'wark* from 95. *44 Vale Road, Mitcham, Surrey CR4 1NN* Tel 0181-679 9329

GOLDING, Piers Edwin Hugh. b 26. RD76. St Aug Coll Cant 48 Edin Th Coll 50. **d** 53 **p** 54. C Guildf Ch Ch *Guildf* 53-55; C Enfield St Andr *Lon* 55-58; Chapl RN 58-62; Chapl RNR 62-93; V S Bermondsey St Aug *S'wark* 62-93; rtd 93; Perm to Offic *S'wark* from 93. *6 White Lion House, Broad Street, Eye, Suffolk IP23 7AF* Tel (01379) 871253

GOLDING, The Ven Simon Jefferies. b 46. Brasted Place Coll 70. Linc Th Coll 72. **d** 74 **p** 75. C Wilton *York* 74-77; Chapl RN from 77; Chapl of the Fleet and Adn for the RN from 97. *Royal Naval Chaplaincy Service, Room 203, Victory Building, HM Naval Base, Portsmouth PO1 3LS* Tel (01705) 727904 Fax 727112

GOLDING, Stephen. b 57. Keele Univ BA79 CertEd79 Lon Bible Coll BA86. Cant Sch of Min 93. **d** 95 **p** 96. NSM Ramsgate St Luke *Cant* from 95; Chapl St Lawr Coll Ramsgate from 95. *28 College Road, Ramsgate, Kent CT11 7AA* Tel (01843) 850592

GOLDING, Canon Terence Brannigan. b 25. Univ of Ottawa MA. Qu Coll Birm 79. **d** 77 **p** 77. Lesotho 77-79; C Walsall *Lich* 79-83; I Currin w Drum and Newbliss *Clogh* 83-86 and from 88; V Eighton Banks *Dur* 86-88; rtd 94. *Scotshouse Rectory, Clones, Co Monagham, Irish Republic* Tel Clones (47) 56103

GOLDINGAY, Dr John Edgar. b 42. Keble Coll Ox BA64 Nottm Univ PhD83. Clifton Th Coll 64. **d** 66 **p** 67. C Finchley Ch Ch *Lon* 66-69; Lect St Jo Coll Nottm 70-75; Dir Studies 76-79; Registrar 79-85; Vice-Prin 85-88; Prin 88-97; Prof OT Studies Fuller Th Sem Pasadena from 97. *111 South Orange Grove, Apartment 108, Pasadena, CA 91105, USA* E-mail johngold@fuller.edu

GOLDSMITH, Brian Derek. b 36. Leeds Univ BA64. Coll of Resurr Mirfield 64. **d** 66 **p** 67. C Littlehampton St Mary *Chich* 66-69; C Guildf St Nic *Guildf* 69-73; V Aldershot St Aug 73-81; C-in-c Leigh Park St Clare CD *Portsm* 82-85; C Rowner 85-96; rtd 97; C Catherington and Clanfield *Portsm* from 97. *27 White Dirt Lane, Catherington, Waterlooville, Hants PO8 0NB* Tel (01705) 599462

GOLDSMITH, John Oliver. b 46. K Coll Lon BD69 AKC69. St Aug Coll Cant 69. **d** 70 **p** 71. C Dronfield *Derby* 70-73; C Ellesmere Port *Ches* 73-74; TV Ellesmere Port 74-81; P-in-c Pleasley *Derby* 81-87; P-in-c Pleasley Hill *S'well* 83-87; V Matlock Bank *Derby* 87-97; RD Wirksworth 92-97; P-in-c Kirk Hallam from 97. *The Vicarage, 71 Ladywood Road, Ilkeston, Derbyshire DE7 4NF* Tel 0115-932 2402

GOLDSMITH, Malcolm Clive. b 39. Birm Univ BSocSc60. Ripon Hall Ox 60. **d** 62 **p** 63. C Balsall Heath St Paul *Birm* 62-64; Chapl Aston Univ 64-72; Bp's Adv on Ind Soc *S'well* 72-78; C Sherwood 78-79; R Nottingham St Pet and St Jas 79-85; P-in-c Nottingham All SS 85; Gen Sec IVS 85-88; Lic to Offic 85-88; Bp's Personal Exec Asst *Bradf* 88-91; Hon C Edin St Jo *Edin* 92-94; R Edin St Cuth from 94. *6 Westgarth Avenue, Edinburgh EH13 0BD* Tel 0131-441 3557

GOLDSMITH, Mrs Mary Louie. b 48. K Coll Lon BA70 AKC70. Qu Coll Birm 91. **d** 93 **p** 94. NSM Matlock Bank *Derby* 93-97; NSM Kirk Hallam from 97. *The Vicarage, 71 Ladywood Road, Ilkeston, Derbyshire DE7 4NF* Tel 0115-932 2402

GOLDSMITH, Mrs Pauline Anne. b 40. Linc Th Coll 82. **dss** 84 **d** 87 **p** 94. Waddington *Linc* 86-88; Par Dn 87-88; Par Dn Gt and Lt Coates w Bradley 88-94; TV 94-96; TV Kidderminster St Mary and All SS w Trimpley etc *Worc* from 96. *The Vicarage, 50 Nursery Grove, Kidderminster, Worcs DY11 5BG* Tel (01562) 748016

GOLDSMITH, Stephen. b 32. Edin Th Coll. **d** 76 **p** 77. SPCK Staff from 53; Bookshops Regional Manager SPCK from 87; NSM Penicuik *Edin* 76-81; NSM Linc St Nic w St Jo Newport *Linc* 81-90; NSM Gt and Lt Coates w Bradley 90-96; NSM Kidderminster St Mary and All SS w Trimpley etc *Worc* from 96. *The Vicarage, 50 Nursery Grove, Kidderminster, Worcs DY11 5BG* Tel (01562) 748016

GOLDSPINK, David. b 35. Open Univ BA81 BAC Acc 88. Lon Coll of Div 62. **d** 65 **p** 66. C Mile Cross *Nor* 65-68; C St Austell *Truro* 68-70; TV Bramerton w Surlingham *Nor* 70-73; Min Gunton St Pet 73-75; R Mutford w Rushmere w Gisleham w N Cove w Barnby 75-81; Asst Chapl HM Pris Man 81-82; Chapl HM Youth Cust Cen Hollesley Bay Colony 82-84; Chapl HM Pris Blundeston 84-88; Perm to Offic *St E* from 87; rtd 88; Perm to Offic *Nor* from 88. *14 Deepdale, Carlton Colville, Lowestoft, Suffolk NR33 8TU* Tel (01502) 537769

GOLDSPINK, Canon Robert William. b 23. Fitzw Coll Cam BA52 MA56. Trin Coll Bris 47. **d** 52 **p** 53. C Blackpool St Mark *Blackb* 52-56; V Erith St Paul *Roch* 56-64; V Tunbridge Wells St Jas 64-83; Lect Lon Coll of Div 65-66; Hon Can Roch Cathl *Roch* 83-87; V Seal St Pet 83-87; rtd 87; Perm to Offic *Nor* from 87. *Bethany, 50 Uplands Close, Carlton Colville, Suffolk NR33 8AD* Tel (01502) 515662

GOLDSTRAW, William Henry. b 15. Lich Th Coll 60. **d** 61 **p** 62. C Stone St Mich *Lich* 61-68; V Alton 68-82; V Bradley-in-the-Moors 68-82; V Alton w Bradley-le-Moors 82-84; rtd 84; Perm to Offic *Lich* from 84. *36 The Avenue, Cheddleton, Leek, Staffs ST13 7BJ* Tel (01538) 360204

GOLDTHORPE, Peter Martin. b 36. AKC61. **d** 62 **p** 63. C Lt Ilford St Barn *Chelmsf* 62-66; C Wickford 66-68; P-in-c Luton St Anne *St Alb* 68-78; P-in-c Linby w Papplewick *S'well* 78-82; Perm to Offic 82-92; Midl Sec CMJ 83-92; Perm to Offic *Birm* 85-92; Perm to Offic *Linc* 86-92; V Leaton and Albrighton w Battlefield *Lich* from 93. *The Vicarage, Baschurch Road, Bomere Heath, Shrewsbury SY4 3PN* Tel (01939) 290259

GOLDTHORPE, Ms Shirley. b 42. Linc Th Coll 70. **dss** 76 **d** 87 **p** 94. Thornhill Lees *Wakef* 76-78; Birkenshaw w Hunsworth 78-80; Batley St Thos 80-85; Batley All SS 80-85; Purlwell 80-92; Par Dn 87-88; D-in-c 88-92; D-in-c Horbury Junction 92-94; P-in-c from 94. *The Vicarage, Millfield Road, Horbury, Wakefield, W Yorkshire WF4 5DU* Tel (01924) 275274

GOLIGHTLY, William Michael. b 43. Chich Th Coll 67. **d** 70 **p** 74. C Sleekburn *Newc* 70-71; C Wallsend St Luke 71; C Shiremoor 74-77; C Delaval 77-81; TV Bellingham/Otterburn Gp 81-89; TV N Shields 89-92; Chapl Winterton Hosp Sedgefield 92-95; Chapl N Durham NHS Trust from 96. *36 Archery Rise, Neville's Cross, Durham DH1 4LA* Tel 0191-378 0845

GOLLEDGE, Christopher John. b 66. St Mich Coll Llan DipTh92. **d** 92 **p** 93. C Newton Nottage *Llan* 92-95; Perm to Offic *Chich* from 95. *32 Bennett Road, Brighton BN3 5JL*

GOLLOP, Michael John. b 58. Keble Coll Ox BA81 MA85. St Mich Coll Llan BD85. **d** 85 **p** 86. C Newport St Mark *Mon* 85-87; C Bassaleg 87-91; V St Hilary Greenway 91-93; V Itton and St Arvans w Penterry and Kilgwrrwg etc from 93. *The Vicarage, St Arvans, Chepstow NP6 6EU* Tel (01291) 622064

GOLTON, Alan Victor. b 29. St Jo Coll Ox BA51 MA54 DPhil54. LNSM course 84. **d** 85 **p** 86. P-in-c Barston *Birm* 87-95; Perm to Offic 95-96. *Address temp unknown*

GOMERSALL, Ian Douglass. b 56. Birm Univ BSc77 Fitzw Coll Cam BA80 MA85 Dur Univ MA94. Westcott Ho Cam 78. **d** 81 **p** 82. C Darlington St Mark w St Paul *Dur* 81-84; C Barnard Castle w Whorlton 84-86; Chapl HM Young Offender Inst Deerbolt 85-90; P-in-c Cockfield *Dur* 86-88; R 88-90; Dep Chapl HM Pris Wakef 90-91; Chapl HM Pris Full Sutton 91-97; P-in-c Kexby w Wilberfoss *York* 93-97; Chapl Man Metrop Univ *Man* from 97; TV Man Whitworth from 97. *11 Mardale Avenue, Withington, Manchester M20 4TU* Tel 0161-434 4071 or 273 1465

GOMERSALL, Richard. b 45. FCA68. N Ord Course 90. **d** 93 **p** 94. NSM Thurcroft *Sheff* from 93. *Dale View House, 14 Wignall Avenue, Wickersley, Rotherham, S Yorkshire S66 0AX* Tel (01709) 546441 or 376313 Fax 703026 or 836008

GOMPERTZ, Canon Peter Alan Martin. b 40. ALCD63. **d** 64 **p** 65. C Eccleston St Luke *Liv* 64-69; Scripture Union 69-73; C Yeovil *B & W* 73-75; V Northampton St Giles *Pet* 75-96; Can Pet Cathl from 88; P-in-c Aynho and Croughton w Evenley 96; R Aynho and Croughton w Evenley etc from 97. *The Rectory, Croughton Road, Aynho, Banbury, Oxon OX17 3BG* Tel (01869) 810903

GONIN, Christopher Willett. b 33. Man Univ DipRS82 DipA&CE87. AKC56. **d** 60 **p** 61. C Camberwell St Geo *S'wark* 60-64; C Stevenage H Trin *St Alb* 64-69; C Bletchley *Ox* 70-73; R Newington St Mary *S'wark* 73-76; Perm to Offic *Bris* 76-77; Hon C Horfield H Trin 77-89; Hon C City of Bris 89-91; V Milton Ernest *St Alb* from 92; V Thurleigh from 92. *The Vicarage, Thurleigh Road, Milton Ernest, Bedford MK44 1RF* Tel (01234) 822885

GOOCH, Michael Anthony. b 44. Nottm Coll of Educn TCert66. Cant Sch of Min 90. **d** 93 **p** 94. NSM New Romney w Old Romney and Midley *Cant* from 93. *Little Owls, Tookey Road, New Romney, Kent TN28 8ET* Tel (01679) 364652

GOOD, Alan Raymond. b 39. Bris Sch of Min 83. **d** 85 **p** 86. NSM Horfield St Greg *Bris* 85-97; Hon Chapl Southmead Health Services NHS Trust Bris from 97. *177 Filton Road, Horfield, Bristol BS7 0XX* Tel 0117-952 1323

GOOD, Andrew Ronald. b 60. Bris Univ BA82. Linc Th Coll 83. **d** 85 **p** 86. C Epping St Jo *Chelmsf* 85-88; C Cheshunt *St Alb* 88-91; R Spixworth w Crostwick *Nor* 91-92; R Frettenham w Stanninghall 91-92; R Spixworth w Crostwick and Frettenham from 92. *The Rectory, Spixworth, Norwich NR10 3PR* Tel (01603) 898258

GOOD, Anthony Ernest. b 28. ARIBA51 Heriot-Watt Univ MSc73. Wells Th Coll 54. **d** 56 **p** 57. C Maidstone All SS *Cant* 56-60; C Reading St Mary V *Ox* 60-62; R Sandhurst 62-70; Perm to Offic *Ex* 71-82; TR Wallingford w Crowmarsh Gifford etc *Ox* 82-92; RD Wallingford 85-91; rtd 92. *Cotts Weir Quay, Bere Alston, Yelverton, Devon PL20 7BX* Tel (01822) 840524

GOOD, David Howard. b 42. Glouc Sch of Min 84. **d** 87 **p** 88. NSM Bromyard *Heref* 87-92; C Pontesbury I and II 92-95; P-in-c Ditton Priors w Neenton, Burwarton etc from 95. *The Vicarage, Ditton Priors, Bridgnorth, Shropshire WV16 6SQ* Tel (01746) 34636

GOOD, Florence Rose. b 10. SRN44. **dss** 78 **d** 87 **p** 94. Upper Holloway St Pet w St Jo *Lon* 84-89; Hon Par Dn 87-89; rtd 89. *221 Salisbury Walk, Magdala Avenue, London N19 5DY* Tel 0171-272 8652

GOOD, Geoffrey. b 27. St Aid Birkenhead. **d** 61 **p** 62. C Roby *Liv* 61-65; V Staincliffe *Wakef* 65-79; V Thornes St Jas w Ch Ch 79-93; rtd 93; Perm to Offic *Wakef* from 93. *147 Thornes Road, Wakefield, W Yorkshire WF2 8QN* Tel (01924) 378273

GOOD, The Very Revd George Fitzgerald. b 19. TCD BA41. CITC 42. **d** 42 **p** 43. C Drumglass *Arm* 42-45; Clerical V Ch Ch Cathl Dublin *D & G* 45-49; I Inniskeel w Lettermacaward *D & R* 49-60; I Raphoe w Raymochy 60-67; Can Raphoe Cathl 60-62; Dean Raphoe 62-67; Dean Derry 67-84; I Templemore 67-84; rtd 84. *Cliff Cottage, Portnoo, Lifford, Co Donegal, Irish Republic* Tel Portnoo (75) 45268

GOOD, John Hobart. b 43. Bps' Coll Cheshunt 66 Coll of Resurr Mirfield 68. **d** 69 **p** 70. C Ex St Jas *Ex* 69-73; C Cockington 73-75; C Wolborough w Newton Abbot 75-78; P-in-c Exminster 78-80; P-in-c Kenn 78-80; R Exminster and Kenn 80-95; RD Kenn 89-95; TR Axminster, Chardstock, Combe Pyne and Rousdon from 95. *The Rectory, Church Street, Axminster, Devon EX13 5AQ* Tel (01297) 32264

GOOD, Kenneth Raymond. b 52. TCD BA74 Nottm Univ BA76 NUI HDipEd81 MEd84. St Jo Coll Nottm 75. **d** 77 **p** 78. C Willowfield *D & D* 77-79; Chapl Ashton Sch Cork 79-84; I Dunganstown w Redcross and Conary *D & G* 84-90; I Lurgan Ch the Redeemer *D & D* from 90; RD Shankill from 92. *Shankill Rectory, 62 Banbridge Road, Lurgan, Craigavon, Co Armagh BT66 7HG* Tel (01762) 323341 or 325673 Fax 325673

GOOD, The Ven Kenneth Roy. b 41. K Coll Lon BD66 AKC66. **d** 67 **p** 68. C Stockton St Pet *Dur* 67-70; Chapl Antwerp Miss to Seamen *Eur* 70-74; Japan 74-79; Hon Can Kobe from 74; Asst Gen Sec Miss to Seamen 79-85; Asst Chapl St Mich Paternoster Royal *Lon* 79-85; V Nunthorpe *York* 85-93; RD Stokesley 90-93; Adn Richmond *Ripon* from 93. *62 Palace Road, Ripon, N Yorkshire HG4 1HA* Tel (01765) 604342 Fax as telephone

GOOD, Robert Stanley. b 24. TCD BA45 BD47 Kent Univ MA82. **d** 47 **p** 48. C Lurgan Ch Ch *D & D* 47-49; CMS 50-60; Kenya 50-60; Sen Div Master Maidstone Gr Sch 62-64; Sen Lect Ch Ch Coll Cant 64-78; Fiji 83-87; rtd 87; Perm to Offic *Cant* from 87. *44 Ivanhoe Road, Herne Bay, Kent CT6 6EG* Tel (01227) 363561

GOOD, Stuart Eric Clifford. b 37. Wycliffe Hall Ox 63. **d** 64 **p** 65. C Walton H Trin *Ox* 64-67; Australia from 66; Sen Chapl Angl Homes Dio Perth from 85. *6 Enright Circuit, Stanford Gardens, Beeliar, W Australia 6164* Tel Perth (9) 370 1199 (Pager) Fax 310 5580

GOOD, Canon William Thomas Raymond. b 13. TCD BA39 MA45. **d** 39 **p** 40. C Castlecomer *C & O* 39-43; Dioc C (Cork) *C, C & R* 43-45; I Kilnagross 45-52; I Castleventry w Kilmean 52-60; I Rathcooney 60-73; Can Cloyne Cathl 67-69; Prec 69-82; I Carrigrohane Union 73-82; Preb Cork Cathl 79-82; rtd 82. *Grange House, Castlemartyr, Co Cork, Irish Republic* Tel Cork (21) 667349

GOODACRE, Canon David Leighton. b 36. Birm Univ DPS69. AKC59. **d** 60 **p** 61. C Stockton St Chad *Dur* 60-63; C Birtley 63-68; Chapl Sunderland Gen Hosp 69-74; P-in-c Ryhope *Dur* 75-81; V Ovingham *Newc* from 81; Hon Can Newc Cathl from 92. *St Mary's Vicarage, 2 Burnside Close, Ovingham, Prudhoe, Northd NE42 6BS* Tel (01661) 832273

GOODACRE, Norman William. b 07. ARIBA32 Liv Univ BArch31 MA33. Westcott Ho Cam 32. **d** 33 **p** 34. C Toxteth Park Ch Ch *Liv* 33-35; C Gt Budworth *Ches* 35-36; C Otley *Bradf* 36-38; V Thornbury 38-45; V Coniston Cold 45-58; Lic to Offic

Ripon 58-75; rtd 75; Perm to Offic *Liv* from 76. *81 Holmefield Road, Liverpool L19 3PF* Tel 0151-724 4176

GOODALL, George. b 24. LCP. **d** 86 **p** 87. NSM Bretby w Newton Solney *Derby* 86-94; Perm to Offic from 94. *6 Brizlincote Lane, Burton-on-Trent, Staffs DE15 0PR* Tel (01283) 562467

GOODALL, John William. b 45. Hull Univ BA69. Ripon Hall Ox 69. **d** 71 **p** 72. C Loughborough Em *Leic* 71-74; C Dorchester *Ox* 74-75; TV Dorchester 75-80; Tutor Sarum & Wells Th Coll 80-88; Vice Prin S Dios Minl Tr Scheme 80-88; P-in-c Gt Wishford *Sarum* 80-83; P-in-c Colehill 88-96; V from 96; Dioc Dir of Readers 88-95. *The Vicarage, Smugglers Lane, Colehill, Wimborne, Dorset BH21 2RY* Tel (01202) 883721

GOODALL, Jonathan Michael. b 61. R Holloway Coll Lon BMus83. Wycliffe Hall Ox 86. **d** 89 **p** 90. C Bicester w Bucknell, Caversfield and Launton *Ox* 89-92; Sacr and Chapl Westmr Abbey from 92; Lic to Offic *Lon* from 94. *4B Little Cloister, Westminster Abbey, London SW1P 3PL* Tel 0171-222 1386 Fax 233 2072

GOODALL, Malcolm. b 39. Carl Dioc Tr Course 80. **d** 85 **p** 86. NSM Crosscanonby *Carl* 85-88; NSM Allonby 85-88; C Auckland St Andr and St Anne *Dur* 88-90; V Grindon and Stillington from 90. *The Vicarage, Thorpe Thewles, Stockton-on-Tees, Cleveland TS21 3JU* Tel (01740) 30549

GOODBURN, David Henry. b 41. S'wark Ord Course 73. **d** 76 **p** 77. NSM Enfield SS Pet and Paul *Lon* 76-82; Perm to Offic 83-85; NSM Potters Bar *St Alb* 85-88; Chapl RN 88-96; V Luton St Sav *St Alb* from 96. *St Saviour's Vicarage, St Saviour's Crescent, Luton LU1 5HG* Tel (01582) 30445

GOODCHILD, Andrew Philip. b 55. Oak Hill Th Coll BA85. **d** 85 **p** 86. C Barnston *Ches* 85-88; C Hollington St Leon *Chich* 88-89; P-in-c Millbrook *Ches* 89-94; Chapl Kimbolton Sch Cambs from 94; Head RE from 94. *Longways, 27 Stow Road, Kimbolton, Huntingdon, Cambs PE18 0HU* Tel (01480) 861221

GOODCHILD, Canon John McKillip. b 42. Clare Coll Cam BA64 MA68 Or Coll Ox CertEd69. Wycliffe Hall Ox 67. **d** 69 **p** 70. C Clubmoor *Liv* 69-72; Nigeria 72-83; Hon Can Aba from 74; V Ainsdale *Liv* 83-89; TR Maghull from 89. *The Rectory, 20 Damfield Lane, Maghull, Liverpool L31 6DD* Tel 0151-526 5017

✠**GOODCHILD, The Rt Revd Ronald Cedric Osbourne.** b 10. Trin Coll Cam BA32 MA35. Bps' Coll Cheshunt 34. **d** 34 **p** 35 **c** 64. C Ealing St Mary *Lon* 34-37; Chapl Oakham Sch 37-42; Chapl RAFVR 42-46; W Germany 46-49; Sch Sec SCM 49-53; P-in-c St Helen Bishopsgate w St Martin Outwich *Lon* 51-53; V Horsham *Chich* 53-59; RD Horsham 54-59; Adn Northn *Pet* 59-64; R Ecton 59-64; Can Pet Cathl 62-64; Suff Bp Kensington *Lon* 64-79; Area Bp Kensington 79-80; rtd 80; Asst Bp Ex from 83. *Mead Farm, Welcombe, Hartland, Bideford, Devon EX39 6HH* Tel (01288) 83241

GOODCHILD, Roy John. b 30. Wycliffe Hall Ox 60. **d** 61 **p** 62. C Hayes *Roch* 61-64; C S w N Bersted *Chich* 64-68; R Birdham w W Itchenor 68-73; V Saltdean 74-83; V Hollington St Jo 83-90; V Ticehurst and Flimwell from 90; RD Rotherfield 95-97. *The Vicarage, Ticehurst, Wadhurst, E Sussex TN5 7AB* Tel (01580) 200316

GOODDEN, John Maurice Phelips. b 34. Sarum & Wells Th Coll 70. **d** 72 **p** 75. C Weymouth H Trin *Sarum* 72-74; C Harlow New Town w Lt Parndon *Chelmsf* 74-78; Ind Chapl 78-82; Chapl Princess Alexandra Hosp Harlow 78-82; V Moulsham St Jo *Chelmsf* 86-90; R Chipstead *S'wark* from 90; Adv Rural Min from 90. *The Rectory, Starrock Lane, Chipstead, Coulsdon, Surrey CR5 3QD* Tel (01737) 552157 or 553527

GOODE, Allan Kenneth. b 37. S'wark Ord Course. **d** 72 **p** 73. C Belmont *Lon* 72-74; V Liv St Bride w St Sav *Liv* 74-78; V Eccleston Park 78-89; C Billinge 89-91; P-in-c Scarisbrick 91-94; V from 94. *St Mark's Vicarage, 458A Southport Road, Ormskirk, Lancs L40 9RF* Tel (01704) 880317

GOODE, Anthony Thomas Ryall. b 42. Ex Coll Ox BA64 MA71. Cuddesdon Coll 65. **d** 67 **p** 68. C Wolvercote *Ox* 67-71; Chapl RAF 71-91; P-in-c Edith Weston w Normanton *Pet* 72-74; Asst Chapl-in-Chief RAF 91-97; rtd 97. *Chaplaincy Services (RAF), HQ, Personnel and Training Command, RAF Innsworth, Gloucester GL3 1EZ* Tel (01452) 712612 ext 5164 Fax 510828

GOODE, John Laurence. b 48. W Cheshire Coll of Tech TEng70 Federal Univ Minas Gerais Brazil DipT78. Chich Th Coll 81. **d** 83 **p** 84. C Crewe St Andr *Ches* 83-86; USPG 87-94; Brazil 91-94; TV Ches Team *Ches* from 94. *Christ Church Vicarage, 5 Gloucester Street, Chester CH1 3HR* Tel (01244) 380625

GOODE, Michael Arthur John. b 40. K Coll Lon BD AKC63. **d** 64 **p** 65. C Sunderland Springwell w Thorney Close *Dur* 64-68; C Solihull *Birm* 68-70; R Fladbury, Wyre Piddle and Moor *Worc* 70-75; P-in-c Foley Park 75-81; V 81-83; RD Kidderminster 81-83; TR Crawley *Chich* 83-93; TR Abingdon *Ox* from 93; V Shippon from 93. *The Rectory, St Helen's Court, Abingdon, Oxon OX14 5BS* Tel (01235) 520144

GOODE, Canon Peter William Herbert. b 23. Oak Hill Th Coll 60. **d** 62 **p** 63. C Woodford Wells *Chelmsf* 62-65; V Harold Hill St Paul 65-76; V Gt Warley Ch Ch 76-93; RD Brentwood 89-93; Hon Can Chelmsf Cathl 90-93; rtd 93. *52 Slimmons Drive, St Albans, Herts AL4 9AP* Tel (01727) 831904

GOODE, William Aubrey. b 08. Bps' Coll Cheshunt 63. **d** 65 **p** 66. C Hessle *York* 65-67; V Kirk Fenton 67-76; rtd 76; Perm to Offic *York* from 76. *Flat 16, Guardian Court, Water Lane, Clifton, York YO3 6PR* Tel (01904) 655199

GOODER, Martin Lee. b 37. Sheff Univ BSc58. Oak Hill Th Coll 58. **d** 60 **p** 61. C Barrow St Mark *Carl* 60-63; C Halliwell St Pet *Man* 63-66; R Chorlton on Medlock St Sav 66-71; R Brunswick 71-92; P-in-c Bacup Ch Ch from 92. *Christ Church Vicarage, Greensnook Lane, Bacup, Lancs OL13 9DQ* Tel (01706) 878293

GOODERHAM, Daniel Charles. b 24. St Fran Coll Brisbane 49 ACT ThL51. **d** 52 **p** 53. Australia 52-60; C Staveley *Derby* 60-61; C Ipswich St Thos *St E* 61-64; V Ipswich St Bart 64-71; R Drinkstone 71-78; R Rattlesden 71-78; RD Lavenham 75-78; V Beckenham St Mich w St Aug *Roch* 78-87; P-in-c Whiteparish *Sarum* 87-89; rtd 89. *58 Millfield, Eye, Suffolk IP23 7DE* Tel (01379) 871589

GOODERICK, Peter Handley. b 26. Down Coll Cam BA50 MA52. Linc Th Coll 51. **d** 53 **p** 54. C Brighouse *Wakef* 53-56; Prec Gib Cathl *Eur* 56-58; Chapl Izmir 58-59; C Wimbledon *S'wark* 59-63; CF (TAVR) 59-74; V Streatham St Paul *S'wark* 63-68; V Merton St Jas 68-80; P-in-c Baginton *Cov* 80-81; P-in-c Stoneleigh w Ashow 80-81; R Stoneleigh w Ashow and Baginton 81-88; RD Kenilworth 83-90; R Berkswell 88-91; rtd 91; Chapl Malaga w Almunecar and Nerja *Eur* 91-92; Perm to Offic *Cov* from 93. *9 Margetts Close, Barrowfield Lane, Kenilworth, Warks CV8 1EN* Tel (01926) 59855

GOODERSON, Canon William Dennis. b 09. St Pet Hall Ox BA35 MA39. Wycliffe Hall Ox 35. **d** 36 **p** 37. Tutor St Aid Birkenhead 36-41; C Rugby St Andr *Cov* 41-44; CMS Nigeria 45-55; Warden Melville Hall 45-56; Hon Can Lagos 49-55; Chapl St Pet Hall Ox 56-57; V Norton w Whittington *Worc* 57-60; Vice-Prin Wycliffe Hall Ox 60-65; V Cumnor *Ox* 66-77; rtd 77. *6 Gouldland Gardens, Headington, Oxford OX3 9DQ* Tel (01865) 62387

GOODEY, Philip Julian Frank (Phil). b 61. Glos Coll of Arts & Tech HND83. Aston Tr Scheme 87 Trin Coll Bris DipTh92. **d** 92 **p** 93. C Iver *Ox* 92-94; C Hornchurch St Andr *Chelmsf* from 94. *85 Kenilworth Gardens, Hornchurch, Essex RM12 4SG* Tel (01708) 442275

GOODFELLOW, Dr Ian. b 37. St Cath Coll Cam BA61 MA65 Lon Univ PGCE76 Dur Univ PhD83. Wells Th Coll 61. **d** 63 **p** 64. C Dunstable *St Alb* 63-67; Chapl Haileybury Coll Herts 67-71; Lect, Chapl and Tutor Bede Coll Dur 71-74; Lect SS Hild and Bede Dur 75-78; Sen Counsellor Open Univ (SW Region) from 79; Perm to Offic *Ex* 80-95. *Crosslea, 206 Whitchurch Road, Tavistock, Devon PL19 9DQ* Tel (01822) 612069

GOODFIELD, Dudley Francis. b 40. AKC65. **d** 66 **p** 67. C Bath Twerton-on-Avon *B & W* 66-69; C Lache cum Saltney *Ches* 69-71; C Portishead *B & W* 71-76; V Weston-super-Mare St Andr Bournville 76-82; V Ruishton w Thornfalcon from 82. *The Vicarage, Church Lane, Ruishton, Taunton, Somerset TA3 5JW* Tel (01823) 442269

GOODHAND, Richard. b 51. Sarum & Wells Th Coll 88. **d** 90 **p** 91. C Wollaton *S'well* 90-93; P-in-c Clarborough w Hayton from 93; Sub-Chapl HM Pris Ranby 93-96; Asst Chapl from 96. *The Vicarage, Church Lane, Clarborough, Retford, Notts DN22 9NA* Tel (01777) 704781 Fax 702691

GOODHEW, David John. b 65. Collingwood Coll Dur BA86 CCC Ox DPhil92 St Jo Coll Dur BA92 DMinlStuds93. Cranmer Hall Dur 90. **d** 93 **p** 94. C Bedminster *Bris* 93-96; Chapl St Cath Coll Cam from 96. *St Catharine's College, Cambridge CB2 1RL, or 8 South Green Road, Cambridge CB3 9JP* Tel (01223) 338346 or 324035 Fax 338340

GOODHEW, Mrs Lindsey Jane Ellin. b 66. UEA BA87 St Jo Coll Dur BA92 DMinlStuds93. Cranmer Hall Dur 90. **d** 93 **p** 94. C Bishopsworth *Bris* 93-96; Perm to Offic *Ely* 96-97; NSM Cambridge St Mark from 97. *8 South Green Road, Cambridge CB3 9JP* Tel (01223) 324035

GOODHEW, Roy William. b 41. Reading Univ BA. S Dios Minl Tr Scheme. **d** 89 **p** 90. C Southampton Maybush St Pet *Win* 89-94; V Hound from 94. *The Vicarage, Grange Road, Netley Abbey, Southampton S03 5FF* Tel (01703) 452209

GOODING, Ian Eric. b 42. MIProdE68 CEng69 Leeds Univ BSc63 BCom65. St Jo Coll Nottm 70 Lon Coll of Div LTh72 DPS73. **d** 73 **p** 74. C Wandsworth All SS *S'wark* 73-77; Bp's Ind Adv *Derby* from 77; P-in-c Stanton-by-Dale w Dale Abbey 77-87; R from 87; P-in-c Risley from 94. *The Rectory, Stanton-by-Dale, Ilkeston, Derbyshire DE7 4QA* Tel 0115-932 4584

GOODING, Ian Peter Slade. b 56. MBCS88 Imp Coll Lon BScEng77. Qu Coll Birm DipTh92. **d** 92 **p** 93. C Swindon Dorcan *Bris* 92-96; TV Langley Marish *Ox* from 96. *St Francis Vicarage, 21 Lynwood Avenue, Slough SL3 7BJ* Tel (01753) 527903

GOODING, John Henry. b 47. St Jo Coll Nottm. **d** 84 **p** 85. C Charles w Plymouth St Matthias *Ex* 84-88; C Leeds St Geo *Ripon* 88-93; TV Liskeard, St Keyne, St Pinnock, Morval etc *Truro* 93-94; Consultant Lon and SE CPAS from 94; Perm to Offic *S'wark* from 94; Hon C Egham *Guildf* from 96. *9 Redwood, Thorpe, Egham, Surrey TW20 8SU* Tel (01932) 560407

GOODLAD, Canon Martin Randall. b 39. Sheff City Coll of Educn TDip60. Linc Th Coll 63. **d** 66 **p** 67. C Bramley *Ripon* 66-69; TV Daventry *Pet* 69-71; Asst Dioc Youth Officer 69-71; Asst Dir of

Educn *Wakef* 71-74; Youth Work Officer Gen Syn Bd of Educn 74-83; P-in-c Cheam Common St Phil *S'wark* 83-85; V 85-97; RD Sutton 90-97; Hon Can S'wark Cathl from 96; V Coulsdon St Andr from 97. *St Andrew's Vicarage, Julien Road, Coulsdon, Surrey CR5 2DN* Tel 0181-660 0398

GOODLEY, Christopher Ronald. b 47. K Coll Lon BD72 AKC72. **d** 73 **p** 74. C Shenfield *Chelmsf* 73-77; C Hanley H Ev *Lich* 77-78; TV 78-83; Chapl Whittington Hosp Lon 83-86; Chapl St Crispin's Hosp Northampton 88-94; Chapl Northn Healthcare NHS Trust from 94. *Princess Marina Hospital, Duston, Northampton NN5 6UN* Tel (01604) 595087 or 752323

GOODMAN, Preb Denys Charles. b 24. Selw Coll Cam BA49 MA56. Linc Th Coll 49. **d** 51 **p** 52. C Leigh St Mary *Man* 51-54; C Pendlebury St Aug 54-57; V Hollinwood 57-70; R Bath Bathwick St Mary *B & W* 70-78; P-in-c Bath Bathwick St Jo 76-78; R Bath Bathwick 78-91; RD Bath 81-90; Preb Wells Cathl 82-96; Sub-Dean Wells 82-96; rtd 91; Perm to Offic *B & W* from 96. *Hollinwood, Johnson Close, Wells, Somerset BA5 3NN* Tel (01749) 675011

GOODMAN, Canon Derek George. b 34. Keble Coll Ox BA57 MA60. Ridley Hall Cam 59. **d** 61 **p** 62. C Attenborough *S'well* 61-65; R Eastwood 65-84; Dioc Insp of Schs 65-89; V Woodthorpe 84-89; Dioc Dir of Educn *Leic* 89-96; Hon Can Leic Cathl 90-96; rtd 96; Perm to Offic *Leic* from 96. *1 Brown Avenue, Quorn, Loughborough, Leics LE12 8RH* Tel (01509) 415692

GOODMAN, Ernest Edwin. b 14. BNC Ox BA49 MA53. Chich Th Coll 53. **d** 54 **p** 55. C Kettering All SS *Pet* 54-57; R Stoke Bruerne w Grafton Regis and Alderton 57-61; India 61-63; USPG 63-67; Perm to Offic *Pet* 66-94; R Clayton w Keymer *Chich* 71-79; rtd 79. *33 Hatton Hall, Hatton Avenue, Wellingborough, Northants NN8 5AP* Tel (01933) 222912

GOODMAN, John. b 20. Selw Coll Cam BA42 MA46. Linc Th Coll 47. **d** 49 **p** 50. C Kidderminster St Jo *Worc* 49-53; C Marlborough *Sarum* 53-56; V Wootton Bassett 56-65; C Broad Town 56-65; C Salisbury St Mark 65-68; V 68-83; R Wool and E Stoke 83-88; rtd 88. *141 Avon Road, Devizes, Wilts SN10 1PY* Tel (01380) 721267

GOODMAN, John Dennis Julian. b 35. Sarum & Wells Th Coll 74. **d** 76 **p** 77. C Cotmanhay *Derby* 76-79; TV Old Brampton and Loundsley Green 79-86; R Finningley w Auckley *S'well* 86-96; rtd 96. *5 Waterhouse Gardens, Barton Seagrave, Kettering, Northants NN15 5TU* Tel (01536) 415571

GOODMAN, Mark Alexander Scott. b 61. Lanc Univ BA84 Nottm Univ BTh90. Linc Th Coll 87. **d** 90 **p** 91. C Denton St Lawr *Man* 90-93; R Dalkeith *Edin* from 93; R Lasswade from 93. *The Rectory, 7 Ancrum Bank, Dalkeith, Midlothian EH22 3AY* Tel 0131-663 7000 Fax as telephone

GOODMAN, Peter William (Bill). b 60. St Cath Coll Cam BA82. St Jo Coll Nottm 85. **d** 89 **p** 90. C Stapenhill w Cauldwell *Derby* 89-92; C Ovenden *Wakef* 92-94; V Halifax St Aug from 94. *St Augustine's Vicarage, Hanson Lane, Halifax, W Yorkshire HX1 5PG* Tel (01422) 65552

GOODMAN, Canon Sidney William. b 10. Kelham Th Coll 27. **d** 33 **p** 34. C Wigan St Mich *Liv* 33-36; C Gt Grimsby St Mary and St Jas *Linc* 36-39; V Fulstow 39-44; V Habrough 44-55; V Immingham 44-55; V Habrough Gp 55-71; Can and Preb Linc Cathl 69-79; P-in-c Wold Newton w Hawerby 71-78; rtd 78; Perm to Offic *Linc* from 78. *28 Grosvenor Road, Louth, Lincs LN11 0BB* Tel (01507) 603798

GOODMAN, Victor Terence (Vic). b 46. MBCS74 CEng92 Liv Univ BSc67. EMMTC 82. **d** 85 **p** 86. NSM Barwell w Potters Marston and Stapleton *Leic* 85-89; NSM Croft and Stoney Stanton 89-94; P-in-c Whetstone from 94. *The Vicarage, Church Lane, Whetstone, Leicester LE8 6LQ* Tel 0116-284 8713

GOODRICH, Derek Hugh. b 27. Selw Coll Cam BA48 MA54. St Steph Ho Ox 50. **d** 52 **p** 53. C Willesden St Andr *Lon* 52-57; Guyana from 57; Adn Berlice 81-84; V Gen Dio Guyana 82-94; Dean Georgetown 84-94; rtd 92. *St Aloysius Chapel, 615/6 Penny Lane, South Ruimveldt Gardens, Georgetown, Guyana*

GOODRICH, Canon Peter. b 36. Dur Univ BA58. Cuddesdon Coll 60. **d** 62 **p** 63. C Walton St Jo *Liv* 62-66; C Prescot 66-68; V Anfield St Marg 68-72; V Gt Crosby St Faith 72-83; P-in-c Seaforth 76-80; RD Bootle 78-83; TR Upholland 83-94; Hon Can Liv Cathl from 89; R Halsall from 94; Dioc Dir LNSM from 94. *Gesterfield Farmhouse, Halsall Road, Halsall, Ormskirk, Lancs L39 8RN* Tel (01704) 841202

✠**GOODRICH, The Rt Revd Philip Harold Ernest.** b 29. St Jo Coll Cam BA52 MA56. Cuddesdon Coll 52. **d** 54 **p** 55 **c** 73. C Rugby St Andr *Cov* 54-57; Chapl St Jo Coll Cam 57-61; R S Ormsby w Ketsby, Calceby and Driby *Linc* 61-68; R Harrington w Brinkhill 61-68; R Oxcombe 61-68; R Ruckland w Farforth and Maidenwell 61-68; R Somersby w Bag Enderby 61-68; R Tetford and Salmonby 61-68; V Bromley SS Pet and Paul *Roch* 68-73; Suff Bp Tonbridge 73-82; Dioc Dir of Ords 74-82; Bp Worc 82-96; rtd 96. *Ordis Farm, Sutton St Nicholas, Hereford HR1 3AY*

GOODRIDGE, Canon Peter David. b 32. Yale Univ STM84 FRSA92. AKC57. **d** 58 **p** 59. C Eastcote St Lawr *Lon* 58-64; V Tottenham St Phil 64-71; V W Drayton 71-85; P-in-c St Michael Penkevil *Truro* 85-88; P-in-c Lamorran and Merther 85-88; Dir of Educn 85-97; Hon Can Truro Cathl 87-97; rtd 97. *16 Crescent Rise, Truro, Cornwall TR1 3ER* Tel (01872) 70940 or 74352 Fax 222510

✠**GOODRIDGE, The Rt Revd Sehon Sylvester.** b 37. K Coll Lon BD66. Huron Coll Ontario DD77 Codrington Coll Barbados 59. **d** 63 **p** 64 **c** 94. St Lucia 64-66; Jamaica 66-71; Warden & Dep Prin United Th Coll W Indies 69-71; Barbados 71-89; Prin Codrington Coll 71-82; Warden, Counsellor & Sen Lect Univ of W Indies 83-89; Hon Can Barbados from 76; Prin Simon of Cyrene Th Inst 89-94; Chapl to The Queen 93-94; Bp Windward Is from 94. *Bishop's House, PO Box 128, Kingstown, St Vincent, West Indies*

GOODRUM, Mrs Alice. b 30. Lightfoot Ho Dur 58. **dss** 80 **d** 87 **p** 94. Fenham St Jas and St Basil *Newc* 80-91; C 87-91; rtd 91; Perm to Offic *Dur* from 91. *58 West Avenue, South Shields, Tyne & Wear NE34 6BD* Tel 0191-427 6746

GOODSELL, Patrick (Pat). b 32. BA88. Linc Th Coll 62. **d** 64 **p** 65. C Thornton Heath St Jude *Cant* 64-65; C Croydon St Jo *S'wark* 65-70; V Tenterden St Mich *Cant* 70-78; P-in-c Sellindge w Monks Horton and Stowting 78-84; P-in-c Lympne w W Hythe 82-84; V Sellindge w Monks Horton and Stowting etc 84-92; V Nonington w Wymynswold and Goodnestone etc from 92. *The Rectory, Vicarage Lane, Nonington, Dover, Kent CT15 4JT* Tel (01304) 840271

GOODWIN, Dr Barry Frederick John. b 48. Birm Univ BSc69 PhD77. St Jo Coll Nottm LTh88. **d** 88 **p** 89. C Ware Ch Ch *St Alb* 88-91; P-in-c Stanstead Abbots 91-96; P-in-c Gt Amwell w St Marg 95-96; V Gt Amwell w St Margaret's and Stanstead Abbots from 96. *The Vicarage, 25 Hoddesdon Road, Stanstead Abbotts, Ware, Herts SG12 8EG* Tel (01920) 870115

GOODWIN, Daphne Mary. **d** 97. NSM Ifield *Chich* from 97. *150 Buckswood Drive, Gossops Green, Crawley, W Sussex RH11 8JF* Tel (01293) 612906

GOODWIN, David Wayne. b 71. Univ of Wales BD95. Cranmer Hall Dur 95. **d** 97. C Ches H Trin *Ches* from 97. *44 Southway, Blacon, Chester CH1 5NN* Tel (01244) 373955

GOODWIN, Canon John Fletcher Beckles. b 20. Jes Coll Cam BA43 MA46. Ridley Hall Cam 42. **d** 45 **p** 46. C Southall H Trin *Lon* 45-48; C Drypool *York* 48-49; Niger 50-57; Vice-Prin Ripon Hall Ox 57-62; V Mert *Ox* 62-70; V Heanor *Derby* 70-74; V Hazelwood 74-85; V Turnditch 74-85; Adv for In-Service Tr and Chapl to Bp 74-88; Hon Can Derby Cathl 81-85; rtd 85; Perm to Offic *Derby* from 85. *63 Ladywood Avenue, Belper, Derbyshire DE56 1HT* Tel (01773) 820844

GOODWIN, Ronald Victor (Ron). b 33. S'wark Ord Course. **d** 86 **p** 87. NSM Wickford and Runwell *Chelmsf* from 86. *164 Southend Road, Wickford, Essex SS11 8EH* Tel (01268) 734447

GOODWIN, Stephen. b 58. Sheff Univ BA80. Cranmer Hall Dur 82. **d** 85 **p** 86. C Lytham St Cuth *Blackb* 85-87; C W Burnley 88-90; TV Headley All SS *Guildf* from 90. *St Mark's Vicarage, 58 Forest Road, Bordon, Hants GU35 0BP* Tel (01420) 477550

GOODWIN, Mrs Susan Elizabeth. b 51. Leeds Poly BSc74 Leeds Univ MSc76. St Jo Coll Dur 82. **dss** 84 **d** 87 **p** 94. Norton Woodseats St Chad *Sheff* 84-87; Par Dn 87; Chapl Scargill Ho 87-89; NSM W Burnley *Blackb* 89-90; NSM Headley All SS *Guildf* from 90; Past Asst Acorn Chr Healing Trust 91-93. *St Mark's Vicarage, 58 Forest Road, Bordon, Hants GU35 0BP* Tel (01420) 477550

GOODWINS, Christopher William Hedley. b 36. St Jo Coll Cam BA58 MA62. Linc Th Coll 62. **d** 64 **p** 65. C Lowestoft Ch Ch *Nor* 64-69; V Tamerton Foliot *Ex* from 69; P-in-c Southway 78-82. *St Mary's Vicarage, Tamerton Foliot, Plymouth PL5 4NH* Tel (01752) 771033

GOODYER, Edward Arthur (Ted). b 42. Witwatersrand Univ BA63 SS Coll Cam BA67 MA70 Rhodes Univ MTh91. St Pet Coll Grahamstown 68. **d** 68 **p** 69. S Africa 69-92; Can Cape Town 80-84; R Alverstoke *Portsm* from 92; P-in-c Gosport Ch Ch from 97. *The Rectory, Little Anglesey Road, Alverstoke, Gosport, Hants PO12 2JA* Tel (01705) 581979

GOOLD, Peter John. b 44. Lon Univ BD74. St Steph Ho Ox 67. **d** 70 **p** 71. C Chiswick St Nic w St Mary *Lon* 70-73; Chapl Asst R Masonic Hosp Lon 73-74; Chapl Asst Basingstoke Distr Hosp 74-77; Chapl R Marsden Hosp Lon and Surrey 77-80; Chapl N Hants Hosp 80-94; Chapl N Hants Hosps NHS Trust from 94; Chapl Loddon Trust Hants from 94; Perm to Offic *Guildf* from 94. *The North Hampshire Hospital, Aldermaston Road, Basingstoke, Hants RG24 9NA* Tel (01256) 473202

GORDON, Canon Alexander Ronald. b 49. Nottm Univ BPharm71 Leeds Univ DipTh76. Coll of Resurr Mirfield 74. **d** 77 **p** 78. C Headingley *Ripon* 77-80; C Fareham SS Pet and Paul *Portsm* 80-83; V Cudworth *Wakef* 83-85; Hon C Tain *Mor* 85-87; P-in-c Lairg Miss from 87; P-in-c Brora from 88; P-in-c Dornoch from 88; Dioc Dir of Ords from 89; Can St Andr Cathl Inverness from 95. *The Grange, Lochside, Lairg, Sutherland IV27 4EG* Tel (01549) 402295 or 402374 Fax 402295

✠**GORDON, The Rt Revd Archibald Ronald McDonald.** b 27. Ball Coll Ox BA50 MA52. Cuddesdon Coll 50. **d** 52 **p** 53 **c** 75. C Stepney St Dunstan and All SS *Lon* 52-55; Chapl Cuddesdon Coll 55-59; Lic to Offic *Ox* 57-59; V Birm St Pet *Birm* 59-68; Lect Qu Coll Birm 60-62; Can Res Birm Cathl *Birm* 67-71; V Ox

St Mary V w St Cross and St Pet *Ox* 71-75; Bp Portsm 75-84; Bp at Lambeth (Hd of Staff) *Cant* 84-91; Asst Bp S'wark 84-91; Bp HM Forces 85-90; Can Res and Sub-Dean Ch Ch *Ox* 91-96; Asst Bp Ox from 91; rtd 96. *16 East St Helen Street, Abingdon, Oxon OX14 5EA* Tel (01235) 526956

GORDON, Bruce Harold Clark. b 40. Hull Univ DipMin87 Edin Univ MTh96. Cranmer Hall Dur 65. **d** 68 **p** 69. C Edin St Jas *Edin* 68-71; C Blackheath St Jo *S'wark* 71-74; R Duns *Edin* 74-90; R Lanark *Glas* from 90; R Douglas from 90. *The Rectory, 1 Cleghorn Road, Lanark ML11 7QT* Tel (01555) 663065

GORDON, David John. b 65. Edin Th Coll CECM93. **d** 93 **p** 94. Chapl St Andr Cathl *Ab* 93-95; P-in-c Alexandria *Glas* from 95. *St Mungo's Rectory, Queen Street, Alexandria, Dunbartonshire G83 0AS* Tel (01389) 752633 Fax as telephone

GORDON, Donald Ian (Don). b 30. Nottm Univ BA52 PhD64. Westcott Ho Cam 71. **d** 71 **p** 72. NSM Newport *Chelmsf* 71-75; NSM Creeksea w Althorne, Latchingdon and N Fambridge from 76. *Holden House, Steeple Road, Latchingdon, Chelmsford CM3 6JX* Tel (01621) 740296

GORDON, Edward John. b 32. Univ of Wales BA52. St Mich Coll Llan 52. **d** 55 **p** 56. C Baglan *Llan* 55-61; C Newcastle w Laleston and Tythegston 61-65; V Ynyshir 65-69; C Bramhall *Ches* 69-72; V Cheadle Hulme All SS 72-79; V Tranmere St Paul w St Luke 79-88; V Sandbach Heath from 88; Chapl Arclid Hosp 90-93; RD Congleton *Ches* 92-97; P-in-c Wheelock 95-97; rtd 97. *55 Greenslade Gardens, Nailsea, Bristol BS19 2BJ*

GORDON, Ms Jennifer Anne. b 60. Hull Univ BSc81. S Dios Minl Tr Scheme 90. **d** 93 **p** 94. C Alverstoke *Portsm* 93-96; C Elson from 97. *1 Newlands Avenue, Alverstoke, Gosport, Hants PO12 3QX* Tel (01705) 522710

GORDON, John Michael. b 30. CITC. **d** 83 **p** 84. NSM Dublin St Geo *D & G* 83-85; NSM Dublin Irishtown w Donnybrook from 85. *Ferndale House, Rathmichael, Shankill, Co Dublin, Irish Republic* Tel Dublin (1) 282 2421 Fax 282 2954

GORDON, Jonathan Andrew. b 61. Keele Univ BA83 Southn Univ BTh88. Sarum & Wells Th Coll. **d** 87 **p** 88. C Wallingford w Crowmarsh Gifford etc *Ox* 87-91; C Tilehurst St Mich 91-93; TV Stoke-upon-Trent *Lich* from 93. *All Saints Vicarage, 540 Leek Road, Hanley, Stoke-on-Trent ST1 3HH* Tel (01782) 205713

GORDON, Canon Kenneth Davidson. b 35. Edin Univ MA57. Tyndale Hall Bris 58. **d** 60 **p** 61. C St Helens St Helen *Liv* 60-66; V Daubhill *Man* 66-71; R Bieldside *Ab* from 71; Can St Andr Cathl from 81; Syn Clerk *St And* from 96. *St Devenick's Rectory, Bieldside, Aberdeen AB1 9AP* Tel (01224) 861552 Fax 869463

GORDON, Robert Andrew. b 42. Llan Dioc Tr Scheme 82. **d** 84 **p** 85. C Bargoed and Deri w Brithdir *Llan* 84-87; V Aberpergwm and Blaengwrach 87-94; R Johnston w Steynton *St D* 94-97; R Cosheston w Nash and Upton from 97. *The Rectory, St Michael's House, Cosheston, Pembroke Dock SA72 4UD* Tel (01646) 682477

GORDON, Robert Douglas (Rob). b 57. Hull Univ BSc. Trin Coll Bris BA87. **d** 87 **p** 88. C Bridgwater St Fran *B & W* 87-90; C Street w Walton 90-93. *1 Newland Avenue, Alverstoke, Gosport, Hants PO12 3QX* Tel (01705) 522710

GORDON, Robert John. b 56. Edin Univ MA81. Wycliffe Hall Ox 87. **d** 89 **p** 90. C Wilnecote *Lich* 89-91; C Bideford *Ex* 91-95; P-in-c Feniton, Buckerell and Escot from 95. *The Rectory, Feniton, Honiton, Devon EX14 0ED* Tel (01404) 850253

GORDON, Thomas William. b 57. QUB BEd80 Univ of Ulster MA86 TCD BTh89 DPS Dip Counselling 96. CITC 85. **d** 89 **p** 90. C Ballymacash *Conn* 89-91; Min Can Belf Cathl 91-95; Chapl and Tutor CITC 91-96; Dir Extra-Mural Studies from 96; PV Ch Ch Cathl Dublin *D & G* from 96. *CITC, Braemor Park, Dublin 14, Irish Republic* Tel Dublin (1) 492 3506 Fax 492 3082

GORDON CLARK, Charles Philip. b 36. Worc Coll Ox BA59 MA61. Cuddesdon Coll 61. **d** 62 **p** 63. C Haslemere *Guildf* 62-65; Chapl Tonbridge Sch 65-68; R Keston *Roch* 68-74; V Tunbridge Wells K Chas 74-86; Perm to Offic *S & B* from 86; rtd 96. *4 Dan yr Allt, Llaneglwys, Builth Wells LD2 3BJ* Tel (01982) 560656

GORDON CLARK, John Vincent Michael. b 29. FCA DipRS. S'wark Ord Course 73. **d** 76 **p** 77. NSM Guildf H Trin w St Mary *Guildf* 76-81; NSM Albury w St Martha 81-92; Dioc Chapl to MU from 92; Perm to Offic 92-96. *Hillfield, 8 Little Warren Close, Guildford GU4 8PW* Tel (01483) 69027

GORDON-CUMMING, Henry Ian. b 28. Called to the Bar (Gray's Inn) 56. Oak Hill Th Coll 54. **d** 57 **p** 58. C Southsea St Jude *Portsm* 57-60; Uganda 61-68; V Virginia Water *Guildf* 68-78; R Busbridge 78-87; V Lynch w Iping Marsh and Milland *Chich* 87-94; rtd 94; Perm to Offic *Chich* from 94. *Bay Cottage, Brookside, Runcton, Chichester, W Sussex PO20 6PX* Tel (01243) 783395

GORDON-KERR, Canon Francis Alexander. b 39. Dur Univ BA64 MA67 Hull Univ PhD81 DipEd. Wycliffe Hall Ox 65. **d** 67 **p** 68. C Heworth St Mary *Dur* 67-70; Chapl Newc Poly *Newc* 70-75; Chapl Hull Univ *York* 75-82; V Welton w Melton 82-92; Clergy Tr Officer E Riding 82-92; AD W Hull 87-96; RD Hull 89-96; Can and Preb York Minster from 89; V Anlaby St Pet from 92. *The Vicarage, Church Street, Anlaby, Hull HU10 7DG* Tel (01482) 653024

GORDON-TAYLOR, Benjamin Nicholas. b 69. St Jo Coll Dur BA90 MA92 Leeds Univ BA94. Coll of Resurr Mirfield 92. **d** 95 **p** 96. C Launceston *Truro* 95-97; C Northampton St Matt *Pet* from 97. *5 Brookland Crescent, Northampton NN1 4SS* Tel (01604) 711467

GORE, Canon John Charles. b 29. Leeds Univ BA52. Coll of Resurr Mirfield 52. **d** 54 **p** 55. C Middlesbrough St Jo the Ev *York* 54-59; N Rhodesia 59-64; Zambia 64-75; Can Lusaka 70-75; R Elland *Wakef* 75-84; TR 84-86; RD Brighouse and Elland 77-86; V Wembley Park St Aug *Lon* 86-95; P-in-c Tokyngton St Mich 89-90; AD Brent 90-95; rtd 95; P-in-c Heptonstall *Wakef* from 95. *16 Hepton Drive, Heptonstall, Hebden Bridge, W Yorkshire HX7 7LU* Tel (01422) 842004

GORE, Canon John Harrington. b 24. Em Coll Cam BA49 MA52. Westcott Ho Cam 49. **d** 51 **p** 52. C Deane *Man* 51-54; C Whitstable All SS w St Pet *Cant* 54-59; CF 59-62; V Womenswold *Cant* 62-67; C-in-c Aylesham CD 62-67; R Deal St Leon 67-75; RD Sandwich 70-78; P-in-c Sholden 74-75; R Deal St Leon w Sholden 75-80; R Southchurch H Trin *Chelmsf* 80-90; RD Southend-on-Sea 84-89; Hon Can Chelmsf Cathl 86-90; rtd 90; Perm to Offic *St E* from 90; Perm to Offic *Chelmsf* from 90. *8 De Burgh Place, Clare, Suffolk CO10 8QL* Tel (01787) 278558

GORHAM, Andrew Arthur. b 51. Bris Univ BA73 Birm Univ DipTh78 MA87. Qu Coll Birm 77. **d** 79 **p** 80. C Plaistow St Mary *Roch* 79-82; Chapl Lanchester Poly *Cov* 82-87; TV Warwick 87-95; Chapl Birm Univ *Birm* from 95. *258 Mary Vale Road, Bournville, Birmingham B30 1PJ* Tel 0121-458 7432 E-mail aagorham@bham.ac.uk

GORHAM, Ms Karen Marisa. b 64. Trin Coll Bris BA95. **d** 95 **p** 96. C Northallerton w Kirby Sigston *York* from 95. *1 Ashlands Road, Northallerton, N Yorkshire DL6 1HA* Tel (01609) 777385

GORICK, David Charles. b 32. Reading Univ BA55 Nottm Univ DipEd72. EMMTC 81. **d** 84 **p** 85. NSM W Bridgford *S'well* 84-89; C Gotham 89-97; C Kingston and Ratcliffe-on-Soar 89-97; C Barton in Fabis 89-97; C Thrumpton 89-97; P-in-c Gotham from 97. *The New Rectory, 39 Leake Road, Gotham, Notts NG11 0JL* Tel 0115-983 0608

GORICK, Janet Margaret. b 30. Reading Univ BA54. EMMTC 84. **dss** 86 **d** 87 **p** 94. Hon Par Dn W Bridgford *S'well* 87-95; NSM Gotham from 95; NSM Barton in Fabis from 95; NSM Kingston and Ratcliffe-on-Soar from 95; NSM Thrumpton from 95. *The New Rectory, 39 Leake Road, Gotham, Nottingham NG11 0JL* Tel 0115-983 0608

GORICK, Martin Charles William. b 62. Selw Coll Cam BA84 MA88. Ripon Coll Cuddesdon 85. **d** 87 **p** 88. C Birtley *Dur* 87-91; Bp's Dom Chapl *Ox* 91-94; V Smethwick *Birm* from 94; RD Warley from 97. *The Vicarage, 93A Church Road, Smethwick, Warley, W Midlands B67 6EE* Tel 0121-558 1763

GORING, Charles Robert (Charlie). b 60. Linc Th Coll CMM93. **d** 93 **p** 94. C Thornbury *Glouc* 93-96; Perm to Offic *Chich* from 96. *6 Toll Wood Road, Horham, Heathfield, E Sussex TN21 0DX*

GORNALL, William Brian. b 36. OStJ SRN58. Ely Th Coll 61. **d** 64 **p** 65. C Blackpool St Mich *Blackb* 64-67; C Cheshunt *St Alb* 67-69; P-in-c Blackb St Pet w All SS *Blackb* 69-75; Hon Chapl and Lect Blackb Coll of Tech 69-75; V Blackb St Pet w All SS 75-79; V Blackpool St Mich 79-84; V Torrisholme 84-91; C Greenhill *Sheff* 91-94; rtd 94. *St George's Presbytery, 1 Sansome Place, Worcester WR1 1UG* Tel (01905) 22574

GORRIE, Richard Bingham. b 27. Univ Coll Ox BA49 MA51. Ridley Hall Cam 49. **d** 51 **p** 52. C Ox St Clem *Ox* 51-54; C Morden *S'wark* 54-56; Scripture Union Rep (Scotland) 56-92; Chapl Fettes Coll Edin 60-74; Dir Inter-Sch Chr Fellowship (Scotland) 74-80; rtd 92; Perm to Offic *Glas* from 92. *5 Ashlea Drive, Giffnock, Glasgow G46 6BX* Tel 0141-637 5946

GORRINGE, Timothy Jervis. b 46. St Edm Hall Ox BA69 MPhil75. Sarum Th Coll 69. **d** 72 **p** 73. C Chapel Allerton *Ripon* 72-75; C Ox St Mary V w St Cross and St Pet *Ox* 76-78; India 79-86; Chapl St Jo Coll Ox 86-96; Reader St Andr Univ from 96. *99 Magdalen Yard Road, Dundee DD2 1BA*

GORTON, Anthony David Trevor. b 39. Lon Univ BSc65. Oak Hill Th Coll 78. **d** 81 **p** 82. Hon C Colney Heath St Mark *St Alb* from 81. *Waterdell, Lane End, Hatfield, Herts AL10 9DU* Tel (01707) 263605

GORTON, Ian Charles Johnson. b 62. Bp Otter Coll BA84 Sarum & Wells Th Coll 86. **d** 89 **p** 90. C Wythenshawe Wm Temple Ch *Man* 89-92; C Man Apostles w Miles Platting 92-95; P-in-c Abbey Hey from 95. *St George's Rectory, 10 Redacre Road, Abbey Hey, Manchester M18 8RD* Tel 0161-223 1624

GORTON, Sarah Helen Buchanan (Sally). b 44. **d** 96. NSM Lenzie *Glas* from 96. *Northbank Gardens, Northbank Road, Kirkintilloch, Glasgow G66 1EZ* Tel 0141-775 1204

GOSDEN, Timothy John. b 50. Open Univ BA86. Chich Th Coll 74. **d** 77 **p** 78. C Cant All SS *Cant* 77-81; Asst Chapl Loughb Univ *Leic* 81-85; Lic to Offic *Cant* 85-87; Chapl Ch Ch Coll Cant 85-87; Sen Chapl Hull Univ 87-94; V Taunton Lyngford *B & W* from 94. *St Peter's Vicarage, Eastwick Road, Taunton, Somerset TA2 7HD* Tel (01823) 275085

GOSHAI, Miss Veja Helena. b 32. SRN57 SCM59 MTD66. Trin Coll Bris 75. **d** 87 **p** 94. Asst Chapl St Bart Hosp Lon from 87; rtd 91. *Box 305, Gloucester House, Little Britain, London EC1A 7DN*

GOSLING, Dr David Lagourie. b 39. MInstP69 CPhys84 Man Univ MSc63 Fitzw Coll Cam MA69 Lanc Univ PhD74. Ridley

Hall Cam 63. **d** 73 **p** 74. Hon C Lancaster St Mary *Blackb* 73-74; Hon C Kingston upon Hull St Matt w St Barn *York* 74-77; Hon C Cottingham 78-83; Lic to Offic *Eur* 83-84 and 88-94; Chapl Geneva 84-88; C Cambridge Gt St Mary w St Mich *Ely* from 89; C Dry Drayton 90-94; India from 95. *Great St Mary's, Cambridge CB2 3PQ, or St Stephen's College, University of Delhi, Delhi 110007, India* Fax (01223) 350914 or Delhi (11) 725 796

GOSLING, James Albert (Jim). b 41. Oak Hill Th Coll. **d** 84 **p** 85. NSM Victoria Docks St Luke *Chelmsf* 84-96; Perm to Offic from 96; Hon C Gt Mongeham w Ripple and Sutton by Dover *Cant* from 96; Hon C Eastry and Northbourne w Tilmanstone etc from 96. *The Rectory, The Street, Northbourne, Deal, Kent CT14 0LG* Tel (01304) 374967

GOSLING, John William Fraser. b 34. St Jo Coll Dur BA58 DipTh60 MA71 Ex Univ PhD78. Cranmer Hall Dur 58. **d** 60 **p** 61. C Plympton St Mary *Ex* 60-68; V Newport 68-78; Org Sec (Dios St Alb and Ox) CECS 78-82; C Stratford sub Castle *Sarum* 83-86; Adv on Cont Minl Educn 83-86; Perm to Offic 86-91; C Swindon Ch Ch *Bris* 91-95; rtd 95. *1 Wiley Terrace, Wilton, Salisbury SP2 0HN* Tel (01722) 742788

GOSNEY, Jeanette Margaret. b 58. Bath Univ BA81 Nottm Univ PGCE82. St Jo Coll Nottm BTh93 MPhil95. **d** 95 **p** 96. C Ipswich St Marg *St E* from 95. *44 Corder Road, Ipswich IP4 2XD* Tel (01473) 231137

GOSS, David James. b 52. Nottm Univ BCombStuds. Linc Th Coll. **d** 83 **p** 84. C Wood Green St Mich w Bounds Green St Gabr etc *Lon* 83-86; TV Gleadless Valley *Sheff* 86-89; TR 89-95; V Wheatley Hills from 95. *The Vicarage, Central Boulevard, Doncaster, S Yorkshire DN2 5PE* Tel (01302) 342047

GOSS, Kevin Ian. b 56. LRAM75 LTCL76 GRSM77 LGSM80 Hughes Hall Cam PGCE78. S Dios Minl Tr Scheme 89. **d** 92 **p** 93. NSM Ardingly *Chich* from 92; Asst Chapl Ardingly Coll Haywards Heath from 92. *11 Gordon Close, Haywards Heath, W Sussex RH16 1ER* Tel (01444) 417187

GOSS, Michael John. b 37. Chich Th Coll 62. **d** 65 **p** 66. C Angell Town St Jo *S'wark* 65-68; C Catford St Laur 68-71; P-in-c Lewisham St Swithun 71-81; V Redhill St Jo 81-88; V Dudley St Thos and St Luke *Worc* from 88. *The Vicarage, King Street, Dudley, W Midlands DY2 8QB* Tel (01384) 252015

GOSS, The Very Revd Thomas Ashworth. b 12. St Andr Univ MA36. Ridley Hall Cam 35. **d** 37 **p** 38. C Frodingham *Linc* 37-41; Chapl RAFVR 41-47; V Sutton le Marsh *Linc* 47-51; Chapl RAF 51-67; QHC 66-67; R Jersey St Sav *Win* 67-71; Dean Jersey 71-85; Hon Can Win Cathl 71-85; R Jersey St Helier 71-85; rtd 85. *Les Pignons, Mont de la Rosière, Jersey JE2 6RG* Tel (01534) 861433

GOSSWINN, Nicholas Simon. b 50. Birm Poly FGA80. St D Coll Lamp DipTh73. **d** 73 **p** 77. C Abergavenny St Mary *Mon* 73-74; C-in-c Bassaleg 74-80; TV Barrow St Geo w St Luke *Carl* 81-87; C Usworth *Dur* 89-90; TV 90-96; P-in-c Sunderland Red Ho from 96. *St Cuthbert's Vicarage, Rotherham Road, Sunderland SR5 5QS* Tel 0191-549 1261

GOSWELL, Geoffrey. b 34. SS Paul & Mary Coll Cheltenham CertEd68. Glouc Th Course 70. **d** 71 **p** 72. C Cheltenham Em *Glouc* 71-73; C Lydney w Aylburton 73-76; P-in-c Falfield w Rockhampton 76-79; Chapl HM Det Cen Eastwood Park 76-79; Area Sec CMS (Dios Linc and Pet) 79-86; (Dio Ely) 79-81; CMS Dep Regional Sec (UK) from 86; P-in-c Orton Waterville *Ely* 90-96; TV The Ortons, Alwalton and Chesterton from 96. *The Rectory, 67 Church Drive, Orton Waterville, Peterborough PE2 5HE* Tel (01733) 238877

GOTELEE, Peter Douglas. b 28. K Coll Lon 50. **d** 54 **p** 55. C Croydon St Pet S End *Cant* 54-57; C Camberley St Paul *Guildf* 57-65; P-in-c Badshot Lea CD 65-75; P-in-c Bisley 75-76; V W End 75-76; R Bisley and W End 76-85; V Yarcombe w Membury and Upottery *Ex* 85-93; P-in-c Cotleigh 85-93; rtd 93; Perm to Offic *Ex* from 93. *3 Sharpiter Close, Paignton, Devon TQ3 1AR* Tel (01803) 559150

GOTT, Joseph Desmond. b 26. Ch Ch Ox BA47 MA51 St Chad's Coll Dur DipTh52. **d** 52 **p** 53. C Horden *Dur* 52-55; C Bishopwearmouth St Mich 55-58; R Bishopwearmouth St Mich w St Hilda 58-66; Prin Argyle Ho Sch Sunderland 59-65; V Down Ampney *Glouc* 66-72; PC Poulton 66-69; V 69-72; V Cheltenham St Steph 72-89; rtd 89. *3 Avonmore, 24 Granville Road, Eastbourne, E Sussex BH20 7HA* Tel (01323) 736222

GOTT, Stephen. b 61. St Jo Coll Nottm DipThMin94. **d** 94 **p** 95. C Mount Pellon *Wakef* 94-97; V Greetland and W Vale from 97. *The Vicarage, 2 Goldfields Way, Greetland, Halifax, W Yorkshire HX4 8LA* Tel (01422) 372802

GOUGH, Andrew Stephen. b 60. Sarum & Wells Th Coll 83. **d** 86 **p** 87. C St Leonards Ch Ch and St Mary *Chich* 86-88; C Broseley w Benthall *Heref* 88-90; V Ketley and Oakengates *Lich* 90-93; TV Bickleigh (Plymouth) *Ex* 93; TV Bickleigh (Roborough) and Shaugh Prior 94; P-in-c St Day *Truro* 94-96; V Chacewater w St Day and Carharrack from 96. *The Vicarage, St Day, Redruth, Cornwall TR16 5LD* Tel (01209) 820275

GOUGH, Andrew Walter. b 55. Bris Univ BA78. Trin Coll Bris ADMT92. **d** 92 **p** 93. C Mossley Hill St Matt and St Jas *Liv* 92-94; C Wavertree H Trin 94-96; Chapl Warw Sch from 96. *9 Griffin Road, Warwick CV34 6QX* Tel (01926) 400533 E-mail agough@trinity.u-net.com

GOUGH, Dr Anthony Walter (Tony). b 31. Lon Univ DipTh68 Leic Univ MA76. Chicago Th Sem DMin81 Oak Hill Th Coll 57. **d** 60 **p** 61. C Southsea St Simon *Portsm* 60-64; R Peldon *Chelmsf* 64-71; V Rothley *Leic* 71-80; USA 80-81; Chapl St Jo Hosp Aylesbury 81-82; Perm to Offic *Leic* 82-96; rtd 96. *410 Hinckley Road, Leicester LE3 0WA* Tel 0116-285 4284 Fax as telephone

GOUGH, Colin Richard. b 47. St Chad's Coll Dur BA69. Cuddesdon Coll 73. **d** 75 **p** 76. C Lich St Chad *Lich* 75-78; C Codsall 78-84; V Wednesbury St Paul Wood Green 84-92; TR Tettenhall Wood from 92. *Christ Church Rectory, 7 Broxwood Park, Tettenhall Wood, Wolverhampton WV6 8LZ* Tel (01902) 751116

GOUGH, David Norman. b 42. Oak Hill Th Coll 70. **d** 70 **p** 71. C Penn Fields *Lich* 70-73; C Stapenhill w Cauldwell *Derby* 73-77; V Heath 77-86; P-in-c Derby St Chad 86-95; TV Walbrook Epiphany from 95. *81 Palmerston Street, Derby DE23 6PF* Tel (01332) 760846

GOUGH, Derek William. b 31. Pemb Coll Cam BA55 MA59. St Steph Ho Ox 55. **d** 57 **p** 58. C E Finchley All SS *Lon* 57-60; C Roxbourne St Andr 60-66; V Edmonton St Mary w St Jo from 66. *St John's Vicarage, Dysons Road, London N18 2DS* Tel 0181-807 2767

GOUGH, Canon Ernest Hubert. b 31. TCD BA53 MA57. **d** 54 **p** 55. C Glenavy *Conn* 54-57; C Lisburn Ch Ch 57-61; P-in-c Belfast St Ninian 61-62; I 62-71; I Belfast St Bart 71-85; I Templepatrick w Donegore 85-97; Can Conn Cathl from 91; rtd 97. *The Cairn, 15 Swilly Road, Portstewart, Co Londonderry BT55 7DJ* Tel (01265) 833253

GOUGH, Frank Peter. b 32. Lon Coll of Div 66. **d** 68 **p** 69. C Weymouth St Mary *Sarum* 68-70; C Attenborough w Chilwell *S'well* 70-73; R Barrow *Ches* 73-77; P-in-c Summerstown *S'wark* 77-88; RD Tooting 80-88; Dioc Past Sec 88-93; Chapl and Tutor Whittington Coll Felbridge from 93. *32 Whittington College, London Road, Felbridge, East Grinstead, W Sussex RH19 2QU* Tel (01342) 322790

✠**GOUGH, The Rt Revd Hugh Rowlands.** b 05. CMG55 OBE45 TD50. Trin Coll Cam BA27 MA31. Lambeth DD59 ACT Hon ThD59 Wycliffe Coll Toronto Hon DD63 Lon Coll of Div 28. **d** 28 **p** 29 **c** 48. C Islington St Mary *Lon* 28-31; V 46-48; R Walcot *B & W* 31-34; V Carlisle St Jas 34-39; V Bayswater *Lon* 39-46; CF (TA) 39-45; RD Islington *Lon* 46-48; Preb St Paul's Cathl 48; Adn W Ham *Chelmsf* 48-58; Suff Bp Barking 48-58; Abp Sydney 58-66; Primate of Australia 59-66; R Freshford w Limpley Stoke *B & W* 67-72; rtd 72. *Forge House, Over Wallop, Stockbridge, Hants SO20 8JF* Tel (01264) 781315

GOUGH, Jonathan Robin Blanning. b 62. Univ of Wales (Lamp) BA83. St Steph Ho Ox 83. **d** 85 **p** 86. C Braunton *Ex* 85-86; C Matson *Glouc* 86-89; CF from 89. *MOD Chaplains (Army), Trenchard Lines, Upavon, Pewsey, Wilts SN9 6BE* Tel (01980) 615804 Fax 615800

GOUGH, Martyn John. b 66. Univ of Wales (Cardiff) 84. St Steph Ho Ox 88. **d** 90 **p** 91. C Port Talbot St Theodore *Llan* 90-92; C Roath St Marg 92-94; Asst Chapl Milan w Genoa and Varese *Eur* from 95. *The European School, Varese, Fermo Pasta 6855, Stabio, Switzerland*

GOUGH, Robert (Bob). b 50. S'wark Ord Course 79. **d** 82 **p** 83. C Heston *Lon* 82-83; C Feltham 83-86; TV Hemel Hempstead *St Alb* 86-90; NSM Kingston All SS w St Jo *S'wark* 90-91; Perm to Offic 91-94. *Pen y Gaer Uchaf, Llanfihangel Glyn Myfr, Corwen LL21 9UH* Tel (01490) 420791

GOUGH, Stephen William Cyprian. b 50. Alberta Univ BSc71. Cuddesdon Coll BA80. **d** 79 **p** 80. C Walton St Mary *Liv* 79-83; V New Springs 83-87; V Childwall St Dav from 87. *St David's Vicarage, Rocky Lane, Liverpool L16 1JA* Tel 0151-722 4549

GOULD, Alan Charles. b 26. Lon Univ DipTh53. **d** 62 **p** 63. C Bromborough *Ches* 62-67; V Audlem and Burleydam 67-80; P-in-c Coreley w Doddington *Heref* 80-83; V Knowbury 80-83; P-in-c Berrington and Betton Strange 83-91; P-in-c Cound 83-91; rtd 91; Perm to Offic *Heref* from 91; Perm to Offic *Lich* from 91. *32 Mytton Oak Road, Shrewsbury SY3 8UD* Tel (01743) 244820

GOULD, Preb Douglas Walter. b 35. St Jo Coll Cam BA59 MA63. Ridley Hall Cam 59. **d** 61 **p** 62. C Clifton *York* 61-64; C Bridgnorth w Tasley *Heref* 64-67; C Astley Abbotts w Linley 64-67; R Acton Burnell w Pitchford 67-73; P-in-c Cound 68-73; Asst Dioc Youth Officer 68-73; P-in-c Frodesley 69-73; V Bromyard from 73; P-in-c Stanford Bishop from 73; RD Bromyard from 73; Chapl Bromyard Hosp from 73; P-in-c Ocle Pychard *Heref* 76-88; P-in-c Ullingswick 76-88; P-in-c Stoke Lacy, Moreton Jeffries w Much Cowarne etc 76-83; Preb Heref Cathl from 83. *The Vicarage, 28 Church Lane, Bromyard, Herefordshire HR7 4DZ* Tel (01885) 482438

GOULD, Gerald. b 37. S Dios Minl Tr Scheme 84. **d** 86 **p** 87. C Hedge End *Win* 86-89; V St Goran w St Mich Caerhays *Truro* 89-93; P-in-c Crook Peak *B & W* 93-94; R from 94. *The Rectory, Sparrow Hill Way, Weare, Axbridge, Somerset BS26 2LE* Tel (01934) 733140

GOULD, Ms Jan. b 63. Westcott Ho Cam 92. **d** 95 **p** 96. C Pet St Mary Boongate *Pet* from 95. *19 Danes Close, Peterborough PE1 5LJ* Tel (01733) 53526

GOULD, John Barry. b 38. MICE68. S'wark Ord Course 77. **d** 77 **p** 78. C Streatham St Leon *S'wark* 77-80; V Upper Tooting H Trin 80-87; P-in-c Brockham Green 87-90; P-in-c Betchworth 87-95; P-in-c Buckland 87-95; C-in-c Roundshaw CD from 95. *St Paul's House, 32 Waterer Rise, Wallington, Surrey SM6 9DN* Tel 0181-773 2842

GOULD, Jonathan George Lillico. b 58. Bris Univ LLB79. Wycliffe Hall Ox 86. **d** 89 **p** 91. Australia 89-93; Schs Worker Scripture Union Independent Schs 93-95; Perm to Offic *S'wark* 93-95; Min Hampstead St Jo Downshire Hill Prop Chpl *Lon* from 95. *64 Pilgrim's Lane, London NE3 1SN* Tel 0171-435 8404 Fax as telephone

GOULD, Peter Richard. b 34. Univ of Wales BA57. Qu Coll Birm DipTh62. **d** 62 **p** 63. C Rothwell *Ripon* 62-68; V Allerton Bywater 68-73; Lic to Offic *S'well* 73-76; Chapl Lic Victuallers' Sch Ascot 76-93; V Aberavon H Trin *Llan* from 93. *Holy Trinity Vicarage, Fairway, Sandfields, Port Talbot SA12 7HG* Tel (01639) 884409

GOULD, Dr Robert Ozburn. b 38. Williams Coll Mass BA59 St Andr Univ PhD63. **d** 78 **p** 83. NSM Edin St Columba *Edin* 78-80; TV from 83; Hon Dioc Supernumerary 80-83. *33 Charterhall Road, Edinburgh EH9 3HS* Tel 0131-667 7230

GOULD, Susan Judith. *See* MURRAY, Mrs Susan Judith

GOULDING, Charles John. b 18. Sarum Th Coll 56. **d** 58 **p** 59. C Beddington *S'wark* 58-61; C Horsell *Guildf* 61-63; V Ardleigh *Chelmsf* 63-72; V Shrub End 72-84; RD Colchester 81-84; rtd 84; Hon C Fovant, Sutton Mandeville and Teffont Evias etc *Sarum* 84-86; Hon C Mayfield *Chich* 86-89; Perm to Offic 89-95; Perm to Offic *Ex* from 95. *Flat 14, Gracey Court, Woodlands Road, Broadclyst, Exeter EX5 3LP* Tel (01392) 462325

GOULDING, Edward William. b 23. St Aid Birkenhead 54. **d** 56 **p** 57. C Ross *Heref* 56-60; V Everton St Chad w Ch Ch *Liv* 60-64; V Knotty Ash St Jo 64-65; V Llangarron w Llangrove *Heref* 65-69; Chapl HM Pris Birm 69-72; V Gt Harwood St Bart *Blackb* 73-76; Lic to Offic 76-78; V Wray w Tatham Fells 78-87; rtd 88. *2 Crag Bank Road, Carnforth, Lancs LA5 9EG* Tel (01524) 735026

GOULDING, John Gilbert. b 29. Univ Coll Dur BA54 MA59. **d** 88 **p** 89. NSM Kemsing w Woodlands *Roch* from 88; Hon Nat Moderator for Reader Tr ACCM 90-91; ABM 91-94; Hon C Sevenoaks St Luke CD 91-96; Perm to Offic from 97. *Springwood, 50 Copperfields, Kemsing, Sevenoaks, Kent TN15 6QG* Tel (01732) 762558

GOULDING, Nicolas John. b 56. Southn Univ BSc78 PhD82. NTMTC 94. **d** 97. NSM Smithfield St Bart Gt *Lon* from 97. *5 Greatfield Close, Harpenden, Herts AL5 3HP* Tel (01582) 461293 Fax 0171-982 6076 E-mail n.j.goulding@mds.qmw.ac.uk

GOULDSTONE, Preb Timothy Maxwell. b 46. Ex Univ BSc68 MSc76. Trin Coll Bris 76. **d** 78 **p** 79. C Ware Ch Ch *St Alb* 78-81; P-in-c Ansley *Cov* 81-82; V 82-85; V St Keverne *Truro* 85-95; Preb St Endellion 90-95; P-in-c St Michael Penkevil from 95; Dioc Tr Officer from 95; RD Powder from 96. *The Rectory, Tresillian, Truro, Cornwall TR2 4AA* Tel (01872) 520431 E-mail gouldstone@btinternet.com

GOULSTONE, The Very Revd Thomas Richard Kerry. b 36. Univ of Wales (Lamp) BA57. St Mich Coll Llan 57. **d** 59 **p** 60. C Llanbadarn Fawr *St D* 59-61; C Carmarthen St Pet 61-64; V 84-93; V Whitchurch w Solva and St Elvis 64-67; V Gors-las 67-76; V Burry Port and Pwll 76-84; Chapl W Wales Gen Hosp Carmarthen 84-93; Can St D Cathl *St D* 86-93; Hon Can St D Cathl from 93; RD Carmarthen 88-92; Adn Carmarthen 91-93; Dean and Lib St As Cathl *St As* from 93. *The Deanery, St Asaph LL17 0RL* Tel (01745) 583597

GOUNDRY, Canon Ralph Walter. b 31. St Chad's Coll Dur BA56 DipTh58. **d** 58 **p** 59. C Harton Colliery *Dur* 58-62; Prec Newc Cathl *Newc* 62-65; V Sighill 65-72; V Long Benton 72-96; Hon Can Newc Cathl 94-96; rtd 96. *Chapter House, The Cloisters, Birker Lane, Wilberfoss, York YO4 5RH* Tel (01759) 388166

GOURLEY, William Robert Joseph. b 48. K Coll Lon BD74. CITC 68. **d** 75 **p** 76. C Newtownards *D & D* 75-78; I Currin w Drum and Newbliss *Clogh* 78-81; I Dublin St Geo and St Thos, Finglas and Free Ch *D & G* 81-88; RD St Mary 86-88; I Dublin Zion Ch from 88. *The Rectory, 18 Bushy Park Road, Rathgar, Dublin 6, Irish Republic* Tel Dublin (1) 492 2365

GOVAN, Kesh Rico. b 66. Bolton Inst of HE HND90. St Jo Coll Dur BA96. **d** 96 **p** 97. C Astley Bridge *Man* from 96. *51 Shoreswood, Bolton BL1 7DD* Tel (01204) 302070

GOVER, Michael Sydney Richard. b 41. Culham Coll Ox BA63. Chich Th Coll 68. **d** 71 **p** 72. C Ryde All SS *Portsm* 71-75; C Waterlooville 75-83; Perm to Offic 83-91; NSM Portsea Ascension from 91. *333 Twyford Avenue, Portsmouth PO2 8PE* Tel (01705) 671161

GOW, Iain Douglas. b 60. Denver Univ USA BA83 MIM85. Trin Coll Bris DipHE92 MA94. **d** 94 **p** 95. C Kenilworth St Jo *Cov* from 94. *14 Siddeley Avenue, Kenilworth, Warks CV8 1EW* Tel (01926) 59992

GOW, Peter Draffin. b 52. Bede Coll Dur BEd76. St Jo Coll Nottm 83. **d** 85. C Kingston Hill St Paul *S'wark* 85-86; rtd 86. *33 Canbury Avenue, Kingston upon Thames, Surrey KT2 6JP* Tel 0181-549 7942 E-mail petergow@waacis.edex.co.uk

GOWDEY, Canon Alan Lawrence. b 25. Trin Coll Toronto BA50 Ridley Hall Cam. **d** 52 **p** 53. C Swindon St Aug *Bris* 52-55; C Marshfield w Cold Ashton 55-57; Bp's Asst Soc and Ind Adv 57-62; Hon C Dartford H Trin *Roch* 62-66; Ind Chapl 62-75; Hon C Gravesend St Geo 66-75; Chapl Heathrow Airport *Lon* 75-82; Hon Can Gib Cathl *Eur* 82-84; Chapl Costa Blanca 82-85; Can Gib Cathl 84-86; Ind Chapl *Roch* 85-86; C Bromley SS Pet and Paul 87-88; rtd 88. *25 Osprey House, Sillwood Place, Brighton BN1 2ND* Tel (01273) 749459

GOWDEY, Michael Cragg. b 32. Or Coll Ox BA56 MA58 Keele Univ CertEd73. Qu Coll Birm DipTh57. **d** 58 **p** 59. C Ashbourne w Mapleton and Clifton *Derby* 58-63; V Chellaston 63-69; Asst Chapl Ellesmere Coll Shropshire 69-74; Chapl Trent Coll Nottm 74-81; Educn Chapl *Worc* 81-97; Chapl K Edw Sixth Form Coll Worc 81-97; rtd 97; P-in-c Beeley and Edensor *Derby* from 97. *The Vicarage, Edensor, Bakewell, Derbyshire DE45 1PH* Tel (01246) 582130

GOWEN, John Frank. b 30. **d** 87 **p** 89. NSM Lecale Gp *D & D* 87-91; NSM Cregagh 87-91; Lic to Offic from 91. *36 Downshire Road, Belfast BT6 9JL* Tel (01232) 701640

GOWER, Christopher Raymond. b 45. FRSA84 Nottm Univ BA73 Heythrop Coll Lon MA96. St Jo Coll Nottm 70. **d** 73 **p** 74. C Hounslow H Trin *Lon* 73-76; Hon C N Greenford All Hallows 76-77; P-in-c Willesden Green St Gabr 77-83; P-in-c Brondesbury St Anne w Kilburn H Trin 81-82; Perm to Offic 82-84; P-in-c Yiewsley 84-96; R St Marylebone w H Trin from 97. *21 Beaumont Street, London W1N 1FF* Tel 0171-935 8965

GOWER, Denys Victor. b 33. Cant Sch of Min 85. **d** 87 **p** 88. NSM Gillingham H Trin *Roch* 87-91; NSM Gillingham St Aug 89-91; C Perry Street 91-93; P-in-c Wateringbury w Teston and W Farleigh 93-96; R from 96. *The Rectory, Church Street, Teston, Maidstone, Kent ME18 5AJ* Tel (01622) 812494

GOWER, Nigel Plested. b 37. SS Coll Cam BA62 MA65 Lon Univ PGCE68. Ridley Hall Cam 61. **d** 63 **p** 64. C Walthamstow St Jo *Chelmsf* 63-66; CMS 67-78; Nigeria 67-78; P-in-c Loscoe *Derby* 78-79; V 79-88; RD Heanor 84-88; R Bamford from 88; Dioc World Development Officer 90-96; P-in-c Bradwell from 96. *The Rectory, Bamford, Sheffield S30 2AY* Tel (01433) 651375

GOWER, Miss Patricia Ann. b 44. Wilson Carlile Coll IDC79 Sarum & Wells Th Coll 88. **d** 88 **p** 94. Chapl Bris Univ *Bris* 88-91; Hon Par Dn Clifton St Paul 88-91; Par Dn Spondon *Derby* 91-94; C 94-95; Asst Chapl HM Open Pris Sudbury from 95; Asst Chapl HM Pris Foston Hall from 95. *The Rectory, Sudbury, Derby DE6 5HS* Tel (01283) 585302

GOWER, Archdeacon of. *See* PIERCE, The Ven Anthony Edward

GOWING, The Ven Frederick William. b 18. OBE85. TCD BA40. CITC 41. **d** 41 **p** 42. C Portadown St Mark *Arm* 41-47; I Woodschapel 47-56; I Mullavilly 56-84; Preb Arm Cathl 73-75; Treas 75-79; Adn Arm 79-84; rtd 84. *40 Old Rectory Park, Portadown, Craigavon, Co Armagh BT62 3QH* Tel (01762) 330933

GOYMOUR, Michael Edwyn. b 29. Selw Coll Cam BA51 McGill Univ Montreal BD53. Montreal Dioc Th Coll 51 Wells Th Coll 53. **d** 53 **p** 54. C Bury St Edmunds St Jo *St E* 53-56; C Ipswich St Bart 56-60; R Gamlingay *Ely* 60-68; rtd 92; Perm to Offic *Ely* from 92; Perm to Offic *Pet* from 92. *56 Church Drive, Orton Waterville, Peterborough PE2 5HE* Tel (01733) 231535

GRACE, Juliet Christine. b 38. Cam Inst of Educn 60. S Dios Minl Tr Scheme 84. **d** 87 **p** 94. NSM Petersfield *Portsm* 87-93; NSM Steep and Froxfield w Privett from 93; Community Mental Health Chapl Petersfield from 93. *33 Woodbury Avenue, Petersfield, Hants GU32 2ED* Tel (01730) 262335

GRACE, Kenneth. b 24. Leeds Univ BA49. Wycliffe Hall Ox 62. **d** 63 **p** 64. C Tonge w Alkrington *Man* 63-66; R Thwing *York* 66-70; V Wold Newton 66-70; Chapl St Andr Sch Worthing 70-76; R Berwick w Selmeston and Alciston *Chich* 76-81; P-in-c Kingston Buci 81-85; R Westbourne 85-90; rtd 90; Perm to Offic *Chich* from 90. *17 Beech Road, Findon, Worthing, W Sussex BN14 0UR* Tel (01903) 877021

GRACE, Richard Maurice. b 29. St Chad's Coll Dur BA53. Chich Th Coll 53. **d** 55 **p** 56. C Toxteth Park St Agnes *Liv* 55-58; C Wolverhampton St Pet *Lich* 58-62; V W Bromwich St Fran 62-78; P-in-c Salt 78-84; P-in-c Sandon w Burston 82-84; V Salt and Sandon w Burston 84-93; rtd 94; Perm to Offic *Ches* from 94. *Little Owls, 1 Trinity Close, Crewe CW2 8FD* Tel (01270) 662221

GRACE, Wilfrid Windsor. b 15. ACA39 FCA60. Westcott Ho Cam 52. **d** 53 **p** 54. C Chippenham St Andr w Tytherton Lucas *Bris* 53-57; V Minety w Oaksey 57-71; V Oldland 71-76; V Abbots Leigh w Leigh Woods 76-80; Chapl Ham Green Hosp 79-87; rtd 80; Perm to Offic *B & W* from 81; Hon Chapl Cheshire Home Axbridge from 81. *Hurn Mead, 71 Woodborough Road, Winscombe, Avon BS25 1BA* Tel (01934) 843362

GRACIE, Anthony Johnstone. b 25. Ch Coll Cam BA48 MA51. Linc Th Coll 57. **d** 59 **p** 60. C Edgbaston St Geo *Birm* 59-62; R Lyndon w Manton and Martinsthorpe *Pet* 62-76; R N Luffenham 66-76; V Odiham w S Warnborough *Win* 76; V Odiham w S Warnborough and Long Sutton 76-85; Perm to Offic *Bris* 85-88; rtd 88. *53 Ashford Road, Swindon SN1 3NS* Tel (01793) 695235

GRACIE, Bryan John. b 45. Open Univ BA81. AKC67. **d** 68 **p** 69. C Whipton *Ex* 68-72; Chapl St Jo Sch Tiffield 72-73; Chapl HM Borstal Stoke Heath 74-78; Asst Chapl HM Pris Liv 74; Chapl HM Youth Cust Cen Feltham 78-85; Chapl HM Pris Birm from 85. *HM Prison, Winson Green Road, Birmingham B18 4AS* Tel 0121-554 3838 Fax 554 7990

GRAEBE, Canon Denys Redford. b 26. Qu Coll Cam BA48 MA51. Westcott Ho Cam 50. **d** 51 **p** 52. C Hitchin St Mary *St Alb* 51-57; R Gt Parndon *Chelmsf* 57-72; V Norton *St Alb* 72-83; R Kimpton w Ayot St Lawrence 83-92; RD Wheathampstead 87-92; Hon Can St Alb Abbey 90-92; rtd 92. *5 Sancroft Way, Fressingfield, Eye, Suffolk IP21 5QN* Tel (01379) 588178

GRAESSER, Adrian Stewart. b 42. Tyndale Hall Bris 63. **d** 67 **p** 68. C Nottingham St Jude *S'well* 67-69; C Slaithwaite w E Scammonden *Wakef* 69-72; CF 72-75; V Earl's Heaton *Wakef* 75-81; R Norton Fitzwarren *B & W* 81-86; R Bickenhill w Elmdon *Birm* 86-90; R Elmdon St Nic from 90. *Elmdon Rectory, Tanhouse Farm Road, Solihull, W Midlands B92 9EY* Tel 0121-743 6336

GRAFTON, Roger Patrick. b 63. Lon Univ BA85. Trin Coll Bris DipHE90. **d** 91 **p** 92. C Kennington St Mark *S'wark* 91-92; C Dulwich St Barn 92-95; C Chasetown *Lich* 95-97. *258A Upland Road, London SE22 0DN*

GRAHAM, Alan Robert. b 44. St Edm Hall Ox BA67 MA71. St Steph Ho Ox 67. **d** 70 **p** 71. C Clifton All SS *Bris* 70-74; C Tadley St Pet *Win* 74-77; P-in-c Upper Clatford w Goodworth Clatford 77-79; R Abbotts Ann and Upper and Goodworth Clatford 79-84; V Lyndhurst and Emery Down 84-92; P-in-c Over Wallop w Nether Wallop from 92. *The Rectory, Over Wallop, Stockbridge, Hants SO20 8HT* Tel (01264) 781345

GRAHAM, Alfred. b 34. Bris Univ BA57. Tyndale Hall Bris. **d** 58 **p** 59. C Chaddesden St Mary *Derby* 58-61; C Bickenhill w Elmdon *Birm* 61-64; V Kirkdale St Lawr *Liv* 64-70; V Stapleford *S'well* 70-83; V Burton Joyce w Bulcote 83-95; V Burton Joyce w Bulcote and Stoke Bardolph from 95. *The Vicarage, 9 Chestnut Grove, Burton Joyce, Nottingham NG14 5DP* Tel 0115-931 2109

✠**GRAHAM, The Rt Revd Andrew Alexander Kenny (Alec).** b 29. St Jo Coll Ox BA52 DipTh53 MA57 Lambeth DD95. Ely Th Coll 53. **d** 55 **p** 56 **c** 77. C Hove All SS *Chich* 55-58; Chapl Lect Th and Tutor Worc Coll Ox 58-70; Can and Preb Linc Cathl *Linc* 70-77; Warden Linc Th Coll 70-77; Suff Bp Bedford *St Alb* 77-81; Bp Newc 81-97; Chmn Selectors ACCM 84-87; Chmn Doctrine Commn 87-97; rtd 97. *Fell End, Butterwick, Penrith, Cumbria CA10 2QQ*

GRAHAM, Canon Anthony Nigel. b 40. Univ of Wales (Abth) BA62 CertEd70. Ripon Hall Ox 62. **d** 64 **p** 65. C Heref H Trin *Heref* 64-67; C Birm St Martin *Birm* 67-69; C Selly Oak St Mary 71-75; V Edgbaston SS Mary and Ambrose 75-83; CMS Miss Partner Nigeria 84-88; Hon Can Jos from 88; V Highworth w Sevenhampton and Inglesham etc *Bris* 88-95; RD Highworth 93-95; P-in-c Coalpit Heath from 95. *The Vicarage, Beesmoor Road, Coalpit Heath, Bristol BS17 2RP* Tel (01454) 775129

GRAHAM, Anthony Stanley David (Tony). b 34. SS Coll Cam BA56 MA60. Cuddesdon Coll 58. **d** 60 **p** 61. C Welwyn Garden City *St Alb* 60-64; Asst Chapl Ipswich Sch 64-65; C Margate St Jo *Cant* 65-68; Chr Aid Area Sec Chich from 68; Perm to Offic *Cant* from 68. *48 Springfield Road, Crawley, W Sussex RH11 8AH* Tel (01293) 526279

GRAHAM, Clifton Gordon. b 53. ARCM72 GRSM74 FRCO75 Coll of Ripon & York St Jo PGCE76. St Steph Ho Ox 90. **d** 92 **p** 93. C Northfield *Birm* 92-93; C Perry Beeches 93-97; P-in-c S Yardley St Mich from 97. *St Michael's Vicarage, 60 Yew Tree Lane, Birmingham B26 1AP* Tel 0121-706 2563

GRAHAM, Canon Douglas Wrixon. b 13. TCD BA39. Div Test40. **d** 41 **p** 43. C Donaghcloney *D & D* 41-42; C Taney *D & G* 42-43; C New Ross *C & O* 43-50; I Killegney Union 50-66; I Roscommon w Donamon, Rathcline, Kilkeevin etc *K, E & A* 66-88; Preb Elphin Cathl 79-88; rtd 88. *6 St Theresa's Terrace, Lis na Nult, Roscommon, Irish Republic* Tel Roscommon (902) 25028

GRAHAM, Canon Frederick Lawrence. b 35. TCD BA65 DChCD88. CITC 66. **d** 66 **p** 67. C Belfast St Matt *Conn* 66-69; TV Chelmsley Wood *Birm* 69-73; Ch of Ireland Youth Officer 73-78; Bp's C Stoneyford *Conn* 78-88; Bp's C Fahan Lower and Upper *D & R* 88-91; RD Innishowen 88-96; Can Raphoe Cathl from 90; I Donagheady from 91; Can Derry Cathl from 95. *Earlsgift Rectory, 33 Longland Road, Donamana, Co Tyrone BT82 0PH* Tel (01504) 398017

GRAHAM, Frederick Louis Roth. b 20. Selw Coll Cam BA47 MA49. Ridley Hall Cam 48. **d** 50 **p** 51. C Shirley *Win* 50-53; R Old Trafford St Jo *Man* 53-61; R Wombwell *Sheff* 61-71; V Thorne 71-77; P-in-c Chilton-super-Polden w Edington *B & W* 77-82; P-in-c Catcott 77-82; V W Poldens 82-86; RD Glastonbury 82-86; rtd 86; Perm to Offic *Win* from 86. *73 Newlands Avenue, Southampton SO15 5EQ* Tel (01703) 789353

GRAHAM, George David. b 42. Jes Coll Cam BA64 MA68. St Jo Coll Nottm LTh Lon Coll of Div 66. **d** 71 **p** 72. C Corby St Columba *Pet* 71-74; C Deptford St Jo *S'wark* 74-77; P-in-c Deptford St Pet 77-82; C-in-c Wheatley Park St Paul CD *Sheff* 82-87; TV Dunstable *St Alb* 87-92; V Bromley Common St Luke *Roch* from 92. *St Luke's Vicarage, 20 Bromley Common, Bromley BR2 9PD* Tel 0181-464 2076

GRAHAM, George Edgar. b 55. QUB BA91. Sarum & Wells Th Coll 74 CITC 77. **d** 78 **p** 79. C Lisburn Ch Ch *Conn* 78-81; C Mossley 81-83; I Broomhedge 83-91; I Derriaghy w Colin 91-96; RD Derriaghy 94-96; I Ballywillan from 96. *The Rectory, 10 Coleraine Road, Portrush, Co Antrim BT56 8EA* Tel (01265) 824298

GRAHAM, George Gordon. b 17. OBE96. St Chad's Coll Dur BA48 DipTh50 MSc71. **d** 50 **p** 51. C Luton Ch Ch *St Alb* 50-53; C Bakewell *Derby* 53-56; P-in-c Wheatley Hill *Dur* 56-69; V Hunwick 69-88; Chapl Homelands Hosp Dur from 80; rtd 88. *3 The Willows, Bishop Auckland, Co Durham DL14 7HH* Tel (01388) 602758

GRAHAM, George Gordon. b 34. Harvard Univ BA55 MDiv JD71. **d** 96 **p** 97. Aux Min Seapatrick *D & D* from 97. *10 Castlebridge Court, Newcastle, Co Down BT32 0RF* Tel (013967) 726175 or (018206) 22612

GRAHAM, Gordon Cecil. b 31. JP. Ch Coll Cam BA53 MA57. Ripon Hall Ox 53. **d** 55 **p** 56. C Didsbury St Jas and Em *Man* 55-58; C Rochdale 58-60; R Heaton Mersey 60-67; Chapl Hulme Gr Sch Oldham 67-74; Lic to Offic *Ches* from 72; rtd 92. *21 The Crescent, Davenport, Stockport, Cheshire SK3 8SL* Tel 0161-483 6011

GRAHAM, Harry John. b 52. Magd Coll Cam BA75 MA86. Trin Coll Bris BA94. **d** 96 **p** 97. C Walkden Moor w Lt Hulton *Man* from 96. *37 Park Road, Worsley, Manchester M28 7DU* Tel 0161-799 1412

GRAHAM, Ian Maxwell. b 50. CertEd76. Chich Th Coll 86. **d** 88 **p** 89. C Middlesbrough St Thos *York* 88-90; C Stainton-in-Cleveland 90-93; V Hemlington from 93. *1 Southdene Drive, Hemlington, Middlesbrough, Cleveland TS8 9HH* Tel (01642) 590496

GRAHAM, James Hamilton. b 54. Solicitor 78 Cam Univ MA76 Ox Univ MA83. Ripon Coll Cuddesdon. **d** 84 **p** 85. C Harlescott *Lich* 84-88; C Moreton Say 88-93; R Hodnet w Weston under Redcastle from 93; RD Hodnet from 97. *The Rectory, Hodnet, Market Drayton, Shropshire TF9 3NQ* Tel (01630) 685491

GRAHAM, John. b 24. **d** 84 **p** 84. Hon C Glas St Kentigern *Glas* from 84; Chapl Glas R Infirmary from 84. *121 Garthland Drive, Glasgow G31 2SQ* Tel 0141-554 5718

GRAHAM, John Francis Ottiwell Skelton. b 15. G&C Coll Cam BA37 MA48. Wells Th Coll 37. **d** 39 **p** 40. C Walton St Mary *Liv* 39-48; V Speke All SS 48-58; V Winterbourne Earls w Winterbourne Dauntsey etc *Sarum* 58-72; R Bincombe w Broadwey 72-80; R Bincombe w Broadwey, Upwey and Buckland Ripers 80-81; rtd 81; Perm to Offic *Win* 81-95. *15A Belmore Lane, Lymington, Hants SO41 3NL* Tel (01590) 673256

GRAHAM, John Galbraith. b 21. K Coll Cam BA43 MA46. Ely Th Coll 46. **d** 48 **p** 49. C E Dulwich St Jo *S'wark* 48-49; Chapl St Chad's Coll *Dur* 49-52; C Aldershot St Mich *Guildf* 52-55; C-in-c Beaconsfield St Mich CD *Ox* 55-62; Chapl Reading Univ 62-72; C Pimlico St Pet w Westmr Ch Ch *Lon* 72-74; R Houghton w Wyton *Ely* 74-78; rtd 86; Lic to Offic *St E* from 86; Lic to Offic *Ely* from 86. *31 Rectory Lane, Somersham, Huntingdon, Cambs PE17 3EL* Tel (01487) 842737

GRAHAM, The Very Revd Malcolm Frederick. b 15. TCD BA37 MA69. **d** 40 **p** 41. C Ballymacarrett St Martin *D & D* 40-45; C Templemore *D & R* 45-47; P-in-c Clondehorkey 47-48; I 48-53; I Belfast St Luke *Conn* 53-60; I Kilbroney *D & D* 60-79; RD Newry and Mourne 61-79; RD Kilbroney 61-79; Preb St Patr Cathl Dublin 69-72; Dean Killala *T, K & A* 79-89; I Killala w Dunfeeny, Crossmolina etc 79-89; rtd 89. *Kilbroney, Rathnamaugh, Crossmolina, Co Mayo, Irish Republic* Tel Ballina (96) 31717

GRAHAM, Mrs Marion McKenzie. b 39. St As Minl Tr Course. **d** 89 **p** 97. NSM Bagillt *St As* 89-93; NSM Flint from 93. *Sharondale, Bryntirion Road, Bagillt CH6 6BZ* Tel (01352) 734139

GRAHAM, Canon Matthew. b 30. Univ Coll Dur BSc54. K Coll (NS) BD71 Ridley Hall Cam 54. **d** 56 **p** 57. C Littleover *Derby* 56-59; C Fazakerley Em *Liv* 59-61; V Huyton St Geo 61-65; Canada 65-71; V Sutton Coldfield St Columba *Birm* 71-85; V Warley Woods 85-95; RD Warley 87-93; Hon Can Birm Cathl 90-95; rtd 95. *18 The Drive, Checketts Lane, Worcester WR3 7JS* Tel (01905) 458151

GRAHAM, Michael. b 30. Westcott Ho Cam 61. **d** 61 **p** 62. C Withington St Paul *Man* 61-64; V Lawton Moor 64-87; R Mobberley *Ches* from 87. *The Rectory, Mobberley, Knutsford, Cheshire WA16 7RA* Tel (01565) 873218

GRAHAM, Michael. b 51. CITC BTh95. **d** 95 **p** 96. C Cork St Fin Barre's Union *C, C & R* from 95; Min Can Cork Cathl from 97. *23 Firgrove Gardens, Bishopstown, Cork, Irish Republic* Tel Cork (21) 345889 E-mail m.graham@iol.ie

GRAHAM, Michael Alistair. b 47. CITC 67. **d** 70 **p** 71. C Dublin Clontarf *D & G* 71-75; C Ox St Mich w St Martin and All SS *Ox* 76-78; P-in-c Dublin Sandymount *D & G* 80-86; I Stillorgan w Blackrock from 86. *The Rectory, Stillorgan, Blackrock, Co Dublin, Irish Republic* Tel Dublin (1) 288 1091

GRAHAM, Peter. b 32. CEng MIMechE. **d** 86 **p** 87. NSM Minchinhampton *Glouc* 86-96; rtd 96; Perm to Offic *Glouc*

from 96. *2 Dr Browns Close, Minchinhampton, Stroud, Glos GL6 9DW* Tel (01453) 886747

GRAHAM, Peter Bartlemy. b 23. K Coll Cam BA47 MA52. Ely Th Coll 50. **d** 52 **p** 53. C St Alb Abbey *St Alb* 52-55; V Eaton Bray 55-64; R Harpenden St Nic 64-73; V Aylesbury *Ox* 73-82; Hon Can Ch Ch 79-82; R Elford *Lich* 82-88; Dioc Adv Past Care and Counselling 82-88; rtd 88. *Carriers Cottage, Buckland Newton, Dorchester, Dorset DT2 7DW* Tel (01300) 345287

GRAHAM, Canon Robert John. b 15. Lon Univ BD54 Hull Univ DipAdEd. Bp Wilson Coll 39. **d** 42 **p** 43. C Ravensthorpe *Wakef* 42-44; C Skipton Ch Ch *Bradf* 44-47; C-in-c Heaton St Martin CD 47-49; V Grimethorpe *Wakef* 49-55; V Beeston Hill St Luke *Ripon* 55-58; V Howden *York* 58-78; V Barmby on the Marsh 62-78; V Wressell 62-78; RD Howden 70-78; Sen Lect Hull Univ 65-80; Can and Preb York Minster 74-78; C Worksop Priory *S'well* 78-80; rtd 80. *Flat 13, Capel Court, The Burgage, Prestbury, Cheltenham, Glos GL52 3EL* Tel (01242) 580608

GRAHAM, Ronald Fleming. b 33. Edin Th Coll 67. **d** 69 **p** 69. Chapl St Andr Cathl *Ab* 69-73; R Glas Gd Shep *Glas* 73-75; R Glas Gd Shep and Ascension 75-76; CF (TA) 74-76; R Peterhead *Ab* 76-80; Chapl RAF 76-80; Bp's Dom Chapl *Arg* 80-84; Itinerant Priest 80-84; R Lanark *Glas* 84-89; R Douglas 84-89; rtd 89; Hon C Glas St Ninian *Glas* from 91. *77 Merryvale Avenue, Merrylee Park, Giffnock, Glasgow G46 6DE* Tel 0141-569 5090

GRAHAM, Ronald Gaven. b 27. **d** 90 **p** 91. NSM Adare w Kilpeacon and Croom *L & K* 90-92; Dioc Info Officer (Limerick) 91-95; NSM Rathkeale w Askeaton and Kilcornan 92-96; NSM Wexford w Ardcolm and Killurin *C & O* from 97. *Woodcock Hollow, Crossabeg, Wexford, Irish Republic* Tel Wexford (53) 28520

GRAHAM, Roy Richard Arthur. b 39. Lon Univ BD63 Open Univ BA78. ALCD62. **d** 63 **p** 64. C Southsea St Jude *Portsm* 63-66; C Morden *S'wark* 66-70; V Tittensor *Lich* 70-79; R Dinsdale w Sockburn *Dur* from 79; R Hurworth from 79. *The Rectory, 3 Croft Road, Hurworth, Darlington, Co Durham DL2 2HD* Tel (01325) 720362

GRAHAM, William Bruce. b 37. **d** 90 **p** 91. Canada 90-97; P-in-c W Poldens *B & W* from 97. *The Vicarage, Holy Well Road, Edington, Bridgwater, Somerset TA7 9LE* Tel (01278) 722055

GRAHAM-BROWN, John George Francis. b 34. CA60. Wycliffe Hall Ox 60. **d** 63 **p** 64. C Darlington St Cuth *Dur* 63-67; C Rufforth w Moor Monkton and Hessay *York* 67-73; Sec York Dioc Redundant Chs Uses Cttee 69-89; Asst Sec DBF 73-84; Dioc Past Cttee 73-89; Hon C York St Barn 73-85; P-in-c 85-92; TV Marfleet from 92. *St Giles' Vicarage, Church Lane, Marfleet, Hull HU9 5RL* Tel (01482) 783690

GRAHAM-ORLEBAR, Ian Henry Gaunt. b 26. New Coll Ox BA49 MA56. Cuddesdon Coll 60. **d** 62 **p** 63. C Hemel Hempstead *St Alb* 62-70; R Barton-le-Cley w Higham Gobion 70-80; R Barton-le-Cley w Higham Gobion and Hexton 80-92; rtd 92; Perm to Offic *Ex* from 94. *Hole Farm, Bickington, Newton Abbot, Devon TQ12 6PE* Tel (01626) 821298

GRAIN, Anthony Ernest. b 07. CCC Cam BA31 MA35. Ely Th Coll 31. **d** 32 **p** 33. C Fulham St Clem *Lon* 32-34; C Cheshunt *St Alb* 35-41; P-in-c Eversholt 41-43; V Stotfold 43-48; Chapl Control Commn Germany 48-52; Chapl Marseille *Eur* 52-55; P-in-c Edin St Barn *Edin* 55-58; Jamaica 61-62; S Rhodesia 63-65; Rhodesia 65-80; Zimbabwe 80-86; rtd 73; Perm to Offic *Chich* from 86. *College of St Barnabas, Blackberry Lane, Lingfield, Surrey RH7 6NJ* Tel (01342) 870260

GRAIN, Canon Keith Charles. b 27. St Boniface Warminster 47 AKC51. **d** 52 **p** 53. C Liversedge *Wakef* 52-55; C Barnsley St Mary 55-60; V Hanging Heaton 60-70; V Heckmondwike 70-82; Hon Can Wakef Cathl 74-82; RD Birstall 79-82; V Gargrave *Bradf* 82-92; rtd 92; Perm to Offic *Bradf* from 92. *2 Holme Ghyll, Colne Road, Glusburn, Keighley, W Yorkshire BD20 8RG* Tel (01535) 630668

GRAINGE, Alan Herbert. b 16. Dur Univ BA49 MA53. Sarum Th Coll 49. **d** 51 **p** 52. C Gainsborough St Jo *Linc* 51-54; Gambia 54-60; Hon Can Bathurst Cathl 56-60; Adn Gambia 58-60; V Immingham *Linc* 61-70; Perm to Offic *Ox* 70-74; Lic to Offic 74-81; SSJE from 76; Lic to Offic *Leic* 80-86; rtd 86; Lic to Offic *Lon* from 86. *St Edward's House, 22 Great College Street, London SW1P 3QA* Tel 0171-222 9234

GRAINGER, Canon Bruce. b 37. Nottm Univ BA62 Hull Univ MA83. Cuddesdon Coll 62. **d** 64 **p** 65. C Bingley All SS *Bradf* 64-67; Chapl K Sch Cant 67-72; Hon Min Can Cant Cathl *Cant* 69-72; V Baildon *Bradf* 72-88; Hon Can Bradf Cathl from 84; V Oxenhope from 88; Dir of Ords 88-95; Dioc Ecum Officer from 96. *The Vicarage, Oxenhope, Keighley, W Yorkshire BD22 9SA* Tel (01535) 642529

GRAINGER, Horace. b 34. Carl Dioc Tr Course 82. **d** 85 **p** 86. NSM Barrow St Matt *Carl* 85-89; C Carl St Herbert w St Steph 89-91; TV Penrith w Newton Reigny and Plumpton Wall 91-96; P-in-c Holme Cultram St Mary from 96; P-in-c Holme Cultram St Cuth from 96. *The Vicarage, Abbeytown, Carlisle CA5 4NQ* Tel (01697) 361246

GRAINGER, Ian. b 66. Barrow-in-Furness Coll of FE BTEC NC86. Cranmer Hall Dur 89. **d** 92 **p** 93. C Whitehaven *Carl* 92-94; C Walney Is 94-97; P-in-c Barrow St Aid from 97. *The Vicarage, 31 Middle Hill, Barrow-in-Furness, Cumbria LA13 9HD* Tel (01229) 830445

GRAINGER, Michael Noel Howard. b 40. Trin Coll Carmarthen. **d** 91 **p** 92. NSM Haverfordwest St Martin w Lambston *St D* 91-95; V Maenclochog and New Moat etc from 95. *The Rectory, New Moat, Clarbeston Road SA63 4RQ* Tel (01437) 532238

GRAINGER, Dr Roger Beckett. b 34. FRAI FRSA Birm Univ MA70 Leeds Univ PhD79 Lon Univ BA80 DD90 Huddersfield Poly MPhil88. Lambeth STh83 Trin Coll Bris PhD92 Lich Th Coll 64. **d** 66 **p** 69. C W Bromwich All SS *Lich* 66-68; C Walsall 69-73; Chapl Stanley Royd Hosp Wakef 73-90; rtd 91; Hon C Wakef St Jo *Wakef* from 93. *7 Park Grove, Horbury, Wakefield, W Yorkshire WF4 6EE* Tel (01924) 272742

GRANDELL, Peter. **d** 95. USA 95-96; C St Jo Wood *Lon* from 96. *3 Cochrane Street, London NW8 7PA* Tel 0171-722 4766

GRANGER, Canon Ronald Harry (Ron). b 22. Selw Coll Cam BA49 MA53. Cuddesdon Coll 49. **d** 51 **p** 52. C Portsea St Mary *Portsm* 51-57; V Lower Sandown St Jo 57-63; V Ryde All SS 63-70; RD E Wight 65-70; Hon Can Portsm Cathl 67-90; V Petersfield 70-90; RD Petersfield 75-80; P-in-c Buriton 79-84; R 84-90; rtd 90. *45 Siskin Close, Bishops Waltham, Hants SO32 1RP* Tel (01489) 894378

GRANT, Alistair Sims. b 25. SS Coll Cam BA49 MA53. Sarum Th Coll 49. **d** 51 **p** 52. V Haddenham *Ely* 58-65; rtd 90. *56 The Causeway, Burwell, Cambridge CB5 0DU* Tel (01638) 741670

GRANT, Andrew Richard. b 40. Univ of Wales BA62. Chich Th Coll 63. **d** 65 **p** 66. C Kennington St Jo *S'wark* 65-68; Hon C 70-72; Hon C Stockwell Green St Andr 68-70; V Nunhead St Antony 72-79; TR N Lambeth 79-92; USPG from 92; Ghana from 92. *PO Box 17, St Monica's Complex, Ashanti-Mattpong, Ghana* Tel 0171-928 8681 Fax 928 2371

GRANT, Antony Richard Charles. b 34. Ch Ch Ox BA59 MA64. Coll of Resurr Mirfield 72. **d** 74 **p** 75. C St Jo Wood *Lon* 74-77; Novice CR 77-79; CR from 79; Lic to Offic *Wakef* from 80. *House of the Resurrection, Mirfield, W Yorkshire WF14 0BN* Tel (01924) 494318

GRANT, Arthur Glyndŵr Webber (Glyn). b 28. K Coll Lon RTC47 St Luke's Coll Ex CertEd49. Wells Th Coll 52. **d** 54 **p** 55. C Cannock *Lich* 54-57; S Rhodesia 57-63; C Paignton St Jo *Ex* 63-68; C Brighton Gd Shep Preston *Chich* 68-76; C Moulsecoomb 76-80; Chapl HM Pris Northeye 80-83; P-in-c Wartling *Chich* 80-83; C Seaford w Sutton 83-87; Sub-Chapl HM Pris Lewes 86-92; rtd 92; Perm to Offic *Ex* 93-95. *33 Occombe Valley Road, Paignton, Devon TQ3 1QX* Tel (01803) 522722

GRANT, David Francis. b 32. Chich Th Coll. **d** 60 **p** 61. C Acton Green St Pet *Lon* 60-63; C Ruislip St Martin 63-68; V Oving w Merston *Chich* 68-75; Bp's Dom Chapl 68-75; R Graffham w Woolavington 75-86; R Hastings St Clem and All SS 86-91; R Petworth 91-94; R Egdean 91-94; RD Petworth 92-94; rtd 97. *Glebeland, Graffham, Petworth, W Sussex GU28 0QE* Tel (01798) 867289

GRANT, Canon Douglas Wyndham Maling. b 22. Trin Coll Cam BA48 MA52. Edin Th Coll 53. **d** 55 **p** 56. Chapl and Prec St Andr Cathl Inverness *Mor* 55-58; R Banff *Ab* 58-61; R Portsoy 58-61; P-in-c Grantown-on-Spey *Mor* 61-65; P-in-c Rothiemurchus 61-65; R Lenzie *Glas* 65-70; R Alyth *St And* 70-78; R Blairgowrie 70-78; R Inverurie *Ab* 78-88; R Auchindoir 78-88; R Alford 78-88; P-in-c Kemnay 78-88; Can St Andr Cathl 87-88; Hon Can St Andr Cathl from 88; rtd 88; Perm to Offic *Mor* from 89. *Shewglie, 8 Ardross Place, Inverness IV3 5EL* Tel (01463) 242870

GRANT, Canon Edward Francis. b 14. TCD BA37. TCD Div Sch Div Test. **d** 40 **p** 41. C New Ross *C & O* 40-43; P-in-c Preban w Moyne 43-46; I Fethard w Tintern and Killesk 46-56; P-in-c Ardcolm 56-70; I Wexford w Ardcolm 70-85; Preb Ferns Cathl 57-63; Treas 64-65; Chan 65-69; Prec 69-85; Preb Stagonil St Patr Cathl Dublin 76-85; rtd 85. *9 Kingston College, Mitchelstown, Co Cork, Irish Republic* Tel Mitchelstown (25) 84214

GRANT, Canon Geoffrey. b 27. Lich Th Coll 55. **d** 58 **p** 59. C Swindon New Town *Bris* 58-62; V Eastville St Thos 62-67; V Sherston Magna w Easton Grey 67-75; P-in-c Luckington w Alderton 71-75; P-in-c Woolcott Park 75-78; V Cotham St Mary 76-78; V Cotham St Sav w St Mary 78-81; TR Yate New Town 81-88; Hon Can Bris Cathl 82-92; Dir St Jo Home Bris 89-92; rtd 92; Perm to Offic *Bris* from 92. *5 Hawthorn Coombe, Worle, Weston-super-Mare, Avon BS22 9EE* Tel (01934) 513295

GRANT, Canon Geoffrey Leslie. b 33. Trin Coll Cam BA57 MA61. Ridley Hall Cam 57. **d** 59 **p** 60. C Chelsea St Luke *Lon* 59-64; Chapl Orwell Park Sch Nacton from 64; R Nacton w Levington *St E* 64-78; P-in-c Bucklesham w Brightwell and Foxhall 75-76; R Nacton and Levington w Bucklesham and Foxhall from 78; RD Colneys from 86; Hon Can St E Cathl from 94; P-in-c Kirton w Falkenham from 96. *The Rectory, Nacton, Ipswich IP10 0HY* Tel (01473) 659232

GRANT, James Neil. b 57. Toorak Coll of Educn BEd80. Trin Coll Melbourne BTh84. **d** 85 **p** 86. Australia 85-87 and from 89; C Feltham *Lon* 87-89. *2/278 Punt Road, South Yarra, Victoria, Australia 3141*

GRANT, Dr John Brian Frederick. b 47. FRCS76 Bris Univ BSc68 MB, ChB71 MD76. Coll of Resurr Mirfield 91. **d** 93 **p** 94. C Doncaster Ch Ch *Sheff* 93-95; C Doncaster H Trin 95-96; Asst

Chapl Salford R Hosps NHS Trust from 96. *23 Sefton Road, Pendlebury, Manchester M27 6DZ, or Hope Hospital, Stott Lane, Salford M6 8HD* Tel 0161-727 8189 or 0161-789 7373

GRANT, John Peter. b 19. TD50. Wycliffe Hall Ox. **d** 62 **p** 63. C Chich St Paul and St Bart *Chich* 62-64; V Adwell w S Weston *Ox* 64-67; V Lewknor 64-67; Chapl Warneford Hosp Ox 67-71; Rhodesia 71-80; V Gayton *Nor* 80-82; rtd 82; S Africa from 82. *96 Protea Heuwelsig, PO Box 15223, Verwoerdburg, 0140 South Africa*

GRANT, Kenneth Gordon. b 21. ARCM54. K Coll Lon. **d** 55 **p** 56. C Wotton-under-Edge *Glouc* 55-58; R Charfield 58-96; rtd 96. *10 Canters Leaze, Wickwar, Wotton-under-Edge, Glos GL12 8LX* Tel (01454) 294660

GRANT, The Very Revd Malcolm Etheridge. b 44. Edin Univ BSc66 BD69. Edin Th Coll 66. **d** 69 **p** 70. C St Mary's Cathl *Glas* 69-72; C Grantham w Manthorpe *Linc* 72; TV Grantham 72-78; P-in-c Invergordon St Ninian *Mor* 78-81; Provost St Mary's Cathl *Glas* 81-91; Can 81-91; R Glas St Mary 81-91; Provost St Andr Cathl Inverness *Mor* from 91; R Inverness St Andr from 91; P-in-c Culloden St Mary-in-the-Fields from 91; R Strathnairn St Paul from 91. *15 Ardross Street, Inverness IV3 5NS* Tel (01463) 233535

GRANT, Murray William. b 36. Chich Th Coll 64. **d** 66 **p** 67. C Stanley *Liv* 66-70; C Munster Square St Mary Magd *Lon* 70-74; C Westmr St Sav and St Jas Less 74-82; P-in-c Albany Street Ch Ch 82; P-in-c Hammersmith H Innocents 83-94; V from 94. *Holy Innocents Vicarage, 35 Paddenswick Road, London W6 0VA* Tel 0181-748 5195 or 748 2286

GRANT, Patrick Iain Douglas. b 67. K Alfred's Coll Win BA88. Cuddesdon Coll BTh93. **d** 96 **p** 97. C Croydon Woodside *S'wark* from 96. *24 Swinburne Crescent, Addiscombe, Croydon CR0 7BY*

GRANT, Canon Rodney Arthur. b 26. AKC52. **d** 53 **p** 54. C Edin St Jas *Edin* 53-56; R 72-80; C Musselburgh 56-59; P-in-c Prestonpans 59-60; P-in-c Edin St Aid Miss Niddrie Mains 60-72; R Edin Ch Ch 72-80; R Edin Ch Ch-St Jas 80-86; R Edin SS Phil and Jas 86-92; Chapl St Columba's Hospice Edin 86-92; Hon Can St Mary's Cathl from 91; rtd 92. *29 Bruntsfield Gardens, Edinburgh EH10 4DY* Tel 0131-229 1857

GRANT, William Frederick (Eric). b 23. Fitzw Ho Cam BA48 MA50 Cam Univ CertEd50. Wycliffe Hall Ox 51. **d** 53 **p** 54. C Islington St Paul Ball's Pond *Lon* 53-57; V Islington All SS 57-60; Head RE Therfield Sch Leatherhead 60-84; Perm to Offic *Guildf* from 66; rtd 88; Perm to Offic *S'wark* from 89. *Kingfishers, 24 The Avenue, Brockham, Betchworth, Surrey RH3 7EN* Tel (01737) 842551

GRANT, The Very Revd William James. b 29. **d** 58 **p** 59. Asst Missr S Ch Miss Ballymacarrett *D & D* 58-60; C Belfast St Geo *Conn* 60-63; Canada 63-66; Miss to Seamen 66-70; I Fethard w Tintern and Killesk *C & O* 70-77; I Cong, Ballinrobe and Aasleagh *T, K & A* 77-81; Adn Tuam 80-93; I Tuam w Cong and Aasleagh 81-93; Dean Tuam 81-93; rtd 93. *48 Brazabon House, Sandymount, Dublin 4, Irish Republic* Tel Dublin (1) 269 5071

GRANTHAM, Michael Paul. b 47. Linc Th Coll. **d** 84 **p** 85. C Gainsborough All SS *Linc* 84-87; R S Kelsey Gp 87-94; R Dunster, Carhampton and Withycombe w Rodhuish *B & W* from 94. *The Rectory, St George's Street, Dunster, Minehead, Somerset TA24 6RS* Tel (01643) 821812

GRANTHAM, Suffragan Bishop of. *Vacant*

GRASBY, Derek. b 56. Bris Univ BA80 MA82. Wesley Coll Bris 77 EAMTC 95. **d** 95 **p** 96. C Harlescott *Lich* 95-96; C W Bromwich St Andr w Ch Ch from 96. *23 Rowley View, West Bromwich, W Midlands B70 8QR* Tel 0121-553 3538

GRATY, Canon John Thomas. b 33. Univ Coll Ox BA58 MA60. Coll of Resurr Mirfield 58. **d** 60 **p** 61. C Cov St Mark *Cov* 60-63; C Hitchin St Mary *St Alb* 63-67; R Cov St Alb *Cov* 67-75; P-in-c Radway w Ratley 75-77; P-in-c Warmington w Shotteswell 75-77; RD Dassett Magna 76-79; R Warmington w Shotteswell and Radway w Ratley 77-84; Hon Can Cov Cathl 80-96; P-in-c Nuneaton St Mary 84-89; V 89-96; rtd 96. *48 Shakespeare Street, Stratford-upon-Avon, Warks CV37 6RN* Tel (01789) 298856

GRAVELL, Canon John Hilary. b 45. Univ of Wales (Abth) BA65 DipEd66. Burgess Hall Lamp 66. **d** 68 **p** 69. C Aberystwyth *St D* 68-72; V Blaenpennal and Llangeitho 72-81; V Betws Leuci 73-81; V Llan-non 81-95; Can St D Cathl from 92; V Llandybie from 95. *The Vicarage, 77 Kings Road, Llandybie, Ammanford SA18 2TL* Tel (01269) 850337

GRAVELLE, John Elmer. b 25. St Jo Coll Dur BA50 DipTh51. **d** 51 **p** 52. C Luton St Mary *St Alb* 51-54; CF 54-58; R Toddington *St Alb* 58-64; V Hatfield Hyde 64-71; P-in-c Gt Munden 71-74; Dep Dir Clinical Th Assn 71-80; P-in-c Fryerning w Margaretting *Chelmsf* 80-87; Dep Dir Cathl Cen for Research and Tr 82-84; Bp's Adv in Care and Counselling 87-90; rtd 90; Perm to Offic *Chelmsf* from 90. *8 Gordon Road, Chelmsford CM2 9LL* Tel (01245) 491795

GRAVES, Jonathan Mark. b 57. BEd. St Steph Ho Ox. **d** 84 **p** 85. C St Leonards Ch Ch and St Mary *Chich* 84-88; C-in-c N Langley CD 88-95; V Stone Cross St Luke w N Langney from 95; Chapl St Wilfrid's Hospice Eastbourne from 94. *The Vicarage, 8 Culver Close, Eastbourne, E Sussex BN23 8EA* Tel (01323) 764473

GRAVES, Peter. b 33. EMMTC 78. **d** 81 **p** 82. NSM Roughey *Chich* 81-89; NSM Itchingfield w Slinfold from 89. *2 Coniston Close, Roffey, Horsham, W Sussex RH12 4GU* Tel (01403) 258363

GRAY, Alan. b 25. LRAM52 DCEd75. Qu Coll Birm 51. **d** 54 **p** 55. C Monkseaton St Pet *Newc* 54-56; C Sighill 56-61; C-in-c Balkwell CD 61-66; R Callander *St And* 66-74; R Killin 66-74; R Lochearnhead 66-74; R Alloa 74-77; Community Educn Officer 76-85; Lic to Offic 77-85; R Alyth 85-90; R Blairgowrie 85-90; R Coupar Angus 85-90; rtd 90. *Ach-na-Coile, Ancaster Road, Callander, Perthshire FK17 8EL* Tel (01877) 330158

GRAY, Alan Eric. b 18. Lich Th Coll 38. **d** 41 **p** 42. C Sampford Peverell *Ex* 41-44; Africa 47-60; V Lower Breeding Chich 61-70; rtd 83. *Appletree Cottage, 81 Belmont Road, Malvern, Worcs WR14 1PN* Tel (01684) 572453

GRAY, Angela Margery. b 46. St D Coll Lamp DipTh73. **dss** 73 **d** 80 **p** 97. Aberystwyth *St D* 73-80; Par Dn Dafen and Llwynhendy 80-90; D-in-c 90-94; D-in-c Llwynhendy 94-97; V from 97. *Clergy House, 10 Bryn Isaf, Llwynhendy, Llanelli SA14 9EX* Tel (01554) 774213

GRAY, Charles Malcolm. b 38. Lich Th Coll 67. **d** 69 **p** 70. C St Geo-in-the-East St Mary *Lon* 69-72; C Bush Hill Park St Mark 72-75; V Winchmore Hill H Trin from 75. *Holy Trinity Vicarage, King's Avenue, London N21 3NA* Tel 0181-360 2947 Fax as telephone

GRAY, Ms Christine Angela (Kit). b 46. Nottm Univ BA67 CertEd68 Dur Univ DipTh73. Cranmer Hall Dur 71. **dss** 80 **d** 87 **p** 94. Rawthorpe *Wakef* 74-81; Chapl Nottm Univ *S'well* 81-88; C Rushmere *St E* 88-94; P-in-c Ringshall w Battisford, Barking w Darmsden etc from 94. *The Rectory, Main Road, Willisham, Ipswich IP8 4SP* Tel (01473) 831274

GRAY, Dale Armitage. b 42. Edin Th Coll 62. **d** 92 **p** 93. Dioc Missr *Arg* from 92; Chapl St Jo Cathl Oban 92-95; P-in-c Cumbrae (or Millport) from 95. *The College, Millport, Isle of Cumbrae KA28 0HE* Tel (01475) 530353

GRAY, David Bryan. b 28. RD77. Roch Th Coll 59. **d** 61 **p** 62. C Linc St Giles *Linc* 61-65; V Thurlby 65-67; P-in-c Ropsley 67-75; P-in-c Sapperton w Braceby 67-75; P-in-c Somerby w Humby 67-75; R Trimley *St E* 75-82; R Orford w Sudbourne, Chillesford, Butley and Iken 82-94; rtd 94. *30 Roman Way, Felixstowe, Suffolk IP11 9NJ* Tel (01394) 285778

GRAY, David Cedric. b 53. RMN77 Hollings Coll Man 79. LNSM course 94. **d** 97. NSM Gorton Em w St Jas *Man* from 97. *Emmanuel Church House, 12 Abbotsbury Close, Manchester M12 5EQ* Tel 0161-231 4701

GRAY, Canon Donald Cecil. b 24. K Coll Lon 46. Linc Th Coll 49. **d** 50 **p** 51. C Abington *Pet* 50-53; C Bedford St Paul *St Alb* 53-56; Chapl Bedf Gen Hosp 53-56; C Wilton Place St Paul *Lon* 56-59; V N Holmwood *Guildf* 59-67; RD Dorking 63-67; Chapl Cobgates Hosp and Farnham Hosp Guildf 67-89; R Farnham 67-89; RD Farnham 69-74; Hon Can Guildf Cathl 71-89; rtd 89. *13 Benenden Green, Alresford, Hants SO24 9PE* Tel (01962) 734234

GRAY, Canon Donald Clifford. b 30. TD70. FRHistS88 Liv Univ MPhil80 Man Univ PhD85. AKC55. **d** 56 **p** 57. C Leigh St Mary *Man* 56-60; CF (TA) 58-67; V Westleigh St Pet *Man* 60-67; V Elton All SS 67-74; CF (TAVR) 67-77; QHC 74-77; R Liv Our Lady and St Nic w St Anne *Liv* 74-87; RD Liv 75-81; Hon Can Liv Cathl 82-87; Chapl to The Queen from 82; Can Westmr Abbey from 87; R Westmr St Marg from 87; Chapl to Speaker of Ho of Commons from 87. *1 Little Cloister, Westminster Abbey, London SW1P 3PL* Tel 0171-222 4027 or 222 5152 Fax 233 2072

GRAY, Evan William. b 43. Oak Hill Th Coll 86. **d** 88 **p** 89. C Street w Walton *B & W* 88-92; V Blackpool St Mark *Blackb* from 92. *St Mark's Vicarage, 163 Kingscote Drive, Blackpool FY3 8EH* Tel (01253) 392895

GRAY, Frank Harold Castell. b 14. ALCD41. **d** 41 **p** 42. C Northwood Em *Lon* 41-45; P-in-c Nottingham St Ann *S'well* 45-47; V Gatten St Paul *Portsm* 47-53; V Prestonville St Luke *Chich* 53-66; V Watford St Luke *St Alb* 66-79; rtd 79; Perm to Offic *B & W* from 80. *9 Southwell Close, Trull, Taunton, Somerset TA3 7EU* Tel (01823) 282567

GRAY, Canon Geoffrey Thomas. b 23. Oak Hill Th Coll 40 and 46. **d** 46 **p** 47. C Havering-atte-Bower *Chelmsf* 46-48; C Dovercourt 48-49; C Ches Square St Mich w St Phil *Lon* 49-51; V Lee Gd Shep *S'wark* 51-56; P-in-c Eltham St Pet 52-56; R Bermondsey St Mary w St Olave and St Jo 56-59; P-in-c Bermondsey St Luke 57-59; V Yalding *Roch* 59-66; RD Malling 64-66; V Gillingham St Mary 66-75; RD Gillingham 66-75; Perm to Offic 75-80; V Strood St Nic w St Mary 80-87; Hon Can Roch Cathl 82-87; Chapl Huggens' Coll Northfleet 87-91; rtd 88; Hon Bp's Chapl *Roch* from 90; Hon PV Roch Cathl from 91. *Deanery Lodge, The Precinct, Rochester, Kent ME1 1TG* Tel (01634) 844165

GRAY, The Ven Hugh Henry James. b 21. TCD BA48 Div Test49 MA64. **d** 49 **p** 50. C Enniscorthy *C & O* 49-51; I Fenagh w Myshall 51-60; I Clonenagh w Roskelton 60-80; RD Baltinglass 62-96; Preb Ossory & Leighlin Cathls 70-78; Treas 78-80; Chan 80-83; I Clonenagh w Offerlane, Borris-in-Ossory etc 80-96; Adn Ossory and Leighlin 83-92; rtd 96. *Old Borris Road, Castletown, Mountrath, Co Laois, Irish Republic* Tel Portlaoise (502) 32196

GRAY, John. ARCM. **d** 89 **p** 90. NSM Tenbury St Mich *Heref* 89-96; Perm to Offic from 96. *Flat 3, Castlemead, Burford, Tenbury Wells, Worcs WR15 8AH* Tel (01584) 810959

GRAY, John David Norman. b 38. Oak Hill Th Coll DipHE86. **d** 86 **p** 87. C Portsdown *Portsm* 86-88; C Worthing St Geo *Chich* 88-91; TV Swanborough *Sarum* from 91. *The Vicarage, Wilcot, Pewsey, Wilts SN9 5NS* Tel (01672) 62282

GRAY, John Howard. b 39. St Aid Birkenhead 61. **d** 65 **p** 66. C Old Trafford St Cuth *Man* 65-68; C Urmston 68-74; V Oldham Moorside from 74. *The Vicarage, 1 Glebe Lane, Moorside, Oldham, Lancs OL1 4SJ* Tel 0161-652 6452

GRAY, Mrs Joy Dora. b 24. SRN46 SCM48 HVCert. Gilmore Ho 79. **dss** 81 **d** 87 **p** 95. Newick *Chich* 81-87; Hon Par Dn 87-94; NSM Fletching from 94. *10 High Hurst Close, Newick, Lewes, E Sussex BN8 4NJ* Tel (01825) 722965

GRAY, Julian Francis. b 64. Univ of Wales (Lamp) BA86. Coll of Resurr Mirfield 86. **d** 88 **p** 89. C Newport St Woolos *Mon* 88-91; Min Can St Woolos Cathl 88-91; C Bassaleg 91-93; V Overmonnow w Wonastow and Michel Troy from 93. *St Thomas's Vicarage, Overmonnow, Monmouth NP5 3ES* Tel (01600) 712869

GRAY, Kenneth Amphlett. b 11. St Jo Coll Dur BA34 MA37 DipTh37. **d** 35 **p** 36. C Dorking St Paul *Guildf* 35-38; C Walcot *B & W* 38-41; V Croydon Ch Ch Broad Green *Cant* 41-47; R Clapham w Patching *Chich* 47-53; Devon and Cornwall Distr Sec BFBS 53-56; NW Regional Sec BFBS 56-62; Dorset and Wilts Distr Sec BFBS 62-75; rtd 75; Perm to Offic *Nor* 81-96. *Windwhistle, Triple Plea Road, Woodton, Bungay, Suffolk NR35 2NS* Tel (01508) 44395

GRAY, Martin Clifford. b 44. Westcott Ho Cam 78. **d** 80 **p** 81. C Gaywood, Bawsey and Mintlyn *Nor* 80-84; V Sheringham 84-94; P-in-c Lowestoft and Kirkley 94; TR Lowestoft St Marg from 94; Chapl Lothingland Hosp from 95; RD Lothingland *Nor* from 97. *St Margaret's Rectory, Hollingsworth Road, Lowestoft, Suffolk NR32 4BW* Tel (01502) 573046

GRAY, Maurice William Halcro. b 27. Hertf Coll Ox BA48 MA60. Coll of Resurr Mirfield. **d** 60 **p** 61. C Cricklade w Latton *Bris* 60-63; Chapl Ellesmere Coll Shropshire 63-92; Lic to Offic *Lich* 63-93; rtd 92; Hon C Ellesmere *Lich* from 93; RD Ellesmere from 95. *The Pynt, Rhosgadfa, Gobowen, Oswestry, Shropshire SY10 7BN* Tel (01691) 661110

GRAY, Melvyn Dixon. b 38. Lon Univ BD86 Dur Univ MA89. NE Ord Course 84. **d** 87 **p** 88. C Richmond w Hudswell *Ripon* 87-90; P-in-c Downholme and Marske 88-90; P-in-c Forcett and Stanwick w Aldbrough 90; P-in-c Forcett and Aldbrough and Melsonby 90-91; R from 91. *The Vicarage, 1 Appleby Close, Aldbrough St John, Richmond, N Yorkshire DL11 7TT* Tel (01325) 374634

GRAY, Michael Frederick Henry. b 36. Southn Univ CQSW78. Lich Th Coll 62. **d** 65 **p** 66. C Victoria Docks Ascension *Chelmsf* 65-67; C Plaistow St Mary 67-70; Chapl RN 70-72; Hon C Whyke w Rumboldswhyke and Portfield *Chich* 84-88; TV Crawley 88-95; rtd 95; Perm to Offic *Chich* from 97. *Flat 14, Sussex Court, Eaton Road, Hove, E Sussex BN3 3AS* Tel (01273) 326677

GRAY, Neil Kenneth. b 48. Kelham Th Coll 67. **d** 71 **p** 72. C Chorley St Laur *Blackb* 71-74; C S Shore H Trin 74-78; P-in-c Preston St Oswald 78-83; C Blackpool St Steph 83-87; Chapl Co-ord Bolton HA 87-90; Chapl Bolton Gen Hosp 87-90; Chapl Bolton R Infirmary 87-90; Chapl Bolton Hosps NHS Trust from 90. *The Chaplain's Office, Bolton General Hospital, Minerva Road, Bolton BL4 0JR* Tel (01204) 390770 or 390390

GRAY, Neil Ralph. b 53. MA. St Steph Ho Ox. **d** 82 **p** 83. C Kennington St Jo w St Jas *S'wark* 82-85; C Somers Town St Mary *Lon* 85-88. *3 Parsonage Close, High Wycombe, Bucks HP13 6DT* Tel (01494) 531875

GRAY, Penelope Jane. *See* GRAYSMITH, Mrs Penelope Jane

GRAY, Percy. b 28. OBE94 TD71. Lon Univ BA53 St Cath Soc Ox BA55 MA59. Oak Hill Th Coll 50. **d** 55 **p** 56. C Sutton *Liv* 55-58; C Chelsea Ch Ch *Lon* 58-59; V Bermondsey St Crispin w Ch Ch *S'wark* from 59; CF (TA) 59-67; CF (TAVR) from 67; CF (ACF) from 76. *St Crispin's Vicarage, 483 Southwark Park Road, London SE16 2HU* Tel 0171-237 5567

GRAY, Philip Charles. b 67. Nottm Univ BA91. St Steph Ho Ox 91. **d** 93 **p** 94. C Scarborough St Martin *York* 93-97; TV Leek and Meerbrook *Lich* from 97. *All Saints' Vicarage, Compton, Leek, Staffs ST13 5PT* Tel (01538) 382588

GRAY, Philip Thomas. b 41. Lon Univ BA65. Chich Th Coll 66. **d** 68 **p** 69. C Leigh St Clem *Chelmsf* 68-74; V Mendlesham *St E* from 74; P-in-c Wickham Skeith from 86. *The Vicarage, Mendlesham, Stowmarket, Suffolk IP14 5RS* Tel (01449) 766359

GRAY, Robert James (Bob). b 70. TCD BA92 HDipEd93 MA95. Irish Sch of Ecum MPhil94. **d** 96 **p** 97. C Clooney w Strathfoyle *D & R* from 96. *11 Mosley Park, Kilfennan, Londonderry BT47 1HR* Tel (01504) 341966

GRAY, Sidney Patrick. b 19. Worc Ord Coll. **d** 63 **p** 63. C Skegness *Linc* 63-65; V Dunholme 65-71; R Cliffe at Hoo w Cooling *Roch* 72-78; V Gillingham St Aug 78-84; rtd 84; Perm to Offic *Cant* from 84; Perm to Offic *Roch* from 84. *September Cottage, 168 Loose Road, Maidstone, Kent ME15 7UD*

GRAY-STACK, Martha Mary Stewart. b 35. QUB BA57. **d** 90 **p** 91. NSM Limerick City *L & K* 90-93; Warden of Readers 90-93; NSM Clara w Liss, Moate and Clonmacnoise *M & K* from 93. *St Bridgit's Rectory, Clara, Co Offaly, Irish Republic* Tel Clara (506) 31406

GRAYSHON, Matthew Richard. b 47. St Jo Coll Nottm BTh81. **d** 81 **p** 82. C Beverley Minster *York* 81-85; V Hallwood *Ches* 85-93; R Hanwell St Mary w St Chris *Lon* from 93. *The Rectory, 91 Church Road, London W7 3BJ* Tel 0181-567 6185

GRAYSHON, Paul Nicholas Walton (Nick). b 50. St Jo Coll Dur 81. **d** 83 **p** 84. C Walkden Moor *Man* 83-87; V Radcliffe St Andr from 87. *St Andrew's Vicarage, St Andrew's View, Radcliffe, Manchester M26 4HE* Tel 0161-723 2427

GRAYSMITH (née GRAY), Mrs Penelope Jane. b 63. SS Hild & Bede Coll Dur BA85 Em Coll Cam MPhil88. Westcott Ho Cam 86. **d** 89 **p** 94. Par Dn Evington *Leic* 89-92; Par Dn Cannock *Lich* 92-94; C 94-96; Chapl Asst Mid Staffs Gen Hosps NHS Trust from 96. *The Vicarage, 226 Hednesford Road, Heath Hayes, Cannock, Staffs WS12 5DZ* Tel (01543) 270107

GRAYSMITH (formerly SMITH), Peter Alexander. b 62. UEA BSc83. Westcott Ho Cam 85. **d** 88 **p** 89. C Tettenhall Regis *Lich* 88-89; C Cannock 89-92; TV from 92. *The Vicarage, 226 Hednesford Road, Heath Hayes, Cannock, Staffs WS12 5DZ* Tel (01543) 270107

GRAYSON, Canon Robert William. b 24. Worc Coll Ox BA48 MA49 DipTh50. Wycliffe Hall Ox 49. **d** 50 **p** 51. C N Meols *Liv* 50-53; India 53-57; P-in-c Litherland St Paul Hatton Hill *Liv* 57-61; V Knowsley 61-66; V Stanwix *Carl* 66-79; RD Carl 71-79; Hon Can Carl Cathl 76-89; V Appleby 79-89; R Ormside 81-89; rtd 89; Perm to Offic *Carl* from 89. *Panorama, North End, Burgh-by-Sands, Carlisle CA5 6BD* Tel (01228) 576863

GREADY, Andrew John. b 63. Univ Coll Lon BSc84. St Jo Coll Nottm DPS89. **d** 89 **p** 90. C Monkwearmouth St Andr *Dur* 89-92; S Africa from 92. *PO Box 39063, Bramley, 2018 South Africa* Tel Johannesburg (11) 786-0656

GREANY, Richard Andrew Hugh. b 44. Qu Coll Ox BA67 MA83. Coll of Resurr Mirfield 67. **d** 69 **p** 70. C Hartlepool St Oswald *Dur* 69-72; C Clifton All SS *Bris* 72-75; Tutor Coll of Resurr Mirfield 75-78; V Whitworth w Spennymoor *Dur* 78-83; P-in-c Byers Green 78-79; Asst Prin St Alb Minl Tr Scheme 83-88; V Flamstead *St Alb* 83-88; V Hessle *York* 88-94; P-in-c Cambridge St Mary Less *Ely* 94-95; V from 95. *St Mary the Less Vicarage, 4 Newnham Terrace, Cambridge CB3 9EX* Tel (01223) 350733

GREASLEY, James Kenneth (Jim). b 39. K Coll Lon BD AKC66. **d** 67 **p** 68. C Stoke upon Trent *Lich* 67-70; Zambia 70-76; Chapl HM Borstal Gaynes Hall 76-81; V Gt Staughton *Ely* 76-81; V Melbourn 81-96; V Meldreth 81-96; RD Shingay 82-96; R Chalfont St Peter *Ox* from 96. *The Vicarage, 4 Austenway, Gerrards Cross, Bucks SL9 8NW* Tel (01753) 882389

GREATBATCH, John Charles. b 56. BA. Coll of Resurr Mirfield. **d** 83 **p** 84. C Wednesbury St Paul Wood Green *Lich* 83-88; C Codsall 88-94; V Tipton St Jo from 94. *St John's Vicarage, Upper Church Lane, Tipton, W Midlands DY4 9ND* Tel 0121-557 1793

GREATREX, Warren Robert. b 21. Qu Univ Kingston Ontario BCom41. Trin Coll Toronto LTh50 BD51. **d** 50 **p** 51. Canada 50-78; Perm to Offic *Heref* from 78. *The Highlands, Symonds Yat, Ross-on-Wye, Herefordshire HR9 6DY* Tel (01600) 890318

GREAVES, Arthur Roy Hurst. b 15. Man Univ BA38. Ridley Hall Cam 38. **d** 40 **p** 41. C New Bury *Man* 40-43; C Lawton Moor 43-45; C Heywood St Jas 45-47; C Stockport St Geo *Ches* 47-50; C Denton Ch Ch *Man* 50-52; V Goodshaw 52-56; Australia 56-68; V Diseworth *Leic* 69-78; R Long Whatton and Diseworth 78-82; rtd 82. *Unit 103, 20 Excelsior Street, Shenton Park, W Australia 6008* Tel Perth (9) 382 1198

GREAVES, Canon John Neville. b 29. AAI56 Lon Univ DipTh60 Newc Univ MA96. St Aid Birkenhead 58. **d** 61 **p** 62. C Pendleton St Ambrose *Man* 61-63; C Benchill 63-65; P-in-c Wythenshawe St Rich 65-71; V 71-73; R Sadberge *Dur* 73-78; V Dur St Cuth 78-94; Chapl New Coll Dur 78-92; Lect NE Ord Course 79-84; Chapl Dur Fire Brigade 85-94; RD Dur 80-93; Hon Can Dur Cathl 91-94; rtd 94; Perm to Offic *Ches* from 94; P-in-c Salt and Sandon w Burston *Lich* from 97. *The Vicarage, Salt, Stafford ST18 0BW* Tel (01889) 508341

GREED, Frederick John. b 44. Trin Coll Bris 79. **d** 81 **p** 82. C Yateley *Win* 81-85; R Ore *Chich* 85-95; R Street w Walton *B & W* from 95. *The Rectory, Vestry Close, Street, Somerset BA16 0HZ* Tel (01458) 442671

GREEDY, Tegryd Joseph (Teg). b 31. St D Coll Lamp 59. **d** 61 **p** 62. C Newbridge *Mon* 61-64; C Bassaleg 64-66; V Newport St Teilo 66-74; Hon C Newport St Mark 80-83; V Goldcliffe and Whiston and Nash 83-90; Ind Chapl 83-90; V Marshfield and Peterstone Wentloog etc 90-96; rtd 96. *42 Churchward Drive, Lliswerry, Newport NP9 0SB*

GREEN, Alan John Enrique. b 56. Worc Coll Ox BA78 MA83. Linc Th Coll 83. **d** 85 **p** 86. C Kirkby *Liv* 85-88; TV 88-94; Chapl Knowsley Community Coll 87-90; Chapl Worc Coll Ox from 94; C Ox St Giles and SS Phil and Jas w St Marg *Ox* from 94. *173 Walton Street, Oxford OX1 2HD* Tel (01865) 54586 or 278371

GREEN, Canon Alan Thomas. b 21. Launde Abbey. **d** 64 **p** 65. C Loughborough All SS *Leic* 64-67; V Oaks (Charnwood Forest) 67-70; R Braunstone 70-74; P-in-c Loddington 74-83; Hon Can Leic Cathl 78-87; P-in-c Knossington and Cold Overton 81-83; P-in-c Owston and Withcote 81-83; V Enderby w Lubbesthorpe and Thurlaston 83-87; rtd 87; Perm to Offic *Leic* from 87. *22 Main Street, Cold Overton, Oakham, Leics LE15 7QB* Tel 0116-445 4345

GREEN, Alfred. b 06. St Aid Birkenhead 47. **d** 48 **p** 49. C Birkenshaw w Hunsworth *Wakef* 48-51; C-in-c Lundwood 51-52; V Low Elswick *Newc* 52-55; V Cullingworth *Bradf* 55-60; V Blackb St Matt *Blackb* 60-66; V Holme-in-Cliviger 66-73; rtd 73; Lic to Offic *Blackb* from 75. *40 Richmond Avenue, Cliviger, Burnley, Lancs BB10 4JL* Tel (01282) 38429

GREEN, Anthony Brian. b 39. Birm Univ CertEd60 Coll of Preceptors ACP66 Sussex Univ MA88 Brighton Univ DipRE95. Bps' Coll Cheshunt 64. **d** 64 **p** 65. C Batheaston w St Cath *B & W* 64-67; Chapl Aiglon Coll and Villars *Eur* 67-71; Hd Master Battisborough Sch Holbeton 71-81; Perm to Offic *Ex* 71-81; Perm to Offic *Worc* 81-83; Chapl R Gr Sch Worc 81-83; Perm to Offic *Glouc* 83-96; Hd Master Frewen Coll Rye 83-96; P-in-c New Groombridge *Chich* from 97. *The Vicarage, Groombridge, Tunbridge Wells, Kent TN3 9SE* Tel (01892) 864265 Fax as telephone

GREEN, Arthur Edward. b 27. Chich Th Coll 58. **d** 59 **p** 60. C Malden St Jas *S'wark* 59-62; C Caterham 62-67; R Burgh Parva w Briston *Nor* 67-75; V Middleton 75-76; V Middleton w E Winch 76-84; R Neatishead w Irstead 84-90; V Barton Turf 84-90; R Neatishead, Barton Turf and Irstead 90-92; rtd 92. *2 Clinton Road, Waterlooville, Hants PO7 6DT* Tel (01705) 240789

GREEN, Barrie. b 51. SS Coll Cam BA72 MA76. Wycliffe Hall Ox 75. **d** 78 **p** 79. C Castle Vale *Birm* 78-81; V W Heath 81-96; RD Kings Norton 87-95; TR Dronfield w Holmesfield *Derby* from 96. *The Rectory, Church Street, Dronfield, Sheffield S18 6QB* Tel (01246) 412328

GREEN, Brian Robert. b 31. Bris Univ BA55. Tyndale Hall Bris 52. **d** 56 **p** 57. C Toxteth Park St Philemon *Liv* 56-58; V Toxteth Park St Philemon w St Silas 58-69; P-in-c Toxteth Park St Gabr 64-69; P-in-c Toxteth Park St Jo and St Thos 64-69; P-in-c Toxteth Park St Jas and St Matt 68-69; V Elsenham *Chelmsf* 69-85; V Henham 69-85; P-in-c Ugley 84-85; V Henham and Elsenham w Ugley 85-89; RD Newport and Stansted 87-89; Perm to Offic *Ex* 90-91; V Tidenham w Beachley and Lancaut *Glouc* 91-97; RD Forest S 95-97; rtd 97. *1 The Square, Offwell, Honiton, Devon EX14 9SA* Tel (01404) 831795

GREEN, Mrs Catherine Isabel (Cathy). b 48. Cant Sch of Min 89. **d** 92 **p** 94. Par Dn Willesborough *Cant* 92-94; C 94-96; Sen Asst P E Dereham and Scarning *Nor* from 96; Asst Chapl HM Pris Wayland from 96. *15 George Eliot Way, Dereham, Norfolk NR19 1EX* Tel (01362) 692982

GREEN, Christopher Frederick. b 46. Nottm Univ BTh75 Birm Univ DipEd85 Univ of Wales (Abth) MEd94. Bp Otter Coll CertEd69 Linc Th Coll 71. **d** 75 **p** 76. C Hodge Hill *Birm* 75-77; C S Lafford *Linc* 77-79; P-in-c Worc St Mich *Worc* 79-82; Hd of Relig Studies and Lib RNIB New Coll Worc 82-96; V Clipstone *S'well* from 96. *The Vicarage, Church Road, Clipstone, Mansfield, Notts NG21 9DG* Tel (01623) 23916

GREEN, Christopher Martyn. b 58. New Coll Edin BD80. Cranmer Hall Dur 82. **d** 83 **p** 84. C Virginia Water *Guildf* 83-87; C Bromley Ch Ch *Roch* 87-91; Study Asst the Proclamation Trust 91-92; C Surbiton Hill Ch Ch *S'wark* from 92. *181 Elgar Avenue, Surbiton, Surrey KT5 9JX* Tel 0181-399 1503

GREEN, Mrs Clare Noreen. b 30. SW Minl Tr Course 84. **d** 88. NSM Bideford *Ex* 88-90; Perm to Offic from 90. *5 St Margarets Court, Lakenham Hill, Northam, Bideford, Devon EX39 1JW* Tel (01237) 472960

GREEN, Clifford. b 28. Leeds Univ BA51. Coll of Resurr Mirfield 51. **d** 53 **p** 54. C Solihull *Birm* 53-56; CR from 58; Lic to Offic *Wakef* 59-62 and from 67; S Africa 63-66; Lic to Offic *Ripon* 75-76. *House of the Resurrection, Mirfield, W Yorkshire WF14 0BN* Tel (01924) 494318

GREEN, David John. b 54. DCR, MU. SW Minl Tr Course 82. **d** 85 **p** 86. C St Marychurch *Ex* 85-89; C Laira 89-90; V Maughold *S & M* from 90. *The Vicarage, Maughold, Ramsey, Isle of Man IM7 1AS* Tel (01624) 812070 E-mail dgreen@mcb.net

GREEN, David Norman. b 37. Magd Coll Cam BA60. Clifton Th Coll 60. **d** 62 **p** 63. SSF from 55; C Islington St Mary *Lon* 62-65; C Burley *Ripon* 65-68; Kenya 69-80; P-in-c Brimscombe *Glouc* 81-90; R Woodchester and Brimscombe 90-96; P-in-c Coberley w Cowley 96-97; P-in-c Colesborne 96-97; Dioc Rural Adv from 96; P-in-c Coberley, Cowley, Colesbourne and Elkstone from 97. *The Rectory, Cowley, Cheltenham, Glos GL53 9NJ* Tel (01242) 870232

GREEN, David William. b 53. CertEd75 Nottm Univ BCombStuds84. Linc Th Coll 81. **d** 84 **p** 85. C S Merstham *S'wark* 84-88; C Walton-on-Thames *Guildf* 88-91; V Gillingham H Trin *Roch* from 91; Chapl to Lennox Wood Elderly People's Home from 91. *Holy Trinity Vicarage, 2 Waltham Road, Gillingham, Kent ME8 6XQ* Tel (01634) 231690 or 231372

GREEN, Canon Dennis John. b 45. Lich Th Coll 69. **d** 72 **p** 73. C Hampton All SS *Lon* 72-74; P-in-c Leverington *Ely* 75-76; R 76-80; Can Res Ely Cathl from 80; Vice-Dean and Treas Ely Cathl from 84; Dioc Development Officer for Par from 80; Dioc Development Consultant from 84; Cathl Development Officer from 92. *The Black Hostelry, The College, Ely, Cambs CB7 4DL* Tel (01353) 662612

GREEN, Canon Derek George Wilson. b 27. Bris Univ BA53 MA58. Tyndale Hall Bris 48. **d** 53 **p** 54. C Weymouth St Mary *Sarum* 53-55; Chapl RAF 55-58; R N Pickenham w Houghton on the Hill *Nor* 58-89; R S Pickenham 58-89; R N Pickenham w S Pickenham etc 89-93; Hon Can Nor Cathl 78-93; E Region Co-ord Scripture Union 80-92; rtd 93. *5 Hawkins Meadow, College Fields, Marlborough, Wilts SN8 1UA* Tel (01672) 511713

GREEN, Donald Henry. b 31. Selw Coll Cam BA54 Lon Inst of Educn PGCE55. Qu Coll Birm 81. **d** 83 **p** 84. C Dudley St Aug Holly Hall *Worc* 83-85; V Dudley St Barn 85-90; rtd 96. *The Cuckoo's Nest, 12 Mill Green, Knighton LD7 1EE* Tel (01547) 528289

GREEN, Donald Pentney (Brother Donald). b 25. Leeds Univ BA50. Coll of Resurr Mirfield 50. **d** 52 **p** 53. C Ardwick St Benedict *Man* 52-55; SSF from 55; Sec for Miss SSF 78-96; Lic to Offic *Chelmsf* 58-60 and 69-72; Papua New Guinea 60-63; Chapl HM Pris Kingston (Portsm) 72-76; Lic to Offic *Edin* 76-77; Org Sec Catholic Renewal 77; Lic to Offic *Lich* from 78; rtd 95. *85 Crofton Road, London E13 8QT* Tel 0171-474 5863 Fax as telephone

GREEN, Mrs Dorothy Mary. b 36. Westf Coll Lon BA58. Selly Oak Coll 60. **dss** 83 **d** 87 **p** 94. Ryde All SS *Portsm* 83-87; C 87-91; Hon C Hempnall *Nor* 91-96; rtd 96; Perm to Offic *B & W* from 97. *Oneida, Charnwood Drive, Cheddar, Somerset BS27 3HD* Tel (01934) 742167

GREEN, Douglas Edward. b 17. Sarum Th Coll 47. **d** 50 **p** 51. C Glouc St Paul *Glouc* 50-53; C Malvern Link St Matthias *Worc* 53-56; R Tolladine 56-58; V Bosbury *Heref* 58-78; R Coddington 59-79; V Wellington Heath 59-79; Hon C Minsterley 78-80; rtd 82; Perm to Offic *Worc* from 83. *St Agnes, Lower Dingle, Malvern, Worcs WR14 4BQ*

GREEN, Duncan Jamie. b 52. Sarum & Wells Th Coll 82. **d** 84 **p** 85. C Uckfield *Chich* 84-87; Dioc Youth Officer *Chelmsf* 87-96; Warden and Chapl St Mark's Coll Res Cen 93-96; TR Saffron Walden w Wendens Ambo and Littlebury from 96. *The Rectory, 17 Borough Lane, Saffron Walden, Essex CB11 4AG* Tel (01799) 500947

GREEN, Edward John. b 35. Lich Th Coll. **d** 59 **p** 60. C Longford *Cov* 59-61; C Wigston Magna *Leic* 61-65; V from 73; V Ellistown 65-73. *The Vicarage, Bushloe End, Wigston, Leics LE18 2BA* Tel 0116-288 3419

GREEN, Edward Marcus. b 66. Mert Coll Ox BA88 MA92. Wycliffe Hall Ox 90. **d** 94 **p** 95. C Glyncorrwg w Afan Vale and Cymmer Afan *Llan* 94-96; C Aberystwyth *St D* from 96. *8 Crynfryn Buildings, Aberystwyth SY23 2BD*

GREEN, Canon Edward Michael Bankes. b 30. Ex Coll Ox BA53 MA56 Qu Coll Cam BA57 MA61 BD66 Toronto Univ DD92 Lambeth DD96. Ridley Hall Cam 55. **d** 57 **p** 58. C Eastbourne H Trin *Chich* 57-60; Tutor Lon Coll of Div 60-69; Prin St Jo Coll Nottm 69-75; Hon Can Cov Cathl *Cov* 70-78; R Ox St Aldate w H Trin *Ox* 75-82; R Ox St Aldate w St Matt 82-86; Canada 87-92; Prof Evang Regent Coll Vancouver 87-92; Abps' Adv Springboard for Decade of Evang 92-96; Six Preacher Cant Cathl *Cant* from 93; rtd 96. *7 Little Acreage, Marston, Oxford OX3 0PS* Tel (01865) 248387

GREEN, Edward Wallace. b 11. K Coll Lon BA32 AKC33. Ripon Hall Ox 33. **d** 35 **p** 36. C Coln St Aldwyn w Hatherop and Quenington *Glouc* 35-39; P-in-c 39-45; Asst Master Hawtreys Sch Savernake 45-46; Chapl The Abbey Ashurst Wood 46-52; Asst Master St Edm Sch Hindhead 52-54; Chapl Oakham Sch 54-58; Asst Master Alleyn Court Sch Westcliff-on-Sea 58-79; rtd 79; Perm to Offic *Win* 81-95. *Day House, Alma Road, Romsey, Hants SO51 8EB* Tel (01703) 557756

GREEN, Mrs Elizabeth Pauline Anne. b 29. Lon Coll of Div DipRK70. **dss** 76 **d** 87 **p** 94. Chorleywood Ch Ch *St Alb* 76-87; Par Dn 87-90; C Chipping Sodbury and Old Sodbury *Glouc* 90-95; Asst Dioc Missr 90-95; rtd 95; NSM Chipping Sodbury and Old Sodbury *Glouc* from 95. *The Old House, Parks Farm, Old Sodbury, Bristol BS17 6PX* Tel (01454) 311936

GREEN, Eric Kenneth. b 18. Tyndale Hall Bris 40. **d** 45 **p** 47. C Heatherlands St Jo *Sarum* 45-48; C Radipole 48-49; C Bucknall and Bagnall *Lich* 49-50; V Halwell w Moreleigh *Ex* 50-53; V Wakef St Mary *Wakef* 53-55; R Peldon *Chelmsf* 55-57; P-in-c Leaden Roding 57-58; R 58-63; V Aythorpe Roding and High Roding 60-63; R All Cannings w Etchilhampton *Sarum* 63-75; V Over Kellet *Blackb* 75-83; rtd 83; Perm to Offic *Bradf* from 91. *1 Hill Crescent, Burley in Wharfedale, Ilkley, W Yorkshire LS29 7QG* Tel (01943) 864538

GREEN, Ernest James. b 31. Pemb Coll Cam BA55 MA62. Linc Th Coll 55. **d** 57 **p** 58. C Rawmarsh *Sheff* 57-60; Sec Th Colls Dept SCM 60-62; Prec and Sacr Bris Cathl *Bris* 62-65; Min Can 62-65; V Churchill *B & W* 65-78; RD Locking 72-78; V

Burrington and Churchill 78-82; Preb Wells Cathl 81-82; V Ryde All SS *Portsm* 82-91; P-in-c Ryde H Trin 82-86; RD E Wight 83-88; TR Hempnall *Nor* 91-96; rtd 96; Perm to Offic *B & W* from 97. *Oneida, Charnwood Drive, Cheddar, Somerset BS27 3HD* Tel (01934) 742167

GREEN, Ernest Swinfen. b 12. Wells Th Coll 66. **d** 67 **p** 67. C Eastbourne St Mary *Chich* 67-70; V Lower Beeding 70-77; rtd 77; Perm to Offic *Chich* from 77. *9 Barleycroft, Cowfold, Horsham, W Sussex RH13 8DP* Tel (01403) 864352

GREEN, Fleur Estelle. b 72. Univ of Wales (Ban) BD94. Ripon Coll Cuddesdon DipMin95. **d** 97. C Blackpool St Jo *Blackb* from 97. *52 Leeds Road, Blackpool FY1 4JH* Tel (01253) 24036

GREEN, Frank Gilbert. b 23. Kelham Th Coll 46. **d** 50 **p** 51. C Sheff Parson Cross St Cecilia *Sheff* 50-56; SSM from 52; C Nottingham St Geo w St Jo *S'well* 56-58; Basutoland 59-62; S Africa 62-69 and 84-88; Lesotho 69-84; Lic to Offic *Ox* from 88; rtd 93. *SSM Priory, Willen, Milton Keynes MK15 9AA* Tel (01908) 663749 Fax 234546

GREEN, Canon Frederick George (Fred). b 40. Nottm Univ BA62 MA67. Linc Th Coll 64. **d** 66 **p** 67. C Warsop *S'well* 66-70; R 76-89; V Clipstone 70-76; P-in-c Norton Cuckney 85-89; TR Hucknall Torkard from 89; Hon Can S'well Minster from 93; RD Newstead from 93. *The Rectory, Annesley Road, Hucknall, Nottingham NG15 7DE* Tel 0115-963 2033

GREEN, Gareth David. b 60. Worc Coll Ox BA82 MA86 FRCO79 FLCM87 ARCM75. N Ord Course 94. **d** 97. NSM Lupset *Wakef* from 97. *7 Belgravia Road, St Johns, Wakefield, W Yorkshire WF1 3JP* Tel (01924) 376848 Fax 380182

GREEN, Gary Henry. b 64. Univ of Wales (Cardiff) BD87 DPT95. St Mich Coll Llan 93. **d** 95 **p** 96. C Baglan *Llan* from 95. *35 Crawford Road, Port Talbot SA12 8ND* Tel (01639) 814116

GREEN, George Henry Langston. b 12. St Aug Coll Cant 38. **d** 41 **p** 42. C Liv St Chris Norris Green *Liv* 41-43; C Garston 43-44; C Aintree St Pet 44-46; CF (EC) 46-47; V Neen Savage w Kinlet *Heref* 47-50; R Ironbridge 50-55; V Frodsham *Ches* 55-78; rtd 78; Perm to Offic *Ches* from 78. *River View, Gwespyr, Holywell CH8 9JS* Tel (01745) 857489

GREEN, George James. b 26. Cuddesdon Coll 69. **d** 69 **p** 70. C Handsworth St Mary *Birm* 69-76; R Croughton w Evenley *Pet* 76-88; R Aynho and Croughton w Evenley 88-95; rtd 95. *Dibbinsdale, Langley Road, Claverdon, Warwick CV35 8PU*

GREEN, Gordon Sydney. b 33. Ridley Hall Cam 77. **d** 79 **p** 80. C Ipswich St Marg *St E* 79-83; TV Barton Mills, Beck Row w Kenny Hill etc 83-85; TV Mildenhall 85-86; Perm to Offic *Pet* from 87; rtd 88. *65 Orwell View Road, Shotley Street, Ipswich IP9 1NW* Tel (01473) 787303

GREEN, Graham Herbert. b 53. City Univ BSc74. Westcott Ho Cam 75. **d** 78 **p** 79. C Hatcham St Cath *S'wark* 78-82; C S Ashford Ch Ch *Cant* 82-88; V Cheriton All So w Newington from 88. *All Souls' Vicarage, 1 Ashley Avenue, Cheriton, Folkestone, Kent CT19 4PX* Tel (01303) 275483

GREEN, Graham Reginald. b 48. Sarum & Wells Th Coll 71. **d** 74 **p** 75. C Chorley St Laur *Blackb* 74-76; C Padiham 76-79; V Osmondthorpe St Phil *Ripon* 79-94. *3 Northwood Gardens, Colton, Leeds LS15 9HH* Tel 0113-264 3558

GREEN, Humphrey Christian (Father Benedict). b 24. Mert Coll Ox BA49 MA52. Cuddesdon Coll 50. **d** 51 **p** 82. C Northolt St Mary *Lon* 51-56; Lect Th K Coll Lon 56-60; Lic to Offic *Wakef* from 61; CR from 62; Vice-Prin Coll of Resurr Mirfield 65-75; Prin 75-84; rtd 94. *House of the Resurrection, Mirfield, W Yorkshire WF14 0BN* Tel (01924) 494318

GREEN, James Hardman. b 19. Open Univ BA74. **d** 52 **p** 53. C Darlington St Paul *Dur* 52-54; C Darlington St Hilda 54-57; V Hunwick 57-60; Chapl RADD 60-65 and 75-77; Perm to Offic *Lon* 60-65; R Morcott w S Luffenham *Pet* 65-75; V E Boldon *Dur* 77-84; rtd 84. *8 Hanover Court, Hawthorn Avenue, Haxby, York YO3 3SS* Tel (01904) 763227

GREEN, James Manton. b 33. EMMTC 82. **d** 85 **p** 86. Hon C Kirby Muxloe *Leic* 85-89; Asst Chapl Glenfield Gen and Glenfrith Hosps from 89. *83 Oakcroft Avenue, Kirby Muxloe, Leicester LE9 2DH* Tel 0116-239 3126

GREEN, Miss Jennifer Mary (Jenny). b 55. SEN78 SRN81 RM84. Trin Coll Bris DipHE88 ADPS89. **d** 90 **p** 95. C Tong *Bradf* 90-93; Chapl Bradf Cathl 93; CMS from 94; Uganda from 94. *Muhabura Diocese, PO Box 22, Kisoro, Uganda*

GREEN, Jeremy Nigel. b 52. St Andr Univ MA Nottm Univ DipTh. St Jo Coll Nottm 80. **d** 83 **p** 84. C Dorridge *Birm* 83-86; V Scrooby *S'well* 86-94; V Bawtry w Austerfield and Misson from 94. *The Vicarage, Martin Lane, Bawtry, Doncaster, S Yorkshire DN10 6NJ* Tel (01302) 710298

GREEN, John. b 28. AKC54. **d** 55 **p** 56. C Poulton-le-Fylde *Blackb* 55-57; C St Annes 57-63; V Inskip 63-75; V Fairhaven 75-87; rtd 87; Perm to Offic *Blackb* from 87. *42 Westwood Road, Lytham, Lytham St Annes, Lancs FY8 5NX* Tel (01253) 739288

GREEN, John. b 53. Nottm Univ BCombStuds83. Linc Th Coll 80. **d** 83 **p** 84. C Watford St Mich *St Alb* 83-86; C St Alb St Steph 86-91; Chapl RN from 91. *Royal Naval Chaplaincy Service, Room 203, Victory Building, HM Naval Base, Portsmouth PO1 3LS* Tel (01705) 727903 Fax 727112

GREEN, John David. b 29. Lon Univ BD66. Roch Th Coll 63. **d** 66 **p** 66. C Roch St Pet w St Marg *Roch* 66-72; V Oxshott *Guildf* 72-85; R Weybridge 85-94; rtd 94; Perm to Offic *Guildf* from 94. *103 Bitterne Drive, Woking, Surrey GU21 3JX* Tel (01483) 727936

GREEN, John Francis Humphrey. b 44. MIL85 Ex Univ BA65 Heythrop Coll Lon MA96. Westcott Ho Cam CTM93. **d** 93 **p** 94. C Tadworth *S'wark* 93-96; Chapl St Geo Sch Harpenden from 96. *9 Stewart Road, Harpenden, Herts AL5 4QE* Tel (01582) 461823

GREEN, Canon John Henry. b 44. K Coll Lon BD72 AKC. **d** 73 **p** 74. C Tupsley *Heref* 73-77; Asst Chapl Newc Univ *Newc* 77-79; V Stevenage St Hugh Chells *St Alb* 79-85; V St Jo in Bedwardine *Worc* 85-92; P-in-c Guarlford and Madresfield w Newland from 92; Dir of Ords from 92; Hon Can Worc Cathl from 94. *The Rectory, Madresfield, Malvern, Worcs WR13 5AB* Tel (01684) 574919

GREEN, John Herbert Gardner-Waterman. b 21. Trin Hall Cam BA48 MA58. Wells Th Coll 58. **d** 59 **p** 60. C New Romney w Hope *Cant* 59-63; V Hartlip 63-68; R Sandhurst w Newenden 68-90; RD W Charing 74-81; rtd 90; Perm to Offic *Cant* from 95. *Littlefield House, Maytham Road, Rolvenden Layne, Cranbrook, Kent TN17 4NS* Tel (01580) 241579

GREEN, Preb John Stanley. b 12. Keble Coll Ox BA33 MA37. Wells Th Coll 33. **d** 35 **p** 36. C Stockport St Matt *Ches* 35-39; C Bournemouth St Mary *Win* 39-46; PV Ex Cathl *Ex* 46-49; Dep PV 49-77; R Ex St Jas 49-77; Preb Ex Cathl 69-84; rtd 77; Perm to Offic *Ex* from 84. *2 Whiteway Drive, Heavitree, Exeter EX1 3AN* Tel (01392) 437291

GREEN, Joseph Hudson. b 28. TD76. Dur Univ TCert73. Kelham Th Coll 48. **d** 53 **p** 54. C Norton St Mich *Dur* 53-56; C Heworth St Mary 56-62; V Harton Colliery 62-69; Chapl S Shields Gen Hosp 62-69; CF (TA) 63-67; CF (TAVR) 67-77; V Leadgate *Dur* 69-78; V Dudleston *Lich* 78-85; V Criftins 78-85; R Hodnet w Weston under Redcastle 85-93; RD Hodnet 86-93; rtd 93; Perm to Offic *Lich* from 93. *3 The Paddocks, Market Drayton, Shropshire TF9 3UE* Tel (01630) 658887

GREEN, Julia Ann. b 58. Nottm Univ BA80. Linc Th Coll 84. **dss** 86 **d** 87 **p** 94. Asst Chapl HM Pris Morton Hall 85-90; Linc St Jo *Linc* 86-87; Hon C 87-88; Hon C Bardney 88-97; Chapl Linc Co Hosp 90-93; Chapl St Geo Hosp Linc 90-93; Chapl Linc Distr Health Services & Hosps NHS Trust 93-97; Chapl S Bucks NHS Trust from 97. *Wycombe General Hospital, Queen Alexandra Road, High Wycombe, Bucks HP11 2TT* Tel (01494) 526161

GREEN, Miss Karina Beverley. b 61. Ripon Coll Cuddesdon 87. **d** 90 **p** 94. C Lee-on-the-Solent *Portsm* 90-93; Dioc Youth Officer *Guildf* from 94. *2 South Hill, Godalming, Surrey GU7 1JT* Tel (01483) 416539

✠**GREEN, The Rt Revd Laurence Alexander (Laurie).** b 45. K Coll Lon BD68 AKC68. DMin82 NY Th Sem STM69 St Aug Coll Cant 70. **d** 70 **p** 71 **c** 93. C Kingstanding St Mark *Birm* 70-73; V Erdington St Chad 73-83; Prin Aston Tr Scheme 83-89; Hon C Birchfield *Birm* 84-89; TR Poplar *Lon* 89-93; Area Bp Bradwell *Chelmsf* from 93. *The Bishop's House, Orsett Road, Horndon-on-the-Hill, Stanford-le-Hope, Essex SS17 8NS* Tel (01375) 673806 Fax 674222 E-mail lauriegr@globalnet.co.uk

GREEN, Mrs Margaret Elizabeth. b 34. DipYL65. St Mich Ho Ox 60. **dss** 84 **d** 87 **p** 94. Ecclesall *Sheff* 84-87; Par Dn 87-90; C Doncaster St Jas 90-94; rtd 95; Perm to Offic *Sheff* from 95. *91 Littemoor Lane, Doncaster, S Yorkshire DN4 0LQ* Tel (01302) 365884

✠**GREEN, The Rt Revd Mark.** b 17. MC45. Linc Coll Ox BA40 MA44 Aston Univ Hon DSc80. Cuddesdon Coll 40. **d** 40 **p** 41 **c** 72. C Glouc St Cath *Glouc* 40-42; CF (EC) 43-46; V Newland St Jo *York* 48-53; CF 53-56; V S Bank *York* 56-58; R Cottingham 58-64; Can and Preb York Minster 63-72; Hon Chapl to Abp York 64-72; V Bishopthorpe 64-72; V Acaster Malbis 64-72; RD Ainsty 64-68; Suff Bp Aston *Birm* 72-82; Dioc Dir of Ords 80-82; rtd 82; Asst Bp Chich from 82. *27 Selwyn House, Selwyn Road, Eastbourne, E Sussex BN21 2LF* Tel (01323) 642707

GREEN, Martin Charles. b 59. Bris Univ BA81 MPhil86. Wycliffe Hall Ox 82. **d** 84 **p** 85. C Margate H Trin *Cant* 84-88; V Kingston upon Hull St Aid Southcoates *York* 88-94; P-in-c Bishop's Itchington *Cov* from 94. *The Vicarage, Bishop's Itchington, Leamington Spa CV33 0QT* Tel (01926) 613466

GREEN, Martyn. b 41. FCA. Ridley Hall Cam 78. **d** 80 **p** 81. C Wetherby *Ripon* 80-83; V Leeds St Cypr Harehills 83-90; V Ossett cum Gawthorpe *Wakef* from 90. *The Vicarage, Fearnley Avenue, Ossett, W Yorkshire WF5 9ET* Tel (01924) 274068

GREEN, Canon Maurice Paul. b 34. MCIMA60. Wells Th Coll 68. **d** 70 **p** 71. C Eaton *Nor* 70-74; R N w S Wootton 74-90; RD Lynn 83-89; Hon Can Nor Cathl 88-96; V Swaffham 90-96; rtd 96. *6 Wimborne Avenue, Ipswich IP3 8QW* Tel (01473) 711061

GREEN, Muriel Hilda. b 38. SEITE 94. **d** 96 **p** 97. NSM Ealing St Barn *Lon* from 96. *1 Maybury Court, 55 Pitshanger Lane, London W5 1RU* Tel 0181-810 9769

GREEN, Neil Howard. b 57. New Coll Ox BA80 PGCE81. Wycliffe Hall Ox 87. **d** 90 **p** 91. C Finchley St Paul and St Luke *Lon* 90-94; C Muswell Hill St Jas w St Matt from 94. *8 St James Lane, London N10 3DB* Tel 0181-883 0636

GREEN, Paul. b 25. RD. Sarum & Wells Th Coll 72. **d** 74 **p** 75. C Pinhoe *Ex* 74-77; P-in-c 77-79; V 79-85; P-in-c Bishopsteignton

85-88; P-in-c Ideford, Luton and Ashcombe 85-88; rtd 88; Perm to Offic *Ex* from 88. *58 Maudlin Drive, Teignmouth, Devon TQ14 8SB* Tel (01626) 777312

GREEN, Paul Francis. b 48. Cranmer Hall Dur BA78. **d** 79 **p** 80. C Cirencester *Glouc* 79-82; C Lydney w Aylburton 82-85; V Westbury-on-Severn w Flaxley and Blaisdon 85-90; Chapl Carlton Hayes Hosp 90-96; Chapl Leics Mental Health Service Unit from 90; Chapl Leics Mental Health Services NHS Trust from 94. *The Bradgate Mental Health Unit, Glenfield General Hospital, Groby Road, Glenfield, Leicester LE3 9EJ* Tel 0116-250 2550

GREEN, Paul John. b 48. Sarum & Wells Th Coll 72. **d** 73 **p** 74. C Tuffley *Glouc* 73-76; C Prestbury 76-82; P-in-c Highnam w Lassington and Rudford 82-83; P-in-c Tibberton w Taynton 82-83; R Highnam, Lassington, Rudford, Tibberton etc 84-92; Hon Min Can Glouc Cathl from 85; V Fairford 92-96; RD Fairford 93-96; rtd 96. *37 Thomas Stock Gardens, Abbeymead, Gloucester GL4 5GH*

GREEN, Peter. b 38. Ex Univ BSc59. Sarum Th Coll 59. **d** 61 **p** 62. C Romford St Edw *Chelmsf* 61-66; Ceylon 66-70; V Darnall H Trin *Sheff* 71-80; TV Stantonbury *Ox* 80-87; TV Stantonbury and Willen 87-91; Dep Chapl HM Pris Belmarsh 91-92; Chapl HM Pris Woodhill from 92. *The Chaplain's Office, HM Prison Woodhill, Tattenhoe Street, Milton Keynes MK4 4DA* Tel (01908) 501999 Fax 505417

GREEN, Canon Peter Edwin. b 33. Lich Th Coll. **d** 62 **p** 63. C Sprowston *Nor* 62-65; C-in-c Heartsease St Fran CD 65-73; V Loddon w Sisland 73-91; Hon Can Nor Cathl 86-92; rtd 92; Perm to Offic *Nor* 92-96. *Ambleside, Lowestoft Road, Beccles, Suffolk NR34 7DG* Tel (01502) 717740

GREEN, Peter Geoffrey. b 59. St Andr Univ MA83. Coll of Resurr Mirfield 85. **d** 88 **p** 89. C Pershore w Pinvin, Wick and Birlingham *Worc* 88-91; V Dudley St Barn from 91. *St Barnabas's Vicarage, Middlepark Road, Dudley, W Midlands DY1 2LD* Tel (01384) 256680

GREEN, Peter Jamie. b 63. Reading Coll of Tech C&G82. Aston Tr Scheme 87 Oak Hill Th Coll BA93. **d** 93 **p** 94. C Brigg *Linc* 93-97; C Brigg, Wrawby and Cadney cum Howsham 97; P-in-c Billinghay from 97. *The Vicarage, 6 Walcot Road, Billinghay, Lincoln LN4 4EH* Tel (01526) 861746

GREEN, Philip Charles. b 53. Wigan Coll of Tech HNC77 IMC81. Nor Ord Course 91. **d** 94 **p** 95. C Southport Em *Liv* from 94. *28 Elswick Green, Southport, Merseyside PR9 9XT* Tel (01704) 27294

GREEN, Canon Philip Harry. b 19. ALCD50. **d** 50 **p** 51. C Keighley *Bradf* 50-53; V Everton St Sav *Liv* 53-57; V Barnoldswick w Bracewell *Bradf* 57-64; V Shipley St Paul 64-77; Hon Can Bradf Cathl 77-82; V Gargrave 77-82; rtd 82; Perm to Offic *Bradf* from 82; Perm to Offic *Carl* from 82. *102 Kentsford Road, Grange-over-Sands, Cumbria LA11 7BB* Tel (015395) 32950

GREEN, Richard Charles. b 49. K Coll Lon 68 St Aug Coll Cant 73. **d** 74 **p** 75. C Broseley w Benthall *Heref* 74-79; TV Heref St Martin w St Fran (S Wye TM) 80-95; C Heref S Wye from 95. *Flat 3, St Martin's Parish Centre, Ross Road, Hereford HR2 7RJ* Tel (01432) 354588 or 353717 Fax 352412

GREEN, Robert Henry. b 57. K Coll Lon BD79. Wycliffe Hall Ox 81. **d** 83 **p** 84. C Norbury *Ches* 83-86 and from 91; C Knutsford St Jo and Toft 86-88; rtd 88. *122 Cavendish Road, Hazel Grove, Stockport, Cheshire SK7 6JH* Tel (01625) 877042

GREEN, Robert Leonard. b 44. Sarum & Wells Th Coll. **d** 84 **p** 85. C Battersea St Luke *S'wark* 84-89; CF from 89. *MOD Chaplains (Army), Trenchard Lines, Upavon, Pewsey, Wilts SN9 6BE* Tel (01980) 615804 Fax 615800

GREEN, Robert Stanley. b 42. Dur Univ BA65. Wells Th Coll 65. **d** 67 **p** 68. C Ashford *Cant* 67-73; R Otham 73-80; V Bethersden w High Halden 80-87; R Winterbourne Stickland and Turnworth etc *Sarum* from 87. *The Rectory, Winterbourne Stickland, Blandford Forum, Dorset DT11 0NL* Tel (01258) 880482

GREEN, Robin Christopher William. b 43. Leeds Univ BA64 Fitzw Ho Cam BA67. Ridley Hall Cam 65. **d** 68 **p** 69. C S'wark H Trin *S'wark* 68-71; C Englefield Green *Guildf* 71-73; Chapl Whitelands Coll of HE *S'wark* 73-78; Team Ldr Dioc Lay Tr Team 78-84; V W Brompton St Mary w St Pet *Lon* 84-87; USPG 87-90; Perm to Offic *S'wark* 88-90; NSM from 91. *2 Church Path, Mitcham, Surrey CR4 3BN* Tel 0181-543 0519

GREEN, Rodney William. b 52. LNSM course 90. **d** 93 **p** 94. NSM Flixton St Jo *Man* from 93. *85 Arundel Avenue, Flixton, Manchester M41 6MG* Tel 0161-748 7238

GREEN, Roger Thomas. b 43. Oak Hill Th Coll DipHE79. **d** 79 **p** 80. C Paddock Wood *Roch* 79-83; R High Halstow w All Hallows and Hoo St Mary 83-89; Chapl HM Pris Brixton 89-90; Chapl HM Pris Standford Hill 90-94; Chapl HM Pris Swaleside from 94. *HM Prison Swaleside, Eastchurch, Sheerness, Kent ME12 4AX* Tel (01795) 880766 Fax 880267

GREEN, Preb Ronald Henry (Ron). b 27. Lambeth MA86 Bps' Coll Cheshunt 53. **d** 55 **p** 56. C St Marylebone Ch Ch w St Barn *Lon* 55-58; R 58-62; Dioc Youth Tr Officer 62-64; C St Andr Holborn 62-64; RE Adv 63-73; V Hampstead St Steph 64-73; RD N Camden (Hampstead) 67-73; V Heston 73-80; Preb St Paul's Cathl 75-83; Jt Dir Lon and S'wark Bd of Educn 79-83; Dir of Educn *Sarum* 83-86; R Chiddingfold *Guildf* 86-91; rtd 91; Perm to Offic *Nor* 91-92; Master St Nic Hosp Salisbury 92-97. *20 Ayleswade Road, Salisbury SP2 8DR* Tel (01722) 327660

GREEN, Ruth Valerie. *See* JAGGER, Mrs Ruth Valerie

GREEN, Sidney Leonard. b 44. Lon Univ DipTh70 BD72 MTh86 Montessori Soc DipEd84. Oak Hill Th Coll 68. **d** 72 **p** 73. C Skelmersdale St Paul *Liv* 72-74; C Denton Holme *Carl* 74-76; In Bapt Ch 76-85; Chapl Qu Eliz Gr Sch Blackb 85-91; Perm to Offic *Blackb* 91; Chapl Epsom Coll from 91; Lic to Offic *Guildf* from 91. *17 Tintagel Close, Epsom, Surrey KT17 4HA* Tel (01372) 742204 E-mail sidney_green@compuserve.com

GREEN, Stephen Keith. b 48. Ex Coll Ox BA69 Mass Inst of Tech MSc75. N Ord Course 84. **d** 87 **p** 88. Hong Kong 87-93. *10 Queen Street Place, London EC4R 1BQ, or 44 Scarsdale Villa, London W8 6PP* Tel 0171-336 3354 or 937 3290 Fax 336 3661

GREEN, Steven Douglas. b 57. Univ of Wales (Ban) DipTh81. Sarum & Wells Th Coll 81. **d** 82 **p** 83. C Hawarden *St As* 82-86; V Mostyn 86-93; V Ffynnongroyw 86-93; V Mostyn w Ffynnongroyw from 93. *The Vicarage, Hafod y Ddol Lane, Mostyn, Holywell CH8 9EJ* Tel (01745) 560513

GREEN, Stuart. b 57. Nottm Univ BA79. Linc Th Coll 83. **d** 85 **p** 86. C Boultham *Linc* 85-88; R Bardney 88-96. *Address temp unknown*

GREEN, Ms Susan Denise. b 66. TCD BA89 HDipEd90. Irish Sch of Ecum MPhil93. **d** 92 **p** 93. C Antrim All SS *Conn* 92-95; Dio Youth Officer (Cashel) *C & O* from 95. *The Rectory, Castlecomer, Co Kilkenny, or St Canice's Library, Kilkenny, Irish Republic* Tel Kilkenny (56) 41677 or 61910 Fax 41677 or 51813

GREEN, Mrs Susan Margaret (Sue). b 54. Univ of Wales (Abth) BSc75. SW Minl Tr Course 92. **d** 95 **p** 96. NSM Wiveliscombe w Chipstable, Huish Champflower etc *B & W* from 95. *North Rodden Cottage, Maundown, Wiveliscombe, Taunton, Somerset TA4 2BU* Tel (01984) 623809

GREEN, Trevor Geoffrey Nash. b 45. BA. Oak Hill Th Coll 81. **d** 84 **p** 85. C Stalybridge H Trin and Ch Ch *Ches* 84-89; V 89-96; V Lache cum Saltney from 96. *St Mark's Vicarage, 5 Cliveden Road, Chester CH4 8DR* Tel (01244) 671702

GREEN, Trevor Howard. b 37. Sarum & Wells Th Coll 72. **d** 74 **p** 75. C Bloxwich *Lich* 74-77; C Willenhall St Steph 77-79; P-in-c 79-80; V 80-82; V Essington 82-90; V Brewood from 90; V Bishopswood from 90; RD Penkridge from 94. *The Vicarage, Sandy Lane, Brewood, Stafford ST19 9ET* Tel (01902) 850368

GREEN, Vivian Hubert Howard. b 15. DD58. **d** 39 **p** 40. Lic to Offic *Cant* 39-47; Perm to Offic *Sarum* 42-51; Chapl Linc Coll Ox 51-79; Rector Linc Coll Ox 83-87; rtd 87. *Calendars, Sheep Street, Burford, Oxon OX18 4LS* Tel (01993) 823214

GREEN, William. b 44. Newc Univ BA66 DipEd67 MA77. N Ord Course 87. **d** 90 **p** 91. NSM Utley *Bradf* from 90. *105 Shann Lane, Keighley, W Yorkshire BD20 6DY* Tel (01535) 605102

GREEN, William John. b 23. Birm Univ BSc43. Roch Th Coll 64. **d** 66 **p** 67. C Minchinhampton *Glouc* 66-68; C Standish w Hardwicke and Haresfield 68-70; R Eastington and Frocester 70-80; P-in-c S Cerney w Cerney Wick 80-84; V S Cerney w Cerney Wick and Down Ampney 84-87; P-in-c Maisemore 87-90; rtd 90. *36 Fairfield, Upavon, Pewsey, Wilts SN9 6DZ* Tel (01980) 630798

GREEN, William Lewis. b 12. St Cath Coll Cam BA34 MA39. Cuddesdon Coll 34. **d** 35 **p** 36. C Hackney Wick St Mary of Eton *Lon* 35-46; C Desborough *Pet* 40-45; Vice-Prin Old Rectory Coll Hawarden 46-47; Chapl and Lect St Mary's Coll Ban 47-62; Kenya 62-70; Nigeria 70-78; Perm to Offic *Ches* 78-79 and from 82; Tanzania 79-82; rtd 82. *20 Dunkirk Drive, Ellesmere Port, South Wirral L65 6QH* Tel 0151-355 5456

GREENACRE, Canon Roger Tagent. b 30. Clare Coll Cam BA52 MA56. Coll of Resurr Mirfield 52. **d** 54 **p** 55. C Hanworth All SS *Lon* 54-59; Chapl Ely Th Coll 59-60; Chapl Summer Fields Sch Ox 60-61; C N Audley Street St Mark *Lon* 62-63; Chapl Liddon Ho Lon 63-65; Chapl Paris St Geo *Eur* 65-75; RD France 70-75; Dioc Ecum Officer *Chich* 75-88; Lect Chich Th Coll 75-89; Can Res and Chan Chich Cathl *Chich* 75-97; Chmn Chich Dioc Eur Ecum Cttee from 89; Can Res and Prec Chich Cathl from 97. *4 Vicars' Close, Canon Lane, Chichester, W Sussex PO19 1PT* Tel (01243) 784244 Fax 536190

GREENALL, Canon Ronald Gilbert. b 41. St Aid Birkenhead 61. **d** 64 **p** 65. C Adlington *Blackb* 64-67; C Ribbleton 67-69; R Coppull St Jo 69-84; V Garstang St Thos from 84; RD Garstang from 89; Hon Can Blackb Cathl from 95. *The Vicarage, Church Street, Garstang, Preston PR3 1PA* Tel (01995) 602162

GREENE, Colin John David. b 50. QUB BA73 Fitzw Coll Cam MA75 Nottm Univ PhD. St Jo Coll Nottm 78. **d** 80 **p** 81. Hon C Sandiacre *Derby* 80-81; C Loughborough Em *Leic* 81-84; V Thorpe Acre w Dishley 84-89; Evang Tr Consultant Bible Soc 89-91; Tutor Trin Coll Bris from 91. *Trinity College, Stoke Hill, Bristol BS9 1JP* Tel 0117-968 2803

GREENE, David Arthur Kirsopp. b 36. St Pet Coll Ox BA60 MA64 FETC81. Tyndale Hall Bris 61. **d** 63 **p** 64. C Southgate *Chich* 63-66; C Kirby Grindalythe *York* 66-69; C N Grimston w Wharram Percy and Wharram-le-Street 66-69; R Folke, N Wootton and Haydon w Long Burton *Sarum* 69-75; R Long Burton, Folke, N Wootton, Haydon etc 75-80; P-in-c Thornford w Beer Hackett 80-84; P-in-c High Stoy 81-84; R Bradford Abbas and Thornford w Beer Hackett from 84. *The Rectory, Church Road, Thornford, Sherborne, Dorset DT9 6QE* Tel (01935) 872382

GREENE, John Howe. b 22. K Coll Lon AKC48 BD49. **d** 49 **p** 50. C Drayton in Hales *Lich* 49-52; C Stoke upon Trent 52-56; V Wilnecote 56-62; V Lodsworth *Chich* 62-69; R Selham 62-69; R Burwash 69-75; R Petworth 75-88; RD Petworth 76-88; P-in-c Egdean 76-80; R 80-88; rtd 88; Perm to Offic *Chich* from 88. *37 Wilderness Road, Hurstpierpoint, Hassocks, W Sussex BN6 9XD* Tel (01273) 833651

GREENE, Paul David O'Dwyer. b 53. Brunel Univ BSc78 Southn Univ DASS81 CQSW81. Oak Hill NSM Course 90. **d** 93 **p** 94. NSM Northwood Em *Lon* from 93. *Orchard House, 50 The Drive, Northwood, Middx HA6 1HP* Tel (01923) 829605

GREENER, Jonathan Desmond Francis. b 61. Trin Coll Cam BA83 MA87. Coll of Resurr Mirfield 89. **d** 91 **p** 92. C S'wark H Trin w St Matt *S'wark* 91-94; Bp's Dom Chapl *Truro* 94-96; V Brighton Gd Shep Preston *Chich* from 96. *The Good Shepherd Vicarage, 272 Dyke Road, Brighton BN1 5AE* Tel (01273) 882987 Fax 386989

GREENFIELD, Canon Martin Richard. b 54. Em Coll Cam MA75. Wycliffe Hall Ox MA78. **d** 79 **p** 80. C Enfield Ch Ch Trent Park *Lon* 79-83; CMS from 84; Nigeria 85-94; Hon Can Aba from 89; C Langdon Hills *Chelmsf* 94-95; R Brampton *Ely* from 95. *The Rectory, 15 Church Road, Brampton, Huntingdon, Cambs PE18 8PF* Tel (01480) 453341

GREENFIELD, Norman John Charles. b 27. Leeds Univ BA51. Chich Th Coll 51. **d** 53 **p** 54. C Portsea St Cuth *Portsm* 53-56; C Whitley Ch Ch *Ox* 56-60; V Moorends *Sheff* 60-65; V Littleworth *Ox* 65-71; Asst Stewardship Adv 65-70; V New Marston 71-79; Dioc Stewardship Adv *Chich* 79-88; P-in-c Amberley w N Stoke 79-83; R Guestling and Pett 88-94; rtd 94; Perm to Offic *Chich* from 94. *5 Marlborough Close, Eastbourne, E Sussex BN23 8AN* Tel (01323) 769494

GREENHALGH, David Murray. b 13. Jes Coll Cam BA34 MA38 Lon Univ BD47. Ridley Hall Cam 34. **d** 36 **p** 37. C Worsley *Man* 36-38; C Pennington 38-43; R Newton Heath St Anne 43-49; V Guilden Morden *Ely* 49-55; V Terrington St Clement 55-59; V Shirley *Win* 59-78; rtd 78; Perm to Offic *Pet* from 84; Perm to Offic *Leic* from 91; Perm to Offic *Linc* from 91. *3 Cricket Lawns, Oakham, Leics LE15 6HT* Tel (01572) 757238

GREENHALGH, Eric. b 20. Tyndale Hall Bris. **d** 63 **p** 64. C Preston St Mary *Blackb* 63-66; P-in-c 66-68; V 68-72; V Partington and Carrington *Ches* 72-81; V Inskip *Blackb* 81-85; rtd 85; Perm to Offic *Blackb* from 85; Perm to Offic *Carl* from 85. *4 Rydal Close, Millom, Cumbria LA18 4QR* Tel (01229) 770995

GREENHALGH, Ian Frank. b 49. Wycliffe Hall Ox 74. **d** 77 **p** 78. C Parr *Liv* 77-80; V Wigan St Barn Marsh Green 80-84; Chapl RAF from 84. *Chaplaincy Services (RAF), HQ, Personnel and Training Command, RAF Innsworth, Gloucester GL3 1EZ* Tel (01452) 712612 ext 5164 Fax 510828

GREENHALGH, Philip Adrian. b 52. Ian Ramsey Coll 75 Wycliffe Hall Ox 76. **d** 79 **p** 80. C Gt Clacton *Chelmsf* 79-82; P-in-c Stalmine *Blackb* 82-86; Perm to Offic *Ely* 86-87; Rep Leprosy Miss E Anglia 86-87; Area Org CECS 88-90; Perm to Offic *Carl* 88-93; NSM Alston Team *Newc* 90-92; NSM Chulmleigh *Ex* 92-93; NSM Chawleigh w Cheldon 92-93; NSM Wembworthy w Eggesford 92-93; P-in-c Gilsland w Nether Denton *Carl* 93-95; V Millom from 95. *The Vicarage, St George's Road, Millom, Cumbria LA18 4JA* Tel (01229) 772889

GREENHALGH, Stephen. b 53. Trin Coll Bris 77 Lon Bible Coll BA80. **d** 81 **p** 82. C Horwich H Trin *Man* 81-84; C Horwich 84-85; Chapl RAF 85-93; Perm to Offic *Blackb* from 93. *88 Full View, Blackburn BB2 4QE*

GREENHILL, Anthony David. b 39. Bris Univ BSc59. Tyndale Hall Bris 61. **d** 63 **p** 64. C Southsea St Jude *Portsm* 63-65; India 65-78; C Kinson *Sarum* 78-81; V Girlington *Bradf* 81-97; C Platt Bridge *Liv* from 97. *28 Stanley Road, Platt Bridge, Wigan, Lancs WN2 3TF* Tel (01942) 747378

GREENHOUGH, Alan Kenneth. b 40. St D Coll Lamp DipTh66. **d** 66 **p** 67. C Allestree *Derby* 66-70; C Ilkeston St Mary 70-73; V Bradwell 73-85; R Twyford w Guist w Bintry w Themelthorpe etc *Nor* 85-95; P-in-c Stibbard 94-95; R Twyford, Guist, Bintree, Themelthorpe etc from 95. *The Rectory, Guist, Dereham, Norfolk NR20 5LU* Tel (01362) 84255

GREENHOUGH, Andrew Quentin (Andy). b 68. E Lon Poly BSc89. Wycliffe Hall Ox BTh94. **d** 94 **p** 95. C Partington and Carrington *Ches* from 94. *18 Langdale Road, Partington, Urmston, Manchester M31 4NE* Tel 0161-775 7666 Fax as telephone

GREENHOUGH, Arthur George. b 30. Fitzw Ho Cam BA52 MA56. Tyndale Hall Bris 55. **d** 57 **p** 58. C Wakef St Andr *Wakef* 57-63; R Birkin w Haddlesey *York* 63-85; RD Selby 77-84; P-in-c Hambleton 84-85; R Haddlesey w Hambleton and Birkin from 85. *The Rectory, Chapel Haddlesey, Selby, N Yorkshire YO8 8QF* Tel (01757) 270245

GREENHOUGH, Geoffrey Herman. b 36. Sheff Univ BA57 Lon Univ BD71. St Jo Coll Nottm 74. **d** 75 **p** 76. C Cheadle Hulme St Andr *Ches* 75-78; R Tilston and Shocklach 78-82; V Hyde St Geo 82-87; V Pott Shrigley from 87. *The Vicarage, Spuley Lane, Pott Shrigley, Macclesfield, Cheshire SK10 5RS* Tel (01625) 573316

GREENISH, Dr Brian Vivian Isitt. b 20. LRCP MRCS Lon Univ MB BSc. **d** 89 **p** 89. NSM Bedford St Pet w St Cuth *St Alb* 89-91; Perm to Offic from 91. *69 Chaucer Road, Bedford MK40 2AW* Tel (01234) 352498

GREENLAND, Clifford James Gomm. b 09. Clifton Th Coll 63. **d** 64 **p** 65. C Woking St Pet *Guildf* 64-67; V Wiggenhall St Mary Magd *Ely* 67-75; rtd 75; Perm to Offic *Chelmsf* from 75. *6 Sunset Avenue, Woodford Green, Essex IG8 0ST* Tel 0181-505 8858

GREENLAND, Martin. b 65. Warw Univ BSc87. Westcott Ho Cam CTM94. **d** 97. C Scarborough St Martin *York* from 97. *St Michael's House, 136 Filey Road, Scarborough, N Yorkshire YO11 3AA* Tel (01723) 378105

GREENLAND, Robin Anthony Clive. b 31. Dur Univ BA53. Linc Th Coll 59. **d** 61 **p** 62. C Marsden *Wakef* 61-63; C Cleethorpes *Linc* 63-65; V Holton-le-Clay 65-70; V Tetney 65-70; V Embsay w Eastby *Bradf* 70-78; V Earby 78-83; V Firbank, Howgill and Killington 83-94; Hon C Sedbergh, Cautley and Garsdale 83-94; rtd 94; Perm to Offic *Heref* from 94. *19 Worcester Road, Ledbury, Herefordshire HR8 1PL* Tel (01531) 631224

GREENLAND, Roy Wilfrid. b 37. St Steph Ho Ox 71. **d** 73 **p** 74. C Wanstead St Mary *Chelmsf* 73-76; V Harlow St Mary Magd 76-83; P-in-c Huntingdon All SS w St Jo *Ely* 83-84; P-in-c Huntingdon St Barn 83-84; P-in-c Huntingdon St Mary w St Benedict 83-84; Bermuda 84-89; V Northampton St Alb *Pet* 89-92; R Waldron *Chich* from 92. *The Rectory, Sheepsetting Lane, Waldron, Heathfield, E Sussex TN21 0UY* Tel (01435) 862816

GREENLEES, Geoffrey Ian Loudon. b 20. Sarum Th Coll 70. **d** 71 **p** 72. C Wilton w Netherhampton and Fugglestone *Sarum* 71-74; R Woodchurch *Cant* 75-85; rtd 85; Perm to Offic *Cant* from 85. *8 Martin's Close, Tenterden, Kent TN30 7AJ* Tel (01580) 762586

GREENMAN, David John. b 35. Lon Univ BA59. Oak Hill Th Coll 57. **d** 61 **p** 62. C Wandsworth St Steph *S'wark* 61-63; C Bishopwearmouth St Gabr *Dur* 63-66; C-in-c Bedgrove CD *Ox* 66-74; P-in-c Macclesfield Ch Ch *Ches* 74-77; V 77-81; P-in-c Glouc All SS *Glouc* 81-85; V Glouc St Jas 81-85; V Bare *Blackb* 85-91; V Market Lavington and Easterton *Sarum* from 91. *The Vicarage, 14 Church Street, Market Lavington, Devizes, Wilts SN10 4DT* Tel (01380) 813914

GREENSLADE, Mrs Gillian Carol. b 43. Leic Univ BA64 Nottm Univ PGCE65 Essex Univ MA78. EAMTC 93. **d** 96 **p** 97. NSM Dovercourt and Parkeston w Harwich *Chelmsf* from 96. *6 St Faith Road, Colchester CO4 4PS* Tel (01206) 843284

GREENSLADE, Keith James Inglis. b 27. St Mich Coll Llan 60. **d** 62 **p** 63. C Bishopsworth *Bris* 62-65; C Chippenham St Paul w Langley Burrell 65-68; V Upper Stratton 68-95; rtd 95; Perm to Offic *Bris* from 95. *65 Shakespeare Road, Wootton Bassett, Swindon SN4 8HF* Tel (01793) 853253

GREENSLADE, Peter Michael. b 37. Bp Burgess Hall Lamp 69. **d** 71 **p** 72. C Llanwnda w Goodwick and Manorowen *St D* 71-73; C Lydiate *Liv* 73-75; V Wigan St Cath 75-76; Chapl Newsham Gen Hosp Liv 76-78; C Knotty Ash St Jo *Liv* 76-78; C Lache cum Saltney *Ches* 78-80; V Barnton 80-84; C Warburton 85-86; Warden Petroc Chr Guest Ho 86-90; rtd 90. *Freshfields, Cenarth, Newcastle Emlyn SA38 9TP*

GREENSLADE, Timothy Julian (Tim). b 63. St Jo Coll Ox BA86. Oak Hill Th Coll BA95. **d** 95 **p** 96. C Broadwater St Mary *Chich* from 95. *30 Fletcher Road, Worthing, W Sussex BN14 8EX* Tel (01903) 526370

GREENSTREET, Mark George. b 68. St Jo Coll Dur BA94. **d** 97. C St Alb St Pet *St Alb* from 97. *33A Catherine Street, St Albans, Herts AL3 5JG* Tel (01727) 832965 or 855485 Mobile 0973-110506 E-mail st.peters.curate@st.albans.clara.net

GREENWAY, John. b 32. Bps' Coll Cheshunt 68 Qu Coll Birm 69. **d** 69 **p** 70. C Luton Ch Ch *St Alb* 69-74; C Pulloxhill w Flitton 75-76; P-in-c Marston Morteyne 76-79; P-in-c Lidlington 77-79; P-in-c Marston Morteyne w Lidlington 80-81; R 81-97; rtd 97. *73 Northmore Road, Locks Heath, Southampton SO3 6LA*

GREENWAY, John Michael. b 34. LNSM course 94. **d** 96. NSM Gt Yarmouth *Nor* from 96. *17 Hamilton Road, Great Yarmouth, Norfolk NR30 4ND* Tel (01493) 853558

GREENWAY, Margaret Hester. b 26. **d** 87. Downend *Bris* 75-79; Oldland 79-82; Stratton St Margaret w S Marston etc 82-86; rtd 86; Perm to Offic *B & W* 87-95. *5 Weston Lodge, Lower Bristol Road, Weston-super-Mare, Avon BS23 2PJ* Tel (01934) 623561

GREENWELL, Christopher. b 49. Linc Th Coll 79. **d** 81 **p** 82. C Scarborough St Martin *York* 81-84; V S Bank 84-89; R Bolton by Bowland w Grindleton *Bradf* 89-92; V Nether Hoyland St Andr *Sheff* 92-96; V Kirkleatham *York* from 96. *Kirkleatham Vicarage, 130 Mersey Road, Redcar, Cleveland TS10 4DF* Tel (01642) 482073

GREENWELL, Paul. b 60. Magd Coll Ox BA81 MA85. St Steph Ho Ox 82. **d** 85 **p** 86. C Hendon and Sunderland *Dur* 85-88; Chapl Univ Coll of Ripon and York St Jo 88-93; Min Can and Prec Ripon Cathl *Ripon* 88-93; V Hunslet St Mary from 93. *The Vicarage, Church Street, Hunslet, Leeds LS10 2QY* Tel 0113-271 9661 or 270 4659

GREENWOOD, Canon Gerald. b 33. Leeds Univ BA57 Sheff Poly MSc83 Surrey Univ Hon MA93. Linc Th Coll 57. **d** 59 **p** 60. C Rotherham *Sheff* 59-62; V Elsecar 62-69; V Wales 70-77; P-in-c Thorpe Salvin 74-77; Dioc Sch Officer 77-84; P-in-c Bramley and Ravenfield 77-78; P-in-c Hooton Roberts 77-78; R 78-84; Hon Can Sheff Cathl 80-84; Dioc Dir of Educn 81-84; Hon Can S'wark Cathl *S'wark* from 84; Dir of Educn from 84. *15C Paveley Drive, Morgan's Walk, London SW11 3TP* Tel 0171-585 1731 or 407 7911

GREENWOOD, Gordon Edwin. b 44. Trin Coll Bris 78. **d** 80 **p** 81. C Bootle St Matt *Liv* 80-83; V Hunts Cross 83-93; V Skelmersdale St Paul from 93. *The Vicarage, Church Road, Skelmersdale, Lancs WN8 8ND* Tel (01695) 722087

GREENWOOD, Hilary Peter Frank. b 29. Nottm Univ BA57. Kelham Th Coll 50. **d** 57 **p** 58. SSM from 54; Tutor Kelham Th Coll 57-59; Warden 70-74; S Africa 59-60; Australia 60-67; Asst Chapl Madrid *Eur* 74-76; Perm to Offic *Blackb* 76-80; Perm to Offic *Man* 80-82; R Longsight St Jo w St Cypr 82-89; rtd 89; Perm to Offic *Dur* from 89; Hon Asst Chapl Prague *Eur* 92-95. *St Anthony's Priory, Claypath, Durham DH1 1QT* Tel 0191-384 3747

GREENWOOD, James Peter. b 61. RIBA87 Univ Coll Lon BSc83 DipArch86 St Jo Coll Dur BA90. Cranmer Hall Dur 88. **d** 91 **p** 92. C Belper *Derby* 91-94; CMS from 95; Pakistan from 95. *St Thomas Church, Luqman Hakim Road, G-7/2, Islamabad, Pakistan*

GREENWOOD, John Newton. b 44. St Chad's Coll Dur BA69 DipTh70. **d** 70 **p** 71. C Hartlepool H Trin *Dur* 70-72; Lic to Offic from 72; Hd Master Archibald Primary Sch Cleveland from 84. *1 Brae Head, Eaglescliffe, Stockton-on-Tees, Cleveland TS16 9HP* Tel (01642) 783200

GREENWOOD, Leslie. b 37. Dur Univ BA59 DipTh61. St Jo Coll Dur. **d** 61 **p** 62. C Birstall *Wakef* 61-63; C Illingworth 64-70; Chapl H Trin Sch Halifax 64-89; V Charlestown 70-91; TV Upper Holme Valley from 91. *The Vicarage, 2 Ashgrove Road, Holmfirth, Huddersfield HD7 1LR* Tel (01484) 683131

GREENWOOD, Michael Eric. b 44. Oak Hill Th Coll 78. **d** 80 **p** 81. C Clubmoor *Liv* 80-83; V Pemberton St Mark Newtown 83-94; V Grassendale from 94. *St Mary's Vicarage, 22 Eaton Road, Liverpool L19 0PW* Tel 0151-427 1474

GREENWOOD, Norman David. b 52. Edin Univ BMus74 Lon Univ BD78 Nottm Univ MPhil90. Oak Hill Th Coll 76. **d** 78 **p** 79. C Gorleston St Andr *Nor* 78-81; SAMS 81-83; C Cromer *Nor* 83-84; R Appleby Magna and Swepstone w Snarestone *Leic* 84-94; P-in-c Chesterfield H Trin *Derby* 94-95; P-in-c Chesterfield Ch Ch 94-95; R Chesterfield H Trin and Ch Ch from 95. *Christ Church Vicarage, 89 Sheffield Road, Chesterfield, Derbyshire S41 7JH* Tel (01246) 273508

GREENWOOD, Robert John Teale. b 28. Leeds Univ BA53. Coll of Resurr Mirfield 53. **d** 55 **p** 56. C S Kirkby *Wakef* 55-60; C Hitchin St Mary *St Alb* 60-63; P-in-c Westgate Common *Wakef* 63-64; V 64-68; Asst Chapl HM Pris Man 68-69; Chapl HM Pris Holloway 69-70; Chapl HM Pris Man 71-77; Chapl HM Pris Styal 77-88; Lic to Offic *Ches* 77-93; Perm to Offic *St As* from 89; Perm to Offic *Ban* from 89; rtd 93. *1 Glanwern, Pentrefoelas, Betws-y-Coed LL24 0LG* Tel (01690) 5313

GREENWOOD, Canon Robin Patrick. b 47. St Chad's Coll Dur BA68 DipTh69 MA71 Birm Univ PhD92. **d** 70 **p** 71. C Adel *Ripon* 70-73; Min Can and Succ Ripon Cathl 73-78; V Leeds Halton St Wilfrid 78-86; Dioc Can Res Glouc Cathl *Glouc* 86-95; Dioc Missr and Dir Lay and Post-Ord Tr 86-95; Dir of Min *Chelmsf* from 95; Hon Can Chelmsf Cathl from 95. *124 Broomfield Road, Chelmsford CM1 1RN* Tel (01245) 353915

GREENWOOD, Roy Douglas. b 27. Tyndale Hall Bris 58. **d** 60 **p** 61. C Ox St Matt *Ox* 60-62; V Ulpha *Carl* 62-63; V Seathwaite w Ulpha 63-72; P-in-c Haverthwaite 72-74; C Ulverston St Mary w H Trin 74-78; V Egton w Newland 78-86; Assoc Chapl Palma de Mallorca and Balearic Is *Eur* 86-93; Assoc Chapl Palma de Mallorca 93-95; rtd 95. *La Finquita, Aptd 78, Pollensa, Palma de Mallorca 07460, Spain* Tel Pollensa (71) 530966

GREER, Eric Gordon. b 52. Pepperdine Univ BA74. Princeton Th Sem MDiv80. **d** 93 **p** 94. C Southgate St Andr *Lon* 93-96; C Camden Square St Paul from 96. *The Vicarage, Camden Square, London NW1 9XG* Tel 0171-485 3147

GREER, Canon Robert Ferguson. b 34. TCD BA56 MA59. **d** 60 **p** 61. C Dundela *D & D* 60-65; I Castlewellan 65-78; I Castlewellan w Kilcoo from 78; RD Kilmegan from 89; Can Dromore Cathl from 90; Prec from 93. *The Rectory, 58 Mill Hill, Castlewellan, Co Down BT31 9NB* Tel (01396) 778306

GREETHAM, Canon William Frederick. b 40. Bede Coll Dur CertEd. Cranmer Hall Dur 63. **d** 66 **p** 67. C St Annes *Blackb* 66-69; C Ashton-on-Ribble St Andr 69-71; Chapl Aysgarth Sch N Yorkshire 71-81; C Bedale *Ripon* 72-75; V Crakehall 75-82; V Hornby 75-82; V Patrick Brompton and Hunton 75-82; V Kirkby Stephen *Carl* 82-90; R Kirkby Stephen w Mallerstang etc 90-96; RD Appleby 86-91; Hon Can Carl Cathl from 89; P-in-c Crosthwaite Kendal from 96; P-in-c Cartmel Fell from 96; P-in-c Winster from 96; P-in-c Witherslack from 96. *The Vicarage, Crosthwaite, Kendal, Cumbria LA8 8HT* Tel (01539) 568276

GREG, John Kennedy. b 24. Trin Coll Cam BA46 MA61. Chich Th Coll 46. **d** 49 **p** 50. C Walmsley *Man* 49-51; C Carl H Trin *Carl* 51-55; V Lanercost w Kirkcambeck 55-62; V Cumwhitton 62-75; C Carl St Barn 75; TV 75-80; Chapl Strathclyde Ho Hosp Carl 80-85; TV Carl H Trin and St Barn *Carl* 80-85; rtd 85; Perm to Offic *Carl* 86-93. *113 Wigton Road, Carlisle CA2 7EL* Tel (01228) 38837

GREGG, David William Austin. b 37. Lon Univ BD66 Bris Univ MA69. Tyndale Hall Bris 63. **d** 68 **p** 69. C Barrow St Mark *Carl* 68-71; P-in-c Lindal w Marton 71-75; Communications Sec Gen Syn Bd for Miss and Unity 76-81; Prin Romsey Ho Coll Cam 81-88; V Haddenham w Cuddington, Kingsey etc *Ox* 88-96; P-in-c Newton Longville w Stoke Hammond and Whaddon from 96. *The Rectory, Drayton Road, Newton Longville, Milton Keynes MK17 0BH* Tel (01908) 377847

GREGORY, Alan Paul Roy. b 55. K Coll Lon BD77 MTh78 AKC. Ripon Coll Cuddesdon 78. **d** 79 **p** 80. C Walton-on-Thames *Guildf* 79-82; Tutor and Dir of Studies Sarum & Wells Th Coll 82-88; USA from 88. *4862 Cambridge Drive, Dunwoody, Atlanta, Georgia 30338, USA*

GREGORY, Brian. b 43. Trin Coll Bris. **d** 82 **p** 83. C Burscough Bridge *Liv* 82-85; V Platt Bridge 85-92; V Ben Rhydding *Bradf* from 92. *The Vicarage, Ben Rhydding, Ilkley, W Yorkshire LS29 8PT* Tel (01943) 607363

GREGORY, Clive Malcolm. b 61. Lanc Univ BA84 Qu Coll Cam BA87 MA89. Westcott Ho Cam 85. **d** 88 **p** 89. C Margate St Jo *Cant* 88-92; Chapl Warw Univ *Cov* from 92. *92 De Montfort Way, Coventry CV4 7DT* Tel (01203) 690216 or 523519

GREGORY, Father. *See* DUDDING, Edward Leslie

GREGORY, Graham. b 36. Open Univ BA78 Lon Univ DipTh65. Tyndale Hall Bris 63. **d** 66 **p** 67. C Wandsworth St Mich *S'wark* 66-71; C Hastings Em and St Mary in the Castle *Chich* 71-75; V Douglas St Ninian *S & M* 75-91; Dioc Youth Officer 78-88; Chapl HM Pris Douglas 82-86; RD Douglas *S & M* 86-91; V Wollaton Park *S'well* 91-95; V Lenton Abbey 91-95; rtd 95. *15 Keble Drive, Bishopthorpe, York YO2 1TA* Tel (01904) 701679

GREGORY, Ian Peter. b 45. Open Univ BA82 Plymouth Univ PGCE92. Bernard Gilpin Soc Dur 66 Chich Th Coll 67. **d** 70 **p** 71. C Tettenhall Regis *Lich* 70-73; C Shrewsbury H Cross 73-76; P-in-c Walsall St Mary and All SS Palfrey 76-80; R Petrockstowe, Petersmarland, Merton, Meeth etc *Ex* 80-87; TV Ex St Thos and Em 87-91; Hon C S Wimbledon All SS *S'wark* from 94. *142 Monkleigh Road, Morden, Surrey SM4 4ER* Tel 0181-401 6148

GREGORY, Ivan Henry. b 31. Leeds Univ BA52. Ely Th Coll 58. **d** 60 **p** 60. C Stoke Newington St Faith, St Matthias and All SS *Lon* 60-63; C Withycombe Raleigh *Ex* 63-67; V Braunton 67-77; V Tintagel *Truro* 77-93; RD Trigg Minor 84-86; rtd 93. *20 Greenfields Avenue, Alton, Hants GU34 2ED* Tel (01420) 542860

GREGORY, John Frederick. b 33. Glouc Sch of Min 75. **d** 78 **p** 78. NSM S Cerney w Cerney Wick *Glouc* 78-81; NSM Coates, Rodmarton and Sapperton etc 81-88; P-in-c Kempsford w Welford from 88. *The Parsonage, Kempsford, Fairford, Glos GL7 4ET* Tel (01285) 810241

GREGORY, Miss Pauline Beatrice Joan (Paula). b 20. SRN43. K Coll Lon 47. **dss** 54 **d** 87 **p** 94. CSA 49-57; Jamaica 58-69; Victoria Docks Ascension *Chelmsf* 70-80; Canning Town St Cedd 80-84; Colchester St Botolph w H Trin and St Giles 84-87; Hon Par Dn 87-94; Hon C from 94. *51 St John's Green, Colchester CO2 7EZ* Tel (01206) 43138

GREGORY, Peter. b 35. Cranmer Hall Dur 59. **d** 62 **p** 63. C Pennington *Man* 62-65; C N Ferriby *York* 65-68; V Tonge Fold *Man* 68-72; V Hollym w Welwick and Holmpton *York* 72-77; P-in-c Foston w Flaxton 77-80; P-in-c Crambe w Whitwell and Huttons Ambo 77-80; R Whitwell w Crambe, Flaxton, Foston etc 81-94; rtd 94. *6 High Terrace, Northallerton, N Yorkshire DL6 1BG* Tel (01609) 776956

GREGORY, Richard Branson. b 33. Fitzw Ho Cam BA58 MA62. Sarum Th Coll 58 Ridley Hall Cam 59. **d** 60 **p** 61. C Sheff St Cuth *Sheff* 60-62; Asst Chapl Leeds Univ *Ripon* 62-64; V Yeadon St Jo *Bradf* 64-71; R Keighley 71-74; TR Keighley St Andr 74-82; Hon Can Bradf Cathl 71-82; RD S Craven 71-73 and 78-82; P-in-c Broadmayne, W Knighton, Owermoigne etc *Sarum* 82-85; R from 85. *The Rectory, Main Street, Broadmayne, Dorchester, Dorset DT2 8EB* Tel (01305) 852435

GREGORY, Canon Stephen Simpson. b 40. Nottm Univ BA62 CertEd63. St Steph Ho Ox. **d** 68 **p** 69. C Aldershot St Mich *Guildf* 68-71; Chapl St Mary's Sch Wantage 71-74; R Edgefield *Nor* 74-88; R Holt 74-94; R Holt w High Kelling 94-95; RD Holt 79-84 and 93-95; Hon Can Nor Cathl 94-95; V Prestbury *Glouc* from 95. *The Vicarage, Prestbury, Cheltenham, Glos GL52 3DQ* Tel (01242) 244373

GREGORY-SMITH, Thomas Gregory. b 08. St Jo Coll Cam BA30 MA34. Lon Coll of Div 33. **d** 34 **p** 35. C Islington St Jude Mildmay Park *Lon* 34-36; C S Croydon Em *Cant* 36-38; CMS Miss Rwanda 38-47 and 52-63; Lic to Offic *Win* 48; Financial Sec Rwanda Miss 49-52; Asst Sec 64-71; Lic to Offic *S'wark* 65-71; Perm to Offic *Guildf* 65-71; Perm to Offic *Win* 77-94; C-in-c Wimbledon Em Ridgway Prop Chpl *S'wark* 71-76; rtd 76. *46 Sea*

Road, Barton-on-Sea, New Milton, Hants BH25 7NG Tel (01425) 610942

GREGSON, Peter John. b 36. Univ Coll Dur BSc61. Ripon Hall Ox 61. **d** 63 **p** 64. C Radcliffe St Thos *Man* 63-65; C Baguley 65-67; Chapl RN 68-91; V Ashburton w Buckland in the Moor and Bickington *Ex* from 91; RD Moreton from 95. *The Vicarage, Copperwood Close, Ashburton, Newton Abbot, Devon TQ13 7JQ* Tel (01364) 652506

GREIG, George Malcolm. b 28. CA53 St Andr Univ BD95. LNSM course 75. **d** 81 **p** 82. NSM Dundee St Mary Magd *Bre* 81-84; NSM Dundee St Jo 82-84; P-in-c Dundee St Ninian 84; Hon Chapl St Paul's Cathl Dundee from 85; NSM Dundee St Paul from 85. *61 Charleston Drive, Dundee DD2 2HE* Tel (01382) 566709

GREIG, John Kenneth. b 38. Natal Univ BA57. St Paul's Grahamstown LTh60. **d** 61 **p** 62. S Africa 61-66 and 71-78; C Friern Barnet St Jas *Lon* 66-69; C Kenton 69-71; Chapl Whitelands Coll of HE *S'wark* 78-84; Area Ecum Officer (Croydon) from 84; V Purley St Swithun from 84. *Windsor Lodge, Purley Rise, Purley, Surrey CR8 3AW* Tel 0181-660 3744

GREIG, Martin David Sandford. b 45. Bris Univ BSc67. St Jo Coll Nottm 72. **d** 75 **p** 76. C Keresley and Coundon *Cov* 75-79; C Rugby St Andr 79-83; TV 83-86; V Cov St Geo 86-93; TV Southgate *Chich* from 93. *St Andrew's Vicarage, Weald Drive, Crawley, W Sussex RH10 6NU* Tel (01293) 531828

GREIG, Michael Lawrie Dickson. b 48. Shuttleworth Agric Coll NDA70. All Nations Chr Coll 78 St Jo Coll Nottm 94. **d** 96 **p** 97. C Hunningham *Cov* from 96; C Wappenbury w Weston under Wetherley from 96; C Offchurch from 96; C Long Itchington and Marton from 96. *The Vicarage, Hunningham, Leamington Spa, Warwickshire CV33 9DS* Tel (01926) 632739

GRELLIER, Brian Rodolph. b 34. AKC61. **d** 62 **p** 63. C Wandsworth St Paul *S'wark* 62-66; Japan 66-72; Miss to Seamen 72-76; V Freiston w Butterwick *Linc* from 76; Chapl HM Pris N Sea Camp 89-96. *Pinchbeck House, Butterwick, Boston, Lincs PE22 0HZ* Tel (01205) 760550 Fax 760098

GRETTON, Tony Butler. b 29. St Jo Coll Dur BA53. **d** 54 **p** 55. C W Teignmouth *Ex* 54-57; R Norton Fitzwarren *B & W* 57-68; rtd 68; Chapl Glouc Docks Mariners' Ch *Glouc* 73-92; P-in-c Brookthorpe w Whaddon 79-82; Hon C The Edge, Pitchcombe, Harescombe and Brookthorpe 82-89; Perm to Offic from 89. *18 Clover Drive, Hardwicke, Gloucester GL2 4TG* Tel (01452) 721505

GREW, Nicholas David. b 52. Surrey Univ BSc74 MSc75. Wycliffe Hall Ox DipMin95. **d** 95 **p** 96. C Biddulph *Lich* from 95. *48 Thames Drive, Biddulph, Stoke-on-Trent ST8 7HL* Tel (01782) 522428

GREW, Richard Lewis. b 32. Clare Coll Cam BA54 MA58. Wycliffe Hall Ox 67. **d** 68 **p** 70. C Repton *Derby* 68-73; Asst Chapl Repton Sch Derby 74-93; Lic to Offic *Derby* 73-93; rtd 93; Perm to Offic *Sarum* from 94. *5 Priory Gardens, Spetisbury, Blandford Forum, Dorset DT11 9DS* Tel (01258) 857613

GREWCOCK, Peter Joseph. b 28. Sarum Th Coll. **d** 58 **p** 59. C Mitcham St Barn *S'wark* 58-60; C Kingswood 60-62; V Howe Bridge *Man* 62-72; P-in-c Werrington, St Giles in the Heath and Virginstow *Truro* 72-73; V Leic St Chad *Leic* 73-76; P-in-c Trotton w Chithurst *Chich* 76-80; C Broadstone *Sarum* 80-84; TV Gillingham 84-88; P-in-c Milborne St Andrew w Dewlish 88-92; rtd 92. *9 Hambledon Close, Blandford Forum, Dorset DT11 7SA* Tel (01258) 450893

GREY, Canon Edward Alwyn. b 23. Univ of Wales (Swansea) BA48. St D Coll Lamp. **d** 50 **p** 51. C Wrexham *St As* 50-58; R Llanfynydd 58-69; R Flint 69-89; RD Holywell 73-89; Can St As Cathl 76-89; rtd 89. *60 Gronant Road, Prestatyn LL19 9NE* Tel (01745) 855302

GREY, Richard Thomas. b 50. St D Coll Lamp BA73 Ripon Hall Ox 73. **d** 75 **p** 76. C Blaenavon w Capel Newydd *Mon* 75-77; Ind Chapl from 77; C Newport St Paul 77-80; CF (TA) from 78; Chapl Aberbargoed Hosp 80-88; V Bedwellty *Mon* 80-88; R Llanwenarth Ultra 88-92; R Govilon w Llanfoist w Llanelen from 92. *The Rectory, Govilon, Abergavenny NP7 9PT* Tel (01873) 830342

GREY, Canon Roger Derrick Masson. b 38. AKC61. **d** 62 **p** 63. C Darlington H Trin *Dur* 62-63; C Bishopwearmouth St Mich 63-67; V Mabe *Truro* 67-70; Dioc Youth Chapl 67-70; Youth Chapl *Glouc* 70-77; V Stroud H Trin 77-82; Dioc Can Res Glouc Cathl from 82; Dir of Educn 82-94; Bp's Chapl from 94. *4A Millers Green, Gloucester GL1 2BN* Tel (01452) 525242

GREY, Stephen Bernard. b 56. Linc Th Coll 86. **d** 88 **p** 89. C Worsley *Man* 88-93; V Bamford from 93. *St Michael's Vicarage, 389 Bury and Rochdale Old Road, Heywood, Lancs OL10 4AT* Tel (01706) 369610

GREY, Canon Thomas Hilton. b 18. St D Coll Lamp BA39 Keble Coll Ox BA41 MA46. St Mich Coll Llan 41. **d** 42 **p** 43. C Aberystwyth H Trin *St D* 42-49; R Ludchurch and Templeton 49-64; R Haverfordwest St Thos and Haroldston E St Issell 64-77; Can St D Cathl 72-84; Treas St D Cathl 80-84; RD Roose 74-84; R Haverfordwest St Mary and St Thos w Haroldston 77-84; rtd 85. *3 Gwscwm Park, Burry Port SA16 0DX* Tel (01554) 833629

GRIBBEN, John Gibson. b 44. Lon Univ DipTh73 K Coll Lon BD75 QUB MTh81. CITC 73. **d** 75 **p** 76. C Dunmurry *Conn* 75-78; CR from 81; Lic to Offic *Wakef* from 83. *College of the Resurrection, Mirfield, W Yorkshire WF14 0BW* Tel (01924) 490441

GRIBBIN, Canon Bernard Byron. b 35. Bradf Univ DipHP76 MPhil84. St Aid Birkenhead 58. **d** 60 **p** 61. C Maghull *Liv* 60-63; C Prescot 63-65; V Denholme Gate *Bradf* 65-71; V Bankfoot 71-79; Dioc Stewardship Adv 79-86; Prec and Chapl Choral Ches Cathl *Ches* 86-91; Hon Can Ches Cathl 91-96; V Ringway 91-96; Dioc Tourism Officer 91-96; rtd 96. *12 Hodgson Fold, Addingham, Ilkley, W Yorkshire LS29 0HA* Tel (01943) 831502

GRIBBLE, Canon Arthur Stanley. b 04. Qu Coll Cam BA27 MA31. Westcott Ho Cam 27. **d** 30 **p** 31. C Applethwaite *Carl* 30-33; C Almondbury *Wakef* 33-36; Chapl Sarum Th Coll 36-38; R Shepton Mallet *B & W* 38-54; RD Shepton Mallet 49-54; Preb Wells Cathl 49-54; Prin Qu Coll Birm 54-67; Hon Can Birm Cathl *Birm* 54-67; Can Res Pet Cathl *Pet* 67-79; rtd 79; Perm to Offic *Pet* from 79; Perm to Offic *Linc* from 80. *2 Colyton Terrace, Bayford Hill, Wincanton, Somerset BA9 9LQ* Tel (01963) 33678

GRIBBLE, Howard Frank. b 27. Magd Coll Cam BA50 MA56. Ely Th Coll 50. **d** 52 **p** 53. C Leytonstone St Marg w St Columba *Chelmsf* 52-56; N Rhodesia 56-59; Metrop Area Sec UMCA 59-62; V Harlow St Mary Magd *Chelmsf* 62-70; R Lawhitton *Truro* 70-81; R Lezant 70-81; RD Trigg Major 75-79; P-in-c S Petherwin w Trewen 77-79; Chapl R Cornwall Hosps NHS Trust 81-84; rtd 84; Perm to Offic *Truro* from 84. *Westerlies, Marine Drive, Widemouth Bay, Bude, Cornwall EX23 0AQ* Tel (01288) 361528

GRIBBLE, Malcolm George. b 44. Chu Coll Cam BA67 MA71. Linc Th Coll 79. **d** 81 **p** 82. C Farnborough *Roch* 81-84; V Bostall Heath 84-90; V Bexleyheath Ch Ch from 90. *The Vicarage, 113 Upton Road, Bexleyheath, Kent DA6 8LS* Tel 0181-303 3260

GRICE, Charles. b 24. MBE83. **d** 58 **p** 59. C Stocksbridge *Sheff* 58-61; R Armthorpe 61-66; Ind Missr 66-69; Ind Chapl 69-76; V Tinsley 69-73; V Oughtibridge 73-76; Gen Sec Ch Lads' and Ch Girls' Brigade 77-91; R Braithwell w Bramley *Sheff* 88-91; rtd 89; Perm to Offic *Sheff* from 89. *57 Deepdale Road, Rotherham, S Yorkshire S61 2NR* Tel (01709) 557551

GRICE, Canon David Richard. b 32. Keble Coll Ox BA55 MA59. St Steph Ho Ox 55. **d** 57 **p** 58. C Leeds St Aid *Ripon* 57-61; C Middleton St Mary 61-62; V Woodlesford 62-69; V Leeds St Wilfrid 69-78; TR Seacroft 78-93; Hon Can Ripon Cathl from 92; P-in-c Thorner 93-95; V from 95. *The Vicarage, Church View, Thorner, Leeds LS14 3ED* Tel 0113-289 2437

GRICE-HUTCHINSON, Canon George Arthur Claude. b 12. Bps' Coll Cheshunt 39. **d** 39 **p** 40. C Shoreditch St Leon *Lon* 39-40; C Seaton Hirst *Newc* 40-41 and 43-46; Asst Chapl Bermondsey Charterho Miss *S'wark* 41-43; C Pershore w Wick *Worc* 46-47; P-in-c Sighill *Newc* 47-49; V Newc St Cuth 49-55; V Newc All SS 50-55; V Newc St Cuth and All SS 55-56; V Blyth St Mary 56-63; V Benwell St Jas 63-74; V N Sunderland 74-79; Hon Can Newc Cathl 77-79; rtd 80. *17 Westacres Crescent, Newcastle upon Tyne NE15 7NY* Tel 0191-274 7975

GRIDLEY, Miss Susan Mary (Sue). b 49. EAMTC 94. **d** 97. NSM Doddinghurst and Mountnessing *Chelmsf* from 97. *11 Worrin Close, Shenfield, Essex CM15 8DG* Tel (01277) 210137

GRIERSON, Peter Stanley. b 42. Lon Univ BD68 Leeds Univ MPhil74. Linc Th Coll 68. **d** 69 **p** 70. C Clitheroe St Mary *Blackb* 69-71; C Aston cum Aughton *Sheff* 71-74; V Preston St Jude w St Paul *Blackb* 74-81; V Blackb St Luke w St Phil from 89; RD Blackb 91-97. *St Luke's Vicarage, Lansdowne Street, Blackburn BB2 1UU* Tel (01254) 581402

GRIEVE, David Campbell. b 51. St Jo Coll Dur BA74. Wycliffe Hall Ox 74. **d** 76 **p** 77. C Upton (Overchurch) *Ches* 76-80; C Selston *S'well* 80-82; V Pelton *Dur* 82-89; rtd 89. *Horn's House Farm, Witton Gilbert, Durham DH7 6TT* Tel 0191-384 1268

GRIEVE (née BELL), Mrs Judith Margaret. b 52. Golds Coll Lon CertEd73. NE Ord Course 91. **d** 94 **p** 96. NSM Choppington *Newc* from 94. *20 Stobhill Villas, Morpeth, Northd NE61 2SH* Tel (01670) 503433

GRIEVE, Robert Andrew Cameron. b 33. ACP65. Edin Th Coll 69. **d** 71 **p** 72. C Leigh St Mary *Man* 71-73; Hon C Chedburgh w Depden and Rede *St E* 73-75; Lic to Offic 75-77; P-in-c Newton 77-79; V Assington 77-79; R Fraserburgh w New Pitsligo *Ab* 79-83; R Corringham *Linc* 83-91; Perm to Offic from 91; V Owston *Sheff* 91-96; rtd 96. *3 Mill Mere Road, Corringham, Gainsborough, Lincs DN21 5QZ*

GRIEVES, Anthony Michael. b 47. St Alb Minl Tr Scheme 81. **d** 84 **p** 85. NSM Stevenage St Mary Shephall *St Alb* 84-86; NSM Stevenage St Mary Sheppall w Aston from 86. *27 Falcon Close, Stevenage, Herts SG2 9PG* Tel (01438) 727204

GRIEVES, Ian Leslie. b 56. Bede Coll Dur CertEd77 BEd78. Chich Th Coll 82. **d** 84 **p** 85. C Darlington St Mark w St Paul *Dur* 84-87; C Whickham 87-89; V Darlington St Jas from 89. *St James's Vicarage, Vicarage Road, Darlington, Co Durham DL1 1JW* Tel (01325) 465980

GRIFFIN, Dr Alan Howard Foster. b 44. TCD BA66 MA69 Peterho Cam PhD71. Sarum & Wells Th Coll 75. **d** 78 **p** 79. Asst to Lazenby Chapl and Lect Ex Univ from 78; Sub-Warden from

78; Warden from 81; Sen Warden from 84; Lic to Offic *Ex* from 78. *Duryard House, Duryard Halls, Lower Argyll Road, Exeter EX4 4RG* Tel (01392) 432164 or 264203

GRIFFIN, Christopher Donald (Chris). b 59. Reading Univ BA80 CertEd81. Wycliffe Hall Ox DipTh85. **d** 85 **p** 86. C Gerrards Cross *Ox* 85-88; Chapl Felsted Sch Essex from 88; Perm to Offic *Chelmsf* from 88. *The Colony, Chelmsford Road, Felstead, Dunmow, Essex CM6 3EP* Tel (01371) 820414 or 820258

GRIFFIN, Dennis Gordon. b 24. Worc Ord Coll 66. **d** 68 **p** 69. C Cradley *Worc* 68-69; V Rainbow Hill St Barn 69-74; R Broughton *Man* 74-79; V Pendlebury Ch Ch 79-86; rtd 89. *Trevean, Goldsithney, Penzance, Cornwall TR20 9JZ* Tel (01736) 711320

GRIFFIN, Gerald Albert Francis. b 31. Qu Coll Birm 74. **d** 77 **p** 78. NSM Bushbury *Lich* 77-83; Ind Chapl *Dur* 83-88; Chapl HM Pris Man 88-89; Chapl HM Pris Featherstone 89-93; C Toxteth St Philemon w St Gabr and St Cleopas *Liv* 93-96; rtd 96. *7 Chartwell Drive, Bushbury, Wolverhampton WV10 8JL*

GRIFFIN, Harold Rodan Bristow. b 12. Jes Coll Cam BA33 LLB34 MA43. Ridley Hall Cam 43. **d** 45 **p** 46. C Kirby Moorside w Gillamoor *York* 45-49; C Linthorpe 49-52; C Boylestone *Derby* 52; R Hulland, Atlow and Bradley 52-61; V Framsden *St E* 61-71; R Helmingham 61-71; rtd 77; Perm to Offic *Ely* from 91. *Flat 17, Gretton Court, Girton, Cambridge CB3 0QN* Tel (01223) 276842

GRIFFIN, Joan Angela. b 35. Qu Coll Birm 82. **dss** 85 **d** 92 **p** 94. Moseley St Mary *Birm* 85-92; NSM from 92. *389 Wake Green Road, Birmingham B13 0BH* Tel 0121-777 8772

GRIFFIN, Canon John Henry Hugh. b 13. St Cath Coll Cam BA35 MA39. Linc Th Coll 35. **d** 38 **p** 39. C Bramford w Burstall *St E* 38-42; P-in-c Halesworth 42-46; R Stratford St Mary 46-72; V Higham 46-72; C Hadleigh w Layham and Shelley 72-73; P-in-c Gt and Lt Glemham 73-79; P-in-c Blaxhall w Stratford St Andrew and Farnham 73-79; Hon Can St E Cathl 78-79; rtd 79. *3 Church Street, Hadleigh, Ipswich IP7 5DT* Tel (01473) 823100

GRIFFIN, Joseph William. b 48. Univ of Wales (Cardiff) DipTh73 DPS74. St Mich Coll Llan 70. **d** 74 **p** 75. C Killay *S & B* 74-78; C Swansea St Thos and Kilvey 78-81; V Troedrhiwgarth *Llan* 81-91; V Llanrhidian w Llanmadoc and Cheriton *S & B* from 91; RD Gower from 94. *The Vicarage, Llanrhidian, Swansea SA3 1EH* Tel (01792) 390144

GRIFFIN, Keith. b 66. Nottm Trent Univ BA88. Cranmer Hall Dur BA94. **d** 95 **p** 96. C Gedling *S'well* from 95. *St George's Rectory, Victoria Road, Nottingham NG4 2NN* Tel 0115-961 5566

GRIFFIN, Kenneth Francis. b 21. Lon Univ BSc64. St Jo Coll Nottm 72. **d** 73 **p** 74. C Bexleyheath Ch Ch *Roch* 73-77; R Kingsdown 77-82; rtd 86. *Woodlands, Palmers Cross Hill, Rough Common, Canterbury, Kent CT2 9BL* Tel (01227) 457314

GRIFFIN, Malcolm Neil. b 36. Leeds Univ BA57. Coll of Resurr Mirfield 57. **d** 59 **p** 60. C Cheadle *Lich* 59-61; C Bloxwich 61-64; P-in-c Willenhall St Anne 64-69; V Stretton w Claymills 69-75; V Baswich 75-85; V Madeley 85-96; V Fulford w Hilderstone from 96. *20 Tudor Hollow, Fulford, Stoke-on-Trent ST11 9NP* Tel (01782) 397073

GRIFFIN, Malcolm Roger. b 46. Open Univ BA DipRS83 DM90. S'wark Ord Course. **d** 83 **p** 84. NSM Romford St Andr *Chelmsf* 83-87; Hon C Romford St Jo 87-90; Hon C Gt Ilford St Alb from 90. *35 Oak Street, Romford RM7 7BA* Tel (01708) 741089

GRIFFIN, Mark Richard. b 68. Trin Coll Bris BA93. Westcott Ho Cam 94. **d** 96 **p** 97. C Walmer *Cant* from 96. *9 Roselands, Walmer, Deal, Kent CT14 7QE* Tel (01304) 368656

GRIFFIN, Canon Michael Richard. b 19. CD78. Trin Coll Bris 43. **d** 44 **p** 44. C Tonbridge St Steph *Roch* 44-45; C Tunbridge Wells H Trin 45-47; V Hindley St Pet *Liv* 47-51; Canada from 51; Can Huron from 64; CStJ from 78. *68 Caledonia Street, Stratford, Ontario, Canada, N5A 5W6*

GRIFFIN, Niall Paul. b 37. TCD BA61 Div Test61. **d** 61 **p** 62. C Newtownards *D & D* 61-63; C Arm St Mark *Arm* 63-64; Jamaica 64-66; C Lurgan Ch Ch *D & D* 66-69; Chapl RAF 69-84; Missr Chr Renewal Cen *D & D* 84-89; Ireland and Scotland Network Ldr SOMA from 89. *7 Cloughmore Park, Rostrevor, Newry, Co Down BT34 3AX* Tel (01693) 738959

GRIFFIN, Nigel Robert. b 50. Univ of Wales (Lamp) BA71. Ripon Hall Ox 71. **d** 73 **p** 74. C Burry Port and Pwll *St D* 73-77; C Carmarthen St Pet 77-79; Youth Chapl 79-96; V Whitland and Kiffig 80-89; Warden of Ords 86-91; V Llangynnwr and Cwmffrwd 89-92; RD Carmarthen 91-92; R Aberporth w Tremain and Blaenporth 92-95; V Aberporth w Tremain w Blaenporth and Betws Ifan 95-96; Chapl Morriston Hosp Swansea from 96. *Morriston Hospital Trust, Heol Maes Eglwys, Cwmrhydyceirw, Swansea SA6 8EL* Tel (01792) 702222

GRIFFIN, Canon Roger Thomas Kynaston. b 14. ALCD41. **d** 41 **p** 42. C Norbiton *S'wark* 41-45; V Gd Easter *Chelmsf* 45-55; R Berners Roding 45-55; R Abbess and Beauchamp Roding 49-55; V Becontree St Alb 55-61; V W Ham 61-82; P-in-c Plaistow St Mary 71-72; Chmn RADD 73-86; Hon Can Chelmsf Cathl 80-82; rtd 82; Perm to Offic *B & W* from 83. *Warrenhurst, Church Street, Minehead, Somerset TA24 5JU* Tel (01643) 706166

GRIFFIN, Canon Rutland Basil. b 16. ALCD41. **d** 41 **p** 42. C Aylesbury *Ox* 41-45; C Hatfield *St Alb* 45-50; V Biggleswade 50-61; V Dartford H Trin *Roch* 61-84; RD Dartford 64-84; Hon Can Roch Cathl 70-84; rtd 84; Perm to Offic *Roch* 84-95; Perm to Offic *Cant* from 84. *94 Stratford Road, Warwick CV34 6BG* Tel (01926) 419582

GRIFFIN, The Very Revd Victor Gilbert Benjamin. b 24. MRIA TCD BA46 MA57 Hon DD92. CITC 47. **d** 47 **p** 48. C Londonderry St Aug *D & R* 47-51; C Londonderry Ch Ch 51-57; I 57-68; RD Londonderry 60-68; Preb Howth St Patr Cathl Dublin 62-68; Dean St Patr Cathl Dublin 68-91; rtd 91. *7 Tyler Road, Limavady, Co Londonderry BT49 0DW* Tel (01504) 762093

GRIFFIN, William George. b 13. St Pet Hall Ox BA36 MA45. Wycliffe Hall Ox 36. **d** 37 **p** 38. C Chatham St Paul *Roch* 37-41; P-in-c Strood St Fran 41-45; V Lozells St Paul *Birm* 45-51; V Birm Bp Ryder 51-56; V Burton All SS *Lich* 56-59; V Bretby w Newton Solney *Derby* 59-66; V Church Broughton w Barton and Sutton on the Hill 66-72; R Brington w Whilton *Pet* 72-78; rtd 78; Perm to Offic *Pet* from 86. *6 Riverside Drive, Weedon, Northampton NN7 4RT* Tel (01327) 41585

GRIFFITH, Brian Vann. b 34. Univ Sch Th Abth & Lamp DipTh82 BTh91 MTh94. **d** 82 **p** 83. NSM Aberystwyth *St D* 82-87; NSM Llanfihangel w Llanafan and Llanwnnws etc 87-88; NSM Llanbadarn Fawr w Capel Bangor and Goginan 88-93; Public Preacher 93-96; NSM Machynlleth w Llanwrin and Penegoes *Ban* from 97. *14 Ystwyth Close, Penparcau, Aberystwyth SY23 3RU*

GRIFFITH, Canon David Vaughan. b 36. Univ of Wales (Lamp) BA60. Lich Th Coll 60. **d** 62 **p** 63. C Llanfairfechan *Ban* 62-66; C Dolgellau 66-70; R Llanfair Talhaiarn *St As* 70-82; P-in-c Llangernyw, Gwytherin and Llanddewi 77-85; R Llanfairtalhaiarn and Llansannan 82-85; V Colwyn from 85; Warden of Readers from 91; Can Cursal St As Cathl from 95. *The Vicarage, 28 Bodelwyddan Avenue, Old Colwyn, Colwyn Bay LL29 9NP* Tel (01492) 518394

GRIFFITH, Canon Dermot George Wallace. b 13. TCD BA35. **d** 36 **p** 37. C Ballymacarrett St Patr *D & D* 36-40; C Belfast St Mark *Conn* 40-42; P-in-c Ardoyne *C & O* 42-47; I Killyman *Arm* 47-86; RD Dungannon 67-86; Can Arm Cathl 73-86; Treas Arm Cathl 83-86; rtd 86. *The Cottage, 38 Drumkee Road, Dungannon, Co Tyrone BT71 6JA* Tel (01868) 748629

GRIFFITH, Donald Bennet. b 17. Dur Univ LTh40. St Aid Birkenhead 36. **d** 40 **p** 41. C Collyhurst St Oswald *Man* 40-43; C Pendlebury St Jo 43-45; P-in-c Pendleton 45-47; V Everton St Cuth *Liv* 47-52; V Lathom 52-58; R Frating w Thorrington *Chelmsf* 58-66; R Lawford 66-73; R Theydon Garnon 73-77; P-in-c Bradfield 77-82; rtd 82; Perm to Offic *Chelmsf* from 82. *Porto Cristo, Mill Lane, Thorpe-le-Soken, Clacton-on-Sea, Essex CO16 0ED* Tel (01255) 861766

GRIFFITH, Frank Michael. b 24. Bris Univ BSc50 Lon Univ DipTh60. St Aid Birkenhead 58. **d** 60 **p** 61. C Leamington Priors H Trin *Cov* 60-63; C Stratford-on-Avon w Bishopton 63-67; V Rounds Green *Birm* 67-70; R Barford *Cov* 70-78; V Wasperton 70-78; RD Stratford-on-Avon 77-79; R Barford w Wasperton and Sherbourne 78-89; RD Fosse 79-87; rtd 90. *Wusi, Armscote Road, Tredington, Shipston-on-Stour, Warks CV36 4NP* Tel (01608) 661621

GRIFFITH, Canon Geoffrey Grenville. b 17. Linc Coll Ox BA48 MA56. Chich Th Coll 48. **d** 50 **p** 51. C Newland St Aug *York* 50-53; R Waddington *Linc* 53-57; Chapl Dur Univ *Dur* 57-66; V Chapel-en-le-Frith *Derby* 66-84; RD Buxton 71-78; Hon Can Derby Cathl 80-84; rtd 84; Perm to Offic *Derby* 84-90; Chapl HM Pris Morton Hall 85-90; Chapl St Barn Hospice Linc 91-94. *292 Hykenham Road, Lincoln LN6 8BJ* Tel (01522) 695683

GRIFFITH, Glyn Keble Gethin. b 37. St D Coll Lamp BA59 Ridley Hall Cam 67. **d** 69 **p** 70. C Derby St Aug *Derby* 69-72; C Coity w Nolton *Llan* 72-75; P-in-c Heage *Derby* 75-81; V Allestree St Nic 81-92; R Wilne and Draycott w Breaston from 92. *The Rectory, 68 Risley Lane, Breaston, Derby DE7 3AU* Tel (01332) 872242

GRIFFITH, Canon Hugh Emrys. b 24. St D Coll Lamp BA53. **d** 54 **p** 55. C Welshpool *St As* 54-56; C Abergele 56-58; R Llanfair Talhaiarn 58-61; R Newborough w Llangeinwen w Llangaffo etc *Ban* 61-75; R Llanllyfni 75-81; R Amlwch 81-94; RD Twrcelyn 82-94; Can Ban Cathl from 89; rtd 94; Lic to Offic *Ban* from 94. *Llys Caerwynt, Rhosybol, Amlwch LL68 9TS* Tel (01407) 830740

GRIFFITH, Canon John Vaughan. b 33. LTh73. St D Coll Lamp 53. **d** 58 **p** 59. C Holyhead w Rhoscolyn *Ban* 58-63; R Maentwrog w Trawsfynydd 63-68; Chapl RAF 68-72; V Winnington *Ches* 72-76; V Northwich St Luke and H Trin 76-81; V Sandiway from 81; Dioc Communications Officer 84-86; Ed Ches Dioc News from 84; Hon Can Ches Cathl from 89. *The Vicarage, Sandiway, Northwich, Cheshire CW8 2JU* Tel (01606) 883286

GRIFFITH, Malcolm. b 43. FRICS71. EAMTC 94. **d** 97. NSM Stilton w Denton and Caldecote etc *Ely* from 97. *40 Chisenhale, Orton Waterville, Peterborough PE2 5FP* Tel (01733) 371065 Mobile 0860-594915

GRIFFITH, Steven Ellsworth. b 63. St Steph Ho Ox. **d** 87 **p** 88. C Holyhead w Rhoscolyn w Llanfair-yn-Neubwll *Ban* 87-90; CF from 90. *MOD Chaplains (Army), Trenchard Lines, Upavon, Pewsey, Wilts SN9 6BE* Tel (01980) 615804 Fax 615800

GRIFFITH, William Stephen. b 50. Univ of Wales (Ban) BA71. Westcott Ho Cam 71. **d** 73 **p** 74. C Llandudno *Ban* 73-76; C Calne and Blackland *Sarum* 76-78; P-in-c Broadwindsor w Burstock and Seaborough 78-79; TV Beaminster Area 79-81; Lic to Offic 81-83; Chapl St Pet Sch York 83-87; C Leeds St Pet *Ripon* 87; Chapl Bearwood Coll Wokingham 87-92; CMS 92-95; Jordan 92-95; Chapl Univ of Wales (Cardiff) *Llan* 95-96; Chapl Damascus from 96. *FCO Damascus, King Charles Street, London SW1 2AH*

GRIFFITH-JONES, Robin Guthrie. b 56. New Coll Ox BA78 Ch Coll Cam BA88. Westcott Ho Cam 86. **d** 89 **p** 90. C Cantril Farm *Liv* 89-92; Chapl Linc Coll Ox from 92. *Lincoln College, Oxford OX1 3DR* Tel (01865) 279800

GRIFFITHS, Alan Charles. b 46. Dur Univ BA67 DipTh69. Cranmer Hall Dur 66. **d** 69 **p** 70. C Leic H Apostles *Leic* 69-72; Lic to Offic *York* 73-77; V Lea Hall *Birm* 77-87; Asst Dir of Educn *Sheff* 87-92; V W Bessacarr from 92. *The Vicarage, 39 Sturton Close, Doncaster, S Yorkshire DN4 7JG* Tel (01302) 538487

GRIFFITHS, Alec. b 42. St Chad's Coll Dur BA63 DipTh65. **d** 65 **p** 66. C Glas St Ninian *Glas* 65-68; C Greenock 68-72; R Glas H Cross 72-79; V Birchencliffe *Wakef* 79-83; Chapl Kingston Hosp Surrey 83-91; Chapl Tolworth Hosp Surbiton 83-93; Chapl Kingston Hosp NHS Trust Surrey from 91. *Kingston Hospital, Galsworthy Road, Kingston-upon-Thames, Surrey KT2 7QB, or 107 Hook Rise South, Tolworth, Surbiton, Surrey KT6 7NA* Tel 0181-546 7711 ext 2429 or 397 1577

GRIFFITHS, Arthur Evan. b 27. ACP66. St Deiniol's Hawarden. **d** 69 **p** 70. Hon C Cleobury Mortimer w Hopton Wafers *Heref* 69-83; C 84-86; P-in-c Coreley w Doddington 86-88; P-in-c Knowbury 86-88; rtd 89; Perm to Offic *Heref* from 93. *Maryn, Catherton Road, Cleobury Mortimer, Kidderminster, Worcs DY14 8EB* Tel (01299) 270489

GRIFFITHS, Beatrice Mary. b 29. Chelsea Coll Lon DipPE50 CertEd60 Lon Univ CertRK60. Westcott Ho Cam 85. **dss** 86 **d** 87 **p** 94. W Bridgford *S'well* 86-87; NSM Wilford Hill from 87. *7 Stella Avenue, Tollerton, Nottingham NG12 4EX* Tel 0115-937 4155

GRIFFITHS, Caroline Heidi Ann. *See* PRINCE, Caroline Heidi Ann

GRIFFITHS, David. b 38. St Mich Coll Llan DipTh67. **d** 67 **p** 68. C Llangollen *St As* 67-71; C Rhyl 71-74; V Kerry 74-77; V Kerry and Llanmerewig 77-82; R Caerwys and Bodfari 82-87; V Gresford from 87; RD Wrexham from 97. *The Vicarage, Gresford, Wrexham LL12 8RG* Tel (01978) 852236

GRIFFITHS, David Bruce. b 44. Sussex Univ BA69 Hull Univ MA83. Linc Th Coll. **d** 82 **p** 83. C Springfield All SS *Chelmsf* 82-84; TV Horwich *Man* 84-92; V Heaton Ch Ch from 92. *The Vicarage, 2 Towncroft Lane, Bolton BL1 5EW* Tel (01204) 840430

GRIFFITHS, David John. b 53. Bromsgrove F E Coll HND76. St Jo Coll Nottm BTh93 DipMM94. **d** 94 **p** 95. C Retford *S'well* 94-96; NSM Thwaites Brow *Bradf* from 96. *2 Prospect Drive, Keighley, W Yorkshire BD22 6DD* Tel (01535) 602682

GRIFFITHS, David Mark. b 41. Univ of Wales (Cardiff) BA67 CertEd71. St Mich Coll Llan 92. **d** 94 **p** 95. C Llwynderw *S & B* 94-96; R Llanbadarn Fawr, Llandegley and Llanfihangel etc from 96. *The Rectory, Rock Road, Cross Gates, Llandrindod Wells, Powys LD1 6AF* Tel (01597) 851204

GRIFFITHS, David Mark. b 59. Kent Univ BA80. Chich Th Coll 81. **d** 83 **p** 84. C Clydach *S & B* 83-84; C Llwynderw 84-88; V Swansea St Nic from 88; Chapl Swansea Inst of HE from 90. *St Nicholas' Vicarage, 58A Dyfed Avenue, Townhill, Swansea SA1 6NG* Tel (01792) 654272

GRIFFITHS, The Ven Dr David Nigel. b 27. RD77. FSA Worc Coll Ox BA52 MA56 Reading Univ PhD91. Linc Th Coll 56. **d** 58 **p** 59. C Northampton St Matt *Pet* 58-61; SPCK HQ Staff 61-67; Chapl RNR 63-77; Hon C Bromley St Andr *Roch* 65-67; V Linc St Mich *Linc* 67-73; R Linc St Mary Magd w St Paul 67-73; Vice Chan and Lib Linc Cathl 67-73; TR New Windsor *Ox* 73-87; RD Maidenhead 77-82 and 84-87; Chapl to The Queen 77-97; Hon Can Ch Ch *Ox* 83-87; Adn Berks 87-92; rtd 92; Chapl St Anne's Bede Houses Linc from 93. *2 Middleton's Field, Lincoln LN2 1QP* Tel (01522) 525753

GRIFFITHS, David Percy Douglas. b 25. St Mich Coll Llan. **d** 78 **p** 79. C Betws w Ammanford *St D* 78-80; V Llanarth w Mydroilyn, Capel Cynon, Talgarreg etc 80-84; V Llanarth and Capel Cynon w Talgarreg etc 84-86; V Newcastle Emlyn w Llandyfriog and Troed-yr-aur 86-95; rtd 95. *The Poplars, Ebenezer Street, Newcastle Emlyn SA38 9BS* Tel (01239) 711448

GRIFFITHS, David Rowson Hopkin. b 38. Oak Hill Th Coll 59. **d** 62 **p** 63. C Barrow St Mark *Carl* 62-65; OMF Internat from 66; Japan 66-88; The Philippines from 88. *c/o OMF, Belmont, The Vine, Sevenoaks, Kent TN13 3TZ* Tel (01732) 450747 Fax 456164

GRIFFITHS, David Wynne. b 47. Univ of Wales (Cardiff) BD73. St Mich Coll Llan 69. **d** 73 **p** 74. Hon C Gabalfa *Llan* 73-76; Lic to Offic 77-79; Hon C Tonypandy w Clydach Vale 79-80; Hon C Pontypridd St Cath 80-87; Perm to Offic from 87. *13 Heol Ty'n-y-Cae, Rhiwbina, Cardiff CF4 6DH*

GRIFFITHS, Garrie Charles. b 53. St Jo Coll Nottm LTh77. **d** 77 **p** 78. Canada 77-78; C Stalybridge H Trin and Ch Ch *Ches* 78-81; C Moreton 81-84; V Godley cum Newton Green 84-89; V Bayston Hill *Lich* from 89. *42 Eric Lock Road West, Bayston Hill, Shrewsbury SY3 0QA* Tel (01743) 872164

GRIFFITHS, Geoffrey Ernest. b 28. AKC52. **d** 53 **p** 54. C Shirehampton *Bris* 53-59; SCM Sec (W England Schs) 58-61; Lic to Offic *Bris* 59-63; Chapl Colston's Sch Bris 59-75; Chapl St Brandon's Sch Clevedon 60-63; V Atworth *Sarum* 63-72; Chapl Stonar Sch Melksham 63-66; P-in-c Shaw and Whitley *Sarum* 69-72; V Atworth w Shaw and Whitley 72-94; NSM Breage w Germoe *Truro* 94-96; rtd 94. *Windrush, Prospect Row, Ashton, Helston, Cornwall TR13 9RR* Tel (01736) 763703

GRIFFITHS, George Brian. b 25. Kelham Th Coll 46. **d** 51 **p** 52. SSM 51-65; Miss P Bloemfontein S Africa 51-60; R and Prior Teyateyaneng Basutoland 60-63; Lic to Offic *S'well* 63-64; C Amersham *Ox* 64-65; P Missr Amersham St Mich CD 66-73; V Amersham on the Hill 73-95; rtd 95. *8 Oak Close, Hexham, Northd NE46 2RE* Tel (01434) 608946

GRIFFITHS, Gerald Lewis. b 38. Qu Coll Birm. **d** 88 **p** 89. C Wrexham *St As* 88-91; TV 91-95; R Hope from 95. *The Rectory, Kiln Lane, Hope, Wrexham LL12 9HN* Tel (01978) 762127

GRIFFITHS, Gordon John. b 31. Univ of Wales (Cardiff) BA53. S'wark Ord Course 72. **d** 75 **p** 76. NSM Sutton St Nic *S'wark* 75-78; Asst Chapl Eastbourne Coll 78-81; NSM Willingdon *Chich* 81-88; Perm to Offic from 88. *15 Buckhurst Close, Willingdon, Eastbourne, E Sussex BN20 9EF* Tel (01323) 505547

GRIFFITHS, Harvey Stephen. b 35. Linc Coll Ox BA58 MA62. Linc Th Coll 62. **d** 62 **p** 63. C Frodingham *Linc* 62-65; P-in-c Darlington St Cuth *Dur* 65-70; Chapl RN 70-92; P-in-c Southwick w Boarhunt *Portsm* from 92. *The White House, High Street, Southwick, Fareham, Hants PO17 6EB* Tel (01705) 377568

GRIFFITHS, Mrs Jean Rose. b 36. Avery Hill Coll TCert56. S'wark Ord Course 93. **d** 95 **p** 96. NSM Charlton St Luke w H Trin *S'wark* from 95; Asst Chapl HM Pris Brixton from 95. *90 Maryon Road, London SE7 8DJ* Tel 0181-317 7467

GRIFFITHS, John Alan. b 48. CPsychol AFBPsS Univ of Wales BSc72 Cape Town Univ MSc76. St Mich Coll Llan 87. **d** 89 **p** 90. C Neath w Llantwit *Llan* 89-93; V Roath St German 93-95. *All Pine Grange, Bath Road, Bournemouth BH1 2PF* Tel (01202) 314120

GRIFFITHS, John Gareth. b 44. Lich Th Coll 68. **d** 71 **p** 72. C Shotton *St As* 71-73; C Rhyl w St Ann 73-76; V Llanasa 76-95; RD Holywell 89-95; V Rhuddlan from 95. *The Vicarage, Vicarage Lane, Rhuddlan, Rhyl LL18 2UE* Tel (01745) 591568

GRIFFITHS, Leonard Lewis Rees. b 09. Lon Coll of Div 27 St Jo Coll Dur BA31 LTh31 MA43. **d** 32 **p** 33. C Leamington Priors St Paul *Cov* 32-35; C-in-c Styvechale w Green Lanes CD 35-38; V Finham 38-39; Chapl RN 39-64; Chapl St Luke's Sch Southsea 64-67; Chapl RN Sch Haslemere 67-75; Antigua 75-76; rtd 76; Perm to Offic *Guildf* from 76; Perm to Offic *Chich* from 76. *9 Rosemary Court, Church Road, Haslemere, Surrey GU27 1BH* Tel (01428) 661391

GRIFFITHS, Lewis Eric Holroyd. b 05. Univ Coll Dur BA29. **d** 29 **p** 30. C Litherland St Andr *Liv* 29-32; C Ches St Paul *Ches* 32-35; C Wisbech St Aug *Ely* 35-37; V Gt Witchingham *Nor* 37-42; R Lt Witchingham 37-42; V Heigham St Phil 42-58; Chapl Hellesdon Hosp Nor 45-59; V Bawburgh *Nor* 58-59; V Lt Melton 58-59; R Tendring *Chelmsf* 59-70; rtd 70. *Palmer House, 1 Ennerdale Road, Kew, Richmond, Surrey TW9 3PG*

GRIFFITHS, Malcolm. b 47. St Alb Minl Tr Scheme. **d** 82 **p** 83. NSM Hemel Hempstead *St Alb* 82-86; C 86-87; TV Liskeard, St Keyne, St Pinnock, Morval etc *Truro* 87-96; V Landrake w St Erney and Botus Fleming from 96. *The Vicarage, School Road, Landrake, Saltash, Cornwall PL12 5EA* Tel (01752) 851801

GRIFFITHS, Margaret. *See* MacLACHLAN, Mrs Margaret

GRIFFITHS, Mrs Margarett. b 29. ATCL47 LRAM48. CA Tr Coll 50. **dss** 81 **d** 87. Hackington *Cant* 81-83; Ashford 84-89; Par Dn 87-89; rtd 89. *39 Newington Way, Craven Arms, Shropshire SY7 9PS* Tel (01588) 673848

GRIFFITHS, Canon Martyn Robert. b 51. Nottm Univ BTh74 St Martin's Coll Lanc PGCE75. Kelham Th Coll 70. **d** 74 **p** 75. C Kings Heath *Birm* 74-77; C-in-c Elmdon Heath CD 77-79; TV Solihull 79-81; Asst Admin Shrine of Our Lady of Walsingham 81-85; V Oldham St Steph and All Martyrs *Man* 85-89; TR Swinton and Pendlebury from 89; Hon Can Man Cathl from 96. *The Rectory, Vicarage Road, Swinton, Manchester M27 3WA* Tel 0161-794 1578 or 727 8175 Fax 728 2553

GRIFFITHS, Meirion. b 38. Clifton Th Coll 63. **d** 66 **p** 67. C Upper Holloway St Pet *Lon* 66-68; C Taunton St Jas *B & W* 68-70; C Radipole *Sarum* 70-74; R Chich St Pancras and St Jo *Chich* 74-82; RD Edeyrnion *St As* 82-88; R Corwen and Llangar 82-88; Australia from 88. *35 Ashington Street, Dianella, W Australia 6062* Tel Perth (9) 275 8635

GRIFFITHS, Mervyn Harrington. b 15. Ripon Hall Ox 53. **d** 54 **p** 55. C Aigburth *Liv* 54-56; C Grassendale 56-58; C Findon *Chich* 58-59; R Bighton *Win* 59-78; V Bishop's Sutton 59-78; rtd

80; Perm to Offic *Ex* from 80. *Kimberley, Clapps Lane, Beer, Seaton, Devon EX12 3HQ* Tel (01297) 22382

GRIFFITHS, Morgan Emlyn. b 17. St D Coll Lamp BA38 St Mich Coll Llan 39. **d** 43 **p** 44. C Lougher *S & B* 43-45; C Defynnog w Rhydybriw and Llandeilo'r Fan 45-47; Barbados 45-59; R Cwmdu and Tretower *S & B* 60-78; V Crickhowell w Cwmdu and Tretower 78-83; rtd 83. *10 St John's, Pendre Close, Brecon LD3 9ED* Tel (01874) 611125

GRIFFITHS, Neville. b 39. Univ of Wales BA63. St D Coll Lamp LTh66. **d** 66 **p** 67. C Newport St Mark *Mon* 66-68; C Cardiff St Jo *Llan* 68-70; Chapl Greystoke Th Tr Coll 70-76; C Greystoke w Matterdale *Carl* 70-75; TV Greystoke, Matterdale and Mungrisdale 75-76; Chapl Grey Coll Dur 76-81; C Croxdale *Dur* 76-81; R Didsbury Ch Ch *Man* 81-83; P-in-c Lowther and Askham *Carl* 83-84; R 84-88; V Guernsey St Matt *Win* 88-93; R Guernsey St Pierre du Bois from 93. *The Rectory, St Peter-in-the-Wood, Guernsey, Channel Islands GY7 9SB* Tel (01481) 63544

GRIFFITHS, Paul Edward. b 48. St Jo Coll Nottm 86. **d** 88 **p** 89. C Ipswich St Andr *St E* 88-92; P-in-c Tollerton *S'well* from 92; P-in-c Plumtree from 95. *The Rectory, Tollerton, Nottingham NG12 4FW* Tel 0115-937 2349

GRIFFITHS, Richard Barre Maw. b 43. CCC Ox BA65 MA69. Cranmer Hall Dur DipTh71 BA71. **d** 71 **p** 72. C Fulwood *Sheff* 71-74; Hon C Sheff St Jo 74-76; Fell Dept of Bibl Studies Sheff Univ 74-76; C Fulham St Matt *Lon* 76-78; P-in-c 78-83; R Chich St Pancras and St Jo *Chich* from 83. *St Pancras's Rectory, 9 St John Street, Chichester, W Sussex PO19 1UR* Tel (01243) 536390 or 536387

GRIFFITHS, Robert Fred. b 20. St Aid Birkenhead 47. **d** 50 **p** 51. C Redditch St Steph *Worc* 50-52; C Hartlebury 52-55; C Droitwich St Nic w St Pet 55-58; R Astley 61-69; C-in-c Fairfield St Rich CD 69-76; rtd 85. *56 Heathfield Road, Norton, Evesham, Worcs WR11 4TQ* Tel (01386) 870198

GRIFFITHS, Robert Herbert. b 53. Univ of Wales (Ban) DipTh75. Chich Th Coll 75. **d** 76 **p** 77. C Holywell *St As* 76-80; CF (TA) 79-87; P-in-c Gyffylliog *St As* 80-84; V Llanfair D C 80-84; V Llanfair, Derwen, Llanelidan and Efenechtyd 84-88; Asst Dioc Youth Chapl 81-86; Dioc Youth Chapl 86-91; PV St As and Tremeirchion w Cefn 88-97; Chapl H M Stanley Hosp 88-97; Bp's Visitor and Dioc RE Adv *St As* 88-93; Chapl Glan Clwyd Distr Gen Hosp 93-97; V Llanrhos *St As* from 97; Chapl Llandudno Gen Hosp from 97. *Llanrhos Vicarage, 2 Vicarage Road, Llandudno LL30 1PT* Tel (01492) 876152

GRIFFITHS, Robert James (Rob). b 52. Nottm Univ BTh82. St Jo Coll Nottm 79. **d** 82 **p** 83. C Kettering St Andr *Pet* 82-85; C Collier Row St Jas *Chelmsf* 85; C Collier Row St Jas and Havering-atte-Bower 86-89; R High Ongar w Norton Mandeville 89-97; P-in-c Ilmington w Stretton-on-Fosse etc *Cov* from 97. *The Rectory, Ilmington, Shipston-on-Stour, Warks CV36 4LB* Tel (01608) 682210

GRIFFITHS, Roger. b 46. Trin Coll Bris 70. **d** 74 **p** 75. C Normanton *Derby* 74-77; C Bucknall and Bagnall *Lich* 77-80; TV 80-83; TV Aberystwyth *St D* 83-86; R Letterston w Llanfair Nant-y-Gof etc from 86. *The Rectory, 22 St David's Road, Letterston, Haverfordwest SA62 5SE* Tel (01348) 840336

GRIFFITHS, Roger Michael. b 47. Wycliffe Hall Ox 83. **d** 86 **p** 87. Min Can St D Cathl *St D* 86-88; V Pen-boyr 88-94; V Fishguard w Llanychar and Pontfaen w Morfil etc from 94. *The Vicarage, High Street, Fishguard SA65 9AU* Tel (01348) 872895

GRIFFITHS, Russell Howard. b 22. Glouc Th Course 75. **d** 77 **p** 78. NSM Fownhope w Fawley *Heref* 77-80; NSM Brockhampton 77-80; P-in-c Bridstow w Peterstow 80-81; TV Ross w Brampton Abbotts, Bridstow and Peterstow 81-87; rtd 87; Perm to Offic *Heref* from 91. *Green Gables, 239 Ledbury Road, Hereford HR1 1QN* Tel (01432) 265362

GRIFFITHS, Shirley Thelma. b 48. Univ of Wales (Ban) CertEd69 Open Univ BA83. St Deiniol's Hawarden 79. **d** 82 **p** 95. NSM Dyserth and Trelawnyd and Cwm *St As* 82-91; RE Officer 89-95; Min Can St As Cathl 91-95; P-in-c The Cowtons *Ripon* from 95; RE Adv from 95. *The Vicarage, East Cowton, Northallerton, N Yorkshire DL7 0BN* Tel (01325) 378230

GRIFFITHS, Simon Mark. b 62. Ch Ch Coll Cant BA84. Chich Th Coll. **d** 87 **p** 88. C Cardiff St Jo *Llan* 87-91; Sub-Chapl HM Pris Cardiff 87-91; Chapl and Succ Roch Cath *Roch* 91-96; Chapl Chich Inst of HE from 96. *Chichester Institute of Higher Education, Bishop Otter College, College Lane, Chichester, W Sussex PO19 4PE* Tel (01243) 787911 Fax 536011

GRIFFITHS, Canon Stanley Arthur. b 17. Lon Univ BSc38. Cuddesdon Coll 46. **d** 47 **p** 48. C Southsea St Matt *Portsm* 47-48; C Southsea H Spirit 48-51; C Cowley St Jas *Ox* 51-55; V Northbourne 55-65; V St Neots *Ely* 65-77; RD St Neots 76-82; Hon Can Ely Cathl 76-82; V Buckden 77-82; rtd 82; Perm to Offic *Ely* from 82; Perm to Offic *York* from 82. *17 York Road, Malton, N Yorkshire YO17 0AX* Tel (01653) 697324

GRIFFITHS, Stephen Mark (Steve). b 67. Nottm Univ BTh93. St Jo Coll Nottm 90. **d** 93 **p** 94. C Glascote and Stonydelph *Lich* 93-96; P-in-c Stratford New Town St Paul *Chelmsf* from 96. *The Vicarage, 65 Maryland Road, London E15 1JL* Tel 0181-534 3640

GRIFFITHS, Mrs Susan Angela. b 61. St Jo Coll Nottm BTh94. **d** 94 **p** 95. C Ingrow cum Hainworth *Bradf* from 94. *Endlich, 2 Prospect Drive, Keighley, W Yorkshire BD22 6DD* Tel (01535) 602682

GRIFFITHS, Miss Sylvia Joy. b 50. Gipsy Hill Coll of Educn CertEd71. St Jo Coll Nottm 85. **dss** 86 **d** 87 **p** 94. Woodthorpe *S'well* 86-90; Par Dn 87-90; Min Bestwood/Rise Park LEP 90-94; TD Bestwood 90-94; TR from 94. *The Rectory, 81 Cherry Orchard Mount, Nottingham NG5 5TJ* Tel 0115-920 2928

GRIFFITHS, Thomas. b 31. AKC57. **d** 58 **p** 59. C Cheadle Hulme All SS *Ches* 58-61; C Oxton 61-63; V Micklehurst 63-72; V Ringway 73-91; V Liscard St Mary w St Columba 91-96; rtd 96; Perm to Offic *Ches* from 96. *14A High Street, Ellesmere, Shropshire SY12 0EP* Tel (01691) 623589

GRIFFITHS, Thomas Wailes (Tom). b 02. Wadh Coll Ox BA25 MA33. St D Coll Lamp 24. **d** 25 **p** 26. C Pembroke Dock *St D* 25-27; C Norwood St Luke *S'wark* 27-29; C Swansea Ch Ch *S & B* 29-33; V Abergavenny H Trin *Mon* 33-37; R St Brides and Marloes *St D* 37-49; P-in-c Dale 39-43; V Southill *St Alb* 49-52; V Combe *Ox* 52-57; V Gt w Lt Tew 57-68; P-in-c Over w Nether Worton 58-67; P-in-c Innerleithen *Edin* 67-71; Perm to Offic *Newc* and *Carl* 72-73; Perm to Offic *Sarum* 73-79; Perm to Offic *B & W* 76-79; P-in-c Lerwick *Ab* 78-79; P-in-c Burravoe 78-79; rtd 79. *115 Banbury Road, Oxford OX2 6LA* Tel (01865) 516461

GRIFFITHS, Trefor Idris. b 51. Univ of Wales (Cardiff) BA73 CertEd76 DPS86. St Mich Coll Llan 84. **d** 86 **p** 87. C Aberdare St Jo *Llan* 86-89; V Port Talbot St Agnes w Oakwood 89-94; V Rhymney *Mon* 94-96. *58 Pantygraigwen Road, Pantygraigwen, Pontypridd CF37 2RS*

GRIFFITHS, Tudor Francis Lloyd. b 54. Jes Coll Ox BA76 MA81. Wycliffe Hall Ox 76. **d** 79 **p** 80. C Brecon w Battle *S & B* 79-81; Min Can Brecon Cathl 79-81; C Swansea St Mary w H Trin 81-83; V Llangattock and Llangynidr 83-88; CMS from 89; Uganda 89-96; C Newton St Pet *S & B* 96; V Goldcliffe and Whiston and Nash *Mon* from 96; Dioc Missr from 96. *The Vicarage, Whiston, Newport NP6 2PG* Tel (01633) 278106

GRIFFITHS, Vyrnach Morgan. b 24. Univ of Wales (Lamp) BA50. St Mich Coll Llan 52. **d** 54 **p** 55. C Llantrisant *Llan* 54-56; C Ystradyfodwg 56-60; C Cwmavon 60-61; V Clydach Vale 61-63; R Llanfair Talhaiarn *St As* 63-69; V Dinas w Penygraig *Llan* 69-74; R Llanddulas *St As* 74-80; R Llanddulas and Llysfaen 80-89; rtd 89. *10 Cilfan, Pensarn, Abergele LL22 7RD*

GRIFFITHS, William Bevan. b 13. AKC37. **d** 37 **p** 38. C Llangyfelach and Morriston *S & B* 37-50; R Llanbadarn Fawr and Llandegley 50-59; R Braunston *Pet* 59-79; rtd 79; Perm to Offic *Llan* from 79. *73 Glannant Way, Cimla, Neath SA11 3YP* Tel (01639) 770527

GRIFFITHS, William David Aled. b 52. Univ of Wales (Abth) BA74 Man Univ AHA77. St Mich Coll Llan DipTh83. **d** 83 **p** 84. C Carmarthen St Pet *St D* 83-87; Asst Warden of Ords 84-91; Warden of Ords from 91; V Llansadwrn w Llanwrda and Manordeilo 87-92; V Llangynnwr and Cwmffrwd from 92. *The Vicarage, Llangynnwr, Carmarthen SA31 2HY* Tel (01267) 236435

GRIFFITHS, William David Maldwyn. b 23. St D Coll Lamp BA47. **d** 50 **p** 51. C Cardigan *St D* 50-54; C Henfynyw w Aberaeron 54-57; P-in-c Llechryd 57-59; V Mathri, St Edrens and Llanrheithan 59-67; V Llanfihangel Geneu'r Glyn 67-89; RD Llanbadarn Fawr 87-89; rtd 89. *Bro Enlli, Lower Regent Street, Aberaeron SA46 0HZ* Tel (01545) 570176

GRIFFITHS, William Thomas Gordon. b 48. York Univ BA70 Fitzw Coll Cam BA79. Ridley Hall Cam 78. **d** 80 **p** 81. C Dulwich St Barn *S'wark* 80-83; C Egglescliffe *Dur* 83-85; Ind Chapl 85-90; V Stockton St Jas from 90. *243 Darlington Lane, Stockton-on-Tees, Cleveland TS19 8AA* Tel (01642) 676323

GRIGG, Simon James. b 61. Warw Univ BA82 MA83 Southn Univ BTh90. Chich Th Coll 87. **d** 90 **p** 91. C Cowley St Jas *Ox* 90-94; C W Hampstead St Jas *Lon* 94-95; V Munster Square Ch Ch and St Mary Magd from 95. *The Mission House, 24 Redhill Street, London NW1 4DQ* Tel 0171-388 2166 or 3095

GRIGG, Canon Terence George. b 34. Kelham Th Coll 54. **d** 59 **p** 60. C Brookfield St Anne, Highgate Rise *Lon* 59-62; Chapl Lee Abbey 63-66; Chapl and Lect St Luke's Coll Ex 66-70; V Stainton-in-Cleveland *York* 70-83; R Cottingham from 83; Hon Can Koforidua from 84; Can and Preb York Minster *York* from 90. *The Rectory, Hallgate, Cottingham, N Humberside HU16 4DD* Tel (01482) 847668

GRIGG, William John Frank. b 27. SSC. Ripon Hall Ox. **d** 66 **p** 67. C Wigan All SS *Liv* 66-67; C Leek St Luke *Lich* 67-69; C Fenton 69-74; C St Stephen by Saltash *Truro* 74-76; TV Redruth 76-79; TV Laneast w St Clether and Tresmere 79-81; P-in-c Wendron 81-85; TV Helston and Wendron 85-91; rtd 91. *St Germoe, 23 Dunheved Fields, Launceston, Cornwall PL15 7HS* Tel (01566) 772878

GRIGGS, Canon Alan Sheward. b 33. Trin Hall Cam BA56 MA60. Westcott Ho Cam 58. **d** 60 **p** 61. C Arnold *S'well* 60-63; Succ S'wark Cathl *S'wark* 63-66; Ind Chapl 66-71; C Leeds H Trin *Ripon* 71-81; V 81-91; Soc and Ind Adv 71-81; Hon Can Ripon Cathl from 84; Soc Resp Officer from 91. *33 Harrowby Road, Leeds LS16 5HZ* Tel 0113-275 8100 or 234 3533

GRIGGS, Frederick John. b 20. Peterho Cam BA48 MA53. Linc Th Coll. **d** 50 **p** 51. C Stand *Man* 50-53; C Writtle *Chelmsf* 53-55; P-in-c The Chignals w Mashbury 55-58; V Chelmsf St Andr 58-62; R Colne Engaine 62-80; P-in-c Frating w Thorrington 80-83; rtd 85. *6 Church View, Holton, Halesworth, Suffolk IP19 8PB* Tel (01986) 875298

✠**GRIGGS, The Rt Revd Ian Macdonald.** b 28. Trin Hall Cam BA52 MA56. Westcott Ho Cam. **d** 54 **p** 55 **c** 87. C Portsea St Cuth *Portsm* 54-59; Youth Chapl *Sheff* 59-64; Bp's Dom Chapl 59-64; V Sheff St Cuth 64-71; V Kidderminster St Mary *Worc* 71-82; Hon Can Worc Cathl 77-84; TR Kidderminster St Mary and All SS, Trimpley etc 82-84; Preb Heref Cathl *Heref* 84-94; Adn Ludlow 84-87; P-in-c Tenbury St Mich 84-87; Suff Bp Ludlow 87-94; rtd 94; Hon Ass Bp Carlisle from 94. *Rookings, Patterdale, Penrith, Cumbria CA11 0NP* Tel (01768) 482064

GRIGGS, Kenneth Courtenay. b 13. Worc Ord Coll 56. **d** 58 **p** 59. C Dudley St Jas *Worc* 58-60; C Kidderminster St Geo 60-64; V Dodford 64-79; rtd 79; Perm to Offic *Worc* 79-82; Perm to Offic *Glouc* 82-92. *Parton House, Parton Road, Churchdown, Gloucester GL3 2JE* Tel (01452) 714775

GRIGOR, Miss Alice Moira (Trish). b 49. Ripon Coll Cuddesdon 94. **d** 96 **p** 97. C Curry Rivel w Fivehead and Swell *B & W* from 96. *44 Stanchester Way, Curry Rivel, Langport, Somerset TA10 0PU* Tel (01458) 253149

GRIGOR, David Alexander. b 29. Lon Univ DipTh54. St Aid Birkenhead 51. **d** 54 **p** 55. C Hengrove *Bris* 54-57; C Marshfield w Cold Ashton 57-60; V Newport *Ex* 60-67; V Paignton St Paul Preston 67-73; Brazil 73-74; Hon C Heavitree *Ex* 74-77; Chapl Ex Sch 74-77; Chapl Brighton Coll 77-89; Chapl Warminster Sch 89-93; rtd 93. *28 Lower Keyford, Frome, Somerset BA11 4AS* Tel (01373) 474147

GRIGSBY, Peter Edward. b 31. Magd Coll Cam MA56 CertEd56. NE Ord Course 85. **d** 88 **p** 89. NSM Haxby w Wigginton *York* 88-90; C Brayton 90-92; TV from 92. *St Francis's Vicarage, 25 Fox Lane, Thorpe Willoughby, Selby, N Yorkshire YO8 9NA* Tel (01757) 703742

GRIGSON, Richard John Stephen. b 60. Man Univ BA83. Qu Coll Birm 86. **d** 88 **p** 89. C W Bromwich St Fran *Lich* 88-92; V Smallthorne from 92. *St Saviour's Vicarage, Smallthorne, Stoke-on-Trent ST6 1NX* Tel (01782) 835941

GRIMASON, Canon Alistair John. b 57. CITC 76. **d** 79 **p** 80. C Belfast H Trin *Conn* 79-82; C Dublin Drumcondra w N Strand *D & G* 82-84; I Navan w Kentstown, Tara, Slane, Painestown etc *M & K* 84-91; Dioc Youth Officer (Meath) 90-94; Dioc Info Officer (Meath) 90-96; I Tullamore w Durrow, Newtownfertullagh, Rahan etc from 91; Preb Tipper St Patr Cathl Dublin from 92; Can Kildare Cathl *M & K* from 92. *The Rectory, Hop Hill, Tullamore, Co Offaly, Irish Republic* Tel Tullamore (506) 21731

GRIME, Arthur Michael. b 28. Kelham Th Coll 48. **d** 52 **p** 53. Basutoland 52-55; C Ealing St Barn *Lon* 55-57; C Pimlico St Gabr 57-59; C Greenford H Cross 59-62; V Fulham St Pet 62-66; V Chiswick St Paul Grove Park 66-88; rtd 89; Perm to Offic *Chich* from 89. *9 Portland Mews, St George's Road, Brighton BN2 1EQ*

GRIME, William John Peter. b 38. St Jo Coll Ox BA60 MA66. Cuddesdon Coll 69. **d** 70 **p** 71. C Blackb St Jas *Blackb* 70-74; Chapl St Martin's Coll of Educn 74-77; V Seascale *Carl* 77-78; P-in-c Irton w Drigg 77-78; V Seascale and Drigg from 78. *The Vicarage, The Banks, Seascale, Cumbria CA20 1QT* Tel (019467) 28217

GRIMES, William Geoffrey. b 33. Cranmer Hall Dur 59. **d** 62 **p** 63. C Preston St Jo *Blackb* 62-65; C Ribbleton 65-68; V New Longton 68-76; Adv on Services for the Deaf Sefton 77-89; Lic to Offic 80-89; Perm to Offic *Liv* from 86; P-in-c Ingol *Blackb* 89-90; C Ashton-on-Ribble St Mich 90; P-in-c 90-91; P-in-c Ashton-on-Ribble St Mich w Preston St Mark 91-92; V from 92. *St Michael's Vicarage, 2 Edgerton Road, Ashton-on-Ribble, Preston PR2 1AJ* Tel (01772) 726157

GRIMLEY, The Very Revd Robert William. b 43. Ch Coll Cam BA66 MA70 Wadh Coll Ox BA68 MA76. Ripon Hall Ox 66. **d** 68 **p** 69. C Radlett *St Alb* 68-72; Hon C Moseley St Mary *Birm* 72-84; Chapl K Edw Sch Birm 72-84; V Edgbaston St Geo *Birm* 84-97; Dean Bris from 97. *The Deanery, 20 Charlotte Street, Bristol BS1 5PZ* Tel 0117-926 2443

GRIMSBY, Suffragan Bishop of. *See* TUSTIN, The Rt Revd David

GRIMSDALE, Mrs Margaret. b 24. STDip48 Lon Univ STD55. Gilmore Course 80. **dss** 82 **d** 87. Stoke Poges *Ox* 82-87; Hon Par Dn 87-88; Hon Par Dn Burrington and Churchill *B & W* 88-90; rtd 90; Perm to Offic *B & W* 90-94. *6 Chapel Close, Castle Cary, Somerset BA7 7AX* Tel (01963) 50866

GRIMSHAW, Canon Eric Fenton Hall. b 34. Bris Univ BA57. Tyndale Hall Bris 54. **d** 58 **p** 59. C Moss Side St Jas *Man* 58-61; C Leyland St Andr *Blackb* 61-64; V Preston St Mark 64-72; V Mirehouse *Carl* 72-91; Hon Can Carl Cathl 86-91; V Knowsley *Liv* from 91. *The Vicarage, Tithebarn Road, Prescot, Merseyside L34 0JA* Tel 0151-546 4266

GRIMSTER, Barry John. b 49. Ex Univ BA70. Trin Coll Bris 72. **d** 74 **p** 75. C S Lambeth St Steph *S'wark* 74-77; C New Malden and Coombe 77-82; P-in-c Deptford St Jo 82-84; V Deptford St Jo w H Trin 84-89; V Woking St Pet *Guildf* from 89. *St Peter's Vicarage, 28 High Street, Old Woking, Woking, Surrey GU22 9ER* Tel (01483) 762707

GRIMWADE, Eric Peter. b 14. AKC37. **d** 37 **p** 38. C Nunhead St Silas *S'wark* 37-39; C Camberwell St Mark 39-40; Chapl RAFVR 40-46; C Redruth *Truro* 46-48; R St Enoder 48-52; V St Clement 52-62; Chapl R Cornwall Infirmary 52-62; Chapl St Lawr Hosp Bodmin 62-69; Chapl Cane Hill Hosp Coulsdon 69-78; C Lee-on-the-Solent *Portsm* 78-79; Hon C 79-81; rtd 79; Perm to Offic *Chich* from 82. *50 Brookway, Lindfield, Haywards Heath, W Sussex RH16 2BP* Tel (01444) 414761

GRIMWADE, Canon John Girling. b 20. Keble Coll Ox BA48 MA52. Cuddesdon Coll 48. **d** 50 **p** 51. C Kingston All SS *S'wark* 50-53; C Ox St Mary V *Ox* 53-56; PC Londonderry *Birm* 56-62; R Caversham *Ox* 62-81; Hon Can Ch Ch 73-90; Chapl to The Queen 80-90; R Caversham and Mapledurham *Ox* 81-83; P-in-c Stonesfield 83-89; rtd 89; Perm to Offic *Ox* from 89; Perm to Offic *Glouc* from 89. *88 Alexander Drive, Cirencester, Glos GL7 1UJ* Tel (01285) 885767

GRIMWADE, Leslie Frank. b 24. FBIM60. Trin Coll Bris 74. **d** 77 **p** 78. C Taunton St Jas *B & W* 77-80; C Polegate *Chich* 80-83; R Swainsthorpe w Newton Flotman *Nor* 83-90; rtd 90; Hon Min Malmesbury Abbey *Bris* from 90; Chapl Malmesbury Hosp from 90. *Drimwal, Common Road, Malmesbury, Wilts SN16 0HN* Tel (01666) 823541

GRIMWOOD, Canon David Walter. b 48. Lon Univ BA70 K Coll Lon BD73 AKC73. **d** 74 **p** 75. C Newc St Geo *Newc* 74-78; C Whorlton 78-80; TV Totton *Win* 80-93; Adv to Coun for Soc Resp (Dios Cant and Roch) *Cant* from 93; Hon Can Roch Cathl *Roch* from 97. *56 Postley Road, Maidstone, Kent ME15 6TR* Tel (01622) 764625

GRINDELL, James Mark. b 43. Nottm Univ BA66 Bris Univ MA69. Wells Th Coll 66. **d** 68 **p** 69. C Bushey Heath *St Alb* 68-72; C Ex St Dav *Ex* 72-74; Chapl St Audries Sch W Quantoxhead 74-83; Chapl Berkhamsted Colleg Sch Herts 83-86; Chapl Denstone Coll Uttoxeter 86-91; Chapl Portsm Gr Sch from 92. *Portsmouth Grammar School, High Street, Portsmouth PO1 2LN* Tel (01705) 819125

✠**GRINDROD, The Rt Revd John Basil Rowland.** b 19. KBE90. Qu Coll Ox BA49 MA53. Linc Th Coll 49. **d** 51 **p** 52 **c** 66. C Hulme St Mich *Man* 51-54; R Ancoats All SS 56-60; Australia from 60; Adn Rockhampton 60-65; Bp Riverina 66-71; Bp Rockhampton 71-80; Abp Brisbane 80-90; rtd 90. *14B Thomas Street, Murwillumbah, NSW, Australia 2484* Tel Murwillumbah (66) 726640

GRINHAM, Garth Clews. b 36. Oak Hill Th Coll 61. **d** 64 **p** 65. C Beckenham Ch Ch *Roch* 64-68; C Wallington H Trin *S'wark* 68-71; V Erith St Paul *Roch* 71-76; Asst Sec CPAS 76-81; Hon C Knockholt *Roch* 76-81; V Southport Ch Ch *Liv* 81-94; V Douglas St Ninian *S & M* from 94. *St Ninian's Vicarage, 58 Ballanard, Douglas, Isle of Man IM2 5HE* Tel (01624) 621694

GRINHAM, Julian Clive. b 39. Birkb Coll Lon BA65. Oak Hill Th Coll 79. **d** 81 **p** 82. C Blackb Ch Ch w St Matt *Blackb* 81-83; Nat Sec Pathfinders CPAS 83-89; Dir CYPECS 89-94; V Normanton *Derby* from 94. *St Giles Vicarage, Browning Street, Normanton, Derby DE23 8DN* Tel (01332) 767483

GRINSTED, Richard Anthony. b 43. Leic Univ BSc65. Oak Hill Th Coll 67. **d** 70 **p** 71. C Egham *Guildf* 70-73; C Woodford Wells *Chelmsf* 73-76; P-in-c Havering-atte-Bower 76-84; R Ditton *Roch* 84-94; R Chulmleigh *Ex* 94-96; R Chawleigh w Cheldon 94-96; R Wembworthy w Eggesford 94-96; R Chulmleigh, Chawleigh w Cheldon, Wembworthy etc from 96. *The Rectory, Chulmleigh, Devon EX18 7NY* Tel (01769) 580537

GRISCOME, David. b 47. Oak Hill Th Coll BA88 TCD Div Sch 89. **d** 89 **p** 90. C Glendermott *D & R* 89-91; I Clondehorkey w Cashel 91-95; I Mevagh w Glenalla 91-95; Bp's C Calry *K, E & A* from 95. *Calry Rectory, The Mall, Sligo, Irish Republic* Tel Sligo (71) 46513

GRITTEN, Desmond Digby. b 17. ALCD54. **d** 54 **p** 55. C Blackheath St Jo *S'wark* 54-58; V Kenilworth St Jo *Cov* 58-87; RD Kenilworth 63-73; rtd 87; Perm to Offic *Cant* from 92; Perm to Offic *Ex* from 92. *22 Rumsay Gardens, Barnstaple, Devon EX32 9EY* Tel (01271) 326794

GROOCOCK, Christopher John (Chris). b 59. St Jo Coll Nottm LTh92 DCM92. **d** 92 **p** 93. C Shawbury *Lich* 92-95; V Hengoed w Gobowen from 95. *The Vicarage, Old Chirk Road, Gobowen, Oswestry, Shropshire SY11 3LL* Tel (01691) 661226

GROOM, Mrs Susan Anne (Sue). b 63. Univ of Wales BA85 Hughes Hall Cam MPhil86 Lon Bible Coll MA94. St Jo Coll Nottm 94. **d** 96 **p** 97. C Harefield *Lon* from 96. *23 High Street, Harefield, Middx UB9 6BX* Tel (01895) 822510

GROSSCURTH, Stephen. b 55. Sarum & Wells Th Coll 81. **d** 84 **p** 85. C Southport H Trin *Liv* 84-87; C Amblecote *Worc* 87-89; V Walton St Jo *Liv* 89-95; Chapl S Man Univ Hosps NHS Trust from 95. *Wythenshawe Hospital, Southmoor Road, Wythenshawe, Manchester M23 9LT, or 68 Lincoln Close, Woolston, Warrington WA1 4LU* Tel (01925) 821124 Fax 0161-946 2603

GROSSE, Anthony Charles Bain. b 30. Oak Hill Th Coll 58. **d** 61 **p** 62. C Chislehurst Ch Ch *Roch* 61-65; C Washfield *Ex* 65-71; TV Washfield, Stoodleigh, Withleigh etc 71-73; R Hemyock 73-86; P-in-c Clayhidon 76-86; R Hemyock w Culm Davy and

Clayhidon 87-93; R Hemyock w Culm Davy, Clayhidon and Culmstock 93-96; rtd 96. *17 Frog Street, Bampton, Tiverton, Devon EX16 9NT* Tel (01398) 331981

GROSSE, Richard William. b 52. Solicitor 77 Mid Essex Tech Coll LLB73. Ridley Hall Cam 86. **d** 88 **p** 89. C Soham *Ely* 88-91; C Bedale *Ripon* 91-93; C-in-c Thornton Watlass w Thornton Steward 91-93; V Barton and Manfield w Cleasby 93-95; V Barton and Manfield and Cleasby w Stapleton from 95. *The Vicarage, Barton, Richmond, N Yorkshire DL10 6JJ* Tel (01325) 377274

GROSU, Iosif. b 60. Iasi Univ BTh92. RC Inst Iasi DipTh89. **d** 89 **p** 89. In RC Ch 89-93; C Darlington St Cuth *Dur* from 96. *9 St Cuthbert's Place, Darlington, Co Durham DL3 7UX* Tel (01325) 365612

GROSVENOR, Royston Johannes Martin. b 47. K Coll Lon BD70 AKC. **d** 71 **p** 72. C Pontesbury I and II *Heref* 71-75; C Bishopston *Bris* 75-79; P-in-c Croydon St Pet S End *Cant* 79-81; V Croydon St Pet 81-84; V Croydon St Pet *S'wark* 85-87; R Merstham and Gatton from 87. *The Rectory, Gatton Bottom, Merstham, Redhill RH1 3BH* Tel (01737) 643755

GROVE, Canon John Montgomery. b 13. Magd Coll Cam BA35 MA39. Westcott Ho Cam 39. **d** 39 **p** 40. Chapl Dover Coll 39-43; Chapl Clifton Coll Bris 43-57; Hd Master Chorister Sch Dur 57-78; rtd 74; Hon Can Dur Cathl *Dur* 74-90. *22 South Street, Durham DH1 4QP* Tel 0191-384 4787

GROVE, Ronald Edward. b 32. Oak Hill Th Coll 60. **d** 63 **p** 64. C Bromley St Jo *Roch* 63-66; V Stratford New Town St Paul *Chelmsf* 66-94; rtd 97; Perm to Offic *Chich* from 97. *Flat 3, Beacon Height, 4 Church Road, Haywards Heath, W Sussex RH16 3PB* Tel (01444) 416892

GROVER, Wilfrid John. b 29. Lich Th Coll 55. **d** 58 **p** 59. C Northampton St Alb *Pet* 58-61; C Boyne Hill *Ox* 61-65; V Cookham 65-85; RD Maidenhead 82-85; Warden Christchurch Retreat Ho *Glouc* 85-93; rtd 89; Hon C Jedburgh *Edin* from 93. *Cairnbrook, Bemersyde, Melrose, Roxburghshire TD6 9DP* Tel (01835) 822054

GROVES, James Alan. b 32. CCC Cam BA58 MA62. Wells Th Coll 58. **d** 60 **p** 61. C Milton next Gravesend Ch Ch *Roch* 60-64; C Beckenham St Jas 64-66; V Orpington St Andr from 66. *St Andrew's Vicarage, Anglesea Road, Orpington, Kent BR5 4AN* Tel (01689) 823775

GROVES, Mrs Jill. b 61. Univ Coll Lon BSc82. St Jo Coll Nottm DTS91 MA93. **d** 93 **p** 94. C Tenbury *Heref* from 93. *23 Castle Close, Burford, Tenbury Wells, Worcs WR15 8AY* Tel (01584) 811975

GROVES, Peter John. b 70. New Coll Ox BA92 MA96 DPhil96. Westcott Ho Cam 95. **d** 97. C Leigh-on-Sea St Marg *Chelmsf* from 97. *45 Eaton Road, Leigh-on-Sea, Essex SS9 3PF* Tel (01702) 77863

GROVES, Philip Neil. b 62. Man Univ BA84. St Jo Coll Nottm 86. **d** 88 **p** 89. C Holbeck *Ripon* 88-91; CMS from 91; Tanzania from 93. *St Philip's Theological College, PO Box 26, Kongwa, Tanzania*

GROVES, Robert John (Bob). b 42. Trin Coll Bris 74. **d** 76 **p** 77. C Norwood St Luke *S'wark* 76-79; P-in-c Clapham Park All SS 79-86; V Anerley *Roch* 86-95; TV Canford Magna *Sarum* from 95. *The Vicarage, Canford Magna, Wimborne, Dorset BH21 3AF* Tel (01202) 883382

GROWNS, John Huntley. b 28. Chich Th Coll 57. **d** 60 **p** 61. C Hayes St Mary *Lon* 60-64; C Addlestone *Guildf* 64-67; C-in-c Kempston Transfiguration CD *St Alb* 67-74; R Stevenage St Geo 74-82; R Felpham w Middleton *Chich* 82-88; P-in-c Westmill w Gt Munden *St Alb* 88-89; Dioc Stewardship Adv 88-93; P-in-c Westmill 89-93; rtd 93; Perm to Offic *Chich* from 93. *45 Lewes Road, Ditchling, Hassocks, W Sussex BN6 8TU* Tel (01273) 846415

GRUBB, Greville Alexander. b 36. Saltley Tr Coll Birm CertEd60 Lon Univ DipPE61 DipRE67. St Jo Coll Nottm 72. **d** 74 **p** 75. C Rushden w Newton Bromswold *Pet* 74-77; Chapl St D Coll Llandudno 77-89; Chapl Casterton Sch Lancs 90-96; Lic to Offic *Carl* 90-96; rtd 96; Perm to Offic *Blackb* from 96. *21 Littledale Road, Brookhouse, Lancaster LA2 9PH* Tel (01524) 770512

GRUNDY, Anthony Brian. b 36. Pemb Coll Cam BA62 MA87. Ridley Hall Cam 61. **d** 63 **p** 64. C Hatcham St Jas *S'wark* 63-66; C Margate H Trin *Cant* 66-68; C Brixton Hill St Sav *S'wark* 68-70; V Assington *St E* 70-76; TV Much Wenlock w Bourton *Heref* 76-81; TV Wenlock 81-82; TR 82-88; RD Condover 86-88; R Burghfield *Ox* from 88. *The Rectory, Hollybush Lane, Burghfield Common, Reading RG7 3BH* Tel (0118) 983 4433

GRUNDY, Christopher John. b 49. Trin Coll Bris 74. **d** 77 **p** 78. C Maidstone St Luke *Cant* 77-81; Argentina 81-82; Chile 82-84; Perm to Offic *Guildf* from 84. *The Lyttons, Seale, Farnham, Surrey GU10 1HR* Tel (01252) 782071

GRUNDY, Jocelyn Pratchitt. b 22. Trin Coll Cam MA. Westcott Ho Cam 64. **d** 66 **p** 67. C Guildf H Trin w St Mary *Guildf* 66-68; R Shere 68-73; V Fleet 73-83; C Aldershot St Mich 83-87; rtd 87; Perm to Offic *Guildf* from 87. *Richmond Cottage, School Hill, Seale, Farnham, Surrey GU10 1HY* Tel (01252) 782238

GRUNDY, Mrs Judith Michal Towers Mynors. b 54. Lady Spencer Chu Coll of Educn CertEd76 Ox Univ BEd77. Trin Coll Bris DipHE87. **d** 93 **p** 94. NSM Kensal Rise St Mark and St Martin *Lon* 93-95; NSM Snettisham w Ingoldisthorpe and Fring *Nor* from 95. *The Vicarage, 18 Park Lane, Snettisham, King's Lynn, Norfolk PE31 7NW* Tel (01485) 541301

GRUNDY, Julian David. b 60. St Andr Univ MA83. Trin Coll Bris BA88. **d** 89 **p** 90. C Lancaster St Thos *Blackb* 89-92; C Kensal Rise St Mark and St Martin *Lon* 92-95; R Snettisham w Ingoldisthorpe and Fring *Nor* from 95. *The Vicarage, 18 Park Lane, Snettisham, King's Lynn, Norfolk PE31 7NW* Tel (01485) 541301

GRUNDY, The Ven Malcolm Leslie. b 44. AKC68 Open Univ BA76. **d** 69 **p** 70. C Doncaster St Geo *Sheff* 69-72; Ind Chapl 72-80; Dir of Educn *Lon* 80-86; TR Huntingdon *Ely* 86-91; Hon Can Ely Cathl 88-94; Dir Avec 91-94; Lic to Offic 91-93; Perm to Offic *Lon* 91-94; Adn Craven *Bradf* from 94. *The Vicarage, Gisburn, Clitheroe, Lancs BB7 4HR* Tel (01200) 445214 Fax 445816

GRUNDY, Paul. b 55. BD77 AKC. Linc Th Coll 79. **d** 80 **p** 81. C Ryhope *Dur* 80-82; C Ferryhill 82-85; TV Cramlington *Newc* 85-87; TV Swinton and Pendlebury *Man* 87-90; V Wingate Grange *Dur* 90-95; R Willington and Sunnybrow from 95. *The Rectory, Willington, Crook, Co Durham DL15 0DE* Tel (01388) 746242

GRÜNEWALD, Gottfried Johannes. b 38. Loyola Univ Chicago MPS93. Th Faculty Frankfurt 66. **d** 69 **p** 69. Denmark 70-95; C Dunbar *Edin* from 95. *St Anne's House, 1 West Gate, Dunbar, East Lothian EH42 1JL* Tel (01368) 865711

GRYLLS, Michael John. b 38. Qu Coll Cam BA62 MA66. Linc Th Coll 62. **d** 64 **p** 65. C Sheff Gillcar St Silas *Sheff* 64-67; C-in-c Dunscroft CD 67-70; V Herringthorpe 70-78; V Amport, Grateley, Monxton and Quarley *Win* 78-89; RD Andover 85-89; V Whitchurch w Tufton and Litchfield from 89. *The Vicarage, Church Street, Whitchurch, Hants RG28 7AS* Tel (01256) 892535

GUBBINS, Andrew Martin. b 65. York Univ BA86 Keele Univ 93. St Jo Coll Nottm LTh93. **d** 96 **p** 97. C Harrogate St Mark *Ripon* from 96. *13 Albany Road, Harrogate, N Yorkshire HG1 4NS* Tel (01423) 566983

GUBBINS (née O'BRIEN), Mrs Mary. b 68. Leeds Univ BSc90. St Jo Coll Nottm BTh93 DipMM94. **d** 94 **p** 95. C Middleton St Mary *Ripon* 94-96; C Bilton from 96. *13 Albany Road, Harrogate, N Yorkshire HG1 4NS* Tel (01423) 566983

GUDGEON, Canon Michael John. b 40. Qu Coll Cam BA63 MA67. Chich Th Coll 65. **d** 66 **p** 67. C Kings Heath *Birm* 66-72; Asst Chapl K Edw Sch Birm 69-72; Chapl and Tutor Cuddesdon Coll 72-75; V Hawley H Trin *Guildf* 75-80; V Minley 75-80; Adult Educn Adv *Chich* 80-87; Can Res Portsm Cathl *Portsm* 87-90; Dioc Dir of Educn 87-90; V Hove St Thos *Chich* 90-93; TV Hove 93-94; Perm to Offic from 94; Bp's Chapl *Eur* from 94; Dir of Ords 94-97; Can Gib Cathl from 96. *46 Blackwater Lane, Worth, Crawley, W Sussex RH10 4RN* Tel (01293) 883051 Fax 884479 E-mail 101741.3160.@compuserve.com

GUERNSEY, Dean of. *See* TRICKEY, The Very Revd Frederick Marc

GUEST, David. b 41. Dur Univ BA62. Coll of Resurr Mirfield 70. **d** 72 **p** 73. C Horsforth *Ripon* 72-75; C Richmond 75-76; C Richmond w Hudswell 76-78; R Middleham 78-81; R Middleham and Coverham w Horsehouse 81-86; R W Rainton *Dur* from 86; V E Rainton from 86; RD Houghton 92-94 and 96-97. *The Rectory, West Rainton, Houghton le Spring, Tyne & Wear DH4 6PA* Tel 0191-584 3263

GUEST, David Andrew. b 61. Portsm Coll of Tech NDTJ82. Chich Th Coll BTh92 CMT92. **d** 92 **p** 93. C Prenton *Ches* 92-94; C Ches H Trin 94-97; Assoc P Douglas St Thos *S & M* from 97; Dioc Communications Officer from 97. *62 Ballabrooie Way, Douglas, Isle of Man IM1 4HB* Tel (01624) 621547

GUEST, Derek William. b 55. N Ord Course 90. **d** 93 **p** 94. C Cheadle Hulme St Andr *Ches* from 93. *33 Kingsley Drive, Cheadle Hulme, Cheadle, Cheshire SK8 5LZ* Tel 0161-486 9306

GUEST, The Ven Frederick William. b 07. St Aug Coll Cant 27. **d** 32 **p** 33. C Tilbury Docks *Chelmsf* 32-34; Australia from 34; Can Perth 51-73; Adn Canning 61-67; Adn Perth 67-73. *203 Riley House, 20 Excelsior Street, Shenton Park, W Australia 6008* Tel Perth (9) 381-7052

GUEST, John. b 36. Trin Coll Bris 59. **d** 61 **p** 62. C Barton Hill St Luke w Ch Ch *Bris* 61-64; C Liv St Sav *Liv* 65-66; USA from 66. *30 Myrtle Hill Road, Sewickley, Pennsylvania 15143, USA*

GUEST, John Andrew Kenneth. b 55. Univ of Wales (Lamp) BA78. Wycliffe Hall Ox 78. **d** 80 **p** 81. C Eastwood *S'well* 80-84; TV Toxteth St Philemon w St Gabr and St Cleopas *Liv* 84-89; C Cranham Park *Chelmsf* 89-93; P-in-c Stanford-le-Hope w Mucking from 93. *The Rectory, The Green, Stanford-le-Hope, Essex SS17 0EP* Tel (01375) 672271

GUEST, Leslie Leonard. b 15. Ripon Hall Ox 62. **d** 63 **p** 64. C Gt Malvern Ch Ch *Worc* 63-66; V Norton and Lenchwick 66-77; R Inkberrow w Cookhill and Kington w Dormston 77-84; rtd 84; Perm to Offic *Worc* from 84. *35 Husum Way, Kidderminster, Worcs DY10 3QJ* Tel (01562) 745722

GUEST, Simon Llewelyn. b 56. Univ of Wales (Lamp) BA78 CertEd79 DipTh85. St Mich Coll Llan 83. **d** 85 **p** 86. C Bassaleg *Mon* 85-88; C Cwmbran 88-89; R 89-90; V Raglan w Llandenny and Bryngwyn from 90. *The Vicarage, Primrose Green, Raglan NP5 2DU* Tel (01291) 690330

GUEST-BLOFELD, Thomas. b 35. St D Coll Lamp BA59 Cranmer Hall Dur 59. **d** 62 **p** 63. C Maltby *Sheff* 62-63; C Goole 63-66; C Pocklington w Yapham-cum-Meltonby, Owsthorpe etc *York* 67-68; C Ely 68-70; C Pemberton St Jo *Liv* 70-72; V Walton St Jo 72-74; V Barkisland w W Scammonden *Wakef* 74-80; V Smallbridge *Man* 80-82; C Irlam 83-86; rtd 87. *38 Richmond Road, Pelynt, Looe, Cornwall PL13 2NH*

GUILDFORD, Bishop of. *See* GLADWIN, The Rt Revd John Warren

GUILDFORD, Dean of. *See* WEDDERSPOON, The Very Revd Alexander Gillan

GUILLAN, Miss Barbara Doris. b 19. S'wark Ord Course 45. **d** 87. NSM St Stythians w Perranarworthal and Gwennap *Truro* 87-89; rtd 89; Perm to Offic *Truro* 89-94. *46 The Embankment, Langport, Somerset TA10 9RZ* Tel (01458) 253492

GUILLE, John Arthur. b 49. Southn Univ BTh79. Sarum & Wells Th Coll 73. **d** 76 **p** 77. C Chandler's Ford *Win* 76-80; P-in-c Bournemouth St Jo 80-84; P-in-c Bournemouth St Mich 83-84; V Bournemouth St Jo w St Mich 84-89; R Guernsey St Andr from 89. *The Rectory, rue des Morts, St Andrew, Guernsey, Channel Islands GY6 8XN* Tel (01481) 38568

GUILLEBAUD, Miss Margaret Jean (Meg). b 43. Edin Univ BSc66. All Nations Chr Coll DipRS79 Cranmer Hall Dur 79. **dss** 80 **d** 87 **p** 94. New Malden and Coombe *S'wark* 80-84; Carlton Colville w Mutford and Rushmere *Nor* 84-91; Par Dn 87-91; Par Dn Rodbourne Cheney *Bris* 91-94; C 94-95; Rwanda from 95. *BP 426, Kigali, Rwanda*

GUILLOTEAU, Claude. b 32. Ripon Coll Cuddesdon 77. **d** 57 **p** 57. In RC Ch 57-76; C Warmsworth *Sheff* 78-80; C Goole 80-86; C Hatfield 86-88; C Ecclesall 88-94; rtd 94. *Residence Frederic Mistral, 3 rue Frederic Mistral, F-81200, Mazamet, France*

GUINNESS, Christopher Paul. b 43. Lon Coll of Div 64. **d** 67 **p** 68. C Farnborough *Guildf* 67-70; C Tulse Hill H Trin *S'wark* 70-74; C Worting *Win* 74-78; P-in-c S Lambeth St Steph *S'wark* 78-89; V 89-91; RD Lambeth 86-90; C Ches Square St Mich w St Phil *Lon* from 91. *4 Victoria Square, London SW1W 0QY* Tel 0171-834 7268

GUINNESS, Garry Grattan. b 40. Em Coll Cam BA64 MA68. Ridley Hall Cam 64. **d** 66 **p** 67. C Wallington H Trin *S'wark* 66-69; C St Marylebone All So w SS Pet and Jo *Lon* 69-72; P-in-c Clifton H Trin, St Andr and St Pet *Bris* 72-79; V Watford St Luke *St Alb* 79-90; TR Worthing Ch the King *Chich* from 90. *4 Shakespeare Road, Worthing, W Sussex BN11 4AL* Tel (01903) 205185

GUINNESS, Graham Alexander. b 60. Jordan Hill Coll Glas DCE82 Edin Univ LTh85. Edin Th Coll 82. **d** 85 **p** 86. Dioc Youth Chapl *Mor* 85-88; C Elgin w Lossiemouth 85-88; P-in-c Glas St Ninian *Glas* 88-90; R Tighnabruaich *Arg* 90-91; R Dunoon from 90; Miss to Seamen from 90. *The Rectory, Kilbride Road, Dunoon, Argyll PA23 7LN* Tel (01369) 702444

GUINNESS, Peter Grattan. b 49. Man Univ BSc71 CertEd73 Nottm Univ DipTh81. St Jo Coll Nottm 80. **d** 82 **p** 83. C Normanton *Wakef* 82-87; V Fletchamstead *Cov* 87-91; V Lancaster St Thos *Blackb* from 91. *St Thomas's Vicarage, 33 Belle Vue Terrace, Lancaster LA1 4TY* Tel (01524) 32134 Fax 846895

GUINNESS, Canon Robin Gordon. b 38. St Jo Coll Cam MA61. Ridley Hall Cam 63. **d** 63 **p** 64. C Bedworth *Cov* 63-66; CMS 66-68; Canada from 68. *47 Prospect Street, Westmount, Quebec, Canada, H3Z 1W5* Tel Westmount (514) 931-6796

GUISE, John Christopher. b 29. MRPharmS Cheltenham & Glouc Coll of HE MA94. WMMTC 80 DipMiss87. **d** 83 **p** 84. NSM Alfrick, Lulsley, Suckley, Leigh and Bransford *Worc* 83-94; NSM Martley and Wichenford, Knightwick etc from 94. *Marsh Cottage, Leigh, Worcs WR6 5LE* Tel (01886) 832336

GUISE, Stephen. b 48. Win Sch of Arts BA75. Chich Th Coll 85. **d** 87 **p** 88. C Bexhill St Pet *Chich* 87-90; TV Haywards Heath St Wilfrid 90-94; V Kirdford 94-97; rtd 97; Perm to Offic *Chich* from 97. *9 Crosbie Close, Donnington, Chichester, W Sussex PO19 2PZ* Tel (01403) 820605

GUITE, Ayodeji Malcolm. b 57. Pemb Coll Cam BA80 MA84 Newc Poly PGCE82. Ridley Hall Cam 88. **d** 90 **p** 91. C Ely 90-93; TV Huntingdon from 93. *The Vicarage, 3A Longstaff Way, Hartford, Huntingdon, Cambs PE18 7XT* Tel (01480) 434463

GUITE, Mrs Margaret Ann (Maggie). b 53. Girton Coll Cam BA74 MA78 St Jo Coll Dur PhD81. Cranmer Hall Dur 75. **dss** 79 **d** 87 **p** 94. Warlingham w Chelsham and Farleigh *S'wark* 79-82; Tutor Westcott Ho Cam 82-90; Cherry Hinton St Jo *Ely* 82-86; Tutor Wesley Ho Cam 87-90; Hon Par Dn Ely 90-93; Hon Par Dn Chettisham 90-93; Hon Par Dn Prickwillow 90-93; NSM Huntingdon from 93. *The Vicarage, 3A Longstaff Way, Hartford, Huntingdon, Cambs PE18 7XT* Tel (01480) 434463

GUIVER, Paul Alfred (George). b 45. St Chad's Coll Dur BA68. Cuddesdon Coll 71. **d** 73 **p** 74. C Mill End and Heronsgate w W Hyde *St Alb* 73-76; P-in-c Bishop's Frome *Heref* 76-82; P-in-c Castle Frome 76-82; P-in-c Acton Beauchamp and Evesbatch w Stanford Bishop 76-82; CR from 85. *House of the Resurrection, Mirfield, W Yorkshire WF14 0BN* Tel (01924) 494318

GUIVER, Roger William Antony. b 53. Edin Univ MA75 St Chad's Coll Dur BA78. Coll of Resurr Mirfield. **d** 82 **p** 83. C Rekendyke *Dur* 82-85; Chapl Middlesb Gen Hosp 85-93; P-in-c Middlesbrough St Columba w St Paul *York* 85-94; V Acomb Moor from 94. *The Vicarage, Thanet Road, Dringhouses, York YO2 2PE* Tel (01904) 706047

GULL, William John. b 42. Ripon Hall Ox 63. **d** 65 **p** 66. C Worksop Priory *S'well* 65-69; C Newark St Mary 69-71; P-in-c Mansfield St Lawr 71-77; V 77-78; Chapl HM Young Offender Inst Lowdham Grange 78-90; R Lambley *S'well* 78-91; Chmn Dioc Bd Soc Resp from 86; V Sneinton St Cypr from 91. *St Cyprian's Vicarage, Marston Road, Nottingham NG3 7AN* Tel 0115-987 3425

GULLAND, John Robertson. b 46. ACIB Avery Hill Coll CertEd70 Open Univ BA76 Chelsea Coll Lon MA82. Oak Hill Th Coll 88. **d** 90 **p** 91. NSM Woodside Park St Barn *Lon* 90-92; NSM Castletown *S & M* from 92; Chapl K Wm Coll from 92. *Anchor House, Queens Road, Port St Mary, Isle of Man IM9 5ES* Tel (01624) 834548

GULLEY, Hubert Edward Raymond. b 06. Bris Univ BA27. Sarum Th Coll 27. **d** 29 **p** 30. C Bedminster St Jo *Bris* 29-31; P-in-c Dalry *Glas* 57-75; rtd 75; Perm to Offic *Chich* 84-92. *College of St Barnabas, Blackberry Lane, Lingfield, Surrey RH7 6NJ* Tel (01342) 870430

GULLIDGE, Philip Michael Nowell. b 60. Univ of Wales (Swansea) BSc82 Univ of Wales (Cardiff) BD93. St Mich Coll Llan 90. **d** 93 **p** 94. C Neath w Llantwit *Llan* 93-97; V Treharris w Bedlinog from 97. *The Vicarage, 13 The Oaks, Ty Llwyd Parc, Quakers Yard, Treharris CF46 5LA* Tel (01443) 410280

GULLIFORD, William Douglas. b 69. Selw Coll Cam BA91. Westcott Ho Cam CTM92. **d** 94 **p** 95. C Banstead *Guildf* from 94. *14 Glenfield Road, Banstead, Surrey SM7 2DQ* Tel (01737) 353938

GULLY, Paul David. b 59. Lon Univ BEd81. Trin Coll Bris BA95. **d** 95 **p** 96. C Radcliffe *Man* from 95. *6 Poolfield Close, Manchester M26 3UE* Tel 0161-723 5860

GULVIN, Philip Christopher. b 53. BSc76. St Jo Coll Nottm 82. **d** 85 **p** 86. C Northwood H Trin *Lon* 85-89; TV Sanderstead All SS *S'wark* 89-96; V Croydon St Matt from 96. *The Vicarage, 7 Brownlow Road, Croydon CR0 5JT* Tel 0181-688 5055

GUMBEL, Nicholas Glyn Paul. b 55. Trin Coll Cam MA76 BA85. Wycliffe Hall Ox 83. **d** 86 **p** 87. C Brompton H Trin w Onslow Square St Paul *Lon* from 86. *13 Macaulay Road, London SW4 0QP* Tel 0171-498 1472

GUMMER, Dudley Harrison. b 28. Roch Th Coll 61. **d** 63 **p** 64. C Deptford St Paul *S'wark* 63-65; C Melton Mowbray w Thorpe Arnold *Leic* 65-68; C-in-c E Goscote CD 68-75; V E Goscote 75-78; V Luton St Anne *St Alb* 78-88; R Albury w St Martha *Guildf* 88-95; rtd 95; Perm to Offic *Chich* from 95. *Wyndham House, The Gardens, West Ashling, Chichester, W Sussex PO18 8DX* Tel (01243) 573002

GUMMER, Selwyn. b 07. Univ of Wales BA34. Wycliffe Hall Ox 39. **d** 39 **p** 40. C Norbury *Ches* 39-41; C Bexley St Mary *Roch* 41-44; V Gillingham H Trin 44-53; R Gravesend St Jas 53-65; RD Gravesend 53-65; V Preston *Chich* 65-70; rtd 71. *Winston Grange, Debenham, Stowmarket, Suffolk IP14 6LE* Tel (01728) 860522

GUNN, Frederick George. b 11. **d** 51 **p** 51. C Bingley H Trin *Bradf* 51-53; C N Lynn w St Marg and St Nic *Nor* 53-55; R Sculthorpe w Dunton and Doughton 55-64; P-in-c Tatterford 56-60; R 60-64; R Witton w Brundall and Braydeston 64-79; RD Blofield 74-79; rtd 80; Perm to Offic *Nor* 80-91; Perm to Offic *Leic* from 93. *Flat 17, Stuart Court, New Road, Kibworth, Leicester LE8 0LE* Tel 0116-279 6367

GUNN, Geoffrey Charles. b 12. Kelham Th Coll 28. **d** 36 **p** 37. C York St Mich-le-Belfrey *York* 36-39; C York St Olave w St Giles 36-39; St Vincent 39-45; Min Can Carl Cathl *Carl* 45-48; C Romsey *Win* 48-51; V Holme Cultram St Cuth *Carl* 51-56; V Shotesham *Nor* 56-77; Chapl Trin Hosp Shotesham 56-77; rtd 77; Min Can Nor Cathl *Nor* from 85. *Shepherd's Close, Priory Lane, Shotesham, Norwich NR15 1YH* Tel (01508) 50285

GUNN, Jeffrey Thomas. b 47. St Chad's Coll Dur BA77 Kent Univ MA95. Coll of Resurr Mirfield 77. **d** 79 **p** 80. C Prestbury *Glouc* 79-82; P-in-c Coldham *Ely* 82-87; P-in-c Elm 82-87; P-in-c Friday Bridge 82-87; V Larkfield *Roch* 87-94; P-in-c Leybourne 87-94; V Petts Wood from 94. *The Vicarage, Willett Way, Orpington, Kent BR5 1QE* Tel (01689) 829971

GUNN, Robert. b 35. Oak Hill Th Coll 59. **d** 62 **p** 63. C Upper Holloway St Jo *Lon* 62-66; C Woking St Jo *Guildf* 66-69; Scripture Union 69-71; R Necton w Holme Hale *Nor* 71-77; V Tottenham St Jo *Lon* 77-81; V Gt Cambridge Road St Jo and St Jas 82-85; V Luton St Fran *St Alb* 85-90; Chapl Luton Airport 90-95; rtd 95. *95 Edgewood Drive, Luton LU2 8ER* Tel (01582) 416151

GUNN-JOHNSON, David Allan. b 49. St Steph Ho Ox 79 Lambeth STh85 MA95. **d** 81 **p** 82. C Oxhey St Matt *St Alb* 81-84; C Cheshunt 84-88; TR Colyton, Southleigh, Offwell, Widworthy etc *Ex* from 88; RD Honiton 90-96. *The Vicarage, Colyton, Devon EX13 6LJ* Tel (01297) 552307

GUNNER, Canon Laurence François Pascal. b 36. Keble Coll Ox BA59 MA63. Wells Th Coll 59. **d** 61 **p** 62. C Charlton Kings

St Mary *Glouc* 61-65; C Hemel Hempstead *St Alb* 65-69; Chapl Bloxham Sch 69-86; Sen Chapl Marlborough Coll 86-96; Can Windsor from 96; Steward from 97. *6 The Cloisters, Windsor Castle, Windsor, Berks SL4 1NJ* Tel (01753) 866313 Fax 866044

GUNNING, George Peter. b 36. Harper Adams Agric Coll NDA58. EMMTC 78. **d** 85 **p** 86. C Winterton Gp *Linc* 85-88; V Alkborough from 88. *The Vicarage, Alkborough, Scunthorpe, S Humberside DN15 9JJ* Tel (01724) 721126

GUNSTONE, Canon John Thomas Arthur. b 27. St Chad's Coll Dur BA48 MA55. Coll of Resurr Mirfield 50. **d** 52 **p** 53. C Walthamstow St Jas Gt *Chelmsf* 52-53; C Forest Gate St Edm 53-58; C-in-c Rush Green St Aug CD 58-71; Chapl Barn Fellowship Winterborne Whitechurch 71-75; Tutor Sarum & Wells Th Coll 71-75; Sec Gtr Man Co Ecum Coun 75-92; Lic to Offic *Man* 75-80; Hon Can Man Cathl 80-92; rtd 92. *12 Deneford Road, Didsbury, Manchester M20 8TD* Tel 0161-434 8351

GUNTER, Timothy Wilson. b 37. Leeds Univ BA59 St Jo Coll Cam BA62 MA66. Ridley Hall Cam 59. **d** 62 **p** 63. C Beverley Minster *York* 62-65; C Hornsea and Goxhill 65-70; V Silsden *Bradf* 70-80; V Sunninghill *Ox* from 80. *Sunninghill Vicarage, Church Lane, Ascot, Berks SL5 7DD* Tel (01344) 20727

GUNYON, Stephen Francis. b 14. Selw Coll Cam BA38 MA48. Linc Th Coll 38. **d** 40 **p** 41. C Greenhill St Jo *Lon* 40-43; SSF 43-44; CF 44-48; C Westmr St Steph w St Jo *Lon* 48-50; V Thornaby on Tees St Paul *York* 50-57; Res Chapl Middx Hosp Lon 57-66; Gen Sec Hosp Chapl Fellowship 57-66; V Hinchley Wood *Guildf* 66-71; V Hindhead 71-80; rtd 80; Perm to Offic *Pet* 80-94. *12 Southgate House, Rougham Road, Bury St Edmunds, Suffolk IP33 2RN* Tel (01284) 703156

GUPPY, Kenneth Henry Stanley. b 29. Univ of Wales (Lamp) BA54. St Mich Coll Llan 54. **d** 56 **p** 57. C Rumney *Mon* 56-61; Chapl Shirley Ho Sch Watford 61-63; V Llangwm Uchaf w Llangwm Isaf w Gwernesney etc *Mon* 63-85; rtd 85; Lic to Offic *Ox* 88-92; Perm to Offic *B & W* from 94. *11 St Thomas's Court, Woodbury Avenue, Wells, Somerset BA5 2XY*

GURD, Brian Charles (Simon). b 44. Sarum & Wells Th Coll 72. **d** 74 **p** 75. OSP from 67; Lic to Offic *Win* 74-82; Prior Alton Abbey 79-82; C Shepherd's Bush St Steph w St Thos *Lon* 82-84; NSM Willesborough *Cant* 85-87; V Bethersden w High Halden 87-95; R Etchingham *Chich* from 95; V Hurst Green from 95. *The Rectory, High Street, Etchingham, E Sussex TN19 7AH* Tel (01580) 819235

GURDON, Mrs June Mary. b 38. Sarum Th Coll 83. **dss** 86 **d** 87 **p** 94. Jersey St Sav *Win* 85-86; Jersey St Mary 86-88; Hon Par Dn 87-88; Hon Par Dn Jersey St Brelade 88-94; Hon C from 94. *The Glade, St Mary, Jersey, Channel Islands* Tel (01534) 864282

GURNEY, Miss Ann. b 27. Lon Univ DipTh48 STh92. Gilmore Ho 45. **dss** 54 **d** 87 **p** 94. Lewisham St Jo Southend *S'wark* 54-56; Warden Berridge Ho Coll of Educn 56-59; Prin Gilmore Ho 59-70; Bp's Adv for Lay Min *Lon* 70-87; rtd 87; Hon C Eltham H Trin *S'wark* from 94. *35 Archery Road, London SE9 1HF* Tel 0181-850 4083

GURNEY, Dennis Albert John. b 31. Lon Coll of Div. **d** 67 **p** 68. C Boscombe St Jo *Win* 67-69; V Hurstbourne Tarrant and Faccombe 70-77; R Jersey St Ouen w St Geo 77-84; Chapl Intercon Ch Soc from 84; Hon Chapl Miss to Seamen from 84; UAE from 84. *PO Box 7415, Dubai, United Arab Emirates* Tel Dubai (4) 374947

GURNEY, Canon Richmond Harptree. b 24. Worc Coll Ox BA48 MA48. Cuddesdon Coll 48. **d** 50 **p** 51. C Bishopwearmouth St Mich *Dur* 50-53; C Beamish 53-55; PC Silksworth 55-66; R Gateshead St Mary 66-72; TR Gateshead 72-75; P-in-c Eskdale, Irton, Muncaster and Waberthwaite *Carl* 75-78; V 78-82; Sec Dioc Past and Redundant Chs Uses Cttees 82-87; R Asby 82-89; V Bolton 82-89; V Crosby Ravensworth 82-89; Hon Can Carl Cathl 84-89; rtd 89; Perm to Offic *Carl* from 89. *Dunelm, Gelt Road, Brampton, Cumbria CA8 1QH* Tel (016977) 2516

GURR, Ralph Sydney. b 27. AKC55. **d** 57 **p** 58. C Lewisham St Mary *S'wark* 57-63; Chapl Lewisham Hosp 61-63; C Cheam *S'wark* 63-69; V Wyke *Bradf* 69-72; V Edmonton St Mich *Lon* 72-79; R Fordingbridge w Ibsley *Win* 79-82; V Fordingbridge 82-84; C N Stoneham 84-94; P-in-c 89-90; rtd 94. *1 Grosvenor Mansions, Grosvenor Square, Polygon, Southampton SO15 2GQ* Tel (01703) 339243

GURR, Stephen John. b 72. Kent Univ BA94. Trin Coll Bris MLitt94. **d** 97. C Ore *Chich* from 97. *Church House, 311 The Ridge, Hastings, E Sussex TN34 2RA* Tel (01424) 754501

GUSH, Laurence Langley. b 23. CChem CEng MICE52 ACGI MRIC Lon Univ BSc44. NW Ord Course 73. **d** 76 **p** 77. NSM Sheff St Matt *Sheff* 76-82; NSM Aston cum Aughton 82-84; NSM Aston cum Aughton and Ulley 84-89; rtd 89; Perm to Offic *Sheff* from 89. *86 Nursery Crescent, Anston, Sheffield S31 7BR* Tel (01909) 567081

GUSSMAN, Robert William Spencer Lockhart. b 50. Ch Ch Ox BA72 MA76. Coll of Resurr Mirfield BA74. **d** 75 **p** 76. C Pinner *Lon* 75-79; C Northolt W End St Jos 79-81; P-in-c Sutton *Ely* 81-82; V 82-89; P-in-c Witcham w Mepal 81-82; R 82-89; RD Ely 86-89; V Alton St Lawr *Win* from 89. *St Lawrence's Vicarage, Church Street, Alton, Hants GU34 2BW* Tel (01420) 83234

GUTCH, John Pitt. b 14. St Edm Hall Ox BA36 MA42. Cuddesdon Coll 37. **d** 38 **p** 39. C Camberwell St Mich *S'wark* 38-41; C Cheshunt *St Alb* 41-43; S Africa 43-59; P-in-c Port Eliz St Mark w St Fran 43-57; P-in-c Port Eliz St Fran 57-59; RD Port Eliz 52-59; Can Grahamstown Cathl 57-59; V Derby St Jas *Derby* 59-67; R Elton *Ely* 67-80; RD Yaxley 72-80; P-in-c Stibbington 75-80; P-in-c Water Newton 76-80; rtd 80. *27 Manor Gardens, Warminster, Wilts BA12 8PN* Tel (01985) 219258

GUTHRIE, Nigel. b 60. LRAM78 ARCO80 ARCM81 Bris Univ BA82 Ox Univ BA87 MA91. Ripon Coll Cuddesdon 85. **d** 88 **p** 89. C Cov St Jo *Cov* 88-91; Chapl Cov Cathl 91-94; V Chellaston *Derby* from 94. *The Vicarage, St Peter's Road, Chellaston, Derby DE7 1UU* Tel (01332) 704835

GUTSELL, Canon David Leonard Nicholas. b 35. Sheff Univ BA59 LTh74. ALCD61. **d** 61 **p** 62. C Clapham Common St Barn *S'wark* 61-65; V Upper Tulse Hill St Matthias 65-76; RD Clapham and Brixton 74-75; V Patcham *Chich* 76-93; Can and Preb Chich Cathl from 89; V Polegate from 93. *St John's Vicarage, 1 Church Road, Polegate, E Sussex BN26 5BX* Tel (01323) 483259

GUTSELL, Eric Leslie. b 44. Golds Coll Lon TCert65 Ox Univ SDES87. Ox NSM Course. **d** 82 **p** 83. NSM Gt Faringdon w Lt Coxwell *Ox* 82-88; NSM Shrivenham w Watchfield and Bourton from 82. *54 Folly View Road, Faringdon, Oxford SN7 7DH* Tel (01367) 240886

GUTTERIDGE, David Frank. b 39. Man Univ BSc61 Lon Inst of Educn PGCE62 DipEd67 Birkb Coll Lon MSc73. WMMTC 82. **d** 85 **p** 87. NSM Droitwich *Worc* 85-87; NSM Droitwich Spa 87-93; C Shrawley, Witley, Astley and Abberley from 93; Chapl Abberley Hall Sch Worc from 93. *The Rectory, Abberley, Worcester WR6 6BN* Tel (01299) 896248 E-mail 100532.2002 @compuserve.com

GUTTERIDGE, John. b 34. Oak Hill Th Coll 60. **d** 63 **p** 64. C Deptford St Luke *S'wark* 63-66; C Southgate *Chich* 66-70; P-in-c Brixton Road Ch Ch *S'wark* 70-73; P-in-c Manuden w Berden *Chelmsf* 73-76; Distr Sec (N Lon, Herts and Essex) BFBS 76-82; Hon C Walthamstow St Gabr 79-82; V 82-95; Chapl Thorpe Coombe Psycho-Geriatric Hosp 83-95; rtd 95; Perm to Offic *Chelmsf* from 95. *52 Hatch Road, Pilgrims Hatch, Brentwood, Essex CM15 9PX* Tel (01277) 375401

GUTTERIDGE, John Philip. b 52. QUB BA74. Chich Th Coll 75. **d** 78 **p** 79. C Leeds St Aid *Ripon* 78-82; C Manston 82-85; P-in-c Beeston Hill H Spirit from 85. *Holy Spirit Vicarage, 114 Stratford Street, Leeds LS11 7EQ* Tel 0113-271 0390

GUTTERIDGE, Richard Joseph Cooke. b 11. Trin Hall Cam BA32 MA36 BD78. Wells Th Coll 34. **d** 35 **p** 36. C Edgbaston St Bart *Birm* 35-38; Tutor Qu Coll Birm 35-37; Lect Qu Coll Birm 37-38; C Bexhill St Pet *Chich* 38-40; C Temple Balsall *Birm* 40-41; Prin Blue Coat Sch Birm 41-45; R Brampton *Ely* 45-52; Chapl RAF 52-68; Fell Ox Univ 69-72; P-in-c Longstowe *Ely* 72-73; Lic to Offic from 73. *1 Croftgate, Fulbrooke Road, Cambridge CB3 9EG* Tel (01223) 352626

GUTTRIDGE, John Arthur. b 26. Trin Hall Cam BA51 MA55. Westcott Ho Cam 51. **d** 53 **p** 54. C Rugby St Andr *Cov* 53-59; Lect Wells Th Coll 59-61; Chapl Wells Th Coll 61-63; Vice-Prin Wells Th Coll 63-66; Bp's Dom Chapl *Wakef* 66-68; Dir of Post Ord Tr 66-68; Dir of Further Tr *Dur* 68-74; Dir of Studies Sarum & Wells Th Coll 74-78; C Bilston St Leon *Lich* 78-79; TV Bilston 80-84; V Wall 84-90; V Stonnall 84-90; rtd 91. *15 St George's Lane North, Worcester WR1 1RD* Tel (01905) 22175

GUY, Dr Ian Towers. b 47. MRCGP MB BS MSc. NE Ord Course. **d** 83 **p** 84. NSM Saltburn-by-the-Sea *York* 83-88; NSM Skelton w Upleatham 88-92; Perm to Offic from 92. *14 North Terrace, Skelton-in-Cleveland, Saltburn-by-the-Sea TS12 2ES* Tel (01287) 650309

GUY, Dr John Richard. b 44. FRHistS80 FRSM81. St D Coll Lamp BA65 PhD85 St Steph Ho Ox 65. **d** 67 **p** 68. C Canton St Cath *Llan* 67-68; C Roath St Sav 68-70; C Machen and Rudry *Mon* 71-74; R Wolvesnewton w Kilgwrrwg and Devauden 74-80; Perm to Offic *B & W* 80-93; V Betws Cedewain and Tregynon and Llanwyddelan *St As* from 93; RD Cedewain from 97. *The Vicarage, Bettws Cedewen, Newtown SY16 3DS* Tel (01686) 650345

GUY, Kate Anne. b 26. LNSM course 87. **d** 88 **p** 94. NSM Welton *Linc* 88-92; NSM Welton and Dunholme w Scothern 92-96. *2 Eastfield Close, Welton, Lincoln LN2 3NB* Tel (01673) 860285

GUY, Simon Edward Walrond. b 39. St Andr Univ MA61. St D Coll Lamp LTh67. **d** 67 **p** 68. C Bris St Mary Redcliffe w Temple etc *Bris* 67-68; C Knowle St Martin 68-71; C Bishopston 71-75; V Westwood *Sarum* 75-81; TV Melksham 81-82; TV Wednesfield *Lich* 82-90; R Heaton Moor *Man* from 90. *St Paul's Rectory, 42 Lea Road, Stockport, Cheshire SK4 4JU* Tel 0161-432 1227

GUYMER, Raymond John. b 41. AKC64. **d** 65 **p** 66. C W Bromwich All SS *Lich* 65-70; Chapl HM Borstal Portland 70-78; Chapl HM Youth Cust Cen Hollesley Bay Colony 78-84; Chapl HM Pris Wormwood Scrubs 84-93; Lic to Offic *Lon* 84-93; Chapl HM Pris Win from 93. *HM Prison Winchester, Romsey Road, Winchester, Hants SO22 5DF* Tel (01962) 854494 Fax 842560

GWILLIAM, Christopher. b 44. St Chad's Coll Dur BA65 DipTh67. **d** 67 **p** 68. C Chepstow *Mon* 67-70; C Risca 70-72; V

Cwmtillery 72-75; V Hartlepool St Oswald *Dur* 75-82; Relig Progr Producer Radio Tees 80-87; C Stockton w St Jo 82-83; R Longnewton w Elton 83-87; Relig Progr Producer Radio Nottm *S'well* 87-93; Relig Progr Producer BBC Radio 4 (Man) from 93. *New Broadcasting House, PO Box 27, Oxford Road, Manchester M60 1SJ* Tel 0161-955 3614

GWILLIM, Allan John. b 51. Coll of Resurr Mirfield 87. **d** 89 **p** 90. C Skerton St Luke *Blackb* 89-94; P-in-c Ellel from 94. *St John's Vicarage, Chapel Lane, Galgate, Ellel, Lancaster LA2 0BW* Tel (01524) 752017

GWILT, Stephen Gary. **d** 88 **p** 89. S Africa 88-94; Chapl Glouc Docks Mariners' Ch *Glouc* from 95. *1 Ladywell Close, Gloucester GL2 6XE* Tel (01452) 501794

GWINN, Brian Harvey. b 35. MIQA75. St Alb Minl Tr Scheme 83. **d** 86 **p** 87. NSM Wheathampstead *St Alb* 86-88; Ind Chapl 88-95; RD Hatfield 93-95; P-in-c Watton at Stone from 95; P-in-c Bramfield w Stapleford and Waterford from 96. *The Rectory, Watton at Stone, Hertford SG14 3RD* Tel (01920) 830262

GWYNN, Phillip John. b 57. Univ of Wales BA87 Univ of Wales (Cardiff) DPS89. St Mich Coll Llan 87. **d** 89 **p** 90. C Clydach *S & B* 89-93; V Swansea St Thos and Kilvey from 93. *The Vicarage, Lewis Street, St Thomas, Swansea SA1 8BP* Tel (01792) 652891

GWYNNE, Robert Durham. b 44. Birm Univ DipTh70. Qu Coll Birm 67. **d** 70 **p** 72. C N Hammersmith St Kath *Lon* 70-75; C Ramsey *Ely* 76-78; TV Old Brumby *Linc* 78-81; C Scartho 81; P-in-c Goxhill 81-83; P-in-c Thornton Curtis 81-83; C Edmonton All SS w St Mich *Lon* 83-84; rtd 86. *Upper Flat, 107-109 Northgate Mews, Louth, Lincs LN11 9QE*

GWYTHER, Geoffrey David. b 51. St D Coll Lamp DipTh73. **d** 74 **p** 75. C Pembroke Dock *St D* 74-77; C Milford Haven 77-81; V Llawhaden w Bletherston and Llanycefn 81-88; R Prendergast w Rudbaxton from 88. *Prendergast Rectory, 5 Cherry Grove, Haverfordwest SA61 2NT* Tel (01437) 762625

GWYTHER, Ronald Lloyd. b 23. Lon Univ BA85 Southn Univ MA97. St Fran Coll Brisbane ThL47. **d** 47 **p** 48. Australia 48-50; Perm to Offic *Ox* 50-51; Australia 51-56; C Broadstairs *Cant* 56-60; R Pinxton *Derby* 60-73; V Swanley St Mary *Roch* 73-89; rtd 89. *20 Maylings Farm Road, Fareham, Hants PO16 7QU* Tel (01329) 230990

GYLE, Alan Gordon. b 65. Aber Univ MA87 Ox Univ BA91. St Steph Ho Ox. **d** 92 **p** 93. C Acton Green *Lon* 92-94; Min Can, Succ and Dean's V Windsor from 94. *3 The Cloisters, Windsor Castle, Windsor, Berks SL4 1NJ* Tel (01753) 868680

GYTON, Robert Wilfred. b 21. N Ord Course. **d** 78 **p** 79. NSM Repps *Nor* 78-79; C Trunch 79-83; TV 83-88; rtd 88; Perm to Offic *Nor* 88-94; P-in-c Castle Acre w Newton, Rougham and Southacre 94-97; Perm to Offic from 97. *Yamato, 47 Fir Park, Ashill, Thetford, Norfolk IP25 7DE* Tel (01760) 440305

H

HABERMEHL, Canon Kenneth Charles. b 22. Em Coll Cam BA46 MA48. Chich Th Coll 47. **d** 49 **p** 50. C Luton St Chris Round Green CD *St Alb* 49-53; C Luton Ch Ch 53-56; V Caddington 56-65; V Kempston 65-87; Hon Can St Alb 81-87; rtd 87; Perm to Offic *St Alb* 87-93. *34 Bedford Road, Aspley Guise, Milton Keynes MK17 8DH* Tel (01908) 584710

HABERSHON, Kenneth Willoughby. b 35. New Coll Ox BA57 DipTh58 MA60. Wycliffe Hall Ox 57. **d** 59 **p** 60. C Finchley Ch Ch *Lon* 59-66; Sec CYFA 66-74; CPAS Staff 74-90; Hon C Slaugham *Chich* 84-88; Ldr Limpsfield CYFA and Sec Ch Patr Trust from 90. *Truckers Ghyll, Horsham Road, Handcross, Haywards Heath, W Sussex RH17 6DT* Tel (01444) 400274

HABGOOD, Simon. b 60. Nottm Univ BTh88. St Jo Coll Nottm 85. **d** 88 **p** 89. C Holbeach *Linc* 88-90; CF (TA) from 89; C Alford w Rigsby *Linc* 90-91; R Rattlesden w Thorpe Morieux and Brettenham *St E* 91-93; V Churchdown *Glouc* 93; V Maenclochog w Henry's Moat and Mynachlogddu etc *St D* 93-94; R Overstrand, Northrepps, Sidestrand etc *Nor* from 95. *The Rectory, 22A Harbord Road, Overstrand, Cromer, Norfolk NR27 0PN* Tel (01263) 579350

HABGOOD, Stephen Roy. b 52. Univ of Wales DipTh77. **d** 77 **p** 78. C Eglwyswen and Llanfair Nant-gwyn *St D* 77-81; Perm to Offic *Worc* 85-91. *Oak Thatch, 76 Main Street, Bretforton, Evesham, Worcs WR11 5JJ* Tel (01386) 830323

✠**HABGOOD of Calverton, The Rt Revd and Rt Hon Lord (John Stapylton).** b 27. PC83. K Coll Cam BA48 MA51 PhD52 Dur Univ Hon DD75 Cam Univ Hon DD84 Aber Univ Hon DD88 Huron Coll Hon DD90. Cuddesdon Coll 53. **d** 54 **p** 55 **c** 73. C Kensington St Mary Abbots w St Geo *Lon* 54-56; Vice-Prin Westcott Ho Cam 56-62; R Jedburgh *Edin* 62-67; Prin Qu Coll Birm 67-73; Hon Can Birm Cathl *Birm* 71-73; Bp Dur 73-83; Abp York 83-95; rtd 95. *18 The Mount, Malton, N Yorkshire YO17 0ND*

HACK, Ms Alison Ruth. b 53. RGN75 RSCN75 RHV80. Sarum & Wells Th Coll 89. **d** 91. Par Dn St Marylebone St Paul *Lon* 91-94; C from 94. *St Paul's House, 9A Rossmore Road, London NW1 6NJ* Tel 0171-402 1000

HACK, Canon Rex Hereward. b 28. ACA56 FCA67 Pemb Coll Cam BA50 MA56. Ripon Hall Ox 58. **d** 59 **p** 60. C Ashton on Mersey St Mary *Ches* 59-62; C Ellesmere Port 62-65; V Norton Cuckney *S'well* 65-69; V Bramhall *Ches* 69-93; RD Cheadle 87-92; Hon Can Ches Cathl 90-93; rtd 93; Perm to Offic *Ches* from 93. *The Oaks, 214 Woodford Road, Woodford, Stockport, Cheshire SK7 1QE* Tel 0161-439 0300

✠**HACKER, The Rt Revd George Lanyon.** b 28. Ex Coll Ox BA52 MA56. Cuddesdon Coll 52. **d** 54 **p** 55 **c** 79. C Bris St Mary Redcliffe w Temple *Bris* 54-59; Chapl St Boniface Coll Warminster 59-64; V Bishopwearmouth Gd Shep *Dur* 64-71; R Tilehurst St Mich *Ox* 71-79; Hon Can Carl Cathl *Carl* 79-94; Suff Bp Penrith 79-94; Episc Adv for the Angl Young People's Assn 87-94; rtd 94; Hon Ass Bp Carlisle from 94. *Keld House, Milburn, Penrith, Cumbria CA10 1TW* Tel (01768) 361506

HACKER HUGHES, Mrs Katherine Lucy (Katy). b 60. York Univ BA81. Westcott Ho Cam 90. **d** 92 **p** 94. Par Dn S Woodham Ferrers *Chelmsf* 92-94; C 94-95; NSM Maldon All SS w St Pet from 95. *Sunnyside, King's Street, Maldon, Essex CM9 5DY* Tel (01621) 850211

HACKETT, Bryan Malcolm. b 66. Magd Coll Ox BA88 MA93 Cam Univ BA92. Westcott Ho Cam 90. **d** 93 **p** 94. C Willington Team *Newc* 93-97; TV Radcliffe *Man* from 97. *The Rectory, Rectory Close, Radcliffe, Manchester M26 9QB* Tel 0161-723 2460

HACKETT, Canon Frank James. b 33. AMIMechE68 MBIM72 MIIM79 HNC54 DMS72 Birm Univ MA77. Bps' Coll Cheshunt 62. **d** 64 **p** 65. C Feltham *Lon* 64-69; Ind Chapl *Lich* 69-73; Ind Chapl Port of Lon *Chelmsf* from 73; P-in-c N Ockendon 79-93; Can Chelmsf Cathl from 93; Ind Chapl from 93. *11 Fairfield Avenue, Upminster, Essex RM14 3AZ* Tel (01708) 221461

HACKETT, John Nigel. b 32. Trin Hall Cam BA55 MA59. Ely Th Coll. **d** 59 **p** 60. C Handsworth St Mary *Birm* 59-66; V Handsworth St Jas 66-82; P-in-c Balsall Common 82-83; V 83-95; Perm to Offic *B & W* from 96. *Honeymead, Duck Lane, Kenn, Clevedon, Avon BS21 6TP* Tel (01275) 876591

HACKETT, Peter Edward. b 25. Magd Coll Ox BA48 MA51 ALCD60. **d** 60 **p** 61. C Lenton *S'well* 60-62; C Attenborough w Bramcote 62-63; V Lenton Abbey 63-67; R Acton Beauchamp and Evesbatch w Stanford Bishop *Heref* 67-71; V Choral Heref Cathl 72-76; P-in-c St Weonards w Orcop 76-79; P-in-c Tretire w Michaelchurch and Pencoyd 76-79; P-in-c Garway 76-79; P-in-c Welsh Newton w Llanrothal 77-79; V Rounds Green *Birm* 79-87; C Sutton Coldfield H Trin 87-90; rtd 90; NSM Shipton Moyne w Westonbirt and Lasborough *Glouc* 91-94; Perm to Offic *Birm* from 94. *58 Lodgefield Road, Halesowen, W Midlands B62 8AT* Tel 0121-561 2365

HACKETT, Ronald Glyndwr. b 47. Hatf Coll Dur BA70. Cuddesdon Coll 70. **d** 72 **p** 73. C Pembroke St Mary and St Mich *St D* 72-75; C Bassaleg *Mon* 75-78; V Blaenavon w Capel Newydd 78-84; Chapl Gwent R Hosp from 84; V Newport St Paul *Mon* 84-90; V Newport Ch Ch from 90. *The Vicarage, Christchurch, Newport NP6 1JJ* Tel (01633) 420701

HACKING, Philip Henry. b 31. St Pet Hall Ox BA53 MA57. Oak Hill Th Coll 53. **d** 55 **p** 56. C St Helens St Helen *Liv* 55-58; C-in-c Edin St Thos *Edin* 59-68; V Fulwood *Sheff* from 68. *The Vicarage, 2 Chorley Drive, Sheffield S10 3RR* Tel 0114-230 1911

HACKING, Rodney Douglas. b 53. K Coll Lon BD74 AKC74 Man Univ MA83. St Aug Coll Cant 75. **d** 76 **p** 78. C Byker St Mich *Newc* 76-77; C Eltham St Jo *S'wark* 77-79; Ind Chapl *Ripon* 80-85; R Upwell St Pet *Ely* 85-88; R Outwell 85-88; Vice Prin S Dios Minl Tr Scheme 89-93; V Bolton le Sands *Blackb* from 93. *The Vicarage, Ancliffe Lane, Bolton-le-Sands, Carnforth, Lancs LA5 8DS* Tel (01524) 822335

HACKING, Stuart Peter. b 60. St Pet Coll Ox BA82 MA. Oak Hill Th Coll 83. **d** 85 **p** 86. C Shipley St Pet *Bradf* 85-88; C Darfield *Sheff* 88-91; V Thornton St Jas *Bradf* from 91. *The Vicarage, 300 Thornton Road, Thornton, Bradford, W Yorkshire BD13 3AB* Tel (01274) 833200

HACKNEY, Bryan William George. b 41. Hull Univ MA80. Linc Th Coll 65. **d** 68 **p** 69. C Baildon *Bradf* 68-71; R Gt and Lt Casterton w Pickworth and Tickencote *Pet* 71-74; Lic to Offic *Linc* 74-77; V Barnetby le Wold 77-81; P-in-c Somerby w Humby 77-81; P-in-c Bigby 77-81; Bp's Ind Adv *Derby* 81-85; R Morton and Stonebroom 85-91; V Mackworth St Fran from 91. *St Francis's Vicarage, 78 Collingham Gardens, Mackworth, Derby DE22 4FQ* Tel (01332) 347690

HACKNEY, Archdeacon of. See YOUNG, The Ven Clive

HACKSHALL, Brian Leonard. b 33. K Coll Lon BD53 AKC53. **d** 57 **p** 58. C Portsea St Mary *Portsm* 57-62; C Westbury-on-Trym St Alb *Bris* 62-64; V Avonmouth St Andr 64-71; Miss to Seamen 71-79; C Crawley *Chich* 79; TV from 79; Ind Chapl from 89. *35 Turnpike Place, Crawley, W Sussex RH11 7UA* Tel (01293) 513264

HACKWOOD, Paul Colin. b 61. Bradf Coll of Educn DSocStuds82 Huddersfield Poly BSc84 Birm Univ DipTh88. Qu Coll Birm 86. **d** 89 **p** 90. C Horton *Bradf* 89-93; Soc Resp Adv *St Alb* 93-97; V Thornbury *Bradf* from 97. *8 The Leaves, Appelley Bridge, Bradford, W Yorkshire BD10 0UW* Tel (01274) 613096

HADDLETON, Peter Gordon. b 53. UEA BA74 Southn Univ BTh80. Sarum & Wells Th Coll 76. **d** 79 **p** 80. C Thamesmead *S'wark* 79-83; TV Bridgnorth, Tasley, Astley Abbotts, Oldbury etc *Heref* 83-91; TV Heref St Martin w St Fran (S Wye TM) 91-95; TV Heref S Wye from 95. *The Vicarage, 1 Holme Lacy Road, Hereford HR2 6DP* Tel (01432) 277234 or 353717 Fax 352142

HADDOCK, Malcolm George. b 27. Univ of Wales (Cardiff) DipTh53 BA56 CertEd73. St Deiniol's Hawarden 87. **d** 80 **p** 81. NSM Newport Ch Ch *Mon* 80-85; NSM Risca 85-87; C 87-89; C Caerleon 89-96; rtd 96. *48 Cambria Close, Caerleon, Newport NP6 1LF* Tel (01633) 422960

HADDON-REECE (née STREETER), Mrs Christine Mary. b 50. St Jo Coll Nottm BTh81 LTh81. **dss** 83 **d** 87 **p** 94. Monkwearmouth St Andr *Dur* 83-85; Stranton 85-87; Par Dn 87-90; Par Dn Lastingham w Appleton-le-Moors, Rosedale etc *York* 90-94; C 94-97; V Topcliffe w Baldersby, Dalton, Dishforth etc from 97. *St Columba's Vicarage, Front Street, Topcliffe, Thirsk, N Yorkshire YO7 3RU* Tel (01845) 577939

HADFIELD, Christopher John Andrew. b 39. Jes Coll Cam BA61. Wells Th Coll 63. **d** 65 **p** 66. C Wigton w Waverton *Carl* 65-68; Teacher Newlands Sch from 70; Lic to Offic *Mor* from 92; Perm to Offic *Chich* from 96. *Newlands School, Seaford, E Sussex BN25 4NP* Tel (01323) 892209

HADFIELD, Douglas. b 22. K Coll Cam BA44 MA49. St Jo Coll Nottm 84. **d** 88 **p** 89. Hon C Lenzie *Glas* 88-92; rtd 92; Perm to Offic *Pet* from 92. *Thelema, 8 Church Street, Helmdon, Brackley, Northants NN13 5QJ* Tel (01295) 760679

HADFIELD, Graham Francis. b 48. Bris Univ BSc69 St Jo Coll Dur DipTh71. **d** 73 **p** 74. C Blackpool St Thos *Blackb* 73-76; CF from 76. *MOD Chaplains (Army), Trenchard Lines, Upavon, Pewsey, Wilts SN9 6BE* Tel (01980) 615804 Fax 615800

HADFIELD, Jonathan Benedict Philip John. b 43. Lon Univ BA64 Jes Coll Cam BA67 MA72. Edin Th Coll 66. **d** 68 **p** 69. C Fort William *Arg* 68-70; Chapl K Sch Glouc from 70; Hon Min Can Glouc Cathl *Glouc* from 70. *Dulverton House, King's School, Pitt Street, Gloucester GL1 2BG* Tel (01452) 521251

HADFIELD, Norman. b 39. Doncaster Coll of Educn TEng78 Univ of Wales (Cardiff) DPS90. St Mich Coll Llan 89 Llan Dioc Tr Scheme 83. **d** 86 **p** 87. NSM Ferndale w Maerdy *Llan* 86-90; C Llanblethian w Cowbridge and Llandough etc 90-92; V Resolven w Tonna from 92. *The Vicarage, Resloven, Neath SA11 4AN* Tel (01639) 710354

HADLEY, Charles Adrian. b 50. Trin Coll Cam BA71 MA75. Cuddesdon Coll 73. **d** 75 **p** 76. C Hadleigh w Layham and Shelley *St E* 75-78; C Bracknell *Ox* 78-82; R Blagdon w Compton Martin and Ubley *B & W* 82-92; RD Chew Magna 88-92; R Somerton w Compton Dundon, the Charltons etc from 92. *The Vicarage, Vicarage Lane, Somerton, Somerset TA11 7NQ* Tel (01458) 72216

HADLEY, Donald Thomas. b 30. Lich Th Coll 55. **d** 58 **p** 59. C Saltley *Birm* 58-61; C-in-c S Yardley St Mich CD 61-66; V S Yardley St Mich 66-70; V Tonge Moor *Man* 70-84; C Selly Oak St Mary *Birm* 85-90; rtd 90; Perm to Offic *Birm* from 90. *83 Grosvenor Road, Birmingham B17 9AL* Tel 0121-426 4450

HADLEY, Miss Elizabeth Ann. b 33. DipTh83. St Jo Coll Nottm 80. **dss** 81 **d** 87 **p** 94. Aspley *S'well* 81-85; Stone St Mich w Aston St Sav *Lich* 85-87; Par Dn 87-92; P-in-c Myddle from 92; P-in-c Broughton from 92; Dioc Voc Officer from 92. *The Rectory, Myddle, Shrewsbury SY4 3RX* Tel (01939) 290811

HADLEY, John Spencer Fairfax. b 47. Ch Ch Ox BA70 MA73. Coll of Resurr Mirfield BA72. **d** 73 **p** 74. C Stoke Newington St Mary *Lon* 73-77; C High Wycombe *Ox* 77-81; TV 82-87; P-in-c Clifton St Paul *Bris* 87-91; Chapl Bris Univ 87-91; Chapl Hengrave Hall Ecum Cen 91-94; Ecum Assoc Min Chelsea Methodist Ch 94-97; Chapl Westcott Ho Cam from 97. *Westcott House, Jesus Lane, Cambridge CB5 8BP* Tel (01223) 741000

HADLEY, Stuart James. b 55. K Coll Lon BD76 AKC76. St Steph Ho Ox 77. **d** 78 **p** 79. C Mansfield St Mark *S'well* 78-82; V Cowbit *Linc* 82-86; Perm to Offic 86-88; NSM W w E Allington and Sedgebrook 88-95; NSM Saxonwell 95-96; NSM Woolsthorpe 88-95; NSM Harlaxton Gp 95-96; Perm to Offic from 97. *35 Wensleydale Close, Grantham, Lincs NG31 8FH*

HADWIN, Alfred. b 34. N Ord Course 85. **d** 88 **p** 89. NSM Lower Darwen St Jas *Blackb* 88-92; NSM Lezayre St Olave Ramsey *S & M* from 92. *St Olave's Vicarage, Ramsey, Isle of Man IM8 3HA* Tel (01624) 812104

HAGAN, Kenneth Raymond. b 40. St Jo Coll Morpeth 62 ACT ThDip64. **d** 64 **p** 65. C Charlestown *Man* 64-69; Australia 69-75 and from 89; C Portsea St Mary *Portsm* 75-78; P-in-c Wolvey, Burton Hastings and Stretton Baskerville *Cov* 78-81; OCF 78-81; P-in-c Withybrook w Copston Magna *Cov* 78-81; P-in-c Shilton w Ansty 78-81; Perm to Offic *Leic* 81-83; Perm to Offic *Lon* 82-89. *148 Denison Street, Hamilton, NSW, Australia 2303* Tel Hamilton (49) 611980

HAGGAN, David Anthony. b 25. Barrister-at-Law 70 QUB LLB49. S'wark Ord Course 87. **d** 89 **p** 90. NSM Reigate St Mary *S'wark* from 89. *2 Fairford Close, Brightlands Road, Reigate, Surrey RH2 0EY* Tel (01737) 246197

HAGGAR, Keith Ivan. b 38. MRPharmS61. Cant Sch of Min 87. **d** 90 **p** 91. NSM Woodnesborough w Worth and Staple *Cant* from 90. *Burtree Cottage, The Street, Worth, Deal, Kent CT14 0DE* Tel (01304) 613599

HAGGARD, Amyand Richard. b 21. Jes Coll Ox MA57. Ripon Hall Ox 56. **d** 58 **p** 59. C Battersea St Luke *S'wark* 58-61; V Battersea St Phil 61-68; rtd 86. *78 Eland Road, London SW11 5LA* Tel 0171-228 8166

✠**HAGGART, The Rt Revd Alastair Iain Macdonald.** b 15. Dur Univ LTh41 BA42 MA45 Dundee Univ Hon LLD70. Edin Th Coll 38. **d** 41 **p** 42 **c** 75. C Glas St Mary *Glas* 41-45; C Hendon St Mary *Lon* 45-48; Prec St Ninian's Cathl Perth *St And* 48-51; R Glas St Oswald *Glas* 51-59; P-in-c Glas St Martin 53-58; Can St Mary's Cathl 58-59; Syn Clerk 58-59; Provost St Paul's Cathl Dundee *Bre* 59-71; R Dundee St Paul 59-71; Prin Edin Th Coll 71-75; Can St Mary's Cathl *Edin* 71-75; Bp Edin 75-85; Primus 77-85; rtd 85. *14/2 St Margaret's Place, Thirlstane Road, Edinburgh EH9 1AY* Tel 0131-446 9052

HAGGER, Jonathan Paul. b 59. St Jo Coll Nottm BTh95. **d** 95 **p** 96. C Newsham *Newc* 95-97; C Newc St Gabr from 97. *33 Swindon Terrace, Heaton, Newcastle upon Tyne NE6 5RB* Tel 0191-224 1596

HAGGIE, Deborah. b 58. **d** 92. NSM Merton St Mary *S'wark* from 94. *31 Dennis Park Crescent, London SW20 8QH* Tel 0181-542 9030

HAGGIS, Richard. b 66. Ch Ch Ox BA88 MA95 Nottm Univ MA95. Linc Th Coll DipMM94. **d** 95 **p** 96. C Romford St Edw *Chelmsf* from 95. *54 Parkside Avenue, Romford RM1 4ND* Tel (01708) 727960

HAGGIS, Timothy Robin. b 52. New Coll Ox BA75 MA79. St Jo Coll Nottm DipTh. **d** 82 **p** 83. C Chilwell *S'well* 82-86; TV Hucknall Torkard 86-94; Chapl Trent Coll Nottm from 94. *Trent College, Long Eaton, Nottingham NG10 4AD* Tel 0115-973 2737

HAGON, Roger Charles. b 58. Nottm Univ BA80. St Steph Ho Ox 82. **d** 85 **p** 86. C Charlton St Luke w H Trin *S'wark* 85-88; C St Helier 88-95; V Kenley from 95. *The Vicarage, 3 Valley Road, Kenley, Surrey CR8 5DJ* Tel 0181-660 3263

HAGUE, David Hallett. b 59. Univ Coll Lon BScEng81 MSc82. Ridley Hall Cam CTM93. **d** 93 **p** 94. C Luton St Mary *St Alb* 93-96; V Stevenage St Pet Broadwater from 96. *St Peter's House, 1 The Willows, Stevenage, Herts SG2 8AN* Tel (01438) 352447

HAGUE, Eric. b 13. Lon Univ BA52. St Aid Birkenhead 36. **d** 39 **p** 40. C Edge Hill St Cypr *Liv* 39-43; CMS Miss China 43-49; Kwangsi-Hunan 43-52; Hong Kong 52-57; V Woking Ch Ch *Guildf* 57-62; V High Wycombe *Ox* 62-69; R Lt Shelford *Ely* 69-76; P-in-c Parr Mt *Liv* 76-77; V 77-79; rtd 79; Perm to Offic *Ely* from 79. *10 Manor Court, Grange Road, Cambridge CB3 9BE* Tel (01223) 355430

HAIG, Alistair Matthew. b 39. K Coll Lon BD63 AKC63. **d** 64 **p** 65. C Forest Gate St Edm *Chelmsf* 64-67; C Laindon w Basildon 67-71; V S Woodham Ferrers 71-78; P-in-c Bath H Trin *B & W* 78-83; R 83-89; R Bocking St Mary *Chelmsf* 89-95; Dean Bocking 89-95. *66 Wimpole Road, Colchester CO1 2DN* Tel (01206) 795275

HAIG, Andrew Livingstone. b 45. Keble Coll Ox BA67. Coll of Resurr Mirfield 67. **d** 69 **p** 70. C Elton All SS *Man* 69-75; R Brantham *St E* 75-76; R Brantham w Stutton 76-82; RD Samford 81-82; P-in-c Haverhill 82; TR Haverhill w Withersfield, the Wrattings etc 82-90; RD Clare 84-87; Chapl Qu Eliz Hosp King's Lynn 90-94; Chapl K Lynn and Wisbech Hosps NHS Trust from 94. *The Chaplain's Office, Queen Elizabeth Hospital, King's Lynn, Norfolk PE30 4ET* Tel (01553) 766266

HAIG, Canon Murray Nigel Francis. b 39. Univ of Wales (Lamp) BA62. Kelham Th Coll 62. **d** 66 **p** 67. C Felixstowe St Jo *St E* 66-72; C Morpeth *Newc* 72-74; V Byker St Mich 74-79; V Byker St Mich w St Lawr 79-81; V Benwell St Jas 81-85; TR Benwell Team 85-91; TR Cramlington 91-97; Hon Can Newc Cathl from 95; P-in-c Alnwick St Mich and St Paul from 97. *The Vicarage, Alnwick, Northd NE66 1LT* Tel (01665) 602184

HAIGH, Alan Bernard. b 42. NE Ord Course 87. **d** 90 **p** 91. NSM Thorner *Ripon* from 90. *4 The Paddock, Thorner, Leeds LS14 3JB* Tel 0113-289 2870

HAIGH, Colin. b 15. St Chad's Coll Dur BA40 DipTh41 MA43. **d** 41 **p** 42. C Linthwaite *Wakef* 41-44; C Featherstone 44-45; C Streatham St Pet *S'wark* 45-48; C Benhilton 48-50; C Ipswich St Bart *St E* 50-52; C Leigh St Clem *Chelmsf* 52-56; R Fobbing 56-64; P-in-c Rawreth 64-68; V Romford St Alb 68-80; rtd 80; Perm to Offic *Chelmsf* from 80. *93 Egremont Street, Glemsford, Sudbury, Suffolk CO10 7SG* Tel (01787) 281173

HAIGH, John Gibson. b 47. Chich Th Coll 88. **d** 90 **p** 91. C Swinton and Pendlebury *Man* 90-93; C Richmond w Hudswell *Ripon* 93-96; C Downholme and Marske 93-96; R Nuthurst *Chich* from 96. *The Rectory, Nuthurst Street, Nuthurst, Horsham, W Sussex RH13 6LH* Tel (01403) 891449

HAIGH, Maurice. b 22. St Cath Coll Cam BA46 MA48 Lon Univ BD60. **d** 60 **p** 61. NSM Marton *Blackb* 60-88; rtd 88; Perm to

Offic *Blackb* from 88. *20 Doncaster Road, Blackpool FY3 9SQ* Tel (01253) 63897

HAIGH, Norman. b 02. Dorchester Miss Coll 27. **d** 30 **p** 31. C Stamford Hill St Jo *Lon* 30-31; C Old St Pancras w Bedford New Town St Matt 31-36; C Slaugham *Chich* 36-39; C Findon 39-42; CF (EC) 42-46; V Ripponden *Wakef* 46-50; Nyasaland 50-54; V Pontefract All SS *Wakef* 54-57; C Stonebridge St Mich *Lon* 58-59; C Wood Green St Mich 60-62; R Aston Somerville *Glouc* 62-72; V Childswyckham 62-72; rtd 72; Perm to Offic *Cov* 72-77. *c/o Mr C P T Walker, Flat 1, 12 Western Place, Worthing, W Sussex BN11 3LU*

HAIGH, Owen Quentin. b 15. St Chad's Coll Dur BA43 MA46. **d** 43 **p** 44. C Birtley *Dur* 43-47; C Billingham St Cuth 47-50; Min Darlington St Mark CD 50-55; R Wiston *Chich* 55-75; V Ashington 55-75; P-in-c Stedham w Iping 75-83; P-in-c Trotton w Chithurst 80-81; rtd 83; Perm to Offic *Chich* from 84. *10 Streetlands, Brede Lane, Sedlescombe, Battle, E Sussex TN33 0PX* Tel (01424) 870761

HAIGH, Richard Michael Fisher. b 30. Dur Univ BA57 Birm Univ DPS71. Cranmer Hall Dur DipTh59. **d** 59 **p** 60. C Stanwix *Carl* 59-62; India 63-67 and 68-70; R Salford St Clem w St Cypr Ordsall *Man* 71-75; R Holcombe 75-85; V Unsworth 85-93; R Brough w Stainmore, Musgrave and Warcop *Carl* 93-97; rtd 97. *21 Templand Park, Allithwaite, Grange-over-Sands, Cumbria LA11 7QS*

HAILES, Derek Arthur. b 38. Coll of Resurr Mirfield. **d** 82 **p** 83. C Sneinton St Cypr *S'well* 82-84; V Kneesall w Laxton 84-85; P-in-c Wellow 84-85; V Kneesall w Laxton and Wellow 85-88; V Sneinton St Steph w St Alb 88-95; P-in-c Bury H Trin *Man* from 95. *Holy Trinity Vicarage, Spring Street, Bury, Lancs BL9 0RW* Tel 0161-764 2006

HAILS, Canon Brian. b 33. JP71. ACMA62 FCMA76. NE Ord Course 77. **d** 81 **p** 82. NSM Harton *Dur* 81-87; Ind Chapl from 87; Hon Can Dur Cathl from 93; TR Sunderland from 96. *Inhurst, 5 Hepscott Terrace, South Shields, Tyne & Wear NE33 4TH* Tel 0191-456 3490

HAILSTONE, Miss Kitty. b 22. St Andr Ho Portsm 49. **dss** 81 **d** 87. W Acklam *York* 60-82; rtd 82; Beverley St Mary *York* 82-87; Hon Par Dn 87-95; Perm to Offic from 95. *26 Corporation Road, Beverley, N Humberside HU17 9HG* Tel (01482) 860223

HAINES, Andrew Philip. b 47. LSE BSc68. Oak Hill Th Coll 84. **d** 87 **p** 88. C Enfield Ch Ch Trent Park *Lon* 87-91; V Hillmorton *Cov* from 91. *The Vicarage, Hoskyn Close, Hillmorton, Rugby, Warks CV21 4LA* Tel (01788) 576279

HAINES, Dr Daniel Hugo. b 43. TD89. MRCS73 DRCOG78 Lon Univ BDS68 Witwatersrand Univ 78. **d** 79 **p** 84. Swaziland 79-80; Falkland Is 80-82; Hon C Hatcham St Cath *S'wark* from 84. *56 Vesta Road, London SE4 2NH* Tel 0171-635 0305

HAINES, Robert Melvin. b 31. Coll of Resurr Mirfield 71. **d** 73 **p** 74. C Derringham Bank *York* 73-76; P-in-c Newport St Steph 76-79; TV Howden TM 80-82; R Turriff *Ab* 82-97; R Cuminestown 82-97; R Banff 82-97; P-in-c Portsoy 94-97; P-in-c Buckie 94-97; rtd 97. *Ceol-na-Mara, 11 Scotstown, Banff AB45 1LA* Tel (01261) 818258

HAINES, Stephen Decatur. b 42. Freiburg Univ MA68 Fitzw Coll Cam BA70 MA74. **d** 71 **p** 72. C Fulham St Dionis Parson's Green *Lon* 71-76; C Finchley St Mary 76-78; Hon C Clapham Old Town *S'wark* 83-87; Hon C Clapham TM 87-88; Hon C Camberwell St Giles w St Matt from 88; Hon PV S'wark Cathl from 92. *3 Lyndhurst Square, London SE15 5AR* Tel 0171-703 4239

HAIR, James Eric. b 48. Lon Univ BA69. St Steph Ho Ox 69. **d** 72 **p** 73. C Fishponds St Jo *Bris* 72-75; C Bushey *St Alb* 75-79; P-in-c Lake *Portsm* 79-82; V 82-89; P-in-c Shanklin St Sav 79-82; V 82-89; TV Totton *Win* 89-95; C Portchester *Portsm* 96; Asst to RD Fareham from 97. *26 Bayly Avenue, Portchester, Fareham, Hants PO16 9LD* Tel (01705) 215832

HAKE, Andrew Augustus Gordon. b 25. Trin Coll Cam BA49 MA54. Wells Th Coll 50. **d** 51 **p** 52. C Filwood Park CD *Bris* 51-54; C Eastville St Thos 54-57; Kenya 57-69; Perm to Offic *Bris* 70-90; rtd 90. *Stotehayes, Yarcombe, Honiton, Devon EX14 9BB* Tel (01404) 881200

HAKES, Leslie John. b 25. CEng MRAeS MBIM. Roch Th Coll 60. **d** 62 **p** 63. C Swansea St Pet *S & B* 62-67; V Griffin *Blackb* 67-71; V Dolphinholme 71-74; V Dolphinholme w Quernmore from 74. *The Vicarage, Dolphinholme, Lancaster LA2 9AH* Tel (01524) 791300

HALAHAN, Maxwell Crosby. b 30. Lon Univ BSc52 Southn Univ CertEd78 W Sussex Inst of HE ACertEd83. Westcott Ho Cam 54. **d** 56 **p** 57. C Forton *Portsm* 56-60; C Liv Our Lady and St Nic *Liv* 60-62; Bahamas 62-64; C Widley w Wymering *Portsm* 64-66; C-in-c Cowes St Faith CD 66-70; V Cowes St Faith 70-77; Hon C Portsea St Sav 77-84; rtd 84; Perm to Offic *Portsm* 84-94. *4 Coach House Mews, Old Canal, Southsea, Hants PO4 8HD*

HALDANE-STEVENSON, James Patrick. b 10. TD50. St Cath Soc Ox BA33 MA41. Bps' Coll Cheshunt 35. **d** 35 **p** 37. C Lambeth St Mary the Less *S'wark* 35-38; CF (TA) 37-45; C Pokesdown St Jas *Win* 38-39; R Hillington *Nor* 39-46; CF 45-55; Australia from 55; Perm to Offic *Chich* 77-78; rtd 83. *3 Argyle Square, Ainslie Avenue, Reid, ACT, Australia 2612* Tel Canberra (6) 257 2681 Fax 248 6951

HALE, Antony Jolyon (Jon). b 56. MRTPI89 Newc Univ BA79. Sarum & Wells Th Coll 86. **d** 88 **p** 89. C Monkseaton St Mary *Newc* 88-92; P-in-c Tandridge *S'wark* 92-97; C Oxted 92-97; C Oxted and Tandridge from 97. *St Peter's Vicarage, Tandridge Lane, Oxted, Surrey RH8 9NN* Tel (01883) 722932

HALE, Dennis Ernest (Jim). b 26. Southn Univ MA(Ed)66. Sarum & Wells Th Coll 74. **d** 77 **p** 78. NSM N Stoneham *Win* 77-86; Assoc Chapl Southn Univ from 86. *12 Field Close, Southampton SO16 3DY* Tel (01703) 554538

HALE, Elsie Amelia. Gilmore Ho 53. **dss** 58 **d** 87. R Devon and Ex Hosps 64-84; Heavitree w Ex St Paul *Ex* 84-88; Perm to Offic from 88. *13 Riverside Court, Colleton Crescent, Exeter EX2 4BZ*

HALE, John. b 37. Ban Coll DBS60 Trin Coll Carmarthen CertEd59. St D Coll Lamp DipTh66. **d** 66 **p** 67. C Tenby and Gumfreston *St D* 66-71; R Burton 71-78; R Burton and Rosemarket from 78. *The Rectory, Burton, Milford Haven SA73 1NX* Tel (01646) 600275

HALE, John Frederick. b 29. Fitzw Ho Cam BA54 MA58. Tyndale Hall Bris. **d** 55 **p** 56. C Heigham H Trin *Nor* 55-58; C Paddington St Jas *Lon* 58-61; V St Leonards St Ethelburga *Chich* 61-79; C Prestonville St Luke 79-90; R Rotherfield w Mark Cross 90-92; rtd 92; Perm to Offic *Chich* from 92. *51 Brangwyn Drive, Brighton BN1 8XB*

HALE, Keith John Edward. b 53. Sheff Poly BSc75. St Jo Coll Nottm DipTh91. **d** 91 **p** 92. C Greasbrough *Sheff* 91-94; P-in-c Tankersley 94-95; R Tankersley, Thurgoland and Wortley from 95. *The Rectory, 9 Chapel Road, Tankersley, Barnsley, S Yorkshire S75 3AR* Tel (01226) 744140

HALE (née McKAY), Mrs Margaret McLeish (Greta). b 37. RN76. W of England Minl Tr Course 92. **d** 95 **p** 96. NSM Bream *Glouc* from 95. *14 Meadow Walk, Sling, Coleford, Glos GL16 8LR* Tel (01594) 834919

HALE, Peter Raymond Latham. b 30. St Pet Hall Ox BA54 MA58. Linc Th Coll 54. **d** 56 **p** 57. C Old Brumby *Linc* 56-59; Prec and Chapl Gib Cathl *Eur* 59-62; V New Cleethorpes *Linc* 62-67; Chapl Sebright Sch Wolverley 67-70; V Dudley St Jas *Worc* 70-76; V Crowthorne *Ox* 76-86; RD Sonning 81-86; P-in-c Cookham 86-90; V Lacey Green 90-95; rtd 95. *3 Rushall Road, Thame, Oxon OX9 3TR* Tel (01844) 216763

HALE, Roger Anthony. b 41. MIH85. Brasted Th Coll 68 Oak Hill Th Coll 70. **d** 72 **p** 73. C Blackb Sav *Blackb* 72-75; C Burnley St Pet 75-77; Chapl Burnley Gen Hosp 75-77; V Fence in Pendle *Blackb* 77-82; Chapl Lancs Ind Miss 77-82; NSM Tottenham St Mary *Lon* 88-91; R Cheddington w Mentmore and Marsworth *Ox* from 91. *The Rectory, 29 Mentmore Road, Cheddington, Leighton Buzzard, Beds LU7 0SD* Tel (01296) 661358

HALES, Ms Janet (Jan). b 65. TCD BEd85. CITC BTh94. **d** 94 **p** 95. C Lisburn Ch Ch Cathl *Conn* from 94. *3 Benford Park, Lisburn, Co Antrim BT27 5HL* Tel (01846) 665979

HALFORD, David John. b 47. JP84. Open Univ DipEd86 Didsbury Coll Man CertEd69 Open Univ BA75 Man Univ MEd79 ACP72. LNSM course 96. **d** 96 **p** 97. NSM Royton St Anne *Man* from 96. *33 Broadway, Royton, Oldham OL2 5DD* Tel 0161-633 4650 Fax as telephone

HALFPENNY, Brian Norman. b 36. CB90. St Jo Coll Ox BA60 MA64. Wells Th Coll 60. **d** 62 **p** 63. C Melksham *Sarum* 62-65; Chapl RAF 65-83; Sen Chapl RAF Coll Cranwell 82-83; Asst Chapl-in-Chief RAF 83-88; Chapl-in-Chief RAF 88-91; QHC 85-91; Offg Chapl RAF from 91; Can and Preb Linc Cathl *Linc* 89-91; TR Redditch, The Ridge *Worc* from 91. *St Luke's Rectory, 69 Evesham Road, Redditch, Worcs B97 4JX* Tel (01527) 545521

HALIFAX, Archdeacon of. *See* INWOOD, The Ven Richard Neil

HALKES, John Stanley. b 39. SW Minl Tr Course 87. **d** 90 **p** 91. NSM St Buryan, St Levan and Sennen *Truro* 90-92; P-in-c Lanteglos by Fowey 92-94; P-in-c from 94. *The Vicarage, Battery Lane, Polruan, Fowey, Cornwall PL23 1PR* Tel (01726) 870213

HALL, Alan Maurice Frank. b 28. FCCA. Sarum & Wells Th Coll 86. **d** 89 **p** 90. NSM Winterbourne Stickland and Turnworth etc *Sarum* from 89. *4 The Knapp, Winterborne Houghton, Blandford Forum, Dorset DT11 0PD* Tel (01258) 880985

✠**HALL, The Rt Revd Albert Peter.** b 30. St Jo Coll Cam BA53 MA56. Ridley Hall Cam 53. **d** 55 **p** 56 **c** 84. C Birm St Martin *Birm* 55-60; S Rhodesia 60-65; Rhodesia 65-70; R Birm St Martin *Birm* 70-84; Hon Can Birm Cathl 75-84; Suff Bp Woolwich *S'wark* 84-91; Area Bp Woolwich 91-96; Chmn ACUPA 90-96; rtd 96; Asst Bp Birm from 96. *27 Jacey Road, Birmingham B16 0LL* Tel 0121-455 9240

HALL, Alfred Christopher. b 35. Trin Coll Ox BA58 MA61. Westcott Ho Cam 58. **d** 61 **p** 62. C Frecheville *Derby* 61-64; C Dronfield 64-67; V Smethwick St Matt *Birm* 67-70; V Smethwick St Matt w St Chad 70-75; Can Res Man Cathl *Man* 75-83; Hon Can 83-90; Dioc Adult Educn Officer 75-83; Dioc World Development Officer 76-88; V Bolton St Pet 83-90; Co-ord Chr Concern for One World from 90; rtd 96. *The Knowle, Deddington, Banbury, Oxon OX15 0TB* Tel (01869) 338225 Fax as telephone

HALL, Mrs Ann Addington. b 34. Ex Univ CertEd71. SW Minl Tr Course 82. **dss** 85 **d** 87 **p** 94. Ex St Mark *Ex* 85-90; Hon Par Dn

87-90; Perm to Offic 90-92; NSM Cen Ex from 92. *33 Union Road, Exeter EX4 6HU* Tel (01392) 78717

HALL, Arthur John. b 23. Bris Univ BSc48. Sarum & Wells Th Coll 74. **d** 76 **p** 77. Hon C Portishead *B & W* 76-88; Perm to Offic from 88; Chapl St Brandon's Sch Clevedon from 86. *34 Beechwood Road, Portishead, Bristol BS20 8EP* Tel (01275) 842603

HALL, Barry George. b 38. Solicitor 62. Oak Hill Th Coll 78. **d** 81 **p** 82. NSM Stock Harvard *Chelmsf* 81-90; NSM W Hanningfield 90-93; P-in-c from 93. *Harvard Cottage, Swan Lane, Stock, Ingatestone, Essex CM4 9BQ* Tel (01277) 840387

HALL, Brian. b 59. Aston Tr Scheme 90 Oak Hill Th Coll DipHE94. **d** 94 **p** 95. C Mansfield St Jo *S'well* 94-96; C Skegby from 96. *The Parsonage, Fackley Road, Teversal, Sutton-in-Ashfield, Notts NG17 3JA* Tel (01623) 550975

HALL, Brian Arthur. b 48. Ex Univ BEd70. Cuddesdon Coll 73. **d** 75 **p** 76. C Hobs Moat *Birm* 75-79; V Smethwick 79-93; R Handsworth St Mary from 93. *Handsworth Rectory, 288 Hamstead Road, Birmingham B20 2RB* Tel 0121-554 3407

HALL, Charles Bryan. b 37. Liv Univ BA59. St Mich Coll Llan 59. **d** 62 **p** 63. C Prestatyn *St As* 62-64; C Cardiff St Mary *Llan* 64-67; V 73-75; C Hawarden *St As* 67-72; TV 72-73 and 84-86; P-in-c Cardiff St Steph *Llan* 73-75; V Cardiff St Mary w St Steph 75-81; V Penycae *St As* 81-84; R Llandegla and Bryneglwys and Llanarmon-yn-Ial 86-87; R Llandegla and Llanarmon yn Ial from 87. *The Rectory, Llandegla, Wrexham LL11 3AW* Tel (01978) 88362

HALL, Charles John. b 40. JP. Lon Coll of Div ALCD68 LTh74. **d** 68 **p** 69. C Upton (Overchurch) *Ches* 68-72; C Morden *S'wark* 72-76; V Hyson Green *S'well* 76-84; V Stapleford 84-97; RD Beeston 90-97; TR Thetford *Nor* from 97. *The Rectory, 6 Redcastle Road, Thetford, Norfolk IP24 3NF* Tel (01842) 762291

HALL, Christine Mary. b 45. K Coll Lon BD67 MPhil86. **d** 87. NSM Bickley *Roch* 87-92; Vice-Prin Chich Th Coll 92-95; Lic to Offic *Chich* from 95. *The Old School, East Marden, Chichester PO18 9JE* Tel (01243) 535244

HALL, David Anthony. b 43. Reading Univ BA66. Qu Coll Birm 79. **d** 81 **p** 82. C Norton *St Alb* 81-85; TV Hitchin 85-93; P-in-c Bidford-on-Avon *Cov* 93; V from 93. *5 Howard Close, Bidford-on-Avon, Alcester, Warks B50 4EL* Tel (01789) 772217

HALL, Denis. b 43. Lon Coll of Div 65. **d** 69 **p** 70. C Netherton *Liv* 69-71; C Roby 72-75; V Wigan St Steph 75-90; V Newton-le-Willows from 90. *The Vicarage, 243 Crow Lane East, Newton-le-Willows, Merseyside WA12 9UB* Tel (01925) 224869

HALL, Derek Guy. b 26. Tyndale Hall Bris 50. **d** 51 **p** 52. C Preston All SS *Blackb* 51-54; C Halliwell St Pet *Man* 54-56; C-in-c Buxton Trin Prop Chpl *Derby* 56-58; V Blackb St Jude *Blackb* 58-67; R Fazakerley Em *Liv* 67-74; TR 74-81; V Langdale *Carl* 81-86; rtd 86; Perm to Offic *Carl* from 86. *14 Gale Park, Ambleside, Cumbria LA22 0BN* Tel (015394) 33144

HALL, Desmond. b 27. St Cuth Soc Dur BSc54 PhD58. NE Ord Course 78. **d** 81 **p** 82. NSM Bishopwearmouth St Mich w St Hilda *Dur* 81-82; C Bishopwearmouth St Mary V w St Pet CD 82-85; V Leadgate 85-94; P-in-c Dipton 93-94; rtd 94; NSM Cornwood *Ex* from 94. *19 Ash Grove, Ivybridge, Devon PL21 0HX* Tel (01752) 837833

HALL, Edwin George. b 40. Sarum & Wells Th Coll 88. **d** 91 **p** 92. NSM Purton *Bris* 91-97. *17 Linley Cottages, Church Path, Purton, Swindon SN5 9DR* Tel (01793) 770520

HALL, Elaine Chegwin. b 59. RGN82 Univ Coll Ches MTh. N Ord Course 94. **d** 97. C Frankby w Greasby *Ches* from 97. *5 Flail Close, Greasby, Wirral, Merseyside L49 2RN* Tel 0151-605 0735

HALL, Ernest. b 10. AKC36. **d** 36 **p** 37. C Kingsbury H Innocents *Lon* 36-40; C Highgate St Mich 40-44; V Enfield St Mich 44-49; V Kingsbury H Innocents 49-59; R Clifton *St Alb* 59-69; RD Shefford 66-69; V Osmotherley *York* 69-75; rtd 75; Perm to Offic *York* from 75. *Dulverton Hall, St Martin's Square, Scarborough, N Yorkshire YO11 2DB* Tel (01723) 373082

HALL, Geoffrey Hedley. b 33. Bris Univ BA55. St Steph Ho Ox 63. **d** 65 **p** 66. C Taunton H Trin *B & W* 65-67; CF 67-80; Sen CF 80-86; P-in-c Ambrosden w Arncot and Blackthorn *Ox* 72-75; V Barnsley St Edw *Wakef* from 86. *St Edward's Vicarage, 186 Racecommon Road, Barnsley, S Yorkshire S70 6JY* Tel (01226) 203919

HALL, George Richard Wyndham. b 49. Ex Univ LLB71. Wycliffe Hall Ox BA74 MA78. **d** 75 **p** 76. C Walton H Trin *Ox* 75-79; C Farnborough *Guildf* 79-84; Bp's Chapl *Nor* 84-87; R Saltford w Corston and Newton St Loe *B & W* from 87; Chapl Bath Coll of HE from 88; RD Chew Magna *B & W* from 97. *The Rectory, 12 Beech Road, Saltford, Bristol BS18 3BE* Tel (01225) 872275

HALL, Canon George Rumney. b 37. Westcott Ho Cam 60. **d** 62 **p** 63. C Camberwell St Phil *S'wark* 62-65; C Waltham Cross *St Alb* 65-67; R Buckenham w Hassingham and Strumpshaw *Nor* 67-74; Chapl St Andr Hosp Thorpe 67-72; Chapl HM Pris Nor 72-74; V Wymondham *Nor* 74-87; RD Humbleyard 86-87; Dom Chapl to The Queen from 87; Chapl to The Queen from 89; R Sandringham w W Newton *Nor* 87-94; P-in-c Flitcham 87-94; P-in-c Wolferton w Babingley 87-94; R Sandringham w W Newton and Appleton etc from 95; P-in-c Castle Rising from 87; P-in-c Hillington from 87; Hon Can Nor Cathl from 87; RD Heacham and Rising from 89. *The Rectory, Sandringham, King's Lynn, Norfolk PE35 6EH* Tel (01485) 540587

HALL, Mrs Gillian Louise. b 45. N Ord Course 87. **d** 90 **p** 94. NSM Earby *Bradf* 90-96; NSM Gisburn from 96; NSM Hellifield from 96. *244 Colne Road, Earby, Colne, Lancs BB8 6TD* Tel (01282) 842593

HALL, Canon Godfrey Charles. b 43. Linc Coll Ox BA66 MA72. Cuddesdon Coll 66. **d** 68 **p** 69. C St Helier *S'wark* 68-72; Asst Chapl Ch Hosp Horsham 72-82; Hd Master Prebendal Sch Chich from 82; Can and Preb Chich Cathl *Chich* from 93. *53 West Street, Chichester, W Sussex PO19 1RT* Tel (01243) 782026

HALL, Harold Henry Stanley Lawson. b 23. Qu Coll Birm 56. **d** 58 **p** 59. C Bishopwearmouth Ch Ch *Dur* 58-61; C Winlaton 61-65; V Cockerton 65-69; V Newton Aycliffe 69-76; R Whitburn 76-89; rtd 89. *9 Balmoral Terrace, East Herrington, Sunderland SR3 3PR* Tel 0191-528 0108

HALL, Harry. b 41. Open Univ BA93. Chich Th Coll CMT91. **d** 91 **p** 92. C Boston *Linc* 91-92; C Bourne 92-94; P-in-c Sutterton w Fosdyke and Algarkirk from 94. *The Vicarage, Station Road, Sutterton, Boston, Lincs PE20 2JH* Tel (01205) 460285

HALL, Herbert Alexander. b 05. **d** 61 **p** 62. C Elloughton *York* 61-64; V Burton Pidsea and Humbleton w Elsternwick 64-70; R Sigglesthorne 70-74; R Sigglesthorne and Rise w Nunkeeling and Bewholme 74-76; rtd 76; Hon C Beverley St Mary *York* from 81. *19 Manor Close, Beverley, N Humberside HU17 7BP* Tel (01482) 867889

HALL, Canon Hubert William Peter. b 35. Ely Th Coll 58. **d** 60 **p** 61. C Louth w Welton-le-Wold *Linc* 60-62; C Gt Grimsby St Jas 62-69; C Gt Grimsby St Mary and St Jas 69-71; Hon Chapl Miss to Seamen from 71; V Immingham *Linc* from 71; RD Haverstoe from 86; Can and Preb Linc Cathl from 89. *The Vicarage, 344 Pelham Road, Immingham, Grimsby, S Humberside DN40 1PU* Tel (01469) 572560

HALL, Ian Michael. b 48. Mansf Coll Ox MA70 Leeds Univ CertEd71. Carl Dioc Tr Course 85. **d** 88 **p** 89. NSM Eskdale, Irton, Muncaster and Waberthwaite *Carl* from 88. *Fisherground Farm, Eskdale, Cumbria CA19 1TF* Tel (01946) 23319

HALL, James. b 28. Wollongong Univ BA78. CITC 53. **d** 56 **p** 57. C Belfast St Mich *Conn* 56-59; I Cleenish *Clogh* 59-62; R Openshaw *Man* 63-68; Australia 68-89; R Morley w Deopham, Hackford, Wicklewood etc *Nor* 89-92; R High Oak 92-93; rtd 93. *174 O'Brien's Road, Figtree, NSW, Australia 2525* Tel Wollongong (42) 283239

HALL, Canon James Robert. b 24. TCD BA48 MA54. **d** 49 **p** 50. C Seagoe *D & D* 49-51; C Lisburn Ch Ch *Conn* 51-59; I Belfast St Mich 59-66; I Finaghy 66-89; Can Belf Cathl 82-89; RD S Belfast *Conn* 83-89; rtd 89. *3 Coachman's Way, Hillsborough, Co Down BT26 6HQ* Tel (01846) 689678

HALL, Mrs Jean Margaret. b 38. Bris Univ CertEd59 DipRE59 ACertEd73. Bris Sch of Min 84. **d** 88 **p** 94. NSM Bris St Andr w St Bart *Bris* 88; NSM E Bris 88-91; Par Dn Plympton St Mary *Ex* 91-93; Asst Chapl Cant and Thanet Community Healthcare Trust from 93. *Thanet Mental Health Unit, Ramsgate Road, Margate, Kent CT9 4BF* Tel (01843) 225544 or 869181

HALL, Jeffrey Ernest. b 42. Linc Th Coll 73. **d** 75 **p** 76. C Brampton St Thos *Derby* 75-78; C New Whittington 78-81; C Whittington 78-81; TV Riverside *Ox* 81-90; R Anstey *Leic* from 90. *The Rectory, 1 Hurd's Close, Groby Road, Anstey, Leicester LE7 7GH* Tel 0116-236 2176

HALL, John Barrie. b 41. Sarum & Wells Th Coll 82. **d** 84 **p** 85. Chapl St Edward's Hosp Cheddleton 84-88; C Cheddleton *Lich* 84-88; V Rocester 88-94; V Rocester and Croxden w Hollington from 94; RD Uttoxeter from 91. *The Vicarage, Church Lane, Rocester, Uttoxeter, Staffs ST14 5JZ* Tel (01889) 590424

HALL, John Bellamy. b 10. Ridley Hall Cam 55. **d** 57 **p** 57. C Tonbridge SS Pet and Paul *Roch* 57-59; V Ickleton *Ely* 59-66; R Daglingworth w the Duntisbournes *Glouc* 66-72; R Daglingworth w the Duntisbournes and Winstone 72-74; P-in-c Kempley w Oxenhall 74-77; rtd 77; Perm to Offic *Chich* 78-83; Perm to Offic *St E* from 83. *14 Riverside, Dunmow, Essex CM6 3AR*

HALL, Dr John Bruce. b 33. St Louis Covenant Th Sem MTh80 DMin85 Lon Coll of Div ALCD60 LTh74. **d** 60 **p** 61. C Kingston upon Hull H Trin *York* 60-67; C Beverley Minster 67-68; V Clapham Park St Steph *S'wark* 68-76; R Tooting Graveney St Nic from 76. *The Rectory, 20A Rectory Lane, London SW17 9QJ* Tel 0181-672 7691

HALL, John Charles. b 46. Hull Univ BA71. Ridley Hall Cam 71. **d** 73 **p** 74. C Bromley Common St Aug *Roch* 73-77; C Westbury-on-Trym St Alb *Bris* 78-80; Oman 80-82; C-in-c Bishop Auckland Woodhouse Close CD *Dur* 82-90; P-in-c Gt and Lt Glemham, Blaxhall etc *St E* 90-91; P-in-c Rodney Stoke w Draycott *B & W* from 91; Dioc Ecum Officer from 91. *The Vicarage, Vicarage Lane, Draycott, Cheddar, Somerset BS27 3SH* Tel (01934) 742315

HALL, John Curtis. b 39. CEng73 MIMechE73. Coll of Resurr Mirfield 80. **d** 82 **p** 83. C Pet Ch Carpenter *Pet* 82-86; TV Heavitree w Ex St Paul *Ex* 86-93; R Bow w Broad Nymet from 93; V Colebrooke from 93; R Zeal Monachorum from 93. *The Rectory, Bow, Crediton, Devon EX17 6HS* Tel (01363) 82566

HALL, Canon John Derek. b 25. St Cuth Soc Dur BA50. Linc Th Coll 50. **d** 52 **p** 53. C Redcar *York* 52-54; C Newland St Jo 54-57; V Boosbeck w Moorsholm 57-61; V Middlesbrough St Oswald 61-68; V York St Chad 68-90; Can and Preb York Minster 85-90; rtd 90; Chapl Castle Howard York from 90. *Chanting Hill Farm, Welburn, York YO6 7EF* Tel (01653) 618345

HALL, John Edmund. b 49. Birm Poly CQSW76 Open Univ BA84. Trin Coll Bris BA89. **d** 89 **p** 90. C Winchmore Hill St Paul *Lon* 89-92; V Edmonton St Aldhelm from 92. *St Aldhelm's Vicarage, Windmill Road, London N18 1PA* Tel 0181-807 5336

HALL, Canon John Kenneth. b 32. Qu Coll Birm 61. **d** 63 **p** 64. C Ilminster w Whitelackington *B & W* 63-66; P-in-c Mackworth St Fran *Derby* 66-69; V Blackford *B & W* 69-76; R Chapel Allerton 69-76; New Zealand from 77; Can St Pet Cathl Waikato from 85; rtd 93. *24 Pohutukawa Drive, Athenree, Katikati RD1, New Zealand* Tel Te Aroha (7) 863 4465 Fax as telephone

HALL, Dr John MacNicol. b 44. MRCGP75 Glas Univ BSc65 MB, ChB69 St Jo Coll Cam BA73 MA76 Nottm Univ MTh88. Westcott Ho Cam 71. **d** 86 **p** 86. NSM Knighton St Jo *Leic* 86; NSM Clarendon Park St Jo w Knighton St Mich 86-89; Perm to Offic *Ely* 89-91; Perm to Offic *St Alb* 90-92; Perm to Offic *Birm* from 91. *HM Prison, Winson Green Road, Birmingham B18 4AS* Tel 0121-554 3838 Fax 554 7990

HALL, John Michael. b 47. BD. Oak Hill Th Coll 68. **d** 73 **p** 74. C Walthamstow St Mary w St Steph *Chelmsf* 73-76; C Rainham 76-79; P-in-c Woodham Mortimer w Hazeleigh 79-93; P-in-c Woodham Walter 79-93; Ind Chapl 79-93; R Fairstead w Terling and White Notley etc from 93. *The Rectory, New Road, Terling, Chelmsford CM3 2PN* Tel (01245) 433256

HALL, John Michael. b 62. Leeds Univ BA. Coll of Resurr Mirfield 83. **d** 86 **p** 87. C Ribbleton *Blackb* 86-89; C Carnforth 89-92; V Lt Marsden from 92. *St Paul's Vicarage, Bentley Street, Nelson, Lancs BB9 0BS* Tel (01282) 615888

HALL, John Redvers. b 25. Dur Univ BA59 DipTh62 Man Univ CertEd74. **d** 61 **p** 62. C Lutterworth w Cotesbach *Leic* 61-63; C Loughborough Em 63-66; Lic to Offic 66-70; Lic to Offic *Blackb* 70-81; P-in-c Ingoldmells w Addlethorpe *Linc* 81-83; V Cholsey *Ox* 83-92; rtd 92; Perm to Offic *Chich* from 92. *9 Ruislip Gardens, Aldwick, Bognor Regis, W Sussex PO21 4LB* Tel (01243) 264865

HALL, Canon John Robert. b 49. St Chad's Coll Dur BA71. Cuddesdon Coll 73. **d** 75 **p** 76. C Kennington St Jo *S'wark* 75-78; P-in-c S Wimbledon All SS 78-84; V Streatham St Pet 84-92; Can Res Blackb Cathl and Dioc Dir of Educn *Blackb* from 92. *St Leonard's House, Potters Lane, Samlesbury, Preston PR5 0UE* Tel (01772) 877229

HALL, Dr Joseph Hayes. b 30. TD71. FGS53 St Jo Coll Dur BSc53 DipTh55 Liv Univ MA73 ThD90. Wycliffe Hall Ox 55. **d** 55 **p** 56. C Wallasey St Hilary *Ches* 55-59; C Macclesfield St Mich 59-60; CF (TA) 59-72; V Barnton *Ches* 60-67; V New Brighton All SS 67-81; V Woodford 81-95; rtd 95; Perm to Offic *Ches* from 95. *13 Briarwood, Wilmslow, Cheshire SK9 2DH*

HALL, Keven Neil. b 47. Auckland Univ BSc PhD74. K Coll Lon BD AKC79. **d** 79 **p** 80. New Zealand 79-87; Chapl Nat Soc for Epilepsy from 91. *1 Coverdale Road, London W12 8JJ* Tel 0181-743 4515

HALL, Leslie. b 37. Man Univ BSc59. EMMTC 83. **d** 86 **p** 87. NSM Freiston w Butterwick *Linc* from 86; Dioc NSM Officer from 94. *29 Brant End Road, Butterwick, Boston, Lincs PE22 0ET* Tel (01205) 760375

HALL, Mrs Linda Charlotte. b 50. Cam Inst of Educn CertEd72. St Alb Minl Tr Scheme 85 Oak Hill Th Coll 91. **d** 92 **p** 94. NSM St Alb St Steph *St Alb* from 92. *15 Nelsons Avenue, St Albans, Herts AL1 5SE* Tel (01727) 869570

HALL, Mrs Margaret Mercia. b 39. Bedf Coll Lon BA61 Cam Univ DipRS78. Gilmore Ho 73. **dss** 80 **d** 87 **p** 94. Gt Chesham *Ox* 81-87; Par Dn 87-94; C from 94. *19 Stanley Avenue, Chesham, Bucks HP5 2JG* Tel (01494) 784479

HALL, Mrs Marigold Josephine. b 29. Linc Th Coll 81. **dss** 83 **d** 87. Chapl Asst Hellesdon Hosp Nor 83-94; Nor St Pet Parmentergate w St Jo *Nor* 83-87; C 87-94; rtd 90; Perm to Offic *Nor* from 94. *11 Stuart Court, Norwich NR1 1NP* Tel (01603) 625933

HALL, Michael Edward. b 32. Fitzw Ho Cam BA57 MA61. Ridley Hall Cam 68. **d** 69 **p** 70. C Aspley *S'well* 69-73; P-in-c Bulwell St Jo 73-75; V 75-81; P-in-c Tylers Green *Ox* 81-90; V from 90. *The Vicarage, Tyler's Green, High Wycombe, Bucks HP10 8HB* Tel (01494) 813367

HALL, Murray. b 34. K Coll Lon. **d** 61 **p** 62. C Eaton *Nor* 61-64; C Shalford *Guildf* 64-67; V Oxshott 67-72; P-in-c Runham *Nor* 72-80; P-in-c Stokesby w Herringby 72-80; R Filby w Thrigby w Mautby 72-80; R Filby w Thrigby, Mautby, Stokesby, Herringby etc 80-94; rtd 94; Perm to Offic *Nor* from 94. *64 Nursery Close, Acle, Norwich NR13 3EH* Tel (01493) 751287

HALL, Nicholas Charles. b 56. **d** 86 **p** 87. C Hyde St Geo *Ches* 86-89; C Cheadle 89-91; NSM from 91. *5 Brooklyn Crescent, Cheadle, Cheshire SK8 1DX* Tel 0161-491 6758

HALL, Canon Nigel David. b 46. Univ of Wales (Cardiff) BA67 BD76 Lon Univ CertEd68. St Mich Coll Llan 73. **d** 76 **p** 77. C Cardiff St Jo *Llan* 76-81; R Llanbadarn Fawr, Llandegley and Llanfihangel etc *S & B* 81-95; RD Maelienydd 89-95; Can Brecon Cathl from 94; V Builth and Llanddewi'r Cwm w Llangynog etc from 95. *The Vicarage, 1 North Road, Builth Wells LD2 3BT* Tel (01982) 552355

HALL (née WANSTALL), Canon Noelle Margaret. b 53. Wolfs Coll Cam BEd76. Sarum & Wells Th Coll 84. **dss** 86 **d** 87 **p** 94. Hythe *Cant* 86-87; Par Dn 87-89; Par Dn Reculver and Herne Bay St Bart 89-94; C 94-95; P-in-c Sittingbourne St Mary from 95; Dioc Adv in Women's Min from 95; Hon Can Cant Cathl from 96. *St Mary's Vicarage, 88 Albany Road, Sittingbourne, Kent ME10 1EL* Tel (01795) 472535

HALL, Peter Douglas. b 60. Ox Poly HND81. Oak Hill Th Coll BA92. **d** 92 **p** 93. C Bromyard *Heref* 92-96; C Dorridge *Birm* from 96. *2 Hurst Green Road, Bentley Heath, Solihull, W Midlands B93 8AE* Tel (01564) 775494

HALL, Philip Edward Robin. b 36. Oak Hill Th Coll 64. **d** 67 **p** 68. C Ware Ch Ch *St Alb* 67-70; C Rayleigh *Chelmsf* 70-73; R Leven w Catwick *York* 73-85; P-in-c Mayfield *Lich* 85-95; P-in-c Ilam w Blore Ray and Okeover 89-95; C Drayton Bassett from 95. *35 Moat Drive, Drayton Bassett, Tamworth, Staffs B78 3UG* Tel (01827) 251620

HALL, Robert Arthur. b 35. Lon Univ BSc66. NW Ord Course 74. **d** 77 **p** 78. C York St Paul *York* 77-79; R Elvington w Sutton on Derwent and E Cottingwith 79-82; Chapl Tiffield Sch Northants 82-84; V Bessingby *York* 84-88; V Carnaby 84-88; V Fulford from 88. *The Vicarage, 1 Fulford Park, Fulford, York YO1 4QE* Tel (01904) 633261

HALL, Roger John. b 53. Linc Th Coll. **d** 84 **p** 85. C Shrewsbury St Giles w Sutton and Atcham *Lich* 84-87; CF from 87. *MOD Chaplains (Army), Trenchard Lines, Upavon, Pewsey, Wilts SN9 6BE* Tel (01980) 615804 Fax 615800

HALL, Ronald Cecil. b 20. St Aid Birkenhead 63. **d** 65 **p** 66. C Tamworth *Lich* 65-69; R Talke 69-74; V Birstwith *Ripon* 74-90; P-in-c Thornthwaite w Thruscross and Darley 76-77; rtd 90. *Wickham House, Kingsmead, Farm Road, Bracklesham Bay, Chichester, W Sussex PO20 8JU* Tel (01243) 671190

HALL, Mrs Sonia Winifred. b 44. Nottm Univ BSc66 Leeds Univ MSc68. Ox Min Course DipMin94. **d** 94 **p** 95. NSM Ox St Andr *Ox* 94-95; C Buckland from 96. *33 Bowness Avenue, Headington, Oxford OX3 0AL* Tel (01865) 63639

HALL, Stephen Clarence. b 23. Kelham Th Coll 46. **d** 51 **p** 52. C Killingworth *Newc* 51-53; C Newc H Cross 53-56; S Rhodesia 56-65; Rhodesia 65-80; Zimbabwe from 80; S Africa from 77. *PO Box 10685, Meer-en-See, Zululand, 3901 South Africa* Tel Richards Bay (351) 32713

HALL, Stephen Philip. b 56. Ripon Coll Cuddesdon. **d** 84 **p** 85. C Camberwell St Giles *S'wark* 84-88; Chapl Brighton Poly *Chich* 88-92; Chapl Brighton Univ 92; TV Bicester w Bucknell, Caversfield and Launton *Ox* from 92; Sub Chapl HM Pris Bullingdon from 92. *75 Ravencroft, Langford Village, Bicester, Oxon OX6 0YQ* Tel (01869) 323635

HALL, Prof Stuart George. b 28. New Coll Ox BA52 MA55 BD72. Ripon Hall Ox 53. **d** 54 **p** 55. C Newark w Coddington *S'well* 54-58; Tutor Qu Coll Birm 58-62; Lect Th Nottm Univ 62-73; Sen Lect 73-78; Prof Ecclesiastical Hist K Coll Lon 78-90; Perm to Offic *St Alb* 80-86; Perm to Offic *S'wark* 86-90; R Pittenweem *St And* from 90; R Elie and Earlsferry from 90; rtd 93. *Hopedene, 15 High Street, Elie, Leven, Fife KY9 1BY* Tel (01333) 330145 Fax as telephone

HALL, Thomas Bartholomew Berners. b 39. St Fran Coll Brisbane 63. **d** 65 **p** 66. Australia 65-75 and from 82; P-in-c Whitehawk *Chich* 75-82. *PO Box 647, Strathpine, Queensland, Australia 4500, or 2 Lindale Court, Cashmere, Queensland, Australia 4500* Tel Brisbane (7) 3881 2090 or 3882 0880

HALL, Timothy Robert. b 52. Dur Univ BA74. St Jo Coll Nottm LTh87. **d** 87 **p** 88. C Hawarden *St As* 87-89; Chapl St D Coll Llandudno from 90. *Woodpecker Cottage, St David's College, Llandudno LL30 1RD* Tel (01492) 581224

HALL, William. b 34. Hull Univ BSc(Econ)56 St Jo Coll Dur CertRS88. NE Ord Course 89. **d** 92 **p** 93. NSM Sunderland *Dur* from 92. *31 Nursery Road, Silksworth Lane, Sunderland SR3 1NT* Tel 0191-528 4843

HALL, Canon William Cameron. b 40. K Coll Lon 60. **d** 65 **p** 66. C Thornaby on Tees St Paul *York* 65-68; Chapl to Arts and Recreation *Dur* from 68; V Grindon 71-80; Hon Can Dur Cathl from 84; Sen Chapl Actors' Ch Union from 89. *59 Western Hill, Durham DH1 4RJ* Tel 0191-386 3177

HALL, William Nawton Sinclair. b 17. Kelham Th Coll 35. **d** 41 **p** 42. C Gateshead St Cuth *Dur* 41-43; C Notting Hill All SS w St Columb *Lon* 43-46; C Clewer St Andr *Ox* 46-50; PC Gateshead St Aid *Dur* 50-55; R Witton Gilbert 55-61; R Lowther w Askham *Carl* 61-84; rtd 83; Perm to Offic *Carl* from 84. *41 Briar Rigg, Keswick, Cumbria CA12 4NN* Tel (017687) 74103

HALL, William Norman. b 30. ARIC74 TCD BA52 MA64 BD65. TCD Div Sch Div Test54. **d** 54 **p** 55. C Dundela *D & D* 54-58; C Holywood 58-63; I Drumgooland 63-66; Chapl St Jas Choir Sch Grimsby 66-70; Asst Master Hautlieu Sch Jersey 70-73; V Jersey St Mark *Win* 73-92; rtd 92. *La Chansonette, 26 Seafield Avenue, Milbrook, Jersey, Channel Islands JE2 3LZ* Tel (01534) 80221

HALL CARPENTER, Leslie Thomas Frank. b 19. Lich Th Coll 55. **d** 57 **p** 58. C Methley w Mickletown *Ripon* 57-59; V Kirkby Ravensworth w Dalton 59-61; India 61-63; V Ellingham w S

Charlton *Newc* 63-67; V Horsford *Nor* 67-69; V Horsham St Faith w Newton St Faith 67-69; R Lochgilphead *Arg* 69-70; Area Sec USPG (York) 70-73; P-in-c Well *Ripon* 73-74; V Kirk Hammerton 74-75; R Hunsingore w Cowthorpe 74-75; V Nun Monkton 74-75; R Kirk Hammerton w Nun Monkton and Hunsingore 75-77; P-in-c Hackness w Harwood Dale *York* 77-79; V Melbecks and Muker *Ripon* 79-82; R Twyford w Guist w Bintry w Themelthorpe etc *Nor* 82-84; rtd 84; Perm to Offic *Nor* 90-96. *Little Cogden, 6 Old Hall Drive, Dersingham, Norfolk PE31 6JT* Tel (01485) 542271

HALL-MATTHEWS, Preb John Cuthbert Berners. b 33. Queensland Univ BA55 K Coll Lon PGCE65. Coll of Resurr Mirfield 58. **d** 60 **p** 61. C Woodley St Jo the Ev *Ox* 60-63; C Is of Dogs Ch Ch and St Jo w St Luke *Lon* 63-65; Asst Chapl Ch Hosp Horsham 65-72; Chapl R Hosp Sch Holbrook 72-75; V Tupsley *Heref* 75-90; P-in-c Hampton Bishop and Mordiford w Dormington 77-90; RD Heref City 84-90; Preb Heref Cathl 85-90; TR Wolverhampton *Lich* from 90. *St Peter's Rectory, 42 Park Road East, Wolverhampton WV1 4QA* Tel (01902) 23140 or 28491

HALL-THOMPSON, Colin Lloyd. b 51. JP. TCD DipTh. **d** 84 **p** 85. C Dublin Rathfarnham *D & G* 84-86; Bp's C Clonmel Union *C, C & R* 86-91; Chapl Fort Mitchel Pris from 86; I Kilbride *Conn* from 91; Hon Chapl Miss to Seamen from 91. *Kilbride Rectory, 7 Rectory Road, Doagh, Co Antrim BT39 0PT* Tel (01960) 340225

HALLAM, Dr Nicholas Francis (Nick). b 48. MRCPath91 Univ Coll Ox BA71 MA81 Glas Univ PhD76 MB, ChB81. Ox NSM Course 84. **d** 87 **p** 88. NSM Ox St Clem *Ox* 87-93; NSM Balerno *Edin* from 93. *11 Ravelrig Park, Edinburgh EH14 7DL* Tel 0131-449 5341 or 536 6329

HALLAM, Canon Peter Hubert. b 33. Trin Hall Cam BA56 MA60. Westcott Ho Cam 56. **d** 58 **p** 59. C St Annes *Blackb* 58-62; Asst Chapl and Tutor St Bede Coll Dur 62-67; V Briercliffe *Blackb* from 67; Hon Can Blackb Cathl from 92. *St James's Vicarage, Briercliffe, Burnley, Lancs BB10 2HU* Tel (01282) 423700

HALLAM, Stanley Bywater. b 16. Wells Th Coll 71. **d** 71 **p** 72. C Haughton le Skerne *Dur* 72-74; R Stanhope 74-82; rtd 82. *8 Low Well Park, Wheldrake, York YO4 6DS* Tel (01904) 448803

✠**HALLATT, The Rt Revd David Marrison.** b 37. Southn Univ BA59 St Cath Coll Ox BA62 MA66. Wycliffe Hall Ox 59. **d** 63 **p** 64 **c** 94. C Maghull *Liv* 63-67; PC Totley *Derby* 67-75; R Didsbury St Jas *Man* 75-80; R Barlow Moor 76-80; TR Didsbury St Jas and Em 80-89; Adn Halifax *Wakef* 89-94; Area Bp Shrewsbury *Lich* from 94. *Athlone House, 68 London Road, Shrewsbury SY2 6PG* Tel (01743) 235867 Fax 243296

HALLATT, John Leighton. b 34. St Pet Coll Ox BA58 MA62. Wycliffe Hall Ox 58. **d** 60 **p** 61. C Ipswich St Jo *St E* 60-63; C Warrington St Paul *Liv* 63-66; V Wadsley *Sheff* 66-72; V Hindley St Pet *Liv* 72-75; Area Sec (Scotland and Dios Newc and Dur) CMS 75-83; N Sec CMS 78-83; TR Cramlington *Newc* 83-90; V Monkseaton St Mary from 90. *The Vicarage, 77 Holywell Avenue, Whitley Bay, Tyne & Wear NE26 3AG* Tel 0191-252 2484

HALLETT, Howard Adrian. b 43. Man Univ MPhil90. Oak Hill Th Coll BA81. **d** 81 **p** 82. C Walshaw Ch Ch *Man* 81-84; V Stoke sub Hamdon *B & W* from 84; RD Ivelchester 91-95. *The Vicarage, 1 East Stoke, Stoke-sub-Hamdon, Somerset TA14 6RQ* Tel (01935) 822529

HALLETT, Miss Jacqueline Victoria (Lyn). b 54. Ex Univ BA75 PGCE76. Linc Th Coll CMinlStuds94. **d** 94 **p** 95. C Crook *Dur* from 94. *Cherry Tree House, Park Avenue, Crook, Co Durham DL15 9HX* Tel (01388) 762451

HALLETT, Keith Philip. b 37. Tyndale Hall Bris 61. **d** 64 **p** 65. C Higher Openshaw *Man* 64-68; C Bushbury *Lich* 68-71; P-in-c Drayton Bassett 71-72; R 72-90; V Fazeley 71-90; P-in-c Hints 78-83; V 83-90; C-in-c Canwell CD 78-83; V Canwell 83-90; RD Tamworth 81-90; P-in-c Buckhurst Hill *Chelmsf* from 90. *St John's Rectory, High Road, Buckhurst Hill, Essex IG9 5RX* Tel 0181-504 1931

HALLETT, Peter. b 49. Bath Univ BSc72. Oak Hill Th Coll DPS. **d** 76 **p** 77. C Brinsworth w Catcliffe *Sheff* 76-79; P-in-c Doncaster St Jas 80-81; V 81-86; R Henstridge and Charlton Horethorne w Stowell *B & W* from 86. *The Vicarage, Henstridge, Templecombe, Somerset BA8 0QE* Tel (01963) 362266

HALLETT, Peter Duncan. b 43. CCC Cam BA66 MA68. Westcott Ho Cam 69. **d** 71 **p** 72. C Sawston *Ely* 71-73; C Lyndhurst and Emery Down *Win* 73-78; C Skegness and Winthorpe *Linc* 78-80; P-in-c Samlesbury *Blackb* 80-91; Asst Dir RE from 80; C Leyland St Ambrose 91-94. *24 Bosburn Drive, Mellor Brook, Blackburn BB2 7PA* Tel (01254) 813544

HALLETT, Raymond. b 44. EMMTC 85. **d** 88 **p** 89. NSM Hucknall Torkard *S'well* from 88. *26 Nursery Close, Hucknall, Nottingham NG15 6DQ* Tel 0115-963 3360

HALLETT, Canon Roy. b 17. St D Coll Lamp BA48. **d** 49 **p** 50. C Llantarnam *Mon* 49-52; C Llanfrechfa All SS 52-58; V Caldicot 58-71; V Rumney 71-87; RD Bassaleg 82-87; Can St Woolos Cathl 86-87; rtd 87. *247 Llantarnam Road, Cwmbran NP44 3BQ* Tel (01633) 874128

HALLIBURTON, Canon Robert John. b 35. Selw Coll Cam BA56 MA60 Keble Coll Ox BA58 DPhil61 MA71. St Steph Ho Ox 58. **d** 61 **p** 62. C Stepney St Dunstan and All SS *Lon* 61-67; Lect St Steph Ho Ox 67-71; Vice-Prin 71-75; Lect Linc Coll Ox 73-75; Prin Chich Th Coll 75-82; Can and Preb Chich Cathl *Chich* 76-82; Wightring Preb and Th Lect 88-90; P-in-c St Margarets on Thames *Lon* 82-90; Can Res and Chan St Paul's Cathl from 90. *1 Amen Court, London EC4M 7BU* Tel 0171-248 1817

HALLIDAY, Christopher Norton Robert. b 48. N Ord Course 82. **d** 85 **p** 86. C Davyhulme St Mary *Man* 85-87; Lect Bolton St Pet 87-90; I Rathdrum w Glenealy, Derralossary and Laragh *D & G* from 90. *The Rectory, Rathdrum, Co Wicklow, Irish Republic* Tel Rathdrum (404) 46160 Mobile 087-444180 Fax 46663

HALLIDAY, Mrs Diana Patricia (Di). b 40. ALA66. N Ord Course 89. **d** 92 **p** 94. NSM Burley in Wharfedale *Bradf* 92-95; NSM Harden and Wilsden from 95. *The Brackens, 6A Walker Road, Baildon, Shipley, W Yorkshire BD17 5BE* Tel (01274) 582859

HALLIDAY, Edwin James. b 35. NW Ord Course 70. **d** 73 **p** 74. C New Bury *Man* 73-76; V Bolton St Phil 76-82; Dioc Communications Officer 82-88; V Radcliffe St Thos and St Jo 82-90; R Gt Lever from 90. *St Michael's Rectory, 130 Green Lane, Bolton BL3 2HX* Tel (01204) 526510

HALLIDAY, Paula Patricia. b 50. MEd83 BTh94. **d** 94 **p** 95. C Killala w Dunfeeny, Crossmolina, Kilmoremoy etc *T, K & A* 94-97; I Crosspatrick Gp *C & O* from 97. *The Rectory, Tinahely, Arklow, Co Wicklow, Irish Republic* Tel Arklow (402) 38178

✠**HALLIDAY, The Rt Revd Robert Taylor.** b 32. Glas Univ MA54 BD57. Edin Th Coll 55. **d** 57 **p** 58 **c** 90. C St Andrews St Andr *St And* 57-60; R 83-90; C Glas St Marg *Glas* 60-63; Lect NT Edin Th Coll 63-74; R Edin H Cross *Edin* 63-83; Tutor Edin Univ 69-71; Can St Mary's Cathl *Edin* 73-83; R St Andrews St Andr *St And* 83-90; Tutor St Andr Univ 84-90; Bp Bre 90-96; rtd 96. *28 Forbes Road, Edinburgh EH10 4ED* Tel 0131-221 1490

HALLIDIE SMITH, Andrew. b 31. Pemb Coll Cam BA54 MA58. Ely Th Coll 55. **d** 56 **p** 57. C Pype Hayes *Birm* 56-58; Sec Albany Trust Lon 58-60; Canada 60-63 and 67-70 and 79-81 and from 91; V Elmstead *Chelmsf* 63-67; R Alresford 70-79; V Elsecar *Sheff* 81-91; rtd 91. *PO Box 765, Big River, Saskatchewan, Canada, S0J 0E0* Tel (306) 469-4417 Fax 469-5662

HALLING, William Laurence. b 43. Linc Coll Ox BA64 DipTh66 MA68 Lon Univ BD68. Tyndale Hall Bris 66. **d** 68 **p** 69. C Beckenham St Jo *Roch* 68-72; C Walton H Trin *Ox* 72-78; V Barrow St Mark *Carl* 78-86; R Kirkheaton *Wakef* from 86; Chapl Mill Hill Hosp Huddersfield from 86. *The Rectory, Church Lane, Kirkheaton, Huddersfield HD5 0JR* Tel (01484) 532410

HALLIWELL, Christopher Eigil. b 57. Newc Univ BA78. Trin Coll Bris DipHE91. **d** 91 **p** 92. C Mildenhall *St E* 91-94; R Wrentham w Benacre, Covehithe, Frostenden etc from 94. *The Vicarage, 52 Main Street, Cossington, Leicester LE7 4UU* Tel (01509) 813455

HALLIWELL, Ivor George. b 33. St Cath Coll Cam BA57 MA60. Wells Th Coll 58. **d** 60 **p** 60. C Hanworth St Geo *Lon* 60-62; C Willenhall *Cov* 62-65; C-in-c Whitley St Jas CD 65-68; V Whitley 68-72; V Corton *Nor* 72-77; P-in-c Hopton 72-74; V 74-77; Asst Chapl HM Pris Pentonville 77; Chapl HM Pris Ex 77-83; Chapl HM Pris Wakef 83-85; P-in-c Bickington *Ex* 85-87; P-in-c Ashburton w Buckland-in-the-Moor 85-87; V Ashburton w Buckland in the Moor and Bickington 87-90; Chapl HM Pris Channings Wood 90-97; Lic to Offic *Ex* from 90; rtd 97. *Anastasis, Avenue Road, Bovey Tracey, Newton Abbot, Devon TQ13 9BQ*

HALLIWELL, Michael Arthur. b 28. St Edm Hall Ox BA50 MA53. Ely Th Coll 52. **d** 54 **p** 55. C Welling *S'wark* 54-57; C Bournemouth St Alb *Win* 57-59; Asst Gen Sec C of E Coun on Foreign Relns 59-62; C St Dunstan in the West *Lon* 60-62; Chapl Bonn w Cologne *Eur* 62-67; Chapl RAF 66-67; V Croydon St Andr *Cant* 67-71; R Jersey St Brelade *Win* 71-96; Chapl HM Pris Jersey 75-80; Vice-Dean Jersey *Win* from 85; Tutor S Dios Minl Tr Scheme 92-96; rtd 96; Hon C Jersey Grouville *Win* from 96. *16 Le Clos du Rivage, Gorey Coast Road, St Martin, Jersey JE3 6EY* Tel (01534) 856506

HALLOWS, John Martin. b 50. Birm Univ BA78 Lon Univ PGCE82 E Lon Univ MSc93. Oak Hill Th Coll 92. **d** 94 **p** 95. C Boxmoor St Jo *St Alb* from 94. *23 Beechfield Road, Boxmoor, Hemel Hempstead, Herts HP1 1PP* Tel (01442) 253102

HALLS, Peter Ernest. b 38. Bris Univ BA62. Tyndale Hall Bris 59. **d** 64 **p** 65. C Blackb St Barn *Blackb* 64-67; C Bromley Ch Ch *Roch* 67-70; V Halvergate w Tunstall *Nor* 70-79; V Freethorpe w Wickhampton 71-79; P-in-c Beighton and Moulton 77-79; V Tuckswood 79-90; RD Nor S 86-90; R Brooke, Kirstead, Mundham w Seething and Thwaite from 90; RD Depwade 91-97. *The Vicarage, Brooke, Norwich NR15 1JV* Tel (01508) 550378

HALMSHAW, Mrs Stella Mary. b 36. Brighton Coll of Educn TCert57 Westmr Coll Lon CertRE58. St Alb Minl Tr Scheme 81. **dss** 84 **d** 87 **p** 96. Radlett *St Alb* 84-87; Par Dn 87-93; Hon C from 93; Chapl Herts Univ 93-96; rtd 96. *13 The Crosspath, Radlett, Herts WD7 8HR* Tel (01923) 854314

HALSALL, Mrs Isobel Joan. b 47. Local Minl Tr Course. **d** 94 **p** 95. C Walshaw Ch Ch *Man* from 94. *42 Knowsley Road, Bolton BL2 5PU* Tel (01204) 894171

HALSALL, Michael John. b 61. Salford Univ BSc83. Wycliffe Hall Ox 88. **d** 91 **p** 92. C Cowley St Jo *Ox* 91-93; CF from 93. *MOD*

Chaplains (Army), Trenchard Lines, Upavon, Pewsey, Wilts SN9 6BE Tel (01980) 615804 Fax 615800

HALSE, Raymond Stafford. b 19. Lon Univ BA49. Oak Hill Th Coll 46. **d** 50 **p** 51. C Rodbourne Cheney *Bris* 50-52; C Farnborough *Guildf* 52-54; V Islington St Jude Mildmay Park *Lon* 54-59; V Over Stowey w Aisholt *B & W* 59-68; V Ramsgate St Luke *Cant* 68-85; P-in-c Ramsgate Ch Ch 85; rtd 85; Hon C Hordle *Win* 86-92. *58 Brunel Drive, Preston, Weymouth, Dorset DT3 6NY* Tel (01305) 833048

HALSEY, Anthony Michael James (Tony). b 35. Solicitor 64 K Coll Cam BA56 MA62. St Jo Coll Nottm 73. **d** 75 **p** 76. C Derby St Werburgh *Derby* 75-77; Chapl Canford Sch Wimborne 78-87; TV Sanderstead All SS *S'wark* 87-89; Perm to Offic *Portsm* from 89. *Woodlands, South Road, Liphook, Hants GU30 7HS* Tel (01428) 724459

HALSEY, George John. b 16. Lon Univ BSc36. Wycliffe Hall Ox 38. **d** 39 **p** 40. C Maidenhead St Andr and St Mary *Ox* 39-43; C Brompton H Trin *Lon* 43-47; V Southall H Trin 47-51; R Ashtead *Guildf* 51-66; V Shelford *S'well* 66-68; V Radcliffe-on-Trent 66-68; Lic to Offic *S'wark* 73-81; rtd 81; Perm to Offic *Guildf* 81-96. *70 Ashcombe Road, Dorking, Surrey RH4 1NA* Tel (01306) 886469

✠**HALSEY, The Rt Revd Henry David.** b 19. K Coll Lon BA38. Sarum Th Coll 40. **d** 42 **p** 43 **c** 68. C Petersfield w Sheet *Portsm* 42-45; Chapl RN 46-47; C Plymouth St Andr *Ex* 47-50; V Netheravon w Fittleton *Sarum* 50-53; C-in-c Chatham St Steph CD *Roch* 53-59; V Chatham St Steph 59-62; V Bromley SS Pet and Paul 62-68; Chapl Bromley Hosp 62-68; Hon Can Roch Cathl *Roch* 64-68; RD Bromley 65-66; Adn Bromley 66-68; Suff Bp Tonbridge 68-72; Bp Carl 72-89; rtd 89; Asst Bp Portsm from 91. *Bramblecross, Gully Road, Seaview, Isle of Wight PO34 5BY* Tel (01983) 613583

HALSEY, Brother John Walter Brooke. b 33. Cam Univ BA57 Edin Univ DPT67. Westcott Ho Cam 61. **d** 61 **p** 62. C Stocksbridge *Sheff* 61-65; Community of the Transfiguration Midlothian from 65; Ind Chapl Edin 65-69. *Hermitage of the Transfiguration, 23 Manse Road, Roslin, Midlothian EH25 9LF*

HALSON, Bryan Richard. b 32. Jes Coll Cam BA56 MA60 Liv Univ MA72. Ridley Hall Cam. **d** 59 **p** 60. C Coulsdon St Andr *S'wark* 59-62; Lic to Offic *Ches* from 63; Tutor St Aid Birkenhead 63-65; Sen Tutor 65-68; Vice-Prin 68-69; Lect Alsager Coll of Educn 69-74; Prin Lect Crewe and Alsager Coll of HE from 74. *11 Winston Avenue, Alsager, Stoke-on-Trent ST7 2BE* Tel (01270) 873998

✠**HAMBIDGE, The Most Revd Douglas Walter.** b 27. Lon Univ BD58. ALCD53 Angl Th Coll (BC) DD70. **d** 53 **p** 54 **c** 69. C Dalston St Mark w St Bart *Lon* 53-56; Canada 56-93; Can Caledonia 65-69; Bp Caledonia 69-80; Bp New Westmr 80; Abp New Westmr and Metrop BC 81-93; Prin St Mark's Th Coll Dar es Salaam from 93. *St Mark's Theological College, PO Box 25017, Dar es Salaam, Tanzania*

HAMBIDGE, John Robert. b 29. Sarum Th Coll. **d** 55 **p** 56. C Tynemouth H Trin W Town *Newc* 55-57; C Middlesbrough St Jo the Ev *York* 58-63; C Clerkenwell H Redeemer w St Phil *Lon* 63-64; C Richmond St Mary *S'wark* 64-66; V Richmond St Jo 66-76; R Swanscombe *Roch* 76-84; V Aberedw w Llandeilo Graban and Llanbadarn etc *S & B* 84-91; P-in-c Sibson w Sheepy and Ratcliffe Culey *Leic* 91-94; P-in-c Orton-on-the-Hill w Twycross etc 92-94; R The Sheepy Gp 95-97; rtd 97. *99 Elizabeth Drive, Tamworth, Staffs BT9 8DE* Tel (01827) 61526

HAMBLEN, John William Frederick. b 24. Sarum Th Coll 64. **d** 65 **p** 66. C Weymouth H Trin *Sarum* 66-68; C Marlborough 68-70; V Chardstock 70-77; P-in-c Lytchett Matravers 77-83; P-in-c Burpham *Chich* 83-89; Dioc Stewardship Adv 83-89; rtd 89; Perm to Offic *Ex* from 89. *73 West Cliff Road, Dawlish, Devon EX7 9QX*

HAMBLETON, Ronald Dalzell. b 27. Ripon Hall Ox 61. **d** 62 **p** 63. C Stokesay *Heref* 62-65; V Knowbury 65-75; P-in-c Weston under Penyard 75-79; P-in-c Hope Mansell 75-79; R Weston-under-Penyard w Hope Mansel and The Lea 79-92; rtd 92; NSM Portree *Arg* 92-95; Perm to Offic *Heref* from 96. *21 Pentaloe Close, Mordiford, Hereford HR1 4LS* Tel (01432) 870622

HAMBLIN, Derek Gordon Hawthorn. b 35. SW Minl Tr Course 94. **d** 96. Hon C S Brent and Rattery *Ex* from 96. *Paddock Retreat, Noland Park, South Brent, Devon TQ10 9DE* Tel (01364) 72388

HAMBLIN, John Talbot. b 38. St Steph Ho Ox 64. **d** 66 **p** 67. C Newc St Jo *Newc* 66-70; C Covent Garden St Paul *Lon* 70-71; C St Marylebone Ch Ch w St Barn 71-72; C St Marylebone Ch Ch w St Paul 72-73; C Hendon St Mary 73-76; P-in-c Hornsey St Pet 76-77; V Tottenham Ch Ch W Green 76-77; V W Green Ch Ch w St Pet 77-96. *8 College Gardens, Brighton BN2 1HP* Tel (01273) 675592

HAMBLIN, Roger Noel. b 42. Ripon Hall Ox 67. **d** 70 **p** 71. C Scotforth *Blackb* 70-73; C Altham w Clayton le Moors 73-76; V Cockerham w Winmarleigh 76-87; V Cockerham w Winmarleigh and Glasson from 87. *The Vicarage, 5 Lancaster Road, Cockerham, Lancaster LA2 0EB* Tel (01524) 791390

HAMBORG, Graham Richard. b 52. Bris Univ BSc73 Nottm Univ BA76 MTh77. St Jo Coll Nottm 74. **d** 77 **p** 78. C Tile Cross *Birm* 77-80; C Upton cum Chalvey *Ox* 80-82; TV 82-86; V Ruscombe and Twyford from 86. *Ruscombe and Twyford Church Office, St Mary's Church Centre, Station Road, Twyford, Reading RG10 9NT* Tel 0118-934 4792

HAMBREY, Canon Frank Bernard. b 14. Leeds Univ BA42. Coll of Resurr Mirfield 43. **d** 44 **p** 45. C W Bromwich St Andr *Lich* 44-46; C Edgmond 46-51; V Bury St Thos *Man* 51-57; Area Sec (Dios Man and Liv) SPG 57-64; USPG 65-68; V Colton *Carl* 68-70; Can Res Bermuda Cathl 70-75; Perm to Offic *Carl* from 77; rtd 79. *Bully Cottage, Embleton, Cockermouth, Cumbria CA13 9YA* Tel (017687) 76379

HAMBREY, Frederick Charles. b 19. Leeds Univ BA41. Coll of Resurr Mirfield 41. **d** 43 **p** 45. C Bloxwich *Lich* 43-45; C Willenhall St Giles 45-49; C Hednesford 49-54; V W Bromwich Gd Shep 54-59; V Hanbury 59-70; V Colton *Carl* 70-71; V Satterthwaite and Rusland 70-71; V Colton w Satterthwaite and Rusland 71-84; rtd 84; Perm to Offic *Carl* from 85. *Underknott, Blease Road, Threlkeld, Keswick, Cumbria CA12 4RY* Tel (017687) 79604

HAMEL COOKE, Christopher Kingston. b 21. CCC Ox BA49 MA52 Birm Univ DPS67. Cuddesdon Coll 49. **d** 50 **p** 51. C Roehampton H Trin *S'wark* 50-53; C Temple Balsall *Birm* 53-57; PV Lich Cathl *Lich* 57-59; Hon PV 59-69; V Cov St Mark *Cov* 59-69; V Bedford St Andr *St Alb* 69-79; P-in-c Bedford St Mary 70-75; R St Marylebone w H Trin *Lon* 79-89; rtd 90; Perm to Offic *Cov* from 90. *The Malt House, Halford, Shipston-on-Stour, Warks CV36 5BT* Tel (01789) 740615

HAMEL COOKE, Ian Kirk. b 17. Birm Univ BA39. Chich Th Coll 39. **d** 41 **p** 42. C Bedminster St Fran *Bris* 41-43; C Alton All SS *Win* 43-48; V N Baddesley 48-55; R Hartest w Boxted *St E* 55-63; V Addlestone *Guildf* 63-75; R Tittleshall w Godwick and Wellingham *Nor* 75-76; R Tittleshall w Godwick, Wellingham and Weasenham 76-82; rtd 82; Perm to Offic *Nor* from 82. *Crugmeer, Croft Yard, Wells-next-the-Sea, Norfolk NR23 1JS* Tel (01328) 710358

HAMER, David Handel. b 41. Cape Town Univ BA61 Trin Coll Ox BA66. Coll of Resurr Mirfield 62. **d** 66 **p** 67. S Africa 66-73; Chapl Blundell's Sch Tiverton from 73; Lic to Offic *Ex* from 73. *Mayfield House, 2 Tidcombe Lane, Tiverton, Devon EX16 4DZ* Tel (01884) 253098

HAMER, Irving David. b 59. **d** 84 **p** 85. C Newton Nottage *Llan* 84-88; C Roath St Marg 88-90; V Llansawel w Briton Ferry from 90; Miss to Seamen from 90. *The Vicarage, 251 Neath Road, Briton Ferry SA11 2SL* Tel (01639) 812200

HAMER, Roderick John Andrew. b 44. K Coll Lon 64. Ridley Hall Cam 67. **d** 68 **p** 69. C Timperley *Ches* 68-72; C Brewood *Lich* 72-74; V Chesterton 74-80; C S Gillingham *Roch* 80-83; Adv Cant and Roch Coun for Soc Resp 83-90; Hon C S Gillingham 83-90; Perm to Offic *Cant* 84-90; ACUPA Link Officer (Dio Roch) 87-90; TR Southend *Chelmsf* 90-94; P-in-c N Woolwich w Silvertown from 94; Ind Chapl from 94. *St John's Vicarage, Manwood Street, London E16 2JY* Tel 0171-476 2388

HAMER, Canon Thomas. b 15. Univ of Wales BA37. St Mich Coll Llan 37. **d** 38 **p** 39. C Llanllwchaiarn *St D* 38-41; C Llandyfaelog 41-47; V Maenclochog w Llanycefn 47-52; V Maenclochog w Llandeilo, Llanycefn, Henry's Moat 52-79; V Maenclochog w Henry's Moat and Mynachlogddu etc 79-80; Hon Can St D Cathl 79-80; rtd 80. *Bryngwyn, The Crescent, Narberth SA67 7DL* Tel (01834) 860455

HAMER, Mrs Valerie Margaret. b 52. Leeds Univ BA74. S'wark Ord Course 83. **dss** 86 **d** 87 **p** 94. Warlingham w Chelsham and Farleigh *S'wark* 86-87; Par Dn 87-88; Par Dn Caterham 88-94; C 94-96; RD Caterham 95-96; V Addiscombe St Mildred from 96. *St Mildred's Vicarage, Sefton Road, Croydon CR0 7HR* Tel 0181-654 3569

HAMERTON, Thomas Patrick. b 13. St Edm Hall Ox BA35 DipTh36 MA50. Cuddesdon Coll 37. **d** 38 **p** 39. C Bury St Mary *Man* 38-40; C Southbourne St Kath *Win* 40-42; India 42-44; C Parkstone St Pet w Branksea *Sarum* 44-52; V Weedon Lois w Plumpton *Pet* 52-58; R Abthorpe 52-58; R Slapton 52-58; V Weedon Lois w Plumpton and Moreton Pinkney 58-63; R Abington 63-76; V Welton w Ashby St Ledgers 76-83; rtd 83; Perm to Offic *Glouc* 83-95. *15 Langton Road, Rugby, Warks CV21 3UA* Tel (01788) 546599

HAMEY, Geoffrey Allan. b 25. Lon Univ BSc47. S'wark Ord Course 75. **d** 78 **p** 79. NSM Pinner *Lon* 78-83; P-in-c Fincham *Ely* 83-84; P-in-c Marham 83-84; P-in-c Shouldham 83-84; P-in-c Shouldham Thorpe 83-84; V 84-88; rtd 88; Hon C Winkleigh *Ex* from 88. *4 East Park Close, Winkleigh, Devon EX19 8LG* Tel (01837) 83455

HAMIL, Sheila. b 49. TCert71. NE Ord Course DipHE95. **d** 95. NSM Wallsend St Luke *Newc* from 95. *5 Kings Road South, Wallsend, Tyne & Wear NE28 7QT* Tel 0191-263 2371

HAMILL-STEWART, Simon Francis. b 32. Pemb Coll Cam BA56. N Ord Course 77. **d** 80 **p** 81. NSM Neston *Ches* 80-83; C 83-86; V Over St Jo from 86; Dioc Ecum Officer from 92. *St John's Vicarage, Delamere Street, Winsford, Cheshire CW7 2LY* Tel (01606) 594651

✠**HAMILTON, The Rt Revd Alexander Kenneth.** b 15. Trin Hall Cam BA37 MA41. Westcott Ho Cam 37. **d** 39 **p** 40 **c** 65. C Birstall *Leic* 39-41; C Whitworth w Spennymoor *Dur* 41-45; Chapl RNVR 45-47; V Bedminster St Fran *Bris* 47-58; V Newc St Jo

Newc 58-65; RD Newc Cen 62-65; Suff Bp Jarrow *Dur* 65-80; rtd 80; Asst Bp B & W from 80. *3 Ash Tree Road, Burnham-on-Sea, Somerset TA8 2LB* Tel (01628) 783823

HAMILTON, Andrew David. b 65. Chester Coll BA86. Oak Hill Th Coll BA92. **d** 92 **p** 93. C Necton w Holme Hale *Nor* 92-94; C Necton, Holme Hale w N and S Pickenham 95-96; Chapl Bp Wand Sch *Lon* 96-97; Chapl HM Pris Bris from 97. *HM Prison Bristol, 19 Cambridge Road, Horfield, Bristol BS7 8PS* Tel 0117-980 8100

HAMILTON, Canon Edgar Reid. b 27. TCD BA49 MA52. CITC 51. **d** 51 **p** 52. C Belfast St Donard *D & D* 51-55; Dean's V Belf Cathl 55-59; C-in-c Stormont *D & D* 60-64; I 64-93; RD Dundonald 77-93; Can Belf Cathl 85-91; Preb Wicklow St Patr Cathl Dublin 90-93; rtd 93. *13 Massey Park, Belfast BT4 2JX* Tel (01232) 763835

HAMILTON, Gerald Murray Percival. b 14. Ch Coll Cam BA37 MA41. Ridley Hall Cam 37. **d** 39 **p** 40. C Shirley *Win* 39-40; Bp's Dom Chapl 40-41; C Odiham w S Warnborough and Long Sutton 41-44; C Leeds St Pet *Ripon* 44-46; V Ashton on Mersey St Mary *Ches* 46-51; Relig Broadcasting Org BBC N Region 52-65; Lic to Offic *Ches* 51-65; Can Res Newc Cathl *Newc* 65-67; Bp's Ind and Community Adv 65-67; Prin Lect Coll of Ripon & York St Jo 67-79; R Crayke w Brandsby and Yearsley *York* 78-82; rtd 82; Perm to Offic *York* from 82. *31 St Andrewgate, York YO1 2BR* Tel (01904) 632506

HAMILTON, Canon James. b 22. Dur Univ LTh48. Tyndale Hall Bris 41. **d** 49 **p** 50. C Carl St Jo *Carl* 49-52; N Area Sec BCMS 52-55; V Southport SS Simon and Jude *Liv* 55-66; V Eccleston Ch Ch 66-87; Hon Can Liv Cathl 76-87; rtd 87; Perm to Offic *Liv* from 87. *6 Freckleton Road, St Helens, Merseyside WA10 3AW* Tel (01744) 57716

HAMILTON, James Davy. b 20. Hatf Coll Dur 38. Edin Th Coll 40. **d** 43 **p** 45. C Kirkcaldy *St And* 43-46; C Wokingham St Paul *Ox* 46-49; Chapl RAF 49-55; C St Athan *Llan* 49-50; C Boscombe Down 50-52; C Amersham *Ox* 55-62; R Sandford w Upton Hellions *Ex* 62-79; P-in-c Ashprington 79-81; P-in-c Cornworthy 79-81; R Ashprington, Cornworthy and Dittisham 81-83; C Weymouth St Paul *Sarum* 83-85; rtd 85; Perm to Offic *Ex* from 85. *21 Langaton Lane, Pinhoe, Exeter EX1 3SP* Tel (01392) 66747

HAMILTON, John Frederick. b 57. Leeds Univ BA78. Edin Th Coll 78. **d** 80 **p** 81. C Whitkirk *Ripon* 80-83; C Leeds Belle Is St Jo and St Barn 83-86; V Oulton w Woodlesford 86-94; V Cookridge H Trin from 94. *Holy Trinity Vicarage, 53 Green Lane, Cookridge, Leeds LS16 7LW* Tel 0113-267 4921

HAMILTON, John Hans Patrick. b 44. MBIM86 BD66 AKC67 DipAdEd76 DMS85. K Coll Lon 66. **d** 67 **p** 68. C Cleobury Mortimer w Hopton Wafers *Heref* 67-69; C Sanderstead All SS *S'wark* 69-73; V Battersea St Mary-le-Park 73-75; Dir of Educn *Derby* 90-95; P-in-c Cliddesden and Ellisfield w Farleigh Wallop etc *Win* from 95. *The Rectory, Ellisfield, Basingstoke, Hants RG25 2QR* Tel (01256) 381217

HAMILTON, John Nicholas. b 49. Trin Coll Cam BA71 MA75. Ridley Hall Cam 72. **d** 75 **p** 76. C Ealing Dean St Jo *Lon* 75-79; C Stoughton *Guildf* 79-83; R Denton St Lawr *Man* 83-88; R The Sherbornes w Pamber *Win* from 88. *The Rectory, Sherborne St John, Basingstoke, Hants RG24 9HX* Tel (01256) 850434

HAMILTON, Canon Noble Ridgeway. b 23. TD66. TCD BA45 MA49. **d** 47 **p** 48. C Dundela *D & D* 47-51; C Holywood 51-55; I Belfast St Clem 55-61; I Seapatrick 61-89; RD Aghaderg 64-88; Can Dromore Cathl 66-89; Prec 75-84; Chan 84-89; rtd 89; Lic to Offic *D & D* from 90. *67 Meadowvale, Waringstown, Craigavon, Co Armagh BT66 7RL* Tel (01762) 882064

HAMILTON, Richard Alexander. b 46. Pemb Coll Cam BA67 MA87. S Dios Minl Tr Scheme 82. **d** 85 **p** 86. NSM Guernsey St Sampson *Win* 85-89; C Highgate St Mich *Lon* 89-91; P-in-c Tottenham H Trin 91-96. *Address temp unknown*

HAMILTON, Robert Hair. b 26. Oak Hill Th Coll 75. **d** 76 **p** 77. C Bootle St Matt *Liv* 76-78; C Horwich H Trin *Man* 78-81; R Whalley Range St Marg 81-86; Perm to Offic *Ches* from 86; rtd 91. *The Leaves, 47 Statham Road, Birkenhead, Merseyside L43 7XS* Tel 0151-653 7110

HAMILTON, Samuel Derek. b 34. Bris Univ BA58. Tyndale Hall Bris 54. **d** 59 **p** 60. C Dublin St Cath *D & G* 59-61; C Dublin Booterstown 61-63; I Drumcliffe w Lissadell *K, E & A* 63-69; I Cahir *C & O* 69-78; Bp's C Sallaghy *Clogh* 79-83; rtd 83. *12 Cairnshill Court, Saintfield Road, Belfast BT8 4TX*

HAMILTON, William Graham. b 63. New Coll Ox BA86. Wycliffe Hall Ox BA95. **d** 95 **p** 96. C Ivybridge w Harford *Ex* from 95. *5 Orchard Court, Ivybridge, Devon PL21 9UB* Tel (01752) 893208

HAMILTON, William Joseph Taylor. **d** 97. NSM Ches Team *Ches* from 97. *35 Sherbourne Avenue, Westminster Park, Chester CH4 7QU* Tel (01244) 678080

HAMILTON-BROWN, James John (Jimmy). b 35. Lon Univ BSc59. Trin Coll Bris ADipTh90 Ridley Hall Cam 59. **d** 61 **p** 62. C Attenborough w Bramcote *S'well* 61-67; V Bramcote 67-76; R and D Officer Abps' Coun on Evang 76-79; Lic to Offic *Sarum* 76-81; TR Dorchester 81-91; Sec Par and People 91-95; P-in-c Tarrant Valley from 95. *The Old Mill, Spetisbury, Blandford Forum, Dorset DT11 9DF* Tel (01258) 453939

HAMILTON MANON, Phillip Robert Christian. b 49. BA88. St Steph Ho Ox 89. **d** 90 **p** 91. C Norton St Mary *Dur* 90-94; P-in-c Cleadon Park 94-95; V from 95. *St Cuthbert's Vicarage, 218 Sunderland Road, South Shields, Tyne & Wear NE34 6AT* Tel 0191-456 0091

HAMLET, Paul Manning. b 42. MCollP Open Univ BA81. Lambeth STh84 Kelham Th Coll 61. **d** 66 **p** 67. C Rumboldswyke *Chich* 66-69; C Ely 69-73; Hon C Ipswich St Bart *St E* 73-84; Chapl Wellington Sch Somerset 84-94; CF (TAVR) from 88; Chapl Ipswich Sch from 94. *Ipswich School, 25 Henley Road, Ipswich IP1 3SG* Tel (01473) 255313

HAMLYN, Canon Eric Crawford. b 37. Dur Univ BA60 MA91. Cranmer Hall Dur DipTh62. **d** 62 **p** 63. C Bushbury *Lich* 62-64; C Whitchurch 64-67; V Burslem St Paul 67-72; V Stafford St Paul Forebridge 72-77; V Trentham 77-85; TR Mildenhall *St E* 85-89; P-in-c Boxford 89-91; R from 91; Clergy Tr Officer from 89; Hon Can St E Cathl from 91. *The Rectory, Boxford, Colchester CO6 5JT* Tel (01787) 210191

HAMMERSLEY, John Goodwin. b 34. Keble Coll Ox BA57 MA60. Westcott Ho Cam 57. **d** 60 **p** 61. C Sheff St Swithun *Sheff* 60-67; Sec Par and People 67-70; P-in-c Linc St Mary-le-Wigford w St Benedict etc *Linc* 70-78; C Tettenhall Regis *Lich* 78-80; TV 80-87; Preb Lich Cathl 81-87; Chapl Metro Cen Gateshead *Dur* 87-94; RD Gateshead W 88-93; TV Langley Marish *Ox* 94-96; Dir Thamesway Progr 94-96; Co-ord Tr Portfolio (Bucks) from 96; Lic to Offic from 96. *Saint Mary's Vicarage, 180 Langley Road, Slough SL3 7EE* Tel (01753) 546659

HAMMERSLEY, Peter. b 41. Lon Univ BD78 Birm Univ MEd87. Kelham Th Coll 60. **d** 65 **p** 66. C Oadby *Leic* 65-69; Jamaica 70-77; Min Can Worc Cathl *Worc* 77-84; Chapl and Hd RE K Sch Worc 77-84; V Foley Park 84-90; TV Kidderminster St Jo and H Innocents 90-91; Vice-Prin Aston Tr Scheme from 91; Warden of Readers *Worc* from 91. *52 Hanbury Road, Droitwich, Worcs WR9 8PD* Tel (01905) 776197

HAMMERSLEY, Peter Angus Ragsdale. b 35. Linc Th Coll 74. **d** 76 **p** 77. C Stafford *Lich* 76-79; P-in-c W Bromwich St Andr 79-83; V 83-88; P-in-c W Bromwich Ch Ch 85-88; V Streetly from 88; RD Walsall from 90. *The Vicarage, 2 Foley Church Close, Sutton Coldfield, W Midlands B74 3JX* Tel 0121-353 2292

HAMMERTON, Canon Howard Jaggar. b 14. Man Univ BA36 Leeds Univ MA44. Ridley Hall Cam 36. **d** 38 **p** 39. C Beeston *Ripon* 38-39; C Armley St Bart 39-42; C Kippax 42-46; V Hunslet St Mary 46-53; P-in-c Hunslet St Silas 47-53; Chapl Rothwell Hosp 46-53; R Garforth 53-59; Lect Leeds H Trin 59-65; Hon Can Ripon Cathl 63-81; V Leeds St Jo Ev 65-75; V Leeds H Trin 75-81; Dir Post-Ord Tr 75-81; rtd 81. *Flat 4, Bramhope Manor, Moor Road, Bramhope, Leeds LS16 9HJ* Tel 0113-284 2142

HAMMETT, Barry Keith. b 47. Magd Coll Ox BA71 MA74. St Steph Ho Ox 71. **d** 74 **p** 75. C Plymouth St Pet *Ex* 74-77; Chapl RN 77-86; Staff Chapl to Chapl of The Fleet from 86. *Royal Naval Chaplaincy Service, Room 203, Victory Building, HM Naval Base, Portsmouth PO1 3LS* Tel (01705) 727903 Fax 727112

HAMMOND, Mrs Barbara Watson. b 33. ACP70 Lanc Univ MA79. Bp Otter Coll TCert53 S'wark Ord Course DipRS92. **d** 92 **p** 94. NSM Upper Norwood St Jo *S'wark* 92-94; Hon C Spring Park All SS 94-97. *27 Maisemore Gardens, Emsworth, Hants PO10 7JU* Tel (01243) 370531 Mobile 0802-482974 E-mail brian@br2811.demon.co.uk

HAMMOND, Canon Betty Marian. b 27. Gilmore Ho. **dss** 84 **d** 87 **p** 94. Gosport Ch Ch *Portsm* 84-87; C 87-93; C 94-95; Par Dn 93-94; Hon Can Portsm Cathl 92-95; rtd 95. *10 Alvara Road, Gosport, Hants PO12 2HY* Tel (01705) 583068

HAMMOND, Canon Brian Leonard. b 31. Bris Univ BSc54. Wells Th Coll 56. **d** 58 **p** 59. C Clapham H Trin *S'wark* 58-62; V Walworth All SS and St Steph 62-72; V S Merstham 72-87; RD Reigate 80-86; Hon Can S'wark Cathl 83-97; V Spring Park All SS 87-97; rtd 97. *27 Maisemore Gardens, Emsworth, Hants PO10 7JU* Tel (01243) 370531 Mobile 0802-482974 E-mail brian@br2811.demon.co.uk

HAMMOND, Charles Kemble. b 10. TCD BA33 MA37. TCD Div Sch Div Test33. **d** 34 **p** 35. C Willowfield *D & D* 35-37; C Belfast St Donard 37; Australia from 37; rtd 78. *36 William Street, Avalon Beach, NSW, Australia 2107* Tel Sydney (2) 9918 8025

HAMMOND, Eric Penharwood. b 08. St Chad's Coll Dur BA31 DipTh32 MA47. **d** 32 **p** 33. C N Gosforth *Newc* 32-36; C Knowle St Martin *Bris* 36-42; C Bath H Trin *B & W* 42-43; R Westborough w Dry Doddington and Stubton *Linc* 43-52; V Mickleton *Glouc* 52-74; rtd 74. *St Francis, Outlands Lane, Curdridge, Southampton SO30 2HD* Tel (01489) 783324

HAMMOND, Frank. b 49. Linc Th Coll 75. **d** 77 **p** 78. C Sutton *Liv* 77-79; C Blundellsands St Nic 80-83. *13 Leicester Avenue, Crosby, Liverpool L22 2BA*

HAMMOND, Lindsay John. b 57. Southn Univ BA83. Sarum & Wells Th Coll 84. **d** 86 **p** 87. C Ashford *Cant* 86-90; V Appledore w Brookland, Fairfield, Brenzett etc from 90; Hon Min Can Cant Cathl from 93; P-in-c Stone-in-Oxney from 95; RD S Lympne from 95. *The Vicarage, Appledore, Ashford, Kent TN26 2DB* Tel (01233) 758250

HAMMOND, Mary. b 15. St Aid Coll Dur BA51 Maria Grey Coll Lon CertEd52. Roch and S'wark Dss Ho 40. **dss** 43 **d** 87.

Australia 68-73; Abp Langton Sch Beare Green 73-75; rtd 75; Perm to Offic *Linc* 75-87; Perm to Offic *Win* 87-89; Perm to Offic *Ex* from 95. *27 Homebourne House, Belle Vue Road, Paignton, Devon TQ4 6PT* Tel (01803) 520249

HAMMOND, Canon Peter. b 21. Mert Coll Ox BA48 MA53 Salonica Univ 48. Cuddesdon Coll 50. **d** 51 **p** 52. C Summertown *Ox* 51-53; Gen Sec Angl and E Chs Assn 53-55; C Soho St Anne w St Thos and St Pet *Lon* 53-55; V Stowe *Ox* 55-56; R Radclive 55-56; R Bagendon *Glouc* 56-61; Lic to Offic *York* 62-83; Perm to Offic *Linc* 83-87; Can and Preb Linc Cathl from 87; rtd 90. *Flat 2, 2 Greestone Place, Lincoln LN2 1PP* Tel (01522) 543047

HAMMOND, Peter Clark. b 27. Linc Coll Ox BA49 MA53. Wells Th Coll 51. **d** 52 **p** 53. C Willesborough *Cant* 52-55; C Croydon 55-59; R Barham 60-66; V Walmer 66-85; V Rolvenden 85-89; rtd 89; Perm to Offic *Ely* from 89. *19 Hardwick Street, Cambridge CB3 9JA* Tel (01223) 467425

HAMNETT, Herbert Arnold. b 22. K Coll Lon BSc49. Qu Coll Birm 49. **d** 51 **p** 52. C Greenhill St Jo *Lon* 51-54; C Horsham *Chich* 55-60; R Yapton w Ford 60-87; rtd 87; Perm to Offic *St E* from 87. *Clarence House, Stradbrooke Road, Fressingfield, Eye, Suffolk IP21 5PP*

HAMPEL, Michael Hans Joachim. b 67. Univ Coll Dur BA89. Westcott Ho Cam CTMin93. **d** 93 **p** 94. C Whitworth w Spennymoor *Dur* 93-97; C Spennymoor, Whitworth and Merrington from 97; Prec, Sacr and Min Can Dur Cathl from 97. *16A The College, Durham DH1 3EQ* Tel 0191-384 2481

HAMPSON, Claude Eric. b 25. Rhodes Univ BA49. St Paul's Grahamstown LTh50. **d** 50 **p** 51. S Africa 50-54; C Greenford H Cross *Lon* 54-58; Sec Fellowship of SS Alb and Sergius 58-60; Australia 60-74; Adn of the W 67-74; Vietnam 74-75; V Kilburn St Aug w St Jo *Lon* 75-77; Australia from 77; rtd 85. *Box 107, Edgecliff, NSW, Australia 2027* Tel Sydney (2) 327 8215 Fax 362 4063

HAMPSON, David. b 46. Chich Th Coll 69. **d** 72 **p** 73. C Penrith *Carl* 72-78; V Crosscrake 78-95; V Crosscrake and Preston Patrick 95; P-in-c Arnside 95-97; rtd 97. *81 Rectory Road, North Ashton, Wigan, Lancs WN4 0QD*

HAMPSON, Miss Judith Elizabeth. b 50. I M Marsh Coll of Physical Educn Liv BEd72 Open Univ BA89. Ripon Coll Cuddesdon 90. **d** 92 **p** 94. C Alnwick St Mich and St Paul *Newc* 92-96; R Allendale w Whitfield from 96. *Allendale Rectory, 16 Forstersteads, Allendale, Hexham, Northd NE47 9DA* Tel (01434) 683336

HAMPSON, Michael John. b 67. Jes Coll Ox BA88. Ripon Coll Cuddesdon 88. **d** 91 **p** 92. C W Burnley *Blackb* 91-93; C Harlow St Mary Magd *Chelmsf* from 93. *39 Hadley Grange, Church Langley, Harlow, Essex CM17 9PQ* Tel (01279) 451382

HAMPSON, Robert Edward. b 58. **d** 97. C Chingford SS Pet and Paul *Chelmsf* from 97. *2 Sunnyside Drive, London E4 7DZ* Tel 0181-529 3929

HAMPSTEAD, Archdeacon of. *See* WHEATLEY, The Ven Peter William

HAMPTON, Canon John Waller. b 28. Linc Coll Ox BA51 MA58. Westcott Ho Cam 51. **d** 53 **p** 54. C Rugby St Andr *Cov* 53-56; Chapl St Paul's Sch Hammersmith 56-65; Chapl St Paul's Girls' Sch Hammersmith 60-65; V Gaydon w Chadshunt *Cov* 65-69; Asst Dir RE 65-70; C-in-c Warwick St Nic 69-75; Fell Qu Coll Birm 75-76; P-in-c Wetton *Lich* 76-82; P-in-c Alstonfield 76-82; P-in-c Sheen 76-80; RD Alstonfield 80-82; P-in-c Butterton 80-82; P-in-c Warslow and Elkstones 80-82; P-in-c Broadway *Worc* 82-91; V 91-93; RD Evesham 87-93; Hon Can Worc Cathl 88-93; rtd 93; Perm to Offic *Ab* from 93. *41 Craigton Terrace, Aberdeen AB1 7RN* Tel (01224) 310074

HAMPTON, Stephen William Peter. b 72. Magd Coll Cam BA93. Wycliffe Hall Ox 95. **d** 96 **p** 97. C St Neots *Ely* from 96. *20 Avenue Road, St Neots, Huntingdon, Cambs PE19 1LJ* Tel (01480) 219207

HAMPTON, Terence Alastair Godfrey Macpherson. b 38. Bris Univ PGCE73. Lon Coll of Div ALCD63 BD68. **d** 64 **p** 65. C Clifton Ch Ch w Em *Bris* 64-66; C Ickenham *Lon* 66-67; C Patchway *Bris* 67-73; TV Jersey St Brelade *Win* 73-83; R Jersey Grouville 83-94. *Address temp unknown*

HAMPTON-SMITH, David Charles. b 22. Ch Ch Ox BA48 MA48. Cuddesdon Coll 48. **d** 50 **p** 51. C Shrewsbury St Chad *Lich* 50-53; C Kingswood *S'wark* 53-56; V Howe Bridge *Man* 56-62; Chapl Woodbridge Sch 62-65; Australia from 65; rtd 87. *139 Esplanade, Port Noarlunga South, S Australia 5167* Tel Adelaide (8) 386 1284

HANCE, Stephen John. b 66. Portsm Poly BSc89 Nottm Univ BTh92 MA93. St Jo Coll Nottm 90. **d** 93 **p** 94. C Southsea St Jude *Portsm* 93-96; TV Tollington *Lon* from 96. *St Saviour's Vicarage, Hanley Road, London N4 3DQ* Tel 0171-272 1246

HANCOCK, Alfred John. b 28. Lon Univ BSc52. Ex & Truro NSM Scheme 74. **d** 77 **p** 78. NSM Phillack w Gwithian and Gwinear *Truro* 77-78 and 86-96; NSM Camborne 78-86; NSM Godrevy from 96; rtd 96. *Redlands, Rosewarne Downs, Camborne, Cornwall TR14 0BD* Tel (01209) 713527

HANCOCK, Mrs Barbara. b 40. TCert60. EMMTC 93. **d** 96. NSM Caythorpe *Linc* from 96. *Fulbeck Cottage, Sudthorpe Hill, Fulbeck, Grantham, Lincs NG32 3LE* Tel (01400) 272644

HANCOCK, Bernard. b 13. Wycliffe Hall Ox 61. **d** 62 **p** 63. C Gt Malvern St Mary *Worc* 62-65; R Peopleton 65-70; R Hagley 70-76; rtd 78. *The Old Post Office, Birlingham, Pershore, Worcs WR10 3AB* Tel (01386) 750641

HANCOCK, Dr Christopher David. b 54. Qu Coll Ox BA75 MA80 St Jo Coll Dur PhD84. Cranmer Hall Dur BA78. **d** 82 **p** 83. C Leic H Trin w St Jo *Leic* 82-85; Chapl Magd Coll Cam 85-88; USA 88-94; V Cambridge H Trin *Ely* from 94. *Holy Trinity Vicarage, 1 Selwyn Gardens, Cambridge CB3 0XG* Tel (01223) 354774

HANCOCK, David Richard. b 48. Chich Th Coll. **d** 89 **p** 90. C Maidstone All SS and St Phil w Tovil *Cant* 89-93; CF 90-93; P-in-c Sellindge w Monks Horton and Stowting etc *Cant* from 93. *The Vicarage, Harringe Lane, Sellindge, Ashford, Kent TN25 6HP* Tel (01303) 813168

HANCOCK, Douglas Charles. b 16. Lon Univ BSc39 PhD52. Wycliffe Hall Ox 59. **d** 60 **p** 61. C Bournemouth St Alb *Win* 60-64; R Baughurst w Ramsdale 64-70; V Bournemouth St Andr 70-79; RD Alresford 79-84; R Hinton Ampner w Bramdean and Kilmeston 79-84; rtd 84; Perm to Offic *Win* from 84; Perm to Offic *Sarum* from 86. *Flat 40, Fairhaven Court, 32/34 Sea Road, Bournemouth BH5 1DG* Tel (01202) 301942

HANCOCK, Preb Frances Margaret. b 34. LMH Ox BA56 MA94 LSE DipPM57. Gilmore Course IDC81. **dss** 81 **d** 87 **p** 94. Isleworth All SS *Lon* 81-87; TD Ross w Brampton Abbotts, Bridstow and Peterstow *Heref* 87-93; Dioc Adv on Women in Min from 93; NSM Peterchurch w Vowchurch, Turnastone and Dorstone from 93; rtd 94; Preb Heref Cathl *Heref* from 96. *Brockwell, Peterchurch, Hereford HR2 0TE* Tel (01981) 550457

HANCOCK, Ivor Michael. b 31. Lon Univ BD60. Linc Th Coll 65. **d** 66 **p** 67. C Havant *Portsm* 66-69; V Gosport Ch Ch 69-76; P-in-c Southend St Alb *Chelmsf* 76-80; V Hawley H Trin *Guildf* 80-96; V Minley 80-96; RD Aldershot 83-88; rtd 96. *Assisi, 15 Whaley Road, Wokingham, Berks RG40 1QA* Tel 0118-962 9976

HANCOCK, John Clayton. b 36. Dur Univ BA58. Cranmer Hall Dur DipTh60. **d** 60 **p** 61. C Newbarns w Hawcoat *Carl* 60-65; V Church Coniston 65-76; R Torver 66-76; P-in-c Heversham 76-77; V 77-93; V Heversham and Milnthorpe from 93. *The Vicarage, Woodhouse Lane, Heversham, Milnthorpe, Cumbria LA7 7EW* Tel (015395) 63125

HANCOCK, Canon John Mervyn. b 38. St Jo Coll Dur BA61 DipTh64 MA70 Hertf Coll Ox BA63 MA66. Cranmer Hall Dur 63. **d** 64 **p** 65. C Bishopwearmouth St Gabr *Dur* 64-67; V Hebburn St Jo 67-87; RD Jarrow 83-92; V S Westoe from 87; Hon Can Dur Cathl from 88; C-in-c S Shields St Aid w St Steph 92-95. *St Michael's Vicarage, Westoe Road, South Shields, Tyne & Wear NE33 3PJ* Tel 0191-425 2074

HANCOCK, John Raymond. b 11. FBOA32. St Boniface Warminster. **d** 62 **p** 63. C Andover St Mich *Win* 62-65; R Guernsey St Michel du Valle 65-79; rtd 79; Perm to Offic *Portsm* 82-94. *Kingsomborne, The Broadway, Totland Bay, Isle of Wight PO39 0BL* Tel (01983) 754321

HANCOCK, Leonard George Edward. b 28. Open Univ BA81 Leic Univ MEd84. ALCD52. **d** 52 **p** 56. C Bilston St Leon *Lich* 52-53; C Sheff St Swithun *Sheff* 56-58; C Ecclesfield 58; C-in-c Ecclesfield St Paul CD 58-63; V Sheff St Mary w St Simon w St Matthias 63-72; V Michael *S & M* 72-76; R Loughborough All SS *Leic* 76-83; R Loughborough All SS and H Trin 83-93; rtd 93; Perm to Offic *Leic* from 93. *5 Rumsey Close, Quorn, Loughborough, Leics LE12 8EZ* Tel (01509) 620012

HANCOCK, Malcolm James. b 50. AGSM73. Sarum & Wells Th Coll 85. **d** 87 **p** 88. C Sandhurst *Ox* 87-90; P-in-c Bradbourne and Brassington *Derby* 90-92; TV Wirksworth 92-95; V Tunbridge Wells K Chas *Roch* from 95. *The Vicarage, 5D Frant Road, Tunbridge Wells, Kent TN2 5TA* Tel (01892) 525455

HANCOCK, Ms Mary Joy. b 40. Auckland Univ BA61 Auckland Teachers' Coll PGCE62 Man Univ CQSW69. S'wark Ord Course 91. **d** 94 **p** 95. NSM Merton St Mary *S'wark* from 94. *55 Huntspill Street, London SW17 0AA* Tel 0181-946 8984

HANCOCK, Michael John. b 33. Lich Th Coll 55. **d** 58 **p** 59. C Rumboldswyke *Chich* 58-62; C Hampstead Garden Suburb *Lon* 63-66; V Cinderford St Jo *Glouc* 66-67; C Brockworth 67-69; C Romsey *Win* 69-72; C Moordown 72-75; C Christchurch 75-78; V Guernsey St Jo 78-89; rtd 89. *10 la rue du Tertre, Vale, Guernsey GY3 5QX* Tel (01481) 48887

HANCOCK, Nigel John. b 35. K Coll Cam BA63 MA67. EAMTC 86. **d** 89 **p** 91. NSM Cambridge St Mary Less *Ely* from 89; PV St Jo Coll Cam from 95. *5 Atherton Close, Cambridge CB4 2BE* Tel (01223) 355828

HANCOCK, Paul. b 43. AKC66. **d** 67 **p** 68. C Wednesbury St Paul Wood Green *Lich* 67-70; C Rugeley 70-73; V Rickerscote 73-75; R Blisland w St Breward *Truro* 75-78; V Mansfield St Lawr *S'well* 78-82; P-in-c Charleton *Ex* 82-83; P-in-c E Portlemouth, S Pool and Chivelstone 82-83; R Charleton w Buckland Tout Saints etc 83-95; RD Woodleigh 88-95; P-in-c Plymouth Crownhill Ascension from 95. *The Vicarage, 33 Tavistock Road, Plymouth PL5 3AF* Tel (01752) 783617

HANCOCK, Paul Byron. b 51. Bris Univ BA71 MA73. Ripon Hall Ox 72. **d** 75 **p** 76. C Croydon *Cant* 75-78; USA from 78. *3200 Woodland Ridge Boulevard, Baton Rouge, Louisiana 70816, USA*

HANCOCK, Canon Peter. b 55. Selw Coll Cam BA76 MA79. Oak Hill Th Coll BA80. **d** 80 **p** 81. C Portsdown *Portsm* 80-83; C Radipole and Melcombe Regis *Sarum* 83-87; V Cowplain *Portsm* from 87; RD Havant from 93; Hon Can Portsm Cathl from 97. *The Vicarage, Padnell Road, Cowplain, Waterlooville, Hants PO8 8DZ* Tel (01705) 262295

HANCOCK, Peter Ernest. b 33. Man Univ BA54. Qu Coll Birm 54. **d** 56 **p** 57. C Wigston Magna *Leic* 56-59; C Hucknall Torkard *S'well* 59-61; V Sutton in Ashfield St Mich 61-65; Dioc Youth Officer *Portsm* 65-73; R Broughton Astley *Leic* 73-86; Dioc Adv for Min of Health and Healing *B & W* 86-93; rtd 94. *24 Mulberry Road, Congresbury, Bristol BS19 5HD* Tel (01934) 838920

HANCOCK, Peter Thompson. b 31. G&C Coll Cam BA54 MA58. Ridley Hall Cam 54. **d** 56 **p** 57. C Beckenham Ch Ch *Roch* 56-59; Chapl St Lawr Coll Ramsgate 59-62; Chapl Stowe Sch Bucks 62-67; Asst Chapl and Lect Emb Ch Paris *Eur* 67-70; V Walton H Trin *Ox* 70-80; Canada 80-84; V Northwood H Trin *Lon* 84-94; rtd 94. *Roughwood Oak, Deadhearn Lane, Chalfont St Giles, Bucks HP8 4HG* Tel (01494) 872324

HANCOCK, Reginald Legassicke (Rex). b 28. Trin Coll Cam BA51 MA57. Clifton Th Coll 60. **d** 61 **p** 62. C Finchley Ch Ch *Lon* 61-63; CF 63-82; R Quantoxhead *B & W* 82-93; rtd 93; Perm to Offic *B & W* from 94. *Stowleys, Bossinton Lane, Porlock, Minehead, Somerset TA24 8HD* Tel (01643) 862327

HANCOCK, Richard Manuel Ashley. b 69. Linc Th Coll 94 Westcott Ho Cam 95. **d** 97. C Didcot St Pet *Ox* from 97. *25 Sovereign Close, Didcot, Oxon OX11 8TR* Tel (01235) 819949

HANCOCK, Ronald Edward. b 24. MRCS49 LRCP49. **d** 78 **p** 79. Hon C Highbury Ch Ch *Lon* 78; Hon C Highbury Ch Ch w St Jo 79-82; R Puddletown and Tolpuddle *Sarum* 82-90; rtd 90. *9 Churchward Avenue, Weymouth, Dorset DT3 6NZ* Tel (01305) 832558

HANCOCKS, Graeme. b 58. Univ of Wales (Ban) BD79. Linc Th Coll 79. **d** 81 **p** 82. C Denbigh and Nantglyn *St As* 81-84; Asst Chapl Oslo St Edm *Eur* 84-88; Chapl Stockholm 88-89; Chapl Marseille w St Raphael Aix-en-Provence etc 89; Chapl Gothenburg w Halmstad, Jönköping etc 90-93; Chapl Southn Univ Hosps NHS Trust from 93. *Chaplaincy Centre, Southampton General Hospital, Tremara Road, Southampton SO19 6TD* Tel (01703) 798517

HANCOX, Granville Leonard. b 32. Lich Th Coll 67. **d** 70 **p** 71. C Caverswall *Lich* 70-73; C Norton in the Moors 73-76; P-in-c Leek St Luke 76-79; TV Leek 79-83; V Priors Lee and St Georges from 83. *The Vicarage, Ashley Road, Telford, Shropshire TF2 9LF* Tel (01952) 612923

✠**HAND, The Most Revd Geoffrey David.** b 18. CBE75. Or Coll Ox BA41 MA46. Cuddesdon Coll 40. **d** 42 **p** 43 **c** 50. C Heckmondwike *Wakef* 42-46; Papua New Guinea 46-83; Bp Coadjutor New Guinea 50-63; Adn N New Guinea 50-63; Bp Papua New Guinea 63-77; Abp Papua New Guinea 77-83; Bp Port Moresby 77-83; rtd 83; P-in-c E w W Rudham *Nor* 83-85; P-in-c Houghton 83-85. *121 Brackenbury Road, London W6 0BQ*

HAND, Michael Anthony (Tony). b 63. SROT York Univ BA84 DipCOT88. St Jo Coll Nottm MA95. **d** 95 **p** 96. C Lutterworth w Cotesbach *Leic* from 95. *The Vicarage, Lutterworth Road, Bitteswell, Lutterworth, Leics LE17 4RX* Tel (01455) 556367

HAND, Nigel Arthur. b 54. St Jo Coll Nottm. **d** 84 **p** 85. C Birm St Luke *Birm* 84-88; C Walton H Trin *Ox* 88-89; TV 89-97; C Selly Park St Steph and St Wulstan *Birm* from 97. *927 Pershore Road, Selly Park, Birmingham B29 7PS* Tel 0121-472 2514

HAND, Peter Michael. b 42. Univ Coll Ox BA63 Lon Univ BSc75. Sarum & Wells Th Coll 77. **d** 80 **p** 81. NSM Shaston *Sarum* 80-81; C Tisbury 81-83; C Glastonbury St Jo w Godney *B & W* 83-84; C Glastonbury w Meare, W Pennard and Godney 84-87; V High Littleton from 87; RD Midsomer Norton from 92. *The Vicarage, High Littleton, Bristol BS18 5HG* Tel (01761) 472097

✠**HANDFORD, The Rt Revd George Clive.** b 37. Hatf Coll Dur BA61. Qu Coll Birm DipTh63. **d** 63 **p** 64 **c** 90. C Mansfield St Pet *S'well* 63-67; Lebanon 67-74; Dean Jerusalem 74-78; UAE 78-83; Adn Gulf 78-83; V Kneesall w Laxton *S'well* 83-84; P-in-c Wellow 83-84; RD Tuxford and Norwell 83-84; Adn Nottingham 84-90; Suff Bp Warw *Cov* 90-96; Bp Cyprus and the Gulf from 96. *2 Grigori Afxentiou Street, PO Box 2075, Nicosia, Cyprus*

HANDFORD, John Richard. b 32. Sydney Univ BSc52 Univ Coll Lon MSc58 Surrey Univ MA84 Lon Univ DipTh67. Lon Coll of Div 68. **d** 69 **p** 70. Asst Chapl Wellington Coll Berks 69-80; Hon C Windlesham *Guildf* 87-92; Perm to Offic from 92. *Desiderata, 33 Chertsey Road, Windlesham, Surrey GU20 6EW* Tel (01276) 472397

HANDFORD, Maurice. b 25. Oak Hill Th Coll 48. **d** 52 **p** 53. C Dublin Miss Ch *D & G* 52-55; Org & Deputation Sec ICM (N & Midl) 55-58; C-in-c Buxton Trin Prop Chpl *Derby* 58-87; I Clondevaddock w Portsalon and Leatbeg *D & R* 87-90; Bp's Dom Chapl 88-90; rtd 90; Perm to Offic *Ches* from 90; Perm to Offic *Derby* from 92. *9 Birtlespool Road, Cheadle Hulme, Cheadle, Cheshire SK8 5JZ* Tel 0161-485 3134

HANDFORTH, Canon Richard Brereton. b 31. St Pet Coll Ox BA55 MA60. Westcott Ho Cam 63. **d** 64 **p** 65. C Hornchurch St Andr *Chelmsf* 64-65; Hong Kong 65-73; Chapl CMS Fellowship Ho Chislehurst 73-75; Hon C Chislehurst St Nic *Roch* 73-75; Home Educn Sec CMS 75-83; Perm to Offic *Roch* 75-83; V Biggin Hill 83-88; Inter-change Adv CMS 88-96; Perm to Offic *Roch* 88-95; Hon C Plaistow St Mary from 95; Hon Can Lagos from 95; rtd 96. *67 Murray Avenue, Bromley BR1 3DJ* Tel 0181-460 0238

HANDLEY, The Ven Anthony Michael. b 36. Selw Coll Cam BA60 MA64. Chich Th Coll 60. **d** 62 **p** 63. C Thorpe *Nor* 62-66; C Gaywood, Bawsey and Mintlyn 66-72; V Hellesdon 72-81; RD Nor N 80-81; Adn Nor 81-93; Adn Norfolk from 93. *40 Heigham Road, Norwich NR2 3AU* Tel (01603) 611808

HANDLEY, Dennis Francis. b 57. MIE79 TEng(CEI)80. Coll of Resurr Mirfield 82. **d** 85 **p** 86. C Headingley *Ripon* 85-88; C Rothwell 88-92; V Liversedge *Wakef* from 92. *Christ Church Vicarage, Knowler Hill, Liversedge, W Yorkshire WF15 6LJ* Tel (01924) 402414

HANDLEY, Harold. b 14. ACIS42 AACCA44 ACWA48. Bps' Coll Cheshunt 62. **d** 63 **p** 64. C Hitchin St Mary *St Alb* 63-65; V Totternhoe 65-79; C Ringwood *Win* 79-80; rtd 79; Perm to Offic *Win* 80-95. *Risdene, 16 Barton Court Avenue, New Milton, Hants BH25 7HD* Tel (01425) 611771

HANDLEY, John. b 38. Oak Hill Th Coll. **d** 83 **p** 84. C Witton w Brundall and Braydeston *Nor* 83-86; R Reedham w Cantley w Limpenhoe and Southwood 86-93; P-in-c E w W Harling and Bridgham w Roudham 93-95; R E w W Harling, Bridgham w Roudham and Larling 95-96; P-in-c Garboldisham w Blo' Norton, Riddlesworth etc 94-96; RD Thetford and Rockland from 95; P-in-c E w W Harling, Bridgham w Roudham and Larling 96-97; R E w W Harling, Bridgham w Roudham, Larling etc from 97. *The Rectory, Church Road, East Harling, Norwich NR16 2NB* Tel (01953) 717235

HANDLEY, Neil. b 40. St Aid Birkenhead 64. **d** 67 **p** 68. C Ashton Ch Ch *Man* 67-70; C Stretford All SS 70-73; C Tonge 73; C-in-c Bolton St Jo Breightmet CD 74-79; V Bolton St Jo 79-80; R Broughton 80-87; Perm to Offic *Eur* from 90. *La Taire du Grel, 24250 Domme, France* Tel France (33) 53 28 23 42

HANDLEY, Terence Anthony. b 55. Trent Poly HNC Open Univ BA89. Trin Coll Bris 85. **d** 87 **p** 88. C Meole Brace *Lich* 87-91; V Stafford St Paul Forebridge 91-94. *8 The Croft, Cheslyn Hay, Staffs WS6 7QB*

HANDLEY, Timothy John. b 63. St Steph Ho Ox 94. **d** 96 **p** 97. C St Marychurch *Ex* from 96. *100 Hartop Road, Torquay TQ1 4QJ* Tel (01803) 311629

HANDLEY MACMATH, Terence. b 59. Golds Coll Lon BA80 K Coll Cam BA93. Westcott Ho Cam 91. **d** 94 **p** 95. NSM Southwold *St E* from 94. *Manor Garden Cottage, Woodley's Yard, Southwold, Suffolk IP18 6HP* Tel (01502) 722153

HANDS, Graeme. b 35. Cranmer Hall Dur. **d** 61 **p** 62. C Atherstone *Cov* 61-63; Chapl Aldwickbury Sch Harpenden 63-66; C Cov St Alb *Cov* 66-68; P-in-c Warwick St Paul 68-80; V Radford from 80; RD Cov N 87-93. *The Vicarage, 21 Tulliver Street, Coventry CV6 3BY* Tel (01203) 598449

HANDSCOMBE, Canon Richard John. b 23. Cuddesdon Coll 58. **d** 60 **p** 61. C Shrub End *Chelmsf* 60-63; V Fingringhoe 63-86; P-in-c E Donyland 75-77; R Fingringhoe w E Donyland 86-90; R Fingringhoe w E Donyland and Abberton etc from 90; Hon Can Chelmsf Cathl from 89. *The Rectory, Fingringhoe, Colchester CO5 7BN* Tel (01206) 729383

HANDY, Canon Maurice Arthur. b 04. TCD BA26 MA34. **d** 27 **p** 28. C Dublin St Steph *D & G* 27-36; Hd TCD Miss Belfast 36-39; C Dublin Donnybrook 40-41; P-in-c Dublin Whitechurch 41-55; I 55-65; Can Ch Ch Cathl Dublin 63-72; Warden of Ch's Min of Healing in Ireland 65-72; I Hacketstown *C & O* 72-76; rtd 76. *Rathfarnham Convalescent Home, Stocking Lane, Rathfarnham, Dublin 16, Irish Republic* Tel Dublin (1) 493 3166

HANFORD, William Richard. b 38. Keble Coll Ox BA60 MA64 Lon Univ BD66. St Steph Ho Ox 60. **d** 63 **p** 64. C Roath St Martin *Llan* 63-66; C Llantwit Major 67-68; PV Llan Cathl 68-72; Chapl RN 72-76; Lic to Offic *Eur* 74-76; Hon C Eastbourne St Sav and St Pet *Chich* 76-77; C Brighton St Pet 77-78; Can Res and Prec Guildf Cathl *Guildf* 78-83; V Ewell from 83. *St Mary's Vicarage, 14 Church Street, Ewell, Epsom, Surrey KT17 2AQ* Tel 0181-393 2643

HANKE, Mrs Hilary Claire. b 53. Qu Coll Birm BTh93. **d** 93 **p** 94. C Kempsey and Severn Stoke w Croome d'Abitot *Worc* 93-97; TV Wordsley from 97. *25 Middleway Avenue, Wordsley, Stourbridge, W Midlands DY8 5NB* Tel (01384) 293350

HANKEY, Miss Dorothy Mary. b 38. CertEd65. Trin Coll Bris 75. **dss** 78 **d** 87 **p** 94. Wigan St Jas w St Thos *Liv* 78-84; Middleton *Man* 84-85; Litherland Ch Ch *Liv* 85-89; Par Dn 87-89; Par Dn Blackpool St Mark *Blackb* 89-94; C 94-95; C Blackpool St Paul from 95. *33 Courtfield Avenue, Blackpool FY2 0UN* Tel (01253) 397735

HANKINS, Clifford James. b 24. Chich Th Coll 70 SSC87. **d** 72 **p** 73. C Henfield *Chich* 72-76; V Fernhurst 76-84; V Mithian w Mt Hawke *Truro* 84-89; rtd 89; Hon C W Wittering and Birdham w Itchenor *Chich* from 90. *2 Kestrel Close, East Wittering, Chichester, W Sussex PO20 8PQ* Tel (01243) 672164

HANLON, Thomas Kyle. b 72. QUB BA94 TCD BTh97. **d** 97. C Bangor *D & D* from 97. *36 Stratford Road, Bangor, Co Down BT19 6ZN* Tel (01247) 273173

HANMER, Canon Richard John. b 38. Peterho Cam BA61 MA65. Linc Th Coll 62. **d** 64 **p** 65. C Sheff St Swithun *Sheff* 64-69; Bp's Chapl *Nor* 69-73; V Cinderhill *S'well* 73-81; V Eaton *Nor* 81-94; Dioc Chapl MU from 91; Hon Can Nor Cathl from 93; Can Res Nor Cathl from 94. *52 The Close, Norwich NR1 4EG* Tel (01603) 665210

HANNA, John. b 44. Trin Coll Bris DipHE82 Lon Bible Coll BA83 Westcott Ho Cam 86. **d** 87 **p** 88. C Denton Ch Ch *Man* 87-91; V Higher Walton *Blackb* from 91. *The Vicarage, Blackburn Road, Higher Walton, Preston PR5 4EA* Tel (01772) 35406

HANNA, Peter Thomas. b 45. ACII66 GIFireE75. CITC 85. **d** 88 **p** 89. NSM Cork St Fin Barre's Union *C, C & R* 88-95; Min Can Cork Cathl from 92; Dio Info Officer 94-95. *Mount Windsor, Farnahoe, Inishannon, Co Cork, Irish Republic* Tel Cork (21) 775470

HANNA, Canon Robert Charles. b 49. Oak Hill Th Coll 75. **d** 77 **p** 78. C Coleraine *Conn* 77-82; I Convoy w Monellan and Donaghmore *D & R* 82-94; Can Raphoe Cathl 88-94; I Drumcliffe w Kilnasoolagh *L & K* from 94. *St Columba's Rectory, Bindon Street, Ennis, Co Clare, Irish Republic* Tel Ennis (65) 20109 Fax as telephone

HANNAFORD, Dr Robert. b 53. Ex Univ BEd76 MA78 PhD87. St Steph Ho Ox 78. **d** 80 **p** 81. C Ex St Jas *Ex* 80-83; Chapl Ex Univ 83-88; Tutor St Steph Ho Ox 89-92; Sen Lect Ch Ch Coll Cant from 92. *25 Goudhurst Close, Canterbury, Kent CT2 7TU* Tel (01227) 784148 or 767700

HANNAH, John Douglas. b 39. St Paul's Grahamstown DipTh71. **d** 71 **p** 72. S Africa 71-85; C Finchley St Mary *Lon* 85-91; V Balsall Heath St Paul *Birm* from 91. *The Vicarage, 26 Lincoln Street, Balsall Heath, Birmingham B12 9EX* Tel 0121-440 2219

HANNAH, Richard. b 24. CCC Ox BA49 MA53. St Mich Coll Llan 49. **d** 51 **p** 52. C Cardiff St Jo *Llan* 51-55; C Usk *Mon* 55-58; V Llanfihangel Crucorney w Oldcastle etc 58-63; R Shenington w Alkerton *Ox* 63-69; R Shenington and Alkerton w Shutford 69-79; RD Deddington 78-84; P-in-c Deddington w Clifton and Hempton 79-80; V Deddington w Barford, Clifton and Hempton 81-89; rtd 89. *Cwm Brynnau, Riverside, Llyswen, Brecon LD3 0LJ* Tel (01874) 754716

HANNAY, Robert Fleming. b 23. Ch Ch Ox MA49. Cuddesdon Coll 63. **d** 65 **p** 66. C Church Stretton *Heref* 65-69; R Garsington *Ox* 69-79; R The Claydons 79-85; rtd 88. *The Old Rectory, Yatesbury, Calne, Wilts SN11 8YE* Tel (01249) 817311

HANNEN, Robert John. b 65. W Glam Inst of HE DipHE87 BEd89. St Mich Coll Llan DipTh91 BTh92. **d** 92 **p** 93. C Gorseinon *S & B* 92-95; P-in-c Swansea St Luke from 95. *St Luke's Rectory, 8 Vicarage Lane, Cwmdu, Swansea SA5 8EU* Tel (01792) 586300

✠**HANNON, The Rt Revd Brian Desmond Anthony.** b 36. TCD BA59 MA62. TCD Div Sch Div Test61. **d** 61 **p** 62 **c** 86. C Clooney *D & R* 61-64; I Desertmartin 64-69; I Londonderry Ch Ch 69-82; RD Londonderry 77-82; I Enniskillen *Clogh* 82-86; Preb Clogh Cathl 82-84; Dean Clogh 85-86; Bp Clogh from 86. *The See House, Fivemiletown, Co Tyrone BT75 0QP* Tel (01365) 521265 Fax as telephone

HANSEN, Harold Percy. b 05. St Chad's Coll Dur BA29 DipTh30 MA32. **d** 30 **p** 31. C Leeds St Aid *Ripon* 30-32; C Keighley *Bradf* 32-35; C Stella *Dur* 35-38; V Cassop cum Quarrington 38-50; CF (EC) 41-46; R Croxdale *Dur* 50-58; V Studham w Whipsnade *St Alb* 58-66; R Campton 66-70; V Shefford 66-70; rtd 70. *Moorlands, Moor Road, Cotherstone, Barnard Castle, Co Durham DL12 9PH* Tel (01833) 650726

HANSEN, Mrs Moira Jacqueline. b 55. K Coll Lon BSc76. Oak Hill Th Coll BA88. **d** 88 **p** 96. Par Dn Finchley Ch Ch *Lon* 88-91; Par Dn Broadwater St Mary *Chich* 91-94; Chapl Oak Hill Th Coll from 94. *4 Farm Lane, London N14 4PP, or Oak Hill College, Chase Side, London N14 4PS* Tel 0181-441 5992 or 449 0467

HANSEN, Neil Bertram. b 29. **d** 53 **p** 54. C Plymouth St Pet *Ex* 53-55; New Zealand from 55. *3 Mascot Street, Tawa, Wellington, New Zealand* Tel Wellington (4) 232 9983

HANSFORD, Gordon John. b 40. Southn Univ BSc61. Trin Coll Bris 77. **d** 79 **p** 80. C Ex St Leon w H Trin *Ex* 79-82; C Shirley *Win* 82-87; R Landcross, Littleham, Monkleigh etc *Ex* 87-96; TV Bideford, Northam, Westward Ho!, Appledore etc from 96; P-in-c Monkleigh from 96; RD Hartland from 96. *The Rectory, Weare Giffard, Bideford, Devon EX39 4QP* Tel (01237) 472017

HANSON, Christopher. b 48. Birm Bible Inst DipMin75 Wycliffe Hall Ox 87. **d** 89 **p** 90. C Heref St Pet w St Owen and St Jas *Heref* 89-91; C Plymouth St Andr w St Paul and St Geo *Ex* 91-93; C Devonport St Mich 93-94; TV Shebbear, Buckland Filleigh, Sheepwash etc from 94. *The Rectory, Petrockstowe, Okehampton, Devon EX20 3HQ* Tel (01837) 810499

HANSON, Dale Robert. b 57. Fitzw Coll Cam BA78 MA81 Univ of BC MA80. Ridley Hall Cam 81. **d** 84 **p** 85. C Much Woolton *Liv* 84-87; Hong Kong 87-91; TV Billingham St Aid *Dur* 91-95; C Dur St Nic from 95. *15 Providence Row, Durham DH1 1RS* Tel 0191-384 1065

HANSON, Canon John Westland. b 19. OBE74. St Jo Coll Dur BA41 DipTh43 MA44. **d** 43 **p** 44. C Louth w Welton-le-Wold *Linc* 43-50; Chapl and Lect RAF Flying Coll Manby 50-76; R Grimoldby w Manby 50-76; RD E Louthesk 60-68; Chief Examiner Relig Studies Cam Univ 66-82; Can and Preb Linc Cathl from 67; RD Louthesk 68-77; V Woodhall Spa and Kirkstead 76-88; P-in-c Langton w Woodhall 76-88; rtd 88. *Brookfield, 28 Tor-o-Moor Road, Woodhall Spa, Lincs LN10 6TD* Tel (01526) 352554

HANSON, Michael Beaumont. b 49. Ox Univ MA. N Ord Course. **d** 84 **p** 85. NSM Leeds St Geo *Ripon* from 84; Chapl Leeds Gr Sch from 84. *The Martlets, 9 Orville Gardens, Leeds LS6 2BS* Tel 0113-278 5370

HANSON, Peter Richard. b 45. ARCM. Chich Th Coll 72. **d** 75 **p** 76. C Forest Gate St Edm *Chelmsf* 75-79; C Chingford SS Pet and Paul 79-81; V Leytonstone H Trin Harrow Green 81-86; Dep Chapl HM Pris Wandsworth 86-88; Chapl HM Pris Lewes 88-91; rtd 91; Perm to Offic *Chich* from 91. *Flat 2, 39 St Anne's Crescent, Lewes, E Sussex BN7 1SB* Tel (01273) 471714

HANSON, Richard. b 14. Wells Th Coll 40. **d** 42 **p** 43. C Penrith St Andr *Carl* 42-45; C Ludlow *Heref* 45-48; W Germany 48-50; Chapl Geneva *Eur* 50-56; V Goole *Sheff* 56-60; RD Snaith and Hatfield 56-60; V Ecclesall 60-67; Chapl Milan *Eur* 67-72; V Harrow Weald All SS *Lon* 72-77; P-in-c Alfrick w Lulsley and Suckley *Worc* 77-78; P-in-c Leigh w Bransford 77-78; P-in-c Alfrick, Lulsley, Suckley, Leigh and Bransford 78; R 78-82; rtd 82; Perm to Offic *Linc* from 82. *The Rectory Bungalow, Horsington, Lincoln LN3 5EX* Tel (01526) 388696

HANSON, Robert Arthur. b 35. Keele Univ BA57 Birm Univ DipPTh96. St Steph Ho Ox 57 St Mich Coll Llan 59. **d** 60 **p** 61. C Longton St Mary and St Chad *Lich* 60-65; Chapl St Mary's Cathl *Edin* 65-69; R Glas St Matt *Glas* 69-79; R Paisley H Trin 79-87; V Walsall St Andr *Lich* 87-93; Perm to Offic *Worc* 94-97; C Kentish Town *Lon* from 97. *St Benets Church House, Ospringe Road, London NW5 2JB* Tel 0171-267 4720

HANSON, Timothy David. b 68. Oak Hill Th Coll BA95. **d** 95 **p** 96. C Boscombe St Jo *Win* from 95. *167 Southcote Road, Bournemouth BH1 3SP* Tel (01202) 397691

HAPGOOD-STRICKLAND, Peter Russell. b 57. BA. St Steph Ho Ox. **d** 83 **p** 84. C Ashford *Cant* 83-86; C Sheerness H Trin w St Paul 86-90; V Blackb St Thos w St Jude *Blackb* from 90. *St Jude's Vicarage, Accrington Road, Blackburn BB1 2AB* Tel (01254) 263259

HARBIDGE, Adrian Guy. b 48. St Jo Coll Dur BA70. Cuddesdon Coll 73. **d** 75 **p** 76. C Romsey *Win* 75-80; V Bournemouth St Andr 80-86; V Chandler's Ford from 86; RD Eastleigh from 93. *The Vicarage, Hursley Road, Eastleigh, Hants SO53 2FT* Tel (01703) 252597

HARBORD, Paul Geoffrey. b 56. Keble Coll Ox BA78 MA86. Chich Th Coll 81. **d** 83 **p** 84. C Rawmarsh w Parkgate *Sheff* 83-86; C Doncaster St Geo 86-90; C-in-c St Edm Anchorage Lane CD 90-95; V Masbrough from 95. *St Paul's Vicarage, 256 Kimberworth Road, Rotherham, S Yorkshire S61 1HG* Tel (01709) 557810

HARBORD, Philip James. b 56. St Cath Coll Ox BA77. Cranmer Hall Dur 78. **d** 80 **p** 81. C Enfield St Andr *Lon* 80-83; CMS 84-88; Pakistan 84-88; C Clay Hill St Jo and St Luke *Lon* 88-91; Chapl Wexham Park Hosp Slough 91-95; Chapl Upton Hosp Slough 91-95; Chapl Leic Gen Hosp NHS Trust from 95. *Leicester General Hospital, Gwendolen Road, Leicester LE5 4PW* Tel 0116-249 0490

HARBOTTLE, Anthony Hall Harrison. b 25. LVO79. Ch Coll Cam BA50 MA53. Wycliffe Hall Ox 50. **d** 52 **p** 53. C Boxley *Cant* 52-54; C St Peter-in-Thanet 54-60; R Sandhurst w Newenden 60-68; Chapl Royal Chpl Windsor Gt Park 68-81; Chapl to The Queen 68-95; R E Dean w Friston and Jevington *Chich* 81-95; rtd 95; P-in-c E Dean w Friston and Jevington *Chich* 95-96. *44 Summerdown Road, Eastbourne, E Sussex BN20 8DQ* Tel (01323) 730881

HARCOURT, Canon Giles Sidford. b 36. Westcott Ho Cam 68. **d** 71 **p** 72. C Bishopwearmouth St Mich w St Hilda *Dur* 71-73; C Fishponds St Mary *Bris* 73-75; Bp's Dom Chapl *S'wark* 75-78; Lic to Offic 78-79; V S Wimbledon H Trin and St Pet 79-88; V Greenwich St Alfege w St Pet and St Paul from 88; Chapl RN Coll Greenwich 89-95; Sub-Dean Greenwich N *S'wark* 94-96; RD Greenwich Thameside from 96; Hon Can S'wark Cathl from 96. *The Vicarage, Park Vista, London SE10 9LZ* Tel 0181-858 6828

HARCOURT, Paul George. b 67. Em Coll Cam BA88 MA92. Wycliffe Hall Ox BA91. **d** 92 **p** 93. C Moreton *Ches* 92-95; C Woodford Wells *Chelmsf* from 95. *7 Marion Grove, Woodford Green, Essex IG8 9TA* Tel 0181-505 1431

HARCOURT-NORTON, Michael Clive. *See* NORTON, Michael Clive Harcourt

HARCUS, Canon Arthur Reginald (Reg). b 38. Lon Univ BD71 MPhil78. Kelham Th Coll 58. **d** 63 **p** 64. C Charlton St Luke w St Paul *S'wark* 63-69; C Felpham w Middleton *Chich* 78-80; P-in-c Donnington 80-85; V Fernhurst 85-91; V Bolney from 91; Tutor Lay Educn & Tr from 91; Hon Can Koforidua from 91. *The Vicarage, Bolney, Haywards Heath, W Sussex RH17 5QR* Tel (01444) 881301

HARDAKER, Canon Ian Alexander. b 32. K Coll Lon BD59 AKC59. **d** 60 **p** 61. C Beckenham St Geo *Roch* 60-65; R Eynsford w Lullingstone 65-70; V Chatham St Steph 70-85; RD Roch 78-85; Hon Can Roch Cathl from 83; Clergy Appts Adv from 86;

Hon Chapl to The Queen from 94. *Fielden House, Little College Street, London SW1P 3SH* Tel 0171-222 9544/5 Fax 233 1104

HARDCASTLE, Frank Rata. b 05. Lon Univ BA24 BD30 AKC30. **d** 30 **p** 31. C S Wimbledon H Trin *S'wark* 30-32; C Norwood St Luke 32-38; C Coulsdon St Andr 38-47; CF (EC) 44-46; Hon CF 46; V Sheff St Cuth *Sheff* 47-48; V Watford St Mich *St Alb* 48-69; Chapl Holywell Hosp 49-69; C Welwyn Garden City 69-71; rtd 71; Perm to Offic *Ex* 72-91. *13 Gracey Court, Woodland Road, Broadclyst, Exeter EX5 3LP*

HARDCASTLE, Nigel John. b 47. Reading Univ BSc68. Qu Coll Birm DipTh71. **d** 72 **p** 73. C Weoley Castle *Birm* 72-75; C Handsworth St Andr 75-78; V Garretts Green 78-86; Exec Sec Ch Computer Project BCC 86-89; R Emmer Green *Ox* from 89. *St Barnabas Vicarage, 20 St Barnabas Road, Emmer Green, Reading RG4 8LG* Tel 0118-947 8239

HARDCASTLE, Roger Clive. b 52. Southn Univ BSc73. Qu Coll Birm DipTh77. **d** 78 **p** 79. C Walton St Mary *Liv* 78-82; V Pemberton St Fran Kitt Green 82-94; TV Padgate 94-96; V Birchwood from 96. *The Vicarage, Admiral's Road, Birchwood, Warrington WA3 6QG* Tel (01925) 811906

HARDIE, John Blair. b 16. MBE46. LDS FDS MRCS38 MRCSE66. Edin Th Coll 73. **d** 76 **p** 76. Chapl St Paul's Cathl Dundee *Bre* 76-86; rtd 86; Hon C Carnoustie *Bre* from 86. *4 Lammerton Terrace, Dundee DD4 7BW* Tel (01382) 452247

HARDIE, Stephen. b 41. AKC67. **d** 68 **p** 69. C Roxbourne St Andr *Lon* 68-73; C Colchester St Mary V *Chelmsf* 73-76; R Wivenhoe 76-92; TR Dovercourt and Parkeston 92-96; P-in-c Harwich 92-96; R Dovercourt and Parkeston w Harwich from 96; RD Harwich from 97. *The Rectory, 51 Highfield Avenue, Dovercourt, Harwich, Essex CO12 4DR* Tel (01255) 552033

HARDING, Dr Alan. b 45. St Jo Coll Ox BA67 MA73 Pemb Coll Ox DPhil92. Oak Hill NSM Course 89. **d** 93 **p** 94. NSM Lt Heath *St Alb* from 93. *White Cottage, 41 Quakers Lane, Potters Bar, Herts EN6 1RH* Tel (01707) 652973

HARDING, Alec James. b 61. St Andr Univ MA83 DTh. Cranmer Hall Dur 86. **d** 89 **p** 90. C Thirsk *York* 89-93; TV Heref St Martin w St Fran (S Wye TM) *Heref* 93-95; TV Heref S Wye from 95. *The Vicarage, 1 Prinknash Close, Belmont, Hereford HR2 7XA* Tel (01432) 277364 or 353717

HARDING, Brenda Kathleen. b 39. Bedf Coll Lon BA60 K Coll Lon BD62. St Deiniol's Hawarden 91. **d** 92 **p** 94. NSM Lancaster Ch Ch w St Jo and St Anne *Blackb* from 92. *14 Ascot Close, Lancaster LA1 4LT* Tel (01524) 66071

HARDING, Canon Brian Edward. b 38. ALCD65. **d** 65 **p** 66. C Chislehurst Ch Ch *Roch* 65-68; P-in-c Baxenden *Blackb* 68-70; V 70-88; V Douglas from 88; Hon Can Blackb Cathl from 96. *The Vicarage, 5 Tan House Lane, Parbold, Wigan, Lancs WN8 7HG* Tel (01257) 462350

HARDING, Clifford Maurice. b 22. Leeds Univ BA47. Coll of Resurr Mirfield 46. **d** 48 **p** 49. C Tonge Moor *Man* 48-54; Nyasaland 54-56; CF 56-59; V Oldham St Jo *Man* 59-65; Lic to Offic *Blackb* from 65; rtd 87. *31 Riley Avenue, St Annes, Lytham St Annes, Lancs FY8 1HZ* Tel (01253) 725138

HARDING, Colin Ronald Stansby. b 32. RGN71 FVCM92. Bp Otter Coll 94. **d** 97. NSM Aldingbourne, Barnham and Eastergate *Chich* from 97. *Fresh Fields, Church Lane, Barnham, Bognor Regis, W Sussex PO22 0DA* Tel (01243) 552579

HARDING, David Anthony. b 30. St Edm Hall Ox BA54 MA58 Dur Univ MPhil85. Ely Th Coll 54. **d** 56 **p** 57. C Fulham All SS *Lon* 56-59; Lect Armenian Sem Istanbul 59-62; Chapl K Sch Cant 63-68; Chapl Westmr Sch 68-74; Chapl St Bede Coll Dur 74-75; SS Hild and Bede Coll 75-80; Lic to Offic *S'well* 80-91; Asst Chapl Worksop Coll Notts 80-82; Chapl 82-91; Chapl Sch of St Mary and St Anne Abbots Bromley 91-95; rtd 95; Perm to Offic *Glouc* from 95. *29 King John's Court, King John's Island, Tewkesbury, Glos GL20 6EG* Tel (01684) 291978

HARDING, Miss Eileen Thelma. b 18. St Mich Ho Ox 58. **dss** 60 **d** 87. Worthing St Geo *Chich* 60-64; Sec Dioc Bd for Women's Min 63-77; Hd Dss 68-81; Dioc Lay Min Adv 77-81; rtd 81; Broadwater St Mary *Chich* 84-87; Hon Par Dn 87-97; Perm to Offic from 97. *199 King Edward Avenue, Worthing, W Sussex BN14 8DW* Tel (01903) 239867

HARDING, Frederick Arthur. b 16. S'wark Ord Course 75. **d** 77 **p** 78. NSM Oxted *S'wark* 77-97; NSM Oxted and Tandridge from 97. *33 Crabwood, 13 Blue House Lane, Oxted, Surrey RH8 0UA* Tel (01883) 716454

HARDING, John James. b 08. BEM. Worc Ord Coll 60. **d** 62 **p** 63. C Highweek *Ex* 62-64; C Blandford Forum *Sarum* 64-66; C Langton Long 64-66; V Stourpaine 66-71; P-in-c Bockleton w Leysters *Heref* 71-76; rtd 76. *Flat 4, Trafalgar Court, 2 Richmond Road, Southsea, Hants PO5 2NU* Tel (01705) 839195

HARDING, John Stuart Michael. b 45. St Jo Coll Nottm 79. **d** 81 **p** 82. C Clifton *S'well* 81-87; V Broxtowe from 87. *The Vicarage, Frinton Road, Nottingham NG8 6GR* Tel 0115-927 8837

HARDING, John William Christopher. b 31. St Jo Coll Dur BA55. **d** 58 **p** 59. C Wigan St Cath *Liv* 58-60; C Much Woolton 60-63; V Whiston 63-73; V Birkdale St Jo 73-97; rtd 97. *17 Baytree Close, Southport, Merseyside PR9 8RE* Tel (01704) 507654

HARDING, Mrs Marion. b 33. Gilmore Course 75. **dss** 85 **d** 87 **p** 94. Hertford St Andr *St Alb* 85-87; Par Dn 87-93; rtd 93; NSM Lt Amwell *St Alb* from 93. *41 Calton Avenue, Hertford SG14 2ER* Tel (01992) 587348

HARDING, Michael Anthony John. b 37. Brasted Th Coll 67 Sarum Th Coll 68. **d** 71 **p** 72. C Forest Hill Ch Ch *S'wark* 71-72; C Catford St Laur 72-74; C Leominster *Heref* 74-77; V Ditton Priors 77-86; R Neenton 77-86; P-in-c Aston Botterell w Wheathill and Loughton 77-86; P-in-c Burwarton w N Cleobury 77-86; R Ditton Priors w Neenton, Burwarton etc 86-94; P-in-c E Budleigh and Bicton *Ex* 94; P-in-c Otterton and Colaton Raleigh 94; V E Budleigh w Bicton and Otterton from 94. *The Vicarage, East Budleigh, Budleigh Salterton, Devon EX9 7EF* Tel (01395) 444060

HARDING, Preb Michael David. b 38. Man Univ BA61. Lich Th Coll 61. **d** 63 **p** 64. C Hednesford *Lich* 63-67; C Blurton 67-70; V Newcastle St Paul from 70; RD Newcastle 87-97; Preb Lich Cathl from 89. *St Paul's Vicarage, Hawkstone Close, Newcastle, Staffs ST5 1HT* Tel (01782) 617913

HARDING, Peter Edward. b 39. Univ Coll Ox BA61 MA69. Wycliffe Hall Ox 62. **d** 64 **p** 65. C Westlands St Andr CD *Lich* 64-67; C Hinckley H Trin *Leic* 67-69; R Sutton cum Duckmanton *Derby* 69-75; P-in-c Elvaston and Shardlow 75-96. *113 Fitzsimmons Court, Shakespeare Crescent, London NW10 8XJ* Tel 0181-961 6558

HARDING, Peter Gordon. b 45. **d** 79 **p** 80. C Kirkheaton *Wakef* 79-82; NSM New Sleaford *Linc* from 90. *67 The Drove, Sleaford, Lincs NG34 7AS* Tel (01529) 307231

HARDING, Peter Richard. b 46. AKC69. St Aug Coll Cant 69. **d** 70 **p** 71. C Chorley St Pet *Blackb* 70-73; C Ribbleton 73-74; C St Marylebone w H Trin *Lon* 74-80; P-in-c St Marylebone St Cypr 80-82; V from 82; AD Westmr St Marylebone 83-92; Sub-Warden Guild of St Raphael from 88. *St Cyprian's Vicarage, 16 Clarence Gate Gardens, London NW1 6AY* Tel 0171-402 6979

HARDING, Richard Michael. b 42. St Alb Minl Tr Scheme. **d** 83 **p** 84. C Pershore w Pinvin, Wick and Birlingham *Worc* 83-86; V Longdon, Castlemorton, Bushley, Queenhill etc 86-95; P-in-c Catshill and Dodford from 95. *The Vicarage, 403 Stourbridge Road, Catshill, Bromsgrove, Worcs B61 9LG* Tel (01527) 579619

HARDING, Rolf John. b 22. Oak Hill Th Coll 41 Lon Coll of Div 46. **d** 49 **p** 50. C Sydenham H Trin *S'wark* 49-52; C Harold Wood *Chelmsf* 52-53; Min Harold Hill St Paul CD 53-61; V Coopersale 61-91; Chapl St Marg Hosp Epping 73-91; Chapl W Essex HA 86-91; rtd 91; Perm to Offic *B & W* from 91. *11 Westbrook Park, Weston, Bath BA1 4DP* Tel (01225) 484968

HARDING, Miss Sylvia. b 23. St Mich Ho Ox 55. **dss** 64 **d** 87. Rodbourne Cheney *Bris* 64-66; Midl Area Sec CPAS 66-71; Patchway 71-78; Sec Coun of Women's Min Bris 77-84; rtd 84; Westbury-on-Trym St Alb *Bris* 86-92; Hon Par Dn 87-92; Perm to Offic from 92; Perm to Offic *B & W* from 92. *24 Woodhill Road, Portishead, Bristol BS20 9EU* Tel (01275) 848638

HARDINGHAM, Paul David. b 52. Lon Univ BSc74 Fitzw Coll Cam BA77. Ridley Hall Cam 75. **d** 78 **p** 79. C Cambridge St Martin *Ely* 78-81; C Jesmond Clayton Memorial *Newc* 81-88; C Harborne Heath *Birm* 88-91; R Ipswich St Matt *St E* from 91. *St Matthew's Rectory, 3 Portman Road, Ipswich IP1 2ES* Tel (01473) 251630

HARDMAN, Dr Bryan Edwin. b 29. Lon Univ BD60 Selw Coll Cam PhD64 K Coll Lon MTh75. Moore Th Coll Sydney ThL54. **d** 55 **p** 55. Australia 55-60 and 68-83; Perm to Offic *Ely* 60-65; V Cambridge St Andr Less 65-68; Bangladesh 83-86; Singapore 87-95; rtd 94. *InterServe Korea, 402 Pierson Building, Sinmuno 2 Ga, Chongno Gu, Seoul, Korea*

HARDMAN, Mrs Christine Elizabeth. b 51. Lon Univ BSc(Econ)73. St Alb Minl Tr Scheme 81. **dss** 84 **d** 87 **p** 94. Markyate Street *St Alb* 84-87; Par Dn 87-88; Tutor St Alb Minl Tr Scheme 88-91; Course Dir St Alb Minl Tr Scheme 91-96; C Markyate Street 94-96; V Stevenage H Trin from 96. *Holy Trinity Vicarage, 18 Letchmore Road, Stevenage, Herts SG1 3JD* Tel (01438) 353229 E-mail chris@hardman.demon.co.uk

HARDMAN, Geoffrey James. b 41. Birm Univ BA63. N Ord Course 77. **d** 80 **p** 81. NSM Latchford St Jas *Ches* 80-93; NSM Haydock St Jas *Liv* from 94. *48 Denbury Avenue, Stockton Heath, Warrington WA4 2BW* Tel (01925) 664064

HARDMAN, Canon Peter George. b 35. Man Univ BSc56. Ridley Hall Cam 58. **d** 60 **p** 61. C Oldham St Paul *Man* 60-63; Lic to Offic 63-67; NW England Area Sec SCM 63-64; NW England Area Sec CEM 64-67; Asst Chapl Marlborough Coll 67-72; Chapl 72-79; P-in-c Wareham *Sarum* 79-80; TR from 80; Chapl Wareham Hosp from 80; Can and Preb Sarum Cathl *Sarum* from 87; RD Purbeck from 89. *The Rectory, 19 Pound Lane, Wareham, Dorset BH20 4LQ* Tel (01929) 552684

HARDWICK, Christopher George. b 57. ACIB79 Open Univ BA94 DASSc94 Birm Univ MA96. Ripon Coll Cuddesdon 90. **d** 92 **p** 93. C Worc SE *Worc* 92-95; R Ripple, Earls Croome w Hill Croome and Strensham from 95; RD Upton from 97. *The Rectory, The Cross, Ripple, Tewkesbury, Glos GL20 6HA* Tel (01684) 592655

HARDWICK, Dennis Egerton. b 27. St Deiniol's Hawarden. **d** 82 **p** 83. NSM Lache cum Saltney *Ches* 82-85; P-in-c Backford 85-88; P-in-c Capenhurst 87-88; R Backford and Capenhurst

88-93; rtd 93; Perm to Offic *Chich* from 93. *11 Prime Close, Walberton, Arundel, W Sussex BN18 0PL*

HARDWICK, Graham John. b 42. Qu Coll Birm 68. **d** 70 **p** 71. C Watford St Mich *St Alb* 70-73; C N Mymms 73-75; Youth Officer Cov Cathl *Cov* 75-81; Chapl Lanchester Poly 76-81; V Nuneaton St Nic 81-95; P-in-c New Bilton from 95. *St Oswald's Vicarage, New Street, Rugby, Warks CV22 7BE* Tel (01788) 544011

HARDWICK, John Audley. b 28. Em Coll Cam BA51 MA55. Westcott Ho Cam 51. **d** 53 **p** 54. C Selby Abbey *York* 53-56; Chapl St Edm Sch Hindhead 56-60; Chapl Aysgarth Sch N Yorkshire 60-62; Chapl St Edm Sch Hindhead 62-86; Asst Hd Master 73-90; Lic to Offic *Guildf* 63-90; rtd 93. *5 Trafalgar Court, Farnham, Surrey GU9 7QE*

HARDWICK, Robert (Rob). b 56. St Jo Coll Nottm DCM93. **d** 93 **p** 94. C Beeston *S'well* 93-97; V Scawby, Redbourne and Hibaldstow *Linc* from 97. *The Vicarage, Scawby, Brigg, S Humberside DN20 9LX* Tel (01652) 654251

HARDWICK, Mrs Susan Frances. b 44. Warw Univ BA81. Qu Coll Birm 82. **dss** 85 **d** 87 **p** 94. Chilvers Coton w Astley *Cov* 85-91; C 87-91; Chapl Hereward Coll 91-96; Hon C New Bilton from 96. *St Oswald's Vicarage, New Street, Rugby, Warks CV22 7BE* Tel (01788) 544011

HARDWICKE, Stephen Michael. b 57. Herts Coll BA85 Lon Bible Coll MA87 K Coll Lon MTh92. Westcott Ho Cam 93. **d** 95 **p** 96. C Leagrave *St Alb* from 95. *St Luke's House, 39 Butley Road, Luton LU4 9EW* Tel (01582) 572054

HARDY, Ms Alison Jane. b 61. **d** 95 **p** 96. C Flixton St Mich *Man* from 95. *350 Church Road, Flixton, Urmston, Manchester M31 3HR* Tel 0161-748 3568

HARDY, Anthony. b 36. **d** 86 **p** 87. Hon C Malden St Jas *S'wark* from 86. *48 Blake's Lane, New Malden, Surrey KT3 6NR* Tel 0181-949 0703

HARDY, Anthony William. b 56. Man Univ BEd79 MEd86. St Jo Coll Nottm LTh88. **d** 88 **p** 89. C Pennington *Man* 88-91; V Eccleston St Luke *Liv* from 91. *St Luke's Vicarage, Mulberry Avenue, St Helens, Merseyside WA10 4DE* Tel (01744) 22456

HARDY, Bertram Frank. b 08. Lich Th Coll 51. **d** 52 **p** 52. C Isham *Pet* 52; C Kettering SS Pet and Paul 52-54; V Mears Ashby 54-57; R Hardwick 54-57; Australia 57-64; R Morchard Bishop *Ex* 64-69; P-in-c N w S Barrow *B & W* 69-74; P-in-c Lovington 69-74; rtd 74; Perm to Offic *B & W* from 74. *7 Churchill Avenue, Wells, Somerset BA5 3JE* Tel (01749) 674696

HARDY, Canon Brian Albert. b 31. St Jo Coll Ox BA54 DipTh55 MA58. Westcott Ho Cam 55. **d** 57 **p** 58. C Rugeley *Lich* 57-62; Chapl Down Coll Cam 62-66; C-in-c Livingston Miss *Edin* 66-74; Preb Heref Cathl *Heref* 74-78; Ch Planning Officer Telford 74-78; RD Telford Severn Gorge 75-78; Chapl Edin Th Coll 78-82; Chapl Edin R Infirmary 82-86; R Edin St Columba *Edin* 82-91; Dean Edin 86-91; Hon Can St Mary's Cathl from 91; R St Andrews All SS *St And* 91-96; rtd 96. *3/3 Starbank Road, Edinburgh EH5 3BN* Tel 0131-551 6783

HARDY, Christopher Richard. b 52. R Holloway Coll Lon BMus77 Southn Univ BTh90. Chich Th Coll 87. **d** 90 **p** 91. C Kenton *Lon* 90-95; V E Finchley All SS from 95. *All Saints' Vicarage, 1 Twyford Avenue, London N2 1NV* Tel 0181-883 9315

HARDY, Prof Daniel Wayne. b 30. Haverford Coll (USA) BA52. Gen Th Sem (NY) STB55 STM63. **d** 55 **p** 56. USA 55-61 and 90-95; Fell and Tutor Gen Th Sem 59-61; Lic to Offic *Ox* 61-65; Lect Modern Th Thought Birm Univ 65-75; Sen Lect 75-86; Hon C Londonderry *Birm* 67-90; Van Mildert Prof Div Dur Univ 86-90; Can Res Dur Cathl *Dur* 86-90; Dir Cen Th Inquiry 90-95; rtd 95. *101 Millington Lane, Cambridge CB3 9HA* Tel (01223) 312302

HARDY, Miss Janet Frances. b 59. Newc Univ BA81 CertEd82. Trin Coll Bris 87. **d** 89 **p** 94. Par Dn Sheff St Paul Wordsworth Avenue *Sheff* 89-92; TD Gt Snaith 92-94; TV 94-96; V Pitsmoor Ch Ch from 96. *The Vicarage, 257 Pitsmoor Road, Sheffield S3 9AQ* Tel (0114) 272 7756

HARDY, John Charles. b 22. Sheff Univ BA48 DipEd49 Lon Univ DipTh53. St Deiniol's Hawarden 66. **d** 67 **p** 68. Hon C Chorley St Laur *Blackb* 67-87; rtd 87; Perm to Offic *Blackb* from 87. *4 Glamis Drive, Chorley, Lancs PR7 1LX* Tel (01257) 265743

HARDY, John Christopher. b 61. St Jo Coll Dur BA83 Dur Univ MA95. Coates Hall Edin BD92. **d** 92 **p** 93. C Walker *Newc* 92-95; Fell Chapl Magd Coll Ox from 95; Lic to Offic *Ox* from 95. *Magdalen College, High Street, Oxford OX1 4AU* Tel (01865) 242141

HARDY, Canon John Lewis Daniel. b 26. St Chad's Coll Dur BA51 DipTh52. **d** 52 **p** 53. C Hucknall Torkard *S'well* 52-58; V Harworth 58-65; V Sutton in Ashfield St Mary 65-85; R Keyworth 85-93; P-in-c Stanton-on-the-Wolds 85-93; RD Bingham S 91-93; Hon Can S'well Minster 92-93; rtd 93. *10 Redhill Lodge Drive, Nottingham NG5 8JH* Tel 0115-926 7370

HARDY, Michael Frederick Bryan. b 36. Selw Coll Cam BA60 MA64. Linc Th Coll 60. **d** 62 **p** 63. C Pontefract St Giles *Wakef* 62-66; C Lightcliffe 66-69; V Hightown 69-78; V Birkby 78-85; C Boultham *Linc* 88-89; V Misterton and W Stockwith *S'well* from 89. *The Vicarage, 5 Minster Road, Misterton, Doncaster, S Yorkshire DN10 4AP* Tel (01427) 890270

HARDY, Michael Henry. b 33. Qu Coll Birm 85. **d** 86 **p** 87. C Leic St Jas *Leic* 86-88; R Arnesby w Shearsby and Bruntingthorpe 88-94; RD Guthlaxton I 91-94; TV Ratby w Groby from 94. *The Vicarage, 15 Groby Road, Ratby, Leicester LE6 0LJ* Tel 0116-239 3009

HARDY, Michael John. b 35. Keble Coll Ox BA58 MA66. Cuddesdon Coll 59. **d** 61 **p** 62. C Dalton-in-Furness *Carl* 61-64; C Harborne St Pet *Birm* 64-68; Min Can Ripon Cathl *Ripon* 68-73; Appt and Tr Sec USPG 73-80; R Stretford St Pet *Man* 80-91; P-in-c Newton Hall *Dur* 91-96; TR Keighley St Andr *Bradf* from 96. *The Rectory, 13 Westview Grove, Keighley, W Yorkshire BD20 6JJ* Tel (01535) 667167

HARDY, Canon Paul Richard. b 30. K Coll Cam BA52 MA56. St Steph Ho Ox 57. **d** 59 **p** 60. C Corringham *Chelmsf* 59-61; C Prittlewell All SS 61-64; USPG 64-95; Tanzania 64-95; Can Dar-es-Salaam 74-88; Can Zanzibar and Tanga 88-95; Hon Can from 95; rtd 95; Perm to Offic *Roch* from 95. *22 Bromley College, London Road, Bromley BR1 1PE* Tel 0181-290 1289

HARDY, Miss Pauline. b 41. CertEd. Linc Th Coll 85. **d** 87 **p** 94. Par Dn Walsall Wood *Lich* 87-89; Par Dn Buckingham *Ox* 89-93; C Buckingham w Radclive cum Chackmore 93-97; C Nash w Thornton, Beachampton and Thornborough 96-97; C Buckingham from 97. *The Rectory, Chapel Lane, Thornborough, Buckingham MK18 2DJ* Tel (01280) 812515

✠**HARDY, The Rt Revd Robert Maynard.** b 36. Clare Coll Cam BA60 MA64. Cuddesdon Coll 60. **d** 62 **p** 63 **c** 80. C Langley St Aid CD *Man* 62-64; C Langley All SS and Martyrs 64-65; Chapl and Lect Th Selw Coll Cam 65-72; V Boreham Wood All SS *St Alb* 72-75; Dir St Alb Minl Tr Scheme 75-80; P-in-c Aspley Guise *St Alb* 75-79; P-in-c Husborne Crawley w Ridgmont 76-79; R Aspley Guise w Husborne Crawley and Ridgmont 80; Suff Bp Maidstone *Cant* 80-87; Bp Linc from 87; Bp HM Pris from 85. *Bishop's House, Eastgate, Lincoln LN2 1QQ* Tel (01522) 534701 Fax 511095

HARDY, Thomas Woodburn. b 26. Bp's Univ Lennoxville BA48. **d** 49 **p** 50. Canada 49-57 and 59-62; C Gt Bookham *Guildf* 57-59; C Fulham St Oswald w St Aug *Lon* 62-68; P-in-c Fulham St Aug 68-73; V 73-91; rtd 91. *58 Boston Gardens, Brentford, Middx TW8 9LP* Tel 0181-847 4533

HARDY, Wallis Bertrand. b 03. Lon Univ BSc24. St Steph Ho Ox 53. **d** 54 **p** 55. C Northam *Ex* 54-59; V Ashbury w Compton Beauchamp *Ox* 59-64; Chapl Community of St Denys Warminster 64-75; rtd 75. *Ingram House, Whiteley Village, Walton-on-Thames, Surrey KT12 4EJ* Tel (01932) 856315

HARDY, William Marshall Conyers. b 25. Linc Th Coll 55. **d** 56 **p** 57. C Newc H Cross *Newc* 56-60; C Wooler 60-62; V Belford 62-77; RD Bamburgh and Glendale 71-77; V Riding Mill 77-90; RD Corbridge 82-88; Hon Can Newc Cathl 88-91; rtd 90. *5 Riding Dene, Mickley, Stocksfield, Northd NE43 7DG* Tel (01434) 682009

HARE, Christopher Sumner. b 49. Solicitor 73. W of England Minl Tr Course 92. **d** 95 **p** 96. NSM Saltford w Corston and Newton St Loe *B & W* from 95. *The Cottage, 84 Norman Road, Saltford, Bristol BS18 3BJ* Tel (01225) 873510

HARE, David (Brother David Columba). b 46. Qu Coll Birm. **d** 83 **p** 83. SSF from 67; Bp's Dom Chapl *Birm* 83-87; V Handsworth St Mich from 87. *St Michael's Vicarage, 20 Soho Avenue, Handsworth, Birmingham B18 5LB* Tel 0121-554 3521 or 4090

HARE, Douglas Stewart. b 27. **d** 96 **p** 97. Hon C Margate H Trin *Cant* from 96. *5 Meadow Road, Margate, Kent CT9 5JJ* Tel (01843) 292528

HARE, Frank Richard Knight. b 22. Trin Hall Cam BA46 MA48. Cuddesdon Coll 46. **d** 48 **p** 49. C Dennington *St E* 48-51; C Eastbourne St Mary *Chich* 51-54; R Rotherfield 54-62; V Steyning 62-70; R Ashurst 62-70; TV Raveningham *Nor* 70-71; TR Barnham Broom 71-79; V Buxton w Oxnead 79-86; R Lammas w Lt Hautbois 79-86; rtd 86; Perm to Offic *St E* from 86. *14 Lee Road, Aldeburgh, Suffolk IP15 5HG* Tel (01728) 453372

HARE, Dr Richard William. b 66. Bris Univ BSc88 PhD94. Cranmer Hall Dur BA95. **d** 95 **p** 96. C Coulsdon St Jo *S'wark* from 95. *8 Waddington Avenue, Coulsdon, Surrey CR5 1QE* Tel (01737) 556043

HARE, Stanley Thomas. b 23. Roch Th Coll. **d** 62 **p** 63. C York St Lawr w St Nic *York* 62; C Newland St Jo 63-65; R Sutton cum Duckmanton *Derby* 65-69; V Sheff St Barn *Sheff* 69-73; Chapl Farnborough and Orpington Hosps 73-85; rtd 85. *17 Gale Garth, Alne, York YO6 2LQ*

✠**HARE, The Rt Revd Thomas Richard.** b 22. Trin Coll Ox BA48 MA53. Westcott Ho Cam 48. **d** 50 **p** 51 **c** 71. C Haltwhistle *Newc* 50-52; Bp's Dom Chapl *Man* 52-59; Can Res Carl Cathl *Carl* 59-65; R Barrow St Geo w St Luke 65-69; Adn Westmorland and Furness 65-71; Hon Can Carl Cathl 65-71; V Winster 69-71; Suff Bp Pontefract *Wakef* 71-92; rtd 92. *Wood Cottage, Mirehouse, Underskiddaw, Keswick, Cumbria CA12 4QE* Tel (017687) 72996

✠**HARE DUKE, The Rt Revd Michael Geoffrey.** b 25. Trin Coll Ox BA49 MA51 St Andr Univ Hon DD94. Westcott Ho Cam 50. **d** 52 **p** 53 **c** 69. C St Jo Wood *Lon* 52-56; V Bury St Mark *Man* 56-62; Past Dir Clinical Th Assn Nottm 62-64; Past Consultant

64-69; V Daybrook *S'well* 64-69; Bp St And 69-94; rtd 94. *2 Balhousie Avenue, Perth PH1 5HN* Tel (01738) 622642

HARES, David Ronald Walter. b 40. Qu Coll Cam BA63 MA67 CertEd. Westcott Ho Cam 64. **d** 66 **p** 67. C Cannock *Lich* 66-69; Chapl Peterho Cam 69-72; Asst Master Chesterton Sch Cam 72-74; V Kesgrave *St E* from 74. *The Vicarage, Kesgrave, Ipswich IP5 7JQ* Tel (01473) 622181

HAREWOOD, John Rupert. b 24. Man Univ BA48. Sarum & Wells Th Coll 76. **d** 79 **p** 80. NSM Taunton St Jas *B & W* 79-82; TV Camelot Par 82-89; rtd 89; Perm to Offic *Ex* from 92. *19 Swains Road, Budleigh Salterton, Devon EX9 6HL* Tel (01395) 445802

HARFORD, Julian Gray. b 29. Univ Coll Ox BA52 MA59 Lon Univ PGCE58. Qu Coll Birm DipTh64. **d** 64 **p** 65. C W End *Win* 64-67; C Chearsley w Nether Winchendon *Ox* 67-77; C Chilton All SS 72-77; R Westbury w Turweston, Shalstone and Biddlesden 77-86; C Chenies and Lt Chalfont 86-87; C Chenies and Lt Chalfont, Latimer and Flaunden 87-95; rtd 95. *14 Dial Close, Seend, Melksham, Wilts SN12 6NP* Tel (01380) 828306

HARFORD, The Ven Michael Rivers Dundas. b 26. Trin Coll Cam BA49 MA51. Westcott Ho Cam 50. **d** 52 **p** 53. C Ashton-on-Ribble St Andr *Blackb* 52-55; Perm to Offic *Edin* 55-56; Malaya 56-63; Malaysia 63-66; V Childwall St Dav *Liv* 66-71; Australia from 71; Adn Albany 76-79; Adn Swan 86-89; Adn Mitchell 90-91; rtd 91. *3B Tamar Street, Palmyra, W Australia 6157* Tel Perth (9) 319 1538

HARFORD, Timothy William. b 58. Nottm Univ BTh89. Linc Th Coll 86. **d** 89 **p** 90. C Minehead *B & W* 89-93; R Knebworth *St Alb* from 93. *The Rectory, 15 St Martin's Road, Knebworth, Herts SG3 6ER* Tel (01438) 812101

HARGER, Robin Charles Nicholas. b 49. BTh. Sarum & Wells Th Coll 78. **d** 81 **p** 82. C Charlton Kings St Mary *Glouc* 81-85; C Folkestone St Mary and St Eanswythe *Cant* 85-89; TV Langley and Parkfield *Man* 89-95; TV Bournemouth St Pet w St Swithun, H Trin etc *Win* from 95. *St Stephen's Vicarage, St Stephen's Way, Bournemouth BH2 6JZ* Tel (01202) 554355

HARGRAVE, Dr Alan Lewis. b 50. Birm Univ BSc73 PhD77. Ridley Hall Cam 87. **d** 89 **p** 90. C Cambridge H Trin w St Andr Gt *Ely* 89-92; C Cambridge H Trin 92-93; C-in-c Fen Ditton 93-94; V Cambridge Holy Cross from 94. *Holy Cross Vicarage, 192 Peverel Road, Cambridge CB5 8RL* Tel (01223) 413343

HARGREAVE, James David. b 44. ALCM89 LTCL90 Lon Univ BA66 CertEd68. Coll of Resurr Mirfield DipTh72. **d** 73 **p** 74. C Houghton le Spring *Dur* 73-77; C Gateshead St Cuth w St Paul 77-79; V Trimdon 79-87; C-in-c Stockton Green Vale H Trin CD 87-94; V Hedon w Paull *York* from 94. *The Vicarage, 44 New Road, Hedon, Hull HU12 8BS* Tel (01482) 897693

HARGREAVES, Arthur Cecil Monsarrat. b 19. Trin Hall Cam BA42 MA46. Westcott Ho Cam 47. **d** 49 **p** 50. C Wembley St Jo *Lon* 49-52; India 52-61 and 70-76; Asia Sec CMS 61-69; Gen Sec Conf of Br Miss Socs 76-79; Hon C Croydon St Aug *Cant* 79-81; V Marden 81-86; rtd 86; Perm to Offic *S'wark* from 86. *Windrush Cottage, 87 Downscourt Road, Purley, Surrey CR8 1BJ* Tel 0181-668 8871

HARGREAVES, Dr Arthur Walsh. b 34. FRCSE FRCS Man Univ MB, ChB. St Deiniol's Hawarden. **d** 90 **p** 91. NSM Baguley *Man* from 90. *Greenways, Woodbourne Road, Sale, Cheshire M33 3SX* Tel 0161-973 7674

HARGREAVES, John. b 43. St Jo Coll Nottm 86. **d** 88 **p** 89. C Werneth *Man* 88-91; TV Rochdale 91-96; C Man Gd Shep 96-97; Perm to Offic *Liv* from 96; C Manchester Gd Shep and St Barn *Man* from 97. *St Barnabas' Rectory, South Street, Openshaw, Manchester M11 2EW* Tel 0161-231 4365

HARGREAVES, Canon John Henry Monsarrat. b 11. Trin Coll Cam BA33 MA37. Westcott Ho Cam 35. **d** 37 **p** 38. C Bishopwearmouth Ch Ch *Dur* 37-39; C Hunslet St Mary *Ripon* 39-43; C Brompton H Trin *Lon* 57-58; CMS (Nigeria) 43-57 and 59-63; SPCK 65-90; C-in-c Sevenoaks St Luke CD *Roch* 65-83; RD Sevenoaks 74-79; Hon Can Roch Cathl 81-83; rtd 83; Perm to Offic *Guildf* from 91. *20 St Pauls Road West, Dorking, Surrey RH4 2HU* Tel (01306) 888648

HARGREAVES, John Rodney. b 36. Open Univ BA74. Didsbury Meth Coll 59 St Deiniol's Hawarden 74. **d** 75 **p** 75. In Meth Ch 63-74; C Pontypool *Mon* 75-77; C Llanedeyrn 77-79; Chapl HM Pris Aylesbury 79-83; Sen Chapl HM Pris Stafford 83-88; Asst Chapl Gen of Pris (N) 88-90; Asst Chapl Gen of Pris 90-96; R Stone St Mich w Aston St Sav *Lich* from 96. *The Rectory, 56 Lichfield Road, Stone, Staffs ST15 8PG* Tel (01785) 812747

HARGREAVES, John Wilson. b 46. Aber Univ BScFor67 Birm Poly DipVG73. Westcott Ho Cam 84. **d** 86 **p** 87. C Rugby St Andr *Cov* 86-90; TV Daventry *Pet* 90-92; P-in-c Welton w Ashby St Ledgers 90-92; TV Daventry, Ashby St Ledgers, Braunston etc from 92; Chapl Daventry Tertiary Coll from 94. *The Vicarage, 19 High Street, Welton, Daventry, Northants NN11 5JP* Tel (01327) 705563

HARGREAVES, Ms Marise. b 60. Leeds Univ BA81. Cranmer Hall Dur 82. **d** 94 **p** 95. NSM Bradf St Clem *Bradf* 94-96; NSM Buttershaw St Paul from 96. *58 Exmouth Place, Undercliffe, Bradford BD3 0NA* Tel (01274) 641551

HARGREAVES, Mark Kingston. b 63. **d** 91 **p** 92. C Highbury Ch Ch w St Jo and St Sav Lon 91-94; C Ealing St Steph Castle Hill 94-96; C Notting Hill St Jo and St Pet from 96. *48 Ladbroke Road, London W11 3NW*

HARGREAVES, Raymond. Open Univ BA79 St Jo Coll York CertEd61. Ripon Hall Ox 72. **d** 73 **p** 74. C Stanwix *Carl* 73-78; Chapl St Olave's Sch York 78-94; Perm to Offic *York* from 94; rtd 96. *21 Oak Tree Lane, Haxby, York YO3 3YL* Tel (01904) 763127

HARGREAVES-STEAD, Terence Desmond. b 32. Edin Th Coll 60. **d** 63 **p** 64. C Walney Is *Carl* 63-66; Chapl Withington Hosp Man 66-72; V Westleigh St Paul *Man* from 72. *St Paul's Vicarage, Westleigh Lane, Leigh, Lancs WN7 5NW* Tel (01942) 882883

HARINGTON, Roger John Urquhart. b 48. Trin Hall Cam BA70 MA71. Coll of Resurr Mirfield 72. **d** 75 **p** 76. C Liv Our Lady and St Nic w St Anne *Liv* 75-78; Asst Chapl Leeds Univ and Poly *Ripon* 78-81; C Moor Allerton 81; TV 81-86; Dioc Drama Adv (Jabbok Theatre Co) 86-95; V Leeds Gipton Epiphany from 95. *227 Beech Lane, Leeds LS9 6SW* Tel 0113-235 1264

HARKER, Harold Aidan. b 35. **d** 82 **p** 83. OSB from 53; C Reading St Giles *Ox* 82-83; Lic to Offic 83-87; C Halstead St Andr w H Trin and Greenstead Green *Chelmsf* 87-89; P-in-c Belchamp St Paul from 89. *The Vicarage, Belchamp St Paul, Sudbury, Suffolk CO10 7BT* Tel (01787) 277210

HARKER, Dr John Hadlett. b 37. Dur Univ BSc59 Newc Univ PhD67 CEng MIChemE64 MInstE64 CChem MRSC65 FIChemE80. NE Ord Course 81. **d** 84 **p** 85. C Earsdon *Newc* 84-87; P-in-c Long Horsley 87-91; V Bassenthwaite, Isel and Setmurthy *Carl* 91-94; TR Howden TM *York* 94-96; P-in-c Willerby w Ganton and Folkton from 96. *Willerby Vicarage, Staxton, Scarborough, N Yorkshire YO12 4SF* Tel (01944) 710364

HARKER, Stephan John. b 47. Em Coll Cam BA68 MA72. Westcott Ho Cam 70. **d** 72 **p** 73. C Marton *Blackb* 72-76; C Preston St Matt 76-79; C Fleetwood 79-80; Chapl Charterhouse Godalming from 81. *Lower Oakhurst, Frith Hill Road, Godalming, Surrey GU7 2ED* Tel (01483) 422155

HARKIN, John Patrick. b 53. Oak Hill Th Coll DipHE89. **d** 89 **p** 90. C Wisley w Pyrford *Guildf* 89-93; P-in-c Mickleham from 93; Chapl Box Hill Sch Surrey from 93. *The Rectory, Mickleham, Dorking, Surrey RH5 6EB* Tel (01372) 378335

HARKIN, Terence James. b 46. Lon Bible Coll BA82 New Coll Edin MTh94. **d** 95 **p** 96. In Bapt Min 86-95; C Edin H Cross *Edin* from 95; C S Queensferry from 95. *12 Springfield Place, South Queensferry, West Lothian EH30 9XE* Tel 0131-319 1099 or 331 5540

HARKINS, Canon James Robert. b 27. Minnesota Univ BA49. Seabury-Western Th Sem MTh53. **d** 52 **p** 52. USA 52-60; 72-79; 91-93; Colombia 60-72; Dominica 79-85; Venezuela 85-91; Chapl Venice w Trieste *Eur* from 94. *253 Dorsoduro, San Gregorio, 30123 Venice, Italy* Tel Venice (41) 520-0571

HARKNESS, Verney Austin Barnett. b 19. Lon Univ BA40 DipTh63. Ridley Hall Cam 46. **d** 47 **p** 48. C Cockermouth All SS w Ch Ch *Carl* 47-50; R The Shelsleys *Worc* 53-56; Egypt 50-53; V Bris H Trin *Bris* 56-60; R Stoke next Guildf St Jo *Guildf* 63-72; Sri Lanka 73-77; P-in-c Walkington *York* 78-79; P-in-c Bishop Burton 78-79; R Bishop Burton w Walkington 79-84; rtd 85; Perm to Offic *York* from 85. *30 Tuart Street, Chester le Street, Co Durham DH3 3EN* Tel 0191-388 9788

HARLAND, Albert Henry. b 17. Oak Hill Th Coll 57. **d** 59 **p** 61. SAMS 59-60; C Jesmond H Trin *Newc* 61-63; P-in-c Dowdeswell *Glouc* 63-68; V Renhold *St Alb* 69-80; rtd 80; Perm to Offic *St Alb* from 80. *123 Putnoe Lane, Bedford MK41 8LB* Tel (01234) 345831

HARLAND, Canon Harold William James. b 35. Hertf Coll Ox BA59 MA63. Clifton Th Coll 59. **d** 61 **p** 62. C Reigate St Mary *S'wark* 61-64; C Farnborough *Guildf* 64-68; V Walmley *Birm* 68-74; V Bromley Ch Ch *Roch* 74-86; V Foord St Jo *Cant* from 86; Dir of Post-Ord Tr from 94; Hon Can Cant Cathl from 94. *St John's Vicarage, 4 Cornwallis Avenue, Folkestone, Kent CT19 5JA* Tel (01303) 253732

✠**HARLAND, The Rt Revd Ian.** b 32. Peterho Cam BA56 MA60. Wycliffe Hall Ox 58. **d** 60 **p** 61 **c** 85. C Melton Mowbray w Thorpe Arnold *Leic* 60-63; V Oughtibridge *Sheff* 63-72; V Sheff St Cuth 72-75; P-in-c Brightside All SS 72-75; RD Ecclesfield 73-75; V Rotherham 75-79; RD Rotherham 76-79; Adn Doncaster 79-85; P-in-c Dunscroft Ch Ch 81-83; Hon Can Blackb Cathl *Blackb* 85-89; Suff Bp Lancaster 85-89; Bp Carl from 89. *Rose Castle, Dalston, Carlisle CA5 7BZ* Tel (016974) 76274 Fax 76550

HARLEY, Dr Anne Marion. b 39. St Hugh's Coll Ox MA64 DPhil65. Sarum & Wells Th Coll 85. **d** 88 **p** 94. Par Dn Isleworth St Jo *Lon* 88-91; Chapl Asst St Thos Hosp Lon 91-94; Chapl Guy's and St Thos' Hosps NHS Trust Lon from 94. *12 Canterbury House, Royal Street, London SE1 7LN* Tel 0171-928 9292 (Office)

HARLEY, Brother Brian Mortimer. b 25. K Coll Lon 48. **d** 53 **p** 54. C Bris St Agnes w St Simon *Bris* 53-56; Lic to Offic *Sarum* 56-62; SSF from 56; Chapl St Fran Sch Hooke 58-61; Papua New Guinea 61-79; Australia from 87; Min Gen SSF from 91; rtd 95. *The Hermitage of St Bernadine, Stroud, NSW, Australia 2425* Tel Cessnock (49) 945372

HARLEY, Canon Brian Nigel. b 30. Clare Coll Cam BA53 MA57. Cuddesdon Coll 53. **d** 55 **p** 56. C Basingstoke *Win* 55-60; TV 71-73; TR 73-80; C W End 60-61; C-in-c Southn St Chris Thornhill CD 61-71; V Eastleigh 80-93; RD Eastleigh 85-93; rtd 93; Bp's Dom Chapl *Win* 94-96. *18 Phillimore Road, Southampton SO16 2NR* Tel (01703) 551049

HARLEY, Dr Christopher David. b 41. Selw Coll Cam BA63 MA69 Bris Univ PGCE64. Columbia Bibl Sem DMin92 Clifton Th Coll 64. **d** 66 **p** 67. C Finchley Ch Ch *Lon* 66-69; Hon C 75-78; Ethiopia 70-75; Hd of UK Miss CMJ 75-78; Lect All Nations Chr Coll Ware 78-85; Prin 85-93; Chmn Lon Inst of Contemporary Christianity 88-89; Chmn CMJ 89-90; Lic to Offic *St Alb* 79-92; Crosslinks from 93; NSM Bromley Ch Ch *Roch* from 94. *5 Ullswater Close, Bromley BR1 4JF* Tel 0181-691 6111 Fax 694 8023

HARLEY, David Bertram. b 22. Down Coll Cam BA50 MA55. Westcott Ho Cam 55. **d** 56 **p** 58. Asst Master Bedf Sch 50-58; C Biddenham *St Alb* 56-58; Chapl Stamford Sch 58-87; Lic to Offic *Linc* from 59; Confrater Browne's Hosp Stamford from 87; rtd 87. *Beggars' Roost, Priory Road, Stamford, Lincs PE9 2ES* Tel (01780) 763403

HARLEY, Michael. b 50. AKC73 Ch Ch Coll Cant CertEd74 Lambeth STh92 Kent Univ MPhil95. St Aug Coll Cant 74. **d** 75 **p** 76. C Chatham St Wm *Roch* 75-78; C-in-c Weeke *Win* 78-81; V Southampton St Mary Extra 81-86; V Hurstbourne Tarrant, Faccombe, Vernham Dean etc from 86; ACORA Link Officer 91-94; Dioc Rural Officer from 95; RD Andover from 95. *The Vicarage, Hurstbourne Tarrant, Andover, Hants SP11 0AH* Tel (01264) 736222 Fax as telephone

HARLEY, Robert Patterson (Bob). b 53. St Andr Univ MA75 Cam Univ CertEd76 Glas Univ PhD89 Edin Univ BD97. **d** 97. C Edin St Thos *Edin* from 97. *81 Glasgow Road, Edinburgh EH12 8LJ* Tel 0131-334 4434

HARLEY, Roger Newcomb. b 38. Ely Th Coll 61. **d** 64 **p** 65. C Plymouth St Pet *Ex* 64-66; C Heston *Lon* 66-69; C Maidstone All SS w St Phil and H Trin *Cant* 69-73; R Temple Ewell w Lydden 73-79; P-in-c Shirley St Geo 79-81; V 81-84; V Croydon H Sav *S'wark* 85-95; V Forest Row *Chich* from 95. *The Vicarage, Lewes Road, Forest Row, E Sussex RH18 5AF* Tel (01342) 822595

HARLOW, Antony Francis. b 24. Pemb Coll Cam BA50 MA55. Oak Hill Th Coll 84. **d** 85 **p** 86. NSM Watford St Luke *St Alb* 85-86; CMS 86-91; Uganda 86-91; Perm to Offic *St Alb* from 90; NSM Watford St Pet 92-94. *23 Elizabeth Court, 170 Hempstead Road, Watford WD1 3LR* Tel (01923) 239111

HARLOW, Canon Derrick Peter. b 30. St Jo Coll Cam BA53 MA57. Ridley Hall Cam 53. **d** 55 **p** 56. C Barking St Marg *Chelmsf* 55-58; V Leyton Em 58-63; V Goodmayes All SS 63-75; R Thundersley 76-83; TR Saffron Walden w Wendens Ambo and Littlebury 83-95; Hon Can Chelmsf Cathl 84-95; rtd 95. *26 Kintbury, Duxford, Cambridge CB2 4RR* Tel (01223) 833891

HARLOW, Mrs Elizabeth Gilchrist. b 27. MSc. DipTh. **d** 91 **p** 94. Par Dn St Alb St Luke *St Alb* from 91. *23 Elizabeth Court, 170 Hempstead Road, Watford WD1 3LR* Tel (01923) 239111

HARLOW-TRIGG, Richard John St Clair. b 63. Cam Univ BA85 MA88. Cranmer Hall Dur 87. **d** 89 **p** 90. C Hyson Green *S'well* 89-91; C Basford w Hyson Green 91-94; C Mansfield St Pet from 94. *85 Delamere Drive, Mansfield, Notts NG18 4DD* Tel (01623) 649119

HARLOW, Archdeacon of. *See* TAYLOR, The Ven Peter Flint

HARMAN, Preb John Gordon Kitchener. b 14. Qu Coll Cam BA36 MA40. Lon Coll of Div 36. **d** 37 **p** 38. C St Marylebone All So w SS Pet and Jo *Lon* 37-38; C Edgware 38-42; Travelling Sec Inter-Univ Fellowship 42-45; China 45-52; R Cheadle *Ches* 54-60; R Edgware *Lon* 60-75; Preb St Paul's Cathl 65-75; C-in-c Westbourne Ch Ch Prop Chpl *Win* 75-81; rtd 79; Perm to Offic *Leic* from 82; Perm to Offic *Lon* 84-92; Perm to Offic *S'well* from 91. *32 Lansdowne Road, Shepshed, Loughborough, Leics LE12 9RS* Tel (01509) 502865

HARMAN, Leslie Davies. b 46. Nottm Univ BTh76. St Jo Coll Nottm LTh75. **d** 76 **p** 77. C Wandsworth All SS *S'wark* 76-78; C Godstone 78-82; V Thorncombe w Winsham and Cricket St Thomas *B & W* 82-87; TV Hitchin *St Alb* 87-95; V Royston from 95; RD Buntingford from 96. *The Vicarage, 31 Baldock Road, Royston, Herts SG8 5BJ* Tel (01763) 243145

HARMAN, Michael John. b 48. Chich Th Coll 71. **d** 74 **p** 75. C Blackpool St Steph *Blackb* 74-79; Chapl RN from 79. *Royal Naval Chaplaincy Service, Room 203, Victory Building, HM Naval Base, Portsmouth PO1 3LS* Tel (01705) 727903 Fax 727112

HARMAN, Canon Robert Desmond. b 41. TCD BA65 MA71. CITC 67. **d** 67 **p** 68. C Taney Ch Ch *D & G* 67-73; I Dublin Santry w Glasnevin 73-86; I Dublin Sandford w Milltown from 86; Can Ch Ch Cathl Dublin from 91. *The Rectory, Sandford Close, Ranelagh, Dublin 6, Irish Republic* Tel Dublin (1) 497 2983 Fax 496 4789

HARMAN, Theodore Allan. b 27. Linc Coll Ox BA52 MA56 Hatf Coll Dur MA90. Wells Th Coll 52. **d** 54 **p** 55. C Hawkshead and Low Wray *Carl* 54-55; C Kirkby Stephen w Mallerstang 55-57; Lic to Offic *Bradf* from 57; Asst Chapl Sedbergh Sch Cumbria 57-84; Sen Chapl 84-87; Asst Master 57-87; Tutor Hatf Coll Dur from 88; Admissions Tutor 89-90; Lib from 91; Coll Officer from 91; rtd 92; Perm to Offic *Dur* from 92. *Flat D1, Hatfield College, North Bailey, Durham DH1 3RQ* Tel 0191-374 3176 Fax 374 7472

HARMER, Timothy James (Tim). b 47. Birm Univ CertEd68. St Jo Coll Nottm BA95. **d** 95 **p** 96. C Studley *Cov* from 95. *3 Westmead Avenue, Studley, Warks B80 7NB* Tel (01527) 857688

HARMSWORTH, Roger James. b 46. Univ of W Ontario BA87. Huron Coll Ontario MDiv90. **d** 90 **p** 90. Canada 90-96; I Maryborough w Dysart Enos and Ballyfin *C & O* from 96. *The Rectory, Coote Street, Portlaoise, Co Laois, Irish Republic* Tel Portlaoise (502) 21154 Fax as telephone E-mail therev@iol.ie

HARNISH, Dr Robert George (Rob). b 64. Univ of Ottawa BSc87 Worc Coll Ox DPhil90 MA92. Wycliffe Hall Ox 90. **d** 93 **p** 94. C Chinnor w Emmington and Sydenham etc *Ox* 93-95; Chapl and Dean of Div New Coll Ox from 96. *New College, Oxford OX1 3BN* Tel (01865) 279541

HARONSKI, Boleslaw. b 46. Pemb Coll Ox BA68 MA72 DPhil73. St Mich Coll Llan 80 Westcott Ho Cam 82. **d** 82 **p** 83. C Maindee *Mon* 82-85; V Llanishen w Trellech Grange and Llanfihangel etc 85-89; V Blackwood 89-92. *45 St Julian's Road, Newport NP9 7GN*

HARPER, The Ven Alan Edwin Thomas. b 44. OBE96. Leeds Univ BA65. CITC 75. **d** 78 **p** 79. C Ballywillan *Conn* 78-80; I Moville w Greencastle, Upper Moville etc *D & R* 80-82; I Londonderry Ch Ch 82-86; I Belfast Malone St Jo *Conn* from 86; RD S Belfast from 89; Preb St Audoen St Patr Cathl Dublin from 90; Adn Conn from 96; Prec Belf Cathl from 96. *St John's Rectory, 86 Maryville Park, Belfast BT9 6LQ* Tel (01232) 666644

HARPER, Alan Peter. b 50. FCA83 Man Univ BA73. Ripon Coll Cuddesdon 86. **d** 88 **p** 89. C Newport w Longford and Chetwynd *Lich* 88-91; P-in-c Wilnecote 91-94; V from 94. *The Vicarage, Glascote Lane, Wilnecote, Tamworth, Staffs B77 2PH* Tel (01827) 280806

HARPER, Brian John. b 61. Liv Univ BA82 TCD DipTh85. **d** 85 **p** 86. C Portadown St Columba *Arm* 85-88; C Drumglass 88-89; I Errigle Keerogue w Ballygawley and Killeshil 89-93; Dioc Info Officer from 90; I Mullavilly from 93. *89 Mullavilly Road, Tandragee, Co Armagh BT62 2LX* Tel (01762) 840221

HARPER, Clive Stewart. b 35. FCIS71. Ridley Hall Cam 80. **d** 82 **p** 83. C Bromyard *Heref* 82-85; P-in-c Bredenbury and Wacton w Grendon Bishop 85-89; P-in-c Edwyn Ralph and Collington w Thornbury 85-89; P-in-c Pencombe w Marston Stannett and Lt Cowarne 85-89; R Bredenbury w Grendon Bishop and Wacton etc 89-92; R Bilton *Cov* from 92. *The Rectory, Church Walk, Rugby, Warks CV22 7RN* Tel (01788) 812613

HARPER, David Laurence. b 51. Qu Coll Cam BA73 MA77 PhD78. Wycliffe Hall Ox BA80. **d** 80 **p** 81. C Mansfield St Pet *S'well* 80-84; C Wollaton 84-87; V Brinsley w Underwood 87-94; R Bingham from 94. *The Rectory, Bingham, Nottingham NG13 8DR* Tel (01949) 837335

HARPER, Donald Morrison. b 10. MBE91. Qu Coll Cam BA36 MA41. Ridley Hall Cam 36. **d** 38 **p** 39. C S Harrow St Paul *Lon* 38-39; Chapl RAF 40-65; P-in-c Brighton St Geo *Chich* 65-70; Nigeria 70-72; Chapl Madeira *Eur* 72-76; rtd 75; Chapl Costa del Sol W *Eur* 76-84; Chapl Tangier 84-85; Chapl Palermo w Taormina 85-90. *Bishop's House, Lansdowne Crescent, Worcester WR3 8JH* Tel (01905) 723972

HARPER, Geoffrey. b 32. Hertf Coll Ox BA55 MA59. Coll of Resurr Mirfield. **d** 57 **p** 58. C Cov St Pet *Cov* 57-60; C Handsworth St Mich *Birm* 60-62; C-in-c Kingstanding St Mark CD 62-71; V Kingstanding St Mark 71-73; R Sheviock *Truro* 73-80; R Antony w Sheviock 80-82; V Paul from 82; Dioc Development Rep from 86. *The Vicarage, Paul, Penzance, Cornwall TR20 8TY* Tel (01736) 731261

HARPER, Geoffrey Roger. b 57. Jes Coll Cam BA MA DipTh. St Jo Coll Nottm 81. **d** 84 **p** 85. C Belper *Derby* 84-87; C Birstall and Wanlip *Leic* 87-90; TV Tettenhall Regis *Lich* from 90. *St Paul's Vicarage, 1 Talaton Close, Pendeford, Wolverhampton WV9 5LS* Tel (01902) 787199

HARPER, Gordon. b 32. Oak Hill Th Coll 64. **d** 66 **p** 67. C Halliwell St Pet *Man* 66-71 and from 84; P-in-c Brinsworth *Sheff* 71-75; V Brinsworth w Catcliffe 76-84. *15 New Church Road, Bolton BL1 5QP* Tel (01204) 849413

HARPER, Dr Gordon William Robert. b 48. Wellington Univ (NZ) BA70 St Chad's Coll Dur BA74 Nottm Univ PhD89. Coll of Resurr Mirfield 74. **d** 75 **p** 76. C Battyeford *Wakef* 75-76; New Zealand 76-80; P-in-c Byers Green *Dur* 80-83; V Evenwood 83-89; R Wolviston from 89. *The Rectory, 1 Clifton Avenue, Billingham, Cleveland TS22 5DE* Tel (01642) 551666

HARPER, Preb Horace Frederic. b 37. Lich Th Coll 58. **d** 60 **p** 61. C Stoke upon Trent *Lich* 60-63; C Fenton 63-66; V Coseley Ch Ch 66-75; V Trent Vale 75-88; P-in-c Dresden 88-89; V from 89; P-in-c Normacot from 94; Preb Lich Cathl from 96. *Dresden Vicarage, 22 Red Bank, Longton, Stoke-on-Trent ST3 4EY* Tel (01782) 321257

HARPER, Ian. b 54. AKC78. Oak Hill Th Coll 79. **d** 80 **p** 81. C Sidcup St Jo *Roch* 80-83; C Bushey *St Alb* 83-87; TV Thamesmead *S'wark* 87-92; TR N Lambeth from 92. *St Anselm's Rectory, Kennington Road, London SE11 5DU* Tel 0171-735 3415 or 735 3403

HARPER, James. b 35. St Luke's Coll Ex TDip57. SW Minl Tr Course DipTh89. **d** 90 **p** 91. NSM Pendeen w Morvah *Truro* from 90. *11 Carrallack Terrace, St Just, Penzance, Cornwall TR19 7LW* Tel (01736) 788574

HARPER, John Anthony. b 46. AKC69. **d** 70 **p** 71. C Pet St Mary Boongate *Pet* 70-73; C Abington 73-75; V Grendon w Castle Ashby 75-82; Asst Dioc Youth Chapl 75-82; R Castor w Sutton and Upton 82-94; TV Riverside *Ox* from 94. *St Andrew's Vicarage, 55 Welley Road, Wraysbury, Staines, Middx TW19 5ER* Tel (01784) 481258

HARPER, John Hugh. b 34. ALAM62 Hertf Coll Ox BA57 MA61. Wells Th Coll 57. **d** 59 **p** 60. C Twerton *B & W* 59-62; R Chapel Allerton 62-69; V Blackford 62-69; V Halsetown *Truro* 69-91; RD Penwith 84-88; P-in-c S Brent *Ex* 91; V S Brent and Rattery from 91. *The Vicarage, Firswood, South Brent, Devon TQ10 9AN* Tel (01364) 72774

HARPER, Joseph Frank. b 38. Hull Univ BA60 MA86. Linc Th Coll 80. **d** 81 **p** 82. C Preston St Cuth *Blackb* 81-83; C Lancaster St Mary 83-87; V Bamber Bridge St Aid 87-92; V Kinsley w Wragby *Wakef* from 92. *The Vicarage, Fitzwilliam, Pontefract, W Yorkshire WF9 5BX* Tel (01977) 610497

HARPER, Canon Malcolm Barry. b 37. Dur Univ BSc59. Wycliffe Hall Ox 59. **d** 61 **p** 62. C Harold Wood *Chelmsf* 61-65; C Madeley *Heref* 65-68; V Slaithwaite w E Scammonden *Wakef* 68-75; V Walmley *Birm* from 75; Hon Can Birm Cathl from 96. *The Vicarage, 2 Walmley Road, Sutton Coldfield, W Midlands B76 1QN* Tel 0121-351 1030

HARPER, Martin Nigel. b 48. FRICS88. S Dios Minl Tr Scheme. **d** 85 **p** 86. NSM St Leonards Ch Ch and St Mary *Chich* 85-94; NSM Rye from 94. *6 St Matthew's Drive, St Leonards-on-Sea, E Sussex TN38 0TR* Tel (01424) 713631

HARPER, Canon Maurice. b 20. St Steph Ho Ox 60. **d** 62 **p** 63. C Upminster *Chelmsf* 62-67; V Gt Ilford St Mary 67-71; R Upminster 71-85; RD Havering 80-85; Hon Can Chelmsf Cathl 84-85; rtd 85; Perm to Offic *Chelmsf* from 85; Perm to Offic *Nor* from 85; Perm to Offic *St E* from 87. *1 Pine Close, Harleston, Norfolk IP20 9DZ* Tel (01379) 853401

HARPER, Michael Sydney. b 36. Portsm Dioc Tr Course 86. **d** 87. NSM Leigh Park St Clare CD *Portsm* 87-88; NSM Warren Park St Clare from 88; NSM Leigh Park from 96. *17 Hampage Green, Warren Park, Havant, Hants PO9 4HJ* Tel (01705) 454275

HARPER, Dr Richard Michael. b 53. Lon Univ BSc75 Univ of Wales PhD78. St Steph Ho Ox BA80. **d** 81 **p** 82. C Holt *Nor* 81-84; C-in-c Grahame Park St Aug CD *Lon* 84-88; Sub-Warden & Dir of Studies St Mich Llan 88-93; Lect Ch Hist Univ of Wales (Cardiff) 88-93; R St Leonards Ch Ch and St Mary *Chich* from 94. *14 Stockleigh Road, St Leonards-on-Sea, E Sussex TN38 0JP* Tel (01424) 422513

HARPER, Robert. b 08. Lon Coll of Div 46. **d** 46 **p** 47. China 46-51; India 52-55; Singapore 55-69; R St Florence and Redberth *St D* 70-78; rtd 78; Hon C Maenclochog w Henry's Moat and Mynachlogddu etc *St D* 95; Hon C New Moat w Llys-y-fran 95. *South Hill Cottages, Talbenny, Haverfordwest SA62 3XA* Tel (01437) 781338

HARPER, Roger. FCA BSc. **d** 87 **p** 88. NSM Onchan *S & M* 87-97; NSM Douglas St Geo and St Barn from 97. *Ballahowin House, St Mark's, Ballasalla, Isle of Man IM9 3AS* Tel (01624) 851251

HARPER, Thomas Reginald. b 31. Dur Univ BA57 MA67. **d** 58 **p** 59. C Corbridge w Halton *Newc* 58-60; C Byker St Mich 60-62; V Ushaw Moor *Dur* 62-67; Asst Chapl HM Pris Dur 62-67; N Sec CMS 67-74; V Thornthwaite *Carl* 74-75; V Thornthwaite cum Braithwaite and Newlands 76-90; TV Bellingham/Otterburn Gp *Newc* 90-91; TV N Tyne and Redesdale Team 91-92; TR from 92; RD Bellingham from 93. *Bellingham Rectory, Hexham, Northd NE48 2JS* Tel (01434) 220019

HARPER, Timothy James Lincoln (Tim). b 54. LRAM Lon Univ BMus76 CertEd DipP&C. Wycliffe Hall Ox 84. **d** 86 **p** 87. C Morden *S'wark* 86-90; V Deptford St Pet 90-97; R Amersham *Ox* from 97. *The Rectory, Church Street, Amersham, Bucks HP7 0DB* Tel (01494) 729380 Fax 724426

HARRAP, William Charles (Bill). b 32. BEM86. **d** 72 **p** 74. Hon C Bethnal Green St Jas Less *Lon* from 72. *12 Wedgewood House, Morpeth Street, London E2 0PZ* Tel 0181-980 6887

HARRATT, Philip David. b 56. Magd Coll Ox BA79 MA83. Ripon Coll Cuddesdon 82. **d** 85 **p** 86. C Ewyas Harold w Dulas, Kenderchurch etc *Heref* 85-88; V Chirbury from 88; V Trelystan from 88; V Marton from 88. *The Vicarage, Chirbury, Montgomery SY15 6BN* Tel (01938) 561218

HARRE, Kenneth Michael. b 25. MA. EAMTC. **d** 84 **p** 85. NSM N Walsham w Antingham *Nor* 84-87; P-in-c Nor St Helen 87-95; Chapl Gt Hosp Nor 87-95; Perm to Offic *Nor* from 95. *65 Yarmouth Road, North Walsham, Norfolk NR28 9AU* Tel (01692) 403362

HARREX, David Brian. b 54. DipHE89. Trin Coll Bris 87. **d** 89 **p** 90. C Bedminster St Mich *Bris* 89-93; V Pilning w Compton Greenfield from 93; RD Westbury and Severnside from 97. *The Vicarage, The Glebe, Pilning, Bristol BS12 3LE* Tel (01454) 633409 E-mail 101352.2157@compuserve.com

HARRIES, Gwilym David. b 41. Univ of Wales (Lamp) BA63. St Mich Coll Llan 63. **d** 65 **p** 66. C Llangiwg *S & B* 65-68; C Llangyfelach and Morriston 68-71; TV Aberystwyth *St D* 71-76; R Hubberston 76-82; R Hubberston w Herbrandston and Hasguard etc 82-84; V Burry Port and Pwll from 84. *The Vicarage, 134 Pencoed Road, Burry Port SA16 0PS* Tel (01554) 832936

HARRIES, Henry Rayner Mackintosh. b 30. MBE67. Chich Th Coll 53. **d** 55 **p** 56. C Hastings H Trin *Chich* 55-58; Chapl RAF 58-79; Asst Chapl-in-Chief RAF 79-84; QHC 83-84; P-in-c Gt Brickhill w Bow Brickhill and Lt Brickhill *Ox* 84-86; R 86-94; RD Mursley 91-94; rtd 95; Perm to Offic *Chelmsf* from 94. *44 Onslow Gardens, Ongar, Essex CM5 9BQ* Tel (01277) 363741

HARRIES, Dr John Edward. b 60. Bris Univ BSc81 PhD84. Wycliffe Hall Ox 94. **d** 96 **p** 97. C Hyde St Geo *Ches* from 96. *121 Dowson Road, Hyde, Cheshire SK14 5HJ* Tel 0161-367 9353

HARRIES, Canon Lewis John. b 27. Univ of Wales BA52. St Mich Coll Llan 51. **d** 53 **p** 54. C Maindee *Mon* 53-58; V Goldcliffe and Whiston and Nash 58-64; V Tredegar St Geo 64-93; RD Bedwellty 78-93; Can St Woolos Cathl 82-93; rtd 93; Hon Can St Woolos Cathl *Mon* from 93; Perm to Offic *St D* from 93. *14 Hendre Road, Llanelli SA14 9LD* Tel (01554) 773039

HARRIES, Malcolm David. b 44. Oak Hill Th Coll 94. **d** 96 **p** 97. C Rock Ferry *Ches* from 96. *13 Graylands Road, Wirral, Merseyside L62 4SB* Tel 0151-643 9292

✠**HARRIES, The Rt Revd Richard Douglas.** b 36. Selw Coll Cam BA61 MA65 FKC83. Cuddesdon Coll 61. **d** 63 **p** 64 **c** 87. C Hampstead St Jo *Lon* 63-69; Chapl Westf Coll Lon 67-69; Tutor Wells Th Coll 69-71; Warden Sarum & Wells Th Coll 71-72; V Fulham All SS *Lon* 72-81; Dean K Coll Lon 81-87; Consultant to Abps Cant and York on Inter-Faith Relns from 86; Bp Ox from 87. *Bishop's House, 27 Linton Road, Oxford OX2 6UL* Tel (01865) 244566 Fax 790470

HARRINGTON, Charles William. b 04. Linc Th Coll. **d** 42 **p** 43. C Gedling *S'well* 42-44; Clerical Dir (W Midl) ICF 44-47; V Woodborough 47-50 and 57-63; V Nottingham All SS 50-55; S Africa 55-57; Chapl HM Borstal Inst Roch 63-65; V Horley w Hornton *Ox* 65-70; P-in-c Hanwell 65-70; V Letcombe Regis w Letcombe Bassett 70-73; rtd 73; Perm to Offic *Cant* 74-88; Perm to Offic *Glouc* from 88. *Broadleas Retirement Home, 9 Eldorado Road, Cheltenham, Glos GL50 2PU* Tel (01242) 583232

HARRINGTON, John Christopher Thomas. b 43. Conf Catholic Colls CertRE63. Qu Coll Birm 71. **d** 74 **p** 75. C Northampton St Mich *Pet* 74-76; CF (TA) 75-85; C Paston *Pet* 76-79; Chapl Doddington Co Hosp 79-83; R Benwick St Mary *Ely* 79-82; R Doddington 79-82; R Doddington w Benwick 82-83; V Eastbourne St Mich *Chich* from 83. *The Vicarage, 15 Long Acre Close, Eastbourne, E Sussex BN21 1UF* Tel (01323) 645740 E-mail harrington@fastnet.co.uk

HARRINGTON, Peter Anthony Saunders. b 30. Fitzw Ho Cam BA52 MA58. Ely Th Coll 53. **d** 55 **p** 56. C Croydon St Mich *Cant* 55-59; Australia 59-62; C W Wycombe *Ox* 63-66; Chapl Dr Challoner's Gr Sch Amersham 67-95; Lic to Offic *Ox* 67-78; Lic to Offic *St Alb* from 78; rtd 95. *5 Linfields, Little Chalfont, Amersham, Bucks HP7 9QH* Tel (01494) 763471

HARRINGTON, William Harry. b 33. AKC57. **d** 58 **p** 59. C Childwall All SS *Liv* 58-60; C Sutton 60-64; V Ditton St Mich 64-76; V Mossley Hill St Barn 76-83; V Highfield from 83. *St Matthew's Vicarage, Highfield, Wigan, Lancs WN3 6BL* Tel (01942) 222121

HARRIS, Arthur Emlyn Dawson. b 27. Ex Univ BSc47 Lon Univ DipRS86. S'wark Ord Course 83. **d** 86 **p** 87. NSM Frant w Eridge *Chich* 86-87; P-in-c Withyham St Mich 87-95; rtd 95. *53A The Close, Salisbury SP1 2EL* Tel (01722) 339886

HARRIS, Bernard Malcolm. b 29. Leeds Univ BA54. Coll of Resurr Mirfield 54. **d** 56 **p** 57. C Shrewsbury St Chad *Lich* 56-60; C Porthill 60-61; V Birches Head 61-66; V W Bromwich St Jas 66-78; V Sedgley All SS 78-93; rtd 93. *6 Beacon Lane, Sedgley, Dudley, West Midlands DY3 1NB* Tel (01902) 663134

HARRIS, Brian. b 33. Man Univ BSc. Qu Coll Birm 79. **d** 80 **p** 81. C Lich St Chad *Lich* 80-81; Perm to Offic *Ches* 82-87; NSM Warburton 87-88; P-in-c 88-92; R Gt and Lt Casterton w Pickworth and Tickencote *Pet* from 92; RD Barnack from 94. *The Rectory, Main Street, Great Casterton, Stamford, Lincs PE9 4AP* Tel (01780) 64036

HARRIS, Brian William. b 38. K Coll Lon BD61 AKC61. St Boniface Warminster 61. **d** 62 **p** 63. C Liversedge *Wakef* 62-65; C Kirkby *Liv* 65-70; V Dalton 70-79; V Aberford w Saxton *York* 79-91; V Hemingbrough 91-95; rtd 95; Perm to Offic *York* from 95; Dom Chapl to Bp Selby from 95. *1 Andrew Drive, Huntington, York YO3 9YF* Tel (01904) 422988

HARRIS, Catherine Elizabeth. *See* EDMONDS, Mrs Catherine Elizabeth

HARRIS, Cedric Herbert. b 13. AKC37. Wycliffe Hall Ox 37. **d** 37 **p** 38. C Normanton *Wakef* 37-42; C Brighouse 42-44; V Barkisland w W Scammonden 44-49; V Thornes St Jas 49-57; V Wakef Ch Ch 50-57; V Thornes St Jas w Ch Ch 57-73; V Shepley 73-78; rtd 78. *44 Rayner Street, Horbury, Wakefield, W Yorkshire WF4 5BD* Tel (01924) 272297

HARRIS, Charles Edward. b 20. Roch Th Coll 63. **d** 65 **p** 66. C Hertford St Andr *St Alb* 65-71; R Sywell w Overstone *Pet* 71-90; rtd 90; Perm to Offic *Chich* from 92. *College of St Barnabas, Blackberry Lane, Lingfield, Surrey RH7 6NJ* Tel (01342) 870607

HARRIS, Claude Anthony. b 16. Dur Univ LTh39. Oak Hill Th Coll 36. **d** 39 **p** 40. C Darlaston St Laur *Lich* 39-45; C Walsall St Matt 45-48; V Wombridge 48-53; V Tipton St Matt 53-60; R Stone St Mich 60-82; V Aston 60-82; rtd 82; Perm to Offic *Lich* from 82. *Hardwick Cottage, 51 Stafford Road, Stone, Staffs ST15 0HE* Tel (01785) 815100

HARRIS, Cyril Evans. b 30. Linc Th Coll 61. **d** 63 **p** 64. C Beaconsfield *Ox* 63-68; V Stoke Poges from 68. *The Vicarage, Park Road, Stoke Poges, Slough SL2 4PE* Tel (01753) 644177

HARRIS, David. b 52. AKC76. St Steph Ho Ox 76. **d** 77 **p** 79. C Wimbledon *S'wark* 77-80; C Coalbrookdale, Iron-Bridge and Lt Wenlock *Heref* 80-82; V Highters Heath *Birm* 82-84; Perm to Offic *Lon* from 85. *35 Paddonswick Road, London W6 0UA* Tel 0181-748 5195

HARRIS, David Rowland. b 46. Ch Ch Ox BA69 DipTh71 MA72. Wycliffe Hall Ox 70. **d** 73 **p** 74. C Virginia Water *Guildf* 73-76; C Clifton Ch Ch w Em *Bris* 76-79; Scripture Union 79-85; V Bedford Ch Ch *St Alb* from 85. *Christ Church Vicarage, 115 Denmark Street, Bedford MK40 3TJ* Tel (01234) 359342

HARRIS, Derrick William. b 21. **d** 63 **p** 64. C Birkdale St Jo *Liv* 63-67; V Billinge 67-81; V Walton *Ches* 81-87; rtd 88; Perm to Offic *Ches* from 88; Perm to Offic *Liv* from 88. *3 Melrose Avenue, Southport, Merseyside PR9 9UY* Tel (01704) 213828

HARRIS, Ernest John. b 46. Lon Univ DipTh74 QUB BD75. **d** 75 **p** 76. C Lisburn Ch Ch *Conn* 75-78; C Coleraine 78-83; I Belfast St Kath 83-90; I Ballinderry from 90. *The Rectory, 124 Ballinderry Road, Ballinderry Upper, Lisburn, Co Antrim BT28 2NL* Tel (01846) 651310

HARRIS, Evan Rufus. b 21. Univ of Wales (Lamp) BA49. Bp Burgess Hall Lamp. **d** 50 **p** 51. C Gt Grimsby St Luke *Linc* 50-52; C Gainsborough All SS 52-54; R Gate Burton 54-57; V Marton 54-57; R Barrowby 57-86; RD Grantham 69-78; Offg Chapl RAF 70-76; rtd 86. *Flat 2, 4 Northumberland Road, Barnet, Herts EN5 1ED* Tel 0181-447 0502

HARRIS, Frank Edward. b 33. ACT ThL69 St Fran Coll Brisbane 65. **d** 68 **p** 69. Australia 68-71 and 73-76; C Plymstock *Ex* 71-72; C E Acton St Dunstan w St Thos *Lon* 72-73; C Bodmin *Truro* 76-77; P-in-c Menheniot 77-79; V Winton *Man* 79-87; Guinea 87-89; R Blisland w St Breward *Truro* 90-96. *4 Gwel Marten, Headland Road, Carbis Bay, St Ives, Cornwall TR26 2PB* Tel (01736) 793280

HARRIS, Geoffrey Daryl. b 39. Lon Univ DipTh66 Open Univ BA83. St Aid Birkenhead 63. **d** 66 **p** 67. C Eston *York* 66-70; C Iffley *Ox* 70-75; V Bubwith *York* 75-78; V Bubwith w Ellerton and Aughton 78-79; P-in-c Stillingfleet w Naburn 79-80; R Escrick and Stillingfleet w Naburn 80-95; Chapl Qu Marg Sch York 83-94; Hon C Okehampton w Inwardleigh, Bratton Clovelly etc *Ex* from 96. *St Bridget's House, Bridestowe, Okehampton, Devon EX20 4ER* Tel (01837) 861612

HARRIS, George. b 36. Sarum Th Coll 66. **d** 68 **p** 69. C Shildon *Dur* 68-70; CF 70-74; P-in-c Doddington *Ely* 74-75; R 75-78; R Benwick St Mary 74-78; V Shotton *Dur* 78-86; V Stockton St Mark 86-87; V Chilton Moor 87-94; P-in-c Lyons 96; R from 96. *The Rectory, High Street, Easington Lane, Houghton le Spring, Tyne & Wear DH5 0JN* Tel 0191-526 5505

HARRIS, Gerald Alfred. b 29. Qu Coll Birm 80. **d** 84 **p** 85. NSM Pedmore *Worc* 84-86; C Christchurch *Win* 86-94; rtd 94. *7 Wych Court, Hawkchurch, Axminster, Devon EX13 5XE* Tel (01297) 678503

HARRIS, Jack Peter Francis. b 49. Barrister-at-Law (Lincoln's Inn) 72 St Cath Coll Ox BA70 MA74 Fitzw Coll Cam BA85 MA89. Westcott Ho Cam 83. **d** 86 **p** 87. C Doncaster Ch Ch *Sheff* 86-91; P-in-c 91-92; V 92-95; V Doncaster H Trin 95-96; V Belsize Park *Lon* from 96. *St Peter's Vicarage, Belsize Square, London NW3 4HY* Tel 0171-794 4020

HARRIS, James Nigel Kingsley. b 37. St D Coll Lamp BA60. Sarum Th Coll. **d** 62 **p** 63. C Painswick *Glouc* 62-65; C Glouc St Paul 65-67; V Slad 67-77; V Cam 77-78; P-in-c Stinchcombe 77-78; V Cam w Stinchcombe 78-82; V Stonehouse from 82; Chapl Standish Hosp Glouc from 92. *The Vicarage, Elms Road, Stonehouse, Glos GL10 2NP* Tel (01453) 822332

HARRIS, James Philip. b 59. Westf Coll Lon BA82. St Mich Coll Llan BD86. **d** 86 **p** 87. C Newport St Paul *Mon* 86-89; C Bedwellty 89-91; V Newport St Matt 91-96. *Address temp unknown*

HARRIS, Jeremy Michael. b 64. Gwent Coll of HE HNC86. St Steph Ho Ox BTh93. **d** 93 **p** 94. C Newport St Julian *Mon* 93-95; C Ebbw Vale 95-97; TV from 97. *Glaslyn, Beaufort Hill, Ebbw Vale NP3 5QR* Tel (01495) 350208

HARRIS, The Very Revd John. b 32. Univ of Wales (Lamp) BA55. Sarum Th Coll 55. **d** 57 **p** 58. V Pontnewynydd *Mon* 57-60; C Bassaleg 60-63; V Penmaen 63-69; V Newport St Paul 69-84; RD Newport 77-93; V Maindee 84-93; Can St Woolos Cathl 84-93; Dean Brecon *S & B* from 93; V Brecon St Mary and Battle w Llanddew 93-95. *The Deanery, Cathedral Close, Brecon LD3 9DP* Tel (01874) 623344

HARRIS, John. b 45. St Steph Ho Ox 72. **d** 75 **p** 76. C Wanstead St Mary *Chelmsf* 75-84; V Penponds *Truro* 84-91; V St Gluvias from 91. *The Vicarage, St Gluvias, Penryn, Cornwall TR10 9LQ* Tel (01326) 373356

HARRIS, John. b 54. Leeds Univ BSc75. St Jo Coll Nottm LTh86. **d** 86 **p** 87. C S Ossett *Wakef* 86-90; V Moldgreen 90-97; P-in-c S Ossett from 97. *36 Manor Road, Ossett, Wakefield, W Yorkshire WF5 0AU* Tel (01924) 263311

HARRIS, John Brian. b 53. Hertf Coll Ox BA76. Ripon Coll Cuddesdon 87. **d** 89 **p** 90. C Witton *Ches* 89-93; R Thurstaston from 93. *The Rectory, Thurstaston Road, Irby, Wirral, Merseyside L61 0HQ* Tel 0151-648 1816

HARRIS, Canon John Peter. b 33. St D Coll Lamp BA57. **d** 58 **p** 59. Chapl St Woolos Hosp Newport 58-63; C Newport St Woolos *Mon* 58-60; Chapl St Woolos Cathl 60-63; CF (TA) 59-63; CF 63-82; V Chepstow *Mon* from 82; RD Chepstow from 85; Can St Woolos Cathl from 93. *The Vicarage, 25 Mount Way, Chepstow NP6 5NF* Tel (01291) 620980

HARRIS, John Stuart. b 29. Hertf Coll Ox BA52 MA56. Wells Th Coll 52. **d** 54 **p** 55. C Epsom St Martin *Guildf* 54-58; C Guildf H Trin w St Mary 58-63; R Bentley 63-72; V Milford 72-87; R Walton-on-the-Hill from 87; Dioc Ecum Officer 87-92. *St Peter's Rectory, Walton-on-the-Hill, Tadworth, Surrey KT20 7SO* Tel (01737) 812105

HARRIS, Mrs Judith Helen. b 42. Chelsea Coll Lon TCert64. St Alb Minl Tr Scheme 83. **dss** 86 **d** 87 **p** 94. Leagrave *St Alb* 86-87; Hon Par Dn 87-91; TD Dunstable 91-94; TV from 94. *95 Evelyn Road, Dunstable, Beds LU5 4NQ* Tel (01582) 476536

HARRIS, Canon Kenneth. b 28. NW Ord Course 70. **d** 72 **p** 73. NSM Upton Ascension *Ches* 72-77; NSM Eccleston and Pulford 77-80; P-in-c Hargrave 80-81; V 81-94; Exec Officer Dioc Bd for Soc Resp 84-94; Hon Can Ches Cathl 91-94; rtd 94; P-in-c Ashton Hayes *Ches* from 96. *Delsa, Willington Road, Willington, Tarporley, Cheshire CW6 0ND* Tel (01829) 751880

HARRIS, Lawrence Rex Rowland. b 35. St Cath Coll Cam BA59 MA63. Ely Th Coll. **d** 61 **p** 62. C Carrington *S'well* 61-63; Chapl Rampton Hosp Retford 63-66; V Sturton w Littleborough *S'well* 66-71; V Bole w Saundby 66-71; R Clowne *Derby* from 71; RD Bolsover and Staveley 81-86. *The Rectory, Rectory Road, Clowne, Chesterfield, Derbyshire S43 4BH* Tel (01246) 810387

HARRIS, Margaret Claire (Novice Sister Margaret Joy). b 53. RGN85 Homerton Coll Cam BEd78. Ridley Hall Cam CTM92. **d** 92. Par Dn Stevenage All SS Pin Green *St Alb* 92-94; C 94-95; CSMV from 95. *St Mary's Convent, Challow Road, Wantage, Oxon OX12 9DJ* Tel (01235) 763141

HARRIS, Martin John. b 54. Trin Coll Cam BA76 MA. Wycliffe Hall Ox 82. **d** 85 **p** 86. C Lindfield *Chich* 85-88; C Galleywood Common *Chelmsf* 88-91; V Southchurch Ch Ch from 91. *Christ Church Vicarage, Warwick Road, Southend-on-Sea SS1 3BN* Tel (01702) 582585

HARRIS, Michael. b 34. ACP65 MIL76 St Mark & St Jo Coll Lon CertEd56. Qu Coll Birm. **d** 83 **p** 84. NSM Bournville *Birm* 83-90; NSM Stirchley from 90; Chapl Univ of Cen England in Birm from 92; Dean NSMs from 96. *3 Teazel Avenue, Bournville, Birmingham B30 1LZ* Tel 0121-459 5236 or 331 5188 Fax 356 2875 E-mail 101736.1423compuserve.com

HARRIS, Michael Andrew. b 53. Ian Ramsey Coll 74 Trin Coll Bris 75. **d** 78 **p** 79. C St Paul's Cray St Barn *Roch* 78-82; C Church Stretton *Heref* 82-87; Res Min Penkridge w Stretton *Lich* 87-90; Res Min Penkridge Team 90-92; V Amington *Birm* from 92. *The Vicarage, 224 Tamworth Road, Amington, Tamworth, Staffs B77 3DE* Tel (01827) 62573

HARRIS, Nicholas Bryan. b 60. Down Coll Cam BA81 MA85. Ridley Hall Cam 82. **d** 85 **p** 86. C Walney Is *Carl* 85-88; C S'wark Ch Ch *S'wark* 88-92; Perm to Offic *Chich* from 92. *82 Hurst Road, Eastbourne, E Sussex BN21 2PW* Tel (01323) 731922

HARRIS, Owen. b 50. Univ of Wales (Swansea) BSc(Econ)71 PGCE72. St Mich Coll Llan DPT94. **d** 94 **p** 95. C Bassaleg *Mon* from 94. *2 High Cross Drive, Rogerstone, Newport NP1 9AB* Tel (01633) 895441

✠**HARRIS, The Rt Revd Patrick Burnet.** b 34. Keble Coll Ox BA58 MA63. Clifton Th Coll 58. **d** 60 **p** 61 **c** 73. C Ox St Ebbe w St Pet *Ox* 60-63; SAMS 63-81; Adn N Argentina 70-73; Bp 73-80; R Kirkheaton *Wakef* 81-85; Asst Bp Wakef 81-85; Sec C of E Partnership for World Miss 86-88; Asst Bp Ox 86-88; Bp S'well from 88. *Bishop's Manor, Southwell, Notts NG25 0JR* Tel (01636) 812112 Fax 815401 E-mail bishop.southwell @john316.com

HARRIS, Paul. b 55. BEd79 DipHE84. Oak Hill Th Coll 82. **d** 84 **p** 85. C Billericay and Lt Burstead *Chelmsf* 84-87; TV Cheltenham St Mary, St Matt, St Paul and H Trin *Glouc* 87-93; V Bitterne *Win* from 93. *The Vicarage, 2 Bursledon Road, Southampton SO19 7LW* Tel (01703) 446488

HARRIS, Paul Ian. b 45. MSc. Qu Coll Birm. **d** 82 **p** 83. C The Quinton *Birm* 82-86; V Atherstone *Cov* from 86. *40 Holte Road, Atherstone, Warks CV9 1HN* Tel (01827) 713200

HARRIS, Paul Michael. b 58. Chelsea Coll Lon BSc79 Bath Coll of HE CertEd82. Oak Hill Th Coll BA89. **d** 89. C Finchley Ch Ch *Lon* 89-90; Teacher St Luke's Sch W Norwood 90-91; The Philippines from 91. *Brent International School, Meralco Avenue, Pasig, Manila, The Philippines* Tel Manila (2) 631-1265

HARRIS, Peter Frank. b 43. WMMTC 89. **d** 92 **p** 93. NSM Lich Ch Ch *Lich* 92-96; NSM Ogley Hay from 96. *94 Ogley Hay Road, Boney Hay, Walsall WS7 8HU* Tel (01543) 675258

HARRIS, Peter Malcolm. b 52. Em Coll Cam BA74 MA79. Trin Coll Bris DipHE80. **d** 80 **p** 81. C Upton (Overchurch) *Ches* 80-83; BCMS 83-93; Crosslinks from 93; Portugal from 83. *Arocha, Cruzinha, Mexilhoeira Grande, 8500 Portimão, Portugal* Tel Portimão (82) 96380

HARRIS, Raymond. b 36. Nottm Univ BA58. Lich Th Coll 58. **d** 60 **p** 61. C Clifton St Fran *S'well* 60-63; C Davyhulme St Mary *Man* 63-66; V Bacup Ch Ch 66-82; R Dunsby w Dowsby *Linc* 82-87; R Rippingale 82-87; R Rippingale Gp 87-94; rtd 94. *2 The Bungalow, High Street, Swaton, Sleaford, Lincs NG34 0JU* Tel (01529) 421343

HARRIS, Canon Raymond John. b 29. Leeds Univ BA51. Coll of Resurr Mirfield 51. **d** 53 **p** 54. C Workington St Mich *Carl* 53-59; V New Swindon St Barn Gorse Hill *Bris* 59-94; Hon Can Bris Cathl 80-94; RD Cricklade 82-88; rtd 94; Perm to Offic *Glouc* from 94. *46 Courtbrook, Fairford, Glos GL7 4BE* Tel (01285) 713965

HARRIS, Rebecca Jane. *See* SWYER, Mrs Rebecca Jane

HARRIS (née LEE), Mrs Rebecca Susan. b 62. Man Univ BA85 S Glam Inst HE 86. Trin Coll Bris DipHE95. **d** 95 **p** 96. C Cirencester *Glouc* from 95. *15 Partridge Way, Cirencester, Glos GL7 1BH* Tel (01285) 654779

HARRIS, The Ven Reginald Brian. b 34. Ch Coll Cam BA58 MA61. Ridley Hall Cam. **d** 59 **p** 60. C Wednesbury St Bart *Lich* 59-61; C Uttoxeter w Bramshall 61-64; V Bury St Pet *Man* 64-70; V Walmsley 70-80; RD Walmsley 70-80; Adn Man from 80; Can Res Man Cathl from 80. *4 Victoria Avenue, Eccles, Manchester M30 9HA* Tel 0161-707 6444 Fax as telephone

HARRIS, Robert Douglas. b 57. BEd. Chich Th Coll 80. **d** 82 **p** 83. C Portsea St Mary *Portsm* 82-87; V Clevedon St Jo *B & W* 87-92; R Felpham w Middleton *Chich* from 92. *The Rectory, 24 Limmer Lane, Felpham, Bognor Regis, W Sussex PO22 7ET* Tel (01243) 842522

HARRIS, Robert James. b 45. ALCD73. St Jo Coll Nottm 69. **d** 72 **p** 73. C Sheff St Jo *Sheff* 72-76; C Goole 76-78; V Bramley and Ravenfield 78-91; P-in-c Boulton *Derby* from 91; RD Melbourne from 96. *The Vicarage, 1 St Mary's Close, Boulton Lane, Alvaston, Derby DE24 0FE* Tel (01332) 571296

HARRIS, Thomas William (Tom). b 54. AKC76. Linc Th Coll 77 Kelham Th Coll. **d** 78 **p** 79. C Norton Woodseats St Chad *Sheff* 78-81; V Barnby Dun 81-91; P-in-c Kirk Bramwith 81-85; P-in-c Fenwick 81-85; Chapl RN 91-94; P-in-c Christian Malford w Sutton Benger etc *Bris* 94; R Draycot from 94. *The Rectory, Church Road, Christian Malford, Chippenham, Wilts SN15 4BW* Tel (01249) 720466

HARRIS, William Edric Mackenzie. b 46. Sarum & Wells Th Coll 72. **d** 75 **p** 76. C Langney *Chich* 75-79; C Moulsecoomb 80-81; TV 81-85; R W Grinstead from 85. *The Rectory, Steyning Road, West Grinstead, Horsham, W Sussex RH13 8LR* Tel (01403) 710339

HARRIS, William Fergus. b 36. CCC Cam BA59 MA63 Edin Univ DipEd70. Yale Div Sch 59 Westcott Ho Cam 60. **d** 62 **p** 63. C St Andrews St Andr *St And* 62-64; Chapl Edin Univ *Edin* 64-71; R Edin St Pet 71-83; R Perth St Jo *St And* 83-90; Hon C from 90; rtd 90. *35 St Mary's Drive, Perth PH2 7BY* Tel (01738) 621379

HARRIS-DOUGLAS, John Douglas. b 34. Ripon Hall Ox 65. **d** 66 **p** 67. C Ringwood *Win* 66-67; C Baswich *Lich* 67-71; R St Tudy *Truro* 71-74; R St Tudy w Michaelstow 74-76; Adv in Children's Work and Asst Dir Educn 71-76; R Fiskerton *Linc* 76-79; Dir of Educn and Adv RE 76-79; P-in-c Thormanby *York* 79-84; V Brafferton w Pilmoor and Myton on Swale 79-84; V Brafferton w Pilmoor, Myton on Swale etc 84-97; rtd 97. *The Vicarage, Brafferton, York YO6 2QB* Tel (01423) 360244

HARRIS-EVANS, Canon Francis Douglas Harris. b 07. Keble Coll Ox BA32 MA39. Linc Th Coll 32. **d** 35 **p** 36. C Birstall *Leic* 35-39; C Ashby-de-la-Zouch St Helen 39-40; C Knighton St Jo 40-41; C Ashby-de-la-Zouch St Helen 41-45; V Horninghold w Blaston 45-51; P-in-c 51-54; RD Gartree III 49-57; R Medbourne w Holt 51-57; Hon Can Leic Cathl 54-74; RD Christianity 62-66; V Knighton St Jo 57-68; V Newtown Linford 68-74; rtd 74; Perm to Offic *Leic* from 74; Perm to Offic *Pet* from 74. *5 Mayflower Mews, Uppingham, Leics LE15 9ZZ* Tel (01572) 823699

HARRIS-EVANS, William Giles. b 46. AKC68. Bangalore Th Coll DipTh70. **d** 70 **p** 71. C Clapham H Trin *S'wark* 70-74; Sri Lanka 75-78; V Benhilton *S'wark* 78-86; TR Cov E *Cov* 86-93; TR Brighouse and Clifton *Wakef* from 93. *The Vicarage, 11 Slead Avenue, Brighouse, W Yorkshire HD6 2JB* Tel (01484) 714032

HARRIS-WHITE, John Emlyn. b 34. St Aid Birkenhead 59. **d** 62 **p** 63. C Cricklade w Latton *Bris* 62-63; C Kingswood 63-66; C Ashton-on-Ribble St Andr *Blackb* 66-69; V Heyhouses 69-71; Chapl Roundway Hosp Devizes 71-77; Chapl R Variety Children's Hosp 77-89; Chapl K Coll and Belgrave Hosps Lon 77-89; Regional Community Relns Co-ord 89-93; rtd 94. *11 Leaside Court, Clifton Gardens, Folkestone, Kent CT20 2ED* Tel (01303) 245184

HARRISON, Alan George. b 20. Leeds Univ BA49. Coll of Resurr Mirfield 49. **d** 51 **p** 52. C Wellingborough St Mary *Pet* 51-55; Br Honduras 55-61; V Bournemouth St Fran *Win* 61-68; V Eastleigh 68-72; Chapl Guild of Health Lon 72-76; Chapl St Mich Convent Ham 73-86; Sec Coun for Relig Communities 76-86; rtd 86; Perm to Offic *S'wark* from 86. *10 The Quadrangle, Morden College, London SE3 0PW* Tel 0181-858 5134

HARRISON, Alan William. b 16. Lich Th Coll 38. **d** 41 **p** 42. C Norbury St Oswald *Cant* 41-43; C Sheff St Cuth *Sheff* 43-49; V Orton-on-the-Hill w Twycross etc *Leic* 49-55; V Somerby, Burrough on the Hill and Pickwell 55-72; R Boxford *St E* 72-82; rtd 82; Perm to Offic *St E* from 82. *10 Meadowlands, Woolpit, Bury St Edmunds, Suffolk IP30 9SE* Tel (01359) 41614

HARRISON, Albert Arthur. b 01. FCIT. **d** 63 **p** 64. Hon C Richmond *Ripon* 63-65; Chapl Aske Chapelry 65-85; NSM Rokeby w Brignall 67-89; rtd 89. *16 Ronaldshay Drive, Richmond, N Yorkshire DL10 5BN* Tel (01748) 823072

HARRISON, Mrs Alison Edwina. b 53. Newc Univ BEd75. Linc Th Coll 84. **dss** 86 **d** 87 **p** 94. Loughborough Em *Leic* 86-87; Par Dn 87-89; C Stockton *Dur* 89-92; P-in-c Lynesack 92-95; P-in-c Cockfield 92-95; P-in-c Ebchester 95-96; R from 96; V Medomsley from 96. *The New Rectory, Shaw Lane, Consett, Co Durham DH8 0PY* Tel (01207) 560301

HARRISON, Alistair Lee. b 22. ALCD51. **d** 51 **p** 52. C Stoke Damerel *Ex* 51-54; Chapl RAF 54-67; Asst Chapl Miss to Seamen 67-77; Lic to Offic *D & G* 77-83; Lic to Offic *M & K* 77-83; C Dublin St Ann w St Mark and St Steph *D & G* 83-92; rtd 92. *8 Grosvenor Place, Rathgar, Dublin 6, Irish Republic* Tel Dublin (1) 497 6053

HARRISON, Mrs Barbara Ann. b 41. Man Univ BA63 Leic Univ CertEd64. EMMTC 85. **d** 88 **p** 94. C Immingham *Linc* 88-94; P-in-c Habrough Gp from 94. *The Vicarage, 29 School Road, South Killingholme, Grimsby, S Humberside DN40 3HS* Tel (01469) 540287

HARRISON, Mrs Barbara Anne. b 34. Westf Coll Lon BA56 CertEd57 Hull Univ MA85. Linc Th Coll 76. **dss** 79 **d** 87 **p** 94. Lakenham St Jo *Nor* 79-80; Chapl York Univ *York* 80-88; TD Sheff Manor *Sheff* 88-93; Par Dn Holts CD *Man* 93-94; C-in-c from 94; Dioc UPA Officer from 93. *St Hugh's Vicarage, Wildmoor Avenue, Oldham OL4 5NZ* Tel 0161-620 1646 or 832 5253 Fax 832 2869

HARRISON, Bernard Charles. b 37. St Mich Coll Llan 61. **d** 64 **p** 65. C Toxteth Park St Marg *Liv* 64-69; C Hindley All SS 69-71; V Wigan St Geo from 71. *St George's Vicarage, 6 Wrightington Street, Wigan, Lancs WN1 2BX* Tel (01942) 44500

HARRISON, Brian John. b 35. FCP. Glouc Sch of Min 83. **d** 86 **p** 89. NSM Broseley w Benthall *Heref* 86-93; Perm to Offic from 94. *17 Hafren Road, Little Dawley, Telford, Shropshire TF4 3HJ* Tel (01952) 591891

HARRISON, Bruce. b 49. Linc Th Coll 86. **d** 88 **p** 89. C Syston *Leic* 88-90; C Whitby *York* 90-93; V Glaisdale from 93. *The Vicarage, Glaisdale, Whitby, N Yorkshire YO21 2PL* Tel (01947) 897214

HARRISON, Bruce Mountford. b 49. AKC71. **d** 72 **p** 73. C Hebburn St Cuth *Dur* 72-75; C Bethnal Green St Jo w St Simon *Lon* 75-77; P-in-c Bethnal Green St Bart 77-78; TV Bethnal Green St Jo w St Bart 78-80; C-in-c Pennywell St Thos and Grindon St Oswald CD *Dur* 80-85; V Sunderland Pennywell St Thos 85-90; V Gateshead St Helen from 90. *The Vicarage, 7 Carlton Terrace, Gateshead, Tyne & Wear NE9 6DE* Tel 0191-487 6510

HARRISON, Cécile. b 29. Bp Lonsdale Coll TCert51 Lon Univ DBRS73. St Steph Ho Ox 97. **d** 97 **p** 97. Lic to Offic *Eur* from 97. *Prasada, Quartier Subrane, Montauroux, 83440 Fayence, France* Tel France (33) 4 94 47 74 26

HARRISON, Christopher Dennis. b 57. Clare Coll Cam BA79 BA86. Westcott Ho Cam 84. **d** 87 **p** 88. C Camberwell St Geo *S'wark* 87-92; V Forest Hill 92-96; P-in-c Fenny Bentley, Kniveton, Thorpe and Tissington *Derby* from 96; P-in-c Parwich w Alsop en le Dale from 96. *The Vicarage, Parwich, Ashbourne, Derbyshire DE6 1QD* Tel (01335) 390226

HARRISON, Christopher Joseph. b 38. AKC61 Bris Univ BEd75. **d** 62 **p** 63. C Bottesford *Linc* 62-67; C Elloughton *York* 67-68; P-in-c Farmington *Glouc* 69-74; C Tredington w Stoke Orchard and Hardwicke 74-86; Perm to Offic from 87. *Appledore, 93 Stoke Road, Bishops Cleeve, Cheltenham, Glos GL52 4RP* Tel (01242) 673452

HARRISON, Colin Charles. b 32. Nottm Univ BA59. Ripon Hall Ox 59. **d** 61 **p** 62. C Everton St Chad w Ch Ch *Liv* 61-64; Japan 64-66; P-in-c Glas St Gabr *Glas* 66-71; R Clarkston 71-74; Area Sec (Inner Lon) Chr Aid 74-84; Hon C St Nic Cole Abbey *Lon* 74-78; Hon C St Botolph without Bishopgate 78-84; Miss to Seamen from 85; Nigeria 85-86; S Africa 87-88; Korea 88-91; Trinidad and Tobago 91-92; Singapore from 92. *291 River Valley Road, Singapore 0923* Tel Singapore (65) 737-2880 Fax 235-3391

HARRISON, David Henry. b 40. Lon Univ DipTh67. Tyndale Hall Bris 65. **d** 68 **p** 69. C Bolton St Paul *Man* 68-72; V Bircle 72-83; V Southport SS Simon and Jude *Liv* 83-91; TR Fazakerley Em from 91. *The Rectory, Higher Lane, Liverpool L9 9DJ* Tel 0151-525 2689

HARRISON, David Robert. b 31. Bris Univ BSc52 CertEd55. Oak Hill Th Coll 56. **d** 58 **p** 59. C Brixton Hill St Sav *S'wark* 58-60; C Harpurhey Ch Ch *Man* 60-62; Singapore 62-67; V Greenfield *Man* 67-78; V Tonge Fold 78-90; R Tasburgh w Tharston, Forncett and Flordon *Nor* 90-93; C Gorleston St Andr 93-96; rtd 96. *7 The Close, Brixham, Devon TQ5 8RE* Tel (01803) 854627

HARRISON, David Samuel. b 44. Univ of Wales (Ban) BSc67. St Mich Coll Llan 67. **d** 70 **p** 71. C Canton St Jo *Llan* 70-74; C

Witton *Ches* 74-78; V Sutton St Geo 78-96; P-in-c Henbury from 96. *The Vicarage, Church Lane, Henbury, Macclesfield, Cheshire SK11 9NN* Tel (01625) 424113

HARRISON, Miss Doreen. b 32. Leeds Univ BA53 PGCE54 DipRE57 Lanc Univ MLitt78 MA79. **d** 92 **p** 94. C Ambleside w Brathay *Carl* 92-96; C Satterthwaite from 96; C Colton from 96; C Rusland from 96. *Fox How, Ambleside, Cumbria LA22 9LL* Tel (01539) 433021

HARRISON, Ernest Wilfrid. b 17. Ox Univ MA Toronto Univ MA. Sarum Th Coll. **d** 40 **p** 41. C Roby *Liv* 40-43; C-in-c St D Huyton w Roby 43-45; C Coulsdon St Jo *S'wark* 45-47; Asst Dioc Missr 48-52; Canada from 52. *Address temp unknown*

HARRISON, Francis Russell. b 20. EAMTC. **d** 82 **p** 83. NSM Felixstowe St Jo *St E* 82-85; Asst Chapl Ipswich Hosp 85-87; rtd 87; Perm to Offic *St E* from 87. *The Strands, London Road, Copdock, Ipswich IP8 3JF* Tel (01473) 730292

HARRISON, Fred Graham. b 41. Lon Univ BSc62. Ridley Hall Cam 80. **d** 82 **p** 83. C Lenton *S'well* 82-85; V Ruddington from 85. *The Vicarage, 62 Musters Road, Ruddington, Nottingham NG11 6HW* Tel 0115-921 1505

HARRISON, Guy Patrick. b 58. DipC91. CA Tr Coll CertRS85 DipEvang85 Sarum & Wells Th Coll DipThMin94. **d** 94 **p** 95. C Wimborne Minster and Holt *Sarum* 94-96; C Wimborne Minster 96-97; Chapl Dorothy House Foundation (Hospice) Winsley from 97. *Dorothy House Foundation, Winsley, Bradford-on-Avon, Wilts BA15 2LE* Tel (01225) 722988 Fax 722907

HARRISON, Herbert Gerald. b 29. Oak Hill Th Coll 53. **d** 56 **p** 57. C Chesterfield H Trin *Derby* 56-59; C Cambridge St Andr Less *Ely* 59-64; Miss to Seamen 64-74; Kenya 64-68; Port Chapl Ipswich 68-74; V Ipswich All SS *St E* 74-81; P-in-c Elmsett w Aldham 81-88; P-in-c Kersey w Lindsey 81-88; R Horringer cum Ickworth 88-94; rtd 94. *15 Lynwood Avenue, Felixstowe, Suffolk IP11 9HS* Tel (01394) 283764

HARRISON, Ian David. b 45. Imp Coll Lon BSc66. Oak Hill Th Coll 93. **d** 96 **p** 97. NSM Tunbridge Wells St Jo *Roch* from 96. *32 Warwick Park, Tunbridge Wells, Kent TN2 5TB* Tel (01892) 527384

HARRISON, Ian Wetherby. b 39. Kelham Th Coll 59. **d** 64 **p** 65. C Kennington Park St Agnes *S'wark* 64-67; C E Ham w Upton Park *Chelmsf* 67-71; V Walthamstow St Mich 71-78; Dioc Ecum Officer *Wakef* 78-87; P-in-c Upper Hopton 78-87; P-in-c Mirfield Eastthorpe St Paul 82-87; Min St D Cathl *St D* 87-90; Succ St D Cathl 87-90; P-in-c Leic Ascension *Leic* 90-92; V Leic St Anne from 92. *St Anne's Vicarage, 76 Letchworth Road, Leicester LE3 6FH* Tel 0116-285 8452

HARRISON, Jack. b 08. Ripon Hall Ox 64. **d** 65 **p** 66. C Strood St Fran *Roch* 65-69; V Downe 69-76; rtd 76; Perm to Offic *Chich* from 76. *Jolly Cottage, Langham Road, Robertsbridge, E Sussex TN32 5DY* Tel (01580) 880374

HARRISON (née HOLLINRAKE), Mrs Jean Margaret. b 28. Leeds Univ DSocStuds51 Bolton Teacher Tr Coll TCert64. Wakef Dioc Reader Tr 82. **d** 93 **p** 96. NSM Perth St Ninian *St And* 93-96; NSM Stanley from 96. *12 South Inch Terrace, Perth PH2 8AN* Tel (01738) 639464

HARRISON, John. b 49. Fitzw Coll Cam BA71 MA74. Westcott Ho Cam 74. **d** 77 **p** 78. C Nunthorpe *York* 77-81; C Acomb St Steph 81-83; C-in-c St Aid 81-83; V Heptonstall *Wakef* 83-91; R Stamford Bridge Gp of Par *York* from 91. *The Rectory, 8 Viking Road, Stamford Bridge, York YO4 1BR* Tel (01759) 371353

HARRISON, Canon John Gordon. b 13. Wadh Coll Ox BA48 MA52. Trin Coll Bris 32. **d** 36 **p** 38. Sudan 35-45; BCMS Miss Kapoeta 35-41; CMS Opari 41-42; Nugent Sch Loka 42-45; C Reading St Jo *Ox* 45-46; Lic to Offic 46-48; V Sevenoaks Weald *Roch* 48-52; V Gerrards Cross *Ox* 52-84; RD Amersham 70-79; Hon Can Ch Ch 75-91; Lic to Offic 84-92; Perm to Offic *Sarum* from 93. *The Clock House, Upton Scudamore, Warminster, Wilts BA12 0AH* Tel (01985) 214744

HARRISON, John Northcott. b 31. St Jo Coll Cam BA54. Westcott Ho Cam 54. **d** 56 **p** 57. C Moor Allerton *Ripon* 56-59; C Bedale 59-61; V Hudswell w Downholme 61-64; Youth Chapl *Dur* 64-68; V Auckland St Andr and St Anne 68-76; Community Chapl Stockton-on-Tees 76-83; TR Southampton (City Cen) *Win* 83-88; V Bris Ch the Servant Stockwood *Bris* 88-96; RD Brislington 89-95; Chapl St Brendan's Sixth Form Coll 90-96; rtd 96; Perm to Offic *B & W* from 96. *8 Moorham Road, Winscombe, Avon BS25 1HS* Tel (01934) 844403

HARRISON, Joseph Benson. b 11. OBE74. Didsbury Meth Coll. **d** 49 **p** 50. C Rushen *S & M* 49-52; C Douglas St Geo 52-53; V Marown 53-55; CF (TA) 52-55; Gen Sec C of E Coun for Soc Aid 55-75; rtd 76; Perm to Offic *Chich* from 76. *50A Sedlescombe Road South, St Leonards-on-Sea, E Sussex TN38 0TJ* Tel (01424) 446241

HARRISON, Josephine Mary. b 42. **d** 97. NSM Yatton Keynell *Bris* from 97. *9 Dallas Road, Chippenham, Wilts SN15 1LE* Tel (01249) 658548

HARRISON, Lyndon. b 47. St D Coll Lamp DipTh91 St Mich Coll Llan DMinlStuds93. **d** 93 **p** 94. C Ebbw Vale *Mon* 93-96; TV from 96. *The Vicarage, 177 Badminton Grove, Beaufort, Ebbw Vale NP3 5UN* Tel (01495) 304516

HARRISON, Martin. b 58. DCR78 BA89. Trin Coll Bris 86. **d** 89 **p** 90. C Heworth *York* 89-94; Chapl York Distr Hosp 89-94; P-in-c Skelton w Shipton and Newton on Ouse *York* 94-95; R from 95. *The Rectory, Church Lane, Skelton, York YO3 6XT* Tel (01904) 470045

HARRISON, Mary Furley. b 21. MBE63. Westf Coll Lon BA42. Moray Ho Edin CertEd43 Edin Dioc NSM Course 79. **dss** 83 **d** 86. Edin H Cross *Edin* 83-86; NSM from 86; rtd 89. *Barnhill, 33 Barnton Avenue, Edinburgh EH4 6JJ* Tel 0131-336 2226

HARRISON, Matthew Henry. b 64. Univ Coll Dur BA85. Union Th Sem (NY) STM93 St Steph Ho Ox BA88 MA92. **d** 89 **p** 90. C Whickham *Dur* 89-92; USA 92-93; C Owton Manor *Dur* 93-95; Asst Chapl Paris St Geo *Eur* from 95. *7 rue Auguste-Vacquerie, 75116 Paris, France* Tel France (33) 47 20 22 51

HARRISON, Michael. **d** 97. NSM Thornhill and Whitley Lower *Wakef* from 97. *66 Wellhouse Lane, Mirfield, W Yorkshire WF14 0BE* Tel (01924) 490823

HARRISON, Michael Burt (Crispin). b 36. Leeds Univ BA59 Trin Coll Ox BA62 MA66. Coll of Resurr Mirfield 62. **d** 63 **p** 64. C W Hartlepool St Aid *Dur* 63-64; C Middlesbrough All SS *York* 64-66; Lic to Offic *Wakef* 67-69 and 78-87; CR from 68; S Africa 69-77 and from 87; Registrar Coll of the Resurr Mirfield 78-84; Vice-Prin 84-87. *St Peter's Priory, PO Box 991, Southdale, 2135 South Africa* Tel Johannesburg (11) 434-2504

HARRISON, Michael Robert. b 63. Selw Coll Cam BA84 MSc85. Ripon Coll Cuddesdon BA89 Union Th Sem (NY) STM90. **d** 90 **p** 91. C S Lambeth St Anne and All SS *S'wark* 90-94; Chapl Bp's Chapl to Students *Bradf* from 94; Chapl Bradf Univ from 94; Chapl Bradf and Ilkley Community Coll from 94. *Anglican Chaplaincy, Michael Ramsey House, 2 Ashgrove, Bradford, W Yorkshire BD7 1BN* Tel (01274) 727034 or 733466 E-mail mrharrison@bradford.ac.uk

HARRISON, Canon Noel Milburn. b 27. Lon Univ DipTh56 Leeds Univ MPhil75 PhD80. St Aid Birkenhead 54. **d** 57 **p** 58. C Doncaster St Jas *Sheff* 57-60; Chapl Yorkshire Res Sch for Deaf Doncaster 60-68; C Woodlands *Sheff* 60-62; Chapl to the Deaf 60-68; Hd Master Elmete Hall Sch Leeds 68-84; Hon C Whitgift w Adlingfleet and Eastoft 83-84; Hon C Abbeydale St Jo 84-86; Dioc Dir of Educn 84-94; R Tankersley 86-94; Hon Can Sheff Cathl 88-94; rtd 94; Perm to Offic *Sheff* from 94; Perm to Offic *Linc* from 95. *Aidan House, 118 High Street, Crowle, Scunthorpe, S Humberside DN17 4DR*

HARRISON, Mrs Nona Margaret. b 50. Open Univ BA80. S Dios Minl Tr Scheme 92. **d** 95 **p** 96. NSM Wellow *Win* from 95. *5 Chichester Close, East Wellow, Romsey, Hants SO51 6EY* Tel (01794) 323101

HARRISON, Oliver. b 71. SS Paul & Mary Coll Cheltenham BA93. St Jo Coll Nottm MA95. **d** 97. Asst Chapl The Hague *Eur* from 97. *Kornalijnhorst 185, 2592 HW, Den Haag, The Netherlands* Tel Den Haag (70) 347 7491 E-mail harri153@emarkt.com

HARRISON, Miss Patricia Mary. b 35. St Kath Coll Lon CertEd65 DPEd70 Open Univ BA74. St Mich Ho Ox IDC59. **dss** 85 **d** 87 **p** 94. Nunthorpe *York* 85-87; NSM from 87; rtd 95. *22 Lamonby Close, Nunthorpe, Middlesbrough, Cleveland TS7 0QG* Tel (01642) 313524

HARRISON, Paul Graham. b 53. Sarum & Wells Th Coll 76. **d** 79 **p** 80. C Brixham w Churston Ferrers *Ex* 79-82; C Portsea N End St Mark *Portsm* 82-87; V Tiverton St Andr *Ex* 87-94; P-in-c Astwood Bank *Worc* from 94; Chapl to the Deaf from 94. *The Vicarage, Church Road, Astwood Bank, Redditch, Worcs B96 6EH* Tel (01527) 892489

HARRISON, Paul Thomas. b 57. Nor Inst of Art & Design BA80 Leeds Poly PGCE88 Leeds Univ DipTh96. Qu Coll Birm 95. **d** 97. C Northallerton w Kirby Sigston *York* from 97. *26 Helmsley Way, Romanby, Northallerton, N Yorkshire DL7 8SX* Tel (01609) 780975

HARRISON, Canon Peter George Stanley. b 22. St Jo Coll Dur BA49 DipTh50. **d** 50 **p** 51. C Birm St Martin *Birm* 50-55; Chapl St Jo Coll Dur 56-59; V W Derby St Jas *Liv* 59-68; P-in-c Routh *York* 68-91; V Beverley Minster 68-91; RD Beverley 73-85; Can and Preb York Minster from 83; rtd 91. *19 Orchard Way, Pocklington, York YO4 2EH* Tel (01759) 304112

HARRISON, Peter Graham. b 12. Ch Ch Ox BA34 MA38. Westcott Ho Cam 34. **d** 35 **p** 36. C St Peter-in-Thanet *Cant* 35-38; C Croydon St Sav 38-41; Chapl RNVR 41-46; V Westgate St Jas *Cant* 45-52; R Hawkinge 52-58; R Acrise 52-58; P-in-c Swingfield 52-56; V Gt Torrington *Ex* 58-78; R Lt Torrington 59-78; RD Torrington 66-77; rtd 78; C-in-c Holne *Ex* 78-85; Perm to Offic *B & W* from 85. *5 The Leat, Bishops Lydeard, Taunton, Somerset TA4 3NY* Tel (01823) 432864

HARRISON, Peter Keith. b 44. Open Univ BA85. St Aid Birkenhead. **d** 68 **p** 69. C Higher Bebington *Ches* 68-71; C Walmsley *Man* 71-74; V Lumb in Rossendale 74-79; V Heywood St Marg 79-87; V Hey 87-95; AD Saddleworth 93-94; Chapl Athens w Kifissia *Eur* from 95. *c/o The British Embassy, Plutarchou 1, 106 75 Athens, Greece* Tel Athens (1) 721-4906

HARRISON, Canon Peter Reginald Wallace. b 39. Selw Coll Cam BA62. Ridley Hall Cam 62. **d** 64 **p** 65. C Barton Hill St Luke w Ch Ch *Bris* 64-69; Chapl Greenhouse Trust 69-77; Dir Northorpe Hall Trust 77-84; Lic to Offic *Wakef* 77-84; TR Drypool *York*

from 84; AD E Hull from 88; Can and Preb York Minster from 94. *The Vicarage, 139 Laburnum Avenue, Hull HU8 8PA* Tel (01482) 74257

HARRISON, Philip Hubert. b 37. Sarum & Wells Th Coll 77. **d** 79 **p** 80. C Wymondham *Nor* 79-83; V Watton w Carbrooke and Ovington 83-92; R Drayton w Felthorpe from 92. *The Rectory, 46 School Road, Drayton, Norwich NR8 6EF* Tel (01603) 868749

HARRISON, Raymond Harold. b 16. Keble Coll Ox BA41 MA45. St Aug Coll Cant. **d** 42 **p** 43. C Balkwell *Newc* 42-45; C Henfield *Chich* 45-46; C Wisbech SS Pet and Paul *Ely* 46-49; R Stow Bardolph w Wimbotsham and Stow Bridge 49-56; R Fen Ditton 56-75; RD Quy 73-75; V W Wratting 75-82; P-in-c Weston Colville 75-76; R 76-82; rtd 82; Perm to Offic *Ely* from 82. *2 Guntons Close, Soham, Ely, Cambs CB7 5DN* Tel (01353) 720774

HARRISON, Richard Crispin. b 57. Plymouth Poly BSc79. Trin Coll Bris 82. **d** 85 **p** 86. C Southway *Ex* 85-89; TV Kinson *Sarum* 89-96; C Petersfield *Portsm* from 96. *41 North Lane, Buriton, Petersfield, Hants GU31 5RS* Tel (01730) 269390

HARRISON, Richard Kingswood. b 61. Linc Coll Ox BA83 MA88 Leeds Univ BA90. **d** 91 **p** 92. C Reading St Giles *Ox* 91-93; Asst Chapl Merchant Taylors' Sch Northwood 93-96; Chapl Ardingly Coll Haywards Heath from 96. *Ardingly College, Haywards Heath, W Sussex RH17 6SQ* Tel (01444) 892273

HARRISON, Robert Peter. b 28. Chich Th Coll. **d** 60 **p** 61. C Ealing Ch the Sav *Lon* 60-64; C Hammersmith SS Mich and Geo White City Estate CD 64-66; P-in-c Fulham St Pet 66-73; V 73-94; rtd 94. *10 Portland Avenue, Hove, E Sussex BN3 5NG* Tel (01273) 416254

HARRISON, Robert William. b 62. Mansf Coll Ox BA84. Qu Coll Birm 87. **d** 89 **p** 90. C Sholing *Win* 89-93; Communications Adv to Bp Willesden *Lon* 93-97; C Cricklewood St Gabr and St Mich 93-97; V Hillingdon St Jo from 97. *St John's Vicarage, Royal Lane, Uxbridge, Middx UB8 3QR* Tel (01895) 233932

HARRISON, Rodney Lovel Neal. b 46. MBE87. Dur Univ BA67. Ripon Coll Cuddesdon DipMin95. **d** 95 **p** 96. C N w S Wootton *Nor* from 95. *Ambleside, Castle Rising Road, South Wootton, King's Lynn, Norfolk PE30 3JB* Tel (01533) 674632

HARRISON, Roger John Orrell. b 54. K Coll Lon BD76 AKC76. Carl Dioc Tr Inst 86. **d** 88 **p** 89. Asst Chapl Sedbergh Sch 88-91; Chapl Trent Coll Nottm 91-94; C Uppingham w Ayston and Wardley w Belton *Pet* 94-95. *41 Ash Close, Uppingham, Oakham, Leics LE15 9PJ* Tel (01572) 822528

HARRISON, Rosemary Jane. b 53. Bradf Coll of Educn CertEd76. Trin Coll Bris DipHE85. **d** 87 **p** 94. NSM Southway *Ex* 87-89; NSM Kinson *Sarum* 89-96. *41 North Lane, Buriton, Petersfield, Hants GU31 5RS* Tel (01730) 269390

HARRISON, Dr Steven John. b 47. FRMetS74 Univ of Wales (Abth) BSc68 PhD74. St And Dioc Tr Course 87. **d** 90 **p** 91. NSM Alloa *St And* 90-94; NSM Bridge of Allan from 94. *46 Westerlea Drive, Bridge of Allan, Stirling FK9 4DQ* Tel (01786) 833482 or 467847 Fax 467843

HARRISON, Walter William. b 28. St Jo Coll Nottm. **d** 71 **p** 72. C Lenton *S'well* 71-74; R Carlton-in-the-Willows 74-93; rtd 93. *20 Conway Gardens, Nottingham NG5 6LR* Tel 0115-920 0766

HARRISON, Canon William Roy. b 34. Dur Univ BA58 DipTh59. Cranmer Hall Dur 57. **d** 59 **p** 60. C Kingswood *Bris* 59-62; Kenya 62-65; P-in-c Gt Somerford *Bris* 66; V Soundwell from 66; Hon Can Bris Cathl from 92. *The Vicarage, 46 Sweets Road, Bristol BS15 1XQ* Tel 0117-967 1511

HARRISON-WATSON, Carole. *See* FORD, Mrs Carole

HARRISSON, John Anthony Lomax. b 47. Ex Univ BA72 DipTh85. Qu Coll Birm 72. **d** 74 **p** 75. C Loughton St Jo *Chelmsf* 74-81; V Chingford St Anne from 81. *St Anne's Vicarage, 200A Larkhall Road, London E4 6NP* Tel 0181-529 4740

HARROLD, Canon Jeremy Robin. b 31. Hertf Coll Ox BA54 BSc56 MA58 DipTh59. Wycliffe Hall Ox. **d** 59 **p** 60. C Rushden *Pet* 59-61; Bp's Chapl *Lon* 61-64; Australia 64-67; V Harlesden St Mark *Lon* 67-72; V Hendon St Paul Mill Hill 72-84; V Stowmarket *St E* 84-96; RD Stowmarket 90-96; Hon Can St E Cathl from 94; rtd 96. *18 Wilkinson Way, Woodbridge, Suffolk IP12 1SS* Tel (01394) 380127

HARRON, Gareth Andrew. b 71. QUB BA92. CITC BTh95. **d** 95 **p** 96. C Willowfield *D & D* from 95. *21 Loopland Crescent, Belfast BT6 9EE* Tel (01232) 452165

HARRON, James Alexander. b 37. GIMechE61 HNC59 St Aid Coll Dur 63. **d** 65 **p** 66. C Willowfield *D & D* 65-69; I Desertmartin *D & R* 69-80; Dep Sec BCMS (Ireland) 80-84; I Aghalee *D & D* from 84; Chapl HM Pris Maghaberry from 86. *39 Soldierstown Road, Aghalee, Craigavon, Co Armagh BT67 0ES* Tel (01846) 651233

HARROP, Douglas. b 21. St Aid Birkenhead 62. **d** 64 **p** 65. C Wombwell *Sheff* 64-67; C Doncaster St Leon and St Jude 67-70; R S Witham *Linc* 70-76; R N Witham 70-76; RD Beltisloe 72-76; V Kirkdale *York* 76-85; rtd 85; Perm to Offic *Linc* from 85. *13 Dovecote, Middle Rasen, Market Rasen, Lincs LN8 3UD* Tel (01673) 843675

HARROP, Preb Joseph Blakemore. b 17. Saltley Tr Coll Birm TCert39. Qu Coll Birm 51. **d** 53 **p** 56. CMS Sudan 48-55; C Stoke upon Trent *Lich* 56-58; V Foxt w Whiston 58-93; P-in-c Oakamoor w Cotton 78-85; Preb Lich Cathl from 93; rtd 93; Hon P-in-c Foxt w Whiston *Lich* from 93. *6 New Cottages, Foxt, Stoke-on-Trent ST10 2HL* Tel (01538) 266656

HARROP, Stephen Douglas. b 48. St Jo Coll York CertEd74 Man Univ DSPT85 DipAdEd90. Edin Th Coll 77. **d** 79 **p** 82. C Middlesbrough St Martin *York* 79-80; C N Hull St Mich 80; C Cayton w Eastfield 80-81; C Oldham *Man* 82-84; V Oldham St Barn 84-89; Hong Kong 89-93; TV Kidderminster St Mary and All SS w Trimpley etc *Worc* 93-95; Ind Chapl 93-95; Chapl Kidderminster Coll 93-95; Sandwell Chs Link Officer *Birm* 95-96; Dep Chapl HM Pris Brixton from 96. *The Chaplain's Office, HM Prison Brixton, Jebb Avenue, London SW2 5XF* Tel 0181-674 9811 Fax 674 6128

HARRY, Bruce David. b 40. JP77. Culham Coll Ox CertEd60. N Ord Course 83. **d** 86 **p** 87. NSM Liscard St Thos *Ches* 86-91; NSM Eastham 91-94; C New Brighton St Jas 94-96; C New Brighton Em 94-96; C New Brighton St Jas w Em from 96. *21 Sandymount Drive, Wallasey, Merseyside L45 0LJ* Tel 0151-639 7232

HART, Allen Sydney George. b 38. Chich Th Coll 64. **d** 67 **p** 68. C N Wembley St Cuth *Lon* 67-71; C W Bromwich All SS *Lich* 71-74; TV Hucknall Torkard *S'well* 74-80; V Annesley Our Lady and All SS 80-86; V Bilborough St Jo from 86; RD Nottingham W from 94. *St John's Vicarage, Graylands Road, Nottingham NG8 4FD* Tel 0115-929 3320

HART, Andre Hendrik. b 62. Cape Town Univ BA86. St Steph Ho Ox 89. **d** 91 **p** 92. C Newbold w Dunston *Derby* 91-95; P-in-c Clifton from 95; P-in-c Norbury w Snelston from 95; Chapl St Osw Hosp Ashbourne from 95. *The Vicarage, Clifton, Ashbourne, Derbyshire DE6 2GJ* Tel (01335) 342199

HART, Anthony. b 35. St Mich Coll Llan 77. **d** 79 **p** 80. NSM Jersey St Helier *Win* 79-81; C Heref All SS *Heref* 81-82; C Kingstone 82-84; C Eaton Bishop 82-84; C Clehonger 82-84; R Sutton St Nicholas w Sutton St Michael 84-88; R Withington w Westhide 84-88; R Jersey St Mary *Win* from 88. *St Mary's Rectory, Jersey, Channel Islands JE3 3DB* Tel (01534) 481410

HART, Colin Edwin. b 45. Leeds Univ BA66 PGCE67 Fitzw Coll Cam BA73 MA77 K Coll Lon MTh76 Leeds Univ MPhil89. Trin Coll Bris 74. **d** 74 **p** 75. C Ware Ch Ch *St Alb* 74-78; TV Sheff Manor *Sheff* 78-80; V Wombridge *Lich* 80-87; Lect St Jo Coll Nottm from 87; Public Preacher *S'well* from 87; Hon C Chilwell 87-91; Hon C Trowell from 91. *St John's College, Chilwell Lane, Bramcote, Nottingham NG9 3DS* Tel 0115-925 1114 or 943 0774 Fax 943 6438

HART, David. b 48. Edge Hill Coll of HE BEd80 Liv Inst of Educn ADEd84 Liv Univ MEd87. Nor Ord Course BPhil94. **d** 94 **p** 95. NSM Ashton-in-Makerfield St Thos *Liv* from 94. *12 Ratcliffe Road, Aspull, Wigan, Lancs WN2 1YE* Tel (01942) 832918

HART, David Alan. b 54. Keble Coll Ox BA75 MPhil78. Union Th Sem (NY) STM79 Westcott Ho Cam 83. **d** 83 **p** 84. Asst Chapl Gresham's Sch Holt 83-84; Chapl K Edw VI Sch Nor 84-85; Chapl Shrewsbury Sch 85-87; Chapl St Jo Coll Sch Cam 87-88; C Camberwell St Giles w St Matt *S'wark* 88-90; Chapl Loughb Univ *Leic* 90-97; Chapl Roehampton Inst from 97. *Whitelands College, West Hill, London SW15 3SN* Tel 0181-392 3516

HART, David John. b 58. K Coll Lon BD80. St Mich Coll Llan. **d** 85 **p** 86. C Denbigh and Nantglyn *St As* 85-88; Chapl RAF 88-89; C Llanrhos *St As* 89-91; V Rhosllannerchrugog from 91. *1 Gerddi, Hall Street, Rhosllanerchrugog, Wrexham LL14 2LG* Tel (01978) 840065

HART, David Leonard. b 42. Ripon Hall Ox 68. **d** 71 **p** 72. C Castle Vale *Birm* 71-73; Chapl All SS Hosp Birm 73-94; Chapl Services Manager N Birm Mental Health Services NHS Trust from 94. *12 Dorchester Drive, Birmingham, B17 0SW, or All Saints' Hospital, Lodge Road, Birmingham B18 5SD* Tel 0121-427 7828 or 523 5151

HART, David Maurice. b 35. Univ Coll Dur BSc57. Clifton Th Coll 59. **d** 61 **p** 62. C Bolton St Paul *Man* 61-64; C Hamworthy *Sarum* 64-70; R W Dean w E Grimstead 70-81; R Farley w Pitton and W Dean w E Grimstead 81-90; V Steeple Ashton w Semington and Keevil from 90. *The Vicarage, Vicarage Lane, Steeple Ashton, Trowbridge, Wilts BA14 6HH* Tel (01380) 870344

HART, Canon Dennis Daniel. b 22. Linc Th Coll 45. **d** 48 **p** 49. C Abbots Langley *St Alb* 48-49; C Bedford St Paul 49-53; CF 53-55; V St Alb St Sav *St Alb* 55-92; Hon Can St Alb 74-92; RD St Alb 84-90; rtd 92. *7 Bassett Close, Redbourn, Herts AL3 7JY* Tel (01582) 794464

HART, Dennis William. b 30. JP. Open Univ BA. Oak Hill Th Coll 75. **d** 78 **p** 79. Hon C Clacton St Paul *Chelmsf* from 78. *15 Albert Gardens, Clacton-on-Sea, Essex CO15 6QN* Tel (01255) 431794

HART, Edwin Joseph. b 21. Oak Hill Th Coll 56. **d** 58 **p** 59. C Harlow New Town w Lt Parndon *Chelmsf* 58-60; C Leyton 60-61; C-in-c Cranham Park St Luke CD 61-69; V Cranham Park 69-71; R Markfield *Leic* 71-89; rtd 89; Perm to Offic *Leic* from 89. *135 Grace Dieu Road, Thringstone, Coalville, Leics LE67 5AP* Tel (01530) 222767

HART, Geoffrey Robert. b 49. **d** 95 **p** 96. P-in-c Edin St Salvador *Edin* from 96; C Edin St Cuth from 96. *The Rectory, 44 Stenhouse Street West, Edinburgh EH11 3QU* Tel 0131-443 2228

HART, Canon Geoffrey William. b 27. Ex Coll Ox BA51 MA55. Ridley Hall Cam 51. **d** 54 **p** 55. C Islington St Mary *Lon* 54-58; C Leeds St Geo *Ripon* 58-59; V Harold Wood *Chelmsf* 59-65; V Southport Ch Ch *Liv* 65-73; R Cheltenham St Mary *Glouc* 73-76; TR Cheltenham St Mary, St Matt, St Paul and H Trin 76-93; Hon Can Glouc Cathl 78-93; rtd 93; Perm to Offic *Ex* from 94. *Little Goosemoor, Branscombe, Seaton, Devon EX12 3BU* Tel (01297) 80271

HART, Mrs Gillian Mary (Gill). b 57. Sheff City Poly BA79. Carl Dioc Tr Inst 92. **d** 95 **p** 96. C Burgh-by-Sands and Kirkbampton w Kirkandrews etc *Carl* from 95; C Aikton from 95; C Orton St Giles from 95. *2 Oaks Lane, Kirkbampton, Carlisle CA5 6HY* Tel (01228) 576048

HART, Graham Cooper. b 36. S Dios Minl Tr Scheme 88. **d** 91 **p** 92. NSM Filton *Bris* 91-93; Hon C Downend from 93. *The Old Post Office, Hambrook, Bristol BS16 1RF* Tel 0117-956 5300

HART, Canon Graham Merril (Merry). b 23. Ridley Coll Melbourne 65. **d** 77 **p** 77. Tanzania 69-84; CMS 72-83; Can Musoma from 85; Chapl Ostend w Knokke and Bruges *Eur* 84-93; Miss to Seamen 84-93; rtd 93; Perm to Offic *S'wark* from 93. *Morden College, 7 Alexander Court, Kidbrook Grove, London SE3 0LH* Tel 0181-858 3731

HART, Henry St John. b 12. St Jo Coll Cam BA34 Qu Coll Cam MA38 BD54. **d** 36 **p** 37. Chapl Qu Coll Cam 36-50; Dean 40-50 and 55-72; Fell from 36; Vice Pres 78-79; Reader in Hebrew Cam Univ 72-79; rtd 80; Lic to Offic *Nor* 80-86; Perm to Offic from 86. *The Retreat, Felbrigg Hall, Norwich NR11 8PR* Tel (01263) 837652

HART, James (Jim). b 53. MIL84 Dur Univ BA75 DipEd76 DipHE88. Oak Hill Th Coll 86. **d** 88 **p** 89. C Starbeck *Ripon* 88-90; SAMS 90-96; Argentina 90-96; Chapl Bishop's Stortford Coll from 96. *The Chaplain's House, Lower Green, Bishop's Stortford College, Bishop's Stortford, Herts CM23 2QZ* Tel (01279) 838621

HART, John Charles. b 11. Worc Coll Ox BA34 MA40. Wycliffe Hall Ox 34. **d** 36 **p** 38. C Eastbourne St Elisabeth *Chich* 36-38; Chapl Chailey Heritage Sch Lewes 38-46; C Chailey *Chich* 42-46; V Wartling 46-53; R Plumpton w E Chiltington 53-66; V Rudgwick 66-77; rtd 77. *68 The Sheeplands, Sherborne, Dorset DT9 4BS* Tel (01935) 813921

HART, John Peter. b 39. Bris Sch of Min 80. **d** 84 **p** 85. NSM Malmesbury w Westport and Brokenborough *Bris* 84-88; C Yatton Moor *B & W* 89-90; V Bridgwater H Trin 90-96; Chapl HM Pris The Mount from 96; P-in-c Sarratt *St Alb* from 96. *The Rectory, The Green, Sarratt, Rickmansworth, Herts WD3 6BP* Tel (01923) 264377

HART, John Richard. b 16. Ox NSM Course 72. **d** 75 **p** 76. NSM Reading St Matt *Ox* 75-77; NSM Grazeley and Beech Hill 77-88; NSM Spencer's Wood 77-88; NSM Beech Hill, Grazeley and Spencers Wood 88-89; Perm to Offic *Portsm* from 89. *14 Elizabeth Court, High Street, Bembridge, Isle of Wight PO35 5SN* Tel (01983) 874509

HART, Michael Anthony. b 50. AKC71. St Aug Coll Cant 72. **d** 73 **p** 74. C Southwick St Columba *Dur* 73-76; C Hendon St Alphage *Lon* 76-78; P-in-c Eltham Park St Luke *S'wark* 78-83; V 83-85; R Newington St Mary 85-96; P-in-c Camberwell St Mich w All So w Em 85-96; RD S'wark and Newington 93-96; P-in-c Caterham from 96; P-in-c Chaldon from 96. *The Rectory, 5 Whyteleafe Road, Caterham, Surrey CR3 5ER* Tel (01883) 342062

HART, Canon Michael Stuart. b 39. Univ of Wales (Lamp) BA61 Lanc Univ MA72. Wycliffe Hall Ox 61. **d** 63 **p** 64. C W Bromwich St Jas *Lich* 63-66; C Tarrington w Stoke Edith *Heref* 66-67; C Putney St Mary *S'wark* 67-70; V Accrington St Mary *Blackb* 70-82; RD Accrington 76-82; Hon Can Blackb Cathl 81-91; V Walton-le-Dale 82-91; P-in-c Samlesbury 91; TR Heavitree w Ex St Paul *Ex* from 91. *The Rectory, 10 Sherwood Close, Exeter EX2 5DX* Tel (01392) 421841

HART, Peter Osborne. b 57. St Jo Coll Nottm DCM92. **d** 92 **p** 93. C Shipley St Pet *Bradf* 92-97; TV Walsall *Lich* from 97. *St Martins House, 17 Daffodil Road, Walsall WS5 3DQ* Tel (01274) 583457

HART, Peter William. b 60. Liv Univ BA82 Université de Haute Normandie MesL84 Univ of Wales (Swansea) MPhil92. Sarum & Wells Th Coll 86. **d** 88 **p** 89. C Llansamlet *S & B* 88-89; C Sketty 89-92; P-in-c Warndon St Nic *Worc* 92-97; R Berkhamsted St Mary *St Alb* from 97. *St Mary's Rectory, 80 High Street, Northchurch, Berkhamsted, Herts HP4 3QW* Tel (01442) 865312

HART, Richard. b 49. Or Coll Ox MPhil84. St D Coll Lamp BA82 Qu Coll Birm 84. **d** 85 **p** 86. C Sketty *S & B* 85-87; P-in-c Llanbister and Llanbadarn Fynydd w Llananno 87-88; V 88-92; P-in-c Dymock w Donnington and Kempley *Glouc* from 92; P-in-c Preston from 92. *The Rectory, Dymock, Glos GL18 2AJ* Tel (01531) 890270

HART, Ronald George (Ron). b 46. BSc Bris Univ DSA72 Lon Univ DASS77 CQSW77. Sarum & Wells Th Coll. **d** 85 **p** 86. C Sittingbourne St Mich *Cant* 85-88; C Walton H Trin *Ox* 88-89; TV 89-96; R Broughton Gifford, Gt Chalfield and Holt *Sarum* from 96. *The Rectory, Ham Green, Holt, Trowbridge, Wilts BA14 7PZ* Tel (01225) 782289

HART, Tony. b 36. CCC Cam BA59 MA63. Cuddesdon Coll 59. **d** 61 **p** 62. C Middlesbrough All SS *York* 61-64; Bp's Dom Chapl *Dur* 64-67; C Owton Manor CD 67-70; V Harton Colliery 70-82; TR S Shields All SS 82-83; RD Jarrow 77-83; Can Res Dur Cathl 83-92; V Easingwold w Raskelfe *York* from 92. *The Vicarage, Easingwold, York YO6 3JT* Tel (01347) 821394

HART, Prof Trevor Andrew. b 61. St Jo Coll Dur BA82 Aber Univ PhD89. **d** 88 **p** 88. NSM Bieldside *Ab* 88-95; NSM St Andrews St Andr *St And* from 95; Prof Div St Mary's Coll St Andr Univ from 95. *St Mary's College, South Street, St Andrews, Fife KY16 9JU* Tel (01334) 462864

HARTE, Frederick George (Fred). b 25. AKC53. **d** 54 **p** 55. C Lewisham St Jo Southend *S'wark* 54-57; C Eltham H Trin 57-60; V Bellingham St Dunstan 60-73; V Plumstead St Nic 73-84; V Sutton Bridge *Linc* 84-90; rtd 90; Master St Jo Hosp Bath and P-in-c of Chpl from 90. *The Master's Lodge, St John's Hospital, Chapel Court, Bath BA1 1SL* Tel (01225) 464972 Fax 481291

HARTE, The Ven Matthew Scott. b 46. TCD BA70 MA74. CITC 71. **d** 71 **p** 72. C Bangor Abbey *D & D* 71-74; C Ballynafeigh St Jude 74-76; I Ardara w Glencolumbkille, Inniskeel etc *D & R* from 76; Adn Raphoe from 83. *The Rectory, Ardara, Lifford, Co Donegal, Irish Republic* Tel Ardara (75) 41124

HARTERINK, Mrs Joy Frances. b 49. DCEG82 Essex Univ BA71 Hughes Hall Cam CertEd72 Lon Univ MSc87. Oak Hill NSM Course 89. **d** 92 **p** 94. NSM Richmond H Trin and Ch Ch *S'wark* from 92. *9 Sandringham House, Courtlands, Sheen Road, Richmond, Surrey TW10 5BG* Tel 0181-948 7579

HARTLAND, David Robson. b 33. Qu Coll Birm 64. **d** 66 **p** 67. C Brierley Hill *Lich* 66-71; V Hartshill 71-76; V Moxley 76-85; V Willenhall St Steph from 85. *St Stephen's Vicarage, Wolverhampton Street, Willenhall, W Midlands WV13 2PS* Tel (01902) 605239

HARTLAND, Ian Charles. b 49. K Coll Lon CertEd BD72 AKC72 MTh76. Sarum & Wells Th Coll 83. **d** 84 **p** 85. C Orpington All SS *Roch* 84-87; Lect Ch Ch Coll Cant from 87. *Ivy Lodge, 4 The Terrace, Canterbury, Kent CT2 7AJ* Tel (01227) 760789

HARTLESS, Mrs Berengaria Isabella de la Tour (Beren). b 52. Univ of Wales (Cardiff) BSc74 Golds Coll Lon PGCE76. Ox Min Course CBTS93. **d** 93 **p** 94. Par Dn High Wycombe *Ox* 93-94; C from 94. *15 Rupert Avenue, High Wycombe, Bucks HP12 3NG* Tel (01494) 534605

HARTLEY, Brian. b 41. N Ord Course 82. **d** 85 **p** 86. NSM Royton St Paul *Man* 85-91; NSM Oldham St Steph and All Martyrs 91-94; TV E Farnworth and Kearsley from 94. *The Vicarage, 93 Bradford Street, Farnworth, Bolton BL4 9JY* Tel (01204) 573843

HARTLEY, David Michael. b 59. RGN85 Edin Univ BD81. St Steph Ho Ox 87. **d** 89 **p** 90. C Kingswinford St Mary *Lich* 89-92; C Wolstanton 92; TV 92-95. *43 St Mary's Road, Oxford OX4 1PY* Tel (01865) 434480

HARTLEY, Mrs Dianna Lynn. b 57. Santa Ana Community Coll AS76 California Univ BA78. S'wark Ord Course DipRS92. **d** 92 **p** 94. NSM Peckham St Sav *S'wark* 92-97; C Dulwich St Barn from 97. *67 Danby Street, London SE15 4BT* Tel 0171-639 6408 or 732 3435

HARTLEY, Godfrey. b 37. Man Univ 58. Cuddesdon Coll 64. **d** 64 **p** 65. C Balderton *S'well* 64-67; Miss to Seamen 67-94; Portuguese E Africa 67-73; Sen Chapl and Sec for Scotland 74-89; P-in-c Glas St Gabr *Glas* 74-89; Chapl RNR from 74; Chapl Cornwall Miss to Seamen 89-94; rtd 95; Perm to Offic *Truro* from 95. *Sandoes Gate, Feock, Truro, Cornwall TR3 6QN* Tel (01872) 865863

HARTLEY, Graham William Harrington. b 21. Ripon Hall Ox 61. **d** 62 **p** 63. C N Meols *Liv* 62-65; Nigeria 65-66; V Knowsley *Liv* 66-72; V Langdale *Carl* 72-81; TV Egremont and Haile 81-85; TV Whitehaven 85-88; rtd 88; Perm to Offic *Carl* from 88. *14 Thrang Brow, Chapel Stile, Ambleside, Cumbria LA22 9JN* Tel (015394) 37322

HARTLEY, Harold Aitken. b 21. Whitaker Sch of Th. **d** 84 **p** 85. USA 84-89; from 92; NSM Fulford *York* 89-92. *1106 Riverview, Rogers City, MI, 49779, USA*

HARTLEY, Canon Harry. b 02. Birm Univ BSc28 Open Univ BA76. St Steph Ho Ox 28. **d** 30 **p** 31. C S Elmsall *Wakef* 30-32; S Africa 32-34; C Prestbury *Ches* 34-35; V Flockton cum Denby Grange *Wakef* 35-44; R Malvern Link St Matthias *Worc* 44-53; R Solihull *Birm* 53-70; Hon Can Birm Cathl 64-70; Perm to Offic *Glouc* from 70; rtd 71. *Flat 1, Capel Court, The Burgage, Prestbury, Cheltenham, Glos GL52 3EL* Tel (01242) 244426

HARTLEY, Herbert. b 28. AKC52 **d** 53 **p** 54. C Blackpool H Cross *Blackb* 53-55; C Reading St Giles *Ox* 55-58; V Ruscombe and Twyford 58-66; Chapl RN 66-73; C Langley Marish *Ox* 73-77; R Hedsor and Bourne End 77-93; rtd 93. *5 Charlotte Way, Marlow, Bucks SL7 1PJ* Tel (01628) 478513

HARTLEY, Dr John Peter. b 56. Cam Univ BA78 Leeds Univ PhD82 Dur Univ BA84. Cranmer Hall Dur 82. **d** 85 **p** 86. C Spring Grove St Mary *Lon* 85-88; C Bexleyheath St Pet *Roch* 88-91; P-in-c Hanford *Lich* from 91; Faith in the City Officer (Potteries) from 91. *The Vicarage, Hanford, Stoke-on-Trent, Staffs ST4 4QD* Tel (01782) 657848

HARTLEY, John William. b 47. St Jo Coll Dur BA69. Linc Th Coll 70. **d** 72 **p** 73. C Poulton-le-Fylde *Blackb* 72-76; C Lancaster

St Mary 76-79; V Barrowford 79-87; V Salesbury from 87. *St Peter's Vicarage, 49A Ribchester Road, Blackburn BB1 9HU* Tel (01254) 248072

HARTLEY, Julian John. b 57. Oak Hill Th Coll BA85. **d** 85 **p** 86. C Eccleston Ch Ch *Liv* 85-89; V Goose Green from 89. *St Paul's Vicarage, Warrington Road, Wigan, Lancs WN1 6QB* Tel (01942) 42984

HARTLEY, Michael Leslie. b 56. Leeds Univ BSc77. Ripon Coll Cuddesdon 87. **d** 89 **p** 90. C Standish *Blackb* 89-93; V Bamber Bridge St Aid from 93. *St Aidan's Vicarage, Longworth Street, Bamber Bridge, Preston PR5 6GN* Tel (01772) 35310

HARTLEY, Nigel John. b 48. Portsm Poly BA. St Jo Coll Nottm. **d** 83 **p** 84. C Ipswich St Marg *St E* 83-86; P-in-c Hintlesham w Chattisham 86-95; Dioc Radio Officer 86-95; P-in-c Gt Finborough w Onehouse and Harleston from 95; Acting RD Stowmarket from 96. *The Rectory, Woodland Close, Onehouse, Stowmarket, Suffolk IP14 3HL* Tel (01449) 614378

HARTLEY, Nigel Rogers. b 65. Mansf Coll Ox BA86 MA90. Chich Th Coll 87. **d** 89 **p** 90. C Borehamwood *St Alb* 89-91; PV Llan Cathl *Llan* 91-93; R Foundn of St Kath in Ratcliffe 93-94. *Address temp unknown*

HARTLEY, Paul. b 51. Nottm Univ BTh88. Linc Th Coll 85. **d** 88 **p** 89. C Clitheroe St Mary *Blackb* 88-91; TV Guiseley w Esholt *Bradf* 91-97; R Ackworth *Wakef* from 97. *The Rectory, Ackworth, Pontefract, W Yorkshire WF7 7EJ* Tel (01977) 780880

HARTLEY, Canon Peter. b 44. Avery Hill Coll PGCE67 Ox Univ DipRE74 St Cath Coll Cam BA66 MA69. Sarum & Wells Th Coll 77. **d** 78 **p** 79. Hon C Freemantle *Win* 78-79; Chr Educn Officer *Pet* 79-81; Dir of Educn 81-90; Dir Coun of Educn and Tr *Chelmsf* from 90; Hon Can Chelmsf Cathl from 92. *St Clare, Links Drive, Chelmsford CM2 9AW* Tel (01245) 251461

HARTLEY, Peter Mellodew. b 41. Qu Coll Cam BA63 MA66 Lon Univ MSc71 DipTh83 FICE. S'wark Ord Course. **d** 83 **p** 84. NSM Salfords *S'wark* 83-97; Chapl E Surrey Hosp and Community Healthcare NHS Trust from 97. *Old Timbers, North Lane, West Hoathly, W Sussex RH19 4QF* Tel (01342) 811238

HARTLEY, Stephen William Mark. b 50. St Chad's Coll Dur BA71. Westcott Ho Cam 72. **d** 74 **p** 75. C Holbrooks *Cov* 74-76; C Styvechale 76-79; P-in-c Snitterfield w Bearley 79-81; V 81-83; V Exhall 83-88; V Tilehurst St Cath *Ox* 88-95; TR Cowley St Jas from 95. *Cowley Rectory, St James House, Beauchamp Lane, Cowley, Oxford OX4 3LF* Tel (01865) 747680

HARTLEY, Stewart John Ridley. b 47. St Jo Coll Nottm 78. **d** 80 **p** 81. C Altham w Clayton le Moors *Blackb* 80-84; P-in-c Nelson St Phil 84-91; V from 91. *St Philip's Vicarage, 1 Victory Close, Chapel Street, Nelson, Lancs BB9 9ED* Tel (01282) 698161

HARTLEY, Canon William Reginald (Rex). b 19. CCC Cam BA41 MA45. Linc Th Coll 41. **d** 42 **p** 43. C Stourbridge St Thos *Worc* 42-46; Lic to Offic *Ox* 46-47; Tutor CA Tr Coll 46-47; C Tardebigge *Worc* 47-50; V White Ladies Aston w Spetchley and Churchill 50-53; V Pendleton St Barn *Man* 53-59; R Birch St Jas 59-74; V Atherton 74-86; Hon Can Man Cathl 76-86; AD Leigh 79-85; rtd 86; Perm to Offic *Bradf* from 86. *21 Easby Close, Ilkley, W Yorkshire LS29 9DJ* Tel (01943) 609005

HARTNELL, Canon Bruce John. b 42. Ex Univ BA64 Linacre Coll Ox BA66 MA. Ripon Hall Ox 64. **d** 66 **p** 67. C S Stoneham *Win* 66-69; Chapl and Tutor Ripon Hall Ox 69-74; V Knowl Hill w Littlewick *Ox* 74-78; Chapl Southn Univ *Win* 78-83; V Sholing from 83; RD Southn from 93; Hon Can Win Cathl from 93. *The Vicarage, 41 Station Road, Southampton SO19 8FN* Tel (01703) 448337

HARTRIDGE, James Bernard Robertson (Jamie). b 44. S Dios Minl Tr Scheme 89. **d** 92 **p** 93. C Portsea St Cuth *Portsm* 92-95. *20 Highgrove Road, Portsmouth PO3 6PR* Tel (01705) 661890

HARVEY, Alan Douglas. b 25. FRSH82. Melbourne Coll of Div 78. **d** 79 **p** 81. Australia 79-86; Perm to Offic *Ely* 86-87; V Wiggenhall St Germans and Islington 88-95; V Wiggenhall St Mary Magd 88-95; rtd 95. *21 Dane Court Gardens, Broadstairs, Kent CT10 2SB* Tel (01843) 864080

HARVEY, The Ven Anthony Ernest. b 30. Worc Coll Ox BA53 MA56 DD83. Westcott Ho Cam 56. **d** 58 **p** 59. C Chelsea Ch Ch *Lon* 58-62; Ch Ch Ox 62-69; Warden St Aug Coll Cant 69-75; Lect Th Ox Univ 76-82; Chapl Qu Coll Ox 77-82; Can and Lib Westmr Abbey from 82; Adn Westmr from 87; Sub-Dean Westmr from 87. *3 Little Cloister, Westminster Abbey, London SW1P 3PL* Tel 0171-222 4174 or 222 5152 Fax 233 2072

HARVEY, Anthony Peter. b 42. Birm Univ BSc63 MSc64. Wycliffe Hall Ox 79. **d** 81 **p** 82. C Stoke Damerel *Ex* 81-84; Canada 84-90; Chapl HM Young Offender Inst Deerbolt 91-92; Chapl HM Pris Leeds 92-95; Chapl HM Pris Kirkham from 95. *HM Prison, Kirkham, Preston PR4 2RA* Tel (01772) 684343 Fax 682855

HARVEY, Arthur Ernest. b 30. Lon Univ DipTh58 MSc80. Oak Hill Th Coll 54. **d** 57 **p** 58. C Rayleigh *Chelmsf* 57-60; C Morpeth *Newc* 60-63; R Pitsea *Chelmsf* 63-74; Bp's Ind Officer 73-80; R Bobbingworth 74-81; Chapl Bordeaux w Riberac, Cahors, Duras etc *Eur* 82-86; V Barnsbury St Andr and H Trin w All SS *Lon* 86-90; TR Barnsbury from 90. *5 Huntingdon Street, London N1 1BU* Tel 0171-607 6895 or 837 6937

HARVEY, The Very Revd Brian. b 16. TCD BA38 BD41. TCD Div Sch Div Test39. **d** 40 **p** 41. C Dublin St Geo *D & G* 40-45; Min Can St Patr Cathl Dublin 42-45; Sec SCM (Ireland) 45-48; Dean of Res QUB 45-48; Min Can Belf Cathl 45-48; India 48-63; Adn Hazaribagh 60-63; Can Th Belf Cathl 63-70; I Kilkenny w Aghour and Kilmanagh *C & O* 70-91; Preb Leighlin Cathl from 70; Dean Ossory 70-91; rtd 91. *Alton, Kilbrittain, Co Cork, Irish Republic* Tel Clonakilty (23) 49686

HARVEY, Charles Alma West. b 07. Glas Univ MA29. Edin Th Coll 29. **d** 31 **p** 32. C Glas Ch Ch *Glas* 31-35; C Edin Ch Ch *Edin* 35-37; R Penicuik 37-57; CF (EC) 40-45; R Gullane *Edin* 57-75; rtd 75. *Flat 23, 17 Kirk Loan, Edinburgh EH12 7HD* Tel 0131-334 7933

HARVEY, Christopher John Alfred. b 41. S'wark Ord Course 66. **d** 69 **p** 70. C Grays Thurrock *Chelmsf* 69-73; C Gt Baddow 73-75; V Berechurch St Marg w St Mich 75-94; R Tendring and Lt Bentley w Beaumont cum Moze from 94. *The Rectory, The Street, Tendring, Clacton-on-Sea, Essex CO16 0BW* Tel (01255) 830586

HARVEY, The Ven Cyril John. b 30. Univ of Wales (Lamp) BA51. Coll of Resurr Mirfield 51. **d** 53 **p** 54. C Caerau w Ely *Llan* 53-57; C Milford Haven *St D* 57-61; V Castlemartin and Warren 61-65; R Begelly w Kilgetty 65-73; V Haverfordwest St Martin w Lambston 73-88; Can St D Cathl from 85; R Tenby 88-96; Adn St D 91-96; rtd 96. *10 Oakwood Grove, Slade Lane, Haverfordwest SA61 2HF*

HARVEY, Debra Eileen. b 54. **d** 94 **p** 95. NSM Camborne *Truro* from 94. *Redwin, 11 Roseland Park, Camborne, Cornwall TR14 8LU* Tel (01209) 716282

HARVEY, Desmond Victor Ross. b 37. QUB BA59 Princeton Th Sem ThM63 Fuller Th Sem California DMin93. St Mich Coll Llan 95. **d** 95 **p** 96. C Cwmbran *Mon* 95-97; TV from 97. *St Mary's Vicarage, 89 Bryn Eglwys, Croesyceiliog, Cwmbran NP44 2LS* Tel (01633) 483425

HARVEY, Geoffrey George (Geoff). b 46. Lon Univ BSc71. Ridley Coll Melbourne BTh82. **d** 82 **p** 83. Australia from 82. *St Luke's Vicarage, 59-61 Police Road, Mulgrave, Victoria, Australia 3170* Tel Melbourne (3) 9546-6533 Fax as telephone

HARVEY, John. b 30. S'wark Ord Course. **d** 65 **p** 66. C Lewisham St Jo Southend *S'wark* 65-73; V Bellingham St Dunstan 73-78; TV Bourne Valley *Sarum* 78-81; TR 81-87; R Kilkhampton w Morwenstow *Truro* 87-90; rtd 90; Perm to Offic *Roch* from 90. *50 Essex Road, Longfield, Dartford DA3 7QL* Tel (01474) 709627

HARVEY, John Christopher. b 65. Univ of Wales (Lamp) BA86 Nottm Univ BTh89. Linc Th Coll 89. **d** 89 **p** 90. C Dwygyfylchi *Ban* 89-93; V Llangrannog w Llandysiliogogo w Penbryn *St D* from 93. *The Vicarage, Pontgarreg, Llangrannog, Llandysul SA44 6AJ* Tel (01239) 654003

HARVEY, John Mark. b 64. QUB BEd87 TCD BTh93. CITC 90. **d** 93 **p** 94. C Portadown St Columba *Arm* 93-96; I Monaghan w Tydavnet and Kilmore *Clogh* from 96. *The Rectory, Clones Road, Monaghan, Irish Republic* Tel Monaghan (47) 81136

HARVEY, John Wilfred. b 05. Lon Coll of Div 37. **d** 39 **p** 40. C Launceston *Truro* 39-45; V Perranzabuloe 45-60; V E and W Looe 60-70; RD W Wivelshire 68-70; Public Preacher 70-77; C-in-c Sheviock 71-72; rtd 73; P-in-c St Martin by Looe *Truro* 77-79. *Chy Morvah, Marine Drive, Looe, Cornwall PL13 2DJ* Tel (01503) 263327

HARVEY, Lance Sydney Crockford. b 25. Ridley Hall Cam 67. **d** 69 **p** 70. C Mortlake w E Sheen *S'wark* 69-74; P-in-c Woolwich St Thos 75-86; V Lee Gd Shep w St Pet 86-92; RD E Lewisham 87-91; rtd 92; Perm to Offic *Truro* from 92. *36 Chapel Street, Penzance, Cornwall TR18 4AQ* Tel (01736) 60967

HARVEY, Margaret Claire. b 41. Univ of Wales (Abth) BA62 DipEd63 Lon Univ BD68. Dalton Ho Bris 66. **dss** 68 **d** 80 **p** 97. Flint *St As* 68-74; Lect Trin Coll Bris 74-80; Connah's Quay *St As* 79-80; C 80-86; Bp's Adv for Continuing Clerical Educn from 86; Hon C Corwen and Llangar 86-87; D-in-c Bryneglwys from 87. *Coleg y Groes, The College, Corwen LL21 0AU* Tel (01490) 412169

HARVEY, Maurice. b 31. **d** 70 **p** 71. C Lisburn St Paul *Conn* 70-72; C Ballymacarrett St Patr *D & D* 72-77; I Ballyphilip w Ardquin 77-79; I Ardmore w Craigavon 79-87; I Killyman *Arm* 87-94; Bp's C Acton w Drumbanagher 94-97; rtd 97. *Flat 1, 16 Cathedral Close, Armagh BT61 7EE* Tel (01861) 523971

HARVEY, Norman Roy. b 43. Nottm Univ DipAE86. Wycliffe Hall Ox 66. **d** 69 **p** 70. C Clay Cross *Derby* 69-72; C Dronfield 72-76; TV 76-79; Dioc Youth Officer 79-83; P-in-c Rowsley 79-89; Dioc Adv in Adult and Youth Educn 83-89; TR Eckington w Handley and Ridgeway from 89. *The Rectory, Eckington, Sheffield S31 9BG* Tel (01246) 432196

HARVEY, Oliver Paul. b 33. Magd Coll Ox BA55 MA59. Cuddesdon Coll 57. **d** 59 **p** 60. C S Norwood St Mark *Cant* 59-61; C Hythe 61-64; Zambia 64-71; Chapl Cant Coll of Tech 71-77; Hon C Cant St Martin and St Paul *Cant* 73-77; Chapl K Sch Roch 77-88; C Roch 88-90; V Gillingham St Mary from 90. *The Vicarage, 27 Gillingham Green, Gillingham, Kent ME7 1SS* Tel (01634) 850529

HARVEY, Miss Pamela Betty (Pam). b 33. Dalton Ho Bris IDC59 CertRK59. **dss** 68 **d** 87 **p** 95. Nottingham St Ann *S'well* 68-72;

Bestwood St Matt 72-76; CPAS Staff 76-93; Dir Consultants Division CPAS from 93; Perm to Offic *Leic* from 92. *37 Tysoe Hill, Leicester LE3 8AR* Tel 0116-287 2670 Fax (01926) 337613

HARVEY, Mrs Patricia Ann (Pat). b 45. Qu Coll Birm. **dss** 82 **d** 87 **p** 94. Gospel Lane St Mich *Birm* 82-85; Exhall *Cov* 85-87; C 87-89; TD Droitwich Spa *Worc* 89-94; TV 94-97; P-in-c Finstall from 97. *The Vicarage, 15 Finstall Road, Bromsgrove, Worcs B60 2EA* Tel (01527) 872459

HARVEY, Canon Patrick Arnold. b 58. TCD BA DipTh MA. **d** 85 **p** 86. C Bandon Union *C, C & R* 85-88; I Limerick St Mich *L & K* 88-90; Dioc Info Officer 88-90; I Abbeyleix w Old Church, Ballyroan etc *C & O* from 90; Preb Ossory Cathl from 96. *The Rectory, Abbeyleix, Portlaoise, Co Laois, Irish Republic* Tel Portlaoise (502) 31243 Fax as telephone

HARVEY, Reginald Darwin. b 28. EAMTC. **d** 82 **p** 83. NSM Gillingham w Geldeston, Stockton, Ellingham etc *Nor* from 82; Perm to Offic *St E* from 86. *Blaenwern, Mill Road, Ellingham, Bungay, Suffolk NR35 2PY* Tel (01508) 518663

HARVEY, Robert Martin. b 30. S'wark Ord Course 69. **d** 70 **p** 71. C Sutton New Town St Barn *S'wark* 70-75; C Leatherhead *Guildf* 76-78; V Wadworth w Loversall *Sheff* 78-96; RD W Doncaster 94-97; rtd 96. *44 Castlegate, Tickhill, Doncaster, S Yorkshire DN11 9QU* Tel (01302) 746532

HARVEY, Robin Grant. b 43. Clare Coll Cam BA64 MA68 Univ of NSW PhD74. Linc Th Coll 85. **d** 87 **p** 88. C Keynsham *B & W* 87-91; R E w W Harptree and Hinton Blewett from 91. *The Rectory, Church Lane, East Harptree, Bristol BS18 6BD* Tel (01761) 221239

HARVEY, Steven Charles. b 58. Reading Univ BA79 Ox Univ BA83 MA88. Ripon Coll Cuddesdon 81. **d** 84 **p** 85. C Oldham *Man* 84-87; Chapl and Hd Relig Studies St Pet Sch York 87-96; Sen Dep Hd Kingswood Sch Bath from 96; Perm to Offic *B & W* from 96. *North Lodge, College Road, Lansdown, Bath BA1 5SD* Tel (01225) 426326

HARVEY, Trevor John. b 43. Sheff Univ BA64. Coll of Resurr Mirfield 64. **d** 66 **p** 67. C Kingswinford St Mary *Lich* 66-72; V Upper Gornal 72-77; V Meir 77-86; Chapl St Geo Sch Windsor from 86; Min Can Windsor from 86. *12 The Cloisters, Windsor Castle, Windsor, Berks SL4 1NJ* Tel (01753) 842086

HARVEY, Victor Llewellyn Tucker. b 16. Ch Coll Cam BA38 MA42. Ridley Hall Cam 38. **d** 39 **p** 40. C W Ham All SS *Chelmsf* 39-41; CF 41-46; Hon CF from 46; V Forest Gate Em *Chelmsf* 46-50; R Sutton *Liv* 50-59; Chapl St Helens Hosp Liv 50-59; R Sanderstead All SS *S'wark* 59-64; R St Marylebone St Mary *Lon* 64-82; Chapl St Marylebone Hosp and W Ophthalmic Hosp 64-82; rtd 82; Perm to Offic *St E* from 82; P-in-c Hasketon 83-89. *The Boot, Great Bealings, Woodbridge, Suffolk IP13 6PQ* Tel (01473) 735382

HARVEY-COOK, Elizabeth Ann. *See* SMITHAM, Mrs Elizabeth Ann

HARVEY-NEILL, Nicola Lisa Jane. b 69. QUB BD91 TCD MPhil95. CITC BTh94. **d** 95 **p** 96. Dioc C *T, K & A* 95-96; C Galway w Kilcummin 96-97; Dioc Youth Adv (Limerick) *L & K* from 97. *14 Springfield Drive, Dooradoyle, Limerick, Irish Republic* Tel Limerick (61) 302038 Mobile 088-500570 Fax as telephone

HARVIE, Paul Johnston. b 36. ARCO74 FTCL73 Melbourne Univ BMusEd80 MMus83. St Mich Th Coll Crafers 58 Trin Coll Melbourne LTh61 ACT ThL. **d** 62 **p** 63. Australia 62-64 and 66-89; C Penton Street St Silas w All SS *Lon* 64-66; Vice-Provost St Paul's Cathl Dundee *Bre* 89-92; R Dundee St Paul 89-92; R Dundee St Salvador from 92. *The Rectory, 9 Minard Crescent, Dundee DD3 6LH* Tel (01382) 221785

HARWOOD, Frederick Ronald (Fred). b 21. Wells Th Coll 61. **d** 63 **p** 64. C Devonport St Mark Ford *Ex* 63-66; V Hessenford *Truro* 66-71; V Hayle 71-87; rtd 87; Hon C Madron *Truro* 88-92; Prec Gib Cathl and Port Chapl *Eur* 92-95; Perm to Offic *Truro* from 95. *Ferncliffe, 5 Harbour View, Hayle, Cornwall TR27 4LB*

HARWOOD, Canon John Rossiter. b 26. Selw Coll Cam BA51 MA55. Wycliffe Hall Ox 51. **d** 53 **p** 54. C Handsworth St Mary *Birm* 53-55; Nigeria 55-64; Sierra Leone 64-67; Home Educn Sec CMS 67-75; V Cheltenham Ch Ch *Glouc* 75-91; RD Cheltenham 84-89; Hon Can Glouc Cathl 85-91; rtd 91; Perm to Offic *Ex* from 91. *29 Clarence Hill, Dartmouth, Devon TQ6 9NY* Tel (01803) 835827

HARWOOD, Dr Peter James. b 64. Birm Univ MB88 ChB88. Wycliffe Hall Ox BA93. **d** 94 **p** 95. C Cov H Trin *Cov* from 94. *85 Stoney Road, Coventry CV3 6HH* Tel (01203) 504141

HARWOOD, Thomas Smith. b 10. St Jo Coll Dur 38. **d** 41 **p** 41. C Kingston upon Hull St Barn *York* 41-43; C Beverley Minster 43-47; Chapl RAF 43-47; R S Milford *York* 47-50; V York St Lawr w St Nic 50-55; V Leake *Linc* 55-59; V Over and Nether Silton *York* 55-59; Area Sec (E Anglia) BFBS 59-62; Perm to Offic *Ely* 59-62; V Middleton St Mary *Ripon* 62-75; V E Winch *Nor* 62-75; rtd 75; Perm to Offic *Nor* 75-96. *8 Beechwood Close, Watlington, King's Lynn, Norfolk PE33 0HP* Tel (01553) 811463

HASELDEN, Canon Eugene John Charles. b 17. Em Coll Cam BA40 MA44. Ridley Hall Cam 40. **d** 42 **p** 43. C Bermondsey St Mary w St Olave and St Jo *S'wark* 42-46; C Ox St Aldate *Ox* 46-49; Chapl RNVR 48-58; Metrop Sec CMS 49-52; V Leic H Trin *Leic* 52-58; Chapl HM Pris Leic 52-58; V Leamington Priors H Trin *Cov* 58-75; RD Leamington 69-75; Hon Can Cov Cathl 69-75; V Lymington *Win* 75-83; RD Lyndhurst 78-82; rtd 83; Perm to Offic *Win* from 83. *1 Ashley Meadows, Romsey, Hants SO51 7LT* Tel (01794) 522688

HASELHURST (née STERLING), Mrs Anne. b 51. Macalester Coll (USA) BA73. EAMTC 89. **d** 92 **p** 94. Par Dn Bury St Edmunds St Jo *St E* 92-94; C 94-95; V Fordham St Pet *Ely* from 95; P-in-c Kennett from 95. *The Vicarage, 24 Mildenhall Road, Fordham, Ely, Cambs CB7 5NR* Tel (01638) 720266

HASELOCK, Canon Jeremy Matthew. b 51. York Univ BA73 BPhil74. St Steph Ho Ox BA82 MA86. **d** 83 **p** 84. C Pimlico St Gabr *Lon* 83-86; C Paddington St Jas 86-88; Bp's Dom Chapl *Chich* 88-91; P-in-c Boxgrove 91-94; V from 94; Dioc Adv on Liturgy from 91; Can and Preb Chich Cathl from 94. *The Vicarage, Boxgrove, Chichester, W Sussex PO18 0ED* Tel (01243) 774045

HASKINS, Thomas. b 41. TCD BA72. CITC 71. **d** 73 **p** 74. C Larne and Inver *Conn* 73-78; C Antrim All SS 78-83; I Belfast St Mark 83-90; RD M Belfast 89-90; I Dublin Clontarf *D & G* from 90; RD Fingal from 95. *15 Seafield Road West, Clontarf, Dublin 3, Irish Republic* Tel Dublin (1) 833 1181

HASLAM, Andrew James. b 57. Univ Coll Dur BSc78 Coll of Ripon & York St Jo PGCE79. Lambeth STh84 Trin Coll Bris 80. **d** 83 **p** 84. C Leyland St Andr *Blackb* 83-86; C Hartford *Ches* 86-88; V Grimsargh *Blackb* from 88. *St Michael's Vicarage, Preston Road, Grimsargh, Preston PR2 5SD* Tel (01772) 653283

HASLAM, Canon David. b 31. St Chad's Coll Dur BA57. Wells Th Coll 57. **d** 59 **p** 60. C Manston *Ripon* 59-62; C Bournemouth St Pet *Win* 62-65; V E and W Worldham, Hartley Mauditt w Kingsley etc 65-71; V Boscombe St Andr 71-92; RD Bournemouth 80-90; Hon Can Win Cathl 84-92; rtd 92. *50 Petersfield Road, Bournemouth BH7 6QJ* Tel (01202) 432330

HASLAM, Canon Frank. b 26. Bris Univ BA50. Tyndale Hall Bris 49. **d** 51 **p** 52. C Halliwell St Paul *Man* 51-55; Uganda 56-60; C Wednesfield Heath *Lich* 60-61; V Wolverhampton St Matt 61-65; V Blackpool Ch Ch *Blackb* 65-70; V Macclesfield St Mich *Ches* 71-80; Dir of Resources 80-91; Hon Can Ches Cathl 81-91; rtd 91; Perm to Offic *Ches* from 91. *Brackendale, Chester Road, Buckley CH7 3AH* Tel (01244) 294544

HASLAM, James Robert. b 31. Open Univ BA74. Bps' Coll Cheshunt 55. **d** 57 **p** 58. C Penwortham St Mary *Blackb* 57-63; V Cockerham 63-74; V Cockerham w Winmarleigh 74-76; V Gt Harwood St Bart 76-88; V Fairhaven 88-95; rtd 95; Perm to Offic *Blackb* from 95. *5 Willowtrees Drive, Blackburn BB1 8LB* Tel (01254) 697092

HASLAM, Mrs Jane. b 70. Leeds Poly BA92. Trin Coll Bris 94. **d** 97. C Minehead *B & W* from 97. *Jordan House, 75 Summerland Avenue, Minehead, Somerset TA24 5BW* Tel (01643) 702868

HASLAM, John Gordon. b 32. Birm Univ LLB53. Qu Coll Birm 75. **d** 77 **p** 77. Hon C Bartley Green *Birm* 77-79; Hon C Moseley St Mary 79-96; Chapl to The Queen from 89; Perm to Offic *Heref* from 97. *16 Mill Street, Ludlow, Shropshire SY8 1BE* Tel (01584) 876663 Fax as telephone

HASLAM, Michael Henry. b 72. Buckm Univ BA93. Trin Coll Bris BA94 MA94. **d** 97. C Minehead *B & W* from 97. *Jordan House, 75 Summerland Avenue, Minehead, Somerset TA24 5BW* Tel (01643) 702868

HASLAM, Robert John Alexander. b 34. CCC Cam BA58. Coll of Resurr Mirfield 58. **d** 60 **p** 61. C Rawmarsh w Parkgate *Sheff* 60-66; Perm to Offic *Edin* 66-73; Perm to Offic *Carl* 73-77; P-in-c Peebles *Edin* 77-81; V Darnall H Trin *Sheff* 81-85; Hon C Bermondsey St Hugh CD *S'wark* 86-88; R Clydebank *Glas* from 88. *21 Dunmore Street, Clydebank, Dunbartonshire G81 1RL* Tel 0141-952 0298

HASLAM-JONES, Christopher John. b 28. ALCD53. **d** 53 **p** 54. C Walthamstow St Jo *Chelmsf* 53-57; C High Wycombe All SS *Ox* 57-62; V Parkfield in Middleton *Man* 62-68; V Radcliffe St Andr 68-86; R Colchester Ch Ch w St Mary V *Chelmsf* 86-93; rtd 93. *Ramia, 4A Belle Vue Road, Poole, Dorset BH14 8TW* Tel (01202) 767674

HASLER, John Joseph (Joe). b 45. Qu Coll Birm 89. **d** 90 **p** 91. C Horfield H Trin *Bris* 90-93; V Bris St Andr Hartcliffe from 93. *St Andrew's Vicarage, Peterson Square, Bristol BS13 0EE* Tel 0117-964 3554

HASSALL, William Edwin. b 41. St Jo Coll Nottm 75. **d** 77 **p** 78. C Wellington w Eyton *Lich* 77-80; C Farewell 80-82; V 82-93; C Gentleshaw 80-82; V 82-93; P-in-c Cheddleton 93-94. *17 Ansty Drive, Heath Hayes, Cannock, Staffs WS12 5TZ* Tel (01543) 275087

HASSELL, David Edwin. b 38. WMMTC 87. **d** 90 **p** 91. NSM Worc SE *Worc* 90-93; C Abberton, Naunton Beauchamp and Bishampton etc 93-94; P-in-c 94; R Abberton, The Flyfords, Naunton Beauchamp etc from 94. *The Rectory, Bishampton, Pershore, Worcs WR10 2LT* Tel (01386) 462648

HASSELL, John Charles. b 44. FCA. Sarum & Wells Th Coll 81. **d** 83 **p** 84. C Tottenham St Paul *Lon* 83-86; C Fingringhoe w E Donyland *Chelmsf* 86-90; V Moulsham St Jo from 90. *St John's Vicarage, Vicarage Road, Moulsham, Chelmsford CM2 9PH* Tel (01245) 352344

HASSEN, Canon Edward William. b 27. TCD. **d** 56 **p** 57. C Larne *Conn* 56-59; C Derriaghy 59-61; Chapl RAF 61-64; C-in-c Muckamore *Conn* 64-67; I 67-94; RD Antrim 74-93; Dioc Stewardship Adv 90-94; Can Belf Cathl 93-94; rtd 94. *Valloire, 8 Parkgate Road, Parkgate, Templepatrick, Co Antrim BT39 0DF* Tel (01849) 432823

HASTED, Canon John Arthur Ord. b 28. Keble Coll Ox BA50 MA54. Wells Th Coll 51. **d** 53 **p** 54. C Cheshunt *St Alb* 53-58; Prec Birm Cathl *Birm* 58-59; V Bulkington *Cov* 59-61; V Styvechale 61-64; V Yoxford *St E* 64-79; V Sibton 64-78; RD Saxmundham 74-79; Hon Can St E Cathl 75-79; rtd 79; Perm to Offic *St Alb* from 82. *1 Eaton Court, Pemberley Avenue, Bedford MK40 2LH* Tel (01234) 341402

HASTEY, Erle. b 44. St Mich Coll Llan 66. **d** 68 **p** 69. C Pontefract St Giles *Wakef* 68-71; C Almondbury 71-74; V Purlwell 74-79; P-in-c Batley Carr 76-79; V Ynyshir *Llan* 79-86; V Tylorstown w Ynyshir 86-87; V Tonyrefail w Gilfach Goch 87-97; P-in-c Llandyfodwg 87-97; V Tonyrefail w Gilfach Goch and Llandyfodwg from 97. *The Vicarage, High Street, Tonyrefail CF39 8PL* Tel (01443) 670330

HASTIE-SMITH, Timothy Maybury (Tim). b 62. Magd Coll Cam MA84. Wycliffe Hall Ox 85. **d** 88 **p** 89. C Ox St Ebbe w H Trin and St Pet *Ox* 88-91; Chapl Stowe Sch Bucks from 91. *New Field House, Stowe School, Buckingham MK18 5DF* Tel (01280) 812446

HASTINGS, David Kerr. b 40. St Luke's Coll Ex CertEd63. Ox NSM Course 84. **d** 87 **p** 88. Hd Master St Edburg's Sch Bicester from 82; Asst Chapl HM Pris Grendon and Spring Hill 87-89; NSM Bicester w Bucknell, Caversfield and Launton *Ox* 87-89; Chapl HM Pris Reading 90-92; P-in-c Gt Wishford *Sarum* 92; P-in-c S Newton 92; P-in-c Stapleford w Berwick St James 92; R Lower Wylye and Till Valley 92-95; Chapl HM Pris Ex from 96. *HM Prison Exeter, New North Road, Exeter EX4 4EX* Tel (01392) 278321 Fax 422647

HASTINGS, Gary Lea. b 56. New Univ of Ulster BA82 MA87 TCD BTh93. CITC 90. **d** 93 **p** 94. C Galway w Kilcummin *T, K & A* 93-95; Dom Chapl to Bp Tuam from 94; I Aughaval w Achill, Knappagh, Dugort etc from 95. *The Rectory, Newport Road, Westport, Co Mayo, Irish Republic* Tel Westport (98) 25127

HASTINGS, Patrick John Alan. b 45. ACIB68 CertEd75 Sussex Univ BEd82. S Dios Minl Tr Scheme 83. **d** 86 **p** 87. NSM Whyke w Rumboldswhyke and Portfield *Chich* 86-87; C Weybridge *Guildf* 87-89; C Verwood *Sarum* 89-93; P-in-c Lytchett Matravers from 93. *The Rectory, Jenny's Lane, Lytchett Matravers, Poole, Dorset BH16 6BP* Tel (01929) 459200

HASTROP, Paul. b 39. Wells Th Coll 70. **d** 72 **p** 73. C Parkstone St Osmund *Sarum* 72-76; C Penzance St Mary w St Paul *Truro* 76-79; V St Blazey 79-87; TV Bournemouth St Pet w St Swithun, H Trin etc *Win* 87-94; TV Thornaby on Tees *York* 94-96; P-in-c N Thornaby 96; P-in-c Portsea St Sav *Portsm* from 96. *St Saviour's Vicarage, Twyford Avenue, Portsmouth PO2 8PB* Tel (01705) 663664

HASTWELL, James Sydney (Jim). b 37. Roch Th Coll 67. **d** 69 **p** 70. C Croydon St Aug *Cant* 69-73; C Hurstpierpoint *Chich* 73-75; P-in-c Twineham 76; P-in-c Sayers Common 76; P-in-c Albourne 76; R Albourne w Sayers Common and Twineham 76-88; V Forest Row 88-94. *4 Park Close, Hurstpierpoint, Hassocks, W Sussex BN6 9XA* Tel (01273) 835954

HATCH, Canon George Andrew. b 29. Leeds Univ BA. Coll of Resurr Mirfield. **d** 53 **p** 54. C S Farnborough *Guildf* 53-55; Windward Is 55-63; Barbados from 63; Assoc Dir Chr Action Development in Caribbean 73-83. *St James, Barbados* Tel Barbados (1809) 432-1580

HATCH, Richard Francis. b 36. Qu Coll Cam BA60 MA64. Cuddesdon Coll 60. **d** 62 **p** 63. C Leigh St Mary *Man* 62-66; PC Peel Green 66-71; V Barton w Peel Green 71-75; Dioc Broadcasting Officer 73-85; R Birch St Jas 75-78; R Fallowfield 75-78; Lic Preacher from 78. *24 Denison Road, Victoria Park, Manchester M14 5RY* Tel 0161-225 0799

HATCHETT, Michael John. b 49. Enfield Coll BSc72 K Coll Lon BD77 AKC77. Linc Th Coll 77. **d** 78 **p** 79. C Halstead St Andr *Chelmsf* 78-79; C Halstead St Andr w H Trin and Greenstead Green 79-81; C Greenstead juxta Colchester 81-85; V Gt Totham from 85. *The Vicarage, 1 Hall Road, Great Totham, Maldon, Essex CM9 8NN* Tel (01621) 893150

HATCHLEY, Canon Walter John. b 24. Lon Univ BA65. Coll of Resurr Mirfield 64. **d** 66 **p** 67. C Monkseaton St Pet *Newc* 66-69; C Gosforth All SS 69-72; C Cullercoats St Geo 72; TV 72-78; V Newc St Fran 78-93; RD Newc E 83-92; Hon Can Newc Cathl 90-93; rtd 93. *4 Woodthorne Road, Jesmond, Newcastle upon Tyne NE2 3PB*

HATCHMAN, Ms Elizabeth Mary (Lizzie). b 63. St Andr Univ MA85 Kent Coll for Careers DCG87. Selly Oak Coll Qu Coll Birm BD92. **d** 93 **p** 94. C Aston SS Pet and Paul *Birm* 93-96; C Rowley Regis from 96. *194 Hanover Road, Rowley Regis, Warley, W Midlands B65 9PQ* Tel 0121-559 3830

HATCHMAN, Hugh Alleyne. b 28. Qu Coll Cam BA52 MA56. Ridley Hall Cam 52. **d** 54 **p** 55. C E Twickenham St Steph *Lon* 54-56; C Morden *S'wark* 56-59; E Midl Area Sec CPAS 59-63; V New Catton St Luke *Nor* 63-79; Chapl Bexley Hosp Kent 79-93; rtd 93. *Braemar, North Lyminge, Lyminge, Folkestone, Kent CT18 8EF* Tel (01303) 862369

HATCLIFFE, Charles John William Coombes. b 26. St Aid Birkenhead 59. **d** 61 **p** 62. C Salford Stowell Memorial *Man* 61-64; V Stubbins 64-71; P-in-c Clifton Green 71-74; V 74-82; P-in-c Acton Burnell w Pitchford *Heref* 82-83; P-in-c Condover 82-83; P-in-c Frodesley 82-83; V Bentley *Lich* 83-89; rtd 89; Perm to Offic *Lich* from 89. *3 Chestnut Drive, Bayston Hill, Shrewsbury SY3 0QQ*

HATFULL, Ronald Stanley. b 22. CChem42 MChemA48 FRSC48 FRSH65. Qu Coll Birm 79. **d** 82 **p** 83. NSM Castle Church *Lich* 82-89; Kingsmead Hosp Stafford 82-89; rtd 89; Perm to Offic *Lich* from 89. *Ridge House, Ridgeway Close, Hyde Lea, Stafford ST18 9BE* Tel (01785) 52992

HATHAWAY, Canon David Alfred Gerald. b 48. DipTh72. St Mich Coll Llan 69. **d** 72 **p** 73. C Newport St Julian *Mon* 72-74; P-in-c Oakham w Hambleton and Egleton *Pet* 74-77; V Newport St Matt *Mon* 77-83; V Abertillery 83-88; V Rumney from 88; Hon Can St Woolos Cathl from 91. *The Vicarage, 702 Newport Road, Rumney, Cardiff CF3 8DF* Tel (01222) 797882

HATHAWAY, John Albert. b 24. Sarum Th Coll 59. **d** 60 **p** 61. C Fleet *Guildf* 60-64; C Cowley St Jas *Ox* 64-66; V Holmwood *Guildf* 66-71; R Westborough 71-74; V Newmarket All SS *St E* 74-82; V Acton w Gt Waldingfield 82-85; R W Downland *Sarum* 85-90; rtd 90. *3 Nettlebed Nursery, Shaftesbury, Dorset SP7 8QS* Tel (01747) 851950

HATHAWAY, Martin Charles. b 48. St Jo Coll Nottm LTh95. **d** 95 **p** 96. C Weddington and Caldecote *Cov* from 95. *62 Castle Road, Nuneaton, Warks CV10 0EW*

HATHERLEY, Peter Graham. b 46. Univ of Wales (Cardiff) BSc67 PhD70. St Mich Coll Llan 70. **d** 72 **p** 73. C Ystrad Mynach *Llan* 72-75; Hon C Tonyrefail 75-88; Perm to Offic from 88. *Treetops, The Derwen, Bridgend CF35 6HD*

HATHERLEY, Victor Charles. b 17. St Aug Coll Cant 63. **d** 64 **p** 64. C Crewkerne *B & W* 64-68; R E Harptree 68-73; R E w W Harptree 73-76; R E w W Harptree and Hinton Blewett 76-82; rtd 82; Perm to Offic *B & W* 83-91. *10 Fairview Road, Broadstone, Dorset BH18 9AX* Tel (01202) 699371

HATHORNE (née MARSH), Mrs Carol Ann. b 44. W Midl Coll of Educn BA82. WMMTC 88. **d** 91 **p** 94. Par Dn Wednesbury St Paul Wood Green *Lich* 91-93; NSM Pensnett *Worc* from 93. *222 High Street, Pensnett, Brierley Hill, W Midlands DY5 4JP* Tel (01384) 78438

HATHWAY, Richard Peter. b 17. Kelham Th Coll 34. **d** 41 **p** 42. C Cleckheaton St Jo *Wakef* 41-44; P-in-c Monk Bretton 44-46; CF 46-66; Chapl Highgate Sch Lon 66-81; rtd 81; Perm to Offic *Nor* from 81; Perm to Offic *St E* from 87. *10 Station Road, Harleston, Norfolk IP20 9ES* Tel (01379) 853590

HATHWAY, Ross Arthur. b 56. DATh87. Moore Th Coll Sydney BTh86. **d** 86 **p** 87. Australia 87-88; C Corby St Columba *Pet* 89-92; R Trull w Angersleigh *B & W* from 92. *The Rectory, Wild Oak Lane, Trull, Taunton, Somerset TA3 7JT* Tel (01823) 253518

HATREY, David Nigel. b 57. SS Mark & Jo Coll Plymouth CertEd79 CertSc87 BEd90. SW Minl Tr Course 90. **d** 93 **p** 94. NSM S Hill w Callington *Truro* from 93. *8 Lowertown Close, Landrake, Saltash, Cornwall PL12 5DG* Tel (01752) 851529

HATT, Michael John. b 34. Sarum Th Coll 67. **d** 69 **p** 70. Hon C Ex St Mary Arches *Ex* 70-73; Hon C Cen Ex from 73. *133 Topsham Road, Exeter EX2 4RE* Tel (01392) 271165

HATTAN, Jeffrey William Rowland. b 49. Cranmer Hall Dur 83. **d** 85 **p** 86. C Eston w Normanby *York* 85-89; TV 89-95; V Hunmanby w Muston from 95. *The Vicarage, 6 Northgate, Hunmanby, Filey, N Yorkshire YO14 0NT* Tel (01723) 890294

HATTER, Canon David George. b 21. Lich Th Coll. **d** 57 **p** 58. C Carrington *S'well* 57-61; V Clipstone 61-67; V Mansfield St Mark 67-81; V Sutton w Carlton and Normanton upon Trent etc 81-86; P-in-c Caunton 84-86; Hon Can S'well Minster 84-86; RD Tuxford and Norwell 84-86; rtd 86; Perm to Offic *S'well* from 86. *1 North End, Farndon, Newark, Notts NG24 3SX* Tel (01636) 76960

HATTON, Jeffrey Charles. b 49. K Coll Lon BD70 Bris Univ MA72. Westcott Ho Cam 73 Episc Th Sch Cam Mass 74. **d** 74 **p** 75. C Nor St Pet Mancroft *Nor* 74-78; C Earlham St Anne 78-79; Relig Broadcasting Asst IBA 79-82; Hon C Kensington St Barn *Lon* 79-84; Hon C Fulham All SS 85-89; R Win All SS w Chilcomb and Chesil *Win* 89-94; Dioc Communications Officer 89-94; P-in-c Salisbury St Thos and St Edm *Sarum* from 94. *The Rectory, St Thomas's Square, Salisbury SP1 1BA* Tel (01722) 322537

HATTON, Michael Samuel. b 44. St Jo Coll Dur BA72 DipTh74. **d** 74 **p** 75. C Dudley St Jas *Worc* 74-75; C N Lynn w St Marg and St Nic *Nor* 75-77; C Walsall Wood *Lich* 78-79; Min Shelfield St Mark CD 79-89; V Middleton St Cross *Ripon* from 89. *St Cross Vicarage, Middleton Park Avenue, Leeds LS10 4HT* Tel 0113-271 6398

HATTON, Trevor. b 55. Oak Hill Th Coll BA86. **d** 86 **p** 87. C Chilwell *S'well* 86-90; R Trowell 90-95; Chapl Nottm Trent Univ from 95. *53 Ashchurch Drive, Wollaton, Nottingham NG8 2RB* Tel 0115-928 3261

HATWELL, Timothy Rex. b 53. Oak Hill Th Coll BA85. **d** 85 **p** 86. C Tonbridge St Steph *Roch* 85-90; V Cudham and Downe from 90. *The Vicarage, Cudham Lane South, Cudham, Sevenoaks, Kent TN14 7QA* Tel (01959) 572445 Fax as telephone E-mail t.hatwell@ndirect.co.uk

HAUGHAN, John Francis (Frank). b 28. Tyndale Hall Bris 56. **d** 60 **p** 61. C Tonbridge St Steph *Roch* 60-63; C Cheltenham St Mark *Glouc* 63-67; V Tewkesbury H Trin 67-92; rtd 92; Perm to Offic *Glouc* from 92. *Beech View, Lower Road, Yorkley, Lydney, Glos GL15 4TQ* Tel (01594) 562066

HAUGHTON, Peter Steele. b 57. K Coll Lon BD84 MA90 Fitzw Coll Cam DipTh85. Westcott Ho Cam 84. **d** 86 **p** 87. C Cheam Common St Phil *S'wark* 86-90; Chapl Lon Univ Medical Schs 90-94; Educn Adv Lon Univ Medical Schs 94-95; P-in-c Kingston Vale St Jo from 95. *St John's Vicarage, Robin Hood Lane, London SW15 3PY* Tel 0181-546 4079

HAVARD, Alan Ernest. b 27. Qu Coll Birm 79. **d** 81 **p** 82. NSM Rugby St Matt *Cov* 81-84; C Portishead *B & W* 84-86; V Mickleover All SS *Derby* 86-96; rtd 96; Perm to Offic *Derby* from 96. *7 Headingley Court, Littleover, Derby DE3 6XS*

HAVARD, David William. b 56. Man Univ BA84. Qu Coll Birm 84. **d** 85. C Man Clayton St Cross w St Paul *Man* 85-88; Canada from 88. *211 Seventh Street, New Westminster, British Columbia, Canada, V3M 3K2*

HAVELL, Edward Michael. b 38. Dur Univ BA65. Ridley Hall Cam 66. **d** 68 **p** 69. C Ecclesall *Sheff* 68-71; C Roch St Justus *Roch* 71-74; P-in-c Holbeach Hurn *Linc* 74-75; C Hollington St Jo *Chich* 75-85; TV Rye 85-92; C E Dereham and Scarning *Nor* 92; rtd 93. *4 Gammons Way, Sedlescombe, Battle, E Sussex TN33 0RQ* Tel (01424) 870864

HAVENS, Mrs Anita Sue. b 44. Mass Univ BSEd67 Clark Univ (USA) MA72 Hughes Hall Cam BA79. Cranmer Hall Dur MA83. **dss** 84 **d** 87 **p** 94. Gateshead Hosps 84-87; Par Dn Cen Telford *Lich* 87-90; Ind Chapl 87-90; Ind Chapl *Liv* 90-96; TV Man Whitworth *Man* from 96; Chapl Man Univ from 96. *354 Wilbraham Road, Manchester M21 1UX* Tel 0161-881 7688 or 273 1465

HAVEY, Kenneth Richard. b 61. St Steph Ho Ox 95. **d** 97. C Corringham *Chelmsf* from 97. *St John's House, Springhouse Road, Corringham, Stanford-Le-Hope, Essex SS17 7LF* Tel (01375) 675463

HAVILAND, Edmund Selwyn. b 24. K Coll Cam BA49 MA51. Wells Th Coll 49. **d** 51 **p** 52. C St Helier *S'wark* 51-55; C-in-c Bermondsey St Hugh CD 55-58; V Ockbrook *Derby* 58-68; V E Peckham *Roch* 68-78; R E Peckham and Nettlestead 78-84; S Africa 84-85; Dep Chapl HM Pris Brixton 85-89; rtd 89; Perm to Offic *Guildf* from 89. *Hill Farm, Thursley, Godalming, Surrey GU8 6QQ* Tel (01252) 702115

HAWES, Andrew Thomas. b 54. Sheff Univ BA77 Em Coll Cam MA79. Westcott Ho Cam 77. **d** 80 **p** 81. FFS from 78; C Gt Grimsby St Mary and St Jas *Linc* 80-84; P-in-c Gedney Drove End 84-86; P-in-c Sutton St Nicholas 84-86; V Lutton w Gedney Drove End, Dawsmere 86-89; V Edenham w Witham-on-the-Hill from 89; RD Beltisloe from 97. *The Vicarage, Church Lane, Edenham, Bourne, Lincs PE10 0LS* Tel (01778) 591358

HAWES, The Ven Arthur John. b 43. UEA BA86 Birm Univ DPS72 DipL&A75. Chich Th Coll 65. **d** 68 **p** 69. C Kidderminster St Jo *Worc* 68-72; P-in-c Droitwich 72-76; R Alderford w Attlebridge and Swannington *Nor* 76-92; Chapl Hellesdon and David Rice Hosps and Yare Clinic 76-92; RD Sparham *Nor* 81-91; Mental Health Act Commr 86-94; Hon Can Nor Cathl *Nor* 88-95; TR Gaywood St Faith 92-95; Adn Linc from 95; Can and Preb Linc Cathl from 95. *Archdeacon's House, Northfield Road, Quarrington, Sleaford, Lincs NG34 8RT* Tel (01529) 304348 Fax 304354

HAWES, Clive. b 37. Univ of Wales BSc59. Coll of Resurr Mirfield 61. **d** 63 **p** 64. C Ynyshir *Llan* 63-65; C Roath St Marg 65-72; V Llanddewi Rhondda w Bryn Eirw 72-75; Chapl Ch Coll Brecon 75-92; V Llantilio Crossenny w Penrhos, Llanvetherine etc *Mon* 92-97. *Caeredin, 1 College Lane, Trefecca, Brecon LD3 0PP* Tel (01874) 711999

HAWES, George Walter. b 10. Lon Coll of Div 39. **d** 41 **p** 42. C Woodford Wells *Chelmsf* 41-48; Chapl Herts Sanatorium 43-46; V E Ham St Paul 48-56; Adn W Kenya 56-60; R Rowner *Portsm* 60-78; rtd 78. *90 Kiln Road, Fareham, Hants PO16 7UJ* Tel (01329) 286309

HAWES, Joseph Patricius. b 65. St Chad's Coll Dur BA87. St Steph Ho Ox 88. **d** 91 **p** 92. C Clapham TM *S'wark* 91-96; P-in-c Barnes St Mich from 96. *St Michael's Vicarage, 39 Elm Bank Gardens, London SW13 0NX* Tel 0181-876 5230

HAWES, Michael Rowell. b 31. AKC61. **d** 62 **p** 63. C Epsom St Martin *Guildf* 62-65; Chapl RAF 65-86; R Newnham w Nately Scures w Mapledurwell etc *Win* from 86. *The Rectory, Up Nateley, Basingstoke, Hants RG27 9PL* Tel (01256) 762021

HAWKEN, Andrew Robert. b 58. K Coll Lon BD81 AKC81. St Steph Ho Ox 83. **d** 85 **p** 86. C Ex St Dav *Ex* 85-88; TV Witney *Ox* 88-93; V Benson from 93. *The Vicarage, Church Road, Benson, Wallingford, Oxon OX9 6SF* Tel (01491) 838254

HAWKER, Canon Alan Fort. b 44. Hull Univ BA65 Lon Univ DipTh68. Clifton Th Coll 65. **d** 68 **p** 69. C Bootle St Leon *Liv* 68-71; C Fazakerley Em 71-73; V Goose Green 73-81; TR Southgate *Chich* from 81; Can and Preb Chich Cathl from 91; RD E Grinstead from 94. *The Rectory, Forester Road, Crawley, W Sussex RH10 6EH* Tel (01293) 523463

HAWKER, Alan John. b 53. BD76 AKC76. Sarum & Wells Th Coll 77. **d** 78 **p** 79. C Coleford w Staunton *Glouc* 78-81; C Up Hatherley 81-84; V Plymouth St Jas Ham *Ex* 84-92; TV Worc SE *Worc* from 92. *The Vicarage, 160 Bath Road, Worcester WR5 3EP* Tel (01905) 357244

HAWKER, Brian Henry. b 34. AKC61 St Boniface Warminster 61. **d** 62 **p** 63. C Hemel Hempstead *St Alb* 62-66; R Stone w Hartwell w Bishopstone *Ox* 66-69; Chapl St Jo Hosp Stone 66-69; V W Wycombe 69-72; Past Consultant Clinical Th Assn 72-83; Past Consultant 83-94; Public Preacher *S'well* 72-76; Perm to Offic *B & W* 76-83; Perm to Offic *Truro* 83-90; rtd 94. *12 Burfield Avenue, Loughborough, Leics LE11 3AZ*

✠**HAWKER, The Rt Revd Dennis Gascoyne.** b 21. Qu Coll Cam BA48 MA53. Cuddesdon Coll 48. **d** 50 **p** 51 **c** 72. C Folkestone St Mary and St Eanswythe *Cant* 50-55; V S Norwood St Mark 55-60; Lic to Offic *Linc* 60-64; Can and Preb Linc Cathl 64-87; V Gt Grimsby St Mary and St Jas 65-72; Suff Bp Grantham 72-87; Dean Stamford 73-87; Chapl RNR from 78; rtd 87; Asst Bp Nor from 93. *Pickwick Cottage, Hall Close, Heacham, King's Lynn, Norfolk PE31 7JT* Tel (01485) 70450

HAWKER, The Ven Peter John. b 37. Ex Univ BA59. Wycliffe Hall Ox 69. **d** 70 **p** 71. Chapl Berne w Neuchatel *Eur* 70-89; Adn Switzerland from 86; Can Brussels Cathl from 86; Chapl Zurich w St Gallen and Winterthur 90-93; Chapl Zurich w Winterthur from 93. *Promenadengasse 9, 8001 Zurich, Switzerland* Tel Zurich (1) 261-2241 or 252-6024 Fax 252-6024

HAWKES, Mrs Elisabeth Anne. b 56. GRNCM78 PGCE80 Kent Univ MA97. Linc Th Coll 86. **d** 88. Hon Par Dn Finham *Cov* 88-90; Hon Par Dn Bexhill St Pet *Chich* 90-97; Asst to RD Oundle *Pet* from 97. *The Vicarage, 12 New Street, Oundle, Peterborough PE8 4EA* Tel (01832) 273595

HAWKES, The Ven Francis George. b 23. LTh50. St Barn Coll Adelaide ACT 50. **d** 51 **p** 51. Australia 51-65 and from 83; CF 65-83; Adn Marsden 82-89; rtd 89. *Kurrajong, PO Box 62, Australia 2758* Tel Kurrajong (45) 731617

HAWKES, Keith Andrew. b 28. Oak Hill Th Coll 72. **d** 74 **p** 75. C Gt Yarmouth *Nor* 74-77; C-in-c Bowthorpe CD 77; Chapl Dusseldorf *Eur* 77-83; TV Quidenham *Nor* 83-88; TR 88-90; RD Thetford and Rockland 86-90; R Wickmere w Lt Barningham, Itteringham etc 90-96; Dioc Rural Officer 90-94; P-in-c Saxthorpe w Corpusty, Blickling, Oulton etc 94-96; R Lt Barningham, Blickling, Edgefield etc from 96. *The Rectory, The Street, Itteringham, Norwich NR11 7AX* Tel (01263) 584262

HAWKES, Ronald Linton. b 54. York Univ CertEd75 Leeds Univ BEd76 Kent Univ MA96. Linc Th Coll 85. **d** 87 **p** 88. C Finham *Cov* 87-90; C Bexhill St Pet *Chich* 90; TV 91-97; V Oundle *Pet* from 97. *The Vicarage, 12 New Street, Oundle, Peterborough PE8 4EA* Tel (01832) 273595

HAWKETT, Graham Kenneth. b 20. Bps' Coll Cheshunt 61. **d** 63 **p** 64. C Farncombe *Guildf* 63-67; V Wyke 67-85; rtd 85; Perm to Offic *Guildf* from 85. *Bede House, Beech Road, Haslemere, Surrey GU27 2BX* Tel (01428) 656430

HAWKINGS, Timothy Denison. b 55. Ex Univ BA78 Nottm Univ BA80. St Jo Coll Nottm 78. **d** 81 **p** 82. C Penn *Lich* 81-85; C Stafford 85; TV 85-94; TR Stratton St Margaret w S Marston etc *Bris* from 94. *The Rectory, Kenwin Close, Swindon SN3 4NB* Tel (01793) 822793

HAWKINS, Alec Borman. b 07. **d** 68 **p** 69. C Boldmere *Birm* 68-79; Perm to Offic from 79. *2 Wrekin Court, Vesey Close, Sutton Coldfield, W Midlands B74 4QN* Tel 0121-308 4625

HAWKINS, Alfred Pryse. b 29. St Mich Coll Llan 57. **d** 59 **p** 60. C Dowlais *Llan* 59-62; C Caerau w Ely 62-66; V Aberaman and Abercwmboi 66-77; R Ebbw Vale *Mon* 77-82; V St Benet Paul's Wharf *Lon* from 82; P-in-c Paddington St Dav Welsh Ch from 82; P-in-c St Jas Garlickhythe w St Mich Queenhithe etc 85-86. *St David's Vicarage, St Mary's Terrace, London W2 1SJ* Tel 0171-723 3104 or 489 8754

HAWKINS, Canon Alun John. b 44. BA66 AKC Univ of Wales (Ban) BD81. St Deiniol's Hawarden 78. **d** 81 **p** 82. C Dwygyfylchi *Ban* 81-84; R Llanberis 84-89; Tutor Ban Dioc NSM Course 85-90; Dir of Ords *Ban* 86-90; V Knighton and Norton *S & B* 89-93; Chapl Knighton Hosp 89-93; R Ban from 93; Can Missr Ban Cathl from 93. *The Canonry, Cathedral Close, Bangor LL57 1LH* Tel (01248) 362840

HAWKINS, Andrew Robert. b 40. St Andr Univ BSc64 Dur Univ BA68 DipTh69. St Chad's Coll Dur 65. **d** 69 **p** 70. C Sutton St Nic *S'wark* 69-73; C Wimbledon 73-77; TV Cramlington *Newc* 77-81; R Clutton w Cameley *B & W* 81-89; Chapl City of Bath Coll of FE from 90; Perm to Offic *B & W* from 90. *18 Wallycourt Road, Chew Stoke, Bristol BS18 8XN* Tel (01275) 332422

HAWKINS, Bruce Alexander. b 44. Qu Coll Ox BA66 MA71. Sarum Th Coll 66. **d** 68 **p** 69. C Epsom St Martin *Guildf* 68-71; Dioc Youth Chapl *Cant* 72-81; Hon Min Can Cant Cathl from 75; Dep Dir of Educn 81-86; V Walmer from 86; RD Sandwich from 94. *The Vicarage, St Mary's Road, Deal, Kent CT14 7NQ* Tel (01304) 374645 Fax as telephone

HAWKINS, Clive Ladbrook. b 53. DHSA79 St Pet Coll Ox BA76 MA79 DipTh82. Trin Coll Bris 80. **d** 82 **p** 83. C Win Ch Ch *Win* 82-86; R Eastrop from 86. *Eastrop Rectory, 2A Wallis Road, Basingstoke, Hants RG21 3DW* Tel (01256) 55507

HAWKINS, Canon David John Leader. b 49. Nottm Univ BTh73 LTh. St Jo Coll Nottm 69 ALCD73. **d** 73 **p** 74. C Bebington *Ches* 73-76; Nigeria 76-82; C Ox St Aldate w St Matt *Ox* 83-86; V Leeds St Geo *Ripon* from 86. *St George's Vicarage, 208 Kirkstall Lane, Leeds LS5 2AB* Tel 0113-274 4367 or 243 8498

HAWKINS, David Kenneth Beaumont. b 36. LTh. Em Coll Saskatoon 63. **d** 63 **p** 64. Canada 63-85; C St Alb St Paul *St Alb* 85-87; C Hednesford *Lich* 87-92; R Buildwas and Leighton w Eaton Constantine etc 92-95; TV Wrockwardine Deanery from 95. *The Vicarage, Eaton Constantine, Shrewsbury SY5 6RF* Tel (01952) 510333

HAWKINS, David Sewell. b 33. Bps' Coll Cheshunt. **d** 58 **p** 59. C Chingford St Anne *Chelmsf* 58-59; C Bridlington Quay Ch Ch *York* 59-63; V Rudston, Grindale and Ergham w Boynton 63-64; P-in-c Boynton 63-64; V Rudston w Boynton 64-68; Chapl RADD 68-77; R Burton Agnes w Harpham *York* 77-80; P-in-c Lowthorpe w Ruston Parva 77-80; P-in-c Kilham 77-80; R Burton Agnes w Harpham, Kilham, Lowthorpe etc 80-85; R Burton Agnes w Harpham and Lowthorpe etc from 85. *The Rectory, Rudston Road, Burton Agnes, Driffield, N Humberside YO25 0NE* Tel (01262) 490293

HAWKINS, Donald John. b 39. K Coll Lon BD62 AKC62. St Boniface Warminster 62. **d** 63 **p** 64. C Winlaton *Dur* 63-66; C Gateshead St Mary 66-69; C Ryhope 69-71; R Cockfield 71-79; Chapl N Staffs R Infirmary Stoke-on-Trent 79-89; Chapl Stoke-on-Trent City Gen Hosp 89-93; Chapl N Staffs Hosp NHS Trust from 93; Chapl Co-ord from 94. *The Chaplain's Office, City General, Newcastle Road, Stoke-on-Trent ST4 6QG* Tel (01782) 552146 or 715444

HAWKINS, Canon Francis John (Frank). b 36. Ex Coll Ox BA61 MA63. Chich Th Coll 59. **d** 61 **p** 62. C Tavistock and Gulworthy *Ex* 61-64; Lect Chich Th Coll 64-73; Vice-Prin 73-75; V E Grinstead St Mary *Chich* 75-81; Can Res and Treas Chich Cathl from 81; V Sidlesham 81-89; Dir of Ords from 89. *12 St Martin's Square, Chichester, W Sussex PO19 1NR* Tel (01243) 783509

HAWKINS, Ian Clinton. b 27. Roch Th Coll 63. **d** 65 **p** 66. C Boulton *Derby* 65-68; V Cotmanhay 68-77; V Ospringe *Cant* 77-85; P-in-c Eastling 77-85; P-in-c Goodnestone H Cross w Chillenden and Knowlton 85; P-in-c Womenswold 85; V Nonington w Wymynswold and Goodnestone etc 85-92; rtd 92; Perm to Offic *Derby* from 92. *7 Main Road, Bradwell, Sheffield S30 2JG* Tel (01433) 621360

HAWKINS, James Reginald. b 39. Ex Univ BA61. Westcott Ho Cam 61. **d** 63 **p** 64. C Cannock *Lich* 63-66; C Wem 66-67; C Cheddleton 67-69; R Yoxall 69-77; R The Quinton *Birm* 77-84; V Bosbury w Wellington Heath etc *Heref* 84-96; P-in-c Ancaster Wilsford Gp *Linc* from 96. *The Rectory, 117 Ermine Street, Ancaster, Grantham, Lincs NG32 3QL* Tel (01400) 230398

HAWKINS, John. b 27. FASI73 Ox Poly DipArch52. S'wark Ord Course 84. **d** 87 **p** 88. Hon C Carshalton Beeches *S'wark* 87-89; Perm to Offic from 89. *44 Castlemaine Avenue, South Croydon, Surrey CR2 7HR* Tel 0181-688 9685

HAWKINS, John Arthur. b 45. Lon Univ DipTh69. Kelham Th Coll 64. **d** 69 **p** 70. C Cov St Alb *Cov* 70-73; C Fletchamstead 73-77; V Whitley 77-81; TV Northampton Em *Pet* 81-90; TV Gt Chesham *Ox* from 90. *Christ Church Vicarage, 95 Latimer Road, Chesham, Bucks HP5 1QQ* Tel (01494) 773318

HAWKINS, John Charles Lacey. b 18. Linc Th Coll 40. **d** 42 **p** 43. C Dalton-in-Furness *Carl* 42-44; C Workington St Mich 44-48; V Allonby w W Newton 48-53; V Thornton w Allerthorpe *York* 53-60; R Stockton-on-the-Forest w Holtby and Warthill 60-77; R Sigglesthorne and Rise w Nunkeeling and Bewholme 77-83; rtd 83; Perm to Offic *York* from 83. *Woodlea, 26 Limekiln Lane, Bridlington, N Humberside YO16 5TH* Tel (01262) 601760

HAWKINS, John Edward Inskipp. b 63. K Coll Lon BD85. Qu Coll Birm 86. **d** 88 **p** 89. C Birchfield *Birm* 88-92; C Poplar *Lon* 92-93; TV from 93. *St Nicholas' Vicarage, Dee Street, London E14 0PT* Tel 0171-515 8405

HAWKINS, Canon John Henry. b 13. TCD BA35 BD51. CITC 37. **d** 37 **p** 38. C Ballymacarrett St Patr *D & D* 37-39; Min Can Down Cathl 39-44; I Ballee 44-50; I Connor w Antrim St Patr *Conn* 50-55; I Antrim St Patr 55-67; I Agherton 67-78; Can Conn Cathl 76-78; rtd 78. *11 Carnreagh Avenue, Hillsborough, Co Down BT26 6LL* Tel (01846) 682565

HAWKINS, Noel. b 46. St Jo Coll Nottm 82. **d** 84 **p** 85. C Worksop St Jo *S'well* 84-86; C Wollaton Park 86-89; TV Billericay and Lt Burstead *Chelmsf* 89-95; TV Keynsham *B & W* from 95. *St Francis Vicarage, Warwick Road, Keynsham, Bristol BS18 2PW* Tel 0117-986 3968

HAWKINS, Paul Henry Whishaw. b 46. Ex Coll Ox BA68 MA74 SS Coll Cam MA84. St Steph Ho Ox 70. **d** 72 **p** 73. C Fawley *Win* 72-75; C Ealing St Steph Castle Hill *Lon* 75-77; P-in-c Dorney *Ox* 77-78; TV Riverside 78-81; Lic to Offic *Ely* 82-87; Chapl SS Coll Cam 82-87; V Plymstock *Ex* 87-97; RD Plymouth Sutton 91-96; TR Plymstock and Hooe from 97. *The Rectory, 5 Cobb Lane, Plymstock, Plymouth PL9 9BQ* Tel (01752) 403126

HAWKINS, Peter Edward. b 35. Leeds Univ BA60. Coll of Resurr Mirfield 60. **d** 62 **p** 63. C Forest Gate St Edm *Chelmsf* 62-65; C Sevenoaks St Jo *Roch* 65-68; Chapl Metrop Police Cadet Corps Tr Sch 68-73; P-in-c Knowle H Nativity *Bris* 73; TV Knowle 73-79; V Westbury-on-Trym H Trin 79-87; TR Solihull *Birm* 87-96; Hon Can Birm Cathl 92-96. *Back Street Cottage, 15 St Andrew's Road, Stogursey, Bridgwater, Somerset TA5 1TE* Tel (01278) 733635

HAWKINS, Peter Michael. b 38. Kelham Th Coll 58. **d** 63 **p** 64. India 63-69; C Manningham St Paul and St Jude *Bradf* 70-72; C Bradf Cathl 72-75; V Allerton 75-90; V Pet H Spirit Bretton *Pet* from 90; P-in-c Marholm 90-95. *23 Westhawe, Bretton, Peterborough PE3 8BE* Tel Peterborough (0733) 264418 or 265705 Fax 332544

✠**HAWKINS, The Rt Revd Richard Stephen.** b 39. Ex Coll Ox BA61 MA65 Ex Univ BPhil76. St Steph Ho Ox 61. **d** 63 **p** 64 **c** 88. C Ex St Thos *Ex* 63-66; C Clyst St Mary 66-75; TV Clyst St George, Aylesbeare, Clyst Honiton etc 75-78; Bp's Officer for Min 78-81; Jt Dir Ex and Truro NSM Scheme 78-81; TV Cen Ex 78-81; Dioc Dir of Ords 79-81; Adn Totnes 81-88; P-in-c Oldridge 81-87; P-in-c Whitestone 81-87; Suff Bp Plymouth 88-96; Suff Bp Crediton from 96. *10 The Close, Exeter EX1 1EZ* Tel (01392) 273509 Fax 431266

HAWKINS, Richard Whishaw. b 51. Coll of Resurr Mirfield 93. **d** 95 **p** 96. C Weymouth H Trin *Sarum* from 95. *1 Ben Nevis Road, Weymouth, Dorset DT4 0DB* Tel (01305) 779088

HAWKINS, Roger David William. b 33. K Coll Lon BD58 AKC58. **d** 59 **p** 60. C Twickenham St Mary *Lon* 59-61; C Heston 61-64; C Dorking w Ranmore *Guildf* 64-65; V Mitcham St Mark *S'wark* 65-74; V Redhill St Matt 74-91; P-in-c Warlingham w Chelsham and Farleigh 91-97; TR from 97. *The Rectory, 15 Chapel Road, Warlingham, Surrey CR6 9LH* Tel (01883) 624125

HAWKINS, Roger Julian. b 32. Ripon Hall Ox 59. **d** 61 **p** 62. C-in-c Newall Green CD *Man* 61-63; Chapl RAF 63-67; R Mawgan in Pyder *Truro* 67-75; R Lanteglos by Camelford w Advent 75-78; R Newmarket St Mary w Exning St Agnes *St E* 78-85; P-in-c Coltishall w Gt Hautbois *Nor* 85-87; R Coltishall w Gt Hautbois and Horstead 87-90; Chapl Whiteley Village *Guildf* 90-94. *26 New Road, Ringwood, Hants BH24 3AU*

HAWKINS, Timothy St John (Tim). b 59. CCC Ox BA82. Trin Coll Bris BA87. **d** 87 **p** 88. C Cheltenham St Mary, St Matt, St Paul and H Trin *Glouc* 87-90; C Cowplain *Portsm* 90-94; V Pennycross *Ex* 94-96; P-in-c St Keverne *Truro* from 96. *The Vicarage, St Keverne, Helston, Cornwall TR12 6NG* Tel (01326) 280227

HAWKINS, William Arthur. b 18. Clifton Th Coll 50. **d** 53 **p** 54. C Ellacombe *Ex* 53-54; C Totnes 54-58; R Ashill w Broadway *B & W* 58-74; R Herstmonceux *Chich* 74-83; rtd 83; Perm to Offic *Chich* from 84. *Three Gables, 17 Heighton Road, Newhaven, E Sussex BN9 0RB* Tel (01273) 513694

HAWKSBEE, Canon Derek John. b 28. Lon Univ BSc49. S'wark Ord Course 70. **d** 71 **p** 72. C Norbiton *S'wark* 71-75; Cand and S Area Sec SAMS 71-79; Overseas Sec 73-79; Hon Can Paraguay from 73; Hon C Tunbridge Wells St Jo *Roch* 75-79; USA 79-87; R Ravendale Gp *Linc* 88-96; rtd 96. *205 Upper Grosvenor Road, Tunbridge Wells, Kent TN1 2EG* Tel (01892) 533485

HAWKSWORTH, Maldwyn Harry. b 45. Aston Univ CertEd74. St Jo Coll Nottm 87. **d** 89 **p** 90. C Penn *Lich* 89-94; TV Bloxwich from 94. *6 Cresswell Crescent, Bloxwich, Walsall WS3 2UW* Tel (01922) 476647

HAWKSWORTH, Peter John Dallas. b 54. Solicitor 79 St Jo Coll Ox BA75 MA79. Sarum & Wells Th Coll 89. **d** 91 **p** 92. C Warminster St Denys, Upton Scudamore etc *Sarum* 91-95; P-in-c Salisbury St Mark from 95. *St Mark's Vicarage, 62 Barrington Road, Salisbury SP1 3JD* Tel (01722) 323767

HAWLEY, Canon Anthony Broughton. b 41. St Pet Coll Ox BA67 MA71 Kent Univ DMS96. Westcott Ho Cam 67. **d** 69 **p** 70. C Wolverhampton St Pet *Lich* 69-72; C-in-c Bermondsey St Hugh CD *S'wark* 73-84; Hon PV S'wark Cathl 83-84; TR Kirkby *Liv* from 84; AD Walton from 93; Hon Can Liv Cathl from 96. *The Rectory, Old Hall Lane, Kirkby, Liverpool L32 5TH* Tel 0151-547 2155 Fax as telephone

HAWLEY, John Andrew. b 50. K Coll Lon BD71 AKC71. Wycliffe Hall Ox 72. **d** 74 **p** 75. C Kingston upon Hull H Trin *York* 74-77; C Bradf Cathl Par *Bradf* 77-80; V Woodlands *Sheff* 80-91; TR Dewsbury *Wakef* from 91. *The Rectory, 16A Oxford Road, Dewsbury, W Yorkshire WF13 4JT* Tel (01924) 465491 or 457057 Fax 465491

HAWLEY, Nigel David. b 51. Coll of Resurr Mirfield 77. **d** 80 **p** 81. C Birch w Fallowfield *Man* 80-84; P-in-c Moston St Jo 84-85; R 85-93; R Reddish from 93. *St Elisabeth's Rectory, Bedford Street, Stockport, Cheshire SK5 6DJ* Tel 0161-432 3033

HAWNT, John Charles Frederick. b 30. St Paul's Cheltenham. Selly Oak Coll 52 Westwood Cen Zimbabwe 72. **d** 75 **p** 76. Rhodesia 75-80; Zimbabwe 80-81; C Rugby St Andr *Cov* 81-85; R Lydeard St Lawrence w Brompton Ralph etc *B & W* from 85. *The Rectory, Lydeard St Lawrence, Taunton, Somerset TA4 3SF* Tel (01984) 667220

HAWORTH, Mrs Betsy Ellen. b 24. Wm Temple Coll Rugby 50. **dss** 80 **d** 89. Walkden Moor *Man* 80-81; Third Ch Estates Commr

81-88; Lic to Offic 88-89; NSM Astley Bridge from 89. *14 Sharples Hall Fold, Bolton BL1 7EH* Tel (01204) 591588

HAWORTH (née ARMSTRONG), Fiona Heather. b 65. Reading Univ BSc86 Nottm Univ PhD90. St Jo Coll Nottm BTh94. **d** 97. C Sutton in Ashfield St Mary *S'well* from 97. *Grosvenor House, Grosvenor Avenue, Sutton-in-Ashfield, Notts NG17 1FG* Tel (01623) 553862

HAWORTH, John Luttrell. b 28. **d** 67 **p** 68. C Kilcommick *K, E & A* 67-70; C Ballymacelligott *L & K* 70-71; TV Tralee w Ballymacelligott, Kilnaughtin etc 71-72; I Kinneigh w Ballymoney *C, C & R* 72-76; I Easkey w Kilglass *T, K & A* 77-83; I Monasterevan w Nurney and Rathdaire *M & K* 83-87; I Kiltegan w Hacketstown, Clonmore and Moyne *C & O* 87-92; I Fermoy Union *C, C & R* 92-96; rtd 96. *Shane Cottage, Fennells Bay, Myrtleville, Co Cork, Irish Republic* Tel Cork (21) 831157

HAWORTH, Mark Newby. b 50. MICFor81 Aber Univ BSc73. Westcott Ho Cam 88. **d** 90 **p** 91. C Cherry Hinton St Andr *Ely* 90-93; C Teversham 90-93; P-in-c Swaffham Bulbeck and Swaffham Prior w Reach 93-94; V from 94; RD Fordham from 96. *St Mary's Vicarage, Swaffham Prior, Cambridge CB5 0JT* Tel (01638) 741409

HAWORTH, Paul. b 47. G&C Coll Cam BA68 MA72. Westcott Ho Cam 75. **d** 78 **p** 79. C Hornchurch St Andr *Chelmsf* 78-81; C Loughton St Mary and St Mich 81-88; C Waltham H Cross 88; TV 88-92; TR Becontree S from 92. *St Alban's Vicarage, Vincent Road, Dagenham, Essex RM9 6AL* Tel 0181-592 5410

HAWORTH, Stanley Robert. b 48. St Jo Coll Dur BA69. Sarum & Wells Th Coll 71. **d** 73 **p** 74. C Skipton H Trin *Bradf* 73-76; C Bradf Cathl 76-78; C Grantham *Linc* 78; TV 78-82; V Deeping St James 82-96; V Middlewich w Byley *Ches* from 96. *St Michael's Vicarage, 37 Queen Street, Middlewich, Cheshire CW10 9AR* Tel (01606) 833124

HAWORTH, Stuart. b 43. Local Minl Tr Course 91. **d** 94 **p** 95. C Bradshaw *Man* from 94. *178 Turton Road, Bolton BL2 3EE* Tel (01204) 594506

HAWTHORN, The Ven Christopher John. b 36. Qu Coll Cam BA60 MA64. Ripon Hall Ox 60. **d** 62 **p** 63. C Sutton St Jas *York* 62-66; V Kingston upon Hull St Nic 66-72; V Coatham 72-79; V Scarborough St Martin 79-91; RD Scarborough 82-91; Can and Preb York Minster from 87; Adn Cleveland from 91. *Park House, Rose Hill, Great Ayton, Middlesbrough TS9 6BH* Tel (01642) 723221

HAWTHORN, David. b 63. Chich Th Coll 87. **d** 90 **p** 91. C Hartlepool H Trin *Dur* 90-94; C Middlesbrough All SS *York* 94-95; P-in-c Thornaby on Tees 95-96; V S Thornaby from 96. *The Rectory, 14 White House Road, Thornaby, Stockton-on-Tees, Cleveland TS17 0AJ* Tel (01642) 761655

HAWTHORNE, Andrew. b 68. Jes Coll Ox BA89 MA93. Chich Th Coll BTh93. **d** 93 **p** 94. C Christchurch *Win* 93-97; TV Dorchester *Sarum* from 97. *St Mary's Vicarage, 17A Edward Road, Dorchester, Dorset DT1 2HL* Tel (01305) 268434

HAWTHORNE, John William. b 32. St Aug Coll Cant 74. **d** 77 **p** 78. C Boxley *Cant* 77-80; P-in-c Langley 80-82; P-in-c Otham 80-82; R Otham w Langley 82-83; TR Preston w Sutton Poyntz and Osmington w Poxwell *Sarum* 83-87; R Tetbury w Beverston *Glouc* from 87. *The Vicarage, The Green, Tetbury, Glos GL8 8DN* Tel (01666) 502333 Fax 505330

HAWTHORNE, Noel David. b 30. BNC Ox BA53 MA58. Ridley Hall Cam 53. **d** 55 **p** 56. C Sheff Abbeydale St Pet *Sheff* 55-58; C Keighley *Bradf* 58-61; V Idle H Trin 61-70; R Colne St Bart *Blackb* 70-91; RD Pendle 85-91; rtd 91. *56 Barrowford Road, Colne, Lancs BB8 9QE* Tel (01282) 869110

HAWTHORNE, William James (Jim). b 46. TCD 66. **d** 69 **p** 70. C Gilnahirk *D & D* 69-72; Asst Chapl Miss to Seamen 72-76; Lic to Offic *Win* 73-76; C Boultham *Linc* 76-78; C Bracebridge Heath 78-90; Dioc Adv for Relig Broadcasting 80-90; Chapl Palma de Mallorca and Balearic Is *Eur* 90-93; Chapl Palma de Mallorca from 93. *Nunez de Balboa 6, Son Armadans, 07014 Palma de Mallorca, Spain* Tel Palma de Mallorca (71) 737279 Fax 454492

HAWTIN, The Ven David Christopher. b 43. Keble Coll Ox BA65 MA70. Wm Temple Coll Rugby 65 Cuddesdon Coll 66. **d** 67 **p** 68. C Pennywell St Thos and Grindon St Oswald CD *Dur* 67-71; C Stockton St Pet 71-74; C-in-c Leam Lane CD 74-79; R Washington 79-88; Dioc Ecum Officer 88-91; Adn Newark *S'well* from 92. *c/o Dunham House, 8 Westgate, Southwell, Notts NG25 0JL* Tel (01636) 814490 Fax 815882

HAY, David Frederick. b 38. MA67. Qu Coll Birm 82. **d** 84 **p** 85. C Prenton *Ches* 84-88; V Stockport St Sav 88-96; P-in-c Gt Saughall from 96. *The Vicarage, Church Road, Saughall, Chester CH1 6EN* Tel (01244) 880213

HAY, Ian Gordon. b 52. Dundee Univ MA73 Edin Univ BD76 CertEd84. Edin Th Coll 73. **d** 76 **p** 77. C Dumfries *Glas* 76-79; Dioc Chapl *Bre* 79-81; R Brechin 81-85; Asst Chapl H Trin Sch Halifax 85-88; Dioc Youth Officer *Carl* from 89. *64 Curwendale, Stainburn, Workington, Cumbria CA14 4UT* Tel (01900) 603213 Fax (01228) 48769

HAY, Jack Barr. b 31. Bps' Coll Cheshunt 57. **d** 60 **p** 61. C Byker St Ant *Newc* 60-63; C Killingworth 63-68; V Cowgate 68-77; V Woodhorn w Newbiggin 77-96; rtd 96. *7 Glebelands, Corbridge, Northd NE45 5DS*

HAY, John. b 43. St D Coll Lamp 63. **d** 67 **p** 68. C Ynyshir *Llan* 67-70; C Cardiff St Mary and St Steph w St Dyfrig etc 70-74; V Llanwynno 74-78; P-in-c Weston-super-Mare All SS *B & W* 78-80; TV Weston-super-Mare Cen Par 80-85; P-in-c Handsworth St Mich *Birm* 85-86; NSM Eastbourne St Sav and St Pet *Chich* 88-91; V Buckley *St As* 91-96; P-in-c Ardwick St Benedict *Man* from 96. *St Benedict's Presbytery, Bennett Street, Ardwick, Manchester M12 5BD* Tel 0161-223 0154

HAY, Canon John. b 45. CITC 77. **d** 79 **p** 80. C Newtownards *D & D* 79-81; I Galloon w Drummully *Clogh* 81-89; I Donacavey w Barr from 89; Preb Clogh Cathl from 91. *Maranatha, The Rectory, Fintona, Co Tyrone BT78 2DA* Tel (01662) 841644

HAY, Kenneth Gordon. b 14. TD50. Worc Ord Coll 63. **d** 65 **p** 66. C Southend St Sav Westcliff *Chelmsf* 65-68; CF (TA) 66-79; R Kelvedon Hatch *Chelmsf* 68-73; P-in-c Prittlewell St Steph 73-78; V 78-79; rtd 79; Perm to Offic *Chelmsf* from 79. *26 Warwick Road, Thorpe Bay, Southend-on-Sea SS1 3BN* Tel (01702) 586496

HAY, Nicholas John. b 56. Sheff Poly BSc85 DPS88. St Jo Coll Nottm 85. **d** 88 **p** 89. C Blackb Redeemer *Blackb* 88-91; C Hellesdon *Nor* 91-95; R Widford *Chelmsf* from 95. *The Rectory, 3 Canuden Road, Widford, Chelmsford CM1 2SU* Tel (01245) 355989

HAY, Richard. b 42. CMG92. Ball Coll Ox BA63. Cranmer Hall Dur 94. **d** 96 **p** 97. C Hastings St Clem and All SS *Chich* from 96. *130 All Saints Street, Hastings, E Sussex TN34 3BG* Tel (01424) 420797

HAYBALL, Douglas Reginald. b 18. Oak Hill Th Coll 66. **d** 68 **p** 69. C Ilkley All SS *Bradf* 68-72; V Parr Mt *Liv* 72-75; P-in-c Sheepey w Ratcliffe Culey *Leic* 75-76; R Sibson w Sheepy and Ratcliffe Culey 76-86; rtd 86; Perm to Offic *B & W* from 86. *57 Parklands Way, Somerton, Somerset TA11 6JG* Tel (01458) 73312

HAYCRAFT, Roger Brian Norman. b 43. Oak Hill Th Coll 69. **d** 73 **p** 74. C Belsize Park *Lon* 73-76; C Yardley St Edburgha *Birm* 76-79; V Hornchurch H Cross *Chelmsf* from 79. *The Vicarage, 260 Hornchurch Road, Hornchurch, Essex RM11 1PX* Tel (01708) 447976

HAYDAY, Alan Geoffrey David. b 46. Kelham Th Coll 65. **d** 69 **p** 70. C Evington *Leic* 69-72; C Spalding *Linc* 72-78; V Cherry Willingham w Greetwell 78-86; RD Lawres 84-86; TR Brumby from 86; RD Manlake from 93. *St Hugh's Rectory, 114 Ashby Road, Scunthorpe, S Humberside DN16 2AG* Tel (01724) 843064

HAYDEN, Canon David Frank. b 47. Lon Univ DipTh69 BD71. Tyndale Hall Bris 67. **d** 71 **p** 72. C Silverhill St Matt *Chich* 71-75; C Galleywood Common *Chelmsf* 75-79; R Redgrave cum Botesdale w Rickinghall *St E* 79-84; RD Hartismere 81-84; V Cromer *Nor* from 84; P-in-c Gresham from 84; Chapl Cromer and Distr Hosp Norfolk from 84; Chapl Fletcher Hosp Norfolk from 85; RD Repps *Nor* from 95; Hon Can Nor Cathl from 96. *The Vicarage, 30 Cromwell Road, Cromer, Norfolk NR27 0BE* Tel (01263) 512000

HAYDEN, Eric Henry Ashmore. b 26. ACII65. Sarum & Wells Th Coll 71. **d** 73 **p** 74. C Horsham *Chich* 73-78; V Cuckfield 78-92; rtd 92; P-in-c Tilshead, Orcheston and Chitterne *Sarum* 92-97. *The Vicarage, High Street, Tilshead, Salisbury SP3 4RZ* Tel (01980) 620517

HAYDEN, Canon John Donald. b 40. Lon Univ BD62. Tyndale Hall Bris 63. **d** 65 **p** 66. C Macclesfield Ch Ch *Ches* 65-68; Tanzania 68-77; Home Sec USCL 77-83; TV Ipswich St Mary at Stoke w St Pet and St Mary Quay *St E* 83-85; TV Ipswich St Mary at Stoke w St Pet 85-94; P-in-c Bury St Edmunds St Mary from 94. *78 Hardwick Lane, Bury St Edmunds, Suffolk IP33 2RA* Tel (01284) 706668

HAYDOCK, Canon Alan. b 41. Kelham Th Coll 60. **d** 65 **p** 66. C Rainworth *S'well* 65-68; C Hucknall Torkard 68-71; TV 71-74; V Bilborough St Jo 74-80; R E Bridgford 80-82; R E Bridgford and Kneeton from 82; RD Bingham 84-94; Hon Can S'well Minster from 86. *The Rectory, Kirk Hill, East Bridgford, Nottingham NG13 8PE* Tel (01949) 20218

HAYDON, Mrs Christine Mary. b 45. K Alfred's Coll Win CertEd66. NTMTC 93. **d** 96 **p** 97. NSM Aylesford *Roch* from 96. *44 Bramley Road, Snodland, Kent ME6 5DY* Tel (01634) 241821

HAYDON, Keith Frank. b 46. Cuddesdon Coll 73. **d** 75 **p** 76. C De Beauvoir Town St Pet *Lon* 75-77; C Wells St Thos w Horrington *B & W* 77-80; TV Weston-super-Mare Cen Par 80-84; TV Cowley St Jas *Ox* 84-87; TR 87-95; V Walsingham, Houghton and Barsham *Nor* 95-96; P-in-c from 96. *The Vicarage, Walsingham, Norfolk NR22 6BL* Tel (01328) 820345

HAYES, Brian Richard Walker. b 33. Qu Coll Birm 81. **d** 83 **p** 84. C Cheadle Hulme All SS *Ches* 83-87; C Sheff Parson Cross St Cecilia *Sheff* 87-88; C Sheff Norwood St Leon 88-91; V Gazeley w Dalham, Moulton and Kentford *St E* from 91. *The Vicarage, Gazeley, Newmarket, Suffolk CB8 8RB* Tel (01638) 552379

HAYES, Christopher John. b 64. Univ of Wales BN RGN Leeds Univ MA. Cranmer Hall Dur. **d** 96 **p** 97. C Burton Fleming w Fordon, Grindale etc *York* from 96. *Westlands, West Lane, Burton Fleming, Driffield, N Humberside YO25 0PW*

HAYES, David Malcolm Hollingworth. b 42. K Coll Lon BD68 AKC68. **d** 69 **p** 70. C Upper Teddington SS Pet and Paul *Lon*

69-70; C Ruislip St Martin 70-75; P-in-c Ludford *Heref* 75-80; P-in-c Ashford Carbonell w Ashford Bowdler 75-80; V Eastcote St Lawr *Lon* 80-90; R Cant St Pet w St Alphege and St Marg etc *Cant* from 90; Master Eastbridge Hosp from 90. *The Master's Lodge, 58 St Peter's Street, Canterbury, Kent CT1 2BE* Tel (01227) 462395

HAYES, David Roland Payton. b 37. Hertf Coll Ox BA62 MA66. Coll of Resurr Mirfield 62. **d** 64 **p** 65. C Woodley St Jo the Ev *Ox* 64-67; C Emscote *Cov* 67-69; C Farnham Royal *Ox* 69-75; P-in-c 75-78; P-in-c Lathbury 78-79; P-in-c Newport Pagnell 78-79; R Newport Pagnell w Lathbury 79-85; RD Newport 80-85; Chapl Renny Lodge Hosp 85-87; R Newport Pagnell w Lathbury and Moulsoe *Ox* 85-86; P-in-c 86-87; P-in-c Bucknell w Buckton, Llanfair Waterdine and Stowe *Heref* 87-91; V Bucknell w Chapel Lawn, Llanfair Waterdine etc 91-94; RD Clun Forest 91-94; P-in-c Presteigne w Discoed, Kinsham and Lingen from 94. *The Rectory, Presteigne LD8 2BP* Tel (01544) 267777

HAYES, John Henry Andrew. b 52. BSc. Wycliffe Hall Ox 82. **d** 84 **p** 85. C Moreton *Ches* 84-87; R Barrow 87-94; Bp's Chapl 87-94; P-in-c Runcorn St Mich from 94; P-in-c Runcorn All SS from 94. *The Vicarage, Highlands Road, Runcorn, Cheshire WA7 4PS* Tel (01928) 575666

HAYES, John Philip. b 52. RMN76. Chich Th Coll 79. **d** 82 **p** 84. C Wigston Magna *Leic* 82-83; C Thurmaston 83-85; TV Shirley *Birm* 85-91; V Lee St Aug *S'wark* 91-93; TV Staveley and Barrow Hill *Derby* 93-96; P-in-c Linc St Botolph by Bargate *Linc* from 96. *St Botolph's Vicarage, 84 Little Bargate Street, Lincoln LN5 8JL* Tel (01522) 520469

HAYES, Kenneth Richard. b 50. Cen Sch of Art Lon DipAD72 RCA(Lon). Qu Coll Birm 95. **d** 97. C Gravesend H Family w Ifield *Roch* from 97. *74 Apsledene, Singlewell, Gravesend, Kent DA12 5EE* Tel (01474) 322827

HAYES, Michael Gordon William. b 48. St Cath Coll Cam BA69 MA73 PhD73. Ridley Hall Cam 73. **d** 75 **p** 76. C Combe Down w Monkton Combe *B & W* 75-78; C Cambridge H Trin *Ely* 78-81; V Bathampton *B & W* 81-88; V Clevedon St Andr and Ch Ch 88-95; C Belper *Derby* from 95. *St Mark's House, Openwoodgate, Belper, Derbyshire DE56 0SD* Tel (01773) 825727

HAYES, Richard. b 39. K Coll Lon BD68 AKC68. **d** 69 **p** 70. C Dartford H Trin *Roch* 69-72; C S Kensington St Steph *Lon* 72-76; V Ruislip Manor St Paul 76-82; V Ealing St Pet Mt Park 82-91; R St Edm the King and St Mary Woolnoth etc from 91. *24 Cinnamon Street, London E1 9NJ* Tel 0171-481 9699

HAYES, Richard Henry. b 65. Bp Otter Coll St Jo Coll Nottm 89. **d** 92 **p** 93. C Southborough St Pet w Ch Ch and St Matt *Roch* 92-95; C Downend *Bris* from 95. *15 Glendale, Downend, Bristol BS16 6EQ* Tel 0117-956 8109

HAYES, Mrs Rosemarie Eveline. b 51. Brighton Coll of Educn CertEd72. N Ord Course 88. **d** 91 **p** 94. Par Dn Manston *Ripon* 91-94; C 94-95; C Beeston from 95. *St Davids House, Waincliffe Drive, Leeds LS11 8ET* Tel 0113-270 2829

HAYES, Timothy James. b 62. **d** 89 **p** 90. C Lache cum Saltney *Ches* 89-94; P-in-c Dukinfield St Jo from 94. *37 Harald Avenue, Dukinfield, Cheshire SK16 5NH* Tel 0161-308 4708

HAYLES, Graham David. b 39. Lon Univ DipTh66. Clifton Th Coll 64. **d** 67 **p** 68. C Gipsy Hill Ch Ch *S'wark* 67-70; C Heatherlands St Jo *Sarum* 70-74; V W Streatham St Jas *S'wark* 74-90; TR Hinckley H Trin *Leic* from 90. *Holy Trinity Vicarage, 1 Cleveland Road, Hinckley, Leics LE10 0AJ* Tel (01455) 635711

HAYLLAR, Bruce Sherwill. b 23. Trin Hall Cam BA47 MA53. Cuddesdon Coll 48. **d** 50 **p** 51. C Almondbury *Wakef* 50-53; India 53-63; V Peacehaven *Chich* 63-72; Zambia 72-75; V Moulsecoomb *Chich* 76-81; TR 81-83; R Rotherfield w Mark Cross 83-90; RD Rotherfield 87-90; rtd 90; Perm to Offic *Chich* from 90. *Moses Farm Cottage, Piltdown, Uckfield, E Sussex TN22 3XN* Tel (01825) 722006

HAYMAN, Mrs Audrey Doris. b 41. St Mary's Coll Cheltenham 61 Bris Univ CertEd61 Cov Coll of Educn 65. Glouc Sch of Min 88. **d** 91 **p** 94. NSM Matson *Glouc* from 91. *32 Corncroft Lane, St Leonard's Park, Gloucester GL4 9XU* Tel (01452) 411786

HAYMAN, Canon Robert Fleming. b 31. Princeton Univ BA53. Gen Th Sem (NY) MDiv56. **d** 56 **p** 56. USA 56-88; I Drumcliffe w Lissadell and Munninane *K, E & A* 88-92; Preb Elphin Cathl 88-92; rtd 92. *Kingsfort House, Ballintogher, Sligo, Irish Republic* Tel Sligo (71) 64622

HAYNES, Miss Catherine Mary. b 68. Man Univ BA90. St Mich Coll Llan BD93 DPT93. **d** 96 **p** 97. C Llantwit Major *Llan* from 96. *8 Illtyd Avenue, Llantwit Major CF61 1TG* Tel (01446) 792476

HAYNES, Clifford. b 33. Cam Univ MA60. Linc Th Coll 80. **d** 82 **p** 83. C Lightcliffe *Wakef* 82-85; V Bradshaw from 85. *The Vicarage, Pavement Lane, Bradshaw, Halifax, W Yorkshire HX2 9JJ* Tel (01422) 244330

HAYNES, Cyril Michael. b 26. Univ of Wales BEd64. **d** 84 **p** 85. NSM Wenlock *Heref* 84-96; Perm to Offic from 96. *8 Forester Avenue, Much Wenlock, Shropshire TF13 6EX* Tel (01952) 727263

HAYNES, Donald Irwin. b 28. Birm Univ BA51. Ripon Hall Ox 59. **d** 59 **p** 60. C Chatham St Mary w St Jo *Roch* 59-66; Hon C Gillingham St Mary 66-71; Lic to Offic *Birm* 71-81; P-in-c Whittington *Derby* 82-85; R 85-90; C Kinver and Enville *Lich* 90-93; rtd 93. *4 Beech Gardens, Codsall, Wolverhampton WV8 2BL*

HAYNES, Canon John Richard. b 35. Ely Th Coll 60. **d** 63 **p** 64. C Bollington St Jo *Ches* 63-67; C Ches St Jo 67-68; C Davenham 68-70; Rhodesia 70-80; Zimbabwe 80-90; Sub-Dean Bulawayo Cathl 78-83; Hon Can Matabeleland from 90; R Bishop's Stortford *St Alb* from 90. *69 Havers Lane, Bishop's Stortford, Herts CM23 3PA* Tel (01279) 656546

HAYNES, John Stanley. b 30. WMMTC. **d** 82 **p** 83. NSM Westwood *Cov* 82-84; C Radford Semele and Ufton 84-85; V 85-95; rtd 95. *64 Rugby Road, Cubbington, Leamington Spa, Warks CV32 7JF* Tel (01926) 330016

HAYNES, Leonard Thomas. b 17. **d** 69 **p** 70. C Lutterworth w Cotesbach *Leic* 69-73; C-in-c Swinford w Catthorpe, Shawell and Stanford 73-74; V 74-83; rtd 83; Perm to Offic *Leic* from 83; Perm to Offic *Birm* from 95. *10 Warwick Way, Ashby-de-la-Zouch, Leics LE65 1WY* Tel (01530) 411466

HAYNES, Canon Michael Thomas Avery. b 32. AKC61. St Boniface Warminster 61. **d** 62 **p** 63. C Hebden Bridge *Wakef* 62-64; C Elland 64-68; V Thornhill Lees 68-82; V Lindley from 82; Hon Can Wakef Cathl 82-97. *The Vicarage, 2 The Clock Tower, Lindley, Huddersfield HD3 3JB* Tel (01484) 650996

HAYNES, The Very Revd Peter. b 25. Selw Coll Cam BA49 MA54. Cuddesdon Coll 50. **d** 52 **p** 53. C Stokesley *York* 52-54; C Hessle 54-58; V Drypool St Jo 58-63; Asst Dir RE *B & W* 63-70; Youth Chapl 63-70; V Glastonbury St Jo 70-72; V Glastonbury St Jo w Godney 72-74; Adn Wells, Can Res and Preb Wells Cathl 74-82; Dean Heref 82-92; V Heref St Jo 82-92; rtd 92; Perm to Offic *B & W* from 92. *23 Conway Crescent, Burnham-on-Sea, Somerset TA8 2SL* Tel (01278) 789048

HAYNES, Peter Nigel Stafford. b 39. Hertf Coll Ox BA62 MA66. Cuddesdon Coll 62. **d** 64 **p** 65. C Norwood All SS *Cant* 64-68; C Portsea N End St Mark *Portsm* 68-72; Asst Chapl Brussels *Eur* 72-76; TV Banbury *Ox* 76-80; Asst Sec (Internat Affairs) Gen Syn Bd Soc Resp 80-85; P-in-c E Peckham and Nettlestead *Roch* 85-92; R Bredgar w Bicknor and Frinsted w Wormshill etc *Cant* from 92. *The Vicarage, Bredgar, Sittingbourne, Kent ME9 8HA* Tel (01627) 884387

HAYNES, Philip Mayo. b 25. St Edm Hall Ox BA50 MA50. Cuddesdon Coll 50. **d** 54 **p** 55. C Richmond St Mary *S'wark* 54-58; C Raynes Park St Sav 58-63; C Limpsfield and Titsey 63-70; V Purley St Mark Woodcote 70-82; R Sherington w Chicheley, N Crawley, Astwood etc *Ox* 82-90; rtd 90. *1 Ridgemont Close, Woodstock Road, Oxford OX2 7PJ* Tel (01865) 58116

HAYNES, Spencer Malcolm. b 46. Sarum & Wells Th Coll DCTM93. **d** 93 **p** 94. C Devonport St Budeaux *Ex* 93-96; C Dunsford and Doddiscombsleigh 96; TV Tedburn St Mary, Whitestone, Oldridge etc from 96. *The Vicarage, Dunsford, Exeter EX6 7AA* Tel (01647) 252898

HAYTER, Mary Elizabeth. *See* BARR, Dr Mary Elizabeth

HAYTER, Canon Michael George. b 18. Ch Ch Ox BA39 MA43. Cuddesdon Coll 40. **d** 41 **p** 42. C Scarborough St Mary *York* 41-46; R Steeple Aston *Ox* 46-77; P-in-c Tackley 76-77; R Steeple Aston w N Aston and Tackley 77-83; RD Woodstock 64-74; Hon Can Ch Ch 75-83; rtd 83; Perm to Offic *Pet* 84-94. *Felden House, Charlton, Banbury, Oxon OX17 3DL* Tel (01295) 811426

HAYTER, Raymond William. b 48. Oak Hill Th Coll 74. **d** 77 **p** 78. C Bermondsey St Jas w Ch Ch *S'wark* 77-80; C Sydenham H Trin 81-83; Asst Chapl HM Pris Brixton 83-84; Chapl HM Youth Cust Cen Stoke Heath 84-88; Chapl HM Pris Maidstone 88-91; CF from 91. *MOD Chaplains (Army), Trenchard Lines, Upavon, Pewsey, Wilts SN9 6BE* Tel (01980) 615804 Fax 615800

HAYTER, Ronald William Joseph. b 19. Keble Coll Ox BA40 MA44. Wells Th Coll 40. **d** 42 **p** 43. C Honiton *Ex* 42-45; C Ex St Mark 45-47; C Ex St Thos 47-51; C Paignton St Jo 51-55; V Countess Wear 55-87; rtd 87; Perm to Offic *Ex* from 92. *85 Swedwell Road, Torquay TQ2 8QL* Tel (01803) 322903

HAYTER, Mrs Sandra (Sandy). b 46. S Dios Minl Tr Scheme 82. **dss** 85 **d** 87 **p** 94. Catherington and Clanfield *Portsm* 85-86; Lee-on-the-Solent 86-87; C 87-89; Par Dn Burnham w Dropmore, Hitcham and Taplow *Ox* 89-94; C 94; TV Wallingford w Crowmarsh Gifford etc from 94. *The Vicarage, 34 Thames Mead, Crowmarsh Gifford, Wallingford, Oxon OX10 8EY* Tel (01491) 837626

HAYTHORNTHWAITE, Alfred Parker. b 10. Wycliffe Hall Ox 29. **d** 35 **p** 36. C Aspatria *Carl* 35-37; C Clifton (Penrith) 37-39; CF 39-45; R Kirkby Thore w Temple Sowerby *Carl* 45-57; V Seascale 57-67; V Allithwaite 67-76; rtd 76; Perm to Offic *Carl* from 80. *St Mary's Cottage, Vicarage Lane, Kirkby Lonsdale, Cumbria LA6 2BA* Tel (01524) 271525

HAYTHORNTHWAITE, Robert Brendan. b 31. Solicitor 59 TCD BA53 LLB56 MA64 QUB DipEd71. Edin Th Coll 63. **d** 64 **p** 65. C Belfast St Jo Laganbank w Orangefield *D & D* 64-66; C Belfast St Thos *Conn* 66-68; Lic to Offic 68-75; C Belfast Malone St Jo 75-89; I Shinrone w Aghancon etc *L & K* from 89; Dom Chapl to Bp of Killaloe and Clonfert from 89. *St Mary's Rectory, Shinrone, Birr, Co Offaly, Irish Republic* Tel Roscrea (505) 47164 Fax as telephone

HAYTON, John Anthony. b 45. TD81. ACII70. Oak Hill Th Coll 93. **d** 96 **p** 97. NSM St Alb St Mich *St Alb* from 96. *89 Harpenden Road, St Albans, Herts AL3 6BY* Tel (01727) 761719

HAYTON, Mark William. b 59. St Steph Ho Ox 85. **d** 88 **p** 89. C Sittingbourne St Mich *Cant* 88-91; C Kennington 91-94; R Broadstairs from 94; RD Thanet from 96. *The Rectory, Nelson Place, Broadstairs, Kent CT10 1HQ* Tel (01843) 862921

HAYTON, Norman Joseph Patrick. b 32. ARICS57. Sarum Th Coll 69. **d** 71 **p** 72. C Lytham St Cuth *Blackb* 71-74; V Wesham 74-79; V Chorley St Geo 79-80; NSM Kells *Carl* 84-85; P-in-c Flimby 85-90; V Barrow St Jas 90-94; TV Egremont and Haile from 94. *The Vicarage, 1 Bridge End Park, Egremont, Cumbria CA22 2RE* Tel (01946) 822051

HAYWARD, Canon Alan Richard. b 25. Open Univ BA72. Wycliffe Hall Ox 54. **d** 56 **p** 57. C Dudley St Fran *Worc* 56-59; C-in-c Wollescote CD 59-65; V Wollescote 65-85; Hon Can Worc Cathl 85-91; R Alvechurch 85-91; rtd 91. *2 St Kenelm's Court, St Kenelm's Road, Romsley, Halesowen, W Midlands B62 0NF* Tel (01562) 710749

HAYWARD, Alfred Ross. b 20. Clifton Th Coll 52. **d** 54 **p** 55. C Attenborough w Bramcote *S'well* 54-56; V Snape w Friston *St E* 56-60; V Willoughby-on-the-Wolds w Wysall *S'well* 60-65; V Woodborough 65-70; Warden Braithwaite Gospel Tr Stathern 73-77; V Tugby and E Norton w Skeffington *Leic* 77-81; R Beeston Regis *Nor* 81-83; rtd 83. *4 Somersby Road, Nottingham NG3 5QY* Tel 0115-920 1406

HAYWARD, Canon Christopher Joseph (Chris). b 38. TCD BA63 MA67. Ridley Hall Cam 63. **d** 65 **p** 66. C Hatcham St Jas *S'wark* 65-69; Warden Lee Abbey Internat Students' Club Kensington 69-74; Chapl Chelmsf Cathl *Chelmsf* 74-77; P-in-c Darlaston All SS *Lich* 77-83; Ind Chapl 77-83; Can Res Bradf Cathl *Bradf* 83-92; Sec Bd Miss 83-92; R Linton in Craven from 92; Hon Can Bradf Cathl from 92; RD Skipton from 93. *The Rectory, Hebden Road, Grassington, Skipton, N Yorkshire BD23 5LB* Tel (01756) 752575 Fax 722898

HAYWARD, Clifford. b 08. St Paul's Grahamstown 51. **d** 52 **p** 53. Portuguese E Africa 52-57; S Africa 57-63 and 64-73; R Kimberley St Alb 68-73; C Coulsdon St Andr *S'wark* 63-65; C Lewisham St Mary 73-78; rtd 78; Hon C E Dulwich St Jo *S'wark* from 78. *The Charterhouse, Charterhouse Square, London EC1M 6AN* Tel 0171-251 6357

HAYWARD, Preb Edwin Calland. b 11. ATCL30 Lon Univ BSc32 Leeds Univ DipEd44. Linc Th Coll 35. **d** 36 **p** 37. C Heaton St Barn *Bradf* 36-41; C-in-c Heaton St Martin CD 41-46; Chan's V Lich Cathl *Lich* 46-49; V Riddlesden *Bradf* 49-52; V W Bromwich St Fran *Lich* 52-62; V Pattingham 62-69; V Burton St Modwen 69-81; RD Tutbury 69-81; Preb Lich Cathl 72-81; P-in-c Burton Ch Ch 76-81; Chapl Burton Gen Hosp 76-81; rtd 81; Perm to Offic *Derby* from 81; Perm to Offic *Lich* from 81. *19 Henhurst Hill, Burton-on-Trent, Staffs DE13 9TB* Tel (01283) 548735

HAYWARD, Canon Jeffrey Kenneth. b 47. Nottm Univ BTh74. St Jo Coll Nottm LTh74. **d** 74 **p** 75. C Stambermill *Worc* 74-77; C Woking St Jo *Guildf* 77-83; V Springfield H Trin *Chelmsf* from 83; Chapl HM Pris Chelmsf from 86; Area RD Chelmsf 86-88; RD Chelmsf 88-93; RD Chelmsf N 93-95; Can Chelmsf Cathl from 93. *The Vicarage, 61 Hill Road, Chelmsford CM2 6HW* Tel (01245) 353389 Fax 493041

HAYWARD, Mrs Jennifer Dawn. b 38. WMMTC 85. **d** 88 **p** 94. NSM Gt Malvern St Mary *Worc* 88-90; NSM Gt Malvern Ch Ch 88-90; Par Dn 90-94; C 94-96; TV Wirksworth *Derby* from 96. *58 Yokecliffe Drive, Wirksworth, Matlock, Derbyshire DE4 4EX* Tel (01629) 822896

HAYWARD, John Andrew. b 63. MHCIMA83 Nottm Univ BTh89. Linc Th Coll 86. **d** 89 **p** 90. C Seaford w Sutton *Chich* 89-92; C St Pancras H Cross w St Jude and St Pet *Lon* 92-95; V Kentish Town St Martin w St Andr from 95. *The Vicarage, 26 Vicars Road, London NW5 4NN* Tel 0171-485 3807

HAYWARD, John David. b 40. AKC63. **d** 65 **p** 66. C Westleigh St Pet *Man* 65-68; C Elton All SS 68-72; R Moston St Chad 72-77; TV Stantonbury *Ox* 74-87; TV Stantonbury and Willen 87-89; P-in-c N Springfield *Chelmsf* from 89. *The Vicarage, 32 Oak Lodge Tye, Chelmsford CM1 5GZ* Tel (01245) 466160

HAYWARD, The Ven John Derek Risdon. b 23. Trin Coll Cam BA56 MA64. Westcott Ho Cam 56. **d** 57 **p** 58. C Sheff St Mary w St Simon w St Matthias *Sheff* 57-59; V Sheff Gillcar St Silas 59-63; V Isleworth All SS *Lon* 64-94; Adn Middx 74-75; Gen Sec Lon Dio 75-93; rtd 94; Perm to Offic *B & W* from 94. *5 Sion Hill Place, Lansdown, Bath BA1 5SJ* Tel (01225) 336305

HAYWARD, Preb John Talbot. b 28. Selw Coll Cam BA52 MA56. Wells Th Coll 52. **d** 54 **p** 55. C S Lyncombe *B & W* 54-58; R Lamyatt 58-71; V Bruton w Wyke Champflower and Redlynch 58-71; RD Bruton 62-71; R Weston-super-Mare St Jo 71-75; Preb Wells Cathl 73-92; TR Weston-super-Mare Cen Par 75-92; rtd 92; Perm to Offic *B & W* from 92. *5 Chelswood Avenue, Weston-super-Mare, Avon BS22 8QP* Tel (01934) 628431

HAYWARD, Ms Pamela Jane. b 52. RGN82. Westcott Ho Cam 84. **d** 87 **p** 94. Par Dn Northampton St Mary *Pet* 87-90; Par Dn Bris St Mary Redcliffe w Temple etc *Bris* 90-94; C 94-96; V Eastville St Anne w St Mark and St Thos from 96. *St Anne's Vicarage, 75 Greenbank Road, Bristol BS5 6HD* Tel 0117-952 0202

HAYWARD, Peter Noel. b 26. Leeds Univ BA48 BD78. Coll of Resurr Mirfield 48. **d** 50 **p** 51. C S Elmsall *Wakef* 50-56; C Sheldon *Birm* 56-60; C-in-c Garretts Green CD 60-69; V Garretts Green 69-70; R Hotham *York* from 70; V N Cave w Cliffe from 70; RD Howden 78-86; P-in-c Newbald from 97. *The Vicarage, North Cave, Brough, N Humberside HU15 2LJ* Tel (01430) 422398

HAYWARD, Roynon Albert Oscar James. b 25. **d** 67 **p** 68. Hon C Glouc St Paul *Glouc* 67-89; rtd 89; Perm to Offic *Glouc* from 89. *37 Forest View Road, Gloucester GL4 0BX* Tel (01452) 521104

HAYWARD, William Richmond. b 42. NY Th Sem BA90. Chich Th Coll 88. **d** 88 **p** 90. Bermuda from 88. *8 Seabright Avenue, Paget DV 04, Bermuda* Tel Bermuda (1-441) 236-3221 Fax as telephone

HAYWOOD, James William. b 36. Chich Th Coll 69. **d** 73 **p** 74. C Leeds Halton St Wilfrid *Ripon* 73-76; C Workington St Jo *Carl* 76-78; V Clifton 78-84; P-in-c Barrow St Jas 84-85; V 85-89; V Crosby Ravensworth 89-94; R Asby 89-94; V Bolton 89-94. *19 Bramham Road, Whitwood, Castleford, W Yorkshire WF10 5PA*

HAYWOOD, Keith Roderick. b 48. Oak Hill Th Coll 84. **d** 86 **p** 87. C Fazeley *Lich* 86-90; TV Leek and Meerbrook from 90. *St Luke's Vicarage, Novi Lane, Leek, Staffs ST13 6NR* Tel (01538) 373306

HAZEL, Sister. *See* SMITH, Sister Hazel Ferguson Waide

HAZELL, The Ven Frederick Roy (Fred). b 30. Fitzw Ho Cam BA53 MA59. Cuddesdon Coll 54. **d** 56 **p** 57. C Ilkeston St Mary *Derby* 56-59; C Heanor 59-62; V Marlpool 62-63; Chapl Univ of W Indies 63-66; C St Martin-in-the-Fields *Lon* 66-68; V Croydon H Sav *Cant* 68-84; RD Croydon 72-78; Hon Can Cant Cathl 73-84; P-in-c Croydon H Trin 77-80; Adn Croydon 84; Adn Croydon *S'wark* 85-93; rtd 93; P-in-c Chard Furnham w Chaffcombe, Knowle St Giles etc *B & W* from 95. *The Rectory, Furnham Road, Chard, Somerset TA20 1AE* Tel (01460) 63167

HAZELL, Thomas Jeremy. b 35. Bris Univ LLB56. St D Coll Lamp 56. **d** 58 **p** 59. C Newport St Paul *Mon* 58-61; C Derby St Jo *Derby* 61-64; V Arksey *Sheff* 64-69; rtd 95. *9 Fairleigh Road, Cardiff CF1 9JT* Tel (01222) 345832

HAZELTON, Edwin Geoffrey. b 08. OBE45. St Geo Windsor 50. **d** 51 **p** 52. C Rotherham *Sheff* 51-53; C Ranmoor 53-56; V Amesbury *Sarum* 56-67; RD Avon 64-67; V Flushing *Truro* 67-69; R Wylye, Stockton and Fisherton Delamere *Sarum* 69-73; R Wylye, Fisherton Delamere and the Langfords 73-76; rtd 76. *c/o Mr P J E Hazelton, 84 Lock Chase, London SE3 9HA* Tel 0181-852 6989 Fax 852 6422

HAZELTON, John. b 35. St Cath Coll Cam BA56 MA60 Bris Univ MLitt74 Newc Univ BPhil80. Wells Th Coll 59. **d** 61 **p** 62. C Twerton *B & W* 61-65; V Pitcombe w Shepton Montague 65-72; Lect SS Hild and Bede *Dur* 72-79; Lic to Offic *Dur* from 74; Dame Allan's Schs Newc 79-89; Chapl from 89; Lic to Offic *Newc* from 89. *36 Orchard Drive, Durham DH1 1LA* Tel 0191-384 6606 or 275 0608

HAZELTON, Dr Michael John. b 53. UEA BA76 Bedf Coll Lon PhD80 Heythrop Coll Lon BD89 Ox Univ 89. **d** 90 **p** 90. Asst Chapl Helsinki *Eur* 94-95; Asst Chapl Zurich w Winterthur from 95. *Promenadengasse 9, 8001 Zurich, Switzerland* Tel Zurich (1) 252-6023 Fax as telephone

HAZELTON, Robert Henry Peter. b 22. Wells Th Coll 65. **d** 67 **p** 68. C Eastover *B & W* 67-69; C Milton 69-76; V Peasedown St John 76-80; V Peasedown St John w Wellow 80-89; rtd 90; Perm to Offic *B & W* from 90. *37 High Meadows, Midsomer Norton, Bath BA3 2RY* Tel (01761) 419675

HAZELWOOD, Ms Jillian. b 32. Bp Otter Coll CertEd52 St Alb Minl Tr Scheme 82. **d** 87 **p** 94. NSM Wheathampstead *St Alb* from 87. *14 Butterfield Road, Wheathampstead, St Albans, Herts AL4 8PU* Tel (01582) 833146

HAZLEDINE, Basil William. b 18. St Pet Hall Ox BA42 MA45. Wycliffe Hall Ox 42. **d** 43 **p** 44. C Highfield *Ox* 43-46; C Gerrards Cross 46-51; V Barking St Patr *Chelmsf* 51-55; V Sayers Common *Chich* 55-60; R Twineham 55-60; V Stoughton *Guildf* 60-70; V Westlands St Andr *Lich* 70-77; P-in-c Whatfield w Semer *St E* 77-78; R 78-81; P-in-c Nedging w Naughton 77-81; R Whatfield w Semer, Nedging and Naughton 81-84; rtd 84; Perm to Offic *Guildf* from 91. *14 Willis Close, Epsom, Surrey KT18 7SS* Tel (01372) 726615

HAZLEHURST, Anthony Robin. b 43. Man Univ BSc64. Tyndale Hall Bris 65. **d** 68 **p** 69. C Macclesfield Ch Ch *Ches* 68-71; C Bushbury *Lich* 71-75; P-in-c New Clee *Linc* 75-85; TV Deane *Man* 85-96; V Harwood from 96. *The Vicarage, Stitch mi Lane, Bolton BL2 4HU* Tel (01204) 525196

HAZLEHURST, David. b 32. Liv Univ BSc54. St Steph Ho Ox 55. **d** 57 **p** 58. C Sheff Arbourthorne *Sheff* 57-59; C Doncaster Ch Ch 59-61; C W Wycombe *Ox* 61-63; P-in-c Collyhurst St Jas *Man* 66-67; V Blackrod 67-79; V Halliwell St Marg 79-84; R Sutton St Nic *S'wark* 84-94; rtd 94; Perm to Offic *S'wark* from 95; Perm to Offic *Guildf* from 95. *48 The Orchard, North Holmwood, Dorking, Surrey RH5 4JT* Tel (01306) 886858

HAZLEHURST, David John Benedict (Benny). b 63. Trin Coll Bris 88. **d** 91 **p** 92. C Plumstead St Jo w St Jas and St Paul *S'wark* from 91. *34 Earl Rise, London SE18 7NH* Tel 0181-855 1311

HAZLETT, Stephen David. b 56. TCD BTh88. CITC. **d** 88 **p** 89. C Ballywillan *Conn* 88-90; I Rathcoole 90-95; I Dunluce from 95. *Dunluce Rectory, 17 Priestlands Road, Bushmills, Co Antrim BT57 8QP* Tel (01256) 731221

HAZLEWOOD, Andrew Lord. b 54. BSc. Wycliffe Hall Ox. **d** 82 **p** 83. C Leckhampton SS Phil and Jas w Cheltenham St Jas *Glouc* 82-85; C Waltham H Cross *Chelmsf* 85-89; R Pedmore *Worc* from 89. *The Rectory, Pedmore Lane, Stourbridge, W Midlands DY9 0SW* Tel (01562) 884856

HAZLEWOOD, Dr David Paul. b 47. Sheff Univ MB, ChB70 Campion Hall Ox BA72 MA77. Wycliffe Hall Ox 70. **d** 73 **p** 74. C Chapeltown *Sheff* 73-75; Singapore 76; Indonesia 76-88; R Ipswich St Helen *St E* 88-97; V Shirley *Win* from 97. *The Vicarage, Wordsworth Road, Southampton SO15 5LX* Tel (01703) 774329

HAZLEWOOD, Canon George Ian. b 28. St Fran Coll Brisbane 52. **d** 55 **p** 56. Australia 55-56; C Poplar All SS w St Frideswide *Lon* 56-62; Bp's Youth Chapl *St Alb* 62-67; V Yeovil H Trin *B & W* 67-74; RD Merston 72-74; V Prestbury *Glouc* 74-94; Hon Can Glouc Cathl 88-94; Hon Can Wangaratta from 88; rtd 94; Perm to Offic *Ex* from 94; Perm to Offic *Truro* from 94. *6 Plymouth Road, Tavistock, Devon PL19 8AY* Tel (01822) 612325

✠**HAZLEWOOD, The Rt Revd John.** b 24. K Coll Cam BA48 MA52. Cuddesdon Coll 48. **d** 49 **p** 50 **c** 75. C Camberwell St Mich *S'wark* 49-50; Australia 50-53 and from 55; C Camberwell St Mich w All So *S'wark* 53-55; Vice Prin St Fran Th Coll Brisbane 55-60; Dean Rockhampton 61-68; Dean Perth 68-75; Bp Ballarat 75-93; rtd 93. *1409 Gregory Street, Ballarat, Victoria, Australia 3350* Tel Ballarat (53) 382392

HEAD, David Nicholas. b 55. Pemb Coll Cam BA77 MA81. Westcott Ho Cam 78. **d** 81 **p** 82. C Surbiton St Andr and St Mark *S'wark* 81-84; C St Marylebone w H Trin *Lon* 84-89; TV Clapham TM *S'wark* 89-96; Chapl Princess Alice Hospice Esher from 96. *73A Pleasant Place, Hersham, Walton-on-Thames, Surrey KT12 4HU* Tel (01932) 243302

HEAD, Canon Derek Leonard Hamilton. b 34. ALCD58. **d** 58 **p** 59. C Bexleyheath Ch Ch *Roch* 58-61; C Wisley w Pyrford *Guildf* 61-66; C-in-c Ewell St Paul Howell Hill CD 66-73; R Headley All SS 73-81; TR 81-82; RD Farnham 80-82; V Chertsey from 82; Hon Can Guildf Cathl from 83; RD Runnymede 88-93; Dir Post-Ord Tr 90-94. *The Vicarage, London Street, Chertsey, Surrey KT16 8AA* Tel (01932) 563141

HEAD, John Leslie. b 06. Dur Univ LTh31. Sarum Th Coll 29. **d** 31 **p** 32. C Kentish Town St Barn *Lon* 31-34; Hon C W Silvertown St Barn *Chelmsf* 34-36; P-in-c Victoria Docks St Mark 36-37; Min Leytonstone St Aug CD 37-41; CF (EC) 41-46; Hon CF 46; R Black Notley *Chelmsf* 46-50; R Leigh St Clem 50-72; rtd 72; Perm to Offic *Chelmsf* from 72. *Flat 13, Waters Mead, 26 Thorpe Hall Avenue, Southend-on-Sea SS1 3DW* Tel (01702) 589108

HEAD, Peter Ernest. b 38. Lon Univ BSc59. Ridley Hall Cam 61. **d** 63 **p** 64. C Fulwood *Sheff* 63-66; C Belper *Derby* 66-68; Head RE Shoeburyness Sch Southend-on-Sea 69-74; Lic to Offic *Chelmsf* 69-74; Head RE Bilborough Coll Nottm 74-79; Public Preacher *S'well* 74-79; NSM Bramcote 74-79; Vice-Prin Totton Coll Southn 79-93; Perm to Offic *Win* 80-93; rtd 93; NSM Hordle *Win* from 94. *44 Lentune Way, Lymington, Hants SO41 3PF* Tel (01590) 678097 Fax as telephone

HEAD, William Peter. b 18. St Edm Hall Ox BA46 MA51. Cuddesdon Coll 46. **d** 48 **p** 49. C Beeston *S'well* 48-52; CF 52-56; V Wellingborough St Barn *Pet* 56-61; Chapl Highfield Sch Liphook 61-74; rtd 83; Perm to Offic *Chich* from 83. *3 Ferndale Road, Chichester, W Sussex PO19 4QJ* Tel (01243) 527075

HEADING, Richard Vaughan. b 43. ARCS65 Lon Univ BSc65. Coll of Resurr Mirfield 66. **d** 68 **p** 69. C Heref St Martin *Heref* 68-75; P-in-c Birches Head *Lich* 75-77; P-in-c Northwood 75-77; TV Hanley H Ev 77-82; V Heref H Trin *Heref* 82-92; TR Bedminster *Bris* from 92. *Bedminster Rectory, 287 North Street, Bristol BS3 1JP* Tel 0117-966 4025

HEADLAND, James Frederick. b 20. Clifton Th Coll 51. **d** 53 **p** 54. C Barnsbury St Andr *Lon* 53-55; C Spitalfields Ch Ch w All SS 55-57; V Upper Tulse Hill St Matthias *S'wark* 57-65; P-in-c Smethcott w Woolstaston *Heref* 65-81; R Church Pulverbatch 65-81; P-in-c Cantley w Limpenhoe and Southwood *Nor* 81; R Reedham 81; R Reedham w Cantley w Limpenhoe and Southwood 81-86; rtd 86; Perm to Offic *Heref* from 86; Perm to Offic *Lich* from 88. *3 Ashford Avenue, Pontesbury, Shrewsbury SY5 0QN* Tel (01743) 790565

HEADLEY, Miss Carolyn Jane. b 50. MCSP71 GDipP71. Lon Bible Coll DipTh76 Oak Hill Th Coll BA83. **dss** 83 **d** 87 **p** 94. Harlesden St Mark *Lon* 83-86; Kensal Rise St Mark and St Martin 86-87; Par Dn 87; Par Dn Uxbridge St Andr w St Jo 87-88; Par Dn Uxbridge 88-90; TD 90-92; Warden of Readers (Willesden Episc Area) 88-92; Tutor Wycliffe Hall Ox from 94. *6 Tanners Court, Dancers Hill, Charlbury, Chipping Norton, Oxon OX7 3RP* Tel (01608) 810799

HEADS, John. b 27. Bps' Coll Cheshunt 60. **d** 62 **p** 63. C Beamish *Dur* 61-64; C Monkwearmouth St Andr 64-65; C Stockton St Chad 65-70; rtd 94. *18 Green Crescent, Golcar, Huddersfield HD7 4RF* Tel (01484) 651232

HEAGERTY, Alistair John. b 42. MBE86. Or Coll Ox BA63 MA67. Lon Coll of Div BD68. **d** 68 **p** 69. C Margate H Trin *Cant* 68-72; CF 72-97; Chapl R Memorial Chpl Sandhurst 92-97; TV Kingswood *Bris* from 97. *60 Lavers Close, Kingswood, Bristol BS15 2ZG* Tel 0117-935 2658

HEAK, Philip George. b 70. QUB BA92. CITC BTh95. **d** 95 **p** 96. C Ballymacash *Conn* from 95. *11 Fulmar Avenue, Lisburn, Co Antrim BT28 3HS* Tel (01846) 678252

HEAL, David Walter. b 37. Ox Univ MA63 Trin Coll Carmarthen 87. **d** 90 **p** 91. NSM Henfynyw w Aberaeron and Llanddewi Aberarth *St D* 90-96; Hon Asst Chapl Algarve *Eur* from 96. *Casa Santa Catarina, Paqua de Praia, Praia da Luz, 8600 Lagos, Portugal* Tel Lagos (82) 789126

HEAL, Miss Felicity Joan. b 42. Brighton Poly DCouns88. Portsm Dioc Tr Course 89. **d** 92. NSM Bramshott and Liphook *Portsm* 92-95; NSM Blendworth w Chalton w Idsworth from 95. *40 Rushes Road, Petersfield, Hants GU32 3BW* Tel (01730) 260410

HEAL, Geoffrey. b 28. Linc Th Coll 54. **d** 56 **p** 57. C Camberwell St Giles *S'wark* 56-59; C Rotherhithe St Mary w All SS 59-62; V Peckham St Jo 62-75; V Southfields St Barn 75-88; rtd 88; Perm to Offic *Ex* from 89. *Digby Cottage, 5 Hind Street, Ottery St Mary, Devon EX11 1BW* Tel (01404) 814729

HEALD, William Roland. b 40. Birm Univ DPS79. St Jo Coll Auckland LTh74. **d** 74 **p** 75. New Zealand 74-78 and 79-93; C Bournville *Birm* 78-79; V S Kensington St Luke *Lon* from 93. *St Luke's Vicarage, 1 Cathcart Road, London SW10 9NL* Tel 0171-352 7553

HEALE, Dr Nicholas James. b 67. St Cath Coll Ox BA89 DPhil95 Leeds Univ BA94. Coll of Resurr Mirfield CPT95. **d** 95 **p** 96. C Syston TM *Leic* from 95. *1121 Melton Road, Syston, Leics LE7 8JS* Tel 0116-260 1670

HEALE, Walter James Grenville. b 40. Wycliffe Hall Ox 77. **d** 79 **p** 80. C Walsall *Lich* 79-82; TV Marfleet *York* 82-89; TR 89-94; R Easington w Skeffling, Kilnsea and Holmpton from 94. *The Rectory, Hull Road, Easington, Hull HU12 0TE* Tel (01964) 650203

HEALES, John. b 48. K Coll Lon BD71 AKC71 PGCE72 DPS76. St Mich Coll Llan 75. **d** 76 **p** 77. C Cwmbran *Mon* 76-78; Chapl Rendcomb Coll Cirencester 78-82; Perm to Offic *Mon* 85-88; V Penhow, St Brides Netherwent w Llandavenny etc from 88. *Flat 1, The Rectory, Llanfaches, Newport NP6 3AY* Tel (01633) 400901

HEALEY, The Very Revd James Christopher. b 44. Linc Th Coll 84. **d** 86 **p** 87. C Boultham *Linc* 86-90; TV Gt Grimsby St Mary and St Jas 90-91; I Narraghmore w Timolin, Castledermot and Kinneagh *D & G* 91-93; I New Ross *C & O* 93-97; Dean Lismore from 97; I Lismore w Cappoquin, Kilwatermoy, Dungarvan etc from 97; Chan Cashel Cathl from 97; Prec Waterford Cathl from 97. *The Deanery, The Mall Rectory, Colleg, Lismore, Co Waterford, Irish Republic* Tel Lismore (58) 54137 Fax as telephone

HEANEY, James Roland. b 59. DipTh85. **d** 85 **p** 86. C Ballynafeigh St Jude *D & D* 85-88; C Lisburn Ch Ch Cathl *Conn* 88-90; I Dunganstown w Redcross and Conary *D & G* from 90. *The Rectory, Redcross, Co Wicklow, Irish Republic* Tel Wicklow (404) 41637

HEANEY, Michael Roger. b 43. TCD BA66 HDipEd67 MA69 DCG83. CITC 74. **d** 76 **p** 77. Chapl St Columba's Coll Dub from 76. *Montana, Scholarstown Road, Dublin 16, Irish Republic* Tel Dublin (1) 493 1167 or 493 2219 Fax 493 6655

HEANEY, Samuel Stewart. b 44. Open Univ BA79 Ulster Univ BEd83 Lon Univ BD93. Pb Coll Belf 85 St Deiniol's Hawarden 92. **d** 92 **p** 93. In Pb Ch 85-92; C Knockbreda *D & D* 92-96; I Belfast H Trin and Ardoyne *Conn* from 96. *313 Ballysillan Road, Belfast BT14 6RD* Tel (01232) 713958

HEANEY, Wendy Anne. b 42. **d** 95 **p** 96. NSM Clifton and Southill *St Alb* from 95. *34 Meadow Way, Letchworth, Herts SG6 3JB* Tel (01462) 482852

HEANS, Simon John. b 56. **d** 94 **p** 95. Asst Chapl Lancing Coll from 94. *Edgewood, Hoe Court, Lancing, W Sussex BN15 0QX* Tel (01903) 767585

HEAP, David Leonard. b 58. Man Univ BA79. Cranmer Hall Dur 82. **d** 85 **p** 86. C Clitheroe St Jas *Blackb* 85-88; C Blackb St Gabr 88-92; V Bare from 92. *St Christopher's Vicarage, 12 Elm Grove, Morecambe, Lancs LA4 6AT* Tel (01524) 411363

HEAPS, Richard Peter. b 35. Qu Coll Birm 58. **d** 61 **p** 62. C Castle Bromwich SS Mary and Marg *Birm* 61-65; C-in-c Erdington St Chad CD 65-70; V Nechells 70-81; RD Aston 75-81; V Marston Green 81-86; P-in-c Shrawley and Witley w Astley *Worc* 86-92; R Shrawley, Witley, Astley and Abberley from 92. *The Rectory, Shrawley, Worcester WR6 6TS* Tel (01905) 620489

HEAPS, William Henry. b 20. St Deiniol's Hawarden 81. **d** 83 **p** 84. NSM Tranmere St Cath *Ches* 83-96; NSM Prenton 86-96; rtd 96. *21 Fisher Green, Honley, Huddersfield HD7 2DU* Tel (01484) 660276

HEARD, Charles. b 19. S'wark Ord Course 62. **d** 65 **p** 66. C Plumstead St Nic *S'wark* 65-71; C Blackheath All SS 71-72; V Barnes H Trin 72-84; rtd 84; Hon C E Wickham *S'wark* from 84.

Flat 5, Elmfield Court, Wickham Street, Welling, Kent DA16 3DF Tel 0181-855 9809

HEARD, Ross McPherson. b 11. Clifton Th Coll 38. **d** 41 **p** 42. C Lyncombe *B & W* 41-42; C Rushden *Pet* 42-44; C Watford *St Alb* 44-47; V Rushden St Pet 47-50; New Zealand 50-54; V Colney Heath St Mark *St Alb* 54-57; R Hatch Beauchamp w Beercrocombe *B & W* 58-76; V W Hatch 62-76; rtd 76; Perm to Offic *Ely* from 76. *235 Queen Edith's Way, Cambridge CB1 4NJ* Tel (01223) 212252

HEARN, John Henry. b 49. Trin Coll Bris. **d** 82 **p** 83. C Epsom Common Ch Ch *Guildf* 82-85; C Ringwood *Win* 85-88; Chapl Basingstoke Distr Hosp 88-91; Chapl Luton and Dunstable Hosp 91-96; C Ampthill w Millbrook and Steppingley *St Alb* from 96. *18 Russell Drive, Ampthill, Bedford MK45 2UA* Tel (01525) 405812

HEARN, Jonathan. b 58. GradIPM85 Leeds Univ BA81. Westcott Ho Cam 89. **d** 91 **p** 92. C Tuffley *Glouc* 91-94; C Milton *Win* from 94. *St Peter's House, 25 Ashley Common Road, New Milton, Hants BH25 5AJ* Tel (01425) 612644

HEARN, Canon Peter Brian. b 31. St Jo Coll Dur 52. **d** 55 **p** 56. C Frodingham *Linc* 55-59; R Belton SS Pet and Paul 59-64; PC Manthorpe w Londonthorpe 59-64; V Billingborough 64-73; V Sempringham w Pointon and Birthorpe 64-73; V Flixborogh w Burton upon Stather 73-96; RD Manlake 87-93; Can and Preb Linc Cathl from 92; rtd 96. *7 St Andrews Drive, Burton-upon-Stather, Scunthorpe, S Humberside DN15 9BY* Tel (01724) 720510

HEARN, Thomas Peter. b 18. Selw Coll Cam BA40 MA45. Linc Th Coll 40. **d** 42 **p** 43. C Oxhey St Matt *St Alb* 42-45; C Cirencester *Glouc* 45-52; V Childswyckham 52-62; R Aston Somerville 52-62; RD Winchcombe 60-62; R Stratton w Baunton 62-75; V France Lynch 75-83; rtd 84; Perm to Offic *Glouc* from 84. *9 Cotswold Close, Cirencester, Glos GL7 1XP* Tel (01285) 655627

HEARN, Trevor. b 36. Sarum Th Coll 61. **d** 64 **p** 65. C Hounslow St Steph *Lon* 64-67; Miss to Seamen from 67; Lic to Offic *St E* 74-80; Lic to Offic *Bris* 80-92; UAE from 92. *Dubai International Seafarers' Centre, Mina Rashid Road, PO Box 5811, Dubai, United Arab Emirates* Tel Dubai (4) 452951 or 452918 Fax 493298

HEARNE, Derrick Kenneth. b 32. FBCS69 K Coll Lon BA68 AKC68. St Mich Coll Llan DMinlStuds. **d** 90 **p** 91. C Llanbadarn Fawr w Capel Bangor and Goginan *St D* 90-91; Miss to Seamen 92-97; Jordan 92-97; rtd 97. *Glenview, Llanglydwen, Hebron, Whitland SA34 0UN*

HEARTFIELD, Canon Peter Reginald. b 27. Chich Th Coll 61. **d** 63 **p** 64. C Hurstpierpoint *Chich* 63-67; V Brighton St Alb Preston 67-73; Chapl Kent and Cant Hosp 73-92; Chapl Nunnery Fields Hosp Cant 73-92; Six Preacher Cant Cathl *Cant* 79-84; Hon Can Cant Cathl 84-92; rtd 92; Abp's Adv for Hosp Chapl *Cant* from 92. *13 Lanfranc Gardens, Harbledown, Canterbury, Kent CT2 8NJ* Tel (01227) 451621

HEASLIP, William John (Jack). b 44. TCD BA66. CITC 79. **d** 80 **p** 81. Chapl Mt Temple Sch Dub 80-86; Bp's C Aughaval w Burrishoole, Knappagh and Louisburgh *T, K & A* 86-88; I Aughaval w Achill, Knappagh, Dugort etc 88-95; Radio Officer (Tuam) 90-95; I Cork St Luke Union *C, C & R* from 95. *St Luke's Rectory, Mahony's Avenue, Summerhill, Cork, Irish Republic* Tel Cork (21) 501672

HEATH, Mrs Cynthia Grace. b 46. ARCM66 Open Univ BA84 St Mark & St Jo Coll Lon TCert68. WMMTC 94. **d** 97. NSM Penkridge Team *Lich* from 97. *2 Hall Farm Road, Brewood, Staffs ST19 9EZ* Tel (01902) 850175

HEATH, Henry. b 40. FCII77. Oak Hill Th Coll 77. **d** 80 **p** 81. Hon C Lexden *Chelmsf* 80-86; C Colne Engaine 86-87; Hon C Halstead St Andr w H Trin and Greenstead Green 87-90; NSM W w E Mersea 91-95; R Stanway from 95. *The Rectory, Church Lane, Stanway, Colchester CO3 5LR* Tel (01206) 210407

HEATH, Mrs Janet. b 45. EMMTC 89. **d** 91 **p** 94. Par Dn Rainworth *S'well* 91-94; C 94-96; C Mansfield Woodhouse from 96. *17 The Hollies, Sherwood Park, Rainworth, Mansfield, Notts NG21 0FZ* Tel (01623) 490422

HEATH, Canon John Gordon. b 08. Lon Univ AKC34. **d** 33 **p** 34. C Bramley *Guildf* 33-36; S Africa from 36; Can Port Elizabeth from 73. *Cottage 10, 77 Water Road, Walmer, Port Elizabeth, 6070 South Africa* Tel Port Elizabeth (41) 515372

HEATH, John Henry. b 41. Chich Th Coll 69. **d** 71 **p** 72. C Crediton *Ex* 71-74; C Tavistock and Gulworthy 74-76; C Brixham 76-77; C Brixham w Churston Ferrers 77-79; R Bere Ferrers 79-85; P-in-c Moretonhampstead, N Bovey and Manaton 85-88; R 88-93; P-in-c Lifton from 93; P-in-c Kelly w Bradstone from 93; P-in-c Broadwoodwidger from 93. *The Rectory, Lifton, Devon PL16 0BJ* Tel (01566) 784291

HEATH, Canon Peter Henry. b 24. Kelham Th Coll 40. **d** 47 **p** 48. C Derby St Anne *Derby* 47-49; C Staveley 49-52; C Brampton St Thos 52-54; C-in-c Brampton St Mark CD 54-59; V New Whittington 59-66; V Glossop 66-92; RD Glossop 83-89; Hon Can Derby Cathl 84-92; rtd 92; Perm to Offic *Derby* from 92. *Birchinlea, 15 Park Crescent, Glossop, Derbyshire SK13 9BQ* Tel (01457) 862047

HEATH, Raymond Walker. b 19. Cuddesdon Coll 46. **d** 47 **p** 48. C Radford *Cov* 47-50; C Tilehurst St Mich *Ox* 50-54; Miss to Seamen 54-58; V Walmer *Cant* 58-66; V Rolvenden 66-75; Perm to Offic *Glouc* from 79; rtd 84. *High Lodge, Kineton, Guiting Power, Cheltenham, Glos GL54 5UG* Tel (01451) 850440

HEATH, William Walter. b 11. St Jo Coll Ox BA32. **d** 72 **p** 73. Hon C Petworth *Chich* 72-90; Perm to Offic from 90. *Malthouse, Lurgashall, Petworth, W Sussex GU28 9ET* Tel (01428) 707212

HEATLEY, David Henry. b 50. Kent Univ BA72. Qu Coll Birm 86. **d** 88 **p** 89. C Liss *Portsm* 88-91; V Newchurch from 91; V Arreton from 91. *The Vicarage, Newchurch, Sandown, Isle of Wight PO36 0NN* Tel (01983) 865504

HEATLEY, Henry David. b 24. CITC 66. **d** 68 **p** 69. C Belfast St Matt *Conn* 68-72; C-in-c Layde 72-78; C Belfast St Mary 78-80; I Belfast St Barn 80-92; rtd 92. *Ebenezer, 91 Larne Road, Carrickfergus, Co Antrim BT38 7NH* Tel (01960) 365382

HEATLEY, William Cecil. b 39. QUB BA61. Ridley Hall Cam 62. **d** 64 **p** 65. C Ballymacarrett St Patr *D & D* 64-69; C Herne Hill St Paul *S'wark* 69-74; TV Sanderstead All SS 75-82; P-in-c Peckham St Sav 82-87; V from 87; RD Dulwich from 97. *173 Choumert Road, London SE15 4AW* Tel 0171-639 5072 or 732 3435

HEATON, Alan. b 36. K Coll Lon BD64 AKC64 Nottm Univ MTh76. **d** 65 **p** 66. C Stockton St Chad *Dur* 65-68; C Englefield Green *Guildf* 68-70; C Winlaton *Dur* 70-74; Chapl Derby Lonsdale Coll *Derby* 74-79; V Alfreton 79-87; RD Alfreton 81-86; TR Clifton *S'well* 87-93; P-in-c Rolleston w Fiskerton, Morton and Upton 93-96; rtd 97. *29 The Parchments, Newton le Willows, Merseyside WA12 0DX* Tel (01925) 292209

HEATON, Julian Roger. b 62. LSE BSc(Econ)83. St Steph Ho Ox BA86 MA92. **d** 87 **p** 88. C Stockport St Thos w St Pet *Ches* 87-90; Chapl Asst Qu Medical Cen Nottm 90-92; Chapl Asst Univ Hosp Nottm 90-92; V Knutsford St Cross *Ches* from 92. *The Vicarage, Mobberley Road, Knutsford, Cheshire WA16 8EL* Tel (01565) 632389

✠**HEAVENER, The Rt Revd Robert William.** b 05. TCD BA28. CITC 29. **d** 29 **p** 30 **c** 73. C Clones *Clogh* 29-31; Dioc C 31-32; C-in-c Lack 32-38; I Derryvullen N 38-46; R Monaghan w Tyholland 46-51; RD Monaghan 46-73; R Monaghan w Tydavnet 51-73; Can St Patr Cathl Dublin 62-68; Adn Clogh 68-73; Bp Clogh 73-80; rtd 80. *12 Church Avenue, Jordanstown, Newtownabbey, Co Antrim BT37 0PJ* Tel (01232) 863242

HEAVER, Derek Cyril. b 47. St Jo Coll Nottm BTh73. **d** 73 **p** 74. C Win Ch Ch *Win* 73-77; CF from 77. *MOD Chaplains (Army), Trenchard Lines, Upavon, Pewsey, Wilts SN9 6BE* Tel (01980) 615804 Fax 615800

HEAVISIDES, Canon Neil Cameron. b 50. Selw Coll Cam BA72 MA76 Ox Univ BA74 MA85. Ripon Hall Ox 72. **d** 75 **p** 76. C Stockton St Pet *Dur* 75-78; Succ S'wark Cathl *S'wark* 78-81; V Seaham w Seaham Harbour *Dur* 81-88; P-in-c Edington and Imber, Erlestoke and E Coulston *Sarum* 88-89; R 89-93; Can Res Glouc Cathl *Glouc* from 93. *7 College Green, Gloucester GL1 2LX* Tel (01452) 523987

HEAWOOD, Canon Alan Richard. b 32. G&C Coll Cam BA54 MA58. Union Th Sem (NY) BD56 Ripon Hall Ox 56. **d** 57 **p** 58. C Horwich H Trin *Man* 57-59; C Weaste 59-60; C Beverley Minster *York* 60-62; Chapl and Lect St Pet Coll Saltley 62-65; R Hockwold w Wilton *Ely* 65-72; R Weeting 65-72; V Melbourn 72-80; V Meldreth 72-80; P-in-c Teversham 80-90; Adult Educn Sec 80-89; Dir of Educn from 80; Hon Can Ely Cathl from 80. *The Rectory, 30 Church Road, Teversham, Cambs CB1 5AW* Tel (01223) 292220

HEBBLETHWAITE, Canon Brian Leslie. b 39. Magd Coll Ox BA61 MA67 Magd Coll Cam BA63 MA68 BD84. Westcott Ho Cam 62. **d** 65 **p** 66. C Elton All SS *Man* 65-68; Chapl Qu Coll Cam 68; Dean of Chpl 69-94; Life Fellow from 94; Asst Lect Cam Univ 73-77; Lect from 77; Can Th Leic Cathl *Leic* from 82. *52 Storey's Way, Cambridge CB3 0DX* Tel (01223) 339561

HEBBLETHWAITE, Dr Emma Sian. b 65. CCC Cam BA88 MA91 PhD92. Westcott Ho Cam CTM94. **d** 94 **p** 95. C Framlingham w Saxtead *St E* 94-96; Chapl K Coll Cam from 96. *52 Storey's Way, Cambridge CB3 0DX* Tel (01223) 331251

HEBBLEWHITE, David Ernest. b 52. Hull Univ BA81 Nottm Univ MA82 CQSW82. St Jo Coll Nottm MA95. **d** 97. C Melton Mowbray *Leic* from 97. *17 Ankle Hill, Melton Mowbray, Leics LE13 0QJ*

HEBBORN, Roy Valentine Charles. S Dios Minl Tr Scheme 83. **d** 86 **p** 87. NSM Lewes All SS, St Anne, St Mich and St Thos *Chich* from 86. *3 St Anne's Terrace, Western Road, Lewes, E Sussex BN7 1RH* Tel (01273) 474063

HEBDEN, Mrs Cynthia Margaret. b 47. Univ of Wales (Ban) BTh94. **d** 94 **p** 97. NSM Llanfairpwll w Penmynydd *Ban* 94-95; C Twrcelyn Deanery 95-96; C Knighton St Mary Magd *Leic* from 96. *41 Cairnsford Road, Leicester LE2 6GC* Tel 0116-288 6097

HEBDEN, John Percy. b 18. Sheff Univ 46 Lon Univ 67. St Aid Birkenhead 58. **d** 60 **p** 60. C Skipton H Trin *Bradf* 60-62; R Kirby Misperton *York* 63-67; V Laxey *S & M* 70-83; V Lonan 80-83; rtd 84; Hon C Douglas St Geo and St Barn *S & M* from 84. *Begra, Clayhead Road, Baldrine, Douglas, Isle of Man IM4 6DN* Tel (01624) 781296

HEBDEN, Peter. b 43. Wigan Coll of Tech MICE67. St As Minl Tr Course 92. **d** 95 **p** 96. NSM Twrcelyn Deanery *Ban* 95-96; NSM

Gt Glen, Stretton Magna and Wistow etc *Leic* from 97. *41 Cairnsford Road, Leicester LE2 6GC* Tel 0116-288 6097

HEBER-PERCY, Christopher John. b 41. St Jo Coll Cam BA64 MA68. Wells Th Coll 66. **d** 68 **p** 69. C Leigh St Mary *Man* 68-71; Asst Ind Chapl 71-80; P-in-c Oldham St Andr 75-78; TV Oldham 78-80; Ind Chapl *Win* 80-90; N Humberside Ind Chapl *York* from 90. *19 Bellfield Avenue, Hull HU8 9DS* Tel (01482) 702033

HECKINGBOTTOM, John Michael. b 33. Leeds Univ BA55. St Steph Ho Ox 55. **d** 57 **p** 58. C Wigan All SS *Liv* 57-59; Min Can and Succ Ripon Cathl *Ripon* 59-63; P-in-c Seacroft 63-66; V Menston w Woodhead *Bradf* 66-82; P-in-c Bishop Monkton and Burton Leonard *Ripon* 82-88; Chapl Scotton Banks Hosp Knaresborough 86-88; V Collingham w Harewood *Ripon* 88-94; Perm to Offic from 94; Perm to Offic *York* from 95. *8 Lawson Road, Dringhouses, York YO2 2NE* Tel (01904) 707916

HECTOR, Noel Antony. b 61. Barrister-at-Law 84 Sheff Univ LLB83. Oak Hill Th Coll BA91. **d** 91 **p** 92. C Rodbourne Cheney *Bris* 91-92; C Bris St Mary Redcliffe w Temple etc 92-95; R Wrington w Butcombe *B & W* from 95. *The Rectory, High Street, Wrington, Bristol BS18 7QD* Tel (01934) 862201

HEDDLE, Dr Duncan. b 34. Wadh Coll Ox BA57 MA61 DPhil64. **d** 86 **p** 86. Chapl Aber Univ *Ab* from 86; P-in-c Bucksburn from 90. *2 Douglas Place, High Street, Aberdeen AB2 3EA* Tel (01224) 485975 or 272888

HEDGCOCK, Dr Walter Paul. b 09. FRCGP Lon Univ MB, BS32 MD34. S'wark Ord Course 69. **d** 72 **p** 73. C Blakeney w Lt Langham *Nor* 72-73; P-in-c Field Dalling w Saxlingham 73-76; Bp's Scientific Resp Adv 76-83; Hon C Wallingford w Crowmarsh Gifford etc *Ox* 84-96. *3 Cherwell Close, Wallingford, Oxon OX10 0HF* Tel (01491) 837684

HEDGE, Peter Andrew. b 62. New Coll Ox MA90. Coll of Resurr Mirfield 90. **d** 93 **p** 94. C Thornbury *Bradf* from 93. *69 Upper Ruston Road, Thornbury, Bradford, W Yorkshire BD3 7EU* Tel (01274) 666875

HEDGER, Graham. b 57. Lon Bible Coll BA Ridley Hall Cam. **d** 83 **p** 84. C Walton *St E* 83-86; TV Mildenhall 86-91; R Swainsthorpe w Newton Flotman *Nor* 91-94; Dioc Evang Officer 91-94. *14 St Peter's Close, Charsfield, Woodbridge, Suffolk IP13 7RG* Tel (01473) 737280

HEDGES, Mrs Anne Violet. b 53. Ripon Coll Cuddesdon 87. **d** 89 **p** 94. C Thetford *Nor* 89-94; Chapl Riddlesworth Hall Sch Nor from 93; P-in-c Garboldisham w Blo' Norton, Riddlesworth etc *Nor* 94-97; R Guiltcross from 97. *The Rectory, Back Street, Garboldisham, Diss, Norfolk IP22 2SD* Tel (01953) 818101

HEDGES, Canon Dennis Walter. b 29. Sarum Th Coll. **d** 62 **p** 63. C Walton-on-Thames *Guildf* 62-66; C Westborough 66-69; V Blackheath and Chilworth 69-79; R Farncombe 79-94; RD Godalming 84-89; Hon Can Guildf Cathl 92-94; rtd 94; Perm to Offic *Guildf* from 94; Perm to Offic *Win* from 94. *21 Lincoln Green, Alton, Hants GU34 1SX* Tel (01420) 542624

HEDGES, Ian Charles. b 55. Sarum & Wells Th Coll 79. **d** 82 **p** 83. C Chessington *Guildf* 82-85; C Fleet 85-90; V S Farnborough from 90. *The Vicarage, 1 St Mark's Close, Farnborough, Hants GU14 6PP* Tel (01252) 544711

HEDGES, Canon Jane Barbara. b 55. St Jo Coll Dur BA78. Cranmer Hall Dur 78. **dss** 80 **d** 87 **p** 94. Fareham H Trin *Portsm* 80-83; Southampton (City Cen) *Win* 83-87; Par Dn 87-88; Dioc Stewardship Adv *Portsm* 88-93; Can Res Portsm Cathl from 93. *51 High Street, Portsmouth PO1 2LU* Tel (01705) 731282

HEDGES, Mrs Jane Rosemary. b 44. RGN65. S Dios Minl Tr Scheme 86. **d** 89 **p** 94. NSM Gillingham *Sarum* from 89; Asst Chapl Westmr Memorial Hosp Shaftesbury from 89. *Dene Hollow, Wyke, Gillingham, Dorset SP8 4NG* Tel (01747) 822812

HEDGES, John Michael Peter. b 34. Leeds Univ BA60. Ripon Hall Ox 60. **d** 61 **p** 62. C Weaste *Man* 61-65; V Ashton St Pet 65-74; C Easthampstead *Ox* 74-85; V Tilehurst St Geo 85-91; C Thatcham 91-94; TV from 94. *1 Cowslip Crescent, Thatcham, Berks RG18 4DE* Tel (01635) 869940

HEDGES, Leslie Norman. b 26. Bris Univ BA51 Lon Univ BD56. Clifton Th Coll 48. **d** 53 **p** 54. C Summerstown *S'wark* 53-55; C Wolverhampton St Luke *Lich* 55-56; C Reigate St Mary *S'wark* 56-59; V Clapham Park All SS 59-70; V Findern *Derby* 70-82; V Willington 70-82; V Trowbridge St Thos and W Ashton *Sarum* 82-91; rtd 91; Perm to Offic *Truro* from 91. *16 Penwerris Road, Truro, Cornwall TR1 3QS* Tel (01872) 79858

HEDLEY, Dr Charles John Wykeham. b 47. R Holloway Coll Lon BSc69 PhD73 Fitzw Coll Cam BA75 MA79. Westcott Ho Cam 73. **d** 76 **p** 77. C Chingford St Anne *Chelmsf* 76-79; C St Martin-in-the-Fields *Lon* 79-84 and 85-86; P-in-c 84-85; Chapl Ch Coll Cam 86-90; TR Gleadless *Sheff* from 90. *The Rectory, 243 Hollinsend Road, Sheffield S12 2EE* Tel 0114-239 0757

HEDLEY, Henry. b 10. St Edm Hall Ox BA32 MA43. Linc Th Coll 33. **d** 34 **p** 35. C Kendal H Trin *Carl* 34-38; C S Shore H Trin *Blackb* 38-42; R St Mary-at-Lambeth *S'wark* 42-63; RD Lambeth 56-63; R Bletchley *Ox* 63-79; rtd 79. *6 Caldersyde, The Banks, Seascale, Cumbria CA20 1QJ* Tel (019467) 28985

HEDLEY, Ronald. b 27. Codrington Coll Barbados. **d** 64 **p** 65. Trinidad and Tobago 64-92; rtd 92; Perm to Offic *Dur* from 92. *6 Ludlow Road, Sunderland SR2 9HH*

HEDLEY, William Clifford. b 35. Tyndale Hall Bris 65. **d** 67 **p** 68. C Hensingham *Carl* 67-69; C Rainhill *Liv* 69-71; C St Helens St Helen 71-73; V Low Elswick *Newc* 73-81; V Kingston upon Hull St Aid Southcoates *York* 81-87; TV Heworth 87-94; V Norton juxta Malton from 94. *The Vicarage, 80 Lanton Road, Norton, Malton, N Yorkshire YO17 9AE* Tel (01653) 692741

HEFFER, Thomas Patrick Peter. b 69. K Coll Lon BD90 AKC90. Cuddesdon Coll 94. **d** 96 **p** 97. C Sprowston w Beeston *Nor* from 96. *6 Wroxham Road, Sprowston, Norwich NR7 8TZ* Tel (01603) 484438 Fax as telephone

HEFFER, William John Gambrell. b 30. AKC55. **d** 56 **p** 57. C Biggleswade *St Alb* 56-59; C Clacton St Jas *Chelmsf* 59-61; V Langford *St Alb* 61-67; V Luton All SS 67-73; P-in-c Eaton Socon 73-75; V 75-77; Lic to Offic 78-81; R Wingrave w Rowsham, Aston Abbotts and Cublington *Ox* 81-88; R Wilden w Colmworth and Ravensden *St Alb* 88-91; C Leighton Buzzard w Eggington, Hockliffe etc 91-94; rtd 94. *35 Pebblemoor, Edlesborough, Dunstable, Beds LU7 2HZ* Tel (01525) 220428

HEFFERNAN, Anna Elizabeth. b 65. Cuddesdon Coll DipMin95. **d** 97. C Limpsfield and Titsey *S'wark* from 97. *Berry House, High Street, Limpsfield, Oxted, Surrey RH8 0DT* Tel (01883) 713836

HEFFERNAN, Ms May Olive. b 52. Maria Grey Coll Lon CertEd74 Lon Univ BD93. Aston Tr Scheme 88 Westcott Ho Cam CTMin93. **d** 93 **p** 94. C Duddeston w Nechells *Birm* from 93. *14 Stanley Road, Birmingham B7 5QS* Tel 0121-328 3781

HEGARTY, Gerald. b 52. QUB BA74 BD81. Union Th Coll Belf 78. **d** 86 **p** 87. NSM Leic H Trin w St Jo *Leic* 86-87; P-in-c Sibson w Sheepy and Ratcliffe Culey 87-90; Tutor Wycliffe Hall Ox 90-95; Chapl St Edm Hall Ox 90-97; Tutor St Alb and Ox Min Course *Ox* from 96. *5 Barns Hay, Old Marston, Oxford OX3 0PN* Tel (01865) 721608

HEGGS, Thomas James. b 40. Inter-American Univ Puerto Rico BA65. Linc Th Coll 75. **d** 77 **p** 78. C Newark St Mary *S'well* 77-80; C Newark w Hawton, Cotham and Shelton 80; R Barwell w Potters Marston and Stapleton *Leic* 80-89; R Upwell St Pet *Ely* 89-94; R Outwell 89-94; P-in-c Yaxley 94-97; P-in-c Holme w Conington 96-97; V Yaxley and Holme w Conington from 97. *The Vicarage, Church Street, Yaxley, Peterborough PE7 3LH* Tel (01733) 240339

HEIDT, John Harrison. b 32. Yale Univ BA54 Ox Univ BLitt67 DPhil75. Nashotah Ho BD57 MDiv69. **d** 56 **p** 57. USA 57-75 and from 96; C Ox St Mary Magd *Ox* 75-80; V Up Hatherley *Glouc* 80-96; P-in-c Cheltenham St Steph 89-95; rtd 97. *204 N Rosemont Avenue, Dallas, Texas 75208, USA* Tel Dallas (214) 948 3442 Fax 941 0339

HEIL, Miss Janet. b 53. Liv Univ BEd75 St Jo Coll Dur BA84. Cranmer Hall Dur. **dss** 85 **d** 87 **p** 94. Ashton Ch Ch *Man* 85-91; Par Dn 87-91; Par Dn Scotforth *Blackb* 91-94; C 94-95; V Gt Harwood St Bart from 95. *St Bartholomew's Vicarage, 1 Church Lane, Great Harwood, Blackburn BB6 7PU* Tel (01254) 884039

HEINZE, Rudolph William. b 31. Concordia Coll (USA) BSc56 CertEd56 De Paul Univ (USA) MA59 Univ of Iowa PhD65. **d** 86 **p** 87. NSM Colney St Pet *St Alb* from 86; Lect Oak Hill Th Coll 86-88; Sen Tutor Oak Hill Th Coll from 88. *3 Farm Lane, Chase Side, London N14 4PP* Tel 0181-449 5969 Fax 441 5996

HELEY, John. b 28. Lon Univ BA72. Bps' Coll Cheshunt 54. **d** 56 **p** 57. S Africa 57-61; C Wimborne Minster *Sarum* 61-62; V Narborough w Narford *Nor* 62-67; V Pentney St Mary Magd w W Bilney 62-67; V Catton 67-69; Lic to Offic *Ox* 69-72; R E w W Rudham *Nor* 72-75; P-in-c Houghton 72-74; V 74-75; V Hunstanton St Edm 75-82; V Hunstanton St Edm w Ringstead 82-83; rtd 88. *Meadow Cottage, Cradle Hall Farm, Burnham Market, Kings Lynn, Norfolk PE31 8JX* Tel (01485) 518686

HELFT, Gunter. b 23. Lon Univ BA48. Ely Th Coll 46. **d** 48 **p** 49. Chapl Essex Home Sch Chelmsf 48-52; C Chelmsf Ascension *Chelmsf* 48-49; C Billesley Common *Birm* 52-53; Miss to Seamen 53-62; Japan 53-57; Sec HQ 57-62; Sudan 57; Bp's Youth Officer *Ox* 62-65; Tr Officer C of E Youth Coun 65-67; Hd Master Abp Temple's Sch Lambeth 67-71; Hd Master Don Valley High Sch S Yorkshire 71-80; rtd 80; Perm to Offic *Worc* from 87. *19 Kenwood Avenue, Worcester WR4 9BD* Tel (01905) 29797

HELLARD, Dawn Yvonne Lorraine. b 47. St Mich Coll Llan 89. **d** 91 **p** 97. C Llantwit Major *Llan* 91-95; TV Cowbridge from 95. *The Vicarage, St Hilary, Cowbridge CF71 7DP* Tel (01446) 772460

HELLEWELL, John. b 63. **d** 94 **p** 95. C Greasbrough *Sheff* from 94. *18 Coach Road, Rotherham, S Yorkshire S61 4ED* Tel (01709) 562378

HELLICAR, Hugh Christopher. b 37. Qu Coll Birm 69. **d** 70 **p** 71. C Bromyard *Heref* 70-73; C Bishop's Castle w Mainstone 73-75; Perm to Offic *S'wark* 77-85; Perm to Offic *Chich* 83-93; NSM Hove All SS 93; NSM Hove from 93. *14 Lewes Crescent, Brighton BN2 1FH* Tel (01273) 676019

HELLIER, Jeremy Peter. b 53. K Coll Lon BD75 AKC75. St Aug Coll Cant 75. **d** 76 **p** 77. C Walton *St E* 76-79; C Ipswich St Fran 79-80; C Wolborough w Newton Abbot *Ex* 80-82; CF 82-84; R Pendine w Llanmiloe and Eglwys Gymyn w Marros *St D* 84-89; TR Widecombe-in-the-Moor, Leusdon, Princetown etc *Ex* 89-94; CF (TAVR) 90-94; RD Moreton *Ex* 91-94; Chapl Wellington Sch Somerset from 94. *Wellington School,*

Wellington, Somerset TA21 8NT Tel (01823) 668827 or 668837 Fax 668844

HELLYER, Ian Anthony. b 66. Plymouth Poly HNC87 Lanc Univ BSc91 Nottm Univ BTh95. Linc Th Coll 92. **d** 95 **p** 96. C Poulton-le-Fylde *Blackb* from 95. *29 Mossbourne Road, Poulton-le-Fylde, Blackpool FY6 7DU* Tel (01253) 884298

HELLYER, Stephen John (Steve). b 56. St Cath Coll Cam BA77 MA81. Wycliffe Hall Ox 82. **d** 84 **p** 85. C Plymouth St Andr w St Paul and St Geo *Ex* 84-88; Chapl Lee Abbey 88-89; Consultant Lon and SE CPAS 90-94; C Nottingham St Nic *S'well* from 94. *4 Balmoral Avenue, West Bridgford, Nottingham NG2 7QU* Tel 0115-981 5665

HELM, Alistair Thomas. b 53. Aston Univ BSc75. EAMTC 88. **d** 91 **p** 92. NSM Leic St Jas *Leic* 91-95; NSM Humberstone from 95. *20 Stoughton Drive North, Leicester LE5 5UB* Tel 0116-273 0613

HELM, Nicholas. b 57. Surrey Univ BSc81. St Jo Coll Nottm 85. **d** 88 **p** 89. C Old Ford St Paul w St Steph and St Mark *Lon* 88-92; TV Netherthorpe *Sheff* 92-93; V Sheff St Bart from 93. *The Vicarage, 73 Burgoyne Road, Sheffield S6 3QB* Tel 0114-233 6977

HELMS, David Clarke. b 50. Boston Univ AB72. Yale Div Sch MDiv77. **d** 97 **p** 77. USA 77-88; Ind Chapl *Worc* 88-97; Chapl NE Worcs Coll 88-97; Ind Chapl Teesside *York* from 97. *26 Chestnut Close, Saltburn-by-the-Sea, Cleveland TS12 1PE*

HELYER, Canon Patrick Joseph Peter. b 15. FRGS83. ALCD39 Wycliffe Hall Ox 38. **d** 38 **p** 39. C Maidstone St Paul *Cant* 38-41; Asst Chapl Miss to Seamen 41-42; Chapl RNVR 42-46; V St Nicholas at Wade w Sarre *Cant* 46-50; Australia 51-61; V Rolvenden *Cant* 62-66; R Frome St Quintin w Evershot and Melbury Bubb *Sarum* 66-71; Falkland Is 71-75; Hon Can Port Stanley 72-75; R Streat w Westmeston *Chich* 75-78; Tristan da Cunha 78-81; rtd 81; Perm to Offic *Heref* from 84; Perm to Offic *Glouc* from 84; Hon C Bishopswood from 93. *Tristan, 4 Gorse Lane, Sling, Coleford, Glos GL16 8JH* Tel (01594) 834990

HEMINGWAY, Peter. b 32. S'wark Ord Course 72. **d** 75 **p** 76. NSM Belmont *S'wark* 75-79; C Herne Hill St Paul 79-81; V Headstone St Geo *Lon* 81-92; V N Harrow St Alb from 87. *St Alban's Vicarage, Church Drive, Harrow, Middx HA2 7NS* Tel 0181-868 6567

HEMMING, Terry Edward. b 47. S Wales Bible Coll DipTh70 Calvin Coll Michigan MA84 S Dios Minl Tr Scheme 88. **d** 90 **p** 91. Hon C Win All SS w Chilcomb and Chesil *Win* from 90; Chapl St Swithun's Sch Win from 95. *15 Gordon Avenue, Winchester, Hants SO23 0QE* Tel (01962) 855701

HEMMING-CLARK, Stanley Charles. b 29. Peterho Cam BA52 MA56. Ridley Hall Cam 52. **d** 54 **p** 55. C Redhill H Trin *S'wark* 54-56; C Woking St Jo *Guildf* 56-59; V Crockenhill All So *Roch* 59-97; rtd 97. *St Anthony's, 22 Ashcroft, Shalford, Guildford, Surrey GU4 8JJ* Tel (01483) 568197

HEMMINGS, Roy Anthony. b 48. Wolv Poly HND69 Univ of Wales (Cardiff) BD85 DPS86. St Mich Coll Llan 82. **d** 86 **p** 87. C Rhyl w St Ann *St As* 86-90; CF from 90. *MOD Chaplains (Army), Trenchard Lines, Upavon, Pewsey, Wilts SN9 6BE* Tel (01980) 615804 Fax 615800

HEMMONS, Laurence John. b 19. Worc Ord Coll 64. **d** 66 **p** 66. C Weston-super-Mare St Jo *B & W* 66-69; R Churchstanton *Ex* 69-70; P-in-c Otterford *B & W* 69-70; R Churchstanton w Otterford 70-82; R Churchstanton, Buckland St Mary and Otterford 80-84; rtd 84; Perm to Offic *Ex* from 88. *7 Westview Close, Whimple, Exeter EX5 2TW* Tel (01404) 822783

HEMPENSTALL, John Albert. b 43. CITC 64. **d** 67 **p** 68. C Carlow w Urglin and Staplestown *C & O* 67-70; Chapl RN from 70. *Royal Naval Chaplaincy Service, Room 203, Victory Building, HM Naval Base, Portsmouth PO1 3LS* Tel (01705) 727903 Fax 727112

HEMPHILL, John James. b 44. TCD BA68 MA72. Oak Hill Th Coll 71. **d** 73 **p** 74. C Dundonald *D & D* 73-78; I Balteagh w Carrick *D & R* from 78. *Balteagh Rectory, 115 Drumsurn Road, Limavady, Co Londonderry BT49 0PD* Tel (01504) 763069

HEMS, Canon Richard Brian. b 30. K Coll Lon BD58. St Aug Coll Cant. **d** 59 **p** 60. C Whitnash *Cov* 59-63; C-in-c Tuckswood CD *Nor* 63-69; V Tuckswood 69-78; R Framingham Earl 78-94; R Gt w Lt Poringland and Howe 78-94; P-in-c Bixley 93-94; R Poringland from 94; Hon Can Nor Cathl from 92. *The Rectory, Rectory Lane, Poringland, Norwich NR14 7SL* Tel (01508) 492215

HEMSLEY, David Ridgway. b 36. AKC61. **d** 61 **p** 62. C Penhill *Bris* 61-64; C Highworth w Sevenhampton and Inglesham etc 64-66; C Surbiton St Andr *S'wark* 67-70; P-in-c Tingewick w Water Stratford *Ox* 70-75; P-in-c Radclive 72-75; PM N Marston w Granborough etc 75-81; P-in-c Quainton 75-81; TV Schorne 81-90; P-in-c Lt Missenden 90-93; V from 93. *The Vicarage, Little Missenden, Amersham, Bucks HP7 0RA* Tel (01494) 862008

HEMSLEY, Susan Mary. b 59. Cranmer Hall Dur 93. **d** 95 **p** 96. C Wilnecote *Lich* from 95. *5 Avill, Hockley, Tamworth, Staffs B77 5QE* Tel (01827) 251816

HEMSTOCK, Julian. b 51. MIProdE CEng Trent Poly BSc74. Sarum & Wells Th Coll 89. **d** 91 **p** 92. C Carrington *S'well* 91-94; C Basford St Aid 94-97; Asst Chapl Qu Medical Cen Nottm Univ Hosp NHS Trust from 97. *St John's House, 65 Osborne Grove, Nottingham NG5 2HE* Tel 0115-985 6980

HEMSTOCK, Mrs Pat. b 51. Sarum & Wells Th Coll 89. **d** 91 **p** 95. Par Dn Carrington *S'well* 91-94; Par Dn Basford St Aid 94-95; C 95-97; P-in-c from 97. *St John's House, 65 Osborne Grove, Nottingham NG5 2HE* Tel 0115-985 6980

HENCHER, John Bredon. b 31. Lich Th Coll 58. **d** 60 **p** 61. C Pershore w Wick *Worc* 60-62; Bp's Dom Chapl 63-64; V Amblecote 64-70; Perm to Offic *Glouc* 72-74; Dioc RE Adv *Heref* 74-80; Lic to Offic 80-87; Perm to Offic *Mon* from 87; Asst Chapl Mon Sch from 87; rtd 96. *The Tank House, Weston, Pembridge, Herefordshire HR6 9JE* Tel (01544) 388540

HENDERSON, Canon Alastair Roy. b 27. BNC Ox BA51 MA54. Ridley Hall Cam 52. **d** 54 **p** 55. C Ex St Leon w H Trin *Ex* 54-57; Travelling Sec IVF 57-60; C St Mary le Bow w St Pancras Soper Lane etc *Lon* 58-60; V Barton Hill St Luke w Ch Ch *Bris* 60-68; P-in-c Bris St Phil and St Jacob w Em 67-68; V Stoke Bishop 68-92; Lect Clifton Th Coll 69-71; Lect Trin Coll Bris 71-73; RD Westbury and Severnside *Bris* 73-79; Hon Can Bris Cathl 80-92; rtd 92; Perm to Offic *Ex* from 92. *3 Garden Court, Cricketfield Lane, Budleigh Salterton, Devon EX9 6PN* Tel (01395) 446147

HENDERSON, Andrew Douglas. b 36. MBASW Trin Coll Cam BA60 MA64 Ox Univ DipPSA63 Liv Univ DASS65. Cuddesdon Coll 60. **d** 62 **p** 63. C Newington St Paul *S'wark* 62-64; Hon C Camberwell St Luke 65-80; Perm to Offic *Lon* from 85. *178 Lancaster Road, London W11 1QU* Tel 0171-229 6790

HENDERSON, David. b 35. Oak Hill NSM Course. **d** 83 **p** 84. NSM Rush Green *Chelmsf* from 83. *196 Marlborough Road, Romford RM7 8AL* Tel (01708) 765955

HENDERSON, The Ven Edward Chance. b 16. Lon Univ BD39. ALCD39. **d** 39 **p** 40. C Low Elswick *Newc* 39-42; NE Area Sec CPAS 42-46; V New Wortley St Mary w Armley Hall *Ripon* 46-52; V Halifax All So *Wakef* 52-59; V Dewsbury All SS 59-68; RD Dewsbury 61-68; Hon Can Wakef Cathl 65-68; Adn Pontefract 68-81; V Darrington w Wentbridge 68-75; rtd 81; Perm to Offic *Wakef* from 81; Perm to Offic *Sheff* from 82. *12 Park Lane, Balne, Goole, N Humberside DN14 0EP* Tel (01405) 861934

HENDERSON, Euan Russell Milne. b 42. St Steph Ho Ox 75. **d** 80 **p** 81. NSM Hambleden Valley *Ox* 80-83; C Reading All SS 83-84; C Maidenhead St Luke 84-86; NSM Swyncombe w Britwell Salome 87-97; NSM Icknield from 97. *The Old Forge, Stonor, Henley-on-Thames, Oxon RG9 6HE* Tel (01491) 638566

HENDERSON, Francis Colin. b 35. St Cath Coll Cam BA59 MA63. Cuddesdon Coll 60. **d** 62 **p** 63. C Croydon *Cant* 62-67; V Westwood *Cov* 67-75; V Chilvers Coton w Astley 75-80; P-in-c Wolston 80; P-in-c Church Lawford w Newnham Regis 80; V Wolston and Church Lawford 80-85; USA from 85. *1364 Katella Street, Laguna Beach, California 92651, USA* Tel Laguna Beach (714) 497-2239

HENDERSON, Ian Robert. b 29. S'wark Ord Course 64. **d** 67 **p** 69. C Ealing St Pet Mt Park *Lon* 67-72; Hon C N Acton St Gabr 72-74; PC Ealing Ascension Hanger Hill 74-88; P-in-c W Twyford 85-88; V Hanger Hill Ascension and W Twyford St Mary 88-90; rtd 90. *5 Croyde Avenue, Greenford, Middx UB6 9LS* Tel 0181-578 8917

HENDERSON, James. b 22. Chich Th Coll 51. **d** 54 **p** 55. C Burnage St Nic *Man* 54-56; C Prestwich St Mary 56-59; V Waterfoot 59-64; P-in-c Rawtenstall St Jo 61-64; V Bolton St Geo 64-70; V Newhey 70-87; rtd 87; Perm to Offic *Man* from 87. *17 Swift Road, Rochdale, Lancs OL11 5RF* Tel (01706) 522228

HENDERSON, Miss Janet. b 57. St Jo Coll Dur BA88 RGN82. Cranmer Hall Dur 85. **d** 88 **p** 94. Par Dn Wisbech SS Pet and Paul *Ely* 88-90; Par Dn Bestwood *S'well* 90-93; Tutor St Jo Coll Nottm 92-93; Lect St Jo Coll Nottm from 93; NSM Bramcote *S'well* from 94. *St John's College, Chilwell Lane, Beeston, Nottingham NG9 3DS* Tel 0115-925 1114 or 922 8356 Fax 943 6438

HENDERSON, John William. b 13. AKC38. **d** 38 **p** 39. C Welling *Roch* 38-41; C Orpington All SS 41-44; R Hartley 44-58; RD Cobham 56-58; R Cliffe at Hoo w Cooling 58-63; V Wateringbury 63-78; rtd 78. *Cumloden, The Triangle, Somerton, Somerset TA11 6QJ* Tel (01458) 273424

HENDERSON, Judith Ann. b 37. **d** 89 **p** 94. NSM Sheringham *Nor* 89-92; NSM Brampton St Thos *Derby* from 92. *Rose Cottage, Cotton Mill Hill, Chesterfield, Derbyshire S42 7EV* Tel (01246) 569106

HENDERSON, Julian Tudor. b 54. Keble Coll Ox BA76 MA81. Ridley Hall Cam 77. **d** 79 **p** 80. C Islington St Mary *Lon* 79-83; V Hastings Em and St Mary in the Castle *Chich* 83-92; V Claygate *Guildf* from 92; RD Emly from 96. *The Vicarage, Church Road, Claygate, Esher, Surrey KT10 0JP* Tel (01372) 463603

HENDERSON, Nicholas Paul. b 48. Selw Coll Cam BA73 MA77. Ripon Hall Ox 73. **d** 75 **p** 76. C St Alb St Steph *St Alb* 75-78; Warden J F Kennedy Ho Cov Cathl 78-79; C Bow w Bromley St Leon *Lon* 79-85; P-in-c W Acton St Martin 85-96; V from 96; P-in-c Ealing All SS 89-95; V from 96. *25 Birch Grove, London W3 9SP* Tel 0181-248 0608 or 992 2333 Fax 993 5812 E-mail 101607.2025@compuserve.com

HENDERSON, Olive Elizabeth. b 48. **d** 97. Aux Min Tallaght *D & G* from 97. *Tyrellstown, Athy, Co Kildare, Irish Republic* Tel Athy (0507) 31891

HENDERSON, The Very Revd Richard Crosbie Aitken. b 57. Magd Coll Ox MA84 DPhil84. St Jo Coll Nottm 83. **d** 86 **p** 87. C Chinnor w Emmington and Sydenham etc *Ox* 86-89; I Abbeystrewry Union *C, C & R* 89-95; Can Cork and Ross Cathls from 93; I Ross Union from 95; Dean Ross from 95; Preb Cork Cathl from 95. *The Deanery, Rosscarbery, Co Cork, Irish Republic* Tel Cork (23) 48166

HENDERSON, Robert. b 43. TCD 66 Ulster Univ DipG&C87 Lambeth STh94. **d** 69 **p** 70. C Drumglass *Arm* 69-72; Chapl Miss to Seamen 72-78; Kenya 77-78; I Mostrim w Granard, Clonbroney, Killoe etc *K, E & A* 78-82; I Belfast St Matt *Conn* 82-92; RD M Belfast 90-93; I Kilroot and Templecorran from 92. *Kilroot Rectory, 29 Downshire Gardens, Carrickfergus, Co Antrim BT38 7LW* Tel (01960) 362387

HENDERSON, Samuel James Noel. b 16. Hertf Coll Ox BA39 MA42. **d** 42 **p** 43. C Seagoe *D & D* 42-45; C Donaghadee 45-46; P-in-c Clabby *Clogh* 46-47; C Ipswich All Hallows *St E* 47-48; C Heacham *Nor* 48-49; C Ingoldisthorpe 48-49; R E w W Lexham 49-53; R Gt w Lt Dunham 49-53; R Nor St Aug w St Mary 53-56; V Eastbourne Ch Ch *Chich* 56-65; V Hickling *Nor* 65-82; rtd 82; Perm to Offic *Nor* from 82. *96 Church Lane, Beeston Regis, Sheringham, Norfolk NR26 8EY* Tel (01263) 825686

HENDERSON, Mrs Shirley Claire. b 49. Bp Otter Coll 94. **d** 96. NSM Shorwell w Kingston *Portsm* from 96; NSM Gatcombe from 96; NSM Chale from 96. *Squirrels, 12 Calbourne Road, Carisbrooke, Isle of Wight PO30 5AP* Tel (01983) 523586

HENDERSON, Terry James. b 45. Warw Univ Dip Counselling 97. St Deiniol's Hawarden 76. **d** 77 **p** 77. C Wrexham *St As* 77-79; CA Wilson Carlile Coll of Evang 79-81; TV Langtree *Ox* 81-87; P-in-c Aston Cantlow and Wilmcote w Billesley *Cov* 87-90; V 90-97; V St Peter-in-Thanet *Cant* from 97. *14 Vicarage Street, St Peters, Broadstairs, Kent CT10 2SG* Tel (01843) 869169 or 866061

HENDERSON, William Desmond. b 27. TCD BA56 MA64. **d** 56 **p** 57. C Derryloran *Arm* 56-59; C Conwall *D & R* 59-62; I Killoughter *K, E & A* 62-64; I Kilrush *C & O* 64-66; I Tubbercurry w Kilmactigue *T, K & A* 66-75; rtd 75. *8 Kingston College, Mitchelstown, Co Cork, Irish Republic*

HENDERSON, William Ernest (Bill). b 53. CEng81 MICE81 Southn Univ BSc75. St Jo Coll Nottm 87. **d** 89 **p** 90. C Win Ch Ch *Win* 89-93; V Stanley *Wakef* from 93. *The Vicarage, 379 Aberford Road, Stanley, Wakefield, W Yorkshire WF3 4HE* Tel (01924) 822143

HENDERSON, William Ralph. b 32. Oak Hill Th Coll 65. **d** 67 **p** 68. C Littleover *Derby* 67-68; C Nottingham St Sav *S'well* 68-74; V Alne *York* 75-92; Chapl York Distr Hosp 86-92; rtd 92. *15 Drakes Close, Bishop's Manor, Huntington, York YO3 9GN* Tel (01904) 761741

HENDERSON-BEGG, Robert John. b 11. Edin Univ MA32. Westcott Ho Cam 32 Qu Coll Birm 37. **d** 37 **p** 39. C Bradford-on-Avon *Sarum* 37-40; CF (EC) 40-46; Asst Master All Hallows Sch 46-47; RAF (Educn Branch) 47-57; Asst Master Beds LEA 57-76; Perm to Offic and Chapter Clerk Newport Deanery *Ox* from 73; Perm to Offic *St Alb* from 73; rtd 76; Hon C Olney w Emberton *Ox* 81-84. *Stone Cottage, High Street, Carlton, Bedford MK43 7LA* Tel (01234) 720366

HENDEY, Clifford. b 30. K Coll Lon BD53 AKC53. **d** 54 **p** 55. C S Wimbledon All SS *S'wark* 54-58; Trinidad and Tobago 58-71 and 81-82; V Spratton *Pet* 72-77; V Leeds All So *Ripon* 77-80; R Corringham *Linc* 80-81; V Alkham w Capel le Ferne and Hougham *Cant* 82-95; rtd 95. *308 Dover Road, Folkestone, Kent CT19 6NZ*

HENDRICKSE, Canon Clarence David. b 41. CEng MIMechE71 Nottm Univ PGCE73. St Jo Coll Nottm 71. **d** 74 **p** 75. C St Helens St Helen *Liv* 74-76; C Netherley Ch Ch CD 76-77; TV 78-87; V Liv Ch Ch Norris Green 87-93; V Eccleston Ch Ch from 93; Hon Can Liv Cathl from 96. *The Vicarage, Chapel Lane, Eccleston, St Helens, Merseyside WA10 5DA* Tel (01744) 22698 Fax as telephone

HENDRY, Mrs Helen Clare. b 58. Lanc Univ BA79 Cam Univ PGCE80. Reformed Th Sem Mississippi MA85 Oak Hill Th Coll 94. **d** 95. NSM Muswell Hill St Jas w St Matt *Lon* from 95. *7 Byre Road, Chase Side, London N14 4PQ* Tel 0181-441 7805

HENDRY, Leonard John. b 34. Univ of Wales CPT68. St D Coll Lamp DipTh68. **d** 68 **p** 69. C Minchinhampton *Glouc* 68-71; C Bishop's Cleeve 71-74; V Cheltenham St Mich 74-78; V Horsley and Newington Bagpath w Kingscote 78-82; Chapl Salonika *Eur* 82-91; rtd 94. *Sebilles 5, Tsinari, Ano Poli, Salonika 546 33, Greece* Tel Salonika (31) 281193

HENDRY, Philip David. b 48. K Coll Lon BD72 AKC72. St Aug Coll Cant 72. **d** 73 **p** 74. C Benhilton *S'wark* 73-78; TV Catford (Southend) and Downham 78-85; Chapl St Andr Sch Croydon from 85; P-in-c Croydon St Andr *S'wark* 85-86; V from 86. *St Andrew's Vicarage, 6 St Peter's Road, Croydon CR0 1HD* Tel 0181-688 6011 Fax 667 9540

HENDY, Graham Alfred. b 45. St Jo Coll Dur BA67 MA75 Fitzw Coll Cam CertEd. Sarum Th Coll 67. **d** 70 **p** 71. C High Wycombe *Ox* 70-75; TV 75-78; R Upton cum Chalvey 78-83; TR 83-90; R S Walsham and Upton *Nor* from 90; Dioc Lay Tr Officer from 90. *The Rectory, The Street, South Walsham, Norfolk NR13 6DQ* Tel (01603) 270455 Fax 270595

HENEY, William Butler. b 22. CITC. **d** 60 **p** 61. C Seagoe *D & D* 60-63; I Carrickmacross *Clogh* 64-73; I Newbridge w Carnalway and Kilcullen *M & K* 73-96; Treas Kildare Cathl 81-86; Can Kildare Cathl 81-96; Adn Kildare 86-94; rtd 96; Chapl Mageough Home *D & G* from 96. *14 Trees Road, Mount Merrion, Blackrock, Co Dublin, Irish Republic* Tel Dublin (1) 288 9773

HENLEY, Claud Michael. b 31. Keble Coll Ox BA55 MA59. Chich Th Coll 55. **d** 57 **p** 58. C Cowley St Jas *Ox* 57-60; C Wetherby *Ripon* 60-63; C Brighton St Pet *Chich* 63-69; V Brighton St Jo 69-75; V New Groombridge 75-96; rtd 96. *12 Barn Stables, De Montfort Road, Lewes, E Sussex BN7 1ST* Tel (01273) 472467

HENLEY, Canon David Edward. b 44. Sarum & Wells Th Coll 69. **d** 72 **p** 73. C Fareham H Trin *Portsm* 72-76; C-in-c Leigh Park St Clare CD 76-78; R Freshwater 78-87; RD W Wight 83-87; R Meonstoke w Corhampton cum Exton from 87; R Droxford from 87; RD Bishops Waltham from 93; Hon Can Portsm Cathl from 96. *The Rectory, Rectory Lane, Meonstoke, Southampton SO32 3NF* Tel (01489) 877512

HENLEY, Dean. b 64. St Chad's Coll Dur BA93. Westcott Ho Cam CTMin95. **d** 95 **p** 96. C Farncombe *Guildf* from 95. *73 Binscombe Crescent, Farncombe, Godalming, Surrey GU7 3RA* Tel (01483) 428972

HENLEY, John Francis Hugh. b 48. SS Mark & Jo Coll Chelsea CertEd69. St Mich Coll Llan DipTh82. **d** 82 **p** 83. C Griffithstown *Mon* 82-85; V St Hilary Greenway 85-90; P-in-c Fulham St Etheldreda w St Clem *Lon* from 90. *St Etheldreda's Vicarage, Doneraile Street, London SW6 6EL* Tel 0171-736 3809

✠**HENLEY, The Rt Revd Michael Harry George.** b 38. CB91. Lon Coll of Div LTh60. **d** 61 **p** 62 **c** 95. C St Marylebone w H Trin *Lon* 61-64; Chapl RN 64-68 and 74-89; Chapl of the Fleet and Adn for the RN 89-93; Dir Gen Naval Chapl Services 92-93; Chapl St Andr Univ *St And* 68-72; Chapl R Hosp Sch Holbrook 72-74; QHC 89-93; Hon Can Gib Cathl *Eur* 89-93; P-in-c Pitlochry *St And* 94-95; Bp St And from 95. *Afton House, Kennedy Gardens, St Andrews KY16 9DJ* Tel (01334) 473167 or (01738) 443173 Fax (01738) 443174

HENLY, Francis Michael. b 25. Sarum Th Coll. **d** 67 **p** 68. C E w W Harnham *Sarum* 67-70; P-in-c Stour Provost w Todbere 70-75; P-in-c Rowde 75-79; V 79-83; R Poulshot 79-83; V Bishop's Cannings, All Cannings etc 83-92; rtd 92. *Oldbury View, Middle Lane, Cherhill, Calne, Wilts SN11 8XX* Tel (01249) 815191

HENNING, Mrs Judy. b 49. S Dios Minl Tr Scheme 85. **d** 88 **p** 97. C Catherington and Clanfield *Portsm* 88-91; C Leigh Park 91-92; Perm to Offic 94-96; Min in Whiteley and Asst to RD Fareham from 96. *20 Sheridan Gardens, Whiteley, Fareham, Hants PO15 7DY* Tel (01489) 881500

HENRY, The Very Revd Bryan George. b 30. St D Coll Lamp BA51 St Mich Coll Llan 51. **d** 53 **p** 54. C Aberdare St Fagan *Llan* 53-57; C Penarth All SS 57-63; Chapl RAF 63-81; Provost Nicosia and Adn Cyprus 81-90; Prov Sec Jerusalem and Middle E 84-90; Exec Officer Ch in Wales 90-95; rtd 95; Perm to Offic *Llan* from 95. *51 Parcau Avenue, Bridgend CF31 4SZ* Tel (01656) 669489

HENRY, Miss Jacqueline Margaret. b 40. Open Univ BA82. Trin Coll Bris DipHE79. **dss** 83 **d** 87 **p** 94. Deptford St Jo *S'wark* 79-82; Catshill and Dodford *Worc* 83-86; The Lye and Stambermill 86-87; Par Dn 87-89; Educn Chapl 89-93; C Tolleshunt Knights w Tiptree and Gt Braxted *Chelmsf* 94-97; Chapl amongst Deaf People 94-97; TV Stantonbury and Willen *Ox* from 97. *The Cross and Stable Church House, Downs Barn, Milton Keynes MK14 7RZ* Tel (01908) 663346

HENRY, Canon Maurice James Birks. b 14. Dorchester Miss Coll 34. **d** 38 **p** 39. C Wakef St Jo *Wakef* 38-41; C Dewsbury 41-43; C Bredbury St Barn *Ches* 43-47; R Taxal 47-56; R Davenham 56-60; R Rode, Rode Hill and Woolverton *B & W* 60-65; V Chelford w Lower Withington *Ches* 65-81; RD Knutsford 73-80; Hon Can Ches Cathl 76-81; rtd 81; Perm to Offic *Ches* from 81. *Norlands, 56 Holly Tree Road, Plumley, Knutsford, Cheshire WA16 0UJ* Tel (01565) 722721

HENRY, Peter. b 49. BTh. St Jo Coll Nottm. **d** 84 **p** 85. C Sinfin Moor *Derby* 84-89; C Blagreaves St Andr CD 84-89; V Guernsey St Jo *Win* from 89. *St John's Vicarage, Les Amballes, St Peter Port, Guernsey, Channel Islands GY1 1WY* Tel (01481) 720879

HENRY, Stephen Kenelm Malim. b 37. Bps' Coll Cheshunt 60. **d** 62 **p** 63. C Leic St Phil *Leic* 62-67; CF 67-70; V Woodhouse *Wakef* from 70. *Christ Church Vicarage, 79 Woodhouse Hill, Huddersfield HD2 1DH* Tel (01484) 424669

✠**HENSHALL, The Rt Revd Michael.** b 28. St Chad's Coll Dur BA54 DipTh56. **d** 56 **p** 57 **c** 76. C Sewerby w Marton *York* 56-59; C Bridlington Quay H Trin 56-59; C-in-c Micklehurst CD *Ches* 59-62; V Micklehurst 62-63; V Altrincham St Geo 63-76; Hon Can Ches Cathl 72-76; Suff Bp Warrington *Liv* 76-96; rtd 96. *28 Hermitage Way, Sleights, Whitby, N Yorkshire YO22 5HG* Tel (01947) 811233

HENSHALL, Nicholas James. b 62. Wadh Coll Ox BA84 MA88. Ripon Coll Cuddesdon 85. **d** 88 **p** 89. C Blyth St Mary *Newc*

88-92; V Scotswood from 92. *St Margaret's Vicarage, 14 Heighley Street, Newcastle upon Tyne NE15 6AR* Tel 0191-274 6322

HENSHALL, Ronald Keith. b 54. Loughb Coll of Educn CertEd76. Chich Th Coll 87. **d** 89 **p** 90. C Ribbleton *Blackb* 89-92; USPG 92-95; St Kitts-Nevis 92-95; TV Ribbleton *Blackb* from 95. *Ascension House, 450 Watling Street Road, Ribbleton, Preston PR2 6UA* Tel (01772) 700568

HENSHAW, George William. b 21. St Edm Hall Ox BA48 MA48. Qu Coll Birm 48. **d** 49 **p** 50. C Stoke upon Trent *Lich* 49-51; C Wednesbury St Bart 51-54; R Longsight St Jo *Man* 54-63; R Man St Paul New Cross 64-70; rtd 86; Perm to Offic *Man* 86-87. *2A Beauchamp Hill, Leamington Spa, Warks CV32 5LS* Tel (01926) 426173

HENSHAW, Nicholas Newell. b 49. Rhodes Univ BA72. Cuddesdon Coll 73. **d** 75 **p** 76. C Beaconsfield *Ox* 75-78; Chapl Wellington Coll Berks 78-80; C Pimlico St Pet w Westmr Ch Ch *Lon* 80-82; Chapl Sevenoaks Sch from 82; Hon C Sevenoaks St Nic *Roch* from 82. *Orchards, Solefields Road, Sevenoaks, Kent TN13 1PF* Tel (01732) 456710

HENSON, Ms Carolyn. b 44. Solicitor 75 Bedf Coll Lon BA65 Nottm Univ MTh88. EMMTC 82. **dss** 85 **d** 87 **p** 94. Braunstone *Leic* 85-87; Hon Par Dn 87; Par Dn 88; Adult Educn and Tr Officer *Ely* 89-91. *Address temp unknown*

HENSON, John Richard. b 40. Selw Coll Cam BA62 MA66. Ridley Hall Cam 62. **d** 65 **p** 66. C Ollerton *S'well* 65-68; Univs Sec CMS 68-73; Chapl Scargill Ho 73-78; V Shipley St Paul *Bradf* 78-83; TR Shipley St Paul and Frizinghall 83-91; V Ilkeston St Mary *Derby* from 91. *St Mary's Vicarage, Ilkeston, Derbyshire DE7 5JA* Tel 0115-932 4725

HENSON, Dr Richard Clive. b 41. Univ of Wales (Cardiff) BSc63 PhD66. S'wark Ord Course 77. **d** 88 **p** 89. Hon C Lee St Mildred *S'wark* 88-97; Res Min Donington *Lich* from 97. *Donington Rectory, Albrighton, Wolverhampton WV7 3EP* Tel (01702) 372279

HENSTRIDGE, Edward John. b 31. FIPM AFBPsS Ex Coll Ox BA55 MA59. Wells Th Coll 55. **d** 57 **p** 58. C Milton *Portsm* 57-62; V Soberton w Newtown 62-69; Lic to Offic *Derby* 69-71; Perm to Offic *Guildf* 72-84; Lic to Offic from 84; rtd 96. *The White House, Thursley Road, Elstead, Godalming, Surrey GU8 6LW* Tel (01252) 702272 Fax 702747

HENTHORNE, Thomas Roger. b 30. EAMTC. **d** 79 **p** 80. Hd Master St Mary's Sch St Neots 67-93; Hon C St Neots *Ely* from 79. *Stapley, 45 Berkeley Street, Eynesbury, St Neots, Huntingdon, Cambs PE19 2NE* Tel (01480) 472548

HENTON, John Martin. b 48. AKC72 St Luke's Coll Ex DipEd73. St Aug Coll Cant 73. **d** 74 **p** 75. C Woolwich St Mary w H Trin *S'wark* 74-77; C Cotham St Mary *Bris* 77-78; C Cotham St Sav w St Mary 78-80; R Filton 80-87; Chapl Ex Sch 87-91; Chapl St Marg Sch Ex 87-91; V Ex St Dav *Ex* from 91. *St David's Vicarage, 95 Howell Road, Exeter EX4 4LH* Tel (01392) 54396

HENWOOD, Gillian Kathleen (Gill). b 56. ABIPP81. Carl and Blackb Tr Inst 94. **d** 97. NSM Whitechapel w Admarsh-in-Bleasdale *Blackb* from 97. *Woodland Farm, Hothersall Lane, Hothersall, Preston PR2 2XB* Tel (01254) 878419 Fax 878936

HENWOOD, Martin John. b 58. Glas Univ BD81. Ripon Coll Cuddesdon. **d** 85 **p** 86. C Dartford H Trin *Roch* 85-88; C St Martin-in-the-Fields *Lon* 88-93; V Dartford H Trin *Roch* from 93. *The Vicarage, High Street, Dartford DA1 1RX* Tel (01322) 222782

HENWOOD, Canon Peter Richard. b 32. St Edm Hall Ox BA55 MA69. Cuddesdon Coll 56. **d** 57 **p** 58. C Rugby St Andr *Cov* 57-62; C-in-c Gleadless Valley CD *Sheff* 62-71; V Plaistow St Mary *Roch* 71-97; RD Bromley 79-96; Hon Can Roch Cathl 88-97; rtd 97. *Wayside, 1 Highfield Close, Sandling Road, Saltwood, Hythe, Kent CT21 4QP* Tel (01303) 230039

HENWOOD (née OAKLEY), Mrs Susan Mary. b 55. Salford Univ BSc76. St Jo Coll Nottm LTh86 DPS87. **d** 87 **p** 94. Par Dn Armthorpe *Sheff* 87-91; C Howell Hill *Guildf* 91-96. *Address temp unknown*

HEPPER, Christopher Michael Alan. b 55. St Jo Coll Nottm 90. **d** 92 **p** 93. C High Harrogate Ch Ch *Ripon* 92-95; Bp's Dom Chapl from 95. *18 Cathedral Close, Ripon, N Yorkshire HG4 1ND* Tel (01765) 604518 or 602045 Fax 600758

HEPPLE, Gordon. b 32. Edin Th Coll. **d** 63 **p** 68. C Billingham St Cuth *Dur* 63-64; C Ryhope 64; Perm to Offic 66-68; C Wingate Grange 68-69; C Heworth St Mary 69; C Gateshead St Mary 69-71; P-in-c Low Team 71-72; R Lyons 72-79; V Basford St Aid *S'well* 79-84; V Blackhill *Dur* 84-95; rtd 97. *66B Ringwood Road, Christchurch, Dorset BH23 5RE* Tel (01425) 279068

HEPWORTH, Canon Ernest John Peter. b 42. K Coll Lon BD65 AKC65 Hull Univ MA87. **d** 66 **p** 67. C Headingley *Ripon* 66-69; Asst Chapl St Geo Hosp Lon 69-71; C Gt Grimsby St Mary and St Jas *Linc* 71-72; TV 72-74; V Crosby 74-80; V Barton upon Humber from 80; RD Yarborough 86-92; Can and Preb Linc Cathl from 94. *The Vicarage, Beck Hill, Barton-on-Humber, S Humberside DN18 5EY* Tel (01652) 632202

HEPWORTH, Michael David Albert. b 37. Em Coll Cam BA59 MA63 Lon Inst of Educn CertEd60. Ridley Hall Cam 65. **d** 67 **p** 68. C Eastbourne All SS *Chich* 67-69; Asst Chapl Bedford Sch 69-72; Chapl 72-83; Hd Master Birkdale Sch from 83; Perm to Offic *Sheff* from 83; Perm to Offic *Derby* from 84. *Birkdale School, 4 Oakholme Road, Sheffield S10 3DH* Tel 0114-266 8408

HEPWORTH, Michael Edward. b 29. Leeds Univ BA51. NW Ord Course 74. **d** 77 **p** 78. Hon C Timperley *Ches* from 77. *56 Ridgway Road, Timperley, Altrincham, Cheshire WA15 7HD* Tel 0161-980 5104

HERBERT, Alan. b 33. FPhS62 Open Univ BA80. Paton Congr Coll Nottm 54 Coll of Resurr Mirfield 67. **d** 68 **p** 68. C Cockermouth All SS w Ch Ch *Carl* 68-71; V Clifton 71-77; V Westf St Mary 77-87; R Long Marton w Dufton and w Milburn from 87. *The Rectory, Long Marton, Appleby-in-Westmorland, Cumbria CA16 6BN* Tel (017683) 61269

HERBERT, Anthony. b 19. Bris Univ. Qu Coll Birm 46. **d** 48 **p** 49. C Frodingham *Linc* 48-51; C Liv St Bride *Liv* 51-54; Chapl Liv Univ 51-54; C Liv St Sav 54-55; C Stapleton *Bris* 55-58; V Hamer *Man* 58-64; Chapl HM Young Offender Inst Buckley Hall 58-64; V Dur St Cuth *Dur* 64-78; Chapl Low Newton Rem Cen 68-77; V Barrow upon Soar *Leic* 78-83; R Barrow upon Soar w Walton le Wolds 83-84; rtd 84; Perm to Offic *B & W* from 85. *12 Valley View, Clutton, Bristol BS18 4SN* Tel (01761) 452494

HERBERT, Canon Charles Vernon. b 18. St Jo Coll Dur BA42 DipTh43 MA45. **d** 43 **p** 44. C Fazakerley Em *Liv* 43-46; C St Helens St Helen 46-49; V Laisterdyke *Bradf* 49-55; Area Sec (Dios Liv, Man and Ches) CMS 55-61; V Portsdown *Portsm* 61-79; RD Havant 72-77; V Hambledon 79-84; rtd 84; Perm to Offic *Portsm* from 84. *6 Farmhouse Way, Horndean, Waterlooville, Hants PO8 9LF* Tel (01705) 571129

HERBERT, Christopher John. b 37. Dur Univ BA60 DipTh62. Cranmer Hall Dur 60. **d** 62 **p** 63. C Huyton Quarry *Liv* 62-65; C Rainford 65-68; V Impington *Ely* 68-78; RD N Stowe 76-78; V Gt Shelford 78-97; RD Shelford 80-85; rtd 97. *North Place, Crown Street, Great Bardfield, Braintree, Essex CM7 4ST* Tel (01371) 810516

✠**HERBERT, The Rt Revd Christopher William (Chris).** b 44. Univ of Wales (Lamp) BA65. Wells Th Coll 65. **d** 67 **p** 68 **c** 95. C Tupsley *Heref* 67-71; Dioc RE Adv 71-76; Dioc Dir RE 76-81; Preb Heref Cathl 76-81; V Bourne *Guildf* 81-90; Hon Can Guildf Cathl 85-95; Adn Dorking 90-95; Bp St Alb from 95. *Abbey Gate House, 4 Abbey Mill Lane, St Albans, Herts AL3 4HD* Tel (01727) 853305 Fax 846715

HERBERT, Clair Geoffrey Thomas (Geoff). b 36. Tyndale Hall Bris 61. **d** 64 **p** 65. C Nottingham St Sav *S'well* 64-67; C Harwell *Ox* 67-70; C Chilton All SS 67-70; V Bucklebury w Marlston 70-80; Chapl Brighton Coll Jun Sch 80-83; Hon C Upton (Overchurch) *Ches* 85-86; C 86-88; V Collier Row St Jas and Havering-atte-Bower *Chelmsf* from 88. *St James's Vicarage, 24 Lower Bedfords Road, Romford RM1 4DG* Tel (01708) 749891

HERBERT, Clare Marguerite. b 54. Bris Univ CASS85 St Hild Coll Dur BA76 New Coll Edin MTh78. Linc Th Coll 79. **d** 87 **p** 94. Hon Par Dn Bris St Mary Redcliffe w Temple etc *Bris* 87-90; Dioc Past Care Adv *Lon* 92-95; Hon C Clapham TM *S'wark* 94-96; C St Martin-in-the-Fields *Lon* from 96. *6 St Martins Place, London WC2N 4JJ* Tel 0171-930 1646

HERBERT, Canon David Alexander Sellars. b 39. Bris Univ BA60. St Steph Ho Ox 65. **d** 67 **p** 68. C St Leonards Ch Ch *Chich* 67-80; C St Leonards Ch Ch and St Mary 81; V Bickley *Roch* from 81; Hon Can Roch Cathl from 92. *The Vicarage, Bickley Park Road, Bromley BR1 2BE* Tel 0181-467 3809

HERBERT, David Roy. b 51. K Coll Lon BD73 AKC73. **d** 74 **p** 75. C Sheff St Aid w St Luke *Sheff* 74-76; C Sheff Manor 76-78; TV Gleadless Valley 78-83; TV Ellesmere Port *Ches* 83-93; V Tarvin from 93. *St Andrew's Vicarage, Tarvin, Chester CH3 8EB* Tel (01829) 740354

HERBERT, Geoffrey William. b 38. Ox Univ MA62 Birm Univ PhD72. Qu Coll Birm DipTh82. **d** 82 **p** 83. C Hall Green Ascension *Birm* 82-85; R Sheldon 85-95; rtd 95; Perm to Offic *Birm* from 95. *28 Lulworth Road, Birmingham B28 8NS*

HERBERT, Graham Paul. b 54. Birm Univ BA75. Wycliffe Hall Ox BA80 MA. **d** 81 **p** 82. C Crowborough *Chich* 81-85; Chapl Monkton Combe Sch Bath from 85. *Croft House, The Croft, Monkton Combe, Bath BA2 7HG* Tel (01225) 721127

HERBERT, Jonathan Patrick. b 62. Bris Univ BA86. Linc Th Coll 86. **d** 88 **p** 89. C Kirkby *Liv* 88-91; TV Blakenall Heath *Lich* 91-96; Pilsdon Community from 96. *Pilsdon Manor, Pilsdon, Bridport, Dorset DT6 5NZ* Tel (01308) 868308

HERBERT, Kenneth Cyril. b 20. Univ of Wales (Abth) BA41. St D Coll Lamp LTh43. **d** 43 **p** 44. C Carmarthen St Pet *St D* 43-56; V Llangorwen 56-89; RD Llanbadarn Fawr 80-86; rtd 89. *68 Ger-y-llan, Penrhyncoch, Aberystwyth SY23 3DW* Tel (01970) 828207

HERBERT, Malcolm Francis. b 53. K Coll Lon BD74 AKC74 St Mary's Coll Cheltenham CertEd75. Trin Coll Bris 76. **d** 77 **p** 78. C Wotton-under-Edge w Ozleworth *Glouc* 77; C Wotton-under-Edge w Ozleworth and N Nibley 77-79; C Milton *B & W* 79-80; C Worle 80-85; V Woking Ch Ch *Guildf* from 86; RD Woking from 94. *Christ Church Vicarage, 10 Russetts Close, Woking, Surrey GU21 4BH* Tel (01483) 762100

HERBERT, Michael. b 35. Nottm Univ BA57. St D Coll Lamp 59. **d** 61 **p** 62. C Paston *Pet* 61-65; C Northampton All SS w St Kath

65-67; R Sutton w Upton 67-72; Asst Youth Chapl 67-72; Ind Chapl 72-84; P-in-c Pitsford 79-84; Ind Chapl Worc from 84; TV Redditch, The Ridge from 84; Chapl NE Worcs Coll from 86. *The Parsonage, Church Road, Webheath, Redditch, Worcs B97 5PD* Tel (01527) 402404

HERBERT, Ronald (Ron). b 53. Worc Coll Ox BA75 MA80 Lon Univ BD78 W Kentucky Univ MA79. Oak Hill Th Coll 75. **d** 79 **p** 80. C Welling Roch 79-89; V Falconwood 89-90; V Becontree St Mary Chelmsf from 90. *The Vicarage, 191 Valence Wood Road, Dagenham, Essex RM8 3AH* Tel 0181-592 2822

HERBERT, Mrs Rosemary. b 44. Westf Coll Lon BSc65. Qu Coll Birm 81. **dss** 85 **d** 87. Malvern Link w Cowleigh Worc 85-87; Hon Par Dn from 87. *4 Cedar Avenue, Malvern, Worcs WR14 2SG* Tel (01684) 572497

HERBERT, Timothy David (Tim). b 57. Man Univ BA78 MPhil88. Ridley Hall Cam 79. **d** 81 **p** 82. C Macclesfield St Mich Ches 81-85; V Wharton 85-93; Asst Continuing Minl Educn Officer 90-93; P-in-c Thanington Cant from 93; Dir of Ords from 93. *The Vicarage, 70 Thanington Road, Canterbury, Kent CT1 3XE* Tel (01227) 464516 or 785894 Fax 785894

✠**HERD, The Rt Revd William Brian.** b 31. Clifton Th Coll 55. **d** 58 **p** 59 **c** 76. C Wolverhampton St Luke Lich 58-61; Uganda 61-77; Adn Karamoja 70-75; Bp Karamoja 76-77; Deputation Sec (Ireland) BCMS 77-89; C Harrow Trin St Mich Lon 89-93; V Gresley Derby from 93. *The Vicarage, 120 Church Street, Church Gresley, Swadlincote, Derbyshire DE11 9NR* Tel (01283) 223983

HEREFORD, Archdeacon of. *See* HOOPER, The Ven Michael Wrenford

HEREFORD, Bishop of. *See* OLIVER, The Rt Revd John Keith

HEREFORD, Dean of. *See* WILLIS, The Very Revd Robert Andrew

HEREWARD, Dr John Owen. b 53. FRCSE82 Lon Univ MB, BS77. Ridley Hall Cam 89. **d** 91 **p** 92. C W Ealing St Jo w St Jas Lon 91-95; P-in-c Hanwell St Mellitus w St Mark from 95. *St Mellitus Vicarage, Church Road, London W7 3BA* Tel 0181-567 6535

HERITAGE, Barry. b 35. Clifton Th Coll 59. **d** 61 **p** 62. C Wolverhampton St Jude Lich 61-65; C Chaddesden St Mary Derby 65-67; V Kidsgrove Lich 67-76; NE Area Sec CPAS 76-89; Perm to Offic Newc 76-89; Lic to Offic York 76-89; V Elloughton and Brough w Brantingham 89-93; C York St Paul from 93. *123 Hamilton Drive, York YO2 4NX* Tel (01904) 785135

HERKLOTS, Canon John Radu. b 31. Trin Hall Cam BA53 MA61. Westcott Ho Cam 54. **d** 55 **p** 56. C Attercliffe w Carbrook Sheff 55-60; C Stoke Damerel Ex 60-65; V Devonport St Bart 65-72; V Denmead Portsm 72-97; RD Havant 82-87; Hon Can Portsm Cathl 86-97; rtd 97. *Stead Cottage, 37 Church Street, Church Stretton, Shropshire SY6 6DO* Tel (01694) 724663

HERNIMAN, The Ven Ronald George. b 23. Birkb Coll Lon BA51. Oak Hill Th Coll. **d** 54 **p** 55. C Enfield Ch Ch Trent Park Lon 54-56; Tutor Oak Hill Th Coll 54-61; R Washfield Ex 61-72; P-in-c Withleigh 61-72; P-in-c Calverleigh 61-72; R Stoodleigh 62-72; P-in-c Oakford 63-72; P-in-c Morebath 63-72; P-in-c Rackenford 65-72; P-in-c Templeton w Loxbeare 66-72; Adn Barnstaple 70-88; R Shirwell w Loxhore 72-82; rtd 89; Perm to Offic B & W from 89; Perm to Offic Ex from 89. *Castleland House, Oakford, Tiverton, Devon EX16 9JA*

HERON, Alexander Francis. b 28. Univ of BC BA60. Angl Th Coll (BC) LTh53. **d** 52 **p** 53. C Bush Hill Park St Mark Lon 52-53; C Beckenham St Barn Roch 54-55; Canada 55-62 and from 77; Chapl RAF 62-77. *address temp unknown*

HERON, David George. b 49. AKC72. **d** 73 **p** 74. C Stockton St Chad Dur 73-77; C Beamish 77-81; R Willington and Sunnybrow 81-95; V Dipton and Leadgate from 95. *The Vicarage, St Ives Road, Leadgate, Consett, Co Durham DH8 7SN* Tel (01207) 503918

HERON, George Dobson. b 34. TD. Cranmer Hall Dur 58. **d** 61 **p** 62. C Benfieldside Dur 61-65; C Winlaton 65-68; V Dunston St Nic 68-77; P-in-c Dunston Ch Ch 74-77; V Dunston 77-82; V Gateshead St Helen 82-89; rtd 94; Perm to Offic Dur from 94. *36 Woodlands Road, Shotley Bridge, Consett, Co Durham DH8 0DE* Tel (01207) 507733

HERON, Nicholas Peter. b 60. Man Univ BA81 Southn Univ BTh86. Sarum & Wells Th Coll. **d** 84 **p** 85. C Brinnington w Portwood Ches 84-87; Chapl RAF from 87. *Chaplaincy Services (RAF), HQ, Personnel and Training Command, RAF Innsworth, Gloucester GL3 1EZ* Tel (01452) 712612 ext 5164 Fax 510828

HERON, Raymond (Ray). b 48. Cranmer Hall Dur St Jo Coll Dur CTM94. **d** 94 **p** 95. C Newc H Cross Newc from 94. *2A Lanercost Drive, Newcastle upon Tyne NE5 2DE* Tel 0191-274 9574

HERRICK, Andrew Frederick. b 58. Univ of Wales (Lamp) BA80. Wycliffe Hall Ox 80. **d** 82 **p** 83. C Aberystwyth St D 82-85; P-in-c Llangeitho and Blaenpennal w Betws Leucu etc 85-86; R 86-88; Youth Chapl 86-88; R Aberporth w Tremain and Blaenporth 88-91; Succ St D Cathl 91-94; Min St D Cathl 91-94; V Betws w Ammanford from 94. *The Vicarage, College Street, Ammanford SA18 3AB* Tel (01269) 592084

HERRICK, David William. b 52. Middx Poly BSc73. St Jo Coll Nottm DipTh80. **d** 82 **p** 83. C Ipswich St Matt St E 82-85; C Nor St Pet Mancroft w St Jo Maddermarket Nor 85-88; V Bury St Edmunds St Geo St E 88-96; P-in-c Gt Barton from 96. *The Vicarage, Church Road, Great Barton, Bury St Edmunds, Suffolk IP31 2QR* Tel (01284) 787274

HERRICK (NEE RENAUT), Mrs Vanessa Anne. b 58. York Univ BA80 LTCL75. St Jo Coll Nottm 80 Ridley Hall Cam MA94. **d** 96 **p** 97. C St E Cathl Distr St E from 96. *The Vicarage, Church Road, Great Barton, Bury St Edmunds, Suffolk IP31 2QR* Tel (01284) 787274

HERRINGTON, Wilfrid Spencer. b 17. Chich Th Coll 72. **d** 72 **p** 72. C Bedhampton Portsm 72-77; P-in-c Holton St Mary w Gt Wenham St E 77-86; P-in-c Raydon 77-86; rtd 86; Perm to Offic Chich from 86. *1 Roffrey Avenue, Eastbourne, E Sussex BN22 0AE* Tel (01323) 503212

HERROD, Mrs Kathryn. b 59. Warw Univ BSc80 Matlock Coll of Educn PGCE81. St Jo Coll Nottm MA97. **d** 97. C Wollaton S'well from 97. *4 Woodbank Drive, Wollaton, Nottingham NG8 2QU* Tel 0115-928 2779

HERRON, Robert Gordon John. b 36. MIPM75. Wycliffe Hall Ox 65. **d** 77 **p** 78. C Ditton St Mich Liv 77-80; C W Kirby St Bridget Ches 80-82; R Gorton Our Lady and St Thos Man from 82. *Our Lady and St Thomas Rectory, 195B Mount Road, Gorton, Manchester M18 7GG* Tel 0161-223 0421

HERSCHEL, Richard J. b 27. **d** 57 **p** 57. USA 57-81 and from 84; TV Cannock Lich 82-84; rtd 92. *99 Bayview Road, Chesapeake City, Maryland 21915, USA*

HERTFORD, Archdeacon of. *See* JONES, The Ven Trevor Pryce

HERTFORD, Suffragan Bishop of. *See* SMITH, The Rt Revd Robin Jonathan Norman

HERVE, John Anthony. b 49. TD94. Open Univ BA81 Birm Univ DPS85 Wolv Univ PGCE95. Lich Th Coll 70. **d** 73 **p** 74. C Middlesbrough All SS York 73-76; CF 76-81; P-in-c Handsworth St Andr Birm 81-86; Hon C Cowley St Jo Ox 86-90; Tutor St Steph Ho Ox 86-90; V Sparkbrook St Agatha w Balsall Heath St Barn Birm from 90. *The Clergy House, 288A Ladypool Road, Birmingham B12 8JU* Tel 0121-449 2790

HERVEY, Mary Diana (Di). b 41. St Hugh's Coll Ox BA63. St And Dioc Tr Course 83. **d** 92 **p** 94. Par Dn Cupar St And from 92; Asst Chapl St Andr Univ from 94. *Lynwood, Back Lebanon, Cupar, Fife KY15 4JW* Tel (01334) 652760

HERYET, Dudley. b 18. AKC42. **d** 42 **p** 43. C Southampton St Alb Win 42-45; C Finsbury Park St Thos Lon 45-48; C Hackney Wick St Mary of Eton w St Aug 48-50; C St Geo-in-the-East St Mary 50-53; V 53-58; V Edmonton St Mich 58-62; V Blean Cant 62-73; V Kennington 73-83; rtd 83; Perm to Offic Cant from 83. *27 Homespire House, Knotts Lane, Canterbury CT1 2AB* Tel (01227) 451511

HESELTINE, Mrs Barbara Joan. b 42. Keele Univ BA65. S'wark Ord Course 85. **d** 88 **p** 94. NSM Addington S'wark from 88. *Little Manor, Manor Park, The Avenue, Whyteleafe, Surrey CR3 0AQ* Tel 0181-668 0476

HESELWOOD, Eric Harold. b 43. Oak Hill Th Coll 84. **d** 86 **p** 87. C Farnborough Roch 86-88; V Biggin Hill 88-96; V Orpington All SS from 96. *The Vicarage, 1A Keswick Road, Orpington, Kent BR6 0EU* Tel (01689) 824624

HESELWOOD, Mrs Hilda. b 39. CA Tr Coll 61. **dss** 85 **d** 87 **p** 94. Bromley Common St Luke Roch 85-87; Par Dn 87-94; Par Dn 94; C from 94. *The Vicarage, 1A Keswick Road, Orpington, Kent BR6 0EU* Tel (01689) 824624

HESKETH, Canon Douglas Campbell. b 09. St Pet Hall Ox BA37 MA44. Wycliffe Hall Ox 37. **d** 38 **p** 39. C Fazakerley Em Liv 38-42; P-in-c Liv St Mich 42-44; V Halifax St Aug Wakef 44-53; V Mossley Hill St Barn Liv 53-75; RD Childwall 69-75; Hon Can Liv Cathl 73-75; rtd 75; Hon C Southport All SS Liv 75-88; Perm to Offic from 88. *52 Skipton Avenue, Southport, Merseyside PR9 8JP* Tel (01704) 29584

HESKETH, Dr Philip John. b 64. K Coll Lon BD86 AKC86 PhD94 Richmond Fellowship Coll DipHRel90. Ripon Coll Cuddesdon DipMin94. **d** 94 **p** 95. C Bearsted w Thurnham Cant from 94. *19 Fulbert Drive, Bearsted, Maidstone, Kent ME14 4PU* Tel (01622) 631192

HESKETH, Robin Adams Lempriere. b 18. St Cath Soc Ox BA43 MA47. St Steph Ho Ox 43. **d** 45 **p** 46. C Babbacombe Ex 45-48; Perm to Offic 48-51; C Dawlish 51-55; C Brixham 55-61; V S Petherwin w Trewen Truro 61-72; V Lewannick 62-71; P-in-c Penponds 72-73; V 73-83; rtd 84; Perm to Offic Truro from 84. *Camelview, Marshall Road, Nanstallon, Bodmin, Cornwall PL30 5LD* Tel (01208) 831892

HESKETH, Ronald David. b 47. Bede Coll Dur BA68. St Mich Coll Llan 69 Ridley Hall Cam. **d** 71 **p** 72. C Southport H Trin Liv 71-74; Asst Chapl Miss to Seamen 74-75; Chapl RAF from 75. *Chaplaincy Services (RAF), HQ, Personnel and Training Command, RAF Innsworth, Gloucester GL3 1EZ* Tel (01452) 712612 ext 5164 Fax 510828

HESKINS, Mrs Georgiana Mary. b 48. K Coll Lon BD81 AKC81 MTh93. Westcott Ho Cam 81. **dss** 83 **d** 87 **p** 94. Cobbold Road St Sav w St Mary Lon 83-85; St Botolph Aldgate w H Trin Minories 85-87; Par Dn 87; Perm to Offic S'wark 88-93; Par Dn Kidbrooke 93-95; Tutor S'wark Ord Course 93-94; Tutor SEITE from 94; PV S'wark Cathl S'wark from 95. *185 Charlton Church Lane, London, SE7 7AA, or SEITE, 27 Blackfriars Road, London SE1 8NY* Tel 0181-305 1297 or 0171-928 4793 Fax 0181-305 1297

HESKINS, Jeffrey George. b 55. AKC78 Heythrop Coll Lon MA94. Chich Th Coll 80. **d** 81 **p** 82. C Primrose Hill St Mary w Avenue Road St Paul *Lon* 81-85; Enfield Deanery Youth Officer 85-88; C Enfield Chase St Mary 85-88; TV Kidbrooke *S'wark* 88-95; R Charlton St Luke w H Trin from 95. *The Rectory, 185 Charlton Church Lane, London SE7 7AA* Tel 0181-858 0791 Fax 305 1297

HESLOP, David Anthony. b 45. BSc DipEd DipTh MTh. St Jo Coll Nottm 81. **d** 83 **p** 84. C Willenhall H Trin *Lich* 83-86; V Gresley *Derby* 86-92; V Marston on Dove w Scropton 92-95; Chapl Derby Univ from 95. *The Vicarage, Hazelwood, Duffield, Belper, Derbyshire DE56 4AL* Tel (01332) 840161 E-mail daheslop@derby.ac.uk

HESLOP, Harold William. b 40. Leeds Univ BA62 Open Univ BA72. Ox NSM Course. **d** 78 **p** 79. NSM Stoke Mandeville *Ox* 78-91; NSM Wendover from 82; NSM Ellesborough, The Kimbles and Stoke Mandeville from 91. *7 Chiltern Road, Wendover, Aylesbury, Bucks HP22 6DB* Tel (01296) 624812

HESLOP, James Alan. b 37. Codrington Coll Barbados 61. **d** 64 **p** 65. Br Guiana 64-66; Guyana 66-68; Bahamas 68-72; C Haxby w Wigginton *York* 72-74; TV 74-76; V York St Olave w St Giles 76-87; V Northampton All SS w St Kath *Pet* 87-88; R Felpham w Middleton *Chich* 88-92; TR Howden TM *York* 92-94; Warden Coll of St Barn Lingfield from 94. *The Lodge, College of St Barnabas, Blackberry Lane, Lingfield, Surrey RH7 6NJ* Tel (01342) 870366 or 870260

HESLOP, Michael Andrew. b 47. Trin Coll Bris 73. **d** 76 **p** 77. C Burmantofts St Steph and St Agnes *Ripon* 76-80; V Thorpe Edge *Bradf* 80-87; TV Penrith w Newton Reigny and Plumpton Wall *Carl* 87-91; V Silloth from 91. *The Vicarage, Wigton Road, Silloth, Carlisle CA5 4NJ* Tel (016973) 31413

HESS, John Peter. b 22. Bp Gray Coll Cape Town 59. **d** 62 **p** 63. C Alverstoke *Portsm* 74-76; C-in-c Gurnard All SS CD 76-78; S Africa from 78; rtd 87. *4 Westlee, 21 Morton Road, Plumstead, 7800 South Africa*

HESS, Paul Austin. b 67. Cape Town Univ BA89. St Bede's Coll Umtata DipTh92. **d** 93 **p** 93. S Africa 92-94; NSM Eythorne and Elvington w Waldershare etc *Cant* 95-96; C Storrington *Chich* from 96. *9 Longland Avenue, Storrington, Pulborough, W Sussex RH20 4HY* Tel (01903) 741272

HESSELGREAVES, Canon Arthur. b 16. Univ Coll Dur BA38 DipTh40 MA41. Qu Coll Birm 39. **d** 40 **p** 41. C Ossett cum Gawthorpe *Wakef* 40-45; C Knottingley 45-49; V Purlwell 49-65; R Cumberworth 65-80; RD Kirkburton 71-80; Hon Can Wakef Cathl 74-81; rtd 81; Perm to Offic *Wakef* from 81. *1 Park Avenue, Thornes, Wakefield, W Yorkshire WF2 8DS* Tel (01924) 381104

HESTER, Canon John Frear. b 27. St Edm Hall Ox BA48 MA52. Cuddesdon Coll 51. **d** 52 **p** 53. C Southall St Geo *Lon* 52-55; C Clerkenwell H Redeemer w St Phil 55-58; Sec Actors' Ch Union 58-63; Sen Chapl 70-75; Chapl Soc of Sisters of Bethany Lloyd Square 59-62; Dep Min Can St Paul's Cathl 62-75; R Soho St Anne w St Thos and St Pet 63-75; P-in-c Covent Garden St Paul 69-75; P-in-c Brighton St Jo *Chich* 75-80; V Brighton St Pet 75-78; Can and Preb Chich Cathl 76-85; Can Res and Prec Chich Cathl 85-97; RD Brighton 76-85; RD Kemp Town 76-83; RD Preston 76-83; P-in-c Brighton Chpl Royal 77-78; V Brighton St Pet w Chpl Royal 78-80; V Brighton St Pet w Chpl Royal and St Jo 80-85; P-in-c Brighton St Nic 84-85; Chapl to The Queen 84-97; rtd 97; Perm to Offic *Chich* from 97. *The Hovel, Church Lane, Oving, Chichester, W Sussex PO20 6DE* Tel (01243) 782071

HETHERINGTON, Andrew. b 50. Sheff Univ BSc71. Wycliffe Hall Ox 71. **d** 74 **p** 75. C Leic H Trin w St Jo *Leic* 74-78; C Leic H Apostles 78-82; V Bootle St Mary w St Paul *Liv* 82-93; TR W Swindon and the Lydiards *Bris* from 93. *The Rectory, Old Shaw Lane, Shaw, Swindon SN5 9PH* Tel (01793) 770568

HETHERINGTON, Dermot Hugh. b 42. SRN63 RMN65 RM72 Worc Coll of Educn BSc. **d** 78 **p** 79. Hon C Raveningham *Nor* 78-90; Perm to Offic from 90. *1 Whiteways, Wheatacre, Beccles, Suffolk NR34 0AU* Tel (01502) 77467

HETHERINGTON, Mrs Glynis Catherine. b 48. EMMTC CTPS93. **d** 93 **p** 94. NSM E and W Leake, Stanford-on-Soar, Rempstone etc *S'well* from 93. *20 Potters Lane, East Leake, Loughborough, Leics LE12 6NQ* Tel (01509) 853344

HETHERINGTON, John Carl. b 52. Linc Th Coll. **d** 84 **p** 85. C Crosby *Linc* 84-88; TV Cleethorpes 88-93; Chapl RAF from 93. *Chaplaincy Services (RAF), HQ, Personnel and Training Command, RAF Innsworth, Gloucester GL3 1EZ* Tel (01452) 712612 ext 5164 Fax 510828

HETLING, William Maurice (Bill). b 37. AKC61. **d** 62 **p** 63. C Eltham St Barn *S'wark* 62-66; C Horley 66-71; Jamaica 71-75; C-in-c Farnham Royal S CD *Ox* 75-78; TV W Slough 78-80 and 88-91; TR 80-88; TV Parkstone St Pet w Branksea and St Osmund *Sarum* 91-96; P-in-c Reading St Barn *Ox* from 96. *St Barnabas' Rectory, 14 Elm Road, Reading RG6 5TS* Tel 0118-987 1718

HEWAT, Patrick Duxbury. b 13. CCC Cam BA35 MA55. K Coll Lon 48. **d** 49 **p** 50. C Nuneaton St Mary *Cov* 49-51; V Binley 51-55; V Grantchester *Ely* 55-70; Perm to Offic from 70; rtd 78. *19 High Street, Bassingbourn, Royston, Herts SG8 5NE* Tel (01763) 247611

HEWER, Sidney Eric. b 24. Nor Ord Course. **d** 78 **p** 79. NSM Grimston w Congham *Nor* 78-91; NSM Grimston, Congham and Roydon 91-92; Perm to Offic from 92. *42 Vong Lane, Pott Row, Grimston, King's Lynn, Norfolk PE32 1BW* Tel (01485) 600635

HEWES, John. b 29. Nottm Univ BA50. Chich Th Coll 79. **d** 81 **p** 82. C Buckland in Dover w Buckland Valley *Cant* 81-84; P-in-c Elmsted w Hastingleigh 84-89; P-in-c Crundale w Godmersham 84-89; RD W Bridge 88-89; R Lydd 89-95; RD S Lympne 89-95; rtd 95; Perm to Offic *Cant* from 95. *Brambledown, Tamley Lane, Hastingleigh, Ashford, Kent TN25 5HW* Tel (01233) 750214

HEWETSON, The Ven Christopher. b 37. Trin Coll Ox BA60 MA64. Chich Th Coll 67. **d** 69 **p** 70. C Leckhampton St Pet *Glouc* 69-71; C Wokingham All SS *Ox* 71-73; V Didcot St Pet 73-82; R Ascot Heath 82-90; RD Bracknell 86-90; P-in-c Headington Quarry 90-94; Hon Can Ch Ch 92-94; RD Cowley 94; Adn Ches from 94. *8 Queen's Park Road, Chester CH4 7AD* Tel (01244) 675417

HEWETSON, David Geoffrey. b 31. S'wark Ord Course 71. **d** 74 **p** 75. NSM Brighton St Mich *Chich* from 74. *Flat 1, 166 Dyke Road, Brighton BN1 5PU* Tel (01273) 564483

HEWETSON, Robin Jervis. b 39. AKC63. **d** 64 **p** 65. C Thorpe *Nor* 64-67; C E Dereham w Hoe 67-69; TV Mattishall w Mattishall Burgh 69-72; R Ingham w Sutton 72-78; R Catfield 75-78; R Taverham w Ringland 78-89; P-in-c Marsham 89-92; P-in-c Burgh 89-92; Dioc Ecum Officer from 89; Exec Officer Norfolk Ecum Coun from 89; R Marsham w Burgh-next-Aylsham from 92. *The Rectory, Marsham, Norwich NR10 5PP* Tel (01263) 733249 Fax 733799

HEWETSON, Valerie Patricia. b 44. St Mary's Coll Dur BSc66 MSc70 Leeds Univ MA75. Linc Th Coll 89. **d** 91 **p** 94. C Kingston upon Hull St Nic *York* 91-94; R Barmby Moor w Allerthorpe, Fangfoss and Yapham from 94. *The Vicarage, Barmby Moor, York YO4 5HF* Tel (01759) 305971

HEWETT, Andrew David. b 63. Univ of Wales (Lamp) BA. Chich Th Coll 84. **d** 86 **p** 87. C Caldicot *Mon* 86-90; Chapl RAF from 90. *Chaplaincy Services (RAF), HQ, Personnel and Training Command, RAF Innsworth, Gloucester GL3 1EZ* Tel (01452) 712612 ext 5164 Fax 510828

HEWETT, Maurice Gordon. b 28. Lon Univ BA53. Oak Hill Th Coll 49. **d** 54 **p** 55. C Gipsy Hill Ch Ch *S'wark* 54-57; C Maidstone St Faith *Cant* 57-60; R Chevening *Roch* 60-95; rtd 95; Perm to Offic *Roch* from 95. *Rosings, 12 The Thicketts, Sevenoaks, Kent TN13 2SZ* Tel (01732) 464734

HEWETT, Roger Leroy. b 45. St Mich Coll Llan DPT95. **d** 95 **p** 96. C Whitchurch *Llan* from 95. *10 Keynsham Road, Whitchurch, Cardiff CF4 1TS* Tel (01222) 611388

HEWISON, Alan Stuart. b 30. SS Mark & Jo Coll Plymouth BEd82. K Coll Lon. **d** 57 **p** 58. C S Mymms K Chas *Lon* 57-60; C Bourne *Guildf* 60-63; Chapl RN 63-79; Perm to Offic *Ex* from 79; rtd 95. *8 Hazelwood Crescent, Plymouth PL9 8BL*

HEWITSON, Denise Ann. b 52. Liv Univ BEd74. St Jo Coll Nottm MA97. **d** 97. C Bootle St Matt *Liv* from 97. *25 Leicester Road, Bootle, Merseyside L20 9BP* Tel 0151-922 5641

HEWITT, Charles David. b 38. Or Coll Ox BA60 MA63. Clifton Th Coll 63. **d** 66 **p** 67. C Southport SS Simon and Jude *Liv* 66-70; C Bethnal Green St Jas Less w Victoria Park *Lon* 70-76; Hon C Old Ford St Paul w St Steph 76-82; Ldr Bridge Ho Chr Cen Shaftesbury Soc 76-90; Hon C Old Ford St Paul w St Steph and St Mark 82-90; V Homerton St Luke from 90. *St Luke's Vicarage, 23 Cassland Road, London E9 7AL* Tel 0181-985 2263

HEWITT, Colin Edward. b 52. Man Poly BA80 Em Coll Cam BA82 MA86. Westcott Ho Cam 80. **d** 83 **p** 84. C Radcliffe St Thos and St Jo *Man* 83-84; C Langley and Parkfield 84-86; R Byfield w Boddington *Pet* 86-89; R Byfield w Boddington and Aston le Walls 89-91; Chapl RAF from 91. *Chaplaincy Services (RAF), HQ, Personnel and Training Command, RAF Innsworth, Gloucester GL3 1EZ* Tel (01452) 712612 ext 5164 Fax 510828

HEWITT, David Warner. b 33. Selw Coll Cam BA56 MA60. Wells Th Coll 57. **d** 59 **p** 60. C Longbridge *Birm* 59-61; C Sheldon 61-64; V Smethwick Old Ch 64-70; V Smethwick 70-78; P-in-c Littlehampton St Jas *Chich* 78-85; P-in-c Wick 78-85; V Littlehampton St Mary 78-85; TR Littlehampton and Wick 86-89; Perm to Offic *Eur* from 95. *Kleious 21A, 54 633 Thessaloniki, Greece*

HEWITT, Canon Francis John Adam. b 42. St Chad's Coll Dur BA64 DipTh66. **d** 66 **p** 67. C Dewsbury Moor *Wakef* 66-69; C Huddersfield St Jo 69-73; V King Cross 73-81; V Lastingham *York* 81; P-in-c Appleton-le-Moors 81; V Lastingham w Appleton-le-Moors 81-84; P-in-c Rosedale 83-84; V Lastingham w Appleton-le-Moors and Rosedale 84-86; RD Helmsley 85-94; V Lastingham w Appleton-le-Moors, Rosedale etc 86-94; V Pickering 94-95; V Pickering w Lockton and Levisham from 95; RD Pickering from 94; Can and Preb York Minster from 97. *The Vicarage, Whitby Road, Pickering, N Yorkshire YO18 7HD* Tel (01751) 472983

HEWITT, Garth Bruce. b 46. St Jo Coll Dur BA68. Lon Coll of Div LTh70. **d** 70 **p** 71. C Maidstone St Luke *Cant* 70-73; Staff Evang CPAS 73-79; Hon C W Ealing St Jo w St Jas *Lon* 73-81; Dir Amos Trust 88-96; Regional Co-ord (Lon and SE) Chr Aid from 96. *Christian Aid, 35 Lower Marsh, London SE1 7RL* Tel 0171-620 4444 Fax 620 0719 E-mail caid@gn.apc.org

HEWITT, Geoffrey Williams. b 48. Leeds Univ BA69. Wells Th Coll 70. **d** 72 **p** 73. C Heywood St Luke *Man* 72-74; Ind Chapl 74-77; P-in-c Hulme St Geo 74-77; V Mamhilad and Llanfihangel Pontymoile *Mon* 77-80; Ind Chapl 77-80; V Arthog w Fairbourne *Ban* 80-89; R Llangelynnin w Rhoslefain 87-89; TV Ban 89-94; Dioc Dir of Soc Resp from 89; P-in-c Pentir from 94. *Pentir Vicarage, Pentir, Bangor LL57 4YB* Tel (01248) 354244 Fax 353360

HEWITT, Canon George Henry Gordon. b 12. BNC Ox BA34 DipTh35 MA38. Wycliffe Hall Ox 34. **d** 36 **p** 37. C Sheepscar *Ripon* 36-39; Chapl Ridley Hall Cam 39-41; C Leeds St Pet *Ripon* 41-42; P-in-c Leeds Em 42-43; P-in-c Leeds H Trin 42-43; Educn Sec United Soc for Chr Lit 43-52; Lect Hart Street St Olave *Lon* 44-52; Educn Sec and Bp's Chapl *Sheff* 52-58; Can Res Sheff Cathl 53-58; V Ox St Andr *Ox* 58-64; Can Res Chelmsf Cathl *Chelmsf* 64-78; Chapl to The Queen 69-82; rtd 78. *Ellesborough Manor, Butlers Cross, Aylesbury, Bucks HP17 0XF* Tel (01296) 696001

HEWITT, Harold William. b 12. Fitzw Ho Cam BA35 MA39. Wycliffe Hall Ox 36. **d** 38 **p** 39. C Westhoughton *Man* 38-40; C Kersal Moor 40-43; V Oldham St Paul 43-52; R Droylsden St Mary 52-66; V Gt Bowden w Welham *Leic* 66-77; rtd 77; Perm to Offic *Ches* from 77. *20 Rectory Close, Bowling Green Court, Nantwich, Cheshire CW5 5SW* Tel (01270) 626660

HEWITT, Canon Henry Thomas Maxwell. b 20. TCD BA44 MA63. **d** 44 **p** 45. C Ardamine w Kiltennel and Killena *C & O* 44-48; I Glascarrig, Monamolin w Kilmuckridge 48-54; C Alperton *Lon* 54-61; V Paddington Em Harrow Road 61-72; I Abbeyleix w Old Church, Ballyroan etc *C & O* 72-90; Chan Leighlin Cathl 83-89; Chan Ossory Cathl 83-89; rtd 90. *St James's Rectory, Stradbally, Co Waterford, Irish Republic* Tel Stradbally (51) 93129

HEWITT, James Herbert. b 17. Ch Coll Cam BA39 MA42. Ridley Hall Cam 40. **d** 41 **p** 42. C Heworth H Trin *York* 41-43; C York St Mary Castlegate w St Mich Spurriergate 41-43; C Tulse Hill H Trin *S'wark* 43-45; CMS India 45-47; Pakistan 47-60; Vice-Prin CMS Tr Coll Chislehurst 61-65; C Spitalfields Ch Ch w All SS *Lon* 64-65; V New Beckenham St Paul *Roch* 65-71; R Mereworth w W Peckham 71-75; V Bradf St Aug Undercliffe *Bradf* 75-82; rtd 82; Perm to Offic *Glas* from 82. *73 Georgetown Road, Dumfries DG1 4DG* Tel (01387) 263973

HEWITT, John Kaffrell. b 34. St Aid Birkenhead 60. **d** 63 **p** 64. C Woking Ch Ch *Guildf* 63-66; P-in-c Sudbury w Ballingdon and Brundon *St E* 66-70; V 70-80; V Portsdown *Portsm* 80-96; rtd 96. *45 Knowland Drive, Milford-on-Sea, Lymington, Hants SO41 0RH* Tel (01590) 644473

HEWITT, Kenneth Victor. b 30. Lon Univ BSc49 CertEd51 MSc53. Cuddesdon Coll 60. **d** 62 **p** 63. C Maidstone St Martin *Cant* 62-64; C Croydon St Mich 64-67; P-in-c S Kensington St Aug *Lon* 67-73; V 73-95; Asst Chapl Lon Univ 67-73; rtd 95; Perm to Offic *Roch* from 95. *Lower Treasurer's House, 41 Bromley College, London Road, Bromley BR1 1PE*

HEWITT, Michael David. b 49. K Coll Lon BD79 AKC79 CertEd. Qu Coll Birm 79. **d** 80 **p** 81. C Bexleyheath Ch Ch *Roch* 80-84; C Buckland in Dover w Buckland Valley *Cant* 84-89; R Ridgewell w Ashen, Birdbrook and Sturmer *Chelmsf* from 89. *The Rectory, Church Lane, Ridgewell, Halstead, Essex CO9 4SA* Tel (01440) 85355

HEWITT, Paul Stephen Patrick. b 59. BA DipTh. **d** 86 **p** 87. C Ballymacash *Conn* 86-89; Bp's C Ballymena w Ballyclug 89-91; I Glencraig *D & D* from 91. *Glencraig Vicarage, 3 Seahill Road, Craigavad, Holywood, Co Down BT18 0DA* Tel (01232) 422225

HEWITT, Robert Samuel. b 51. QUB BSc73. CITC 77. **d** 80 **p** 81. C Dundela *D & D* 80-84; I Donaghadee 84-92. *3 The Trees, New Road, Donaghadee, Co Down BT21 0EJ* Tel (01247) 882594

HEWITT, Stephen Wilkes. b 49. Fitzw Coll Cam BA71. St Jo Coll Nottm DipTh90. **d** 90 **p** 91. C Eaton *Nor* 90-93; V Warwick St Paul *Cov* from 93. *St Paul's Vicarage, 33 Stratford Road, Warwick CV34 6AS* Tel (01926) 419814

HEWITT, Thomas Peter James. b 24. St Andr Univ MA50. St Steph Ho Ox 50. **d** 52 **p** 53. C Ellesmere Port *Ches* 52-56; C Leytonstone St Marg w St Columba *Chelmsf* 56-60; V Barlby *York* 60-65; V Godshill *Portsm* 65-93; rtd 93. *Blue Nile, 14 Fairfield Way, Totland Bay, Isle of Wight PO39 0EF*

HEWITT, Timothy James. b 67. St D Coll Lamp BD. Ripon Coll Cuddesdon. **d** 91 **p** 92. C Milford Haven *St D* 91-94; C Llanelli 94-96; P-in-c Llan-non from 96. *Y Gorlan, 146 Heol Bryngwili, Cross Hands, Llanelli SA14 6LY*

HEWITT, William Patrick (Paddy). b 48. Nottm Univ BTh79. Linc Th Coll 75. **d** 79 **p** 80. C Workington St Jo *Carl* 79-83; V Flookburgh 83-87; V Barrow St Matt 87-90; V Lowick and Kyloe w Ancroft *Newc* 90-96; R Ford and Etal 90-96; RD Norham 91-96; I Fanlobbus Union *C, C & R* from 96. *The Rectory, Sackville Street, Dunmanway, Co Cork, Irish Republic* Tel Bandon (23) 45151 Fax as telephone

HEWLETT, David Bryan. b 49. Bris Univ BEd72. Qu Coll Birm 77. **d** 79 **p** 80. C Ludlow *Heref* 79-81; TV 81-84; V Marden w Amberley and Wisteston 84-92; Lect Glouc Sch for Min 84-92; Field Officer for Lay Min *Heref* 84-91; Continuing Minl Educn Adv 86-92; Dir Post-Ord Tr 91-92; Perm to Offic *Sarum* 92-94; Hd Master St Fran Sch Pewsey 92-94; Co-ord Chapl Frenchay Healthcare NHS Trust Bris from 94. *The Chaplaincy, Blackberry Hill Hospital, Manor Road, Fishponds, Bristol BS16 1LE* Tel 0117-965 6061 ext 4232 E-mail david.hewlett@virgin.net

HEWLETT, Dr David Jonathon Peter. b 57. Dur Univ BA79 PhD83. Ridley Hall Cam 82. **d** 83 **p** 84. C New Barnet St Jas *St Alb* 83-86; Lect CITC 86-90; P-in-c Feock *Truro* 91-95; Jt Dir SW Minl Tr Course 91-95; Prin SW Minl Tr Course *Truro* from 95; Adv Local Ord Min 91-95. *The Whisperings, Petherwin Gate, North Petherwin, Launceston, Cornwall PL15 8LW* Tel (01566) 785545

HEWLETT, Guy Edward. b 59. Thames Poly CertEd89 Open Univ BA90. Oak Hill Th Coll 96. **d** 96 **p** 97. NSM Sudbury St Andr *Lon* from 96. *9 Ventnor Avenue, Stanmore, Middx HA7 2HX* Tel 0181-907 1196

HEWLETT, Michael Edward. b 16. Mert Coll Ox BA39 MA46. Qu Coll Birm 46. **d** 48 **p** 49. C Brighton Gd Shep Preston *Chich* 48-51; C Crawley 51-56; V Malden St Jo *S'wark* 56-69; C Woolfardisworthy w Kennerleigh *Ex* 69-72; TV Cheriton Fitzpaine, Woolfardisworthy etc 72-76; TV N Creedy 76-86; rtd 86; Perm to Offic *Ex* 86-87; Perm to Offic *St Alb* from 87. *Jasmine Cottage, 3 The Green, Sarratt, Rickmansworth, Herts WD3 6AY* Tel (01923) 263803

HEWLINS, Pauline Elizabeth. b 47. **d** 96 **p** 97. NSM Radley and Sunningwell *Ox* from 96; Chapl SS Helen and Kath Sch Abingdon from 96. *10 Lumberd Road, Abingdon, Oxon OX14 2QH* Tel (01235) 520380

HEWSON, Thomas Robert (Tom). b 45. Man Univ BA66. S'wark Ord Course 85. **d** 89 **p** 90. C Chinnor w Emmington and Sydenham etc *Ox* 89-92; TV Burnham w Dropmore, Hitcham and Taplow from 92. *Hitcham Vicarage, 1 The Precinct, Burnham, Slough SL1 7HU* Tel (01628) 602881

HEYCOCKS, Christian John. b 71. Univ of Wales (Ban) BA93 MA96. Westcott Ho Cam 94 CITC 97. **d** 97. C Rhyl w St Ann *St As* from 97. *The Close, Paradise Street, Rhyl LL18 3LW* Tel (01745) 350862

HEYES, Andrew Robin. b 61. Man Univ BA93. St Steph Ho Ox 93. **d** 95 **p** 96. C Tonge Moor *Man* from 95. *182 Tonge Moor Road, Bolton BL2 2HN* Tel (01204) 365247

HEYGATE, Dr Stephen Beaumont. b 48. Loughb Univ BSc71 CQSW73 PhD89. St Jo Coll Nottm LTh88. **d** 88 **p** 89. C Aylestone St Andr w St Jas *Leic* 88-90; V Cosby from 90. *Cosby Vicarage, Main Street, Cosby, Leicester LE9 1UU* Tel 0116-286 2313

HEYHOE, Jonathan Peter. b 53. Man Univ BA75. Trin Coll Bris 77. **d** 80 **p** 81. C Woking St Pet *Guildf* 80-83; C Heatherlands St Jo *Sarum* 83-91; Chr Renewal Cen Newry 91-95; Perm to Offic *D & D* from 91. *11 Rowallon, Warrenpoint, Newry, Co Down BT34 3TR* Tel (016937) 53595

✠**HEYWARD, The Rt Revd Oliver Spencer.** b 26. Univ of Tasmania BA49 Or Coll Ox BA53 MA56. Cuddesdon Coll 51. **d** 53 **p** 54 **c** 75. C Brighton St Pet *Chich* 53-56; Australia from 56; Bp Bendigo 75-91; rtd 91. *7 Waltham Street, Richmond, Victoria, Australia 3121* Tel Melbourne (3) 9429 2806

HEYWOOD, Mrs Anne Christine. **d** 97. C Talbot Village *Sarum* from 97. *St Saviour's House, 18 Hillside Road, Poole, Dorset BH12 5DY* Tel (01202) 548694

HEYWOOD, David Stephen. b 55. Selw Coll Cam BA76 MA80 SS Hild & Bede Coll Dur PhD89. St Jo Coll Dur 80. **d** 86 **p** 87. C Cheltenham St Luke and St Jo *Glouc* 86-90; TV Sanderstead All SS *S'wark* from 90. *35 Audley Drive, Warlingham, Surrey CR6 9AH* Tel 0181-657 5505

HEYWOOD, Geoffrey Thomas. b 26. St Mich Coll Llan 60. **d** 62 **p** 63. C Porthmadog *Ban* 62-64; C Llandudno 64-67; V Caerhun w Llangelynin 67-74; Asst Chapl HM Pris Liv 74-75; Chapl HM Pris Ex 75-77; Chapl HM Pris Wakef 77-79; Chapl HM Young Offender Inst Eastwood Park 79-90; Chapl HM Pris Leyhill 79-90; rtd 90; Perm to Offic *Glouc* from 94. *5 Meadow Road, Leyhill, Wotton-under-Edge, Glos GL12 8HW*

HEYWOOD, Michael Herbert. b 41. Liv Univ BSc63. Clifton Th Coll 63. **d** 65 **p** 66. C Low Elswick *Newc* 65-68; C St Helens St Mark *Liv* 68-75; Lic to Offic *Dur* 75-85; Leprosy Miss Area Org NE & Cumbria 75-85; S Lon, Surrey and Berks from 85; Lic to Offic *S'wark* from 85. *3 Valerie Court, 33 Worcester Road, Sutton, Surrey SM2 6PU* Tel 0181-643 4896

HEYWOOD, Peter. b 46. Cranmer Hall Dur 72. **d** 75 **p** 76. C Blackley St Andr *Man* 75-78; C Denton Ch Ch 78-80; V Constable Lee from 80. *St Paul's Vicarage, Hollin Lane, Rawtenstall, Rossendale, Lancs BB4 8HT* Tel (01706) 228634

HEZEL, Adrian. b 43. Chelsea Coll Lon BSc64 PhD67. N Ord Course 78. **d** 81 **p** 82. NSM Mirfield *Wakef* 81-89; C 89-90; V Shelley and Shepley from 90. *The Vicarage, 6 Stonecroft Gardens, Shepley, Huddersfield HD8 8EX* Tel (01484) 602640

HIBBERD, Brian Jeffery. b 35. Fitzw Coll Cam MA62 Southn Univ MA84. Ridley Hall Cam 58. **d** 60 **p** 61. C Cambridge H Trin *Ely* 60-63; C Doncaster St Mary *Sheff* 63-66; Asst Master Price's Sch Fareham 66-69; Warblington Sch Havant 69-71; Hd Soc and Relig Studies Carisbrooke High Sch 71-84; Distr Health Promotion Officer Is of Wight 84-88; SW Herts 88-90; Hd Relig Studies Goffs Sch Cheshunt 90-95; rtd 95; Teacher Qu Sch

Bushey from 95. *50 Rosehill Gardens, Abbots Langley, Herts WD5 0HF*

HIBBERD, Carol Anne. b 59. Kent Univ BA80. S'wark Ord Course 89. **d** 92 **p** 94. NSM Gospel Lane St Mich *Birm* 92-94; C from 94. *12 Elmcroft Road, Birmingham B26 1PJ* Tel 0121-784 8677

HIBBERD, John. b 60. Wadh Coll Ox MA82. Trin Coll Bris BA89. **d** 89 **p** 90. C Northolt St Mary *Lon* 89-92; C-in-c Southall Em CD 92-94; Min of Miss Through Faith Miss *Ely* from 95. *63 Wertheim Way, Stukeley Meadows, Huntingdon, Cambs PE18 6UH* Tel (01480) 433718

HIBBERD, John Charles. b 38. Chich Th Coll 63. **d** 66 **p** 67. C W Drayton *Lon* 66-70; C Noel Park St Mark 70-72; C Ealing St Steph Castle Hill 72-75; V Gunnersbury St Jas 75-84; V Whitton SS Phil and Jas 84-86; Finance and Trust Sec Lon Dioc Fund from 87; Perm to Offic 87-93. *London Diocesan House, 30 Causton Street, London SW1P 4AU* Tel 0171-821 9351 Fax 821 0424

HIBBERT, Miss Anne Mary Elizabeth. b 59. Southn Univ BA81. Trin Coll Bris 81. **dss** 83 **d** 87 **p** 94. Muswell Hill St Jas w St Matt *Lon* 83-86; Leic H Trin w St Jo *Leic* 86-87; Par Dn 87-90; Evang Co-ord and Adv CPAS from 90; Perm to Offic *Cov* from 90. *7 Suffolk Street, Leamington Spa, Warks CV32 5TG* Tel (01926) 888210

HIBBERT, Charles Dennis. b 24. Linc Th Coll 69. **d** 70 **p** 71. C Radcliffe-on-Trent *S'well* 70-73; P-in-c Ladybrook 73-77; V 77-79; V Boughton 79-85; V Ollerton 79-85; R Nuthall 85-89; rtd 89. *27 Nottingham Road, Kimberley, Nottingham NG16 2NB* Tel 0115-938 6302

HIBBERT, James Raymond. b 10. St Pet Coll Ox BA32 MA36. Wycliffe Hall Ox 32. **d** 34 **p** 35. C Southport Em *Liv* 34-37; C Lancaster St Mary *Blackb* 37-45; CF (TA - R of O) 39-56; V Fulwood Ch Ch *Blackb* 45-75; rtd 75; Lic to Offic *Blackb* from 75. *c/o Mr K Bretherton, 27 Kingswood Road, Central Park, Leyland, Preston PR5 5PX*

HIBBERT, Peter John. b 43. Hull Univ BA71 Lon Univ CertEd72 MA79. Sarum & Wells Th Coll 85. **d** 88 **p** 89. C Newsome and Armitage Bridge *Wakef* 88-92; P-in-c Newton Flowery Field *Ches* from 92; P-in-c Hyde St Thos from 97. *St Stephen's Vicarage, 154 Bennett Street, Hyde, Cheshire SK14 4SS* Tel 0161-368 3333

HIBBERT, Richard Charles. b 62. Trin Coll Bris BA93. **d** 96 **p** 97. C Luton St Mary *St Alb* from 96. *34 Wychwood Avenue, Luton, Beds LU2 7HU* Tel (01582) 29902

HIBBERT, Preb Roy Trevor. b 30. AKC54. **d** 55 **p** 56. C W Bromwich St Fran *Lich* 55-58; C Cannock 58-60; C-in-c Sneyd Green CD 60-62; V Sneyd Green 62-67; V Harlescott 67-81; R Newport w Longford and Chetwynd 81-96; RD Edgmond 82-96; P-in-c Forton 84-96; Preb Lich Cathl 87-97; R Newport w Longford, Chetwynd and Forton 96-97; rtd 97. *6 Coppice Drive, Newport, Shropshire TF10 7HU*

HIBBINS, Neil Lance. b 60. St Anne's Coll Ox BA82 MA87. St Mich Coll Llan DPS83. **d** 85 **p** 86. C Griffithstown *Mon* 85-87; C Pontypool 87-88; TV Pontypool 88-92; Walsall Hosps NHS Trust 92-96; Asst Chapl Manor Hosp Walsall 92-96; R Norton Canes *Lich* from 96. *The Rectory, 81 Church Road, Norton Canes, Cannock, Staffs WS11 3PQ* Tel (01543) 278969

HIBBS, Canon Lawrence Winston. b 14. Kelham Th Coll 31. **d** 37 **p** 38. C Walworth St Jo *S'wark* 37-39; C Hendon St Alphage *Lon* 39-46; R Jersey H Trin *Win* 46-55; V Bournemouth St Alb 55-68; V Chandler's Ford 68-75; R Jersey Grouville 75-83; Hon Can Win Cathl 76-83; rtd 83; Perm to Offic *Win* from 83. *13 Rectory Close, St Clement, Jersey, Channel Islands JE2 6RF* Tel (01534) 851394

HICHENS, Anthony. b 29. AKC59. **d** 60 **p** 61. C Ashford St Hilda *Lon* 60-64; C Leeds St Wilfrid *Ripon* 64-66; Guyana 67-75; P-in-c Stratton Audley w Godington *Ox* 76-83; P-in-c Finmere w Mixbury 76-78; P-in-c Fringford w Hethe and Newton Purcell 76-83; R Stratton Audley and Godington, Fringford etc 83-95; rtd 95; Perm to Offic *Pet* from 95. *86 Horton Drive, Middleton Cheney, Banbury, Oxon OX17 2LL* Tel (01295) 712826

HICKES, Roy Edward. b 31. Lon Univ DipTh60. St Aid Birkenhead 56. **d** 59 **p** 60. C New Bury *Man* 59-63; C Wyther Ven Bede *Ripon* 63-65; R Oldham St Andr *Man* 65-69; V Smallbridge 69-79; R Winford *B & W* 79-81; R Winford w Felton Common Hill 81-88; RD Chew Magna 85-88; Chapl Costa Blanca *Eur* 88-92; rtd 92; Perm to Offic *Bris* from 92; Perm to Offic *B & W* from 92. *Church Farm Bungalow, Chelwood, Bristol BS18 4NW* Tel (01767) 490923

HICKEY, Canon Francis Joseph. b 20. AKC49. **d** 50 **p** 51. C Portsea St Mary *Portsm* 50-58; V Tilbury Docks *Chelmsf* 58-87; RD Orsett and Grays 70-83; Hon Can Chelmsf Cathl 79-87; rtd 87; Perm to Offic *Guildf* from 95. *202 Parkside House, Malvern Road, Southsea, Hants PO5 2LD* Tel (01705) 750301

HICKFORD, Michael Francis. b 53. Edin Th Coll 84. **d** 86 **p** 87. Chapl St Jo Cathl Oban *Arg* 86-89; R Alexandria *Glas* 89-95; P-in-c Dingwall *Mor* from 95; P-in-c Strathpeffer from 95. *The Parsonage, 4 Castle Street, Dingwall, Ross-shire IV15 9HU* Tel (01349) 862204

HICKIN, Maurice Whitehouse. b 09. St Cath Coll Cam BA32 MA38 Bonn Univ DPhil33. Ely Th Coll 33. **d** 34 **p** 35. C Fulham St Andr Fulham Fields *Lon* 34-35; C London Docks St Pet 35-36; Ghana 36-38; C Paddington St Mary *Lon* 40-46; C Beckenham St Mich *Roch* 46-48; C Worthing St Andr *Chich* 48-51; C Clewer St Andr *Ox* 51-55; Perm to Offic 55-58; C Kirkley *Nor* 58-61; R Runwell *Chelmsf* 61-75; rtd 75. *Calle De Murillo 6, Benidoleig, Alicante 03759, Spain* Tel Alicante (6) 558-3266

HICKLEY, Peter Michael. b 28. Ely Th Coll 56. **d** 59 **p** 60. C Shepherd's Bush St Steph *Lon* 59-62; C Lee Gd Shep w St Pet *S'wark* 62-66; V Carlton *Wakef* 66-68; C Is of Dogs Ch Ch and St Jo w St Luke *Lon* 68-70; R S Hackney St Jo w Ch Ch 70-77; R Euston w Barnham and Fakenham *St E* 77-80; TR Fenny Stratford and Water Eaton *Ox* 80-88; R Benington w Walkern *St Alb* 88-91; rtd 91; Perm to Offic *Birm* 91-96; Perm to Offic *Nor* from 96. *12 Newark Road, Lowestoft, Suffolk NR33 0LY* Tel (01502) 514525

HICKLING, Canon Colin John Anderson. b 31. K Coll Cam BA53 MA57. Chich Th Coll 56. **d** 57 **p** 58. C Pallion *Dur* 57-61; Asst Tutor Chich Th Coll 61-65; Asst Lect K Coll Lon 65-68; Lect 68-84; Hon C Munster Square St Mary Magd *Lon* 68-69; Dep Min Can St Paul's Cathl 69-78; Hon C E Dulwich St Jo *S'wark* 70-84; Dep P in O 71-74; P-in-O 74-84; Can Th Leic Cathl *Leic* from 81; Tutor Qu Coll Birm 84-85; Lect Linc Th Coll 85-86; V Arksey *Sheff* from 86; Hon Lect Bibl Studies Sheff Univ from 86. *The Vicarage, Station Road, Arksey, Doncaster, S Yorkshire DN5 0SP* Tel (01302) 874445

HICKLING, John. b 34. Launde Abbey. **d** 69 **p** 70. C Melton Mowbray w Thorpe Arnold *Leic* 69-71; TV 71-75; R Waltham on the Wolds w Stonesby and Saltby 75-84; R Aylestone St Andr w St Jas 84-93; R Husbands Bosworth w Mowsley and Knaptoft etc 93-96; rtd 96. *28 Oxford Drive, Melton Mowbray, Leics LE13 0AL* Tel (01664) 60770

HICKMAN, George May. b 11. AKC33. **d** 35 **p** 36. C Hayes St Mary *Lon* 35-36; C Stepney St Aug w St Phil 36-39; C Bray *Ox* 40-41; V Beedon 41-45; V Rotherhithe H Trin *S'wark* 45-50; R Nettlecombe *B & W* 50-68; R Withycombe 68-84; rtd 84; Perm to Offic *B & W* 85-91. *1 The Causeway, Withycombe, Minehead, Somerset TA24 6PZ* Tel (01984) 640227

HICKMAN, John William. b 38. Barrister-at-Law (Middle Temple) 69 Qu Coll Cam LLM81. Oak Hill Th Coll 92. **d** 95 **p** 96. NSM Sevenoaks St Nic *Roch* from 95. *26 The Rise, Sevenoaks, Kent TN13 1RQ* Tel (01732) 454546

HICKS, Miss Barbara. b 42. Cranmer Hall Dur BA71. **dss** 85 **d** 87 **p** 94. Norton Woodseats St Paul *Sheff* 85-87; Par Dn Sheff St Jo 87-94; C from 94; Chapl Shrewsbury Hosp from 96. *Chaplain's House, The Shrewsbury Hospital, Norfolk Road, Sheffield S2 2SU, or 15 Benson Road, Sheffield S2 5EU* Tel 0114-272 0574 or 275 9997

HICKS, Francis Fuller (Frank). b 28. Sarum & Wells Th Coll 71. **d** 74 **p** 75. C Broadstone *Sarum* 74-78; P-in-c Kington Magna and Buckhorn Weston 78-79; TV Gillingham 79-86; P-in-c Portland St Jo 86-89; V 89-93; rtd 93; Perm to Offic *B & W* from 93. *Windyridge, 21 Castle Road, Sherborne, Dorset DT9 3RW* Tel (01935) 814837

HICKS, Herbert. b 10. Bede Coll Dur BA32 MA47. Ridley Hall Cam 34. **d** 36 **p** 37. C Humberstone *Leic* 36-38; C Knighton St Mary Magd 38-43; V Starbeck *Ripon* 43-55; V Bramhope 55-74; rtd 74. *2 Larkfield Drive, Harrogate, N Yorkshire HG2 0BX* Tel (01423) 508675

HICKS, Mrs Joan Rosemary. b 60. Homerton Coll Cam BEd83. Westcott Ho Cam 87. **d** 90 **p** 94. Par Dn Wendover *Ox* 90-94; C 94-95; C Earley St Pet from 95. *33 Clevedon Drive, Reading RG6 2XF* Tel 0118-987 1396

HICKS, Richard Barry. b 32. Dur Univ BA55. Sarum Th Coll 59. **d** 61 **p** 62. C Wallsend St Luke *Newc* 61-64; C Tynemouth Ch Ch 64-69; V Tynemouth St Jo 69-75; V Prudhoe 75-82; TV Swanborough *Sarum* 82-86; R Hilperton w Whaddon and Staverton etc from 86. *The Rectory, Hilperton, Trowbridge, Wilts BA14 7RL* Tel (01225) 752804

HICKS, Stuart Knox. b 34. Univ of W Ontario BA56 Huron Coll LTh59 Ox Univ DipEd67. **d** 58 **p** 60. Canada 58-65; C Allerton *Liv* 65-66; Hon C Rye Park St Cuth *St Alb* 68-72; Lic to Offic *B & W* 72-87 and 88-95; Chapl Magdalen Chpl Bath 80-86; Chapl Partis Coll Bath 88-91. *Folly Orchard, The Folly, Saltford, Bristol BS18 3JW* Tel (01225) 873391

HICKS, Mrs Valerie Joy. b 47. SRN69 HVCert70. Cant Sch of Min 82. **dss** 85 **d** 87 **p** 94. Roch 85-87; Hon Par Dn 87-89; Par Dn Thatcham *Ox* 89-93; TD Aylesbury w Bierton and Hulcott 93-94; TV from 94. *St Peter's House, 18 Bronte Close, Aylesbury, Bucks HP19 3LF* Tel (01296) 432677

HICKS, William Trevor. b 47. Hull Univ BA68 Fitzw Coll Cam BA70 MA74. Westcott Ho Cam 68. **d** 70 **p** 71. C Cottingham *York* 70-73; C Elland *Wakef* 73-76; V Walsden 76-81; V Knottingley 81-92; R Castleford All SS 92-96; RD Pontefract from 94; P-in-c Womersley and Kirk Smeaton from 96. *The Vicarage, Womersley, Doncaster, S Yorkshire DN6 9BG* Tel (01977) 620436

HIDER, David Arthur. b 46. Lon Univ BSc67. Sarum & Wells Th Coll 86. **d** 89 **p** 90. NSM Southbourne w W Thorney *Chich* 89-91; C Goring-by-Sea 91-94; P-in-c Peacehaven from 94; P-in-c Telscombe w Piddinghoe and Southease from 94. *Peacehaven*

Vicarage, 41 Bramber Avenue, Peacehaven, E Sussex BN10 8HR Tel (01273) 583149

HIGDON, Lewis George. b 36. Dur Univ BA58. Cranmer Hall Dur DipTh60. **d** 60 **p** 61. C Leeds St Pet *Ripon* 60-65; C Shipley St Paul *Bradf* 65-66; V Esholt 67-75; V Kirkstall *Ripon* 75-79; V Stanwix *Carl* 79-87; V Ambleside w Brathay 87-95; rtd 95. *Springtime, 17 Priory Crescent, Grange-over-Sands, Cumbria LA11 7BL* Tel (015395) 32864

HIGGINBOTTOM, Richard. b 48. Lon Univ BD74. Oak Hill Th Coll DipTh72. **d** 74 **p** 75. C Kenilworth St Jo *Cov* 74-77; C Finham 77-79; P-in-c Attleborough 79-81; V 81-84; Asst Chapl HM Pris Brixton 84-85; Chapl HM Pris Roch 85-92; Chapl HM Pris Camp Hill from 92. *HM Prison, Camp Hill, Newport, Isle of Wight PO30 5PB* Tel (01983) 527661 Fax 520505

HIGGINBOTTOM, Richard William. b 51. Man Univ BA73 MA75. Edin Th Coll 83. **d** 85 **p** 86. C Knighton St Mary Magd *Leic* 85-87; C Northleach w Hampnett and Farmington *Glouc* 87-89; V Hayfield *Derby* 89-93; Consultant NW England and Scotland CPAS from 93; Perm to Offic *Blackb* from 93. *60 Huntsfield, Clayton-le-Woods, Chorley, Lancs PR6 7TT* Tel (01772) 315825

HIGGINS, Anthony Charles. b 46. LNSM course 96. **d** 97. NSM Swanage and Studland *Sarum* from 97. *19 Ballard Estate, Swanage, Dorset BH19 1QZ* Tel (01929) 424711

HIGGINS, Dr Bernard. b 42. MRPharmS68 Leic Poly BPharm63 PhD66. St Jo Coll Nottm 89. **d** 91 **p** 92. C Stockport St Geo *Ches* 91-94; C Stockport SW 94-95; P-in-c Dunham Massey St Marg and St Mark from 95. *St Margaret's Vicarage, Dunham Road, Altrincham, Cheshire WA14 4AQ* Tel 0161-928 1609

HIGGINS, Bernard George. b 27. Wycliffe Hall Ox 68. **d** 70 **p** 72. C Surbiton St Matt *S'wark* 70-72; C Battersea St Mary 72-76; C Warblington and Emsworth *Portsm* 76-81; C Milton 81-91; rtd 91; Perm to Offic *Portsm* from 91. *49 Queens Crescent, Stubbington, Fareham, Hants PO14 2QG* Tel (01329) 667905

HIGGINS, Frank Roylance. b 34. Open Univ BA74 MEd83. Bps' Coll Cheshunt 59. **d** 62 **p** 63. C Sunderland *Dur* 62-64; C S Westoe 64-66; P-in-c Smethwick St Mich *Birm* 66-67; V 67-70; V Garretts Green 70-75; Lic to Offic *Worc* 76-84; Perm to Offic *Birm* 81-87; Hon C Feckenham w Bradley *Worc* 84-87; R Ripple, Earls Croome w Hill Croome and Strensham 87-95; RD Upton 92-95; rtd 95; P-in-c Church Lench w Rous Lench and Abbots Morton *Worc* from 95. *The Rectory, Church Lench, Evesham, Worcs WR11 4UB* Tel (01386) 870345

HIGGINS, Geoffrey Minta. b 27. New Coll Ox BA52 MA56. Cuddesdon Coll 52. **d** 54 **p** 55. C Pet St Mary Boongate *Pet* 54-56; CF 56-77; Hong Kong from 77. *12-C Far East Consortium Building, Main Road, Yuen Long, New Territories, Hong Kong* Tel Hong Kong (852) 479-9374

HIGGINS, Canon Godfrey. b 39. St Chad's Coll Dur BA61 DipTh62 DipEd63. **d** 63 **p** 64. C Brighouse *Wakef* 63-66; C Huddersfield St Jo 66-68; R High Hoyland w Clayton W 68-75; V Marsden 75-84; V Pontefract St Giles from 84; Hon Can Wakef Cathl from 93. *The Vicarage, The Mount, Pontefract, W Yorkshire WF8 1NE* Tel (01977) 706803

HIGGINS, John. b 44. Trin Coll Bris 71. **d** 73 **p** 74. C Clapham St Jas *S'wark* 73-74; C Ruskin Park St Sav and St Matt 74-77; C Hamworthy *Sarum* 77-80; V Bordesley St Andr *Birm* 80-83; V Bishop Sutton and Stanton Drew and Stowey *B & W* from 83. *The Vicarage, Sutton Hill Road, Bishop Sutton, Bristol BS18 4UR* Tel (01275) 333385

HIGGINS, Canon John Leslie. b 43. BA CQSW Birm Univ MEd89. Lich Th Coll 64. **d** 66 **p** 67. C Sale St Anne *Ches* 66-69; C Bredbury St Mark 69-72; V Wharton 72-74; Hon C Annan *Glas* 75-79; Hon C Lockerbie 75-79; V Coseley Ch Ch *Lich* 79-89; R Arthuret *Carl* 89-96; Soc Resp Officer from 96; C Brampton and Farlam and Castle Carrock w Cumrew from 96; Hon Can Carl Cathl from 96. *The Rectory, Castle Carrock, Carlisle CA4 9LZ* Tel (01228) 70120

HIGGINS, Canon John Norman. b 14. Em Coll Cam BA36 MA40. Wells Th Coll 39. **d** 40 **p** 41. C Thornaby on Tees St Paul *York* 40-42; Chapl RNVR 42-46; C Fulham All SS *Lon* 46-47; V Wilton *B & W* 47-51; V Twerton 51-58; V Greenwich St Alfege w St Pet *S'wark* 58-63; V Redcar *York* 64-67; V Kirkleatham 64-67; RD Guisborough 64-67; R Sutton St Nic *S'wark* 67-77; Hon Can S'wark Cathl 76-82; R Limpsfield and Titsey 77-82; rtd 82; Perm to Offic *B & W* from 84. *Robin House, 28 College Road, Wells, Somerset BA5 2TB* Tel (01749) 676416

HIGGINS, Kenneth. b 56. TCD BTh93. CA Tr Coll DipEvang83 CITC 90. **d** 93 **p** 94. C Cregagh *D & D* 93-96; Bp's C Movilla from 96. *34 Hollymount Road, Newtownards, Co Down B23 3DL* Tel (01247) 810787

HIGGINS, The Very Revd Michael John. b 35. Birm Univ LLB57 G&C Coll Cam LLB59 PhD62. Ridley Hall Cam 63. **d** 65 **p** 65. C Ormskirk *Liv* 65-67; Selection Sec ACCM 67-74; Hon C St Marylebone St Mark w St Luke *Lon* 69-74; P-in-c Woodlands *B & W* 74-80; V Frome St Jo 74-80; TR Preston St Jo *Blackb* 80-91; Dean Ely from 91. *The Deanery, The College, Ely, Cambs CB7 4DN* Tel (01353) 662432

HIGGINS, Richard Ellis. b 63. Univ of Wales BA84. St Mich Coll Llan DipTh88 DPS89. **d** 89 **p** 90. C Bargoed and Deri w Brithdir *Llan* 89-92; Zimbabwe 92-94; V Penmaen and Crumlin *Mon* from 94. *The Vicarage, Central Avenue, Oakdale, Blackwood NP2 0JS* Tel (01495) 223043

HIGGINS, Rupert Anthony. b 59. Man Univ BA80. Wycliffe Hall Ox 82. **d** 85 **p** 86. C Plymouth St Andr w St Paul and St Geo *Ex* 85-90; C-in-c St Paul 88-90; Assoc V Clifton Ch Ch w Em *Bris* 90-95; V S Croydon Em *S'wark* from 95. *Emmanuel Vicarage, 38 Croham Manor Road, South Croydon, Surrey CR2 7BE* Tel 0181-688 2478 or 688 6676

HIGGINS, Timothy John. b 45. Bris Univ BEd70 Lanc Univ MA74 St Jo Coll Dur DipTh79. **d** 79 **p** 80. C Northampton All SS w St Kath *Pet* 79-82; V Whitton St Aug *Lon* 82-90; AD Hampton 86-90; TR Aylesbury w Bierton and Hulcott *Ox* from 90; RD Aylesbury from 94. *The Vicarage, Parson's Fee, Aylesbury, Bucks HP20 2QZ* Tel (01296) 24276

HIGGINSON, Arthur Rothwell. b 14. Edin Th Coll 48. **d** 51 **p** 52. C Glas Ch Ch *Glas* 51-52; C St Mary's Cathl 52-54; R Gt Weldon *Pet* 55-64; RD Weldon 62-64; V Northampton Ch Ch 64-74; V Whitewell *Blackb* 74-79; P-in-c Hurst Green and Mitton *Bradf* 76-79; rtd 79; Lic to Offic *Blackb* from 80. *24 Moorlands, Garstang Road, Preston PR1 1NN* Tel (01772) 251660

HIGGINSON, Gerald Scott. b 29. Keele Univ BA54 Birm Univ PhD57. NW Ord Course 73. **d** 76 **p** 77. NSM York St Mary Bishophill Junior w All SS *York* 76-84; P-in-c 84-86; P-in-c York H Trin w St Jo Micklegate and St Martin 84-86; R Micklegate H Trin and Bishophill Junior St Mary from 86. *Holy Trinity Rectory, Micklegate, York YO1 1LE* Tel (01904) 623798

HIGGINSON, Richard Edwin. b 15. St Jo Coll Dur BA39 MA42 Lon Univ BD51. Tyndale Hall Bris 35. **d** 39 **p** 40. C Preston All SS *Blackb* 39-42; C Chadderton Ch Ch *Man* 42-44; V Chadderton Em 44-47; V Halliwell St Pet 47-56; V Redland *Bris* 56-69; V S Croydon Em *Cant* 69-78; P-in-c Weeton *Blackb* 78-80; rtd 80; Lic to Offic *Blackb* from 81. *30 Pennine Way, Great Eccleston, Preston PR3 0YS* Tel (01995) 70634

HIGGS, Allan Herbert Morris. b 22. St Jo Coll Dur BA48 DipTh50. **d** 50 **p** 51. C Morpeth *Newc* 50-54; V Amble 54-61; V Fenham St Jas and St Basil 61-75; Adult Educn Adv *Linc* 75-80; V Stamfordham w Matfen *Newc* 80-88; rtd 88; Perm to Offic *Bradf* from 88. *3 Southfield Lane, Addingham, Ilkley, W Yorkshire LS29 0NX* Tel (01943) 830167

HIGGS, Andrew Richard Bowen (Andy). b 53. Man Univ BSc75. St Jo Coll Nottm 81. **d** 85 **p** 86. C Droylsden St Mary *Man* 85-88; C Harlow Town Cen w Lt Parndon *Chelmsf* 88-95; TV from 95. *4A The Drive, Netteswell, Harlow, Essex CM20 3QD* Tel (01279) 437717

HIGGS, Michael John. b 53. Sarum & Wells Th Coll 76. **d** 80 **p** 81. C Cant St Martin and St Paul *Cant* 80-84; C Maidstone St Martin 84-88; R Egerton w Pluckley from 88. *St James's Vicarage, Glebeland, Egerton, Ashford, Kent TN27 9DH* Tel (01233) 706224

HIGGS, Owen Christopher Goodwin. b 63. St Anne's Coll Ox BA84 MA88. St Steph Ho Ox 90. **d** 93 **p** 94. C Teddington St Mark and Hampton Wick St Jo *Lon* 93-96; C Lon Docks St Pet w Wapping St Jo from 96. *St Peter's Mission House, Wapping Lane, London E1 9RW* Tel 0171-702 2307

HIGHAM, Gerald Norman. b 40. St Aid Birkenhead 64. **d** 68 **p** 69. C Garston *Liv* 68-71; C Blundellsands St Nic 71-73; V Bolton All So w St Jas *Man* 73-78; V Tonge w Alkrington 78-84; P-in-c Edenfield 84-86; P-in-c Stubbins 84-86; V Edenfield and Stubbins from 86. *St Philip's Vicarage, Chatterton Road, Ramsbottom, Bury, Lancs BL0 0PQ* Tel (01706) 822079

HIGHAM, Canon Jack. b 33. Linc Coll Ox BA56 MA60 Birm Univ DipTh59. Union Th Sem (NY) STM61 Qu Coll Birm 58. **d** 60 **p** 61. C Handsworth *Sheff* 60-64; V Handsworth Woodhouse 64-70; USA 70-78; R Stoke Bruerne w Grafton Regis and Alderton *Pet* 78-83; RD Towcester 82-83; Can Res, Chan and Lib Pet Cathl from 83. *Canonry House, Minster Precincts, Peterborough PE1 1XX* Tel (01733) 62125

HIGHAM, John Leonard. b 39. Liv Univ DipSocSc71. Wycliffe Hall Ox 62. **d** 65 **p** 66. C Prescot *Liv* 65-71; V Hollinfare 71-74; Adult and Youth Service Adv Knowsley 74-76; TV Padgate 76-84; V Farnworth 84-89; TR Sutton from 89. *Sutton Rectory, Eaves Lane, St Helens, Merseyside WA9 3UB* Tel (01744) 812347

HIGHAM (née ANNS), Mrs Pauline Mary. b 49. Bris Univ BEd71. EMMTC 87. **d** 90 **p** 94. Par Dn Wirksworth w Alderwasley, Carsington etc *Derby* 90-92; Par Dn Wirksworth 92; Par Dn Lt Berkhamsted and Bayford, Essendon etc *St Alb* 92-94; C 94-96; P-in-c from 96. *The Rectory, 1 Berkhamsted Lane, Little Berkhamsted, Hertford SG13 8LU* Tel (01707) 875940

HIGHTON, William James. b 31. St Deiniol's Hawarden. **d** 82 **p** 83. NSM Thornton Hough *Ches* 82-84; C Cheadle 84-88; V Walton from 88. *St John's Vicarage, Chester Road, Higher Walton, Warrington WA4 6TJ* Tel (01925) 662939

HIGTON, Anthony Raymond (Tony). b 42. Lon Univ BD65. Oak Hill Th Coll 65. **d** 67 **p** 68. C Newark Ch Ch *S'well* 67-69; C Cheltenham St Mark *Glouc* 70-75; R Hawkwell *Chelmsf* from 75. *The Rectory, Ironwell Lane, Hawkwell, Hockley, Essex SS5 4JY* Tel (01702) 203870 Fax 207753 E-mail 101343.164@compuserve.com

HILARY, Sister. *See* HOPKINS, Hilda

HILARY, Sister. *See* JORDINSON, Vera

HILDAGE, James Francis. b 18. Univ of Wales BA44. Coll of Resurr Mirfield 44. **d** 46 **p** 47. C Long Eaton St Laur *Derby* 46-51; C Chesterfield St Mary and All SS 51-54; P-in-c Earl Sterndale and Monyash 54-56; V 56-87; Lect Matlock Coll of HE 66-83; rtd 87; Perm to Offic *Ban* from 88. *Llangwyfan Isaf, Ty Croes, Anglesey LL63 5YP* Tel (01407) 810756

HILDITCH, Dr Janet. b 59. St Andr Univ MTh81 PhD87. N Ord Course 92. **d** 94 **p** 95. C Kirkholt *Man* from 94. *58 Friars Crescent, Rochdale, Lancs OL11 2SF* Tel (01706) 353916

HILDRED, David. b 61. Bath Univ BSc83 CertEd83. Wycliffe Hall Ox 86. **d** 89 **p** 90. C Westcliff St Mich *Chelmsf* 89-92; C Rayleigh 92-96; V Sidcup St Andr *Roch* from 96. *The Vicarage, St Andrew's Road, Sidcup, Kent DA14 4SA* Tel 0181-300 4712

HILES, John Michael. b 32. Qu Coll Cam BA57 MA61. Sarum Th Coll 57. **d** 59 **p** 60. C Clifton St Jas *Sheff* 59-62; V Bramley St Fran 62-69; Hon C Holmfirth *Wakef* 69-89; Hon C Upper Holme Valley 89-91; Lic to Offic from 91. *Rosehill, Parkhead Lane, Holmfirth, Huddersfield HD7 1LB* Tel (01484) 683045

HILL, Alexander Francis. b 71. Leeds Univ BA94. Coll of Resurr Mirfield 95. **d** 97. C Notting Hill All SS w St Columb *Lon* from 97. *The Curate's Flat, 12 Powis Gardens, London W11 1JG* Tel 0171-221 2857

HILL, Mrs Anne Doreen. b 40. **d** 88 **p** 94. Par Dn Bexleyheath St Pet *Roch* 88-90; Sub-Chapl HM Pris Belmarsh 91-93; Dep Chapl from 93; Hon C Lee St Mildred *S'wark* from 93. *The Chaplain's Office, HM Prison Belmarsh, Western Way, London SE28 0EB* Tel 0181-317 2436 Fax 317 2421

HILL, Mrs Bridget Ann. b 54. Open Univ BA82 CertEd75. EMMTC 83. **dss** 86 **d** 87 **p** 94. Gt and Lt Coates w Bradley *Linc* 86-87; NSM 87-88; Par Dn Louth 88-91; TD 91-94; Chapl Louth Co Hosp from 89; TV Louth *Linc* from 94. *Holy Trinity Vicarage, 24 Grosvenor Road, Louth, Lincs LN11 0BB* Tel (01507) 607991

HILL, Dr Charles Bernard. b 50. Sheff Univ BA71 Qu Coll Ox DPhil76. Cant Sch of Min 91. **d** 94 **p** 95. NSM Sandgate St Paul w Folkestone St Geo *Cant* from 94. *18 Audley Road, Folkestone, Kent CT20 3QA* Tel (01303) 253270 E-mail cbh@cbhill.demon.co.uk

HILL, Charles Merrick (Charlie). b 52. Strathclyde Univ BA74. Qu Coll Birm DipTh79. **d** 80 **p** 81. C Silksworth *Dur* 80-83; C Stockton St Pet 83-85; TV Southampton (City Cen) *Win* 85-87; V Portsea St Geo *Portsm* 87-94; P-in-c Bodenham w Hope-under-Dinmore, Felton etc *Heref* from 94. *The Vicarage, Bodenham, Hereford HR1 3JX* Tel (01568) 84370

✠**HILL, The Rt Revd Christopher John.** b 45. K Coll Lon BD67 AKC67 MTh68. **d** 69 **p** 70 **c** 96. C Tividale *Lich* 69-73; C Codsall 73-74; Abp's Asst Chapl on Foreign Relns *Cant* 74-81; ARCIC from 74; Sec 74-90; Hon Can Cant Cathl *Cant* 82-89; Abp's Sec for Ecum Affairs 82-89; Chapl to The Queen from 87; Can Res and Prec St Paul's Cathl *Lon* 89-96; Select Preacher Ox Univ from 90; Area Bp Stafford *Lich* from 96. *Ash Garth, Broughton Crescent, Barlaston, Stoke-on-Trent ST12 9DD* Tel (01782) 373308 Fax 373705

HILL, Canon Colin. b 42. Leic Univ BSc64 Open Univ PhD88. Ripon Hall Ox 64. **d** 66 **p** 67. C Leic Martyrs *Leic* 66-69; C Braunstone 69-71; Lect Ecum Inst Thornaby Teesside 71-72; V Worsbrough St Thos and St Jas *Sheff* 72-78; Telford Planning Officer *Lich* 78-96; RD Telford 80-96; RD Telford Severn Gorge *Heref* 80-96; Preb Heref Cathl 83-96; Can Res Carl Cathl *Carl* from 96; Dioc Sec from 96. *4 The Abbey, Carlisle CA3 8TZ* Tel (01228) 590778 or 22573 Fax 48769

HILL, Canon Colin Arnold Clifford. b 29. Bris Univ 52. Ripon Hall Ox 55. **d** 57 **p** 58. C Rotherham *Sheff* 57-61; V Brightside St Thos 61-64; R Easthampstead *Ox* 64-73; Chapl RAF Coll Bracknell 68-73; V Croydon *Cant* 73-84; Chapl Abp Jo Whitgift Foundn 73-84; Hon Can Cant Cathl 75-84; V Croydon St Jo *S'wark* 85-94; Hon Can S'wark Cathl 85-94; Chapl to The Queen 90-94; rtd 94. *Silver Birches, 70 Preston Crowmarsh, Wallingford, Oxon OX10 6SL*

HILL, Canon David. b 25. AKC54. **d** 55 **p** 56. C Kingsbury H Innocents *Lon* 55-58; C Putney St Mary *S'wark* 58-62; V Battersea St Mich 62-89; RD Battersea 69-76; Hon Can S'wark Cathl 74-89; rtd 89; Perm to Offic *Chelmsf* from 89. *70 Gloucester Avenue, Maldon, Essex CM9 6LA* Tel (01621) 855384

HILL, David Rowland. b 34. Lon Univ BSc55. Qu Coll Birm. **d** 59 **p** 60. C Upper Tooting H Trin *S'wark* 59-61; C Cheam 61-63; C Richmond St Mary 63-68; V Sutton St Nicholas *Linc* 68-82; V Pinchbeck from 82. *The Vicarage, Spalding Road, Pinchbeck, Spalding, Lincs PE11 3ND* Tel (01775) 768710

HILL, Canon Derek Ingram. b 12. FSA74 Trin Coll Ox BA34 MA38 Kent Univ Hon DD83. Wells Th Coll 34. **d** 35 **p** 36. C Buckland in Dover *Cant* 35-39; C Croydon St Andr 39-43; P-in-c S Norwood H Innocents 43-49; V 49-57; V Cant St Greg 57-65; R Cant St Pet and St Alphege w St Marg 65-74; P-in-c Cant St Mildred w St Mary de Castro 72-74; R Cant St Pet w St Alphege and St Marg etc 74-76; Can Res Cant Cathl 76-83; rtd 83. *2 St John's House, 40 Northgate, Canterbury, Kent CT1 1BE* Tel (01227) 761954

HILL, Derek Stanley. b 28. AKC53. **d** 53 **p** 54. C Rushmere *St E* 53-55; S Africa 55-57; C Boreham Wood All SS *St Alb* 57-59; V Crowfield *St E* 59-67; P-in-c Stonham Aspal 59-61; R 61-67; V Bury St Edmunds St Geo 67-73; P-in-c Ampton w Lt Livermere and Ingham 68-73; V Gazeley w Dalham 73-75; P-in-c Lidgate w Ousden 73-74; P-in-c Gt Bradley 74-78; V Gazeley w Dalham and Moulton 75-78; V Gt Barton 78-86; V Bury St Edmunds All SS 86-93; rtd 93. *Whinwillow, 38 Maltings Garth, Thurston, Bury St Edmunds, Suffolk IP31 3PP* Tel (01359) 30770

HILL, Elizabeth Jayne Louise. *See* DAVENPORT, Ms Elizabeth Jayne Louise

HILL, Eugene Mark. b 48. Univ of Wales (Lamp) BA71. Sarum Th Coll 71. **d** 73 **p** 74. C Sutton St Nic *S'wark* 73-77; Hon C 77-80; Asst Chapl Em Sch Wandsworth 77-87; Chapl from 87; Hon C St Helier *S'wark* 83-84; Hon C Caterham from 84; Dir Chr Studies Course from 85. *The Rectory, 5 Whyteleafe Road, Caterham, Surrey CR3 5EG* Tel (01883) 342062

HILL, Frederick Ashton. b 13. Ch Coll Cam BA34 MA38. Chich Th Coll 36. **d** 38 **p** 39. C Beckenham St Barn *Roch* 38-44; C Swindon New Town *Bris* 44-50; R Letchworth *St Alb* 50-69; R Gt and Lt Ryburgh w Gateley and Testerton *Nor* 69-93; R Stibbard 69-93; rtd 93. *3B Stibbard Road, Fulmodeston, Fakenham, Norfolk NR21 0LZ* Tel (01328) 878717

HILL, Geoffrey Dennison. b 31. Tyndale Hall Bris DipTh55. **d** 56 **p** 57. C Denton Holme *Carl* 56-59; R Asby w Ormside 59-63; R Arthuret 63-71; V Arnside 71-76; P-in-c Torver 76-79; rtd 91. *Holywath, Coniston, Cumbria LA21 8HN*

HILL, George Ernest. b 25. St Jo Coll Nottm. **d** 85 **p** 87. NSM Selston *S'well* from 85. *105 Main Road, Jacksdale, Nottingham NG16 5HR* Tel (01773) 603446

HILL, Mrs Gillian Beryl (Gill). b 53. Open Univ BA86. S Dios Minl Tr Scheme 87. **d** 90 **p** 94. NSM Southsea St Jude *Portsm* 90-95; C Southsea St Pet from 95. *27 Inglis Road, Southsea, Hants PO5 1PB* Tel (01705) 811233

HILL, Harold Gordon Haynes. b 15. Tyndale Hall Bris 36. **d** 39 **p** 40. C Aldridge *Lich* 39-42; Org Sec (N and Midl) ICM 42-46; Cen Sec S 46-48; R Whinburgh w Westfield *Nor* 48-81; R Reymerston 48-81; P-in-c Cranworth w Letton and Southbergh 78-79; rtd 81. *34 Morley Road, Sheringham, Norfolk NR26 8JE* Tel (01263) 824965

HILL, Harry Baxter. b 19. St Alb Minl Tr Scheme 76. **d** 79 **p** 80. Hon C Mill End and Heronsgate w W Hyde *St Alb* 79-84; Asst Chapl Amersham Hosp from 79; Perm to Offic from 84. *Stelling, 66 Quickley Lane, Chorleywood, Rickmansworth, Herts WD3 5AF* Tel (01923) 282309

HILL, Ian Maxwell. b 60. Loughb Univ BSc81 MCIT85. EMMTC DipTh95. **d** 95 **p** 96. NSM Thurnby Lodge *Leic* from 95. *4 Sturrock Close, Thurnby, Leics LE7 9QP* Tel 0116-243 1609

HILL, James Arthur. b 47. Ulster Univ BEd85. CITC. **d** 72 **p** 73. C Ballymena w Ballyclug *Conn* 72-74; C Arm St Mark w Aghavilly *Arm* 74-78; C Derg w Termonamongan *D & R* 78-79; I Inver w Mountcharles, Killaghtee and Killybegs 79-87. *53 Dufferin Avenue, Bangor, Co Down BT20 3AB* Tel (01247) 469090

HILL, James Reginald. b 06. Man Univ BA29. S'wark Ord Course 67. **d** 69 **p** 70. C Purley Ch Ch *S'wark* 69-77; Perm to Offic *Chich* 77-82 and from 88; Perm to Offic *St Alb* 82-88. *Bethany, Rosemary Avenue, Steyning, W Sussex BN44 3YS* Tel (01903) 816102

HILL, Mrs Jennifer Clare. b 50. City Univ BSc71 FBCO72. EAMTC 94. **d** 97. NSM Bottesford and Muston *Leic* from 97. *The Ridings, 3 Blacksmiths Close, Nether Broughton, Melton Mowbray, Leics LE14 3EW* Tel (01664) 823294

HILL, John. b 56. S'wark Ord Course. **d** 89 **p** 90. NSM Upper Norwood St Jo *S'wark* 89-94; Chapl RN from 94. *Royal Naval Chaplaincy Service, Room 203, Victory Building, HM Naval Base, Portsmouth PO1 3LS* Tel (01705) 727903 Fax 727112

HILL, John Michael. b 34. FCA. Oak Hill NSM Course 81. **d** 85 **p** 86. NSM Rayleigh *Chelmsf* 85-96; Perm to Offic *Lon* 86-94; NSM Rochford *Chelmsf* from 96. *8 High Road, Hockley, Essex SS5 4SX* Tel (01702) 203287

HILL, Kenneth. b 27. Wycliffe Coll Toronto LTh. **d** 58 **p** 59. Canada 58-61; C Newc St Matt w St Mary *Newc* 61-62; SSF 62-64; C Burslem St Werburgh *Lich* 64-67; C Walsall St Gabr Fulbrook 67-70; P-in-c Hanley St Jude 70-79; P-in-c Chacewater *Truro* 79-92; rtd 92; Perm to Offic *Truro* from 92. *Delmore, Sparnon Close, Redruth, Cornwall TR15 2RJ* Tel (01209) 219318

HILL, Kenneth James. b 43. Leic Univ BA64 Lon Univ BD68. Oak Hill Th Coll 65. **d** 69 **p** 70. C Southall Green St Jo *Lon* 69-72; C Blackheath Park St Mich *S'wark* 72-75; C Bath Abbey w St Jas *B & W* 75-83; P-in-c Bath St Mich w St Paul 75-82; R 82-83; R Huntspill 83-91; Perm to Offic from 91; Omega Order from 91. *The Omega Order, Winford Manor, Winford, Bristol BS18 8DW* Tel (01275) 472262

HILL, Laurence Bruce. b 43. AKC67. **d** 69 **p** 70. C Feltham *Lon* 69-72; C-in-c Hampstead St Steph 72-77; V Finchley H Trin from 77. *Holy Trinity Vicarage, 91 Church Lane, London N2 0TH* Tel 0181-883 8720

HILL, Leslie Hugh. b 23. Westcott Ho Cam 73. **d** 73 **p** 74. NSM Holbrook and Lt Eaton *Derby* 73-79; NSM Loscoe 79-85; P-in-c Denby 85-88; P-in-c Horsley Woodhouse 87-88; rtd 88; Perm to Offic *Derby* from 88. *1 Hunter Drive, Kilburn, Derby DE56 0ND* Tel (01332) 881081

HILL, Malcolm Crawford. b 43. Lon Univ DipTh70. Oak Hill Th Coll 68. **d** 71 **p** 72. C Maidstone St Luke *Cant* 71-74; C Longfleet *Sarum* 74-79; V Bexleyheath St Pet *Roch* 79-90; V Lee St Mildred

S'wark from 90. *The Vicarage, 1A Helder Grove, London SE12 0RB* Tel 0181-857 5205

HILL, Mrs Marjorie Ann. b 38. MCSP60. St Jo Coll Nottm 92. **d** 94 **p** 95. Par Dn Hull St Martin w Transfiguration *York* 94; C from 94. *87 Parkfield Drive, Hull HU3 6TF* Tel (01482) 566706

HILL, Dr Martyn William. b 43. MInstP68 CPhys85 Man Univ BSc64 Univ of Wales (Ban) PhD70. Westcott Ho Cam CTM92. **d** 92 **p** 93. C Horninglow *Lich* 92-95; TV Hawarden *St As* from 95. *St Mary's Vicarage, Church Road, Broughton, Chester CH4 0QB* Tel (01244) 520148

HILL, Matthew Anthony Robert. b 71. Leeds Univ BA93 Univ of Wales (Cardiff) BD96. St Mich Coll Llan 94. **d** 97. C Cardiff St Jo *Llan* from 97. *17 Brithdir Street, Cathays, Cardiff CF2 4LE* Tel (01222) 390703

HILL, Michael. b 32. TD77. AKC55. **d** 56 **p** 57. C Tynemouth Cullercoats St Paul *Newc* 56-59; C Drayton in Hales *Lich* 59-61; V Milton 61-64; V Preston Gubbals 64-73; V Leaton 64-76; CF (TA) 65-67; CF (TAVR) 67-87; V Oswestry St Oswald *Lich* 76-87; P-in-c Trefonen 80-83; V Sunningdale *Ox* 87-97; rtd 97. *The Vicarage, Sidbury Close, Sunningdale, Ascot, Berks SL5 0PD* Tel (01344) 20061

HILL, The Ven Michael Arthur. b 49. Ridley Hall Cam 74. **d** 77 **p** 78. C Addiscombe St Mary *Cant* 77-81; C Slough *Ox* 81-83; P-in-c Chesham Bois 83-90; R 90-92; RD Amersham 89-92; Adn Berks from 92. *Foxglove House, Love Lane, Donnington, Newbury, Berks RG13 2JG* Tel (01635) 552820 Fax 522165

HILL, The Rt Revd Michael John Giles. b 43. S Dios Minl Tr Scheme 82. **d** 84 **p** 86. Community of Our Lady and St John from 67; Abbot from 90; Perm to Offic *Win* 84-92; Lic to Offic from 92. *Alton Abbey, Abbey Road, Beech, Alton, Hants GU34 4AP* Tel (01420) 562145 or 563575 Fax 561691

HILL, Norman. b 20. St Chad's Coll Dur LTh48. Linc Th Coll 45. **d** 49 **p** 50. C Swinton *Sheff* 49-59; V Mosborough 59-72; P-in-c Codnor and Loscoe *Derby* 73-79; V 79-85; rtd 85. *10 The Hill, Walsingham, Norfolk NR22 6DP* Tel (01328) 820859

HILL, Norman William. b 14. Ch Coll Cam BA36 MA40. Linc Th Coll 43. **d** 45 **p** 46. C Hitchin St Mary *St Alb* 45-49; C St Alb Abbey 49-60; V Rickmansworth 60-74; P-in-c Northill 74-78; P-in-c Moggerhanger 74-78; P-in-c Northill w Moggerhanger 78-79; RD Biggleswade 75-79; rtd 80. *West Sillywrea, Langley-on-Tyne, Hexham, Northd NE47 5NE* Tel (01434) 684635

HILL, Canon Peter. b 36. AKC60. St Boniface Warminster 60. **d** 61 **p** 62. C Gt Berkhamsted *St Alb* 61-67; R Bedford St Mary 67-69; P-in-c 69-70; V Goldington 69-79; V Biggleswade 79-90; RD Biggleswade 80-85; Hon Can St Alb 85-90; V Holbeach *Linc* from 90; RD Elloe E from 94. *The Vicarage, Holbeach, Spalding, Lincs PE12 7DT* Tel (01406) 22185

HILL, Peter. b 50. Man Univ BSc71 Nottm Univ MTh90. Wycliffe Hall Ox 81. **d** 83 **p** 84. C Porchester *S'well* 83-86; V Huthwaite 86-95; P-in-c Calverton from 95; RD S'well from 97. *The Vicarage, Crookdale Lane, Calverton, Nottingham NG14 6GF* Tel 0115-965 2552 E-mail peter.hill@icthus.demon.co.uk

HILL, Ralph Jasper. b 15. Tyndale Hall Bris 38. **d** 41 **p** 42. C Stambermill *Worc* 41-44; C Harmondsworth *Lon* 44-45; C Wandsworth St Steph *S'wark* 45-48; Org Sec SAMS 49-59; Asst Master Hove Gr Sch 65-78; rtd 80; Perm to Offic *Chich* from 82. *29 Gorham Way, Telscombe Cliffs, Newhaven, E Sussex BN10 7BA* Tel (01273) 583729

HILL, Raymond John Walter. b 09. AKC34. **d** 34 **p** 35. C Bishopston *Bris* 34-37; C Henleaze 36-37; Jamaica 37-38; C Chertsey *Guildf* 38-41; C Pontesbury I and II *Heref* 41-45; C Ludlow 45-47; V Elmsted w Hastingleigh *Cant* 47-50; R Adisham 50-54; R Kingsnorth 54-65; R Shadoxhurst 54-65; V Westbury and Turweston *Ox* 65-77; P-in-c Shalstone w Biddlesden 68-77; rtd 77; Perm to Offic *Glouc* from 78. *15 Shepherds Way, Stow on the Wold, Cheltenham, Glos GL54 1EA* Tel (01451) 831028

HILL, Richard Brian. b 47. Dur Univ BA68 DipTh70. Cranmer Hall Dur 68 Westcott Ho Cam 70. **d** 71 **p** 72. C Cockermouth All SS w Ch Ch *Carl* 71-74; C Barrow St Geo w St Luke 74-76; V Walney Is 76-83; Dir of Clergy Tr 83-90; P-in-c Westward, Rosley-w-Woodside and Welton 83-90; V Gosforth All SS *Newc* from 90. *All Saints' Vicarage, 33 Brackenfield Road, Newcastle upon Tyne NE3 4DX* Tel 0191-285 6345

HILL, Preb Richard Hebert. b 11. Linc Th Coll 34. **d** 36 **p** 37. C Moor Allerton *Ripon* 36-39; CF (R of O) 39-45; R Berrington and Betton Strange *Heref* 45-61; V Bromyard 61-72; RD Bromyard 61-72; Preb Heref Cathl 65-78; C-in-c Pencombe w Marston Stannett and Lt Cowarne 69-72; R Ledbury 72-78; RD Ledbury 72-78; P-in-c Eastnor 73-78; rtd 78; Perm to Offic *Heref* from 79. *4 Old School, Henley Road, Ludlow, Shropshire SY8 1RA* Tel (01584) 874332

HILL, Richard Hugh Oldham. b 52. CCC Ox BA74 BA77 MA78. Wycliffe Hall Ox 75. **d** 78 **p** 79. C Harold Wood *Chelmsf* 78-81; C Hampreston *Sarum* 81-86; TV N Ferriby *York* from 86. *The Vicarage, St Barnabas Drive, Swanland, North Ferriby, N Humberside HU14 3RL* Tel (01482) 631271

HILL, Robert Joseph. b 45. Oak Hill Th Coll BA81. **d** 81 **p** 82. C W Derby St Luke *Liv* 81-84; P-in-c Devonport St Mich *Ex* from 84. *St Michael's Vicarage, 41 Albert Road, Plymouth PL2 1AB* Tel (01752) 562967

HILL, Robin. b 35. Cranmer Hall Dur 59. **d** 62 **p** 63. C Aspley *S'well* 62-65; V Mansfield St Aug 65-71; R Hulland, Atlow and Bradley *Derby* 71-76; Australia 76-86; P-in-c Alkmonton, Cubley, Marston, Montgomery etc *Derby* 86-93; P-in-c Ticknall, Smisby and Stanton by Bridge from 93; P-in-c Barrow-on-Trent w Twyford and Swarkestone from 94. *The Vicarage, 7 Church Lane, Ticknall, Derby DE7 1JU* Tel (01332) 862549

HILL, Roger Anthony John. b 45. Liv Univ BA67 Linacre Coll Ox BA69 MA. Ripon Hall Ox 67. **d** 70 **p** 71. C St Helier *S'wark* 70-74; C Dawley Parva *Lich* 74-75; C Cen Telford 76-77; TV 77-81; TR 81-88; TR Newark w Hawton, Cotham and Shelton *S'well* 88-89; TR Newark from 89; RD Newark 90-95. *The Rectory, 6 Bede House Lane, Newark, Notts NG24 1PY* Tel (01636) 704513

HILL, Simon George. b 53. Reading Univ BSc75 MSc78 Lon Univ DipRS82. S'wark Ord Course 80. **d** 83 **p** 84. Hon C Croydon St Aug *Cant* 83-84; Swaziland 84-86; Fiji 86-88; Hon C Croydon St Aug *S'wark* 88-90; Tanzania 90-94; Uganda from 94. *23 Godstone Road, Oxted, Surrey RH8 9JS*

HILL, Simon James. b 64. Sheff Univ BA85 Ex Univ PGCE88. Ripon Coll Cuddesdon BA84 DipMin95. **d** 95 **p** 96. C Manston *Ripon* from 95. *2 Manston Avenue, Leeds LS15 8BT* Tel 0113-264 1301

HILL, Stuart Graeme. b 64. Ripon Coll Cuddesdon BTh94. **d** 97. C Usworth *Dur* from 97. *55 Laurens Court, Washington, Tyne & Wear NE37 2EF* Tel 0191-416 1284 E-mail stuart.hill@virgin.net

HILL, Canon Thomas Henry. b 19. Univ of Wales BA41 BD45. **d** 66 **p** 67. C Roath St Marg *Llan* 66-67; P-in-c Cymmer and Abercregan 67-71; P-in-c Glyncorrwg 67-71; P-in-c Afan Vale 67-71; R Glyncorrwg w Afan Vale and Cymmer Afan 71-74; V Pembroke St Mary and St Mich *St D* 74-84; Can St D Cathl 80-84; rtd 84. *29 Mortimer Hill, Tring, Herts HP23 5JB* Tel (01442) 826558

HILL, Trevor Walton. b 30. Leeds Univ BA57. Coll of Resurr Mirfield. **d** 59 **p** 60. C Bollington St Jo *Ches* 59-62; C Woodchurch 62-64; V Addingham *Carl* 64-67; V Carl H Trin 67-71; R Wetheral w Warw 71-80; P-in-c Doddington w Wychling *Cant* 80-82; P-in-c Newnham 80-82; rtd 95. *59 Medina Avenue, Newport, Isle of Wight PO30 1HG*

HILL, William Henry George. b 21. S'wark Ord Course 66. **d** 69 **p** 70. C Welling *S'wark* 69-73; C Reigate St Luke S Park 73-76; V Lynsted w Kingsdown *Cant* 76-87; R Norton 76-87; rtd 87. *Little Orchard, 15 Bramley Hill, Bridport, Dorset DT6 3DP* Tel (01308) 423915

HILL, William James. b 13. Ripon Hall Ox 60. **d** 61 **p** 62. C Breaston *Derby* 61-63; C Darley w S Darley 63-66; V Chinley w Buxworth 68-74; R Whitwell 74-77; P-in-c Denby 77-79; rtd 79; Perm to Offic *Derby* from 79. *Greenstile, 15 Harewood Road, Allestree, Derby DE22 2JP* Tel (01332) 556135

HILL-BROWN, Timothy Duncan. b 65. Westmr Coll Ox BA87. Wycliffe Hall Ox DPS92. **d** 93 **p** 94. C Sparkhill w Greet and Sparkbrook *Birm* 93-97; C Sutton Coldfield H Trin from 97. *1 Trinity Hill, Sutton Coldfield, West Midlands B72 1GH* Tel 0121-355 3352

HILL-TOUT, Mark Laurence. b 50. AKC73. **d** 74 **p** 75. C Brighton Resurr *Chich* 74-77; C New Shoreham 77-79; C Old Shoreham 77-79; Dioc Stewardship Adv Lewes and Hastings 79-84; P-in-c Stonegate 79-83; R Horsted Keynes 84-89; V St Helens *Portsm* 89-95; V Sea View 89-95; P-in-c Widley w Wymering from 95. *The Vicarage, Medina Road, Portsmouth PO6 3NH* Tel (01705) 376307

HILLARY, Leslie Tyrone James. b 59. Cranmer Hall Dur 84. **d** 87 **p** 88. C Middlesbrough All SS *York* 87-89; C Stainton-in-Cleveland 89-91; CF from 91. *MOD Chaplains (Army), Trenchard Lines, Upavon, Pewsey, Wilts SN9 6BE* Tel (01980) 615804 Fax 615800

HILLEBRAND, Frank David. b 46. AKC68. St Boniface Warminster 68. **d** 69 **p** 70. C Wood Green St Mich *Lon* 69-72; C Evesham *Worc* 72-75; V Worc H Trin 75-80; P-in-c Kidderminster St Jo 80-81; V 81-90; TR Kidderminster St Jo and H Innocents 90-91; TV High Wycombe *Ox* 91-95; TR from 95. *The Vicarage, 6 Priory Avenue, High Wycombe, Bucks HP13 6SH* Tel (01494) 525602

HILLIAM, Mrs Cheryl. b 49. EMMTC DipTh94. **d** 94 **p** 95. C Linc St Faith and St Martin w St Pet *Linc* from 94. *46 Yarborough Crescent, Lincoln LN1 3LU* Tel (01522) 512650

HILLIARD, David. b 57. BTh. **d** 91 **p** 92. C Holywood *D & D* 91-94; C Seagoe 94-96; I Tartaraghan w Diamond *Arm* from 96. *Tartaraghan Rectory, 5 Tarthlogue Road, Portadown, Co Armagh BT62 1RB* Tel (01762) 851289

HILLIARD, The Very Revd George Percival St John. b 45. TCD BA67. **d** 69 **p** 70. C Seapatrick *D & D* 69-73; C Carrickfergus *Conn* 73-76; I Fanlobbus Union *C, C & R* 76-85; Prec Cork Cathl from 85; I Cloyne Union from 85; Dean Cloyne from 85. *The Deanery, Dungourney Road, Midleton, Co Cork, Irish Republic* Tel Cork (21) 631449

HILLIARD, John William Richard (Jack). b 19. St Jo Coll Morpeth 54. **d** 55 **p** 56. Australia 55-68; I Carbury *M & K* 68-72; C W Bridgford *S'well* 72-78; V Mansfield St Aug 78-84; P-in-c Everton and Mattersey w Clayworth 84-87; rtd 87. *Flat 4,*

Spencer Court, Merton Road, Southsea, Hants PO5 2AJ Tel (01705) 293918

HILLIARD, Robert Godfrey. b 52. Univ of Wales DipTh75 Portsm Univ BEd97. St Mich Coll Llan. **d** 75 **p** 76. C Whitchurch *Llan* 75-80; Chapl RN from 80. *Royal Naval Chaplaincy Service, Room 203, Victory Building, HM Naval Base, Portsmouth PO1 3LS* Tel (01705) 727903 Fax 727112

HILLIER, Derek John. b 30. Sarum Th Coll 61. **d** 63 **p** 64. C Salisbury St Mark *Sarum* 63-65; C Weymouth H Trin 65-66; R Caundle Bishop w Caundle Marsh and Holwell 66-75; P-in-c Pulham 70-78; R The Caundles and Holwell 75-81; R The Caundles w Folke and Holwell from 81. *The Rectory, Bishops Caundle, Sherborne, Dorset DT9 5ND* Tel (01963) 23243

HILLIER, Timothy John. b 55. Westmr Coll Ox CertEd77. Oak Hill Th Coll 94. **d** 96 **p** 97. C Chertsey *Guildf* from 96. *18 Weymead Close, Chertsey, Surrey KT16 8PG* Tel (01932) 566328

HILLMAN, Clive Ralph. b 71. York Univ BSc92. St Steph Ho Ox BA93. **d** 96 **p** 97. C Kingston upon Hull St Alb *York* from 96. *4 Moorbeck Close, Hull HU6 8QT*

HILLMAN, Jesse James. b 22. S'wark Ord Course 83. **d** 86 **p** 87. Communications Sec CMS 86; NSM Kidbrooke *S'wark* 86; NSM Peterchurch w Vowchurch, Turnastone and Dorstone *Heref* 86-93; rtd 93; Perm to Offic *Heref* from 93. *Wesley Place, Peterchurch, Hereford HR2 0RY* Tel (01981) 550609

HILLMAN, John Anthony. b 32. St Chad's Coll Dur BA53. St Mich Coll Llan 54. **d** 55 **p** 56. C Llangollen *St As* 56-60; S Africa 60-86; TV Wolstanton *Lich* 86-91; P-in-c E Goscote w Ratcliffe and Rearsby *Leic* 91-93; TV Syston TM from 93. *The Vicarage, 25 Ling Dale, East Goscote, Leicester LE7 3XW* Tel 0116-260 5938

HILLS, John Bucknell. b 21. Glouc Sch of Min. **d** 89 **p** 89. NSM Moreton-in-Marsh w Batsford, Todenham etc *Glouc* 89-94; Perm to Offic from 94. *3 Bowling Green Court, Hospital Road, Moreton-in-Marsh, Glos GL56 0BX* Tel (01608) 651507

HILLS, Kenneth Hugh. b 30. Univ of NZ BCom54. Ripon Hall Ox 55. **d** 57 **p** 58. C Handsworth St Mary *Birm* 57-59; New Zealand 59-67; Ind Chapl *Birm* 67-74; Chapl Aston Univ 74-82; rtd 91; Community Member Cluny Hill Coll from 93. *The Park, Forres, Morayshire IV36 0TZ* Tel (01309) 672288

HILLS, Mervyn Hyde. b 19. Ch Coll Cam BA40 MA44. Westcott Ho Cam 40. **d** 42 **p** 43. C Croydon St Sav *Cant* 42-44; C Boyne Hill *Ox* 44-49; C Whitley Ch Ch 49-53; V Bourn *Ely* 53-86; R Kingston 53-86; rtd 86; Perm to Offic *Ely* from 87. *13 Bakers' Close, Comberton, Cambridge CB3 7DJ* Tel (01223) 262993

HILLS, Michael John. b 58. BA82. Westcott Ho Cam 87. **d** 88 **p** 89. C Workington St Jo *Carl* 88-91; C Gosforth All SS *Newc* 91-93; TV Seaton Hirst from 93. *St Andrew's Vicarage, Hawthorn Road, Ashington, Northd NE63 9AU* Tel (01670) 818691

HILLS, Michael Rae Buchanan. b 52. CQSW83 Univ of Wales (Lamp) BA81 Ex Univ BPhil83. St Steph Ho Ox DipMin94. **d** 94 **p** 95. C Kingston upon Hull St Nic *York* 94-97; V Newington w Dairycoates from 97. *St John's Vicarage, 203 St George's Road, Hull HU3 3SP* Tel (01482) 214551

HILLS, Michael William John. b 54. Univ of Wales (Lamp) BA84. Westcott Ho Cam 85. **d** 87 **p** 88. C Reddish *Man* 87-91; V Bolton St Phil from 91. *St Philip's Vicarage, 453 Bridgeman Street, Bolton BL3 6TH* Tel (01204) 61533

HILLS, Richard Leslie. b 36. FMA83 Qu Coll Cam MA63 DIC64 Man Univ PhD68. St Deiniol's Hawarden 85. **d** 87 **p** 88. C Urmston *Man* 87-89; C Gt Yarmouth *Nor* 89-90; NSM Mottram in Longdendale w Woodhead *Ches* 90-93; NSM Mottram in Longdendale from 93. *Stamford Cottage, 47 Old Road, Mottram, Hyde, Cheshire SK14 6LW* Tel (01457) 763104

HILLS, Roger Malcolm. b 42. Oak Hill Th Coll 83. **d** 86 **p** 87. Hon C Mill Hill Jo Keble Ch *Lon* from 86; NSM Mill Hill St Mich from 86. *22 Sefton Avenue, London NW7 3QD* Tel 0181-959 1931

HILLS, Rowland Jonathan. b 12. Selw Coll Cam BA35 MA39. Cuddesdon Coll 36. **d** 37 **p** 38. C Hampton All SS *Lon* 37-39; C Forest Row *Chich* 39-40; P-in-c 40-44; V 44-48; V Brighton Gd Shep Preston 48-59; V Iffley *Ox* 59-75; rtd 75; Perm to Offic *Ox* from 76; Chapl Venice w Trieste *Eur* 79-80; Chapl San Remo w Bordighera 81. *St John's Home, St Mary's Road, Oxford OX4 1QE*

HILLYER, Charles Norman. b 21. Lon Univ BD48. Lambeth STh67 ALCD48. **d** 48 **p** 49. C Finchley Ch Ch *Lon* 48-51; C New Malden and Coombe *S'wark* 51-54; V Hanley Road St Sav w St Paul *Lon* 54-59; Chapl City of Lon Maternity Hosp 54-59; V Ponsbourne *St Alb* 59-70; Chapl Tolmers Park Hosp 59-70; Lib Tyndale Ho Cam 70-73; Org Ed UCCF 73-79; Sec Tyndale Fellowship Bibl Research Cam 73-75; P-in-c Hatherleigh *Ex* 79-81; V 81-86; rtd 86; Perm to Offic *Sarum* from 89. *Charters, The Avenue, Sherborne, Dorset DT9 3AJ* Tel (01935) 813357

HILTON, Clive. b 30. K Coll Lon 54. **d** 58 **p** 59. C Wythenshawe Wm Temple Ch CD *Man* 58-61; C Newton Heath All SS 61-62; C-in-c Oldham St Chad Limeside CD 62-65; V Oldham St Chad Limeside 65-70; P-in-c Gravesend H Family *Roch* 70-71; R Killamarsh *Derby* 71-88; R Broughton w Loddington and Cransley etc *Pet* 88-91; rtd 92; Perm to Offic *Man* from 92. *7 Chudleigh Close, Altrincham, Cheshire WA14 4XE* Tel 0161-941 3010

HILTON, Ian Anthony. b 57. St Jo Coll Nottm 83. **d** 86 **p** 87. C Nottingham St Sav *S'well* 86-90; C Aspley 90-97; P-in-c Colchester, New Town and The Hythe *Chelmsf* from 97. *The Rectory, 24 New Town Road, Colchester CO1 2EF* Tel (01206) 570442

HILTON, John. b 49. Ex Univ BA70. Cuddesdon Coll 71. **d** 73 **p** 74. C W Derby (or Tuebrook) St Jo *Liv* 73-79; V Orford St Andr 79-96; V Leeds St Wilfrid *Ripon* from 96. *St Wilfrid's Vicarage, Chatsworth Road, Leeds LS8 3RS* Tel 0113-249 7724

HILTON, John Read. b 41. Lon Univ BD63 AKC65 LSE BSc73. **d** 65 **p** 66. C Cov H Trin *Cov* 65-69; C Hemel Hempstead *St Alb* 69-70; Hon C Catford St Andr *S'wark* 70-81. *89 Arngask Road, London SE6 1XZ* Tel 0181-698 1965

HILTON-TURVEY, Geoffrey Michael. b 34. Oak Hill Th Coll 80. **d** 81 **p** 82. C Bispham *Blackb* 81-85; V Inskip from 85. *St Peter's Vicarage, Preston Road, Inskip, Preston PR4 0TT* Tel (01772) 690316

HINCHCLIFFE, Garry Anthony Frank. b 68. New Coll Edin BD94. Edin Th Coll CECM93. **d** 94 **p** 95. C Dumfries *Glas* from 94. *39 Barnton Road, Georgetown, Dumfries DG1 4HN* Tel (01387) 252158

HINCHEY, Peter John. b 30. LTCL53. Chich Th Coll 55. **d** 58 **p** 59. C Malden St Jo *S'wark* 58-61; V Rosherville *Roch* 61-67; V Gillingham St Aug 67-72; V Bromley St Andr 72-74; Hon Chapl to Bp 74-78; Hon C Lamorbey H Redeemer 76-78; R Foots Cray 78-81; Perm to Offic *Chich* 92-94; rtd 94; Perm to Offic *S'wark* from 94; Hon C Rotherhithe St Mary w All SS from 94; Perm to Offic *Chelmsf* from 95. *2 Elizabeth Avenue, Ilford, Essex IG1 1TU* Tel 0181-478 5723

HINCKLEY, Paul Frederick. b 61. Cranfield Inst of Tech MSc85 Farnborough Tech Coll HND83. Ridley Hall Cam CTM94. **d** 94 **p** 95. C Ovenden *Wakef* from 94. *82 Ashfield Drive, Ovenden, Halifax, W Yorkshire HX3 5PG* Tel (01422) 353502

✠**HIND, The Rt Revd John William.** b 45. Leeds Univ BA66. Cuddesdon Coll 70. **d** 72 **p** 73 **c** 91. C Catford (Southend) and Downham *S'wark* 72-76; V Forest Hill Ch Ch 76-82; P-in-c Forest Hill St Paul 81-82; Wiccamical Preb Chich Cathl *Chich* 82-91; Prin Chich Th Coll 82-91; Area Bp Horsham *Chich* 91-93; Bp Eur from 93; Asst Bp Chich from 93. *Bishop's Lodge, Worth, Crawley, W Sussex RH10 7RT, or 14 Tufton Street, London SW1P 3QZ* Tel (01293) 883051 or 0171-976 8001 Fax (01293) 884479 or 0171-976 8002 E-mail 101741.3160@compuserve.com

HIND, Canon Stanley Maurice. b 29. AKC53. **d** 54 **p** 55. C Haydock St Jas *Liv* 54-57; C Elland *Wakef* 57-60; V Mirfield Eastthorpe St Paul 60-67; V Carleton 67-78; V E Hardwick 72-78; V Morley St Pet w Churwell 78-86; V Womersley 86-87; P-in-c Kirk Smeaton 86-87; V Womersley and Kirk Smeaton 87-94; Hon Can Wakef Cathl 89-94; rtd 94; Perm to Offic *Wakef* from 94. *1 The Lilacs, Carleton Road, Pontefract, W Yorkshire WF8 3RW* Tel (01977) 700386

HINDLE, Miss Penelope Jane Bowyn. b 45. Trin Coll Bris 76. **dss** 84 **d** 87 **p** 94. Stoneycroft All SS *Liv* 84-89; Par Dn 87-89; Chapl R Free Hosp Lon 89-93; Asst Chapl N Herts NHS Trust from 93. *Oakland, 19 Park Lane, Knebworth, Herts SG3 6PD* Tel (01438) 811584 or 781518

HINDLEY, Canon Andrew David. b 59. Univ of Wales (Lamp) BA. Sarum & Wells Th Coll. **d** 82 **p** 83. C Huddersfield St Pet *Wakef* 82-84; C Huddersfield St Pet and All SS 84-86; P-in-c Holmfield 86-91; R Ribchester w Stidd *Blackb* 91-96; Bp's Adv for Leisure and Tourism 91-96; Chapl Ribchester Hosp from 91; Hon Can Blackb Cathl 96; Can Res Blackb Cathl from 96. *23 Billinge Avenue, Blackburn BB2 6SD* Tel (01254) 261152

HINDLEY, Anthony Talbot. b 41. Bernard Gilpin Soc Dur 61 Oak Hill Th Coll 62. **d** 66 **p** 67. C Stoke next Guildf St Jo *Guildf* 66-69; Kenya 70-78; C Redhill H Trin *S'wark* 78-79; P-in-c Eastbourne All So *Chich* 79-83; V 83-86; V S Malling from 86. *The Vicarage, Church Lane, South Malling, Lewes, E Sussex BN7 2JA* Tel (01273) 474387

HINDLEY, John. b 32. UWIST BSc71. **d** 84 **p** 85. NSM Llantilio Crossenny w Penrhos, Llanvetherine etc *Mon* 85-88; P-in-c Tilbrook *Ely* from 88; P-in-c Covington from 88; P-in-c Keyston and Bythorn from 88; P-in-c Catworth Magna from 88; RD Leightonstone from 89; P-in-c Gt w Lt Gidding and Steeple Gidding 94-96. *The Rectory, Church Lane, Tilbrook, Huntingdon, Cambs PE18 0JS* Tel (01480) 860147

HINDLEY, Roger Dennis. b 48. Birm Univ BA70 Ox Univ BA77 MA83. Ripon Coll Cuddesdon 75 Qu Coll Birm 77. **d** 78 **p** 79. C Rubery *Birm* 78-81; C Henbury *Bris* 81-83; V Erdington St Chad *Birm* 83-89; V Hill from 89; RD Sutton Coldfield from 96. *61 Mere Green Road, Sutton Coldfield, W Midlands B75 5BW* Tel 0121-308 0074

HINDLEY, Thomas Richard. b 31. ARIBA54 Sheff Univ BA53 Lon Univ BD66. Clifton Th Coll 61. **d** 63 **p** 64. C Kenilworth St Jo *Cov* 63-67; C Cheadle *Ches* 67-70; R Harpurhey Ch Ch *Man* 70-95; R Harpurhey St Steph 72-95; rtd 96; Perm to Offic *Man* from 96. *15 Twyford Close, Didsbury, Manchester M20 2YR* Tel 0161-438 0387

HINDS, Kenneth Arthur Lancelot. b 30. Bps' Coll Cheshunt. **d** 64 **p** 65. C Sawbridgeworth *St Alb* 64-67; C Gt Berkhamsted 67-71; V Boreham Wood St Mich 71-75; Trinidad and Tobago 75-79; P-in-c Gt Ilford St Luke *Chelmsf* 79-81; V 81-95; rtd 95; Perm to Offic *Chelmsf* from 95. *214 Aldborough Road South, Ilford, Essex IG3 8HF* Tel 0181-598 2963

HINDS, Paul Anthony. b 62. CA Tr Coll DipEvang94 St Mich Coll Llan DipTh88. **d** 88 **p** 89. C Skewen *Llan* 88-90; C Roath St Marg 90-91; C Stockland Green *Birm* 94-96; P-in-c from 96. *St Mark's Vicarage, Bleak Hill Road, Birmingham B23 7EL* Tel 0121-373 0130

HINE, Canon John Timothy Matusch. b 27. TCD BA51 MA54. Linc Th Coll 53. **d** 55 **p** 56. C Boston *Linc* 55-57; PV, Sacr and Succ Lin Cathl 57-60; C Bray and Braywood *Ox* 60-61; Min Can Windsor 60-62; V Laneast w St Clether *Truro* 62-65; V Tresmere 62-65; V Fareham H Trin *Portsm* 65-67; V Asthall and Swinbrook w Widford *Ox* 67-94; RD Witney 76-81 and 87-89; Hon Can Ch Ch 88-94; rtd 94. *Cheriton, Ring Street, Stalbridge, Sturminster Newton, Dorset DT10 2LZ* Tel (01963) 363813

HINE, John Victor. b 36. Open Univ BA82. Carl Dioc Tr Course 85. **d** 88 **p** 89. NSM Dean *Carl* 88-92; NSM Clifton 88-92; C Millom 92-94; P-in-c Gt Broughton and Broughton Moor from 94. *The Vicarage, The Green, Little Broughton, Cockermouth, Cumbria CA13 0YG* Tel (01900) 825317

HINE, Keith Ernest. b 50. Bradf Univ BA Leeds Univ CertEd. N Ord Course 89. **d** 89 **p** 90. C Wilmslow *Ches* 89-94; V Bowdon from 94. *The Vicarage, Church Brow, Bowdon, Altrincham, Cheshire WA14 2SG* Tel 0161-928 2468

HINES, Dr Richard Arthur. b 49. Imp Coll Lon MSc73 PhD76 K Coll Lon MTh89. Oak Hill Th Coll 82. **d** 84 **p** 85. C Mile Cross *Nor* 84-87; Lect Oak Hill Th Coll 87-97; Vice-Prin N Thames Minl Tr Course 94-97; R Happisburgh, Walcott, Hempstead w Eccles etc *Nor* from 97. *The Rectory, The Hill, Happisburgh, Norwich NR12 0PW* Tel (01692) 650313

HINEY, Thomas Bernard Felix (Tom). b 35. MC61. RMA 56. Ridley Hall Cam DipTh69. **d** 69 **p** 70. C Edgbaston St Aug *Birm* 69-71; CF 71-91; Chapl R Hosp Chelsea from 91. *The Royal Hospital Chelsea, Royal Hospital Road, London SW3 4SL* Tel 0171-730 0161 Fax 823 6871

HINGE, Canon David Gerald Francis. b 30. FRSA57. Wells Th Coll 64. **d** 66 **p** 67. C Brookfield St Anne, Highgate Rise *Lon* 66-69; C N Greenford All Hallows 69-71; V Winton *Man* 71-78; R Etherley *Dur* 78-96; Hon Can Dur Cathl from 90; rtd 96. *9 Hillside, Ingleton, Darlington, Co Durham DL2 3JH* Tel (01325) 732002

HINGE, Derek Colin. b 36. CChem60 MRSC60 Imp Coll Lon BSc58. St Alb Minl Tr Scheme 84. **d** 88 **p** 89. NSM Bishop's Stortford St Mich *St Alb* from 88. *12 Avenue Road, Bishop's Stortford, Herts CM23 5NU* Tel (01279) 652173

HINGLEY, Christopher James Howard. b 48. Trin Coll Ox BA69 MA71. Wycliffe Hall Ox 81. **d** 80 **p** 81. Zimbabwe 80-81 and from 87; Lic to Offic *Ox* 85-87. *Whitestone School, Postbag 4, Hillside, Bulawayo, Zimbabwe*

HINGLEY, Robert Charles. b 46. Ball Coll Ox BA69 MA74 Birm Univ CertEd73. Qu Coll Birm DipTh72. **d** 73 **p** 74. C Charlton St Luke w St Paul *S'wark* 73-76; Asst Warden Iona Abbey 76-77; TV Langley Marish *Ox* 77-83; V Balsall Heath St Paul *Birm* 83-90; Perm to Offic 90-91; V Birm St Luke 91-96; Lic to Offic from 96; Asst P Moseley St Agnes from 96. *40 Grove Avenue, Moseley, Birmingham B13 9RY* Tel 0121-449 0624

HINGLEY, Roderick Stanley Plant. b 51. St Chad's Coll Dur BA72. St Steph Ho Ox 74. **d** 75 **p** 76. C Lower Gornal *Lich* 75-79; C Tividale 79-82; C Broseley w Benthall *Heref* 82-84; C Wanstead St Mary *Chelmsf* 84-92; V Romford St Alb from 92. *St Alban's Vicarage, 3 Francombe Gardens, Romford RM1 2TH* Tel (01708) 473580

HINKES, Sidney George Stuart. b 25. Lon Univ BA50 BD70. St Steph Ho Ox 50. **d** 52 **p** 53. C Burton St Paul *Lich* 52-54; C Leigh St Clem *Chelmsf* 54-58; C Upton cum Chalvey *Ox* 58-66; C-in-c Bayswater St Mary CD 66-82; V Headington St Mary 83-90; rtd 90; Perm to Offic *B & W* 90-91; Perm to Offic *Bris* 92-93; Rtd Clergy Officer Swindon Adnry from 93. *1 The Bungalow, Bremilham Road, Malmesbury, Wilts SN16 0DQ* Tel (01666) 825249

HINKSMAN, Barrie Lawrence James. b 41. K Coll Lon BD64 AKC64. St Boniface Warminster 61. **d** 65 **p** 66. C Crosby *Linc* 65-67; Ecum Development Officer Scunthorpe Coun of Chs 67-69; C Chelmsley Wood *Birm* 69-72; TV 72-75; P-in-c Offchurch *Cov* 75-79; Bp's Adv for Lay Tr 75-79; Perm to Offic 89-90; Hon Chapl Cov Cathl from 90. *67 Cubbington Road, Lillington, Leamington Spa, Warks CV32 7AQ* Tel (01926) 832312 Fax as telephone

HINTON, David Hugh. b 31. Tyndale Hall Bris. **d** 63 **p** 64. C Belper *Derby* 63-67; C Bowling St Steph *Bradf* 67-71; V Denholme Gate 71-79; P-in-c Morton St Luke 79-85; V 85-86; rtd 86; Perm to Offic *Bradf* from 86. *9 Sydenham Place, Bradford, W Yorkshire BD3 0LB* Tel (01274) 643460

HINTON, Mrs Frances Mary. b 43. EN(G)85. EMMTC 89. **d** 92 **p** 94. Par Dn Hornsey Rise Whitehall Park Team *Lon* 92-94; C 94-97; C Upper Holloway from 97. *6 Zoffany Street, London N19 3ER* Tel 0171-263 4217

HINTON, John Dorsett Owen. b 21. Wells Th Coll 59. **d** 61 **p** 62. C Littleham w Exmouth *Ex* 61-67; V Pucklechurch and Abson w Dyrham *Bris* 67-86; rtd 86; Perm to Offic *Bris* from 86; Perm to Offic *B & W* from 86. *Tower House, Clifton Down Road, Bristol BS8 4AG* Tel 0117-973 9298

HINTON, Michael George. b 27. Mert Coll Ox BA48 MA51 Reading Univ PhD59. S Dios Minl Tr Scheme 81. **d** 83 **p** 84. NSM Weston-super-Mare St Paul *B & W* 83-85; NSM Sibertswold w Coldred *Cant* 85-87; NSM Eythorne and Elvington w Waldershare etc 87-95. *212 The Gateway, Dover, Kent CT16 1LL* Tel (01304) 830245

HINTON, Nigel Keith. b 49. Univ Coll Lon BSc70 Worc Coll of Educn PGCE73 Lon Univ MA87. Oak Hill NSM Course 89. **d** 92 **p** 93. NSM Cudham and Downe *Roch* from 92. *218 Swievelands Road, Biggin Hill, Westerham, Kent TN16 3QS* Tel (01959) 573017

HINTON, Robert Matthew. b 69. Lanc Univ BA91. Cranmer Hall Dur 94. **d** 97. C Lache cum Saltney *Ches* from 97. *69 Sandy Lane, Saltney, Chester CH2 8UB* Tel (01244) 683225

HINTON, Roger Amos. b 33. Keble Coll Ox BA56 MA60. Ridley Hall Cam 56. **d** 58 **p** 59. C Drypool St Columba *York* 58-61; CMS 62-76; India 62-67; Tutor CMS Tr Coll Chislehurst 67-69; Pakistan 69-76; V Coalville *Leic* 76-78; V Coalville and Bardon Hill 78-85; RD Akeley S 81-84; TR Bushbury *Lich* from 85. *The Rectory, Bushbury Lane, Bushbury, Wolverhampton WV10 8JP* Tel (01902) 782226

HIPKINS, Leslie Michael. b 35. ACIS60 Univ Coll Dur BA57. Westcott Ho Cam 89 Oak Hill Th Coll 78. **d** 81 **p** 82. NSM Halstead St Andr w H Trin and Greenstead Green *Chelmsf* 81-87; C Tolleshunt Knights w Tiptree and Gt Braxted 87-89; P-in-c Cratfield w Heveningham and Ubbeston etc *St E* from 89. *The Vicarage, Cratfield, Halesworth, Suffolk IP19 0BU* Tel (01986) 798564

HIPPLE, Maureen Atlee. b 53. **d** 94 **p** 94. NSM Portarlington w Cloneyhurke and Lea *M & K* 96-97; USA from 97. *Address temp unknown*

HIRONS, Malcolm Percy. b 36. Or Coll Ox BA59 MA62. Wycliffe Hall Ox 59. **d** 61 **p** 62. C Edgbaston St Aug *Birm* 61-64; Chapl Warw Sch 64-65; C Beverley Minster *York* 65-69; V Barnby upon Don *Sheff* 69-80; P-in-c Kirk Bramwith 75-80; P-in-c Fenwick 75-80; V Norton Woodseats St Paul from 80. *St Paul's Vicarage, 6 Angerford Avenue, Sheffield S8 9BG* Tel 0114-255 1945

HIRST, Alan. b 44. Leeds Univ CQSW74. Linc Th Coll 79. **d** 81 **p** 82. C Newton Heath All SS *Man* 81-84; Chapl to the Deaf 84-88; V Oldham St Chad Limeside 88-91; Dep Chapl HM Pris Liv 91-92; Chapl HM Pris Ranby 92-96; Chapl HM Pris Wakef from 96. *HM Prison, Love Lane, Wakefield, W Yorkshire WF2 8AG* Tel (01924) 378282 Fax 384391

HIRST, Anthony Melville. b 50. Keele Univ BA73. Cuddesdon Coll 74. **d** 77 **p** 78. C S Gillingham *Roch* 77-80; C Coity w Nolton *Llan* 80-83; OSB from 81; R Hallaton w Horninghold, Allexton, Tugby etc *Leic* 83-90; V Arthog w Fairbourne w Llangelynnin w Rhoslefain *Ban* 90-97; R Montgomery and Forden and Llandyssil *St As* from 97. *The Rectory, Lions Bank, Montgomery SY15 6PT* Tel (01686) 668243 Fax as telephone E-mail ahirst@avnet.co.uk

HIRST, David William. b 37. Man Univ BA78. Brasted Th Coll 59 St Aid Birkenhead 61. **d** 63 **p** 64. C Clayton *Man* 63-64; C Bury St Jo 64-66; C Wythenshawe Wm Temple Ch 67-70; V Oldham St Chad Limeside 70-79; V Friezland 79-91; R Ashton St Mich 91-95; Chapl HM Pris Buckley Hall from 95; Lic Preacher *Man* from 95. *HM Detention Centre, Buckley Hall, Buckley Road, Rochdale, Lancs OL12 9DT* Tel (01706) 861610

HIRST, Douglas. b 33. Oak Hill Th Coll 89. **d** 91 **p** 93. NSM Thorley *St Alb* 91-95. *Axholme, 68 Cannons Close, Bishop's Stortford, Herts CM23 2BQ* Tel (01279) 651345

HIRST, Canon Godfrey Ian. b 41. MBIM Univ of Wales (Lamp) BA63. Chich Th Coll 63. **d** 65 **p** 66. C Brierfield *Blackb* 65-68; Ind Chapl *Liv* 68-71; TV Kirkby 71-75; Ind Chapl *Blackb* 75-94; P-in-c Treales 75-87; Hon Can Blackb Cathl from 83; Can Res Blackb Cathl 87-94; V Lytham St Cuth from 94. *The Vicarage, Church Road, Lytham St Annes, Lancs FY8 5PX* Tel (01253) 736168

HIRST, John Adrian. b 49. St Jo Coll Nottm BTh78. **d** 78 **p** 79. C Cheltenham St Mark *Glouc* 78-84; TV 84-85; TV Swan *Ox* 85-89; R Denham from 89. *The Rectory, Ashmead Lane, Denham, Uxbridge, Middx UB9 5BB* Tel (01895) 832771

HIRST, Mrs Judith (Judy). b 54. St Mary's Coll Dur BA76 LMH Ox PGCE77 Hull Univ MA86. Cranmer Hall Dur BA94. **d** 94 **p** 95. C Dur St Oswald *Dur* from 94; Bp's Adv in Pastoral Care and Counselling from 94. *1 Mill Hill Lane, Durham DH1 3LQ* Tel 0191-374 3979

HIRST, Peter Thornton. b 34. Leeds Univ BA59. Ely Th Coll 59. **d** 61 **p** 62. C Brierley Hill *Lich* 61-64; C Wednesfield St Thos 64-66; R Salford St Bart *Man* 66-71; V Sedgley St Mary *Lich* 71-77; TR Billingham St Aid *Dur* 77-86; TR Elland *Wakef* 86-90; Ind Chapl *Ripon* 93-96; C Headingley 93-96; rtd 96. *33 Bent Lea, Bradley Road, Huddersfield HD2 1QW* Tel (01484) 427058

HIRST, Reginald Arnold Archer. b 36. St Paul's Grahamstown. **d** 60 **p** 61. S Africa 60-88; R Wickham *Portsm* from 88. *The*

Rectory, Southwick Road, Wickham, Fareham, Hants PO17 6HR Tel (01329) 832134

HIRST, Wilfrid. b 11. Roch Th Coll 65. **d** 66 **p** 67. C Woodmansterne *S'wark* 66-69; C Shere *Guildf* 69-71; R Lifton *Ex* 71-74; R Kelly w Bradstone 71-74; R Exbourne w Jacobstowe 74-77; rtd 77; Perm to Offic *Chich* from 77. *3 Park Drive, Felpham, Bognor Regis, W Sussex PO22 7RD* Tel (01243) 584058

HISCOCK, David Alan. b 52. Sarum & Wells Th Coll. **d** 85 **p** 86. C Charlton Kings St Mary *Glouc* 85-89; TV Swan *Ox* from 89. *The Rectory, Marsh Gibbon, Bicester, Oxon OX6 0HJ* Tel (01869) 277297

HISCOCK, Donald Henry. b 26. St Mich Th Coll Crafers 50 ACT ThL56. **d** 53 **p** 54. Australia 53 and from 65; SSM from 54; C Averham w Kelham *S'well* 56-58; Lic to Offic 58-59; S Africa 59-60; Basutoland 60-61; rtd 92. *12 Charsley Street, Willagee, W Australia 6156* Tel Adelaide (8) 9314 5192 or 9364 8472

HISCOCK, Gary Edward. b 43. DipDrama68 Lon Univ DipRS88. Oak Hill Th Coll BA90. **d** 90 **p** 91. C Cheltenham St Luke and St Jo *Glouc* 90-94; C Hardwicke, Quedgeley and Elmore w Longney 95-96; rtd 96. *25 Bournside Road, Cheltenham, Glos GL51 5AL* Tel (01242) 513002

HISCOCK, Peter George Harold. b 31. Wadh Coll Ox BA54 MA66. Ely Th Coll 54. **d** 58 **p** 59. C Edge Hill St Dunstan *Liv* 58-61; C Kirkby 61-64; C Southport St Luke 64-66; Asst Dean of Residence TCD 66-68; Dean of Res TCD 68-73; India 73-76; TV Jarrow *Dur* 77-82; Chapl Univ Coll Dur 82-87; RD Newc Cen *Newc* 87-94; P-in-c Dinnington 87-88; TV Ch the King in the Dio of Newc 88-94; rtd 94. *8 Banbury Road, London E9 7DU* Tel 0181-986 2252

HISCOX, Jonathan Ronald James. b 64. Univ of Wales (Cardiff) DipTh85. Qu Coll Birm 87. **d** 89 **p** 90. C Wiveliscombe *B & W* 89-93; P-in-c Donyatt w Horton, Broadway and Ashill 93-94; TV Ilminster and District from 94. *The Rectory, Broadway, Ilminster, Somerset TA19 9RE* Tel (01460) 52559

HITCH, Kim William. b 54. Leic Univ BSc75 K Coll Lon MA94. Trin Coll Bris 76. **d** 78 **p** 79. C Becontree St Mary *Chelmsf* 78-80; C Huyton Quarry *Liv* 80-83; V Hatcham St Jas *S'wark* 83-91; TR Kidbrooke from 91. *St James's Rectory, 62 Kidbrooke Park Road, London SE3 0DU* Tel 0181-856 3438

HITCHCOCK, David. b 37. MIEH. S'wark Ord Course 70. **d** 73 **p** 74. NSM Milton next Gravesend Ch Ch *Roch* 73-94; NSM Chalk from 96; Chapl ACF from 79; Asst ChStJ from 94. *148 Old Road East, Gravesend, Kent DA12 1PF* Tel (01474) 361091

HITCHINS, Graham Edward David. b 54. S Dios Minl Tr Scheme 91. **d** 94 **p** 95. C Bishops Waltham *Portsm* from 94; C Upham from 94. *15 Denewulf Close, Bishops Waltham, Southampton SO32 1GZ* Tel (01489) 894729

HITCHINSON, Preb William Henry. b 12. Chich Th Coll 51. **d** 53 **p** 54. C Twickenham St Mary *Lon* 53-56; V Eastcote St Lawr 56-80; Preb St Paul's Cathl 76-80; rtd 80. *66 Waller Drive, Northwood, Middx HA6 1BW* Tel (01923) 829778

HITCHMAN, Keith John. b 62. Middx Univ BSc90. Trin Coll Bris BA95. **d** 95 **p** 96. C Bestwood *S'well* from 95. *17 Harvest Close, Nottingham NG5 9BW* Tel 0115-975 3378

HITCHMOUGH, William. b 30. N Ord Course. **d** 81 **p** 82. NSM Penketh *Liv* 81-83; Perm to Offic from 83; Chapl Warrington Distr Gen Hosp from 83. *15 Beecroft Close, Warrington WA5 5QX* Tel (01925) 650541

HIZA, Douglas William. b 38. Richmond Univ Virginia BA60 MDiv63 Mankato State Univ MS70. Virginia Th Sem 60. **d** 63 **p** 64. USA 63-79; Chapl Hackney Hosp Gp Lon 80-95; Chapl Homerton Hosp Lon 80-95. *International Counselling Skills, 140 Tabernacle Street, London EC2A 4SD* Tel 0171-336 6197

HJORTH, Rolf Gunnar Leer. b 25. AMICE St Jo Coll Ox BA46 MA50. Wycliffe Hall Ox 61. **d** 62 **p** 63. C Cumnor *Ox* 62-65; V Bramfield and Walpole *St E* 65-69; V Oulton *Lich* 69-78; Chapl Ostend w Knokke and Bruges *Eur* 78-84; Chapl Düsseldorf 85-90; rtd 90. *Sa Fontansa 104, Begur, 17255 Girona, Spain*

HOAD, Anne Elizabeth. b 42. Bris Univ BA63. **dss** 69 **d** 94 **p** 95. Asst Chapl Imp Coll *Lon* 69-74; S'wark Lay Tr Scheme 74-77; Brixton St Matt *S'wark* 77-80; Charlton St Luke w H Trin 80-94; Project Worker Community of Women and Men 88-91; Voc Adv Lewisham from 91; Chapl Lewisham Hosp from 92; Hon C Lee Gd Shep w St Pet from 94. *14 Silk Close, Dorville Road, London SE12 8DL* Tel 0181-297 8761

HOAD, Miss Rosemary Claire. b 60. Cranmer Hall Dur 92. **d** 94 **p** 95. C Epsom St Martin *Guildf* from 94. *115 Albert Road, Epsom, Surrey KT17 4EN* Tel (01372) 741739

HOAR, George Stanley. b 20. Chich Th Coll 47. **d** 50 **p** 53. C Cullercoats St Geo *Newc* 50-52; C Old Brumby *Linc* 53-56; V Alvingham w N and S Cockerington 56-60; V Leake 60-71; V Castle Bytham 71-91; R Careby w Holywell and Aunby 73-91; R Lt Bytham 73-91; rtd 91; Perm to Offic *Pet* from 91. *1 Sulthorpe Road, Ketton, Stamford, Lincs PE9 3SN* Tel (01780) 720817

HOARE, Carol. b 46. Lon Univ BA68 Birm Univ CertEd69. Qu Coll Birm 86 WMMTC 86. **d** 91 **p** 94. NSM Curdworth *Birm* from 91. *14 Elms Road, Sutton Coldfield, W Midlands B72 1JF* Tel 0121-354 1117

HOARE, David Albert Sylvester. b 47. **d** 95. Asst Chapl Gib Cathl *Eur* from 95. *The Old Deanery Flat, 3 Governor's Lane, Gibraltar*

HOARE, Canon David Marlyn. b 33. Bps' Coll Cheshunt 60. **d** 63 **p** 64. C Ampthill w Millbrook and Steppingley *St Alb* 63-67; C Bushey 67-70; V Harlington 70-76; V Oxhey All SS 76-81; V Hellesdon *Nor* from 81; Hon Can Nor Cathl from 95. *The Vicarage, Broom Avenue, Hellesdon, Norwich NR6 6LG* Tel (01603) 426902

HOARE, Janet Francis Mary. *See* MILES, Ms Janet Francis Mary

HOARE, Patrick Reginald Andrew Reid (Toddy). b 47. TD80 and Bar 88. Hull Univ MA90. Wycliffe Hall Ox 77. **d** 80 **p** 81. C Guisborough *York* 80-83; CF (TA) from 82; P-in-c Felixkirk w Boltby *York* from 83; P-in-c Kirby Knowle from 83; P-in-c Leake w Over and Nether Silton and Kepwick from 83; P-in-c Cowesby from 83. *The Vicarage, Knayton, Thirsk, N Yorkshire YO7 4AZ* Tel (01845) 537277

HOARE, Patrick Vernon Keymer. b 35. Oak Hill NSM Course 90. **d** 93 **p** 94. NSM Staines St Mary and St Pet *Lon* 93-96; P-in-c Littleton from 96. *Littleton Rectory, Squire Bridge Road, Shepperton, Middx TW17 0QE* Tel (01932) 562249

HOARE, Roger John. b 38. Tyndale Hall Bris 63. **d** 66 **p** 67. C Stoughton *Guildf* 66-70; C Chesham St Mary *Ox* 70-73; V Bath St Bart *B & W* 73-83; V Gt Faringdon w Lt Coxwell *Ox* 83-89; Deputation Appeals Org (NE Lon) Children's Soc 89-93; P-in-c Lambourne w Abridge and Stapleford Abbotts *Chelmsf* from 93; Ind Chapl from 93. *The Rectory, 39 Hoe Lane, Abridge, Romford RM4 1AU* Tel (01992) 813424 Fax as telephone

✠**HOARE, The Rt Revd Rupert William Noel.** b 40. Trin Coll Ox BA61 MA66 Fitzw Ho Cam BA64 MA84 Birm Univ PhD73. Westcott Ho Cam 62. **d** 64 **p** 65 **c** 93. C Oldham St Mary w St Pet *Man* 64-67; Lect Qu Coll Birm 68-72; Can Th Cov Cathl *Cov* 70-76; R Man Resurr *Man* 72-78; Can Res Birm Cathl *Birm* 78-81; Prin Westcott Ho Cam 81-93; Area Bp Dudley *Worc* from 93. *Bishop's House, 366 Halesowen Road, Cradley Heath, Warley, W Midlands B64 7JF* Tel 0121-550 3407

HOARE, Canon Simon Gerard. b 37. AKC61. **d** 62 **p** 63. C Headingley *Ripon* 62-65; C Adel 65-68; R Spofforth 68-71; R Spofforth w Kirk Deighton 71-77; V Rawdon *Bradf* 77-85; Hon Can Bradf Cathl from 85; R Carleton and Lothersdale from 85; Dioc Ecum Officer 85-94. *The Rectory, Carleton, Skipton, N Yorkshire BD23 3BY* Tel (01756) 792789

HOBBS, Antony Ewan Talbot. b 25. Ripon Hall Ox 58. **d** 60 **p** 61. C Cuckfield *Chich* 62-64; V Staplefield Common 64-89; rtd 89; Perm to Offic *Chich* from 89. *Chippers, Chalvington, Hailsham, E Sussex BN27 3TE* Tel (01321) 811243

HOBBS, Basil Ernest William. b 22. St Chad's Coll Dur BA49 DipTh50. **d** 51 **p** 52. C Mitcham St Mark *S'wark* 51-54; CF 54-68; Hon C Paddington H Trin w St Paul *Lon* 70-72; Asst Chapl St Mary's Hosp Praed Street Lon 69-72; Novice CR 72-74; Past Consultant Clinical Th Assn 74-84; Lic to Offic *S'well* 74-83; Chapl HM Pris Nottm 81-84; Hon C Nottingham St Andr *S'well* 83-84; C 84-86; TV Clifton 86-87; rtd 87; Perm to Offic *S'well* from 87. *10 New Vale Road, Nottingham NG4 2LB* Tel 0115-987 0460

HOBBS, Christopher Bedo. b 61. Jes Coll Cam BA83 BTh90. Ridley Hall Cam 88. **d** 91 **p** 92. C Langham Place All So *Lon* 91-95; C Hull Newland St Jo *York* from 95. *75 Desmond Avenue, Hull HU6 7JX* Tel (01482) 343789

HOBBS, Christopher John Pearson. b 60. Sydney Univ BA82 K Coll Lon BD89 AKC89. Wycliffe Hall Ox 89. **d** 91 **p** 92. C S Mimms Ch Ch *Lon* 91-94; C Jesmond Clayton Memorial *Newc* from 94. *56 Holly Avenue, Jesmond, Newcastle upon Tyne NE2 2QA* Tel 0191-281 9046

HOBBS, James (Jim). b 42. K Alfred's Coll Win CertEd64 C of E Bd Educn RTC 64 Open Univ BA89 Hull Univ MA94 Cert Counselling 97. Linc Th Coll 66. **d** 68 **p** 69. C Moseley St Mary *Birm* 68-73; V Kingstanding St Mark 73-77; R Rushbrooke *St E* 77-78; R Bradfield St Geo 77-80; P-in-c Bradfield St Clare 77-80; P-in-c Felsham w Gedding 77-80; R Bradfield St George w Bradfield St Clare etc 80-84; P-in-c Gt and Lt Whelnetham 84-85; R Gt and Lt Whelnetham w Bradfield St George 85-90; Ecum Chapl for F&HE Grimsby *Linc* 90-97; Chapl Lincs and Humberside Univ (Grimsby Campus) 90-97; Gen Preacher from 92; P-in-c Ingham w Cammeringham w Fillingham from 97. *The Vicarage, Ingham, Lincoln LN1 2YW* Tel (01522) 730519

HOBBS, John Antony. b 36. S Dios Minl Tr Scheme. **d** 87 **p** 88. NSM Crowborough *Chich* from 87. *May Cottage, Alice Bright Lane, Crowborough, E Sussex TN6 3SQ* Tel (01892) 653909

HOBBS, Canon Keith. b 25. Ex Coll Ox BA46 MA51. Wells Th Coll 56. **d** 58 **p** 59. C Clewer St Steph *Ox* 58-60; C Soho St Anne w St Thos and St Pet *Lon* 60-62; Hon C S Kensington St Steph 62-71; C 71-78; Acting Gen Sec Ch Union 78; Bp's Dom Chapl *Chich* 78-81; Adn Chich 81-91; rtd 91; Perm to Offic *Chich* from 91. *10 St Martin's Square, Chichester, W Sussex PO19 1NR* Tel (01243) 784260

HOBBS, Kenneth Ian. b 50. Oak Hill Th Coll 74. **d** 77 **p** 78. C Southborough St Pet w Ch Ch and St Matt *Roch* 77-80; C Hoole *Ches* 80-84; V Barnston 84-95; P-in-c Bedworth *Cov* 95; TR from 95. *The Rectory, 1 Linden Lea, Bedworth, Nuneaton, Warks CV12 8ES* Tel (01203) 310219

HOBBS, Ms Maureen Patricia. b 54. Surrey Univ BSc76 Warw Univ 92. Westcott Ho Cam 95. **d** 97. C Shrewsbury St Chad w

St Mary *Lich* from 97. *1 St Chad's Terrace, Shrewsbury SY1 1JL* Tel (01743) 232194

HOBBS, Michael Bedo. b 30. Fitzw Ho Cam BA58 MA62. Clifton Th Coll 58. **d** 60 **p** 61. C Southsea St Jude *Portsm* 60-63; Paraguay 63-65; Argentina 65-67; V Potters Green *Cov* 68-75; Distr Sec BFBS 75-82; R Plaxtol *Roch* 82-96; Dioc Miss Audits Consultant 90-96; rtd 96. *Falcons, Barkers Hill, Donhead St Andrew, Shaftesbury, Dorset SP7 9EB*

HOBBS, Canon Philip Bertram. b 20. MBE81. Wells Th Coll 46. **d** 48 **p** 49. C Glouc Ch Ch *Glouc* 48-51; R Boxwell w Leighterton 51-60; P-in-c Ozleworth 58-60; P-in-c Newington Bagpath w Kingscote 58-60; V Glouc St Jas 60-74; Chapl HM Pris Glouc 61-82; V Sevenhampton w Charlton Abbots and Hawling *Glouc* 74-75; P-in-c Whittington 74-75; V Sevenhampton w Charlton Abbotts and Hawling etc 75-95; Hon Can Glouc Cathl 77-95; rtd 95; Perm to Offic *Glouc* from 95. *5 Woodlands View, Hobbs Lane, Woodmancote, Cirencester, Glos GL7 7EQ* Tel (01285) 831846

HOBBS, Simon John. b 59. Ox Univ MA82. St Steph Ho Ox 80. **d** 83 **p** 84. C Middlesbrough Ascension *York* 83-85; C Stainton-in-Cleveland 85-88; C St Marylebone All SS *Lon* 88-90; P-in-c Paddington St Pet 90-94; C-in-c Grosvenor Chpl from 94; C Hanover Square St Geo w St Mark from 94. *13 North Audley Street, London W1Y 1WF* Tel 0171-629 3891

HOBDAY, Walter William Henry. b 10. Ely Th Coll 56. **d** 57 **p** 58. C Perivale *Lon* 57-59; R 59-72; P-in-c Lichborough w Maidford *Pet* 72-74; R 74-76; R Lichborough w Maidford and Farthingstone 76-79; rtd 79; Lic to Offic *Pet* 80-86; Perm to Offic 86-94; Perm to Offic *St Alb* from 88. *Hardwicke Cottage, 13 The Green, Bromham, Bedford MK43 8JS* Tel (01234) 824542

HOBDEN, Brian Charles. b 38. Oak Hill Th Coll 63. **d** 66 **p** 67. C S Lambeth St Steph *S'wark* 66-70; C Cheadle *Ches* 70-76; USA from 76. *3215 Lilac Drive, Portsmouth, Virginia 23703, USA*

HOBDEN, Christopher Martin. b 49. Lon Univ BSc71. Oak Hill Th Coll 80. **d** 87 **p** 88. NSM St Marylebone All So w SS Pet and Jo *Lon* 87-88; NSM Langham Place All So 88-95. *Soldier's Field, Nepcote Lane, Findon, Worthing, W Sussex BN14 0SH* Tel (01903) 872222

HOBDEN, David Nicholas. b 54. K Coll Lon BD76 AKC76 Cam Univ PGCE. Ripon Coll Cuddesdon 77. **d** 78 **p** 79. C Marlborough *Sarum* 78-80; C Salisbury St Thos and St Edm 81-85; V Shalford *Guildf* from 85. *The Vicarage, East Shalford Lane, Shalford, Guildford, Surrey GU4 8AE* Tel (01483) 562396

HOBDEN, Geoffrey William. b 46. DipTh. Trin Coll Bris 80. **d** 82 **p** 83. C Ex St Leon w H Trin *Ex* 82-86; V Weston-super-Mare Ch Ch *B & W* from 86; RD Locking from 93. *Christ Church Vicarage, 18 Montpelier, Weston-super-Mare, Avon BS23 2RH* Tel (01934) 624376

HOBSON, Anthony John. b 42. Univ of Wales (Abth) BSc64 Birm Univ MSc65. Qu Coll Birm 79. **d** 81 **p** 82. NSM Bilton *Cov* 81-88; P-in-c Grandborough w Willoughby and Flecknoe from 88. *4 Juliet Drive, Rugby, Warks CV22 6LY* Tel (01788) 810416

HOBSON, Anthony Peter. b 53. St Jo Coll Cam BA74. St Jo Coll Nottm 75. **d** 77 **p** 78. C Brunswick *Man* 77-82; R Stretford St Bride 82-92; TR Hackney Marsh *Lon* from 92. *St Barnabas' Vicarage, 111 Homerton High Street, London E9 6DL* Tel 0181-985 2764

HOBSON, Herbert Leslie. b 09. St Aid Birkenhead 37. **d** 39 **p** 40. C Newark Ch Ch *S'well* 39-42; C Bulwell St Mary 42-47; V Awsworth w Cossall 47-59; V Mansfield St Jo 59-68; Chapl Mansfield Gen Hosp 59-68; V Heath *Derby* 68-75; rtd 75; Perm to Offic *Derby* from 75; Perm to Offic *S'well* from 75. *40 High Tor, Skegby, Sutton-in-Ashfield, Notts NG17 3EX* Tel (01623) 557083

HOBSON, Canon Patrick John Bogan. b 33. MC53. Magd Coll Cam BA56 MA60. S'wark Ord Course 75 Qu Coll Birm 77. **d** 79 **p** 80. C St Jo in Bedwardine *Worc* 79-81; R Clifton-on-Teme, Lower Sapey and the Shelsleys 81-88; TR Waltham H Cross *Chelmsf* from 88; Hon Can Chelmsf Cathl from 95. *The Rectory, Highbridge Street, Waltham Abbey, Essex EN9 1DG* Tel (01992) 762115

HOCKEN, Glen Rundle. b 59. ACA84 Kent Univ BA80 Southlands Coll Lon PGCE90. Wycliffe Hall Ox 90. **d** 92 **p** 93. C Cogges *Ox* 92-94; C Cogges and S Leigh 94-96; C Boldmere *Birm* from 96. *St Michael's House, 46 Redacre Road, Sutton Coldfield, W Midlands B73 5EA* Tel 0121-354 8432

HOCKEY, Paul Henry. b 49. Oak Hill Th Coll BA86. **d** 86 **p** 87. C Dalton-in-Furness *Carl* 86-89; R Clifton, Brougham and Cliburn 89-94; V Fremington *Ex* from 94. *The Vicarage, Fremington, Barnstaple, Devon EX31 2NX* Tel (01271) 73879

HOCKING, Canon Hugh Michael Warwick. b 12. VRD54. Ch Coll Cam BA34 MA38. Westcott Ho Cam 34. **d** 36 **p** 37. C Hackney St Jo *Lon* 36-37; C Stoke Damerel *Ex* 37-39; Chapl RNVR 39-46; V Madron w Morvah *Truro* 46-54; Chapl Poltair Hosp 50-54; V Bris St Ambrose Whitehall *Bris* 54-62; R Guildf H Trin w St Mary *Guildf* 62-77; Chapl St Luke's Hosp Guildf 63-77; Hon Can Guildf Cathl 68-77; rtd 77; Chapl W Cornwall Hosp Penzance 78-97; Perm to Offic *Ex* from 97. *Flat 23, Gracey Court, Woodland Road, Broadclyst, Exeter EX5 3LP* Tel (01392) 465170

HOCKING, John Theodore. b 28. Oak Hill Th Coll 61. **d** 63 **p** 64. C Woodford Wells *Chelmsf* 63-67; N Area Sec BCMS 67-71; Hon C Preston All SS *Blackb* 67-71; V Hoghton 71-78; V Blawith w Lowick *Carl* 78-86; rtd 86; Perm to Offic *Blackb* from 93. *161 Watling Street Road, Fulwood, Preston PR2 8AE* Tel (01772) 795058

HOCKING, Paul Frederick. b 43. Chich Th Coll 84. **d** 86 **p** 87. C Whitton and Thurleston w Akenham *St E* 86-89; V Ipswich All Hallows 89-91; P-in-c Gt Cornard from 91. *The Vicarage, 95 Bures Road, Great Cornard, Sudbury, Suffolk CO10 0JE* Tel (01787) 373579

HOCKLEY, Paul William. b 47. Chu Coll Cam BA68 MA72 Nottm Univ BA73. St Jo Coll Nottm 71. **d** 74 **p** 75. C Chatham St Phil and St Jas *Roch* 74-78; C Tunbridge Wells St Jo 78-81; V Penketh *Liv* from 81. *St Paul's Vicarage, 6 Poplar Avenue, Penketh, Warrington WA5 2EH* Tel (01925) 723492

HOCKLEY, Canon Raymond Alan. b 29. LRAM53 Em Coll Cam MA71. Westcott Ho Cam 56. **d** 58 **p** 59. C Endcliffe *Sheff* 58-61; P-in-c Wicker w Neepsend 61-63; Chapl Westcott Ho Cam 63-68; Chapl Em Coll Cam 68-76; Can Res and Prec York Minster *York* 76-95; rtd 95; Perm to Offic *York* from 95. *2A Sycamore Terrace, York YO3 7DN* Tel (01904) 646702

HOCKNULL, Dr Mark Dennis. b 63. Surrey Univ BSc85 Univ Coll Lon PhD89. Cranmer Hall Dur BA93. **d** 94 **p** 95. C Prenton *Ches* 94-96; C Runcorn All SS from 96; C Runcorn St Mich from 96. *The Vicarage, 145 Greenway Road, Runcorn, Cheshire WA7 4NR* Tel (01928) 576168

HOCKRIDGE, Joan. b 25. Girton Coll Cam BA47 MA50. St Steph Ho Ox 82. **dss** 83 **d** 87 **p** 94. Ealing Ascension Hanger Hill *Lon* 83-88; Hon C 87-88; Hon C Hanger Hill Ascension and W Twyford St Mary 88-92; Hon C Hillingdon St Jo 92-95; Perm to Offic from 95. *17 Mead Way, Ruislip, Middx HA4 7QW* Tel (01895) 622643

HODDER, John Kenneth. b 45. Edin Univ MA68. Cuddesdon Coll 71. **d** 73 **p** 74. C Kibworth Beauchamp *Leic* 73-76; C Whittlesey *Ely* 76-80; P-in-c Coveney 80-81; R 81-87; R Downham 80-87; R Nunney and Witham Friary, Marston Bigot etc *B & W* from 87. *The Rectory, High Street, Nunney, Frome, Somerset BA11 4LZ* Tel (01373) 836732

HODDER, Trevor Valentine. b 31. Bps' Coll Cheshunt 65. **d** 67 **p** 68. C Oxhey All SS *St Alb* 67-70; C Digswell 70-73; V Colchester St Anne *Chelmsf* 74-96; rtd 96. *30 Drury Road, Colchester CO2 7UX* Tel (01206) 766480

HODGE, Albert. b 40. N Ord Course 84. **d** 87 **p** 88. C Huyton St Geo *Liv* 87-89; P-in-c Widnes St Paul from 89; Chapl Halton Coll of FE from 89. *St Paul's Vicarage, Victoria Square, Widnes, Cheshire WA8 7QU* Tel 0151-424 2221

HODGE, Anthony Charles. b 43. AKC66. **d** 67 **p** 68. C Carrington *S'well* 67-69; C Bawtry w Austerfield 69-72; C Misson 69-72; Grenada 72-74; Trinidad and Tobago 74-76; V Tuckingmill *Truro* 76-78; V Worksop St Paul *S'well* 78-81; P-in-c Patrington w Hollym, Welwick and Winestead *York* 81-86; R 86-88; V York St Olave w St Giles from 88; Chapl York Coll for Girls 88-96. *St Olave's Vicarage, 52 Bootham, York YO3 7BZ* Tel (01904) 625186 E-mail provis@msn.com

HODGE, Colin. b 39. Sarum & Wells Th Coll. **d** 83 **p** 84. NSM Wareham *Sarum* 84-87; C Parkstone St Pet w Branksea and St Osmund 87-89; V Lilliput from 89. *The Vicarage, 55 Lilliput Road, Poole, Dorset BH14 8JX* Tel (01202) 708567

HODGE, Graham Anthony. b 49. Linc Th Coll 79. **d** 80 **p** 81. C Hale *Guildf* 80-82; C Christchurch *Win* 82-86; R Chawton and Farringdon 86-96; rtd 96. *6 Reads Field, St Aubin's Close, Four Marks, Alton, Hants GU34 5DS* Tel (01420) 588395

HODGE, John Shaw. b 30. Chich Th Coll 78. **d** 80 **p** 81. C Furze Platt *Ox* 80-83; V Kirkwhelpington, Kirkharle, Kirkheaton and Cambo *Newc* 83-84; TV Langley Marish *Ox* 84-87; rtd 87; Perm to Offic *Cant* from 87. *St Peter's, 15 The Street, Ash, Canterbury, Kent CT3 2HH* Tel (01227) 813347

HODGE, Marilyn Elizabeth. *See* IVEY, Mrs Marilyn Elizabeth

HODGE, Canon Michael Robert. b 34. Pemb Coll Cam BA57 MA61. Ridley Hall Cam 57. **d** 59 **p** 60. C Harpurhey Ch Ch *Man* 59; C Blackpool St Mark *Blackb* 59-62; V Stalybridge Old St Geo *Man* 62-67; R Cobham w Luddesdowne and Dode *Roch* 67-81; Hon Can Roch Cathl from 81; R Bidborough from 81. *The Rectory, Rectory Drive, Bidborough, Tunbridge Wells, Kent TN3 0UL* Tel (01892) 528081 Fax as telephone E-mail michaelhodge@cix.compulink.co.uk

HODGE, Nigel John. b 61. BTh83 Univ of Wales DPS85. St Mich Coll Llan 83. **d** 85 **p** 86. C Mynyddislwyn *Mon* 85-87; C Machen 87-89; TV Ebbw Vale 89-91; V Abercarn from 91. *The Vicarage, Abercarn NP1 5GU* Tel (01495) 243919

HODGES, Francis Reginald. b 26. Selw Coll Cam BA48 MA61. Chich Th Coll 48. **d** 50 **p** 51. C Portsea St Alb *Portsm* 50-56; Prior Ho of the Resurr Mirfield 56-58; C Heref All SS *Heref* 58-61; R St Breoke *Truro* 61-76; rtd 76; C St Kew *Truro* 77-78; P-in-c 78-80. *Tregellist Cottage, St Kew, Bodmin, Cornwall PL30 3HG* Tel (01208) 880083

HODGES, Jasper Tor. b 62. Leeds Univ BSc84 Sheff Univ MEng85 Lon Univ PGCE87. Trin Coll Bris BA94. **d** 94 **p** 95. C Holbeck *Ripon* from 94. *23 Park View, Leeds LS11 7AY* Tel 0113-277 7528

HODGES, Keith Michael. b 53. Southn Univ BTh82. Chich Th Coll 77. **d** 80 **p** 81. C Sydenham St Phil *S'wark* 80-84; Perm to

Offic 85; C Leatherhead *Guildf* 86-89; V Aldershot St Aug from 89. *St Augustine's Vicarage, Holly Road, Aldershot, Hants GU12 4SE* Tel (01252) 20840

HODGES, Murray Knowles. b 02. K Coll Cam BA24 MA29. Ridley Hall Cam. **d** 25 **p** 26. C Cockermouth Ch Ch *Carl* 25-26; C Newton Heath St Wilfrid *Man* 26-27; C Kendal H Trin *Carl* 27-31; V Mungrisdale 31-34; V Loweswater 34-45; V Muncaster 45-57; V Muncaster w Waberthwaite 57-75; rtd 75; Perm to Offic *Carl* 77-93. *Eskside, Ravenglass, Cumbria CA18 1SF* Tel (01229) 717259

HODGES, Miss Stephanie Margaret. b 54. Trin Coll Bris DipHE95. **d** 97. C Croydon Ch Ch *S'wark* from 97. *9 Berry Lane, London SE21 8AR* Tel 0181-355 4185

HODGETTS, Alan Paul. b 54. BSc78. St Steph Ho Ox 79. **d** 82 **p** 83. C Perry Barr *Birm* 82-85; C Broseley w Benthall *Heref* 85-87; V Effingham w Lt Bookham *Guildf* 87-96; R Merrow from 96. *The Rectory, 232 Epsom Road, Merrow, Guildford, Surrey GU4 7AA* Tel (01483) 504311

HODGETTS, Colin William. b 40. St D Coll Lamp BA61 Ripon Hall Ox 61. **d** 63 **p** 64. C Hackney St Jo *Lon* 63-68; Hon C St Martin-in-the-Fields 70-76; C Creeksea w Althorne *Chelmsf* 76-79; Perm to Offic *Ex* from 84. *The Small School, Fore Street, Hartland, Bideford, Devon EX39 6AB* Tel (01237) 441672

HODGETTS, Harry Samuel. b 30. Chich Th Coll 63. **d** 65 **p** 66. C Harton Colliery *Dur* 65-68; C Penzance St Mary *Truro* 68-70; V Penwerris 70-79; V Kettering St Mary *Pet* 79-94; rtd 95. *20 Crofton Close, Christchurch, Dorset BH23 2JN* Tel (01202) 474456

HODGINS, George Eric. b 12. ALCD39. **d** 39 **p** 40. C Colchester St Botolph w H Trin and St Giles *Chelmsf* 39-40; C Gidea Park 40-42; P-in-c Springfield H Trin 42-45; C Guernsey St Sampson *Win* 46-50; V Forest Gate All SS *Chelmsf* 50-54; R Highnam w Lassington and Rudford *Glouc* 54-56; R Wivenhoe *Chelmsf* 56-59; V White Ladies Aston w Spetchley and Churchill *Worc* 59-60; R Wakes Colne w Chappel *Chelmsf* 60-63; R Lt Easton 63-73; P-in-c Alphamstone w Lamarsh 73; R Alphamstone w Lamarsh and Pebmarsh 74-77; rtd 77; Perm to Offic *Chelmsf* from 77. *Candles, 23 Church Street, Colne Engaine, Colchester CO6 2EX* Tel (01787) 223776

HODGINS, John Henry. b 21. TCD BA43 BD48. TCD Div Sch Div Test44. **d** 45 **p** 46. Educn Org Ch of Ireland 69-71; Can Th Belf Cathl 71-76; Dean Killala *T, K & A* 76-79; Area Sec (Dios Ripon and York) CMS 79-83; C Acomb St Steph *York* 83-86; rtd 86. *57 Sandhurst Drive, Belfast BT9 5AZ* Tel (01232) 668990

HODGINS, The Ven Michael Minden. b 12. Lambeth Hon MA60 Cuddesdon Coll 38. **d** 39 **p** 40. C Northolt Park St Barn *Lon* 39-43; Asst Sec Lon Dioc Fund 43-46; Sec 46-74; Lic to Offic 47-51; Adn Hackney 51-71; Lic to Offic 71-77; rtd 77; Perm to Offic *Cant* from 77. *Flat 5, Up The Quadrangle, Morden College, London SE3 0PU* Tel 0181-858 4762

HODGINS, Philip Arthur. b 57. Lanc Univ BA78 Nottm Univ DipTh83 Bradf Univ MBA90 GradIPM91. Linc Th Coll 82. **d** 85 **p** 86. C Norton *Ches* 85-88; C Whitkirk *Ripon* 88-89; Perm to Offic *Bradf* 89-90; Perm to Offic *Chich* from 91; Jo Grooms Assn for Disabled People from 91. *Little Becks, Batts Bridge Road, Maresfield, Uckfield, E Sussex TN22 2HJ* Tel (01825) 762767

HODGKINSON, Canon Arthur Edward. b 13. Dur Univ LTh42. Edin Th Coll 36. **d** 39 **p** 40. C Glas St Geo *Glas* 39-43; Choir Chapl St Ninian's Cathl Perth *St And* 43-44; Prec 44-47; P-in-c Lochgelly 47-52; R 52-54; R Motherwell *Glas* 54-65; Can St Mary's Cathl 63-65; Provost St Andr Cathl *Ab* 65-78; Hon Can from 81; Hon Can Ch Ch Cathl Connecticut 65-78; Area Sec (S Wales) USPG 78-82; rtd 82; Hon C Eyemouth *Edin* 82-86; Perm to Offic *Llan* 86-89. *36 Forbes Road, Edinburgh EH10 4ED* Tel 0131-229 7593

HODGKINSON, Frank Cyril. b 18. Lon Univ BA50. Oak Hill Th Coll 46. **d** 51 **p** 52. C Gaywood, Bawsey and Mintlyn *Nor* 51-53; C Hall Green Ascension *Birm* 53-55; V W Bromwich St Paul Golds Hill *Lich* 55-57; V Donington 57-65; R Aldham *St E* 65-68; R Elmsett 65-68; V Barkby *Leic* 68-74; V Leic St Chris 74-77; V Ryhall w Essendine *Pet* 77-83; rtd 83; Perm to Offic *Nor* from 84. *16 Waveney Close, Wells-next-the-Sea, Norfolk NR23 1HU*

HODGKINSON, Canon John. b 27. Trin Hall Cam BA51 MA55. Linc Th Coll 51. **d** 53 **p** 54. C Penrith St Andr *Carl* 53-56; C Linc St Nic w St Jo Newport *Linc* 56-58; C-in-c Lin St Jo Bapt CD 58-63; V Linc St Jo 63-66; R Old Brumby 66-71; V Kendal H Trin *Carl* 71-90; Hon Can Carl Cathl 84-90; rtd 90; Perm to Offic *Carl* from 90. *Boxtree Barn, Levens, Kendal, Cumbria LA8 8NZ* Tel (015395) 60806

HODGKINSON, John David. b 57. Birm Univ BA78 Edin Univ BD89. Edin Th Coll 86. **d** 89 **p** 90. C Briercliffe *Blackb* 89-92; C Darwen St Cuth w Tockholes St Steph 92-94; R Harrington *Carl* from 94. *The Rectory, Rectory Close, Harrington, Workington, Cumbria CA14 5PN* Tel (01946) 830215

HODGKINSON, Oswald Merchant. b 21. Qu Coll Birm 68. **d** 69 **p** 70. C Shard End *Birm* 69-74; V 74-80; TV Wrexham *St As* 80-86; rtd 86; Perm to Offic *St As* from 86; Perm to Offic *Ban* from 86. *12 Arfryn, Llanrhos, Llandudno LL30 1PB* Tel (01492) 584419

HODGSON, Ms Amanda Jane Mandy. b 66. Westmr Coll Ox BA88 St Andr Univ 93. Westcott Ho Cam 94. **d** 96 **p** 97. C Epping Distr *Chelmsf* from 96. *Vicarage Cottage, Hartland Road, Epping, Essex CM16 4PD* Tel (01992) 572906

HODGSON, Anthony Owen Langlois. b 35. Ripon Hall Ox 60. **d** 62 **p** 63. C Blakeney w Lt Langham *Nor* 62-65; C Stiffkey w Morston 62-65; C Paddington Ch Ch *Lon* 66-70; Area Sec (Beds & Cambs) Chr Aid 70-74; (Herts & Hunts) 70-73; (Rutland & Northants) 73-74; V Gt w Lt Gidding and Steeple Gidding *Ely* 77-81; Warden Dovedale Ho 81-89; P-in-c Ilam w Blore Ray and Okeover *Lich* 81-89; Dir Chr Rural Cen 89-91; C Checkley 91-97; C Stramshall 91-97; TV Uttoxeter Area from 97. *The New Rectory, Church Lane, Checkley, Stoke-on-Trent ST10 4NJ* Tel (01538) 722732

HODGSON, Anthony William. b 35. Dur Univ BSc56. Wells Th Coll 58. **d** 60 **p** 61. C Gateshead St Mary *Dur* 60-62; C Leeds All SS *Ripon* 62-66; V Hartlepool St Oswald *Dur* 66-75; C-in-c Stockton St Jas CD 75-81; V Easington Colliery 81-89; V Eighton Banks from 89. *St Thomas's Vicarage, 8 Norwood Court, Gateshead, Tyne & Wear NE9 7XF* Tel 0191-487 6927

HODGSON, Antony Robert. b 66. Westcott Ho Cam 90. **d** 93 **p** 94. C Chorley St Geo *Blackb* 93-96; C Lytham St Cuth from 96. *11 Milner Road, Lytham-St-Annes, Lancs FY8 4EY* Tel (01253) 733782

HODGSON, Canon Charles. b 16. St Aid Coll Dur LTh42 St Jo Coll Dur BA43 MA45. St Aid Birkenhead 39. **d** 43 **p** 44. C Chorley St Laur *Blackb* 43-46; C Preston St Mary 46-49; V Preston St Thos 50-55; V Idle H Trin *Bradf* 55-60; V Middleton *Birm* 60-70; R Wishaw 60-70; Dioc Adult Educn Officer 60-70; Dioc Missr and Tr Officer Ox 70-82; Hon Can Ch Ch *Ox* 81; RD Witney 81-86; rtd 82. *40 Wykeham Way, Haddenham, Aylesbury, Bucks HP17 8BX* Tel (01844) 292593

HODGSON, Christopher. b 24. Or Coll Ox BA49 MA54. Qu Coll Birm 50. **d** 52 **p** 53. C Cheltenham Ch Ch *Glouc* 52-55; C Liv Our Lady and St Nic *Liv* 55-57; V Anfield St Columba 57-64; V Pembury *Roch* 64-82; Chapl Pembury Hosp Tunbridge Wells 66-82; R Aynho w Newbottle and Charlton *Pet* 82-85; Chapl Burrswood Cen for Divine Healing 85-94; C Castle Bromwich St Clem *Birm* 86-94; rtd 94. *Lightwood, 37 Heath Road East, Petersfield, Hants GU31 4HR*

HODGSON, David George. b 54. Coll of Resurr Mirfield. **d** 82 **p** 83. C Stainton-in-Cleveland *York* 82-87; R Loftus 87; P-in-c Carlin How w Skinningrove 87; R Loftus and Carlin How w Skinningrove 87-93; V Middlesbrough Ascension from 93. *The Ascension Vicarage, Penrith Road, Middlesbrough TS3 7SR* Tel (01642) 244857

HODGSON, David Peter. b 56. Fitzw Coll Cam BA77 MA81 Nottm Univ BA82 MTh85. St Jo Coll Nottm 80. **d** 83 **p** 84. C Guiseley w Esholt *Bradf* 83-86; Asst Chapl Loughb Univ *Leic* 86-89; P-in-c Hatfield Broad Oak *Chelmsf* 89-90; P-in-c Bush End 89-90; P-in-c Hatfield Broad Oak and Bush End 90-97; Ind Chapl to Harlow 89-97; P-in-c Wokingham All SS *Ox* 97; R from 97. *23 Tickenor Drive, Finchampstead, Wokingham, Berks RG40 4UD*

HODGSON, Derek Cyril. b 29. Hatf Coll Dur BA50 St Chad's Coll Dur DipTh54. **d** 54 **p** 55. C Lindley *Wakef* 54-58; C-in-c Mixenden CD 58-62; V Thurlstone 62-75; V Mytholm Royd 75-97; rtd 97. *The Autumn Barn, Bishop Walton, York YO4 1SF*

HODGSON, George. b 36. Qu Coll Birm 75. **d** 78 **p** 79. NSM Wordsley *Lich* 78-93; NSM Wordsley *Worc* from 93; Perm to Offic 84-93. *1 Newfield Drive, Kingswinford, W Midlands DY6 8HY* Tel (01384) 292543

HODGSON, John. b 35. St Jo Coll Cam MA62 Lon Univ BD61. St Deiniol's Hawarden 80. **d** 81 **p** 82. Hon C Padiham *Blackb* 81-84; C W Burnley 85-87; V 87-95; rtd 95. *1 Riversway, Broadway Park, Childswickham Road, Broadway, Worcs WR12 7HB* Tel (01386) 853049

HODGSON, The Ven John Derek. b 31. St Jo Coll Dur BA53. Cranmer Hall Dur DipTh59. **d** 59 **p** 60. C Stranton *Dur* 59-62; C Monkwearmouth St Andr 62-64; V Stillington 64-66; V Consett 66-75; TR Gateshead 75-83; RD Gateshead 76-83; Hon Can Dur Cathl 78-83; Can Res Dur Cathl 83-97; Adn Auckland 83-93; Adn Dur 93-97; rtd 97. *45 Woodside, Barnard Castle, Durham DL12 8DZ* Tel (01833) 690557

HODGSON, Matthew William. b 13. Lich Th Coll 40. **d** 44 **p** 45. C N Gosforth *Newc* 44-47; C Wallsend St Luke 47-49; C Haltwhistle 49-50; C Winlaton *Dur* 50-51; Chapl Aberlour Orphanage 51-53; R Jarrow Grange *Dur* 54-60; Chapl Palmer Memorial Hosp 54-60; R Nairn *Mor* 60-64; V Byker St Laur *Newc* 64-71; V Woodhorn w Newbiggin 71-77; rtd 77; Lic to Offic *Newc* 77-93. *5 Cumming Street, Nairn, Inverness IV12 4NQ* Tel (01667) 56719

HODGSON, Peter Richard. b 23. Dur Univ BA50. Bps' Coll Cheshunt 49. **d** 52 **p** 53. C Redcar *York* 52-55; C Beverley Minster 55-57; V Lythe 57-61; V Bolsterstone *Sheff* 61-80; V Kirton in Holland *Linc* 80-86; rtd 86; Perm to Offic *Linc* from 86. *Omega, Littlemoor Lane, Sibsey, Boston, Lincs PE22 0TU* Tel (01205) 750167

HODGSON, Roger Vaughan. b 27. Magd Coll Cam BA49 MA54. Cuddesdon Coll 55. **d** 56 **p** 57. C Westmr St Matt *Lon* 56-59; C Pimlico St Pet w Westmr Ch Ch 59-65; R Lt Hadham *St Alb* 65-78; Chapl Oporto *Eur* 78-80; Chapl and Lect St Deiniol's Lib Hawarden 81-82; V Coldwaltham *Chich* 82-92; rtd 92; Asst

Chapl Costa Blanca *Eur* 92-94; Perm to Offic *Chich* from 94. *21 Maltravers Street, Arundel, W Sussex BN18 9AP* Tel (01903) 884708

HODGSON, The Ven Thomas Richard Burnham. b 26. FRMetS88. Lon Coll of Div BD52 ALCD52. **d** 52 **p** 53. C Crosthwaite Kendal *Carl* 52-55; C Stanwix 55-59; V Whitehaven St Nic 59-65; R Aikton 65-67; V Raughton Head w Gatesgill 67-73; Bp's Dom Chapl 67-73; Dir of Ords 70-74; Hon Can Carl Cathl 72-91; V Grange-over-Sands 73-79; RD Windermere 76-79; P-in-c Mosser 79; V 79-83; Adn W Cumberland 79-91; rtd 91; Perm to Offic *Carl* from 91. *58 Greenacres, Wetheral, Carlisle CA4 8LD* Tel (01228) 561159

HODGSON, Vernon Charles. b 34. MRPharmS58 Lon Univ BPharm58 Univ of Wales (Cardiff) DPS91. St Mich Coll Llan 90 Llan Dioc Tr Scheme 83. **d** 86 **p** 87. NSM Roath St Marg *Llan* 86-91; C Caerphilly 91-93; V Llanbister and Llanbadarn Fynydd w Llananno etc *S & B* from 93. *The Vicarage, Llanbister, Llandrindod Wells LD1 6TN* Tel (01597) 83333

HODKINSON, George Leslie. b 48. Qu Coll Birm 86. **d** 88 **p** 89. C Hall Green St Pet *Birm* 88-91; TV Solihull 91-96; P-in-c Billesley Common from 96. *Holy Cross Vicarage, 29 Beauchamp Road, Birmingham B13 0NS* Tel 0121-444 1737

HODSON, Gordon George. b 35. St Chad's Coll Dur BA59 DipTh60. **d** 60 **p** 61. C Tettenhall Regis *Lich* 60-64; C Rugeley 64-68; V Shrewsbury St Mich 68-74; V Kinnerley w Melverley 74-87; P-in-c Knockin w Maesbrook 75-87; P-in-c Chebsey 87-91; P-in-c Seighford, Derrington and Cresswell 87-91; V Chebsey, Ellenhall and Seighford-with-Creswell from 91. *The Vicarage, Seighford, Stafford ST18 9PQ* Tel (01785) 282829

HODSON, Keith. b 53. Hatf Coll Dur BA74. Wycliffe Hall Ox 77. **d** 80 **p** 81. C Ashton on Mersey St Mary *Ches* 80-84; C Polegate *Chich* 84-92; V Baddesley Ensor w Grendon *Birm* from 92. *The Vicarage, Baddesley Ensor, Atherstone, Warks CV9 2BY* Tel (01827) 715327

HODSON, Miss Margaret Christina. b 39. Linc Th Coll 88. **d** 90 **p** 94. Par Dn Old Trafford St Jo *Man* 90-94; C 94-95; P-in-c Calderbrook from 95; P-in-c Shore from 95. *St James's Vicarage, 4 Stansfield Hall, Littleborough, Lancs OL15 9RH* Tel (01706) 378414

HODSON, Raymond Leslie. b 42. St Chad's Coll Dur BSc64 DipTh66. **d** 66 **p** 67. C Adlington *Blackb* 66-68; C Cleveleys 68-72; V Ewood 72-77; V Nazeing *Chelmsf* 77-84; R Ampthill w Millbrook and Steppingley *St Alb* 84-95; Chapl Madrid *Eur* from 95. *General Oraa 16, eseB, 6B, 28006 Madrid, Spain*

HODSON, William. b 42. Man Univ BA. Cranmer Hall Dur 81. **d** 82 **p** 83. C Ashton St Mich *Man* 82-86; V Tintwistle *Ches* 86-93; P-in-c Weston from 93. *All Saints' Vicarage, 13 Cemetery Road, Weston, Crewe CW2 5LQ* Tel (01270) 582585

HOEY, Canon David Paul. b 57. QUB BD79. CITC 79. **d** 81 **p** 82. C Belfast Whiterock *Conn* 81-83; C Portadown St Mark *Arm* 83-84; I Cleenish w Mullaghdun *Clogh* 84-90; I Magheracross from 90; Dir of Ords from 91; Preb Clogh Cathl from 95. *The Rectory, Ballinamallard, Co Fermanagh BT94 2BT* Tel (01365) 388238 Fax as telephone

HOEY, The Ven Raymond George. b 46. TCD BA70 MA. **d** 72 **p** 73. C Portadown St Mark *Arm* 72-78; I Camlough w Mullaglass from 78; Dom Chapl to Abp Arm from 86; RD Mullabrack 88-92; Adn Arm from 92. *2 Maytown Road, Bessbrook, Newry, Co Down BT35 7LY* Tel (01693) 830301 Fax as telephone

HOEY, William Thomas. b 32. CITC 64. **d** 66 **p** 67. C Belfast St Mary *Conn* 66-68; C Lisburn Ch Ch 69-72; I Ballinderry 72-78; I Belfast St Simon w St Phil from 78. *St Simon's Rectory, 106 Upper Lisburn Road, Belfast BT10 0BB* Tel (01232) 617562

HOFFMAN, Canon Stanley Harold. b 17. St Edm Hall Ox BA39 MA43 Kent Univ MA82. Linc Th Coll 40. **d** 41 **p** 42. C New Windsor *Ox* 41-44; C Weston All SS *B & W* 44-47; C Chertsey *Guildf* 47-51; V Shottermill 51-65; Dir of Educn *Roch* 65-80; Hon Can Roch Cathl 65-80; Warden of Readers 73-80; Chapl to The Queen 76-88; rtd 80; Perm to Offic *Guildf* 82-93; Perm to Offic *Truro* from 93; Hon C Padstow from 93. *Zansizzey, Trevone, Padstow, Cornwall PL28 8QJ* Tel (01841) 520864

HOFFMANN, Jonathan Mark. b 60. Cranmer Hall Dur 95. **d** 97. C Eaton *Nor* from 97. *12 Fulton Close, Eaton, Norwich NR4 6HX* Tel (01603) 454078

HOGAN, Edward James Martin. b 46. Trin Coll Bris. **d** 85 **p** 86. C St Austell *Truro* 85-88; V Gt Broughton and Broughton Moor *Carl* 88-94; V St Stythians w Perranarworthal and Gwennap *Truro* from 94. *The Vicarage, Old Vicarage Close, Stithians, Truro, Cornwall TR3 7DZ* Tel (01209) 860123

HOGAN, John James. b 24. St Edm Hall Ox BA51 MA56. Wells Th Coll 51. **d** 53 **p** 54. C Cannock *Lich* 53-55; C Drayton in Hales 55-58; V Woore 58-84; P-in-c Norton in Hales 82-84; V Woore and Norton in Hales 84-89; rtd 89; Perm to Offic *Lich* from 89. *Wrekin Prospect, Audlem Road, Woore, Crewe CW3 9RJ* Tel (01630) 647677

HOGAN, William Riddell. b 22. Qu Coll Birm 48. **d** 51 **p** 52. C Brighouse *Wakef* 51-54; Singapore 55-58; V Greetland *Wakef* 59-73; V Greetland and W Vale 73-80; V Kellington w Whitley 80-87; rtd 87. *15 The Pastures, Carlton, Goole, N Humberside DN14 9QF* Tel (01405) 862233

HOGARTH, Alan Francis. b 58. Oak Hill Th Coll BA89. **d** 89 **p** 90. C Felixstowe SS Pet and Paul *St E* 89-93; R Beckington w Standerwick, Berkley, Rodden etc *B & W* from 93. *8 Church Street, Beckington, Bath BA3 6TG* Tel (01373) 830314

HOGARTH, Foley James Myddelton. b 16. Ch Ch Ox BA38 MA42. Wells Th Coll 38. **d** 39 **p** 40. C Rainbow Hill St Barn *Worc* 39-41; C Charlton Kings H Apostles *Glouc* 41-42; CF 42-46; V Fordcombe *Roch* 47-52; Asst Hd Master Holmewood Ho Sch Kent 52-53; Australia from 53; rtd 81. *9 Northumberland Street, Heathpool, S Australia 5068* Tel Adelaide (8) 316318

HOGARTH, Joseph. b 32. Edin Th Coll 65. **d** 67 **p** 67. C Walney Is *Carl* 67-71; V Whitehaven St Jas 71-76; V Millom H Trin w Thwaites 76-82; V Maryport 82-91; V Consett *Dur* 91-97; rtd 97. *81 High Street, Crayford, Dartford DA1 4EJ* Tel (01322) 526733

HOGBEN, The Ven Peter Graham. b 25. Bps' Coll Cheshunt 60. **d** 61 **p** 62. C Hale *Guildf* 61-64; R Westborough 64-71; V Ewell 71-82; Hon Can Guildf Cathl 79-90; RD Epsom 80-82; Adn Dorking 82-90; rtd 90; Perm to Offic *Guildf* from 90. *3 School Road, Rowledge, Farnham, Surrey GU10 4EJ* Tel (01252) 793533

HOGG, Anthony. b 42. Univ of Wales (Lamp) BA63. Linc Th Coll 64 Chich Th Coll 78. **d** 78 **p** 79. NSM Ridgeway *Ox* 78-86; C 90-91; NSM W w E Hanney 86-88; Hd Master New Coll Sch Ox 88-89; P-in-c Hanney, Denchworth and E Challow *Ox* 91-92; V from 92. *The Vicarage, Winter Lane, West Hanney, Wantage, Oxon OX12 0LF* Tel (01235) 868863

HOGG, Neil Richard. b 46. BSc69. Ridley Hall Cam 82. **d** 84 **p** 85. C Bingham *S'well* 84-87; TV Bushbury *Lich* from 87. *The Vicarage, 17 Goodyear Avenue, Low Hill, Wolverhampton WV10 9JX* Tel (01902) 731713

HOGG, Peter Stuart. b 42. Ch Coll Cam BA65 MA68. NW Ord Course 74. **d** 77 **p** 78. NSM Bollington St Jo *Ches* 77-88; Chapl Wells Cathl Sch from 88. *18 Vicars' Close, Wells, Somerset BA5 2UJ* Tel (01749) 674527

HOGG, William John. b 49. New Coll Ox MA71 Lon Univ CertEd72 Crewe & Alsager Coll MSc88. Edin Th Coll 86. **d** 88 **p** 89. C Oxton *Ches* 88-93; R Bromborough from 93. *The Rectory, Mark Rake, Bromborough, Wirral, Merseyside L62 2DH* Tel 0151-334 1466

HOGG, William Ritson. b 47. Leeds Univ BSc69. Qu Coll Birm DipTh71. **d** 72 **p** 73. C Bordesley St Oswald *Birm* 72-76; TV Seacroft *Ripon* 76-82; V Hunslet St Mary 82-88; V Catterick from 88. *The Vicarage, High Green, Catterick, Richmond, N Yorkshire DL10 7LN* Tel (01748) 811462

HOGGARD, Mrs Jean Margaret. b 36. NW Ord Course 76. **dss** 79 **d** 87 **p** 94. Northowram *Wakef* 79-87; Par Dn 87-94; C from 94. *13 Joseph Avenue, Northowram, Halifax, W Yorkshire HX3 7HJ* Tel (01422) 201475

HOGGETT, Robert William John. b 13. Worc Ord Coll 65. **d** 67 **p** 68. C Bromsgrove St Jo *Worc* 67-71; V Keelby *Linc* 71-87; V Riby 74-87; PC Aylesby 77-87; RD Haverstoe 81-86; rtd 87; Perm to Offic *Linc* from 88. *Lauriston, North Halls, Binbrook, Lincoln LN3 6BW* Tel (01472) 398157

HOGWOOD, Brian Roy. b 38. Bps' Coll Cheshunt. **d** 65 **p** 92. NSM Thetford *Nor* 91-93; Hon C from 93. *31 Byron Walk, Thetford, Norfolk IP24 1JX* Tel (01842) 753915

HOLBROOK, Colin Eric Basford. *See* BASFORD HOLBROOK, Colin Eric

HOLBROOK, John Edward. b 62. St Pet Coll Ox BA83 MA87. Ridley Hall Cam 82. **d** 86 **p** 87. C Barnes St Mary *S'wark* 86-89; C Bletchley *Ox* 89-93; C N Bletchley CD 89-93; V Adderbury w Milton from 93. *The Vicarage, 13 Dog Close, Adderbury, Banbury, Oxon OX17 3EF* Tel (01295) 810309

HOLBROOKE-JONES, Canon Stanley Charles. b 27. Dur Univ BA58 DipTh60 MA77. Cranmer Hall Dur 58. **d** 60 **p** 61. C Gravesend St Jas *Roch* 60-63; C Streatham Immanuel w St Anselm *S'wark* 63-66; V W Bromwich H Trin *Lich* 66-79; V W Exe *Ex* 79-88; R Poole *Sarum* from 88; Miss to Seamen from 88; Can and Preb Sarum Cathl *Sarum* from 96. *The Rectory, 10 Poplar Close, Poole, Dorset BH15 1LP* Tel (01202) 672694

HOLCOMBE, Graham William Arthur. b 50. ARCM69. St Mich Coll Llan DipTh80. **d** 80 **p** 81. C Neath w Llantwit *Llan* 80-84; Asst Youth Chapl 81-84; PV Llan Cathl 84-86; V Pentyrch from 86. *The Vicarage, Pentyrch, Cardiff CF4 8QF* Tel (01222) 890318

HOLDAWAY, Graham Michael. b 51. Southn Univ BSc73. Sarum & Wells Th Coll 74. **d** 77 **p** 78. C Walton-on-Thames *Guildf* 77-81; TV Westborough 81-86; Perm to Offic from 86. *2 Sheerwater Cottages, Sheerwater Road, West Byfleet, Surrey KT14 6AB* Tel (01932) 340396

HOLDAWAY, Dr Simon Douglas. b 47. Lanc Univ BA73 Sheff Univ PhD81. N Ord Course 78. **d** 81 **p** 82. NSM Gleadless *Sheff* from 81; Sen Lect in Sociology Sheff Univ from 81. *136 Totley Brook Road, Sheffield S17 3QU* Tel 0114-236 3711

HOLDAWAY, Stephen Douglas. b 45. Hull Univ BA67. Ridley Hall Cam 67. **d** 70 **p** 71. C Southampton Thornhill St Chris *Win* 70-73; C Tardebigge *Worc* 73-78; Ind Chapl 73-78; Ind Chapl *Linc* 78-93; Co-ord City Cen Group Min 81-93; TR Louth from 93; RD Louthesk from 95. *The Rectory, Westgate, Louth, Lincs LN11 9YE* Tel (01507) 610247

HOLDCROFT, Ian Thomas. b 46. St Jo Coll Cam BA68 MA71. Westcott Ho Cam 72. **d** 73 **p** 74. C Bris St Mary Redcliffe w Temple etc *Bris* 73-76; Th Educn Sec Chr Aid 76-80; Exec Sec 80-82; Hon C Battersea St Mary *S'wark* 81-86; Dep Sec Gen Syn Bd for Miss and Unity 82-86; V Whitchurch *Bris* 86-92; V Almondsbury 92-96; P-in-c Olveston 92-95; P-in-c Littleton on Severn w Elberton 92-96. *2 Goldney Road, Clifton, Bristol BS8 4RB* Tel 0117-909 9232

HOLDEN, Canon Arthur Stuart James. b 23. ALCD51. **d** 51 **p** 52. C Barking St Marg *Chelmsf* 51-54; P-in-c Berechurch 54-55; V 55-61; V Earls Colne 61-82; P-in-c White Colne 66-67; V 68-82; V Earls Colne and White Colne 82-88; Hon Can Chelmsf Cathl 80-88; rtd 88; Perm to Offic *Chelmsf* from 88. *10 Wroxham Close, Colchester CO3 3RQ* Tel (01206) 560845

HOLDEN, Geoffrey. b 26. FCII54. Oak Hill Th Coll 57. **d** 59 **p** 60. C Crookes St Thos *Sheff* 59-61; C Belper *Derby* 61-63; C Woking St Jo *Guildf* 63-66; R Bath St Mich w St Paul *B & W* 66-73; Chapl Bath Gp Hosps 73-91; rtd 91; Perm to Offic *B & W* from 91. *10 Marlborough Lane, Bath BA1 2NQ* Tel (01225) 427933

HOLDEN, Geoffrey Ralph. b 25. Ripon Hall Ox 64. **d** 65 **p** 66. C Sparkhill St Jo *Birm* 65-68; C Walsall *Lich* 68-71; R Longton St Jas 71-75; rtd 90. *Aberscethin, Talybont LL43 2AR* Tel (01341) 247538

HOLDEN, Jack Crawford (Simon). b 30. Leeds Univ BA59. Coll of Resurr Mirfield 59. **d** 61 **p** 61. C Middlesbrough All SS *York* 61-64; Lic to Offic *Wakef* 65-69; CR from 67; Asst Chapl Univ Coll *Lon* 69-74; Lic to Offic 70-74. *House of the Resurrection, Mirfield, W Yorkshire WF14 0BN* Tel (01924) 494318

HOLDEN, Canon John. b 33. MBE76. Selly Oak Coll 71 Ridley Hall Cam 65. **d** 67 **p** 68. C Flixton St Jo CD *Man* 67-71; Uganda 71-75; V Aston SS Pet and Paul *Birm* 75-87; RD Aston 86-87; Hon Can Birm Cathl 86-87; R Ulverston St Mary w H Trin *Carl* from 87; RD Furness 90-94; Hon Can Carl Cathl 91-94. *The Rectory, 15 Ford Park Crescent, Ulverston, Cumbria LA12 7JR* Tel (01229) 584331

HOLDEN, John Norman. b 35. Heythrop Coll Lon 96. Oak Hill Th Coll 91. **d** 95 **p** 96. NSM Codicote *St Alb* 95-96. *4 Chapel Row, Upper Dean, Huntingdon, Cambs PE18 0LZ* Tel (01234) 708928

HOLDEN, John Worrall. b 44. K Coll Lon AKC67 DPS. **d** 70 **p** 71. C Derby St Bart *Derby* 70-72; Lic to Offic 72-74; Hon C St Helier *S'wark* 74-77; Hon C St Marylebone All SS *Lon* 80-83; Hon C St Botolph Aldgate w H Trin Minories from 84. *St Botolph's Vestry, London EC3N 1AB* Tel 0171-283 1670

HOLDEN, Mark Noel. b 61. Collingwood Coll Dur BA82 Edin Univ CQSW85 Warw Univ TCert93 Birm Univ MA95. Qu Coll Birm 93. **d** 95 **p** 96. C Brumby *Linc* from 95. *32 Alvington Road, Scunthorpe, S Humberside DN16 2HD* Tel (01724) 840616

HOLDEN, Paul Edward. b 53. CEng79 MIM MIBF BSc75 DipHE84. Trin Coll Bris 82. **d** 86 **p** 87. C Harpurhey Ch Ch *Man* 86-88; C Harpurhey St Steph 88-93; Min Harpurhey LEP 88-93. *2 Baywood Street, Harpurhey, Manchester M9 1XX* Tel 0161-205 2938

HOLDER, John William. b 41. Chester Coll CertEd61 Open Univ BA73 Bath Univ MEd85. Trin Coll Bris MA94. **d** 87 **p** 88. C Brockworth *Glouc* 87-91; P-in-c Avening w Cherington 91-95; V Cinderford St Jo from 95. *St John's Vicarage, 1 Abbots View, Cinderford, Glos GL14 3EG* Tel (01594) 825446

HOLDER, Kenneth William (Ken). b 29. Sarum Th Coll 60. **d** 61 **p** 62. C Crawley *Chich* 61-65; C-in-c Wick CD 65-73; V Hangleton 73-79; R Rotherfield 79-81; R Rotherfield w Mark Cross 81-83; Chapl Eastbourne Coll 83-84; C Farnborough *Roch* 85; TV Mildenhall *St E* 87-92; R Redgrave cum Botesdale w Rickinghall from 92. *The Rectory, Bury Road, Rickinghall, Diss, Norfolk IP22 1HA* Tel (01379) 898685

HOLDER, Rodney Dennis. b 50. Trin Coll Cam BA71 MA75 Ch Ch Ox MA75 DPhil78 FRAS75 CPhys91 MInstP91 CMath95 FIMA95. Wycliffe Hall Ox 94. **d** 97. C Long Compton, Whichford and Barton-on-the-Heath *Cov* from 97; C Wolford w Burmington from 97; C Cherington w Stourton from 97; C Barcheston from 97. *The Vicarage, Great Wolford, Shipston-on-Stour, Warks CV36 5NQ* Tel (01608) 674361 Fax as telephone

HOLDING, Kenneth George Frank. b 27. Sarum & Wells Th Coll 75. **d** 77 **p** 78. C Bexley St Mary *Roch* 77-80; Min Joydens Wood St Barn CD 80-85; R Mereworth w W Peckham 85-92; rtd 92; Perm to Offic *York* from 92. *121 Burden Road, Beverley, N Humberside HU17 9LW* Tel (01482) 872609

HOLDRIDGE, The Ven Bernard Lee. b 35. Lich Th Coll 64. **d** 67 **p** 68. C Swinton *Sheff* 67-71; V Doncaster St Jude 71-81; R Rawmarsh w Parkgate 81-88; RD Rotherham 86-88; V Worksop Priory *S'well* 88-94; Adn Doncaster *Sheff* from 94. *Fairview House, 14 Armthorpe Lane, Doncaster, S Yorkshire DN2 5LZ* Tel (01302) 325787

HOLDSTOCK, Godfrey. b 48. St Jo Coll Cam BA69 MA72 Ox Univ BA77 MA81. St Steph Ho Ox 76. **d** 78 **p** 79. C Chislehurst Annunciation *Roch* 78-81; Hon C Richmond St Mary w St Matthias and St Jo *S'wark* 82-85; V Billesdon and Skeffington *Leic* 85-89; TV High Wycombe *Ox* 89-91; Chapl St Paul's Prep Sch Barnes 91-92; NSM Terriers *Ox* 92-93; P-in-c Barnes H Trin *S'wark* from 93. *Holy Trinity Vicarage, 162 Castelnau, London SW13 9ET* Tel 0181-748 5744

HOLDSWORTH, Ian Scott. b 52. Sheff Poly BA75. Oak Hill Th Coll BA81. **d** 81 **p** 82. C Denham *Ox* 81-84; P-in-c S Leigh 84-89; P-in-c Cogges 84-88; V 88-89. *Address temp unknown*

HOLDSWORTH, John Ivor. b 49. Univ of Wales (Abth) BA70 Univ of Wales (Cardiff) BD73 MTh75. St Mich Coll Llan 70. **d** 73 **p** 74. C Newport St Paul *Mon* 73-77; CF (TAVR) 75-90; V Abercraf and Callwen *S & B* 77-86; Bp's Chapl for Th Educn from 80; V Gorseinon from 86; Hon Lect Th Univ of Wales (Swansea) from 88. *The Vicarage, 42 Princess Street, Gorseinon, Swansea SA4 4US* Tel (01792) 892849

HOLDSWORTH, Kelvin. b 66. Man Poly BSc89 St Andr Univ BD92 Edin Univ MTh96. Edin Th Coll 95. **d** 97. C Perth St Ninian *St And* from 97. *28B Balhousie Street, Perth PH1 5HJ*

HOLDSWORTH, Michael Andrew. b 65. Univ Coll Dur BA88. Ripon Coll Cuddesdon BA92. **d** 93 **p** 94. C Cannock *Lich* from 93. *44 Manor Avenue, Cannock, Staffs WS11 1AA* Tel (01543) 502896

HOLE, The Very Revd Derek Norman. b 33. Linc Th Coll 57. **d** 60 **p** 61. C Knighton St Mary Magd *Leic* 60-62; S Africa 62-64; C Kenilworth St Nic *Cov* 64-67; R Burton Latimer *Pet* 67-73; V Leic St Jas *Leic* 73-92; Hon Can Leic Cathl 83-92; RD Christianity S 83-92; Provost Leic from 92; Chapl to The Queen 85-93. *The Provost's House, 1 St Martin's East, Leicester LE1 5FX* Tel 0116-262 5294 Fax 262 5295

HOLFORD, Andrew Peter. b 62. Nottm Univ BSc84. Cranmer Hall Dur 87. **d** 90 **p** 91. C Waltham Cross *St Alb* 90-93; C Northampton St Benedict *Pet* 93-95; V Pet Ch Carpenter from 95. *The Vicarage, Chestnut Avenue, Peterborough PE1 4PE* Tel (01733) 67140

HOLFORD, John Alexander. b 40. Chich Th Coll 65. **d** 67 **p** 68. C Cottingley *Bradf* 67-71; C Baildon 71-73; P-in-c Bingley H Trin 73-74; V 74-86; V Woodhall 86-93; C Shelf 93-94; TV Shelf St Mich w Buttershaw St Aid from 94. *91A Mandale Road, Bradford, W Yorkshire BD6 3JS* Tel (01274) 675015

HOLGATE, Dr David Andrew. b 54. Cape Town Univ BA77 Port Eliz Univ BA89 Rhodes Univ MTh90 PhD94. All Nations Chr Coll DipTh82. **d** 82 **p** 84. S Africa 82-93; P-in-c Felsted *Chelmsf* 93-96; Continuing Minl Educn Officer 93-96; V Felsted and Lt Dunmow 96-97; Dean of Studies S Th Educn and Tr Scheme from 97. *19 The Close, Salisbury SP1 2EE* Tel (01722) 412996 Fax 338508

✠HOLLAND, The Rt Revd Alfred Charles. b 27. St Chad's Coll Dur BA50 DipTh52. **d** 52 **p** 53 **c** 70. C W Hackney St Barn *Lon* 52-54; Australia 55-93; from 94; Asst Bp Perth 70-77; Bp Newcastle 78-92; rtd 92; Jerusalem 93-94. *21 Sullivan Crescent, Wanniassa, ACT, Australia 2903* Tel Canberra (6) 231 8368

✠HOLLAND, The Rt Revd Edward. b 36. AKC64. **d** 65 **p** 66 **c** 86. C Dartford H Trin *Roch* 65-69; C Mill Hill Jo Keble Ch *Lon* 69-72; Prec Gib Cathl *Eur* 72-74; Chapl Naples Ch Ch 74-79; Chapl Bromley Hosp 79-86; V Bromley St Mark *Roch* 79-86; Suff Bp Eur 86-95; Dean Brussels 86-95; Area Bp Colchester *Chelmsf* from 95. *1 Fitzwalter Road, Colchester CO3 3SS* Tel (01206) 576648 Fax 763868

HOLLAND, Glyn. b 59. Hull Univ BA Bris Univ CertEd. Coll of Resurr Mirfield 83. **d** 85 **p** 86. C Brighouse St Martin *Wakef* 85-89; V Ferrybridge 89-96; Chapl Pontefract Gen Infirmary Wakef 89-96; V Middlesbrough All SS *York* from 96. *All Saints' Vicarage, Grange Road, Middlesbrough, Cleveland TS1 2LR* Tel (01642) 245035

HOLLAND, Dr Henry Bowlby Tristram. b 11. Edin Univ MB, ChB34. Edin Th Coll 52. **d** 66 **p** 67. Pakistan 66-71; C Edin SS Phil and Jas *Edin* 71-77; C W Linton 77-88; C Penicuik 77-88; rtd 88. *Cuaig, Linton Bank Drive, West Linton, Peeblesshire EH46 7DT* Tel (01968) 60454

HOLLAND, John Stuart. b 52. Sarum & Wells Th Coll 77. **d** 80 **p** 81. C Wylde Green *Birm* 80-83; C Swanage and Studland *Sarum* 83-85; P-in-c Handley w Gussage St Andrew and Pentridge 85-88; TV Preston w Sutton Poyntz and Osmington w Poxwell 88-95; P-in-c Failsworth St Jo *Man* from 95. *St John's Rectory, Pole Lane, Manchester M35 9PB* Tel 0161-681 2734 Mobile 0468-203925

HOLLAND, Laurence Frederick Alfred (Fred). b 21. Sarum & Wells Th Coll. **d** 87 **p** 88. NSM Beaminster Area *Sarum* 87-92; Perm to Offic from 94. *18 St Mary Well Street, Beaminster, Dorset DT8 3BB* Tel (01308) 862426

HOLLAND, Mrs Linda (Lynne). b 48. Sarum & Wells Th Coll DCM93. **d** 93 **p** 94. Par Dn Queensbury All SS *Lon* 93-94; C 94-96; C Enfield St Jas from 96. *170 Addison Road, Enfield, Middx EN3 5LE* Tel 0181-805 1271

HOLLAND, Matthew Francis. b 52. Lon Univ BA73. Qu Coll Birm DipTh78. **d** 79 **p** 80. C Ecclesall *Sheff* 79-83; TV Gleadless Valley 83-86; TR 86-88; V Sheff Gillcar St Silas 88-92; V Sheff St Silas Broomhall from 92. *St Silas's Vicarage, 40 Hanover Street, Sheffield S3 7WT* Tel 0114-272 5300

HOLLAND, Paul William. b 55. Coll of Resurr Mirfield 78. **d** 80 **p** 81. C Parkstone St Pet w Branksea and St Osmund *Sarum* 80-83; CR 85-93; Asst Chapl Musgrove Park Hosp 93; Asst Chapl St Helier Hosp Carshalton 93-96; C Croydon St Jo *S'wark* from 96. *37 Alton Road, Croydon CR0 4LZ* Tel 0181-760 9629

HOLLAND, Peter Christie. b 36. St Andr Univ BSc60 Dur Univ DipTh62. Cranmer Hall Dur 60. **d** 62 **p** 63. C Darlington St Jo *Dur* 62-64; C Bishopwearmouth Ch Ch 64-69; V Tudhoe 69-77; V New Seaham 77-89; V Totternhoe, Stanbridge and Tilsworth *St Alb* from 89. *The Vicarage, Mill Road, Stanbridge, Leighton Buzzard, Beds LU7 9HX* Tel (01525) 210253

HOLLAND, Simon Geoffrey. b 63. MHCIMA83 Dorset Inst of HE OND81. Trin Coll Bris DipHE90. **d** 91 **p** 92. C Reigate St Mary *S'wark* 91-95; Chapl Lee Abbey from 95. *Lee Abbey, Lynton, Devon EX35 6JJ* Tel (01598) 752621 Fax 752619

HOLLAND, Simon Paul. b 56. Univ Coll Lon LLB77 Qu Coll Cam BA80 MA84 Edin Univ MTh94. Westcott Ho Cam 79. **d** 81 **p** 82. C Uckfield *Chich* 81-84; TV Lewes All SS, St Anne, St Mich and St Thos 84-88; TR 88-91; R Glas St Matt *Glas* 91-95; P-in-c Glas St Kentigern 95-96; R Aldingbourne, Barnham and Eastergate *Chich* from 96. *The Rectory, 97 Barnham Road, Barnham, Bognor Regis, W Sussex PO22 0EQ* Tel (01243) 554077

HOLLAND, William Geoffrey Bretton. b 36. Magd Coll Cam BA59 MA63. Westcott Ho Cam 61. **d** 63 **p** 64. C Cannock *Lich* 63-66; C Paddington Ch Ch *Lon* 66-69; Chapl Magd Coll Cam 69-73; V Twyford *Win* 74-78; V Twyford and Owslebury and Morestead 78-84; Chapl Twyford Sch Win from 84. *Twyford School, Searles Hill, Twyford, Winchester, Hants SO21 1NW* Tel (01962) 712269

HOLLAND, William Michael Tristram. b 26. Jes Coll Cam BA50 MA52. St Steph Ho Ox 79. **d** 81 **p** 82. C High Wycombe *Ox* 81-84; R Steeple Aston w N Aston and Tackley 84-94; rtd 94. *10 Tree Lane, Iffley, Oxford OX4 4EY*

HOLLANDS, Albert William. b 17. Roch Th Coll 60. **d** 62 **p** 63. C Aylsham *Nor* 62-66; R Syderstone 66-77; R Tattersett 67-83; P-in-c Tatterford 76-83; R Syderstone w Barmer 77-79; R Syderstone w Barmer and Bagthorpe 79-83; rtd 83; Perm to Offic *Nor* from 84. *25 Renwick Park East, West Runton, Cromer, Norfolk NR27 9LY* Tel (01263) 837352

HOLLANDS, Derek Gordon. b 45. Chich Th Coll 72. **d** 74 **p** 75. C Banstead *Guildf* 74-77; C Cranleigh 77-79; C Haywards Heath St Wilfrid *Chich* 79-80; TV 80-82; Chapl Hillingdon Area HA 82-86; Chapl W Suffolk Hosp Bury St Edm 86-95; Pres Coll Health Care Chapls 92-94; Sen Chapl R Cornwall Hosps NHS Trust from 95. *Royal Cornwall Hospital Trust, Treliske Hospital, Truro, Cornwall TR1 3LJ* Tel (01872) 74242

HOLLANDS, Percival Edwin Macaulay. b 36. Edin Th Coll 57. **d** 60 **p** 61. C Greenock *Glas* 60-64; C Aberdeen St Mary *Ab* 64-65; P-in-c Aberdeen St Clem 65-68; R Cruden Bay 68-70; CF 70-82; C Ribbleton *Blackb* 82-83; TV 83-88; C Longton 88; C Penwortham St Mary 88-92; V Farington from 92. *St Paul's Vicarage, 150 Croston Road, Farington, Preston PR5 3PR* Tel (01772) 38999

HOLLANDS, Ray Leonard. b 42. AMRSH OSB. S'wark Ord Course 68. **d** 71 **p** 72. NSM Hanworth All SS *Lon* 71-77 and 85-91; NSM Hanworth St Geo 77-85; NSM Marshwood Vale TM *Sarum* 81-91. *4 Priscilla House, Staines Road West, Sunbury-on-Thames, Middx TW16 7BE* Tel (01932) 781080

HOLLETT, Catherine Elaine. *See* DAKIN, Mrs Catherine Elaine

HOLLEY, Canon Geoffrey Raymond. b 28. AKC51. **d** 52 **p** 53. C Gt Ilford St Clem *Chelmsf* 52-53; C Gt Burstead 53-56; V 56-75; Bp's Ecum Officer 71-82; R Loughton St Jo 75-91; TR 91-92; Can Chelmsf Cathl 78-92; RD Epping Forest 82-92; rtd 92; Perm to Offic *Chelmsf* from 92. *5 The Maltings, Park Street, Thaxted, Dunmow, Essex CM6 2NB* Tel (01371) 830902

HOLLEY, Preb Graham Frank. b 29. Sarum Th Coll 60. **d** 61 **p** 62. C Heref All SS *Heref* 61-63; C W Wycombe *Ox* 63-67; V Much Marcle *Heref* 67-94; P-in-c Lt Marcle 84-86; RD Ledbury 87-90; Preb Heref Cathl 87-94; rtd 94. *40 Barrhill Road, Gourock, Renfrewshire PA1 1LB* Tel (01475) 632487

HOLLEY, Paul Robert. b 65. St Jo Coll Dur 91. **d** 94 **p** 95. C Tonge w Alkrington *Man* from 94. *18 Highfield Drive, Middleton, Manchester M24 1DJ* Tel 0161-653 0543

HOLLIDAY, Andrew. b 62. St Steph Ho Ox 89. **d** 92 **p** 93. C Marton *Blackb* 92-95; C Poulton-le-Fylde 95-97; V Leyland St Jas from 97. *St James's Vicarage, 201 Slater Lane, Leyland, Preston PR5 3SH* Tel (01772) 421034

HOLLIDAY, Arthur. b 22. St Jo Coll Dur 80. **d** 81 **p** 82. Hon C Allerton *Bradf* 81-84; Hon C Thornton St Jas from 84. *9 Alston Close, Bradford, W Yorkshire BD9 6AN* Tel (01274) 487331

HOLLIDAY, Eric Hedley. b 13. ARCS34 Lon Univ BSc35. Ridley Hall Cam 35. **d** 37 **p** 38. C Deptford St Luke *S'wark* 37-40; C Woking St Jo *Guildf* 40-44; V W Thurrock *Chelmsf* 44-55; V Islington St Paul Ball's Pond *Lon* 55-78; rtd 78; Perm to Offic *Ely* from 78. *4 George Place, Eynesbury, St Neots, Huntingdon, Cambs PE19 2QG* Tel (01480) 215703

HOLLIDAY, Peter Leslie. b 48. FCA79 Birm Univ BCom70 MA92. Qu Coll Birm 81. **d** 83 **p** 84. C Burton *Lich* 83-87; P-in-c Longdon 87-93; PV and Subchanter Lich Cath 87-93; R Stratford-on-Avon w Bishopton *Cov* from 93. *Stratford Vicarage, Old Town, Stratford-upon-Avon, Warks CV37 6BG* Tel (01789) 293098

HOLLIDAY, William (Bill). b 33. Qu Coll Cam BA56 MA60 McGill Univ Montreal BD58 LTh58. Montreal Dioc Th Coll 56 Linc Th Coll 58. **d** 58 **p** 59. C Stanningley St Thos *Ripon* 58-63; C Romaldkirk 63-64; India 64-77; V Thwaites Brow *Bradf* 77-86; RD S Craven 82-86; P-in-c Horton from 86; P-in-c Bradf St Oswald Chapel Green from 91; RD Bowling and Horton from 95. *Faith Sawrey's House, 41 Little Horton Green, Bradford, W Yorkshire BD5 0NG* Tel (01274) 727976

HOLLIMAN, The Ven John James. b 44. St D Coll Lamp BA66. **d** 67 **p** 68. C Tideswell *Derby* 67-71; CF 71-95; Dep Chapl Gen from 96; Adn for the Army from 96. *MOD Chaplains (Army), Trenchard Lines, Upavon, Pewsey, Wilts SN9 6BE* Tel (01980) 615802 Fax 615800

HOLLIN, Ian. b 40. Open Univ BA76 Inst of Counselling DCC91. Sarum Th Coll 67. **d** 70 **p** 71. C Lancaster Ch Ch *Blackb* 70-72; C S Shore H Trin 72-75; C Marton Moss 72-75; V Morecambe St Lawr 75-78; V Blackpool St Mary 78-83; PV and Succ Ex Cathl *Ex* 83-87; Counsellor Coun for Chr Care and Tr 87-91; Admin Boniface Cen Ex 91-93; TV Maltby *Sheff* 93-96; R Handsworth from 96. *The Rectory, Handsworth Road, Handsworth, Sheffield S13 9BZ* Tel 0114-269 2403

HOLLINGDALE, Derek Leslie. b 32. Ex & Truro NSM Scheme. **d** 83 **p** 84. NSM Tuckingmill *Truro* 83-85; NSM Illogan 85-92; NSM Treslothan from 92. *St Margaret's, 11 Atlantic Terrace, Camborne, Cornwall TR14 7AW* Tel (01209) 612938 or 890501

HOLLINGHURST, Mrs Anne Elizabeth. b 64. Trin Coll Bris BA93. **d** 96 **p** 97. C Nottingham St Sav *S'well* from 96. *Glebe House, 2 The Vicarage, Arkwright Walk, Nottingham NG2 2JU* Tel 0115-985 0931

HOLLINGHURST, Stephen. b 59. Univ of Wales DipTh. St Jo Coll Nottm 81. **d** 83 **p** 84. C Hyde St Geo *Ches* 83-86; C Cropwell Bishop w Colston Bassett, Granby etc *S'well* 86-90; R Pembridge w Moorcourt, Shobdon, Staunton etc *Heref* from 90; RD Kington and Weobley from 95. *The Rectory, Pembridge, Leominster, Herefordshire HR6 9EB* Tel (01544) 388998

HOLLINGHURST, Stephen Patrick. b 63. Hull Univ BA84. Trin Coll Bris BA93 MA93. **d** 96 **p** 97. C Nottingham St Sav *S'well* from 96. *Glebe House, 2 The Vicarage, Arkwright Walk, Nottingham NG2 2JU* Tel 0115-985 0931

HOLLINGS, Miss Patricia Mary. b 39. CertEd59. S'wark Ord Course 84. **d** 87. Par Dn Wyke *Bradf* 87-94; C 94-96; rtd 96; Perm to Offic *Bradf* from 96. *1 Greenacre Way, Wyke, Bradford, W Yorkshire BD12 9DJ* Tel (01274) 677439

HOLLINGS, Robert George (Bob). b 48. St Jo Coll Nottm DipThMin94. **d** 94 **p** 95. C Cotmanhay *Derby* 94-97; TV Godrevy *Truro* from 97. *The Vicarage, St Erth, Hayle, Cornwall TR27 6HN* Tel (01736) 753194

HOLLINGSHEAD, Miss Pauline Carol. b 49. Local Minl Tr Course. **d** 94 **p** 95. NSM Colsterworth Gp *Linc* from 94. *The Lodge, Little Ponton, Grantham, Lincs NG33 5BS* Tel (01476) 530382

HOLLINGSHURST, Robert Peter. b 38. Ridley Hall Cam 64. **d** 67 **p** 68. C Roxeth Ch Ch *Lon* 67-70; C Attenborough w Chilwell *S'well* 70-73; C Ramsgate St Luke *Cant* 74-75; Chapl to the Deaf 78-80; TV Louth *Linc* 80-84; Chapl to the Deaf *Sarum* 84-87; P-in-c Odstock w Nunton and Bodenham 84-96; P-in-c Britford 89-96; P-in-c Charlton All Saints 89-96; P-in-c Gt and Lt Gaddesden *St Alb* from 96. *The Vicarage, Piper's Hill, Great Gaddesden, Hemel Hempstead, Herts HP1 3BY* Tel (01442) 252672

HOLLINGSWORTH, Geoffrey. b 53. MIPM85 Leeds Poly 74. N Ord Course 86. **d** 86 **p** 87. C Thorne *Sheff* 86-89; V Rawcliffe 89-96; V Airmyn, Hook and Rawcliffe from 96. *The Vicarage, 12 Church Lane, Hook, Goole, N Humberside DN14 5PN* Tel (01405) 763654

HOLLINGSWORTH, Canon Gerald Frank Lee. b 26. Lon Univ BA53. Oak Hill Th Coll 49. **d** 54 **p** 55. C Sutton *Liv* 54-57; C Ipswich All Hallows *St E* 57-59; V Yoxford 59-64; P-in-c Sibton 59-62; V 62-64; Dioc Youth Chapl 60-62; Bp's Ind Adv 64-75; V Ipswich H Trin 64-72; R Ipswich St Clem w H Trin 72-75; R Gt and Lt Bealings w Playford and Culpho 75-90; RD Woodbridge 76-84; Hon Can St E Cathl 76-90; rtd 90; Perm to Offic *St E* from 90. *The Conifers, Ipswich Road, Grundisburgh, Woodbridge, Suffolk IP13 6TJ* Tel (01473) 735232

HOLLINGSWORTH, James William. b 69. Southn Univ BA91 SS Coll Cam BA96. Aston Tr Scheme 92 Ridley Hall Cam 94. **d** 97. C Mildenhall *St E* from 97. *103 Melbourne Drive, Mildenhall, Suffolk IP28 7BP* Tel (01638) 715112

HOLLINGSWORTH, Miss Paula Marion. b 62. Van Mildert Coll Dur BSc83. Trin Coll Bris BA91. **d** 91 **p** 94. C Keynsham *B & W* 91-95; C Balsall Heath St Paul *Birm* from 95. *51 Alpha Close, Balsall Heath, Birmingham B12 9HF* Tel 0121-440 7867

HOLLINGTON, David Mark. b 61. DipEH83 MIEH83. Trin Coll Bris BA94. **d** 94. C Wednesbury St Paul Wood Green *Lich* 94-95; C Cannock 95-96. *19 Rylands Drive, Wolverhampton WV4 5SQ*

HOLLINGWORTH, Martin Douglas. b 50. RMCM GRSM73. Trin Coll Bris 73. **d** 77 **p** 78. C Hartford *Ches* 77-78; C Knowle *Birm* 79-81; S Africa 81-93; Chapl Hong Kong Cathl from 93. *Flat D-2, On Lee, 2 Mount Davis Road, Hong Kong* Fax Hong Kong (852) 521-7830

HOLLINRAKE, Jean Margaret. *See* HARRISON, Mrs Jean Margaret

HOLLINS, John Edgar. b 35. St Jo Coll Cam BA58 MA62. Oak Hill Th Coll 58. **d** 60 **p** 61. C Whalley Range St Edm *Man* 60-63;

C Highbury Ch Ch *Lon* 63-66; C St Alb St Paul *St Alb* 66-71; Hon C Halliwell St Paul *Man* 71-72; C Ravenhill St Jo 72-73; Perm to Offic *Birm* 79-81; V Millbrook *Ches* 81-89; rtd 89. *Tresuan, Meadway, Looe, Cornwall PL13 1JT* Tel (01503) 264062

HOLLIS, Anthony Wolcott Linsley. b 40. McGill Univ Montreal BA61 Long Is Univ MA76. Gen Th Sem NY MDiv64. **d** 64 **p** 65. USA 64-92; Bermuda from 92. *PO Box GE 85, St George's GE BX, Bermuda* Tel Bermuda (1-441) 297-0216 Fax 297-8256

HOLLIS, The Ven Arnold Thaddeus. b 33. JP87. Stockton State Coll New Jersey BA74 NY Th Sem MDiv74 STM76 DMin78. Codrington Coll Barbados 56. **d** 59 **p** 60. C Wakef St Jo *Wakef* 60-62; Br Guiana 62-64; P-in-c Horbury Bridge *Wakef* 64-66; C Loughton St Jo *Chelmsf* 66-69; USA 69-77; Bermuda from 77; Hon Chapl RN from 77; Chapl HM Pris from 77; Chapl Miss to Seamen from 90; Hon Can Bermuda Cathl from 87; Adn Bermuda from 96. *PO Box MA 74, Sandys MA BX, Bermuda* Tel Bermuda (1-441) 234-0834 or 2025 Fax 234-2723

HOLLIS, Christopher Barnsley. b 28. Clare Coll Cam BA52 MA59. Wells Th Coll 60. **d** 62 **p** 63. C Baildon *Bradf* 62-64; V Esholt 64-66; V Heaton St Barn 66-85; RD Airedale 73-82; Hon Can Bradf Cathl 77-85; Chapl HM Young Offender Inst Medomsley 85-90; V Medomsley *Dur* 85-90; P-in-c Denholme Gate *Bradf* 90-95; rtd 95; Perm to Offic *Bradf* from 95. *52 Wilmer Drive, Bradford, W Yorkshire BD9 4AS* Tel (01274) 546722

HOLLIS, Derek. b 60. Loughb Univ BA82. Cranmer Hall Dur 83. **d** 86 **p** 87. C Evington *Leic* 86-89; C Arnold *S'well* 89-93; V Beckingham w Walkeringham from 93; P-in-c Gringley-on-the-Hill from 95. *The Vicarage, Beckingham, Doncaster, S Yorkshire DN10 4PJ* Tel (01427) 84266

HOLLIS, Douglas John. b 32. S Dios Minl Tr Scheme. **d** 84 **p** 85. NSM Haywards Heath St Wilfrid *Chich* from 84. *2 Northlands Avenue, Haywards Heath, W Sussex RH16 3RT* Tel (01444) 453688

HOLLIS, Canon Gerald. b 19. Ch Ch Ox BA42 MA45. Wells Th Coll 45. **d** 47 **p** 48. C Stepney St Dunstan and All SS *Lon* 47-50; C Rossington *Sheff* 50-54; R Armthorpe 54-60; V Rotherham 60-74; Hon Can Sheff Cathl 70-74; Adn Birm 74-84; Hon Can Birm Cathl 74-84; rtd 84; Perm to Offic *Sarum* from 87. *68 Britford Lane, Salisbury SP2 8AH* Tel (01722) 338154

HOLLIS, Howard Charles. b 16. Melbourne Univ MusBac40. Trin Coll Melbourne ThL43. **d** 45 **p** 46. Australia 45-47; C Croydon Woodside *Cant* 47-49; C S Kensington St Steph *Lon* 49-51; Min Can Westmr Abbey 51-59; Dep P in O 54-59; Chapl Westmr Sch 57-59; Australia 59-65 and from 76; V Primrose Hill St Mary w Avenue Road St Paul *Lon* 65-76; rtd 83. *18 Maud Street, North Balwyn, Victoria, Australia 3104* Tel Melbourne (3) 9859 3213

HOLLIS, Jeffrey Norman. b 30. Qu Coll Birm 71. **d** 74 **p** 75. C Inkberrow *Worc* 74-76; C Eastleigh *Win* 76-79; V Jersey St Jas 79-85; V Jersey St Luke 79-85; R Jersey St Sav 85-91; rtd 91. *12 Hill Farm, Stonepit Lane, Inkberrow, Worcester WR7 4EX* Tel (01386) 793334

HOLLIS, Peter. b 20. Jes Coll Cam BA49. Wells Th Coll 49. **d** 51 **p** 52. C Yardley St Edburgha *Birm* 51-55; C Coleshill 55-57; V Kingshurst 57-67; R Sudbury St Greg and St Pet *St E* 67-81; R Sudbury and Chilton 81-86; rtd 86. *1 New Cottages, Brundon, Sudbury, Suffolk CO10 6XS* Tel (01787) 370447

HOLLIS, Timothy Knowles (Tim). b 28. RN Coll Dartmouth 45. St Steph Ho Ox 54. **d** 58 **p** 59. C Oatlands *Guildf* 58-60; C Crawley *Chich* 60-63; C Sotterley w Willingham *St E* 63-69; R Sotterley, Willingham, Shadingfield, Ellough etc 69-76; Gen Sec L'Arche UK 77-93; Perm to Offic from 77; rtd 93; Perm to Offic *Chich* from 93. *Padwicks Farm, Bepton, Midhurst, W Sussex GU29 0LY* Tel (01730) 815495

HOLLIS, Mrs Valerie Elizabeth. b 40. **d** 92 **p** 94. NSM Kempston Transfiguration *St Alb* from 92. *33 Silverdale Street, Kempston, Bedford MK42 8BE* Tel (01234) 853397

HOLLOWAY, Canon Alan James. b 23. FPhS64 Lon Univ BD58 MTh67. Oak Hill Th Coll 53. **d** 56 **p** 57. C Tonbridge St Steph *Roch* 56-58; C Chalk 58-59; V 59-62; Tutor Oak Hill Th Coll 62-68; Chapl and Lect St Paul's Coll Cheltenham 69-73; V Maisemore *Glouc* 73-76; Dir of Educn 74-82; Can Res Glouc Cathl 74-82; R Glouc St Mary de Crypt w St Jo and Ch Ch 82-88; rtd 88; Bp's Personal Asst *Glouc* 88-92. *42 Stancliffe Road, Bedford MK41 9AP* Tel (01234) 261566

HOLLOWAY, Canon David Dennis. b 43. Lich Th Coll 65. **d** 68 **p** 69. C Cricklade w Latton *Bris* 68-71; C Bris St Agnes w St Simon 71-72; C Bris St Agnes and St Simon w St Werburgh 72-74; V Bitton 74-78; TV E Bris 78-80; P-in-c Tormarton w W Littleton 80-83; Sub Chapl HM Pris Bris 80-92; Dioc Ecum Officer 83-93; Hon C Bris St Mich 89-93; Hon Can Bris Cathl from 92; V Horfield St Greg from 93; RD Horfield from 97. *St Gregory's Vicarage, Filton Road, Horfield, Bristol BS7 0PD* Tel 0117-969 2839

HOLLOWAY, David Ronald James. b 39. Univ Coll Ox BA62 MA66. Ridley Hall Cam 65. **d** 67 **p** 68. C Leeds St Geo *Ripon* 67-71; Tutor Wycliffe Hall Ox 71-72; V Jesmond Clayton Memorial *Newc* from 73. *The Vicarage, 7 Otterburn Terrace, Jesmond, Newcastle upon Tyne NE2 3AP* Tel 0191-281 2001

HOLLOWAY, Graham Edward. b 45. Chich Th Coll 69. **d** 72 **p** 73. C W Drayton *Lon* 72-75; P-in-c Hawton *S'well* 75-80; TV Newark w Hawton, Cotham and Shelton 80; V Ladybrook 80-85; P-in-c Babworth 85-87; R Babworth w Sutton-cum-Lound 87-97; RD Retford 88-93; C Mansfield Woodhouse from 97. *13 Church Hill Avenue, Mansfield Woodhouse, Notts NG19 9JU*

HOLLOWAY, Howard Robinett. b 06. Keble Coll Ox BA27 MA31. Wells Th Coll 27. **d** 29 **p** 30. C Newport St Paul *Mon* 29-32; C Birm Cathl *Birm* 32-38; V E Bedfont *Lon* 38-48; V Hounslow Heath St Paul 48-65; V Treleigh *Truro* 65-70; R Perranuthnoe 70-72; rtd 72. *Verona Villa, Canossa Complex, 169 Rocks Road, Oxley, Brisbane, Australia 4075*

HOLLOWAY, Keith Graham. b 45. Linc Coll Ox BA67 St Jo Coll Dur DipTh72. **d** 73 **p** 74. C Gt Ilford St Andr *Chelmsf* 73-78; Hon C Squirrels Heath 78-80; Min Chelmer Village CD 80-87; V E Springfield 87-89; P-in-c Gt Dunmow 89-96; R Gt Dunmow and Barnston from 96. *The Vicarage, 3 The Charters, Church End, Dunmow, Essex CM6 2SJ* Tel (01371) 872504

✠**HOLLOWAY, The Most Revd Richard Frederick.** b 33. FRSA92 Lon Univ BD63 Aber Univ Hon DD95. NY Th Sem STM68 Edin Th Coll 58. **d** 59 **p** 60 **c** 86. C Glas St Ninian *Glas* 59-63; P-in-c Glas St Marg 63-68; R Edin Old St Paul *Edin* 68-80; USA 80-84; V Ox St Mary Magd *Ox* 84-86; Bp Edin from 86; Primus from 92. *3 Eglinton Crescent, Edinburgh EH12 5DH, or Diocesan Centre, 21A Grosvenor Crescent, Edinburgh EH2 5EL* Tel 0131-226 5099 or 538 7044 Fax 225 3181

HOLLOWAY, Roger Graham. b 33. OBE97. Selw Coll Cam BA58 MA61. S'wark Ord Course 75. **d** 78 **p** 80. Hong Kong 78-80 and 85-88; Japan 80-84; PV Westmr St Marg from 88; Nat Dir ICF 91-96; Lic to Offic *Lon* from 94; Preacher Gray's Inn from 97; Lic Preacher *Lon* from 97. *Flat 6, 2 Porchester Gardens, London W2 6JL* Tel 0171-402 4937 Fax 402 4683

HOLLOWAY, Simon Anthony. b 50. Sussex Univ BSc72. Trin Coll Bris 76. **d** 79 **p** 81. C Bushbury *Lich* 79-81; C Castle Church 81-84; P-in-c Sparkbrook Ch Ch *Birm* 84-91; V from 91; RD Bordesley from 92. *Christ Church Vicarage, 34 Grantham Road, Birmingham B11 1LU* Tel 0121-772 6558

HOLLOWOOD, Christopher George. b 54. K Alfred's Coll Win BEd76. Ripon Coll Cuddesdon 83. **d** 86 **p** 87. C Tupsley *Heref* 86-89; R Much Birch w Lt Birch, Much Dewchurch etc 89-92; Hd of Relig Studies Haywood High Sch Heref from 92. *41 Harold Street, Hereford HR1 2QU*

HOLLOWOOD, Lewis William Rye. b 17. Dur Univ 37. Edin Th Coll 37. **d** 40 **p** 41. C St Paul's Cathl Dundee *Bre* 40-41; Chapl 41-43; C Ches St Jo *Ches* 43-44; R Fortrose *Mor* 44-46; R Cromarty 44-46; R Paisley H Trin *Glas* 46-47; R Renfrew 46-47; R Carnoustie *Bre* 47-49; Chapl K Coll Hosp Lon 49-50; V Mark Beech *Roch* 50-59; V New Groombridge *Chich* 59-67; V Hadlow Down 67-74; R Buxted St Marg 72-74; V Bexhill St Barn 75-81; Chapl Community Servants of the Cross Lindfield 81-97; rtd 82. *Convent of the Holy Rood, Lindfield, Haywards Heath, W Sussex RH16 2QY* Tel (01444) 482095

HOLMAN, Francis Noel. b 37. DSPT90. Sarum Th Coll 62. **d** 65 **p** 66. C Weston Favell *Pet* 65-68; C Eckington *Derby* 68-71; Asst Chapl St Thos Hosp Lon 72-77; Chapl Hope Hosp and Ladywell Hosp Salford 77-94; Chapl Salford R Hosp 77-93; Chapl Man and Salford Skin Hosp 88-94; Chapl Salford R Hosps NHS Trust from 94. *90 Rocky Lane, Monton, Eccles, Manchester M30 9LY* Tel 0161-707 1180 or 787 5167

HOLMAN, Geoffrey Gladstone. b 32. AKC56. **d** 57 **p** 58. C Eltham St Barn *S'wark* 57-60; CF 60-73; Dep Asst Chapl Gen 73-80; Asst Chapl Gen 80-84; QHC 82-84; V Wetwang and Garton-on-the-Wolds w Kirkburn *York* 84-92; RD Harthill 87-92; rtd 92; NSM Askham Bryan *York* from 93. *20 North Parade, Bootham, York YO3 7AB* Tel (01904) 624419

HOLMDEN, Miss Maria Irene. b 50. Trent Poly TCert72 BEd73 Golds Coll Lon DPEd84. Oak Hill Th Coll DipHE92. **d** 92 **p** 94. Par Dn Stratford St Jo and Ch Ch w Forest Gate St Jas *Chelmsf* 92-94; C 94-96; P-in-c Leyton All SS from 96. *All Saints' Vicarage, 47 Melbourne Road, London E10 7HF* Tel 0181-539 2170

HOLME, Thomas Edmund. b 49. Selw Coll Cam BA71 MA75. Coll of Resurr Mirfield 71. **d** 73 **p** 74. C Wyther Ven Bede *Ripon* 73-76; C Wimbledon *S'wark* 76-78; TV 78-79; V Bermondsey St Anne 79-81; V Stamford Baron *Pet* 83-89; P-in-c Tinwell 83-89; Hon Min Can Pet Cathl 84-89; Prec Worc Cathl *Worc* 89-95; P-in-c Penshurst and Fordcombe *Roch* from 95. *The Rectory, Penshurst, Tonbridge, Kent TN11 8BN* Tel (01892) 870316

HOLMES, Alan Stewart. b 57. MInstPkg88 St Andr Univ BSc80. Ox NSM Course 85. **d** 88 **p** 89. NSM Shinfield *Ox* 88-95; NSM Beech Hill, Grazeley and Spencers Wood from 95. *The Cottage, Church Lane, Three Mile Cross, Reading RG7 1HB* Tel 0118-988 2436

HOLMES, Andrew Keith. b 69. Univ of Wales BEng93. St Mich Coll Llan BTh93. **d** 96 **p** 97. C Clydach *S & B* from 96. *37 Kelvin Road, Clydach, Swansea SA6 5JP* Tel (01792) 845397

HOLMES, Anthony David Robert. b 38. Oak Hill Th Coll 75. **d** 77 **p** 78. C Iver *Ox* 77-81; V Bucklebury w Marlston from 81. *The Vicarage, Bucklebury, Reading RG7 6PL* Tel (0118) 971 3193

HOLMES, Brian. b 41. NE Ord Course DipHE95. **d** 95 **p** 96. NSM Darlington St Matt and St Luke *Dur* from 95. *24 Coniston Street, Darlington, Co Durham DL3 6DJ* Tel (01325) 354669

HOLMES, Clive Horace. b 31. Ox NSM Course. **d** 83 **p** 84. NSM Cumnor *Ox* from 83. *62 Westminster Way, Oxford OX2 0LW* Tel (01865) 249640

HOLMES, David Roy. b 34. FIPM75. Ox NSM Course 81. **d** 84 **p** 85. NSM Ox SS Phil and Jas w St Marg *Ox* 84-85; NSM Ox St Giles and SS Phil and Jas w St Marg from 85. *48 Charlbury Road, Oxford OX2 6UX* Tel (01865) 510061

HOLMES, Frank. b 22. NW Ord Course 75. **d** 78 **p** 79. NSM Hyde St Geo *Ches* 78-81; C Poynton 81-87; rtd 87; Perm to Offic *Ches* from 87. *277 Stockport Road, Marple, Stockport, Cheshire SK6 6ES* Tel 0161-449 9289

HOLMES, Geoffrey Robert. b 67. Nottm Univ BSc89. Ridley Hall Cam BA92. **d** 93 **p** 94. C Clifton St Jas *Sheff* from 93. *26 Greenwich Court, Rotherham, S Yorkshire S65 1BU* Tel (01709) 372079

HOLMES, Grant Wenlock. b 54. St Steph Ho Ox BA78 MA83. **d** 79 **p** 80. C Benhilton *S'wark* 79-82; C-in-c S Kenton Annunciation CD *Lon* 82-86; Tutor Chich Th Coll 86-87; Bp's Dom Chapl *Chich* 86-88; V Mayfield from 88. *The Vicarage, High Street, Mayfield, E Sussex TN20 6AB* Tel (01435) 873180

HOLMES, Canon John Robin. b 42. Leeds Univ BA64. Linc Th Coll 64. **d** 66 **p** 67. C Wyther Ven Bede *Ripon* 66-69; C Adel 69-73; V Beeston Hill St Luke 73-76; V Holbeck 76-86; RD Armley 82-86; V Manston 86-93; Hon Can Ripon Cathl from 89; Dioc Missr from 93. *Churchfields, Main Street, Darley, Harrogate, N Yorkshire HG3 2QF* Tel (01423) 780771

HOLMES, Jonathan Michael. b 49. MRCVS73 Qu Coll Cam BA70 VetMB73 MA74 PhD78. Ridley Hall Cam 87. **d** 88 **p** 89. Chapl Qu Coll Cam from 88; Dean of Chpl from 94. *Queens' College, Cambridge CB3 9ET* Tel (01223) 335545 Fax 335522 E-mail 115@cam.ac.uk

HOLMES, Nigel Ernest Hartley. b 37. Em Coll Cam BA58 MA64 Lon Hosp BChir61 MB62. Ridley Hall Cam 62. **d** 64 **p** 65. C Cambridge St Phil *Ely* 64-68; I Jersey St Paul Prop Chpl *Win* 68-77; C Cambridge H Sepulchre w All SS *Ely* 78-80; Perm to Offic *St E* 80-86; Perm to Offic *Ely* 80-86; P-in-c Brinkley, Burrough Green and Carlton 86-92; P-in-c Westley Waterless 86-92; NSM in Evang from 92; Perm to Offic *Nor* from 97; rtd 97. *133 Coleridge Road, Cambridge CB1 3PN* Tel (01223) 771903

HOLMES, Nigel Peter. b 48. Nottm Univ BTh72 Lanc Univ CertEd72 Lon Univ BD76 Sheff Univ MEd84. Kelham Th Coll. **d** 72 **p** 73. C Barrow St Matt *Carl* 72-75; C Derby St Bart *Derby* 75-78; P-in-c Gt Barlow 78-84; V Carl St Herbert w St Steph *Carl* 84-91; V Keswick St Jo 91-94; V Mexborough *Sheff* 94-97; P-in-c Nether Hoyland St Pet from 97. *The Vicarage, 104 Hawshaw Lane, Hoyland, Barnsley, S Yorkshire S74 0HH* Tel (01226) 749231

HOLMES, Mrs Patricia Ann (Pat). b 52. N Ord Course 96. **d** 97. C Almondbury w Farnley Tyas *Wakef* from 97. *30 Benomley Road, Almondbury, Huddersfield HD5 8LS* Tel (01484) 537773

HOLMES, Peter Anthony. b 55. Univ of Wales (Ban) BA77 Brighton Poly CertEd78. Trin Coll Bris DipHE. **d** 88 **p** 89. C Croydon Ch Ch *S'wark* 88-93; V Norbiton from 93; RD Kingston from 97. *The Vicarage, 21 Wolsey Close, Kingston upon Thames, Surrey KT2 7ER* Tel 0181-942 8330

HOLMES, Dr Peter Geoffrey. b 32. Bris Univ BSc59 MSc69 Leic Univ PhD74. St Deiniol's Hawarden 74. **d** 76 **p** 77. NSM Glen Parva and S Wigston *Leic* from 76; Prof Nottm Poly 85-92; Prof City Univ Nottm from 92. *19 Windsor Avenue, Glen Parva, Leicester LE2 9JQ* Tel 0116-277 4534

HOLMES, Robert John Geoffrey. b 28. TCD BA53 MA57. Ely Th Coll 56. **d** 57 **p** 58. C Whitton St Aug CD *Lon* 57-59; C St Pancras w St Jas and Ch Ch 59-63; C Stepney St Dunstan and All SS 63-66; Chapl The Lon Hosp (Whitechapel) 63-68; C Stepney St Aug w St Phil *Lon* 66-68; S Africa 68-74; Perm to Offic *Ely* 74; Perm to Offic *Chich* 74-76; R Telscombe w Piddinghoe and Southease 76-93; P-in-c Barlavington, Burton w Coates, Sutton and Bignor 93-96; rtd 95; Perm to Offic *Chich* from 95. *8 Bishops Courtyard, The Hornet, Chichester, W Sussex PO19 4GT*

HOLMES, Roger Cockburn. b 46. Jes Coll Ox BA70 MA84 Edin Univ BD76. Edin Th Coll 73. **d** 84 **p** 85. Canada 84-88; R Ditchingham w Pirnough *Nor* 88-90; R Hedenham 88-90; R Broome 88-90; R Ditchingham, Hedenham and Broome 90-93; V Helmsley *York* 93-97. *Address temp unknown*

HOLMES, Roy Grant. b 37. Ox NSM Course 83. **d** 86 **p** 87. NSM Wokingham St Paul *Ox* from 86. *58 Copse Drive, Wokingham, Berks RG41 1LX* Tel (0118) 978 4141

HOLMES, Stanley Thomas. b 11. Selw Coll Cam BA34 MA46. St Steph Ho Ox 34. **d** 36 **p** 37. C Headington *Ox* 36-48; V Goring 48-84; rtd 84; Perm to Offic *Ox* from 84. *Lower Farm, 8 Dunstan Road, Old Headington, Oxford OX3 9BY* Tel (01865) 62657

HOLMES, Stephen. b 54. St Andr Univ MTh84. Chich Th Coll 84. **d** 86 **p** 87. C Croydon St Jo *S'wark* 86-89; C Tewkesbury w Walton Cardiff *Glouc* 89-92; P-in-c Bournemouth St Luke *Win* 92-94; V from 94. *St Luke's Vicarage, 31 Lonsdale Road, Bournemouth BH3 7LY* Tel (01202) 516653

HOLMES, Stephen John. b 50. CertEd72 DipHE83. Trin Coll Bris 81 Sarum & Wells Th Coll 88. **d** 89 **p** 90. C Skegness and Winthorpe *Linc* 89-93; P-in-c Mablethorpe w Trusthorpe 93-97; V Hadleigh St Barn *Chelmsf* from 97. *St Barnabas' Vicarage, 169 Church Road, Hadleigh, Essex SS7 2EJ* Tel (01702) 554658

HOLMES, William John. b 49. **d** 97. Aux Min Billy w Derrykeighan *Conn* from 97. *14 Glenlough Park, Coleraine, Co Londonderry BT52 1TY* Tel (01265) 55993

HOLNESS, Edwin Geoffrey Nicholas. b 39. RGN BTA. Sarum Th Coll 68. **d** 71 **p** 72. C Upper Beeding *Chich* 71-74; C Bramber w Botolphs 71-74; C Munster Square St Mary Magd *Lon* 74-75; Perm to Offic *Chich* 75-76; C Brighton Annunciation 76-77; Chapl Brighton Hosp Gp 77-94; Chapl R Sussex Co Hosp Brighton 77-94; Perm to Offic *Chich* from 77. *1 Belgrave Place, Brighton BN2 1EL* Tel (01273) 686830

HOLROYD, Gordon Eric. b 31. SSM. **d** 76 **p** 76. Asst Chapl St Martin's Coll Lanc 76-77; Chapl 77-78; Hon C Sheff St Matt *Sheff* 78-80; Lic to Offic *Man* 80-81; P-in-c Willen *Ox* 81-84; Perm to Offic *Blackb* 84-95; NSM Middlesbrough All SS *York* 89-95; Australia from 95. *St John's Priory, 14 St John Street, Adelaide, S Australia 5000* Tel Adelaide (8) 223 2348 Fax 223 1014

HOLROYD, John Richard. b 54. Liv Univ BA75 PGCE77. Wycliffe Hall Ox 78. **d** 81 **p** 82. C Gt Stanmore *Lon* 81-84; Min Can, V Choral and Prec St E Cathl *St E* 84-89; TV Wolverton *Ox* 89-96; P-in-c Maidenhead St Luke from 96. *St Luke's Vicarage, 26 Norfolk Road, Maidenhead, Berks SL6 7AX* Tel (01628) 783033

HOLROYD, Stephen Charles. b 56. UEA BA79. St Jo Coll Nottm 84. **d** 87 **p** 88. C Barton Seagrave w Warkton *Pet* 87-91; V Eye 91-97; V Silsoe, Pulloxhill and Flitton *St Alb* from 97. *Little Gable, 21 West End Road, Bedford MK45 4DU*

HOLT, Alan Leonard. b 12. Dur Univ LTh42. Edin Th Coll 39. **d** 42 **p** 43. C Ulverston St Mary *Carl* 42-44; C Carl St Aid and Ch Ch 44-46; C W Bromwich All SS *Lich* 46-50; V Streetly 50-77; rtd 77; Perm to Offic *B & W* from 77. *Old Vicarage, Rectory Way, Lympsham, Weston-super-Mare, Avon BS24 0EW* Tel (01934) 750527

HOLT, Brian. b 30. BMin73. Huron Coll Ontario. **d** 70 **p** 71. Canada 70-78; V Glodwick *Man* 78-83; TV E Farnworth and Kearsley 83-87; R Abbey Hey 87-94; rtd 95; Perm to Offic *Blackb* from 95. *79 Lennox Road, Todmorden, Lancs OL14 8PS* Tel (01706) 819672

HOLT, David. b 44. St Jo Coll Dur BSc67 DipTh69. **d** 70 **p** 71. C Blackley St Pet *Man* 70-73; C Radcliffe St Thos 73-74; C Radcliffe St Thos and St Jo 74-75; V Ashton St Pet 75-79; Dioc Youth Officer *Guildf* 80-85; V Bagshot 85-97; RD Surrey Heath 92-97; V Fleet from 97. *The Vicarage, Branksomewood Road, Fleet, Hants GU13 8JU* Tel (01252) 616361

HOLT, Douglas Robert. b 49. MA. Ridley Hall Cam. **d** 82 **p** 83. C Cambridge St Barn *Ely* 82-84; P-in-c 84-86; V 86-91; V Ealing St Mary *Lon* from 91. *St Mary's Vicarage, 11 Church Place, London W5 4HN* Tel 0181-567 0414 or 579 7134 Fax 840 4534

HOLT, Francis Thomas (Frank). b 38. Edin Th Coll 79. **d** 81 **p** 82. C Cullercoats St Geo *Newc* 81-83; C Ponteland 83-86; Chapl Worc Coll of HE 86-89; R Worc St Clem *Worc* 86-93; V Finstall 93-96; Chapl Menorca *Eur* 96-97. *c/o 85 Fruitlands, Malvern, Worcs WR14 4XB*

HOLT, Harold. b 20. **d** 52 **p** 52. Dioc Supernumerary *Ab* 52; P-in-c Burravoe 52-56; R Strichen 56-60; V Haslingden St Jo Stonefold *Blackb* 60-72; V Blackb St Aid 72-85; rtd 85; Perm to Offic *Blackb* from 85. *24 Scott Avenue, Baxenden, Accrington, Lancs BB5 2XA* Tel (01254) 396474

HOLT, Jack Derek. b 38. Trin Coll Bris 71. **d** 73 **p** 74. C Daubhill *Man* 73-76; P-in-c Thornham w Gravel Hole 76-79; V 79-83; R Talke *Lich* 83-93; V Cotmanhay *Derby* from 93; Chapl Ilkeston Community Hosp from 93. *Cotmanhay Vicarage, Vicarage Street, Cotmanhay, Ilkeston, Derbyshire DE7 8QL* Tel 0115-932 5670

HOLT, Keith. b 37. S'wark Ord Course. **d** 82 **p** 83. NSM Selsdon St Jo w St Fran *Cant* 82-84; NSM Selsdon St Jo w St Fran *S'wark* from 85. *12 Ridge Langley, South Croydon, Surrey CR2 0AR* Tel 0181-651 1815 or 0171-215 8200

HOLT, Michael. b 38. Univ of Wales (Lamp) BA61 DipTh63. **d** 63 **p** 64. C Stand *Man* 63-69; V Bacup St Jo from 69. *St John's Vicarage, Bankside Lane, Bacup, Lancs OL13 8HG* Tel (01706) 873275

HOLT, Norman Botterill. b 16. Worc Ord Coll 60. **d** 60 **p** 61. C-in-c Dines Green St Mich CD *Worc* 60-62; R Earls Croome w Hill Croome and Strensham 62-83; rtd 83. *19 Nelson Road, Sheringham, Norfolk NR26 8BU* Tel (01263) 822624

HOLT, Paul William Charles. b 53. St Jo Coll Dur BA75. Oak Hill Th Coll 75 Ridley Hall Cam 76. **d** 77 **p** 78. C Bexleyheath Ch Ch *Roch* 77-80; C Frimley *Guildf* 80-84; P-in-c Badshot Lea CD 84-91; P-in-c Lt Marlow *Ox* 91-93; V Flackwell Heath 93-94; Perm to Offic *Birm* from 96. *119 Barnes Hill, Weoley Castle, Birmingham B29 5UN* Tel 0121-427 1730

HOLT, Stuart Henry. b 57. Bath Univ BEd78. Ridley Hall Cam 84. **d** 87 **p** 88. C Locks Heath *Portsm* 87-90; Chapl RAF 89-91; C Worthing St Geo *Chich* 91-93; C Portchester *Portsm* 93-95. *11 Old Garden Close, Locks Heath, Southampton SO31 6RN* Tel (01489) 885805

HOLT, Susan. **d** 97. NSM Longwood *Wakef* from 97. *229/231 Stainland Road, Holywell Green, Halifax, W Yorkshire HX4 9AJ*

HOLTAM, Nicholas Roderick. b 54. Collingwood Coll Dur BA75 K Coll Lon BD78 AKC78 Dur Univ MA89. Westcott Ho Cam 78. **d** 79 **p** 80. C Stepney St Dunstan and All SS *Lon* 79-83; Tutor Linc Th Coll 83-88; V Is of Dogs Ch Ch and St Jo w St Luke *Lon* 88-95; V St Martin-in-the-Fields from 95. *6 St Martin's Place, London WC2N 4JH* Tel 0171-930 1862

HOLTBY, The Very Revd Robert Tinsley. b 21. FSA St Edm Hall Ox BA43 MA46 BD57 K Coll Cam BA47 MA52. Cuddesdon Coll 43 Westcott Ho Cam 44. **d** 46 **p** 47. C Pocklington w Yapham-cum-Meltonby, Owsthorpe etc *York* 46-48; CF 48-52; Malaya 50-52; Chapl Malvern Coll 52-54; Lic to Offic *Worc* 52-54; Chapl St Edw Sch Ox 54-59; Lic to Offic *Ox* 55-59; Can Res Carl Cathl *Carl* 59-67; Dir RE 59-67; Sec C of E Schs Coun 67-74; Gen Sec Nat Soc 67-77; Lic to Offic *S'wark* 68-77; Gen Sec Gen Syn Bd of Educn 74-77; Dean Chich 77-89; rtd 89; Perm to Offic *Carl* from 89; Perm to Offic *York* from 90. *4 Hutton Hall, Huttons Ambo, York YO6 7HW* Tel (01653) 696366

HOLTH, Oystein Johan. b 31. Open Univ BA75. AKC54. **d** 54 **p** 55. C Greenford H Cross *Lon* 54-56; Br N Borneo and Sarawak 56-63; E Malaysia 63-67; Chapl OHP 67-75; Chapl St Hilda's Sch Whitby 67-75; P-in-c Pimlico St Barn *Lon* 75-97; Ind Chapl 75-97; rtd 97. *The Clergy House, St Barnabas Street, London SW1W 8PF* Tel 0171-730 5054

HOLYER, Vincent Alfred Douglas. b 28. Ex Univ BA54. Oak Hill Th Coll 54. **d** 56 **p** 57. C Bethnal Green St Jas Less *Lon* 56-58; C Braintree *Chelmsf* 58-61; V Islington All SS *Lon* 61-65; R St Ruan w St Grade *Truro* 65-85; V Constantine 85-91; rtd 91; Perm to Offic *Truro* from 91. *The Cornerstone, 7 Tregenning Park, St Keverne, Helston, Cornwall TR12 6QT* Tel (01326) 280691

HOLYHEAD, Rex Noel Humphrey. b 32. **d** 68 **p** 69. C Glouc St Mary de Lode and St Nic *Glouc* 68-70; C Christchurch *Win* 70-77; V Win St Jo cum Winnall 77-81; P-in-c Millbrook 81-82; R from 82. *The Rectory, 115 Regents Park Road, Southampton SO15 8NZ* Tel (01703) 773417

HOLZAPFEL, Peter Rudolph. b 51. St Jo Coll Nottm 84. **d** 86 **p** 87. C St Jo in Bedwardine *Worc* 86-89; V Worc St Mich from 89. *St Michael's Vicarage, Burleigh Road, Worcester WR2 5QT* Tel (01905) 421986

HOMER, Alan Fellows. b 30. Ridley Hall Cam 61. **d** 63 **p** 64. C Heref St Jas *Heref* 63-66; Dep Chapl HM Pris Brixton 66-70; V Brixton Hill St Sav *S'wark* 66-73; CF (TA) 70-73; CF 73-76; V Heeley *Sheff* 75-87; R Cheveley *Ely* 87-95; R Ashley w Silverley 87-95; V Wood Ditton w Saxon Street 87-95; V Kirtling 87-95; RD Linton 94-95; rtd 95; Perm to Offic *Bris* from 95; Perm to Offic *Glouc* from 95. *62 The Willows, Highworth, Swindon SN6 7PH* Tel (01793) 764023

HOMEWOOD, Michael John. b 33. Wells Th Coll 69. **d** 71 **p** 72. C Ilfracombe H Trin *Ex* 71-72; C Ilfracombe, Lee and W Down 72-75; P-in-c Woolacombe 76-78; TV Ilfracombe, Lee, W Down, Woolacombe and Bittadon 78-82; TR S Molton w Nymet St George, High Bray etc 82-97; RD S Molton 93-95; rtd 97. *5 Avon Drive, Northmoor Park, Wareham, Dorset BH20 4EL*

HOMEWOOD, Peter Laurence de Silvie. b 58. Or Coll Ox BA80 MA84. St Steph Ho Ox 90. **d** 92 **p** 93. C Ruislip St Martin *Lon* 92-96; R Hayes St Mary from 96. *The Rectory, 170 Church Road, Hayes, Middx UB3 2LR* Tel 0181-573 2470

HOMFRAY, John Bax Tayler. b 29. Keble Coll Ox BA52 MA. Ridley Hall Cam 52. **d** 54 **p** 55. C Kingswood *Bris* 54-57; C Leckhampton St Pet *Glouc* 57-64; V Staverton w Boddington 64-86; V Staverton w Boddington and Tredington etc 87-95; rtd 95; Perm to Offic *Glouc* from 95. *Bowness, 1 The Hyde, Winchcombe, Cheltenham, Glos GL54 5QR* Tel (01242) 680307

HONE, Canon Frank Leslie. b 11. Kelham Th Coll 32. **d** 38 **p** 39. C Sheff Arbourthorne *Sheff* 38-40; CF (EC) 40-45; C Sheff St Anne and St Phil *Sheff* 45-46; C Rotherham 46-49; V Brightside St Thos 49-53; R Attercliffe w Carbrook 53-60; P-in-c Sheff St Swithun 60-66; V Frodingham *Linc* 66-78; RD Manlake 69-76; Can and Preb Linc Cathl 72-78; rtd 78; Perm to Offic *Linc* from 78. *Morcote, 13 Roselea Avenue, Welton, Lincoln LN2 3RT* Tel (01673) 861548

HONES, Simon Anthony. b 54. Sussex Univ BSc75. Qu Coll Birm DipTh78. **d** 79 **p** 80. C Win Ch Ch *Win* 79-82; C Basing 82-88; Min Chineham CD 88-90; V Surbiton St Matt *S'wark* from 90. *St Matthew's Vicarage, 20 Kingsdowne Road, Surbiton, Surrey KT6 6JZ* Tel 0181-399 4853

HONEY, Canon Frederick Bernard. b 22. Selw Coll Cam BA48 MA72. Wells Th Coll 48. **d** 50 **p** 51. C S'wark St Geo *S'wark* 50-52; C Claines St Jo *Worc* 52-55; V Wollaston 55-87; RD Stourbridge 72-83; Hon Can Worc Cathl 75-87; rtd 87. *38 Park Farm, Bourton-on-the-Water, Cheltenham, Glos GL54 2YF* Tel (01451) 822218

HONEY, Thomas David (<u>Tom</u>). b 56. Lon Univ BA78. Ripon Coll Cuddesdon 80. **d** 83 **p** 84. C Mill End and Heronsgate w W Hyde *St Alb* 83-86; C Stepney St Dunstan and All SS *Lon* 86-89; TV High Wycombe *Ox* 89-95; P-in-c Headington Quarry from 95. *The Vicarage, Headington Quarry, Oxford OX3 8NU* Tel (01865) 62931

HONNER, Canon Robert Ralph. b 15. St Chad's Coll Dur BA37 DipTh38 MA40. **d** 38 **p** 39. C Gt Crosby St Faith *Liv* 38-41; P-in-c Wigan St Andr 41-44; C Rugby St Andr *Cov* 44-49; V Derby St Barn *Derby* 49-53; V Melbourne 54-72; RD Melbourne 54-67; Hon Can Derby Cathl 58-80; V Beeley and Edensor 72-80; RD Bakewell and Eyam 73-78; rtd 80; Perm to Offic *Derby* from 80. *5 Castle Mews, Blackwell Lane, Melbourne, Derby DE73 1LW* Tel (01332) 864356

HONNOR, Mrs Marjorie Rochefort. b 27. Birm Univ BA48. Cranmer Hall Dur 79. **dss** 81 **d** 87 **p** 94. Church Oakley and Wootton St Lawrence *Win* 81-87; Par Dn 87-89; rtd 89. *33C Surrey Road, Bournemouth BH4 9BJ* Tel (01202) 761021

HONOUR, Colin Reginald. b 44. Lanc Univ CertEd69 Man Univ ADEd75 Newc Univ MEd80. N Ord Course 88. **d** 91 **p** 92. NSM Walmsley *Man* 91; C Middleton 92-94; R Holcombe from 94. *The Rectory, 12 Carrwood Hey, Ramsbottom, Bury, Lancs BL0 9QT* Tel (01706) 822312

HONOUR, Derek. b 59. Bath Univ BSc84. St Jo Coll Nottm. **d** 89 **p** 90. C High Wycombe *Ox* 89-91; C Brightside w Wincobank *Sheff* 91-94; P-in-c Dawley St Jerome *Lon* from 94. *St Jerome's Lodge, 42 Corwell Lane, Uxbridge, Middx UB8 3DE* Tel 0181-573 1895

HONOUR, Ms Joanna Clare (<u>Jo</u>). b 61. Westmr Coll Ox BEd83. St Jo Coll Nottm LTh88 DPS89. **d** 89 **p** 94. Par Dn High Wycombe *Ox* 89-91; Par Dn Brightside w Wincobank *Sheff* 91-94; C 94; Perm to Offic *Lon* 94-96 and from 97; Dep Chapl HM Pris Wandsworth 96-97; NSM Dawley St Jerome *Lon* 96-97; Chapl HM Pris The Mount from 97; Lic to Offic *St Alb* from 97. *42 Corwell Lane, Uxbridge, Middx UB8 3DE* Tel 0181-573 1895

HOOD, Mrs Doreen. b 38. Open Univ BA90. NE Ord Course 90. **d** 93 **p** 94. NSM Cullercoats St Geo *Newc* from 93. *24 Keswick Drive, North Shields, Tyne & Wear NE30 3EW* Tel 0191-253 1762

HOOD, Leslie. b 23. NE Ord Course. **d** 85 **p** 85. NSM Seaham w Seaham Harbour *Dur* 85-90; NSM Dalton le Dale 90-93; NSM Hawthorn 90-93; rtd 93; Perm to Offic *Dur* from 93. *3 Queen Street, Seaham, Co Durham SR7 7SR* Tel 0191-581 2658

HOOD, Peter Michael. b 47. Sheff Univ BSc68 St Pet Coll Ox DipTh72. Wycliffe Hall Ox 70. **d** 73 **p** 74. C Soundwell *Bris* 73-76; P-in-c Walcot St Andr CD 76-77; TV Swindon St Jo and St Andr 77-80; V Esh *Dur* 80-88; V Hamsteels 80-88; V Stockton St Paul from 88. *65 Bishopton Road, Stockton-on-Tees, Cleveland TS18 4PE* Tel (01642) 617869

HOOD, Robert Ernest Nathaniel. b 12. TCD BA34 MA42. **d** 37 **p** 38. C Belfast St Aid *Conn* 37-39; Org Sec ICM 39-41; C Brixton Road Ch Ch *S'wark* 41-42; V Skellingthorpe *Linc* 42-46; V S Lambeth St Steph *S'wark* 46-57; V Holloway Em w Hornsey Road St Barn *Lon* 57-77; rtd 77; Perm to Offic *Cant* 79-93. *25 Bromley College, London Road, Bromley BR1 1PE* Tel 0181-464 2694

HOOD, Canon Thomas Henry Havelock. b 24. Chich Th Coll 51. **d** 54 **p** 55. C Stella *Dur* 54-57; Australia from 57; Hon Can Brisbane from 88; rtd 93. *18 Moonyean Street, Bellbird Park, Queensland, Australia 4300* Tel Brisbane (7) 3288 5106

HOOGERWERF, John Constant. b 50. MIH86 Bris Poly BA85. Oscott Coll (RC) 68. **d** 73 **p** 74. In RC Ch 73-84; Hon C Davyhulme Ch Ch *Man* 84-93; Perm to Offic *Heref* from 93. *14 Foster Road, Bridgnorth, Shropshire WV16 4LS* Tel (01746) 766328

HOOK, Ian Kevin. b 57. Trin Coll Bris DipHE95. **d** 95 **p** 96. C Dalton-in-Furness *Carl* from 95. *4 Fair View, Dalton-in-Furness, Cumbria LA15 8RZ* Tel (01229) 464402

HOOK, Neil. b 73. Univ of Wales (Swansea) BA94 Univ of Wales (Cardiff) BD96. St Mich Coll Llan 94. **d** 97. C Brecon St Mary and Battle w Llanddew *S & B* from 97; Min Can Brecon Cathl from 97. *The Clergy House, Cathedral Close, Brecon LD3 9DP* Tel (01874) 623776

HOOK, Ronald Arthur. b 10. Or Coll Ox BA33 MA46. Sarum Th Coll 33. **d** 34 **p** 35. C Cowley St Jas *Ox* 34-39 and 45-46; CF (R of O) 39-45; V Luton St Andr *St Alb* 46-54; R Lewes St Anne *Chich* 54-65; R Hurstpierpoint 65-75; R Albourne 71-75; rtd 75; Perm to Offic *Chich* from 76. *6 Cheviot Close, Tonbridge, Kent TN9 1NH* Tel (01732) 356941

HOOKER, Canon Roger Hardham. b 34. St Edm Hall Ox BA58 Ox Univ DipTh59. Wycliffe Hall Ox 58. **d** 60 **p** 61. C Stockton *Dur* 60-63; India 65-78; Tutor Crowther Hall CMS Tr Coll Selly Oak 79-82; Dioc Missr *Birm* from 82; Miss Partner CMS from 82; Hon Can Birm Cathl *Birm* from 89. *30 Little Moor Hill, Smethwick, W Midlands B67 7BG* Tel 0121-558 3386

HOOLE, Charles. b 33. St Aid Birkenhead 61. **d** 63 **p** 64. C Skerton St Luke *Blackb* 63-65; P-in-c Preston St Jas 65-69; V Lostock Hall 69-73; Chapl HM Pris Eastchurch 74-75; V St Annes St Marg *Blackb* 75-81; V S Shore St Pet 81-92; C Laneside 92-94; rtd 95; Perm to Offic *Blackb* from 95. *32 Hanover Crescent, Blackpool FY2 9DL* Tel (01253) 853564

HOOLEY, John Philip. b 45. Hartley Victoria Coll 69 St Deiniol's Hawarden 78. **d** 79 **p** 79. In Meth Ch 73-78; C Heref St Martin *Heref* 79-81; CF from 81. *MOD Chaplains (Army), Trenchard Lines, Upavon, Pewsey, Wilts SN9 6BE* Tel (01980) 615804 Fax 615800

HOOPER, Miss Catherine Margaret. b 58. Leic Univ BSc81 St Jo Coll Dur BA84. **dss** 85 **d** 87 **p** 94. Houghton le Spring *Dur* 85-87; Par Dn 87-88; C Millfield St Mark 88-94; D-in-c Heworth St Alb

94; P-in-c from 94. *The Vicarage, Coldwell Park Drive, Felling, Gateshead, Tyne & Wear NE10 9BX* Tel 0191-438 1720

HOOPER, Canon Charles. b 24. Witwatersrand Univ BA46. Coll of Resurr Mirfield 49. **d** 51 **p** 52. S Africa 51-68; Swaziland 68-86; Can Swaziland 71-86; CR from 89. *House of the Resurrection, Mirfield, W Yorkshire WF14 0BN* Tel (01924) 494318

HOOPER, Preb Derek Royston. b 33. St Edm Hall Ox BA57 MA65. Cuddesdon Coll 57. **d** 59 **p** 60. C Gt Walsingham *Nor* 59-62; C Townstall w Dartmouth *Ex* 62-65; V Lynton and Brendon 65-69; C Littleham w Exmouth 70-72; TV 72-79; R Wrington w Butcombe *B & W* 79-94; Preb Wells Cathl 93-94; rtd 94; Perm to Offic *Ex* from 95; Perm to Offic *B & W* from 95. *Beckington, 7 Cyprus Road, Exmouth, Devon EX8 2DZ* Tel (01395) 272831

HOOPER, Geoffrey Michael. b 39. K Coll Lon 61. **d** 66 **p** 67. C Chesterfield St Mary and All SS *Derby* 66-69; Chapl RAF 69-74; P-in-c Hook Norton w Swerford and Wigginton *Ox* 74-80; P-in-c Gt Rollright 75-80; R Hook Norton w Gt Rollright, Swerford etc 80-82; Warden Mansf Ho Univ Settlement Plaistow from 82; Dir from 86. *Mansfield House, 30 Avenons Road, London E13 8HT* Tel 0171-476 2375 or 476 1505

HOOPER, Ian. b 44. St Jo Coll York CertEd67. Trin Coll Bris DipHE88. **d** 88 **p** 89. C Martlesham w Brightwell *St E* 88-92; V Pakenham w Norton and Tostock from 92. *The Vicarage, Church Hill, Pakenham, Bury St Edmunds, Suffolk IP31 2LN* Tel (01359) 30287

HOOPER, The Ven Michael Wrenford. b 41. Univ of Wales (Lamp) BA63. St Steph Ho Ox 63. **d** 65 **p** 66. C Bridgnorth St Mary *Heref* 65-70; P-in-c Habberley 70-78; R 78-81; V Minsterley 70-81; RD Pontesbury 75-80; Preb Heref Cathl from 81; V Leominster 81-85; TR Leominster from 85; P-in-c Eyton 81-85; RD Leominster 81-97; P-in-c Eye, Croft w Yarpole and Lucton 91-97; Adn Heref from 97. *The Archdeacon's House, The Close, Hereford HR1 2NG* Tel (01432) 272873

HOOPER, Paul Denis Gregory. b 52. Man Univ BA75 Ox Univ BA80 MA87. Wycliffe Hall Ox 78. **d** 81 **p** 82. C Leeds St Geo *Ripon* 81-84; Dioc Youth Officer 84-87; Bp's Dom Chapl 87-95; Dioc Communications Officer from 87; V Harrogate St Mark from 95. *The Vicarage, 13 Wheatlands Road, Harrogate, N Yorkshire HG2 8BB* Tel (01423) 504959

HOOPER, Peter Guy. b 30. K Coll Lon 51. **d** 55 **p** 56. C Huddersfield St Pet *Wakef* 55-60; C Brompton H Trin *Lon* 60-67; R Hazelbury Bryan w Stoke Wake etc *Sarum* 72-84; R Yetminster w Ryme Intrinseca and High Stoy 84-93; RD Sherborne 87-91; rtd 93; Perm to Offic *B & W* from 93. *Rose Villa, Long Street, Sherborne, Dorset DT9 3DD* Tel (01935) 816819

HOOPER, Sydney Paul. b 46. Lanc Univ BA68 CertEd69 QUB. **d** 85 **p** 87. NSM Killaney w Carryduff *D & D* 85-91; Lic to Offic from 91. *26 Manse Park, Baronscourt, Carryduff, Belfast BT8 8RX* Tel (01232) 815607

HOOPER, William Gilbert. b 38. Ex Univ BA60. St Mich Coll Llan DipTh82. **d** 82 **p** 83. C Hubberston w Herbrandston and Hasguard etc *St D* 82-85; R Llangwm and Freystrop 85-97; R Llangwm w Freystrop and Johnston from 97. *The Rectory, Four Winds, Llangwm, Haverfordwest SA62 4NG* Tel (01437) 891317

HOOTON, Arthur Russell. b 23. Moore Th Coll Sydney ACT ThL51. **d** 52 **p** 52. Australia 52-61 and 63-65; C Styvechale *Cov* 62-63; V Stockingford 65-89; rtd 89; Perm to Offic *Leic* from 89. *18 Chetwynd Drive, Nuneaton, Warks CV11 4TF* Tel (01203) 343281

HOOTON, David James. b 50. St Kath Coll Liv CertEd73 DipRE81. N Ord Course 83. **d** 86 **p** 87. NSM Pemberton St Mark Newtown *Liv* 86-89; C Ashton-in-Makerfield St Thos 89-92; V Bryn from 92. *The Vicarage, 12 Bryn Road, Ashton-in-Makerfield, Wigan, Lancs WN4 0AA* Tel (01942) 727114

HOPCRAFT, Jonathan Richard. b 34. Or Coll Ox BA55 DipEd66 MA66. Westcott Ho Cam 57. **d** 59 **p** 60. C Cannock *Lich* 59-63; N Rhodesia 63-64; S Rhodesia 64-65; Hon C Olton *Birm* 66-68; Antigua 68-72; C Gt Grimsby St Mary and St Jas *Linc* 72; TV 72-76; P-in-c E Stockwith 76-84; V Blyton w Pilham 76-84; P-in-c Laughton w Wildsworth 76-84; TV Bilston *Lich* 84-90; P-in-c Wolverhampton St Jo from 90; C Wolverhampton from 97. *St John's Vicarage, St John's Square, Wolverhampton WV2 4AT* Tel (01902) 713041

HOPE, Charles Henry. b 64. FRGS89 Regent's Park Coll Ox BA87 MA90. St Jo Coll Dur BA90. **d** 90 **p** 91. C Tynemouth St Jo *Newc* 90-94; V from 94. *St John's Vicarage, Percy Main, North Shields, Tyne & Wear NE29 6HS* Tel 0191-257 1819

HOPE, Colin Frederick. b 49. St Mich Coll Llan 73. **d** 76 **p** 77. C Warrington St Elphin *Liv* 76-80; V Newton-le-Willows 80-84; CSWG from 84; Lic to Offic *Chich* from 88. *The Monastery, Crawley Down, Crawley, W Sussex RH10 4LH* Tel (01342) 712074

HOPE, Cyril Sackett. b 24. St Edm Hall Ox BA49 MA54. Ely Th Coll 50. **d** 51 **p** 52. C Wigston Magna *Leic* 51-55; C Hawley H Trin *Guildf* 55-58; R Clayhidon *Ex* 58-63; R Dunchideock and Shillingford 63-77; Asst Dir of Educn 73-90; P-in-c Stockland w Dalwood 77-79; V 79-90; rtd 90; Perm to Offic *Ex* from 90. *Verbena, Hind Street, Ottery St Mary, Devon EX11 1BW* Tel (01404) 815028

✠**HOPE, The Most Revd and Rt Hon David Michael.** b 40. KCVO95 PC91. Nottm Univ BA62 Linacre Ho Ox DPhil65. St Steph Ho Ox 62. **d** 65 **p** 66 **c** 85. C W Derby (or Tuebrook) St Jo *Liv* 65-67 and 68-70; Chapl Bucharest *Eur* 67-68; V Orford St Andr *Liv* 70-74; Prin St Steph Ho Ox 74-82; V St Marylebone All SS *Lon* 82-85; Master of Guardians Shrine Our Lady Walsingham 82-93; Bp Wakef 85-91; Bp Lon 91-95; Dean of HM Chpls Royal and Prelate of OBE 91-95; Abp York from 95. *The Palace, Bishopthorpe, York YO2 1QE* Tel (01904) 707021 or 707022 Fax 709204

HOPE, Miss Edith. b 43. SRN64 SCM66 HVCert72 Lanc Univ MA86. Wycliffe Hall Ox 89. **d** 91 **p** 94. Par Dn Droylsden St Mary *Man* 91-94; Par Dn Ecclesall *Sheff* 94; C from 94. *11 Mylor Road, Sheffield S11 7PF* Tel 0114-266 2313

HOPE, Robert. b 36. Dur Univ BSc61. Clifton Th Coll 61. **d** 63 **p** 64. C Woking St Mary *Guildf* 63-66; C Surbiton Hill Ch Ch *S'wark* 66-68; Th Students' Sec IVF 68-71; Hon C Wallington H Trin *S'wark* 69-71; C Ox St Ebbe w St Pet *Ox* 71-74; V Walshaw Ch Ch *Man* 74-87; TR Radipole and Melcombe Regis *Sarum* 87-93; rtd 93; Perm to Offic *St D* from 93. *1A Swiss Valley, Felinfael, Llanelli SA14 8BS* Tel (01554) 759199

HOPE, Miss Susan. b 49. St Jo Coll Dur BA83. Cranmer Hall Dur 80. **dss** 83 **d** 87 **p** 94. Boston Spa *York* 83-86; Brightside w Wincobank *Sheff* 86-87; Par Dn 87-89; D-in-c 89-94; V 94-97; V Chapeltown from 97. *St John's Vicarage, 23 Housley Park, Chapeltown, Sheffield S30 4UE* Tel 0114-257 0966

HOPEWELL, Jeffery Stewart. b 52. ACA79 Leic Univ BA75. EMMTC 82. **d** 85 **p** 86. NSM Houghton on the Hill w Keyham *Leic* 85-88; NSM Houghton-on-the-Hill, Keyham and Hungarton 88-91; C Syston 91-93; TV Syston TM from 93; Bp's Ecum Adv from 91. *The Vicarage, Brookside, Barkby, Leicester LE7 3QD* Tel 0116-269 5539

HOPKIN, Gerallt. b 12. Univ of Wales BA36. Sarum Th Coll 37. **d** 38 **p** 39. C Aberdare St Fagan *Llan* 38-40; C Caerau St Cynfelin 40-44; C Gelligaer 44-50; V Penrhiwceiber 50-55; V Penrhiwceiber and Tyntetown w Ynysboeth 55-68; R St Fagans w Michaelston-super-Ely 68-77; rtd 77; Perm to Offic *Llan* from 79. *25B Tangmere Drive, Fairwood Chase, Cardiff CF5 2PP* Tel (01222) 553985

HOPKIN, Neil Richard. b 67. ONC86 Trent Poly HNC88. St Jo Coll Nottm BTh95. **d** 95. C Easton H Trin w St Gabr and St Lawr and St Jude *Bris* 95. *13 Kingsley Crescent, Long Eaton, Nottingham NG10 3DA* Tel 0115-973 5090

HOPKINS, Mrs Angela Joan. b 42. Bp Otter Coll Chich CertEd64. S Dios Minl Tr Scheme 92. **d** 95 **p** 96. NSM Kingsbury H Innocents *Lon* from 95. *3 Regal Way, Harrow, Middx HA3 0RZ* Tel 0181-907 1045

HOPKINS, Miss Barbara Agnes. b 28. Lon Univ BSc60 Imp Coll Lon DIC66 MPhil67 DipRS80. St Alb Minl Tr Scheme 82. **dss** 85 **d** 87. Bedford All SS *St Alb* 85-86; Chapl Asst Bedf Gen Hosp 86-88; Bedford St Mich *St Alb* 86-88; Hon Par Dn 87-88; Chapl Asst St Jo Hosp Linc 89-91; Perm to Offic *Linc* 92-95. *14 Woburn Avenue, Lincoln LN1 3HJ* Tel (01522) 513359

HOPKINS, Brenda Alison. b 63. St Martin's Coll Lanc BA95 Anglia Poly Univ MA97. Westcott Ho Cam 95. **d** 97. C Camberwell St Geo *S'wark* from 97. *131 Coleman Road, London SE5 7TF* Tel 0171-703 2704

HOPKINS, Christopher Freeman. b 41. Dur Univ BA63. Wells Th Coll 63. **d** 65 **p** 66. C Spring Park *Cant* 65-69; S Africa 69-78; Botswana 78-81; R Beckley and Peasmarsh *Chich* from 81. *The Rectory, School Lane, Peasmarsh, Rye, E Sussex TN31 6UW* Tel (01797) 230255

HOPKINS, Ernest. b 16. Tyndale Hall Bris 68. **d** 69 **p** 70. C Walton Breck *Liv* 69-70; P-in-c Everton St Chrys 70-74; P-in-c Everton St Jo 70-74; P-in-c Everton Em 70-74; V Everton St Chrys 74-79; RD Walton 76-79; V Eccleston St Luke 79-83; rtd 83; Perm to Offic *St As* from 84; Perm to Offic *Ches* from 88. *12 Shetland Drive, Bromborough, Wirral, Merseyside L62 7JZ* Tel 0151-334 4044

HOPKINS, Henry Charles (Harry). b 46. RD87. Edin Th Coll 65. **d** 71 **p** 72. C Dundee St Salvador *Bre* 71-74; C Dundee St Martin 71-74; Chapl RNVR from 72; R Monifieth *Bre* 74-78; Chapl Miss to Seamen Kenya 78-85; Singapore 85-92; Offg Chapl NZ Defence Force 89-92; Chapl Miss to Seamen Teesside 92-94; V Middlesbrough St Thos *York* 94-97; V N Thornaby from 97. *St Paul's Vicarage, 60 Lanehouse Road, Thornaby, Stockton-on-Tees, Cleveland TS17 8EA* Tel (01642) 868086 Fax 868087

HOPKINS, Hilda (Sister Hilary). **dss** 33 **d** 87. CSA from 49. *St Andrew's House, 2 Tavistock Road, London W11 1BA* Tel 0171-229 2662

HOPKINS, Hugh. b 33. TCD BA. **d** 62 **p** 63. C Ballymena *Conn* 62-64; C Belfast Ch Ch 64-67; I Ballintoy 67-72; I Belfast St Ninian 72-81; I Mossley 81-86; I Ballywillan 86-96; Miss to Seamen from 86; Can Belf Cathl 94-96; rtd 96. *2 Bush Gardens, Ballyness, Bushmills, Co Antrim BT57 8AE* Tel (01265) 732981

HOPKINS, Canon Hugh Graham Beynon. b 18. Jes Coll Ox BA40 MA45. St Mich Coll Llan 40. **d** 42 **p** 43. C Cardigan *St D* 42-45; C Canton St Jo *Llan* 45-52; R Dowlais 52-59; V Aberavon 59-86; Can Llan Cathl 81-86; RD Margam 81-85; rtd 86; Perm to Offic *Llan* from 86. *25B Mary Street, Porthcawl CF36 3YL* Tel (01656) 771651

HOPKINS, John Alun. b 33. Univ of Wales (Lamp) BA55. St Steph Ho Ox 55. **d** 57 **p** 58. C Aberystwyth St Mich *St D* 57-59; C Llanelli St Paul 59-62; V 76-94; R Eglwys Gymyn and Marros 62-76; rtd 94. *5 Langland Mews, Langland Road, Llanelli SA15 1BR* Tel (01554) 773865

HOPKINS, John Dawson. b 39. Chich Th Coll 85. **d** 87 **p** 88. C Walker *Newc* 87-89; C Newc St Fran 89-92; V Horton from 92. *St Benedict's Vicarage, Brierley Road, Cowpen, Blyth, Northd NE24 5AU* Tel (01670) 367035

HOPKINS, John Edgar Alexander. b 19. TD65. Jes Coll Cam BA46 MA48. Wells Th Coll 46. **d** 48 **p** 49. C Forest Gate Em *Chelmsf* 48-50; P-in-c Nursling and Rownhams *Win* 50-55; Min Maybush St Pet CD Win 50-59; V Southampton Maybush St Pet 59-65; V Holdenhurst 65-71; C-in-c Holdenhurst St Barn CD 65-71; Chapl Stonar Sch Melksham 71-80; P-in-c Clyffe Pypard and Tockenham *Sarum* 80-81; P-in-c Broad Town 80-81; R Broad Town, Clyffe Pypard and Tockenham 81-85; rtd 85. *17 Coxstalls, Wootton Bassett, Swindon SN4 7AW* Tel (01793) 854091

HOPKINS, Canon John Howard Edgar Beynon. b 14. Univ Coll Ox BA36 MA39. St Mich Coll Llan 36. **d** 37 **p** 38. C Pontyberem *St D* 37-39; C Llanedy 39-41; CF (EC) 41-46; C Pontardawe All SS *S & B* 46-49; R Glas All SS *Glas* 49-62; R Kilmacolm 62-75; R Bridge of Weir 62-75; R Glas St Marg 75-84; Can St Mary's Cathl 79-84; rtd 84; Hon Can St Mary's Cathl *Glas* from 84. *156 Drymen Road, Bearsden, Glasgow G61 3RE* Tel 0141-942 6013

HOPKINS, Dr Kenneth Victor John. b 45. Univ Coll Lon BA66 Lon Univ BD69 Hull Univ PhD84. Tyndale Hall Bris 66. **d** 69 **p** 70. C S Mimms Ch Ch *Lon* 69-72; C Parkstone St Luke *Sarum* 72-76; P-in-c Trowbridge St Thos 76; V 76-81; R Wingfield w Rowley 76-81; Chapl and Lect NE Surrey Coll of Tech Ewell 81-84; Hd Student Services Essex Inst of HE 84-88; Kingston Poly 88-92; Kingston Univ from 92. *Kingston University, Penrhyn Road, Kingston-upon-Thames, Surrey KT1 2EE* Tel 0181-549 1366

HOPKINS, Lionel. b 48. Open Univ BA82. St D Coll Lamp DipTh70. **d** 71 **p** 72. C Llandeilo Tal-y-bont *S & B* 71-74; C Morriston 74-78; P-in-c Waunarllwydd 78-80; V 80-86; Youth Chapl 84-86; V Llangyfelach 86-96; P-in-c Swansea Ch Ch from 96; Chapl HM Pris Swansea from 96. *Christ Church Vicarage, 226 Oystermouth Road, Swansea SA1 3UH* Tel (01792) 52606

HOPKINS, Miss Patricia Mary. b 46. Kingston Poly BEd78. Trin Coll Bris 83. **dss** 85 **d** 87 **p** 94. Gorleston St Andr *Nor* 85-87; C 87-88; C Woking St Jo *Guildf* 88-90; TD Barnham Broom *Nor* 90-94; TV 94-97; V Otford *Roch* from 97. *The Vicarage, The Green, Otford, Sevenoaks, Kent TN14 5PD* Tel (01959) 523185

HOPKINS, Peter. b 54. Nottm Univ BSc75 Imp Coll Lon MSc79. Oak Hill Th Coll BA86. **d** 86 **p** 87. C Gee Cross *Ches* 86-90; R Gt Gonerby *Linc* 90-95; R Barrowby and Gt Gonerby from 95. *The Rectory, 7 Long Street, Great Gonerby, Grantham, Lincs NG31 8LN* Tel (01476) 565737

HOPKINS, Robert James Gardner. b 42. St Alb Minl Tr Scheme. **d** 79 **p** 80. NSM Chorleywood Ch Ch *St Alb* 79-83; NSM Parr Mt *Liv* from 83. *38 Lascelles Street, St Helens, Merseyside WA9 1BA* Tel (01744) 758886 Fax 23433

HOPKINSON, Preb Alfred Stephan. b 08. Wadh Coll Ox BA30 MA35. Linc Th Coll 34. **d** 35 **p** 36. C Putney St Mary *S'wark* 35-39; V Barrow St Jo *Carl* 39-43; V Battersea St Mary *S'wark* 43-52; RD Battersea 48-52; P-in-c St Mary Woolnoth *Lon* 52-54; V 54-59; P-in-c Tollington Park St Anne 55-56; Gen Dir ICF 58-63; V St Kath Cree 59-63; Preb St Paul's Cathl 60-63; Angl Adv ATV 60-68; Ind Adv to Bp Chelmsf 63-73; R Bobbingworth *Chelmsf* 63-73; rtd 73; Asst Chapl Win Coll 73-90; Hon C Cambridge Gt St Mary w St Mich *Ely* 90-93; Perm to Offic *Chich* from 93. *c/o S Thistleton-Smith Esq, Down Place, South Harting, Petersfield, Hants GU31 5PN* Tel (01730) 825374

HOPKINSON, The Ven Barnabas John (Barney). b 39. Trin Coll Cam BA63 MA67. Linc Th Coll 63. **d** 65 **p** 66. C Langley All SS and Martyrs *Man* 65-67; C Cambridge Gt St Mary w St Mich *Ely* 67-71; Asst Chapl Charterhouse Godalming 71-75; P-in-c Preshute *Sarum* 75-76; TV Marlborough 76-81; RD Marlborough 77-81; TR Wimborne Minster and Holt 81-86; Can and Preb Sarum Cathl from 83; RD Wimborne 85-86; Adn Sarum from 86; P-in-c Stratford sub Castle from 87. *Russell House, Stratford sub Castle, Salisbury SP1 3LG* Tel (01722) 328756

HOPKINSON, Benjamin Alaric (Ben). b 36. Trin Coll Ox BA59. Chich Th Coll 59. **d** 61 **p** 62. C Pallion *Dur* 61-66; Rhodesia 66-67; Botswana 67-74; Hon C Sherwood *S'well* 74-77; Hon C Carrington 74-77; V Lowdham 77-85; R Whitby *York* 85-95; Miss to Seamen from 85; V Stainton w Hilton *York* from 95; Chapl Cleveland Constabulary from 95. *The Vicarage, 21 Thornton Road, Stainton, Middlesbrough, Cleveland TS8 9BS* Tel (01642) 590423

HOPKINSON, Colin Edward. b 57. BA LLB. Ridley Hall Cam. **d** 84 **p** 85. C Chadwell *Chelmsf* 84-87; C Canvey Is 87-90; P-in-c E Springfield from 90; RD Chelmsf N from 95. *The Vicarage, Ashton Place, Chelmsford CM2 6ST* Tel (01245) 469316

HOPKINSON, David John. b 47. Ox NSM Course. **d** 79 **p** 80. NSM Wardington *Ox* 79-80; Hon C Didcot St Pet 80-83; C Headingley *Ripon* 83-87; P-in-c Leeds All So 87-91; R Middleton Tyas w Croft and Eryholme 91-95; V Leeds Belle Is St Jo and St Barn from 95. *The Vicarage, Low Grange View, Leeds LS10 3DT* Tel 0113-271 7821

HOPKINSON, William Humphrey. b 48. ARIC73 Lon Univ BSc69 Dur Univ MA78 Nottm Univ MPhil84 Man Poly MSc90. St Jo Coll Dur DipTh76. **d** 77 **p** 78. C Normanton *Derby* 77-80; C Sawley 80-82; V Birtles *Ches* 82-87; Dir Past Studies N Ord Course 82-94; Dir of Course Development 90-94; Continuing Minl Educn Officer *Ches* 87-94; P-in-c Tenterden St Mich *Cant* 94-96; Dir of Min and Tr from 96. *Berkley, Greenside, High Halden, Ashford, Kent TN26 3LT* Tel (01233) 850952

HOPLEY, David. b 37. Wells Th Coll 62. **d** 65 **p** 66. C Frome St Mary *B & W* 65-68; R Staunton-on-Arrow w Byton and Kinsham *Heref* 68-81; P-in-c Lingen 68-81; P-in-c Aymestrey and Leinthall Earles w Wigmore etc 72-81; R Dungeon Hill *Sarum* from 81. *The Rectory, Buckland Newton, Dorchester, Dorset DT2 7BY* Tel (01300) 345456

HOPLEY, Gilbert. b 40. Univ of Wales (Ban) BA62. St D Coll Lamp LTh65. **d** 65 **p** 66. C St As and Tremeirchion *St As* 65-73; Warden Ch Hostel Ban 73-76; Chapl Univ of Wales (Ban) *Ban* 73-76; V Meifod and Llangynyw *St As* 76-79; Chapl St Marg Sch Bushey 79-87; Hd Master St Paul's Cathl Choir Sch from 87. *Flat 2, 173 Queenstown Road, London SW8 3RJ*

HOPLEY, William James Christopher (Bill). b 50. AKC74. St Aug Coll Cant 74. **d** 75 **p** 76. C Kidderminster St Jo *Worc* 75-78; Ind Chapl 78-85; Co-ord Ind Chapl 85-94; TV Worc St Martin w St Pet, St Mark etc 85-86; TV Worc SE 86-94; Sen Chapl W Midl Police *Birm* from 94. *5 Masshouse Lane, Birmingham B38 9AS* Tel 0426-958158 (pager)

HOPPER, Bernard. b 20. Leeds Univ BA42. Coll of Resurr Mirfield. **d** 44 **p** 45. C Fulham St Pet *Lon* 44-46; C Cowley St Jo *Ox* 46-48; C Clewer St Steph 48-50; Chapl Sandleford Priory and St Gabr Sch Newbury 50-55; V Sparkbrook St Agatha *Birm* 55-67; V Brighton St Mich *Chich* 67-85; rtd 85; Perm to Offic *Chich* from 85. *64 Warren Drive, Lewes, E Sussex BN7 1HD* Tel (01273) 475303

HOPPER, Peter John. b 37. Univ Coll Dur BSc59 Lon Univ PGCE60. N Ord Course 89. **d** 91 **p** 91. C Aston cum Aughton and Ulley *Sheff* 91-93; C Aston cum Aughton w Swallownest, Todwick etc 93-94; P-in-c Braithwell w Bramley 94-95; TV Bramley and Ravenfield w Hooton Roberts etc from 95. *The Rectory, Micklebring Lane, Braithwell, Rotherham, S Yorkshire S66 7AS* Tel (01709) 812665

HOPPER, Robert Keith. b 45. St Jo Coll Dur 74. **d** 77 **p** 78. C Oxclose *Dur* 77-80; C Hebburn St Jo 80-82; V Lobley Hill from 82. *The Vicarage, Rowanwood Gardens, Gateshead, Tyne & Wear NE11 0DB* Tel 0191-460 4409

HOPPERTON, Thomas. b 33. Chich Th Coll 71. **d** 73 **p** 74. C Cheam *S'wark* 73-89; P-in-c St Alb Ch 76-89; P-in-c Rotherhithe St Kath w St Barn 89-92; P-in-c S Bermondsey St Bart 91-92; V Bermondsey St Kath w St Bart from 92. *St Katharine's Vicarage, 92 Eugenia Road, London SE16 2RA* Tel 0171-237 3679

HOPWOOD, Adrian Patrick. b 37. CBiol MIBiol MIWEM N Lon Poly BSc61. Ox Min Course 87. **d** 90 **p** 91. NSM Chesham Bois *Ox* 90-93; NSM Amersham 93-95; NSM Ridgeway from 95. *The Glebe House, Childrey, Wantage, Oxon OX12 9UP* Tel (01235) 751518

HOPWOOD OWEN, Mrs Karen. b 58. Padgate Coll of Educn CertEd79 St Martin's Coll Lanc DASE90. LNSM course 92. **d** 95 **p** 96. NSM Peel *Man* from 95. *168 Manchester Road, Tyldesley, Manchester M29 8WY* Tel (01942) 894850

HORBURY, Dr William. b 42. Or Coll Ox BA64 MA67 Clare Coll Cam BA66 PhD71. Westcott Ho Cam 64. **d** 69 **p** 70. Fell Clare Coll Cam 68-72; CCC Cam from 78; Lic to Offic *Ely* 69-72 and 78-90; R Gt w Lt Gransden 72-78; Lect Div Cam Univ from 84; NSM Cambridge St Botolph *Ely* from 90. *5 Grange Road, Cambridge CB3 9AS* Tel (01223) 63529

HORDER, Mrs Catharine Joy. b 51. Battersea Coll of Educn CertEd72. S Dios Minl Tr Scheme 92. **d** 95 **p** 96. C Burrington and Churchill *B & W* from 95. *31 Garstons, Wrington, Bristol BS18 7QW* Tel (01934) 863493

HORDER, Peter Alan Trahair. b 43. LNSM course 95. **d** 97. NSM Madron *Truro* from 97. *Kurion, 38 Boscathoe Way, Heamoor, Cornwall TR18 3JS* Tel (01736) 60813

HORDERN, Peter John Calveley. b 35. Jes Coll Cam BA59 MA64. Linc Th Coll. **d** 61 **p** 62. C Billingham St Aid *Dur* 61-65; Canada from 65. *346 Aberdeen Avenue, Brandon, Manitoba, Canada, R7A 1N4*

HORE, Michael John. b 50. Man Univ BSc71. Linc Th Coll 75. **d** 78 **p** 79. C Maidstone St Martin *Cant* 78-81; C St Peter-in-Thanet 81-83; R Storrington *Chich* 83-93; RD Storrington 90-93; V Goring-by-Sea from 93. *The Vicarage, 12 Compton Avenue, Goring-by-Sea, Worthing, W Sussex BN12 4UJ* Tel (01903) 242525

HORLESTON, Kenneth William. b 50. BA86. Oak Hill Th Coll 84. **d** 86 **p** 87. C Wednesfield Heath *Lich* 86-89; V Blagreaves *Derby* from 89. *St Andrew's Vicarage, 5 Greenburn Close, Littleover, Derby DE23 7FF* Tel (01332) 773877

HORLOCK, The Very Revd Brian William. b 31. OBE78. Univ of Wales (Lamp) BA55. Chich Th Coll 55. **d** 57 **p** 58. C Chiswick St Nic w St Mary *Lon* 57-61; C Witney *Ox* 61-62; V N Acton St Gabr *Lon* 62-68; Chapl Oslo w Bergen, Trondheim and Stavanger *Eur* 68-89; RD Scandinavia 75-79; Adn 80-89; Hon Can Brussels Cathl 80-89; Dean Gib from 89; Chapl Gib from 89. *The Deanery, Bomb House Lane, Gibraltar* Tel Gibraltar (350) 78377

HORN, Colin Clive. b 39. CEng MIMechE. Cant Sch of Min. **d** 83 **p** 84. NSM Yalding w Collier Street *Roch* 83-91; V Kemsing w Woodlands from 91; RD Shoreham from 94. *The Vicarage, High Street, Kemsing, Sevenoaks, Kent TN15 6PY* Tel (01732) 761351

HORN, David Randolph. b 47. Nottm Univ BA69 CQSW71. Qu Coll Birm. **d** 82 **p** 83. C Hamstead St Paul *Birm* 82-84; V Aston St Jas 84-94; Sec Inner Cities Relig Coun from 94; Perm to Offic *Chelmsf* from 94. *49 Cranmer Road, London E7 0JL, or Room P2/125, Department of the Environment, 2 Marsham Street, London SW1P 3EB* Tel 0181-257 1162 or 0171-276 4430 Fax 0171-276 0767

HORN, Michael Leonard. b 32. Oak Hill Th Coll 56. **d** 59 **p** 60. C Ealing All SS *Lon* 59-62; India 62-75; New Zealand 77-86; rtd 94. *903 Dominion Road, Mount Roskill, Auckland 4, New Zealand*

HORNBY, John Hulme. b 24. AKC47. Qu Coll Birm 48. **d** 49 **p** 50. C N Harrow St Alb *Lon* 49-51; C Hackney St Jo 51-53; V Old Ford St Paul 53-57; USA 57-58; R Croydon w Clopton *Ely* 59-66; V Tadlow w E Hatley 59-66; R Hatley 59-66; R Stretham w Thetford 66-74; P-in-c Bratton Fleming *Ex* 74-89; P-in-c Stoke Rivers 74-89; P-in-c Challacombe 75-89; RD Shirwell 77-80; rtd 89; Perm to Offic *Ex* from 89. *6 Barbican Terrace, Barnstaple, Devon EX32 9HQ* Tel (01271) 75463

HORNE, Anthony Cedric. b 26. MIMechE61 MIEE67. **d** 77 **p** 78. NSM Kingsdown *Bris* 77-83; C Soundwell 83-85; P-in-c Bris St Andr w St Bart 85-92; rtd 92; Perm to Offic *Bris* from 92. *88 Church Road, Soundwell, Bristol BS16 4RG* Tel 0117-970 1007

HORNE, Dr Brian Edward. b 37. CEng68 MRAeS68 MIEE68 EurIng92 Lon Univ BSc62 PhD78. W of England Minl Tr Course 92. **d** 95 **p** 96. NSM Cheltenham St Mark *Glouc* from 95. *87A Rowanfield Road, Cheltenham, Glos GL51 8AF* Tel (01242) 236786

HORNE, Brian Lawrence. b 39. FRSA Natal Univ BA60 Dur Univ DipTh62 MLitt68 Lon Univ PhD71. Gen Th Sem (NY) MDiv63 St Chad's Coll Dur 60. **d** 62 **p** 63. Tutor St Chad's Coll Dur 63-66; Lect K Coll Lon from 66. *King's College, Strand, London WC2R 2LS* Tel 0171-274 6222

HORNE, Jack Kenneth. b 20. Linc Th Coll 68. **d** 70 **p** 71. C Danbury *Chelmsf* 70-75; V Frampton *Linc* 75-85; rtd 85; Perm to Offic *Linc* from 85. *154 Kenilworth Road, Grantham, Lincs NG31 9UH* Tel (01476) 578867

HORNE, Simon Timothy. b 62. Ball Coll Ox BA86 MA90 Southn Univ RNMH89. Qu Coll Birm BD94. **d** 95 **p** 96. C Basingstoke *Win* from 95. *1 The Glebe, Church Square, Basingstoke, Hants RG21 7QW* Tel (01256) 466694

HORNER, Eric. b 43. EMMTC 87. **d** 90 **p** 91. C Boultham *Linc* 90-93; P-in-c Kirton in Holland 93-95; P-in-c Frampton 93-95; P-in-c Frampton w Kirton in Holland from 95. *The Vicarage, Willington Road, Kirton, Boston, Lincs PE20 1EH* Tel (01205) 722380

HORNER, Graham. b 57. ACA81 Grey Coll Dur BSc78. St Jo Coll Nottm DTS93. **d** 93 **p** 94. C Longdon-upon-Tern, Rodington, Uppington etc *Lich* 93-95; C Wrockwardine Deanery 95-96; TV from 96. *The Vicarage, Church Road, High Ercall, Telford, Shropshire TF6 6AF* Tel (01952) 770206

HORNER, John Henry. b 40. Leeds Univ BA62 Lon Univ DipRS74 Middx Poly MA87. Oak Hill Th Coll 76. **d** 79 **p** 80. Hon C Datchworth w Tewin *St Alb* 79-85; Hon C Ware St Mary 85-91; C S Ashford Ch Ch *Cant* 91-94; C Hatfield *St Alb* from 94. *St John's House, Bishop's Rise, Hatfield, Herts AL10 9BZ* Tel (01707) 262689

HORNER, Philip David Forster. b 30. Tyndale Hall Bris BDip67. **d** 67 **p** 68. C Ulverston St Mary w H Trin *Carl* 67-71; C Princes Risborough w Ilmer *Ox* 71-76; C Wendover 76-89; P-in-c Ellesborough 76-89; P-in-c Gt and Lt Kimble 82-89; C Walton H Trin 89-92; TV 92-95; rtd 95; P-in-c Cowden w Hammerwood *Chich* from 95. *The Rectory, Cowden, Edenbridge, Kent TN8 7JE* Tel (01342) 850221

HORNER, Richard Murray. b 61. Dur Univ BSc83. NTMTC 93. **d** 96 **p** 97. C Sherborne w Castleton and Lillington *Sarum* from 96. *32 Abbots Way, Sherborne, Dorset DT9 6TD* Tel (01935) 817142

HORNER, Robert William. b 17. RD. St Pet Hall Ox MA46 DipEd. Ripon Hall Ox 56. **d** 57 **p** 58. C Paignton Ch Ch *Ex* 57-60; V Bickleigh (Plymouth) 60-66; Chapl RNR 63-74; R Chinnor *Ox* 66-73; R Emmington 66-73; V Sydenham 66-73; R Chinnor w Emmington and Sydenham 73-84; rtd 84; Perm to Offic *Ex* from 84. *29 Lammas Lane, Paignton, Devon TQ3 1PS* Tel (01803) 528426

HORNSBY, Edgar. b 23. AKC50. **d** 51 **p** 52. C Portsea St Mary *Portsm* 51-55; Chapl RAF 55-69; St Mary's Hall and Brighton Coll 69-74; Chapl St Swithun's Sch Win 74-88; rtd 88; Perm to Offic *B & W* from 88. *The Manor Farmhouse, Littlewindsor, Beaminster, Dorset DT8 3QU*

HOROBIN, Hector Stanley. b 09. Kelham Th Coll 30 Edin Th Coll 46. **d** 46 **p** 47. C Burntisland *St And* 46-47; C Winlaton *Dur* 47-50; V Coundon 50-57; V Birtley 57-62; V Petts Wood *Roch* 62-88; rtd 88; Perm to Offic *Cant* from 89. *23 Wentworth Close, Lyminge, Folkestone, Kent CT18 8HL* Tel (01303) 863095

HOROBIN, Timothy John (Tim). b 60. St Jo Coll Nottm DipThMin94. **d** 94 **p** 95. C Nelson St Phil *Blackb* from 94. *412 Leeds Road, Nelson, Lancs BB9 8ET* Tel (01282) 697327

HORREX, Mrs Gay Lesley. b 42. Guildf Dioc Min Course 90. **d** 96 **p** 97. NSM Walton-on-Thames *Guildf* from 96. *173 Sidney Road, Walton-on-Thames, Surrey KT12 3SB* Tel (01932) 225742

HORROCKS, Mrs Judith Anne (Judie). b 53. Univ of Calgary BSc76. St Jo Coll Nottm DPS82. **dss** 82 **d** 87 **p** 94. Denton Ch Ch *Man* 82-85; Whalley Range St Edm 85-87; Par Dn 87-94; C from 94; Chapl Man R Infirmary 88-90; Chapl S Man Univ Hosps NHS Trust from 95. *St Edmund's Rectory, 1 Range Road, Whalley Range, Manchester M16 8FS* Tel 0161-226 1291 Pager via 161-446 3000

HORROCKS, Oliver John. b 30. Clare Coll Cam BA53 MA57. Westcott Ho Cam 53. **d** 55 **p** 56. C Moss Side Ch Ch *Man* 55-58; C Arnold *S'well* 58-60; R Ancoats *Man* 60-67; R Barthomley *Ches* 67-96; rtd 96. *36 Station Road, Alsager, Stoke-on-Trent ST7 2PD* Tel (01270) 877284

HORROCKS, Robert James. b 56. Grey Coll Dur BSc78. St Jo Coll Nottm DipTh80 DPS82. **d** 82 **p** 83. C Denton Ch Ch *Man* 82-85; R Whalley Range St Edm from 85. *St Edmund's Rectory, 1 Range Road, Whalley Range, Manchester M16 8FS* Tel 0161-226 1291

HORROCKS, Stanley. b 22. Man Univ BA76. Coll of Resurr Mirfield 77. **d** 78 **p** 79. Hon C Man Miles Platting *Man* 78-81; Hon C Lower Broughton St Clem w St Matthias 81-87; rtd 87; NSM Higher Broughton *Man* 87-92; NSM Broughton St Jas w St Clem and St Matthias 92-93; Perm to Offic from 93. *80 Northumberland Street, Salford M7 0DG* Tel 0161-792 1037

HORSEMAN, Christopher Michael. b 54. Bris Sch of Min 84 Trin Coll Bris 87. **d** 88 **p** 89. C Weston-super-Mare Cen Par *B & W* 88-92; TV Yatton Moor from 92. *6 Westaway Park, Yatton, Bristol BS19 4JU* Tel (01934) 834537

HORSEMAN, Colin. b 46. Lon Coll of Div ALCD69 BD70 STh75. **d** 70 **p** 71. C Higher Openshaw *Man* 70-74; C Darfield *Sheff* 75-78; V Stainforth 78-88; V Heeley 88-95; P-in-c Ducklington *Ox* from 95. *The Rectory, 6 Standlake Road, Ducklington, Witney, Oxon OX8 7XG* Tel (01993) 776625

HORSEY, Maurice Alfred. b 30. AIB. S'wark Ord Course 61. **d** 64 **p** 65. C Oxhey All SS *St Alb* 64-67; C Coulsdon St Jo *S'wark* 67-71; P-in-c Champion Hill St Sav 71-76; Hon C Lewisham St Swithun 84-86; P-in-c Woolwich St Thos 86-90; R 90-94; rtd 94; Spain from 94; Chapl Costa del Sol W *Eur* from 94. *Apartado 106, 29670 San Pedro de Alcantara, Malaga, Spain* Tel Malaga (52) 886091

HORSEY, Stanley Desmond. b 20. Ely Th Coll 46. **d** 49 **p** 50. C S Clevedon *B & W* 49-51; C Leigh-on-Sea St Marg *Chelmsf* 51-53; C Barbourne *Worc* 53-55; V Edgbaston St Jas *Birm* 55-60; V Brighton St Martin *Chich* 60-67; V Hove St Barn 67-77; V Hove St Barn and St Agnes 77-85; rtd 85; Perm to Offic *Chich* from 85. *27A Amesbury Crescent, Hove, E Sussex BN3 5RD* Tel (01273) 732081

HORSFALL, David John. b 55. Bris Poly BA77. Trin Coll Bris DipHE82 St Jo Coll Nottm DPS89. **d** 89 **p** 90. C Chaddesden St Mary *Derby* 89-92; V Swadlincote from 92. *The Vicarage, Church Street, Swadlincote, Derbyshire DE11 8LF* Tel (01283) 217756

HORSFALL, Keith. b 39. Tyndale Hall Bris 62. **d** 65 **p** 66. C Walton Breck *Liv* 65-68; C Fazakerley Em 68-70; C Mile Cross *Nor* 70-73; V Gayton 73-80; TR Parr *Liv* 80-90; V Leyland St Andr *Blackb* from 90. *St Andrew's Vicarage, Crocus Field, Leyland, Preston PR5 2DY* Tel (01772) 621645

HORSFIELD, Preb Robert Alan. b 38. Leeds Univ BA60 MA66. Coll of Resurr Mirfield 61. **d** 63 **p** 64. C Lower Gornal *Lich* 63-66; C Bridlington Quay H Trin *York* 66-68; C Sewerby w Marton 66-68; C-in-c Gt Grimsby St Matt Fairfield CD *Linc* 68-73; R Scartho 73-79; R Cleobury Mortimer w Hopton Wafers *Heref* 79-94; P-in-c Neen Sollars w Milson 81-94; P-in-c Neen Savage w Kinlet 91-94; R Cleobury Mortimer w Hopton Wafers etc from 95; P-in-c Knowbury 84-86; P-in-c Coreley w Doddington 84-86; RD Ludlow 89-96; Preb Heref Cathl from 92. *The Rectory, The Hurst, Cleobury Mortimer, Kidderminster, Worcs DY14 8EG* Tel (01299) 270264

HORSHAM, Archdeacon of. *See* FILBY, The Ven William Charles Leonard

HORSHAM, Area Bishop of. *See* URWIN, The Rt Revd Lindsay Goodall

HORSINGTON, Timothy Frederick. b 44. Dur Univ BA66. Wycliffe Hall Ox 67. **d** 69 **p** 70. C Halewood *Liv* 69-72; C Farnworth 72-75; P-in-c Llangarron w Llangrove *Heref* 75-82; P-in-c Whitchurch w Ganarew 77-82; R Llangarron w Llangrove, Whitchurch and Ganarew 83-84; R Highclere and Ashmansworth w Crux Easton *Win* from 84. *The Rectory,*

2 Flexford Close, Highclere, Newbury, Berks RG15 9PE Tel (01635) 253991

HORSLEY, Canon Alan Avery. b 36. St Chad's Coll Dur BA58 Pacific State Univ MA84 PhD85. Qu Coll Birm 58. **d** 60 **p** 61. C Daventry *Pet* 60-63; C Reading St Giles *Ox* 63-64; C Wokingham St Paul 64-66; V Yeadon St Andr *Bradf* 66-71; R Heyford w Stowe Nine Churches *Pet* 71-78; RD Daventry 76-78; V Oakham w Hambleton and Egleton 78-81; Can Pet Cathl 79-86; V Oakham, Hambleton, Egleton, Braunston and Brooke 81-86; V Lanteglos by Fowey *Truro* 86-88; Provost St Andr Cathl Inverness *Mor* 88-91; R Inverness St Andr 88-91; P-in-c Culloden St Mary-in-the-Fields 88-91; P-in-c Strathnairn St Paul 88-91; V Mill End and Heronsgate w W Hyde *St Alb* from 91. *St Peter's Vicarage, Berry Lane, Rickmansworth, Herts WD3 2HQ* Tel (01923) 772785

HORSMAN, Andrew Alan. b 49. Otago Univ BA70 Man Univ MA72 PhD75. St Steph Ho Ox BA80 MA87. **d** 81 **p** 82. C Hillingdon All SS *Lon* 81-84; C Lt Stanmore St Lawr 84-87; TV Haxby w Wigginton *York* from 87. *The Vicarage, 5 Back Lane, Wigginton, York YO3 3ZH* Tel (01904) 768178

HORSWELL, Kevin George. b 55. Jes Coll Cam BA77 MA81 Nottm Univ BA81. St Jo Coll Nottm. **d** 82 **p** 83. C Bootle Ch Ch *Liv* 82-86; Chapl LMH Ox 86-91; C Ox St Giles and SS Phil and Jas w St Marg *Ox* 86-91; R Dodleston *Ches* from 91. *St Mary's Rectory, Pulford Lane, Dodleston, Chester CH4 9NN* Tel (01244) 660257

HORTA, Nelson Pinto. b 40. Lisbon Univ Lic80 Cath Univ of Portugal LicTh92. **d** 65 **p** 69. Portugal from 65; I Sétubal H Spirit *Eur* 69-71; Chapl Lisbon St Paul from 71. *Quinta da Cerieira, rua C, Lote 261, Vale de Figueira-Sobreda, 2800 Almada, Portugal* Tel Almada (1) 295 7943

HORTON, Alan Michael. b 47. Univ of Wales BScTech71. Linc Th Coll CMinlStuds92. **d** 92 **p** 93. C Bexleyheath Ch Ch *Roch* 92-95; P-in-c Slade Green from 95. *The Vicarage, Slade Green Road, Erith, Kent DA8 2HX* Tel (01322) 333970

HORTON, Andrew Charles. b 50. Ex Univ BA71. Sarum Th Coll 71. **d** 73 **p** 74. C Westbury-on-Trym St Alb *Bris* 73-76; USA 76-90; P-in-c Battersea St Mich *S'wark* 90-92; V from 92; Local Min Officer Kingston Episc Area from 94. *St Michael's Vicarage, 93 Bolingbroke Grove, London SW11 6HA* Tel 0171-228 1990

HORTON, Canon Christopher Peter. b 26. Leeds Univ BA49. Coll of Resurr Mirfield 49. **d** 51 **p** 52. C Blyth St Mary *Newc* 51-55; C Delaval 55-59; V Grangetown *York* 59-91; Can and Preb York Minster 85-91; rtd 91. *51 Well Ridge Close, Seaton Grange, Whitley Bay, Tyne & Wear NE25 9PN* Tel 0191-251 0742

HORTON, David Harold. b 49. St Jo Coll Dur BA72. NE Ord Course 82. **d** 86 **p** 87. C Enfield St Jas *Lon* 86-90; Min Joydens Wood St Barn CD *Roch* 90-93; V Joydens Wood St Barn from 93. *The Vicarage, 6 Tile Kiln Lane, Bexley, Kent DA5 2BD* Tel (01322) 528923

HORTON, Jeremy Nicholas Orkney. b 44. Cranmer Hall Dur 64. **d** 68 **p** 69. C Dalton-in-Furness *Carl* 68-70; C Penrith 70-73; V Hudswell w Downholme and Marske *Ripon* 73-75; R Middleton Tyas and Melsonby 75-81; P-in-c Croft 78-81; P-in-c Eryholme 78-81; V Wortley de Leeds 81-93; V Middleton St Mary from 93; RD Armley from 96. *Middleton Vicarage, 198 Town Street, Leeds LS10 3TJ* Tel 0113-270 5689

HORTON, John Ward. b 27. Leeds Univ BA50. Coll of Resurr Mirfield 50. **d** 52 **p** 53. C Balkwell CD *Newc* 52-55; C Coatham *York* 55-58; C-in-c Acomb Moor CD 58-71; V Acomb Moor 71-93; rtd 93. *39 Billy Mill Lane, North Shields, Tyne & Wear NE26 8BZ* Tel 0191-296 4082

HORTON, Melanie Jane. **d** 96 **p** 97. C Lich St Chad *Lich* from 96. *38 St Chad's Road, Lichfield, Staffs WS13 7MD* Tel (01543) 251009

HORTON, Michael John. b 56. St Jo Coll Cam BA80 MA83 Univ of Wales (Swansea) PGCE83 Ox Univ BA88 MA92. Wycliffe Hall Ox 86. **d** 89 **p** 90. C Northallerton w Kirby Sigston *York* 89-92; C Ulverston St Mary w H Trin *Carl* 92-94; V Lightwater *Guildf* from 94. *The Vicarage, 28 Broadway Road, Lightwater, Surrey GU18 5SJ* Tel (01276) 472270

HORTON, Ralph Edward. b 41. S'wark Ord Course 75. **d** 78 **p** 79. C Streatham St Leon *S'wark* 78-81; TV Catford (Southend) and Downham 81-88; V Ashford St Matt *Lon* from 88. *The Vicarage, 99 Church Road, Ashford, Middx TW15 2NY* Tel (01784) 252459

HORTON, Canon Roberta Anne. b 44. Leic Univ BSc66 CertEd67 Nottm Univ BCombStuds82. Linc Th Coll 79. **dss** 82 **d** 87 **p** 94. Cambridge St Jas *Ely* 82-86; Beaumont Leys *Leic* 86-87; Par Dn 87-91; Dioc Dir of Tr from 91; P-in-c Swithland from 94; Hon Can Leic Cathl from 94. *The Rectory, 157 Main Street, Swithland, Loughborough, Leics LE12 8QT* Tel (01509) 891173

HORWOOD, Graham Frederick. b 34. Univ of Wales (Cardiff) BA55. Coll of Resurr Mirfield 55. **d** 57 **p** 58. C Llantrisant *Llan* 57-61; C Roath St Sav 61-62; C Roath St Marg 62-66; V Clydach *S & B* 66-77; V Canton St Luke *Llan* from 77. *St Luke's Vicarage, 12 Thompson Avenue, Cardiff CF5 1EY* Tel (01222) 562022

HOSKIN, David James. b 63. Hull Univ BA86. Trin Coll Bris BA94. **d** 94 **p** 95. C Southway *Ex* from 94. *5 Treago Gardens, Plymouth PL6 7EJ* Tel (01752) 787065

HOSKIN, David William. b 49. Hatf Coll Dur BSc71. Wycliffe Hall Ox 72. **d** 75 **p** 76. C Bridlington Priory *York* 75-78; C Rodbourne Cheney *Bris* 78-79; C Bebington *Ches* 79-82; R Lockington and Lund and Scorborough w Leconfield *York* 82-88; V Beverley St Mary from 88. *The Vicarage, 15 Molescroft Road, Beverley, N Humberside HU17 7DX* Tel (01482) 881437

HOSKIN, Canon Eric James. b 28. St Chad's Coll Dur BA50 DipTh52. **d** 52 **p** 53. C Coney Hill *Glouc* 52-54; C Stroud 54-57; R Ruardean 57-63; P-in-c Lydbrook 61-63; V Cheltenham Em 63-70; R Dursley 70-86; RD Dursley 77-85; Hon Can Glouc Cathl 81-86; R Easington w Liverton *York* 86-96; rtd 96. *37A Algarth Rise, Pocklington, York YO4 2HX* Tel (01759) 305798

HOSKIN, Henry Brian. b 32. NW Ord Course 72. **d** 75 **p** 76. NSM Chesterfield St Aug *Derby* 75-79; NSM Bolsover 79-83; NSM Old Brampton and Loundsley Green 83-88; P-in-c Gt Barlow 88-94; rtd 97; Perm to Offic *Derby* from 97. *25 Barn Close, Chesterfield, Derbyshire S41 8BD* Tel (01246) 201550

HOSKING, Canon Harold Ernest. b 19. Lich Th Coll 51. **d** 53 **p** 54. C Penwerris *Truro* 53-56; R Mawgan in Pyder 56-61; V Newlyn St Pet 61-69; V Newquay 69-74; TR Redruth 74-80; R Redruth w Lanner 80-84; Hon Can Truro Cathl 78-84; rtd 84; Perm to Offic *Ex* from 84; Perm to Offic *Truro* from 84. *28 Chantry Close, Teignmouth, Devon TQ14 8FE* Tel (01626) 770329

HOSKINS, Hugh George. b 46. S Dios Minl Tr Scheme. **d** 84 **p** 85. NSM Hilperton w Whaddon and Staverton etc *Sarum* 84-87; C Calne and Blackland 87-90; R W Lavington and the Cheverells 90-97; P-in-c Heytesbury and Sutton Veny from 97. *The Rectory, Best's Lane, Sutton Veny, Warminster, Wilts BA12 7AU* Tel (01985) 840014

HOSKYNS, John Algernon Peyton. b 20. Pemb Coll Cam BA41 MA45. Westcott Ho Cam 47. **d** 49 **p** 50. C Eastleigh *Win* 49-52; C Brompton H Trin *Lon* 52-54; V Hartley Wintney and Elvetham *Win* 54-62; R Worplesdon *Guildf* 62-72; V St Weonards w Orcop *Heref* 73-76; P-in-c Linton w Upton Bishop 76-78; P-in-c How Caple w Sollers Hope 76-85; P-in-c Sellack and King's Caple w Foy 81-85; rtd 85; Perm to Offic *Heref* from 85. *Tump House, Woolhope, Hereford HR1 4QP* Tel (01432) 860301

HOST, Mrs Charmaine Anne. b 54. WMMTC 87. **d** 90 **p** 94. C Westwood *Cov* 90-94; C Whitnash 94-96; V Kineton from 96; V Combroke w Compton Verney from 96. *The Vicarage, Southam Street, Kineton, Warwick CV35 0LL* Tel (01926) 640248

HOTCHEN, Stephen Jeffrie. b 50. Bradf Coll of Educn. Linc Th Coll 85. **d** 87 **p** 88. C Morpeth *Newc* 87-90; TV High Wycombe *Ox* 90-91; R Dingwall *Mor* 91-94; R Strathpeffer 91-94; V Rickerscote *Lich* from 94. *St Peter's Vicarage, 106 Rickerscote Road, Stafford ST17 4HB* Tel (01785) 52878

HOTCHIN, Mrs Hilary Moya. b 52. Birm Univ CertEd73. WMMTC 85. **d** 88 **p** 94. NSM Redditch St Steph *Worc* 88-91; Par Dn Handsworth *Sheff* 91-94; C 94-96; TV Maltby from 96. *The Vicarage, 5 Haids Road, Maltby, Rotherham, S Yorkshire S66 8BH* Tel (01709) 814951

HOUGH, Dr Adrian Michael. b 59. MRSC CChem AMITD Hertf Coll Ox BA81 MA84 DPhil84. Ripon Coll Cuddesdon BA91. **d** 92 **p** 93. C Martley and Wichenford, Knightwick etc *Worc* 92-96; AP Evesham Deanery 96-97; V Badsey w Aldington and Offenham and Bretforton from 97. *The Vicarage, Badsey, Evesham, Worcs WR11 5EW* Tel (01386) 830343

HOUGH, Miss Carole Elizabeth. b 59. Lon Hosp SRN81. St Jo Coll Nottm DipMin91. **d** 91 **p** 94. Par Dn Beoley *Worc* 91-94; C 94-95; Asst Chapl Addenbrooke's NHS Trust Cam from 95. *Addenbrooke's Hospital, Hills Road, Cambridge CB2 2QQ* Tel (01223) 217769 or 245151

HOUGH, Edward Lewis. b 38. Univ of Wales (Lamp) BA60. St Mich Coll Llan 60. **d** 62 **p** 63. C Baglan *Llan* 62-69; Ind Chapl *York* 69-72; R Cilybebyll *Llan* 72-93; RD Neath 84-89; Ind Chapl Port Talbot 92-95; V Cadoxton-juxta-Neath 93-95; rtd 95. *14 Alderwood Close, Crynant, Neath SA10 8PY* Tel (01639) 750006

HOUGH, Michael. b 49. Man Univ. St Jo Coll Nottm. **d** 84 **p** 85. C Newbottle *Dur* 84-87; V Felling 87-96; R Gateshead Fell from 96. *The Rectory, 45 Shotley Gardens, Low Fell, Gateshead, Tyne & Wear NE9 5DP* Tel 0191-487 3537

HOUGH, Peter George. b 40. Dur Univ BA62. Wells Th Coll 62. **d** 64 **p** 65. C Stocking Farm CD *Leic* 64-68; V Leic St Aid 68-76; V Knutton *Lich* from 76; P-in-c Silverdale and Alsagers Bank 93-95. *The Vicarage, Church Lane, Newcastle, Staffs ST5 6DU* Tel (01782) 624282

HOUGH, Sidney Stephen Valentine. b 27. G&C Coll Cam BA50 MA54. Ripon Hall Ox 55. **d** 57 **p** 58. C Goodmayes All SS *Chelmsf* 57-60; C Warwick St Mary *Cov* 60-62; V Messing *Chelmsf* 62-72; R Inworth 62-72; V Messing w Inworth 72-77; Chapl Warley Hosp Brentwood 78-79; R Alphamstone w Lamarsh and Pebmarsh *Chelmsf* 79-88; rtd 88. *27 Weavers Court, Weavers Lane, Sudbury, Suffolk CO10 6HY* Tel (01787) 374812

HOUGHTBY, Frank. b 12. Chich Th Coll 41. **d** 41 **p** 42. C Daventry *Pet* 41-44 and 46-47; Chapl RAFVR 43-47; R Wittering w Thornhaugh and Wansford *Pet* 47-56; V E

Carlton 57-58; C Leamington Priors All SS *Cov* 58-60; R N Runcton w Hardwick and Setchey *Nor* 60-91; rtd 91. *29 Lodge Way, Grantham, Lincs NG31 8DD* Tel (01476) 592282

HOUGHTON, Christopher Guy. b 64. W Surrey Coll of Art & Design BA86. Oak Hill Th Coll DipHE88 BA89. **d** 89 **p** 90. C Mossley Hill St Matt and St Jas *Liv* 89-92; C Ashton-in-Makerfield St Thos 92-95; C Southport St Phil and St Paul 95-96; Chapl Chorley and S Ribble NHS Trust from 96. *The Chaplain's Office, Chorley and South Ribble NHS Trust, Preston Road, Chorley, Lancs PR7 1PP* Tel (01257) 247171

HOUGHTON, David John. b 47. Edin Univ BSc(Econ)68. Cuddesdon Coll 69. **d** 71 **p** 72. C Prestbury *Glouc* 71-74; Prec Gib Cathl *Eur* 74-76; Chapl Madrid 76-78; C Croydon *Cant* 78-80; Chapl Warw Sch 80-85; P-in-c Isleworth St Fran *Lon* 85-90; USA 90-91; TV Clapham TM *S'wark* from 91; RD Clapham from 93. *15 Elms Road, London SW4 9ER* Tel 0171-622 8703 Fax as telephone

HOUGHTON, Edward Johnson. b 23. Keble Coll Ox BA48 MA48. Linc Th Coll 48. **d** 50 **p** 51. C Nelson in Lt Marsden *Blackb* 50-52; C Lancaster St Mary 52-55; Chapl R Albert Hosp Lanc 52-61; Chapl Ripley Sch Lanc 52-56; R Quernmore *Blackb* 55-61; CF (TA) 56-62; Chapl Hellingly and Amberstone Hosps 61-90; rtd 88; Perm to Offic *Chich* from 88. *1 Nursery Close, Osborne Park, Hailsham, E Sussex BN27 2PX* Tel (01323) 442126

HOUGHTON, Mrs Evelyn Mabel. b 44. Stockwell Coll of Educn TCert65. Oak Hill NSM Course 92. **d** 94 **p** 95. NSM Bedford St Jo and St Leon *St Alb* from 94. *29 Turner Way, Bedford MK41 7ND* Tel (01234) 212525

HOUGHTON, Geoffrey John. b 59. Ridley Hall Cam 87. **d** 90 **p** 91. C Sholing *Win* 90-94; P-in-c Jersey All SS from 94. *All Saints Vicarage, Saville Street, St Helier, Jersey, Channel Islands JE2 3XF* Tel (01534) 68538

HOUGHTON, Ian David. b 50. Lanc Univ BA71 Newc Univ CertEd74 Man Univ CertRS90. Sarum & Wells Th Coll 80. **d** 82 **p** 83. C Newc St Geo *Newc* 82-85; Chapl Newc Poly 85-92; Chapl Univ of Northumbria at Newc 92-95; Master Newc St Thos Prop Chpl 90-95; Black Country Urban Ind Miss *Lich* from 95; Res Min Bilston from 95. *24 Overfield Drive, Bilston, W Midlands WV14 9XW* Tel (01902) 662443

HOUGHTON, James Robert. b 44. AKC67. **d** 68 **p** 69. C Herrington *Dur* 68-70; Asst Dioc Youth Chapl *Bris* 70-72; Perm to Offic *Ex* 73-74; C Heavitree 74-77; Perm to Offic *Lon* 78-80 and 83-88; C Heavitree w Ex St Paul *Ex* 78; Hon C W Drayton *Lon* 80-83; Chapl Greycoat Hosp Sch 83-88; Chapl Stonar Sch Melksham 88-95; Chapl Sch of St Mary and St Anne Abbots Bromley from 95. *St Mary's Lodge, High Street, Abbots Bromley, Rugeley, Staffs WS15 3BW* Tel (01283) 840225

HOUGHTON, Canon John Caswell. b 16. Dur Univ BA38 LTh38. St Boniface Warminster 34. **d** 39 **p** 40. C Wolverton St Geo *Ox* 39-42; Zambia 42-74; Warden Dioc Th Sem N Rhodesia 47-52; Can N Rhodesia 60-62; Adn N Rhodesia 62-64; Adn S Zambia 64-70; Can Lusaka 71-74; Promotions Sec Feed the Minds 74-81; rtd 81; Perm to Offic *Ox* from 82. *18 Cornelia Close, Bletchley, Milton Keynes MK2 3LX* Tel (01908) 370526

HOUGHTON, Canon Michael Alan. b 49. Lanc Univ BA70 Dur Univ PGCE71 Southn Univ BTh83. Chich Th Coll 78. **d** 80 **p** 81. C Wellingborough All Hallows *Pet* 80-84; St Helena 84-89; Hon Can from 94; Tutor Coll of Ascension Selly Oak 90; V Folkestone St Pet *Cant* from 90. *St Peter's Vicarage, The Durlocks, Folkestone, Kent CT19 6AL* Tel (01303) 254472

HOUGHTON, Michael Richard. b 29. CCC Cam BA52 MA56. Cuddesdon Coll 52. **d** 54 **p** 55. C Portsea N End St Mark *Portsm* 54-57; New Zealand from 57; Adn Tamaki 77-81. *Private Bag 12, Papakura, New Zealand* Tel Auckland (9) 292 2432

HOUGHTON, Peter Graham. b 51. St Jo Coll Nottm. **d** 87 **p** 88. C Toxteth Park St Clem *Liv* 87-91; Chapl Winwick Hosp Warrington 91-94; Chapl Warrington Community Healthcare NHS Trust from 94. *The Chaplain's Office, Winwick Hospital, Warrington WA2 8RR* Tel (01925) 655221

HOUGHTON, Reginald Leighton. b 10. St Chad's Coll Dur BA33 DipTh34 MA36. **d** 34 **p** 35. C Billingham St Cuth *Dur* 34-38; C Hunslet St Mary *Ripon* 38-42; V S Benfleet *Chelmsf* 42-50; V Bassingbourn *Ely* 50-60; P-in-c Whaddon 52-54; V 54-60; V Bartley Green *Birm* 60-75; rtd 75; Perm to Offic *Lich* from 77. *Flat 204, The Cedars, Abbey Foregate, Shrewsbury SY2 6BY* Tel (01743) 246482

HOUGHTON, Robert Sherwood. b 26. **d** 52 **p** 53. C Howe Bridge *Man* 52-54; Australia from 60; rtd 95. *40 Canning Street, North Melbourne, Victoria, Australia 3051* Tel Melbourne (3) 9328 1419

HOUGHTON, Thomas. b 17. NW Ord Course 71. **d** 74 **p** 75. NSM Newcastle w Butterton *Lich* 74-82; Perm to Offic from 82. *Fernyhough, Crewe CW3 9JT* Tel (01782) 750275

HOUGHTON, Timothy John. b 56. Kingston Poly BSc88. Oak Hill Th Coll BA93. **d** 97. C Normanton *Derby* from 97. *211 Village Street, Normanton, Derby DE23 8DE* Tel (01332) 767407

HOULDEN, Prof James Leslie. b 29. Qu Coll Ox BA52 MA56. Cuddesdon Coll 53. **d** 55 **p** 56. C Hunslet St Mary and Stourton *Ripon* 55-58; Tutor Chich Th Coll 58-59; Chapl 59-60; Chapl Trin Coll Ox 60-70; Prin Cuddesdon Coll 70-75; V Cuddesdon *Ox* 70-77; Prin Ripon Coll Cuddesdon 75-77; Hon Can Ch Ch *Ox* 76-77; Sen Lect NT Studies K Coll Lon 77-87; Prof Th K Coll Lon 87-94; rtd 94; Perm to Offic *S'wark* from 94. *33 Raleigh Court, Lymer Avenue, London SE19 1LS* Tel 0181-265 9869

HOULDING, David Nigel Christopher. b 53. AKC76. **d** 77 **p** 78. C Hillingdon All SS *Lon* 77-81; C Holborn St Alb w Saffron Hill St Pet 81-85; V Hampstead St Steph w All Hallows from 85. *All Hallows' House, 52 Courthope Road, London NW3 2LD* Tel 0171-267 7833

HOULDSWORTH, Raymond Clifford. b 30. Bps' Coll Cheshunt 64. **d** 66 **p** 67. C Egham Hythe *Guildf* 66-70; C Cranbrook *Cant* 70-76; V Hernhill 76-82; V Minster w Monkton 82-95; rtd 95. *11 Craig Road, Six Bells, Abertillery NP3 2LR* Tel (01495) 321934

HOULT, Roy Anthony. b 35. AKC58. **d** 59 **p** 60. C Walton St Mary *Liv* 59-63; Canada from 63; Hon Can Koot 75-79. *381 Huron Street, Toronto, Ontario, Canada, M5S 2G5*

HOUNSFIELD, Thomas Paul. b 15. Lon Coll of Div 46. **d** 47 **p** 48. C Penn Fields *Lich* 47-50; R Treeton *Sheff* 50-61; V Donington *Lich* 61-80; rtd 80; Perm to Offic *Win* from 81. *10 Widden Close, Sway, Lymington, Hants SO41 6AX* Tel (01590) 682399

HOUSE, The Ven Francis Harry. b 08. OBE55. Wadh Coll Ox BA30 MA34. Cuddesdon Coll 34. **d** 35 **p** 36. Pemb Coll Miss Walworth *S'wark* 35-37; Sec World Student Chr Federation Geneva 38-40; Lic to Offic *Eur* 38-40; C Leeds St Pet *Ripon* 40-42; Overseas Relig Broadcasting Org BBC 42-44; Rep World Student Relief (Greece) 44-46; Lic to Offic *Eur* 44-46; Hd of Relig Broadcasting BBC 47-55; Sec Youth Dept WCC Geneva 46-47; Hon C Hampstead Garden Suburb *Lon* 47-55; Select Preacher Cam Univ 49; Assoc Gen Sec WCC Geneva 55-62; V Pontefract St Giles *Wakef* 62-67; R Gawsworth *Ches* 67-78; Adn Macclesfield 67-78; rtd 78. *11 Drummond Court, Drummond Avenue, Leeds LS16 5QE* Tel 0113-278 3646

HOUSE, Graham Ivor. b 44. BA80. Oak Hill Th Coll 77. **d** 80 **p** 81. C Ipswich St Jo *St E* 80-84; V Ipswich St Andr from 84. *286 Britannia Road, Ipswich IP4 5HF* Tel (01473) 728204

HOUSE, Jack Francis. b 35. Bris Univ BEd70 Lon Univ MA80 Univ of Wales MTh94. Bris & Glouc Tr Course 79. **d** 80 **p** 81. NSM Bedminster *Bris* 80-92; Perm to Offic 92-94; NSM Knowle H Nativity from 94. *48 Hendre Road, Bristol BS3 2LR* Tel 0117-966 1144

HOUSE, Mrs Janet. b 45. E Anglia Univ BA67 Keswick Hall Coll PGCE68 Sussex Univ MA80. Ripon Coll Cuddesdon 93. **d** 95 **p** 96. C Swindon Ch Ch *Bris* from 95. *58 Upham Road, Swindon SN3 1DN* Tel (01793) 521296

HOUSE, Simon Hutchinson. b 30. Peterho Cam BA65 MA67. Cuddesdon Coll 61. **d** 64 **p** 65. C Sutton St Jas *York* 64-67; C Acomb St Steph 67-69; V Allestree St Nic *Derby* 69-81; RD Duffield 74-81; V Bitterne Park *Win* 81-91; rtd 91. *22 Stanley Street, Southsea, Hants PO5 2DS* Tel (01705) 838592

HOUSE, Vickery Willis. b 45. MA. Kelham Th Coll. **d** 69 **p** 70. C Crediton *Ex* 69-76; TV Sampford Peverell, Uplowman, Holcombe Rogus etc 76-81; R Berwick w Selmeston and Alciston *Chich* 81-90; Chapl Ardingly Coll Haywards Heath 90-94; V Brighton St Bart *Chich* from 94. *16 Richmond Terrace, Brighton BN2 2NA* Tel (01273) 685142

HOUSEMAN, Patricia Adele. *See* CAMPION, Ms Patricia Adele

HOUSMAN, Arthur Martin Rowand. b 53. MA CertEd. Trin Coll Bris 81. **d** 83 **p** 84. C Croydon Ch Ch Broad Green *Cant* 83-84; C Croydon Ch Ch *S'wark* 85-87; TV Stratton St Margaret w S Marston etc *Bris* 87-93; Zimbabwe from 94. *Peterhouse, Private Bag 3741, Marondera, Zimbabwe*

HOUSTON, Canon Arthur James. b 54. Trin Coll Bris BA87. **d** 87 **p** 88. C Chatham St Phil and St Jas *Roch* 87-91; I Carrigaline Union *C, C & R* from 91; Preb Cork Cathl from 95; Preb Ross Cathl from 95. *The Rectory, Carrigaline, Co Cork, Irish Republic* Tel Cork (21) 372224

HOUSTON, Edward Davison. b 31. TCD BA56. **d** 57 **p** 58. C Conwall Union *D & R* 57-59; India 59-88; V Whittlebury w Paulerspury *Pet* from 89; P-in-c Wicken from 89. *The Rectory, 2 Tews End Lane, Paulerspury, Towcester, Northants NN12 7NQ* Tel (01327) 333670

HOUSTON (née LOVELL), Mrs Helen Sarah. b 70. Bris Univ BA91. St Jo Coll Nottm MA95. **d** 95 **p** 96. C Bourne *Guildf* from 95. *64 Weydon Hill Road, Farnham, Surrey GU9 8NY* Tel (01252) 715250

HOUSTON, Michael Alexander (Mike). b 46. Lanc Univ MA92. Linc Th Coll 86. **d** 88 **p** 89. C Longton *Blackb* 88-91; C Woughton *Ox* 91-92; TV from 92. *2 Braunston, Woughton Park, Milton Keynes MK6 3AU* Tel (01908) 674742

HOUSTON, Michael James. b 41. **d** 95 **p** 97. Aux Min *D & D* from 95. *73 Milecross Road, Newtownards, Co Down BT23 4SR* Tel (01247) 813397

HOUSTON, Prof Samuel Kenneth (Ken). b 43. FIMA73 QUB BSc64 PhD67. CITC 81. **d** 85 **p** 86. NSM Belfast St Jas w St Silas *Conn* 85-91; NSM Belfast St Andr from 91; Prof Mathematical Studies NUU from 96. *29 North Circular Road, Belfast BT15 5HB* Tel (01232) 771830

HOUSTON, William Paul. b 54. QUB BSSc76 TCD BTh78. CITC 78. **d** 81 **p** 82. C Carrickfergus *Conn* 81-83; C Bangor St Comgall *D & D* 83-86; I Gilford 86-90; I Carnalea from 90. *St Gall's*

Rectory, 171 Crawfordsburn Road, Bangor, Co Down BT19 1BT Tel (01247) 853366

HOVENDEN, Gerald Eric. b 53. York Univ BA75 Ox Univ MA85. Wycliffe Hall Ox 78. **d** 81 **p** 82. C Pitsmoor w Ellesmere *Sheff* 81-85; Chapl Lyon w Grenoble and St Etienne *Eur* 85-90; TV S Gillingham *Roch* from 90. *26 Pear Tree Lane, Hempstead, Gillingham, Kent ME7 3PT* Tel (01634) 387892

HOVEY, Richard Michael. b 58. Imp Coll Lon BSc79 ACGI79 Cranfield Inst of Tech MBA84 CEng83 MIEE83. Cranmer Hall Dur CTM95. **d** 95 **p** 96. C Cheddar *B & W* from 95. *19 Silver Street, Cheddar, Somerset BS27 3LE* Tel (01934) 743527

HOVIL, Richard Guy. b 29. Ex Coll Ox BA51 MA57. Ridley Hall Cam. **d** 55 **p** 56. C Finchley Ch Ch *Lon* 55-58; Staff Worker Scripture Union 58-71; Chapl Monkton Combe Sch Bath 71-83; V Fremington *Ex* 83-94; rtd 94. *37 Upper Marsh Road, Warminster, Wiltshire BA12 9PN* Tel (01985) 214337

HOVIL, Richard Jeremy Guy. Wycliffe Hall Ox. **d** 95 **p** 96. C Kensington St Barn *Lon* from 95. *17 Devonport Road, London W12 8NZ* Tel 0181-743 2784

HOW, Canon John Maxloe. b 15. Magd Coll Cam BA37 MA49. Westcott Ho Cam 39. **d** 39 **p** 40. C Norton St Mary *Dur* 39-44; P-in-c W Pelton 44-45; P-in-c Stella 46-47; V Thornley 47-51; V Monkwearmouth St Andr 51-59; V Barton w Pooley Bridge *Carl* 59-73; RD Penrith 61-73; Hon Can Carl Cathl 72-81; V Kirkby Lonsdale w Mansergh 73-76; TR Kirkby Lonsdale 76-81; rtd 81; Perm to Offic *Carl* from 81. *4 Kilmidyke Drive, Grange-over-Sands, Cumbria LA11 7AL* Tel (015395) 34117

HOWARD, Alan James. b 45. Bris Univ BA69. Clifton Th Coll. **d** 71 **p** 72. C Welling *Roch* 71-74; C Cromer *Nor* 74-78; V Sidcup St Andr *Roch* 78-86; V Leyton St Cath *Chelmsf* 86-93; V Leyton, St Cath and St Paul from 93. *St Catherine's Vicarage, Fairlop Road, London E11 1BL* Tel 0181-539 6361

HOWARD, Andrew. b 63. Man Univ BA95 Leeds Univ MA97. Coll of Resurr Mirfield 95. **d** 97. C Worksop Priory *S'well* from 97. *268 Kilton Road, Worksop, Notts S80 2DZ* Tel (01909) 484720

HOWARD, Charles William Wykeham. b 52. Southn Univ BTh81. Sarum & Wells Th Coll 76. **d** 79 **p** 80. C St Mary-at-Latton *Chelmsf* 79-82; Chapl RN from 82. *Royal Naval Chaplaincy Service, Room 203, Victory Building, HM Naval Base, Portsmouth PO1 3LS* Tel (01705) 727903 Fax 727112

HOWARD, David John. b 47. Ripon Hall Ox 70. **d** 72 **p** 73. C Benchill *Man* 72-75; C Sedgley All SS *Lich* 75-77; C-in-c Lostock CD *Man* 77-85; V Lt Hulton 85-88; Perm to Offic 90-91; C E Leake *S'well* 91-92; C Costock 91-92; C Rempstone 91-92; C Stanford on Soar 91-92; C W Leake w Kingston-on-Soar and Ratcliffe-on-Soar 91-92; C E and W Leake, Stanford-on-Soar, Rempstone etc 92-94; P-in-c Bilborough w Strelley from 94. *St Martin's Rectory, 11 St Agnes Close, Nottingham NG8 4BJ* Tel 0115-929 1874

HOWARD, David John. b 51. Lon Univ BSc73. Oak Hill Th Coll 74. **d** 77 **p** 78. C Radipole and Melcombe Regis *Sarum* 77-83; R Tredington and Darlingscott w Newbold on Stour *Cov* 83-90; P-in-c Binley 90-94; V from 94; RD Cov E from 95. *Binley Vicarage, 68 Brandon Road, Coventry CV3 2JF* Tel (01203) 636334

HOWARD, David William. b 43. K Coll Lon 63. **d** 67 **p** 68. C Skegness *Linc* 67-69; C Gainsborough All SS 69-72; Jamaica from 72. *Address temp unknown*

HOWARD, Canon Donald. b 27. K Coll Lon BD58 AKC58. **d** 59 **p** 60. C Saltburn-by-the-Sea *York* 59-62; S Africa 62-72; R Haddington *Edin* 72-78; Can St Andr Cathl *Ab* 78-91; Provost St Andr Cathl 78-91; R Aberdeen St Andr 78-91; Chapl Aber Univ 78-82; P-in-c Aberdeen St Ninian 80-91; Angl Adv Grampian TV 84-88; rtd 91; Hon Can St Andr Cathl *Ab* from 91; Perm to Offic *Ripon* from 91. *42 Waterside, Ripon, N Yorkshire HG4 1RA* Tel (01765) 692144

HOWARD, Mrs Erika Kathryn. b 49. SRN70 SCM72. S Dios Minl Tr Scheme 88. **d** 91 **p** 94. NSM New Shoreham *Chich* 91-94; NSM Old Shoreham 91-94; C Kingston Buci from 94. *207 Upper Shoreham Road, Shoreham-by-Sea, W Sussex BN43 6BE* Tel (01273) 881585

HOWARD, Francis Curzon. b 27. St Aid Birkenhead DipTh57. **d** 57 **p** 58. C Claughton cum Grange *Ches* 57-60; C Cheltenham St Paul *Glouc* 60-62; V Sheff St Barn *Sheff* 62-65; Bermuda 65-71; USA from 71; rtd 92. *Trinity Episcopal Church, PO Box 127, Church Street, Tariffville, Connecticut 06081, USA*

HOWARD, Frank Thomas. b 36. Lon Univ BSc57. Bps' Coll Cheshunt 59. **d** 61 **p** 62. C Macclesfield St Mich *Ches* 61-64; C Claughton cum Grange 64-66; V Lache cum Saltney 66-76; R Stanton *St E* from 76; RD Ixworth 79-85. *The Rectory, The Street, Stanton, Bury St Edmunds, Suffolk IP31 2DQ* Tel (01359) 50239

HOWARD, Geoffrey. b 30. Barrister-at-Law 83 Lon Univ LLB77. EMMTC. **d** 85 **p** 86. NSM Barton *Ely* 85-87; NSM Coton 85-87; C W Walton 87-92; TV Daventry, Ashby St Ledgers, Braunston etc *Pet* 92-97; rtd 97. *11 Porson Court, Porson Road, Cambridge CB2 2ER* Tel (01223) 300738

HOWARD, George Granville. b 47. Trin Coll Bris. **d** 88 **p** 89. C Downend *Bris* 88-92; V Clifton H Trin, St Andr and St Pet from 92; Bp's Officer for Miss & Evang from 92. *Holy Trinity Vicarage, 6 Goldney Avenue, Clifton, Bristol BS8 4RA* Tel 0117-973 4751

HOWARD, John Alexander. b 27. Wesley Coll Leeds 48 Coll of Resurr Mirfield 66. **d** 67 **p** 68. C Almondbury *Wakef* 67-71; V Skelmanthorpe 71-81; R Fortrose *Mor* 81-94; R Cromarty 81-94; R Arpafeelie 81-94; rtd 94; Perm to Offic *Glouc* from 94. *2 Webbs Cottages, Stratford Road, Mickleton, Chipping Campden, Glos GL55 6SW* Tel (01386) 438787

HOWARD, John Robert. b 60. NUI BA HDipEd TCD DipTh. **d** 84 **p** 85. C Donaghcloney w Waringstown *D & D* 84-88; I Belfast St Ninian *Conn* 88-94; Bp's Dom Chapl 88-94; Chapl Ulster Univ from 88; I Annahilt w Magherahamlet *D & D* from 94. *Annahilt Rectory, 2 Loughaghery Road, Hillsborough, Co Down BT26 6DB* Tel (01846) 638218

HOWARD, Keith. b 55. Univ of Wales (Ban) DipTh81. St Jo Coll Nottm 81. **d** 84 **p** 85. C Llanidloes w Llangurig *Ban* 84-87; R Llansantffraid Glan Conway and Eglwysfach *St As* from 87. *The Rectory, Glan Conway, Colwyn Bay LL29 5ST* Tel (01492) 580279

HOWARD, Malcolm. b 29. St Deiniol's Hawarden. **d** 73 **p** 74. NSM Birstall *Leic* 73-82; NSM Birstall and Wanlip 82-90; Chapl Leics Hospice 89-90; rtd 90. *65 Fielding Road, Birstall, Leicester LE4 3AH* Tel 0116-267 3046

HOWARD, Martin John Aidan. b 68. Lon Univ BA90 Open Univ MA96. St Jo Coll Nottm MA94. **d** 97. C Billericay and Lt Burstead *Chelmsf* from 97. *9 Arundel Close, Queens Park, Billericay, Essex CM12 0FN* Tel (01277) 632822

HOWARD, Canon Michael Charles. b 35. Selw Coll Cam BA58 MA63. Wycliffe Hall Ox 58. **d** 60 **p** 61. C Stowmarket *St E* 60-64; Nigeria 64-71; Hon Can Ondo 70-71; Hon C Southborough St Pet w Ch Ch and St Matt *Roch* 72-73; Lic to Offic *Ox* from 73. *17 Milton Road, Bloxham, Banbury, Oxon OX15 4JD*

HOWARD, Canon Michael Paul Penrose. b 40. Keele Univ BA62 Lon Univ BD69. Lon Coll of Div 66. **d** 69 **p** 70. C Nottingham St Nic *S'well* 69-72; C Ox St Aldate w H Trin *Ox* 72-77; Chapl CCC Ox 75-77; V Dartford Ch Ch *Roch* 77-90; Chapl W Hill Hosp Dartford 77-90; P-in-c Cobham w Luddesdowne and Dode *Roch* 90-96; Dioc Adv on Evang from 90; Hon Can Roch Cathl from 92; P-in-c Sevenoaks Weald from 96. *St George's Vicarage, Church Road, Weald, Sevenoaks, Kent TN14 6LT* Tel (01732) 463291 Fax as telephone

HOWARD, Nicolas John. b 61. Nottm Univ BTh90. Aston Tr Scheme 85 Linc Th Coll 87. **d** 90 **p** 91. C Bracknell *Ox* 90-94; P-in-c Oldham St Chad Limeside *Man* 94-96; Perm to Offic *Birm* from 96. *100 Teignmouth Road, Birmingham B29 7AY* Tel 0121-471 4420

HOWARD, Norman. b 26. AKC57. St Boniface Warminster 57. **d** 58 **p** 59. C Friern Barnet St Jas *Lon* 58-62; Jamaica 62-69; USA from 69; rtd 91. *766 Lake Forest Road, Clearwater, Florida 34625, USA* Tel Clearwater (813) 799-3929

HOWARD, Mrs Patricia Anne (Pat). b 38. Ox Min Course CertBS92. **d** 92 **p** 94. NSM Winslow w Gt Horwood and Addington *Ox* from 92. *Rotherby House, Singleborough, Milton Keynes MK17 0RF* Tel (01296) 712648

HOWARD, Paul David. b 47. Lanchester Poly BA69. St Jo Coll Nottm 74. **d** 77 **p** 78. C Bedworth *Cov* 77-83; V Newchapel *Lich* 83-93; V Stretton w Claymills from 93. *The Vicarage, Church Road, Stretton, Burton-on-Trent, Staffs DE13 0HD* Tel (01283) 565141

HOWARD, Peter Leslie. b 48. Nottm Univ BTh77 Birm Univ MA80 Leeds Univ MEd91. St Jo Coll Nottm LTh77. **d** 77 **p** 78. C Gospel Lane St Mich *Birm* 77-81; P-in-c Nechells 81-85; V Stanley *Wakef* 85-92; P-in-c Nor Heartsease St Fran *Nor* from 92. *The Vicarage, 100 Rider Haggard Road, Norwich NR7 9UQ* Tel (01603) 702799

HOWARD, Reginald James (Reg). b 33. AKC60. **d** 61 **p** 62. C Shildon *Dur* 61-64; C Hurworth 64-66; V Morley St Paul *Wakef* 66-75; V Westgate Common 75-93; rtd 93. *41 Oakleigh Avenue, Wakefield, W Yorkshire WF2 9DF* Tel (01924) 373020

HOWARD, Canon Robert Weston. b 28. Pemb Coll Cam BA49 MA53. Westcott Ho Cam 51. **d** 53 **p** 54. C Bishopwearmouth St Mich *Dur* 53-56; C Cambridge Gt St Mary w St Mich *Ely* 56-60; Hong Kong 60-66; V Prenton *Ches* 66-75; RD Frodsham 74-82; P-in-c Dunham-on-the-Hill 75-77; V Helsby and Ince 75-77; V Helsby and Dunham-on-the-Hill 77-82; Hon Can Ches Cathl 78-82; V Moseley St Mary *Birm* 82-88; V Chalke Valley W *Sarum* 88-93; rtd 93; Perm to Offic *St D* from 93; Perm to Offic *Heref* from 93. *The Coach House, 13 Clun Road, Aston-on-Clun, Craven Arms, Shropshire SY7 8EW* Tel (01588) 660630

HOWARD, Ronald. b 40. AMIBF65 EngTech91. Cranmer Hall Dur 86. **d** 88 **p** 89. C Baildon *Bradf* 88-92; P-in-c Sutton 92-96; P-in-c St Tudy w St Mabyn and Michaelstow *Truro* from 96. *The Rectory, Glebe Parc, St Tudy, Bodmin, Cornwall PL30 3AS* Tel (01208) 850374

HOWARD, Canon Ronald Trevor. b 19. Pemb Coll Cam BA41 MA45. Wells Th Coll 52. **d** 54 **p** 55. C Moulsham St Jo *Chelmsf* 54-59; R Belchamp Otten w Belchamp Walter and Bulmer 59-93; RD Belchamp 75-90; Hon Can Chelmsf Cathl 79-93; rtd 93; Perm to Offic *Nor* from 93; Perm to Offic *Chelmsf* from 93. *The Old Rectory, Mendham, Harleston, Norfolk IP20 0NH* Tel (01379) 852327

HOWARD, Simon Charles. b 60. Birm Univ BA81 Westhill Coll Birm CYCW86. Ridley Hall Cam CTM92. **d** 92 **p** 93. C Cambridge St Martin *Ely* 92-96; Chapl St Bede's Sch Cam 92-96; P-in-c Earley Trinity *Ox* from 96. *15 Caraway Road, Reading RG6 2XR* Tel 0118-986 8615

HOWARD, Stanley Reginald Kekewich. b 10. St Pet Hall Ox BA31 MA35. Ridley Hall Cam 31. **d** 33 **p** 34. C Battersea St Mich *S'wark* 33-36; C Watford St Andr *St Alb* 36-39; C Margate H Trin *Cant* 39-40; R Cuxton *Roch* 40-51; V Cheltenham St Paul *Glouc* 51-76; Chapl St Cath Ho 51-68; Chapl Cheltenham Boys' Home 51-56; Chapl Cheltenham Maternity and St Paul's Hosps 61-76; rtd 76; Perm to Offic *Win* from 81. *Selah, 3 Montague Road, Bournemouth BH5 2EW* Tel (01202) 427376

HOWARD, Ms Susan. b 65. Lanc Univ BA86. Ripon Coll Cuddesdon 88. **d** 91 **p** 94. C Ditton St Mich *Liv* 91-94; C Kirkby 94-97; Adv for Youth and Young Adults *Man* from 97. *St James's Vicarage, 280 Walshaw Road, Bury, Lancs BL1 1PY* Tel 0161-764 6217

HOWARD, Thomas Norman. b 40. St Aid Birkenhead 64. **d** 67 **p** 68. C Farnworth and Kearsley *Man* 67-70; C Prestwich St Marg 70-73; V Heyside 73-85; Warden Lamplugh Ho Angl Conf Cen Thwing 85-90; Hon C Langtoft w Foxholes, Butterwick, Cottam etc *York* 85-87; C 87-90; V Fence and Newchurch-in-Pendle *Blackb* from 90; Dioc Ecum Officer 90-95. *The Vicarage, 12 Wheatcroft Avenue, Fence, Burnley, Lancs BB12 9QL* Tel (01282) 617316

HOWARD, William Alfred. b 47. St Jo Coll Dur BA69. Wycliffe Hall Ox 74. **d** 77 **p** 79. C Norbiton *S'wark* 77-80; C Mile Cross *Nor* 80-84; R Grimston w Congham 84-91; R Grimston, Congham and Roydon from 91. *The Rectory, Grimston, King's Lynn, Norfolk PE32 1BQ* Tel (01485) 600335

HOWARD-COWLEY, Joseph Charles. b 27. Trin Coll Cam BA53 MA56. Wells Th Coll 53. **d** 55 **p** 56. C Newmarket All SS *St E* 55-58; Chapl Aycliffe Approved Sch Co Dur 58-61; V Aldringham *St E* 61-86; rtd 86; Perm to Offic *St E* 86-93; Perm to Offic *Truro* from 93. *Lower Penquite, St Ive, Liskeard, Cornwall PL14 3NE* Tel (01579) 83469

HOWARD JONES, Preb Raymond Vernon. b 31. AKC54. **d** 55 **p** 56. C Hutton *Chelmsf* 55-58; CF 58-62; V Walpole St Andrew *Ely* 62-64; Chapl St Crispin's Hosp Northampton 64-70; V Brockhampton w Fawley *Heref* 70-86; V Fownhope 70-86; RD Heref Rural 77-81; Preb Heref Cathl 81-97; Communications Adv and Bp's Staff Officer 86-97; rtd 97. *Kingfishers, Breinton, Hereford HR4 7PP* Tel (01432) 279371

HOWARTH, Arthur. b 14. Dur Univ 36. **d** 37 **p** 38. C Aylesbury *Ox* 37-40; C W Wycombe 41-42; C Acton Vale St Thos *Lon* 42-43; C Fulham All SS 43-44; C Hornsey St Mary 44-46; St Vincent 46-51; Perm to Offic *Ox* 51-54; Perm to Offic *Guildf* 54; Nigeria from 55. *Bishop Lasbrey College Irete, PO Box 68, Owerri, Nigeria*

HOWARTH, Christopher. b 47. S Dios Minl Tr Scheme. **d** 83 **p** 84. NSM Uckfield *Chich* from 83; NSM Lt Horsted from 83; NSM Isfield from 83. *137 Rocks Park Road, Uckfield, E Sussex TN22 2BD* Tel (01825) 765352

HOWARTH, Geoffrey Gifford. b 21. Oak Hill Th Coll 65. **d** 66 **p** 67. C Woodford Wells *Chelmsf* 66-69; P-in-c Bootle St Mary w St Jo *Liv* 69-73; V Newburn *Newc* 73-86; rtd 86; Perm to Offic *York* from 91. *Beeches, Pickering Road East, Snainton, Scarborough, N Yorkshire YO13 9AF* Tel (01723) 859148

HOWARTH, Jack Raymond. b 13. Leeds Univ BSc34. Coll of Resurr Mirfield 34. **d** 36 **p** 37. C Anfield St Columba *Liv* 36-39 and 46-47; C Illingworth *Wakef* 39-43; Chapl RAFVR 43-46; C Birstall *Wakef* 47-48; V Harley Wood 48-52; V Manningham St Jude *Bradf* 52-63; RD Bradf 58-63; R Elland *Wakef* 63-75; RD Brighouse and Elland 70-73; V Halifax St Jo 75-78; rtd 78; Hon C Haydock St Jas *Liv* 78-86; Chapl Wigan R Infirmary 86-88. *13/4 Ladywell Road, Edinburgh EH12 7TA* Tel 0131-334 0594

HOWARTH, Leslie John. b 22. MIEH MRSH. Sarum & Wells Th Coll 75. **d** 78 **p** 79. NSM Plymouth St Gabr *Ex* from 78. *1 Wardlow Gardens, Trevannion Park, Plymouth PL6 5PU* Tel (01752) 773641

HOWARTH, Robert Francis Harvey. b 31. S'wark Ord Course 71. **d** 72 **p** 73. C St Marylebone All So w SS Pet and Jo *Lon* 72-73; C St Helen Bishopsgate w St Martin Outwich 73-78; V Harlow St Mary and St Hugh w St Jo the Bapt *Chelmsf* 78-88; P-in-c Victoria Docks Ascension 88-96; rtd 96. *Lochhill, Palnackle, Castle Douglas, Kirkudbrightshire DG7 2PW* Tel (01556) 6200363

HOWARTH, Canon Ronald. b 26. TCD BA51 MA54. Linc Th Coll 50. **d** 52 **p** 53. C Gannow *Blackb* 52-55; Nigeria 55-89; rtd 91. *4 Kingston Court, Walton Street, Oxford OX2 6ES* Tel (01865) 53046

HOWARTH, Toby Matthew. b 62. Yale Univ BA86 Birm Univ MA91. Wycliffe Hall Ox 89 Qu Coll Birm 90. **d** 92 **p** 93. C Derby St Aug *Derby* 92-95; Crosslinks from 95. *Henry Martyn Institute, 5-8-660/1/B/1 Chirag Ali Lane, PO Box 153, Hyderabad 500001, India* Tel Hyderabad (40) 201134 Fax 222483

HOWAT, Jeremy Noel Thomas. b 35. Em Coll Cam BA59 MA63. Ridley Hall Cam 59. **d** 63 **p** 64. C Sutton *Liv* 63-65; C Kirk Ella *York* 65-66; C Bridlington Quay Ch Ch 66-69; R Wheldrake 69-78; Dioc Youth Officer 70-74; SAMS from 78; Argentina 78-81 and from 90; P-in-c Newton upon Ouse *York* 81-82; V Shipton w Overton 81-82; P-in-c Skelton by York 81-82; R Skelton w Shipton and Newton on Ouse 82-89. *Almte Brown 2577, (1832) Lomas de Zamora, Prov de Buenos Aires, Argentina*

HOWDEN, Canon John Travis. b 40. RIBA62. Sarum Th Coll 66. **d** 69 **p** 70. C S Gillingham *Roch* 69-72; C Banbury *Ox* 72-73; Lic to Offic *York* 73-74; Hon C Hull Newland St Jo 74-81; Hon C Stock Harvard *Chelmsf* 82-86; R Doddinghurst and Mountnessing 86-91; P-in-c Pleshey from 91; Warden Pleshey Retreat Ho from 91; Hon Can Chelmsf Cathl *Chelmsf* from 97. *The Vicarage, The Street, Pleshey, Chelmsford CM3 1HA* Tel (01245) 237251

HOWE, Alan Raymond. b 52. Nottm Univ BTh79. St Jo Coll Nottm 76. **d** 80 **p** 81. C Southsea St Simon *Portsm* 80-83; C Bexleyheath St Pet *Roch* 83-86; TV Camberley St Paul *Guildf* 86-93; P-in-c Mansfield St Jo *S'well* 93-96; P-in-c Wollaton Park from 96. *St Mary's Vicarage, Wollaton Park, Nottingham NG8 1AF* Tel 0115-978 6988

HOWE, Charles. b 30. Lon Univ BD65 Open Univ BA79. Tyndale Hall Bris 55. **d** 58 **p** 59. C Willowfield *D & D* 58-60; C Derryloran *Arm* 60-64; C Belfast St Bart *Conn* 64-65; I Tullyaughnish w Kilmacrennan and Killygarvan *D & R* 65-72; I Londonderry St Aug 73-95; Can Derry Cathl 85-95; Dioc Org and Tutor for Aux Min 93-95; rtd 95. *2 Dunwood Park, Londonderry BT47 2NN* Tel (01504) 312305

HOWE, Canon David Randall. b 24. St Jo Coll Cam BA51 MA55. Wells Th Coll 51. **d** 53 **p** 54. C Basingstoke *Win* 53-59; V Rotherwick, Hook and Greywell 59-70; R Bossington w Broughton 70-81; R Broughton w Bossington and Mottisfont 81-86; R Broughton, Bossington, Houghton and Mottisfont 86-89; Hon Can Win Cathl 87-89; rtd 89. *Little Orchard, Hilldrop Lane, Ramsbury, Marlborough, Wilts SN8 2RB* Tel (01672) 20326

HOWE, Miss Frances Ruth. b 28. ACIB67 GSSR91. Cranmer Hall Dur IDC80. **dss** 80 **d** 87 **p** 94. Newc St Andr *Newc* 80-82; Chapl Asst R Victoria Infirmary Newc 80-87; Chapl Wylam and Fleming Ch Hosp 82-87; Chapl St Oswald's Hospice Newc 86-92; C Newc Epiphany *Newc* 87-90; rtd 92; Hon C Delaval *Newc* from 92. *18 Mason Avenue, Whitley Bay, Tyne & Wear NE26 1AQ* Tel 0191-252 5163

HOWE, Canon George Alexander. b 52. St Jo Coll Dur BA73. Westcott Ho Cam 73. **d** 75 **p** 76. C Peterlee *Dur* 75-79; C Norton St Mary 79-81; V Hart w Elwick Hall 81-85; R Sedgefield 85-91; RD Sedgefield 89-91; V Kendal H Trin *Carl* from 91; RD Kendal from 94; Hon Can Carl Cathl from 94. *Holy Trinity Vicarage, 2 Lynngarth Drive, Kendal, Cumbria LA9 4JA* Tel (01539) 721541 or 721248

HOWE, Harry Norman. b 10. United Th Coll Limuru. **d** 73 **p** 74. Kenya 73-75; C Fringford w Hethe and Newton Purcell *Ox* 75-76; rtd 76; Perm to Offic *York* 76-80; Perm to Offic *Lich* 80-93; Perm to Offic *Wakef* 84-93. *25 Brian Street, Lindley, Huddersfield HD3 3JU* Tel (01484) 648298

HOWE, Canon John. b 36. Ex Coll Ox BA58 MA63. St Steph Ho Ox 58. **d** 61 **p** 62. C Horninglow *Lich* 61-64; C Sedgley All SS 64-66; V Ocker Hill 66-73; V Gnosall 73-79; P-in-c Hoar Cross 79-82; Preb Lich Cathl 83-88; V Hoar Cross w Newchurch 83-88; Can Res Lich Cathl 88-96; I St Jo Hosp Lich from 96. *The Master's House, St John's Hospital, St John Street, Lichfield, Staffs WS13 6PB* Tel (01543) 264169

✠**HOWE, The Rt Revd John William Alexander.** b 20. St Chad's Coll Dur BA43 MA48 BD48. Gen Th Sem (NY) Hon DD74 Lambeth DD78. **d** 43 **p** 44 **c** 55. C Scarborough All SS *York* 43-46; Ghana 46-50; Vice-Prin Edin Th Coll 50-55; Hon Chapl St Mary's Cathl *Edin* 51-55; Bp St And 55-69; Exec Officer Angl Communion 69-71; Hon Can St Mary's Cathl *Glas* from 69; Sec Gen ACC 71-82; Research Fell 83-85; Can Jerusalem 76-82; rtd 85; Asst Bp Ripon from 85; Perm to Offic *Leic* from 95. *Flat 6, Stuart Court, High Street, Kibworth, Leicester LE8 0LE* Tel 0116-279 6205

HOWE, Nicholas Simon. b 60. Man Univ BA81 K Coll Lon MTh85. Ridley Hall Cam 86. **d** 88 **p** 89. C Lich St Chad *Lich* 88-92; TV Leeds City *Ripon* from 92. *Holy Trinity Vicarage, 28 Hawkswood Avenue, Leeds LS5 3PN* Tel 0113-259 0031

HOWE, Canon Rex Alan. b 29. Ch Coll Cam BA53 MA57. Coll of Resurr Mirfield 53. **d** 55 **p** 56. C Barnsley St Pet *Wakef* 55-57; C Helmsley *York* 57-60; V Middlesbrough St Martin 60-67; V Redcar 67-73; V Kirkleatham 67-73; RD Guisborough 67-73; Dean Hong Kong 73-76; Adn 75-76; TR Grantham *Linc* 77-85; RD Grantham 78-85; Can and Preb Linc Cathl 81-85; V Canford Cliffs and Sandbanks *Sarum* 85-94; RD Poole 92-94; rtd 94. *Little Over, Mead Road, Corfe Castle, Wareham, Dorset BH20 5EW* Tel (01929) 480528

HOWE, Canon Ronald Douglas. b 38. K Coll Lon BD62 AKC62 LSE DSA63 Leic Univ MA95. **d** 64 **p** 65. C Hendon All SS Childs Hill *Lon* 64-67; C Northampton St Mary *Pet* 67-69; V Potterspury w Furtho and Yardley Gobion 69-81; R Corby Epiphany w St Jo 81-86; RD Corby 81-90 and from 95; V Brigstock w Stanion 86-95; P-in-c Lowick w Sudborough and Slipton 94-95; R Brigstock w Stanion and Lowick and

Sudborough from 95; Can Pet Cathl from 95. *The Rectory, Brigstock, Kettering, Northants NN14 3EX* Tel (01536) 373371

HOWE, Roy William. b 38. ALCD67. **d** 66 **p** 67. C Bradf Cathl *Bradf* 66-70; C Barnoldswick w Bracewell 70-72; V Yeadon St Jo 72-79; P-in-c Bainton *York* 79-86; P-in-c Middleton-on-the-Wolds 79-86; P-in-c N Dalton 79-86; RD Harthill 81-87; C Watton w Beswick and Kilnwick 82-86; R Bainton w N Dalton, Middleton-on-the-Wolds etc 86-87; TV Penrith w Newton Reigny and Plumpton Wall *Carl* 87-92; Dioc Chapl to Agric and Rural Life 87-92; V Cornhill w Carham *Newc* from 92; V Branxton from 92. *The Vicarage, The Old School House, Branxton, Cornhill-on-Tweed, Northd TD12 4SW* Tel (01890) 820368

HOWE, William Ernest. b 25. ARICS51. Westcott Ho Cam 68. **d** 70 **p** 71. C Anston *Sheff* 70-73; V 84-92; C Woodsetts 70-73; V Greasbrough 73-84; rtd 92; Perm to Offic *Sheff* from 92. *18 New Cottages, Worksop, Notts S80 3PE* Tel (01909) 479618

HOWELL, Alfred. b 32. Wells Th Coll 57. **d** 59 **p** 60. C Ferryhill *Dur* 59-61; C Tankersley *Sheff* 61-63; V New Edlington 63-66; V Sparkbrook Ch Ch *Birm* 66-73; Lic to Offic *Chelmsf* 73-83; P-in-c Brentwood St Geo 83-88; rtd 88; Perm to Offic *Chich* from 88. *Windy Corner, Grove Lane, Iden, Rye, E Sussex TN31 7QA* Tel (01797) 280564

HOWELL, Andrew John. b 44. Clifton Th Coll 68. **d** 71 **p** 72. C Halliwell St Pet *Man* 71-77; V Facit 77-95; P-in-c Smallbridge and Wardle from 95. *The Vicarage, 151 Wardle Road, Rochdale, Lancs OL12 9JA* Tel (01706) 713529

HOWELL, Canon Basil Rayson. b 20. St Pet Hall Ox BA49 MA53. Wycliffe Hall Ox 49. **d** 51 **p** 52. C Worksop St Jo *S'well* 51-54; C-in-c Worksop St Paul CD 54-61; V Blundellsands St Nic *Liv* 61-81; RD Bootle 69-78; Hon Can Liv Cathl 78-81; rtd 81; Perm to Offic *Cov* from 81. *9 Arlington Court, Arlington Avenue, Leamington Spa, Warks CV32 5HR* Tel (01926) 314746

HOWELL, David. b 29. Clifton Th Coll 56. **d** 59 **p** 60. C Tipton St Martin *Lich* 59-62; V W Bromwich St Paul Golds Hill 62-71; V Deptford St Jo *S'wark* 71-81; Dir and Chapl Home of Divine Healing Crowhurst 81-89; rtd 90; Dir Ch Coun for Health and Healing 91-93; Hon Dioc Adv on Health and Healing *B & W* from 93. *60 Andrew Allan Road, Rockwell Green, Wellington, Somerset TA21 9DY* Tel (01823) 664529

HOWELL (formerly WILLIAMS), David Paul. b 61. Coll of Resurr Mirfield 91. **d** 93 **p** 94. C Leic St Aid *Leic* from 93. *26 Chevin Avenue, Braunstone, Leicester LE3 6PZ* Tel 0116-287 2558

HOWELL, Donald Martin. b 32. Lon Univ BD56. **d** 95 **p** 96. NSM Aylmerton w Runton *Nor* 95-96; NSM Holt w High Kelling from 96. *8 The Beeches, Station Road, Holt, Norfolk NR25 6AU* Tel (01263) 713397

HOWELL, Geoffrey Peter. b 52. LTCL82 Selw Coll Cam BA75 MA78. Cranmer Hall Dur 85. **d** 87 **p** 88. C Hartlepool St Luke *Dur* 87-90; TV Burford I *Heref* 90-94; TV Burford II w Greete and Hope Bagot 90-94; TV Burford III w Lt Heref 90-94; TV Tenbury 90-94; TV Tenbury St Mich 94; P-in-c Cradley w Mathon and Storridge from 94. *The Rectory, Cradley, Malvern, Worcs WR13 5LQ* Tel (01886) 880438

HOWELL, John Anthony Neil Belville. b 39. Man Univ BA64. St Deiniol's Hawarden 77. **d** 79 **p** 81. C Wistaston *Ches* 79-82; P-in-c Derry Hill *Sarum* 82-83; V Clayton *Bradf* from 83. *The Vicarage, Clayton Lane, Clayton, Bradford, W Yorkshire BD14 6AX* Tel (01274) 880373

HOWELL, Martin John Hope. b 38. Bris Univ BA62. Tyndale Hall Bris 59. **d** 64 **p** 65. C Bolton St Paul *Man* 64-67; C Bishopsworth *Bris* 67-70; V Swindon St Aug 70-81; TR Stratton St Margaret w S Marston etc 81-93; RD Cricklade 88; RD Highworth 88-93; Chapl Lee Abbey from 93; Lic to Offic *Ex* from 93. *Lee Abbey Fellowship, Lynton, Devon EX35 6JJ* Tel (01598) 752621 Fax 752619

HOWELL, Roger Brian. b 43. ALCD67. **d** 67 **p** 68. C Battersea Park St Sav *S'wark* 67-71; C Southgate *Chich* 71-76; V Pendeen *Truro* 76-81; P-in-c Sancreed 76-81; V Bedgrove *Ox* 81-91; R Purley from 91; RD Bradfield from 94. *The Rectory, 1 Westridge Avenue, Purley, Reading RG8 8DE* Tel 0118-941 7727

HOWELL, Ronald William Fullerton. b 51. Man Univ BA72 CertEd Ox Univ BA78 MA. Ripon Coll Cuddesdon 76. **d** 79 **p** 80. C Newc St Fran *Newc* 79-81; C Warmsworth *Sheff* 81-82; Dioc Educn Officer 82-85; V Millhouses H Trin 85-93; R Thornhill and Whitley Lower *Wakef* 93-96. *East House, 10 Woodbridge Road East, Ipswich IP4 5PA* Tel (01473) 727309

HOWELL, Preb Walter Ernest. b 17. St D Coll Lamp BA49. **d** 50 **p** 51. C Bromley St Mich *Lon* 50-56; V Somers Town St Mary 56-68; V Kentish Town St Benet and All SS 68-79; Preb St Paul's Cathl 78-84; V Alexandra Park St Sav 79-84; rtd 84; Perm to Offic *York* from 90. *6 Wattlers Close, Copmanthorpe, York YO2 3XR* Tel (01904) 702615

HOWELL-JONES, Peter. b 62. Huddersfield Poly BMus84 Bretton Hall Coll PGCE85. St Jo Coll Nottm DTS92 DipMM93 MA96. **d** 93 **p** 94. C Walsall *Lich* from 93. *164 Birmingham Road, Walsall WS1 2NJ* Tel (01922) 645445

HOWELLS, Alun. b 24. St D Coll Lamp 62. **d** 64 **p** 65. C Carmarthen St Dav *St D* 64-70; V Llandyssilio and Egremont 70-71; V Llanboidy and Meidrim 71-81; V Meidrim and Llanboidy and Merthyr 81-88; rtd 88. *Aweltwywi Residential Home, Bethlehem Road, Ffairfach, Llandeilo SA19 6SY* Tel (01558) 822556

HOWELLS, Canon Arthur Glyn. b 32. Univ of Wales (Lamp) BA54. St Mich Coll Llan 54. **d** 56 **p** 57. C Oystermouth *S & B* 56-58; C Llangyfelach and Morriston 58-64; R Llandefalle and Llyswen w Boughrood etc 64-69; Youth Chapl 67-71; V Landore 70-80; Dioc Missr 80-89; Can Brecon Cathl 80-89; Can Treas 89-94; Dir St Mary's Coll Swansea 82-89; V Swansea St Jas *S & B* from 89; Chan Brecon Cathl from 94; RD Swansea from 96. *The Vicarage, 1 Ffynone Drive, Swansea SA1 6DB* Tel (01792) 470532

HOWELLS, David. b 55. Grey Coll Dur BA78. Ripon Coll Cuddesdon 79. **d** 81 **p** 82. C Birtley *Dur* 81-84; Canada from 84. *127 Glasgow Street North, Guelph, Ontario, Canada N1H 4W5*

HOWELLS, David Morgan. b 24. Qu Coll Birm 72. **d** 75 **p** 76. NSM Radford *Cov* 75-87; rtd 87; Perm to Offic *Cov* from 87. *21 Banks Road, Coventry CV6 1JT* Tel (01203) 598118

HOWELLS, Canon Donald Lockwood. b 20. Lon Univ BA43. Oak Hill Th Coll 39. **d** 43 **p** 44. C Wandsworth St Mich *S'wark* 43-45; C Foord St Jo *Cant* 45-48; C Watford St Mary *St Alb* 48-49; V Weston 49-54; C Stevenage 54-57; R Knebworth 57-66; R Tring 66-80; P-in-c Aldbury 78-80; P-in-c Puttenham w Long Marston 79-80; Hon Can St Alb 80-85; RD Berkhamsted 80-85; TR Tring 80-85; rtd 85; Perm to Offic *Cant* from 85. *10 Cadram Close, Canterbury, Kent CT2 7SD* Tel (01227) 462835

HOWELLS, Euryl. b 60. Univ of Wales (Cardiff) BD93. St Mich Coll Llan 90. **d** 93 **p** 94. C Newcastle Emlyn w Llandyfriog etc *St D* 93-97; V Llangeler w Pen-Boyr from 97. *The Vicarage, Llangeler, Llandysul SA44 5EX* Tel (01559) 371170

HOWELLS, Garfield Edwin (Gary). b 18. K Coll Lon 53 St Boniface Warminster 53. **d** 54 **p** 55. C Sanderstead All SS *S'wark* 54-57; CF 57-60; R Kingsdown *Roch* 60-64; Australia from 64; rtd 83. *137 Fendam Street, Warnbro, W Australia 6169* Tel Perth (9) 593 1819

HOWELLS, Gordon. b 39. Univ of Wales (Cardiff) BSc61 DipEd62. Ripon Coll Cuddesdon 86. **d** 88 **p** 89. C Atherstone *Cov* 88-89; C Lillington 89-92; V Clymping and Yapton w Ford *Chich* 92-97; P-in-c Rackheath and Salhouse *Nor* from 97; Chapl to the Deaf from 97. *The Rectory, Stone Hill, Rackheath, Norwich NR13 6NG* Tel (01603) 720097

HOWELLS, Lucinda Jane Reid. b 57. Dur Univ BA78. Ripon Coll Cuddesdon 79. **dss** 81 **d** 85 **p** 85. Birtley *Dur* 81-84; Canada from 84. *127 Glasgow Street North, Guelph, Ontario, Canada N1H 4W5*

HOWELLS, Neil. b 23. Qu Mary Coll Lon BSc48. Bps' Coll Cheshunt 48. **d** 50 **p** 51. C Cowley St Jas *Ox* 50-54; C Forest Hill 54-56; Min Headington St Mary 56-60; V Maidenhead St Luke 60-68; Chapl Maidenhead Gen Hosp 60-68; R Welford w Wickham 68-73; R Welford w Wickham and Gt Shefford 73-77; RD Newbury 73-77; V Bray and Braywood 77-84; rtd 84; Perm to Offic *Sarum* from 85. *19 Loders, Bridport, Dorset DT6 3SA* Tel (01308) 456490

HOWELLS, Richard Grant. b 62. Univ of Wales (Lamp) BA83. Westcott Ho Cam 83 and 92. **d** 93 **p** 94. NSM Harston w Hauxton *Ely* from 93. *The Old School House, 8 High Street, Harston, Cambridge CB2 5PX* Tel (01223) 871902

HOWELLS, Mrs Sandra Jane. b 52. FBDO77. LNSM course. **d** 93 **p** 97. NSM Caerwent w Dinham and Llanfair Discoed etc *Mon* from 93. *3 Lancaster Way, Chepstow NP6 5SJ* Tel (01291) 620460

HOWELLS, William Gordon. b 26. **d** 61 **p** 62. C Aberdare St Jo *Llan* 61-64; C Coity w Nolton 64-67; C Northam *Ex* 67-71; V Bishops Tawton 71-76; V Cofton w Starcross 76-80; R Aveton Gifford 80-86; V Modbury 80-86; TV Lynton, Brendon, Countisbury, Lynmouth etc 86-91; rtd 91; Perm to Offic *Ex* from 91. *Umtali, Golf Links Road, Westward Ho!, Bideford, Devon EX39 1HH* Tel (01237) 473578

HOWES, Alan. b 49. Chich Th Coll 76. **d** 79 **p** 80. C Bilborough St Jo *S'well* 79-82; TV Newark w Hawton, Cotham and Shelton 82-89; TV Newark 89-94; P-in-c Coseley St Chad *Worc* 94-96; V from 96. *St Chad's Vicarage, 3 Oak Street, Coseley, Bilston, W Midlands WV14 9TA* Tel (01902) 882285

HOWES, David. b 30. Open Univ BA75. Roch Th Coll 62. **d** 64 **p** 65. C Highweek *Ex* 64-67; C Clyst St George 67-71; P-in-c Woolfardisworthy w Kennerleigh 71-72; P-in-c Washford Pyne w Puddington 71-72; TR N Creedy 72-73; Perm to Offic 74-77; C Walworth *S'wark* 77-78; C-in-c Roundshaw CD 78-83; R S'wark St Geo 83-90; P-in-c S'wark St Jude 84-90; P-in-c Risley *Derby* 90-93; Bp's Ind Adv 90-93; Perm to Offic from 93; rtd 93. *44 Ash Grove, Stapleford, Nottingham NG9 7EL* Tel 0115-939 3041

HOWES, Miss Judith Elizabeth. b 44. SRN RSCN. Ripon Coll Cuddesdon 83. **d** 89 **p** 94. Par Dn Ex St Sidwell and St Matt *Ex* 89-92; Par Dn Brixham w Churston Ferrers and Kingswear 92-94; C 94-95; TV E Darlington *Dur* from 95. *St John's House, 58 Windermere Court, Darlington, Co Durham DL1 4YW* Tel (01325) 360798

HOWES, Michael John Norton. b 43. Hull Univ BA66. Linc Th Coll 66. **d** 68 **p** 69. C Gt Berkhamsted *St Alb* 68-71; C Ampthill w Millbrook and Steppingley 71-72; Chapl RAF 72-88; V Thurlby w Carlby *Linc* 88-95; V Ness Gp 95-97; R Bassingham from 97; V

Aubourn w Haddington from 97; V Carlton-le-Moorland w Stapleford from 97; R Thurlby w Norton Disney from 97. *The Rectory, Torgate Lane, Bassingham, Lincoln LN5 9HF* Tel (01522) 788383 or 750952

HOWES, Canon Norman Vincent. b 36. AKC61. **d** 62 **p** 63. C Radford *Cov* 62-66; V Napton on the Hill 66-72; V Exhall 72-83; R Walton D'Eiville from 83; V Wellesbourne from 83; RD Fosse 87-93; Hon Can Cov Cathl from 89. *The Vicarage, Wellesbourne, Warwick CV35 9LS* Tel (01789) 840262

✠**HOWES, The Rt Revd Peter Henry Herbert.** b 11. OBE61 PBS63. Kelham Th Coll 29. **d** 34 **p** 35 **c** 76. C Norton St Mich *Dur* 34-37; Sarawak 37-38 and 40-63; Br N Borneo 38-40; Malaysia 63-81; Can Borneo 55-62; Adn Sarawak 61-62; Adn Kuching 62-65; Can Kuching 62-71; Adn Brunei and N Sarawak 65-71; Asst Bp Kuching 76-81; rtd 81; Perm to Offic *York* from 91. *7 Tower Place, York YO1 1RZ* Tel (01904) 638050

HOWITT, Ivan Richard. b 56. Kent Univ BA81. Sarum & Wells Th Coll 83. **d** 85 **p** 86. C Herne Bay Ch Ch *Cant* 85-87; C St Laurence in the Isle of Thanet 87-90; R Owmby and Normanby w Glentham *Linc* 90-91; P-in-c Spridlington w Saxby and Firsby 90-91; R Owmby Gp from 91; P-in-c Hackthorn w Cold Hanworth from 93; RD Lawres from 96. *The Rectory, Owmby-by-Spital, Market Rasen, Lincs LN8 2HL* Tel (01673) 878275

HOWITT, John Leslie. b 28. Lon Coll of Div 60. **d** 62 **p** 63. C Attenborough w Bramcote *S'well* 62-66; Chapl Rampton Hosp Retford 66-71; P-in-c Treswell and Cottam *S'well* 68-71; Chapl HM Pris Cardiff 71-75; Chapl HM Youth Cust Cen Dover 75-79; Chapl HM Pris Dartmoor 79-83; Chapl HM Pris Cant 83-87; Chapl HM Det Cen Aldington 83-87; Perm to Offic *Cant* 87-88; V Shobnall *Lich* 88-94; rtd 94; Perm to Offic *Chich* from 94. *6 Park View Road, Hove, E Sussex BN3 7BF*

HOWLAND, Miss Ada Lilian. b 08. St Andr Ho Portsm 47. **dss** 50 **d** 87. Edge Hill St Cath *Liv* 50-52; Australia 52-59; Southsea St Pet *Portsm* 60-74; rtd 74; Portsm Cathl *Portsm* 74-87; Perm to Offic from 87. *The Home of Comfort, 17/19 Victoria Grove, Southsea, Hants PO5 1NF* Tel (01705) 753480

HOWLAND, Ms Pamela Isobel. b 29. Lady Mabel Coll CertEd71. Qu Coll Birm 79. **dss** 82 **d** 87. Thorpe Edge *Bradf* 82-89; Par Dn 87-89; rtd 89. *308 Moorview Way, Skipton, N Yorkshire BD23 2TW* Tel (01756) 700725

HOWLDEN, Paul Wilfrid. b 41. Trin Coll Cam BA63 MA67. Cuddesdon Coll 64. **d** 66 **p** 67. C Paulsgrove *Portsm* 66-73; Hon C Ealing Ascension Hanger Hill *Lon* 75-87; R Bishops Waltham *Portsm* 87-88; Perm to Offic 89-91; Perm to Offic *Chich* from 91. *33 Chamberlain Grove, Fareham, Hants PO14 1HH* Tel (01329) 233035

HOWLES, Kenneth. b 56. Oak Hill Th Coll DipHE93. **d** 93 **p** 94. C Leyland St Andr *Blackb* 93-96; C Livesey from 96; C Ewood from 96. *Elwood Vicarage, Bolton Road, Blackburn BB2 4LA* Tel (01254) 51206 E-mail 100657.3100@compuserve.com.

HOWLETT, Richard Laurence. b 56. Trin Coll Bris. **d** 94 **p** 95. C Louth *Linc* from 94. *15 Grosvenor Crescent, Louth, Lincs LN11 0BD* Tel (01507) 603635

HOWLETT, Victor John. b 43. S Dios Minl Tr Scheme 90. **d** 93 **p** 94. NSM Bris St Andr w St Bart *Bris* 93-95; Hon C Bris St Matt and St Nath 95-96; Hon C Bishopston 95-96; C Gtr Corsham from 96. *7B Lypiatt Road, Corsham, Wilts SN13 9JB* Tel (01249) 712619

HOWSE, Elizabeth Ann. *See* SMITH, Mrs Elizabeth Ann

HOWSON, Canon George Webster. b 15. Man Univ BA46. Sarum Th Coll 47. **d** 49 **p** 50. C Liscard St Mary *Ches* 49-52; C Astbury 52-53; V Seacombe 53-60; V Over St Chad 60-80; RD Middlewich 74-80; rtd 80; Perm to Offic *Ches* from 80. *58 Mount Drive, Nantwich, Cheshire CW5 6JQ* Tel (01270) 627870

HOY, Michael John. b 30. Reading Univ BSc52. Oak Hill Th Coll 57. **d** 59 **p** 60. C Worthing St Geo *Chich* 59-62; C Tulse Hill H Trin *S'wark* 62-66; R Danby Wiske w Yafforth and Hutton Bonville *Ripon* 66-76; V Camelsdale *Chich* 76-87; V Gt Marsden *Blackb* 87-96; rtd 96. *35 Hardwick Park, Banbury, Oxon OX16 7YF* Tel (01295) 268744

HOY, Stephen Anthony. b 55. Leeds Poly BA76. Linc Th Coll 92. **d** 94 **p** 95. C Glen Parva and S Wigston *Leic* from 94. *163 Little Glen Road, Leicester LE2 8TX* Tel 0116-277 4275

HOYAL, Richard Dunstan. b 47. Ch Ch Ox BA67 MA71 BA78. Ripon Coll Cuddesdon 76. **d** 79 **p** 80. C Stevenage St Geo *St Alb* 79-83; V Monk Bretton *Wakef* 83-89; V Ilkley St Marg *Bradf* from 89; Dir of Ords from 96. *St Margaret's Vicarage, 14 Queen's Road, Ilkley, W Yorkshire LS29 9QJ* Tel (01943) 607015

HOYE, Reginald George. b 16. Tyndale Hall Bris 58. **d** 60 **p** 61. C Penn Fields *Lich* 60-62; V Nottingham St Sav *S'well* 62-82; rtd 82; Perm to Offic *S'well* from 82. *1 White Acre, Burton Joyce, Nottingham NG14 5BU* Tel 0115-931 2485

HOYLAND, John Gregory. b 50. Sussex Univ BEd73. Wycliffe Hall Ox 75. **d** 78 **p** 79. C Pudsey St Lawr *Bradf* 78-81; P-in-c Long Preston 81-84; P-in-c Long Preston w Tosside 84; V 84; CPAS Staff 85-87; Chapl Univ Coll of Ripon and York St Jo from 87. *College of Ripon and York, Lord Mayor's Walk, York YO3 7EX* Tel (01904) 656771

HOYLE, Dr David Michael. b 57. CCC Cam BA80 MA83 DPhil91. Ripon Coll Cuddesdon 84. **d** 86 **p** 87. C Chesterton Gd Shep *Ely* 86-88; Chapl and Fell Magd Coll Cam 88-91; Dean and Fell 91-95; V Southgate Ch Ch *Lon* from 95. *Christ Church Vicarage, 1 The Green, London N14 7EG* Tel 0181-886 0384

HOYLE, Lawrence. b 27. St Aid Birkenhead 52. **d** 55 **p** 56. C Halifax All So *Wakef* 55-57; C Bromley SS Pet and Paul *Roch* 57-59; V Widnes St Ambrose *Liv* 59-61; R Lanteglos by Camelford w Advent *Truro* 61-66; V Wrose *Bradf* 66-70; R Thwing *York* 70-81; V Wold Newton 71-81; Warden Lamplugh Ho Conf Cen 72-85; Dir Angl Renewal Min 81-89; Hon C Starbeck *Ripon* 87-89; rtd 89; Perm to Offic *Ex* from 92. *30 Highfield Drive, Waterside Park, Kingsbridge, Devon TQ7 1JR* Tel (01548) 856109

HOYLE, Pamela Margaret. *See* CLOCKSIN, Mrs Pamela Margaret

HRYZIUK, Petro. b 57. Lanc Univ BEd80. St Jo Coll Nottm DipTh89. **d** 90 **p** 91. C Huyton St Geo *Liv* 90-93; C Goose Green 93-96; C Wavertree H Trin from 96. *24 Orford Street, Liverpool L15 8HX* Tel 0151-733 1989

HUARD, The Ven Geoffrey Robert. b 43. Lon Univ DipTh71. Clifton Th Coll 64. **d** 70 **p** 71. C Barking St Marg *Chelmsf* 70-73; C Everton St Ambrose w St Tim *Liv* 73-74; C Everton St Pet 74-76; Australia from 76; Adn Sydney and Cumberland 89-93; Adn Liverpool from 93. *27 Hurlstone Avenue, Hurlstone Park, Sydney, NSW, Australia 2193* Tel Sydney (2) 265 1555 Fax 558 3817

HUBAND, Eric Bob. b 27. Bris Univ BSc50. Sarum Th Coll 50. **d** 52 **p** 53. C Lockleaze St Fran CD *Bris* 52-56; C Bishopsworth 56-60; V Greenbank 60-67; V Hengrove 67-77; R E Horsley *Guildf* 77-92; rtd 92; Perm to Offic *Bris* from 92. *23 Hardens Mead, Chippenham, Wilts SN15 3AE* Tel (01249) 661219

HUBAND, Richard William. b 39. Trin Coll Cam BA62 MA66. Qu Coll Birm 76. **d** 78 **p** 79. C Norton *St Alb* 78-81; R Aspley Guise w Husborne Crawley and Ridgmont 81-91; V Elstow from 91. *The Abbey Vicarage, Elstow, Bedford MK42 9XT* Tel (01234) 261477

HUBBARD, Christopher Maurice. b 25. Trin Coll Cam BA49 MA69. Chich Th Coll 51. **d** 53 **p** 54. C Ringwood *Win* 53-56; Canada 56-60; C Holdenhurst *Win* 60; C-in-c Holdenhurst St Barn CD 61-65; V Wymeswold *Leic* 65-72; R Lambley *S'well* 72-77; Chapl HM Youth Cust Cen Lowdham Grange 74-77; P-in-c Chilbolton cum Wherwell *Win* 77-79; R 79-90; rtd 90. *Bridge House, High Street, Stockbridge, Hants SO20 6HB* Tel (01264) 810302

HUBBARD, David Harris. b 33. St Pet Hall Ox BA57 MA61 K Coll Lon MTh88. Ridley Hall Cam 59. **d** 60 **p** 61. C Dalston St Mark w St Bart *Lon* 60-63; C Stoke Newington St Olave 63-67; Hon C 67-68; Hon C Hornsey Ch Ch 69-70; V 70-82; AD W Haringey 78-85; V Highgate All SS from 82. *All Saints' Vicarage, 1B Church Road, London N6 4QH* Tel 0181-340 1123

HUBBARD, Mrs Elisabeth Ann. b 41. EAMTC 82. **dss** 85 **d** 87 **p** 94. Cambridge H Trin w St Andr Gt *Ely* 85-86; Cherry Hinton St Jo 86-87; Par Dn 87-92; Par Dn Milton 92-94; C 94-95; R Willingham from 95; R Rampton from 95. *The Rectory, Willingham, Cambridge CB4 5ES* Tel (01954) 261225

HUBBARD, Ian Maxwell. b 43. FCollP83 ACP83 Surrey Univ BEd84 Golds Coll Lon MA86. Sarum & Wells Th Coll 69. **d** 73 **p** 74. Hon C S'wark H Trin w St Matt *S'wark* 73-78; Hon C Camberwell St Mich w All So w Em 78-87; Hon C Dulwich St Barn 87-90; C Battersea St Mary 90-91; C Battersea St Mary 91-92; V Winscombe *B & W* from 92. *The Vicarage, Winscombe Hill, Winscombe, Avon BS25 1DE* Tel (01934) 843164

HUBBARD, Julian Richard Hawes. b 55. Em Coll Cam BA76 MA81. Wycliffe Hall Ox BA80 MA85. **d** 81 **p** 82. C Fulham St Dionis Parson's Green *Lon* 81-84; Tutor Wycliffe Hall Ox 84-89; Chapl Jes Coll Ox 84-89; Selection Sec ACCM 89-91; Sen Selection Sec ABM 91-93; Perm to Offic *Guildf* 89-93; V Bourne from 93; RD Farnham from 96. *The Vicarage, 2 Middle Avenue, Farnham, Surrey GU9 8JL* Tel (01252) 715505

HUBBARD, Laurence Arthur (Laurie). b 36. Qu Coll Cam BA60 MA64. Wycliffe Hall Ox 60 CMS Tr Coll Chislehurst 65 CMS Tr Coll Selly Oak 93. **d** 62 **p** 63. C Widcombe *B & W* 62-65; Kenya 66-73; V Pype Hayes *Birm* 73-79; P-in-c Norwich-over-the-Water Colegate St Geo *Nor* 79-85; P-in-c Nor St Aug w St Mary 79-85; CMS from 85; Area Sec (Dios Cant and Roch) CMS 85-93; Perm to Offic *Cant* 85-93; Syria from 93. *All Saints Community Church, PO Box 11129, Damascus, Syria*

HUBBARD, Roy Oswald. b 32. Lich Th Coll 62. **d** 64 **p** 65. C Baswich *Lich* 64-68; P-in-c Ash 68-70; V Stevenage St Pet Broadwater *St Alb* 71-78; V Flitwick 78-90; RD Ampthill 87-90; R Sharnbrook and Knotting w Souldrop 90-96; rtd 96. *11 Cowslip Close, Rushden, Northants NN10 0UD* Tel (01933) 419210

HUBBARD-JONES, Ms Judith Frances. b 49. St Alb Minl Tr Scheme 79. **dss** 82 **d** 87 **p** 94. Hemel Hempstead *St Alb* 82-86; Longden and Annscroft w Pulverbatch *Heref* 86-87; NSM 87-97; Vice-Prin Glouc and Heref Sch for Min 92-94; Acting Prin W of England Minl Tr Course 94-95; Vice-Prin 95-97; Cathl Chapl and Visitors' Officer *Glouc* from 97. *10 College Green, Gloucester GL1 2LX* Tel (01452) 300655 Fax as telephone

HUBBLE, Canon Raymond Carr (Ray). b 30. Wm Temple Coll Rugby 60. **d** 61 **p** 62. C Newbold w Dunston *Derby* 61-64; Chapl RAF 64-80; Asst Chapl-in-Chief RAF 80-85; QHC 84-85; P-in-c Odiham w S Warnborough and Long Sutton *Win* 85; P-in-c Odiham 85-86; V 86-95; RD Odiham 88-95; Hon Can Win Cathl 94-95; rtd 95. *Dormers, Centre Lane, Everton, Lymington, Hants SO41 0JP*

HUBBLE, Trevor Ernest. b 46. Chich Th Coll 70. **d** 76 **p** 77. C Eltham St Barn *S'wark* 76-79; Lesotho 80-87; Adn S Lesotho 84-87; S Africa from 87. *PO Box 33, Matatiele, 4730 South Africa* Tel Matatiele (373) 3589

HUBERT, Brother. *See* COPINGER, Stephen Hubert Augustine

HUCKETT, Andrew William. b 50. AKC72. St Aug Coll Cant 72. **d** 73 **p** 74. C Chipping Sodbury and Old Sodbury *Glouc* 73-76; Miss to Seamen from 76; Chapl Flushing Miss to Seamen *Eur* 76-79; Teesside 79-82; Chapl and Hon Sec Milford Haven 86-92; Perm to Offic *St D* 86-92; Chapl Medway Ports from 92; Perm to Offic *Cant* from 92. *27 The Finches, Sittingbourne, Kent ME10 4PY* Tel (01795) 472851 Fax as telephone

HUCKLE, John Walford. b 39. EMMTC. **d** 89 **p** 90. C Nottingham St Pet and St Jas *S'well* from 89; Commercial Chapl Nottingham City Cen from 89; Dioc Adv on Ind Soc from 96. *43 Bingham Road, Radcliffe-on-Trent, Nottingham NG12 2FY* Tel 0115-933 2278 or 948 3658

HUCKLE, Peter. b 46. Ox Univ Inst of Educn CertEd69 Auckland Univ DipPE71 DipEd71. **d** 90 **p** 91. New Zealand 90-91; Hon C N Walsham w Antingham *Nor* 91-92; C Gt Yarmouth 92-94; TV 94-96; Min Can and Chapl St Paul's Cathl *Lon* 96-97; Perm to Offic *Eur* from 97. *c/o The British Embassy, 1 Ploutarchou Street, Athens, Greece* Tel Athens (1) 801-5335

HUCKLE, Stephen Leslie. b 48. Ch Ch Ox BA70 BA72 MA74. Coll of Resurr Mirfield 73. **d** 75 **p** 76. C Wednesbury St Paul Wood Green *Lich* 75-78; C Aylesbury *Ox* 78-85; C Farnham Royal w Hedgerley 85-88; V Fenny Stratford from 88. *The Vicarage, Manor Road, Fenny Stratford, Milton Keynes MK2 2HW* Tel (01908) 372825

HUCKLE, Sydney George. b 16. Oak Hill Th Coll 76. **d** 79 **p** 80. Hon C Wakes Colne w Chappel *Chelmsf* 79-80; Hon C Aldham 80-81; Hon C Marks Tey 80-81; Hon C Marks Tey w Aldham and Lt Tey from 81. *5 Orchard Close, Hallow, Worcester WR2 6LA* Tel (01905) 640818

HUDD, Philip Simon. b 68. Westmr Coll Ox BA90. Westcott Ho Cam 91. **d** 93 **p** 94. C Kirkby *Liv* from 93. *St Mark's Vicarage, Brook Hay Drive, Kirkby, Liverpool L33 9TE* Tel 0151-546 2645

HUDDLESON, Robert Roulston. b 32. QUB BA55 TCD Div Test57. **d** 57 **p** 58. C Ballymena *Conn* 57-59; C Belfast St Jas 59-63; Ethiopia 65-69; Exec Asst WCC Geneva 69-75; Dep Sec Gen Syn Bd for Miss and Unity 75-81; Admin Sec *Dur* 81-86; Lic to Offic 81-86; Dioc Sec *Ex* 86-97; Lic to Offic 86-97; rtd 97. *Yelverton, Bugford, Lapford, Crediton, Devon EX17 6AA*

✠**HUDDLESTON, The Most Revd Ernest Urban Trevor.** b 13. Ch Ch Ox BA34 MA38 Aber Univ Hon DD56 Lanc Univ Hon DLitt72. Wells Th Coll 35. **d** 36 **p** 37 **c** 60. C Swindon New Town *Bris* 36-39; CR from 41; Novice Guardian CR Mirfield 56-58; Prior Lon Ho 58-60; S Africa 43-56; Bp Masasi 60-68; Suff Bp Stepney *Lon* 68-78; Bp Mauritius 78-83; Abp Indian Ocean 78-83; rtd 83. *House of the Resurrection, Mirfield, W Yorkshire WF14 0BN* Tel (01924) 494318

HUDDLESTON, Geoffrey Roger. b 36. TCD BA63 MA67. Ridley Hall Cam 63. **d** 65 **p** 66. C Tonbridge SS Pet and Paul *Roch* 65-69; Chapl RAF 69-85; V Lyonsdown H Trin *St Alb* from 85; RD Barnet from 94. *Holy Trinity Vicarage, 18 Lyonsdown Road, Barnet, Herts EN5 1JE* Tel 0181-449 0382

HUDGHTON, John Francis. b 56. BA. Cranmer Hall Dur 81. **d** 83 **p** 84. C Stockport St Geo *Ches* 83-85; C Witton 85-87; C Stockport St Alb Hall Street 87-90; V Thornton le Moors w Ince and Elton 90-95; Chapl RAF from 95; Perm to Offic *Llan* from 95. *Chaplaincy Services (RAF), HQ, Personnel and Training Command, RAF Ainsworth, Gloucester GL3 1EZ* Tel (01452) 712612 ext 5164 Fax 510828

HUDSON, Andrew Julian. b 57. Cranmer Hall Dur CTMin93. **d** 93 **p** 94. C Moldgreen *Wakef* from 93. *3 Forest Road, Huddersfield HD5 8EU* Tel (01484) 514203

HUDSON, Anthony George. b 39. N Ord Course. **d** 84 **p** 85. C Harrogate St Mark *Ripon* 84-87; P-in-c Hampsthwaite 87-96; P-in-c Killinghall 87-94; V Hampsthwaite and Killinghall from 96. *The Vicarage, Church Lane, Hampsthwaite, Harrogate, N Yorkshire HG3 2HB* Tel (01423) 770337

HUDSON, Brainerd Peter de Wirtz Goodwin. b 34. K Coll Lon BD57 AKC57. Westcott Ho Cam 57. **d** 59 **p** 60. C Morden *S'wark* 59-60; Australia 61-65; Asst Sec CCCS 65-68; Lic to Offic *Lon* 65-68; Chapl St Lawr Coll Ramsgate 68-74; Lic to Offic *Cant* 68-74; Chapl Repton Sch Derby 74-94; Lic to Offic *Derby* 74-94; Chile from 94. *Casilla 16144, Santiago 9, Chile*

HUDSON, Christopher John. b 45. Lon Univ BSc68 MIH73. Cranmer Hall Dur DipTh77. **d** 77 **p** 78. C Bath Weston St Jo *B & W* 77-80; P-in-c Baltonsborough w Butleigh and W Bradley 80-84; V 84-87; P-in-c Shirwell w Loxhore *Ex* 87-89; P-in-c Kentisbury, Trentishoe, E Down and Arlington 88-89; RD Shirwell 88-91; TR Shirwell, Loxhore, Kentisbury, Arlington, etc 90-91; P-in-c Trentishoe 90-91; R Huntspill *B & W* 91-94. *28 Laburnham Road, Wellington, Somerset TA21 8EL* Tel (01823) 664968

HUDSON, Canon Gerald Ernest. b 20. Ex Coll Ox BA42 MA46. Westcott Ho Cam 42. **d** 43 **p** 44. C Deptford St Paul *S'wark* 43-47; C Raynes Park St Sav 47-51; V Catford St Laur 51-60; V Roehampton H Trin 60-71; Hon Can S'wark Cathl 68-80; Prin S'wark Ord Course 71-80; R St Mary le Bow w St Pancras Soper Lane etc *Lon* 80-85; rtd 85; Perm to Offic *Cant* from 85; Dir of Post-Ord Tr 86-88. *10 Medina Avenue, Whitstable, Kent CT5 4EN* Tel (01227) 276548

HUDSON, Harold Paige. b 05. New Coll Ox BA28 MA32. Westcott Ho Cam 32. **d** 34 **p** 35. C St Marylebone Em *Lon* 34-36; C Handsworth *Sheff* 36-39; I Ashby Magna *Leic* 39-45; R Kirby Muxloe 45-50; Perm to Offic *Glouc* 51-53; rtd 75. *La Mouette, Pontac, St Clement, Jersey JE2 6SE* Tel (01534) 851684

HUDSON, John. b 47. FRSA CSocStuds. Linc Th Coll. **d** 83 **p** 84. C Merton St Mary *S'wark* 83-86; C Kirk Ella *York* 86-88; P-in-c Lenborough *Ox* 88-93; V Lenborough from 93; P-in-c Tingewick w Water Stratford, Radclive etc 89-93; P-in-c Water Stratford from 93. *The Rectory, Thornborough Road, Padbury, Buckingham MK18 2AH* Tel (01280) 813162

HUDSON, John. b 51. Oak Hill Th Coll 84. **d** 86 **p** 87. C Leyland St Andr *Blackb* 86-89; V Coppull from 89. *The Vicarage, Chapel Lane, Coppull, Chorley, Lancs PR7 4NA* Tel (01257) 791218

HUDSON, Canon John Cecil. b 22. Selw Coll Cam BA46 MA48. Qu Coll Birm BD51. **d** 48 **p** 49. C Darlington St Cuth *Dur* 48-53; CF (TA) 50-57; TR Usworth *Dur* 53-57; V Padiham *Blackb* 57-68; RD Burnley 65-68; RD Whalley 68-83; V Clitheroe St Mary 68-85; Hon Can Blackb Cathl 79-85; rtd 85; Perm to Offic *Blackb* from 85; Perm to Offic *Bradf* from 85. *29 Eastfield Drive, West Bradford, Clitheroe, Lancs BB7 4TQ* Tel (01200) 23531

HUDSON, John Leonard. b 44. AKC66. **d** 67 **p** 68. C Dodworth *Wakef* 67-70; Prec Wakef Cathl 70-73; V Ravensthorpe 73-80; V Royston from 80; P-in-c Carlton from 90; RD Barnsley from 93. *The Clergy House, Church Street, Royston, Barnsley, S Yorkshire S71 4QZ* Tel (01226) 722410

HUDSON, John Peter. b 42. AKC64. St Boniface Warminster 64. **d** 65 **p** 66. C S Shields St Hilda w St Thos *Dur* 65-68; Chapl RN 68-84; V Mellor *Blackb* from 84. *The Vicarage, Church Lane, Mellor, Blackburn BB2 7JL* Tel (01254) 812324 E-mail peter.h6@ukonline.com.

HUDSON, John Stephen Anthony. b 49. S Dios Minl Tr Scheme 85 Chich Th Coll 86. **d** 88 **p** 89. C Horsham *Chich* 88-91; TV Littlehampton and Wick from 91. *The Vicarage, 40 Beaconsfield Road, Wick, Littlehampton, W Sussex BN17 6LN* Tel (01903) 724990

HUDSON, Mrs Mary Gertrude. b 29. Univ Coll Lon BA51 CertEd52. Qu Coll Birm 82. **dss** 85 **d** 87 **p** 94. Kings Norton *Birm* 85-87; NSM from 87. *67 Wychall Lane, Birmingham B38 8TB* Tel 0121-458 3128

HUDSON, Philip Howard. b 50. St Steph Ho Ox 89. **d** 91 **p** 92. C Poulton-le-Fylde *Blackb* 91-95; V Blackpool St Wilfrid from 95. *St Wilfrid's Vicarage, 8 Langdale Road, Blackpool FY4 4RT* Tel (01253) 761532

HUDSON, Canon Thomas George. b 32. TCD BA54. CITC Div Test54. **d** 55 **p** 56. C Belfast St Matt *Conn* 55-58; C Belfast Ch Ch 58-60; C Carlow *C & O* 60-61; I Hacketstown 61-69; I Kinneigh Union *C, C & R* 69-72; I Monasterevan *M & K* 72-83; I Mostrim w Granard, Clonbroney, Killoe etc *K, E & A* from 83; Preb Elphin Cathl from 86. *The Rectory, Edgeworthstown, Co Longford, Irish Republic* Tel Longford (43) 71172

HUDSON, Trevor. b 32. Dur Univ BA56. Cranmer Hall Dur DipTh. **d** 58 **p** 59. C Doncaster St Mary *Sheff* 58-62; C Attercliffe 62-64; V Stannington 64-79; V Abbeydale St Jo 79-88; V Worsbrough 88-95; rtd 95; Perm to Offic *Sheff* from 95. *Spring Villa Garden, 136A Langsett Road South, Oughtibridge, Sheffield S30 3HA* Tel 0114-286 3559

HUDSON, Wilfred. b 23. St Jo Coll Dur BA49 DipTh. **d** 51 **p** 52. C Doncaster St Mary *Sheff* 51-56; V Brampton Bierlow 56-64; V Anston 64-74; V Woodsetts 64-74; V Sheff Sharrow 74-88; rtd 88. *128 Totley Brook Road, Sheffield S17 3QU* Tel 0114-236 5558

HUDSON, Wilfrid Reginald. b 17. Clifton Th Coll 48 St Aid Birkenhead 49. **d** 51 **p** 52. C Fazakerley Em *Liv* 51-55; C Heatherlands St Jo *Sarum* 55-58; V Hatherleigh *Ex* 58-63; V Scarisbrick *Liv* 63-78; New Hall Hosp Scarisbrick 63-78; P-in-c Creacombe *Ex* 78; P-in-c Meshaw 78; P-in-c Thelbridge 78; P-in-c W w E Worlington 78; P-in-c Witheridge 78; P-in-c Witheridge, Thelbridge, Creacombe, Meshaw etc 79; V 79-86; rtd 86; Perm to Offic *Ex* from 86. *19 Beech Hill, Wellington, Somerset TA21 8ER* Tel (01823) 662642

HUDSON-WILKIN, Mrs Rose Josephine. b 61. WMMTC 89. **d** 91 **p** 94. Par Dn Wolverhampton St Matt *Lich* 91-94; C 94-95; C W Bromwich Gd Shep w St Jo from 95; Black Anglican Concern from 95. *St Andrew's Vicarage, Oakwood Street, West Bromwich, W Midlands B70 9SN* Tel 0121-553 1871

HUDSPITH, Colin John. b 46. Nottm Univ BA67. SW Minl Tr Course 93. **d** 96. C Pilton w Ashford *Ex* from 96. *28 Old School Road, Barnstaple, Devon EX32 9DP* Tel (01271) 25553

HUDSPITH, Ernest. b 26. Open Univ BA73 Birm Univ DipTh64. Qu Coll Birm 61. **d** 64 **p** 65. PV S'well Minster *S'well* 64-67; Prec Gib Cathl *Eur* 67-68; NSM Twickenham St Mary *Lon* 69-74; rtd 94. *Flat 3, 68 Warrior Square, St Leonards-on-Sea, E Sussex TN37 6BP* Tel (01424) 441760

HUDSPITH, Mrs Susan Mary. b 49. St Alb Minl Tr Scheme 79. **dss** 82 **d** 87 **p** 94. Luton St Chris Round Green *St Alb* 82-87; Par Dn 87-88; NSM 88-92; Perm to Offic 92-94; C Luton St Mary from 94. *171 Hart Lane, Luton LU2 0JH* Tel (01582) 34948

HUETT, Basil George Pringle. b 19. Lon Univ BA39 Man Univ BD42. Roch Th Coll. **d** 62 **p** 62. Ind Chapl *Roch* 62-72; C Erith St Jo 62-72; rtd 84; Perm to Offic *Roch* 84-95. *Hazelcroft, Stonehouse Road, Halstead, Sevenoaks, Kent TN14 7HN* Tel (01689) 855471

HUGGETT, Christopher Roy. b 49. Hull Univ BA72 CertEd73. Linc Th Coll 79. **d** 93 **p** 94. C Accrington St Jo w Huncoat *Blackb* 93-95; C Cleveleys 95-97; P-in-c Scorton from 97. *St Peter's Vicarage, Snow Hill Lane, Scorton, Preston PR3 1AY* Tel (01524) 791229

HUGGETT, Dr David John. b 34. Lon Univ BSc56 Southn Univ PhD59. Clifton Th Coll 64. **d** 67 **p** 68. C Heatherlands St Jo *Sarum* 67-70; C Cambridge St Sepulchre *Ely* 70-73; R Nottingham St Nic *S'well* 73-92; Cyprus from 93. *PO Box 80, Polis Chrysochous, Cyprus*

HUGGETT, John Victor James. b 39. Dur Univ BA64. Tyndale Hall Bris 64. **d** 66 **p** 67. C Hailsham *Chich* 66-69; C Worthing St Geo 69-71; C Woking St Pet *Guildf* 71-73; C Buckhurst Hill *Chelmsf* 73-76; V Meltham Mills *Wakef* 76-78; V Wilshaw 76-78; rtd 79; Ldr Breath Fellowship 79-84; Perm to Offic *Wakef* 79-84; Perm to Offic *Roch* from 84. *3 Wells Close, Clarence Road, Tunbridge Wells, Kent TN1 1HF*

HUGGETT, Kevin John. b 62. St Jo Coll Dur BA83. Trin Coll Bris DipHE90 ADPS91. **d** 91 **p** 92. C Gt Ilford St Andr *Chelmsf* 91-94; CMS from 94. *49 St Andrew's Road, Ilford, Essex IG1 3PF* Tel 0181-554 7523

HUGGETT, Michael George. b 38. Bris Univ BA60 Birm Univ CertEd61 Nottm Univ DCE83. EMMTC 85. **d** 88 **p** 89. C Sawley *Derby* 88-92; C Chaddesden St Phil 92-93; P-in-c Alkmonton, Cubley, Marston, Montgomery etc from 93. *The Vicarage, Cubley, Ashbourne, Derbyshire DE6 3DL* Tel (01335) 330680

HUGGILL, Cyril Howard. b 20. St Cath Soc Ox BA42 MA46 AKC44. **d** 44 **p** 45. C Macclesfield St Mich *Ches* 44-47; Chapl RNVR 47-49; C Prenton *Ches* 49-51; R Delamere 51-66; RD Middlewich 61-65; Chapl and Lect Bp Lonsdale Coll Derby 66-70; V Biggin *Derby* 70-76; V Hartington 70-76; V Goostrey *Ches* 76-85; rtd 85. *The Granary, Silver Street, Kirkby Stephen, Cumbria CA17 4RB* Tel (017683) 71068

HUGGINS, John Henry William. b 24. Wadh Coll Ox MA. Cuddesdon Coll 49. **d** 51 **p** 52. R Esher *Guildf* 55-57; rtd 90. *2 The Malthouse, 3 Willow Vale, Frome, Somerset BA11 1BG* Tel (01373) 465845

HUGHES, Adrian John. b 57. Newc Univ BA78 Dur Univ BA82. Cranmer Hall Dur 80. **d** 83 **p** 84. C Shard End *Birm* 83-86; TV Solihull 86-90; TV Glendale Gp *Newc* 90-94; P-in-c Belford 94-95; V Belford and Lucker from 95; V Ellingham from 95; RD Bamburgh and Glendale from 97. *The Vicarage, North Bank, Belford, Northd NE70 7LT* Tel (01668) 213545

HUGHES, Alan. b 34. St D Coll Lamp BA54 St Mich Coll Llan 58. **d** 60 **p** 61. C Aberavon *Llan* 60-62; Chapl RAF 62-66; CF 66-76; USA from 76. *1408 South West 20th Street, Gresham, OR, 07030 USA*

HUGHES, Alan. b 46. TD. Edin Th Coll 71. **d** 74 **p** 75. C Edin St Cuth *Edin* 74-76; P-in-c Edin St Luke 76-78; C Marske in Cleveland *York* 78-81; V New Marske 81-84; V Kirkbymoorside w Gillamoor, Farndale etc 84-94; CF 84-94; V Berwick H Trin and St Mary *Newc* from 94. *The Vicarage, Parade, Berwick-upon-Tweed TD15 1DF* Tel (01289) 306136

HUGHES, Albert Ashbden. b 10. Univ of Wales BA37. St Mich Coll Llan 38. **d** 39 **p** 40. C Llangeinwen *Ban* 39-42; CF 43-44; C Llanfachraeth *Ban* 42-45; C Llandegai 45-49; R Blaina *Mon* 49-55; V Harlech and Llanfair juxta Harlech *Ban* 55-58; V Coldhurst *Man* 58-64; Chapl Oldham and Distr Gen Hosp 57-64; V Goostrey *Ches* 64-76; rtd 76; Perm to Offic *Ches* from 76. *50 Preston Road, Lytham, Lytham St Annes, Lancs FY8 5AA* Tel (01253) 795108

HUGHES, Albert William. b 48. S Dios Minl Tr Scheme 90. **d** 92 **p** 93. Community of Our Lady and St John from 70; Prior from 90; Perm to Offic *Win* from 96. *Alton Abbey, Abbey Road, Beech, Alton, Hants GU34 4AP* Tel (01420) 562145 or 563575 Fax 561691

HUGHES, Andrew Terrell. b 29. Bris Univ BA56 DipEd. Coll of Resurr Mirfield 64. **d** 66 **p** 67. C Weston-super-Mare St Sav *B & W* 66-70; C Yeovil St Jo w Preston Plucknett 70-73; TV Yeovil 73-83; R Wincanton 83-88; rtd 89. *2 Cove Street, Weymouth, Dorset DT4 8TS* Tel (01305) 778639

HUGHES, Miss Angela Mary. b 52. Avery Hill Coll CertEd75. St Steph Ho Ox 90. **d** 92 **p** 94. Par Dn Kidderminster St Mary and All SS w Trimpley etc *Worc* 92-94; C 94-96; P-in-c Gilmorton w Peatling Parva and Kimcote etc *Leic* from 96. *The Rectory, Church Lane, Gilmorton, Lutterworth, Leics LE17 5LU* Tel (01455) 552119

HUGHES, Arthur Lewis. b 36. St Deiniol's Hawarden 65. **d** 68 **p** 69. C Holywell *St As* 68-71; Lect St Mary Watford 71-75; V Thornton in Lonsdale w Burton in Lonsdale *Bradf* 75-84; V Daubhill *Man* 84-89; V Castle Town *Lich* from 89; Chapl Staffs Univ from 91. *St Thomas's Vicarage, Doxey, Stafford ST16 1EQ* Tel (01785) 58796

HUGHES, Arthur William Ronald. b 14. Ch Coll Cam BA36 MA40. St Mich Coll Llan 37. **d** 39 **p** 41. C Rhosddu *St As* 39-40; C Minera 40-42; C Wrexham 42-49; R Llangynyw 49-53; R Moston St Jo *Man* 53-57; V Coalbrookdale *Heref* 57-67; V Arthog w Fairbourne *Ban* 67-74; R Machynlleth and Llanwrin 74-77; rtd 77; Perm to Offic *St D* from 77. *4 Clos y Drindod, Buarth Road, Aberystwyth SY23 1LR* Tel (01970) 623779

HUGHES, Bernard Patrick. b 35. DipTh64. Oak Hill Th Coll 62. **d** 65 **p** 66. C Fulham St Matt *Lon* 65-69; Chapl St Steph Hosp Lon 69-89; Chapl St Mary Abbots Hosp Lon 69-97; Chapl Westmr Hosp Lon 89-94; Sen Chapl Chelsea and Westmr Healthcare NHS Trust 94-97; rtd 97. *9 Walham Grove, London SW6 1QP* Tel 0171-385 1348

HUGHES, Bertram Arthur Edwin. b 23. Clifton Th Coll 64. **d** 66 **p** 67. C Taunton St Jas *B & W* 66-68; C Ramsgate St Luke *Cant* 68-70; Australia 70-76; P-in-c Swanton Abbott w Skeyton *Nor* 76-80; P-in-c Scottow 76-80; Australia 80-83; R Reymerston w Cranworth, Letton, Southburgh etc *Nor* 83-84; rtd 84; Perm to Offic *Ex* from 90. *88 Winslade Road, Sidmouth, Devon EX10 9EZ* Tel (01395) 512452

HUGHES, Miss Carol Lindsay. b 51. Cam Inst of Educn CertEd72 Nottm Univ BEd86. Trin Coll Bris DipHE93. **d** 93 **p** 94. C Ilkeston St Mary *Derby* 93-97; P-in-c Langley Mill from 97. *The Vicarage, 214 Cromford Road, Langley Mill, Nottingham NG16 4HB* Tel (01773) 712441

HUGHES, Christopher. b 45. CQSW81. Sarum & Wells Th Coll 86. **d** 88 **p** 89. C Handsworth *Sheff* 88-91; TV Wombourne w Trysull and Bobbington *Lich* 91-96; TR from 96. *The Vicarage, School Road, Wombourne, Wolverhampton WV5 9ED* Tel (01902) 892234

HUGHES, Christopher Clarke. b 40. Lon Coll of Div ALCD65 LTh. **d** 65 **p** 66. C Broadclyst *Ex* 65-68; C Chenies and Lt Chalfont *Ox* 68-70; TV Lydford w Bridestowe and Sourton *Ex* 70-72; TV Lydford, Brent Tor, Bridestowe and Sourton 72-74; V Buckland Monachorum 74-83; R Ashtead *Guildf* from 83. *The Rectory, Dene Road, Ashtead, Surrey KT21 1ED* Tel (01372) 272135

HUGHES, Clive. b 54. Univ of Wales BA77 MA82. St Mich Coll Llan BD95. **d** 95 **p** 96. C Carmarthen St Dav *St D* 95-97; TV Aberystwyth from 97. *St Anne's Vicarage, Penparcau, Aberystwyth SY23 1RZ* Tel (01970) 617819

HUGHES, David Anthony. b 25. Trin Coll Cam BA48 MA55. Linc Th Coll 74. **d** 76 **p** 77. C Boston *Linc* 76-78; V Graffoe 78-90; rtd 90; Perm to Offic *Linc* from 91. *27 St Clement's Road, Ruskington, Sleaford, Lincs NG34 9AF* Tel (01526) 832618

HUGHES, David Howard. b 55. Univ of Wales (Ban). St Mich Coll Llan. **d** 79 **p** 80. C Llanrhos *St As* 79-82; C Eckington w Handley and Ridgeway *Derby* 82-83; C Staveley and Barrow Hill 83-85; TV 85-89; V Whitworth *Man* from 89. *St Bartholomew's House, 1 Beech Close, Whitworth, Rochdale, Lancs OL12 8AR* Tel (01706) 853551

HUGHES, David Michael. b 41. Oak Hill Th Coll BD67. **d** 68 **p** 69. C Tunbridge Wells St Jo *Roch* 68-73; C Crookes St Thos *Sheff* 73-81; V Normanton *Wakef* 81-90; TR Didsbury St Jas and Em *Man* from 90. *St James's Rectory, 9 Didsbury Park, Manchester M20 0LH* Tel 0161-434 2178

HUGHES, Debbie Ann. *See* PEATMAN, Mrs Debbie Ann

HUGHES, Denis Charles. b 27. LNSM course 92. **d** 95 **p** 96. NSM S Merstham *S'wark* from 95; Asst Chapl E Surrey Hosp Redhill 95. *1 South Close Green, Merstham, Redhill RH1 3DU* Tel (01737) 642652

HUGHES, Douglas. b 25. Lon Coll of Div BD54 ALCD54. **d** 54 **p** 55. C Ravenhead *Liv* 54-57; C Bunbury *Ches* 57-60; V Cotmanhay *Derby* 60-68; R Risley 68-77; P-in-c Horsley 77-87; P-in-c Kirk Langley 87-91; P-in-c Mackworth All SS 87-91; P-in-c Mugginton and Kedleston 89-91; rtd 91; Perm to Offic *Derby* from 91. *44 Chapel Lane, Spondon, Derby DE21 7JU* Tel (01332) 660561

HUGHES, Elfed. b 53. St Mich Coll Llan BD75. **d** 77 **p** 78. C Skewen *Llan* 77-80; TV Ystradyfodwg w Gelli, Rhigos and Tonpentre 80-81; P-in-c Pentre CD 81-85; V Pentre 85-87; Chapl Wales Poly 87-91; V Llantrisant 91-97; rtd 97. *The Vicarage, Coed yr Esgob, Llantrisant CF7 8EL* Tel (01443) 223356

HUGHES, Mrs Elizabeth Jane. b 58. K Coll Lon BD81 AKC81. Ripon Coll Cuddesdon 81. **dss** 83 **d** 87 **p** 94. Chipping Barnet w Arkley *St Alb* 83-86; Dunstable 86-87; Hon Par Dn 87-93; NSM Boxmoor St Jo from 93. *St John's Vicarage, 10 Charles Street, Hemel Hempstead, Herts HP1 1JH* Tel (01442) 255382

HUGHES, Ms Eunice Nesta. b 14. K Coll Lon 38 CertEd51. Lambeth DipTh40 St Chris Coll Blackheath 34. **dss** 61 **d** 87. RE Teacher Darley Gate 62-64; Cheltenham Ladies' Coll 65-74; Cant St Martin and St Paul *Cant* 76-80; Westgate St Sav 80-87; Hon Par Dn 87; Perm to Offic from 87. *Flat 1, 4 Cedric Road, Westgate-on-Sea, Kent CT8 8NZ* Tel (01843) 831746

HUGHES, The Ven Evan Arthur Bertram. b 25. St D Coll Lamp BA48 LTh50. **d** 50 **p** 51. C Abergwili w Llanfihangel-uwch-Gwili *St D* 50-53; C Llanelli 53-58; India 59-69; Adn Bhagalpur 65-66; C Llanstadwel *St D* 70-73; Pakistan 73-74; R Johnston w Steynton *St D* 74-80; Can St D Cathl 80-85; V Newcastle Emlyn 80-81; V Newcastle Emlyn w Llandyfriog and Troed-yr-aur 81-86; Adn Carmarthen 85-91; V Llanegwad w Llanfynydd 86-88; V Cynwil Elfed and Newchurch 88-91; rtd 91. *104 Bronwydd Road, Carmarthen SA31 2AW* Tel (01267) 237155

HUGHES, Canon Evelyn. b 31. Gilmore Ho 73. **dss** 79 **d** 87 **p** 94. Fetcham *Guildf* 79-82; Dioc Adv Lay Min 82-86; Farnborough 83-87; C 87-92; Bp's Adv for Women's Min 87-96; D-in-c Badshot Lea CD 92-94; C-in-c 94-96; Hon Can Guildf Cathl 94-96; TV Hale 96; rtd 96. *4 Oaklands, Haslemere, Surrey GU27 3RQ* Tel (01428) 651576

HUGHES, Canon Geraint Morgan Hugh. b 34. Keble Coll Ox BA58 MA63. St Mich Coll Llan 58. **d** 59 **p** 60. C Gorseinon *S & B* 59-63; C Oystermouth 63-68; R Llanbadarn Fawr, Llandegley and Llanfihangel etc 68-76; R Llandrindod w Cefnllys 76-87; R Llandrindod w Cefnllys and Disserth from 87; Can Brecon Cathl from 89; Prec Brecon Cathl from 95; RD Maelienydd from 95. *The Rectory, Broadway, Llandrindod Wells LD1 5HT* Tel (01597) 822043

HUGHES, Canon Gerald Thomas. b 30. Lon Univ BD63 MTh. Qu Coll Birm 72. **d** 72 **p** 73. Lic to Offic *Cov* 72-80; P-in-c Birdingbury 80-81; P-in-c Leamington Hastings 80-81; V Leamington Hastings and Birdingbury 81-82; V Dunchurch 82-89; RD Rugby 85-89; Can Res Cov Cathl 89-94; rtd 94; Perm to Offic *Cov* from 94. *Loafers' Cottage, Lazy Lane, Fladbury, Pershore, Worcs WR10 2QL* Tel (01386) 860650

HUGHES, Gwilym Berw. b 42. St Mich Coll Llan DipTh68. **d** 68 **p** 69. C Conwy w Gyffin *Ban* 68-71; V Llandinorwig w Penisarwaun and Llanddeiniolen 71-75; TV Llandudno 75-80; V Dwygyfylchi 80-96; RD Arllechwedd 88-96; V Bodelwyddan *St As* from 96. *The Vicarage, Bodelwyddan, Rhyl LL18 5UR* Tel (01745) 583034

HUGHES, Gwyndaf Morris. b 36. Univ of Wales (Lamp) BA57. St Steph Ho Ox 58 St Mich Coll Llan 59. **d** 59 **p** 60. C Glanogwen *Ban* 59-62; Chapl RN 62-78; R Llanfairpwll w Penmynydd *Ban* 78-90; RD Tindaethwy from 88; R Beaumaris from 90; Can Ban Cathl 95-97; Prec from 97. *The Rectory, 5 Tros-y-Afon, Beaumaris LL58 8BN* Tel (01248) 811402

HUGHES, Canon Harold Mervyn. b 13. St D Coll Lamp BA34. **d** 37 **p** 38. C Glouc St Cath *Glouc* 37-40; P-in-c Churchdown 40; CF (EC) 40-46; V Hucclecote *Glouc* 46-78; rtd 78; Perm to Offic *Glouc* from 83. *13 Woodland Green, Upton St Leonards, Gloucester GL4 8DB* Tel (01452) 618301

HUGHES, Canon Hazel. b 45. St Jo Coll Dur 75. **dss** 78 **d** 87 **p** 94. Lower Mitton *Worc* 78-81; Worc St Martin w St Pet, St Mark etc 82-87; Par Dn Worc SE 87-88; D-in-c Wribbenhall 88-94; V 94; P-in-c from 94; Chapl to Mentally Handicapped from 94; Hon Can Worc Cathl from 95. *Wribbenhall Vicarage, Trimpley Lane, Bewdley, Worcs DY12 1JJ* Tel (01299) 402196

HUGHES, Canon Henry. b 18. Kelham Th Coll 35. **d** 41 **p** 42. C Tonge Moor *Man* 41-45; C Wigston Magna *Leic* 45-50; V Holbrooks *Cov* 50-89; Hon Can Cov Cathl 73-89; rtd 89; P-in-c Hoar Cross w Newchurch *Lich* 89-95; Perm to Offic from 95. *15 Swan Pool Grove, Shelfield, Walsall WS4 1TD* Tel (01922) 694398

HUGHES, Henry Charles William. b 30. K Coll Lon 58. Roch Th Coll 59. **d** 61 **p** 62. C Forest Gate Em w Upton Cross *Chelmsf* 61-64; C Woodford St Barn 64-72; Lic to Offic 72-95; rtd 95. *99 St Anthony's Drive, Chelmsford CM2 9EH* Tel (01245) 265230

HUGHES, Hugh. b 13. St D Coll Lamp BA35 St Mich Coll Llan 35. **d** 36 **p** 37. C Llanfaethlu w Llanfwrog *Ban* 36-41; C Holyhead 41-45; V Dolwyddelan 45-56; R Llanbeulan w Llanfaelog and Tal-y-Llyn 56-69; R Llaneugrad w Llanallgo and Penrhosllugwy etc 73-82; RD Twrcelyn 80-82; rtd 82; Perm to Offic *Ban* from 86. *50 Craig-y-Don, Tyn-y-Gongl LL74 8SN* Tel (01248) 853500

HUGHES, Chan Hywel Maldwyn. b 20. Univ of Wales (Swansea) BA42. St Mich Coll Llan 42. **d** 44 **p** 45. C Llangyfelach and Morriston *S & B* 44-47; C Builth w Alltmawr and Llanynys 46-48; Min Can Brecon Cathl 48-53; R Llanfeugan w Llanddetty and Glyncollwg 53-59; R Ystradgynlais 59-68; V Killay 68-87; RD Clyne 79; Can Brecon Cathl from 81; Treas Brecon Cathl 81; Chan 83-87; rtd 88; Canada from 95; Perm to Offic Toronto from 95. *142 Three Valleys Drive, Don Mills, Ontario, Canada, M3A 3B9* Tel Ontario (416) 445 8571

HUGHES, Ivor Gordon. b 45. Culham Coll of Educn CertEd68 Westmr Coll Ox MTh94. Ripon Coll Cuddesdon 75. **d** 77 **p** 78. C Newport w Longford *Lich* 77-79; Children's Work Officer CMS 79-82; V Gt and Lt Bedwyn and Savernake Forest *Sarum* 82-86; P-in-c Urchfont w Stert 86-90; TR Redhorn 90-92; Nat Children's Officer Gen Syn Bd of Educn 92-95; R Yeovil w Kingston Pitney *B & W* from 95. *The Rectory, 5 West Park, Yeovil, Somerset BA20 1DE* Tel (01935) 75396

HUGHES, Mrs Jackie Louise. b 50. ACP81 Birm Poly BEd86. WMMTC 89. **d** 92. NSM Edgbaston St Geo *Birm* 92-95; Tutor Qu Coll Birm from 96. *267 Stoney Lane, Yardley, Birmingham B25 8YG* Tel 0121-628 4184

HUGHES, Miss Jacqueline Monica (Jackie). b 36. Lon Univ TCert56. Dalton Ho Bris 59. **dss** 77 **d** 88. Redditch St Steph *Worc* 77-79; Worc H Trin 79-82; Chapl Asst Worc R Infirmary 82-94; Asst Chapl Worc R Infirmary NHS Trust from 94. *38 Cockshute Hill, Droitwich, Worcs WR9 7QP* Tel (01905) 775153 or 763333

HUGHES, John Chester. b 24. St Jo Coll Dur BA48 DipTh50 MA51. **d** 50 **p** 51. C Southend St Sav Westcliff *Chelmsf* 50-53; Succ Chelmsf Cathl 53-55; V New Humberstone *Leic* 55-61; V Croxton Kerrial w Branston by Belvoir 61-63; Provost Leic 63-78; ChStJ from 74; V Bringhurst w Gt Easton *Leic* 78-87; rtd 87; Perm to Offic *Leic* from 87. *29 High Street, Hallaton, Market Harborough, Leics LE16 8UD* Tel (01858) 89622

HUGHES, Canon John Herbert Vivian. b 28. St D Coll Lamp BA51 LTh53. **d** 53 **p** 54. C Abergwili w Llanfihangel-uwch-Gwili *St D* 53-58; C Llanelli 58-62; V Newchurch and Merthyr 62-71; V Abergwili w Llanfihangel-uwch-Gwili etc 71-89; RD Carmarthen 82-88; Can St D Cathl 87-89; rtd 89. *104 Bronwydd Road, Carmarthen SA31 2AR* Tel (01267) 237155

HUGHES, John Malcolm. b 47. Man Univ BSc68 Leeds Univ DipTh70. Coll of Resurr Mirfield 68. **d** 71 **p** 72. C Newton Nottage *Llan* 71-78; V Llanwynno 78-92; R Cadoxton-juxta-Barry from 92. *The Rectory, 21 Rectory Road, Cadoxton, Barry CF63 3QB* Tel (01446) 733041

HUGHES, John Patrick. b 41. Oak Hill Th Coll DipTh66. **d** 67 **p** 68. C Chorleywood St Andr *St Alb* 67-71; C E Twickenham St Steph *Lon* 71-76; TV High Wycombe *Ox* 77-92; Chapl Wycombe Hosp 77-83; V Harborne Heath *Birm* from 92. *St John's Vicarage, 99 Wentworth Road, Birmingham B17 9ST* Tel 0121-428 2093 Fax 428 1934

HUGHES, John Stunt Dickson. b 01. Keble Coll Ox BA25 MA48. Cuddesdon Coll 25. **d** 26 **p** 27. C Burnham *Ox* 26-31; C Shoreham *Roch* 31-42; V Washington *Chich* 42-70; rtd 70; Perm to Offic *Chich* from 70. *5 West Preston Manor, Rustington, Littlehampton, W Sussex BN16 3AX* Tel (01903) 786062

✠**HUGHES, The Rt Revd John Taylor.** b 08. CBE75. Bede Coll Dur BA31 DipTh32 MA35. **d** 31 **p** 32 **c** 56. Asst Chapl and Tutor St Bede Coll Dur 31-34; Lect 34-35; C Shildon *Dur* 34-37; V Hartlepool St Jas 37-48; Warden S'wark Dioc Ho Blackheath and St Sav Coll 48-56; Can Miss S'wark Cathl 48-56; Suff Bp Croydon *Cant* 56-77; Bp HM Forces 66-75; Adn Croydon *Cant* 67-77; rtd 77; Asst Bp Cant 77-86; Asst Bp S'wark from 86. *Hospital of the Holy Trinity, Croydon CR0 1UB* Tel 0181-686 8313

HUGHES, John Tudor. b 59. Nottm Univ BSc81 Univ of Wales (Cardiff) BD84. St Mich Coll Llan 81. **d** 84 **p** 85. C Mold *St As* 84-88; Asst Dioc Youth Chapl from 86; Min Can St As Cathl 88-90; Min St As and Tremeirchion 88-90; V Holt 90-96; V Buckley from 96. *St Matthew's Vicarage, 114 Church Road, Buckley CH7 3JN* Tel (01244) 550645

HUGHES, John William George. b 48. MBE93. St Mich Coll Llan DipTh72. **d** 72 **p** 73. C Swansea St Pet *S & B* 72-76; V Cwmddauddwr w St Harmon's and Llanwrthwl 76-79; P-in-c Caereithin 79; V 80-86; Chapl RAF from 86. *Chaplaincy Services (RAF), HQ, Personnel and Training Command, RAF Innsworth, Gloucester GL3 1EZ* Tel (01452) 712612 ext 5164 Fax 510828

HUGHES, Leonard Mordecai. b 50. St Jo Coll Nottm 95. **d** 97. NSM N Evington *Leic* from 97. *68 Trevino Drive, Leicester LE4 7PH* Tel 0116-266 9979

HUGHES, Martin Conway. b 40. Ex Coll Ox BA61 MA67. Chich Th Coll. **d** 63 **p** 64. C Roehampton H Trin *S'wark* 63-67; C Addlestone *Guildf* 67-71; V Burpham 71-88; V Shamley Green from 88; RD Cranleigh 90-95. *The Vicarage, Church Hill, Shamley Green, Guildford, Surrey GU5 0UD* Tel (01483) 892030

HUGHES, Martyn Lawrence. b 19. Magd Coll Ox BA42 MA46 K Coll Cam BA43 MA52. Westcott Ho Cam. **d** 44 **p** 45. V Eltham St Jo *S'wark* 44-46; China 47-53; Chapl K Coll Cam 53-56; Asst Chapl Uppingham Sch Leics 56-61; Chapl Harrow Sch 61-73; Perm to Offic *Chich* from 73; Hd Relig Studies Rich Collyer Coll Horsham 73-84; Chapl St Mich Sch Petworth 85-87; rtd 87. *20 Normandy Court, West Parade, Worthing, W Sussex BN11 3QY* Tel (01903) 200531

HUGHES, Matthew James. b 66. K Coll Lon BD88. Westcott Ho Cam 89. **d** 91 **p** 92. C Heston *Lon* 91-94; C Fulham All SS 94-96; TV St Laur in Thanet *Cant* from 96. *St Christopher's Vicarage, Kimberley Road, Newington, Folkstone, Kent CT12 6HH* Tel (01843) 594160

HUGHES, Dr Michael John Minto. b 50. Liv Univ MB, ChB74 DRCOG87 Ox Univ MTh94. Wycliffe Hall Ox 76. **d** 79 **p** 80. C Stranton *Dur* 79-82; Peru 82-86; Hon C Gosforth w Nether Wasdale and Wasdale Head *Carl* 87-89; TV Thetford *Nor* from 89. *44 Nunsgate, Thetford, Norfolk IP24 3EL* Tel (01842) 752075

HUGHES, Neville Joseph. b 52. NUU BA79 MBIM93. **d** 91 **p** 92. NSM Mullabrack w Markethill and Kilcluney *Arm* from 91. *109 Markethill Road, Portadown, Co Armagh BT62 3SL* Tel (01762) 841500

HUGHES, Owen. b 17. Univ of Wales BA39. St Mich Coll Llan 39. **d** 40 **p** 41. C Heneglwys w Tregwalchmai *Ban* 40-42; C

Llanfairisgaer 42-45; Chapl RNVR 45-47; C Llandudno *Ban* 47-50; C Halsall *Liv* 50-53; V Stanley 53-57; V Lydiate 57-62; V Wesham *Blackb* 62-70; R Llanbeulan w Llanfaelog and Tal-y-Llyn *Ban* 70-71; R Church Kirk *Blackb* 71-74; V Oswaldtwistle All SS 74-82; rtd 82; Lic to Offic *Blackb* from 82. *57 Blackburn Road, Rishton, Blackburn BB1 4EU* Tel (01254) 884165

HUGHES, Paul Vernon. b 53. Ripon Coll Cuddesdon 79. **d** 82 **p** 83. C Chipping Barnet w Arkley *St Alb* 82-86; TV Dunstable 86-93; P-in-c Boxmoor St Jo from 93; RD Hemel Hempstead from 96. *St John's Vicarage, 10 Charles Street, Hemel Hempstead, Herts HP1 1JH* Tel (01442) 255382

HUGHES, Peter John. b 43. Melbourne Univ BA67 Ch Ch Ox BPhil77. Trin Coll Melbourne 64 ACT 70. **d** 70 **p** 70. Australia 70-74 and from 84; Perm to Offic *Ox* 75-77; Lic to Offic 77-79; Chapl Lon Univ *Lon* 79-84. *Level 3, 169-171 Phillip Street, Sydney, NSW, Australia 2000* Tel Sydney (2) 232 3022 or 363 3335 Fax 232 4182

HUGHES, Peter John. b 59. Wolv Poly BA83 Lon Univ PGCE85 Inst of Marketing DipM. Wycliffe Hall Ox 90. **d** 92 **p** 93. C Ecclesall *Sheff* 92-96; V Kimberworth from 96. *The Vicarage, 331 Kimberworth Road, Rotherham, S Yorkshire S61 1HD* Tel (01709) 554441

HUGHES, Peter Knowles. b 61. Sarum & Wells Th Coll 87. **d** 90 **p** 91. C Whitchurch *Bris* 90-93. *75 Geraldine Road, Malvern, Worcs WR14 3NX*

HUGHES, Philip. b 47. St Jo Coll Nottm 79. **d** 81 **p** 82. C Dolgellau w Llanfachreth and Brithdir etc *Ban* 81-83; Youth Chapl 82-83; R Llaneugrad w Llanallgo and Penrhosllugwy etc 83-95; R Llanberis w Llanrug from 95. *The Rectory, Llanberis, Caernarfon LL55 4TF* Tel (01286) 870285

HUGHES, Philip Geoffrey John (Phil). b 60. Nottm Univ BCombStuds82 Birm Univ DipTh88. Aston Tr Scheme 84 Qu Coll Birm 86. **d** 89 **p** 90. C Sedgley All SS *Lich* 89-93; C Sedgley All SS *Worc* 93-94; V Boscoppa *Truro* 94-96; Chapl Gatwick Airport *Chich* from 96; C Crawley from 96. *Address excluded by request* Tel (01293) 503857 Fax 505540

HUGHES, Philip Stephen. b 34. Dur Univ BA59. Coll of Resurr Mirfield 59. **d** 62 **p** 63. C Horfield St Greg *Bris* 62-66; C Bedminster St Mich 66-69; P-in-c Chippenham St Pet 69-71; V 71-83; TR Bedminster 83-91; V Ashton Keynes, Leigh and Minety from 91. *The Vicarage, 23 Richmond Court, Ashton Keynes, Swindon SN6 6PP* Tel (01285) 861566

HUGHES, Richard Clifford. b 24. Pemb Coll Cam BA57 MA59. Ely Th Coll 48. **d** 50 **p** 51. C Wandsworth St Anne *S'wark* 50-53; S Rhodesia 53-65; S Africa 65-86; Adn Pinetown 75-80; Australia from 86; rtd 89. *54 Mersey Street, Box Hill North, Victoria, Australia 3129* Tel Melbourne (3) 9898 5335

HUGHES, Richard Jeffrey. b 47. Trin Coll Carmarthen CertEd68. St Mich Coll Llan 74. **d** 76 **p** 77. C Llanbeblig w Caernarfon and Betws Garmon etc *Ban* 76-78; Dioc Youth Chapl 78-82; TV Holyhead w Rhoscolyn w Llanfair-yn-Neubwll 78-83; R Llanfachraeth 83-92; R Llangefni w Tregaean and Llangristiolus etc 92-95; R Llanbeblig w Caernarfon and Betws Garmon etc from 95. *Hafoty, Bryn Rhos, Rhosbodrual, Caernarfon LL55 2BT* Tel (01286) 674181

HUGHES, Richard Millree. b 33. Univ of Wales BA56 MA79. St Mich Coll Llan 56. **d** 58 **p** 59. C Mold *St As* 58-61; V Choral St As Cathl 61-64; V Towyn 64-67; Asst Master Marlborough Sch Woodstock 77-79; R Whitchurch St Mary *Ox* from 79. *The Rectory, Whitchurch, Reading RG8 7DF* Tel (0118) 984 3219

HUGHES, Robert Elistan-Glodrydd. b 32. Trin Coll Ox BA54 MA58 Birm Univ MLitt85. Westcott Ho Cam 55. **d** 57 **p** 58. C Stoke *Cov* 57-61; Ind Chapl *S'wark* 61-64; Birm Univ *Birm* 64-87; Chapl 64-69; Lodgings Warden and Student Welfare Adv 69-87; Dir Housing Study Overseas Students Trust 88-91; Perm to Offic *Ban* 88-94; V Harlech and Llanfair-juxta-Harlech etc from 94. *Clogwyn Melyn, Talsarnau LL47 6TP* Tel (01766) 780383

HUGHES, Dr Robert Guy. b 64. York Univ BSc86 Reading Univ PhD89. Ripon Coll Cuddesdon BA92. **d** 93 **p** 94. C Sandhurst *Ox* 93-95; Chapl K Sch Ely from 95. *59 Silver Street, Ely, Cambs CB7 4JD* Tel (01353) 668691

HUGHES, Rodney Thomas. b 39. Dur Univ BA60 St Cath Coll Ox DipTh61. Wycliffe Hall Ox 60. **d** 62 **p** 63. C Edin St Thos *Edin* 62-65; C Harlow New Town w Lt Parndon *Chelmsf* 65-67; R Haworth *Bradf* 67-74; R W Knighton w Broadmayne *Sarum* 74-77; R Broadmayne, W Knighton, Owermoigne etc 77-82; V Crosthwaite Keswick *Carl* from 82. *Crosthwaite Vicarage, Vicarage Hill, Keswick, Cumbria CA12 5QB* Tel (017687) 72509

HUGHES, Mrs Sheila. b 52. N Ord Course 92. **d** 95 **p** 96. NSM Birkenhead Priory *Ches* from 95. *33 Farndon Way, Birkenhead, Merseyside L43 2NW* Tel 0151-653 9434

HUGHES, Steven Philip. b 52. St Jo Coll Dur BA. Ridley Hall Cam. **d** 82 **p** 83. C Chilvers Coton w Astley *Cov* 82-86; TV Kings Norton *Birm* 86-91; Asst Chapl Bucharest *Eur* from 96. *Cisnadioara nr 38, C-P 2438, Jud Sibiu, Romania, or PO Box 2368, Kings Norton, Birmingham B38 8RZ* Tel Sibiu (69) 561126 or 415181 Fax as telephone

HUGHES, Ms Valerie Elizabeth (Val). b 53. Birm Univ BA75 CertEd76. Wycliffe Hall Ox DipTh86. **d** 87 **p** 94. C Hallwood *Ches* 87-90; Par Dn Garston *Liv* 90-93; TD Gateacre 93-94; TV from 94; Asst Chapl Liv Univ 93. *St Mark's Vicarage, Cranwell Road, Liverpool L25 1NX* Tel 0151-487 9634

HUGHES, William Roger. b 47. Trin Coll Carmarthen. **d** 91 **p** 92. NSM Llan-non *St D* 91-93; Dio Officer for Soc Resp from 93; V Llangathen w Llanfihangel Cilfargen etc from 93. *The Vicarage, Llangathen, Carmarthen SA32 8QD* Tel (01558) 668455

HUGHMAN, Dr June Alison. b 58. Kingston Poly BSc81 Southn Univ PhD84. Trin Coll Bris DipHE88. **d** 89 **p** 94. Par Dn Penge St Jo *Roch* 89-93; C Woking Ch Ch *Guildf* from 93. *4 Orchard Drive, Woking, Surrey GU21 4BN* Tel (01483) 771551

HUGO, Canon Keith Alan. b 41. Nottm Univ BA62. Chich Th Coll 62. **d** 64 **p** 65. C Pontefract St Giles *Wakef* 64-68; C Chesterfield St Mary and All SS *Derby* 68-71; V Allenton and Shelton Lock 71-77; Dioc Communications Officer *Sarum* 77-89; V Worton 77-84; V Potterne 77-84; Can and Preb Sarum Cathl from 84; V Potterne w Worton and Marston 84-89; R Wyke Regis from 89; RD Weymouth from 94. *The Rectory, 1 Portland Road, Weymouth, Dorset DT4 9ES* Tel (01305) 784649

HUITSON, Christopher Philip. b 45. Keble Coll Ox BA66 MA70. Cuddesdon Coll 67. **d** 69 **p** 70. C Croydon St Sav *Cant* 69-71; Soc Service Unit St Martin-in-the-Fields Lon 71-73; C St Alb St Pet *St Alb* 73-77; V Cople 77-78; P-in-c Willington 77-78; V Cople w Willington 78-89; V Leavesden All SS 89-96; V Totteridge from 96. *The Vicarage, 44 Totteridge Village, London N20 8PR* Tel 0181-445 6787

HULBERT, Charles Donald. b 09. Linc Th Coll 37. **d** 38 **p** 39. C Beccles St Mich *St E* 38-40; R Halesworth 40-56; Chapl RAFVR 42-46; Bp's Hon Chapl 54-57; Area Sec (E Anglia) BFBS 56-58; V Norton Subcourse *Nor* 58-62; R Thurlton w Thorpe next Haddiscoe 58-62; R Plaxtol *Roch* 62-74; rtd 74; Perm to Offic *Nor* 74-96. *31 Holt Road, Weybourne, Holt, Norfolk NR25 7SU* Tel (01263) 70384

HULBERT, Hugh Forfar. b 22. Bris Univ BA49. Tyndale Hall Bris 46. **d** 50 **p** 51. C Summerstown *S'wark* 50-53; C Felixstowe SS Pet and Paul *St E* 53-55; Min Collier Row ED Chelmsf 55-59; SW Area Sec CPAS 59-63; V Portsea St Luke *Portsm* 63-75; V Worthing H Trin *Chich* 75-81; C-in-c Hove H Trin CD 81-85; C Hailsham 86-87; rtd 87; Perm to Offic *Chich* from 87. *43 Milland Road, Hailsham, E Sussex BN27 1TQ* Tel (01323) 842215

HULBERT, Canon John Anthony Lovett. b 40. Trin Coll Cam BA63 MA67. Wells Th Coll 64. **d** 66 **p** 67. C Fareham H Trin *Portsm* 66-70; R Wickham 70-79; RD Bishops Waltham 74-79; V Bedford St Andr *St Alb* 79-92; RD Bedford 87-92; Hon Can St Alb from 91; V Leighton Buzzard w Eggington, Hockliffe etc from 92. *The Vicarage, Pulford Road, Leighton Buzzard, Beds LU7 7AB* Tel (01525) 373217

HULBERT, Canon Martin Francis Harrington. b 37. Dur Univ BSc58 MA62. Ripon Hall Ox 58. **d** 60 **p** 61. C Buxton *Derby* 60-63; C Eglingham *Newc* 63-67; C-in-c Loundsley Green Ascension CD *Derby* 67-71; P-in-c Frecheville 71-73; R Frecheville and Hackenthorpe *Sheff* 73-77; P-in-c Hathersage *Derby* 77-83; V 83-90; RD Bakewell and Eyam 81-90; Hon Can Derby Cathl from 89; R Brailsford w Shirley and Osmaston w Edlaston 90-93; V Tideswell from 93; RD Buxton from 96. *The Vicarage, Pursglove Drive, Tideswell, Buxton, Derbyshire SK17 8PA* Tel (01298) 871317 Fax 872621

HULETT, Mrs Janet Elizabeth Mary. b 48. **d** 91 **p** 96. NSM Broadwater St Mary *Chich* 91-95; NSM Thame w Towersey *Ox* from 96. *24 Clarendon Drive, Thame, Oxon OX9 3XP* Tel (01844) 216457

HULETT, Peter. b 31. CEng MIMechE62 Leeds Univ CertEd74. Wycliffe Hall Ox 75. **d** 77 **p** 78. C Eastwood *S'well* 77-80; C Granby w Elton 80-83; V Gilling and Kirkby Ravensworth *Ripon* 83-90; P-in-c Bishop Monkton and Burton Leonard 90-96; rtd 96. *2 Carden Drive, Ben Rhydding, Ilkley, W Yorkshire LS29 8PH* Tel (01943) 604202

HULL, David John. b 44. Linc Th Coll 88. **d** 90 **p** 91. C Mansfield Woodhouse *S'well* 90-93; P-in-c Mansfield St Lawr from 93. *St Lawrence's Vicarage, 3 Shaw Street, Mansfield, Notts NG18 2NP* Tel (01623) 23698

HULL, John Hammond. b 36. Sarum Th Coll 60. **d** 61 **p** 62. C Gt Clacton *Chelmsf* 61-66; Lic to Offic 66-75; Area Chapl (E Anglia) Toc H 66-70; (Midl Region) 70-75; Lic to Offic *Ox* from 75; Chapl Toc H HQ 75-82. *66 Grenville Avenue, Wendover, Aylesbury, Bucks HP22 6AL* Tel (01296) 624487

HULL, Theodore James Nesbitt (Theo). b 57. Southn Univ BTh84. Sarum & Wells Th Coll 80. **d** 82 **p** 83. C Plumstead St Mark and St Marg *S'wark* 82-84; C Surbiton St Andr and St Mark 84-87; V Balham St Mary and St Jo 87-93; Chapl Lt Plumstead Hosp from 94; Hon C Freethorpe w Wickhampton, Halvergate etc *Nor* from 97; Hon C Reedham w Cantley w Limpenhoe and Southwood from 97. *Little Plumstead Hospital, Hospital Road, Little Plumstead, Norwich NR13 5EW*

HULL, Thomas Henry. b 55. QUB BD79. NTMTC ADPS94. **d** 97. C Kidbrooke *S'wark* from 97. *252 Wricklemarsh Road, London SE3 8DW* Tel 0181-856 1775

HULL, Timothy David. b 60. Lon Bible Coll 87. St Jo Coll Nottm BTh90. **d** 90 **p** 91. C Leyton St Mary w St Edw *Chelmsf* 90-95; Chapl Havering Coll of F&HE from 94; C Harold Hill St Geo *Chelmsf* from 95. *18 Petersfield Avenue, Romford RM3 9PA* Tel (01708) 374388

HULL, Suffragan Bishop of. *See* JONES, The Rt Revd James Stuart

HULLAH, Canon Peter Fearnley. b 49. FRSA93 K Coll Lon BD71 AKC71. Cuddesdon Coll 73. **d** 74 **p** 75. Asst Chapl St Edw Sch Ox 74-77; C Summertown *Ox* 74-76; C Wolvercote w Summertown 76-77; Chapl Sevenoaks Sch 77-82; Hon C Sevenoaks St Nic *Roch* 77-82; Ho Master Internat Cen Sevenoaks Sch 82-87; Hon C Kippington 82-87; Sen Chapl K Sch Cant 87-92; Hon Min Can Cant Cathl *Cant* 87-92; Hd Master Chetham's Sch of Music from 92; Lic Preacher *Man* from 93; Perm to Offic *Carl* from 87; Hon Can Man Cathl *Man* from 96. *Chetham's School of Music, Long Millgate, Manchester M3 1SB* Tel 0161-834 9644 Fax 839 3609

HULLETT, Frederick Graham. b 32. St Jo Coll York CertEd53 Leeds Univ BA58. Coll of Resurr Mirfield 58. **d** 60 **p** 61. C Acton Green St Pet *Lon* 60-61; C W Hackney St Barn 61-64; C Paddington St Mary 64-67; Hon C 67-69; P-in-c Haggerston St Aug w St Steph 69-73; Lic to Offic 73-84; Perm to Offic *Linc* from 84; rtd 91. *2 Ryland Road, Welton, Lincoln LN2 3LU* Tel (01673) 860839

HULLYER, Paul Charles. b 68. Anglia Poly Univ DipTh97. Aston Tr Scheme 92 Westcott Ho Cam CTM94. **d** 97. C Stoke Newington St Mary *Lon* from 97. *The Rectory Flat, Stoke Newington Church Street, London N16 9ES* Tel 0171-249 6138

HULME, Alan John. b 60. Birm Univ BSc81. Wycliffe Hall Ox BA90. **d** 91 **p** 92. C Chilwell *S'well* 91-96; TV Roxeth *Lon* from 96. *St Paul's Vicarage, Findon Close, off Corbins Lane, South Harrow, Middx HA2 8NJ* Tel 0181-422 2991

HULME, Ms Juliette Mary. b 57. Whitelands Coll Lon BEd81. Cranmer Hall Dur CTMin94. **d** 94 **p** 95. C Crayford *Roch* from 94. *1A Iron Mill Place, Crayford, Dartford DA1 4RT* Tel (01322) 558789

HULME, Norman. b 31. Kelham Th Coll 50. **d** 54 **p** 55. C Blackb St Pet *Blackb* 54-57; C Blakenall Heath *Lich* 57-59; V Gannow *Blackb* 59-64; V Anwick *Linc* 64-74; V S Kyme 64-74; V Moulton 74-83; V Earl Shilton w Elmesthorpe *Leic* 83-88; Chapl Harperbury Hosp Radlett 88-96; rtd 96. *9 Sunningdale, Luton LU2 7TF* Tel (01582) 451748

HULME, Suffragan Bishop of. *See* SCOTT, The Rt Revd Colin John Fraser

HULSE, William John (Bill). b 42. Dur Univ BA65. Linc Th Coll 65. **d** 67 **p** 68. C S Westoe *Dur* 67-70; Lic to Offic *Newc* 70-72; C Far Headingley St Chad *Ripon* 72-76; R Swillington 76-88; V Shadwell 88-95; V Oulton w Woodlesford from 95. *The Vicarage, 46 Holmsley Lane, Woodlesford, Leeds LS26 8RY* Tel 0113-282 0411

HUME, Miss Clephane Arrol. b 46. Edin Occupational Therapy Tr Cen DipOT68 Jordan Hill Coll Glas CertFE83 Open Univ BA87. Edin Dioc NSM Course 88. **d** 92 **p** 94. NSM Edin St Jo *Edin* from 92. *30 Findhorn Place, Edinburgh EH9 2JP* Tel 0131-667 2996 Fax 317 3256

HUME, Ernest. b 45. Linc Th Coll 77. **d** 79 **p** 80. C Ilkeston St Mary *Derby* 79-81; C Sheff Manor *Sheff* 81-82; TV 82-88; V Norton Woodseats St Chad from 88. *The Vicarage, 9 Linden Avenue, Sheffield S8 0GA* Tel 0114-274 5086

HUME, Leslie Paul. b 09. Kelham Th Coll 27. **d** 32 **p** 33. SSM from 32; C Liv St Nic *Liv* 32-37; Chapl Kelham Th Coll 37-41; C Nottingham St Geo w St Jo *S'well* 41-43; S Africa 43-49 and 51-52 and 66-76; Basutoland 50-51 and 62-66; Dir SSM 52-62; Lic to Offic *S'well* 52-62; Perm to Offic *Ox* 76-83. *SSM Priory, Willen, Milton Keynes MK15 9AA* Tel (01908) 663749

HUME, Martin. b 54. Grimsby Coll of Tech HND75. Coll of Resurr Mirfield 89. **d** 91 **p** 92. C Brentwood St Thos *Chelmsf* 91-94; P-in-c Corringham from 94. *The Rectory, Church Road, Corringham, Stanford-le-Hope, Essex SS17 9AP* Tel (01375) 673074

HUMMERSTONE, Jeremy David. Mert Coll Ox BA65 MA70. Wells Th Coll 70. **d** 72 **p** 73. C Helmsley *York* 72-75; C Pockley cum E Moors 72-75; P-in-c Manningford Bruce w Manningford Abbots *Sarum* 75; TV Swanborough 75-80; P-in-c Frithelstock *Ex* 80-81; P-in-c Gt Torrington 80-81; P-in-c Lt Torrington 80-81; V Gt and Lt Torrington and Frithelstock from 81. *The Vicarage, Calf Street, Torrington, Devon EX38 8EA* Tel (01805) 622166

HUMPHREY, Mrs Betty. b 37. St Mich Ho Ox 59. **d** 90 **p** 94. C Hardwicke, Quedgeley and Elmore w Longney *Glouc* 90-93; D-in-c Swindon w Uckington and Elmstone Hardwicke 93-94; P-in-c 94-96; R from 96. *The Rectory, Swindon, Cheltenham, Glos GL51 9RD* Tel (01242) 329069

HUMPHREY, David Lane. b 57. Maine Univ BA79. St Jo Coll Nottm 84. **d** 88 **p** 89. C Springfield All SS *Chelmsf* 88-91; C Thundersley 91-96; V Standon *St Alb* from 96. *The Vicarage, Kents Lane, Standon, Ware, Herts SG11 1PJ* Tel (01920) 821390

HUMPHREY, Derek Hollis. b 37. Chich Th Coll 69. **d** 72 **p** 73. C Havant *Portsm* 72-75; C Southsea H Spirit 75-78; V Finsbury Park St Thos *Lon* 78-88; V S Patcham *Chich* from 88. *10 Church Close, Brighton BN1 8HS* Tel (01273) 502385

HUMPHREY, Canon George William. b 38. Lon Bible Coll BD61 Lon Univ CertEd74 Man Univ DipEdG75. Oak Hill Th Coll 61. **d** 62 **p** 63. C Heigham H Trin *Nor* 62-64; P-in-c Buckenham w Hassingham and Strumpshaw 64-67; Chapl St Andr Hosp Norwich 64-67; Asst Master Mexborough Gr Sch 67-69; Hd RE Cheadle Gr Sch 69-76; Hon C Cheadle Hulme St Andr *Ches* 70-76; P-in-c Kellington w Whitley *Wakef* 76-80; Teacher Thurnscoe Comp Sch 76-80; RE Insp Glos Co Coun and Dio *Glouc* 80-93; Dioc RE Adv from 93; Hon Can Glouc Cathl from 95. *The Rectory, Swindon, Cheltenham, Glos GL51 9RD* Tel (01242) 329069

HUMPHREY, Heather Mary. b 46. CertEd68. WMMTC 87. **d** 90 **p** 94. NSM Overbury w Teddington, Alstone etc *Worc* from 90. *2/3 Saunders Cottages, Kinsham, Tewkesbury, Glos GL20 8HP* Tel (01684) 72816

HUMPHREY, Timothy Martin. b 62. Ex Univ BA83. St Jo Coll Nottm DipTh87. **d** 89 **p** 90. C Wallington H Trin *S'wark* 89-97; C Church Oakley and Wootton St Lawrence *Win* from 97. *19 Sainfoin Lane, Oakley, Basingstoke, Hants RG23 7HZ* Tel (01256) 782790

HUMPHREYS, Mrs Anne-Marie (Anna). b 44. K Coll Lon BD92 AKC92 SRN67. N Ord Course 92. **d** 95 **p** 96. NSM Man Gd Shep *Man* 95-97; NSM Manchester Gd Shep and St Barn from 97; Chapl Cen Man Healthcare NHS Trust from 96. *16 Clothorn Road, Manchester M20 6BQ* Tel 0161-434 2164

HUMPHREYS, Brian Leonard. **d** 87 **p** 88. NSM Maughold *S & M* 87-92; NSM S Ramsey St Paul 92-94; Perm to Offic from 94. *Lewaigue Lodge, Port Lewaigue, Maughold, Isle of Man IM7 1AG* Tel (01624) 813694

HUMPHREYS, George Bernard. b 10. AKC36. **d** 36 **p** 37. C Leigh St Mary *Man* 36-38; C Streatham St Pet *S'wark* 38-41; C Tarporley *Ches* 42-48; R Moreton Corbet *Lich* 48-53; V Dawley Parva 53-65; R Fobbing *Chelmsf* 65-78; rtd 78; Perm to Offic *Ex* from 78. *Prestercot, Butts Lane, Christow, Exeter EX6 7NN* Tel (01647) 52595

HUMPHREYS, Dr James Graham. b 36. Liv Univ BEng57 PhD60. Trin Coll Bris 61. **d** 63 **p** 64. C Denton Holme *Carl* 63-66; C St Helens St Mark *Liv* 66-68; V Houghton *Carl* 68-79; V Bramcote *S'well* 79-93; RD Beeston 85-90; rtd 93. *43 Ribblesdale Road, Nottingham NG5 3GY* Tel 0115-926 3471

HUMPHREYS, Canon John Elwyn Price. b 15. OBE77 Portuguese Order of Merit 94. Univ of Wales BA37. St Mich Coll Llan 38. **d** 39 **p** 41. C Newtown *St As* 39-42; C Rhosymedre 42-43; Chapl RNVR 43-46; Chapl RN 46-51; Chapl Santa Cruz *Eur* 51-52; Chapl and Asst Master Reed's Sch Cobham 53-57; Lic to Offic *Guildf* 53-57; Chapl Estoril *Eur* 57-80; Can Gib Cathl 67-80; rtd 80. *Casa Contente, Monte Estoril, 2765 Estoril, Portugal* Tel Lisbon (1) 468-3238

HUMPHREYS, John Louis. b 51. Jes Coll Cam BA72 MA76 Nottm Univ BA75. St Jo Coll Nottm 73. **d** 76 **p** 77. C W Bromwich Gd Shep w St Jo *Lich* 76-79; C Woodford Wells *Chelmsf* 79-83; V Werrington *Lich* from 83; Chapl HM Young Offender Inst Werrington Ho from 83. *The Vicarage, 360 Ash Bank Road, Werrington, Stoke-on-Trent ST9 0JS* Tel (01782) 302441 Fax 302504

HUMPHREYS, Canon Kenneth Glyn (Ken). b 28. Bps' Coll Cheshunt 64. **d** 66 **p** 67. C New Windsor St Jo *Ox* 66-67; C Whitley Ch Ch 67-70; V Compton 70-74; V Compton w E Ilsley 74-75; R E Ilsley 74; C Wokingham All SS 75-77; Chapl Lucas Hosp Wokingham (Almshouses) 77-81; V California *Ox* 81-94; RD Sonning 86-88; Hon Can Ch Ch 91-94; rtd 95. *17 Snowberry Close, Wokingham, Berks RG41 4AQ* Tel (0118) 977 2096

HUMPHREYS, Mrs Lydia Ann. b 60. CCSk90. Sarum & Wells Th Coll DCM93. **d** 93 **p** 94. C Gaywood St Faith *Nor* 93-95 and 95-97; TV Cov E *Cov* from 97. *St Margaret's Vicarage, 18 South Avenue, Coventry CV2 4DR* Tel (01203) 457344

HUMPHREYS, Canon Neil Edgar. b 20. St Pet Hall Ox BA48 MA52. Linc Th Coll 48. **d** 50 **p** 51. C Wigan St Geo *Liv* 50-53; C Liv Our Lady and St Nic 53-56; V Dalston *Carl* 56-64; Ghana 64-69; Asst Chapl Liv Univ *Liv* 69-78; Dioc Planning Officer 72-78; Bp's Planning Adv 78-79; Hon Can Liv Cathl 78-89; TV W Derby St Mary 79-89; rtd 89; Perm to Offic *Liv* from 89. *109 Thingwall Road, Liverpool L15 7JX* Tel 0151-722 4114

HUMPHREYS, Canon Philip Noel. b 34. Bps' Coll Cheshunt 62. **d** 64 **p** 65. C Plymouth St Andr *Ex* 64-68; Chapl Lee Abbey 68-73; V Porchester *S'well* 73-82; RD Bingham W 82-87; P-in-c W Leake w Kingston-on-Soar and Ratcliffe-on-Soar 82-87; R W Bridgford from 82; Hon Can S'well Minster from 93. *The Rectory, Church Drive, West Bridgford, Nottingham NG2 6AX* Tel 0115-981 1112

HUMPHREYS, Roger John. b 45. CertEd66 Open Univ BA76. Wycliffe Hall Ox 81. **d** 83 **p** 84. Chapl Dragon Sch Ox 83-87; C Ox St Andr *Ox* 83-87; V Carterton 87-94; R Bladon w Woodstock from 94. *The Rectory, Woodstock, Oxford OX20 1UQ* Tel (01993) 811415

HUMPHREYS, Stephen Robert Beresford. b 52. K Coll Lon 74. **d** 76 **p** 77. C Northwood Hills St Edm *Lon* 76-79; C Manningham St Mary and Bradf St Mich *Bradf* 79-81; C Manningham St Paul and St Jude 82; Chapl Bradf R Infirmary 82-86; C Leeds St Pet *Ripon* 87-90; Perm to Offic *B & W* from 94. *Stowey Farm, Timberscombe, Minehead, Somerset TA24 7BW* Tel (01643) 841265

HUMPHREYS, William Alfred. b 18. Lich Th Coll 54. **d** 56 **p** 57. C Stone St Mich *Lich* 56-60; V Fazeley 60-65; V Prees 65-83; P-in-c Fauls 66-70; V 70-83; RD Wem and Whitchurch 80-83; rtd 83;

Perm to Offic *Heref* from 83. *Bryncroft, 4 Seabridge Meadow, Bucknell, Shropshire SY7 0AP* Tel (01547) 530597

HUMPHREYS, William Haydn. b 09. AKC36. St D Coll Lamp 29. **d** 36 **p** 37. C Kirkheaton *Wakef* 36-43; CF (EC) 43-47; V Dewsbury St Mark *Wakef* 48-78; Chapl Dewsbury Gen Hosp 50-78; rtd 78. *Flat 24, Marion Court, Lisvane Road, Cardiff CF4 5RZ* Tel (01222) 757158

HUMPHRIES, Anthony Roy (Tony). b 49. Lon Univ BSc73. Wycliffe Hall Ox DipMin94. **d** 94 **p** 95. C Worksop St Jo *S'well* 94-96; C Retford from 96. *1 Chapelgate, Retford, Notts DN22 6PL* Tel (01777) 706792

HUMPHRIES, Benjamin Paul. b 56. FRGS Man Univ BA Birm Univ DipTh. Qu Coll Birm 82. **d** 85 **p** 86. C Hall Green Ascension *Birm* 85-88; P-in-c Belmont *Man* 88-96; USPG Fieldworker (Blackb, Bradf, Carl and Wakef) from 96; Perm to Offic *Blackb* from 96; Perm to Offic *Carl* from 96. *6 Higher Bank Road, Fulwood, Preston PR2 4PD* Tel (01772) 713044 Fax as telephone

HUMPHRIES, Miss Catherine Elizabeth. b 53. Anglia Poly Univ MA95. Trin Coll Bris BA87. **d** 87 **p** 94. C Bath Twerton-on-Avon *B & W* 87-90; Personnel Manager and Tr Officer TEAR Fund 90-95; Tr Manager for UK and Overseas Personnel 95; Asst C (MSE) Norbiton *S'wark* 91-96; Perm to Offic *Ely* 95-97; Tutor E Anglian Minl Tr Course from 97. *9 Minster Precincts, Peterborough PE1 1XS* Tel (01733) 897795

HUMPHRIES, Christopher William. b 52. St Jo Coll Cam BA73 MA77 CertEd DipTh. St Jo Coll Nottm 76. **d** 79 **p** 80. C Eccleshill *Bradf* 79-82; Chapl Scargill Ho 82-86; TV Guiseley w Esholt *Bradf* 86-91; V Filey *York* from 91. *The Vicarage, 5 Belle Vue Crescent, Filey, N Yorkshire YO14 9AD* Tel (01723) 512745

HUMPHRIES, David Graham. b 48. Univ of Wales (Cardiff) DipTh70. St Mich Coll Llan 67. **d** 71 **p** 72. C Neath w Llantwit *Llan* 71-72; C Bishop's Cleeve *Glouc* 81-83; C Cirencester 83-87; V Glouc St Steph 87-96; P-in-c Mickleton from 96. *50 Ballards Close, Mickleton, Chipping Campden, Glos GL55 6TN* Tel (01386) 438846

HUMPHRIES, David John. b 51. BSc CertEd BD. Edin Th Coll. **d** 84 **p** 85. C Styvechale *Cov* 84-88; V Greetland and W Vale *Wakef* 88-96; V Shawbury *Lich* from 96; V Stanton on Hine Heath from 96. *The Vicarage, Shawbury, Shrewsbury SY4 4NH* Tel (01939) 250419

HUMPHRIES, Donald. b 43. Bris Univ BA66. Clifton Th Coll 66. **d** 68 **p** 69. C Selly Hill St Steph *Birm* 68-74; Chapl Warw Univ *Cov* 74-79; V Bedford Ch Ch *St Alb* 79-85; V Cambridge H Trin w St Andr Gt *Ely* 85-92; V Cambridge H Trin 92-94; rtd 94; Perm to Offic *Ely* from 94. *56 The Rowans, Milton, Cambridge CB4 6YU*

HUMPHRIES, Miss Dorothy Maud. b 22. Bedf Coll Lon BA44 Lon Univ DipEd45 Cam Univ DipTh50. Gilmore Course 85. **dss** 79 **d** 87 **p** 94. Kidderminster Deanery *Worc* from 79; NSM from 87. *26 Linden Avenue, Kidderminster, Worcs DY10 3AB* Tel (01562) 824459

HUMPHRIES, Frank Charles. b 40. St Chad's Coll Dur BA61 DipTh63. **d** 63 **p** 64. C Tottenham All Hallows *Lon* 63-66; C S Harrow St Paul 66-71; V Hillingdon All SS 71-80; V Preston Ascension from 80; Dir of Ords from 86. *The Vicarage, 319 Preston Road, Harrow, Middx HA3 0QQ* Tel 0181-904 4062

HUMPHRIES, Grahame Leslie. b 44. Lon Coll of Div ALCD70 LTh. **d** 71 **p** 72. C Wandsworth St Mich *S'wark* 71-74; C Slough *Ox* 74-77; P-in-c Arley *Cov* 77-82; R 82-84; Norfolk Churches' Radio Officer *Nor* 84-96; P-in-c Bawdeswell w Foxley 84-96; P-in-c Mayfield *Lich* from 96; Stoke-on-Trent Local Min Adv from 96. *The Vicarage, Church Lane, Mayfield, Ashbourne, Derbyshire DE6 2JR* Tel (01335) 342855

HUMPHRIES, Harold Joseph. b 14. MIEE52. S'wark Ord Course 70. **d** 70 **p** 71. C Merton St Mary *S'wark* 70-71; C Glouc All SS *Glouc* 71-75; Hon C 78-82; C Glouc St Jas 75-77; Hon Min Can Glouc Cathl from 77. *Monument House, St Mary's Street, Gloucester GL1 2QR* Tel (01452) 520449

HUMPHRIES, John. b 49. Univ of Wales (Cardiff) DipTh76. St Mich Coll Llan 73. **d** 76 **p** 77. C Pontnewynydd *Mon* 76-78; C Ebbw Vale 78-81; V Pet Ch Carpenter *Pet* 81-86; P-in-c Kings Cliffe 86-87; R King's Cliffe w Apethorpe 87-93; R King's Cliffe from 93. *The Rectory, 3 Hall Yard, King's Cliffe, Peterborough PE8 6XQ* Tel (01780) 470314

HUMPHRIES, Miss Marion Betty. b 29. K Coll Lon DipTh50 Open Univ BA84. Selly Oak Coll 51. **dss** 80 **d** 87 **p** 94. Newmarket St Mary w Exning St Agnes *St E* 80-82; Acomb St Steph *York* 83-86; Scarborough St Martin 86-87; Par Dn 87-93; C Cayton w Eastfield 94; rtd 94; Perm to Offic *Nor* from 95. *27 Wells Road, Walsingham, Norfolk NR22 6DL* Tel (01328) 820489

HUMPHRIES, William David. b 57. QUB BEd DipTh. **d** 86 **p** 87. C Ballyholme *D & D* 86-90; Min Can Belf Cathl from 89; V Choral Belf Cathl 90-93; C Belfast St Anne *Conn* 90-93; I Stormont *D & D* from 93. *St Molua's Rectory, 64 Wandsworth Road, Belfast BT4 3LU* Tel (01232) 657667

HUMPHRISS, Canon Reginald George (Reg). b 36. Kelham Th Coll 56. **d** 61 **p** 62. C Londonderry *Birm* 61-63; Asst Dir RE *Cant* 63-66; Dioc Youth Chapl 63-66; V Preston next Faversham 66-72; P-in-c Goodnestone St Bart and Graveney 71-72; V Spring Park 72-76; R Cant St Martin and St Paul 76-90; RD Cant 82-88; Hon Can Cant Cathl from 85; R Saltwood from 90; RD Elham from 93. *The Rectory, Saltwood, Hythe, Kent CT21 4QA* Tel (01303) 266932

HUMPHRY, Toby Peter. b 66. Man Univ BA88. Ripon Coll Cuddesdon BA90 Qu Coll Birm 92. **d** 93 **p** 94. C Westhoughton *Man* 93-96; C Westhoughton and Wingates from 97. *1 Furze Avenue, Westhoughton, Bolton BL5 2NW* Tel (01942) 818030

HUMPHRYES, Garry James. b 62. Coll of Resurr Mirfield 92. **d** 95 **p** 96. C Lt Marsden *Blackb* from 95. *3 Rickards Road, Nelson, Lancs BB9 0RN* Tel (01282) 614451

HUMPLEBY, Peter. b 40. Open Univ BA76 Hull Univ DipTh82. Linc Th Coll 75. **d** 77 **p** 78. C Todmorden *Wakef* 77-80; V Bruntcliffe 80-88; R Aldingham and Dendron and Rampside *Carl* 88-92; V Dodworth *Wakef* from 92. *The Vicarage, Green Road, Dodworth, Barnsley, S Yorkshire S75 3TY* Tel (01226) 203838

HUNDLEBY, Alan. b 41. LNSM course 86. **d** 86 **p** 87. NSM Fotherby *Linc* from 86. *35 Cheapside, Waltham, Grimsby, S Humberside DN37 0HE* Tel (01472) 827159

HUNG, Frank Yu-Chi. b 45. Birm Univ BSc68 BA75 Liv Univ MSc71 Ox Univ DipTh77. Wycliffe Hall Ox 76. **d** 78 **p** 79. C Walton H Trin *Ox* 78-82; C Spring Grove St Mary *Lon* 82-85; TV Wexcombe *Sarum* 85-92; V Hatcham St Jas *S'wark* from 92; Chapl Golds Coll Lon from 95. *St James's Vicarage, St James's, London SE14 6AD* Tel 0181-692 7774

HUNGERFORD, Robin Nicholas. b 47. CertEd74. Trin Coll Bris DipHE88. **d** 88 **p** 89. C Swindon Dorcan *Bris* 88-92; TV Melbury *Sarum* from 92. *The Vicarage, Corscombe, Dorchester, Dorset DT2 0NU* Tel (01935) 891247

HUNNISETT, John Bernard. b 47. AKC73. **d** 73 **p** 74. C Charlton Kings St Mary *Glouc* 73-77; C Portsea St Mary *Portsm* 77-80; V Badgeworth w Shurdington *Glouc* 80-87; R Dursley from 87. *The Rectory, The Broadwell, Dursley, Glos GL11 4JE* Tel (01453) 542053 E-mail hunnisett@dial.pipex.com

HUNNYBUN, Martin Wilfrid. b 44. Oak Hill Th Coll 67. **d** 70 **p** 71. C Ware Ch Ch *St Alb* 70-74; C Washfield, Stoodleigh, Withleigh etc *Ex* 74-75; TV Washfield, Stoodleigh, Withleigh etc 75-80; R Braunston *Pet* 80-85; Australia from 85. *284-288 Castle Hill Road, Castle Hill, NSW, Australia 2154* Tel Sydney (2) 634 0530 or 899 8706 Fax 634 0533

HUNT, Alan. b 31. GIMechE51 GIPE51. St Mich Coll Llan 65. **d** 67 **p** 68. C Standish *Blackb* 67-72; V Clitheroe St Paul Low Moor 72-76; Lic to Offic 76-85; rtd 85; Perm to Offic *Blackb* from 85. *68 Coniston Drive, Walton-le-Dale, Preston PR5 4RQ* Tel (01772) 39554

HUNT, Ashley Stephen. b 50. St Jo Coll Nottm 81. **d** 83 **p** 84. C Southchurch H Trin *Chelmsf* 83-86; TV Droitwich *Worc* 86-87; USA 88-91; TV Melton Gt Framland *Leic* 92-93; TV Melton Mowbray from 93. *1 Palmerston Road, Melton Mowbray, Leics LE13 0SS* Tel (01664) 64229

HUNT, Bruce Allan. b 32. Nottm Univ BA54 DipEd55 Leic Univ CCouns90. ALCD59. **d** 61 **p** 62. C Watford St Mary *St Alb* 61-64; C Rayleigh *Chelmsf* 64-69; V Lepton *Wakef* 69-81; V Worksop St Jo *S'well* 81-91; rtd 91; Perm to Offic *S'well* from 91; Perm to Offic *Sheff* from 91. *14 Dunstan Crescent, Worksop, Notts S80 1AF* Tel (01909) 478214

HUNT, Charles Evans. b 13. Dur Univ LTh44. ALCD37. **d** 37 **p** 38. C Doncaster St Jude *Sheff* 37-41; C Wadsley 41-47; C Doncaster St Geo 47-49; V Masbrough St Paul 49-73; P-in-c Masbrough St Jo 56-73; V Wentworth 73-79; rtd 79; Lic to Offic *Ely* from 79. *1 Vicarage Lane, Whittlesford, Cambridge CB2 4NA* Tel (01223) 833402

HUNT, Mrs Christina. b 24. Qu Mary Coll Lon BSc45. S Dios Minl Tr Scheme 78. **dss** 81 **d** 87 **p** 94. Alderbury and W Grimstead *Sarum* 81-87; Hon Par Dn 87-91; Hon Par Dn Alderbury Team 91-94; rtd 94; Perm to Offic *Sarum* from 94. *The Heather, Southampton Road, Alderbury, Salisbury SP5 3AF* Tel (01722) 710601

HUNT, Christopher Paul Colin. b 38. Ch Coll Cam BA62 MA62. Clifton Th Coll 63. **d** 65 **p** 66. C Widnes St Paul *Liv* 65-68; Singapore 68-70; Malaysia 70-71; Hon C Foord St Jo *Cant* 72-73; Iran 74-80; Overseas Service Adv CMS 81-91; Lic to Offic *S'wark* 81-91; P-in-c Claverdon w Preston Bagot *Cov* from 91. *The Vicarage, Church Road, Claverdon, Warks CV35 8PD* Tel (01926) 842256

HUNT, David John. b 35. Kelham Th Coll 60. **d** 65 **p** 66. C Bethnal Green St Jo w St Simon *Lon* 65-69; C Mill Hill St Mich 69-73; R Staple Fitzpaine, Orchard Portman, Thurlbear etc *B & W* 73-79; P-in-c E Coker w Sutton Bingham 79-88; V E Coker w Sutton Bingham and Closworth from 88; RD Merston 85-94. *The Vicarage, East Coker, Yeovil, Somerset BA22 9JG* Tel (01935) 862125

HUNT, Derek Henry. b 38. ALCD61. **d** 62 **p** 63. C Roxeth Ch Ch *Lon* 62-66; C Radipole *Sarum* 66-70; P-in-c Shalbourne w Ham 70-72; V Burbage 72-73; V Burbage and Savernake Ch Ch 73-78; P-in-c Hulcote w Salford *St Alb* 78-88; R Cranfield 78-88; R Cranfield and Hulcote w Salford 88-95; rtd 95. *26 Jowitt Avenue, Kempston, Bedford MK42 8NW*

HUNT, Canon Edward Trebble (Ted). b 31. St Mich Coll Llan 56. **d** 58 **p** 59. C Swansea St Thos *S & B* 58-62; C Swansea St Mary and H Trin 62-65; P-in-c Glantawe 65-72; V 72-76; V Swansea Ch

Ch 76-96; Chapl HM Pris Swansea 76-96; Hon Can Brecon Cathl *S & B* from 96; rtd 96. *16 Coedmor, Sketty, Swansea SA2 8BQ*

HUNT, Ernest Gary. b 36. Univ Coll Dur BA57 DipEd58. Carl Dioc Tr Inst 90. **d** 93 **p** 94. NSM Salesbury *Blackb* 93-95; NSM Blackb St Mich w St Jo and H Trin from 95. *Dunelm, 10 Pleckgate Road, Blackburn BB1 8NN* Tel (01254) 52531

HUNT, Ernest William. b 09. St Jo Coll Dur BA31 MA34 Birm Univ BD46 St Cath Soc Ox BLitt51 Ox Univ MLitt90. St Jo Coll Dur DipTh32. **d** 32 **p** 33. C Gateshead Fell *Dur* 32-37; V Dunston Ch Ch 37-43; Succ Birm Cathl *Birm* 43-51; Lect Qu Coll Birm 46-51; Vice-Prin Lich Th Coll 51-57; Prof St D Coll Lamp 57-69; rtd 75. *16 Peachcroft Road, Abingdon, Oxon OX14 2NA* Tel (01235) 521549

HUNT, Giles Butler. b 28. Trin Hall Cam BA51 MA55. Cuddesdon Coll 51. **d** 53 **p** 54. C N Evington *Leic* 53-56; C Northolt St Mary *Lon* 56-58; Bp's Dom Chapl *Portsm* 58-59; Bp's Chapl *Nor* 59-62; R Holt 62-67; R Kelling w Salthouse 63-67; C Pimlico St Pet w Westmr Ch Ch *Lon* 67-72; V Barkway w Reed and Buckland *St Alb* 72-79; V Preston next Faversham, Goodnestone and Graveney *Cant* 79-92; rtd 92; Perm to Offic *Nor* from 92. *The Cottage, The Fairstead, Cley-next-the-Sea, Holt, Norfolk NR25 7RJ* Tel (01263) 740471

HUNT, Canon Ian Carter. b 34. Chich Th Coll 61. **d** 64 **p** 65. C Plymouth St Pet *Ex* 64-67; C Daventry *Pet* 67-70; V Northampton St Paul 70-91; Can Pet Cathl from 81; V Wellingborough All Hallows from 91. *The Vicarage, Church Street, Wellingborough, Northants NN8 3PA* Tel (01933) 222002

HUNT, James Allen (Jim). b 49. Linc Th Coll CMinlStuds92. **d** 92 **p** 93. C Huddersfield St Pet and All SS *Wakef* 92-95; V Longwood from 95. *St Mark's Vicarage, 313 Vicarage Road, Huddersfield HD3 4HJ* Tel (01484) 653576

HUNT, Jeremy Mark Nicholas. b 46. FRGS70 Open Univ BA73 Bris Univ DipEd. Ridley Hall Cam 83. **d** 85 **p** 86. C Leckhampton SS Phil and Jas w Cheltenham St Jas *Glouc* 85-87; Asst Chapl Vevey w Chateau d'Oex and Villars *Eur* 87-90; Asst Chapl Chapl Berne w Neuchatel 89-90; Chapl HM Pris Pentonville 94-95; Chapl HM Pris Highpoint from 95. *The Chaplain's Office, HM Prison, Highpoint, Stradishall, Newmarket, Suffolk CB8 9YG* Tel (01440) 820611 Fax 820203

HUNT, John Barry. b 46. Lich Th Coll 70 Qu Coll Birm 72. **d** 73 **p** 74. C Auckland St Andr and St Anne *Dur* 73-77; C Consett 77-79; R Lyons 79-89; P-in-c Hebburn St Cuth from 89. *St Cuthbert's Vicarage, Cosserat Place, Hebburn, Tyne & Wear NE31 1RD* Tel 0191-483 2038

HUNT, John Edwin. b 38. ARCO Dur Univ BA60 DipEd. EMMTC 78. **d** 81 **p** 82. NSM Newbold w Dunston *Derby* 81-92; NSM Chesterfield St Mary and All SS from 92. *4 Ardsley Road, Ashgate, Chesterfield, Derbyshire S40 4DG* Tel (01246) 275141

HUNT, John Stewart. b 37. Nor Ord Course 75. **d** 78 **p** 79. NSM Hunstanton St Edm *Nor* 78-81; NSM Hunstanton St Mary w Ringstead Parva, Holme etc 81-86; NSM Sedgeford w Southmere 84-86; C Lowestoft and Kirkley 86-89; R Blundeston w Flixton and Lound 89-93; P-in-c Kessingland w Gisleham from 93. *The Rectory, 1 Wash Lane, Kessingland, Lowestoft, Suffolk NR33 7QZ* Tel (01502) 740256

HUNT, Dr Judith Mary. b 57. MRCVS80 Bris Univ BVSc80 Lon Univ PhD85 Fitzw Coll Cam BA90. Ridley Hall Cam 88. **d** 91 **p** 94. Par Dn Heswall *Ches* 91-94; C 94-95; P-in-c Tilston and Shocklach from 95. *The Rectory, Inveresk Road, Tilston, Malpas, Cheshire SY14 7ED* Tel (01829) 250289

HUNT, Kevin. b 59. St Jo Coll Dur BA80 Ox Univ BA84 MA88. St Steph Ho Ox 81. **d** 84 **p** 85. C Mansfield St Mark *S'well* 84-85; C Hendon and Sunderland *Dur* 85-88; V Sunderland Springwell w Thorney Close 88-95; V Sunderland St Mary and St Pet 95; TR Jarrow from 95; Chapl Monkton and Primrose Hill Hospitals from 95. *St Peter's House, York Avenue, Jarrow, Tyne & Wear NE32 5LP* Tel 0191-489 0946

HUNT, Canon Michael Francis. b 26. Wadh Coll Ox BA49 MA50. St Steph Ho Ox 49. **d** 51 **p** 52. C E Clevedon All SS *B & W* 51-55; C-in-c Broxtowe CD *S'well* 56-62; R Auchterarder *St And* 62-66; R Dumfries *Glas* 66-73; R Arbroath *Bre* 73-78; R Inverness St Mich *Mor* 78-80; R Inverness St Jo 78-80; Papua New Guinea 80-91; Hon Can St Jo Cathl Port Moresby 89-91; rtd 91; P-in-c Tain *Mor* from 91. *St Andrew's Rectory, Manse Street, Tain, Ross-shire IV19 1HE* Tel (01862) 892193

HUNT, Miss Nicola Mary. b 54. SRN77 RSCN77 RHV87. Ripon Coll Cuddesdon DipMin95. **d** 95 **p** 96. C Broughton Astley and Croft w Stoney Stanton *Leic* from 95. *1 Aland Gardens, Broughton Astley, Leicester LE9 6NE* Tel (01455) 286210

HUNT, Paul Edwin. b 47. Ripon Coll Cuddesdon DipMin95. **d** 95 **p** 96. C Cleobury Mortimer w Hopton Wafers etc *Heref* from 95. *The Glebe, New Road Gardens, Cleobury Mortimer, Kidderminster, Worcs DY14 8AW* Tel (01299) 270559

HUNT, Paul Firth. b 62. Ox Univ MA89 Edin Univ BD89. Edin Th Coll 86. **d** 89 **p** 90. C Leeds Halton St Wilfrid *Ripon* 89-92; C Leeds City 92-95; V Leeds Richmond Hill from 95. *All Saints' Vicarage, Pontefract Lane, Leeds LS9 9AE* Tel 0113-248 0971

HUNT, Paul Michael. b 57. St Chad's Coll Dur BA79 K Coll Lon PGCE80 K Coll Lon MA96. Chich Th Coll 91. **d** 92 **p** 93. Chapl Brighton Coll 92-93; NSM St Leonards SS Pet and Paul *Chich* 92-93; Chapl Mill Hill Sch Lon from 93; Hon C Hendon St Paul Mill Hill *Lon* from 95; P in O from 96. *The Bungalow, The Ridgeway, London NW7 1QX* Tel 0181-201 1397 or 959 1176 Fax 201 0663

HUNT, Canon Peter John. b 35. AKC58. St Boniface Warminster. **d** 59 **p** 60. C Chesterfield St Mary and All SS *Derby* 59-61; C Matlock and Tansley 61-63; Chapl Matlock Hosp 61-63; Lect Matlock Teacher Tr Coll 61-63; V Tottington *Man* 63-69; CF (TA) 65-67 and from 75; V Bollington St Jo *Ches* 69-76; R Wilmslow from 76; Hon Can Ches Cathl from 94. *The Rectory, 12 Broadway, Wilmslow, Cheshire SK9 1NB* Tel (01625) 523127 or 520309

HUNT, Philip Lacey Winter. b 09. St Steph Ho Ox. **d** 68 **p** 69. Chapl to the Deaf *Ox* 68-75; Hon Chapl from 75. *13 Wingfield Court, Glebe Street, Oxford OX4 1DG* Tel (01865) 248385

HUNT, Richard William. b 46. G&C Coll Cam BA67 MA71. Westcott Ho Cam 68. **d** 72 **p** 73. C Bris St Agnes and St Simon w St Werburgh *Bris* 72-77; Chapl Selw Coll Cam 77-84; V Birchfield *Birm* from 84. *Holy Trinity Vicarage, 213 Birchfield Road, Birmingham B20 3DG* Tel 0121-356 4241

HUNT, Ms Rosalind (Ros). b 55. Man Univ BA76. St Steph Ho Ox 86. **d** 88 **p** 94. Chapl Jes Coll Cam 88-92; Hon Chapl to the Deaf *Ely* from 92. *107 Hemingford Road, Cambridge CB1 3BY* Tel (01223) 575778

HUNT, Canon Russell Barrett. b 35. NY Univ Virginia Univ Fitzw Ho Cam. Westcott Ho Cam 73. **d** 75 **p** 76. C Leic St Mary *Leic* 75-78; V Leic St Gabr 78-82; Chapl Leic Gen Hosp 82-95; Hon Can Leic Cathl *Leic* 88-95; rtd 95. *33 Braunstone Avenue, Leicester LE3 0JH* Tel 0116-254 9101

HUNT, Simon John. b 60. Pemb Coll Ox BA81 MA85. St Jo Coll Nottm 87. **d** 90 **p** 91. C Stalybridge St Paul *Ches* 90-93; C Heysham *Blackb* from 93. *Blomidon House, 11 Heysham Mossgate Road, Morecambe, Lancs LA3 2JU* Tel (01524) 853846

HUNT, Stephen. b 38. Man Univ BSc61 MSc62 PhD64 DSc80. Carl Dioc Tr Inst 88. **d** 91 **p** 92. C Broughton *Blackb* 91-95; Chapl Preston Acute Hosps NHS Trust from 94; V Preston Em *Blackb* from 95. *Emmanuel Vicarage, 2 Cornthwaite Road, Preston PR2 3DA* Tel (01772) 717136

HUNT, Timothy Collinson. b 65. ASVA91 Univ of Wales (Cardiff) BD95. Ripon Coll Cuddesdon 95. **d** 97. C Ex St Dav *Ex* from 97. *44 Wrefords Close, Exeter EX4 5AY* Tel (01392) 211482

HUNT, Vera Susan Henrietta. b 33. S Dios Minl Tr Scheme 88. **d** 91 **p** 94. Hon Chapl RAD from 91. *27 Redriff Close, Maidenhead, Berks SL6 4DJ* Tel (01628) 23909

HUNTER, Allan Davies. b 36. Univ of Wales (Lamp) BA57. Coll of Resurr Mirfield 57. **d** 59 **p** 60. C Cardiff St Jo *Llan* 59-68; V Llansawel 68-76; Youth Chapl 71-77; V Llansawel w Briton Ferry 76-79; V Canton St Cath from 79. *The Vicarage, 22A Romilly Crescent, Canton, Cardiff CF1 9NR* Tel (01222) 382796

✠**HUNTER, The Rt Revd Anthony George Weaver.** b 16. Leeds Univ BA39. Coll of Resurr Mirfield 39. **d** 41 **p** 42 **c** 68. C Newc St Geo *Newc* 41-43 and 48-49; S Africa 43-48; V Ashington *Newc* 49-60; V Huddersfield St Pet and St Paul *Wakef* 60-68; RD Huddersfield 60-68; Hon Can Wakef Cathl 62-68; Bp Swaziland 68-75; R Hexham *Newc* 75-79; Asst Bp Newc 76-81; rtd 81. *The West Wing, Sandwood House, Spaldington, Goole, N Humberside DN14 7NG* Tel (01430) 432434

HUNTER, Cyril Stanley Maurice. b 18. Worc Ord Coll 67. **d** 69 **p** 70. C Guisborough *York* 69-72; C Northallerton w Kirby Sigston 72-75; P-in-c Thornton-le-Street w Thornton-le-Moor etc 75-79; R Thornton le Street w N Otterington etc 79-85; rtd 85; Perm to Offic *York* from 85. *Linden, Upsall Road, South Kilvington, Thirsk, N Yorkshire YO7 2NQ* Tel (01845) 522829

HUNTER, David. b 30. Edin Th Coll 60. **d** 64 **p** 65. C Glas Ch Ch *Glas* 64-67; R 67-70 and 75-78; R Coatbridge 70-73; Chapl HM Pris Glas (Barlinnie) 72-84; P-in-c Glas H Trin *Glas* 73-84; R Glas All SS 84-95; rtd 95. *5/12 Anniesland Court, 843 Crow Road, Glasgow G13 1LG* Tel 0141-959 4943

HUNTER, David Matheson. b 46. K Coll Lon BD69 AKC69. **d** 76 **p** 77. C Paignton St Jo *Ex* 76-80; C Plymstock 80-82; Jerusalem 82-84; P-in-c Brinkley, Burrough Green and Carlton *Ely* 84-86; P-in-c Westley Waterless 84-86; R Bressingham w N and S Lopham and Fersfield *Nor* 87-96; rtd 96; Chapl and Lect Wymondham Coll *Nor* from 96. *2 Cavick Cottages, Cavick Road, Wymondham, Norfolk NR18 9PJ* Tel (01953) 605672

HUNTER, Edwin Wallace. b 43. FCIM NUI BA83 DipCatech DipCIM. **d** 94 **p** 95. NSM Cork St Fin Barre's Union *C, C & R* from 94; Min Can Cork Cathl from 95. *Cedar Lodge, Church Road, Carrigaline, Co Cork, Irish Republic* Tel Cork (21) 372338

HUNTER, Canon Frank Geoffrey. b 34. Keble Coll Ox BA56 MA60 Fitzw Coll Cam BA58 MA62. Ridley Hall Cam 57. **d** 59 **p** 60. C Bircle *Man* 59-62; C Jarrow Grange *Dur* 62-65; V Kingston upon Hull St Martin *York* 65-72; V Linthorpe 72-76; V Heslington from 76; RD Derwent from 78; Can and Preb York Minster from 85. *The Rectory, Heslington, York YO1 5EE* Tel (01904) 410389

HUNTER, Harold Hamilton. b 23. Dur Univ BSc48. NE Ord Course 76. **d** 79 **p** 80. NSM Corbridge w Halton *Newc* 79-82;

NSM Corbridge w Halton and Newton Hall from 82. *15 Carham Close, Corbridge, Northd NE45 5NA* Tel (01434) 632748

HUNTER, Ian Paton. b 20. Em Coll Cam BA46 MA50. Tyndale Hall Bris 40. **d** 43 **p** 47. C Harrington *Pet* 43-47; C Portman Square St Paul *Lon* 47-50; V Furneux Pelham w Stocking Pelham *St Alb* 50-54; V Moulton *Pet* 54-60; V Danehill *Chich* 60-67; R Plumpton w E Chiltington 67-77; V Burwash Weald 77-83; P-in-c Stonegate 83-85; rtd 85; Perm to Offic *Chich* from 86. *Edzell, 15 Harrow Close, Seaford, E Sussex BN25 3PE* Tel (01323) 899871

HUNTER, James. b 38. Bible Tr Inst Glas DipTh65 Union Th Coll Belf BD90. **d** 92 **p** 92. In Pb Ch of Ireland 82-92; V Werneth *Man* from 92. *St Thomas's Vicarage, 3 Regency Close, Oldham OL8 1SS* Tel 0161-678 8926

HUNTER, Canon John Gaunt. b 21. St Jo Coll Dur BA49 Leeds Univ MA94. Ridley Hall Cam 49. **d** 51 **p** 52. C Bradf Cathl *Bradf* 51-54; C Compton Gifford *Ex* 54-56; V Bootle St Matt *Liv* 56-62; Uganda 62-65; Prin Bp Tucker Coll 62-65; Dioc Missr *Liv* 65-71; V Altcar 65-78; Abp York's Adv in Miss 71-78; Hon Can Liv Cathl 71-78; R Buckhurst Hill *Chelmsf* 78-79; TR 79-89; Dioc Adv in Evang *Bradf* 89-92; rtd 92; Perm to Offic *Bradf* from 92. *Westhouse Lodge, Westhouse, Carnforth, Lancs LA6 3NZ* Tel (01524) 241305

HUNTER, Lionel Lawledge Gleave. b 24. Liv Coll of Art NDD50. ALCD53. **d** 53 **p** 54. C Leic H Trin *Leic* 53-56; C Northampton St Giles *Pet* 56-58; C Everton St Chrys *Liv* 58-59; P-in-c Liv St Mich 59-61; Chile 61-72; R Diddlebury w Bouldon and Munslow *Heref* 72-75; P-in-c Abdon w Clee St Margaret 73-75; P-in-c Holdgate w Tugford 73-75; Canada 75-85; V N Elmham w Billingford *Nor* 85-89; R N Elmham w Billingford and Worthing 89-90; rtd 90; Perm to Offic *Heref* from 93. *Araucana, Wyson Lane, Brimfield, Ludlow, Shropshire SY8 4AN* Tel (01584) 711463

HUNTER, Dr Michael John. b 45. CCC Cam BA67 MA71 PhD71 Ox Univ BA75. Wycliffe Hall Ox 73. **d** 76 **p** 77. C Partington and Carrington *Ches* 76-79; CMS 80-90; Uganda 80-89; C Penn Fields *Lich* from 90; RD Trysull from 97. *100 Bellencroft Gardens, Wolverhampton WV3 8DU* Tel (01902) 763603

HUNTER, Canon Michael Oram. b 40. K Coll Lon BD64 AKC64. **d** 65 **p** 66. C Tividale *Lich* 65-68; C Harrogate St Wilfrid *Ripon* 68-70; V Hawksworth Wood 70-78; V Whitkirk 78-86; TR Gt Grimsby St Mary and St Jas *Linc* from 86; Can and Preb Linc Cathl from 89. *49 Park Drive, Grimsby, S Humberside DN32 0EG* Tel (01472) 342933

HUNTER, Paul. b 55. Huddersfield Poly BEd82. Chich Th Coll 86. **d** 88 **p** 90. C Weymouth H Trin *Sarum* 88-92; P-in-c Hucknall Torkard *S'well* 92; TV 92-96; V Thurcroft *Sheff* from 96. *The Vicarage, 122 Green Arbour Road, Thurcroft, Rotherham, S Yorkshire S66 9ED* Tel (01709) 542261

HUNTER, Peter Wells. b 52. Bris Univ BSc73. Trin Coll Bris BA91. **d** 91 **p** 92. C New Borough and Leigh *Sarum* 91-97; P-in-c Warminster Ch Ch from 97. *The Vicarage, 13 Avon Road, Warminster, Wilts BA12 9PR* Tel (01985) 212219

HUNTER, Robert. b 36. Man Univ BSc60. Clifton Th Coll. **d** 63 **p** 64. C Chadderton Ch Ch *Man* 63-65; C Balderstone 65-69; C Newburn *Newc* 69-73; TV Sutton St Jas and Wawne *York* 73-81; V Bilton St Pet 81-82; Hon C N Hull St Mich 82-91; TV Howden TM from 91. *3 Thimblehall Lane, Newport, Brough, N Humberside HU15 2PX* Tel (01430) 440546

HUNTER, Rodney Squire. b 33. Ox Univ BA56 MA61. Coll of Resurr Mirfield 56. **d** 58 **p** 59. C Forest Gate St Edm *Chelmsf* 58-61; Lib Pusey Ho Ox 61-65; Zambia 65-74; Malawi from 74. *Box 130, Zomba, Malawi* Tel Malawi (265) 522419

HUNTER-BAILEY, James Ralph. b 11. Ripon Hall Ox 55. **d** 56 **p** 57. C St Jo in Bedwardine *Worc* 56-58; C Ealing St Pet Mt Park *Lon* 58-59; C Pershore w Wick *Worc* 59-61; V Skegby *S'well* 61-64; R Wychbold and Upton Warren *Worc* 64-71; Lic to Offic *Sarum* 71-78; rtd 76; Perm to Offic *Win* 78-95. *46 Erica Drive, Corfe Mullen, Wimborne, Dorset BH21 3TQ* Tel (01202) 602260

HUNTER SMART, Ian Douglas. b 60. St Jo Coll Dur BA83. Edin Th Coll 83. **d** 85 **p** 86. C Cockerton *Dur* 85-89; TV Jarrow 89-92; TV Sunderland from 92; Chapl Sunderland Univ from 92. *2 Thornhill Terrace, Sunderland SR2 7JL* Tel 0191-510 8267 E-mail ian.hunter-smart@sunderland.ac.uk

HUNTINGDON, Archdeacon of. *See* BEER, The Ven John Stuart

HUNTINGDON, Suffragan Bishop of. *See* FLACK, The Rt Revd John Robert

HUNTLEY, David Anthony. Lon Univ BA60. **d** 64 **p** 65. OMF Internat from 65; Singapore 68-77; Hong Kong 77-81; Thailand from 81. *c/o OMF, Belmont, The Vine, Sevenoaks, Kent TN13 3TZ* Tel (01732) 450747 Fax 456164

HUNTLEY, Denis Anthony. b 56. Qu Coll Birm 77. **d** 80 **p** 81. C Llanblethian w Cowbridge and Llandough etc *Llan* 80-83; TV Glyncorrwg w Afan Vale and Cymmer Afan 83-86; R 86-89; Chapl Asst Walsgrave Hosp Cov 89-92; Chapl Halifax Gen Hosp 92-94; Chapl Calderdale Healthcare NHS Trust 94-97; C Leeds City *Ripon* from 97; Chapl to the Deaf from 97. *11 Bedford View, Leeds LS16 6DL* Tel 0113-267 2599

HUNTRESS, Franklin Elias. b 33. Berkeley Div Sch STM62. **d** 62 **p** 63. USA 62-65 and 73-77 and 81-91; C Ches St Mary *Ches* 65-68; C Waltham Abbey *Chelmsf* 68-73; V Leic St Gabr *Leic* 77-81; C Skegness and Winthorpe *Linc* 91-93; P-in-c Long Bennington w Foston 93-94. *c/o The Revd Canon R Rodger, Bishop's House, Eastgate, Lincoln LN2 1QQ* Tel (01522) 534701

HUNWICKE, John William. b 41. Hertf Coll Ox BA64 MA67. St Steph Ho Ox. **d** 67 **p** 68. C Beaconsfield *Ox* 67-70; C Newington St Paul *S'wark* 70-73; Asst Chapl Lancing Coll from 73. *Hoe Court House, Lancing, W Sussex BN15 0QX* Tel (01903) 752145

HURCOMBE, Thomas William (Tom). b 45. BD74 AKC76. **d** 76 **p** 77. C Hampstead All So *Lon* 76-79; C Is of Dogs Ch Ch and St Jo w St Luke 79-83; C Bromley All Hallows 83-89; C E Greenwich Ch Ch w St Andr and St Mich *S'wark* 89-96; Ind Chapl from 89; Dioc Urban Missr 90-96; Greenwich Waterfront Chapl from 96. *81 Charlton Road, London SE3 8TH* Tel 0181-858 9521

HURD, Alun John. b 52. Avery Hill Coll DipHE83. Trin Coll Bris BA86. **d** 86 **p** 87. C Chertsey *Guildf* 86-90; Chapl St Pet Hosp Chertsey 86-90; V W Ewell *Guildf* from 90. *All Saints' Vicarage, 7 Church Road, Epsom, Surrey KT19 9QY* Tel 0181-393 4357

HURD, Arthur Edward Stanley. b 12. St Jo Coll Dur LTh41 BA42 MA45. Tyndale Hall Bris 38. **d** 42 **p** 43. C Broadwater St Mary *Chich* 42-45; BCMS 45-57; Ethiopia 45-57; Kenya 57-62; Adn Maralal 59-62; V Gen 61-62; R Southover *Chich* 63-77; rtd 77; Perm to Offic *Chich* from 77; Perm to Offic *B & W* 77-95. *9 Wiltons, Wrington, Bristol BS18 7LS* Tel (01934) 862382

HURD, Brenda Edith. b 44. Sittingbourne Coll DipEd75. Cant Sch of Min 87. **d** 92 **p** 94. NSM Birling, Addington, Ryarsh and Trottiscliffe *Roch* from 92. *Southview, London Road, Ryarsh, West Malling, Kent ME19 5AW* Tel (01732) 842588

HURD, John Patrick. b 37. CertEd65 Open Univ BA73 Kent Univ MA92. S Dios Minl Tr Scheme 77. **d** 80 **p** 81. NSM Billingshurst *Chich* 80-82 and 89-94; NSM Itchingfield w Slinfold 82-89. *Groomsland Cottage, Parbrook, Billingshurst, W Sussex RH14 9EU* Tel (01403) 782167

HURDMAN, William Richard. b 40. AKC66 Hull Univ MA84. **d** 67 **p** 72. C Portsea St Mary *Portsm* 67-68; C N Walsham w Antingham *Nor* 71-74; V Friskney *Linc* 74-81; TR Bottesford w Ashby 81-88; TR Hackney *Lon* 88-95; P-in-c King's Lynn St Marg w St Nic *Nor* from 95. *St Margaret's Vicarage, St Margaret's Place, King's Lynn, Norfolk PE30 5DL* Tel (01553) 772858

HURFORD, Colin Osborne. b 33. Qu Coll Ox BA55 MA59. Wells Th Coll 55. **d** 57 **p** 58. C Barnoldswick w Bracewell *Bradf* 57-61; C Warrington St Elphin *Liv* 61-63; Malaysia 63-70; P-in-c Annscroft *Heref* 71-79; P-in-c Longden 71-79; P-in-c Pontesbury III 71-79; R Longden and Annscroft 79-85; P-in-c Church Pulverbatch 81-85; R Longden and Annscroft w Pulverbatch 85-86; Tanzania 86-87; TR Billingham St Aid *Dur* 87-96; rtd 96. *4 Manor Park, Pontesbury, Shrewsbury SY5 0RH*

HURFORD, The Ven Richard Warwick. b 44. St Jo Coll Auckland DipTh70. **d** 69 **p** 70. Australia 69-71; P-in-c Tisbury *Sarum* 71-73; R 73-75; R Tisbury and Swallowcliffe w Ansty 75-76; P-in-c Chilmark 76-78; TR Tisbury 76-78; Australia from 78; Adn The Clarence and Hastings 85-87; Dean Grafton from 83; Adn 87-92. *The Deanery, 2 Duke Street, Grafton, NSW, Australia 2460* Tel Grafton (66) 422844 or 431745 Fax 432519

HURLE, Anthony Rowland (Tony). b 54. Lon Univ BSc Em Coll Cam PGCE. Wycliffe Hall Ox 80. **d** 83 **p** 84. C Ipswich St Mary at Stoke w St Pet *St E* 83-87; TV Barking St Marg w St Patr *Chelmsf* 87-92; V St Alb St Paul *St Alb* from 92; RD St Alb from 95. *St Paul's Vicarage, 7 Brampton Road, St Albans, Herts AL1 4PN* Tel (01727) 836810 or 846281

HURLE (née POWNALL), Mrs Lydia Margaret. b 53. Wycliffe Hall Ox 78. **dss** 81 **d** 94 **p** 95. Ipswich St Mary at Stoke w St Pet & St Mary Quay *St E* 81-83; NSM St Alb St Paul *St Alb* from 93. *St Paul's Vicarage, 7 Brampton Road, St Albans, Herts AL1 4PN* Tel (01727) 836810

HURLEY, Daniel Timothy. b 37. St Mich Coll Llan 68. **d** 70 **p** 71. C Llanfabon *Llan* 70-73; CF 73-79; R W Walton *Ely* 79-86; V Cwmddauddwr w St Harmon's and Llanwrthwl *S & B* from 86. *The Vicarage, Cwmdeuddwr, Rhayader LD6 5AP* Tel (01597) 810574

HURLEY, Mark Tristan. b 57. Trin Coll Bris DipHE88 BA89 Sarum & Wells Th Coll 89. **d** 91 **p** 92. C Gainsborough All SS *Linc* 91-94; TV Grantham from 94. *The Vicarage, The Grove, Grantham, Lincs NG31 7PU* Tel (01476) 71270

HURLEY, Robert. b 64. Univ of Wales (Cardiff) BD86. Ridley Hall Cam 88. **d** 90 **p** 91. C Dagenham *Chelmsf* 90-93; C Egg Buckland *Ex* 93-96; C Devonport St Budeaux 96; P-in-c Camberwell All SS *S'wark* from 96; Camberwell Deanery Missr from 96. *36 Finsen Road, London SE5 9AX*

HURLOCK, Ronald James. b 31. BSc PhD. St Deiniol's Hawarden. **d** 83 **p** 84. C Oxton *Ches* 83-87; Chapl Asst Man R Infirmary 87-91; rtd 91. *78 Garwood Close, Westbrook, Warrington WA5 5TF* Tel (01925) 444583

HURLSTON, Ronald Wilcox. b 30. St Deiniol's Hawarden 84. **d** 86 **p** 87. NSM Timperley *Ches* 86-90; C 90-95; rtd 95; Perm to Offic *Ches* from 95. *1 Heath Road, Timperley, Altrincham, Cheshire WA15 6BH* Tel 0161-973 9205

HURN, Mrs June Barbara. b 32. Birm Univ CertEd53. Cant Sch of Min 87. **d** 90 **p** 94. NSM Chislehurst St Nic *Roch* from 90.

Hawkswing, Hawkswood Lane, Chislehurst, Kent BR7 5PW Tel 0181-467 2320

HURRELL, John William. b 25. Ripon Hall Ox 65. **d** 66 **p** 67. C Painswick *Glouc* 66-68; C Glouc St Geo 68-70; C Thornbury 70-73; V Glouc St Steph 73-86; V Deerhurst, Apperley w Forthampton and Chaceley 86-90; rtd 90; Perm to Offic *B & W* from 90. *1 Church View, Porlock, Minehead, Somerset TA24 8NA* Tel (01643) 862488

HURRELL, Canon Lionel Rex. b 41. Southn Univ BA64. Coll of Resurr Mirfield 64. **d** 66 **p** 67. C St Marychurch *Ex* 66-69; C Dawlish 69-71; Dioc Youth Officer *Cov* 71-75; V Porthleven *Truro* 75-80; RD Kerrier 78-80; P-in-c Sithney 78-80; V Swindon New Town *Bris* 80-88; TR 88-97; RD Wroughton 93-97; Hon Can Bris Cathl 94-97; rtd 97. *331 Seaside, Eastbourne, E Sussex BN22 7PA*

HURST, Alaric Desmond St John. b 24. New Coll Ox BA50 MA70. Wells Th Coll 48. **d** 51 **p** 53. C Huddersfield H Trin *Wakef* 51-52; C Leeds St Geo *Ripon* 52-54; Bp's Chapl for Rehabilitation *Roch* 55-56; C St Steph Walbrook and St Swithun etc *Lon* 57-59; V Pudsey St Paul *Bradf* 59-63; V Writtle *Chelmsf* 63-69; rtd 89. *9 Ganderton Court, Pershore, Worcs WR10 1AW* Tel (01905) 840939

HURST, Antony. b 38. MA MSc. S'wark Ord Course 79. **d** 83 **p** 84. NSM S'wark H Trin w St Matt *S'wark* 83-89; NSM S'wark Ch Ch from 89. *33 Hugh Street, London SW1V 1QT* Tel 0171-828 2844

HURST, Brian Charles. b 58. Nottm Univ BA. Ripon Coll Cuddesdon 82. **d** 84 **p** 85. C Cullercoats St Geo *Newc* 84-87; C Prudhoe 87-88; TV Willington Team 88-95; V Denton from 95; RD Newc W from 97. *The Vicarage, Dunblane Crescent, Newcastle upon Tyne NE5 2BE* Tel 0191-267 4376

HURST, Colin. b 49. Linc Th Coll 88. **d** 90 **p** 91. C Wavertree H Trin *Liv* 90-93; C Croft and Stoney Stanton *Leic* 93-95; TV Broughton Astley and Croft w Stoney Stanton 95-97; V Wigan St Andr *Liv* from 97. *St Andrew's Vicarage, 3A Mort Street, Wigan, Lancs WN6 7AU* Tel (01942) 43514

HURST, Colin. b 58. Westmr Coll Ox BA90. St Jo Coll Nottm MA95. **d** 95 **p** 96. C Warboys w Broughton and Bury w Wistow *Ely* from 95. *78 Humberdale Way, Warboys, Huntingdon, Cambs PE17 2TP* Tel (01487) 823878

HURST, Geoffrey. b 30. St Aid Birkenhead 59. **d** 64 **p** 65. C Sheff Parson Cross St Cecilia *Sheff* 64-69; V Wellingborough St Mark *Pet* 69-77; P-in-c Leic St Mark *Leic* 77-82; TV Leic Resurr 82-83; V Willenhall St Steph *Lich* 83-85; V Nether Hoyland St Andr *Sheff* 85-91; V Moorends 91-94; rtd 95. *80 Sunnyvale Road, Sheffield S17 4FB* Tel 0114-236 1407

HURST, Jeremy Richard. b 40. FCP Trin Coll Cam BA61 MA MPhil. Linc Th Coll 62. **d** 64 **p** 65. C Woolwich St Mary w H Trin *S'wark* 64-69; Perm to Offic *Ex* 69-76; Perm to Offic *Ox* 76-84; TV Langley Marish 84-85; TR from 85; Chapl Thames Valley Univ *Lon* from 92. *The Rectory, 3 St Mary's Road, Langley, Berks SL3 7EN* Tel (01753) 542068

HURST, John. b 31. NW Ord Course 76. **d** 79 **p** 80. C Flixton St Jo *Man* 79-82; P-in-c Hindsford 82-86; V 86-88; V Halliwell St Paul 88-93; rtd 93. *6 Barrisdale Close, Bolton BL3 4TR* Tel (01204) 654863

HURST, John Cecil. b 08. Trin Coll Cam BA30 MA37. Westcott Ho Cam 31. **d** 32 **p** 33. C Camberwell St Geo *S'wark* 32-36; Perm to Offic *Leic* 36-37; C Rye *Chich* 37-41; R Yoxall *Lich* 41-50; R W Meon *Portsm* 50-63; R W Meon and Warnford 63-73; RD Petersfield 57-62; rtd 73. *Middle Butts, Rectory Lane, Meonstoke, Southampton SO32 3NF* Tel (01489) 877309

HURST-BANNISTER, Michael Barnabas St Leger. b 19. Dorchester Miss Coll 41. **d** 44 **p** 45. C Machen *Mon* 45-46; C W Wycombe *Ox* 46-48; C Hendford *B & W* 48-49; V Pilton 49-56; R Fugglestone w Bemerton *Sarum* 56-63; R Gt Wishford 63-67; R Lt Langford 63-67; CECS Clerical Org Sec Dios Win, Sarum and Portsm 67-78; Sen Chapl Actors' Ch Union 75-89; P-in-c Soho St Anne w St Thos and St Pet *Lon* 78-84; rtd 84. *Barford Lodge, West Street, Barford St Martin, Salisbury SP3 4AS* Tel (01722) 742630

HURT, Arnould Herbert. b 04. Man Univ BSc24. Cuddesdon Coll 28. **d** 28 **p** 29. C Blackb St Jo *Blackb* 28-32; C Sunderland *Dur* 32-37; V Shirebrook *Derby* 37-45; V Woodville 45-53; V New Cleethorpes *Linc* 53-62; Prin St Mich Coll Belize 62-68; V Scunthorpe Resurr 69-71; rtd 71; P-in-c Innerleithen *Edin* 73-77 and 82-92; Hon C Anfield St Marg *Liv* 77-82. *41 St Augustine's Avenue, Grimsby, S Humberside DN32 0LD* Tel (01472) 752349

HUSBAND, Terence. b 26. NW Ord Course 72. **d** 75 **p** 76. C Weaste *Man* 75-78; R Gorton St Phil 78-81; V Belford *Newc* 81-88; Lic to Offic from 88; rtd 91. *11 Carham Close, Corbridge, Northd NE45 5NA* Tel (01434) 633274

HUSBANDS, Canon Norman. b 03. AKC32. St Steph Ho Ox 32. **d** 32 **p** 33. C Northampton St Edm *Pet* 32-37; C Richmond St Jo *S'wark* 37-41; V Roade *Pet* 41-76; P-in-c Courteenhall 47-54; RD Wootton 63-69; Can Pet Cathl 67-76; rtd 76; Lic to Offic *Pet* 76-86; Perm to Offic from 86. *47 Ridge Way, Weston Favell, Northampton NN3 3AP* Tel (01604) 408024

HUSSELL, Thomas Stanley (Stan). b 13. Univ of Wales BSc34. Sarum Th Coll 35. **d** 37 **p** 38. C Morley St Paul *Wakef* 37-42; C Liversedge 42-44; V W Vale 44-50; V Thornbury *Bradf* 50-57; C Wakef Cathl *Wakef* 57-61; Asst Master Qu Eliz Gr Sch Wakef 57-78; V Wragby 61-71; Lic to Offic 71-95; rtd 78; Perm to Offic *Wakef* from 78. *22 St John's Grove, Wakefield, W Yorkshire WF1 3SA* Tel (01924) 377891

HUSSEY, William Kenneth Alfred. b 27. St Jo Coll Ox BA48 DipEd49 MA52. Wycliffe Hall Ox 51. **d** 52 **p** 53. Asst Chapl Wrekin Coll Shropshire 55-60; Chapl Ipswich Sch 60-72; Hd Master Ches Cathl Choir Sch 72-74; Chapl Rendcomb Coll Cirencester 74-78; P-in-c Rendcomb *Glouc* 74-78; Chapl Berkhamsted Colleg Sch Herts 78-83; TV Redruth w Lanner *Truro* 83-84; V St Goran w St Mich Caerhays 84-89; rtd 89; Perm to Offic *Truro* from 89. *20 Albany Road, Falmouth, Cornwall TR11 3RW* Tel (01326) 312343

HUTCHEON, Mrs Elsie. b 39. RGN63 SCM65 RCN79. EAMTC 89. **d** 92 **p** 94. NSM Heigham St Thos *Nor* from 92. *Beech Cottage, 103 Norwich Road, Tacolneston, Norwich NR16 1BP* Tel (01508) 41424

HUTCHIN, David William. b 37. LRAM ARCM LTCL Man Univ MusB58 CertEd59 DipEd59. Glouc Sch of Min 85. **d** 88 **p** 89. NSM Northleach w Hampnett and Farmington *Glouc* 88-94; NSM Cold Aston w Notgrove and Turkdean 88-94; NSM Chedworth, Yanworth and Stowell, Coln Rogers etc from 94; RD Northleach from 96. *The Vicarage, Chedworth, Cheltenham, Glos GL54 4AE* Tel (01285) 720392

HUTCHINGS, Colin Michael. b 36. Clifton Th Coll 66. **d** 68 **p** 69. C Worksop St Jo *S'well* 68-71; C Hampreston *Sarum* 71-76; TV Tisbury 76-82; R Waddesdon w Over Winchendon and Fleet Marston *Ox* from 82. *The Rectory, Waddesdon, Aylesbury, Bucks HP18 0JQ* Tel (01296) 651312

HUTCHINGS, Ian James. b 49. Lon Univ DipTh72. Clifton Th Coll 69 Trin Coll Bris 72. **d** 73 **p** 74. C Parr *Liv* 73-77; C Timperley *Ches* 77-81; V Partington and Carrington 81-96; V Huntington from 96; Chapl Bp's Blue Coat C of E High Sch from 96. *St Luke's Vicarage, 14 Celandine Close, Huntington, Chester CH3 6DT* Tel (01244) 347345 Fax as telephone

HUTCHINGS, John Denis Arthur. b 29. Keble Coll Ox BA53 MA59 MSc59. Chich Th Coll 58. **d** 60 **p** 61. C St Pancras w St Jas and Ch Ch *Lon* 60-63; Asst Chapl Denstone Coll Uttoxeter 63-67 and 79-83; C Stepney St Dunstan and All SS *Lon* 67-78; V Devonport St Boniface *Ex* 83-86; TR Devonport St Boniface and St Phil 86-93; P-in-c Lydford and Brent Tor 93-95; rtd 96; Perm to Offic *Ex* from 96. *Flat above 40 Brook Street, Tavistock, Devon PL19 0HE* Tel (01822) 616946

HUTCHINGS, Norman Leslie. b 09. MVI. Wycliffe Hall Ox 42. **d** 43 **p** 43. C Tonbridge SS Pet and Paul *Roch* 43-46; V Islington St Steph w St Bart and St Matt *Lon* 46-53; PC Dollis Hill St Paul 53-62; V Ore Ch Ch *Chich* 62-77; Chapl Mt Pleasant Hosp 65-77; Chapl Ledsham Court Sch 65-77; rtd 77; Perm to Offic *Chich* from 77; Perm to Offic *Roch* from 77. *6 Sunnyside Road, Rusthall, Tunbridge Wells, Kent TN4 8RB* Tel (01892) 533264

HUTCHINGS, Robert Henry. b 45. Nottm Univ DTPS88. EMMTC 85. **d** 88 **p** 89. NSM Kibworth and Smeeton Westerby and Saddington *Leic* 88-90; NSM Swinford w Catthorpe, Shawell and Stanford 90-92; NSM Newtown Linford 92-94; NSM Husbands Bosworth w Mowsley and Knaptoft etc from 94. *16 Highcroft, Husbands Bosworth, Lutterworth, Leics LE17 6LF* Tel (01858) 880131

HUTCHINSON, Alison Joyce. b 62. Leeds Univ BA84 RMN90. Aston Tr Scheme 92 Ripon Coll Cuddesdon 94. **d** 97. C Benfieldside *Dur* from 97. *36 Barley Mill Crescent, Bridgehill, Consett, Co Durham DH8 8JX* Tel (01207) 590650

HUTCHINSON, Andrew Charles. b 63. Univ of Wales (Ban) BA84 MEd96. Aston Tr Scheme 85 Chich Th Coll 87. **d** 89 **p** 90. C Burnley St Cath w St Alb and St Paul *Blackb* 89-92; C Shrewsbury St Chad w St Mary *Lich* 92-94; Chapl Heref Cathl Sch from 94; Succ Heref Cathl *Heref* from 94. *3 Castle Street, Hereford HR1 2NL* Tel (01432) 273708

HUTCHINSON, Andrew Paul. b 65. Trin Hall Cam BA87 MA91 Ox Univ BTh97 Solicitor 90. Aston Tr Scheme 92 Ripon Coll Cuddesdon 94. **d** 97. C Stanley *Dur* from 97. *36 Barley Mill Crescent, Bridgehill, Consett, Co Durham DH8 8JX* Tel (01207) 590650

HUTCHINSON, Canon Cyril Peter. b 37. Dur Univ BA61. Wm Temple Coll Rugby 61. **d** 63 **p** 64. C Birm St Paul *Birm* 63-67; Prin Community Relns Officer 66-69; Perm to Offic 67-69; Dir Bradf SHARE 69-76; Perm to Offic *Bradf* 69-75; Hon C Manningham 75-76; V Clayton 76-83; RD Bowling and Horton 80-83; TR Keighley St Andr 83-94; Hon Can Bradf Cathl 84-94; rtd 94; Hon C Keighley All SS *Bradf* from 94. *Wellcroft, Laycock, Keighley, W Yorks BD22 0PN* Tel (01535) 606145

HUTCHINSON, David Bamford. b 29. QUB BSc53 TCD Div Test55 QUB DipEd57. **d** 55 **p** 56. C Lisburn Ch Ch *Conn* 55-57; Uganda 57-65; I Kilkeel *D & D* 66-75; I Willowfield 75-82; V Longfleet *Sarum* 82-94; rtd 94. *68 Bracken Road, Ferndown, Dorset BH22 9PF* Tel (01202) 664964

HUTCHINSON, Harold. b 36. NE Ord Course. **d** 84 **p** 85. C Auckland St Andr and St Anne *Dur* 84-87; V Coundon from 87. *2 Collingwood Street, Coundon, Bishop Auckland, Co Durham DL14 8LG* Tel (01388) 603312

HUTCHINSON, Hugh Edward. b 27. CEng FICE. Bps' Coll Cheshunt. **d** 61 **p** 62. C Limehouse St Anne *Lon* 61-64; C Townstall w Dartmouth *Ex* 64-67; V Ex St Mark 67-75; P-in-c Foston on the Wolds *York* 75-77; P-in-c N Frodingham 75-77; R Beeford w Lissett 75-77; R Beeford w Frodingham and Foston 77-80; RD N Holderness 79-80; P-in-c Appleton Roebuck w Acaster Selby 80-84; P-in-c Etton w Dalton Holme 84-91; rtd 91; Perm to Offic *York* from 91. *33 Limestone Grove, Burniston, Scarborough, N Yorkshire YO13 0DH* Tel (01723) 871116

HUTCHINSON, Jeremy Olpherts. b 32. Or Coll Ox BA55 MA60 St Jo Coll Dur DipTh57. **d** 57 **p** 58. C Shoreditch St Leon *Lon* 57-60; V Hoxton St Jo w Ch Ch 60-78; Hon C Hackney 78-85; C Highbury Ch Ch w St Jo and St Sav Lon 85-91; P-in-c Hanley Road St Sav w St Paul 91-92; TV Tollington 92-96; rtd 96. *8 Casimir Road, London E5 9NU* Tel 0181-806 6492

HUTCHINSON, John Charles. b 44. K Coll Lon 64. **d** 69 **p** 70. C Portsea All SS *Portsm* 69-73; TV Fareham H Trin 73-78; P-in-c Pangbourne *Ox* 78-86; P-in-c Tidmarsh w Sulham 84-86; R Pangbourne w Tidmarsh and Sulham 86-96. *The Coombe House, Streatley, Reading RG8 9QL*

HUTCHINSON, Jonathan Mark. b 45. Cant Sch of Min 85. **d** 89 **p** 90. NSM Wickham Market w Pettistree and Easton *St E* 89-93; V Thorington w Wenhaston, Bramfield etc 94-97; TV Ipswich St Mary at Stoke w St Pet from 97. *St Peter's House, Stoke Park Drive, Ipswich IP2 9TH* Tel (01473) 603421

HUTCHINSON, Julie Lorraine. b 55. WMMTC 90. **d** 93 **p** 94. C Northampton St Mary *Pet* 93-95; P-in-c Morcott w Glaston and Bisbrooke from 95. *109 Brooke Road, Oakham, Leics LE15 6HQ* Tel (01572) 756330

HUTCHINSON, Paul Edward. b 33. K Coll Lon. **d** 59 **p** 60. C Bromley St Mich *Lon* 59-63; C Mill Hill St Mich 63-66; C Sandridge *St Alb* 66-73; V St Alb St Mary Marshalswick 73-80; V Tunstall *Lich* 80-91; RD Stoke N 82-91; V Lower Gornal 91-93; V Lower Gornal *Worc* from 93. *The Vicarage, Church Street, Lower Gornal, Dudley, W Midlands DY3 2PF* Tel (01902) 882023

HUTCHINSON, Miss Pauline. b 49. St Jo Coll Nottm 88. **d** 90 **p** 94. Par Dn Sherwood *S'well* 90-94; C 94-95; TV Newark from 95. *St Leonard's Vicarage, Lincoln Road, Newark, Notts NG24 2DQ* Tel (01636) 703691

HUTCHINSON, Peter Francis. b 52. Portsm Poly HND74. Sarum & Wells Th Coll 87. **d** 89 **p** 90. C Honiton, Gittisham, Combe Raleigh, Monkton etc *Ex* 89-93; V Valley Park *Win* from 93. *35 Raglan Close, Eastleigh, Hants SO53 4NH* Tel (01703) 255749

HUTCHINSON, Philip Sheldon. b 32. Pemb Coll Cam BA56 MA59. Chich Th Coll 56. **d** 58 **p** 59. C Plumstead St Nic *S'wark* 58-60; C Roehampton H Trin 60-64; USA 64-65; R Charlton St Luke w St Paul *S'wark* 65-69; Australia from 69. *14 Acland Street, St Kilda, Victoria, Australia 3182* Tel Melbourne (3) 9534 3892

HUTCHINSON, Raymond. b 30. Lon Univ DipTh59. Richmond Th Coll 53. **d** 56 **p** 58. India 56-60; C Wooburn *Ox* 60-63; C Caversham 63-65; R Duror *Arg* 65-70; R Portnacrois 65-70; R Partney w Dalby *Linc* 70-73; R Ashby by Partney 70-73; V Skendleby 70-73; R Candlesby w Scremby 72-73; Canada from 78; rtd 95. *CP 157, R R 2, Arundel, Quebec, Canada, J0T 1A0*

HUTCHINSON, Raymond John. b 51. Liv Univ BSc73. Westcott Ho Cam 73. **d** 76 **p** 77. C Peckham St Jo *S'wark* 76-78; C Peckham St Jo w St Andr 78-79; C Prescot *Liv* 79-81; V Edge Hill St Dunstan 81-87; P-in-c Waterloo Park 87-89; P-in-c Litherland Ch Ch 87-89; V Waterloo Ch Ch and St Mary 90-97; Chapl Wigan and Leigh Health Services NHS Trust from 97. *85 Winwick Road, Newton-le-Willows, Merseyside WA12 8DB, or Royal Albert Edward Infirmary, Wigan Lane, Wigan WN1 2NN* Tel (01925) 225800

HUTCHINSON, The Very Revd Roland Louis. b 29. TCD BA51 MA61. **d** 52 **p** 53. C Mullabrack w Kilcluney *Arm* 52-54; C Dromore Cathl *D & D* 54-62; C-in-c Rathmullan w Tyrella 62-65; I 65-74; I Magheralin w Dollingstown 74-95; Treas Dromore Cathl 86-90; Prec 90-93; Dean Dromore 93-95; rtd 95. *Summerhill Lodge, 22 Summerhill, Lurgan, Craigavon, Co Armagh BT66 7AW* Tel (01762) 881789

HUTCHINSON, Canon Stephen. b 38. St Chad's Coll Dur BA60 DipTh62. **d** 62 **p** 63. C Tividale *Lich* 62-68; V Walsall St Andr 68-73; R Headless Cross *Worc* 73-81; TR Redditch, The Ridge 81-91; RD Bromsgrove 85-91; Hon Can Worc Cathl from 88; V Stourbridge St Thos from 91. *St Thomas's Vicarage, 34 South Road, Stourbridge, W Midlands DY8 3TB* Tel (01384) 392401

HUTCHINSON, Canon William David. b 27. Wycliffe Hall Ox 55. **d** 57 **p** 58. C Ipswich St Jo *St E* 57-60; R Combs 60-65; V Ipswich St Aug 65-76; R Ewhurst *Guildf* 76-81; V Aldeburgh w Hazlewood *St E* 81-92; RD Saxmundham 83-88; Hon Can St E Cathl 87-92; rtd 92. *Hazelwood, 3 Birch Close, Woodbridge, Suffolk IP12 4UA* Tel (01394) 383760

HUTCHINSON-CERVANTES, Ian Charles. b 62. Cant Univ (NZ) BSc84 Reading Univ MSc86 Jes Coll Cam BA88. Westcott Ho Cam 86. **d** 89 **p** 90. C Iffley *Ox* 89-92; USPG from 92; Venezuela from 93. *c/o USPG, Partnership House, 157 Waterloo Road, London SE1 8XA* Tel 0171-928 8681 Fax 928 2371

HUTCHISON, Geoffrey John. b 52. Trin Hall Cam MA76 Lon Univ CertEd76. Ridley Hall Cam 77. **d** 79 **p** 80. C Harold Wood *Chelmsf* 79-83; CF 83-89; Warden Viney Hill Chr Adventure Cen 89-96; P-in-c Viney Hill *Glouc* 89-96; V Wadsley *Sheff* from 96. *The Vicarage, 91 Airedale Road, Sheffield S6 4AW* Tel 0114-234 8481

HUTCHISON, Henry Peter. b 20. FIChemE CCC Ox MA49 TCD MA52 SS Coll Cam MA55. Linc Th Coll 80. **d** 81 **p** 82. Hon C Cambridge St Barn *Ely* 81-83; Hon C Ashley w Silverley 83-85; P-in-c Abbots Ripton w Wood Walton 85-90; P-in-c Kings Ripton 85-90; rtd 90; Perm to Offic *Nor* from 90. *Meadow Lodge, Church Farm Lane, Scarning, Dereham, Norfolk NR19 2NN* Tel (01362) 698860

HUTT, Colin Villette. b 32. FCA. Glouc Sch of Min 87. **d** 89 **p** 90. NSM Ludlow *Heref* 89-93; C Ludlow, Ludford, Ashford Carbonell etc 93-94; TV Tenbury from 94. *Old Yew Tree Farmhouse, Ashford Bowdler, Ludlow, Shropshire SY8 4DJ* Tel (01584) 831513

HUTT, Canon David Handley. b 38. AKC68. **d** 69 **p** 70. C Bedford Park *Lon* 69-70; C Westmr St Matt 70-73; PV and Succ S'wark Cathl *S'wark* 73-78; Chapl K Coll Taunton 78-82; V Bordesley SS Alb and Patr *Birm* 82-86; V St Marylebone All SS *Lon* 86-95; Can Steward Westmr Abbey from 95. *5 Little Cloister, London SW1P 3PL* Tel 0171-222 6939 or 222 5152 Fax 233 2072

HUTTON, Brian Allan. b 40. Bps' Coll Cheshunt. **d** 69 **p** 70. C Newc St Matt w St Mary *Newc* 69-72; C Blyth St Mary 72-75; V Sheff St Cath Richmond Road *Sheff* 75-85; R Paisley St Barn *Glas* from 85; R Paisley H Trin from 87. *11 Tantallon Drive, Paisley, Renfrewshire PA2 9JT* Tel (01505) 812359

HUTTON, Canon David James. b 40. Dur Univ BA64 Kent Univ MA79. Coll of Resurr Mirfield 64. **d** 66 **p** 67. C Kirkby *Liv* 66-70; Asst Chapl Kent Univ *Cant* 70-73; Chapl 73-78; Six Preacher Cant Cathl 74-80; Chapl The Lon Hosp (Whitechapel) 78-83; Can Res and Chan Liv Cathl *Liv* from 83. *4 Cathedral Close, Liverpool L1 7BR* Tel 0151-709 6271 or 708 0938

HUTTON, Griffith Arthur Jeremy. b 31. Trin Hall Cam BA56 MA59. Linc Th Coll 56. **d** 58 **p** 59. C Hexham *Newc* 58-60; C Gosforth All SS 60-65; V Whitegate *Ches* 65-71; V Whitegate w Lt Budworth 71-78; R Dowdeswell and Andoversford w the Shiptons etc *Glouc* 78-91; V Newnham w Awre and Blakeney 91-96; rtd 96. *Hill House, Stoke Lacy, Bromyard, Herefordshire HR7 4RE* Tel (01432) 820423

HUTTON, John Alexander. b 26. LNSM course 73. **d** 77 **p** 78. Hon C Edin St Mary *Edin* 77-89; NSM Glenurquhart *Mor* from 89; Dioc Chapl from 89. *St Ninian's House, Glenurquhart, Inverness IV3 6TN* Tel (01456) 476264

HUTTON, Joseph Charles. b 21. DFC41. Westcott Ho Cam 63. **d** 65 **p** 66. C St Marychurch *Ex* 65-67; V Warborough *Ox* 67-70; V Earley St Pet 70-75; R Ludgvan *Truro* 75-79; rtd 79. *2 Baines Close, Bourton-on-the-Water, Cheltenham, Glos GL54 2PU*

HUTTON, Patrick George. b 41. Open Univ BA87. Chich Th Coll 65. **d** 68 **p** 69. C Palmers Green St Jo *Lon* 68-71; Guyana 71-80; P-in-c Stow Bardolph w Wimbotsham and Stow Bridge *Ely* 80-88; P-in-c Nordelph 80-88; V E Bedfont *Lon* from 88; AD Hounslow 93-97. *St Mary's Vicarage, 9 Hatton Road, Feltham, Middx TW14 8JR* Tel 0181-751 0088

HUTTON, Canon Stanley Peart. b 15. St Jo Coll Dur BA37 DipTh38 MA40. **d** 38 **p** 39. C Beamish *Dur* 38-40; C Jarrow St Paul 40-42; Chapl RAFVR 42-46; V New Malton *York* 47-54; V Hessle 54-62; R Stevenage *St Alb* 62-69; Hon Can St Alb 66-80; R Knotting w Souldrop 69-80; V Sharnbrook 69-80; rtd 80; Perm to Offic *Ex* from 80. *Flat 2, Coly House, Rosemary Lane, Colyton, Devon EX13 6LS* Tel (01297) 552744

HUTTON, Miss Susan Elizabeth. b 70. Univ of Wales (Cardiff) BD91. Ripon Coll Cuddesdon 93. **d** 95 **p** 96. C W Parley *Sarum* from 95. *48 Cammel Road, West Parley, Ferndown, Dorset BH22 8SB* Tel (01202) 871459

HUTTON-BURY, David. b 44. **d** 94 **p** 95. NSM Geashill w Killeigh and Ballycommon *M & K* 94-97; NSM Clane w Donadea and Coolcarrigan from 97. *Chorleyville Farm, Tullamore, Co Offaly, Irish Republic* Tel Offaly (506) 21813

HUXHAM, Hector Hubert. b 29. Bris Univ BA55. Tyndale Hall Bris 52. **d** 56 **p** 57. C Eccleston St Luke *Liv* 56-58; C Heworth H Trin *York* 59-60; V Burley *Ripon* 61-66; Chapl St Jas Univ Hosp Leeds 67-94; rtd 94; Perm to Offic *Bradf* from 94. *3 Oakwell Oval, Leeds LS8 4AL* Tel 0113-266 8851

HUXHAM, Canon Peter Richard. b 38. Worc Coll Ox BA61 MA74. St Steph Ho Ox 61. **d** 63 **p** 64. C Gillingham *Sarum* 63-67; C Osmondthorpe St Phil *Ripon* 67-70; V Parkstone St Osmund *Sarum* 70-75; TR Parkstone St Pet w Branksea and St Osmund 75-92; RD Poole 85-92; Can and Preb Sarum Cathl 85-92; Chapl Taunton and Somerset NHS Trust from 92. *The Chaplain's Office, Musgrove Park Hospital, Taunton, Somerset TA1 5DA* Tel (01823) 333444

HUXLEY, Keith. b 33. Ch Coll Cam BA57 MA61. Cuddesdon Coll 57. **d** 59 **p** 60. C Bowdon *Ches* 59-61; C Crewe Ch Ch 61-62; C Ches St Pet 62-64; Youth Chapl 62-68; Asst Chapl Ches Cathl 65-68; V Grange St Andr 68-73; TR E Runcorn w Halton 73-77; Home Sec Gen Syn Bd for Miss and Unity 77-83; Chapl to The Queen from 81; TR Gateshead *Dur* from 83; RD Gateshead

88-92. *The Rectory, 91 Old Durham Road, Gateshead, Tyne & Wear NE8 4BS* Tel 0191-477 3990

HUXLEY, Canon Stephen Scott. b 30. Linc Th Coll 53. **d** 56 **p** 57. C Cullercoats St Geo *Newc* 56-59; C Eglingham 59-60; C N Gosforth 60-63; V Hartburn and Meldon 63-65; V Nether Witton 63-65; V Tynemouth Priory 65-74; V Warkworth and Acklington 74-78; P-in-c Tynemouth St Jo 78-81; V 81-87; Hon Can Newc Cathl 82-92; V Wylam 87-92; rtd 92. *35 Castle Street, Norham, Berwick-upon-Tweed TD15 2LQ* Tel (01289) 382356

HUXTABLE, Christopher Michael Barclay. b 61. Ex Univ BA83 Qu Coll Cam PGCE84. St Steph Ho Ox DipMin95. **d** 95 **p** 96. C Chichester *Chich* from 95. *St Paul's House, 37 Somerstown, Chichester, W Sussex PO19 4AL* Tel (01243) 775199

HUXTABLE, Michael George. b 29. St Jo Coll Cam BA50 MA54. S Dios Minl Tr Scheme 87. **d** 90 **p** 91. NSM Fisherton Anger *Sarum* from 90. *124 Bouverie Avenue South, Salisbury SP2 8EA* Tel (01722) 334364

HUYTON, Stuart. b 37. St D Coll Lamp BA62 DipTh63. **d** 63 **p** 64. C Kingswinford H Trin *Lich* 63-66; C Leek St Edw 66-69; V Wigginton 69-76; V Wombourne 76-89; RD Trysull 79-84; P-in-c Bobbington 85-89; TR Wombourne w Trysull and Bobbington 89-95; V Lt Aston from 95. *The Vicarage, 3 Walsall Road, Sutton Coldfield, W Midlands B74 3BD* Tel 0121-353 0356

HUYTON, Susan Mary. b 57. Birm Univ BA79 DipTh86. Qu Coll Birm 83. **d** 86 **p** 97. C Connah's Quay *St As* 86-89; C Wrexham 89-90; D-in-c 90-91; TD from 91. *The Vicarage, 55 Princess Street, Wrexham LL13 7US* Tel (01978) 266145

HUZZEY, Peter George. b 48. Trin Coll Bris 74. **d** 76 **p** 77. C Bishopsworth *Bris* 76-79; V 86-96; C Downend 79-80; TV Kings Norton *Birm* 80-86; V Bishopsworth and Bedminster Down *Bris* from 97. *St Peter's Vicarage, 61 Fernsteed Road, Bristol BS13 8HE* Tel 0117-964 2734

HYATT, Robert Keith (Bob). b 34. Em Coll Cam BA59 MA63. Ridley Hall Cam 58. **d** 60 **p** 61. C Cheltenham St Mary *Glouc* 60-63; Asst Chapl K Edw Sch Witley 63-65; C Godalming *Guildf* 65-69; Hong Kong 69-78; V Claygate *Guildf* 78-91; TV Whitton *Sarum* 91-96; TR from 96. *The Rectory, Back Lane, Ramsbury, Marlborough, Wilts SN8 2QH* Tel (01672) 520235

HYDE, Alan. b 09. Lon Univ BSc33. St Aid Birkenhead 46. **d** 48 **p** 51. C Seacombe *Ches* 48-49; C Hanwell St Chris CD *Lon* 49-51; C Ealing St Barn 51-52; Asst Master St Olave's Gr Sch Tower Bridge 51-56; Acton Co Sch 56-70; Hon C Greenford H Cross 52-54; Perm to Offic 56-70; V Satley *Dur* 70-77; rtd 77. *7 Selby Gardens, Consett, Co Durham DH8 8AS* Tel (01207) 501441

HYDE, Dennis Hugh. b 23. Leeds Univ BA56. Sarum Th Coll 60. **d** 60 **p** 61. C Farncombe *Guildf* 60-62; C Burgh Heath 62-65; V Shottermill 65-74; Past Consultant Clinical Th Assn 74-80; rtd 88. *32 Amis Avenue, New Haw, Addlestone, Surrey KT15 3ET* Tel (01932) 345526

HYDE, Edgar Bonsor. b 29. Clifton Th Coll 59. **d** 61 **p** 62. C Weston-super-Mare Ch Ch *B & W* 61-66; C Chipping Campden *Glouc* 66-70; R Longborough w Condicote and Sezincote 70-78; R Longborough, Sezincote, Condicote and the Swells from 78. *The Rectory, Longborough, Moreton-in-the-Marsh, Glos GL56 0QF* Tel (01451) 830447

HYDE-DUNN, Keith Frederick. b 43. Sarum Th Coll. **d** 69 **p** 70. Rhodesia 69-72; C Horsham *Chich* 73-77; P-in-c Fittleworth 77-86; P-in-c Graffham w Woolavington from 86. *The Rectory, Graffham, Petworth, W Sussex GU28 0NL* Tel (01798) 867247

HYDER, Geoffrey Frank. b 28. St Jo Coll Dur 49. **d** 53 **p** 54. C Kingston upon Hull H Trin *York* 53-56; C Southend St Sav Westcliff *Chelmsf* 56-59; V Haggerston All SS *Lon* 59-65; V Southwick St Pet *Chich* 65-68; Regional Org (Gtr Lon) Chr Aid 68-74; R Keston *Roch* 74-83; R Speldhurst w Groombridge and Ashurst 83-93; RD Tunbridge Wells 86-91; rtd 93; Perm to Offic *Chich* from 93; Perm to Offic *Roch* from 93. *2 Holland House, 16 Pevensey Road, St Leonards-on-Sea, E Sussex TN38 0JY* Tel (01424) 715350

HYDER-SMITH, Brian John. b 45. MBIM MInstAM. EAMTC 84. **d** 87 **p** 88. NSM Huntingdon *Ely* 87-90; P-in-c Abbots Ripton w Wood Walton from 90; P-in-c Kings Ripton from 90. *The Rectory, Abbots Ripton, Huntingdon, Cambs PE17 2LE* Tel (01487) 3260

HYDON, Ms Veronica Weldon. b 52. N Lon Poly BA73 Maria Grey Coll Lon CertEd74. Aston Tr Scheme 87 Westcott Ho Cam 89. **d** 91 **p** 94. Par Dn Poplar *Lon* 91-94; C 94-95; P-in-c Roxwell *Chelmsf* from 95; Dio Lay Development Officer from 95. *The Vicarage, Vicarage Road, Roxwell, Chelmsford CM1 4NB* Tel (01245) 248644

HYLAND, Canon Cecil George. b 38. TCD BA62 MA78. **d** 63 **p** 64. C Belfast St Nic *Conn* 63-66; C Monkstown *D & G* 66-68; Ch of Ireland Youth Officer 68-73; Chapl TCD 73-79; I Tullow *D & G* 79-90; RD Killiney from 86; I Howth from 90; Dir of Ords (Dub) from 91; Can Ch Ch Cathl Dublin 91-95; Preb from 95. *The Rectory, Howth Road, Dublin 13, Irish Republic* Tel Dublin (1) 832 3019 Fax as telephone

HYNDMAN, David Jonathan. b 65. Man Univ BA95. Wycliffe Hall Ox MTh95. **d** 97. C Cockermouth w Embleton and Wythop *Carl* from 97. *35 Gable Road, Cockermouth, Cumbria CA13 9BU* Tel (01900) 824843

HYSLOP, Mrs Catherine Graham Young (Katie). b 53. St Andr Univ CPSS75. Carl Dioc Tr Inst 90. **d** 92 **p** 94. NSM St Bees *Carl* 92-95; NSM Carl St Jo from 95. *St John's Vicarage, Manor Road, Carlisle CA2 4LH* Tel (01228) 23380

HYSLOP, James Stott Davidson. b 09. Edin Th Coll 60. **d** 62 **p** 63. C Arbroath *Bre* 62-65; C Edin St Mich and All SS *Edin* 65-68; C Dundee St Ninian *Bre* 68-69; R Galashiels *Edin* 69-76; rtd 76. *22/6 Ferry Road Avenue, Edinburgh EH4 4BL* Tel 0131-332 9277

HYSLOP, Thomas James (Jim). b 54. St Andr Univ BD76. Edin Th Coll 76. **d** 78 **p** 79. C Whitehaven *Carl* 78-81; C Walney Is 81-83; P-in-c Gt Broughton and Broughton Moor 83-85; V 85-88; V Kells 88-95; P-in-c Upperby St Jo 95-97; V from 97. *St John's Vicarage, Manor Road, Carlisle CA2 4LH* Tel (01228) 23380

HYSON, Peter Raymond. b 51. Open Univ BA80 BA87. Oak Hill Th Coll 85. **d** 87 **p** 88. C Billericay and Lt Burstead *Chelmsf* 87-92; TV Whitton *Sarum* from 92. *The Vicarage, St Michael's Mount, Aldbourne, Marlborough, Wilts SN8 2BP* Tel (01672) 40261

I

I'ANSON, Frederic Mark. b 43. R Agric Coll Cirencester MRAC68. Carl Dioc Tr Inst 89. **d** 92 **p** 93. NSM Sedbergh, Cautley and Garsdale *Bradf* from 92. *The Bowers, Firbank, Sedbergh, Cumbria LA10 5EG* Tel (01539) 620826

IBALL, Charles Martin John. b 40. Lich Th Coll 67. **d** 69 **p** 70. C Dudley St Edm *Worc* 69-73; C W Bromwich St Jas *Lich* 73-76; V Oxley 76-80; Hon C Whittington w Weeford from 86; Hon C Clifton Campville w Edingale and Harlaston from 96. *75 Carlcroft, Stoneydelph, Tamworth, Staffs B77 4DW* Tel (01827) 896644

ICELY, Lawrence Valentine. b 07. Cuddesdon Coll 40. **d** 40 **p** 41. C Penistone w Midhope *Wakef* 40-41; Chapl Mersey Miss to Seamen 41-46; Min Four Marks CD *Win* 47-48; C Wybunbury *Ches* 48-51; V Dukinfield Ch Ch 51-56; V Hargrave 56-74; rtd 74; Perm to Offic *Ches* from 74. *61 Oxford Road, Runcorn, Cheshire WA7 4NU* Tel (01928) 577147

IDDON, Roy Edward. b 40. TCert61 Lanc Univ MA88. N Ord Course 83. **d** 83 **p** 84. Hd Teacher St Andr Primary Sch Blackb from 83; NSM Bolton St Matt w St Barn *Man* 83-88; Lic to AD Walmesley 88-93; NSM Walmsley from 93. *28 New Briggs Fold, Egerton, Bolton BL7 9UL* Tel (01204) 306589

IDLE, Christopher Martin. b 38. St Pet Coll Ox BA62. Clifton Th Coll 62. **d** 65 **p** 66. C Barrow St Mark *Carl* 65-68; C Camberwell Ch Ch *S'wark* 68-71; P-in-c Poplar St Matthias *Lon* 71-76; R Limehouse 76-89; P-in-c Palgrave w Wortham and Burgate *St E* 89; P-in-c Thrandeston, Stuston and Brome w Oakley 89; R N Hartismere 89-95; Perm to Offic *S'wark* from 95. *13 Unwin Close, Haymerle Road, London SE15 6SH* Tel 0171-732 8584

IENT, Peter. b 25. Leeds Univ BA49. Coll of Resurr Mirfield 49. **d** 51 **p** 52. C King Cross *Wakef* 51-55; C Helmsley *York* 55-57; C Seamer w E Ayton 57-60; V Batley Carr *Wakef* 60-64; V Bradf St Columba *Bradf* 64-66; V Bradf St Columba w St Andr 66-69; Chapl HM Rem Cen Warrington 69-74; Chapl HM Pris Albany 74-79; Chapl HM Pris Birm 80-84; Chapl HM Pris Coldingley 84-88; rtd 88; Perm to Offic *Guildf* from 88. *61 Whites Road, Farnborough, Hants GU14 6PB* Tel (01252) 540982

IEVINS, Peter Valdis. b 54. Solicitor 79 St Jo Coll Ox BA75 MA81. Westcott Ho Cam 86. **d** 88 **p** 89. C Sawston *Ely* 88-91; C Babraham 88-91. *32 Ledbury Road, Peterborough PE3 9RH* Tel (01733) 269029

IKIN, Gordon Mitchell. b 30. AKC57. **d** 58 **p** 59. C Leigh St Mary *Man* 58-61; V Westleigh St Paul 61-72; V Thornham St Jas 72-95; rtd 95; Perm to Offic *Man* from 95. *3 Thornham Old Road, Royton, Oldham OL2 5UN* Tel 0161-624 2428

ILES, Canon Paul Robert. b 37. FRCO65 Fitzw Coll Cam BA59 MA64 St Edm Hall Ox MA80. Sarum Th Coll 59. **d** 61 **p** 62. Chapl Bp Wordsworth Sch Salisbury 61-67; C Salisbury St Mich *Sarum* 61-64; Min Can Sarum Cathl 64-67; C Bournemouth St Pet *Win* 67-72; R Filton *Bris* 72-79; V Ox SS Phil and Jas w St Marg *Ox* 79-83; Can Res and Prec Heref Cathl *Heref* from 83. *The Canon's House, The Close, Hereford HR1 2NG* Tel (01432) 266193

ILLING, Eric James. b 33. Kelham Th Coll 54 Chich Th Coll 55. **d** 57 **p** 58. C Leeds St Aid *Ripon* 57-60; C Leeds All SS 60-62; C E Grinstead St Swithun *Chich* 62-65; V Middleton St Mary *Ripon* 65-74; R Felpham w Middleton *Chich* 74-81; Chapl R Devon and Ex Hosp (Wonford) 81-94; TR Heavitree w Ex St Paul *Ex* 81-91; R Bradninch and Clyst Hydon 91-94; rtd 94; Clergy Retirement and Widows' Officer *B & W* from 94; Perm to Offic from 94; Perm to Offic *Chich* from 94. *25 Pikes Crescent, Taunton, Somerset TA1 4HS* Tel (01823) 289203

ILLINGWORTH, John Patrick Paul. b 34. New Coll Ox BA59 DipTh61 MA63. Chich Th Coll 61. **d** 63 **p** 64. C Brighouse *Wakef*

63-66; C Willesden St Andr *Lon* 66-70; Chapl Gothenburg w Halmstad and Jönköping *Eur* 70-74; Perm to Offic *Chich* 74; V Ryhill *Wakef* 74-82; R Weston Longville w Morton and the Witchinghams *Nor* from 82; P-in-c Alderford w Attlebridge and Swannington from 94; RD Sparham from 95. *The Rectory, Weston Longville, Norwich NR9 5JU* Tel (01603) 880163

ILOTT, Philip Edwin. b 36. Roch Th Coll 66. **d** 68 **p** 69. C Leavesden All SS *St Alb* 68-71; C-in-c Godshill CD *Portsm* 71-77; V Mayfield *Chich* 77-81; V Bexhill St Barn 81-84; rtd 84; Perm to Offic *Chich* from 85. *Albany House, 11 Albany Road, Bexhill-on-Sea, E Sussex TN40 1BY*

ILSON, John Robert. b 37. Leeds Univ BSc59 Lon Univ BD64 CertEd65. ALCD63. **d** 64 **p** 65. C Kennington St Mark *S'wark* 64-67; C Sydenham H Trin 67-70; Asst Dir RE *Sheff* 70-77; R Hooton Roberts 70-75; R Hooton Roberts w Ravenfield 75-77; P-in-c Kidderminster St Geo *Worc* 77-81; TR 81-85; P-in-c Powyke 85-96; Chapl N Devon Distr Hosp Barnstaple from 97. *North Devon District Hospital, Raleigh Park, Barnstaple, Devon EX31 4JB, or 88 Chanters Hill, Barnstaple, Devon EX32 8DG* Tel (01271) 22577 or 79163

ILTON, Mrs Jennifer Jane. b 38. Chelsea Coll Lon DipT60. S Dios Minl Tr Scheme 92. **d** 95 **p** 96. NSM Jersey St Sav *Win* from 95. *38 Maison St Louis, St Saviour, Jersey JE2 7LX* Tel (01534) 22327

ILYAS, Marilyn. b 51. Oak Hill Th Coll 92. **d** 95 **p** 96. C Roch from 95. *47 Roebuck Road, Rochester, Kent ME1 1UE* Tel (01634) 826821

IMMS, William George Law. b 11. Lich Th Coll 64. **d** 64 **p** 65. C Penhill *Bris* 64-69; C Swindon New Town 69-76; Hon C Cricklade w Latton 76-81; rtd 77. *29 Trewartha Park, Weston-super-Mare, Avon BS23 2RR* Tel (01934) 627586

IMPEY, Miss Joan Mary. b 35. Lon Univ CertRK69. Dalton Ho Bris 65. **dss** 74 **d** 87 **p** 94. Kennington St Mark *S'wark* 67-75; Barking St Marg w St Patr *Chelmsf* 75-81; Harwell w Chilton *Ox* 81-87; Par Dn 87-92; Par Dn Didcot All SS 92-94; C from 94. *12 Trent Road, Ladygrove, Didcot, Oxon OX11 7RB* Tel (01235) 819036

IMPEY, Mrs Patricia Irene. b 45. Birm Univ BA67. Carl Dioc Tr Course 88. **d** 90 **p** 94. Par Dn Blackpool St Paul *Blackb* 90-94; C 94-95; Chapl Asst Victoria Hosp Blackpool 94-95; Asst Chapl Norfolk and Nor Hosp 95-96; Hon C Sprowston w Beeston *Nor* 96; R Felmingham, Skeyton, Colby, Banningham etc from 96. *The Rectory, Aylsham Road, North Walsham, Norfolk NR28 0LD* Tel (01692) 402382

IMPEY, Richard. b 41. Em Coll Cam BA63 MA67 Harvard Univ ThM67. Ridley Hall Cam 67. **d** 68 **p** 69. C Birm St Martin *Birm* 68-72; Dir of Tr *B & W* 72-79; Dir of Ords 76-79; V Blackpool St Jo *Blackb* 79-95; RD Blackpool 84-90; Hon Can Blackb Cathl 89-95; Dioc Dir of Tr *Nor* from 95. *The Rectory, Aylsham Road, North Walsham, Norfolk NR28 0LD* Tel (01692) 402382

INALL, Mrs Elizabeth. b 47. MCSP69. St As Minl Tr Course 88. **d** 92 **p** 94. NSM Tring *St Alb* from 92. *Jordans, 27 Park Road, Tring, Herts HP23 6BN* Tel (01442) 823718

INCE, Preb Edgar Kenelm Peter. b 16. DFC45. Wells Th Coll 54. **d** 56 **p** 57. C Littleham w Exmouth *Ex* 56-58; R Burghclere w Newtown *Win* 58-66; R Ashwater *Ex* 66-73; R Ashwater w Halwill and Beaworthy 73-86; RD Holsworthy 74-80; Preb Ex Cathl 85-86; rtd 86; Perm to Offic *Ex* from 86. *Prispen, Longmeadow Road, Lympstone, Exmouth, Devon EX8 5LF* Tel (01395) 266597

INCE, Peter Reginald. b 26. Bp's Coll Calcutta 48. **d** 51 **p** 52. India 51-55; C Leek St Luke *Lich* 55-57; C Milton 57-59; C Lewisham St Jo Southend *S'wark* 59-62; R Loddington w Cransley *Pet* 62-75; V Snibston *Leic* 75-79; R Mickleham *Guildf* 79-92; rtd 92; Perm to Offic *Guildf* from 92. *Bickerton, 8 Rockdale, Headley Road, Grayshott, Hindhead, Surrey GU26 6TU* Tel (01428) 604694

IND, Dominic Mark. b 63. Lanc Univ BA87. Ridley Hall Cam 87. **d** 90 **p** 91. C Birch w Fallowfield *Man* 90-93; SSF 93-95; Perm to Offic *Glas* 95-96; C Byker St Martin *Newc* from 96; C Walker from 96. *St Martin's Vicarage, 152 Roman Avenue, Newcastle upon Tyne NE6 2RJ* Tel 0191-265 5931

IND, Philip William David. b 35. K Coll Lon BD82. Wycliffe Hall Ox 74 Cranmer Hall Dur 59. **d** 65 **p** 66. C Ipswich St Jo *St E* 65-67; C Charlton Kings St Mary *Glouc* 67-71; R Woolstone w Gotherington and Oxenton 71-74; Chapl Alleyn's Sch Dulwich 76-81; C Beckenham St Geo *Roch* 83-85; V Bromley St Jo 85-87; Perm to Offic *Ox* 88-91; P-in-c Hurley 91-92; P-in-c Stubbings 91-92; rtd 92. *Stilegate, Tugwood Common, Cookham, Maidenhead, Berks SL6 9TT* Tel (01628) 477425

✠**IND, The Rt Revd William.** b 42. Leeds Univ BA64. Coll of Resurr Mirfield 64. **d** 66 **p** 67 **c** 87. C Feltham *Lon* 66-71; C Northolt St Mary 71-73; TV Basingstoke *Win* 73-87; Vice-Prin Aston Tr Scheme 79-82; Dioc Dir of Ords *Win* 82-87; Hon Can Win Cathl 84-87; Suff Bp Grantham *Linc* 87-97; Dean Stamford 87-97; Can and Preb Linc Cathl 87-97; Bp Truro from 97. *Lis Escop, Feock, Truro, Cornwall TR3 6QQ* Tel (01872) 862657 Fax 862037

INDER, Patrick John. b 30. K Coll Lon BD54 AKC54. St Boniface Warminster. **d** 55 **p** 56. C St Margarets on Thames *Lon* 55-57; C Golders Green 57-61; V Hanwell St Mellitus 61-77; R Rawmarsh w Parkgate *Sheff* 77-80; rtd 80; Hon C Sheff St Matt *Sheff* 82-88; Perm to Offic *Win* 90-92. *7 Woodlands, Triangle, Sowerby Bridge, W Yorkshire HX6 3PD* Tel (01422) 831003

INESON, David Antony. b 36. DPS. ALCD62. **d** 62 **p** 63. C Sandal St Helen *Wakef* 62-65; C Birm St Geo *Birm* 66-71; V Horton *Bradf* 71-80; RD Bowling and Horton 78-80; V Sedbergh, Cautley and Garsdale 80-86; C Firbank, Howgill and Killington 81-86; TV Langley and Parkfield *Man* 86-88; TR Banbury *Ox* from 92. *The Vicarage, 89 Oxford Road, Banbury, Oxon OX16 9AJ* Tel (01295) 262370

INGALL, Heber Doveton. b 18. ALCD43. **d** 43 **p** 44. C Gt Clacton *Chelmsf* 43-46; C Brixton Road Ch Ch *S'wark* 46-49; C Aylesford *Roch* 49-51; C Rusthall 51-52; R Coates *Ely* 52-56; R Benefield *Pet* 56-70; P-in-c Stoke Doyle 63-67; rtd 70. *10 Pilgrims Lodge, Pilgrims Way, Canterbury, Kent CT1 1XT*

INGAMELLS, Harold Frankish. b 34. Codrington Coll Barbados 56. **d** 59 **p** 60. Barbados 59-64; P-in-c Horbury Bridge *Wakef* 64-73; V Horbury Junction 65-75; V Monk Bretton 75-83; P-in-c Hoyland Swaine 83-84; V Thurlstone 83-84; Chapl Community of St Pet Woking 84-95; rtd 95; Perm to Offic *York* from 95. *20 Corbie Way, Pickering, N Yorkshire YO18 7JS* Tel (01751) 477759

INGAMELLS, Ronald Sidney. b 32. MITD. AKC56. **d** 57 **p** 58. C Leeds Gipton Epiphany *Ripon* 57-59; C Gt Yarmouth *Nor* 59-64; Dioc Youth Officer 64-79; Hon C Nor St Pet Mancroft 64-79; P-in-c Lemsford *St Alb* from 79; Sec Tr Development and Chr Educn Nat Coun YMCAs 79-92; Consultant to Romania Euro Alliance YMCAs 93-97. *7 High Oaks Road, Welwyn Garden City, Herts AL8 7BJ* Tel (01707) 327621 Fax as telephone

INGE, Canon John Geoffrey. b 55. St Chad's Coll Dur BSc77 Keble Coll Ox PGCE79 Dur Univ MA94. Coll of Resurr Mirfield. **d** 84 **p** 85. Asst Chapl Lancing Coll 84-86; Jun Chapl Harrow Sch 86-89; Sen Chapl 89-90; V Wallsend St Luke *Newc* 90-96; Can Res Ely Cathl *Ely* from 96. *Powcher's Hall, The College, Ely, Cambs CB7 4DL* Tel (01353) 663662

INGHAM, John Edmund. b 34. Reading Univ BA56. Clifton Th Coll 58. **d** 60 **p** 61. C Rodbourne Cheney *Bris* 60-63; C Tunbridge Wells St Jo *Roch* 63-67; V Sevenoaks Weald 67-82; V Farrington Gurney *B & W* 82-92; V Paulton 82-92; RD Midsomer Norton 88-91; R Aspley Guise w Husborne Crawley and Ridgmont *St Alb* from 92. *The Rectory, Aspley Guise, Milton Keynes MK17 8HN* Tel (01908) 583169

INGHAM, Mrs Pamela. b 47. MBE96. NE Ord Course 93. **d** 96 **p** 97. C Newc Epiphany *Newc* from 96. *15 Neptune Road, Newcastle upon Tyne NE15 7QN* Tel 0191-264 4861

INGHAM, Russell Edward. b 39. Glas Univ MA61 Keble Coll Ox BA63 MA67. Cuddesdon Coll 63. **d** 64 **p** 65. Chapl St Mary's Cathl *Glas* 64-69; Warden St John's Youth Cen Tuebrook Liv 69-71; R Port Glas 71-77; R St Andrews All SS *St And* 77-91; V Ruislip St Martin *Lon* 91-94; Chapl Ankara *Eur* from 96. *c/o The British Embassy, FCO (Ankara), King Charles Street, London SW1A 2AH*

INGHAM, Stephen Charles. b 49. S'wark Ord Course 75. **d** 78 **p** 79. C Lee St Aug *S'wark* 78-82; R Gt w Lt Yeldham *Chelmsf* 82-84; TV Rye *Chich* 84-90; V Alderney *Win* from 90. *The Vicarage, Alderney, Guernsey, Channel Islands GY9 3UE* Tel (01481) 822335

INGLEBY, Anthony Richard. b 48. Keele Univ BA72. Trin Coll Bris. **d** 83 **p** 84. C Plymouth St Jude *Ex* 83-88; R Lanreath *Truro* 88-97; V Pelynt 88-97; RD W Wivelshire 96-97; P-in-c Stoke Climsland from 97. *The Rectory, Stoke Climsland, Callington, Cornwall PL17 8NZ* Tel (01579) 370501

INGLEDEW, Peter David Gordon. b 48. Jo Dalton Coll Man CertEd73 Croydon Coll DASS92 CQSW92. AKC77 St Steph Ho Ox 77. **d** 78 **p** 79. C Whorlton *Newc* 78-81; C Poplar *Lon* 81-83; TV 83-85; V Tottenham H Trin 85-90; Perm to Offic *Chich* from 93. *Flat 3, 18 Chesham Place, Kemptown, Brighton BN2 1FB*

INGLESBY, Eric Vredenburg (Paul). b 15. Qu Coll Ox BA46 MA63. Wycliffe Hall Ox 63. **d** 64 **p** 64. C Plymouth Crownhill Ascension *Ex* 64-66; R Caythorpe *Linc* 66-70; C Scilly Is *Truro* 70-73; C Plymouth St Andr w St Paul and St Geo *Ex* 73-76; rtd 76. *St Helen's House, 7 Magdalene Street, Glastonbury, Somerset BA6 9EW* Tel (01458) 831596 or 831678

INGLESBY, Richard Eric. b 47. Birm Univ BSc69 Bris Univ CertEd74. Wycliffe Hall Ox 85. **d** 87 **p** 88. C Cheltenham Ch Ch *Glouc* 87-92; P-in-c Paulton *B & W* 92-94; V from 94; P-in-c Farrington Gurney 92-94; V from 94. *The Vicarage, Church Street, Paulton, Bristol BS18 5LG* Tel (01761) 416581

INGRAM, Bernard Richard. b 40. Lon Coll of Div 66. **d** 66 **p** 67. C Bromley Common St Aug *Roch* 66-70; C Gravesend St Geo 70-74; Chapl Joyce Green Hosp Dartford 75-83; V Dartford St Edm *Roch* 75-83; V Strood St Fran from 83; RD Strood 91-97. *St Francis's Vicarage, Galahad Avenue, Strood, Rochester, Kent ME2 2YS* Tel (01634) 717162

INGRAM, Miss Emmeline Jessica Anne (Emily). b 26. Gilmore Ho 53. **dss** 54 **d** 87. Ind Chapl *Chelmsf* 68-82; rtd 86; Leigh-on-Sea St Jas *Chelmsf* 86-87; Hon Par Dn from 87. *73 Bohemia Chase, Leigh-on-Sea, Essex SS9 4PW* Tel (01702) 520276

INGRAM, Gary Simon. b 58. K Coll Lon BD AKC. Ripon Coll Cuddesdon. **d** 83 **p** 84. Chapl Nelson and Colne Coll from 92; C Spalding *Linc* 83-87; C Heaton Ch Ch *Man* 87-89; V Colne H Trin *Blackb* from 89; RD Pendle from 96. *Holy Trinity Vicarage, 49 Penrith Crescent, Colne, Lancs BB8 8JS* Tel (01282) 863431

INGRAM, Michael. b 28. St Jo Coll Dur 49. **d** 53 **p** 54. C Southend St Sav Westcliff *Chelmsf* 53-56; C Stoke Damerel *Ex* 56-60; Chapl RAF 60-76; P-in-c St Enoder *Truro* 76-79; rtd 90. *FCO (New Delhi), King Charles Street, London SW1A 2AH*

INGRAM, Peter Anthony. b 53. N Ord Course 83. **d** 86 **p** 87. C Maltby *Sheff* 86-89; TV Gt Snaith 89-92; R Adwick-le-Street w Skelbrooke from 92. *The Rectory, Village Street, Adwick-le-Street, Doncaster, S Yorkshire DN6 7AD* Tel (01302) 723224

INGRAMS, Peter Douglas. b 56. Wheaton Coll Illinois BA77 Ox Univ BA80. Wycliffe Hall Ox 78. **d** 83 **p** 84. C Rowner *Portsm* 83-86; C Petersfield w Sheet 86-90; V Sheet 90-96; V Locks Heath from 96. *The Vicarage, 125 Locks Heath Park Road, Locks Heath, Southampton SO31 6LY* Tel (01489) 572497

INKPEN, Richard John. b 28. AKC56. **d** 58 **p** 59. C Willesden St Mary *Lon* 58-61; C Hendon St Mary 61-66; C-in-c S Kenton Annunciation CD 66-69; Chapl Montreux w Gstaad *Eur* 69-70; V Blackmoor *Portsm* 70-93; RD Petersfield 80-85; rtd 94; Perm to Offic *Ex* from 94. *69 St Luke's Road, Newton Abbot, Devon TQ12 4ND* Tel (01626) 65510

INKPIN, David Leonard. b 32. CChem MRSC55 Liv Univ BSc54. EMMTC 83. **d** 86 **p** 87. NSM Market Rasen *Linc* from 86; NSM Legsby from 86; NSM Linwood from 86. *Weelsby House, Legsby Road, Market Rasen, Lincs LN8 3DY* Tel (01673) 843360

INKPIN, Jonathan David Francis. b 60. Mert Coll Ox MA81. Ripon Coll Cuddesdon BA85. **d** 86 **p** 87. C Hackney *Lon* 86-88; Tutor Ripon Coll Cuddesdon 88-90; C Cuddesdon *Ox* 88-90; TV Gateshead *Dur* 90-95; C Stanhope w Frosterley from 95; C Eastgate w Rookhope from 95; Dioc Rural Development Adv from 95. *12 Kirk Rise, Frosterley, Bishop Auckland, Co Durham DL13 2SF* Tel (01388) 526580

INMAN, John Phillip. b 12. St Jo Coll Dur BA35 DipTh36 MA38. **d** 36 **p** 37. C Crook *Dur* 36-39; C Monkwearmouth St Andr 39-40; C Esh 40-43; V Cleadon 43-50; V St John in Weardale 50-56; P-in-c Westgate 50-56; V Grindon 56-60; Lect Charlotte Mason Coll Ambleside 60-73; rtd 77; Perm to Offic *Carl* 77-95. *16 Collingwood Close, Coniston, Cumbria LA21 8DZ* Tel (015394) 41629

INMAN, Malcolm Gordon. b 33. Edin Th Coll 58. **d** 60 **p** 61. C Lundwood *Wakef* 60-63; C Heckmondwike 63-70; V Wrenthorpe 70-75; Chapl Cardigan Hosp 70-73; Asst Chapl Pinderfields Gen Hosp Wakef 72-73; V Cleckheaton St Jo *Wakef* from 75. *St John's Vicarage, 33 Ashbourne Avenue, Cleckheaton, W Yorkshire BD19 5JH* Tel (01274) 874896

INMAN, Mark Henry. b 31. Lon Univ BSc53. EAMTC 80. **d** 83 **p** 84. Hon C Orford w Sudbourne, Chillesford, Butley and Iken *St E* 83-85; Chapl HM Young Offender Inst Hollesley Bay Colony 85-91; Hon C Alderton w Ramsholt and Bawdsey *St E* 85-92; P-in-c from 92; P-in-c Shottisham w Sutton from 92. *The Rectory, Church Lane, Shottisham, Woodbridge, Suffolk IP12 3HG* Tel (01394) 411748

INMAN, Martin. b 50. K Coll Lon BD72 AKC73. St Aug Coll Cant 72. **d** 73 **p** 74. C Bridgnorth St Mary *Heref* 73-77; C Parkstone St Pet w Branksea and St Osmund *Sarum* 77-79; V Willenhall St Anne *Lich* 79-85; Chapl Yeovil Distr Gen Hosp 85-91; TV Yeovil *B & W* 85-88; R Barwick 88-91; Chapl St Helier Gen Hosp from 91. *The Chaplain's Office, General Hospital, St Helier, Jersey, Channel Islands JE2 3QS* Tel (01534) 59000

INMAN, Paul Stuart. b 60. R Agric Coll Cirencester HND82 DipAI83 Nottm Univ BTh90 Man Univ MA95. Linc Th Coll 87. **d** 90 **p** 91. C Hulme Ascension *Man* 90-94; CMS from 94; Dioc Missr (Owerri) Nigeria from 94; V in charge Cathl of Transfiguration from 95. *Bishop's House, Transfiguration Road, PO Box 31, Owerri, Imo State, Nigeria* Tel Owerri (83) 230417

INMAN, Thomas Jeremy (Tom). b 45. Rhodes Univ BA67. St Steph Ho Ox 67. **d** 69 **p** 70. C Deptford St Paul *S'wark* 69-72; S Africa 72-76; P-in-c Donnington *Chich* 76-80; V Hangleton 80-86; V Bosham from 86; RD Westbourne from 91. *The Vicarage, Bosham, Chichester, W Sussex PO18 8HX* Tel (01243) 573228

INNES, Donald John. b 32. St Jo Coll Ox BA54 MA. Westcott Ho Cam 56. **d** 56 **p** 57. C St Marylebone St Mark Hamilton Terrace *Lon* 56-58; C Walton-on-Thames *Guildf* 58-67; Chapl Moor Park Coll Farnham 67-76; P-in-c Tilford *Guildf* 76-97; rtd 97. *Watchetts, 67A Upper Hale Road, Farnham, Surrey GU9 0PA* Tel (01252) 734597

INNES, Donald Keith. b 33. St Jo Coll Ox BA56 MA60 Lon Univ BD58. Clifton Th Coll 56. **d** 58 **p** 59. C Harold Hill St Paul *Chelmsf* 58-61; C Ealing Dean St Jo *Lon* 61-65; V Westacre *Nor* 65-70; R Gayton Thorpe w E Walton 65-70; V Woking St Paul *Guildf* 70-78; R Alfold and Loxwood 78-88; V Doddington w Wychling *Cant* 88-90; V Newnham 88-90; V Doddington, Newnham and Wychling 90-97; rtd 97. *High Elms, Lewes Road, Ringmer, Lewes, E Sussex BN8 5NE* Tel (01273) 814995

INNES, James Michael. b 32. Lon Univ BA56 BD59. Clifton Th Coll 59. **d** 59 **p** 60. C Blackpool St Thos *Blackb* 59-62; Tutor Clifton Th Coll 62-65; V Burton All SS *Lich* 65-73; V Ashton on Mersey St Mary *Ches* 73-90; P-in-c Brereton w Swettenham 90-91; R from 91; Dioc Clergy Widows and Retirement Officer from 93. *The Rectory, Brereton, Sandbach, Cheshire CW11 9RY* Tel (01477) 533263

INNES, Robert Neil. b 59. K Coll Cam BA82 MA85. St Jo Coll Dur BA91 DMinlStuds92. **d** 95 **p** 96. C Dur St Cuth *Dur* from 95; Lect St Jo Coll Dur from 95. *Grosvenor House, Farley Mount, Durham DH1 4DZ* Tel 0191-383 5150

INSLEY, Canon Michael George Pitron. b 47. Trin Coll Ox BA69 MA70 Nottm Univ MPhil85. Wycliffe Hall Ox 69. **d** 72 **p** 73. C Beckenham Ch Ch *Roch* 72-76; P-in-c Cowden 76-79; Lect St Jo Coll Nottm 79-85; Lic to Offic *S'well* 79-85; V Tidebrook *Chich* from 85; V Wadhurst from 85; Can and Preb Chich Cathl from 94; P-in-c Stonegate from 95. *The Vicarage, High Street, Wadhurst, E Sussex TN5 6AA* Tel (01892) 782083

INSTRELL, Robert Llewellyn (Rob). b 65. Portsm Poly BSc87 Birm Univ DipTh92. Qu Coll Birm 89. **d** 92 **p** 93. C Acocks Green *Birm* 92-95; Chapl Northn Gen Hosp NHS Trust from 95. *Chaplain's Office, Northampton General Hospital, Cliftonville, Northampton NN1 5RD* Tel (01604) 34700

INVERNESS, Provost of. *See* GRANT, The Very Revd Malcolm Etheridge

INWOOD, The Ven Richard Neil. b 46. Univ Coll Ox BSc70 MA73 Nottm Univ BA73. St Jo Coll Nottm 71. **d** 74 **p** 75. C Fulwood *Sheff* 74-78; C St Marylebone All So w SS Pet and Jo *Lon* 78-81; V Bath St Luke *B & W* 81-89; R Yeovil w Kingston Pitney 89-95; Preb Wells Cathl 90-95; Adn Halifax *Wakef* from 95. *2 Vicarage Gardens, Brighouse, W Yorkshire HD6 3HD* Tel (01484) 714553 Fax 711897

ION, Robert Henry. b 18. Pemb Coll Ox BA41 MA44 BD47. Ripon Hall Ox 41. **d** 42 **p** 49. C Allerton *Liv* 42-43; C Bromborough *Ches* 49-52; V Tintwistle 52-53; V Crewe St Mich 53-59; Hd Div Crewe Coll of Educn 56-65; Sen Lect 65-73; R Church Lawton 73-78; rtd 78. *25 Leachfield Road, Galgate, Lancaster LA2 0NX* Tel (01524) 751653

IORNS, Derrick John. b 11. AKC33. **d** 34 **p** 35. C Rainham *Roch* 34-38; C-in-c Bentley Common CD *Chelmsf* 38-51; V Bentley Common 51-53; V Maldon All SS w St Pet 53-71; RD Maldon 56-70; R Gt Warley St Mary 71-72; P-in-c Childerditch w Lt Warley 71-72; R Gt Warley w Childerditch 72-81; P-in-c Ingrave 79-81; rtd 81; Perm to Offic *Chelmsf* from 91. *45 South Drive, Brentwood, Essex CM1 4DL* Tel (01277) 220777

IPGRAVE, Canon Michael Geoffrey. b 58. Or Coll Ox BA78. Ripon Coll Cuddesdon 79. **d** 82 **p** 83. C Oakham, Hambleton, Egleton, Braunston and Brooke *Pet* 82-85; Japan 85-87; TV Leic Ascension *Leic* 87-90; Dioc Chapl Relns w People of Other Faiths from 91; C Leic H Trin w St Jo 91-92; Bp's Dom Chapl from 92; TV Leic H Spirit 94-95; TR from 95; Hon Can Leic Cathl from 94. *27 Tudor Road, Leicester LE3 5JF* Tel 0116-262 2628

IPSWICH, Archdeacon of. *See* GIBSON, The Ven Terence Allen

IREDALE, Simon Peter. b 56. Cam Univ BA78 MPhil80. Wycliffe Hall Ox 83. **d** 86 **p** 87. C Thirsk *York* 86-89; Asst Chapl Norfolk and Nor Hosp 89-90; P-in-c Kexby w Wilberfoss *York* 90-93; Sub-Chapl HM Pris Full Sutton 90-93; Chapl RAF from 93. *Chaplaincy Services (RAF), HQ, Personnel and Training Command, RAF Innsworth, Gloucester GL3 1EZ* Tel (01452) 712612 ext 5164 Fax 510828

IRELAND, David Arthur. b 45. MICFRM87 Mert Coll Ox BA67 MA71. Cuddesdon Coll 67. **d** 69 **p** 70. C Chapel Allerton *Ripon* 69-72; C Harpenden St Nic *St Alb* 72-76; R Clifton 76-84; Perm to Offic *Guildf* from 91. *43 Harefield Avenue, Cheam, Surrey SM2 7ND* Tel 0181-642 3781

IRELAND, Leslie Sydney. b 55. York Univ BA76. St Jo Coll Nottm 83. **d** 86 **p** 87. C Harwood *Man* 86-89; C Davyhulme St Mary 89-90; V Bardsley from 90. *The Vicarage, Byrth Road, Oldham OL8 2TJ* Tel 0161-624 9004

IRELAND, Mrs Lucy Annabel. b 53. Univ of Zimbabwe BSc74. St Jo Coll Nottm 81. **dss** 85 **d** 87 **p** 95. Mansfield St Jo *S'well* 85-87; Hon Par Dn Harwood *Man* 87-89; Hon Par Dn Bardsley 90-95; Hon C from 95. *The Vicarage, Byrth Road, Oldham OL8 2TJ* Tel 0161-624 9004

IRELAND, Mark Campbell. b 60. St Andr Univ MTh81. Wycliffe Hall Ox 82. **d** 84 **p** 85. C Blackb St Gabr *Blackb* 84-87; C Lancaster St Mary 87-89; Chapl HM Pris Lanc 87-89; V Baxenden *Blackb* from 89. *The Vicarage, Langford Street, Baxenden, Accrington, Lancs BB5 2RF* Tel (01254) 232471 E-mail the.vic@baxvic.airtime.co.uk

IRESON, Brian Walter. b 41. St Mich Coll Llan DMinlStuds93. **d** 93 **p** 94. C Pembroke St Mary and St Mich *St D* 93-96; TV Ebbw Vale *Mon* from 96. *The Vicarage, Cwm Road, Waunlwyd, Ebbw Vale NP3 6TR* Tel (01495) 371258

IRESON, David Christopher. b 45. Man Univ TCert67 Birm Univ BEd80. St Steph Ho Ox DipTh93. **d** 93 **p** 94. C Minehead *B & W* 93-97; V St Decumans from 97. *St Decuman's Vicarage, 47A Brendon Road, Watchet, Somerset TA23 0HU* Tel (01984) 631228

IRESON, Ms Gillian Dorothy. b 39. Gilmore Ho 67. **dss** 72 **d** 87 **p** 94. Stepney St Dunstan and All SS *Lon* 72-87; Par Dn 87-94; C from 94. *St Faith's House, Shandy Street, London E1 4ST* Tel 0171-790 4194

IRESON, Philip. b 52. Newc Univ BSc73. St Jo Coll Nottm LTh84. **d** 84 **p** 85. C Owlerton *Sheff* 84-87; V The Marshland 87-94; Perm to Offic *Linc* 90-93; Chapl HM Young Offender Inst Hatf 91-92; R Firbeck w Letwell *Sheff* from 94; V Woodsetts from 94. *The Rectory, Letwell, Worksop, Notts S81 8DF* Tel (01909) 730346

IRESON, Richard Henry. b 46. Linc Th Coll 69. **d** 71 **p** 72. C Spilsby w Hundleby *Linc* 71-74; TV Grantham w Manthorpe 74-76; R Claypole 76-79; P-in-c Westborough w Dry Doddington and Stubton 76-77; R 77-79; R Bratoft w Irby-in-the-Marsh 79-86; V Burgh le Marsh 79-86; V Orby 79-86; R Welton-le-Marsh w Gunby 79-86; R Wyberton from 86; RD Holland W 95-97. *The Rectory, Wyberton, Boston, Lincs PE21 7AF* Tel (01205) 353593

IRETON, Robert John. b 56. Bris Univ BEd. Oak Hill Th Coll BA. **d** 84 **p** 85. C Bromley Ch Ch *Roch* 84-87; TV Greystoke, Matterdale, Mungrisdale etc *Carl* 87-90; V Falconwood *Roch* from 90. *The Vicarage, The Green, Welling, Kent DA16 2PG* Tel 0181-298 0065

IRONS, Barry. b 39. Wilson Carlile Coll 57 Coll of Resurr Mirfield 82. **d** 83 **p** 84. CA from 57; C Willersey, Saintbury, Weston-sub-Edge etc *Glouc* 83-85; R Scalford w Goadby Marwood and Wycombe etc *Leic* 85-88; P-in-c Clun w Chapel Lawn, Bettws-y-Crwyn and Newcastle *Heref* 88-91; Bp's Officer for Evang 91-94; P-in-c Breinton 91-94; P-in-c Weston-super-Mare Cen Par *B & W* 94-95; R Weston super Mare St John from 96. *The Rectory, 24 All Saints Road, Weston-super-Mare, Avon BS23 2NN* Tel (01934) 621958

IRONS, Nigel Richard. b 55. Aston Univ BSc77. St Jo Coll Nottm MA95. **d** 97. C Newchapel *Lich* from 97. *21 Powderham Close, Packmoor, Stoke-on-Trent ST6 6XN*

IRONSIDE, John Edmund. b 31. Peterho Cam BA55 MA59. Qu Coll Birm 55. **d** 57 **p** 58. C Spring Park *Cant* 57-60; C Guernsey St Sampson *Win* 60-63; Thailand 63-66; V Guernsey St Jo *Win* 66-72; V Sholing 72-82; R Guernsey St Sampson from 82; Miss to Seamen from 82. *The Rectory, Grandes Maisons Road, St Sampson, Guernsey, Channel Islands GY2 4JS* Tel (01481) 44710

IRVINE, Christopher Paul. b 51. Nottm Univ BTh75 Lanc Univ MA76 St Martin's Coll Lanc PGCE77. Kelham Th Coll 73. **d** 76 **p** 76. Chapl Lanc Univ *Blackb* 76-77; C Stoke Newington St Mary *Lon* 77-80; Chapl Sheff Univ *Sheff* 80-85; Chapl St Edm Hall Ox 85-90; Tutor St Steph Ho Ox 85-90; Vice-Prin St Steph Ho Ox 91-94; V Cowley St Jo *Ox* from 94. *The Vicarage, 271 Cowley Road, Oxford OX4 2AJ* Tel (01865) 242396

IRVINE, David John. b 50. Trin Coll Cam BA72 MA75. NE Ord Course 91. **d** 94 **p** 95. C Hexham *Newc* from 94. *3 Dipton Close, Hexham, Northd NE46 1UG* Tel (01434) 604935

IRVINE, Donald Andrew (Don). b 45. Trin Coll Bris DipHE94. **d** 96 **p** 97. C Allington and Maidstone St Pet *Cant* from 96. *30 Poplar Grove, Maidstone, Kent ME16 0AE* Tel (01622) 662209

IRVINE, Gerard Philip. b 30. QUB BA52. Edin Th Coll 56. **d** 56 **p** 57. Chapl St Andr Cathl *Ab* 56-58; Prec St Andr Cathl 58-59; C Belfast Malone St Jo *Conn* 61-66; Chapl Community of St Jo Ev Dublin 67-77; C Dublin Sandymount *D & G* from 77. *c/o YWCA of Ireland, Trench House, 22-24 Crosthwaite Park East, Dun Laoghaire, Co Dublin, Irish Republic* Tel Dublin (1) 280 7463

IRVINE, James Clyde. b 35. QUB BA57 NUU BPhil(Ed)83. CITC 59. **d** 59 **p** 60. C Belfast St Luke *Conn* 59-62; C Lisburn Ch Ch Cathl 62-65; R Duneane w Ballyscullion 65-69; I Kilbride 69-74; Chapl Ballyclare High Sch from 73. *1A Rathmena Avenue, Ballyclare, Co Antrim BT39 9HX* Tel (01960) 322933

IRVINE, John Dudley. b 49. Sussex Univ BA70. Wycliffe Hall Ox BA80. **d** 81 **p** 82. C Brompton H Trin w Onslow Square St Paul *Lon* 81-85; P-in-c Kensington St Barn 85-94; V from 94. *St Barnabas's Vicarage, 23 Addison Road, London W14 8LH* Tel 0171-471 7000

IRVINE, Preb John Graham Gerard Charles. b 20. Mert Coll Ox BA42 MA46. St Steph Ho Ox 42. **d** 45 **p** 46. C Knowle H Nativity *Bris* 45-48; C Longton St Mary and St Chad *Lich* 48-51; C Soho St Anne w St Thos and St Pet *Lon* 51-53; LDHM Cranford 53-61; V Earl's Court St Cuth w St Matthias 61-69; V Westmr St Matt 69-86; Preb St Paul's Cathl 82-86; rtd 86; Perm to Offic *Chich* from 86. *42 Montpelier Road, Brighton, E Sussex BN1 3BA* Tel (01273) 730039

IRVINE, The Very Revd John Murray. b 24. Magd Coll Cam BA45 MA49. Ely Th Coll 46. **d** 48 **p** 49. C Poplar All SS w St Frideswide *Lon* 48-53; Chapl SS Coll Cam 53-60; Selection Sec CACTM 60-65; Can Res and Chan Heref Cathl *Heref* 65-78; Dir of Ords 65-78; Provost S'well 78-91; P-in-c Edingley w Halam 78-91; P-in-c Rolleston w Fiskerton, Morton and Upton 90-91; rtd 91; Perm to Offic *Ex* from 92. *9 Salston Barton, Strawberry Lane, Ottery St Mary, Devon EX11 1RG* Tel (01404) 815901

IRVINE, Stanley. b 35. TCD DipTh83. **d** 83 **p** 84. C Arm St Mark w Aghavilly *Arm* 83-85; I Kilmoremoy w Castleconnor, Easkey, Kilglass etc *T, K & A* 85-94; Dom Chapl to Bp Tuam 88-94; I Stranorlar w Meenglas and Kilteevogue *D & R* from 94. *The Rectory, Stranorlar, Co Donegal, Irish Republic* Tel Ballybofey (74) 31081

IRVINE, William Barry. b 48. QUB BD75. St Jo Coll Nottm 75. **d** 76 **p** 77. C Belfast St Mich *Conn* 76-80; C Mansfield St Pet *S'well* 80-84; V Chapel-en-le-Frith *Derby* 84-90; Chapl Cheltenham Gen Hosp 90-94; Chapl Delancey Hosp 90-94; Chapl E Glos NHS Trust from 94. *29 Brookway Drive, Charlton Kings, Cheltenham, Glos GL53 8AJ* Tel (01242) 581649 or 222222

IRVING, Canon Andrew. b 27. St Deiniol's Hawarden 62. **d** 65 **p** 66. C Benwell St Jas *Newc* 65-69; C Langley Marish *Ox* 69-73; V Moulsford 73-81; Canada from 81; rtd 92. *204-4630 Ponderosa Drive, Peachland, British Columbia, Canada, V0H 1X0* Tel Peachland (604) 767-9582

IRVING, Canon Donald Richard (Don). b 31. Lon Univ BSc56. Lon Coll of Div 66. **d** 68 **p** 69. C Leic H Trin *Leic* 68-71; Asst Chapl HM Pris Leic 70-71; Chapl to Leic Students 70-71; E Regional Co-ord CPAS 71-76; Dir Ch Soc 76-82; Gen Sec Intercon Ch Soc 82-92; Hon Can Brussels Cathl *Eur* from 83; rtd 92. *83 Alfred Street, Alfreton, Derby DE55 7JD* Tel (01773) 520116

IRVING, Leslie. b 09. Keble Coll Ox BA30 DipTh31 MA46. Wycliffe Hall Ox 30. **d** 32 **p** 33. C Neston *Ches* 32-35; C Hawarden *St As* 35-36; S Africa 36-56; V Aldborough w Dunsforth *Ripon* 56-57; Chapl Dover Coll 57-63; R Risby *St E* 63-65; Lic to Offic *Guildf* 65-67; Chapl St Cath Sch Bramley 67-74; rtd 74; Perm to Offic *Chich* 74-83; Perm to Offic *Nor* 83-88. *2 Capel Court, The Burgage, Prestbury, Cheltenham, Glos GL52 3EL* Tel (01242) 576426

IRVING, Canon Michael John Derek. b 43. BEd80. Qu Coll Birm 80. **d** 81 **p** 82. C Coleford w Staunton *Glouc* 81-84; V Dean Forest H Trin 84-91; RD Forest S 88-91; P-in-c Hempsted 91-96; Dir of Ords 91-96; Hon Can Glouc Cathl from 94; R Minchinhampton from 96. *The Rectory, Butt Street, Minchinhampton, Stroud, Glos GL6 9JP* Tel (01453) 882289

IRWIN, Albert Samuel. b 14. TCD BA38 MA44. CITC 38. **d** 38 **p** 39. C Bury St Pet *Man* 38-42; C Bolton St Pet 42-45; Lect 45-47; Chapl RNVR 47-48; C Gillingham *Sarum* 48-49; Argentina 49-54; V Apethorpe w Woodnewton *Pet* 54-59; R Clyst St Mary *Ex* 59-61; R Clyst St George 59-61; V Stamford Baron *Pet* 61-81; P-in-c Tinwell 77-81; rtd 81; Lic to Offic *Pet* 81-85; Perm to Offic from 85; Perm to Offic *Linc* from 91. *19 Water Street, Stamford, Lincs PE9 2NJ*

IRWIN, John Nesbitt Cottier. b 27. SEN79 Mert Coll Ox BA50 MA53. SW Minl Tr Course 86. **d** 87 **p** 88. NSM Buckfastleigh w Dean Prior *Ex* from 87. *56 Plymouth Road, Buckfastleigh, Devon TQ11 0DH* Tel (01364) 43044

IRWIN, Patrick Alexander. b 55. BNC Ox BA77 MA81 Edin Univ BD81. Edin Th Coll 77 Liturgisches Inst Trier 79. **d** 81 **p** 82. Hon C Cambridge St Botolph *Ely* 81-84; Chapl BNC Ox 84-92; Lect Th 86-92; Lic to Offic *Ox* 85-92; Lic to Offic *B & W* 87-92; Perm to Offic *D & G* from 87; CF from 92; Chapl Udruga Hvrata Sv Dominik Gorazde 94-95; Perm to Offic *Arm* from 96. *MOD Chaplains (Army), Trenchard Lines, Upavon, Pewsey, Wilts SN9 6BE* Tel (01980) 615804 Fax 615800

IRWIN, Stewart. b 53. Sarum & Wells Th Coll 80. **d** 83 **p** 84. C Brighouse *Wakef* 83-87; V Stockton St Jo *Dur* 87-95; V Howden-le-Wear and Hunwick from 95. *The Vicarage, Hunwick, Crook, Co Durham DL15 0JU* Tel (01388) 604456

IRWIN, Miss Susan Elizabeth (Sue). b 47. Cam Univ DipRS79. St Jo Coll Dur 77. **dss** 79 **d** 87 **p** 94. Harborne St Faith and St Laur *Birm* 79-82; Caterham *S'wark* 82-88; Par Dn 87-88; Par Dn Kidlington w Hampton Poyle *Ox* 88-94; C 94-95; TV Gt Marlow w Marlow Bottom, Lt Marlow and Bisham from 95. *18 Oak Tree Road, Marlow, Bucks SL7 5EE* Tel (01628) 481722

IRWIN, Victor. b 32. Lon Coll of Div 64. **d** 66 **p** 67. C Leic H Trin *Leic* 66-68; CF 68-72; V Quarry Bank *Lich* 72-81; P-in-c Hopesay w Edgton *Heref* 81-85; V Lydbury N 81-85; R Wickenby Gp *Linc* 85-88; R Gartcosh *Glas* 88-91; R Airdrie 88-91; I Garrison w Slavin and Belleek *Clogh* 91-97; rtd 97. *2 Cowan Heron House, Dromara Road, Dromore, Co Down BT25*

IRWIN, William George. b 53. QUB BSc77. CITC 80. **d** 80 **p** 81. C Lisburn St Paul *Conn* 80-83; C Seagoe *D & D* 83-85; C Newtownards w Movilla Abbey 85-88; I Ballymacash *Conn* from 88; RD Lisburn from 91. *St Mark's Rectory, 97 Antrim Road, Lisburn, Co Antrim BT28 3EA* Tel (01846) 662393

IRWIN-CLARK, Peter Elliot. b 49. Univ Coll Lon LLB71 St Jo Coll Dur BA81. Cranmer Hall Dur 81. **d** 81 **p** 82. C Kirkheaton *Wakef* 81-86; V Shirley *Win* 86-96; Perm to Offic *Chich* from 96; Perm to Offic *S'wark* from 97. *Desmonds Castle, Hyde Estate, Handcross, Haywards Heath, W Sussex RH17 6HA* Tel (01444) 400307

ISAAC, Arthur Kenneth. b 12. St Aug Coll Cant. **d** 62 **p** 63. C Combe Down *B & W* 62-65; R Rode, Rode Hill and Woolverton 65-72; R Hutton 72-77; rtd 77; Perm to Offic *Ex* 77-86; Perm to Offic *Chich* from 86. *Bungalow No 2, Terry's Cross, Woodmancote, Henfield, W Sussex BN5 9SX* Tel (01273) 493006

ISAAC, Bryan Raymund. b 09. MBE46. Ch Coll Cam BA31 MA35. Wycliffe Hall Ox 31. **d** 33 **p** 34. C Ealing Dean St Jo *Lon* 33-36; C Walcot *B & W* 36-38; V Battersea Park St Sav *S'wark* 38-43; CF (EC) 43-46; Home Sec Rwanda Miss CMS 46-62; V Cudham *Roch* 62-73; S Area Sec Rwanda Miss CMS 73-75; rtd 74. *Delapre*

House, St Andrew's Road, Bridport, Dorset DT6 3BZ Tel (01308) 425246

ISAAC, Canon David Thomas. b 43. Univ of Wales BA65. Cuddesdon Coll 65. **d** 67 **p** 68. C Llan w Capel Llanilltern *Llan* 67-71; P-in-c Swansea St Jas *S & B* 71-73; Chapl Ch in Wales Youth Coun 73-77; V Llangiwg *S & B* 77-79; Dioc Youth Officer *Ripon* 79-83; Nat Officer for Youth Work Gen Syn Bd of Educn 83-90; Dioc Dir of Educn *Portsm* from 90; Can Res Portsm Cathl from 90. *1 Pembroke Close, Portsmouth PO1 2NX* Tel (01705) 818107 or 822053 Fax 295081

ISAAC, Edward Henry. b 20. Qu Coll Cam BA42 MA46. Ridley Hall Cam 45. **d** 47 **p** 48. C Wednesbury St Bart *Lich* 47-51; V Liv St Phil *Liv* 51-56; V Knowsley 56-61; V Garston 61-66; V Millom St Geo *Carl* 66-85; rtd 85; Perm to Offic *Carl* from 86. *31 Lowther Road, Millom, Cumbria LA18 4PE* Tel (01229) 772332

ISAACS, John Kenneth. b 36. Cam Univ MA. EAMTC. **d** 82 **p** 83. NSM Ely 82-85; Chapl K Sch Ely 85-94; Lic to Offic *Ely* 85-94; P-in-c Denver from 94; P-in-c Ryston w Roxham from 94; P-in-c W Dereham from 94. *Denver Rectory, Downham Market, Norfolk PE38 0DP* Tel (01366) 382127

ISAACSON, Alan Timothy. b 55. York Univ BA77 Sheff Univ PGCE84 Leeds Univ MA97. N Ord Course 94. **d** 96 **p** 97. C Kimberworth *Sheff* from 96. *32 Hill View Road, Rotherham, S Yorkshire S61 2AJ* Tel (01709) 559010

ISAM, Miss Margaret Myra Elizabeth. b 35. Nottm Univ BEd73. EMMTC 78. **dss** 81 **d** 87 **p** 94. Humberston *Linc* 81-84; Gt Grimsby St Andr and St Luke 85-87; D-in-c 87-93; D-in-c Gt Grimsby St Andr w St Luke and All SS 94; P-in-c 94-97; V from 97. *St Luke's Vicarage, 17 Heneage Road, Grimsby, S Humberside DN32 9DZ* Tel (01472) 358007

ISBISTER, Charles. b 27. Chich Th Coll 58. **d** 60 **p** 61. C Tynemouth Ch Ch *Newc* 60-64; C Boyne Hill *Ox* 64-67; V Cookridge H Trin *Ripon* 67-93; rtd 93. *2 Church Mount, Horsforth, Leeds LS18 5LE* Tel 0113-239 0813

ISDELL-CARPENTER, Philip Wynn Howard. b 11. St Jo Coll Ox BA33 MA37. Westcott Ho Cam 35. **d** 36 **p** 37. C Leatherhead *Guildf* 36-39; C Frimley 39-44; R Winterslow *Sarum* 44-48; TR Preston w Sutton Poyntz and Osmington w Poxwell 48-60; R Frimley *Guildf* 60-72; rtd 76; Perm to Offic *B & W* 86-95. *6 Gracey Court, Broadclyst, Exeter EX5 3LP*

ISHERWOOD, David Owen. b 46. BA68 Lon Univ MA95 MPhil87. Ridley Hall Cam 76. **d** 78 **p** 79. C Sanderstead All SS *S'wark* 78-82; C Horley 82-84; TV 84-88; P-in-c Streatham Immanuel and St Andr 88-89; V 89-95; TR Clapham TM from 95. *25 The Chase, London SW4 0NP* Tel 0171-498 6879 or 627 0941

ISHERWOOD, Robin James. b 56. Hull Univ BA78 Uppsala Univ MDiv92. Ripon Coll Cuddesdon DipMin94. **d** 94 **p** 95. C Bramhall *Ches* from 94. *33 Dawlish Close, Bramhall, Stockport, Cheshire SK7 2JD* Tel 0161-440 8415

ISHERWOOD, Samuel Peter. b 34. Lon Coll of Div ALCD62 LTh74. **d** 62 **p** 63. C Bacup St Sav *Man* 62-65; C Man Albert Memorial Ch 65-67; V Livesey *Blackb* 67-79; V Handforth *Ches* from 79; RD Cheadle from 92. *The Vicarage, 36 Sagars Road, Handforth, Wilmslow, Cheshire SK9 3EE* Tel (01625) 524119 or 532145

ISIORHO, Father The Chief David John Phillip. b 58. Liv Poly BA80 Wolv Poly DipPsych89 Warw Univ MA93. Westcott Ho Cam 87. **d** 90 **p** 91. C Nuneaton St Mary *Cov* 90-93; P-in-c Bradf St Oswald Chapel Green *Bradf* 93-96; P-in-c Brereton *Lich* from 96. *The Vicarage, Brereton, Rugeley, Staffs WS15 1DU* Tel (01889) 582466

ISIORHO (née NORTHALL), Mrs Linda Barbara. b 50. Birm Univ BA72 Worc Coll of Educn PGCE75. Qu Coll Birm 88. **d** 90 **p** 94. C Wood End *Cov* 90-91; Perm to Offic 91-93; Perm to Offic *Bradf* 93-94; NSM Low Moor St Mark 94-96; Perm to Offic *Lich* from 96. *The Vicarage, Brereton, Rugeley, Staffs WS15 1DU* Tel (01889) 582466

ISITT, Canon David Edgar Reid. b 28. K Coll Cam BA49 MA53. Wells Th Coll 51. **d** 53 **p** 54. C Westbury-on-Trym H Trin *Bris* 53-56; Chapl K Coll Cam 56-60; V Haslingfield *Ely* 60-68; R Harlton 60-68; Chapl St Edw K and Martyr Cam 68-77; Asst Chapl Trin Hall Cam 68-77; Can Res Bris Cathl *Bris* 77-86; Dir Dioc Sch of Min 77-86; P-in-c Bris Ch Ch w St Ewen and All SS 80-82; Dioc Dir of Ords 81-86; Lic to Offic *Ely* from 87; Acting Dean Trin Hall Cam 89; Tutor Westcott Ho 90; Chapl Fitzw Coll Cam 90-93; rtd 93. *41 Fulbrooke Road, Cambridge CB3 9EE* Tel (01223) 358522

ISITT, Norman. b 34. St Jo Coll Dur BA56. Cranmer Hall Dur DipTh59. **d** 59 **p** 60. C Loughton St Mary *Chelmsf* 59-62; C Moulsham St Jo 62-64; Billericay Co Sch 64-90; Squirrels Heath Sch Romford 64-90; Althorpe and Keadby Co Sch 66-95; rtd 95. *21 Cambridge Avenue, Bottesford, Scunthorpe, S Humberside DN16 3LT* Tel (01724) 851489

ISLE OF WIGHT, Archdeacon of. *See* BANTING, The Ven Kenneth Mervyn Lancelot Hadfield

ISON, Canon David John. b 54. Leic Univ BA76 Nottm Univ BA78 K Coll Lon PhD85. St Jo Coll Nottm 76. **d** 79 **p** 80. C Deptford St Nic and St Luke *S'wark* 79-85; Lect CA Tr Coll Blackheath 85-88; V Potters Green *Cov* 88-93; Jt Dir SW Min Tr Course *Ex* 93-95; Dioc Officer for Continuing Minl Educn from 93; Can Res Ex Cathl from 95. *12 The Close, Exeter EX1 1EZ* Tel (01392) 275745

ISON, Mrs Hilary Margaret. b 55. Leic Univ BA76 Nottm Univ DipTh78. Gilmore Course 77 St Jo Coll Nottm DPS79. **d** 87 **p** 94. NSM Deptford St Nic and St Luke *S'wark* 87-88; NSM Potters Green *Cov* 88-90; C Rugby St Andr 90-93; Chapl Exeter Hospicare from 93; Lic to Offic *Ex* from 93. *12 The Close, Exeter EX1 1EZ* Tel (01392) 275745

ISON, John. b 20. Alnwick Tr Coll TCert46. Cranmer Hall Dur 81. **d** 81 **p** 82. NSM Stockton St Jo CD *Dur* 81-83; NSM Hawthorn 83-86; rtd 86; Perm to Offic *Dur* from 86. *32 Limbrick Court, Fairfield, Stockton-on-Tees, Cleveland TS19 7QF* Tel (01642) 588525

ISRAEL, Dr Martin Spencer. b 27. Witwatersrand Univ MB49 MRCP52. **d** 74 **p** 75. Hon C St Mich Cornhill w St Pet le Poer etc *Lon* 74-77; Hon C S Kensington H Trin w All SS 77-82; P-in-c 83-96; rtd 96. *Flat 2, 26 Tregunter Road, London SW10 9LS* Tel 0171-370 5160

ISSBERNER, Cllr Norman Gunther Erich. b 34. Fitzw Ho Cam BA58 MA61. Clifton Th Coll 57. **d** 59 **p** 60. C Croydon Ch Ch Broad Green *Cant* 59-61; C Surbiton Hill Ch Ch *S'wark* 61-66; V Egham *Guildf* 66-75; V Wallington H Trin *S'wark* 75-86; UK Chmn Africa Inland Miss from 77; Adv on Miss and Evang *Chelmsf* 86-91; P-in-c Castle Hedingham 91-93; V Clacton St Paul from 93; RD St Osyth from 94. *The Vicarage, 7 St Alban's Road, Clacton-on-Sea, Essex CO15 6BA* Tel (01255) 424760

ITALY AND MALTA, Archdeacon of. *Vacant*

IVE, Dr Jeremy George Augustus. b 57. Rhodes Univ BA81 Ch Coll Cam PhD87 K Coll Lon MPhil95. Wycliffe Hall Ox DipTh91. **d** 91 **p** 92. NSM Ivybridge w Harford *Ex* 91-95; P-in-c Abbotskerswell from 95. *The Vicarage, Church Path, Abbotskerswell, Newton Abbot, Devon TQ12 5NY* Tel (01626) 334445

IVE (née KNOTT), Mrs Pamela Frances. b 58. Bedf Coll of Educn BEd79. Wycliffe Hall Ox 88. **d** 90. Par Dn Ivybridge w Harford *Ex* 90-95; C Abbotskerswell from 95. *The Vicarage, Church Path, Abbotskerswell, Newton Abbot, Devon TQ12 5NY* Tel (01626) 334445

IVELL, Robert William. b 45. Lon Univ BSc71 Liv Univ CertEd Sheff Univ DBS83. Ridley Hall Cam 83. **d** 85 **p** 86. C Wadsley *Sheff* 85-88; V Laughton w Throapham 88-96; V Wadworth w Loversall from 96. *The Vicarage, Vicarage Drive, Wadworth, Doncaster, S Yorkshire DN11 9BW* Tel (01302) 851974

IVENS, Edmund Masters. b 11. Edin Th Coll 37. **d** 37 **p** 38. C Fort William *Arg* 37-39; C Kirkcaldy *St And* 39-44; R Kinross 44-52; R Dunbar *Edin* 52-79; rtd 79. *28 Kingsburgh Gardens, East Linton, East Lothian EH40 3BZ* Tel (01620) 860283

IVES, Raymond Charles. b 27. St Mark & St Jo Coll Lon CertEd50. LNSM course 92. **d** 95 **p** 96. NSM Croydon St Pet *S'wark* from 95. *60 Windermere Road, West Wickham, Kent BR4 9AW* Tel 0181-777 4956

IVESON, Mrs Patricia Jill (Pat). b 35. Cam Univ CertEd55 K Coll Lon DipTh70 BD76 AKC76. **dss** 81 **d** 87 **p** 94. Wilmington *Roch* 81-87; Hon Par Dn 87-94; Hon C from 94; Chapl W Hill Hosp Dartford from 87. *Branksome, Church Hill, Wilmington, Dartford DA2 7EH* Tel (01322) 279100

IVEY (née HODGE), Mrs Marilyn Elizabeth. b 52. Wilson Carlile Coll IDC82 Carl Dioc Tr Course. **d** 89 **p** 94. CA from 82; Par Dn Millom *Carl* 89-92; Par Dn Egremont and Haile 92-94; C from 94. *St John's House, Bigrigg, Egremont, Cumbria CA22 2TU* Tel (01946) 811155

IVIN, Miss Maureen. b 34. Gilmore Ho 60. **dss** 85 **d** 87 **p** 94. Grays Thurrock *Chelmsf* 85-87; Par Dn 87-94; TV from 94. *Wendover, College Avenue, Grays, Essex RM17 5UW* Tel (01375) 373468

IVISON, Norman William. b 54. Hull Univ BA75 DipEd76. Trin Coll Bris DipHE81 DipTh82. **d** 82 **p** 83. Ecum Liaison Officer BBC Radio Furness 82-85; C Barrow St Mark *Carl* 82-85; Chapl Barrow Sixth Form Coll 83-85; Dioc Broadcasting Officer *Lich* 85-91; Relig Progr Producer BBC Radio Stoke 85-91; Hon C Bucknall and Bagnall *Lich* 85-91; Asst Producer Relig Progr BBC TV Man 91-93; Producer Relig Progr BBC TV Man from 93; Perm to Offic *Man* 92-95; Lic to Offic from 95. *6 Bournelea Avenue, Burnage, Manchester M19 1AF* Tel 0161-442 6490 or 244 3238 Mobile 0585-866317 Fax 244 3232

IVORY, Christopher James. b 54. Reading Univ BSc76. Qu Coll Birm DipTh80. **d** 81 **p** 82. C Waltham Cross *St Alb* 81-84; C Is of Dogs Ch Ch and St Jo w St Luke *Lon* 84-88; V Streatham Ch Ch *S'wark* from 88; Lambeth Adnry Ecum Officer from 90. *Christ Church Vicarage, 3 Christchurch Road, London SW2 3ET* Tel 0181-674 5723

IZZARD, David Antony. b 55. Trin Coll Bris DipHE94. **d** 94 **p** 95. C E Bris from 94. *34 Thurstons Barton, Whitehall, Bristol BS5 7BQ* Tel 0117-951 1300

IZZARD, Mrs Susan Amanda. b 59. Hatf Poly BA82. Trin Coll Bris BA86. **dss** 86 **d** 87. Birm St Martin w Bordesley St Andr *Birm* 86-89; Par Dn 87-89; C Handsworth St Jas 89-91; Asst Chapl Qu Eliz Hosp Birm 90-91. *40 Hay Green Lane, Birmingham B30 1UN* Tel 0121-451 2057

J

JACK, Alexander Richard (Alex). b 30. Leeds Univ BSc55 MSc66. Oak Hill Th Coll 69. **d** 71 **p** 72. C Penn Fields *Lich* 71-78; P-in-c 78-83; R Barnston and Lt Dunmow *Chelmsf* 83-95; RD Dunmow 88-95; rtd 95; Perm to Offic *Lich* from 95. *30 Bellencroft Gardens, Wolverhampton WV3 8DT* Tel (01902) 763481

JACK, Canon Henry Graham. b 21. K Coll Lon AKC48 BD49. **d** 49 **p** 50. C Hornsey Ch Ch *Lon* 49-50; C Steyning *Chich* 52-56; R Warbleton 56-61; V Alfriston and Lullington 61-65; RD Seaford 64-65; Chile 65-74; Hon Can Chile 66-74; R Trowbridge St Jas *Sarum* 74-87; Can and Preb Sarum Cathl 83-87; rtd 87. *285A The Common, Holt, Trowbridge, Wilts BA14 6QJ* Tel (01225) 782776

JACK, Paul Pembroke. b 19. SS Coll Cam BA41. Linc Th Coll 41. **d** 42 **p** 43. C Prittlewell St Mary *Chelmsf* 42-45; Chapl Chigwell Sch Essex 45-47; Min Can Heref Cathl *Heref* 47-50; Chapl Heref Cathl Sch 47-50; Asst Chapl Br Emb Ch Paris *Eur* 50-52; C St Giles-in-the-Fields *Lon* 52-54; C Guernsey St Peter Port *Win* 54-55; V Primrose Hill St Mary *Lon* 55-57; rtd 84. *39 Warren Hill Road, Woodbridge, Suffolk IP12 4DY* Tel (01394) 386562

JACK, Robin Watson. b 43. Westcott Ho Cam. **d** 90 **p** 91. C Debenham w Aspall and Kenton *St E* 90-93; P-in-c Bacton w Wyverstone and Cotton from 93. *The Rectory, Church Road, Bacton, Stowmarket, Suffolk IP14 4LJ* Tel (01449) 781245

JACKLIN, John Frederick. b 30. Oak Hill Th Coll 72. **d** 72 **p** 72. Chile 72-75; C Roxeth Ch Ch *Lon* 75-78; V Selston *S'well* 78-95; rtd 95. *5 Rose Avenue, Borrowash, Derby DE7 3GA* Tel (01332) 669670

JACKS, David. b 59. Nottm Univ BTh87 Birm Univ MA95. Linc Th Coll 84. **d** 87 **p** 88. C Oakham, Hambleton, Egleton, Braunston and Brooke *Pet* 87-90; V Weedon Bec w Everdon from 90. *The Vicarage, Church Street, Weedon, Northampton NN7 4PL* Tel (01327) 340359 Mobile 0850-597891 Fax as telephone

JACKSON, Alan. b 44. Newc Univ BA67 DipEd68 MEd79. NE Ord Course 79. **d** 81 **p** 82. NSM Jesmond H Trin *Newc* 81-82; Chapl Bp Wand's Sch Sunbury-on-Thames 82-89; V Hanworth St Rich *Lon* from 89. *St Richard's Vicarage, 35 Forge Lane, Hanworth, Middx TW13 6UN* Tel 0181-898 0241

JACKSON, Canon Arthur Malcolm. b 31. TCD BA54 MA60. CITC 54. **d** 54 **p** 55. C Templecorran Union *Conn* 54-57; C Dublin Santry Union *D & G* 57-58; Bp's V and Registrar *C & O* 58-61; I Monasterevan *M & K* 61-68; I Narraghmore w Fontstown and Timolin *D & G* 68-88; I Narraghmore w Timolin, Castledermot and Kinneagh 88-91; I Killanne w Killegney, Rossdroit and Templeshanbo *C & O* from 91; Preb Ferns Cathl 93-96; Bp's Dom Chapl from 93; Chan Ferns Cathl from 96. *The Rectory, Clonroche, Enniscorthy, Co Wexford, Irish Republic* Tel Enniscorthy (54) 44180

JACKSON, Barry. b 30. St Jo Coll Cam BA53 DipEd54 MA57. Westcott Ho Cam 63. **d** 65 **p** 66. C Stockport St Geo *Ches* 65-68; C Bridgwater St Mary, Chilton Trinity and Durleigh *B & W* 68-70; P-in-c Thurloxton 70-75; Chapl Wycliffe Coll Glos 75-88; V Heathfield *Chich* 88-97; rtd 97. *11 Glenleigh Walk, Robertsbridge, E Sussex TN32 5DQ* Tel (01580) 880067

JACKSON, The Very Revd Brandon Donald. b 34. Liv Univ LLB56 Bradf Univ Hon DLitt90. Wycliffe Hall Ox DipTh59. **d** 58 **p** 59. C New Malden and Coombe *S'wark* 58-61; C Leeds St Geo *Ripon* 61-65; V Shipley St Pet *Bradf* 65-77; Relig Adv Yorkshire TV 69-79; Provost Bradf 77-89; Dean Linc 89-97; rtd 97. *c/o The Revd R B Jackson, Kimbers, Lord Wandsworth College, Long Sutton, Hook, Hants RG29 1TB*

JACKSON, Christopher John Wilson. b 45. St Pet Coll Ox BA67 MA87. Ridley Hall Cam 69. **d** 72 **p** 73. C Putney St Marg *S'wark* 72-76; C Battersea St Pet and St Paul 76-79; TV Preston St Jo *Blackb* 79-87; P-in-c Sandal St Cath *Wakef* 87-90; V Shenley Green *Birm* from 90; RD Kings Norton from 95. *St David's Vicarage, 49 Shenley Green, Birmingham B29 4HH* Tel 0121-475 4874

JACKSON, Miss Cynthia. b 42. CertMS90. S'wark Ord Course 93. **d** 96. NSM Wimbledon *S'wark* from 96. *39 Panmuir Road, London SW20 0PZ* Tel 0181-947 5940

JACKSON, Canon David. b 33. Leeds Univ BA60. Coll of Resurr Mirfield 60. **d** 62 **p** 63. C Lewisham St Steph *S'wark* 62-65; P-in-c New Charlton H Trin 65-69; C Charlton St Luke w St Paul 69-72; Sen Tutor Coll of the Resurr Mirfield 72-75; R Clapham H Trin 75-78; P-in-c Clapham St Pet 76-78; TR Clapham Old Town 78-84; Hon Can S'wark Cathl 80-96; V Battersea St Mary-le-Park 84-89; V Surbiton St Andr and St Mark 89-96; rtd 96; Chapl St Mich Convent Ham from 96. *43 Ham Common, Richmond, Surrey TW10 7JG* Tel 0181-948 0775

JACKSON, David. b 48. Open Univ BA85. Nazarene Th Coll Man DipTh73 St Deiniol's Hawarden 91. **d** 91 **p** 92. In Nazarene Ch 73-90; C Scotforth *Blackb* 91-95; C Banbury *Ox* from 95. *4 Longfellow Road, Banbury, Oxon OX16 9LB* Tel (01295) 264961

JACKSON, David Hilton. b 62. Stanford Univ BA84 Ox Univ MSt94. Princeton Th Sem MDiv90 Wycliffe Hall Ox DipTh95. **d** 95 **p** 96. C Ox St Andr *Ox* from 95. *5 Squitchey Lane, Oxford OX2 7LD* Tel (01865) 53944

JACKSON, David Reginald Estcourt. b 25. OBE. Qu Coll Cam BA45 MA49. St Jo Coll Dur 80. **d** 81 **p** 82. Hon C Douglas *Blackb* 81-82; C 82-87; rtd 90. *64 The Common, Parbold, Wigan, Lancs WN8 7EA* Tel (01257) 462671

JACKSON, David Robert. b 51. Lon Univ BDS. Linc Th Coll 81. **d** 83 **p** 84. C Hatcham St Cath *S'wark* 83-87; V Sydenham St Bart 87-93. *23 Birkdale Court, Buckland Road, Maidstone, Kent ME16 0UH* Tel (01622) 662483

JACKSON, David William. b 53. Golds Coll Lon BA75 PGCE76. Cranmer Hall Dur 90. **d** 92 **p** 93. C Desborough *Pet* 92-95; C Eastham *Ches* from 95. *107 Eastham Rake, Eastham, Wirral, Merseyside L62 9AW* Tel 0151-327 7533

JACKSON, Canon Derek. b 26. Ex Coll Ox BA51 MA55. Westcott Ho Cam 51. **d** 53 **p** 54. C Radcliffe-on-Trent *S'well* 53-56; C Frome St Jo *B & W* 56-57; V Eaton Socon *St Alb* 57-63; V Boxmoor St Jo 63-74; V Bishop's Stortford St Mich 74-85; Hon Can St Alb 82-85; Bermuda 85-89; P-in-c Cerne Abbas w Godmanstone and Minterne Magna *Sarum* 89-95; rtd 95; Chapl Menorca *Eur* 95-96; Perm to Offic *Chelmsf* from 97. *88 Stansted Road, Bishop's Stortford, Herts CM23 2DZ* Tel (01279) 652664

JACKSON, Canon Derek Reginald. b 49. K Coll Lon BD72 AKC72. **d** 73 **p** 74. C Westhoughton *Man* 73-75; C Kendal H Trin *Carl* 75-78; V Pennington w Lindal and Marton 78-83; Warden of Readers 82-92; V Kendal St Geo 83-94; Hon Can Carl Cathl from 89; V Applethwaite 94-96; P-in-c Troutbeck 94-96; V Windermere St Mary and Troutbeck from 96. *St Mary's Vicarage, Ambleside Road, Windermere, Cumbria LA23 1BA* Tel (01539) 443032

JACKSON, Derrick Raymond. b 20. ALAM. Worc Ord Coll 63. **d** 65 **p** 66. C Old Swinford *Worc* 65-68; C Headless Cross 68-70; R Mamble w Bayton 70; TV Steeple Morden *Ely* 71-80; V Hunningham *Cov* 80-85; V Wappenbury w Weston under Wetherley 80-85; rtd 85; Perm to Offic *Ex* from 85. *9 Cauleston Close, Exmouth, Devon EX8 3LU* Tel (01395) 266615

JACKSON, Doreen May. S Dios Minl Tr Scheme. **d** 88 **p** 94. NSM Fareham H Trin *Portsm* from 88. *134 Oak Road, Fareham, Hants PO15 5HR* Tel (01329) 841429

JACKSON, Mrs Elizabeth Mary. b 41. Man Univ BA67. Ox Min Course 90. **d** 92 **p** 94. Chapl Asst R Berks Hosp Reading 86-95; Chapl R Berks and Battle Hosps NHS Trust from 95; Chapl Asst Reading Hosps 86-95; NSM Reading St Luke w St Bart *Ox* from 92. *2 Belle Avenue, Reading RG6 2BL, or Royal Berkshire Hospital, London Road, Reading RG1 5AN* Tel 0118-926 4149 or 987 5111

JACKSON, Mrs Frances Anne (Peggy). b 51. FCA81 ACA76 Somerville Coll Ox BA72 MA76. Ripon Coll Cuddesdon 85. **d** 87 **p** 94. C Ilkeston St Mary *Derby* 87-90; TD Hemel Hempstead *St Alb* 90-94; TV from 94. *St Paul's Vicarage, 23 Saturn Way, Hemel Hempstead, Herts HP2 5NY* Tel (01442) 255023

JACKSON, Miss Freda. b 41. Bp Otter Coll TCert61 LNSM course 89. **d** 92 **p** 94. NSM Middleton *Man* 92-94; NSM Middleton w Thornham from 94. *783 Manchester Old Road, Middleton, Manchester M24 4RE* Tel 0161-653 5876

JACKSON, George. b 10. St Jo Coll Dur LTh33 BA35 MA39. St Aid Birkenhead 30. **d** 35 **p** 36. C Preston St Cuth *Blackb* 35-37; C Accrington St Jas 38-40; V Haslingden St Jo Stonefold 40-43; V Blackb St Mich 43-53; V Woodplumpton 53-74; C Broughton 74-77; rtd 75; Perm to Offic *Blackb* from 75. *Fosbrooke House, 8 Clifton Drive, Lytham St Annes, Lancs FY8 5RE* Tel (01253) 737680

JACKSON, Harry Francis. b 30. FBOA FSMC FBCO K Coll Lon BD61 AKC61. Sarum Th Coll 61. **d** 62 **p** 62. Bermuda 62-65; C Cobham *Guildf* 65-69; R Ash 69-96; Chapl RAF Farnborough 80-96; rtd 96; P-in-c Mawnan *Truro* from 96. *The Rectory, Old Church Road, Mawnan Smith, Falmouth, Cornwall TR11 5HY* Tel (01326) 250280

JACKSON, Hilary Walton. b 17. St Chad's Coll Dur BA40 MA48. **d** 46 **p** 47. C Selby Abbey *York* 46-49; C Middlesbrough All SS 49-51; V Thornley *Dur* 51-56; V Beamish 56-66; V Heighington 66-82; rtd 82. *127 Bates Avenue, Darlington, Co Durham DL3 0UE* Tel (01325) 482746

JACKSON, Ian. b 53. Jes Coll Ox BA75. Linc Th Coll 76. **d** 78 **p** 79. C Holbeach *Linc* 78-82; V Newsome *Wakef* 82-85; V Newsome and Armitage Bridge from 85. *The Vicarage, Newsome, Huddersfield HD4 6QU* Tel (01484) 420664

JACKSON, Mrs Janet Lesley. b 45. Newc Poly CQSW78. NE Ord Course 93. **d** 96 **p** 97. NSM Whorlton *Newc* from 96. *The Vicarage, Thornhill Road, Ponteland, Newcastle upon Tyne NE20 9PZ* Tel (01661) 822140

JACKSON, John Edward. b 29. K Coll Lon BD57 AKC57. St Boniface Warminster 57. **d** 58 **p** 59. C Crofton Park St Hilda w St Cypr *S'wark* 58-61; V Bremhill w Foxham *Sarum* 61-69; V Netheravon w Fittleton 69-73; V Netheravon w Fittleton and Enford 73-85; OCF 69-85; V Salisbury St Mark *Sarum* 85-92; P-in-c Bryngwyn and Newchurch and Llanbedr etc *S & B* 92-96; rtd 96. *The Cloister, 1 Herman Villas, Rhosgoch, Builth Wells LD2 3JY* Tel (01497) 851660

JACKSON, John Reginald. b 25. Selw Coll Cam BA45 MA49. Ridley Hall Cam 45. **d** 48 **p** 49. C Doncaster St Jas *Sheff* 48-50; C Walcot *B & W* 50-53; C Cheltenham St Mark *Glouc* 53-56; R Down *Ex* 56-67; R Georgeham 67-73; V Abbotsley *Ely* 73-79; V Everton w Tetworth 73-79; V Waresley 73-79; P-in-c Garway *Heref* 79-85; P-in-c St Weonards w Orcop 79-85; P-in-c Tretire w Michaelchurch and Pencoyd 79-85; P-in-c Welsh Newton w Llanrothal 79-85; rtd 85; Perm to Offic *Heref* from 85. *4 Rosemary Gardens, Hereford HR1 1UP* Tel (01432) 270271

JACKSON, Preb John Wilson. b 14. St Jo Coll Dur BA38. Wycliffe Hall Ox 38. **d** 40 **p** 41. C Bordesley H Trin *Birm* 40-41; C Sparkhill St Jo 41-44; C Walsall St Matt *Lich* 44-46; R Birm All SS *Birm* 46-50; V Bromley Common St Aug *Roch* 50-52; V Sparkhill St Jo *Birm* 52-64; Chapl Birm Women's Hosp 52-64; Hon Can Birm Cathl *Birm* 61-64; V Swindon Ch Ch *Bris* 64-68; Chapl Swindon Hosps 64-68; V Walsall *Lich* 68-81; RD Walsall 68-81; Preb Lich Cathl 72-81; rtd 81; Perm to Offic *Birm* from 82. *6 Arnold Grove, Shirley, Solihull, W Midlands B90 3JR* Tel 0121-744 1288

JACKSON, Miss Kathryn Dianne. b 64. Leeds Univ BA87. St Steph Ho Ox 87. **d** 90 **p** 94. Par Dn Headingley *Ripon* 90-94; C 94; C Hawksworth Wood from 94. *St Andrew's House, Butcher Hill, Leeds LS16 5BG* Tel 0113-278 4560

JACKSON, Kenneth Evans. b 30. Kelham Th Coll 50. **d** 54 **p** 55. C Coppenhall *Ches* 54-57; C Stockport St Alb Hall Street 57-60; CF 60-67; R Lewtrenchard w Thrushelton *Ex* 67-77; P-in-c Stowford 73-77; P-in-c Malborough w S Huish 77-83; P-in-c W Alvington w S Milton 82-83; V Malborough w S Huish, W Alvington and Churchstow 83-86; P-in-c Lustleigh 86-95; NSM 95-96; rtd 95; NSM Moretonhampstead, Manaton, N Bovey and Lustleigh *Ex* from 96. *28 Staddons View, Bovey Tracey, Newton Abbot, Devon TQ13 9HN* Tel (01626) 832736

JACKSON, Kenneth William (Ken). b 30. MCSP53. Chich Th Coll 70. **d** 72 **p** 73. C Eastney *Portsm* 72-74; C Portchester 75-79; V Elson 79-95; rtd 95. *13 Jellicoe Avenue, Gosport, Hants PO12 2PA* Tel (01705) 587089

JACKSON, The Very Revd Lawrence. b 26. AKC50. **d** 51 **p** 52. C Leic St Marg *Leic* 51-55; V Wymeswold 55-59; V Leic St Jas 59-65; V Cov H Trin *Cov* 65-73; Hon Can Cov Cathl 67-73; RD Cov N 68-73; Provost Blackb 73-92; rtd 92; Perm to Offic *Cov* from 93. *Northcot, Brook Lane, Newbold on Stour, Stratford-upon-Avon, Warks CV37 8UA* Tel (01789) 450721

JACKSON, Margaret Elizabeth. b 47. Lon Univ BSc68 MSc95 FIPD91. S'wark Ord Course DipRS83. **dss** 83 **d** 92 **p** 94. Surbiton Hill Ch Ch *S'wark* 83-84; Saffron Walden w Wendens Ambo and Littlebury *Chelmsf* 84-85; Dulwich St Barn *S'wark* 86-92; Hon C from 92; Personal Asst to Bp S'wark 92-94; Selection Sec ABM from 96. *4 Ferrings, College Road, London SE21 7LU* Tel 0181-299 1872 or 0171-222 9011 Fax 0181-299 1872

JACKSON, Mrs Margaret Elizabeth. b 47. Mon Dioc Tr Scheme. **d** 87 **p** 94. C Chepstow *Mon* 87-90; C Exhall *Cov* 90-92; C Leamington Priors All SS 92-96; R Hulme Ascension *Man* from 96. *The Ascension Rectory, Royce Road, Hulme, Manchester M15 5FQ* Tel 0161-226 5568

JACKSON, Mrs Margaret Jane. b 50. RGN72 S Bank Poly HDipHV75. S'wark Ord Course 89. **d** 92 **p** 94. Par Dn Hatcham St Cath *S'wark* 92-94; C from 94. *26 Millmark Grove, London SE14 6RQ* Tel 0181-692 4645 or 732 4343

JACKSON, Mark Harding. b 51. Open Univ BA87. Sarum & Wells Th Coll 76. **d** 79 **p** 80. C Hobs Moat *Birm* 79-83; Chapl RN from 83. *Royal Naval Chaplaincy Service, Room 203, Victory Building, HM Naval Base, Portsmouth PO1 3LS* Tel (01705) 727903 Fax 727112

JACKSON, Martin. b 56. Clare Coll Cam BA77 MA81. Cranmer Hall Dur BA80. **d** 81 **p** 82. C Houghton le Spring *Dur* 81-84; C Bishopwearmouth St Mich w St Hilda 84-86; TV Winlaton 86; V High Spen and Rowlands Gill 86-94; P-in-c Benfieldside 94-97; V from 97. *St Cuthbert's Vicarage, Church Bank, Consett, Co Durham DH8 0NW* Tel (01207) 503019

JACKSON, The Very Revd Michael Geoffrey St Aubyn. b 56. TCD BA79 MA82 St Jo Coll Cam BA81 MA85 PhD86 Ch Ch Ox MA89 DPhil89. CITC 86. **d** 86 **p** 87. C Dublin Zion Ch *D & G* 86-89; Chapl Ch Ch Ox 89-97; I Cork St Fin Barre's Union *C, C & R* from 97; Dean Cork from 97. *The Deanery, 9 Dean Street, Cork, Irish Republic* Tel Cork (21) 964742 Fax as telephone

JACKSON, Michael James. b 44. CEng69 MICE69 Liv Univ BEng65 Newc Univ PhD84. NE Ord Course 82. **d** 84 **p** 85. C Houghton le Spring *Dur* 84-87; V Millfield St Mark 87-95; V Ponteland *Newc* from 95. *The Vicarage, Thornhill Road, Ponteland, Newcastle upon Tyne NE20 9PZ* Tel (01661) 822140

JACKSON, Michael Richard. b 31. Selw Coll Cam BA54 MA58. Westcott Ho Cam 54. **d** 56 **p** 57. C Gosforth All SS *Newc* 56-62; R Dinnington *Sheff* 62-76; V Swinton 76-97; rtd 97. *10 Elmhirst Drive, Rotherham, S Yorkshire S65 3ED*

JACKSON, Canon Noel Benjamin. b 26. TCD BA50 MA55. **d** 51 **p** 52. C Conwall Union *D & R* 51-55; I Laghey 55-59; I Dromore *Clogh* 59-66; I Belfast Upper Malone (Epiphany) *Conn* 66-82; RD S Belfast 79-82; I Carnmoney 82-94; Preb Castleknock St Patr Cathl Dublin 86-94; rtd 94. *6 Kingsfort Lodge, Moira, Craigavon, Co Armagh BT67 0GQ* Tel (01846) 619802

JACKSON, Norman. b 14. St Jo Coll Dur BA39 DipTh40 MA42. **d** 40 **p** 41. C Chorley St Geo *Blackb* 40-42; C Poulton-le-Fylde 42-45; Distr Sec (Man Area) BFBS 45-49; V Bolton H Trin *Man* 49-53; V Norden w Ashworth 53-69; R St Mewan *Truro* 69-79; rtd 80; Perm to Offic *Carl* 82-93. *23 Riverbank Road, Kendal, Cumbria LA9 5JS*

JACKSON, Norman. b 20. CEng MIMechE53. S'wark Ord Course 74. **d** 77 **p** 78. NSM Erith Ch Ch *Roch* 77-82; NSM Bishopstoke *Win* 82-95; rtd 95. *7 Otter Close, Eastleigh, Hants SO50 8NF* Tel (01703) 695045

JACKSON, Peter. b 39. Open Univ BA81. St Jo Coll Nottm LTh85. **d** 85 **p** 86. C Clifton *York* 85-88; Chapl Clifton Hosp York 85-88; TV Moor Allerton *Ripon* from 88. *73 The Avenue, Leeds LS17 7NP* Tel 0113-267 8487

JACKSON, Peter Jonathan Edward. b 53. St Pet Coll Ox BA74 MA78 PGCE78. St Steph Ho Ox 79. **d** 79 **p** 80. C Malvern Link w Cowleigh *Worc* 79-82; Hon C Ox St Mich w St Martin and All SS *Ox* 79-80; Chapl Aldenham Sch Herts 82-89; Chapl and Hd RE Harrow Sch from 89; Perm to Offic *Lon* from 89. *Field House South, West Street, Harrow, Middx HA1 3ER* Tel 0181-869 1225

JACKSON, Peter Lewis. b 34. Bps' Coll Cheshunt 63. **d** 66 **p** 67. C Stockingford *Cov* 66-67; C Kenilworth St Nic 67-72; P-in-c Napton on the Hill 72-75; V 75-89; V Lower Shuckburgh 75-89; R Napton-on-the-Hill, Lower Shuckburgh etc from 89. *The Vicarage, Napton, Rugby, Warks CV23 8NE* Tel (01926) 812383

JACKSON, Peter William. b 35. Sarum Th Coll 67. **d** 68 **p** 69. C Skelton in Cleveland *York* 68-69; C Upleatham 68-70; Chapl RN 70-92; Miss to Seamen from 92; Japan from 92. *Port PO Box 709, Kobe 651-01, Japan* Tel Kobe (78) 331-1696 Fax 331-1612

JACKSON, Reginald. b 05. Lon Coll of Div 44. **d** 45 **p** 46. C Maidstone St Faith *Cant* 45-48; C Woking St Jo *Guildf* 48-52; R Thetford St Pet w St Nic *Nor* 52-58; V Sissinghurst *Cant* 58-70; rtd 70; Master St Jo Hosp Bath 70-75; Perm to Offic *B & W* 70-91. *Suddon House, Suddon, Wincanton, Somerset BA9 8BP*

JACKSON, Reginald Grant. b 03. Birm Univ BA29. Ripon Hall Ox 28. **d** 29 **p** 30. C Bordesley St Andr *Birm* 29-31; C Moseley St Mary 31-32; C Keston *Roch* 32-35; I Saul *D & D* 35-37; I Saul w Whitminster 37-43; V Painswick *Glouc* 43-54; Canada from 62. *200 Main Street, Ailsa Craig, Ontario, Canada, N0M 1A0*

JACKSON, Richard Charles. b 61. Ch Ch Ox BA83 Cranfield Inst of Tech MSc85. Trin Coll Bris DipHE94. **d** 94 **p** 95. C Lindfield *Chich* from 94. *2 Church Close, Frances Road, Lindfield, Haywards Heath, W Sussex RH16 2JB* Tel (01444) 483945

JACKSON, Robert Brandon. b 61. Lanchester Poly BA86 Ox Univ BA88 MA95. Wycliffe Hall Ox 86. **d** 89 **p** 90. C Bromley Common St Aug *Roch* 89-92; P-in-c Stowe *Ox* 92-97; Asst Chapl Stowe Sch Bucks 92-97; Chapl Lord Wandsworth Coll from 97. *Kimbers, Lord Wandsworth College, Long Sutton, Hook, Hants RG29 1TB* Tel (01256) 862206

JACKSON, Robert Fielden. b 35. St D Coll Lamp BA57. Sarum Th Coll 57. **d** 59 **p** 60. C Altham w Clayton le Moors *Blackb* 59-62; C Lytham St Cuth 62-64; V Skerton St Chad 64-69; V Preesall 69-90; RD Garstang 85-89; V Wray w Tatham and Tatham Fells from 90. *The Vicarage, Main Street, Wray, Lancaster LA2 8QF* Tel (01524) 221030

JACKSON, Robert Stewart. ALCM48 TCD BA53 MA56. CITC 54. **d** 54 **p** 55. C Aghalee *D & D* 54-57; I Derrybrusk *Clogh* 57-61; I Magheracross 61-68; I Lisnaskea 68-91; Chapl to Bp Clogh 73-80; Preb Clogh Cathl 79-85; Preb Donaghmore St Patr Cathl Dublin 85-91; Dioc Registrar *Clogh* 89-91; Preb Elphin Cathl *K, E & A* 91-97; Adn Elphin and Ardagh 91-97; I Templemichael w Clongish, Clooncumber etc 91-96; P-in-c Roscommon w Donamon, Rathcline, Kilkeevin etc 92-97; Dir of Ords 93-97; rtd 97. *The Cairn, Castlebalfour Park, Lisnaskea, Enniskillen, Co Fermanagh BT92 0GD*

JACKSON, Robert William. b 49. K Coll Cam MA73 Man Univ MA. St Jo Coll Nottm 78. **d** 81 **p** 82. C Fulwood *Sheff* 81-84; V Grenoside 84-92; Chapl Grenoside Hosp Sheff 84-92; V Scarborough St Mary w Ch Ch and H Apostles *York* from 92. *The Vicarage, The Crescent, Scarborough, N Yorkshire YO11 2PP* Tel (01723) 371354

JACKSON, Roger. b 57. Chich Th Coll 85. **d** 88 **p** 89. C Hale *Guildf* 88-92; V Barton w Peel Green *Man* 92-95; P-in-c Long Crendon w Chearsley and Nether Winchendon *Ox* from 95. *The Vicarage, Long Crendon, Aylesbury, Bucks HP18 9AL* Tel (01844) 208363

JACKSON, Canon Roger Brumby. b 31. Dur Univ BSc53 DipEd54. Ridley Hall Cam 57. **d** 59 **p** 60. C Rowner *Portsm* 59-61; C Drypool St Columba w St Andr and St Pet *York* 61-64; Asst Chapl HM Pris Hull 61-64; V Plumstead St Jas w St Jo *S'wark* 65-68; P-in-c Plumstead St Paul 65-68; V Plumstead St Jo w St Jas and St Paul 68-74; Sub-Dean Woolwich 71-74; Chapl Hulton Hosp Bolton from 74; V Deane *Man* 74-80; TR from 80; AD Deane 80-85; Hon Can Man Cathl from 90. *Deane Rectory, 234 Wigan Road, Bolton BL3 5QE* Tel (01204) 61819

JACKSON, Preb Roland Francis. b 20. Univ of Wales (Lamp) BA42. St Mich Coll Llan 42. **d** 44 **p** 45. C Risca *Mon* 44-49; C Chepstow St Arvan's w Penterry 49-54; R Haughton *Lich* 54-61; V Stafford St Paul Forebridge 61-72; RD Eccleshall 72-82; Chapl HM Pris Drake Hall 75-85; V Eccleshall *Lich* 72-85; Preb Lich Cathl 82-85; rtd 85; Perm to Offic *Lich* from 85. *Treginnis,*

29 Meadow Drive, Haughton, Stafford ST18 9HQ Tel (01785) 780571

JACKSON, Canon Ronald William (Ron). b 37. ALCD. **d** 69 **p** 70. C Crofton *Portsm* 69-74; V Wolverhampton St Matt *Lich* 74-85; V Bloxwich 85-89; C Tamworth 89-92; Bp's Officer for Par Miss and Development *Bradf* from 92; Hon Can Bradf Cathl from 94. *6 Woodvale Crescent, Bingley, W Yorkshire BD16 4AL* Tel (01274) 565789 Fax 510556 E-mail rjackson@woodvale.u-net.com

JACKSON, Canon Stanley. b 21. St Cath Soc Ox BA48 MA52. Linc Th Coll 48. **d** 50 **p** 51. C Swinton St Pet *Man* 50-52; C Skegness *Linc* 52-56; CF 56-68; R Lt Coates *Linc* 68-77; R Bradley 75-77; TR Gt and Lt Coates w Bradley 78; R Ruskington 78-86; V Dorrington 78-82; Can and Preb Linc Cathl from 79; rtd 86. *73A Lincoln Road, Ruskington, Sleaford, Lincs NG34 9AR* Tel (01526) 832821

JACKSON, Canon Stephen Alexander. b 18. Keble Coll Ox BA40 MA44. Cuddesdon Coll 40. **d** 42 **p** 43. C Hatfield *St Alb* 42-45; C Welwyn Garden City 45-49; Youth Chapl *Leic* 49-52; R Asfordby 52-58; P-in-c Frisby-on-the-Wreake w Kirby Bellars 52-54; V Quorndon 58-65; R Aylestone 65-83; RD Christianity S 74-81; Hon Can Leic Cathl 74-81; rtd 83; Perm to Offic *Leic* from 83. *34 Bradgate Drive, Wigston, Leics LE18 1HA* Tel 0116-288 1564

JACKSON, Thomas Peter. b 27. Univ of Wales (Lamp) BA50. St Mich Coll Llan 50. **d** 52 **p** 53. C Swansea St Mary and H Trin *S & B* 52-58; Area Sec (S Midl and S Wales) UMCA 58-60; V Glouc St Steph *Glouc* 60-73; R Upton St Leonards 73-92; RD Glouc N 82-91; rtd 92; Perm to Offic *Glouc* from 92. *44 Grebe Close, Gloucester GL4 9XL* Tel (01452) 306634

JACKSON, William Stafford. b 48. Sunderland Poly DCYW83. Linc Th Coll. **d** 89 **p** 90. C Heworth St Mary *Dur* 89-91; C Tudhoe Grange 91-92. *10 Merrington Close, Kirk Merrington, Spennymoor, Co Durham DL16 7HU* Tel (01388) 815061

JACKSON, Canon William Stanley Peter. b 39. Univ of Wales DipTh66. St Mich Coll Llan 63. **d** 66 **p** 67. C Llandrindod w Cefnllys *S & B* 66-69; C Gowerton w Waunarlwydd 69-73; V Crickadarn w Gwenddwr and Alltmawr 73-79; V Llanfeugan and Llanthetty and Glyncollwng etc from 79; Dioc GFS Chapl from 84; Can Res Brecon Cathl from 90. *The Rectory, Talybont-on-Usk, Brecon LD3 7UX* Tel (01874) 87243

JACKSON-STEVENS, Preb Nigel. b 42. St Steph Ho Ox. **d** 68 **p** 69. C Babbacombe *Ex* 68-73; P-in-c W Buckland 73-75; V Swimbridge 73-75; V Swimbridge and W Buckland 75-84; P-in-c Mortehoe 84-85; P-in-c Ilfracombe, Lee, W Down, Woolacombe and Bittadon 84-85; TR Ilfracombe, Lee, Woolacombe, Bittadon etc from 85; RD Barnstaple from 93; Preb Ex Cathl from 95. *The Vicarage, St Brannock's Road, Ilfracombe, Devon EX34 8EG* Tel (01271) 863467

JACOB, Mrs Amelia Stanley. b 52. Punjab Univ BA73. Oak Hill Th Coll. **d** 90 **p** 94. NSM Asian Chr Congr All SS Tufnell Park *Lon* 90-92; NSM Alperton from 92. *62 Clifford Road, Wembley, Middx HA0 1AE* Tel 0181-902 4592

JACOB, John Lionel Andrew. b 26. Selw Coll Cam BA50 MA54. Westcott Ho Cam 50. **d** 52 **p** 53. C Brightside St Thos *Sheff* 52-55; C Maltby 55-58; V Doncaster Intake 58-67; V Sheff St Aid w St Luke 67-75; TR Sheff Manor 75-82; R Waddington *Linc* 82-91; rtd 91; Perm to Offic *Linc* from 91. *1 Woburn Avenue, Lincoln LN1 3HJ* Tel (01522) 513772

JACOB, Canon Joseph. b 38. CITC 65. **d** 68 **p** 69. C Belfast St Aid *Conn* 68-70; Bp's Dom Chapl 70-71; I Kilscoran *C & O* 71-80; I Geashill *M & K* 80-83; Asst Warden Ch's Min of Healing from 83; Gen Sec (Ireland) CMJ 87-91; I Ardamine w Kiltennel, Glascarrig etc *C & O* from 91; Preb Ferns Cathl from 96. *Ardamine Rectory, Courtown Harbour, Gorey, Co Wexford, Irish Republic* Tel Gorey (55) 25423

JACOB, Neville Peter. b 60. Kent Univ BA82 Leeds Metrop Univ PGCE86. Cuddesdon Coll 94. **d** 96 **p** 97. C Market Harborough *Leic* from 96; C Market Harborough Transfiguration from 96. *5 Ashfield Road, Market Harborough, Leics LE16 7LX* Tel (01858) 431977

JACOB, The Ven William Mungo. b 44. Hull Univ LLB66 Linacre Coll Ox BA69 MA73 Ex Univ PhD. St Steph Ho Ox 70. **d** 70 **p** 71. C Wymondham *Nor* 70-73; Asst Chapl Ex Univ *Ex* 73-75; Dir Past Studies Sarum & Wells Th Coll 75-80; Vice-Prin 77-80; Selection Sec and Sec Cttee for Th Educn ACCM 80-86; Warden Linc Th Coll 85-96; Can and Preb Linc Cathl *Linc* 86-96; Hon C Linc Minster Gp 88-96; Adn Charing Cross *Lon* from 96; Bp's Sen Chapl from 96. *4 Cambridge Place, London W8 5PB* Tel 0171-937 2560

JACOBS, Michael David. b 41. Ex Coll Ox BA63 MA67. Chich Th Coll 63. **d** 65 **p** 66. C Walthamstow St Pet *Chelmsf* 65-68; Chapl Sussex Univ *Chich* 68-72; Student Counsellor Leic Univ 72-84; Lect Adult Educn Dept from 84; Dir Cen for Past Care and Counselling 84-91. *Vaughan College, St Nicholas' Circle, Leicester LE1 4LB* Tel 0116-251 7368

JACOBS, Neville Robertson Eynesford. b 32. Lon Coll of Div ALCD59 LTh74. **d** 59 **p** 60. C Chesham St Mary *Ox* 59-62; CMS 62-67; C Keynsham *B & W* 67-71; R Croscombe and Dinder 72-80; R Pilton w Croscombe, N Wootton and Dinder 80-83; V Biddenham *St Alb* 83-89; V Chipping Sodbury and Old Sodbury *Glouc* 89-97; RD Hawkesbury 91-94; rtd 97. *33A Bakers Lane, Lingfield, Surrey RH7 6HE* Tel (01342) 836271

JACOBS, Peter John. **d** 96 **p** 97. Hon C Boughton under Blean w Dunkirk and Hernhill *Cant* from 96. *182 Dargate Road, Yorkletts, Whitstable, Kent CT5 3AH* Tel (01227) 751115

JACOBSON, William Walter. b 24. Cant Univ (NZ) LTh51. **d** 51 **p** 52. New Zealand 51-58; P-in-c Poughill w Stockleigh English *Ex* 58-59; V Shiphay Collaton 59-77; TV Clyst St George, Aylesbeare, Clyst Honiton etc 77-78 and 80-84; R Clyst St Mary, Clyst St George etc 85-89; C Ottery St Mary 79-80; Dioc Communications Officer 83-89; rtd 89; Perm to Offic *Ex* from 89. *5 Clyst Valley Road, Clyst St Mary, Exeter EX5 1DD* Tel (01392) 874304

JACQUET, Trevor Graham. b 56. Man Univ BSc77. Oak Hill Th Coll BA88. **d** 88 **p** 89. C Deptford St Nic and St Luke *S'wark* 88-92; Chapl HM Pris Brixton 92-95; Chapl HM Pris Elmley from 95; Perm to Offic *S'wark* from 96. *HM Prison Elmley, Eastchurch, Sheerness, Kent ME12 4DZ* Tel (01795) 880808 Fax 880118

JACSON, Edward Shallcross Owen. b 38. St Steph Ho Ox 61. **d** 64 **p** 65. C Yate *Glouc* 64-67; C Churchdown 67-71; P-in-c Sandhurst 71-75; V Sherborne w Windrush and the Barringtons 75-76; V Sherborne, Windrush, the Barringtons etc 76-80; TV Shaston *Sarum* 80-87; Perm to Offic from 88. *Grove Farm, Melbury Abbas, Shaftesbury, Dorset SP7 0DE* Tel (01747) 853688

JAGE-BOWLER, Christopher William. b 61. Nottm Univ BA83 Ch Ch Ox PGCE84 Down Coll Cam BA89. Ridley Hall Cam 87. **d** 90 **p** 91. C Downend *Bris* 90-94; Chapl Bris Univ 94-96; C Bris St Mich and St Paul 94-96; Asst Chapl Berlin *Eur* from 96. *Garibaldistrasse 47, 13158 Berlin, Germany* Tel Berlin (30) 917-2248 Fax 301-4646

JAGGER, Ian. b 55. K Coll Cam BA77 MA81 St Jo Coll Dur BA80 MA87. Cranmer Hall Dur 78. **d** 82 **p** 83. C Twickenham St Mary *Lon* 82-85; P-in-c Willen *Ox* 85-87; TV Stantonbury and Willen 87-94; TR Fareham H Trin *Portsm* from 94; Dioc Ecum Officer 94-96; RD Fareham from 96. *The Rectory, 9 Brook Meadow, Fareham, Hants PO15 5JH* Tel (01329) 280180

JAGGER, Dr Peter John. b 38. FRHistS78 Leeds Univ MPhil76 PhD87. Lambeth MA71 Wesley Coll Leeds 62 Coll of Resurr Mirfield 67. **d** 68 **p** 69. C Leeds All SS *Ripon* 68-71; V Bolton w Redmire 71-77; Warden and Chief Lib St Deiniol's Lib Hawarden 77-97; Dir of Self Supporting Min 77-97; Perm to Offic *Ches* from 77; Lic to Offic *St As* from 77; Perm to Offic *Ban* from 77; rtd 97. *6 Coed-y-Glyn, Llanberis, Caernarfon LL55 4PX* Tel (01286) 871726

JAGGER (née GREEN), Mrs Ruth Valerie. b 56. Ex Univ CertEd77. Ox NSM Course 87. **d** 90 **p** 94. NSM Stantonbury and Willen *Ox* 90-94; NSM Fareham H Trin *Portsm* from 94. *The Rectory, 9 Brook Meadow, Fareham, Hants PO15 5JH* Tel (01329) 280180

JAGGS, Michael Richard Moore. b 37. Toronto Univ PhD67 FBDO85. S Dios Minl Tr Scheme 93. **d** 95 **p** 96. NSM Hook *Win* from 95. *Turnpike Field, London Road, Hartley Wintney, Hook, Hants RG27 8HY* Tel (01252) 842658 Fax as telephone

JAGO, Alfred Douglas James. b 08. Leeds Univ BA30. Coll of Resurr Mirfield 30. **d** 32 **p** 33. C Plymouth St Pet *Ex* 32-42; C-in-c Honicknowle CD 42-57; V Honicknowle 57; V Penwerris *Truro* 57-65; RD Carnmarth S 63-65; R St Stephen in Brannel 65-76; RD St Austell 71-76; rtd 76; Hon C Charlestown *Truro* from 77. *22 Fairbourne Road, St Austell, Cornwall PL25 4NR* Tel (01726) 75208

JAGO, Christine May. b 52. **d** 94 **p** 95. NSM St Buryan, St Levan and Sennen *Truro* from 94. *Boscarne House, St Buryan, Penzance, Cornwall TR19 6HU*

JAGO, David. b 48. Shoreditch Coll Lon CertEd69 Birm Univ BPhil77 Hull Univ DipC93. St Steph Ho Ox DipMin95. **d** 97. C S Bank *York* from 97. *13 Poplar Grove, South Bank, Middlesbrough TS6 6SY* Tel (01642) 458589

JAKEMAN, Francis David. b 47. Leeds Univ BSc69 Ealing Coll of Educn DMS81. Cuddesdon Coll 71. **d** 74 **p** 75. C Gt Grimsby St Mary and St Jas *Linc* 74-77; Ind Chapl *Lon* 77-88; V Harrow Weald All SS from 88; Chapl Weald Coll from 88. *The Vicarage, 175 Uxbridge Road, Harrow, Middx HA3 6TP* Tel 0181-954 0247

JALLAND, Hilary Gervase Alexander. b 50. FRSA Ex Univ BA72. Coll of Resurr Mirfield 74. **d** 76 **p** 77. C Ex St Thos *Ex* 76-80; C Ex St Thos and Em 80; C Portsea St Mary *Portsm* 80-86; V Hempton and Pudding Norton *Nor* 86-90; TV Hawarden *St As* 90-93; R Llandysilio and Penrhos and Llandrinio etc from 93. *The Rectory, Rhos Common, Four Crosses, Llanymynech SY22 6RW* Tel (01691) 830533

JAMES, Andrew Nicholas. b 54. BSc76. Trin Coll Bris 77. **d** 80 **p** 81. C Prescot *Liv* 80-83; C Upholland 83-85; V Hindley Green 85-91; V Dean Forest H Trin *Glouc* from 91; RD Forest S from 97. *Holy Trinity Vicarage, Oakland Road, Harrow Hill, Drybrook, Glos GL17 9JX* Tel (01594) 542232

JAMES, Anne Loraine. b 45. St Jo Coll Nottm CertCS. **d** 90 **p** 94. NSM Ellon *Ab* from 90; NSM Cruden Bay from 90. *Millhouse, Nethermill, Hatton, Peterhead, Aberdeenshire AB42 7SN* Tel (01779) 812609

JAMES, Arthur Kenneth. b 14. St Chad's Coll Dur BA35 DipTh35 MA38. **d** 37 **p** 38. C Bedwas *Mon* 37-39; C Newport St Paul 39-42; CF (EC) 42-46; CF 46-64; V Marshfield and Peterstone Wentloog etc *Mon* 64-79; rtd 79. *3 Ellis Avenue, Onslow Village, Guildford, Surrey GU2 5SR* Tel (01483) 38582

JAMES, Barry Paul. b 49. BSc. Sarum & Wells Th Coll. **d** 82 **p** 83. C Bitterne Park *Win* 82-86; V Southampton St Mary Extra from 86. *The Vicarage, 65 Peartree Avenue, Southampton SO19 7JN* Tel (01703) 448353

JAMES, Brian Percival Harold. b 26. Southn Univ BSc53. Wycliffe Hall Ox 62. **d** 64 **p** 65. C Hartley Wintney and Elvetham *Win* 64-66; C Shelf *Bradf* 66-71; V Oldham St Ambrose *Man* from 71. *The Vicarage, Prince Charlie Street, Oldham OL1 4HJ* Tel 0161-624 7122

JAMES, Brother. *See* PICKEN, James Hugh

JAMES, Miss Carolyn Anne. b 65. Coll of Ripon & York St Jo BA87 Nottm Univ BTh91. Linc Th Coll 88. **d** 91 **p** 94. Par Dn Middleton St Mary *Ripon* 91-94; C Wetherby from 94. *53 Barleyfields Road, Wetherby, W Yorkshire LS22 7PT* Tel (01937) 583628

✠**JAMES, The Rt Revd Colin Clement Walter.** b 26. K Coll Cam BA49 MA51. Cuddesdon Coll 50. **d** 52 **p** 53 **c** 73. C Stepney St Dunstan and All SS *Lon* 52-55; Asst Chapl Stowe Sch Bucks 55-56; Chapl 56-59; Asst in Relig Broadcasting BBC 59-60; Relig Broadcasting Org W Region BBC 60-67; V Bournemouth St Pet *Win* 67-73; P-in-c Bournemouth St Steph 70-73; Dir of Tr 72-77; Can Res Win Cathl 73-77; Suff Bp Basingstoke 73-77; Bp Wakef 77-85; Bp Win 85-95; rtd 95; Asst Bp B & W from 95. *5 Hermitage Road, Lansdown, Bath BA1 5SN* Tel (01225) 312702

JAMES, Colin Robert. b 34. IPFA. St Deiniol's Hawarden 84. **d** 87 **p** 88. NSM Llanwnda w Llanfaglan *Ban* 87-88; NSM Arfon Deanery 88-90; NSM Bistre *St As* from 90. *1 Lea Drive, Buckley CH7 2BQ* Tel (01244) 544392

JAMES, Colin Robert. b 39. Magd Coll Ox BA61 MA65 DipEd62. St Alb and Ox Min Course 93. **d** 96 **p** 97. NSM Wokingham All SS *Ox* from 96. *7 Sewell Avenue, Wokingham, Berks RG41 1NT* Tel (0118) 978 1515

JAMES, The Ven David Brian. b 30. FCA52 Univ of Wales (Swansea) BA63. St Mich Coll Llan 55. **d** 57 **p** 58. C Llandeilo Tal-y-bont *S & B* 57-59; C Newport Ch Ch *Mon* 59-63; V Bryngwyn and Newchurch and Llanbedr etc *S & B* 63-70; V Llanfeugan and Llanthetty and Glyncollwng etc 70-79; V Ilston w Pennard 79-94; Hon Can Brecon Cathl 87-89; RD Gower 89-94; Can Brecon Cathl 89-94; Chan Brecon Cathl 93-94; Adn Brecon from 94; P-in-c Llanllyr-yn-Rhos w Llanfihangel Helygen from 94. *The Vicarage, Highbury, Llanyre, Llandrindod Wells LD1 6NF* Tel (01597) 822472

JAMES, David Charles. b 45. Ex Univ BSc66 PhD71. St Jo Coll Nottm BA73. **d** 73 **p** 74. C Portswood Ch Ch *Win* 73-76; V from 90; C Goring-by-Sea *Chich* 76-78; Chapl UEA *Nor* 78-82; V Ecclesfield *Sheff* 82-90; RD Ecclesfield 87-90. *The Vicarage, 36 Brookvale Road, Southampton SO2 1QR* Tel (01703) 554277

JAMES, David Clive. b 40. Bris Univ BA61 K Coll Lon DipEd87. St Steph Ho Ox 64. **d** 65 **p** 66. C Portslade St Nic *Chich* 65-68; C Haywards Heath St Wilfrid 68-71; Chapl Brighton Poly 71-76; Perm to Offic from 76. *22 Bradford Road, Lewes, E Sussex BN7 1RB* Tel (01273) 471851

JAMES, David Howard. b 47. Ex Univ BA70 MA73 Pemb Coll Cam CertEd72. Linc Th Coll 81. **d** 83 **p** 84. C Tavistock and Gulworthy *Ex* 83-86; C E Teignmouth 86-88; C W Teignmouth 86-88; P-in-c Bishopsteignton 88-89; P-in-c Ideford, Luton and Ashcombe 88-89; TV Teignmouth, Ideford w Luton, Ashcombe etc 90-95; P-in-c Sidmouth, Woolbrook, Salcombe Regis, Sidbury etc 95-97; TR from 97. *The Rectory, Glen Road, Sidmouth, Devon EX10 8RW* Tel (01395) 514223

JAMES, Canon David Walter Skyrme. b 36. Nottm Univ BA61. Wells Th Coll 61. **d** 63 **p** 64. C Sneinton St Cypr *S'well* 63-66; C Newark St Mary 66-69; V Kirkby in Ashfield St Thos 69-77; P-in-c Rempstone 76-84; P-in-c Costock 76-84; P-in-c Stanford on Soar 76-84; R E Leake 77-84; R Wollaton from 84; Hon Can S'well Minster from 88; AD Nottingham W 90-91. *St Leonard's Rectory, Russell Drive, Nottingham NG8 2BD* Tel 0115-928 1798

JAMES, David William. b 55. CA Tr Coll CertRS77 Coll of Resurr Mirfield 86. **d** 88 **p** 88. C New Rossington *Sheff* 88-90; V Yardley Wood *Birm* 90-95; P-in-c Allens Cross from 95. *St Bartholomew's Vicarage, 148 Frankley Beeches Road, Birmingham B31 5LW* Tel 0121-475 8329

JAMES, Derek George. b 27. Sarum & Wells Th Coll 72. **d** 74 **p** 75. C Petersfield w Sheet *Portsm* 74-77; P-in-c Gosport Ch Ch 77-81; V 81-96; RD Gosport 90-96; rtd 96. *2 Pyrford Close, Alverstoke, Gosport, Hants PO12 2RA*

JAMES, Dewi Hirwaun. b 41. St Mich Coll Llan 66 Lich Th Coll 67. **d** 70 **p** 72. C Porthmadog St Jo w Borth-y-Gest and Tremadog *Ban* 70-73; C Llanbeblig w Caernarfon and Betws Garmon etc 83-85; C Ban 88-89 and 90-94; C Sheff Parson Cross St Cecilia *Sheff* 89-90; Min Can Ban Cathl *Ban* 90-94; C Holyhead w Rhoscolyn w Llanfair-yn-Neubwll 94-95; C Holyhead 95-96. *Address temp unknown*

JAMES, The Ven Douglas Gordon. b 22. Univ of Wales (Abth) BA47. Qu Coll Birm 74. **d** 75 **p** 76. C Cwmbach *Llan* 75-77; C Aberdare St Jo 77-82; V 82-92; Hon Can Llan Cathl 87-92; Adn Margam 88-92; rtd 92; Perm to Offic *Llan* from 92. *31 Abernant Road, Aberdare CF44 0PY* Tel (01685) 872559

JAMES, Canon Eric Arthur. b 25. K Coll Lon AKC50 BD51 FKC78 Trin Coll Cam MA55 Lambeth DD93 FRSA92. **d** 51 **p** 52. C Westmr St Steph w St Jo *Lon* 51-55; Chapl Trin Coll Cam 55-59; Warden Trin Coll Miss Camberwell 59-64; V Camberwell St Geo *S'wark* 59-64; Dir Par and People 64-69; Can Res and Prec S'wark Cathl 66-73; Dioc Missr *St Alb* 73-83; Can Res St Alb 73-83; Hon Can 83-90; Preacher Gray's Inn 78-96; Dir Chr Action 79-90; Hon Dir from 90; Chapl to The Queen 84-95; Extra Chapl to The Queen from 95; rtd 90; Perm to Offic *S'wark* from 90. *11 Denny Crescent, London SE11 4UY, or 125 Kennington Road, London SE11 6SF* Tel 0171-582 3068 or 735 2372

JAMES, Gareth Hugh. b 40. St D Coll Lamp DipTh66. **d** 66 **p** 67. C Llandaff N *Llan* 66-68; C Whitchurch 68-71; Chapl Llan Cathl Sch 71-93; rtd 93. *Address temp unknown*

JAMES, Canon Godfrey Walter. b 36. Univ of Wales (Lamp) BA58 Univ of Wales (Cardiff) MA60 St Pet Coll Ox DipEd61 BA63 MA67. St Mich Coll Llan 63. **d** 64 **p** 65. C Canton St Jo *Llan* 64-71; V Williamstown 71-85; V Kenfig Hill from 85; Can Llan Cathl from 96. *The Vicarage, Kenfig Hill, Bridgend CF33 6DR* Tel (01656) 740856

JAMES, Gordon Cecil. b 35. Sarum Th Coll 66. **d** 67 **p** 68. C Kew *S'wark* 67-72; P-in-c Weston Longville w Morton and the Witchinghams *Nor* 72-81; R Diss from 81. *The Rectory, 26 Mount Street, Diss, Norfolk IP22 3QG* Tel (01379) 642072

✠**JAMES, The Rt Revd Graham Richard.** b 51. Lanc Univ BA72 Ox Univ DipTh74. Cuddesdon Coll 72. **d** 75 **p** 76 **c** 93. C Pet Ch Carpenter *Pet* 75-79; C Digswell *St Alb* 79-82; TV Digswell and Panshanger 82-83; Lic to Offic 83-93; Sen Selection Sec and Sec Cand Cttee ACCM 83-87; Abp's Chapl *Cant* 87-93; Hon Can Dallas from 89; Suff Bp St Germans *Truro* from 93. *32 Falmouth Road, Truro, Cornwall TR1 2HX* Tel (01872) 73190 Fax 77883

JAMES, Henley George. b 31. Sarum & Wells Th Coll 79. **d** 81 **p** 82. C Tottenham H Trin *Lon* 81-85; C Cricklewood St Pet 85-88; P-in-c 88-89; V Bearwood *Birm* 89-97; rtd 97. *51 Cedar Garden Road, Cedar Grove, Mandeville PO, Manchester, Jamaica*

JAMES, Henry Glyn. b 26. Keble Coll Ox BA50 DipTh51 MA62 Toronto Univ MEd74. Wycliffe Hall Ox 50. **d** 52 **p** 53. C Edgbaston St Aug *Birm* 52-54; C Surbiton St Matt *S'wark* 54-57; Kingham Hill Sch 57-62; Chapl St Lawr Coll Ramsgate 62-68; Canada 68-73; Hon C Kidmore End *Ox* 74-77; K Jas Coll of Henley 74-87; Hon C Remenham *Ox* 77-88; Chapl The Henley Coll 87-88; Chapl Toulouse *Eur* 88-91; rtd 91; Hon C Bournemouth St Pet w St Swithun, H Trin etc *Win* from 93. *13 Harbour Road, Bournemouth BH6 4DD* Tel (01202) 427697

JAMES, Herbert Royston Joseph. b 22. Sarum Th Coll 65. **d** 67 **p** 68. C Whipton *Ex* 67-75; V Shaugh Prior 75-83; V Ipplepen w Torbryan 83-87; rtd 87; Perm to Offic *Ex* from 90. *188 Hamlin Lane, Exeter EX1 2SH*

JAMES, Howard. b 19. Chich Th Coll. **d** 87. Hon C Whitton St Aug *Lon* 87-94; Perm to Offic from 94. *95 Lyndhurst Avenue, Twickenham TW2 6BH* Tel 0181-898 1190

JAMES, Idris Frank. b 20. MISM69 AMBIM70. St D Coll Lamp 52. **d** 55 **p** 59. C Llangynwyd w Maesteg *Llan* 55-59; C Plaistow St Andr *Chelmsf* 59-61; C Chadwell Heath 61-62; V Dunton 62-79; P-in-c Bulphan 62-64; R 64-77; rtd 85. *39 Cae Fardre, Church Village, Pontypridd CF38 1DS* Tel (01443) 202834

JAMES, Jeremy Richard. b 52. Jes Coll Cam BA73 MA77 York Univ CertEd77. St Jo Coll Dur 86. **d** 88 **p** 89. C Broxbourne w Wormley *St Alb* 88-91; C Hailsham *Chich* from 91. *15 Howlett Drive, Hailsham, E Sussex BN27 1QW* Tel (01323) 846680

JAMES, John Charles. b 37. Keble Coll Ox BA59. Linc Th Coll 68. **d** 70 **p** 71. C S Shields St Hilda w St Thos *Dur* 70-77; P-in-c Jarrow Docks 77-78; Adn Seychelles 78-92; V Mylor w Flushing *Truro* from 92. *The Vicarage, Mylor, Falmouth, Cornwall TR11 5UD* Tel (01326) 374408

JAMES, John David. b 23. CCC Cam MA. Wells Th Coll. **d** 50 **p** 51. C Romford St Edw *Chelmsf* 50-54; C Cannock *Lich* 54-56; R Wickham Bishops *Chelmsf* 56-61; V Stansted Mountfitchet 61-71; V Clacton St Jas 71-84; R Poulshot *Sarum* 84; V Rowde 84; R Rowde and Poulshot 84-88; rtd 88; Perm to Offic *Heref* from 92. *15 Beaconsfield Park, Ludlow, Shropshire SY8 4LY* Tel (01584) 873754

JAMES, John Hugh Alexander. b 56. St Jo Coll Dur BA78 Univ of Wales DipTh81. St Mich Coll Llan. **d** 81 **p** 82. C Newton Nottage *Llan* 81-84; Prov Youth and Children's Officer Ch in Wales 84-92; V Llanfihangel-ar-arth *St D* 92-97; V Llanfihangel-ar-arth w Capel Dewi from 97. *The Vicarage, Llanfihangel-ar-arth, Pencader SA39 9HU* Tel (01559) 384858

JAMES, John Morgan. b 21. Lon Univ BD43 MTh45. ALCD43. **d** 44 **p** 45. C Leyton St Mary w St Edw *Chelmsf* 44-47; C Southend St Sav Westcliff 47-50; Prec Chelmsf Cathl 50-53; V Kemp Town St Mark *Chich* 53-65; R Balcombe 65-67; V Sunbury *Lon* 67-77; RD Kemp Town *Chich* 55-65; Dir Coll of Preachers 77-85; rtd 85. *Fair Winds, 126 Pagham Road, Pagham, Bognor Regis, W Sussex PO21 4NN* Tel (01243) 264250

JAMES, John Paul. b 30. Sarum Th Coll 58. **d** 60 **p** 61. C Milton *Portsm* 60-65; C Stanmer w Falmer and Moulsecoomb *Chich* 65-69; PC Brighton H Trin 69-71; Canada from 71; Dean Quebec 77-87; rtd 96. *Little Portion, 51 rue Principale, Beebe Plain, Quebec City, Canada, J0B 1E0* Tel Quebec City (819) 876 2147 Fax 876 5088

JAMES, Joshua John Gerwyn. b 31. St D Coll Lamp BA52. **d** 54 **p** 55. C Haverfordwest St Mary w St Thos *St D* 54-56; C Llanaber w Caerdeon *Ban* 56-57; CF 57-76; V Tidenham w Beachley and Lancaut *Glouc* 76-80; R Aberdovey *Ban* 80-82; V Quinton w Marston Sicca *Glouc* 82-90; RD Campden 88-90; P-in-c Upper Chelsea St Simon *Lon* 90-96; rtd 96. *Updown, 31 The Downs, London SW20 8HG*

JAMES, Keith Edwin Arthur. b 38. Sarum & Wells Th Coll 85. **d** 87 **p** 88. C Hempnall *Nor* 87-91; R Roughton and Felbrigg, Metton, Sustead etc from 91. *The Rectory, Church Loke, Roughton, Norwich NR11 8SZ* Tel (01263) 768075

JAMES, Keith Nicholas. b 69. Leeds Univ BA91 Nottm Univ MA93. St Jo Coll Nottm 91. **d** 93 **p** 94. C Crosby *Linc* 93-96; P-in-c Cherry Willingham w Greetwell from 96. *The Vicarage, 14 Church Lane, Cherry Willingham, Lincoln LN3 4AB* Tel (01522) 750356

JAMES, Lewis John. b 20. St D Coll Lamp BA42. **d** 48 **p** 49. C Llangiwg *S & B* 48-55; C Clydach 55-57; R Whitton w Pilleth 57-60; V Smalley *Derby* 60-85; P-in-c Morley 72-81; rtd 85; Perm to Offic *Derby* 85-87. *78 Waun Daniel, Rhos, Pontardawe, Swansea SA8 5HR* Tel (01792) 830796

JAMES, Lionel Dennis. b 07. Qu Coll Birm. **d** 62 **p** 63. C Kingsthorpe *Pet* 62-65; V Weedon Bec 65-74; R Dodford w Brockhall 66-74; rtd 74. *7 Springfield Park, Mylor Bridge, Falmouth, Cornwall TR11 5SJ* Tel (01326) 373743

JAMES, Malcolm. b 37. CEng MICE MIStructE. N Ord Course. **d** 83 **p** 84. NSM Ripponden *Wakef* from 83. *Lower Stones, Bar Lane, Rishworth, Sowerby Bridge, W Yorkshire HX6 4EY* Tel (01422) 822483

JAMES, Martin. b 40. ACII. **d** 94 **p** 95. NSM N Farnborough *Guildf* from 94. *43 Ashley Road, Farnborough, Hants GU14 7HB* Tel (01252) 544698

JAMES, Michael John. b 29. ALA53 Strathclyde Univ CYCW74 Heriot-Watt Univ CQSW81. Ho of Resurr Mirfield 57. **d** 59 **p** 60. C Applethwaite *Carl* 59-61; C Carl H Trin 61-63; C-in-c Carl St Luke Morton CD 63-67; R Lambley w Knaresdale *Newc* 67-72; Rossie Sch Montrose 75-83; Prin Redding Ho Falkirk 83-86; rtd 93. *28 Windsor Street, Edinburgh EH7 5JR* Tel 0131-556 4935

JAMES, Noel Beddoe Walters. b 39. St Mich Coll Llan DipTh68. **d** 68 **p** 69. C Swansea St Nic *S & B* 68-70; C Swansea St Pet 70-72; Chapl RAF 72-93; P-in-c The Heyfords w Rousham and Somerton *Ox* from 93. *The Rectory, Station Road, Lower Heyford, Bicester, Oxon OX6 3PD* Tel (01869) 340733

JAMES, Paul Dominic Denis. b 48. AKC71 Westmr Coll Ox DipApTh90. **d** 72 **p** 73. C Leytonstone St Marg w St Columba *Chelmsf* 72-74; C Leigh-on-Sea St Marg 74-79; V Walthamstow St Sav from 79. *St Saviour's Vicarage, 210 Markhouse Road, London E17 8EP* Tel 0181-520 2036

JAMES, Paul Maynard. b 31. Univ of Wales (Ban) BA52 Fitzw Ho Cam BA54 MA58. Ridley Hall Cam 56. **d** 57 **p** 58. C Newhaven *Chich* 57-60; Kenya 60-65; SW Area Sec CCCS 65-68; V Shrewsbury St Julian *Lich* 68-76; V Shrewsbury H Trin w St Julian 76-90; P-in-c Woore and Norton in Hales from 90; Adn Salop's Adv on Evang from 90; RD Hodnet 93-97. *The Vicarage, Woore, Crewe CW3 9SA* Tel (01630) 647316

JAMES, Peter David. b 42. Keble Coll Ox BA63 Lon Univ BD67. Tyndale Hall Bris 64. **d** 67 **p** 68. C Haydock St Mark *Liv* 67-69; C Ashton-in-Makerfield St Thos 69-74; V Whiston 74-80; V Harlech and Llanfair-juxta-Harlech etc *Ban* 80-94; R Botwnnog w Bryncroes from 94. *The Rectory, Botwnnog, Pwllheli LL53 8PY* Tel (01758) 730450

JAMES, Peter Heppell. b 19. Tyndale Hall Bris 39. **d** 42 **p** 43. C Castle Town *Lich* 42-44; Chapl RAFVR 44-47; C Bucknall and Bagnall *Lich* 47-49; C Watford St Mary *St Alb* 49-51; V Braintree *Chelmsf* 51-60; R Lt Leighs 60-70; rtd 84. *57 Tynedale Road, Loughborough, Leics LE11 3TA* Tel (01509) 266940

JAMES, Raymond John. b 36. Linc Th Coll 85. **d** 87 **p** 88. C Cov E *Cov* 87-91; V Wolvey w Burton Hastings, Copston Magna etc from 91. *St John's Vicarage, School Lane, Wolvey, Hinckley, Leics LE10 3LH* Tel (01455) 220385

JAMES, Richard Andrew. b 44. Mert Coll Ox BA67 MA70. Tyndale Hall Bris DipTh69. **d** 70 **p** 71. C Bebington *Ches* 70-73; C Histon *Ely* 73-77; Chapl Guildf Coll of Tech 77-80; C Guildf St Sav w Stoke-next-Guildford *Guildf* 77-80; Chapl Bedf Coll of HE *St Alb* 81-83; TV Ipsley *Worc* 84-89; R Mulbarton w Kenningham *Nor* 89-92; rtd 93. *5 Kirkby Close, Ripon, N Yorkshire HG4 2DS* Tel (01765) 604511

JAMES, Richard David. b 45. Lon Coll of Div 67. **d** 70 **p** 71. C Boultham *Linc* 70-74; C Waltham 74-77; C New Waltham 74-77; TV Cleethorpes 77-87; TR E Bris from 87. *St Ambrose Vicarage, Stretford Avenue, Bristol BS5 7AN* Tel 0117-951 7299

JAMES, Dr Richard David. b 65. Clare Coll Cam MA88 Lon Hosp MB90 BChir90. Ridley Hall Cam CTM95. **d** 95 **p** 96. C Clifton Ch Ch w Em *Bris* from 95. *First Floor Flat, Linden Gate, Clifton Down Road, Bristol BS8 4AH* Tel 0117-973 2128

JAMES, Richard William. b 47. St D Coll Lamp DipTh75. **d** 75 **p** 76. C Hubberston *St D* 75-78; R Pendine w Llanmiloe and Eglwys Gymyn w Marros 78-83; V Caerwent w Dinham and Llanfair Discoed etc *Mon* 83-84; Chapl Gothenburg w Halmstad, Jonkoping etc *Eur* 84-89; P-in-c Shooters Hill Ch Ch *S'wark* 89-97; V Plumstead St Mark and St Marg from 97. *St Mark's Vicarage, 11 Old Mill Road, London SE18 1QE* Tel 0181-854 2973

JAMES, Roger Michael. b 44. K Coll Lon BD66 AKC66. **d** 69 **p** 70. C Frindsbury w Upnor *Roch* 69-72; Lic to Offic *St Alb* 73-78; C Digswell 78-81; R Knebworth 81-92; P-in-c Upper Tean *Lich* from 92; Stoke-on-Trent Local Min Adv from 92. *The Vicarage, Vicarage Road, Tean, Stoke-on-Trent ST10 4LE* Tel (01538) 722227

JAMES, Stephen Lynn. b 53. Middx Poly DipHCM74 DipPM75. Oak Hill Th Coll BA86. **d** 86 **p** 87. C Heigham H Trin *Nor* 86-89; Canada 89-93; R Bebington *Ches* from 93. *The Rectory, Church Road, Bebington, Wirral, Merseyside L63 3EX* Tel 0151-645 6478 Fax 643 9664

JAMES, William Arthur. b 10. Univ of Wales BA40. St Mich Coll Llan 40. **d** 42 **p** 43. C Johnston w Steynton *St D* 42-44; C Llanstephan *S & B* 44-45; C Llanybri w Llandilo Abercowin *St D* 45-46; C Maindee *Mon* 46-54; R Bedwas 54-77; rtd 77. *c/o Mrs Stephens, 50 Castle View, Simpson Cross, Haverfordwest SA62 6ES* Tel (01437) 710681

JAMES, William Glynne George. b 39. Trin Coll Carmarthen 82. **d** 85 **p** 86. NSM Gorseinon *S & B* from 85. *23 Cecil Road, Gowerton, Swansea SA4 3DF* Tel (01792) 872363

JAMESON, David Kingsbury. b 28. Mert Coll Ox BA50 MA55. Qu Coll Birm 50. **d** 53 **p** 54. C Leominster *Heref* 53-56; C Portsm Cathl *Portsm* 56-60; Dioc Youth Officer 58-61; V Gosport Ch Ch 60-65; V Portsea St Cuth 65-70; V Enfield Jes Chpl *Lon* 70-74; RD Nuneaton *Cov* 74-79; V Nuneaton St Nic 74-80; Org Sec (Leics and Northants) CECS 80-82; P-in-c Forty Hill Jes Ch *Lon* 82-87; V 87-91; rtd 91; Hon C Okehampton w Inwardleigh, Bratton Clovelly etc *Ex* 94-96; Hon C St Giles-in-the-Fields *Lon* from 96. *Flat 1, 26 West Street, London WC2H 9NA* Tel 0171-836 3667

JAMESON, Canon Dermot Christopher Ledgard. b 27. TCD BA49 MA54. CITC 49. **d** 50 **p** 51. C Seagoe *D & D* 50-53; C Holywood 53-57; I Kilkeel 57-62; I Donaghcloney w Waringstown 62-79; Can Dromore Cathl 77-93; I Kilbroney 79-93; Treas Dromore Cathl 81-83; Prec Dromore Cathl 83-90; Chan Dromore Cathl 90-93; rtd 93. *Concord, 10B Kilbroney Road, Rostrevor, Co Down BT34 3BH* Tel (01693) 739728

JAMESON, Geoffrey Vaughan. b 27. Culham Coll Ox CertEd51 St Luke's Coll Ex ACertEd52. Wycliffe Hall Ox 68. **d** 70 **p** 71. C Buckingham *Ox* 70-73; R Exton w Whitwell *Pet* 73-86; V Marystowe, Coryton, Stowford, Lewtrenchard etc *Ex* 86-90; rtd 90; Perm to Offic *Portsm* from 91. *18 Eglantine Walk, Cowplain, Waterlooville, Hants PO8 9BG* Tel (01705) 571112

JAMESON, Canon John Edward. b 16. Kelham Th Coll 34. **d** 39 **p** 40. C Haltwhistle *Newc* 39-47; C Seaton Hirst 47-52; V Sugley 52-62; V Gosforth All SS 62-76; Hon Can Newc Cathl 72-83; R Rothbury 76-83; rtd 83. *Abbeyfield House, Dial Place, Warkworth, Morpeth, Northd NE65 0UR* Tel (01665) 712510

JAMESON, Peter. b 31. Trin Coll Cam BA54 MA60. Linc Th Coll. **d** 62 **p** 63. C Earl's Court St Cuth w St Matthias *Lon* 62-68; C Notting Hill St Clem 68-72; C Notting Hill St Clem and St Mark 72-74; TV Notting Hill 74-77; V Stoke Newington St Olave 77-95; rtd 95; Perm to Offic *Chich* from 95. *Colemans, Warren Lane, Cross in Hand, Heathfield, E Sussex TN21 0TB* Tel (01435) 863414

JAMIESON, Hugh Gollan. b 20. TCD BA49. CITC 49. **d** 49 **p** 50. C Limerick St Lawr w H Trin and St Jo *L & K* 49-51; I Ballynaclough Union 51-53; Sec BCMS 53-56; I Murragh Union *C, C & R* 56-60; R Birkin w Haddlesey *York* 60-63; I Derralossary *D & G* 63-69; I Mothel *C & O* 69-76; I Badoney Lower *D & R* 76-78; I Donagh w Tyholland and Errigal Truagh *Clogh* 78-82; I Killeshandra w Killegar and Derrylane *K, E & A* 82-87; rtd 87. *Rose Cottage, Killyboley, Glaslough, Monaghan, Irish Republic* Tel Monaghan (47) 88231

JAMIESON, Kenneth Euan Oram. b 24. Lon Univ DipTh68. Roch Th Coll 60. **d** 62 **p** 63. C Bromley SS Pet and Paul *Roch* 62-66; R Colchester St Mary Magd *Chelmsf* 66-71; V Bexleyheath St Pet *Roch* 71-78; P-in-c Maidstone St Faith *Cant* 78-83; P-in-c Maidstone St Paul 78-83; Ind Chapl *St Alb* 83-89; rtd 89; Lic to Offic *B & W* from 89. *4 Ashley Road, Taunton, Somerset TA1 5BP* Tel (01823) 289367

JAMIESON, Mrs Marilyn. b 52. Cranmer Hall Dur IDC80. **d** 91 **p** 94. Par Dn Gateshead St Cuth w St Paul *Dur* 91; Par Dn Bensham 91-93; Par Dn Ryton w Hedgefield 93-94; C 94; Chapl Metro Cen Gateshead from 94. *The Rectory, Barmoor House, Main Road, Ryton, Tyne & Wear NE40 3AJ* Tel 0191-413 4592

JAMIESON, Peter Grant. b 64. Liv Univ BA87. Coll of Resurr Mirfield CPT93. **d** 93 **p** 94. C Charlton Kings St Mary *Glouc* 93-96. *Broncroft Castle, Broncroft, Craven Arms, Shropshire SY7 9HL* Tel (01584) 841203

JAMIESON, Miss Rosalind Heather. b 49. CertEd71. St Jo Coll Dur 79. **dss** 81 **d** 87 **p** 94. Queensbury All SS *Lon* 81-85; Richmond H Trin and Ch Ch *S'wark* 85-87; Par Dn 87-91; Par Dn Burmantofts St Steph and St Agnes *Ripon* 91-94; C from 94. *52 Shakespeare Grange, Leeds LS9 7VA* Tel 0113-248 2606

JAMIESON, Thomas Lindsay. b 53. N Lon Poly BSc74. Cranmer Hall Dur DipTh76. **d** 77 **p** 78. C Gateshead Fell *Dur* 77-80; C Gateshead 80-84; TV 84-90; P-in-c Gateshead St Cuth w St Paul 90-91; TV Bensham 91-93; P-in-c Ryton w Hedgefield 93-95; R from 95; RD Gateshead W from 94. *The Rectory, Barmoor House, Main Road, Ryton, Tyne & Wear NE40 3AJ* Tel 0191-413 4592

JAMIESON, William Douglas. b 38. Oak Hill Th Coll 63. **d** 66 **p** 67. C Shrewsbury St Julian *Lich* 66-68; C Bucknall and Bagnall 68-70; C Otley *Bradf* 70-74; TV Keighley 74-81; V Utley from 81. *St Mark's Vicarage, Greenhead Road, Keighley, W Yorkshire BD20 6ED* Tel (01535) 607003

JAMIESON-HARVEY, Neil Benedict. b 44. Chich Th Coll 89. **d** 91 **p** 92. Bahamas 91-95; C Meir Heath *Lich* 95-96; P-in-c Cross Heath from 96. *St Michael's Presbytery, Linden Grove, Newcastle, Staffs ST5 9LJ* Tel (01782) 617241

JANES, David Edward. b 40. Lon Univ BSc67. Glouc Sch of Min 86. **d** 89 **p** 90. NSM Church Stretton *Heref* from 89. *15 Watling Street South, Church Stretton, Shropshire SY6 7BG* Tel (01694) 722253

JANICKER, Laurence Norman. b 47. SS Mark & Jo Coll Chelsea DipEd69. Ridley Coll Melbourne 77 St Jo Coll Nottm 83. **d** 85 **p** 86. C Beverley Minster *York* 85-89; R Lockington and Lund and Scorborough w Leconfield 89-94; V Cov St Geo *Cov* from 94. *St George's Vicarage, 101 Moseley Avenue, Coventry CV6 1HR* Tel (01203) 591994

JANSMA, Dr Henry Peter. b 57. NE Bible Coll (USA) BA79 Dur Univ PhD91. Westmr Th Sem (USA) MA85 Linc Th Coll CMM91. **d** 91 **p** 92. C Spalding *Linc* 91-96; P-in-c Cleethorpes St Aid 96-97; V from 97. *St Aidan's Vicarage, Hart Street, Cleethorpes, S Humberside DN35 7RQ* Tel (01472) 692989

JANVIER, Philip Harold. b 57. Trin Coll Bris BA87. **d** 87 **p** 88. C Much Woolton *Liv* 87-90; TV Toxteth St Philemon w St Gabr and St Cleopas 90-97; TR Gateacre from 97. *St Stephen's Rectory, Belle Vale Road, Gateacre, Liverpool L25 2PQ* Tel 0151-487 9338

JAONA, Ramahalefitra Hyacinthe Arsène. b 70. MADAGASCAR CAP94. **d** 94 **p** 96. Madagascar 94-97; C Caldicot *Mon* from 97. *143 Elan Way, Caldicot, Newport NP6 4QB* Tel (01291) 430586

JAQUES, Geoffrey Sanderson. b 48. HND70. NE Ord Course 94. **d** 97. NSM Gt Ayton w Easby and Newton in Cleveland *York* from 97. *132 Roseberry Crescent, Great Ayton, Middlesbrough, Cleveland TS9 6EW* Tel (01642) 722979

JAQUET, Peter Michael. b 23. ARIBA51. Wells Th Coll 56. **d** 57 **p** 58. C Hythe *Cant* 57-60; V Sellindge w Monks Horton and Stowting 60-78; C Drypool St Columba w St Andr and St Pet *York* 78-80; TV Drypool 80-86; rtd 86; Perm to Offic *York* from 86. *20 Harthill Avenue, Leconfield, Beverley, N Humberside HU17 7LN* Tel (01964) 550108

JARAM, Peter Ellis. b 45. MIEE77 CEng77 MBIM88 Lon Univ BSc70. Linc Th Coll CMinlStuds94. **d** 94 **p** 95. C Bridlington Priory *York* 94-96; P-in-c Healaugh w Wighill, Bilbrough and Askham Richard from 96; P-in-c Rufforth w Moor Monkton and Hessay from 96. *The Rectory, Back Lane, Bilbrough, York YO2 3PL* Tel (01937) 833527

JARDIN, Kenneth. b 35. TCD 67. **d** 69 **p** 70. Chapl R Sch Arm 69-72; C Arm St Mark *Arm* 69-72; Chapl RAF 72-78; V Barlings *Linc* 78-83; P-in-c Stainton-by-Langworth 78; P-in-c Scothern w Sudbrooke 78; Chapl Monte Carlo *Eur* 83-87; P-in-c Sudbury and Somersal Herbert *Derby* 87-92; Dep Chapl HM Open Pris Foston Hall and Sudbury 87-92; P-in-c Mackworth All SS from 92; P-in-c Mugginton and Kedleston from 92; P-in-c Kirk Langley from 92. *The Vicarage, 4 Church Lane, Kirk Langley, Ashbourne, Derbyshire DE6 4NG* Tel (01332) 824729

JARDINE, Anthony. b 38. Lon Univ DipTh70. Qu Coll Birm 64. **d** 67 **p** 68. C Baldock w Bygrave and Clothall *St Alb* 67-71; C N Stoneham *Win* 71-73; P-in-c Ecchinswell cum Sydmonton 73-79; P-in-c Burghclere w Newtown 78-79; R Burghclere w Newtown and Ecchinswell w Sydmonton 79-87; P-in-c Wonston 87; R Wonston and Stoke Charity w Hunton from 87. *The Rectory, Wonston, Sutton Scotney, Winchester, Hants SO21 3PA* Tel (01962) 760240

JARDINE, David Eric Cranswick. b 30. CCC Ox BA53 DipTh54 MA57. Wycliffe Hall Ox 53. **d** 55 **p** 56. C Wavertree St Mary *Liv* 55-58; C Liv All So Springwood 58-62; C Horley *S'wark* 62-65; V Mitcham Ch Ch 65-72; V Iford *Win* 72-89; R Smannell w Enham Alamein 89-96; rtd 96. *44 Tapton Hill Road, Crosspool, Sheffield S10 5QA* Tel 0114-266 5064

JARDINE, David John (Brother David). b 42. QUB BA65. CITC 67. **d** 67 **p** 68. C Ballymacarrett St Patr *D & D* 67-70; Asst Chapl QUB 70-73; SSF from 73; Asst Chapl HM Pris Belf 75-79; Chapl 79-85; USA 85-88; Sen Asst Warden Ch of Ireland Min of Healing 88-92. *St Francis House, 75 Deerpark Road, Belfast BT14 7PW* Tel (01232) 351480

JARDINE, Norman. b 47. QUB BSc72. Trin Coll Bris 74. **d** 76 **p** 77. C Magheralin *D & D* 76-78; C Dundonald 78-80; Bp's C Ballybeen 80-88; I Willowfield from 88. *The Rectory, 149 My Lady's Road, Belfast BT6 8FE* Tel (01232) 457654

JARDINE, Thomas Parker. b 44. Oak Hill Th Coll BA87. **d** 87 **p** 88. C Crowborough *Chich* 87-91; R Dersingham w Anmer and Shernborne *Nor* from 91. *The Vicarage, Dersingham, King's Lynn, Norfolk PE31 6JA* Tel (01485) 540214

JARMAN, Christopher. b 38. QUB BA63. Wells Th Coll 69. **d** 71 **p** 72. C Leckhampton SS Phil and Jas *Glouc* 71-73; Chapl RN 73-94; R Stirling *Edin* from 94; Hon Chapl RAF from 97. *29 Parkdyke, Stirling FK7 9LS* Tel (01786) 471755

JARMAN, John Geoffrey. b 31. IEng. S'wark Ord Course 75. **d** 78 **p** 79. NSM Chigwell *Chelmsf* 78-81; NSM Leytonstone St Marg w St Columba 81-87; C Walthamstow St Sav 87-89; V Gt Bentley 89-92; P-in-c Frating w Thorrington 89-92; C Wanstead St Mary 92-93; C Wanstead St Mary w Ch Ch 93-95; rtd 95; Perm to Offic *Chelmsf* from 95. *20 Stevens Way, Chigwell, Essex IG7 6HR* Tel 0181-500 2161

JARMAN, Robert Joseph (Bob). b 59. Van Mildert Coll Dur BA90 Univ of Wales (Cardiff) DPS91. **d** 92 **p** 93. C Llanishen and Lisvane *Llan* 92-93; C Whitchurch 93-94. *47 Penydre, Rhiwbina, Cardiff CF4 6EJ*

JARMY, David Michael. b 49. Cam Univ PGCE90. Chich Th Coll 76. **d** 79 **p** 80. C St Leonards Ch Ch *Chich* 79-80; C St Leonards Ch Ch and St Mary 81-82; C St Leonards SS Pet and Paul 82-85; V Sidley 85-89; Perm to Offic *Pet* 89-90; Lt Gidding Community 89-90; NSM Oundle *Pet* from 90. *27 Lower Benefield, Oundle, Peterborough PE8 5AE* Tel (01832) 275287

JARRATT, Canon Robert Michael. b 39. K Coll Lon BD62 AKC62. NY Th Sem DMin85. **d** 63 **p** 64. C Corby St Columba *Pet* 63-67; Lay Tr Officer *Sheff* 67-71; Ind Chapl *S'wark* 72-80; P-in-c Betchworth 76-80; V Ranmoor *Sheff* from 80; RD Hallam 87-94; Hon Can Sheff Cathl from 95. *The Vicarage, 389A Fulwood Road, Sheffield S10 3GA* Tel 0114-230 1671 or 230 1199

JARRATT, Stephen. b 51. Edin Univ BD76 St Kath Coll Liv CertEd77. **d** 78 **p** 79. C Horsforth *Ripon* 78-81; C Stanningley St Thos 81-84; P-in-c Fishponds St Jo *Bris* 84-85; V 85-92; V Chapel Allerton *Ripon* from 92. *The Vicarage, Wood Lane, Chapel Allerton, Leeds LS7 3QF* Tel 0113-268 3072

✠**JARRETT, The Rt Revd Martyn William.** b 44. Hull Univ MPhil91. K Coll Lon BD67 AKC67. **d** 68 **p** 69 **c** 94. C Bris St Geo *Bris* 68-70; C Swindon New Town 70-74; C Northolt St Mary *Lon* 74-76; V Northolt W End St Jos 76-81; V Hillingdon St Andr 81-83; P-in-c Uxbridge Moor 82-83; V Uxbridge St Andr w St Jo 83-85; Lic to Offic 85-91; Selection Sec ACCM 85-88; Sen Selection Sec 89-91; V Chesterfield St Mary and All SS *Derby* 91-94; Hon Can Blackb Cathl *Blackb* from 93; Suff Bp Burnley from 94. *Dean House, 449 Padiham Road, Burnley, Lancs BB12 6TD* Tel (01282) 423564 Fax 835496

JARRETT, Rene Isaac Taiwo. b 49. TCert79 Lon Inst of Educn BEd94. Sierra Leone Th Hall CPS83. **d** 83 **p** 85. Sierra Leone 83-89; Hon C St Pancras w St Jas and Ch Ch *Lon* from 89. *2 Woburn Mansions, Torrington Place, London WC1E 7HL* Tel 0171-580 5165

JARROW, Suffragan Bishop of. *See* SMITHSON, The Rt Revd Alan

JARVIS, David Thomas. b 15. St D Coll Lamp BA36. **d** 38 **p** 39. C Sheringham *Nor* 38-39; C Reepham and Hackford w Whitwell and Kerdiston 39-41; C Paddington St Steph *Lon* 41-42; C St Marylebone w H Trin 42-45; R Gt and Lt Bealings *St E* 45-53; V Hampstead Ch Ch *Lon* 53-69; Jerusalem 69-71; V Turnham Green Ch Ch *Lon* 72-85; rtd 85; Perm to Offic *Heref* from 85. *28 Penn Grove Road, Hereford HR1 2BH* Tel (01432) 270196

JARVIS, Canon Eric Thomas Noel. b 24. Qu Coll Cam BA52 MA54. Ridley Hall Cam 52. **d** 54 **p** 55. C Stratford St Jo *Chelmsf* 54-57; V Ansley *Cov* 57-64; V Woodbridge St Jo *St E* 64-68; V Roundhay St Edm *Ripon* 68-86; RD Allerton 79-84; Hon Can Ripon Cathl 81-86; R St Olave Hart Street w All Hallows Staining etc *Lon* 86-90; V St Marg Pattens 86-90; rtd 90; Perm to Offic *Ely* from 90. *38 Doggett Road, Cherry Hinton, Cambridge CB1 4LF* Tel (01223) 213387

JARVIS, Graham Michael. b 60. Golds Coll Lon BMus81 PGCE83. Trin Coll Bris BA91. **d** 91 **p** 92. C St Keverne *Truro* 91-94; Sweden from 94. *Address temp unknown*

JARVIS, Ian Frederick Rodger. b 38. Bris Univ BA60. Tyndale Hall Bris 61. **d** 63 **p** 64. C Penge Ch Ch w H Trin *Roch* 63-67; C Bilston St Leon *Lich* 67-71; V Lozells St Silas *Birm* 71-76; V Chaddesden St Mary *Derby* 76-95; V Newhall from 95. *The Vicarage, Church Street, Newhall, Swadlincote, Derbyshire DE11 0HY* Tel (01283) 214685

JARVIS, Jeffrey Wallace. b 45. Sarum & Wells Th Coll 73. **d** 75 **p** 76. C Cherry Hinton St Andr *Ely* 76-77; C Nottingham St Mary *S'well* 77-78; Australia from 78. *25 Corfield Street, Point Vernon, Hervey Bay, Queensland, Australia 4655* Tel Bundaberg (71) 24 5411

JARVIS, Miss Mary. b 35. Leeds Univ BA57 Lon Univ CertEd59. Cranmer Hall Dur 78. **dss** 80 **d** 87 **p** 94. Low Harrogate St Mary *Ripon* 80-84; Wortley de Leeds 84-87; C 87-88; C Upper Armley 88-94; C Holbeck 94-95; rtd 95. *71 Burnsall Croft, Leeds LS12 3LH* Tel 0113-279 7832

JASPER, Dr David. b 51. Jes Coll Cam BA72 MA76 Keble Coll Ox BD80 Dur Univ PhD83. St Steph Ho Ox BA75 MA79. **d** 76 **p** 77. C Buckingham *Ox* 76-79; C Dur St Oswald *Dur* 80; Chapl Hatf Coll Dur 81-88; Dir Cen Study of Lit and Th Dur 88-91; Prin St Chad's Coll Dur 88-91; Reader and Dir Cen Study of Lit and Th Glas Univ from 91; Vice-Dean of Div from 95; Lic to Offic *Glas* from 91. *Netherwood, 124 Old Manse Road, Wishaw, Lanarkshire ML2 0EP* Tel (01698) 373286 Fax as telephone

JASPER, David Julian McLean. b 44. Dur Univ BA66 Nottm Univ DipTh68. Linc Th Coll 66. **d** 68 **p** 69. C Redruth *Truro* 68-72; R 72-74; TV 74-75; V St Just in Penwith 75-86; P-in-c Sancreed 82-86; Hon C Reading St Matt *Ox* from 96. *St Matthew's Vicarage, 205 Southcote Lane, Reading RG30 3AX* Tel 0118-957 3755

JASPER, James Roland. b 32. CA Tr Coll 56 NE Ord Course 82. **d** 84 **p** 84. C Newburn *Newc* 84-86; V Ansley *Cov* 86-97; rtd 97. *69 Desford Road, Newbold Verdon, Leics LE9 9LG* Tel (01203) 396403

JASPER, Jonathan Ernest Farley. b 50. AKC72 DPMSA85. St Aug Coll Cant 73. **d** 73 **p** 74. C Cheshunt *St Alb* 73-75; C Bedford St Paul 75-77; C Bedford St Pet w St Cuth 75-77; Chapl Southn Univ *Win* 77-80; Chapl Lon Univ Medical Students *Lon* 80-86; PV Chich Cathl *Chich* 86-89; P-in-c Earls Colne and White Colne *Chelmsf* 89-94; P-in-c Colne Engaine 89-94; R Earls Colne w White Colne and Colne Engaine from 95. *St Andrew's Rectory, 5 Shut Lane, Earls Colne, Colchester CO6 2RE* Tel (01787) 222262

JAUNDRILL, John Warwick. b 47. MInstM81. Qu Coll Birm 86. **d** 88 **p** 89. C Bistre *St As* 88-91; P-in-c Towyn and St George 91-92; V from 92. *The Vicarage, 11 Chester Avenue, Kinmel Bay, Rhyl LL18 5LA* Tel (01745) 350119

JAY, Colin. b 62. Keble Coll Ox BA85 St Jo Coll Dur BA89. Cranmer Hall Dur 87. **d** 90 **p** 91. C Bishopwearmouth St Gabr *Dur* 90-94; C Newton Aycliffe 94; TV 94-96; TV Gt Aycliffe from 96. *20 Haslewood Road, Newton Aycliffe, Co Durham DL5 4XF* Tel (01325) 320112

JAY, Edmund Arthur. b 41. St Chad's Coll Dur BA63. **d** 65 **p** 66. C Bishopwearmouth Gd Shep *Dur* 65-69; C Southwick St Columba 69-70; Hon C Westbury-on-Trym H Trin *Bris* 72-73; P-in-c S Shields St Fran *Dur* 73-76; C S Shields St Hilda w St Thos 76-79; Chapl S Shields Gen Hosp 79-85; rtd 88. *9 Broadmeadows, East Herrington, Sunderland SR3 3RF* Tel 0191-522 6938

JAY, Ms Nicola Mary. b 37. SRN58 ONC61. NE Ord Course 88. **d** 91 **p** 94. Par Dn Whitburn *Dur* 91-94; C 94-95; P-in-c Sacriston and Kimblesworth from 95. *The Vicarage, 1A Church Parade, Sacriston, Durham DH7 6AD* Tel 0191-371 1853

JAY, Richard Hylton Michael. b 31. Bris Univ BEd75. Sarum & Wells Th Coll 77. **d** 79 **p** 80. NSM Bath St Barn w Englishcombe *B & W* 79-81; NSM Saltford w Corston and Newton St Loe 81-88; R Hatch Beauchamp w Beercrocombe, Curry Mallet etc 89-97; rtd 97. *Stableside, 5 Princess Road, Taunton, Somerset TA1 4SY*

JAYNE, Martin Philip. b 49. MRTPI73 Man Univ BA71 Preston Poly DMS80. Carl Dioc Tr Course 87. **d** 90 **p** 91. NSM Natland *Carl* from 90. *12 Longmeadow Lane, Natland, Kendal, Cumbria LA9 7QZ* Tel (015395) 60942

JEANES, Gordon Paul. b 55. Ox Univ BA79 MA82 BD90. St Steph Ho Ox 80. **d** 82 **p** 83. C S Wimbledon H Trin and St Pet *S'wark* 82-85; C Surbiton St Andr and St Mark 85-90; Chapl St Chad's Coll Dur 90-93; Sub-Warden St Mich Coll Llan from 94. *Sub-Warden's Flat, St Michael's College, Llandaff, Cardiff CF5 2YJ* Tel (01222) 563379

JEANS, Alan Paul. b 58. MIAAS84 MIBCO84 Southn Univ BTh89. Sarum & Wells Th Coll 86. **d** 89 **p** 90. C Parkstone St Pet w Branksea and St Osmund *Sarum* 89-93; P-in-c Bishop's Cannings, All Cannings etc from 93. *The Vicarage, The Street, Bishop's Cannings, Devizes, Wilts SN10 2LD* Tel (01380) 860650

JEANS, David Bockley. b 48. Mert Coll Ox BA71 MA80 PGCE73. Trin Coll Bris DipHE85. **d** 85 **p** 86. C Clevedon St Andr and Ch Ch *B & W* 85-88; V Wadsley *Sheff* 88-96; Prin CA Wilson Carlile Coll of Evang from 96. *Wilson Carlile College of Evangelism, 50 Cavendish Street, Sheffield S3 7RZ* Tel 0114-278 7020

JEAPES (née PORTER), Mrs Barbara Judith. b 47. Cam Inst of Educn TCert68. Carl Dioc Tr Inst 91. **d** 94 **p** 95. NSM Egremont and Haile *Carl* from 94. *15 Millfields, Beckermet, Cumbria CA21 2YY* Tel (01946) 841489

JEAVONS, Maurice. b 32. Ely Th Coll 60. **d** 62 **p** 63. C Longton St Jo *Lich* 62-68; V Wednesfield St Greg 68-81; V Lower Gornal 81-90; NSM Willenhall St Anne 92-93; C Tunstall from 93. *7 Park Terrace, Stoke-on-Trent ST6 6BP* Tel (01782) 819175

JEE, Colin Scott. b 32. Worc Coll Ox BA55 MA59. Clifton Th Coll 55. **d** 57 **p** 58. C Spitalfields Ch Ch w All SS *Lon* 57-62; C New Malden and Coombe *S'wark* 62-66; R Ludgershall *Ox* 66-78; P-in-c Oakley 73-82; RD Waddesdon 73-78; R Ludgershall w Wotton Underwood and Ashendon from 78. *The Rectory, Ludgershall, Aylesbury, Bucks HP18 9PG* Tel (01844) 238335

JEE, Jonathan Noel. b 63. BNC Ox BA84 MA88. Wycliffe Hall Ox 85. **d** 88 **p** 89. C Brampton St Thos *Derby* 88-92; TV Hinckley H Trin *Leic* from 92. *7 Rosemary Way, Hinckley, Leics LE10 0LN* Tel (01455) 890473

JEFF, Canon Gordon Henry. b 32. St Edm Hall Ox BA56 MA60. Wells Th Coll 59. **d** 61 **p** 62. C Sydenham St Bart *S'wark* 61-64; C Kidbrooke St Jas 64-66; V Clapham St Paul 66-72; V Raynes Park St Sav 73-79; RD Merton 77-79; V Carshalton Beeches 79-86; P-in-c Petersham 86-90; Chapl St Mich Convent 90-96; Hon Can S'wark Cathl 93-96; rtd 96. *9 Barnetts Well, Draycott, Cheddar, Somerset BS27 3TF* Tel (01934) 744943

JEFFERIES, Cecil Arthur. b 11. Glouc Th Course 68. **d** 69 **p** 70. Hon C Rodborough *Glouc* 69-78; Hon C Cainscross w Selsley 78-89; rtd 89. *Address temp unknown*

JEFFERIES, Michael Lewis (Mike). b 45. St Jo Coll Nottm. **d** 87 **p** 88. C Pudsey St Lawr and St Paul *Bradf* 87-93; V Beckenham St Jo *Roch* from 93. *St John's Vicarage, 249 Eden Park Avenue, Beckenham, Kent BR3 3JN* Tel 0181-650 6110

JEFFERIES, Phillip John. b 42. St Chad's Coll Dur BA65 DipTh67 MA91. **d** 67 **p** 68. C Tunstall Ch Ch *Lich* 67-71; C Wolverhampton St Pet 71-74; P-in-c Oakengates 74-80; V 80-82; P-in-c Ketley 78-82; V Horninglow from 82; Bp's Adv on Hosp Chapl from 82; RD Tutbury from 97. *Horninglow Vicarage, Rolleston Road, Burton-on-Trent, Staffs DE13 0JZ* Tel (01283) 568613

JEFFERSON, Charles Dudley. b 55. St Pet Coll Ox BA78 MA81. Ridley Hall Cam 79. **d** 81 **p** 82. C Chadkirk *Ches* 81-84; C Macclesfield St Pet 84-85; C Macclesfield Team Par 85-89; R Elworth and Warmingham from 89. *The Rectory, 38 Roman Way, Sandbach, Cheshire CW11 9EW* Tel (01270) 762415

JEFFERSON, David Charles. b 33. Leeds Univ BA57. Coll of Resurr Mirfield 57. **d** 59 **p** 60. C Kennington Cross St Anselm *S'wark* 59-62; C Richmond St Mary 62-64; Public Preacher from 64; Chapl Wilson's Gr Sch Camberwell 64-93; Chapl Wilson's Sch Wallington from 75; rtd 93. *15 Sandown Drive, Stanley Road, Carshalton, Surrey SM5 4LN* Tel 0181-669 0640

JEFFERY, Arthur Francis. b 11. St D Coll Lamp BA33 St Mich Coll Llan 33. **d** 35 **p** 36. C Penydarren *Llan* 35-39; C Eglwysilan 39-40; C Penarth w Lavernock 40-44; C Llanharan 44-50; C Garw Valley w Blaengarw 50-53; V Buttington *St As* 53-68; V Rhydymwyn 68-78; rtd 78; Perm to Offic *St As* from 78. *36 Llys Alyn, Rhydymwyn, Mold CH7 5HW* Tel (01352) 741435

JEFFERY, Graham. b 35. Qu Coll Cam BA58. Wells Th Coll 58. **d** 60 **p** 61. C Southampton Maybush St Pet *Win* 60-63; Australia 63-66; C E Grinstead St Swithun *Chich* 66-68; C-in-c The Hydneye CD 68-74; V Wick 74-76; C Hove 76-78; P-in-c Newtimber w Pyecombe 78-82; R Poynings w Edburton, Newtimber and Pyecombe 82-92; P-in-c Sullington and Thakeham w Warminghurst 92-95; rtd 96. *Meyrick, Rock Road, Ashington, Pulborough, W Sussex RH20 3AG*

JEFFERY, Jonathan George Piers. b 63. Man Univ LLB84. Ripon Coll Cuddesdon 95. **d** 97. C Lee-on-the-Solent *Portsm* from 97. *85 Seymour Road, Lee-on-the-Solent, Hants BO13 9EQ* Tel (01705) 552108

JEFFERY, Kenneth Charles. b 40. Univ of Wales BA64 Linacre Coll Ox BA67 MA70. St Steph Ho Ox 64. **d** 67 **p** 68. C Swindon New Town *Bris* 67-68; C Summertown *Ox* 68-71; C Brighton St Pet *Chich* 71-77; V Ditchling from 77. *The Vicarage, Ditchling, Hassocks, W Sussex BN6 8TS* Tel (01273) 843165

JEFFERY, Michael Frank. b 48. Linc Th Coll 74. **d** 76 **p** 77. C Caterham Valley *S'wark* 76-79; C Tupsley *Heref* 79-82; P-in-c Stretton Sugwas 82-84; P-in-c Bishopstone 83-84; P-in-c Kenchester and Bridge Sollers 83-84; V Whiteshill *Glouc* 84-92; P-in-c Randwick 92; V Whiteshill and Randwick from 93. *The Vicarage, Farmhill Lane, Stroud, Glos GL5 4DD* Tel (01453) 764757

JEFFERY, Norman. b 42. Bps' Coll Cheshunt. **d** 67 **p** 68. C Putney St Marg *S'wark* 67-71; C Hoddesdon *St Alb* 71-74; P-in-c Roxton w Gt Barford 74-79; V 79-86; V Woburn Sands from 86; RD Ampthill from 96. *The Vicarage, Church Road, Woburn Sands, Milton Keynes MK17 8TR* Tel (01908) 582581

JEFFERY, Peter James. b 41. Leeds Univ BSc63. Oak Hill Th Coll 64. **d** 66 **p** 67. C Streatham Park St Alb *S'wark* 66-70; C Northampton St Giles *Pet* 70-73; C Rushden St Pet 73-76; C Rushden w Newton Bromswold 77-78; V Siddal *Wakef* 78-85; V Sowerby Bridge w Norland from 85. *The Vicarage, Park Road, Sowerby Bridge, W Yorkshire HX6 2PG* Tel (01422) 831253

JEFFERY, Peter Noel. b 37. Pemb Coll Ox BA60 MA64. Linc Th Coll 60. **d** 62 **p** 63. C W Smethwick *Birm* 62-64; P-in-c Bordesley St Andr 64-69; R Turvey *St Alb* from 69; P-in-c Stevington from 79. *The Rectory, Turvey, Bedford MK43 8DB* Tel (01234) 881210

JEFFERY, Richard William Christopher. b 43. Ex Univ BA65. Coll of Resurr Mirfield 66. **d** 68 **p** 69. C Widley w Wymering *Portsm* 68-71; C Salisbury St Mich *Sarum* 71-74; TV Ridgeway 74-80; V Stanford in the Vale w Goosey and Hatford *Ox* 80-89; V Topsham *Ex* from 89. *The Vicarage, Globefields, Topsham, Exeter EX3 0EZ* Tel (01392) 876120

JEFFERY, The Very Revd Robert Martin Colquhoun. b 35. K Coll Lon BD58 AKC58 FRSA91. **d** 59 **p** 60. C Grangetown *Dur* 59-61; C Barnes St Mary *S'wark* 61-63; Asst Sec Miss and Ecum Coun Ch Assembly 64-68; Sec Dept Miss and Unity BCC 68-71; V Headington *Ox* 71-78; RD Cowley 73-78; P-in-c Tong *Lich* 78-83; V 83-87; Dioc Missr 78-80; Adn Salop 80-87; Dean Worc

87-96; Can Res and Sub-Dean Ch Ch *Ox* from 96. *Christ Church, Oxford OX1 1DP* Tel (01865) 276278 or 276155 Fax 276277

JEFFERYES, June Ann. b 37. Dur Univ BA58. WMMTC 87. **d** 90 **p** 94. NSM Caverswall *Lich* 90-92; NSM Caverswall and Weston Coyney w Dilhorne from 92. *8 Vicarage Crescent, Caverswall, Stoke-on-Trent ST11 9EW* Tel (01782) 393309

JEFFERYES, Neil. b 37. St Andr Univ BSc60 Lon Univ BD62. Tyndale Hall Bris 60. **d** 63 **p** 64. C St Helens St Helen *Liv* 63-68; V Barrow St Mark *Carl* 68-77; RD Furness 74-77; P-in-c Tetsworth *Ox* 77-81; P-in-c Adwell w S Weston 77-81; P-in-c Stoke Talmage w Wheatfield 77-81; RD Aston 81-85; R Tetsworth, Adwell w S Weston, Lewknor etc 81-86; V Caverswall *Lich* 86-92; P-in-c Dilhorne 86-92; RD Cheadle from 91; V Caverswall and Weston Coyney w Dilhorne from 92. *8 Vicarage Crescent, Caverswall, Stoke-on-Trent ST11 9EW* Tel (01782) 393309

JEFFORD, Brian Harrison. b 30. S Dios Minl Tr Scheme 79. **d** 81 **p** 82. NSM Eastbourne St Jo *Chich* from 81. *Flat 1, 20 Derwent Road, Eastbourne, E Sussex BN20 7PH* Tel (01323) 730265

JEFFORD, Mrs Margaret June. b 50. Univ of Wales RGN81. St Mich Coll Llan 94. **d** 96 **p** 97. C Risca *Mon* from 96. *The Rectory, Bryn Goleu, Bedwas, Newport NP1 8AU*

JEFFORD, Peter Ernest. b 29. AKC53. **d** 54 **p** 55. C Berkeley *Glouc* 54-57; C Petersfield w Sheet *Portsm* 57-61; R Rollesby w Burgh w Billockby *Nor* 62-71; V Watton 71-81; V Watton w Carbrooke and Ovington 81-82; P-in-c Brampford Speke *Ex* 82-83; P-in-c Cadbury 82-83; P-in-c Thorverton 82-83; P-in-c Upton Pyne 82-83; TR Thorverton, Cadbury, Upton Pyne etc 83-92; rtd 92. *27 Ashlong Road, Marston, Oxford OX3 0NH* Tel (01865) 60593

JEFFORD, Ronald (Ron). b 46. Univ of Wales (Lamp) Univ of Wales (Cardiff) DPS. St Mich Coll Llan DMinlStuds. **d** 91 **p** 92. C Ebbw Vale *Mon* 91-94; TV 94-95; R Bedwas and Rudry from 95. *The Rectory, Bryn Goleu, Bedwas, Newport NP1 8AU* Tel (01222) 885220

JEFFREE, Robin. b 29. AKC54. **d** 55 **p** 56. C N Harrow St Alb *Lon* 55-59; C Hendon St Mary 59-62; V Manea *Ely* 62-67; V Hartford 67-83; P-in-c Denver 83; R 83-94; P-in-c Ryston w Roxham 83; V 83-94; V W Dereham 83-94; rtd 94; Perm to Offic *Nor* from 94. *3 Church Lane, Hindolveston, Dereham, Norfolk NR20 5BT* Tel (01263) 861857

JEFFREYS, David John. b 45. S Dios Minl Tr Scheme 89. **d** 92 **p** 93. NSM Bexhill St Barn *Chich* 92-95; Chapl Hastings and Rother NHS Trust from 95. *Conquest Hospital, The Ridge, St Leonards-on-Sea, E Sussex TN37 7RD* Tel (01424) 843672

JEFFREYS, Timothy John. b 58. Man Univ BSc79. Cranmer Hall Dur 83. **d** 86 **p** 87. C Goodmayes All SS *Chelmsf* 86-88; Perm to Offic *S'wark* from 92; Hon C S Lambeth St Anne and All SS 93-96; C Croydon St Jo from 96. *Church House, Barrow Road, Croydon CR0 4EZ* Tel 0181-688 7006

JEFFRIES, Keith. b 48. St Steph Ho Ox DipMin93. **d** 93 **p** 94. C St Marychurch *Ex* 93-96; TV Wood Green St Mich w Bounds Green St Gabr etc *Lon* from 96. *27 Collings Close, London N22 4RL* Tel 0181-881 9836

JEFFRIES, Canon Peter George Charles. b 28. Qu Coll Birm 54. **d** 56 **p** 57. C Slad *Glouc* 56-59; C Tuffley 59-62; V Clearwell 62-69; R The Ampneys w Driffield and Poulton 69-93; RD Fairford 86-93; Hon Can Glouc Cathl 89-93; rtd 93; Perm to Offic *Heref* from 93. *14 Lambourne Close, Ledbury, Herefordshire HR8 2HW* Tel (01531) 636105

JELBART, Alexander Parismas. b 21. Oak Hill Th Coll DipTh53. **d** 53 **p** 54. C Bucknall and Bagnall *Lich* 53-56; V Walthamstow St Steph *Chelmsf* 56-62; TR Chell *Lich* 62-70; V Madeley *Heref* 70-78; V St Helens St Mark *Liv* 78-86; rtd 86; Perm to Offic *Leic* from 86. *7 Stuart Court, High Street, Kibworth Beauchamp, Leics LE8 0LE* Tel 0116-279 6340

JELF, Miss Pauline Margaret. b 55. Chich Th Coll 88. **d** 90 **p** 94. Par Dn Clayton *Lich* 90-94; C Knutton from 94; C Silverdale and Alsagers Bank 94-95; P-in-c from 95. *St John's Presbytery, High Street, Alsagers Bank, Stoke-on-Trent ST7 8BQ* Tel (01782) 721259

JELLEY, David. b 25. St Deiniol's Hawarden 86. **d** 87 **p** 88. NSM Evington *Leic* 87-93; rtd 93; P-in-c New Galloway *Glas* from 93. *The Rectory, New Galloway, Castle Douglas, Kirkcudbrightshire DG7 3RP* Tel (01644) 4202235

JELLEY, Ian. b 54. NE Ord Course. **d** 91 **p** 92. C Jarrow *Dur* 91-95; P-in-c Leam Lane 95-96; Chapl HM Pris Holme Ho from 96. *HM Prison Holme House, Stockton-on-Tees, Cleveland TS18 2QU* Tel (01642) 673759 Fax 674598

JELLEY, James Dudley (Jim). b 46. Linc Th Coll 78. **d** 80 **p** 81. C Stockwell Green St Andr *S'wark* 80-85; V Camberwell St Phil and St Mark 85-93; Perm to Offic 93-96; V Camberwell St Luke from 96. *St Luke's Vicarage, 123 Farnborough Way, London SE15 6HL* Tel 0171-703 5587

JENKIN, Hon Charles Alexander Graham. b 54. BScEng. Westcott Ho Cam 81. **d** 84 **p** 85. C Binley *Cov* 84-88; TV Canvey Is *Chelmsf* 88-94; TR Melton Mowbray *Leic* from 94. *The Rectory, 67 Dalby Road, Melton Mowbray, Leics LE13 0BQ* Tel (01664) 480923

JENKIN, Christopher Cameron. b 36. BNC Ox BA61 MA64. Clifton Th Coll 61. **d** 63 **p** 64. C Walthamstow St Mary *Chelmsf* 63-68; C Surbiton Hill Ch Ch *S'wark* 68-78; V Newport St Jo *Portsm* 78-88; R Newbarns w Hawcoat *Carl* from 88. *St Paul's Rectory, 353 Abbey Road, Barrow-in-Furness, Cumbria LA13 9JY* Tel (01229) 821546

JENKINS, Alan David. b 60. Bris Poly BA83 Wolv Poly DipTM87 DipM90. ASCAT DipApTh85 Wycliffe Hall Ox 93. **d** 95 **p** 96. C Tunbridge Wells St Jas w St Phil *Roch* from 95. *3 Andrews Close, Tunbridge Wells, Kent TN2 3PA* Tel (01892) 531297

JENKINS, Dr Allan Kenneth. b 40. Lon Univ BD63 AKC63 MTh69 PhD85. St Mich Coll Llan 63. **d** 64 **p** 65. C Llanblethian w Cowbridge *Llan* 64-70; India 70-76; V Llanarth w Clytha, Llansantffraed and Bryngwyn *Mon* 76-78; Dir of Studies Chich Th Coll 78-83; P-in-c Fowlmere *Ely* 83-87; P-in-c Thriplow 83-87; Sen Tutor E Anglian Minl Tr Course 84-87; Sen Chapl Cardiff Colls 87-95; Dioc Dir Post-Ord Tr *Llan* 88-95; P-in-c Sidlesham *Chich* from 95; Tutor Bp Otter Coll Chich from 95. *The Vicarage, Church Farm Lane, Sidlesham, Chichester, W Sussex PO20 7RE* Tel (01243) 641237

JENKINS, Miss Anne Christina. b 47. Birm Univ BA70 Hull Univ CertEd71 St Jo Coll Dur BA77 DipTh78. Cranmer Hall Dur 75. **dss** 78 **d** 87 **p** 94. Coatham *York* 78-81; OHP 81-87; Perm to Offic *York* 81-87; Ghana 87-88; Par Dn Beeston *Ripon* 88-93; Par Dn Leeds Gipton Epiphany 93-94; V Leeds St Marg and All Hallows from 94. *The Vicarage, 24 Regent Terrace, Leeds LS6 1NP* Tel 0113-242 2205

JENKINS, Clifford Thomas. b 38. IEng MIElecIE. Sarum & Wells Th Coll. **d** 77 **p** 78. Chapl Yeovil Coll 77-92; Hon C Yeovil *B & W* 77-87; Perm to Offic 87-92; Chs FE Liason Officer (Dios B & W, Bris & Glouc) 87-92; FE Adv Gen Syn Bd of Educn & Meth Ch from 90; Perm to Offic *B & W* from 93. *Bethany, 10 Grove Avenue, Yeovil, Somerset BA20 2BB* Tel (01935) 75043 or 0171-222 9011 Fax 0171-233 1094

JENKINS, Clive Ronald. b 57. Ripon Coll Cuddesdon 81. **d** 84 **p** 85. C E Grinstead St Swithun *Chich* 84-87; C Horsham 87-88; TV 88-90; Dioc Youth Chapl 90-96; P-in-c Amberley w N Stoke and Parham, Wiggonholt etc 93-96; V Southbourne w W Thorney from 96. *The Vicarage, 271 Main Road, Southbourne, Emsworth, Hants PO10 8JE* Tel (01243) 372436

JENKINS, Cyril. b 27. Univ of Wales (Lamp) BA53. Wells Th Coll 53. **d** 55 **p** 56. C Uttoxeter w Bramshall *Lich* 55-57; C Shrewsbury St Alkmund 57-60; V Essington 60-69; V Gnosall 69-72; Chapl St Alb Sch Chorley 72-79; Lic to Offic *Blackb* from 73; Hd of Relig Studies Runshaw Coll 74-84; Lect Runshaw Tertiary Coll 84-86; rtd 86. *55 Church Walk, Euxton, Chorley, Lancs PR7 6HL* Tel (01257) 263973

✠**JENKINS, The Rt Revd David Edward.** b 25. Qu Coll Ox BA51 MA54 Dur Univ DD87. Linc Th Coll 52. **d** 53 **p** 54 **c** 84. C Birm Cathl *Birm* 53-54; Lect Qu Coll Birm 53-54; Chapl Qu Coll Ox 54-69; Lect Th Ox Univ 55-69; Can Th Leic Cathl *Leic* 66-82; Dir WCC Humanum Studies 69-73; Dir Wm Temple Foundn Man 73-78; Jt Dir 79-94; Prof Th and Relig Studies Leeds Univ 79-84; Bp Dur 84-94; rtd 94; Hon Asst Bp Ripon from 94. *Ashbourne, Cotherstone, Barnard Castle, Co Durham DL12 9PR* Tel (01833) 650804

JENKINS, David Harold. b 61. SS Coll Cam BA84 MA87 Ox Univ BA88 MA94. Ripon Coll Cuddesdon 86. **d** 89 **p** 90. C Chesterton Gd Shep *Ely* 89-91; C Earley St Pet *Ox* 91-94; V Blackpool St Mich *Blackb* from 94. *St Michael's Vicarage, Calvert Place, Blackpool FY3 7RU* Tel (01253) 397755

JENKINS, Canon David Myrddin. b 30. Univ of Wales BEd76. St Mich Coll Llan 59. **d** 61 **p** 62. C Haverfordwest St Mary w St Thos *St D* 61-63; C Pembroke Dock 63-67; Japan 67-69; Miss to Seamen 69-71; V Llansteffan and Llan-y-bri etc *St D* 71-78; R Llantwit Major *Llan* from 78; Can Llan Cathl from 89. *The Rectory, Llantwit Major CF61 1SS* Tel (01446) 792324 Fax 795551

JENKINS, David Noble. b 25. CCC Cam BA47 MA50. Cuddesdon Coll 48. **d** 50 **p** 51. C Northampton St Matt *Pet* 50-54; Chapl Hurstpierpoint Coll Hassocks 54-59; USPG 60-65; Chapl Eastbourne Coll 66-74; V Jarvis Brook *Chich* 75-90; rtd 90; USA 90-92; Perm to Offic *Chich* from 92. *2 Littlebourne Cottages, London Road, Crowborough, E Sussex TN6 1SR* Tel (01892) 661179

JENKINS, David Roland. b 32. Kelham Th Coll 55. **d** 59 **p** 60. C Middlesbrough St Jo the Ev *York* 59-60; C Kingston upon Hull St Alb 60-64; C Roehampton H Trin *S'wark* 64-68; V Dawley St Jerome *Lon* 68-73; R Harlington from 73. *The Rectory, St Peter's Way, Hayes, Middx UB3 5AB* Tel 0181-759 9569

JENKINS, David Thomas. b 43. RIBA70 Lon Univ DipTh79. S'wark Ord Course 76. **d** 79 **p** 80. NSM Merthyr Tydfil and Cyfarthfa *Llan* 79-86; NSM Brecon St David w Llanspyddid and Llanilltyd *S & B* 86-91; P-in-c Llangiwg 91-92; V from 92. *The Vicarage, 10 Uplands, Pontardwe, Swansea SA5 9PA* Tel (01792) 862003

JENKINS, The Ven David Thomas Ivor. b 28. Birm Univ MA63 K Coll Lon BD52 AKC52. **d** 53 **p** 54. C Bilton *Cov* 53-56; V Wolston 56-61; Asst Dir RE *Carl* 61-63; V Carl St Barn 63-72; V Carl St Cuth 72-76; P-in-c Carl St Mary w St Paul 72-76; Hon Can Carl Cathl 76-91; V Carl St Cuth w St Mary 76-91; Dioc Sec 84-95; Can Res Carl Cathl 91-95; Adn Westmorland and Furness from 95. *Woodcroft, Levens, Kendal, Cumbria LA8 8NQ* Tel (01539) 561281

JENKINS, Canon Eric Neil. b 23. Univ of Wales BSc43 MSc47. Wycliffe Hall Ox 60. **d** 62 **p** 63. C Allerton *Liv* 62-65; V Hale 65-73; Bp's Adv on Soc and Scientific Affairs 73-88; V Hightown 73-88; Hon Can Liv Cathl 83-89; rtd 89; Perm to Offic *Liv* from 89. *51 Oulton Road, Liverpool L16 8NP* Tel 0151-722 5515

JENKINS, Ernest Dennis. b 28. S Dios Minl Tr Scheme 80. **d** 83 **p** 84. NSM Lancing St Mich *Chich* 83-86; C E Grinstead St Swithun 86-89; C Portslade St Nic and St Andr 89-94; rtd 94; Perm to Offic *Chich* from 94. *61A Upton Road, Worthing, W Sussex BN13 1BY* Tel (01903) 263911

JENKINS, The Very Revd Frank Graham. b 23. St D Coll Lamp BA47 Jes Coll Ox BA49 MA53. St Mich Coll Llan 49. **d** 50 **p** 51. C Llangeinor *Llan* 50-53; Min Can Llan Cathl 53-60; CF (TA) 56-61; V Abertillery *Mon* 60-64; V Risca 64-75; Can St Woolos Cathl 67-76; V Caerleon 75-76; Dean Mon 76-90; rtd 90. *Rivendell, 209 Christchurch Road, Newport NP9 7QL* Tel (01633) 255278

JENKINS, Frederick Llewellyn. b 14. St D Coll Lamp BA35 St Mich Coll Llan 36. **d** 37 **p** 38. C Gilfach Goch w Llandyfodwg *Llan* 37-40; C Bishop's Castle w Mainstone *Heref* 40-45; CF 45-64; CF (R of O) 64-69; Chapl R Masonic Sch Bushey 64-77; rtd 77; Perm to Offic *Lich* 77-95. *Plas Uchaf, Trefonen, Oswestry, Shropshire SY10 9DT* Tel (01691) 653918

JENKINS, Garry Frederick. b 48. Southn Univ BTh79. Chich Th Coll 75. **d** 79 **p** 80. C Kingsbury St Andr *Lon* 79-84; C Leigh St Clem *Chelmsf* 84-88; P-in-c Brentwood St Geo 88-94; V from 94. *The Vicarage, 28 Robin Hood Road, Brentwood, Essex CM15 9EN* Tel (01277) 213618

JENKINS, Gary John. b 59. York Univ BA80 CertEd81. Oak Hill Th Coll BA89. **d** 89 **p** 90. C Norwood St Luke *S'wark* 89-94; P-in-c St Helier 94-95; V from 95. *St Peter's Vicarage, Bishopsford Road, Morden, Surrey SM4 6BH* Tel 0181-648 6050

JENKINS, Canon George Patrick. b 36. Univ of Wales (Lamp) BA61. Lich Th Coll 61. **d** 63 **p** 64. C Dursley *Glouc* 63-66; C Stroud H Trin 66-69; V Churcham w Bulley 69-81; V Churcham w Bulley and Minsterworth from 81; RD Forest N 79-95; Hon Can Glouc Cathl from 90. *The Vicarage, Church Lane, Churcham, Gloucester GL2 8AF* Tel (01452) 750252

JENKINS, Jeanette. b 42. St Jo Coll Nottm 83. **dss** 84 **d** 86 **p** 94. NSM Kilmarnock *Glas* 84-94; NSM Irvine St Andr LEP 84-94; NSM Ardrossan 84-94; Asst Chapl Crosshouse Hosp 86-94; Chapl Ayrshire Hospice from 90. *4 Gleneagles Avenue, Kilwinning, Ayrshire KA13 6RD* Tel (01294) 553383

JENKINS, John Francis. b 46. Ripon Hall Ox 77 Ripon Coll Cuddesdon 75. **d** 77 **p** 78. C Filton *Bris* 77-79; C Bris St Andr Hartcliffe 79-84; P-in-c Bris H Cross Inns Court 84-85; V 85-95; R Odcombe, Brympton, Lufton and Montacute *B & W* from 95. *The Rectory, Street Lane, Higher Odcombe, Yeovil, Somerset BA22 8UP* Tel (01935) 863034

JENKINS, John Howard David. b 51. Birm Univ BA72. St Steph Ho Ox 72. **d** 74 **p** 75. C Milford Haven *St D* 74-77; PV Llan Cathl *Llan* 77-81; Chapl Lowther Coll St As 81-84; V Choral St As Cathl *St As* 81-84; C Neath w Llantwit *Llan* 84-86; Chapl Colston's Sch Bris 86-91; Chapl Blue Coat Sch Birm from 91. *Blue Coat School, Metchley Lane, Birmingham B17 0HR* Tel 0121-454 1425

JENKINS, John Morgan. b 33. Mon Dioc Tr Scheme 82. **d** 85 **p** 86. NSM Cwmbran *Mon* from 85. *5 Ridgeway Avenue, Newport NP9 5AF* Tel (01633) 259979

JENKINS, John Raymond. b 26. K Coll Lon 52. **d** 53 **p** 54. C Wrexham *St As* 53-56; Hon C 77-82; C Welshpool 56-57; V Mochdre 57-65; V Llandysul *St D* 65-67; V Llanfair Caereinion w Llanllugan *St As* 67-70; V Llanychaearn w Llanddeiniol *St D* 82-91; rtd 91; Chapl Lanzarote *Eur* 95-97. *Address temp unknown*

JENKINS, John Richard. b 68. Dundee Univ LLB90. St Steph Ho Ox BA94 DipMin94. **d** 94 **p** 95. C Brighouse and Clifton *Wakef* 94-97; C Barnsley St Mary from 97. *33 Queens Drive, Barnsley, S Yorkshire S75 2UG* Tel (01226) 284775

JENKINS, Lawrence Clifford. b 45. AKC70 Open Univ BA77. St Aug Coll Cant. **d** 71 **p** 72. C Osmondthorpe St Phil *Ripon* 71-74; C Monkseaton St Mary *Newc* 75-78; V Shiremoor 78-84; V Wheatley Hills *Sheff* 84-95; RD Doncaster 92-95; V Greenhill from 95. *St Peter's Clergy House, Reney Avenue, Sheffield S8 7FN* Tel 0114-237 2311

JENKINS, Paul Morgan. b 44. Sussex Univ BEd68 Fitzw Coll Cam BA73 MA76. Westcott Ho Cam 71. **d** 74 **p** 75. C Forest Gate St Edm *Chelmsf* 74-77; P-in-c Stourpaine, Durweston and Bryanston *Sarum* 77-83; Perm to Offic 83-85; Chapl Bryanston Sch Dorset 77-85; Lic to Offic *Derby* 84-91; Asst Chapl and Housemaster Repton Sch Derby 84-89; Dean of Chpl 89-91; R Singleton *Chich* from 91; V E Dean from 91; V W Dean from 91. *The Rectory, Singleton, Chichester, W Sussex PO18 0EZ* Tel (01243) 811213

JENKINS, The Ven Raymond Gordon Finney. b 98. TCD BA23 MA32 BD36. CITC 28 TCD Div Sch Div Test28. **d** 30 **p** 31. C Dublin St Thos *D & G* 30-33; Hon Clerical V Ch Ch Cathl Dublin from 31; C Dublin St Bart 33-34; Warden Div Hostel Dublin 34-39; Dean of Res TCD 35-40; Lect TCD 39-70; I Dublin Grangegorman 39-76; Chapl St Brendan's Hosp 39-76; Treas St Patr Cathl Dublin 52-62; Chan 62-76; Adn Dublin *D & G* 61-74; rtd 76. *4 Damer Court, Upper Wellington Street, Dublin 7, Irish Republic* Tel Dublin (1) 830 1156 or 830 7145

JENKINS, Preb Richard David. b 33. Magd Coll Cam BA58 MA. Westcott Ho Cam 59. **d** 61 **p** 62. C Staveley *Derby* 61-64; C Billingham St Aid *Dur* 64-68; V Walsall Pleck and Bescot *Lich* 68-73; R Whitchurch from 73; RD Wem and Whitchurch 85-95; P-in-c Tilstock and Whixall 92-95; Preb Lich Cathl from 93. *The Rectory, Church Street, Whitchurch, Shropshire SY13 1LB* Tel (01948) 892342

JENKINS, Richard Morvan. b 44. St Mich Coll Llan DipTh68 DPS69. **d** 69 **p** 70. C Tenby *St D* 69-73; V Llanrhian w Llanhywel and Carnhedryn 73-77; V Llanrhian w Llanhywel and Carnhedryn etc 77-80; R Johnston w Steynton 80-93; V St Ishmael's w Llan-saint and Ferryside from 93. *The Vicarage, Water Street, Ferryside SA17 5RT* Tel (01267) 267288

JENKINS, Canon Robert Francis. b 33. BNC Ox BA57 MA59. Wycliffe Hall Ox 57. **d** 59 **p** 60. C Hall Green Ascension *Birm* 59-63; V Dosthill and Wood End 63-71; V Brandwood 71-85; V Sutton Coldfield St Columba 85-97; Hon Can S Malawi from 87; rtd 97. *4 The Pines, Lichfield, Staffs WS14 9XA* Tel (01543) 252176

JENKINS, Thomas Glennard Owen. b 22. St Jo Coll Ox BA48 MA52. Wells Th Coll 49 Wycliffe Hall Ox 50. **d** 50 **p** 51. Min Can St D Cathl *St D* 50-54; Chapl RN 54-58; Prec and Sacr Worc Cathl *Worc* 58-60; V Hailey w Crawley *Ox* 60-79; V Penbryn and Betws Ifan w Bryngwyn *St D* 79-87; rtd 87. *24 Anwylfan, Aberporth, Cardigan SA43 2EL* Tel (01239) 811402

JENKINS, Thomas William. b 14. Univ of Wales BA40. St Mich Coll Llan 40. **d** 42 **p** 43. C Newport St Mark *Mon* 42-46; C Kidderminster St Mary and All SS, Trimpley etc *Worc* 46-48; V Walsall Pleck and Bescot *Lich* 48-67; V Shrewsbury H Trin w St Julian 67-75; Chapl Manor Hosp and St Jo Hosp 48-67; V Ruyton 75-80; rtd 80; Perm to Offic *Lich* from 80. *4 Larkhill Road, Park Hall, Oswestry, Shropshire SY11 4AW* Tel (01691) 659304

JENKINS, Timothy David. b 52. Pemb Coll Ox BA73 MLitt77 MA82 St Edm Ho Cam BA84. Ridley Hall Cam 82. **d** 85 **p** 86. C Kingswood *Bris* 85-87; Sen Chapl Nottm Univ *S'well* 88-92; Dean Jes Coll Cam from 92. *4 Claremont, Hills Road, Cambridge CB2 1PA* Tel (01223) 363185 or 339339

JENKINS, William David. b 42. Birm Univ BA63. St D Coll Lamp LTh65. **d** 65 **p** 66. C Gorseinon *S & B* 65-67; C Llanelli *St D* 67-72; V Clydach *S & B* 72-82; Chapl Llandudno Gen Hosp 82-97; V Llanrhos *St As* 82-97; RD Llanrwst 84-96; Hon Can St As Cathl 93-97; TR Tenby *St D* from 97. *The Rectory, Church Park, Tenby SA70 7EE* Tel (01834) 842068

JENKINS, William Frederick. b 08. St Jo Coll Dur BA33 MA38. **d** 35 **p** 36. C Blackb Sav *Blackb* 35-38; C Chadderton Ch Ch *Man* 38-40; V Hougham in Dover Ch Ch *Cant* 40-44; V Blackb Sav *Blackb* 44-53; V Hyson Green *S'well* 53-60; V Histon *Ely* 60-75; rtd 75; Lic to Offic *Blackb* from 75. *6 Arden Moor Way, North Hykeham, Lincoln LN6 9PP* Tel (01522) 682396

JENKINSON, Margaret. b 40. MCSP62. Carl Dioc Tr Inst 89. **d** 92 **p** 94. NSM Preesall *Blackb* from 92. *10 Spruce Cottages, The Conifers, Hambleton, Poulton-le-Fylde, Lancs FY6 9EP* Tel (01253) 701788

JENKYNS, Preb Henry Derrik George. b 30. Sarum Th Coll 57. **d** 60 **p** 61. C Kettering SS Pet and Paul *Pet* 60-64; V Shrewsbury St Geo *Lich* 64-71; V Wednesbury St Paul Wood Green 71-76; V Stokesay *Heref* 76-86; P-in-c Acton Scott 76-86; RD Condover 80-86; Preb Heref Cathl 83-96; R Kington w Huntington, Old Radnor, Kinnerton etc 86-96; rtd 96. *Llantroft, Newcastle, Craven Arms, Shropshire SY7 8PD* Tel (01588) 640314

JENKYNS, John Thomas William Basil. b 30. Univ of Wales (Lamp) BA54 St Cath Coll Ox BA57 MA62. Wycliffe Hall Ox 54. **d** 57 **p** 58. C Neasden cum Kingsbury St Cath *Lon* 57-60; C S Lyncombe *B & W* 60-64; V Gt Harwood St Bart *Blackb* 64-66; R Colne St Bart 66-69; V Chard St Mary *B & W* 69-87; Preb Wells Cathl 87; V Swaffham *Nor* 87-89; V Overbury w Teddington, Alstone etc *Worc* 89-95; rtd 95. *Isfryn, Caerbont, Abercrave, Swansea SA9 1SW* Tel (01639) 730108

JENKYNS, Thomas John Blackwell. b 31. St D Coll Lamp BA52. **d** 54 **p** 55. C Llanelli St Paul *St D* 54-58; C New Windsor St Jo *Ox* 58-64; Chapl RAF 64-85; P-in-c Herriard w Winslade and Long Sutton etc *Win* 85-86; V from 86. *The Vicarage, Upton Grey, Basingstoke, Hants RG25 2RB* Tel (01256) 862469

JENNER, Miss Brenda Ann. b 54. Culham Coll Ox BEd80. St Jo Coll Nottm DPS88. **d** 88. Par Dn Leigh St Mary *Man* 88-92; Par Dn Leic Ch Sav *Leic* 92-94; rtd 94. *18 Chatsworth Avenue, Wigston, Leicester LE18 4LF*

JENNER, Michael Albert. b 37. Oak Hill Th Coll 75. **d** 77 **p** 78. C Mile Cross *Nor* 77-80; P-in-c Easton *Ely* 80-86; P-in-c Ellington 80-86; P-in-c Grafham 80-86; P-in-c Spaldwick w Barham and Woolley 80-86. *Hope Cottage, 12 Main Street, Greetham, Leics LE15 7NL* Tel (01572) 813415

JENNER, Dr Peter John. b 56. Chu Coll Cam BA77 PhD80 MA81. St Jo Coll Nottm 82. **d** 85 **p** 86. C Upperby St Jo *Carl* 85-88; Chapl Reading Univ *Ox* 88-96; P-in-c Mellor *Derby* from 96. *The Vicarage, Church Road, Mellor, Stockport, Cheshire SK6 5LX* Tel 0161-427 1203

JENNETT, Maurice Arthur. b 34. St Jo Coll Dur BA60. Cranmer Hall Dur 60. **d** 62 **p** 63. C Marple All SS *Ches* 62-67; V Withnell *Blackb* 67-75; V Stranton *Dur* 75-91; BCMS 91-93; Crosslinks from 93; Zimbabwe from 91. *St Mary Magdalene's Mission, Post Bag 2005, Nyanga, Zimbabwe*

JENNINGS, Miss Anne. b 41. CertEd63 STh Cam Univ CertRK67. Gilmore Ho 65. **dss** 71 **d** 87 **p** 94. Barton w Peel Green *Man* 71-76; Wythenshawe Wm Temple Ch 76-79; Rochdale 79-83; Chapl Rochdale Colls of FE 79-83; Hillock *Man* 83-87; D-in-c 87-88; Chapl Wakef Cathl *Wakef* 88-96; P-in-c Whitwell *Derby* from 96. *The Rectory, Whitwell, Worksop, Notts S80 4RE* Tel (01909) 720220

JENNINGS, The Ven David Willfred Michael. b 44. AKC66. **d** 67 **p** 68. C Walton St Mary *Liv* 67-69; C Christchurch *Win* 69-73; V Hythe 73-80; V Romford St Edw *Chelmsf* 80-92; RD Havering 85-92; Hon Can Chelmsf Cathl 87-92; Adn Southend from 92. *136 Broomfield Road, Chelmsford CM1 1RN* Tel (01245) 258257 Fax 250845

JENNINGS, Frederick David. b 48. K Coll Lon BD73 AKC73. St Aug Coll Cant 73. **d** 74 **p** 75. C Halesowen *Worc* 74-77; Perm to Offic *Birm* 78-80; Perm to Offic *Leic* 78-80 and 85-87; P-in-c Snibston 80-85; Community Relns Officer 81-84; P-in-c Burbage w Aston Flamville 87-91; R from 91. *The Rectory, New Road, Burbage, Hinkley, Leics LE10 2AW* Tel (01455) 230512

JENNINGS, George. b 20. Lon Univ BD64. Lambeth STh89 Oak Hill Th Coll 46. **d** 51 **p** 52. C Laisterdyke *Bradf* 51-53; C Morden *S'wark* 53-56; V Houghton *Carl* 56-66; V Haydock St Mark *Liv* 66-77; V Newburgh 77-89; rtd 89; Perm to Offic *Liv* from 89; Perm to Offic *Heref* from 90. *97 Watling Street South, Church Stretton, Shropshire SY6 7BH* Tel (01694) 722145

JENNINGS, Harold Andrew. b 15. ATCL35 LTCL36 FTCL37 MRST39 LRAM39. St Deiniol's Hawarden 63. **d** 63 **p** 64. C Swansea St Gabr *S & B* 63-67; R Aberedw w Llandeilo Graban etc 67-79; V Knighton and Norton 79-85; Hon C Llanbister and Llanbadarn Fynydd w Llananno 85-87; rtd 87. *Finsbury, Beaufort Road, Llandrindod Wells LD1 5EL* Tel (01597) 824892

JENNINGS, Ian. N Ord Course. **d** 97. NSM Hackenthorpe *Sheff* from 97. *162 Birley Spa Lane, Hackenthorpe, Sheffield S12 4BQ*

JENNINGS, Janet. b 38. SCM71 SRN74. Oak Hill Th Coll BA87. **d** 88 **p** 97. Par Dn Stevenage St Pet Broadwater *St Alb* 88-90; Perm to Offic *St As* from 92. *Pound House, Forden, Welshpool SY21 8NU* Tel (01938) 580400

JENNINGS, Jonathan Peter. b 61. Lon Univ BD. Westcott Ho Cam. **d** 86 **p** 87. C Peterlee *Dur* 86-89; C Darlington St Cuth 89-92; Dioc Communications Officer *Man* 92-95; Broadcasting Officer Gen Syn from 95; Perm to Offic *S'wark* from 95. *19 Hanford Close, London SW18 5AU, or Church House, Great Smith Street, London SW1P 3NZ* Tel 0181-871 1178 or 0171-222 9011 Fax 0171-233 2660

JENNINGS, The Very Revd Kenneth Neal. b 30. CCC Cam BA54 MA58. Cuddesdon Coll 54. **d** 56 **p** 57. C Ramsgate H Trin *Cant* 56-59; India 59-66; Vice-Prin Cuddesdon Coll 67-73; V Hitchin St Mary *St Alb* 73-76; TR Hitchin 77-83; Dean Glouc 83-96; rtd 96. *The School House, Keasden, Clapham, Lancaster LA2 8EY* Tel (01524) 251455

JENNINGS, Mervyn. b 39. Sarum & Wells Th Coll 83. **d** 85 **p** 86. C Knowle *Bris* 85-89; P-in-c Cressing *Chelmsf* 89-93; Rural Youth Development Officer from 89; V Barkingside St Fran from 93. *St Francis's Vicarage, 144 Fencepiece Road, Ilford, Essex IG6 2LA* Tel 0181-500 2970

JENNINGS, Paul Warwick. b 55. Birm Univ BSc77. Coll of Resurr Mirfield 77. **d** 80 **p** 81. C Dudley St Jas *Worc* 80-83; TV Halesowen 83-87; Chapl St Marg Hosp Birm 88-89. *220 Birmingham Road, Walsall WS1 2NY* Tel (01922) 720656

JENNINGS, Peter James. b 28. Univ of Wales (Lamp) BA56. St D Coll Lamp LTh57. **d** 57 **p** 58. C Dudley St Jo *Worc* 57-60; C Dudley St Thos 61-64; Chapl HM Borstal Portland 64-66; Chapl HM Pris Wakef 66-70; Chapl HM Pris Liv 70-76; RD Walton *Liv* 75-76; Chapl HM Pris Styal 76-77 and 88-92; N Regional Chapl 76-82; Asst Chapl Gen (N) 82-88; Perm to Offic *Man* from 77; Perm to Offic *Ches* from 79; rtd 93. *6 St Anns Road South, Cheadle, Cheshire SK8 3DZ* Tel 0161-437 8828

JENNINGS, Robert Henry. b 46. St Jo Coll Dur BA69 MA79. Qu Coll Birm DipTh71. **d** 72 **p** 73. C Dursley *Glouc* 72-74; C Coleford w Staunton 75-78; TV Bottesford w Ashby *Linc* 78-83; TV Witney *Ox* 83-89; V Lane End w Cadmore End from 89. *The Vicarage, 7 Lammas Way, Lane End, High Wycombe, Bucks HP14 3EX* Tel (01494) 881913

JENNINGS, Thomas Robert. b 24. TCD BA47 MA51. **d** 48 **p** 49. C Drumragh *D & R* 48-51; CF 51-67; I Killeshandra *K, E & A* 67-70; I Newcastle w Newtownmountkennedy and Calary *D & G* 70-92; Can Ch Ch Cathl Dublin from 88; rtd 92. *Cedarwood House, Woodstock Road, Kilcoole, Greystones, Co Wicklow, Irish Republic* Tel Dublin (1) 287 5807

JENNINGS, Walter James. b 37. Birm Univ BMus60 MA90. Qu Coll Birm 77. **d** 80 **p** 81. Hon C Hampton in Arden *Birm* 80-84; Chapl St Alb Aided Sch Highgate Birm 84-86; C Wotton-under-Edge w Ozleworth and N Nibley *Glouc* 86-89; V Cheltenham All SS from 89. *All Saints Vicarage, 66 All Saints Road, Cheltenham, Glos GL52 2HA* Tel (01242) 523341

JENNISON, Ronald Bernard (Ron). b 27. Chich Th Coll 57. **d** 59 **p** 60. C Thornaby on Tees St Paul *York* 59-62; V N Hull St Mich 62-69; V Bridlington Quay H Trin 69-77; V Sewerby w Marton 69-77; V Bridlington H Trin and Sewerby w Marton 77-79; Chapl Marseille w St Raphael Aix-en-Provence etc *Eur* 79-82; Chapl Nice w Vence 82-84; R Finmere w Mixbury, Cottisford, Hardwick etc *Ox* 84-92; RD Bicester and Islip 85-92; rtd 92. *12 St Mary's Court, Church Lane, Tingewick, Buckingham MK18 4AT* Tel (01280) 848815

JENNO, Charles Henry. b 25. Wells Th Coll 65. **d** 66 **p** 67. C Shirehampton *Bris* 66-69; C Fishponds St Mary 69-73; V Thornes St Jas w Ch Ch *Wakef* 73-78; V Carleton 78-82; V E Hardwick 78-82; rtd 82; Perm to Offic *Wakef* from 82. *32 Tower Avenue, Upton, Pontefract, W Yorkshire WF9 1EE* Tel (01977) 640925

JENSON, Philip Peter. b 56. Ex Coll Ox BA78 MA82 Down Coll Cam BA80 MA86 PhD88. Ridley Hall Cam 80. **d** 87 **p** 88. C Gt Warley Ch Ch *Chelmsf* 87-89; Lect Trin Coll Bris from 89. *77 Reedley Road, Bristol BS9 3TB, or Trinity College, Stoke Hill, Bristol BS9 1JP* Tel 0117-968 2880 or 968 2803

JEPHSON, Douglas Ronald Shipstone. b 17. St Jo Coll Dur BA38 MA43. **d** 40 **p** 41. C Wortley de Leeds *Ripon* 40-43; C Armley St Bart 43-45; C Woodhouse St Mark 45-47; V Riddings *Derby* 47-54; V Elmton 54-70; R Tysoe w Compton Winyates and Oxhill *Cov* 70-81; R Whatcote 76-81; V Tysoe w Oxhill and Whatcote 81-82; rtd 82; Perm to Offic *York* from 92. *The Old School House, 42 The Village, Thorp Arch, Wetherby, W Yorkshire LS23 7AG* Tel (01937) 845955

JEPPS, Philip Anthony. b 34. BNC Ox BA58 MA68. Wycliffe Hall Ox 58. **d** 60 **p** 73. C Elton All SS *Man* 60; Perm to Offic *Pet* 70-73; R Church w Chapel Brampton 74-80; P-in-c Harlestone 79-80; V Kettering St Andr 80-94; V Conisbrough *Sheff* from 94. *St Peter's Vicarage, 8 Castle Avenue, Conisbrough, Doncaster, S Yorkshire DN12 3BT* Tel (01709) 864695

JERMAN, Cecil Maldwyn. b 13. St D Coll Lamp BA34 St Mich Coll Llan 34. **d** 36 **p** 37. C Harlech and Llanfair juxta Harlech *Ban* 36-37; C Llanfechell w Bodewryd, Rhosbeirio etc 37-38; C Llandegai 38-41; P-in-c Llandegai St Ann, Bethesda w Tregarth 41-44; C Hoylake *Ches* 45-48; V Crewe St Barn 48-55; V New Brighton St Jas 55-74; Lic to Offic *Ban* from 75; rtd 78. *Bryn Haul, Llaneilian, Amlwch LL68 9LR* Tel (01407) 830977

JERMAN, Edward David. b 40. Trin Coll Carmarthen CertEd61. **d** 87 **p** 88. NSM Llandrygarn w Bodwrog and Heneglwys etc *Ban* from 87. *Tryfan, Trefor, Holyhead LL65 3YT* Tel (01407) 720856

JERMY, Jack. b 22. ACP65. Ripon Hall Ox 64. **d** 65 **p** 66. Hd Master SS Simon and Jude Primary Sch Bolton 62-80; C Bolton SS Simon and Jude *Man* 65-74; P-in-c Rivington 74-93; NSM Horwich and Rivington 93-95; Perm to Offic from 95. *8 Mill Lane, Horwich, Bolton BL6 6AT* Tel (01204) 696198

JERSEY, Dean of. *See* SEAFORD, The Very Revd John Nicholas

JERUSALEM, Bishop of. *See* KAFITY, The Rt Revd Samir

JERUSALEM, Dean of. *See* SELLORS, The Very Revd Michael Harry

JERVIS, Christopher. b 53. BEd Cam Univ DipTh. Wycliffe Hall Ox. **d** 82 **p** 83. C Woodford Wells *Chelmsf* 82-85; Chapl Felsted Sch Essex 85-87; Chapl Canford Sch Wimborne from 87. *Merryvale, Canford Magna, Wimborne, Dorset BH21 2AF* Tel (01202) 887722 or 841254

JERVIS, Preb Horace Roland. b 14. St Jo Coll Dur LTh38 BA39. St Aid Birkenhead 35. **d** 39 **p** 40. C Cannock *Lich* 39-43; P-in-c 43-49; V Donnington Wood 49-79; Preb Lich Cathl 77-79; rtd 79; Perm to Offic *Lich* from 79. *88 Crossbush Road, Felpham, Bognor Regis, W Sussex PO22 7LZ* Tel (01630) 654293

JERVIS, William Edward. b 47. ARICS74. Linc Th Coll 74. **d** 77 **p** 78. C W Bromwich All SS *Lich* 77-80; C Horsham *Chich* 80-86; R W Tarring from 86. *West Tarring Rectory, Glebe Road, Worthing, W Sussex BN14 7PF* Tel (01903) 235043

JESSETT, David Charles. b 55. K Coll Lon BD77 AKC77 MTh. Westcott Ho Cam 78. **d** 79 **p** 80. C Aveley *Chelmsf* 79-82; C Walthamstow St Pet 82-85; P-in-c Hunningham *Cov* 85-91; P-in-c Wappenbury w Weston under Wetherley 85-91; Progr Dir Exploring Chr Min Scheme 85-91; Dir CME 87-90; Perm to Offic 90-97; P-in-c Barford w Wasperton and Sherbourne from 97. *The Rectory, Barford, Warwick CV35 8ES* Tel (01926) 624238

JESSIMAN, Timothy Edward. b 58. Oak Hill Th Coll DipHE91. **d** 91 **p** 92. C Baldock w Bygrave *St Alb* 91-95; C Bideford *Ex* 95-96; TV Bideford, Northam, Westward Ho!, Appledore etc from 96. *The Vicarage, Mines Road, Bideford, Devon EX39 4BZ* Tel (01237) 477036

JESSON, Alan Francis. b 47. MBIM82 FLA91 Ealing Coll of Educn ALA70 Loughb Univ MLS77 Cam Univ MA87. EAMTC 88. **d** 91 **p** 92. NSM Swavesey *Ely* 91-95; NSM Fen Drayton w Conington and Lolworth etc from 95; Chapl ACF from 92. *25 Market Street, Swavesey, Cambridge CB4 5QG* Tel (01954) 30337

JESSON, George Albert Oswald (Ossie). b 54. NCA73. Trin Coll Bris DipHE92. **d** 92 **p** 93. C Thorpe Acre w Dishley *Leic* from 92. *19 Cothelstone Avenue, Thorpe Acre, Loughborough, Leics LE11 0TS* Tel (01509) 265986

JESSOP, Mrs Gillian Mary. b 48. Hatf Poly BSc71 Nottm Univ MEd85 Homerton Coll Cam PGCE80. EAMTC 91. **d** 94 **p** 95. C Gt Yarmouth *Nor* 94-97; R Gt w Lt Addington and Woodford *Pet* from 97. *The Rectory, Church Street, Woodford, Kettering, Northants NN14 4EX* Tel (01832) 732478

JESSOP, John Edward. b 46. RMCS BScEng71. S Dios Minl Tr Scheme 87 Ridley Coll Melbourne DBS89. **d** 90 **p** 90. Australia from 90. *5 Queen Street, Blackburn, Victoria, Australia 3130* Tel Melbourne (3) 9878 8536

JESSUP, Gordon Ernest. b 36. Lon Univ BA59. Oak Hill Th Coll 57. **d** 61 **p** 62. C Barnehurst *Roch* 61-64; C Rushden St Pet 64-67; SE Sec CMJ 67-72; Youth Sec CMJ 68-78; Tr Officer CMJ 78-83; Hon C Woodside Park St Barn *Lon* 78-83; TV Bramerton w Surlingham *Nor* 83-88; P-in-c Framingham Pigot 88; P-in-c Bergh Apton w Yelverton 88; P-in-c Ashby w Thurton, Claxton and Carleton 88; R Thurton 88-97; rtd 97; Perm to Offic *Nor* from 97. *4 Homestead Close, Lingwood, Norwich NR13 4AT*

JESSUP, William Roy. b 27. Lon Univ BSc48 CertEd. Ridley Hall Cam 59. **d** 61 **p** 62. C Walton *St E* 61-64; R Tuddenham St Mary w Cavenham 64-83; P-in-c Eriswell 75-78; Assoc Min Ipswich All SS 83-85; R Toppesfield and Stambourne *Chelmsf* 85-92; rtd 92; Perm to Offic *Chelmsf* from 92. *41 Ashpole Road, Braintree, Essex CM7 5LW* Tel (01376) 322554

JESTY, Mrs Helen Margaret. b 51. York Univ BA72. Cranmer Hall Dur BA81. **dss** 82 **d** 87. S Lambeth St Steph *S'wark* 82-86; Norbiton 86-93; Par Dn 87-90; Hon Par Dn 91-93. *Fairfield, 1 Downside Road, Winchester, Hants SO22 5LT* Tel (01962) 849190

JEVONS, Alan Neil. b 56. Ex Univ BA77 Selw Coll Cam BA80 MA84. Ridley Hall Cam. **d** 81 **p** 82. C Halesowen *Worc* 81-84; C Heywood St Luke w All So *Man* 84-87; TV Heref St Martin w St Fran (S Wye TM) *Heref* 87-93; P-in-c Much Birch w Lt Birch, Much Dewchurch etc from 93. *The Rectory, Much Birch, Hereford HR2 8HT* Tel (01981) 540558

JEWELL, Alan David John. b 59. St Cath Coll Ox MA86. Wycliffe Hall Ox 83. **d** 86 **p** 87. C Walton H Trin *Ox* 86-91; TV Sutton *Liv* 91-97; TV Halewood from 97. *The Rectory, 3 Rectory Drive, Halewood, Liverpool L26 6LJ* Tel 0151-487 5610 E-mail alanjewell@aol.com

JEWELL, Charles John. b 15. Bps' Coll Cheshunt 46. **d** 49 **p** 50. C Swindon St Aug *Bris* 49-52; CF 52-58; C-in-c Patchway CD *Bris* 58-61; Tristan da Cunha 61 and 71-74; Area Sec (Ireland) USPG 62-69; Area Sec (Dios Ex and Truro) USPG 69-71; S Africa 74-87; rtd 87; Perm to Offic *Ex* from 87. *13 Fairfield Avenue, Plymouth PL2 3QF* Tel (01752) 777169

JEWELL, Mrs Maureen Ann. b 34. Reading Univ CertEd72. Chich Th Coll 90. **d** 91 **p** 95. NSM Parklands St Wilfrid CD *Chich* 91-94; NSM Storrington 94-97; Perm to Offic from 97. *3 Garden Close, Storrington, Pulborough, W Sussex RH20 4PL* Tel (01903) 742780

JEWITT, Martin Paul Noel. b 44. AKC69. St Aug Coll Cant. **d** 70 **p** 71. C Usworth *Dur* 70-74; TV 77-78; Papua New Guinea 74-77; V Balham Hill Ascension *S'wark* 78-93; R N Reddish *Man* from 93. *St Agnes Rectory, 551 Gorton Road, Stockport, Cheshire SK5 6NF* Tel 0161-223 0692

JEYNES, Anthony James. b 44. AKC68. **d** 69 **p** 70. C Ellesmere Port *Ches* 69-73; C Birkenhead St Pet w St Matt 73-75; R Oughtrington 75-80; C Timperley 80-85; C Eastham 85-89; V New Brighton St Jas 89-96; P-in-c New Brighton Em 94-96; R Tarleton *Blackb* from 96. *The Rectory, Blackgate Lane, Tarleton, Preston PR4 6UT* Tel (01772) 812614

JIGNASU, Nallinkumar Hiralal. b 28. Bombay Univ BA48. Bp Tucker Coll Mukono 68. **d** 68 **p** 69. Uganda 68-73; C Leamington Priors St Mary *Cov* 73-75; Nigeria 75-79; P-in-c New Humberstone *Leic* 80-94; rtd 94; Perm to Offic *Leic* from 94. *8 Somerby Road, Thurnby, Leicester LE7 9PR* Tel 0116-241 8541

JINMAN, Cecil Alfred Keith. b 20. Keble Coll Ox BA48 MA51. Wycliffe Hall Ox 48. **d** 50 **p** 51. C Southall H Trin *Lon* 50-52; C St Marylebone St Mary 52-54; R Bruntingthorpe *Leic* 54-56; Min Stourbridge St Mich Norton CD *Worc* 57-59; V Claines St Geo 59-76; rtd 76; Perm to Offic *Worc* from 76. *11 Diglis Avenue, Worcester WR1 2NS* Tel (01905) 351736

JOACHIM, Dr Margaret Jane. b 49. FGS91 St Hugh's Coll Ox BA70 MA74 W Midl Coll of Educn PGCE71 Birm Univ PhD77. S Dios Minl Tr Scheme 91. **d** 94 **p** 95. NSM Ealing St Barn *Lon* 94-97; Perm to Offic from 97. *8 Newburgh Road, London W3 6DQ* Tel 0181-723 4514 E-mail msuksp01.tz5thv@eds.com

JOAN, Sister. *See* DAVIES, Sister Joan Margaret

JOB, Evan Roger Gould. b 36. ARCM55 Magd Coll Ox BA60 MA64. Cuddesdon Coll 60. **d** 62 **p** 63. C Liv Our Lady and St Nic *Liv* 62-65; V New Springs 65-70; Min Can and Prec Man Cathl *Man* 70-74; Prec and Sacr Westmr Abbey 74-79; Can Res, Prec and Sacr Win Cathl *Win* 79-94; Vice-Dean Win 91-94; Perm to Offic from 94. *Kitwood Farmhouse, Kitwood Lane, Ropley, Alresford, Hants SO24 0DB* Tel (01962) 772303

JOBSON, Clifford Hedley. b 31. St Jo Coll Dur BA54 DipTh56 MA81. **d** 56 **p** 57. C Hall Green Ascension *Birm* 56-59; C Ambleside w Rydal *Carl* 59-60; R Arthuret 60-62; CF 62-73; Dep Asst Chapl Gen 73-78; Asst Chapl Gen 78-84; QHC from 80; V Fleet *Guildf* 84-96; rtd 96; Perm to Offic *B & W* from 96. *Vine Cottage, 25 Silver Street, South Petherton, Somerset TA13 5AL* Tel (01460) 241783

JOBSON, Canon Paul. b 39. Wells Th Coll 62. **d** 65 **p** 66. C Woolwich St Mary w H Trin *S'wark* 65-68; Chapl Culham Coll Abingdon 68-72; P-in-c Walworth St Pet *S'wark* 72-75; P-in-c Walworth All SS and St Steph 73-75; TR Walworth 75-89; Hon Can S'wark Cathl 83-89; RD S'wark and Newington 85-88; V Seaham w Seaham Harbour *Dur* from 89; Hon Chapl Miss to Seamen from 89. *The Vicarage, Seaham, Co Durham SR7 7SN* Tel 0191-581 3385

JOHANSEN, Paul Charles. b 33. Miami Univ BEd60. Yale Div Sch 61. **d** 64 **p** 64. USA 64-96; rtd 96; P-in-c Adare w Kilpeacon and Croom *L & K* from 96. *The Rectory, Kilmallock, Co Limerick, Irish Republic* Tel Rathluire (63) 98334 Fax as telephone

JOHN, Andrew Thomas Griffith. b 64. Univ of Wales LLB. St Jo Coll Nottm BA DPS. **d** 89 **p** 90. C Cardigan and Mwnt and Y Ferwig *St D* 89-91; C Aberystwyth 91-92; TV from 92. *The Vicarage, Buarth Road, Aberystwyth SY23 1NB* Tel (01970) 617015

JOHN, Barbara. b 34. Cam Univ DipTh67. Gilmore Ho. **dss** 67 **d** 80 **p** 97. Merthyr Tydfil *Llan* 67-71; Loughton St Jo *Chelmsf* 71-73; Newport St Woolos *Mon* 73-78; Asst Chapl Univ Hosp of Wales Cardiff 78-85; C Radyr *Llan* from 85. *14 Pace Close, Danescourt, Llandaff, Cardiff CF5 2QZ* Tel (01222) 552989

JOHN, Beverley Hayes. b 49. Qu Coll Birm 83. **d** 85 **p** 86. C Oystermouth *S & B* 85-87; C Morriston 87-88; V Cefn Coed and Capel Nantddu w Vaynor etc from 88. *The Vicarage, Somerset Lane, Cefn Coed, Merthyr Tydfil CF48 2PA* Tel (01685) 374253

JOHN, Caroline Victoria. b 64. Cam Univ BA86 MA90. St Jo Coll Nottm DPS90. **d** 90. NSM Cardigan and Mwnt and Y Ferwig *St D* 90-91; NSM Aberystwyth 91-96. *The Vicarage, Buarth Road, Aberystwyth SY23 1NB* Tel (01970) 617015

JOHN, David Llewelyn. b 43. FCCA80. W of England Minl Tr Course 93. **d** 96. Hon C Bath St Sav w Swainswick and Woolley *B & W* from 96. *Musetta Lodge, Leigh Close, Bath BA1 6LB* Tel (01225) 337469

JOHN, Canon David Michael. b 36. Univ of Wales (Lamp) BA57. St Mich Coll Llan 57. **d** 59 **p** 60. C Pontypool *Mon* 59-61; C Roath St Marg *Llan* 61-66; Asst Chapl HM Pris Liv 66-67; Chapl HM Pris Ex 67-68; V Ystrad Rhondda *Llan* 68-76; V Pontyclun w Talygarn 76-84; R Newton Nottage 84-91; Can Llan Cathl 85-91; rtd 91; Perm to Offic *Llan* from 91. *1 Hornbeam Close, St Mellons, Cardiff CF3 0JA* Tel (01222) 797496

JOHN, Canon Elwyn Crebey. b 36. Univ of Wales (Lamp) BA57. St Mich Coll Llan 57. **d** 59 **p** 60. C Llangiwg *S & B* 59-62; C Llandrindod w Cefnllys 62-66; V Beguildy and Heyope 66-79; Youth Chapl 72-79; Chapl Agric and Rural Soc from 77; V Builth and Llanddewi'r Cwm w Llangynog etc 79-95; Can Brecon Cathl 88-95; Can Res Brecon Cathl from 95; Prec 94-95; Treas from 95; V Brecon St Mary and Battle w Llanddew from 95. *The Almonry, Cathedral Close, Brecon LD3 9DP*

JOHN, The Ven Islwyn David. b 33. St D Coll Lamp BA56. **d** 58 **p** 59. C Brynamman *St D* 58-61; C Carmarthen St Dav 61-64; V 83-93; V Penbryn and Blaenporth 64-68; V Llandysul 68-83; Can St D Cathl 88-93; RD Carmarthen 92-93; Adn Carmarthen from 93; V Cynwil Elfed and Newchurch from 93. *The Vicarage, Cynwyl Elfed, Carmarthen SA33 6TU* Tel (01267) 281605

JOHN, Canon James Richard (Dick). b 21. Ch Coll Cam BA47 MA49. Cuddesdon Coll 47. **d** 49 **p** 50. C Sidcup Ch Ch *Roch* 49-52; V Gillingham St Mary 52-66; RD Gillingham 60-66; V Bolton St Jas w St Chrys *Bradf* 66-78; R Guiseley 78-83; RD Otley 80-86; P-in-c Esholt 82-83; TR Guiseley w Esholt 83-87; Hon Can Bradf Cathl 83-87; rtd 87; Perm to Offic *Bradf* from 87. *37 Croft House Drive, Otley, W Yorkshire LS21 2ER* Tel (01943) 461998

JOHN, Dr Jeffrey Philip Hywel. b 53. Hertf Coll Ox BA75 Magd Coll Ox DPhil84. St Steph Ho Ox BA77 MA78 CPTS78. **d** 78 **p** 79. C Penarth w Lavernock *Llan* 78-80; Asst Chapl Magd Coll Ox 80-82; Chapl and Lect BNC Ox 82-84; Fell and Dean of Div Magd Coll Ox 84-91; V Eltham H Trin *S'wark* from 91. *Holy Trinity Vicarage, 59 Southend Crescent, London SE9 2SD* Tel 0181-850 1246 or 316 8150

JOHN, Mark Christopher. b 61. SS Mark & Jo Coll Plymouth BA83. St Steph Ho Ox 84. **d** 87 **p** 88. C Treboeth *S & B* 87-90; V Swansea St Mark and St Jo 90-94; Chapl HM Pris Swansea 91-95; Chapl HM Young Offender Inst Usk and Prescoed from 95. *HM Prison Usk, 45 Maryport Street, Usk NP5 1XP* Tel (01291) 32411 Fax 33800

JOHN, Meurig Hywel. b 46. St D Coll Lamp 67. **d** 71 **p** 72. C Llanelli Ch Ch *St D* 71-74; V Penrhyncoch and Elerch 74-79; V Llanfihangel Aberbythych 79-81; R Cilgerran w Bridell and Llantwyd 81-83; V Gwaun-cae-Gurwen 83-89; V Llanfihangel Genau'r-glyn and Llangorwen 89-95; V Newcastle Emlyn w Llandyfriog etc from 95. *The Vicarage, Newcastle Emlyn SA38 9LL* Tel (01239) 710385

JOHN, Napoleon. b 55. Punjab Univ BA76. Lahetysteologisen Inst Ryttyla Finland DipHE85 Oak Hill Th Coll BA93. **d** 93 **p** 94. C Leyton St Mary w St Edw *Chelmsf* 93-96; C Leyton St Mary w St Edw and St Luke 96-97; P-in-c Becontree St Elisabeth from

97. *The Vicarage, Hewett Road, Dagenham, Essex RM8 2XT* Tel 0181-517 0355

JOHN, Nigel. b 59. Univ of Wales (Cardiff) BA87 Selw Coll Cam MPhil90. Westcott Ho Cam 88. **d** 91 **p** 92. C Carmarthen St Pet *St D* 91-94; Chapl Roehampton Inst *S'wark* 94-96; V Gors-las *St D* from 96. *48 Swansea Road, Llanelli SA15 3YT* Tel (01554) 756270

JOHN, Robert Michael. b 46. Edin Univ BSc67 Man Univ MSc68 PhD70 Otago Univ BD78. St Jo Coll Auckland 76. **d** 78 **p** 79. New Zealand 78-87 and from 88; C Swansea St Jas *S & B* 87-88. *1 Barrymore Road, Mount Albert, Auckland 1003, New Zealand* Tel Auckland (9) 846 4812 or 379 7440

JOHN, Sidney Arthur Charles Bernard. b 13. Jes Coll Ox BA35 MA39. **d** 38 **p** 39. C Newington St Paul *S'wark* 38-40; C Rotherhithe St Barn 40; C Mitcham St Olave 41-44; PV Wells Cathl *B & W* 44-47; C Landore *S & B* 47-49; C Belvedere St Aug *Roch* 49-50; C Eltham H Trin *S'wark* 51; C E Dulwich St Clem 51-55; V Sydenham St Phil 55-58; R Syderstone *Nor* 58-65; V Gt Barlow *Derby* 65-78; rtd 78; Chapl Chesterfield R Hosp 80-87; Perm to Offic *Ox* from 87. *2 Willow Road, Chinnor, Oxon OX9 4RA* Tel (01844) 352321

JOHN, Stephen Michael. b 63. Univ of Wales BA85. Coll of Resurr Mirfield 87. **d** 89 **p** 90. C Coity w Nolton *Llan* 89-91; C Merthyr Dyfan 91-94; V Tredegar St Geo *Mon* from 94. *St George's Vicarage, Church Street, Tredegar NP2 3DU* Tel (01495) 252672

JOHN, William Glyndwr (Glyn). b 21. Roch Th Coll 60. **d** 60 **p** 61. C Streatham St Leon *S'wark* 60-64; V Castleton *Derby* 64-69; V Frizinghall *Bradf* 69-73; V Long Preston 73-80; V Sutton 80-84; rtd 84; Perm to Offic *Bradf* from 84. *110 Princes Drive, Skipton, N Yorkshire BD23 1HW* Tel (01756) 793003

JOHN-CHARLES, Brother. *See* VOCKLER, The Rt Revd John Charles

JOHN-FRANCIS, Brother. *See* FRIENDSHIP, Roger Geoffrey

JOHNES, Philip Sydney. b 45. St Mich Coll Llan DMinlStuds92. **d** 92 **p** 93. C Cardigan and Mwnt and Y Ferwig *St D* 92-95; V Llanegwad w Llanfynydd from 95. *Llanegwad Vicarage, Heol Alltyferin, Nantgaredig, Carmarthen SA32 7NE* Tel (01267) 290142

JOHNS, Adam Aubrey. b 34. TCD BA57 MA76 NUU BA75. CITC 58. **d** 58 **p** 59. C Aghalee *D & D* 58-61; C Derriaghy *Conn* 61-63; I Billy 63-77; I Billy w Derrykeighan from 77. *321 Castlecat Road, Dervock, Ballymoney, Co Antrim BT53 8BP* Tel (01265) 741241

JOHNS, Canon Bernard Thomas. b 36. Birm Univ BSc58. St Mich Coll Llan 61. **d** 63 **p** 64. C Aberavon *Llan* 63-65; C St Andrew's Major and Michaelston-le-Pit 65-70; V Cardiff St Andr and St Teilo 70-76; Asst Dioc Dir of Educn 72-91; V Roath St Marg 76-88; R Wenvoe and St Lythans from 88; Dioc Dir Community Educn from 91; Can Llan Cathl from 96. *The Rectory, 2 Port Road, Wenvoe, Cardiff CF5 6DF* Tel (01222) 593392 Fax as telephone

JOHNS, James Dudley. b 09. Selw Coll Cam BA34 MA38. Ridley Hall Cam 34. **d** 36 **p** 37. C Moulsham St Jo *Chelmsf* 36-39; C Grays Thurrock 39-41; V Forest Gate All SS 41-49; Dioc Insp of Schs 46-53; Res Chapl Butlin's Camp Clacton 47-48; Chapl and Dean Selw Coll Cam 49-53; Staff Sec SCM (Cam Univ) 49-51; Chapl Barnard Castle Sch 53-64; Chapl St Geo Sch Hardenden 64-69; Chapl Harpenden St Jo *St Alb* 64-69; Lic to Offic *Dur* 53-64; Lic to Offic *St Alb* 64-69; Perm to Offic *Chelmsf* 49-69; R Gt w Lt Wymondley *St Alb* 70-80; R Gt and Lt Wymondley w Graveley and Chivesfield 80-81; rtd 81; Perm to Offic *Nor* 82-94; Perm to Offic *Chelmsf* from 95. *25A Beeches Close, Saffron Walden, Essex CB11 4BU* Tel (01799) 527119

JOHNS, Mrs Patricia Holly (Pat). b 33. Girton Coll Cam BA56 MA60 Hughes Hall Cam PGCE57. Ox NSM Course 87. **d** 90 **p** 94. NSM Wantage *Ox* 90-94; NSM Marlborough *Sarum* from 94. *15 Blowhorn Street, Marlborough, Wilts SN8 1BU* Tel (01672) 515897

JOHNS, Canon Ronald Charles (Ron). b 37. TD. Dur Univ BA59. Wells Th Coll 59. **d** 61 **p** 62. C Wigan All SS *Liv* 61-66; TV Kirkby 66-75; Ho Master Ruffwood Sch Kirkby 70-75; TV Maghull 75-79; Dep Hd Master Maghull Old Hall High Sch 75-79; P-in-c Borrowdale *Carl* 79-84; V 84-89; RD Derwent 81-89; Hon Can Carl Cathl 87-89; Can Res Carl Cathl 89-94; R Caldbeck, Castle Sowerby and Sebergham from 94. *The Rectory, Caldbeck, Wigton, Cumbria CA7 8EW* Tel (016974) 78233

JOHNS, Thomas Morton (Tom). b 43. Oak Hill Th Coll 67. **d** 70 **p** 71. C N Meols *Liv* 70-73; C Farnborough *Guildf* 73-76; P-in-c Badshot Lea CD 76-83; Lic to Offic *Pet* 83-90; Chapl HM Youth Cust Cen Wellingborough 83-88; Chapl HM Young Offender Inst Swinfen Hall 88-90; Chapl Tr Officer 88-95; Chapl HM Pris Service Coll 90-95; Lic to Offic *Cov* 90-95; Asst Chapl Gen of Pris (HQ) from 95. *Room 715, Abell House, John Islip Street, London SW1P 4LH* Tel 0171-217 2024

JOHNS, Trevor Charles. b 33. St D Coll Lamp BA58. **d** 58 **p** 59. C Pembroke St Mary and St Mich *St D* 58-61; R Walwyn's Castle w Robeston W 61-67; CF 67-75; V Spittal and Treffgarne *St D* 75-79; C Tring *St Alb* 79-80; TV Tring 80-85; V Knighton and Norton *S & B* 85-86; V Merthyr Cynog and Dyffryn Honddu etc from 86. *The Vicarage, Lower Chapel, Brecon LD3 9RE* Tel (01874) 89238

JOHNS, Canon Vernon. b 12. St D Coll Lamp BA33 St Mich Coll Llan 34. **d** 35 **p** 36. C Llanstadwel *St D* 35-38; C Pembroke Dock 38-40; P-in-c Freystrop and Haroldston E St Issell 40-41; R Cosheston 41-52; CF (EC) 43-46; V Llanwnda w Goodwick and Manorowen *St D* 52-67; RD Fishguard 59-65; RD Dewisland and Fishguard 65-67; R Prendergast 67-69; R Prendergast w Rudbaxton 69-72; Can St D Cathl 70-78; R Tenby w Gumfreston and Penally 72-78; rtd 78. *78 Laws Street, Pembroke Dock SA72 6DQ* Tel (01646) 686149

JOHNS, William Price. b 28. Keble Coll Ox BA51 DipTh52 MA56. St Mich Coll Llan 52. **d** 53 **p** 54. C Whitchurch *Llan* 53-56; C Pontypridd St Cath 56-59; Min Can Brecon Cathl *S & B* 59-62; V Wellington *Heref* 62-78; R Wellington w Pipe-cum-Lyde and Moreton-on-Lugg 78-93; P-in-c Ford 63-69; rtd 93; Perm to Offic *Llan* from 93. *12 Deepdale Close, Cardiff CF2 5LR* Tel (01222) 483762

JOHNSEN, Edward Andrew. b 67. Birm Univ BTh89. Qu Coll Birm 95. **d** 97. C Birm St Luke *Birm* from 97. *63 Princess Road, Edgbaston, Birmingham B5 7PZ* Tel 0121-440 6794

JOHNSON, Andrew Paul. b 56. W Surrey Coll of Art & Design BA79 Kent Coll for Careers CertEd82 TCD BTh96. CITC 93. **d** 96 **p** 97. C Penarth w Lavernock *Llan* from 96. *Church House, 153 Windsor Road, Penarth CF64 1JF* Tel (01222) 701144

JOHNSON, Miss Annie. b 26. Trin Coll Bris 70. **dss** 75 **d** 87 **p** 94. Barnsbury St Andr *Lon* 75-78; Newark Ch Ch *S'well* 79-80; Newark w Hawton, Cotham and Shelton 80-87; Par Dn 87-88; rtd 88; Perm to Offic *S'well* from 88. *1 Carswell Close, Newark, Notts NG24 4HW* Tel (01636) 704299

JOHNSON, Anthony Arthur Derry. b 15. Kelham Th Coll 31. **d** 39 **p** 40. C Pinner *Lon* 39-42; C Willesden St Andr 42-44; C Winchmore Hill H Trin 44-49; V Brookfield St Anne, Highgate Rise 49-60; V Mill Hill St Mich 60-73; R Chalfont St Giles *Ox* 73-80; rtd 80. *Garden Close, Long Street, Sherborne, Dorset DT9 3DD* Tel (01935) 813469

JOHNSON, Anthony Peter. b 45. Lon Univ DipTh71 AKC76 BD76 MTh79. Wells Th Coll 67. **d** 70 **p** 71. C Goldington *St Alb* 70-73; C Hainault *Chelmsf* 73-76; TV Loughton St Mary 76-81; V Scunthorpe All SS *Linc* 81-85; V Alkborough 85-87; Chapl Man Univ *Man* 87-96; TV Man Whitworth 87-96; P-in-c Chorlton-cum-Hardy St Werburgh from 96. *St Werburgh's Rectory, 388 Wilbraham Road, Manchester M21 0UH* Tel 0161-881 1642

JOHNSON, Canon Anthony Trevor. b 27. CCC Ox BA51 MA55. Cuddesdon Coll 51. **d** 53 **p** 54. C Wareham w Arne *Sarum* 53-57; C Melksham 57-60; R Tarrant Gunville, Tarrant Hinton etc 60-67; R Upton Scudamore 67-85; V Warminster St Denys 67-85; RD Heytesbury 71-76; Can and Preb Sarum Cathl 75-92; P-in-c Horningsham 76-85; P-in-c Semley and Sedgehill 85-86; R E Knoyle, Semley and Sedgehill 86-92; rtd 92. *Coombe Warren, Hindon Lane, Tisbury, Salisbury SP3 6QQ* Tel (01747) 870130

JOHNSON, Anthony Warrington. b 40. Golds Coll Lon CertEd60. St Jo Coll Nottm 86. **d** 88 **p** 89. C Lutterworth w Cotesbach *Leic* 88-92; V Countesthorpe w Foston from 92; P-in-c Arnesby w Shearsby and Bruntingthorpe from 94. *The Vicarage, 102 Station Road, Countesthorpe, Leicester LE8 5TB* Tel 0116-278 4442 or 277 8643

JOHNSON, Arthur Victor. b 19. St Aid Birkenhead 62. **d** 64 **p** 65. C Kirkham *Blackb* 64-66; C Padiham 66-69; V Oswaldtwistle All SS 69-73; V Lancaster St Jo w St Anne 73-79; V Out Rawcliffe 79-84; rtd 84; Perm to Offic *Blackb* from 84. *25 Heysham Park, Morecambe, Lancs LA3 2UD* Tel (01524) 852794

JOHNSON, Brian. b 42. DipRS87. S'wark Ord Course 84. **d** 87 **p** 88. NSM Dulwich St Barn *S'wark* 87-92; NSM Herne Hill 92-94; Perm to Offic 94-96; Chapl HM Pris Man from 96. *The Chaplain's Office, HM Prison, Southall Street, Manchester M60 9AH* Tel 0161-834 8626 Fax 834 0443

JOHNSON, Canon Charles Edmund. b 15. Em Coll Cam BA40 MA42. Ridley Hall Cam 40. **d** 42 **p** 43. C Woking Ch Ch *Guildf* 42-44; Hd Master Seaford Coll E Sussex 44-90; Provost from 90; Can and Preb Chich Cathl *Chich* 84-85. *Seaford College, Lavington Park, Petworth, W Sussex GU28 0NB* Tel (01798) 6392

JOHNSON, Christopher Dudley. b 26. Worc Coll Ox BA44 MA51. Cuddesdon Coll 53. **d** 56 **p** 57. C Basingstoke *Win* 56-61; V Bethnal Green St Barn *Lon* 61-67; V Eton w Eton Wick and Boveney *Ox* 67-88; rtd 91. *White Wings, West Bexington, Dorchester, Dorset DT2 9DE*

JOHNSON, Christopher Frederick. b 43. ARICS67. Ripon Hall Ox 71. **d** 74 **p** 75. C Chatham St Steph *Roch* 74-78; V Slade Green 78-85; V Wilmington 85-95; R Chevening from 95. *Chevening Rectory, Homedean Road, Chipstead, Sevenoaks, Kent TN13 2RU* Tel (01732) 453555

JOHNSON, Christopher Paul. b 47. St Jo Coll Nottm BTh74. **d** 74 **p** 75. C Normanton *Wakef* 74-78; P-in-c Dewsbury St Mark 78-82; V Harden and Wilsden *Bradf* 82-88; P-in-c Holbeck *Ripon* 88-97; Asst Chapl United Leeds Teaching Hosps NHS Trust from 97. *The Chaplaincy Department, Leeds General Infirmary, George Street, Leeds LS1 3EX* Tel 0113-292 3527

JOHNSON, Christopher Robert. b 43. Lon Coll of Div 66. **d** 70 **p** 71. C Everton St Geo *Liv* 70-71; C Childwall All SS 71-75; TV Gateacre 75-76; TV Bushbury *Lich* 76-87; R Burslem from 87. *The Rectory, 16 Heyburn Crescent, Burslem, Stoke-on-Trent ST6 4DL* Tel (01782) 88932

JOHNSON, Canon Colin Gawman. b 32. Leeds Univ BA59. Coll of Resurr Mirfield 59. **d** 61 **p** 62. C Barrow St Matt *Carl* 61-67; V 90-96; V Addingham 67-71; V Carl H Trin 71-80; V Wigton 80-90; Hon Can Carl Cathl 85-96; rtd 96; Perm to Offic *Carl* from 97. *Hemp Garth, Ireby, Carlisle CA5 1EA*

JOHNSON, Colin Leslie. b 41. Trin Coll Cam MA65. Cheshunt Coll Cam 62. **d** 93 **p** 94. Publications Dir Chr Educn Movement from 89; NSM Brailsford w Shirley and Osmaston w Edlaston *Derby* from 93. *33 The Plain, Brailsford, Ashbourne, Derbyshire DE6 3BZ* Tel (01335) 60591

JOHNSON, Cyril Francis. b 22. St Cath Coll Cam BA49 MA54. Ely Th Coll 50. **d** 52 **p** 53. C Twickenham All Hallows *Lon* 52-56; C Kingsthorpe *Pet* 56-61; R Harpole 61-87; rtd 87. *16 Blake's Way, Eastbourne, E Sussex BN23 6EW* Tel (01323) 723491

JOHNSON, David Alan. b 43. Lon Univ BSc63 PhD67. Trin Coll Bris 78. **d** 80 **p** 81. C Watford *St Alb* 80-85; V Idle H Trin *Bradf* from 85. *The Vicarage, 470 Leeds Road, Thackley, Bradford, W Yorkshire BD10 9AA* Tel (01274) 613300

JOHNSON, David Bryan Alfred. b 36. Kelham Th Coll 56. **d** 61 **p** 62. C Streatham St Paul *S'wark* 61-63; Malaysia 63-71; V Worc St Mich *Worc* 71-74; Warden Lee Abbey Internat Students' Club Kensington 74-77; V Plumstead St Mark and St Marg *S'wark* 77-86; Chapl W Park Hosp Epsom 86-96; Chapl Laslett's *Worc* from 96; rtd 96. *The Chaplain's House, Laslett's Almshouses, Union Street, Worcester WR1 2AS* Tel (01905) 24743

JOHNSON, David Clark. b 15. Tyndale Hall Bris 61. **d** 62 **p** 63. C Chippenham St Paul *Bris* 62-64; C Chippenham St Paul w Langley Burrell 64-65; V Bishopsworth 65-74; V Stratton St Margaret 75-78; TR Stratton St Margaret w S Marston etc 78-80; rtd 80; Perm to Offic *Bris* from 80. *13 High Kingsdown, Bristol BS2 8EN* Tel 0117-929 8894

JOHNSON, David Francis. b 32. Univ Coll Ox BA55 MA59. Westcott Ho Cam 55. **d** 57 **p** 58. C Earlsdon *Cov* 57-59; C Willenhall 59-61; C Attenborough w Bramcote *S'well* 61-62; V Ravenstone w Weston Underwood *Ox* 62-66; V Crewe Ch Ch *Ches* 66-70; P-in-c Crewe St Pet 67-70; V Thornton w Allerthorpe *York* 70-79; V N Hull St Mich 79-81; V Leyburn w Bellerby *Ripon* 81-88; V Coxwold and Husthwaite *York* from 88. *The Vicarage, Coxwold, York YO6 4AD* Tel (01347) 868301

JOHNSON, David John. b 49. Lanc Univ BA72. Linc Th Coll 78. **d** 81 **p** 82. C Stockport St Thos *Ches* 81-84; OGS from 83; C Stockton Heath *Ches* 84-88; V Tranmere St Paul w St Luke from 88. *St Paul's Vicarage, Old Chester Road, Birkenhead, Merseyside L42 3XD* Tel 0151-645 3547

JOHNSON, David Richard. b 67. Birm Univ BSc88. Ripon Coll Cuddesdon BA92. **d** 94 **p** 95. C Horfield H Trin *Bris* from 94. *31 Rosling Road, Bristol BS7 8SX* Tel 0117-951 9771

JOHNSON, David William. b 40. Lon Univ BD64. Oak Hill Th Coll 60. **d** 65 **p** 66. C Tunbridge Wells St Jas *Roch* 65-68; C Kirby Muxloe *Leic* 68-72; V Burton Joyce w Bulcote *S'well* 72-83; Chapl Northgate Mental Handicap Unit Morpeth 83-87; V Mitford *Newc* 83-87; Asst Chapl R Victoria Infirmary Newc 87-89; Chapl R Hosp Shrewsbury from 89. *Royal Shrewsbury Hospital, Mytton Oak Road, Shrewsbury SY3 8XF* Tel (01743) 261000

JOHNSON, David William. b 53. Selw Coll Cam BA76. Ripon Coll Cuddesdon 76. **d** 78 **p** 79. C Fulham St Etheldreda w St Clem *Lon* 78-82; Communications Sec Gen Syn Bd for Miss and Unity 82-87; PV Westmr Abbey 85-87; R Gilmorton w Peatling Parva and Kimcote etc *Leic* 87-91; R Cogenhoe *Pet* 91-95; R Whiston 93-95; rtd 95. *Seaview Cottage, 115 Hurst Street, Oxford OX4 1HE* Tel (01865) 793393

JOHNSON, Preb Derek John. b 36. St Aid Birkenhead 65. **d** 68 **p** 69. C Eccleshall *Lich* 68-73; C Stafford St Mary 73-75; Chapl New Cross Hosp Wolv 75-96; Preb Lich Cathl *Lich* 83-96; rtd 96; Perm to Offic *St E* from 96. *6 St Paul's Close, Aldeburgh, Suffolk IP15 5BQ* Tel (01728) 452474

JOHNSON, Miss Diana Margaret. b 46. MCSP68 SRP68 GDipP68. Cranmer Hall Dur CTM94. **d** 94 **p** 95. C Birtley *Dur* from 94. *21 Lavers Road, Birtley, Chester le Street, Co Durham DH3 1HH* Tel 0191-492 0884

JOHNSON, Canon Donald Arnold. b 28. Linc Coll Ox BA51 MA59. Cuddesdon Coll 51. **d** 53 **p** 54. C Henfield *Chich* 53-55; C Horsham 55-59; V Oving w Merston 59-68; Bp's Dom Chapl 59-68; V Hellingly 68-78; V Upper Dicker 68-78; R W Stoke from 78; V Funtington and Sennicotts from 78; Can and Preb Chich Cathl from 96. *The Vicarage, Funtington, Chichester, W Sussex PO19 0LH* Tel (01243) 575257

JOHNSON, Mrs Dorothy (Dorrie). Leic Univ BSc89 Ox Univ MTh95 RGN NDN80 FRSH91. Qu Coll Birm 77. **dss** 80 **d** 87 **p** 94. Coventry Caludon *Cov* 80-81; Wolston and Church Lawford 81-86; NSM Stoneleigh w Ashow and Baginton from 87; Bp's Asst Officer for Soc Resp from 87. *The Firs, Stoneleigh Road, Bubbenhall, Coventry CV8 3BS* Tel (01203) 303712 Fax as telephone

JOHNSON, Douglas Leonard. b 45. Trin Coll Bris 70 Lon Bible Coll MA95. **d** 73 **p** 74. C New Malden and Coombe *S'wark* 73-76; P-in-c Upper Tulse Hill St Matthias 76-82; CPAS Staff 82-88; Lect and Tutor CA Coll from 88; Hon C Wimbledon Em Ridgway Prop Chpl *S'wark* from 92. *11 Preston Road, London SW20 0SS* Tel 0181-946 2136

JOHNSON, Edward Anthony (Tony). b 32. Univ of Wales (Swansea) BSc54. St Steph Ho Ox 79. **d** 81 **p** 82. C Wolvercote w Summertown *Ox* 81-84; P-in-c Ramsden 84-87; P-in-c Finstock and Fawler 84-87; P-in-c Wilcote 84-87; V Ramsden, Finstock and Fawler, Leafield etc 87-92; rtd 92; Hon C Kennington *Ox* from 92. *15 Cranbrook Drive, Kennington, Oxford OX1 5RR* Tel (01865) 739751

JOHNSON, Mrs Elizabeth. b 47. St Hilda's Coll Ox MA69. Wycliffe Hall Ox 84. **dss** 86 **d** 87 **p** 94. NSM Ox St Aldate w St Matt *Ox* 86-91; NSM Marston 91-94; NSM Ox St Clem 94-95; NSM Islip w Charlton on Otmoor, Oddington, Noke etc 95-97; C from 97. *St Mary's House, High Street, Charlton on Otmoor, Kidlington, Oxon OX5 2UG* Tel (01865) 331513

JOHNSON, Eric. b 38. Nottm Univ BSc60 Leeds Univ DipFE73 Open Univ BA92 SS Paul & Mary Coll Cheltenham MA94. Qu Coll Birm 74. **d** 77 **p** 78. Sen Lect Cov Tech Coll 66-91; NSM Earlsdon *Cov* 77-81; NSM Wolston and Church Lawford 81-86; NSM Stoneleigh w Ashow and Baginton from 90; FE Liaison Officer Dios B & W and Glouc 91-93; Dioc Dir of Educn *Worc* from 93. *The Firs, Stoneleigh Road, Bubbenhall, Coventry CV8 3BS* Tel (01203) 303712 Fax as telephone

JOHNSON, Geoffrey Kemble. b 22. RD71. Roch Th Coll 62. **d** 64 **p** 65. C Hayes *Roch* 64-68; R Worlingham *St E* 68-84; rtd 84; Perm to Offic *Nor* from 84; Perm to Offic *St E* from 84. *53 St Walstans Road, Taverham, Norwich NR8 6NG* Tel (01603) 860626

JOHNSON, Geoffrey Stuart. b 39. ALCD65 Wolv Poly DipEd. **d** 65 **p** 66. C Worksop St Jo *S'well* 65-68; Taiwan 68-71; Singapore 71-76; Aber Univ *Ab* 76-78; Perm to Offic *Heref* 78-82; P-in-c Hoarwithy, Hentland and Sellack 82-84; Chapl Horton Hosp Epsom 84-90; Distr Chapl Brighton HA 90-94; Managing Chapl Brighton Healthcare NHS Trust from 94; Managing Chapl S Downs Health NHS Trust from 94. *The Royal Sussex County Hospital, Eastern Road, Brighton BN2 5BE* Tel (01273) 696955 ext 4122

JOHNSON, Gordon. b 20. **d** 43 **p** 44. C Glouc St Steph *Glouc* 43-46; C Halifax St Jo Bapt *Wakef* 46-48; C-in-c Seacroft CD *Ripon* 48-52; V N Grimston w Wharram Percy and Wharram-le-Street *York* 52-54; V Finchingfield *Chelmsf* 59-62; R Horseheath *Ely* 64-71; R Bartlow 65-71; Hon C S Kensington St Aug *Lon* 79-85; rtd 85; Perm to Offic *Glouc* from 85. *Rosemary Topping, English Bicknor, Coleford, Glos GL16 7PF* Tel (01594) 861181

JOHNSON, Gordon Edward. b 27. Oak Hill Th Coll 76. **d** 77 **p** 78. C Scarborough St Mary w Ch Ch and H Apostles *York* 77-82; V Hutton Cranswick w Skerne 82-86; P-in-c Watton w Beswick and Kilnwick 82-86; V Hutton Cranswick w Skerne, Watton and Beswick 86-88; V Bubwith w Skipwith 88-93; rtd 93; Perm to Offic *York* from 93. *Greenacres, Lovesome Hill, Northallerton, N Yorkshire DL6 2PB* Tel (01609) 881512

JOHNSON, Graham. b 37. Westcott Ho Cam 66. **d** 68 **p** 69. C Stafford St Mary *Lich* 68-71; C Wombourne 71-74; Youth Chapl 74-77; P-in-c Tong 76-77; Res Min Wednesfield St Thos 77-78; TV 79-82; P-in-c Gayton w Fradswell 84-88; P-in-c Milwich 82-88; P-in-c Weston upon Trent 82-88; V Fradswell, Gayton, Milwich and Weston 88-90; TV Wolstanton 90-96; V Oxley from 96. *The Vicarage, Lymer Road, Oxley, Wolverhampton WV10 6AA* Tel (01902) 783342

JOHNSON, Graham James. b 43. Leeds Univ BA67. Coll of Resurr Mirfield DipTh69. **d** 70 **p** 71. C Heckmondwike *Wakef* 70-73; C Pet St Jude *Pet* 73-76; V Gt w Lt Harrowden and Orlingbury 76-83; R Daventry 83-92; TR Daventry, Ashby St Ledgers, Braunston etc 92; Chapl Danetre Hosp 83-93; RD Daventry *Pet* 88-92; P-in-c Loddington *Leic* from 93; Warden Launde Abbey from 93; RD Framland *Leic* 94-96. *Launde Abbey, East Norton, Leicester LE7 9XB* Tel (01572) 717254

JOHNSON, Harold Barnett. b 10. Ex Coll Ox BA34 MA37. Cuddesdon Coll 34. **d** 35 **p** 36. C Wolverton St Geo *Ox* 35-36; C Cov St Marg *Cov* 36-40; C Wimbledon *S'wark* 40-47; V Southwick w Glapthorn *Pet* 47-60; R Waldron *Chich* 60-75; rtd 75; Hon C Eastbourne St Sav and St Pet *Chich* 75-83; Perm to Offic from 83. *Flat 1, Morley House, College of St Barnabas, Lingfield, Surrey RH7 6NJ* Tel (01342) 870440

JOHNSON, Harriet Etta. LRAM DipEd40. Trin Coll Bris. **dss** 76 **d** 87. Burundi 76-80; Ipplepen w Torbryan *Ex* 81-87; Hon Par Dn 87-90; Perm to Offic from 90. *10 Fairfield West, Huxtable Hill, Torquay TQ2 6RN* Tel (01803) 690115

JOHNSON, Mrs Hilary Ann. b 51. RGN72 RHV74 DipRS85. S'wark Ord Course 82. **dss** 85 **d** 87 **p** 94. Hon Par Dn Salfords *S'wark* 85-90; Chapl St Geo Hosp Lon 90-94; Chapl St Geo's Healthcare NHS Trust Lon from 94; NSM Wimbledon *S'wark* from 95. *St George's Hospital, Blackshaw Road, London SW17 0QT, or 111 Mortimer Crescent, Worcester Park, Surrey KT4 7QN* Tel 0181-725 3070 or 330 2060 Fax 725 1621

JOHNSON, Ian Lawrence. b 44. Wells Th Coll 68. **d** 71 **p** 72. C Benhilton *S'wark* 71-73; C Weymouth H Trin *Sarum* 73-76; R

Pewsey 76-81; R Compton Abbas W w Wynford Eagle etc 81; P-in-c Maiden Newton w Frome Vauchurch 81; R Maiden Newton and Valleys 81-83; Sherborne Episc Area Youth Officer 81-83; Dioc Youth Officer 83-88; TR Langley and Parkfield *Man* 88-95; P-in-c Haughton St Anne from 95; Dioc Adv on Evang from 95. *St Anne's Rectory, St Anne's Drive, Denton, Manchester M34 3EB* Tel 0161-336 2374 Fax 320 1827

JOHNSON, Ian Leslie. b 51. Bede Coll Dur TCert73. Wycliffe Hall Ox DipMin93. **d** 93 **p** 94. C Evington *Leic* 93-96; C Foxton w Gumley and Laughton and Lubenham from 96; Sub Chapl HM Pris Gartree from 96. *The Vicarage, Vicarage Drive, Foxton, Market Harborough, Leics LE16 7RJ* Tel (01858) 545245

✠**JOHNSON, The Rt Revd James Nathaniel.** b 32. Wells Th Coll 63. **d** 64 **p** 65 **c** 85. C Lawrence Weston *Bris* 64-66; St Helena 66-72; Hon Can from 75; Area Sec (Dios Ex and Truro) USPG 72-74; R Combe Martin *Ex* 74-80; V Thorpe Bay *Chelmsf* 80-85; Bp St Helena 85-91; R Byfield w Boddington and Aston le Walls *Pet* 91-92; Asst Bp Pet 91-92; V Hockley *Chelmsf* 92-97; Asst Bp Chelmsf 92-97; Can Chelmsf Cathl 94-97; rtd 97; Hon Asst Bp Chelmsf from 97. *St Helena, 249 Woodgrainge Drive, Southend-on-Sea SS1 2SQ* Tel (01702) 613429

JOHNSON, John Alan. b 51. Ripon Coll Cuddesdon 75. **d** 77 **p** 78. C Boreham Wood All SS *St Alb* 77-79; C Borehamwood 79-80; TV Dunstable 80-85; Toc H from 85; Nat Chapl from 89. *Carreg-y-Saeth, 40 Lionel Avenue, Wendover, Aylesbury, Bucks HP22 6LP* Tel (01296) 696431 or 623911 Fax 696137

JOHNSON, Canon John Anthony. b 18. Selw Coll Cam BA48 MA53 St Jo Coll Dur DipTh51. **d** 51 **p** 52. C Battersea St Mary *S'wark* 51-54; C Merton St Mary 54-56; V Balderton *S'well* 56-60; V Mansfield Woodhouse 60-70; V Beeston 70-85; RD Beeston 81-85; Hon Can S'well Minster 82-85; rtd 86; Perm to Offic *Blackb* from 90. *7 The Spinney, Cranwell Avenue, Lancaster LA1 4JQ* Tel (01524) 65137

JOHNSON, John Cecil. b 23. Peterho Cam BA48. Ely Th Coll 57. **d** 59 **p** 60. C Whitton SS Phil and Jas *Lon* 59-70; P-in-c Fulham St Andr Fulham Fields 70-73; V 73-88; rtd 88; Perm to Offic *Lich* from 88; Perm to Offic *Heref* from 90. *13 Selkirk Drive, Telford, Shropshire TF7 4JE* Tel (01952) 588407

JOHNSON, John David. b 38. St Deiniol's Hawarden 71. **d** 71 **p** 72. C Heref St Martin *Heref* 71-73; P-in-c Ewyas Harold w Dulas 73-79; P-in-c Kilpeck 73-79; P-in-c St Devereux w Wormbridge 73-79; P-in-c Kenderchurch 73-79; P-in-c Bacton 78-79; TR Ewyas Harold w Dulas, Kenderchurch etc 79-81; R Kentchurch w Llangua, Rowlestone, Llancillo etc 79-81; Chapl Napsbury Hosp St Alb 81-96; Chapl Horizon NHS Trust Herts from 96; Lic to Offic *St Alb* from 81. *Napsbury Hospital, Napsbury, St Albans, Herts AL2 1AB* Tel (01727) 823333

JOHNSON, Joseph Clarke. b 10. Bps' Coll Cheshunt 46. **d** 48 **p** 49. C Carl H Trin *Carl* 48-50; V St Johns-in-the-Vale w Wythburn 51-57; V Beckermet St Bridget w Ponsonby 57-78; rtd 78; Perm to Offic *Carl* from 78. *High Moss, Calderbridge, Seascale, Cumbria CA20 1DQ* Tel (01946) 841289

JOHNSON, Keith Henry. b 64. Keele Univ BA91 CQSW91. Coll of Resurr Mirfield BA97. **d** 97. C W Bromwich St Fran *Lich* from 97. *207 Hydes Road, West Bromwich, W Midlands B71 2EF*

JOHNSON, Keith Winton Thomas William. b 37. K Coll Lon BD63 AKC63. **d** 64 **p** 65. C Dartford H Trin *Roch* 64-69; Kuwait 69-73; V Erith St Jo *Roch* 73-80; V Bexley St Jo 80-91; V Royston *St Alb* 91-94; R Sandon, Wallington and Rushden w Clothall 94-97; Bahrain from 97. *St Christopher's Cathedral, PO Box 36, Manama, Bahrain*

JOHNSON, Kenneth William George. b 53. Hull Univ BA76 PGCE77. EMMTC 92. **d** 95 **p** 96. NSM Ilkeston H Trin *Derby* from 95. *18 Park Avenue, Awsworth, Nottingham NG16 2RA* Tel 0115-930 7830

JOHNSON, Malcolm Arthur. b 36. Univ Coll Dur BA60 MA64. Cuddesdon Coll 60. **d** 62 **p** 63. C Portsea N End St Mark *Portsm* 62-67; Chapl Qu Mary Coll *Lon* 67-74; V St Botolph Aldgate w H Trin Minories 74-92; P-in-c St Ethelburga Bishopgate 85-89; AD The City 85-90; Master R Foundn of St Kath in Ratcliffe 93-97; Bp's Adv for Past Care and Counselling *Lon* from 97. *Swan House, 43 Strawberry Vale, Twickenham TW1 4RX* Tel 0181-891 3363 Fax 891 2359

JOHNSON, Malcolm Stuart. b 35. AKC60. **d** 61 **p** 62. C Catford St Laur *S'wark* 61-64; Hon C Hatcham St Cath 66-76; P-in-c Kingstanding St Luke *Birm* 76-77; V 77-82; P-in-c Peckham St Jo w St Andr *S'wark* 82-92; V from 92. *St John's Vicarage, 10A Meeting House Lane, London SE15 2UN* Tel 0171-639 0084

JOHNSON, Ms Margaret Anne Hope. b 52. Homerton Coll Cam Open Univ BA81 Fitzw Coll Cam BA95. Ridley Hall Cam 93. **d** 95 **p** 96. C Northampton Em *Pet* from 95. *4 Booth Lane North, Northampton NN3 6JG* Tel (01604) 648974

JOHNSON, Margaret Joan (Meg). b 41. S'wark Ord Course 92. **d** 95 **p** 96. NSM Sanderstead St Mary *S'wark* from 95. *Flat 2, 16 Lancaster Road, London SE25 4AJ* Tel 0181-653 5322

JOHNSON, Dr Mark. b 62. Leic Poly BSc84 Loughb Univ PhD88. Ripon Coll Cuddesdon 88. **d** 94 **p** 95. C Bishop's Cleeve *Glouc* from 94. *2A Orchard Road, Bishops Cleeve, Cheltenham, Glos GL52 4LX* Tel (01242) 675431 Fax 673612

JOHNSON, Michael. b 42. Birm Univ BSc63. S'wark Ord Course 68. **d** 71 **p** 72. C Kidbrooke St Jas *S'wark* 71-74; Hon C Eynsford w Farningham and Lullingstone *Roch* 74-90; Hon C Selling w Throwley, Sheldwich w Badlesmere etc *Cant* from 90. *1 Halke Cottages, North Street, Sheldwich, Faversham, Kent ME13 0LR* Tel (01795) 536583

JOHNSON, Michael Anthony. b 51. Ex Univ BA76. Ripon Coll Cuddesdon 76 Ch Div Sch of the Pacific (USA) 78. **d** 78 **p** 79. C Primrose Hill St Mary w Avenue Road St Paul *Lon* 78-81; C Hampstead St Jo 81-85; TV Mortlake w E Sheen *S'wark* 85-93; R Wroughton *Bris* from 93; RD Wroughton from 97. *The Vicarage, Church Hill, Wroughton, Swindon SN4 9JS* Tel (01793) 812301 Fax 813273

JOHNSON, Michael Colin. b 37. Lon Univ DipRS80. S'wark Ord Course 77. **d** 80 **p** 81. NSM New Eltham All SS *S'wark* 80-84; NSM Woldingham from 84. *The Rectory, Station Road, Woldingham, Caterham, Surrey CR3 7DD* Tel 0181-905 2192

JOHNSON, Michael Gordon. b 45. Lon Univ DipTh68. Kelham Th Coll 64. **d** 68 **p** 69. C Holbrooks *Cov* 68-72; C Cannock *Lich* 72-75; V Coseley Ch Ch 75-79; P-in-c Sneyd 79-82; R Longton 82-88; Chapl Pilgrim Hosp Boston 88-96; TV Jarrow *Dur* from 96; Chapl Monkton and Primrose Hill Hosps from 96. *St John the Baptist House, Iona Road, Jarrow, Tyne & Wear NE32 4HX* Tel 0191-489 2043

JOHNSON, Nigel Edwin. b 41. AKC64 St Boniface Warminster 64. **d** 65 **p** 66. C Poulton-le-Sands *Blackb* 65-68; Chapl RN 68-93; Perm to Offic *Cant* from 93. *Marlborough House, Duke of York's Royal Military School, Dover, Kent CT15 5DS* Tel (01304) 211688

JOHNSON, Nigel Victor. b 48. ARCM68 LTCL75 Cam Univ DipEd69. Linc Th Coll 80. **d** 82 **p** 83. C Lindley *Wakef* 82-85; P-in-c Upperthong 85-87; Perm to Offic *Derby* 88-89; NSM Calow and Sutton cum Duckmanton 89-90; R from 90. *The Rectory, Top Road, Calow, Chesterfield S44 5AF* Tel (01246) 273486

JOHNSON, Paul Anthony. b 56. Leeds Univ BA77 Kent Coll for Careers DCG81. Linc Th Coll CMM87. **d** 88 **p** 89. C Glouc St Jas and All SS *Glouc* 88-91; C Leckhampton SS Phil and Jas w Cheltenham St Jas 91-93; Perm to Offic from 93. *4 Windermere Road, Gloucester GL2 0HN* Tel (01452) 419114

JOHNSON, Canon Peter Frederick. b 41. Melbourne Univ BA63 Ch Ch Ox BA68 MA72. St Steph Ho Ox 68. **d** 69 **p** 70. C Banbury *Ox* 69-71; Tutor St Steph Ho Ox 71-74; Chapl St Chad's Coll Dur 74-80; Vice-Prin 78-80; Chapl K Sch Cant 80-90; Perm to Offic *Cant* 80-81; Hon Min Can Cant Cathl 81-90; Can Res Bris Cathl *Bris* from 90. *41 Salisbury Road, Bristol BS6 7AR* Tel 0117-944 4464

JOHNSON (née DAVIES), Rhiannon Mary Morgan. b 69. St Anne's Coll Ox BA90 MA96 Univ of Wales (Cardiff) PhD94 BD96 DPT97. St Mich Coll Llan 94. **d** 97. C Whitchurch *Llan* from 97. *16 St John's Crescent, Whitchurch, Cardiff CF4 7AI* Tel (01222) 625947

JOHNSON, Richard Le Bas. b 22. TCD BA50 MA58. Sarum Th Coll 50. **d** 52 **p** 53. C Hugglescote w Donington *Leic* 52-55; C Hinckley St Mary 55-57; Min Can, Prec and Sacr Pet Cathl *Pet* 57-62; S Rhodesia 62-65; Rhodesia 65-72; C King's Worthy *Win* 72-74; R Crawley w Littleton 74-84; R Crawley and Littleton and Sparsholt w Lainston 84-90; rtd 90. *The College of St Barnabas, Blackberry Lane, Lingfield, Surrey RH7 6NJ* Tel (01342) 870002 Fax 870193 E-mail lerr_barr@compuserve.com

JOHNSON, Richard Miles. b 59. Bris Univ BSc82. St Jo Coll Nottm 87. **d** 90 **p** 91. C Bromley SS Pet and Paul *Roch* 90-94. *13 Rochester Avenue, Bromley BR1 3DB* Tel 0181-464 9532

JOHNSON, Robert Kenneth. b 48. N Ord Course 83. **d** 86 **p** 87. C Hattersley *Ches* 86-88; C Brinnington w Portwood 88-90; V Gospel Lane St Mich *Birm* from 90. *St Michael's Vicarage, 237 Lakey Lane, Birmingham B28 8QT* Tel 0121-777 6132 or 777 8443

JOHNSON, Canon Robin Edward Hobbs. b 39. Fitzw Ho Cam BA61 MA65. Ripon Hall Ox 61. **d** 63 **p** 64. C Tyldesley w Shakerley *Man* 63-66; Lic to Offic *Leic* 66-71; V Castleton Moor *Man* 71-77; Dir of Ords 76-81; V Prestwich St Gabr 77-81; V Heaton Ch Ch 81-91; Hon Can Man Cathl 86-91; TR Dorchester *Sarum* from 91. *The Rectory, 56 Prince of Wales Road, Dorchester, Dorset DT1 1PP* Tel (01305) 268837

JOHNSON, Ronald. b 40. Wycliffe Hall Ox 69. **d** 72 **p** 73. C Deane *Man* 72-74; C N Meols *Liv* 74-75; Chapl St Jo Sch Tiffield 75-82; Warden Eton Coll Dorney Project 82-84; Asst Chapl Eton Coll 82-84; TV Riverside *Ox* 82-84; Chapl Eastbourne Coll from 85. *16 Grange Road, Eastbourne, E Sussex BN21 4HJ* Tel (01323) 734329

JOHNSON, Ronald Alan (Ron). b 32. MITSA. Ox NSM Course 84. **d** 86 **p** 87. NSM Beaconsfield *Ox* from 86. *7 Northcroft, Wooburn Green, High Wycombe, Bucks HP10 0BP* Tel (01628) 527141

JOHNSON, Ronald George (Ron). b 33. Chich Th Coll 75. **d** 76 **p** 77. Hon C Shipley *Chich* 76-79; C Brighton St Matthias 79-82; P-in-c Barlavington 82; P-in-c Burton w Coates 82; P-in-c Sutton w Bignor 82; R Barlavington, Burton w Coates, Sutton and Bignor 82-93; rtd 93; Perm to Offic *Chich* from 93. *First Floor Flat, 36 South Terrace, Littlehampton, W Sussex BN17 5NU*

JOHNSON, The Very Revd Samuel Hugh Akinsope. b 30. K Coll Lon BD61. Lich Th Coll 52. **d** 55 **p** 56. C Whitechapel St Paul w

St Mark *Lon* 55-58; C Sunbury 58-59; C Lisson Grove w St Marylebone St Matt w Em 59-60; C St Martin-in-the-Fields 60-62; Nigeria from 63; Provost Lagos Cathl 70-95; rtd 95. *3 Oba Nle Aro Crescent, Ilupeju, PO Box 10021, Marina, Lagos, Nigeria* Fax Lagos (1) 496-0779

JOHNSON, Mrs Shiela. b 43. CertCC66. CITC 93. **d** 96 **p** 97. Aux Min Urney w Denn and Derryheen *K, E & A* 96-97; Aux Min Boyle and Elphin w Aghanagh, Kilbryan etc from 97; Aux Min Roscommon w Donamon, Rathcline, Kilkeevin etc from 97. *St John's Rectory, Battery Road, Longford, Irish Republic* Tel Longford (43) 46442

JOHNSON, The Ven Stanley. b 42. QUB BSc63 TCD BTh89. CITC 86. **d** 89 **p** 90. C Kilmore w Ballintemple, Kildallon etc *K, E & A* 89-97; Adn Elphin and Ardagh from 97; Preb Elphin Cathl from 97; I Templemichael w Clongish, Clooncumber etc from 97. *St John's Rectory, Battery Road, Longford, Irish Republic* Tel Longford (43) 46442

JOHNSON, Terence John. b 44. Cov Poly BA89. Lon Coll of Div ALCD70 LTh74. **d** 69 **p** 70. C Woodside *Ripon* 69-72; C Leeds St Geo 72-76; C Heworth *York* 76-81; V Budbrooke *Cov* 81-97; Chapl Wroxall Abbey Sch 83-93; V Stone Ch Ch and Oulton *Lich* from 97. *Christ Church Vicarage, Bromfield Court, Stone, Staffs ST15 8DA* Tel (01785) 812669

JOHNSON, Thomas Bernard (Tom). b 44. BA CertEd. Oak Hill Th Coll. **d** 84 **p** 85. C Birkenhead St Jas w St Bede *Ches* 84-88; R Ashover and Brackenfield *Derby* from 88; Hon Chapl Derbyshire St Jo Ambulance from 91; RD Chesterfield from 97. *The Rectory, Narrowleys Lane, Ashover, Chesterfield, Derbyshire S45 0AU* Tel (01246) 590246

JOHNSON, Victor Edward. b 45. Linc Th Coll 83. **d** 85 **p** 86. C Garforth *Ripon* 85-90; Dioc Video Officer 90-92; V Wyther Ven Bede from 92. *Wyther Vicarage, Houghley Lane, Leeds LS13 4AU* Tel 0113-279 8014

JOHNSON, Walter. b 21. St Aid Birkenhead. **d** 59 **p** 60. C W Bridgford *S'well* 59-62; V Bracebridge *Linc* 62-73; R Weston sub Edge and Aston sub Edge *Glouc* 73-77; R Willersey, Saintbury, Weston-sub-Edge etc 77-86; rtd 86; Perm to Offic *Win* from 87. *15 Beechey Road, Bournemouth BH8 8LL* Tel (01202) 557063

JOHNSTON, Alan Beere. b 14. Leeds Univ BA36. Coll of Resurr Mirfield 36. **d** 38 **p** 39. C Manningham St Chad *Bradf* 38-40; C Middlesbrough St Paul *York* 40-43; Perm to Offic 43-45; C Crawley *Chich* 45-47; C Portsea N End St Mark *Portsm* 47-48; C Marske in Cleveland *York* 48-50; P-in-c Carlin How w Skinningrove 50-52; V 52-57; V Clifton 57-62; V Kingston upon Hull St Mary 62-68; Asst Master Sir Henry Cooper High Sch Hull 68-70; Waltham Toll Bar Sch Waltham 70-71; Tutor Workers' Educn Assn 71-81; rtd 81; Perm to Offic *Chich* from 93. *6 Arlington Close, Goring-by-Sea, Worthing, W Sussex BN12 4ST* Tel (01903) 426590

JOHNSTON, Alexander Irvine (Alec). b 47. LRAM Keele Univ BA70. St Alb Minl Tr Scheme 77. **d** 80 **p** 81. NSM Hockerill *St Alb* 80-95; NSM High Wych and Gilston w Eastwick 95-96; TV Bottesford w Ashby *Linc* from 96. *Holy Spirit Vicarage, 180 Enderby Road, Scunthorpe, S Humberside DN17 2JX* Tel (01724) 842083

JOHNSTON, Allen Niall. b 61. AMBIM87 MISM87 Southn Univ BTh92. Sarum & Wells Th Coll 89. **d** 92 **p** 93. C Roehampton H Trin *S'wark* 92-95; Dir Past Services RTR Healthcare NHS Trust from 95; Tutor SEITE from 95. *Queen Mary's University Hospital, Roehampton Lane, London SW15 5PN* Tel 0181-789 6611 Fax 780 1089

JOHNSTON, Austin. b 50. Huddersfield Poly CertEd76 BEd90. Chich Th Coll DipThMin94. **d** 94 **p** 95. C Peterlee *Dur* 94-97; C Stockton St Pet from 97. *55 Kensington Road, Stockton-on-Tees, Cleveland TS18 4DQ*

JOHNSTON, Donald Walter. b 28. **d** 64 **p** 65. C Cottingham *York* 64-66; Australia from 66; rtd 91. *22 Albert Street, PO Box 114, Point Lonsdale, Victoria, Australia 3225* Tel Geelong (52) 582139 Fax 583994

JOHNSTON, Duncan Howard. b 63. Hull Univ BA85 Nottm Univ MA93. St Jo Coll Nottm 91. **d** 93 **p** 94. C Werrington *Pet* 93-96; V Gt Doddington and Wilby from 96. *The Vicarage, 72 High Street, Great Doddington, Wellingborough, Northants NN9 7TH* Tel (01933) 226711

JOHNSTON, Edith Violet Nicholl. b 28. **d** 87. Par Dn Bentley *Sheff* 87-88; rtd 88; Perm to Offic *Sheff* from 88. *32 Tennyson Avenue, Mexborough, S Yorkshire S64 0AX* Tel (01709) 570189

JOHNSTON, Elizabeth Margaret. b 37. QUB BA58 DipTh69 Serampore Univ BD87. **dss** 81 **d** 87 **p** 94. BCMS 81-93; Crosslinks 93; India 81-93; C Belfast St Chris *D & D* 93-94; Bp's C from 94. *St Christopher's Rectory, 412 Upper Newtownards Road, Belfast BT4 3EZ* Tel (01232) 471522

JOHNSTON, The Very Revd Frederick Mervyn Kieran. b 11. TCD BA33 MA52. **d** 34 **p** 36. C Castlecomer *C & O* 34-36; C Cork St Luke *C, C & R* 36-38; I Kilmeen 38-40; I Drimoleague 40-45; I Cork St Mich 45-58; Can Cork and Cloyne Cathls 55-59; I Bandon 58-67; Treas Ross Cathl 59-60; Adn Cork 59-66; Dean Cork 66-71; rtd 71. *24 Lapps Court, Hartlands Avenue, Cork, Irish Republic* Tel Cork (21) 313264

JOHNSTON, Geoffrey Stanley. b 44. Aston Univ MBA81 Lon Univ DipTh68 Birm Univ CertEd78. Kelham Th Coll 64. **d** 68 **p** 69. C Blakenall Heath *Lich* 68-72 and 73-75; C St Buryan, St Levan and Sennen *Truro* 72-73; P-in-c Willenhall St Steph *Lich* 75-76; C W Bromwich All SS 76-77; Lect W Bromwich Coll of Commerce and Tech 78-82; Ind Chapl *Worc* 82-94; TV Halesowen 82-94; NSM Dudley St Fran from 94. *37 Blagdon Road, Halesowen, W Midlands B63 3PT* Tel 0121-602 2080

JOHNSTON, James. b 19. FCIB70. Carl Dioc Tr Course. **d** 82 **p** 83. NSM Kendal St Geo *Carl* 82-89; Perm to Offic from 89. *8 Sedbergh Drive, Kendal, Cumbria LA9 6BJ* Tel (01539) 725422

JOHNSTON, Michael David Haigh. b 44. MBCS. S Dios Minl Tr Scheme. **d** 91 **p** 92. NSM Wootton *Portsm* 91-95; NSM Ryde H Trin from 95; NSM Swanmore St Mich and All Angels from 95. *7 Dover Street, Ryde, Isle of Wight PO33 2AQ* Tel (01983) 611291

JOHNSTON, Canon Robert John. b 31. Oak Hill Th Coll 64. **d** 64 **p** 65. C Bebington *Ches* 64-68; I Lack *Clogh* from 68; RD Kesh from 87; Can Clogh Cathl 89-91; Preb Clogh Cathl from 91. *The Rectory, Lack, Enniskillen, Co Fermanagh BT93 0DN* Tel (01365) 6360

JOHNSTON, Thomas Cosbey. b 15. Em Coll Cam BA40 MA44. Ridley Hall Cam 40. **d** 42 **p** 43. C Handsworth St Mary *Birm* 42-48; New Zealand from 48. *254 Main Road, Moncks Bay, Christchurch 8008, New Zealand* Tel Christchurch (3) 384 1224

JOHNSTON, Canon Wilfred Brian. b 44. TCD BA67 MA70. **d** 68 **p** 70. C Seagoe *D & D* 68-73; I Inniskeel *D & R* 73-82; I Castlerock w Dunboe and Fermoyle from 82; Dioc Registrar *D & D* from 89; RD Dungiven and Limavady 91-94; Can Derry Cathl *D & R* from 92. *The Rectory, 52 Main Street, Castlerock, Coleraine, Co Londonderry BT51 4RA* Tel (01265) 848242

JOHNSTON, The Ven William Derek. b 40. CITC 68. **d** 68 **p** 69. V Choral Derry Cathl *D & R* 68-70; I Swanlinbar w Templeport *K, E & A* 70-73; I Billis Union 73-84; Glebes Sec (Kilmore) from 77; I Annagh w Drumaloor and Cloverhill 84-87; Preb Kilmore Cathl 85-89; I Annagh w Drumgoon, Ashfield etc from 87; Adn Kilmore from 89. *The Rectory, Belturbet, Co Cavan, Irish Republic* Tel Cavan (49) 22142

JOHNSTON, William Francis (Frank). b 30. CB83. TCD BA55 MA69. **d** 55 **p** 56. C Orangefield *D & D* 55-59; CF 59-77; Asst Chapl Gen 77-80; Chapl Gen 80-87; P-in-c Winslow *Ox* 87-91; RD Claydon 89-94; R Winslow w Gt Horwood and Addington 91-95; rtd 95; Perm to Offic *Ex* from 95. *Lower Axehill, Chard Road, Axminster, Devon EX13 5ED* Tel (01297) 33259

JOHNSTON, William John. b 35. Lon Univ DipTh72 BA85 MA90. CITC 67. **d** 70 **p** 71. C Belfast St Donard *D & D* 70-72; C Derg *D & R* 72-78; I Drumclamph w Lower and Upper Langfield 78-91; I Kilskeery w Trillick *Clogh* from 91. *The Rectory, 130 Kilskeery Road, Trillick, Omagh, Co Tyrone BT78 3RJ* Tel (01365) 561228

JOHNSTON, William Malcolm. b 48. St Alb and Ox Min Course 92. **d** 95 **p** 96. NSM Banbury *Ox* from 95. *59 Queensway, Banbury, Oxon OX16 9NF* Tel (01295) 263542

JOHNSTON-HUBBOLD, Clifford Johnston. b 19. Lon Univ BA76 BD80. St Aid Birkenhead 49. **d** 52 **p** 53. C Stanwix *Carl* 52-55; V Gt Broughton 55-59; R Sedgeberrow *Worc* 59-73; P-in-c Hinton-on-the-Green 72-73; R Sedgeberrow w Hinton-on-the-Green 73-92; rtd 92. *2 Mills Close, Broadway, Worcs WR12 7RB* Tel (01386) 852199

JOHNSTONE, Ian Douglas. b 42. St Jo Coll Morpeth 67. **d** 70 **p** 70. Australia 70-88; V Morley St Paul *Wakef* 88-95; rtd 96. *14 Newlands Walk, Stanley, Wakefield, W Yorkshire WF3 4DT*

JOHNSTONE, Leslie William. b 20. ALCD49. **d** 49 **p** 50. C Claughton cum Grange *Ches* 49-52; C Crawley *Chich* 52-56; R Bexhill St Mark 56-85; rtd 85; Perm to Offic *Chich* from 86. *4 Fitzgerald Park, Seaford, E Sussex BN25 1AX* Tel (01323) 899708

JOHNSTONE, Peter Verney Lovett. b 37. Trin Coll Cam BA61 MA65. Cuddesdon Coll 61. **d** 63 **p** 64. C Kennington St Jo *S'wark* 63-66; Asst Chapl Southn Univ *Win* 66-70; P-in-c Earlsfield St Jo *S'wark* 70-79; V Eltham St Jo from 79. *The Vicarage, Sowerby Close, London SE9 6HB* Tel 0181-850 2731 or 859 1242

JOHNSTONE, William James. b 70. Dur Univ BA91. St Steph Ho Ox 93. **d** 95 **p** 96. C Plymouth St Pet *Ex* from 95. *261 North Road West, Plymouth PL1 5DH* Tel (01752) 227640

JOHNSTONE, William John Richard. b 13. Leeds Univ BA48. Coll of Resurr Mirfield. **d** 50 **p** 51. C Cockington *Ex* 50-54; C Wolborough w Newton Abbot 54-57; V Westgate Common *Wakef* 57-63; V St Neot *Truro* 63-71; V Ruislip Manor St Paul *Lon* 71-76; C Honicknowle *Ex* 76-77; rtd 78; Perm to Offic *Ex* from 82. *c/o Miss A B Smyth, Syon Abbey, South Brent, Devon TQ10 9JX* Tel (01364) 72256

JOINT, Capt Michael John. b 39. Sarum & Wells Th Coll 79. **d** 79 **p** 79. CA from 61; Hon C Chandler's Ford *Win* 79-83; Youth Chapl 79-83; V Lymington 83-95; Chapl R Bournemouth and Christchurch Hosps NHS Trust from 96. *Royal Bournemouth General Hospital, Castle Lane East, Bournemouth BH7 1DW* Tel (01202) 303626

JOLLY, Leslie Alfred Walter. b 16. AKC40. **d** 40 **p** 41. C Bow w Bromley St Leon *Lon* 40-42; C Cheam Common St Phil *S'wark* 42-50; C Mottingham St Andr 50-52; V Newington St Matt

52-57; R Chaldon 57-85; rtd 85; Perm to Offic *S'wark* 85-94; Perm to Offic *York* from 85. *62 Wharfedale, Filey, N Yorkshire YO14 0DP* Tel (01723) 514591

JONAS, Alan Charles. b 56. Leeds Univ BA79 Univ of Wales (Abth) PGCE80. Wycliffe Hall Ox DipMin94. **d** 94 **p** 95. C Hersham *Guildf* from 94. *3 Burwood Road, Walton-on-Thames, Surrey KT12 4AA* Tel (01932) 247868

JONAS, Ian Robert. b 54. St Jo Coll Nottm BTh80. **d** 80 **p** 81. C Portadown St Mark *Arm* 80-82; C Cregagh *D & D* 82-85; BCMS Sec *D & G* 85-90; V Langley Mill *Derby* 90-97; I Kilgariffe Union *C, C & R* from 97. *The Rectory, Gullanes, Clonakilty, Co Cork, Irish Republic* Tel Cork (23) 33357

JONES, Adrian Alfred Burkett. b 37. St Aid Birkenhead 61. **d** 64 **p** 65. C Derby St Aug *Derby* 64-68; Chapl RAF 68-87; R Worlingham w Barnby and N Cove *St E* from 87. *The Rectory, Lowestoft Road, Beccles, Suffolk NR34 7DZ* Tel (01502) 715403

JONES, Alan. b 28. Man Univ LLB48 LLM50. Coll of Resurr Mirfield 53. **d** 56 **p** 57. C Streatham St Pet *S'wark* 56-59; C Hornsey St Luke *Lon* 59-60; Miss to Seamen 60-61; Chapl RN 61-65; rtd 94. *73 Mousehole Lane, Southampton SO18 4FB* Tel (01703) 550008

JONES, Alan David. b 32. Lon Coll of Div ALCD58 DipTh70 LTh74. **d** 58 **p** 59. C Ipswich All SS *St E* 58-60; C Southend St Jo *Chelmsf* 60-64; CF (TA) 60-62; CF (TA - R of O) 62-67; V Leyton St Cath *Chelmsf* 64-70; V Hatfield Broad Oak 70-77; P-in-c Bush End 77-79; V Theydon Bois 77-88; P-in-c Finchingfield and Cornish Hall End 88-93; rtd 94. *3A Priory Road, Sudbury, Suffolk CO10 6LB* Tel (01787) 370864

JONES, Alan John. b 47. Nottm Univ BA71. Coll of Resurr Mirfield 71. **d** 73 **p** 74. C Sedgley St Mary *Lich* 73-76; C Cov St Jo *Cov* 76-78; V W Bromwich St Fran *Lich* 78-94; V Ettingshall from 94. *The Vicarage, Ettingshall, Wolverhampton WV4 6QH* Tel (01902) 884616

JONES, Alban Vaughan. b 24. St D Coll Lamp BA51. **d** 52 **p** 53. C Llandeilo Tal-y-bont *S & B* 52-55; C Swansea St Pet 55-59; R Llangammarch w Garth, Llanlleonfel etc 59-65; Area Sec (Dios Ches, Ban, St As and S & M) CMS 65-72; V Ventnor H Trin *Portsm* 72-79; V Ventnor St Cath 72-79; V Marshfield and Peterstone Wentloog etc *Mon* 79-90; RD Bassaleg 87-90; rtd 90. *40 St Hilary Drive, Killay, Swansea SA2 7EH* Tel (01792) 208178

JONES, Albert. b 13. K Coll Lon 37. **d** 41 **p** 42. C Farnworth and Kearsley *Man* 41-46; P-in-c 45-46; C Felixstowe St Jo *St E* 46-47; C Headstone St Geo *Lon* 47-49; R Stretford All SS *Man* 49-52; Trinidad and Tobago 52-56; V Farnworth St Pet *Man* 56-58; Area Sec (Dio York) USPG 58-63; V Tillingham *Chelmsf* 63-66; R Dengie w Asheldham 63-66; R Stifford 66-72; P-in-c Stondon Massey 72-79; R Doddinghurst 72-79; rtd 79; Perm to Offic *Chelmsf* from 79. *29 Seaview Road, Brightlingsea, Colchester CO7 0PP* Tel (01206) 303994

JONES, Alfred Albert. b 36. St D Coll Lamp BA59. **d** 61 **p** 62. C Treherbert w Tynewydd and Ynsfeio *Llan* 61-64; C Horsham *Chich* 64-82; V Shipley 82-86; Chapl Hillingdon Hosp & Mt Vernon Hosp Uxbridge 86-87. *Chantry House, Nuthurst Road, Monks Gate, Horsham, W Sussex RH13 6LG* Tel (01403) 891218

JONES, Alun. b 52. Leeds Univ BA96. Cuddesdon Coll DipMin94. **d** 96 **p** 97. C Newc St Geo *Newc* from 96. *Close House, St George's Close, Newcastle upon Tyne NE2 2TF* Tel 0191-281 3871

JONES, Alwyn Humphrey Griffith. b 30. Leeds Univ BSc51. Coll of Resurr Mirfield 53. **d** 55 **p** 56. C W Hackney St Barn *Lon* 55-58; E Pakistan 58-64; India 65-73; P-in-c Bedminster St Fran *Bris* 73-75; TR Bedminster 75-83; TV Langport Area Chs *B & W* 83-85; Dep Chapl HM Pris Nor 85; Chapl HM Pris Preston 85-89; Chapl HM Pris Ashwell 89-91; C Acton Green *Lon* 91-93; rtd 93; Hon C Langport Area Chs *B & W* from 93. *The Vicarage, New Street, Long Sutton, Langport, Somerset TA10 9JW* Tel (01458) 241260

✠**JONES, The Most Revd Alwyn Rice.** b 34. Univ of Wales (Lamp) BA55 Fitzw Ho Cam BA57 MA61. St Mich Coll Llan 57. **d** 58 **p** 59 **c** 82. C Llanfairisgaer *Ban* 58-62; N Wales Sec SCM 60-62; Staff Sec SCM 62-65; Chapl St Winifred's Sch Llanfairfechan 65-68; Dir RE *Ban* 65-75; Dioc Youth Officer 66-72; Dir of Ords 70-75; Asst Tutor Univ of Wales (Ban) 73-76; V Porthmadog *Ban* 75-79; Hon Can Ban Cathl 75-78; Preb 78-79; Dean Brecon *S & B* 79-82; V Brecon w Battle 79-82; Bp St As from 82; Abp Wales from 91. *Esgobty, St Asaph LL17 0TW* Tel (01745) 583503 Fax 584301

JONES, Alyson Elizabeth. *See* DAVIE, Mrs Alyson Elizabeth

JONES, Mrs Andrea Margaret. b 46. Qu Coll Birm 88. **d** 90 **p** 94. Par Dn Kidderminster St Geo *Worc* 90-94; C 94; TV 94-95; C Penn Fields *Lich* from 95. *149 Mount Road, Penn, Wolverhampton WV4 5RS* Tel (01902) 34537

JONES, Andrew. b 61. Univ of Wales (Ban) BD82 PGCE82 TCD BTh85 MA91 Univ of Wales MPhil93. CITC 83 St Geo Coll Jerusalem 84. **d** 85 **p** 86. Min Can Ban Cathl *Ban* 85-88; R Dolgellau w Llanfachreth and Brithdir etc 88-92; Chapl Dolgellau Hosp 88-92; Lect Th Univ of Wales (Cardiff) *Llan* 92-93; Dir Past Studies St Mich Coll Llan 92-96; R Llanbedrog w Llannor w Llanfihangel etc *Ban* from 96. *Ty'n Llan Rectory, Llanbedrog, Pwllheli LL53 7TU*

JONES, Andrew. b 64. York Univ BA85. Westmr Th Sem (USA) MDiv91 St Jo Coll Nottm 92. **d** 94 **p** 95. C Win Ch Ch *Win* from 94. *18 Sparkford Close, Winchester, Hants SO22 4NH* Tel (01962) 865051

JONES, Dr Andrew Christopher. b 47. Southn Univ BA69 PhD75. Ridley Hall Cam 78. **d** 80 **p** 81. C Wareham *Sarum* 80-83; P-in-c Symondsbury 83; P-in-c Chideock 83; R Symondsbury and Chideock 84-91; V Shottermill *Guildf* from 91. *The Vicarage, Vicarage Lane, Shottermill, Haslemere, Surrey GU27 1LQ* Tel (01428) 642057

JONES, Andrew Collins. b 62. Univ Coll Dur BA83 MA84 MLitt92. St Steph Ho Ox 88. **d** 90 **p** 91. C Llangefni w Tregaean and Llangristiolus etc *Ban* 90-94; C Hartlepool St Aid *Dur* from 94; Chapl Hartlepool Gen Hosp from 94. *St Aidan's Clergy House, St Aidan's Street, Hartlepool, Cleveland TS25 1SN* Tel (01429) 273539

JONES, Preb Andrew Theodore Hugh. b 22. St Cath Soc Ox BA49 MA53. St Steph Ho Ox. **d** 50 **p** 51. C Hartland and Welcombe *Ex* 50-54; V 54-66; V Witheridge 66-77; V Creacombe 67-77; R Thelbridge 67-77; R W w E Worlington 67-77; P-in-c Meshaw 69-77; RD S Molton 72-74; P-in-c Limington *B & W* 77-78; P-in-c Ilchester w Northover 77-78; P-in-c Yeovilton 78; R Ilchester w Northover, Limington, Yeovilton etc 78-80; V Bishops Tawton *Ex* 80-85; V Newport 80-85; RD Barnstaple 81-83; Preb Ex Cathl 82-87; TR Newport, Bishops Tawton and Tawstock 85-87; rtd 87; Perm to Offic *Ex* from 87. *Belmont House, King Street, Combe Martin, Ilfracombe, Devon EX34 0AH* Tel (01271) 883135

JONES, Canon Anthony Spacie (Tony). b 34. AKC58. **d** 59 **p** 60. C Bedford St Martin *St Alb* 59-63; Br Guiana 63-66; Guyana 66-71; V Ipswich All Hallows *St E* 72-80; RD Ipswich 78-86; Bp's Dom Chapl 80-82; V Rushmere 82-91; Hon Can St E Cathl from 83; R Brantham w Stutton from 91; P-in-c Bentley w Tattingstone from 95. *The Rectory, Rectory Lane, Brantham, Manningtree, Essex CO11 1PZ* Tel (01206) 392646

JONES, Canon Arthur Alexander. b 10. Birm Univ BA35 MA48 Lon Univ BD45 PhD53. **d** 52 **p** 53. C Cov Cathl *Cov* 53-57; V Nunhead St Silas *S'wark* 57-62; Prin Lect RE Avery Hill Coll 62-75; Hon C Eltham St Sav 71-75; Chapl RAEC Wilton Park 75-80; rtd 75; Tutor K Coll Lon 75-80. *16 Heath Road, Beaconsfield, Bucks HP9 1DD* Tel (01494) 676746

JONES, Barry Mervyn. b 46. St Chad's Coll Dur BA68 DipTh69. **d** 70 **p** 71. C Bloxwich *Lich* 70-72; C Norwood All SS *Cant* 72-76; C New Addington 76-78; Chapl Mayday Univ Hosp Thornton Heath 78-86; Chapl Qu and St Mary's Hosps Croydon 78-86; Chapl Bromsgrove and Redditch DHA 86-94; Chapl Alexandra Hosp Redditch 86-94; Chapl Alexandra Healthcare NHS Trust Redditch from 94. *The Alexandra Hospital, Woodrow Drive, Redditch, Worcs B98 7UB* Tel (01527) 503030

JONES, Canon Basil Henry. b 26. Bps' Coll Cheshunt 63. **d** 64 **p** 65. C Gt Berkhamsted *St Alb* 64-67; V Leagrave 68-74; RD Luton 71-74; P-in-c Bedford St Paul 74-75; V Wigginton 75-93; Hon Can St Alb 82-93; rtd 93. *17 Lochnell Road, Northchurch, Berkhamsted, Herts HP4 3QD* Tel (01442) 864485

JONES, The Ven Benjamin Jenkin Hywel. b 39. Univ of Wales BA61. St Mich Coll Llan 61. **d** 64 **p** 65. C Carmarthen St Pet *St D* 64-70; V Cynwyl Gaeo w Llansawel and Talley 70-79; R Llanbadarn Fawr 79-82; V Llanbadarn Fawr w Capel Bangor and Goginan 82-92; Can St D Cathl 86-90; RD Llanbadarn Fawr 89-90; Adn Cardigan from 90; V Llanychaearn w Llanddeiniol from 92. *The Vicarage, Llanfarian, Aberystwyth SY23 4BX* Tel (01970) 617100

JONES, Benjamin Tecwyn. b 17. Univ of Wales BA38. K Coll Lon 38. **d** 40 **p** 41. C Hawarden *St As* 40-45; C Pleasley *Derby* 45-46; C Ormskirk *Liv* 46-49; R Rufford *Blackb* 49-55; V S Shore St Pet 55-65; C Oldham St Mary w St Pet *Man* 65-69; Hd Master and Chapl St Mary's Sch Bexhill-on-Sea 69-71; V Blackb St Luke *Blackb* 71-72; P-in-c Griffin 71-72; V Blackb St Luke w St Phil 72-83; rtd 83; Lic to Offic *Blackb* from 83. *527A Livesey Branch Road, Feniscowles, Blackburn BB2 5DB* Tel (01254) 209206

JONES, Bernard Lewis. b 48. Llan Dioc Tr Scheme 89. **d** 93 **p** 94. NSM Aberaman and Abercwmboi w Cwmaman *Llan* from 93. *21 Gladstone Street, Aberaman, Aberdare CF44 6SB* Tel (01685) 881994

JONES, Brian H. d 94 **p** 96. Lic to Offic *D & D* from 94. *16 Massey Avenue, Belfast BT4 2JS*

JONES, Canon Brian Howell. b 35. Univ of Wales MPhil96. St Mich Coll Llan DipTh61. **d** 61 **p** 62. C Llangiwg *S & B* 61-63; C Swansea St Mary and H Trin 63-70; R New Radnor w Llanfihangel Nantmelan etc 70-75; V Llansamlet 75-89; Dioc Dir of Stewardship 82-89; P-in-c Capel Coelbren 89-95; Dioc Missr 89-95; Can Res Brecon Cathl from 89; RD Cwmtawe 89-93; V Killay from 95. *The Vicarage, 30 Goetre Fach Road, Killay, Swansea SA2 7SG* Tel (01792) 204233

JONES, Brian Michael. b 34. Trin Coll Bris DipHE81 Oak Hill Th Coll BA82. **d** 84 **p** 84. CMS 82-93; Sierra Leone 84-93; C Frimley *Guildf* from 93. *Church House, 4 Warren Rise, Frimley, Camberley, Surrey GU16 5SH* Tel (01276) 66740

JONES, Canon Brian Noel. b 32. Edin Th Coll 59. **d** 62 **p** 63. C Monkseaton St Mary *Newc* 62-65; C Saffron Walden *Chelmsf* 65-69; P-in-c Swaffham Bulbeck *Ely* 69-75; Dioc Youth Officer 69-75; RD St Ives 75-83 and 87-89; V Ramsey 75-89; V Upwood w Gt and Lt Raveley 75-89; P-in-c Ramsey St Mary's 82-89; Hon Can Ely Cathl 85-97; V Cherry Hinton St Jo 89-97; RD Cambridge 94-97; rtd 97; Perm to Offic *Nor* from 97. *11 Winns Close, Holt, Norfolk NR25 6MQ* Tel (01263) 713645

JONES, Brinley Morgan. b 13. St D Coll Lamp BA37. **d** 40 **p** 41. C Tylorstown *Llan* 40-43; C Penarth All SS 43-47; Australia 47-52; C Llwynypia *Llan* 52-54; V Pwllgwaun 54-71; R Eglwysbrewis and St Athan 71-78; rtd 78; Perm to Offic *Llan* from 78. *228 New Road, Porthcawl CF36 5BA* Tel (01656) 716123

JONES, Canon Bryan Maldwyn. b 32. St Mich Coll Llan DipTh62. **d** 62 **p** 63. C Swansea St Barn *S & B* 62-69; V Trallwng and Betws Penpont 69-75; V Trallwng, Bettws Penpont w Aberyskir etc from 75; RD Brecon II 80-91; RD Brecon from 91; Hon Can Brecon Cathl from 92. *The Vicarage, Trallwng, Brecon LD3 8HP* Tel (01874) 636549

JONES, Bryan William. b 30. Selw Coll Cam BA53 MA57. Linc Th Coll 53. **d** 55 **p** 56. C Bedminster Down *Bris* 55-58; C Filton 58-62; P-in-c Bedminster St Mich 62-65; V 65-72; P-in-c Moorfields 72-75; TV E Bris 75-95; rtd 95; Perm to Offic *Bris* from 95. *89 Canterbury Close, Yate, Bristol BS17 5TU* Tel (01454) 316795

JONES, Bryon. b 34. Open Univ BA84. St D Coll Lamp 61. **d** 64 **p** 65. C Port Talbot St Theodore *Llan* 64-67; C Aberdare St Jo 68-69; C Up Hatherley *Glouc* 69-71; C Oystermouth *S & B* 71-74; V Camrose *St D* 74-77; V Camrose and St Lawrence w Ford and Haycastle from 77. *The Vicarage, Camrose, Haverfordwest SA62 6JE* Tel (01437) 710501

JONES, Charles Derek. b 37. K Coll Lon BD60 AKC60. **d** 61 **p** 62. C Stockton St Chad *Dur* 61-64; C Becontree St Elisabeth *Chelmsf* 64-66; C S Beddington St Mich *S'wark* 66-73; Lic to Offic *Ex* 73-77; Perm to Offic *Liv* from 77. *8 Millfield Close, Barton Park, Farndon, Chester CH3 6PW* Tel (01829) 270554

JONES, Charles Emerson Glynne. b 08. Univ of Wales 27. **d** 31 **p** 32. C Bistre *St As* 31-35; C Broughton 35-36; C Northop 36-40; Chapl RAFVR 40-47; Chapl RAF 47-52; R Middleton Cheney w Chacombe *Pet* 52-75; rtd 75; Hon C N Huish *Ex* 75-83. *31 Y Berllan, Dunvant, Swansea SA2 8RD* Tel (01792) 201886

JONES, Charles Eurwyn. b 27. Univ of Wales BSc48 DipEd51. St Mich Coll Llan 53. **d** 55 **p** 56. C Brecon St Dav *S & B* 55-57; C Carmarthen St Dav *St D* 57-61; Tutor Old Cath Sem Bonn 61-64; Tutor Bps' Coll Cheshunt 64-67; V Carlton *S'well* 67-75; P-in-c Colwick 69-75; V Bunny w Bradmore 75-95; rtd 95. *9 Wentworth Way, Edwalton, Nottingham NG12 4DJ* Tel 0115-923 4119

JONES, Charles Harold Lloyd. b 08. St D Coll Lamp DipTh59. **d** 59 **p** 60. C Henfynyw w Aberaeron and Llanddewi Aberarth *St D* 59-61; R Llanfairorllwyn and Llangynllo 61-70; V Llanllawddog w Capel-y-Groes 70-79; rtd 79. *15 Bro Nantlais, Gwyddgrug, Pencader SA39 9BQ* Tel (01559) 384884

JONES, Charles John Llewelyn. b 11. Jes Coll Cam BA32 MA36. St Aug Coll Cant 56. **d** 56 **p** 57. C Warsop *S'well* 56-59; V Bole w Saundby 59-65; V Sturton w Littleborough 59-65; V Whittlesford *Ely* 65-84; rtd 84; Perm to Offic *Ely* from 86. *Brook House, Seymour Street, Cambridge CB1 3DJ*

JONES, Christopher Howell. b 50. FCCA BA. Oak Hill Th Coll 80. **d** 83 **p** 84. C Leyton St Mary w St Edw *Chelmsf* 83-86; C Becontree St Mary 86-90; P-in-c Bootle St Matt *Liv* 90-93; V from 93; AD Bootle from 97. *St Matthew's Vicarage, 418 Stanley Road, Bootle, Merseyside L20 5AE* Tel 0151-922 3316

JONES, Christopher John Stark. b 39. Lon Univ BA60 AKC60. Wells Th Coll 63. **d** 65 **p** 66. C Stanmore *Win* 65-67; C Bournemouth St Pet 67-71; C W Wycombe *Ox* 71-75; TV High Wycombe 75-77; V Wokingham St Sebastian 77-84; R Didsbury Ch Ch *Man* from 84. *Christ Church Rectory, 35 Darley Avenue, Manchester M20 2ZD* Tel 0161-445 4152

JONES, Christopher Mark. b 54. St Pet Coll Ox BA75 DipTh77 MA79 Selw Coll Cam MPhil80. Ridley Hall Cam 77. **d** 80 **p** 81. C Putney St Marg *S'wark* 80-83; C Ham St Andr 83-86; Chapl HM Rem Cen Latchmere Ho 83-86; Chapl St Jo Coll Dur 87-93; Tutor Cranmer Hall Dur 87-93; Chapl and Fell St Pet Coll Ox from 93. *St Peter's College, Oxford OX1 2DL* Tel (01865) 278900

JONES, Christopher Mark. b 56. St Jo Coll Cam BA78 MA82 Ox Univ BA81 MA85. Wycliffe Hall Ox 79. **d** 82 **p** 83. C Walsall *Lich* 82-84; Chapl St Jo Coll Cam 84-89; Chapl Eton Coll from 89. *Eton College, Windsor, Berks SL4 6DW* Tel (01753) 862062

JONES, Clifford Albert. b 20. Edin Th Coll 54. **d** 56 **p** 57. C Dundee St Salvador *Bre* 56-58; C Linc St Swithin *Linc* 58-59; C Grantham St Wulfram 59-60; R Dundee St Salvador *Bre* 60-69; V Bradford *B & W* 69-74; V Bridgwater St Jo 74-78; RD Bridgwater 76-80; R Bridgwater St Jo w Chedzoy 78-80; P-in-c Timsbury 80-85; R Timsbury and Priston 85; rtd 85; P-in-c Nor St Geo Tombland *Nor* 85-90; Hon C St Marylebone All SS *Lon* 90-94. *188 John Aird Court, St Mary's Terrace, London W2 1UX* Tel 0171-262 9295

JONES, Clive. b 51. BA82. Oak Hill Th Coll 79. **d** 82 **p** 83. C Brunswick *Man* 82-85; V Pendlebury St Jo 85-96; V Attleborough *Cov* from 96. *Attleborough Vicarage, 5 Fi-Field Close, Nuneaton, Warks CV11 4JS* Tel (01203) 354114

JONES, Clive Morlais Peter. b 40. LTCL71 Univ of Wales (Cardiff) BA63 CertEd64. Chich Th Coll 64. **d** 66 **p** 67. C Llanfabon *Llan* 66-70; PV Llan Cathl 70-75; R Gelligaer 75-85; Prec and Can Llan Cathl 84-85; R Tilehurst St Mich *Ox* 85-94; Chapl Costa Blanca *Eur* 94-97; V Newton St Pet *S & B* from 97. *The Vicarage, Mary Twill Lane, Newton, Swansea SA3 4RB* Tel (01792) 368348

JONES, Colin Stuart. b 56. Southn Univ LLB77. Coll of Resurr Mirfield 81. **d** 84 **p** 85. C Mountain Ash *Llan* 84-86; C Castle Bromwich SS Mary and Marg *Birm* 86-89; V Kingshurst 89-94; V Perry Barr from 94. *Perry Barr Vicarage, Church Road, Birmingham B42 2LB* Tel 0121-356 7998

JONES, Cyril. b 27. Linc Th Coll 67. **d** 69 **p** 70. C Milnrow *Man* 69-71; C Chorlton-cum-Hardy St Werburgh 71-73; V Chadderton St Mark 73-75; R Didsbury Ch Ch 75-81; V Farlam and Nether Denton *Carl* 81-85; P-in-c Kirkbride w Newton Arlosh 85-89; rtd 89. *81 Newlands Avenue, Cheadle Hulme, Cheadle, Cheshire SK8 6NE*

JONES, Cyril Ernest. b 29. St D Coll Lamp BA54. **d** 56 **p** 57. C Llanedy *St D* 56-60; C Llanelli 60-63; V Mydroilyn w Dihewyd 63-66; V Llanybydder 66-73; V Llanybydder and Llanwenog w Llanwnnen 73-78; V Betws w Ammanford 78-81; V Cynwyl Gaeo w Llansawel and Talley 81-94; rtd 94. *21 Pontardulais Road, Tycroes, Ammanford SA18 3QD* Tel (01269) 596421

JONES, David. b 55. St Steph Ho Ox. **d** 85 **p** 86. C Fleur-de-Lis *Mon* 85-87; V Ynysddu 87-93; V Blackwood from 93. *The Vicarage, South View Road, Blackwood NP2 1HR* Tel (01495) 224214

JONES, David Arthur. b 44. Liv Univ BA66 Sussex Univ MA68. St D Coll Lamp LTh74. **d** 74 **p** 75. C Tenby *St D* 74-76; C Chepstow *Mon* 76-78; P-in-c Teversal *S'well* 78-81; R 81-91; Chapl Sutton Cen 78-89; V Radford All So w Ch Ch and St Mich from 91; Adv to Urban Priority Parishes from 96. *All Souls' Vicarage, 164 Lenton Boulevard, Nottingham NG7 2BZ* Tel 0115-978 5364

JONES, David Emrys. b 21. Lon Univ BD69 Univ of Wales MA74. St D Coll Lamp BA42. **d** 47 **p** 48. C Llandinorwic *Ban* 47-50; C Conwy w Gyffin 50-57; V Beddgelert 57-72; R Llangystennin *St As* 72-91; rtd 91. *The Rectory, Llanfor, Bala LL23 7YA* Tel (01678) 520080

JONES, Chan David Frederick Donald. b 19. Univ of Wales (Abth) BA41. Westcott Ho Cam 41. **d** 43 **p** 44. C Henfynyw w Aberaeron *St D* 43-46; C Carmarthen St Pet 46-53; V Pencarreg 53-64; Lect Bp Burgess Th Hall Lamp 59-72; V Betws w Ammanford 64-78; RD Dyffryn Aman 72-78; Can St D Cathl 75-88; Chan St D Cathl 83-88; V Felin-foel 78-88; rtd 88. *93 Nun Street, St Davids, Haverfordwest SA62 6NU* Tel (01437) 720359

JONES, David Hugh. b 34. St D Coll Lamp BA56. St Mich Coll Llan 58. **d** 58 **p** 59. C Swansea St Mary and H Trin *S & B* 58-61; Inter-Colleg Sec SCM (Liv) 61-63; Hon Chapl Liv Univ 61-63; C Swansea St Pet *S & B* 63-69; V Llanddewi Ystradenni and Abbey Cwmhir 69-75; V Port Eynon w Rhosili and Llanddewi and Knelston 75-83; V Swansea St Barn 83-92; rtd 92. *16 Lon Ger-y-Coed, Cockett, Swansea SA2 0YH*

✠**JONES, The Rt Revd David Huw.** b 34. Univ of Wales (Ban) BA55 Univ Coll Ox BA58 MA62. St Mich Coll Llan 58. **d** 59 **p** 60 **c** 93. C Aberdare St Jo *Llan* 59-61; C Neath w Llantwit 61-65; V Crynant 65-69; V Cwmavon 69-74; Lect Th Univ of Wales (Cardiff) 74-78; Sub-Warden St Mich Coll Llan 74-78; V Prestatyn *St As* 78-82; Dioc Ecum Officer 78-82; Dean Brecon *S & B* 82-93; V Brecon w Battle 82-93; V Brecon St Mary and Battle w Llanddew 83-93; Asst Bp St As 93-96; Bp St D from 96. *Llys Esgob, Abergwili, Carmarthen SA31 2JG* Tel (01267) 236597

JONES, David Ian Stewart. b 34. Selw Coll Cam BA57 MA61. Westcott Ho Cam 57. **d** 59 **p** 60. C Oldham *Man* 59-63; V Elton All SS 63-66; Chapl Eton Coll 66-70; Sen Chapl 70-74; Hd Master Bryanston Sch Dorset 74-82; P-in-c Bris Ch Ch w St Ewen and All SS *Bris* 82-84; P-in-c Bris St Steph w St Nic and St Leon 82-84; P-in-c City of Bris 84; Soc Resp Adv 84-85; Dir Lambeth Endowed Charities 85-94; Hon PV S'wark Cathl *S'wark* 85-94; rtd 94. *24 Wincott Street, London SE11 4NT* Tel 0171-735 2531

JONES, David James Hammond. b 45. Kelham Th Coll DipTh69. **d** 70 **p** 70. C Cheadle *Lich* 70-73; Hon C W Bromwich All SS 78-83; NSM Primrose Hill St Mary w Avenue Road St Paul *Lon* from 91. *14 Dundonald Road, London NW10 3HR* Tel 0181-969 1580 Fax 830 2317

JONES, David John. b 06. St D Coll Lamp 55. **d** 57 **p** 58. C Pen-bre *St D* 57-59; V Brawdy w Haycastle and Llandeloy 59-71; RD Dewisland and Fishguard 68-71; V Llangyndeyrn 71-76; rtd 76. *73 Heol Marlais, Trimsaran, Kidwelly SA17 4DF* Tel (01554) 810611

JONES, Chan David John. b 18. St D Coll Lamp BA51. **d** 52 **p** 53. C Brynamman *St D* 52-54; C Aberystwyth H Trin 54-57; Min Can St D Cathl 58-60; V Blaenpennal and Llangeitho 60-72; R Llanllwchaiarn 72-79; V Llanfihangel Ystrad w Cribyn and Cilcennin 79-82; Can St D Cathl 82-89; V Llanfihangel Ystrad and Cilcennin w Trefilan etc 82-89; RD Glyn Aeron 85-89; Chan St D Cathl 88-89; rtd 89. *Maerdy, 14 Harford Row, Lampeter SA48 7DG* Tel (01570) 423292

JONES, David Jonathan. b 04. St D Coll Lamp BA34. **d** 34 **p** 35. C Llanllyfni *Ban* 34-38; Min Can Ban Cathl 38-42; R Llanymawddwy 42-48; R Cemmaes 48-55; R Nefyn, Edern and Ceidio 55-59; R Nefyn w Pistyll 60-73; rtd 73; Lic to Offic *Ban* from 73. *Glanrhos Nursing Home, Brynsiencyn, Llanfairpwll-gwyngyll LL62 5PR* Tel (01248) 750162

JONES, David Michael. b 48. Chich Th Coll 75. **d** 78 **p** 79. C Yeovil *B & W* 78-84; C Barwick 81-84; V Cleeve w Chelvey and Brockley 84-92; V Heigham St Barn w St Bart *Nor* from 92. *The Vicarage, Russell Street, Norwich NR2 4QT* Tel (01603) 627859

JONES, David Noel. b 29. St Deiniol's Hawarden 69. **d** 71 **p** 72. C Llandegfan w Beaumaris and Llanfaes *Ban* 71-74; TV Amlwch, Rhosybol, Llandyfrydog etc 74-77; R Llanfair Mathafarn Eithaf w Llanbedrgoch 77-82; V Porthmadog 82-84; V Ynyscynhaearn w Penmorfa and Porthmadog 84-86; R Llanllyfni 86-95; RD Arfon 89-92; rtd 95; Lic to Offic *Ban* from 95. *3 Rhosfryn, Penrhosgarnedd, Bangor LL54 2DL* Tel (01248) 872765

JONES, David Ormond. b 46. Llan Dioc Tr Scheme 90. **d** 94 **p** 95. NSM Resolven w Tonna *Llan* from 94. *30 Henfaes Road, Tonna, Neath SA11 3EX* Tel (01639) 633642

JONES, David Raymond (Ray). b 34. Univ of Wales (Lamp) BA54 St Cath Coll Ox BA57 MA61. Wycliffe Hall Ox 58. **d** 58 **p** 59. C Ex St Dav *Ex* 58-60; C Bideford 60-63; Chapl Grenville Coll Bideford 63-66; Chapl RN 66-89; Hon Chapl to The Queen 84-89; Warden and Dir Ch Min of Healing Crowhurst 89-97; rtd 97; Perm to Offic *Chich* from 97. *Mill View, North Fields Lane, Westergate, Chichester, W Sussex PO20 6UH* Tel (01243) 543179

JONES, David Robert. b 37. MBIM83 Dur Univ BA59 QUB MA83. Cranmer Hall Dur DipTh69. **d** 69 **p** 70. C Middleton *Man* 69-72; CF 72-92; V Staindrop *Dur* from 92. *St Mary's Vicarage, 7 Beechside, Staindrop, Darlington, Co Durham DL2 3PE* Tel (01833) 60237

JONES, David Robert Deverell. b 50. Sarum & Wells Th Coll 72. **d** 75 **p** 78. C Altrincham St Geo *Ches* 75-76; C Clayton *Lich* 77-80; Carriacou 80-81; P-in-c Baschurch *Lich* 81-83; R Baschurch and Weston Lullingfield w Hordley 83-96; RD Ellesmere 85-95; P-in-c Criftins 94-96; P-in-c Dudleston 94-96; P-in-c Jersey St Luke *Win* from 96; P-in-c Jersey St Jas from 96. *The Vicarage, Longueville Farm, Longueville Road, St Saviour, Jersey JE2 7WG* Tel (01534) 851445

JONES, David Roy. b 47. CQSW76 Hull Univ BA74 Man Univ DipAdEd76 Bradf Univ MA85 Leic Univ DipIR91. Bernard Gilpin Soc Dur 69 N Ord Course 77. **d** 80 **p** 81. C New Bury *Man* 80-83; NSM Ringley w Prestolee 92-97; NSM Belmont from 97. *The Vicarage, High Street, Bemont, Bolton BL7 8AP* Tel (01204) 811221

JONES, David Sebastian. b 43. St Cath Coll Cam BA67 MA73. Linc Th Coll 66. **d** 68 **p** 69. C Baguley *Man* 68-71; C Bray and Braywood *Ox* 71-73; V S Ascot from 73; Chapl Heatherwood Hosp E Berks 81-94; Chapl Heatherwood and Wexham Park Hosp NHS Trust from 94; RD Bracknell *Ox* from 96. *The Vicarage, Vicarage Gardens, South Ascot, Berks SL5 9DX* Tel (01344) 22388 Fax as telephone

JONES, David Victor. b 37. Dur Univ BA59. Cranmer Hall Dur DipTh60. **d** 62 **p** 63. C Farnworth *Liv* 62-65; CF 65-68; Asst Master Hutton Gr Sch Preston from 68; Lic to Offic *Blackb* from 70. *10 Houghton Close, Penwortham, Preston PR1 9HT* Tel (01772) 745306

JONES, Capt Derek John. b 43. CA Tr Coll 64 Sarum & Wells Th Coll 82. **d** 83 **p** 84. CA from 66; C Fleur-de-Lis *Mon* 83-85; V Rhymney 85-93; R Ebbw Vale from 93; RD Blaenau Gwent from 94; Can St Woolos Cathl from 96. *The Rectory, Eureka Place, Ebbw Vale NP3 6PN* Tel (01495) 301723

JONES, Miss Diana. b 46. Qu Coll Birm 89. **d** 91 **p** 94. Par Dn Harnham *Sarum* 91-94; C 94-95; C Tidworth, Ludgershall and Faberstown from 95. *The Rectory, St Georges Road, Tidworth, Hants SP9 7EW* Tel (01980) 843889

JONES, Canon Dick Heath Remi. b 32. Jes Coll Cam BA56. Linc Th Coll 56. **d** 58 **p** 59. C Ipswich St Thos *St E* 58-61; C Putney St Mary *S'wark* 61-65; P-in-c Dawley Parva *Lich* 65-75; P-in-c Lawley 65-75; RD Wrockwardine 70-72; P-in-c Malins Lee 72-75; RD Telford 72-80; P-in-c Stirchley 74-75; TR Cen Telford 75-80; Preb Lich Cathl 76-80; TR Bournemouth St Pet w St Swithun, H Trin etc *Win* 80-96; RD Bournemouth 90-95; Hon Can Win Cathl 91-96; Chapl Bournemouth and Poole Coll of FE *Sarum* 94-96; rtd 96. *Maltings, Church Street, Fontmell Magna, Shaftesbury, Dorset SP7 0NY* Tel (01747) 812071

JONES, Donald (Don). b 50. BA BSc. St Jo Coll Nottm 79. **d** 82 **p** 83. C Hutton *Chelmsf* 82-86; C E Ham w Upton Park St Alb 86-88; TV 88-96; V Nuneaton St Nic *Cov* from 96. *61 Ambleside Way, Nuneaton, Warks CV11 6AU* Tel (01203) 346900

JONES, Canon Douglas Rawlinson. b 19. St Edm Hall Ox BA41 MA45. Lambeth DD Wycliffe Hall Ox 41. **d** 42 **p** 43. C Windmill Hill *Bris* 42-45; Lect Wycliffe Hall Ox 45-50; Chapl Wadh Coll Ox 45-50; Lect Th Dur Univ 51-64; Lect Th Dur Univ 51-64; Prof Div 64-85; Can Res Dur Cathl *Dur* 64-85; rtd 85; Lic to Offic *Edin* from 85. *Whitefriars, King's Road, Longniddry, E Lothian EH32 0NN* Tel (01875) 52149

JONES, Edgar John. Univ of Wales (Lamp) BA53. St Mich Coll Llan 53. **d** 55 **p** 56. C Holyhead w Rhoscolyn w Llanfair-yn-Neubwll *Ban* 55-61; R Bodedern and Llechcynfarwy 61-70; V Bodedern w Llechgynfarwy and Llechylched etc 70-73; Perm to Offic 73-96; C Llangefni w Tregaean and Llangristiolus etc from 96. *5 Glan Llyn, Llanfachraeth, Holyhead LL65 4UW* Tel (01407) 742322

JONES, Edgar Joseph Basil. b 14. Univ of Wales LLB37 St Jo Coll Ox BA40 MA43. Ripon Hall Ox 40. **d** 41 **p** 42. C Rhyl *St As* 41-49; V Llangower and Llanuwchllyn 49-53; V Altrincham St Jo *Ches* 53-61; V Sandiway 61-80; rtd 80; Perm to Offic *Ches* from 80; Perm to Offic *Ban* from 80. *Fron, 29 Church Walks, Llandudno LL30 2HL* Tel (01492) 876125

JONES, Edward. b 36. Dur Univ BA60. Ely Th Coll 60. **d** 62 **p** 63. C S Shields St Hilda w St Thos *Dur* 62-65; C Cleadon Park 65-68; V Hebburn St Cuth 68-79; R Winlaton from 79. *The Rectory, Winlaton, Tyne & Wear NE21 6PL* Tel 0191-414 3165

JONES, Edward Gareth. b 36. St D Coll Lamp BA59. **d** 61 **p** 62. C Llanbadarn Fawr *St D* 61-66; V Mydroilyn w Dihewyd 66-69; Missr to the Deaf *Mon* 69-70; V Tregaron *St D* 70-75; Chapl to the Deaf (Dios Llan and Mon) 75-83; V Llanilar w Rhostie and Llangwyryfon etc *St D* from 83; RD Llanbadarn Fawr 90-94. *The Vicarage, Llanilar, Aberystwyth SY23 4PD* Tel (01974) 241659

JONES, Canon Edward Graham. b 25. St Deiniol's Hawarden 62. **d** 64 **p** 65. C Bargoed w Brithdir *Llan* 64-70; V Caerau St Cynfelin 70-95; Hon Can Llan Cathl 93-95; rtd 95. *41 Tywith Bungalows, Nantyffryllon, Maesteg, Bridgend CF34 0TT* Tel (01656) 723988

JONES, Edward Harries. b 16. St D Coll Lamp BA38 Ely Th Coll 38. **d** 39 **p** 40. C Rhyl *St As* 39-52; V Ffynnongroyw 52-81; rtd 81. *16 Coed Pella Road, Colwyn Bay LL29 7BA* Tel (01492) 532997

JONES, Edward Wynne. b 45. OBE93. Univ of Wales (Abth) LLB71. St Mich Coll Llan 72. **d** 74 **p** 75. C Llandegfan w Beaumaris and Llanfaes *Ban* 74-76; V Aberffraw and Llangwyfan w Llangadwaladr 76-78; Chapl RN from 78. *Royal Naval Chaplaincy Service, Room 203, Victory Building, HM Naval Base, Portsmouth PO1 3LS* Tel (01705) 727903 Fax 727112

JONES, Mrs Elaine Joan. b 50. Oak Hill Th Coll. **d** 87 **p** 94. Par Dn Tottenham H Trin *Lon* 87-92; Par Dn Clay Hill St Jo and St Luke 92-94; C St Botolph Aldgate w H Trin Minories 94-96; V Hackney Wick St Mary of Eton w St Aug from 96. *St Mary's House, Eastway, London E9 5JA* Tel 0181-986 8159

JONES, Elidyr Price. b 26. St D Coll Lamp BA51. **d** 53 **p** 54. C Brecon w Battle *S & B* 53-59; Min Can Brecon Cathl 55-59; Chapl St Pet Sch York 59-65; Chapl Kelly Coll Tavistock 65-86; rtd 86; Perm to Offic *St D* from 86. *Bronderi, Pontrhydfendigaid, Ystrad Meurig SY25 6EN* Tel (01974) 831313

JONES, Mrs Elizabeth Mary. b 48. QUB BA69. N Ord Course 88. **d** 91 **p** 94. Par Dn Kippax w Allerton Bywater *Ripon* 91-94; C 94-95; R Swillington from 95. *The Rectory, Wakefield Road, Swillington, Leeds LS26 8DS* Tel 0113-286 0172

JONES, Elizabeth Somerset. b 49. St Jo Coll Nottm CertCS84. **d** 88 **p** 94. NSM Duns *Edin* from 88; NSM Selkirk from 89; Dioc Dir of Ords from 95. *Ellem Lodge, Duns, Berwickshire TD11 3SG* Tel (01361) 890316 Fax 890329 E-mail 100633.2065 @compuserve.com

JONES, Elwyn. b 09. Univ of Wales BA35. St Mich Coll Llan 35. **d** 36 **p** 37. C Towyn *Ban* 36-39; C Dwygyfylchi 39-46; V Llanfihangel-y-Pennant 46-53; V Penycae *St As* 53-61; V Rhosymedre 61-72; V Meliden and Gwaenysgor 72-77; rtd 77. *35 Llys Charles, Towyn, Abergele LL22 9NP* Tel (01745) 355967

JONES, Emile Conrad Modupe Kojo. Univ of Sierra Leone BA74 MA BD **d** 77 **p** 78. Sierra Leone 77-86; C Kissy St Patr 77-78; Freetown H Trin 78-81; Asst Chapl and Lect OT Studies Fourah Bay Coll 81-85; Chapl Heidelberg *Eur* 94-97; Miss Partner CMS from 97; C Holloway St Mary *Lon* from 97. *59 Bride Street, London N7 8RN* Tel 0171-607 2984

JONES, Emmanuel Thomas (Tom). b 19. S Dios Minl Tr Scheme. **d** 81 **p** 82. NSM Fareham H Trin *Portsm* 81-89; rtd 89; Perm to Offic *Portsm* from 89. *24 Maylings Farm Road, Fareham, Hants PO16 7QU* Tel (01329) 310137

JONES, Eric Alexander. b 19. TCD BA40 MA45 BD45. **d** 42 **p** 43. C Belfast St Matt *Conn* 42-45 and 48-51; C Belfast St Jas 45-47; C Belfast St Nic 47-48; I Larne and Inver 51-59; I Jordanstown 59-68; RD N Belfast 65-70; I Carnmoney 68-76; V Hensall *Sheff* 76-84; RD Snaith and Hatfield 79-84; rtd 84. *2 Wilson Crescent, Mount Merrion, Blackrock, Co Dublin, Irish Republic* Tel Dublin (1) 288 0136

JONES, Canon Eric Vernon. b 26. Ely Th Coll 57. **d** 59 **p** 60. C S Shore H Trin *Blackb* 59-63; V Preston St Matt 64-77; R Chorley St Laur 77-91; Hon Can Blackb Cathl 81-91; rtd 91; Perm to Offic *Blackb* from 91. *8 Glamis Driue, Chorley, Lancs PR7 1LX* Tel (01257) 230660

JONES, Eric Walter Nathaniel. b 26. Wells Th Coll. **d** 61 **p** 62. C Buckfastleigh w Dean Prior *Ex* 61-64; Warden Trin Youth Cen Ex 64-67; PV Ex Cathl *Ex* 64-67; Lic to Offic from 67. *Mar-y-*

Vela, 20A Wallaford Road, Buckfastleigh, Devon TQ11 0AR Tel (01364) 43260

JONES, Canon Eric Wilfred. b 22. Linc Coll Ox BA48 MA53. Cuddesdon Coll 48. **d** 50 **p** 51. C E Dulwich St Jo *S'wark* 50-56; V Cov St Pet *Cov* 56-65; Fiji 65-68; Solomon Is 69-74; V Binley *Cov* 74-82; Hon Can Cov Cathl 80-87; RD Cov E 80-82; V Hatton w Haseley and Rowington w Lowsonford 82-87; P-in-c Honiley 85-87; R Hatton w Haseley, Rowington w Lowsonford etc 87; rtd 87; Perm to Offic *Bradf* from 87. *13 Park Avenue, Skipton, N Yorkshire BD23 1PN* Tel (01756) 793302

JONES, Ernest Edward Stephen. b 39. Lon Univ BD76. St D Coll Lamp DipTh66. **d** 66 **p** 67. C N Meols *Liv* 66-69; C Kirkby 69-71; V Farnworth All SS *Man* 71-75; P-in-c Bempton *York* 75-78; R Rufford *Blackb* 78-84; V Cropredy w Gt Bourton and Wardington *Ox* 84-90; R York St Clem w St Mary Bishophill Senior *York* from 90; P-in-c York All SS N Street from 90. *St Clement's Rectory, 13 Nunthorpe Avenue, York YO2 1PF* Tel (01904) 624425

JONES, Evan Hopkins. b 38. St Mich Coll Llan 65. **d** 67 **p** 68. C Churston Ferrers w Goodrington *Ex* 67-70; C Tavistock and Gulworthy 70-73; R Ashprington 73-78; V Cornworthy 73-78; R S Hackney St Jo w Ch Ch *Lon* 78-92; AD Hackney 84-89; V Islington St Jas w St Pet from 92. *St James's Vicarage, Arlington Square, London N1 7DS* Tel 0171-226 4108

JONES, Evan Merfyn. b 40. **d** 97. NSM Ystradyfodwg *Llan* from 97. *71 Tyntyla Road, Llwynypia, Tonypandy CF40 2SR*

JONES, Canon Evan Trefor. b 32. Univ of Wales (Ban) BA54 HospCC82. Coll of Resurr Mirfield 54. **d** 56 **p** 57. C Ban St Mary *Ban* 56-62; V Llandinorwic 62-71; TV Llanbeblig w Caernarfon and Betws Garmon etc 71-84; Ed Dioc Link Magazine 79-89; R Llanfairfechan w Abergwyngregyn 84-97; Can Ban Cathl from 95; rtd 97. *Flat 19, Marlborough Place, Vaughan Street, Llandudno LL30 1AE*

JONES, Canon Evan Trevor. b 18. Univ of Wales BA40. St Mich Coll Llan 40. **d** 42 **p** 43. C Pontyberem *St D* 42-48; C Llanedy 48-56; V Nevern w Cilgwyn and Bayvil 56-69; V Nevern, Bayvil, Moelgrove and Monington 69-77; V Nevern and Bayvil w Eglwyswrw and Meline 77-83; RD Cemais and Sub-Aeron 80-87; V Nevern and Y Beifil w Eglwyswrw and Meline etc 83-87; Can St D Cathl 86-87; rtd 87. *Nyfer, 73 Pontwillem, Brecon LD3 9BS* Tel (01874) 622353

JONES, Frank Llewellyn. b 12. St Pet Hall Ox BA36 MA42. Wycliffe Hall Ox DipTh37. **d** 37 **p** 38. C Deal St Geo *Cant* 37-40; C Guildf St Sav *Guildf* 40-43; R Wick w Doynton *Bris* 43-45; Org Sec (Dios Bradf, Blackb and Carl) CMS 45-49; V Parr *Liv* 49-56; V Liv St Phil 56-69; V Widnes St Paul 69-77; rtd 77; Perm to Offic *Nor* from 77. *14 Stigands Gate, East Dereham, Norfolk NR19 2HF* Tel (01362) 693304

JONES, Canon Fred Leslie. b 12. Univ of Wales (Lamp) BA34. St Mich Coll Llan 34. **d** 35 **p** 36. C Llanfrechfa All SS *Mon* 35-37; C New Tredegar 37-44; R Bettws Newydd w Trostrey and Kemeys Commander 44-51; V Mynyddislwyn 51-67; V Newport St Mark 67-77; Can St Woolos Cathl 67-79; rtd 77. *9 Kingsgate, 7 The Avenue, Branksome Park, Poole, Dorset BH13 6AE*

JONES, Frederick. b 33. FRHistS76 Man Univ BA54 Selw Coll Cam PhD72 LSE MSc82. St Steph Ho Ox 56. **d** 58 **p** 59. C Belfield *Man* 58-59; C Westmr St Matt *Lon* 59-60; Hon C Cambridge St Mary Less *Ely* 71-72; Perm to Offic *Win* 72-74; Lic to Offic 74-89. *Casa Renate, Carrer del Pinsa 86, Port de Pollenca, Mallorca, Spain*

JONES, Frederick John. b 32. Wells Th Coll 57. **d** 60 **p** 61. C Tottington *Man* 60-63; C Horwich H Trin 63-65; R Heaton Norris All SS 65-76; R Heaton Norris Ch w All SS 76-77; V Castleton Moor 77-88; C Greenfield 88-93; rtd 93. *69 Manchester Road, Greenfield, Oldham OL3 7SE* Tel (01457) 873954

JONES, Frederick Morgan. b 19. Univ of Wales (Lamp) BA40 BD49. St Mich Coll Llan 42. **d** 42 **p** 43. C Llanelli St Paul *St D* 42-50; Org Sec (Wales) Ind Chr Fellowship 50-53; C-in-c Llwynhendy CD *St D* 52-56; C Llanelli 56-57; V Penrhyncoch and Elerch 57-61; R Llanbedrog and Penrhos *Ban* 61-74; R Llanbedrog w Llannor w Llanfihangel etc 74-84; C Llangefni w Tregaean and Llangristiolus etc 84-85; rtd 85; Perm to Offic *Ban* from 85. *15 Ponc-y-Fron, Llangefni LL77 7NY* Tel (01248) 722850

JONES, Gareth. b 35. St Aid Birkenhead 59. **d** 61 **p** 62. C Doncaster Ch Ch *Sheff* 61-65; Min Can Ripon Cathl *Ripon* 65-68; Chapl RAF 68-85; Hong Kong 85-89; R Spofforth w Kirk Deighton *Ripon* from 89. *The Rectory, Church Lane, Spofforth, Harrogate, N Yorkshire HG3 1AF* Tel (01937) 590251

JONES, Gareth Lewis. b 42. K Coll Lon BD64 AKC64. **d** 65 **p** 66. C Risca *Mon* 65-70; Perm to Offic *Win* 70-74; Perm to Offic *Newc* 74-75; Perm to Offic *Sarum* 75; C Pontesbury I and II *Heref* 75-77; P-in-c Presteigne w Discoed 77-79; TV Hemel Hempstead *St Alb* 79-86; R Longden and Annscroft w Pulverbatch *Heref* 86-93; TV Leominster from 93. *118 Buckfield Road, Leominster, Herefordshire HR6 8SQ* Tel (01568) 612124

JONES, Chan Gareth Lloyd. b 38. Univ of Wales BA61 Selw Coll Cam BA63 MA67 Yale Univ STM69 TCD BD70 Lon Univ PhD75. Episc Sem Austin Texas Hon DD90 Westcott Ho Cam 62. **d** 65 **p** 66. C Holyhead w Rhoscolyn *Ban* 65-68; USA 68-70; P-in-c Mert *Ox* 70-72; Tutor Ripon Hall Ox 72; Sen Tutor 73-75; Lect Ex Coll Ox 73-77; Tutor and Lib Ripon Coll Cuddesdon 75-77; Lect Th Univ of Wales (Ban) 77-89; Sen Lect from 89; Sub-Dean Faculty of Th 80-89; Dean from 89; Chan Ban Cathl *Ban* from 90; Select Preacher Ox Univ 89. *Nettuno, Mount Street, Menai Bridge LL59 5BW* Tel (01248) 712786

JONES, Glyn Evan. b 44. Lon Coll of Div ALCD67 LTh. **d** 67 **p** 68. C Gt Horton *Bradf* 67-70; SAMS 71-78; Argentina 71-78; V Idle H Trin *Bradf* 78-84; V Hyson Green *S'well* 84-87; V Nottingham St Steph 84-87; V Hyson Green St Paul w St Steph 87-89; V Hyson Green 89-91; V Basford w Hyson Green 91-92; V Worksop St Jo from 92; RD Worksop from 93. *St John's Vicarage, Shepherd's Avenue, Worksop, Notts S81 0JD* Tel (01909) 489868 Fax as telephone Mobile (0585) 816697

JONES, Preb Glyn Owen. b 16. St D Coll Lamp BA37 St Mich Coll Llan 38. **d** 39 **p** 40. C Wrexham *St As* 39-47; CF (EC) 44-47; C Connah's Quay *St As* 47-49; V Whixall *Lich* 49-53; V Hengoed 53-75; Preb Lich Cathl 73-81; V Baschurch 75-81; rtd 81; Perm to Offic *Lich* from 81. *6 Larkhill Road, Park Hall, Oswestry, Shropshire SY11 4AW* Tel (01691) 662739

JONES, Canon Glyndwr (Glyn). b 35. St Mich Coll Llan DipTh62. **d** 62 **p** 63. C Clydach *S & B* 62-64; C Llangyfelach 64-67; C Sketty 67-70; V Bryngwyn and Newchurch and Llanbedr etc 70-72; Miss to Seamen from 72; Aux Min Sec from 81; Asst Gen Sec 85-90; Gen Sec from 90; Hon Can Kobe Japan from 88; Chapl to The Queen from 90; V St Mich Paternoster Royal *Lon* from 91; Perm to Offic *Chelmsf* from 91. *5 The Close, Grays, Essex RM16 2XU, or St Michael Paternoster Royal, College Hill, London EC4R 2RL* Tel 0171-248 5202 or 248 7442 Fax 248 4761

JONES, Glynn. b 56. NE Ord Course 91. **d** 94 **p** 95. NSM Glendale Gp *Newc* 94-97; Dep Chapl HM Pris Leeds from 97. *HM Prison, Armley, Leeds LS12 2TJ* Tel 0113-263 6411 Fax 279 0151

JONES, Godfrey Caine. b 36. Dur Univ BA59 Lon Univ CertEd60 Birm Univ MEd71. St Deiniol's Hawarden 76. **d** 78 **p** 79. NSM Ruthin w Llanrhydd *St As* 78-81; C 83-84; Lic to Offic *Derby* 81-83; P-in-c Llanfwrog and Clocaenog and Gyffylliog *St As* 84-85; R 85-93; V Ruabon from 93; RD Llangollen from 93. *The Vicarage, Rark Street, Ruabon, Wrexham LL14 6LF* Tel (01978) 810176

JONES, Gordon Howlett. b 26. G&C Coll Cam BA47 MA51. Westcott Ho Cam 49. **d** 51 **p** 52. C Milton *Win* 51-54; Study Sec SCM 54-58; C St Helen Bishopsgate w St Martin Outwich *Lon* 54-58; V Claremont H Angels *Man* 58-63; R Northenden 63-79; P-in-c Hilmarton and Highway *Sarum* 79-83; V Bremhill w Foxham and Hilmarton 83-92; RD Calne 84-88; rtd 92. *63 New Park Street, Devizes, Wilts SN11 8SB* Tel (01380) 720950

JONES, Gordon Michael Campbell. b 33. St D Coll Lamp BA56 St Jo Coll Dur 56. **d** 58 **p** 59. C Maindee *Mon* 58-60; C Penhow, St Brides Netherwent w Llandavenny etc 60-63; V Magor w Redwick and Undy 63-68; Australia 68-71; R Kirkby Thore w Temple Sowerby *Carl* 72-73; R Kirkby Thore w Temple Sowerby and Newbiggin 73-79; P-in-c Accrington St Jas *Blackb* 79-81; P-in-c Accrington St Andr 81-83; Kuwait 83-91; R Swardeston w E Carleton, Intwood, Keswick etc *Nor* 91-96; Miss to Seamen from 96; Chapl Limassol St Barn from 96. *St Barnabas' Church, PO Box 1494, 3506 Limassol, Cyprus* Tel Limassol (5) 362713 Fax 747211

JONES, Graham Frederick. b 37. Leeds Univ BA60 GradIPM63. ALCD66. **d** 66 **p** 67. C Chesterfield H Trin *Derby* 66-70; C Leeds St Geo *Ripon* 70-73; P-in-c Newcastle St Geo *Lich* 73-83; New Zealand 83-87; P-in-c Westcote w Icomb and Bledington *Glouc* 89-94; rtd 94. *7 Keynsham Bank, Cheltenham, Glos GL52 6ER* Tel (01242) 238680

JONES, Griffith Bernard. b 20. Univ of Wales (Lamp) BA42. St Mich Coll Llan 42. **d** 44 **p** 45. C Ynyshir *Llan* 44-51; C Handsworth St Jas *Birm* 51-56; V Smethwick St Matt 56-60; V Swalcliffe w E Shutford *Ox* 60-64; Perm to Offic *Pet* 64-82; Perm to Offic *St Alb* 74-82; R Llanfallteg w Clunderwen and Castell Dwyran etc *St D* 82-88; rtd 88. *17 Heol Ceirios, Llandybie, Ammanford SA18 2SR* Tel (01269) 851060

JONES, Griffith Trevor. b 56. BSc MPS Univ of Wales BD. **d** 87 **p** 88. C Llandrygarn w Bodwrog and Heneglwys etc *Ban* 87-89; R Llangefni w Tregaean and Llangristiolus etc 89-91; TV Ban 91-94; Chapl Ysbyty Gwynedd 91-94; NSM Arfon Deanery from 94. *8 Carreg-y-Gad, Llanfairpwllgwyngyll LL61 5QF* Tel (01248) 713094

JONES, Griffith Walter Hywyn. b 24. St Mich Coll Llan 47. **d** 50 **p** 51. C Llanaber *Ban* 50-52; Chapl RAF 52-67; V Bettws y Coed *Ban* 67-69; V Bettws y Coed and Capel Curig 70-78; R Holyhead w Rhoscolyn w Llanfair-yn-Neubwll 78-87; Can and Preb Ban Cathl 78-90; RD Llifon and Talybolion 80-85; Spiritual Dir Cursillo Cymru 81-90; V Ynyscynhaearn w Penmorfa and Porthmadog *Ban* 87-90; rtd 90; Lic to Offic *Ban* from 90. *The Vicarage, Glyn Ceiriog, Llangollen LL20 7EH* Tel (01691) 718245

JONES, Canon Griffith William. b 31. St D Coll Lamp BA53 LTh55. **d** 55 **p** 56. C Llanycil w Bala and Frongoch *St As* 55-58; V Llandrillo 58-66; V Llandrillo and Llandderfel 66-96; RD Penllyn 83-96; Can Cursal St As Cathl from 87; rtd 96. *45 Yr Hafan, Bala LL23 7AU*

JONES, Gwyn Harris. b 19. Univ of Wales (Lamp) BA42. K Coll Lon 42. **d** 43 **p** 44. C Pembroke Dock *St D* 43-44; C Letterston

44-46; Uganda 46-53; C Llanelli *St D* 53-54; V Wolverhampton St Paul *Lich* 54-56; V Burton St Chad 56-79; V Shrewsbury St Geo 79-87; rtd 87; Perm to Offic *Lich* from 87. *18 Kenwood Gardens, Shrewsbury SY3 8AQ* Tel (01743) 351057

JONES, Gwynfryn Lloyd. b 35. Univ of Wales (Lamp) BA59. St Mich Coll Llan 59. **d** 61 **p** 62. C Rhyl w St Ann *St As* 61-64; C Prestatyn 64-67; V Whitford 67-75; V Llay 75-83; V Northop from 83. *The Vicarage, Northop, Mold CH7 6BS* Tel (01352) 840235

JONES, Gwynn Rees. b 32. St D Coll Lamp BA55. **d** 57 **p** 58. C Llangystennin *St As* 57-59; C Llanrhos 59-64; R Cefn 64-68; R Llanfyllin 68-80; V Bistre 80-89; R Flint from 89. *The Rectory, Allt Goch, Flint CH6 5NF* Tel (01352) 733274

JONES, Gwynne Ifor. b 10. Jes Coll Ox BA36 MA38. **d** 70 **p** 71. Hon C Llangefni w Tregaean and Llangristiolus etc *Ban* 70-81; rtd 81; Lic to Offic *Ban* from 81. *Bryn Horton, Greenfield Avenue, Llangefni LL77 7NU* Tel (01248) 723295

JONES, Canon Harold Desmond. b 22. Sarum Th Coll 52. **d** 55 **p** 56. C Bushey Heath *St Alb* 55-58; C Stevenage 58-64; V Thurleigh 64-80; V Milton Ernest 64-80; RD Sharnbrook 70-81; Hon Can St Alb 78-90; P-in-c Knotting w Souldrop 80-82; V Sharnbrook 80-82; R Sharnbrook and Knotting w Souldrop 82-90; P-in-c Felmersham 82-87; RD Sharnbrook 86-90; rtd 90. *24 Towns End Road, Sharnbrook, Bedford MK44 1HY* Tel (01234) 782524

JONES, Harold Philip. b 49. Leeds Univ BA72 St Jo Coll Dur BA84. Cranmer Hall Dur 82. **d** 85 **p** 86. C Scartho *Linc* 85-88; V Dodworth *Wakef* 88-91; C Penistone and Thurlstone 91-95; C Scunthorpe All SS *Linc* 95-96; TV Brumby from 96. *All Saints Vicarage, 159 Warwick Road, Scunthorpe, S Humberside DN16 1HH* Tel (01724) 869081

JONES, Harry Gordon. b 18. Bps' Coll Cheshunt 49. **d** 52 **p** 53. C Goldington *St Alb* 52-56; V Hurley *Ox* 64-70; V Salcombe *Ex* 70-79; P-in-c Abbotsham 79-83; rtd 83; Perm to Offic *Ex* 83-90. *Highfield Manor Nursing Home, Bayview Road, Northam, Bideford, Devon EX39 1AY* Tel (01237) 474563

JONES, Haydn Llewellyn. b 42. Edin Th Coll 63. **d** 65 **p** 66. C Towcester w Easton Neston *Pet* 65-68; C Northampton St Matt 68-72; CF 72-97; rtd 97; Perm to Offic *Roch* from 97. *11 Lady Park Road, Torquay TQ2 6UA* Tel (01803) 605890

✠**JONES, The Rt Revd Haydon Harold.** b 20. **d** 47 **p** 48 **c** 76. C Heaton St Barn *Bradf* 47-49; C Tormohun *Ex* 49-51; C Cov St Pet *Cov* 63-64; R Clutton *B & W* 64-75; R Clutton w Cameley 75-76; Bp Venezuela 76-86; rtd 86. *Apartado 17 467, 1015-A, Caracas, Venezuela*

JONES, Mrs Helen Alison. b 59. St Andr Univ BSc81. EMMTC 93. **d** 96 **p** 97. C Limber Magna w Brocklesby *Linc* 96-97; C Brocklesby Park from 97. *The Glebe House, Great Limber, Grimsby, S Humberside DN37 8JN* Tel (01469) 561082

JONES, Howell Arfon. b 31. St Deiniol's Hawarden. **d** 83 **p** 84. Hon C Northwich St Luke and H Trin *Ches* 83-84; C Bromborough 84-86; C Nantwich 86-87; V Church Minshull w Leighton and Minshull Vernon 87-89; rtd 89. *8 Marton Close, Hough, Crewe CW2 5RD* Tel (01270) 841389

JONES, Hugh Owen. b 14. Coates Hall Edin 45. **d** 47 **p** 48. C Dundee St Mary Magd *Bre* 47-50; P-in-c Airdrie *Glas* 50-52; CF 52-58; R Hope w Shelve *Heref* 58-63; V Bodenham w Hope-under-Dinmore 63-78; R Bodenham w Hope-under-Dinmore, Felton etc 78-80; rtd 80; Perm to Offic *Ban* from 96. *24 Tudor Court, Tudor Road, Llandudno LL30 1BU* Tel (01492) 872849

JONES, Humphrey Ingham. b 20. St Pet Coll Ox BA42 MA46. Cuddesdon Coll 42. **d** 43 **p** 44. C High Elswick St Phil *Newc* 43-47; C Haltwhistle 47-49; C Cullercoats St Geo 49-50; C-in-c Newc St Fran High Heaton CD 50-55; V Newc St Fran 55-61; V Monkseaton St Mary 61-67; Tutor and Registrar Richmond Fellowship 68-85; Hon C Bermondsey St Mary w St Olave, St Jo etc *S'wark* 73-78; Perm to Offic *Lon* 79-96; rtd 85. *Flat 1, Emden House, Barton Lane, Headington, Oxford OX3 9JU* Tel (01865) 308180

JONES, Ian. **d** 97. NSM Tycoch *S & B* from 97. *15 Lon Masarn, Sketty, Swansea SA2 9EL* Tel (01792) 298926

JONES, Ian Andrew. b 65. Lanc Univ BA87. St Mich Coll Llan DPS90. **d** 90 **p** 91. C Caerphilly *Llan* 90-96; Chapl RAF from 96. *Chaplaincy Services (RAF), HQ, Personnel and Training Command, RAF Innsworth, Gloucester GL3 1EZ* Tel (01452) 712612 ext 5164 Fax 510828

JONES, Idris. b 31. **d** 88 **p** 94. NSM Llanfihangel Ysgeifiog and Llanffinan etc *Ban* from 88. *Rhoslyn, Gaerwen LL60 6HR* Tel (01248) 421797

JONES, Idris. b 43. Univ of Wales (Lamp) BA64 Edin Univ LTh67. Edin Th Coll 64 NY Th Sem DMin86. **d** 67 **p** 68. C Stafford St Mary *Lich* 67-70; Prec St Paul's Cathl Dundee *Bre* 70-73; P-in-c Gosforth All SS *Newc* 73-80; R Montrose *Bre* 80-89; R Inverbervie 80-89; Can St Paul's Cathl Dundee 84-92; Chapl Angl Students Dundee Univ 89-92; P-in-c Invergowrie 89-92; R Ayr *Glas* from 92. *12 Barns Terrace, Ayr KA7 2DB* Tel (01292) 262482 Fax as telephone E-mail adia@mail.globalnet.co.uk

JONES, Canon Idwal. Univ of Wales BA36. St Mich Coll Llan 36. **d** 38 **p** 39. C Llanllyfni *Ban* 38-40; C Colwyn Bay *St As* 40-44; CF (EC) 44-47; CF 47-50; Hon CF 50; V Cuddington *Guildf* 50-63; V Leamington Priors All SS *Cov* 63-79; Hon Can Cov Cathl 72-79; rtd 80; Perm to Offic *Cov* from 80. *Leam Cottage, Main Street, Birdingbury, Rugby, Warks CV23 8EL* Tel (01926) 632896

JONES, Ioan Wynne. b 66. Univ of Wales (Ban) DipTh. St Mich Coll Llan. **d** 91 **p** 92. C Llanbeblig w Caernarfon and Betws Garmon etc *Ban* 91-95; P-in-c Glanogwen 95-97. *Address temp unknown*

JONES, Iorwerth Owen. b 24. St D Coll Lamp BA51. **d** 53 **p** 55. C Rhosymedre *St As* 53-57; C Prestatyn 57-59; R Nantglyn 59-63; C Adwick-le-Street *Sheff* 63-68; V Tickhill w Stainton 68-80; R Elworth and Warmingham *Ches* 80-89; rtd 89; Perm to Offic *Ches* from 89. *22 Kings Oak Court, Wrexham LL13 8QH* Tel (01978) 353779

JONES, Ivor Wyn. b 56. Trin Coll Bris DipHE94. **d** 94 **p** 95. C Gabalfa *Llan* 94-97; TV Daventry, Ashby St Ledgers, Braunston etc *Pet* from 97. *The Vicarage, 19 Church Street, Staverton, Daventry, Northants NN11 6JJ*

JONES, Jack Kenneth. b 23. DGA MIPD. EAMTC 83. **d** 84 **p** 85. C Fakenham w Alethorpe *Nor* 84-88; C Gt w Lt Snoring w Kettlestone and Pensthorpe 84-93; Perm to Offic from 93. *The Tunns, Great Snoring, Fakenham, Norfolk NR21 0HN* Tel (01328) 820441

✠**JONES, The Rt Revd James Stuart.** b 48. Ex Univ BA70 PGCE71. Wycliffe Hall Ox 81. **d** 82 **p** 83 **c** 94. C Clifton Ch Ch w Em *Bris* 82-90; V S Croydon Em *S'wark* 90-94; Suff Bp Hull *York* from 94. *Hullen House, Woodfield Lane, Hessle, N Humberside HU3 0ES* Tel (01482) 649019 or 863171 Fax 647449

JONES, Miss Jaqueline Dorian. b 58. K Coll Lon BD80 AKC80 MTh81. Westcott Ho Cam 84. **dss** 86 **d** 87 **p** 94. Epsom St Martin *Guildf* 86-87; C 87-91; Chapl Chelmsf Cathl *Chelmsf* 91-97; V Bridgemary *Portsm* from 97. *St Matthew's Vicarage, 7 Duncton Way, Gosport, Hants PO13 0FD* Tel (01329) 235288

JONES, Jeffrey Lloyd. b 66. Univ of Wales (Abth) BD87 PGCE90. Wycliffe Hall Ox DipMin95. **d** 97. C Lampeter Pont Steffan w Silian *St D* from 97. *Brongest, Heol Llanfair, Lampeter SA48 8JX*

JONES, Jennifer Margaret. b 49. Lon Univ CertEd. Cranmer Hall Dur 87. **d** 89 **p** 94. C Musselburgh *Edin* 89-93; D-in-c 93-94; P-in-c 94-95; R from 95; C Prestonpans 89-93; D-in-c 93-94; P-in-c 94-95; R from 95. *12 Windsor Gardens, Musselburgh, Midlothian EH21 7LP* Tel 0131-665 2925

JONES, John Bernard. b 49. Qu Coll Birm 86. **d** 88 **p** 89. C Mold *St As* 88-91; P-in-c Treuddyn and Nercwys and Eryrys 91-92; V Treuddyn w Nercwys from 92; RD Mold from 95. *The Vicarage, Treuddyn, Mold CH7 4LN* Tel (01352) 770919

JONES, John David Emrys. b 36. Univ of Wales (Abth). Trin Coll Carmarthen. **d** 96 **p** 97. NSM Llanfihangel Ystrad and Cilcennin w Trefilan etc *St D* from 96. *Dolfor, Ciliau Aeron, Lampeter SA48 8DE*

JONES, John Douglas Mathias. b 24. Clare Coll Cam BA49 MA51. Chich Th Coll 49. **d** 51 **p** 52. C Battersea Park All SS *S'wark* 51-54; C Caversham *Ox* 54-59; Chapl RAF 59-66; C Harrogate St Wilfrid *Ripon* 66-67; V Cross Stone *Wakef* 67-76; V Hepworth 76-89; Chapl Storthes Hall Hosp Wakef 81-89; rtd 89. *59 Luke Lane, Holmfirth, Huddersfield HD7 2SZ* Tel (01484) 681036

JONES, Canon John Francis Williams. b 26. St D Coll Lamp 48. **d** 52 **p** 53. C Glanadda *Ban* 52-55; V Porthmadog 55-57; V Llandrygarn w Bodwrog 57-62; V Llandrygarn and Bodwrog w Heneglwys 62-74; V Llandrygarn w Bodwrog and Heneglwys etc 74-96; RD Menai and Malltraeth from 75; Hon Can Ban Cathl 81-83; Can from 83; Preb from 90; rtd 96. *The Vicarage, Llandrygarn, Llanerchymedd LL65 3AZ* Tel (01407) 720234

JONES, John Harries. b 11. **d** 60 **p** 61. C Dwygyfylchi *Ban* 60-64; P-in-c Tudweiliog w Llandudwen, Edern and Ceidio 64-67; R Llanbedr y Cennin w Dolgarrog 67-71; R Llanbedr y Cennin w Dolgarrog, Trefriw etc 71-74; R Llanbeulan w Llanfaelog and Tal-y-Llyn 74-81; rtd 81; Lic to Offic *Ban* from 81. *1 Cerrig-y-Gad, Llanfairpwllgwyngyll, Gwynedd LL61 5QF* Tel (01248) 713756

JONES, John Hellyer. b 20. Birm Univ LDS43. Westcott Ho Cam 65. **d** 67 **p** 68. C Haddenham *Ely* 67-70; P-in-c Lolworth 70-79 and 81-85; P-in-c Fen Drayton w Conington 75-79; R Houghton w Wyton 79; rtd 85; Perm to Offic *Ely* from 85. *13 High Street, Haddenham, Ely, Cambs CB6 3XA* Tel (01353) 740530

JONES, John Howard. b 48. New Coll Ox BA69 MA73 K Coll Cam CertEd70. Sarum & Wells Th Coll 76. **d** 77 **p** 78. C Salisbury St Mark *Sarum* 77-78; C Morriston *S & B* 78-80; Dir of Ords 80-83; V Gowerton 80-83; V Swansea St Jas 85-89; Chapl Alleyn's Foundn Dulwich from 89. *53 Gilkes Crescent, London SE21 7BP* Tel 0181-299 4826

JONES, John Idris. b 16. St D Coll Lamp BA41. **d** 43 **p** 44. C Towyn *Ban* 43-45; C Llanaber 45-48; C Blaenau Ffestiniog 48-50; V Choral St As Cathl *St As* 50-54; V Kerry 54-66; V Llay 66-75; rtd 75. *7 Patricia Drive, Shrewsbury SY2 5YU*

JONES, John Morgan. b 17. Univ of Wales BA39. Ely Th Coll 39. **d** 40 **p** 41. C Chirk *St As* 40-43; C Colwyn Bay 43-50; C Brymbo 46-50; R Pontfadog 50-59; C Rawmarsh *Sheff* 59-60; R Adwick-le-Street 60-63; Asst Master Bentley Sch 63-65; Hatfield Sch 66-80; rtd 82; Perm to Offic *St As* from 82. *3 Heol Awel, Abergele LL22 7UQ* Tel (01745) 823515

JONES, John Samuel. b 11. Univ of Wales BA36. St D Coll Lamp 36. **d** 38 **p** 40. C Llawr-y-Betws *St As* 38-43; P-in-c Llanarmon

Dyffryn Ceiriog 43-57; R Pont Robert and Pont Dolanog 57-66; C Hoylake *Ches* 66-69; R Llwydiarth and Llanfihangel yng Nghwynfa *St As* 69-72; V Llanfair D C 72-79; rtd 79. *51 Snowden Drive, Ty Gwyn, Wrexham LL11 2YD* Tel (01978) 364914

JONES, The Ven John Samuel. b 16. Univ of Wales (Lamp) BA37 BD42. St Mich Coll Llan 38. **d** 39 **p** 40. C Llandysul *St D* 39-42; C Llandybie 42-49; V Llanllwni 49-86; RD Lampeter 64-68; RD Lampeter and Ultra-Aeron 68-82; Can St D Cathl 72-82; Chan 78-82; Adn Cardigan 82-86; rtd 86. *Brynheulwen, Bryn Road, Lampeter SA48 7EE* Tel (01570) 423278

JONES, John Trevor. b 14. St D Coll Lamp BA42. **d** 43 **p** 44. C Rhosddu *St As* 43-52; C Timperley *Ches* 52-53; V Barnton 53-60; V Poulton 60-81; rtd 81; Perm to Offic *Ches* from 82. *21 Sandy Lane, Wallasey, Merseyside L45 3JY* Tel 0151-639 4794

JONES, Joyce Rosemary. b 54. Newnham Coll Cam BA76 MA82 Solicitor 79. Nor Ord Course MA94. **d** 97. C Pontefract All SS *Wakef* from 97. *Stonehouse Farm, New Road, Old Snydale, Pontefract, W Yorkshire WF7 6EZ* Tel (01924) 894003

JONES, Judith Frances. *See* HUBBARD-JONES, Ms Judith Frances

JONES, The Very Revd Keith Brynmor. b 44. Selw Coll Cam BA65 MA69. Cuddesdon Coll 67. **d** 69 **p** 70. C Limpsfield and Titsey *S'wark* 69-72; Dean's V St Alb Abbey *St Alb* 72-76; P-in-c Boreham Wood St Mich 76-79; TV Borehamwood 79-82; V Ipswich St Mary le Tower w St Lawr and St Steph *St E* 82-84; V Ipswich St Mary-le-Tower 84-96; RD Ipswich 92-96; Hon Can St E Cathl 93-96; Dean Ex from 96. *The Deanery, Cathedral Close, Exeter EX1 1HT* Tel (01392) 52891 or 72697

JONES, Keith Bythell. b 35. ACP BA DipHE CertEd. Trin Coll Bris. **d** 83 **p** 84. C Bris St Mary Redcliffe w Temple etc *Bris* 83-86; C Filton 86-88; TV Yate New Town 88-95; rtd 95; Perm to Offic *Mon* from 97. *3 The Woodlands, St Arvans, Chepstow NP6 6EF* Tel (01291) 622377

JONES, Keith Ellison. b 47. Wycliffe Hall Ox 72. **d** 75 **p** 76. C Everton St Chrys *Liv* 75-79; C Buckhurst Hill *Chelmsf* 79-81; TV 81-88; TR Leek and Meerbrook *Lich* from 88. *The Vicarage, 6 Church Street, Leek, Staffs ST13 6AB* Tel (01538) 382515

JONES, Kenneth Elwyn. b 32. Nottm Univ BA54 Sheff Univ CertEd55 DipEd55. Linc Th Coll 80. **d** 82 **p** 83. C Rotherham *Sheff* 82-85; R Harthill and Thorpe Salvin 85-93; V Millhouses H Trin from 93; RD Ecclesall 94-97. *Holy Trinity Vicarage, 80 Millhouses Lane, Sheffield S7 2HB* Tel 0114-236 2838

JONES, Kenneth John. b 26. ALCD53. **d** 53 **p** 54. C Roxeth Ch Ch *Lon* 53-57; C Woking St Jo *Guildf* 57-59; R S Normanton *Derby* 59-65; V Creech St Michael *B & W* 65-91; rtd 91; Perm to Offic *B & W* from 91. *43 Wansbeck Green, Taunton, Somerset TA1 2RE* Tel (01823) 331149

JONES, Canon Kenneth William. b 14. TD61. St D Coll Lamp BA36 St Mich Coll Llan 36. **d** 38 **p** 39. C Oswestry H Trin *Lich* 38-40; CF (EC) 40-47; CF (TA) 49-65; CF (TA - R of O) from 65; R Birdsall w Langton *York* 47-53; R Trowell *S'well* 53-58; Bp's Chapl to Ind *Roch* 58-63; Dir Adult Relig Educn 60-63; Dir Chr Stewardship *Chich* 63-66; V Wilmington 63-66; R Folkington 63-66; V Hove St Jo 66-77; Hon Can Albuquerque from 69; R Buxted St Marg *Chich* 77-81; P-in-c High Hurstwood 78-81; rtd 82; Perm to Offic *Chich* from 82. *2/13 Grange Gardens, Eastbourne, E Sussex BN20 7DA* Tel (01323) 641096

JONES, Kingsley Charles. b 45. Birm Univ BSc66 Open Univ BA75. Sarum Th Coll 66. **d** 69 **p** 70. C Penwortham St Mary *Blackb* 69-72; C Broughton 72-74; P-in-c Gt Wollaston *Heref* 74-77; Chapl RAF 77-83; V Colwich w Gt Haywood *Lich* 83-94; V Winshill *Derby* from 94. *The Vicarage, Mill Hill Lane, Burton-on-Trent, Staffs DE15 0BB* Tel (01283) 545043

JONES, Leslie Joseph. b 23. Linc Th Coll. **d** 57 **p** 58. C Penhill *Bris* 57-60; C-in-c Lockleaze St Mary CD 60-62; V Bris Lockleaze St Mary Magd w St Fran 62-69; V Bedminster St Aldhelm 69-75; TV Bedminster 75-80; V Abbots Leigh w Leigh Woods 80-88; rtd 88; Perm to Offic *Bris* from 88. *4 Summerleaze, Bristol BS16 4ER* Tel 0117-965 3597

JONES, Leslie Lloyd. b 13. OBE. BA. **d** 39 **p** 41. C Pontlottyn *Llan* 39-42; CF 42-73; Chapl Gov of Gib 68-72; V Yarcombe w Membury *Ex* 73-83; V Yarcombe w Membury and Upottery 83-84; rtd 84; Perm to Offic *Ex* from 84. *Lower Farway, Chardstock, Axminster, Devon EX13 7DD* Tel (01460) 20397

JONES, Miss Mair. b 41. Cartrefle Coll of Educn TCert61 DSpEd73. St Mich Coll Llan DipPTh93. **d** 93 **p** 97. C Llangollen w Trevor and Llantysilio *St As* 93-97; V Llandrillo and Llandderfel from 97. *The Vicarage, Llandrillo, Corwen LL21 0SW* Tel (01490) 84224

JONES, Malcolm Francis. b 44. Open Univ BA88 Hull Univ MA96. Chich Th Coll 67. **d** 70 **p** 71. C Prestbury *Ches* 70-73; Chapl RAF 73-81; Perm to Offic *Ox* 75-77; R Heaton Reddish *Man* 81-84; CF (TA) 82-84; Chapl ACF 82-84; OStJ from 84; CF 84-93; Perm to Offic *Guildf* 88-93; TV Cleethorpes *Linc* 93-97; V Ryde H Trin *Portsm* from 97; V Swanmore St Mich and All Angels from 97. *The Vicarage, Wray Street, Swanmore, Ryde, Isle of Wight PO33 3ED* Tel (01983) 562984

JONES, Malcolm Stuart. b 41. Sheff Univ BA62. Linc Th Coll 64. **d** 66 **p** 67. C Monkseaton St Mary *Newc* 66-69; C Ponteland 69-72; Venezuela 73-75; C Hexham *Newc* 75-77; P-in-c Killingworth 77-92; V Delaval from 92. *The Vicarage, Seaton Sluice, Whitley Bay, Tyne & Wear NE26 4QW* Tel 0191-237 1982

JONES, Maldwyn Lloyd. b 17. St D Coll Lamp BA39. **d** 40 **p** 41. C Gorseinon *S & B* 40-43; Lic to Offic *Ox* 43-46; Brazil 46-50; Falkland Is 50-51; Chapl RN 52-68; USA 68-70; Chapl Lon Nautical Sch 71-72; Lic to Offic *Ban* 72-82; rtd 82; Perm to Offic *Ban* from 82. *Clover Cottage, Ledbury Road, Tirley, Gloucester GL19 4ES*

JONES, Ms Margaret. b 28. TCD BA53 Lon Univ BD66. **d** 87 **p** 94. NSM Stanstead Abbots *St Alb* 87-88; NSM Grappenhall *Ches* from 89. *19 Hill Top Road, Grappenhall, Warrington WA4 2ED* Tel (01925) 261992

JONES, Margaret Mary (Maggi). b 47. Oak Hill Th Coll 92. **d** 95 **p** 96. C Sydenham H Trin *S'wark* from 95. *56 Sydenham Park Road, London SE26 4DY* Tel 0181-473 3397

JONES, Mark Andrew. b 60. Southn Univ BSc82 Sussex Univ PGCE83. Oak Hill Th Coll BA91. **d** 91 **p** 92. C Wolverhampton St Luke *Lich* 91-96; I Inishmacsaint *Clogh* from 96. *The Rectory, Derrygonnelly, Enniskillen, Co Fermanagh BT93 6HW* Tel (01365) 641638 Fax as telephone

JONES, Mark Vincent. b 60. Univ of Wales (Cardiff) DipTh84. St Mich Coll Llan 81. **d** 84 **p** 85. C Whitchurch *Llan* 84-89; V Pwllgwaun w Llanddewi Rhondda 89-90; CF from 90. *MOD Chaplains (Army), Trenchard Lines, Upavon, Pewsey, Wilts SN9 6BE* Tel (01980) 615804 Fax 615800

JONES, Mrs Mary Nerissa Anna. b 41. Qu Mary Coll Lon BA86 FRSA91. Ripon Coll Cuddesdon 86. **d** 88 **p** 94. Par Dn St Botolph Aldgate w H Trin Minories *Lon* 88-93; P-in-c Wood End *Cov* 93-95; V from 95. *St Chad's Vicarage, Hillmorton Road, Coventry CV2 1FY* Tel (01203) 612909

JONES, Mary Valerie. b 37. Univ of Wales (Ban) BD84. St Deiniol's Hawarden 84. **d** 85 **p** 97. C Holyhead w Rhoscolyn w Llanfair-yn-Neubwll *Ban* 85-87; C Ynyscynhaearn w Penmorfa and Porthmadog 87-90; D-in-c Llansantffraid and Llanarmon and Pontfadog *St As* 90-97; V from 97. *The Vicarage, Glyn Ceiriog, Llangollen LL20 7EH* Tel (01691) 718245

JONES, Maurice Hughes Rowlestone. b 06. **d** 47 **p** 48. C Ox St Matt *Ox* 47-50; Area Sec CMS Dios Derby, Linc & S'well 50-55; Birm, Cov, Leic, Pet 55-62; Lic Preacher *Linc* 50-55; Lic Preacher *Cov* 55-62; Perm to Offic *Birm* 55-62; Perm to Offic *Leic* 55-62; Perm to Offic *Pet* 55-62; Area Sec CMS (Midl Region) 55-62; Chapl Mt Pleasant Hosp 62-75; V Southall H Trin *Lon* 62-75; rtd 75; Perm to Offic *Glouc* 75-90. *75 Medoc Close, Wymans Brook, Cheltenham, Glos GL50 4SP* Tel (01242) 230328

JONES, Maurice Maxwell Hughes. b 32. Lon Univ DipTh58 Univ of Wales (Cardiff) DPS72. Clifton Th Coll 56. **d** 60 **p** 61. C Islington St Andr w St Thos and St Matthias *Lon* 60-63; Argentina 63-71; C Whitchurch *Llan* 72-73; Area Sec (NW England) SAMS 73-77; V Haydock St Mark *Liv* 78-87; V Paddington Em Harrow Road *Lon* from 87. *Emmanuel Vicarage, 44C Fernoy Road, London W9 3NH* Tel 0181-969 0438

JONES, Melville Kenneth. b 40. Open Univ BA82. St D Coll Lamp DipTh66. **d** 66 **p** 67. C Aberdare St Jo *Llan* 66-71; C Caerau w Ely 71-72; Chapl Pontypridd Hosps 72-89; V Graig *Llan* 72-89; P-in-c Cilfynydd 86-89; V Llantwit Fadre from 89; Chapl E Glam Hosp from 89. *The Vicarage, Upper Church Village, Pontypridd CF38 1EP* Tel (01443) 202538

JONES, Michael. b 49. Leeds Univ BA71 Man Univ MA73. Qu Coll Birm 83. **d** 85 **p** 86. C Leigh St Mary *Man* 85-88; C-in-c Holts CD 88-93; V Hamer from 93. *All Saints' Vicarage, Foxholes Road, Rochdale, Lancs OL12 0EF* Tel (01706) 355591

JONES, Michael Denis Dyson. b 39. CCC Cam BA62 MA66 Lon Univ MSc73. Wycliffe Hall Ox DipTh75. **d** 76 **p** 77. C Plymouth St Andr w St Paul and St Geo *Ex* 76-81; V Devonport St Budeaux from 81; RD Plymouth Devonport 93-95. *The Vicarage, Agaton Road, Plymouth PL5 2EW* Tel (01752) 361019

JONES, Dr Michael Emlyn. b 47. MRCP75 Aber Univ MB, ChB72. **d** 79 **p** 79. Tanzania 79-82; Hon C Duns *Edin* from 83. *Ellem Lodge, Duns, Berwickshire TD11 3SG* Tel (01361) 890316 Fax 890329 E-mail 100633.2065@compuserve.com

JONES, Canon Neil Crawford. b 42. Univ of Wales BA63 K Coll Lon BD66 AKC66. **d** 67 **p** 68. C Holywell *St As* 67-69; C Rhyl w St Ann 69-73; C Christchurch *Win* 73-77; V Stanmore 77-84; RD Win 82-84; V Romsey from 84; RD Romsey 89-94; Hon Can Win Cathl from 93. *The Vicarage, Romsey, Hants SO51 8EP* Tel (01794) 513125

JONES, Canon Neville Charles. b 29. Selw Coll Cam BA52 MA57. Linc Th Coll 52. **d** 54 **p** 55. C Grangetown *Dur* 54-58; C Norton St Mary 58-60; V Greenside 60-69; V Stockton H Trin 69-73; TR Cen Stockton 73-76; P-in-c Elton 75-76; R Longnewton 76; R Longnewton w Elton 76-83; P-in-c 87-93; RD Stockton 77-83; Hon Can Dur Cathl 81-93; Chapl Camerton Hosp Hartlepool 83-85; V Heighington *Dur* 83; Bp's Dom Chapl 85-93; Hon C Norton St Mary 85-87; rtd 93; Perm to Offic *Pet* from 93. *10 Angus Court, Peterborough PE3 6BE* Tel (01733) 69830

JONES, Canon Neville George. b 36. Univ of Wales (Ban) BA59. St Mich Coll Llan 59. **d** 61 **p** 62. C Broughton *St As* 61-65; C Newcastle *Llan* 65-68; V Laleston w Tythegston and Merthyr Mawr 68-84; V Llanishen and Lisvane 84-93; V Llanishen from

93; Can Llan Cathl from 96. *The Vicarage, 2 The Rise, Llanishen, Cardiff CF4 5RA* Tel (01222) 752545

JONES, Nicholas Godwin. b 58. St Jo Coll Cam BA81 MA84 Hughes Hall Cam PGCE90. Ridley Hall Cam CTM93. **d** 93 **p** 94. C Cambridge H Trin *Ely* from 93. *42 Pretoria Road, Cambridge CB4 1HE* Tel (01223) 311144

JONES, Nicholas Newman. b 51. K Coll Lon 71 St Aug Coll Cant 74. **d** 75 **p** 76. C Derringham Bank *York* 75-78; C Stokesley 78-81; P-in-c Kirby Misperton 81-85; R Normanby w Edston and Salton 83-85; R Kirby Misperton w Normanby, Edston and Salton 85-87; V Eskdaleside w Ugglebarnby and Sneaton from 87; RD Whitby from 92. *The Vicarage, 22 Eskdaleside, Sleights, Whitby, N Yorkshire YO22 5EP* Tel (01947) 810349

JONES, Nicholas Peter. b 55. St Mich Coll Llan DipTh82. **d** 82 **p** 83. C St Andrew's Major and Michaelston-le-Pit *Llan* 82-84; C Aberdare St Jo 84-88; Youth Chapl 85-89; V Abercynon 88-96; R Llanilid w Pencoed from 96. *The Rectory, 60 Coychurch Road, Pencoed, Bridgend CF35 5NA* Tel (01656) 860337

JONES, Nigel Ivor. b 54. Birm Univ CPS89. WMMTC 91. **d** 94 **p** 95. C Shirley *Birm* from 94. *20 Clifton Crescent, Solihull, W Midlands B91 3LG* Tel 0121-705 6586

✠**JONES, The Rt Revd Noel Debroy.** b 32. CB86. Univ of Wales (Lamp) BA53. Wells Th Coll 53. **d** 55 **p** 56 **c** 89. C Tredegar St Jas *Mon* 55-57; C Newport St Mark 57-60; Nigeria 60-62; Chapl RN 62-84; Chapl of the Fleet and Adn for the RN 84-89; QHC 83-89; Hon Can Gib Cathl *Eur* 86-89; Bp S & M from 89. *The Bishop's House, Quarterbridge Road, Douglas, Isle of Man IM2 3RF* Tel (01624) 622108 Fax 672890

JONES, Norman. b 35. St Deiniol's Hawarden 83. **d** 85 **p** 86. C Brecon St Mary and Battle w Llanddew *S & B* 85-91; Min Can Brecon Cathl 85-91; V Brynmawr from 91. *The Vicarage, Dumfries Place, Brynmawr NP3 2RA* Tel (01495) 312297

JONES, Norman. b 50. Oak Hill Th Coll BA83. **d** 83 **p** 84. C Ulverston St Mary w H Trin *Carl* 83-87; Hong Kong 88-92; P-in-c Patricroft *Man* 95-96; TR Eccles 92-96; TR Eccles from 96; AD Eccles from 95. *The Rectory, 12B Westminster Road, Eccles, Manchester M30 9EB* Tel 0161-789 1034 Fax 789 1034

JONES, Mrs Patricia Ann. b 43. LNSM course 96. **d** 97. NSM Bincombe w Broadwey, Upwey and Buckland Ripers *Sarum* from 97. *23 Camedown Close, Weymouth, Dorset DT3 5RB* Tel (01305) 813056

JONES, Mrs Patricia Anne. b 55. NNEB75 CSS81. Oak Hill Th Coll 92. **d** 95. NSM Mill Hill Jo Keble Ch *Lon* from 95. *The Flat, St Paul's School, The Ridgeway, London NW7 1QU* Tel 0181-201 1583

JONES, Patrick Geoffrey Dickson. b 28. Ch Ch Ox MA55. St Deiniol's Hawarden 79. **d** 82 **p** 83. Hon C Sandbach *Ches* 82-84; P-in-c Braemar *Ab* 84-94; R Aboyne 84-94; R Ballater 84-94; rtd 94. *12 Bain Terrace, Mintlaw, Peterhead, Aberdeenshire AB42 8EW* Tel (01771) 622553

JONES, Patrick George. b 42. Lich Th Coll 69. **d** 72 **p** 73. C Chesterton St Geo *Ely* 72-75; P-in-c Waterbeach 75-78; P-in-c Landbeach 76-78; R Charlton-in-Dover *Cant* 78-90; Cautley Trust from 90. *Cautley House, 95 Seabrook Road, Seabrook, Hythe, Kent CT21 5QV* Tel (01303) 230762

JONES, Paul Harwood. b 20. Qu Coll Birm 51. **d** 53 **p** 54. C Queensbury All SS *Lon* 53-57; C Enfield Jes Chpl 57-59; V Upper Holloway St Steph 59-68; V White Notley w Faulkbourne *Chelmsf* 68-81; P-in-c Cressing 75-80; V Finchingfield and Cornish Hall End 81-88; RD Braintree 83-87; rtd 88; Perm to Offic *Chelmsf* from 88. *83 Kenworthy Road, Braintree, Essex CM7 7JJ* Tel (01376) 343047

JONES, Paul Terence. b 35. Dur Univ BA60. Qu Coll Birm 60. **d** 62 **p** 63. C Rainford *Liv* 62-65; C Skelmersdale St Paul 65-68; V Huyton Quarry 68-78; V Widnes St Ambrose from 78. *St Ambrose Vicarage, Hargreaves Court, Widnes, Cheshire WA8 0QA* Tel 0151-420 8044

JONES, Ms Penelope Howson. b 58. LGSM79 Girton Coll Cam BA80 MA83. Ripon Coll Cuddesdon BA85 MA88. **dss** 86 **d** 87 **p** 94. Hackney *Lon* 86-87; Par Dn 87-88; Tutor Ripon Coll Cuddesdon 88-90; Par Dn Cuddesdon *Ox* 88-90; Perm to Offic *Dur* 92-93; Dir of Practical Th NE Ord Course *Newc* from 93; Hon C Eastgate w Rookhope *Dur* from 93; Hon C Stanhope w Frosterley from 93. *12 Kirk Rise, Frosterley, Bishop Auckland, Co Durham DL13 2SF* Tel (01388) 526580

JONES, Peter Anthony Watson. b 53. AKC75. Sarum & Wells Th Coll 76. **d** 77 **p** 78. C Hessle *York* 77-81; C Stainton-in-Cleveland 81-82; P-in-c Weston Mill *Ex* 82-84; Chapl Plymouth Poly 82-90; V Gt Ayton w Easby and Newton in Cleveland *York* 90-92; C Devonport St Aubyn *Ex* from 92. *12 Cumberland Street, Plymouth PL1 4DX* Tel (01752) 509605

JONES (formerly TITCOMBE), Peter Charles. b 57. St Mich Coll Llan DipTh83. **d** 83 **p** 84. C Pontnewynydd *Mon* 83-85; C Bassaleg 85-86; C Cwmbran 87; TV 87-94; V Blaenavon w Capel Newydd from 94. *The Vicarage, Llanover Road, Blaenavon NP4 9BE* Tel (01495) 790292

JONES, Peter David. b 48. S'wark Ord Course 89. **d** 92 **p** 93. Hon C Caterham *S'wark* from 92. *79 Beverley Road, Whyteleafe, Surrey CR3 0DG* Tel 0181-668 6398

JONES, Peter Gordon Lewis. b 31. **d** 82 **p** 83. NSM Llangynwyd w Maesteg *Llan* 82-84; Deputation Appeals Org (S & M Glam) CECS 84-87; Appeals Manager (Wales and Glouc) Children's Soc 87-97; NSM Pyle w Kenfig *Llan* 89-97; rtd 97. *18 Fulmar Road, Porthcawl CF36 3UL* Tel (01656) 715455

JONES, Peter Robin. b 42. BA CertEd. EMMTC 79. **d** 82 **p** 83. NSM Doveridge *Derby* from 82; Perm to Offic *Lich* from 93. *4 Cross Road, Uttoxeter, Staffs ST14 7BN* Tel (01889) 565123

JONES, Peter Russell. b 48. St Jo Coll Cam BA71 MA75 Univ of Wales MTh86. Wycliffe Hall Ox DipTh72. **d** 75 **p** 76. C Northampton All SS w St Kath *Pet* 75-79; C Ban Cathl Par *Ban* 79-81; Min Can Ban Cathl 79-81; R Pentraeth and Llanddyfnan 81-85; V Conwy w Gyffin from 85; Lect Univ of Wales (Ban) from 89; RD Arllechwedd *Ban* from 96. *The Vicarage, Rose Hill Street, Conwy LL32 8LD* Tel (01492) 593402

JONES, Canon Philip Bryan. b 34. St Mich Coll Llan DipTh61. **d** 61 **p** 62. C Hope *St As* 61-64; C Llanrhos 64-67; V Kerry 67-74; R Newtown w Llanllwchaiarn w Aberhafesp from 74; RD Cedewain 76-97; Sec Ch in Wales Prov Evang Cttee 80-83; Hon Can St As Cathl *St As* 86-93; Can from 93. *The Rectory, Old Kerry Road, Newtown SY16 1BP* Tel (01686) 625795

JONES, Philip Hugh. b 51. Solicitor. Chich Th Coll 92. **d** 94 **p** 95. C Horsham *Chich* 94-97; V Southwater from 97. *The Vicarage, Southwater, Horsham, W Sussex RH13 7BT* Tel (01403) 730229

JONES, Phillip Edmund. b 56. Man Poly BA78 Fitzw Coll Cam BA84 MA88. Westcott Ho Cam 82. **d** 85 **p** 86. C Stafford St Jo and Tixall w Ingestre *Lich* 85-89; TV Redditch, The Ridge *Worc* 89-95; Ind Chapl from 89; TV Worc SE from 95. *The Vicarage, Walkers Lane, Whittington, Worcs WR5 2RE* Tel (01905) 355989

JONES, Phillip Thomas Henry. b 34. Qu Coll Birm 58. **d** 60 **p** 61. C Castle Bromwich SS Mary and Marg *Birm* 60-67; C Reading St Mary V *Ox* 67-72; C-in-c Reading All SS CD 72-75; V Reading All SS 75-95; Perm to Offic *Portsm* from 97; Hon Chapl Portsm Cathl from 97. *13 Oyster Street, Portsmouth PO1 2HZ* Tel (01705) 756676

JONES, Raymond Blake. b 29. K Coll Lon BD54 AKC54. **d** 55 **p** 56. C Fenny Stratford *Ox* 55-58; C Lt Brickhill 55-58; C Wooburn 58-60; C Southbourne St Kath *Win* 60-66; R Braiseworth *St E* 66-76; V Eye 66-76; P-in-c Yaxley 74-77; RD Hartismere 76-77; V Eye w Braiseworth and Yaxley 77; R Ufford 77-82; V Southbourne St Kath *Win* 82-95; rtd 95. *4 Russell Drive, Riverslea, Christchurch, Dorset BH23 3PA* Tel (01202) 473205

JONES, Raymond Powell. b 21. JP63. St D Dioc Tr Course. **d** 82 **p** 83. NSM Betws w Ammanford *St D* 82-86; rtd 86. *227 Pen-y-Banc Road, Ammanford SA18 3QP* Tel (01269) 592069

JONES, Raymond Sydney. b 35. MSERT71. Glouc Th Course 85. **d** 87 **p** 88. NSM Madley *Heref* 87-89; NSM Preston-on-Wye w Blakemere 87-89; NSM Madley w Tyberton, Preston-on-Wye and Blakemere from 89. *Birch Hill, Clehonger, Hereford HR2 9SY* Tel (01981) 250452

JONES, Raymond Trevor (<u>Ray</u>). b 35. Linc Th Coll. **d** 82 **p** 83. C Rushmere *St E* 82-85; Bp's Dom Chapl 85-86; CF 86-91; TV Ridgeway *Sarum* 91-97; Relig Programmes Producer BBC Wiltshire Sound 91-97; Chapl Fuengirola St Andr *Eur* from 97. *Calle Paulino Uzcudun 16, 29640 Torreblanca, Fuengirola, Malaga* Tel Malaga (52) 47 21 40 Fax as telephone

JONES, Richard. b 23. St Deiniol's Hawarden 74. **d** 76 **p** 77. NSM Welshpool w Castle Caereinion *St As* 76-94; rtd 94. *Sherwood, Rhos Common, Llandrinio, Llanymynech SY22 6RN* Tel (01691) 830534

JONES, Canon Richard. b 28. St D Coll Lamp 54. **d** 56 **p** 57. C Llanaber w Caerdeon *Ban* 56-61; R Aberffraw w Llangwyfan 61-74; CF (TA) 61-71; V Llanfairisgaer *Ban* 74-79; Bp's Private Chapl 78-82; V Llanfair-is-gaer and Llanddeiniolen 79-89; RD Arfon 82-89; Can Ban Cathl from 86; V Llandegfan w Llandysilio 89-96; Chapl ATC from 90; rtd 96. *Bryn Hedydd, Cildwrn Road, Llangefni, Anglesey LL77 7NN* Tel (01248) 750546

JONES, Canon Richard. b 36. Ely Th Coll 61. **d** 64 **p** 65. C Blyth St Mary *Newc* 64-67; C Wallsend St Pet 67-69; R Paisley H Trin *Glas* 69-78; R Monifieth *Bre* from 78; Hon Can St Paul's Cathl Dundee from 93. *The Rectory, 29 Princes Street, Monifieth, Angus DD5 4AW* Tel (01382) 532266

JONES, Richard Eifion. b 23. St D Dioc Tr Course 80 St Mich Coll Llan 84. **d** 82 **p** 83. NSM Llangennech and Hendy *St D* 82-84; C Llanbadarn Fawr w Capel Bangor and Goginan 84-86; V Llangadog and Gwynfe w Llanddeusant 86-91; rtd 91. *Ynysdawel, Church Street, Llangadog SA19 9AA* Tel (01550) 777061

JONES, Richard Keith. b 40. Jes Coll Ox BA63. Wycliffe Hall Ox 61. **d** 63 **p** 64. C Blaenavon w Capel Newydd *Mon* 63-67; C Mynyddislwyn 67-71; C Pontypool 71; V Abercarn 71-81; V Penhow, St Brides Netherwent w Llandavenny etc 81-88. *14 Marine Drive, Burnham-on-Sea, Somerset TA8 1QJ*

JONES, Richard Martin Hugh. b 31. St D Coll Lamp 56. **d** 58 **p** 59. C Swansea St Pet *S & B* 58-63; R Llangynllo and Bleddfa 63-70; R Llandefalle w Llyswen, Boughrood etc 70-83; RD Hay 81-85 and 87-90; R Llandefalle and Llyswen w Boughrood etc 83-96; rtd 96. *Nant yr Hafod, Brook Street, Hay-on-Wye, Hereford HR3 5BQ* Tel (01497) 820158

JONES, Robert. b 26. Lon Univ BA52 K Coll Lon BD65 Hull Univ MA82. St Deiniol's Hawarden 79. **d** 80 **p** 81. NSM Doncaster St Mary *Sheff* 80-81; C Halifax St Jo Bapt *Wakef* 81-82; C Halifax 83; P-in-c Dewsbury St Mark 83-84; TV Dewsbury 84-92; rtd 92; NSM Halifax St Jo *Wakef* 92-95; Perm to Offic from 95. *4 Lidget Street, Huddersfield HD3 3JB* Tel (01484) 316276

JONES, Robert. b 40. **d** 80 **p** 81. C St Laurence in the Isle of Thanet *Cant* 80-83. *76 Southwood Gardens, Ramsgate, Kent CT11 0BQ*

JONES, Robert (Bob). b 45. Culham Coll Ox CertEd67. St Steph Ho Ox. **d** 85 **p** 86. C High Wycombe *Ox* 85-89; V Beckenham St Barn *Roch* 89-90; C Swanley St Mary 90-91; C Edenbridge from 91; C Crockham Hill H Trin from 91. *The Vicarage, Crockham Hill, Edenbridge, Kent TN8 6RL* Tel (01732) 866515

JONES, Robert Bernard. b 24. St Jo Coll Dur BA48. Wycliffe Hall Ox. **d** 50 **p** 51. C Ecclesall *Sheff* 50-53; C Apsley End *St Alb* 53-58; C Christchurch *Win* 58-61; V Ringwood 61-75; R N Stoneham 75-89; rtd 89. *4 Rowden Close, West Wellow, Romsey, Hants SO51 6RF* Tel (01794) 22966

JONES, Robert Cecil. b 32. Univ of Wales (Abth) BA54 DipEd55. Qu Coll Birm 84. **d** 86 **p** 87. C Llanbadarn Fawr w Capel Bangor and Goginan *St D* 86-88; R Llanllwchaearn and Llanina 88-91; R Newport w Cilgwyn and Dinas w Llanllawer from 91. *The Rectory, Long Street, Newport SA42 0TY* Tel (01239) 820380

JONES, Canon Robert Dwyfor. b 20. Univ of Wales (Ban) BA41. St Mich Coll Llan 46. **d** 47 **p** 48. C Llandudno *Ban* 47-55; R Cemmaes 55-58; R Llanenddwyn 58-65; V Glanogwen 65-69; V Conwy w Gyffin 69-85; Can and Treas Ban Cathl 76-85; rtd 85; Perm to Offic *St As* from 85; Perm to Offic *Ban* from 85. *Ormlea, 12 Hywel Place, Llandudno, Gwynedd LL30 1EF* Tel (01492) 874390

JONES, Robert George. b 42. Univ of Wales (Lamp) 87. St Mich Coll Llan DipMin93. **d** 95 **p** 96. NSM Treboeth *S & B* from 95. *Green Gables, 42 Heol Fach, Treboeth, Swansea SA5 9DE* Tel (01792) 774229

JONES, Robert George. b 55. Hatf Coll Dur BA77 Ox Univ BA79 MA87. Ripon Coll Cuddesdon 77. **d** 80 **p** 81. C Foley Park *Worc* 80-84; V Dudley St Fran 84-92; TR Worc St Barn w Ch Ch from 92. *St Barnabas' Vicarage, Church Road, Worcester WR3 8NX* Tel (01905) 23785

JONES, Robert Ivan. b 33. CertEd CertRK. Westcott Ho Cam 85. **d** 85 **p** 86. NSM Wymondham *Nor* 85-86; C Epsom St Martin *Guildf* 87-89; V Hutton Cranswick w Skerne, Watton and Beswick *York* 89-94; RD Harthill 92-97; V Wetwang and Garton-on-the-Wolds w Kirkburn from 94. *The Vicarage, Wetwang, Driffield, N Humberside YO25 9XT* Tel (01377) 236410

JONES, Robert William. b 55. **d** 79 **p** 80. C Seapatrick *D & D* 79; C Bangor Abbey 81-83; I Drumgath w Drumgooland and Clonduff 83-89; I Finaghy *Conn* 89-93; I Kilwaughter w Cairncastle and Craigy Hill from 94. *Cairncastle Rectory, 15 Cairncastle Road, Ballygally, Larne, Co Antrim BT40 2RB* Tel (01574) 583220

JONES, Robert William Aplin. b 32. Univ of Wales (Cardiff) BSc52 MSc65 FRSC71 CChem72. St Deiniol's Hawarden 72. **d** 73 **p** 74. C Bassaleg *Mon* 73-77; V Nantyglo 77-82; Perm to Offic 82-86; R Colwinston w Llandow and Llysworney *Llan* 86-95; rtd 95. *Swn-y-Don, Parrog, Newport SA42 0RX* Tel (01239) 820297

JONES, Canon Robin Lang Wilson. b 07. Worc Coll Ox BA28 MA33. St Mich Coll Llan 41. **d** 41 **p** 42. C Monmouth *Mon* 41-44; Canada 44-48; C Newport St Woolos *Mon* 48-49; Chapl St Woolos Hosp Newport 48-49; C Risca *Mon* 49-50; R Caldbeck w Castle Sowerby *Carl* 50-59; RD Wigton 55-59; R Warcop w Musgrave 59-72; RD Appleby and Kirkby Stephen 60-66; Hon Can Carl Cathl 64-72; rtd 72; Perm to Offic *Carl* 77-93. *Abbeyfield, The Gables, Kirkby Lonsdale, Carnforth, Lancs LA6 2BD* Tel (015242) 71576

JONES, Roderick (Rod). b 48. Leeds Univ BA70 PGCE72. Oak Hill Th Coll 74 Westmr Th Sem (USA) 73. **d** 76 **p** 77. C Beckenham Ch Ch *Roch* 76-80; C Uphill *B & W* 80-84; R Springfield All SS *Chelmsf* 84-90; Selection Sec ABM 91-96; V Horsell *Guildf* from 96. *Heathlands, Castle Road, Woking, Surrey GU21 4EU* Tel (01483) 727443

JONES, Roger. b 49. St Mich Coll Llan 84. **d** 86 **p** 87. C Llangynwyd w Maesteg *Llan* 86-90; V Wiston w Walton E and Clarbeston *St D* from 90. *The Vicarage, Wiston, Haverfordwest SA62 4PL* Tel (01437) 731266

JONES, Ronald Thomas. b 19. Aristotelian Soc 64 Univ of Wales BA41. Westcott Ho Cam 41. **d** 43 **p** 44. C Betws w Ammanford *St D* 43-48; Chapl Oakham Sch 48-51; Perm to Offic *Pet* 48-51; Chapl Ipswich Sch 51-60; Perm to Offic *St E* 51-60; Sen Lect Keswick Hall Coll of Educn 60-64; Prin Lect 64-80; Hd Relig Studies 64-80; Lic to Offic *Nor* 60-84; rtd 84. *Bissom Bungalow, Penryn, Cornwall TR10 9LQ* Tel (01326) 372205

JONES, Russell Frederick. b 55. Edin Univ BD84. Edin Th Coll 81. **d** 84 **p** 85. C Croxteth *Liv* 84-87; V Edge Hill St Dunstan from 87. *St Dunstan's Vicarage, Earle Road, Liverpool L7 6HD* Tel 0151-733 4385

JONES, Samuel. b 44. CITC. **d** 86 **p** 87. C Agherton *Conn* 86-88; I Connor w Antrim St Patr 88-97; I Whitehead w Islandmagee from 97. *St Patrick's Rectory, 74 Cable Road, Whitehead, Carrickfergus, Co Antrim BT38 9SJ* Tel (01960) 373300

JONES, Mrs Sharon Ann. b 60. Liv Univ BA82. Cranmer Hall Dur 83. **dss** 85 **d** 87 **p** 94. Rubery *Birm* 85-87; Par Dn 87-89; C-in-c Chelmsley Wood St Aug CD 89-92; Perm to Offic *Newc* 92-93; Chapl HM Pris Acklington from 93. *HM Prison Acklington, Morpeth, Northd NE65 9XF* Tel (01670) 760411 Fax 761362

JONES, Miss Sian Eira. b 63. Univ of Wales (Lamp) BA84 Southn Univ BTh88. Sarum & Wells Th Coll 85. **d** 88 **p** 97. C Llan-llwch w Llangain and Llangynog *St D* 88-93; D-in-c Llansteffan and Llan-y-bri etc 93-97; V from 97. *The Vicarage, Llansteffan, Carmarthen SA33 5JT* Tel (01267) 241807

JONES, Sian Hilary. *See* WIGHT, Mrs Sian Hilary

JONES, Simon. b 63. Trin Coll Bris BA89. **d** 89 **p** 90. C Hildenborough *Roch* 89-93; C Crofton *Portsm* 93-96; C Northwood Em *Lon* from 96. *4 Church Close, Northwood, Middx HA6 1SG* Tel (01923) 835255

JONES, Stephen Frederick. b 43. Wells Th Coll 68. **d** 71 **p** 72. C-in-c Stockton St Jas CD *Dur* 71-74; Chapl Asst St Ebba's Hosp Epsom 74-79; Chapl Warley Hosp Brentwood 79-87; R Leigh St Clem *Chelmsf* from 87. *St Clement's Rectory, 80 Leigh Hill, Leigh-on-Sea, Essex SS9 1AR* Tel (01702) 75305

JONES, Stephen Frederick. b 53. Magd Coll Ox BA75 MA79 Lon Univ BD89. Linc Th Coll 81. **d** 84 **p** 85. C Kingswinford St Mary *Lich* 84-87; Min Can, Succ and Dean's V Windsor 87-94; C Howden TM *York* 94-96; Chapl St Elphin's Sch Matlock from 96; Perm to Offic *Derby* from 96. *Grove Cottage, St Elphin's School, Darley Dale, Matlock, Derbyshire DE4 2HA* Tel (01629) 735718

JONES, Stephen Leslie. b 59. Hull Univ BA80. Sarum & Wells Th Coll 82. **d** 85 **p** 86. C Perry Barr *Birm* 85-88; C Blackpool St Steph *Blackb* 88-90; V Greenlands 90-95; V Carnforth from 95. *The Vicarage, North Road, Carnforth, Lancs LA5 9LJ* Tel (01524) 732948

JONES, Stephen Richard. b 49. Oak Hill Th Coll 72. **d** 75 **p** 76. C Welling *Roch* 75-79; C Cheltenham St Mark *Glouc* 79-82; V Shiregreen St Jas and St Chris *Sheff* 82-86; P-in-c Harold Hill St Geo *Chelmsf* 86-88; V 88-97; P-in-c Harold Hill St Paul 94-95; V Kippington *Roch* from 97. *The Vicarage, 59 Kippington Road, Sevenoaks, Kent TN13 2LL* Tel (01732) 452112

JONES, Stephen William. b 46. K Coll Lon BD70 AKC70. **d** 71 **p** 72. C Streatham St Pet *S'wark* 71-76; C Leeds St Pet *Ripon* 76-79; C Leeds Richmond Hill 79-85; R Gourock *Glas* 85-88; V Porthleven w Sithney *Truro* 88-94; Miss to Seamen 88-94; P-in-c Portsea Ascension *Portsm* from 96. *The Vicarage, 98 Kirby Road, Portsmouth PO2 0PP* Tel (01705) 660123

JONES, Stewart William. b 57. Heriot-Watt Univ BA79 Bris Univ DSA81. Trin Coll Bris DipHE87 BA88. **d** 88 **p** 89. C Stoke Bishop *Bris* 88-92; P-in-c Brislington St Luke from 92. *The Vicarage, St Luke's Gardens, Church Hill, Bristol BS4 4NW* Tel 0117-977 7633

JONES, Susan Helen. b 60. Trin Coll Carmarthen MPhil94 BEd92. Ripon Coll Cuddesdon DipMin93. **d** 95 **p** 97. Chapl Univ of Wales (Swansea) *S & B* from 95; NSM Sketty from 95. *189 Glanmor Road, Sketty, Swansea SA2 0RR* Tel (01792) 202537

JONES, Mrs Susan Jean. b 47. Bp Grosseteste Coll CertEd69. St Alb and Ox Min Course 93. **d** 96. C S Ascot *Ox* from 96. *The Vicarage, Vicarage Gardens, South Ascot, Berks SL5 9DX* Tel (01344) 22388 Fax as telephone

JONES, Sydney Clarence. b 21. St Cath Soc Ox BA42 MA46 CertEd. Linc Th Coll 43. **d** 44 **p** 45. C Weymouth H Trin *Sarum* 44-50; C-in-c Wrangbrook w N Elmsall CD *Wakef* 50-52; V Sowerby St Mary 52-56; V Drighlington 56-63; V Dewsbury Moor 63-67; Children's Officer Gen Syn Bd of Educn 67-69; Lic to Offic *Bradf* 69-71; V Sharow *Ripon* 71-74; Chapl Dame Allan's Schs Newc 74-79; P-in-c Chollerton w Thockrington *Newc* 79-80; V Scholes *Wakef* 80-86; rtd 86; Perm to Offic *Wakef* from 86. *52 Blacksmith Fold, Almondbury, Huddersfield HD5 8XH* Tel (01484) 541608

JONES, Tegid Owen. b 27. Univ of Wales (Abth) LLB47. St Deiniol's Hawarden. **d** 68 **p** 69. C Rhosddu *St As* 68-71; C Wrexham 71-75; R Marchwiel 75-83; R Marchwiel and Isycoed 83-92; RD Ban Isycoed 86-92; rtd 92. *Teglys, 2 Bungalow, Pentre, Chirk, Wrexham LL14 5AW*

JONES, Canon Thomas Graham. b 33. St D Coll Lamp BA57. **d** 59 **p** 60. C Llanelli *St D* 59-64; V Ysbyty Cynfyn 64-69; V Ysbyty Cynfyn w Llantrisant 69-72; V Llanelli Ch Ch 72-94; RD Cydweli 89-93; Hon Can St D Cathl from 93; V Carmarthen St Dav from 94. *St David's Vicarage, 4 Penllwyn Park, Carmarthen SA31 3BU* Tel (01276) 234183

JONES, The Ven Thomas Hughie. b 27. FRSA Univ of Wales BA49 Lon Univ BD53 Leic Univ MA72. St Deiniol's Hawarden. **d** 66 **p** 67. Hon C Evington *Leic* 66-76; Hon C Kirby Muxloe 76-81; Dioc Adult Educn Officer 81-85; R Church Langton w Thorpe Langton and Tur Langton 81-85; Hon Can Leic Cathl 83-86; R Church Langton w Tur Langton, Thorpe Langton etc 85-86; Adn Loughborough 86-92; rtd 92; Perm to Offic *Leic* from 92. *Four Trees, 68 Main Street, Thorpe Satchville, Melton Mowbray, Leics LE14 2DQ* Tel (01664) 840262

JONES, Thomas John Rhidian. b 54. Univ of Wales (Abth) LLB75 BA81. Wycliffe Hall Ox 81. **d** 83 **p** 84. C St D Cathl *St D* 83-86; Min Can St D Cathl 83-86; V Llanpumsaint w Llanllawddog

86-95. *St Theosevia Centre, 2 Canterbury Road, Oxford OX2 6LU*

JONES, Thomas Percy Norman Devonshire (Tom). b 34. St Jo Coll Ox BA58 MA61. Cuddesdon Coll 58. **d** 60 **p** 61. C Portsea St Cuth *Portsm* 60-61; C Portsea N End St Mark 61-67; Asst Chapl Portsm Tech Coll 67-70; Chapl Portsm Poly *Portsm* 70-73; USA 73-74; V Folkestone St Sav *Cant* 75-81; V Regent's Park St Mark *Lon* from 81; Dir Art and Chr Enquiry Trust from 94. *4 Regent's Park Road, London NW1 7TX* Tel 0171-485 3077 or 586 1694

JONES, Canon Thomas Peter. b 20. Ex Coll Ox BA43 MA46. St Mich Coll Llan 43. **d** 45 **p** 46. C Wrexham *St As* 45-48; C Llandrillo-yn-Rhos 48-57; R Erbistock and Overton 57-83; Can St As Cathl 78-84; Preb and Prec St As Cathl 84-86; RD Ban Isycoed 80-86; R Overton and Erbistock and Penley 83-86; rtd 86; Perm to Offic *Cov* from 86. *49 Oakleigh Road, Stratford-upon-Avon, Warks CV37 0DP* Tel (01789) 269340

JONES, Timothy Llewellyn. b 67. York Univ BA90. Ripon Coll Cuddesdon BA94 DipMin94. **d** 94 **p** 95. C Middlesbrough St Martin *York* 94-96; P-in-c Rounton w Welbury from 96; Chapl HM Young Offender Inst Northallerton from 96. *St Leonard's House, 7 Spring Hill, Welbury, Northallerton, N Yorkshire DL6 2SQ* Tel (01909) 882401

JONES, Timothy Richard Nigel (Tim). b 54. Collingwood Coll Dur BSc75 Birm Univ MSc76. Trin Coll Bris DipHE86. **d** 86 **p** 87. C Hailsham *Chich* 86-91; V Madley w Tyberton, Preston-on-Wye and Blakemere *Heref* from 91. *The Vicarage, Madley, Hereford HR2 9LP* Tel (01981) 250245

JONES, Trevor Blandon. b 43. Oak Hill Th Coll 77. **d** 80 **p** 81. Hon C Homerton St Barn w St Paul *Lon* 80-83; Hon C Harlow New Town w Lt Parndon *Chelmsf* 83-90; C 90-92; V Leyton Em from 92. *Emmanuel Vicarage, 149 Hitcham Road, London E17 8HL* Tel 0181-539 2200

JONES, Trevor Charles. b 50. Oak Hill Th Coll DipHE91. **d** 91 **p** 92. C Goodmayes All SS *Chelmsf* 91-93; C Widford 93-96; C Stowmarket *St E* 96; V from 96. *The Vicarage, 7 Lockington Road, Stowmarket, Suffolk IP14 1BQ* Tel (01449) 613576

JONES, Trevor Edwin. b 49. Ripon Coll Cuddesdon 74. **d** 76 **p** 77. C Cannock *Lich* 76-79; C Middlesbrough Ascension *York* 79-81; V Oldham St Steph and All Martyrs *Man* 81-84; V Perry Beeches *Birm* 84-90; P-in-c Saltley 90-93; P-in-c Shaw Hill 90-93; V Saltley and Shaw Hill 93-97; R Lon Docks St Pet w Wapping St Jo *Lon* from 97. *St Peter's Clergy House, Wapping Lane, London E1 9RW* Tel 0171-481 2985

JONES, The Ven Trevor Pryce. b 48. Southn Univ BEd76 BTh79. Sarum & Wells Th Coll 73. **d** 76 **p** 77. C Glouc St Geo *Glouc* 76-79; Warden Bp Mascall Cen *Heref* 79-84; Dioc Communications Officer 81-86; TR Heref St Martin w St Fran (S Wye TM) 84-95; R Dewsall w Callow 84-95; V Holme Lacy w Dinedor 84-95; V Lt Dewchurch, Aconbury w Ballingham and Bolstone 84-95; V Upper and Lower Bullinghope w Grafton 84-95; Preb Heref Cathl 93-97; TR Heref S Wye 95-97; Adn Hertford *St Alb* from 97. *St Mary's House, Church Lane, Stapleford, Hertford SG14 3NB* Tel (01992) 581169 Fax 558745

JONES, Tudor Howell. b 39. St Mich Coll Llan DipTh67 DPS68. **d** 68 **p** 69. C Clydach *S & B* 68-72; C Swansea St Pet 72-75; V Ystradfellte 75-79; V Llangiwg 79-91; V Manselton from 91. *The Vicarage, Manor Road, Manselton, Swansea SA5 9PA* Tel (01792) 654848

JONES, Victor Harvey. b 25. St D Coll Lamp BA53 Coll of Resurr Mirfield. **d** 55 **p** 56. C Canton St Luke *Llan* 55-57; C Caerau w Ely 57-61; Chapl RN 62-76; Perm to Offic *Truro* 77-80; C Portishead *B & W* 80-83; rtd 83; Perm to Offic *Ex* from 92. *3 Ael y Glyn, Nant Road, Harlech LL46 2UJ*

JONES, Canon Victor Howell. b 18. Univ of Wales BA41. St Mich Coll Llan 41. **d** 43 **p** 45. C Llanelli St Paul *St D* 43-46; Min Can St D Cathl 46-54; V Laugharne 54-72; Chapl St D Hosp Carmarthen 72-85; V Llanllwch *St D* 72-77; V Llanllwch w Llangain 77-83; Can St D Cathl 80-85; V Llan-llwch w Llangain and Llangynog 83-85; rtd 85. *Ty Clyd, 13 Picton Terrace, Carmarthen SA31 3BX* Tel (01267) 232352

JONES, Preb Wilfred David. b 22. Keble Coll Ox BA47 MA48. St Mich Coll Llan 47. **d** 48 **p** 49. C Aberaman *Llan* 48-50; C Cardiff St Jo 50-55; Chapl Kelly Coll Tavistock 55-62; V St Decumans *B & W* 62-76; V Ilminster w Whitelackington 76-92; RD Ilminster 78-87; Preb Wells Cathl 81-92; rtd 92; Perm to Offic *B & W* from 92. *Dragons, Lambrook Road, Shepton Beauchamp, Ilminster, Somerset TA19 0NA* Tel (01460) 40967

JONES, Wilfred Lovell. b 39. Lon Univ BD71 CertEd. St D Coll Lamp DipTh63. **d** 63 **p** 64. C Llanllyfni *Ban* 63-65; C Llanbeblig w Caernarfon 65-68; V Llanwnog w Penstrowed 68-73; V Llanwnnog and Caersws w Carno 73-75; Asst Chapl Dover Coll 77-90; Wrekin Coll Shropshire 91-94; V Llangollen w Trevor and Llantysilio *St As* from 94. *The Vicarage, Abbey Road, Llangollen LL20 8SN* Tel (01978) 860231

JONES, Canon William. b 30. Univ of Wales (Ban) DipTh54. St Mich Coll Llan 54 BTh92. **d** 55 **p** 56. C Denio w Abererch *Ban* 55-60; V Aberdaron and Bodferin 60-66; V Llandwrog 66-71; R Llanstumdwy, Llangybi w Llanarmon 71-74; R Dolbenmaen w Llanystymdwy w Llangybi etc from 74; RD Eifionydd from 75; Can Ban Cathl 84-93; Can and Treas Ban Cathl from 93. *The Rectory, Llanystumdwy, Criccieth LL52 0SS* Tel (01766) 522325

JONES, William Alexander. b 13. Univ of Wales BA35. **d** 69 **p** 70. Hon C Llandegfan w Beaumaris and Llanfaes *Ban* 69-75; C 75-76; P-in-c Penmon and Llangoed w Llanfihangel Dinsylwy 76-77; TV Llandegfan and Beaumaris w Llanfaes w Penmon etc 77-81; rtd 81; Lic to Offic *Ban* from 81. *23 Pont y Brenin, Llangoed, Beaumaris LL58 8LS*

JONES, Canon William David. b 28. Lon Univ BD57 Leeds Univ MA73. St D Coll Lamp BA48 St Mich Coll Llan 48. **d** 51 **p** 52. C Risca *Mon* 51-54; C Chepstow St Arvan's w Penterry 54-55; C St Geo-in-the-East w Ch Ch w St Jo *Lon* 55-59; C Farnham Royal *Ox* 59-64; Lect Div Culham Coll 65-67; Hd of Relig Studies Doncaster Coll of Educn 67-74; Lic to Offic *Sheff* 67-74; Vice-Prin St Bede Coll Dur 74; Vice-Prin SS Hild and Bede Coll Dur 75-89; Lect Th Dur Univ 75-89; Lic to Offic *Dur* 80-85; Dir of Miss Ch in Wales 89-93; Hon Can St D Cathl *St D* 90-93; rtd 93; Perm to Offic *Glouc* from 93. *Hatfield Cottage, 14 Bath Road, Tetbury, Glos GL8 8EF* Tel (01666) 504050

JONES, William Douglas. b 28. St Fran Coll Brisbane ThL56. **d** 56 **p** 58. Australia 56-58; Papua New Guinea 58-72; C Manston *Ripon* 72-75; V Middleton St Mary 75-87; V Ireland Wood 87-94; rtd 94. *6 Willow Court, Pool in Wharfedale, Otley, W Yorkshire LS21 1RX* Tel 0113-284 2028

JONES, William Edward Benjamin. b 19. TCD BA43 MA53. TCD Div Sch Div Test44. **d** 44 **p** 45. C Belfast St Thos *Conn* 44-47; C Sudbury St Andr *Lon* 47-50; CF 50-54; V Edmonton St Pet w St Martin *Lon* 54-59; V N Wembley St Cuth 59-81; V Ripley *Guildf* 81-87; Chapl HM Pris Send 81-87; rtd 87; Perm to Offic *Nor* from 87. *37 Bircham Road, Reepham, Norfolk NR10 4NG* Tel (01603) 870738

JONES, Canon William Glyndwr. b 17. St D Coll Lamp BA39. **d** 42 **p** 43. C Monkton *St D* 42-48; C Betws w Ammanford 48-51; R Granston w St Nic 51-86; V Mathry w St Edrens 69-86; R Jordanston 78-86; Hon Can St D Cathl from 84; rtd 86. *Pencraig, Sladeway, Fishguard SA65 9NY* Tel (01348) 874673

JONES, William John. b 59. St Mich Coll Llan DMinlStuds93. **d** 93 **p** 94. C Pembroke Dock w Cosheston w Nash and Upton *St D* 93-96; C Tenby 96; TV from 96. *The Vicarage, Penally, Tenby SA70 7PN* Tel (01834) 842416

JONES, William Lincoln. b 19. St D Coll Lamp BA41 St Mich Coll Llan 41. **d** 43 **p** 44. C Roath St Marg *Llan* 43-47; C Wooburn *Ox* 47-50; C Bridgwater w Chilton *B & W* 50-55; V Langford Budville w Runnington 55-60; V Winscombe 60-71; V Bishops Lydeard 71-73; V Bishops Lydeard w Cothelstone 73-80; P-in-c Bagborough 78-80; R Bishops Lydeard w Bagborough and Cothelstone 80-84; rtd 84; Perm to Offic *Ex* from 86. *Holme Lea, Well Mead, Kilmington, Axminster, Devon EX13 7SQ* Tel (01297) 32744

JONES, Canon William Lloyd. b 36. Univ of Wales (Lamp) BA59. Wycliffe Hall Ox 59. **d** 61 **p** 62. C Holyhead w Rhoscolyn *Ban* 61-65; C Porthmadog 65-67; R Llanfaethlu w Llanfwrog and Llanrhuddlad etc 67-74; R Llanengan and Llangian from 74; RD Llyn from 90; Can Ban Cathl from 97. *The Rectory, Abersoch, Pwllheli LL53 7EA* Tel (01758) 712871

JONES-CRABTREE, Stephen. b 56. Nottm Univ BTh80. Linc Th Coll 76. **d** 80 **p** 81. C Chorley St Pet *Blackb* 80-83; C Blackpool St Steph 83-84; C Penwortham St Mary 84-88; R Mareham-le-Fen and Revesby *Linc* from 88. *The Rectory, Mareham le Fen, Boston, Lincs PE22 7QU* Tel (01507) 568502

JORDAN, Anthony John (Tony). b 50. Birm Univ BEd73. LNSM course. **d** 83 **p** 84. Asst Chapl Uppingham Sch Leics 83-86; Hon C Uppingham w Ayston and Wardley w Belton *Pet* 83-86; Asst Chapl Sherborne Sch 86-87; NSM Bournemouth St Fran *Win* from 88. *Flat 8, Alverton Court, 26A Wimborne Road, Bournemouth BH2 6NU* Tel (01202) 318346

JORDAN, Miss Avril Marilyn. b 35. Lon Univ DipEd56. SW Minl Tr Course 79. **dss** 82 **d** 87 **p** 94. Highweek and Teigngrace *Ex* 82-87; Par Dn 87-88; Par Dn Ottery St Mary, Alfington, W Hill, Tipton etc 88-94; C from 94. *9 Washbrook View, Ottery St Mary, Exeter EX11 1EP* Tel (01404) 814849

JORDAN, Mrs Elizabeth Ann. b 58. New Hall Cam MA82. St Jo Coll Nottm DipTh84. **d** 87 **p** 94. Par Dn Blackpool St Jo *Blackb* 87-90; Par Dn Ewood 90-94; C 94-95; Asst Dir of Ords 90-95; Min Shelfield St Mark CD *Lich* from 95; Lich Local Min Adv from 95. *Church House, 25 Green Lane, Shelfield, Walsall WS4 1RN*

JORDAN, John. b 37. CQSW81. N Ord Course 84. **d** 87 **p** 88. C Southport Em *Liv* 87-90; V Abram 90-95; V Bickershaw 90-95; V Bempton w Flamborough, Reighton w Speeton *York* from 95. *The Vicarage, Church Street, Flamborough, Bridlington, N Humberside YO15 1PE*

JORDAN, Kenneth John. b 31. K Coll Lon. **d** 69 **p** 70. Guyana 69-74; C Roath St Marg *Llan* 74-76; V Nantymoel w Wyndham 76-81; V Cardiff St Mary w St Steph 81-83; V Cardiff St Mary and St Steph w St Dyfrig etc from 83; Miss to Seamen from 83. *St Mary's Vicarage, Bute Street, Cardiff CF1 5HE* Tel (01222) 487777

JORDAN, Peter Harry. b 42. Leeds Univ BA64. Cranmer Hall Dur 70. **d** 73 **p** 74. C Nottingham St Ann w Em *S'well* 73-77; C Edgware *Lon* 77-82; V Everton St Chrys *Liv* 82-94; V Bootle

St Mary w St Paul from 94; Dioc Ev from 94. *The Vicarage, 70 Merton Road, Bootle, Merseyside L20 7AT* Tel 0151-922 1315

JORDAN, Richard William. b 56. Lanchester Poly BSc78. St Jo Coll Nottm DipTh84. **d** 87 **p** 88. C Blackpool St Jo *Blackb* 87-90; V Ewood 90-95. *Church House, 25 Green Lane, Shelfield, Walsall WS4 1RN*

JORDAN, Robert Brian. b 43. Qu Coll Birm 68. **d** 69 **p** 70. C Norton St Mich *Dur* 69-73; C Hastings St Clem and All SS *Chich* 73-74; C Carshalton *S'wark* 74-81; V Catford St Andr from 81. *The Vicarage, 135 Wellmeadow Road, London SE6 1HP* Tel 0181-697 2600

JORDAN, Ronald Henry. b 30. K Coll Lon. **d** 57 **p** 58. C Clerkenwell H Redeemer w St Phil *Lon* 57-58; C Southgate Ch Ch 58-59; C Edmonton St Mary w St Jo 62-69; Hon C 86-94; V Wood Green St Mich 69-73; Hon C Finchley H Trin 80-86; Perm to Offic from 94; rtd 95. *120 Church Lane, London N2 0TB* Tel 0181-883 7828

JORDAN, Thomas. b 36. Man Univ DSPT91. NW Ord Course 76. **d** 79 **p** 80. NSM Prenton *Ches* 79-84; NSM Egremont St Jo 84-91; C 91-96; Ind Chapl 91-96; TV Birkenhead Priory from 96. *31 Willowbank Road, Devonshire Park, Birkenhead, Merseyside L42 7JU* Tel 0151-652 4212

JORDINSON, Vera (Sister Hilary). b 37. Liv Univ BA60 CertEd61. Westcott Ho Cam 88. **d** 89 **p** 94. CSF from 74; Prov Sec from 90; Gen Sec from 96; Sec for Miss SSF from 96; Lic to Offic *Heref* 89-92; Perm to Offic *Lich* 90-92; Perm to Offic *Birm* 92-94; NSM Birchfield 94-96; Perm to Offic from 97. *St Francis House, 113 Gillott Road, Birmingham B16 0ET* Tel 0121-454 8302 Fax 455 9784

JORY, Joseph Nicholls. b 07. Lon Univ DipTh31. St Andr Whittlesford 40. **d** 40 **p** 41. C High Harrogate St Pet *Ripon* 40-42; Chapl RNVR 42-46; R Spennithorne *Ripon* 46-66; R Finghall 54-66; R Hauxwell 64-66; rtd 72; Perm to Offic *Ex* from 79. *Shilstone, Chagford, Newton Abbot, Devon TQ13 8JX* Tel (01647) 231307

JORYSZ, Ian Herbert. b 62. Van Mildert Coll Dur BSc84 MA95 Liv Univ PhD87. Ripon Coll Cuddesdon BA89 MA95. **d** 90 **p** 91. C Houghton le Spring *Dur* 90-93; C Ferryhill 93-95; P-in-c S Weald *Chelmsf* from 95. *The Vicarage, Wigley Bush Lane, South Weald, Brentwood, Essex CM14 5QP* Tel (01277) 212054

JOWETT, The Very Revd Alfred. b 14. CBE72. St Cath Coll Cam BA35 MA59 Sheff Univ Hon DLitt82. Linc Th Coll 43. **d** 44 **p** 45. C Goole *Sheff* 44-47; Sec Sheff Coun of Chs and Sheff Marriage Guidance Coun 47-51; V Sheff St Geo and St Steph 51-60; V Doncaster St Geo 60-64; Hon Can Sheff Cathl 60-64; Select Preacher Ox Univ 64 and 79; Dean Man 64-83; rtd 83; Perm to Offic *Sheff* from 84. *37 Stone Delf, Sheffield S10 3QX* Tel 0114-230 5455

JOWETT, Ms Hilary Anne. b 54. Hull Univ BA75. Cranmer Hall Dur IDC80. **dss** 82 **d** 87 **p** 94. Sheff St Jo *Sheff* 82-83; Brampton Bierlow 83-87; Par Dn 87-89; Hon Par Dn Sheff Sharrow 89-95; Chapl Nether Edge Hosp Sheff 89-95; C Sheff St Mark Broomhill *Sheff* 95-97; C Mosborough from 97. *Sharrow Vicarage, 45 St Andrew's Road, Sheffield S11 9AL* Tel 0114-255 0533 or 248 7729

JOWETT, Nicholas Peter Alfred. b 44. St Cath Coll Cam BA66 MA Bris Univ CertEd67 Birm Univ DipTh74. Qu Coll Birm 72. **d** 75 **p** 76. C Wales *Sheff* 75-78; TV Sheff Manor 78-83; V Brampton Bierlow 83-89; V Sheff Sharrow from 89. *Sharrow Vicarage, 45 St Andrew's Road, Sheffield S11 9AL* Tel 0114-255 0533

JOWITT, Andrew Robert Benson. b 56. Down Coll Cam BA78 MA81 PGCE79. Wycliffe Hall Ox 88. **d** 90 **p** 91. C Northampton Em *Pet* 90-94; C Barking St Marg w St Patr *Chelmsf* from 94. *79 Sparsholt Road, Barking, Essex IG11 7YG* Tel 0181-594 1960

JOWITT, Canon David Arthur Benson. b 25. St Jo Coll Ox BA49 MA53. Sarum Th Coll 49. **d** 51 **p** 52. C Heckmondwike *Wakef* 51-56; C Harrogate St Wilfrid *Ripon* 56-59; V Kirkby Fleetham 60-69; R Langton on Swale 60-69; OGS from 65; Superior OGS 75-81; P-in-c Edin St Ninian *Edin* 69-77; Dioc Supernumerary 77-80; Chapl Edin R Infirmary 77-80; Syn Clerk *Edin* 77-90; Can St Mary's Cathl 77-90; Vice-Provost 81-86; P-in-c S Queensferry 86-90; rtd 90; Hon C Edin Old St Paul *Edin* from 91. *2 Marchmont Crescent, Edinburgh EH9 1HN* Tel 0131-229 0106

JOWITT, John Frederick Benson. b 23. Oak Hill Th Coll 57. **d** 59 **p** 59. Uganda 59-63; CF 63-73; R Thrandeston, Stuston and Brome w Oakley *St E* 73-82; V Docking *Nor* 82-83; P-in-c Gt Bircham 82-83; R Docking w the Birchams 83-88; P-in-c Stanhoe w Barwick 85-88; R Docking w The Birchams and Stanhoe w Barwick 88; rtd 88; Perm to Offic *Nor* from 88; Perm to Offic *St E* from 90. *White Lodge, The Street, North Cove, Beccles, Suffolk NR34 7PN* Tel (01502) 76404

JOY, Bernard David. b 50. Sarum & Wells Th Coll 90. **d** 92 **p** 93. C Shortlands *Roch* 92-94; C Henbury *Bris* 94-96; V Bristol St Aid w St Geo from 96. *St Aidan's Vicarage, 2 Jockey Lane, St George, Bristol BS5 8NZ* Tel 0117-967 7812

JOY, Canon Leslie John Clifton. b 09. AKC33. St Steph Ho Ox 33. **d** 33 **p** 34. C Byker St Laur *Newc* 33-40; C-in-c Balkwell CD 40-48; V Newc St Matt 48-61; V Newc St Matt w St Mary 61-64; V Blyth St Mary 64-83; RD Bedlington 69-83; Hon Can Newc Cathl 70-83; rtd 83; Perm to Offic *Newc* from 86; Perm to Offic *Ox* 94; Hon C Reading St Giles from 94. *31 Emmbrook Court, Reading RG6 2TZ* Tel 0118-987 3855

JOY, Canon Matthew Osmund Clifton. b 40. St Edm Hall Ox BA62 MA66. St Steph Ho Ox 62. **d** 64 **p** 65. C Brinksway *Ches* 64-66; C Southwick St Columba *Dur* 66-69; V Hartlepool H Trin 69-85; V Rotherham Ferham Park *Sheff* 85-88; V Masbrough 88-95; RD Rotherham 88-93; P-in-c Bordesley St Benedict *Birm* from 95; Bp's Adv on Christian/Muslim relns from 95. *St Benedict's Vicarage, 55 Hob Moor Road, Birmingham B10 9AY* Tel 0121-772 2726

JOYCE, Mrs Alison Jane. b 59. Univ of Wales (Swansea) BA81 SS Coll Cam PGCE84 Bris Univ MLitt87. Ripon Coll Cuddesdon BA87 MA94. **d** 88 **p** 94. Par Dn Chalgrove w Berrick Salome *Ox* 88-90; Tutor WMMTC 90-95; Tutor Qu Coll Birm 95-96; NSM Moseley St Anne *Birm* from 96. *88 Willows Road, Balsall Heath, Birmingham B12 9QD* Tel 0121-440 5171

JOYCE, Anthony Owen (Tony). b 35. Selw Coll Cam BA60 MA64. Wycliffe Hall Ox 60. **d** 62 **p** 63. C Birm St Martin *Birm* 62-67; Rhodesia 67-70; V Birm St Luke *Birm* 70-79; V Downend *Bris* from 79; RD Stapleton 83-89. *The Vicarage, 63 Downend Road, Bristol BS16 5UF* Tel 0117-956 8064

JOYCE, Ernest Thomas Chancellor. b 16. Lon Univ LLB67. Chich Th Coll 68. **d** 70 **p** 71. C Southsea H Spirit *Portsm* 70-75; V New Southgate St Paul *Lon* 75-77; Chantry Priest Chpl St Mich and H So Walsingham 77-81; Perm to Offic *Nor* from 77; rtd 81. *16 Cleaves Drive, Walsingham, Norfolk NR22 6EQ* Tel (01328) 820612

JOYCE, Gordon Franklin. b 51. Birm Univ BA72. St Jo Coll Nottm 86. **d** 88 **p** 89. C Didsbury St Jas and Em *Man* 88-92; V Tonge w Alkrington from 92. *St Michael's Vicarage, 184 Kirkway, Middleton, Manchester M24 1LN* Tel 0161-643 2891

JOYCE, Graham Leslie. b 49. Lon Univ CertEd71. Trin Coll Bris DipHE89. **d** 89 **p** 90. C Heald Green St Cath *Ches* 89-93; R Church Lawton from 93. *The Rectory, 1 Liverpool Road West, Church Lawton, Stoke-on-Trent ST7 3DE* Tel (01270) 882103

JOYCE, John Barnabas Altham. b 47. St Chad's Coll Dur BA69 Lon Univ DipEd86. St Steph Ho Ox 72. **d** 74 **p** 75. C Reading St Giles *Ox* 74-77; C Cowley St Jo 77-80; Dioc Youth and Community Officer 80-87; V Hangleton *Chich* 87-94; Dioc Adv for Schools and Dir Educn from 94. *2 Windlesham Road, Brighton BN1 3AG* Tel (01273) 778083

JOYCE, Kingsley Reginald. b 49. Man Univ BSc70. Cuddesdon Coll 70. **d** 73 **p** 74. C High Wycombe *Ox* 73-76; C Fingest 76-79; C Hambleden 76-79; C Medmenham 76-79; C Fawley (Bucks) 76-79; C Turville 76-79; P-in-c Hambleden Valley 79-80; R 80-87; R Friern Barnet St Jas *Lon* 87-91; CF from 91. *MOD Chaplains (Army), Trenchard Lines, Upavon, Pewsey, Wilts SN9 6BE* Tel (01980) 615804 Fax 615800

JOYCE, Margaret. b 47. Oak Hill NSM Course 86. **d** 89 **p** 94. NSM Chadwell Heath *Chelmsf* 89-92; NSM Bath Odd Down w Combe Hay *B & W* from 92. *69 Bloomfield Rise, Bath BA2 2BN* Tel (01225) 840864

JOYCE, Martin Ernest Chancellor. b 50. K Coll Lon 69. **d** 73 **p** 74. C Leigh Park *Portsm* 73-77; C Milton 77-83; TV Cambridge Ascension *Ely* 83-85; V Blackpool St Mich *Blackb* 85-87. *44 Mulben Crescent, Glasgow G53 7EH* Tel 0141-954 6078

JOYCE, Dr Melville Henry Bushell. b 14. MRCPsych71 St D Coll Lamp BA39 Bris Univ MB, ChB52 DPM54. Ely Th Coll 40. **d** 41 **p** 42. C Abergavenny H Trin *Mon* 41-43; C St Winnow *Truro* 43-45; C Westbury-on-Trym H Trin *Bris* 45-46; C Henleaze 46-52; Public Preacher 52-69; Perm to Offic *Lon* 55-69; Lic to Offic from 69; Lect Psychiatry Lon Univ 58-61; Surrey Univ 61-79. *7 Stanhope Terrace, London W2 2UB* Tel 0171-262 3718

JOYCE, Canon Norman. b 14. St Jo Coll Dur BA35 MA38 DipTh38. **d** 37 **p** 38. C Monkwearmouth All SS *Dur* 37-40; C W Hartlepool St Paul 40-43; V Monkwearmouth All SS 43-53; R Bowness *Carl* 53-57; R N Wingfield *Derby* 57-73; TR N Wingfield, Pilsley and Tupton 73-80; Hon Can Derby Cathl 77-80; rtd 80; Perm to Offic *Carl* from 80. *Fell View, Thurstonfield, Carlisle CA5 6HG* Tel (01228) 576471

JOYCE, Raymond. b 37. Keele Univ BA60 MA67 Linc Coll Ox BA62 MA68. St Steph Ho Ox 78. **d** 80 **p** 81. NSM Normanton *Derby* 80-83; NSM Derby St Alkmund and St Werburgh 83-87; Lic to Offic from 87. *4 South Avenue, Littleover, Derby DE23 6BA* Tel (01332) 768681

JOYCE, Sister. *See* CROSSLAND, Sister Joyce

JOYCE, Terence Alan. b 57. St Jo Coll Nottm BTh84. **d** 84 **p** 85. C Mansfield St Pet *S'well* 84-88; V Greasley from 88. *The Vicarage, 36 Moorgreen, Newthorpe, Notts NG16 2FB* Tel (01773) 712509

JUBB, William Arthur. b 21. Kelham Th Coll 39. **d** 45 **p** 46. C Whitwood Mere *Wakef* 45-47; C Royston 47-52; V Monk Bretton 52-74; rtd 86. *5 Mauds Terrace, Barnsley, S Yorkshire S71 2EA* Tel (01226) 247286

JUCKES, Jonathan Sydney. b 61. St Andr Univ MA83. Ridley Hall Cam BA87. **d** 88 **p** 89. C Sevenoaks St Nic *Roch* 88-92; Proclamation Trust 92-95; C St Helen Bishopsgate w St Andr Undershaft etc *Lon* from 95. *The Old Rectory, Merrick Square, London SE1 4JB* Tel 0171-378 8186

JUDD, Adrian Timothy. b 67. Lanc Univ BA88. Cranmer Hall Dur BA92 Trin Coll Singapore 92 St Jo Coll Dur DMinlStuds93. **d** 93 **p** 94. C Dudley St Aug Holly Hall *Worc* 93-97; V Cantril Farm *Liv* from 97. *St Jude's Vicarage, 168 Round Hey, Liverpool L28 1RQ* Tel 0151-220 4524

JUDD, Colin Ivor. b 35. Dur Univ BA61. Ridley Hall Cam 61. **d** 63 **p** 64. C Stratford St Jo w Ch Ch *Chelmsf* 63-66; C Kimberworth *Sheff* 66-68; Area Sec (Dios Bradf and Wakef) CMS 68-80; V Bradf St Columba w St Andr *Bradf* from 80. *St Columba's Vicarage, 163 Horton Grange Road, Bradford, W Yorkshire BD7 2DN* Tel (01274) 571975

JUDD, Eric Sinclair Alderton. b 04. **d** 43 **p** 44. C Gt Barr *Lich* 43-45; C Bridlington Priory *York* 45-47; P-in-c Harewood *Ripon* 47-49; R Hinderclay w Wattisfield *St E* 49-55; R Belleau w Aby and Claythorpe *Linc* 55-60; R Muckton w Burwell and Walmsgate 57-60; V Anwick 60-64; V N Willingham w Legsby 64-73; rtd 73; Perm to Offic *Linc* from 73. *5 Baildon Crescent, North Hykeham, Lincoln LN6 8HU* Tel (01522) 687442

JUDD, Mrs Nicola Jane (Nicky). b 51. Birm Coll of Educn CertEd72. S Dios Minl Tr Scheme 87. **d** 90 **p** 94. NSM Abbotts Ann and Upper and Goodworth Clatford *Win* from 90. *13 Belmont Close, Andover, Hants SP10 2DE* Tel (01264) 363364

JUDD, The Very Revd Peter Somerset Margesson. b 49. Trin Hall Cam BA71. Cuddesdon Coll 71. **d** 74 **p** 75. C Salford St Phil w St Steph *Man* 74-76; Chapl Clare Coll Cam 76-81; C Burnham *Ox* 81-82; TV Burnham w Dropmore, Hitcham and Taplow 82-88; V Iffley 88-97; RD Cowley 94-97; Provost Chelmsf from 97. *The Provost's House, 3 Harlings Grove, Chelmsford CM1 1YQ* Tel (01245) 354318

JUDGE, James Arthur. b 20. Lon Univ BD50. ALCD50. **d** 50 **p** 51. C Southsea St Jude *Portsm* 50-52; Australia 52-62; R Street *B & W* 62-77; V Banwell 77-88; rtd 88. *512 Gipps House, 270 Jersey Road, Woollahra, NSW, Australia 2025*

JUDGE, Mark Rollo. b 60. Chich Th Coll BTh92. **d** 92 **p** 93. C Forest Gate St Edm *Chelmsf* 92-96; V Gt Ilford St Luke from 96. *60 Dalkeith Road, Ilford, Essex IG1 1JE* Tel 0181-478 4486

JUDGE, Michael Charles. b 42. Southn Univ BTh79. Chich Th Coll 71. **d** 74 **p** 75. C Eastbourne St Mary *Chich* 74-78; C Seaford w Sutton 79-81; R Hurstpierpoint 81-89; V Easebourne from 89; Chapl K Edw VII Hosp Midhurst from 89; RD Midhurst *Chich* from 90. *The Priory, Easebourne, Midhurst, W Sussex GU29 0AJ* Tel (01730) 813341

JUDGE, Ralph Stanley. b 13. TCD BA35 MA58. TCD Div Sch Div Test36. **d** 36 **p** 37. C Clonmel *C & O* 36-39; I Kilkeevin w Kiltullagh *K, E & A* 39-45; I Castlebar *T, K & A* 45-51; Australia from 51; rtd 83. *11 Troon Avenue, Seaton, S Australia 5023* Tel Adelaide (8) 356 5131

JUDSON, Mrs Mary Ruth. b 47. Bretton Hall Coll DipEd68. NE Ord Course 89. **d** 92 **p** 94. Par Dn Lobley Hill *Dur* 92; Par Dn Chester le Street 92-94; C 94-96; V Millfield St Mark and Pallion from 96. *The Vicarage, St Mark's Terrace, Sunderland SR4 7BN* Tel 0191-565 6372

JUDSON, Paul Wesley. b 46. Leic Poly DipAD69 ATD71. Cranmer Hall Dur 87. **d** 89 **p** 90. C Lobley Hill *Dur* 89-92; C Chester le Street 92-96; Sec Dioc Bd of Soc Resp from 96; C Millfield St Mark and Pallion from 96. *The Vicarage, St Mark's Terrace, Sunderland SR4 7BN* Tel 0191-565 6372

JUKES, Preb Keith Michael. b 54. Leeds Univ BA76. Linc Th Coll 77. **d** 78 **p** 79. C Wordsley *Lich* 78-81; C Wolverhampton 81-83; C-in-c Stoneydelph St Martin CD 83-90; TR Glascote and Stonydelph 90-91; RD Tamworth 90-91; TR Cannock 91-97; V Hatherton 91-97; Preb Lich Cathl 96-97; P-in-c Selby Abbey *York* from 97. *The Abbey Vicarage, 32A Leeds Road, Selby, N Yorkshire YO8 0HX* Tel (01757) 709218 or 703123

JULIAN, Sister. *See* WALSH, Julia Christine

JUPE, Canon Derek Robert. b 26. TCD BA53 Div Test54 MA67. **d** 54 **p** 55. C Lurgan Ch Ch *D & D* 54-57; C Dublin Harold's Cross *D & G* 57-60; I Easkey w Kilglass *T, K & A* 60-65; Deputation Sec (Ireland) BCMS 65-72; R Man St Jerome w Ardwick St Silas *Man* 72-78; V Ardsley *Sheff* 78-83; I Tempo and Clabby *Clogh* 83-92; Can Clogh Cathl 89-92; rtd 92. *29 St Andrew's Drive, Whitstone, Nuneaton, Warks CV11 6NQ* Tel (01203) 386880

JUPE, Martin Roy. b 27. Lon Univ BD63. St Deiniol's Hawarden. **d** 61 **p** 62. C Camborne *Truro* 61-64; V Penzance St Jo 64-92; RD Penwith 73-76; rtd 92; Perm to Offic *Truro* from 92. *25 Nancherrow Terrace, St Just, Penzance, Cornwall TR19 7LA* Tel (01736) 788320

JUSTICE, Keith Leonard. b 42. CEng83 MIMechE83 Wolv Univ BSc68. Wycliffe Hall Ox DipMin93. **d** 93 **p** 94. C Penwortham St Mary *Blackb* 93-96; C Dovercourt and Parkeston *Chelmsf* 96; C Dovercourt and Parkeston w Harwich from 96. *19 Beacon Hill Avenue, Harwich, Essex CO12 3NR* Tel (01255) 240886

JUSTICE, Peter John Michael. b 37. Chich Th Coll 60. **d** 63 **p** 64. C Digswell *St Alb* 63-67; C Guildf St Nic *Guildf* 67-68; C Mill End *St Alb* 68-70; V Eaton Bray 70-73; Hon C Prestwood *Ox* 73-84; Chapl to the Deaf 84-90; rtd 90; Perm to Offic *Ox* 90-93; RD Perm to Offic *Ex* 94-95. *8 Theatre Street, Woodbridge, Suffolk IP12 4NE* Tel (01394) 380899

JUSTICE, Simon Charles. b 66. Univ of Wales (Lamp) BD88 Edin Univ MTh90. Cranmer Hall Dur 90. **d** 92 **p** 93. C Tilehurst St Mich *Ox* 92-95; USA from 95. *58 Third Street, Troy, NY 12180, USA* Tel New York (518) 273-7351

JUTSUM, Linda Mary. *See* ELLIOTT, Mrs Linda Mary

K

KAENEL, Brian Herbert. b 19. Coll of Resurr Mirfield 57. **d** 59 **p** 60. C Nunhead St Antony *S'wark* 59-61; Australia 61-67; Asst Master Eccles Hall Sch Quidenham 67-69; St Aug Sch Kilburn 69-70; Ravensbourne Sch Bromley 71-79; Perm to Offic *Roch* from 72; rtd 84. *11 Bromley College, London Road, Bromley BR1 1PE* Tel 0181-290 1660

✠KAFITY, The Rt Revd Samir. Beirut Univ BA57. Near E Sch of Th 57. **d** 57 **p** 58 **c** 86. Jerusalem 57-59; Jordan 59-75; Adn Beirut 74-77; Gen Sec Cen Syn of Episc Ch in JEM 77-86; Adn Jerusalem 77-86; Bp Jerusalem from 86. *St George's Close, PO Box 1248, Jerusalem 91109, Israel* Fax Jerusalem (2) 273847

KAGGWA, Nelson Sonny. b 58. E Lon Univ BA91. Bible Tr Inst Tennessee DipTh84 Bp Tucker Coll Mukono 77. **d** 80 **p** 80. Kenya 80-83; USA 83; Hon C Ox SS Phil and Jas w St Marg *Ox* 84-85; C W Ham *Chelmsf* 86-87; TV Walthamstow St Mary w St Steph 87-92; Perm to Offic *Sheff* 92-95; V Sheff St Paul Wordsworth Avenue from 96. *St Paul's Vicarage, Wheata Road, Sheffield S5 9FP* Tel 0114-246 8137

KAMRAN, Ernest P. b 58. **d** 90. C Shoreditch St Leon and Hoxton St Jo *Lon* from 94. *2 Lorden Walk, London E2 6NL* Tel 0171-739 6234

KANE, Margaret. b 15. LNSM course. **d** 87 **p** 94. NSM Billingham St Aid *Dur* 87-95; Perm to Offic from 95. *218 Kennedy Gardens, Billingham, Cleveland TS23 3RL* Tel (01642) 553940

KANERIA, Rajni. b 57. Bath Univ BPharm82. Wycliffe Hall Ox 83. **d** 86 **p** 87. C Hyson Green *S'well* 86-87; C Hyson Green St Paul w St Steph 87-89; C Harold Hill St Geo *Chelmsf* 89-91; TV Oadby *Leic* from 91. *St Paul's House, Hamble Road, Oadby, Leicester LE2 4NX* Tel 0116-271 0519

KARRACH, Dr Herbert Adolf. b 24. TCD BA46 MB48 BCh48 BAO48 LSHTM DTM&H55. EAMTC 85. **d** 88 **p** 89. Hon C Snettisham w Ingoldisthorpe and Fring *Nor* 88-95; Perm to Offic from 95. *Narnia, 5 Docking Road, Fring, King's Lynn, Norfolk PE31 6SQ* Tel (01485) 518346

KARUNARATNA, Charles Winston. b 28. FPhS FRSA Serampore Coll BD60 DTh84 K Coll Lon MTh66 PhD74 Lon Inst of Educn MA90. ALCD51. **d** 51 **p** 52. C Croydon St Matt *Cant* 51-53; NSM Gt Ilford St Jo *Chelmsf* 89-93; Perm to Offic from 93. *2 Lancelot Road, Ilford, Essex IG6 3BE* Tel 0181-500 4751

KASHOURIS, Peter Zacharias. b 66. Peterho Cam BA89 MA93. St Steph Ho Ox 92. **d** 94 **p** 95. C Hampstead St Jo *Lon* 94-97; R Hartlepool St Hilda *Dur* from 97. *The Rectory, Church Close, Hartlepool, Cleveland TS24 0PW* Tel (01429) 267030

KASIBANTE, Amos Sebadduka. b 54. Trin Coll Cam BA83 MA87 Yale Univ STM89. Bp Tucker Coll Mukono DipTh80. **d** 79 **p** 80. Uganda 79-92; Tutor Coll of the Ascension Selly Oak 93-95; Prin Simon of Cyrene Th Inst from 95. *Simon of Cyrene Theological Institute, 2 St Anne's Crescent, London SW18 2LR* Tel 0181-874 1353 Fax 875 9079

KASSELL, Colin George Henry. b 42. DCC90. Valladolid Spain 63 Ripon Coll Cuddesdon 76. **d** 68 **p** 69. In RC Ch 69-75; Perm to Offic *Ox* 76-77; C Denham 77-80; V Brotherton *Wakef* 80-84; Chapl and Past Ldr St Cath Hospice Crawley 84-91; R Rogate w Terwick and Trotton w Chithurst *Chich* 91-94; C Heene from 94; Chapl Worthing Hosp from 94. *34 Ingleside Crescent, Lancing, W Sussex BN15 8EN* Tel (01903) 764400 Mobile 0802-259310

KAUNHOVEN, Anthony Peter. b 55. Leeds Univ BA78 PGCE79 Edin Univ DipMin80. Edin Th Coll 79. **d** 81 **p** 82. C Leeds St Aid *Ripon* 81-84; C Hawksworth Wood 84-89; V Upper Nidderdale 89-91. *29 St James Road, Ilkley, W Yorkshire LS29 9PY* Tel (01943) 817659

KAVANAGH, Michael Lowther. b 58. CPsychol90 MBPsS90 York Univ BA80 Newc Univ MSc82 Leeds Univ BA86. Coll of Resurr Mirfield 84. **d** 87 **p** 88. C Boston Spa *York* 87-91; V Beverley St Nic from 91; RD Beverley from 95. *St Nicholas' Vicarage, 72 Grovehill Road, Beverley, N Humberside HU17 0ER* Tel (01482) 881458

KAY, Canon Cyril John. b 05. St Aid Birkenhead 44. **d** 46 **p** 47. C Lupset *Wakef* 46-48; C Portland All SS w St Pet *Sarum* 48-54; Chapl HM Borstal Portland 48-54; V Welland *Worc* 54-74; RD Upton 59-73; Hon Can Worc Cathl 69-74; rtd 74; Perm to Offic *Glouc* 80-92. *c/o Mrs E Gibbons, Bromsash House, Bromsash, Ross-on-Wye, Herefordshire HR9 7PL*

KAY, George Ronald. b 24. Sarum & Wells Th Coll 74. **d** 77 **p** 78. NSM Bemerton *Sarum* 77-87; rtd 87. *1 Victoria Close, Wilton, Salisbury SP2 0ET* Tel (01722) 743884

KAY, Ian Geoffrey. **d** 89 **p** 90. NSM Rochdale *Man* 89-91 and from 95; NSM Heywood St Luke w All So 91-95. *92 Albion Street, Castleton, Rochdale, Lancs OL11 2UL* Tel (01706) 39497

KAY, Ronald William. b 28. Liv Univ BEng49 MEng51. Tyndale Hall Bris 59. **d** 61 **p** 62. C Sparkbrook Ch Ch *Birm* 61-65; V Westcombe Park St Geo *S'wark* 65-76; R Doddington *Linc* 76-78; V Skellingthorpe 76-78; R Skellingthorpe w Doddington 78-91; rtd 91; Perm to Offic *Linc* from 91. *18 Abingdon Avenue, Lincoln LN6 3LE* Tel (01522) 696275

KAYE, Alistair Geoffrey. b 62. Reading Univ BSc85. St Jo Coll Nottm DPS90 DTS90. **d** 90 **p** 91. C Gt Horton *Bradf* 90-94; C Rushden w Newton Bromswold *Pet* from 94. *24 Lodge Road, Rushden, Northants NN10 9HA* Tel (01933) 316834

KAYE, Bruce Norman. b 39. Lon Univ BD64 Sydney Univ BA66. Moore Th Coll Sydney ThL64. **d** 64 **p** 65. Australia 64-66 and from 83; Perm to Offic *Dur* 67-69; Tutor St Jo Coll Dur 68-75; Sen Tutor 75-83; Vice Prin 79-83. *General Synod Office, PO Box Q190, Queen Victoria Buildings, Sydney, NSW, Australia 2000* Tel Sydney (2) 265 1525 Fax 264 6552

KAYE, Canon Gerald Trevor. b 32. Man Univ BSc54. Oak Hill Th Coll. **d** 56 **p** 57. C Widnes St Ambrose *Liv* 56-58; C St Helens St Mark 58-62; V Brixton Hill St Sav *S'wark* 62-65; Canada 65-85; Hon Can Keew 70-75; Adn Patricia 75-78; V Slough *Ox* from 85. *St Paul's Vicarage, 196 Stoke Road, Slough SL2 5AY* Tel (01753) 521497

KAYE, Norman. b 15. St Chad's Coll Dur BA47. **d** 49 **p** 50. C Morley St Paul *Wakef* 49-51; C Mexborough *Sheff* 51-54; V Dalton 54-59; V Liv St Paul Stanley *Liv* 59-68; R Leighton w Eaton Constantine *Lich* 68-80; P-in-c Wroxeter 68-80; rtd 80. *7 Rope Lane, Shavington, Crewe CW2 5DT* Tel (01270) 664170

KAYE, Peter Alan. b 47. K Coll Lon BD71 AKC71 Birm Univ DipPastS80 Leic Univ MA82 CQSW82. St Aug Coll Cant 71. **d** 72 **p** 73. C Fulham All SS *Lon* 72-74; Chapl Jo Conolly Hosp Birm 74-80; Rubery Hill and Jos Sheldon Hosps 74-80; Hon C Northfield *Birm* 80-83. *Hildegarden, 99 Bunbury Road, Northfield, Birmingham B31 2ND* Tel 0121-624 8399

KAYE, Timothy Henry. b 52. Linc Th Coll 77. **d** 80 **p** 81. C Warsop *S'well* 80-83; C Far Headingley St Chad *Ripon* 83-86; P-in-c Birkby *Wakef* 86; TV N Huddersfield 86-91; R Stone St Mich w Aston St Sav *Lich* 91-95; V S Kirkby *Wakef* from 95. *The Vicarage, Bull Lane, South Kirkby, Pontefract, W Yorkshire WF9 3QD* Tel (01977) 642795

KEANE, Canon James Goldsworthy. b 23. OBE84 JP71. Selw Coll Cam BA47 MA49. Cuddesdon Coll 47. **d** 49 **p** 50. C Penarth w Lavernock *Llan* 49-56; Org Sec Ch in Wales Prov Youth Coun 56-65; Dir Ch in Wales Publications 65-79; Gen Sec Ch in Wales Prov Educn Coun 65-79; Hon Can Llan Cathl *Llan* 73-92; R St Andrew's Major and Michaelston-le-Pit 79-92; Chan Llan Cathl 90-92; rtd 92; Perm to Offic *Llan* from 92. *3 Tudor Close, Westbourne Road, Penarth CF64 5BR*

KEARNS, Mrs Mary Leah. b 38. **d** 87 **p** 94. Par Dn Morden *S'wark* 87-88; Asst Chapl HM Pris Holloway from 88. *25 Leafield Road, London SW20 9AG* Tel 0181-540 1594 Fax 0171-700 0297

KEARNS, Philip Gillin. b 59. Ripon Coll Cuddesdon 90. **d** 92 **p** 93. C Winchmore Hill St Paul *Lon* 92-97; V N Shoebury *Chelmsf* from 97. *The Vicarage, 2 Weare Gifford, Shoeburyness, Southend-on-Sea SS3 8AB* Tel (01702) 584053

KEARON, Canon Kenneth Arthur. b 53. TCD BA76 MA79 MPhil91. CITC 78. **d** 81 **p** 82. C Raheny w Coolock *D & G* 81-84; Lect TCD 82-90; Dean of Res TCD 84-90; I Tullow *D & G* from 90; Can Ch Ch Cathl Dublin from 95. *Tullow Rectory, Brighton Road, Carrickmines, Dublin 18, Irish Republic* Tel Dublin (1) 289 3135 Fax as telephone E-mail kkearon@iol.ie

KEAST, William. b 43. Univ Coll Ox BA65 DipEd66. LNSM course 86. **d** 88 **p** 89. NSM Scotton w Northorpe *Linc* from 88. *4 Crapple Lane, Scotton, Gainsborough, Lincs DN21 3QT* Tel (01724) 763190

KEATING, Christopher Robin. b 39. K Coll Lon BD AKC84. Sarum Th Coll 62. **d** 65 **p** 66. C Baildon *Bradf* 65-67; CF 67-72; V Thornton Heath St Paul *Cant* 72-79; C Harold Hill St Geo *Chelmsf* 85-89; V Goodmayes All SS from 89. *All Saints' Vicarage, Broomhill Road, Ilford, Essex IG3 9SJ* Tel 0181-590 1476

KEATING, Geoffrey John. b 52. Liv Poly HND79 Open Univ BA94. St Steph Ho Ox 81. **d** 84 **p** 85. C Lancaster Ch Ch w St Jo and St Anne *Blackb* 84-85; C Rotherham *Sheff* 85-87; C Mexborough 87; V Bentley 87-91; V Penponds *Truro* 91-96; V Pet St Jude *Pet* from 96. *St Jude's Vicarage, 49 Atherstone Avenue, Peterborough PE3 6TZ* Tel (01733) 264169 or 268816

KEATING, William Edward. b 10. Trin Coll Ox BA32. Lich Th Coll 33. **d** 33 **p** 34. Dioc Missr *Chelmsf* 33-35; C Gt Yarmouth *Nor* 35-37; C Battersea St Geo w St Andr *S'wark* 37-40; Lic to Offic *Ox* 40-41; V Northbourne 41-55; RD Wallingford 53-55; R Welford w Wickham 55-61; R Welford w Wickham and Gt Shefford 61-63; Chapl Hurstwood Park Hosp Haywards Heath 63-75; Chapl St Fran Hosp Haywards Heath 63-75; rtd 75. *Manormead, Tilford Road, Hindhead, Surrey GU26 6RP* Tel (01428) 607539

KEAY, Alfred David. b 26. Aston Univ MSc72. Qu Coll Birm 76. **d** 79 **p** 80. Hon C Penkridge w Stretton *Lich* 79-82; C Rugeley 82-85; V Cheswardine 85-95; V Hales 85-95; rtd 95. *2 The Coppice, Farcroft Gardens, Market Drayton, Shropshire TF9 3UA* Tel (01630) 657924

KEDDIE, Canon Tony. b 37. Qu Coll Birm 63. **d** 66 **p** 67. C Barnoldswick w Bracewell *Bradf* 66-69; C New Bentley *Sheff* 69-71; TV Seacroft *Ripon* 71-79; V Kippax 79-85; TR Kippax w Allerton Bywater 85-92; R Fountains Gp from 92; Hon Can Ripon Cathl from 94. *Fountains Rectory, Winksley, Ripon, N Yorkshire HG4 3NR* Tel (01765) 658260

KEEBLE, Dorothy Deborah. b 20. **d** 87. NSM Glas H Cross *Glas* from 87. *12 Housel Avenue, Glasgow G13 3UR* Tel 0141-959 3102

KEEBLE, Stephen Robert. b 56. K Coll Lon BD84 AKC84 Selw Coll Cam DipTh86. Westcott Ho Cam 85. **d** 87 **p** 88. C Lt Stanmore St Lawr *Lon* 87-90; C Headstone St Geo 90-93; P-in-c from 93. *The Vicarage, 96 Pinner View, Harrow, Middx HA1 4RJ* Tel 0181-427 1253

KEECH, April Irene. b 52. Pennsylvania Univ BA76. Trin Coll Bris BA89. **d** 89 **p** 92. C Walthamstow St Luke *Chelmsf* 89-92; USA 92-95; V Deptford St Jo w H Trin *S'wark* from 95. *St John's Vicarage, St John's Vale, London SE8 4EA* Tel 0181-692 2857

KEEGAN, The Ven Donald Leslie. b 37. ACII. CITC 65. **d** 68 **p** 69. C Drumragh w Mountfield *D & R* 68-72; I Birr w Lorrha, Dorrha and Lockeen *L & K* from 72; Can Killaloe Cathl 80-82; Treas Killaloe Cathl 82-87; Prec Limerick and Killaloe Cathls 87-89; Adn Killaloe, Kilfenora, Clonfert etc from 89. *The Rectory, Birr, Co Offaly, Irish Republic* Tel Birr (509) 20021 Fax 21547

KEEGAN, Graham Brownell. b 40. Nottm Univ CertEd68. N Ord Course 81. **d** 84 **p** 85. C Highfield *Liv* 84-87; V Ince St Mary 87-95; V Newton in Makerfield St Pet from 95. *St Peter's Vicarage, Church Street, Newton-le-Willows, Merseyside WA12 9SR* Tel (01925) 224815

KEELER, Alan. b 58. MIEE87 CEng88 City Univ BSc81. St Jo Coll Nottm DTS90. **d** 90 **p** 91. C Paddock Wood *Roch* 90-94; V Blendon from 94. *The Vicarage, 37 Bladindon Drive, Bexley, Kent DA5 3BS* Tel 0181-301 5387

KEELEY, John Robin. b 38. G&C Coll Cam BA62. Clifton Th Coll 62. **d** 64 **p** 65. C Onslow Square St Paul *Lon* 64-66; C Hove Bp Hannington Memorial Ch *Chich* 66-69; C Harborne Heath *Birm* 69-72; V Leic H Trin *Leic* 72-74; P-in-c Leic St Jo 72-74; V Leic H Trin w St Jo 74-80; Perm to Offic *St Alb* 81-86; NSM Carterton *Ox* 89-95; Tutor E Anglian Minl Tr Course *Ely* from 95; Lic to Offic from 95. *11 Townsend, Little Downham, Ely, Cambs CB6 2TA* Tel (01353) 698209

KEELEY, Keith Morgan. b 12. Man Univ BA33 MA36. **d** 49 **p** 50. C Shipley St Paul *Bradf* 49-52; C Gt Barr *Lich* 52-53; C Blakenall Heath 53-55; V Tipton St Jo 55-59; R Hinstock 59-64; rtd 77. *36 College Road, Newport, Isle of Wight PO30 1HB* Tel (01983) 523465

KEELING, Brian Arnold. b 35. Coll of Resurr Mirfield. **d** 86 **p** 87. NSM Derby St Mark *Derby* 86-96; Perm to Offic from 96. *31 Highfield Lane, Chaddesden, Derby DE21 6DE* Tel (01332) 668987

KEELING, Peter Frank. b 34. Kelham Th Coll. **d** 58 **p** 59. C S Elmsall *Wakef* 58-63; C Barnsley St Mary 63-67; V Ravensthorpe 67-73; V Cudworth 73-83; R Downham Market w Bexwell *Ely* from 83; RD Fincham 83-94; V Crimplesham w Stradsett from 85. *The Rectory, Downham Market, Norfolk PE38 9LE* Tel (01366) 382187

KEEN, Michael Spencer. b 41. GRSM62 ARCM St Pet Coll Ox BA68 MA72 Reading Univ CertEd. Westcott Ho Cam 68. **d** 73 **p** 74. Hon C W Derby (or Tuebrook) St Jo *Liv* 73-74; Hon C Stanley 74-76; Chs Youth and Community Officer Telford *Lich* 77-82; Dioc Unemployment Officer *Sheff* 82-89; Hon C Brixton Road Ch Ch *S'wark* 89-92; Employment Development Officer 89-92; Perm to Offic from 92. *114 Lowden Road, London SE24 0BQ* Tel 0171-274 2206

KEENAN, Leslie Herbert. b 32. Cranmer Hall Dur. **d** 66 **p** 67. C Anston *Sheff* 66-70; C Woodsetts 66-70; Chapl HM Borstal Pollington 70-78; V Balne *Sheff* 70-78; V Poughill *Truro* from 78. *The Vicarage, Poughill, Bude, Cornwall EX23 9ER* Tel (01288) 355183

KEENE, Canon David Peter. b 32. Trin Hall Cam BA56 MA60. Westcott Ho Cam. **d** 58 **p** 59. C Radcliffe-on-Trent *S'well* 58-61; C Mansfield St Pet 61-64; V Nottingham St Cath 64-71; R Bingham 71-81; Dioc Dir of Ords 81-90; Can Res S'well Minster from 81. *2 Vicar's Court, Southwell, Notts NG25 0HP* Tel (01636) 813188 or 812649

KEENE, Mrs Muriel Ada. b 35. **dss** 83 **d** 87 **p** 94. Dioc Lay Min Adv *S'well* 87-88; Asst Dir of Ords 88-90; D-in-c Oxton 90-93; D-in-c Epperstone 90-94; D-in-c Gonalston 90-94; NSM Lowdham w Caythorpe, and Gunthorpe from 94; rtd 95. *2 Vicar's Court, Southwell, Notts NG25 0HP* Tel (01636) 813188

KEEP, Andrew James. b 55. Collingwood Coll Dur BA77 Yale Univ STM84. Sarum & Wells Th Coll 78. **d** 80 **p** 81. C Banstead *Guildf* 80-83; Chapl Qu Eliz Hosp Banstead 80-83; USA 83-84; Chapl Cranleigh Sch Surrey from 84; Lic to Offic *Guildf* from 84; Perm to Offic *Win* 84-95. *Cranleigh School, Cranleigh, Surrey GU6 8QQ* Tel (01483) 274561

KEEP, Hugh Charles John Martin. b 45. Qu Coll Birm 90. **d** 92 **p** 93. C Aston Cantlow and Wilmcote w Billesley *Cov* 92-95; P-in-c Hampton Lucy w Charlecote and Loxley from 95. *The Vicarage, Charlecote, Warwick CV35 9EW* Tel (01789) 840244

KEETON, Barry. b 40. Dur Univ BA61 MA69 MLitt78 K Coll Lon BD63 AKC63. **d** 64 **p** 65. C S Bank *York* 64-67; C Middlesbrough St Cuth 67-69; C Kingston upon Hull St Alb 70-71; V Appleton-le-Street w Amotherby 71-74; Dioc Ecum Adv 74-81; R Ampleforth w Oswaldkirk 74-78; P-in-c Barmby on the Marsh 78-79; P-in-c Laxton w Blacktoft 78-79; P-in-c Wressell 78-79; V Howden 78-79; TR Howden TM 80-91; Can and Preb York Minster 85-91; RD Howden 86-91; TR Lewes All SS, St Anne, St Mich and St Thos *Chich* 91-96; R Cov St Jo *Cov* from 96; RD Cov N from 97. *St John's Rectory, 9 Davenport Road, Coventry CV5 6QA* Tel (01203) 673203

KEFFORD, Peter Charles. b 44. Nottm Univ BTh74. Linc Th Coll 70. **d** 74 **p** 75. C W Wimbledon Ch Ch *S'wark* 74-77; C All Hallows by the Tower etc *Lon* 77-81; C-in-c Pound Hill CD *Chich* 81; TV Worth 82-83; TR 83-92; V Henfield w Shermanbury and Woodmancote from 92. *The Vicarage, Church Lane, Henfield, W Sussex BN5 9NY* Tel (01273) 492017

KEGG, Gordon Rutherford. b 45. Reading Univ BSc66 Imp Coll Lon PhD71 DIC71 Lon Univ CertEd74. Oak Hill Th Coll DipHE90. **d** 90 **p** 91. C Luton Lewsey St Hugh *St Alb* 90-94; TV Hemel Hempstead from 94. *St Barnabas Vicarage, Everest Way, Hemel Hempstead, Herts HP2 4HY* Tel (01442) 253681

KEIGHLEY, Andrew. b 62. **d** 97. C Pimlico St Jas the Less *Lon* from 97. *90 Abercrombie Street, London SW11 2JD*

KEIGHLEY, David John. b 48. CertEd Open Univ BA88. Sarum & Wells Th Coll 82. **d** 83 **p** 84. C Sawbridgeworth *St Alb* 83-86; TV Saltash *Truro* 86-89; V Lanlivery w Luxulyan from 89. *The Vicarage, Luxulyan, Bodmin, Cornwall PL30 5EE* Tel (01726) 850880

KEIGHLEY, Martin Philip. b 61. Edin Univ MA83. Westcott Ho Cam 86. **d** 88 **p** 89. C Lytham St Cuth *Blackb* 88-91; C Lancaster St Mary 91-93; R Halton w Aughton from 93. *The Rectory, 110 High Road, Halton, Lancaster LA2 6PU* Tel (01524) 811370

KEIGHTLEY, Canon Peter Edward. b 17. Leeds Univ BA41. Coll of Resurr Mirfield 41. **d** 43 **p** 44. C Wellingborough All Hallows *Pet* 43-45; C Solihull *Birm* 45-49; C Cirencester *Glouc* 50-53; V Glouc St Paul 53-59; V Widley w Wymering *Portsm* 59-67; V Southsea H Spirit 67-76; Chapl St Mary's Hosp Portsm 76-82; Hon Can Portsm Cathl *Portsm* 81-82; rtd 82; Perm to Offic *Portsm* from 83. *11 Dolphin Court, St Helen's Parade, Southsea, Hants PO4 0QL* Tel (01705) 816697

KEIGHTLEY, Canon Thomas. b 44. CITC 79. **d** 79 **p** 80. C Seagoe *D & D* 79-83; I Belvoir from 83; Preb Down Cathl from 95. *3 Brerton Crescent, Belfast BT8 4QD* Tel (01232) 643777

KEILLER, Mrs Jane Elizabeth. b 52. Westmr Coll Ox BEd74 St Jo Coll Dur DipTh78 Bangalore Univ DipTh79. Cranmer Hall Dur 76. **dss** 80 **d** 87 **p** 94. Cambridge H Trin w St Andr Gt *Ely* 80-86; Cambridge St Barn 86-87; NSM from 87; Chapl Ridley Hall Cam from 96. *Chestnut Cottage, 38 Pierce Lane, Cambridge CB1 5DL* Tel (01223) 881444

KEIRLE, Michael Robert. b 62. Trin Coll Bris BA89. **d** 89 **p** 90. C Orpington Ch Ch *Roch* 89-92; Zimbabwe 92-95; R Keston *Roch* from 95. *The Rectory, 24 Commonside, Keston, Kent BR2 6BP* Tel (01689) 853186

KEITH, Andrew James Buchanan. b 47. Qu Coll Cam BA69 MA73. Wycliffe Hall Ox 71. **d** 74 **p** 75. C Warrington St Elphin *Liv* 74-77; C Southgate *Chich* 77-80; C-in-c Broadfield CD 80-82; P-in-c Walberton w Binsted 82-85; P-in-c Aldingbourne 83-85; Chapl Oswestry Sch 85-95; Chapl HM Pris Liv 95-96; Chapl HM Pris Preston from 96. *HM Prison, 2 Ribbleton Lane, Preston PR1 5AB* Tel (01772) 257734

KEITH, John. b 25. LRAM50 LGSM50 AGSM51. Cuddesdon Coll 60. **d** 62 **p** 63. C Lee-on-the-Solent *Portsm* 62-65; C Raynes Park St Sav *S'wark* 65-68; rtd 90. *Leaning Tree, Inchlaggan, Invergarry, Inverness-shire PH35 4HR*

KELK, Michael Anthony. b 48. Sarum & Wells Th Coll. **d** 83 **p** 84. C Ross w Brampton Abbotts, Bridstow and Peterstow *Heref* 83-86; P-in-c Burghill 86-97; P-in-c Stretton Sugwas 86-97; P-in-c Walford and St John w Bishopswood, Goodrich etc from 97. *The Vicarage, Walford, Ross-on-Wye, Herefordshire HR9 5QP* Tel (01989) 562703

KELLAM, Miss Margaret June. b 32. Trin Coll Bris IDC70. **dss** 77 **d** 87 **p** 94. Heeley *Sheff* 77-89; Par Dn 87-89; Asst Chapl R Hallamshire Hosp and Jessop Women's Hosp 89-96; Chapl Cen Sheff Univ Hosps NHS Trust from 96; Chapl Sheff Children's Hosp 89-97. *170 Westwick Road, Sheffield S8 7BX* Tel 0114-237 6773

KELLAND, Kenneth William Jerome. b 16. S'wark Ord Course 63. **d** 66 **p** 67. C Addlestone *Guildf* 66-69; C Sholing *Win* 69-74; V Weston 74-82; rtd 82; Hon C Odiham w S Warnborough and Long Sutton *Win* 82-85; Hon C Herriard w Winslade and Long Sutton etc 85-86. *50 Wooteys Way, Alton, Hants GU34 2JZ* Tel (01420) 85325

KELLEN, David. b 52. Univ of Wales (Cardiff) DipTh73. St Mich Coll Llan 70. **d** 75 **p** 76. C Mynyddislwyn *Mon* 75-77; C Risca 77-78; C Malpas 78-81; V Newport All SS 81-88; V St Mellons and Michaelston-y-Fedw 88-96; V St Mellons from 96. *The Vicarage, Tyr Winch Road, St Mellons, Cardiff CF3 9UP* Tel (01222) 796560

KELLETT, Colin. b 25. Worc Ord Coll 65. **d** 67 **p** 68. C E Ardsley *Wakef* 67-69; C Dewsbury Moor 69-72; V Lundwood 72-77; V Gawber 77-88; rtd 88; Perm to Offic *Wakef* from 88; Perm to Offic *York* from 96. *11 Hurrell Court, Hurrell Lane, Thornton Dale, Pickering, N Yorkshire YO18 7QR* Tel (01751) 476487

KELLETT, Neil. b 41. Bps' Coll Cheshunt 64. **d** 66 **p** 67. C Ex St Thos *Ex* 66-72; C Win H Trin *Win* 72-74; P-in-c Redditch St Geo *Worc* 74-77; Canada from 77. *39 Fox Avenue, St John's, Newfoundland, Canada, A1B 2H8* Tel St John's (709) 726-2883

KELLETT, Richard. b 64. Leeds Univ BSc85 PhD89. St Jo Coll Nottm BTh95 MA96. **d** 96 **p** 97. C Nottingham St Jude *S'well* from 96. *St Jude's House, 19 Kent Road, Mapperley, Nottingham NG3 6BE* Tel 0115-962 0281 Fax as telephone

KELLEY, Neil George. b 64. ARCM85 DipRCM87. Westcott Ho Cam 88. **d** 91 **p** 92. C E Bedfont *Lon* 91-93; C Chiswick St Nic w St Mary 93-97; C Kirkby *Liv* from 97. *45 Alvanley Road, Kirkby, Liverpool L32 0SZ* Tel 0151-547 2769 Fax as telephone

KELLY, Canon Albert Norman. b 21. TCD BA43 MA63. **d** 44 **p** 45. C Donaghcloney *D & D* 44-46; C Belfast Malone St Jo *Conn* 46-55; I Billy 55-63; C Dorking w Ranmore *Guildf* 63-66; C-in-c New Haw CD 66-72; V New Haw 72-78; RD Chertsey 73-75; RD Runnymede 75-78; V Egham Hythe 78-86; Hon Can Guildf Cathl 80-86; rtd 86; USPG Area Sec 88-93. *21 Rosetta Road, Belfast BT6 0LQ* Tel (01232) 693921

KELLY, Dr Brian Eugene. b 56. Otago Univ BA77 Dunedin Coll PGCE79 Bris Univ PhD93. Trin Coll Bris BA89. **d** 90 **p** 91. NSM Redland *Bris* 90-93; C Scarborough St Mary w Ch Ch and H Apostles *York* 93-96; Dean Chpl Ch Ch Coll Cant from 96. *Canterbury Christ Church College, North Holmes Road, Canterbury, Kent CT1 1QU* Tel (01227) 767700 E-mail bek1@cant.ac.uk

KELLY, Canon Brian Horace. b 34. St Jo Coll Dur BA57 DipTh58 MA69. **d** 58 **p** 59. C Douglas St Geo and St Barn *S & M* 58-61; V Foxdale 61-64; V Bolton All So w St Jas *Man* 64-73; V Maughold *S & M* 73-77; Dir of Ords 76-93; V German from 77; Can and Prec St German's Cathl from 80; RD Castletown and Peel from 97. *The Cathedral Vicarage, Albany Road, Peel, Isle of Man IM5 1JS* Tel (01624) 842608

KELLY, Christopher Augustine (Kit). b 15. Croix de Guerre 45 TD65. Keble Coll Ox BA37. Ripon Hall Ox 37. **d** 45 **p** 46. C Aston SS Pet and Paul *Birm* 45-51; V Habergham Eaves H Trin *Blackb* 51-57; V Knuzden 57-67; V Bolton Breightmet St Jas *Man* 67-76; V Nelson in Lt Marsden *Blackb* 76-83; rtd 83; Perm to Offic *Bradf* from 83. *33 River Place, Gargrave, Skipton, N Yorkshire BD23 3RY* Tel (01756) 748247

KELLY, Canon Dennis Charles. b 31. Liv Univ BA52. Lich Th Coll 54. **d** 56 **p** 57. C Tranmere St Paul *Ches* 56-59; C-in-c Grange St Andr CD 59-63; P-in-c Grange St Andr 63-65; V 65-67; R Coppenhall 67-82; R W Kirby St Andr from 82; Hon Can Ches Cathl from 86. *St Andrew's Vicarage, 2 Lingdale Road, West Kirby, Wirral, Merseyside L48 5DQ* Tel 0151-632 4728

KELLY, Desmond Norman (Des). b 42. Oak Hill Th Coll DipHE90. **d** 90 **p** 91. C Braintree *Chelmsf* 90-94; P-in-c Castle Hedingham 94-95; P-in-c Sible Hedingham 94-95; R Sible Hedingham w Castle Hedingham from 95. *The Vicarage, 15 Queen Street, Castle Hedingham, Halstead, Essex CO9 3EZ* Tel (01787) 60274

KELLY, Canon Edward William Moncrieff (Ted). b 28. AKC57. **d** 57 **p** 58. C Petersfield w Sheet *Portsm* 57-60; Papua New Guinea 60-65; V Gosport Ch Ch *Portsm* 65-69; Hon C Eltham St Jo *S'wark* 69-87; Org Sec New Guinea Miss 69-77; Org Sec Papua New Guinea Ch Partnership 77-87; Hon Can Papua New Guinea from 78; TR Trowbridge H Trin *Sarum* 87-94; Chapl St Jo Hosp Trowbridge 87-94; rtd 94; Perm to Offic *Portsm* from 94. *133 Borough Road, Petersfield, Hants GU32 3LP* Tel (01730) 260399

KELLY, James Ganly Marks. b 16. TCD BA39 MA50. CITC 39. **d** 39 **p** 40. C Ballymoney *Conn* 39-42; Chapl RAFVR 42-46; P-in-c Aghancon w Kilcolman and Seir-Keiran *L & K* 46-47; P-in-c Clanabogan *D & R* 47-49; CF 49-71; R Siddington w Preston *Glouc* 71-81; rtd 82. *34 Henry Avenue, Rustington, Littlehampton, W Sussex BN16 2PA* Tel (01903) 770635

KELLY, John Adrian. b 49. Qu Coll Birm 70. **d** 73 **p** 74. C Formby St Pet *Liv* 73-77; Perm to Offic from 77; Perm to Offic *Blackb* from 77; Org Sec (Dios Liv, Blackb and S & M) CECS 77-92; Deputation Appeals Org (Lancs and Is of Man) 88-92; Perm to Offic *Man* from 88. *159 Forrest Drive, South Park, Lytham, Lytham St Annes, Lancs FY8 4QG* Tel (01253) 730083

KELLY, John Bernal. b 35. K Coll Cam BA57 MA61. Qu Coll Birm 58. **d** 60 **p** 61. C Huyton St Mich *Liv* 60-62; C Gateshead Fell *Dur* 64-68; R Openshaw *Man* 68-75; V Hey 75-87; V Bury St Jo w St Mark 87-93; V Rochdale St Geo w St Alb from 93. *St George's Vicarage, 13 Brooklands Court, Bury Road, Rochdale, Lancs OL11 4EJ* Tel (01706) 39743

KELLY, John Dickinson. b 42. Nottm Univ BA63. Ripon Hall Ox 63. **d** 65 **p** 66. C Egremont *Carl* 65-67; C Upperby St Jo 67-70; V Arlecdon 70-73; V Barrow St Aid 73-79; V Milnthorpe 79-83; V Beetham and Milnthorpe 83-85; V Camerton St Pet 85-88; P-in-c Camerton H Trin W Seaton 86-88; V Camerton, Seaton and W

Seaton from 88. *The Vicarage, Ling Beck Park, Seaton, Workington, Cumbria CA14 1JQ* Tel (01900) 602162

KELLY, John Graham. b 60. Lanc Univ LLB82 Man Poly Solicitor 84. St Jo Coll Nottm BTh91. **d** 94 **p** 95. C Normanton *Derby* 94-97; P-in-c Ockbrook from 97. *The Vicarage, 265 Victoria Avenue, Ockbrook, Derby DE72 3RL* Tel (01332) 662352

KELLY, John Henry. b 20. Vancouver Sch of Th STh65. **d** 55 **p** 59. Australia 55-58; Canada 58-68; C Hall Green St Pet *Birm* 69-70; V Smethwick St Mich 71-78; P-in-c Smethwick St Steph 72-78; V Selly Oak St Wulstan 78-80; R Over Whitacre w Shustoke 80-86; rtd 86; Perm to Offic *Ches* from 86. *61 Hallfields Road, Tarvin, Chester CH3 8ET* Tel (01829) 741218

KELLY, John Rowe. b 32. Edin Th Coll. **d** 85 **p** 86. C Blyth St Mary *Newc* 85-88; C Slaley 88-91; C Healey 88-91; TV Alston Team 91-96; Chapl Alston Cottage Hosp from 91; P-in-c Alston Team from 96. *The Parsonage, Brampton Road, Alston, Cumbria CA9 3AA* Tel (01434) 381458

KELLY, Malcolm Bernard. b 46. St Mich Coll Llan 72. **d** 74 **p** 75. C Tranmere St Paul w St Luke *Ches* 74-77; Chapl Bebington Hosp from 76; C Barnston *Ches* 77-80; R Thurstaston 80-92; R Grappenhall from 92. *The Rectory, 17 Hill Top Road, Stockton Heath, Warrington WA4 2ED* Tel (01925) 261546

KELLY, Martin Herbert. b 55. Selw Coll Cam MA90. Aston Tr Scheme 78 Ripon Coll Cuddesdon 80. **d** 83 **p** 84. C Clapham Old Town *S'wark* 83-87; Chapl and Fell Selw Coll Cam 87-92; Chapl Newnham Coll Cam 87-92; C Limpsfield and Titsey *S'wark* from 95; Chapl St Piers Hosp Sch Lingfield from 95. *St Andrew's House, Limpsfield Chart, Oxted, Surrey RH8 0TB* Tel (01883) 723153

KELLY, Nigel James. b 60. N Staffs Poly BSc83. Ripon Coll Cuddesdon 83. **d** 86 **p** 87. C Cen Telford *Lich* 86-90; TV 90-92; Chapl RN from 92. *Royal Naval Chaplaincy Service, Room 203, Victory Building, HM Naval Base, Portsmouth PO1 3LS* Tel (01705) 727903 Fax 727112

KELLY, Norman James. b 11. K Coll Lon BD36 AKC36. Wycliffe Hall Ox 36. **d** 36 **p** 37. C Champion Hill St Sav *S'wark* 36-39; C Newhaven *Chich* 39-40; C E Grinstead St Swithun 40-46; V Westf 46-50; New Zealand 50-57; V Canewdon w Paglesham *Chelmsf* from 57. *The Vicarage, High Street, Canewdon, Rochford, Essex SS4 3QA* Tel (01702) 258217

KELLY, Paul Maitland Hillyard. b 24. Ball Coll Ox BA50 MA54. Wells Th Coll 50. **d** 52 **p** 53. C Epsom St Martin *Guildf* 52-57; C-in-c New Cathl CD 57-61; R Abinger cum Coldharbour 61-67; P-in-c Preston St Pet *Blackb* 67-70; V Ottershaw *Guildf* 70-77; R Ickenham *Lon* 77-94; rtd 94; Perm to Offic *B & W* from 94. *37 Dodd Avenue, Wells, Somerset BA5 3JU* Tel (01749) 673334

KELLY, Peter Hugh. b 46. Sarum & Wells Th Coll 81. **d** 84 **p** 85. C Fareham H Trin *Portsm* 84-87; Chapl and Prec Portsm Cathl 87-90; V Eastney 90-97; P-in-c Swanmore St Barn from 97. *The Vicarage, Church Road, Swanmore, Southampton SO32 2PA* Tel (01489) 892105

KELLY, Richard Peter. b 47. BA PhD. CITC BTh90. **d** 90 **p** 91. C Dromore Cathl *D & D* 90-93; C Gweedore, Carrickfin and Templecrone *D & R* from 93; Bp's Dom Chapl from 96. *The Rectory, Bunbeg, Letterkenny, Co Donegal, Irish Republic* Tel Bunbeg (75) 31043

KELLY, Stephen Paul. b 55. Keble Coll Ox BA77. Linc Th Coll 77. **d** 79 **p** 80. C Illingworth *Wakef* 79-82; C Knottingley 82-84; V Alverthorpe 84-93; Dioc Ecum Officer 88-93; TR Bingley All SS *Bradf* from 93. *The Vicarage, Hallbank Drive, Bingley, W Yorkshire BD16 4BZ* Tel (01274) 563113

KELLY, Canon William. b 35. Dur Univ BA58 St Cath Coll Ox DipTh59. Lambeth STh75 Wycliffe Hall Ox 58. **d** 60 **p** 61. C Walney Is *Carl* 60-66; R Distington 66-71; V Barrow St Matt 71-81; RD Furness 77-81; Hon Can Carl Cathl from 79; Dir of Ords 81-97; V Dalston 81-92; RD Carl 83-88; P-in-c Raughton Head w Gatesgill 86-92; P-in-c Maryport 92-97; P-in-c Flimby 93-96; P-in-c Arthuret from 97; P-in-c Nicholforest and Kirkandrews on Esk from 97. *Arthuret Rectory, Arthuret Drive, Longtown, Carlisle CA6 5SG* Tel (01228) 791338

KELLY, William Edward (Bill). b 31. Univ of Wales (Lamp) BA57 St Cath Soc Ox BA59 MA63. St Steph Ho Ox 57. **d** 60 **p** 61. C S Bank *York* 60-63; C Ingoldisthorpe *Nor* 63-66; C Heacham 63-66; Chapl RAF 66-82; Chapl Woodbridge Sch 82-88; V Newport St Paul *Mon* from 90. *11B Victoria Place, Newport NP9 4DZ* Tel (01633) 266657

KELLY, William Frederick Paul. b 12. Ch Ch Ox BA35 MA49. Sarum Th Coll 63. **d** 64 **p** 65. C Barnham Broom w Kimberley, Bixton etc *Nor* 64-68; R Reepham and Hackford w Whitwell and Kerdiston 68-80; P-in-c Salle 68-72; rtd 80; P-in-c Thurning w Wood Dalling *Nor* 80-81; Chapl to Rtd Clergy and Clergy Widows Officer from 81. *40 Catton Grove Road, Norwich NR3 3NW* Tel (01603) 424961

KELLY, William Norman. b 21. St Aid Birkenhead. **d** 64 **p** 65. Miss to Seamen 64-66; C Douglas St Geo and St Barn *S & M* 66-69; V Wingates *Man* 69-75; Perm to Offic 76-84; Chapl HM Pris Liv 77-78; Chapl HM Borstal Stoke Heath 78-84; V Castletown *S & M* 84-92; rtd 92; Perm to Offic *S & M* from 92. *Crossag Villa, St Mark's Road, Ballasalla, Isle of Man IM9 3EF* Tel (01624) 825582

KELLY, William Ralston. b 27. TCD BA52 MA55. Lich Th Coll 52. **d** 54 **p** 55. C Ashton on Mersey St Mary *Ches* 54-60; Hd of RE Bablake Sch Cov 60-92; rtd 92. *108 Duncroft Avenue, Coventry CV6 2BW* Tel (01203) 336807

KELLY, Canon William Robert. b 28. QUB BSc57 BTh. CITC 62. **d** 62 **p** 63. C Lurgan Ch Ch *D & D* 62-66; I Clondehorkey *D & R* 66-70; I Raheny w Coolock *D & G* 70-75; Peru 75-83; I Ballinderry *Conn* 83-89; Hon Can Peru 83; I Belfast St Aid *Conn* 89-96; Can Belf Cathl from 94; rtd 96. *17 College Avenue, Bangor, Co Down BT20 5HJ* Tel (01247) 473679

KELSEY, George Robert. b 61. Imp Coll Lon BSc83 Newc Univ MSc84 PhD92. Cranmer Hall Dur 95. **d** 97. C Denton *Newc* from 97. *8 Fenton Close, Newcastle upon Tyne NE5 1EA* Tel 0191-267 2315

KELSEY, Michael Ray. b 22. FEPA57. Wycliffe Hall Ox 60. **d** 62 **p** 63. C Lower Broughton St Clem *Man* 62-64; V Ingleby Greenhow *York* 64-68; V Scarborough St Jas 68-71; Asst to the Gen Sec USCL 71-74; V Blackheath St Jo *S'wark* 74-87; rtd 87; Perm to Offic *St E* from 88. *25 Prospect Place, Leiston, Suffolk IP16 4AL* Tel (01728) 830975

✠**KELSHAW, The Rt Revd Terence.** b 36. Lon Univ DipTh67 Pittsburgh Th Sem DMin86. Oak Hill Th Coll. **d** 67 **p** 68 **c** 89. C Clifton Ch Ch w Em *Bris* 67-71; C Woking St Jo *Guildf* 71-73; V Bris H Trin *Bris* 73-75; P-in-c Easton St Gabr w St Laur 73-75; V Easton H Trin w St Gabr and St Lawr 75-80; P-in-c Barton Hill St Luke w Ch Ch 76-80; USA from 80; Bp Rio Grande from 89. *4304 Carlisle Northeast, Albuquerque, New Mexico 87107-4811, USA* Tel Albuquerque (505) 881-0636 Fax 883-9048

KELSO, Andrew John (Andy). b 47. LRAM73 Lon Univ BA70. St Jo Coll Nottm 83. **d** 85 **p** 86. C Gorleston St Mary *Nor* 85-87; C Hellesdon 87-90; TV Ipsley *Worc* from 90. *Matchborough Vicarage, Winward Road, Redditch, Worcs B98 0SX* Tel (01527) 29098

KELSO, William Thomas Proctor. b 19. TCD BA41 MA45. CITC 43. **d** 43 **p** 44. C Spring Grove St Mary *Lon* 43-45; C Gt Yarmouth *Nor* 45-48; V W Twyford *Lon* 48-53; V Isleworth St Jo 53-63; R Blendworth, Chalton and Idsworth *Portsm* 63-70; V Balham Hill Ascension *S'wark* 70-78; Perm to Offic *Chich* 78-84; Chapl and Tutor Whittington Coll Felbridge 78-84; rtd 84; Perm to Offic *S'wark* 84-92. *12 Brunswick Place, Lymington, Hants SO41 9EQ* Tel (01590) 677939

KEMM, William St John (Bill). b 39. Birm Univ BA62 MA65. Ridley Hall Cam 62. **d** 64 **p** 65. C Kingswinford H Trin *Lich* 64-68; C Hednesford 68-71; V Hanbury 71-76; R Berrow and Breane *B & W* 76-92; V Hertford All SS *St Alb* from 92. *All Saints' Vicarage, Churchfields, Hertford SG13 8AE* Tel (01992) 582096

KEMP, Allan. b 43. Bps' Coll Cheshunt 65 Oak Hill Th Coll 67. **d** 68 **p** 69. C Tunbridge Wells St Jas *Roch* 68-76; V Becontree St Mary *Chelmsf* 76-90; RD Barking and Dagenham 81-86; V Gt w Lt Chesterford from 90. *The Vicarage, Great Chesterford, Saffron Walden, Essex CB10 1NP* Tel (01799) 530317

KEMP, Ms Audrey. b 26. MSR49. Gilmore Ho 62. **dss** 69 **d** 87 **p** 94. S Ockendon Hosp 70-71; N Greenford All Hallows *Lon* 71-72; Feltham 72-80; Brentford St Faith 80-83; Hanworth All SS 83-85; Hanworth St Geo 85-87; Par Dn 87-88; rtd 88; Perm to Offic *B & W* 88-89; Hon Par Dn Ditcheat w E Pennard and Pylle 89-94; P-in-c 94-95. *5 Adams House, Adams Way, Alton, Hants GU34 2UY* Tel (01420) 80257

KEMP, Barry. b 48. St Edm Hall Ox BA70 MA75 Nottm Univ DipTh73 Newc Univ CertEd82. Linc Th Coll 71. **d** 74 **p** 75. C Ashton Ch Ch *Man* 74-77; CF 77-81; C Dunston *Dur* 81-83; Perm to Offic *Newc* 83-87; C Monkseaton St Mary 88; Chapl Ld Wandsworth Coll Basingstoke from 92. *Kimbers, Lord Wandsworth College, Long Sutton, Basingstoke, Hants RG25 1TB* Tel (01256) 862201

KEMP, Canon Bernard Henry. b 06. St Chad's Coll Dur BA26 MA46 DipTh46. **d** 29 **p** 30. C Sydenham All SS *S'wark* 29-32; Camberwell Deanery Missr 32-35; C Bedford Park *Lon* 35-41; CF (EC) 41-46; V Isleworth St Fran *Lon* 46-50; Mauritius 50-63; Adn Mauritius 54-63; Hon Can Mauritius from 63; V Guernsey St Steph *Win* 63-81; rtd 81; Perm to Offic *Win* from 81. *Carrefour, La Haye du Puits, Castel, Guernsey, Channel Islands GY5 7HX* Tel (01481) 56081

KEMP, Christopher Michael. b 48. K Coll Lon BD71 AKC71. St Aug Coll Cant 75. **d** 76 **p** 77. C Weaverham *Ches* 76-79; C Latchford St Jas 79-82; P-in-c Sandbach Heath 82-88; V Macclesfield St Paul 88-89; C Cheadle Hulme All SS 89-93; C Oxton from 93. *36 Noctorum Dell, Birkenhead, Merseyside L43 9UL* Tel 0151-652 8050

KEMP, Clive Warren. b 36. Sheff Univ BSc60. Clifton Th Coll 62. **d** 64 **p** 65. C Wandsworth All SS *S'wark* 64-67; C Normanton *Wakef* 67-71; V Sandal St Cath 71-76; C Chapeltown *Sheff* 85-87; V Sheff St Jo from 87. *49 Norfolk Park Avenue, Sheffield S2 2RA* Tel 0114-275 9998

✠**KEMP, The Rt Revd Eric Waldram.** b 15. FRHistS51 Ex Coll Ox BA36 MA40 BD44 DD61 Sussex Univ Hon DLitt. St Steph Ho Ox 36. **d** 39 **p** 40 **c** 74. C Newtown St Luke *Win* 39-41; Lib Pusey Ho 41-46; Chapl Ch Ch Ox 43-46; Tutor and Chapl Ex Coll Ox 46-69; Can and Preb Linc Cathl *Linc* from 52; Chapl to The Queen 67-69; Dean Worc 69-74; Bp Chich from 74. *The Palace,*

Chichester, W Sussex PO19 1PY Tel (01243) 782161 Fax 531332

KEMP, Geoffrey Bernard. b 20. Lon Univ BD43. ALCD42. **d** 43 **p** 44. C Leyton All SS *Chelmsf* 43-46; C Woodford St Mary 46-49; V Barkingside St Laur 49-60; V Hadleigh St Barn 60-79; R Kelvedon Hatch 79-86; V Navestock 79-86; rtd 86; Perm to Offic *St E* from 86; Perm to Offic *Chelmsf* from 86. *24 Roman Way, Felixstowe, Suffolk IP11 9NJ* Tel (01394) 276691

KEMP, Jack Noel. b 14. Univ Coll Lon BA36 MA38. Wycliffe Hall Ox 55. **d** 55 **p** 56. C Harborne Heath *Birm* 55-58; PC Tyseley 58-64; V St Mary Cray and St Paul's Cray *Roch* 64-68; Lect Brasted 67-74; V Four Elms 68-80; rtd 80; Perm to Offic *Cant* from 81. *L'Ancresse, 16 Church Street, Whitstable, Kent CT5 1PJ* Tel (01227) 265379

KEMP, John Graham Edwin. b 29. Bris Univ BA51 PGCE52 Lon Univ BD65. Wells Th Coll 63. **d** 65 **p** 66. C Maidenhead St Luke *Ox* 65-70; R Rotherfield Greys 70-78; V Highmore 70-78; Dep Dir Tr Scheme for NSM 78-84; P-in-c Taplow 78-82; TV Burnham w Dropmore, Hitcham and Taplow 82-84; Prin E Anglian Minl Tr Course 84-92; rtd 92. *Lea Cottage, Middleton, Saxmundham, Suffolk IP17 3NJ* Tel (01728) 648324

KEMP, John Robert Deverall. b 42. City Univ BSc65 BD69. Oak Hill Th Coll 66. **d** 70 **p** 71. C Fulham Ch Ch *Lon* 70-73; C Widford *Chelmsf* 73-79; P-in-c New Thundersley 79-84; V from 84; Chapl HM Pris Bullwood Hall from 79. *St George's Vicarage, 89 Rushbottom Lane, Benfleet, Essex SS7 4DN* Tel (01268) 792088 Fax (01702) 207464

KEMP, William Frederick. b 13. St Aug Coll Cant 38. **d** 40 **p** 41. C Wolverhampton *Lich* 40-46; C Norbury St Steph *Cant* 46-51; C Stoke upon Trent *Lich* 51-53; V Gosberton Clough *Linc* 53-64; R Denton w Wootton and Swingfield *Cant* 64-79; rtd 79; Perm to Offic *Cant* 79-80; Hon Min Can Cant Cathl from 80. *12 Chantry Court, St Radigund's Street, Canterbury, Kent CT1 2AD* Tel (01227) 462261

KEMPSTER, Robert Alec. b 29. Selw Coll Cam MA53. Coll of Resurr Mirfield 53. **d** 55 **p** 56. C W Hackney St Barn *Lon* 55-57; C-in-c S'wark All Hallows CD *S'wark* 57-70; PV S'wark Cathl 57-60; Chapl Evelina Children's Hosp 57-70; Chapl Guy's Hosp Lon 70-81; Chapl Nat Hosp for Nervous Diseases Lon 81-89; Chapl Convent Companions Jes Gd Shep W Ogwell 89; rtd 90; Perm to Offic *Ex* from 90. *15A Seymour Road, Newton Abbot, Devon TQ12 2PT* Tel (01626) 61720

KEMPTHORNE, Renatus. b 39. Wadh Coll Ox BA60 DipTh61 MA64. Wycliffe Hall Ox 60. **d** 62 **p** 63. C Stoke *Cov* 62-65; New Zealand 65-68 and from 83; R Wytham *Ox* 68-75; Chapl Bp Grosseteste Coll Linc 75-83. *140 Nile Street, Nelson, New Zealand* Tel Christchurch (3) 546 7447

KENCHINGTON (née BALLANTYNE), Mrs Jane Elizabeth Ballantyne. b 58. Hull Univ BSc79 Cam Univ PGCE83. Westcott Ho Cam 88. **d** 90 **p** 94. C Winchcombe, Gretton, Sudeley Manor etc *Glouc* 90-96; Perm to Offic from 96. *7 Warren Croft, North Nibley, Dursley, Glos GL11 6EN* Tel (01453) 546509

KENCHINGTON, Paul Henry. b 54. Worc Coll Ox MA76. St Jo Coll Nottm BA81. **d** 82 **p** 83. C Scarborough St Mary w Ch Ch and H Apostles *York* 82-85; C Caversham and Mapledurham *Ox* 85-89; V Hucclecote *Glouc* from 89. *128 Hucclecote Road, Gloucester GL3 3SB* Tel (01452) 610568

KENDAL, Gordon McGregor. b 46. Dundee Univ MA70 Mansf Coll Ox BA72 MA76 Lon Univ BA73 PhD79. Edin Th Coll 72. **d** 74 **p** 75. C Bracknell *Ox* 74-77; C Wokingham All SS 77-79; Chapl and Fell Linc Coll Ox 79-83; R Edin St Pet *Edin* 83-87; Manchester Grammar Sch 88-92; Gen Sec Fellowship of St Alb and St Sergius 92-96; V S Lambeth St Anne and All SS *S'wark* from 96. *The Vicarage, 179 Fentiman Road, London SW8 1JY* Tel 0171-735 3191

KENDAL, Henry David. b 59. Bris Poly DipVal&EstM80 ASVA83. Lon Bible Coll 90 Oak Hill NSM Course 92. **d** 94 **p** 95. NSM Roxeth *Lon* 94-95; C from 95. *21 Butler Avenue, Harrow, Middx HA1 4EJ* Tel 0181-422 5270

KENDAL, Stephen. b 35. Leeds Univ BA59. Coll of Resurr Mirfield 59. **d** 61 **p** 62. C Seaton Hirst *Newc* 61-63; C Newc St Geo 63-66; C Gosforth All SS 66-70; Ind Chapl *Llan* 70-78; Ind Chapl *Dur* 78-91; Hon C Houghton le Spring 78-90; Ind Chapl *Worc* from 91. *15 St John's Avenue, Kidderminster, Worcs DY11 6AT* Tel (01562) 823929

KENDALL, Alastair Geoffrey. b 55. BSc DipTh. St Jo Coll Nottm DPS. **d** 84 **p** 85. C Glouc St Aldate *Glouc* 84-87; C Sheff St Jo *Sheff* 87-92; V Bream *Glouc* from 92. *The Vicarage, Bream, Lydney, Glos GL15 6ES* Tel (01594) 562376

KENDALL, Edward Oliver Vaughan (Ted). b 33. Dur Univ BA59. Ridley Hall Cam 59. **d** 61 **p** 62. C Corsham *Bris* 61-64; C Portsea St Mary *Portsm* 64-67; Asst Chapl HM Pris Pentonville 67-68; Chapl HM Borstal Portland 68-71; Lic to Offic *Bradf* from 71; rtd 94. *10 Halsteads Cottages, Settle, N Yorkshire BD24 9QJ* Tel (01729) 822860

KENDALL, Frank. b 40. FRSA90 CCC Cam BA62 MA68. S'wark Ord Course 74. **d** 74 **p** 75. NSM Lingfield *S'wark* 74-75 and 78-82; NSM Sketty *S & B* 75-78; NSM Limpsfield and Titsey *S'wark* 82-84; Lic to Offic *Man* 84-89; Lic to Offic *Liv* from 89. *Cromwell Villa, 260 Prescot Road, St Helens, Merseyside WA10 3HR* Tel (01744) 27626

KENDALL, George Vincent. b 21. Edin Th Coll 46. **d** 48 **p** 49. C Dundee St Marg *Bre* 48-50; C Glas Gd Shep *Glas* 50-53; P-in-c Glas St Serf 53-56; P-in-c Gretna 56-90; P-in-c Langholm 56-90; rtd 90; Perm to Offic *Glas* from 90. *9 Kestrel Hill, Gretna, Dumfriesshire DG16 5DH* Tel (01461) 338268

KENDALL, Gordon Sydney. b 41. **d** 72 **p** 74. Hon C Old Ford St Paul w St Steph and St Mark *Lon* 72-82; Hon C Homerton St Luke 86-92; Chapl Hackney Hosp Gp Lon 87-92; Chapl Asst Homerton Hosp Lon 87-92; Chapl Torbay Hosp Torquay 92-94; Lic to Offic *Ex* from 92; Chapl S Devon Healthcare NHS Trust from 94. *Torbay Hospital, Lawes Bridge, Newton Road, Torquay TQ2 7AA, or 19 Arden Drive, Torquay TQ2 6DZ* Tel (01803) 614567 or 616119

KENDALL, Miss Jacqueline Ann. b 63. Univ of Wales (Abth) BA85. Cranmer Hall Dur 88. **d** 91 **p** 94. Par Dn Stockport St Sav *Ches* 91-94; C 94-95; C Acton and Worleston, Church Minshull etc 95-96; C Helsby and Dunham-on-the-Hill from 96; C Alvanley from 96. *47 Ardern Lea, Helsby, Warrington WA6 9EQ* Tel (01928) 722012

KENDALL, Michael Peter (Mike). b 71. St Jo Coll Dur BTh92 Oak Hill Th Coll MPhil94. **d** 96 **p** 97. C Stapenhill w Cauldwell *Derby* from 96. *3 Stapenhill Road, Stapenhill, Burton-on-Trent, Staffs DE15 9AF* Tel (01283) 515125

KENDRA, Kenneth Ernest. b 13. OBE66. Leeds Univ BA41 MA48. Linc Th Coll 40. **d** 42 **p** 43. C Pocklington and Kilnwick Percy *York* 42-46; CF 46-71; QHC 70-71; V Lee-on-the-Solent *Portsm* 71-80; RD Alverstoke 77-79; rtd 80. *Bookers Barn, Bolney, Haywards Heath, W Sussex RH17 5NB*

KENDRA, Dr Neil Stuart. b 46. FITD84 Leeds Univ BA67 Univ of Wales (Swansea) DipAD72 Bradf Univ MSc80 PhD84. Linc Th Coll 67. **d** 69 **p** 70. C Allerton *Liv* 69-72; Ldr Leeds City Cen Detached Youth Work Project 73-75; Dioc Youth Officer *Ripon* 75-77; Lect Ilkley Coll 77-78; Sen Lect Bradf and Ilkley Community Coll 78-88; Hd Community and Youth Studies St Martin's Coll from 88. *St Martin's College, Lancaster LA1 3JD* Tel (01524) 63446

KENDREW, Geoffrey David. b 42. K Coll Lon BD66 AKC66. **d** 67 **p** 68. C Bourne *Guildf* 67-70; C Haslemere 70-76; V Derby St Barn *Derby* 76-95; R Deal St Leon and St Rich and Sholden *Cant* from 95. *St Leonard's Rectory, Addelam Road, Deal, Kent CT14 9BZ* Tel (01304) 374076

KENDRICK, Dale Evans. b 62. Ch Ch Coll Cant BA86 Nottm Univ MA87 Leeds Univ MA95. Coll of Resurr Mirfield CPT94. **d** 95 **p** 96. C Tividale *Lich* 95-96; C Blakenall Heath 96-97; C Stafford from 97. *14 Darnford Close, Stafford ST16 1LR* Tel (01922) 612081

KENDRICK, Canon Desmond Max. b 22. Leeds Univ BA47. Wycliffe Hall Ox 50. **d** 52 **p** 53. C Glodwick St Mark *Man* 52-54; Chapl Leeds Road Hosp Bradf 54-77; V Bradf St Clem *Bradf* 54-77; RD Bradf 63-73; Hon Can Bradf Cathl 64-89; V Otley 77-89; Chapl Wharfdale Gen Hosp 77-90; rtd 89; Perm to Offic *Bradf* from 89. *26 Ashtofts Mount, Guiseley, W Yorkshire LS20 9DB* Tel (01943) 870430

KENDRICK, Ronald Horace. b 35. Univ of Wales (Ban) BD78 DPS79. St Deiniol's Hawarden. **d** 82 **p** 83. C Wrexham *St As* 82-85; R Llanelian and Betws-yn-Rhos from 85. *The Rectory, Rhodfa Sant Elian, Colwyn Bay LL29 1XX* Tel (01492) 517274

KENNARD, Mark Philip Donald. b 60. Man Univ BSc82. Cranmer Hall Dur 85. **d** 88 **p** 89. C Newark w Hawton, Cotham and Shelton *S'well* 88-89; C Newark 89-91; C Cropwell Bishop w Colston Bassett, Granby etc 91-93; P-in-c Shireoaks from 93; Chapl Bassetlaw Hosp and Community Services NHS Trust 93-96. *1 Potters Nook, Shireoaks, Worksop, Notts S81 8NF* Tel (01909) 486537

KENNARD, Ronald Malcolm. b 15. ACA39 FCA60. Chich Th Coll 74. **d** 75 **p** 76. Hon C Cuckfield *Chich* 75-79; P-in-c Elsted w Treyford and Didling 79-83; Perm to Offic from 83. *22 Wentworth Close, Barnham, Bognor Regis, W Sussex PO22 0HS* Tel (01243) 553215

KENNEDY, Anthony Reeves. b 32. Lon Univ DipTh67. Roch Th Coll 64. **d** 67 **p** 68. C Ross *Heref* 67-69; C Marfleet *York* 69-71; TV 72-76; V Lightwater *Guildf* 76-83; V W Ham *Chelmsf* 83-89; V Lutton w Gedney Drove End, Dawsmere *Linc* 89-94; Perm to Offic *Chich* from 94; rtd 97. *40 Haydock Close, Alton, Hants GU34 2TL* Tel (01420) 549860

KENNEDY, Arthur. b 57. St Pet Coll Ox BA79 MA83. St Jo Coll Nottm 83. **d** 85 **p** 86. C Nor Heartsease St Fran *Nor* 85-89; C Tadley St Pet *Win* 89-91; R Farmborough, Marksbury and Stanton Prior *B & W* from 91. *The Rectory, Church Lane, Farmborough, Bath BA3 1AN* Tel (01761) 470727

KENNEDY, Miss Carolyn Ruth. b 59. Univ of Wales (Ban) BA81 GradCertEd(FE)85. Ripon Coll Cuddesdon BA90. **d** 91 **p** 94. C Frodingham *Linc* 91-95; Chapl Cov Univ *Cov* from 95. *The Chaplaincy, Coventry University, Priory Street, Coventry CV1 5FB* Tel (01203) 838315 or 670124 Fax 838074 E-mail c.r.kennedy@coventry.ac.uk

KENNEDY, David George. b 46. Hull Univ BEd71 MA76. Linc Th Coll 77. **d** 79 **p** 80. C Linc St Faith and St Martin w St Pet *Linc* 79-82; V Bilton St Pet *York* 82-90; V New Seaham *Dur* 90-92;

Chapl Lincs and Humberside Univ *York* 92-97; P-in-c Barrow St Matt *Carl* from 97; Chapl Furness Coll from 97. *The Vicarage, Highfield Road, Barrow-in-Furness, Cumbria LA14 5NZ* Tel (01229) 823569

KENNEDY, Dr David John. b 57. St Jo Coll Dur BA78 Nottm Univ MTh81 Birm Univ PhD96. St Jo Coll Nottm 79. **d** 81 **p** 82. C Tudhoe Grange *Dur* 81-87; C Merrington 84-87; Tutor Qu Coll Birm 88-96; R Haughton le Skerne *Dur* from 96. *The Rectory, Haughton Green, Darlington, Co Durham DL1 2DD* Tel (01325) 468142

KENNEDY, Francis Robert Dixon. b 14. Wadh Coll Ox BA38 MA43. Wycliffe Hall Ox 42. **d** 43 **p** 44. C Gt Malvern Ch Ch *Worc* 43-47; Hd Master Lyttelton Sch Malvern 44-47; C Stroud H Trin *Glouc* 48-49; Chapl Shoreham Gr Sch 49-71; R Caythorpe *Linc* 71-81; rtd 81; Perm to Offic *Chich* 81-93. *8 Ripley Road, Worthing, W Sussex BN11 5NQ* Tel (01903) 249498

KENNEDY, James Ernest. b 20. TCD BA46 MA51. CITC 46. **d** 46 **p** 47. C Kilnamanagh w Kilcormack, Castle Ellis etc *C & O* 46-48; C Ahoghill *Conn* 48; P-in-c Portglenone 48-51; I 51-60; I Agherton 60-67; I Errigal w Desertoghill *D & R* 67-81; rtd 81. *38 Prospect Road, Portstewart, Co Derry BT55 7LQ* Tel (01265) 832052

KENNEDY, Canon Michael Charles. b 39. TCD BA63 MA79 BD79 Open Univ PhD87. TCD Div Sch 61. **d** 63 **p** 64. C Drumglass *Arm* 63-66; I Lisnadill w Kildarton from 66; Warden Dioc Guild of Lay Readers from 74; Hon V Choral Arm Cathl from 75; Tutor for Aux Min (Arm) from 82; Preb Yagoe St Patr Cathl Dublin from 92. *Lisnadill Rectory, 60 Newtownhamilton Road, Armagh BT60 2PW* Tel (01861) 523630

KENNEDY, Paul Alan. b 67. ACA92 Brighton Poly. St Steph Ho Ox BA95. **d** 95 **p** 96. C Romford St Andr *Chelmsf* from 95. *24 Eastbury Road, Romford RM7 9AL* Tel (01708) 734047 Fax 737791

KENNEDY, Paul Joseph Alan. b 57. Newc Univ MA93. Sarum & Wells Th Coll. **d** 84 **p** 85. C Shildon *Dur* 84-85; C Shildon w Eldon 85-86; C Shotton *St As* 86-88; V Waterhouses *Dur* 88-93; V Denton *Newc* 93-95; CF from 95. *MOD Chaplains (Army), Trenchard Lines, Upavon, Pewsey, Wilts SN9 6BE* Tel (01980) 615804 Fax 615800

KENNEDY, Ross Kenneth. b 40. Edin Th Coll 83. **d** 85 **p** 86. C Hexham *Newc* 85-89; TV Glendale Gp 89-93; TR Ch the King in the Dio of Newc from 93. *North Gosforth Vicarage, Wideopen, Newcastle upon Tyne NE13 6NH* Tel 0191-236 2280

KENNEDY, William Edmund. b 20. QUB BA43 TCD BA45 MA48. **d** 45 **p** 46. C Seagoe *D & D* 45-48; C Ballynafeigh St Jude 48-57; I Ballyculter w Kilclief 57-85; rtd 85. *Shalom, 8 Dunnanew Road, Seaforde, Downpatrick, Co Down BT30 6PJ* Tel (01396) 811706

KENNEDY-BELL, Preb Winnington Douglas. b 15. Keble Coll Ox BA38 MA42. Wells Th Coll 38. **d** 39 **p** 40. C E Wickham *S'wark* 39-41; V Richmond Ch Ch 41-44; V St Martin-in-the-Fields *Lon* 44-48; Overseas Relig Broadcasting Org BBC 48-75; Reader of The Temple from 55; Preb St Paul's Cathl *Lon* from 73; Dep P in O 76-86; rtd 80. *1 Victoria Cottages, Kew Gardens, Richmond, Surrey TW9 3NW* Tel 0181-940 5385

KENNERLEY, Canon Katherine Virginia (Ginnie). Somerville Coll Ox BA58 MA65 Irish Sch of Ecum DipEcum84 TCD BA86. CITC 86. **d** 88 **p** 90. Lect Applied Th CITC 88-93; NSM Bray *D & G* 88-93; I Narraghmore w Timolin, Castledermot and Kinneagh from 93; Can Ch Ch Cathl Dublin from 96. *The Rectory, Timolin, Co Kildare, Irish Republic* Tel Athy (507) 24278 E-mail kennerly@indigo.ie

KENNETT-ORPWOOD, Jason Robert. b 55. St Mich Coll Llan DipTh77 DPS78. **d** 78 **p** 79. Chapl St Woolos Cathl *Mon* 78-82; Chapl St Woolos Hosp Newport 79-82; Dioc Youth Chapl *Mon* 82-85; V Cwmcarn 82-85; TV Wrexham *St As* 85-89; V Bistre from 89. *Bistre Vicarage, Mold Road, Buckley CH7 2NH* Tel (01244) 550947

KENNEY, Peter. b 50. Edin Univ BD75. Edin Th Coll 73. **d** 76 **p** 77. C Cullercoats St Geo *Newc* 76-81; TV Whorlton 81-88; P-in-c N Gosforth 88; TR Ch the King in the Dio of Newc 88-93; P-in-c Newc St Jo from 93. *3 Crossway, Jesmond, Newcastle upon Tyne NE2 3QH* Tel 0191-212 0181

KENNING, Michael Stephen. b 47. St Chad's Coll Dur BA68. Westcott Ho Cam 69. **d** 71 **p** 72. C Hythe *Cant* 71-75; TV Bow w Bromley St Leon *Lon* 75-77; C-in-c W Leigh CD *Portsm* 77-81; V Lee-on-the-Solent 81-92; R N Waltham and Steventon, Ashe and Deane *Win* from 92. *The Rectory, North Waltham, Basingstoke, Hants RG25 2BQ* Tel (01256) 379256

KENNINGTON, John Paul. b 61. Collingwood Coll Dur BA85. St Steph Ho Ox BA87 MA92. **d** 88 **p** 89. C Headington *Ox* 88-91; C Dulwich St Clem w St Pet *S'wark* 91-94; TV Mortlake w E Sheen from 94. *All Saints' Vicarage, 86 East Sheen Avenue, London SW14 8AU* Tel 0181-876 4201

KENNY, Canon Charles John. b 39. LGSM74 QUB BA61 MEd78. CITC 69. **d** 69 **p** 70. C Belfast St Paul *Conn* 69-71; Hd of RE Grosvenor High Sch 71-94; Lic to Offic from 84; V Choral Belf Cathl from 94; Can Treas from 95. *45 Deramore Drive, Belfast BT9 5JS* Tel (01232) 669632

KENNY, Frederick William Bouvier. b 28. TCD BA53 DipEd54 MA56 LTh. **d** 56 **p** 57. C Ballymacarrett St Patr *D & D* 56-58; C Blackpool St Jo *Blackb* 58-61; Chapl Preston Hosp N Shields 61-66; V Preston St Paul *Blackb* 61-66; Youth Adv CMS (Lon) 66-70; Youth Sec (Ireland) CMS 70-75; I Belfast St Clem *D & D* 75-80; V Preston St Cuth *Blackb* 80-86; TV Bushbury *Lich* 86-90; P-in-c Stambridge *Chelmsf* from 90; Chapl Rochford Hosp from 90. *The Rectory, Stambridge, Rochford, Essex SS4 2AR* Tel (01702) 258272

KENNY, Thomas Patrick Francis. b 49. Univ of Wales (Cardiff) DipTh76. St Mich Coll Llan 73. **d** 76 **p** 77. C Rochdale *Man* 76-80; R Abbey Hey 80-86; V Stockton Heath *Ches* from 86. *The Vicarage, 91 Walton Road, Stockton Heath, Warrington WA4 6NR* Tel (01925) 661396

KENNY, Canon Thomas Percival Robert. b 27. TCD BA48 MA51. **d** 50 **p** 51. C Drumglass *Arm* 50-53; I Derrynoose w Middletown 53-56; I Aghavilly w Derrynoose 56-62; I Portadown St Sav 62-66; I Magherafelt 66-74; I Derryloran 74-82; CMS 83-88; Nigeria 83-88; Hon Can Owerri from 84; I ClooncIare w Killasnett and Drumlease *K, E & A* 88-90; rtd 90. *26 Clanbrassil Drive, Portadown, Craigavon, Co Armagh BT63 5EH* Tel (01762) 336479

KENRICK, Kenneth David Norman. b 44. Liv Univ RMN. Ripon Hall Ox 70 NW Ord Course 77. **d** 77 **p** 78. C Stockport St Geo *Ches* 77-83; R Stockport St Thos 83-85; R Stockport St Thos w St Pet from 86; Chapl St Thos and Cheadle Royal Hospitals from 88. *St Thomas's Rectory, 25 Heath Road, Stockport, Cheshire SK2 6JJ* Tel 0161-483 2483

KENSINGTON, Area Bishop of. *See* COLCLOUGH, The Rt Revd Michael John

KENT, Dr Christopher Alfred. b 48. CEng77 MIChemE77 Birm Univ BSc69 PhD72 Nottm Univ DipTh83. St Jo Coll Nottm 82. **d** 84 **p** 85. C Bucknall and Bagnall *Lich* 84-86; Hon C Halesowen *Worc* from 86. *40 County Park Avenue, Halesowen, W Midlands B62 8SP* Tel 0121-550 3132

KENT, David. b 44. CEng MIMechE. N Ord Course. **d** 83 **p** 84. NSM Huddersfield St Pet and All SS *Wakef* from 83. *118 Woodside Road, Huddersfield HD4 5JW* Tel (01484) 654058

KENT, Frank. b 44. ARCM76 Open Univ BA82. Ridley Hall Cam. **d** 86 **p** 87. C Faversham *Cant* 86-89; R Lyminge w Paddlesworth, Stanford w Postling etc from 89. *The Rectory, Rectory Lane, Lyminge, Folkestone, Kent CT18 8EG* Tel (01303) 862432

KENT, Keith Meredith. b 32. Lon Univ DipTh57. St Aid Birkenhead 55. **d** 58 **p** 59. C Fulwood Ch Ch *Blackb* 58-60; C Everton St Chrys *Liv* 60-62; C Litherland St Phil 64-68; P-in-c Everton St Polycarp 68-74; V Liv All So Springwood 74-78; V Carr Mill 78-86; V Beddgelert *Ban* 86-91; rtd 91; Perm to Offic *Blackb* from 91. *73 Egerton Road, Ashton-on-Ribble, Preston PR2 1AL* Tel (01772) 722508

KENT, Canon Michael Patrick. b 27. St Edm Hall Ox BA50 MA52. Cuddesdon Coll 50. **d** 52 **p** 53. C W Hartlepool St Aid *Dur* 52-57; C-in-c Pennywell St Thos and Grindon St Oswald CD 57-70; V Cockerton 70-93; RD Darlington 79-84; Hon Can Dur Cathl 83-93; rtd 93; Chapl St Chad's Coll *Dur* from 94. *5 Ferens Close, Durham DH1 1JX* Tel 0191-386 2835

KENT, Preb Neville. b 40. Sarum & Wells Th Coll 70. **d** 72 **p** 73. C Taunton St Andr *B & W* 72-77; R Bradford w Oake, Hillfarrance and Heathfield 77-89; Adv on Soc Concerns 80-87; RD Tone 87-89; V Worle 89-93; TR from 93; Preb Wells Cathl from 94; Perm to Offic *Bris* from 97. *The Vicarage, 93 Church Road, Worle, Weston-super-Mare, Avon BS22 9EA* Tel (01934) 510694 or 515922

KENT, Richard Hugh. b 38. Worc Coll Ox BA61 MA63. Chich Th Coll 61. **d** 63 **p** 64. C Emscote *Cov* 63-66; C Finham 66-70; V Dean Forest St Paul *Glouc* 70-75; V Glouc St Aldate 75-86; Chapl and Warden Harnhill Healing Cen 86-96; R N Buckingham *Ox* from 96. *The Rectory, Main Street, Maids Moreton, Buckingham MK18 1QD* Tel (01280) 813246

KENT, Roger Anthony Edward. b 56. Kent Univ BA78. St Steph Ho Ox 79. **d** 81 **p** 82. C Ipswich All Hallows *St E* 81-84; C Poplar *Lon* 84-88; V Newington w Hartlip and Stockbury *Cant* 88-95; Chapl Prague *Eur* from 95. *Terronska 536/10, 160 00 Praha 6, Czech Republic* Tel Prague (2) 312 4208

KENT, Ronald. b 21. St Jo Coll Dur BA43 MA46. St Steph Ho Ox 79. **d** 45 **p** 46. C Norton St Mary *Dur* 45-50; P-in-c Cassop cum Quarrington 50-55; V Darlington St Luke 55-65; Chapl Univ Coll of Ripon and York St Jo 65-76; Lic to Offic *Dur* 76-88; rtd 86; P-in-c Nidd *Ripon* 88-95. *1 Spring Bank Close, Ripon, N Yorkshire HG4 1ER* Tel (01765) 606114

KENTIGERN-FOX, Canon William Poyntere Kentigern. b 38. AKC63. **d** 64 **p** 65. C S Mimms St Mary and Potters Bar *Lon* 64-67; C S Tottenham 67-70; P-in-c Duddington w Tixover *Pet* 70-76; R Barrowden and Wakerley 70-76; P-in-c Morcott w S Luffenham 75-77; R Barrowden and Wakerley w S Luffenham 77-79; R Byfield w Boddington 79-86; V Northampton St Mich w St Edm 86-95; Can Pet Cathl from 94; V Raunds from 95. *The Vicarage, High Street, Raunds, Wellingborough, Northants NN9 6HS* Tel (01933) 461509

KENWARD, Roger Nelson. b 34. Selw Coll Cam BA58 MA62. Ripon Hall Ox 58. **d** 60 **p** 61. C Paddington St Jas *Lon* 60-63; Chapl RAF 64-82; Asst Chapl-in-Chief RAF 82-89; P-in-c Lyneham w Bradenstoke *Sarum* 72-76; Hon Chapl to The Queen

85-89; R Laughton w Ripe and Chalvington *Chich* 90-95; Chapl Laughton Lodge Hosp 90-95; rtd 95; NSM Chiddingly w E Hoathly *Chich* 96; Perm to Offic from 96. *The Coach House, School Hill, Old Heathfield, Heathfield, E Sussex TN21 9AE* Tel (01435) 862618

KENWAY, Dr Ian Michael. b 52. Leeds Univ BA74 Bris Univ PhD86. Coll of Resurr Mirfield 74. **d** 76 **p** 77. C Cov E *Cov* 76-79; C Southmead *Bris* 79-81; P-in-c Shaw Hill *Birm* 82-88; Asst Sec Gen Syn Bd for Soc Resp 88-93; Chapl Essex Univ *Chelmsf* from 93; Dir of Studies Cen for the Study of Th from 93. *Mariners, Rectory Hill, Wivenhoe, Colchester CO7 9LB* Tel (01206) 823549 E-mail iank@essex.ac.uk

KENWAY, Robert Andrew. b 56. Bris Univ BA78. Westcott Ho Cam 80. **d** 82 **p** 83. C Birchfield *Birm* 82-85; C Queensbury All SS *Lon* 87-89; R Birm St Geo *Birm* 89-97; V Calne and Blackland *Sarum* from 97. *The Vicarage, Vicarage Close, Calne, Wilts SN11 8DD* Tel (01249) 812340

KENYON, Stanley Robert. b 31. Kelham Th Coll 51. **d** 55 **p** 56. C Eckington *Derby* 55-57; C Derby St Andr 57-59; C Lullington 59-61; C Nether and Over Seale 59-61; P-in-c Grimsby St Steph *Linc* 61-71; V Habrough 71-82; V E Halton 73-82; V Killingholme 73-82; V Barnetby le Wold Gp 82-94; rtd 94; Perm to Offic *Linc* from 94. *Machindor, 47 Highfields, Crowle, S Humberside DN17 4NP* Tel (01724) 711435

KEOGH, Anthony. b 35. St Mich Coll Llan 63. **d** 66 **p** 67. C Aberaman and Abercwmboi *Llan* 66-70; Hon C Penarth All SS 70-76; R Jersey H Trin *Win* from 76. *Holy Trinity Rectory, Jersey JE3 5JB* Tel (01534) 861110

KEOGH, Canon Henry James. b 39. TCD BA61 NUI BMus65. **d** 62 **p** 63. C Cork St Fin Barre's Cathl *C, C & R* 62-65; C Belfast St Luke *Conn* 65-66; C Dromore Cathl *D & D* 66-68; I Castlecomer *C & O* 68-85; I Kilscoran w Killinick and Mulrankin from 85; Hon Chapl Miss to Seamen from 85; Preb Ferns Cathl *C & O* from 96. *The Rectory, Killinick, Co Wexford, Irish Republic* Tel Wexford (53) 58989

KEOGH, Robert Gordon. b 56. TCD DipTh84. **d** 84 **p** 85. C Mossley *Conn* 84-87; I Taunagh w Kilmactranny, Ballysumaghan etc *K, E & A* 87-90; I Swanlinbar w Tomregan, Kinawley, Drumlane etc from 90. *The Rectory, Swanlinbar, Co Cavan, Irish Republic* Tel Swanlinbar (49) 21404

KER, Desmond Agar-Ellis. b 15. Wells Th Coll 58. **d** 58 **p** 60. C Wyken *Cov* 58-59; C Dawlish *Ex* 60-61; C Cockington 61-69; V Bovey Tracey St Jo 69-80; rtd 80; Perm to Offic *S'wark* 84-92; Perm to Offic *Chich* from 92. *Flat 36, St Clements Court, Wear Bay Crescent, Folkestone, Kent CT19 6BP*

KERLEY, Brian Edwin. b 36. St Jo Coll Cam BA57 MA61. Linc Th Coll 59. **d** 61 **p** 62. C Sheerness H Trin w St Paul *Cant* 61-64; C St Laurence in the Isle of Thanet 64-69; C Coulsdon St Andr *S'wark* 69-76; P-in-c Fulbourn *Ely* 76-77; R from 77; RD Quy 83-93; P-in-c Gt Wilbraham from 86; P-in-c Lt Wilbraham from 86. *The Rectory, Apthorpe Street, Fulbourn, Cambridge CB1 5EY* Tel (01223) 880337

KERLEY, Patrick Thomas Stewart. b 42. Linc Th Coll. **d** 85 **p** 86. Hon C Thorpe *Nor* 85-90; C Wymondham 90-94; Gt Yarmouth 94-95; TV from 95. *18 Royal Avenue, Great Yarmouth, Norfolk NR30 4EB* Tel (01493) 855693

KERR, Andrew Harry Mayne. b 41. TCD BA63 Birm Univ DPS72. **d** 65 **p** 66. C Belfast St Luke *Conn* 65-68; SCM Sec (Ireland) 68-72; C Clooney *D & R* 72-74; Australia from 74. *8 Filippin Court, Werribee, Victoria, Australia 3030* Tel Melbourne (3) 9741 2893

KERR, Anthony. b 43. Sheff Univ BA64 Man Univ CertEd65. N Ord Course. **d** 85 **p** 86. NSM Greenfield *Man* 85-87; NSM Leesfield 87-97; P-in-c Oldham St Steph and All Martyrs from 97. *16 Netherlees, Spring Lane, Oldham OL4 5BA* Tel 0161-620 6512

KERR, Arthur Henry. LRAM47 TCD BA48 DA65. **d** 49 **p** 50. C Templemore *D & R* 49-50; C Dublin Harold's Cross *D & G* 50-57; ICM 57-60; Chapl Rotunda Hosp 60-75; Lic to Offic *Conn* 88-94; P-in-c Clondevaddock w Portsalon and Leatbeg *D & R* from 94. *Halothane, 172 Mountsandel Road, Coleraine, Co Londonderry BT52 1JE* Tel (01265) 44940

KERR, Bryan Thomas. b 70. QUB BD91 TCD MPhil96. CITC 94. **d** 96 **p** 97. C Enniskillen *Clogh* from 96. *The Curatage, 2 Halls Lane, Enniskillen, Co Fermanagh BT74 7DR* Tel (01365) 325882

KERR, Charles Alexander Gray. b 33. Open Univ BA75 Birm Univ MA83 MA88. Edin Th Coll 63. **d** 67 **p** 68. C Hawick *Edin* 67-70; C Edgbaston St Geo *Birm* 70-72; Chapl Birm Skin Hosp 70-75; P-in-c Quinton Road W St Boniface *Birm* 72-79; V 79-84; R Musselburgh *Edin* 84-86; P-in-c Prestonpans 84-86; NSM Reighton w Speeton *York* 89-91; P-in-c Burton Pidsea and Humbleton w Elsternwick 91-95; V Anlaby Common St Mark 95; rtd 96; Perm to Offic *York* from 96. *311 Filey Road, Scarborough, N Yorkshire YO11 3AF* Tel (01723) 501865

KERR, David James. b 36. TCD BA58 MA61 BD61 HDipEd. **d** 60 **p** 61. C Belfast Trin Coll Miss *Conn* 60-63; Dean's V St Patr Cathl Dublin 63-66; Chapl Beechwood Park Sch St Alb from 66; C Flamstead *St Alb* from 74. *Beechwood Park School, Markyate, St Albans, Herts AL3 8AW* Tel (01582) 841191

KERR, Derek Preston. b 64. TCD BTh90. Oak Hill Th Coll. **d** 90 **p** 91. C Belfast St Donard *D & D* 90-93; C Carrickfergus *Conn* 93-96; I Devenish w Boho *Clogh* from 96. *Monea Rectory, Monea, Enniskillen, Co Fermanagh BT74 8GE* Tel (01365) 341228

KERR, Miss Dora Elizabeth. b 41. QUB BA65 Southn Univ DipEd66 Nottm Univ DipTh83. St Jo Coll Nottm 82. **dss** 84 **d** 87 **p** 94. Becontree St Mary *Chelmsf* 84-87; Par Dn 87-88; Par Dn Rushden w Newton Bromswold *Pet* 88-93; Par Dn Finham *Cov* 94; Chapl Cov and Warks Hosp from 94; C Finham *Cov* from 94. *145 Green Lane, Coventry CV3 6EB* Tel (01203) 413674

KERR, George Cecil. b 36. TCD BA60 MA65. CITC 60. **d** 60 **p** 61. C Coleraine *Conn* 60-63; Div Master Annandale Gr Sch Belf 63-65; Dean of Res QUB 65-74; Lic to Offic *D & D* from 75. *Christian Renewal Centre, Shore Road, Rostrevor, Co Down BT34 3ET* Tel (01693) 38492 Fax 738996

KERR, Mrs Jean. b 46. SS Hild & Bede Coll Dur CertEd69. N Ord Course 84. **d** 87 **p** 94. NSM Peel *Man* 87-93; Par Dn Dixon Green 88-89; Par Dn New Bury 89-93; Par Dn Gillingham St Mark *Roch* 93-94; C from 94. *The Garden House, Vicarage Road, Gillingham, Kent ME7 5JA* Tel (01634) 853687

KERR, John Maxwell. b 43. MSOSc88 Toronto Univ BSc66 Leeds Univ MSc70 Nottm Univ DipTh76. Linc Th Coll 75. **d** 77 **p** 78. C New Windsor *Ox* 77-80; Asst Chapl Cheltenham Coll 80-81; Chapl 81-82; Asst Chapl Win Coll 82-93; Hon C Win St Lawr and St Maurice w St Swithun *Win* from 84. *68 Kingsgate Street, Winchester, Hants SO23 9PE* Tel (01962) 862317

KERR, Joseph Reid. b 43. St Steph Ho Ox 70. **d** 72 **p** 73. C Ox SS Phil and Jas *Ox* 72-73; USA from 73. *Box 158, Stafford, VA 22554, USA*

KERR, Nicholas Ian. b 46. Em Coll Cam BA68 MA72. Westcott Ho Cam 74. **d** 77 **p** 78. C Merton St Mary *S'wark* 77-80; C Rainham *Roch* 80-84; Chapl Joyce Green Hosp Dartford 84-90; V Dartford St Edm *Roch* 84-90; V Lamorbey H Redeemer from 90. *The Vicarage, 64 Days Lane, Sidcup, Kent DA15 8JR* Tel 0181-300 1508

KERR, Paul Turner. b 47. Cranmer Hall Dur 68. **d** 71 **p** 72. C Kingston upon Hull St Martin *York* 71-72; C Linthorpe 72-76; C Cherry Hinton St Jo *Ely* 76-78; Chapl Addenbrooke's Hosp Cam 76-78; TV Rochdale *Man* 78-84; Chapl Birch Hill Hosp Rochdale 78-84; V New Bury 84-87; TR 87-93; C Gillingham St Mark *Roch* from 93; RD Gillingham from 96. *The Garden House, Vicarage Road, Gillingham, Kent ME7 5JA* Tel (01634) 853687

KERR, Peter Albert Calvin. b 09. MC40. Called to the Bar (Gray's Inn) 62 Lon Univ BD30 LLB60 St Cath Soc Ox BA32 MA37. Qu Coll Birm 37. **d** 37 **p** 37. C Aston SS Pet and Paul *Birm* 37-39; CF (TA - R of O) 39-59; Perm to Offic *Mon* from 81. *Hillside, Llanishen, Chepstow NP6 6QD* Tel (01600) 860723

KERR, Canon Stephen Peter. b 46. TCD BA68 Edin Univ BD71 MPhil80. **d** 71 **p** 72. C Belfast H Trin *Conn* 72-76; C Ballywillan 76-78; Lect Linc Th Coll 78-87; Dioc Officer for Adult Educn and Minl Tr *Worc* from 87; P-in-c Ombersley w Doverdale from 87; Hon Can Worc Cathl from 92. *The Rectory, Ombersley, Droitwich, Worcs WR9 0EW* Tel (01905) 620950

KERRIDGE, Donald George. b 32. Bede Coll Dur CertEd72 Hull Univ BA84. Wesley Coll Leeds 57 Bps' Coll Cheshunt 61. **d** 62 **p** 63. C Manston *Ripon* 62-66; C Hawksworth Wood 66-71; Asst Chapl Brentwood Sch Essex 72-74; Lic to Offic *Linc* 81-89; R Tetney, Marshchapel and N Coates 89-91; P-in-c Linc St Swithin 91-95; P-in-c Linc St Swithin w All SS from 95; Asst Chapl Linc Co Hosp 91-94. *St Swithin's Vicarage, Croft Street, Lincoln LN2 5AZ* Tel (01522) 527540

KERRIN, Albert Eric. b 26. Aber Univ MA51. Edin Th Coll 51. **d** 53 **p** 54. C Dumfries *Glas* 53-55; P-in-c Cambuslang w Newton Cathl Miss 55-57; R Alford *Ab* 57-69; P-in-c Portpatrick *Glas* 69-91; P-in-c Stranraer 69-91; rtd 91. *15 London Road, Stranraer, Wigtownshire DG9 8AF* Tel (01776) 702822

KERRISON, Mrs Anne Edmonstone. b 23. Cranmer Hall Dur 69. **dss** 77 **d** 87 **p** 94. Hellesdon *Nor* 77-78; Ind Miss 78-79; Lic to Offic 79-88; Perm to Offic 88-94; NSM Hevingham w Hainford and Stratton Strawless 94-96; Perm to Offic from 96. *Sloley Lodge, Sloley, Norwich NR12 8HE* Tel (01692) 538253

KERRY, Martin John. b 55. Ox Univ MA78 Nottm Univ BA81 MTh83. St Jo Coll Nottm 79. **d** 82 **p** 83. C Everton St Geo *Liv* 82-85; Lic to Offic *S'well* from 85; Chapl Asst Nottm City Hosp 85-89; Chapl 89-94; Chapl Nottm City Hosp NHS Trust from 94. *The Chaplains' Office, City Hospital, Hucknall Road, Nottingham NG5 1BP* Tel 0115-969 1169 or 962 7616

KERSHAW, John Harvey. b 51. Coll of Resurr Mirfield 84. **d** 86 **p** 87. C Hollinwood *Man* 86-89; V Audenshaw St Hilda from 89; Chapl Tameside Gen Hosp 90-94; Chapl Tameside and Glossop NHS Trust from 94. *St Hilda's Vicarage, Denton Road, Audenshaw, Manchester M34 5BL* Tel 0161-336 2310

KERSHAW, Savile. b 37. Bernard Gilpin Soc Dur 60 Chich Th Coll 61. **d** 64 **p** 65. C Staincliffe *Wakef* 64-66; C Saltley *Birm* 66-68; C Birm St Aid Small Heath 68-72; NSM Bordesley SS Alb and Patr 88-93; Perm to Offic from 93. *74 Longmore Road, Shirley, Solihull, W Midlands B90 3EE* Tel 0121-744 3470

KERSLEY, Stuart Casburn. b 40. CEng MIEE. Trin Coll Bris. **d** 82 **p** 83. C Lancing w Coombes *Chich* 82-87; TV Littlehampton and Wick 87-90; R Kingston Buci from 90. *The Rectory, Rectory*

Road, Shoreham-by-Sea, W Sussex BN43 6EB Tel (01273) 592591

KERSWILL, Anthony John. b 39. Lambeth STh85 Linc Th Coll 72. **d** 73 **p** 73. C Boultham *Linc* 73-76; P-in-c N Kelsey 76-83; P-in-c Cadney 76-83; V Gainsborough St Geo 83-91; V Bracebridge from 91; RD Christianity from 96. *The Vicarage, 60 Chiltern Road, Bracebridge, Lincoln LN5 8SE* Tel (01522) 532636 Fax as telephone

KESLAKE, Peter Ralegh. b 33. Sarum & Wells Th Coll. **d** 83 **p** 84. C Glouc St Geo w Whaddon *Glouc* 83-86; P-in-c France Lynch 86-91; V Chalford and France Lynch from 91. *The Vicarage, Brantwood Road, Chalford Hill, Stroud, Glos GL6 8BS* Tel (01453) 883154

KESSLER, Edward Scharps. b 26. Princeton Univ BA47 Chicago Univ MA51 St Chad's Coll Dur DipTh66. **d** 66 **p** 67. C Pallion *Dur* 66-68; C Hendon St Ignatius 68-70; Dioc Planning Officer 70-75; P-in-c Kimblesworth 74-80; Perm to Offic *Sheff* from 87; rtd 89. *44 Hinde Street, Sheffield S4 8HJ* Tel 0114-244 6827

KESTER, Jonathan George Frederick. b 66. Ex Univ BA90. Coll of Resurr Mirfield CPT93. **d** 93 **p** 94. C Cheshunt *St Alb* 93-96; Chapl to Bp Edmonton *Lon* from 96; Hon C Munster Square Ch Ch and St Mary Magd from 96. *4 Silsoe House, Park Village East, London NW1 7QH* Tel 0171-388 2166

KESTERTON, David William. b 59. Man Univ BSc80. Cranmer Hall Dur 85. **d** 88 **p** 89. C Cheddleton *Lich* 88-92; TV Dunstable *St Alb* 92-97; Chapl Dunstable Coll 92-97. *Address temp unknown*

KESTON, Dr Marion. b 44. Glas Univ MB, ChB68. St And Dioc Tr Course 87. **d** 90 **p** 94. NSM Dunfermline *St And* 90-96; NSM W Fife Team Min 90-96; Priest Livingston LEP *Edin* from 96. *12B Carrick Gardens, Livingston, West Lothian EH54 9ET* Tel (01506) 410668 Fax 416436

KETLEY, Christopher. b 62. Aston Tr Scheme 91 Coll of Resurr Mirfield 93. **d** 95 **p** 96. C Gt Crosby St Faith *Liv* from 95. *31 Allenby Road, Liverpool L23 0SU*

KETLEY, Michael James. b 39. DipHE81. Oak Hill Th Coll 79. **d** 81 **p** 82. C Bedhampton *Portsm* 81-85; R St Ive w Quethiock *Truro* 85-86; NSM Basildon St Andr w H Cross *Chelmsf* 89-90; C Barkingside St Cedd 90-92; P-in-c 92-95; R Hadleigh St Jas from 95. *The Rectory, 50 Rectory Road, Hadleigh, Benfleet, Essex SS7 2ND* Tel (01702) 558992

KETTLE, Alan Marshall. b 51. Leeds Univ BA72. Wycliffe Hall Ox MA78. **d** 78 **p** 79. C Llantwit Fadre *Llan* 78-81; Prov RE Adv Ch in Wales 81-84; Chapl Llandovery Coll 84-92; P-in-c Cil-y-Cwm and Ystrad-ffin w Rhandir-mwyn etc *St D* 85-92; Chapl W Buckland Sch Barnstaple from 92; Lic to Offic *Ex* from 92. *2 West Close, West Buckland, Barnstaple, Devon EX32 0ST* Tel (01598) 760314 or 760560

KETTLE, David John. b 47. Bris Univ BSc69 MLitt86 Fitzw Coll Cam BA75 MA79. Westcott Ho Cam 73. **d** 76 **p** 77. C Bris St Andr Hartcliffe *Bris* 76-79; C Fishponds All SS 79-80; P-in-c 81-83; Perm to Offic *St E* from 83; New Zealand from 91. *22 Goodwyn Crescent, Palmerston North, New Zealand* Tel Levin (6) 357 8749 or 357 9099 ext 8325

KETTLE, Martin Drew. b 52. New Coll Ox BA74 Selw Coll Cam BA76 Cam Univ MA85. Ridley Hall Cam 74. **d** 77 **p** 78. C Enfield St Andr *Lon* 77-80; Chapl Ridley Hall Cam 80-84; V Hendon St Paul Mill Hill *Lon* from 85; AD W Barnet 90-95. *St Paul's Vicarage, Hammers Lane, London NW7 4EA* Tel 0181-959 1856 or 959 8551

KETTLE, Mrs Patricia Mary Carole. b 41. Worc Coll of Educn CertEd61 Lon Univ DipTh68. Dalton Ho Bris 66. **d** 87 **p** 94. C Wonersh *Guildf* from 87. *Wakehurst Cottage, Links Road, Bramley, Surrey GU5 0AL* Tel (01483) 898856

KETTLE, Peter. b 51. K Coll Lon BD74 AKC74. St Aug Coll Cant 74. **d** 75 **p** 76. C Angell Town St Jo *S'wark* 75-78; C Putney St Mary 78-80; V Raynes Park St Sav 80-85; Perm to Offic from 85. *46 Allenswood, Albert Drive, London SW19 6JX* Tel 0181-785 3797

KEULEMANS, Andrew Francis Charles. b 68. Univ of Wales (Abth) BSc90. St Jo Coll Nottm BTh93. **d** 94 **p** 95. C Mold *St As* from 94. *2 Harrowby Road, Mold CH7 1DN* Tel (01352) 753624

KEVILL-DAVIES, Christopher Charles. b 44. AKC69. St Aug Coll Cant 70. **d** 70 **p** 71. C Folkestone St Sav *Cant* 70-75; V Yaxley *Ely* 75-78; R Chevington w Hargrave and Whepstead w Brockley *St E* 78-86; Appeals Manager Dr Barnardos 86-88; Appeals Manager St Nic Hospice Bury St Edmunds 88-89; Perm to Offic *St Alb* 86-89; NSM Stansted Mountfitchet *Chelmsf* 87-89; R Barkway, Reed and Buckland w Barley *St Alb* 89-97; R Chelsea St Luke and Ch Ch *Lon* from 97. *The Rectory, 64A Flood Street, London SW3 5TE* Tel 0171-376 5492

KEVIS, Lionel William Graham. b 55. York Univ BA. Wycliffe Hall Ox 83. **d** 86 **p** 87. C Plaistow St Mary *Roch* 86-90; R Ash from 90; R Ridley from 90. *The Rectory, The Street, Ash, Sevenoaks, Kent TN15 7HA* Tel (01474) 872209

KEW, William Richard. b 45. Lon Univ BD69. Lon Coll of Div LTh68. **d** 69 **p** 70. C Finchley St Paul Long Lane *Lon* 69-72; C Stoke Bishop *Bris* 72-76; USA from 76. *1015 Old Lascassas Road, Murfreesboro, Tennessee 37130, USA*

KEY, Christopher Halstead (Chris). b 56. St Jo Coll Dur BA77 K Coll Lon MTh78. Ridley Hall Cam 79. **d** 81 **p** 82. C Balderstone *Man* 81-84; C Wandsworth All SS *S'wark* 84-88; C-in-c W Dulwich Em CD 88-93; V W Dulwich Em 93-95; R Ore *Chich* from 95. *St Helen's Rectory, 266 Elphinstone Road, Hastings, E Sussex TN34 2AG* Tel (01424) 425172

KEY, John Christopher. b 36. Pemb Coll Cam BA60 MA65. Westcott Ho Cam 60. **d** 62 **p** 63. C Rugby St Andr *Cov* 62-67; Papua New Guinea 68-71; V Cov St Geo *Cov* 71-76; RD Cov N 73-76; V Redditch St Steph *Worc* 76-81; Dioc Ecum Officer 80-81; Australia from 81; rtd 96. *5/167 North Rocks Road, North Rocks, NSW, Australia 2151* Tel Sydney (2) 9683 1771

KEY, Robert Frederick. b 52. Bris Univ BA73. Oak Hill Th Coll 74. **d** 76 **p** 77. C Ox St Ebbe w St Pet *Ox* 76-80; C Wallington H Trin *S'wark* 80-85; P-in-c Eynsham *Ox* 85; V Eynsham and Cassington 85-91; V Ox St Andr from 91. *The Vicarage, 46 Charlbury Road, Oxford OX2 6UX, or St Andrew's Church, Linton Road, Oxford OX2 6UG* Tel (01865) 311695 or 311212

KEY, Roderick Charles (Rod). b 57. MTh. **d** 84 **p** 85. C Up Hatherley *Glouc* 84-87; V Glouc St Paul from 87. *St Paul's Vicarage, 2 King Edward's Avenue, Gloucester GL1 5DA* Tel (01452) 523732

KEYES, Alfred Edward de Hault. b 18. Keble Coll Ox BA39. Lich Th Coll 40. **d** 41 **p** 42. C Newland St Aug *York* 41-42; C Drypool St Andr and St Pet 42-47; C Scarborough St Mary 47-48; C Beverley St Mary 48-53; V Old Malton 53-63; V Goathland 63-73; R Rockbourne w Whitsbury *Win* 73-83; rtd 83; Perm to Offic *Ex* from 84. *7 Seaway Gardens, Paignton, Devon TQ3 2PE* Tel (01803) 550303

KEYES, Graham George. b 44. St Cath Coll Cam BA65 MA68 Lanc Univ MA74 Nottm Univ MTh85 MPhil92. EMMTC 82. **d** 84 **p** 85. C Evington *Leic* 84-86; Vice-Prin NE Ord Course 86-89; C Monkseaton St Mary *Newc* 86-89; P-in-c Newc St Hilda 89-94; TV Ch the King in the Dio of Newc from 94. *27 Polwarth Drive, Newcastle upon Tyne NE3 5NH* Tel 0191-236 4995

KEYES, Mrs Iris Doreen. b 28. SRN. Gilmore Ho 69. **dss** 76 **d** 87 **p** 94. Egham Hythe *Guildf* 76-78; Chapl Asst St Pet Hosp Chertsey 78-82; Addlestone 83-86; Walton-on-Thames 86-87; C 87-89; rtd 89; NSM Addlestone *Guildf* 94-95; Perm to Offic from 95. *36 Finlay Gardens, Addlestone, Surrey KT15 2XN* Tel (01932) 846912

KEYES, William Pascall. b 68. Heythrop Coll Lon BD90. Chich Th Coll 92 St Steph Ho Ox DipMin95. **d** 95 **p** 96. C Pimlico St Pet w Westmr Ch Ch *Lon* from 95. *3 St Peter's House, 119 Eaton Square, London SW1W 9AL* Tel 0171-235 4480

KEYS, John Francis. b 47. Goethe Inst Lon DipGL73. S Dios Minl Tr Scheme CECM93. **d** 93 **p** 94. NSM Brighton St Mich *Chich* from 93. *64 Victory Mews, Brighton Marina, Brighton BN2 5XB* Tel (01273) 818812

KEYT, Fitzroy John. b 34. Linc Th Coll. **d** 67 **p** 68. C Highters Heath *Birm* 67-70; Hon C Sheldon 70-73; Australia from 73. *30 Toolona Street, Tugun, Queensland, Australia 4224* Tel Brisbane (7) 5534 2115

KEYTE, Douglas Joseph Henry. b 18. St Jo Coll Cam BA40 MA46. Wycliffe Hall Ox 46. **d** 48 **p** 49. C Kersal Moor *Man* 48-51; C Newall Green 51-54; Chapl K Wm's Coll Is of Man 55-57; Ghana 57-61; Asst Master Co Gr Sch for Girls Sale 61-75; Hon C Charlestown *Man* 75-89; rtd 83; Hon C Pendleton St Thos w Charlestown *Man* 89-95; Hon C Pendleton from 95. *26 Heathfield Close, Sale, Cheshire M33 2PQ* Tel 0161-973 2844

KHAKHRIA, Rohitkumar Prabhulal (Roy). b 60. Sheff Univ BSc82 PGCE83. Oak Hill Th Coll 94. **d** 96 **p** 97. C Muswell Hill St Jas w St Matt *Lon* from 96. *Flat 2, 40 Colney Hatch Lane, London N10 1DU* Tel 0181-365 3194

KHAMBATTA, Neville Holbery. b 48. St Chad's Coll Dur BA74. S'wark Ord Course 81. **d** 84 **p** 85. NSM Thornton Heath St Jude w St Aid *S'wark* 84-87; Asst Chapl Em Sch Wandsworth 84-87; Asst Warden Horstead Cen from 87; NSM Coltishall w Gt Hautbois and Horstead *Nor* from 87. *Horstead Conference Centre, Rectory Road, Horstead, Norwich NR12 7EP* Tel (01603) 737215

KHOO, Boon-Hor. b 31. FBCO. Llan Dioc Tr Scheme. **d** 87 **p** 88. NSM Llan w Capel Llanilltern *Llan* 87-96. *38 The Cathedral Green, Llandaff, Cardiff CF5 2EB* Tel (01222) 561478

KICHENSIDE, Mark Gregory. b 53. Nottm Univ BTh83. St Jo Coll Nottm 80. **d** 83 **p** 84. C Orpington Ch Ch *Roch* 83-86; C Bexley St Jo 86-90; V Blendon 90-93; V Welling from 93. *St John's Vicarage, Danson Lane, Welling, Kent DA16 2BQ* Tel 0181-303 1107

KIDD, Anthony John Eric (Tony). b 38. Solicitor. Oak Hill NSM Course. **d** 89 **p** 90. NSM Rawdon *Bradf* 89-91; C Ilkley All SS 91-93; Perm to Offic 93-95; Perm to Offic *York* 95-96; Hon C Gt and Lt Driffield from 96. *Woodford House, Middle Street, Kilham, Driffield, N Humberside YO25 0RL* Tel (01262) 420792

KIDD, Miss Carol Ivy. b 47. Trent Park Coll of Educn CertEd69. Oak Hill Th Coll DipHE94. **d** 95 **p** 96. C Bootle St Mary w St Paul *Liv* from 95. *35 Jersey Close, Bootle, Merseyside L20 4BP* Tel 0151-922 8119

KIDD, John Alan. b 32. Pemb Coll Cam BA58 MA61. Ridley Hall Cam 57. **d** 61 **p** 62. C Onslow Square St Paul *Lon* 61-65; S Africa 65-67; Uganda 67-69; P-in-c Mayfair Ch Ch *Lon* 69-75; V 75-79; V Virginia Water *Guildf* 79-88; Lic to Offic 88-94; rtd 94. *2 Chapel Street, Easingwold, York YO6 3AE* Tel (01347) 823201

KIDD, Maurice Edward. b 26. Lon Coll of Div ALCD54 LTh. **d** 55 **p** 56. C Wembley St Jo *Lon* 55-58; C Middleton *Man* 58-61; Chapl Pastures Hosp Derby 61-69; Chapl Guild of Health Lon 69-72; R Hanworth St Geo *Lon* 72-82; R Chartham *Cant* 82-91; rtd 91; Perm to Offic *Cant* from 91. *Harvest View, The Mint, Harbledown, Canterbury, Kent CT2 9AA*

KIDD, Timothy. b 24. St Chad's Coll Dur BA48 DipTh50 MA53 Nottm Univ MA57 MPhil71 MEd80. Lambeth STh74. **d** 50 **p** 51. C Mexborough *Sheff* 50-52; Lect Boston 52-56; C Boston *Linc* 52-56; Offg Chapl RAF 56-65; V Grantham St Anne *Linc* 56-65; Asst Dioc Youth Chapl 59-65; Prin Lect Kesteven Coll of Educn 65-79; Hon C Harlaxton 66-72; Hon C Lt Ponton 66-72; Hon C Stroxton 66-72; Gen Preacher from 73; Visiting Lect Univ Evansville (USA) 79-86; Teacher K Sch Grantham 80-90; Perm to Offic *Leic* from 89; rtd 90. *14 Woodlands Drive, Grantham, Lincs NG31 9DJ* Tel (01476) 563273

KIDDLE, John. b 58. Qu Coll Cam BA80 MA83. Ridley Hall Cam 79. **d** 82 **p** 83. C Ormskirk *Liv* 82-86; V Huyton Quarry 86-91; V Watford St Luke *St Alb* from 91. *St Luke's Vicarage, Devereux Drive, Watford WD1 3DD* Tel (01923) 231205

KIDDLE, Mark Brydges. b 34. ACP61. Wycliffe Hall Ox. **d** 63 **p** 64. C Scarborough St Luke *York* 63-66; C Walthamstow St Sav *Chelmsf* 66-71; V Nelson St Bede *Blackb* 71-76; V Perry Common *Birm* 76-79; R Grayingham *Linc* 79-84; V Kirton in Lindsey 79-84; R Manton 79-84; Hon C St Botolph Aldgate w H Trin Minories *Lon* 85-91; Hon C St Clem Eastcheap w St Martin Orgar from 91. *188 Corfield Street, London E2 0DN* Tel 0171-613 1113

KIDDLE, Martin John. b 42. Lon Univ DipTh75 Open Univ BA80. St Jo Coll Nottm 74. **d** 76 **p** 77. C Gt Parndon *Chelmsf* 76-80; Asst Chapl HM Pris Wakef 80-81; Asst Chapl HM Youth Cust Cen Portland 81-88; Chapl HM Pris Cardiff from 88. *HM Prison Cardiff, Knox Road, Cardiff CF2 1UG* Tel (01222) 491212 Fax 489079

KIDDLE, Canon Peter. b 22. Fitzw Ho Cam BA50 MA54. Clifton Th Coll 57. **d** 57 **p** 58. Kenya 57-72; Hon Can Nairobi Cathl 72; V Worthing St Paul *Chich* 73-87; rtd 87; P-in-c Milton Lilbourne w Easton Royal *Sarum* 87-90. *64 Damask Way, Warminster, Wilts BA12 9PP* Tel (01985) 214572

KIDDLE, Miss Susan Elizabeth. b 44. Birm Univ BSc66 Nottm Univ CertEd67. LNSM course 86. **d** 89 **p** 95. NSM Waddington *Linc* from 89. *16 Sycamore Drive, Brant Road, Lincoln LN5 9DR* Tel (01522) 722010

KIDNER, Frank Derek. b 13. ARCM33 Ch Coll Cam BA40 MA44. Ridley Hall Cam 40. **d** 41 **p** 42. C Sevenoaks St Nic *Roch* 41-47; V Felsted *Chelmsf* 47-51; Sen Tutor Oak Hill Th Coll 51-64; Warden Tyndale Ho Cam 64-78; rtd 78; Perm to Offic *Ely* from 79. *56 Manor Park, Histon, Cambridge CB4 4JT* Tel (01223) 232579

KIGHTLEY, David John. b 39. AKC67. **d** 68 **p** 69. C Plymouth St Andr *Ex* 68-70; C Ex St Dav 70-73; Chapl Greenwich Distr Hosp & Brook Gen Hosp Lon 73-76; P-in-c Chippenham *Ely* 76-96; P-in-c Snailwell 76-96; P-in-c Isleham 76-96; RD Fordham 95-96; P-in-c Feltwell from 96; P-in-c Methwold from 96; RD Feltwell from 96. *The Rectory, 7 Oak Street, Feltwell, Thetford, Norfolk IP26 4DD* Tel (01842) 828104

KILBEY, Mrs Sarah. b 39. Edin Univ MA75 Man Poly CertEdD82. Bp Otter Coll TDip59 Edin Dioc NSM Course 84. **d** 93 **p** 97. NSM Edin St Columba *Edin* 93-96; NSM Edin St Martin from 96. *15 Cluny Avenue, Edinburgh EH10 4RN* Tel 0131-447 2378

KILDARE, Archdeacon of. *See* LAWRENCE, The Ven Patrick Henry Andrew

KILDARE, Dean of. *See* TOWNLEY, The Very Revd Robert Keith

KILFORD, John Douglas. b 38. Oak Hill Th Coll 73. **d** 75 **p** 76. C Beckenham St Jo *Roch* 75-80; P-in-c Sinfin Moor *Derby* 80-83; V Penge St Jo *Roch* 83-92; Staff Member Ellel Min from 92. *6 Milford Close, Catterall, Preston PR3 0GE* Tel (01995) 604656

KILFORD, William Roy. b 38. BA. Sarum & Wells Th Coll. **d** 84 **p** 85. C Herne *Cant* 84-87; Chapl Wm Harvey Hosp Ashford 87-93; R Mersham w Hinxhill *Cant* 87-93; P-in-c Sevington 87-93; V Reculver and Herne Bay St Bart 93-95; Chapl Paphos from 95. *c/o The Anglican Church, PO Box 1083, Paphos, Cyprus* Fax Paphos (6) 653090

KILGOUR, Richard Eifl. b 57. Edin Univ BD85. Edin Th Coll 81. **d** 85 **p** 86. C Wrexham *St As* 85-88; V Whitford from 88; Ind Chapl from 89. *The Vicarage, Upper Downing Road, Whitford, Holywell CH8 9AJ* Tel (01745) 560976

KILLALA AND ACHONRY, Archdeacon of. *See* STRATFORD, The Ven Ralph Montgomery

KILLALA, Dean of. *See* ARDIS, The Very Revd Edward George

KILLALOE, KILFENORA AND CLONFERT, Dean of. *See* CUMMINS, The Very Revd Nicholas Marshall

KILLALOE, KILFENORA, CLONFERT AND KILMACDUAGH, Archdeacon of. *See* KEEGAN, The Ven Donald Leslie

KILLE, Canon Vivian Edwy. b 30. Tyndale Hall Bris 60. **d** 62 **p** 63. C Dublin Miss Ch *D & G* 62-66; I Emlaghfad *T, K & A* 66-74; I Aghadrumsee w Clogh and Drumsnatt *Clogh* from 74; Preb Clogh Cathl from 93. *Sunshine Rectory, 16 Dernawilt Road, Rosslea, Enniskillen, Co Fermanagh BT92 7QY* Tel (01365) 751206

KILLICK, Brian Anthony Hugh. b 29. Sarum Th Coll 69. **d** 70 **p** 71. C Kingsbury St Andr *Lon* 70-74; C Selston *S'well* 74-76; P-in-c Scarcliffe *Derby* 76-77; P-in-c Sutton cum Duckmanton 77-80; V Stanley 80-94; rtd 94; Perm to Offic *Derby* from 94. *40 Oakover Drive, Allestree, Derby DE22 2PR* Tel (01332) 550562

KILLINGBACK, Oliver Edwin. b 44. S'wark Ord Course 75. **d** 77 **p** 78. C Kingston All SS w St Jo *S'wark* 77-80; C Horley 80-82; NSM Weston Favell *Pet* 87-93; Perm to Offic from 93. *18 Wansford Walk, Northampton NN3 4YF*

KILLOCK, Alfred Kenneth. b 26. Cranmer Hall Dur 72. **d** 74 **p** 75. C Moor Allerton *Ripon* 74-79; Hon C Bolton St Jas w St Chrys *Bradf* 79-83; P-in-c Oakenshaw cum Woodlands 84-90; P-in-c Allerton 90-91; rtd 91; Perm to Offic *Bradf* from 91. *15 Warwick Road, Bradford, W Yorkshire BD4 7RA* Tel (01274) 394492

KILLWICK, Simon David Andrew. b 56. K Coll Lon BD80 AKC80. St Steph Ho Ox 80. **d** 81 **p** 82. C Worsley *Man* 81-84; TV 84-97; P-in-c Moss Side Ch Ch from 97. *Christ Church Rectory, Monton Street, Manchester M14 4LT* Tel 0161-226 2476

KILMORE, Archdeacon of. *See* JOHNSTON, The Ven William Derek

KILMORE, Dean of. *See* GODFREY, The Very Revd David Samuel George

KILMORE, ELPHIN AND ARDAGH, Bishop of. *See* MAYES, The Rt Revd Michael Hugh Gunton

KILNER, Canon Frederick James (Fred). b 43. Qu Coll Cam BA65 MA69. Ridley Hall Cam 67. **d** 70 **p** 71. C Harlow New Town w Lt Parndon *Chelmsf* 70-74; C Cambridge St Andr Less *Ely* 74-79; P-in-c Milton 79-88; R 88-94; Hon Can Ely Cathl from 88; RD Quy from 93; P-in-c Ely 94-96; P-in-c Chettisham 94-96; P-in-c Prickwillow 94-96; P-in-c Stretham w Thetford 94-96; P-in-c Stuntney 95-96; TR Ely from 96. *The Rectory, St Mary's Street, Ely, Cambs CB7 4ER* Tel (01353) 662308

KILPATRICK, Alan William. b 64. Bournemouth Univ HND85. Birm Bible Inst 94 Oak Hill Th Coll BA94. **d** 96 **p** 97. C Ealing St Paul *Lon* from 96. *15A Erlesmere Gardens, London W13 9TZ* Tel 0181-441 4591

KILSBY, Alfred Daniel Joseph. b 29. St Chad's Coll Dur BA54 Golds Coll Lon PGCE64 Lon Univ BA68 MSc75. Westcott Ho Cam 54. **d** 56 **p** 57. C E Wickham *S'wark* 56-59; C Upper Tooting H Trin 59-63; Lic to Offic *St E* 62-65; Master Hornchurch Gr Sch 64-66; Lect Educn Battersea Coll of Educn 66-75; Lic to Offic *Chich* 68-83; Chapl Forest Boys' Sch Horsham 76-83; Perm to Offic *Win* from 85; rtd 94. *Orange Cottage, Brookley Road, Brockenhurst, Hants SO42 7RR* Tel (01590) 623701

KIMBER, Geoffrey Francis (Geoff). b 46. Univ Coll Lon BA67 PGCE70 DipTh74. St Jo Coll Nottm 86. **d** 88 **p** 89. C Buckhurst Hill *Chelmsf* 88-92; R Arley *Cov* from 92. *The Rectory, Arley, Coventry CV7 8FL* Tel (01676) 40378

KIMBER, Mrs Gillian Margaret. b 48. Bedf Coll Lon BA70. Oak Hill Th Coll 89. **d** 91. NSM Buckhurst Hill *Chelmsf* 91-92; C Arley *Cov* from 92. *The Rectory, Arley, Coventry CV7 8FL* Tel (01676) 40378

KIMBER, Mrs Hazel Olive. b 33. Lon Univ CertEd73. LNSM course 92. **d** 95 **p** 96. Hon C W Dulwich Em *S'wark* from 95. *18 Michaelston House, Kingswood Estate, London SE21 8PX* Tel 0181-670 5298

KIMBER, John Keith. b 45. Bris Univ BSc66. St Mich Coll Llan. **d** 69 **p** 70. C Caerphilly *Llan* 69-72; Chapl Birm Univ *Birm* 72-75; TR Bris St Agnes and St Simon w St Werburgh *Bris* 75-82; P-in-c Bris St Paul w St Barn 80-82; Hon C Westbury-on-Trym H Trin 82-83; Area Sec (Wales) USPG 83-89; TR Halesowen *Worc* 89-92; Chapl Geneva *Eur* from 92. *15 Chemin du Vieux Port, 1290 Versoix, Geneva, Switzerland* Tel Geneva (22) 755-4883 or 731-5155

KIMBER, Stuart Francis. b 53. Qu Eliz Coll Lon BSc74 Fitzw Coll Cam BA79 MA83. Ridley Hall Cam 77. **d** 80 **p** 81. C Edgware *Lon* 80-83; C Cheltenham St Mark *Glouc* 83-84; TV 84-92; C Hawkwell *Chelmsf* from 92. *Golden Cross House, 171 Ashingdon Road, Rochford, Essex SS4 1RP* Tel (01702) 540522

KIMBERLEY, John Harry. b 49. Brasted Th Coll 72 St Steph Ho Ox 74. **d** 76 **p** 77. C W Tarring *Chich* 76-79; C Portslade St Nic 79-82; C-in-c Findon Valley CD 82-89; V Findon Valley 89-90; V E Preston w Kingston 90-95; Chapl Eastbourne Hosps NHS Trust from 95. *Eastbourne District General Hospital, Kings Drive, Eastbourne, E Sussex BN21 2UD* Tel (01323) 417400

KIMBERLEY, The Ven Owen Charles Lawrence. b 27. Univ of NZ BCom53. Tyndale Hall Bris 57. **d** 59 **p** 60. C Higher Openshaw *Man* 59-62; New Zealand from 62; Adn Waimea 78-92; Egypt from 95. *Church of the Epiphany, PO Box 842, Port Said, Egypt* Tel Port Said (66) 206 622 1617

KIMBERLEY, Canon Wilfred Harry. b 19. St Steph Ho Ox 51. **d** 53 **p** 54. C Wallingford St Mary w All Hallows and St Leon *Ox* 53-55; C Newbury St Jo 55-57; V Highters Heath *Birm* 57-65; V Marsworth *Ox* 65-72; P-in-c Slapton 65-72; P-in-c Cheddington w Mentmore 68-72; V Buckingham 72-78; RD Buckingham 76-78; TR High Wycombe 78-84; Hon Can Ch Ch 79-84; rtd 84; Perm to Offic *Glouc* from 85; Perm to Offic *Ox* from 86.

Rosemary Cottage, Naunton, Cheltenham, Glos GL54 3AA Tel (01451) 850711

KIME, Thomas Frederick. b 28. Linc Coll Ox BA50 MA53. Cuddesdon Coll 54. **d** 56 **p** 57. C Forest Gate St Edm *Chelmsf* 56-58; S Africa 58-74; R Ellisfield w Farleigh Wallop and Dummer *Win* 74-83; P-in-c Cliddesden 82-83; R Cliddesden and Ellisfield w Farleigh Wallop etc 83-94; rtd 94. *7 Sparkford Close, Winchester, Hants SO22 4NH* Tel (01962) 870240

KINAHAN, Timothy Charles. b 53. Jes Coll Cam BA75. CITC 77. **d** 78 **p** 79. C Carrickfergus *Conn* 78-81; Papua New Guinea 81-84; I Belfast Whiterock *Conn* 84-90; I Gilnahirk *D & D* from 90. *237 Lower Braniel Road, Belfast BT5 7NQ* Tel (01232) 791748 Mobile 0374-681898 Fax 792413

KINCHIN-SMITH, John Michael. b 52. Fitzw Coll Cam MA. Ridley Hall Cam 79. **d** 82 **p** 83. C Sanderstead All SS *S'wark* 82-87; TV Halesworth w Linstead, Chediston, Holton etc *St E* 87-92; R Mursley w Swanbourne and Lt Horwood *Ox* from 92. *The Rectory, Mursley, Milton Keynes MK17 0RT* Tel (01296) 720056

KINDER, Mark Russell. b 66. Univ of Wales (Swansea) BA(Econ)88. St Jo Coll Nottm 91. **d** 94 **p** 95. C Pheasey *Lich* from 94. *33 Morland Road, Great Barr, Birmingham B43 7JH* Tel 0121-360 1723

KING, Anthony Richard. b 34. Trin Hall Cam BA58. Ely Th Coll 58 Linc Th Coll 61. **d** 62 **p** 63. C Benwell St Jas *Newc* 62-64; C Thirsk w S Kilvington *York* 64-67; V Halifax St Aug *Wakef* 67-74; R Upton-upon-Severn *Worc* from 74; RD Upton 86-92. *The Rectory, Old Street, Upton-upon-Severn, Worcester WR8 0JQ* Tel (01684) 592148

KING, Brian Henry. b 39. Chich Th Coll 63. **d** 65 **p** 66. C Castle Bromwich SS Mary and Marg *Birm* 65-67; C Southwick *Chich* 68-70; V Southwater 70-73; C Brighton St Alb Preston 73-74; TV Brighton Resurr 74-75; V Eastbourne St Elisabeth 75-96; rtd 96; Perm to Offic *Chich* from 96. *7 Bracken Road, Eastbourne, E Sussex BN20 8SH* Tel (01323) 431118

KING, Caroline Naomi. b 62. New Coll Edin BD94. Ripon Coll Cuddesdon DipMin94. **d** 97. NSM Wheatley *Ox* from 97. *109 High Street, Wheatley, Oxon OX33 1XP* Tel (01865) 875625

KING, Cecil John. b 46. Selw Coll Cam BA67 MA71. Coll of Resurr Mirfield 81. **d** 81 **p** 84. Zambia 81-85; SSF from 85; Ghana 86-88; C N Harrow St Alb *Lon* 88-89; C Leeds Gipton Epiphany *Ripon* 91-93. *30 Pembroke Grange, Leeds LS9 6RH* Tel 0113-240 2319

KING, Charles John. b 14. CEng46 MIEE Lon Univ BSc39. Ox NSM Course 73. **d** 76 **p** 77. NSM Cuddesdon *Ox* 76-78; NSM Wantage Downs from 78. *48 Ardington, Wantage, Oxon OX12 8PY* Tel (01235) 833671

KING, Christopher John. b 56. Chelsea Coll Lon BSc78 CertEd79. St Jo Coll Nottm LTh87. **d** 88 **p** 89. C Wandsworth All SS *S'wark* 88-92; Canada from 92. *PO Box 233, 228 Power Street, Geraldton, Ontario, Canada, P0T 1M0*

KING, Clare Maria. b 68. St Andr Univ BD91. Westcott Ho Cam 91. **d** 94. Hon C Norbury St Phil *S'wark* 94-96; Chapl Croydon Coll 95-96; Asst Chapl Cen Sheff Univ Hosps NHS Trust from 96. *The Vicarage, 30 Cedar Street, Hollingwood, Chesterfield, Derbyshire S43 2LE* Tel (01246) 472175

KING, Mrs Daphne Eileen. b 37. EMMTC 78. **dss** 81 **d** 87 **p** 94. Theddlethorpe *Linc* 84-87; D-in-c 87-89; Saltfleetby 84-87; D-in-c 87-89; D-in-c Healing and Stallingborough 89-94; P-in-c from 94. *The Rectory, 1A The Avenue, Healing, Grimsby, S Humberside DN37 7NA* Tel (01472) 883481

KING, David Charles. b 52. K Coll Lon 73 Coll of Resurr Mirfield 77. **d** 78 **p** 79. C Saltburn-by-the-Sea *York* 78-81; Youth Officer 81-85; P-in-c Crathorne 81-85; Par Educn Adv *Wakef* 85-91; Min Coulby Newham Ecum Project *York* 91-94; V Egton w Grosmont from 94. *St Hilda's Vicarage, Egton, Whitby, N Yorkshire YO21 1UT* Tel (01947) 895315

KING, David Frederick. b 32. Southn Coll of Tech DMA70. Sarum Th Coll 59. **d** 61 **p** 72. C Hanworth All SS *Lon* 60-62; Hon C Andover St Mich *Win* 71-83; P-in-c 83-88; V 88-90; Chapl R S Hants Hosp 90-92; Chapl Countess Mountbatten Hospice 90-92; Perm to Offic *Win* 92-97; rtd 97; P-in-c Smannell w Enham Alamein *Win* from 97. *The Rectory, Dunhills Lane, Andover, Hants SP11 6HU* Tel (01264) 352827

KING, David Russell. b 42. Univ of Wales (Lamp) BA67. St D Coll Lamp DipTh68. **d** 68 **p** 69. C Barrow St Geo w St Luke *Carl* 68-72; P-in-c Kirkland 72-74; V Edenhall w Langwathby 72-73; P-in-c Culgaith 72-73; V Edenhall w Langwathby and Culgaith 73-74; V Flookburgh 75-79; V Barrow St Jas 79-82; P-in-c Bolton w Ireby and Uldale 82-83; R 83-90; R Burgh-by-Sands and Kirkbampton w Kirkandrews etc from 90. *The Rectory, Burgh-by-Sands, Carlisle CA5 6AW* Tel (01228) 576324

KING, David William Anthony. b 42. Ch Ch Ox BA63 MA68. Westcott Ho Cam 63. **d** 65 **p** 66. C Cayton w Eastfield *York* 65-68; C Southbroom *Sarum* 68-71; R Hinton Parva 71-72; V Holt St Jas 71-72; V Holt St Jas and Hinton Parva 72-75; P-in-c Horton and Chalbury 73-75; R Holt St Jas, Hinton Parva, Horton and Chalbury 75-79; TV Melton Mowbray w Thorpe Arnold *Leic* 79-83; V Foxton w Gumley and Laughton and Lubenham 83-90; P-in-c Boreham *Chelmsf* from 90. *The Vicarage, Church Road, Boreham, Chelmsford CM3 3EG* Tel (01245) 467281

KING, Dennis. b 31. ACA53 FCA64. EMMTC 73. **d** 76 **p** 77. NSM Chesterfield St Mary and All SS *Derby* from 76. *Hillcrest, Stubben Edge, Ashover, Chesterfield, Derbyshire S45 0EU* Tel (01246) 590279

KING, Dennis Charles. b 27. Chich Th Coll 53. **d** 55 **p** 56. C Luton Ch Ch *St Alb* 55-58 and 59-63; USA 58-59; Bahamas 63-66; Jamaica 66-77; V Bromham w Oakley *St Alb* 77-84; TR St Marylebone Ch Ch *Lon* 84-89; V Flamstead *St Alb* 89-93; rtd 93. *Te Deum, 36 Manor Road, Toddington, Dunstable, Beds LU5 6AH* Tel (01525) 873557

KING, Dennis Keppel. b 33. Lich Th Coll 63. **d** 65 **p** 66. C Eccleston St Thos *Liv* 65-68; C W Derby St Mary 68-71; V Aintree St Giles 71-96; rtd 96. *8 Whiteoak Avenue, Easingwold, York Y06 3GB* Tel (01347) 822625

KING, Dr Derek Edwin Noel. b 31. Qu Mary Coll Lon BSc54 Birkb Coll Lon PhD60. LNSM course 91. **d** 93 **p** 94. NSM Nacton and Levington w Bucklesham and Foxhall *St E* from 93. *Vindelis, 1 Eastcliff, Felixstowe, Suffolk IP11 9TA* Tel (01394) 270815

KING, Donald (Don). b 32. Chich Th Coll. **d** 86. NSM Forton *Portsm* from 86. *8 Burnett Road, Gosport, Hants PO12 3AH* Tel (01705) 523440

KING, Ernest Cuthbert. b 12. Univ of W Aus BA33. Wells Th Coll 35. **d** 36 **p** 37. C Northampton St Jas *Pet* 36-46; CF (EC) 39-46; V Desborough *Pet* 46-49; Australia from 49; rtd 78. *Cottage 113, Hollywood Village, 31 Williams Road, Nedlands, W Australia 6009* Tel Perth (9) 380 5113

KING, Fergus John. b 62. St Andr Univ MA Edin Univ BD89. Edin Th Coll 86. **d** 89 **p** 90. Chapl St Jo Cathl Oban *Arg* 89-92; C Oban St Jo 89-92; Tanzania from 92. *St Mark's Theological College, PO Box 25017, Dar es Salaam, Tanzania*

KING, Frederick William. b 24. CertEd74. Richmond Th Coll 46 Qu Coll Birm 49. **d** 50 **p** 51. C Kimberworth *Sheff* 50-52; C Luton St Mary *St Alb* 52-55; Chapl RAF 55-70; Chapl The Leas Sch Hoylake 70-72; Chapl Wirral Gr Sch 74-75; Chapl Summer Fields Sch Ox 75; rtd 89. *31 Saint Yves, 22580 Plouha, France*

KING, George Henry. b 24. MRHS55 NDH55. St Alb Minl Tr Scheme. **d** 79 **p** 80. Hon C Flamstead *St Alb* from 79; Dioc Agric Chapl from 90. *Chad Lane Farm, Chad Lane, Flamstead, St Albans, Herts AL3 8HW* Tel (01582) 841648

KING, Mrs Gillian Daphne. b 38. EMMTC 79. **dss** 83 **d** 87 **p** 94. Knighton St Jo *Leic* 83-85; Clarendon Park St Jo w Knighton St Mich 86-87; Par Dn 87-89; Chapl Kingston and Esher Mental Health Services 89-93; Chapl Kingston and Esher Community Health Unit 93-97; Chapl Long Grove Hosp Epsom 90-92; Chapl Tolworth Hosp Surbiton 91-97; Chapl Kingston and Distr Community NHS Trust 94-97; TV Hale *Guildf* from 97. *8 Badshot Park, Badshot Lea, Farnham, Surrey GU9 9JZ* Tel (01252) 331370

KING, Harry William. b 15. Oak Hill Th Coll 38. **d** 41 **p** 42. C Upper Holloway St Jo *Lon* 41-44; C Tooting Graveney St Nic *S'wark* 44-46; Perm to Offic *Lon* 46-64 and from 67; Chapl Buckingham Coll Harrow 56-64; Perm to Offic *St Alb* 58-64; from 67; V Sandon 64-67; R Wallington w Rushden 64-67; Asst Master Greenway Sch Hillingdon 72-80; rtd 80. *36 The Gables, Ransome Close, Watford WD1 4NG* Tel (01923) 232360

KING, Canon Jeffrey Douglas Wallace. b 43. AKC67. **d** 68 **p** 69. C S Harrow St Paul *Lon* 68-71; C Garforth *Ripon* 71-74; V Potternewton 74-83; TR Moor Allerton from 83; RD Allerton 85-89; Hon Can Ripon Cathl from 90. *St John's Vicarage, Fir Tree Lane, Leeds LS17 7BZ* Tel 0113-268 4598

KING, Dr Jennifer Mary. b 41. Lon Univ BDS65 MSc75 PhD. Ripon Coll Cuddesdon 86. **d** 88 **p** 94. NSM S Hackney St Mich w Haggerston St Paul *Lon* from 88; Chapl Qu Mary and Westf Coll from 91. *5 Louisa Gardens, London E1 4NS* Tel 0171-982 6325 or 980 1204

KING, Jeremy Norman. *See* CLARK-KING, Jeremy Norman

KING, John. b 38. S'wark Ord Course DipRS77. **d** 80 **p** 81. C S Gillingham *Roch* 80-85; Min Joydens Wood St Barn CD 85-90; V Borstal from 90; Chapl HM Pris Cookham Wood from 90; Chapl The Foord Almshouses from 90. *The Vicarage, 76 Borstal Street, Rochester, Kent ME1 3HL* Tel (01634) 845948 Fax 828921

KING, John Andrew. b 50. Qu Coll Birm 72. **d** 75 **p** 76. C Halesowen *Worc* 75-77; C Belper Ch Ch and Milford *Derby* 78-81; Perm to Offic from 87. *11 Well Lane, Milford, Belper, Derbyshire DE56 0QQ* Tel (01332) 841810

KING, John Charles. b 27. St Pet Hall Ox BA51 MA55. Oak Hill Th Coll 51. **d** 53 **p** 54. C Slough *Ox* 53-57; V Ware Ch Ch *St Alb* 57-60; Ed C of E Newspaper 60-68; Lic to Offic *St Alb* 60-70; Teacher St Fran Bacon Sch St Alb 68-71; Boston Gr Sch 71-88; Lic to Offic *Linc* from 74; rtd 92. *6 Somersby Way, Boston, Lincs PE21 9PQ* Tel (01205) 363061

KING, John Colin. b 39. Cuddesdon Coll 69. **d** 71 **p** 72. C Cookham *Ox* 71-75; Youth Chapl *B & W* 75-80; P-in-c Merriott 76-80; P-in-c Hinton w Dinnington 79-80; R Merriott w Hinton, Dinnington and Lopen from 80. *The Vicarage, Church Street, Merriott, Somerset TA16 5PS* Tel (01460) 73226

KING, John David. b 37. Univ of Wales DipTh63. St Aid Birkenhead 67. **d** 69 **p** 70. C Whitfield *Derby* 69-71; C

St Laurence in the Isle of Thanet *Cant* 71-76; V Alkham w Capel le Ferne and Hougham 76-82; R Deal St Andr from 82. *St Andrew's Rectory, St Andrew's Road, Deal, Kent CT14 6AS* Tel (01304) 374354

KING, John Michael Stuart. b 22. St Edm Hall Ox BA48 MA52. Cuddesdon Coll 48. **d** 50 **p** 51. C Ryhope *Dur* 50-53; C Guisborough *York* 53-56; V High and Low Worsall 56-60; V Kirklevington 56-60; R Hinderwell w Roxby 60-71; V Hibaldstow *Linc* 71-88; rtd 88; Perm to Offic *Linc* from 88. *Old School House, Church Lane, Saxby-All-Saints, Brigg, S Humberside DN20 0QE* Tel (01652) 61693

KING, Joseph Stephen. b 39. St Chad's Coll Dur BA62 DipTh63 MPhil83. **d** 64 **p** 65. C Lewisham St Mary *S'wark* 64-69; Hon C Milton next Gravesend Ch Ch *Roch* 70-85; V from 85. *The Vicarage, 48 Old Road East, Gravesend, Kent DA12 1NR* Tel (01474) 352643

KING, Mrs Katharine Mary. b 63. St Hugh's Coll Ox BA85 MA89 SS Coll Cam BA88. Ridley Hall Cam 86. **d** 89 **p** 94. C Ipswich St Aug *St E* 89-91; NSM Bures from 92. *The Vicarage, Church Square, Bures, Suffolk CO8 5AA* Tel (01787) 227315

KING, Lawrence Norman. b 38. FRICS. St Deiniol's Hawarden. **d** 80 **p** 81. NSM Lt Bowden St Hugh *Leic* 80-84; NSM Fleckney and Kilby 84-89; R Scalford w Goadby Marwood and Wycombe etc from 89. *The Rectory, 16 Church Street, Scalford, Melton Mowbray, Leics LE14 4DL* Tel (01664) 76319

KING, Malcolm Charles. b 37. Chich Th Coll 67. **d** 70 **p** 71. C Mill End *St Alb* 70-72; Chapl RAF 72-76; R W Lynn *Nor* 76-81; V Croxley Green All SS *St Alb* 81-90; V Grimsby St Aug *Linc* from 90; Asst Local Min Officer 90-95; OGS from 90. *St Augustine's Vicarage, 145 Legsby Avenue, Grimsby, S Humberside DN32 0LA* Tel (01472) 877109

KING, Malcolm Stewart. b 56. Sarum & Wells Th Coll 77. **d** 80 **p** 81. C Farnham *Guildf* 80-83; C Chertsey 83-86; Chapl St Pet Hosp Chertsey 83-86; V Egham Hythe *Guildf* 86-91; P-in-c Cove St Jo 91; TR from 91; RD Aldershot from 93. *The Rectory, 55 Cove Road, Farnborough, Hants GU14 0EX* Tel (01252) 544544

KING, Martin Quartermain. b 39. Reading Univ BA61. Cuddesdon Coll 62. **d** 64 **p** 65. C S Shields St Hilda w St Thos *Dur* 64-66; C Newton Aycliffe 66-71; V Chilton Moor 71-78; R Middleton St Geo 78-91; R Sedgefield from 91; RD Sedgefield 91-96. *The Rectory, Sedgefield, Stockton-on-Tees, Cleveland TS21 3DW* Tel (01740) 20274

KING, Maurice Charles Francis. b 32. ACP58 Em Coll Cam BA55 MA59. Chich Th Coll 78. **d** 79 **p** 80. C Burnley St Cath *Blackb* 79-81; C Burnley St Cath w St Alb and St Paul 81-83; C Sheff Parson Cross St Cecilia *Sheff* 83-88; V New Bentley 88-94; rtd 94; Perm to Offic *Carl* from 94. *204 Wordsworth Court, Cockermouth, Cumbria CA13 0EB* Tel (01900) 827503

KING, Michael Charles. Worc Coll Ox BA56 MA60. Coll of Resurr Mirfield. **d** 62 **p** 63. Hon C Hampstead All So *Lon* 62-65; C Thorpe *Nor* 66-69; Ed Sec BRF 69-90; NSM Queensbury All SS *Lon* 69-79; Hon C Lt Stanmore St Lawr 80-90; R Cawston w Haveringland, Booton and Brandiston *Nor* 91-96; P-in-c Saxthorpe w Corpusty, Blickling, Oulton etc 94; R Cawston w Booton and Brandiston etc from 96. *The Rectory, Ames Court, Cawston, Norwich NR10 4AN* Tel (01603) 871282

KING, Nathan Richard. b 68. Whitelands Coll Lon BA89 Liv Univ DipSocSc91. St Mich Coll Llan DipTh93 BTh94. **d** 94 **p** 95. C Hawarden *St As* from 94. *1 Church Cottage, Rectory Lane, Hawarden, Deeside CH5 3NN* Tel (01244) 538715

KING, Nicholas Bernard Paul. b 46. Wycliffe Hall Ox 72. **d** 75 **p** 76. C Pitsmoor w Wicker *Sheff* 75-78; C Erdington St Barn *Birm* 78-80; C Sutton Coldfield H Trin 80-84; V Lynesack *Dur* 84-92; rtd 93. *21 Arthur Terrace, Bishop Auckland, Co Durham DL14 6BL* Tel (01388) 605614

KING, Peter Duncan. b 48. TD. K Coll Lon LLB70 AKC70 Fitzw Coll Cam BA72 MA77. Westcott Ho Cam 70. **d** 80 **p** 81. Hon C Notting Hill *Lon* 80-84; Hon C Mortlake w E Sheen *S'wark* from 84. *49 Leinster Avenue, London SW14 7JW* Tel 0181-876 8997

KING, Peter George. b 24. Lon Univ LLB52. ALCD55. **d** 55 **p** 56. C Chitts Hill St Cuth *Lon* 55-59; C Woking St Pet *Guildf* 59-61; V Toxteth Park St Bede *Liv* 61-68; V Leyton St Paul *Chelmsf* 68-85; rtd 85; Perm to Offic *Ex* from 85. *10 Barrington Mead, Sidmouth, Devon EX10 8QW* Tel (01395) 578172

KING, Canon Philip David. b 35. Keble Coll Ox BA57 MA61. Tyndale Hall Bris 58. **d** 60 **p** 61. C Redhill H Trin *S'wark* 60-63; C Wallington H Trin 63-68; V Fulham Ch Ch *Lon* 68-74; Lic to Offic *S'wark* 74-86; Gen Sec SAMS 74-86; V Roxeth Ch Ch and Harrow St Pet *Lon* 86-89; Gen Sec Gen Syn Bd for Miss from 89. *31 Myrtle Avenue, Ruislip, Middx HA4 8SA* Tel 0171-429 0636 or 222 9011 Fax 799 2714

KING, Miss Philipa Ann. b 65. Heythrop Coll Lon. Westcott Ho Cam CTM95. **d** 95 **p** 96. C Cambridge Ascension *Ely* from 95. *36 Alpha Road, Cambridge CB4 3DG*

KING, Rawlins Henry Pyne. b 16. ALCD42. **d** 42 **p** 43. C Hove Bp Hannington Memorial Ch *Chich* 42-44; C Southborough St Pet *Roch* 44-47; V Ore Ch Ch *Chich* 47-55; Chapl Fairlight Sanatorium 49-55; Chapl Osborne Ho 51-55; Sec CPAS Metrop Area 55-60; Perm to Offic Chelmsf, Chich, Lon, Ox and S'wark 55-60; V Virginia Water *Guildf* 60-68; V Hailsham *Chich* 68-81; rtd 81; Perm to Offic *Chich* from 81. *Ramsay Hall, 9-13 Byron Road, Worthing, W Sussex BN11 3HN*

KING, Richard Andrew. b 51. Linc Th Coll. **d** 84 **p** 85. C Bramhall *Ches* 84-87; V Heald Green St Cath 87-92; P-in-c Ashprington, Cornworthy and Dittisham *Ex* from 92. *The Rectory, Prior View, Cornworthy, Totnes, Devon TQ9 7HN* Tel (01803) 732384

KING, Richard David. b 63. Oak Hill Th Coll 87. **d** 90 **p** 91. C Foord St Jo *Cant* 90-94; P-in-c Orlestone w Snave and Ruckinge w Warehorne from 94; Dioc Ecum Officer from 97. *The Rectory, Cock Lane, Ham Street, Ashford, Kent TN26 2HU* Tel (01233) 732274

KING, Robert Dan (Bob). b 57. Sarum & Wells Th Coll 92. **d** 94 **p** 95. C Heref H Trin *Heref* 94-97; P-in-c from 97. *The Vicarage, 164 Whitecross Road, Hereford HR4 0DH* Tel (01432) 273086

KING, Robin Lucas Colin. b 59. Dundee Univ MA81. Ridley Hall Cam 87. **d** 89 **p** 90. C Ipswich St Aug *St E* 89-92; V Bures from 92. *The Vicarage, Church Square, Bures, Suffolk CO8 5AA* Tel (01787) 227315

KING, Canon Stuart John Langley. b 33. Selw Coll Cam BA57 MA61. Linc Th Coll 57. **d** 59 **p** 60. C Plymouth Crownhill Ascension *Ex* 59-62; C Horsham *Chich* 62-67; V Devonport St Mark Ford *Ex* 67-77; RD Plymouth 74-77; Can Res Cov Cathl *Cov* 77-84; V Tooting All SS *S'wark* 84-96; rtd 96. *12 Lowertown Close, Landrake, Saltash, Cornwall PL12 5DG* Tel (01752) 851512

KING, Terence Reginald. b 33. St Steph Ho Ox 58. **d** 61 **p** 62. C Thornhill Lees *Wakef* 61-65; V Glasshoughton 65-77; V W Ardsley from 77. *St Mary's Vicarage, Woodkirk, Dewsbury, W Yorkshire WF12 7JL* Tel (01924) 472375

KING, Thomas James Richard. b 27. LGSM64 ACP66. St Jo Coll Nottm. **d** 85 **p** 86. Hon C Enderby w Lubbesthorpe and Thurlaston *Leic* from 85. *6 Copt Oak Road, Narborough, Leicester LE9 5EF* Tel 0116-286 4250

KING, Timothy William. b 52. CertEd. Ripon Coll Cuddesdon. **d** 81 **p** 82. C Ludlow *Heref* 81-83; C Walton-on-Thames *Guildf* 83-86; C Hammersmith St Paul *Lon* 86-88; V Send *Guildf* 88-95; R Farncombe from 95. *The Rectory, 38 Farncombe Hill, Godalming, Surrey GU7 2AU* Tel (01483) 416091

KING, Tony Christopher. b 62. Lanc Univ BA83. Coll of Resurr Mirfield 83. **d** 86 **p** 87. C Stansted Mountfitchet *Chelmsf* 86-89; USPG 89-92; Botswana 90-92; C Chingford SS Pet and Paul *Chelmsf* 92-93. *12 Livingstone Road, London E17 9AX*

KING, Preb Walter Raleigh. b 45. New Coll Ox BA67 MA74. Cuddesdon Coll 71. **d** 74 **p** 75. C Wisbech SS Pet and Paul *Ely* 74-77; C Barrow St Geo w St Luke *Carl* 77-79; P-in-c Clifford *Heref* 79-83; P-in-c Cusop 79-83; P-in-c Hardwick 79-83; P-in-c Whitney w Winforton 81-84; R Cusop w Clifford, Hardwicke, Bredwardine etc 83-86; R Heref St Nic 86-92; Dir of Ords 86-92; Preb Heref Cathl 86-92; TR Huntingdon *Ely* from 92; RD Huntingdon from 94. *The Rectory, 1 The Walks East, Huntingdon, Cambs PE18 6AP* Tel (01480) 412674

KING-SMITH, Giles Anthony Beaumont. b 53. Univ Coll Ox BA75. Trin Coll Bris DipHE88. **d** 88 **p** 89. C Gtr Corsham *Bris* 88-92; V Two Mile Hill St Mich 92-96; TV Ilfracombe, Lee, Woolacombe, Bittadon etc *Ex* from 96. *The Vicarage, Springfield Road, Woolacombe, North Devon EX34 7BX* Tel (01271) 870467

KING-SMITH, Philip Hugh (Brother Robert Hugh). b 28. CCC Cam BA52 MA56. Cuddesdon Coll 52. **d** 54 **p** 55. C Stockton St Pet *Dur* 54-59; V Bishopwearmouth Gd Shep 59-64; SSF from 64; USA from 66. *San Damiano, 573 Dolores Street, San Francisco, California 94110, USA* Tel San Francisco (415) 861-1372

KINGCOME, John Parken. b 18. CEng50 MIMechE50. Sarum Th Coll 65. **d** 67 **p** 68. C Melksham *Sarum* 67-70; P-in-c Woodborough w Manningford Bohun etc 70-72; R Swanborough 72-75; TR Swanborough 75-79; RD Pewsey 75-84; Custos St Jo Hosp Heytesbury 79-84; rtd 84; Perm to Offic *B & W* 85-95; Perm to Offic *Bris* from 92. *Stonecrop, The Butts, Biddestone, Chippenham, Wilts SN14 7DY* Tel (01249) 713412

KINGHAM, Derek Henry. b 29. Oak Hill Th Coll 56. **d** 58 **p** 59. C Deptford St Jo *S'wark* 58-60; C Normanton *Derby* 60-63; R Gaulby w Kings Norton and Stretton Parva *Leic* 63-73; V Bacup St Sav *Man* 73-95; rtd 95; Perm to Offic *Carl* from 95. *12 Castle Green Close, Kendal, Cumbria LA9 6AT* Tel (01539) 727008

KINGHAM, Canon John Arthur. b 14. Ch Coll Cam BA36 MA40. Ridley Hall Cam 36. **d** 38 **p** 39. C Roxeth Ch Ch *Lon* 38-40; C Fisherton Anger *Sarum* 40-43; R Hamworthy 44-51; V Gt Baddow *Chelmsf* 51-82; RD Chelmsf 67-77; Hon Can Chelmsf Cathl 75-82; rtd 82; Perm to Offic *Chelmsf* from 82. *63 Tensing Gardens, Billericay, Essex CM12 9JY* Tel (01277) 652475

KINGHAM, Mair Josephine. *See* TALBOT, Mrs Mair Josephine

KINGHORN, Richard. b 16. CCC Cam BA38 MA42. Linc Th Coll 39. **d** 40 **p** 46. C Eastleigh *Win* 40-41; Chapl Stamford Sch 46-58; P-in-c Stamford Baron *Linc* 46-47; Chapl K Coll Sch Wimbledon 58-77; rtd 77; Tutor Open Univ 78-89. *14 Pentewand Road, St Austell, Cornwall PL25 5BX* Tel (01736) 72351

KINGMAN, Paul Henry Charles. b 64. Reading Univ BSc86. Wycliffe Hall Ox BTh95. **d** 95 **p** 96. C Whitton *Sarum* from 95. *8 Knowledge Crescent, Ramsbury, Marlborough, Wilts SN8 2QZ* Tel (01672) 521282

KINGS, Canon Graham Ralph. b 53. Hertf Coll Ox BA77 MA80 Selw Coll Cam DipTh80. Ridley Hall Cam 78. **d** 80 **p** 81. C Harlesden St Mark *Lon* 80-84; CMS 85-91; Kenya 85-91; Dir Studies St Andr Inst Kabare 85-88; Vice Prin 89-91; Lect Missiology Cam Federation Th Colls from 91; Overseas Adv Henry Martyn Trust from 91. *York House, 43 Belvoir Road, Cambridge CB4 1JH* Tel (01223) 353040 or 355397

KINGS, Mrs Jean Alison. b 63. RGN85. Cranmer Hall Dur BA90. **d** 91 **p** 94. Chapl Bris Poly *Bris* 91-92; Chapl Univ of the W of England 92-95; Hon C Bris Lockleaze St Mary Magd w St Fran 91-95; C Fishponds All SS 95-96; Hon C from 96. *36 Timberdene, Trendlewood, Bristol BS16 1TJ* Tel 0117-965 6725

KINGS, Peter Robert. b 33. AKC61. **d** 62 **p** 63. C Moorfields *Bris* 62-65; Dep Dir of Educn *Lon* 66-70; Dep Dir of Educn *S'wark* 66-70; Lic to Offic *Nor* 79-95; rtd 86. *113 Gaywood Road, King's Lynn, Norfolk PE30 2PU* Tel (01553) 772404

KINGSBURY, Canon Richard John. b 41. Lon Univ BA63. Linc Th Coll 65. **d** 67 **p** 68. C Wallsend St Luke *Newc* 67-69; C Monkseaton St Mary 69-70; Chapl K Coll Lon 70-75; V Hungerford and Denford *Ox* 75-83; R Caversham and Mapledurham from 83; Hon Can Ch Ch from 92. *The Rectory, 20 Church Road, Reading RG4 7AD* Tel 0118-947 9130 or 947 1703

KINGSLAND, Desmond George. b 23. Sarum Th Coll 75. **d** 78 **p** 79. Hon C Bournemouth H Epiphany *Win* from 78. *Windy Ridge, 23 Granby Road, Bournemouth BH9 3NZ* Tel (01202) 526011

KINGSLEY, Brian St Clair. b 26. St Steph Ho Ox 56. **d** 59 **p** 60. C Tilehurst St Mich *Ox* 59-63; CSWG from 63; Prior from 85; Lic to Offic *Chich* from 66; rtd 96. *The Monastery of Christ the Saviour, 23 Cambridge Road, Hove, E Sussex BN3 1DE* Tel (01273) 726698

KINGSLEY-SMITH, John Sydney. b 45. ARCM. Ridley Hall Cam 78. **d** 80 **p** 81. C Nailsea H Trin *B & W* 80-84; TV Whitton *Sarum* 84-91; V Chorleywood Ch Ch *St Alb* from 91. *Christ Church Vicarage, Chorleywood Common, Rickmansworth, Herts WD3 5SG* Tel (01923) 282149

KINGSNORTH, Canon Eric John. b 11. FIA38. Wells Th Coll 45. **d** 47 **p** 48. C Upper Norwood St Jo *Cant* 47-50; C Maidstone All SS 50-53; V Yeovil H Trin *B & W* 53-63; Dir of Ords 61-63; Preb Wells Cathl 61-63; V Newark St Mary *S'well* 63-74; RD Newark 63-74; P-in-c Cotham 63-74; P-in-c Hawton 64-74; P-in-c Shelton 64-74; P-in-c Sibthorpe 65-66; Hon Can S'well Minster 66-74; P-in-c Newark St Leon 72-74; P-in-c Bradpole *Sarum* 74-78; rtd 78; Perm to Offic *Win* from 78. *11 The Cloisters, Belmore Lane, Lymington, Hants SO41 3QX* Tel (01590) 678397

KINGSTON, Canon Albert William (Bertie). b 47. Bernard Gilpin Soc Dur 68 Oak Hill Th Coll 69. **d** 72 **p** 73. C Walton Breck *Liv* 72-74; C Templemore *D & R* 74-76; I Kildallon w Newtowngore and Corrawallen *K, E & A* 76-82; Bp's C Ardagh w Tashinny, Shrule and Kilcommick from 82; Preb Elphin Cathl from 95. *The Rectory, Tashinny, Colehill, Ballymahon, Co Longford, Irish Republic* Tel Mullingar (44) 57434

KINGSTON, Mrs Avril Dawson. b 34. Local Minl Tr Course 91. **d** 94 **p** 95. Aux Min Douglas Union w Frankfield *C, C & R* from 94. *Ballymartin House, Glencairn, Co Waterford, Irish Republic* Tel Waterford (58) 56227

KINGSTON, Canon Eric. b 24. **d** 69 **p** 70. C Ballymacarrett St Patr *D & D* 69-72; C Knock 72-76; I Annahilt w Magherahamlet 76-93; rtd 93; Can and Prec Dromore Cathl *D & D* 93. *38 Kinedale Park, Ballynahinch, Co Down BT24 8YS* Tel (01238) 565715

KINGSTON, George Mervyn. b 47. CITC 70. **d** 73 **p** 74. C Comber *D & D* 73-77; C Belfast St Donard 77-80; Min Can Down Cathl 80-84; I Ardglass w Dunsford 82-84; Bp's C Belfast St Andr *Conn* 84-90; I Ballymascanlan w Creggan and Rathcor *Arm* from 90. *1 Whitemill Road, Lower Faughart, Dundalk, Co Louth, Irish Republic* Tel Dundalk (42) 71921

KINGSTON, John Desmond George. b 40. TCD BA63 MA66. CITC 64. **d** 64 **p** 65. C Arm St Mark *Arm* 64-70; Hon V Choral Arm Cathl 69-70; Chapl Portora R Sch Enniskillen from 70; Lic to Offic *Clogh* from 70. *Ambleside, 45 Old Rossory Road, Enniskillen, Co Fermanagh BT74 7LF* Tel (01365) 324493

KINGSTON, Canon Kenneth Robert. b 42. TCD BA65 MA69. **d** 66 **p** 67. C Enniscorthy *C & O* 66-69; C Ballymena *Conn* 70-72; C Drumragh w Mountfield *D & R* 72-78; I Badoney Lower w Greenan and Badoney Upper 78-84; I Desertmartin w Termoneeny from 84; Can Derry Cathl from 97. *25 Dromore Road, Desertmartin, Magherafelt, Co Londonderry BT45 5JZ* Tel (01648) 32455

KINGSTON, Michael Joseph. b 51. K Coll Lon BD73 AKC73. St Aug Coll Cant 73. **d** 74 **p** 75. C Reading H Trin *Ox* 74-77; C New Eltham All SS *S'wark* 77-83; V Plumstead Ascension 83-94; Sub-Dean Greenwich N 92-94; V Sydenham St Bart from 94. *St Bartholomew's Vicarage, 4 Westwood Hill, London SE26 6QR* Tel 0181-778 5290

KINGSTON, Michael Marshall. b 54. St Jo Coll Nottm MA94. **d** 96 **p** 97. C Drayton w Felthorpe *Nor* from 96. *6 Cricket Close, Thorpe Marriott, Norwich NR8 6YA*

KINGSTON, Robert George. b 46. TCD BA68 Div Test69. **d** 69 **p** 72. C Belfast St Thos *Conn* 69-72; C Kilkenny St Canice Cathl *C & O* 72-75; I Ballinasloe w Taughmaconnell *L & K* 77-79; I Maryborough w Dysart Enos and Ballyfin *C & O* 79-85; I Lurgan w Billis, Killinkere and Munterconnaught *K, E & A* 85-88; Registrar Kilmore 87-92; I Lurgan etc w Ballymachugh, Kildrumferton etc 88-92; I Tallaght *D & G* from 92; Warden of Readers from 93. *6 Sally Park, Firhouse Road, Tallaght, Dublin 24, Irish Republic* Tel Dublin (1) 462 1044 or 462 6006 Fax 462 1044

KINGSTON, Roy William Henry. b 31. Chich Th Coll 60. **d** 62 **p** 63. C Leeds St Aid *Ripon* 62-66; S Africa 66-73; V Bramley *Ripon* 74-81; TR Hemel Hempstead *St Alb* 81-85; TR Fareham H Trin *Portsm* 85-93; RD Alverstoke 89-90; RD Fareham 90-93; P-in-c Hambledon 93-97; rtd 97. *8 Pengilly Road, Farnham, Surrey GU9 7XG* Tel (01252) 711371

KINGSTON, Mrs Shirley Alexandra. b 42. Ch of Ireland Tr Coll DPEd61 TCD BA68 HDipEd70. CITC 90. **d** 93 **p** 94. NSM Castlemacadam w Ballinaclash, Aughrim etc *D & G* 93-95; NSM Rathdrum w Glenealy, Derralossary and Laragh 95-97; NSM Bray from 97. *Kilpatrick House, Redcross, Wicklow, Irish Republic* Tel Wicklow (404) 47137

KINGSTON, William Ypres. b 19. TCD BA40 MA43 BD46. TCD Div Sch. **d** 43 **p** 44. C Ballywillan *Conn* 43-47; C Brompton H Trin *Lon* 47-51; CF 51-54; V Albany Street Ch Ch *Lon* 55-80; C Weeke *Win* 80-85; rtd 85; Perm to Offic *Guildf* from 85. *20 Cedar Court, Crown Street, Egham, Surrey TW20 9DB* Tel (01784) 431605

KINGSTON-UPON-THAMES, Area Bishop of. *Vacant*

KINGTON, David Bruce. b 45. Trin Coll Bris 72. **d** 72 **p** 73. C Wellington w Eyton *Lich* 72-77; C Boscombe St Jo *Win* 77-81; R Michelmersh, Timsbury, Farley Chamberlayne etc from 81; RD Romsey from 95. *The Rectory, Braishfield, Romsey, Hants SO51 0PR* Tel (01794) 368335

KINNA, Michael Andrew. b 46. Chich Th Coll 84. **d** 86 **p** 87. C Leominster *Heref* 86-90; TV Wenlock 90-93; P-in-c Broseley w Benthall 93; P-in-c Jackfield 93; P-in-c Linley w Willey and Barrow 93; R Broseley w Benthall, Jackfield, Linley etc from 94. *The Rectory, Church Street, Broseley, Shropshire TF12 5DA* Tel (01952) 882647

KINNAIRD, Jennifer. b 41. Hull Univ BA62 Ex Univ PGCE63. NE Ord Course DipHE94. **d** 97. NSM Corbridge w Halton and Newton Hall *Newc* from 97. *17 Glebelands, Corbridge, Northd NE45 5DS* Tel (01434) 632695

KINNAIRD, Keith. b 42. Chich Th Coll 72. **d** 75 **p** 76. C Didcot St Pet *Ox* 75-78; C Abingdon w Shippon 78-82; Chapl Abingdon Hosp 79-92; P-in-c Sunningwell *Ox* 82-90; P-in-c Radley 88-90; R Radley and Sunningwell 90-95; SBStJ from 91; Oxon Co Chapl OStJ 91-95; V Old Shoreham *Chich* from 95; V New Shoreham from 95. *The Vicarage, Church Street, Shoreham-by-Sea, W Sussex BN43 5DQ* Tel (01273) 452109

KINSEY, Bruce Richard Lawrence. b 59. K Coll Lon BD81 AKC81 MTh86 MA94. Wycliffe Hall Ox. **d** 84 **p** 85. C Gt Stanmore *Lon* 84-88; C Shepherd's Bush St Steph w St Thos 88-91; Chapl and Fell Down Coll Cam from 91. *Downing College, Cambridge CB2 1DQ* Tel (01223) 334800 Fax 337334 E-mail brlk1@cam.ac.uk

KINSEY, Paul. b 56. Nottm Univ BTh89. Linc Th Coll 86. **d** 89 **p** 90. C Connah's Quay *St As* 89-91; Min Can St As Cathl 91-94; Asst Chapl Middx Hosp Lon from 94. *Middlesex Hospital, Mortimer Street, London W1N 8AA* Tel 0171-636 8333

KINSEY, Russell Frederick David. b 34. Sarum Th Coll 59. **d** 62 **p** 63. C Twerton *B & W* 62-66; C N Cadbury 66-76; C Yarlington 66-76; P-in-c Compton Pauncefoot w Blackford 66-76; P-in-c Maperton 66-76; P-in-c N Cheriton 66-76; TV Camelot Par 76-79; V Pill 79-82; P-in-c Easton in Gordano w Portbury and Clapton 80-82; V Pill w Easton in Gordano and Portbury 82-92; rtd 94. *25 Newbourne Road, Weston-super-Mare, Avon BS22 8NF*

KINSMEN, Barry William. b 40. Chan Sch Truro. **d** 74 **p** 75. NSM Padstow *Truro* 74-78; Dioc Adv in RE 79-95; P-in-c St Issey 80-81; P-in-c Lt Petherick 80-81; R St Issey w St Petroc Minor 81-95; rtd 95; Perm to Offic *Truro* from 95. *14 Old School Court, School Hill, Padstow, Cornwall PL28 8ED* Tel (01841) 532507

KIPPAX, Michael John. b 48. Open Univ BA82. SW Minl Tr Course 89. **d** 92 **p** 93. C Camborne *Truro* 92-95; C Woughton *Ox* 95-96; TV from 96. *49 Garraways, Coffee Hall, Milton Keynes MK6 5DD* Tel (01908) 670427

KIRBY, Bernard William Alexander (Alex). b 39. Keble Coll Ox BA62. Coll of Resurr Mirfield 62. **d** 65 **p** 72. C Is of Dogs Ch Ch and St Jo w St Luke *Lon* 65-66; Hon C Battersea St Phil *S'wark* 72; Hon C Battersea St Phil w St Bart 73-76; Perm to Offic 76-78 and from 83. *31 Ashness Road, London SW11 6RY* Tel 0171-223 4000

KIRBY, David Anthony. b 42. Dur Univ BA64 PhD68. N Ord Course 84. **d** 87 **p** 88. NSM Crosland Moor *Wakef* from 87. *9 Fenay Crescent, Almondbury, Huddersfield HD5 8XY* Tel (01484) 533312

KIRBY, David Graham. b 58. Univ of Wales (Cardiff) BA80 Ox Univ BA85. Wycliffe Hall Ox 83. **d** 86 **p** 87. C Northallerton w Kirby Sigston *York* 86-89; C Southport Ch Ch *Liv* 89-92; R Bishop Burton w Walkington *York* from 92. *The Rectory,*

Walkington, Beverley, N Humberside HU17 8SP Tel (01482) 868379

KIRBY, Mrs Joan Florence. b 32. St Hugh's Coll Ox MA57 Lon Univ BA66. St Alb Minl Tr Scheme 79. **d** 87 **p** 94. NSM Hemel Hempstead *St Alb* 87-90; C Blisland w St Breward *Truro* 90-94; NSM Cardynham 94-96; rtd 96; Perm to Offic *Truro* from 96. *Penrose, Tresarrett, Blisland, Bodmin, Cornwall PL30 4QY* Tel (01208) 851003

KIRBY, John Patrick. b 24. Leeds Univ BA50. Coll of Resurr Mirfield 50. **d** 52 **p** 53. C Birm St Aid Small Heath *Birm* 52-55; Swaziland 55-59; C Solihull *Birm* 59-63; Namibia 63-68; P-in-c Buildwas *Lich* 68-77; P-in-c Lt Wenlock *Heref* 68-77; V Coalbrookdale 68-77; C S Gillingham *Roch* 77-83; V New Brompton St Luke 83-89; rtd 89; Perm to Offic *Ely* from 91. *2 Allen Court, Hauxton Road, Cambridge CB2 2LU* Tel (01223) 845303

KIRBY, Maurice William Herbert. b 31. K Coll Lon DipTh CertEd AKC. **d** 55 **p** 56. C Eltham Park St Luke *S'wark* 55-56; C Horley 56-59; C Westbury *Sarum* 59-62; R Poulshot w Worton 62-66; P-in-c Gt Cheverell 65; P-in-c Burcombe 66-68; V 68-70; V Salisbury St Mich 70-73; Chapl SS Helen and Kath Sch Abingdon 73-79; Chapl Wrekin Coll Shropshire 79-84; Hd of Relig Studies 79-84; V Frensham *Guildf* 84-93; Dir of Reader Tr 84-93; rtd 93; Perm to Offic *Ex* 93-94; Perm to Offic *Chich* from 94. *Flat 7, 37 Clermont Terrace, Brighton BN1 6SJ*

KIRBY, Paul Michael. b 51. Wycliffe Hall Ox 74. **d** 76 **p** 77. C Gateacre *Liv* 76-79; C Barton Seagrave w Warkton *Pet* 79-83; V Bidston *Ches* 83-93; V Ormskirk *Liv* from 93. *The Vicarage, Park Road, Ormskirk, Lancs L39 3AJ* Tel (01695) 572143

KIRBY, Stennett Roger. b 54. St Pet Coll Ox BA75 MA79. Sarum & Wells Th Coll 75. **d** 77 **p** 78. C Belsize Park *Lon* 77-79; NSM Plumstead St Nic *S'wark* 88; C Leic Ch Sav *Leic* 90-91; TV Hanley H Ev *Lich* 91-95; P-in-c Walsall St Pet from 95. *St Peter's Vicarage, 22 Bloxwich Road, Walsall WS2 8DB* Tel (01922) 23995

KIRK, Gavin John. b 61. Southn Univ BTh. Chich Th Coll 83. **d** 86 **p** 87. C Seaford w Sutton *Chich* 86-89; Chapl and Succ Roch Cath *Roch* 89-91; Min Can Roch Cathl 89-91; Hon PV Roch Cathl from 91; Asst Chapl K Sch Roch from 91. *5 St Margaret's Street, Rochester, Kent ME1 1TU* Tel (01634) 814479

KIRK, Geoffrey. b 45. Keble Coll Ox BA67. Coll of Resurr Mirfield 71. **d** 72 **p** 73. C Leeds St Aid *Ripon* 72-74; C St Marylebone St Mark w St Luke *Lon* 74-76; C Kennington St Jo *S'wark* 77-79; C Kennington St Jo w St Jas 79-81; P-in-c Lewisham St Steph and St Mark 81-87; V from 87. *St Stephen's Vicarage, Cressingham Road, London SE13 5AG* Tel 0181-318 1295

KIRK, George. b 14. Kelham Th Coll 32. **d** 38 **p** 39. C Norbury St Oswald *Cant* 38-41; C Sheff St Cuth *Sheff* 41-43; Chapl City Gen Hosp 41-43; P-in-c Brightside St Thos 43-44; V 44-48; V Bentley 48-56; R Aston cum Aughton 56-80; P-in-c Ulley 57-65; V 65-80; RD Laughton 72-79; rtd 80; Chapl to Rtd Clergy and Clergy Widows Officer *Sheff* 80-86; Lic to Offic from 86. *3 Borrowdale Crescent, North Anston, Sheffield S25 4JW* Tel (01909) 566774

KIRK, Miss Geraldine Mercedes. b 49. Hull Univ MA89. **d** 87 **p** 94. Ind Chapl *Linc* from 87. *364 Laceby Road, Grimsby, S Humberside DN34 5LU* Tel (01472) 873435

KIRK, Henry Logan. b 52. Adelaide Univ BA74 New Coll Edin BD77. **d** 80 **p** 81. S Africa 80-85; Asst Master Haileybury Sch Herts 86; Asst Chapl Rugby Sch 86-93; Dep Hd Dulwich Coll Prep Sch 93-94; NSM S Dulwich St Steph *S'wark* 93-94; C Linslade *Ox* 94-96; Chapl Birkenhead Sch Merseyside from 96. *61 Shrewsbury Road, Birkenhead, Merseyside L43 2JA*

KIRK, John Andrew. b 37. Lon Univ BD61 AKC61 MPhil75 Fitzw Ho Cam BA63. Ridley Hall Cam 61. **d** 63 **p** 64. C Finchley Ch Ch *Lon* 63-66; Argentina 66-79; SAMS 79-81; CMS 82-90; Dean of Miss Selly Oak Coll Birm from 90. *Department of Mission, Selly Oak Colleges, Birmingham B29 6LQ* Tel 0121-472 4231

KIRK, Peter Fenwick. b 30. **d** 83 **p** 84. NSM Bathgate *Edin* 83-91; NSM Linlithgow 83-91; NSM Bathgate from 92. *18 Inch Crescent, Bathgate, West Lothian EH48 1EU* Tel (01506) 655369

KIRK, Steven Paul. b 59. Ex Univ LLB80 Univ of Wales (Cardiff) BD87 LLM94. St Mich Coll Llan 84. **d** 87 **p** 88. C Ebbw Vale *Mon* 87-89; PV Llan Cathl *Llan* 89-91; PV and Succ 91-94; V Port Talbot St Agnes w Oakwood from 94. *St Agnes Vicarage, 29 Ynys Street, Port Talbot SA13 1YW* Tel (01639) 883630

KIRK-DUNCAN, The Ven Brian Andrew Campbell. Pemb Coll Ox BA46 MA47 TCD MA59 DPhil64. Cuddesdon Coll 39. **d** 41 **p** 42. C Summertown *Ox* 41-43; Asst Master Dragon Sch Ox 41-43; C Headington Quarry 43-44; V Sevenhampton w Charlton Abbots and Hawling *Glouc* 44-47; R Bredon w Bredon's Norton *Worc* 47-62; R St Mary at Hill w St Andr Hubbard etc *Lon* from 62; Prin Becket Coll Lon 63-67; Dep Min Can St Paul's Cathl *Lon* from 69; Perm to Offic *St E* from 91; Perm to Offic *Chelmsf* from 92. *The Rectory, St Mary-at-Hill, London EC3R 8EE* Tel 0171-626 4184 Fax 283 4421

KIRK-SMITH, Harold. b 17. Sheff Univ BA39 MA46 PhD53. Lich Th Coll 39. **d** 41 **p** 42. C Heeley *Sheff* 41-43; C Owlerton 43-46; V Sheff St Bart 46-51; V Wadsley 51-58; Chapl Rossall Junior Sch Fleetwood 58-60; Chapl Rossall Sch Fleetwood 60-72; Hd of Relig Instruction Qu Mary Sch Lytham 72-82; rtd 82; Perm to Offic *Blackb* from 93. *20 Lowick Drive, Poulton-le-Fylde, Lancs FY6 8HB* Tel (01253) 886709

KIRKBY, John Victor Michael. b 39. Lon Univ BScEng62 DipMaths64 BD73. Ridley Hall Cam 65. **d** 67 **p** 68. C Muswell Hill St Jas *Lon* 67-70; Chapl Hatf Poly *St Alb* 71-75; V Wootton 75-86; RD Elstow 82-86; R Byfleet *Guildf* 86-92; P-in-c Potten End w Nettleden *St Alb* 92-97; V from 97. *The Vicarage, Church Road, Potten End, Berkhamsted, Herts HP4 2QY* Tel (01442) 865217

KIRKBY, Reginald Gresham. b 16. Leeds Univ BA40. Coll of Resurr Mirfield 40. **d** 42 **p** 43. C Gorton Our Lady and St Thos *Man* 42-44; C Middlesbrough All SS *York* 44-46; C Becontree St Pet *Chelmsf* 46-48; C Notting Hill St Mich and Ch Ch *Lon* 48-51; V Bow Common 51-94; rtd 94. *7 St James' Court, Bishop Street, London N1 8PH* Tel 0171-226 6992

KIRKE, Clive Henry. b 51. Ridley Hall Cam. **d** 83 **p** 84. C Ainsdale *Liv* 83-86; Gen Asst Bootle Deanery 86-89; P-in-c Litherland St Andr from 89. *St Andrew's Vicarage, St Andrew's Road, Bootle, Merseyside L20 5EX* Tel 0151-922 7916

KIRKER, Richard Ennis. b 51. Sarum & Wells Th Coll 72. **d** 77. C Hitchin *St Alb* 77-78; Gen Sec LGCM from 79. *Oxford House, Derbyshire Street, London E2 6HG* Tel 0171-739 1249 or 791 1802 Fax 0171-739 1249 E-mail lgcm@churchnet.ucsm.ac.uk

KIRKHAM, Clifford Gerald Frank. b 34. Open Univ BA90. Sarum & Wells Th Coll 72. **d** 74 **p** 75. C Worle *B & W* 74-76; C E Preston w Kingston *Chich* 76-78; C Goring-by-Sea 78-80; C-in-c Maybridge CD 80-82; V Maybridge 82-88; R N Chapel w Ebernoe from 88; Chapl for Rural Affairs from 89. *The Rectory, Northchapel, Petworth, W Sussex GU28 9HP* Tel (01428) 707373 E-mail g.kirkham@john316.com

✠**KIRKHAM, The Rt Revd John Dudley Galtrey.** b 35. Trin Coll Cam BA59 MA63. Westcott Ho Cam 60. **d** 62 **p** 63 **c** 76. C Ipswich St Mary le Tower *St E* 62-65; Bp's Chapl *Nor* 65-69; P-in-c Rockland St Mary w Hellington 67-69; Papua New Guinea 69-70; C St Martin-in-the-Fields *Lon* 70-72; C Westmr St Marg 70-72; Abp's Dom Chapl *Cant* 72-76; Suff Bp Sherborne *Sarum* 76-81; Area Bp Sherborne from 81; Can and Preb Sarum Cathl from 77; Abp's Adv to the Headmasters' Conf from 90; Bp HM Forces from 92. *Little Bailie, Dullar Lane, Sturminster Marshall, Wimborne, Dorset BH21 4AD* Tel (01258) 857659 Fax 857961

KIRKLAND, Richard John. b 53. Leic Univ BA75. St Jo Coll Dur 76. **d** 79 **p** 80. C Knutsford St Jo and Toft *Ches* 79-82; C Bebington 82-89; V Poulton Lancelyn H Trin 89-95; V Hoole from 95. *All Saints' Vicarage, 2 Vicarage Road, Chester CH2 3HZ* Tel (01244) 322056

KIRKMAN, Canon Harold. b 11. Man Univ BA43 BD47. Man Egerton Hall 35. **d** 36 **p** 37. C Moss Side Ch Ch *Man* 36-43; V Roundthorn 43-47; V Halliwell St Thos 47-55; V Oldham St Mary w St Pet 55-72; Hon Can Man Cathl 59-76; RD Oldham 63-76; Perm to Offic *Wakef* from 72; rtd 76; Perm to Offic *Man* from 76. *3 Black Dyke, Mankinholes Bank, Todmorden, Lancs OL14 6JA* Tel (01706) 813499

KIRKMAN, Richard Marsden. b 55. Cranmer Hall Dur. **d** 87 **p** 88. C Bridlington Priory *York* 87-90; TV Thirsk 90-96; R Escrick and Stillingfleet w Naburn from 96. *The Rectory, Escrick, York YO4 6EX* Tel (01904) 728406

KIRKMAN, Trevor Harwood. b 51. Trin Hall Cam BA73 MA76. EMMTC 94. **d** 96. NSM Hickling w Kinoulton and Broughton Sulney *S'well* from 96. *The Old Vicarage, 43 Church Lane, Long Clawson, Melton Mowbray, Leics LE14 4ND* Tel (01664) 822270 Fax 63014

KIRKPATRICK, Errol Francis. b 28. TCD. **d** 52 **p** 53. C Enniscorthy *C & O* 52-55; Dioc C (Ferns) 55-56; C Wexford St Iberius 55-56; C Bridgwater St Mary w Chilton Trinity *B & W* 56-59; R Bromley All Hallows *Lon* 59-66; R Kentchurch w Llangua *Heref* 66-77; V Rowlestone w Llancillo 66-77; V Walterstone 66-77; RD Abbeydore 72-77; R Porlock w Stoke Pero *B & W* 77-83; R Lapworth *Birm* 83-89; R Baddesley Clinton 83-89; rtd 89; Perm to Offic *B & W* from 89. *51 Runnymede Road, Yeovil, Somerset BA21 5RY* Tel (01935) 31713

KIRKPATRICK, The Very Revd Jonathan Richard. b 58. CA81 Golds Coll Lon BA85. Wilson Carlile Coll IDC81 S'wark Ord Course 83. **d** 85 **p** 85. C Lewisham St Mary *S'wark* 85-87; Chapl Lewisham Hosp 85-87; Selection Sec and Voc Adv ACCM 88-91; Sec Aston Tr Scheme 89-91; Hon C Noel Park St Mark *Lon* 88-91; New Zealand from 91; Dean Dunedin from 96; V Gen from 97. *PO Box 5205, Dunedin, New Zealand* Tel Christchurch (3) 477 2336 Fax as telephone E-mail jrk@nevill.earthlight.co.nz

KIRKPATRICK, Nigel David Joseph. b 68. CITC BTh96. **d** 96 **p** 97. C Portadown St Columba *Arm* from 96. *14 Ardmore Crescent, Portadown, Craigavon, Co Armagh BT62 4DU* Tel (01762) 331916 Fax as telephone E-mail hillwalker@aol.com

KIRKPATRICK, Roger James (Brother Damian). b 41. FCA. **d** 86 **p** 87. SSF from 66; Guardian Belf Friary 80-88; Birm 89-93; Prov Min from 91; NSM Belfast St Pet *Conn* 86-88; Chapl R Victoria Hosp Belf 86-88; Lic to Offic *Linc* 94-96; Lic to Offic *Lon* from 97. *110 Ellesmere Road, London NW10 1JS* Tel 0181-452 7285 Fax as telephone

KIRKPATRICK, William John Ashley. b 27. SEN SRN RMN. Sarum Th Coll 63. **d** 68 **p** 70. NSM St Mary le Bow w St Pancras Soper Lane etc *Lon* 68-70; NSM Soho St Anne w St Thos and St Pet 70-75; SSF 76-79; NSM S Kensington St Aug *Lon* 79-80; NSM Earl's Court St Cuth w St Matthias from 80. *Flat 3B, Langham Mansions, Earl's Court Square, London SW5 9UP* Tel 0171-373 1330

KIRKUP, Nigel Norman. b 54. K Coll Lon BD79 AKC79. **d** 80 **p** 80. Hon C Catford (Southend) and Downham *S'wark* 80-83; Hon C Surbiton St Andr and St Mark 83-85; Hon C Shirley St Geo from 85. *The Vicarage, The Glade, Croydon CR0 7QJ* Tel 0181-654 8747

KIRKWOOD, Alexander David. b 58. Ex Coll Ox BA81 Dur Univ CertEd82. Linc Th Coll 83. **d** 85 **p** 86. C Linc St Faith and St Martin w St Pet *Linc* 85-88; C Farnborough *Roch* 88-91; V Mitcham St Barn *S'wark* from 91. *St Barnabas' Vicarage, Thirsk Road, Mitcham, Surrey CR4 2BD* Tel 0181-648 2571

KIRKWOOD, David Christopher. b 40. Pemb Coll Ox BA63. Clifton Th Coll 63. **d** 65 **p** 66. C Wilmington *Roch* 65-68; C Green Street Green 68-72; Youth and Area Sec BCMS 72-73; Educn and Youth Sec 73-80; Hon C Sidcup Ch Ch *Roch* 74-80; V Rothley *Leic* 80-92; RD Goscote II 84-88; RD Goscote 88-90; P-in-c Toxteth St Philemon w St Gabr and St Cleopas *Liv* 92-95; TR from 95; AD Toxteth and Wavertree from 96. *St Philemon's Vicarage, 40 Devonshire Road, Liverpool L8 3TZ* Tel 0151-727 1248

KIRKWOOD, Jack. b 21. Worc Ord Coll 62. **d** 63 **p** 64. C Penwerris *Truro* 63-66; V Torpoint 66-73; V Turton *Man* 73-81; P-in-c Castleton All So 81-82; Hon C Heywood St Luke 82-84; rtd 86; Perm to Offic *Blackb* from 86; Perm to Offic *York* 89-94. *2 Westover Grove, Warton, Carnforth, Lancs LA5 9QR* Tel (01524) 732552

KIRTLEY, Georgina. b 44. St Jo Coll Dur BA94. Cranmer Hall Dur. **d** 95 **p** 96. NSM Barnard Castle w Whorlton *Dur* from 95. *Ryelands, Stainton, Barnard Castle, Co Durham DL12 8RB* Tel (01833) 631192

KIRTON, Canon Richard Arthur. b 43. Dur Univ BA67 MA73 DipTh68. Wycliffe Hall Ox 68. **d** 69 **p** 70. C Warsop *S'well* 69-72; C Newark St Mary 72-75; Malaysia 75-83; Dean of Studies Th Sem Kuala Lumpur 79-82; P-in-c Bleasby w Halloughton *S'well* 83-89; V Thurgarton w Hoveringham 83-89; V Thurgarton w Hoveringham and Bleasby etc 89-91; Bp's Adv on Overseas Relns 85-91; Hon Can St Mary's Cathl Kuala Lumpur from 88; Tutor CA Wilson Carlile Coll of Evang from 91. *Wilson Carlile College of Evangelism, 50 Cavendish Street, Sheffield S3 7RZ* Tel 0114-278 7020

KISSELL, Barrington John. b 38. Lon Coll of Div 64. **d** 67 **p** 68. C Camborne *Truro* 67-71; C Chorleywood St Andr *St Alb* from 71; Dir Faith Sharing Min from 74. *Wick Cottage, Quickley Lane, Chorleywood, Rickmansworth, Herts WD3 5AF* Tel (01923) 282188

KITCHEN, Alan. b 39. Coll of Resurr Mirfield 72. **d** 74 **p** 75. C Shelf *Bradf* 74-77; P-in-c Tong 77-79; TR 79-84; TR Manningham 84-92; P-in-c Embsay w Eastby 92-95; rtd 95; P-in-c Embsay w Eastby *Bradf* from 95. *The Vicarage, 21 Shires Lane, Skipton, N Yorkshire BD23 6SB* Tel (01756) 792755

KITCHEN, Leslie Wilson. b 16. Man Univ BA38 MA39. Bps' Coll Cheshunt 39. **d** 41 **p** 42. C Chapel Allerton *Ripon* 41-45; C Barnsley St Mary *Wakef* 45-50; V Skelmanthorpe 50-55; Chapl Wakefield Hosps 55-60; R Garforth *Ripon* 60-72; R Cockley Cley w Gooderstone *Nor* 72-78; V Didlington 72-78; R Gt and Lt Cressingham w Threxton 72-78; R Hilborough w Bodney 72-78; R Oxborough w Foulden and Caldecote 72-78; V Pool w Arthington *Ripon* 78-84; rtd 84; Chapl Ripon Hosps 89-91. *3 West Terrace, Burton Leonard, Harrogate, N Yorkshire HG3 3RR* Tel (01765) 677396

KITCHEN, Canon Dr Martin. b 47. N Lon Poly BA71 K Coll Lon BD76 AKC77 Man Univ PhD88. S'wark Ord Course 77. **d** 79 **p** 80. Lect CA Tr Coll Blackheath 79-83; Hon C Kidbrooke St Jas *S'wark* 79-83; Chapl Man Poly *Man* 83-88; TV Man Whitworth 83-86; TR 86-88; Adv In-Service Tr *S'wark* from 88; Can Res S'wark Cathl from 88. *17 Stradella Road, London SE24 9HN* Tel 0171-274 4918

KITCHENER, Christopher William. b 46. Open Univ BA. Sarum & Wells Th Coll 82. **d** 84 **p** 85. C Bexleyheath Ch Ch *Roch* 84-88; V Gravesend St Mary 88-97; V Biggin Hill from 97. *St Mark's Vicarage, 10 Church Road, Biggin Hill, Westerham, Kent TN16 3LB* Tel (01959) 540482

KITCHENER, Mrs Evarina Carol. b 51. Stockwell Coll of Educn CertEd70. Cant Sch of Min 89. **d** 92 **p** 94. NSM Gravesend St Mary *Roch* 92-97. *St Mark's Vicarage, 10 Church Road, Biggin Hill, Westerham, Kent TN16 3LB* Tel (01959) 540482

KITCHENER, Canon Michael Anthony. b 45. Trin Coll Cam BA67 MA70 PhD71. Cuddesdon Coll 70. **d** 71 **p** 72. C Aldwick *Chich* 71-74; C Caversham *Ox* 74-77; Tutor Coll of Resurr Mirfield 77-83; Prin NE Ord Course *Dur* 83-90; Hon Can Newc Cathl *Newc* 84-90; Can Res and Chan Blackb Cathl *Blackb* 90-95; Warden Rydal Hall *Carl* from 95; P-in-c Rydal from 95. *The Warden's House, Rydal Hall, Ambleside, Cumbria LA22 9LX* Tel (015394) 32050 Fax 34887

KITCHIN, Kenneth. b 46. Trin Coll Bris. **d** 89 **p** 90. C Barrow St Mark *Carl* 89-93; C Dalton-in-Furness 93-95; P-in-c Dearham from 95. *The Vicarage, Church Street, Dearham, Maryport, Cumbria CA15 7HX* Tel (01900) 812320

KITCHING, David Monro. b 26. New Coll Ox BA49. Ridley Hall Cam 80. **d** 82 **p** 83. C Hornchurch St Andr *Chelmsf* 82-86; P-in-c Graveley w Papworth St Agnes w Yelling etc *Ely* 86-90; rtd 91; Perm to Offic *Ely* from 91. *20 Victoria Park, Cambridge CB4 3EL* Tel (01223) 65687

KITCHING, Paul. b 53. GTCL LTCL. Coll of Resurr Mirfield 80. **d** 83 **p** 84. C Hessle *York* 83-86; Youth Officer from 86; P-in-c Crathorne from 86. *The Rectory, Crathorne, Yarm, Cleveland TS15 0BB* Tel (01642) 701158

KITELEY, Robert John. b 51. Hull Univ BSc73 Univ of Wales (Abth) MSc75 Lon Univ PhD82. Trin Coll Bris DipTh83. **d** 83 **p** 84. C Bebington *Ches* 83-88; C Hoole 88-91; V Plas Newton from 91. *22 Plas Newton Lane, Chester CH2 1PA* Tel (01244) 319677

KITLEY, David Buchan. b 53. St Jo Coll Dur BA. Trin Coll Bris 78. **d** 81 **p** 82. C Tonbridge St Steph *Roch* 81-84; C-in-c Southall Em CD *Lon* 84-91; V Dartford Ch Ch *Roch* from 91. *The Vicarage, 67 Shepherds Lane, Dartford DA1 2NS* Tel (01322) 220036

KITNEY, Miss Joan Olive Lily. b 22. Gilmore Ho 50. **dss** 60 **d** 87. Hermitage and Hampstead Norreys, Cold Ash etc *Ox* 80-84; NSM Staines St Mary and St Pet *Lon* 87-89; rtd 89. *54 Newtown Road, Newbury, Berks RG14 7BT* Tel (01635) 36416

KITTERINGHAM, Canon Ian. b 35. CCC Cam BA59 MA63. Westcott Ho Cam 59. **d** 61 **p** 62. C Rotherham *Sheff* 61-64; C Eltham H Trin *S'wark* 64-66; V Battersea St Mary-le-Park 66-73; V Reigate St Mark 73-80; V Caterham Valley 80-85; RD Caterham 84-85; V Wandsworth Common St Mary from 85; RD Tooting 88-93; Hon Can S'wark Cathl from 95. *The Vicarage, 291 Burntwood Lane, London SW17 0AP* Tel 0181-874 4804

KITTS, Joseph. b 27. Tyndale Hall Bris 59. **d** 60 **p** 61. C Parr *Liv* 60-63; C Bootle St Leon 63-66; V Southport SS Simon and Jude 66-74; USA 74-94; rtd 92. *Windyridge, Cottage Lane, St Martin's, Oswestry, Shropshire SY11 3BL* Tel (01691) 777090

KITWOOD, Thomas Morris. b 37. K Coll Cam BA60 MA64. Wycliffe Hall Ox 62. **d** 63 **p** 64. Asst Chapl Sherborne Sch 63-69; Uganda from 69. *PO Box 14123, Kampala, Uganda*

KIVETT, Michael Stephen. b 50. Bethany Coll W Virginia BA72. Chr Th Sem Indiana MDiv76 Sarum & Wells Th Coll 76. **d** 77 **p** 78. C Harnham *Sarum* 77-80; C E Dereham *Nor* 80-83; R S Walsham 83-88; V Upton 83-88; Chapl Lt Plumstead Hosp 84-88; V Chard St Mary *B & W* from 88; RD Crewkerne and Ilminster from 93. *The Vicarage, 2 Forton Road, Chard, Somerset TA20 2HJ* Tel (01460) 62320

KLIMAS, Miss Lynda. b 58. Jes Coll Cam BA89 MA93. Cranmer Hall Dur 89. **d** 90 **p** 94. Par Dn Sandy *St Alb* 90-93; Par Dn Bishop's Stortford St Mich 93-94; C from 94. *Cowell House, 24 Apton Road, Bishop's Stortford, Herts CM23 3SM* Tel (01279) 654414

KNAPMAN, Preb Hugh William Hartly. b 07. St D Coll Lamp BA33. **d** 32 **p** 33. C Henleaze *Bris* 32-36; C Woolcott Park 36-38; CF (TA) 33-37; V Long Ashton *B & W* 38-55; V Glastonbury St Jo 55-69; RD Glastonbury 56-59; P-in-c Greinton 60-68; Preb Wells Cathl 67-87; R Charlton Adam w Charlton Mackrell 69-75; rtd 75; Perm to Offic *B & W* 75-94. *24 Kings Gardens, Honiton, Devon EX14 8FL* Tel (01404) 44743

KNAPP, Antony Blair. b 48. Imp Coll Lon BSc68. N Ord Course 86. **d** 89 **p** 90. C Bolton St Jas w St Chrys *Bradf* 89-92; V Kettlewell w Conistone, Hubberholme etc from 92. *The Vicarage, Kettlewell, Skipton, N Yorkshire BD23 5QU* Tel (01756) 760237

KNAPP, Bryan Thomas. b 61. Trin Coll Bris DipHE90 BA91. **d** 91 **p** 92. C S Gillingham *Roch* 91-95; V Chatham St Paul w All SS from 95. *The Vicarage, 2A Waghorn Street, Chatham, Kent ME4 5LT* Tel (01634) 845419

KNAPP (née STOCKER), Mrs Rachael Ann. b 64. Bris Univ BA86. Trin Coll Bris DipHE90 BA91. **d** 91 **p** 94. C Ditton *Roch* 91-95; C Chatham St Paul w All SS from 95. *The Vicarage, 2A Waghorn Street, Chatham, Kent ME4 5LT* Tel (01634) 845419

✠KNAPP-FISHER, The Rt Revd Edward George. b 15. Trin Coll Ox BA36 MA40 Cam Univ MA49. Wells Th Coll 38. **d** 39 **p** 40 **c** 60. C Brighouse *Wakef* 40-42; Chapl RNVR 42-46; Chapl Cuddesdon Coll 46-49; Prin 52-60; Lic to Offic *Ely* 49-52; Chapl St Jo Coll Cam 49-52; V Cuddesdon *Ox* 52-60; RD Cuddesdon 58-60; S Africa 60-75; Bp Pretoria 60-75; Adn Westmr 75-87; Can Westmr Abbey 75-87; Asst Bp S'wark 75-87; Asst Bp Lon 76-86; Sub-Dean Westmr 82-87; rtd 87; Asst Bp Chich from 87; Custos St Mary's Hosp Chich from 87. *2 Vicars' Close, Canon Lane, Chichester, W Sussex PO19 1PT* Tel (01243) 789219

KNAPPER, Peter Charles. b 39. Lon Univ BA61. St Steph Ho Ox 61. **d** 63 **p** 64. C Carl H Trin *Carl* 63-68; V Westf St Mary 68-76; V Bridekirk 76-83; P-in-c Blackheath Ascension *S'wark* 83-96; P-in-c Holmwood *Guildf* from 96. *The Vicarage, South Holmwood, Dorking, Surrey RH5 4JX* Tel (01306) 889118

KNARESBOROUGH, Suffragan Bishop of. *Vacant*

KNEE, Geoffrey. b 31. Whitelands Coll Lon CertEd71. CA Tr Coll 56 Glouc Sch of Min 91. **d** 92 **p** 93. SSF from 86; NSM Hampton *Worc* from 92. *8 Mayfair, Fairfield, Evesham, Worcs WR11 6JJ* Tel (01386) 443574

KNEE, Jacob Samuel. b 66. LSE BSc(Econ)87 MSc(Econ)88 Ox Univ BA92. Ripon Coll Cuddesdon 90. **d** 93 **p** 94. C Ashby-de-la-Zouch St Helen w Coleorton *Leic* 93-96; C Boston *Linc* from 96; Chapl Boston Coll of FE from 96. *Hazelwood, 5 Irby Street, Boston, Lincs PE21 8SA* Tel (01205) 369266

KNEEN, Michael John. b 55. Univ Coll Lon BSc76 MSc77 St Jo Coll Dur BA85. Cranmer Hall Dur 83. **d** 86 **p** 87. C Bishop's Castle w Mainstone *Heref* 86-90; TV Bridgnorth, Tasley, Astley Abbotts, Oldbury etc from 90. *41 Innage Lane, Bridgnorth, Shropshire WV16 4HS* Tel (01746) 766418 or 767174

KNELL, John George. b 35. Cant Sch of Min. **d** 82 **p** 83. NSM Sheerness H Trin w St Paul *Cant* 82-87; NSM Minster in Sheppey from 87. *11 Uplands Way, Queenborough Road, Sheerness, Kent ME12 3EF* Tel (01795) 665945

KNELL, Canon Raymond John. b 27. Qu Coll Cam BA48 MA52. Ridley Hall Cam 50. **d** 52 **p** 53. C Bishopwearmouth St Gabr *Dur* 52-57; C S Shields St Hilda 57-58; P-in-c Hebburn St Oswald 58-67; V Castleside 67-76; V Heworth St Mary 76-93; RD Gateshead 83-87; Hon Can Dur Cathl 87-93; rtd 93. *40 St Andrew's Drive, Low Fell, Gateshead, Tyne & Wear NE9 6JU* Tel 0191-487 6958

KNIBBS, Norman Vivian. b 27. Ely Th Coll 61. **d** 63 **p** 64. C Reading St Giles *Ox* 63-67; V Northampton St Dav *Pet* 67-73; TV Kingsthorpe w Northn St Dav 73-79; R Brington w Whilton and Norton 79-92; rtd 92; Perm to Offic *Pet* from 92. *18 Harbridges Lane, Long Buckby, Northampton NN6 7QL* Tel (01327) 842857

KNICKERBOCKER, Driss Richard. b 39. Univ of Michigan BA63 MDiv68 Ox Univ DPhil81. **d** 68 **p** 69. USA 68-76 and from 85; C St Marylebone w H Trin *Lon* 78-81; C Chelsea St Luke 81-83; P-in-c Isleworth St Fran 83-85. *4700 Cumberland Street, Harrisburg, PA 17111-2725, USA*

KNIGHT, The Ven Alexander Francis (Alec). b 39. St Cath Coll Cam BA61 MA65. Wells Th Coll. **d** 63 **p** 64. C Hemel Hempstead *St Alb* 63-68; Chapl Taunton Sch 68-75; Dir Bloxham Project 75-81; Dir of Studies Aston Tr Scheme 81-83; P-in-c Easton and Martyr Worthy *Win* 83-91; Adn Basingstoke from 90; Can Res Win Cathl from 91. *1 The Close, Winchester, Hants SO23 9LS* Tel (01962) 869374 Fax 841815

KNIGHT, Andrew James. b 50. Grey Coll Dur BA72 Ox Univ BA74 MA81. Wycliffe Hall Ox 72. **d** 75 **p** 76. Min Can Brecon Cathl *S & B* 75-78; C Brecon w Battle 75-78; C Morriston 78-82; V from 89; V Llanwrtyd w Llanddulas in Tir Abad etc 82-89. *The Vicarage, Vicarage Road, Morriston, Swansea SA6 6DR* Tel (01792) 771329

KNIGHT, Mrs Ann. b 54. Lanc Univ CertEd75. Trin Coll Bris DipHE83 DPS84. **dss** 84 **d** 87 **p** 94. Wigan St Jas w St Thos *Liv* 84-87; Par Dn 87-90; C Costessey *Nor* 90-96; R Gt and Lt Ellingham, Rockland and Shropham etc from 96. *The Rectory, Rectory Lane, Great Ellingham, Attleborough, Norfolk NR17 1LD* Tel (01953) 453200

KNIGHT, Arthur Clifford Edwin. b 42. Univ of Wales BSc64. Wells Th Coll 64. **d** 66 **p** 67. C Llangyfelach and Morriston *S & B* 66-68; C Oystermouth 68-73; Chapl RAF 73-95; Perm to Offic *Heref* 95-97; P-in-c Brant Broughton and Beckingham *Linc* from 97. *The Rectory, Church End, Leadenham, Lincoln LN5 0PX* Tel (01400) 273253

KNIGHT, Mrs Barbara. b 46. St Alb Minl Tr Scheme 86. **d** 90 **p** 94. NSM Weston *St Alb* 90-95; NSM Ardeley 90-95; C Norton 95-97; R Barkway, Reed and Buckland w Barley from 97. *The Rectory, 135 High Street, Barkway, Royston, Herts SG8 8ED* Tel (01763) 848077

KNIGHT, Mrs Barbara Mary. b 43. SRN64. EMMTC 94. **d** 97. NSM Market Harborough *Leic* from 97. *10 Harrison Close, Market Harborough, Leics LE16 9LZ* Tel (01858) 467621 Mobile 0802-717476

KNIGHT, Benjamin Edward. b 10. St Cath Coll Cam BA34 MA38. Wells Th Coll 34. **d** 36 **p** 37. C Streatham Hill St Marg *S'wark* 36-39; Chapl RAF 39-53; Asst Chapl-in-Chief RAF 53-65; Hon Chapl to The Queen 60-65; R Symondsbury *Sarum* 65-78; V Chideock 72-78; rtd 78. *The Coach House, Bothenhampton Old Rectory, Bridport, Dorset DT6 4BT* Tel (01308) 424909

KNIGHT, Christopher. b 61. Inst of Marketing BA84. Wycliffe Hall Ox 94. **d** 96 **p** 97. C Banbury *Ox* from 96. *10 Hardwick Park, Banbury, Oxon OX16 7YD* Tel (01295) 278368

KNIGHT, Dr Christopher Colson. b 52. MSOSc Ex Univ BSc73 Man Univ PhD77 SS Coll Cam MA90. Sarum & Wells Th Coll BTh83. **d** 81 **p** 82. Chapl St Mary's Cathl *Edin* 81-84; V Chesterton *Cov* 84-87; R Lighthorne 84-87; V Newbold Pacey w Moreton Morrell 84-87; Chapl, Fellow and Dir Studies in Th SS Coll Cam 87-92; Sen Research Assoc St Edm Coll Cam from 92. *Hope Cottage, Hindringham Road, Great Walsingham, Norfolk NR22 6DR* Tel (01328) 820108

KNIGHT, David Alan. b 59. Lanc Univ BA81. Ripon Coll Cuddesdon 82. **d** 85 **p** 86. C Stretford All SS *Man* 85-88; C Charlestown 88-89; TV Pendleton St Thos w Charlestown 89-94; V Tysoe w Oxhill and Whatcote *Cov* from 94. *The Vicarage, Peacock Lane, Tysoe, Warwick CV35 0SE* Tel (01295) 680201

KNIGHT, David Charles. b 32. Clare Coll Cam BA55 MA59. Tyndale Hall Bris 55. **d** 57 **p** 58. C Cambridge St Paul *Ely* 57-58; C St Alb Ch Ch *St Alb* 58-61; C-in-c Wimbledon Em Ridgway Prop Chpl *S'wark* 61-67; Publications Sec BCMS 67-68; Ed Asst The Christian 68-69; V Lannarth *Truro* 69-75; RD Carnmarth N 72-75; V Fremington *Ex* 75-83; C Edmonton All SS w St Mich *Lon* 83; Chapl N Middx Hosp 83; rtd 94; Perm to Offic *Chelmsf* from 94. *Magnolia Cottage, Cage End, Hatfield Broad Oak, Bishop's Stortford, Herts CM22 7HT* Tel (01279) 718650

KNIGHT, Canon David Charles. b 45. ATCL63 Lon Univ BA66 St Edm Hall Ox BA68 MA73. St Steph Ho Ox 68. **d** 70 **p** 71. C Northwood H Trin *Lon* 70-73; C Stevenage All SS Pin Green *St Alb* 73-77; C Cippenham CD *Ox* 77-78; TV W Slough 78-83; Dep Min Can Windsor from 81; Ecum Officer to Bp Willesden 83-91; R Lt Stanmore St Lawr *Lon* 83-91; Prec and Can Res Chelmsf Cathl *Chelmsf* from 91. *The Precentor's House, Rainsford Avenue, Chelmsford CM1 2PJ* Tel (01245) 257306

KNIGHT, David Lansley. b 33. Em Coll Cam BA58 MA61 PGCE76. Ridley Hall Cam 57. **d** 59 **p** 60. C Chatham St Steph *Roch* 59-63; C Plymouth St Andr *Ex* 63-65; V Gravesend St Aid *Roch* 65-71; V Bexley St Mary from 71; RD Sidcup from 93. *The Vicarage, 29 Hill Crescent, Bexley, Kent DA5 2DA* Tel (01322) 523457

KNIGHT, Donald. b 31. Bris Univ BA55 Man Univ DASE73. Tyndale Hall Bris 51 Qu Coll Birm 82. **d** 83 **p** 84. C Chell *Lich* 83-87; R St Ruan w St Grade and Landewednack *Truro* 87-91; R High Offley and Norbury *Lich* from 91. *The Rectory, Newport Road, Woodseaves, Stafford ST20 0NP* Tel (01785) 284747

KNIGHT, Canon Donald Martin. b 13. Lon Univ BSc34 St Cath Soc Ox DipTh39. Wycliffe Hall Ox 38. **d** 39 **p** 41. C Chesham St Mary *Ox* 39; Jerusalem 39-42; C Tulse Hill H Trin *S'wark* 42-43; Chapl RAFVR 43-46; Vice-Prin CA Tr Coll 46-49; V New Beckenham St Paul *Roch* 49-57; Chapl for Evang 49-57; R Harlow New Town w Lt Parndon *Chelmsf* 57-86; RD Harlow 60-73; Chapl Harlow Hosp 65-78; Hon Can Chelmsf Cathl *Chelmsf* 71-86; rtd 86; Perm to Offic *Ox* from 86. *Flat 65, The Cloisters, White House Road, Oxford OX1 4QQ* Tel (01865) 202050

KNIGHT, Eric Frank Walter. b 19. St Paul's Grahamstown. **d** 51 **p** 52. S Africa 51-59; R Wick *Mor* 61-63; R Girvan *Glas* 63-68; V Charlton All Saints *Sarum* 68-89; rtd 89. *9 Constable Way, Salisbury SP2 8LN* Tel (01722) 334870

KNIGHT, Henry Christian. b 34. Lon Univ HNC57 Fitzw Ho Cam BA62 MA66. Ridley Hall Cam 62. **d** 63 **p** 64. Succ Bradf Cathl *Bradf* 63-64; Chapl 64-66; Israel 67-79; CMJ 79-86; V Allithwaite *Carl* 86-93; rtd 93; Perm to Offic *Leic* from 93. *20 Saxon Way, Ashby-de-la-Zouch, Leics LE65 2JR* Tel (01530) 560180

KNIGHT, John Bernard. b 34. ACIS60. Oak Hill Th Coll 61 Fuller Th Sem California DMin91. **d** 65 **p** 66. C Morden *S'wark* 65-69; USA 69-71; V Summerfield *Birm* from 71. *Christ Church Vicarage, 64 Selwyn Road, Birmingham B16 0SW* Tel 0121-454 2689

KNIGHT, John Francis Alan MacDonald. b 36. Coll of Resurr Mirfield 59. **d** 61 **p** 62. S Rhodesia 61-65; Rhodesia 65-80; Zimbabwe 80-87; Dean Mutare 81-87; TR Northampton Em *Pet* from 87; RD Northn 88-92. *12 Jersey Court, Northampton NN3 3TB* Tel (01604) 414136 or 402150

KNIGHT, Jonathan Morshead. b 59. Wycliffe Hall Ox 86. **d** 88 **p** 89. C Hillingdon St Jo *Lon* 88-91; NSM Baslow *Derby* 91-92; NSM Curbar and Stoney Middleton 91-92; Lect Bibl Studies Sheff Univ 91-92; Research Fell 92-94; NSM Sheff St Paul Wordsworth Avenue *Sheff* 92-94; Bp's Research Asst *Ely* from 94. *Farthing Cottage, 38 High Street, Harston, Cambridge CB2 5PX* Tel (01223) 870914

KNIGHT, Mrs June. b 28. Glouc Sch of Min 85. **d** 87 **p** 94. NSM Leckhampton SS Phil and Jas w Cheltenham St Jas *Glouc* 87-96; rtd 96; Perm to Offic *Glouc* from 96. *31 St Michael's Road, Woodlands, Cheltenham, Glos GL51 5RP* Tel (01242) 517911

KNIGHT, Mrs June Elizabeth. b 42. St Alb Minl Tr Scheme 90. **d** 93 **p** 94. NSM Stanstead Abbots *St Alb* 93-96; NSM Gt Amwell w St Margaret's and Stanstead Abbots from 96. *The White Cottage, Albury Hall Park, Albury, Ware, Herts SG11 2HX* Tel (01279) 771756

KNIGHT, Keith Kenneth. b 36. Southn Univ BSc58. Wycliffe Hall Ox 59. **d** 62 **p** 63. C Lower Darwen St Jas *Blackb* 62-64; C Leyland St Andr 64-68; P-in-c Blackb All SS 68-71; Dioc Youth Chapl 71-88; Hon C Burnley St Pet 71-74; Warden Scargill Ho from 88; Lic to Offic *Bradf* from 88. *Scargill House, Kettlewell, Skipton, N Yorkshire BD23 5HU* Tel (01756) 760234 or 760315

KNIGHT, Kenneth William. b 15. TD50. Wycliffe Hall Ox. **d** 61 **p** 62. C Paignton Ch Ch *Ex* 61-63; V Holbeton 63-91; rtd 91; Perm to Offic *Ex* from 91. *Buckleberry, Shebbear, Beaworthy, Devon EX21 5SA* Tel (01409) 281423

KNIGHT, Mrs Margaret Owen. b 34. Oak Hill Th Coll 78. **dss** 80 **d** 87 **p** 94. Chorleywood St Andr *St Alb* 80-87; Par Dn 87-94; C from 94; rtd 94. *15A Blacketts Wood Drive, Chorleywood, Rickmansworth, Herts WD3 5PY* Tel (01923) 283832

KNIGHT, Michael Richard. b 47. St Jo Coll Dur BA69 MA79 Fitzw Coll Cam BA73 MA78 St Cross Coll Ox MA92. Westcott

Ho Cam 71. **d** 74 **p** 75. C Bishop's Stortford St Mich *St Alb* 74-75; C Bedford St Andr 75-79; Chapl Angl Students Glas 79-86; V Riddings and Ironville *Derby* 86-91; Lib Pusey Ho 91-94; Fell St Cross Coll Ox 92-94; V Chesterfield St Mary and All SS *Derby* from 94. *28 Cromwell Road, Chesterfield, Derbyshire S40 4TH* Tel (01246) 232937 or 206506 Fax 231993

KNIGHT, Paul James Joseph. b 50. Oak Hill Th Coll. **d** 84 **p** 85. C Broadwater St Mary *Chich* 84-87; R Itchingfield w Slinfold 87-92; Chapl Highgate Sch Lon from 92. *15A Bishopswood Road, London N6 4PB* Tel 0181-348 9211 or 340 1524

KNIGHT, Capt Paul Jeremy. b 53. **d** 94 **p** 95. CA from 77; C Moreton Say *Lich* 94-97; C Adderley, Ash, Calverhall, Ightfield etc from 97. *The Rectory, Moreton Say, Market Drayton, Shropshire TF9 3RS* Tel (01630) 638110

KNIGHT, Peter John. b 51. Lon Univ AKC73 CertEd77. Sarum & Wells Th Coll 79. **d** 80 **p** 81. C Greenford H Cross *Lon* 80-83; C Langley Marish *Ox* 83; NSM W Acton St Martin *Lon* 89-90; C E Acton St Dunstan w St Thos 90-92; V Malden St Jo *S'wark* from 92. *The Vicarage, 329 Malden Road, New Malden, Surrey KT3 6AL* Tel 0181-942 3297

KNIGHT, Dr Peter Malcolm. b 55. DA81 DRCOG83 MRCGP85 DTM&H86 Cam Univ BA76 Lon Hosp MB, BS76. Trin Coll Bris BA94. **d** 94 **p** 95. C Quidenham *Nor* 94-97; C Quidenham Gp from 97. *The Vicarage, Mill Road, Old Buckenham, Attleborough, Norfolk NR17 1SG* Tel (01953) 860047

KNIGHT, Peter Michael. b 47. St Luke's Coll Ex BEd71. Trin Coll Bris DipHE92. **d** 92 **p** 93. C Bris Ch the Servant Stockwood *Bris* 92-95; Chapl St Brendan's Sixth Form Coll 92-94; C W Swindon and the Lydiards *Bris* 95-96; TV from 96. *The Vicarage, The Butts, Lydiard Millicent, Swindon SN5 9LR* Tel (01793) 772417

KNIGHT, Philip Stephen. b 46. Oak Hill Th Coll 75. **d** 77 **p** 78. C Pennycross *Ex* 77-80; C Epsom St Martin *Guildf* 80-83; V Clay Hill St Jo *Lon* 83-86; TV Washfield, Stoodleigh, Withleigh etc *Ex* 86-90; Chapl S Warks Hosps 90-94; Chapl Asst RAF from 94; Chapl S Warks Health Care NHS Trust from 94. *37 Lodge Crescent, Warwick CV34 6BB, or Warwick Hospital, Lakin Road, Warwick CV34 5BW* Tel (01926) 403053 or 495321 ext 4121 Fax 482603

KNIGHT, Canon Roger George. b 41. Culham Coll Ox CertEd63. Linc Th Coll 65. **d** 67 **p** 68. C Bris St Andr Hartcliffe *Bris* 67-69; Hd Master Twywell Sch Kettering 69-74; Lic to Offic *Pet* 69-74; V Naseby 74-79; P-in-c Haselbeech 74-79; R Clipston w Naseby and Haselbech 79-82; P-in-c Kelmarsh 79-82; TR Corby SS Pet and Andr w Gt and Lt Oakley 82-88; R Irthlingborough from 88; RD Higham 89-94; Can Pet Cathl from 92. *The Rectory, 79 Finedon Road, Irthlingborough, Wellingborough NN9 5TY* Tel (01933) 650278

KNIGHT, Roger Ivan. b 54. K Coll Lon BD79 AKC79. Ripon Coll Cuddesdon 79. **d** 80 **p** 81. C Orpington All SS *Roch* 80-84; C St Laurence in the Isle of Thanet *Cant* 84-87; R Cuxton and Halling *Roch* from 87. *The Rectory, Rochester Road, Cuxton, Rochester, Kent ME2 1AF* Tel (01634) 717134

KNIGHT, Canon Sydney Frederick Harrold. b 06. Leeds Univ BA29. Coll of Resurr Mirfield 25. **d** 33 **p** 34. C Haydock St Jas *Liv* 33-37; S Africa from 37; Hon Can St John's from 86. *PO Box 334, George, 6530 South Africa* Tel George (441) 5472

KNIGHT, Thomas. b 20. OBE60. Linc Th Coll 69. **d** 71 **p** 72. C Earlsdon *Cov* 71-74; R Southam 74-77; RD Southam 77-82; R Southam w Stockton 77-82; rtd 82; Perm to Offic *York* from 90. *5 Cedar Vale, Kirkbymoorside, York YO6 6BU* Tel (01751) 31922

KNIGHT, William Lawrence (Bill). b 39. Univ Coll Lon BSc61 PhD65. Coll of Resurr Mirfield 75. **d** 77 **p** 78. C Hatfield *St Alb* 77-81; Asst Chapl Brussels Cathl *Eur* 81-84; V Pet H Spirit Bretton *Pet* 84-89; P-in-c Marholm 84-89; TR Riverside *Ox* from 89. *St Mary's Vicarage, London Road, Datchet, Slough SL3 9JW* Tel (01753) 580467

KNIGHTS, Dr Christopher Hammond. b 61. St Jo Coll Dur BA83 PhD88. Linc Th Coll 87. **d** 89 **p** 90. C Stockton St Pet *Dur* 89-92; C Chich St Paul and St Pet *Chich* 92-94; Tutor Chich Th Coll 92-94; V Ashington *Newc* from 94. *Holy Sepulchre Vicarage, Wansbeck Road, Ashington, Northd NE63 8HZ* Tel (01670) 813358

KNIGHTS, James William. b 34. AKC66. **d** 67 **p** 68. C Kettering St Andr *Pet* 67-71; V Braunston w Brooke 71-81; V Dudley St Jo *Worc* from 81. *St John's Vicarage, 8A New Rowley Road, Dudley, W Midlands DY2 8AS* Tel (01384) 253807

KNIGHTS JOHNSON, Nigel Anthony. b 52. BA75. Wycliffe Hall Ox 78. **d** 80 **p** 81. C Beckenham Ch Ch *Roch* 80-84; CF from 84. *MOD Chaplains (Army), Trenchard Lines, Upavon, Pewsey, Wilts SN9 6BE* Tel (01980) 615804 Fax 615800

KNILL-JONES, Jonathan Waring (Jack). b 58. Univ Coll Lon BSc79. St Jo Coll Nottm DTS90. **d** 90 **p** 91. C Northolt W End St Jos *Lon* 90-94; C Hayes St Nic CD from 94. *St Nicholas Vicarage, Raynton Drive, Hayes, Middx UB4 8BG* Tel 0181-573 4122

KNOCK, Dr Andrew Henry Drysdale. b 49. Lon Univ BA71 Stirling Univ PhD78 Edin Univ BD78. Edin Th Coll 75. **d** 78 **p** 79. Chapl St Ninian's Cathl Perth *St And* 78-80; C Alloa 80-84; P-in-c 85-86; R from 86; Chapl Stirling Univ 80-84; C Bridge of Allan 80-84; C Dollar 81-84. *St John's Rectory, 29 Redwell Place, Alloa, Clackmannanshire FK10 2BT* Tel (01259) 215113 or 724550 Fax 215113 E-mail andrewknock.@enterprise.net

KNOPP, Alexander Edward Robert. b 09. St Jo Coll Cam BA33 MA37. Ridley Hall Cam 32. **d** 34 **p** 35. C Loughton St Mary *Chelmsf* 34-38; C Prittlewell St Mary 38-40; R Nevendon 40; R N Benfleet w Nevendon 41-48; V Walthamstow St Jo 48-50; V Pampisford *Ely* 50-59; V Babraham 50-59; R Quendon w Rickling *Chelmsf* 59-68; R Gt Yeldham 68-73; R Gt w Lt Snoring *Nor* 73-76; rtd 76; Perm to Offic *Ely* from 77. *6 Rose Lane, Melbourn, Royston, Herts SG8 6AD* Tel (01763) 262143

KNOTT, Christopher Rodney. b 42. Open Univ BA77. Kelham Th Coll 64. **d** 68 **p** 69. C Withycombe Raleigh *Ex* 68-72; TV Aylesbeare and Farringdon 72-75; TV Woodbury Salterton 72-75; TV Clyst St George, Aylesbeare, Clyst Honiton etc 75-76; TR Lynton, Brendon, Countisbury, Lynmouth etc 76-81; R Highweek and Teigngrace from 81. *The Rectory, 15 Stoneleigh Close, Newton Abbot, Devon TQ12 1PX* Tel (01626) 54949

KNOTT, Mrs Gladys Phoebe. b 15. Wolsey Hall DipRS64 Glouc Sch of Min 80. **dss** 81 **d** 87. Stroud H Trin *Glouc* 81-85; Minchinhampton 85-87; Hon C from 87. *7 Dr Brown's Close, Minchinhampton, Stroud, Glos GL6 9DG* Tel (01453) 885259

KNOTT, Graham Keith. b 53. Oak Hill Th Coll BA80. **d** 80 **p** 81. C Normanton *Derby* 80-83; C Ripley 83-87; TV Newark w Hawton, Cotham and Shelton *S'well* 87-89; TV Newark 89-97; P-in-c Mansfield St Jo from 97. *The Vicarage, St John Street, Mansfield, Notts NG18 1QH* Tel (01623) 25999

KNOTT, Janet Patricia. b 50. Avery Hill Coll CertEd71. S Dios Minl Tr Scheme MTS91. **d** 92 **p** 94. NSM Clutton w Cameley *B & W* from 92; Chapl R Sch Bath from 94. *3/4 Sunnyside, Clutton Hill, Clutton, Bristol BS18 4QG* Tel (01761) 452597

KNOTT, John Wensley. b 51. FIA84 Fitzw Coll Cam MA75. S Dios Minl Tr Scheme 87. **d** 90 **p** 91. NSM Canford Magna *Sarum* 90-94; Perm to Offic *St Alb* from 94. *11 Shrublands Road, Berkhamsted, Herts HP4 3JH* Tel (01442) 875005

KNOTT, Montague Hardwick. b 05. Oak Hill Th Coll 54. **d** 55 **p** 56. C Walthamstow St Mary *Chelmsf* 55-57; V Blackmore 57-80; P-in-c Stondon Massey 80; V Blackmore and Stondon Massey 80-85; rtd 85; Perm to Offic *Chelmsf* from 85. *1 Wadham Close, Ingatestone, Essex CM4 0DL* Tel (01277) 352024

KNOTT, Pamela Frances. *See* IVE, Mrs Pamela Frances

KNOTT, Robert Michael. b 35. MCIBSE MRIPHH. Clifton Th Coll 67. **d** 70 **p** 70. C Rolleston *Lich* 70-72; C Anslow 70-72; C Uphill *B & W* 73-75; C Weston-super-Mare St Paul 77-79; P-in-c Burgate *St E* 79-82; P-in-c Palgrave 79-82; P-in-c Wortham 79-82; P-in-c Palgrave w Wortham and Burgate 82-87; rtd 88; Perm to Offic *Nor* from 91. *Oak Dene Luana, High Road, Bressingham, Diss, Norfolk IP22 2AT*

KNOWD, George Alexander. St Deiniol's Hawarden. **d** 88 **p** 89. NSM Aghalurcher w Tattykeeran, Cooneen etc *Clogh* 88-91; Dioc Info Officer 89-90 and 92-97; NSM Ballybay w Mucknoe and Clontibret 91-92; C 92-94; I 94-97; I Clonmel w Innislounagh, Tullaghmelan etc *C & O* from 97. *The Rectory, 7 Lindenlea, Silversprings, Clonmel, Co Tipperary, Irish Republic* Tel Clonmel (52) 26643 Fax 29230

KNOWERS, Stephen John. b 49. K Coll Lon BD72 AKC72. **d** 73 **p** 74. C Hatfield *St Alb* 73-77; C Cheshunt 77-81; P-in-c Barnet Vale St Mark 81-83; V 83-85; Hon PV S'wark Cathl *S'wark* from 85; Chapl S Bank Poly 85-92; Chapl S Bank Univ 92-94; V Croydon St Pet from 94. *20 Haling Park Road, South Croydon, Surrey CR2 6NE* Tel 0181-688 4715

KNOWLES, Andrew William Allen. b 46. St Cath Coll Cam BA68 MA72. St Jo Coll Nottm 69. **d** 71 **p** 72. C Leic H Trin *Leic* 71-74; C Cambridge H Trin *Ely* 74-77; C Woking St Jo *Guildf* 77-81; V Goldsworth Park 81-93; V Wyke from 93; Dioc Officer Educn and Development of Lay People from 93. *Wyke Vicarage, Guildford Road, Normandy, Guildford, Surrey GU3 2DA* Tel (01483) 811332

KNOWLES, Charles Howard. b 43. Sheff Univ BSc65 Fitzw Coll Cam BA69 MA73. Westcott Ho Cam 67. **d** 69 **p** 70. C Bilborough St Jo *S'well* 69-72; V Choral S'well Minster 72-82; V Cinderhill 82-94; AD Nottingham W 91-94; V Cov St Mary *Cov* from 94; AD Cov S from 96. *St Mary Magdalen's Vicarage, Craven Street, Coventry CV5 8DT* Tel (01203) 675838

KNOWLES, Clifford. b 35. Open Univ BA82. NW Ord Course 74. **d** 77 **p** 78. C Urmston *Man* 77-80; V Chadderton St Luke 80-87; V Heywood St Luke w All So 87-95; AD Heywood and Middleton 92-95; Perm to Offic *Linc* from 95. *12B Far Lane, Coleby, Lincoln LN5 0AH* Tel (01522) 810720

KNOWLES, Dorothy Joy. b 20. MCThA. Gilmore Ho 64. **dss** 69 **d** 89. Finham *Cov* 69-72; Canley 72-76; Styvechale 76-84; rtd 84; Asst Chapl Harnhill Cen for Chr Healing 88-93; Perm to Offic *Ex* from 95. *8 Station Road, Topsham, Exeter EX3 0DT* Tel (01392) 874708

KNOWLES, Eric Gordon. b 44. WMMTC. **d** 82 **p** 83. NSM Gt Malvern St Mary *Worc* 82-83; NSM Malvern H Trin and St Jas 83-90; NSM Lt Malvern, Malvern Wells and Wyche from 90. *45 Wykewane, Malvern, Worcs WR14 2XD* Tel (01684) 567439

KNOWLES, George. b 37. **d** 95 **p** 96. NSM Hucknall Torkard *S'well* from 95. *8 North Hill Avenue, Hucknall, Nottingham NG15 7FE* Tel 0115-955 9822

KNOWLES, The Ven George Woods Atkin. b 21. TCD BA44 MA47. **d** 44 **p** 45. C Ardoyne *C & O* 44-46; C Knockbreda *D & D* 46-49; I Ballyscullion *D & R* 49-63; I Drumachose 63-89; Can Derry Cathl 75-86; Adn Derry 86-89; rtd 89. *22 Shanreagh Park, Limavady, Co Londonderry BT49 0SF* Tel (01504) 722298

KNOWLES, The Ven Graeme Paul. b 51. AKC73. St Aug Coll Cant 73. **d** 74 **p** 75. C St Peter-in-Thanet *Cant* 74-79; C Leeds St Pet *Ripon* 79-81; Chapl and Prec Portsm Cathl *Portsm* 81-87; Chapter Clerk 85-87; V Leigh Park 87-93; RD Havant 90-93; Adn Portsm from 93. *Victoria Lodge, 36 Osborn Road, Fareham, Hants PO16 7DS* Tel (01329) 280101 Fax 281603

KNOWLES, Mrs Jane Frances. b 44. GGSM66 Lon Inst of Educn TCert67. Ox Min Course CBTS93. **d** 93 **p** 94. NSM Sandhurst *Ox* from 93. *75 Mickle Hill, Little Sandhurst, Camberley, Surrey GU17 8QU* Tel (01344) 774593

KNOWLES, Melvin Clay. b 43. Stetson Univ (USA) BA66 Ex Univ MA73 Ox Univ DipTh76. Ripon Coll Cuddesdon 75. **d** 77 **p** 78. C Minchinhampton *Glouc* 77-80; St Helena 80-82; TV Haywards Heath St Wilfrid *Chich* 82-88; Adult Educn Adv 88-94; TR Burgess Hill St Jo w St Edw from 94. *St John's Vicarage, 68 Park Road, Burgess Hill, W Sussex RH15 8HG* Tel (01444) 232582

KNOWLES, The Very Revd Philip John. b 48. MA BTh. CITC 76. **d** 76 **p** 77. C Lisburn St Paul *Conn* 76-79; I Clooclare w Killasnett and Lurganboy *K, E & A* 79-87; I Gorey w Kilnahue *C & O* 87-89; I Gorey w Kilnahue, Leskinfere and Ballycanew 89-95; Preb Ferns Cathl 91-95; Dean Cashel from 95; I Cashel w Magorban, Tipperary, Clonbeg etc from 95; Chan Waterford Cathl from 95; Chan Lismore Cathl from 95; Preb Ossory and Leighlin Cathls from 96. *The Deanery, Cashel, Co Tipperary, Irish Republic* Tel Tipperary (62) 61232

KNOWLES, Stephen. b 56. Dur Univ BA81 Ox Univ MSc88. Coll of Resurr Mirfield. **d** 83. C Denton *Newc* 83; C Tynemouth Cullercoats St Paul 84. *53 Hotspur Road, Wallsend, Tyne & Wear NE28 9HB* Tel 0191-234 3626

KNOWLES-BROWN, Canon John Henry. b 30. AKC53. **d** 54 **p** 55. C Hertford St Andr *St Alb* 54-58; C Bushey 58-61; Chapl RAF 61-65; C-in-c Farley Hill St Jo CD *St Alb* 65-69; V Farley Hill St Jo 69-72; V Totteridge 72-95; RD Barnet 79-89; Hon Can St Alb 85-95; rtd 95. *1 Ascerton Close, Sidmouth, Devon EX10 9BS* Tel (01395) 579286

KNOWLING, Richard Charles. b 46. K Coll Lon BSc67 St Edm Hall Ox BA70 MA89. St Steph Ho Ox 69. **d** 71 **p** 72. C Hobs Moat *Birm* 71-75; C Shrewsbury St Mary w All SS and St Mich *Lich* 75-77; V Rough Hills 77-83; Dir Past Th Coll of Resurr Mirfield 83-90; V Palmers Green St Jo *Lon* from 90; AD Enfield from 96. *St John's Vicarage, 1 Bourne Hill, London N13 4DA* Tel 0181-886 1348

KNOX, Geoffrey Martin. b 44. Dur Univ BA66 DipTh67 Sheff City Coll of Educn DipEd73. St Chad's Coll Dur 63. **d** 67 **p** 68. C Newark St Mary *S'well* 67-72; Perm to Offic *Derby* 72-74; V Woodville 74-81; RD Repton 79-81; V Long Eaton St Laur from 81. *The Vicarage, Regent Street, Long Eaton, Nottingham NG10 1JX* Tel 0115-973 3154

KNOX, Iain John Edward. b 46. TCD BA70 MA74 Hull Univ BPhil76. Irish Sch of Ecum 74 CITC 71. **d** 71 **p** 72. C Belfast Malone St Jo *Conn* 71-74; Bp's Dom Chapl 72-74; Perm to Offic *D & R* 74-76; I Gweedore Union 76-80; I Clonmel w Innislounagh, Tullaghmelan etc *C & O* 80-96; Bp's Dom Chapl from 82; Press & Radio Officer (Cashel) from 90; Dioc Info Officer (Cashel and Waterford) from 92. *Rossnowlagh, Heywood Road, Clonmel, Co Tipperary, Irish Republic* Tel Clonmel (52) 27107

KNOX, Canon Ian Carroll. b 32. St Jo Coll Dur BA54 DipTh55. **d** 55 **p** 56. C Illingworth *Wakef* 55-58; C Lightcliffe 58-60; V Rastrick St Matt 60-77; Hon Can Wakef Cathl 76-89; RD Huddersfield 77-89; V Huddersfield St Pet 77-84; V Huddersfield St Pet and All SS 84-89; Can Res Wakef Cathl 89-97; Dir of Educn 89-96; Dir Ecum Affairs 94-97; Dioc Adult Educn Officer 96-97; Chapl to The Queen 96-97; rtd 97. *12 Inglemere Gardens, Arnside, Cumbria LA5 0BX*

KNOX, Thomas Anthony. b 31. BA. Ely Th Coll. **d** 56 **p** 57. C Poplar All SS w St Frideswide *Lon* 56-59; C Eastbourne St Andr *Chich* 59-61; C Welwyn *St Alb* 61-66; V Boreham Wood St Mich 66-71; R Puttenham w Long Marston 71-79; R Toddington 79-96; rtd 96. *Croft Cottage, Little Blenheim, Yarnton, Oxford OX5 1LX*

KOHNER, Canon Jeno George. b 31. K Coll Lon BD56 AKC56. Westcott Ho Cam 56. **d** 57 **p** 58. C Eccleston St Thos *Liv* 57-60; Canada from 60; Hon Can Montreal from 75. *31 Prince Edward Avenue, Point Clare, Quebec, Canada, H9R 4C4*

KOLOGARAS, Mrs Linda Audrey. b 48. Humberside Univ BA97. EMMTC 89. **d** 95 **p** 96. NSM Gt and Lt Coates w Bradley *Linc* from 95. *4 Church Avenue, Humberston, Grimsby, S Humberside DN36 4DB* Tel (01472) 815354

KOMOR, Michael. b 60. Univ of Wales BSc83. Chich Th Coll 83. **d** 86 **p** 87. C Mountain Ash *Llan* 86-89; C Llantwit Major 89-91; TV from 91. *The Vicarage, Trepit Road, Wick, Cowbridge CF71 7QL* Tel (01656) 890471

KONIG, Peter Montgomery. b 44. Westcott Ho Cam 80. **d** 82 **p** 83. C Oundle *Pet* 82-86; Chapl Westwood Ho Sch Pet 86-92; Lic to Offic *Pet* 86-94; Chapl Pet High Sch 92-95; Chapl Worksop Coll Notts from 95. *Worksop College, Worksop, Notts S80 3AP* Tel (01909) 479306

KOPSCH, Hartmut. b 41. Sheff Univ BA63 Univ of BC MA66 Lon Univ PhD70 DipHE. Trin Coll Bris 78. **d** 80 **p** 81. C Cranham Park *Chelmsf* 80-85; V Springfield *Birm* 85-92; V Dover St Martin *Cant* 92-96; R Bath Walcot *B & W* from 96. *The Rectory, 6 Rivers Street, Bath BA1 2PZ* Tel (01225) 425570

KORNAHRENS, Wallace Douglas. b 43. The Citadel Charleston BA66 Gen Th Sem (NY) STB69. **d** 69 **p** 70. USA 69-72; C Potters Green *Cov* 72-75; Chapl Community of Celebration Wargrave Oxon 75-76; P-in-c Cumbrae (or Millport) *Arg* 76-78; R Grantown-on-Spey *Mor* 78-83; R Rothiemurchus 78-83; R Edin H Cross *Edin* from 83. *Holy Cross Rectory, 18 Barnton Gardens, Edinburgh EH4 6AF* Tel 0131-336 2311

KOTHARE, Jayant. b 41. Bombay Univ BA Heidelberg Univ MDiv. **d** 86 **p** 87. C Handsworth St Mich *Birm* 86-89; C Southall St Geo *Lon* 89-92; TV Thamesmead *S'wark* from 92. *15 Camelot Close, London SE28 0ES* Tel 0181-854 2382 or 310 6814

KOVOOR, George Iype. b 57. Delhi Univ BA77 Serampore Univ BD80 Chr Medical Assn of India DCHospC85. Union Bibl Sem Yavatmal 78. **d** 80 **p** 80. India 80-90; Dean St Paul's Cathl Ambala 84-88; C Derby St Aug *Derby* 90-94; Min Derby Asian Chr Min Project 90-94; Tutor Crowther Hall CMS Tr Coll Selly Oak from 94. *Crowther Hall, Weoley Park Road, Selly Oak, Birmingham B29 6QT* Tel 0121-472 4228 or 415 5738

KROLL, Dr Una Margaret Patricia. b 25. Girton Coll Cam MB51 BChir51. S'wark Ord Course 68. **d** 88 **p** 97. Par Dn Monmouth *Mon* from 88. *St Mary's Lodge, Priory Street, Monmouth NP5 3BR* Tel (01600) 713465

KRONENBERG, Selwyn Thomas Denzil. b 32. Univ of Wales BA54 St Cath Soc Ox BA57 MA60 Leic Univ MA73. Wycliffe Hall Ox. **d** 57 **p** 58. C Surbiton St Matt *S'wark* 57-60; C Luton w E Hyde *St Alb* 60-62; P-in-c Loscoe *Derby* 62-65; Lect RE Bulmershe Coll 65-67; Whitelands Coll from 67; Perm to Offic *Guildf* from 77. *58 Woodfield Lane, Ashtead, Surrey KT21 2BS* Tel (01372) 272505

KRZEMINSKI, Stefan. b 51. Nottm Univ BTh77. Linc Th Coll 74. **d** 77 **p** 78. C Sawley *Derby* 77-79; Asst Chapl Blue Coat Sch Nottm from 79; Hon C W Hallam and Mapperley *Derby* 84-96; Hd of RE Nottm High Sch from 88; Perm to Offic from 96. *12 Newbridge Close, West Hallam, Ilkeston, Derbyshire DE7 6LY* Tel 0115-930 5052

KUHRT, The Ven Gordon Wilfred. b 41. Lon Univ BD63. Oak Hill Th Coll. **d** 67 **p** 68. C Illogan *Truro* 67-70; C Wallington H Trin *S'wark* 70-73; V Shenstone *Lich* 73-79; P-in-c S Croydon Em *Cant* 79-81; V S Croydon Em *S'wark* 81-89; RD Croydon Cen *Cant* 81-86; Hon Can S'wark Cathl *S'wark* 87-89; Adn Lewisham 89-96; Chief Sec ABM from 96. *6 Layzell Walk, London SE9 4QD* Tel 0181-857 3476

KUHRT, Martin Gordon. b 66. Nottm Univ LLB88. Trin Coll Bris 93. **d** 96 **p** 97. C Morden *S'wark* from 96. *23 Cedars Road, Morden, Surrey SM4 5AB*

KURRLE, Canon Stanley Wynton. b 22. Melbourne Univ BA47 St Cath Soc Ox BA50 MA54. Wycliffe Hall Ox 49. **d** 52 **p** 53. C Sutton *Liv* 52-54; Australia from 54; Can Sydney from 81. *3 Mildura Street, Killara, NSW, Australia 2071* Tel Sydney (2) 9654 1334

KURTI, Peter Walter. b 60. Qu Mary Coll Lon LLB82 K Coll Lon MTh89. Ripon Coll Cuddesdon 83. **d** 86 **p** 87. C Prittlewell *Chelmsf* 86-90; Chapl Derby Coll of HE *Derby* 90-92; Chapl Derby Univ 92-94; Dep Hd Relig Resource and Research Cen 90-94; Australia from 94. *PO Box 1072, Morley, W Australia 6493* Tel Perth (9) 279 3039 or 325 5766 Fax 221 4289

KYBIRD, Paul. b 49. Selw Coll Cam BA72 MA75. Qu Coll Birm 72. **d** 74 **p** 76. C Loughborough Em *Leic* 74-78; Overseas 78-81; Tutor Crowther Hall CMS Tr Coll Selly Oak 82-86; P-in-c Wreay *Carl* from 86; Lay Tr Adv from 86; P-in-c Dalston from 92; P-in-c Raughton Head w Gatesgill from 92. *The Vicarage, Townhead Road, Dalston, Carlisle CA5 7JF* Tel (01228) 710215 or 38086 Fax 48769

KYLE, Laurence Arthur Nelson. b 14. S'wark Ord Course 64. **d** 67 **p** 68. C Bromley Common St Luke *Roch* 67-70; R Hopton w Market Weston *St E* 70-72; P-in-c Barningham w Coney Weston 70-72; R Hopton, Market Weston, Barningham etc 72-79; RD Ixworth 73-79; rtd 79; Perm to Offic *Nor* from 79. *Flat 3, Ellesborough Manor, Butlers Cross, Aylesbury, Bucks HP17 0XF* Tel (01296) 696047

KYLE, Miss Sharon Patricia Culvinor. b 55. Aber Coll of Comm HND75 Open Univ BA90 Edin Univ BD94 MTh96. Coates Hall Edin 91. **d** 94 **p** 95. C Edin SS Phil and Jas *Edin* 94-96; C Neston *Ches* from 96. *26 Stratford Road, Little Neston, South Wirral L64 0SH* Tel 0151-336 4544

KYRIACOU, Brian George. b 42. Lon Univ LLB64. Oak Hill Th Coll 79. **d** 81 **p** 82. C Becontree St Mary *Chelmsf* 81-83; C Becontree St Cedd 83-85; C Becontree W 85; TV 85-87; V Shiregreen St Jas and St Chris *Sheff* 87-92; TV Schorne *Ox* from 92. *The Vicarage, Church Street, North Marston, Bucks MK18 3PH* Tel (01296) 670298

KYRIAKIDES-YELDHAM, Anthony Paul Richard (Tony). b 48. CPsychol91 Birkb Coll Lon BSc82 Golds Coll Lon DASS83

CQSW83 Warw Univ MSc90. K Coll Lon BD73 AKC73. **d** 74 **p** 75. C Dalston H Trin w St Phil *Lon* 74-78; NSM Lon Docks St Pet w Wapping St Jo 79-81; NSM Hackney Wick St Mary of Eton w St Aug 81-85; NSM Wandsworth Common St Mary *S'wark* 85-87; Chapl Wandsworth HA Mental Health Unit 87-93; Chapl Springfield Hosp Lon 87-93; Lect and Co-ord Dip in Counselling Plymouth Univ from 93; Perm to Offic *Ex* from 94. *Liesse, Grange Road, Buckfast, Buckfastleigh, Devon TQ11 0EH* Tel (01364) 42189

L

LA TOUCHE, Francis William Reginald. b 51. Linc Th Coll 73. **d** 76 **p** 77. C Yate *Bris* 76-77; C Yate New Town 77-79; Chapl Vlissingen (Flushing) Miss to Seamen *Eur* 79-83; Lic to Offic *York* 83-91; Miss to Seamen 83-91; V Burstwick w Thorngumbald *York* from 91. *The Vicarage, Main Road, Thorngumbald, Hull HU12 9NA* Tel (01964) 626509

LABDON, John. b 32. Oak Hill Th Coll. **d** 84 **p** 85. C Formby H Trin *Liv* 84-87; P-in-c St Helens St Mark from 87. *St Mark's Vicarage, 160 North Road, St Helens, Merseyside WA10 2TZ* Tel (01744) 23806

LACEY, Allan John. b 48. Wycliffe Hall Ox. **d** 82 **p** 83. C Greasbrough *Sheff* 82-85; R Treeton 85-92; V Thorpe Hesley from 92. *The Vicarage, 30 Barnsley Road, Thorpe Hesley, Rotherham, S Yorkshire S61 2RR* Tel 0114-246 3487 or 245 7564

LACEY, Eric. b 33. Cranmer Hall Dur 69. **d** 71 **p** 72. C Blackpool St Jo *Blackb* 71-75; V Whittle-le-Woods 75-88; R Heysham from 88. *St Peter's Rectory, Main Street, Morecambe, Lancs LA3 2RN* Tel (01524) 851422

LACEY, Canon Frank Gordon. b 26. Magd Coll Cam BA47 MA51. Ely Th Coll 48. **d** 50 **p** 51. C Nottingham St Cath *S'well* 50-53; C Mansfield Woodhouse 53-56; V Rubery *Birm* 56-64; PC Dethick, Lea and Holloway *Derby* 64-69; V Ockbrook 69-73; Dir Past Studies N Ord Course 73-81; V Birtles *Ches* 73-82; Can Res Sheff Cathl *Sheff* 82-91; rtd 91; Perm to Offic *Sheff* from 91; Perm to Offic *Derby* from 91. *6 Barnes Avenue, Dronfield Woodhouse, Sheffield S18 5YG* Tel (01246) 416589

LACEY, Graeme Alexander Warner. b 15. Wycliffe Hall Ox. **d** 63 **p** 64. C Meopham *Roch* 63-67; C Bexley St Jo 67-73; R Cuxton 73-76; R Cuxton and Halling 76-80; rtd 80; Perm to Offic *Chich* from 80. *122 Westminster Drive, Bognor Regis, W Sussex PO21 3RZ* Tel (01243) 266631

LACEY, Nigel Jeremy. b 59. St Jo Coll Nottm BTh94. **d** 94 **p** 95. C Mildenhall *St E* 94-97; C Selly Park St Steph and St Wulstan *Birm* from 97. *76 Bournbrook Road, Birmingham B29 7BU* Tel 0121-414 0089

LACK, Catherine Mary. b 59. Clare Coll Cam BA81. Qu Coll Birm 90. **d** 92 **p** 94. Par Dn Leiston *St E* 92-94; C 94-95; TV Ipswich St Mary at Stoke w St Pet from 95. *St Mary's House, 6 Stone Lodge Lane, Ipswich IP2 9PA* Tel (01473) 601617

LACK, Leonard James Westbrook. b 16. Ripon Hall Ox 65. **d** 66 **p** 67. C Leighton Buzzard *St Alb* 66-81; rtd 81; Perm to Offic *Bris* 81-92. *1 Pulford Road, Leighton Buzzard, Beds LU7 7AB* Tel (01525) 850480

LACK, Martin Paul. b 57. St Jo Coll Ox MA79 MSc80. Linc Th Coll 83. **d** 86 **p** 87. C E Bowbrook *Worc* 86-89; C W Bowbrook 86-89; C Bowbrook S 89-90; C Bowbrook N 89-90; R Teme Valley S from 90. *Hanley Rectory, Broadheath, Tenbury Wells, Worcs WR15 8QW* Tel (01886) 853286

LACKEY, Michael Geoffrey Herbert. b 42. Oak Hill Th Coll 73. **d** 75 **p** 76. C Hatcham St Jas *S'wark* 75-81; V New Barnet St Jas *St Alb* 81-91; V Hollington St Jo *Chich* from 91. *The Vicarage, 94 Lower Glen Road, St Leonards-on-Sea, E Sussex TN37 7AR* Tel (01424) 751103

LACKEY, William Terence Charles. b 32. St Mich Coll Llan 80. **d** 82 **p** 83. C Wrexham *St As* 82-85; V Gwersyllt 85-93; R Trefnant from 93. *The Rectory, Denbigh Road, Trefnant, Denbigh LL16 5UG* Tel (01745) 730584

LACY, Sarah Frances Sally. b 49. Sarum Th Coll 93. **d** 96 **p** 97. NSM Weston Zoyland w Chedzoy *B & W* 96-97; C from 97. *16 Peach Tree Close, Bridgwater, Somerset TA6 4XF* Tel (01278) 457889

LADD, Mrs Anne de Chair. b 56. Nottm Univ BA78 Birm Univ CQSW80 DipSocWork80. St Jo Coll Nottm LTh DPS86. **dss** 86 **d** 87 **p** 94. Bucknall and Bagnall *Lich* 86-87; Par Dn 87-91; NSM Bricket Wood *St Alb* from 91. *20 West Riding, Bricket Wood, St Albans, Herts AL2 3QP* Tel (01923) 681107 or 676401

LADD, John George Morgan. b 36. Univ of Wales (Ban) BA58 MA65. Trin Coll Carmarthen St Mich Coll Llan. **d** 90 **p** 91. NSM Nevern and Y Beifil w Eglwyswrw and Meline etc *St D* 90-92; NSM Llandysilio w Egremont and Llanglydwen etc 92-93; V Gwaun-cae-Gurwen from 93. *The Vicarage, 118 Heol Cae Gurwen, Gwaun-cae-Gurwen, Ammanford SA18 1PD* Tel (01269) 822430

LADD, Nicholas Mark. b 57. Ex Univ BA78 Selw Coll Cam BA81. Ridley Hall Cam 79. **d** 82 **p** 83. C Aston SS Pet and Paul *Birm* 82-86; TV Bucknall and Bagnall *Lich* 86-91; V Bricket Wood *St Alb* from 91. *20 West Riding, Bricket Wood, St Albans, Herts AL2 3QP* Tel (01923) 681107 or 676401

LADDS, Reginald. b 25. ACP LCP. St D Coll Lamp BA50 Westcott Ho Cam 60. **d** 60 **p** 61. Chapl Canon Slade Sch Bolton 60-85; C Bolton St Pet *Man* 60-62; C Bolton All So w St Jas 62-69; Hon C Farnworth and Kearsley 76-78; C E Farnworth and Kearsley 78-84; Chapl Townleys Hosp Bolton from 87; Hon C Turton *Man* from 88. *53 Hillside Avenue, Bromley Cross, Bolton BL7 9NQ* Tel (01204) 306271

LADDS, Canon Robert Sidney. b 41. LRSC72 Lon Univ BEd71. Cant Sch of Min 79. **d** 80 **p** 81. C Hythe *Cant* 80-83; R Bretherton *Blackb* 83-91; Chapl Bp Rawstorne Sch Preston 83-87; Bp's Chapl for Min and Adv Coun for Min *Blackb* 86-91; P-in-c Preston St Jo 91-96; Hon Can Blackb Cathl from 93; R Preston St Jo and St Geo from 96. *The Rectory, 13 Ribblesdale Place, Preston PR1 3NA* Tel (01772) 252528

LADIPO, Canon Adeyemi Olalekan. b 37. Trin Coll Bris 63. **d** 66 **p** 76. C Bilston St Leon *Lich* 66-68; Nigeria 68-84; V Canonbury St Steph *Lon* 85-87; BCMS Sec for Internat Miss 87-90; Hon C Bromley SS Pet and Paul *Roch* 89-90; V Herne Hill *S'wark* from 90; Hon Can Jos from 95. *8 Ruskin Walk, London SE24 9LZ* Tel 0171-274 5741

LAING, Canon Alexander Burns. b 34. RD90. Edin Th Coll 57. **d** 60 **p** 61. C Falkirk *Edin* 60-62; C Edin Ch Ch 62-70; Chapl RNR 64-91; P-in-c Edin St Fillan *Edin* 70-74; Chapl Edin R Infirmary 74-77; Dioc Supernumerary *Edin* from 77; R Helensburgh *Glas* from 77; Can St Mary's Cathl from 87. *The Rectory, 16 William Street, Helensburgh, Dunbartonshire G84 8BD* Tel (01436) 672500

LAING, Canon William Sydney. b 32. TCD BA54 MA62. CITC 55. **d** 55 **p** 56. C Crumlin *Conn* 55-59; C Dublin St Ann *D & G* 59-65; I Carbury *M & K* 65-68; I Dublin Finglas *D & G* 68-80; I Tallaght 80-91; Can Ch Ch Cathl Dublin 90-94; Preb from 94; I Dublin Crumlin w Chapelizod from 91. *St Mary's Rectory, Kimmage Road West, Dublin 12, Irish Republic* Tel Dublin (1) 455 5639

LAIRD, Alisdair Mark. b 60. Auckland Univ BA84. Trin Coll Bris BA92. **d** 92 **p** 93. C Linthorpe *York* from 92. *23 Linden Grove, Middlesbrough, Cleveland TS5 5NF* Tel (01642) 815961

LAIRD, Canon John Charles. b 32. Sheff Univ BA53 MA54 St Cath Coll Ox BA58 MA62 Lon Univ DipEd70. Ripon Hall Ox 56. **d** 58 **p** 59. C Cheshunt *St Alb* 58-62; Chapl Bps' Coll Cheshunt 62-64; Vice-Prin 64-67; Prin 67-69; V Keysoe w Bolnhurst and Lt Staughton *St Alb* from 69; Hon Can St Alb from 87. *The Vicarage, Church Road, Keysoe, Bedford MK44 2HW* Tel (01234) 708251

LAIRD, Robert George (Robin). b 40. TCD Div Sch 58 Edin Th Coll 63. **d** 65 **p** 66. C Drumragh *D & R* 65-68; CF 68-93; QHC 91-93; Sen Chapl Sedbergh Sch from 93; Lic to Offic *Bradf* from 93. *Sedbergh School, Sedbergh, Cumbria LA10 5HG* Tel (015396) 20983 Fax 21301

LAIRD, Stephen Charles Edward. b 66. Or Coll Ox BA88 MA92 MSt93 K Coll Lon MTh91. Wycliffe Hall Ox DipMin94 MPhil96. **d** 94 **p** 95. C Ilfracombe, Lee, Woolacombe, Bittadon etc *Ex* from 94. *St Peter's House, Highfield Road, Ilfracombe, Devon EX34 9LH* Tel (01271) 864119

LAISTER, Peter. b 27. St D Coll Lamp BA54. St Steph Ho Ox 54. **d** 56 **p** 57. C Victoria Docks Ascension *Chelmsf* 56-60; Chapl RN 60-65; C Munster Square St Mary Magd *Lon* 65-66; Chapl Middx Hosp Lon 66-70; V Clerkenwell H Redeemer w St Phil *Lon* 70-86; USA 86-93; rtd 92. *6 Bishop Street, London N1 8PH* Tel 0171-354 2741

LAKE, Canon David Eurwyn. b 17. TD60. St D Coll Lamp BA39. **d** 40 **p** 41. C Miskin *Llan* 40-43; C Cardiff St Jo 43-50; CF (TA) 48-67; P-in-c Llansawel w Briton Ferry *Llan* 50-56; V 56-62; V Skewen 62-84; RD Neath 76-84; rtd 84; Perm to Offic *Llan* from 84. *Fairwell, 42 Brecon Road, Ystradgynlais, Swansea SA9 1HF* Tel (01792) 849541

LAKE, Miss Eileen Veronica. b 58. Lon Univ CCouns93. Aston Tr Scheme 83 Sarum & Wells Th Coll 85. **d** 88 **p** 94. Par Dn Islington St Mary *Lon* 88-92; Asst Chapl Homerton Hosp Lon 92-94; Asst Chapl Hackney Hosp Gp 92-94; P-in-c Brondesbury Ch Ch and St Laur *Lon* from 94. *The Rectory, Chevening Road, London NW6 6DU* Tel 0181-969 5961

LAKE, Stephen David. b 63. Chich Th Coll 85. **d** 88 **p** 89. C Sherborne w Castleton and Lillington *Sarum* 88-92; P-in-c Branksome St Aldhelm 92-96; V from 96. *The Vicarage, St Aldhelm's Road, Poole, Dorset BH13 6BT* Tel (01202) 764420

LAKE, Vivienne Elizabeth. b 38. Lon Univ DHistA78. Westcott Ho Cam 84. **dss** 86 **d** 87 **p** 94. Chesterton Gd Shep *Ely* 86-90; C 87-90; NSM Bourn Deanery from 90. *The Vicarage Flat, School Lane, Barton, Cambridge CB3 7BG* Tel (01223) 264147

LAKER, Mrs Grace. b 39. SRN63. Sarum & Wells Th Coll BTh91. **d** 91 **p** 94. C Helston and Wendron *Truro* 91-95; Chapl Havering Hosps NHS Trust from 95. *Oldchurch Hospital, Oldchurch Road,*

Romford RM7 0BE, or 14 Hillcourt, Main Road, Romford RM1 3DA Tel (01708) 746090

LAKER, Leopold Ernest. b 38. Sarum & Wells Th Coll 77. **d** 77 **p** 78. C Rainham *Roch* 77-80; V Horton Kirby from 80. *The Vicarage, Horton Kirby, Dartford DA4 9BN* Tel (01322) 862201

LAMB, Bruce. b 47. Keble Coll Ox BA69 MA73 Leeds Univ DipTh72. Coll of Resurr Mirfield 70. **d** 73 **p** 74. C Romford St Edw *Chelmsf* 73-76; C Canning Town St Cedd 76-79; V New Brompton St Luke *Roch* 79-83; Chapl RN 83-87; C Rugeley *Lich* 87-88; V Trent Vale 88-92. *16 Epworth Road, Portsmouth PO2 0HD*

LAMB, Bryan John Harry. b 35. Leeds Univ BA60 Aston Univ DCouns72. Coll of Resurr Mirfield 60. **d** 62 **p** 63. C Solihull *Birm* 62-65 and 88-89; Asst Master Malvern Hall Sch Solihull 65-74; Alderbrook Sch & Hd of Light Hall Adult Ed Cen 74-88; V Wragby *Linc* 89; Dioc Dir of Readers 89; Perm to Offic *Birm* from 89; rtd 95. *35 Rectory Road, Solihull, W Midlands B91 3RJ* Tel 0121-705 2489

LAMB, Canon Christopher Avon. b 39. Qu Coll Ox BA61 MA65 Birm Univ MA78 PhD87. Wycliffe Hall Ox BA63. **d** 63 **p** 64. C Enfield St Andr *Lon* 63-69; Pakistan 69-75; Tutor Crowther Hall CMS Tr Coll Selly Oak 75-78; Lic to Offic *Birm* 75-87; Co-ord BCMS/CMS Other Faiths Th Project 78-87; Dioc Community Relns Officer *Cov* 87-92; Can Th Cov Cathl from 92; Sec Inter-Faith Relns Bd of Miss and Unity from 92. *5 Waterloo Street, Coventry CV1 5JS* Tel (01203) 257523 E-mail lamb@easynet.co.uk

LAMB, David Andrew. b 60. Liv Inst of Educn BA94. Nor Ord Course 90. **d** 94 **p** 95. C Formby H Trin *Liv* from 94. *19 Hampton Road, Formby, Liverpool L37 6EJ* Tel (01704) 876557

LAMB, Ms Jean Evelyn. b 57. Reading Univ BA79 Nottm Univ MA88. St Steph Ho Ox 81. **dss** 84 **d** 88. Leic H Spirit *Leic* 84; Beeston *S'well* 88; Par Dn 88-91; Hon C Nottingham St Mary and St Cath from 92. *13 Melbourne Road, Nottingham NG2 5BG* Tel 0115-981 2478

LAMB, John Romney. b 21. Ch Ch Ox BA48 MA53. Wells Th Coll 49. **d** 50 **p** 51. C Tenterden St Mildred w Smallhythe *Cant* 50-53; C Hythe 53-55; CF 55-70; V Horsell *Guildf* 70-76; V Dorking w Ranmore 76-82; P-in-c Charing Heath w Egerton *Cant* 82-83; P-in-c Pluckley w Pevington 82-83; R Egerton w Pluckley 84-87; rtd 87; Perm to Offic *Chich* from 87. *Wayside, Budds Hill, Singleton, Chichester, W Sussex PO18 0HD* Tel (01243) 811516

LAMB, Peter Francis Charles. b 15. St Cath Coll Cam BA37 MA41. Wells Th Coll 37. **d** 38 **p** 39. C Wellingborough All Hallows *Pet* 38-42; C Somersham w Pidley and Colne *Ely* 42-48; Chapl RNVR 46-48; C Sherborne w Castleton and Lillington *Sarum* 48-51; Gambia 51-57; V Winkleigh *Ex* 57-70; RD Chulmleigh 62-63; R Mells w Vobster, Whatley and Chantry *B & W* 70-77; rtd 77; Perm to Offic *B & W* from 77. *6 Parsons Close, Long Sutton, Langport, Somerset TA10 9LN* Tel (01458) 241481

LAMB, Philip Richard James. b 42. Sarum & Wells Th Coll. **d** 83 **p** 84. C Wotton-under-Edge w Ozleworth and N Nibley *Glouc* 83-86; TV Worc SE *Worc* 86-91; R Billingsley w Sidbury, Middleton Scriven etc *Heref* 91-96; R St Dominic, Landulph and St Mellion w Pillaton *Truro* from 96. *The Rectory, St Mellion, Saltash, Cornwall PL12 6RN* Tel (01579) 350061

LAMB, Scott Innes. b 64. Edin Univ BSc86 Fitzw Coll Cam BA92. Aston Tr Scheme 88 Ridley Hall Cam CTMin93. **d** 93 **p** 94. NSM Harrow Trin St Mich *Lon* 93; C E Ham w Upton Park St Alb *Chelmsf* from 93. *281 Central Park Road, London E6 3AF* Tel 0181-471 4243

LAMB, William Robert Stuart. b 70. Ball Coll Ox BA91 MA95 Peterho Cam MPhil94. Westcott Ho Cam CTM95. **d** 95 **p** 96. C Halifax *Wakef* from 95. *15 Savile Drive, Halifax, W Yorkshire HX1 2EU* Tel (01422) 346027

LAMBERT, David Francis. b 40. Oak Hill Th Coll 72. **d** 74 **p** 75. C Paignton St Paul Preston *Ex* 74-77; C Woking Ch Ch *Guildf* 77-84; P-in-c Willesden Green St Gabr *Lon* 84-91; P-in-c Cricklewood St Mich 85-91; V Cricklewood St Gabr and St Mich 92-93; R Chenies and Lt Chalfont, Latimer and Flaunden *Ox* from 93. *The Rectory, Chenies, Rickmansworth, Herts WD3 6ER* Tel (01923) 284433

LAMBERT, David Hardy. b 44. AKC66. **d** 67 **p** 68. C Marske in Cleveland *York* 67-72; V from 85; V N Ormesby 73-85; RD Guisborough 86-91. *The Vicarage, 6 Windy Hill Lane, Marske-by-the-Sea, Redcar, Cleveland TS11 7BN* Tel (01642) 482896

LAMBERT, David Nathaniel. b 34. Headingley Meth Coll 58 Linc Th Coll 66. **d** 66 **p** 67. In Meth Ch 58-66; C Canwick *Linc* 66-68; C-in-c Bracebridge Heath CD 68-69; R Saltfleetby All SS w St Pet 69-73; R Saltfleetby St Clem 70-73; V Skidbrooke 70-73; V Saltfleetby 73-80; R Theddlethorpe 74-80; RD Louthesk 76-82; R N Ormsby w Wyham 80; R Fotherby 81-94; rtd 94; Perm to Offic *Linc* from 94. *The Rowans, 17 Stenton Lane, Louth, Lincs LN11 8RZ* Tel (01507) 606220

LAMBERT, Donald William. b 19. Keble Coll Ox BA40 MA44. St Steph Ho Ox 40. **d** 43 **p** 44. C Worthing St Andr *Chich* 43-47; C Ox St Barn *Ox* 47-51; Bahamas 51-56; V Bathwick St Jo *B & W* 56-66; R Digswell *St Alb* 66-70; C St Alb St Sav 70; V Acton Green St Pet *Lon* 71-77; rtd 77; Perm to Offic *Chich* from 77. *8 Christ Church House, 34 Christ Church Road, Worthing, W Sussex BN11 1JA* Tel (01903) 206978

LAMBERT, Gordon. b 32. Univ of Wales (Lamp) BA56. Wycliffe Hall Ox 56. **d** 58 **p** 59. C Newbarns w Hawcoat *Carl* 58-63; C-in-c Barrow St Aid CD 63-67; V Barrow St Aid 67-68; R Ousby w Melmerby 68-71; V Farlam 71-76; TV Thirsk w S Kilvington and Carlton Miniott etc *York* 76-77; TV Thirsk 77-89; RD Thirsk 81-89; V Belvedere All SS *Roch* 89-96; rtd 96. *19 The Barnhams, Little Common, Bexhill-on-Sea, E Sussex TN39 4RE* Tel (01424) 844443

LAMBERT, Ian Anderson. b 43. Lon Univ BA72 Nottm Univ MTh87. Ridley Hall Cam 66. **d** 67 **p** 68. C Bermondsey St Mary w St Olave, St Jo etc *S'wark* 67-70; Jamaica 71-75; Chapl RAF from 75. *Chaplaincy Services (RAF), HQ, Personnel and Training Command, RAF Innsworth, Gloucester GL3 1EZ* Tel (01452) 712612 ext 5164 Fax 510828

LAMBERT, John Clement Antony. b 28. St Cath Coll Cam BA48 MA52. Cuddesdon Coll 50. **d** 52 **p** 53. C Hornsea and Goxhill *York* 52-55; C Leeds St Pet *Ripon* 55-59; R Carlton-in-Lindrick *S'well* 59-93; rtd 93; Perm to Offic *Derby* from 93. *139 Longedge Lane, Wingerworth, Chesterfield, Derbyshire S42 6PR* Tel (01246) 551774

LAMBERT, Malcolm Eric. b 58. RMN84 Leic Univ BSc80 Fitzw Coll Cam BA89. Ridley Hall Cam 87. **d** 90 **p** 91. C Humberstone *Leic* 90-94; R S Croxton Gp from 94; Warden of Readers from 97. *The Rectory, 19 Main Street, South Croxton, Leicester LE7 3RJ* Tel (01664) 840245

LAMBERT, Michael Roy. b 25. Univ Coll Dur BSc49. Cuddesdon Coll 52. **d** 52 **p** 53. C Middlesbrough St Oswald *York* 52-56; C Romsey *Win* 56-59; C Cottingham *York* 59-64; Chapl Hull Univ 59-64; V Saltburn-by-the-Sea 64-72; P-in-c Shaftesbury H Trin *Sarum* 72-73; R Shaston 74-78; R Corfe Mullen 78-91; rtd 91; Perm to Offic *Glouc* from 91. *16 Pheasant Way, Cirencester, Glos GL7 1BL* Tel (01285) 654657

LAMBERT, Norman. b 39. ACP66 Ch Ch Coll Cant 62 Lon Inst of Educn TCert65. Chich Th Coll 67. **d** 70 **p** 71. C Ocker Hill *Lich* 70-73; C Dudley St Edm *Worc* 73-76; P-in-c Darby End 76-77; V from 77. *St Peter's Vicarage, 25 Brooksbank Drive, Gawne Lane, Cradley Heath, W Midlands B64 5QG* Tel (01384) 637662

LAMBERT, Miss Olivia Jane. b 48. Matlock Coll of Educn BEd70. Trin Coll Bris DipHE86. **dss** 86 **d** 87 **p** 94. York St Luke *York* 86-87; Par Dn 87-90; Chapl York Distr Hosp 86-90; Par Dn Huntington *York* 90-94; C 94-95; TV from 95. *22 Park Avenue, New Earswick, York YO3 8DB* Tel (01904) 764306

LAMBERT, Peter George. b 29. Coll of Resurr Mirfield 86. **d** 87 **p** 88. NSM Rothwell w Orton, Rushton w Glendon and Pipewell *Pet* 87-93; P-in-c Corby Epiphany w St Jo 93-96; rtd 96; Perm to Offic *Pet* from 96. *4 Cogan Crescent, Rothwell, Kettering, Northants NN14 6AS* Tel (01536) 710692

LAMBERT, Philip Charles. b 54. St Jo Coll Dur BA75 Fitzw Coll Cam BA77 MA81. Ridley Hall Cam 75. **d** 78 **p** 79. C Upper Tooting H Trin *S'wark* 78-81; C Whorlton *Newc* 81-84; P-in-c Alston cum Garrigill w Nenthead and Kirkhaugh 84-87; TV Alston Team 87-89; R Curry Rivel w Fivehead and Swell *B & W* from 89. *The Rectory, Curry Rivel, Langport, Somerset TA10 0HQ* Tel (01458) 251375

LAMBERT, Sydney Thomas. b 17. Keble Coll Ox BA39 MA44. Wells Th Coll 40. **d** 41 **p** 42. C Poplar *Lon* 41-44; C Ox St Barn *Ox* 44-45; India 45-49; USA 49-50; CF 50-67; R Rendcomb *Glouc* 67-74; V Colesborne 67-74; P-in-c Cheltenham St Pet 74-78; P-in-c Todenham w Lower Lemington 78-83; P-in-c Bourton on the Hill 78-83; rtd 83; Perm to Offic *Worc* from 83. *97 Elm Road, Evesham, Worcs WR11 5DR* Tel (01386) 446725

LAMBETH, Archdeacon of. *See* BIRD, The Ven Colin Richard Bateman

LAMBOURNE, John Brian. b 36. Chich Th Coll 62. **d** 65 **p** 66. C Cant St Greg *Cant* 65-67; C St Mary in the Marsh 67-68; C E Grinstead St Swithun *Chich* 68-70; C Storrington 70-76; C Sullington 70-76; V Salehurst from 76; CF (TA) from 87; Bp's Adv on Rural Affairs *Chich* from 89; Agric Chapl from 89. *St Mary's Vicarage, Fair Lane, Robertsbridge, E Sussex TN32 5AR* Tel (01580) 880408

LAMDIN, Canon Keith Hamilton. b 47. Bris Univ BA69. Ripon Coll Cuddesdon 86. **d** 86 **p** 87. Adult Educn Officer *Ox* from 86; Team Ldr Par Resources Dept from 88; Dioc Dir Tr from 94; Hon Can Ch Ch from 97. *41 Stapleton Road, Headington, Oxford OX3 3LX* Tel (01865) 67160

LAMMAS, Miss Diane Beverley (Di). b 47. Trin Coll Bris 76. **dss** 79 **d** 87 **p** 94. Lenton Abbey *S'well* 79-84; Wollaton Park 79-84; E Regional Co-ord CPAS 84-89; Sec for Voc and Min CPAS 84-89; Hon C Cambridge St Paul *Ely* 87-90; Voc and Min Adv CPAS 89-92; Sen Voc and Min Adv CPAS 92-95; R Hethersett w Canteloff w Lt and Gt Melton *Nor* from 95. *The Rectory, 27 Norwich Road, Hethersett, Norwich NR9 3AR* Tel (01603) 810273

LAMONT, Roger. b 37. Jes Coll Ox BA60 MA62. St Steph Ho Ox 59. **d** 61 **p** 62. C Northampton St Alb *Pet* 61-66; V Mitcham St Olave *S'wark* 66-73; V N Sheen St Phil and All SS 73-85; P-in-c Richmond St Luke 82-85; Chapl St Lawr Hosp Caterham 85-91; Chapl Lifecare NHS Trust (Caterham) from 91. *Lifecare*

NHS Trust, Coulsdon Road, Caterham, Surrey CR3 5YA Tel (01883) 340803 or 346411

LAMONT, Ms Veronica Jane (Ronni). b 56. Bp Grosseteste Coll CertEd77. St Jo Coll Nottm 90. **d** 92 **p** 94. Par Dn St Alb St Pet *St Alb* 92-94; C 94-96; TV Hemel Hempstead from 96. *St Peter's Vicarage, 7 Tollpit End, Hemel Hempstead, Herts HP1 3NT* Tel (01442) 254061

LANCASHIRE, Allan. b 32. Birm Univ BA54. Lich Th Coll. **d** 63 **p** 64. C Birstall *Wakef* 63-67; V Wrenthorpe 67-70; P-in-c Wolverton H Trin *Ox* 70-73; TV 73-76; Educn Officer 73-76; Dioc Schs Officer *Lich* 76-85; P-in-c Drayton St Pet (Oxon) *Ox* 85-90; P-in-c Horley w Hornton 85-90; R Horley w Hornton and Hanwell, Shenington etc 90-96; rtd 96. *38 Cambrai Drive, Hall Green, Birmingham B28 9AD* Tel 0121-777 8328

LANCASHIRE, Douglas. b 26. SOAS Lon BA50 MA58 K Coll Lon BD55. **d** 61 **p** 79. USA 61-62; Australia 62-65; New Zealand 65-81; R Boxted w Langham *Chelmsf* 81-91; rtd 91. *15 Cecil Avenue, Enfield, Middx EN1 1PT* Tel 0181-363 0718

LANCASTER, Frederick Charles Thomas. b 16. Bps' Coll Cheshunt 48. **d** 51 **p** 52. C Nuneaton St Mary *Cov* 51-54; C Upton cum Chalvey *Ox* 54-57; V Drayton St Pet (Berks) 57-67; R Ascot Heath 67-81; rtd 81; Perm to Offic *Ox* 82-94. *College of St Barnabas, Blackberry Lane, Lingfield, Surrey RH7 6NJ* Tel (01342) 870260

LANCASTER, John Rawson. b 47. BSc. N Ord Course. **d** 82 **p** 83. C Bolton St Jas w St Chrys *Bradf* 82-86; V Barnoldswick w Bracewell from 86. *The Vicarage, 131 Gisburn Road, Barnoldswick, Colne, Lancs BB8 5JU* Tel (01282) 812028

LANCASTER, Norman. b 13. Leeds Univ BA36. Coll of Resurr Mirfield 36. **d** 38 **p** 39. C Skegness *Linc* 38-41; C New Cleethorpes 41-42; C Gt Grimsby St Jas 42-47; V Caistor w Holton le Moor and Clixby 47-52; PC Louth H Trin 52-57; V Keddington 52-57; V Hogsthorpe 57-62; Chapl Butlin's Holiday Camps 59-62; R Panton w Wragby 62-71; V Langton by Wragby 62-71; R Gt Coates 71-77; PC Aylesby 71-77; rtd 77; Perm to Offic *Linc* 77-95. *Fosbrooke House, 8 Clifton Drive, Lytham St Annes, Lancs FY8 5RE* Tel (01253) 738812

LANCASTER, Ronald. b 31. MBE93. FRSC83 CChem83 St Jo Coll Dur BA53 MA56. Cuddesdon Coll 55. **d** 57 **p** 58. C Morley St Pet w Churwell *Wakef* 57-60; C High Harrogate St Pet *Ripon* 60-63; Lic to Offic *Ely* 63-88; Chapl Kimbolton Sch Cambs 63-88; Asst Chapl 88-91; Perm to Offic *Ely* from 88; rtd 96. *7 High Street, Kimbolton, Huntingdon, Cambs PE18 0HB* Tel (01480) 860498 Fax 861277

LANCASTER, Mrs Susan Louise. b 47. Leic Univ BA79 CPES81. EMMTC 88. **d** 93 **p** 94. NSM Clarendon Park St Jo w Knighton St Mich *Leic* 93-97; Perm to Offic from 97. *5 Hartopp Road, Leicester LE2 1WE* Tel 0116-270 9726

LANCASTER, Archdeacon of. *Vacant*

LANCASTER, Suffragan Bishop of. *Vacant*

LAND, Michael Robert John. b 43. Ripon Hall Ox 70. **d** 72 **p** 73. C Newbury St Nic *Ox* 72-75; TV Chigwell *Chelmsf* 75-80; V Walthamstow St Andr from 80. *St Andrew's Vicarage, 37 Sutton Road, London E17 5QA* Tel 0181-527 3969

LANDALL, Richard. b 57. St Jo Coll Dur 85. **d** 88 **p** 89. C Nailsea H Trin *B & W* 88-92; CF from 92. *MOD Chaplains (Army), Trenchard Lines, Upavon, Pewsey, Wilts SN9 6BE* Tel (01980) 615804 Fax 615800

LANDEN, Edgar Sydney. b 23. ARCM46 FRCO46 St Jo Coll Dur BA54 BMus55 DipTh55. **d** 55 **p** 56. Succ Leeds 55-58; Prec Chelmsf Cathl *Chelmsf* 58-60; V Bathampton *B & W* 60-65; Perm to Offic *Glouc* 65-69; C Cirencester 69-76; Min Can Ch Ch *Ox* 76-88; R Wytham 76-88; rtd 88; Perm to Offic *B & W* from 88. *The Old Vicarage, Bakers Hill, Tiverton, Devon EX16 5NE* Tel (01884) 256815

LANDMAN, Denis Cooper. b 21. MBE60 OM(Ger)80. DipEd52. St Deiniol's Hawarden 79. **d** 82 **p** 83. Hon C Tranmere St Paul w St Luke *Ches* 82-86; Australia from 86; rtd 92. *1/24 Stretton Drive, Helensvale, Queensland, Australia 4210* Tel Brisbane (7) 5573 4660

LANDRETH, Canon Derek. b 20. TD63. K Coll Cam BA47 MA52. Bps' Coll Cheshunt 47. **d** 48 **p** 49. C Crofton Park St Hilda *S'wark* 48-49; C Camberwell St Geo 49-52; CF (TA) 51-75; C Tulse Hill H Trin *S'wark* 52-53; V Battersea Rise St Mark 53-59; V Richmond St Mary 59-70; Hon Can S'wark Cathl 68-76; R Sanderstead All SS 70-74; TR 74-77; Can Res S'wark Cathl 77-82; Vice-Chmn Dioc Past Cttee 77-82; Chapl to The Queen 80-90; P-in-c Icklesham *Chich* 82-83; V 83-88; RD Rye 84-88; P-in-c Fairlight 84-86; rtd 89; Perm to Offic *Chich* from 89. *Gossamer Cottage, Slindon, Arundel, W Sussex BN18 0QT* Tel (01243) 814224

LANDRETH, Mrs Mavis Isabella (Isabel). b 32. SEN81. Gilmore Ho 67. **dss** 74 **d** 87. Walthamstow St Sav *Chelmsf* 70-75; Sanderstead All SS *S'wark* 76-79; Sheff St Cuth *Sheff* 84-85; N Gen Hosp Sheff 84-85; Icklesham *Chich* 86-87; Hon Par Dn 87-89; Perm to Offic from 89. *Gossamer Cottage, Slindon, Arundel, W Sussex BN18 0QT* Tel (01243) 814224

LANE, Andrew Harry John. b 49. Lanc Univ BA71. Cuddesdon Coll 71. **d** 73 **p** 74. C Abingdon w Shippon *Ox* 73-78; Chapl Abingdon Sch 75-78; Chapl RAF 78-94; rtd 94; Perm to Offic *Nor* from 94. *32B Beeston Common, Sheringham, Norfolk NR26 8ES* Tel (01263) 825623

LANE, Anthony James. b 29. Leeds Univ BA53. Coll of Resurr Mirfield 53. **d** 55 **p** 56. C Tilehurst St Mich *Ox* 55-60; Min Can Win Cathl *Win* 60-63; R Handley w Gussage St Andrew and Pentridge *Sarum* 64-80; V Thurmaston *Leic* 80-85; TV Bournemouth St Pet w St Swithun, H Trin etc *Win* 85-93; rtd 93. *5 Richards Way, Salisbury SP2 8NT* Tel (01722) 332163

LANE, Antony Kenneth. b 58. Ripon Coll Cuddesdon 84. **d** 87 **p** 88. C Crediton and Shobrooke *Ex* 87-90; C Amblecote *Worc* 90-94; C Sedgley All SS 94-95; TV from 95. *St Andrew's Vicarage, 22 The Straits, Lower Gornal, Dudley, W Midlands DY3 3AB* Tel (01902) 885508

LANE, Christopher George (Chris). b 48. NDH. Sarum & Wells Th Coll 84. **d** 86 **p** 87. C Petersfield *Portsm* 86-90; P-in-c Barton 90-95; Perm to Offic from 95. *Carisbrooke Priory, 39 Whitcombe Road, Carisbrooke, Newport, Isle of Wight PO30 1YS* Tel (01983) 523354

LANE, David John. b 35. Magd Coll Ox BA58 MA62 BD89. Coll of Resurr Mirfield 60. **d** 62 **p** 62. Barbados 61-65; C Wolvercote *Ox* 65-66; Asst Chapl Pemb Coll Ox 66-68; Lect 68-71; Tutor St Steph Ho Ox 68-71; Canada 71-83; Assoc Prof Univ of Toronto 71-83; Tutor Coll of Resurr Mirfield 83-97; Dir of Studies from 84; Vice-Prin 87-90; Prin 90-97; rtd 97. *Lark Rise, Mickley, Ripon, N Yorkshire HG4 3JE*

LANE, Denis John Victor. b 29. Lon Univ LLB49 BD55. Oak Hill Th Coll 50. **d** 53 **p** 54. C Deptford St Jo *S'wark* 53-56; C Cam St Steph CD *Ely* 56-59; OMF 60-94; Malaysia 60-66; Singapore 66-94; Lic to Offic *Chich* 91-94; rtd 94; Perm to Offic *Chich* from 94. *2 Parry Drive, Rustington, Littlehampton, W Sussex BN16 2QY* Tel (01903) 785430 Fax as telephone

LANE, Dennis Charles William. b 17. Lon Univ BD40 AKC40. **d** 40 **p** 41. C Chipping Campden *Glouc* 40-43 and 47-49; Chapl RNVR 43-47; R Blaisdon w Flaxley *Glouc* 49-55; R Woodmansterne *S'wark* 55-64; Dioc Dir of Ords 61-67; V Tandridge 64-91; RD Godstone 71-76; rtd 91. *7 Branksome Close, New Milton, Hants BH25 6BQ* Tel (01425) 613302

LANE, Mrs Elizabeth Jane Holden (Libby). b 66. St Pet Coll Ox BA89. Cranmer Hall Dur DMinlStuds93. **d** 93 **p** 94. C Blackb St Jas *Blackb* 93-96. *38 Highgate, Beverley, N Humberside HU17 0DN* Tel (01482) 862656

LANE, George David Christopher. b 68. St Pet Coll Ox BA89. Cranmer Hall Dur DMinlStuds93. **d** 93 **p** 94. C Blackb St Jas *Blackb* 93-96; C Beverley Minster *York* from 96. *38 Highgate, Beverley, N Humberside HU17 0DN* Tel (01482) 862656

LANE, Canon Gerald. b 29. Bede Coll Dur BA52 MA96. Sarum Th Coll 52. **d** 54 **p** 55. C Camberwell St Giles *S'wark* 54-58; C Gillingham St Aug *Roch* 58-59; V 73-78; V Camberwell St Phil and St Mark *S'wark* 59-67; V Plumstead St Nic 67-73; V Hadlow *Roch* 78-94; Hon Can Roch Cathl 87-94; rtd 94; Perm to Offic *Roch* 94-95. *The Vicarage, Clay Hall Road, Kensworth, Dunstable, Beds LU6 3RF* Tel (01582) 872223

LANE, Canon Harold. b 09. MBE56. St Chad's Coll Dur BA33 LTh33 MA47. St Paul's Coll Burgh 27. **d** 33 **p** 35. C Armley St Bart *Ripon* 33-36; Adn Antigua 62-65; Bahamas 67-80; rtd 80; Perm to Offic *York* from 90. *20 Mallard Way, Haxby, York YO3 3NG* Tel (01904) 763558

LANE, Iain Robert. b 61. CCC Ox BA83. Ripon Coll Cuddesdon BA86 MA88. **d** 87 **p** 88. C Rotherhithe St Mary w All SS *S'wark* 87-91; V Bierley *Bradf* from 91. *St John's Vicarage, Bierley Lane, Bierley, Bradford, W Yorkshire BD4 6AA* Tel (01274) 681397

LANE, John Dormon. b 28. CEng67 MIMechE61 MIProdE61 MBIM75 FBPICS75 FAA77 FIIM81 FICM81 MIEE91 MIMfgE91 Lon Univ BScEng54. LNSM course. **d** 92 **p** 93. NSM Northill w Moggerhanger *St Alb* from 92. *11 Garner Close, Northill, Biggleswade, Beds SG18 9AF* Tel (01767) 627354 Fax (01480) 216319

LANE, John Ernest. b 39. OBE94. MBIM76 Cranfield Inst of Tech MSc80. Handsworth Coll Birm 58. **d** 80 **p** 80. In Meth Ch 62-80; Hon C Peckham St Jo w St Andr *S'wark* from 80; Dir St Mungo Housing Assn from 80. *24 Harcourt Road, London SE4 2AJ* Tel 0181-692 9959 or 0171-286 1358

LANE, Mrs Linda Mary. b 41. ACIB66 Lon Univ BD87. Gilmore Ho DipRK67. **dss** 82 **d** 87 **p** 94. Hadlow *Roch* 82-94; Hon Par Dn 87-94; Perm to Offic 94-96; C Dartford H Trin 96-97; V Kensworth, Studham and Whipsnade *St Alb* from 97. *The Vicarage, Clay Hall Road, Kensworth, Dunstable, Beds LU6 3RF* Tel (01582) 872223

LANE, Martin John. b 69. Coll of Resurr Mirfield 92. **d** 95 **p** 96. C Liss *Portsm* from 95. *13 Woodbourne Close, Liss, Hants GU33 7BA* Tel (01730) 892764

LANE, Richard Peter. b 60. Linc Th Coll 85. **d** 88 **p** 89. C Towcester w Easton Neston *Pet* 88-91; Asst Chapl Oslo w Bergen, Trondheim, Stavanger etc *Eur* 91-93; V Writtle w Highwood *Chelmsf* from 93. *The Vicarage, 19 Lodge Road, Writtle, Chelmsford CM1 3HY* Tel (01245) 421282

LANE, Ms Rosalind Anne. b 69. Trevelyan Coll Dur BA91 Heythrop Coll Lon MTh93. Westcott Ho Cam CTM95. **d** 95 **p** 96. C Huddersfield St Pet and All SS *Wakef* from 95. *41 West View, Paddock, Huddersfield HD1 4HX* Tel (01484) 544473

LANE, Roy Albert. b 42. Bris Sch of Min 82. **d** 85 **p** 86. NSM Bedminster *Bris* 85-97; Perm to Offic from 97. *20 Ashton Drive, Bristol BS3 2PW* Tel 0117-983 0747

LANE, Simon. *See* DOUGLAS LANE, Charles Simon Pellew

LANE, Stephen Toller. b 29. SS Coll Cam BA52 MA56. Lon Coll of Div ALCD54 LTh74. **d** 54 **p** 55. C Heworth H Trin *York* 54-57; V Everton St Cuth *Liv* 57-63; V Eccleston St Luke 63-71; R Bradfield *Ox* 71-85; R Snettisham w Ingoldisthorpe and Fring *Nor* 85-94; rtd 94. *3 Meadow Road, Newbury, Berks RG14 7AH* Tel (01635) 528257

LANE, Terry. S Tr Scheme. **d** 97. NSM Freemantle *Win* from 97. *24 Claremont Crescent, Regents Park, Southampton SO15 4GS* Tel (01703) 361193

LANE, William Michael. b 19. BNC Ox MA47. **d** 79 **p** 80. Asst Chapl Clifton Coll Bris 79-82; P-in-c Bris St Mich *Bris* 82-88; C 88-89; rtd 89; Perm to Offic *Bris* 89-95. *8 Fremantle Square, Bristol BS6 5TL* Tel 0117-924 7925

LANG, Geoffrey Wilfrid Francis. b 33. St Jo Coll Ox BA56 MA61. Cuddesdon Coll 56. **d** 58 **p** 59. C Spalding *Linc* 58-61; Asst Chapl Leeds Univ *Ripon* 61-62; C Chesterton St Luke *Ely* 62-63; C-in-c Chesterton Gd Shep CD 63-69; V Chesterton Gd Shep 69-72; V Willian *St Alb* 72-76; Dioc Dir of Educn 72-76; R N Lynn w St Marg and St Nic *Nor* 77-86; V Hammersmith St Pet *Lon* from 86. *17 Ravenscourt Road, London W6 0UH* Tel 0181-748 1781 or 741 4848 Fax 748 6610

LANG, The Very Revd Dr John Harley. b 27. LRAM Em Coll Cam MA60 K Coll Lon AKC49 BD60 Keele Univ DLitt88. St Boniface Warminster 49. **d** 52 **p** 53. C Portsea St Mary *Portsm* 52-57; PV and Sacr S'wark Cathl *S'wark* 57-60; Chapl Em Coll Cam 60-64; Asst Hd Relig Broadcasting BBC 64-67; Hd of Relig Progr BBC Radio 67-71; Hd of Relig Broadcasting BBC 71-80; C Sacombe *St Alb* 73-80; Chapl to The Queen 77-80; Dean Lich 80-93; rtd 93; Perm to Offic *Glouc* from 93. *South Barn, Stanway Road, Stanton, Broadway, Worcs WR12 7NQ* Tel (01386) 584251

LANG, William David. b 51. K Coll Lon BD74 AKC74. St Aug Coll Cant 74. **d** 75 **p** 76. C Fleet *Guildf* 75-79; C Ewell St Fran 79-82; C W Ewell 79-82; V Holmwood 82-92; R Elstead from 92; V Thursley from 92. *The Rectory, Thursley Road, Elstead, Godalming, Surrey GU8 6DG* Tel (01252) 703251

LANGAN, Mrs Eleanor Susan. b 56. Homerton Coll Cam BEd78. Ripon Coll Cuddesdon 84. **d** 87 **p** 94. Hon Par Dn Grays Thurrock *Chelmsf* 87-89; Lic to Offic 89-94; NSM Creeksea w Althorne, Latchingdon and N Fambridge 94-95; NSM S Woodham Ferrers from 95. *The Vicarage, 18 Victoria Road, South Woodham Ferrers, Chelmsford CM3 5LR* Tel (01245) 320201

LANGAN, Michael Leslie. b 54. Cam Univ BA PGCE. Cranmer Hall Dur. **d** 84 **p** 85. C Grays Thurrock *Chelmsf* 84-89; V Creeksea w Althorne, Latchingdon and N Fambridge 89-95; RD Maldon and Dengie 92-95; P-in-c S Woodham Ferrers from 95. *The Vicarage, 18 Victoria Road, South Woodham Ferrers, Chelmsford CM3 5LR* Tel (01245) 320201

LANGDON, John Bonsall. b 21. Linc Coll Ox BA51 MA55. Ripon Hall Ox 52. **d** 54 **p** 55. C Erith St Jo *Roch* 54-57; C Christchurch *Win* 57-60; Min Can Ripon Cathl *Ripon* 60-63; R Swillington 63-75; P-in-c Wrangthorn 75-76; V Leeds All Hallows w St Simon 75-76; V Leeds All Hallows w Wrangthorn 76-87; P-in-c Woodhouse St Mark 85-87; V Woodhouse and Wrangthorn 87-92; rtd 92. *32 Magdalene Road, Ripon, N Yorkshire HG4 1HT* Tel (01765) 606814

LANGDON, Canon William Ancell Martin. b 14. Selw Coll Cam BA36 MA41. Wells Th Coll 36. **d** 38 **p** 39. C Sydenham St Bart *S'wark* 38-40; C Putney St Mary 40-42; C Worplesdon *Guildf* 42-45; Chapl HM Borstal Portland 45-49; R Portland All SS w St Pet *Sarum* 48-51; Chapl HM Pris The Verne 49-51; R Langton Matravers *Sarum* 51-61; Hon Chapl to Bp Sarum 53-62; R Melksham 61-69; RD Bradford 67-69; Can and Preb Sarum Cathl 68-81; V Charminster 69-81; rtd 81. *32B Burlington Road, Swanage, Dorset BH19 1LT* Tel (01929) 424167

LANGFORD, David Laurence. b 51. LNSM course 86. **d** 88 **p** 89. NSM Scotton w Northorpe *Linc* from 88. *1 Westgate, Scotton, Gainsborough, Lincs DN21 3QX* Tel (01724) 763139

LANGFORD, Prof Michael John. b 31. New Coll Ox BA54 MA58 Cam Univ MA59 Lon Univ PhD66. Westcott Ho Cam 55. **d** 56 **p** 57. C Bris St Nath w St Kath *Bris* 56-59; Chapl Qu Coll Cam 59-63; C Hampstead St Jo *Lon* 63-67; Canada 67-96; Prof Philosophy Newfoundland Univ 82-96; Prof Medical Ethics 87-96; rtd 96. *90 Field View, Bar Hill, Cambridge CB3 8SY* Tel (01954) 789593

LANGFORD, Peter Francis. b 54. Sarum & Wells Th Coll 76. **d** 79 **p** 80. C N Ormesby *York* 79-82; Ind Chapl 83-91; V Middlesbrough St Chad 91-96; R Easington w Liverton from 96. *The Rectory, Easington, Saltburn-by-the-Sea, Cleveland TS13 4NT* Tel (01287) 641348

LANGFORD, Peter Julian. b 33. Selw Coll Cam BA58. Westcott Ho Cam 59. **d** 60 **p** 61. C E Ham St Mary *Chelmsf* 60-67; Hon C 67-71; Hon C Beccles St Mich *St E* 71-76; Warden Ringsfield Hall Suffolk 71-87; P-in-c Ringsfield w Redisham *St E* 76-80; TV Seacroft *Ripon* from 87. *St Richard's Vicarage, Ramshead Hill, Leeds LS14 1BX* Tel 0113-265 6388

LANGHAM, John Godfrey. b 22. Lon Univ DipTh60. Oak Hill Th Coll. **d** 60 **p** 61. C Rushden St Pet 60-63; V Burton in Kendal *Carl* 63-79; rtd 79; Perm to Offic *Ex* from 80. *61 Holmdale, Sidmouth, Devon EX10 8DN* Tel (01395) 516417

LANGHAM, Paul Jonathan. b 60. Ex Univ BA81 DipTh83 Fitzw Coll Cam BA86 MA91. Ridley Hall Cam 84. **d** 87 **p** 88. C Bath Weston All SS w N Stoke *B & W* 87-91; Chapl and Fell St Cath Coll Cam 91-96; V Combe Down w Monkton Combe and S Stoke *B & W* from 96. *The Vicarage, 141 Bradford Road, Combe Down, Bath BA2 5BS* Tel (01225) 833152

LANGLEY, Canon Myrtle Sarah. b 39. FRAI TCD BA61 HDipEd62 MA67 Bris Univ PhD76 Lon Univ BD66. Dalton Ho Bris 64. **d** 88 **p** 94. Dir Chr Development for Miss *Liv* 87-89; Dir of Tr Inst *Carl* from 90; Dioc Dir of Tr from 90; Hon Can Carl Cathl from 91. *92 Greenacres, Wetheral, Carlisle CA4 8LD* Tel (01228) 561478 or 22573 Fax 48769

LANGLEY, Canon Robert (Bob). b 37. St Cath Soc Ox BA61. St Steph Ho Ox. **d** 63 **p** 64. C Aston cum Aughton *Sheff* 63-68; Midl Area Sec Chr Educn Movement 68-71; HQ Sec Chr Educn Movement 71-74; Prin Ian Ramsey Coll Brasted 74-77; Dir St Alb Minl Tr Scheme 77-85; Can Res St Alb 77-85; Can Res Newc Cathl *Newc* from 85. *16 Towers Avenue, Jesmond, Newcastle upon Tyne NE2 3QE* Tel 0191-281 0714

LANGMAN, Barry Edward. b 46. Master Mariner 73. Cant Sch of Min 87. **d** 90 **p** 91. NSM St Margarets-at-Cliffe w Westcliffe etc *Cant* 90-92; C Sandgate St Paul 92; C Sandgate St Paul w Folkestone St Geo 92-95; P-in-c Headcorn from 95. *The Vicarage, 64 Oak Lane, Headcorn, Ashford, Kent TN27 9TB* Tel (01622) 890342

LANGRELL, Gordon John. b 35. Cant Univ (NZ) BA58. Ridley Hall Cam 65. **d** 67 **p** 68. C Tonbridge SS Pet and Paul *Roch* 67-71; New Zealand from 71. *46A Greenhurst Street, Upper Riccarton, Christchurch 8004, New Zealand* Tel Christchurch (3) 348 9554 or 384 1737 Fax 348 9554

✠**LANGRISH, The Rt Revd Michael Laurence.** b 46. Birm Univ BSocSc67 Fitzw Coll Cam BA73 MA77. Ridley Hall Cam 71. **d** 73 **p** 74 **c** 93. C Stratford-on-Avon w Bishopton *Cov* 73-76; Chapl Rugby Sch 76-81; P-in-c Offchurch *Cov* 81-87; Dioc Dir of Ords 81-87; P-in-c Rugby St Andr 87-91; Hon Can Cov Cathl 90-93; TR Rugby St Andr 91-93; Suff Bp Birkenhead *Ches* from 93. *Bishop's House, 67 Bidston Road, Birkenhead, Merseyside L34 6TA* Tel 0151-652 2741 Fax 651 2330

LANGSTAFF, James Henry. b 56. St Cath Coll Ox BA77 MA81 Nottm Univ BA80. St Jo Coll Nottm 78. **d** 81 **p** 82. C Farnborough *Guildf* 81-84; P-in-c 84-85; C 85-86; P-in-c Duddeston *Birm* 86; P-in-c Duddeston w Nechells 86; V 87-96; RD Birm City 95-96; Bp's Dom Chapl from 96. *East Wing, Bishop's Croft, Old Church Road, Harborne, Birmingham B17 0BG* Tel 0121-427 2295

LANGSTON, Clinton Matthew. b 62. Derby Coll of Educn BCombStuds86. Qu Coll Birm 87. **d** 90 **p** 91. C Shirley *Birm* 90-94; CF from 94. *MOD Chaplains (Army), Trenchard Lines, Upavon, Pewsey, Wilts SN9 6BE* Tel (01980) 615804 Fax 615800

LANGTON, Canon Kenneth. b 26. Open Univ BA76. St Aid Birkenhead 52. **d** 55 **p** 56. C Oldham St Paul *Man* 55-57; C Ashton Ch Ch 57-58; P-in-c 58; V Stalybridge New St Geo 58-69; P-in-c Stalybridge Old St Geo 67-69; V Stalybridge 69-71; R Radcliffe St Mary 71-83; Hon Can Man Cathl 80-91; V Tyldesley w Shakerley 83-91; rtd 91; Perm to Offic *Man* from 91. *889 Walmersley Road, Bury, Lancs BL9 5LE* Tel 0161-764 1552

LANGTON, Canon Maurice Charles. b 09. Trin Coll Cam BA30 MA34. Sarum Th Coll 33. **d** 34 **p** 35. C Horsham *Chich* 34-37; India 37-52; V Billingshurst *Chich* 52-56; Dir RE and Tr of Ord Cand 56-77; Can and Preb Chich Cathl 63-77; rtd 77; Perm to Offic *Linc* 77-86. *3 Caithness Road, Stamford, Lincs PE9 2TE* Tel (01780) 51004

LANHAM, Geoffrey Peter. b 62. Cam Univ MA84 Ox Univ MPhil86. Wycliffe Hall Ox 86. **d** 89 **p** 90. C Southborough St Pet w Ch Ch and St Matt *Roch* 89-92; C Harborne Heath *Birm* from 92. *33 Margaret Road, Birmingham B17 0EU*

LANHAM, Richard Paul White. b 42. Dur Univ BA64. Wycliffe Hall Ox 65. **d** 67 **p** 68. C Gerrards Cross *Ox* 67-69; C Horwich H Trin *Man* 69-72; C Worsley 72-74; V Accrington St Andr *Blackb* 74-80; V Shillington *St Alb* 80-85; V Upper w Lower Gravenhurst 80-85; rtd 85; Perm to Offic *St Alb* from 85. *10 Alexander Close, Clifton, Shefford, Beds SG17 5RB* Tel (01462) 813520

LANKEY, David. b 41. MBCS68 CEng88 Southn Univ BSc62. S'wark Ord Course 79. **d** 82 **p** 83. NSM W Wimbledon Ch Ch *S'wark* 82-92; C Tooting All SS 92-95; R Long Ditton from 95. *The Rectory, 67 St Mary's Road, Surbiton, Surrey KT6 5HB* Tel 0181-398 1583

LANSDALE, Charles Roderick. b 38. Leeds Univ BA59. Coll of Resurr Mirfield 59. **d** 61 **p** 62. C Nunhead St Antony *S'wark* 61-65; Swaziland 65-71; V Benhilton *S'wark* 72-78; TR Catford (Southend) and Downham 78-87; TR Moulsecoomb *Chich* from 87. *St Andrew's Rectory, Hillside, Brighton BN2 4TA* Tel (01273) 680680

LANSLEY, Paul Sanford. b 33. Trin Coll Cam BA56 MA61. St Steph Ho Ox 56. **d** 58 **p** 59. C N Acton St Gabr *Lon* 58-60;

Hon C Colchester St Jas, All SS, St Nic and St Runwald *Chelmsf* 69-95; Asst Chapl Colchester Hosps 86-94; Asst Chapl Essex Rivers Healthcare NHS Trust from 94. *31A King Coel Road, Colchester CO3 5AQ* Tel (01206) 562813

LANTSBERY, Colin. b 39. Chich Th Coll 70. **d** 72 **p** 73. C Wednesfield St Thos *Lich* 72-75; C W Bromwich All SS 75-77; V Normacot 77-84; V Longton St Mary and St Chad 84-94. *18 Riverside View, Truro, Cornwall TR1 1UZ* Tel (01872) 70155

LANYON JONES, Keith. b 49. Southn Univ BTh79. Sarum & Wells Th Coll 74. **d** 77 **p** 78. C Charlton Kings St Mary *Glouc* 77-81; Sen Chapl Rugby Sch from 81; Lic to Offic *Truro* from 83. *11 Horton Crescent, Rugby, Warks CV22 5DJ* Tel (01788) 544939

LAPAGE, Michael Clement. b 23. Selw Coll Cam BA47 MA73. Clifton Th Coll 60. **d** 61 **p** 62. Kenya 61-72; Chapl Bedford Sch 73-75; Chapl Lyon w Grenoble *Eur* 76-79; V Walford w Bishopswood *Heref* 79-88; P-in-c Goodrich w Welsh Bicknor and Marstow 83-88; rtd 88; Perm to Offic *Ex* from 88. *Moorlands, 20 Watts Road, Tavistock, Devon PL19 8LG* Tel (01822) 615901

LAPAGE, Canon Peter Reginald. b 17. MC45. Selw Coll Cam BA41 MA44. Ridley Hall Cam 46. **d** 48 **p** 49. C Reading St Jo *Ox* 48-50; CMS 50-65; Nigeria 50-65; Area Sec (Dios Lon and S'wark) CMS 66-82; rtd 82; Perm to Offic *S'wark* 82-94. *37A Trinity Road, London SW19 8QS* Tel 0181-542 9737

LAPHAM, Canon Fred. b 31. Univ of Wales (Lamp) BA53. Vancouver Sch of Th LTh55 BD58. **d** 55 **p** 55. Canada 55-59; C Wallasey St Hilary *Ches* 59-62; V Over St Jo 62-70; V Upton Ascension 70-82; R Grappenhall 82-91; RD Gt Budworth 85-91; Hon Can Ches Cathl 88-91; rtd 91; Perm to Offic *Ches* from 91; Perm to Offic *Heref* from 91. *1 Coppice Gate, Lyth Hill, Shrewsbury SY3 0BT* Tel (01743) 722284

LAPWOOD, Robin Rowland John. b 57. Selw Coll Cam MA. Ridley Hall Cam 80. **d** 82 **p** 83. C Bury St Edmunds St Mary *St E* 82-86; P-in-c Bentley w Tattingstone 86-93; P-in-c Copdock w Washbrook and Belstead 86-93; TV High Wycombe *Ox* 93-96; P-in-c Marcham w Garford from 96. *The Vicarage, 24 Church Street, Marcham, Abingdon, Oxon OX13 6NP* Tel (01865) 391319

LARCOMBE, Paul Richard. b 57. Portsm Poly BSc79 CEng MIEE. Trin Coll Bris 94. **d** 96 **p** 97. C Werrington *Pet* from 96. *66 Barbers Hill, Werrington, Peterborough PE4 5ED* Tel (01733) 323146

LARGE, Preb Denis Henry. b 18. Sarum Th Coll 39. **d** 42 **p** 43. C Warminster St Denys *Sarum* 42-44; C Kingston All SS *S'wark* 44-48; Min Merton St Jas CD 48-51; V Merton St Jas 51-56; R Sandford w Upton Hellions *Ex* 56-61; R Clyst St Mary 61-75; R Clyst St George 61-75; Adv Chr Stewardship 64-81; P-in-c Woodbury Salterton 66-67; V 67-75; P-in-c Rockbeare 66-67; V 67-75; P-in-c Aylesbeare and Farringdon 66-67; R 67-75; R Clyst Honiton 67-75; R Sowton 67-75; RD Aylesbeare 73-76; TR Clyst St George, Aylesbeare, Clyst Honiton etc 75-83; rtd 83; Perm to Offic *Ex* from 83. *30 Higher Shapter Street, Topsham, Devon EX3 0AW* Tel (01392) 873295

LARGE, William Roy. b 40. Dur Univ BA DipEd. Edin Th Coll 82. **d** 84 **p** 85. C Leamington Priors All SS *Cov* 84-88; V Bishop's Tachbrook from 88; Warden of Readers and Sen Tutor from 88. *The Vicarage, 24 Mallory Road, Bishop's Tachbrook, Leamington Spa, Warks CV33 9QX* Tel (01926) 426922

LARK, William Donald Starling. b 35. Keble Coll Ox BA59 MA63. Wells Th Coll 59. **d** 61 **p** 62. C Wyken *Cov* 61-64; C Christchurch *Win* 64-66; V Yeovil St Mich *B & W* 66-75; V Earley St Pet *Ox* 75-85; V Prittlewell *Chelmsf* 85-88; V Dawlish *Ex* from 88. *The Vicarage, 13 West Cliff Road, Dawlish, Devon EX7 9EB* Tel (01626) 862204

LARKIN, Peter John. b 39. ALCD62. **d** 62 **p** 63. C Liskeard w St Keyne *Truro* 62-65; C Rugby St Andr *Cov* 65-67; Sec Bp Cov Call to Miss 67-68; V Kea *Truro* 68-78; P-in-c Bromsgrove St Jo *Worc* 78-81; R Torquay St Matthias, St Mark and H Trin *Ex* from 81; Can Sokoto Nigeria from 91. *The Rectory, Wellswood Avenue, Torquay TQ1 2QE* Tel (01803) 293280

LARKINS, Mary Herve. b 14. IDC. Coll of Ascension 39. **dss** 46 **d** 87. Gt Ayton w Easby and Newton in Cleveland *York* 46-73; rtd 74; Perm to Offic *Guildf* 76-86; Perm to Offic *Glouc* from 87. *25 Capel Court, The Burgage, Prestbury, Cheltenham, Glos GL52 3EL* Tel (01242) 576460

LARNER, Gordon Edward Stanley. b 30. Brasted Th Coll 54 Oak Hill Th Coll 55. **d** 59 **p** 60. C Peckham St Mary Magd *S'wark* 59-62; C Luton w E Hyde *St Alb* 62-68; V Lower Sydenham St Mich *S'wark* 68-73; Ind Chapl 73-84; Lic to Offic *S'well* 84-92; Chapl HM Pris Ranby 84-92; rtd 92. *8 Little Hayes, Fishponds, Bristol BS16 2LD*

LARSEN, Clive Erik. b 55. St Jo Coll Nottm LTh90. **d** 90 **p** 91. C Weaverham *Ches* 90-92; C Helsby and Dunham-on-the-Hill 92-95; P-in-c Cheadle Heath from 95. *The Vicarage, 8 Tillard Avenue, Stockport, Cheshire SK3 0UG* Tel 0161-477 3541

LARTER, John William. b 29. Lon Univ BSc51. Coll of Resurr Mirfield. **d** 54 **p** 55. C Redcar *York* 54-56; C Thornaby on Tees St Paul 56-59; C Boreham Wood All SS *St Alb* 59-62; Perm to Offic *Ox* 62-65; R Middleton Stoney 65-70; P-in-c Bucknell 65-69; R 69-70; V N Hinksey 70-77; V Eye w Braiseworth and Yaxley *St E* 77-84; RD Hartismere 78-81; P-in-c Occold w Redlingfield 80-84; V Hunstanton St Edm w Ringstead *Nor* 84-91; V Wormingford, Mt Bures and Lt Horkesley *Chelmsf* 91-94; rtd 94; Perm to Offic *Nor* from 94; Perm to Offic *S'well* from 94; Perm to Offic *St E* from 95. *16 Highfield, Eye, Suffolk IP23 7BP*

LASHBROOKE, David. b 60. Ex Univ BA87. Ripon Coll Cuddesdon 90. **d** 92 **p** 93. C Sherborne w Castleton and Lillington *Sarum* 92-95; P-in-c Weymouth St Paul from 95. *St Paul's Vicarage, 58 Abbotsbury Road, Weymouth, Dorset DT4 0BJ* Tel (01305) 771217

LASHBROOKE, John. b 28. Kelham Th Coll 49. **d** 53 **p** 54. C Kennington St Jo *S'wark* 53-57; Br Guiana 57-59; V Sydenham St Phil *S'wark* 59-69; R Corby Epiphany w St Jo *Pet* 69-80; V Rubery *Birm* 80-88; V Horam *Chich* 88-93; rtd 93; Perm to Offic *Ex* from 94. *Applegarth, Longmeadow Road, Lympstone, Exmouth, Devon EX8 5LF* Tel (01395) 268594

LASKEY, Cyril Edward. b 44. RMN71 RGN74. Llan Dioc Tr Scheme 85. **d** 88 **p** 89. NSM Troedrhiwgarth *Llan* 88-93; NSM Caerau St Cynfelin from 94. *207 Bridgend Road, Maesteg CF34 0NL* Tel (01656) 734639

LAST, Eric Cyril. b 30. Oak Hill Th Coll 77. **d** 79 **p** 80. C Wandsworth All SS *S'wark* 79-83; V Earlsfield St Andr 83-88; V S Merstham 88-96; Asst RD Reigate 92-96; rtd 96; Hon C Upper Tean *Lich* from 96. *29 Vicarage Road, Tean, Stoke-on-Trent ST10 4LE* Tel (01538) 723551

LAST, Harold Wilfred. b 17. ARCM52 ARCO53 CCC Cam BA38 MA42. Linc Th Coll 39. **d** 40 **p** 41. C Bolton St Jas *Bradf* 40-44; C Woodbridge St Mary *St E* 44-45; Lect K Coll Lon 45-53; Dir of Music St Bees, St Olave's & Felstead Schs 53-73; rtd 73. *Flat 1, Knapton House, North Walsham Road, Knapton, North Walsham, Norfolk NR28 0RT* Tel (01263) 720084

LAST, Michael Leonard Eric. b 60. St Jo Coll Nottm DipThMin94. **d** 94 **p** 95. C Tettenhall Wood *Lich* from 94. *283 Henwood Road, Wolverhampton WV6 8PU* Tel (01902) 746481

LAST, Norman Percy George. b 31. BA CertEd ATPL. Sarum & Wells Th Coll 77 Wycliffe Hall Ox 80. **d** 81 **p** 82. C Walton-on-Thames *Guildf* 81-83; C Farnham 83-87; R Monks Eleigh w Chelsworth and Brent Eleigh etc *St E* 87-90; P-in-c Bradworthy *Ex* from 91. *Church Lodge, West Street, Kilkhampton, Cornwall EX23 9QW*

LATHAM, Christine Elizabeth. b 46. S'wark Ord Course 87. **d** 90 **p** 94. Par Dn Battersea St Pet and St Paul *S'wark* 90-94; Par Dn S'wark Ch Ch 94; C 94-97; C Merstham and Gatton from 97; Chapl E Surrey Learning Disability NHS Trust from 97. *Epiphany House, Mansfield Drive, Merstham, Surrey RH1 3SP* Tel (01737) 642628

LATHAM, Henry Nicholas Lomax (Harry). b 64. Reading Univ BA86. Wycliffe Hall Ox BTh93. **d** 93 **p** 94. C Aberystwyth *St D* from 93. *Ael-y-Bryn, 25 High Street, Aberystwyth SY23 1JG* Tel (01970) 624537

LATHAM, John Montgomery. b 37. **d** 62 **p** 63. C Camberwell St Geo *S'wark* 62-65; New Zealand from 71. *43 Rugby Street, Christchurch 8001, New Zealand* Tel Christchurch (3) 355 6654 or 379 3090 Fax 355 6658 E-mail latham@xtra.co.nz

LATHAM, John Westwood. b 31. Ely Th Coll 57. **d** 60 **p** 61. C Cleckheaton St Jo *Wakef* 60-63; C Hemel Hempstead *St Alb* 63-65; C Wakef Cathl *Wakef* 65-67; V Outwood 67-72; TV Daventry w Norton *Pet* 72-79; V Flore w Dodford and Brockhall 79-96; rtd 96. *53 Lubenham Hill, Market Harborough, Leics LE16 9DG* Tel (01858) 469023

LATHAM, Robert Norman. b 53. Qu Coll Birm 82. **d** 85 **p** 86. C Tamworth *Lich* 85-89; TV Wordsley 89-93; TV Wordsley *Worc* 93-96; P-in-c Hallow 96-97; R Hallow and Grimley w Holt from 97. *Hallow Vicarage, 26 Baveney Road, Worcester WR2 6PF*

LATHAM, Trevor Martin. b 56. BD84. Ripon Coll Cuddesdon 84. **d** 86 **p** 87. C Cantril Farm *Liv* 86-89; TV W Derby St Mary from 89. *The Vicarage, 1 Sandicroft Road, Liverpool L12 0LX* Tel 0151-549 2202

LATHE, Canon Anthony Charles Hudson. b 36. Jes Coll Ox BA59 MA64 UEA DipSoc68. Lich Th Coll 59. **d** 61 **p** 62. C Selby Abbey *York* 61-63; V Hempnall *Nor* 63-72; R Woodton w Bedingham 63-72; R Fritton w Morningthorpe w Shelton and Hardwick 63-72; R Topcroft 63-72; R Banham 72-76; TR Quidenham 76-83; P-in-c New Buckenham 78-79; V Heigham St Thos 83-94; Hon Can Nor Cathl from 87; RD Nor S 90-94; P-in-c Sheringham from 94. *The Vicarage, 10 North Street, Sheringham, Norfolk NR26 8LW* Tel (01263) 822089

LATTIMORE, Anthony Leigh. b 35. Dur Univ BA57. Lich Th Coll 60. **d** 62 **p** 63. C Aylestone *Leic* 62-66; C-in-c Eyres Monsell CD 66-69; V Eyres Monsell 69-73; V Somerby, Burrough on the Hill and Pickwell 73-86; RD Goscote I 80-86; R Glenfield 86-95; rtd 95; Perm to Offic *Leic* from 95; Perm to Offic *Pet* from 95. *28 Elizabeth Way, Uppingham, Oakham, Leics LE15 9PQ* Tel (01572) 823193

LAUGHTON, Derek Basil. b 24. Worc Coll Ox BA49 MA52. Westcott Ho Cam 49. **d** 51 **p** 52. C Wareham w Arne *Sarum* 51-53; CF 53-56; C Hemel Hempstead St Mary *St Alb* 56-59; V Stretton cum Wetmoor *Lich* 59-64; Chapl Wellington Sch Somerset 64-73; Chapl Ardingly Coll Haywards Heath 73-77; R Plumpton w E Chiltington *Chich* 77-88; Perm to Offic *B & W* from 88; rtd 89. *13 Pyles Thorne Road, Wellington, Somerset TA21 8DX* Tel (01823) 667386

LAURENCE, The Ven John Harvard Christopher. b 29. Trin Hall Cam BA53 MA57. Westcott Ho Cam 53. **d** 55 **p** 56. C Linc St Nic w St Jo Newport *Linc* 55-59; V Crosby 59-74; Can and Preb Linc Cathl 74-79 and 85-94; Dioc Missr 74-79; Bp's Dir of Clergy Tr *Lon* 80-85; Adn Lindsey *Linc* 85-94; rtd 94; Perm to Offic *Linc* from 94. *5 Haffenden Road, Lincoln LN2 1RP* Tel (01522) 531444

LAURENCE, Julian Bernard Vere. b 60. Kent Univ BA82. St Steph Ho Ox 86. **d** 88 **p** 89. C Yeovil St Mich *B & W* 88-91; Chapl Yeovil Coll 90-91; Chapl Yeovil Distr Gen Hosp 91; P-in-c Barwick *B & W* 91-94; V Taunton H Trin from 94. *Holy Trinity Vicarage, 18 Holway Avenue, Taunton, Somerset TA1 3AR* Tel (01823) 337890

LAURENCE, Vere Deacon. b 11. Ex Coll Ox BA33 BSc34 MA37. Sarum Th Coll 34. **d** 36 **p** 37. C Horfield St Greg *Bris* 36-42; Dioc Sec for war damage payments 42-43; C Fishponds St Jo 42-43; C Knowle St Barn 43-47; Chapl HM Pris Stafford 47-52; V Upper Sunbury St Sav *Lon* 53-74; R Jacobstow w Warbstow and Treneglos *Truro* 74-83; RD Stratton 77-83; rtd 83; Perm to Offic *B & W* from 85. *12 Westbrook Road, Weston-super-Mare, Avon BS22 8JU* Tel (01934) 415143

LAURIE, Donovan Hugh (Don). b 40. Man Univ MSc. Oak Hill NSM Course. **d** 82 **p** 83. NSM Cudham and Downe *Roch* 82-84; C Tunbridge Wells St Jas 84-88; P-in-c Ventnor St Cath *Portsm* from 88; P-in-c Ventnor H Trin from 88. *The Vicarage, Park Avenue, Ventnor, Isle of Wight PO38 1LD* Tel (01983) 852130

LAURIE, James Andrew Stewart (Jim). b 26. Selw Coll Cam BA51 MA55. Ridley Hall Cam 51. **d** 53 **p** 54. C Neasden cum Kingsbury St Cath *Lon* 53-56; C Cricklewood St Pet 56-59; C Lancing St Jas *Chich* 59-61; V Freehay *Lich* 61-65; P-in-c Ilam w Blore Ray and Okeover 65-71; V Wetton 65-71; V Alstonfield 65-71; P-in-c Calton 66-71; V Charsfield w Debach and Monewden w Hoo *St E* 83-86; V Charsfield w Debach, Monewden, Hoo etc 86-90; rtd 90. *Richmond Grove, Birds Green, Bury St Edmunds, Suffolk IP30 0RT* Tel (01449) 736165

LAUT, Graham Peter. b 37. Chich Th Coll 63. **d** 67 **p** 68. C Corringham *Chelmsf* 67-68; C Leytonstone St Marg w St Columba 68-71; P-in-c Leytonstone St Andr 71-75; V 75-80; V Romford Ascension Collier Row from 80. *The Ascension Vicarage, 68 Collier Row Road, Romford RM5 2BA* Tel (01708) 741658

LAVERACK, John Julian. b 51. Keele Univ BA CertEd Bris Univ BA. Bris Bapt Coll 76 Ex & Truro NSM Scheme 81. **d** 82 **p** 83. In Bapt Ch 79-81; C Braunton *Ex* 82-84; V Ex St Mark 84-92; Perm to Offic from 92. *4 Coronation Terrace, Starcross, Exeter EX6 8QA*

LAVERTY, Canon Walter Joseph Robert. b 49. CITC 70 Glouc Th Course 73. **d** 73 **p** 74. C Belfast St Donard *D & D* 73-77; C Ballymacarrett St Patr 77-82; I Kilwarlin Upper w Kilwarlin Lower 82-86; I Orangefield w Moneyreagh from 86; RD Dundonald from 91; Warden of Readers from 96; Preb Down Cathl from 97. *397 Castlereagh Road, Belfast BT5 6AB* Tel (01232) 704493

LAVERY, Canon Edward Robinson. Lon Univ BA DipTh. St Aid Birkenhead 65. **d** 67 **p** 68. C Belfast Trin Coll Miss *Conn* 67-69; C Belfast St Mary Magd 69-71; CF (TA) from 70; I Belfast St Phil *Conn* 71-74; I Craigs w Dunaghy and Killagan 74-83; I Ballymoney w Finvoy and Rasharkin from 83; Dioc Info Officer from 83; RD Coleraine from 94; Preb Conn Cathl from 96. *The Rectory, Queen Street, Ballymoney, Co Antrim BT53 6JA* Tel (01265) 662149

LAVERY, Leonard. b 06. St Aid Birkenhead 49. **d** 50 **p** 51. C Hensingham *Carl* 50-53; R Moresby 53-59; V Treleigh *Truro* 59-64; V Kenwyn St Jo 64-73; rtd 73. *Glan-Mor, Falmouth Road, Truro, Cornwall TR1 2BL* Tel (01872) 72895

LAVILLE, Jocelyn Roger (Jo). b 30. Ball Coll Ox BA52 MA63. ALCD64. **d** 64 **p** 65. C Gillingham St Mark *Roch* 64-69; C Thorpe Edge *Bradf* 69-72; The Philippines from 72; rtd 95. *PO Box 464, Greenhills, Manila, The Philippines 1502* Tel Manila (2) 922-7259 Fax as telephone

LAW, Andrew Philip. b 61. BNC Ox BA83 MA93 G&C Coll Cam PGCE86. W of England Minl Tr Course 90. **d** 93 **p** 94. C Tupsley w Hampton Bishop *Heref* 93-95; Chapl Heref Sixth Form Coll 94-95; Chapl City of Lon Freeman's Sch Ashtead Park 95-97; Lic to Offic *Guildf* 95-97; Chapl and Hd RS Heref Cathl Sch from 97. *4 Harley Court, Hereford HR1 2NA* Tel (01432) 363509

LAW, Bryan. b 36. Leeds Univ BA59 Lon Univ BD76. Coll of Resurr Mirfield 59. **d** 61 **p** 62. C Winshill *Derby* 61-64; R Gorton St Phil *Man* 64-70; Lic to Offic 70-71; Perm to Offic *Ox* from 71; Hd Master Page Hill Co Middle Sch Buckm from 81. *35 Little Meadow, Loughton, Milton Keynes MK5 8EH* Tel (01908) 661333

LAW, Canon Donald Edward Boughton. b 22. Lon Coll of Div 67. **d** 69 **p** 70. C Leic H Apostles *Leic* 69-73; V Cosby 73-81; RD Guthlaxton I 75-81; V Melton Mowbray w Thorpe Arnold 81-86; Hon Can Leic Cathl 81-88; RD Framland II 84-88; TR Melton Gt Framland 86-88; rtd 88; Perm to Offic *Leic* from 88; Perm to Offic *Pet* from 88. *36 Mill Grove, Whissendine, Oakham, Leics LE15 7EY* Tel (01664) 79411

LAW, Gordon James. b 19. Worc Ord Coll 67. **d** 69 **p** 70. C Hillingdon St Jo *Lon* 69-72; C Brixham *Ex* 72-76; R Drewsteignton 76-79; V Hittisleigh 76-79; V Spreyton 76-79; C Aldershot St Mich *Guildf* 79-82; rtd 82; Perm to Offic *Ex* 83-89; Perm to Offic *Ab* from 83. *69 Maunsell Way, Wroughton, Swindon SN4 9JF* Tel (01793) 812948

LAW, Gordon Peter. b 35. Bernard Gilpin Soc Dur 59 Chich Th Coll 60. **d** 64 **p** 65. C Walthamstow St Barn and St Jas Gt *Chelmsf* 64-67; C Southchurch H Trin 67-68; C Plaistow St Andr 68-69; Chapl Aldersbrook Medical Unit 69-83; P-in-c Forest Gate All SS 69-74; V 74-83; V Romford St Jo from 83. *St John's Vicarage, Mawney Road, Romford RM7 7BH* Tel (01708) 742265

LAW, Herbert James Wentworth. b 12. Dur Univ BA39 DipTh39 MA42. **d** 40 **p** 41. C Monkwearmouth All SS *Dur* 40-43; P-in-c Felling 43-46; C-in-c Lobley Hill CD 46-49; V Lobley Hill 49-52; V Stoke Ferry w Wretton *Ely* 52-58; V Whittington 52-58; R Welney 58-69; V Barton 69-78; RD Barton 72-76; rtd 78; Perm to Offic *Ely* from 78. *37 Westlands, Comberton, Cambridge CB3 7EH* Tel (01223) 263406

LAW, Jeremy Thomson. b 61. Univ of Wales (Abth) BSc82 Southn Univ BTh89. Sarum & Wells Th Coll 84. **d** 87 **p** 88. C Wimborne Minster and Holt *Sarum* 87-90; C Highfield *Ox* 90-94; Chapl Ex Univ *Ex* from 94. *University of Exeter, Theology Department, Queens Building, Queens Drive, Exeter EX4 4QE* Tel (01392) 264240 or 435384 Fax 264377

LAW, Jim. b 20. Lon Coll of Div 49. **d** 52 **p** 53. C Altham w Clayton le Moors *Blackb* 52-55; C Bispham 55-56; V Over Darwen St Jas 56-61; V Gt Singleton 61-87; rtd 87; Perm to Offic *Blackb* from 87. *30 Cedar Avenue, Poulton-le-Fylde, Lancs FY6 8DQ* Tel (01253) 886188

LAW, John Francis. b 35. Bps' Coll Cheshunt 65. **d** 67 **p** 68. C Styvechale *Cov* 67-71; P-in-c Cov St Anne and All SS 71-73; TV Cov E 73-77; P-in-c Fillongley 77-82; P-in-c Corley 77-82; V Fillongley and Corley from 82; RD Nuneaton 90-95. *The Vicarage, Holbeche Crescent, Fillongley, Coventry CV7 8ES* Tel (01676) 40320

LAW, John Michael. b 43. Open Univ BA79. Westcott Ho Cam 65. **d** 68 **p** 69. C Chapel Allerton *Ripon* 68-72; C Ryhope *Dur* 72-73; Lic to Offic *Ely* from 74; Chapl Fulbourn Hosp Cam 74-94; Chapl Ida Darwin Hosp Cam 74-96; Mental Health Chapl Addenbrooke's NHS Trust Cam from 94; Mental Health Fell Bethlem R and Maudsley Hosps 82. *Fulbourn Hospital, Fulbourn, Cambridge CB1 5EF, or 1 The Maples, Fulbourn, Cambridge CB1 5DW* Tel (01223) 218598 or 218591

LAW, Kenneth. b 16. St Jo Coll Dur LTh39 BA40 MA43. St Aid Birkenhead 36. **d** 40 **p** 41. C Bootle St Matt *Liv* 40-41; C Blundellsands St Nic 41-43; C Keighley *Bradf* 43-47; V Allerton 47-50; V Horwich St Cath *Man* 50-54; V Ossett cum Gawthorpe *Wakef* 54-81; CF (TA - R of O) 48-64; CF (TA) 64-81; rtd 81; Perm to Offic *Wakef* from 81. *Heathdene, Cromwell Place, Ossett, W Yorkshire WF5 9LP* Tel (01924) 218992

LAW, Nicholas Charles. b 58. BA89. Trin Coll Bris 86. **d** 89 **p** 90. C Goldington *St Alb* 89-92; C Teignmouth, Ideford w Luton, Ashcombe etc *Ex* 92-97; R Bere Ferrers from 97. *The Rectory, Bere Alston, Yelverton, Devon PL20 7HH* Tel (01822) 840229

LAW, Peter James. b 46. Ridley Hall Cam 85. **d** 87 **p** 88. C Bournemouth St Jo w St Mich *Win* 87-91; V Chineham 91-96; V Luton Lewsey St Hugh *St Alb* from 96. *St Hugh's Vicarage, 367 Leagrave High Street, Luton LU4 0ND* Tel (01582) 605297

LAW, Peter Leslie. b 25. Bede Coll Dur BA48 DipEd49. Qu Coll Birm 53. **d** 55 **p** 56. C Tooting All SS *S'wark* 55-57; C Frome St Jo *B & W* 57-59; V Battersea St Mary-le-Park *S'wark* 59-65; R Brampton Ash w Dingley *Pet* 65-69; Chapl St Luke's Sch Southsea 69-79; Chapl Portsm Cathl *Portsm* 69-79; V Eastney 79-90; rtd 90; Perm to Offic *Portsm* from 90. *123 Hayling Avenue, Portsmouth PO3 6DY* Tel (01705) 619913

LAW, Robert Frederick. b 43. St Aid Birkenhead 67. **d** 69 **p** 70. C Bengeo *St Alb* 69-72; C Sandy 72-76; P-in-c St Ippolyts 76-81; Chapl Jersey Gp of Hosps 81-84; V Crowan w Godolphin *Truro* 84-92; RD Kerrier 90-91; R St Columb Major w St Wenn from 92. *The Rectory, St Columb, Cornwall TR9 6AE* Tel (01637) 880252

LAW, Dr Robert James. b 31. Lon Univ MB, BS55. Ridley Hall Cam 62. **d** 64 **p** 65. C Barnehurst *Roch* 64-66; C Edgware *Lon* 66-72; V Halwell w Moreleigh *Ex* 72-94; P-in-c Woodleigh and Loddiswell 76-79; R 79-94; rtd 96. *38 Wheatlands Road, Paignton, Devon TQ4 5HU* Tel (01803) 559450

LAW, Simon Anthony. b 55. Middx Univ BA93 DipHE79. Oak Hill Th Coll 94. **d** 96 **p** 97. NSM Forest Gate St Mark *Chelmsf* from 96. *236 Sebert Road, London E7 0NP* Tel 0181-257 9754 or 534 8500

LAW-JONES, Peter Deniston. b 55. Newc Univ BA77 Man Univ CertEd81 Nottm Univ BTh87. Linc Th Coll 84. **d** 87 **p** 88. C Chorley St Laur *Blackb* 87-91; V Feniscliffe 91-96; V St Annes from 96. *The Vicarage, St Thomas Road, Lytham St Annes, Lancs FY8 1JL* Tel (01253) 723750

LAWES, David Alan. b 33. Lon Bible Coll BD57 PGCE58 AcDipEd66 Lon Inst of Educn MA70. Cranmer Hall Dur 90. **d** 91 **p** 92. NSM Shaston *Sarum* 91-94; Hon C Diptford, N

Huish, Harberton and Harbertonford *Ex* from 94. *The Vicarage, Harberton, Totnes, Devon TQ9 7SA* Tel (01803) 867117

LAWES, Geoffrey Hyland. b 37. St Jo Coll Dur BA58 DipTh62 Hertf Coll Ox BA60 MA64 Newc Univ PGCE76 MEd79. Cranmer Hall Dur 61. **d** 63 **p** 64. C Millfield St Mark *Dur* 63-66; C Jarrow Grange 66-69; Hon C 69-86; Lic to Offic 86-90; V Collierley w Annfield Plain from 90. *Collierley Vicarage, Annfield Plain, Stanley, Co Durham DH9 8QS* Tel (01207) 236254

LAWES, Stephen George. b 40. Nottm Univ PGCE75. St Jo Coll Nottm BTh74. **d** 82 **p** 83. NSM Hillmorton *Cov* 82-86; Perm to Offic *Pet* 85-94. *Oak Tree Cottage, 34 Stowe Nine Churches, Northampton NN7 4SQ* Tel (01327) 40401

LAWES, Timothy Stanley. b 57. Nottm Univ BTh88. Linc Th Coll 85. **d** 88 **p** 89. C Wymondham *Nor* 88-92; R Felmingham, Skeyton, Colby, Banningham etc 92-96; Sweden from 96. *Timotejvagen 57, 93145 Skelleftea, Sweden*

LAWLESS, Mrs Patricia Elizabeth (Pat). b 36. Bris Univ BA58 PGCE59 Lon Univ DipSocSc77. S Dios Minl Tr Scheme 91. **d** 93 **p** 94. NSM Frome Ch Ch *B & W* 93-95; NSM Mells w Buckland Dinham, Elm, Whatley etc 96; NSM Frome St Jo and St Mary from 96; Chapl Victoria Hosp Frome from 96. *9 Sunnyside, Frome, Somerset BA11 1LD* Tel (01373) 463204

LAWLEY, Peter Gerald Fitch. b 52. Chich Th Coll 77. **d** 80 **p** 81. C Pet St Jo *Pet* 80-83; C Daventry 83-87; P-in-c Syresham w Whitfield 87-90; TV Cen Telford *Lich* from 90. *15 Carwood, Stirchley, Telford TF3 1VA* Tel (01952) 595482

LAWLOR, Colin Robert. b 63. Lanc Univ BA89 St Martin's Coll Lanc PGCE90. Chich Th Coll DMinlTh93. **d** 93 **p** 94. C Moulsecoomb *Chich* from 93. *Church House, Selham Drive, Brighton BN1 9EL* Tel (01273) 601854

LAWRANCE, David. b 26. Man Univ BA51 BD66 St Cath Soc Ox BA53 MA57. Wycliffe Hall Ox 51. **d** 53 **p** 54. C Oldham St Mary *Man* 53-55; Chapl RAF 55-58; Jordan 58-61; V Oldham Moorside *Man* 61-73; Ind Chapl *Sheff* 74-85; C Wetherby *Ripon* 85-91; Chapl HM Young Offender Inst Wetherby 89-93; rtd 91. *Kinver House, The Green, Kirklington, Bedale, N Yorkshire DL8 2NQ* Tel (01845) 567431

LAWRANCE, Hugh Norcliffe. b 49. N Riding Coll of Educn BEd79. Linc Th Coll 83. **d** 85 **p** 86. C Lindley *Wakef* 85-87; C Barkisland w W Scammonden 87-92; C Ripponden 87-92; V Knottingley from 92. *The Vicarage, Chapel Street, Knottingley, W Yorkshire WF11 9AN* Tel (01977) 672267

LAWRANCE, Robert William. b 63. Jes Coll Ox BA85 MA89. Ripon Coll Cuddesdon BA87. **d** 88 **p** 89. C Astley *Man* 88-91; Lect Bolton St Pet 91-94; V Bury St Jo w St Mark from 94. *St John's Vicarage, 270 Walmersley Road, Bury, Lancs BL9 6NH* Tel 0161-764 3412

LAWRENCE, Charles Anthony Edwin. b 53. AKC75. St Aug Coll Cant 75. **d** 76 **p** 77. C Mitcham St Mark *S'wark* 76-80; C Haslemere *Guildf* 80-82; P-in-c Ashton H Trin *Man* 82-84; V 84-93; AD Ashton-under-Lyne 91-97; V Saddleworth 93-97; V Effingham w Lt Bookham *Guildf* from 97. *High Limes, 4 Fiona Close, Bookham, Surrey KT23 3JU* Tel (01372) 458314

LAWRENCE, David Ian. b 48. AIMLS71 MIBiol76 Univ Coll Lon BSc74. Glouc Sch of Min 84 Sarum & Wells Th Coll 87. **d** 88 **p** 89. C Wotton St Mary *Glouc* 88-91; P-in-c Cheltenham St Mich 91-93; V from 93. *St Michael's Vicarage, Severn Road, Cheltenham, Glos GL52 5QA* Tel (01242) 222644

LAWRENCE, David John. b 53. Leeds Poly BEd77. Linc Th Coll. **d** 86 **p** 87. C Gt and Lt Coates w Bradley *Linc* 86-89; P-in-c Hemingby 89-91; R from 91. *The Rectory, Hemingby, Horncastle, Lincs LN9 9QF* Tel (01472) 354240

LAWRENCE, George Leslie. b 11. Bp Wilson Coll 38. **d** 41 **p** 42. C Hartlepool St Hilda *Dur* 41-46; C Darlington St Cuth 46-48; R Jarrow Grange 48-53; CF (TA) 49-64; V Bradley *Wakef* 53-60; V Newsome 60-69; R Crofton 69-78; rtd 79; Perm to Offic *Wakef* from 79. *702 Doncaster Road, Crofton, Wakefield, W Yorkshire WF4 1PX* Tel (01924) 862174

LAWRENCE, Canon Harold. b 12. Univ Coll Dur LTh35 BA36. St Aug Coll Cant 31. **d** 36 **p** 37. C Gt Stanmore *Lon* 36-38; S Africa from 39; Adn Durban 61-74; Hon Can Natal from 74. *7 Chapter Close, Pietermaritzburg, 3201 South Africa* Tel Pietermaritzburg (331) 945686

LAWRENCE, Miss Helen. b 30. St Mich Ho Ox 62. **dss** 74 **d** 87 **p** 94. Braintree *Chelmsf* 74-87; Par Dn 87-90; rtd 90; Perm to Offic *Chelmsf* from 90. *6 Reynards Close, Kirby Cross, Frinton-on-Sea, Essex CO13 0RA* Tel (01255) 673837

LAWRENCE, Miss Ida Eugenia Laura. b 14. Open Univ BA81. Gilmore Ho 45. **dss** 78 **d** 87 **p** 94. Rayleigh *Chelmsf* 78-87; NSM from 87. *Dilkusha, Hardwick Close, Rayleigh, Essex SS6 7QP* Tel (01268) 773059

LAWRENCE, James Conrad. b 62. St Jo Coll Dur BA85. Ridley Hall Cam 85. **d** 87 **p** 88. Min Bar Hill LEP *Ely* 87-93; Deanery Adv in Evang 90-93; CPAS Evang from 93; Perm to Offic *Cov* from 93. *236 Cubbington Road, Leamington Spa, Warks CV32 7AY* Tel (01926) 316368 or 334242 Fax 337613

LAWRENCE, Mrs Janet Maureen. b 43. Hockerill Teacher Tr Coll TCert64. Ox Min Course CBTS92. **d** 92 **p** 94. Hon Par Dn Bletchley *Ox* 92-94; NSM N Bletchley CD from 94. *20 The Elms, Bletchley, Milton Keynes MK3 6DB* Tel (01908) 377660

LAWRENCE, John Graham Clive. b 47. ACIB. Trin Coll Bris DipTh78. **d** 78 **p** 79. C Chatham St Phil and St Jas *Roch* 78-83; V Roch St Justus from 83; Asst Chapl HM Pris Roch from 83. *St Justus's Vicarage, 1 Binnacle Road, Rochester, Kent ME1 2XR* Tel (01634) 841183

LAWRENCE, John Shaw. b 27. WMMTC. **d** 81. NSM Birm St Martin *Birm* 81-85; Chapl Coun for Soc Aid 84-89; NSM Birm St Martin w Bordesley St Andr 85-89; rtd 89. *208 Hay Green Lane, Birmingham B30 1SG* Tel 0121-451 3425

LAWRENCE, Canon Leonard Roy. b 31. Keble Coll Ox BA56 MA59. Westcott Ho Cam 56. **d** 58 **p** 59. C Stockport St Geo *Ches* 58-62; V Thelwall 62-68; V Hyde St Geo 68-75; V Prenton 75-96; Hon Can Ches Cathl 86-96; rtd 96. *39 Mockbeggar Drive, Wallasey, Merseyside L45 3NN*

LAWRENCE, Leslie. b 44. Lon Univ DipRS84. S'wark Ord Course 86. **d** 88 **p** 89. NSM Stanwell *Lon* 88-92; C Hounslow H Trin w St Paul 92-97; P-in-c Norwood St Mary from 97. *The Rectory, 26 Tentelow Lane, Norwood Green, Southall, Middx UB2 4LE* Tel 0181-574 1362

LAWRENCE, Martin Kenneth Borrom. b 59. Univ Coll Dur BA82. St Steph Ho Ox 94. **d** 96 **p** 97. C Wanstead St Mary w Ch Ch *Chelmsf* from 96. *13 Wanstead Place, London E11 2SW* Tel 0181-530 4970

LAWRENCE, Norman. b 45. Lon Univ BEd75. S'wark Ord Course 77. **d** 80 **p** 81. NSM Hounslow H Trin *Lon* 80-88; NSM Hounslow H Trin w St Paul from 88. *89 Bulstrode Avenue, Hounslow TW3 3AN* Tel 0181-572 6292

LAWRENCE, The Ven Patrick Henry Andrew. b 51. TCD BA81. CITC 76. **d** 81 **p** 82. C Templemore *D & R* 81-84; C Kilkenny St Canice Cathl *C & O* 84-85; I Templebreedy w Tracton and Nohoval *C, C & R* 85-92; I Geashill w Killeigh and Ballycommon *M & K* from 92; Can Kildare Cathl from 92; Adn Kildare from 93; Adn Meath from 97; Warden of Readers from 97. *The Rectory, Geashill, Co Offaly, Irish Republic* Tel Tullamore (506) 43879 Fax as telephone

LAWRENCE, Canon Peter Anthony. b 36. Lich Th Coll 67. **d** 69 **p** 70. C Oadby *Leic* 69-74; P-in-c Northmarston and Granborough *Ox* 74-81; P-in-c Hardwick St Mary 74-81; P-in-c Quainton 76-81; P-in-c Oving w Pitchcott 76-81; TR Schorne 81-91; RD Claydon 84-88; V Ivinghoe w Pitstone and Slapton from 91; Hon Can Ch Ch from 97. *The Vicarage, Station Road, Ivinghoe, Leighton Buzzard, Beds LU7 9EB* Tel (01296) 668260

LAWRENCE, Peter Halliday. b 47. ALCM K Alfred's Coll Win CertEd69 Nottm Univ BTh76. St Jo Coll Nottm 72. **d** 76 **p** 77. C Birm St Luke *Birm* 76-79; V Burney Lane 79-93; TV Canford Magna *Sarum* 93-95; TR from 95. *The Vicarage, 359 Sopwith Crescent, Wimborne, Dorset BH21 1XQ* Tel (01202) 886320

LAWRENCE, Ralph Guy. b 55. Trin Coll Bris DipHE89. **d** 89 **p** 90. C Cotmanhay *Derby* 89-93; P-in-c Tansley, Dethick, Lea and Holloway from 93. *Lea Vicarage, Matlock, Derbyshire DE4 5JP* Tel (01629) 534275

LAWRENCE, Timothy Hervey. b 25. Ripon Hall Ox 58. **d** 60 **p** 61. C Newmarket All SS *St E* 60-62; V Kentford w Higham Green 62-84; P-in-c Herringswell 78-84; rtd 84. *13 South Street, Risby, Bury St Edmunds, Suffolk IP28 6QU* Tel (01284) 810083

LAWRENCE, Victor John. b 43. ACII. Oak Hill Th Coll. **d** 83 **p** 84. C Paddock Wood *Roch* 83-87; R Milton next Gravesend w Denton from 87. *The Rectory, Church Walk, Milton, Gravesend, Kent DA12 2QU* Tel (01474) 533434

LAWRENCE-MARCH, David Lawrence. b 61. Univ of Wales (Lamp) BA83. Coll of Resurr Mirfield 83. **d** 85 **p** 86. C Pet St Jude *Pet* 85-89; Chapl St Aug Sch Kilburn 89-92; C Kilburn St Aug w St Jo *Lon* 89-90; C Paddington St Mary 90-92; Chapl Bearwood Coll Wokingham 92-96; R Holt w High Kelling *Nor* from 96. *The Rectory, Church Street, Holt, Norfolk NR25 6BB* Tel (01263) 712048 Fax 711397

LAWRENSON, James Percival. b 12. Kelham Th Coll 30. **d** 36 **p** 37. C Atherton *Man* 36-39; Chapl Toc H (E Yorks) 39-40; C Portland All SS w St Pet *Sarum* 40-42; Acting Chapl HM Borstal Inst Portland 40-42; Chapl 42-45; Chapl HM Borstal Inst Roch 45-50; Asst Sec Lon Police Court Miss 50-56; Hon C Wandsworth St Anne *S'wark* 50-52; Public Preacher 52-56; Chapl Berkhamsted Colleg Sch Herts 56-78; rtd 78; Perm to Offic *St Alb* from 78; Perm to Offic *Ox* 87-90. *Downside, Torrington Road, Berkhamsted, Herts HP4 3DD* Tel (01442) 865999

LAWRENSON, Michael. b 35. Leeds Univ BA60 Liv Univ CSocStuds65 Newc Univ DASS69. Coll of Resurr Mirfield 60. **d** 74 **p** 74. NSM Glenrothes *St And* 74-90; Dioc Supernumerary from 90; Chapl HM Pris Perth from 91. *Hollyburn, West Port, Falkland, Cupar, Fife KY7 7BW* Tel (01337) 857311 E-mail 100522.3005@compuserve.com

LAWRENSON, Ronald David. b 41. CITC 68. **d** 71 **p** 72. C Seapatrick *D & D* 71-78; Min Can Down Cathl 78-79; V Choral Belf Cathl 79-86; Bp's C Tynan w Middletown *Arm* 86-93; Hon V Choral Arm Cathl from 87; I Arm St Mark w Aghavilly 92-93; I Donaghmore w Upper Donaghmore from 93; RD Aghaloo from 94. *St Michael's Rectory, 66 Main Street, Castlecaulfield, Dungannon, Co Tyrone BT70 3NP* Tel (01868) 761214

LAWREY, Leslie John. b 18. Em Coll Cam MA45 Lon Univ CertEd65 DipSocWork69. Ridley Hall Cam 45. **d** 47 **p** 48. C Southport Ch Ch *Liv* 47-50; C Morden *S'wark* 50-53; Hon C Beckenham Ch Ch *Roch* 53-63; Travelling Sec Inter-Sch Chr Fellowship 53-63; Perm to Offic *Win* 60-68; Perm to Offic *Sarum* 67-70; Perm to Offic *Ex* 70-73; NSM Tredington and Darlingscott w Newbold on Stour *Cov* 73-82; Warden Shaftesbury Soc from 83; rtd 93. *c/o P A Toombs Esq, High Pavement, Trent, Sherborne, Dorset DT9 4SW* Tel (01935) 851341

LAWRIE, Paul Edward. b 12. Freiburg Univ LLD35 St Cath Soc Ox BA48 MA53. Wycliffe Hall Ox 46. **d** 48 **p** 49. C Walkley *Sheff* 48-51; C Thrybergh 51-54; V Drax 54-64; R Todwick 64-78; rtd 78; Chapl Rotherham Distr Gen Hosp 78-85; Hon C Handsworth Woodhouse *Sheff* 85-88; Hon C Aston cum Aughton w Swallownest, Todwick etc 88-92; Perm to Offic from 92. *15 Haddon Way, Aston, Sheffield S26 2EH* Tel 0114-287 4864

LAWRIE, Peter Sinclair. b 39. Clifton Th Coll 62. **d** 65 **p** 66. C Derby St Chad *Derby* 65-68; C Toxteth Park St Philemon w St Silas *Liv* 68-71; V Ramsey St Mary's w Ponds Bridge *Ely* 71-81; V Whitwick St Jo the Bapt *Leic* 81-96; P-in-c Felixstowe SS Pet and Paul *St E* from 96. *The Vicarage, 14 Picketts Road, Felixstowe, Suffolk IP11 7JT* Tel (01394) 284135

LAWRY, Mrs Fianach Alice Moir. b 35. St And Dioc Tr Course 85. **d** 88 **p** 94. NSM Dollar *St And* from 88; Chapl HM Pris Glenochil from 91. *Sunnybank, Muckhart, Dollar, Clackmannanshire FK14 7JN* Tel (01259) 781426

LAWRY, Samuel John Lockhart. b 11. CCC Cam BA33 MA38. Wells Th Coll 34. **d** 35 **p** 36. C Abington *Pet* 35-40; Chapl RNVR 40-47; C Portsea St Mary *Portsm* 47-48; V Portsea St Cuth 48-57; V E Meon 57-68; Perm to Offic from 68; rtd 76. *Broadlands House, Petersfield, Hants GU31 4BA* Tel (01730) 262134

LAWS, Clive Loudon. b 54. UEA BEd76 Leeds Univ CertEd75. Wycliffe Hall Ox 79. **d** 82 **p** 83. C Newcastle w Butterton *Lich* 82-85; C Gabalfa *Llan* 85-88; R Pendine w Llanmiloe and Eglwys Gymyn w Marros *St D* 89-94; CF 89-94; Perm to Offic *B & W* 95-96; C Portishead from 96. *24 St Mary's Park Road, Portishead, Bristol BS20 8QL* Tel (01275) 848934

LAWS, Edwin Kingsley. b 06. LVO53 KPM39. Bps' Coll Cheshunt 56. **d** 57 **p** 58. C Shaftesbury H Trin w St Pet *Sarum* 57-60; R Winterborne Whitechurch w Clenston 60-72; R Milton Abbas w Winterborne Whitechurch etc 72-74; RD Milton 66-73; Custos St Jo Hosp Heytesbury 74-79; rtd 79; Perm to Offic *B & W* from 79. *9 Stoberry Crescent, Wells, Somerset BA5 2TG* Tel (01749) 673544

LAWSON, Preb Clifford John. b 21. St Cath Soc Ox BA45 MA47. Qu Coll Birm 45. **d** 47 **p** 48. C Gt Barr *Lich* 47-50; C Hednesford 50-52; V Shrewsbury St Mich 52-57; V Eccleshall 57-71; Chapl HM Pris Drake Hall 58-71; RD Eccleshall *Lich* 65-71; Preb Lich Cathl 70-86; R Stafford St Mary 72-74; P-in-c Stafford St Chad 72-74; RD Stafford 72-77; R Stafford St Mary and St Chad 74-77; RD Oswestry 77-82; R Rhydycroesau 77-86; R Selattyn 77-86; rtd 86; Perm to Offic *Lich* from 86; Perm to Offic *Heref* from 90. *The Burwains, 22 Port Hill Drive, Shrewsbury SY3 8RS* Tel (01743) 354085

LAWSON, David McKenzie. b 47. Glas Univ MA69 Edin Univ BD76. Edin Th Coll 73. **d** 76 **p** 77. C Glas St Mary *Glas* 76-82; V Keighley All SS *Bradf* 82-85; Chapl Asst Univ Coll Hosp Lon 85-91; Hon C St Pancras w St Jas and Ch Ch *Lon* 86-91; R Smithfield St Bart Gt 91-93. *All Saints' House, 82 Margaret Street, London W1N 8LA* Tel 0171-636 2898

LAWSON, David William. b 50. ACA DipHE. Linc Th Coll. **d** 82 **p** 83. C Stafford *Lich* 82-85; TV Redruth w Lanner *Truro* 85-87; Chapl Whitley Hosp Cov 87-94; Chapl Gulson Road Hosp Cov 87-94; Chapl Cov and Warks Hosp 87-94; P-in-c Whitley *Cov* 87-93; V S Leamington St Jo from 93. *St John's Vicarage, Tachbrook Street, Leamington Spa, Warks CV31 3BN* Tel (01926) 422208

LAWSON, Canon Frederick Quinney. b 45. Leic Univ BA. St Steph Ho Ox. **d** 83 **p** 84. Hon C Loughborough Em *Leic* 83-86; NSM Somerby, Burrough on the Hill and Pickwell 86-87; NSM Burrough Hill Pars 87; USA from 87; Hon Can Salt Lake City from 87; Perm to Offic *Leic* 88. *4294 Adonis Drive, Salt Lake City, Utah 84124, USA* Tel Salt Lake City (801) 277-9623 Fax 278-5903

LAWSON, Gary Austin. b 53. Man Univ BA80. Ripon Coll Cuddesdon 80. **d** 82 **p** 83. C Nunhead St Antony *S'wark* 82-86; Hon C Reddish *Man* 86-87; Hon C Longsight St Jo w St Cypr 87-88; V Wythenshawe St Rich from 88. *St Richard's Vicarage, 42 Lomond Road, Manchester M22 5JD* Tel 0161-499 2022

LAWSON, John Alexander. b 62. Sheff Univ BA84. St Jo Coll Nottm DPS87. **d** 87 **p** 88. C Wellington, All SS w Eyton *Lich* 87-92; TV Dewsbury *Wakef* from 92. *St John's Vicarage, 68 Staincliffe Road, Dewsbury, W Yorkshire WF13 4EF* Tel (01924) 463131

LAWSON, Jonathan Halford (Jon). b 68. St Chad's Coll Dur BA90. Westcott Ho Cam CTM93. **d** 93 **p** 94. C Sedgefield *Dur* 93-96; C Usworth 96-97; TV from 97. *St Michael's Vicarage, 14 Prestwick Close, Washington, Tyne & Wear NE37 2LP* Tel 0191-416 1895

LAWSON, Matthew James. b 67. St Andr Univ MTh91 Ox Univ. Ripon Coll Cuddesdon 92. **d** 94 **p** 95. C Bedford St Andr *St Alb* 94-97; Chapl St Jo Sch Leatherhead from 97. *The Chaplain's House, 4 Linden Pit Path, Leatherhead, Surrey KT22 7JD* Tel (01372) 361665 Mobile 0468-515950 E-mail frlawson@aol.com

LAWSON, Michael Charles. b 52. Sussex Univ BA75. Trin Coll Bris 75. **d** 78 **p** 79. C Horsham *Chich* 78-81; C St Marylebone All So w SS Pet and Jo *Lon* 81-87; V Bromley Ch Ch *Roch* from 87. *Christ Church Vicarage, 18 Highland Road, Bromley BR1 4AD* Tel 0181-313 9882 or 464 1898 Fax 464 5846

LAWSON-TANCRED, Christopher. b 24. Trin Coll Cam BA49 MA65. Chich Th Coll 63. **d** 65 **p** 66. C Uckfield *Chich* 65-70; R Wrington *B & W* 70-73; R Wrington w Butcombe 73-79; Perm to Offic *Chich* 80-92; Hon C Battersea St Luke *S'wark* 83-89; rtd 89. *Flat 3, Minterne House, Dorchester, Dorset DT2 7AX* Tel (01300) 341328

LAXON, Colin John. b 44. Cant Sch of Min 86. **d** 89 **p** 90. C Folkestone St Mary and St Eanswythe *Cant* 89-94; P-in-c Barrow St Jas *Carl* from 94. *St James's Vicarage, 150 Abbey Road, Barrow-in-Furness, Cumbria LA14 5AB* Tel (01229) 821475

LAY, Brian Robert. b 37. Bernard Gilpin Soc Dur 59 Chich Th Coll 60. **d** 63 **p** 64. C Battyeford *Wakef* 63-66; C Belhus Park *Chelmsf* 66-73; P-in-c Sutton on Plym *Ex* 73-80; V from 80. *St John's Vicarage, 3 Alma Street, Cattedown, Plymouth PL4 0NL* Tel (01752) 664191

LAY, Geoffrey Arthur. b 54. Leic Poly BA77 Man Univ MA83 Lon Univ BD88. Ridley Hall Cam CTM92. **d** 92 **p** 93. C St Neots *Ely* 92-95; P-in-c Long Stanton w St Mich from 95; P-in-c Dry Drayton 95-97. *The Chalet, St Michael's Road, Longstanton, Cambridge CB4 5BZ* Tel (01954) 782580

LAYBOURNE, Michael Frederick. b 37. Qu Coll Birm 81. **d** 83 **p** 84. C High Elswick St Phil *Newc* 83-85; C High Elswick St Phil and Newc St Aug 86; C Cramlington 86-87; TV 87-95; C Killingworth from 95. *27 Mount Close, Killingworth, Newcastle upon Tyne NE12 0GE* Tel 0191-268 8788

LAYCOCK, Charles. b 37. Open Univ BA88. N Ord Course. **d** 83 **p** 84. C Astley Bridge *Man* 83-86; R Crumpsall 86-94; V Ashton Ch Ch from 94. *The Vicarage, Vicarage Road, Ashton-under-Lyne, Lancs OL7 9QY* Tel 0161-330 1601

LAYCOCK, Lawrence. b 42. HNC. St Deiniol's Hawarden 86. **d** 89 **p** 90. C Blackpool St Mich *Blackb* 89-94; P-in-c Worsthorne from 94; P-in-c Holme-in-Cliviger from 96. *The Vicarage, Gorple Road, Worsthorne, Burnley, Lancs BB10 3NN* Tel (01282) 428478

LAYTON, Miss Norene. b 39. Trin Coll Bris DipHE86. **dss** 86 **d** 87 **p** 94. Lindfield *Chich* 86-87; Par Dn 87-92; Par Dn Loughborough Em *Leic* 92-94; C Loughborough Em and St Mary in Charnwood 94-96; V Hengrove *Bris* from 96. *Christ Church Vicarage, 7 Petherton Road, Bristol BS14 9BP* Tel (01275) 832346

LAZONBY, Canon Alan Frederick. b 19. TD64. St Jo Coll Dur BA40 DipTh41 MA43. **d** 42 **p** 43. C Auckland St Helen *Dur* 42-46; C Horden 46-50; CF (TA) 49-67; CF (TAVR) 67-77; V Witton Park *Dur* 50-57; Bp's Dom Chapl 53-57; R Haughton le Skerne 57-84; RD Darlington 74-78; Hon Can Dur Cathl from 75; rtd 84. *16 Loraine Crescent, Darlington, Co Durham DL1 5TF* Tel (01325) 485876

LE CRAS, Allan. b 20. Linc Th Coll 83. **d** 84 **p** 85. Hon C Toynton All Saints w Toynton St Peter *Linc* 84-88; Hon C Marden Hill Gp 88-90; Perm to Offic from 90. *Snipe Dales Cottage, Lusby, Spilsby, Lincs PE23 4JB* Tel (01507) 588636

LE DIEU, Miss Heather Muriel. b 41. Birm Univ BA62 MA67 DipTh. St Jo Coll Dur 77. **dss** 79 **d** 87. Birchfield *Birm* 79-82; Kings Heath 82-84; Walsall Pleck and Bescot *Lich* 84-88; Par Dn 87-88; rtd 88. *159 Swarthmore Road, Selly Oak, Birmingham B29 4NW*

LE FEUVRE, Henry Mauger. b 21. Lich Th Coll. **d** 62 **p** 63. C Cheam *S'wark* 62-65; C Dulwich St Barn 65-69; P-in-c Dorrington *Heref* 69-72; P-in-c Stapleton 69-72; P-in-c Cardington 69-72; R Jersey St Lawr *Win* 72-80; R Risby w Gt and Lt Saxham and Westley *St E* 80-85; rtd 85; Perm to Offic *St E* from 85. *18 Southgate Street, Bury St Edmunds, Suffolk IP33 2AF* Tel (01284) 703524

LE GRICE, Elizabeth Margaret. b 53. Man Univ BA75 MA(Theol)78. Nor Bapt Coll 75 Westcott Ho Cam 87. **d** 88 **p** 97. In Bapt Ch 78-82; C Whitchurch *Llan* 88-95; Chapl Among the Deaf SE Wales *Mon* from 95. *9 Hawarden Road, Newport NP9 8JP*

LE GRYS, Alan Arthur. b 51. K Coll Lon BD73 AKC73 MTh90. St Aug Coll Cant 73. **d** 74 **p** 75. C Harpenden St Jo *St Alb* 74-77; C Hampstead St Jo *Lon* 77-81; Chapl Westf Coll and Bedf Coll 81-84; V Stoneleigh *Guildf* 84-91; Lect Ripon Coll Cuddesdon 91-96; Prin SEITE from 96; Lic to Offic *S'wark* from 96. *South East Institute for Theological Education, Deanery Gate, The Precinct, Rochester, Kent ME1 1SJ* Tel (01634) 832299

LE PAGE, Canon Dallas Arthur des Reaux. b 17. Keble Coll Ox BA49 MA53. Cuddesdon Coll 49. **d** 51 **p** 52. C Mill Hill Jo Keble Ch *Lon* 51-53; C Hampstead St Steph 53-58; S Africa from 58; rtd 86. *24 Maynard Street Gardens, Cape Town, 8001 South Africa* Tel Cape Town (21) 452221

LE PREVOST, Carl Andrew. b 63. Sarum & Wells Th Coll 85. **d** 88 **p** 89. C Chandler's Ford *Win* 88-91; C Southampton Maybush St Pet 91; Asst Chapl Bryanston Sch Dorset 91-93; R Burghclere w Newtown and Ecchinswell w Sydmonton *Win* from 93. *The Rectory, Well Street, Burghclere, Newbury, Berks RG15 9HS* Tel (01635) 278470

LE ROSSIGNOL, Richard Lewis. b 52. Aston Univ BSc75. Oak Hill Th Coll BA79. **d** 79 **p** 80. C E Ham St Paul *Chelmsf* 79-81; C Willesborough w Hinxhill *Cant* 81-85; Perm to Offic 85-94; Hon C Brabourne w Smeeth from 94. *64 Osborne Road, Willesborough, Ashford, Kent TN24 0EF* Tel (01233) 625193

LE SAUX, Pierre Marie. b 13. Lon Univ BA56 MA57 PGCE57. **d** 36 **p** 37. In RC Ch 36-47; St Mich Coll Llan 49-50; C Roath St Sav *Llan* 49-51; C Milford Haven *St D* 51-52; C Cardiff St Mary *Llan* 52-53; Coll of Resurr Mirfield 53-55; P-in-c Bryn *Llan* 59-66; Switzerland 66-90; Chapl Montreux w Gstaad *Eur* 79-87; rtd 87; Perm to Offic *Eur* from 87. *rue du Guic 15, Belle-Isle-en-Terre, F-22810 France* Tel France (33) 96 43 00 38

LE SUEUR, Paul John. b 38. Lon Univ BSc59. Wycliffe Hall Ox 60. **d** 62 **p** 63. C Mortlake w E Sheen *S'wark* 62-65; C Witney *Ox* 65-69; R Sarsden w Churchill 69-74; P-in-c Clifton Hampden 74-77; P-in-c Rotherfield Greys H Trin 77-82; V 82-90; V Blacklands Hastings Ch Ch and St Andr *Chich* from 90. *Christ Church Vicarage, 28 Laton Road, Hastings, E Sussex TN34 2ES* Tel (01424) 421821

LE VASSEUR, Mrs Linda Susan. b 48. Shenstone Coll of Educn CertEd70. S Dios Minl Tr Scheme 92. **d** 95 **p** 96. NSM Guernsey Ste Marie du Castel *Win* from 95; NSM Guernsey St Matt from 95. *Coin des Arquets, Les Arquets, St Pierre du Bois, Guernsey GY7 9HE* Tel (01481) 64047

LE VAY, Dr Clare Forbes Agard Bramhall Joanna. b 41. St Anne's Coll Ox BA64 MA66 Univ of Wales (Abth) MSc72 PhD86. Westcott Ho Cam 86. **d** 88 **p** 94. C Stamford Hill St Thos *Lon* 88-89; C Hackney 89-92; Asst Chapl Brook Gen Hosp Lon 92-95; Asst Chapl Greenwich Distr Hosp Lon 92-95; Chapl Greenwich Healthcare NHS Trust from 95. *Greenwich District Hospital, Vanbrugh Hill, London SE10 9HE* Tel 0181-858 8141 Fax 312 6248

LEA, His Honour Christopher Gerald. b 17. MC. RMC Called to the Bar (Inner Temple) 48. Ox Min Course 91. **d** 92 **p** 93. NSM Stratfield Mortimer *Ox* from 92. *Simms Farm House, Simms Lane, Mortimer, Reading RG7 2JP* Tel (0118) 933 2360

LEA, Canon Montague Brian. b 34. St Jo Coll Cam BA55 Lon Univ BD71. St Jo Coll Nottm 68. **d** 71 **p** 72. C Northwood Em *Lon* 71-74; Chapl Barcelona *Eur* 74-79; V Hove Bp Hannington Memorial Ch *Chich* 79-86; Adn N France *Eur* 86-94; Chapl Paris St Mich 86-94; Hon Can Gib Cathl from 95; R Chiddingly w E Hoathly *Chich* 94-96; Chapl The Hague *Eur* from 96. *Riouwstraat 2, 2585 HA The Hague, The Netherlands* Tel The Hague (70) 355-5359

LEA, Norman. b 42. Univ of Wales (Lamp) BA67. Coll of Resurr Mirfield 66. **d** 68 **p** 69. C Newton St Pet *S & B* 68-71; C Oystermouth 71-73; C Brecon w Battle 73-74; TV Cwmbran *Mon* 74-77; V Talgarth and Llanelieu *S & B* 77-84; V Port Talbot St Theodore *Llan* 84-95; Hon Chapl Miss to Seamen from 84; V Cadoxton-juxta-Neath *Llan* from 95. *The Vicarage, Cadoxton, Neath SA10 8AS* Tel (01639) 644625

LEA, Canon Richard John Rutland. b 40. Trin Hall Cam BA63 MA67. Westcott Ho Cam 63. **d** 65 **p** 66. C Edenbridge *Roch* 65-68; C Hayes 68-71; V Larkfield 71-86; P-in-c Leybourne 76-86; RD Malling 79-84; V Chatham St Steph 86-88; Can Res and Prec Roch Cathl from 88. *2 Kings Orchard, The Precinct, Rochester, Kent ME1 1TG* Tel (01634) 841491

LEACH, Alan William Brickett. b 28. CEng FIStructE FASI FICE MSc. S'wark Ord Course. **d** 89 **p** 90. NSM Forest Row *Chich* from 89. *Hathaway, Ashdown Road, Forest Row, E Sussex RH18 5BN* Tel (01342) 823778

LEACH, Miss Bethia Morag (Beth). b 62. Sheff Univ BA84 Liv Inst of Educn PGCE85. Ripon Coll Cuddesdon 95. **d** 97. C Stafford *Lich* from 97. *9 Brunswick Terrace, Staffs ST16 1BB* Tel (01785) 243995

LEACH, Gerald. b 27. Sarum & Wells Th Coll 85. **d** 73 **p** 74. NSM Cyncoed *Mon* 73-86; C 86-87; V Dingestow and Llangovan w Penyclawdd etc 87-94; rtd 94; Perm to Offic *Heref* from 95. *19 Grange Park, Whitchurch, Ross-on-Wye, Herefordshire HR9 6EA* Tel (01600) 890397

LEACH, John. b 52. K Coll Lon BD79 AKC79 St Jo Coll Dur MA. **d** 81 **p** 82. C N Walsham w Antingham *Nor* 81-85; C Crookes St Thos *Sheff* 85-89; V Styvechale *Cov* from 89. *The Vicarage, 16 Armorial Road, Coventry CV3 6GJ* Tel (01203) 692299

LEACH, Robert Neville. b 54. Trin Coll Bris DipHE93. **d** 93 **p** 94. C Towcester w Easton Neston *Pet* 93-96; P-in-c Cowley *Lon* from 96. *The Rectory, Church Road, Uxbridge, Middx UB8 3NB* Tel (01895) 232728

LEACH, Stephen Lance. b 42. St Steph Ho Ox 66. **d** 69 **p** 70. C Higham Ferrers w Chelveston *Pet* 69-72; TV Ilfracombe H Trin *Ex* 72-74; V Barnstaple St Mary 74-77; R Goodleigh 74-77; P-in-c Barnstaple St Pet w H Trin 76-77; P-in-c Landkey 77-79; TR Barnstaple and Goodleigh 77-79; TR Barnstaple, Goodleigh and Landkey 79-82; V Paignton St Jo 82-95; Gen Sec ACS from 95; Public Preacher *Birm* from 95. *Gordon Browning House, 8 Spitfire Road, Birmingham B24 9PB* Tel 0121-382 5533 or 354 9885 Fax 382 6999

LEACH, Stephen Windsor. b 47. St Chad's Coll Dur BSc70 Linacre Coll Ox BA72 MA76. Ripon Hall Ox 70. **d** 73 **p** 74. C Swinton St Pet *Man* 73-77; C Oldham St Chad Limeside 77-79; V Shaw 79-87; V St Just in Penwith *Truro* from 87; V Sancreed from 87. *The Vicarage, St Just, Penzance, Cornwall TR19 7UB* Tel (01736) 788672

LEACH, Timothy Edmund (Tim). b 41. Dur Univ BA63. Ridley Hall Cam 63. **d** 65 **p** 66. C Ecclesfield *Sheff* 65-68; C Stocksbridge 68-71; C-in-c W Bessacarr CD 71-80; V Goole 80-95; Hon Chapl Miss to Seamen 80-95; V Wath-upon-Dearne *Sheff* from 95. *The Vicarage, Church Street, Wath-upon-Dearne, Rotherham, S Yorkshire S63 7RD* Tel (01709) 872299

LEADBEATER, Canon Nicolas James. b 20. Univ of Wales BA43. St Steph Ho Ox 43. **d** 45 **p** 46. C Abergavenny H Trin *Mon* 45-47; C Coleford w Staunton *Glouc* 47-55; PC Moreton Valence and V Whitminster 55-67; V Westcote 67-72; P-in-c Icomb 67-72; V Westcote w Icomb 72-79; V Westcote w Icomb and Bledington 79-88; Hon Can Glouc Cathl 83-88; rtd 88; Perm to Offic *Glouc* from 88. *39 Park Farm, Bourton-on-the-Water, Cheltenham, Glos GL54 2HF* Tel (01451) 810192

LEADER, Miss Janette Patricia. b 46. Cam Coll of Art and Tech DipHCM66. EAMTC CertHE97. **d** 97. C Desborough *Pet* from 97. *St Giles House, 5 Cromwell Close, Desborough, Kettering, Northants NN14 2PJ* Tel (01536) 761809

LEAH, William Albert. b 34. K Coll Lon BA56 AKC57 K Coll Cam MA63. Ripon Hall Ox 60. **d** 62 **p** 63. C Falmouth K Chas *Truro* 62-63; Chapl K Coll Cam 63-67; Min Can Westmr Abbey 67-74; V Hawkhurst *Cant* 74-83; Hon Min Can Cant Cathl 78-83; V St Ives *Truro* 83-94. *Trerice Cottage, Sancreed Newbridge, Penzance, Cornwall TR20 8QR* Tel (01736) 810987

LEAHY, David Adrian. b 56. Open Univ BA90. Qu Coll Birm. **d** 85 **p** 86. C Tile Cross *Birm* 85-88; C Warley Woods 88-91; V Hobs Moat from 91. *St Mary's House, 30 Hobs Meadow, Solihull, W Midlands B92 8PN* Tel 0121-743 4955

LEAK, Adrian Scudamore. b 38. Ch Ch Ox BA60 MA65 BD89. Cuddesdon Coll 64. **d** 66 **p** 67. C Cov St Mark *Cov* 66-69; C Dorchester *Ox* 69-73; V Badsey *Worc* 73-80; V Wickhamford 73-80; P-in-c Monkwearmouth St Pet *Dur* 80-81; V Choral and Archivist York Minster *York* 81-86; Can Res and Prec Guildf Cathl *Guildf* 86-90; Hon C Guildf H Trin w St Mary from 96. *8 King's Road, Guildford, Surrey GU1 4JW* Tel (01483) 579669

LEAK, Harry Duncan. b 30. St Cath Coll Cam BA53 MA57. Ely Th Coll 53. **d** 54 **p** 55. S Africa 54-57; Portuguese E Africa 57-61; C Eccleshall *Lich* 62-64; V Normacot 64-66; C Stoke upon Trent 66-68; V Hanley All SS 68-71; R Swynnerton 71-80; Perm to Offic from 80; rtd 92. *15 Sutherland Road, Tittensor, Stoke-on-Trent ST12 9JQ*

LEAK, John Michael. b 42. St Jo Coll Nottm. **d** 84 **p** 85. NSM Beeston *Ripon* 84-87; C Far Headingley St Chad 87-88; Hon C 88-90; C Headingley 90-95; TV Bramley from 95. *St Margaret's Vicarage, Newlay Lane, Bramley, Leeds LS13 2AJ* Tel 0113-257 4811

✠LEAKE, The Rt Revd David. b 35. ALCD59. **d** 59 **p** 60 **c** 69. C Watford *St Alb* 59-61; Lect 61-63; SAMS from 63; Argentina 63-69; Asst Bp Paraguay 69-73; Asst Bp N Argentina 69-80; Bp 80-90; Bp Argentina from 90. *Iglesia Anglicana, Casilla 4293, Correo Central, 100 Buenos Aires, Argentina* Tel Buenos Aires (1) 344618

LEAKE, Duncan Burton. b 49. Leeds Univ BA71 Leeds and Carnegie Coll PGCE72 Birm Univ ADipRE78 Keele Univ MA85. Oak Hill Th Coll 90. **d** 92 **p** 93. C Stanwix *Carl* 92-97; C Chasetown *Lich* from 97. *The Vicarage, Chapel Street, Chase Terrace, Staffs WS7 8ND*

LEAKEY, Ian Ramond Arundell. b 24. K Coll Cam BA47 MA49. Ridley Hall Cam 48. **d** 50 **p** 51. C Litherland St Jo and St Jas *Liv* 50-53; Rwanda Miss 53-73; Can Burundi 66; V Cudham *Roch* 73-76; P-in-c Downe 76; V Cudham and Downe 76-89; rtd 89. *5 Pine Close, Beech Grange, Landford, Salisbury SP5 2AW* Tel (01794) 390561

LEAKEY, Peter Wippell. b 39. Lon Univ BSc60. Trin Coll Bris 73. **d** 75 **p** 76. C Colne St Bart *Blackb* 75-79; V Copp 79-85; V Pennington *Man* from 85; AD Leigh from 93. *The Vicarage, Schofield Street, Leigh, Lancs WN7 4HT* Tel (01942) 673619

LEAL, Malcolm Colin. b 33. Chich Th Coll 72. **d** 75 **p** 76. Hon C Shoreham St Giles CD *Chich* 75-87; Chapl NE Surrey Coll Ewell 87-95; Hon C Arundel w Tortington and S Stoke *Chich* 88-95; Perm to Offic from 95. *8 West Park Lane, Goring-by-Sea, Worthing, W Sussex BN12 4EK* Tel (01903) 244160

LEAMING, Ralph Desmond. b 21. Ripon Coll Cuddesdon 79. **d** 81 **p** 82. C Darlington H Trin *Dur* 81-84; V Hamsterley 84-92; rtd 92. *3 Farnley Ridge, Durham DH1 4HB* Tel 0191-384 2049

LEAMY, Stuart Nigel. b 46. Pemb Coll Ox BA68 MA73 ACA76 FCA81. Sarum Th Coll 68. **d** 70 **p** 71. C Upholland *Liv* 70-78; Lic to Offic *Lon* 78-83 and from 94. *92 Gloucester Road, Hampton, Middx TW12 2UJ* Tel 0181-979 9068 Fax 255 1112

LEAN, David Jonathan Rees. b 52. Univ of Wales (Lamp) DipTh74. Coll of Resurr Mirfield 74. **d** 75 **p** 76. C Tenby *St D* 75-81; V Llanrhian w Llanhywel and Carnhedryn etc 81-88; V

Haverfordwest St Martin w Lambston from 88. *St Martin's Vicarage, Barn Street, Haverfordwest SA61 1TD* Tel (01437) 762509

LEANING, The Very Revd David. b 36. Lich Th Coll 58. **d** 60 **p** 61. C Gainsborough All SS *Linc* 60-65; R Warsop *S'well* 65-76; RD Kington and Weobley *Heref* 76-80; R Kington w Huntington 76-80; Adn Newark *S'well* 80-91; Provost S'well from 91; P-in-c Rolleston w Fiskerton, Morton and Upton 91-93. *The Residence, Southwell, Notts NG25 0HP* Tel (01636) 812593 or 812649 Fax 815904

LEARMOUTH, Michael Walter. b 50. FCA. Oak Hill Th Coll 84. **d** 84 **p** 85. C Harlow St Mary and St Hugh w St Jo the Bapt *Chelmsf* 84-89; V Hainault from 89. *St Paul's Vicarage, Arrowsmith Road, Chigwell, Essex IG7 4NZ* Tel 0181-500 3366

LEARY, Thomas Glasbrook. b 42. AKC66. **d** 67 **p** 68. C W Bromwich All SS *Lich* 67-70; TV Croydon *Cant* 70-75; C Limpsfield and Titsey *S'wark* 75-83; V Sutton New Town St Barn 83-92; V Merton St Mary from 92. *The Vicarage, 3 Church Path, London SW19 3HJ* Tel 0181-543 6192

LEATHARD, Brian. b 56. Sussex Univ BA Cam Univ MA Loughb Univ PhD91. Westcott Ho Cam 79. **d** 82 **p** 83. C Seaford w Sutton *Chich* 82-85; Chapl Loughb Univ *Leic* 85-89; V Hampton Hill *Lon* from 89. *The Vicarage, 46 St James's Road, Hampton, Middx TW12 1DQ* Tel 0181-979 2069

LEATHERBARROW, Ronald. b 35. Chester Coll TCert59. NW Ord Course 71. **d** 75 **p** 76. C Eccleston Ch Ch *Liv* 75-80; C Eccleston St Thos 80-83; R Kirklinton w Hethersgill and Scaleby *Carl* 83-86; R Blackley White Moss St Mark *Man* from 86. *St Mark's Rectory, 70 Booth Hall Road, Manchester M9 2BL* Tel 0161-740 7558

LEATHERS, Brian Stanley Peter. b 61. Nottm Univ BSc83. Oak Hill Th Coll BA89. **d** 89 **p** 90. C Watford *St Alb* 89-92; C Welwyn w Ayot St Peter 92-96; V Heacham *Nor* from 96. *The Vicarage, Heacham, King's Lynn, Norfolk PE31 7HJ* Tel (01485) 570268

LEATHES, David Burlton de Mussenden. b 49. R Agric Coll Cirencester DipEM70. St Jo Coll Nottm DCM92. **d** 92 **p** 93. C Kirkby Stephen w Mallerstang etc *Carl* from 92; C Brough w Stainmore, Musgrave and Warcop from 94. *Low Beck House, Rookby, Kirkby Stephen, Cumbria CA17 4HX* Tel (017683) 71713

LEATHLEY, Susan Mary (Sue). b 57. Bath Univ BPharm78 MRPharmS. Oak Hill Th Coll DTPS94. **d** 94 **p** 97. C Weston-super-Mare Ch Ch *B & W* 94-95. *Address temp unknown*

LEAVER, David Noel. b 63. Hatf Coll Dur BA85. Wycliffe Hall Ox 89. **d** 91 **p** 92. C Blackheath Park St Mich *S'wark* 91-95; C Upton (Overchurch) *Ches* from 95. *43 Grafton Drive, Upton, Wirral, Merseyside L49 0TX* Tel 0151-678 1235

LEAVER (née SMYTH), Lucinda Elizabeth Jane (Liz). b 67. New Hall Cam BA88 MA92. Wycliffe Hall Ox BTh93. **d** 93 **p** 94. C Cambridge St Barn *Ely* 93-97; Chapl St Kath Hall Liv Inst of HE from 97. *43 Grafton Drive, Upton, Wirral, Merseyside L49 0TX* Tel 0151-678 1235

LEAVER, Prof Robin Alan. b 39. Clifton Th Coll 62. **d** 64 **p** 65. C Gipsy Hill Ch Ch *S'wark* 64-67; C Gt Baddow *Chelmsf* 67-71; C-in-c Reading St Mary Castle Street Prop Chpl *Ox* 71-77; Chapl Luckley-Oakfield Sch Wokingham 73-75; P-in-c Cogges *Ox* 77-84; USA from 84; Prof Ch Music Westmr Choir Coll from 84. *Westminster Choir College, Princeton, New Jersey 08540, USA*

LEAVES (née CRAIG), Julie Elizabeth. b 63. Southn Univ BTh87. Sarum & Wells Th Coll 82. **dss** 86 **d** 87 **p** 92. Thatcham *Ox* 86-87; Par Dn 87-88; Hong Kong 88-92; Australia from 92. *Sambell Centre, 42 Colin Street, West Perth, W Australia 6005* Tel Perth (9) 325 7455 or 321 3253 Fax 325 6741

LEAVES, Nigel. b 58. Keble Coll Ox MA80 K Coll Lon MA86. Sarum & Wells Th Coll 84. **d** 86 **p** 87. C Boyne Hill *Ox* 86-88; Hong Kong 88-92; Australia from 92. *Sambell Centre, 42 Colin Street, West Perth, W Australia 6005* Tel Perth (9) 325 7455 or 321 3253 Fax 325 6741

LEAWORTHY, John Owen. b 40. Univ of Wales (Swansea) BSc62. Oak Hill Th Coll DipHE82. **d** 82 **p** 83. C Compton Gifford *Ex* 82-85; C Plymouth Em w Efford 85-86; P-in-c Marks Tey w Aldham and Lt Tey *Chelmsf* 86-88; R 88-89; Chapl HM Pris Full Sutton 89-91; Perm to Offic *Ely* 96; NSM Portree *Arg* from 96. *Mo Dhachaidh, Fiscavaig Road, Portnalong, Carbost, Isle of Skye IV47 8SL* Tel (01478) 640492

LECKEY, The Very Revd Hamilton. b 29. TCD BA51 MA58. **d** 51 **p** 52. C Ballymacarrett St Martin *D & D* 51-55; C Bangor Abbey 55-60; I 79-96; I Drumgooland w Kilcoo 60-62; Private Chapl Bp Down 62-73; Dir of Ords 62-87; I Comber 62-79; Can Down Cathl from 74; Dean Down 87-96; I Down Cathl 87-96. *34 Beechfield Drive, Bangor, Co Down BT19 7ZW* Tel (01247) 469370

LECKEY, Paul Robert. b 61. QUB. Ripon Coll Cuddesdon Aston Tr Scheme. **d** 96 **p** 97. C Eastleigh *Win* from 96. *St Francis House, Nightingale Avenue, Eastleigh, Hants SO50 9JB* Tel (01703) 619949

LEDGARD, Canon Frank William Armitage. b 24. Wells Th Coll 49. **d** 52 **p** 53. C Ipswich St Mary le Tower *St E* 52-55; V Tottington *Man* 55-62; V Kirkby Malzeard w Dallow Gill *Ripon* 62-66; R Bedale 66-87; RD Wensley 79-85; Hon Can Ripon Cathl 80-89; Bp's Adv on Chr Healing 87-89; rtd 89. *Bridge House, 19 Swinton Terrace, Masham, Ripon, N Yorkshire HG4 4HS* Tel (01765) 689375

LEDGARD, Canon Thomas Callinan. b 16. St Jo Coll Cam BA38 MA50. Westcott Ho Cam 38. **d** 39 **p** 40. C Bishopwearmouth St Mich *Dur* 39-42; C Ryhope 42-44; V Norton St Mich 44-46; R Warcop w Musgrave *Carl* 46-50; R Fulbourn *Ely* 50-56; V Kirkby Lonsdale w Mansergh *Carl* 56-69; RD Kirkby Lonsdale 64-69; V Cartmel 69-79; RD Cartmel 69-70; Hon Can Carl Cathl 70-82; P-in-c Warcop, Musgrave, Soulby and Crosby Garrett 79-82; rtd 82; Perm to Offic *Carl* from 83. *Tetley Cottage, Allithwaite Road, Cartmel, Grange-over-Sands, Cumbria LA11 7SB* Tel (01539) 536455

LEDGER, James Henry. b 23. Oak Hill Th Coll 68. **d** 70 **p** 71. C Spitalfields Ch Ch w All SS *Lon* 70-75; V Chitts Hill St Cuth 75-91; rtd 91. *6 Acorn Street, Hunsdon, Ware, Herts SG12 8PB* Tel (01279) 842878

LEDWARD, John Archibald. b 30. FRSA85 Lon Univ BD58 Man Univ DSPT78 MA81 ThD. ALCD57. **d** 58 **p** 59. C St Helens St Helen *Liv* 58-62; V Dearham *Carl* 62-66; V Mirehouse 66-71; V Daubhill *Man* 71-77; R Newcastle w Butterton *Lich* 77-88; P-in-c Rockland St Mary w Hellington *Nor* 88; R Rockland St Mary w Hellington, Bramerton etc 88-94; P-in-c Kirby Bedon w Bixley and Whitlingham 92-94; R Rockland St Mary w Hellington, Bramerton etc 94-95; RD Loddon 92-95; rtd 95; Perm to Offic *Nor* from 95. *41 Lackford Close, Brundall, Norwich NR13 5NL* Tel (01603) 714745

LEE, Mrs Anne Louise. b 65. St Jo Coll Nottm BTh90 Wycliffe Hall Ox 94. **d** 95 **p** 96. C Wembley St Jo *Lon* 95-97; C from 97. *50 Fairfield Crescent, Edgware, Middx HA8 9AH* Tel 0181-952 1342

LEE, Anthony Maurice. b 35. Bps' Coll Cheshunt 62. **d** 65 **p** 66. C Pinner *Lon* 65-71; Asst Youth Chapl *Glouc* 71-72; V Childswyckham 72-73; R Aston Somerville 72-73; V Childswyckham w Aston Somerville 73-91; P-in-c Buckland 88-91; P-in-c Stanton w Snowshill 88-91; R Childswyckham w Aston Somerville, Buckland etc 91-94; RD Winchcombe 86-94; rtd 94. *Little Copse, Stockland, Honiton, Devon EX14 9DY*

LEE, Arnold John. b 17. St Edm Hall Ox BA40 DipTh41 MA43. Wycliffe Hall Ox 40. **d** 42 **p** 43. C Claygate *Guildf* 42-45; China 45-51; Malaysia 51-69; V Ox St Andr *Ox* 69-78; V E Boldre w S Baddesley *Win* 78-82; rtd 82; Perm to Offic *Ox* 82-95; Perm to Offic *Glouc* from 95. *30 Capel Court, The Burgage, Prestbury, Cheltenham, Glos GL52 3EL* Tel (01242) 518625

LEE, Canon Arthur Gordon. b 32. Univ of Wales (Swansea) BA52. St Mich Coll Llan 53. **d** 55 **p** 56. C Brynmawr *S & B* 55-57; C Llangyfelach and Morriston 57-60; V Llanddewi Ystradenni and Abbey Cwmhir 60-69; V Swansea St Pet from 69; RD Penderi from 90; Hon Can Brecon Cathl 91-95; Can Res Brecon Cathl from 95. *The Vicarage, 59 Station Road, Fforestfach, Swansea SA5 5AU* Tel (01792) 581514

LEE, Brian. b 37. Linc Th Coll 78. **d** 80 **p** 81. C Duston *Pet* 80-84; P-in-c Spratton 84-89; V from 89; Jt P-in-c Maidwell w Draughton, Lamport w Faxton from 89; Jt P-in-c Cottesbrooke w Gt Creaton and Thornby from 89; RD Brixworth from 94. *The Vicarage, 2 Church Road, Spratton, Northampton NN6 8HR* Tel (01604) 847212

LEE, Canon Brian Ernest. b 32. ACA59 FCA70. Linc Th Coll 60. **d** 62 **p** 63. C Birch St Jas *Man* 62-65; C Withington St Paul 65-66; R Abbey Hey 66-70; Hon C Gatley *Ches* 86-88; V Egremont St Jo from 88; RD Wallasey 91-96; OGS from 92; Hon Can Ches Cathl *Ches* from 96. *St John's Vicarage, 7 Silverbeech Road, Wallasey, Merseyside L44 9BT* Tel 0151-638 4360

LEE, Brian John. b 51. K Coll Lon BD78 AKC78. Coll of Resurr Mirfield 78. **d** 79 **p** 80. C Ham St Rich *S'wark* 79-82; C Surbiton St Andr and St Mark 82-85; V Shirley St Geo 85-93; V St Botolph Aldgate w H Trin Minories *Lon* from 93. *St Botolph's Vestry, Aldgate, London EC3N 1AB* Tel 0171-283 1670 or 283 1950 Fax 283 9302

LEE, Christopher Garfield (Chris). b 41. St Deiniol's Hawarden 80. **d** 80 **p** 81. C Swansea St Pet *S & B* 80-81; C Oystermouth 81-83; R Cromhall w Tortworth and Tytherington *Glouc* 83-93; R Bishopston *S & B* from 93; UK Field Dir Educn for Min Progr from 93. *The Rectory, 4 Portway, Bishopston, Swansea SA3 3JR* Tel (01792) 232140 Fax 233123

LEE, Clifford Samuel (Sam). b 53. **d** 95 **p** 96. NSM S Elmham and Ilketshall *St E* from 95. *Packway Lodge, Flixton, Bungay, Suffolk NR35 1NR* Tel (01986) 782300

LEE, Colin John Willmot. b 21. Wycliffe Hall Ox 57. **d** 59 **p** 59. C Gravesend St Jas *Roch* 59-62; V Dartford St Edm 62-67; Bp's Ind Adv *Derby* 67-91; C-in-c Ilkeston St Bart CD 67-69; P-in-c Stanton by Dale 69-76; V Ilkeston St Jo 76-91; rtd 91; Perm to Offic *S'well* from 91. *3 Buttermead Close, Trowell, Nottingham NG9 3QT* Tel 0115-949 0100

LEE, Cyril Herbert. b 16. St Jo Coll Dur BA38 DipTh39 MA41. **d** 39 **p** 40. C Cheadle Hulme All SS *Ches* 39-42; Chapl Oakwood Hosp Maidstone 64-66; Perm to Offic *Ches* 42-45; C Kelsall 45-48; PC Milnthorpe *Carl* 48-55; Chapl Milnthorpe Hosp 48-55; V Chelford w Lower Withington *Ches* 55-64; Chapl Oakwood Hosp Maidstone 64-66; Perm to Offic *Cant* from 74; rtd 81;

Chapl HM Pris Standford Hill 81-82. *80 Church Lane, Newington, Sittingbourne, Kent ME9 4JU* Tel (01795) 842704

LEE, David Hartley. b 28. St Deiniol's Hawarden 61. **d** 63 **p** 64. C Merthyr Dyfan *Llan* 63-65; C Penarth All SS 65-70; Miss to Seamen from 70; Canada 70-84 and from 90. *c/o Herring Cove PO, Halifax, Nova Scotia, Canada, B0J 1S0*

LEE, Canon David John. b 46. Bris Univ BSc67 Lon Univ DipTh73 Fitzw Coll Cam BA76 Cam Univ MA79 Birm Univ PhD96. Ridley Hall Cam 74. **d** 77 **p** 78. C Putney St Marg *S'wark* 77-80; Uganda 80-86; Tutor Crowther Hall CMS Tr Coll Selly Oak 86-91; Lic to Offic *Birm* 87-91; P-in-c Wishaw 91-96; P-in-c Middleton 91-96; Can Res Birm Cathl from 96; Dir Dioc Bd for Miss from 96. *134 Oakfield Road, Selly Park, Birmingham B29 7ED* Tel 0121-472 0715 Fax as telephone E-mail dirmission@aol.com

LEE, The Ven David Stanley. b 30. Univ of Wales (Cardiff) BSc51. St Mich Coll Llan 56. **d** 57 **p** 58. C Caerau w Ely *Llan* 57-60; C Port Talbot St Agnes 60-70; Ind Chapl 60-70; R Merthyr Tydfil 70-72; Chapl Merthyr Tydfil Hosp 70-91; R Merthyr Tydfil and Cyfarthfa *Llan* 72-91; RD Merthyr Tydfil 82-91; Can Llan Cathl from 84; Adn Llan from 91; R Llanfabon from 91. *Llanfabon Rectory, High Street, Nelson CF46 6HA* Tel (01443) 450335

LEE, David Wight Dunsmore. b 39. Wells Th Coll 61. **d** 63 **p** 64. C Middlesbrough St Oswald *York* 63-67; C Northallerton w Kirby Sigston 67-69; Malawi 69-75; V Newington Transfiguration *York* 76-81; P-in-c Sheriff Hutton 81-85; P-in-c Sheriff Hutton and Farlington 85-97; V Sheriff Hutton, Farlington, Stillington etc from 97. *The Vicarage, New Lane, Sheriff Hutton, York YO6 1QU* Tel (01347) 870336

LEE, Edmund Hugh. b 53. Trin Coll Ox BA75 Golds Coll Lon BMus83. Ripon Coll Cuddesdon 93. **d** 95 **p** 96. C Malden St Jas *S'wark* from 95. *15 Knightwood Crescent, New Malden, Surrey KT3 5SR*

LEE, Frederick Roydon. b 13. OBE69. S'wark Ord Course 76. **d** 77 **p** 78. NSM Sundridge w Ide Hill *Roch* 77-81; rtd 81; Perm to Offic *Roch* from 81. *Tranquil, Combe Bank, Sundridge, Sevenoaks, Kent TN14 6AD* Tel (01959) 563552

LEE, Frederick William Maxwell. b 15. Dur Univ LTh40 St Pet Hall Ox BA47 MA51 Ox Univ Inst of Educn CertEd68. Lambeth STh89 St Aid Birkenhead 37. **d** 40 **p** 41. C Flixton St Mich *Man* 40-43; C Whalley Range St Marg 43-44; Perm to Offic *Ox* 44-47; Trinidad and Tobago 47-50; Area Sec (York) SPG 50-53; Teaching Service Rhodesia 53-66; Perm to Offic *Ox* 67-68; Perm to Offic *Nor* 68-70; Asst Master Thorpe Gr Sch 68-70; Hitchin Girls' Gr Sch 70-80; Hon C Hitchin St Mary *St Alb* 70-74; C St Alb St Sav 74-80; rtd 80; Perm to Offic *St Alb* 80-97. *13 Sandpit Lane, St Albans, Herts AL1 4DY* Tel (01727) 857353

LEE, Gilbert (Sai Kuen). b 51. Hong Kong BD80. **d** 80 **p** 81. Hong Kong 80-88; NSM St Martin-in-the-Fields *Lon* from 88; Chapl to Chinese in London from 88. *3 Strutton Court, 54 Great Peter Street, London SW1P 2HH* Tel 0171-233 0723

LEE, Hector. b 33. Leeds Univ CertEd60. Kelham Th Coll 53. **d** 57 **p** 58. SSM from 58; Tutor Kelham Th Coll 60-63; Basutoland 63-66; Lesotho 66-69; S Africa 69-88; Can Bloemfontein Cathl 80-88; V Burnley St Cuth *Blackb* from 88. *The Vicarage, Barbon Street, Burnley, Lancs BB10 1TS* Tel (01282) 424978

LEE, Henry. b 31. St Chad's Coll Dur BA53 DipTh55 CertEd. **d** 55 **p** 56. C Hendon St Ignatius *Dur* 55-60; C Dur St Marg 60-65; V Medomsley 65-75; Chapl Darlington Memorial Hosp 75-79; V Darlington H Trin *Dur* 75-82; V Brompton w Deighton *York* 82-90; rtd 90. *103 Benfieldside Road, Consett, Co Durham DH8 0RS* Tel (01207) 592170

LEE, Miss Hoe Lynley. b 52. St Jo Coll Nottm BTh89 K Coll Lon MA93. **d** 90 **p** 94. Par Dn Pitsea *Chelmsf* 90-95; Singapore from 95. *Block 608, Clement Street 1, 08-74, Singapore 0512*

LEE, Hugh Gordon Cassels. b 41. St Andr Univ BSc64. Edin Th Coll 64. **d** 67 **p** 68. C Dumfries *Glas* 67-70; C Totteridge *St Alb* 70-73; R Glas St Jas *Glas* 73-80; R Bishopbriggs 80-86; R St Fillans *St And* 86-89; P-in-c Muthill 86-90; R Comrie from 86; R Crieff from 86; P-in-c Lochearnhead from 89. *Fisherman's Hill, Lechin, Comrie, Crieff, Perthshire PH6 2LX* Tel (01764) 679750

LEE, Miss Iris Audrey Olive. b 26. St Andr Coll Southsea 54. **dss** 76 **d** 87. N Weald Bassett *Chelmsf* 76-87; rtd 87; NSM Clacton St Jas *Chelmsf* from 87. *30 Marine Court, Marine Parade West, Clacton-on-Sea, Essex CO15 1ND* Tel (01255) 423719

LEE, John Charles Hugh Mellanby. b 44. Trin Hall Cam BA66 MA69 Brunel Univ MTech71. Ox NSM Course 78. **d** 81 **p** 82. NSM Amersham on the Hill *Ox* 81-88; NSM Ox St Aldate w St Matt 88-93; NSM Wheatley from 93; Development Officer for Miss in Work and Economic Life from 95. *12 Walton Street, Oxford OX1 2HG* Tel (01865) 511382

LEE, John Foden. b 34. AKC61. **d** 61 **p** 62. C Pet All SS *Pet* 61-63; C Sudbury St Andr *Lon* 63-65; C Sherborne w Castleton and Lillington *Sarum* 65-67; V Erlestoke 67-68; R Gt Cheverell 67; V Erlestoke and Gt Cheverell 68-79; V Seend and Bulkington 79-86; Ind Chapl *Derby* from 86; V Derby St Paul from 86. *St Paul's Vicarage, Old Chester Road, Chester Green, Derby DE1 3SA* Tel (01332) 381116

LEE, John Michael Andrew. b 62. Leeds Univ BA84. Trin Coll Bris 88. **d** 90 **p** 91. C Norbiton *S'wark* 90-94; C Leic H Trin w St Jo *Leic* from 94. *25 Holbrook Road, Leicester LE2 3LG* Tel 0116-270 0732

LEE, John Royden. b 47. MInstGA87 Univ of Wales (Swansea) BSc70 MSc73. Ripon Hall Ox 73. **d** 75 **p** 76. C Swansea St Pet *S & B* 75-78; C St Botolph Aldgate w H Trin Minories *Lon* 79-84; P-in-c Chiddingstone w Chiddingstone Causeway *Roch* 84-89; R from 89. *The Rectory, Chiddingstone, Edenbridge, Kent TN8 7AH* Tel (01892) 870478

LEE, John Samuel. b 47. Chich Th Coll 74. **d** 77 **p** 78. C Bramley *Ripon* 77-80; C Bideford *Ex* 81-84; TV Littleham w Exmouth 84-90; P-in-c Sidbury 90-91; TV Sidmouth, Woolbrook, Salcombe Regis, Sidbury etc 91-97; TV Sidmouth, Woolbrook, Salcombe Regis, Sidbury etc from 97. *The Vicarage, Harcombe Lane, Sidford, Sidmouth, Devon EX10 9QN* Tel (01395) 579520

LEE, Kenneth Peter. b 45. Em Coll Cam BA67 MA71. Cuddesdon Coll 67. **d** 69 **p** 70. C Stoke Poges *Ox* 69-72; C Witton *Ches* 72-74; V Frankby w Greasby 74-92; R Christleton from 92. *The Rectory, Birch Heath Lane, Christleton, Chester CH3 7AP* Tel (01244) 335663

LEE, Luke Gun-Hong. b 37. Univ of Yon Sei BTh62. St Jo Coll Morpeth 64. **d** 67 **p** 68. Korea 67-79; C Bloxwich *Lich* 79-83; TV Dunstable *St Alb* 83-90; V Croxley Green All SS from 90. *All Saints' Vicarage, Croxley Green, Rickmansworth, Herts WD3 3HJ* Tel (01923) 772109

LEE, Martin Paul. b 66. Aston Tr Scheme 91 Linc Th Coll 93 St Steph Ho Ox 94. **d** 96 **p** 97. C Wells St Thos w Horrington *B & W* from 96. *9 Dodd Avenue, Wells, Somerset BA5 3JU* Tel (01749) 673533

LEE, Nicholas Knyvett. b 54. MA. Cranmer Hall Dur. **d** 85 **p** 86. C Brompton H Trin w Onslow Square St Paul *Lon* from 85. *St Paul's Church House, Onslow Square, London SW7 3NX* Tel 0171-589 3933

LEE, Peter Alexander. b 44. Hull Univ BSc(Econ)65. Ex & Truro NSM Scheme 80. **d** 83 **p** 84. NSM Ex St Sidwell and St Matt *Ex* 83-89; NSM Ex St Dav from 90. *Windyridge, Beech Avenue, Exeter EX4 6HF* Tel (01392) 54118

✠**LEE, The Rt Revd Peter John.** b 47. St Jo Coll Cam BA69 CertEd70 MA73. Ridley Hall Cam 70 St Jo Coll Nottm 72. **d** 73 **p** 74 **c** 90. C Onslow Square St Paul *Lon* 73-76; S Africa from 76; V-Gen and Bp Ch the K from 90. *PO Box 1653, Rosettenville, 2130 South Africa* Tel Johannesburg (11) 435-0097

LEE, Peter Kenneth. b 44. Selw Coll Cam BA66 MA69. Cuddesdon Coll 67. **d** 69 **p** 70. C Manston *Ripon* 69-72; C Bingley All SS *Bradf* 72-77; Chapl Bingley Coll of Educn 72-77; V Cross Roads cum Lees *Bradf* 77-90; V Auckland St Pet *Dur* from 90; Tutor NE Ord Course from 91. *St Peter's Vicarage, 39 Etherley Lane, Bishop Auckland, Co Durham DL14 7QZ* Tel (01388) 661856

LEE, Canon Raymond John. b 30. St Edm Hall Ox BA53 MA57. Tyndale Hall Bris 54. **d** 56 **p** 57. C Tooting Graveney St Nic *S'wark* 56-59; C Muswell Hill St Jas *Lon* 59-62; V Woking St Mary *Guildf* 62-70; V Gt Crosby St Luke *Liv* 70-82; Dioc Adv NSM 79-95; V Allerton 82-94; Hon Can Liv Cathl 89-95; rtd 95; P-in-c Altcar *Liv* from 94. *15 Barkfield Lane, Formby, Liverpool L37 1LY* Tel (01704) 872670

LEE, Richard Alexander. b 63. St Jo Coll Nottm BTh91. **d** 91 **p** 92. C Gt Stanmore *Lon* 91-95; C Edgware from 95. *50 Fairfield Crescent, Edgeware, Middx HA8 9AH* Tel 0181-952 1342

LEE, Robert David. b 53. QUB BD75. CITC 77. **d** 77 **p** 78. C Comber *D & D* 77-83; I Mt Merrion 83-87; CMS 89-92; Egypt 89-97; R Peebles *Edin* from 97; P-in-c Innerleithen from 97. *36 Wemyss Place, Peebles EH45 8JT* Tel (01721) 720571 Fax as telephone

LEE, Robert William. b 31. Keele Univ BA54 St Cath Soc Ox BA58 MA63. Ripon Hall Ox 56. **d** 59 **p** 60. C Dawley St Jerome *Lon* 59-62; C Bromley H Trin *Roch* 62-65; R Clayton *Man* 65-70; P-in-c Man St Paul 65-70; TV Hemel Hempstead *St Alb* 70-72; TV Corby SS Pet and Andr w Gt and Lt Oakley *Pet* 72-80; V Weedon Lois w Plumpton and Moreton Pinkney etc 80-88; R Thornhams Magna and Parva, Gislingham and Mellis *St E* 88-96; rtd 96; Perm to Offic *Carl* from 96. *2 Guldrey Fold, Sedbergh, Cumbria LA10 5DY* Tel (01539) 621907

LEE, Roderick James. b 50. Linc Th Coll 88. **d** 90 **p** 91. C Rushden w Newton Bromswold *Pet* 90-93; C Kingsthorpe w Northn St Dav 93-95; TV from 95. *42 Fallow Walk, Northampton NN2 8DE* Tel (01604) 846215

LEE, Simon Margeison. b 43. Brighton Coll of Educn TCert66. Cant Sch of Min 90. **d** 93 **p** 94. NSM Walmer *Cant* from 93. *26 Greenacre Drive, Deal, Kent CT14 7UQ* Tel (01304) 362585

LEE, Steven Michael. b 56. Dur Univ BA. Trin Coll Bris 80. **d** 83 **p** 84. C Beckenham St Jo *Roch* 83-86; C Leic Martyrs *Leic* 86-90; V Coalville and Bardon Hill 90-95; P-in-c Kibworth and Smeeton Westerby and Saddington from 95; P-in-c Foxton w Gumley and Laughton and Lubenham from 96. *The Rectory, 25 Church Road, Kibworth, Leicester LE8 0NB* Tel (0116) 279 9244

LEE, Terence. b 46. FCA. Ox NSM Course. **d** 83 **p** 84. NSM Calcot *Ox* 83-87; NSM Burghfield 87-88. *45 Christchurch Road, Reading RG2 7AN* Tel 0118-931 2512

LEE, Thomas Richard. b 52. AKC73. St Aug Coll Cant 74. **d** 75 **p** 76. C Leam Lane CD *Dur* 75-80; Chapl RAF from 80. *Chaplaincy Services (RAF), HQ, Personnel and Training*

Command, RAF Innsworth, Gloucester GL3 1EZ Tel (01452) 712612 ext 5164 Fax 510828

LEE, William George. b 11. TCD BA33 MA48. **d** 34 **p** 35. C Southport St Andr *Liv* 34-37; C Cambridge St Paul *Ely* 37-44; V Matlock Bath *Derby* 44-49; V Deptford St Jo *S'wark* 49-61; RD Greenwich and Deptford 60; V Chislehurst Ch Ch *Roch* 61-76; rtd 76. *Dale Garth, Harmby, Leyburn, N Yorkshire DL8 5PD* Tel (01969) 622649

LEE WARNER, Canon Theodore John. b 22. Univ Coll Ox BA49 MA54. Wells Th Coll 50. **d** 51 **p** 52. C S Westoe *Dur* 51-55; P-in-c Cassop cum Quarrington 55-59; V Peterlee 59-63; V Darlington H Trin 63-74; Chapl Darlington Memorial Hosp 63-74; V Norton St Mary *Dur* 74-80; RD Barnard Castle 80-87; V Gainford 80-87; R Winston 80-87; Hon Can Dur Cathl 83-87; rtd 87. *112 Cleveland Terrace, Darlington, Co Durham DL3 8JA* Tel (01325) 467585

LEECE, Roderick Neil Stephen. b 59. ARCM85 Wadh Coll Ox BA81 MA85 Leeds Univ BA84. Coll of Resurr Mirfield 82. **d** 85 **p** 86. C Portsea St Mary *Portsm* 85-91; V Stamford Hill St Bart *Lon* from 91. *St Bartholomew's Vicarage, Craven Park Road, London N15 6AA* Tel 0181-800 1554

LEECH, Christopher. b 16. Linc Th Coll 37. **d** 39 **p** 40. C Cudworth *Wakef* 39-41; C Twerton *B & W* 41-43; R Walcot 43-47; S Rhodesia 47-52 and 54-57; V Easton *B & W* 53-54; V Wigan St Geo *Liv* 57-60; R Combe Pyne w Rousdon *Ex* 60-76; P-in-c 76-82; C Axminster 77-79; rtd 82; Perm to Offic *Ex* from 82. *Nestor, Hillhead, Colyton, Devon EX13 6HH* Tel (01297) 552034

LEECH, Kenneth. b 39. Lon Univ BA61 AKC61 Trin Coll Ox BA63 MA71. St Steph Ho Ox 62. **d** 64 **p** 65. C Hoxton H Trin w St Mary *Lon* 64-67; C Soho St Anne w St Thos and St Pet 67-71; Tutor St Aug Coll Cant 71-74; R Bethnal Green St Matt *Lon* 74-79; Field Officer Community & Race Relns Unit BCC 80; Race Relns Officer Gen Syn Bd for Soc Resp 81-87; Hon C Notting Hill St Clem and St Mark *Lon* 82-85; Hon C Notting Dale St Clem w St Mark and St Jas 85-88; Dir Runnymede Trust 87-90; St Botolph Aldgate w H Trin Minories *Lon* from 91. *St Botolph's Vestry, Aldgate, London EC3N 1AB* Tel 0171-377 0721

LEECH, Miss Peggy Irene. b 29. CA Tr Coll 56. **dss** 85 **d** 87 **p** 94. Oxhey All SS *St Alb* 86-87; C from 87; rtd 91. *9 The Mead, Carpenters Park, Watford WD1 5BY* Tel 0181-428 6136

LEEDS, Archdeacon of. *See* OLIVER, The Ven John Michael

LEEFIELD, Michael John. b 37. Liv Univ BA60 K Coll Lon BD65 AKC65. St Boniface Warminster 62. **d** 66 **p** 67. C Gt Yarmouth *Nor* 66-70; V Trowse 70-75; V Arminghall 70-75; R Caistor w Markshall 70-75; Chapl Norfolk and Nor Hosp 70-75; V Lydney w Aylburton *Glouc* 75-84; RD Forest S 82-84; Lic to Offic from 85. *Brays Court, Awre, Newnham, Glos GL14 1EP* Tel (01594) 510483

LEEKE, Canon Charles Browne. b 39. TCD DipTh CertEd. **d** 83 **p** 84. C Ballymoney w Finvoy and Rasharkin *Conn* 83-86; I Faughanvale *D & R* 86-97; Miss to Seamen from 92; Bp's Dom Chapl *D & R* 92-96; Can Derry Cathl from 96; I Drumragh w Mountfield from 97. *Drumragh Rectory, 21 Church Street, Omagh, Co Tyrone BT78 1DG* Tel (01662) 242130 Fax as telephone

LEEKE, Stephen Owen. b 50. EAMTC 82 Ridley Hall Cam 83. **d** 84 **p** 85. C Cherry Hinton St Andr *Ely* 84-87; P-in-c Warboys 87-91; P-in-c Wistow 87-91; P-in-c Bury 87-91; R Warboys w Broughton and Bury w Wistow from 91; RD St Ives from 92. *The Rectory, 15 Church Road, Warboys, Huntingdon, Cambs PE17 2RJ* Tel (01487) 822237

LEEMAN, John Graham. b 41. N Ord Course 78. **d** 80 **p** 81. NSM Hull St Mary Sculcoates *York* 80-96; Perm to Offic from 96. *1 Snuff Mill Lane, Cottingham, N Humberside HU16 4RY* Tel (01482) 840355

LEEMING, Jack. b 34. Kelham Th Coll 56. **d** 61 **p** 62. C Sydenham St Phil *S'wark* 61-64; Chapl RAF 64-84; Chapl Salisbury Gen Infirmary 84-89; R Barford St Martin, Dinton, Baverstock etc *Sarum* from 89. *The Rectory, Barford St Martin, Salisbury SP3 4AS* Tel (01722) 743385

LEEMING, John Maurice. b 24. CEng MIMechE MIProdE FIED. NW Ord Course 72. **d** 75 **p** 76. NSM Endcliffe *Sheff* 75-78; C Norton 78-80; V Bolsterstone 80-89; Jt Min Stocksbridge Chr Cen LEP 80-89; Ind Chapl 81-89; rtd 89; Perm to Offic *S'well* from 89. *Beck House, Toftdyke Lane, Clayworth, Retford, Notts DN22 9AH* Tel (01777) 817795

LEEMING, Peter. b 23. Leeds Univ BA50. Bps' Coll Cheshunt 50. **d** 52 **p** 53. C Riddlesdown *S'wark* 52-56; C Richmond St Mary 56-62; C Sundon w Streatley *St Alb* 62-68; C Moordown *Win* 68-71; C Hawarden *St As* 71-78; TV 78-89; rtd 89. *2 Church Cottages, Rectory Drive, Hawarden, Deeside CH5 3NN* Tel (01244) 531186

LEES, Charles Alan. b 38. RGN OND FETC. WMMTC 78. **d** 81 **p** 82. NSM Yardley St Cypr Hay Mill *Birm* 81-84 and 86-87; Hon C Dorridge 84-86; Chapl E Birm Hosp 85-87; Hon C Leamington Spa and Old Milverton *Cov* 89-90; Perm to Offic *Birm* 95-96. *49 Gordon Street, Leamington Spa, Warks CV31 1HR* Tel (01926) 332199

LEES, John Raymond. b 57. Selw Coll Cam BA78 MA82. St Steph Ho Ox 89. **d** 91 **p** 92. C Eastbourne St Mary *Chich* 91-93; Min Can and Succ St Paul's Cathl *Lon* from 93. *8A Amen Court, London EC4M 7BU* Tel 0171-248 6115

LEES, Mrs Kathleen Marion. b 30. Birkb Coll Lon BA60 DipRS80. S'wark Ord Course 77. **dss** 80 **d** 87 **p** 94. Epping St Jo *Chelmsf* 80-86; Hon C Hunstanton St Mary w Ringstead Parva, Holme etc *Nor* 87-88; Perm to Offic 88-94; NSM Gaywood St Faith 94-95 and from 95; Chapl K Lynn and Wisbech Hosps NHS Trust from 94. *12 Cherry Tree Road, Snettisham, King's Lynn, Norfolk PE31 7NZ* Tel (01485) 540364

LEES, Peter John. b 39. **d** 95 **p** 96. NSM Buckie *Ab* from 95; NSM Turriff from 95. *7 Whitefield Court, Buckpool, Buckie, Banff AB56 1EY* Tel (01542) 835261 or (01542) 835011

LEES, Stephen. b 55. St Jo Coll York CertEd77 BEd78 Nottm Univ MA96. St Jo Coll Nottm 88. **d** 90 **p** 91. C Mansfield St Jo *S'well* 90-93; TV Bestwood from 93. *45 Pine Hill Close, Nottingham NG5 9DA* Tel 0115-927 7229

LEES, Stuart Charles Roderick. b 62. Trin Coll Bris BA. **d** 89 **p** 90. C Woodford Wells *Chelmsf* 89-93; C Brompton H Trin w Onslow Square St Paul *Lon* 93-97; Chapl Stewards Trust 93-97; P-in-c Fulham Ch Ch from 97. *Christ Church Vicarage, 40 Clancarty Road, London SW6 3AA* Tel 0171-736 4261 Fax as telephone

LEES-SMITH, Christopher John (Brother Edward). b 21. CCC Ox BA49 MA65. Cuddesdon Coll 48. **d** 50 **p** 51. C Pallion *Dur* 50-54; SSF from 54; Lic to Offic *Sarum* 57-62; Perm to Offic *Newc* 62-74; Guardian Alnmouth Friary 65-74; Chapl Third Order SSF 74-91; rtd 91. *The Friary, Alnmouth, Alnwick, Northd NE66 3NJ* Tel (01665) 830213

LEESE, Arthur Selwyn Mountford. b 09. K Coll Lon BD31 AKC31 St Cath Soc Ox BA33 MA44. Ripon Hall Ox 31. **d** 33 **p** 34. C Bexleyheath Ch Ch *Roch* 33-37; C Cockington *Ex* 37-39; C Langley Mill *Derby* 39-51; V Hawkhurst *Cant* 51-74; rtd 74; Perm to Offic *Chich* from 75; Perm to Offic *Cant* from 77. *84 Wickham Avenue, Bexhill-on-Sea, E Sussex TN39 3ER* Tel (01424) 213137

LEESE, Frederick Henry Brooke. b 24. AKC47. **d** 47 **p** 48. C Mitcham St Mark *S'wark* 47-50; C Bourne *Guildf* 50-54; V Croydon St Martin *Cant* 54-60; V Pagham *Chich* 60-70; V Chorley *Ches* 70-82; R Rogate w Terwick and Trotton w Chithurst *Chich* 82-90; RD Midhurst 85-90; rtd 90; Perm to Offic *B & W* from 90. *Treetops, Furnham Crescent, Chard, Somerset TA20 1AZ* Tel (01460) 65524

LEESE, Mrs Jane Elizabeth. b 50. Man Univ BA(Econ)72 Avery Hill Coll PGCE73. Sarum Th Coll 93. **d** 96 **p** 97. NSM Kempshott *Win* from 96. *7 Greenbirch Close, Kempshott, Basingstoke, Hants RG22 5JL* Tel (01256) 468884

LEESON, Bernard Alan. b 47. MIMgt92 FCollP92 FRSA92 Bris Univ CertEd68 Open Univ BA75 Southn Univ MA78 Sheff Univ PhD97. EMMTC 84. **d** 87 **p** 88. Dep Hd Master Ripley Mill Hill Sch 80-91; NSM Breadsall *Derby* 87-91; Hd St Aid CE High Sch Lancs from 91; Perm to Offic *Blackb* 91-92; Lic to Offic from 92; NSM Officer 92-96. *The Lodge, Daggers Lane, Preesall, Poulton-le-Fylde, Lancs FY6 0QN* Tel (01253) 811020 or 810504 Fax 810244

LEESON, David Harry Stanley. b 45. Glouc Th Course 82. **d** 85 **p** 86. NSM Stratton w Baunton *Glouc* 85-94; NSM N Cerney w Bagendon 91-94; NSM Stratton, N Cerney, Baunton and Bagendon from 95. *83 Cheltenham Road, Stratton, Cirencester, Glos GL7 2JB* Tel (01285) 651186

LEESON, Mrs Sally Elizabeth. b 57. Sussex Univ BA79. Westcott Ho Cam 83. **dss** 85 **d** 87 **p** 94. Battersea St Pet and St Paul *S'wark* 85-87; Par Dn 87-90; Par Dn Limpsfield and Titsey 90-94; C 94; Perm to Offic from 94. *32 Albany Road, New Malden, Surrey KT3 3NY*

LEFEVER, Dr Henry Charles. b 06. Lon Univ BA30 BD32 Tubingen Univ PhD34. **d** 65 **p** 66. Hon C S'wark St Sav w All Hallows *S'wark* 65-69; Hon C Blackheath Ascension 69-75; rtd 75; Perm to Offic *Cant* from 76. *10 Mulberry Court, Stour Street, Canterbury, Kent CT1 2NT* Tel (01227) 768304

LEFFLER, Christopher. b 33. Em Coll Cam BA57 MA61. Linc Th Coll. **d** 59 **p** 60. C Bermondsey St Mary w St Olave and St Jo *S'wark* 59-60; C Herne Hill St Paul 60-63; C-in-c Canley CD *Cov* 63-67; R Gt and Lt Glemham *St E* 67-72; R Badwell Ash w Gt Ashfield, Stowlangtoft etc 72-82; R Trimley from 82. *The Rectory, Church Lane, Trimley, Ipswich IP10 0SW* Tel (01394) 286188

LEFFLER, Jeremy Paul (Jem). b 62. Westmr Coll Ox BEd88. Wycliffe Hall Ox BTh94. **d** 94 **p** 95. C Ormskirk *Liv* 94-97; C Much Woolton from 97. *46 Linkstor Road, Woolton, Liverpool L25 6DH* Tel 0151-428 3339

LEFROY, Christopher John Elton. b 25. Clare Coll Cam BA46 MA49. Ridley Hall Cam 47. **d** 49 **p** 50. C W Ham St Matt *Chelmsf* 49-51; Asst Chapl Bradfield Coll Berks 51-54; C St Marylebone All So w SS Pet and Jo *Lon* 54-65; V Highbury Ch Ch 65-78; V Highbury Ch Ch w St Jo 79-82; V Highbury Ch Ch w St Jo and St Sav Lon 82-90; rtd 90; Perm to Offic *Chich* from 90. *12 Rodmill Drive, Eastbourne, E Sussex BN21 2SG* Tel (01323) 640294

LEFROY, John Perceval. b 40. Trin Coll Cam BA62. Cuddesdon Coll 64. **d** 66 **p** 67. C Maidstone St Martin *Cant* 66-69; C

St Peter-in-Thanet 69-74; V Barming Heath 74-82; V Upchurch w Lower Halstow from 82; P-in-c Iwade from 95. *The Vicarage, 15 Oak Lane, Upchurch, Sittingbourne, Kent ME9 7AT* Tel (01634) 387227

LEFROY (née CLARK), Mrs Kathleen Christine. b 33. Newton Park Coll Bris TCert53 Lon Univ DipTh58. St Mich Ho Ox 56 Trin Coll Bris 90. **d** 90. Personnel Sec SAMS 83-91; Asst Gen Sec 87-92; NSM Eastbourne H Trin *Chich* from 90; Chmn SEAN (Internat) and SOMA (UK) from 91; rtd 92; Dioc Voc Adv *Chich* from 92. *12 Rodmill Drive, Eastbourne, E Sussex BN21 2SG* Tel (01323) 640294

LEGG, Adrian James. b 52. St Jo Coll Nottm LTh82 BTh82. **d** 82 **p** 83. C Haughton le Skerne *Dur* 82-85; C Llanishen and Lisvane *Llan* 85-89; V Llanwddyn and Llanfihangel and Llwydiarth *St As* 89-93; V Llansadwrn w Llanwrda and Manordeilo *St D* from 93. *The Vicarage, Llanwrda SA19 8HD* Tel (01550) 777343

LEGG, Joanna Susan Penberthy. *See* PENBERTHY, Ms Joanna Susan

LEGG, John Andrew Douglas. b 32. Selw Coll Cam BA55 MA57. Wells Th Coll 57. **d** 59 **p** 59. Australia 59-63; Chapl Rugby Sch 63-64; P-in-c Ashford w Sheldon *Derby* 64-67; Kuwait 67-69; Solomon Is 70-71; Asst Master Lt Ilford Comp Sch 72-83; P-in-c Stapleford Tawney w Theydon Mt *Chelmsf* 78-83; R Hemingby *Linc* 83-88; Greece from 88; rtd 92. *Prastos, Kynorias, Arkadia, Greece 22006* Tel Arkadia (755) 51693

LEGG, Reginald John. b 26. LRAM50 TCert45. Wells Th Coll 61. **d** 63 **p** 64. C Prestbury *Glouc* 63-66; V Milnsbridge *Wakef* 66-67; Miss to Seamen 67-74; V Methwold *Ely* 74-80; RD Feltwell 75-80; P-in-c Preston *Glouc* 80-91; P-in-c Dymock w Donnington and Kempley 80-91; rtd 91. *3 Shottsford Close, Swanage, Dorset BH19 2LH* Tel (01929) 427989

LEGG, Dr Richard. b 37. Selw Coll Cam BA62 MA66 Brunel Univ MPhil77. NY Th Sem DMin Coll of Resurr Mirfield 63. **d** 65 **p** 66. C Ealing St Pet Mt Park *Lon* 65-68; Chapl Brunel Univ 68-78; C Chipping Barnet w Arkley *St Alb* 81-83; TV 83-85; R St Buryan, St Levan and Sennen *Truro* 85-93; Subwarden St Deiniol's Lib Hawarden 93; Perm to Offic *Ches* 93; TV Beaminster Area *Sarum* from 93. *The Vicarage, 20 Orchard Way, Mosterton, Beaminster, Dorset DT8 3LT* Tel (01308) 868090

LEGG, Robert Richard. b 16. MBE45. Open Univ BA78. St Aug Coll Cant 36. **d** 59 **p** 60. C Andover w Foxcott *Win* 59-62; V W w E Tytherley 62-71; V Kingsclere 71-83; rtd 83; Perm to Offic *Win* from 83. *The Furrow, Evingar Road, Whitchurch, Hants RG28 7EU* Tel (01256) 892126

LEGG, Roger Keith. b 35. Lich Th Coll 61. **d** 63 **p** 64. C Petersfield w Sheet *Portsm* 63-66; C Portsea St Mary 66-70; Rhodesia 70-75; V Clayton *Lich* from 75. *The Vicarage, Clayton Lane, Newcastle, Staffs ST5 3DW* Tel (01782) 614500

LEGG, Miss Ruth Helen Margaret. b 52. Hull Univ BA74 Homerton Coll Cam CertEd75. Trin Coll Bris DipHE88. **d** 88 **p** 94. C Clevedon St Andr and Ch Ch *B & W* 88-92; C Nailsea Ch Ch 92-96; C Nailsea Ch Ch w Tickenham 96-97; V Pill w Easton in Gordano and Portbury from 97. *The Rectory, 17 Church Road, Easton in Gordano, Bristol BS20 0PQ* Tel (01275) 372804

LEGGATE, Colin Archibald Gunson. b 44. Bris Sch of Min 86. **d** 88 **p** 89. NSM Brislington St Luke *Bris* 88-97; Asst Chapl Frenchay Healthcare NHS Trust Bris from 97. *Frenchay Hospital, Frenchay, Bristol BS16 1LE* Tel 0117-970 1212

LEGGE, Frederick John (Fred). b 10. Ridley Hall Cam 58. **d** 59 **p** 59. C Addiscombe St Mildred *Cant* 59-60; V Porchester *S'well* 60-63; R E Leake 63-76; P-in-c Rempstone 70-76; P-in-c Costock 70-76; P-in-c Stanford on Soar 70-76; rtd 76. *1 Stuart Court, High Street, Kibworth, Leics LE8 0LE* Tel 0116-279 6347

LEGGETT, James Henry Aufrere. b 61. Oak Hill Th Coll DipHE93. **d** 93 **p** 94. C Hensingham *Carl* from 93. *13 West View, Hensingham, Whitehaven, Cumbria CA28 8QY* Tel (01946) 67030

LEGGETT, Vanessa Gisela. *See* CATO, Ms Vanessa Gisela

LEGOOD, Giles Leslie. b 67. K Coll Lon BD88 AKC88. Ripon Coll Cuddesdon 90. **d** 92 **p** 93. C N Mymms *St Alb* 92-95; Chapl R Veterinary Coll *Lon* from 95; Chapl R Free Medical Sch from 95; Chapl Univ Coll Medical Sch from 95. *15 Ormonde Mansions, 106 Southampton Row, London WC1B 4BP* Tel 0171-242 2574 E-mail glegood@rvc.ac.uk

LEICESTER, Archdeacon of. *See* EDSON, The Ven Michael

LEICESTER, Bishop of. *See* BUTLER, The Rt Revd Thomas Frederick

LEICESTER, Provost of. *See* HOLE, The Very Revd Derek Norman

LEIGH, Mrs Alison Margaret. b 40. CertEd63 Golds Coll Lon BEd75. Sarum & Wells Th Coll 85. **d** 87 **p** 94. C Chessington *Guildf* 87-90; C Green Street Green *Roch* 90-92; D-in-c E Peckham and Nettlestead 92-94; P-in-c 94-95; R from 95. *The Rectory, Bush Road, East Peckham, Tonbridge, Kent TN12 5LL* Tel (01622) 871278

LEIGH, Arnold Robert. b 36. AKC60. **d** 61 **p** 62. C Lewisham St Mary *S'wark* 61-66; C Stockwell Green St Andr 66-69; V 69-72; TV Withycombe Raleigh *Ex* 72-74; TR 74-80; V Devonport St Bart 80-93; P-in-c Moretonhampstead, N Bovey and Manaton 93-96; R Moretonhampstead, Manaton, N Bovey and Lustleigh from 96. *The Rectory, 3 Grays Meadow, Moretonhampstead, Newton Abbot, Devon TQ13 8NB* Tel (01647) 440977

LEIGH, Dennis Herbert. b 34. Lon Univ BSc56 DipTh68. Chich Th Coll 58. **d** 60 **p** 61. C Roehampton H Trin *S'wark* 60-62; C E Wickham 62-67; C Plumstead St Mark and St Marg 67-73; C Corby Epiphany w St Jo *Pet* 73-74; C Paston 84-86; C Aylestone St Andr w St Jas *Leic* 86-95; rtd 95; Perm to Offic *Pet* from 95. *14 Willowbrook Road, Corby, Northants NN17 2EB* Tel (01536) 263405

LEIGH, Canon James Ronald. b 32. S'wark Ord Course 63. **d** 67 **p** 68. C Purley St Barn *S'wark* 67-71; Prec St Ninian's Cathl Perth *St And* 71-73; R Leven 73-79; R Kirkcaldy from 79; R Kinghorn from 81; Can St Ninian's Cathl Perth from 90. *1 Longbraes Gardens, Kirkcaldy, Fife KY2 5YJ* Tel (01592) 263314

LEIGH, Martin Francis. b 40. Sheff Univ BSc63. Cuddesdon Coll 65. **d** 67 **p** 68. C St Mary-at-Lambeth *S'wark* 67-70; C Bakewell *Derby* 70-74; V Ockbrook 74-82; RD Ilkeston 78-82; V Baslow 82-92; Bp's Ecum Officer 82-92; TR Kings Norton *Birm* from 92. *The Rectory, 273 Pershore Road South, Birmingham B30 3EX* Tel 0121-458 7522 or 458 3289

LEIGH, Mrs Mary Elizabeth. b 42. K Coll Lon BA64 LSE DSA65. Westcott Ho Cam 89. **d** 91 **p** 94. NSM Chesterfield St Mary and All SS *Derby* 91-92; C Hall Green Ascension *Birm* 92-94; C Yardley St Edburgha from 94; Chapl and Tutor N Ord Course from 97. *Luther King House, Brighton Grove, Manchester M14 5JP* Tel 0161-225 6668 Fax 248 9201

LEIGH, Raymond. b 37. Lon Univ BEd81. Clifton Th Coll 65. **d** 68 **p** 69. C Chadwell *Chelmsf* 68-71; Chapl RAF 71-77; NSM Hillingdon St Jo *Lon* 87-88; C Rowley Regis *Birm* 88-90; V Londonderry 90-95; R Westbury w Turweston, Shalstone and Biddlesden *Ox* from 95. *The Vicarage, Westbury, Brackley, Northants NN13 5JT* Tel (01280) 704964

LEIGH, Roy Stephen. b 28. Imp Coll Lon BSc49. S'wark Ord Course 87. **d** 90 **p** 92. NSM Green Street Green *Roch* 90-92; NSM E Peckham and Nettlestead from 92. *The Rectory, Bush Road, East Peckham, Tonbridge, Kent TN12 5LL* Tel (01622) 871278

LEIGH-HUNT, Edward Christopher. b 22. Univ Coll Dur BA47. Ely Th Coll 48. **d** 50 **p** 51. C Wandsworth St Anne *S'wark* 50-54; C Bethnal Green St Matt *Lon* 54-56; C Lewisham St Jo Southend *S'wark* 56-57; C Ealing St Barn *Lon* 57-66; Chapl Asst St Bart Hosp Lon 66-73; C St Bart Less *Lon* 66-73; Chapl Middx Hosp 73-86; rtd 87. *14 Cain Court, Castlebar Mews, London W5 1RY* Tel 0181-991 1171

LEIGH-HUNT, Nicolas Adrian. b 46. MIEx70. Qu Coll Birm 85. **d** 87 **p** 88. C Tilehurst St Geo *Ox* 87-91; TV Wexcombe *Sarum* from 91. *The Vicarage, 5 Eastcourt, Burbage, Marlborough, Wilts SN8 3AG* Tel (01672) 810258

LEIGH-WILLIAMS, Owen Charles. b 32. BNC Ox BA56 MA60. Wycliffe Hall Ox 56. **d** 58 **p** 59. C Southgate *Chich* 64-62; C Gt Warley Ch Ch *Chelmsf* 64-68; Asst Chapl Warley Hosp Brentwood 64-68; C Dagenham *Chelmsf* 68-72; P-in-c Basildon St Andr 72-86; rtd 96. *309A Church Road, Basildon, Essex SS14 2NE* Tel (01268) 521628

LEIGHLIN, Dean of. *See* FAULL, The Very Revd Cecil Albert

LEIGHTON, Adrian Barry. b 44. LTh. Lon Coll of Div 65. **d** 69 **p** 70. C Erith St Paul *Roch* 69-72; C Ipswich St Marg *St E* 72-75; P-in-c Ipswich St Helen 75-82; R 82-88; P-in-c Holbrook w Freston and Woolverstone from 88; RD Samford 90-93; P-in-c Wherstead from 94. *The Rectory, Holbrook, Ipswich IP9 2QZ* Tel (01473) 328900

LEIGHTON, Alan Granville Clyde. b 37. MInstM AMIDHE Lon Univ DipRS. S'wark Ord Course 73. **d** 76 **p** 77. C Silverhill St Matt *Chich* 76-79; C Eston *York* 79-82; V 82-84; TR Eston w Normanby from 84. *429 Normanby Road, Normanby, Middlesbrough, Cleveland TS6 0ED* Tel (01642) 460613

LEIGHTON, Canon Anthony Hindess. b 23. Lon Univ BSc44. Wells Th Coll 47. **d** 49 **p** 50. C Melton Mowbray w Burton Lazars, Freeby etc *Leic* 49-54; V Thorpe Acre w Dishley 54-61; R Girton *Ely* 61-88; RD N Stowe 68-76; Hon Can Ely Cathl 82-88; rtd 88; Perm to Offic *Ely* from 88. *Eastleigh, Parkhall Road, Somersham, Huntingdon, Cambs PE17 3HF* Tel (01487) 842750

LEIGHTON, Anthony Robert (Tony). b 56. Trin Coll Bris BA88. **d** 88 **p** 89. C Harrow Trin St Mich *Lon* 88-92; TV Ratby w Groby *Leic* 92-94; TR from 94; P-in-c Newtown Linford from 95. *The Rectory, 58 Pymm Ley Lane, Groby, Leicester LE6 0GZ* Tel 0116-231 3090

LEIGHTON, John Thomas. b 08. **d** 76 **p** 77. C W Derby St Mary *Liv* 76-77; Hon C Knowsley from 77; Hon C Litherland St Phil from 84. *22 Newlyn Avenue, Litherland, Liverpool L21 9LD* Tel 0151-928 1957

LEIGHTON, Mrs Susan. Bretton Hall Coll BEd80. Trin Coll Bris BA89. **d** 89 **p** 94. Par Dn Harrow Weald All SS *Lon* 89-92; NSM Ratby w Groby *Leic* 92-96; C from 96. *The Rectory, 58 Pymm Ley Lane, Groby, Leicester LE6 0GZ* Tel 0116-231 3090

LEIPER, Nicholas Keith. b 34. SS Coll Cam BA55 MB58 BChir58 MA65. St Jo Coll Nottm LTh82. **d** 84 **p** 85. C Bidston *Ches* 84-87; TV Gateacre *Liv* 87-92; P-in-c Bickerstaffe 92-94; P-in-c Melling 92-94; V Bickerstaffe and Melling from 94. *The Vicarage, Intake Lane, Bickerstaffe, Ormskirk, Lancs L39 0EB* Tel (01695) 22304

LEITCH, Peter William. b 36. FCA58 ATII59. Coll of Resurr Mirfield 83. **d** 85 **p** 86. C Newsome *Wakef* 85; C Newsome and Armitage Bridge 85-88; P-in-c Upper Hopton 88-91; P-in-c Mirfield Eastthorpe St Paul 88-91; Chapl Rouen Miss to Seamen *Eur* 92-94; Sen Chapl 94-95; Chapl Pernis Miss to Seamen from 95. *The Missions to Seamen, Vondelingenweg 524, 319 KK Rotterdam, The Netherlands* Tel Rotterdam (10) 438-7043

LEMMON, Canon Rowland. b 09. Keble Coll Ox BA31 MA40. Wells Th Coll 31. **d** 32 **p** 33. C Barrow St Jas *Carl* 32-36; C Carl St Aid and Ch Ch 36-40; V Beckermet St Bridget 40-49; V Ponsonby 41-49; V Millom H Trin 49-62; RD Gosforth 51-62; Hon Can Carl Cathl 60-62; R Hexham *Newc* 62-75; Hon Can Newc Cathl 70-75; rtd 75; Perm to Offic *Ex* from 82. *4 Arundel Close, Alphington, Exeter EX2 8UQ* Tel (01392) 270365

LEMPRIERE, Norman Everard. b 28. Liv Univ BEng54. Ridley Hall Cam 55. **d** 57 **p** 58. C Ware Ch Ch *St Alb* 57-61; R Lt Munden 61-64; R Sacombe 61-64; Lee Abbey 64-66; Perm to Offic *Ex* 64-66; C Witheridge 66-69; R Nymet Rowland w Coldridge 69-75; R Denton w S Heighton and Tarring Neville *Chich* 75-81; R Sullington and Thakeham w Warminghurst 81-92; rtd 92; Perm to Offic *B & W* from 92. *38 Woodbury Avenue, Wells, Somerset BA5 2XP* Tel (01749) 673368

LENDRUM, Canon William Henry. b 24. TCD BA50 MA62. CITC 50. **d** 50 **p** 51. C Belfast St Mich *Conn* 50-53; C Lisburn Ch Ch Cathl 53-61; P-in-c Belfast Whiterock 61-69; I Belfast St Mary Magd 69-91; Can Conn Cathl from 87; rtd 91. *38 Lancefield Road, Belfast BT9 6LL* Tel (01232) 665872

LENG, Bruce Edgar. b 38. St Aid Birkenhead 68. **d** 69 **p** 70. C Sheff St Swithun *Sheff* 69-74; TV Speke St Aid *Liv* 74-78; TV Yate New Town *Bris* 78-82; R Handsworth *Sheff* 82-95; P-in-c Thrybergh w Hooton Roberts 95; R Thrybergh from 95; Warden for Pastoral Workers from 96. *The Rectory, 14 Manor Farm Court, Thrybergh, Rotherham, S Yorkshire S65 4NZ* Tel (01709) 580336

LENNARD, Edward Stuart Churchill. b 21. Ex Coll Ox MA42. Cuddesdon Coll 47. **d** 54 **p** 55. SSJE from 54; Lic to Offic *Ox* 54-57; S Africa 57-59; Lic to Offic *Ox* 59-86; Perm to Offic 86-96; rtd 88. *Green Gates Nursing Home, 2 Hernes Road, Summertown, Oxford OX2 7PT* Tel (01865) 58815

LENNARD, Mrs Elizabeth Jemima Mary Patricia. b 21. Edin Dioc NSM Course 78. **dss** 82 **d** 86 **p** 94. Falkirk *Edin* 82-86; Hon C 86-91; Asst Dioc Supernumerary 91-96; Hon C Grangemouth from 96; Hon C Bo'ness from 96. *36 Heugh Street, Falkirk FK1 5QR* Tel (01324) 623240

LENNARD, Thomas Jay. b 21. MBE54. Edin Dioc NSM Course 74. **d** 76 **p** 77. Hon C Kelso *Edin* 76-82; Hon C Falkirk 82-91; Asst Dioc Supernumerary 91-96; Hon C Grangemouth from 96; Hon C Bo'ness from 96. *36 Heugh Street, Falkirk FK1 5QR* Tel (01324) 623240

LENNON, Alfred Dennis. b 32. Oak Hill Th Coll 72. **d** 74 **p** 74. C Cambridge H Sepulchre w All SS *Ely* 74-77; P-in-c Cambridge St Barn 77-83; R Edin St Thos *Edin* 83-90; P-in-c Burghwallis *Sheff* from 90; Dioc Adv for Evang from 90. *St Helen's Rectory, Burghwallis, Doncaster, S Yorkshire DN6 9JL* Tel (01302) 700227

LENNOX, James. b 12. TCD BA36 MA40. Div Test 37. **d** 38 **p** 39. C Houghton le Spring *Dur* 38-43; C Darlington St Cuth 43-47; V Woodhouse *Wakef* 47-63; V Bingley All SS *Bradf* 63-77; rtd 77; Perm to Offic *Bradf* from 77. *30 Hazel Beck, Cottingley Bridge, Bingley, W Yorkshire BD16 1LZ* Tel (01274) 560189

LENNOX, Joan Baxter. b 50. Strathclyde Univ BA70 DipC94. St Jo Coll Nottm 90. **d** 96. C Baillieston *Glas* from 96. *14 Kildare Drive, Lanark ML11 7AQ* Tel (01555) 662673 Fax as telephone

LENNOX, William Ernest Michael. b 28. Selw Coll Cam BA52 MA63 Leeds Univ CertEd55. K Coll Lon 62. **d** 63 **p** 64. C Bramley *Ripon* 63-66; C Margate St Jo *Cant* 66-71; R Kingsnorth 71-73; R Shadoxhurst 71-73; R Kingsnorth w Shadoxhurst 73-93; rtd 93. *6 Rue Aux Savons, Le Boisle, 80150 Crecy en Ponthieu, France*

LENON, Philip John FitzMaurice. b 24. ARIBA52 Lon Univ BD60. Wycliffe Hall Ox 55. **d** 57 **p** 58. C Hornsey Ch Ch *Lon* 57-60; C-in-c Sidcup St Andr CD *Roch* 60-67; V Crowborough *Chich* 67-89; rtd 89. *Snowhill Cottage, Dinton, Salisbury SP3 5HN* Tel (01722) 716754

LENOX-CONYNGHAM, Andrew George. b 44. Magd Coll Ox BA65 MA73 CCC Cam PhD73. Westcott Ho Cam 72. **d** 74 **p** 75. C Poplar *Lon* 74-77; TV Poplar 77-80; Chapl Heidelberg *Eur* 80-82 and 91-96; Chapl Ch Coll Cam 82-86; Chapl and Fell St Cath Coll Cam 86-91; V Birm St Luke *Birm* from 96. *St Luke's Vicarage, 10 St Luke's Road, Birmingham B5 7DA* Tel 0121-622 2435

LENS VAN RIJN, Robert Adriaan. b 47. St Jo Coll Nottm 78. **d** 80 **p** 81. C Gt Baddow *Chelmsf* 80-83; C Edgware *Lon* 83-86; C Derby St Pet and Ch Ch w H Trin *Derby* 86-90; Chapl Eindhoven *Eur* from 91. *Chopinlaan 41, 5653 ET Eindhoven, The Netherlands* Tel Eindhoven (40) 573523

LENTON, Colin William. b 23. CertEd. Cuddesdon Coll 80. **d** 81 **p** 81. Hon C Cowley St Jo *Ox* 81-82; Hon C Oakley 82-85; V Langtoft w Foxholes, Butterwick, Cottam etc *York* 85-89; rtd 89. *Flat 3, 24 South Drive, Harrogate HG2 8AU* Tel (01423) 564751

LENTON, Robert Vincent. b 15. Clifton Th Coll 62. **d** 63 **p** 63. Kenya 63-71; V Lacock w Bowden Hill *Bris* 71-83; rtd 83; Perm to Offic *Liv* 83-95. *College of St Barnabas, Blackberry Lane, Lingfield, Surrey RH7 6NJ* Tel (01342) 870260

LENYGON, Canon Herbert Edward. b 11. Lon Univ BD53. Kelham Th Coll 32. **d** 38 **p** 39. C Wallsend St Pet *Newc* 38-41; C Newc St Gabr 41-49; Chapl Newc United Hosps 49-74; Hon Can Newc Cathl *Newc* 70-74; rtd 74; Perm to Offic *Cov* 74-93. *48 Foxes Way, Warwick CV34 6AY* Tel (01926) 493954

LEONARD, Ms Ann Cressey. b 50. Open Univ BA90. S Dios Minl Tr Scheme 90. **d** 94 **p** 95. C Portsea St Cuth *Portsm* 94-96; C Farlington from 96. *23 Court Close, Cosham, Portsmouth PO6 2LU* Tel (01705) 385054

LEONARD, John Francis. b 48. Lich Th Coll 69. **d** 72 **p** 73. C Chorley St Geo *Blackb* 72-75; C S Shore H Trin 75-80; V Marton Moss 81-89; V Kingskerswell w Coffinswell *Ex* from 89. *The Vicarage, Pound Lane, Kingskerswell, Newton Abbot, Devon TQ12 5DW* Tel (01803) 872305

LEONARD, Canon John James. b 41. Southn Univ BSc62. Sarum Th Coll 63. **d** 65 **p** 66. C Loughborough Em *Leic* 65-70; V New Humberstone 70-78; C-in-c Rushey Mead CD 78-85; V Leic St Theodore from 85; Hon Can Leic Cathl from 97; RD Christianity N from 97. *St Theodore's House, 4 Sandfield Close, Leicester LE4 7RE* Tel 0116-266 9956

LEONARD, Peter Michael. b 47. MRTPI Portsm Poly BSc Trent Poly DipTP. Sarum & Wells Th Coll 82. **d** 84 **p** 85. C Llantwit Major *Llan* 84-88; V Cymmer and Porth 88-96; R Colwinston w Llandow and Llysworney from 96. *The Rectory, Llandow, Cowbridge CF71 7NT* Tel (01656) 890205

LEONARD, Peter Philip. b 70. Trin Coll Bris BA94. **d** 97. C Haslemere *Guildf* from 97. *16 Chatsworth Avenue, Haslemere, Surrey GU27 1BA* Tel (01428) 643928

LEONARD, Vaughan Thomas. b 51. Coll of Resurr Mirfield 94. **d** 96 **p** 97. C Broadstone *Sarum* from 96. *1A Mission Road, Broadstone, Dorset BH18 8SS* Tel (01202) 603840

LEONARD-JOHNSON, Canon Philip Anthony. b 35. Selw Coll Cam BA58 MA60. Linc Th Coll 63. **d** 65 **p** 66. C Wymondham *Nor* 65-68; Zimbabwe 69-82; V Drayton in Hales *Lich* 82-92; R Adderley 82-92; P-in-c Moreton Say 88-92; S Africa from 92; rtd 97; Hon Can Grahamstown from 97. *PO Box 256, Prince Alfred Square, King William's Town, 5600 South Africa* Tel (45) 962 1105

LEONARDI, Jeffrey. b 49. Warw Univ BA71 Aston Univ DCouns79. Carl Dioc Tr Course 85. **d** 88 **p** 89. C Netherton *Carl* 88-91; V Crosscanonby from 91; V Allonby from 91. *Crosscanonby Vicarage, Crosby, Maryport, Cumbria CA15 6SJ* Tel (01900) 814192

LEPINE, Jeremy John. b 56. BA. St Jo Coll Nottm 82. **d** 84 **p** 85. C Harrow Trin St Mich *Lon* 84-88; TV Horley *S'wark* 88-95; Croydon Evang Team from 95. *Merrow, The Avenue, South Nutfield, Redhill RH1 5RY* Tel (01737) 822322

LEPINE, Peter Gerald. b 27. St Fran Coll Brisbane ThL56. **d** 57 **p** 58. Australia 57-62 and 65-67; SSF 63-91; Perm to Offic *Sarum* 63-65; Perm to Offic *Worc* 63-65; Papua New Guinea 67-76; Solomon Is 76; Perm to Offic *Conn* 76-80; P-in-c Belfast H Redeemer 80-87; Lic to Offic *Newc* from 88; rtd 92. *Flat 1, 2 Queen's Road, Jesmond, Newcastle upon Tyne NE2 2PP* Tel 0191-281 1156

LEPPARD, Miss Myra Anne. b 47. Chich Th Coll. **d** 90. Asst Chapl Brighton Hosp Gp 90-96; Par Dn Brighton Gd Shep Preston *Chich* 91-92; Par Dn S Patcham 92-94; C Rustington 94-96. *47 Brangwyn Drive, Brighton BN1 8XB*

LEPPINGTON, Ms Dian. b 46. Leeds Univ BA85. Cranmer Hall Dur 81. **dss** 83 **d** 87 **p** 94. Potternewton *Ripon* 83-87; Par Dn from 88; Ind Chapl from 85. *52 Newton Court, Leeds LS8 2PH* Tel 0113-248 5011 or 242 4886

LERRY, Keith Doyle. b 49. Univ of Wales (Cardiff) DipTh72. St Mich Coll Llan 69. **d** 72 **p** 73. C Caerau w Ely *Llan* 72-75; C Roath St Martin 75-84; V Glyntaff from 84. *The Vicarage, Glyntaff Road, Pontypridd CF37 4AS* Tel (01443) 402535

LERVY, Hugh Martin. b 68. **d** 91 **p** 92. C Brecon St Mary and Battle w Llanddew *S & B* 91-93; C Oystermouth 93-95; V Glantawe from 95. *The Vicarage, 122 Mansell Road, Bon-y-Maen, Swansea SA1 7JR* Tel (01792) 652839

LESITER, The Ven Malcolm Leslie. b 37. Selw Coll Cam BA61 MA65. Cuddesdon Coll 61. **d** 63 **p** 64. C Eastney *Portsm* 63-66; C Hemel Hempstead *St Alb* 66-71; TV 71-73; V Leavesden All SS 73-88; RD Watford 81-88; V Radlett 88-93; Hon Can St Alb Abbey 90-93; Adn Bedford from 93. *17 Lansdowne Road, Luton LU3 1EE* Tel (01582) 30722 Fax as telephone

LESLIE, David Rodney. b 43. AKC67. **d** 68 **p** 69. C Belmont *Lon* 68-71; C St Giles Cripplegate w St Bart Moor Lane etc 71-75; TV Kirkby *Liv* 76-84; TR Ditton St Mich from 84. *339 Ditchfield Road, Widnes, Cheshire WA8 8XR* Tel 0151-424 2502

LESLIE, Richard Charles Alan. b 46. ACIB71. St Alb Minl Tr Scheme 76. **d** 79 **p** 91. NSM Redbourn *St Alb* 79-88; Hon C Newport Pagnell w Lathbury and Moulsoe *Ox* 88-94; Stewardship Adv St Alb Adnry *St Alb* 94-97; TV

Borehamwood from 97. *St Michael's Vicarage, 142 Brook Road, Borehamwood, Herts WD6 5EQ* Tel 0181-953 2362

LESTER, Preb Geoffrey. b 16. Trin Coll Cam BA39 MA43. Wycliffe Hall Ox 41. **d** 42 **p** 43. C St Marylebone All So w SS Pet and Jo *Lon* 42-47; Chapl Westmr Abbey 43-44; C Bywell St Andr *Newc* 47-48; Kenya 48-60; Provost Nairobi 55-60; R Bath Abbey w St Jas *B & W* 60-89; RD Bath 61-71; Preb Wells Cathl 62-93; rtd 89. *29 Woodland Grove, Claverton Down, Bath BA2 7AT* Tel (01225) 469860

LESTER, Trevor Rashleigh. b 50. CITC 83 St Deiniol's Hawarden 92. **d** 89 **p** 90. NSM Douglas Union w Frankfield *C, C & R* 89-93; C Kilkenny w Aghour and Kilmanagh *C & O* 93-95; Bp's V Ossory Cathl 93-95; Dioc Registrar (Ossory, Ferns and Leighlin) 93-95; Dioc Lib St Canice's Lib 93-95; I Abbeystrewry Union *C, C & R* from 95. *The Rectory, Coronea Drive, Skibbereen, Co Cork, Irish Republic* Tel Cork (28) 21234

L'ESTRANGE, Canon Guy James Albert. b 24. TCD BA47 MA50. CITC. **d** 47 **p** 48. C Ballymacarrett St Martin *D & D* 47-51; Dean's V St Patr Cathl Dublin 51-63; News and Info Officer for Ch of Ireland 61-63; Hd Master Cant Cathl Choir Sch 63-64; Min Can and Prec Cant Cathl *Cant* 63-68; R Saltwood 68-89; RD Elham 74-80; Hon Can Cant Cathl 81-89; Sec to Dioc Bd of Min 86-89; rtd 89; Perm to Offic *Cant* from 89; Guardian Greyfriars from 93. *36 St Stephen's Hill, Canterbury, Kent CT2 7AX* Tel (01227) 763226

L'ESTRANGE, Canon Hilary Cecil Hurford. b 21. St Paul's Coll Barton 42. **d** 45 **p** 46. C Newry St Mary *D & D* 45-47; C Belfast St Luke *Conn* 47-51; C Edin St Salvador *Edin* 51-54; S Africa from 54; Hon Can George from 85; rtd 88. *51 Drostdy Street, Swellendam, 6740 South Africa* Tel Swellendam (291) 42326

L'ESTRANGE, Timothy John Nicholas. b 67. Surrey Univ BA90 Ox Univ BA92 MA96. St Steph Ho Ox 90. **d** 93 **p** 94. C Halesworth w Linstead, Chediston, Holton etc *St E* 93-96; Dom Chapl to Area Bp Horsham *Chich* from 96. *Bishop's House, 21 Guildford Road, Horsham, or St John Bosco House, 108 Clarence Road, Horsham, W Sussex RH13 5SG* Tel (01403) 211139 or 242759 Fax 217349

LETALL, Ronald Richard. b 29. ACII76. Linc Th Coll 82. **d** 84 **p** 85. C Scarborough St Martin *York* 84-86; C Middlesbrough St Thos 86-88; R Kirby Misperton w Normanby, Edston and Salton 88-90; TV Louth *Linc* 90-94; rtd 94; Perm to Offic *Sheff* from 94; Perm to Offic *Wakef* from 95; Perm to Offic *Chich* from 97. *4 Pavilion Close, Brierley, Barnsley, S Yorkshire S72 9LR* Tel (01226) 715433

LETCHER, Canon David John. b 34. K Coll Lon 54. Chich Th Coll 56. **d** 58 **p** 59. C St Austell *Truro* 58-62; C Southbroom *Sarum* 62-64; R Odstock w Nunton and Bodenham 64-72; RD Alderbury 68-73 and 77-82; V Downton 72-85; Can and Preb Sarum Cathl from 79; TV Dorchester 85-97; RD Dorchester 89-95; rtd 97. *Dormers, 6 Longmoor Street, Poundbury, Dorchester, Dorset DT1 3GN* Tel (01305) 257764

LETFORD, Peter Arthur. b 36. Oak Hill Th Coll 68. **d** 70 **p** 71. C Maidstone St Faith *Cant* 70-72; CF 72-75; C Ramsgate St Luke *Cant* 75-77; P-in-c Eastling 77-79; P-in-c Becontree St Elisabeth *Chelmsf* 79-84; P-in-c Clay Cross *Derby* 84-90; TV N Wingfield, Clay Cross and Pilsley 90-94; Chapl Casablanca *Eur* from 94. *Place Leclerc, Angle rue des Vanneaux 1, Casablanca, Morocco* Tel Morocco (2) 257120 Fax as telephone

LETHBRIDGE, Christopher David. b 43. N Ord Course 90. **d** 93 **p** 94. NSM S Elmsall *Wakef* 93-95; C Knottingley from 95. *Mylor, Chapel Lane, Knottingley, W Yorkshire WF11 9AN* Tel (01977) 677010

LETHEREN, William Neils. b 37. Lon Univ DipTh63. St Aid Birkenhead 61. **d** 64 **p** 65. C Liv St Mich *Liv* 64-67; V 71-75; C Kirkdale St Athanasius 67-69; C Walsall Wood *Lich* 69-71; V W Derby St Jas *Liv* 75-84; R Newton in Makerfield Em 84-88; V Garston from 88. *The Vicarage, Horrocks Avenue, Garston, Liverpool L19 5NY* Tel 0151-427 4204

LETSON, Barry. b 55. Univ of Wales (Lamp) BA77. St Deiniol's Hawarden 82. **d** 83 **p** 84. C Flint *St As* 83-86; V Llansantffraid and Llanarmon and Pontfadog 86-89; R Montgomery and Forden and Llandyssil 89-96; RD Pool 92-96; V Mountain Ash *Llan* from 96. *The Vicarage, Duffryn Road, Mountain Ash CF45 4DA* Tel (01443) 473700

LETTON, Stanley Gladstone. b 17. LNSM course 81. **d** 82 **p** 94. NSM Brechin *Bre* from 82; NSM Tarfside from 82; NSM Auchmithie from 82. *12 Latch Road, Brechin, Angus DD9 6JE* Tel (01356) 622519

LETTS, Gerald Vincent. b 33. Univ of Wales BA63 Birm Univ DipTh65. NY Th Sem DMin Qu Coll Birm 63. **d** 65 **p** 66. C Birstall *Leic* 65-68; V Belgrave St Mich 68-75; V Sheff St Cuth *Sheff* 75-91; R Bradfield from 91. *The Rectory, Bradfield, Sheffield S6 6LG* Tel 0114-285 1225

LETTS, Kenneth John (Ken). b 42. Melbourne Univ BA65 Leeds Univ DipTh71 Melbourne Univ DipEd67. Coll of Resurr Mirfield 68. **d** 71 **p** 72. Australia 71-94; Chapl Nice w Vence *Eur* from 94. *11 rue de la Buffa, 06000 Nice, France* Tel France (33) 93 87 19 83

LEUNG, Dr Peter. Trin Coll Singapore BTh60 St Andr Univ PhD73. SE Asia Sch of Th MTh69. **d** 60 **p** 61. Singapore 60-62 and 65-76; Br N Borneo 62-63; Malaysia 63-65; Lect Congr Coll Man 76-77; USPG 77-83; Perm to Offic *Roch* 83-89; BCC 83-90; CCBI from 90; Perm to Offic *S'wark* 88-94; Hon C Shortlands *Roch* from 90; Regional Sec (S and E Asia) CMS from 91. *14 Uplands, Beckenham, Kent BR3 3NB* Tel 0181-650 4157 or 0171-928 8681 Fax 0171-401 3215

LEVER, Edmund Arthur (Ted). b 23. Sarum Th Coll 55. **d** 57 **p** 58. C Chorlton-cum-Hardy St Werburgh *Man* 57-59; C Farnworth and Kearsley 59-60; Hon C Leigh-on-Sea St Jas *Chelmsf* 60-63; V Brentwood St Geo 64-73; Chapl S Ockendon Hosp 73-78; rtd 88; Perm to Offic *Chelmsf* from 88. *42 Pear Tree Close, South Ockendon, Essex RM15 6PR* Tel (01708) 852933

LEVER, Julian Lawrence Gerrard. b 36. Fitzw Coll Cam BA60 MA64. Sarum Th Coll 60. **d** 62 **p** 63. C Amesbury *Sarum* 62-66; R Corfe Mullen 66-78; RD Wimborne 73-75; P-in-c Wilton w Netherhampton and Fugglestone 78-82; R 82-86; R Salisbury St Martin 86-94. *6 St John's Close, Wimborne, Dorset BH21 1LY* Tel (01202) 848249

LEVERTON, Michael John. b 52. K Coll Lon BD76 AKC76 MTh77. Cant Sch of Min 84. **d** 87 **p** 88. NSM Elham w Denton and Wootton *Cant* 87-92; C Yelverton, Meavy, Sheepstor and Walkhampton *Ex* 92-93; TV from 93. *The Vicarage, 1 Manor Farm, Dousland, Yelverton, Devon PL20 6NR* Tel (01822) 855076

LEVERTON, Peter James Austin (Jim). b 33. Nottm Univ BA55. Ripon Coll Cuddesdon 79. **d** 81 **p** 82. C St Jo in Bedwardine *Worc* 81-84; V Worc St Mich 84-88; TR Worc St Barn w Ch Ch 88-92; V Riddings and Ironville *Derby* from 92. *The Vicarage, Vicarage Lane, Ironville, Nottingham NG16 5PT* Tel (01773) 602241

LEVERTON, Peter Robert. b 25. Lich Th Coll 59. **d** 60 **p** 61. C Shepshed *Leic* 60-64; Australia 64-69; V Marshchapel *Linc* 70-73; V Grainthorpe w Conisholme 70-73; R N Coates 70-73; Miss to Seamen 73-77; P-in-c Brislington St Luke *Bris* 77-84; V Avonmouth St Andr 84-87; Ind Chapl 84-87; P-in-c Ugborough *Ex* 87-91; P-in-c Ermington 88-91; rtd 91; Perm to Offic *Ex* 91-95. *4 Drakes Avenue, Sidford, Sidmouth, Devon EX10 9QY* Tel (01395) 579835

LEVETT, Colin Andrew. b 13. **d** 69 **p** 71. Par Dn Hatch End St Anselm *Lon* 69-71; Asst P N Wembley St Cuth 71-73; P-in-c Dollis Hill St Paul 73-78; rtd 78. *32 Hillstead Court, Basingstoke, Hants RG21 3PT* Tel (01256) 333405

LEVETT, Canon Howard. b 44. K Coll Lon AKC67. **d** 68 **p** 69. C Rotherhithe St Mary w All SS *S'wark* 68-72; P-in-c Walworth St Jo 72-77; V Walworth St Jo 77-80; P-in-c Walworth Lady Marg w St Mary 78; RD S'wark and Newington 78-80; Adn Egypt 80-94; Miss to Seamen from 80; JMECA from 80; V Holborn St Alb w Saffron Hill St Pet *Lon* from 94. *St Alban's Clergy House, Brooke Street, London EC1N 7RD* Tel 0171-405 1831 Fax as telephone

LEVEY, Canon Colin Russell. b 35. Open Univ BA76. S'wark Ord Course 63. **d** 66 **p** 67. C Rusthall *Roch* 66-71; Youth Chapl 71-75; Hon C Riverhead 71-75; V Lamorbey H Redeemer 75-81; V Milton next Gravesend Ch Ch 81-85; P-in-c Elmley Lovett w Hampton Lovett and Elmbridge etc *Worc* 87-91; P-in-c Hartlebury 87-91; P-in-c Wilden 87-91; R Orton and Tebay w Ravenstonedale etc *Carl* from 91; RD Appleby from 93; Hon Can Carl Cathl from 94. *The Vicarage, Orton, Penrith, Cumbria CA10 3RQ* Tel (015396) 24532

LEVICK, Brian William. b 30. Westcott Ho Cam 63. **d** 64 **p** 65. C Bourne *Linc* 64-69; C Deeping St James 69-70; C Hemel Hempstead *St Alb* 70-71; TV 71-77; Hon C Sedbergh, Cautley and Garsdale *Bradf* 77-83; V Firbank, Howgill and Killington 77-83; V Cononley w Bradley 83-90; C Kettlewell w Conistone, Hubberholme etc 90-93; rtd 93; Hon C New Sleaford *Linc* from 93; Dioc Ecum Officer from 93. *11 Rowan Drive, Silk Willoughby, Sleaford, Lincs NG34 8PQ* Tel (01529) 303207

LEVICK, Canon Frank Hemsley. b 29. Kelham Th Coll 49. **d** 54 **p** 55. C Anfield St Marg *Liv* 54-58; V 58-67; V Ribbleton *Blackb* 67-80; TR 80-85; Hon Can Blackb Cathl 75-90; R Ribchester w Stidd 85-90; rtd 90. *The Old Nurseries, Low Street, Beckingham, Doncaster, S Yorkshire DN10 4PS* Tel (01427) 848668

LEVY, Christopher Charles. b 51. Southn Univ BTh82. Sarum & Wells Th Coll 79. **d** 82 **p** 83. C Rubery *Birm* 82-85; C Stratford-on-Avon w Bishopton *Cov* 85-87; TV Clifton *S'well* 87-95; V Egmanton from 95; R Kirton from 95; V Walesby from 95. *St Edmund's Vicarage, Walesby, Newark, Notts NG22 9PA* Tel (01623) 860522

LEW, Harry E A. b 39. **d** 96. NSM Dublin Whitechurch *D & G* from 96. *51 Butterfield Park, Rathfarnham, Dublin 14, Irish Republic* Tel Dublin (1) 493 1483

LEWERS, The Very Revd Benjamin Hugh (Ben). b 32. Selw Coll Cam BA60 MA64. Linc Th Coll. **d** 62 **p** 63. C Northampton St Mary *Pet* 62-65; C Hounslow Heath St Paul *Lon* 65-68; C-in-c Hounslow Gd Shep Beavers Lane CD 65-68; Chapl Heathrow Airport 68-75; V Newark St Mary *S'well* 75-80; TR Newark w Hawton, Cotham and Shelton 80-81; P-in-c Averham w Kelham 79-81; Provost Derby from 81. *Provost's House, 9 Highfield Road, Derby DE22 1GX* Tel (01332) 341201 or 342971

LEWES AND HASTINGS, Archdeacon of. *See* READE, The Ven Nicholas Stewart

LEWES, Area Bishop of. *See* BENN, The Rt Revd Wallace Parke

LEWIS, The Ven Albert John Francis. b 21. Univ Coll of S Wales BA(Econ)45. St Mich Coll Llan 46. **d** 48 **p** 49. C Cardiff St Jo *Llan* 48-61; Dioc Dir RE 60-91; V Pendoylan 61-73; P-in-c Welsh St Donats 70-73; V Pendoylan and Welsh St Donats 73-81; RD Llan 69-81; Can Llan Cathl 76-81; Treas 81-88; Adn Margam 81-88; Adn Llan 88-91; rtd 91; Chapl to Rtd Clerics and Widows of Clergy *Llan* from 91; Perm to Offic from 91. *11 Downs View Close, Aberthin, Cowbridge CF7 7HG* Tel (01446) 773320

LEWIS, Canon Alexander Thomas (Alex). b 20. Univ of Wales (Ban) BA51. St Mich Coll Llan 50. **d** 52 **p** 53. C Llanaber *Ban* 52-56; V Llandegai St Ann, Bethesda w Tregarth 56-89; RD Arllechwedd 73-89; Hon Can Ban Cathl 82-84; Can 84-89; rtd 89; Lic to Offic *Ban* from 89; Perm to Offic *Liv* from 89. *91 Wellfield Road, Culcheth, Warrington WA3 4BX* Tel (01925) 762899

LEWIS, Ann Theodora Rachel. b 33. Univ of Wales (Ban) BA55. Qu Coll Birm 78. **d** 80 **p** 97. C Swansea St Mary w H Trin *S & B* 80-96; Chapl St Mary's Coll 90-96; rtd 96; Public Preacher *St D* from 96. *Fisherywish, Maes yr Eglwys, Llansaint, Kidwelly SA17 5JE* Tel (01267) 267386

LEWIS, Canon Arthur Griffith. b 15. Univ of Wales (Lamp) BA40. **d** 47 **p** 48. C Clydach *S & B* 47-55; R Aberyscir and Llanfihangel Nantbran 55-63; V Ystalyfera 63-87; RD Cwmtawe 79-85; Hon Can Brecon Cathl 80-89; Can 81-85; P-in-c Capel Coelbren 85-89; rtd 89. *14 Pontwillim, Brecon LD3 9BT* Tel (01874) 622869

LEWIS, Arthur Jenkin Llewellyn. b 42. Univ of Wales (Cardiff) MPS67 BPharm. Coll of Resurr Mirfield 71. **d** 73 **p** 74. C Cardiff St Jo *Llan* 73-78; C Christchurch *Win* 78-82; R Lightbowne *Man* from 82. *St Luke's Rectory, Kenyon Lane, Manchester M10 9HS* Tel 0161-681 1308

LEWIS, Arthur Roland. b 20. St Edm Hall Ox BA41 MA45. St Steph Ho Ox 41. **d** 43 **p** 44. C Sutton in Ashfield St Mich *S'well* 43-45; C Stirchley *Birm* 45-47; Zanzibar and Tanganyika 47-58; S Rhodesia 58-65; Rhodesia 65-80; Adn Inyanga 66-69; S Africa 80-87; rtd 87; Perm to Offic *Birm* from 88. *54 Lyndon Road, Solihull, W Midlands B92 7RQ*

LEWIS, The Ven Benjamin Alec. b 12. St D Coll Lamp BA34. **d** 36 **p** 37. C Cardigan *St D* 36-40; C Ammanford 40-41; Bp's Messenger 41-46; V Llanelli Ch Ch 46-56; R Hubbertson 56-70; Adn St D 70-82; Can St D Cathl 70-82; Dir Relig Educn 70-82; rtd 82. *4 St Non's Close, St Davids, Haverfordwest SA62 6RL* Tel (01437) 720446

LEWIS, The Very Revd Bertie. b 31. Univ of Wales (Lamp) BA54 St Cath Soc Ox BA57 MA60. Wycliffe Hall Ox 54. **d** 57 **p** 58. C Cwmaman *St D* 57-60; C Aberystwyth St Mich 60-62; V Llanddewi Brefi w Llanbadarn Odwyn 62-65; V Henfynyw w Aberaeron and Llanddewi Aberarth 65-75; V Lampeter 75-80; Can St D Cathl 78-86; Chapl Abth Hosps 80-88; R Aberystwyth *St D* 80-88; Adn Cardigan 86-90; V Nevern and Y Beifil w Eglwyswrw and Meline etc 88-90; V 94-96; Dean St D 90-94; V St D Cathl 90-94; Hon Can St D Cathl 94-97; rtd 96. *Bryn Golau, Llanfarian, Aberystwyth SY23 4BT* Tel (01970) 612492

LEWIS, Brian James. b 52. Cant Univ (NZ) BA75. St Jo Coll Auckland 76. **d** 78 **p** 79. New Zealand 78-80; C Shrub End *Chelmsf* 80-82; P-in-c Colchester St Barn 82-84; V 84-88; P-in-c Romford St Andr 88-90; R from 90; RD Havering from 93. *St Andrew's Rectory, 119 London Road, Romford RM7 9QD* Tel (01708) 764192

LEWIS, The Very Revd Christopher Andrew. b 44. Bris Univ BA69 CCC Cam PhD74. Westcott Ho Cam 71. **d** 73 **p** 74. C Barnard Castle *Dur* 73-76; Dir Ox Inst for Ch and Soc 76-79; Tutor Ripon Coll Cuddesdon 76-79; P-in-c Aston Rowant w Crowell *Ox* 78-81; Sen Tutor Ripon Coll Cuddesdon 79-81; Vice-Prin 81-82; V Spalding *Linc* 82-87; Can Res Cant Cathl *Cant* 87-94; Dir of Minl Tr 89-94; Dean St Alb from 94. *The Deanery, Sumpter Yard, St Albans, Herts AL1 1BY* Tel (01727) 852120 E-mail cathedra@alban.u-net.com

LEWIS, Canon Christopher Gouldson. b 42. K Coll Cam BA64 MA68. Cuddesdon Coll 65. **d** 67 **p** 68. C Gosforth All SS *Newc* 67-71; Sarawak 71-74; V Luton St Chris Round Green *St Alb* 74-80; RD Reculver *Cant* 80-86 and 92-93; V Whitstable All SS w St Pet 80-84; TR Whitstable 84-93; Dir of Post-Ord Tr 88-93; Hon Can Cant Cathl 91-93; Can Res Bradf Cathl *Bradf* from 93; Bp's Officer for Min and Tr from 93. *2 Cathedral Close, Bradford, W Yorkshire BD1 4EG* Tel (01274) 727806

LEWIS, David Antony. b 48. Dur Univ BA69 Nottm Univ MTh84. St Jo Coll Nottm 81. **d** 83 **p** 84. C Gateacre *Liv* 83-86; V Toxteth St Cypr w Ch Ch from 86; AD Liv N from 94. *The Vicarage, 48 John Lennon Drive, Liverpool L6 9HT* Tel 0151-260 3262

LEWIS, David Glyn. b 09. Univ of Wales BA36. Ripon Hall Ox 36. **d** 39 **p** 40. C Acocks Green *Birm* 39-45; Dioc Chapl in charge of Birm St Laur 45-49; V Butlers Marston w Pillerton Hersey etc *Cov* 49-55; V Long Itchington 55-68; P-in-c Ufton 67-68; V Cubbington 68-79; rtd 80; Perm to Offic *Cov* from 80. *4 St James Close, Stratford-upon-Avon, Warks CV37 7RH* Tel (01789) 205559

LEWIS, David Hugh. b 45. Oak Hill Th Coll 88. **d** 90 **p** 91. C Oakham, Hambleton, Egleton, Braunston and Brooke *Pet* 90-94; R Ewhurst *Guildf* from 94. *The Rectory, Ewhurst, Cranleigh, Surrey GU6 7PX* Tel (01483) 277584

LEWIS, David Roy. b 18. Univ of Wales (Lamp) BA39. St Mich Coll Llan 40. **d** 40 **p** 41. C Cardiff St Jo *Llan* 40-46; Br Guiana 46-54; Trinidad and Tobago 54-66; V Seven Sisters *Llan* 66-77; R Colwinston w Llandow and Llysworney 77-86; rtd 86. *Rockleigh, Colwinstone, Cowbridge CF7 7NL* Tel (01656) 654797

LEWIS, David Tudor. b 61. Jes Coll Cam BA83. Trin Coll Bris BA88. **d** 88 **p** 89. C Tile Cross *Birm* 88-91; C Woking St Jo *Guildf* 91-95; TV Carl H Trin and St Barn *Carl* 95-97; Asst Chapl Oslo w Bergen, Trondheim and Stavanger *Eur* from 97. *Valhallveien 9, 4043 Håfrsfjord, Norway* Tel Håfrsfjord (51) 556712

LEWIS, David Tudor Bowes. b 63. Keele Univ BA85 Univ of Wales (Cardiff) BTh90. St Mich Coll Llan 87. **d** 90 **p** 91. C Llangollen w Trevor and Llantysilio *St As* 90-93; C Bistre 93-97; V Berse and Southsea from 97. *The Vicarage, Smithy Lane, Southsea, Wrexham LL11 6PN* Tel (01978) 750150

LEWIS, Canon David Vaughan. b 36. Trin Coll Cam BA60 MA64. Ridley Hall Cam 60. **d** 62 **p** 63. C Rugby St Matt *Cov* 62-65; Asst Chapl K Edw Sch Witley 65-71; Hon C Rainham *Chelmsf* 71-76; V Stoke Hill *Guildf* 76-87; V Wallington H Trin *S'wark* from 87; Hon Can S'wark Cathl from 95; RD Sutton from 97. *Holy Trinity Vicarage, Maldon Road, Wallington, Surrey SM6 8BL* Tel 0181-647 7605

LEWIS, David Watkin. b 40. Univ of Wales (Lamp) BA61 Univ of Wales (Swansea) DipYL65. Wycliffe Hall Ox 61. **d** 63 **p** 64. C Skewen *Llan* 63-66; Field Tr Officer Prov Youth Coun Ch in Wales 66-68; C Gabalfa 68-71; P-in-c Marcross w Monknash and Wick 71-73; R 73-83; RD Llantwit Major and Cowbridge 81-83; V Baglan from 83. *The Vicarage, 29 Church Road, Port Talbot SA12 8ST* Tel (01639) 812199

LEWIS, Canon Donald Edward (Don). b 30. Univ of Wales (Lamp) BA53. Wycliffe Hall Ox 53. **d** 55 **p** 56. C Wrexham *St As* 55-59; R Castle Caereinion 59-62; Area Sec (Dios Ches, Ban, St As and S & M) CMS 62-65; India 62-65; V Hale *Ches* 65-77; V Swansea St Mary and H Trin *S & B* 77-79; V Swansea St Mary w H Trin and St Mark 79-83; V Swansea St Mary w H Trin 83-96; RD Swansea 78-96; Hon Can Brecon Cathl 79-81; Can 81-95; Treas 94-95; Prec Brecon Cathl 90-94; rtd 96. *Fisherywish, Maes yr Eglwys, Llansaint, Kidwelly SA17 5JE* Tel (01267) 267386

LEWIS, Edward John. b 15. Qu Coll Cam BA36 MA40. Ridley Hall Cam 36. **d** 38 **p** 39. C Litherland St Phil *Liv* 38-41; C Prescot 41-43; Chapl RNVR 43-46; R Brechin *Bre* 47-53; V Copt Oak *Leic* 53-56; V Swanwick and Pentrich *Derby* 56-74; P-in-c Longstone 74-80; rtd 80; Perm to Offic *Derby* 80-95; Perm to Offic *Liv* from 80. *5 Old Hall Gardens, Rainford, St Helens, Merseyside WA11 8NS* Tel (01744) 882242

LEWIS, Edward John. b 58. Univ of Wales BEd80 BA82. Chich Th Coll 82. **d** 83 **p** 84. C Llangiwg *S & B* 83-85; C Morriston 85-87; V Tregaron w Ystrad Meurig and Strata Florida *St D* 87-89; Chapl Manor Hosp Walsall 89-92; Distr Co-ord Chapl Walsall Hosps 90-92; Sen Chapl Walsall Hosps NHS Trust from 92; Chapl Walsall Community Health Trust from 92; Asst RD Walsall from 95. *The Chaplain's Office, Manor Hospital, Moat Road, Walsall WS2 9PS* Tel (01922) 721172 or 656834

LEWIS, Elinor Glenys. b 11. CBE93. SRN34 SCM35. St Chris Coll Blackheath 44. **dss** 49 **d** 78 **p** 78. New Zealand from 60; rtd 71. *10A Heybridge Lane, Christchurch 8002, New Zealand* Tel Christchurch (3) 332 6808

LEWIS, Elsie Leonora. b 26. Cranmer Hall Dur 72. **dss** 78 **d** 87 **p** 94. S Westoe *Dur* 78-80; Ryton 80-86; rtd 86. *53 Cushy Cow Lane, Ryton, Tyne & Wear NE40 3NL* Tel 0191-413 5845

LEWIS, Eric. b 36. Sarum & Wells Th Coll 74. **d** 77 **p** 78. NSM Oldbury *Sarum* 77-92; C Weymouth St Paul 92-94; P-in-c Portland St Jo from 94; Chapl Weymouth Coll 94-97; Chapl RN from 95; Chapl Portland Hosp Weymouth from 95. *St John's Vicarage, Ventnor Road, Portland, Dorset DT5 1JE* Tel (01305) 820103

LEWIS, Evan David Dyfrig. b 17. TD67. Univ of Wales BA47. St Mich Coll Llan 47. **d** 49 **p** 50. C Llantwit Major *Llan* 49-52; C Cardiff St Jo 52-58; CF (TA) 52-88; R Llanmaes and Llanmihangel *Llan* 58-88; rtd 88; Perm to Offic *Llan* from 88. *5 Oak Grove, Eglwysbrewis, St Athan, Barry CF62 4QR* Tel (01446) 750123

LEWIS, Evan Edgar. b 07. K Coll Cam BA31 MA35. St D Coll Lamp BA28. **d** 31 **p** 32. C Henfynyw w Aberaeron *St D* 31-32; Chapl St D Cathl 32-35; C Roundhay St Edm *Ripon* 35-36; C Worthing H Trin *Chich* 36-40; V Isleham *Ely* 40-45; V Kirknewton *Newc* 45-50; V Bettws-y-Crwyn w Newcastle *Heref* 50-54; R Taynton *Glouc* 54-57; V Tibberton 54-57; V Stoke St Milburgh w Heath *Heref* 57-73; R Abdon w Clee St Margaret 57-73; R Cold Weston 57-73; rtd 73; Perm to Offic *Heref* 73-90. *The Granary, Stoke St Milborough, Ludlow, Shropshire SY8 2EJ* Tel (01584) 75219

LEWIS, Evan Thomas Derwen. b 10. Univ of Wales BA34. St D Coll Lamp 34. **d** 35 **p** 36. C Llansamlet *S & B* 35-40; CF (EC) 40-46; V Glasbury St Pet *S & B* 46-83; RD Hay 60-62; rtd 83. *55 Gwernyfed Avenue, Three Cocks, Brecon LD3 0RT* Tel (01497) 847229

LEWIS, Francis Edward Walter. b 17. Univ of Wales BA40. St Mich Coll Llan 41. **d** 42 **p** 43. C Newport St Jo Bapt *Mon* 42-46; C Bracknell *Ox* 46-51; R Watlington *Ely* 51-65; V Linslade *Ox* 65-73; V Maidenhead St Luke 73-81; rtd 81. *13 Courtlands*

Road, Shipton-under-Wychwood, Chipping Norton, Oxon OX7 6DF Tel (01993) 830604

LEWIS, Frederick. b 09. FRAI40 Univ of Wales BA31. St Mich Coll Llan 30. **d** 32 **p** 33. C Holyhead *Ban* 32-34; C Llanaber 34-38; C Norwood All SS *Cant* 38-41; V Womenswold 41-44; C-in-c Aylesham CD 41-44; V Abercynon *Llan* 44-53; I St Padarn's Welsh Ch Islington 53-55; Chapl and Tutor Whittington Coll Felbridge 55-68; rtd 68. *7 Shearman Road, Hadleigh, Suffolk IP7 3JW* Tel (01473) 827089

LEWIS, Frederick Norman. b 23. Leeds Univ BA47. Coll of Resurr Mirfield 47. **d** 49 **p** 50. C Haydock St Jas *Liv* 49-51; C Dresden *Lich* 51-55; C Stafford St Mary 55-56; V Wednesfield St Thos 56-65; V Shrewsbury St Chad 65-69; V Kingswinford St Mary 69-88; rtd 88; Perm to Offic *Lich* from 88. *27 Bramblewood Drive, Finchfield, Wolverhampton WV3 9DB* Tel (01902) 334934

LEWIS, Gary. b 61. Lanc Univ BA85. Ripon Coll Cuddesdon 86. **d** 89 **p** 90. C Blackb St Mich w St Jo and H Trin *Blackb* 89-92; C Altham w Clayton le Moors 92-95; V Lea from 95. *St Christopher's Vicarage, 848 Blackpool Road, Lea, Preston PR2 1XL* Tel (01772) 729716

LEWIS, Ms Hannah Margaret. b 71. CCC Cam BA93 Cam Univ MA96. Qu Coll Birm 95. **d** 97. C Cannock *Lich* from 97. *100 Bond Way, Hednesford, Staffs WS11 4SN*

LEWIS, Hubert Godfrey. b 33. Univ of Wales (Lamp) BA59 DipTh60. **d** 60 **p** 61. C Merthyr Tydfil *Llan* 60-64; C Caerphilly 64-66; Perm to Offic *S'wark* 66-76; Perm to Offic *Cant* 76-82; Hon C Shirley St Jo *S'wark* from 82. *4 East Way, Croydon CR0 8AH* Tel 0181-777 6587

LEWIS, Hywel Gwynne. b 37. FCA75. St D Dioc Tr Course 94. **d** 97. NSM Henfynyw w Aberaeron and Llanddewi Aberarth *St D* from 97. *Danycoed, Lampeter Road, Aberaeron SA46 0ED* Tel (01545) 570577

LEWIS, Dr Ian. b 33. MRCS LRCP Lon Univ MB, BS57. Oak Hill Th Coll 61. **d** 63 **p** 64. C Heatherlands St Jo *Sarum* 63-66; Ethiopia 66-73; Hon C Bath Walcot *B & W* 75-77; Lic to Offic 78-84. *22C Ashley Road, Bathford, Bath BA1 7TT* Tel (01225) 859818

LEWIS, Ian Richard. b 54. Sheff Univ BA76 Ox Univ BA83 MA87. Wycliffe Hall Ox 81. **d** 84 **p** 85. C Rusholme H Trin *Man* 84-88; C Sandal St Helen *Wakef* 88-91; V Bath St Bart *B & W* from 91. *St Bartholomew's Vicarage, 5 Oldfield Road, Bath BA2 3NB* Tel (01225) 422070

LEWIS, James Edward. b 22. St D Coll Lamp BA50. **d** 51 **p** 52. C Gorseinon *S & B* 51-52; C Defynnog 52-56; R Llangynllo w Troed-yr-aur *St D* 56-61; V Brynamman 61-72; R Llangathen w Llanfihangel Cilfargen 72-82; V Llangathen w Llanfihangel Cilfargen etc 82-90; RD Llangadog and Llandeilo 85-89; rtd 90. *The Flat, 3 St Mary Street, Carmarthen SA31 1TN* Tel (01267) 221660

LEWIS, Dr Jocelyn Vivien. b 49. Trevelyan Coll Dur BSc70 Sheff Univ PhD75. EMMTC DTPS94. **d** 94 **p** 95. NSM Brimington *Derby* from 94. *10 Rother Avenue, Brimington, Chesterfield, Derbyshire S43 1LE* Tel (01246) 279050

LEWIS, The Ven John Arthur. b 34. Jes Coll Ox BA56 MA60. Cuddesdon Coll 58. **d** 60 **p** 61. C Prestbury *Glouc* 60-63; C Wimborne Minster *Sarum* 63-66; R Eastington and Frocester *Glouc* 66-70; V Nailsworth 70-78; Chapl Memorial and Querns Hosp Cirencester 78-88; V Cirencester *Glouc* 78-88; RD Cirencester 84-88; Hon Can Glouc Cathl from 85; Adn Cheltenham from 88. *Westbourne, 283 Gloucester Road, Cheltenham GL51 7AD* Tel (01242) 522923 Fax 235925

LEWIS, John Edward. b 31. SS Mark & Jo Coll Chelsea CertEd53. Qu Coll Birm 83. **d** 85 **p** 86. C Leominster *Heref* 85-87; TV 87-95; rtd 95. *The Holms, 253 Godiva Road, Leominster, Herefordshire HR6 8TB* Tel (01568) 612280

LEWIS, John Herbert. b 42. Selw Coll Cam BA64 MA68. Westcott Ho Cam 64. **d** 66 **p** 67. C Wyken *Cov* 66-70; C Bedford St Andr *St Alb* 70-73; Lib Pusey Ho 73-77; Bp's Chapl for Graduates *Ox* 73-77; TV Woughton 78-82; TV Gt Chesham 82-88; P-in-c Newport Pagnell w Lathbury and Moulsoe 88-91; R from 91. *New Rectory, 81 High Street, Newport Pagnell, Bucks MK16 8AB* Tel (01908) 611145

LEWIS, John Horatio George. b 47. Southn Univ BEd72 MA85. Ox NSM Course 86. **d** 89 **p** 90. NSM Newbury *Ox* from 89. *36 Glendale Avenue, Newbury, Berks RG14 6RU* Tel (01635) 34721

✠**LEWIS, The Rt Revd John Hubert Richard.** b 43. AKC66. **d** 67 **p** 68 **c** 92. C Hexham *Newc* 67-70; Ind Chapl 70-77; Communications Officer *Dur* 77-82; Chapl for Agric *Heref* 82-87; Adn Ludlow 87-92; Suff Bp Taunton *B & W* 92-97; Bp St E from 97. *The Bishop's House, 4 Park Road, Ipswich IP1 3ST* Tel (01473) 252829 Fax 232552

LEWIS, John Malcolm. b 41. Reading Univ BEd. Trin Coll Bris. **d** 82 **p** 83. C Kingswood *Bris* 82-85; TV Weston-super-Mare Cen Par *B & W* 85-91; Dioc Children's Adv *Nor* 91-97; TV Bishopsworth and Bedminster Down *Bris* from 97. *St Oswald's Vicarage, Cheddar Grove, Bedminster Down, Bristol BS13 7EN* Tel 0117-964 2649

LEWIS, The Very Revd John Percival. b 19. TCD BA44. CITC 47. **d** 47 **p** 48. C Galway *T, K & A* 47-51; I Knappagh 51-74; RD Tuam 56-91; Can Tuam Cathl from 70; I Omey w Ballynakill, Errislannan and Roundstone 73-91; Provost Tuam 73-91; rtd 91. *Albany, Pheasant Hill, Castlebar, Co Mayo, Irish Republic* Tel Castlebar (94) 22747

LEWIS, John Pryce. b 65. Trin Coll Carmarthen BA87. Wycliffe Hall Ox 92. **d** 94 **p** 95. C Carmarthen St Pet *St D* 94-97; V Nevern and Y Beifil w Eglwyswrw and Meline etc from 97. *The Vicarage, Nevern, Newport SA42 0NF* Tel (01239) 820427

LEWIS, John Thomas. b 47. Jes Coll Ox BA69 MA73 St Jo Coll Cam BA72 MA92. Westcott Ho Cam 71. **d** 73 **p** 74. C Whitchurch *Llan* 73-77; C Llanishen and Lisvane 77-80; Asst Chapl Univ of Wales (Cardiff) 80-85; Warden of Ords 81-85; V Brecon St David w Llanspyddid and Llanilltyd *S & B* 85-91; Sec Prov Selection Panel and Bd Ch in Wales 87-94; V Bassaleg *Mon* 91-96; TR from 96. *The Vicarage, 1 Church View, Bassaleg, Newport NP1 9ND* Tel (01633) 893258

LEWIS, Kenneth Lionel. b 22. Keble Coll Ox BA50 MA54 Ch Coll Cam CertEd52. Wycliffe Hall Ox 52. **d** 52 **p** 53. C Bromley St Jo *Roch* 52-55; C Streatham Hill St Marg *S'wark* 55-57; R Tatsfield 57-72; Lic to Offic 72-78 and from 89; Perm to Offic *Roch* 75-78 and 83-93; Perm to Offic *Cant* 75-78. *9 Nostle Road, Northleach, Cheltenham, Glos GL54 3PF* Tel (01451) 860118

LEWIS, Leslie. b 25. Qu Coll Birm 82. **d** 83 **p** 84. NSM Garretts Green *Birm* 83-88; NSM Coleshill 88-92; NSM Maxstoke 88-92; rtd 92; Perm to Offic *Birm* from 92. *54 Bellevue Road, Birmingham B26 2QA* Tel 0121-742 3662

LEWIS, Leslie. b 28. LRAM56. St Aid Birkenhead 61. **d** 63 **p** 64. C Eastham *Ches* 63-66; C W Kirby St Bridget 66-72; V Rainow w Saltersford 72-73; V Rainow w Saltersford and Forest from 73; Dioc Clergy Widows and Retirement Officer 88-93. *The Vicarage, Rainow, Macclesfield, Cheshire SK10 5TZ* Tel (01625) 572013

LEWIS, Maureen. b 50. Chester Coll BA92. St Jo Coll Nottm DipMM94. **d** 94 **p** 95. C Ellesmere Port *Ches* from 94. *The Vicarage, Seymour Drive, Ellesmere Port, South Wirral L65 9LZ* Tel 0151-355 3988

LEWIS, Michael Augustine Owen. b 53. Mert Coll Ox BA75 MA79. Cuddesdon Coll 75. **d** 78 **p** 79. C Salfords *S'wark* 78-80; Chapl Thames Poly 80-84; V Welling 84-91; TR Worc SE *Worc* from 91; RD Worc E from 93. *The Rectory, 6 St Catherine's Hill, Worcester WR5 2EA* Tel (01905) 355119 or 358083

LEWIS, Michael David Bennett. b 41. Univ of Wales DipTh68. St Mich Coll Llan 65. **d** 68 **p** 69. C Penarth w Lavernock *Llan* 68-72; Chapl RAF 72-74; C Llanishen and Lisvane *Llan* 74-77; V Penyfai w Tondu 77-82; Chapl Ardingly Coll Haywards Heath 82-90; R Merrow *Guildf* 90-95; RD Guildf 94-95; V Southsea H Spirit *Portsm* from 95. *The Vicarage, 26 Victoria Grove, Southsea, Hants PO5 1NF* Tel (01705) 736063

LEWIS, Michael John. b 37. LLAM86. St Aid Birkenhead 64. **d** 66 **p** 67. C Whitnash *Cov* 66-69; C Nuneaton St Nic 69-73; TV Basildon St Martin w H Cross and Laindon *Chelmsf* 73-79; V W Bromwich St Jas *Lich* 79-85; TV Buxton w Burbage and King Sterndale *Derby* 85-95; P-in-c Brampton St Mark from 95. *The Vicarage, 15 St Mark's Road, Chesterfield, Derbyshire S40 1DH* Tel (01246) 234015

LEWIS, Norman Eric. b 34. SRN55 Open Univ BA77. Roch Th Coll 59 Lich Th Coll 60. **d** 63 **p** 64. C Hope St Jas *Man* 63-67; V Hindsford 67-77; V Bolton SS Simon and Jude 77-90; rtd 90; Perm to Offic *York* from 90. *Millbank Cottage, Kirby Misperton, Malton, N Yorkshire YO17 0XZ* Tel (01653) 86526

LEWIS, Paul Wilfred. b 37. Ch Ch Ox BA60 DipEd61 MA64 DipTh72. Chich Th Coll 62. **d** 64 **p** 65. C St Pancras H Cross w St Jude and St Pet *Lon* 64-66; C Tottenham St Jo 66-68; Barbados 68-71; Lect Sarum & Wells Th Coll 72-74; Chapl Sarum & Wells Th Coll 73-74; Chapl LSE *Lon* 74-80; Chapl St Chris Hospice Lon 80-86; C St Giles Cripplegate w St Bart Moor Lane etc *Lon* 86-89; Chapl Nat Hosp for Neurology and Neurosurgery Lon from 89. *The National Hospital, Queen Square, London WC1N 3BG* Tel 0171-837 3611 or 278 3706

LEWIS, Peter Andrew. b 67. Pemb Coll Ox MA PhD Univ of Wales (Abth). Trin Coll Bris. **d** 96 **p** 97. C Cardigan and Mwnt and Y Ferwig *St D* from 96. *8 Heol y Wern, North Park, Cardigan SA43 1NE*

LEWIS, Peter Anthony. b 25. Sarum & Wells Th Coll 76. **d** 79 **p** 80. Hon C Southsea St Simon *Portsm* from 79. *2 Selsey Avenue, Southsea, Hants PO4 9QL* Tel (01705) 732394

LEWIS, Canon Peter Goulstone. b 25. Univ of Wales (Lamp) BA48. **d** 50 **p** 51. C Aberystwyth H Trin *St D* 50-54; C Caerphilly *Llan* 54-60; V Cwmbach 60-66; V Tongwynlais 66-79; V Llantrisant 79-90; Can Llan Cathl 85-91; RD Pontypridd 88-90; rtd 91; Perm to Offic *Llan* from 91. *73 Pinecroft Avenue, Cwmbach, Aberdare CF44 0NB* Tel (01685) 882257

LEWIS, Peter Richard. b 40. Dur Univ BA62 Birm Univ DipTh64. Qu Coll Birm 62. **d** 64 **p** 65. C Moseley St Mary *Birm* 64-67; C Sherborne w Castleton and Lillington *Sarum* 67-71; P-in-c Bishopstone w Stratford Tony 72-80; V Amesbury from 80; Offg Chapl RAF from 80. *The Vicarage, Church Street, Amesbury, Salisbury SP4 7EU* Tel (01980) 623145

LEWIS, Miss Rachel Veronica Clare. b 59. St Jo Coll Dur BA80 Man Univ PGCE81 Univ of Wales (Cardiff) MSc. Sarum & Wells Th Coll 86. **d** 86 **p** 94. C Caereithin *S & B* 86-88; Par Dn Bolton St Pet *Man* 88-91; Chapl Bolton Colls of FE 88-91; Chapl

Trin Coll Carmarthen 91-94; C Yatton Keynell *Bris* 94-97; C Nettleton w Littleton Drew 94-97; C Biddestone w Slaughterford 94-97; C Castle Combe 94-97; C W Kington 94-97; P-in-c Grittleton and Leigh Delamere from 95; P-in-c Yatton Keynell from 97; P-in-c Biddestone w Slaughterford from 97; P-in-c Castle Combe from 97; P-in-c W Kington from 97; P-in-c Nettleton w Littleton Drew from 97. *The Rectory, Yatton Keynell, Chippenham, Wilts SN14 7BA* Tel (01249) 782236

LEWIS, Ray Arthur. b 63. Oak Hill Th Coll 87. **d** 90 **p** 91. C Holloway St Mary Magd *Lon* 90-93; TV W Ham *Chelmsf* from 93. *St Matthew's Vicarage, 38 Dyson Road, London E15 4JX* Tel 0181-519 2504

LEWIS, Raymond James. b 34. Univ of Wales (Cardiff) BA Open Univ BSc. St Mich Coll Llan. **d** 91 **p** 92. C Llanelli *St D* 91-94. *4 Hedley Terrace, Llanelli SA15 3RE* Tel (01554) 750355

LEWIS, The Very Revd Richard. b 35. Fitzw Ho Cam BA78 MA63. Ripon Hall Ox 58. **d** 60 **p** 61. C Hinckley St Mary *Leic* 60-63; C Sanderstead All SS *S'wark* 63-66; V S Merstham 67-72; V S Wimbledon H Trin 72-74; P-in-c S Wimbledon St Pet 72-74; V S Wimbledon H Trin and St Pet 74-79; V Dulwich St Barn 79-90; Chapl Alleyn's Foundn Dulwich 79-90; RD Dulwich *S'wark* 83-90; Hon Can S'wark Cathl 87-90; Dean Wells *B & W* from 90; Warden of Readers from 91. *The Dean's Lodging, 25 The Liberty, Wells, Somerset BA5 2SU* Tel (01749) 670278 Fax 679184

LEWIS, Canon Richard Charles. b 44. Lon Univ DipTh68 DipSocSc78. ALCD69. **d** 69 **p** 70. C Kendal H Trin *Carl* 69-72; C Chipping Barnet *St Alb* 72-76; V Watford Ch Ch from 76; Hon Can St Alb Abbey from 90. *Christ Church Vicarage, Leggatts Way, Watford WD2 6BQ* Tel (01923) 672240

LEWIS, Robert (Bob). b 38. St Pet Coll Ox BA62 MA66. Cuddesdon Coll 62. **d** 64 **p** 65. C Kirkby *Liv* 64-67 and 70-71; TV 71-75; Chapl St Boniface Coll Warminster 68-69; Tutor St Aug Coll Cant 69-70; Abp's Dom Chapl *York* 76-79; Dir of Ords 76-79; TR Thirsk 79-92; Chapl Oslo w Bergen, Trondheim, Stavanger etc *Eur* 93-96; P-in-c Danby *York* from 96. *The Vicarage, Danby, Whitby, N Yorkshire YO21 2NQ* Tel (01287) 660388

LEWIS, Robert George. b 53. Lanc Univ BEd76. Ripon Coll Cuddesdon. **d** 78 **p** 79. C Liv Our Lady and St Nic w St Anne *Liv* 78-81; Asst Dir of Educn 81-88; P-in-c Newchurch 88-89; R Newchurch 94; P-in-c Glazebury 88-89; R Newchurch and Glazebury 89-94; R Winwick from 94. *The Rectory, Golborne Road, Winwick, Warrington WA2 8SZ* Tel (01925) 632760

LEWIS, Canon Robert Hugh Cecil. b 25. New Coll Ox BA50 MA50. Westcott Ho Cam 50. **d** 52 **p** 53. C Crumpsall St Matt *Man* 52-54; C New Bury 54-56; V Bury St Pet 56-63; V Poynton *Ches* 63-91; RD Stockport 72-85; Hon Can Ches Cathl 75-91; RD Cheadle 85-87; Dioc Ecum Officer 87-91; Chapl to The Queen from 85; rtd 91; Perm to Offic *Ches* from 91. *78 Dean Drive, Wilmslow, Cheshire SK9 2EY* Tel (01625) 524761

LEWIS, Roger Edward. b 24. Qu Coll Cam BA45 MA49. Ridley Hall Cam 47. **d** 49 **p** 50. C Handsworth St Mary *Birm* 49-52; R Hadleigh St Jas *Chelmsf* 52-58; V Clacton St Paul 58-71; V Surbiton St Matt *S'wark* 71-89; rtd 89; Perm to Offic *S'wark* from 89. *Rose Cottage, 40 Grove Road, Horley, Surrey RH6 8EL* Tel (01293) 771197

LEWIS, Roger Gilbert. b 49. St Jo Coll Dur BA70. Ripon Hall Ox 70. **d** 72 **p** 73. C Boldmere *Birm* 72-76; C Birm St Pet 76-77; TV Tettenhall Regis *Lich* 77-81; V Ward End *Birm* 81-91; rtd 91; Perm to Offic *Birm* from 91. *8 Tudor Terrace, Ravenhurst Road, Birmingham B17 8SB* Tel 0121-427 4915

LEWIS, Preb Ronald Llewellyn. b 12. Leeds Univ BSc35. Coll of Resurr Mirfield 35. **d** 37 **p** 38. C Brislington St Cuth *Bris* 37-40; C Montpelier St Andr 41-46; SW Area Dir ICF 46-49; V Kingston St Mary *B & W* 49-63; PC Broomfield 53-63; V Taunton H Trin 63-77; RD Taunton N 60-63; RD Taunton S 65-71; Preb Wells Cathl from 73; rtd 77; Perm to Offic *B & W* from 77. *Rose Cottage, 23 Burton Place, Taunton, Somerset TA1 4HE* Tel (01823) 274778

LEWIS, Stuart William. b 54. Newc Poly PGCE80 Newc Univ BA79. Edin Th Coll 86. **d** 86 **p** 87. C Ledbury w Eastnor *Heref* 86-89; Chapl Malvern Coll 89-96; Chapl and Prec Portsm Cathl *Portsm* from 96. *15 Grays Court, Portsmouth PO1 2PN* Tel (01705) 733575 Fax 829718

LEWIS, Terence Arnold. b 15. Jes Coll Ox BA37 MA41 BD51. St Mich Coll Llan 38. **d** 39 **p** 40. R Aston Clinton w Buckland and Drayton Beauchamp *Ox* 64-86; rtd 86; Perm to Offic *Ox* 86-87 and from 90. *5 Villiers Close, Moreton Grange, Buckingham MK18 1JH* Tel (01280) 815849

LEWIS, Thomas Peter. b 45. Selw Coll Cam BA67 MA. Ripon Hall Ox 68. **d** 70 **p** 71. C Hatfield *St Alb* 70-74; C Boreham Wood All SS 74-78; Chapl Haileybury Coll Herts 78-85; Chapl Abingdon Sch from 86. *25 Park Road, Abingdon, Oxon OX14 1DA* Tel (01235) 526034

LEWIS, Timothy John. b 56. Univ of Wales (Swansea) BA76. Sarum & Wells Th Coll 83. **d** 86 **p** 87. C Taunton St Mary *B & W* 86-89; Chapl RN from 89. *Royal Naval Chaplaincy Service, Room 203, Victory Building, HM Naval Base, Portsmouth PO1 3LS* Tel (01705) 727903 Fax 727112

LEWIS, Trevor Charlton Haselden. b 22. Qu Coll Birm 49. **d** 51 **p** 52. C Glouc St Aldate *Glouc* 51-54; C Cirencester 54-55; C-in-c Churchdown St Jo CD 55-64; V Churchdown St Jo 64-65; R Dursley 65-70; Chapl RN 70-71; USA from 71; rtd 94. *115 Alpine, Carbondale, Colorado 81623, USA*

LEWIS, Vera Elizabeth. b 45. Lon Univ BA66 Univ of Wales (Abth) DipEd67 DipLib73. St As Minl Tr Course 82. **d** 85 **p** 97. NSM Garthbeibio and Llanerfyl and Llangadfan *St As* 85-86; C 87-88; NSM Llanfair Caereinion w Llanllugan 85-86; C 87-88; D-in-c Llanrhaeadr-ym-Mochnant and Llanarmon etc 88-96; D-in-c Llanddulas and Llysfaen 96-97; R from 97. *The Vicarage, 2 Rhodfa Wen, Llysfaen, Colwyn Bay LL29 8LE* Tel (01492) 516728

LEWIS, Canon Walter Arnold. b 45. NUI BA68 TCD MPhil91. TCD Div Sch 71. **d** 71 **p** 72. C Belfast Whiterock *Conn* 71-73; C Belfast St Mark 73-80; Bp's C Belfast St Andr 80-84; I Belfast St Thos from 84; Can Belf Cathl from 97. *St Thomas's Rectory, 1A Eglantine Avenue, Belfast BT9 6DW* Tel (01232) 668360 Fax as telephone

LEWIS, William George Melville. b 31. Open Univ BA. S'wark Ord Course. **d** 69 **p** 70. C Coulsdon St Jo *S'wark* 69-71; C Perry Hill St Geo 71-74; V Eltham St Barn 74-80; V Reigate St Mark 80-89; V Ham St Rich 89-97; rtd 97. *17 Fellbrook, Richmond, Surrey TW10 7UN*

LEWIS, William George Rees. b 35. Hertf Coll Ox BA59 MA63. Tyndale Hall Bris 61. **d** 63 **p** 64. C Tenby w Gumfreston *St D* 63-66; C Llanelli St Paul 66-69; R Letterston 69-84; R Jordanston w Llanstinan 73-78; R Punchestown and Lt Newc 78-84; R Hubberston w Herbrandston and Hasguard etc 84-90; Prov Officer for Evang and Adult Educn 90-94; V Gabalfa *Llan* from 94. *St Mark's Vicarage, 208 North Road, Cardiff CF4 3BL* Tel (01222) 613286

LEWIS, William Rhys. b 20. St Mich Coll Llan 53. **d** 55 **p** 56. C Ystrad Mynach *Llan* 55-58; C Bassaleg *Mon* 58-59; V Cwmtillery 59-62; V Newport St Andr 62-64; R Ebbw Vale 64-73; V Llangattock and Llangyndir *S & B* 73-78; V Swansea St Luke 78-85; rtd 85; Perm to Offic *Llan* from 85. *6 Beech Avenue, Llantwit Major CF61 1RT* Tel (01446) 796741

LEWIS-ANTHONY, Justin Griffith. b 64. LSE BA86. Ripon Coll Cuddesdon BA91. **d** 92 **p** 93. C Cirencester *Glouc* from 92. *32 Watermoor Road, Cirencester, Glos GL7 1JR* Tel (01285) 652299

LEWIS-JENKINS, Christopher Robin. b 50. St Mich Coll Llan 94. **d** 96 **p** 97. C Barry All SS *Llan* from 96. *4 Alwen Drive, Cwm Talwg, Barry CF62 7LH* Tel (01446) 722548

LEWIS LLOYD, Canon Timothy David (Tim). b 37. Clare Coll Cam BA58 MA62. Cuddesdon Coll 58. **d** 60 **p** 61. C Stepney St Dunstan and All SS *Lon* 60-64; C St Alb Abbey *St Alb* 64-67; Prec St Alb Abbey 67-69; V St Paul's Walden 69-78; V Braughing w Furneux Pelham and Stocking Pelham 78-79; P-in-c Lt Hadham 78-79; V Braughing, Lt Hadham, Albury, Furneux Pelham etc 79-82; V Cheshunt 82-95; RD Cheshunt 89-94; Hon Can St Alb from 94; V Sawbridgeworth from 95. *The Vicarage, 144 Sheering Mill Lane, Sawbridgeworth, Herts CM21 9ND* Tel (01279) 723305

LEWIS-NICHOLSON, Russell John. b 45. Caulfield Inst of Tech DipCivEng68. Oak Hill Th Coll DipTh81. **d** 81 **p** 82. C Clayton *Bradf* 81-84; Australia from 84. *25 Little Myers Street, Geelong, Victoria, Australia 3220* Tel Geelong (52) 232338

LEWISHAM, Archdeacon of. *See* ATKINSON, The Ven David John

LEWORTHY, Graham Llewelyn. b 47. Reading Univ BA69. S Dios Minl Tr Scheme 91. **d** 94 **p** 95. NSM Sark *Win* 94-96; C from 96. *La Baleine, Sark, Guernsey GY9 0SB* Tel (01481) 832140

LEWTHWAITE, David. b 39. K Coll Lon BD75. St Aid Birkenhead 63. **d** 65 **p** 66. C Standish *Blackb* 65-68; S Africa 68-71; P-in-c Blackb All SS *Blackb* 71-72; C Kentish Town St Jo *Lon* 72-75; P-in-c Wilden w Colmworth and Ravensden *St Alb* 75-79; V Knottingley *Wakef* 79-81; R Maulden *St Alb* from 81; RD Ampthill 90-96. *The Rectory, Clophill Road, Maulden, Bedford MK45 2AA* Tel (01525) 403139

LEY, John Andrew. b 16. St Deiniol's Hawarden 70. **d** 72 **p** 73. Hon C Leintwardine *Heref* 72-76; Hon C Wigmore Abbey 76-77; AP Pulloxhill w Flitton *St Alb* 77-79; Lic to Offic *Blackb* 80-81; C Stoke Lacy, Moreton Jeffries w Much Cowarne etc *Heref* 81-87; rtd 87; Perm to Offic *Lich* from 87. *4 Winchester Close, Lichfield, Staffs WS13 7SL* Tel (01543) 255941

LEYLAND, Derek James. b 34. Lon Univ BSc55 Birm Univ DipTh60. Qu Coll Birm 58. **d** 60 **p** 61. C Ashton-on-Ribble St Andr *Blackb* 60-63; V 80-87; C Salesbury 63-65; V Preston St Oswald 65-67; V Pendleton 67-74; Dioc Youth Chapl 67-69; Ind Youth Chapl 70-74; R Brindle 74-80; V Garstang St Helen Churchtown 87-94; Sec SOSc 90-94; rtd 94; Perm to Offic *Blackb* from 94. *Greystocks, Goosnargh Lane, Goosnargh, Preston PR3 2BP*

LEYLAND, Tyrone John. b 49. Aston Univ BSc68. St Jo Coll Nottm 89. **d** 91 **p** 92. C Lich St Mary w St Mich *Lich* 91-94; TV Willenhall H Trin from 94. *The Vicarage, 129 Essington Road, Willenhall, W Midlands WV12 5DT* Tel (01922) 475321 Fax as telephone

LEYSHON, Simon. b 63. Trin Coll Carmarthen BA86 Southn Univ BTh89. Sarum & Wells Th Coll. **d** 89 **p** 90. C Tenby *St D* 89-92; TV 92-96; Chapl Llandovery Coll from 96. *Llandovery College, Queensway, Llandovery SA20 0EE* Tel (01550) 20315

LIBBY, John Ralph. b 55. Trin Coll Cam BA(Econ)83. Ridley Hall Cam 89. **d** 91 **p** 92. C Enfield St Andr *Lon* 91-93; C Northwood Em 93-96; V Denton Holme *Carl* from 96. *St James's Vicarage, Goschen Road, Carlisle CA2 5PF* Tel (01228) 515639 or 810616

LICHFIELD, Archdeacon of. *See* NINIS, The Ven Richard Betts

LICHFIELD, Bishop of. *See* SUTTON, The Rt Revd Keith Norman

LICHFIELD, Dean of. *See* WRIGHT, The Very Revd Nicholas Thomas

LICHTENBERGER, Miss Ruth Eileen. b 34. NY Th Sem 64 Nor Ord Course 95. **d** 96 **p** 97. NSM Warrington H Trin *Liv* from 96. *8 Towers Court, Warrington WA5 5AH* Tel (01925) 656763 Fax as telephone

LICKESS, Canon David Frederick. b 37. St Chad's Coll Dur BA63 DipTh65. **d** 65 **p** 66. C Howden *York* 65-70; V Rudby in Cleveland w Middleton from 70; Can and Preb York Minster from 90; RD Stokesley from 93. *The Vicarage, Hutton Rudby, Yarm, Cleveland TS15 0HY* Tel (01642) 700223

LIDDELL, Peter Gregory. b 40. St Andr Univ MA63 Linacre Ho Ox BA65 MA70. Andover Newton Th Coll DMin75 Ripon Hall Ox 63. **d** 65 **p** 66. C Hatfield *St Alb* 65-71; USA 71-76; P-in-c Kimpton w Ayot St Lawrence *St Alb* 77-83; Dir of Past Counselling from 80. *The Coach House, The Old Vicarage, Kimpton, Hitchin, Herts SG4 8EF* Tel (01438) 832266

LIDDELOW, Peter William. b 33. Oak Hill NSM Course. **d** 82 **p** 83. NSM Finchley Ch Ch *Lon* 82-84; NSM S Mimms Ch Ch from 84. *23 King's Road, Barnet, Herts EN5 4EP* Tel 0181-441 2968

LIDDLE, George. b 48. NE Ord Course 88. **d** 90 **p** 91. C Auckland St Andr and St Anne *Dur* 90-92; C Crook 92-94; C Stanley 92-94; P-in-c Evenwood 94-96; V from 96. *St Paul's Vicarage, Evenwood, Bishop Auckland, Co Durham DL14 9RA* Tel (01388) 832348

LIDDLE, Harry. b 36. Wadh Coll Ox BA57 MA61. Wycliffe Hall Ox 62. **d** 64 **p** 65. C Withington St Paul *Man* 64-68; R Broughton 68-73; V Balby *Sheff* 73-82; R Firbeck w Letwell 82-94; V Woodsetts 82-94; TV Aston cum Aughton w Swallownest, Todwick etc from 94. *9 Horbiry End, Todwick, Sheffield S31 0HH* Tel (01909) 515360

LIDDLE, Stephen John. b 60. St Jo Coll Ox BA81 PGCE82. Linc Th Coll 88. **d** 91 **p** 92. C Morpeth *Newc* 91-95; P-in-c Byker St Mich w St Lawr from 95. *St Michael's Vicarage, Headlam Street, Newcastle upon Tyne NE6 2DX* Tel 0191-265 3720

LIDSTONE, Vernon Henry. b 43. SW Minl Tr Course 89. **d** 92 **p** 93. NSM Bovey Tracey SS Pet, Paul and Thos w Hennock *Ex* 92-94; Sub-Chapl HM Pris Channings Wood 92-96; Asst Dioc Stewardship Adv 92-93; Dioc Stewardship Adv 93-96; Dioc Officer for Par Development *Glouc* from 96. *Church House, College Green, Gloucester GL1 2LY* Tel (01452) 410022

LIDWILL, Mark Robert. b 57. TCD DipTh87. **d** 87 **p** 88. C Annagh w Drumgoon, Ashfield etc *K, E & A* 87-90; I Urney w Denn and Derryheen from 90; Dioc Youth Adv from 92. *The Rectory, Co Cavan, Irish Republic* Tel Cavan (49) 61016

LIFTON, Norman Reginald. b 22. ALSM. Worc Ord Coll 62. **d** 64 **p** 65. C Coleford w Staunton *Glouc* 64-66; C Hersham *Guildf* 66-68; C Milford Haven *St D* 68-70; R Spexhall w Wissett *St E* 70-77; V Berkeley *Glouc* 77-84; C Malborough w S Huish, W Alvington and Churchstow *Ex* 84-87; V Ticknall, Smisby and Stanton by Bridge *Derby* 87-92; rtd 92; Perm to Offic *Ex* 92-95. *Woodleigh, 6 Cotmore Way, Chillington, Kingsbridge, Devon TQ7 2HU* Tel (01548) 580264

LIGHTFOOT, The Very Revd Vernon Keith. b 34. St Jo Coll Dur BA58. Ripon Hall Ox 58. **d** 60 **p** 61. C Rainhill *Liv* 60-62; C Liv Our Lady and St Nic 62-65; V Stanley 65-75; New Zealand from 75; Dean Waikato from 86. *The Deanery, 6 Tisdall Street, Hamilton, PO Box 338, New Zealand* Tel Hamilton (7) 839 3551 or 839 4683 Fax 839 4683

LIGHTOWLER, Joseph Trevor. b 33. **d** 79 **p** 80. Hon C Leverstock Green *St Alb* 79-80; Hon C Chambersbury (Hemel Hempstead) 80-84; C Woodmansterne *S'wark* 84-88; R Odell and Pavenham *St Alb* from 88. *The Rectory, 3 Church Lane, Odell, Bedford MK43 7AA* Tel (01234) 720234

LIKEMAN, Canon Martin Kaye. b 34. St Mich Coll Llan 55. **d** 57 **p** 58. C Llanwnog w Penstrowed *Ban* 57-60; C Llandudno 60-64; V Llanrhian w Llanhywel and Carnhedryn *St D* 64-73; RD Dewisland and Fishguard 71-73; V Llanstadwel from 73; Can St D Cathl from 88. *The Vicarage, Llanstadwel, Milford Haven SA73 1AW* Tel (01646) 600227

LILES, Malcolm David. b 48. Nottm Univ BA69. St Steph Ho Ox 69. **d** 71 **p** 72. C Corby Epiphany w St Jo *Pet* 71-74; C New Cleethorpes *Linc* 74-76; TV Lt Coates 76-77; TV Gt and Lt Coates w Bradley 78-82; Soc Resp Sec 82-93; Hon C Gt Grimsby St Mary and St Jas 82-93; P-in-c Grimsby All SS 88-93; TV Dronfield w Holmesfield *Derby* from 93. *The Vicarage, Main Road, Holmesfield, Sheffield S18 5WT* Tel 0114-289 0243

LILEY, Christopher Frank (Chris). b 47. Nottm Univ BEd70. Linc Th Coll 72. **d** 74 **p** 75. C Kingswinford H Trin *Lich* 74-79; TV Stafford 79-84; V Norton *St Alb* 84-96; RD Hitchin 89-94; V Shrewsbury St Chad w St Mary *Lich* from 96; P-in-c Shrewsbury St Alkmund from 96. *St Chad's Vicarage, Claremont Hill, Shrewsbury SY1 1RD* Tel (01743) 343761

LILEY, Peter James. b 60. Liv Univ BA82 Westmr Coll Ox PGCE83. Oak Hill Th Coll DipHE93. **d** 93 **p** 94. C Exning St Martin w Landwade *St E* 93-96; V Acton w Gt Waldingfield from 96. *The Vicarage, Melford Road, Acton, Sudbury, Suffolk CO10 0BA* Tel (01787) 377287

LILLEY, Christopher Howard (Chris). b 51. FCA75 FTII83. St Jo Coll Bramcote DCM93 LNSM course 83. **d** 85 **p** 86. Hon C Skegness and Winthorpe *Linc* 85-93; Perm to Offic *S'well* from 93; C Limber Magna w Brocklesby *Linc* 93-96; P-in-c Middle Rasen Gp 96-97; R from 97. *The Vicarage, North Street, Middle Rasen, Market Rasen, Lincs LN8 3TS* Tel (01673) 842249

LILLEY, Ivan Ray. b 32. Bps' Coll Cheshunt 58. **d** 61 **p** 62. C Kettering SS Pet and Paul *Pet* 61-64; C Gt Yarmouth *Nor* 64-75; P-in-c Tottenhill w Wormegay *Ely* 76-83; P-in-c Watlington 76-83; P-in-c Holme Runcton w S Runcton and Wallington 76-83; V Tysoe w Oxhill and Whatcote *Cov* 83-86; C Langold *S'well* 87-91; P-in-c from 91. *St Luke's Vicarage, Church Street, Langold, Worksop, Notts S81 9NW* Tel (01909) 730398

LILLIAN, Sister. *See* MORRIS, Sister Lillian Rosina

LILLIE, Judith Virginia. *See* THOMPSON, Mrs Judith Virginia

LILLINGTON, Brian Ray. b 36. RMN60 FRSH84 Ex Univ DSA65 Lon Univ DipMentH67. S Dios Minl Tr Scheme 87. **d** 90 **p** 91. NSM Yateley *Win* from 90. *Kaos, Little Vigo, Yateley, Camberley, Surrey GU17 7ES* Tel (01252) 872760

LILLINGTON (née POLLIT), Mrs Ruth Mary. b 65. SS Paul & Mary Coll Cheltenham BA88. St Jo Coll Nottm DPS90. **d** 90 **p** 94. Par Dn Caverswall *Lich* 90-92; Par Dn Caverswall and Weston Coyney w Dilhorne 92-93; Par Dn Luton St Mary *St Alb* 93-94; C 94-97; Chapl Luton Univ from 93. *72 Crawley Green Road, Luton LU2 0QU* Tel (01582) 35548

LILLISTONE, Brian David. b 38. SS Coll Cam BA61 MA65. St Steph Ho Ox 61. **d** 63 **p** 64. C Ipswich All Hallows *St E* 63-66; C Stokesay *Heref* 66-71; P-in-c Lyonshall w Titley 71-76; R Martlesham w Brightwell *St E* from 76. *The Rectory, 17 Lark Rise, Martlesham Heath, Ipswich IP5 7SA* Tel (01473) 622424

LIMBERT, Kenneth Edward. b 25. CEng69 MIMechE. S'wark Ord Course 72. **d** 75 **p** 76. NSM Northwood Hills St Edm *Lon* 75-90; Perm to Offic from 90. *55 York Road, Northwood, Middx HA6 1JJ* Tel (01923) 825791

LIMBRICK, Gordon. b 36. Open Univ BA88. St Jo Coll Nottm CertCS90. **d** 87 **p** 91. Hon C Troon *Glas* 87-90; Hon C Yaxley *Ely* 90-97; Hon C Yaxley and Holme w Conington from 97. *271 Broadway, Yaxley, Peterborough PE7 3NR* Tel (01733) 243170

LIMERICK AND ARDFERT, Dean of. *See* SIRR, The Very Revd John Maurice Glover

LIMERICK, Archdeacon of. *See* NUTTALL, The Ven Michael John Berkeley

LIMERICK, ARDFERT, AGHADOE, KILLALOE, KILFENORA, CLONFERT, KILMACDUAGH AND EMLY, Bishop of. *See* DARLING, The Rt Revd Edward

LINAKER, David Julian John Ramage. b 65. Ripon Coll Cuddesdon BTh95. **d** 95 **p** 96. C Colehill *Sarum* from 95. *37 Bridle Way, Colehill, Wimborne, Dorset BH21 2UP* Tel (01202) 849364

LINCOLN, Archdeacon of. *See* HAWES, The Ven Arthur John

LINCOLN, Bishop of. *See* HARDY, The Rt Revd Robert Maynard

LINCOLN, Dean of. *Vacant*

LIND-JACKSON, Peter Wilfrid. b 35. Leeds Univ BA67. Linc Th Coll 67. **d** 68 **p** 69. C Heref St Martin *Heref* 68-71; P-in-c Burghill 71-78; V 78-82; P-in-c Whorlton *Dur* 82-83; V Barnard Castle 82-83; V Barnard Castle w Whorlton from 83. *The Vicarage, Barnard Castle, Co Durham DL12 8NW* Tel (01833) 37018

LINDARS, Frank. b 23. Wycliffe Hall Ox 54. **d** 56 **p** 57. C Beeston Hill St Luke *Ripon* 56-59; C Harrogate St Wilfrid 59-61; V Shadwell 61-80; RD Allerton 73-78; V Masham and Healey 80-88; rtd 88. *Hope Cottage, Reeth, Richmond, N Yorkshire DL11 6SF* Tel (01748) 884685

LINDECK, Peter Stephen. b 31. Oak Hill Th Coll 57. **d** 59 **p** 60. C Homerton St Luke *Lon* 59-62; C Salterhebble All SS *Wakef* 62-63; C Islington St Andr w St Thos and St Matthias *Lon* 64-67; V Toxteth Park St Bede *Liv* 68-74; Nigeria 74-76; C Netherton *Liv* 76-77; C Ollerton *S'well* 77-80; C Boughton 77-80; V Whitgift w Adlingfleet and Eastoft *Sheff* 80-86; P-in-c Swinefleet 81-86; V Kilnhurst 86-94; Chapl Montagu Hosp Mexborough 86-94; rtd 94; Perm to Offic *Sheff* from 94. *41 Church Lane, Doncaster, S Yorkshire DN4 0XB* Tel (01302) 855957

LINDEN, Gregory. b 25. Roch Th Coll. **d** 65 **p** 66. C Roundhay St Edm *Ripon* 65-68; C Highweek *Ex* 68-72; V Brampford Speke 72-82; R Upton Pyne 72-82; R Middleton-in-Teesdale *Dur* 82-85; V Eggleston 85-95; R Middleton-in-Teesdale w Forest and Frith 85-95; rtd 95. *15 Ashdown Court, Little Crakehall, Bedale, N Yorkshire DL8 1LQ* Tel (01677) 426380

LINDISFARNE, Archdeacon of. *See* BOWERING, The Ven Michael Ernest

LINDLEY, Geoffrey. b 22. St Jo Coll Ox BA45 MA47. Westcott Ho Cam 47. **d** 47 **p** 48. C E Wickham *S'wark* 47-51; C Welling 51-52; V Lambeth St Phil 52-56; V Ox St Marg *Ox* 56-72; P-in-c Pyrton w Shirburn 72-79; P-in-c Lewknor 72-79; P-in-c Milton-under-Wychwood 79-80; P-in-c Shipton-under-Wychwood 79-80; V Shipton-under-Wychwood w Milton-under-Wychwood 80-85; Perm to Offic from 86; rtd 87. *St John's Home, St Mary's Road, Oxford OX4 1QE* Tel (01865) 247725

LINDLEY, Graham William. b 47. Man Poly CIPFA77. LNSM course 94. **d** 97. NSM E Crompton *Man* from 97. *37 Jordan Avenue, Shaw, Oldham, Lancs OL2 8DQ* Tel (01706) 845677

LINDLEY, Harold Thomas. b 28. St Jo Coll Ox BA51 MA73. Wells Th Coll 51. **d** 53 **p** 54. C Normanton *Wakef* 53-57; C-in-c Rawthorpe CD 57-63; P-in-c Longstone *Derby* 63-67; V 68-74; P-in-c Barrow w Twyford 74-84; V Barrow-on-Trent w Twyford and Swarkestone 84-93; rtd 93. *Gorwel, 35 Nant Bychan, Moelfre LL72 8HE* Tel (01248) 410484

LINDLEY, The Ven Ralph Adrian. b 20. CBE75. St Jo Coll Dur BA51 DipTh53. **d** 53 **p** 54. C Burnley St Steph *Blackb* 53-55; Chapl RAF 55-70; UAE 70-78; Adn Gulf 70-78; Gen Sec JMECA 78-85; rtd 86; Perm to Offic *Glouc* from 86. *Taffrail, Lower Road, St Briavels, Lydney, Glos GL15 6SA* Tel (01594) 530230

LINDLEY, Richard Adrian. b 44. Hull Univ BA65 Birm Univ DPS68 Man Univ MA79 Birm Poly DMS91. Cuddesdon Coll 66. **d** 68 **p** 69. C Ingrow cum Hainworth *Bradf* 68-70; Perm to Offic *Birm* 70-74; TV Ellesmere Port *Ches* 74-79; R Westborough *Guildf* 79-80; TR 80-84; Dir of Educn *Birm* 84-96; Hon Can Birm Cathl 96; Dir of Educn *Win* from 96. *Church House, 9 The Close, Winchester, Hants SO23 9LS* Tel (01962) 844644 Fax 841815

LINDO, Leithland Oscar. b 29. St Aug Coll Cant 57 St Pet Coll Jamaica 53. **d** 56 **p** 57. Jamaica 56-58; C Edmonton St Mary w St Jo *Lon* 58-62; C Heston 62-66; V Staines Ch Ch from 66. *Christ Church Vicarage, Kenilworth Gardens, Staines, Middx TW18 1DR* Tel (01784) 455457

LINDOP, Andrew John. b 57. Cam Univ MA. Cranmer Hall Dur 80. **d** 82 **p** 83. C Brinsworth w Catcliffe *Sheff* 82-85; C S Shoebury *Chelmsf* 85-89; V Mosley Common *Man* from 89. *St John's Vicarage, Mosley Common Road, Worsley, Manchester M28 4AN* Tel 0161-790 2957

LINDOP, Kenneth. b 45. Linc Th Coll 71. **d** 74 **p** 75. C Leic St Phil *Leic* 74-77; C Cov H Trin *Cov* 77-80; P-in-c Cubbington 80-82; V from 82; RD Warwick and Leamington 91-96. *The Vicarage, Rugby Road, Cubbington, Leamington Spa, Warks CV32 7JL* Tel (01926) 423056

LINDSAY, Alexandra Jane (Sandra). b 43. CITC 90. **d** 93 **p** 94. Lic to Offic *K, E & A* 93-94; NSM Bailieborough w Knockbride, Shercock and Mullagh from 94. *Clementstown House, Cootehill, Co Cavan, Irish Republic* Tel Cootehill (49) 52207 Fax as telephone

LINDSAY, Anthony. b 38. Trin Coll Bris DipHE93 St Jo Coll Nottm CertCS88. **d** 89 **p** 90. CMS 76-92; Sierra Leone 88-92; C Rainham w Wennington *Chelmsf* 93-96; R Quendon w Rickling and Wicken Bonhunt etc from 96. *The Rectory, Cambridge Road, Quendon, Saffron Walden, Essex CB11 3XJ* Tel (01799) 543238

LINDSAY, Cecil. b 43. Iona Coll (NY) BBA68. CITC 85. **d** 88 **p** 88. NSM Kilmore w Ballintemple, Kildallon etc *K, E & A* 88-90; Lic to Offic 90-92; NSM Roscommon w Donamon, Rathcline, Kilkeevin etc 92-96; NSM Boyle and Elphin w Aghanagh, Kilbryan etc 96; NSM Killeshandra w Killegar and Derrylane from 96; Dioc Registrar from 97. *Clementstown House, Cootehill, Co Cavan, Irish Republic* Tel Cootehill (49) 52207 Fax as telephone

LINDSAY, David Macintyre. b 46. Trin Hall Cam BA68 MA72 Ox Univ DipTh70. Cuddesdon Coll 68. **d** 71 **p** 72. C Gosforth All SS *Newc* 71-74; C Keele *Lich* 74-78; Perm to Offic *St E* 79-80; Chapl Haberdashers' Aske's Sch Elstree from 80. *36 Cranbourne Drive, Harpenden, Herts AL5 1RU* Tel (01582) 765660

LINDSAY, Eric Graham. b 30. Witwatersrand Univ BA51 Lon Univ DipAdEd78 MA80 Heythrop Coll Lon DipTh82. Coll of Resurr Mirfield 55. **d** 57 **p** 59. C Stella *Dur* 57-58; C W Hartlepool St Aid 58-60; Grenada 60-61; Perm to Offic *Win* 61-65; Perm to Offic *Roch* 65-72; Perm to Offic *Chelmsf* 72-84; C Stepney St Dunstan and All SS *Lon* 84-85; R Bridge of Weir *Glas* from 85; R Kilmacolm from 85. *St Fillan's Rectory, 4 Balmore Court, Kilmacolm, Renfrewshire PA13 4LX* Tel (01505) 872961

LINDSAY, John Carruthers. b 50. Edin Univ MA72 BD82. Edin Th Coll 79. **d** 82 **p** 83. C Broughty Ferry *Bre* 82-84; C Edin St Hilda *Edin* 84-85; TV 85-88; C Edin St Fillan 84-85; TV 85-88; R N Berwick from 88; R Gullane from 88. *The Rectory, 2 May Terrace, North Berwick, East Lothian EH39 4BA* Tel (01620) 892154 Fax as telephone

LINDSAY, Richard John. b 46. Sarum & Wells Th Coll 74. **d** 78 **p** 79. C Aldwick *Chich* 78-81; C Almondbury *Wakef* 81-82; C Almondbury w Farnley Tyas 82-84; V Mossley *Man* from 84. *The Vicarage, Stamford Street, Mossley, Ashton-under-Lyne, Lancs OL5 0LP* Tel (01457) 832219

LINDSAY, Canon Richard John Alan. b 24. TCD BA46 BD52. **d** 49 **p** 50. C Denton Holme *Carl* 49-52; CMS 52-64; Burundi 52-64; Chapl and Tutor CMS Tr Coll Chislehurst 65-68; R Chich St Pancras and St Jo *Chich* 68-74; Chapl Maisons-Laffitte *Eur* 74-82; Can Brussels Cathl 81-89; Chapl The Hague w Leiden and Voorschoten 82-89; rtd 89; Perm to Offic *Heref* from 89. *Japonica Cottage, King's Acre Road, Breinton, Hereford HR4 0SG* Tel (01432) 50230

LINDSAY, Canon Robert. b 16. St Jo Coll Dur BA37 DipTh38 MA40. **d** 39 **p** 40. C Gateshead St Mary *Dur* 39-43; P-in-c Sacriston 43-45; P-in-c Benfieldside 45-46; V Lanercost w Kirkcambeck *Carl* 46-55; V Hawkshead and Low Wray 55-70; R Dean 70-74; RD Derwent 70-81; Hon Can Carl Cathl 72-81; V Loweswater w Buttermere 74-81; rtd 81; Perm to Offic *Ex* from 81. *58 Primley Road, Sidmouth, Devon EX10 9LF* Tel (01395) 577882

LINDSAY, Robert Ashley Charles. b 43. Leeds Univ BA66 Ex Univ BPhil81. Coll of Resurr Mirfield 66. **d** 68 **p** 69. C Mill Hill Jo Keble Ch *Lon* 68-72; C Sherborne w Castleton and Lillington *Sarum* 73-78; Chapl Coldharbour Hosp Dorset 73-78; Perm to Offic *Leic* 87-92. *79 Castledine Street, Loughborough, Leics LE11 2DX* Tel (01509) 264360

LINDSAY-PARKINSON, Michael. b 28. Edin Th Coll 66. **d** 67 **p** 68. C Edin Ch Ch *Edin* 67-70; C Helensburgh *Glas* 70-72; R Lockerbie 72-83; R Annan 72-83; S Africa 83-88; V Alsager St Mary *Ches* 88-93; rtd 93; Perm to Offic *Ches* from 93. *10 Cherry Tree Avenue, Church Lawton, Stoke-on-Trent ST7 3EL* Tel (01270) 875574

LINDSEY, Archdeacon of. *Vacant*

LINES, John Anthony. b 31. Man Univ BA54 MA55 Birm Univ PhD74. St Jo Sem Wonersh 80 EMMTC. **d** 84 **p** 85. NSM Derby St Bart *Derby* 84-87; C Market Bosworth, Cadeby w Sutton Cheney etc *Leic* 87-90; C Wigston Magna 90-91; R Happisburgh w Walcot, Hempstead, Lessingham etc *Nor* 91-95; R Happisburgh, Walcott, Hempstead w Eccles etc 95-96; rtd 96. *1A Queen Street, Worksop, Notts S80 2AN* Tel (01909) 472882

LINES, Nicholas David John (Nick). b 64. St Jo Coll Nottm 94. **d** 96 **p** 97. C Burton All SS w Ch Ch *Lich* from 96. *1A Moor Street, Burton-on-Trent, Staffs DE14 3SU* Tel (01283) 538149

LINFORD, Preb John Kenneth. b 31. Liv Univ BA52. Chich Th Coll 54. **d** 56 **p** 57. C Stoke upon Trent *Lich* 56-61; V Tunstall Ch Ch 61-70; V Sedgley All SS 70-78; Chapl Chase Hosp Cannock 78-91; TR Cannock *Lich* 78-91; V Hatherton 80-91; Preb Lich Cathl from 88; rtd 91; Perm to Offic *Lich* from 91. *16 School Lane, Hill Ridware, Rugeley, Staffs WS15 3QN* Tel (01543) 492831

LING, Andrew Joyner. b 35. ACP69 St Luke's Coll Ex TCert63 Open Univ BA80. SW Minl Tr Course 83. **d** 86 **p** 87. NSM St Mellion w Pillaton *Truro* 86-87; NSM Landulph 86-87; NSM St Dominic 86-87; NSM St Dominic, Landulph and St Mellion w Pillaton 87-90; C Saltash 90-94; TV from 94. *The Vicarage, St Stephens, Saltash, Cornwall PL12 4AB* Tel (01752) 842323

LING, Timothy Charles. b 61. Ex Univ BA85 Selw Coll Cam BA91. Ridley Hall Cam CTM92. **d** 92 **p** 93. C Gerrards Cross and Fulmer *Ox* 92-96; C Woking St Pet *Guildf* from 96. *12 Vicarage Road, Woking, Surrey GU22 9BP* Tel (01483) 764134

LINGARD, Colin. b 36. Kelham Th Coll 58. **d** 63 **p** 64. C Middlesbrough St Martin *York* 63-66; C Stainton-in-Cleveland 66-71; V Eskdaleside w Ugglebarnby 71-77; P-in-c Redcar w Kirkleatham 77; V Kirkleatham 78-86; RD Guisborough 83-86; V Linc St Botolph by Bargate *Linc* 86-89; Dioc Dir of Readers 86-89; R Washington *Dur* 89-93; P-in-c Middleton St Geo 93-97; R from 97. *The Rectory, 8 Westacres, Neasham Road, Middleton St George, Darlington, Co Durham DL2 1LJ* Tel (01325) 332557

LINGARD, Keith Patrick. b 30. AKC53. **d** 54 **p** 55. C Bedford Park *Lon* 54-56; C Ruislip St Martin 56-58; C Kempston *St Alb* 58-63; Metrop Area Sec UMCA 63-65; V S Farnborough *Guildf* 65-75; R Glaston w Bisbrooke *Pet* 75-76; R Morcott w Glaston and Bisbrooke 77-95; rtd 95; Perm to Offic *Linc* from 95. *13 Woodside East, Thurlby, Bourne, Lincs PE10 0HT* Tel (01778) 425572

LINGS, George William. b 49. Nottm Univ BTh74 Ox Univ PGCE75. Lambeth Hon MLitt93 St Jo Coll Nottm 70. **d** 75 **p** 76. C Harold Wood *Chelmsf* 75-78; C Reigate St Mary *S'wark* 78-85; V Deal St Geo *Cant* 85-97; First Dir CA Inst for Evang and Ch Planning from 97. *28 Norfolk Road, Norfolk Park, Sheffield S2 2SX* Tel 0114-270 1780

LINGWOOD, David Peter. b 51. Lon Univ BEd73 Southn Univ BTh80. Sarum & Wells Th Coll 75. **d** 78 **p** 79. C Ashford St Hilda *Lon* 78-81; C Astwood Bank w Crabbs Cross *Worc* 81; TV Redditch, The Ridge 81-86; TR Blakenall Heath *Lich* 86-96; V Rushall from 96. *Rushall Vicarage, 10 Tetley Avenue, Walsall WS4 2HE* Tel (01922) 24677

LINN, Frederick Hugh. b 37. Em Coll Cam BA61 MA65. Ripon Hall Ox 61. **d** 63 **p** 64. C Bramhall *Ches* 63-68; V Liscard St Mary 68-71; V Liscard St Mary w St Columba 71-74; V Wybunbury 74-82; R Eccleston and Pulford from 82. *The Rectory, Eccleston, Chester CH4 9HT* Tel (01244) 674703

LINNEGAN, Canon John McCaughan. ACCS48 ACIS70 TCD BA55. **d** 57 **p** 58. C Billis *K, E & A* 57-59; I Cappagh *D & R* 59-80; I Cappagh w Lislimnaghan 80-90; Can Derry Cathl 82-90; rtd 90. *46 Lisanelly Park, Omagh, Co Tyrone BT79 7DE* Tel (01662) 249643

LINNEGAR, George Leonard. b 33. CGA. Kelham Th Coll 63. **d** 62 **p** 63. C Wellingborough St Mary *Pet* 62-65; Lic to Offic *Lich* 65-69; Lic to Offic *B & W* 69-80; Hon C Lewes All SS, St Anne,

St Mich and St Thos *Chich* 80-86; C from 87. *20 Morris Road, Lewes, E Sussex BN7 2AT* Tel (01273) 478145

LINNEY, The Ven Gordon Charles Scott. b 39. CITC 66. **d** 69 **p** 70. C Agherton *Conn* 69-72; Min Can Down Cathl *D & D* 72-75; I Dublin St Cath w St Jas *D & G* 75-80; Preb Tipperkevin St Patr Cathl Dublin 77-80; I Glenageary *D & G* from 80; Adn Dublin from 88; Lect CITC 89-93. *St Paul's Vicarage, Silchester Road, Glenageary, Co Dublin, Irish Republic* Tel Dublin (1) 280 1616 Fax 280 9459

LINNING, Alexander. b 19. Birm Univ BA40 Lon Univ BD42. **d** 61 **p** 62. Hon C W Bridgford *S'well* 61-80; Lic to Offic from 80. *7 Kingston Road, Nottingham NG2 7AQ* Tel 0115-981 2959

LINSKILL, Martin Paul Richard. b 50. Magd Coll Ox BA72 MA75. St Steph Ho Ox 73. **d** 75 **p** 76. C Pinner *Lon* 75-80; C Greenhill *Sheff* 80-82; C Penistone *Wakef* 82-83; Tutor St Steph Ho Ox 84-91; Chapl Bede Ho Staplehurst 91; V Bedford St Martin *St Alb* from 91. *St Martin's Vicarage, 76 Clapham Road, Bedford MK41 7PN* Tel (01234) 357862

LINTERN, John. b 61. Linc Th Coll BTh93. **d** 93 **p** 94. C Preston on Tees *Dur* 93-96; P-in-c W Pelton from 96. *The Vicarage, West Pelton, Stanley, Co Durham DH9 6RT* Tel 0191-370 2146 Fax as telephone

LINTON, Alan Ross. b 28. Lon Univ DipTh60. St Aid Birkenhead 57. **d** 60 **p** 61. C Blundellsands St Nic *Liv* 60-62; C Southport St Phil 62-63; C Aigburth 63-66; V Glazebury 66-67; C Formby St Pet 67-69; C Douglas *Blackb* 69-71; P-in-c Appley Bridge All SS CD 71-76; P-in-c Scorton 76-85; P-in-c Calder Vale w Admarsh 76-85; R Hoole 85-93; rtd 93; Perm to Offic *Blackb* from 93. *12 Clive Road, Penwortham, Preston PR1 0AT* Tel (01772) 747813

LINTON, Joseph Edmund. b 19. St Andr Univ MA46. Sarum Th Coll 46. **d** 48 **p** 49. C Monkseaton St Mary *Newc* 48-53; CF (TA) 50-54; C-in-c Lynemouth St Aid CD *Newc* 53-59; V Beltingham w Henshaw 59-93; rtd 93. *4 Dipton Close, Eastwood Grange, Hexham, Northd NE46 1UG* Tel (01434) 601457

LINTON, Sydney. b 07. Pemb Coll Ox BA30 MA34. Westcott Ho Cam 31. **d** 32 **p** 33. C Morley St Pet w Churwell *Wakef* 32-39; Hon Chapl Helsinki w Moscow 48-51; C Limpsfield and Titsey *S'wark* 51-57; V Barnes H Trin 57-71; R Codford *Sarum* 71-73; R Upton Lovell 71-73; R Codford, Upton Lovell and Stockton 73-77; rtd 77. *c/o Lord Harris Court, Wokingham, Berks RG41 5EA* Tel (0118) 978 7496

LINTOTT, William Ince. b 36. St Cath Coll Cam BA58. Ely Th Coll 58. **d** 60 **p** 61. C Brighton St Wilfrid *Chich* 60-62; C Chingford SS Pet and Paul *Chelmsf* 62-66; Lic to Offic *Ely* from 66; Chapl Fulbourn Hosp Cam 66-73. *7 Haverhill Road, Stapleford, Cambridge CB2 5BX* Tel (01223) 842008

LINZEY, Prof Andrew. b 52. FRSA93 K Coll Lon BD73 AKC73 Univ of Wales (Cardiff) DPS74 PhD86. St Aug Coll Cant 75. **d** 75 **p** 76. C Charlton-by-Dover SS Pet and Paul *Cant* 75-77; Chapl and Lect Th NE Surrey Coll of Tech 77-81; Chapl Essex Univ *Chelmsf* 81-92; Dir of Studies Cen for Study of Th 87-92; Sen Research Fell Mansf Coll Ox from 92; Tutor Chr Ethics from 93; Special Prof Th Nottm Univ 92-96; Special Prof St Xavier Univ Chicago from 96. *Mansfield College, Oxford OX1 3TF* Tel (01865) 270999

LIPP-NATHANIEL, Julie Christiane. b 41. Melbourne Univ BA63 MA72 DipSocSc63 Lon Univ 93. **d** 95 **p** 95. Lic to Offic *Birm* from 96; Tutor Coll of the Ascension Selly Oak from 96. *College of the Ascension, Weoley Park Road, Birmingham B29 6RD* Tel 0121-472 1667 Fax 472 4320

LIPPIATT, Michael Charles. b 39. Oak Hill Th Coll BD71. **d** 71 **p** 72. C Ardsley *Sheff* 71-74; C Lenton *S'well* 74-78; V Jesmond H Trin *Newc* 78-96; rtd 96. *3 St George's Crescent, Carlisle CA3 9NL* Tel (01228) 37080

LIPPIETT, Dr Peter Vernon. b 47. DRCOG79 MRCGP80 Lon Univ MB, BS73. Ripon Coll Cuddesdon 86. **d** 88 **p** 89. C Pinner *Lon* 88-91; V Twyford and Owslebury and Morestead *Win* from 91. *The Vicarage, Church Lane, Twyford, Winchester, Hants SO21 1NT* Tel (01962) 712208

LIPSCOMB, Ian Craig. b 30. ACT ThL67 Wells Th Coll 61. **d** 63 **p** 64. C Feltham *Lon* 63-65; Australia from 65; rtd 94. *PO Box 118, Goulburn, NSW, Australia 2580* Tel Goulburn (48) 219591

LIPSCOMB, Timothy William. b 52. Chich Th Coll 82. **d** 85 **p** 86. C Sevenoaks St Jo *Roch* 85-89; C Stanningley St Thos *Ripon* 89-92; V Armley w New Wortley from 92. *Armley Vicarage, Wesley Road, Leeds LS12 1SR* Tel 0113-263 8620

LIPSCOMBE, Brian. b 37. Bris Univ BA62. Tyndale Hall Bris 62. **d** 64 **p** 65. C Eccleston Ch Ch *Liv* 64-66; C Halliwell St Pet *Man* 66-69; C Frogmore *St Alb* 69-72; V Richmond Ch Ch *S'wark* 72-75; TV Mortlake w E Sheen 76-80; P-in-c Streatham Vale H Redeemer 80-88; V 85-91; R Norris Bank *Man* 91-96; V Droylsden St Martin from 96. *St Martin's Vicarage, Greenside Lane, Droylsden, Manchester M43 7QS* Tel 0161-370 9833

LISEMORE, Canon Frederick John Henry. b 11. St Cath Soc Ox BA37 MA38. Ripon Hall Ox 36. **d** 37 **p** 38. C Ipswich St Jo *St E* 37-39; CF 39-45; Hon CF 45; C Rugby St Andr *Cov* 46-48; V Radford 48-57; V Ashbourne w Mapleton and Clifton *Derby* 57-70; V Foremark 70-77; V Repton 70-77; Perm to Offic *Lich* from 78; rtd 78; Perm to Offic *Derby* from 78. *36 Church Lane, Barton under Needwood, Burton-on-Trent, Staffs DE13 8HU* Tel (01283) 712554

LISK, Stewart. b 62. Regent's Park Coll Ox BA84 MA88 Univ of Wales (Cardiff) DPS87. St Mich Coll Llan 86. **d** 88 **p** 89. C Glan Ely *Llan* 88-92; Chapl Cardiff Inst of HE 92-96; Chapl Welsh Coll of Music and Drama from 92; Asst Chapl Univ of Wales (Cardiff) 92-96; V Glan Ely from 96. *Church House, Grand Avenue, Ely, Cardiff CF5 4HX* Tel (01222) 591633

LISMORE, Dean of. *See* HEALEY, The Very Revd James Christopher

LISTER, Anthony Galen. b 27. RIBA DipArch. NE Ord Course. **d** 83 **p** 84. Hon C Anlaby St Pet *York* 83-87. *Ballachan, Glenuig, Lochailort, Inverness-shire PH38 4NB* Tel (01687) 7242

LISTER, David Ian. b 26. Roch Th Coll 61. **d** 62 **p** 64. C Scarborough St Mary w Ch Ch, St Paul and St Thos *York* 62-66; C Buttershaw St Aid *Bradf* 66-68; V Tufnell Park St Geo *Lon* 68-83; V Tufnell Park St Geo and All SS 83-92; rtd 92; Perm to Offic *York* from 92. *8 Stonethwaite, Woodthorpe, York YO2 2SY* Tel (01904) 704586

LISTER, Edmund. b 08. AKC35. **d** 35 **p** 36. C Birkenhead St Pet *Ches* 35-36; C Broadheath 36-40; Chapl RNVR 40-46; C Stalybridge St Paul *Ches* 47-48; R Cotleigh w Monkton *Ex* 48-50; V Bickleigh (Plymouth) 50-60; V Bishops Nympton 60-67; R Rose Ash 60-67; P-in-c Creacombe 65-67; RD S Molton 65-67; R Dunsfold *Guildf* 67-73; rtd 73; C Bladon w Woodstock *Ox* 73-75. *The Leys, Ware Lane, Lyme Regis, Dorset DT7 3EL* Tel (01297) 443060

LISTER, Mrs Jennifer Grace (Jenny). b 44. Totley Hall Coll CertEd65. Nor Ord Course 87. **d** 92 **p** 94. C Cowgate *Newc* 92-95; C Lich St Mary w St Mich *Lich* 95-96; C Wall 95-96; P-in-c Yoxall from 96; C The Ridwares and Kings Bromley from 96. *The Rectory, Savey Lane, Yoxall, Burton-on-Trent, Staffs DE13 8PD* Tel (01543) 472528

LISTER (née AISBITT), Mrs Joanne. b 69. St Jo Coll Dur BA91. St Steph Ho Ox 91. **d** 93. NSM Mill End and Heronsgate w W Hyde *St Alb* 93-96. *6 Old Coach Road, Beachley, Chepstow NP6 7HL*

LISTER, The Very Revd John Field. b 16. Keble Coll Ox BA38 MA42. Cuddesdon Coll 38. **d** 39 **p** 41. C Radford *Cov* 39-44; C Cov St Jo 44-45; V Huddersfield St Jo *Wakef* 45-54; V Brighouse 54-71; Adn Halifax 61-72; Chapl to The Queen 66-72; RD Wakef 72-80; Provost Wakef 72-82; rtd 82; Perm to Offic *Cant* from 82. *5 Larkscliff Court, The Parade, Birchington, Kent CT7 9NB* Tel (01843) 42543

LISTER, Joseph Hugh. b 38. Tyndale Hall Bris. **d** 64 **p** 65. C Pemberton St Mark Newtown *Liv* 64-68; Hon C Braintree *Chelmsf* 68-71; Hon C Darfield *Sheff* 71-73; P-in-c Sheff St Swithun 73-76; TV Sheff Manor 76-80; P-in-c Burston *Nor* 80-81; P-in-c Tivetshall 80-81; P-in-c Gissing 80-81; TR Winfarthing w Shelfanger 80-81; R Winfarthing w Shelfanger w Burston w Gissing etc 81-88; P-in-c Sandon, Wallington and Rushden w Clothall *St Alb* 88-89; R 89-93; R Nether and Over Seale *Derby* 93-96; V Lullington 93-96; R Seale and Lullington from 96; RD Repton from 96. *The Rectory, Netherseal, Swadlincote, Derbyshire DE12 9AF* Tel (01524) 761179

LISTER, Miss Mary Phyllis. b 28. St Andr Ho Portsm 52. **dss** 80 **d** 87. Inkberrow w Cookhill and Kington w Dormston *Worc* 80-82; Ancaster *Linc* 82-87; C 87-88; rtd 88; Perm to Offic *Worc* from 88. *7 Byfield Rise, Worcester WR5 1BA* Tel (01905) 29683

LISTER, Peter. b 42. Leeds Univ BA64 Newc Univ PGCE75. Coll of Resurr Mirfield 63. **d** 65 **p** 66. C Monkseaton St Pet *Newc* 65-68; C Cramlington 68-70; Hon C 71-78; C Morpeth 79-83; V Shilbottle 83-88; Asst Dioc Dir of Educn 83-88; Dir of Educn 88-95; Hon Can Newc Cathl 88-95; Dioc Dir of Educn *Lich* from 95. *The Rectory, Savey Lane, Yoxall, Burton-on-Trent, Staffs DE13 8PD* Tel (01543) 472528

LISTER, Father William Bernard. b 67. Keble Coll Ox BA88 MA92. St Steph Ho Ox BA91. **d** 92 **p** 93. C Mill End and Heronsgate w W Hyde *St Alb* 92-96; CF from 96. *MOD Chaplains (Army), Trenchard Lines, Upavon, Pewsey, Wilts SN9 6BE* Tel (01980) 615804 Fax 615800

LISTON, Scott Carnie. b 62. Edin Univ BD87. Edin Th Coll. **d** 88 **p** 88. C Edin St Martin *Edin* 88-91; C Edin St Luke 88-91; C Edin St Dav 91-92; Chapl HM Young Offender Inst Guys Marsh from 92; Perm to Offic *B & W* from 92. *HM Young Offender Institution, Guys Marsh, Shaftesbury, Dorset SP7 0AH* Tel (01747) 853344 Fax 851584

LITHERLAND, Norman Richard. b 30. Lon Univ BA51 Man Univ MEd72. N Ord Course 78. **d** 81 **p** 82. NSM Flixton St Mich *Man* 81-94; rtd 94; Perm to Offic *Man* from 94. *1 Overdale Crescent, Urmston, Manchester M31 3GR* Tel 0161-748 4243

LITHERLAND, Terence (Terry). b 46. LNSM course 90. **d** 93 **p** 94. NSM Horwich and Rivington *Man* from 93. *61 Tomlinson Street, Horwich, Bolton BL6 5QR* Tel (01204) 692201

LITJENS, Shan Elizabeth. b 55. **d** 95. C Fareham SS Pet and Paul *Portsm* 95-96; C Fareham H Trin from 96. *61 Oak Road, Fareham, Hants PO15 5HH*

LITTLE, Andrew. b 27. Open Univ BA83. AKC51. **d** 52 **p** 53. C Fulham All SS *Lon* 52-54; C Epsom St Barn *Guildf* 54-61; V Northwood *Lich* 61-72; P-in-c Hixon 72-86; V Stowe 72-86; V Hixon w Stowe-by-Chartley 86-89; rtd 89; Perm to Offic *Nor*

from 89. *5 Damocles Court, Norwich NR2 1HN* Tel (01603) 662241

LITTLE, Ms Christine. b 60. Lanc Univ BA83. St Jo Coll Nottm DTS90 DPS91. **d** 91 **p** 94. Par Dn Meltham *Wakef* 91-94; C Hatcham St Jas *S'wark* from 94. *Flat 3, St Michael's Centre, Desmond Street, London SE14 6JF* Tel 0181-691 2167

LITTLE, David John. b 65. Oak Hill Th Coll BA94. **d** 94 **p** 95. C Chislehurst Ch Ch *Roch* from 94. *56 Walden Road, Chislehurst, Kent BR7 5DL* Tel 0181-402 2321

LITTLE, Denis Theodore. b 15. St Jo Coll Dur BA36 MA39. **d** 39 **p** 40. C Bishopwearmouth St Mich *Dur* 39-42; C Tudhoe 42-46; C Whitby *York* 46-49; V Kexby 49-54; V Wilberfoss 49-54; V Huntington 54-61; V Lythe 61-72; R Dunnington 72-80; RD Bulmer 78-80; rtd 80; P-in-c Bulmer w Welburn 84-86; Perm to Offic *York* from 86. *92 The Village, Strensall, York YO3 5BX* Tel (01904) 490695

LITTLE, Derek Peter. b 50. St Jo Coll Dur BA72 DipTh75. Trin Coll Bris. **d** 75 **p** 76. C Bradley *Wakef* 75-78; C Kidderminster St Geo *Worc* 78-82; V Lepton *Wakef* 82-85; E Regional Sec CPAS 85-88; Lic to Offic *Ely* 86-88; V Canonbury St Steph *Lon* 88-96; R Bedhampton *Portsm* from 96. *The Rectory, Bidbury Lane, Bedhampton, Havant, Hants PO9 3JG* Tel (01705) 483013

LITTLE, Canon George Nelson. b 39. CITC 70. **d** 72 **p** 73. C Portadown St Mark *Arm* 72-76; I Newtownhamilton w Ballymoyer and Belleek 76-80; I Aghaderg w Donaghmore *D & D* 80-81; I Aghaderg w Donaghmore and Scarva from 81; RD Aghaderg from 88; Can Dromore Cathl from 93; Treas from 93. *Aghaderg Rectory, 32 Banbridge Road, Loughbrickland, Banbridge, Co Down BT32 3YB* Tel (01820) 624073

LITTLE, Harold Clifford. b 18. Lon Univ BD42. ALCD42. **d** 42 **p** 43. C Gt Ilford St Jo *Chelmsf* 42-44; C Loughton St Mary 44-48; V Billesley Common *Birm* 48-56; V S Dulwich St Steph *S'wark* 56-87; Lect Bibl and Relig Studies Lon Univ 61-87; rtd 87; Perm to Offic *Ex* from 88. *Howden Lodge, Willand Old Village, Cullompton, Devon EX15 2RJ* Tel (01884) 32663

LITTLE, Herbert Edwin Samuel. b 21. Lon Univ BA54 BD68. NE Ord Course 79. **d** 80 **p** 81. NSM Dur St Cuth *Dur* 80-88; rtd 88. *3 Whitesmocks Avenue, Durham DH1 4HP* Tel 0191-384 2897

LITTLE, Ian Arthur Langley. b 24. ARICS52. S'wark Ord Course 63. **d** 66 **p** 67. NSM Bickley *Roch* 66-69; NSM Bromley St Andr 69-77; Perm to Offic 77-95; rtd 86. *23 Vale Road, Bickley, Kent BR1 2AL* Tel 0181-467 4899

LITTLE, Ian Dawtry Torrance. b 49. SW Minl Tr Course. **d** 85 **p** 86. NSM St Stythians w Perranarworthal and Gwennap *Truro* from 85. *Kernyk, Crellow Fields, Stithians, Truro, Cornwall TR3 7RE*

LITTLE, James Harry. b 57. York Univ BA79 Birm Univ DipTh86. Qu Coll Birm 84. **d** 87 **p** 88. C Wollaton *S'well* 87-90; C N Wheatley, W Burton, Bole, Saundby, Sturton etc 90-93; R E Markham w Askham, Headon w Upton and Grove from 93. *The Rectory, Lincoln Road, East Markham, Newark, Notts NG22 0SH* Tel (01777) 871731

LITTLE, Canon John Richardson. b 28. Magd Coll Ox BA49 MA53 DipTh50. Westcott Ho Cam 52. **d** 54 **p** 55. C Moss Side Ch Ch *Man* 54-57; C Billingham St Aid CD *Dur* 57-60; V New Springs *Liv* 60-65; V Newc H Cross *Newc* 65-77; RD Newc W 74-77; V Gosforth All SS 77-89; Hon Can Newc Cathl 82-93; V Heddon-on-the-Wall 89-93; rtd 93. *34 Winchester Walk, Woodlands Park, Newcastle upon Tyne NE13 6JP* Tel 0191-236 6535

LITTLE, Rebekah Mary. Oak Hill Th Coll. **d** 97. NSM Chislehurst Ch Ch *Roch* from 97. *56 Walden Road, Chislehurst, Kent BR7 5DL* Tel 0181-402 2321

LITTLE, Stephen Clifford. b 47. Man Univ MEd81. AKC72. **d** 72 **p** 73. C Grange St Andr *Ches* 72-73; C E Runcorn w Halton 73-75; P-in-c Newbold *Man* 75-77; P-in-c Broughton and Milton Keynes *Ox* 77-82; Sector Min Milton Keynes Chr Coun 77-84; TR Warwick *Cov* 84-93; R Harvington and Norton and Lenchwick *Worc* from 93. *The Rectory, Station Road, Harvington, Evesham, Worcs WR11 5NJ* Tel (01386) 871068

LITTLECHILD, William Bryant. b 02. St Geo Windsor 52. **d** 53 **p** 54. C Kenilworth St Nic *Cov* 53-55; V Sutton Courtenay w Appleford *Ox* 55-67; RD Abingdon 57-62; rtd 67; P-in-c Chaffcombe *B & W* 76-77; P-in-c Knowle St Giles w Cricket Malherbie 76-77; Perm to Offic 77-94. *Oak Lodge Nursing Home, Lordleaze Lane, Chard, Somerset TA20 2HN*

LITTLEFAIR, David. b 38. ACCA71 FCCA85 Lon Univ BD79. Trin Coll Bris 76. **d** 79 **p** 80. C Bursledon *Win* 79-82; V Charles w Plymouth St Matthias *Ex* 82-89; Warden Lee Abbey Internat Students' Club Kensington 89-94; V Malmesbury w Westport and Brokenborough *Bris* from 94. *The Abbey Vicarage, Holloway, Malmesbury, Wilts SN16 9BA* Tel (01666) 823126

LITTLER, Eric Raymond. b 36. AMIC93 Lon Univ DipTh67. Roch Th Coll 65. **d** 68 **p** 69. C Hatfield Hyde *St Alb* 68-73; Chapl Welwyn Garden City Hosp 70-73; TV Pemberton St Jo *Liv* 73-78; Chapl Billinge Hosp Wigan 76-81; V Pemberton St Fran Kitt Green *Liv* 78-81; V White Notley, Faulkbourne and Cressing *Chelmsf* 81-88; V Westcliff St Andr 81-96; Chapl Westcliff Hosp 88-96; Chapl Southend HA 89-96; R E and W Tilbury and Linford *Chelmsf* from 96; Chapl Orsett Hosp from 96; RD Thurrock *Chelmsf* from 96. *The Rectory, Princess Margaret Road, East Tilbury, Grays, Essex RM18 8PB* Tel (01375) 842220

LITTLER, Dr Keith Trevor. b 35. Lon Univ BSc(Soc)63 TCert64 York Univ MA82 Hull Univ PhD88 Trin Coll Carmarthen 89. LNSM course 89. **d** 92 **p** 93. NSM Betws w Ammanford *St D* 92-94; C 94; R Pendine w Llanmiloe and Eglwys Gymyn w Marros from 94. *The Rectory, Pendine, Carmarthen SA33 4PD* Tel (01994) 453405

LITTLER, Malcolm Kenneth. b 34. Univ of Wales (Lamp) BA55. **d** 57 **p** 58. C Llanelli *St D* 57-60; C Llandeilo Fawr 60-61; R Puncheston, Lt Newcastle and Castle Bythe 61-64; R Lamp Velfrey 64-68; V Llanwnda w Goodwick and Manorowen 68-74; V Llanfynydd 74-78; V The Suttons w Tydd *Linc* 87-90; V Graffoe 90-94; rtd 94; Perm to Offic *Linc* from 94. *Ivy Cottage, 11 Chapel Lane, Lincoln LN1 3BA*

LITTLEWOOD, Alan James. b 51. Man Poly BEd77. LNSM course 91. **d** 95 **p** 96. NSM Gosberton *Linc* 95-97; NSM Gosberton, Gosberton Clough and Quadrin from 97. *14 Medway Close, Gosberton, Spalding, Lincs PE11 4HS* Tel (01775) 840388

LITTLEWOOD, Alistair David. b 68. St Cath Coll Ox BA89. Qu Coll Birm 93. **d** 96 **p** 97. C Keyworth *S'well* from 96. *10 Moor Lane, Bunny, Nottingham NG11 6QX* Tel 0115-925 7805

LITTLEWOOD, Miss Jacqueline Patricia. b 52. Linc Th Coll 77. **dss** 80 **d** 87 **p** 94. Crayford *Roch* 80-84; Gravesend H Family w Ifield 84-87; Par Dn 87-93; rtd 93; NSM Gravesend St Aid *Roch* from 93. *25 Beltana Drive, Gravesend, Kent DA12 4BT* Tel (01474) 560106

LITTLEWOOD, John Edward. b 50. UEA BSc71. Ridley Hall Cam 72. **d** 75 **p** 76. C Hellesdon *Nor* 75-78; C Eaton 78-81; Hon C S Hill w Callington *Truro* 83-89; Hon C Linkinhorne 86-89; Hon C Stoke Climsland 89-91; Perm to Offic *Ex* from 95. *18 Langdon Court, Elburton, Plymouth PL9 8UH* Tel (01752) 662211

LITTLEWOOD, John Richard. b 37. Ridley Hall Cam 69. **d** 72 **p** 73. C Rushden w Newton Bromswold *Pet* 72-75; Chapl Scargill Ho 75-77; V Werrington *Pet* 77-91; V Highbury Ch Ch w St Jo and St Sav Lon from 91. *Christ Church Vicarage, 155 Highbury Grove, London N5 1SA* Tel 0171-226 4544

LITTLEWOOD, Philip Nigel. b 59. Sarum & Wells Th Coll 87. **d** 90 **p** 91. C Frome St Jo and St Mary *B & W* 90-95; P-in-c Keinton Mandeville w Lydford-on-Fosse etc from 95. *The Rectory, Church Street, Keinton Mandeville, Somerton, Somerset TA11 6EP* Tel (01458) 223216

LITTON, Alan. b 42. Ridley Hall Cam 66. **d** 69 **p** 70. C Bolton St Bede *Man* 69-71; C Ashton St Mich 71-73; V Haslingden St Jo Stonefold *Blackb* 73-77; Ind Chapl *York* 77-81; V Crewe All SS and St Paul *Ches* 81-84; Ind Chapl *Liv* 84-89; V Spotland *Man* 89-94; R Newchurch *Liv* from 94. *The Rectory, 17 Jackson Avenue, Newchurch, Culcheth, Warrington WA3 4DZ* Tel (01925) 766300

LIVERPOOL, Archdeacon of. *See* METCALF, The Ven Robert Laurence

LIVERPOOL, Bishop of. *Vacant*

LIVERPOOL, Dean of. *See* WALTERS, The Very Revd Rhys Derrick Chamberlain

LIVERSUCH, Ian Martin. b 56. St Jo Coll Dur BA79 Univ of Wales (Cardiff) DPS84. Wycliffe Hall Ox 79. **d** 83 **p** 84. C Newport St Mark *Mon* 83-85; C Risca 85-88; P-in-c Newport All SS 88-91; Canada from 91. *567 Champlain, Hemmingford, Quebec, Canada, J0L 1H0* Tel Montreal (514) 247-2880

LIVESEY, Kenneth. b 29. Codrington Coll Barbados 57. **d** 59 **p** 60. Br Guiana 59-66; Guyana 66-72 and 84-89; P-in-c Royton St Paul *Man* 72-73; V 73-81; P-in-c Bury H Trin 81-82; TR Bury Ch King w H Trin 82-84; V Oldham St Steph and All Martyrs 89-91; rtd 91; Perm to Offic *Man* from 91. *2 Malvern Close, Royton, Oldham OL2 5HH* Tel 0161-628 8617

LIVINGSTON, Bertram. TCD BA56. **d** 57 **p** 58. C Enniscorthy *C & O* 57-59; I Carrickmacross *Clogh* 59-61; I Carrickmacross w Magheracloone 61-63; C-in-c Derryvolgie *Conn* 63-78; I 78-79; I Monaghan *Clogh* 79-86; I Desertlyn w Ballyeglish *Arm* 86-94; rtd 94. *40 Ballynagamick Road, Portadown, Craigavon, Co Armagh BT63 5NR* Tel (01762) 831859

LIVINGSTON, Richard. b 46. Qu Coll Birm. **d** 83 **p** 84. C Hobs Moat *Birm* 83-87; V Droylsden St Martin *Man* 87-95; P-in-c Wolverton w Norton Lindsey and Langley *Cov* from 95. *The Rectory, Wolverton, Stratford-upon-Avon, Warks CV37 0HF* Tel (01789) 731278

LIVINGSTONE, Canon Francis Kenneth. b 26. TCD BA48 MA64. TCD Div Sch Div Test49. **d** 49 **p** 50. C Dublin Santry Union w Coolock *D & G* 49-52; C Dublin St Geo 52-57; I Castledermot Union 57-62; C Arm St Mark *Arm* 62-66; Hon V Choral Arm Cathl 63-92; I Portadown St Sav 66-78; I Kilmore St Aid w St Sav 78-83; I Donaghmore w Upper Donaghmore 83-92; Preb Yagoe St Patr Cathl Dublin 85-92; rtd 92. *9 Castle Parade, Richhill, Armagh BT61 9QQ* Tel (01762) 871574

LIVINGSTONE, Canon John Morris. b 28. Peterho Cam BA53 MA56. Cuddesdon Coll 53. **d** 55 **p** 56. C Hunslet St Mary and Stourton *Ripon* 55-60; Chapl Liddon Ho Lon 60-63; V Notting Hill St Jo *Lon* 63-74; P-in-c Notting Hill St Mark 66-73; P-in-c

Notting Hill All SS w St Columb 67-74; P-in-c Notting Hill St Clem 68-74; TR Notting Hill 74-75; Chapl Paris St Geo *Eur* 75-84; Adn N France 79-84; Adn Riviera 84-93; Chapl Nice w Vence 84-93; Chapl Biarritz from 93; rtd 93. *47 Perspective de la Côte des Basques, 64200 Biarritz, France* Tel France (33) 59 24 71 18 Fax as telephone

LIVINGSTONE, John Philip. b 51. Univ of Wales (Abth) BA. **d** 96 **p** 97. NSM Maenclochog and New Moat etc *St D* from 96. *Clydfan, Llysyfran, Clarbeston Road SA63 4RR*

LLANDAFF, Archdeacon of. *See* LEE, The Ven David Stanley

LLANDAFF, Bishop of. *See* DAVIES, The Rt Revd Roy Thomas

LLANDAFF, Dean of. *See* ROGERS, The Very Revd John

✠**LLEWELLIN, The Rt Revd John Richard Allan.** b 38. Fitzw Ho Cam BA64 MA78. Westcott Ho Cam 61. **d** 64 **p** 65 **c** 85. C Radlett *St Alb* 64-68; S Africa 68-71; V Waltham Cross *St Alb* 71-79; R Harpenden St Nic 79-85; Hon Can Truro Cathl *Truro* 85-92; Suff Bp St Germans 85-92; Suff Bp Dover *Cant* from 92. *Upway, 52 St Martin's Hill, Canterbury, Kent CT1 1PR* Tel (01227) 464537 or 459382 Fax 784985

LLEWELLYN, Brian Michael. b 47. ARICS73. Sarum & Wells Th Coll 78. **d** 80 **p** 81. C Farncombe *Guildf* 80-83; Chapl RAF 83-87; R Hethersett w Canteloff w Lt and Gt Melton *Nor* 87-95; RD Humbleyard 94-95; P-in-c Smallburgh w Dilham w Honing and Crostwight from 95. *The Rectory, Honing, North Walsham, Norfolk NR28 9AB* Tel (01692) 536466

LLEWELLYN, Christine Ann. b 46. Univ of Wales (Ban) BA69 DipEd70. **d** 89 **p** 97. NSM Arthog w Fairbourne w Llangelynnin w Rhoslefain *Ban* 90-93; NSM Holyhead w Rhoscolyn w Llanfair-yn-Neubwll 93-94; C 94-95; C Holyhead 95-97; TV from 97. *The Old School, Rhoscolyn, Holyhead LL65 2RQ* Tel (01407) 741593

LLEWELLYN, David John Patrick. b 16. AKC40. Wells Th Coll. **d** 46 **p** 47. C Dorking *Guildf* 46-49; C Dudley St Fran *Worc* 49-50; C Redditch St Steph 50-52; V Bretforton 52-59; V Wolverley 59-60; S Africa 60-65; Rhodesia 65-69; I Kinneigh Union *C, C & R* 76-83; rtd 83. *Anne's Cottage, Hamilton Row, Courtmacsherry, Bandon, Co Cork, Irish Republic* Tel Courtmacsherry (23) 46381

LLEWELLYN, Neil Alexander. b 55. LWCMD78. Westcott Ho Cam 79 Sarum & Wells Th Coll 83. **d** 84 **p** 85. C Heref St Martin *Heref* 84-86; Chapl Rotterdam Miss to Seamen *Eur* 86-89; R Docking w The Birchams and Stanhoe w Barwick *Nor* 89-92; Chapl Ypres *Eur* 92-95; Toc H 92-95; CF from 95. *MOD Chaplains (Army), Trenchard Lines, Upavon, Pewsey, Wilts SN9 6BE* Tel (01980) 615804 Fax 615800

LLEWELLYN, Richard Morgan. b 37. CB91 OBE79 MBE76. FIMgt81. Sarum & Wells Th Coll DCTM93. **d** 93 **p** 94. C Brecon St Mary and Battle w Llanddew *S & B* 93-95; Min Can Brecon Cathl 93-95; Chapl Ch Coll Brecon from 95. *Llangattock Court, Llangattock, Crickhowell NP8 1PH*

LLEWELLYN, William David. b 22. Univ of Wales (Lamp) BA43. **d** 48 **p** 49. C Llanishen and Lisvane *Llan* 48-51; C Whitchurch 51-63; V Treharris 63-70; V Penmaen *Mon* 70-77; V St Mellons 77-87; rtd 87. *262 Cardiff Road, Newport NP9 3AH*

✠**LLEWELLYN, The Rt Revd William Somers.** b 07. Ball Coll Ox BA29 DipTh34 MA37. Wycliffe Hall Ox. **d** 35 **p** 36 **c** 63. C Chiswick St Nic w St Mary *Lon* 35-37; V Badminton w Acton Turville *Glouc* 37-49; CF (EC) 40-46; CF (TA) 48-51; R Tetbury w Beverston *Glouc* 49-61; Hon C 77-85; CF (R of O) 51-62; RD Tetbury *Glouc* 56-61; Adn Lynn *Nor* 61-72; C Blakeney w Lt Langham 62-63; C Stiffkey w Morston 62-63; Suff Bp Lynn 63-72; rtd 73; Asst Bp Glouc from 73; P-in-c Boxwell w Leighterton 73-76. *Glebe House, Leighterton, Tetbury, Glos GL8 8UN* Tel (01666) 890236

LLEWELYN, John Dilwyn. b 18. St D Coll Lamp BA40 AKC42. **d** 42 **p** 43. C Battersea Rise St Mark *S'wark* 42-45; C Thame *Ox* 45-47; C Towersey w Aston Sandford 45-47; C Maidenhead St Andr and St Mary 47-51; P-in-c Devonport St Aubyn *Ex* 51-56; C Merton St Mary *S'wark* 56-61; V Plymouth St Simon *Ex* 61-82; rtd 82; Perm to Offic *Ex* from 84. *25 Oakley Close, Pinhoe, Exeter EX1 3SB* Tel (01392) 467169

LLEWELYN, Robert Charles. b 09. Pemb Coll Cam BA32 MA36. **d** 36 **p** 37. Asst Master Westmr Sch 32-47; Chapl 46-47; C Westmr St Steph w St Mary *Lon* 36-40; India 41-45; Bahamas 47-51; India 51-71; Adn Poona 69-71; Warden Bede Ho Staplehurst 72-75; rtd 74; Chapl Shrine of St Julian 76-90. *80A King Street, Norwich NR1 1PQ* Tel (01603) 662600

LLEWELYN, Canon Robert John. b 32. Keble Coll Ox BA54 MA58. Cuddesdon Coll 65. **d** 66 **p** 67. C Bedford St Andr *St Alb* 66-69; C Cheltenham St Luke and St Jo *Glouc* 69-75; V S Cerney w Cerney Wick 75-80; V Glouc St Cath from 80; P-in-c Glouc St Mark 87-89; Hon Can Glouc Cathl from 94. *St Catharine's Vicarage, 29 Denmark Road, Gloucester GL1 3JQ* Tel (01452) 524497

LLOYD, Canon Bernard James. b 29. AKC56. **d** 57 **p** 58. C Laindon w Basildon *Chelmsf* 57-65; V E Ham St Geo 65-82; RD Newham 76-82; Hon Can Chelmsf Cathl 82-94; R Danbury 82-94; P-in-c Woodham Ferrers 87-90; rtd 94; Perm to Offic *Chelmsf* from 94. *Chanterelle, 47 Seaview Avenue, West Mersea, Colchester CO5 8HE* Tel (01206) 383892

LLOYD, Bertram John (Bert). b 26. DipTh83. St Mich Coll Llan. **d** 83 **p** 84. C Malpas *Mon* 83-85; V Blaenavon w Capel Newydd 85-93; rtd 93. *22 St Helen's Crescent, Llanellen, Abergavenny NP7 9HN* Tel (01873) 857003

LLOYD, The Ven Bertram Trevor. b 38. Hertf Coll Ox BA60 MA64. Clifton Th Coll 62. **d** 64 **p** 65. C S Mimms Ch Ch *Lon* 64-70; V Wealdstone H Trin 70-84; RD Harrow 77-82; P-in-c Harrow Weald St Mich 80-84; V Harrow Trin St Mich 84-89; Adn Barnstaple *Ex* from 89. *Stage Cross, Whitemoor Hill, Bishops Tawton, Barnstaple, Devon EX33 0BE* Tel (01271) 75475 Fax as telephone

LLOYD, Canon Charles Henry. b 13. TCD BA34. CITC 36. **d** 36 **p** 37. C Dublin St Geo *D & G* 36-39; C Dublin Rathfarnham 39-43; I Moynalty w Moybologue *M & K* 43-54; Gen Sec Hibernian CMS 54-70; I New Ross *C & O* 70-82; Dioc Sec (Ferns) 72-80; Preb Tassagard St Patr Cathl Dublin 73-82; rtd 82. *74 The Rise, Woodpark, Ballinteer, Dublin 16, Irish Republic* Tel Dublin (1) 295 1181

LLOYD, Crewdson Howard. b 31. Ex Coll Ox BA54 MA64. Wells Th Coll 64. **d** 66 **p** 67. C Ex St Dav *Ex* 66-69; C Cirencester *Glouc* 69-72; Perm to Offic *Ox* from 72; Summoner of Preachers Ox Univ 81-89; rtd 96. *36 Thackley End, 119 Banbury Road, Oxford OX2 6LB* Tel (01865) 511032

LLOYD, David John. b 52. Lon Univ BD82. St D Coll Lamp DipTh76. **d** 76 **p** 77. C Pembroke St Mary and St Mich *St D* 76-77; C Llanelli 77-80; V Cil-y-Cwm and Ystrad-ffin w Rhandir-mwyn etc 80-82; Oman 82-84; R Llanllwchaearn and Llanina *St D* 84-88; V Llangennech and Hendy 88-90; Perm to Offic *St Alb* 91-95; P-in-c Bampton w Clanfield *Ox* 96-97; V from 97. *5 Deanery Court, Broad Street, Bampton, Oxford OX18 2LY* Tel (01993) 851222

LLOYD, David John Silk. b 37. Univ of Wales (Lamp) BA62. St Steph Ho Ox 71. **d** 73 **p** 74. C Brentwood St Thos *Chelmsf* 73-77; C Hockley 77-80; C Wickford 80-81; C Wickford and Runwell 81-83; TV 83-88; Chapl Runwell Hosp Essex 81-88; S Africa from 88; Perm to Offic *Chelmsf* from 88; rtd 97. *D4 Argyll House, Seaforth Road, Westcliff-on-Sea, Essex SS0 7SJ*

LLOYD, David Peter. b 58. Kingston Poly BA81 DipArch84. Sarum & Wells Th Coll 88. **d** 90 **p** 91. C N Dulwich St Faith *S'wark* 90-94; TV Bedminster *Bris* from 94. *St Dunstan's Vicarage, 66 Bedminster Down Road, Bristol BS13 7AA* Tel 0117-963 5977

LLOYD, Dr Dennis John. b 46. BSc70 MSc74 PhD81. S Dios Minl Tr Scheme. **d** 90 **p** 91. C Hamworthy *Sarum* 90-92; Chapl UEA *Nor* 92-97; P-in-c Malvern St Andr *Worc* from 97. *St Andrew's Vicarage, 48 Longridge Road, Malvern, Worcs WR14 3JB* Tel (01684) 573912

LLOYD, Edward Gareth. b 60. K Coll Cam BA81 MA85. Ridley Hall Cam 85. **d** 88 **p** 89. C Jarrow *Dur* 88-91; C Monkwearmouth St Pet 91-92; P-in-c 92-96; TV Monkwearmouth from 97. *St Peter's Vicarage, St Peter's Way, Sunderland SR6 0DY* Tel 0191-567 3726

LLOYD, Miss Eileen. b 50. FIBMS74 Liv Poly HNC72. N Ord Course 88. **d** 91 **p** 94. C Heref St Martin w St Fran (S Wye TM) *Heref* 91-95; P-in-c Bucknell w Chapel Lawn, Llanfair Waterdine etc from 95. *The Vicarage, Bucknell, Shropshire SY7 0AD* Tel (01547) 4340

LLOYD, Mrs Elizabeth Jane. b 52. CChem GRIC74 MRIC77 HND73 Nottm Univ DipTh79. Linc Th Coll 77. **dss** 80 **d** 87 **p** 94. Linc St Nic w St Jo Newport *Linc* 80-81; Lic to Offic *Sarum* 81-87; Chapl Poole Gen Hosp 85-94; Chapl Poole Hosp NHS Trust from 94; Hon Par Dn Lytchett Matravers *Sarum* 87-92. *The Rectory, 19 Springfield Road, Poole, Dorset BH14 0LG* Tel (01202) 748860 or 442167

LLOYD, Graham. b 36. Brasted Th Coll 62 St Aid Birkenhead 64 Glouc Sch of Min 86. **d** 89 **p** 90. NSM Churchstoke w Hyssington and Sarn *Heref* from 89. *The Pullets Cottage, Church Stoke, Montgomery SY15 6TL* Tel (01588) 620285

LLOYD, Gwilym Wyn. b 50. Leic Univ BA72 Birm Univ MSc73 Lon Univ LLB78. Trin Coll Bris DipHE85. **d** 87 **p** 88. C Bexleyheath Ch Ch *Roch* 87-91; R Darlaston St Lawr *Lich* from 91. *The Rectory, Darlaston, Wednesbury, W Midlands WS10 8AA* Tel 0121-526 2240

LLOYD, Hamilton William John Marteine. b 19. Jes Coll Ox BA41 MA45. Ripon Hall Ox. **d** 43 **p** 44. C Falmouth K Chas *Truro* 43-47; R Gerrans w St Antony in Roseland 47-51; Min Bournemouth H Epiphany Conv Distr 51-53; V Bournemouth H Epiphany *Win* 53-60; V Whitchurch w Tufton 60-68; V Whitchurch w Tufton and Litchfield 68-71; V Lyndhurst 71-73; V Lyndhurst and Emery Down 73-84; rtd 84; Perm to Offic *Win* from 86. *Post Office House, North Litchfield, Whitchurch, Hants RG28 7PR* Tel (01256) 893507

LLOYD, Harry James. b 22. Univ of Wales (Lamp) BA50. **d** 51 **p** 52. C Hay *S & B* 51-55; C Llanigon 51-55; C Hillingdon St Jo *Lon* 55-56; C Marlborough *Sarum* 56-60; V Kingston 60-83; V Worth Matravers 60-83; C Milton Abbas, Hilton w Cheselbourne etc 83-87; rtd 87. *Linden, Streetway Lane, Cheselbourne, Dorchester, Dorset DT2 7NU* Tel (01258) 87331

LLOYD, The Very Revd Henry Morgan. b 11. DSO41 OBE59. Or Coll Ox BA33 MA37. Cuddesdon Coll 33. **d** 35 **p** 36. C Hendon St Mary *Lon* 35-40; Chapl RNVR 40-45; Prin Old Rectory Coll

Hawarden 46-48; Sec CACTM 48-50; Dean Gib *Eur* 50-60; Dean Truro 60-81; R Truro St Mary 60-81; rtd 81; Perm to Offic *Truro* from 81. *10 Waters Road, Kingston upon Thames, Surrey KT1 3LP*

LLOYD, Canon Herbert James. b 31. TD. St D Coll Lamp BA57. **d** 58 **p** 59. C Wrexham *St As* 58-65; TV 71-74; R Llanferres 65-67; R Llanferres, Nercwys and Eryrys 67-71; V Rhyl w St Ann 74-96; CF (TA) from 74; Can St As Cathl *St As* from 81; Prec St As Cathl from 89. *The Orchard, 8 Stoneby Drive, Prestatyn LL19 9PE*

LLOYD, John Everard. b 27. FCMA60 LSE BSc50. St Alb Minl Tr Scheme 84. **d** 87 **p** 88. NSM Harpenden St Nic *St Alb* 87-90; Hon C Addingham *Bradf* from 90. *2 High Springs, Owler Park Road, Ilkley, W Yorkshire LS29 0BG* Tel (01943) 609267

LLOYD, John James. b 14. St D Coll Lamp BA36. **d** 37 **p** 38. C Ferndale *Llan* 37-38; C Grangetown 38-41; C Aberavon 41-50; V Porth 50-63; V Cadoxton-juxta-Neath 63-79; rtd 79; Perm to Offic *Llan* from 79. *16 Spoonbill Close, Rest Bay, Porthcawl CF36 3UR* Tel (01656) 715470

LLOYD, John Philip. b 15. St Chad's Coll Dur BA37 DipTh38 MA40. **d** 38 **p** 39. C Anfield St Columba *Liv* 38-41; C Builth Wells w Alltmawr 41-46; C Llanafan Fawr w Llanfihangel-Bryn-Pabuan 41-46; V Bettws Disserth w Llansantffraed in Elwell *S & B* 46-51; V Eglwys Oen Duw and Llanfihangel Abergwessin etc 51-64; V Gatley *Ches* 64-69; V Bickerton 69-77; rtd 77; Perm to Offic *Ches* from 77. *17 Wesley Close, Bowling Green Court, Nantwich, Cheshire CW5 5SN* Tel (01270) 626771

LLOYD, Jonathan Wilford. b 56. Surrey Univ and City of Lon Poly BSc80 Golds Coll Lon CQSW82 DASS82 N Lon Poly MA86. S'wark Ord Course 87. **d** 90 **p** 91. Hon C Sydenham St Bart *S'wark* 90-94; Dir of Soc Resp 91-95; PV S'wark Cathl 91-97; Bp's Officer for Ch in Soc 95-97; Chapl Bath Univ *B & W* from 97. *Chaplain's House, The Avenue, Claverton Down, Bath BA2 7AX* Tel (01225) 466114 or 826458 Fax 462508 E-mail j.w.lloyd@bath.ac.uk

LLOYD, Michael Francis. b 57. Down Coll Cam BA79 MA82 St Jo Coll Dur BA83. Cranmer Hall Dur 81. **d** 84 **p** 85. C Locks Heath *Portsm* 84-87; Asst Chapl Worc Coll Ox 89-90; Chapl Ch Coll Cam 90-94. *Address temp unknown*

LLOYD, Nigel James Clifford. b 51. Nottm Univ BTh81 Lambeth STh90. Linc Th Coll 77. **d** 81 **p** 82. C Sherborne w Castleton and Lillington *Sarum* 81-84; R Lytchett Matravers 84-92; TR Parkstone St Pet w Branksea and St Osmund from 92; Ecum Officer (Sherborne Deanery) from 92. *The Rectory, 19 Springfield Road, Poole, Dorset BH14 0LG* Tel (01202) 748860

LLOYD, Oscar Wynn. b 17. St D Coll Lamp BA43. **d** 45 **p** 47. C Minera *St As* 45-48; C Cerrigydrudion and Llanfihangel Glyn Myfyr etc 48-50; C Witton *Ches* 50-52; V Pott Shrigley 52-60; V Birkenhead St Mark 60-66; V Helsby 66-74; V Ince 66-74; RD Frodsham 72-74; R Dodleston 74-82; rtd 82; Perm to Offic *Ches* from 82. *12 Hawarden Drive, Drury, Buckley CH7 3ED* Tel (01244) 549650

LLOYD, Mrs Pamela Valpy. b 25. Gilmore Ho 48 St Aug Coll Cant 76. **dss** 76 **d** 87 **p** 94. Chartham *Cant* 76-78; Cant All SS 78-85; rtd 85; Chapl Asst Kent and Cant Hosp 87; Chapl Chaucer Hosp Cant 87-90; NSM Elham w Denton and Wootton *Cant* 87-93; Sub-Chapl HM Pris Cant 88-96; Hon C Cant St Martin and St Paul *Cant* 93-95. *Cavendish House, 9 North Holmes Road, Canterbury, Kent CT1 1QJ* Tel (01227) 457782

LLOYD, Canon Peter John. b 32. TD78. Leic Univ DipSocSc53. Wells Th Coll 59. **d** 61 **p** 62. C Walmer *Cant* 61-63; CF (TA) 62-73 and 77-87; C Maidstone All SS w St Phil *Cant* 63-66; V Milton next Sittingbourne 66-69; R Brinkley, Burrough Green and Carlton *Ely* 69-73; CF 73-77; V Chessington *Guildf* 77-85; RD Epsom 82-87; V Epsom St Martin 85-92; rtd 92; Perm to Offic *B & W* from 92. *74 Southover, Wells, Somerset BA5 1UH* Tel (01749) 672213

LLOYD, Peter Vernon James. b 36. St Jo Coll Cam BA60 MA. Ridley Hall Cam 60. **d** 62 **p** 63. C Keynsham w Queen Charlton *B & W* 62-65; Perm to Offic *Sarum* from 65; NSM Bournemouth St Jo w St Mich *Win* 87-91; NSM Bournemouth St Pet w St Swithun, H Trin etc 90-91; Perm to Offic 91-95. *18 Cornelia Crescent, Branksome, Poole, Dorset BH12 1LU* Tel (01202) 741422

LLOYD, Raymond David (Brother Ramon). b 35. Univ of Wales (Cardiff) DipTh61 Edin Univ MPhil74. Zurich Th Sem BD69 Edin Th Coll 71. **d** 72 **p** 72. C Glas St Mary *Glas* 72-76; Chapl Glas Univ 74-76; SSF from 78. *St Mary at the Cross, Glasshampton, Shrawley, Worcester WR6 6TQ* Tel (01299) 896345

LLOYD, Richard Leslie Harris. b 09. Peterho Cam BA31 MA35 Mert Coll Ox BA32 MA36 BLitt36. St Steph Ho Ox 32. **d** 36 **p** 37. C Middlesbrough St Hilda w St Pet *York* 36-38; C Northallerton 38-41; V Dishforth 41-43; V York St Hilda 43-50; V Coxwold 50-56; V Bishopthorpe 56-63; V Acaster Malbis 56-63; RD Ainsty 59-63; Chapl St Bede Coll Dur 63-74; rtd 74. *Dulverton Hall, St Martin's Square, Scarborough, N Yorkshire YO11 2DB* Tel (01723) 371076

LLOYD, Robert Graham. b 42. St Jo Coll Nottm 82. **d** 84 **p** 85. C Tonyrefail *Llan* 84-87; V Martletwy w Lawrenny and Minwear and Yerbeston *St D* 87-91; V Monkton 91-96; V Cymmer and Porth *Llan* from 96. *The Vicarage, Maesgwyn, Cymmer, Porth CF39 9HW* Tel (01443) 682219

LLOYD, Robert James Clifford. b 18. Selw Coll Cam BA41 MA49. Linc Th Coll 46. **d** 47 **p** 48. C Clapham H Trin *S'wark* 47-50; C High Wycombe All SS *Ox* 50-53; CF (TA) 50-53; C Hampstead St Jo *Lon* 53-55; V Wellington w W Buckland *B & W* 55-66; P-in-c Nynehead 56-57; V 57-66; RD Wellington 59-66; R Chartham *Cant* 66-81; RD W Bridge 75-81; Hon C Elham w Denton and Wootton 81-92; rtd 92; Perm to Offic *Cant* from 83. *Cavendish House, 9 North Holmes Road, Canterbury, Kent CT1 1QJ* Tel (01227) 457782

LLOYD, Roger Bernard. b 58. K Coll Lon BA. Cranmer Hall Dur. **d** 84 **p** 85. C Hornchurch St Andr *Chelmsf* 84-87; C Gt Parndon 87-94; V Elm Park St Nic Hornchurch from 94. *The Vicarage, 17 St Nicholas Avenue, Elm Park, Hornchurch, Essex RM12 4PT* Tel (014024) 51451

LLOYD, Ronald. b 37. St Mich Coll Llan. **d** 83 **p** 84. C Penarth All SS *Llan* 83-85; V Cwmbach 85-91; Perm to Offic from 91. *23 Teilo Street, Cardiff CF1 9JN*

LLOYD, Ronald Henry. b 32. Univ of Wales (Lamp) BA52 LTh54. **d** 54 **p** 56. C Manselton *S & B* 54-56; C Sketty 56-59; C Swansea St Mary 59-63; CF (TA) 59-65; V Elmley Castle w Netherton and Bricklehampton *Worc* 63-69; Chapl Dragon Sch Ox 69-82; Chapl St Hugh's Coll Ox 75-80; P-in-c Ox St Marg *Ox* 75-76; Chapl Magd Coll Ox 75-82; Prec and Chapl Ch Ch *Ox* 82-87; R Alvescot w Black Bourton, Shilton, Holwell etc 87-95; P-in-c Broughton Poggs w Filkins, Broadwell etc 94-95; R Shill Valley and Broadshire from 95. *The Rectory, Shilton, Burford, Oxon OX18 4AE* Tel (01993) 845954

LLOYD, Mrs Sandra Edith. b 48. Sarum & Wells Th Coll 83. **dss** 86 **d** 87 **p** 94. Freshwater *Portsm* 86-87; C 87-89; C Whitwell 89-95; V from 95; C Niton 89-95; P-in-c from 95. *The Rectory, Pan Lane, Niton, Ventnor, Isle of Wight PO38 2BT* Tel (01983) 730595

LLOYD, Simon David. b 58. Portsm Poly BA. Wycliffe Hall Ox. **d** 83 **p** 84. C Cotmanhay *Derby* 83-85; Chapl Asst Nottm City Hosp 85-87; Chapl Basford Hosp Nottm 85-87; Perm to Offic *Birm* from 91. *2 Ash Mews, Acocks Green, Birmingham B27 6TB* Tel 0121-706 5784

LLOYD, Stephen Russell. b 47. Worc Coll Ox BA69 MA77 CertEd DipTh. Oak Hill Th Coll 76. **d** 77 **p** 78. C Canonbury St Steph *Lon* 77-80; C Braintree *Chelmsf* 80-92; V Braintree St Paul from 92. *St Paul's Parsonage, Hay Lane, Braintree, Essex CM7 6DY* Tel (01376) 325095

LLOYD, Canon Stuart George Errington. b 49. TCD BA72. **d** 75 **p** 76. C Cloughfern *Conn* 75-79; C Cregagh *D & D* 79-82; I Eglantine *Conn* 82-89; I Ballymena w Ballyclug from 89; Preb Conn Cathl from 97. *St Patrick's Rectory, 102 Galgorm Road, Ballymena, Co Antrim BT42 1AE* Tel (01266) 652253

LLOYD, Timothy David Lewis. *See* LEWIS LLOYD, Canon Timothy David

LLOYD, William Geoffrey. b 48. Man Univ BA70. Oak Hill Th Coll 92. **d** 95 **p** 96. C Plaistow St Mary *Roch* from 95. *31 Fairfield Road, Bromley BR1 3QN* Tel 0181-464 2181

LLOYD-DAVIES, Arthur (Lloyd). b 31. Univ of Wales BA55. Cuddesdon Coll 55. **d** 57 **p** 58. C Tonypandy w Clydach Vale *Llan* 57-59; C Merthyr Dyfan 59-62; C Amersham *Ox* 62-65; V Tilehurst St Geo 65-73; R Wokingham St Paul 73-84; R Nuthurst *Chich* 84-90; I Fiddown w Clonegam, Guilcagh and Kilmeaden *C & O* 90-96; rtd 96; Hon C Bratton, Edington and Imber, Erlestoke etc *Sarum* from 96. *The Vicarage, 1A The Weir, Edington, Westbury, Wilts BA13 4PX*

LLOYD-JAMES, Duncan Geraint. b 66. St Steph Ho Ox BTh94. **d** 94 **p** 96. C St Leonards Ch Ch and St Mary *Chich* 94-96; C Rottingdean from 96. *St Margaret's Cottage, The Green, Rottingdean, Brighton BN2 7HA*

LLOYD-JAMES, John Eifion. b 39. Clifton Th Coll 63. **d** 65 **p** 66. C Burgess Hill St Andr *Chich* 65-68; C-in-c Portslade Gd Shep CD 68-74; V Lancing St Mich 74-88; V Billingshurst 88-93; V Kemp Town St Mary from 93. *St Mary's Vicarage, 11 West Drive, Brighton BN2 2GD* Tel (01273) 698601

LLOYD JONES, Ieuan. b 31. FBIM St Cath Coll Cam BA51 MA54. Sarum & Wells Th Coll 80. **d** 83 **p** 84. Hon C Claygate *Guildf* 83-89; Perm to Offic *Ox* from 89. *11 Southcroft, Old Marston, Oxford OX3 0PF* Tel (01865) 793098

LLOYD-RICHARDS, David Robert. b 48. Open Univ BA84 Hull Univ MA87. St D Coll Lamp DipTh70. **d** 71 **p** 72. C Skewen *Llan* 71-73; C Neath w Llantwit 73-76; Miss to Seamen 76-77; V Pontlottyn w Fochriw *Llan* 77-84; R Merthyr Dyfan 84-90; Chapl Barry Neale-Kent Hosp 84-90; Tutor Open Univ from 85; Sen Chapl Univ Hosp of Wales Cardiff from 90; Chapl Cardiff Royal Infirmary from 95. *University Hospital of Wales, Heath Park, Cardiff CF4 4XW, or 77 Rhydhelig Avenue, Heath Park, Cardiff CF4 4DB* Tel (01222) 743230 or 747747

LLOYD WILLIAMS, Martin Clifford. b 65. Westmr Coll Lon BEd87. Trin Coll Bris BA93. **d** 93 **p** 94. C Bath Walcot *B & W* 93-97; R Bath St Mich w St Paul from 97. *71 Priory Close, Combe Down, Bath BA2 5AP* Tel (01225) 835490

lo POLITO, Nicola. b 59. Catholic Th Union Chicago MDiv85 MA(Theol)87. Comboni Miss. **d** 85 **p** 86. In RC Ch 85-94; Egypt 86-88; Sudan 88-91; Italy 91-94; Asst Chapl Malta and Gozo *Eur* from 94. *Il-Gardina/2, Constitution Street, Mosta MST 03, Malta* Tel Malta (356) 414474 Fax 225714

LOAT, Andrew Graham. b 61. Aber Univ BD83. St Jo Coll Nottm DPS87. **d** 87 **p** 88. C Llangynwyd w Maesteg *Llan* 87-90; C Llansamlet *S & B* 90-91; V Whitton and Pilleth and Cascob etc from 91; Dioc Officer for CME from 97. *The Rectory, Whitton, Knighton LD7 1NP* Tel (01547) 560231

LOBANOV-ROSTOVSKY, Andrew Russell. b 17. Qu Coll Ox BA38 MA55. Cuddesdon Coll 56. **d** 57 **p** 58. C Cheltenham All SS *Glouc* 57-60; P-in-c Milton *Portsm* 60-64; Chapl St Bede's Ch for the Deaf Clapham 64-75; Chapl to the Deaf *Guildf* 75-82; rtd 82; Perm to Offic *Chich* 82-89; Perm to Offic *Glas* 89-96. *10 Aikenhead House, Kings Park, Carmunnock Road, Glasgow G44 5HL* Tel 0141-633 0479

LOBB, Edward Eric. b 51. Magd Coll Ox BA74 MA76. Wycliffe Hall Ox 73. **d** 76 **p** 77. C Haughton St Mary *Man* 76-80; C Rusholme H Trin 80-84; P-in-c Whitfield *Derby* 84-90; V 90-92; V Stapenhill w Cauldwell from 92. *6 Clay Street, Stapenhill, Burton-on-Trent, Staffs DE15 9BB* Tel (01283) 561437

LOBB, Miss Josephine Mary (Josie). b 57. SRN83 Plymouth Univ DipNursing89. LNSM course 94. **d** 96 **p** 97. NSM St Germans *Truro* from 96. *19 Lowertown Close, Landrake, Saltash, Cornwall PL12 5DG* Tel (01752) 851488

LOCK, David Stephen. b 28. **d** 63 **p** 64. C Streatham Vale H Redeemer *S'wark* 63-66; C Hatcham St Jas 66-75; V Leyton All SS *Chelmsf* 75-95; rtd 95; Perm to Offic *Roch* from 95. *26 Eldred Drive, Orpington, Kent BR5 4PF* Tel (01689) 601726

LOCK, Graham Robert. b 39. Hertf Coll Ox BA63. Ridley Hall Cam 62. **d** 64 **p** 65. C Bexleyheath St Pet *Roch* 64-66; C Roch St Justus 66-71; C St Mary Cray and St Paul's Cray 71-75; V Chatham St Paul w All SS 75-83; R Lambourne w Abridge and Stapleford Abbotts *Chelmsf* 83-92; V Barkingside St Laur from 92. *St Laurence's Vicarage, Donington Avenue, Ilford, Essex IG6 1AJ* Tel 0181-554 2003

LOCK, Paul Alan. b 65. St Chad's Coll Dur BA86. Coll of Resurr Mirfield 87. **d** 89 **p** 90. C Upholland *Liv* 89-92; C Teddington SS Pet and Paul and Fulwell *Lon* 92-95; V from 95. *The Vicarage, 1 Bychurch Road, Teddington, Middx TW11 8PS* Tel 0181-977 3330

LOCK, Canon Peter Harcourt D'Arcy. b 44. AKC67. **d** 68 **p** 69. C Meopham *Roch* 68-72; C Wigmore w Hempstead 72; C S Gillingham 72-77; R Hartley 77-83; R Fawkham and Hartley 83-84; V Dartford H Trin 84-93; Hon Can Roch Cathl from 90; V Bromley SS Pet and Paul from 93; RD Bromley from 96. *The Vicarage, 9 St Paul's Square, Bromley BR2 0XH* Tel 0181-460 6275

LOCKE, Brian Henry. b 38. AKC61. **d** 62 **p** 63. C Westleigh St Pet *Man* 62-65; C Marske in Cleveland *York* 65-68; V Boosbeck w Moorsholm 68-72; Perm to Offic *Man* 78-82; P-in-c Kirkholt 82-86; V 86-97; Chapl HM Young Offender Inst Buckley Hall 85-89; AD Rochdale *Man* 92-97; P-in-c Hey from 97. *Abinger Place, 1 Den Lane, Lees, Oldham* Tel 0161-626 3630

LOCKE, Richard Nigel. b 61. Coll of Resurr Mirfield 92. **d** 94 **p** 95. C Middlesbrough Ascension *York* 94-97; C Paignton St Jo *Ex* from 97. *6 Tower Road, Paignton, Devon TQ3 3EP* Tel (01803) 521859

LOCKE, Robert Andrew. b 62. St Steph Ho Ox 89. **d** 92 **p** 93. C Colchester St Jas, All SS, St Nic and St Runwald *Chelmsf* 92-95; CF from 95. *MOD Chaplains (Army), Trenchard Lines, Upavon, Pewsey, Wilts SN9 6BE* Tel (01980) 615804 Fax 615800

LOCKE, Stephen John. b 60. St Chad's Coll Dur BA82. Sarum & Wells Th Coll 84. **d** 86 **p** 87. C Blackb St Mich w St Jo and H Trin *Blackb* 86-89; C Oswaldtwistle Immanuel and All SS 89-92; V Blackb St Mich w St Jo and H Trin from 92. *St Michael's Vicarage, Whalley New Road, Blackburn BB1 6LB* Tel (01254) 257121

LOCKER, Dorothea Isobel Leslie. b 19. MRPharmS41 Heriot-Watt Coll PhC41. LNSM course 79. **dss** 85 **d** 87. NSM Edin St Pet *Edin* 85-91; rtd 91. *27/220 West Saville Terrace, Edinburgh EH9 3DR* Tel 0131-667 3509

LOCKETT, Paul. b 48. Sarum & Wells Th Coll 73. **d** 76 **p** 77. C Horninglow *Lich* 76-78; C Tewkesbury w Walton Cardiff *Glouc* 78-81; P-in-c W Bromwich St Pet *Lich* 81-90; R Norton Canes 90-95; Dean's V Lich Cathl from 91; V Longton St Mary and St Chad from 95. *St Mary and St Chad's Presbytery, 269 Anchor Road, Stoke-on-Trent ST3 5DH* Tel (01782) 313142

LOCKETT, Canon William Ernest Alfred. b 16. ARCA39 ATD51 FRSA70 FIBD NRD Florence Academy. Linc Th Coll 44. **d** 45 **p** 46. C Beddington *S'wark* 45-47; Lect Bath Tr Coll 48-50; Chapl and Lect St Kath Coll Liv 50-56; Sen Lect Liv Univ 56-82; Can Th Liv Cathl *Liv* 72-82; rtd 82; Perm to Offic *Liv* 82-96. *The Croft, Ruff Lane, Ormskirk, Lancs L39 4QZ* Tel (01695) 572119

LOCKEY, Malcolm. b 45. FRSA75 Sunderland Poly BA67 Newc Univ DipEd68. NE Ord Course 87. **d** 90 **p** 91. NSM Yarm *York* from 90. *26 Blackfriars, Yarm, Cleveland TS15 9HG* Tel (01642) 782696

LOCKHART, Antony William Castleton. b 25. GIMechE. Wells Th Coll 63. **d** 65 **p** 66. C Hale *Guildf* 65-69; C Worplesdon 69-73; V Weston 73-79; TV Westborough 79-84; V Shamley Green 84-87; RD Cranleigh 85-87; Dioc Widows Officer *Cant* 89-90; Perm to Offic from 88; rtd 90. *10 Beverley Road, Canterbury, Kent CT2 7EN* Tel (01227) 760980

LOCKHART, Clare Patricia Anne (Sister Clare). b 44. Bris Univ BA74. St Jo Coll Dur 84. **d** 87 **p** 94. Sisters of Charity from 63; Chapl Asst Sunderland Distr Gen Hosp 84-89; Chapl 89-95; NSM N Hylton St Marg Castletown *Dur* 87-95; P-in-c from 95. *St Margaret's Presbytery, Hylton Castle Road, Sunderland SR5 3ED* Tel 0191-516 0191

LOCKHART, David. b 68. QUB BSc90 TCD BTh93. CITC 90. **d** 93 **p** 94. C Belfast St Mary w H Redeemer *Conn* 93-96; I Belfast St Steph w St Luke from 96. *92 Lansdowne Road, Belfast BT15 4AB* Tel (01232) 774119

LOCKHART, Ms Michelle. b 68. Man Univ BA89. Ripon Coll Cuddesdon 90. **d** 92 **p** 94. Par Dn Leigh St Mary *Man* 92-94; Asst Chapl HM Pris Full Sutton 95-97; V York St Hilda *York* from 97. *St Hilda's Vicarage, 155 Tang Hall Road, York YO1 3SD* Tel (01904) 413150

LOCKHART, Raymond William. b 37. Qu Coll Cam BA58 LLB60 MA61. St Jo Coll Nottm 72. **d** 74 **p** 75. C Aspley *S'well* 74-76; V 81-88; R Knebworth *St Alb* 76-81; Dir CMJ Stella Carmel from 88; Jerusalem from 88. *c/o CMJ, 30C Clarence Road, St Albans, Herts AL1 4JJ* Tel (01727) 833114

LOCKHART, The Very Revd Robert Joseph Norman. b 24. TCD BA46 MA53. **d** 46 **p** 48. C Belfast St Mary Magd *Conn* 46-49; C Knockbreda *D & D* 49-54; P-in-c Killaney w Carryduff 54-60; I Comber 60-62; I Belfast St Donard 62-70; I Lurgan Ch the Redeemer 70-89; Prec Dromore Cathl 71-75; Dean Dromore 75-89; rtd 89; Lic to Offic *D & D* from 90. *30 Church Road, Belfast BT8 4AQ* Tel (01232) 491588

LOCKLEY, The Ven Harold. b 16. Lon Univ BA37 BD43 MTh49 Nottm Univ PhD55 Em Coll Cam MLitt91. Westcott Ho Cam 46. **d** 46 **p** 47. Chapl Loughb Coll 46-51; C Loughborough All SS *Leic* 46-48; V Glen Parva and S Wigston 51-58; Dir of Ords 51-79; Can Res and Chan Leic Cathl 58-63; V Leic All SS 63-78; Adn Loughborough 63-86; rtd 86; Perm to Offic *Leic* from 86. *21 Saxon Close, Market Harborough, Leics LE16 7PR* Tel (01858) 465605

LOCKWOOD, David Nicholas. b 23. Birm Univ MA81. St D Coll Lamp BA51 Qu Coll Birm 51. **d** 53 **p** 54. C Halesowen *Worc* 53-57; C Ribbesford w Bewdley and Dowles 57-60; R Gt w Lt Witley 60-64; V Hanley Castle w Hanley Swan 64-79; V Hanley Castle, Hanley Swan and Welland 79-81; Perm to Offic *S & B* from 81; rtd 88. *Church Row, Llowes, Hereford HR3 5JB* Tel (01497) 847664

LOCKWOOD, Wilfred Eric. b 18. Leeds Univ BA49. Coll of Resurr Mirfield 49. **d** 51 **p** 52. C Tettenhall Regis *Lich* 51-53; C Bournemouth St Fran *Win* 53-57; V Wardleworth St Mary *Man* 57-62; V Leeds Ch Ch and St Jo and St Barn Holbeck *Ripon* 62-71; R Ducklington *Ox* 71-83; CF (ACF) 62-83; rtd 83; Perm to Offic *Nor* from 83. *15A Wells Road, Walsingham, Norfolk NR22 6DL* Tel (01328) 820723

LOCKYER, David Ralph George. b 41. Wells Th Coll 65. **d** 67 **p** 68. C Bottesford *Linc* 67-69; C Eling *Win* 69-73; TV Eling, Testwood and Marchwood 73-77; TR Speke St Aid *Liv* 77-84; V Halifax St Jude *Wakef* 84-96; Chapl Halifax R Infirmary 84-96; V Banwell *B & W* from 96. *The Vicarage, 3 East Street, Banwell, Weston-super-Mare, Avon BS24 6BN* Tel (01934) 822320

LOCKYER, Desmond Edward Weston. b 18. AKC49. **d** 50 **p** 51. C Norwood St Luke *S'wark* 50-52; C Surbiton St Matt 52-54; Chapl Asst United Sheff Hosps 54-56; C Sheff St Anne and St Phil *Sheff* 54-56; C Eastbourne St Mary *Chich* 56-59; V Hellingly 59-68; V Upper Dicker 62-68; V Eastbourne St Mich 68-75; V Preston 75-87; rtd 87; Perm to Offic *Chich* from 87. *Pilgrims, Nep Town Road, Henfield, W Sussex BN5 9DY* Tel (01273) 493681

LOCKYER, Maurice David. b 19. AKC43. **d** 43 **p** 44. C Talbot Village *Sarum* 43-46; C Laindon w Basildon *Chelmsf* 46-50; C Horfield H Trin *Bris* 50-64; V Huncote *Leic* 64-77; rtd 77. *21 Smith Close, London SE16 1PB*

LOCKYER, Peter Weston. b 60. Linc Coll Ox BA80 MA87. St Jo Coll Nottm 84. **d** 87 **p** 88. C Rowner *Portsm* 87-90; C Beaconsfield *Ox* 90-91; TV 91-95; Dep Chapl HM Young Offender Inst Glen Parva 95; Chapl Wellingborough Sch from 96. *Wellingborough School, Wellingborough, Northants NN8 2BX* Tel (01933) 222427

LOCOCK, Jillian Maud (Jill). b 33. Lon Univ BSc55. N Ord Course 81. **dss** 84 **d** 87 **p** 95. Didsbury Ch Ch *Man* 84-86; Chapl Asst Man R Infirmary 85-87; Chapl Asst Withington Hosp 86-88; Chapl Asst RN 88-93; NSM Dumbarton *Glas* from 93. *20C Queen Street, Helensburgh, Dunbartonshire G84 9LG* Tel (01436) 671252

LODER, Sister Helen. b 43. Golds Coll Lon 65. S'wark Ord Course 91. **d** 94 **p** 95. SSM from 70; NSM S Hackney St Mich w Haggerston St Paul *Lon* from 94. *St Saviour's Priory, 18 Queensbridge Road, London E2 8NS* Tel 0171-739 9976

LODGE, Anthony William Rayner. b 26. Wadh Coll Ox BA51 MA55. Cuddesdon Coll 65. **d** 66 **p** 67. Asst Chapl Forest Sch Snaresbrook 66-68; C Walthamstow St Pet *Chelmsf* 66-68; Chapl Ripon Gr Sch 68-91; rtd 91; Perm to Offic *Heref* from 92. *Church Cottage, Diddlebury, Craven Arms, Shropshire SY7 9DH* Tel (01584) 841340

LODGE, Canon John Alfred Ainley. b 29. Wells Th Coll 54. **d** 57 **p** 58. C Huddersfield St Jo *Wakef* 57-60; V Shepley 60-64; V Salterhebble St Jude 64-69; C-in-c Mixenden CD 69-75; V Mixenden 75-76; V Almondbury 76-79; RD Almondbury 76-79; V Warmfield 79-88; Bp's Dom Chapl 79-87; Hon Can Wakef Cathl 85-92; RD Kirkburton 88-92; P-in-c Emley 88-92; R 92; rtd 92; Perm to Offic *Ripon* from 92; Perm to Offic *Wakef* from 92. *Bygate, 2 Station Court, Morton on Swale, Northallerton, N Yorkshire DL7 9TQ* Tel (01609) 778551

LODGE, Michael John. b 53. Wycliffe Hall Ox 87. **d** 89 **p** 90. C Highworth w Sevenhampton and Inglesham etc *Bris* 89-93; P-in-c Cheltenham St Luke and St Jo *Glouc* from 93. *St Luke's Vicarage, 38 College Road, Cheltenham, Glos GL53 7HX* Tel (01242) 513940

LODGE, Robin Paul. b 60. Bris Univ BA82 Ch Ch Coll Cant PGCE83. Chich Th Coll 88. **d** 90 **p** 91. C Calne and Blackland *Sarum* 90-94; Asst Chapl St Mary's Sch Calne 90-94; TV Wellington and Distr *B & W* from 94. *All Saints Vicarage, 8 Exeter Road, Wellington, Somerset TA21 9DH* Tel (01823) 472742

LODGE, Roy Frederick. b 38. MBE97. BTh Birm Univ DipSoc62 DPhil92. Tyndale Hall Bris 63. **d** 66 **p** 67. C Tardebigge *Worc* 66-67; Chapl and Warden Probation Hostel Redditch 67-69; Chapl RAF 69-75; C Kinson *Sarum* 76; Lic to Offic *Pet* 76-77; Asst Chapl HM Pris Stafford 77-78; Chapl HM Pris Ranby 78-84; Chapl HM Pris Long Lartin 84-93; Chapl HM Pris Service Coll 87-93; Chapl HM Pris Hewell Grange from 93; Chapl HM Pris Brockhill from 93. *HM Prison, Brockhill, Redditch, Worcs B97 6RD* Tel (01527) 550314 Fax 550169

LODWICK, Canon Brian Martin. b 40. Leeds Univ BA61 MPhil76 Linacre Coll Ox BA63 MA67 Univ of Wales PhD87. St Steph Ho Ox 61. **d** 64 **p** 65. C Aberaman *Llan* 64-66; C Newton Nottage 66-73; R Llansannor and Llanfrynach w Penllyn etc 73-94; RD Llantwit Major and Cowbridge 83-94; Chan Llan Cathl from 92; R Llandough w Leckwith from 94. *The Rectory, Llandough Hill, Llandough, Penarth CF64 2NA* Tel (01222) 703349

LODWICK, Stephen Huw. b 64. Plymouth Univ BSc85. St Mich Coll Llan DipTh94. **d** 94 **p** 95. C Clydach *S & B* 94-95; Chapl St Woolos Cathl *Mon* from 95. *10 Clifton Road, Newport NP9 4EW*

LOEWENDAHL, David Jacob (Jake). b 50. SS Coll Cam BA74 MA77. Ripon Coll Cuddesdon 75. **d** 77 **p** 78. C Walworth *S'wark* 77-80; Chapl St Alb Abbey *St Alb* 80-83; Chapl St Alb Sch 80-83; Team Ldr Community Service Volunteers 84-90; Perm to Offic *Lon* 83-90; R E and W Tilbury and Linford *Chelmsf* 90-95; V Menheniot *Truro* from 95; RD W Wivelshire from 97. *The Vicarage, Menheniot, Liskeard, Cornwall PL14 3SU* Tel (01579) 342195

LOFT, Edmund Martin Boswell. b 25. St Jo Coll Cam BA49 MA55. Ely Th Coll 49. **d** 51 **p** 52. C Carl H Trin *Carl* 51-54; C Barrow St Geo 54-56; V Allonby w W Newton 56-62; V Fillongley *Cov* 62-77; V Earlsdon 77-90; rtd 90; Perm to Offic *Sheff* from 90. *10 Quarry Road, Sheffield S17 4DA* Tel 0114-236 0759

LOFTHOUSE, Canon Alexander Francis Joseph. b 30. Keble Coll Ox BA54 MA58. St Steph Ho Ox 54. **d** 56 **p** 57. C Barrow St Jas *Carl* 56-59; C Castleford All SS *Wakef* 59-60; V Airedale w Fryston 60-70; V Maryport *Carl* 70-78; P-in-c Helsington 78; V 78-95; P-in-c Underbarrow 78; V 78-95; P-in-c Levens 78; V 78-95; Hon Can Carl Cathl 85-95; rtd 95; Perm to Offic *Blackb* from 95; Perm to Offic *Carl* from 95. *Hazel Grove House, Yealand Redmayne, Carnforth, Lancs LA5 9RW*

LOFTHOUSE, Miss Brenda. b 33. RGN60 RM62 RNT69. N Ord Course 84. **d** 87 **p** 94. Hon Par Dn Greengates *Bradf* 87-89; Par Dn Farsley 89-94; V Bolton St Jas w St Chrys from 94. *St James's Vicarage, 1056 Bolton Road, Bradford, W Yorkshire BD2 4LH* Tel (01274) 637193

LOFTUS, Francis. b 52. Newc Univ BA73 St Andr Univ BPhil76 Coll of Ripon & York St Jo PGCE76 FRSA94. NE Ord Course 93. **d** 96 **p** 97. Hd Master Barlby High Sch from 90; NSM Barlby w Riccall *York* from 96. *19 Green Lane, North Duffield, Selby, N Yorkshire YO8 7RR* Tel (01757) 288030 Fax 213699

LOGAN, Kevin. b 43. Oak Hill Th Coll 73. **d** 75 **p** 76. C Blackb Sav *Blackb* 75-78; C Leyland St Andr 78-82; V Gt Harwood St Jo 82-91; V Accrington Ch Ch from 91. *Christ Church Vicarage, 3 Bentcliff Gardens, Accrington, Lancs BB5 2NX* Tel (01254) 235089

LOGAN, Samuel Desmond. b 39. TEng. CITC. **d** 78 **p** 79. NSM Belvoir *D & D* 78-85; NSM Knock 85-87; NSM Belfast St Brendan 87-91; Lic to Offic 91-95; C Bangor Abbey from 95. *8 Casaeldona Crescent, Belfast BT6 9RE* Tel (01232) 795473

LOGUE, Mrs Rosemary Christine. TCD BTh93. CITC 90. **d** 93 **p** 94. C Clooney w Strathfoyle *D & R* 93-96; I Londonderry St Aug from 96. *St Augustine's Rectory, 4 Bridgwater, Caw, Londonderry BT4 7YA* Tel (01504) 47532

LOMAS, David Xavier. b 39. St Jo Coll Dur BA78. Cranmer Hall Dur 75. **d** 78 **p** 79. C Chester le Street *Dur* 78-81; C-in-c Newton Hall LEP 81-85; Gen Preacher *Linc* from 85; Chapl Scunthorpe Distr HA 85-93; Chapl Linc Distr Health Services & Hosps NHS Trust from 93. *The County Hospital, Greetwell Road, Lincoln LN2 5QY* Tel (01522) 573402 or 512512

LOMAS, John Derrick. b 58. St Mich Coll Llan DPT94. **d** 94 **p** 95. C Rhyl w St Ann *St As* from 94. *8 Grange Court, Larkmount Road, Rhyl LL18 4DF* Tel (01745) 337130

LOMAS, Paul Roy. b 54. Man Univ TCert75. N Ord Course 86. **d** 89 **p** 90. C Hollinwood *Man* 89-92; R Failsworth H Family from 92. *The Rectory, 190 Lord Lane, Failsworth, Manchester M35 0PG* Tel 0161-681 3644 Mobile 0973-239942

LOMAX, Canon Barry Walter John. b 39. Lambeth STh Lon Coll of Div 63. **d** 66 **p** 67. C Sevenoaks St Nic *Roch* 66-71; C Southport Ch Ch *Liv* 71-73; V Bootle St Matt 73-78; P-in-c Litherland St Andr 76-78; V New Borough and Leigh *Sarum* 78-94; Can and Preb Sarum Cathl from 91; R Blandford Forum and Langton Long from 94. *The Rectory, 2 Portman Place, Deer Park, Blandford Forum, Dorset DT11 7DG* Tel (01258) 480092

LOMAX, Eric John. b 64. Cranmer Hall Dur BA93 Wilson Carlile Coll DipEvang88. **d** 96 **p** 97. C Goodshaw and Crawshawbooth *Man* from 96. *St John's Vicarage, 508 Burnley Road, Rossendale, Lancs BB4 8LZ* Tel (01706) 212340

LOMAX, Canon Frank. b 20. Leeds Univ BA42. Coll of Resurr Mirfield 42. **d** 44 **p** 45. V Prudhoe *Newc* 64-74; Singapore from 75; Hon Can Singapore from 75; rtd 87. *142 Killiney Road, 04-146 Devonshire Court, Singapore 0923* Tel Singapore (65) 737-8329

LONDON (St Paul's), Dean of. *See* MOSES, The Very Revd Dr John Henry

LONDON, Archdeacon of. *See* CASSIDY, The Ven George Henry

LONDON, Bishop of. *See* CHARTRES, The Rt Revd and Rt Hon Richard John Carew

LONG, Canon Anne Christine. b 33. Leic Univ BA56 Ox Univ DipEd57 Lon Univ BD65. **dss** 80 **d** 87 **p** 94. Lect St Jo Coll Nottm 73-84; Acorn Chr Healing Trust from 85; Stanstead Abbots *St Alb* 85-92; Hon Par Dn 87-92; Hon Par Dn Camberley St Paul *Guildf* 92-94; Hon C from 94; Hon Can Guildf Cathl from 96. *8 Loweswater Walk, Camberley, Surrey GU15 1BH* Tel (01276) 677591 Fax (01420) 478122

LONG, Anthony Auguste (Tony). b 45. Linc Th Coll 79. **d** 81 **p** 82. C Kingswinford St Mary *Lich* 81-84; TV Ellesmere Port *Ches* 84-87; V Witton from 87. *The Vicarage, 61 Church Road, Northwich, Cheshire CW9 5PB* Tel (01606) 42943

LONG, Anthony Robert. b 48. SS Mark & Jo Coll Chelsea CertEd70 Southn Univ BTh93 UEA MA96. Chich Th Coll 74. **d** 77 **p** 78. C Chiswick St Nic w St Mary *Lon* 77-80; C Earley St Pet *Ox* 80-85; P-in-c Worstead w Westwick and Sloley *Nor* 85-92; P-in-c Tunstead w Sco' Ruston from 85; R Worstead, Westwick, Sloley, Swanton Abbot etc from 92; Chapl Nor Cathl from 85. *The Vicarage, Worstead, North Walsham, Norfolk NR28 9SE* Tel (01692) 536800

LONG, Christopher William. b 47. OBE94. Nottm Univ BTh78 Open Univ BA80. Linc Th Coll 75. **d** 78 **p** 79. C Shiregreen St Jas and St Chris *Sheff* 78-81; V 81-82; Chapl RAF from 82; Perm to Offic *St E* from 91. *Chaplaincy Services (RAF), HQ, Personnel and Training Command, RAF Innsworth, Gloucester GL3 1EZ* Tel (01452) 712612 ext 5164 Fax 510828

LONG, Canon Colin Angus. b 17. St D Coll Lamp BA38 St Mich Coll Llan 39. **d** 40 **p** 43. C Beaufort *Mon* 40; C Panteg 42-47; C Newport St Paul 47-51; V Ynysddu 51-56; V Pontypool 52-62; V Maindee 62-83; Can St Woolos Cathl 77-83; rtd 83. *18 Newport Road, New Inn, Pontypool NP4 0NT* Tel (01495) 753624

LONG, David William. b 47. K Coll Lon 67. St Aug Coll Cant 70. **d** 72 **p** 73. C Stanley *Liv* 72-73; C W Derby St Luke 73-76; C Cantril Farm 76-79; V Warrington St Barn 79-81; V Westbrook St Jas 82-96; V Ince St Mary from 96. *St Mary's Vicarage, Warrington Road, Wigan, Lancs WN3 4NH* Tel (01942) 864383

LONG, Edward Percy Eades (Bill). b 14. Liv Univ BA36 MA38. Linc Th Coll 73. **d** 73 **p** 74. C Sedbergh, Cautley and Garsdale *Bradf* 73-84; rtd 85; Perm to Offic *Bradf* from 85. *4 Derry Cottages, Sedbergh, Cumbria LA10 5SN* Tel (015396) 20577

LONG, Frederick Hugh. b 43. EMMTC 90. **d** 90 **p** 91. NSM Grantham *Linc* from 90. *65 Barrowby Road, Grantham, Lincs NG31 8AB* Tel (01476) 67278

LONG, Geoffrey Lawrence. Portsm Dioc Tr Course 88. **d** 89. NSM Whippingham w E Cowes *Portsm* from 89. *10 Minerva Road, East Cowes, Isle of Wight PO32 6DH* Tel (01983) 295917

LONG, Harry. b 27. BEM. QUB DBS. **d** 79 **p** 80. NSM Carryduff *D & D* 79-86; NSM Newtownards 86; NSM Belvoir 87-91; Lic to Offic from 91. *28 Cadger Road, Carryduff, Belfast BT8 8AU* Tel (01232) 812348

LONG, The Ven John Sanderson. b 13. Qu Coll Cam BA35 MA39. Cuddesdon Coll 35. **d** 36 **p** 37. C Folkestone St Mary and St Eanswythe *Cant* 36-41; Chapl RNVR 41-46; C St Peter-in-Thanet *Cant* 46; Abp's Dom Chapl 46-53; V Bearsted 53-59; V Petersfield w Sheet *Portsm* 59-70; RD Petersfield 62-70; Hon Can Portsm Cathl 67-70; Adn Ely 70-81; R Cambridge St Botolph 70-81; Hon Can Ely Cathl 70-81; rtd 81; Perm to Offic *Ely* from 81. *23 Thornton Road, Girton, Cambridge CB3 0NP* Tel (01223) 276421

LONG, Canon John Sydney. b 25. Lon Univ BSc49. Wycliffe Hall Ox 50. **d** 51 **p** 52. C Plaistow St Andr *Chelmsf* 51-54; C Keighley *Bradf* 54-57; C-in-c Horton Bank Top CD 57-59; V Buttershaw St Aid 59-64; V Barnoldswick w Bracewell 64-85; Hon Can Bradf Cathl 77-91; RD Skipton 83-90; R Broughton, Marton and Thornton 85-91; rtd 91; Perm to Offic *Bradf* from 91. *1 Church*

Villa, Carleton, Skipton, N Yorkshire BD23 3DQ Tel (01756) 799095

LONG, Kingsley Edward. b 41. CITC 90. **d** 93 **p** 94. NSM Howth *D & G* 93-96; NSM Swords w Donabate and Killsallaghan from 96. *Crimond, 125 Seapark, Malahide, Co Dublin, Irish Republic* Tel Dublin (1) 845 3179

LONG, Canon Michael David Barnby. b 32. AKC55. **d** 56 **p** 57. C Whitby *York* 56-59; C Cottingham 59-61; V Elloughton 61-66; P-in-c Brantingham 61-66; V Sheff Parson Cross St Cecilia *Sheff* 66-68; V Flamborough *York* 68-73; R Litcham w Kempston w E and W Lexham *Nor* 73-75; P-in-c York St Luke *York* 75-77; V 77-80; V Hatton w Haseley and Rowington w Lowsonford *Cov* 80-82; V Derringham Bank *York* 82-85; V Castle Acre w Newton *Nor* 85; R Southacre 85; R Castle Acre w Newton, Rougham and Southacre 85-86; TV Grantham *Linc* 86-89; V Cayton w Eastfield *York* from 89; RD Scarborough from 94; Can and Preb York Minster from 97. *The Vicarage, Eastfield, Scarborough, N Yorkshire YO11 3EE* Tel (01723) 582428

LONG, Peter Ronald. b 48. Nottm Univ BA69 Man Univ CertEd70 DPT71. Cuddesdon Coll 71. **d** 73 **p** 74. Chapl RAFVR from 74; C Bodmin *Truro* 73-75; C Newquay 75-76; Asst Youth Chapl 75-76; Dioc Youth Chapl 76-79; Perm to Offic *Eur* 76 and 78-85 and from 87; P-in-c Mawgan w St Martin-in-Meneage *Truro* 76 and 79-82; Chapl Helston-Meneage Community and Geriatric Hosp 80-95; Miss to Seamen from 80; P-in-c Cury w Gunwalloe *Truro* 80-82; R Cury and Gunwalloe w Mawgan from 83; Perm to Offic *Ex* 82-93. *The Rectory, Mawgan, Helston, Cornwall TR12 6AD* Tel (01326) 221293 Telex 45622 HYDCOR G Fax 240478

LONG, Dr Roger Eric. b 36. Univ Coll Dur BSc59 PhD62. NE Ord Course 90. **d** 93 **p** 94. C Street TM *York* from 93. *The Vicarage, Church Lane, Amotherby, Malton, N Yorkshire YO17 0NT* Tel (01653) 693503

LONG, Canon Samuel Ernest. b 18. JP68. ALCD50. **d** 49 **p** 50. C Belfast St Clem *D & D* 49-52; C Willowfield 52-56; I Dromara w Garvaghy 56-85; Can Dromore Cathl 81-85; Treas 82-85; rtd 85. *9 Cairnshill Court, Saintfield Road, Belfast BT8 4TX* Tel (01232) 793401

LONG, Simon Richard. b 40. Birm Univ DPS69. Bernard Gilpin Soc Dur 61 Ely Th Coll 62 Coll of Resurr Mirfield 64. **d** 65 **p** 66. C Bournemouth St Fran *Win* 65-68; Belgium 68; USA 69-88; P-in-c Medbourne cum Holt w Stockerston and Blaston *Leic* 88-89; P-in-c Bringhurst w Gt Easton 88-89; R Six Saints circa Holt from 90; RD Gartree I from 93. *The Rectory, Rectory Lane, Medbourne, Market Harborough, Leics LE16 8DZ* Tel (01858) 83419

LONG, William Thomas. b 53. TCD DipTh81 Dur Univ MA88. **d** 81 **p** 82. C Orangefield *D & D* 81-84; C Portadown St Mark *Arm* 84-86; I Dromara w Garvaghy *D & D* 86-91; I Aghalurcher w Tattykeeran, Cooneen etc *Clogh* 91-96; I Annalong *D & D* from 96. *173 Kilkeel Road, Annalong, Newry, Co Down BT34 4TN* Tel (01396) 768246

LONGBOTHAM, Richard Ashley. b 14. AKC36. Sarum Th Coll 37. **d** 37 **p** 38. C Eastbourne Ch Ch *Chich* 37-40; S Africa 41-46 and from 62; S Rhodesia 46-54 and 59-60; C Durban St Paul 41-44; C Pietermaritzburg St Pet 44-46; R Gatooma 47-52; R Salisbury S 53-54; CF 54-57; V Aldingbourne *Chich* 57-59; R Gwanda 59-60; V Aston w Benington *St Alb* 60-62; R Irene 62-72; R Richmond 72-74; R Eersterust Gd Shep w Silverton All SS 75-80; rtd 80. *Braehead House, Auburn Road, Kenilworth, Cape Town, 7700 South Africa*

LONGBOTTOM, Canon Frank. b 41. Lon Univ DipTh68 Birm Univ DPS74. Ripon Hall Ox 65. **d** 68 **p** 69. C Epsom St Martin *Guildf* 68-72; Asst Chapl St Ebbas Hosp Epsom 68-72; Asst Chapl Qu Mary's Hosp Carshalton 68-72; Asst Chapl Henderson Hosp Sutton 68-72; Chapl Highcroft Hosp Birm 72-94; Chapl Northcroft Hosp Birm 74-94; Dioc Adv for Past Care of Clergy & Families from 89; Bp's Adv from 94; Hon Can Birm Cathl *Birm* from 91. *46 Sunnybank Road, Sutton Coldfield, W Midlands B73 5RE* Tel 0121-350 5823 or 378 2211

LONGBOTTOM, Canon Paul Edward. b 44. AKC67. **d** 68 **p** 69. C Rainham *Roch* 68-71; C Riverhead 71-75; C Dunton Green 71-75; V Penge Lane H Trin 75-84; V Chatham St Wm 84-94; V Shorne from 94; Dioc Dir of Ords from 94; Hon Can Roch Cathl from 96. *The Vicarage, Butchers Hill, Shorne, Gravesend, Kent DA12 3EB* Tel (01474) 822239

LONGFOOT, Richard. b 46. Oak Hill Th Coll 76. **d** 78 **p** 79. C Chaddesden St Mary *Derby* 78-81; C Cambridge St Martin *Ely* 81-83; R Folksworth w Morborne 83-89; R Stilton w Denton and Caldecote 83-89; R Stilton w Denton and Caldecote etc from 90. *The Rectory, Stilton, Peterborough PE7 3RF* Tel (01733) 240282

LONGFORD, Canon Edward de Toesny Wingfield. b 25. Ch Ch Ox BA48 MA53. Wells Th Coll 49. **d** 51 **p** 52. C Stevenage *St Alb* 51-54; PC Chettisham 55-68; Min Can, Prec and Sacr Ely Cathl *Ely* 55-68; P-in-c Everton w Tetworth 68-71; V 71-73; R Gamlingay 68-80; P-in-c Hatley 78-80; Hon Can Ely Cathl 79-90; R Gamlingay w Hatley St Geo and E Hatley 80-90; RD St Neots 82-90; rtd 90; Perm to Offic *Ely* from 90. *9 Philippa Close, Ely, Cambs CB6 1BT* Tel (01353) 667495

LONGMAN, Edward. b 37. Hatf Coll Dur BSc62 Fitzw Ho Cam BA66. Clifton Th Coll 62 Ridley Hall Cam 64. **d** 66 **p** 67. C Lower Homerton St Paul *Lon* 66-72; C Parr *Liv* 72-73; TV 74-85; Perm to Offic from 86. *66 Hard Lane, Dentons Green, St Helens, Merseyside WA10 2LA* Tel (01744) 55667

LONGMAN, Edward George (Ted). b 35. St Pet Hall Ox BA58 MA62. Westcott Ho Cam 59. **d** 61 **p** 62. C Sheff St Mark Broomhall *Sheff* 61-65; V Brightside St Thos 65-74; V Yardley St Edburgha *Birm* 74-84; RD Yardley 77-84; Hon Can Birm Cathl 81-96; R Sutton Coldfield H Trin 84-96; Chapl Gd Hope Distr Gen Hosp Sutton Coldfield 84-90; RD Sutton Coldfield *Birm* 94-96; P-in-c Cerne Abbas w Godmanstone and Minterne Magna *Sarum* from 96. *The Vicarage, 4 Back Lane, Cerne Abbas, Dorchester, Dorset DT2 7LW* Tel (01300) 341251

LONGRIDGE, Richard Nevile. b 15. Sarum Th Coll 46. **d** 48 **p** 49. C Portsea N End St Mark *Portsm* 48-51; R Bourton w Silton *Sarum* 51-63; R Okeford Fitzpaine 63-67; R Spetisbury w Charlton Marshall 67-77; rtd 77; Perm to Offic *Ex* from 78. *The Lodge, 22 Spicer Road, Exeter EX1 1SY* Tel (01392) 435866

LONGUET-HIGGINS, John. b 62. Leeds Univ BA85. St Jo Coll Nottm DTS90 DPS91. **d** 91 **p** 92. C Kidlington w Hampton Poyle *Ox* 91-95; TV N Huddersfield *Wakef* from 95. *8 Oakdean, Huddersfield HD2 2FA* Tel (01484) 425545

LONGWORTH, Arthur Victor. b 24. Trin Coll Ox BA48 MA51. St Steph Ho Ox 48. **d** 49 **p** 50. C Daybrook *S'well* 49-51; Lic to Offic *Wakef* 51-68; CR from 54; Vice-Prin Coll of Resurr Mirfield 56-58; Tutor 58-64; Lect 64-68; C Clifton All SS *Bris* 68-69; Lect Bps' Coll Cheshunt 68; C Rubery *Birm* 69-70; Vice-Prin Chich Th Coll 70-73; V Walsgrave on Sowe *Cov* 73-75; Dioc Dir of Ords 73-80; V Bishop's Tachbrook 75-80; V Sheff St Matt *Sheff* 80-89; Ind Chapl 80-87; rtd 89; Perm to Offic *Blackb* from 89; Perm to Offic *Sheff* from 89. *18 Sycamore Avenue, Garstang, Preston PR3 1FR* Tel (01995) 603145

LONGWORTH-DAMES, Canon Francis Robert. b 12. Jes Coll Cam BA34 MA38. Westcott Ho Cam 36. **d** 37 **p** 38. C Deptford St Paul *S'wark* 37-43; P-in-c Bermondsey St Paul 43-48; Bermondsey Charterho Miss 43-48; V Middlesbrough St Jo the Ev *York* 48-55; V Lewisham St Mary *S'wark* 55-65; Hon Can S'wark Cathl 60-81; RD Lewisham 62-65; R Warlingham w Chelsham and Farleigh 65-73; V Catford St Andr 74-81; rtd 81; Perm to Offic *Glouc* from 81. *17 Capel Court, The Burgage, Prestbury, Cheltenham, Glos GL52 3EL* Tel (01242) 239830

LONSDALE, Canon Rupert Philip. b 05. Ridley Hall Cam 47. **d** 48 **p** 49. C Rowner *Portsm* 49-51; V Morden w Almer and Charborough *Sarum* 51-53; Kenya 53-58 and 61-65; Can Maseno 64-65; R Bentworth cum Shalden *Win* 58-61; V Thornham w Titchwell *Nor* 65-70; rtd 70; Chapl Puerto de la Cruz Tenerife *Eur* 70-73. *Hotel Bristowe, Grange Road, Bournemouth BH6 3NY*

LOOKER, Miss Clare Margaret. b 55. Liv Univ CertEd DipRE. Westcott Ho Cam 85. **d** 87. Par Dn Prestwood and Gt Hampden *Ox* 87-90; rtd 90; Hon C Olney *Ox* from 90. *13 Willoughby Close, Great Barford, Bedford MK44 3LD*

LOOMES, Gaenor Mary. b 65. Hull Univ BA92 RGN86. St Jo Coll Nottm MPhil93. **d** 96. C Charles w Plymouth St Matthias *Ex* from 96. *18 Dale Gardens, Mutley, Plymouth PL4 6PX* Tel (01752) 669087

LOONE, Sean Joseph Patrick. b 60. Cov Poly BA83 Wolv Poly CertEd84 Leeds Univ BA88. Coll of Resurr Mirfield 86. **d** 89 **p** 90. C Solihull *Birm* 89-92; Hd RE Bromsgrove Jun Sch from 93. *9 Broomfield Road, Solihull, W Midlands B91 2ND* Tel 0121-705 5117

LOPDELL-BRADSHAW, Canon Humphrey Maitland. b 32. Edin Th Coll 58. **d** 61 **p** 62. C Edin H Cross *Edin* 61-65; C Edin St Barn 65-67; P-in-c Oldbury *Birm* 67-68; V 68-72; R Edin St Hilda *Edin* 72-77; R Hawick 77-88; R Huntly *Mor* from 88; R Aberchirder from 88; R Keith from 88; Can St Andr Cathl Inverness from 91. *The Rectory, Seafield Avenue, Keith, Banffshire AB55 3BS* Tel (01542) 882782

LOPEZ-FERREIRO, Serafin Julio. b 35. Dur Univ BA74 DipTh71. St Jo Coll Dur. **d** 71 **p** 72. C S Lambeth St Steph *S'wark* 71-75; C Upper Tooting H Trin 76-78; P-in-c Tooting St Aug 78-83; V from 83. *St Augustine's Vicarage, 99 Broadwater Road, London SW17 0DY* Tel 0181-672 4712

LORAINE, Kenneth. b 34. Cranmer Hall Dur 63. **d** 66 **p** 67. C Hartlepool All SS Stranton *Dur* 66-69; C Darlington St Cuth 69-72; V Preston on Tees 72-79; V Staindrop 79-87; P-in-c Haynes *St Alb* 87-96; Dioc Stewardship Adv 87-96; rtd 96. *116 Turker Lane, Northallerton, N Yorkshire DL6 1QD* Tel (01609) 771277

LORD, Alexander. b 13. ALCD43. **d** 43 **p** 44. C Wakef St Mary *Wakef* 43-45; P-in-c Thornham St Jas *Man* 45-47; R Clitheroe St Jas *Blackb* 47-55; V Madeley *Heref* 55-69; R Illogan *Truro* 70-81; rtd 81; C Letton w Staunton, Byford, Mansel Gamage etc *Heref* 81-84. *43 Narrow Lane, Llandudno Junction LL31 9SZ* Tel (01492) 584647

LORD, Clive Gavin. b 69. **d** 96 **p** 97. C Penwortham St Leon *Blackb* from 96. *17 Alderfield, Penwortham, Preston PR1 9HB* Tel (01772) 749866

LORD, Canon John Fairbourne. b 19. Kelham Th Coll 38. **d** 43 **p** 44. C Dallington *Pet* 43-45; C Langley Marish *Ox* 47-51; RD Holt *Nor* 64-79; R Thornage w Brinton w Hunworth and Stody 64-84; Hon Can Nor Cathl 77-84; rtd 84; Perm to Offic *Nor* from 84.

25 Melton Road, Hindolveston, Dereham, Norfolk NR20 5DB Tel (01263) 860819

LORD, Kenneth Frank. b 14. Clifton Th Coll 34. **d** 38 **p** 40. C Sheff St Cuth *Sheff* 38-40; C Walkley 40-42; C Moreton *Ches* 42-44; V Laithkirk *Ripon* 44-53; V Skelton cum Newby 53-81; rtd 81. *The Vicarage, Skelton-on-Ure, Ripon, N Yorkshire HG4 5AJ* Tel (01423) 322864

LORD, Stuart James. b 59. K Coll Lon BD81 AKC81. Sarum & Wells Th Coll 83. **d** 85 **p** 86. C Darwen St Pet w Hoddlesden *Blackb* 85-88; C Otley *Bradf* 88-93; P-in-c Low Moor St Mark from 93. *St Mark's Vicarage, 1 Park Bottom, Low Moor, Bradford, W Yorkshire BD12 0UA* Tel (01274) 677754

LORIMER, Eileen Jean. b 35. CertEd56. Dalton Ho Bris 62. **dss** 84 **d** 89 **p** 94. Chiddingstone w Chiddingstone Causeway *Roch* 84-89; NSM from 89. *The Nursery Flat, Hoath House, Chiddingstone Hoath, Edenbridge, Kent TN8 7DB* Tel (01342) 850784

LOSACK, Marcus Charles. b 53. Ch Coll Cam BA76 MA78 MPhil. Sarum & Wells Th Coll 78. **d** 80 **p** 81. C Hattersley *Ches* 80-82; C Dublin Zion Ch *D & G* 83-86; Libya 86-89; CMS 89-92; Jerusalem 89-92; P-in-c Dublin Sandymount *D & G* 92-93; I Newcastle w Newtownmountkennedy and Calary 93-95. *Céile Dé, Castlekevin, Annamoe, Bray, Co Wicklow, Irish Republic* Tel Wicklow (404) 45595 Fax as telephone

LOSEBY, Everitt James Carnall. b 22. Launde Abbey. **d** 66 **p** 67. C Thurmaston *Leic* 66-70; R Seagrave w Walton le Wolds 70-75; V Thurnby Lodge 75-84; V Swinford w Catthorpe, Shawell and Stanford 84-87; rtd 87; Perm to Offic *Leic* from 87. *63 Willow Road, Blaby, Leicester LE8 4BG* Tel 0116-277 1983

LOTT, Dr Eric John. b 34. Lon Univ BA65 Lanc Univ MLitt70 PhD77. Richmond Th Coll BD59. **d** 60 **p** 61. India 60-88; Prof United Th Coll Bangalore 77-88; Wesley Hall Ch and Community Project Leics 88-94; rtd 94; Perm to Offic *Leic* from 94. *16 Main Road, Old Dalby, Melton Mowbray, Leics LE14 3LR* Tel (01664) 822405

LOUDEN, Canon Terence Edmund (Terry). b 48. Ch Coll Cam BA70 MA74. Sarum & Wells Th Coll 72. **d** 75 **p** 76. C Portsea N End St Mark *Portsm* 75-78; C-in-c Leigh Park St Clare CD 78-81; R Chale 81-88; R Niton 81-88; P-in-c Whitwell 82-84; V Cosham 88-96; Hon Can Portsm Cathl from 92; V E Meon from 96; V Langrish from 96; Dir Continuing Minl Educn from 96. *The Vicarage, East Meon, Petersfield, Hants GU32 1NH* Tel (01730) 823221

LOUGHBOROUGH, Archdeacon of. *See* STANES, The Ven Ian Thomas

LOUGHEED, Canon Brian Frederick Britain. b 38. TCD BA60. CITC 61. **d** 61 **p** 62. C Dublin St Pet w St Audoen *D & G* 61-63; C Glenageary 63-66; I Rathmolyon Union *M & K* 66-79; I Killarney w Aghadoe and Muckross *L & K* from 79; Can Limerick and Killaloe Cathls 87-95; Preb Taney St Patr Cathl Dublin from 89; Dioc Info Officer (Limerick) *L & K* 90-91; Radio Officer from 91. *St Mary's Rectory, Rookery Road, Ballycasheen, Killarney, Co Kerry, Irish Republic* Tel Killarney (64) 31832 Fax as telephone E-mail brianfbl@iol.ie

LOUGHLIN, Canon Alfred. b 10. Clifton Th Coll 37. **d** 39 **p** 40. C Preston St Mark *Blackb* 39-44; Chapl RAFVR 41-43; Org Sec (SE Area) CPAS 44-48; V Sneinton St Chris *S'well* 48-54; R Kinson *Sarum* 54-81; Can and Preb Sarum Cathl 75-81; rtd 81. *18 Donnelly Road, Bournemouth BH6 5NW* Tel (01202) 422306

LOUGHLIN, George Alfred Graham. b 43. Lon Univ DipTh68. Clifton Th Coll 65. **d** 69 **p** 70. C Plumstead All SS *S'wark* 69-73; C Bromley Ch Ch *Roch* 73-76; P-in-c Bothenhampton w Walditch *Sarum* 76-79; TV Bridport 79-83; V Heatherlands St Jo from 83. *St John's Vicarage, 72 Alexandra Road, Poole, Dorset BH14 9EW* Tel (01202) 741276

LOUGHTON, Michael. b 34. K Coll Lon BD58 AKC58. **d** 59 **p** 60. C Chingford SS Pet and Paul *Chelmsf* 59-62; C Eastbourne St Elisabeth *Chich* 62-65; R Lewes St Jo sub Castro 65-74; Perm to Offic from 87. *Follers Manor, Seaford Road, Alfriston, Polegate, E Sussex BN26 5TT* Tel (01323) 870252

LOUIS, Peter Anthony. b 41. St Cath Coll Ox BA63 MA77 Jes Coll Cam CertEd64 Man Univ MPhil85. Wells Th Coll 66. **d** 68 **p** 70. C E Grinstead St Mary *Chich* 68-75; C Radcliffe-on-Trent *S'well* 75-80; Hd Master Blue Coat Comp Sch Cov 80-85; V Welwyn Garden City *St Alb* from 85; Chapl Oaklands Coll from 93. *The Vicarage, 48 Parkway, Welwyn Garden City, Herts AL8 6HH* Tel (01707) 323316

LOUW, Paul Leonard. b 32. Leeds Univ BA56 Port Eliz Univ MA79. Coll of Resurr Mirfield 56. **d** 58 **p** 59. C Solihull *Birm* 58-61; S Africa from 61. *55 Main Road, Walmer, Port Elizabeth, 6070 South Africa* Tel Port Elizabeth (41) 513588

LOVATT, Bernard James. b 31. Lich Th Coll 64. **d** 65 **p** 66. C Burford III w Lt Heref 65-67; C Cleobury Mortimer w Hopton Wafers 67-68; C Bradford-on-Avon *Sarum* 68-69; C Wootton Bassett 69-72; C Broad Town 69-72; R Bishopstrow and Boreham 72-79; P-in-c Brighton St Geo *Chich* 79-83; V Brighton St Anne 79-83; V Brighton St Geo and St Anne 83-86; P-in-c Kemp Town St Mark and St Matt 85-86; V Brighton St Geo w St Anne and St Mark 86-95; rtd 95; Perm to Offic *Ex* from 95. *7 Cambridge Terrace, Salcombe Road, Sidmouth, Devon EX10 8PL* Tel (01395) 514154

LOVATT, William Robert. b 54. SS Coll Cam MA75 K Coll Lon PGCE77 MA78. Oak Hill Th Coll 85. **d** 87 **p** 88. C Devonport St Budeaux *Ex* 87-90; Asst Chapl Paris St Mich *Eur* 90-94; P-in-c Lenton *S'well* from 94. *The Vicarage, 35A Church Street, Nottingham NG7 2FH* Tel 0115-970 1059

LOVE, Ms Anette. b 53. Matlock Coll of Educn CertEd74 Nottm Univ BEd75. St Jo Coll Dur 88. **d** 90 **p** 94. Par Dn Gresley *Derby* 90-92; C Heanor 92-94; C Loscoe from 94. *The Vicarage, High Street, Loscoe, Heanor, Derbyshire DE75 7LE* Tel (01773) 765631

LOVE, Richard Angus. b 45. AKC67. **d** 68 **p** 69. C Balham Hill Ascension *S'wark* 68-71; C Amersham *Ox* 71-73; R Scotter w E Ferry *Linc* 73-79; P-in-c Petham w Waltham and Lower Hardres w Nackington *Cant* 79-85; R Petham and Waltham w Lower Hardres etc 85-90; V Sittingbourne H Trin w Bobbing from 90. *Holy Trinity Vicarage, 47 London Road, Sittingbourne, Kent ME10 1NQ* Tel (01795) 472724

LOVE, Dr Robert (Bob). b 45. Bradf Univ BSc68 PhD74 NE Lon Poly PGCE89. Trin Coll Bris DipTh75. **d** 75 **p** 76. C Bowling St Jo *Bradf* 75-79; TV Forest Gate St Sav w W Ham St Matt *Chelmsf* 79-85; P-in-c Becontree St Elisabeth 85-96; V S Hornchurch St Jo and St Matt from 96. *St John's Parsonage, South End Road, Hornchurch, Essex RM13 7XT* Tel (01708) 555260

LOVEDAY, Joseph Michael. b 54. AKC75. St Aug Coll Cant 75. **d** 78 **p** 79. C Kettering SS Pet and Paul *Pet* 78-81; C Upper Teddington SS Pet and Paul *Lon* 81-84; CF from 84. *MOD Chaplains (Army), Trenchard Lines, Upavon, Pewsey, Wilts SN9 6BE* Tel (01980) 615804 Fax 615800

LOVEGROVE, Mrs Anne Maureen. b 44. DipHE90. Oak Hill Th Coll 88. **d** 90 **p** 94. Par Dn Thorley *St Alb* 90-94; C 94-95; V Croxley Green St Oswald from 95. *The Vicarage, 159 Baldwins Lane, Croxley Green, Rickmansworth, Herts WD3 3LL* Tel (01923) 232387

LOVEGROVE, Walter John. b 19. Dur Univ LTh44. St Aug Coll Cant 38. **d** 42 **p** 43. C Ogley Hay *Lich* 42-43; C Willenhall St Giles 43-45; C Gt Yarmouth *Nor* 45-47; S Africa 47-72 and 83-93; V Chaddesden St Phil *Derby* 72-75; P-in-c Tintinhull *B & W* 75; R Tintinhull w Chilthorne Domer, Yeovil Marsh etc 75-80; RD Martock 78-80; P-in-c Norbury St Phil *Cant* 80-81; V 81-83; rtd 86. *37 Vicarage Lane, Charminster, Dorchester, Dorset DT2 9QF* Tel (01305) 264677

LOVEJOY, Geoffrey William. b 08. St Chad's Coll Dur BA31 LTh31 MA47. Dorchester Miss Coll 28. **d** 32 **p** 33. C Hendford *B & W* 32-34; Australia 34-40; India 40-44; C Tottenham All Hallows *Lon* 45-46; S Rhodesia 46-52; C St Marychurch *Ex* 52-54; P-in-c Shiphay Collaton 54-57; V 57-59; R Cumberworth *Wakef* 59-65; R Stoke Goldington w Gayhurst *Ox* 65-72; P-in-c Ravenstone w Weston Underwood 67-72; rtd 73; Chapl Sevenoaks Hosp 73-78; Hon C Sevenoaks St Jo *Roch* 73-88; Perm to Offic 88-93. *61 Old Mill Close, Eynsford, Dartford DA4 0BN* Tel (01322) 866186

LOVEJOY, John Geoffrey. b 35. K Coll Lon BD60 AKC60. **d** 61 **p** 62. C Byker St Laur *Newc* 61-64; C Choppington 64-66; C Usworth *Dur* 66-70; Perm to Offic *Carl* 73-77; Algeria 77-78; Australia 79-84 and 86-88; NSM Isla-Deveron *Mor* 85-86; Perm to Offic *S'wark* from 88. *30 Woodside Road, Sutton, Surrey SM1 3SU* Tel 0181-644 4151

LOVELAND, John Michael. b 30. Roch Th Coll 65. **d** 67 **p** 68. C Ashford St Hilda CD *Lon* 67-71; P-in-c Earley St Nic *Ox* 71-76; V 76-79; V Kennington 79-84; V Reading St Mark 84-89; P-in-c Drayton St Pet (Berks) 89-92; rtd 92. *Chantry House, Radley Road, Abingdon, Oxon OX14 3SN*

LOVELESS, Christopher Hugh. b 61. Trin Coll Ox BA84 MA91. Linc Th Coll 89. **d** 91 **p** 92. C Willingdon *Chich* 91-95; C Goring-by-Sea from 95. *19 Angus Road, Goring-by-Sea, Worthing, W Sussex BN12 4BL* Tel (01903) 241052

LOVELESS, Martin Frank. b 46. Wycliffe Hall Ox 72. **d** 75 **p** 76. C Caversham *Ox* 75-81; V Carterton 81-86; Chapl RAF from 86. *Chaplaincy Services (RAF), HQ, Personnel and Training Command, RAF Innsworth, Gloucester GL3 1EZ* Tel (01452) 712612 ext 5164 Fax 510828

LOVELESS, Robert Alfred. b 43. Birm Univ BA66. Westcott Ho Cam 66. **d** 68 **p** 69. C Kenilworth St Nic *Cov* 68-72; C Costessey *Nor* 73-75; R Colney 75-80; R Lt w Gt Melton, Marlingford and Bawburgh 75-80; V Lt and Gt Melton w Bawburgh 80-82; P-in-c Westwood *Sarum* 82-83; Chapl Stonar Sch Melksham 82-87; P-in-c Wingfield w Rowley *Sarum* 82-83; R Westwood and Wingfield 83-87; R Paston *Pet* 87-93; V Nassington w Yarwell and Woodnewton from 93. *The Vicarage, 34 Station Road, Nassington, Peterborough PE8 6QG* Tel (01780) 782271

LOVELESS, Canon William Harry. b 21. Lon Univ BSc60. Ridley Hall Cam 61. **d** 63 **p** 64. C Danbury *Chelmsf* 63-65; C Cambridge Gt St Mary w St Mich *Ely* 65-67; V Cambridge St Mark 67-87; RD Cambridge 81-84; Hon Can Ely Cathl 81-87; rtd 87; Perm to Offic *Ely* from 87. *103 High Street, Swaffham Bulbeck, Cambridge CB5 0LX*

LOVELL, Charles Nelson. b 34. Or Coll Ox BA57 MA61. Wycliffe Hall Ox. **d** 59 **p** 60. C Walsall St Matt *Lich* 59-63; C St Giles-in-the-Fields *Lon* 63; Argentina 64-67; C Cambridge H Trin *Ely* 64; V Esh *Dur* 67-75; V Hamsteels 67-75; Chapl Winterton Hosp

Sedgefield 75-83; R Stanhope *Dur* 83-86; Chapl Horn Hall Hosp Weardale 83-97; R Stanhope w Frosterley *Dur* 86-97; V Eastgate w Rookhope 86-97; RD Stanhope 87-97; rtd 97. *10 Riverside, Wolsingham, Co Durham DL13 3BP* Tel (01388) 527038

LOVELL, David John. b 38. JP89. Univ of Tasmania BEcon86. Qu Coll Birm 60. **d** 60 **p** 62. C Glouc St Steph *Glouc* 60-64; C Lower Tuffley St Geo CD 64-67; V Lydbrook 67-73; Australia from 73. *Address temp unknown*

LOVELL, Helen Sarah. *See* HOUSTON, Mrs Helen Sarah

LOVELL, Keith Michael Beard. b 43. K Coll Lon 67. **d** 68 **p** 69. C Romford St Edw *Chelmsf* 68-73; P-in-c Elmstead 73-79; V Tollesbury w Salcot Virley from 79. *The Vicarage, 12 King's Walk, Tollesbury, Maldon, Essex CM9 8XH* Tel (01621) 869393 or 868441

LOVELL, Laurence John. b 31. St D Coll Lamp BA54 Tyndale Hall Bris 54. **d** 56 **p** 57. C Penge Ch Ch w H Trin *Roch* 56-61; C Illogan *Truro* 61-63; V St Keverne 63-68; Australia from 68; rtd 95. *1/64 Cambridge Street, Penshurst, NSW, Australia 2222* Tel Sydney (2) 580 7454

LOVELUCK, Allan (Illtyd). b 30. Queensland Univ MSocWork79 BSocWork74. St D Coll Lamp BA52 St Mich Coll Llan 54. **d** 55 **p** 56. C Dowlais *Llan* 55-58; SSF 58-79; Lic to Offic *Chelmsf* 62-64; Australia from 64; rtd 95. *16 Clinton Court, Palmview, Queensland, Australia 4553* Tel Palmview (74) 945305

LOVELUCK, Dr Graham David. b 34. CChem FRSC Univ of Wales (Abth) BSc55 PhD58. St Deiniol's Hawarden 77. **d** 78 **p** 79. Hon C Llanfair Mathafarn Eithaf w Llanbedrgoch *Ban* 78-87; NSM Llaneugrad w Llanallgo and Penrhosllugwy etc 87-96; C from 96; Dioc Dir of Educn from 92. *Gwenallt, Marianglas LL73 8PE* Tel (01248) 853741

LOVELY, Leslie Walter. b 09. Dur Univ LTh32. **d** 32 **p** 33. C Southampton St Alb *Win* 32-35; Egypt 35-43; S Africa from 43. *158 Darrenwood Village, Private Bag X5, Linden, 2014 South Africa* Tel Johannesburg (11) 678-7303

LOVERIDGE, Douglas Henry. b 52. Sarum & Wells Th Coll. **d** 84 **p** 85. C Earley St Pet *Ox* 84-88; V Hurst from 88. *The Vicarage, Church Hill, Hurst, Reading RG10 0SJ* Tel (0118) 934 0017

LOVERING, Mrs Jennifer Mary (Jen). b 39. Eastbourne Tr Coll CertEd59. Wycliffe Hall Ox 81. **dss** 84 **d** 87 **p** 94. Abingdon w Shippon *Ox* 84-87; Par Dn Abingdon 87-94; C from 94. *39 The Mote, Abingdon, Oxon OX14 3NZ* Tel (01235) 521371

LOVERING, Martin. b 35. Imp Coll Lon BScEng57 DMS66. Wycliffe Hall Ox 82. **d** 84 **p** 85. NSM Abingdon w Shippon *Ox* 84-88; C Abingdon 88-89; TV from 89. *39 The Mote, Abingdon, Oxon OX14 3NZ* Tel (01235) 521371

LOVETT, Francis Roland. b 25. Glouc Th Course. **d** 85 **p** 86. NSM Ludlow *Heref* 85-91; rtd 92; Perm to Offic *Heref* from 96. *7 Poyner Road, Ludlow, Shropshire SY8 1QT* Tel (01584) 872470

LOVETT, Ian Arthur. b 43. NE Lon Poly BSc74 Ox Poly DipTP78. Linc Th Coll 85. **d** 87 **p** 88. C Uppingham w Ayston and Wardley w Belton *Pet* 87-91; R Polebrook and Lutton w Hemington and Luddington from 91. *The Rectory, Polebrook, Peterborough PE8 5LN* Tel (01832) 274941

LOVETT, Ian James. b 49. S'wark Ord Course 73. **d** 76 **p** 77. NSM Gravesend St Geo *Roch* 76-77; NSM Willesborough w Hinxhill *Cant* 77-83; Perm to Offic *Ex* 83-85; C Compton Gifford 85; C Plymouth Em w Efford 85-86; TV 86-92; TV Plymouth Em, St Paul Efford and St Aug from 93. *28A Sefton Avenue, Lipson, Plymouth PL4 7HB* Tel (01752) 663484

LOVEWELL, Robert Antony. b 34. Lich Th Coll. **d** 62 **p** 63. C Endcliffe *Sheff* 62-65; Miss to Seamen 65-79; Portuguese E Africa 65-73; V Wilton *York* 73-79; TV Thornaby on Tees 79-81; Ind Chapl *Ex* from 81. *65 Easterdown Close, Plymstock, Plymouth PL9 8SR* Tel (01752) 552323 or 402103

LOVITT, Gerald Elliott. b 25. St Mich Coll Llan 59. **d** 61 **p** 62. C Aberdare St Jo *Llan* 61-66; C Whitchurch 66-71; V Grangetown 71-76; V Rockfield and Llangattock w St Maughan's *Mon* 76-83; V Rockfield and St Maughen's w Llangattock etc 83-93; rtd 93; Perm to Offic *Llan* from 93. *78 Ninian Road, Penylan, Cardiff CF2 5EN*

LOW, Dr Alastair Graham. b 43. Brunel Univ BSc68 Reading Univ PhD74. Ripon Coll Cuddesdon 90. **d** 92 **p** 93. C Brighton Gd Shep Preston *Chich* 92-96; TV Ifield from 96. *St Leonard's House, 10 Martyrs Avenue, Crawley, W Sussex RH11 7RZ* Tel (01293) 518419

LOW, David Anthony. b 42. AKC66. **d** 67 **p** 68. C Gillingham St Barn *Roch* 67-70; V 82-88; C Wallingford *Ox* 70-73; V Spencer's Wood 73-82; P-in-c Grazeley and Beech Hill 77-82; Chapl Medway Hosp Gillingham 86-88; V Hoo St Werburgh *Roch* from 88; RD Strood from 97. *The Vicarage, Vicarage Lane, Hoo, Rochester, Kent ME3 9BB* Tel (01634) 250291

LOW, David John. b 32. Bris Univ BA53. Wells Th Coll 55. **d** 57 **p** 58. C Bradford Ch Ch *Man* 57-59; C Benchill 59-62; V Newbold 62-75; R Moston St Mary from 75. *St Mary's Rectory, 47 Nuthurst Road, Moston, Manchester M10 0EW* Tel 0161-681 1201

LOW, David Michael. b 39. Cape Town Univ BA60. Cuddesdon Coll 61. **d** 63 **p** 64. C Portsea St Cuth *Portsm* 63-65; S Africa 65-69; C Havant *Portsm* 69-72; V St Helens 72-88; P-in-c Sea View 80-81; V 81-88; V Sandown Ch Ch 88-95; V Lower Sandown St Jo 88-95; R Brading w Yaverland from 95. *The Vicarage, Mall Road, Brading, Sandown, Isle of Wight PO36 0DE* Tel (01983) 407262

LOW, Peter James. b 52. Nottm Univ BTh89. Linc Th Coll 86. **d** 89 **p** 90. C Dartford H Trin *Roch* 89-92; C Plympton St Mary *Ex* 92-94; TR Devonport St Boniface and St Phil from 94. *St Boniface Vicarage, 1 Normandy Way, Plymouth PL5 1SW* Tel (01752) 361137

LOW, Stafford. b 42. N Lon Poly BSc65. Trin Coll Bris 82. **d** 85 **p** 86. C Yeovil *B & W* 85-88; C Glastonbury w Meare, W Pennard and Godney 88-92; R Berrow and Breane from 92. *The Rectory, 1 Manor Way, Coast Road, Berrow, Burnham-on-Sea, Somerset TA8 2RG* Tel (01278) 751744

LOW, Terence John Gordon (Terry). b 37. Oak Hill Th Coll 75. **d** 77 **p** 78. C Kensal Rise St Martin *Lon* 77-79; C Longfleet *Sarum* 79-83; P-in-c Maiden Newton and Valleys 83-84; TV Melbury 84-88; TV Buckhurst Hill *Chelmsf* 88-92; R Gt Hallingbury and Lt Hallingbury from 92. *The Rectory, Wright's Green Lane, Little Hallingbury, Bishop's Stortford, Herts CM22 7RE* Tel (01279) 723341

LOW, William Roberson (Robbie). b 50. MFFS Pemb Coll Cam BA73 MA77. Westcott Ho Cam 76. **d** 79 **p** 80. FFS from 78; C Poplar *Lon* 79-83; Chapl St Alb Abbey *St Alb* 83-88; V Bushey Heath from 88. *St Peter's Vicarage, 19 High Road, Bushey Heath, Watford WD2 1EA* Tel 0181-950 1424 Fax 950 1547

LOWATER, Canon Jennifer Blanche (Jenny). b 34. Eastbourne Tr Coll TCert54. Sarum & Wells Th Coll 82. **dss** 85 **d** 87 **p** 94. Locks Heath *Portsm* 85-87; Hon C 87-88; NSM Southsea St Pet 88-94; Asst Dir of Ords 91-97; NSM Hook w Warsash 94-97; Hon Can Portsm Cathl 95-97; rtd 97. *Lower Gubbles, Hook Lane, Warsash, Southampton SO31 9HH* Tel (01489) 572156

LOWCOCK, Brian Walter. b 23. Man Univ LLB43. Linc Th Coll 56. **d** 57 **p** 58. C S Ormsby w Ketsby, Calceby and Driby *Linc* 57-62; V Gedney Drove End 62-67; P-in-c Sutton St Nicholas 62-65; P-in-c Holbeach Hurn 62-65; V Sutton St Nicholas 65-67; V Holbeach Hurn 65-67; Perm to Offic 68-73; Lic to Offic *Ely* 70-74; P-in-c Holbeach Marsh *Linc* 74-81; P-in-c Witham on the Hill 81; P-in-c Edenham 81; V Edenham w Witham-on-the-Hill 82-85; rtd 85; Perm to Offic *Ely* from 86. *2 The Chase, Ely, Cambs CB6 3DS* Tel (01353) 667641

LOWE, Miss Alison Margaret. b 56. Linc Th Coll. **dss** 84 **d** 89. Knottingley *Wakef* 84-86; Par Educn Adv 86-90; Par Dn Edin Ch Ch *Edin* 90-91. *10 Heath Park Place, Selkirk TD7 4DN*

LOWE, Anthony Richard (Tony). b 45. York Univ BA66 Birm Univ DipTh68. Qu Coll Birm 66. **d** 69 **p** 70. C Greasbrough *Sheff* 69-71; C Thrybergh 71-75; P-in-c Sheff St Mary w St Simon w St Matthias 75-78; V Shiregreen St Hilda 78-85; V Hoxne w Denham St Jo and Syleham *St E* 85-89; P-in-c Wingfield 86-89; R Hoxne w Denham, Syleham and Wingfield from 90. *The Vicarage, Church Hill, Hoxne, Eye, Suffolk IP21 5AT* Tel (01379) 75246

LOWE, Mrs Brenda June. b 53. Cranmer Hall Dur 75. **d** 88 **p** 94. Chapl to Families Trin Coll and Mortimer Ho Bris 88-91; NSM Marple All SS *Ches* from 91; Perm to Offic *Man* from 91. *The Vicarage, 155 Church Lane, Marple, Stockport, Cheshire SK6 7LD* Tel 0161-449 0950 or 998 7070 Fax 449 0950

LOWE, David Charles. b 43. Kelham Th Coll 62. **d** 67 **p** 68. C Wingerworth *Derby* 67-70; C Greenhill St Pet 70-73; TV Eckington 73-74; TV Eckington w Handley and Ridgeway 74-78; V Bury St Edmunds St Geo *St E* 78-86; V Leiston from 86; RD Saxmundham 88-96. *St Margaret's Vicarage, 2 King Edward Road, Leiston, Suffolk IP16 4HQ* Tel (01728) 831059

LOWE, David Reginald. b 42. K Coll Lon BD65 AKC65. St Boniface Warminster 65. **d** 66 **p** 67. C Tupsley *Heref* 66-69; C Lewes St Anne *Chich* 69-73; C Heref H Trin *Heref* 73-77; P-in-c Lyonshall w Titley 77-88; V Lyonshall w Titley, Almeley and Kinnersley 88-96; rtd 97. *The Vicarage, Lyonshall, Kington, Herefordshire HR5 3LN* Tel (01544) 340212

LOWE, Donald. b 33. Lich Th Coll 57. **d** 60 **p** 61. C Horwich H Trin *Man* 60; C Wythenshawe St Martin CD 60-62; C Bury St Paul 62-65; S Africa 65-69 and 73-81; V Gannow *Blackb* 70-73; V Colne H Trin 81-89; TV Melbury *Sarum* 89-94; RD Beaminster 93-94; rtd 94; Perm to Offic *Bradf* from 94. *28 High Bank, Threshfield, Skipton, N Yorkshire BD23 5BU* Tel (01756) 752344

LOWE, Canon Eric. b 29. Trin Coll Ox BA50 MA54. St Steph Ho Ox 50. **d** 52 **p** 53. C Ellesmere Port *Ches* 52-55; C Hucknall Torkard *S'well* 55-56; C Solihull *Birm* 56-58; Area Sec (NW England) UMCA 58-65; Lic to Offic *Ches* 65-88; Lic to Offic *Ban* 65-88; Area Sec (Dios Ches, Ban and St As) USPG 65-88; (Dio Liv) 73-85; Perm to Offic *Liv* 73-88; V Frodsham *Ches* 88-95; Can Ndola (Zambia) from 88; rtd 95. *55 Wetherby Way, Little Sutton, South Wirral L66 4TB* Tel 0151-339 1468

LOWE, The Ven Frank McLean Rhodes. b 26. ACT 59. **d** 61 **p** 63. Australia 61-86 and from 87; Hon Can Gippsland 73-81; Adn Latrobe Valley 81-86; Adn Gippsland 81-86; P-in-c Kirkby in Ashfield St Thos *S'well* 86-87; C Mansfield Woodhouse 87; rtd 91. *12A Lysbeth Street, McKinnon, Victoria, Australia 3204* Tel Melbourne (3) 9569 5893

LOWE, Canon John Bethel. b 30. TCD BA52 BD65. Ridley Hall Cam 55. **d** 55 **p** 56. C Belfast St Mary Magd *Conn* 55-57; Sudan

59-64; Uganda 64-74; Warden CMS Fellowship Ho Foxbury 74-76; V Kippington *Roch* 76-96; Dioc Dir of Ords 82-96; Hon Can Roch Cathl 85-96; rtd 96. *228 Cambridge Road, Great Shelford, Cambridge CB2 5JU* Tel (01223) 840019

LOWE, John Forrester. b 39. Nottm Univ BA61. Lich Th Coll 61. **d** 64 **p** 65. C N Woolwich *Chelmsf* 64-70; V Marks Gate 70-74; V Moulsham St Jo 74-79; V N Woolwich w Silvertown 79-82; V Birm St Pet *Birm* 82-86; Gen Sec SOMA 86-91; V Heckmondwike *Wakef* from 92. *The Vicarage, Church Street, Heckmondwike, W Yorkshire WF16 0AX* Tel (01924) 405881

LOWE, Keith Gregory. b 50. Sarum & Wells Th Coll DCM93. **d** 93 **p** 94. C Wallasey St Hilary *Ches* 93-94; C W Kirby St Bridget from 94. *13 Caldy Road, West Kirby, Wirral, Merseyside L48 2HE* Tel 0151-625 2731

LOWE, Michael Arthur (Mike). b 46. Lon Univ BD67 Hull Univ MA85. Cranmer Hall Dur DipTh75. **d** 76 **p** 77. C Thorpe Edge *Bradf* 76-79; C N Ferriby *York* 79-84; TV 84-86; Dir Past Studies Trin Coll Bris 86-91; V Marple All SS *Ches* from 91; RD Chadkirk from 95. *The Vicarage, 155 Church Lane, Marple, Stockport, Cheshire SK6 7LD* Tel 0161-449 0950 or 427 2378 Fax 449 0950

LOWE, Michael Sinclair. b 35. Open Univ BA75. AKC61. **d** 62 **p** 63. C Wythenshawe Wm Temple Ch CD *Man* 62-66; V Facit 66-70; V Bath St Barn w Englishcombe *B & W* 70-79; V Bathford 79-86; V Branksome Park All SS *Sarum* 86-95; C Christchurch *Win* from 95. *All Saints House, 22 Kestrel Drive, Christchurch, Dorset BH23 4DE* Tel (01425) 276267

LOWE, Raymond John. b 12. OBE67. St Edm Hall Ox BA34 MA38. Sarum Th Coll 34. **d** 36 **p** 37. C Hoxton St Andr *Lon* 36-38; Chapl RN 38-67; QHC 65-67; R Padworth *Ox* 70-77; V Mortimer W End 70-77; rtd 77; Perm to Offic *Ox* 77-93. *Flat 11, Stuart Court, Kibworth Beauchamp, Leics LE8 0LE* Tel 0116-279 2508

LOWE, Canon Reginald Kenneth William. b 09. TCD BA31. **d** 32 **p** 33. C Dublin Drumcondra w N Strand *D & G* 32-42; I Dunlavin 42-50; I Rathdrum w Glenealy 50-65; I Blessington w Kilbride 65-79; Can Ch Ch Cathl Dublin 58-79; Treas 74-79; rtd 79. *Glenbride Cottage, Kilpedder, Co Wicklow, Irish Republic* Tel Dublin (1) 281 9211

LOWE, Richard (Christopher). b 23. Birm Univ BSc44. Coll of Resurr Mirfield 46. **d** 48 **p** 49. C Victoria Docks Ascension *Chelmsf* 48-51; C Swindon New Town *Bris* 51-56; R Corringham *Chelmsf* 56-65; Lic to Offic *Wakef* 66-69 and 86-95; CR from 67; Lic to Offic *Lon* 69-93; Master R Foundn of St Kath in Ratcliffe 82-92; Warden Community of St Denys Warminster 83-87; rtd 93. *St Michael's Priory, 14 Burleigh Street, London WC2E 7PX* Tel 0171-379 6669

LOWE, Samuel (Sam). b 35. St D Coll Lamp. **d** 65 **p** 66. C Tenby w Gumfreston *St D* 65-67; C Lower Mitton *Worc* 67-69; C Halesowen 69-72; R Droitwich St Nic w St Pet 72-73; TV Droitwich 73-77; P-in-c Claines St Geo 77-78; P-in-c Worc St Mary the Tything 77-78; P-in-c Worc St Geo w St Mary Magd 78-84; V from 84. *St George's Vicarage, St George's Square, Worcester WR1 1HX* Tel (01905) 22698

LOWE, Stephen Arthur. b 49. Nottm Univ BSc71 DipTh. Cuddesdon Coll 71. **d** 74 **p** 75. C Mansfield St Mark *S'well* 74-77; Papua New Guinea 77-79; V Kirkby Woodhouse *S'well* 80-86; V Beeston from 86. *The Vicarage, Middle Street, Beeston, Nottingham NG9 1GA* Tel 0115-925 4571

LOWE, The Ven Stephen Richard. b 44. Lon Univ BSc66. Ripon Hall Ox 68. **d** 68 **p** 69. C Gospel Lane St Mich *Birm* 68-72; C-in-c Woodgate Valley CD 72-75; V E Ham w Upton Park *Chelmsf* 75-76; TR E Ham w Upton Park St Alb 76-88; Hon Can Chelmsf Cathl 85-88; Adn Sheff from 88. *23 Hill Turretts Close, Sheffield S11 9RE* Tel 0114-235 0191 Fax 235 2275

LOWELL, Ian Russell. b 53. AKC75. St Aug Coll Cant 75. **d** 76 **p** 77. C Llwynderw *S & B* 76-79; C Swansea St Mary w H Trin and St Mark 79-81; Chapl Ox Hosps 81-83; TV Gt and Lt Coates w Bradley *Linc* 83-88; V Wellingborough St Mark *Pet* from 88; Chapl Northants Ambulance Service from 92. *St Mark's Vicarage, Queensway, Wellingborough, Northants NN8 3SD* Tel (01933) 673893

LOWEN, David John. b 42. Sussex Univ BSc74 Univ of Wales (Lamp) MA84. Llan Dioc Tr Scheme 86. **d** 88 **p** 89. C Carmarthen St Pet *St D* 88-90; P-in-c Walwyn's Castle w Robeston W 90-92; R from 92. *The Rectory, Walwyn's Castle, Haverfordwest SA62 3ED* Tel (01437) 781257

LOWEN, John Michael. b 47. Nottm Univ BTh77. Linc Th Coll 73. **d** 77 **p** 78. C Beeston *S'well* 77-80; C Stratford-on-Avon w Bishopton *Cov* 80-82; V Monkseaton St Mary *Newc* 82-90; V Ponteland 90-95; Chapl HM Pris Leeds 95; P-in-c Sutton St Mary *Linc* from 95. *The Vicarage, Market Place, Long Sutton, Spalding, Lincs PE12 9JJ* Tel (01406) 362033

LOWERSON, John Ridley. b 41. FRHistS83 Leeds Univ BA62 MA65. S Dios Minl Tr Scheme 85. **d** 88 **p** 89. NSM Ringmer *Chich* from 88; Chapl Sussex Univ from 92. *9 Bradford Road, Lewes, E Sussex BN7 9RB* Tel (01273) 473413

LOWLES, Martin John. b 48. Thames Poly BSc72. St Jo Coll Dur DipTh78. **d** 78 **p** 79. C Leyton St Mary w St Edw *Chelmsf* 78-81; C Waltham Abbey 81-85; V E Ham St Paul 85-95; Asst AD Newham 91-95; TR N Huddersfield *Wakef* from 95. *The Vicarage, 75 St John's Road, Huddersfield HD1 5EA* Tel (01484) 427071

LOWMAN, Canon David Walter. b 48. K Coll Lon BD73 AKC73. St Aug Coll Cant 73. **d** 75 **p** 76. C Notting Hill *Lon* 75-78; C Kilburn St Aug w St Jo 78-81; Selection Sec and Voc Adv ACCM 81-86; TR Wickford and Runwell *Chelmsf* 86-93; Dioc Dir of Ords from 93; C Chelmsf All SS from 93; C Chelmsf Ascension from 93; Hon Can Chelmsf Cathl from 93. *25 Roxwell Road, Chelmsford CM1 2LY* Tel (01245) 264187 Fax 348789

LOWNDES, Charles. b 22. MISW57 CQSW72 Rotherham Poly DDW57. **d** 87 **p** 88. NSM Hanley H Ev *Lich* from 87. *7 Beacon Rise, Stone, Staffs ST15 0AL* Tel (01785) 812698

LOWNDES, Richard Owen Lewis. b 63. Univ of Wales (Ban) BD86. Coll of Resurr Mirfield 87. **d** 89 **p** 90. C Milford Haven *St D* 89-91; C Roath St German *Llan* 91-94; Chapl Cardiff R Infirmary 91-94; V Tylorstown w Ynyshir 94-96; Perm to Offic *S'wark* from 96; Asst Chapl St Helier NHS Trust Surrey from 96. *St Helier Hospital, Carshalton, Surrey SM5 1AA, or 21 Kestral Court, Carew Road, Wallington, Surrey SM6 8PW* Tel 0181-644 4343 or 669 7379

LOWRIE, Robert Colledge. b 33. Leeds Univ DipTh57. Chich Th Coll 68. **d** 69 **p** 70. C Sidmouth St Nic *Ex* 69-73; C Sidmouth, Woolbrook and Salcombe Regis 73-74; V W Hill 74-81; RD Ottery 77-82; TR Sidmouth, Woolbrook and Salcombe Regis 81-86; V Redlynch and Morgan's Vale *Sarum* 86-97; rtd 97. *The Farthings, The Copse, Alderbury, Salisbury SP5 3BL* Tel (01722) 711418

LOWRIE, Ronald Malcolm (Ron). b 48. Ripon Hall Ox 70. **d** 72 **p** 73. C Knowle *Birm* 72-75; C Bourton-on-the-Water w Clapton *Glouc* 75-79; R Broadwell, Evenlode, Oddington and Adlestrop 79-81; TV Trowbridge H Trin *Sarum* 81-88; P-in-c Westwood and Wingfield 88-90; R from 90; Chapl Westwood Hosp from 88. *The Rectory, Westwood, Bradford-on-Avon, Wilts BA15 2AF* Tel (01225) 863109

LOWRY, Canon Christopher Somerset. TCD BA47 MA65. **d** 47 **p** 48. C Errigle Keerogue w Ballygawley and Killeshil *Arm* 47-52; I Grange 52-80; Chapl St Luke's Mental Hosp Arm 56-96; RD Tynan 71-91; Can Arm Cathl from 79; Treas 86-88; Prec 88-91; I Loughgall w Grange 80-91; rtd 91. *Fairlow, 10 Mellifont Drive, Armagh BT61 9ES* Tel (01861) 527704

LOWRY, Canon Robert Harold. b 19. TCD BA44 MA49. CITC 44. **d** 44 **p** 45. C Belfast St Mary Magd *Conn* 44-48; C Belfast St Donard *D & D* 48-52; I Drumgooland w Kilcoo 52-59; I Aghalee 59-62; I Willowfield 62-75; RD Hillsborough 70-75; I Lambeg *Conn* 75-89; Can Conn Cathl from 82; rtd 90; Lic to Offic *D & D* from 90. *9 Innisfayle Park, Bangor, Co Down BT19 1DP* Tel (01247) 472423

LOWRY, Stephen Harold. QUB BSc CertEd TCD DipTh. **d** 85 **p** 86. C Coleraine *Conn* 85-88; Bp's Dom Chapl from 87; I Greenisland from 88. *The Rectory, 4 Tinamara, Upper Station Road, Greenisland, Carrickfergus, Co Antrim BT38 8FE* Tel (01232) 863421

LOWSON, Christopher. b 53. AKC75 Heythrop Coll Lon MTh96. Pacific Sch of Religion Berkeley STM78 St Aug Coll Cant 76. **d** 77 **p** 78. C Richmond St Mary *S'wark* 77-79; C Richmond St Mary w St Matthias and St Jo 79-82; P-in-c Eltham H Trin 82-83; V 83-91; R Buriton *Portsm* from 91; V Petersfield from 91; RD Petersfield from 95. *The Vicarage, Shackleford House, 12 Dragon Street, Petersfield, Hants GU31 1AB, or St Peter's Office, Church Path, The Square, Petersfield, Hants GU32 3HS* Tel (01730) 264138 or 260213 Fax 262867

LOWTON, Nicholas Gerard. b 53. St Jo Coll Ox BA76 FRSA94. Glouc Sch of Min 86. **d** 89 **p** 90. Chapl Cheltenham Coll from 89; NSM Prestbury *Glouc* 89-94. *Hazelwell, College Road, Cheltenham, Glos GL53 7JD* Tel (01242) 522665

LOXHAM, Geoffrey Richard. b 40. Hull Univ BA62. Cranmer Hall Dur. **d** 65 **p** 66. C Darwen St Barn *Blackb* 65-68; C Leyland St Andr 68-72; V Preston St Mark 72-79; V Edgeside *Man* 79-91; P-in-c Withnell *Blackb* 91; P-in-c Heapey St Barnabas and Withnell St Paul 91-92; V from 92. *1 Balmoral Drive, Brinscall, Chorley, Lancs PR6 8ST* Tel (01254) 832017

LOXLEY, Deirdre (Dee). b 41. DipEd72. LNSM course 94. **d** 96. NSM Heacham *Nor* from 96. *51 Marram Way, Heacham, Kings Lynn, Norfolk PE31 7AH* Tel (01485) 570994

LOXLEY, Harold. b 43. N Ord Course 79. **d** 82 **p** 83. NSM Sheff Parson Cross St Cecilia *Sheff* 82-87; C Gleadless 87-90; V Sheff St Cath Richmond Road from 90. *St Catherine's Vicarage, 300 Hastilar Road South, Sheffield S13 8EJ* Tel 0114-239 9598

LOXLEY, Ronald Alan Keith. b 26. St Jo Coll Ox BA51 MA55. Wm Temple Coll Rugby 66 Cuddesdon Coll 67. **d** 68 **p** 69. C Swindon Ch Ch *Bris* 68-71; Ind Chapl *Lon* 71-83; Ind Chapl *Chelmsf* 83-92; P-in-c Theydon Garnon 83-92; rtd 92; Perm to Offic *Linc* from 92. *15 Wainwell Mews, Winnowsty Lane, Lincoln LN2 4BF* Tel (01522) 511738

LOXTON, John Sherwood. b 29. Bris Univ BSc50 Birm Univ BA53. Handsworth Coll Birm 50 Chich Th Coll 80. **d** 80 **p** 81. In Meth Ch 50-80; C Haywards Heath St Wilfrid *Chich* 80-82; TV 82-89; V Turners Hill 89-96; rtd 96; Perm to Offic *Chich* from 96. *3 Ashurst Drive, Worth, Crawley, W Sussex RH10 7FS* Tel (01293) 887762

LUBBOCK, David John. b 34. S'wark Ord Course. **d** 87 **p** 88. NSM Tulse Hill H Trin and St Matthias *S'wark* from 87. *78 Claverdale Road, London SW2 2DL* Tel 0181-674 6146

LUCAS, Anthony Stanley. b 41. Man Univ BA62. Qu Coll Birm 63. **d** 65 **p** 66. C N Hammersmith St Kath *Lon* 65-69; C W Wimbledon Ch Ch *S'wark* 69-74; C Caterham 74-78; P-in-c Stockwell St Mich 78-86; V 86-91; P-in-c S'wark St Geo 91; R S'wark St Geo the Martyr w St Jude 91-94; P-in-c S'wark St Alphege 92-94; R S'wark St Geo the Martyr w St Alphege & St Jude from 95. *St George's Rectory, Manciple Street, London SE1 4LW* Tel 0171-407 2796

LUCAS, Arthur Edgar. b 24. Clifton Th Coll 60. **d** 62 **p** 63. C Hyson Green *S'well* 62-66; V Willoughby-on-the-Wolds w Wysall 66-74; P-in-c Widmerpool 71-74; R Collyhurst *Man* 75-80; V Heapey *Blackb* 80-91; rtd 91; Perm to Offic *Blackb* from 91; Perm to Offic *Liv* from 91. *18 Parkway, Standish, Wigan, Lancs WN6 0SJ*

LUCAS, The Ven Brian Humphrey. b 40. CB93. FRSA93 Univ of Wales (Lamp) BA62. St Steph Ho Ox 62. **d** 64 **p** 65. C Llan w Capel Llanilltern *Llan* 64-67; C Neath w Llantwit 67-70; Chapl RAF 70-87; Asst Chapl-in-Chief RAF 87-91; Chapl-in-Chief RAF 91-95; QHC from 88; Perm to Offic *Llan* from 88; Can and Preb Linc Cathl *Linc* 91-95; rtd 95; P-in-c Caythorpe *Linc* from 96. *Pen-y-Coed, 6 Arnhem Drive, Caythorpe, Grantham, Lincs NG32 3DQ* Tel (01400) 272085

LUCAS, Mrs Janet Rosemary. b 46. Open Univ BA76. S Dios Minl Tr Scheme 83. **dss** 86 **d** 87 **p** 94. N Wembley St Cuth *Lon* 86-87; Par Dn 87-88; Par Dn Northolt W End St Jos 88-90; Asst Chapl Ealing Gen Hosp from 90; Par Dn Hanwell St Mary 90-91; Par Dn Hanwell St Chris 90-91; Par Dn Hanwell St Mary w St Chris 91-94; C from 94. *117 Wood End Lane, Northolt, Middx UB5 4JP* Tel 0181-422 4543

LUCAS, Canon John Arthur. b 07. Keble Coll Ox BA29 MA45. Cuddesdon Coll 29. **d** 33 **p** 34. C Ox St Thos *Ox* 33-35; C Brighton St Wilfrid *Chich* 35-37; C London Docks St Pet *Lon* 37-39; V Swanley St Mary *Roch* 39-47; V Ox St Thos *Ox* 47-74; P-in-c 74-79; Hon Can Ch Ch 70-85; rtd 74; Hon C Ox St Mary V w St Cross and St Pet *Ox* 78-85; Perm to Offic 85-96. *12 Lucas Place, Iffley, Oxford OX4 4HA* Tel (01865) 774508

LUCAS, John Kenneth. b 32. LNSM course 92. **d** 95 **p** 96. NSM Deptford St Nic and St Luke *S'wark* 95-97; Perm to Offic from 97. *4 The Colonnade, Grove Street, London SE8 3AY* Tel 0181-691 3161

LUCAS, John Maxwell. b 34. TD85. Cranmer Hall Dur 59. **d** 62 **p** 63. C Lancaster St Mary *Blackb* 62-65; C Lytham St Cuth 65-68; V Blackb St Aid 68-72; V Sparkhill St Jo *Birm* 72-78; CF (TAVR) from 73; V Edgbaston St Aug *Birm* 78-85; V Slyne w Hest *Blackb* 85-89; Chapl HM Young Offender Inst Stoke Heath 89-93; rtd 93. *2 Glendon Close, Market Drayton, Shropshire TF9 1NX* Tel (01630) 652977

LUCAS, Kenneth Ashley. b 18. Wells Th Coll 68. **d** 69 **p** 70. C Rye w Rye Harbour and Playden *Chich* 69-73; R W Chiltington 74-83; rtd 83; Perm to Offic *Chich* from 83. *12 Delves House West, Delves Close, Ringmer, Lewes, E Sussex BN8 5EW* Tel (01273) 813150

LUCAS, Mark Wesley. b 62. Man Univ BSc83. Oak Hill Th Coll BA94. **d** 94 **p** 95. C Harold Wood *Chelmsf* from 94. *8 Archibald Road, Harold Wood, Romford RM3 0RH* Tel (01708) 370977

LUCAS, Canon Paul de Neufville. b 33. Ch Ch Ox BA59 MA59 Cam Univ MA63. Cuddesdon Coll 57. **d** 59 **p** 60. C Westmr St Steph w St Jo *Lon* 59-63; Chapl Trin Hall Cam 63-69; V Greenside *Dur* 69-73; Chapl Shrewsbury Sch 73-77; V Batheaston w St Cath *B & W* 78-88; Preb Wells Cathl 87-88; Can Res and Prec from 88. *4 The Liberty, Wells, Somerset BA5 2SU* Tel (01749) 673188

LUCAS, Peter Stanley. b 21. Sarum Th Coll 48. **d** 50 **p** 51. C Gillingham *Sarum* 50-53; Min Heald Green St Cath CD *Ches* 53-58; V Heald Green St Cath 58-62; V Egremont St Jo 62-65; Canada from 66. *Apt 404, 1241 Fairfield Road, Victoria, British Columbia, Canada, V8V 3B3*

LUCAS, Raymond Charles Henry. b 15. ALCD41. **d** 41 **p** 42. C Southborough St Pet *Roch* 41-43; C Bris H Trin *Bris* 43-47; C Worthing H Trin *Chich* 47-50; V Islington St Jude Mildmay Park *Lon* 50-54; V Southborough St Matt *Roch* 54-61; R Branston *Linc* 61-76; R Parkham, Alwington and Buckland Brewer *Ex* 76-79; rtd 80. *3 Walnut Court, Walnut Road, Chelston, Torquay TQ2 6HS* Tel (01803) 606703

LUCAS, Preb Richard Charles (Dick). b 25. Trin Coll Cam BA49 MA57. Ridley Hall Cam. **d** 51 **p** 52. C Sevenoaks St Nic *Roch* 51-55; Cand Sec CPAS 55-61; Asst Sec 61-67; R St Helen Bishopsgate w St Martin Outwich *Lon* 61-80; P-in-c St Andr Undershaft w St Mary Axe 77-80; R St Helen Bishopsgate w St Andr Undershaft etc from 80; Preb St Paul's Cathl from 85. *The Rectory, 33 Great St Helen's, London EC3A 6AT* Tel 0171-283 2231 Fax 626 0911

LUCAS, Ronald James. b 38. St Aid Birkenhead 64. **d** 67 **p** 68. C Swindon Ch Ch *Bris* 67-71; C Knowle St Martin 71-74; V Swindon St Jo 74-77; TR Swindon St Jo and St Andr 77-81; R Wroughton 81-83; TV Liskeard w St Keyne, St Pinnock and Morval *Truro* 83-87; R St Ive w Quethiock 87-91; R St Ive and Pensilva w Quethiock from 91. *The Rectory, St Ive, Liskeard, Cornwall PL14 3LX* Tel (01579) 382327

LUCAS, Mrs Vivienne Kathleen. b 44. Sarum & Wells Th Coll 84. **d** 87 **p** 94. Chapl Asst W Middx Univ Hosp Isleworth 87-92; Par Dn Whitton St Aug *Lon* 87-94; C Isleworth St Jo from 94. *St Mary's Vicarage, 11 Paget Lane, Isleworth, Middx TW7 6ED* Tel 0181-560 6166

LUCAS, William Wallace. b 29. Sarum Th Coll 56. **d** 59 **p** 60. C Stockton St Jo *Dur* 59-63; V Norton St Mich 63-81; R Broseley w Benthall *Heref* 81-93; P-in-c Jackfield 81-93; P-in-c Linley w Willey and Barrow 81-93; rtd 93; Perm to Offic *Dur* from 93. *105 Side Cliff Road, Sunderland SR6 9JR* Tel 0191-549 1573

LUCK, Benjamin Paul. b 53. BD. St Mich Coll Llan 80. **d** 83 **p** 84. C Blakenall Heath *Lich* 83-87; C Torpoint *Truro* 87-89; V Tuckingmill 89-96; C Knowle St Barn and Holy Cross Inns Court *Bris* from 96. *Holy Cross Vicarage, Inns Court Green, Bristol BS4 1TF* Tel 0117-966 4123

LUCKCUCK, Anthony Michael. b 47. Lon Univ BA70. Wycliffe Hall Ox 70. **d** 77 **p** 78. C Mansfield Woodhouse *S'well* 77-79; C Beeston 79-82; V Harworth 82-85; V Carlton from 85. *St John's Vicarage, 261 Oakdale Road, Nottingham NG4 1BP* Tel 0115-987 4882

LUCKRAFT, Christopher John. b 50. K Coll Lon BD80 AKC80. Ripon Coll Cuddesdon. **d** 81 **p** 82. C Sherborne w Castleton and Lillington *Sarum* 81-84; Bermuda 84-87; Chapl RN from 87. *Royal Naval Chaplaincy Service, Room 203, Victory Building, HM Naval Base, Portsmouth PO1 3LS* Tel (01705) 727903 Fax 727112

LUDLOW, Canon Arthur Percival. b 26. Chich Th Coll 48. **d** 51 **p** 52. C Manston *Ripon* 51-54; C Seacroft 54-58; V Stanground *Ely* 58-72; R Somersham w Pidley and Oldhurst 72-88; P-in-c Gt w Lt Stukeley 88-95; Chapl Hinchingbrooke Hosp 88-95; Hon Can Ely Cathl *Ely* 89-95; rtd 95. *18/20 High Street, Manea, March, Cambs PE15 0JA*

LUDLOW, Christopher George. b 18. AKC42. **d** 42 **p** 43. C N Harrow St Alb *Lon* 42-45; C Gt Stanmore 45-49; Min Can Cant Cathl *Cant* 49-54; Asst Master K Sch Cant 50-54; V Canewdon w Paglesham *Chelmsf* 54-57; Chapl K Alfred Coll *Win* 57-70; Prin Lect Relig Studies 57-76; rtd 83. *23 Penair View, Truro, Cornwall TR1 1XR* Tel (01872) 41898

LUDLOW, Archdeacon of. *See* SAXBEE, The Rt Revd John Charles

LUDLOW, Suffragan Bishop of. *See* SAXBEE, The Rt Revd John Charles

LUFF, Canon Alan Harold Frank. b 28. ARCM77 Univ Coll Ox DipTh52 MA54. Westcott Ho Cam 54. **d** 56 **p** 57. C Stretford St Matt *Man* 56-59; C Swinton St Pet 59-61; Prec Man Cathl 61-68; V Dwygyfylchi *Ban* 68-79; Prec and Sacr Westmr Abbey 79-86; Prec 86-92; Can Res Birm Cathl *Birm* 92-96; rtd 96. *12 Heol Ty'n-y-Cae, Cardiff CF4 6DJ* Tel (01222) 616023

LUFF, Mrs Caroline Margaret Synia. b 44. St Hild Coll Dur BA65 Bris Univ CertEd66. SW Minl Tr Course 87. **d** 90 **p** 94. Par Dn Teignmouth, Ideford w Luton, Ashcombe etc *Ex* from 90. *The Rectory, 30 Dawlish Road, Teignmouth, Devon TQ14 8TG* Tel (01626) 774495

LUFF, Philip Garth. b 42. St Chad's Coll Dur BA63 DipTh64. **d** 65 **p** 66. C Sidmouth St Nic *Ex* 65-69; C Plymstock 69-71; Asst Chapl Worksop Coll Notts 71-74; V Gainsborough St Jo *Linc* 74-80; V E Teignmouth *Ex* 80-89; P-in-c W Teignmouth 85-89; TR Teignmouth, Ideford w Luton, Ashcombe etc from 90. *The Rectory, 30 Dawlish Road, Teignmouth, Devon TQ14 8TG* Tel (01626) 774495

LUGG, Donald Arthur. b 31. St Aid Birkenhead 56. **d** 59 **p** 60. C Folkestone H Trin w Ch Ch *Cant* 59-62; V Seasalter 62-66; Iran 67-73; V Cliftonville *Cant* 74-94; rtd 94; Perm to Offic *Cant* from 94; Reculver from 94. *Redcroft, Vulcan Close, Whitstable, Kent CT9 1DF* Tel (01227) 770434

LUGG, Stuart John. b 26. Glouc Th Course 74. **d** 76 **p** 77. NSM Fairford *Glouc* 76-79; P-in-c Kempsford w Welford 80-88; Perm to Offic from 88. *Content, Station Road, South Cerney, Cirencester, Glos GL7 5UB* Tel (01285) 860498

LUKE, Anthony (Tony). b 58. Down Coll Cam BA81 MA85 Geneva Univ CES84. Ridley Hall Cam 82. **d** 84 **p** 85. C Allestree *Derby* 84-87; C Oakham, Hambleton, Egleton, Braunston and Brooke *Pet* 87-88; V Allenton and Shelton Lock *Derby* from 88; Dir Reader Tr 95-97; Warden of Readers from 97. *St Edmund's Vicarage, Sinfin Avenue, Allenton, Derby DE24 9JA* Tel (01332) 701194

LUMB, David Leslie. b 28. Jes Coll Cam BA52 MA56. Oak Hill Th Coll 52. **d** 54 **p** 55. C Walcot *B & W* 54-58; C Lenton *S'well* 58-60; V Handforth *Ches* 60-71; V Plymouth St Jude *Ex* 71-87; V Southminster *Chelmsf* 87-93; rtd 93. *13 Glebe Close, Redditch, Worcs B98 0AW* Tel (01527) 28623

LUMB, Dennis. b 36. Oak Hill Th Coll 77. **d** 79 **p** 80. C Penn Fields *Lich* 79-84; P-in-c Tibberton, Kinnersley and Preston Wealdmoors 84-89; R Tibberton w Bolas Magna and Waters Upton 89-91; P-in-c Saltfleetby *Linc* 91-96; P-in-c Theddlethorpe 91-96; rtd 96; NSM Wombourne w Trysull and Bobbington *Lich* from 96. *59 Six Ashes Road, Bobbington, Stourbridge, Staffs DY7 5BT*

LUMBY, Jonathan Bertram. b 39. Em Coll Cam BA62 MA66 Lon Univ PGCE66. Ripon Hall Ox 62. **d** 64 **p** 65. C Moseley St Mary *Birm* 64-65; Asst Master Enfield Gr Sch 66-67; C Hall Green

Ascension 67-70; V Melling *Liv* 70-81; P-in-c Milverton w Halse and Fitzhead *B & W* 81-82; R 82-86; P-in-c Gisburn *Bradf* 90-93; Dioc Rural Adv 90-93; P-in-c Easton w Colton and Marlingford *Nor* from 95; Dioc Missr from 95. *The Vicarage, 107 Dereham Road, Easton, Norwich NR9 5ES* Tel (01603) 880197

LUMGAIR, Michael Hugh Crawford. b 43. Lon Univ BD71. Oak Hill Th Coll 66. **d** 71 **p** 72. C Chorleywood Ch Ch *St Alb* 71-74; C Prestonville St Luke *Chich* 74-75; C Attenborough *S'well* 75-80; R Tollerton 80-91; V Bexleyheath St Pet *Roch* from 91. *St Peter's Vicarage, 50 Bristow Road, Bexleyheath, Kent DA7 4QA* Tel 0181-303 8713

LUMLEY, William. b 22. TCD BA44 MA49 BD49 QUB PhD77. Edgehill Th Coll Belf 49. **d** 50 **p** 51. C Dublin Drumcondra w N Strand *D & G* 50-52; Clerical V Ch Ch Cathl Dublin 52-53; C Clooney *D & R* 55-59; I Aghabog *Clogh* 59-63; V Newhey *Man* 63-66; I Ballybay *Clogh* 66-73; I Derryvullen S w Garvary 73-82; I Killucan w Clonard and Castlelost *M & K* 82-88; rtd 88. *Gallows Hill, 104 Ballyquinn Road, Limavady, Co Londonderry BT49 9EY* Tel (01504) 766174

LUMMIS, Elizabeth Howieson. *See* McNAB, Mrs Elizabeth Howieson

LUMSDEN, Frank. b 20. Edin Th Coll 51. **d** 53 **p** 54. C Usworth *Dur* 53-56; V Lynesack 56-76; R Castle Eden w Monkhesleden 76-86; rtd 86; Perm to Offic *Dur* from 86; Perm to Offic *Ripon* from 90. *Cloud High, Eggleston, Barnard Castle, Co Durham DL12 0AU* Tel (01833) 50644

LUMSDON, Keith. b 45. Linc Th Coll 68. **d** 71 **p** 72. C S Westoe *Dur* 71-74; C Jarrow St Paul 74-77; TV Jarrow 77-88; V Ferryhill from 88. *St Luke's Vicarage, Church Lane, Ferryhill, Co Durham DL17 8LT* Tel (01740) 651438

LUND, David Peter. b 46. N Ord Course 88. **d** 91 **p** 92. C Maghull *Liv* 91-94; V Hindley All SS from 94. *The Vicarage, 192 Atherton Road, Hindley, Wigan, Lancs WN2 3XA* Tel (01942) 551757

LUND, John Edward. b 48. St Jo Coll Dur 78. **d** 80 **p** 81. C Peterlee *Dur* 80-83; C Bishopton w Gt Stainton 83-85; C Redmarshall 83-85; C Grindon and Stillington 83-85; V Hart w Elwick Hall from 85; Hon Chapl Miss to Seamen from 85. *The Vicarage, Hart, Hartlepool, Cleveland TS27 3AP* Tel (01429) 262340

LUNGLEY, Canon John Sydney. b 41. St Pet Coll Ox BA64 MA70. St Steph Ho Ox 64. **d** 66 **p** 67. C Burslem St Werburgh *Lich* 66-70; C Codsall 70-73; V Ocker Hill 73-88; RD Wednesbury 84-88; V Kingswinford St Mary 88-93; V Kingswinford St Mary *Worc* 93-96; TR from 96; Hon Can Worc Cathl from 94. *The Vicarage, 17 Penzer Street, Kingswinford, W Midlands DY6 7AA* Tel (01384) 273716

LUNN, Preb Brooke Kingsmill. b 32. TCD BA62 MA66. Chich Th Coll 62. **d** 64 **p** 65. C Northolt Park St Barn *Lon* 64-66; C N St Pancras All Hallows 66-68; P-in-c Hornsey St Luke 68-79; V Stroud Green H Trin from 79; AD W Haringey 90-95; Preb St Paul's Cathl from 96. *The Vicarage, Granville Road, London N4 4EL* Tel 0181-340 2051

LUNN, Christopher James Edward. b 34. AKC58. **d** 59 **p** 60. C Clapham H Trin *S'wark* 59-62; C Cranleigh *Guildf* 63-64; C Ham St Andr *S'wark* 64-66; V Ham St Rich 66-75; V Coulsdon St Andr 75-96; rtd 96. *Ty Newydd, Cilgerran, Cardigan SA43 2SN* Tel (01239) 614514

LUNN, David. b 47. Bris Univ BSc69 Dur Univ BA73 DipTh74. St Jo Coll Dur 71. **d** 74 **p** 75. C Aigburth *Liv* 74-77; C Slough *Ox* 77-81; P-in-c Haversham w Lt Linford 81-84; R Haversham w Lt Linford, Tyringham w Filgrave 84-93; RD Newport 86-92; TR Walton Milton Keynes from 93. *The Rectory, Walton Road, Wavendon, Milton Keynes MK17 8LW* Tel (01908) 582839

✠**LUNN, The Rt Revd David Ramsay.** b 30. K Coll Cam BA53 MA57. Cuddesdon Coll 53. **d** 55 **p** 56 **c** 80. C Sugley *Newc* 55-59; C N Gosforth 59-63; Chapl Linc Th Coll 63-66; Sub-Warden 66-70; V Cullercoats St Geo *Newc* 71-72; TR 72-80; RD Tynemouth 75-80; Bp Sheff 80-97; rtd 97. *Rivendell, 28 Southfield Road, Wetwang, Driffield, N Humberside YO25 9XX*

LUNN, Leonard Arthur. b 42. Trin Coll Bris 69. **d** 72 **p** 73. C Walthamstow St Mary w St Steph *Chelmsf* 72-75; V Collier Row St Jas 75-85; V Collier Row St Jas and Havering-atte-Bower 86-87; Sen Chapl St Chris Hospice Sydenham *S'wark* from 87. *St Christopher's Hospice, 51-59 Lawrie Park Road, London SE26 6DZ* Tel 0181-778 9252 or 699 3305 Fax 659 8680

LUNN, Canon William Bell. b 21. Edin Th Coll 47. **d** 50 **p** 51. C Stirling *Edin* 50-53; P-in-c Bo'ness 53-57; P-in-c Linlithgow 53-57; R Edin St Mark 57-75; Can St Mary's Cathl 68-75; R Fochabers *Mor* 75-86; R Aberlour 75-86; Can St Andr Cathl Inverness 79-86; Hon Can from 86; rtd 86. *67 Woodside Drive, Forres, Morayshire IV36 0UF* Tel (01309) 675208

LUNNEY, Canon Henry. b 31. ACIB57. Wycliffe Hall Ox 73. **d** 74 **p** 75. C Ipswich St Aug *St E* 74-77; P-in-c Westerfield w Tuddenham St Martin 77-83; R Westerfield and Tuddenham w Witnesham from 83; Asst Dioc Chr Stewardship Adv 78-83; Hon Can St E Cathl from 92. *The Rectory, Westerfield, Ipswich IP6 9AG* Tel (01473) 251073

LUNNON, Canon Robert Reginald. b 31. K Coll Lon BD55 AKC55. St Boniface Warminster 55. **d** 56 **p** 57. C Maidstone St Mich *Cant* 56-58; C Deal St Leon 58-62; V Sturry 63-68; V Norbury St Steph 68-77; V Orpington All SS *Roch* 77-96; RD Orpington 79-95; Hon Can Roch Cathl 96; rtd 96; Perm to Offic *Cant* from 96. *10 King Edward Road, Deal, Kent CT14 6QL* Tel (01304) 364898

LUNT, Colin Peter. b 54. York Univ BA75 Leeds Poly DipLib77. Trin Coll Bris 95. **d** 97. C Westbury-on-Trym H Trin *Bris* from 97. *16 Southfield Road, Westbury-on-Trym, Bristol BS9 3BH* Tel 0117-962 1336 Fax as telephone E-mail cplunt@aol.com

LUNT, Derek. b 32. St Jo Coll Dur 51. St Aid Birkenhead 55. **d** 57 **p** 58. C Toxteth St Cypr w Ch Ch *Liv* 57-59; C Prescot 59-61; R Much Dewchurch w Llanwarne and Llandinabo *Heref* 61-67; R Pembridge w Moor Court and Shobdon 67-74; Chapl Lucton Sch Herefordshire 71-74; rtd 91; Perm to Offic *Worc* from 93. *The Firs, 243 West Malvern Road, Malvern, Worcs WR14 4BE* Tel (01684) 573932

LUNT, Dr Margaret Joan. b 44. Leeds Univ MBChA68. Cranmer Hall Dur CTMin91. **d** 94 **p** 95. C Stanford-le-Hope w Mucking *Chelmsf* from 94. *Glebe House, Wharf Road, Stanford-le-Hope, Essex SS17 0BY*

LUNT, Canon Ronald Sowden. b 30. Leeds Univ BA56. Ely Th Coll 56. **d** 58 **p** 59. C Stockport St Thos *Ches* 58-61; C Ellesmere Port 61-65; V Newton in Mottram 65-78; RD Ches 78-95; TR Ches Team 78-96; Hon Can Ches Cathl 82-96; rtd 96; Perm to Offic *Ches* from 96. *Walsingham, 23 Edinburgh Way, Chester CH4 7AS* Tel (01244) 679523

LURIE, Miss Gillian Ruth (Gill). b 42. LRAM62 GNSM63 ACertCM80. Gilmore Ho 68. **dss** 74 **d** 87 **p** 94. Camberwell St Phil and St Mark *S'wark* 74-76; Haddenham *Ely* 76-79; Dioc Lay Min Adv 79-86; Longthorpe *Pet* 79-81; Pet H Spirit Bretton 81-86; Bramley *Ripon* 86-87; C 87-88; TD 88-93; P-in-c Methley w Mickletown from 93. *The Rectory, Church Side, Methley, Leeds LS26 9BJ* Tel (01977) 515278

LURKINGS, Edward Henry. b 28. AKC53 Lon Univ BSc68 MSc70 PhD81. **d** 54 **p** 55. C Brookfield St Mary *Lon* 54-59; C Cricklewood St Pet 59-62; Ind Chapl 62-71; Hon C Luton St Mary *St Alb* 72-84; V Potterspury, Furtho, Yardley Gobion and Cosgrove *Pet* 84-92; rtd 92. *Glasfryn, Abercych, Boncath SA37 0JL* Tel (01239) 87576

LURY, Anthony Patrick. b 49. K Coll Lon BD71 AKC71. St Aug Coll Cant 71. **d** 72 **p** 73. C Richmond St Mary *S'wark* 72-76; P-in-c Streatham Hill St Marg 76-81; V Salfords 81-90; V Emscote *Cov* from 90. *All Saints' Vicarage, Vicarage Fields, Warwick CV34 5NJ* Tel (01926) 492073

LURY, Denys Patrick. b 15. Dur Univ LTh48. Bps' Coll Cheshunt 36. **d** 38 **p** 39. C Bromley St Mich *Lon* 38-40; V Maidstone St Mich *Cant* 63-72; Chapl St Monica Home Westbury-on-Trym 72-80; rtd 80; Perm to Offic *Bris* from 80. *8 Avon Court, Lawn Road, Bristol BS16 5BL* Tel 0117-958 6673

LUSBY, Dennis John. b 27. Brentwood Coll of Educn CertEd70. **d** 93 **p** 94. NSM Grayshott *Guildf* from 93. *Squirrels Dray, Waggoners Way, Grayshott, Hindhead, Surrey GU26 6DX* Tel (01428) 604419

LUSCOMBE, John Nickels. b 45. AKC68. **d** 69 **p** 70. C Stoke Newington St Faith, St Matthias and All SS *Lon* 69-74; V Tottenham St Phil 74-81; Zimbabwe 82-86; V Queensbury All SS *Lon* from 86. *The Vicarage, Waltham Drive, Edgware, Middx HA8 5PQ* Tel 0181-952 4536 or 952 0744

✠**LUSCOMBE, The Rt Revd Lawrence Edward (Ted).** b 24. ACA52 FSA80 Dundee Univ LLD87 MPhil91 PhD93. K Coll Lon 63. **d** 63 **p** 64 **c** 75. C Glas St Marg *Glas* 63-66; R Paisley St Barn 66-71; Provost St Paul's Cathl Dundee *Bre* 71-75; R Dundee St Paul 71-75; Bp Bre 75-90; Primus 85-90; OStJ from 85; rtd 90; Perm to Offic *Bre* from 90. *Woodville, Kirkton of Tealing, Dundee DD4 0RD* Tel (01382) 380331

LUSTED, Jack Andrew. b 58. Sussex Univ BSc79 PGCE81. St Steph Ho Ox 88. **d** 90 **p** 91. C Moulsecoomb *Chich* 90-93; C Southwick 93-97; R Lurgashall, Lodsworth and Selham from 97. *The Vicarage, Lodsworth, Petworth, W Sussex GU28 9DE* Tel (01798) 861274

LUSTY, Ronald Henry. b 23. Ox NSM Course. **d** 84 **p** 85. NSM Tilehurst St Mary *Ox* 84-88; NSM Reading H Trin from 88. *St Benedict's, 11 Juniper Way, Tilehurst, Reading RG3 6NB* Tel 0118-942 8669

LUTES, David Martin. **d** 97. NSM Whittle-le-Woods *Blackb* from 97. *16 Homestead, Clayton Brook, Preston PR5 8BA* Tel (01772) 313890

LUTHER, Richard Grenville Litton (Dick). b 42. Lon Univ BD64. Tyndale Hall Bris 66. **d** 68 **p** 69. C Preston St Mary *Blackb* 68-70; C Bishopsworth *Bris* 70-71; C Radipole *Sarum* 72-76; TV Radipole and Melcombe Regis 77-90; TR Hampreston from 90. *The Rectory, 9 Pinewood Road, Ferndown, Wimborne, Dorset BH22 9RW* Tel (01202) 872084

LUTTON, Percy Theodore Bell Boyce. b 24. TCD BA45 MA48. **d** 46 **p** 48. C Whitehouse *Conn* 47-49; C Dudley St Jo *Worc* 49-52; V Stambermill 52-61; V Wribbenhall 61-80; R Castlemorton, Hollybush and Birtsmorton 80-89; rtd 89; Perm to Offic *Lich* from 90. *23 Bridgeman Road, Oswestry, Shropshire SY11 2JP* Tel (01691) 656425

✠**LUXMOORE, The Rt Revd Christopher Charles.** b 26. Trin Coll Cam BA50 MA54. Chich Th Coll 50. **d** 52 **p** 53 **c** 84. C Newc St Jo *Newc* 52-55; C-in-c Newsham St Bede CD 55-57; V Newsham 57-58; Trinidad and Tobago 58-66; V Headingley *Ripon* 67-81; Hon Can Ripon Cathl 80-81; Can Res and Prec Chich Cathl

Chich 81-84; Bp Bermuda 84-89; Adn Lewes and Hastings *Chich* 89-91; rtd 91; Provost Woodard Corp (S Division) 89-96; Asst Bp Chich from 91. *42 Willowbed Drive, Chichester, W Sussex PO19 2JB* Tel (01243) 784680

LYALL, Canon Graham. b 37. Univ of Wales (Lamp) BA61 Birm Univ DipTh63. Qu Coll Birm 61. **d** 63 **p** 64. C Middlesbrough Ascension *York* 63-67; C Kidderminster St Mary *Worc* 67-72; V Dudley St Aug Holly Hall 72-79; P-in-c Barbourne 79-81; V 81-93; RD Worc E 83-89; Hon Can Worc Cathl from 85; TR Malvern Link w Cowleigh from 93. *St Matthias' Rectory, 12 Lambourne Avenue, Malvern, Worcs WR14 1NL* Tel (01684) 573834

LYDDON, David Andrew. b 47. LDSRCSEng70 Lon Univ BDS70. SW Minl Tr Course 90. **d** 93 **p** 94. NSM Tiverton St Pet *Ex* 93-95; NSM Tiverton St Pet and Chevithorne w Cove from 95. *Hightrees, 19 Patches Road, Tiverton, Devon EX16 5AH* Tel (01884) 257250

LYDON, Mrs Barbara. b 34. Gilmore Ho 64. **dss** 72 **d** 87 **p** 94. Rastrick St Matt *Wakef* 72-85; Upper Hopton 85-87; Par Dn 87; D-in-c Kellington w Whitley 87-94; P-in-c 94-95; rtd 95; Perm to Offic *Wakef* from 95. *17 Garlick Street, Brighouse, W Yorkshire HD6 3PW* Tel (01484) 722704

LYES-WILSDON, Mrs Patricia Mary (Pat). b 45. ALA65 Open Univ BA86. Glouc Th Course 84 Qu Coll Birm 86. **d** 87 **p** 94. C Thornbury *Glouc* 87-94; P-in-c Cromhall w Tortworth and Tytherington from 94; Dioc Voc Officer from 94. *The New Rectory, Rectory Lane, Cromhall, Wotton-under-Edge, Glos GL12 8AN* Tel (01454) 294767

LYNAS, Mrs Judith (Judy). b 53. Hollings Coll Man HND74. S Dios Minl Tr Scheme 89. **d** 92 **p** 94. Par Dn Lytchett Minster *Sarum* 92-94; C 94-96. *14 Belle Vue Road, Lower Parkstone, Poole, Dorset BH14 8TW*

LYNAS, The Very Revd Norman Noel. b 55. St Andr Univ MTh78. CITC 78. **d** 79 **p** 80. C Knockbreda *D & D* 79-81; C Holywood 81-85; I Portadown St Columba *Arm* 85-91; Dioc Info Officer 86-89; Tutor for Aux Min (Arm) 88-91; Radio Officer (Arm) 90-91; I Kilkenny w Aghour and Kilmanagh *C & O* from 91; Dean Ossory from 91. *The Deanery, Kilkenny, Irish Republic* Tel Kilkenny (56) 21516 Fax 51817

LYNAS, Stephen Brian. b 52. St Jo Coll Nottm BTh77. **d** 78 **p** 79. C Penn *Lich* 78-81; Relig Progr Org BBC Radio Stoke-on-Trent 81-84; C Hanley H Ev 81-82; C Edensor 82-84; Relig Progr Producer BBC Bris 85-88; Lic to Offic *Bris* 85-92; Relig Progr Sen Producer BBC S & W England 88-91; Hd Relig Progr TV South 91-92; Community (and Relig) Affairs Ed Westcountry TV from 92; Perm to Offic *Cant* 91-92; Perm to Offic *Ex* from 92. *Shippen House, Brownston, Rattery, South Brent, Devon TQ10 9LQ* Tel (01364) 642015

LYNCH, Preb Donald MacLeod. b 11. CBE72. Pemb Coll Cam BA34 MA37. Wycliffe Hall Ox. **d** 35 **p** 36. C Chelsea Ch Ch *Lon* 35-38; Public Preacher *St Alb* 38-40; Tutor Oak Hill Th Coll 38-40; C Stonebridge St Mich *Lon* 40-42; Min Queensbury All SS 42-50; V Tunbridge Wells St Luke *Roch* 50-53; Prin CA Tr Coll 53-61; Lic to Offic *Lon* 53-76; Chief Sec CA 60-76; Preb St Paul's Cathl *Lon* 64-76; Chapl to The Queen 69-81; P-in-c Seal St Lawr *Roch* 74-85; rtd 76; RD Sevenoaks *Roch* 79-84; P-in-c Underriver 80-85; Perm to Offic *Chich* from 86; Perm to Offic *Roch* 86-93. *Flat 2, 20 Grassington Road, Eastbourne, E Sussex BN20 7BJ* Tel (01323) 720849

LYNCH, Mrs Eithne Elizabeth Mary. b 45. CITC BTh94. **d** 97. C Douglas Union w Frankfield *C, C & R* from 97. *64 Willow Bank, Church Road, Blackrock, Cork, Irish Republic* Tel Cork (21) 358226 Mobile 087-535002

LYNCH, James. EAMTC 93. **d** 96 **p** 97. NSM High Oak *Nor* from 96. *Beechenlea, Church Lane, Wicklewood, Wymondham, Norfolk NR18 9QH*

LYNCH-WATSON, Graham Leslie. b 30. AKC55. **d** 56 **p** 57. C New Eltham All SS *S'wark* 56-60; C W Brompton St Mary *Lon* 60-62; V Camberwell St Bart *S'wark* 62-66; V Purley St Barn 67-77; C Caversham *Ox* 77-81; C Caversham and Mapledurham 81-85; P-in-c Warwick St Paul *Cov* 85-86; V 86-92; rtd 92. *11 Crouch Street, Banbury, Oxon OX16 9PP* Tel (01295) 263172

LYNDS, Thomas George. b 34. Lon Coll of Div ALCD62 LTh74. **d** 62 **p** 63. C Eastbourne All So *Chich* 62-65; C Edgware *Lon* 65-72; V Wimbledon St Luke *S'wark* 72-85; P-in-c Rainham *Chelmsf* 85-92; P-in-c Wennington 85-92; R Rainham w Wennington 92-95; P-in-c Gt Canfield 95-96; R Gt Canfield w High Roding and Aythorpe Roding from 96. *The Rectory, Great Canfield, Dunmow, Essex CM6 1JX* Tel (01279) 871300

LYNE, Peter. b 27. Sheff Univ BA51. Qu Coll Birm 51. **d** 53 **p** 54. C Newland St Aug *York* 53-55; C Harworth *S'well* 55-56; C Burbage *Derby* 56-58; V Horsley Woodhouse 58-62; V Rawcliffe *Sheff* 62-69; V Elvaston and Shardlow *Derby* 69-74; P-in-c Ashbourne St Jo 74-80; P-in-c Kniveton w Hognaston 75-80; P-in-c Fenny Bentley, Thorpe and Tissington 77-78; P-in-c Osmaston w Edlaston 78-80; P-in-c Lt Eaton 80-84; P-in-c Holbrooke 80-84; V Holbrook and Lt Eaton 84-91; rtd 91; Perm to Offic *Derby* from 91. *3 Vicarage Close, High Street, Belper, Derbyshire DE56 1TB* Tel (01773) 829188

LYNE, Roger Howard. b 28. Mert Coll Ox BA52 MA56. Oak Hill Th Coll 52. **d** 54 **p** 55. C Rugby St Matt *Cov* 54-58; C Weymouth St Jo *Sarum* 58-61; V Newchapel *Lich* 61-65; C Bucknall and Bagnall 76-81; Perm to Offic *Win* from 82; rtd 88. *21 Copse Road, Burley, Ringwood, Hants BH24 4EG* Tel (01425) 402232

LYNESS, Nicholas Jonathan. b 55. **d** 97. C Reading Greyfriars *Ox* from 97. *26 Prospect Street, Reading RG1 7YG* Tel 0118-959 9930

LYNETT, Anthony Martin (Tony). b 54. K Coll Lon BD75 AKC75 Darw Coll Cam PGCE76. Sarum & Wells Th Coll 77. **d** 78 **p** 79. C Swindon Ch Ch *Bris* 78-81; C Leckhampton SS Phil and Jas w Cheltenham St Jas *Glouc* 81-83; Asst Chapl HM Pris Glouc 83-88; Chapl from 91; V Coney Hill *Glouc* 83-88; Chapl HM Young Offender Inst Deerbolt 88-91; P-in-c Glouc St Mark *Glouc* from 91. *St Mark's Vicarage, Sandhurst Lane, Gloucester GL2 9AB* Tel (01452) 523843 Fax 310302

LYNN, Mrs Antonia Jane. b 59. Girton Coll Cam BA80 MA84. St Steph Ho Ox 82. **dss** 84 **d** 87. Portsm Cathl *Portsm* 84-87; D-in-c Camberwell St Mich w All So w Em *S'wark* 87-91; Par Dn Newington St Mary 87-91; Perm to Offic 91-94; Chapl Horton Hosp Epsom 91-94; Hon Par Dn Ewell *Guildf* from 94; Perm to Offic *Lon* from 94. *7 Kingsmead Close, West Ewell, Epsom, Surrey KT19 9RD* Tel 0181-786 8983 or 0171-580 2492

LYNN, Dixon. b 09. Wesley Coll Leeds 34 Ely Th Coll 46. **d** 47 **p** 48. Meth Min 38-45; C Newc St Gabr *Newc* 47-52; V Ulgham 52-55; V Whittonstall 55-57; R Lerwick *Ab* 57-62; R Wark *Newc* 62-75; V Birtley 62-75; rtd 75; Perm to Offic *Newc* from 75. *Bridge House, Newbrough, Hexham, Northd NE47 5AR* Tel (01434) 674219

LYNN, Frank Trevor. b 36. Keble Coll Ox BA61 MA63. St Steph Ho Ox 61. **d** 63 **p** 64. C W Derby St Mary *Liv* 63-65; C Chorley *Ches* 65-68; V Altrincham St Jo 68-72; Chapl RN 72-88; Hon C Walworth St Jo *S'wark* 88-90; C Cheam 90-96. *7 Kingsmead Close, West Ewell, Epsom, Surrey KT19 9RD* Tel 0181-786 8983

LYNN, Jeffrey. b 39. Moore Th Coll Sydney EMMTC 76. **d** 79 **p** 80. C Littleover *Derby* 79-80; Hon C Allestree 80-85; Chapl HM Pris Man 85-86; Chapl HM Pris Kirkham 86-93; Chapl HM Pris Wakef 93-95; Chapl HM Open Pris Sudbury 95-96; Chapl HM Pris Foston Hall 95-96; rtd 96. *Address temp unknown*

LYNN, John Cairns. b 40. Surrey Univ BSc63 Lon Univ MSc66. NW Ord Course 73. **d** 76 **p** 77. NSM Hunts Cross *Liv* 76-80; Chapl Liv Cathl from 80. *2 Bancroft Close, Hunts Cross, Liverpool L25 0LS* Tel 0151-486 7833

LYNN, Peter Anthony. b 38. Keele Univ BA62 St Jo Coll Cam BA64 MA68 PhD72. Westcott Ho Cam 67. **d** 68 **p** 69. C Soham *Ely* 68-72; Min Can St Paul's Cathl *Lon* 72-78; Perm to Offic *St Alb* 78-86; Min Can and Sacr St Paul's Cathl *Lon* 86-88; C Westmr St Matt 89-91; V Glynde, W Firle and Beddingham *Chich* from 91. *The Parsonage, Firle, Lewes, E Sussex BN8 6NP* Tel (01273) 858227

LYNN, Archdeacon of. *See* FOOTTIT, The Ven Anthony Charles

LYNN, Suffragan Bishop of. *See* CONNER, The Rt Revd David John

LYON, Adrian David. b 55. Coll of Resurr Mirfield 84. **d** 87 **p** 88. C Crewe St Andr *Ches* 87-90; C Altrincham St Geo 90-91; TV Accrington *Blackb* from 91. *St Peter's Vicarage, 151 Willows Lane, Accrington, Lancs BB5 0LN* Tel (01254) 382173

LYON, Christopher David. b 55. Strathclyde Univ LLB75 Edin Univ BD81. Edin Th Coll 78. **d** 81 **p** 82. C Dumfries *Glas* 81-84; P-in-c Alexandria 84-88; R Greenock from 88. *St John's Rectory, 24 Forsyth Street, Greenock, Renfrewshire PA16 9DZ* Tel (01475) 720750

LYON, Dennis. b 36. Lon Univ DipTh66. Wycliffe Hall Ox 64. **d** 67 **p** 68. C Woodthorpe *S'well* 67-70; Warden Walton Cen 70-72; V W Derby Gd Shep *Liv* 72-81; V Billinge from 81; AD Wigan W from 89. *91 Newton Road East, Billinge, Wigan, Lancs WN5 7LB* Tel (01744) 892210

LYON, Canon Donald Robert. b 20. Trin Coll Cam BA41 PhD44 MA45. Linc Th Coll 46. **d** 47 **p** 48. C Dursley *Glouc* 47-51; C Brislington St Luke *Bris* 51-52; V Glouc St Mark *Glouc* 52-85; Hon Can Glouc Cathl 74-85; RD Glouc City 77-83; rtd 85; Perm to Offic *Glouc* from 86. *12 Doverdale Drive, Longlevens, Glos GL2 0NN* Tel (01452) 524070

LYON, John Forrester. b 39. Edin Th Coll CertEd95. **d** 95 **p** 96. C Greenock *Glas* from 95; C Gourock from 95; Chapl Ardgowan Hospice from 95. *St Bartholomew's Rectory, 86 Albert Road, Gourock, Renfrewshire PA19 1NN* Tel (01475) 631828

LYON, John Harry. b 51. S Dios Minl Tr Scheme 86. **d** 89 **p** 90. NSM S Patcham *Chich* 89-91; C Chich St Paul and St Pet 91-94; R Earnley and E Wittering from 94. *The Rectory, East Wittering, Chichester, W Sussex PO20 8PS* Tel (01243) 672260

LYON, Stephen Paul. b 49. Univ of Wales (Swansea) BSc71. Trin Coll Bris 74. **d** 77 **p** 78. C Hull Newland St Jo *York* 77-81; Chapl Lee Abbey 81-84; V Norbiton *S'wark* 84-92; RD Kingston 88-92; Prin S'wark LNSM Scheme from 92. *11 Cupar Road, London SW11 4JW* Tel 0171-622 4925 or 378 7506 Fax 403 6497

LYONS, Bruce Twyford. b 37. K Alfred's Coll Win CertEd61. Tyndale Hall Bris DipTh69. **d** 70 **p** 71. C Virginia Water *Guildf* 70-73; Chapl Ostend w Knokke and Bruges *Eur* 73-78; V E Ham St Paul *Chelmsf* 78-85; V St Alb Ch Ch *St Alb* 85-91; Chapl Wellingborough Sch 92-95; P-in-c Stogumber w Nettlecombe and Monksilver *B & W* from 96. *The Rectory, Vellow Road, Stogumber, Taunton, Somerset TA4 3TL* Tel (01984) 656221

LYONS, Edward Charles. b 44. Nottm Univ BTh75 LTh. St Jo Coll Nottm 71. **d** 75 **p** 76. C Cambridge St Martin *Ely* 75-78; P-in-c Bestwood Park *S'well* 78-85; R W Hallam and Mapperley *Derby* from 85. *The Rectory, The Village, West Hallam, Ilkeston, Derbyshire DE7 6GR* Tel 0115-932 4695

LYONS, Margaret Rose Marie. b 47. LNSM course 89. **d** 89. NSM Gainsborough All SS *Linc* 89-91. *1C Common Road, Low Moor, Bradford BD12 0NT*

LYONS, Paul Benson. b 44. Qu Coll Birm 68. **d** 69 **p** 70. C Rugby St Andr *Cov* 69-70; C Moston St Jo *Man* 70-72; PV Llan Cathl *Llan* 73-74; C Brookfield St Anne, Highgate Rise *Lon* 74-75; Perm to Offic 76-82; C Westmr St Sav and St Jas Less 82-86; V Gt Cambridge Road St Jo and St Jas from 86. *St John's Vicarage, 113 Creighton Road, London N17 8JS* Tel 0181-808 4077

LYONS, William. b 22. LNSM course 78. **d** 80 **p** 81. NSM Glenrothes *St And* 80-81; NSM Kirkcaldy 81-91; NSM Kinghorn 81-91; rtd 91. *44 Annandale Gardens, Glenrothes, Fife KY6 1JD* Tel (01592) 751905

✠LYTH, The Rt Revd Richard Edward. b 16. St Edm Hall Ox BA38 MA55. Oak Hill Th Coll. **d** 56 **p** 57 **c** 67. C Arthuret *Carl* 56-59; Uganda 59-72; Bp Kigezi 67-72; C Chorleywood St Andr *St Alb* 74-81; rtd 81. *31 Backwoods Lane, Lindfield, Haywards Heath, W Sussex RH16 2EQ* Tel (01444) 482500

LYTLE, Canon John Deaville. b 23. Wadh Coll Ox BA50 MA52. Wycliffe Hall Ox 50. **d** 51 **p** 52. C Ilkeston St Mary *Derby* 51-56; P-in-c Brassington 56-59; V Bradbourne and Brassington 59-89; RD Wirksworth 78-88; Hon Can Derby Cathl 82-89; rtd 89; Perm to Offic *Derby* from 89. *14 Manor Road, Ashbourne, Derbyshire DE6 1EH* Tel (01335) 346588

M

MABBS, Miss Margaret Joyce. b 24. St Hilda's Coll Ox BA45 MA47 DipEd46 DipRS82. S'wark Ord Course 79. **dss** 82 **d** 87 **p** 94. Eltham Park St Luke *S'wark* 82-87; NSM from 87. *70 Westmount Road, London SE9 1JE* Tel 0181-850 4621

McADAM, Alexander William. b 15. Univ of Wales BA37 Jes Coll Ox BA40 MA43. St Mich Coll Llan 39. **d** 41 **p** 42. C Bedwas *Mon* 41-44; C Pontnewynydd 44-50; V Grosmont and Skenfrith 50-85; rtd 85. *Sally Ruck, Rectory Lane, Grosmont, Abergavenny NP7 8LW* Tel (01981) 240421

McADAM, Gordon Paul. b 66. QUB BSc88 TCD BTh93. CITC 90. **d** 93 **p** 94. C Drumglass w Moygashel *Arm* 93-96; I Dungiven w Bovevagh *D & R* from 96. *14 Main Street, Dungiven, Londonderry BT47 4LB* Tel (01504) 741226

McADAM, Canon Michael Anthony. b 30. K Coll Cam BA52 MA56. Westcott Ho Cam 54. **d** 56 **p** 57. C Towcester w Easton Neston *Pet* 56-59; Chapl Hurstpierpoint Coll Hassocks 60-68; Bp's Chapl *Lon* 69-73; R Much Hadham *St Alb* 73-95; Hon Can St Alb 89-95; rtd 95; RD Oundle *Pet* from 96. *Parkers Patch, 55 Barnwell, Peterborough PE8 5PG* Tel (01832) 273451

✠McADOO, The Most Revd Henry Robert. b 16. TCD BA38 PhD40 BD48 DD49. Seabury-Western Th Sem Hon STD62. **d** 39 **p** 40 **c** 62. C Waterford H Trin *C & O* 39-43; I Castleventry w Ardfield *C, C & R* 43-48; I Kilmocomogue 48-52; RD Glansalney W and Bere 48-52; Preb Cork Cathl 49-52; Can Cloyne Cathl 49-52; Dean Cork 52-62; Can St Patr Cathl Dublin 59-62; Bp Ossory, Ferns and Leighlin 62-77; Dean Leighlin *C & O* 62-63; Abp Dublin *D & G* 77-85; rtd 85. *2 The Paddocks, Dalkey, Co Dublin, Irish Republic* Tel Dublin (1) 280 0063

McALEESE, William Henry. b 27. TCD BA53. St Aug Coll Cant 60. **d** 60 **p** 61. C Donaghadee *D & D* 60-62; S Africa 62-66; C Dorking w Ranmore *Guildf* 66-68; I Billis *K, E & A* 68-71; C W Byfleet *Guildf* 71-74; C Gt Bookham 74-77; C Epsom Common Ch Ch 77-80; C Leatherhead 80-86; rtd 86; Perm to Offic *D & D* from 87; Perm to Offic *Conn* from 90. *Hollygate Lodge, 21 Hollygate Park, Carryduff, Belfast BT8 8DN*

McALISTER, David. b 39. St Jo Coll Nottm 83. **d** 87 **p** 88. NSM Arpafeelie *Mor* 87-93; NSM Cromarty 87-93; NSM Fortrose 87-93; C Broughty Ferry *Bre* 93-95; P-in-c Nairn *Mor* from 95. *1 Clova Crescent, Nairn IV12 4TE* Tel (01667) 452458

McALISTER, Kenneth Bloomer. b 25. TCD BA51. **d** 51 **p** 53. C Cregagh *D & D* 51-54; C Monaghan *Clogh* 54-57; C Portadown St Mark *Arm* 57-62; R Ripley *Ripon* 62-91; rtd 91. *31 Wetherby Road, Knaresborough, N Yorkshire HG5 8LH* Tel (01423) 860705

MacALISTER, Randall George Leslie. b 41. TCD BA63 MA66. **d** 64 **p** 66. C Portadown St Mark *Arm* 64-67; I Keady w Armaghbreague and Derrynoose 67-74; R Kirriemuir *St And* 74-81; R Greenock *Glas* 81-87; R Forfar *St And* 87-95; R Lunan Head 87-95; Chapl Sophia Antipolis *Eur* from 95. *6 Traverse deî Tourdres, Haut Sartoux, 06560 Valbourne, France* Tel France (33) 93 65 38 63

McALISTER, Thomas George. b 20. TCD BA42 MA47. **d** 43 **p** 44. C Aghalee *D & D* 43-45; C Belfast St Pet *Conn* 45-53; V Southport St Andr *Liv* 53-59; V Spring Grove St Mary *Lon* 59-69; Chapl Wispers Sch Surrey 69-79; R Haslemere *Guildf* 69-79; V Slyne w Hest *Blackb* 79-85; rtd 85; Perm to Offic *Guildf* 86-96; Perm to Offic *Portsm* from 86; P-in-c Linchmere *Chich* 92-93. *Bywoods, Bunch Lane, Haslemere, Surrey GU27 1ET* Tel (01428) 643516

McALLEN, James. b 38. Lon Univ BD71. Oak Hill Th Coll 63. **d** 66 **p** 67. C Blackheath St Jo *S'wark* 66-69; C Edin St Thos *Edin* 69-73; V Selby St Jas *York* 73-80; V Wistow 75-80; V Houghton *Carl* 80-91; Gen Sec Lon City Miss 92-93; Dir 93-94; Hon C Blackheath St Jo *S'wark* from 94. *192 Charlton Road, London SE7 7DW* Tel 0181-856 7306

McALLEN, Robert. b 41. Bps' Coll Cheshunt 62. **d** 65 **p** 66. C Seagoe *D & D* 65-68; C Knockbreda 68-70; CF 70-96; Chapl R Memorial Chpl Sandhurst 87-92; rtd 96. *MOD Chaplains (Army), Trenchard Lines, Upavon, Pewsey, Wilts SN9 6BE* Tel (01980) 615804 Fax 615800

MACAN, Peter John Erdley. b 36. Bp Gray Coll Cape Town 58 LTh60. **d** 60 **p** 61. S Africa 60-67; C S Lambeth St Ann *S'wark* 68-71; V Nunhead St Silas 72-81; P-in-c Clapham H Spirit 81-87; TV Clapham TM 87-90; V Dulwich St Clem w St Pet from 90. *St Clement's Vicarage, 140 Friern Road, London SE22 0AY* Tel 0181-693 1890

McARTHUR, Duncan Walker. b 50. Strathclyde Univ BSc73 Melbourne Univ BD82. **d** 82 **p** 82. Australia 82-90 and from 93; P-in-c Harraby *Carl* 90-93. *23 King Creek Road, Wauchope, NSW, Australia 2446* Tel Wauchope (65) 851147

MACARTNEY, Prof Fergus James. b 40. MRCP68 FACC76 FRCP77 Qu Coll Cam BA62 MA84 St Thos Hosp Cam BCh66 MB67. EAMTC 86 SW Minl Tr Course 88. **d** 90 **p** 91. Chapl Lee Abbey 90-91; NSM Shirwell, Loxhore, Kentisbury, Arlington, etc *Ex* 90-91; Asst Chapl Amsterdam w Den Helder and Heiloo *Eur* from 91. *Angsteloord 46, 1391 EG Abcoude, The Netherlands* Tel Abcoude (2946) 4233

McATEER, John Alexander. b 18. TCD BA44 MA50. CITC 44. **d** 44 **p** 45. C Limerick Cathl *L & K* 44-47; C Dublin St Bart *D & G* 47-51; C S Kensington St Steph *Lon* 51-52; C Notting Hill All SS w St Columb 52-59; V Hammersmith H Innocents 59-83; rtd 83; Perm to Offic *Lon* 83-93. *162 Sutton Court Road, London W4 3HR* Tel 0181-995 5317

MACAULAY, John Roland. b 39. Man Univ BSc61 Liv Inst of Educn PGCE80. Wells Th Coll 61. **d** 63 **p** 64. C Padgate Ch Ch *Liv* 63-66; C Upholland 66-73; TV 73-75; V Hindley St Pet 75-81; Chapl Liv Coll 81-96; Sub-Chapl HM Pris Risley from 85; R Lowton St Luke *Liv* from 96. *The Rectory, 246 Slag Lane, Lowton, Warrington WA3 2ED* Tel (01942) 728434

MACAULAY, Kenneth Lionel. b 55. Edin Univ BD78. Edin Th Coll 74. **d** 78 **p** 79. C Glas St Ninian *Glas* 78-80; Dioc Youth Chapl 80-87; P-in-c Glas St Matt 80-87; R Glenrothes *St And* 87-89; Chapl St Mary's Cathl *Glas* 89-92; Min Glas St Mary 89-92; Min Glas St Serf 92-94; Perm to Offic from 94. *90 Wellshot Road, Glasgow G32 7DA* Tel 0141-778 0188

McAUSLAND, Canon William James. b 36. Edin Th Coll 56. **d** 59 **p** 60. C Dundee St Mary Magd *Bre* 59-64; R 71-79; R Glas H Cross *Glas* 64-71; Chapl St Marg Old People's Home 79-85; R Dundee St Marg *Bre* from 79; Chapl St Mary's Sisterhood 82-87; Chapl Dundee Hosps from 85; Hon Can St Paul's Cathl Dundee *Bre* from 93. *St Margaret's Rectory, 19 Ancrum Road, Dundee DD2 2JL* Tel (01382) 667227

McAVOY, George Brian. b 41. MBE78. TCD BA61 MA72. **d** 63 **p** 65. C Cork St Luke w St Ann *C, C & R* 63-66; I Timoleague w Abbeymahon 66-68; Chapl RAF 68-88; Asst Chapl-in-Chief RAF 88-95; QHC 91-95; Chapl Fosse Health NHS Trust from 95; Perm to Offic *Pet* from 95. *The Crescent, King Street, Leicester LE1 6RX* Tel 0116-223 2427 Fax 223 2441

McAVOY, Philip George. b 63. Imp Coll Lon BSc85 SS Coll Cam BA90. Westcott Ho Cam 88. **d** 91 **p** 92. C W End *Win* 91-95; TV Swanage and Studland *Sarum* from 95. *The Vicarage, 130 Victoria Avenue, Swanage, Dorset BH19 1AX* Tel (01929) 422916

McBAY, Canon Walter Ernest. b 17. St Aid Birkenhead 47. **d** 49 **p** 50. C Droitwich St Nic w St Pet *Worc* 49-51; Benin 51-59; P-in-c Shrawley *Worc* 59-62; Nigeria 62-67; Hon Can Owerri 66-67; R The Shelsleys *Worc* 67-72; V Farndon *S'well* 72-78; R Thorpe 72-78; V Swinefleet *Sheff* 78-80; C Cleethorpes *Linc* 80-83; rtd 83; Perm to Offic *Ex* 83-93. *Flat 10, Ellesborough Manor, Butlers Cross, Aylesbury, Bucks HP17 0XF* Tel (01296) 622324

McBRIDE, Stephen Richard. b 61. QUB BSc84 TCD DipTh87 BTh89 QUB PhD. CITC 84. **d** 87 **p** 88. C Antrim All SS *Conn* 87-90; I Belfast St Pet 90-95; Bp's Dom Chapl from 94; I Antrim All SS from 95. *The Vicarage, 10 Vicarage Gardens, Antrim BT41 4JP* Tel (01849) 462186

McCABE, Alan. b 37. Lon Univ BScEng61. Ridley Hall Cam 61. **d** 63 **p** 64. C Bromley SS Pet and Paul *Roch* 63-67; PV Roch Cathl

67-70; V Bromley H Trin 70-77; V Westerham 77-88; V Eastbourne St Jo *Chich* from 88. *St John's Vicarage, 9 Buxton Road, Eastbourne, E Sussex BN20 7LL* Tel (01323) 721105

McCABE, The Ven John Trevor. b 33. RD78. Nottm Univ BA55 St Cath Soc Ox DipTh59. Wycliffe Hall Ox 57. **d** 59 **p** 60. C Compton Gifford *Ex* 59-63; P-in-c Ex St Martin, St Steph, St Laur etc 63-66; Chapl RNR from 63; Chapl Ex Sch 64-66; V Capel *Guildf* 66-71; V Scilly Is *Truro* 71-74; TR Is of Scilly 74-81; Can Res Bris Cathl *Bris* 81-83; V Manaccan w St Anthony-in-Meneage and St Martin *Truro* 83-96; RD Kerrier 87-90 and 94-96; Chmn Cornwall NHS Trust for Mental Handicap from 91; Hon Can Truro Cathl from 93; Adn Cornwall from 96. *Archdeacon's House, Knights Hill, Kenwyn, Truro, Cornwall TR1 3UY* Tel (01872) 72866

McCABE, Terence John. b 46. Sarum Th Coll 71. **d** 74 **p** 75. C Radford *Cov* 74-77; P-in-c Bris St Paul w St Barn *Bris* 77-80; TV E Bris 80-84; USA 84-90; R Eynesbury *Ely* from 90. *The Rectory, 7 Howitt's Lane, Eynesbury, St Neots, Huntingdon, Cambs PE19 2AJ* Tel (01480) 403884

McCABE, Thomas Stephen (Tom). b 56. QUB BSc77. St Jo Coll Nottm DTS91. **d** 91 **p** 92. C Broadheath *Ches* 91-95; C Bramhall from 95. *17 Syddal Road, Bramhall, Stockport, Cheshire SK7 1AB* Tel 0161-439 0994

McCABE, Dr William Alexander Beck. b 27. QUB BA50 PhD65. **d** 74 **p** 74. Sec Sheff Coun of Chs 74-80; Hon C Millhouses H Trin *Sheff* 74-80; TV Sheff Manor 80-83; C Mosborough 83; C Portsea St Cuth *Portsm* 83-86; C S w N Hayling 86-87; V Mickleover St Jo *Derby* 87-91; rtd 91; Perm to Offic *Derby* from 91. *Tawelfan, Ruthin Road, Cadole, Mold CH7 5LQ* Tel (01352) 810435

McCAFFERTY, Canon Christine Ann. b 43. FCA76. Gilmore Course 76. **dss** 79 **d** 87 **p** 94. Writtle *Chelmsf* 79-81; Writtle w Highwood 81-87; C 87-94; NSM Officer from 88; Bp's Dom Chapl (Bradwell) from 88; Hon Can Chelmsf Cathl from 91; TR Wickford and Runwell from 94. *The Rectory, 120 Southend Road, Wickford, Essex SS11 8EB* Tel (01268) 733147

McCAFFERTY (née BACK), Mrs Esther Elaine. b 52. Saffron Walden Coll CertEd74. Trin Coll Bris 79 Oak Hill Th Coll BA81. **dss** 81 **d** 87 **p** 94. Collyhurst *Man* 81-84; Upton (Overchurch) *Ches* 84-88; Par Dn 87-88; Par Dn Upper Holloway St Pet w St Jo *Lon* 88-90; Min in charge 90-97; P-in-c Pitsea w Nevendon *Chelmsf* from 97. *The Rectory, Rectory Road, Pitsea, Basildon, Essex SS13 2AA* Tel (01268) 553240 Fax as telephone

McCAGHREY, Mark Allan. b 66. Warw Univ BSc87. St Jo Coll Nottm BTh93. **d** 94 **p** 95. C Byfleet *Guildf* from 94. *118 Rectory Lane, Byfleet, Surrey KT14 7LY* Tel (01932) 354627

McCALLA, Robert Ian. b 31. AKC55. St Boniface Warminster 52. **d** 56 **p** 57. C Barrow St Jo *Carl* 56-58; C Penrith St Andr 58-61; R Greenheys St Clem *Man* 61-64; V Glodwick 64-71; R Distington *Carl* 71-73; V Howe Bridge *Man* 73-87; Chapl Atherleigh Hosp from 75; R Heaton Mersey *Man* 87-92; V Tyldesley w Shakerley from 92. *St George's Vicarage, 203 Manchester Road, Tyldesley, Manchester M29 8WT* Tel (01942) 882914

MacCALLUM, Canon Norman Donald. b 47. Edin Univ LTh70. Edin Th Coll 67. **d** 71 **p** 72. TV Livingston LEP *Edin* 71-82; P-in-c Bo'ness from 82; R Grangemouth from 82; Miss to Seamen from 82; Syn Clerk *Edin* from 96; Can St Mary's Cathl from 96. *33 Carronflats Road, Grangemouth, Stirlingshire FK3 9DG* Tel (01324) 482438

McCAMLEY, The Ven Gregor Alexander. b 42. TCD BA64 MA67. CITC 65. **d** 65 **p** 66. C Holywood *D & D* 65-68; C Bangor St Comgall 68-72; I Carnalea 72-80; I Knock from 80; Stewardship Adv from 89; Can Down Cathl from 90; Dioc Registrar 90-95; Adn Down from 95. *The Rectory, 29 King's Road, Belfast BT5 6JG* Tel (01232) 471514

McCAMMON, Canon John Taylor. b 42. QUB BSc65 Lon Univ BD70. Clifton Th Coll 67. **d** 71 **p** 72. C Lurgan Ch Ch *D & D* 71-75; I Kilkeel 75-82; I Lisburn Ch Ch Cathl *Conn* from 82; Treas 94-96; Prec 96; Chan from 96; Can Conn Cathl from 85. *Cathedral Rectory, 2 Clonevin Park, Lisburn, Co Antrim BT28 3BL* Tel (01846) 662865

McCANDLESS, John Hamilton Moore. b 24. QUB BA Ulster Poly BEd. **d** 63 **p** 64. C Belfast St Matt *Conn* 63-66; I Termonmaguirke *Arm* 66-69; C Jordanstown *Conn* 69-70; I Ballinderry w Tamlaght and Arboe *Arm* 70-74; I Kilbarron w Rossnowlagh and Drumholm *D & R* 84-87; rtd 87. *10 Drumvale Road, Bendooragh, Ballymoney, Co Antrim BT53 7TD* Tel (01265) 662078

McCANN, Michael Joseph. b 61. Man Univ BSc82 TCD BTh91. **d** 91 **p** 92. C Derryloran *Arm* 91-94; I Dunmurry *Conn* from 94. *27 Church Avenue, Dunmurry, Belfast BT17 9RS* Tel (01232) 610984

McCANN, Roland Neil. b 39. Serampore Coll BD73. Bp's Coll Calcutta DipTh70. **d** 70 **p** 73. India 70-74; C Earley St Bart *Ox* 74-77; C-in-c Harlington Ch Ch CD *Lon* from 77. *192 Waltham Avenue, Hayes, Middx UB3 1TF* Tel 0181-573 0112

McCANN, Thomas Alan George. b 66. CITC 90. **d** 93 **p** 94. C Carrickfergus *Conn* from 93. *20 Meadow Hill Close, Carrickfergus, Co Antrim BT38 9RQ* Tel (01960) 362126

McCARRAHER, Seymour. b 26. Magd Coll Cam BA48 MA55. St Steph Ho Ox. **d** 55 **p** 56. C Southwick St Columba *Dur* 55-59; Chapl RN 59-75; C Christchurch *Win* 75-81; V Darton *Wakef* 81-92; rtd 92; Perm to Offic *York* from 93. *34 Moorside, Boston Spa, Wetherby, W Yorkshire LS23 6PN* Tel (01937) 843948

McCARTHY, David William. b 63. Edin Th Coll BD88. **d** 88 **p** 89. C Edin St Paul and St Geo *Edin* 88-91; P-in-c S Queensferry 91-95; R Glas St Silas *Glas* from 95. *77 Southbrae Drive, Glasgow G13 1PU* Tel 0141-954 9368 E-mail 101466.416@compuserve.com

McCARTHY, The Very Revd John Francis. b 38. TCD BA61 MA72. **d** 62 **p** 63. C Seapatrick *D & D* 62-66; C Seagoe 66-71; I Moira 71-75; I Dundalk *Arm* 75-86; I Enniskillen *Clogh* 86-94; Dean Clogh 89-94; USA from 94. *St John's Anglican Church, 7th and Hampshire Street, Quincy, Illinois 62301, USA*

McCARTHY, Peter James. b 25. OBE. Cranmer Hall Dur. **d** 85 **p** 86. Hon C Farnham w Scotton, Staveley, Copgrove etc *Ripon* 85-87; V Startforth w Bowes 87-92; rtd 92; C Dufftown *Ab* 92-95. *Manderley, Farnham Lane, Ferrensby, Knaresborough, N Yorkshire HG5 9JG*

MacCARTHY, The Very Revd Robert Brian. b 40. TCD BA63 MA66 PhD83 NUI MA65 Ox Univ MA82. Cuddesdon Coll 77. **d** 79 **p** 80. C Carlow w Urglin and Staplestown *C & O* 79-81; Lic to Offic (Cashel, Waterford and Lismore) 81-86; Lib Pusey Ho 81-82; Fell St Cross Coll Ox 81-82; C Bracknell *Ox* 82-83; TV 83-86; C Kilkenny w Aghour and Kilmanagh *C & O* 86-88; Bp's V and Lib Kilkenny Cathl 86-88; Chapl Kilkenny Coll 86-88; Bp's Dom Chapl 86-89; I Castlecomer w Colliery Ch, Mothel and Bilbo 88-95; RD Carlow 88-95; Dioc Info Officer (Ossory and Leighlin) 88-90; Glebes Sec (Ossory and Leighlin) 92-94; Preb Monmohenock St Patr Cathl Dublin from 94; Provost Tuam *T, K & A* from 95; I Galway w Kilcummin from 95; Chapl Univ Coll Galway from 95. *The Rectory, Taylor's Hill, Galway, Irish Republic* Tel Galway (91) 521914 or 64648

McCARTHY, Miss Sandra Ellen. b 56. ARCM75 FRCO77 GRNCM78 Man Univ BMus77 Golds Coll Lon PGCE79. S'wark Ord Course 92. **d** 95 **p** 96. C Beckenham St Geo *Roch* from 95. *2 Durban Road, Beckenham, Kent BR3 4EZ* Tel 0181-663 1706 Fax as telephone

McCARTHY, Terence Arthur (Terry). b 46. Kelham Th Coll 66. **d** 70 **p** 71. C Gt Burstead *Chelmsf* 70-74; C Wickford 74-76; TV E Runcorn w Halton *Ches* 76-80; V Runcorn H Trin 80-84; Chapl HM Pris Liv 84; Chapl HM Pris Acklington 84-92; Chapl HM Pris Holme Ho from 92. *The Chaplain's Office, HM Prison Holme House, Stockton-on-Tees, Cleveland TS18 2QU* Tel (01642) 673759 Fax 674598

McCARTNEY, Adrian Alexander. b 57. Stranmillis Coll BEd79 TCD BTh88. St Jo Coll Nottm LTh86. **d** 88 **p** 89. C Jordanstown w Monkstown *Conn* 88-91; Bp's C Monkstown 91-94; I 94-96. *22 Rosemount Crescent, Jordanstown, Newtownabbey, Co Antrim BT37 0NH* Tel (01232) 865160

McCARTNEY, Ellis. b 47. Univ Coll Lon BSc73 Golds Coll Lon DipRE80 Lon Inst of Educn MA82 Cert Counselling 94. NTMTC 94. **d** 97. NSM Tollington *Lon* from 97. *6 Elfort Road, London N5 1AZ* Tel 0171-226 1533

McCARTNEY, Robert Charles. TCD DipTh85. **d** 85 **p** 85. C Portadown St Mark *Arm* 85-88; I Erringle Keerogue w Ballygawley and Killeshil 88-89; CF from 89. *MOD Chaplains (Army), Trenchard Lines, Upavon, Pewsey, Wilts SN9 6BE* Tel (01980) 615804 Fax 615800

McCARTY, Dr Colin Terence. b 46. Loughb Univ BTech68 PhD71 Lon Univ PGCE73 FRSA89. EAMTC 91. **d** 94 **p** 95. NSM Exning St Martin w Landwade *St E* from 94. *1 Seymour Close, Newmarket, Cambs CB8 8EL* Tel (01638) 669400 Fax (01223) 325537

MacCARTY, Paul Andrew. b 34. Sarum & Wells Th Coll 73. **d** 75 **p** 76. Ind Chapl *Win* 75-80; C Bournemouth St Andr 75-84; Hon C Christchurch 80-91; C from 91. *3 Douglas Avenue, Christchurch, Dorset BH23 1JT* Tel (01202) 483807

McCAUGHEY, Canon Robert Morley. b 07. MA35. **d** 35 **p** 36. C Walker *Newc* 35-38; C Ponteland 38-41; C Benwell St Jas 41-43; V Wallsend St Luke 43-52; V Berwick H Trin 52-61; V Wisbech SS Pet and Paul *Ely* 61-74; RD Wisbech 62-72; Hon Can Ely Cathl 72-74; rtd 74; Perm to Offic *D & R* from 76. *51 Ballinahone House, Knockcloughrim, Magherafelt, Co Londonderry BT45 8PT* Tel (01648) 42110

McCAUSLAND, Norman. b 58. TCD BTh89. CITC 89. **d** 89 **p** 90. C Portadown St Columba *Arm* 89-91; P-in-c Clonmel Union *C, C & R* 91-94; Miss to Seamen 91-94; CMS 94-95; Bp's V and Lib Ossory Cathl *C & O* 96; Chapl and Tutor CITC from 96; PV Ch Ch Cathl Dublin *D & G* from 96. *18 Marley Close, Rathfarnham, Dublin 16, Irish Republic* Tel Dublin (1) 492 3082 or 492 3852 Fax 492 3082

McCLATCHEY, Alfred Henry Bailey. b 20. BNC Ox BA48 MA48. **d** 67 **p** 68. C Lambeth St Mary the Less *S'wark* 67-69; V Escomb *Dur* 69-74; V Witton Park 69-74; Bp's Dom Chapl 69-74; Bp's Dom Chapl *Worc* 74-79; R Hartlebury 74-86; rtd 86; Perm to Offic *Worc* from 86. *10 Bellars Lane, Malvern, Worcs WR14 2DN* Tel (01684) 560336

McCLAUGHRY, Victor Thomas. b 13. TCD BA34 MA46. **d** 36 **p** 37. C Cork St Fin Barre's Cathl *C, C & R* 36-41; C Taney *D & G* 41-45; C S'wark Cathl *S'wark* 45-48; Chapl Guy's Hosp Lon 45-48; Chapl Holloway Sanatorium Virginia Water 48-54; V

Gaydon w Chadshunt *Cov* 54-56; Chapl Mickleover Hosp Derby 56-60; PC Derby St Jo *Derby* 60-63; Chapl The Dorothy Kerin Trust Burrswood 63-66; V Peasmarsh *Chich* 66-70; V E Preston w Kingston 70-79; rtd 79; Perm to Offic *Chich* from 79. *16 Woodland Avenue, High Salvington, Worthing, W Sussex BN13 3AF* Tel (01903) 692971

McCLAY, David Alexander. b 59. TCD DipTh87. **d** 87 **p** 88. C Magheralin w Dollingstown *D & D* 87-90; I Kilkeel from 90. *The Rectory, 44 Manse Road, Kilkeel, Newry, Co Down BT34 4BN* Tel (01693) 762300

McCLEAN, Lydia Margaret Sheelagh. b 72. Ball Coll Ox BTh94. Cuddesdon Coll 94. **d** 96 **p** 97. C Brackley St Pet w St Jas *Pet* from 96. *12 Bannerman Drive, Brackley, Northants NN13 6HS* Tel (01280) 704263

McCLEAN, Robert Mervyn. b 38. Greenwich Univ BTh91. Edgehill Th Coll Belf 57. **d** 85 **p** 88. NSM Seapatrick *D & D* from 85. *2 Kiloanin Crescent, Lurgan Road, Banbridge, Co Down BT32 4NU* Tel (01820) 627419

McCLOUGHLIN, Joshua. b 27. CITC 69. **d** 70 **p** 71. C Magheraculmoney *Clogh* 70-72; C Cloughfern *Conn* 73-77; I Dunfanaghy *D & R* 77-79; I Drumkeeran w Templecarne and Muckross *Clogh* 79-83; I Aghavea 83-96; rtd 96. *109 Ballagh Road, Fivemiletown, Co Tyrone BT75 0DL* Tel (01365) 521120

McCLURE, Robert (Roy). b 30. Open Univ BA92. TCD Div Sch 68. **d** 70 **p** 71. C Monaghan *Clogh* 70-72; C Belfast St Matt *Conn* 72-76; Chapl HM Pris Liv 76-77; Chapl HM Pris Preston 77-82; V Foulridge *Blackb* 82-88; rtd 88; Perm to Offic *Liv* from 89. *4 Mill Lane Crescent, Southport, Merseyside PR9 7PF* Tel (01704) 27476

McCLURE, Canon Timothy Elston (Tim). b 46. St Jo Coll Dur BA68. Ridley Hall Cam 68. **d** 70 **p** 71. C Kirkheaton *Wakef* 70-73; C Chorlton upon Medlock *Man* 74-79; Chapl Man Poly 74-82; TR Man Whitworth 79-82; Gen Sec SCM 82-92; Perm to Offic *Birm* 83-92; Bp's Soc & Ind Adv & Team Ldr Soc & Ind Min LEP *Bris* from 92; Hon Can Bris Cathl from 92; Hon C Cotham St Sav w St Mary from 96; Chapl Lord Mayor's Chpl from 96. *7 South Road, Bristol BS6 6QP* Tel 0117-955 7430 or 942 5264 E-mail isrbristol@gn.apc.org

McCLUSKEY, Miss Lesley. b 45. Hull Univ LLB72 Bolton Coll of Educn PGCE77. N Ord Course 89. **d** 92 **p** 94. C Bootle St Mary w St Paul *Liv* 92-94; C Wigan St Anne from 94. *33 Guildford Crescent, Beech Hill, Wigan, Lancs WN6 8NG* Tel (01942) 33794

McCOLLUM, Alastair Colston. b 69. Whitelands Coll Lon BA91. Westcott Ho Cam 95. **d** 96 **p** 97. C Hampton All SS *Lon* from 96. *Westwood Cottage, 44 The Avenue, Hampton, Middx TW12 3RG* Tel 0181-255 6119 E-mail acmccollum@ad.com

McCOLLUM, Charles James. b 41. TCD BTh89. CITC 85. **d** 89 **p** 90. C Larne and Inver *Conn* 89-91; Bp's C Belfast Whiterock 91-96; I Belfast St Pet from 96. *The Rectory, 17 Waterloo Park South, Belfast BT15 5HX* Tel (01232) 777053 Fax as telephone

McCOLLUM, Robert George. b 20. TCD BA43 MA60. **d** 44 **p** 45. C Dublin Santry w Glasnevin *D & G* 44-48; C Taney 48-54; I Donabate w Lusk 54-62; I Dublin Clontarf 62-89; Can Ch Ch Cathl Dublin 83-89; RD Fingal 84-89; I Rathmolyon w Castlerickard, Rathcore and Agher *M & K* 89-94; rtd 94. *16 Park View, Athboy, Co Meath, Irish Republic* Tel Meath (46) 32938

McCOMB, Samuel. b 33. CITC 70. **d** 71 **p** 72. C Belfast St Mich *Conn* 71-74; C Lisburn Ch Ch 74-79; I from 83; I Ballinderry *Arm* 79-83. *Christ Church Rectory, 27 Hillsborough Road, Lisbury, Co Antrim BT28 1JL* Tel (01846) 662163

McCONACHIE, Robert Noel. b 40. Golds Coll Lon BA86. Oak Hill Th Coll 86. **d** 88 **p** 89. C Larkfield *Roch* 88-93; R Mereworth w W Peckham from 93. *The Rectory, The Street, Mereworth, Maidstone, Kent ME18 5NA* Tel (01622) 812214

McCONKEY, Brian Robert. b 62. Carl Dioc Tr Inst 92. **d** 95 **p** 96. C Blackb St Gabr *Blackb* from 95. *St Gabriel's House, 100 Highbank, Blackburn BB1 9SX* Tel (01254) 662818

McCONNELL, Canon Brian Roy. b 46. St Paul's Grahamstown DipTh71. **d** 71 **p** 72. S Africa 71-77 and 79-85; C Prestwich St Marg *Man* 77-79; V Liscard St Mary w St Columba *Ches* 85-90; V Altrincham St Geo from 90; RD Bowdon from 95; Hon Can Ches Cathl from 97. *St George's Vicarage, Townfield Road, Altrincham, Cheshire WA14 4DS* Tel 0161-928 1279

McCONNELL, Peter Stuart. b 54. Linc Th Coll 89. **d** 91 **p** 92. C N Shields *Newc* 91-95; V Balkwell from 95. *St Peter's Vicarage, The Quadrant, North Shields, Tyne & Wear NE29 7JA* Tel 0191-257 0952

McCONNELL, Robert Mark. b 60. Oak Hill Th Coll BA88. **d** 89 **p** 90. C Bedford Ch Ch *St Alb* 89-92; C Bangor St Comgall *D & D* 92-94; I Killyleagh from 94. *The Rectory, 34 Irishbeg, Killyleagh, Downpatrick, Co Down BT30 9TR* Tel (01396) 828231

McCORMACK, Dr Alan William. b 68. Jes Coll Ox BA90 MA94 DPhil94. CITC 93. **d** 96 **p** 97. C Knock *D & D* from 96. *The Curate's Residence, 3 Sandown Park South, Belfast BT5 6HE* Tel (01232) 653370

McCORMACK, Canon David Eugene. b 34. Wells Th Coll 66. **d** 68 **p** 69. C Lillington *Cov* 68-71; C The Lickey *Birm* 71-75; V Highters Heath 75-82; V Four Oaks from 82; Hon Can Birm Cathl from 95. *The Vicarage, 2 Walsall Road, Sutton Coldfield, W Midlands B74 4QJ* Tel 0121-308 5315

McCORMACK, George Brash. b 32. ACIS65 FCIS75 Lon Univ DipRS85. S'wark Ord Course 82. **d** 85 **p** 86. Hon C Crofton St Paul *Roch* 85-89; C Crayford 89-91; R Fawkham and Hartley from 91. *The Rectory, 3 St John's Lane, Hartley, Dartford DA3 8ET* Tel (01474) 703819

McCORMACK, John Heddon. b 58. Chich Th Coll 85. **d** 88 **p** 89. C Cleobury Mortimer w Hopton Wafers *Heref* 88-90; C Lymington *Win* 90-92; C Portsea N End St Mark *Portsm* 92-95; Chapl St Barn Hospice Worthing from 95. *St Barnabas Hospice, Columbia Drive, Worthing, W Sussex BN13 2QF, or, 17 St Elmo Road, Worthing BN14 7EJ* Tel (01903) 264221

McCORMACK, Kevan Sean. b 50. Chich Th Coll 77. **d** 80 **p** 81. C Ross *Heref* 80-81; C Ross w Brampton Abbotts, Bridstow and Peterstow 81-83; C Leominster 83; TV 84-87; Chapl R Hosp Sch Holbrook from 87. *The Housemaster's Flat, Nelson House, Royal Hospital School, Holbrook, Ipswich IP9 2RX* Tel (01473) 328851

McCORMACK, Mrs Lesley Sharman. b 50. EAMTC. **d** 88 **p** 94. Hon Par Dn Chevington w Hargrave and Whepstead w Brockley *St E* 88-95; Asst Chapl W Suffolk Hosp Bury St Edm 88-95; Chapl Kettering Gen Hosp NHS Trust from 95. *Kettering General Hospital, Rothwell Road, Kettering, Northants NN16 8UZ* Tel (01536) 492000

McCORMICK, Mrs Anne Irene. b 67. Sheff Univ BA89 Hull Univ PGCE90. Ripon Coll Cuddesdon 90. **d** 92 **p** 94. C Spalding *Linc* 92-96; C Gt Grimsby St Mary and St Jas 96-97; NSM from 97. *St Hugh's Parsonage, 4 Freshney Drive, Grimsby, S Humberside DN31 1TP* Tel (01472) 359332

McCORMICK, David Mark. b 68. Univ of Wales (Ban) BD89. Ripon Coll Cuddesdon 90. **d** 92 **p** 93. C Holbeach *Linc* 92-96; TV Gt Grimsby St Mary and St Jas from 96. *St Hugh's Parsonage, 4 Freshney Drive, Grimsby, S Humberside DN31 1TP* Tel (01472) 359332

McCOSH, Duncan Ian. b 50. Edin Dioc NSM Course 82. **d** 91 **p** 92. C Dalkeith *Edin* 91-96; C Lasswade 91-96; P-in-c Falkirk from 96. *The Rectory, 55 Kerse Lane, Falkirk FK1 1RX* Tel (01324) 623709

McCOUBREY, Prof Hilaire. b 53. Trin Coll Cam BA75 MA78 Nottm Univ PhD90 Solicitor 78. EMMTC 92. **d** 95 **p** 96. Prof Law Hull Univ from 95; NSM Rowley w Skidby *York* from 95. *University of Hull Law School, Hull HU6 7RX* Tel (01482) 466323 Fax 466388

McCOUBREY, William Arthur. b 36. CEng MIMechE. Sarum & Wells Th Coll 86. **d** 89 **p** 90. C Bedhampton *Portsm* 89-92; V Stokenham w Sherford *Ex* 92-96; R Stokenham w Sherford and Beesands, and Slapton from 96. *The Vicarage, Stokenham, Kingsbridge, Devon TQ7 2ST* Tel (01548) 580385

McCOULOUGH, David. b 61. Man Univ BA84 St Jo Coll Dur BA88. Cranmer Hall Dur 86. **d** 89 **p** 90. C Man Apostles w Miles Platting *Man* 89-92; C Elton All SS 92-94; V Halliwell St Marg from 94. *The Vicarage, 1 Somerset Road, Bolton BL1 4NE* Tel (01204) 840880

McCOULOUGH, Thomas Alexander. b 32. AKC59. **d** 60 **p** 61. C Norton St Mich *Dur* 60-63; India 63-67; P-in-c Derby St Jas *Derby* 67-72; Ind Chapl *York* 72-82; P-in-c Sutton on the Forest 82-96; Dioc Sec for Local Min 82-89; Lay Tr Officer 89-96; rtd 96. *1 Horsley Gardens, Holywell, Whitley Bay, Tyne & Wear NE25 0TU* Tel 0191-298 0332

McCREA, Basil Wolfe. b 21. QUB BA49. Wycliffe Hall Ox 51. **d** 53 **p** 54. C Kingston upon Hull H Trin *York* 53-56; C Dundela *D & D* 56-59; C Cork H Trin w St Paul, St Pet and St Mary *C, C & R* 59-61; I Tullyaughnish *D & R* 61-65; I Rathkeale *L & K* 65-68; I Cork H Trin *C, C & R* 68-72; I Carrigaline Union 72-90; rtd 90. *30 Somerville, Carrigaline, Co Cork, Irish Republic* Tel Cork (21) 371538

McCREA, Francis. b 53. BTh. **d** 91 **p** 92. C Dundonald *D & D* 91-94; I Belfast St Brendan from 94. *St Brendan's Rectory, 36 Circular Road, Belfast BT4 2GA* Tel (01232) 763458

McCREADY, Kennedy Lemar. b 26. FIEE56 Garnett Coll Lon TCert54 Woolwich Poly CEng56 Birkb Coll Lon BSc59 Sussex Univ DBS92. Chich Th Coll 91. **d** 92. NSM Mayfield *Chich* 92-97; Perm to Offic from 97. *Quarry House, Groomsbridge, Tunbridge Wells, Kent TN3 9PS* Tel (01892) 864297

McCREADY, Marcus Diarmuid Julian. b 63. NUU BA85 TCD BTh88 MA MPhil. **d** 88 **p** 89. C Seagoe *D & D* 88-91; I Clonallon w Warrenpoint 91-96; Chapl Liv Coll from 96. *Liverpool College, North Mossley Hill Road, Liverpool L18 8BE* Tel 0151-724 1563

McCREADY, Maurice Shaun. b 55. MA. Ripon Coll Cuddesdon. **d** 83 **p** 84. C Bridgwater St Fran *B & W* 83-86; C Walton-on-Thames *Guildf* 86-88; C Elm Park St Nic Hornchurch *Chelmsf* 88-93; NSM from 93. *39 Woodcote Avenue, Elm Park, Hornchurch, Essex RM12 4PY* Tel (01708) 452740

McCREERY, Canon William Robert Desmond. b 35. QUB BD. Oak Hill Th Coll 59. **d** 62 **p** 63. C Dundonald *D & D* 62-66; C Belfast St Donard 66-69; I Annalong 69-78; I Knockbreda 78-89; Can Belf Cathl from 88; I Bangor St Comgall *D & D* from 89. *2 Raglan Road, Bangor, Co Down BT20 3TL* Tel (01247) 465230

McCRORY, Canon Peter. b 34. Chich Th Coll 63. **d** 67 **p** 68. C St Marychurch *Ex* 67-72; R Kenn w Mamhead 72-76; R Kenn 76-78; Bp's Dom Chapl *S'wark* 78-81; V Kew from 81; RD

Richmond and Barnes 84-89; Hon Can S'wark Cathl from 90. *The Vicarage, 278 Kew Road, Kew, Richmond, Surrey TW9 3EE* Tel 0181-940 4616

McCRORY, Walter Edward. b 38. TCD 66. **d** 69 **p** 70. C Carrickfergus *Conn* 69-73; C Ballywillan 73-76; I Armoy w Loughguile and Drumtullagh from 76. *The Rectory, 181 Glenshesk Road, Armoy, Ballymoney, Co Antrim BT53 8RJ* Tel (01265) 751226

McCRUM, Michael Scott. b 35. Glas Univ BSc57 UNISA BTh85. **d** 85 **p** 85. S Africa 85-89; Kerygma Internat Chr Min 89-92; Perm to Offic *Nor* 93-94; NSM Chesham Bois *Ox* 94-95; NSM Chorleywood St Andr *St Alb* from 95. *Woodstock, North Road, Chorleywood, Rickmansworth, Herts WD3 5LE* Tel (01923) 285562 Fax as telephone E-mail misamccrum@aol.com

McCUBBIN, The Very Revd David. b 29. AKC54. St Boniface Warminster 54. **d** 55 **p** 56. C Frome Ch Ch *B & W* 55-57; C Glastonbury St Jo 57-60; R Dunoon *Arg* 60-63; R Kirkcaldy *St And* 63-70; R Wallsend St Pet *Newc* 70-79; R Aberdeen St Jo *Ab* 79-81; R Glas St Bride *Glas* 81-87; Provost Cumbrae Cathl *Arg* 87-94; R Cumbrae (or Millport) 87-94; Can St Jo Cathl Oban 87-94; Syn Clerk 88-94; rtd 94. *137 Marlborough Avenue, Glasgow G11 7JE* Tel 0141-357 1553

McCULLAGH, Ms Elspeth Jane Alexandra. b 68. Man Univ BSc90. Wycliffe Hall Ox BTh95. **d** 95 **p** 96. C Huddersfield H Trin *Wakef* from 95. *60 Imperial Road, Huddersfield HD1 4PG* Tel (01484) 548340

McCULLAGH, John Eric. b 46. TCD BA68 BTh88 QUB DipEd70. **d** 88 **p** 89. C Stillorgan w Blackrock *D & G* 88-91; Chapl and Hd of RE Newpark Sch Dub from 90; I Clondalkin w Rathcoole from 91. *The Rectory, Monastery Road, Clondalkin, Dublin 22, Irish Republic* Tel Dublin (1) 459 2160

McCULLAGH, Mervyn Alexander. b 44. TCD BA68 BEng68. CITC 79. **d** 79 **p** 80. C Larne and Inver *Conn* 79-83; C Ballymacash 83-85; C Dublin St Ann w St Mark and St Steph *D & G* 85-88; I Baltinglass w Ballynure etc *C & O* from 88; Warden of Readers from 90; Preb Ossory and Leighlin Cathls 92-96; Treas Ossory and Leighlin Cathls from 96. *The Rectory, Baltinglass, Co Wicklow, Irish Republic* Tel Baltinglass (508) 81321

McCULLOCH, Alistair John. b 59. Univ of Wales (Lamp) BA81 Leeds Univ BA86. Coll of Resurr Mirfield 84. **d** 87 **p** 88. C Portsm Cathl *Portsm* 87-90; C Portsea St Mary 90-94; V Reading St Matt *Ox* 94-95. *Address temp unknown*

MacCULLOCH, Dr Diarmaid Ninian John. b 51. FSA78 FRHistS82 Chu Coll Cam BA72 MA76 PhD77 Liv Univ DAA72. Ripon Coll Cuddesdon DipTh87. **d** 87. NSM Clifton All SS w St Jo *Bris* 87-88. *28 William Street, Bristol BS3 4TT* Tel 0117-971 2422

McCULLOCH, Geoffrey Kenneth. b 10. OBE57. Lon Coll of Div 62. **d** 64 **p** 65. C Kingston upon Hull H Trin *York* 64-67; P-in-c Kingston upon Hull St Matt 68-71; P-in-c Kingston upon Hull St Barn 70-71; V Kingston upon Hull St Matt w St Barn 71-79; rtd 79; Perm to Offic *Lon* from 79. *5 Roy Road, Northwood, Middx HA6 1EQ* Tel (01923) 827438

✠**McCULLOCH, The Rt Revd Nigel Simeon.** b 42. Selw Coll Cam BA64 MA69. Cuddesdon Coll 64. **d** 66 **p** 67 **c** 86. C Ellesmere Port *Ches* 66-70; Dir Th Studies Ch Coll Cam 70-75; Chapl 70-73; Dioc Missr *Nor* 73-78; P-in-c Salisbury St Thos and St Edm *Sarum* 78-81; R 81-86; Adn Sarum 79-86; Can and Preb Sarum Cathl 79-86; Suff Bp Taunton *B & W* 86-92; Preb Wells Cathl 86-92; Bp Wakef from 92. *Bishop's Lodge, Woodthorpe Lane, Wakefield, W Yorkshire WF2 6JL* Tel (01924) 255349 Fax 250202

McCULLOCK, Mrs Patricia Ann. b 46. CertEd72. EMMTC 87. **d** 90 **p** 94. C Bottesford w Ashby *Linc* 90-95; P-in-c Wragby from 95. *The Rectory, Snelland Road, Wickenby, Lincoln LN3 5AB* Tel (01673) 885721

McCULLOUGH, Roy. b 46. Linc Th Coll 70. **d** 73 **p** 74. Chapl Highfield Priory Sch Lancs 73-77; C Ashton-on-Ribble St Andr *Blackb* 73-77; V Rishton 77-86; V Burnley (Habergham Eaves) St Matt w H Trin 86-97; RD Burnley 91-97; V Walton-le-Dale St Leon w Samlesbury St Leon from 97. *The Vicarage, Church Brow, Preston PR5 4BH* Tel (01772) 880233

McCULLOUGH, Sidney. b 31. QUB BA53 DipEd61 MEd74. CITC. **d** 89 **p** 91. NSM Glencraig *D & D* 89-91; Lic to Offic 91; I Ballyphilip w Ardquin from 91. *The Rectory, 8 Cloughey Road, Portaferry, Newtownards, Co Down BT22 1ND* Tel (01247) 728349

McCURDY, Hugh Kyle. b 58. Portsm Poly BA Univ of Wales (Cardiff) PGCE. Trin Coll Bris. **d** 85 **p** 86. C Egham *Guildf* 85-88; C Woking St Jo 88-91; V Histon *Ely* from 91; RD N Stowe from 94. *The Vicarage, 9A Church Street, Histon, Cambridge CB4 4EP* Tel (01223) 232255

McDERMID, The Ven Norman George Lloyd Roberts. b 27. St Edm Hall Ox BA49 MA52. Wells Th Coll 49. **d** 51 **p** 52. C Leeds St Pet *Ripon* 51-56; V Bramley 56-64; Dioc Stewardship Adv 64-76; R Kirkby Overblow 64-80; Hon Can Ripon Cathl 72-93; Dioc Stewardship Adv *Wakef* 73-76; Dioc Stewardship Adv *Bradf* 73-76; RD Harrogate *Ripon* 77-83; V Knaresborough 80-83; Adn Richmond 83-93; rtd 93. *Greystones, 10 North End, Bedale, N Yorkshire DL8 1AB* Tel (01677) 422210

McDERMOTT, Christopher Francis Patrick. b 54. Southeastern Coll USA BA84 Wheaton Coll Illinois MA87. EAMTC. **d** 95 **p** 96. C Gt Ilford St Clem and St Marg *Chelmsf* from 95. *25 Valentines Road, Ilford, Essex IG1 4RZ* Tel 0181-518 3982

MACDONALD, Alan Hendry. b 49. St Steph Ho Ox 86. **d** 88 **p** 89. C Heavitree w Ex St Paul *Ex* 88-91; C Withycombe Raleigh 91-92; TV 92-95; R Silverton, Butterleigh, Bickleigh and Cadeleigh from 95. *The Rectory, 21A King Street, Silverton, Exeter EX5 4JG* Tel (01392) 860350

MACDONALD, Alastair Douglas. b 48. St Jo Coll Dur 71. **d** 74 **p** 75. C Mottingham St Andr *S'wark* 74-78; C Woolwich St Mary w St Mich 78-81; V S Wimbledon St Andr 81-89; V Brighton St Matthias *Chich* 89-94; Chapl Southampton Community Services NHS Trust from 94. *Royal South Hampshire Hospital, Brinton Terrace, Southampton SO14 0YG* Tel (01703) 822666

MACDONALD, Cameron. b 51. Open Univ BA89. Wilson Carlile Coll 76 NE Ord Course 89. **d** 90 **p** 91. CA from 76; C Nairn *Mor* 90-92; P-in-c 92-95; CF from 95. *MOD Chaplains (Army), Trenchard Lines, Upavon, Pewsey, Wilts SN9 6BE* Tel (01980) 615804 Fax 615800

MACDONALD, Christopher Kenneth. b 57. Ex Univ BA79 PGCE80. Trin Coll Bris DipHE93. **d** 93 **p** 94. C Eastbourne All SS *Chich* 93-96; C Polegate from 96. *St Wilfrid's House, 90 Broad Road, Lower Willingdon, Eastbourne, E Sussex BN20 9RA* Tel (01323) 482088

MACDONALD, Colin. b 47. St Jo Coll Nottm 87. **d** 89 **p** 90. C Limber Magna w Brocklesby *Linc* 89-92; P-in-c Barrow and Goxhill 92-97; V from 97. *The Vicarage, Thornton Street, Barrow-on-Humber, S Humberside DN19 7DG* Tel (01469) 30357

MACDONALD, Canon Donald Courtenay. b 45. Nottm Univ BTh74 St Martin's Coll Lanc CertEd75. Kelham Th Coll 70. **d** 75 **p** 76. C Clifton All SS w Tyndalls Park *Bris* 75-78; C Clifton All SS w St Jo 78-79; Chapl Derby Lonsdale Coll *Derby* 79-84; V Derby St Andr w St Osmund from 84; RD Derby S from 89; Dioc Communications Officer 89-93; Hon Can Derby Cathl from 95. *St Osmund's Vicarage, London Road, Derby DE24 8UW* Tel (01332) 571329

McDONALD, Douglas Mark. b 28. Linc Coll Ox BA54 MA59. Wells Th Coll 68. **d** 69 **p** 70. C Horsham *Chich* 69-76; TV Kirkby Lonsdale *Carl* 76-79; P-in-c Tidmarsh w Sulham *Ox* 79-83; Chapl St Audries Sch W Quantoxhead 83-91; rtd 91; Perm to Offic *B & W* from 91. *18 Lower Park, Minehead, Somerset TA24 8AX* Tel (01643) 703104

McDONALD, Gordon James Joseph. b 17. Wycliffe Hall Ox 50. **d** 52 **p** 53. C Southall H Trin *Lon* 52-55; CMS 55-59; Uganda 56-59; P-in-c Dallam CD *Liv* 59-63; V Pemberton St Mark Newtown 63-80; R Easton w Letheringham *St E* 80-83; rtd 83. *Flat 21, Capel Court, The Burgage, Cheltenham, Glos GL52 3EL* Tel (01242) 579463

MACDONALD, Henry George Warren. b 20. TCD BA42 MA46 BD46. Div Test43. **d** 43 **p** 44. C Dublin St Thos w St Barn *D & G* 43-47; Chapl RNVR 47-49; Chapl RN 49-75; QHC from 74; C Fulford *York* 75-79; Perm to Offic *Ex* from 79; OCF from 87; rtd 92. *12 Little Ash Road, Plymouth PL5 1JT* Tel (01752) 361271

McDONALD, Canon Ian Henry. b 40. TD. St Aid Birkenhead 65. **d** 68 **p** 69. C Kingston upon Hull H Trin *York* 68-70; C Drumglass *Arm* 70-73; I Eglish w Killylea 73-80; I Maghera w Killelagh *D & R* 80-91; I Killowen from 91; CF (TAVR) from 91; Can Derry Cathl *D & R* from 94. *St John's Rectory, Laurel Hill, Coleraine, Co Londonderry BT51 3EE* Tel (01265) 42629

McDONALD, James Damian (Jack). b 66. Pemb Coll Cam BA87 MA91 SS Hild & Bede Coll Dur PGCE88 K Coll Lon MA96. Qu Coll Birm 90. **d** 92 **p** 93. C Camberwell St Geo *S'wark* 92-95; Chapl G&C Coll Cam from 95; Lic to Offic *Ely* from 95. *Gonville and Caius College, Cambridge CB2 1TA* Tel (01223) 332408 Fax 332456 E-mail jdm39@cam.ac.uk

MacDONALD, John. b 16. St Cath Soc Ox BA38 MA42 BLitt58. St Steph Ho Ox 39. **d** 41 **p** 42. C Birkdale St Jo *Liv* 41-44; C Walton St Mary 44-49; Chapl St Steph Ho Ox 49-54; Chapl Ch Ch Ox 51-60; Chapl New Coll Ox 52-60; Lib Pusey Ho 54-60; Chapl Burgess Hall Lamp 60-76; Sub-Warden 62-76; V Edstaston *Lich* 76-82; V Whixall 76-82; Chapl Choral Ches Cathl *Ches* 82-85; rtd 85. *47 The Links, Gwernaffield, Mold CH7 5DZ* Tel (01352) 740015

MACDONALD, John Alexander. b 07. Tyndale Hall Bris. **d** 41 **p** 42. C Burnage St Marg *Man* 41-44; C Man Albert Memorial Ch 44-46; V Wakef St Mary *Wakef* 46-53; V Byker St Mark *Newc* 53-80; rtd 80. *137 Bewick Park, Wallsend, Tyne & Wear NE28 9RY*

McDONALD, John Richard Burleigh. b 17. TCD BA40 BD41 MA. **d** 41 **p** 42. C Belfast St Pet *Conn* 41-45; Uganda 46-61; Educn Officer Ch of Ireland 61-64; Hd of RE Stranmills Coll of Educn Belf 66-86; Dir Post-Ord Tr *Conn* 86-94; rtd 94. *76 Osborne Drive, Belfast BT9 6LJ* Tel (01232) 666737

McDONALD, Lawrence Ronald. b 32. St Alb Minl Tr Scheme 84. **d** 87 **p** 88. NSM Sharnbrook and Knotting w Souldrop *St Alb* 87-90; C Bromham w Oakley and Stagsden 90-93; P-in-c Renhold from 93. *The Vicarage, 46 Church End, Renhold, Bedford MK41 0LU* Tel (01234) 771317

MACDONALD, Malcolm James. b 42. Sarum Th Coll 70. **d** 71 **p** 73. C Hounslow St Steph *Lon* 71-72; C Hammersmith St Sav 72-76; P-in-c Hammersmith St Luke 76-79; V 79-87; V Kirkby Woodhouse *S'well* from 87. *The Vicarage, 57 Skegby Road, Kirkby-in-Ashfield, Nottingham NG17 9JE* Tel (01623) 759094

MACDONALD, Canon Murray Somerled. b 23. Pemb Coll Cam BA46 MA49. Ely Th Coll 47. **d** 48 **p** 49. C Hendon St Mary *Lon* 48-51; C Hanover Square St Geo 51-53; P-in-c Upton and Copmanford *Ely* 53-54; R Sawtry 53-54; R Sawtry, Upton and Copmanford 54-57; V Upwood w Gt and Lt Raveley 57-62; R Wood Walton 57-62; V Fenstanton 62-70; V Hilton 62-70; RD Huntingdon 69-76; R Huntingdon All SS w St Jo 70-82; R Huntingdon St Mary w St Benedict 71-82; Hon Can Ely Cathl 72-82; Can Res 82-88; rtd 89; Perm to Offic *Linc* from 89; Perm to Offic *Ely* from 89. *4 Hacconby Lane, Morton, Bourne, Lincs PE10 0NT* Tel (01778) 570711

MACDONALD, Ranald Alexander (Alec). b 23. Fitzw Ho Cam BA50 MA55. Westmr Coll Cam 48 Lon Coll of Div 63. **d** 63 **p** 63. C Headstone St Geo *Lon* 63-67; In Pb Ch 51-62; R Parham & Wiggonholt w Greatham *Chich* 67-83; P-in-c Bolam w Whalton *Newc* 83-86; P-in-c Hartburn and Meldon 83-86; P-in-c Nether Witton 83-88; R Bolam w Whalton and Hartburn w Meldon 86-88; rtd 88; Perm to Offic *Chich* 88-93. *2 Redbarn Cottages, High Street, Henfield, W Sussex BN5 9HP* Tel (01273) 493370

MACDONALD, Stephen Calliss. b 35. Selw Coll Cam BA58. Westcott Ho Cam 58. **d** 60 **p** 61. C Norwood All SS *Cant* 60-64; Chapl Cov Cathl *Cov* 64-68; Chr Aid 68-70; rtd 96. *Crossways, Breachwood Green, Hitchin, Herts SG4 8PL* Tel (01438) 833210

MacDONALD, Trevor John. b 33. Hertf Coll Ox BA55 MA59. Chich Th Coll 92. **d** 93 **p** 94. NSM Hove St Barn and St Agnes *Chich* from 93. *31 Orchard Gardens, Hove, E Sussex BN3 7BH* Tel (01273) 771228

MACDONALD, Warren. Melbourne Univ BEng MPhil. Trin Coll Bris DipHE95. **d** 95 **p** 96. NSM Iford *Win* from 95. *40 Abinger Road, Bournemouth BH7 6LX* Tel (01202) 422131

MACDONALD-MILNE, Brian James. b 35. CCC Cam BA58 MA62 St Pet Coll Ox MA81. Cuddesdon Coll 58. **d** 60 **p** 61. C Fleetwood *Blackb* 60-63; Solomon Is 64-78; New Hebrides 78-80; Acting Chapl Trin Coll Ox 81; Acting Chapl St Pet Coll Ox 81-82; Asst Chapl HM Pris Grendon and Spring Hill 81-82; Research Fell Qu Coll Birm 82-83; Hon AP Bordesley SS Alb and Patr *Birm* 82-83; R Landbeach *Ely* 83-88; V Waterbeach 83-88; OCF 83-88; R Radwinter w Hempstead *Chelmsf* from 88; RD Saffron Walden 91-97; P-in-c The Sampfords 95-97; rtd 97. *39 Way Lane, Waterbeach, Cambridge CB5 9NQ* Tel (01223) 861631

McDONOUGH, David Sean. b 55. **d** 89 **p** 90. C Moseley St Mary *Birm* 89-92; TV Glascote and Stonydelph *Lich* from 92. *90 Briar, Tamworth, Staffs B77 4DZ* Tel (01827) 52754

McDONOUGH, Terence. b 57. St Jo Coll Nottm LTh86. **d** 89 **p** 90. C Linthorpe *York* 89-94; TV Heworth from 94. *6 Forest Way, Stockton Lane, York YO3 0BJ* Tel (01904) 425678

McDOUGAL, John Anthony Phelps Standen. *See* STANDEN McDOUGAL, Canon John Anthony Phelps

McDOUGALL, David Robin. b 61. Avery Hill Coll CertEd BEd84. Ridley Hall Cam 85. **d** 87 **p** 88. C Bletchley *Ox* 87-91; C High Wycombe 91-93; C E Twickenham St Steph *Lon* from 93. *17 Sandycoombe Road, Twickenham TW1 2LU* Tel 0181-891 0729

MacDOUGALL, Iain Ferguson. b 27. OBE JP. Clare Coll Cam BA51 MA55. Sarum & Wells Th Coll 85. **d** 86 **p** 87. NSM Langport Area Chs *B & W* 86-88; NSM Sedbergh, Cautley and Garsdale *Bradf* 88-90; NSM Appleby Deanery *Carl* 90-91; NSM Kirkby Stephen w Mallerstang etc from 91; OCF from 90. *Sandford Lodge, Sandford, Appleby-in-Westmorland, Cumbria CA16 6NR* Tel (017683) 52978

MacDOUGALL, Canon Iain William. b 20. TCD BA43 MA59. CITC 43. **d** 43 **p** 44. C Belfast St Steph *Conn* 43-45; C Enniskillen and Trory *Clogh* 45-48; I Drumlane *K, E & A* 48-50; I Ballinaclash *D & G* 51-54; I Moate *M & K* 54-58; I Ballyloughloe 54-58; I Ferbane 54-58; I Mullingar, Portnashangan, Moyliscar, Kilbixy etc 58-85; RD Duleek and Slane 58-85; Can Meath 81-85; rtd 85. *18 Denville Court, Killiney, Co Dublin, Irish Republic* Tel Dublin (1) 285 4751

McDOUGALL, Stuart Ronald. b 28. Leeds Univ DipAdEd MEd84. Roch Th Coll 64. **d** 66 **p** 67. C Gravesend St Aid *Roch* 66-69; C Wells St Thos w Horrington *B & W* 69-70; TV Tong *Bradf* 70-73; V Cononley w Bradley 73-82; C Thornthwaite w Thruscross and Darley *Ripon* 82-83; P-in-c Dacre w Hartwith 83-86; rtd 86. *Portman Chase Lodge, Chalbury, Wimborne, Dorset BH21 7EU* Tel (01258) 840558

MACDOUGALL, William Duncan. b 47. Nottm Univ BTh74 LTh74. St Jo Coll Nottm 69. **d** 74 **p** 75. C Highbury New Park St Aug *Lon* 74-77; C Tunbridge Wells St Jo *Roch* 78; SAMS 77 and 78-82; Argentina 78-82; V Rashcliffe and Lockwood *Wakef* 83-87; V Tonbridge St Steph *Roch* from 87. *St Stephen's Vicarage, 6 Brook Street, Tonbridge, Kent TN9 2PJ* Tel (01732) 353079

McDOWALL, Julian Thomas. b 39. CCC Cam BA62 MA67. Linc Th Coll 62. **d** 64 **p** 65. C Rugby St Andr *Cov* 64-70; C-in-c Stoke Hill CD *Guildf* 70-72; V Stoke Hill 72-76; R Elstead 76-91; V Thursley 82-91; TV Wellington and Distr *B & W* 91-93; C Lymington *Win* from 93. *20 Solent Avenue, Lymington, Hants SO41 3SD* Tel (01590) 676750

McDOWALL, Robert Angus (Robin). b 39. AKC66. **d** 67 **p** 68. C Bishopwearmouth St Mich w St Hilda *Dur* 67-69; CF from 69; Sen CF 80-91; Asst Chapl Gen 91-94; QHC from 93. *MOD Chaplains (Army), Trenchard Lines, Upavon, Pewsey, Wilts SN9 6BE* Tel (01980) 615804 Fax 615800

McDOWALL, Roger Ian. b 40. AKC64. **d** 65 **p** 66. C Peterlee *Dur* 65-68; C Weaste *Man* 68-70; C Tonge Moor 70-73; V Whitworth 73-80; TV Torre *Ex* 80-88; V Torre All SS from 88. *All Saints' Vicarage, 45 Barton Road, Torquay TQ1 4DT* Tel (01803) 328865

McDOWELL, Francis John. b 56. QUB BA78 LSE DipBS84. CITC BTh93. **d** 96 **p** 97. C Antrim *Conn* from 96. *28 Steeple Green, Antrim BT41 1BP* Tel (01849) 460107

McDOWELL, Ian. b 67. Ch Coll Cam MA88 BA92. Westcott Ho Cam CTM93. **d** 93 **p** 94. C Hackney *Lon* 93-96; Asst Chapl Homerton Hosp NHS Trust Lon from 96. *25 Strand Building, Urswick Road, London E9 6DW* Tel 0181-985 4683 or 919 7738 E-mail mcdow@dircon.co.uk

McDOWELL, Peter Kerr. b 69. QUB BA91. CITC BTh94. **d** 94 **p** 95. C Lisburn St Paul *Conn* from 94. *12 Belvoir Crescent, Lisburn, Co Antrim BT28 1VA* Tel (01846) 664189

McEACHRAN, Peter. b 20. **d** 75 **p** 76. Pakistan 75-79; Area Sec (Dios Ox and St Alb) CMS 79-97; Hon C Haddenham w Cuddington, Kingsey etc *Ox* 79-97; rtd 86. *15 Allens Lane, Wells, Somerset BA5 3NQ* Tel (01749) 672469

McELHINNEY, Mrs Mary Elizabeth Ellen (Liz). b 45. TCD BSSc67 BA67. CITC BTh94. **d** 97. C Magheralin w Dollingstown *D & D* from 97. *47 Cottage Road, Dollingsdown, Lurgan, Co Armagh BT67 9ND* Tel (01762) 322721

McENDOO, Canon Neil Gilbert. b 50. TCD BA72. CITC 75. **d** 75 **p** 76. C Cregagh *D & D* 75-79; C Dublin St Ann *D & G* 79-82; I Dublin Rathmines w Harold's Cross from 82; Can Ch Ch Cathl Dublin from 92. *The Rectory, Purser Gardens, Church Avenue, Rathmines, Dublin 6, Irish Republic* Tel Dublin (1) 497 1797

McENERY, Michael Joseph (Mike). b 35. Cant Sch of Min 77. **d** 80 **p** 81. C Smarden *Cant* 80-83; P-in-c 83-85; P-in-c Biddenden 83-85; P-in-c Harrietsham 85-86; P-in-c Ulcombe 85-86; R Harrietsham w Ulcombe 86-90; R Willesborough from 90. *The Rectory, 66 Church Road, Willesborough, Ashford, Kent TN24 0JG* Tel (01233) 624064

McEVITT, Peter Benedict. b 58. Coll of Resurr Mirfield 91. **d** 93 **p** 94. C Swinton and Pendlebury *Man* 93-96; TV from 96. *St Augustine's Vicarage, 23 Hospital Road, Pendlebury, Manchester M27 1EY* Tel 0161-794 2962

McFADDEN, Canon Ronald Bayle. b 30. TCD BA53 MA55. **d** 54 **p** 55. C Drumglass *Arm* 54-58; S Africa 58-62; Bp's Dom Chapl *D & D* 62-64; C Dundela 62-64; V Pateley Bridge and Greenhow Hill *Ripon* 64-73; V Knaresborough St Jo 73-79; P-in-c Knaresborough H Trin 78-79; Can Res Ripon Cathl 79-90; rtd 90; Chapl Qu Mary's Sch Baldersby Park 90-97. *12 Ure Bank Terrace, Ripon, N Yorkshire HG4 1JG* Tel (01765) 604043

McFADYEN, Canon Phillip. b 44. K Coll Lon BD69 AKC69 MTh70 ATD. St Aug Coll Cant 69. **d** 71 **p** 72. C Sheff St Mark Broomhall *Sheff* 71-74; Chapl Keswick Hall Coll Nor 74-79; V Swardeston *Nor* 79-81; P-in-c E Carleton 79-81; P-in-c Intwood w Keswick 79-81; R Swardeston w E Carleton w Intwood and Keswick 81-85; R Swardeston w E Carleton, Intwood, Keswick etc 85-90; V Ranworth w Panxworth and Woodbastwick from 90; Dioc Clergy Tr Officer from 90; Hon Can Nor Cathl from 97. *The Vicarage, Ranworth, Norwich NR13 6HT* Tel (01603) 270263 Fax 270597

McFARLAND, Alan Malcolm. b 24. Lon Univ BA53. Bris Sch of Min 82. **d** 85 **p** 86. NSM Westbury-on-Trym H Trin *Bris* 85-88; Asst Lect Bris Sch of Min 85-88; Perm to Offic *Glouc* 88-89; NSM Lechlade 89-93; Perm to Offic *Lon* from 92; Perm to Offic *Sarum* from 93. *11 The Sea Horse, Higher Sea Lane, Charmouth, Bridport, Dorset DT6 6BB* Tel (01297) 560414

McFARLAND, Darren William. b 71. QUB BA93. CITC BTh93. **d** 96. C Greystones *D & G* from 96; PV Ch Ch Cathl Dublin from 97. *192 Heatherview, Greystones, Co Wicklow, Irish Republic* Tel Dublin (1) 287 1336

McFARLANE, Beverly. b 50. RGN. Edin Th Coll 90 Brechin NSM Ord Course 85. **d** 87. NSM Dundee St Martin *Bre* 87-90; Par Dn Edin H Cross *Edin* 92-94; All SS Convent Ox from 94. *All Saints Convent, St Mary's Road, Oxford OX4 1RU* Tel (01865) 249127

McFARLANE, Ms Janet Elizabeth. b 64. Sheff Univ BMedSci87 St Jo Coll Dur BA92. Cranmer Hall Dur DMinlStuds93. **d** 93 **p** 94. Par Dn Stafford *Lich* 93-94; C 94-96; Chapl and Min Can Ely Cathl *Ely* from 96. *The Porta, The College, Ely, Cambs CB7 4DL* Tel (01353) 666781

McFARLANE, Percival Alan Rex. b 28. Columbia Univ (NY) BSc61 MA62. Montreal Dioc Th Coll 50. **d** 51 **p** 52. Canada 51-55 and 66-74; USA 55-66; Perm to Offic *Lon* from 86. *13 Formosa Street, London W9 2JS* Tel 0171-289 9922

MACFARLANE, William Angus. b 17. Worc Coll Ox BA39 MA43. Wycliffe Hall Ox 39. **d** 40 **p** 41. C Charles w Plymouth St Luke *Ex* 40-45; C Reading St Jo *Ox* 45-47; CMS Tr Coll Blackheath 47-48; C Brompton H Trin *Lon* 48-49; R Bighton

Win 49-52; V Bishop's Sutton 49-52; V Southwold *St E* 52-59; V Plaistow St Mary *Roch* 59-71; V Bexleyheath Ch Ch 71-79; Perm to Offic *B & W* 79-95; Chapl Sandhill Park Hosp Taunton 80-87; rtd 82. *Moorlands, Blue Anchor, Minehead, Somerset TA24 6JZ* Tel (01643) 821564

McFIE, Canon James Ian. b 28. Lich Th Coll 59. **d** 61 **p** 62. C Salford St Phil w St Steph *Man* 61-65; V Hey 65-75; V Elton All SS 75-85; V Walmsley 85-95; AD Walmsley 85-95; Hon Can Man Cathl 90-95; rtd 95; Perm to Offic *Carl* from 95. *4 Devonshire Road, Millom, Cumbria LA18 4JF* Tel (01229) 775192

McGANITY, Steven. b 61. Nottm Univ BTh93. St Jo Coll Nottm 90. **d** 93 **p** 94. C Gateacre *Liv* 93-97; V Clubmoor from 97. *St Andrew's Vicarage, 176 Queen's Drive, Liverpool L13 0AL* Tel 0151-226 1977

McGARAHAN, Kevin Francis. b 51. Oak Hill Th Coll BA84. **d** 84 **p** 85. C Balderstone *Man* 84-87; Sports Chapl from 86; C Stoughton *Guildf* 87-89; C Ashton St Mich *Man* 89-92; TV Madeley *Heref* 92-96; CF from 96. *MOD Chaplains (Army), Trenchard Lines, Upavon, Pewsey, Wilts SN9 6BE* Tel (01980) 615804 Fax 615800

McGEARY, Peter. b 59. K Coll Lon BD AKC. Chich Th Coll 84. **d** 86 **p** 87. C Brighton St Pet and St Nic w Chpl Royal *Chich* 86-90; C St Marylebone All SS *Lon* 90-95; P-in-c Hayes St Anselm 95-97; V from 97. *St Anselm's Vicarage, 101 Nield Road, Hayes, Middx UB3 1SQ* Tel 0181-573 0958

McGEE, Preb Peter John. b 36. Trin Coll Cam BA60 MA. Chich Th Coll 60. **d** 62 **p** 63. C N Keyham *Ex* 62-63; C St Marychurch 63-65; C Townstall w Dartmouth 65-68; C Cockington 68-71; V Exminster 71-78; V Alfington 78-82; V Ottery St Mary 78-82; RD Ottery 82-90; Preb Ex Cathl from 82; TR Ottery St Mary, Alfington and W Hill 82-87; TR Ottery St Mary, Alfington, W Hill, Tipton etc 87-96; P-in-c Woodbury from 96. *The Vicarage, Woodbury, Exeter EX5 1EF* Tel (01395) 232315

McGEE, The Very Revd Stuart Irwin. b 30. TCD BA53 MA68. **d** 53 **p** 54. C Belfast St Simon *Conn* 53-55; Singapore 55-58; I Drumholm and Rossnowlagh *D & R* 58-65; CF 65-77; Dep Asst Chapl Gen 77-88; Can Achonry Cathl *T, K & A* 89-92; I Achonry w Tubbercurry and Killoran 89-92; Dean Elphin and Ardagh *K, E & A* from 92; I Sligo w Knocknarea and Rosses Pt from 92. *The Cathedral Rectory, Strandhill Road, Sligo, Irish Republic* Tel Sligo (71) 62263

McGHIE, Clinton Adolphus. b 44. Univ of W Indies. CA Tr Coll. **d** 78 **p** 79. Jamaica 78-96; Perm to Offic *Chelmsf* 96-97; P-in-c Highams Park All SS from 97. *All Saints' Vicarage, 12A Castle Avenue, London E4 9QD* Tel 0181-527 3269

McGILL, Francis Leonard (Frank). b 31. **d** 93 **p** 94. NSM Howell Hill *Guildf* from 93. *27 Hampton Grove, Ewell, Epsom, Surrey KT17 1LA* Tel 0181-393 2226

MacGILLIVRAY, Canon Alexander Buchan. b 33. Edin Univ MA55 Aber Univ DipEd67. Edin Th Coll 55. **d** 57 **p** 58. Chapl St Ninian's Cathl Perth *St And* 57-59; Chapl Aberlour Orphanage 59-62; C Aberlour *Mor* 59-62; R Oldmeldrum *Ab* from 62; R Whiterashes from 62; R Fyvie from 74; R Insch from 74; Can St Andr Cathl from 78. *The Rectory, Oldmeldrum, Inverurie, Aberdeenshire AB51 0AD* Tel (01651) 872208

MacGILLIVRAY, Jonathan Martin. b 53. Aber Univ MA75. Coll of Resurr Mirfield. **d** 80 **p** 81. C Hulme Ascension *Man* 80-84; P-in-c Birch St Agnes 84-85; R 85-91; V Hurst 91-96; Chapl Tameside Gen Hosp 92-96; Dir of Ords *Man* from 96; LNSM Officer from 96. *2 Hamilton Road, Prestwich, Manchester M25 8GG* Tel 0161-773 0675 or 708 9366 Fax 792 6829

McGINLEY, Jack Francis. b 36. ALCD65. **d** 65 **p** 66. C Erith St Paul *Roch* 65-70; C Morden *S'wark* 70-74; V New Catton Ch Ch *Nor* 74-94; RD Nor N 84-89; Hon Can Nor Cathl 90-94; R Carlton-in-the-Willows *S'well* from 94; R Colwick from 96. *St Paul's Rectory, Church Street, Nottingham NG4 1BJ* Tel 0115-961 6169

McGINLEY, John Charles. Trin Coll Bris. **d** 96 **p** 97. C Hounslow H Trin w St Paul *Lon* from 96. *183 Bath Road, Hounslow TW3 3BU*

McGIRR, Canon William Eric. b 43. CITC 68. **d** 71 **p** 72. C Carrickfergus *Conn* 71-74; C Mt Merrion *D & D* 74-77; I Donacavey w Barr *Clogh* 77-88; RD Kilskeery 86-88; I Ballybeen *D & D* 88-94; I Magheraculmoney *Clogh* from 94; Can Clogh Cathl from 95. *The Rectory, Kesh, Enniskillen, Co Fermanagh BT93 1TF* Tel (01365) 632221

McGLASHAN, Alastair Robin. b 33. MSAnPsych90 Ch Ch Ox BA57 MA58 St Jo Coll Cam BA59 MA63. Ridley Hall Cam 58. **d** 60 **p** 61. C St Helens St Helen *Liv* 60; C Ormskirk 60-62; India 63-74; USA 74-75; C Lamorbey H Redeemer *Roch* 75-77; Chapl W Park Hosp Epsom 77-85; Chapl Maudsley Hosp Lon 85-87; Perm to Offic *S'wark* from 86. *102 Westway, London SW20 9LS* Tel 0181-542 2125

McGLINCHEY, Patrick Gerard. b 59. **d** 95 **p** 96. C Kettering Ch the King *Pet* 95-97; C Gorleston St Andr *Nor* from 97. *1 South Garden, Gorleston, Great Yarmouth, Norfolk NR31 6TL* Tel (01493) 699401

McGONIGLE, Canon Thomas. b 22. TCD BA45 MA65. TCD Div Sch 43. **d** 46 **p** 47. C Drumglass *Arm* 46-50; I Clogherney 50-53; I Magherafelt 53-61 and 74-88; I Portadown St Mark 61-74; Can Arm Cathl 72-88; Treas 79-83; Chan 83-88; Prec 88; rtd 88; Lic to Offic *Arm* from 88. *91 Kernan Gardens, Portadown, Craigavon, Co Armagh BT63 5RA* Tel (01762) 330892

McGOWAN, Anthony Charles. b 57. Jes Coll Cam BA79 MA. Coll of Resurr Mirfield. **d** 82 **p** 83. C Milford Haven *St D* 82-85; C Penistone *Wakef* 85-86; C Thurlstone 85-86; C Penistone and Thurlstone 86-88; CR from 88; Asst Chapl Radcliffe Infirmary Ox 91-94; Chapl Radcliffe Infirmary NHS Trust from 94. *Radcliffe Infirmary, Woodstock Road, Oxford OX2 6HE* Tel (01865) 224664 or 311188

McGOWAN, Preb Michael Hugh. b 35. St Cath Coll Cam BA58 MA62. Clifton Th Coll. **d** 60 **p** 61. C Islington St Mary *Lon* 60-63; Chapl Lyon w Grenoble and Aix-les-Bains *Eur* 63-67; Chapl Chantilly, Rouen, Caen and Le Havre 63-65; Asst Chapl Chapl Paris St Mich 63-67; V Maidenhead St Andr and St Mary *Ox* 68-81; V S Mimms Ch Ch *Lon* 82-96; AD Cen Barnet 91-96; Preb St Paul's Cathl from 96; P-in-c Upper Chelsea St Simon from 96; P-in-c Upper Chelsea St Sav from 96. *St Simon Zelotes Vicarage, 34 Milner Street, London SW3 2QF* Tel 0171-589 5747

McGOWN, Robert Jackson. b 20. Keble Coll Ox BA42 MA46. Linc Th Coll 42. **d** 45 **p** 46. C Ipswich St Mary le Tower *St E* 45-47; Chapl Brockhurst Sch 47-49; Perm to Offic *Ox* 49-50; C Astbury *Ches* 50-51; C Glouc St Mary de Lode and St Nic *Glouc* 51-54; Min Can Glouc Cathl 51-54; C W Kirby St Bridget *Ches* 64-71; Perm to Offic from 76; rtd 85. *16 Church Road, West Kirby, Wirral, Merseyside L48 0RW* Tel 0151-625 9481

McGRANAGHAN, Patrick Joseph Colum. b 46. Glas Univ BSc68 Lanc Univ MA72. St Alb Minl Tr Scheme. **d** 85 **p** 86. NSM Markyate Street *St Alb* 85-94. *Clovelly Court, Glencairn Road, Kilmacolm, Renfrewshire PA13 4NR* Tel (01505) 872733 Fax 874164 E-mail cmcgranagh@aol.com

McGRATH, Prof Alister Edgar. b 53. Wadh Coll Ox BA75 Mert Coll Ox MA78 DPhil78 BD83. Westcott Ho Cam 78. **d** 80 **p** 81. C Wollaton *S'well* 80-83; Tutor Wycliffe Hall Ox from 83; Prin from 95; Chapl St Hilda's Coll Ox 83-87; Research Lect in Th Ox Univ from 93; Prof Systematic Th Regent Coll Vancouver from 93. *Wycliffe Hall, 54 Banbury Road, Oxford OX2 6PW* Tel (01865) 274209 or 244658 Fax 311346 or 274215

McGRATH, Dr Gavin John. b 53. Marietta Coll (USA) BA76 Trin Episc Sch for Min MDiv81 Dur Univ PhD90. **d** 81 **p** 82. USA 81-87; C Fulwood *Sheff* 87-95. *c/o The L'Abri Fellowship, The Manor House, Greatham, Liss, Hants GU33 6HP* Tel (01420) 538436

McGRATH, Ian Denver. b 47. Leeds Univ CertEd72. LNSM course 85. **d** 87 **p** 88. NSM Ancaster *Linc* 87-89; NSM Ancaster Wilsford Gp 89-92; C Spilsby w Hundleby 92-95; P-in-c Asterby Gp from 95. *The Rectory, Butt Lane, Goulceby, Louth, Lincs LN11 9UP* Tel (01507) 343345

McGRATH, John. b 49. Salford Univ BSc78 Man Poly CertEd79. N Ord Course 82. **d** 85 **p** 86. C Horwich *Man* 85-88; P-in-c Hillock 88-89; V 89-94; V York St Luke *York* from 94. *St Luke's Vicarage, 79 Burton Stone Lane, York YO3 6BZ* Tel (01904) 630354

McGRATH, Patrick Desmond. b 64. Liv Univ LLB86. Wycliffe Hall Ox 92. **d** 96 **p** 97. C Netherton *Liv* from 96. *57 Park Lane West, Bootle, Merseyside L30 3SX* Tel 0151-521 5977

MACGREGOR, Alan John. S Tr Scheme. **d** 97. NSM Worting *Win* from 97. *65 Oakridge Road, Basingstoke, Hants RG21 2SF*

McGREGOR, Alistair Darrant. b 45. ALCD69. **d** 69 **p** 70. C Streatham Immanuel w St Anselm *S'wark* 69-73; Bermuda 73-76; Warden St Mich Cen New Cross 76-80; C Hatcham St Jas *S'wark* 76-80; V Nor Heartsease St Fran *Nor* 80-87; TR Thetford 87-96; P-in-c Kilverstone 87-90; P-in-c Croxton 87-90; RD Thetford and Rockland 90-95; TR Gt Baddow *Chelmsf* from 96. *The Vicarage, 12 Church Street, Great Baddow, Chelmsford CM2 7HZ* Tel (01245) 471740

MacGREGOR, Colin Highmoor. b 19. Lon Univ BSc45 Magd Coll Cam BA47 MA50. Wells Th Coll 54. **d** 56 **p** 57. C Camberwell St Giles *S'wark* 56-60; V Clapham St Pet 60-73; V Riddlesdown 73-87; rtd 87. *Flat 3, Longacre Court, 21 Mayfield Road, South Croydon, Surrey CR2 0BG* Tel 0181-651 2615

MACGREGOR, Donald Alexander Thomson (Don). b 52. Loughb Univ BSc75 Leic Univ CertEd78. St Jo Coll Nottm DTS93. **d** 93 **p** 94. C Walmley *Birm* 93-96; C Braunstone *Leic* 96-97; TV from 97. *36 Woodcote Road, Leicester LE3 2WD* Tel 0116-282 5272

✠MACGREGOR, The Rt Revd Gregor. b 33. St Andr Univ MA64 BD67. **d** 77 **p** 77 **c** 94. NSM Elie and Earlsferry *St And* 77-81; NSM Pittenweem 77-81; R Glenrothes 81-86; C Cumbrae (or Millport) *Arg* 86; P-in-c Dollar *St And* 87-90; Wester Hailes St Luke *Edin* 91-94; Bp Mor from 94. *Bishop's House, 34 Rangemore Road, Inverness IV3 5EA* Tel (01463) 231059 or 226255

MacGREGOR, Neil. b 35. Keble Coll Ox BA60 MA80. Wells Th Coll. **d** 65 **p** 66. C Bath Bathwick St Mary w Woolley *B & W* 65-70; R Oare w Culbone 70-74; C Lynton, Brendon, Countisbury and Lynmouth *Ex* 70-74; P-in-c Kenn w Kingston Seymour *B & W* 74-76; R 76-80; V Lee Brockhurst *Lich* from 80; R Wem from 80; P-in-c Loppington w Newtown from 95; RD Wem and Whitchurch from 95. *The Rectory, Ellesmere Road, Wem, Shrewsbury SY4 5TU* Tel (01939) 232550

McGREGOR, Nigel Selwyn. b 47. FCA69. Sarum & Wells Th Coll 87. **d** 89 **p** 90. C Charlton Kings St Mary *Glouc* 89-92; P-in-c Seale *Guildf* 92-95; P-in-c Puttenham and Wanborough 92-95; R Seale, Puttenham and Wanborough from 95. *The Rectory, Seale, Farnham, Surrey GU10 1JA* Tel (01252) 782302

McGUFFIE, Dr Duncan Stuart. b 45. Man Univ MA70 Regent's Park Coll Ox DPhil80. S Dios Minl Tr Scheme 84. **d** 85 **p** 85. C Sholing *Win* 85-89; V Clavering w Langley and Arkesden *Chelmsf* from 89. *The Vicarage, 54 Pelham Road, Clavering, Saffron Walden, Essex CB11 4PQ* Tel (01799) 550703

McGUINNESS, Gordon Baxter. b 57. St Andr Univ BSc79 BNC Ox MSc80. Oak Hill NSM Course 86. **d** 89 **p** 90. NSM Loudwater *Ox* 89-92; C Chilwell *S'well* from 92. *Church House, Barncroft, Chilwell, Nottingham NG9 4HU* Tel 0115-922 1879

McGUIRE, Alec John. b 51. Societas Liturgica 85 MRSH86 BAC Acc 90 K Coll Cam BA73 MA76. Westcott Ho Cam 74. **d** 78 **p** 79. C Hungerford and Denford *Ox* 78-81; Prec Leeds St Pet *Ripon* 81-86; Perm to Offic 86-90. *34 Gledhow Wood Road, Leeds LS8 4BZ* Tel 0113-240 0336

McGUIRE, John. b 31. Oak Hill Th Coll 59. **d** 62 **p** 65. C Tooting Graveney St Nic *S'wark* 62-64; C Normanton *Derby* 64-67; N Area Sec ICM 67-71; Chapl RNR 67-81; R Biddulph Moor *Lich* from 71. *The Rectory, Hot Lane, Biddulph Moor, Stoke-on-Trent ST8 7HP* Tel (01782) 513323

MACHA, David. b 65. Keele Univ BA88 St Jo Coll Dur BA94. **d** 97. C Loughborough Em and St Mary in Charnwood *Leic* from 97. *47 Brookfield Avenue, Loughborough, Leics LE11 3LN* Tel (01509) 261070

McHAFFIE, Alistair. b 57. Oak Hill Th Coll DipHE94. **d** 94 **p** 95. C Braintree *Chelmsf* from 94. *183 Notley Road, Braintree, Essex CM7 3HG* Tel (01376) 322578

McHARDY, Canon Iain William Thomson Duff. b 13. St Andr Univ MA36. Ely Th Coll 37. **d** 38 **p** 39. C S Kirkby *Wakef* 38-45; C Cantley *Sheff* 45-52; P-in-c Invergordon St Ninian *Mor* 52-74; Can St Andr Cathl Inverness 64-80; R Fortrose 74-80; Dean Mor 77-80; rtd 80; Hon Can St Andr Cathl Inverness *Mor* from 80. *Beech Tree Cottage, Navity, Cromarty, Ross-shire IV11 8XY* Tel (01381) 600451

McHUGH, Brian Robert. b 50. FSS77 AFIMA83 York Univ BA72 Keele Univ CertEd73 Southn Univ CEurStuds78 Portsm Poly CertComp84 DPSE90. S Dios Minl Tr Scheme 79. **d** 82 **p** 83. NSM Sarisbury *Portsm* 82-86; NSM Shedfield from 86. *28 Siskin Close, Bishops Waltham, Southampton SO32 1RQ* Tel (01489) 896658

MACINNES, Canon David Rennie. b 32. Jes Coll Cam BA55 MA59. Ridley Hall Cam 55. **d** 57 **p** 58. C Gillingham St Mark *Roch* 57-61; C St Helen Bishopsgate w St Martin Outwich *Lon* 61-67; Prec Birm Cathl *Birm* 67-78; Angl Adv ATV 67-82; Angl Adv Cen TV from 82; Dioc Missr *Birm* 79-87; Hon Can Birm Cathl 81-87; R Ox St Aldate w St Matt *Ox* 87-94; R Ox St Aldate from 95. *St Aldate's Parish Centre, 40 Pembroke Street, Oxford OX1 1BP* Tel (01865) 244713

MACINNES, Harry Campbell. b 67. Nottm Poly BA89. Wycliffe Hall Ox BTh94. **d** 97. C E Twickenham St Steph *Lon* from 97. *308 Richmond Road, Twickenham, Middx TW1 2NH* Tel 0181-891 3504

MACINTOSH, Andrew Alexander. b 36. St Jo Coll Cam BA59 MA63 BD80. Ridley Hall Cam 60. **d** 62 **p** 63. C S Ormsby Gp *Linc* 62-64; Lect St D Coll Lamp 64-67; Lic to Offic *Ely* from 67; Chapl St Jo Coll Cam 67-69; Asst Dean 69-79; Dean from 79; Lect Th from 70. *St John's College, Cambridge CB2 1TP* Tel (01223) 338600

McINTOSH, Andrew Malcolm Ashwell. b 43. Chich Th Coll 67. **d** 70 **p** 71. C Brentwood St Thos *Chelmsf* 70-74; C Chingford SS Pet and Paul 74-79; P-in-c Maldon St Mary w Mundon 79-83; R from 83. *St Mary's Rectory, Park Drive, Maldon, Essex CM9 7JG* Tel (01621) 857191

MacINTOSH, George Grant. b 41. St Jo Coll Dur BA75 DipTh76. **d** 76 **p** 77. C Ecclesall *Sheff* 76-79; Hon C Sheff St Oswald 79-81; Dioc Adult Educn Officer from 81; V Crookes St Tim 81-88; V Abbeydale St Jo from 88; RD Ecclesall 89-94. *The Rectory, Deveron Road, Turriff, Aberdeenshire AB53 4BB* Tel (01888) 563238

McINTOSH, Canon Hugh. b 14. Hatf Coll Dur LTh41 BA42 MA45. Edin Th Coll 38. **d** 42 **p** 42. C St Paul's Cathl Dundee *Bre* 42-46; Chapl St Mary's Cathl *Edin* 46-49; C Edin St Salvador 49-51; R Gullane 51-54; R Dumfries *Glas* 54-66; Can St Mary's Cathl 59-66 and 70-83; Syn Clerk 59-66; Provost 66-70; R Lanark 70-83; rtd 83; Hon Can St Mary's Cathl *Glas* from 83. *2 Ridgepark Drive, Lanark ML11 7PG* Tel (01555) 663458

McINTOSH, Ian MacDonald. b 64. Jes Coll Cam BA86. Trin Coll Bris BA90. **d** 90 **p** 91. C Belmont *Lon* 90-92; C Pinner 92-95; Chapl Leic Univ *Leic* from 96; TV Leic H Spirit from 96. *290 Victoria Park Road, Leicester LE2 1ZE* Tel 0116-285 6493 E-mail imm4@le.ac.uk

McINTOSH, Mrs Nicola Ann. b 60. Trin Coll Bris DipHE89 ADPS90. **d** 90 **p** 94. Par Dn Queensbury All SS *Lon* 90-93; Par Dn Ruislip Manor St Paul 93-94; C 94-95; NSM Clarendon Park St Jo w Knighton St Mich *Leic* from 96. *290 Victoria Park Road, Leicester LE2 1ZE* Tel 0116-285 6493

MACINTYRE, Angus Greer. b 14. Linc Coll Ox BA36 DipTh39 MA41. Wycliffe Hall Ox 38. **d** 39 **p** 40. C Sheepscar *Ripon* 39-40; Chapl RAFVR 40-46; C Edin St Jo *Edin* 46-48; R Edin Ch Ch-St Jas 48-52; Chapl Trin Coll Glenalmond 52-68; Can St Ninian's Cathl Perth *St And* 66-68; V Harborne St Pet *Birm* 68-76; St Helena 76-79; rtd 79; Hon C Edin Ch Ch *Edin* 79-90. *12 Inverleith Place, Edinburgh EH3 5PZ* Tel 0131-551 3287

McINTYRE, James Whitelaw. b 37. Lon Univ BD66. Edin Th Coll 59. **d** 62 **p** 63. C Dumfries *Glas* 62-66; P-in-c Cumbernauld 66-74; R Stirling *Edin* 74-93; rtd 93. *24 Cedar Avenue, Stirling FK8 2PQ* Tel (01786) 474380

McINTYRE, Robert Mark. b 69. Nottm Univ BA91. Coll of Resurr Mirfield 92. **d** 94 **p** 95. C Wednesbury St Jas and St Jo *Lich* 94-97; C Wolstanton from 97. *14 Dorrington Grove, Porthill, Newcastle, Staffs ST5 0HY*

McKAE, William John. b 42. Liv Univ BSc63 St Mark & St Jo Coll Lon PGCE64 Bris Univ DipTh70. Wells Th Coll 68. **d** 71 **p** 72. C Tranmere St Paul w St Luke *Ches* 71-74; C Midsomer Norton *B & W* 74-75; TV Birkenhead Priory *Ches* 75-80; R Oughtrington 80-91; Chapl Asst Hope, Salford R and Ladywell Hosps Man 91-92; Lic Preacher *Man* 91-92; R Heaton Reddish from 92. *The Rectory, St Mary's Drive, Stockport, Cheshire SK5 7AX* Tel 0161-477 6702

McKAVANAGH, Dermot James. b 51. TCD BA75 MA78 K Coll Lon BD78 AKC78. **d** 78 **p** 79. C Croydon H Sav *Cant* 78-82; Asst Chapl Wellington Coll Berks 82-87; Lic to Offic *Ox* 85-87; Chapl RAF from 87; Perm to Offic *Nor* from 95. *Chaplaincy Services (RAF), HQ, Personnel and Training Command, RAF Innsworth, Gloucester GL3 1EZ* Tel (01452) 712612 ext 5164 Fax 510828

McKAY, Brian Andrew. b 39. Sarum Th Coll 69. **d** 71 **p** 72. C Walker *Newc* 71-74; C Wooler Gp 74-77; TV 77-81; V Long Benton St Mary 81-89; TV Bellingham/Otterburn Gp 89-91; TV N Tyne and Redesdale Team from 91. *The Vicarage, Otterburn, Newcastle upon Tyne NE19 1NP* Tel (01830) 520212

MACKAY, Canon Douglas Brysson. b 27. Edin Th Coll 56. **d** 58 **p** 59. Prec St Andr Cathl Inverness *Mor* 58-61; P-in-c Fochabers 61-70; R 70-72; Chapl Aberlour Orphanage 64-67; P-in-c Aberlour 64-72; Syn Clerk 65-72; Can St Andr Cathl Inverness 65-72; Hon Can from 72; R Carnoustie *Bre* from 72; Can St Paul's Cathl Dundee from 81; Syn Clerk from 81. *Holyrood Rectory, Carnoustie, Angus DD7 6AB* Tel (01241) 852202

MACKAY, Hedley Neill. b 27. St Aid Birkenhead 53. **d** 56 **p** 57. C Beverley St Mary *York* 56-59; C Scarborough St Mary 59-60; Nigeria 61-70; C Wawne *York* 70-71; TV Sutton St Jas and Wawne 72-76; V Huntington 76-82; TR 82-93; Perm to Offic from 93; rtd 93; Dioc Rtd Clergy and Widows Officer *York* from 94. *2 Elmfield Terrace, Heworth, York YO3 0EH* Tel (01904) 412971

MACKAY, Ian Stuart Reay. b 31. St Aid Birkenhead 56. **d** 58 **p** 59. C Selly Oak St Mary *Birm* 58-60; Ind Chapl *Sheff* 60-66; C Pitsmoor 61-63; C Rotherham 63-66; V Bolton Sav *Man* 66-71; Lect Liv Educn Authority 71-74; Regional Officer Nat Assn for Teachers in F&HE 75-91; rtd 92. *5 East Meade, Chorltonville, Manchester M21 2DX* Tel 0161-881 1228

MACKAY, James Alexander Nigel. b 11. TCD BA38. Edin Th Coll 38. **d** 41 **p** 42. C Edin All SS *Edin* 41-45; R Alexandria *Glas* 45-51; V Kelstern, Calcethorpe and E Wykeham *Linc* 51-59; R Ludford Magna w Ludford Parva 51-59; P-in-c Kentish Town St Benet and All SS *Lon* 60-62; V Weasenham *Nor* 62-67; V Rougham 62-67; Perm to Offic *Lon* 72-76; rtd 76. *33 Russell Court, Bushmead Avenue, Bedford MK40 3RW*

McKAY, John Andrew. b 38. HDipEd. Chich Th Coll. **d** 74 **p** 75. C Primrose Hill St Mary w Avenue Road St Paul *Lon* 74-77; V Battersea Ch Ch and St Steph *S'wark* 77-82; I Rathkeale w Askeaton and Kilcornan *L & K* 82-85; I Dublin St Bart w Leeson Park *D & G* from 85. *12 Merlyn Road, Ballsbridge, Dublin, Irish Republic* Tel Dublin (1) 269 4813

McKAY, John William. b 41. Aber Univ MA62 Keble Coll Ox BA64 Selw Coll Cam PhD69. Ridley Hall Cam 66. **d** 70 **p** 71. Lect Th Hull Univ 69-82; Hon C Cottingham *York* 70-79; Hon C Willerby 79-82; R Prestwick *Glas* 82-85; Dir of Studies Roffey Place Chr Tr Cen Horsham from 85; Lic to Offic *Chich* from 85. *Kingdom Faith Ministries, Roffey Place, Crawley Road, Faygate, Horsham, W Sussex RH12 4SA* Tel (01293) 851543 Fax 851330

McKAY, Margaret McLeish. *See* HALE, Mrs Margaret McLeish

McKEACHIE, William Noble. b 43. **d** 70 **p** 70. Chapl St Jo Coll Ox 70-72; USA 73 and from 78; Canada 74-78. *126 Coming Street, Charleston, South Carolina 29403, USA*

McKEARNEY, Andrew Richard. b 57. Selw Coll Cam MA. Edin Th Coll 81. **d** 82 **p** 83. Prec St Ninian's Cathl Perth *St And* 82-84; Chapl St Mary's Cathl *Edin* 84-88; R Hardwick *Ely* 88-94; R Toft w Caldecote and Childerley 88-94; V Chesterton Gd Shep from 94. *The Good Shepherd Vicarage, 51 Highworth Avenue, Cambridge CB4 2BQ* Tel (01223) 312933

McKECHNIE, John Gregg. b 30. Em Coll Cam BA54 MA57. Ridley Hall Cam 54. **d** 55 **p** 56. C Morden *S'wark* 55-57; Tutor Clifton Th Coll 57-62; R Chich St Pancras and St Jo *Chich* 62-68; V Reading St Jo *Ox* 68-85; RD Reading 83-85; V Lindfield *Chich* 85-95; rtd 95; Perm to Offic *Chich* from 95. *3 The Courtyard,*

Stockbridge Road, Chichester, W Sussex PO19 2GP Tel (01243) 531703

McKEE, Douglas John Dunstan. b 34. Univ of W Aus BA65. St Mich Th Coll Crafers 54. **d** 57 **p** 58. Australia 57-72 and from 85; SSM from 58; Lic to Offic *S'well* 73-85. *St John's College, College Road, St Lucia, Queensland, Australia 4067* Tel Brisbane (7) 3871 8377

McKEE, Canon Harold Denis. b 30. TCD BA53 MA57. **d** 54 **p** 55. C Dublin Donnybrook *D & G* 54-58; Treas V St Patr Cathl Dub 56-61; C Dublin St Bart 58-61; Succ Sheff Cathl *Sheff* 61-65; Can Res and Prec Sheff Cathl 65-86; C Preston St Jo *Blackb* 86-87; TV 87-92; rtd 92; Perm to Offic *Sheff* from 92. *200 Cobden View Road, Sheffield S10 1HT* Tel 0114-267 8214

McKEE, Patrick Joseph. b 49. Ripon Coll Cuddesdon DipMin94. **d** 94 **p** 95. C Oakham, Hambleton, Egleton, Braunston and Brooke *Pet* 94-97; V Ryhall w Essendine and Carlby from 97. *The Vicarage, Church Street, Ryhall, Stamford, Lincs PE9 4HR* Tel (01780) 62398

McKEE, William Thomas. b 18. CITC 64. **d** 65 **p** 66. C Ballymena *Conn* 65-68; C Willowfield *D & D* 68-73; Bp's C Magherally w Annaclone 73-77; I 77-85; rtd 85. *Flat 15, Fold Mews, 22 Ballyholme Road, Bangor, Co Down BT20 5JS* Tel (01247) 459598

McKEEMAN, David Christopher. b 36. AKC58 DipEd76. **d** 60 **p** 61. C Catford St Andr *S'wark* 60-64; P-in-c W Dulwich Em 64-69; Lic to Offic *Win* 70-82; R Silchester from 82. *The Rectory, Silchester, Reading RG7 2LU* Tel (0118) 970 0322

McKEGNEY, John Wade. b 47. TCD BA70 MA81. CITC 70. **d** 72 **p** 73. C Ballynafeigh St Jude *D & D* 72-75; C Bangor St Comgall 75-80; I Drumgath w Drumgooland and Clonduff 80-83; I Gilnahirk 83-90; I Arm St Mark w Aghavilly *Arm* from 90. *St Mark's Rectory, 14 Portadown Road, Armagh BT61 9EE* Tel (01861) 522970

MACKEITH (née GODFREY), Mrs Ann Veronica. b 35. Bris Univ BSc57 CertEd. Gilmore Course 78. **dss** 79 **d** 87 **p** 94. Bishopwearmouth Ch Ch *Dur* 79-83; Bishopwearmouth St Gabr 83-86; Ryhope 86-88; Par Dn 87-88; Par Dn Darlington H Trin 88-94; C 94-95; Family Life Officer from 95. *135 Hummersknott Avenue, Darlington, Co Durham DL3 8RR* Tel (01325) 463481

McKELLAR, John Lorne. b 19. Sarum Th Coll 70. **d** 72 **p** 73. C Warminster St Denys *Sarum* 72-75; USA 75-79 and 81-84; P-in-c Colchester St Barn *Chelmsf* 79-81; rtd 84. *Corrie, 105A Clay Street, Crockerton, Warminster, Wilts BA12 8AG* Tel (01985) 213161

McKELVEY, Mrs Jane Lilian. b 48. Liv Inst of Educn BA94. Nor Bapt Coll 94. **d** 97. C Aughton St Mich *Liv* from 97. *92 Delph Park Avenue, Aughton, Ormskirk, Liverpool L39 6SB* Tel 0151-228 4159

McKELVEY, Canon Robert Samuel James Houston. b 42. QUB BA65 MA(Ed)88. CITC 67. **d** 67 **p** 68. C Dunmurry *Conn* 67-70; CF (TAVR) from 70; P-in-c Kilmakee *Conn* 70-77; I 77-81; N Ireland Educn Org from 81; Preb Newcastle St Patr Cathl Dublin from 89. *19 Upper Lisburn Road, Belfast BT10 0GW* Tel (01232) 619008 or 301130

McKELVIE, Canon Alfred. b 10. TCD BA34 MA43. CITC 35. **d** 35 **p** 36. C Lisburn Ch Ch *Conn* 35-38; C Ballynafeigh St Jude *D & D* 38-42; I Templecorran w Islandmagee *Conn* 42-46; I Belfast St Donard *D & D* 46-56; I Ballynafeigh St Jude 56-80; Adn Down 70-75; Chan Down Cathl 75-80; rtd 80. *50 Blenheim Park, Carryduff, Belfast BT8 8NN* Tel (01232) 812682

McKEMEY, Alfred Douglas. b 18. Tyndale Hall Bris 38. **d** 42 **p** 43. C Upper Holloway St Pet *Lon* 42-45; C Heatherlands St Jo *Sarum* 45-48; SE Area Sec CPAS 48-51; V Plumstead St Paul *S'wark* 51-57; V Eastbourne All SS *Chich* 57-68; V Burgess Hill St Andr 68-84; RD Hurst 80-84; rtd 84; Perm to Offic *Chich* from 85; P-in-c Henfield w Shermanbury and Woodmancote 91-92. *45 Parsonage Road, Henfield, W Sussex BN5 9JG* Tel (01273) 493222

McKEMEY, Canon Robert. b 15. St Aid Birkenhead 50. **d** 52 **p** 53. C Blackb Ch Ch *Blackb* 52-53; PC Blackb St Barn 53-57; Kenya 57-69; Schs Supervisor 57-64; Adn Nakuru 64-69; I Kilrea *D & R* 69-73; R Meysey Hampton w Marston Meysey *Glouc* 73-81; RD Fairford 77-81; I Clondevaddock *D & R* 81-85; rtd 85. *3 Sevenoaks Road, Reading RG6 7NT* Tel 0118-966 0501

McKENNA, Dermot William. TCD BA63 MA66. CITC 64. **d** 64 **p** 65. C Enniscorthy *C & O* 64-66; I Killeshin 66-84; rtd 84. *20 Sherwood, Pollerton, Carlow, Irish Republic* Tel Carlow (503) 32003

McKENNA, Lindsay Taylor. b 62. Glas Univ MA83 Aber Univ BD86. Edin Th Coll 87. **d** 87 **p** 88. C Broughty Ferry *Bre* 87-90; C Wantage *Ox* 90-93; V Illingworth *Wakef* from 93. *St Mary's Vicarage, 157 Keighley Road, Illingworth, Halifax, W Yorkshire HX2 9LL* Tel (01422) 244322

MACKENNA, Richard William. b 49. Pemb Coll Cam BA71 MA75. Ripon Coll Cuddesdon BA77 MA81. **d** 78 **p** 79. C Fulham St Dionis Parson's Green *Lon* 78-81; C Paddington St Jas 81-85; Tutor Westcott Ho Cam 85-89; V Kingston All SS w St Jo *S'wark* 90-91. *187 Lichfield Court, Sheen Road, Richmond, Surrey TW9 1BB* Tel 0181-940 0893

MACKENNA, Robert Christopher Douglass (Chris). b 44. Or Coll Ox BA72 MA75 MBAP85. Cuddesdon Coll 71. **d** 73 **p** 74. C Farncombe *Guildf* 73-77; C Tattenham Corner and Burgh Heath 77-80; P-in-c Hascombe 80-90; R from 90; RD Godalming 91-96. *The Rectory, The Street, Hascombe, Godalming, Surrey GU8 4JA* Tel (01483) 208362

MACKENZIE, Alfred Arthur. b 25. Bps' Coll Cheshunt 61. **d** 61 **p** 62. C Waltham Abbey *Chelmsf* 61-64; V Barking St Erkenwald 64-72; V Broomfield 72-83; P-in-c Willerby w Ganton and Folkton *York* 83-91; R 91-95; rtd 95. *41 Suggitts Lane, Cleethorpes, S Humberside DN35 7JG*

MACKENZIE, Andrew John Kett. b 46. Southn Univ BA68. LNSM course 88. **d** 91 **p** 92. Fullbrook Sch New Haw from 76; NSM Woodham *Guildf* from 91. *250 Albert Drive, Sheerwater, Woking, Surrey GU21 5TY* Tel (01932) 346712

MACKENZIE, Miss Ann. b 54. CertEd76 DipHE82 DPS86. Trin Coll Bris 82. **dss** 85 **d** 87 **p** 94. Normanton *Wakef* 85-87; Par Dn 87-90; Par Dn Bletchley *Ox* 90-94; C from 94. *13 Burns Road, Bletchley, Milton Keynes MK3 5AN* Tel (01908) 366729

MACKENZIE, David Stuart. b 45. Linc Th Coll 66. **d** 69 **p** 70. C Bishopwearmouth St Mary V w St Pet CD *Dur* 69-72; C Pontefract St Giles *Wakef* 72-74; Chapl RAF from 74. *Chaplaincy Services (RAF), HQ, Personnel and Training Command, RAF Innsworth, Gloucester GL3 1EZ* Tel (01452) 712612 ext 5164 Fax 510828

MACKENZIE, George. b 09. MBE46 TD50. Worc Coll Ox BA31 MA35. Wells Th Coll 32. **d** 33 **p** 34. C Whalley *Blackb* 33-36; C Ashton-on-Ribble St Andr 36-44; CF (TA) 35-59; CF (TA - R of O) 59-64; V Whaddon w Tattenhoe *Ox* 45-47; R W Grinstead *Chich* 47-52; R Sullington 52-74; R Storrington 53-74; RD Storrington 63-70; rtd 74; Perm to Offic *Chich* from 74. *21 The Martlets, West Chiltington, Pulborough, W Sussex RH10 2QB* Tel (01798) 812771

MacKENZIE, Canon Iain MacGregor. b 37. Qu Coll Ox BA59 MA63 BD91 Edin Univ MTh69. Wycliffe Hall Ox. **d** 63 **p** 64. C Southampton St Mary w H Trin *Win* 63-66; C Christchurch 66-69; R Dunoon *Arg* 69-75; V Pokesdown All SS *Win* 75-78; C Woolston 78-79; C St Giles-in-the-Fields *Lon* 79-82; R St Marylebone St Mary 82-89; Can Res Worc Cathl *Worc* from 89; Select Preacher Ox Univ 96. *2 College Green, Worcester WR1 2LH* Tel (01905) 25238 or 28854 Fax 611139

McKENZIE, Ian Colin. b 31. CA56 Nottm Univ CTPS92. EMMTC 89. **d** 93. NSM Edin St Mark *Edin* from 93; NSM Edin St Andr and St Aid from 93. *7 Highfield Close, Ravenshead, Nottingham NG15 9DZ* Tel (01623) 792162

MACKENZIE, Ian William (Bill). b 46. Trin Coll Bris DipHE95. **d** 95 **p** 96. C Bideford *Ex* 95-96; C Bideford, Northam, Westward Ho!, Appledore etc from 96. *61 Hanson Park, Bideford, Devon EX39 3SB* Tel (01237) 477482

McKENZIE, Jack Llewellyn. b 29. FRSH AMIEHO MAMIT. S'wark Ord Course. **d** 79 **p** 80. Hon C Stonebridge St Mich *Lon* 79-88; Hon C Willesden St Mary from 88. *2 Beckett Square, Chiltern Park, Berkhamsted, Herts HP4 1BZ* Tel (01442) 874265

MACKENZIE, Preb Lawrence Duncan. b 30. St Aid Birkenhead 52. **d** 55 **p** 56. C Blackb St Gabr *Blackb* 55-58; C Burnley St Pet 58-60; C St Giles-in-the-Fields *Lon* 60-63; V Queensbury All SS 63-85; V Hillingdon St Jo 85-96; Preb St Paul's Cathl 89-96; rtd 96; NSM Gt Stanmore *Lon* from 96. *16 The Chase, Stanmore, Middx HA7 3RY* Tel 0181-954 4616

MACKENZIE, Peter Sterling. b 65. Univ Coll Lon BSc88. Oak Hill Th Coll BA95. **d** 95 **p** 96. C Roxeth *Lon* from 95. *69 Southdown Crescent, Harrow, Middx HA2 0QT*

MACKENZIE, Canon Peter Thomas. b 44. Lon Univ LLB67 Nottm Univ DipTh68 Westmr Coll Ox MTh97. Cuddesdon Coll 68. **d** 70 **p** 71. C Leigh Park *Portsm* 70-75; P-in-c Sittingbourne St Mary *Cant* 75-82; V Folkestone St Sav 82-90; RD Elham 89-90; R Cant St Martin and St Paul from 90; RD Cant from 95; Hon Can Cant Cathl from 97. *The Rectory, 13 Ersham Road, Canterbury, Kent CT1 3AR* Tel (01227) 462686

McKENZIE, Mrs Priscilla Ann (Cilla). b 47. St Jo Coll Nottm 87. **d** 93 **p** 94. NSM Ellon *Ab* 93-96; NSM Cruden Bay 93-96; Perm to Offic *Roch* from 96. *Iona, Linton Hill, Linton, Maidstone, Kent ME17 4AW* Tel (01622) 741318

MACKENZIE, Reginald James Sterling. b 11. Sarum Th Coll 55. **d** 57 **p** 57. C Bognor St Jo *Chich* 57-59; R Tillington 59-67; V St Kew *Truro* 67-73; P-in-c St Hilary 73-78; P-in-c Perranuthnoe 73-78; P-in-c St Hilary w Perranuthnoe 78-81; rtd 81. *7 Lindsey Court, Bognor Regis, W Sussex PO22 8JQ*

MACKENZIE, Richard Graham. b 49. St Aug Coll Cant 72. **d** 73 **p** 74. C Deal St Leon *Cant* 73-75; C Deal St Leon w Sholden 75-78; C Herne 78-81; Canada from 81. *46 Victoria Street, Petawawa, Ontario, Canada, K8H 2G6*

MACKENZIE, Simon Peter Munro. b 52. Univ Coll Ox BA74. Coll of Resurr Mirfield 82. **d** 85 **p** 86. C Tipton St Jo *Lich* 85-91; V Perry Beeches *Birm* from 91. *St Matthew's Vicarage, 313 Beeches Road, Birmingham B42 2QR* Tel 0121-360 2100

McKEON, Canon James Ernest. b 22. TCD BA45 HDipEd49 Div Test. **d** 46 **p** 47. C Dundalk *Arm* 46-48; C Dublin St Geo *D & G* 48-52; I Kilsaran w Drumcar, Dunleer and Dunany *Arm* 52-59; I Drogheda 59-64; P-in-c Termonfeckin and Beaulieu

62-64; Warden Wilson's Hosp Sch Multyfarnham 64-83; Can Kildare Cathl *M & K* 83-88; Prec 87-88; P-in-c Geashill w Killeigh and Ballycommon 83-88; rtd 88; Dioc Info Officer (Meath) *M & K* 90-91; Radio Officer 91-96. *Church House, Collinstown, Mullingar, Co Westmeath, Irish Republic* Tel Collinstown (44) 66229

McKEON, Canon Victor Edward Samuel. b 39. FCA65 Lon Univ BD. CITC. **d** 68 **p** 69. C Enniskillen *Clogh* 68-72; Accountant to Conn & D & D 72-79; P-in-c Magherahamlet *D & D* 77-79; I Derryvullen N w Castlearchdale *Clogh* 79-91; Dioc Treas from 83; Can Clogh Cathl 86-89; Preb 89-95; Chan from 95; I Monaghan w Tydavnet and Kilmore 91-95; RD Monaghan 91-95; I Trory w Killadeas from 95. *Trory Rectory, Rossfad, Ballinamallard, Co Fermanagh BT94 2LS* Tel (01365) 388477

MACKERACHER, Alasdair John. b 22. Linc Th Coll 69. **d** 71 **p** 72. C Oakdale St Geo *Sarum* 71-73; C Swanage 73-78; V W Alvington w S Milton *Ex* 78-81; R Ashreigney 81-85; R Broadwoodkelly 81-85; V Brushford 81-85; V Winkleigh 81-85; V Swimbridge and W Buckland 85-88; rtd 88. *2 Peak Coach House, Cotmaton Road, Sidmouth, Devon EX10 8SY*

MACKEY, John. b 34. Lich Th Coll. **d** 64 **p** 65. C Kells *Carl* 64-67; C Barrow St Matt 67-70; R Clayton *Man* 70-75; V Low Marple *Ches* 75-83; R Coppenhall from 83. *The Rectory, Coppenhall, Crewe CW1 3TN* Tel (01270) 215151

MACKEY, Lionel John. b 47. FCA76 AITI78 TCD BTh93. CITC 90. **d** 93 **p** 94. C Raheny w Coolock *D & G* 93-96; I Templebreedy w Tracton and Nohoval *C, C & R* from 96. *The Rectory, Crosshaven, Cork, Irish Republic* Tel Cork (21) 831236 Fax as telephone E-mail mackeyl@tinet.ie

McKIBBIN, Gordon. b 29. Lon Univ DipTh57. St Aid Birkenhead 55. **d** 58 **p** 59. C Dundela *D & D* 58-60; C Knotty Ash St Jo *Liv* 61-64; V Gt Sankey from 64. *The Parsonage, Parsonage Way, Great Sankey, Warrington WA5 1RP* Tel (01925) 723235

MacKICHAN, Gillian Margaret (Gill). b 34. Bedf Teacher Tr Coll DipPE56 Cam Univ CertEd56 Lon Univ DSocStuds76 CQSW80. S Dios Minl Tr Scheme 90. **d** 93 **p** 94. NSM Upper Kennet *Sarum* from 93. *West Bailey, Lockeridge, Marlborough, Wilts SN8 4ED* Tel (01672) 861629

MACKIE, Ian William. b 31. Lon Univ BSc53 Ex Univ PGCE54. Linc Th Coll 81. **d** 83 **p** 84. C Market Rasen *Linc* 83-87; V Bracebridge Heath 87-96; RD Christianity 92-96; rtd 96. *57 Bridle Crescent, Chapeltown, Sheffield S30 4QX* Tel (0114) 284 4073

McKIE, Kenyon Vincent. b 60. Aus Nat Univ BA83 Canberra Coll DipEd84. ACT BTh88 DipMin89. **d** 86 **p** 87. Australia 86-89; Hon C Coulsdon St Andr *S'wark* from 89. *23 Rickman Hill, Coulsdon, Surrey CR5 3DS* Tel (01737) 557732

McKINLEY, Canon Arthur Horace Nelson. b 46. TCD BA69 MA79. CITC 70. **d** 70 **p** 71. C Taney Ch Ch *D & G* 71-76; I Dublin Whitechurch from 76; Preb Dunlavin St Patr Cathl Dublin from 91. *Whitechurch Vicarage, Whitechurch Road, Rathfarnham, Dublin 16, Irish Republic* Tel Dublin (1) 493 3953

McKINLEY, George Henry. b 23. TCD BA44 MA51. **d** 46 **p** 47. C Waterford Ch Ch *C & O* 46-49; I Fiddown 49-51; I Fiddown w Kilmacow 51-54; C S Harrow St Paul *Lon* 54-58; V Stonebridge St Mich 58-65; R Hackney St Jo 65-72; TR Hackney 72-77; V Painswick w Sheepscombe *Glouc* 77-83; Bp's Chapl 83-87; C Sandhurst 83-85; C Twigworth, Down Hatherley, Norton, The Leigh etc 85-87; rtd 88; Perm to Offic *Heref* from 96. *Middlemarch, 2 Old Barn Court, Bircher, Leominster, Herefordshire HR6 0AU* Tel (01568) 780795

McKINNEL, Nicholas Howard Paul. b 54. Qu Coll Cam BA75 MA79. Wycliffe Hall Ox BA79 MA86. **d** 80 **p** 81. C Fulham St Mary N End *Lon* 80-83; Chapl Liv Univ *Liv* 83-87; P-in-c Hatherleigh *Ex* 87-88; R Hatherleigh, Meeth, Exbourne and Jacobstowe 88-94; P-in-c Plymouth St Andr w St Paul and St Geo 94-95; TR Plymouth St Andr and St Paul Stonehouse from 95. *St Andrew's Vicarage, 13 Bainbridge Avenue, Plymouth PL3 5QZ* Tel (01752) 772139 or 661414

McKINNEY, James Alexander. b 52. Ex Univ BA74 Hull Univ MA87. Ripon Coll Cuddesdon 75. **d** 78 **p** 79. C Wath-upon-Dearne w Adwick-upon-Dearne *Sheff* 78-82; V Doncaster Intake 82-87; Ind Chapl 84-87; Chapl Bramshill Police Coll *Win* 87-92; V Cleator Moor w Cleator *Carl* 92-96; Chapl Cumbria Constabulary 93-96; P-in-c Frizington and Arlecdon 94-96; V Roehampton H Trin *S'wark* from 96. *The Vicarage, 7 Ponsonby Road, London SW15 4LA* Tel 0181-788 9460

McKINNEY, Mervyn Roy. b 48. St Jo Coll Nottm. **d** 81 **p** 82. C Tile Cross *Birm* 81-84; C Bickenhill w Elmdon 84-89; V Addiscombe St Mary *S'wark* 89-93; V Addiscombe St Mary Magd w St Martin from 93. *St Mary Magdalene Vicarage, Canning Road, Croydon CR0 6QD* Tel 0181-654 3459

McKINNON, Archibald Vincent. b 07. **d** 77 **p** 78. Hon C Tranmere St Paul w St Luke *Ches* 77-79; Hon C W Kirby St Bridget 79-88; rtd 88; Perm to Offic *Ches* from 88. *4 Caldy Court, Caldy Road, Wirral, Merseyside L48 2HG*

MacKINNON, Mrs Karen Audrey. b 64. Ex Univ BA85. Linc Th Coll CMM92. **d** 92 **p** 94. Par Dn Filton *Bris* 92-93; Par Dn Bris Lockleaze St Mary Magd w St Fran 93-94; C 94-96; P-in-c from 96. *The Parsonage, Copley Gardens, Bristol BS7 9YE* Tel 0117-951 2516

McKINNON, Neil Alexander. b 46. Wycliffe Hall Ox 71. **d** 74 **p** 75. C Deptford St Nic w Ch Ch *S'wark* 74-76; C St Helier 76-79; Min W Dulwich All SS and Em 79-81; TV Thamesmead 87-95; V S'wark H Trin w St Matt from 95. *The Rectory, Meadow Row, London SE1 6PQ* Tel 0171-407 1707

MACKINNON, Ross Cameron. b 52. St Steph Ho Ox 86. **d** 88 **p** 89. C Monk Bretton *Wakef* 88-91. *4 Cornwall Close, Barnsley, S Yorkshire S71 2ND* Tel (01226) 281275

MACKINTOSH, AEneas. b 27. Kelham Th Coll 44. **d** 52 **p** 53. Prec St Andr Cathl Inverness *Mor* 52-55; C Wisbech St Aug *Ely* 55-57; P-in-c Glas St Matt *Glas* 57-60; R 60-61; R Haddington *Edin* 61-65; C Edin St Jo 65-69; R 69-81; Can St Mary's Cathl 75-87; R Gullane 81-87; R N Berwick 81-87; Info Officer & Communications Adv to the Gen Syn 87-92; rtd 92. *31 St Albans Road, Edinburgh EH9 2LT* Tel 0131-667 4160

MACKINTOSH, Robin Geoffrey James. b 46. Rhodes Univ BCom71 Cranfield Inst of Tech MBA78 Ox Univ BA85 MA91. Ripon Coll Cuddesdon 83. **d** 86 **p** 87. C Cuddesdon *Ox* 86; C Cannock *Lich* 86-89; R Girton *Ely* from 89. *The Rectory, 40 Church Lane, Girton, Cambridge CB3 0JP* Tel (01223) 276235 Fax as telephone

McKITTRICK, Douglas Henry. b 53. St Steph Ho Ox 74. **d** 77 **p** 78. C Deptford St Paul *S'wark* 77-80; C W Derby (or Tuebrook) St Jo *Liv* 80-81; TV St Luke in the City 81-89; V Toxteth Park St Agnes and St Pancras from 89. *St Agnes's Vicarage, 1 Buckingham Avenue, Liverpool L17 3BA* Tel 0151-733 1742

McKITTRICK, Noel Thomas Llewellyn. b 28. TCD BA50 MA57 BD71. **d** 51 **p** 53. C Londonderry Ch Ch *D & R* 51-52; C Belfast St Aid *Conn* 52-54; C Knockbreda *D & D* 54-58; C Keynsham w Queen Charlton *B & W* 58-59; V Glastonbury St Benedict 59-82; V Weston-super-Mare St Paul 82-92; rtd 93; Perm to Offic *Ex* from 94. *Priory Lodge, Latimer Road, Exeter EX4 7JP* Tel (01392) 496744

McKNIGHT, John Andrew. b 49. **d** 78 **p** 79. Australia 78-89; C Eltham St Sav *S'wark* 89-90; C Catford St Laur 91-93; C Bellingham St Dunstan 91-93. *75 Bexhill Road, London SE4 1SJ* Tel 0181-690 2904

McKNIGHT, Thomas Raymond. b 48. QUB BEd71. CITC 74. **d** 77 **p** 78. C Lisburn Ch Ch Cathl *Conn* 77-80; C Carrickfergus 80-82; I Kilcronaghan w Draperstown and Sixtowns *D & R* 82-86; I Magheragall *Conn* 86-91; RD Lisburn 88-91; CF from 91. *MOD Chaplains (Army), Trenchard Lines, Upavon, Pewsey, Wilts SN9 6BE* Tel (01980) 615804 Fax 615800

MACKRIELL, Peter John. b 64. Mansf Coll Ox BA85 MA93 Man Univ PGCE87. St Jo Coll Nottm BTh93 MA94. **d** 94 **p** 95. C Hale and Ashley *Ches* 94-96; C Marple All SS from 96. *125 Church Lane, Marple, Stockport, Cheshire SK6 7LD* Tel 0161-427 1467

MACKRILL, Robert John (Bob). b 51. RIBA79 Univ Coll Lon BSc73 DipArch76. EMMTC 92. **d** 93 **p** 94. NSM Stamford All SS w St Jo *Linc* 93-97; P-in-c Stamford Ch Ch from 97. *110 Lonsdale Road, Stamford, Lincs PE9 2SF* Tel (01780) 754490

MacLACHLAN (née GRIFFITHS), Mrs Margaret. b 44. SRN67 Birm Poly CertEd81 Open Univ BA82. WMMTC 92. **d** 95 **p** 96. NSM Tile Cross *Birm* from 95. *Wayside, 17 Chester Road, Birmingham B36 9DA* Tel 0121-747 2340

MACLACHLAN, Michael Ronald Frederic. b 39. Wycliffe Hall Ox 75. **d** 77 **p** 78. C Mansfield St Pet *S'well* 77-80; P-in-c Newark Ch Ch 80; TV Newark w Hawton, Cotham and Shelton 80-86; P-in-c Sparkhill St Jo *Birm* 86-90; P-in-c Sparkbrook Em 86-90; V Sparkhill w Greet and Sparkbrook 90-92; RD Bordesley 90-92; Canada from 92. *St Andrew's Mission, Box 296, Kugluktuk, NWT, Canada, XOE OEO* Tel Kugluktuk (403) 982 3073 Fax 982 3487

McLACHLAN, Ms Sheila Elizabeth. b 52. SRN73 Kent Univ MA89. Wycliffe Hall Ox 80. **dss** 83 **d** 87 **p** 94. Chapl Kent Univ *Cant* 83-94; Dep Master Rutherford Coll 87-94; D-in-c Kingsnorth w Shadoxhurst 94; P-in-c from 94. *The Rectory, Church Hill, Kingsnorth, Ashford, Kent TN23 3EG* Tel (01233) 620433

MacLAREN, Ms Clare. b 67. Edin Univ LLB88. Linc Th Coll BTh95. **d** 95 **p** 96. C Benchill *Man* from 95. *St Luke's House, Brownley Road, Manchester M22 4PT* Tel 0161-945 7399

MacLAREN, Duncan Arthur Spencer. b 69. Or Coll Ox BA90 MA96. Oak Hill Th Coll 92. **d** 94 **p** 95. C Ox St Clem *Ox* 94-97; Chapl St Edm Hall Ox from 97. *12A Morrell Avenue, Oxford OX4 1NE* Tel (01865) 790837

MACLAREN, Grant. b 12. St Cath Coll Cam BA37 MA41. Wycliffe Hall Ox 37. **d** 39 **p** 40. C Greenwich H Trin and St Paul *S'wark* 39-42; C Gipsy Hill Ch Ch 42-45; C Beccles St Mich *St E* 45-48; V Oulton Broad *Nor* 48-56; PC Derby Ch Ch *Derby* 56-57; P-in-c Derby H Trin 56-57; PC Derby Ch Ch and H Trin 57-73; V Stanley 73-80; rtd 80; Perm to Offic *Derby* from 80. *21 Tennessee Road, Chaddesden, Derby DE21 6LE* Tel (01332) 661226

MACLAREN (née ALEXANDER), Mrs Jane Louise. b 69. LMH Ox BA90 MA96. Oak Hill Th Coll BA95. **d** 95 **p** 96. C Ox St Clem *Ox* from 95. *12A Morrell Avenue, Oxford OX4 1NE* Tel (01865) 790837

McLAREN, Mrs Jeanette Moira. b 59. **d** 95 **p** 96. C Dulwich St Clem w St Pet *S'wark* from 95. *9 Grass Mount, London SE23 3UW*

McLAREN, Richard Francis. b 46. Mansf Coll Ox DSocStuds69. S'wark Ord Course 72. **d** 75 **p** 76. C Charlton St Luke w H Trin *S'wark* 75-78; C Kensington St Mary Abbots w St Geo *Lon* 78-81; Hon C St Marylebone w H Trin 82-96; P-in-c 96-97. *Church Urban Fund, 2 Great Peter Street, London SW1P 3LX* Tel 0171-222 7011 ext 4361

McLAREN, Robert Ian (Rob). b 62. Bris Univ BSc84 St Jo Coll Dur BA87. Cranmer Hall Dur 85. **d** 88 **p** 89. C Birkenhead Ch Ch *Ches* 88-90; C Bebington 90-95; V Cheadle All Hallows from 95. *All Hallows' Vicarage, 222 Councillor Lane, Cheadle, Cheshire SK8 2JG* Tel 0161-428 9071

McLAREN, Ronald. b 31. Kelham Th Coll. **d** 59 **p** 60. C Redcar *York* 59-62; C Hornsea and Goxhill 62-65; V Middlesbrough St Thos 65-70; Chapl RN 70-73; Australia from 73; rtd 96. *16 Moselle Drive, Thornlands, Queensland, Australia 4164*

McLAREN, William Henry. b 27. OBE94. Edin Th Coll 55. **d** 56 **p** 57. C Skipton H Trin *Bradf* 56-60; V Bingley H Trin 60-65; V Allerton 65-68; R Aberdeen St Mary *Ab* 68-73; P-in-c Newland St Aug *York* 73-74; V 74-75; V Hull St Cuth 75-81; V Hedon w Paull 81-94; RD S Holderness 84-94; rtd 94; Perm to Offic *York* from 94. *Kirklea, Ottringham Road, Keyingham, Hull HU12 9RX* Tel (01964) 624159

McLARNON, Mrs Sylvia Caroline Millicent. b 45. S Dios Minl Tr Scheme 92. **d** 95 **p** 96. NSM Burgess Hill St Andr *Chich* from 95. *75 Cants Lane, Burgess Hill, W Sussex RH15 0LX* Tel (01444) 233902

McLAUGHLIN, Hubert James Kenneth. Greenwich Univ BTh93. **d** 88 **p** 89. NSM Donagheady *D & R* 88-89; NSM Glendermott from 89. *9 Cadogan Park, Kilfennan, Londonderry BT47 1QW* Tel (01504) 48916

McLAUGHLIN, Michael Anthony. b 48. **d** 97. C Gt Chart *Cant* from 97. *5 Yeoman's Square, Hoppers Way, Chartfield Hamlet, Ashford, Kent TN23 4GH*

MCLAY, Robert James. b 49. **d** 73 **p** 74. New Zealand 73-75 and from 77; Hon C Yardley St Edburgha *Birm* 75-77. *4 Livet Place, Papakowhai, Porihua, New Zealand* Tel Wellington (4) 233 1211 or 233 9781

MACLEAN, Alexander James. b 28. CEng MIStructE53. St Aid Birkenhead 52. **d** 55 **p** 56. C Wigan St Cath *Liv* 55-57; C Rainford 57-60; V Chadderton Em *Man* 60-69; R Largs *Glas* 69-71; V E Crompton *Man* 71-79; V Turners Hill *Chich* 79-89; rtd 89; Perm to Offic *Chich* from 89. *22 College Road, Ardingly, Haywards Heath, W Sussex RH17 6TY* Tel (01444) 892199

MACLEAN, The Very Revd Allan Murray. b 50. Edin Univ MA72. Cuddesdon Coll 72. **d** 76 **p** 77. Chapl St Mary's Cathl *Edin* 76-81; Tutor Edin Univ 77-80; R Dunoon *Arg* 81-86; R Tighnabruaich 84-86; Provost St Jo Cathl Oban from 86; Can from 86; Can Cumbrae from 86; R Oban St Jo from 86; R Ardbrecknish from 86; R Ardchattan from 89; Miss to Seamen from 86. *The Rectory, Ardconnel Terrace, Oban, Argyll PA34 5DJ* Tel (01631) 562323

McLEAN, Dr Bradley Halstead. b 57. McMaster Univ Ontario BSc Toronto Univ MDiv MTh PhD. **d** 83 **p** 84. C Dur St Giles *Dur* 83-84; Canada from 84. *38 Tweedsmuir Road, Winnipeg, Manitoba, Canada, R3P 1Z2, or St John's College, 400 Dysart Road, Winnipeg, Manitoba, Canada R3T 2M5*

MACLEAN, Donald Allan Lachlan. b 05. Linc Coll Ox BA27 MA31. Linc Th Coll 27. **d** 28 **p** 29. C Frodingham *Linc* 28-33; C Farnham Royal *Ox* 33-35; C Edin St Jo *Edin* 35-39; R Galashiels 39-43; R Fort William *Arg* 43-44; R Highnam w Lassington and Rudford *Glouc* 44-50; R Greystoke *Carl* 50-53; R Aylton w Pixley and Munsley *Heref* 53-63; R Pitlochry *St And* 63-70; rtd 70; Perm to Offic *Mor* from 70. *Hazelbrae House, Glenurquhart, Inverness IV3 6TJ* Tel (01456) 476267

McLEAN, The Ven Donald Stewart. b 48. TCD BA70. CITC 70. **d** 72 **p** 73. C Glendermott *D & R* 72-75; I Castledawson 75-87; Dioc Dir of Ords from 79; I Londonderry Ch Ch from 87; Can Derry Cathl from 91; Adn Derry from 96. *Christ Church Rectory, 80 Northland Road, Londonderry BT48 0AL* Tel (01504) 263279

MACLEAN, Dorothy. b 31. Dundee Coll DipEd70. **d** 86. NSM Kirriemuir *St And* from 82. *84 Slade Gardens, Kirriemuir, Angus DD8 5AG* Tel (01575) 72396

McLEAN, Mrs Eileen Mary. b 44. City Univ BSc67. N Ord Course 85. **d** 88 **p** 94. Par Dn Burley in Wharfedale *Bradf* 88-92; Par Dn Nottingham St Pet and St Jas *S'well* 92-94; C from 94. *15 Hamilton Drive, The Park, Nottingham NG7 1DF* Tel 0115-924 3354

McLEAN, Miss Frances Ellen. b 21. RGN44 SCM45. Edin Dioc NSM Course 85. **d** 88 **p** 94. NSM Penicuik *Edin* from 88; NSM W Linton from 88. *56 Cuikenburn, Penicuik, Midlothian EH26 0JQ* Tel (01968) 675029

MACLEAN, John Raglan. b 19. Univ of NZ BA47. Cuddesdon Coll 47. **d** 50 **p** 51. C Moorfields *Bris* 50-53; New Zealand from 53. *PO Box 87 193, Auckland 1130, New Zealand* Tel Auckland (9) 528 9768

MACLEAN, Kenneth John Forbes. b 31. St Deiniol's Hawarden 80. **d** 81 **p** 82. C Sedgley All SS *Lich* 81-85; V Shareshill 85-90; R Bicton, Montford w Shrawardine and Fitz 90-96; rtd 96. *7 The Armoury, Wenlock Road, Shrewsbury SY2 6PA* Tel (01743) 243308

McLEAN, Ms Margaret Anne (Maggie). b 62. Birm Univ BA91. Qu Coll Birm 88. **d** 91 **p** 94. Par Dn Bedford All SS *St Alb* 91-94; C 94; Chapl St Alb High Sch for Girls from 94. *4 High Street, Colney Heath, St Albans, Herts AL4 0NU* Tel (01727) 821647

McLEAN, Canon Michael Stuart. b 32. Dur Univ BA57. Cuddesdon Coll 57. **d** 59 **p** 60. C Camberwell St Giles *S'wark* 59-61; Lic to Offic *Nor* 61-68; R Marsham 68-74; R Burgh 68-74; RD Ingworth 70-74; P-in-c Nor St Pet Parmentergate w St Jo 74-75; TV 75-78; TR 78-86; Hon Can Nor Cathl 82-86; Can Res Nor Cathl 86-94; P-in-c Nor St Mary in the Marsh 87-94; Perm to Offic from 94. *10 Fountain Court, Ipswich Road, Norwich NR1 2QA* Tel (01603) 630398

McLEAN, Peter. **d** 94 **p** 95. C Mold *St As* from 94. *Trelawney, Bryn Coch Lane, Mold CH7 1PS* Tel (01352) 757337

McLEAN, Robert Hedley. b 47. St Jo Coll Dur BA69. Ripon Hall Ox 69. **d** 71 **p** 72. C Redhill St Jo *S'wark* 71-74; C S Beddington St Mich 74-77; C-in-c Raynes Park H Cross CD 77; P-in-c Motspur Park 77-80; V 80-84; V Tadworth from 84; Asst RD Reigate 92-93; RD Reigate from 93. *The Vicarage, The Avenue, Tadworth, Surrey KT20 5AS* Tel (01737) 813152

McLEAN-REID, Robert. b 43. Oak Hill Th Coll DipHE83. **d** 83 **p** 84. C Rainham *Chelmsf* 83-86; R Challoch w Newton Stewart *Glas* 86-87; R Aberdeen St Pet *Ab* 87-90; P-in-c Aberdeen St Clem 89-90; V Easington Colliery *Dur* 90-95; rtd 95. *37 Middleton Close, Seaton, Seaham, Co Durham SR7 0PQ* Tel 0191-581 1729

MacLEAY, Angus Murdo. b 59. Solicitor 83 Univ Coll Ox BA81 MA86 Man Univ MPhil92. Wycliffe Hall Ox 85. **d** 88 **p** 89. C Rusholme H Trin *Man* 88-92; V Houghton *Carl* from 92. *The Vicarage, Houghton, Carlisle CA6 4HZ* Tel (01228) 810076 or 515972

MACLEAY, The Very Revd John Henry James. b 31. St Edm Hall Ox BA54 MA60. Coll of Resurr Mirfield 55. **d** 57 **p** 58. C E Dulwich St Jo *S'wark* 57-60; C Inverness St Mich *Mor* 60-62; R 62-70; P-in-c Grantown-on-Spey 70-78; P-in-c Rothiemurchus 70-78; Can St Andr Cathl Inverness 77-78; R Fort William *Arg* from 78; Can St Jo Cathl Oban 80-87; Can Cumbrae from 80; Syn Clerk 80-87; Dean Arg from 87. *St Andrew's Rectory, Parade Road, Fort William, Inverness-shire PH33 6BA* Tel (01397) 702979

McLELLAN, Andrew Thomas. b 72. Pemb Coll Ox BA94. CITC BTh94. **d** 97. C Dublin Ch Ch Cathl Gp *D & G* from 97. *32 Shandon Drive, Phibsborough, Dublin 7, Irish Republic* Tel Dublin (1) 838 0469

McLELLAN, Eric Macpherson Thompson. b 16. St Jo Coll Dur BA38 DipTh39 MA41. **d** 39 **p** 40. C Byker St Mark *Newc* 39-44; C Fazakerley Em *Liv* 44-45; V Everton Em 45-54; R Sevenoaks St Nic *Roch* 54-70; Hon Can Roch Cathl 68-70; Chapl Br Emb Ch Paris *Eur* 70-80; RD France 75-79; Adn N France 79-80; Perm to Offic *Chich* from 80; Perm to Offic *Roch* from 80; rtd 81. *7 Stainer Road, Tonbridge, Kent TN10 4DS* Tel (01732) 356491

MACLEOD, Alan Roderick Hugh (Roddie). b 33. St Edm Hall Ox BA56 MA61 Ox Univ DipEd62 Lon Univ DipCD69. Wycliffe Hall Ox 56. **d** 58 **p** 59. C Bognor St Jo *Chich* 58-61; Chapl Wadh Coll Ox 62; Hd of RE Picardy Boys' Sch Erith 62-68; C Erith St Jo *Roch* 63-69; Dean Lonsdale Coll Lanc Univ 70-72; Lic to Offic *Blackb* 70-72; Hd of RE K Edw VI Sch Totnes 72-73; Perm to Offic *Ex* 72-73; St Helier Boys' Sch Jersey 73-84; Lic to Offic *Win* 73-84; V Shipton Bellinger from 84. *St Peter's Vicarage, Shipton Bellinger, Tidworth, Hants SP9 7UF* Tel (01980) 842244

McLEOD, Everton William. b 57. DCR78. Oak Hill Th Coll DipHE91. **d** 91 **p** 92. C New Ferry *Ches* 91-93; C Moreton from 93. *40 Carnsdale Road, Moreton, Wirral, Merseyside L46 9QR* Tel 0151-605 1241

MacLEOD, John Malcolm (Jay). b 61. Harvard Univ BA84 Pemb Coll Ox BA87. Linc Th Coll MDiv93. **d** 93 **p** 94. C Chesterfield St Aug *Derby* 93-96; C Stalybridge St Paul *Ches* from 96. *69 Fistral Crescent, Stalybridge, Cheshire SK15 3HN* Tel 0161-303 8453

McLEOD, Kenneth. b 22. St Chad's Coll Dur BA50 DipTh52. **d** 52 **p** 53. C Holsworthy w Cookbury *Ex* 52-55; C Braunton 55-58; R Milton Damerel and Newton St Petrock etc 58-70; RD Holsworthy 66-70; V Kirkby Fleetham *Ripon* 70-89; R Langton on Swale 70-89; P-in-c Scruton 88-89; R Kirkby Fleetham w Langton on Swale and Scruton 90-96; rtd 96. *14 The Green, Kirkby Fleetham, Northallerton, N Yorkshire DL7 0SB*

McLEOD, Canon Ronald. b 17. Lon Univ BA39 BA50 BD71 Ex Univ BA56 Man Univ MA59. Bps' Coll Cheshunt 39. **d** 41 **p** 42. C Plymouth St Pet *Ex* 41-44; Chapl RAF 44-69; Prin RAF Chapl Sch and Asst Chapl-in-Chief 69-73; QHC 72-73; R Itchen Abbas cum Avington *Win* 73-91; Hon Can Win Cathl 84-91; rtd 91; Perm to Offic *Ex* from 92. *Melfort, High Wall, Barnstaple, Devon EX31 2DP* Tel (01271) 43636

McLEOD, Ms Susan Margaret. b 48. SEN69 Sheff Poly CQSW89 DipSocWork89. N Ord Course MTh95. **d** 95 **p** 96. NSM Charlesworth and Dinting Vale *Derby* from 95. *30 Lee Vale Drive, Charlesworth, Broadbottom, Hyde, Cheshire SK14 6HD* Tel (01457) 866640

McLOUGHLIN, Ian Livingstone. b 38. CEng MICE64. Carl Dioc Tr Course 78. **d** 83 **p** 84. NSM Stanwix *Carl* 83-88; C Barrow St Geo w St Luke 88-90; R Kirkby Thore w Temple Sowerby and Newbiggin from 90. *The Rectory, Kirkby Thore, Penrith, Cumbria CA10 1UR* Tel (017683) 61248

McLUCKIE, John Mark. b 67. St Andr Univ BD89. Edin Th Coll MTh91. **d** 91 **p** 92. C Perth St Ninian *St And* 91-94; Chapl K Coll Cam 94-96; TV Baillieston *Glas* from 96. *21 Swinton Road, Baillieston, Glasgow G69 6DS* Tel 0141-771 3000

McMAHON, Brian Richard. b 39. ACII. Oak Hill NSM Course 84. **d** 87 **p** 88. NSM Colney Heath St Mark *St Alb* from 87. *23 Bluebridge Avenue, Brookmans Park, Hatfield, Herts AL9 7RY* Tel (01707) 655351

McMANN, Duncan. b 34. Jes Coll Ox BA55 MA60. Clifton Th Coll 55. **d** 58 **p** 59. C Newburn *Newc* 58-60; C Bishopwearmouth St Gabr *Dur* 60-62; N Area Sec BCMS 62-66; Midl and E Anglia Area Sec 66-92; Support Co-ord 84-92; Lic to Offic *Man* 62-66; Lic to Offic *Cov* 66-92; P-in-c Awsworth w Cossall *S'well* from 92; Chapl Notts Constabulary from 93. *The Vicarage, The Lane, Awsworth, Nottingham NG16 2QP* Tel 0115-944 4887

McMANNERS, John. b 16. FRHistS73 FBA78 St Edm Hall Ox BA39 MA45 DLitt77 St Chad's Coll Dur DipTh47 Hon DLitt84. **d** 47 **p** 48. C Leeds St Pet *Ripon* 47-48; Chapl St Edm Hall Ox 48-56; Dean 51-56; Australia 56-67; Regius Prof Ecclesiastical Hist Ox Univ 72-84; Can Res Ch Ch *Ox* 72-84; rtd 84; Chapl All So Coll Ox from 85. *71 Cunliffe Close, Oxford OX2 7BJ, or All Souls College, Oxford OX1 4AL* Tel (01865) 279368

McMANUS, James Robert. b 33. Man Univ DipS&PT82. Wycliffe Hall Ox 56. **d** 58 **p** 59. C Leic H Trin *Leic* 58-60; C Aylestone 60-63; India 66-79; V Oldham St Barn *Man* 79-83; Asst Regional Sec CMS 83-85; V Wolverhampton St Matt *Lich* 85-93; V Lapley w Wheaton Aston from 93; P-in-c Blymhill w Weston-under-Lizard from 93. *Lapley Vicarage, Pinfold Lane, Wheaton Aston, Stafford ST19 9PD* Tel (01785) 840395 Fax as telephone

McMASTER, James Alexander. b 43. **d** 69 **p** 70. C Dundonald *D & D* 69-73; C Antrim All SS *Conn* 73-78; I Tempo and Clabby *Clogh* 78-83; I Knocknamuckley *D & D* 83-95; I Carrickfergus *Conn* from 95. *The Rectory, 12 Harwood Gardens, Carrickfergus, Co Antrim BT38 7US* Tel (01960) 363244

McMASTER, Richard Ian. b 32. Edin Th Coll 57. **d** 60 **p** 61. C Carl H Trin *Carl* 60-63; Tanganyika 63-64; Tanzania 64-66; V Broughton Moor *Carl* 66-69; V Burnley St Steph *Blackb* 69-77; V New Longton 77-89; P-in-c Woodhall Spa and Kirkstead *Linc* 89-91; P-in-c Langton w Woodhall 89-91; P-in-c Bucknall w Tupholme 89-91; P-in-c Horsington w Stixwould 89-91; R Woodhall Spa Gp from 92. *The Vicarage, Alverston Avenue, Woodhall Spa, Lincs LN10 6SL* Tel (01526) 353856

McMASTER, William Keith. b 57. TCD. **d** 82 **p** 84. C Portadown St Columba *Arm* 82-84; C Erdington St Barn *Birm* 84-87; TV Shirley from 87. *1 Mappleborough Road, Shirley, Solihull, Birmingham B90 1AG* Tel 0121-744 3123

McMICHAEL, Andrew Hamilton. b 48. Univ of Wales (Ban) BA77 Mansf Coll Ox DSocStuds74. Chich Th Coll 87. **d** 89 **p** 90. C Chorley St Geo *Blackb* 89-92; C Burnley St Andr w St Marg 92-94; Chapl Burnley Healthcare NHS Trust 92-94; R Eccleston *Blackb* from 94. *The Rectory, Eccleston, Chorley, Lancs PR7 6NA* Tel (01257) 451206

McMONAGLE, William Archibald. b 36. CITC 65. **d** 68 **p** 69. C Magheralin *D & D* 68-71; C Bangor Abbey 71-81; I Grey Abbey w Kircubbin from 81. *90 Newtownards Road, Greyabbey, Co Down BT22 2QJ* Tel (012477) 88216

✠**McMULLAN, The Rt Revd Gordon.** b 34. ACIS57 QUB BSc61 PhD71 Cam Univ DipRS78 Irish Sch of Ecum ThD87 TCD MPhil90 Univ of the South (USA) DMin. Ridley Hall Cam 61. **d** 62 **p** 63 **c** 80. C Ballymacarrett St Patr *D & D* 62-67; Cen Adv on Chr Stewardship to Ch of Ireland 67-70; C Knock 70-71; I 76-80; I Belfast St Brendan 71-76; Offg Chapl RAF 71-78; Bp's Dom Chapl *D & D* 73-78; Adn Down 79-80; Bp Clogh 80-86; Bp D & D 86-97; rtd 97. *26 Wellington Park, Bangor, Co Down BT20 4PJ* Tel (01247) 460821

McMULLEN, Alan John. b 14. K Coll Cam BA36 MA41. Cuddesdon Coll 39. **d** 40 **p** 41. C St Marylebone St Cypr *Lon* 40-49; Chapl K Coll Cam 41-43; V Choral York Minster *York* 49-81; rtd 81; Perm to Offic *York* from 81. *2 Ramsey Avenue, Acaster Lane, Bishopthorpe, York YO2 1SQ* Tel (01904) 701121

McMULLEN, Philip Kenneth. b 55. RMN80 Glam Univ DMS92. St Mich Coll Llan DipTh95. **d** 95 **p** 96. C Coity w Nolton *Llan* from 95. *100 Fairfield Road, Bridgend CF31 3DS* Tel (01656) 652948

McMULLEN, Ronald Norman. b 36. TCD BA61 MA66 Liv Univ DSocStuds73 York Univ DipCommW74 BAC Acc 89 California Inst of Integral Studies MA92. Ridley Hall Cam 61. **d** 63 **p** 64. C Fulham St Mary N End *Lon* 63-67; C Cambridge St Sepulchre *Ely* 67-70; C Everton St Ambrose w St Tim *Liv* 70-73; Community Work Course & Research Asst York Univ 73-75; P-in-c Heanor *Derby* 75-79; V 79-88; RD Heanor 76-83; USA 88-93. *18 Fleetwood Avenue, Holland-on-Sea, Clacton-on-Sea, Essex CO15 5SD* Tel (01255) 815364

McMULLON, Andrew Brian. b 56. Sheff Univ BSc DipTh. St Jo Coll Nottm. **d** 83 **p** 84. C Stainforth *Sheff* 83-86; V Blackb Redeemer *Blackb* 86-90; Chapl RAF from 90. *Chaplaincy Services (RAF), HQ, Personnel and Training Command, RAF Innsworth, Gloucester GL3 1EZ* Tel (01452) 712612 ext 5164 Fax 510828

McNAB (née LUMMIS), Mrs Elizabeth Howieson. b 44. Lon Univ LDSRCSEng68 BDS68. St Jo Coll Nottm CertCS88. **d** 88 **p** 95. NSM Lerwick *Ab* from 88; NSM Burravoe from 88. *9 Blydoit, Scalloway, Shetland ZE1 0UG* Tel (01595) 880327 Fax as telephone

MACNAB, Kenneth Edward. b 65. LMH Ox BA87 MA91. Coll of Resurr Mirfield 89. **d** 91 **p** 92. C Northampton All SS w St Kath *Pet* 91-93; Lib Pusey Ho from 93. *Pusey House, Oxford OX1 3LZ* Tel (01865) 278415

McNAMARA, Michael Ian. b 59. Van Mildert Coll Dur BA81. Ridley Hall Cam 83. **d** 85 **p** 86. C Bedford Ch Ch *St Alb* 85-89; BCMS 89-92; Tanzania 89-92; TV Bolton St Paul w Em *Man* 93-97; C Galleywood Common *Chelmsf* from 97. *St Michael's House, 13 Roughtons, Galleywood, Chelmsford CM2 8PE* Tel (01245) 474695

McNAMEE, William Graham. b 38. Birm Univ BSocSc59. Cranmer Hall Dur BA74 DipTh. **d** 75 **p** 76. C Tonbridge St Steph *Roch* 75-78; C Fazeley *Lich* 78-87; Chapl Staffs Poly 87-92; Chapl Staffs Univ from 92. *19 Paragon Avenue, Westbury Park, Clayton, Newcastle, Staffs ST5 4EX* Tel (01782) 625544

MACNAUGHTON, Alexander. b 15. SS Coll Cam BA37 MA41. Linc Th Coll 40. **d** 41 **p** 42. C Melksham *Sarum* 41-44; C Long Benton *Newc* 44-47; India 48-73; C Derby St Thos *Derby* 74-80; Chapl Derbyshire R Infirmary 75-80; rtd 80; Perm to Offic *Derby* 80-92. *Flat 10, 40 Drummond Place, Edinburgh EH3 6NR* Tel 0131-558 1700

MACNAUGHTON, Canon Donald Allan. b 17. Or Coll Ox BA40 MA43. Westcott Ho Cam 40. **d** 41 **p** 42. C Tynemouth Ch Ch *Newc* 41-45; C Leeds St Pet *Ripon* 45-49; V Pendleton St Barn *Man* 49-53; V Wallsend St Luke *Newc* 53-58; V Wooler 58-71; RD Glendale 58-71; P-in-c Branxton 60-67; P-in-c Ingram 61-71; P-in-c Ilderton 61-71; P-in-c Kirknewton 68-71; P-in-c Doddington 69-71; V Berwick H Trin 71-82; P-in-c Berwick St Mary 71-82; RD Norham 71-82; Hon Can Newc Cathl 71-82; rtd 82; Chapl Marseille w St Raphael Aix-en-Provence etc *Eur* 82-87. *Flat 2, 18 Fidra Road, North Berwick, East Lothian EH39 4NG* Tel (01620) 892841

MACNAUGHTON, James Alastair. b 54. St Jo Coll Ox BA78 Fitzw Coll Cam BA80. Ridley Hall Cam 78. **d** 81 **p** 82. C Rounds Green *Birm* 81-85; TV Bestwood Park *S'well* 85-86; TV Bestwood 86-90; V Amble *Newc* 90-97; TR Cramlington from 97. *33 Twyford Close, Cramlington, Northd NE23 9PH* Tel (01670) 712259

McNAUGHTON, John. b 29. St Chad's Coll Dur DipTh54. **d** 54 **p** 55. C Thorney Close CD *Dur* 54-58; C-in-c E Herrington St Chad CD 58-62; PC E Herrington 62-66; CF 66-94; V Hutton Cranswick w Skerne, Watton and Beswick *York* from 94. *47 Southgate, Hutton Cranswick, Driffield, N Humberside YO25 9QX* Tel (01377) 270869

MACNAUGHTON, William Malcolm. b 57. Qu Coll Cam BA80. Ridley Hall Cam 79. **d** 81 **p** 82. C Haughton le Skerne *Dur* 81-85; P-in-c Newton Hall 85-90; TV Shoreditch St Leon and Hoxton St Jo *Lon* from 90; AD Hackney from 94. *St John's Vicarage, Crondall Street, London N1 6PT* Tel 0171-739 9823

McNEE, William Creighton. FIPM TCD DipTh Univ of Wales (Cardiff) DipPM Ulster Univ MA NUU MA. **d** 82 **p** 83. C Larne and Inver *Conn* 82-84; I Donagheady *D & R* 84-91; I Kilwaughter w Cairncastle and Craigy Hill *Conn* 91-93; I Ardstraw w Baronscourt, Badoney Lower etc *D & R* from 93; Bp's Dom Chapl from 96. *2 Bunbeg Road, Newtownstewart, Omagh, Co Tyrone BT78 4NQ* Tel (01662) 661342 Fax as telephone

McNEIGHT, Herbert Frank. b 14. Chich Th Coll. **d** 79 **p** 80. Hon C Southwick *Chich* from 79; Chapl Southlands Hosp Shore by Sea from 83. *12 Mile Oak Crescent, Southwick, Brighton BN42 4QP* Tel (01273) 592765

McNEIL, Mrs Ann. b 41. **d** 89 **p** 94. NSM Henfield w Shermanbury and Woodmancote *Chich* from 89. *Lancasters, West End Lane, Henfield, W Sussex BN5 9RB* Tel (01273) 492606

McNEILE, Donald Hugh. b 30. Trin Coll Cam BA53. Coll of Resurr Mirfield 53. **d** 55 **p** 56. C Wigan All SS *Liv* 55-57; C W Derby Gd Shep 57-61; rtd 95. *Manor Farm Household, North Hinksey, Oxford OX2 0NA* Tel (01865) 245473

MACNEILL, Nicholas Terence. b 62. St Steph Ho Ox BTh93. **d** 93 **p** 94. C Ex St Thos and Em *Ex* from 93. *St Andrew's Vicarage, 78 Queens Road, Exeter EX2 9EW* Tel (01392) 433656

McNEISH, Canon John. b 34. Edin Th Coll 58. **d** 61 **p** 62. C Kirkcaldy *St And* 61-64; Prec St Andr Cathl *Ab* 64-66; Chapl RAF 66-72; C Wootton Bassett *Sarum* 72-75; P-in-c Stour Provost w Todbere 75-79; TR Gillingham from 79; RD Blackmore Vale 81-86; Can and Preb Sarum Cathl from 92. *The Rectory, High Street, Gillingham, Dorset SP8 4AH* Tel (01747) 822435

McNICOL, Andrew Keith. b 45. Westmr Coll of Educn CertEd69 Westmr Coll Ox DipApTh89 MA90 Open Univ BA79. Westmr Coll Cam 70 Westcott Ho Cam 92. **d** 92 **p** 93. In URC 73-92; C Whitstable *Cant* 92-95; V Ferring *Chich* from 95. *The Vicarage, 19 Grange Park, Ferring, Worthing, W Sussex BN12 5LS* Tel (01903) 241645

McNIVEN, Mrs Betty. b 47. Lanc Univ BA68. N Ord Course 83. **dss** 86 **d** 87 **p** 94. Baguley *Man* 86-87; Hon Par Dn 87-88; Par Dn Newton Heath All SS 88-91; Par Dn E Farnworth and Kearsley 91-94; TV 94-95; P-in-c Spotland from 95. *The Vicarage, 10 Little Flatt, Rochdale, Lancs OL12 7AU* Tel (01706) 48972

MACONACHIE, Canon Alwyn. b 21. TCD BA43 MA47 BD47. CITC 44. **d** 44 **p** 45. C Londonderry Ch Ch *D & R* 44-47; I Killowen 47-64; RD Limavady 60-65; N Sec (Ireland) CMS 64-70; Gen Sec 70-74; I Glencraig *D & D* 74-91; RD Bangor 78-91; Can Down Cathl 82-91; Prec 87-90; Chan 90-91; rtd 91. *16 Springhill Road, Bangor, Co Down BT20 3NR* Tel (01247) 466999

MACONACHIE, Canon Charles Leslie. b 27. TCD BA71 MA74 MDiv85 PhD90. Em Coll Saskatoon 47. **d** 50 **p** 51. C Clooney *D & R* 50-54; P-in-c Lower Tamlaght O'Crilly 54-61; Chapl Newsham Gen Hosp Liv 61-63; Chapl RAF 63-67; C Londonderry Ch Ch *D & R* 69-75; I Belmont 75-78; Warden for Min of Healing 75-96; I Culmore w Muff and Belmont 78-96; Warden Irish Internat Order of St Luke Physician from 82; Can Derry Cathl from 85; Chmn Ch's Min of Healing from 96. *3 Broomhill Court, Waterside, Londonderry BT47 1WP* Tel (01504) 48942

MACOURT, The Ven William Albany. b 19. TCD BA40 MA46. **d** 42 **p** 43. C Ballymena *Conn* 42-46; C Belf Cathl 46-48; I Duneane w Ballyscullion *Conn* 48-51; I Belfast St Mark 51-64; I Ballymacarrett St Patr *D & D* 64-89; Preb Swords St Patr Cathl Dublin 75-89; Adn Down *D & D* 80-89; Chan Belf Cathl 85-89; rtd 89; Dioc Info Officer *D & D* 89-97. *4 Barnett's Road, Belfast BT5 7BA* Tel (01232) 794282

McPHATE, Dr Gordon Ferguson. b 50. Aber Univ MB, ChB74 Fitzw Coll Cam BA77 MA81 MD88 Surrey Univ MSc86 Edin Univ MTh94. Westcott Ho Cam 75. **d** 78 **p** 79. Hon C Sanderstead All SS *S'wark* 78-81; Hon PV S'wark Cathl 81-86; Lect Lon Univ 81-86; Hon C Edin St Mich and All SS *Edin* 86-89; Chapl and Lect St Andr Univ *St And* from 86; Sen Lect from 93. *68 Winram Place, St Andrews, Fife KY16 8XH* Tel (01334) 476983

MacPHEE, Roger Hunter. b 43. Leeds Univ BSc65. EAMTC. **d** 86 **p** 87. NSM Trunch *Nor* from 86. *8 Lawn Close, Knapton, North Walsham, Norfolk NR28 0SD* Tel (01263) 720045

McPHERSON, Andrew Lindsay (Andy). b 58. MIPM84 St Jo Coll Dur BA79. St Jo Coll Nottm DPS88. **d** 88 **p** 89. C Bitterne *Win* 88-92; V Weston from 92. *The Vicarage, Weston Lane, Southampton SO19 9HG* Tel (01703) 448421

MACPHERSON, Anthony Stuart. b 56. Qu Coll Birm 77. **d** 80 **p** 81. C Morley St Pet w Churwell *Wakef* 80-84; C Penistone 84-85; P-in-c Thurlstone 85-86; TV Penistone and Thurlstone 86-88; V Grimethorpe 88-95; P-in-c Westgate Common 95-96; V from 96. *St Michael's Vicarage, 166 Horbury Road, Wakefield, W Yorkshire WF2 8BQ* Tel (01924) 380689

MACPHERSON, Archibald McQuarrie. b 27. Edin Th Coll 50. **d** 52 **p** 53. Asst Chapl St Andr Cathl *Ab* 52-55; Prec 55-56; P-in-c Airdrie *Glas* 56-63; R Dumbarton 63-92; rtd 92. *29 Bramblehedge Path, Alexandria, Dunbartonshire G83 8PH* Tel (01389) 753981

MacPHERSON, David Alan John. b 42. Lon Univ DipTh71 BD75 Open Univ BA83 Hatf Poly MSc89. Clifton Th Coll 69 Trin Coll Bris 72. **d** 72 **p** 73. C Drypool St Columba w St Andr and St Pet *York* 72-76; Asst Chapl HM Pris Hull 72-76; P-in-c Bessingby *York* 76-78; P-in-c Carnaby 76-78; Chapl RAF 78-83; P-in-c Chedgrave w Hardley and Langley *Nor* 83-87; R 87-97; Chapl Langley Sch Nor 83-97; P-in-c Brington w Whilton and Norton *Pet* from 97. *The New Rectory, Great Brington, Northampton NN7 4JB* Tel (01604) 770402

MACPHERSON, Ewan Alexander. b 43. Toronto Univ BA74. Wycliffe Coll Toronto MDiv78. **d** 78 **p** 79. Canada 78-86; V Westbury sub Mendip w Easton *B & W* from 86; V Priddy from 86. *The Vicarage, Crow Lane, Westbury sub Mendip, Wells, Somerset BA5 1HL* Tel (01749) 870293

MACPHERSON, John. b 28. Lon Univ BSc50 Ex Univ DipEd51 Univ of W Indies HDipEd65. St Alb Minl Tr Scheme 82. **d** 89 **p** 90. NSM Gt Berkhamsted *St Alb* from 89. *Southways, 5 Kingsdale Road, Berkhamsted, Herts HP4 3BS* Tel (01442) 866262

MACPHERSON, Peter Sinclair. b 44. Lich Th Coll 68. **d** 71 **p** 72. C Honiton, Gittisham and Combe Raleigh *Ex* 71-72; C Bideford 72-74; C Devonport St Mark Ford 74-75; V Thorncombe *Sarum* 75-79; TV Dorchester 79-85; Chapl Jersey Gp of Hosps 85-90; Chapl Derriford Hosp Plymouth from 90; Lic to Offic *Ex* from 90. *Bymoor House, Down Lane, Buckland Monachorum, Yelverton, Devon PL20 7LN* Tel (01752) 777111

McQUADE, William. b 09. BSP46. **d** 49 **p** 50. Canada 49-51; C Newtownforbes *K, E & A* 51-52; P-in-c Glencolumbkille *D & R* 52-54; P-in-c Preban w Moyne *C & O* 54; I Dingle *L & K* 54-56; I Ballinaclash *D & G* 56-57; R Bewcastle *Carl* 57-66; V Allhallows 66-76; rtd 76; Perm to Offic *K, E & A* from 76. *Ballinafad, Via Boyle, Co Sligo, Irish Republic* Tel Sligo (71) 66291

MacQUAIDE, Arthur John Allan. b 13. TCD BA37. **d** 38 **p** 39. Dioc C *Clogh* 38-39; C Enniskillen 39-41; P-in-c Lack 41-46; P-in-c Derryvullen S w Garvary 46-58; C Flint *St As* 58-60; I Garrison w Slavin and Belleek *Clogh* 60-80; Bp Dom Chapl 67-73; Preb Clogh Cathl 73-80; rtd 80; C Steeton *Bradf* 84-89. *1 Moyle Height, Clare Road, Ballycastle, Co Antrim BT54 6DB* Tel (01265) 769895

MACQUARRIE, Canon John. b 19. TD62. FBA84 Glas Univ MA40 BD43 PhD54 DLitt64 Hon DD69 Ox Univ MA70 DD81. **d** 65 **p** 65. USA 65-70; Lady Marg Prof Div Ox Univ 70-86; Can Res Ch Ch *Ox* 70-86; rtd 86. *206 Headley Way, Oxford OX3 7TA* Tel (01865) 61889

MACQUIBAN, Gordon Alexander. b 24. Univ of Wales (Lamp) BA49 Crewe Coll of Educn CertEd72. Ely Th Coll 49. **d** 51 **p** 52. C Christleton *Ches* 51-53; C Disley 53-55; C Heswall 55-58; Chapl R Liv Children's Hosp 55-58; V Norley *Ches* 58-64; V Ches Ch Ch 64-71; Hon C Ches H Trin 71-85; Hon C Runcorn All SS 85-87; Hon C Frodsham 87-88; rtd 88; Perm to Offic *B & W* from 88. *12 Langham Gardens, Taunton, Somerset TA1 4PE* Tel (01823) 282602

McQUILLAN, Miss Martha. b 33. St Mich Ho Ox 66. **dss** 70 **d** 87 **p** 94. Barnsbury St Andr *Lon* 70-72; Nottingham St Ann w Em *S'well* 72-79; Chapl Asst Univ Hosp Nottm 79-90; Chapl Asst Nottm Gen Hosp 79-90; rtd 90. *27 Penarth Rise, Nottingham NG5 4EE* Tel 0115-962 1760

McQUILLEN, Brian Anthony. b 45. Ripon Hall Ox 73. **d** 75 **p** 76. C Northfield *Birm* 75-78; C Sutton Coldfield H Trin 78-80; V Bearwood 80-89; V Glouc St Geo w Whaddon *Glouc* 89-96; R St Martin w E and W Looe *Truro* from 96. *St Martin's Rectory, Barbican Road, Looe, Cornwall PL13 1NX* Tel (01503) 263070

McQUILLEN-WRIGHT, Christopher Charles (Chris). b 71. Kent Univ BA92. Westcott Ho Cam CTM95. **d** 95 **p** 96. C Phillack w Gwithian and Gwinear *Truro* 95-96; C Hayle 95-96; C St Erth 95-96; C Godrevy from 96. *Godrevy House, Penpol Avenue, Hayle, Cornwall TR27 4NQ* Tel (01736) 755870

MACRAE, Charles. b 27. RD71. Edin Univ BDS62. S Dios Minl Tr Scheme 88. **d** 91 **p** 92. NSM Heene *Chich* 91-94; NSM Portsea St Alb *Portsm* 94-96; Perm to Offic *Chich* from 96. *64 Stone Lane, Worthing, W Sussex BN13 2BQ* Tel (01903) 693877

McRAE, Keith Alban. b 44. S'wark Ord Course 68. **d** 73 **p** 74. NSM Crawley *Chich* 73-78; NSM Ifield 78-90. *Plough Cottage, Ifield Street, Ifield, Crawley, W Sussex RH10 0NN* Tel (01293) 513629

MacRAE, Mrs Rosalind Phyllis (Ros). b 41. Sarum & Wells Th Coll 81. **dss** 84 **d** 87 **p** 94. Feltham *Lon* 84-87; Par Dn 87; Asst Chapl R Cornwall Hosps NHS Trust 87-88; Chapl Mt Edgcumbe Hospice 88-92; Chapl St Austell Hosp 88-92; Chapl Penrice Hosp St Austell 88-92; NSM St Austell *Truro* 88-92; Chapl R Cornwall Hosps NHS Trust 92-95; rtd 95. *Christmas Cottage, 7 Church Lane, Mevagissey, St Austell, Cornwall PL26 6SX* Tel (01726) 844353

McREYNOLDS, Kenneth Anthony. b 48. TCD DipTh83. **d** 83 **p** 84. C Ballymena w Ballyclug *Conn* 83-86; I Rathcoole 86-90; I Lambeg from 90. *Lambeg Rectory, 58 Belfast Road, Lisburn, Co Antrim BT27 4AT* Tel (01846) 663872

MACROW-WOOD, Anthony Charles. b 60. ACA86 York Univ BA82 Jes Coll Cam BA91. Westcott Ho Cam CTM92. **d** 92 **p** 93. C Swindon St Jo and St Andr *Bris* 92-96; TV Preston w Sutton Poyntz and Osmington w Poxwell *Sarum* from 96. *The Vicarage, 58 Littlemoor Road, Weymouth, Dorset DT3 6AA* Tel (01305) 833704

McSPARRON, Cecil. b 35. Regent Coll Vancouver MCS87 Bible Tr Inst Glas DipMin63 Trin Th Coll Singapore DipMin68 MMin77 MDiv86. **d** 68 **p** 69. C Glendermott *D & R* 68-70; Singapore 70-77 and 83-89; C Portadown St Mark *Arm* 78-80; UK Regional Dir OMF 80-82; Tutor Miss Studies Lon Bible Coll 90-93. *London Bible College, Green Lane, Northwood, Middx HA6 2UW* Tel (01923) 826061

McTEER, Robert Ian. b 56. Chich Th Coll 90. **d** 92 **p** 93. C S Shields All SS *Dur* 92-95; P-in-c Auckland St Helen 95-97; V from 97; Chapl Tindale Crescent Hosp Dur from 95. *The Vicarage, 8 Manor Road, Bishop Auckland, Co Durham DL14 9EN* Tel (01388) 604152

McVEAGH, Paul Stuart. b 56. Southn Univ BA78. Oak Hill Th Coll BA88. **d** 88 **p** 89. C Bebington *Ches* 88-92; BCMS 92-93; Crosslinks 93-95; Portugal 92-95; R High Halstow w All Hallows and Hoo St Mary *Roch* from 95. *The Rectory, Cooling Road, High Halstow, Rochester, Kent ME3 8SA* Tel (01634) 250637 Fax as telephone E-mail pmcveagh@aol.com

McVEETY, Ian. b 46. N Ord Course 82. **d** 85 **p** 86. NSM Langley and Parkfield *Man* 85-86; C 87-89; V Castleton Moor from 89; AD Heywood and Middleton from 95. *The Vicarage, Vicarage Road North, Rochdale, Lancs OL11 2TE* Tel (01706) 32353

McVEIGH, Miss Dorothy Sarah. b 67. QUB BA89 TCD BTh93. CITC 90. **d** 93 **p** 94. C Belfast St Matt *Conn* 93-96; C Carrickfergus from 96. *7 Macroom Gardens, Carrickfergus, Co Antrim BT38 8NB* Tel (01960) 367739

McVEIGH, Samuel. b 49. CITC 77. **d** 79 **p** 80. C Drumragh w Mountfield *D & R* 79-82; I Dromore *Clogh* 82-90; RD Kilskeery 89-90; I Drumachose *D & R* from 90. *49 Killane Road, Limavady, Co Londonderry BT49 0DJ* Tel (01504) 762680

McVEIGH, Sandra. *See* BUTLER, Mrs Sandra

MACVICAR, Miss Mary. b 23. Edin Univ MA44 Ox Univ DipEd45. Ripon Coll Cuddesdon 85. **dss** 86 **d** 87 **p** 94. Bishops Waltham *Portsm* 86-89; Hon C 87-89; Perm to Offic 89-94; Hon C Portsm Cathl 94-95; rtd 95; Perm to Offic *Portsm* from 95.

15 Roman Row, Bank Street, Bishops Waltham, Southampton SO32 1RW Tel (01489) 895955

McWATT, Glenn Ellsworth. b 48. Birkb Coll Lon DipRS92. Lon Bible Coll 70 S'wark Ord Course 89. **d** 92 **p** 93. Hon C Tulse Hill H Trin and St Matthias *S'wark* from 92. *32 Brockwell Court, Effra Road, London SW2 1NA* Tel 0171-274 5521 or 620 4444

MacWILLIAM, The Very Revd Alexander Gordon. b 23. Univ of Wales BA43 Lon Univ BD47 PhD52. St Mich Coll Llan 43. **d** 45 **p** 46. C Llanllyfni *Ban* 46-49; Min Can Ban Cathl 49-55; C Ban St Mary 50-53; C Ban St Jas 53-55; R Llanfaethlu w Llanfwrog 55-56; R Llanfaethlu w Llanfwrog and Llanrhuddlad etc 56-58; Lect Trin Coll Carmarthen 58-84; Lic to Offic *St D* 60-78; Can St D Cathl 78-84; Prec, V, and Dean 84-90; rtd 90. *Pen Parc, Smyrna Road, Llangain, Carmarthen SA33 5AD* Tel (01267) 241333

McWILLIAM, Charles Denis. b 24. Clare Coll Cam BA49 MA52. Cuddesdon Coll 49. **d** 51 **p** 52. Tutor Cuddesdon Coll 51-54; C Cuddesdon *Ox* 51-54; S Africa 54-66; Perm to Offic *Sarum* 67-73; Perm to Offic *Eur* 73-80; V Heyhouses *Blackb* 80-88; V Sabden and Pendleton 88-89; rtd 89; Perm to Offic *Blackb* from 89. *Österkamp 14, 26209 Kirchhatten, Germany*

MACCLESFIELD, Archdeacon of. *See* GILLINGS, The Ven Richard John

MACE, Alan Herbert. b 28. Lon Univ BA49 Ex Inst of Educn TCert50. Wycliffe Hall Ox 59. **d** 60 **p** 61. C Disley *Ches* 60-63; C Folkestone H Trin w Ch Ch *Cant* 63-67; Lic to Offic *Win* from 67; rtd 93. *15 Bassett Heath Avenue, Southampton SO16 7GP* Tel (01703) 768161

MACE, David Sinclair. b 37. **d** 95 **p** 96. NSM Godalming *Guildf* from 95. *Torridon, Grosvenor Road, Godalming, Surrey GU7 1NZ* Tel (01483) 414646

MACE, Mrs Helen Elizabeth. b 31. Ox Univ MA52 Solicitor 56. Coll of Ascension 62. **dss** 74 **d** 87 **p** 94. Tadcaster *York* 77-84; Asst Chapl Leeds Gen Infirmary 84-94; rtd 91; C Woodhouse and Wrangthorn *Ripon* 94-96. *25 Grosvenor Park Gardens, Leeds LS6 2PL* Tel 0113-276 0645

MACE, Robert Alfred Beasley. b 16. Leeds Univ BA49. Coll of Resurr Mirfield 48. **d** 50 **p** 51. C Callander *St And* 50-53; C Newc St Mary *Newc* 53-54; C Penton Street St Silas w All SS *Lon* 54-56; C Aylesbury *Ox* 56-59; P-in-c Glas St Gabr *Glas* 59-61; R Campbeltown *Arg* 61-65; V Barnsley St Pet *Wakef* 65-72; V Barnsley St Pet and St Jo 72-84; rtd 85; Perm to Offic *Wakef* from 85. *90 Blenheim Road, Barnsley, S Yorkshire S70 6AS* Tel (01226) 283831

MACEY, Anthony Keith Frank. b 46. Univ of Wales (Cardiff) DipTh69. St Steph Ho Ox 69. **d** 71 **p** 72. C Ex St Thos *Ex* 71-76; V Wembury 76-88; RD Ivybridge 83-91; V Cockington from 88. *The Vicarage, 22 Monterey Close, Torquay TQ2 6QW* Tel (01803) 607957

MACEY, Ralph Arthur. b 14. TD63. Leeds Univ BA38. Coll of Resurr Mirfield 38. **d** 40 **p** 41. C Tynemouth H Trin W Town *Newc* 40-42; C Hexham 42-45; C Chollerton 45-47; C Sighill 47-50; V High Elswick St Phil 50-60; CF (TA) 50-69; V N Gosforth *Newc* 60-67; Hd of RE Newc Ch High Sch 67-80; Hon C Gosforth All SS 67-76; Hon C Cullercoats St Geo from 76; rtd 79. *13 Sandyford Park, Sandyford Road, Newcastle upon Tyne NE2 1TA* Tel 0191-281 2860

MACHIN, Roy Anthony. b 38. BA79. Oak Hill Th Coll 76. **d** 79 **p** 80. C Halliwell St Pet *Man* 79-83; V Eccleston St Luke *Liv* 83-91; V Kendal St Thos *Carl* from 91; V Crook from 91. *St Thomas's Vicarage, South View Lane, Kendal, Cumbria LA9 4PL* Tel (01539) 721509

MACK, Mrs Gillian Frances (Gill). b 50. SCM72. Cant Sch of Min 84. **d** 87 **p** 94. NSM Deal St Geo *Cant* 87-88; NSM Deal St Leon and St Rich and Sholden 88-92; Par Dn 93-94; C from 94. *St Richard's Lodge, 7 St Richard's Road, Deal, Kent CT14 9JR* Tel (01304) 374674

MACKLIN, Reginald John. b 29. Bris Univ BA52. Ely Th Coll 54. **d** 55 **p** 56. C W Hackney St Barn *Lon* 55-58; C E Ham St Mary *Chelmsf* 58-61; C Northolt St Mary *Lon* 61-64; Jordan 64-68; Palma de Mallorca and Balearic Is *Eur* 68-69; P-in-c Hammersmith St Matt *Lon* 69-70; V Stanwell 70-82; V Kimbolton *Ely* 82-88; V Stow Longa 82-88; RD Leightonstone 82-88; P-in-c Keyston and Bythorn 85-88; P-in-c Catworth Magna 85-88; P-in-c Tilbrook 85-88; P-in-c Covington 85-88; R Coveney 88-96; R Downham 88-96; RD Ely 89-96; rtd 96. *11 Castelhythe, Ely, Cambs CB7 4BU* Tel (01353) 662205

MACKNEY, John Pearson. b 17. Univ of Wales BA39 Lon Univ MA81 PGCE73. St D Coll Lamp 39. **d** 41 **p** 42. C Gelligaer *Llan* 41-44; CF 44-47; C Llangeinor *Llan* 47-49; P-in-c Cardiff All SS 49-58; Chapl HM Pris Cardiff 49-58; V Mountain Ash *Llan* 58-69; Hon C Streatley w Moulsford *Ox* from 81. *Merlebank, Reading Road, Moulsford, Wallingford, Oxon OX10 9JG* Tel (01491) 651347

MADDEN, Robert Willis. b 14. TCD BA36 MA40. CITC 38. **d** 39 **p** 40. Tutor Wycliffe Hall Ox 39-40; Lic to Offic *Ox* 39-40; C Bangor *D & D* 40-42; I Ballyfin *C & O* 42-49; C Taunton St Jas *B & W* 49-52; V Mayfield *Lich* 52-61; V Thurnby w Stoughton *Leic* 61-66; R Misterton w Walcote 66-79; rtd 79; Perm to Offic *Derby* from 79. *22A Duffield Road, Little Eaton, Derby DE21 5DS* Tel (01332) 832388

MADDEX, Patrick John. b 31. Edin Univ BSc54. Bps' Coll Cheshunt 55. **d** 57 **p** 58. C Baldock w Bygrave and Clothall *St Alb* 57-61; C Oxhey All SS 61-64; V Codicote 64-82; R Gt and Lt Wymondley w Graveley and Chivesfield 82-96; rtd 96. *19 Bramber Road, Seaford, E Sussex BN25 1AG*

MADDISON, Norman. b 12. St Jo Coll Dur BA34. **d** 35 **p** 36. C Dalton le Dale *Dur* 35-37; C Bishopwearmouth St Mich 37-43; V Barrow St Jo *Carl* 43-48; V Seaham w Seaham Harbour *Dur* 48-60; R Wolsingham 61-64; R Wolsingham and Thornley 64-77; rtd 77. *Whitfield Place, Wolsingham, Bishop Auckland, Co Durham DL13 3AJ* Tel (01388) 527127

MADDOCK, Mrs Audrey. b 27. Lon Univ CertEd79 Open Univ BA80. Bris Sch of Min 81. **dss** 84 **d** 87 **p** 94. Stanton St Quintin, Hullavington, Grittleton etc *Bris* 84-87; Par Dn 87-94; C 94; P-in-c Littleton Drew from 95. *1 Brookside, Hullavington, Chippenham, Wilts SN14 6HD* Tel (01666) 837275

MADDOCK, David John Newcomb. b 36. Qu Coll Cam BA60 MA64. Oak Hill Th Coll 60. **d** 62 **p** 63. C Bispham *Blackb* 62-65; R 82-93; Canada 65-70; R Walsoken *Ely* 70-77; V Ore Ch Ch *Chich* 77-82; RD Blackpool *Blackb* 90-93; V Fowey *Truro* from 93. *The Vicarage, Church Avenue, Fowey, Cornwall PL23 1BU* Tel (01726) 833535

MADDOCK, Francis James Wilson. b 14. Bris Univ BA36 Wadh Coll Ox BA38 MA42. Cuddesdon Coll 39. **d** 40 **p** 41. C Southfields St Barn *S'wark* 40-44; C Horfield H Trin *Bris* 44-49; PC Brislington St Anne 49-56; V Newlyn St Pet *Truro* 56-60; Perm to Offic 60-64; R Forrabury w Minster and Trevalga 64-74; P-in-c Davidstow w Otterham 64-74; RD Trigg Minor 66-69; TR Boscastle w Davidstow 74-78; P-in-c Port Isaac 78-79; rtd 79; Perm to Offic *Ex* from 87. *8 Sylvan Close, Exmouth, Devon EX8 3BQ* Tel (01395) 274381

MADDOCK, Nicholas Rokeby. b 47. ABSM72 Birm Coll of Educn CertEd73. Linc Th Coll 82. **d** 82 **p** 83. C Romford St Edw *Chelmsf* 82-87; V Sway *Win* 87-94; V Taunton St Mary *B & W* from 94. *St Mary's Vicarage, Church Square, Taunton, Somerset TA1 1SA* Tel (01823) 272441

MADDOCK, Philip Arthur Louis. b 47. Open Univ BA82. Oak Hill Th Coll 75. **d** 78 **p** 79. C New Ferry *Ches* 78-81; C Barnston 81-82; V Over St Jo 82-85; Chapl to the Deaf 85-88; V Norley 85-88; P-in-c Treales *Blackb* 88-96; Chapl to the Deaf 88-96; Chapl to the Deaf *Lich* from 96. *56 Uttoxeter Road, Rugeley, Staffs WS15 3QU*

MADDOCK, Canon Philip Lawrence. b 20. Bris Univ BA42. Cuddesdon Coll 42. **d** 43 **p** 44. C Kilburn St Aug *Lon* 43-48; C Weston-super-Mare All SS *B & W* 48-57; Chapl Community of the Epiphany Truro 57-60; Sub-Warden 60-63; Chapl HM Pris Wandsworth 63-64; HM Pris Birm 64-67; Ex 67-69; Chapl St Lawr Hosp Bodmin 69-76; Can Res and Treas Truro Cathl *Truro* 76-88; rtd 88; Perm to Offic *Truro* from 88. *31 Trenethick Avenue, Helston, Cornwall TR13 8LU* Tel (01326) 564909

✠**MADDOCKS, The Rt Revd Morris Henry St John.** b 28. Trin Coll Cam BA52 MA56. Chich Th Coll 52. **d** 54 **p** 55 **c** 72. C Ealing St Pet Mt Park *Lon* 54-55; C Uxbridge St Andr w St Jo 55-58; V Weaverthorpe w Helperthorpe and Luttons *York* 58-61; V Scarborough St Martin 61-71; Suff Bp Selby 72-83; Adv Min Health and Healing to Abps Cant and York 83-95; Asst Bp B & W 83-87; Asst Bp Chich from 87; Jt Founding Dir Acorn Chr Healing Trust from 91; Can and Preb Chich Cathl from 92; rtd 95; Perm to Offic *Guildf* from 95. *3 The Chantry, Cathedral Close, Chichester, W Sussex PO19 1PZ* Tel (01243) 788888

MADDOX, David John. b 34. AIMLS58. Sarum & Wells Th Coll 92. **d** 81 **p** 93. In RC Ch 81-91; NSM Wimborne Minster and Holt *Sarum* 93-95; NSM Broadstone from 95. *298 Wimborne Road, Poole, Dorset BH15 3EG* Tel (01202) 672597

MADDOX, Edwin Joseph Crusha. b 09. Dorchester Miss Coll 38. **d** 41 **p** 42. C Wakef St Jo *Wakef* 41-43; C Canning Town St Cedd *Chelmsf* 43-46; C Gt Ilford St Clem 46-50; P-in-c Gt Ilford St Alb CD 46-50; V Leytonstone H Trin Harrow Green 50-61; P-in-c Leytonstone St Aug CD 59-61; V Walthamstow St Sav 61-71; V Leigh-on-Sea St Jas 71-77; rtd 77; Perm to Offic *Chelmsf* from 77. *43 Barnard Road, Leigh-on-Sea, Essex SS9 3PH* Tel (01702) 76822

MADDOX, Goronwy Owen. b 23. Univ of Wales (Swansea) BA52 DipEd53. Sarum Th Coll 67. **d** 70 **p** 71. Hd Master H Trin Sch Calne 57-82; Hon C Calne and Blackland *Sarum* 70-82; C 82-83; V Llywel and Traean-glas w Llanulid *S & B* 83-92; rtd 92. *4 St Matthews Close, Rowde, Devizes, Wilts SN10 2PG* Tel (01380) 728965

MADDOX, Hugh Inglis Monteath. b 37. CCC Cam BA60. Westcott Ho Cam 61. **d** 63 **p** 64. C Attercliffe *Sheff* 63-66; C Maidstone All SS w St Phil *Cant* 66-67; C Folkestone St Mary and St Eanswythe 67-69; C St Martin-in-the-Fields *Lon* 69-73; R Sandwich *Cant* 73-81; V St Peter-in-Thanet 81-84; V Red Post *Sarum* from 84. *The Vicarage, Morden, Wareham, Dorset BH20 7DR* Tel (01929) 459244

MADDY, Kevin. b 58. GRNCM79 Selw Coll Cam BA83 FRSA96. Westcott Ho Cam 81. **d** 85 **p** 86. C St Peter-in-Thanet *Cant* 85-88; Perm to Offic *Nor* from 88; Chapl RAF from 88. *Chaplaincy Services (RAF), HQ, Personnel and Training Command, RAF Innsworth, Gloucester GL3 1EZ* Tel (01452) 712612 ext 5164 Fax 510828

MADELEY, Mark Keith. b 68. DipHE92 AVCM96. Oak Hill Th Coll BA93. **d** 93 **p** 94. C Mickleover All SS *Derby* 93-96; C Charlesworth and Dinting Vale from 96. *7 Burwell Close, Glossop, Derbyshire SK13 9PG* Tel (01457) 856833 Mobile 0705-0021860 Fax as telephone E-mail revmadeley@aol.com

MADGE, Francis Sidney. b 35. AKC58. **d** 59 **p** 60. C York St Mary Bishophill Senior *York* 59-62; C Sutton St Mich 62-64; C Ex St Jas *Ex* 64-69; R Sutton by Dover w Waldershare *Cant* 69-78; P-in-c W Wickham St Mary 78-81; V 81-84; V W Wickham St Mary *S'wark* from 85. *St Mary's Vicarage, The Avenue, West Wickham, Kent BR4 0DX* Tel 0181-777 3137

MAGAHY, Canon Gerald Samuel. b 23. TCD BA45 MA61 LLD80 Univ Coll Galway HDipEd55. **d** 53 **p** 54. Dioc Chapl and Hd Master Villiers Sch Limerick 53-61; Chapl and Hd Master K Hosp Sch Dub 61-83; Treas St Patr Cathl Dublin 80-89; Chan 89-91; Prec 91-95; rtd 95. *Seacrest, Bray Heaf, Co Wicklow, Irish Republic* Tel Skibbereen (28) 67231

MAGEE, Francis Malcolm. b 24. Edin Univ MA49. **d** 54 **p** 55. Lic to Offic *S'wark* 71-75; Hon C Abbey Wood 75-78; C Mottingham St Andr 79-81; C Rotherhithe St Mary w All SS 81-83; C Rotherhithe St Kath w St Barn 83-89; rtd 89; Perm to Offic *Ely* from 93. *33 Apthorpe Street, Fulbourn, Cambs CB1 5EY* Tel (01223) 880218

MAGEE, Frederick Hugh. b 33. Yale Univ BA57. Westcott Ho Cam 58. **d** 59 **p** 60. C Bury St Mark *Man* 59-62; USA 63-64 and from 87; Chapl St Paul's Cathl Dundee *Bre* 74-79; P-in-c Invergowrie 76-79; R St Andrews St Andr *St And* 79-83; R Lunan Head 83-87; R Forfar 83-87. *220 Cottage Avenue, Box 351, Cashmere, Washington 98815-1004, USA* Tel Cashmere (509) 782-2786

MAGEE, John Lawrence. b 19. Lon Univ BA52. **d** 78 **p** 78. Hon C Westbury-on-Severn w Flaxley and Blaisdon *Glouc* 78-89; rtd 89; Perm to Offic *Glouc* from 89. *Sharon, Blaisdon, Longhope, Glos GL17 0AL* Tel (01452) 831217

MAGEE, Canon Patrick Connor. b 15. K Coll Cam BA37 MA41. Westcott Ho Cam 38. **d** 39 **p** 40. C King Cross *Wakef* 39-42; Chapl RNVR 43-46; Chapl K Coll Cam 46-52; V Kingston All SS *S'wark* 52-60; Chapl Bryanston Sch Dorset 60-70; V Ryde All SS *Portsm* 70-72; Chapl Tiffin Sch Kingston 72-73; V Salisbury St Mich *Sarum* 73-75; TR Bemerton 75-84; rtd 84. *16A Donaldson Road, Salisbury SP1 3AD* Tel (01722) 324278

MAGILL, Robert James Henderson (Bobby). b 59. Paisley Coll of Tech BSc81. Sarum & Wells Th Coll DipThMin94. **d** 94 **p** 95. C W Moors *Sarum* from 94. *21 Weavers Close, West Moors, Ferndown, Dorset BH22 0PG* Tel (01202) 891816

MAGILL, Waller Brian Brendan. b 20. TCD BA42 BD45. **d** 44 **p** 45. C Knock *D & D* 44-47; C Holywood 47-50; Vice-Prin Qu Coll Birm 50-55; Chapl Rugby Sch 55-62; Lect Div Nottm Coll of Educn 62-75; Hd of Dept Trent Poly 75-85; Lic to Offic *S'well* from 66; rtd 85. *16 Parkcroft Road, Nottingham NG2 6FN* Tel 0115-923 3293

MAGNESS, Anthony William John. b 37. New Coll Ox BA62 MA65. Coll of Resurr Mirfield 78. **d** 80 **p** 81. C Gt Crosby St Faith *Liv* 80-83; C Newc St Jo *Newc* 83-85; P-in-c Newc St Luke 85-88; P-in-c Newc St Andr 88; V Newc St Andr and Newc St Luke from 89; Chapl Hunter's Moor Hosp 89-95. *The Vicarage, 15 Claremont Street, Newcastle upon Tyne NE2 4AH* Tel 0191-232 3341 Fax as telephone

MAGOR, Robert Jolyon. b 47. Wilson Carlile Coll IDC82 Sarum & Wells Th Coll DCTM93. **d** 93 **p** 94. C Plaistow *Chelmsf* 93-96; TV Plaistow and N Canning Town from 96. *The Rectory, 19 Abbey Street, London E13 8DT* Tel 0171-476 9920

MAGOWAN, Alistair James. b 55. Leeds Univ BSc77 DipHE. Trin Coll Bris 78. **d** 81 **p** 82. C Owlerton *Sheff* 81-84; C Dur St Nic *Dur* 84-89; Chapl St Aid Coll 85-89; V Egham *Guildf* from 89; RD Runnymede from 93. *The Vicarage, Vicarage Road, Egham, Surrey TW20 9JN* Tel (01784) 432066

MAGOWAN, Harold Victor. b 34. ACII69 FCII73 Chartered Insurance Practitioner 89 QUB BA55 BSc(Econ)66 DipEd69. TCD Div Sch Div Test57. **d** 57 **p** 58. C Antrim All SS w Muckamore *Conn* 57-59. *95A Groomsport Road, Bangor, Co Down BT20 5NG*

MAGSON, Thomas Symmons. b 09. MA. **d** 75 **p** 76. NSM Highworth w Sevenhampton and Inglesham etc *Bris* 75-88; Perm to Offic from 88. *21 Cricklade Road, Highworth, Swindon SN6 7BW* Tel (01793) 762579

MAGUIRE, Canon Brian William. b 33. Hull Univ BTh84 MA88. Coll of Resurr Mirfield 70. **d** 72 **p** 73. C Guisborough *York* 72-76; TV Haxby w Wigginton 76-77; TR 78-89; V Huddersfield St Pet and All SS *Wakef* from 89; Hon Can Wakef Cathl from 94. *59 Lightridge Road, Huddersfield HD2 2HF* Tel (01484) 544558 or 427964

MAHONEY, William Denis. b 35. Sem of the Immaculate Conception (NY) 77. **d** 79 **p** 95. In RC Ch 79-87; USA 79-87; NSM Egremont and Haile *Carl* 92-93; NSM Kells from 93. *Valley View, 30 Abbey Vale, St Bees, Cumbria CA27 0EF* Tel (01946) 822543

MAHONY, Conal Martin. b 38. Pontificio Ateneo Antoniano Rome LicSTh64 Lateran Univ Rome ThD66. Franciscan Ho of Studies 57. **d** 62 **p** 63. In RC Ch 62-89; Dir Folkestone Family Care Cen 86-92; Lic to Offic *Cant* 89-92; C Hempnall *Nor* 92-94; TV 94-97; TR from 97. *The Rectory, The Street, Hempnall, Norwich NR15 2AD* Tel (01508) 498157

MAHOOD, Canon Brian Samuel. b 12. St Jo Coll Dur BA39 MA42. **d** 39 **p** 40. C Barkingside St Laur *Chelmsf* 39-41; CF 41-46; V Hatfield Peverel *Chelmsf* 46-53; V Squirrels Heath 53-79; Hon Can Chelmsf Cathl 76-79; rtd 79; Perm to Offic *Chelmsf* from 79. *Jesmond Dene Cottages, 79 Tenterfield Road, Maldon, Essex CM9 5EN* Tel (01621) 855366

MAIDEN, Charles Alistair Kingsley. b 60. Trent Poly BSc84. St Jo Coll Nottm LTh88. **d** 89 **p** 90. C Porchester *S'well* 89-93; C Selston 93-96; P-in-c Huthwaite from 96. *The Vicarage, Blackwell Road, Huthwaite, Sutton-in-Ashfield, Notts NG17 2QT* Tel (01623) 555053

MAIDMENT, Thomas John Louis (Tom). b 43. Lon Univ BSc65. St Steph Ho Ox. **d** 67 **p** 68. C Westmr St Steph w St Jo *Lon* 67-73; P-in-c Twickenham Common H Trin 73-77; V 77-80; V Heston from 80. *The Vicarage, 147 Heston Road, Hounslow TW5 0RD* Tel 0181-570 2288

MAIDSTONE, Archdeacon of. *See* EVANS, The Ven Patrick Alexander Sidney

MAIDSTONE, Suffragan Bishop. *See* REID, The Rt Revd Gavin Hunter

MAIN, Clive Timothy. b 53. St Andr Univ MA75 Cam Univ PGCE76. Oak Hill Th Coll BA94. **d** 96 **p** 97. C Alperton *Lon* from 96. *19 Bowrons Avenue, Wembley, Middx HA0 4QS* Tel 0181-902 5997

MAIN, David. b 16. Man Univ BA40 St Jo Coll Ox BA48 MA53. Cuddesdon Coll 40. **d** 41 **p** 42. C Blackb St Jo *Blackb* 41-42; CF 42-46; Perm to Offic *Ox* 46-48; Chapl and Educn Officer SPCK 48-52; Egypt 48-57; R Bracon Ash w Hethel *Nor* 57-73; rtd 73. *3 Low Farm Cottages, Keswick Road, Norwich NR4 6TX* Tel (01603) 58109

MAIN, Canon David Murray. b 28. Univ Coll Ox BA52 MA56. St Deiniol's Hawarden 73. **d** 73 **p** 74. C Glas St Marg *Glas* 73-75; R Challoch w Newton Stewart 75-79; R Kilmarnock 79-93; Can St Mary's Cathl 85-93; rtd 93; Hon Can St Mary's Cathl *Glas* from 93. *Sunnybrae, 50 Abercromby Road, Castle Douglas, Kirkcudbrightshire DG7 1BA* Tel (01556) 504669

MAINA, Simon Mwangi. b 52. Nairobi Univ 85. **d** 80 **p** 81. Kenya 80-95; C Acton St Mary *Lon* from 95. *39 Derwentwater Road, London W3 6DF* Tel 0181-993 8201

MAINES, Trevor. b 40. Leeds Univ BSc63. Ripon Hall Ox 63. **d** 65 **p** 66. C Speke All SS *Liv* 65-70; C Stevenage St Geo *St Alb* 70-73; V Dorridge *Birm* 73-78; Org Sec (Dio Ex) CECS 79-80; Hon C Tiverton St Pet *Ex* 79-80; Org Sec (Wales) CECS 80-87; Hon C Newton Nottage *Llan* 81-83; Perm to Offic *Mon* 83-87; V Arlesey w Astwick *St Alb* 87-95; RD Shefford 91-95; V Goldington from 95. *St Mary's Vicarage, Church Lane, Goldington, Bedford MK41 0EX* Tel (01234) 355024

MAINEY, Ian George. b 51. CertEd73. Oak Hill Th Coll DipHE86 BA87. **d** 87 **p** 88. C Denton Holme *Carl* 87-91; V Hensingham from 91. *The Vicarage, Egremont Road, Hensingham, Whitehaven, Cumbria CA28 8QW* Tel (01946) 692822

MAINWARING, Islwyn Paul. b 52. Univ of Wales (Swansea) BD75 DPS79. St Mich Coll Llan 77. **d** 79 **p** 80. C Llanilid w Pencoed *Llan* 79-82; C Llanishen and Lisvane 82-85; TV Cwmbran *Mon* 85-88; V Troedyrhiw w Merthyr Vale *Llan* 88-91. *Pennant, 109 Penygroes Road, Blaenau, Ammanford SA18 3BZ* Tel (01269) 850350

MAINWARING, William Douglas. b 26. Univ of Wales (Swansea) DipTh73. St Mich Coll Llan 72. **d** 74 **p** 75. C Aberdare St Fagan *Llan* 74-78; V Seven Sisters 78-80; rtd 80; Perm to Offic *Llan* from 80. *3 Rhiw Nant, Abernant, Aberdare CF44 0QB* Tel (01685) 878409

MAIR, Canon James Fraser. b 24. St Pet Hall Ox BA49 MA53. Wycliffe Hall Ox 49. **d** 51 **p** 52. C Stockport St Geo *Ches* 51-55; V Hollingworth 55-67; R Bacton w Wyverstone *St E* 67-80; V Thurston 80-89; Hon Can St E Cathl 87-89; rtd 89; Perm to Offic *St E* from 90. *The Maltings, Shop Green, Bacton, Stowmarket, Suffolk IP14 4LF* Tel (01449) 781896

MAIRS, Adrian Samuel. b 43. DipHE. Oak Hill Th Coll 76. **d** 78 **p** 79. C Rugby St Matt *Cov* 78-82; P-in-c Mancetter 82-84; V from 84; P-in-c Hartshill from 97. *The Vicarage, Quarry Lane, Mancetter, Atherstone, Warks CV9 1NL* Tel (01827) 713266

MAITIN, Ito. b 36. Lon Univ DipTh67 BA. Kelham Th Coll 63. **d** 68 **p** 69. C Longton St Jo *Lich* 68-69; C Leek St Edw 69-71; C Lich St Chad 71-74; C Tamworth 74-81; V Penkhull from 81. *The Vicarage, 214 Queen's Road, Stoke-on-Trent ST4 7LG* Tel (01782) 414092

MAITLAND, Sydney Milivoge Patrick. b 51. Edin Univ BSc Strathclyde Univ DipTP. **d** 86 **p** 87. Hon C Glas St Geo *Glas* from 86. *14 Kersland Street, Glasgow G12 8BL* Tel 0141-339 4573

MAJOR, Maurice Edward. b 23. EAMTC. **d** 84 **p** 85. NSM Field Dalling w Saxlingham *Nor* 84-87; NSM Sharrington 84-87; NSM Gunthorpe w Bale 84-87; NSM Gunthorpe w Bale w Field Dalling, Saxlingham etc 87-89; Perm to Offic *St As* 89-93; Perm to Offic *Nor* from 93. *Endymion, Creake Road, Burnham Market, King's Lynn, Norfolk PE31 8EW* Tel (01328) 738757

MAJOR, Richard James Edward. b 54. DipTh. Trin Coll Bris 78. **d** 81 **p** 82. C Parr *Liv* 81-84; V Burton Fleming w Fordon *York*

84-85; V Grindale and Ergham 84-85; P-in-c Wold Newton 84-85; V Burton Fleming w Fordon, Grindale etc 85-91; V Bilton St Pet from 91. *The Vicarage, Swine, Hull HU11 4AD* Tel (01482) 811441

MAJOR, Dr Richard John Charles. b 63. Ex Coll Ox BA91 MA93 Magd Coll Ox DPhil91 Massey Univ (NZ) MA85. St Steph Ho Ox 92. **d** 94 **p** 95. C Truro Cathl *Truro* 94-97; C Putney St Mary *S'wark* from 97. *17 Fanthorpe Street, London SW15 1BZ* Tel 0181-788 7164

MAKAMBWE, Francis James. b 40. St Jo Sem Lusaka. **d** 65 **p** 67. Zambia 65-91; Miss Partner CMS from 91; C Waterloo St Jo w St Andr *S'wark* 91-96; V Hatcham St Cath from 96. *St Catherine's Vicarage, 102 Pepys Road, London SE14 5SG* Tel 0171-639 1050 Fax 401 3215

MAKEL, Arthur. b 39. Sheff Poly DMS75. AKC63. **d** 64 **p** 65. C Beamish *Dur* 64-68; Ind Chapl *York* 68-72; P-in-c Scotton w Northorpe *Linc* 72-81; Ind Chapl 72-81; R Epworth 81-89; P-in-c Wroot 81-89; R Epworth and Wroot 89-92; R Sigglesthorne and Rise w Nunkeeling and Bewholme *York* from 92. *The Rectory, Sigglesthorne, Hull HU11 5QA* Tel (01964) 533033

MAKEPEACE, David Norman Harry. b 51. Magd Coll Ox BA74. Trin Coll Bris 83. **d** 85 **p** 86. C Romford Gd Shep Collier Row *Chelmsf* 85-88; Tanzania 88-89; C York St Paul *York* 89-91; TV Radipole and Melcombe Regis *Sarum* from 91. *The Vicarage, 106 Spa Road, Weymouth, Dorset DT3 5ER* Tel (01305) 771938

MAKEPEACE, Preb James Dugard. b 40. Keble Coll Ox BA63 MA67. Cuddesdon Coll 63. **d** 65 **p** 66. C Cullercoats St Geo *Newc* 65-68; Chapl Wadh Coll Ox 68-72; Lib Pusey Ho 68-72; V Romford St Edw *Chelmsf* 72-79; V Tettenhall Regis *Lich* 79-80; TR from 80; RD Trysull 87-97; Preb Lich Cathl from 96. *The Vicarage, 2 Lloyd Road, Tettenhall, Wolverhampton WV6 9AU* Tel (01902) 751622

MAKIN, Hubert. b 18. ACP66 Open Univ BA74. NW Ord Course. **d** 78 **p** 79. Hon C Mount Pellon *Wakef* 78-91; Hon C King Cross 91-94; Perm to Offic from 94. *46 Upper Highfield, Mount Tabor, Halifax, W Yorkshire HX2 0UG* Tel (01422) 244642

MAKIN, Miss Pauline. b 45. Cranmer Hall Dur 75. **dss** 78 **d** 87 **p** 94. Ashton-in-Makerfield St Thos *Liv* 78-87; Par Dn 87-89; Par Dn Rainford 89-94; C 94-95; Asst Dioc Chapl to the Deaf 89-95; C Farnworth from 95. *43 Hampton Drive, Widnes, Cheshire WA8 5DA*

MAKIN, Valerie Diana. Lon Univ DipRS83. S'wark Ord Course 86. **d** 88 **p** 94. Hon Par Dn Bryanston Square St Mary w St Marylebone St Mark *Lon* 88-95; Chapl St Marylebone Healing and Counselling Cen 88-94; NSM Godalming *Guildf* 94-95; Perm to Offic from 95; Perm to Offic *Lon* from 95. *Crowts, Tuesley, Godalming, Surrey GU7 1UD* Tel (01483) 416613

MAKOWER, Canon Dr Malory. b 38. TCD BA61 MA68 St Jo Coll Ox MA64 DPhil64. Ridley Hall Cam 64. **d** 66 **p** 67. C Onslow Square St Paul *Lon* 66-69; Tutor Ridley Hall Cam 69-71; Sen Tutor 71-76; P-in-c Lode and Longmeadow *Ely* 76-84; Warden E Anglian Minl Tr Course 77-79; Prin 79-84; Dir of Post-Ord Tr for NSM *Nor* 84-90; C Gt Yarmouth 84-89; TV 89-95; Dioc NSM Officer 88-95; Hon Can Nor Cathl from 94; Prin LNSM Tr Scheme from 95. *9 Duverlin Close, Norwich NR4 6HS* Tel (01603) 454087

MALAN, Victor Christian de Roubaix. b 39. Cape Town Univ BA60 Linacre Coll Ox BA63 MA68. Wycliffe Hall Ox 61. **d** 63 **p** 64. C Springfield *Birm* 63-66; P-in-c 66-67; C New Windsor *Ox* 67-69; Chapl St Jo Coll Cam 69-74; V Northampton All SS w St Kath *Pet* 74-86; V Stockport St Geo *Ches* 86-89; R N Mundham w Hunston and Merston *Chich* from 89. *The Rectory, Church Lane, Hunston, Chichester, W Sussex PO20 6AJ* Tel (01243) 782003

MALBON, Canon John Allin. b 36. Oak Hill Th Coll 62. **d** 65 **p** 66. C Wolverhampton St Jude *Lich* 65-68; C Hoole *Ches* 68-71; P-in-c Crewe Ch Ch 71-75; V 75-79; V Plemstall w Guilden Sutton from 79; Hon Can Ches Cathl from 96. *The Vicarage, Guilden Sutton, Chester CH3 7EL* Tel (01244) 300306

MALCOLM, Brother. *See* FOUNTAIN, David Roy

MALCOLM, Miss Mercia Alana. b 54. St Andr Univ MA77 Lon Univ DipRS87. S'wark Ord Course 84. **d** 87 **p** 94. C Dartford Ch Ch *Roch* 87-91; Par Dn Stockport St Geo *Ches* 91-94; C 94; C Stockport SW 94; Chapl Ulster Univ from 95; C Jordanstown *Conn* from 95. *6 Mount Pleasant Road, Jordanstown, Newtownabbey, Co Antrim BT37 0NQ* Tel (01232) 853524

MALDOOM, Ms Julie Marilyn. b 65. Jes Coll Ox BA88 PGCE89. Cuddesdon Coll BTh93. **d** 96 **p** 97. C Chinnor w Emmington and Sydenham etc *Ox* from 96. *44 Cowleaze, Chinnor, Oxon OX9 4TB* Tel (01844) 353763

MALE, David Edward. b 62. Southn Univ BA83. St Jo Coll Dur BA90 Cranmer Hall Dur 88. **d** 91 **p** 92. C Leic St Chris *Leic* 91-94; C Kirkheaton *Wakef* from 94. *423 Wakefield Road, Huddersfield HD5 8DB* Tel (01484) 429885

MALES, Dr Jeanne Margaret. b 49. Reading Univ BA71 Lon Univ MPhil73 Surrey Univ PhD86 AFBPsS75 CPsychol88. S'wark Ord Course 93. **d** 96. NSM Caterham *S'wark* from 96. *17 Town End, Caterham, Surrey CR3 5UJ* Tel (01883) 340063

MALINS, Peter. b 18. Down Coll Cam BA40 MA47. Ridley Hall Cam 40. **d** 42 **p** 43. C Earlsdon *Cov* 42-44; CF (EC) 44-47; CF 47-73; QHC 72-73; V Greenwich St Alfege w St Pet and St Paul *S'wark* 73-87; P-in-c Greenwich H Trin and St Paul 76-84; Sub-Dean Greenwich 79-81; rtd 87; Perm to Offic *Guildf* from 87. *12 Ridgeway Drive, Dorking, Surrey RH4 3AN* Tel (01306) 882035

MALKINSON, Christopher Mark. b 47. Chich Th Coll 84. **d** 86 **p** 87. C Stroud and Uplands w Slad *Glouc* 86-89; V Cam w Stinchcombe from 89. *The Vicarage, Church Road, Cam, Dursley, Glos GL11 5PQ* Tel (01453) 542084

MALKINSON, Michael Stephen. b 43. St Steph Ho Ox 65. **d** 68 **p** 69. C New Addington *Cant* 68-71; C Blackpool St Steph *Blackb* 71-74; V Wainfleet St Mary *Linc* 74-81; R Wainfleet All SS w St Thos 74-81; P-in-c Croft 80-81; V Lund *Blackb* 81-93; V Heyhouses on Sea from 93. *St Annes Vicarage, 4 Oxford Road, Lytham St Annes, Lancs FY8 2EA* Tel (01253) 722725

MALLESON, Michael Lawson. b 42. Univ of Wales (Swansea) BA64 Nottm Univ DipTh68. Linc Th Coll 67. **d** 70 **p** 71. C Wakef St Jo *Wakef* 70-73; C-in-c Holmfield St Andr CD 73-75; V Holmfield 75-80; V Heworth St Alb *Dur* 80-93; V Killingworth *Newc* from 93. *The Vicarage, West Lane, Killingworth, Newcastle upon Tyne NE12 0BL* Tel 0191-268 3242

MALLETT, John Christopher. b 44. EAMTC. **d** 82 **p** 83. NSM Hethersett w Canteloff *Nor* 82-85; NSM Hethersett w Canteloff w Lt and Gt Melton 85-90; Chapl Wayland Hosp Norfolk from 88. *2 Bailey Close, Hethersett, Norwich NR9 3EU* Tel (01603) 811010

MALLETT, Michael William. b 18. St Deiniol's Hawarden. **d** 69 **p** 70. C Hyde St Geo *Ches* 69-75; V Broadheath 75-84; rtd 84; Perm to Offic *Carl* 84-94. *3 Ellesborough Manor, Butlers Cross, Aylesbury, Bucks HP17 0XF* Tel (01296) 696018

MALLETT, Mrs Pamela Joan. b 26. LNSM course 93. **d** 96. NSM Long Ditton *S'wark* from 96. *109 Ditton Hill, Long Ditton, Surbiton, Surrey KT6 5EJ* Tel 0181-398 5189

MALLIN, The Very Revd Stewart Adam Thomson. b 24. Edin Th Coll 59. **d** 61 **p** 62. Prec St Andr Cathl Inverness *Mor* 61-64; Itinerant Priest 64-68; P-in-c Thurso 68-77; R Wick 68-77; CSG from 74; Can St Andr Cathl Inverness *Mor* 74-91; R Dingwall 77-91; R Strathpeffer 77-91; Syn Clerk 81-83; Dean Mor 83-91; rtd 91; Hon Can St Andr Cathl Inverness *Mor* from 91; Hon C Strathnairn St Paul from 91. *St Paul's Parsonage, Croachy, Strathnairn, Inverness IV1 2UB* Tel (01808) 521397

MALLINSON, Canon Ralph Edward. b 40. Or Coll Ox BA63 MA66. St Steph Ho Ox 63. **d** 66 **p** 67. C Bolton St Pet *Man* 66-68; C Elton All SS 68-72; V Bury St Thos 72-76; V Bury Ch King 76-81; P-in-c Goodshaw 81-82; V 82-84; V Goodshaw and Crawshawbooth 84-93; AD Rossendale 83-93; Hon Can Man Cathl from 92; V Unsworth from 93. *St George's Vicarage, Hollins Lane, Bury, Lancs BL9 8JJ* Tel 0161-766 2429

MALLOCH, Elizabeth Gilmour. b 10. Edin Univ MA33 DipEd34. **dss** 85 **d** 86 **p** 94. NSM Edin St Mary *Edin* 85-95; rtd 95. *Flat 10, 23 Salisbury Road, Edinburgh EH16 5AA* Tel 0131-668 4238

MALLON, Allister. b 61. Sheff Univ BA83 TCD DipTh87 BTh89 MA. CITC. **d** 87 **p** 88. C Ballymoney w Finvoy and Rasharkin *Conn* 87-90; C Belfast St Mary w H Redeemer 90-92; Bp's C Belfast St Mary Magd from 92. *St Mary Magdalene Rectory, 56 Windsor Avenue, Belfast BT9 6EJ* Tel (01232) 667516

MALLORY, George Henry. b 14. JP. Lon Univ BSc63. St Deiniol's Hawarden. **d** 80 **p** 81. NSM Oaks in Charnwood and Copt Oak *Leic* 80-88; rtd 88; Perm to Offic *Leic* 88-91; Perm to Offic *Worc* from 91. *Claudina, Bewdley Road North, Stourport-on-Severn, Worcs DY13 8PX* Tel (01299) 827969

MALONEY, Ms Fiona Elizabeth. b 60. Bradf Univ BSc82. Cranmer Hall Dur BA91 N Ord Course 91. **d** 92 **p** 94. Par Dn Castleton Moor *Man* 92-94; C 94-96; Hon C Pendlebury St Jo 96-97; C from 97. *St John's Vicarage, 27 Bolton Road, Pendlebury, Manchester M27 8XS* Tel 0161-925 0171

MALONEY, Terence Mark. b 63. York Univ BSc84. Cranmer Hall Dur 88. **d** 91 **p** 92. C Blackley St Andr *Man* 91-96; P-in-c Pendlebury St Jo from 96. *St John's Vicarage, 27 Bolton Road, Pendlebury, Manchester M27 2XS* Tel 0161-736 2176

MALPASS, Clive William. b 36. AKC60. **d** 61 **p** 62. C Malden St Jo *S'wark* 61-64; C Horley 64-69; Youth Chapl *Dur* 69-72; Adv in Lay Tr 72-76; V Wyther Ven Bede *Ripon* 76-82; V Askrigg w Stallingbusk from 82; RD Wensley from 94. *The Vicarage, Askrigg, Leyburn, N Yorkshire DL8 3HZ* Tel (01969) 650301

MALSOM, Laurence Michael. b 31. Selw Coll Cam BA55 MA59. Cuddesdon Coll 55. **d** 57 **p** 58. C Crediton *Ex* 57-60; C Plymouth St Gabr 60-62; C Sidmouth St Nic 62-64; V Harberton 64-71; V Harbertonford 64-71; RD Totnes 70-75; V S Brent 71-75; V St Marychurch 75-79; P-in-c Plymouth Crownhill Ascension 79-80; V 80-94; rtd 94; Perm to Offic *Truro* from 94. *The Village, St Mellion, Saltash, Cornwall PL12 6RJ* Tel (01579) 51219

MALTBY, Geoffrey. b 38. Leeds Univ BA62 Nottm Univ DipRE72 Glas Coll of Ed CSpPastCat92. Wells Th Coll 68. **d** 70 **p** 71. C Mansfield St Mark *S'well* 70-73; V Skegby 73-78; V Carrington 78-87; C Rainworth 87-90; Chapl for People w Learning Disability (Mental Handicap) from 90. *18 Beverley Close, Rainworth, Mansfield, Notts NG21 0LW* Tel (01623) 797095

MALTBY, Dr Judith Diane. b 57. Illinois Univ BA79 Newnham Coll Cam PhD92. S Dios Minl Tr Scheme 89. **d** 92 **p** 94. Tutor Sarum & Wells Th Coll 87-93; Hon Par Dn Wilton w

Netherhampton and Fugglestone *Sarum* 92-93; Chapl and Fell CCC Ox from 93. *Corpus Christi College, Oxford OX1 4JF* Tel (01865) 276722 E-mail judith.maltby@ccc.ox.ac.uk

MALTIN, Basil St Clair Aston. b 24. Qu Coll Cam BA49 MA54. Westcott Ho Cam 50. **d** 51 **p** 52. C Dursley *Glouc* 51-53; C Bathwick w Woolley *B & W* 53-57; V Frome Ch Ch 57-63; P-in-c Marston Bigot 57-59; V Bishops Lydeard 63-71; R Pulborough *Chich* 71-90; RD Storrington 84-89; rtd 90; Perm to Offic *Chich* from 90. *13 Somerstown, Chichester, W Sussex PO19 4AG* Tel (01243) 786740

MAN, Archdeacon of. *See* PARTINGTON, The Ven Brian Harold

MANCE, Herbert William. b 19. St Jo Coll Cam BA40 MA44. Oak Hill Th Coll 47. **d** 49 **p** 50. C Leeds St Geo *Ripon* 49-53; CF 53-57; Nigeria 58-71; Can Ibadan 70-71; C Buckhurst Hill *Chelmsf* 71-75; P-in-c Roydon 75-79; V 79-85; rtd 85; Perm to Offic *Lich* from 85. *52 Redwood Avenue, Stone, Staffs ST15 0DB* Tel (01785) 816128

MANCHESTER, Canon Charles. b 28. Univ Coll Lon BD54. Oak Hill Th Coll 50. **d** 55 **p** 56. C Nottingham St Nic *S'well* 55-58; C Kinson *Sarum* 58-61; R Haworth *Bradf* 61-67; V Aldershot H Trin *Guildf* 67-87; RD Aldershot 73-78; R Newdigate 87-93; Hon Can Guildf Cathl 89-93; rtd 93; Perm to Offic *Guildf* from 93. *12 Fulmar Road, Christchurch, Dorset BH23 4BJ*

MANCHESTER, John Charles. b 45. Lon Univ BD69. ALCD68. **d** 69 **p** 70. C Scarborough St Martin *York* 69-73; C Selby Abbey 73-76; P-in-c Old Malton 76-79; V from 79; RD Bulmer and Malton 85-91. *The Gannock House, Old Malton, Malton, N Yorkshire YO17 0HB* Tel (01653) 692121

MANCHESTER, Simon Lorimer. b 53. Univ of NSW BA. Moore Th Coll Sydney ThL79. **d** 80 **p** 80. Australia 80-82 and from 84; C St Helen Bishopsgate w St Andr Undershaft etc *Lon* 82-84. *The Rectory, PO Box 132, McLaren Street, North Sydney, NSW, Australia 2059* Tel Sydney (2) 9929 4807 Fax 955 5180

MANCHESTER, Archdeacon of. *See* HARRIS, The Ven Reginald Brian

MANCHESTER, Bishop of. *See* MAYFIELD, The Rt Revd Christopher John

MANCHESTER, Dean of. *See* RILEY, The Very Revd Kenneth Joseph

MANDER, Dennis Stanley. b 18. Bps' Coll Cheshunt 60. **d** 62 **p** 63. C Moulsham St Jo *Chelmsf* 62-64; R Didmarton w Oldbury-on-the-Hill and Sopworth *Glouc* 64-69; S Africa 69-78; R Lanteglos by Camelford w Advent *Truro* 78-85; rtd 85; Perm to Offic *Truro* from 85. *12 Menheniot Crescent, Langore, Launceston, Cornwall PL15 8PD* Tel (01566) 772853

MANDER, Peter John. b 52. Liv Univ BA85. Sarum & Wells Th Coll 85. **d** 87 **p** 88. C Hale and Ashley *Ches* 87-90; TV Grantham *Linc* from 90. *114 Manthorpe Road, Grantham, Lincs NG31 8DL* Tel (01476) 576047

MANDER, Canon Thomas Leonard Frederick. b 33. Ely Th Coll 60. **d** 62 **p** 63. C Cov St Mary *Cov* 62-66; V Bishop's Tachbrook 66-70; V Earlsdon 70-76; V Chesterton 76-83; R Lighthorne 76-83; V Newbold Pacey w Moreton Morrell 76-83; Hon Can Cov Cathl 80-92; P-in-c S Leamington St Jo 83-84; V 84-92; rtd 92; Perm to Offic *Cov* from 92. *59 Murcott Road East, Whitnash, Leamington Spa, Warks CV31 2JJ* Tel (01926) 339950

MANDERSON, Dr Robert Dunlop (Leslie). b 35. FDS68 FRCSEd68 Dur Univ LDS59. Ox Min Course 92. **d** 94 **p** 95. NSM Maidenhead St Andr and St Mary *Ox* from 94. *Squirrels, Sandisplatt Road, Maidenhead, Berks SL6 4NB* Tel (01628) 38505

MANHIRE, Ashley Lewin. b 31. AKC55. **d** 56 **p** 57. C Plymouth St Gabr *Ex* 56-59; C Cockington 59-66; V Torquay St Martin Barton 66-83; RD Ipplepen 82-87; V Shaldon from 83. *The Vicarage, Torquay Road, Shaldon, Teignmouth, Devon TQ14 0AX* Tel (01626) 872396

MANHOOD, Canon Phyllis. b 32. Aston Tr Scheme 78 Qu Coll Birm 79. **dss** 82 **d** 87 **p** 94. Harwich *Chelmsf* 82-83; Dovercourt and Parkeston 83-85; Fawley *Win* 85-87; Par Dn 87-92; P-in-c Bournemouth St Aug from 92; Hon Can Win Cathl from 96. *St Augustine's Vicarage, 2A St Anthony's Road, Bournemouth BH2 6PD* Tel (01202) 556861

✠**MANKTELOW, The Rt Revd Michael Richard John.** b 27. Ch Coll Cam BA48 MA52. Chich Th Coll 51. **d** 53 **p** 54 **c** 77. C Boston *Linc* 53-56; Chapl Ch Coll Cam 57-61; Chapl Linc Th Coll 61-63; Sub-Warden 64-66; V Knaresborough St Jo *Ripon* 66-73; RD Harrogate 72-77; V Harrogate St Wilfrid 73-77; P-in-c Harrogate St Luke 75-77; Hon Can Ripon Cathl 75-77; Suff Bp Basingstoke *Win* 77-93; Can Res Win Cathl 77-91; Hon Can 91-93; Vice-Dean 87-93; rtd 93; Asst Bp Chich from 94; Asst Bp Eur from 94; Wiccamical Preb Chich Cathl *Chich* from 97. *2 The Chantry, Canon Lane, Chichester, W Sussex PO19 1PZ* Tel (01243) 531096

MANLEY, Canon Gordon Russell Delpratt. b 33. Ch Coll Cam BA56 MA60. Linc Th Coll 57. **d** 59 **p** 60. C Westbury-on-Trym St Alb *Bris* 59-61; Chapl Ch Coll Cam 61-66; V Radlett *St Alb* 66-75; V Faversham *Cant* from 75; RD Ospringe 84-90; Hon Can Cant Cathl from 90. *The Vicarage, Preston Street, Faversham, Kent ME13 8PG* Tel (01795) 532592

MANLEY, Michael Alan. b 60. SS Hild & Bede Coll Dur BA82. Trin Coll Bris DipTh86. **d** 86 **p** 87. C Accrington St Jo *Blackb* 86-89; C Huncoat 88-89; C Accrington St Jo w Huncoat 89-90; V Preston St Luke and St Oswald 90-96; V Blackpool St Jo from 96. *St John's Vicarage, 19 Leamington Road, Blackpool FY1 4HD* Tel (01253) 20626

MANLEY-COOPER, Simon James. b 46. S Dios Minl Tr Scheme 91. **d** 94 **p** 95. NSM Soho St Anne w St Thos and St Pet *Lon* 94-96; Ind Chapl 94-96; Perm to Offic *St Alb* 94-96; P-in-c Bedford St Mich from 96; Ind Chapl from 96. *St Michael's Vicarage, Faldo Road, Bedford MK42 0EH* Tel (01234) 266920

MANN, Ms Angela. b 58. Bath Univ BA80 Bris Univ PGCE83. Trin Coll Bris DipHE94. **d** 94 **p** 95. C Marlborough *Sarum* from 94. *10 Alexandra Terrace, Marlborough, Wilts SN8 1DA* Tel (01672) 515244

MANN, Lt Comdr Anthony James. b 34. Open Univ BA76. St Jo Coll Nottm 85. **d** 88 **p** 89. NSM Helensburgh *Glas* from 88. *The Anchorage, Portkil, Kilcreggan, Helensburgh, Dunbartonshire G84 0LF* Tel (01436) 842623

MANN, Canon Charmion Anne Montgomery. b 36. Liv Univ BA57 CertEd62 DipEd79. Trin Coll Bris 80. **dss** 82 **d** 87 **p** 94. Bris St Nath w St Kath *Bris* 82-84; Bris St Matt and St Nath 84-85; Asst Chapl City Cen Hosps Bris 85-88; Chapl Bris Maternity Hosp 88-94; Chapl Bris R Hosp for Sick Children 88-94; Chapl Bris R Infirmary 88-94; Hon Can Bris Cathl *Bris* from 93; P-in-c Lacock w Bowden Hill from 94. *The Vicarage, Folly Lane, Lacock, Chippenham, Wilts SN15 2LL* Tel (01249) 730272 Fax 730130

MANN, Christopher John. b 57. Glas Univ BSc79. Westcott Ho Cam 83. **d** 86 **p** 87. C Worc SE *Worc* 86-89; Min Can and Sacr St Paul's Cathl *Lon* 89-96; R Upminster *Chelmsf* from 96. *The Rectory, Gridiron Place, Upminster, Essex RM14 2BE* Tel (01708) 220174

MANN, David. b 57. BA. Ridley Hall Cam. **d** 82 **p** 83. C Monkwearmouth St Andr *Dur* 82-86; Chapl Sheff Cathl *Sheff* 86-87; C Leeds St Geo *Ripon* 87-94; V Ripon H Trin from 94. *Holy Trinity Vicarage, College Road, Ripon, N Yorkshire HG4 2AE* Tel (01765) 605865

MANN, Donald Leonard. b 22. Westcott Ho Cam. **d** 47 **p** 48. C S'well Minster *S'well* 47-49; C Edwinstowe w Carburton 49-51; C St Alb St Paul *St Alb* 51-54; C Baldock w Bygrave and Clothall 54-56; V Guilden Morden *Ely* 56-59; V Rocester *Lich* 59-63; V Gnosall w Knightley 63-69; V Sheen 69-76; P-in-c Calton 72-76; P-in-c Ellastone 76; rtd 76; Perm to Offic *Ches* from 93. *Bungalow 24, Lyme Green Settlement, Macclesfield, Cheshire SK11 0LD* Tel (01260) 252209

MANN, Gary. b 63. Nottm Univ BTh90. Linc Th Coll 87. **d** 90 **p** 91. C Knottingley *Wakef* 90-93; TV Brighouse and Clifton from 93. *The Vicarage, 31 Robin Hood Way, Brighouse, W Yorkshire HD6 4LA* Tel (01484) 713290

MANN, Ivan John. b 52. Brunel Univ BTech74 Southn Univ BTh80. Sarum & Wells Th Coll 75. **d** 78 **p** 79. C Hadleigh w Layham and Shelley *St E* 78-81; C Whitton and Thurleston w Akenham 81-83; V Leiston 83-86; Perm to Offic 86-89; R Aldringham w Thorpe, Knodishall w Buxlow etc 89-93; V Ipswich St Jo 93-96; Chapl St Mary's Convent Wantage from 96. *St Mary's Convent, Wantage, Oxon OX12 9DJ* Tel (01235) 763141

MANN, John. b 35. ISO91. Lon Univ DipEcon66. Oak Hill NSM Course 89. **d** 92 **p** 93. NSM Springfield All SS *Chelmsf* from 92. *18 Humber Road, Chelmsford CM1 5PE* Tel (01245) 259596

MANN, John Owen. b 55. QUB BD77 MTh86. CITC 79. **d** 79 **p** 81. C Cloughfern *Conn* 79-82; C Knock *D & D* 82-85; I Ballyrashane w Kildollagh *Conn* 85-89; R Bentworth and Shalden and Lasham *Win* 89-93; RD Alton 92-93; I Cloughfern *Conn* from 93. *Cloughfern Rectory, 126 Doagh Road, Newtownabbey, Co Antrim BT37 9QR* Tel (01232) 862437

MANN, Julian Farrer Edgar. b 64. Peterho Cam MA90. Oak Hill Th Coll BA93. **d** 96 **p** 97. C Hoole *Ches* from 96. *8 Park Drive, Hoole, Chester CH2 3JS* Tel (01244) 311104

✠**MANN, The Rt Revd Michael Ashley.** b 24. KCVO89. CBIM RMA 42 Harvard Univ AMP73. Wells Th Coll 55. **d** 57 **p** 58 **c** 74. C Wolborough w Newton Abbot *Ex* 57-59; V Sparkwell 59-62; Nigeria 62-67; Home Sec Miss to Seamen 67-69; Can Res Nor Cathl *Nor* 69-74; Vice-Dean 73-74; Dioc Ind Adv 69-74; Suff Bp Dudley *Worc* 74-76; Dean of Windsor and Dom Chapl to The Queen 76-89; rtd 89. *Lower End Farm Cottage, Eastington, Northleach, Glos GL54 3PN* Tel (01451) 860767

MANN, Canon Peter Eric. b 51. St Jo Coll Dur BA73. Westcott Ho Cam 73. **d** 75 **p** 76. C Barrow St Jo *Carl* 75-78; C Egremont 78-80; V Carl St Luke Morton 80-86; TR Egremont and Haile 86-93; P-in-c Barrow St Geo w St Luke from 93; RD Furness from 94; Hon Can Carl Cathl from 95. *The Rectory, 98 Roose Road, Barrow-in-Furness, Cumbria LA13 9RL* Tel (01229) 821641

MANN, Ralph Norman. b 27. BNC Ox BA51 MA55 DipEd52. Ox NSM Course 79. **d** 82 **p** 83. NSM Kingham w Churchill, Daylesford and Sarsden *Ox* 82-85; S Area Sec BCMS 82-89; P-in-c Broadwell, Evenlode, Oddington and Adlestrop *Glouc* 89-97; rtd 97; P-in-c Upton St Leonards *Glouc* from 97. *The Rectory, 12 Bondend Road, Upton St Leonards, Gloucester GL4 8AG* Tel (01452) 618432

MANN, Robin. b 45. MRTPI73 DipTP72 Fitzw Coll Cam BA76 MA80. Ridley Hall Cam 73. **d** 77 **p** 78. C Wetherby *Ripon* 77-80;

V Hipswell 80-86; V Mamble w Bayton, Rock w Heightington etc *Worc* 86-96; V Avon Valley *Sarum* from 96. *The Vicarage, Netheravon, Salisbury SP4 9QP* Tel (01980) 670326

MANN, Terence John (Terry). b 47. GGSM68 LRSM79 Lon Univ PGCE69 Trin Coll Cam FTCL79 Miami Univ MA80. Ox Min Course CBTS94. **d** 94 **p** 95. NSM Kingham w Churchill, Daylesford and Sarsden *Ox* from 94. *The Baliffe's House, Kingham Hill, Kingham, Chipping Norton, Oxon OX7 6TE* Tel (01608) 658450 Fax 658658

MANNALL, Michael John Frederick. b 37. St Mich Coll Llan 61. **d** 63 **p** 64. C Clapham H Spirit *S'wark* 63-66; C Brighton St Bart *Chich* 66-68; C Willesden St Matt *Lon* 68-69; C-in-c Cricklewood St Pet CD 69-73; R Broughton *Pet* 73-75; Hon C Kingston St Luke *S'wark* 76-94; rtd 84; Perm to Offic *Nor* 95-96. *The Blessings, 55 Sculthorpe Road, Fakenham, Norfolk NR21 9ET* Tel (01328) 863496

MANNERS, Kenneth. b 29. N Ord Course. **d** 84 **p** 85. NSM Brayton *York* from 84. *16 Wistow Road, Selby, N Yorkshire YO8 0LY* Tel (01757) 702129

MANNING, Adrian Peter. b 63. St Cath Coll Cam MA88 K Coll Lon PGCE88 St Cath Coll Cam BA84. Ridley Hall Cam CTM95. **d** 95 **p** 96. C Oxhey All SS *St Alb* 95-97; Asst Chapl Bedford Sch from 97. *2 Burnaby Road, Bedford MK40 2TT* Tel (01234) 344243

MANNING, Mrs Ann. b 42. Liv Univ CertEd75. St Jo Coll Nottm CTM94 N Ord Course 94. **d** 95 **p** 96. NSM Grasmere *Carl* 95-96. *12 Butterbache Road, Huntington, Chester CH3 6BZ* Tel (01244) 400138

MANNING, Arthur Philip. b 35. Chester Coll BEd74. St Jo Coll Nottm 88. **d** 89 **p** 90. C Eastham *Ches* 89-90; NSM Lache cum Saltney 91-95; NSM Langdale *Carl* 95-96; P-in-c Barnton *Ches* from 97. *12 Butterbache Road, Huntington, Chester CH3 6BZ* Tel (01244) 400138

MANNING, Brian Hawthorne. b 29. AMCT52 CEng59 MIStructE59. NW Ord Course 70. **d** 73 **p** 74. NSM Birch St Jas *Man* 73-75; NSM Prestwich St Gabr 75-80; NSM Prestwich St Mary 80-85; NSM Marple All SS *Ches* 85-88; R Cockfield w Bradfield St Clare, Felsham etc *St E* 88-95; RD Lavenham 93-95; rtd 95. *Edale House, The Street, Woolpit, Bury St Edmunds, Suffolk IP30 9SA* Tel (01359) 242519

MANNING, David Godfrey. b 47. Trin Coll Bris 73. **d** 76 **p** 77. C Richmond H Trin and Ch Ch *S'wark* 76-79; C Anston *Sheff* 79-83; V Blackpool St Mark *Blackb* 83-91; V Creech St Michael *B & W* from 91. *The Vicarage, Creech St Michael, Taunton, Somerset TA3 5PP* Tel (01823) 442237

MANNING, Neville Alexander. b 41. Lon Univ BD68. ALCD68. **d** 68 **p** 69. C Belvedere All SS *Roch* 68-71; C Hollington St Leon *Chich* 71-73; C Hersham *Guildf* 73-77; V Dawley St Jerome *Lon* 77-94; R Denton w S Heighton and Tarring Neville *Chich* from 94. *The Rectory, 6 Heighton Road, Newhaven, E Sussex BN9 0RB* Tel (01273) 514319

✠**MANNING, The Rt Revd William James.** b 16. TCD BA44 MA47 Or Coll Ox MA50. TCD Div Sch Div Test44. **d** 44 **p** 45 **c** 78. C Dublin Donnybrook *D & G* 44-47; C Cork St Fin Barre's Cathl *C, C & R* 47-49; Chapl Thos Coram Sch Berkhamsted 49-51; Bermuda 51-64; Can Res Bermuda Cathl 53-64; Zürich *Eur* 64-66; S Africa from 67; Dean George 72-77; Bp George 78-87. *Liamslea, 10 Dalmore Road, Tokai, 7945 South Africa* Tel Cape Town (21) 757811

MANNINGS, Andrew James. b 52. Trent Park Coll of Educn CertEd73. St Jo Coll Nottm DCM92. **d** 92 **p** 94. C Over St Chad *Ches* 92-93; C Sale St Anne 93-96; C Timperley from 96. *St Catherine's House, 97 Park Road, Timperley, Altrincham, Cheshire WA15 6QG* Tel 0161-962 3017

MANNS, Edwin Ernest (Eddie). b 30. Portsm Dioc Tr Course 84. **d** 85. C Paulsgrove *Portsm* 85-95; Chapl St Mary's Hosp Portsm 90-91; Team Chapl Portsm Hosp 91-95; rtd 95. *17 Kelvin Grove, Portchester, Fareham, Hants PO16 8LQ* Tel (01705) 324818

MANSBRIDGE, The Ven Michael Winstanley. b 32. Southn Univ BA54. Ridley Hall Cam 56. **d** 58 **p** 59. C Ware St Mary *St Alb* 58-60; C Claverdon w Preston Bagot *Cov* 60-62; Kenya 62-65; V Chilvers Coton w Astley *Cov* 65-75; RD Nuneaton 66-73; V Leamington Priors H Trin 75-83; Adn Cyprus and the Gulf from 83; Chapl Abu Dhabi St Andr UAE 83-97; Can Bahrain from 87; Provost Nicosia from 97. *PO Box 2014, Nicosia CY1516, Cyprus* Tel Nicosia (2) 467897 Fax 442241

MANSELL, Clive Neville Ross. b 53. Solicitor 77 Leic Univ LLB74. Trin Coll Bris DipHE81. **d** 82 **p** 83. C Gt Malvern St Mary *Worc* 82-85; Min Can Ripon Cathl *Ripon* 85-89; R Kirklington w Burneston and Wath and Pickhill from 89. *The Rectory, Kirklington, Bedale, N Yorkshire DL8 2NJ* Tel (01845) 567429

MANSFIELD, Gordon Reginald. b 35. Lon Univ DipTh61 CertEd BA. Clifton Th Coll 58. **d** 63 **p** 64. C Carl St Jo *Carl* 63-65; C Westcombe Park St Geo *S'wark* 65-68; C Rashcliffe *Wakef* 68-70; V Woodlands *Sheff* 70-80; V Steeple Bumpstead and Helions Bumpstead *Chelmsf* from 80. *The Vicarage, Church Street, Steeple Bumpstead, Haverhill, Suffolk CB9 7EA* Tel (01440) 730257

MANSFIELD, Julian Nicolas (Nick). b 59. K Coll Lon BD AKC. Edin Th Coll 83. **d** 85 **p** 86. C Kirkby *Liv* 85-89; TV Ditton St Mich 89-96; P-in-c Preston St Luke and St Oswald *Blackb* from 96. *The Vicarage, 60 Harewood Road, Preston PR1 6XE* Tel (01772) 795395

MANSFIELD, Robert William. b 45. LNSM course 89. **d** 88 **p** 89. NSM Louth *Linc* from 88. *The Old Railway House, Stewton, Louth, Lincs LN11 8SD* Tel (01507) 327533

MANSFIELD, Simon David. b 55. Brunel Univ BSc81 Lon Univ MA94. Ripon Coll Cuddesdon 88. **d** 90 **p** 91. C N Harrow St Alb *Lon* 90-93; C Birchington w Acol and Minnis Bay *Cant* from 93. *29 Hunting Gate, Birchington, Kent CT7 9JA* Tel (01843) 843750

MANSFIELD, Stephen McLaren. b 59. FGA DipRJ GDip. Cranmer Hall Dur 86. **d** 89 **p** 90. C Poynton *Ches* 89-92; C Bromborough 92-94; V Bidston from 94. *The Vicarage, 6 Statham Road, Birkenhead, Merseyside L43 7XS* Tel 0151-652 4852

MANSHIP, Canon David. b 27. ARCO Keble Coll Ox BA52 MA58. Qu Coll Birm 52. **d** 54 **p** 55. C Hackney St Jo *Lon* 54-58; C Preston Ascension 58-61; C St Andr Holborn 61-65; Members' Tr Officer C of E Youth Coun 65-68; Clergy Tr Officer 68-70; Dir of Educn *Win* 70-79; Hon Can Win Cathl 74-79; R Old Alresford 76-79; V Abingdon w Shippon *Ox* 79-89; TR Abingdon 89-93; V Shippon 89; RD Abingdon 87-90; rtd 93. *Woodlyn, Faringdon Road, Southmoor, Abingdon, Oxon OX13 5AF* Tel (01865) 820885

MANSLEY, Colin Edward. b 56. Edin Univ MA80 BA85. Ripon Coll Cuddesdon 83. **d** 86 **p** 87. C Worle *B & W* 86-89; C Baguley *Man* 89-91; C Radcliffe St Mary 91; TV Radcliffe 91-96; V Bartley Green *Birm* from 96. *The Vicarage, 96 Romsley Road, Birmingham B32 3PS* Tel 0121-475 1508

MANSON-BRAILSFORD, Andrew Henry. b 64. NUU BA86. Ripon Coll Cuddesdon 87. **d** 90 **p** 91. C Warrington St Elphin *Liv* 90-93; C Torrisholme *Blackb* 93-96; V Brighton St Geo w St Anne and St Mark *Chich* from 96. *22 Seymour Square, Kemp Town, Brighton BN2 1DW*

MANTLE, John Ambrose Cyril. b 46. St Andr Univ MTh74 CertEd75 Kent Univ MA90. Edin Th Coll 66. **d** 69 **p** 70. C Broughty Ferry *Bre* 69-71; Perm to Offic 71-75; Perm to Offic *Edin* 75-77; Chapl St Andr Univ *St And* 77-80; P-in-c Pittenweem 78-80; P-in-c Elie and Earlsferry 78-80; Chapl and Fell Fitzw Coll Cam 80-86; Tutor Cant Sch of Min 86-91; Vice Prin 91-93; C Boxley w Detling *Cant* 86-93; Lect Rob Gordon Univ Aber 94; Dioc Avd for Educn and Tr of Adults *Chich* from 94. *18 Nizells Avenue, Hove, E Sussex BN3 1PL* Tel (01273) 736389

MANTLE, Canon Rupert James. b 15. Edin Univ MA37. Edin Th Coll 38. **d** 40 **p** 41. C Paisley H Trin *Glas* 40-42; C Lenzie 43; Chapl St Andr Cathl *Ab* 44-46; R Bucksburn 46-50; R Inverness St Jo *Mor* 50-55; C-in-c Dundee St Ninian *Bre* 55-67; R Aberdeen St Pet *Ab* 67-81; Hon C 84-87; Can St Paul's Cathl Dundee *Bre* 70-76; Can St Andr Cathl *Ab* 78-81; rtd 81; Hon Can St Andr Cathl *Ab* from 81; Perm to Offic from 81. *32 Craigiebuckler Terrace, Aberdeen AB15 8SX* Tel (01224) 316636

MAPLE, David Charles. b 34. Sarum Th Coll 64. **d** 66 **p** 66. C Buckland in Dover *Cant* 66-67; C St Laurence in the Isle of Thanet 67-71; Chapl RAF 71-75; P-in-c Ivychurch 75-76; P-in-c Newchurch *Cant* 75-78; P-in-c Burmarsh 75-78; P-in-c St Mary in the Marsh 75-76; R Dymchurch 76-78; R Dymchurch w Burmarsh and Newchurch 78-81; Hon Min Can Cant Cathl from 79; Abp's Dioc Chapl 81-91; Chapl St Jo Hosp Cant 91-95; rtd 95. *1 Mount Pleasant, Blean, Canterbury, Kent CT2 9EU* Tel (01227) 459044

MAPLE, John Philip (Jack). b 50. Chich Th Coll 71. **d** 74 **p** 79. C Notting Hill St Mich and Ch Ch *Lon* 74-75; Lic to Offic 78-79; C Barnsbury St Dav w St Clem 79-80; C Cotham St Sav w St Mary *Bris* 80-83; TV St Marylebone Ch Ch *Lon* 83-91; R St Marylebone St Paul from 91. *St Paul's House, 9 Rossmore Road, London NW1 6NJ* Tel 0171-262 9443

MAPLES, The Ven Jeffrey Stanley. b 16. Down Coll Cam BA38 MA46. Chich Th Coll 39. **d** 40 **p** 41. C Milton *Portsm* 40-46; C Watlington *Ox* 46-48; V Swinderby *Linc* 48-50; V Linc St Mich 50-56; Youth Chapl and Asst Dir Educn 48-50; Dir of Educn 50-56; Can and Preb Linc Cathl 54-56; Dioc Dir RE *Sarum* 56-63; Can and Preb Sarum Cathl 57-60; Can Res and Chan Sarum Cathl 60-67; Dir BRF 63-67; V Milton *Portsm* 67-73; RD Portsm 68-73; Hon Can Portsm Cathl 72-73; Adn Swindon *Bris* 74-82; rtd 82. *Flat 1, 95 Crane Street, Salisbury SP1 2PU* Tel (01722) 323848

MAPLEY, Mrs Barbara Jean. b 46. Guy's Hosp Medical Sch MCSP69. Oak Hill NSM Course 86. **d** 89 **p** 94. NSM Kelvedon *Chelmsf* 89-93; C Witham 93-94; TV from 94. *2 Janmead, Witham, Essex CM8 2EN* Tel (01376) 516872

MAPPLEBECKPALMER, Richard Warwick. b 32. CCC Cam BA56 MA60. Cuddesdon Coll 56. **d** 58 **p** 59. C Redcar *York* 58-60; C Drypool St Jo 61-63; V Pendleton St Ambrose *Man* 63-77; P-in-c Piddington *Ox* 77; P-in-c Ambrosden w Arncot and Blackthorn 77; P-in-c Mert 77; V Ambrosden w Mert and Piddington 77-88; USA from 88; rtd 97. *472 Dale Road, Martinez, CA 94553-4829, USA* Tel Martinez (510) 228 5252

MAPSON, Preb John Victor. b 31. Lon Univ BA60. Oak Hill Th Coll 55. **d** 60 **p** 61. C Littleover *Derby* 60-62; C Wandsworth

St Mich *S'wark* 62-65; R Willand *Ex* 65-71; P-in-c Axmouth 71-72; V 72-75; V Axmouth w Musbury 75-77; RD Honiton 76-77; V Cullompton 77-89; R Kentisbeare w Blackborough 77-89; RD Cullompton 81-89; P-in-c Sidmouth All SS 89-96; Preb Ex Cathl from 91; RD Ottery 94-96; rtd 96. *Gospel Hall Cottage, 4 Gospel Hall Terrace, North Street, Axminster, Devon EX13 5QA* Tel (01297) 35023

MAPSTONE, Trevor Anthony. b 63. Lanc Univ BSc84 MA96. St Jo Coll Nottm LTh88 DPS89. **d** 89 **p** 90. C Hoole *Ches* 89-92; C Lancaster St Thos *Blackb* 92-96; V Harrow Trin St Mich *Lon* from 96. *The Vicarage, 39 Rusland Park Road, Harrow, Middx HA1 1UN* Tel 0181-427 2616 or 863 6131

MARAJH, Brian Melvin. BA. **d** 86 **p** 87. S Africa 86-94; Perm to Offic *Glas* from 94. *c/o The Diocesan Office, 5 St Vincent Place, Glasgow G1 2DH* Tel 0141-221 5720

MARCER, Graham John. b 52. Ripon Coll Cuddesdon 75. **d** 78 **p** 79. C Sherborne w Castleton and Lillington *Sarum* 78-81; C Christchurch *Win* 81-84; V Southampton St Jude 84-90; P-in-c Moordown 90-91; C Sheff Parson Cross St Cecilia *Sheff* 91-93; V Balby from 93; RD W Doncaster from 97. *St John's Vicarage, 6 Greenfield Lane, Doncaster, S Yorkshire DN4 0PT* Tel (01302) 853278

MARCETTI, Alvin Julian. b 41. San Jose State Univ BA66 Santa Clara Univ MA76. Cranmer Hall Dur 85. **d** 87 **p** 88. C Stepney St Dunstan and All SS *Lon* 87-91; Chapl City of Lon Poly 91-92; Chapl Lon Guildhall Univ 92-96; Chapl Homerton Hosp NHS Trust Lon from 96; Chapl City and Hackney Community Services NHS Trust from 96. *Homerton Hospital, Homerton Row, London E9 6SR* Tel 0181-985 5555

MARCH, Charles Anthony Maclea (Tony). b 32. CCC Cam BA55 MA70. Oak Hill Th Coll 55. **d** 57 **p** 58. C S Croydon Em *Cant* 57-60; C Eastbourne H Trin *Chich* 60-63; V Whitehall Park St Andr Hornsey Lane *Lon* 63-67; V Tunbridge Wells H Trin w Ch Ch *Roch* 67-82; V Prestonville St Luke *Chich* 82-97; rtd 97. *The Barn, 2 Town Farm Dairy, Brenchley Road, Brenchley, Tonbridge, Kent TN12 7PA* Tel (01892) 722802

MARCH, Gerald. b 44. Nottm Univ BA75. Oak Hill Th Coll 92. **d** 95 **p** 96. C Sandgate St Paul w Folkestone St Geo *Cant* from 95. *The Vicarage, 10 Meadowbrook, Sandgate, Folkestone, Kent CT20 3NY* Tel (01303) 248675

MARCH, John Vale. b 39. CCC Cam BA62 MA76. Linc Th Coll 62. **d** 64 **p** 65. C Sheldon *Birm* 64-68; C Hodge Hill 68-72; TV 72-85; C Handsworth St Jas from 85. *168 Albert Road, Birmingham B21 9JT* Tel 0121-523 0317

MARCHAND, Canon Rex Anthony Victor (Toby). b 47. K Coll Lon BD69 AKC69. St Aug Coll Cant 69. **d** 70 **p** 71. C Leigh Park *Portsm* 70-73; C Hatfield *St Alb* 73-80; R Deal St Leon and St Rich and Sholden *Cant* 80-95; RD Sandwich 91-94; Hon Can Cant Cathl 94-95; V Bishop's Stortford St Mich *St Alb* from 95. *St Michael's Vicarage, 8 Larkspur Road, Bishop's Stortford, Herts CM23 4LL* Tel (01279) 651415

MARCHANT, The Ven George John Charles. b 16. St Jo Coll Dur LTh38 BA39 MA42 BD64. Tyndale Hall Bris 35. **d** 39 **p** 40. C Whitehall Park St Andr Hornsey Lane *Lon* 39-41; Lic to Offic 41-44; C Cambridge St Andr Less *Ely* 44-48; V Skirbeck H Trin *Linc* 48-54; V Dur St Nic *Dur* 54-74; RD Dur 64-74; Hon Can Dur Cathl 72-74; Adn Auckland 74-83; Can Res Dur Cathl 74-83; rtd 83; Perm to Offic *Nor* from 83. *28 Greenways, Eaton, Norwich NR4 6PE* Tel (01603) 58295

MARCHANT, Canon Iain William. b 26. Wells Th Coll 59. **d** 60 **p** 61. C Dalston *Carl* 60-63; V Hawkesbury *Glouc* 63-76; R Newent 76-85; Hon Can Glouc Cathl 84-92; R Newent and Gorsley w Cliffords Mesne 85-92; rtd 92; Perm to Offic *Glouc* from 92. *Daisy Green, Daisy Lane, Howley, Wotton-under-Edge, Glos GL12 7PF* Tel (01453) 844779

MARCHANT, Canon Ronald Albert. b 26. Em Coll Cam BA50 MA52 PhD57 BD64. Ridley Hall Cam 50. **d** 54 **p** 55. C Acomb St Steph *York* 54-57; C Willian *St Alb* 57-59; V Laxfield *St E* 59-92; RD Hoxne 73-78; Hon Can St E Cathl 75-92; P-in-c Wilby w Brundish 86-92; rtd 92. *34 The Paddock, Boroughbridge Road, York YO2 6AW* Tel (01904) 798446

MARCUS, The Very Revd Justus Mauritius. b 55. Cape Town Univ BA78. St Pet Coll Natal 77. **d** 78 **p** 79. S Africa 78-86 and from 89; C Wimbledon *S'wark* 87-89; Dean Kimberley from 91. *The Deanery, 4 Park Road, Kimberley, 8301 South Africa* Tel Kimberley (531) 33436 or 33437

MARGAM, Archdeacon of. *See* WILLIAMS, The Ven Martin Inffeld

MARGARET JOY, Sister. *See* HARRIS, Margaret Claire

MARINER, Aris. b 43. Alexandria Univ BSc65. St Alb Minl Tr Scheme 84. **d** 87. NSM Stevenage H Trin *St Alb* from 87. *13 Church Lane, Stevenage, Herts SG1 3QS* Tel (01438) 365596

MARION EVA, Sister. *See* RECORD, Sister Marion Eva

MARK, Brother. *See* SHARPE, John Brebber

MARK, Timothy John. b 34. Bris Univ BA57 MLitt68 MEd71 Leeds Univ PhD79. Didsbury Meth Coll 54. **d** 59 **p** 61. India 59-64 and 65-69; Perm to Offic *Sheff* from 73. *15 Fieldhouse Road, Sprotborough, Doncaster, S Yorkshire DN5 7RN* Tel (01302) 853022

MARKBY, Archibald Campbell. b 15. Em Coll Cam BA37 MA41. Ridley Hall Cam 37. **d** 39 **p** 39. C Bradf St Clem *Bradf* 39-42; C Ox St Aldate *Ox* 42-46; V Kilburn St Mary *Lon* 46-53; V Hornsey Ch Ch 53-64; R Ickenham 64-68; V Crowfield w Stonham Aspal *St E* 68-71; V Damerham *Sarum* 71-80; V Martin 71-80; rtd 80. *2 Church Farm, Church Street, Fordingbridge, Hants SP6 1BQ* Tel (01425) 656141

MARKBY, Peter John Jenner. b 38. Em Coll Cam BA60. Clifton Th Coll 62. **d** 64 **p** 65. C Tufnell Park St Geo *Lon* 64-68; C Crowborough *Chich* 68-73; C Polegate 73-77; R Southover from 77. *The Rectory, Southover High Street, Lewes, E Sussex BN7 1HT* Tel (01273) 472018

MARKE, Christopher Andrew Burrows. b 42. MIElecIE FRSA93 Open Univ BA81. Oak Hill NSM Course. **d** 84 **p** 85. NSM Brighstone and Brooke w Mottistone *Portsm* 84-86; NSM Shorwell w Kingston 85-93; NSM Gatcombe 87-93; NSM Chale 89-93; Asst Chapl Dunkerque Miss to Seamen *Eur* 94; Chapl Rouen Miss to Seamen 94-97; Singapore from 97. *291 River Valley Road, Singapore 238332* Tel Singapore (65) 737 2880 Fax 235 3391

MARKHAM, Deryck O'Leary. b 28. Oak Hill Th Coll 66. **d** 68 **p** 69. C Purley Ch Ch *S'wark* 68-72; V E Budleigh and Bicton *Ex* 72-93; RD Aylesbeare 89-93; rtd 93; Perm to Offic *Ex* from 93. *86 Granary Lane, Budleigh Salterton, Devon EX9 6ER* Tel (01395) 443340

MARKHAM, Canon Gervase William. b 10. Trin Coll Cam BA32 MA36. Westcott Ho Cam 34. **d** 36 **p** 37. C Bishopwearmouth St Mich *Dur* 36-39; Bp's Dom Chapl 39-40; CF (EC) 40-46; V Burnley St Steph *Blackb* 46-52; CF (TA) 50-52; CF (TA - R of O) from 52; V Gt Grimsby St Jas *Linc* 52-65; Can and Preb Linc Cathl 56-65; RD Grimsby and Cleethorpes 62-64; V Morland w Thrimby and Gt Strickland *Carl* 65-84; RD Lowther 65-69; Hon Can Carl Cathl 72-84; rtd 84; Perm to Offic *Carl* from 84. *The Garden Flat, Morland House, Penrith, Cumbria CA10 3AZ* Tel (01931) 714654

MARKHAM, John Gabriel. b 06. Linc Coll Ox BA30 MA70. Ely Th Coll 30. **d** 31 **p** 32. C Kennington St Jo *S'wark* 31-37; R Walworth St Pet 37-44; R Caister *Nor* 44-60; Chapl Reading and Distr Hosps 60-74; rtd 74. *22 Watlington Road, Benson, Oxford OX10 6LS* Tel (01491) 835397

MARKLAND, Vincent Hilton. b 33. Univ of Wales (Lamp) BA55 Leic Univ PGCE58. Ripon Hall Ox 67. **d** 68 **p** 69. C Worsley *Man* 68-83; V Monton 83-95; AD Eccles 93-95; rtd 95; Perm to Offic *Man* from 95. *50 Knowsley Drive, Swinton, Manchester M27 0FA*

MARKS, Alfred Howard. b 02. Qu Coll Cam BA25 MA29. Ridley Hall Cam 25. **d** 26 **p** 27. C Aston SS Pet and Paul *Birm* 26-29; C Surbiton St Matt *S'wark* 29-33; C St Marylebone H Trin *Lon* 33-35; V Birmingham St Asaph *Birm* 35-40; CF 40-45; Hon CF 45; V Charles w Plymouth St Luke *Ex* 46-48; V Shirley *Win* 48-59; V Ipswich St Marg *St E* 59-70; rtd 70; Lic to Offic *St E* 70-80; Lic to Offic *Lich* 81-84; Lic to Offic *Worc* 84-91. *28 Stuart Court, High Street, Kibworth, Leicester LE8 0LE* Tel 0116-279 6357

MARKS, Allan Willi. b 56. Cranmer Hall Dur CTM94. **d** 94 **p** 95. C Barnoldswick w Bracewell *Bradf* 94-96; C Willington Team *Newc* from 96. *47 Norman Terrace, Wallsend, Tyne & Wear NE28 6SP* Tel 0191-262 3574

MARKS, Anthony Alfred (Tony). b 28. AKC53. **d** 54 **p** 55. C Fleetwood *Blackb* 54-58; V Burnley St Cuth 58-63; Chapl RN 63-83; QHC from 81; P-in-c Bradninch *Ex* 83-88; R Bradninch and Clyst Hydon 88-90; rtd 90; Perm to Offic *B & W* from 90. *Bryony Cottage, The Combe, Compton Martin, Bristol BS18 6JD*

MARKS, Anthony Wendt. b 43. G&C Coll Cam BA63 MA67 PhD70 BNC Ox DPhil72. St Steph Ho Ox 70. **d** 72 **p** 73. C Withington St Crispin *Man* 72-75; Chapl Lon Univ Medical Students *Lon* 75-80; Warden Liddon Ho Lon 80-92; C-in-c Grosvenor Chpl *Lon* 80-92; V Shrewsbury All SS w St Mich *Lich* from 92. *All Saints Presbytery, 5 Lingen Close, Shrewsbury SY1 2UN* Tel (01743) 358820

MARKS, David Frederick. b 14. Univ of Wales BA37 Jes Coll Ox BA40 MA45. St Mich Coll Llan 40. **d** 41 **p** 42. C Llandeilo Fawr *St D* 41-49; R Llangathen w Llanfihangel Cilfargen 49-56; Lect St D Coll Lamp 56-74; Sen Lect 74-82; P-in-c Llanycrwys 57-64; rtd 82. *Wyngarth, Bryn Road, Lampeter SA48 7EF* Tel (01570) 422474

MARKS, John Alexander Rishworth. b 19. TCD BA41 MA61. CITC 43. **d** 43 **p** 44. C Dublin Sandford *D & G* 43-45; Chapl RNVR 45-46; Chapl RN 46-69; rtd 69; Perm to Offic *St Alb* from 77. *1 Linten Close, Hitchin, Herts SG4 9PA*

MARKS, Timothy John. b 45. Man Univ BA76 Cert Counselling 94 Anglia Poly Univ MA97. **d** 88 **p** 89. NSM Burton and Sopley *Win* 88-91; R Croxton and Eltisley *Ely* 91-96; R Graveley w Papworth St Agnes w Yelling etc 91-96; Dir Network Counselling and Tr 96-97. *8 Arundell Road, Weston-super-Mare, Avon BS23 2QQ* Tel (01934) 415807

MARKWELL, Donald Stanley. b 30. Victoria Univ Wellington MA53. **d** 79 **p** 80. Hon C Kingston Hill St Paul *S'wark* 79-82; Hon C Ham St Andr from 82. *12 Albany Mews, Albany Park Road, Kingston upon Thames, Surrey KT2 5SL* Tel 0181-546 0740

MARLEY, Alan Gordon. b 59. Birm Univ BA89. **d** 89 **p** 90. C Blandford Forum and Langton Long *Sarum* 89-93; Chapl HM Young Offender Inst Aylesbury 93-97; I Fermoy Union *C, C & R*

from 97. *The Rectory, Forglen Terrace, Fermoy, Co Cork, Irish Republic* Tel Cork (21) 31016

MARLEY, Neville William Arthur. b 24. Em Coll Cam BA46 MA51. Ridley Hall Cam 48. **d** 50 **p** 51. C Chester le Street *Dur* 50-53; C Darlington St Cuth 53-54; C Bury St Edmunds St Mary *St E* 54-56; V Telford Park St Thos *S'wark* 56-89; CF (TA) 59-64; CF (TA - R of O) 64-67; rtd 89; Perm to Offic *Dur* from 89. *12 The Headlands, Darlington, Co Durham DL3 8RP* Tel (01325) 357559

MARLOW (née SIBBALD), Mrs Olwyn Eileen. b 57. Linc Th Coll 87. **d** 89 **p** 94. Par Dn Wythenshawe St Martin *Man* 89-93; Par Dn Baguley 93-94; C 94-95; Asst Chapl Cen Man Healthcare NHS Trust from 95; NSM Newall Green *Man* from 97. *28 Arcadia Avenue, Sale, Cheshire M33 3SA*

MARLOW, Walter Geoffrey. b 29. AKC57. **d** 57 **p** 58. C Long Eaton St Laur *Derby* 57-61; C Mackworth St Fran 61-63; R Stoke Albany w Wilbarston *Pet* 63-68; PC Calow *Derby* 68-73; R Wingerworth 73-82; P-in-c Islington St Jas w St Phil *Lon* 82-87; P-in-c Islington St Pet 82-87; V Islington St Jas w St Pet 87-92; AD Islington 84-90; Preb St Paul's Cathl 87-92; Bp's Dom Chapl *B & W* 92-96; Preb Wells Cathl 92-96; rtd 96. *Taverners Cottage, Park Road, Wells-next-the-Sea, Norfolk NR23 1DQ* Tel (01328) 710432

MARNHAM, Charles Christopher. b 51. Jes Coll Cam BA73 MA77. Cranmer Hall Dur DipTh76. **d** 77 **p** 78. C Brompton H Trin *Lon* 77-78; C Brompton H Trin w Onslow Square St Paul 78-80; C Linthorpe *York* 80-84; R Haughton le Skerne *Dur* 84-95; V Ches Square St Mich w St Phil *Lon* from 95. *St Michael's Vicarage, 4 Chester Square, London SW1W 9HH* Tel 0171-730 8889

MARNS, Nigel Geoffrey. b 63. Univ of Wales (Abth) BSc(Econ)85 Birm Univ BD92. Qu Coll Birm 90. **d** 93 **p** 94. C Addington *S'wark* 93-96; P-in-c W Bromwich Gd Shep w St Jo *Lich* from 96. *The Vicarage, 4 Bromford Lane, West Bromwich, W Midlands B70 7HP* Tel 0121-525 5530

MARQUEZ, Edilberto (Eddie). b 57. Instituto Biblico Alianza Lima BA80 Westmr Coll Ox MA93. St Steph Ho Ox 92. **d** 94 **p** 95. C Reading St Jo *Ox* from 94. *1 Church House, Orts Road, Reading RG1 3JN* Tel 0118-966 9545

MARR (née PARKER), Mrs Anne Elizabeth. b 46. Hull Univ BSc67 CertEd68. NE Ord Course 91. **d** 96. NSM Whorlton *Newc* from 96. *26 The Chesters, Newcastle upon Tyne NE5 1AF* Tel 0191-267 4808

MARR, Canon Donald Radley. b 37. K Coll Lon 57. St Aid Birkenhead 61. **d** 64 **p** 65. C Macclesfield St Mich *Ches* 64-66; C Sale St Anne 66-67; V Marthall 67-72; C W Kirby St Bridget 72-76; R Waverton 76-83; R Nantwich 83-87; RD Nantwich 86-87; RD Malpas 87-91; V Bunbury 87-91; Hon Can Ches Cathl 91-92; Dioc Rural Officer from 91; rtd 91; Perm to Offic *Truro* from 94. *5 Hockenhull Crescent, Tarvin, Chester CH3 8LJ, or The Parsonage, Tresco, Isles of Scilly TR24 0QQ* Tel (01829) 741302 or (01720) 423176

MARR, Mrs Joan Mary. b 36. SRN58 SCM75 HVCert78 NDN79. St Jo Coll Nottm CertCS91. **d** 91. Par Dn Moffat *Glas* from 91. *Auburn Cottage, Templand, Lockerbie, Dumfriesshire DG11 1TG* Tel (01387) 810734

MARR, Peter. b 36. Reading Univ PhD78. Ox NSM Course 84. **d** 87 **p** 88. NSM Reading St Giles *Ox* 87-89; C Beverley Minster *York* 90-92; P-in-c Beckenham St Barn *Roch* 92-96; V from 96. *St Barnabas' Vicarage, Oakhill Road, Beckenham, Kent BR3 6NG* Tel 0181-650 3332

MARRETT, Hedley Charles Guille. b 09. St Boniface Warminster 29. **d** 34 **p** 35. C Woolwich H Trin *S'wark* 34-37; S Africa 37-47; V Holbrooks *Cov* 47-50; V Jersey St Simon *Win* 50-77; P-in-c Jersey All SS 67-77; rtd 77. *11 Bell Meadow, Hook, Basingstoke, Hants RG27 9HB* Tel (01256) 763176

MARRIOTT (née REID), Mrs Amanda Joy (Mandy). b 63. DipRSAMDA83 Nottm Univ BTh92. Linc Th Coll 89. **d** 92 **p** 96. Par Dn Rothwell *Ripon* 92-94; C 94-95; C Manston from 95. *21 Pendas Grove, Leeds LS15 8HE* Tel 0113-264 9666

MARRIOTT, Frank Lewis. b 29. Lich Th Coll 57. **d** 60 **p** 61. C Earlsdon *Cov* 60-64; R Tysoe w Compton Winyates and Oxhill 64-70; P-in-c Cov St Marg 70-77; R Ufton 77-83; V Long Itchington 77-83; RD Southam 82-89; V Long Itchington and Marton 83-95; rtd 95; Perm to Offic *Heref* from 95. *12 Traherne Close, Ledbury, Herefordshire HR8 2JF* Tel (01531) 634576

MARRIOTT, Stanley Richard. b 36. AKC60 Warw Univ MA92. **d** 61 **p** 62. C Coleshill *Birm* 61-64; C Maxstoke 61-64; V Ansley *Cov* 64-78; Org Sec (E Midl) CECS 79-83; P-in-c Baxterley *Birm* 83; P-in-c Merevale w Bentley 83; P-in-c Baxterley w Hurley and Wood End and Merevale etc 83-84; R 84-87; R Newton Regis w Seckington and Shuttington 87-97; rtd 97; Perm to Offic *B & W* from 97. *Dunkery Pleck, Wootton Courtenay, Minehead, Somerset TA24 8RH* Tel (01643) 841058

MARRISON, Geoffrey Edward. b 23. Lon Univ BA48 PhD67. Bps' Coll Cheshunt 49 Kirchliche Hochschule Th Coll Berlin 50. **d** 51 **p** 52. C Wormley *St Alb* 51-52; Malaya 52-55; Singapore 55-56; C Radlett *St Alb* 56-57; C St Botolph Aldgate w H Trin Minories *Lon* 57-58; V Crookes St Tim *Sheff* 58-61; India 62-64; Perm to Offic *Cant* 64-69; Lic to Offic 69-82; Perm to Offic *Carl* from 83; Tutor Carl Dioc Tr Course from 83. *1 Ainsworth Street, Ulverston, Cumbria LA12 7EU* Tel (01229) 586874

MARROW, David Edward Armfield. b 42. Nottm Univ BA65 MA. Tyndale Hall Bris 65. **d** 67 **p** 68. C Clifton Ch Ch w Em *Bris* 67-70; Ethiopia 70-75; N Area Sec BCMS 75-77; C-in-c Ryde St Jas Prop Chpl *Portsm* 77-84; V Worthing St Geo *Chich* from 84. *The Vicarage, 20 Seldon Road, Worthing, W Sussex BN11 2LN* Tel (01903) 203309

MARSDEN, Andrew Philip. b 63. Keble Coll Ox BA85 MA90 Birm Univ MA86. Wycliffe Hall Ox BA90. **d** 91 **p** 92. C Newport St Jo *Portsm* 91-94; C Cowplain from 94. *24 Wincanton Way, Cowplain, Waterlooville, Hants PO7 8NW* Tel (01705) 257915

MARSDEN, Andrew Robert. b 49. AKC71. St Aug Coll Cant 68. **d** 72 **p** 73. C New Addington *Cant* 72-75; C Prudhoe *Newc* 75-77; Asst Chapl HM Pris Wakef 77; Chapl HM Borstal Portland 77-82; Chapl HM Young Offender Inst Onley 82-89; V Ulceby Gp *Linc* from 89. *The Vicarage, Church Lane, Ulceby, S Humberside DN39 6TB* Tel (01469) 588239

MARSDEN, Mrs Carole. b 44. Avery Hill Coll TCert65 Sheff Poly DipEd87. N Ord Course 88. **d** 91 **p** 94. NSM Saddleworth *Man* 91-92; Par Dn 92-94; C 94-95; P-in-c Oldham St Paul from 95. *St Paul's Vicarage, 55 Belgrave Road, Oldham OL8 1LU* Tel 0161-624 1068

MARSDEN, Geoffrey (Geoff). b 26. Lon Univ CertEd50 DipTh54 Open Univ BA79. EAMTC. **d** 86 **p** 87. NSM Higham *St E* 86-89; NSM Stratford St Mary 86-89; P-in-c Polstead 89-94; rtd 95; Perm to Offic *Chelmsf* from 95. *Mwaiseni, 5 Upper Street, Stratford St Mary, Colchester CO7 6LR* Tel (01206) 322316

MARSDEN, John Joseph. b 53. York Univ BA74 Nottm Univ DipTh78 MTh81 Kent Univ PhD88. St Jo Coll Nottm 77. **d** 80 **p** 81. C Leigh St Mary *Man* 80-83; Hon C Chatham St Steph *Roch* 83-91; Ind Chapl 83-91; Lect Systematic Th CITC from 91. *3 Somerton, Upper Dargle Road, Bray, Co Wicklow, Irish Republic*

MARSDEN, John Robert. b 22. Linc Coll Ox BA48 MA49. Ripon Hall Ox 57. **d** 58 **p** 59. C Dur St Cuth *Dur* 58-61; Chapl Dur Sch 61-85; rtd 85. *Prebends, High Kilburn, York YO6 4AJ* Tel (01347) 868597

MARSDEN, Miss Joyce. b 47. Trin Coll Bris DipHE80. **dss** 83 **d** 87 **p** 94. Wavertree H Trin *Liv* 83-85; Much Woolton 85-87; Par Dn 87-94; C from 94. *25 Linkside Road, Liverpool L25 9NX* Tel 0151-428 6935

MARSDEN, Michael John. b 59. St Mich Coll Llan 78. **d** 82 **p** 83. C Neath w Llantwit *Llan* 82-85; Asst Chapl Univ Hosp of Wales Cardiff 85-89; V Graig *Llan* 89-93; P-in-c Cilfynydd 89-93; R Merthyr Tydfil St Dav from 93. *The Rectory, Bryntirion Road, Thomastown, Merthyr Tydfil CF47 0ER* Tel (01685) 722992

MARSDEN, Robert. b 59. Ch Ch Ox BA81 PGCE82. Oak Hill Th Coll BA92. **d** 92 **p** 93. C Sevenoaks St Nic *Roch* 92-95; Chapl Fettes Coll Edin from 95. *6 Westwoods, Edinburgh EH4 1RA*

MARSDEN, Robert James. b 56. Ch Ch Coll Cant BEd79. Oak Hill Th Coll DipHE92. **d** 94 **p** 95. C Margate H Trin *Cant* from 94. *84 Millmead Road, Cliftonville, Margate, Kent CT9 3LP* Tel (01843) 224408

MARSDEN, Canon Robert William. b 24. TCD BA49 MA52. CITC 50. **d** 50 **p** 51. C Dublin St Jas *D & G* 50-54; Asst Chapl Miss to Seamen 54-58; I Currin w Drum *Clogh* 58-66; I Clones w Killeevan 66-94; Prec Clogh Cathl 86-94; rtd 94. *30 Claremont Park, Sandymount, Dublin 4, Irish Republic* Tel Dublin (1) 668 0210

MARSDEN, Samuel Edward. b 44. Keble Coll Ox BA66 MA85. Linc Th Coll 66. **d** 68 **p** 69. C Liskeard w St Keyne *Truro* 68-72; R Gerrans w St Antony in Roseland 72-77; Hong Kong 77-81; P-in-c Ingrave *Chelmsf* 81-82; P-in-c Gt Warley w Childerditch 81-82; R Gt Warley w Childerditch and Ingrave 82-89; Australia from 89. *The Rectory, Gilmour Street, Kelso, NSW, Australia 2795* Tel Orange (63) 324606

MARSDEN-JONES, Watkin David. b 22. Univ of Wales (Lamp) BA48. **d** 49 **p** 50. C Flint *St As* 49-54; C Forest Row *Chich* 54-56; V Copthorne 56-70; RD E Grinstead 66-70; V Bosham 70-86; rtd 86; Perm to Offic *Chich* from 86. *10 Fairfield Road, Bosham, Chichester, W Sussex PO18 8JH* Tel (01243) 575053

MARSH, Anthony David. b 29. Roch Th Coll 64. **d** 66 **p** 67. C Liskeard w St Keyne *Truro* 66-69; R Wrentham w Benacre and Covehithe *St E* 69-75; R Wrentham w Benacre, Covehithe, Frostenden etc 75-80; P-in-c Beyton and Hessett 80-86; C Felixstowe St Jo 86-88; rtd 88. *7 Lime Tree Avenue, Felixstowe Beach Holiday Park, Walton Avenue, Felixstowe IP11 8HE* Tel (01394) 283393

MARSH, Carol Ann. *See* HATHORNE, Mrs Carol Ann

MARSH, Colin Arthur. b 54. St Jo Coll Nottm. **d** 82 **p** 83. C Kirkby *Liv* 82-86; TV St Luke in the City 86-91; USPG from 91; Zambia from 91. *c/o USPG, Partnership House, 157 Waterloo Road, London SE1 8XA* Tel 0171-928 8681 Fax 928 2371

MARSH, David. b 32. St Jo Coll Dur BA54 DipTh57. **d** 57 **p** 58. C Bilston St Leon *Lich* 57-62; Kenya 63-66 and 70-72; Chapl Scargill Ho 67-69; Adn S Maseno 70-72; V Meole Brace *Lich* 72-77; V Westlands St Andr 77-86; V Trentham 86-96; P-in-c Alstonfield, Butterton, Warslow w Elkstone etc from 96. *The Vicarage, Alstonefield, Ashbourne, Derbyshire DE6 2FX* Tel (01335) 310216

MARSH, Donald. b 35. WMMTC. **d** 90 **p** 91. NSM Wednesbury St Bart *Lich* from 90. *Holly Rise, 19 Trouse Lane, Wednesbury, W Midlands WS10 7HR* Tel 0121-556 0095

MARSH, The Ven Francis John. b 47. ATCL ARCM ARCO York Univ BA69 DPhil76 Selw Coll Cam 73. Oak Hill Th Coll 72. **d** 75 **p** 76. C Cambridge St Matt *Ely* 75-78; C Pitsmoor w Wicker *Sheff* 79; C Pitsmoor w Ellesmere 79-81; C Crookes St Thos 81-85; V S Ossett *Wakef* 85-96; RD Dewsbury 93-96; Adn Blackb from 96; Bp's Adv on Hosp Chapls from 96. *19 Clarence Park, Blackburn BB2 7FA* Tel (01254) 263394 E-mail vendocjon @aol.com

MARSH, Geoffrey John. b 38. K Coll Lon BD60 AKC60 Birm Univ PGCE67. **d** 61 **p** 62. C Upper Teddington SS Pet and Paul *Lon* 61-63; C Brierley Hill *Lich* 63-66; Asst Master Borough Green Sch 67-69; P-in-c Bracknell *Ox* 69-73; P-in-c Speen 73-74; P-in-c Stockcross 73-74; R Boxford w Stockcross and Speen 74-80; PV Truro Cathl *Truro* 80-82; Chapl Truro Cathl Sch 80-82; Chapl Sch of St Mary and St Anne Abbots Bromley 82-85; Chapl Heref Cathl Sch 85-96; rtd 97; Chapl Beauchamp Community from 97. *The Chaplain's House, The Beauchamp Community, Newland, Malvern, Worcs WR13 5AX* Tel (01684) 893243

MARSH, Gordon Bloxham. b 25. Cant Sch of Min 82. **d** 85 **p** 86. NSM Loose *Cant* 85-86; NSM New Romney w Old Romney and Midley 86-90; NSM Asst to RD S Lympne 90-94; rtd 94; Perm to Offic *Cant* from 94. *Westleton, St John's Road, New Romney, Kent TN28 8EN* Tel (01797) 366506

MARSH, Harry Carter. b 14. Chich Th Coll 48. **d** 49 **p** 50. C Portswood Ch Ch *Win* 49-51; C Win St Thos and St Clem w St Mich etc 51-52; V Corby St Columba *Pet* 52-60; V Sholing *Win* 60-71; R Michelmersh w Eldon w Timsbury 71-74; R Michelmersh w Mottisfont, Timsbury and Eldon 74-79; Perm to Offic 79-94; rtd 80; Perm to Offic *Portsm* 82-94. *Manormead Residential Home, Tilford Road, Hindhead, Surrey GU26 6RA* Tel (01428) 604780

MARSH, Jack Edmund Bruce. b 08. MA. **d** 73 **p** 74. NSM Yatton Keynell *Bris* 73-88; NSM Biddestone w Slaughterford 73-88; NSM Castle Combe 73-88; NSM W Kington 73-88; Perm to Offic from 88. *St Peter's House, The Green, Biddestone, Chippenham, Wilts SN14 7DG* Tel (01249) 712835

MARSH, Lawrence Allan. b 36. Sarum Th Coll 66. **d** 67 **p** 68. C Waterlooville *Portsm* 67-70; V Shedfield 70-76; R Fen Ditton *Ely* from 76; P-in-c Horningsea from 83. *The Rectory, 16 High Street, Fen Ditton, Cambridge CB5 8ST* Tel (01223) 293257

MARSH, Leonard Stuart Alexander. b 55. Hull Univ BA77. Linc Th Coll 77. **d** 79 **p** 80. C Eltham St Barn *S'wark* 79-81; C Camberwell St Giles 81-83; Hon C Clifton St Paul *Bris* 83-86; Chapl Bris Univ 83-86; Area Sec (Dio S'wark) USPG 86-91; Chapl City Univ *Lon* from 91; NSM Clerkenwell H Redeemer and St Mark 94-95; P-in-c Finsbury St Clem w St Barn and St Matt from 95. *The Vicarage, King Square, Lever Street, London EC1V 8DA* Tel 0171-253 9140

MARSH, Mrs Margaret Ann. b 37. Nottm Univ BSc59 Ox Univ DipEd60 Newc Univ MA93. Carl Dioc Tr Course 86 Lambeth STh87. **d** 87. Asst Chapl Garlands Hosp 87-92; Dn Carl Cathl *Carl* 87-93; NSM Carl St Luke Morton 93-94; NSM Cumbria Ind Chapl Team from 94. *34 Moorville Drive South, Carlisle CA3 0AW* Tel (01228) 45717

MARSH, Miss Maxine Dorothy. b 49. Bretton Hall Coll TCert72. Westcott Ho Cam 90. **d** 92 **p** 94. C Kings Norton *Birm* 92-95; P-in-c Kingsbury 95-96; V from 96. *The Vicarage, Church Lane, Kingsbury, Tamworth, Staffs B78 2LR* Tel (01827) 873500

MARSH, Ralph. b 42. ACP65 Chester Coll CertEd63 Birm Univ BPhil77. St Deiniol's Hawarden 86. **d** 88 **p** 89. NSM Tranmere St Paul w St Luke *Ches* 88-90; C Guiseley w Esholt *Bradf* 90-92; V Broughton *St As* 92-94; C Ribbleton *Blackb* from 94. *St Anne's House, Waddington Road, Preston PR2 6HU* Tel (01772) 792993

MARSH, Dr Richard St John Jeremy. b 60. Keble Coll Ox BA82 MA86 Dur Univ PhD91. Coll of Resurr Mirfield 83. **d** 85 **p** 86. C Grange St Andr *Ches* 85-87; Fell and Chapl Univ Coll Dur 87-92; Abp's Asst Sec for Ecum Affairs *Cant* 92-95; Abp's Sec for Ecum Affairs from 95; Lic to Offic *Lon* from 93; Hon C Westmr St Steph w St Jo from 94. *Cottage 3, Lambeth Palace, London SE1 7JU* Tel 0171-928 8282

MARSH, Robert Christopher. b 53. Ex Univ BEd76. St Steph Ho Ox 86. **d** 88 **p** 89. C St Leonards Ch Ch and St Mary *Chich* 88-91; TV Crawley from 91. *Peterhouse, 128 Ifield Road, Crawley, W Sussex RH11 7BW* Tel (01293) 520921

MARSH, Roger Philip. b 44. K Coll Lon BD72 AKC72 Sussex Univ MA95. St Aug Coll Cant 73. **d** 73 **p** 74. C Leagrave *St Alb* 73-76; Asst Youth Officer 76-77; Resources Officer 77-80; Chapl Marlborough Coll 80-86; Master Ardingly Coll Jun Sch Haywards Heath 86-95; Hd Master St Geo Sch Windsor from 95. *The Headmaster's House, St George's School, Windsor Castle, Berks SL4 1QF* Tel (01753) 620123 or 865553 Fax 842093

MARSH, Mrs Shelley Ann. b 54. SRN75 SCM76. St Jo Coll Nottm CertCS87. **d** 89 **p** 94. Hon C Glas Gd Shep and Ascension *Glas* 89-96; P-in-c Johnstone from 96; P-in-c Renfrew from 96. *44 Atholl Crescent, Paisley, Renfrewshire PA1 3AW* Tel 0141-883 8668

MARSH, Simon Robert. b 59. Sarum & Wells Th Coll 79. **d** 82 **p** 83. C Mottram in Longdendale w Woodhead *Ches* 82-85; Bp's Dom Chapl *Bradf* 85-87; V Ashton Hayes *Ches* 87-90; V Macclesfield St Paul 90-96; V Ringway from 96. *Ringway Vicarage, Wicker Lane, Altrincham, Cheshire WA15 0HQ* Tel 0161-980 3955

MARSHALL, Alan John. b 48. Carl Dioc Tr Course. **d** 89 **p** 90. NSM Carl St Luke Morton *Carl* 89-92. *12 Thornton Road, Stanwix, Carlisle CA3 9HZ* Tel (01228) 25338

MARSHALL, Alexander John. **d** 95 **p** 96. NSM Holbrook w Freston and Woolverstone *St E* from 95; NSM Wherstead from 95. *1 The Street, Freston, Ipswich IP9 1AF* Tel (01473) 780738

MARSHALL, Alexander Robert. b 43. Glouc Sch of Min 84. **d** 87 **p** 88. NSM Newtown w Llanllwchaiarn w Aberhafesp *St As* from 87. *42 Churchill Drive, Newtown SY16 2LQ* Tel (01686) 628375

MARSHALL, Ms Alison Rose Marie. b 60. Leic Univ BA83 Birkb Coll Lon MA86 E Anglia Univ PGCE87. Ridley Hall Cam CTM95. **d** 95 **p** 96. C Whittlesey, Pondersbridge and Coates *Ely* from 95. *The Vicarage, St Mary's Street, Whittlesey, Peterborough PE7 1BG* Tel (01733) 203676

MARSHALL, Mrs Angela. b 48. Trin Coll Bris 74. **d** 88 **p** 96. Hon Par Dn Newcastle St Geo *Lich* 88-92; Lic to Offic *Eur* 92-94; Dn Versailles St Mark from 94. *31 rue du Pont Colbert, 78000 Versailles, France* Tel France (331) 39 02 79 45

MARSHALL, Basil Eustace Edwin. b 21. OBE69. Westcott Ho Cam 71. **d** 73 **p** 74. C Edenbridge *Roch* 73-78; P-in-c Matfield 78-85; P-in-c Lamberhurst 78-85; C Farnborough 85-86; rtd 86; Hon C Speldhurst w Groombridge and Ashurst *Roch* from 86. *7 Boyne Park, Tunbridge Wells, Kent TN4 8EL* Tel (01892) 521664

MARSHALL, Bernard Godfrey Graham. b 35. Birm Univ BA56. Qu Coll Birm DipTh59. **d** 60 **p** 61. C Hampton *Worc* 60-63; P-in-c Fairfield St Rich CD 63-65; Deanery Youth Chapl 62-65; Chapl RN 65-91; V Ashford Hill w Headley *Win* from 91. *The Vicarage, Ashford Hill, Thatcham, Berks RG19 8AZ* Tel (01635) 268217

MARSHALL, Canon Bryan John. b 40. Chich Th Coll 63. **d** 65 **p** 66. C Poulton-le-Fylde *Blackb* 65-68; C S Shore H Trin 68-70; V Wesham 70-74; PV Chich Cathl *Chich* 74-82; V Boxgrove 82-91; P-in-c Tangmere 82-84; R 84-91; R Westbourne 91-95; Can and Preb Chich Cathl from 94; V E Preston w Kingston from 95. *The Vicarage, 33 Vicarage Lane, East Preston, Littlehampton, W Sussex BN16 2SP* Tel (01903) 783318

MARSHALL, Mrs Christine Anne. **d** 95 **p** 96. NSM Holbrook w Freston and Woolverstone *St E* from 95; NSM Wherstead from 95. *1 The Street, Freston, Ipswich IP9 1AF* Tel (01473) 780734

MARSHALL, Christopher John. b 56. Edge Hill Coll of HE BEd79. St Alb Minl Tr Scheme 83. **d** 86 **p** 87. C Biggleswade *St Alb* 86-89; Chapl Asst S Beds Area HA 89-91; Chapl St Helier Hosp Carshalton 91-93; Sen Chapl St Helier NHS Trust Surrey from 93. *32 Gauntell Road, Sutton, Surrey SM1 4RY, or St Helier Hospital, Carshalton, Surrey SM5 1AA* Tel 0181-296 2306 or 644 4343

MARSHALL, Preb Christopher John Bickford (Chris). b 32. TD78. AKC56. **d** 57 **p** 58. C Leatherhead *Guildf* 57-60; C Crewkerne *B & W* 60-63; V Long Sutton 63-72; V Long Sutton w Long Load 72-76; V Wiveliscombe 76-93; RD Tone 78-87; Preb Wells Cathl 88-96; P-in-c Chipstable w Huish Champflower and Clatworthy 93; R Wiveliscombe w Chipstable, Huish Champflower etc 93-96; rtd 96; Perm to Offic *B & W* from 96. *Tap Cottage, High Street, Milverton, Taunton, Somerset TA4 1LL* Tel (01823) 400419

MARSHALL, Christopher Robert. b 49. St Chad's Coll Dur BA71. Sarum & Wells Th Coll 72. **d** 74 **p** 75. C Sheff Parson Cross St Cecilia *Sheff* 74-77; C Walsall St Gabr Fulbrook *Lich* 77-78; C Upper Gornal 78-80; V Walsall St Andr 80-86; V Willenhall St Giles from 86. *St Giles's Vicarage, Walsall Street, Willenhall, W Midlands WV13 2ER* Tel (01902) 605722

MARSHALL, David. b 66. St Kath Coll Liv CertRS88 Liv Univ BA88. Ripon Coll Cuddesdon 89. **d** 92 **p** 93. C Dovecot *Liv* 92-96; Dioc Communications Officer from 95; P-in-c Westbrook St Jas from 96. *The Vicarage, 302 Hood Lane North, Great Sankey, Warrington WA5 1UQ* Tel (01925) 633873 Fax as telephone E-mail onetenprod@msn.com

MARSHALL, David Charles. b 52. St Chad's Coll Dur BA73. Trin Coll Bris 74. **d** 76 **p** 77. C Meole Brace *Lich* 76-78; C W Teignmouth *Ex* 78-80; C Broadwater St Mary *Chich* 80-84; V Newcastle St Geo *Lich* 84-92; Chapl Versailles w Chevry *Eur* from 92. *31 rue du Pont Colbert, 78000 Versailles, France* Tel France (331) 39 02 79 45 Fax 39 50 97 29

MARSHALL, David Evelyn. b 63. New Coll Ox BA85 Birm Univ MA88. Ridley Hall Cam 88. **d** 90 **p** 91. C Roundhay St Edm *Ripon* 90-92; Chapl Ex Coll Ox from 95. *Exeter College, Oxford OX1 3DP* Tel (01865) 279600 E-mail david.marshall@exeter.ox.ac.uk

MARSHALL, Eric. b 20. EMMTC. **d** 82 **p** 83. Chapl Grimsby Distr Hosps from 82; Hon C Gt Grimsby St Mary and St Jas *Linc* from 85. *Morn Tide, Waithe Lane, Grimsby, S Humberside DN37 0RJ* Tel (01472) 823681

MARSHALL, Canon Geoffrey Osborne (Geoff). b 48. St Jo Coll Dur BA71. Coll of Resurr Mirfield 71. **d** 73 **p** 74. C Waltham Cross *St Alb* 73-76; C Digswell 76-78; P-in-c Belper Ch Ch and

Milford *Derby* 78-86; V Spondon 86-93; Chapl Derby High Sch for Girls from 87; RD Derby N *Derby* 90-95; Can Res Derby Cathl from 93; Dioc Dir of Ords from 95. *24 Kedleston Road, Derby DE22 1GU* Tel (01332) 343144 E-mail geoffrey @canonry.demon.co.uk

MARSHALL, Mrs Gillian Kathryn. b 54. Glouc Sch of Min 84. **d** 87 **p** 97. NSM Newtown w Llanllwchaiarn w Aberhafesp *St As* from 87. *42 Churchill Drive, Newtown SY16 2LQ* Tel (01686) 628375

MARSHALL, Graham George. b 38. Dur Univ BA60 St Chad's Coll Dur DipTh65. **d** 65 **p** 66. C Ashton-on-Ribble St Mich *Blackb* 65-67; C Lancaster St Mary 67-71; R Church Eaton *Lich* 71-75; Prec Man Cathl *Man* 75-78; R Reddish 78-85; V Chadderton St Luke from 87. *St Luke's Vicarage, Queen's Road, Chadderton, Oldham OL9 9HU* Tel 0161-624 3562

MARSHALL (née CHADWICK), Mrs Helen Jane. b 63. UEA BA84 Nottm Univ MTh91. St Jo Coll Nottm LTh88 DPS91. **d** 91 **p** 94. Par Dn Easton H Trin w St Gabr and St Lawr and St Jude *Bris* 91-94; C 94-95. *6 Stanley Road, Oxford OX4 1QZ* Tel (01865) 242831

MARSHALL, Canon Hugh Phillips. b 34. SS Coll Cam BA57 MA61. Linc Th Coll 57. **d** 59 **p** 60. C Westmr St Steph w St Jo *Lon* 59-65; V Tupsley *Heref* 65-74; V Wimbledon *S'wark* 74-78; TR 78-87; RD Merton 79-86; V Mitcham SS Pet and Paul 87-90; Hon Can S'wark Cathl 89-90; Perm to Offic from 90; Chief Sec ABM 90-96; V Wendover *Ox* from 96; P-in-c Halton from 96; Hon Can Bulawayo from 96. *The Vicarage, 34 Dobbins Lane, Wendover, Aylesbury, Bucks HP22 6DH* Tel (01296) 622230

MARSHALL, Mrs Jean. b 36. SW Minl Tr Course 84. **d** 87 **p** 94. NSM Stratton *Truro* 87-89; NSM Bodmin w Lanhydrock and Lanivet 89-94; NSM Lezant w Lawhitton and S Petherwin w Trewen from 94. *The Vicarage, South Petherwin, Launceston, Cornwall PL15 7JA* Tel (01566) 773782

MARSHALL, John. b 37. Kelham Th Coll 53. **d** 62 **p** 63. C Winshill *Derby* 62-64; C Chaddesden St Phil 64-65; Chapl HM Borstal Morton Hall 65-75; V Swinderby *Linc* 66-77; R Church Aston *Lich* 77-84; V Auckland St Andr and St Anne *Dur* from 84; P-in-c Hunwick 88-90; Chapl Bishop Auckland Gen Hosp from 84. *St Andrew's Vicarage, Park Street, Bishop Auckland, Co Durham DL14 7JS* Tel (01388) 604397

MARSHALL, John. b 50. St Luke's Coll Ex CertEd74 W Lon Inst of HE DipEdHChild79. S'wark Ord Course 88. **d** 91 **p** 92. Hon C Brixton Hill St Sav *S'wark* 91-95; Hon C Clapham St Jas from 95. *57A Kingscourt Road, London SW16 1JA* Tel 0181-769 3665

MARSHALL, John Dixon. b 17. Dur Univ LTh43. Edin Th Coll 40. **d** 43 **p** 44. C Edin Old St Paul *Edin* 43-47; CF (EC) 47-53; Min Can Ripon Cathl *Ripon* 53-54; R Kirkwall *Ab* 54-59; R Galashiels *Edin* 59-65; R Fortrose *Mor* 65-74; R Cromarty 65-74; R Baillieston *Glas* 74-82; R Glas St Serf 74-82; rtd 82; Perm to Offic *Mor* from 82. *17 Mackenzie Terrace, Rosemarkie, Fortrose, Ross-shire IV10 8UH* Tel (01381) 20924

MARSHALL, John Douglas. b 23. Univ of Wales (Cardiff) BA43. **d** 79 **p** 80. Hon C Radlett *St Alb* 79-86; Lic to Offic *Llan* from 86. *Meiros, 3 River Walk, Cowbridge CF7 7DW* Tel (01446) 773930

MARSHALL, John Linton. b 42. Worc Coll Ox BA64 MA68 Bris Univ MLitt75. Wells Th Coll 66. **d** 68 **p** 69. C Bris St Mary Redcliffe w Temple etc *Bris* 68-71; Tutor Sarum & Wells Th Coll 71-73; Perm to Offic *Pet* 74-77; Lic to Offic *S'well* 77-81; V Choral S'well Minster 79-81; R Ordsall 81-88; P-in-c Grove 84-88; RD Retford 84-88; V Northowram *Wakef* from 88. *The Vicarage, Back Clough, Northowram, Halifax, W Yorkshire HX3 7HH* Tel (01422) 202551

MARSHALL, John William. b 24. St And NSM Tr Scheme. **d** 73 **p** 74. NSM Inverkeithing *St And* 73-90; NSM Lochgelly 73-90; NSM Rosyth 73-90; rtd 90. *St Ronan's, 72 Lumphinnans Road, Lochgelly, Fife KY5 9AR* Tel (01592) 780769

MARSHALL, Kirstin Heather. b 64. St Jo Coll Nottm 90. **d** 93 **p** 95. NSM Glas St Marg *Glas* 93-96; Hon Asst P Glas St Mary from 96. *19 Kirkoswald Road, Glasgow G43 2YH* Tel 0141-633 1437

MARSHALL, Lionel Alan. b 41. TEng. St Deiniol's Hawarden 84 Qu Coll Birm 86. **d** 87 **p** 88. C Llandudno *Ban* 87-90; V Rhayader and Nantmel *S & B* from 90. *The Vicarage, Dark Lane, Rhayader LD6 5DA* Tel (01597) 810223

MARSHALL, Canon Maurice Peter. b 23. Oak Hill Th Coll 59. **d** 61 **p** 62. C Haydock St Mark *Liv* 61-64; V New Ferry *Ches* 64-79; V Hartford 79-89; Hon Can Ches Cathl 87-89; rtd 89; Perm to Offic *Ches* from 89. *27 East Lane, Sandiway, Northwich, Cheshire CW8 2QQ* Tel (01606) 888591

MARSHALL, Michael David. b 51. BSc. Trin Coll Bris. **d** 84 **p** 85. C Kennington St Mark *S'wark* 84-88; V Streatham Park St Alb 88-96; RD Tooting 93-96; V Blackheath St Jo from 96. *146 Langton Way, London SE3 7JS* Tel 0181-293 1248

✠**MARSHALL, The Rt Revd Michael Eric.** b 36. Ch Coll Cam BA58 MA60. Cuddesdon Coll 58. **d** 60 **p** 61 **c** 75. C Birm St Pet *Birm* 60-62; Tutor Ely Th Coll 62-64; Min Can Ely Cathl *Ely* 62-64; Chapl Lon Univ *Lon* 64-69; V St Marylebone All SS 69-75; Suff Bp Woolwich *S'wark* 75-84; Asst Bp Lon from 84; Episc Dir Angl Inst Missouri 84-92; Can and Preb Chich Cathl *Chich* 90-97; Asst Bp Chich from 92; Abps' Adv Springboard for Decade of Evang from 92; P-in-c Upper Chelsea H Trin w St Jude *Lon* from 97. *Upper Chelsea Rectory, 97A Cadogan Lane, London SW1X 9DU* Tel 0171-628 0847 Mobile 0410-215131

MARSHALL, Canon Peter Arthur. b 31. AKC58. **d** 59 **p** 60. C Hutton *Chelmsf* 59-61; C Rickmansworth *St Alb* 61-66; Chapl Orchard View and Kingsmead Court Hosps 66-94; R Lexden *Chelmsf* 66-94; RD Colchester 88-93; Hon Can Chelmsf Cathl 90-94; rtd 94. *21 Manor Close, Wickham, Fareham, Hants PO17 5BZ* Tel (01329) 832988

MARSHALL, Peter James. b 48. Qu Coll Birm 78. **d** 80 **p** 81. C Ormskirk *Liv* 80-83; V Dallam from 83. *St Mark's Vicarage, Longshaw Street, Warrington WA5 5DY* Tel (01925) 631193

MARSHALL, The Very Revd Peter Jerome. b 40. McGill Univ Montreal. Westcott Ho Cam 61. **d** 63 **p** 64. C E Ham St Mary *Chelmsf* 63-66; C Woodford St Mary 66-71; C-in-c S Woodford 66-71; V Walthamstow St Pet 71-81; Dep Dir of Tr 81-84; Can Res Chelmsf Cathl 81-85; Dioc Dir of Tr *Ripon* 85-97; Can Res Ripon Cathl 85-97; Dean Worc from 97. *The Deanery, 10 College Green, Worcester WR1 2LH* Tel (01905) 27821

MARSHALL, Peter John. b 33. K Coll Lon 56. Codrington Coll Barbados 57. **d** 61 **p** 62. Trinidad and Tobago 61-64; Singapore 64-67; CF 67-88; rtd 88. *MOD Chaplains (Army), Trenchard Lines, Upavon, Pewsey, Wilts SN9 6BE* Tel (01980) 615804 Fax 615800

MARSHALL, Peter John Charles. b 35. Bris Univ BA60. Ridley Hall Cam 60. **d** 62 **p** 63. C Lindfield *Chich* 62-65; Travelling Sec Scripture Union 65-83; Hon C Nottingham St Nic *S'well* 65-67; Hon C Cheadle Hulme St Andr *Ches* 67-83; V Ilkley All SS *Bradf* from 83; RD Otley from 92. *The Vicarage, 58 Curly Hill, Ilkley, W Yorkshire LS29 0BA* Tel (01943) 607537

MARSHALL, Robert Paul (Rob). b 60. Sheff Univ BA81 Dur Univ MA85. Cranmer Hall Dur 81. **d** 83 **p** 84. C Kirkstall *Ripon* 83-85; C Otley *Bradf* 85-87; Dioc Communications Officer 87-91; P-in-c Embsay w Eastby 87-91; Dioc Communications Officer *Lon* 91-95; V S Kensington St Aug from 95; Media Adv to Abp *York* from 95. *St Augustine's House, 117 Queen's Gate, London SW7 2LW* Tel 0171-581 1877

MARSHALL, Simon. b 54. Kingston Poly BSc77 Leeds Univ PGCE78 MA(Ed)79. Qu Coll Birm DipTh93. **d** 93 **p** 94. C Gt Clacton *Chelmsf* 93-97; TV Chigwell and Chigwell Row from 97. *All Saints' Vicarage, Romford Road, Chigwell Row, Essex IG7 4QD* Tel 0181-501 5150

MARSHALL, Susan. *See* PANTER MARSHALL, Mrs Susan Lesley

MARSHALL, Canon Timothy James. b 26. Barrister-at-Law (Middle Temple) 50 BNC Ox BA48 BCL49 MA53. St Steph Ho Ox DipTh51. **d** 52 **p** 53. C Staveley *Derby* 52-60; V Shirebrook 60-92; Hon Can Derby Cathl 86-92; rtd 92. *43 Charleston Road, Penrhyn Bay, Llandudno LL30 3HB* Tel (01492) 543541

MARSHALL, Timothy John. b 53. GRSM74. Oak Hill Th Coll BA79. **d** 79 **p** 80. C Muswell Hill St Jas w St Matt *Lon* 79-85; V Hammersmith St Simon 85-92; V Bovingdon *St Alb* from 92. *The Vicarage, Bovingdon, Hemel Hempstead, Herts HP3 0LP* Tel (01442) 833298

MARSHALL, Canon William John. b 35. TCD BA57 BD61 PhD75. TCD Div Sch 59. **d** 59 **p** 60. C Ballyholme *D & D* 59-61; India 62-72; Asst Dean of Residence TCD 73-76; I Rathmichael *D & G* 76-92; Can Ch Ch Cathl Dub from 90; Chan from 91; Vice-Prin CITC from 92. *99 Landscape Park, Churchtown, Dublin 14, Irish Republic* Tel Dublin (1) 298 6989 or 492 3506 Fax 492 3082

MARSHALL, William Michael (Bill). b 30. Pemb Coll Ox BA53 MA57 DipEd65 Lon Univ DipTh67 Bris Univ MLitt72 PhD79 DipTh. Sarum & Wells Th Coll 79. **d** 80 **p** 81. Asst Chapl Millfield Sch Somerset 65-96; Hon C Glastonbury St Jo w Godney *B & W* 80-84; Hon C Glastonbury w Meare, W Pennard and Godney 84-96; rtd 96; Perm to Offic *Portsm* from 96; Perm to Offic *Win* from 96. *33 White Hart Road, King James's Quay, Portsmouth PO1 2TP* Tel (01705) 861543

MARSTON, David Howarth. b 48. St Jo Coll Dur BA69. Edin Th Coll 69. **d** 71 **p** 72. C Kendal H Trin *Carl* 71-75; Perm to Offic *Glas* 75-78; Hon C Barrow St Matt *Carl* 79-93; NSM Southport All SS *Liv* 93-94; NSM Southport All So 93-94; NSM Southport All SS and All So from 94. *28 Hillsview Road, Southport, Merseyside PR8 3PN* Tel (01704) 576138

MARSTON, William Thornton. b 59. Worc Coll Ox BA81 MA85 Cam Univ CertEd83. St Steph Ho Ox BA87. **d** 88 **p** 89. C Beckenham St Geo *Roch* 88-92; TV Ifield *Chich* 92-97; C-in-c Middleton-on-Sea CD from 97. *St Nicholas House, 106 Elmer Road, Middleton-on-Sea, Bognor Regis, W Sussex PO22 6LJ* Tel (01243) 586348

MART, Terence Eugene. b 47. CertEd76 BA82. St Jo Coll Nottm LTh87. **d** 87 **p** 88. C Prestatyn *St As* 87-91; Chapl Theatr Clwyd Mold 87-91; R Llangystennin from 91; RD Llanrwst from 96. *The Rectory, Glyn y Marl Road, Llandudno Junction LL31 9NS* Tel (01492) 583579

MARTIN, Alexander Lewendon. b 26. Em Coll Cam BA47 MA51. Ridley Hall Cam 56. **d** 57 **p** 58. C Ashtead *Guildf* 57-59; Asst Chapl Tonbridge Sch 59-64; Chapl Felsted Sch Essex 64-74; Chapl Sedbergh Sch 74-84; R Askerswell, Loders and Powerstock *Sarum* 84-89; RD Lyme Bay 86-89; rtd 89; Perm to

Offic *Ex* from 89. *Thirtover, 7 Alexandra Way, Crediton, Devon EX17 2EA* Tel (01363) 776206

MARTIN, Canon Anthony Bluett. b 29. St Jo Coll Cam BA52 MA56. Ridley Hall Cam 52. **d** 54 **p** 55. C Rushden *Pet* 54-57; C Worthing St Geo *Chich* 57-59; CSSM 59-63; Lic to Offic *Man* 59-63; V Hoole *Ches* 63-84; Hon Can Ches Cathl 83-94; V Bowdon 84-94; rtd 94; Perm to Offic *Ches* from 94. *8 Eaton Mews, Chester CH4 7EJ* Tel (01244) 680307

MARTIN, Anthony George. b 20. Nottm Univ LTh74. ALCD42. **d** 43 **p** 45. C Salisbury St Edm *Sarum* 43-46; C Bradford-on-Avon 46-48; C Sherborne w Castleton and Lillington 48-50; C Keynsham w Queen Charlton *B & W* 50-53; V Puriton 53-58; V Wookey 58-69; R Ilchester w Northover 69-72; R Limington 69-72; R Axbridge 72-74; R Axbridge w Shipham and Rowberrow 74-80; rtd 81; Perm to Offic *B & W* from 81. *5 Lawpool Court, Wells, Somerset BA5 2AN* Tel (01749) 675739

MARTIN, Brother. *See* COOMBE, John Morrell

MARTIN, Christopher John. b 45. Ball Coll Ox BA67 MA87. Wycliffe Hall Ox 86. **d** 88 **p** 89. C Edin St Thos *Edin* 88-90; R Duns from 90. *The Rectory, Wellfield, Duns, Berwickshire TD11 3EH* Tel (01361) 882209

MARTIN, Christopher John Neville. b 32. Trin Coll Ox BA54 MA57. St Deiniol's Hawarden 82 S'wark Ord Course. **d** 83 **p** 84. NSM Man St Ann *Man* 83-84; NSM N Sheen St Phil and All SS *S'wark* 84-87; NSM Petersham 87-89; C Fryerning w Margaretting *Chelmsf* 89-92; P-in-c St Ippolyts *St Alb* 92-96; V from 96. *The Vicarage, Stevenage Road, St Ippolyts, Hitchin, Herts SG4 7PE* Tel (01462) 457552

MARTIN, Prof David Alfred. b 29. LSE BSc PhD. Westcott Ho Cam. **d** 83 **p** 84. Hon C Guildf Cathl *Guildf* from 83. *174 St John's Road, Woking, Surrey GU21 1PQ* Tel (01483) 762134

MARTIN, David Geoffrey. b 34. K Coll Lon BD60 AKC61. **d** 61 **p** 62. C Liv Our Lady and St Nic *Liv* 61-63; Australia 63-66; Chapl and Lect K Coll Lon 66-70; V Kennington St Jo *S'wark* 70-77; P-in-c Camberwell St Jas 76-77; Hon C Clapham Ch Ch and St Jo 77-81; Lic to Offic 81-85; V S Wimbledon All SS 85-90; V Upper Norwood St Jo from 90. *St John's Vicarage, 2 Sylvan Road, London SE19 2RX* Tel 0181-653 0378

MARTIN, David Howard. b 47. Worc Coll Ox BEd79. AKC70 St Aug Coll Cant 70. **d** 71 **p** 72. C Sedgley All SS *Lich* 71-75; Dioc Youth Chapl *Worc* 75-81; P-in-c Worc St Andr and All SS w St Helen 75-81; R Newland, Guarlford and Madresfield 81-91; R Alvechurch from 91. *The Rectory, Alvechurch, Birmingham B48 7SB* Tel 0121-445 1087

MARTIN, Donald Dales. b 30. Sarum Th Coll 53. **d** 55 **p** 56. C Guiseley *Bradf* 55-60; V Manfield w Cleasby *Ripon* 60-73; V Melbecks and Muker 73-78; R Romaldkirk w Laithkirk 78-83; V Broughton and Duddon *Carl* 83-89; rtd 89; R Iona *Arg* 89-95; Lic to Offic from 95; Lic to Offic *Mor* from 89. *The Grove, Ewanfield, Crieff, Perthshire PH7 3DA* Tel (01764) 652228

MARTIN, Donald Philip Ralph. b 30. Trin Coll Toronto MA55 STB55. **d** 54 **p** 55. Canada 54-57; Tutor Kelham Th Coll 57-73; SSM from 60; P-in-c Willen *Ox* 73-81; Japan 81-82; Ghana 83-89; Dir Cleveland Lay Tr Course from 89; C Middlesbrough All SS *York* 89-91; NSM 91-92. *Box 1735, Maseru, Lesotho*

MARTIN, Edward Eldred William. b 37. Cranfield Inst of Tech MSc84. S'wark Ord Course 65. **d** 68 **p** 69. C Greenwich St Alfege w St Pet *S'wark* 68-71; C Kidbrooke St Jas 71-75; V Peckham St Jo 75-78; P-in-c Peckham St Andr w All SS 76-78; V Peckham St Jo w St Andr 78-81; Hon PV S'wark Cathl from 81; Chapl Guy's Hosp Lon 81-88. *22 Jerningham Road, London SE14 5NX* Tel 0171-639 1402

MARTIN, Edwin John. b 43. JP89. TEng MIIExE89. **d** 83 **p** 84. NSM Cwmbran *Mon* 83-85; NSM Griffithstown 85-87; NSM Cwmbran from 87. *168 Rowleaze, Greenmeadow, Cwmbran NP44 4LG* Tel (01633) 485575

MARTIN, Miss Eileen Susan Kirkland. b 45. LCST66. Lon Bible Coll DipTh71 Cranmer Hall Dur 77. **dss** 83 **d** 86. Kilmarnock *Glas* 84-86; Par Dn Heanor *Derby* 87-92; Perm to Offic from 92. *20 The Nook, Loscoe, Heanor, Derbyshire DE75 7LQ* Tel (01773) 760220

MARTIN, George Cobain. b 34. TCD BA57 MA65. **d** 57 **p** 58. C Bangor St Comgall *D & D* 57-64; I Kircubbin 64-74; R Ashby by Partney *Linc* 75-78; R Partney w Dalby 75-78; V Skendleby 75-78; P-in-c Candlesby w Scremby 77-78; R Partney 78-95; rtd 95; Perm to Offic *Linc* from 95. *Southwold, Main Road, East Keal, Spilsby, Lincs PE23 4BA* Tel (01790) 752988

MARTIN, Glenn. b 52. Qu Coll Birm 84. **d** 86 **p** 87. C Chatham St Wm *Roch* 86-89; Chapl Pastures Hosp Derby 89-94; Chapl Kingsway Hosp Derby 89-94; Sen Chapl S Derbys Mental Health NHS Trust from 94. *14 Barnwood Close, Mickleover, Derby DE3 5QY, or Kingsway Hospital, Kingsway, Derby DE22 3LZ* Tel (01332) 510869 or 362221

MARTIN, Canon Gordon Albion John. b 30. AKC54. **d** 55 **p** 56. C Enfield Chase St Mary *Lon* 55-59; C Palmers Green St Jo 59-61; V Edmonton St Martin 61-64; V Culham *Ox* 64-67; Bp's Youth Chapl *St Alb* 67-73; P-in-c Wareside 69-73; V Harpenden St Jo 73-96; RD Wheathampstead 76-87; Hon Can St Alb 85-96; rtd 96; Perm to Offic *Ex* from 96. *2 Pottery Court, Church Road, Dartmouth, Devon TQ6 9SN* Tel (01803) 835628

MARTIN, Graham Rowland. b 39. LCP FRSA Liv Univ CertEd58 Nottm Univ DipRE65 Lon Univ DipTh BD70 Bris Univ BEd73 Bris Poly DipEdMan80. Wells Th Coll 71. **d** 71 **p** 72. Hon C Glouc St Cath *Glouc* 71-76; P-in-c Brookthorpe w Whaddon 76-78; Perm to Offic 78-80; Hon C Hucclecote 80-82; Hon C Tuffley 82-88; NSM Hardwicke, Quedgeley and Elmore w Longney 88-89; V Kemble, Poole Keynes, Somerford Keynes etc 89-96; P-in-c Bibury w Winson and Barnsley from 96; Dioc Ecum Officer from 96. *The Vicarage, Bibury, Cirencester, Glos GL7 5NT* Tel (01285) 740387

MARTIN, Henry Rowland Felix. b 67. Leeds Univ BA89 SS Coll Cam BA95. Ridley Hall Cam CTM93. **d** 96 **p** 97. C Becontree St Mary *Chelmsf* from 96. *104 Temple Avenue, Dagenham, Essex RM8 1LS* Tel 0181-595 8625

MARTIN, Dr James Davidson. b 35. Glas Univ MA57 BD60 PhD70. **d** 89 **p** 89. NSM St Andrews St Andr *St And* 89-94; Chapl St Andr Univ 89-94; TV Glenrothes from 94; TV Leven from 94; TV Lochgelly from 94. *32 Craigievar Drive, Glenrothes, Fife KY7 4PH* Tel (01592) 772956

MARTIN, James Smiley. b 32. TCD 65. **d** 67 **p** 68. C Glenavy *Conn* 67-70; C Belfast St Mary 70-73; I Carnmoney 73-74; I Mallusk 74-94; rtd 94. *21 Dundesert Road, Nutts Corner, Crumlin, Co Antrim BT29 4SL* Tel (01232) 825636

MARTIN, John Albert. TCD DipTh85. **d** 85 **p** 86. C Drumachose *D & R* 85-88; I Cumber Upper w Learmount from 88; Bp's Dom Chapl from 91. *Alla Rectory, 87 Cumber Road, Claudy, Co Londonderry BT47 4JA* Tel (01504) 338214

MARTIN, John Henry. b 42. St Jo Coll Cam BA63 MA67. St Jo Coll Nottm BA73. **d** 73 **p** 74. C Ecclesall *Sheff* 73-77; C Hednesford *Lich* 77-82; V Walsall Pleck and Bescot 82-92; V Whittington w Weeford from 92. *The Vicarage, Whittington, Lichfield, Staffs WS14 9LH* Tel (01543) 432233

MARTIN, John Hunter. b 42. AKC64. **d** 65 **p** 66. C Mortlake w E Sheen *S'wark* 65-69; C-in-c Bermondsey St Hugh CD 69-72; V Bermondsey St Anne 72-78; P-in-c Lt Ouse *Ely* 78; V Littleport 78-89; V Attercliffe *Sheff* 89-90; P-in-c Darnall H Trin 89-90; TR Darnall-cum-Attercliffe 90-96; TR Attercliffe, Darnall and Tinsley 96; R Kirk Sandall and Edenthorpe from 96. *The Rectory, 31 Doncaster Road, Kirk Sandall, Doncaster, S Yorkshire DN3 1HP* Tel (01302) 882861

MARTIN, John Keith. b 32. Sarum & Wells Th Coll 76. **d** 79 **p** 80. C Bath Bathwick *B & W* 79-82; V Weston-super-Mare St Andr Bournville 82-85; V Cinderford St Jo *Glouc* 85-94; rtd 97. *Glen Cairn, 39 Laflouder Fields, Mullion, Helston, Cornwall TR12 7EJ* Tel (01326) 240613

MARTIN, Canon John Pringle. b 24. Bris Univ BA50. Clifton Th Coll 50. **d** 52 **p** 53. C Braintree *Chelmsf* 52-56; C St Alb St Paul *St Alb* 56-59; V Congleton St Pet *Ches* 59-81; RD Congleton 74-85; Hon Can Ches Cathl 80-90; R Brereton w Swettenham 81-90; rtd 90; Perm to Offic *B & W* from 90. *49 Parkhouse Road, Minehead, Somerset TA24 8AD* Tel (01643) 706769

MARTIN, John Stuart. b 11. St Jo Coll Dur BA34. Wycliffe Hall Ox. **d** 35 **p** 36. C Mansfield St Pet *S'well* 35-37; C Newhaven *Chich* 37-39; C Barcombe 39-43; V Ox H Trin *Ox* 43-46; V Leafield w Wychwood 46-51; R Rotherfield Greys 51-63; V Highmore 55-63; R Bow w Broad Nymet *Ex* 63-65; V Upottery 65-72; TV Farway w Northleigh and Southleigh 72-73; rtd 73. *Church Villa, 8 Church Road, Bawdrip, Bridgwater, Somerset TA7 8PU* Tel (01278) 684092

MARTIN, Canon John Tidswell. b 24. Em Coll Cam BA48 MA52. Kelham Th Coll 48. **d** 53 **p** 54. C Yardley Wood *Birm* 53-55; Asst Gen Sec and Sec Th Colls Dept SCM 55-58; Gen Sec 58-62; R Withington St Chris *Man* 62-68; V Kingston All SS *S'wark* 68-76; V Kingston All SS w St Jo 76-89; Hon Can S'wark Cathl 87-89; rtd 89; Perm to Offic *S'wark* from 89. *175 Lincoln Avenue, Twickenham TW2 6NL*

MARTIN, Jonathan Patrick McLeod. b 55. Leic Univ BA81. Sarum & Wells Th Coll 84. **d** 86 **p** 87. C Southampton Thornhill St Chris *Win* 86-89; Perm to Offic 89-92; C Heatherlands St Jo *Sarum* 92-97; Dioc Link Officer for ACUPA 95-97; Lic to Offic *Portsm* from 97. *80 Kingston Road, Poole, Dorset BH15 2LS* Tel (01202) 687180

MARTIN, Joseph Edward. b 35. NDD55. Bps' Coll Cheshunt 58. **d** 60 **p** 61. C Short Heath *Birm* 60-62; C Caterham Valley *S'wark* 63-66; R W Hallam and Mapperley *Derby* 66-70; P-in-c Mapperley 66-67; V Wykeham and Hutton Buscel *York* 71-78; Chapl HM Pris Askham Grange 78-82; V Askham Bryan w Askham Richard *York* 78-82; R Amotherby w Appleton and Barton-le-Street 82-84; C Banbury *Ox* 85-88; C Warsop *S'well* 88-90; V Tuxford w Weston and Markham Clinton from 90. *The Vicarage, Lincoln Road, Tuxford, Newark, Notts NG22 0HP* Tel (01777) 870497

MARTIN, Kenneth. b 20. Univ of Wales (Lamp) BA47. **d** 48 **p** 49. C Rumney *Mon* 48-49; C Griffithstown 49-51; CF (TA) from 52; Perm to Offic *Llan* from 51. *21 Earls Court Road, Penylan, Cardiff CF3 7DE* Tel (01222) 493796

MARTIN, Kenneth Cyril. b 31. AIGCM53. S'wark Ord Course 71. **d** 73 **p** 74. C Hollington St Leon *Chich* 73-76; C Horsham 76-79; P-in-c Broadwaters *Worc* 79-81; V 81; P-in-c Worc H Trin 81-86; R Stoulton w Drake's Broughton and Pirton etc 86-91; rtd 91;

Perm to Offic *Chich* from 95. *190 Gossops Drive, Crawley, W Sussex RH11 8LD* Tel (01293) 529172

MARTIN, Canon Kenneth Roger. b 16. Solicitor. AKC40. **d** 40 **p** 41. C Ex St Thos *Ex* 40-45; Perm to Offic *Cant* 45-46; C Upper Norwood St Jo 46-47; C Sidmouth St Nic *Ex* 47-51; Perm to Offic *Wakef* 51-53; C Whitley Ch Ch *Ox* 53-56; V Summertown 56-63; R Rotherfield Greys 63-69; V Highmore 63-69; R Wokingham All SS 69-81; RD Sonning 78-81; Hon Can Ch Ch 80-81; rtd 81; Perm to Offic *Ex* from 81; Perm to Offic *Ox* from 81. *1 Indio Road, Bovey Tracey, Newton Abbot, Devon TQ13 9BT* Tel (01626) 832605

MARTIN, Miss Marion. b 47. Oak Hill Th Coll DipHE85. **dss** 86 **d** 87. Ditton *Roch* 86-88; C 87-88; rtd 88; Perm to Offic *Glouc* 89-95. *33 Campden Road, Cheltenham, Glos GL51 6AA* Tel (01242) 239477

MARTIN, Nicholas Roger. b 53. St Jo Coll Dur BA74. Ripon Coll Cuddesdon 75. **d** 77 **p** 78. C Wolvercote w Summertown *Ox* 77-80; C Kidlington 80-82; TV 82-84; V Happisburgh w Walcot *Nor* 84-85; P-in-c Hempstead w Lessingham and Eccles 84-85; R Happisburgh w Walcot, Hempstead, Lessingham etc 85-89; R Blakeney w Cley, Wiveton, Glandford etc from 89. *The Rectory, Wiveton Road, Blakeney, Holt, Norfolk NR25 7NJ* Tel (01263) 740686

MARTIN, Nicholas Worsley. b 52. Sarum & Wells Th Coll 71. **d** 75 **p** 76. C Llan w Capel Llanilltern *Llan* 75-79; C Cardiff St Jo 79; C Caerphilly 79-83; TV Hemel Hempstead *St Alb* 83-93; Chapl Hemel Hempstead Gen Hosp 83-93; Perm to Offic *Chich* from 94. *Pilgrims Cottage, The Street, Graffham, Petworth, W Sussex GU28 0NP* Tel (01798) 867397

MARTIN, Norman George. b 22. Sarum & Wells Th Coll 74. **d** 77 **p** 78. NSM Long Ashton *B & W* 77-81; NSM Walton in Gordano 81-82; NSM E Clevedon and Walton w Weston w Clapton 82-87; Perm to Offic from 87; Chapl Barrow Hosp from 87; Chapl Farleigh Hosp from 87. *7 Clynder Grove, Castle Road, Clevedon, Avon BS21 7DF* Tel (01275) 873124

MARTIN, Paul Dexter. b 50. Wabash Coll (USA) BA72 Univ of the South (USA) MDiv75. **d** 75 **p** 76. Educn Tutor Cov Cathl 75-76; C Norbury St Phil *Cant* 76-80; USA from 80. *705 Bonin Road, Lafayette, Louisiana 70508, USA*

MARTIN, Mrs Penelope Elizabeth. b 44. Cranmer Hall Dur 83. **dss** 86 **d** 87 **p** 94. Seaham w Seaham Harbour *Dur* 86-87; Par Dn 87-89; Par Dn Cassop cum Quarrington 89-93; Par Dn Sherburn w Pittington 93-94; C 94-95; V from 95; R Shadforth from 95. *The Vicarage, 89 Front Street, Sherburn, Durham DH6 1HD* Tel 0191-372 0374

MARTIN, Peter. b 50. MIH75. Linc Th Coll 82. **d** 84 **p** 85. C Taunton H Trin *B & W* 84-86; C Bath Bathwick 86-88; R Cannington, Otterhampton, Combwich and Stockland from 88; Chapl Cannington Coll from 89; Chapl Somerset Coll of Agric and Horticulture from 89. *The Rectory, 27 Brook Street, Cannington, Bridgwater, Somerset TA5 2HP* Tel (01278) 652953

MARTIN, Peter. b 66. Univ of Wales (Ban) BD89. Qu Coll Birm 90. **d** 92 **p** 93. C Kingswinford St Mary *Lich* 92-93; C Kingswinford St Mary *Worc* 93-95; Chapl Redbridge Healthcare NHS Trust from 95. *The Chaplain's Office, King George Hospital, Eastern Avenue, Ilford, Essex IG2 7RL* Tel 0181-983 8000

MARTIN, Philip James. b 58. Cam Univ BA. Coll of Resurr Mirfield. **d** 84 **p** 85. C Pontefract St Giles *Wakef* 84-88; C Wantage *Ox* 88-90; C Didcot All SS 90; V Alderholt *Sarum* from 90; Dioc USPG Rep from 90. *The Vicarage, Draggons Road, Alderholt, Fordingbridge, Hants SP6 3DN* Tel (01425) 653179

MARTIN, Raymond William. b 32. MBIM Lon Univ BSc66 DMA. Glouc Th Course 73. **d** 76 **p** 76. C Glouc St Mary de Lode and St Nic *Glouc* 76-77; Hon C Redmarley D'Abitot, Bromesberrow w Pauntley etc 77-84; R 84-91; P-in-c Falfield w Rockhampton from 91; P-in-c Oldbury-on-Severn from 91; Chapl HM Pris Eastwood Park 91-96. *The Vicarage, Sundayshill Lane, Falfield, Wotton-under-Edge, Glos GL12 8DQ* Tel (01454) 260033

MARTIN, Richard. b 34. Rhodes Univ BA54 Em Coll Cam BA57 MA58. Wells Th Coll 57. **d** 59 **p** 60. C Portsea St Mary *Portsm* 59-60; S Africa 60-87; C Aldershot St Mich *Guildf* 87-94; R Wick *Mor* from 94; P-in-c Thurso from 94. *5 Navier Place, Thurso, Caithness KW14 7PZ* Tel (01847) 893393

MARTIN, Richard Charles de Villeval. b 41. St Jo Coll Ox BA63 MA67. Ox Ord Course. **d** 84 **p** 85. NSM Ox St Thos w St Frideswide and Binsey *Ox* from 84; Asst Chapl Highgate Sch Lon 86-92; Magd Coll Sch Ox from 92; Chapl from 94. *11 Benson Place, Oxford OX2 6QH* Tel (01865) 510694

MARTIN, Richard Hugh. b 55. Dur Univ BA78. St Jo Coll Nottm BA81 DPS82. **d** 82 **p** 83. C Gateshead *Dur* 82-85; C Redmarshall 85-88; V Scarborough St Jas w H Trin *York* 88-96; Chapl R Wolv Hosps NHS Trust from 96. *The Chaplain's House, New Cross Hospital, Wednesfield Road, Wolverhampton WV10 0QP* Tel (01902) 307999

MARTIN, Robert David Markland. b 49. FCA80 Trin Coll Cam BA71 MA74. Trin Coll Bris BA91. **d** 91 **p** 92. C Kingswood *Bris* 91-95; V Frome H Trin *B & W* from 95. *Holy Trinity Vicarage, Orchard Street, Frome, Somerset BA11 3BX* Tel (01373) 462586

MARTIN, Robert Paul Peter. b 58. Chich Th Coll. **d** 83 **p** 84. C Anfield St Columba *Liv* 83-86; C Orford St Marg 86-87; R Blackley H Trin *Man* 87-90; C Oseney Crescent St Luke *Lon* 90-93; C Kentish Town 93-96; V Harringay St Paul from 96. *St Paul's Vicarage, Wightman Road, London N4 1RW* Tel 0181-340 5299

MARTIN, Robin Hugh. b 35. Rhodes Univ BA56 Birm Univ DipTh57. **d** 58 **p** 59. C Darnall H Trin *Sheff* 58-62; C-in-c Kimberworth Park 62-65; Lic to Offic *Sarum* 65-66; Lic to Offic *Newc* 67-71; Perm to Offic *Man* 79-93; rtd 93. *Address temp unknown*

MARTIN, Roger Ivor. b 42. DMS76 MIMgt. Cant Sch of Min. **d** 85 **p** 86. NSM Saltwood *Cant* 85-90; P-in-c Crundale w Godmersham from 90; Dioc Exec Officer for Adult Educn and Lay Tr 90-96; CME Officer 94-96; Chapl to Bp Maidstone from 96. *The Forge, Godmersham Park, Godmersham, Canterbury, Kent CT4 7DT* Tel (01227) 738177 Fax as telephone

MARTIN, Mrs Rosanna Stuart. b 60. Bris Univ BA81. Wycliffe Hall Ox 89. **d** 92 **p** 94. Par Dn Stanford in the Vale w Goosey and Hatford *Ox* 92-94; C 94-96; C Abingdon from 96. *7 Limetrees, Chilton, Didcot, Oxon OX11 1AH* Tel (01235) 821861

MARTIN, Roy Ernest. b 29. FCA54. Qu Coll Birm 74. **d** 77 **p** 77. NSM Marston Green *Birm* 77-85; NSM Sheldon 85-89; Perm to Offic from 89. *14 Walcot Green, Dorridge, Solihull, W Midlands B93 8BU* Tel (01564) 772943

MARTIN, Rupert Gresley. b 57. Worc Coll Ox BA78 Ox Univ MA95. Trin Coll Bris DipHE91. **d** 91 **p** 92. C Yateley *Win* 91-95; V Sandal St Helen *Wakef* from 95. *The Vicarage, 333 Barnsley Road, Wakefield, W Yorkshire WF2 6FL* Tel (01924) 255441

MARTIN, Russell Derek. b 47. St Jo Coll Dur 71. **d** 74 **p** 75. C Hartlepool H Trin *Dur* 74-78; C Swindon St Jo and St Andr *Bris* 78-79; V Penhill 79-91; V Haselbury Plucknett, Misterton and N Perrott *B & W* from 91. *The Rectory, North Perrott, Crewkerne, Somerset TA18 7TB* Tel (01460) 72063

MARTIN, Mrs Sara Galloway. b 19. MCSP40. N Ord Course 71. **dss** 79 **d** 87 **p** 94. Ainsworth *Man* 79-82; Tottington 82-87; Par Dn 87-88; Hon C from 94; rtd 89; Perm to Offic *Man* 89-94. *36 Victoria Street, Tottington, Bury, Lancs BL8 4AG* Tel (01204) 882868

MARTIN, Miss Susan (Sue). b 56. Nottm Univ BA77. Edin Th Coll 86. **d** 88 **p** 94. C Leigh Park *Portsm* 88-91; C Sandown Ch Ch 91-94; C Portsea St Cuth 94-95; rtd 95; Perm to Offic *Portsm* from 95. *7 Farthingdale Terrace, Peacock Lane, Portsmouth PO1 2TL* Tel (01705) 297994

MARTIN, Sylvia. **d** 97. NSM Locks Heath *Portsm* from 97. *9 Harvester Drive, Catisfield, Fareham, Hants PO15 5NR*

MARTIN, Sylvia. b 24. **dss** 75 **d** 87 **p** 94. NSM Selsdon St Jo w St Fran *S'wark* from 87. *42 Upper Selsdon Road, Selsdon, Croydon CR2 8DE* Tel 0181-657 3422

MARTIN, Thomas Robin. b 40. Bps' Coll Cheshunt 64. **d** 67 **p** 68. C Ripley *Derby* 67-70; C Ilkeston St Mary 70-74; V Chinley w Buxworth 74-83; V Knighton St Mich *Leic* 83-85; V Thurmaston from 85. *The Vicarage, 828 Melton Road, Thurmaston, Leicester LE4 8BE* Tel 0116-269 2555

MARTIN, William Harrison. b 38. **d** 87 **p** 88. NSM Rushen *S & M* 87-92; C German 92-97; V Lonan from 97; V Laxey from 97. *The Vicarage, 56 Ard Reayrt, Ramsey Road, Laxey, Isle of Man IM4 7QQ* Tel (01624) 862050

MARTIN, William Henry Blyth. b 10. Keble Coll Ox BA33 MA36. Cuddesdon Coll 35. **d** 36 **p** 37. C S Shields St Mary *Dur* 36-39; Chapl Bps' Coll Cheshunt 39-45; Vice-Prin Bp's Coll Cheshunt 45-48; CF (EC) 41-45; V Chesterfield St Aug *Derby* 49-62; V Long Eaton St Laur 62-80; rtd 81; Perm to Offic *Cov* from 81; Perm to Offic *Pet* 85-94. *93 Crick Road, Hillmorton, Rugby, Warks CV21 4DZ*

MARTIN, William Matthew (Bill). b 28. C&G81 FETC81 Ch Coll Cam BA52 MA56. Ridley Hall Cam 52. **d** 54 **p** 55. C Weaste *Man* 54-56; V 56-61; CF (TA) 58-61; CF 61-82; Dep Asst Chapl Gen 73-82; Asst Master St Jo Southworth RC High Sch Preston 82-88; Lic to Offic *Blackb* from 82; rtd 93. *40 Jepps Avenue, Barton, Preston PR3 5AS* Tel (01772) 862166

MARTIN-DOYLE, Mrs Audrey Brenda. b 35. Cranmer Hall Dur 80. **dss** 82 **d** 87 **p** 95. The Lye and Stambermill *Worc* 82-86; Chapl Lee Abbey 86-88; Ldr Aston Cottage Community from 88; NSM Cheltenham St Mark *Glouc* 94; NSM Cheltenham St Mary, St Matt, St Paul and H Trin from 94. *4 Jenners Walk, St George's Place, Cheltenham, Glos GL50 3LD* Tel (01242) 514419

MARTIN-SMITH, Paul. b 38. TCD BA64 Lon Univ MSc67 FIPEM88. WMMTC 94. **d** 97. NSM Tile Hill *Cov* from 97. *74 Stoneleigh Avenue, Earlsdon, Coventry CV5 6BZ* Tel (01203) 673829

MARTINDALE, Mrs Patricia Ann. b 24. Qu Coll Birm. **dss** 84 **d** 87 **p** 94. Rugby St Andr *Cov* 84-87; NSM from 87. *54 Hillmorton Road, Rugby, Warks CV22 5AD* Tel (01788) 543038

MARTINEAU, Canon Christopher Lee (Chris). b 16. Trin Hall Cam BA38 MA70. Linc Th Coll 39. **d** 41 **p** 42. C Hinckley St Mary *Leic* 41-43; Chapl RNVR 43-46; C St Alb Abbey *St Alb* 46-48; V Balsall Heath St Paul *Birm* 48-54; P-in-c Shard End 54-58; V 58-65; R Skipton H Trin *Bradf* 65-83; rtd 83; Perm to Offic *Bradf* from 83. *6 Greenhead Avenue, Utley, Keighley, W Yorkshire BD20 6EY* Tel (01535) 609247

MARTINEAU, Canon David Richards Durani. b 36. AKC59. **d** 60 **p** 61. C Ches St Jo *Ches* 60-64; S Africa 64-69; C Jarrow St Paul *Dur* 69-72; TV 72-75; TR Jarrow 76-85; V Gildersome *Wakef* from 85; Hon Can Wakef Cathl from 94. *St Peter's House, 2A Church Street, Gildersome, Morley, Leeds LS27 7AF* Tel 0113-253 3339

MARTINEAU, Jeremy Fletcher. b 40. K Coll Lon BD65 AKC65. **d** 66 **p** 67. C Jarrow St Paul *Dur* 66-73; Bp's Ind Adv 69-73; P-in-c Raughton Head w Gatesgill *Carl* 73-80; Chapl to Agric 73-80; Ind Chapl *Bris* 80-90; Abps' Rural Officer *Cant* 90-93; Nat Rural Officer Gen Syn Bd of Miss from 94. *The Arthur Rank Centre, National Agricultural Centre, Stoneleigh Park, Kenilworth, Warks CV8 2LZ* Tel (01203) 696460 Fax 696460 E-mail j.martineau@midnet.com

✠**MARTINEAU, The Rt Revd Robert Arnold Schurhoff.** b 13. Trin Hall Cam BA35 MA39. Westcott Ho Cam 36. **d** 38 **p** 39 **c** 66. C Melksham *Sarum* 38-41; Chapl RAFVR 41-46; V Ovenden *Wakef* 46-52; V Allerton *Liv* 52-66; Hon Can Liv Cathl 61-66; RD Childwall 64-66; Suff Bp Huntingdon *Ely* 66-72; Bp Blackb 72-81; rtd 81. *Gwenallt, Park Street, Denbigh LL16 3DB* Tel (01745) 814089

MARTLEW, Andrew Charles. b 50. Nottm Univ BTh76 Lanc Univ MA80. Linc Th Coll 72. **d** 76 **p** 77. C Poulton-le-Fylde *Blackb* 76-79; Hon C Lancaster Ch Ch 79-80; Malaysia 81-83; V Golcar *Wakef* 83-89; Dioc Schs Officer 89-95; V Warmfield 89-95; Dioc Dir of Educn *York* from 95. *The Vicarage, Crayke, York YO6 4TA*

MARVELL, John. b 32. Lon Univ BD63 Leic Univ MEd73 PhD85. Oak Hill Th Coll 79. **d** 80 **p** 81. NSM Colchester Ch Ch w St Mary V *Chelmsf* 80-85; Perm to Offic 85-87; P-in-c Stisted w Bradwell and Pattiswick from 87. *The Rectory, Water Lane, Stisted, Braintree, Essex CM7 8AP* Tel (01376) 551839

MARVIN, David Arthur. b 51. HND73. St Jo Coll Nottm 96. **d** 97. C Mansfield St Jo *S'well* from 97. *131 Beardall Street, Hucknall, Notts NG15 7RH*

MARWOOD, Timothy John Edmonds (Tim). b 51. Whitelands Coll Lon CertEd72 Open Univ BA89 Lon Inst of Educn MA91. S'wark Ord Course 92. **d** 95 **p** 96. NSM Putney St Mary *S'wark* from 95. *54 Eversleigh Road, London SW11 5XA* Tel 0171-223 0510

MASCALL, Mrs Margaret Ann. b 43. LRAM64 Bris Univ CertEd65 St Jo Coll Dur BA71 MA79. Cranmer Hall Dur 69. **dss** 76 **d** 87 **p** 94. Hertford St Andr *St Alb* 75-79; Herne Bay Ch Ch *Cant* 79-82; Seasalter 82-84; Whitstable 84-87; Par Dn 87-90; Perm to Offic 91-94; Hon C Hackington 94-95; V Newington w Hartlip and Stockbury from 95. *The Vicarage, Church Lane, Newington, Sittingbourne, Kent ME9 7JU* Tel (01795) 844345

MASDING, John William. b 39. Magd Coll Ox BA61 MA65 DipEd63 Univ of Wales (Cardiff) LLM94 FRSA96. Ridley Hall Cam 63. **d** 65 **p** 66. C Boldmere *Birm* 65-71; V Hamstead St Paul from 71. *Hamstead Vicarage, 840 Walsall Road, Birmingham B42 1ES* Tel 0121-357 1259 Fax 357 8328

MASH, William Edward John (Bill). b 54. ARCS MCIT81 Imp Coll Lon BSc75. St Jo Coll Nottm 87. **d** 89 **p** 90. C Beverley Minster *York* 89-93; V Elloughton and Brough w Brantingham from 93. *The Vicarage, Church Lane, Elloughton, Brough, N Humberside HU15 1HN* Tel (01482) 667431

MASHEDER, Peter Timothy Charles. b 49. AKC71. St Aug Coll Cant 71. **d** 72 **p** 73. C Barkingside St Fran *Chelmsf* 72-75; C Chingford SS Pet and Paul 75-91; P-in-c High Laver w Magdalen Laver and Lt Laver etc from 91. *The Lavers Rectory, Magdalen Laver, Ongar, Essex CM5 0ES* Tel (01279) 426774

MASHEDER, Richard. b 36. AKC59. **d** 60 **p** 61. C Preston St Matt *Blackb* 60-62; C Padiham 62-65; P-in-c Worsthorne 65; V 65-74; CF (TA) 65-67; P-in-c Blackb St Jude *Blackb* 74-78; V Blackb St Thos 76-78; V Blackb St Thos w St Jude 78-82; V Silverdale from 82. *The Vicarage, St John's Grove, Silverdale, Carnforth, Lancs LA5 0RH* Tel (01524) 701268

MASKELL, John Michael. b 45. Sarum & Wells Th Coll 86. **d** 88 **p** 89. C Swanborough *Sarum* 88-91; Chapl RAF 91-95; P-in-c Ollerton w Boughton *S'well* 95-97; P-in-c Capel *Guildf* from 97. *The Vicarage, Capel, Dorking, Surrey RH5 5LN* Tel (01306) 711260

MASKREY, Mrs Susan Elizabeth. b 43. Cranmer Hall Dur IDC70 St Jo Coll Dur CertRK70. **dss** 76 **d** 92 **p** 94. Littleover *Derby* 76-77; Sec to Publicity Manager CMS Lon 77-78; Stantonbury and Willen *Ox* 78-88; Billingham St Aid *Dur* 88-95; C 92-95; Asst Chapl HM Pris Holme Ho 94-95; Asst Chapl HM Pris Preston from 95. *HM Prison, 2 Ribbleton Lane, Preston PR1 5AB* Tel (01772) 57734 Fax 556643

MASLEN (formerly CHILD), Mrs Margaret Mary. b 44. ALA76 Open Univ BA79. S Dios Minl Tr Scheme 89. **d** 92 **p** 94. C Portishead *B & W* 92-93; C Ilminster w Whitelackington 93-94; C Ilminster and District 94-96; C Tatworth from 96. *The Vicarage, Tatworth, Chard, Somerset TA20 2PD* Tel (01460) 220404

MASLEN, Richard Ernest. b 34. S Dios Minl Tr Scheme 89. **d** 92 **p** 93. NSM Sherston Magna, Easton Grey, Luckington etc *Bris* 92-93; NSM Ilminster w Whitelackington *B & W* 93-94; NSM Ilminster and District 94-96; P-in-c Tatworth from 96. *The Vicarage, Tatworth, Chard, Somerset TA20 2PD* Tel (01460) 220404

MASLEN, Canon Stephen Henry. b 37. CCC Ox BA62 MA65. Ridley Hall Cam 62. **d** 64 **p** 65. C Keynsham w Queen Charlton *B & W* 64-67; C Cheltenham St Mary *Glouc* 67-71; P-in-c St Mary-at-Lambeth *S'wark* 72-74; TV N Lambeth 74-79; V Horley 79-84; TR 84-94; RD Reigate 86-91; R Coulsdon St Jo from 94; Hon Can S'wark Cathl from 95. *232 Coulsdon Road, Coulsdon, Surrey CR5 1EA* Tel (01737) 552152

MASLEN, Trevor. b 51. Chich Th Coll 77. **d** 80 **p** 81. C Harlow St Mary Magd *Chelmsf* 80-83; C Huntingdon St Barn *Ely* 83-86; P-in-c Huntingdon 86-87; TV 87-92; V Southampton St Jude *Win* 92-97. *116 Fotheringham Road, Enfield, Middx EN1 1QE*

MASON, Adrian Stanley. b 54. Hatf Poly BSc77. Ripon Coll Cuddesdon 77. **d** 80 **p** 81. C Mill End and Heronsgate w W Hyde *St Alb* 80-83; P-in-c Chardstock *Ex* 83; TV Axminster, Chardstock, Combe Pyne and Rousdon 83-87; TV Halesworth w Linstead, Chediston, Holton etc *St E* 87-88; R Brandon and Santon Downham 88-91; R Glem Valley United Benefice 91-95; NSM Clare Deanery from 95. *The Rectory, Glemsford, Sudbury, Suffolk CO10 7RF* Tel (01787) 280361

MASON, Alan Hambleton. b 27. Lon Univ BD59. Wycliffe Hall Ox 56. **d** 59 **p** 60. C Norbiton *S'wark* 59-63; V Thornton St Jas *Bradf* 63-73; V Norbiton *S'wark* 73-84; V Wavertree St Thos *Liv* 84-92; rtd 92; Perm to Offic *Liv* from 92. *17 Lovelace Road, Liverpool L19 1QE* Tel 0151-427 5678

MASON, Charles Godfrey. b 24. CEng71 FInstE74 Open Univ BA84. CITC 85 D & D Ord Course 85. **d** 87 **p** 89. NSM Bangor St Comgall *D & D* 87-90; NSM Lecale Gp 87-91; NSM Donaghadee 90-91; rtd 91; Lic to Offic *D & D* from 91. *20 Seymour Avenue, Bangor, Co Down BT19 1BN* Tel (01247) 465096

MASON, Charles Oliver. b 51. Jes Coll Cam BA73 St Jo Coll Dur BA79. **d** 80 **p** 81. C Cheltenham St Mary, St Matt, St Paul and H Trin *Glouc* 80-84; C Enfield Ch Ch Trent Park *Lon* 84-88; P-in-c W Hampstead St Cuth 88-93; V from 93. *St Cuthbert's Vicarage, 13 Kingscroft Road, London NW2 3QE* Tel 0181-452 1913

MASON, Dr Christina. b 42. Univ of Wales BMus63 MA65 BSc(Econ)70 CertCS82 Dundee Univ PhD84 MSW91 CQSW91. **dss** 82 **d** 86. Lic to Offic *Bre* from 82. *Maywood, Main Street, Longforgan, Dundee DD2 5EP* Tel (01826) 22337

MASON, Mrs Christine Mary. b 43. Sarum & Wells Th Coll 91. **d** 93 **p** 94. Par Dn Blakenall Heath *Lich* 93-94; C from 94. *27 Smithfield Road, Walsall WS3 1ND* Tel (01922) 477013

MASON, Christopher David. b 51. Lanc Univ BA72 MEd82. EAMTC 91. **d** 94 **p** 95. NSM Pet St Mary Boongate *Pet* from 94. *21 Bakers Lane, Woodston, Peterborough PE2 9QW* Tel (01733) 342116

MASON, Clive Ray. b 34. St Chad's Coll Dur BA57. Qu Coll Birm 57. **d** 59 **p** 60. C Gateshead St Mary *Dur* 59-62; C Bishopwearmouth Ch Ch 62-64; V Darlington St Jo 64-74; P-in-c Southwick H Trin 75-84; R 84-89; V Bearpark 89-95; rtd 95; Perm to Offic *Dur* from 95. *41 Harbour View, Littlehaven, South Shields, Tyne & Wear NE33 1LS* Tel 0191-454 0234

MASON, David Gray. b 37. MPhil LDS. **d** 95 **p** 95. NSM Biddenham *St Alb* from 95. *2A Devon Road, Bedford MK40 3DF* Tel (01234) 357036

MASON, Dawn Lavinia. b 53. Ripon Coll Cuddesdon 95. **d** 97. C Wisbech St Aug *Ely* from 97. *19 Waterlees Road, Wisbech, Cambs PE13 3HE*

MASON, Dennis Wardell. b 28. Ox NSM Course 83. **d** 86 **p** 87. NSM Ox St Barn and St Paul *Ox* from 86. *26 John Lopes Road, Eynsham, Witney, Oxon OX8 1JR* Tel (01865) 880440

MASON, Mrs Elizabeth Ann. b 42. Cam Inst of Educn TCert64 Open Univ BA90. Ox Min Course CBTS94. **d** 94 **p** 95. NSM Worminghall w Ickford, Oakley and Shabbington *Ox* from 94. *20 Clifden Road, Wormingham, Aylesbury, Bucks HP18 9JP* Tel (01844) 339640

MASON, Ernest Walter. b 20. S'wark Ord Course 74. **d** 77 **p** 78. NSM Clapham H Spirit *S'wark* 77-87; NSM Clapham TM 87-88; rtd 88; Perm to Offic *S'wark* from 88. *35 Klea Avenue, London SW4 9HG* Tel 0181-673 5575

MASON, Francis Robert Anthony. b 56. Trin Coll Bris BA90. **d** 90 **p** 91. C Denham *Ox* 90-94; P-in-c Jersey Grouville *Win* from 94. *The Rectory, Grouville, Jersey, Channel Islands JE3 9DA* Tel (01534) 853073

MASON, Frederic. b 13. SS Coll Cam MA38 Malaya Univ LLD60. St Aug Coll Cant 60. **d** 61 **p** 62. Prin Ch Ch Coll Cant 61-75; Hon C Hackington *Cant* 61-67; Lic to Offic 67-75; Perm to Offic *Ex* 75-88; Perm to Offic *Sarum* from 88. *Downsview House, 63 St Mark's Avenue, Salisbury SP1 3DD* Tel (01722) 325165

MASON, Frederick Michael Stewart. b 15. Kelham Th Coll 32. **d** 39 **p** 40. C Swindon New Town *Bris* 39-49; C Ox St Paul *Ox* 49-51; C Heref All SS *Heref* 51-56; Min Cov St Fran N Radford CD *Cov* 56-59; V Cov St Fran N Radford 59-86; rtd 86; Perm to Offic *Glouc* from 86. *Brinsworth, 2 Mercia Road, Winchcombe, Cheltenham, Glos GL54 5QD* Tel (01242) 602709

MASON, Geoffrey Charles. b 48. K Coll Lon BD74 AKC74. St Aug Coll Cant 74. **d** 75 **p** 76. C Hatcham Park All SS *S'wark* 75-78; V Bellingham St Dunstan 78-87; RD E Lewisham 82-87; C Catford (Southend) and Downham 87-88; Bp's Adv for Min

Development from 88. *32 King's Orchard, London SE9 5TJ* Tel 0181-859 7614 or 0171-378 7506 Fax 0171-403 6497

MASON, John Evans. b 32. RD. Linc Th Coll 57. **d** 59 **p** 60. C Putney St Mary *S'wark* 59-62; C Berry Pomeroy *Ex* 62-64; Chapl RN 64-68; V Hopton *Nor* 68-72; Chapl RNR 69-82; P-in-c Roydon St Remigius *Nor* 72-76; R Diss 72-80; Dir YMCA Cam 80-85; Prin YMCA Dunford Coll 85-88; Perm to Offic *Glouc* from 88; Perm to Offic *Ox* from 89; rtd 96. *Westerley Cottage, Burford Street, Lechlade, Glos GL7 3AP* Tel (01367) 252642

MASON, John Martin. b 41. UMIST BSc63. Glouc Sch of Min 80 Qu Coll Birm 82. **d** 84 **p** 85. C Tuffley *Glouc* 84-87; P-in-c Willersey, Saintbury, Weston-sub-Edge etc 87-92; R 92-96; P-in-c Selling w Throwley, Sheldwich w Badlesmere etc *Cant* from 96; Dioc Rural Officer from 96. *The Rectory, Vicarage Lane, Selling, Faversham, Kent ME13 9RD* Tel (01227) 752221

MASON, Jonathan Patrick. b 55. Edin Th Coll 90. **d** 92 **p** 93. C Edin Ch Ch *Edin* 92-94; C Edin Old St Paul 94-96; R St Andrews All SS *St And* from 96. *All Saints' Rectory, North Street, St Andrews, Fife KY16 9AQ* Tel (01334) 473193

MASON, Ms Josephine Margaret. b 41. Edin Univ BMus64. WMMTC 88. **d** 93 **p** 94. Chapl Asst Highcroft and Northcroft Hosps *Birm* from 91; C Birm St Jo Ladywood from 93. *340 Selly Oak Road, Birmingham B30 1HP* Tel 0121-451 1412

MASON, Julia Ann. b 43. St Jo Coll Nottm 89. **d** 91 **p** 95. NSM Troon *Glas* 91-93; NSM Ayr from 93; NSM Maybole from 93; NSM Girvan from 93. *2 Balcomie Crescent, Troon, Ayrshire KA10 7AR* Tel (01292) 311707

MASON, Canon Kenneth Staveley. b 31. ARCS53 Lon Univ BSc53 BD64. Wells Th Coll 56. **d** 58 **p** 59. C Kingston upon Hull St Martin *York* 58-61; C Pocklington w Yapham-cum-Meltonby, Owsthorpe etc 61-63; C Millington w Gt Givendale 61-63; V Thornton w Allerthorpe 63-69; Sub-Warden St Aug Coll Cant 69-76; Abp's Adv in Past Min 76-77; Dir Cant Sch of Min 77-81; Sec to Dioc Bd of Min *Cant* 77-87; Six Preacher Cant Cathl 79-84; Prin Cant Sch of Min 81-89; Hon Can Cant Cathl 84-89; Prin Edin Th Coll 89-95; Can St Mary's Cathl *Edin* 89-96; rtd 95; Perm to Offic *Ripon* from 96. *2 Williamson Close, Ripon, N Yorkshire HG4 1AZ* Tel (01765) 607041

MASON, Nigel Frederick. b 60. Wycliffe Hall Ox DipMin95. **d** 95 **p** 96. C Highbury Ch Ch w St Jo and St Sav Lon from 95. *7 Lyndon Court, Kelvin Road, London N5 2PP* Tel 0171-359 1799

MASON, Nigel James. b 56. Culham Coll of Educn BEd78 DipLaw84. St Steph Ho Ox 95. **d** 97. C Hove *Chich* from 97. *Church House Flat, Wilbury Road, Hove, E Sussex BN3 3PB* Tel (01273) 736643

MASON, Paul. b 51. Cranmer Hall Dur CTMin93. **d** 93 **p** 94. C Handforth *Ches* 93-97; V Partington and Carrington from 97. *St Mary's Vicarage, Manchester Road, Partington, Manchester M31 4FB* Tel 0161-775 3542 Fax as telephone

MASON, Peter Charles. b 45. K Coll Lon BD72 AKC72 Birm Univ PGCE89. St Aug Coll Cant 72. **d** 73 **p** 74. C Ilkeston St Mary *Derby* 73-76; C Bridgnorth St Mary *Heref* 76-78; TV Bridgnorth, Tasley, Astley Abbotts, Oldbury etc 78-88; RE Teacher from 89; Perm to Offic from 89. *4 Woodberry Close, Bridgnorth, Shropshire WV16 4PT*

MASON, Canon Peter Joseph. b 34. Lon Univ BA58. Coll of Resurr Mirfield 58. **d** 60 **p** 61. C Belhus Park CD *Chelmsf* 60-63; Lic to Offic *Eur* 63-64; Asst Chapl Lon Univ *Lon* 64-70; Chapl City Univ 66-70; R Stoke Newington St Mary 70-78; V Writtle *Chelmsf* 78-81; P-in-c Highwood 78-81; V Writtle w Highwood 81-86; R Shenfield 86-93; Hon Can Chelmsf Cathl from 89; P-in-c Maldon All SS w St Pet 93-95; V from 95; RD Maldon and Dengie from 95. *All Saints' Vicarage, Church Walk, Maldon, Essex CM9 7PY* Tel (01621) 854179

MASON, The Ven Richard John. b 29. Linc Th Coll 55. **d** 58 **p** 59. C Hatfield *St Alb* 58-64; Bp's Chapl *Lon* 64-69; V Riverhead *Roch* 69-73; P-in-c Dunton Green 69-73; V Edenbridge 73-83; Hon Can Roch Cathl 77-95; Adn Tonbridge 77-95; P-in-c Crockham Hill H Trin 81-83; C-in-c Sevenoaks St Luke CD 83-95; rtd 95. *61 Nelson Road, Ipswich IP4 4DU* Tel (01473) 726350

MASON, Robert Herbert George (Bob). b 48. Oak Hill Th Coll 82. **d** 84 **p** 85. C Ware Ch Ch *St Alb* 84-88; V Eastbourne All So *Chich* from 88. *The Vicarage, 53 Susan's Road, Eastbourne, E Sussex BN21 3TH* Tel (01323) 731366

MASON, Roger Arthur. b 41. Lon Univ BSc65 K Coll Lon BD68 AKC68. **d** 69 **p** 70. C Enfield St Andr *Lon* 69-72; P-in-c Westbury *Heref* 72-78; P-in-c Yockleton 72-78; P-in-c Gt Wollaston 77-78; V Willesden St Mary *Lon* 78-88; V Prittlewell *Chelmsf* from 88; P-in-c Prittlewell St Steph from 92. *Prittlewell Vicarage, 489 Victoria Avenue, Southend-on-Sea SS2 6NL* Tel (01702) 343470

MASON, Simon Duncan. b 61. Strathclyde Univ BA83 St Jo Coll Dur PhD89 Nottm Univ BTh92. Linc Th Coll 89. **d** 92 **p** 93. C Grays Thurrock *Chelmsf* 92-96; TV Plaistow and N Canning Town from 96. *45 Mafeking Road, London E16 4NS* Tel 0171-511 7848

MASON, Stephen David. b 65. Univ of Wales (Lamp) BA87. Ripon Coll Cuddesdon 89. **d** 92 **p** 93. C Gt Grimsby St Mary and St Jas *Linc* 92-97; V Southborough St Thos *Roch* from 97. *The Vicarage, 28 Pennington Road, Southborough, Tunbridge Wells, Kent TN4 0SL* Tel (01892) 529624

MASON, Terry Mathew. b 56. Trin Coll Bris 94. **d** 96 **p** 97. C Bexleyheath Ch Ch *Roch* from 96. *50 Martin Dene, Bexleyheath, Kent DA6 8NA* Tel 0181-298 1355

MASON, Thomas Edward. b 52. Bris Univ MEd80. Trin Coll Bris BA91. **d** 91 **p** 92. C Glouc St Jas and All SS *Glouc* 91-94; V Churchdown from 94. *The Vicarage, 5 Vicarage Close, Churchdown, Gloucester GL3 2NE* Tel (01452) 713203

MASON, Thomas Henry Ambrose. b 51. BA86. **d** 86 **p** 87. C W Drayton *Lon* 86-89; Field Officer Oak Hill Ext Coll 89-94; Eur Sec Intercon Ch Soc 94-95; Dir of Tr *Eur* from 95. *72 Byne Road, London SE26 5JD, or 14 Tufton Street, London SW1P 3QZ* Tel 0181-659 3249 or 0171-976 8001 Fax 0171-976 8002

MASON, William Frederick. b 48. Linc Th Coll 75. **d** 78 **p** 79. C Ipswich St Aug *St E* 78-81; TV Dronfield *Derby* 81-88; V Ellesmere St Pet *Sheff* 88-91; V Bedgrove *Ox* from 91. *The Vicarage, 252 Wendover Road, Aylesbury, Bucks HP21 9PD* Tel (01296) 22214

MASSEY, George Douglas. b 44. St Jo Coll Nottm DCM93. **d** 93 **p** 94. C Higher Bebington *Ches* from 93. *Christ Church House, 3 Beech Road, Bebington, Wirral, Merseyside L63 8PE* Tel 0151-645 9074

MASSEY, Keith John. b 46. Oak Hill Th Coll 69. **d** 72 **p** 73. C Bermondsey St Jas w Ch Ch *S'wark* 72-76; C Benchill *Man* 76-82; V Clifton Green 82-97; V Flixton St Jo from 97. *St John's Vicarage, Irlam Road, Flixton, Manchester M41 6AP* Tel 0161-748 6754

MASSEY, Nigel John. b 60. Birm Univ BA81 MA82. Wycliffe Hall Ox. **d** 87 **p** 88. C Bearwood *Birm* 87-90; C Warley Woods 90; C Tottenham St Paul *Lon* 91-94; USA from 94. *French Church Du St Spirit, 111 East 60th Street, New York 10022, USA* Tel Bronx (212) 838-5680

MASSEY, Paul Daniel Shaw. b 70. Nottm Univ BA93. Westcott Ho Cam 94. **d** 96 **p** 97. C Ashby-de-la-Zouch St Helen w Coleorton *Leic* from 96. *38 Avenue Road, Ashby-de-la-Zouch, Leics LE6 5FE* Tel (01530) 411721 Fax as telephone

MASSEY, Preb William Cyril. b 32. Lich Th Coll 58. **d** 61 **p** 62. C Heref St Martin *Heref* 61-66; V Kimbolton w Middleton-on-the-Hill 66-75; V Alveley 75-83; P-in-c Quatt 81-83; R Alveley and Quatt 84-85; R Llangarron w Llangrove, Whitchurch and Ganarew 85-97; Preb Heref Cathl 92-97; rtd 97. *Hollybush Cottage, Pencombe, Bromyard, Herefordshire HR7 4RW* Tel (01885) 400713

MASSHEDAR, John Frederick. b 50. Dur Univ BEd74. Linc Th Coll 76. **d** 78 **p** 79. C Pocklington w Yapham-cum-Meltonby, Owsthorpe etc *York* 78-81; C Middlesbrough Ascension 81-82; V 82-85; V Eskdaleside w Ugglebarnby and Sneaton 85-87; V Shotton *Dur* from 87. *The Vicarage, Shotton Colliery, Durham DH6 2JW* Tel 0191-526 1156

MASSHEDAR, Richard Eric. b 57. Nottm Univ BTh86. Linc Th Coll 83. **d** 86 **p** 87. C Cassop cum Quarrington *Dur* 86-89; C Ferryhill 89-91; V Leam Lane 91-94; P-in-c Hartlepool St Paul 94-96; V from 96. *St Paul's Vicarage, 6 Hutton Avenue, Hartlepool, Cleveland TS26 9PN* Tel (01429) 272934

MASSINGBERD-MUNDY, John. b 07. Pemb Coll Cam BA30 MA46. Cuddesdon Coll 31. **d** 32 **p** 33. C Dagenham St Martin *Chelmsf* 32-34; C Sheff St Cuth *Sheff* 34-37; C Linthorpe *York* 37-40; V Sewerby cum Marton and Grindale 40-43; V Market Weighton 43-50; R Goodmanham 46-50; P-in-c Bedale *Ripon* 50-59; R 59-65; V Limber Magna w Brocklesby *Linc* 65-72; V Kirmington 65-72; rtd 72. *79 Wolverton Road, Newport Pagnell, Bucks MK16 8BH* Tel (01908) 617242

MASSINGBERD-MUNDY, Roger William Burrell. b 36. TD. Univ of Wales (Lamp) BA59. Ridley Hall Cam 59. **d** 61 **p** 62. C Benwell St Jas *Newc* 61-64; CF (TA) 63-68; CF (TAVR) 71-83; C Whorlton *Newc* 64-72; TV 73; P-in-c Healey 73-85; Dioc Stewardship Adv 73-85; Hon Can Newc Cathl 82-85; R S Ormsby w Ketsby, Calceby and Driby *Linc* 85-86; P-in-c Harrington w Brinkhill 85-86; P-in-c Haugh 85-86; P-in-c Oxcombe 85-86; P-in-c Ruckland w Farforth and Maidenwell 85-86; P-in-c Somersby w Bag Enderby 85-86; P-in-c Tetford and Salmonby 85-86; R S Ormsby Gp 86-96; RD Bolingbroke 88-96; rtd 96. *Bates Hill, Ninebanks, Hexham, Northd NE47 8DB*

MASSON, Philip Roy. b 52. Hertf Coll Ox BA75 Leeds Univ BA77. Coll of Resurr Mirfield 75. **d** 78 **p** 79. C Port Talbot St Theodore *Llan* 78-82; V Penyfai w Tondu 82-92; Dioc Dir Post-Ord Tr 85-88; Warden of Ords from 88; R Newton Nottage from 92. *The Rectory, 64 Victoria Avenue, Porthcawl CF36 3HE* Tel (01656) 782042

MASTERMAN, Malcolm. b 49. K Coll Lon 73. Chich Th Coll 76. **d** 77 **p** 78. C Peterlee *Dur* 77-80; Chapl Basingstoke Distr Hosp 80-85; Chapl Freeman Hosp Newc 85-95; Tr and Development Officer Hosp Chapl Council from 96; Perm to Offic *Newc* from 96; Perm to Offic *Dur* from 96. *Hospital Chaplaincies Council, Fielden House, Little College Street, London SW1P 3SH* Tel 0171-222 5090 Fax 222 5156

MASTERMAN, Miss Patricia Hope (Pat). b 28. St Mich Ho Ox 59. **dss** 79 **d** 87. Asst CF 79-90; rtd 90; Perm to Offic *Chich* from 90. *33 Sea Lane Gardens, Ferring, Worthing, W Sussex BM12 5EQ* Tel (01903) 245231

✠MASTERS, The Rt Revd Brian John. b 32. Qu Coll Cam BA55 MA59. Cuddesdon Coll 62. d 64 p 65 c 82. C Stepney St Dunstan and All SS *Lon* 64-69; V Hoxton H Trin w St Mary 69-82; P-in-c Hoxton St Anne w St Sav and St Andr 69-75; P-in-c Hoxton St Anne w St Columba 75-80; Suff Bp Fulham 82-84; Area Bp Edmonton from 85. *1 Regent's Park Terrace, London NW1 7EE* Tel 0171-267 4455 Fax 267 4404

MASTERS, Kenneth Leslie (Ken). b 44. Leeds Univ BA68. Cuddesdon Coll 68. **d** 70 **p** 71. C Wednesbury St Paul Wood Green *Lich* 70-71; C Tettenhall Regis 71-75; TV Chelmsley Wood *Birm* 75-79; R Harting *Chich* 79-87; V Rustington from 87. *The Vicarage, Claigmar Road, Rustington, Littlehampton, W Sussex BN16 2NL* Tel (01903) 784749

MASTERS, Leslie. b 31. Ripon Hall Ox 73. **d** 75 **p** 76. C Hanham *Bris* 75-78; TV Bris St Agnes and St Simon w St Werburgh 78-84; Asst Chapl HM Pris Man 84; Chapl HM Pris Northeye 84-88; Chapl HM Pris Littlehey 88-94; rtd 94; NSM St Goran w St Mich Caerhays *Truro* from 94. *The Vicarage, Gorran, St Austell, Cornwall PL26 6HN* Tel (01726) 842229

MASTERS, Canon Raymond Austin. b 26. Kelham Th Coll 45. **d** 52 **p** 53. SSM from 51; S Africa 52-65; Can Bloemfontein Cathl 58-65; Perm to Offic *Blackb* 66-68; Chapl St Martin's Coll of Educn Lanc 68-70; Asst Sec Gen Syn Bd for Miss and Unity 71-77; Hon C Harrow St Pet *Lon* 72-77; TV Cen Ex 78-82; Dioc Miss and Ecum Officer 78-82; Warden Windsor Convent 79-95; Can Res Heref Cathl *Heref* 82-93; Treas 85-93; Bp's Co-ord for Min 82-93; rtd 95. *2 Whitehall, South Petherton, Somerset TA13 5AQ* Tel (01460) 242272

MASTERS, Stephen Michael. b 52. St Chad's Coll Dur BA75. Coll of Resurr Mirfield 85. **d** 87 **p** 88. C Primrose Hill St Mary w Avenue Road St Paul *Lon* 87-90; C Hornsey St Mary w St Geo 90-91; Bp's Dom Chapl *Chich* 91-96; V Brighton St Mich from 96. *St Michael's Clergy House, 6 Montpelier Villas, Brighton BN1 3DH* Tel (01273) 727362

MASTERTON, Paul Robert. b 35. Clifton Th Coll 63. **d** 66 **p** 67. C Selly Hill St Steph *Birm* 66-68; C Sutton Coldfield H Trin 68-72; C Aldridge *Lich* 72-74; C Gt Crosby St Luke *Liv* 74-76; P-in-c Manuden w Berden *Chelmsf* 76-86; R Helpringham w Hale *Linc* 86-97; rtd 97. *65 Pilleys Lane, Boston, Lincs PE21 9RA* Tel (01205) 354753

MASTIN, Brian Arthur. b 38. Peterho Cam BA60 MA63 BD80 Mert Coll Ox MA63. Ripon Hall Ox 62. **d** 63 **p** 64. Asst Lect Hebrew Univ Coll of N Wales (Ban) 63-65; Lect Hebrew 65-82; Sen Lect from 82; Chapl Ban Cathl *Ban* 63-65; Lic to Offic from 65. *Department of Religious Studies, University College, Bangor LL57 2DG* Tel (01248) 351151

MATCHETT, Edward James Boyd. b 19. TCD BA43 MA60. **d** 43 **p** 44. C Belfast St Mary *Conn* 43-45; Miss to Seamen from 45; Iraq 47-50; New Zealand 64-69; Regional Dir Miss to Seamen (E Region) 69-74; Hong Kong 74-83; Chapl Cornish Ports 83-86; Perm to Offic *Nor* from 86. *10 Southern Reach, Mulbarton, Norwich NR14 8BU* Tel (01508) 70337

MATHER, Bernard Herbert. b 26. Univ Coll Dur BA51. Sarum Th Coll 53. **d** 55 **p** 56. C Wallsend St Luke *Newc* 55-60; USPG 60-94; India 60-94; rtd 94. *9 Lindisfarne Road, Shipley, W Yorkshire BD18 4RD* Tel (01274) 583693

MATHER, Cuthbert. b 15. Tyndale Hall Bris 36. **d** 40 **p** 41. C Bebington *Ches* 40-42; C Stapenhill w Cauldwell *Derby* 43-51; C Cambridge St Andr Less *Ely* 51-52; C Dagenham *Chelmsf* 53-57; V Needham w Rushall *Nor* 57-80; rtd 80; Perm to Offic *Nor* from 80. *2 Church Close, Hunstanton, Norfolk PE36 6BE* Tel (01485) 533084

MATHER, David Jonathan. b 65. New Coll Ox BA88 MA95. St Steph Ho Ox BTh95. **d** 95 **p** 96. C Pickering w Lockton and Levisham *York* from 95. *74 Eastgate, Pickering, N Yorkshire YO18 7DY* Tel (01751) 475472

MATHER, Mrs Elizabeth Ann (Libby). b 45. Dalton Ho Bris IDC70 St Jo Coll Nottm 92. **d** 94 **p** 95. NSM Littleover *Derby* from 94. *The Vicarage, 35 Church Street, Littleover, Derby DE23 6GF* Tel (01332) 767802

MATHER, James Malcolm. b 31. Trin Coll Cam BA54 MA59. Cuddesdon Coll 54. **d** 56 **p** 57. C S Bank *York* 56-60; C Sutton St Mich 60-61; C Hanwell St Thos *Lon* 61-63; V Ilkeston H Trin *Derby* 63-72; P-in-c Upper Langwith 73-77; R 77-80; P-in-c Whaley Thorns 77-80; R Upper Langwith w Langwith Bassett etc 80; P-in-c Watlington *Ox* 80-81; V Watlington w Pyrton and Shirburn 81-86; R Harome w Stonegrave, Nunnington and Pockley *York* 86-96; rtd 96; P-in-c Penponds *Truro* from 96. *The Vicarage, Mill Road, Penponds, Camborne, Cornwall TR14 0QH* Tel (01209) 712329

MATHER, James William. b 63. Sheff Univ BA86. St Steph Ho Ox 88. **d** 91 **p** 92. C Doncaster St Leon and St Jude *Sheff* 91-94; C Cantley 94-95; V Lakenheath *St E* from 95. *The Vicarage, Lakenheath, Brandon, Suffolk IP27 9EW* Tel (01842) 860683

MATHER, Stephen Albert. b 54. Qu Coll Birm 85. **d** 87 **p** 88. C Sutton *Liv* 87-90; TV 90-96; V Abram from 96; V Bickershaw from 96. *The Vicarage, 9 Lee Lane, Abram, Wigan, Lancs WN2 5QU* Tel (01942) 866396

MATHER, William Bernard George. b 45. St Jo Coll Nottm 77. **d** 79 **p** 80. C St Leonards St Leon *Chich* 79-82; TR Netherthorpe *Sheff* 82-90; V Littleover *Derby* from 90. *The Vicarage, 35 Church Street, Littleover, Derby DE23 6GF* Tel (01332) 767802

MATHERS, Alan Edward. b 36. FPhS Lon Univ BA. Oak Hill Th Coll 61. **d** 64 **p** 65. C Ox St Matt *Ox* 64-66; C Bootle St Leon *Liv* 66-68; C Hampreston *Sarum* 68-70; P-in-c Damerham 70-71; V Queniborough *Leic* 71-76; USA 76-77; P-in-c Tipton St Paul *Lich* 77-84; V 85-86; V Tipton St Matt 77-86; V Sutton Ch Ch *S'wark* 86-95; Chapl Cannes *Eur* from 95. *Residence Kent, 4 rue du General Ferrie, 06400 Cannes, France* Tel France (33) 93 94 54 61

MATHERS, David Michael Brownlow. b 43. Em Coll Cam BA65 MA69. Clifton Th Coll 65. **d** 67 **p** 68. C Branksome St Clem *Sarum* 67-70; C Bromley Ch Ch *Roch* 70-73; V Bures *St E* 73-80; Brazil 80-82; P-in-c Old Newton w Stowupland *St E* 82-86; V 87-90; V Thurston from 90; RD Ixworth from 94. *Thurston Vicarage, Bury St Edmunds, Suffolk IP31 3RU* Tel (01359) 30301

MATHERS, Derek. b 48. N Ord Course 82. **d** 85 **p** 86. C Huddersfield St Jo *Wakef* 85-86; C N Huddersfield 86-88; TV Almondbury w Farnley Tyas 88-92; V Marsden from 92. *The Vicarage, 20A Station Road, Marsden, Huddersfield HD7 6DG* Tel (01484) 847864

MATHERS, Kenneth Ernest William. b 56. Portsm Coll of Tech TDip82 HND84. Trin Coll Bris DipHE95. **d** 95 **p** 96. C Bournemouth St Jo w St Mich *Win* from 95. *7 Bournewood Drive, Bounemouth BH4 9JP* Tel (01202) 760412

MATHERS (née STEWART), Mrs Kim Deborah. b 61. Southn Univ LLB82. ASCAT DipApTh86 Trin Coll Bris DipHE88 ADPS89. **d** 89 **p** 94. Par Dn Bitterne *Win* 89-93; Hon C Stoke Bishop *Bris* 93-95; Hon C Bournemouth St Jo w St Mich *Win* from 95. *7 Bournewood Drive, Bournemouth BH4 9JP* Tel (01202) 760412

MATHESON, Alexander. **d** 97. NSM Cowplain *Portsm* from 97. *11 Kitwood Green, Havant, Hants PO9 5QN* Tel (01705) 471987

MATHESON, David Melville. b 23. McGill Univ Montreal BA55 BD61. Linc Th Coll 77. **d** 77 **p** 78. Chapl Blue Coat Sch Reading 77-85; Hon C Verwood *Sarum* 85-88; C Stratfield Mortimer *Ox* 88-92; Perm to Offic 93-94. *7 Highfield Court, Reading Road, Reading RG7 3YP* Tel 0118-983 4039

MATHESON, Canon Ronald Stuart. b 29. Lon Univ BA50. Ely Th Coll 52. **d** 54 **p** 55. C Byker St Ant *Newc* 54-57; C Hedworth *Dur* 57-59; V S Hylton 59-65; P-in-c Glenrothes *St And* 65-69; R 69-73; R Dundee St Marg *Bre* 73-78; Belize 79-80; Chapl Sliema *Eur* 81-82 and 94-97; Chapl Costa del Sol E 82-94; Hon Can Gib Cathl 90-97; rtd 94. *c/o Bohn, 1013 Buchanan Street, Fairfield, CA 94533 4656, USA*

MATHEWS, Richard Twitchell. b 27. Bps' Coll Cheshunt 57. **d** 59 **p** 60. C Leic St Phil *Leic* 59-62; Chapl Beirut 62-63; Qatar 63-67; V Riddlesden *Bradf* 67-74; Australia 74-78; P-in-c Medbourne cum Holt w Stockerston and Blaston *Leic* 78-82; Chapl Alassio *Eur* 82-83; Chapl San Remo 82-83; Chapl Palma and Balearic Is w Ibiza etc 83-87; P-in-c Witchford w Wentworth *Ely* 87-91; rtd 91. *Rosecroft, Church Lane, Ringwould, Deal, Kent CT14 8HR* Tel (01304) 367554

MATHEWS, Ronald Peel Beresford. b 24. TCD DBS DipYL. **d** 64 **p** 65. C Waterford w Killea, Drumcannon and Dunhill *C & O* 64-66; I Clonbroney w Killoe *K, E & A* 66-71; I Drumgoon and Ashfield 71-74; Dep Sec Leprosy Miss 74-84; I Kinneigh Union *C, C & R* 84-93; rtd 93. *19 Kingston College, Mitchelstown, Co Cork, Irish Republic* Tel Cork (25) 84779

MATHEWS, Trevor John. b 50. HonLMStJ83. Golds Coll Lon MSc98 CACP95 UEA PPAC94. St Steph Ho Ox 87. **d** 89 **p** 90. C Cheltenham St Steph *Glouc* 89-91; C Up Hatherley 89-91. *Community Drug Team, Baddow Road, Chelmsford CM2 9QU* Tel (01245) 351441

MATHIAS, John Maelgwyn. b 15. St D Coll Lamp BA38 St Mich Coll Llan 40. **d** 40 **p** 41. C Ban St Mary *Ban* 40-44; C Swansea St Pet *S & B* 44-49; V Mydroilyn w Dihewyd *St D* 49-54; R Cellan w Llanfair Clydogau 54-83; Lect St Jo Ch Coll Ystrad Meurig 67-77; rtd 83. *Bronallt, Capel Seion Road, Drefach, Llanelli SA14 4BN*

MATHIAS, Ms Lesley. b 49. Portsm Poly BA72 Nottm Univ MTh90. EMMTC 93. **d** 96 **p** 97. C Oadby *Leic* from 96. *62 Fairstone Hill, Oadby, Leicester LE2 5RJ* Tel 0116-271 6474

MATHIAS-JONES, Edward Lloyd. b 71. Univ of Wales (Lamp) BA93. St Mich Coll Llan BD94. **d** 97. C Llanelli *St D* from 97. *44 Coldstream Street, Llanelli SA15 3BH* Tel (01554) 752056

MATHIE, Patricia Jean (Mother Donella). b 22. Worc Coll of Educn CertEd49. CertRK74. **dss** 79 **d** 87. CSA 74-92; Asst Superior 82-94; Mother Superior from 94; Notting Hill St Jo *Lon* 79-80; Abbey Ho Malmesbury 81-82; Notting Hill St Clem and St Mark 82-84; Kensal Town St Thos w St Andr and St Phil 85-87; Hon C from 87; rtd 96. *St Andrew's House, 2 Tavistock Road, London W11 1BA* Tel 0171-229 2662

MATON, Oswald. b 24. St Aug Coll Cant 75. **d** 77 **p** 78. Hon C Chatham St Steph *Roch* from 77. *304 Maidstone Road, Chatham, Kent ME4 6JJ* Tel (01634) 843568

MATTEN, Derek Norman William. b 30. Man Univ BA51. Wycliffe Hall Ox 54. **d** 56 **p** 57. C Farnworth *Liv* 56-59; C Walton H Trin *Ox* 59-62; Uganda 62-69; W Germany 69-90; Germany 90-93; Lic to Offic *Eur* 69-93; Perm to Offic *Ex* 90-93;

rtd 93. *The Church House, Ringmore, Kingsbridge, Devon TQ7 4HR* Tel (01548) 810565

MATTHEW, Canon Andrew Foster. b 45. Oak Hill Th Coll 68. **d** 70 **p** 71. C St Alb St Paul *St Alb* 70-74; C Harwell *Ox* 74-76; C Chilton All SS 74-76; C Harwell w Chilton 76-77; V St Keverne *Truro* 77-84; RD Kerrier 81-84; V St Austell from 84; Hon Can Truro Cathl from 89. *The Vicarage, 1 Carnsmerry Crescent, St Austell, Cornwall PL25 4NA* Tel (01726) 73839

MATTHEWS, Adrian. d 96. NSM Tonge w Alkrington *Man* from 96. *102 Andover Avenue, Alkrington, Middleton, Manchester M24 1JW*

MATTHEWS, Anita Kathryn. b 70. Dur Univ BTh91. Ripon Coll Cuddesdon DipMin93. **d** 97. C E Barnet *St Alb* from 97. *31 Church Hill Road, East Barnet, Herts EN4 8SY* Tel 0181-441 2698

MATTHEWS, Barry Alan. b 46. AKC68. St Boniface Warminster St Paul's Grahamstown. **d** 69 **p** 70. S Africa 69-74 and 77-83; C Leeds St Aid *Ripon* 74-77; C Shotton *St As* 83-84; Zimbabwe from 84. *St Margaret's Rectory, 2 Greenfield Square, North End, Bulawayo, Zimbabwe*

MATTHEWS, Brian. b 32. ARIC55. Cranmer Hall Dur 59. **d** 62 **p** 63. C Belgrave St Pet *Leic* 62-65; C Whitwick St Jo the Bapt 65-69; C Kirby Muxloe 69-71; P-in-c Bardon Hill 71-78; V Thringstone St Andr from 78. *The Vicarage, 49 Loughborough Road, Thringstone, Coalville, Leics LE67 8LQ* Tel (01530) 222380

MATTHEWS, Canon Campbell Thurlow. b 33. Lon Univ BA56 Dur Univ DipEd57. St Jo Coll Nottm 70. **d** 71 **p** 72. C Ryton *Dur* 71-74; Chapl R Victoria Infirmary Newc 74-82; V Greenside *Dur* 74-82; R Wetheral w Warw *Carl* 82-93; RD Brampton 83-91; P-in-c Farlam and Nether Denton 87-93; P-in-c Gilsland 87-93; Hon Can Carl Cathl from 87; P-in-c Thornthwaite cum Braithwaite and Newlands from 93. *Thornthwaite Vicarage, Braithwaite, Keswick, Cumbria CA12 5RY* Tel (01768) 78243 Fax (01228) 48769

MATTHEWS, Celia Inger. b 30. St Chris Coll Blackheath 50. **d** 86 **p** 94. Dioc Missr *St And* from 86. *24 Barossa Place, Perth PH1 5HH* Tel (01738) 623578

MATTHEWS, Preb Clarence Sydney. b 11. Lon Univ BA30 AKC32 BD38. **d** 34 **p** 35. C Stamford Hill St Ann *Lon* 34-38; C Barnes St Mary *S'wark* 38-40; V Fulham St Oswald w St Aug *Lon* 40-54; V Ealing St Steph Castle Hill 54-81; RD Ealing E 68-79; rtd 81; Perm to Offic *Cant* 81-92; Perm to Offic *Lon* 84-93; Perm to Offic *Ox* from 93. *8 Swanbrook Court, Bridge Avenue, Maidenhead, Berks SL6 1YZ* Tel (01628) 789287

MATTHEWS, Colin John. b 44. Jes Coll Ox BA67 MA71 Fitzw Coll Cam BA70 MA74. Ridley Hall Cam 68. **d** 71 **p** 72. C Onslow Square St Paul *Lon* 71-74; C Leic H Apostles *Leic* 74-78; Bible Use Sec Scripture Union 78-89; Dir St Sav Ch Cen Guildf 89-95; V Burpham *Guildf* from 95. *The Vicarage, 5 Orchard Road, Burpham, Guildford, Surrey GU4 7JH* Tel (01483) 300858

MATTHEWS, David Charles. b 61. TCD BA84 HDipEd86 MA87 Lille Univ LesL85 TCD BTh95. CITC. **d** 95 **p** 96. C Arm St Mark w Aghavilly *Arm* 95-97; Hon V Choral Arm Cathl 96-97; Chapl St Woolos Cathl *Mon* from 97. *Hebron, 9 Clifton Road, Newport NP9 4EW* Tel (01633) 267191

MATTHEWS, Mrs Diana Elizabeth Charlotte. b 43. MCSP65. LNSM course 92. **d** 93 **p** 96. NSM Merrow *Guildf* from 93. *Ravenswood, 22 Tangier Road, Guildford, Surrey GU1 2DF* Tel (01483) 839738

MATTHEWS, Mrs Francilla Lacey (Cilla). b 37. S'wark Ord Course 83. **dss** 86 **d** 87 **p** 94. Bromley St Mark *Roch* 86-87; Hon Par Dn 87-90; Par Dn Hayes 90-94; C from 94. *71 Hayes Road, Bromley BR2 9AE* Tel 0181-464 4083

MATTHEWS, Frederick Peter. b 45. Grey Coll Dur BA66 MA68 K Coll Lon PGCE68 Lon Univ BSc(Econ)75. Sarum & Wells Th Coll 70. **d** 72 **p** 73. C W Wickham St Jo *Cant* 72-74; C Sholing *Win* 74-77; Lic to Offic 78-79; V Woolston from 79. *St Mark's Vicarage, 117 Swift Road, Southampton SO19 9ER* Tel (01703) 326908

MATTHEWS, George Charles Wallace. b 27. Sarum Th Coll 58. **d** 60 **p** 61. C Coppenhall St Paul *Ches* 60-63; C Lewes St Anne *Chich* 63-67; V Wheelock *Ches* 67-76; V Mossley 76-93; rtd 93; Perm to Offic *Ches* from 93. *20 Leyland Grove, Haslington, Crewe CW1 1ZE* Tel (01270) 587463

MATTHEWS, Gerald Lancelot. b 31. Bris Univ LLB50. Ripon Hall Ox 55. **d** 57 **p** 58. C The Quinton *Birm* 57-60; C Olton 60-63; V Brent Tor *Ex* 63-72; P-in-c Lydford w Bridestowe and Sourton 70-72; TR Lydford, Brent Tor, Bridestowe and Sourton 72-78; P-in-c Black Torrington, Bradf w Cookbury etc 78-90; Perm to Offic from 90; rtd 94. *The Larches, Black Torrington, Beaworthy, Devon EX21 5PU* Tel (01409) 231228

MATTHEWS, Gilbert Brian Reeves. b 19. Keble Coll Ox BA42 MA48. St Steph Ho Ox 41. **d** 44 **p** 45. C Brighton St Wilfrid *Chich* 44-49; C St Leonards Ch Ch 49-55; C Finedon *Pet* 55-58; Youth Chapl 58-64; R Rushton and Glendon 58-79; P-in-c Thorpe Malsor 76-79; R Rushton and Glendon w Thorpe Malsor 79-81; C Spondon *Derby* 81-87; rtd 87; Perm to Offic *B & W* from 87. *Christchurch Parsonage, Redhill, Bristol BS18 7SL*

MATTHEWS, Harold James. b 46. Leeds Univ BSc68 Fitzw Coll Cam BA70 MA74. Westcott Ho Cam 68. **d** 71 **p** 72. C Mossley Hill St Matt and St Jas *Liv* 71-74; C Stanley 74-76; TV Hackney *Lon* 76-78; Chapl Forest Sch Snaresbrook 78-83; Hd Master Vernon Holme Sch Cant 83-88; Perm to Offic *Cant* 83-88; Hd Master Heath Mt Sch Hertf from 88; Perm to Offic *St Alb* from 88. *Heath Mount School, Woodhall Park, Watton at Stone, Hertford SG14 3NG* Tel (01920) 830230 or 830541

MATTHEWS, Mrs Heather Ann. b 49. Bris Univ BA71 Lon Univ CertEd72. Trin Coll Bris 87. **d** 89 **p** 94. C Blagdon w Compton Martin and Ubley *B & W* 89-93; D-in-c 93-94; P-in-c 94; R from 94. *The Rectory, High Street, Blagdon, Bristol BS18 6TA* Tel (01761) 462495

MATTHEWS, Mrs Joan Muriel. b 53. N Ord Course 89. **d** 92 **p** 94. C Aughton St Mich *Liv* 92-97; R Wavertree St Mary from 97. *St Mary's Rectory, 1 South Drive, Wavertree, Liverpool L15 8JJ* Tel 0151-734 3103

MATTHEWS, Canon John. b 22. TD66. Trin Coll Cam BA48 MA51. Bps' Coll Cheshunt 49. **d** 51 **p** 52. C Woodlands *Sheff* 51-54; CF (TA) from 53; C Sheff Sharrow *Sheff* 54-57; V Sheff St Barn 57-62; P-in-c Lt Canfield *Chelmsf* 62-70; V Gt Dunmow 62-88; P-in-c Gt Easton 70-83; RD Dunmow 75-88; Hon Can Chelmsf Cathl 85-88; rtd 88. *Moorside Cottage, The Common, Walberswick, Southwold, Suffolk IP18 6TE* Tel (01502) 722783

MATTHEWS, Lewis William (Bill). b 29. St Jo Coll Dur BA53 DipTh55 MSc76. **d** 55 **p** 56. C Eston *York* 55-57; C Wicker w Neepsend *Sheff* 57; Ind Chapl 57-61; V Copt Oak *Leic* 61-64; R Braunstone 64-70; V Thornaby on Tees St Paul *York* 70-72; TR Thornaby on Tees 72-78; Dir Dioc Bd for Soc Resp *Lon* 79-84; Perm to Offic 84-94; Warden Durning Hall Chr Community Cen Forest Gate 84-94; rtd 94. *Gouray Vicarage, Gorey Village, Grouville, Jersey JE3 6EB* Tel (01534) 853255

MATTHEWS, Melvyn William. b 40. St Edm Hall Ox BA63 MA68. K Coll Lon BD66 AKC67. **d** 67 **p** 68. C Enfield St Andr *Lon* 67-70; Asst Chapl Southn Univ *Win* 70-73; Kenya 75-76; V Highgate All SS *Lon* 76-79; P-in-c Clifton St Paul *Bris* 79-87; Sen Chapl Bris Univ 79-87; Dir Ammerdown Cen for Study and Renewal 87-93; V Chew Magna w Dundry *B & W* from 93. *The Vicarage, 24 High Street, Chew Magna, Bristol BS18 8PW* Tel (01275) 332199

MATTHEWS, Oswald John. b 13. St Edm Hall Ox BA37 MA40. Ripon Hall Ox 35. **d** 37 **p** 38. C Beverley Minster *York* 37-41; V Drypool St Andr and St Pet 41-48; Chapl RAF 41-45; V Fridaythorpe w Fimber and Thixendale *York* 48-52; Miss to Seamen 52-64; Argentina 52-54; New Zealand from 54. *12 Kenneth Small Crescent, Point Chevalier, Auckland 2, New Zealand* Tel Auckland (9) 815 3846

MATTHEWS, Paul. b 47. Brunel Univ BTech70 S Bank Poly DipEEngD72. S Dios Minl Tr Scheme 89. **d** 92 **p** 93. Hon C Goring-by-Sea *Chich* from 92. *Rose Cottage, The Court House, Sea Lane, Goring-by-Sea, Worthing, W Sussex BN12 4NY* Tel (01903) 502011

MATTHEWS, Canon Percival Charles Halls. b 15. Em Coll Cam BA37 MA41. Wycliffe Hall Ox 37. **d** 38 **p** 39. C Selly Hill St Steph *Birm* 38-41; Org Sec (Midl) CPAS 41-45; Public Preacher *Birm* 42-44; V Birm St Chrys 44-49; PC N Harborne 49-53; V Douglas St Geo *S & M* 53-57; V Douglas St Geo and St Barn 57-80; RD Douglas 71-80; Can St German's Cathl 75-80; rtd 80; Perm to Offic *S & M* 80-81 and from 94; Hon C German St Jo 81-94. *Edelweiss, Glen Lough Circle, Glen Vine, Douglas, Isle of Man IM4 4AX* Tel (01624) 851860

MATTHEWS, Peter Henry. b 22. Sarum Th Coll 62. **d** 64 **p** 65. C Wareham w Arne *Sarum* 64-67; P-in-c Houghton 67; C Sholing *Win* 67-69; R Hilperton w Whaddon *Sarum* 70-78; P-in-c Staverton 71-72; V 72-78; P-in-c Milborne St Andrew w Dewlish 78-87; rtd 87; Perm to Offic *B & W* from 87. *Holmlands, Lambrook Road, Shepton Beauchamp, Ilminster, Somerset TA19 0LZ* Tel (01460) 40938

MATTHEWS, Rodney Charles. b 36. Sarum Th Coll 62. **d** 64 **p** 65. C Gt Clacton *Chelmsf* 64-68; C Loughton St Mary 68-74; TV 74-76; V Goodmayes All SS 76-87; V Woodford Bridge from 87; Hon Chapl Sail Tr Assn from 89; P-in-c Barkingside St Cedd 90-92. *St Paul's Vicarage, 4 Cross Road, Woodford Green, Essex IG8 8BS* Tel 0181-504 3815

MATTHEWS, Roger Charles. b 54. MBCS82 CEng90 Man Univ BSc75 CDipAF78. Trin Coll Bris 87. **d** 89 **p** 90. C Gt Baddow *Chelmsf* 89-93; P-in-c Chigwell Row 93-94; TV Chigwell and Chigwell Row 94-96; Dioc Miss Officer from 96. *Glebelands, Boreham Road, Great Leighs, Chelmsford CM3 1PP* Tel (01245) 362644

MATTHEWS, Canon Roy Ian John. b 27. TD71. St Cath Soc Ox BA52 MA56. St Steph Ho Ox 52. **d** 54 **p** 55. C Barnsley St Mary *Wakef* 54-58; V Staincliffe 58-65; CF (TA) 58-92; V Penistone w Midhope *Wakef* 65-72; V Brighouse 72-84; Hon Can Wakef Cathl 76-92; V Darrington w Wentbridge 84-92; Dioc Schs Officer 84-89; Dep Dir of Educn 85-89; rtd 92; Perm to Offic *Wakef* from 92; Perm to Offic *York* from 92; P-in-c Selby Abbey from 96. *14 Spring Walk, Brayton, Selby, N Yorkshire YO8 9DS* Tel (01757) 707259

MATTHEWS, Royston Peter. b 39. Univ of Wales (Lamp) BA61 DipTh64. St Mich Coll Llan 61. **d** 64 **p** 65. C Fairwater CD *Llan* 64-67; C Cadoxton-juxta-Barry 67-71; V Bettws *Mon* 71-84; V

Abergavenny H Trin from 84. *Holy Trinity Vicarage, Baker Street, Abergavenny NP7 5BH* Tel (01873) 853203

MATTHEWS, Canon Stuart James. b 37. St Jo Coll Dur BA60. Bps' Coll Cheshunt 60. **d** 62 **p** 63. C Horsham *Chich* 62-65; C Rednal *Birm* 65-67; Min Brandwood St Bede Statutory Distr 67-68; C Northfield 68-73; V Thurcroft *Sheff* 73-82; RD Laughton 79-82; R Sprotbrough from 82; RD Adwick 84-89; Hon Can Sheff Cathl from 92. *The Rectory, 42A Spring Lane, Sprotborough, Doncaster, S Yorkshire DN5 7QG* Tel (01302) 853203

MATTHEWS, Terence Leslie. b 35. Handsworth Coll Birm 55. **d** 61 **p** 62. C W Acklam *York* 61-64; V Horden *Dur* 64-72; R Witton Gilbert 72-77; P-in-c Grangetown 77-85; V Cleadon 85-86; V Hebburn St Cuth 86-88; rtd 88. *7 Holmlands Park South, Sunderland SR2 7SG* Tel 0191-522 6466

MATTHEWS, Canon William Andrew (Bill). b 44. Reading Univ BA65 MA94. St Steph Ho Ox 65. **d** 67 **p** 68. C Westbury-on-Trym St Alb *Bris* 67-70; C Marlborough *Sarum* 70-73; P-in-c Winsley 73-75; V 75-81; V Bradford-on-Avon from 81; RD Bradford 84-94; Can and Preb Sarum Cathl from 88. *Holy Trinity Vicarage, 18A Woolley Street, Bradford-on-Avon, Wilts BA15 1AF* Tel (01225) 864444 Fax 863623

MATTHEWS, William Temple Atkinson. b 47. EMMTC 86. **d** 83 **p** 83. SSF 83-86; C Brinsley w Underwood *S'well* 86-89; TV Hitchin *St Alb* 89-97; R Toddington from 97. *The Rectory, 41 Leighton Road, Toddington, Dunstable, Beds LU5 6AL* Tel (01525) 872298

MATTHEWS-LOYDALL, Mrs Elaine. b 63. Bp Otter Coll BA85 St Jo Coll Nottm LTh89 DPS90. **d** 90 **p** 94. Par Dn Nottingham All SS *S'well* 90-94; C 94-95; Asst Chapl to the Deaf 91-93; Chapl to the Deaf from 93. *Pumpkin Cottage, 54 Wilne Road, Sawley, Notts NG10 3AN* Tel 0115-972 8943

MATTHEWS-PAYNE, James. b 19. St D Coll Lamp BA41. Lich Th Coll 41 St Mich Coll Llan 46. **d** 46 **p** 47. C Barry All SS *Llan* 46-51; C Canton St Cath 51; P-in-c Aberavon 51-55; Bermuda 55-60; V Woolston *Win* 60-65; Australia from 65; rtd 80. *22/11 Freedman Road, Mount Lawley, W Australia 6050* Tel Adelaide (8) 9272 5253

MATTHIAE, David. b 40. Fitzw Ho Cam BA63 MA69. Linc Th Coll 63. **d** 65 **p** 66. C New Addington *Cant* 65-70; C Charlton-by-Dover SS Pet and Paul 70-75; V Cant All SS 75-84; P-in-c Tunstall 84-87; R Tunstall w Rodmersham from 87; RD Sittingbourne 88-94. *The Rectory, Tunstall, Sittingbourne, Kent ME9 8DU* Tel (01795) 423907

MATTHIAS, Edwin (Eddie). b 23. AKC50. **d** 51 **p** 52. C Hinckley St Mary *Leic* 51-54; C Putney St Mary *S'wark* 54-58; V Bolney *Chich* 58-65; R Chailey 65-92; rtd 92; Perm to Offic *Chich* from 92. *Oak Cottage, Hunters End, Lewes, E Sussex BN8 4AT* Tel (01273) 400894

MATTHIAS, George Ronald. b 30. CertEd51. St Deiniol's Hawarden 76. **d** 78 **p** 79. NSM Broughton *St As* 78-83; NSM Wrexham 83-85; C 85-87; V Brymbo 87-95; rtd 95. *Bryn Adref, Pisgah Hill, Pentre Hill, Wrexham LL11 5DB*

MATTHIAS, John Rex. b 61. St Mich Coll Llan DMS94. **d** 94 **p** 95. C Llandrillo-yn-Rhos *St As* from 94. *5 Conway Close, Rhos-on-Sea, Colwyn Bay LL28 4JE* Tel (01492) 546373

MATTHIAS, Paul. b 47. Philippa Fawcett Coll CertEd75 Kent Univ DipEd84. Cant Sch of Min 92. **d** 94 **p** 95. Head RE Hever Sch Maidstone 80-94; NSM Gillingham St Aug *Roch* from 94; Chapl Ch Ch High Sch Ashford from 94. *Ashford Christ Church High School, Millbank Road, Kingsnorth, Ashford, Kent TN23 3HG* Tel (01233) 623465

MATTOCK, Colin Graham. b 38. Chich Th Coll. **d** 84 **p** 85. C Hove All SS *Chich* 84-87; C Bexhill St Pet 87-90; V Henlow *St Alb* 90-96; V Linslade *Ox* from 96. *The Vicarage, Vicarage Road, Leighton Buzzard, Beds LU7 7LP* Tel (01525) 372149

MATTY, Horace Anthony (Tony). b 36. Ely Th Coll 61. **d** 63 **p** 64. C Minchinhampton *Glouc* 63-66; C Hunslet St Mary and Stourton *Ripon* 66-69; TV Wendy w Shingay *Ely* 69-71; V Parson Drove 71-74; V Southea cum Murrow 71-74; V Coven *Lich* 74-82; TV Hednesford 82-85; TV Basildon St Martin w Nevendon *Chelmsf* 85-92; P-in-c Basildon St Andr w H Cross 85-92; P-in-c Sandon from 92; P-in-c E Hanningfield from 92. *The Rectory, Sandon, Chelmsford CM2 7SQ* Tel (01245) 472262

MAUCHAN, Andrew. b 44. Hertf Coll Ox BA65 MA69 Man Univ CertEd66. Oak Hill Th Coll DipHE90. **d** 90 **p** 91. C Bridlington Priory *York* 90-94; V Alverthorpe *Wakef* from 94. *The Vicarage, St Paul's Drive, Wakefield, W Yorkshire WF2 0BT* Tel (01924) 371300

MAUDE, Canon Alan. b 41. Lon Univ DipTh67 BD69 Newc Univ MSc90. Lambeth STh74 Oak Hill Th Coll 66. **d** 69 **p** 70. C Balderstone *Man* 69-73; Asst Chapl Crumpsall and Springfield Hosps 73-75; C Crumpsall St Matt 73-75; Chapl R Victoria Infirmary Newc 75-94; Chapl R Victoria Infirmary and Assoc Hosps NHS Trust from 94; Hon Can Newc Cathl *Newc* from 88. *Royal Victoria Infirmary, Queen Victoria Road, Newcastle upon Tyne NE1 4LP* Tel 0191-284 4966 or 232 5131

MAUDE, Ralph Henry Evelyn. b 09. St Pet Hall Ox BA33 MA37. St Steph Ho Ox 32. **d** 33 **p** 34. C Bris St Geo *Bris* 33-36; C Bournemouth St Steph *Win* 36-45; R Shaftesbury St Jas *Sarum* 45-57; V Weymouth St Paul 57-66; V Devizes St Pet 66-74; rtd 74. *4 Manor Court, Swan Road, Pewsey, Wilts SN9 5DW* Tel (01672) 63186

MAUDLIN, David. b 39. EAMTC 92. **d** 95 **p** 96. NSM Bury St Edmunds St Jo *St E* from 95. *The Rorty Crankle, 6 Norton Road, Thurston, Bury St Edmunds, Suffolk IP31 3PB* Tel (01359) 231772

MAUDSLEY, Canon George Lambert. b 27. St Jo Coll Nottm 74. **d** 75 **p** 76. C Binley *Cov* 75-77; Chapl Barn Fellowship Winterborne Whitechurch 77-83; V Salford Priors *Cov* 83-94; RD Alcester 87-92; Hon Can Cov Cathl 91-94; rtd 94. *7 Flax Piece, Upton Snodsbury, Worcester WR7 4PA* Tel (01905) 381034

MAUDSLEY, Keith. b 51. York Univ BA72. Ripon Hall Ox 72. **d** 75 **p** 76. C Rugby St Andr *Cov* 75-79; C Cambridge Gt St Mary w St Mich *Ely* 79-82; Chapl Girton Coll 79-82; P-in-c Binley *Cov* 82-89; RD Cov E 87-89; P-in-c Leek Wootton 89-91; Dioc Policy Development Adv 89-91; Dioc Adv on UPA *Liv* from 91; Soc Resp Officer from 91. *8 The Parchments, Newton-le-Willows, Merseyside WA12 0DY* Tel (01925) 220586

MAUDSLEY, Michael Peter. b 38. St Andr Univ BSc61. Oak Hill Th Coll 65. **d** 67 **p** 68. C Blackpool St Mark *Blackb* 67-70; C Hartford *Ches* 70-72; R Balerno *Edin* 72-82; V Stapenhill w Cauldwell *Derby* 82-91; TV Edin St Paul and St Geo *Edin* 91-95; R from 95. *21 Barony Street, Edinburgh EH3 6PD* Tel 0131-558 1157

MAUGHAN, Angela. b 54. Newc Univ 93. NE Ord Course 94. **d** 97. C Willington Team *Newc* from 97. *10 Church Street, Wallsend, Tyne & Wear NE28 7SJ* Tel 0191-263 6140

MAUGHAN, Geoffrey Nigel (Geoff). b 48. CCC Cam BA69 MA73. Oak Hill Th Coll 75. **d** 77 **p** 78. C New Malden and Coombe *S'wark* 77-81; C Abingdon w Shippon *Ox* 81-89; TV Abingdon from 89. *69 Northcourt Road, Abingdon, Oxon OX14 1NR* Tel (01235) 520115 or 522549

MAUGHAN, John. b 28. Keble Coll Ox BA51 MA55. Linc Th Coll 51. **d** 53 **p** 54. C Heworth St Mary *Dur* 53-56; C Winlaton 56-59; R Penshaw 59-72; V Cleadon Park 72-93; rtd 93. *2 Struddar's Farm Court, Bates Lane, Blaydon-on-Tyne, Tyne & Wear NE21 5TF* Tel 0191-414 8350

✠**MAUND, The Rt Revd John Arthur Arrowsmith.** b 09. CBE75 MC46. Leeds Univ BA31. Coll of Resurr Mirfield 31. **d** 33 **p** 34 **c** 50. C Evesham *Worc* 33-36; C Blackheath All SS *S'wark* 36-38; S Africa 39-50; Bp Basutoland 50-66; Bp Lesotho 66-76; Asst Bp St E 76-83; Asst Bp Worc from 84; rtd 86. *1 Warden's Lodge, Beauchamp Community, The Quadrangle, Newland, Malvern, Worcs WR13 5AX* Tel (01684) 568072

MAUND, Mrs Margaret Jennifer. b 42. RGN64 RM65 DTM66 MTD72. Llan Dioc Tr Scheme 89. **d** 94 **p** 97. NSM Cymmer and Porth *Llan* from 94. *27 Mill Street, Tonyrefail, Porth CF39 8AB* Tel (01443) 670085

MAUNDER, Alan John. b 52. UWIST BSc74. Oak Hill Th Coll DipHE88. **d** 90 **p** 91. C Birkenhead Ch Ch *Ches* 90-95; P-in-c Poulton from 95. *St Luke's Vicarage, Mill Lane, Wallasey, Merseyside L44 3BP* Tel 0151-638 4663

MAUNDRELL, Canon Wolseley David. b 20. New Coll Ox BA41 DipTh42 MA45. **d** 43 **p** 44. C Haslemere *Guildf* 43-49; Bp's Dom Chapl *Chich* 49-50; V Sparsholt w Lainston *Win* 50-56; R Weeke 56-61; Can Res and Treas Win Cathl 61-70; Vice-Dean Win 66-70; Asst Chapl Brussels *Eur* 70-71; V Icklesham *Chich* 72-82; RD Rye 78-84; Can and Preb Chich Cathl 81-89; TR Rye 82-89; rtd 89; P-in-c Stonegate *Chich* 89-95; Perm to Offic from 95. *13 North Walls, Chichester, W Sussex PO19 1DA* Tel (01243) 537359

MAUNSELL, Colin Wray Dymock. b 33. Pemb Coll Cam BA56 MA59 Lon Univ DipTh58. Tyndale Hall Bris 56. **d** 58 **p** 59. C Virginia Water *Guildf* 58-60; BCMS 60-93; Ethiopia 61-79 and from 91; Portugal 81-91; Crosslinks 93-94; rtd 94. *c/o St Matthew's Church, PO Box 109, Addis Ababa, Ethiopia* Tel Addis Ababa (1) 112623

MAURICE, John Kenneth Williams. b 07. St D Coll Lamp BA34. **d** 33 **p** 34. C Wembdon *B & W* 33-35; C Dawlish *Ex* 35-36; C Sidmouth St Nic 36-39; R Buckerell 39; Perm to Offic 42-45; C Dawlish 45-46; Chapl Lausanne *Eur* 46-47; Chapl Estoril 48-49; Perm to Offic *B & W* 49 and 51-57; Perm to Offic *Heref* 50-51; R Cruwys Morchard *Ex* 57-68; rtd 68; Perm to Offic *Ex* from 85. *Little Knowle, Hillside Road, Sidmouth, Devon EX10 8JD*

MAURICE, Peter David. b 51. St Chad's Coll Dur BA72. Coll of Resurr Mirfield. **d** 75 **p** 76. C Wandsworth St Paul *S'wark* 75-79; TV Mortlake w E Sheen 79-85; V Rotherhithe H Trin 85-96; RD Bermondsey 91-96; V Tooting All SS from 96. *All Saints' Vicarage, 84 Franciscan Road, London SW17 8DQ* Tel 0181-672 3706

MAWBEY, Miss Diane. b 55. Cranmer Hall Dur. **d** 89 **p** 94. Par Dn Menston w Woodhead *Bradf* 89-92; C Barnoldswick w Bracewell 92-93; Chapl Asst Birm Children's Hosp 93-96; Chapl Asst Birm Maternity Hosp 93-96; Chapl Birm Women's Health Care NHS Trust from 96. *101 Leahurst Crescent, Birmingham B17 0LD* Tel 0121-428 1624 or 472 1377

MAWDITT, Stephen Donald Harvey. b 56. LNSM course 94. **d** 96. NSM Ashill w Saham Toney *Nor* from 96. *Cutbush House, Whitehall Lane, Saham Toney, Thetford, Norfolk IP25 7HB* Tel (01953) 883390

MAWER, Canon David Ronald. b 32. Keble Coll Ox BA55 MA58 Dur Univ BA57 McGill Univ Montreal PhD77. Wells Th Coll 58. **d** 59 **p** 60. C Cullercoats St Geo *Newc* 59-61; Canada 61-92; Co-ord Angl Studies St Paul Univ Ottawa 81-92; Can Ottawa from 85; rtd 92. *Moorside, Church Lane, Thropton, Morpeth, Northd NE65 7JA* Tel (01669) 620597

MAWSON, Canon Arthur Cyril. b 35. St Pet Coll Ox BA56 MA61. Wycliffe Hall Ox 61. **d** 62 **p** 63. C Walsall *Lich* 62-66; V Millhouses H Trin *Sheff* 66-73; Selection Sec ACCM 73-79; Can Res and Treas Ex Cathl *Ex* from 79; Dioc Dir of Ords 81-87. *9 The Close, Exeter EX1 1EZ* Tel (01392) 279367

MAWSON, David Frank. b 44. Selw Coll Cam BA65 MA69. Linc Th Coll 79. **d** 80 **p** 81. C Tunstall *Lich* 80-83; C Blakenall Heath 83-84; TV 84-90; Chapl Goscote Hosp Walsall 87-90; V Pelsall *Lich* 90-94; V Tividale from 94. *St Michael's Vicarage, Tividale, Warley, W Midlands B69 2LQ* Tel 0121-520 7766

MAWSON, Frank. b 18. ACIS70. NW Ord Course 74. **d** 77 **p** 78. NSM Stockport St Mary *Ches* 77-79; P-in-c Harthill and Burwardsley 79-82; rtd 82; Perm to Offic *Ches* from 82; Perm to Offic *St As* from 82; Perm to Offic *Lich* from 88; Perm to Offic *Heref* from 95. *Flat 16, College Court, Ludlow, Shropshire SY8 1BZ* Tel (01584) 873869

MAXTED, Neil Andrew. b 58. GradIMI80. Sarum & Wells Th Coll CMinlStuds92 Aston Tr Scheme 88. **d** 92 **p** 93. C Folkestone St Sav *Cant* 92-96; CF from 96. *Chaplain's School of Aviation, Middle Wallop, Stockbridge, Hants SO20 8YY*

MAXWELL, Christopher John Moore (Bill). b 31. MRCS59 LRCP59 Qu Coll Cam MA75. Trin Coll Bris 74. **d** 75 **p** 76. Chile 75-81; C Clevedon Ch Ch *B & W* 75; Hon C Homerton St Luke *Lon* 81-94; Chapl Ibiza *Eur* from 94. *c/o Supermercado Magon, Port des Torrent, 07820 San Antonio, Ibiza, Spain*

MAXWELL, Ian Charles. b 17. Ch Coll Cam BA40 MA44. Ridley Hall Cam 40. **d** 42 **p** 43. C Dartford Ch Ch *Roch* 42-45; CF (EC) 45-47; V Aston St Jas *Birm* 47-51; CMS 51-55; V Belvedere All SS *Roch* 55-61; R Stanhope *Dur* 61-74; R Gt w Lt Somerford and Seagry *Bris* 74-82; rtd 82; Perm to Offic *Chich* from 82. *22 Hastings Avenue, Seaford, E Sussex BN25 3LQ* Tel (01323) 890453

MAXWELL, Marcus Howard. b 54. Liv Univ BSc76 Man Univ MPhil89. St Jo Coll Nottm BA79. **d** 80 **p** 81. C Chadderton St Matt *Man* 80-84; V Bircle 84-93; P-in-c Heaton Mersey from 93. *St John's Rectory, 15 Priestnall Road, Stockport, Cheshire SK4 3HR* Tel 0161-432 2165

MAXWELL, Ralph. b 21. CEng MIMechE. **d** 86 **p** 87. NSM Belfast St Mich *Conn* 86-87; Lic to Offic 87-89; NSM Belfast St Jas w St Silas 89-97; NSM Belfast St Pet from 97. *69 Woodvale Road, Belfast BT13 3BN* Tel (01232) 742421

MAXWELL, Richard Renwick. b 23. Mert Coll Ox BA49 MA49. Westcott Ho Cam 49. **d** 51 **p** 52. C Moordown *Win* 51-55; N Rhodesia 55-64; Zambia 64-65; C N Holmwood *Guildf* 65-67; R Harrietsham *Cant* 67-73; V Blean 73-84; Hon C Hindhead *Guildf* 84-88; Perm to Offic *Cant* from 85; rtd 88; Perm to Offic *Guildf* from 88. *4 St Birinus Road, Woodfalls, Salisbury SP5 2LE* Tel (01725) 22037

MAY, Anthony John (Tony). b 30. Sarum Th Coll 62. **d** 63 **p** 64. C Bridport *Sarum* 63-67; Min Belhus Park CD *Chelmsf* 63-68; C Kirkby *Liv* 67-69; P-in-c Woolwich St Thos *S'wark* 69-74; Chapl Warlingham Park Hosp Croydon 74-81; Field Worker Surrey Community Development Trust 81-85; Admin Nat Assn for Voluntary Hostels 85-92; rtd 93. *Summerland, St James, South Elmham, Halesworth, Suffolk IP19 0HS*

MAY, Arthur John. b 16. Linc Th Coll 40. **d** 42 **p** 43. C Stepney St Matt *Lon* 42-46; C Plaistow St Andr *Chelmsf* 46-48; P-in-c N Woolwich 48-53; V W Silvertown St Barn 48-53; V Upton Park 53-63; V Belhus Park 68-83; rtd 83; Perm to Offic *Chelmsf* from 83. *19 Warriner Avenue, Hornchurch, Essex RM12 4LH* Tel (01708) 458421

MAY, Charles Henry. b 29. Lon Coll of Div ALCD58 LTh74. **d** 58 **p** 59. C Bethnal Green St Jas Less *Lon* 58-61; C Woking St Pet *Guildf* 61-64; Area Sec (W Midl) CPAS 64-67; V Homerton St Luke *Lon* 67-80; Home Sec SAMS 80-84; V Fulham Ch Ch *Lon* 84-94; rtd 94; Perm to Offic *Ely* from 94; Perm to Offic *Pet* from 94; Perm to Offic *Linc* from 95. *16 Kilverstone, Werrington, Peterborough PE4 5DX* Tel (01733) 328108

MAY, Denis Harry. b 31. ARICS56. S'wark Ord Course. **d** 63 **p** 64. C Eltham St Jo *S'wark* 63-65; Hon C Charing w Lt Chart *Cant* 66-70; Lic to Offic from 70. *19 Malvern Road, Ashford, Kent TN24 8JA* Tel (01233) 638816

MAY, Donald Charles Leonard. b 25. Chich Th Coll 72. **d** 73 **p** 74. C Barkingside H Trin *Chelmsf* 73-77; V Aldersbrook 77-91; rtd 92; Perm to Offic *Chelmsf* from 92. *236 Prospect Road, Woodford Green, Essex IG8 7NQ* Tel 0181-504 6119

MAY, George Louis. b 27. Selw Coll Cam BA52 MA55 Cam Univ PGCE67 ADEd78. Ridley Hall Cam 52. **d** 54 **p** 55. C St Mary Cray and St Paul's Cray *Roch* 54-56; C St Paul's Cray St Barn CD 56-57; C-in-c Elburton CD *Ex* 57-66; Asst Master Guthlaxton Sch Wigston 67-70; Ixworth Sch 70-72; Thurston Upper Sch 73-74; Perias Sch New Alresford 75-85; Hon C Ropley w W Tisted *Win* 78-79; Perm to Offic 79-96; rtd 92. *Oven House, Water Lane, Eyam, Sheffield S30 1RG* Tel (01433) 630599

MAY, John Alexander Cyril. b 52. K Coll Lon BD77 Ox Univ PGCE78. Linc Th Coll 79. **d** 80 **p** 81. C Tynemouth Ch Ch *Newc* 80-82; C Tynemouth Ch Ch w H Trin 82-85; C Tynemouth St Aug 82-85; TV Glendale Gp 85-90; V Wotton-under-Edge w Ozleworth and N Nibley *Glouc* from 90. *The Vicarage, Culverhay, Wotton-under-Edge, Glos GL12 7LS* Tel (01453) 842175

MAY, Peter Dudfield. b 12. St Jo Coll Cam BA34 LLB35 LLM. Ripon Hall Ox 38. **d** 39 **p** 40. C Gravelly Hill *Birm* 39-43; C Trowbridge St Jas *Sarum* 43-46; V Preshute 46-53; Chapl Marlborough Children's Convalescent Hosp 46-53; R Stoke Abbott 53-82; V Netherbury 54-82; rtd 82. *Parsonage Farmhouse, Dinnington, Hinton St George, Somerset TA17 8SU* Tel (01460) 53880

MAY, Peter Richard. b 43. MICE70 St Jo Coll Cam BA64 MA68. Trin Coll Bris 77. **d** 79 **p** 80. C Lancaster St Thos *Blackb* 79-85; V Darwen St Barn 85-91; Chapl Lyon w Grenoble *Eur* 91-92; Chapl Lyon 92-94; Perm to Offic *S'wark* 94-95; TR Horley from 95. *4 Russells Crescent, Horley, Surrey RH6 7DN* Tel (01293) 783509

MAY, Simon George. b 47. FCA77 Ex Univ BA69 Univ of Wales (Ban) CertEd72. Sarum & Wells Th Coll 86. **d** 88 **p** 89. C Tamworth *Lich* 88-92; V Whitchurch *Ex* from 92. *The Vicarage, 204 Whitchurch Road, Tavistock, Devon PL19 9DQ* Tel (01822) 610364

MAY, Dr Stephen Charles Arthur. b 52. Mert Coll Ox BA73 Edin Univ BD78 Aber Univ PhD86. Ridley Hall Cam 84. **d** 86 **p** 87. C Sawley *Derby* 86-88; Lect Systematic Th St Jo Coll Auckland from 88. *179B St John's Road, Auckland 5, New Zealand* Tel Auckland (9) 521-0063

MAYBURY, David Kaines. b 32. G&C Coll Cam BA55 MA59. Ridley Hall Cam 55. **d** 57 **p** 58. C Sydenham H Trin *S'wark* 57-60; C Rainham *Chelmsf* 60-63; R Edin St Jas *Edin* 63-75; R Jedburgh 75-84; NSM Duns 84-91; Warden Whitchester Conf Cen 84-91; NSM Hawick *Edin* 91-97; Warden Whitchester Chr Guest Ho and Retreat Cen 91-97; rtd 97. *DaDo Heights, Borthaugh, Hawick, Roxburghshire TD9 7LN* Tel (01450) 370809

MAYBURY, Doreen Lorna. b 33. RGN54 SCM56. Edin Th Coll 76. **dss** 81 **d** 95 **p** 95. Jedburgh *Edin* 81-84; Duns 84-91; Warden Whitchester Conf Cen 84-91; Hawick *Edin* 91-95; NSM 95-97; rtd 97. *DaDo Heights, Borthaugh, Hawick, Roxburghshire TD9 7LN* Tel (01450) 370809

MAYBURY, Canon John Montague. b 30. G&C Coll Cam BA53 MA57. Ridley Hall Cam 53. **d** 55 **p** 56. C Allerton *Liv* 55-59; C Rowner *Portsm* 59-62; V Wroxall 62-67; V Southsea St Simon 67-78; V Crofton 78-91; Hon Can Portsm Cathl 81-95; C Locks Heath 91-95; rtd 95. *19 Netley Road, Titchfield Common, Fareham, Hants PO14 4PE* Tel (01489) 584168

MAYBURY, Paul. b 31. St Deiniol's Hawarden 87. **d** 88 **p** 90. NSM Sutton St Geo *Ches* 88-94; rtd 94; Perm to Offic *Ches* from 94. *29 Westbury Drive, Macclesfield, Cheshire SK11 8LR* Tel (01625) 424475

MAYBURY, Paul Dorian. b 58. Trin Coll Bris DipHE95. **d** 95 **p** 96. C Spondon *Derby* from 95. *Prospect House, 27 Park Road, Spondon, Derby DE21 7LN* Tel (01332) 662990

MAYCOCK, Ms Jane Ellen. b 66. Somerville Coll Ox BA90 Ox Univ MA95. Cranmer Hall Dur 90. **d** 92 **p** 94. Par Dn Harrow Trin St Mich *Lon* 92-94; C 94-95; C Kendal H Trin *Carl* from 95. *7 Wattsfield Road, Kendal, Cumbria LA9 5JH* Tel (01539) 729572

MAYELL, Howard John. b 50. Bris Sch of Min 81. **d** 84 **p** 88. NSM Patchway *Bris* 84-86; NSM Weston-super-Mare Cen Par *B & W* 87-88; C N Stoneham *Win* 88-91; P-in-c Black Torrington, Bradf w Cookbury etc *Ex* from 91. *The Rectory, Black Torrington, Beaworthy, Devon EX21 5PU* Tel (01409) 231279

MAYER, Alan John. b 46. AKC70. St Aug Coll Cant 70. **d** 71 **p** 72. C Stanningley St Thos *Ripon* 71-74; C St Helier *S'wark* 74-79; TV Wimbledon 79-85; V Reigate St Luke S Park from 85. *St Luke's Vicarage, Church Road, Reigate, Surrey RH2 8HY* Tel (01737) 246302

MAYER, Graham Keith. b 46. St Cath Coll Ox BA68 Nottm Univ PGCE69 Ex Univ MA93 Plymouth Univ DCouns95. Linc Th Coll 78. **d** 80 **p** 81. C Paignton St Jo *Ex* 80-93; Perm to Offic 93-96; P-in-c Christow, Ashton, Trusham and Bridford from 96. *The Rectory, Dry Lane, Christow, Exeter EX6 7PE* Tel (01647) 252845

MAYER, Mrs Paula Denise. b 45. St Hilda's Coll Ox BA68 Nottm Univ CertEd69. SW Minl Tr Course 84. **d** 88. Hon Par Dn Paignton St Jo *Ex* 88-90; Par Dn 90-93; Perm to Offic from 93. *367A Torquay Road, Paignton, Devon TQ3 2BJ*

MAYERSON, Dr Paul Strom. b 28. PhD MEd MusBac. Ridley Hall Cam 80. **d** 82 **p** 83. C New Romney w Old Romney and Midley *Cant* 82-85; P-in-c Ospringe 85; P-in-c Eastling 85; R Eastling w Ospringe and Stalisfield w Otterden 85-90; rtd 90; Perm to Offic *Cant* from 90. *168 Piper Hill Road, Ashland, New Hampshire NH03217, USA*

MAYES, Andrew Dennis. b 56. K Coll Lon BD79 AKC79. St Steph Ho Ox 80. **d** 81 **p** 82. C Hendon St Alphage *Lon* 81-84; C Hockley *Chelmsf* 84-87; V Kingstanding St Mark *Birm* 87-92; V Saltdean *Chich* from 92. *St Nicholas' Vicarage, Saltdean, Brighton BN2 8HE* Tel (01273) 302345

MAYES, The Very Revd Gilbert. b 15. TCD BA43 MA61. CITC 44. **d** 44 **p** 45. C Arm St Mark *Arm* 44-47; Hd Master Cathl Sch Arm 47-48; Dioc C 47-48; I Upper Donaghmore w Pomeroy 48-52; I Dundalk 52-61; Dean Lismore *C & O* 61-87; I Lismore w Cappoquin, Kilwatermoy, Dungarvan etc 61-87; Prec Waterford Cathl 84-87; Preb Stagonil St Patr Cathl Dublin 85-87; rtd 87. *Woodford, Ballybride Road, Rathmichael, Shankill, Co Dublin, Irish Republic* Tel Dublin (1) 282 4089

MAYES, Canon John Charles Dougan. b 44. Bps' Coll Cheshunt 63. **d** 67 **p** 68. C Portadown St Mark *Arm* 67-74; I Aghadowey w Kilrea *D & R* 74-86; USPG Area Sec 77-94; I Clooney w Strathfoyle from 86; Can Derry Cathl from 92. *All Saints' Rectory, 20 Limavady Road, Londonderry BT47 1JD* Tel (01504) 44306

MAYES, Leonard Harry. b 25. Ely Th Coll 59. **d** 61 **p** 62. C Norton *St Alb* 61-65; C Biscot 65-69; V Watford St Mich 69-78; V Liscard St Mary w St Columba *Ches* 78-82; R Moreton and Church Eaton *Lich* 82-90; rtd 90; Perm to Offic *Lich* from 90. *11 Covert Close, Great Haywood, Stafford ST18 0RN* Tel (01889) 882994

✠**MAYES, The Rt Revd Michael Hugh Gunton.** b 41. TCD BA62 Lon Univ BD85. TCD Div Sch Div Test64. **d** 64 **p** 65 **c** 93. C Portadown St Columba *Arm* 64-68; Japan 68-74; Area Sec (Dios Cashel, Cork, Lim and Tuam) USPG 75-93; I Cork St Mich Union *C, C & R* 75-86; I Moviddy Union 86-88; Adn Cork, Cloyne and Ross 86-93; I Rathcooney Union 88-93; Preb Elphin Cathl *K, E & A* from 93; Bp K, E & A from 93. *The See House, Kilmore, Cavan, Irish Republic* Tel Cavan (49) 31336 Fax 62829

MAYES, Stephen Thomas. b 47. St Jo Coll Nottm 67. **d** 71 **p** 72. C Cullompton *Ex* 71-75; C Cheltenham St Mark *Glouc* 76-84; P-in-c Water Orton *Birm* 84-91; V from 91. *The Vicarage, Water Orton, Birmingham B46 1RX* Tel 0121-747 2751

✠**MAYFIELD, The Rt Revd Christopher John.** b 35. G&C Coll Cam BA57 MA61 Linacre Ho Ox DipTh63 Cranfield Inst of Tech MSc83. Wycliffe Hall Ox 61. **d** 63 **p** 64 **c** 85. C Birm St Martin *Birm* 63-67; Lect 67-71; V Luton St Mary *St Alb* 71-80; RD Luton 74-80; Adn Bedford 80-85; Suff Bp Wolverhampton *Lich* 85-92; Area Bp Wolverhampton 92-93; Bp Man from 93. *Bishopcourt, Bury New Road, Manchester M7 0LE* Tel 0161-792 2096 Fax 792 6826

MAYFIELD, Timothy James Edward (Tim). b 60. LMH Ox BA82. Trin Coll Bris BA88. **d** 88 **p** 89. C Ovenden *Wakef* 88-92; V Mount Pellon from 92. *The Vicarage, Church Lane, Halifax, W Yorkshire HX2 0EF* Tel (01422) 365027

MAYHEW, Canon Charles. b 40. K Coll Lon BD64 AKC64. **d** 65 **p** 66. C Nottingham St Mary *S'well* 65-69; R Cawston *Nor* 69-74; P-in-c Felthorpe w Haveringland 69-74; R Barnack w Ufford and Bainton *Pet* 74-86; RD Barnack 77-86; Can Pet Cathl 83-94; V Oakham, Hambleton, Egleton, Braunston and Brooke 86-94; Chapl Catmose Vale & Rutland Memorial Hosps 86-94; rtd 94. *Thorndon Green, Church Road, Lyndon, Oakham, Leics LE15 8TU* Tel (01572) 722108

MAYHEW, David Francis. b 51. Ch Ch Ox BA72 MA76 Newc Poly DCG76. Wycliffe Hall Ox BA75 NE Ord Course 89. **d** 91 **p** 92. NSM High Elswick St Paul *Newc* 91-94; Toc H 91-94; V Mitford *Newc* from 94; Chapl Northgate Mental Handicap Unit Morpeth from 94. *The Vicarage, Stable Green, Mitford, Morpeth, Northd NE61 3PZ* Tel (01670) 512527

MAYHEW, Peter. b 10. MBE46. Lon Univ BSc31 Ox Univ MLitt79. Ely Th Coll 34. **d** 35 **p** 36. C Cheetwood St Alb *Man* 35-38; C Shrewsbury St Mary *Lich* 38-39; CF (TA - R of O) 39-46; V Leeds St Aid *Ripon* 46-53; Australia 53-62; Adn of the W 59-62; V Kennington St Jo *S'wark* 62-69; Australia 70-74; Chapl Soc of All SS Sisters of the Poor Ox 74-84; rtd 84; Perm to Offic *Ox* from 84. *St John's Home, St Mary's Road, Oxford OX4 1QE* Tel (01865) 724309

MAYLAND, Mrs Jean Mary. b 36. JP77. TCert60 LMH Ox BA58 DipTh59 MA61. St Deiniol's Hawarden 91. **d** 91 **p** 94. NSM York Minster *York* 91-93; Lect and Tutor N Ord Course 91-96; Dioc Ecum Officer *Dur* 93-96; Local Unity Officer Dur Ecum Relns Gp 93-96; Assoc Sec CCBI from 96. *Inter-Church House, 35-41 Lower Marsh, London SE1 7RI*

MAYLAND, Canon Ralph. b 27. VRD63. Ripon Hall Ox 57. **d** 59 **p** 60. C Lambeth St Andr w St Thos *S'wark* 59-62; Chapl RNR 61-94; C-in-c Worksop St Paul CD *S'well* 62-68; V Brightside St Marg *Sheff* 68-72; Ind Chapl 68-81; V Ecclesfield 72-81; Can Res and Treas York Minster *York* 82-94; rtd 94; Hon C Brancepeth *Dur* 94-96. *Minster Cottage, 51 Sands Lane, Barmston, Driffield, N Humberside YO25 8PQ* Tel (01262) 468709

MAYLOR, David Charles. b 59. Lanc Univ BSc80 Edge Hill Coll of HE PGCE81. St Jo Coll Nottm 89. **d** 91 **p** 92. C Hindley All SS *Liv* 91-94; P-in-c Spalding St Paul *Linc* from 94. *St Paul's Vicarage, 65 Holbeach Road, Spalding, Lincs PE11 2HY* Tel (01775) 722532

MAYNARD, John William. b 37. Lon Univ BSc58. Ripon Hall Ox 60. **d** 62 **p** 63. C St Laurence in the Isle of Thanet *Cant* 62-67; C S Ashford Ch Ch 67-70; V Pagham *Chich* from 70. *The Vicarage, Church Lane, Pagham, Bognor Regis, W Sussex PO21 4NX* Tel (01243) 262713

MAYNARD, Raymond. b 30. S'wark Ord Course 75 Ox Ord Course 76. **d** 77 **p** 78. NSM Hedsor and Bourne End *Ox* 77-80; C Newport Pagnell w Lathbury 80-83; P-in-c Lacey Green 83-89; V 89; Perm to Offic *Guildf* from 90. *9 Forestdale, Grayshott, Hindhead, Surrey GU26 6TA* Tel (01428) 604565

MAYNARD, Canon Richard Edward Buller. b 42. AKC66. **d** 67 **p** 68. C St Ives *Truro* 67-71; C Falmouth K Chas 71-74; V St Germans 74-84; V Tideford 74-84; RD E Wivelshire 81-85; Hon Can Truro Cathl from 82; V St Germans 84-85; TR Saltash from 85; Chapl St Barn Hosp Saltash from 90. *The Vicarage, 11 Higher Port View, Saltash, Cornwall PL12 4BU* Tel (01752) 843142

MAYNE, Brian John. b 52. LTCL75 ARICS81 Univ of Wales (Cardiff) BA73. NE Ord Course 82 Coll of Resurr Mirfield 84. **d** 85 **p** 86. C Stainton-in-Cleveland *York* 85-89; P-in-c Rounton w Welbury 89-96; Chapl HM Young Offender Inst Northallerton 89-96; Chapl HM Young Offender Inst Lanc Farms from 96. *HM Young Offender Institution, Lancaster Farms, Stone Row Head, Lancaster LA1 3QZ* Tel (01524) 848745

MAYNE, Canon John Andrew Brian. b 34. QUB BA55 Lon Univ BD62. TCD Div Sch Div Test 57. **d** 57 **p** 58. C Ballymoney *Conn* 57-60; C Knock *D & D* 60-62; P-in-c Knocknagoney 62-68; P-in-c Belvoir 68-71; I 71-80; Dean Waterford *C & O* 80-84; I Lecale Gp *D & D* from 84; Can Down Cathl from 87; Prec Down Cathl from 91; Sec Gen Syn Liturg Cttee from 89. *Saul Rectory, 9 Quoile Road, Downpatrick, Co Down BT30 6SE* Tel (01396) 613101 or 614922 Fax 614456

MAYNE, The Very Revd Michael Clement Otway. b 29. KCVO96. CCC Cam BA55 MA56. Cuddesdon Coll 55. **d** 57 **p** 58. C Harpenden St Jo *St Alb* 57-59; Bp's Dom Chapl *S'wark* 59-65; V Norton *St Alb* 65-72; Hd of Relig Progr BBC Radio 72-79; Hon Can S'wark Cathl *S'wark* 75-79; V Cambridge Gt St Mary w St Mich *Ely* 79-86; Dean Westmr 86-96; rtd 96; Perm to Offic *Sarum* from 97. *37 St Mark's Road, Salisbury SP1 3AY* Tel (01722) 331069

MAYO, Christopher Paul (Chris). b 68. Heythrop Coll Lon BD91. Qu Coll Birm 91. **d** 93 **p** 94. C Wednesfield *Lich* 93-94; C Bilston 94-95. *Newman RC Teacher Training College, Genners Lane, Birmingham B32 3NT* Tel 0121-476 1186

MAYO, Mrs Deborah Ann. b 67. Newc Univ BA89 Birm Univ BD92. Qu Coll Birm 90. **d** 93 **p** 94. Par Dn Bloxwich *Lich* 93-94; C 94-97; TV Gt Grimsby St Mary and St Jas *Linc* from 97. *St Martin's Vicarage, Scartho Road, Grimsby, S Humberside DN33 2AD* Tel (01472) 752340

MAYO, Canon Gordon Edwin. b 18. St Jo Coll Dur LTh42 BA45 MA61. Oak Hill Th Coll. **d** 42 **p** 43. C Cheadle *Ches* 42-44; C Dur St Nic *Dur* 44-45; Chapl RAFVR 45-48; C St Marylebone All So w SS Pet and Jo *Lon* 48-50; Kenya 50-59; Can Mombasa 57-59; Asst Warden Lee Abbey 60-64; Warden Lee Abbey Internat Students' Club Kensington 64-71; R Coulsdon St Jo *S'wark* 71-78; Dir of Chr Stewardship 78-85; Hon Can S'wark Cathl 83-85; rtd 85; P-in-c Limpsfield and Titsey *S'wark* 85-89; Perm to Offic *Chich* 90-94. *160 New Street, Horsham, W Sussex RH13 5EG* Tel (01403) 273508

MAYO, Inglis John. b 46. FCA. Ripon Coll Cuddesdon 74. **d** 77 **p** 78. C Bitterne Park *Win* 77-81; C Christchurch 81-86; P-in-c Sturminster Marshall *Sarum* 86-89; P-in-c Kingston Lacy and Shapwick 86-89; V Sturminster Marshall, Kingston Lacy and Shapwick from 89. *The Vicarage, Newton Road, Sturminster Marshall, Wimborne, Dorset BH21 4BT* Tel (01258) 857255

MAYO, Robert William (Bob). b 61. Keble Coll Ox BA83. Cranmer Hall Dur 85. **d** 87 **p** 88. C Luton Lewsey St Hugh *St Alb* 87-90; Hd Cam Univ Miss 90-95; Hon C Bermondsey St Jas w Ch Ch *S'wark* 90-95; Chapl S Bank Univ from 95. *1 St Alphege Clergy House, Pocock Street, London SE16 0BJ* Tel 0171-928 8912

MAYOH, John Harrison. b 23. Southn Univ BA50. Wycliffe Coll Toronto 50 Wycliffe Hall Ox 52. **d** 53 **p** 54. C Litherland St Jo and St Jas *Liv* 53-55; CMS 57-60; India 57-60; C Upton (Overchurch) *Ches* 60-62; V Everton Em *Liv* 62-69; V Bridlington Quay Ch Ch *York* 69-80; R Aythorpe w High and Leaden Roding *Chelmsf* 80-87; rtd 87; Perm to Offic *Ches* from 91. *5 Keswick Close, Chester CH2 2PP* Tel (01244) 328789

MAYOH, Margaret Evelyn. b 38. Open Univ BA87. Trin Coll Bris DipHE82. **dss** 82 **d** 87 **p** 94. Halliwell St Paul *Man* 82-87; Hon Par Dn 87-91; Hon Par Dn Walmersley 91-94; Hon C 94-97; NSM Heaton Ch Ch from 97. *40 Hillside Avenue, Bromley Cross, Bolton BL7 9NJ* Tel (01204) 305423

MAYOR, Henry William. b 39. Or Coll Ox BA62 Birm Univ DPS67. Westcott Ho Cam 62. **d** 64 **p** 65. C The Quinton *Birm* 64-66; C Dudley St Thos *Worc* 67-71; R Birch St Agnes *Man* 71-83; Community Chapl Aylesbury *Ox* 83-89; Community Chapl Aylesbury w Bierton and Hulcott 89; R Cheetham St Luke and Lower Crumpsall St Thos *Man* 89-96; R Cheetham and Lower Crumpsall from 97. *26 Saltire Gardens, Tetlow Lane, Salford M7 0BG* Tel 0161-792 3123

MAYOSS, Anthony (Aidan). b 31. Leeds Univ BA55. Coll of Resurr Mirfield 55. **d** 57 **p** 58. C Meir *Lich* 57-62; Lic to Offic *Wakef* 62-72 and from 78; CR from 64; S Africa 73-75; Asst Chapl Lon Univ *Lon* 76-78; Bursar CR 84-90. *House of the Resurrection, Mirfield, W Yorkshire WF14 0BN* Tel (01924) 494318

MAYOSS-HURD, Mrs Susan Patricia. b 59. Lanc Univ BA81. Cranmer Hall Dur 82. **dss** 84 **d** 87 **p** 94. Ribbesford w Bewdley and Dowles *Worc* 84-88; Par Dn 87-88; Chapl W Heath Hosp 88-96; C W Heath *Birm* 88-96; V from 96. *St Anne's Vicarage, Lilley Lane, Birmingham B31 3JT* Tel 0121-475 5587

MDUMULLA, Jonas Habel. b 50. Nairobi Univ Hull Univ BTh87 MA89. St Phil Coll Kongwa DipTh74. **d** 74 **p** 75. Tanzania 74-82; C Sutton St Jas and Wawne *York* 82-96; P-in-c Carlton and Drax from 96. *The Vicarage, 2 Church Dike Lane, Drax, Selby, N Yorkshire YO8 8NZ* Tel (01757) 618313

MEACHAM, John David. b 24. AKC51 Open Univ MPhil90. Lambeth STh77. **d** 52 **p** 53. C Maidenhead St Luke *Ox* 52-55; C Croydon *Cant* 55-58; V Sittingbourne St Mich 58-74; V Brenchley *Roch* 74-83; Bp's Chapl and Research Asst 83-86; P-in-c Gt Wishford *Sarum* 83-88; P-in-c S Newton 83-88; Sec C of E Doctrine Commn 84-89; rtd 88. *20 Chiselbury Grove, Salisbury SP2 8EP* Tel (01722) 332217

MEAD, Arthur Hugh. b 39. K Coll Cam BA60 MA64 New Coll Ox BLitt66. St Steph Ho Ox 61. **d** 80 **p** 80. NSM Hammersmith St Jo *Lon* from 80; Chapl St Paul's Sch Barnes 82-97; Dep P in O 85-90 and from 95; P in O 90-95; Reader of The Temple from 95; rtd 97. *11 Dungarvan Avenue, London SW15 5QU* Tel 0181-876 5833

MEAD, Colin Harvey. b 26. FCA. S Dios Minl Tr Scheme. **d** 84 **p** 85. NSM Talbot Village *Sarum* 84-96; rtd 96; Perm to Offic *Sarum* from 96. *59 Alyth Road, Bournemouth BH3 7HB* Tel (01202) 763647

MEAD, Canon John Harold. b 37. Wells Th Coll 69. **d** 71 **p** 72. C Charlton Kings St Mary *Glouc* 71-75; R Stratton w Baunton 75-82; R Bishop's Cleeve from 82; RD Tewkesbury 88-97; Hon Can Glouc Cathl from 90. *The Rectory, Bishops Cleeve, Cheltenham, Glos GL52 4NG* Tel (01242) 675103

MEAD, Nicholas Charles. b 50. Newc Univ BEd73 Reading Univ MA76. Ridley Hall Cam 83. **d** 85 **p** 86. C Bilton *Cov* 85-88; C Whittlesey *Ely* 88-89; Hd of Relig Studies Neale-Wade Community Coll March 89-97; Sen Lect RE Westmr Coll Ox from 97. *Westminster College, Harcourt Hill, Oxford OX2 9AT* Tel (01865) 247644

MEAD, Nigel Gerrish. b 31. Tyndale Hall Bris 62. **d** 64 **p** 65. C Shirley *Win* 64-67; C Alverdiscott w Huntshaw *Ex* 67-71; C Yarnscombe 67-71; C Beaford and Roborough 67-71; C St Giles in the Wood 67-71; R Shebbear, Buckland Filleigh, Sheepwash etc 71-88; TR 89-95; P-in-c Langtree 85-86; RD Torrington 86-93; rtd 96; Perm to Offic *Truro* from 96. *18 Lundy Drive, Crackington Haven, Bude, Cornwall EX23 0PA* Tel (01840) 230477

MEADEN, Philip George William. b 40. Open Univ BA75. Lich Th Coll 64. **d** 66 **p** 67. C Aston SS Pet and Paul *Birm* 66-70; V Lozells St Paul 70-76; Asst Chapl HM Pris Brixton 76-77; Chapl HM Pris Lewes 77-84; Chapl HM Pris Aylesbury 84-88; Chapl HM Pris Wandsworth from 88. *HM Prison Wandsworth, PO Box 757, Heathfield Road, London SW18 3HS* Tel 0181-874 7292 Fax 877 0358

MEADER, Philip John. b 44. Oak Hill Th Coll 73. **d** 75 **p** 76. C E Ham St Paul *Chelmsf* 75-77; CMJ 77-90; TV Lowestoft and Kirkley *Nor* 90-94; V Lowestoft St Andr 94-96; R Panfield and Rayne *Chelmsf* from 96. *The Rectory, Shalford Lane, Rayne, Braintree, Essex CM7 5BT* Tel (01376) 21938

MEADOWS, Mrs Freda Angela. b 46. CertEd68. Oak Hill Th Coll 93. **d** 96 **p** 97. NSM N Wembley St Cuth *Lon* from 96. *48 Torrington Drive, Harrow, Middx HA2 8NF* Tel 0181-248 3523

MEADOWS, John Michael. b 27. St Jo Coll Cam BA50. Ridley Hall Cam 51. **d** 53 **p** 54. C Daubhill *Man* 53-55; Overseas Miss Fellowship 56-87; Malaya 57-61; Vietnam 62-75; Refugee Reception Cen Sopley *Win* 79-82; NSM Canford Magna *Sarum* 86-88; C Radipole and Melcombe Regis 89-94; rtd 94. *18 Wellington Avenue, Southampton SO18 5DD* Tel (01703) 465167

MEADOWS, Canon Stanley Percival. b 14. TD61. St D Coll Lamp BA46. **d** 47 **p** 48. C Worsley *Man* 47-49; C Littleborough 49-51; V Charlestown 51-61; R Man St Geo w St Barn 61-72; R Man Miles Platting 72-82; RD Ardwick 77-82; rtd 82; Perm to Offic *Man* from 82. *20 Dantall Avenue, Manchester M9 7BH* Tel 0161-795 9478

MEADS, William Ivan. b 35. ACIS67 ACMA75 Qu Mary Coll Lon BA56. Linc Th Coll 75. **d** 77 **p** 78. C Cheltenham St Luke and St Jo *Glouc* 77-81; Chapl HM Pris Pentonville 81-82; Preston 82-85; Wakef 85-88; P-in-c Wroxton w Balscote and Shenington w Alkerton *Ox* 88-90; R Broughton w N Newington and Shutford etc 90-95; P-in-c Week St Mary w Poundstock and Whitstone *Truro* from 95. *The Rectory, The Glebe, Week St Mary, Holsworthy, Devon EX22 6UY* Tel (01288) 84265

MEADWAY, Dr Jeanette Valerie. b 47. FRCP87 FRCPEd87 Edin Univ MB, ChB69. Oak Hill NSM Course 89. **d** 93 **p** 94. NSM Stratford St Jo and Ch Ch w Forest Gate St Jas *Chelmsf* from 93. *4 Glebe Avenue, Woodford Green, Essex IG8 9HB* Tel 0181-504 1958

MEAGER, Frederick William. b 18. St Mich Coll Llan 46. **d** 48 **p** 49. C Aberdare St Fagan *Llan* 48-51; C Hawarden *St As* 51-54; C Willian *St Alb* 54-56; V Wildmore *Linc* 56-59; V Old Warden *St Alb* 59-64; C-in-c Watford St Pet CD 64-67; V Watford St Pet 67-83; RD Watford 70-75; rtd 83; Perm to Offic *St Alb* from 83; Perm to Offic *Ely* from 84. *31 Home Manor House, Cassio Road, Watford WD1 7BS* Tel (01932) 237032

MEAKIN, Canon Anthony John (Tony). b 28. TD76. Down Coll Cam BA52 MA56. Westcott Ho Cam 52. **d** 54 **p** 55. C Gosforth All SS *Newc* 54-60; V Alnwick St Paul 60-71; V Edlingham 62-71; CF (TA) 63-83; R Whickham *Dur* 71-88; RD Gateshead W 78-88; Hon Can Dur Cathl 83-93; Bp's Sen Chapl and Exec Officer for Dioc Affairs 88-93; rtd 93. *73 Oakfields, Burnopfield, Newcastle upon Tyne NE16 6PQ* Tel (01207) 70429

MEAKIN, David John. b 61. Hull Univ BA82 Hughes Hall Cam PGCE83 Lambeth STh88. Westcott Ho Cam 86. **d** 88 **p** 89. C Upminster *Chelmsf* 88-92; Prec and Sacr Dur Cathl *Dur* from 92. *8 The College, Durham DH1 3EQ* Tel 0191-386 4733

MEAKIN, The Ven John Ernest. b 13. Kelham Th Coll 30. **d** 36 **p** 37. C Stepney St Matt *Lon* 36-39; C Cheltenham St Steph *Glouc* 39-41; C Knottingley *Wakef* 41-43; P-in-c Stepney St Phil *Lon* 43-46; Argentina 46-51; Singapore 51-55; Australia from 55; Adn Eyre Peninsula 68-70; Adn Willoch 70-80; Adn Willoch (Outer) 80-87; rtd 87. *Staddle Stones, Elder Street, Moonta Mines, S Australia 5558* Tel Moonta Mines (8) 8825 2816

MEANLEY, Hubert Edward Sylvester. b 10. Trin Coll Cam BA32. **d** 34 **p** 35. C Sandal St Helen *Wakef* 34-38; C Penistone w Midhope 38-40; C Huddersfield St Pet 40-44; V Cawthorne 44-53; V Barnsley St Geo 53-62; V Askham Bryan *York* 62-68; V Askham Richard 62-68; R Settrington 68-76; P-in-c Thorpe Bassett 72-76; rtd 76. *5 Cherry Tree Close, Skelton-on-Ure, Ripon, N Yorkshire HG4 5AL*

MEARA, David Gwynne. b 47. Or Coll Ox BA70 MA73. Lambeth STh76 Cuddesdon Coll 71. **d** 73 **p** 74. C Whitley Ch Ch *Ox* 73-77; Chapl Reading Univ 77-82; V Basildon 82-87; P-in-c Aldworth and Ashampstead 85-87; V Basildon w Aldworth and Ashampstead 87-94; RD Bradfield 90-94; V Buckingham w Radclive cum Chackmore 94-97; RD Buckingham from 95; P-in-c Nash w Thornton, Beachampton and Thornborough 96-97; R Buckingham from 97. *The Rectory, 39 Fishers Field, Buckingham MK18 1SF* Tel (01280) 813178

MEARDON, Dr Brian Henry. b 44. Reading Univ BSc66 PhD71. Oak Hill Th Coll DipHE79 MPhil84. **d** 79 **p** 80. C Reading St Jo *Ox* 79-82; V Warfield from 82. *The Vicarage, Church Lane, Warfield, Bracknell, Berks RG42 6EE* Tel (01344) 882228

MEARNS, Christopher Lee. b 30. Worc Coll Ox BA54 MA58. Ripon Hall Ox BTh56. **d** 57 **p** 58. C Greenhill St Jo *Lon* 57-60; Canada 60-62; Lect Ripon Coll of Educn 63-75; Sen Lect Coll of Ripon and York St Jo 75-85; USA 87 and 89; Tutor Ridley Hall Cam 88; Seychelles 88 and 89-90; Perm to Offic *Ripon* from 90. *14 Primrose Drive, Ripon, N Yorkshire HG4 1EY* Tel (01765) 602695

✠**MEARS, The Rt Revd John Cledan.** b 22. Univ of Wales (Abth) BA43 Univ of Wales MA48. Wycliffe Hall Ox 43. **d** 47 **p** 48 **c** 82. C Mostyn *St As* 47-49; C Rhosllannerchrugog 49-56; V Cwm 56-59; Lic to Offic *Llan* 59-73; Chapl St Mich Coll Llan 59-67; Lect Th Univ of Wales (Cardiff) 59-73; Sub-Warden St Mich Coll Llan 67-73; V Gabalfa *Llan* 73-82; Hon Can Llan Cathl 81-82; Bp Ban 82-92; rtd 92; Perm to Offic *Llan* from 92. *Isfryn, 23 Avonridge, Cardiff CF4 9AU* Tel (01222) 615505

MEARS, Phillip David. b 40. Dur Univ BA62 DipTh63. **d** 65 **p** 66. C Sandylands *Blackb* 65-68; C Chorley St Geo 68-71; V Leyland St Ambrose 71-81; Perm to Offic *Ches* from 81; Chapl Warrington Distr Gen Hosp from 81. *Warrington District General Hospital, Lovely Lane, Warrington WA5 1QC* Tel (01925) 664082 or 35911

MEASEY, George. b 08. Roch Th Coll 67. **d** 68 **p** 69. C Rowner *Portsm* 68-72; C Worthing St Geo *Chich* 72-78; rtd 78; Perm to Offic *Chich* from 78. *15 Westbrooke Court, Crescent Road, Worthing, W Sussex BN11 1RG*

MEATH AND KILDARE, Bishop of. *See* CLARKE, The Most Revd Richard Lionel

MEATH, Archdeacon of. *See* LAWRENCE, The Ven Patrick Henry Andrew

MEATS, Canon Alan John. b 41. Univ of Wales (Cardiff) BA62 DipEd63 Lon Univ BD70. St Mich Coll Llan 68. **d** 70 **p** 71. C Pontypridd St Cath *Llan* 70-73; TV Ystradyfodwg 73-75; Dioc Insp of Schs 73-75 and 83-89; V Llandeilo Tal-y-bont *S & B* 75-83; RD Llwchwr 81-83; V Aberdare St Fagan *Llan* 83-89; V Felin-foel *St D* from 89; Asst Dioc Dir of Educn 89-92; Dioc Dir of Educn from 92; Can St D Cathl from 94. *The Vicarage, Swiss Valley Road, Felinfoel, Llanelli SA14 8BS* Tel (01554) 773559

MEDCALF, James Gordon (Jim). b 31. CB. Solicitor 63. S'wark Ord Course 87. **d** 90 **p** 91. NSM Shortlands *Roch* from 90. *14B Bromley Grove, Bromley BR2 0LN* Tel 0181-464 2211

MEDCALF, John Edward. b 19. Oak Hill Th Coll 47. **d** 50 **p** 51. C Rugby St Matt *Cov* 50-53; TR Chell *Lich* 53-61; V Wednesfield Heath 61-85; rtd 85; Perm to Offic *Heref* from 86. *Clee View, Kilforge, Bolstone, Hereford HR2 6NE* Tel (01432) 840339

MEDCALF, William Henry. b 15. TCD BA45 MA49. CITC 46. **d** 46 **p** 47. C Belfast St Mich *Conn* 46-48; C Bedford St Pet *St Alb* 48-50; SE Sec CMJ 50-63; Dir Exhibitions CMJ 63-80; rtd 80; Perm to Offic *Lon* from 80. *185 Dibdin House, London W9 1QQ* Tel 0171-328 3133

MEDFORTH, Allan Hargreaves. b 27. Qu Coll Cam BA48 MA52. Westcott Ho Cam 50. **d** 51 **p** 52. C Hexham *Newc* 51-55; PV S'well Minster *S'well* 55-59; V Farnsfield 59-72; RD S'well 66-72; V St Alb St Pet *St Alb* 72-95; RD St Alb 74-84; rtd 95. *62 Cuckman's Drive, St Albans, Herts AL2 3AF* Tel (01727) 836437

MEDHURST, Prof Kenneth Noel (Ken). b 38. Edin Univ MA61 Man Univ PhD69. **d** 91 **p** 93. NSM Baildon *Bradf* from 91. *100 Langley Lane, Baildon, Shipley, W Yorkshire BD17 6TD* Tel (01274) 598273

MEDHURST, Dr Leslie John. b 56. TCD DipTh85 BTh90 MA93 Open Univ BA91 Greenwich Univ PhD93. **d** 85 **p** 86. C Seapatrick *D & D* 85-90; I Belfast St Mark *Conn* 90-97; I Helen's Bay *D & D* from 97. *2 Woodland Avenue, Helens Bay, Bangor, Co Down BT19 1TX* Tel (01247) 853601

MEDLEY, Philip Roger. b 46. ANCA FTC69 Birm Univ CertEd73. SW Minl Tr Course. **d** 85 **p** 86. NSM Ottery St Mary, Alfington and W Hill *Ex* 85-86; C S Hill w Callington *Truro* 86-89; C Linkinhorne 86-89; V from 89; Dioc Officer for Evang from 93; Warden Cornwall Preachers' Coll from 93. *The Vicarage, Linkinhorne, Callington, Cornwall PL17 7LY* Tel (01579) 362560 Fax as telephone

MEE, Colin Henry. b 36. Reading Univ BSc58. Bris Sch of Min 83. **d** 85 **p** 86. NSM Stanton St Quintin, Hullavington, Grittleton etc *Bris* 85-87; C Swindon Ch Ch 88-90; TV Washfield, Stoodleigh, Withleigh etc *Ex* 90-95; TR from 95. *The Rectory, Withleigh, Tiverton, Devon EX16 8JG* Tel (01884) 252357

MEEHAN, Cyril Frederick. b 52. St Jo Coll Nottm BTh80. **d** 80 **p** 81. C Keresley and Coundon *Cov* 80-83; P-in-c Linton and Castle Gresley *Derby* 83-90; P-in-c Alvaston from 90. *The Vicarage, 8 Church Street, Alvaston, Derby DE24 0PR* Tel (01332) 571143

MEEK, Anthony William (Tony). b 45. ACIB. Ox NSM Course 80. **d** 83 **p** 84. NSM Gt Chesham *Ox* from 83. *Elmcroft, Ley Hill, Chesham, Bucks HP5 3QR* Tel (01494) 772816

MEEK, George Edward. b 08. Leeds Univ BA30. Coll of Resurr Mirfield 26. **d** 32 **p** 33. C Glouc St Mark *Glouc* 32-35; C Stroud 35-37; C Cirencester 37-39; V Ixworth *St E* 39-48; CF (R of O) from 39; P-in-c Ixworth Thorpe *St E* 46-48; R W Monkton *B & W* 48-53; R Byfleet *Guildf* 53-58; V Wombourne *Lich* 58-68; P-in-c Newton Longville *Ox* 68-75; P-in-c Whaddon w Tattenhoe 68-75; RD Mursley 73-77; R Newton Longville w Stoke Hammond, Whaddon etc 75-77; rtd 77; Perm to Offic *Chich* from 77. *28 Titian Road, Hove, E Sussex BN3 5QS* Tel (01273) 773065

MEEK, Canon John Conway. b 33. Lon Univ BSc55 AKC56 St Cath Soc Ox BA59 MA63. Wycliffe Hall Ox 57. **d** 59 **p** 60. C Streatham Immanuel w St Anselm *S'wark* 59-62; C Bilston St Leon *Lich* 63-65; Chapl Kent and Cant Hosp 65-73; V Cant St Mary Bredin *Cant* 65-82; RD Cant 76-82; Hon Can Cant Cathl 79-82; R Bridlington Priory *York* from 82; RD Bridlington from 83; Can and Preb York Minster from 94. *The Rectory, Church Green, Bridlington, N Humberside YO16 5JX* Tel (01262) 672221

MEERE, Mrs Alison Elizabeth. b 44. SRN65 HVCert67. Ripon Coll Cuddesdon 85. **d** 87 **p** 94. Par Dn Hengrove *Bris* 87-88; Par Dn Winterbourne 88-91; Par Dn Southmead 91-93; Par Dn Hackney *Lon* 93-94; TV 94-95; Asst Chapl R Berks Hosp Reading 95-96; Asst Chapl Battle Hosp Reading 95-96. *Camden and Islington NHS Trust, 112 Hampstead Road, London NW1* Tel 0171-380 0717

MEERING, Laurence Piers Ralph. b 48. Man Univ BSc70. Trin Coll Bris 79. **d** 81 **p** 82. C Downend *Bris* 81-84; C Crofton *Portsm* 84-87; V Witheridge, Thelbridge, Creacombe, Meshaw etc *Ex* 87-94; TV Southgate *Chich* from 94. *21 Anglesey Close, Crawley, W Sussex RH11 9HG* Tel (01293) 537976

MEGAHEY, Alan John. b 44. Selw Coll Cam BA65 MA69 QUB PhD69. Westcott Ho Cam 69. **d** 70 **p** 71. Asst Chapl Wrekin Coll Shropshire 70-72; Ho Master Cranleigh Sch Surrey 72-83; Zimbabwe 83-93; Chapl Uppingham Sch Leics from 93. *Pentire House, 48 High Street West, Uppingham, Oakham, Leics LE15 9QD* Tel (01572) 822144

✠**MEHAFFEY, The Rt Revd Dr James.** b 31. TCD BA52 MA56 BD56 QUB PhD75. **d** 54 **p** 55 **c** 80. C Ballymacarrett St Patr *D & D* 54-56; C Deptford St Jo *S'wark* 56-58; C Down Cathl *D & D* 58-60; C-in-c Ballymacarrett St Chris 60-62; I Kilkeel 62-66; I Cregagh 66-80; Bp's Private Chapl 72-76; Preb Down Cathl 76-80; Dioc Missr 76-80; Bp D & R from 80. *The See House, 112 Culmore Road, Londonderry BT48 8JF* Tel (01504) 262440 Fax 352554

MEIKLE, Canon David Skene. b 39. St Cath Coll Cam BA60 MA89. Westcott Ho Cam. **d** 63 **p** 64. C Hawick *Edin* 63-67; C Edin SS Phil and Jas 67-72; C Banbury *Ox* 72-73; TV 74-78; R Ipswich St Matt *St E* 78-91; Hon Can St E Cathl from 90; TR Mildenhall from 91. *The Vicarage, Barton Mills, Bury St Edmunds IP28 6AP* Tel (01638) 716044

MEIN, Canon James Adlington. b 38. Nottm Univ BA60. Westcott Ho Cam 61. **d** 63 **p** 64. C Edin St Columba *Edin* 63-67; Bp's Dom Chapl 65-67; Malawi 67-72; R Grangemouth *Edin* 72-82; P-in-c Bo'ness 76-82; TV Livingston LEP 82-90; R Edin Ch Ch from 90; Can St Mary's Cathl from 90. *4 Morningside Road, Edinburgh EH10 4DD* Tel 0131-229 6556

MEIN, Canon Peter Simon. b 27. Nottm Univ BA55 MA59. Kelham Th Coll 48. **d** 55 **p** 01. SSM 54-70; Chapl Kelham Th Coll 55-61; Warden 62-70; Prior 64-70; USA from 71; Chapl St Andr Sch Delaware from 71; Hon Can Delaware 89; rtd 92; Assoc Member S Delaware TM 92. *St Andrew's School, 350 Noxontown Road, Middletown, DE 19709, USA* Tel Wilmington (302) 378-9511 Fax 378-7120

MEIRION-JONES, Huw Geraint. b 39. R Agric Coll Cirencester NDA61 MRAC61 K Coll Lon AKC69 BD71 MA84. St Aug Coll Cant 69. **d** 70 **p** 71. C Harlescott *Lich* 70-73; C Worplesdon *Guildf* 73-77; V Ash Vale 77-85; TR Westborough 85-96; Dioc Press Officer 85-94; P-in-c Shere from 96. *The Rectory, Spinning Walk, Shere, Guildford, Surrey GU5 9HN* Tel (01483) 202394

MEISSNER, Canon Charles Ludwig Birbeck Hill. b 26. TCD 60. **d** 62 **p** 63. C Monaghan *Clogh* 62-64; C Kildallon *K, E & A* 64-65; I 65-71; I Kinawley w H Trin 71-85; I Mohill w Farnaught, Aughavas, Oughteragh etc 85-96; Preb Elphin Cathl 87-96; rtd 96. *Millview, Laragh, Ballycassidy, Enniskillen, Co Fermanagh BT94 2JT* Tel (01365) 323842

MELANIPHY, Miss Angela Ellen. b 55. SRN79. Cranmer Hall Dur 87. **d** 90 **p** 94. Par Dn Leytonstone St Jo *Chelmsf* 90-94; C 94-95; TV Harlow Town Cen w Lt Parndon from 95. *41 Sharpecroft, Harlow, Essex CM19 4AB*

MELBOURNE, Brian Kenneth. b 45. York Univ Toronto 77. Trin Coll Toronto LTh82. **d** 82 **p** 82. Canada 82-87; Bermuda 88-94; P-in-c Biddenden and Smarden *Cant* 94-97. *21 The Gardens, Stockett Lane, Maidstone, Kent ME17 4PU*

MELBOURNE, Miss Thelma. b 08. Dalton Ho Bris 68. **dss** 77 **d** 87 **p** 94. Earlham St Anne *Nor* 77-87; Perm to Offic 87-94; C Earlham St Anne 94-96; Perm to Offic from 96. *333 Earlham Road, Norwich NR2 3RQ* Tel (01603) 53008

MELDRUM, Andrew John Bruce. b 66. Univ of Wales (Abth) LLB89. Westcott Ho Cam CTM94. **d** 94 **p** 95. C Paddington St Jas *Lon* from 94. *8 St James's Court, 75 Gloucester Terrace, London W2 3DH* Tel 0171-706 2796

MELHUISH, Douglas. b 12. St Pet Hall Ox BA34 MA38. Wycliffe Hall Ox 39. **d** 39 **p** 40. Asst Master Haberdashers' Aske's Sch Hampstead 37-40; St Jo Sch Leatherhead 37-40; Lic to Offic *Guildf* 40-42; Asst Master Bedford Sch 42-46; Chapl 43-46; Lic to Offic *St Alb* 42-46; Lect and Tutor Trin Coll Carmarthen 46-48; Prin CMS Buwalasi Coll Uganda 48-53; Colonial Service (Educn) Kenya 53-67; Perm to Offic *Win* 69-74; P-in-c St Lawrence *Portsm* 74-79; Perm to Offic *Sarum* from 79; Perm to Offic *B & W* from 85. *12 Woodcock Gardens, Warminster, Wilts BA12 9JG* Tel (01985) 219467

MELINSKY, Canon Michael Arthur Hugh. b 24. Ch Coll Cam BA47 MA49. Ripon Hall Ox 57. **d** 57 **p** 59. C Wimborne Minster *Sarum* 57-59; C Wareham w Arne 59-61; V Nor St Steph *Nor* 61-68; Chapl Norfolk and Nor Hosp 61-68; Hon Can Nor Cathl and Can Missr *Nor* 68-73; Chief Sec ACCM 73-78; Prin N Ord Course 78-88; rtd 88; Perm to Offic *Nor* from 88. *15 Parson's Mead, Norwich NR4 6PG* Tel (01603) 55042

MELLERUP, Miss Eiler Mary. b 37. Saffron Walden Coll CertEd58. LNSM course 94. **d** 96. NSM Happisburgh, Walcott, Hempstead w Eccles etc *Nor* from 96. *Channings, The Crescent, Walcott, Norwich NR12 0NH* Tel (01692) 651393

MELLING, John Cooper. b 44. ALCD73. St Jo Coll Nottm 68. **d** 72 **p** 73. C Enfield St Andr *Lon* 72-76; C Didsbury St Jas and Em *Man* 76-79; R Gt Lever 79-84; V Seamer w E Ayton *York* 84-97; P-in-c Londesborough from 97; P-in-c Burnby from 97; P-in-c Nunburnholme and Warter from 97; P-in-c Shiptonthorpe w Hayton from 97. *The Vicarage, Fairview, Shiptonthorpe, York YO4 3PE* Tel (01430) 872513

MELLING, Canon Leonard Richard. b 13. St Aid Birkenhead 38. **d** 41 **p** 42. C W Acklam *York* 41-45; C Scarborough St Mary 45-48; V Newby 48-54; Borneo 54-59; Area Sec (Dios Ox and Cov) USPG 59-64; Dio York 64-67; V Osbaldwick w Murton *York* 67-78; RD Bulmer 72-78; Malaysia 78-81; Dean Kuching 78-81; rtd 81. *12 Heslington Road, York YO1 5AT* Tel (01904) 627593

MELLISH, John. b 26. Cranmer Hall Dur 67. **d** 69 **p** 70. C Ulverston St Mary w H Trin *Carl* 69-72; V Bromfield 72-73; V Bromfield w Waverton 73-79; P-in-c Allonby w W Newton 77-79; V Shap w Swindale 79-86; RD Appleby 82-86; V Bassenthwaite, Isel and Setmurthy 86-90; rtd 90; Perm to Offic *Carl* from 90. *Wyndham, 3 Old Road, Longtown, Cumbria CA6 5TH* Tel (01228) 791441

MELLISS, Laurence John Albert. b 21. DSM45 RD69. AKC52. **d** 53 **p** 54. C Norbury St Steph *Cant* 53-56; C Folkestone St Mary and St Eanswythe 56-60; Chapl RNVR 56-59; Chapl RNR 59-76; R Upper St Leonards St Jo *Chich* 60-64; V Littlehampton St Mary 64-76; RD Arundel 75-76; V Findon 76-81; R Catsfield and Crowhurst 81-86; rtd 86; Perm to Offic *Sarum* from 95. *4 St Osmond Close, Yetminster, Sherborne, Dorset DT9 6LU* Tel (01935) 872536

MELLOR, Miss Dorothy Lilian. b 38. Birm Univ BA61. N Ord Course 86. **d** 89 **p** 94. NSM Stockton Heath *Ches* from 89; Chapl HM Young Offender Inst Thorn Cross from 92. *100 Bridge*

Lane, Appleton, Warrington, Cheshire WA4 3AL Tel (01925) 267683 Fax 262153

MELLOR, Frederick Charles Walter (Tony). b 24. Oak Hill NSM Course 80. **d** 83 **p** 84. NSM Loughton St Jo *Chelmsf* 83-93; Chapl Asst Whipps Cross Hosp Lon from 87; Perm to Offic from 93. *4 Scotland Road, Buckhurst Hill, Essex IG9 5NR* Tel 0181-504 6203

MELLOR, Canon Kenneth Paul. b 49. Southn Univ BA71 Leeds Univ MA72. Cuddesdon Coll 72. **d** 73 **p** 74. C Cottingham *York* 73-76; C Ascot Heath *Ox* 76-80; V Tilehurst St Mary 80-85; V Menheniot *Truro* 85-94; RD W Wivelshire 88-96; Hon Can Truro Cathl from 90; Can Treas from 94; Can Res and Treas Truro Cathl from 94. *Lemon Lodge, Lemon Street, Truro, Cornwall TR1 2PE* Tel (01872) 72094

MELLOR, Roy. b 52. Lanc Univ BA92. Cuddesdon Coll 94. **d** 96 **p** 97. C Oakdale *Sarum* from 96. *328 Wimborne Road, Poole, Dorset BH15 3EG* Tel (01202) 673296

MELLORS, Derek George. b 38. Bris Univ CertEd60 Lon Univ BSc71 Nottm Univ DipEd74 Liv Univ MEd83. N Ord Course 81. **d** 84 **p** 85. NSM Eccleston Ch Ch *Liv* 84-92; C Lowton St Mary 92-93; V Ashton-in-Makerfield St Thos from 93. *The Vicarage, 18 Warrington Road, Ashton-in-Makerfield, Wigan, Lancs WN4 9PL* Tel (01942) 727275

MELLORS, James. b 32. Kelham Th Coll 52. **d** 56 **p** 57. C Horbury *Wakef* 56-61; V Scholes 61-72; V Mirfield 72-88; Hon Can Wakef Cathl 83-88; V Leyburn w Bellerby *Ripon* 88-93; rtd 93. *Langthwaite Cottage, Main Street, West Witton, Leyburn, N Yorkshire DL8 4LR* Tel (01969) 622452

MELLOWS, Canon Alan Frank. b 23. Qu Coll Cam BA45 MA49. Tyndale Hall Bris 47. **d** 49 **p** 50. C Morden *S'wark* 49-54; V Brimscombe *Glouc* 54-62; R Mileham *Nor* 62-74; P-in-c Beeston next Mileham 62-66; R 66-74; P-in-c Stanfield 62-74; P-in-c Gt w Lt Dunham 70-73; R Ashill 74-79; P-in-c Saham Toney 78-79; R Ashill w Saham Toney 79-88; Hon Can Nor Cathl 82-88; rtd 88; Perm to Offic *Nor* from 88. *8 Smugglers Close, Hunstanton, Norfolk PE36 6JU* Tel (01485) 534271

MELLOWSHIP, Robert John (Rob). b 52. St Mich Coll Llan BD92. **d** 92 **p** 93. C Brecon St Mary and Battle w Llanddew *S & B* 92-94; Min Can Brecon Cathl 92-94; C Pontypool *Mon* 94-95; TV 95-97; P-in-c Bressingham w N and S Lopham and Fersfield *Nor* from 97. *The Rectory, High Street, Bressingham, Diss, Norfolk IP22 2AT* Tel (01379) 688267 Fax as telephone

MELLUISH, Mark Peter. b 59. Oak Hill Th Coll. **d** 89 **p** 90. C Ashtead *Guildf* 89-93; V Ealing St Paul *Lon* from 93. *St Paul's Vicarage, 102 Elers Road, London W13 9QE* Tel 0181-567 4628 or 579 5953

MELLUISH, Stephen. b 60. Trin Coll Bris DipHE93. **d** 93 **p** 94. C Gipsy Hill Ch Ch *S'wark* 93-96; V Wandsworth St Steph from 96. *St Stephen's Vicarage, 2A Oakhill Road, London SW15 2QU* Tel 0181-874 5610

MELLY, Aleck Emerson. b 24. Oak Hill Th Coll 50. **d** 53 **p** 54. C Chadderton Ch Ch *Man* 53-56; C Cheltenham St Mark *Glouc* 56-59; V Tipton St Paul *Lich* 59-68; R Kemberton w Sutton Maddock 68-80; P-in-c Stockton 74-80; R Kemberton, Sutton Maddock and Stockton 81-89; rtd 89; Perm to Offic *Lich* from 89; Perm to Offic *Heref* from 90. *47 Greenfields Road, Bridgnorth, Shropshire WV16 4JG* Tel (01746) 762711

MELROSE, Kenneth Mark Cecil. b 15. Ex Coll Ox BA37 DipTh38 MA41. Ripon Hall Ox 37. **d** 39 **p** 40. C Clifton St Jo *Bris* 39-41; Lic to Offic *Glouc* 41-42; Chapl RNVR 42-46; Lic to Offic *St Alb* 47-49; V Bedminster St Aldhelm *Bris* 49-55; V Hurstbourne Tarrant *Win* 55-63; V Portswood St Denys 63-71; V Bovey Tracey SS Pet and Paul *Ex* 71-85; rtd 85; Perm to Offic *Cant* from 85. *88 Wells Way, Faversham, Kent ME13 7QU* Tel (01795) 536115

MELROSE, Michael James Gervase. b 47. St Chad's Coll Dur BA69 DipTh70. **d** 71 **p** 72. C Chelmsf All SS *Chelmsf* 71-74; C Pimlico St Pet w Westmr Ch Ch *Lon* 74-80; R Man Victoria Park *Man* 80-94; P-in-c Cheetwood St Alb 85-91; R Reading St Giles *Ox* from 94. *St Giles's Rectory, Church Street, Reading RG1 2SB* Tel 0118-957 2831

MELTON, Mrs Anne. b 44. N Riding Coll of Educn CertEd65. St Jo Coll Dur 80. **dss** 83 **d** 87 **p** 94. Newton Aycliffe *Dur* 83-87; Par Dn 87-88; Par Dn Shildon w Eldon 88-94; Asst Dir of Ords 88-94; C Shildon w Eldon 94; P-in-c Usworth 94-96; TR from 96. *4 Highbury Close, Springwell, Gateshead, Tyne & Wear NE9 7PU* Tel 0191-416 3533

MELVILLE, Dominic. b 63. Sussex Univ BA84 Southn Univ BTh90. Sarum & Wells Th Coll 87. **d** 90 **p** 91. C Willenhall H Trin *Lich* 90-94; V Wednesfield St Greg from 94. *St Gregory's Vicarage, 112 Long Knowle Lane, Wednesfield, Wolverhampton WV11 1JQ* Tel (01902) 731677

MELVILLE, Malcolm Charles Crompton. b 13. Birm Univ BSc36. Lich Th Coll 37. **d** 39 **p** 40. C Swindon St Paul *Bris* 39-42; C Lich St Mich *Lich* 42-43; PV Lich Cathl 42-46; Treas and Sacr 42-43; Chan 43-46; Chapl RNVR 46-48; Brazil 48-52; Chapl St Paul's Sch St Paulo 48-52; C St Marylebone All SS *Lon* 52-63; Hd Master All SS Choir Sch 52-63; P-in-c Clifton w Glapton *S'well* 63-65; C Heacham *Nor* 65-67; Perm to Offic *St Alb* from 67; rtd 78. *45 Beverley Crescent, Bedford MK40 4BX* Tel (01234) 266060

MELVIN, Gordon Thomas. b 55. BA86. Sarum & Wells Th Coll 86. **d** 88 **p** 89. C Linc St Faith and St Martin w St Pet *Linc* 88-91; TV Horsham *Chich* 91-94; Chapl Horsham Gen Hosp 91-94; Chapl Ipswich Hosp from 94. *50 Constable Road, Ipswich IP4 2UZ, or Ipswich Hospital, Heath Road, Ipswich IP4 5PD* Tel (01473) 704100 or 712233

MEMBERY, Donald Percy. b 20. K Coll Lon BSc50 DipEd51 AKC51. Ox NSM Course. **d** 79 **p** 80. NSM Aston Rowant w Crowell *Ox* 79-81; P-in-c Swyncombe 81-85; R Swyncombe w Britwell Salome 85-88; rtd 88; Perm to Offic *Ripon* from 88. *11 Carr Manor Gardens, Leeds LS17 5DQ* Tel 0113-269 1578

MENDEL, Thomas Oliver (Tom). b 57. Down Coll Cam BA79 MA82. Cranmer Hall Dur 79. **d** 81 **p** 82. Lic to Offic *Ely* 81-86; Chapl Down Coll Cam 81-86; Hon C Ely 81-86; V Minsterley *Heref* 86-92; Chapl Costa del Sol W *Eur* 92-93; Chapl Shrewsbury Sch 93-95; Chapl Milan w Genoa and Varese *Eur* 95-96; Chapl Copenhagen w Aarhus from 96. *St Alban's House, Stigaardsvej 6, DK-2900 Hellerup, Denmark* Tel Denmark (45) 39 62 77 36

MENEY, Brian James. b 42. Glas Univ MA63. Edin Th Coll 63. **d** 65 **p** 66. C Dundee St Paul *Bre* 65-69; Lic to Offic *Edin* 69-71; C Edin H Cross 71-73; Asst Sec Rep Ch Coun 73-81; P-in-c Edin St Barn 73-81; Chapl Bede Ho Staplehurst 81-82; P-in-c Plaistow SS Phil and Jas w St Andr *Chelmsf* 82-83; TR Plaistow 83-90; V Leeds Gipton Epiphany *Ripon* 90-95; rtd 95. *Spofforth Hall Cheshire Home, Wetherby Road, Harrogate, W Yorkshire HG3 1BX* Tel (01937) 590669

✠**MENIN, The Rt Revd Malcolm James.** b 32. Univ Coll Ox BA55 MA59. Cuddesdon Coll 55. **d** 57 **p** 58 **c** 86. C Southsea H Spirit *Portsm* 57-59; C Fareham SS Pet and Paul 59-62; V Nor St Jas w Pockthorpe *Nor* 62-72; P-in-c Nor St Martin 62-74; P-in-c Nor St Mary Magd 68-72; V Nor St Mary Magd w St Jas 72-86; RD Nor E 81-86; Hon Can Nor Cathl 82-86; Suff Bp Knaresborough *Ripon* 86-97; rtd 97; Perm to Offic *Nor* from 97. *32C Bracondale, Norwich NR1 2AN* Tel (01603) 627987

MENNISS, Andrew Philip. b 49. Univ of Wales (Swansea) BSc73. Sarum & Wells Th Coll 83. **d** 85 **p** 86. C Horsell *Guildf* 85-89; V Bembridge *Portsm* from 89; RD E Wight from 95. *The Vicarage, Church Road, Bembridge, Isle of Wight PO35 5NA* Tel (01983) 872175

MENON, Nicholas Anthony Thotekat. b 39. Mert Coll Ox BA61 MA65 DipTh62. St Steph Ho Ox 61. **d** 63 **p** 64. C Paddington Ch Ch *Lon* 63-66; Hon C 66-70; V Thorpe *Guildf* 70-76; V Ox SS Phil and Jas w St Marg *Ox* 76-79; Chapl Surrey Univ *Guildf* 79-81; Asst Chapl and Ho Master Cranleigh Sch Surrey from 82. *Loveday House, Cranleigh School, Cranleigh, Surrey GU6 8PZ* Tel (01483) 272510

MENSINGH, Gregg Richard. b 69. Portsm Univ BSc94. Westcott Ho Cam 95. **d** 97. C Birchfield *Birm* from 97. *48 Leonard Road, Handsworth, Birmingham B19 1JU* Tel 0121-551 6125

MENTZEL, Kevin David. b 60. Reading Univ BSc82 Down Coll Cam BA87 MA91. Ridley Hall Cam 85. **d** 88 **p** 89. C Ditton *Roch* 88-91; Asst Chapl Eton Coll 91-93; Asst Chapl R Hosp Sch Holbrook 93-94; Sen C Fulham St Dionis Parson's Green *Lon* from 94. *16 Parson's Green, London SW6 4TS* Tel 0171-736 4849

MEPHAM, Kevin Aubrey. b 55. Sarum & Wells Th Coll 85. **d** 88 **p** 89. NSM Sidley *Chich* 88-90; C Hollington St Leon 90-94; V Horam from 94. *The Vicarage, Horebeech Lane, Horam, Heathfield, E Sussex TN21 0DT* Tel (01435) 812563

MEPHAM, Stephen Richard. b 64. K Coll Lon BD85 AKC85. Linc Th Coll 87. **d** 89 **p** 90. C Newark *S'well* 89-92; C Cheshunt *St Alb* 92-95; Min Turnford St Clem CD 95; P-in-c from 95. *St Clement's House, 44 Hillview Gardens, Cheshunt, Waltham Cross, Herts EN8 0PE* Tel (01992) 625098

MEPSTED, Leonard Charles. b 34. Leeds Univ BA61. Coll of Resurr Mirfield 61. **d** 63 **p** 64. C Goldthorpe *Sheff* 63-65; C S Shields St Hilda w St Thos *Dur* 65-69; C Woodston *Ely* 69-71; V Friday Bridge 71-72; C Moss Side Ch Ch *Man* 72-74; P-in-c Farnworth All SS 75-76; C Lawton Moor 76-78; P-in-c Falinge 78-87; R Eastchurch w Leysdown and Harty *Cant* from 87. *The Rectory, Warden Road, Eastchurch, Sheerness, Kent ME12 4EJ* Tel (01795) 880205

✠**MERCER, The Rt Revd Eric Arthur John.** b 17. Kelham Th Coll. **d** 47 **p** 48 **c** 65. C Coppenhall *Ches* 47-51; C-in-c Heald Green St Cath CD 51-53; R Stockport St Thos 53-59; R Ches St Bridget w St Martin 59-65; Dioc Missr 59-65; Hon Can Ches Cathl 64-65; Suff Bp Birkenhead 65-73; Bp Ex 73-85; rtd 85; P-in-c E Knoyle, Hindon w Chicklade and Pertwood *Sarum* 85-86; P-in-c Hindon w Chicklade and Pertwood 86-88. *Frickers House, Cow Drove, Chilmark, Salisbury SP3 5AJ* Tel (01722) 716400

MERCER, Canon John James Glendinning. b 20. TCD BA49 MA55. **d** 50 **p** 51. C Newtownards *D & D* 50-53; C Bangor St Comgall 53-55; I Ballyholme 55-90; Can Belf Cathl 76-88; Preb Wicklow St Patr Cathl Dublin 88-90; rtd 90. *6 Hillfoot, Groomsport, Bangor, Co Down BT19 6JJ* Tel (01247) 472979

MERCER, Nicholas Stanley (Nick). b 49. Selw Coll Cam BA72 PGCE73 MA76. Spurgeon's Coll BA78 Lon Bible Coll MPhil86 Cranmer Hall Dur 95. **d** 95 **p** 95. C Northwood Hills St Edm *Lon*

from 95. *128 Pinner View, Harrow, Middx HA1 4RN* Tel 0181-723 2658 Fax 723 2658

✠**MERCER, The Rt Revd Robert William Stanley.** b 35. St Paul's Grahamstown LTh59. **d** 59 **p** 60 **c** 77. S Rhodesia 59-63; Lic to Offic *Wakef* 64-66; CR from 65; Perm to Offic *Llan* 66-68; S Africa 68-70; Rhodesia 70-80; Zimbabwe 80-87; Sub-Prelate OStJ from 80; Bp Matabeleland 77-87; Canada from 87; Asst Bp Angl Catholic Ch of Canada 88-89; Dioc Bp from 89. *225 First Avenue, Ottawa, Ontario, Canada K1S 2G5, or House of the Resurrection, Mirfield, W Yorkshire WF14 0DN* Tel Kingston (613) 594 8637 Fax 233 4399

MERCER, Timothy James. b 54. Fitzw Coll Cam BA76 MA80. Westcott Ho Cam 78. **d** 81 **p** 82. C Bromley SS Pet and Paul *Roch* 81-85; R Swanscombe 85-96; Chapl Bromley Hosps NHS Trust from 96. *75 Tintagel Road, Orpington, Kent BR5 4LH* Tel (01689) 821171

MERCER-LESLIE, Shirley Vera. b 62. Linc Th Coll DMS94. **d** 96 **p** 97. C Frodingham *Linc* from 96. *66 Church Lane, Scunthorpe, S Humberside DN15 7AF* Tel (01724) 848171

MERCERON, Daniel John. b 58. Lon Univ BA81. Westcott Ho Cam 88. **d** 90 **p** 91. C Clevedon St Jo *B & W* 90-94; CF from 94. *MOD Chaplains (Army), Trenchard Lines, Upavon, Pewsey, Wilts SN9 6BE* Tel (01980) 615804 Fax 615800

MERCHANT, David Clifford. b 17. Univ of Wales BA37 Birm Univ MA70. St Mich Coll Llan 45. **d** 46 **p** 47. C Newport St Julian *Mon* 46-48; C Hawarden *St As* 48-50; V Choral St As Cathl 50-53; Area Sec (Midl) SPG 53-57; V W Bromwich St Jas *Lich* 57-65; Chapl Westhill Coll of HE Birm 65-82; Hon C Northfield *Birm* 74-92; rtd 82; Perm to Offic *Birm* from 92. *28 Weoley Park Road, Birmingham B29 6QU* Tel 0121-472 0910

MERCIER, David Cuthbert. b 10. St Pet Hall Ox BA32 MA36. Wycliffe Hall Ox 35. **d** 37 **p** 38. C Edge Hill St Mary *Liv* 37-41; C Gt Sankey 41-44; C Parr 44-49; V Langford Budville w Runnington *B & W* 49-54; R Phillack w Gwithian *Truro* 55-59; New Zealand from 59. *44 Haumoana Road, Haumoana, Hawkes Bay, New Zealand* Tel Levin (6) 875 0147

MERCURIO, Frank James Charles. b 46. Webster Univ (USA) BA73 MA75. St Alb Minl Tr Scheme 87. **d** 89 **p** 90. C Cheshunt *St Alb* 89-93; TV Hitchin from 93; RD Hitchin from 94. *Holy Saviour Vicarage, St Anne's Road, Hitchin, Herts SG5 1QB* Tel (01462) 456140

MEREDITH, Andrew James MacPherson. b 59. St Jo Coll Nottm DCM93. **d** 93 **p** 94. C Killay *S & B* 93-97; V Waunarllwydd from 97. *St Barnabas' Vicarage, 59 Victoria Road, Waunarlwydd, Swansea SA5 4SY* Tel (01792) 206631

MEREDITH, James Noel Michael Creed. b 17. Keble Coll Ox BA40 MA43. Westcott Ho Cam 39. **d** 40 **p** 42. C Woolwich St Mary w H Trin *S'wark* 40-44; CF 44-47; Chapl St Jo Sch Leatherhead 47-48; R Moss Side Ch Ch *Man* 48-56; Jamaica 56-61; R Stoke *Cov* 61-71; RD Cov E 69-71; V Hessle *York* 71-78; R Milton Abbas, Hilton w Cheselbourne etc *Sarum* 78-80; TV Llandudno *Ban* 80-84; rtd 82. *11 Pascoe Close, Poole, Dorset BH14 0NT* Tel (01202) 737108

MEREDITH, Robert. b 21. Bps' Coll Cheshunt 56. **d** 58 **p** 59. C Bedford St Andr *St Alb* 58-61; V Luton All SS 61-67; V Kimpton 67-75; RD Wheathampstead 72-76; R Kimpton w Ayot St Lawrence 75-76; R Hunsdon 76-80; R Widford 76-80; R Hunsdon w Widford and Wareside 80-84; P-in-c Braughing, Lt Hadham, Albury, Furneux Pelham etc 84-88; R Braughing w Furneux Pelham and Stocking Pelham 88-90; rtd 90; Perm to Offic *St Alb* from 90. *19 Cowper Crescent, Hertford SG14 3DZ* Tel (01992) 558847

MEREDITH, Canon Roland Evan. b 32. Trin Coll Cam BA55 MA59. Cuddesdon Coll 55. **d** 57 **p** 58. C Bishopwearmouth St Mich *Dur* 57-59; Dioc Chapl *Birm* 59-60; C Kirkby *Liv* 60-63; V Hitchin St Mary *St Alb* 63-72; V Preston St Jo *Blackb* 72-76; TR 76-79; RD Preston 72-79; Hon Can Blackb Cathl 77-79; TR Witney *Ox* 79-94; P-in-c Hailey w Crawley 79-82; RD Witney 89-97; Hon Can Ch Ch 92-97; rtd 94. *1 Deanery Court, Broad Street, Bampton, Oxford OX18 2LY* Tel (01993) 851142

MEREDITH, Ronald Duncan d'Esterre. b 09. K Coll Lon BD32 AKC32. **d** 32 **p** 33. C Milton Regis St Mary *Cant* 32-35; C Croydon St Sav 35-39; C St Peter-in-Thanet 32-42; C-in-c 42-44; Chapl RNVR 44-45; V Chislet *Cant* 45-50; V Sittingbourne H Trin 50-62; R Dymchurch w Eastbridge, Orgarswick etc 62-63; R Dymchurch 63-68; V Seasalter 68-76; Six Preacher Cant Cathl 73-76; rtd 76; Perm to Offic *Cant* from 76. *64 Beacon Road, Broadstairs, Kent CT10 3DG* Tel (01843) 869883

MEREDITH-JONES, Richard. b 26. JP79. K Coll Lon 50. **d** 54 **p** 55. C Perry Hill St Geo *S'wark* 54-56; P-in-c New Charlton H Trin 56-58; V Cinderford St Jo *Glouc* 58-62; Chapl Dilke Hosp Cinderford 58-62; V Richmond St Jo *S'wark* 62-66; Chapl Royal Hosp Richmond 62-66; Ind Chapl *Wakef* 66-70; Chapl Glenside Hosp Bris 70-92; Perm to Offic *Glouc* 70-88; CF (TAVR) 78-91; Perm to Offic *Ban* 88-93; rtd 91; Perm to Offic *St D* and *B & W* from 91. *18 Wetlands Lane, Portishead, Bristol BS20 8NA* Tel (01275) 817217

MERIONETH, Archdeacon of. See DAVIES, The Ven Francis James Saunders

MERIVALE, Charles Christian Robert. b 44. Cranmer Hall Dur 76. **d** 78 **p** 79. C Highbury Ch Ch *Lon* 78; C Highbury Ch Ch w St Jo 79-81; P-in-c Hawes *Ripon* 81-82; P-in-c Hardrow and St Jo w Lunds 81-82; V Hawes and Hardraw 82-84; Chapl R Cornwall Hosps NHS Trust 85-92; Lic to Offic *Truro* 85-92; rtd 92; Perm to Offic *B & W* from 92. *Welham House, Welham, Castle Cary, Somerset BA7 7NE* Tel (01963) 350264

MERRETT, Jonathan Charles. b 55. Univ of Wales (Ban) BMus77 MMus78. Ripon Coll Cuddesdon 78. **d** 81 **p** 82. C Kenilworth St Nic *Cov* 81-84; C Grandborough w Willoughby and Flecknoe 84-87; Asst Dioc Educn Officer from 87. *18 St Mary's Crescent, Leamington Spa, Warks CV31 1JL* Tel (01926) 885146

MERRICK, John. b 51. New Univ of Ulster BA72 DipAdEd75 TCD HDipEd73. CITC 89. **d** 92 **p** 93. Hd Master Sligo Gr Sch from 92; Lic to Offic *K, E & A* from 92. *The Headmaster's Residence, Sligo Grammar School, The Mall, Sligo, Irish Republic* Tel Sligo (71) 42775

MERRINGTON, Bill. b 55. BSc. Cranmer Hall Dur. **d** 83 **p** 84. C Harborne Heath *Birm* 83-88; V Leamington Priors St Paul *Cov* from 88; RD Warwick and Leamington from 97. *The Vicarage, 15 Lillington Road, Leamington Spa, Warks CV32 5YS* Tel (01926) 335331

MERRY, David Thomas (Tom). b 48. St Chad's Coll Dur BA70. AKC73. **d** 74 **p** 75. C Cirencester *Glouc* 74-78; TV Bridgnorth, Tasley, Astley Abbotts and Oldbury *Heref* 78-83; P-in-c Quatford 81-83; P-in-c Stroud H Trin *Glouc* from 83; Chapl Stroud Gen Hosp from 83. *Holy Trinity Vicarage, 10 Bowbridge Lane, Stroud, Glos GL5 2JW* Tel (01453) 764551

MERRY, Ivor John. b 28. WMMTC. **d** 87 **p** 88. NSM Redditch, The Ridge *Worc* 87-94; NSM Astwood Bank from 94. *5 Church Road, Astwood Bank, Redditch, Worcs B96 6EH* Tel (01527) 892887

MERRY, Canon James Thomas Arthur. b 38. Toronto Univ BA58 Saskatchewan Univ LLB74. Wycliffe Coll Toronto BTh62. **d** 61 **p** 62. Canada 61-89; I Ematris w Rockcorry, Aghabog and Aughnamullan *Clogh* from 89; Dioc Registrar from 91; Can Clogh Cathl from 95. *The Rectory, Dartrey, Cootehill, Co Cavan, Irish Republic* Tel Castleblayney (42) 42484

MERRY, Rex Edwin. b 38. AKC67. **d** 68 **p** 69. C Spalding St Jo *Linc* 68-73; C Boxmoor St Jo *St Alb* 73-83; TV Hemel Hempstead 83-95; V Farley Hill St Jo from 95. *The Vicarage, 47 Rotheram Avenue, Luton LU1 5PP* Tel (01582) 29466

MERWOOD, Raymond George. b 27. K Coll Lon. **d** 54 **p** 56. C Wareham w Arne *Sarum* 54-55; C Rawmarsh *Sheff* 55-58; C Thrybergh 58-62; C Brixham *Ex* 62-67; V Newton Poppleford w Harpford 67-91; rtd 91; Perm to Offic *Ex* from 92. *53 Carter Avenue, Exmouth, Devon EX8 3EF* Tel (01395) 279432

MESSENGER, Paul. b 38. Univ of Wales (Lamp) BA63. Coll of Resurr Mirfield 63. **d** 65 **p** 66. C Battersea St Luke *S'wark* 65-69; C Ainsdale *Liv* 69-71; V Wigan St Steph 71-74; Asst Chapl St Marg Convent E Grinstead 74-76; Chapl Kingsley St Mich Sch W Sussex 74-76; P-in-c Southwater *Chich* 76-81; V 81-97; R Sullington and Thakeham w Warminghurst from 97. *The Rectory, Thakeham, Pulborough, W Sussex RH20 3EP* Tel (01798) 813121

MESSENGER, Canon Reginald James. b 13. Univ Coll Dur LTh38 BA39 MA57. St Aug Coll Cant 35. **d** 39 **p** 40. India 39-80; rtd 80; Perm to Offic *Chich* from 80. *58 Oakcroft Gardens, Littlehampton, W Sussex BN17 6LT* Tel (01903) 715982

MESSOM, Alan George. b 42. St Chad's Coll Dur BA63 DipTh65. **d** 65 **p** 66. C Newc St Gabr *Newc* 65-68; Korea 69-77; V Derby St Bart *Derby* from 78. *St Bartholomew's Vicarage, Addison Road, Derby DE24 8FH* Tel (01332) 347709

METCALF, Preb Michael Ralph. b 37. Clare Coll Cam BA61 MA65 Birm Univ MA80. Ridley Hall Cam 63. **d** 64 **p** 65. C Downend *Bris* 64-67; Perm to Offic *Birm* 68-78; Perm to Offic *Lich* 72-81; Dioc Dir of Educn 83-94; Perm to Offic *Heref* from 87; Preb Lich Cathl *Lich* from 91; V Stafford St Paul Forebridge from 94. *St Paul's Vicarage, 31 The Oval, Stafford ST17 4LQ* Tel (01785) 51683

METCALF, The Ven Robert Laurence (Bob). b 35. Dur Univ BA60. Cranmer Hall Dur DipTh62. **d** 62 **p** 63. C Bootle Ch Ch *Liv* 62-65; C Farnworth 65-67; V Wigan St Cath 67-75; R Wavertree H Trin 75-94; Chapl Blue Coat Sch Liv 75-94; Dir of Ords *Liv* from 82; Hon Can Liv Cathl from 87; Adn Liv from 94. *38 Menlove Avenue, Allerton, Liverpool L18 2EF* Tel 0151-734 3956

METCALFE, Alan. b 22. St Aid Birkenhead 49. **d** 52 **p** 53. C Cleckheaton St Jo *Wakef* 52-55; C Todmorden 55-56; C Thornhill Lees 56-58; V Middlestown 58-60; V S Crosland 60-64; V Upwood w Gt and Lt Raveley *Ely* 64-69; Chapl RAF 64-68; V Dewsbury St Matt and St Jo *Wakef* 69-71; Warden Bridgehead Hostel Cardiff 71-73; Field View Hostel Stoke Prior 73-75; McIntyre Ho Nuneaton 75-79; C Southam w Stockton *Cov* 79-84; P-in-c Kinwarton w Gt Alne and Haselor 84-87; rtd 87; Hon C Yarcombe w Membury and Upottery *Ex* 89-92. *32 High Road, Trimley, Ipswich IP10 0SZ* Tel (01394) 271585

METCALFE, James. b 17. St Pet Hall Ox BA39 MA44. Wycliffe Hall Ox 39. **d** 41 **p** 42. C Dartford Ch Ch *Roch* 41-43; CF (EC) 43-47; C Goole *Sheff* 47-49; V Batley St Thos *Wakef* 49-55; V Mexborough *Sheff* 55-71; R Wickersley 71-82; rtd 82; Perm to Offic *Bradf* from 83. *Scar Fields, The Mains, Giggleswick, Settle, N Yorkshire BD24 0AX* Tel (01729) 823983

METCALFE, Reginald Herbert. b 38. **d** 79. Hon C Aspley Guise *St Alb* 79; Hon C Aspley Guise w Husborne Crawley and Ridgmont 80-84; Hon C Bovingdon from 84. *30 Manorville Road, Aspley, Hemel Hempstead, Herts HP3 0AP* Tel (01442) 242952

METCALFE, Canon Ronald. b 41. BA. Edin Th Coll 67. **d** 69 **p** 70. C Saltburn-by-the-Sea *York* 69-72; P-in-c Crathorne 73-77; Youth Officer 73-77; Dioc Adult Tr Officer 78-88; Can Res York Minster from 88; Sec for Miss and Min from 88. *5 Minster Yard, York YO1 2JE* Tel (01904) 642542

METCALFE, William Bernard. b 47. St Jo Coll Cam BA69 MA73 Ball Coll Ox BA71. Ripon Hall Ox 70. **d** 72 **p** 73. C Caversham *Ox* 72-75; C Aylesbury 75-79; Ind Chapl 75-79; TV Thamesmead *S'wark* 79-84; TR Totton *Win* 84-94; R Gt Bentley and Frating w Thorrington *Chelmsf* from 94. *The Rectory, Moors Close, Great Bentley, Colchester CO7 8QL* Tel (01206) 250476

METCALFE, Canon William Nelson. b 15. St Jo Coll Dur BA39 MA54. St Aid Birkenhead LTh38. **d** 39 **p** 40. C Basford St Leodegarius *S'well* 39-42; Chapl RAF 42-46; C Melton Mowbray w Burton Lazars, Freeby etc *Leic* 47; V Bunny w Bradmore *S'well* 47-59; R Bottesford *Leic* 59-62; R Bottesford and Muston 62-82; RD Framland I 60-80; Hon Can Leic Cathl 75-82; rtd 82; Perm to Offic *Linc* from 82. *62 Church Lane, Sutton-on-Sea, Mablethorpe, Lincs LN12 2JB* Tel (01507) 442331

METHUEN, The Very Revd John Alan Robert. b 47. BNC Ox BA69 MA74. Cuddesdon Coll 69. **d** 71 **p** 72. C Fenny Stratford *Ox* 71-73; C Fenny Stratford and Water Eaton 74; Asst Chapl Eton Coll 74-77; P-in-c Dorney *Ox* 74-77; Warden Dorney/Eton Coll Conf Cen 74-77; V Reading St Mark 77-83; R Hulme Ascension *Man* 83-95; Dean Ripon from 95. *The Minster House, Ripon, N Yorkshire HG4 1PE* Tel (01765) 603615

METHVEN, Alexander George. b 26. Lon Univ BD52 Em Coll Cam BA54 MA58. ACT ThL47 Lon Coll of Div 50. **d** 53 **p** 53. C Cambridge St Andr Less *Ely* 52-54; Chapl RAF 55-60; V Lower Sydenham St Mich *S'wark* 60-67; Australia from 68; rtd 91. *PO Box 494, Belgrave, Victoria, Australia 3160* Tel Victoria (3) 9754 8056

METIVIER, Robert John. b 31. Lon Univ BA68. Lambeth STh61 Ch Div Sch of the Pacific (USA) BD66 MDiv69 Codrington Coll Barbados 56. **d** 60 **p** 61. Trinidad and Tobago 61-64 and 68-78; USPG 66-67; C Gt Berkhamsted *St Alb* 78-82; V Goff's Oak St Jas 82-90; V Tokyngton St Mich *Lon* from 90. *The Vicarage, St Michael's Avenue, Wembley, Middx HA9 6SL* Tel 0181-902 3290

METTERS, Anthony John Francis. b 43. AKC65. **d** 68 **p** 69. C Heavitree *Ex* 68-74; V Plymouth Crownhill Ascension 74-79; RD Plymouth 77-79; Chapl RN from 79. *Royal Naval Chaplaincy Service, Room 203, Victory Building, HM Naval Base, Portsmouth PO1 3LS* Tel (01705) 727903 Fax 727112

METTHAM, Maurice Desmond. b 20. Sarum & Wells Th Coll 73. **d** 74 **p** 75. C Guernsey St Sav *Win* 74-81; Perm to Offic 81-96. *La Masse Residential Home, Grande Capelles Road, St Sampsons, Guernsey* Tel (01481) 49334

MEW, Ms Jacqueline Mary (Jackie). b 57. Southn Univ MPhil90 MBCS83. S Dios Minl Tr Scheme 92. **d** 95 **p** 96. NSM Hythe *Win* from 95. *9 Birchdale, Hythe, Southampton SO45 3HX* Tel (01703) 840132 Fax as telephone

MEWIS, David William. b 47. Leeds Inst of Educn CertEd68 Leeds Poly BEd83. N Ord Course 87. **d** 90 **p** 91. C Skipton Ch Ch *Bradf* 90-92; R Bolton by Bowland w Grindleton from 92. *The Rectory, Sawley Road, Grindleton, Clitheroe, Lancs BB7 4QS* Tel (01200) 41154

MEWS, Stuart Paul. b 44. Leeds Univ BA64 MA67 Trin Hall Cam PhD74 FRHistS75. Westcott Ho Cam 86. **d** 87 **p** 88. Lect Lanc Univ 68-92; NSM Caton w Littledale *Blackb* 87-90; Hon C Lancaster St Mary 88-92; Reader Relig Studies Chelt & Glouc Coll of HE from 92; Perm to Offic *Glouc* from 93. *Cheltenham and Gloucester College, PO Box 220, The Park Campus, Cheltenham, Glos GL50 2QF* Tel (01242) 543358

MEYER, Stuart Thomas. b 45. GLCM69 Open Univ BA85. Trin Coll Bris 76. **d** 78 **p** 79. C Heref St Pet w St Owen *Heref* 78-79; C Heref St Pet w St Owen and St Jas 79-80; Chapl K Coll Cam 80-84; Chapl Lon Univ Medical Schs *S'wark* 84-87; Chapl Dulwich Hosp 87-93; Chapl Camberwell Distr HA 90-93; Chapl K Coll Hosp Lon 90-93; Sen Chapl King's Healthcare NHS Trust from 93. *King's College Hospital, Denmark Hill, London SE5 9PJ* Tel 0171-346 3522

MEYER, William John. b 46. ACIB. Cranmer Hall Dur 83. **d** 85 **p** 86. C Merrow *Guildf* 85-89; V Grayshott from 89. *The Vicarage, Grayshott, Hindhead, Surrey GU26 6NH* Tel (01428) 604540

MEYNELL, Andrew Francis. b 43. Westcott Ho Cam 70. **d** 73 **p** 74. C Cowley St Jas *Ox* 73-79; TV 79-81; P-in-c Halton 81-95; V Wendover 81-95; P-in-c Monks Risborough from 95. *The Rectory, Mill Lane, Monks Risborough, Princes Risborough, Bucks HP27 9JE* Tel (01844) 342556

MEYNELL, Mrs Honor Mary. b 37. EMMTC 84. **d** 87 **p** 94. NSM Kirk Langley *Derby* from 87. *Meynell Langley, Kirk Langley, Ashbourne, Derbyshire DE6 4NT* Tel (01332) 824207

MEYNELL, Canon Mark. b 14. Ch Ch Ox BA37 MA44. Cuddesdon Coll. **d** 40 **p** 41. C St Alb Abbey *St Alb* 40-46; R Folkington *Chich* 46-49; R Marlesford *St E* 49-56; R Campsey Ashe 51-56; R Cogenhoe *Pet* 56-63; V Leamington Hastings *Cov* 65-79; R Birdingbury 74-79; Can Th Cov Cathl 73-78; rtd 79; Perm to Offic *St E* from 80. *2 Double Street, Framlingham, Woodbridge, Suffolk IP13 9BN* Tel (01728) 723898

MEYNELL, Mark John Henrik. b 70. New Coll Ox MA93. Ridley Hall Cam MA95. **d** 97. C Fulwood *Sheff* from 97. *Stumperlowe Lodge, Stumperlowe Hall Road, Sheffield S10 3QS* Tel 0114-230 1911 Fax 230 6568

MEYRICK, Cyril Jonathan. b 52. St Jo Coll Ox BA73 MA77. Sarum & Wells Th Coll 74. **d** 76 **p** 77. C Bicester *Ox* 76-78; Bp's Dom Chapl 78-81; Barbados 81-84; TV Burnham w Dropmore, Hitcham and Taplow *Ox* 84-90; TR Tisbury *Sarum* from 90; Link Officer Black Anglican Concerns from 90. *The Rectory, Park Road, Tisbury, Salisbury SP3 6LF* Tel (01747) 870312

MEYRICK, Thomas Henry Corfe. b 67. Magd Coll Ox BA88 MA92. St Steph Ho Ox BA94. **d** 95 **p** 96. C Bierley *Bradf* from 95. *12 Thurley Road, Bradford, W Yorkshire BD4 7AT* Tel (01274) 729084

MIALL, Peter Brian. b 30. Scawsby Coll of Educn TCert69. **d** 89 **p** 89. Hon C Bolsterstone *Sheff* from 89. *Waldershaigh Cottage, Heads Lane, Bolsterstone, Sheffield S30 5ZH* Tel 0114-288 5558

MICHAEL, Brother. *See* FISHER, The Rt Revd Reginald Lindsay

MICHAEL, Ian MacRae. b 40. Aber Univ MA62 Hertf Coll Ox DPhil66. Westcott Ho Cam 77. **d** 79 **p** 80. C Kings Heath *Birm* 79-82; Vice-Provost St Paul's Cathl Dundee *Bre* 82-88; V Harborne St Faith and St Laur *Birm* from 88; RD Edgbaston from 91. *The Vicarage, 115 Balden Road, Birmingham B32 2EL* Tel 0121-427 2410

MICHAELS, David Albert Emmanuel. b 49. Barrister-at-Law (Inner Temple) 73 Bede Coll Dur BA72. Westcott Ho Cam 86. **d** 88 **p** 89. C Hampstead St Jo *Lon* 88-91; TV Wolvercote w Summertown *Ox* from 91. *The Vicarage, 2 Mere Road, Wolvercote, Oxford OX2 8AN* Tel (01865) 515640 Fax 516440

MICHELL, Canon Douglas Reginald. b 19. St Jo Coll Dur BA41 MA44. Westcott Ho Cam 41. **d** 43 **p** 44. C Wanstead H Trin Hermon Hill *Chelmsf* 43-45; Chapl St Jo Coll Dur 45-48; Lic to Offic *Dur* 45-48; R Moss Side St Jas *Man* 48-53; V Horwich H Trin 53-61; V Evington *Leic* 61-80; Hon Can Leic Cathl 67-84; RD Christianity N 74-79; V Billesdon w Goadby and Rolleston 80-82; RD Gartree I 81-84; V Billesdon and Skeffington 82-84; rtd 85; Perm to Offic *St Alb* from 85; Perm to Offic *Chich* from 97. *2 Ravens Court, St John's Road, Eastbourne, E Sussex BN20 7HY* Tel (01323) 640682

MICHELL, Francis Richard Noel. b 42. St Cath Coll Cam BA64 MA68. Tyndale Hall Bris 64. **d** 66 **p** 67. C Northampton St Giles *Pet* 66-69; C Gateacre *Liv* 69-72; V Litherland St Paul Hatton Hill 72-79; V Rainhill 79-88; V Rainford from 88. *The Vicarage, Church Road, Rainford, St Helens, Merseyside WA11 8HD* Tel (01744) 882200

MICKLETHWAITE, Andrew Quentin. b 67. Univ Coll Dur BA89. Trin Coll Bris BA94. **d** 94 **p** 95. C Abington *Pet* 94-97; TV Duston Team from 97. *7 Pine Copse Close, New Dunston, Northampton NN5 6NF* Tel (01604) 590256

MICKLETHWAITE, Jane Catherine. b 56. Lanc Univ BSc78. Trin Coll Bris DipHE94. **d** 95 **p** 96. NSM Kings Heath *Pet* 95-96; C from 96; Chapl Nene Coll of HE Northn from 97. *7 Pine Copse Close, New Dunston, Northampton NN5 6NF* Tel (01604) 590256

MICKLETHWAITE, Peter William. b 62. Peterho Cam BA84 MA88. St Jo Coll Nottm DipTh89 DPS90. **d** 90 **p** 91. C Leatherhead *Guildf* 90-93; C Wisley w Pyrford 93-97; R Windlesham from 97. *The Rectory, Windlesham, Surrey GU20 6AA* Tel (01276) 472363

MIDDLEBROOK, Bryan. b 33. Dur Univ BA55 DipEd58 Newc Univ MEd74. NE Ord Course 85. **d** 88 **p** 88. NSM Dur St Cuth *Dur* from 88. *5 Fieldhouse Terrace, Durham DH1 4NA* Tel 0191-386 6665

MIDDLEDITCH, Terry Gordon. b 30. Univ of Wales (Lamp) BA62. **d** 63 **p** 64. C Poulton-le-Fylde *Blackb* 63-67; C-in-c Heysham 65-67; C Cheltenham St Pet *Glouc* 75-77; Perm to Offic 77-82; Hon C Badgeworth w Shurdington 82-87; C Poulton-le-Sands w Morecambe St Laur *Blackb* 88-91; V Stalmine from 91. *The Vicarage, Carr End Lane, Stalmine, Blackpool FY6 0LQ* Tel (01253) 702538

MIDDLEMISS, Fritha Leonora. b 47. Man Univ BA68 CertEd69. Glouc Sch of Min 86. **d** 89 **p** 94. NSM Bengeworth *Worc* 89-94; NSM Stoulton w Drake's Broughton and Pirton etc 94-96; Chapl Malvern Girls' Coll from 96. *Malvern Girls' College, 15 Avenue Road, Malvern, Worcs WR14 3BA*

MIDDLESEX, Archdeacon of. *See* COLMER, Malcolm John

MIDDLETON, Alan Derek. b 46. St Jo Coll Dur BA68 MA85. Qu Coll Birm DipTh71 DPS72. **d** 72 **p** 73. C Cannock *Lich* 72-76; Warden St Helen's Youth & Community Cen Bp Auckd 76-79; V Darlington St Jo *Dur* 79-89; TR E Darlington 89-90; V Upper Norwood All SS *S'wark* from 90. *All Saints' Vicarage, 12 Beulah Hill, London SE19 3LS* Tel 0181-653 2820

MIDDLETON, Barry Glen. b 41. Lich Th Coll 68. **d** 70 **p** 71. C Westhoughton *Man* 70-73; C Prestwich St Marg 73-74; TV

Buxton w Burbage and King Sterndale *Derby* 74-77; Chapl Worc R Infirmary 77-83; Fairfield Hosp Hitchin 83-85; P-in-c Erpingham w Calthorpe *Nor* 85-86; R Erpingham w Calthorpe, Ingworth, Aldborough etc 86-92; R Badingham w Bruisyard, Cransford and Dennington *St E* 92-96; V Sidcup St Jo *Roch* from 96. *St John's Vicarage, 13 Church Avenue, Sidcup, Kent DA14 6BU* Tel 0181-300 0383

MIDDLETON, Hugh Charles. b 50. Nottm Univ BTh77. Linc Th Coll 73. **d** 77 **p** 78. C New Sleaford *Linc* 77-81; C Grantham 81; TV 81-83; R Caythorpe 83-95; P-in-c Bracebridge Heath from 97. *54 Wolsey Way, Lincoln LN2 4QH* Tel (01522) 540460

MIDDLETON, Kenneth Frank. b 28. Keble Coll Ox BA52 MA64. St Steph Ho Ox 52. **d** 55 **p** 56. C Leic St Matt *Leic* 55-58; C W Hackney St Barn *Lon* 58-60; V Leic St Matt and St Geo *Leic* 60-82; RD Christianity N 79-82; P-in-c Leic St Alb 80-82; Hon Can Leic Cathl 80-82; P-in-c Belgrave St Mich 81-82; TR Bridgnorth, Tasley, Astley Abbotts, Oldbury etc *Heref* 82-87; P-in-c Quatford 83; RD Bridgnorth 83-87; TR Littleham w Exmouth *Ex* from 87. *The Rectory, 1 Maer Road, Exmouth, Devon EX8 2DA* Tel (01395) 272227

MIDDLETON, Leonard James. b 33. Bps' Coll Cheshunt 55. **d** 58 **p** 59. C Beckenham St Geo *Roch* 58-60; C Wallingford St Mary w All Hallows and St Leon *Ox* 60-64; V Codnor and Loscoe *Derby* 64-71; P-in-c W Tilbury *Chelmsf* 71-77; V E Tilbury 71-77; R Copford w Easthorpe 77-91; R Gayton Gp of Par *Nor* 91-96; rtd 96; Perm to Offic *Nor* from 96. *Santiago, 7 Clipped Hedge Lane, Southrepps, Norwich NR11 8NS* Tel (01263) 834202

MIDDLETON, The Ven Michael John. b 40. Dur Univ BSc62 Fitzw Ho Cam BA66 MA70. Westcott Ho Cam 63. **d** 66 **p** 67. C Newc St Geo *Newc* 66-69; V 77-85; S Africa 69-72; Chapl K Sch Tynemouth 72-77; R Hexham *Newc* 85-92; Hon Can Newc Cathl 90-92; Adn Swindon *Bris* from 92. *2 Louviers Way, Swindon SN1 4DU* Tel (01793) 644556 Fax 495352

MIDDLETON, Rodney. b 54. St Andr Univ BD80. St Steph Ho Ox 80. **d** 82 **p** 83. C Walton St Mary *Liv* 82-87; C-in-c Kew St Fran CD 87-94; V Kew 94-95; Chapl Southport and Formby Distr Gen Hosp 87-95; V Haydock St Jas from 95. *The Vicarage, 169 Church Road, Haydock, St Helens, Merseyside WA11 0NJ* Tel (01942) 727956

MIDDLETON, Thomas Arthur. b 36. AKC61. **d** 62 **p** 63. C Sunderland *Dur* 62-63; C Auckland St Helen 63-67; C Winlaton 67-70; C-in-c Pennywell St Thos and Grindon St Oswald CD 70-79; R Boldon from 79; Adv in Stewardship Dur Adnry from 87. *Boldon Rectory, Rectory Green, West Boldon, Tyne & Wear NE36 0QD* Tel 0191-536 7370

MIDDLETON-DANSKY, Brother Serge Wladimir. b 45. Cuddesdon Coll 74. **d** 77 **p** 78. C Wisbech SS Pet and Paul *Ely* 77-79; Lic to Offic Adnry Riviera *Eur* from 80; C Ox St Giles and SS Phil and Jas w St Marg *Ox* 83-86; Perm to Offic 86-88; Perm to Offic *Truro* 88-90; P-in-c Zennor 90-96; P-in-c Towednack 90-96; rtd 96; Perm to Offic *Truro* from 97. *The Old Vicarage, Zennor, St Ives, Cornwall TR26 3BY* Tel (01736) 796955

MIDDLETON, Suffragan Bishop of. *See* VENNER, The Rt Revd Stephen Squires

MIDDLEWICK, Robert James. b 44. K Alfred's Coll Win CertEd67 Lon Univ BD76. Ripon Coll Cuddesdon 75. **d** 77 **p** 78. C Bromley SS Pet and Paul *Roch* 77-81; C Belvedere All SS 81-84; P-in-c Lamberhurst 85-88; P-in-c Matfield 85-88; V Lamberhurst and Matfield from 88. *The Vicarage, Old Town Hill, Lamberhurst, Tunbridge Wells, Kent TN3 8EL* Tel (01892) 890324

MIDGLEY, Edward Graham. b 23. St Edm Hall Ox BA47 MA48 BLitt50. Cuddesdon Coll 56. **d** 56 **p** 57. Lic to Offic *Ox* 56-89; Dean St Edm Hall Ox 56-78; Vice-Prin 70-78; Chapl 78-86; Chapl St Hugh's Coll Ox 86-89. *4 St Lawrence Road, South Hinksey, Oxford OX1 5AZ* Tel (01865) 735460

MIDGLEY, George William. b 38. N Ord Course. **d** 83 **p** 84. C Penistone and Thurlstone *Wakef* 88-89; TV 89-94; TR from 94. *The Vicarage, Shrewbury Road, Penistone, Sheffield S30 6DY* Tel (01226) 763241

MIDGLEY, Stephen Nicholas. b 60. Jes Coll Cam MA86 Lon Hosp MB86 BS86. Wycliffe Hall Ox DipMin95. **d** 97. C Hove Bp Hannington Memorial Ch *Chich* from 97. *53 Quarry Road, Headington, Oxford OX3 8NK* Tel (01865) 742651

MIDLANE, Colin John. b 50. Qu Mary Coll Lon BA72. Westcott Ho Cam 73 Sarum & Wells Th Coll 77. **d** 78 **p** 79. C Bethnal Green St Pet w St Thos *Lon* 78-82; P-in-c Haggerston All SS 82-88; Chapl Hengrave Hall Ecum Cen 88-89; Priest Counsellor St Botolph Aldgate *Lon* 89-94; C St Botolph Aldgate w H Trin Minories 93-94; TV Haywards Heath St Wilfrid *Chich* 94-97; C Brighton St Geo w St Anne and St Mark from 97. *28 Henley Road, Kemp Town, Brighton BN2 5NA* Tel (01273) 696796

MIDWINTER, Sister Josie Isabel. b 46. Open Univ BA84. CA Tr Coll IDC71 ACT DipTh77. **d** 87. CA from 71; CMS 84-93; Uganda 85-91; Kenya from 92. *Church Army Training College, PO Box 72584, Nairobi, Kenya* Tel Nairobi (2) 558596 or 554970 Fax 554970

MIDWOOD, Peter Stanley. b 47. Linc Th Coll 80. **d** 82 **p** 83. C Garforth *Ripon* 82-85; C-in-c Grinton w Arkengarthdale, Downholme and Marske 85-86; C-in-c Melbecks and Muker 85-86; P-in-c Swaledale 86; V from 86. *The Vicarage, Reeth, Richmond, N Yorkshire DL11 6TR* Tel (01748) 884706

MIELL, David Keith. b 57. BSc PhD BA. Westcott Ho Cam 83. **d** 86 **p** 87. C Blackbird Leys CD *Ox* 86-89; C Walton 89-90; TV Walton Milton Keynes 90-96; RD Milton Keynes 93-95; TR Upton cum Chalvey from 96. *The Rectory, 18 Albert Street, Slough SL1 2BU* Tel (01753) 529988

MIER, Ms Catherine Elizabeth (Kate). b 60. Bris Univ BSc81 Chelsea Coll Lon MSc84 Dur Univ BA95. Cranmer Hall Dur 93. **d** 96 **p** 97. C Royston *St Alb* from 96. *12 Prince Andrew's Close, Royston, Herts SG8 9DZ* Tel (01763) 243265

MIGHALL, Robert. b 33. St Pet Coll Ox BA57 MA61. Wycliffe Hall Ox 57. **d** 58 **p** 59. C Stoke *Cov* 58-62; C Rugby St Andr 62-64; V Newbold on Avon 64-76; V Combroke w Compton Verney 76-96; V Kineton 76-96; rtd 96. *Leasowe Bank, Hoo Lane, Chipping Campden, Glos GL55 6AZ* Tel (01386) 841321

MIHILL, Dennis George. b 31. St Alb Minl Tr Scheme 78. **d** 81 **p** 82. NSM Harpenden St Nic *St Alb* 81-86; C Sawbridgeworth 86-89; V Motspur Park *S'wark* 89-96; rtd 96. *1 Holden Close, Biddenham, Bedford MK40 4QY* Tel (01234) 349364

MILBURN, John Frederick. b 56. Westmr Coll Ox BA84. Sarum & Wells Th Coll 84. **d** 86 **p** 87. C Leavesden All SS *St Alb* 86-89; C Broxbourne w Wormley 89-93; CF (TA) 90-94; Australia from 94. *PO Box 106, 29 Broadway Street, Texas, Queensland, Australia 4385* Tel Toowoomba (76) 531175

MILBURN, The Very Revd Robert Leslie Pollington. b 07. FSA SS Coll Cam BA30 MA34. **d** 34 **p** 35. Chapl Worc Coll Ox 34-57; Tutor 45-57; Select Preacher Ox Univ 42-44; Univ Lect Ch Hist 47-59; Dean Worc 57-68; Master of The Temple 68-80; rtd 80; Perm to Offic *Heref* 81-88; Perm to Offic *Worc* from 85. *Highwell House, Highwell Lane, Bromyard, Herefordshire HR7 4DG* Tel (01885) 488544

MILES, Canon Charles Reginald (Reg). b 12. Tyndale Hall Bris 36. **d** 39 **p** 40. C Wolverhampton St Luke *Lich* 39-43; C Bucknall and Bagnall 43-46; R Dibden *Win* 46-92; Hon Can Win Cathl 75-92; rtd 92. *10 Redwood Close, Dibden Purlieu, Southampton SO45 5SN* Tel (01703) 848202

MILES, Gerald Christopher Morgan. b 36. CEng MIEE Peterho Cam BA57 MA72 Cranfield Inst of Tech MSc72. Wycliffe Hall Ox 74. **d** 76 **p** 77. C Tunbridge Wells St Jas *Roch* 76-80; V Leigh 80-90; R Addington w Trottiscliffe 90-91; P-in-c Ryarsh w Birling 90-91; R Birling, Addington, Ryarsh and Trottiscliffe from 91. *The Vicarage, Birling Road, Ryarsh, West Malling, Kent ME19 5LS* Tel (01732) 842249

MILES (née HOARE), Ms Janet Francis Mary. b 48. St Aid Coll Dur BA70 Bris Univ MEd84. Sarum & Wells Th Coll DipMin93. **d** 93 **p** 94. C Bruton and Distr *B & W* from 93. *30 Priory Mead, Bruton, Somerset BA10 0DZ* Tel (01749) 813822

MILES, Malcolm Robert. b 36. AKC60. **d** 61 **p** 62. C Northampton St Mary *Pet* 61-63; C E Haddon 63-67; R Broughton 67-73; Asst Chapl Nottm Univ *S'well* 73-74; V Northampton H Trin *Pet* 75-84; V Painswick w Sheepscombe *Glouc* 84-97; RD Bisley 90-94; V Painswick w Sheepscombe and Cranham from 97. *The Vicarage, Orchard Mead, Painswick, Stroud, Glos GL6 6YD* Tel (01452) 812334

MILES, Mrs Marion Claire. b 41. S Dios Minl Tr Scheme 86. **d** 88 **p** 94. Hon Par Dn Blandford Forum and Langton Long *Sarum* 88-94; Hon C from 94; Chapl Blandford Community Hosp from 88. *20 Alexandra Street, Blandford Forum, Dorset DT11 7JE* Tel (01258) 452010

MILES, Canon Robert William. b 27. Magd Coll Cam BA50 MA55. Westcott Ho Cam 50. **d** 52 **p** 53. C Bury St Mary *Man* 52-55; Bp's Dom Chapl *Chich* 55-58; Kenya 58-63; Provost Mombasa 58-63; R Dalmahoy *Edin* 65-70; R Batsford w Moreton-in-Marsh *Glouc* 70-77; rtd 77; Perm to Offic *Glouc* from 79. *Boilingwell, Winchcombe, Cheltenham, Glos GL54 5JB* Tel (01242) 603337

MILES, Miss Ruth Cecilia. b 11. St Cath Ho Lon 37 St Mich Ho Ox 38. **dss** 40 **d** 87. Byker St Ant *Newc* 40-44; Stocksbridge *Sheff* 44-47; Attercliffe w Carbrook 47-52; Dioc Adv in Children's Voluntary RE 52-60; Adv in Children's RE *Linc* 60-71; Sec Bd of Women's Work 60-71; rtd 71; Perm to Offic *Glouc* from 83. *The Abbeyfield House, 326 Prestbury Road, Cheltenham, Glos GL52 3DD* Tel (01242) 516357

MILES, Stephen John. b 44. Monash Univ Aus BA66 Ox Univ DipEd68 Lon Univ MA75 California Univ PhD80. Melbourne Coll of Div BTh86. **d** 87 **p** 88. Australia 87-97; Asst Chapl Bonn w Cologne *Eur* from 97. *Friesdorferstrasse 57, 53173 Bonn, Germany*

MILFORD, Mrs Catherine Helena. b 39. LMH Ox BA61 DipTh62 MA65 FRSA92. Gilmore Course 81. **dss** 82 **d** 87 **p** 94. Heaton St Barn *Bradf* 82-87; Par Dn 87-88; Adult Educn Adv *Win* 88-96; TR Barnham Broom *Nor* from 96; P-in-c Reymerston w Cranworth, Letton, Southburgh etc from 96. *The Vicarage, Barnham Broom, Norwich NR9 4DB* Tel (01603) 759204

MILLAM, Peter John. b 36. Univ of Wales (Lamp) BA58. Ridley Hall Cam 58. **d** 63 **p** 64. C Cheltenham Ch Ch *Glouc* 63-66; Falkland Is 66-70; V Pulloxhill w Flitton *St Alb* 70-79; V Luton St Paul 79-89; V Chipping Campden w Ebrington *Glouc* 89-94; rtd 94; Perm to Offic *Chich* from 94. *22 Willowhale Avenue,*

Aldwick, Bognor Regis, W Sussex PO21 4AY Tel (01243) 268316

MILLAR, Alan Askwith. b 26. Qu Coll Birm 59. **d** 60 **p** 61. C Redcar *York* 60-64; C Kirkleatham 60-64; V Middlesbrough St Aid 64-72; V Cayton w Eastfield 72-88; Chapl to RD of Scarborough 88-89; rtd 89; Perm to Offic *Bradf* from 89. *23 Rowan Court, Old Bridge Rise, Ilkley, W Yorkshire LS29 9HH* Tel (01943) 602081

MILLAR, Andrew Charles (Andy). b 48. Hull Univ BSc69. Cuddesdon Coll 71. **d** 73 **p** 74. C Rushmere *St E* 73-76; C Ipswich All Hallows 76-79; Youth Chapl *Sheff* 79-83; Youth Chapl *Win* 83-92; V Colden from 92. *The Vicarage, Colden Common, Winchester, Hants SO21 1TL* Tel (01962) 712505

MILLAR, Christine. *See* WHEELER, Mrs Christine

MILLAR, Frank. b 38. N Lon Poly CQSW63. Sarum Th Coll 67. **d** 69 **p** 70. C S'wark H Trin *S'wark* 69-72; C Saltdean *Chich* 72-74; CECS 74-75; P-in-c Beaumont and Moze *Chelmsf* 76-80; P-in-c Gt Oakley 76-77; P-in-c Tendring 76-80; R Tendring and Lt Bentley w Beaumont cum Moze 80-83; R Rivenhall 83-87; Chapl Palma de Mallorca w Menorca *Eur* 87-90; Perm to Offic *S'wark* 90-94; P-in-c Takeley w Lt Canfield *Chelmsf* from 94. *The Rectory, Parsonage Road, Takeley, Bishop's Stortford, Herts CM22 6QX* Tel (01279) 870837

MILLAR, Gary. b 67. Wales Poly HND88. St Mich Coll Llan 88. **d** 91 **p** 92. C Tonyrefail w Gilfach Goch *Llan* 91-93; C Barry All SS 93-95; TV Cowbridge from 95. *The Vicarage, 2 Court Close, Aberthin, Cowbridge CF7 7EH* Tel (01446) 773889

MILLAR, John Alexander Kirkpatrick (Sandy). b 39. Trin Coll Cam BA62 MA66. St Jo Coll Dur 74. **d** 76 **p** 77. C Brompton H Trin *Lon* 76-78; C Brompton H Trin w Onslow Square St Paul 78-85; V from 85; AD Chelsea 89-94. *Holy Trinity Vicarage, 73 Prince's Gate Mews, London SW7 2PP* Tel 0171-584 8957 or 581 8255

MILLARD, Albert George. b 17. Chich Th Coll. **d** 64 **p** 65. C Wokingham All SS *Ox* 64-71; V Kintbury w Avington 71-82; rtd 82. *8 Crown Mews, 15 Clarence Road, Gosport, Hants PO12 1DH* Tel (01705) 511934

MILLARD, Canon Jane Mary. b 43. Open Univ BA80. Edin Dioc NSM Course 81. **d** 90 **p** 94. NSM Edin St Mary *Edin* from 90; Chapl HIV/AIDS from 90; Can St Mary's Cathl from 95. *Honeybrae, Ninemileburn, Penicuik, Midlothian EH26 9NB*

MILLARD, Jonathan Neil. b 62. Barrister-at-Law (Gray's Inn) 84 Aston Univ BSc83. Wycliffe Hall Ox 89. **d** 92 **p** 93. C Haddenham w Cuddington, Kingsey etc *Ox* 92-94; USA from 94. *23 Stonemarker Drive, Washington, PA 15301-2745, USA*

MILLARD, Malcolm Edoric. b 38. Lon Univ BA60 AKC60 Lon Inst of Educn PGCE61. St Jo Coll Nottm 88. **d** 77 **p** 81. Gambia 77-95; CMS 89-94; C S Shoebury *Chelmsf* from 95. *Shalom, 56 Wakering Road, Shoeburyness, Southend-on-Sea SS3 9SY* Tel (01702) 292078

MILLARD, Canon Murray Clinton. b 29. Ex Coll Ox BA50 DipTh52 MA58. St Steph Ho Ox 51. **d** 53 **p** 54. C Horfield St Greg *Bris* 53-55; C Guernsey St Steph *Win* 55-61; R Jersey St Mary 61-71; R Guernsey St Sampson 71-82; V Guernsey St Steph from 82; Hon Can Win Cathl from 83. *St Stephen's Vicarage, De Beauvoir, St Peter Port, Guernsey, Channel Islands GY1 1RN* Tel (01481) 720268

MILLARD, Richard Stuart Marsh. b 33. St Pet Coll Ox BA57 MA. Oak Hill NSM Course 90. **d** 93 **p** 94. NSM Laleham *Lon* 93-94; Hon C Neatishead, Barton Turf and Irstead *Nor* from 94; NSM C to RD Tunstead from 94. *The Rectory, Butcher's Common, Neatishead, Norwich NR12 8XH* Tel (01602) 630645

MILLER, Alan James (Brother Alan). b 52. NE Ord Course 93. **d** 96 **p** 97. C Walker *Newc* from 96. *24 Berry Close, Walker, Newcastle upon Tyne NE6 3UW* Tel 0191-262 1946

MILLER, Anthony Talbot. b 37. Univ of Wales (Lamp) BA59. Coll of Resurr Mirfield. **d** 61 **p** 62. C Panteg w Llanddewi Fach and Llandegfeth *Mon* 61-63; C Monmouth 63-65; V Holme Cultram St Mary *Carl* 65-76; Lic to Offic *Lich* 76-78; P-in-c Wrockwardine Wood 78-80; R 80-94; OCF 92-94; rtd 94. *7 Bron yr Afon, Conwy, Llandudno LL32 8LP* Tel (01492) 573757

MILLER, Barry. b 42. Bede Coll Dur TCert63 Open Univ BA79 Leic Univ MEd86. Linc Th Coll 63. **d** 65 **p** 66. C Greenside *Dur* 65-68; C Auckland St Andr and St Anne 68-71; Adv in Educn *Leic* 71-77; C Leic St Nic 77-80; Asst Chapl Leic Univ 77-80; Lect Relig Studies Leic Poly 77-80; Children's Officer Gen Syn Bd of Educn 80-84; Hd of Relig Studies W Midl Coll of HE 84-89; Hd of Initial Teacher Educn Wolv Poly 89-92; Wolv Univ 92-93; Hd of Teacher Educn Bradf and Ilkley Community Coll from 94. *Greystoke, Victoria Avenue, Ilkley, W Yorkshire LS29 9BL* Tel (01943) 604156

MILLER, Charles Irvine. b 35. Nottm Univ BEd76. Bps' Coll Cheshunt 61. **d** 63 **p** 64. C Anlaby Common St Mark *York* 63-66; C Whitby 66-68; R Ingoldmells w Addlethorpe *Linc* 68-72; P-in-c Bishop Norton 72-76; V Scunthorpe St Jo 76-83; Chapl Manor Hosp Walsall 83-89; rtd 89; Perm to Offic *Ely* from 89. *68 Station Road, Kennett, Newmarket, Suffolk CB8 7QF* Tel (01638) 552576

MILLER, Darren Noel. b 67. Birm Univ BSocSc89. Chich Th Coll BTh95 Coll of Resurr Mirfield 94. **d** 95 **p** 96. C Weoley Castle *Birm* from 95. *34 Shenley Lane, Birmingham B29 5PL* Tel 0121-476 3990

MILLER, David George. b 54. Or Coll Ox BA76 MA80. Ripon Coll Cuddesdon 78. **d** 81 **p** 82. C Henfield w Shermanbury and Woodmancote *Chich* 81-84; C Monk Bretton *Wakef* 84-87; V Rastrick St Jo 87-93; TR Helston and Wendron *Truro* from 93. *St Michael's Rectory, Church Lane, Helston, Cornwall TR13 8PF* Tel (01326) 572516

MILLER, David James Tringham. b 45. AKC70. Sarum & Wells Th Coll 76. **d** 77 **p** 78. C Abington *Pet* 77-80; TV Corby SS Pet and Andr w Gt and Lt Oakley 80-83; V Kettering All SS 83-94; RD Kettering 87-94; V Pet All SS from 94. *All Saints' Vicarage, 208 Park Road, Peterborough PE1 2UJ* Tel (01733) 54130

MILLER, David John. b 37. Louvain Univ Belgium LicScCat67. Chich Th Coll 60. **d** 62 **p** 63. C Southsea H Spirit *Portsm* 62-65; C Roehampton H Trin *S'wark* 67-68; Chapl Luxembourg *Eur* 68-72; Chapl Lausanne 72-91; Asst Chapl Lausanne 91-93; Perm to Offic from 94. *Avenue de l'Eglise Anglaise 1 bis, 1006 Lausanne, Switzerland* Tel Lausanne (21) 616-2636

MILLER, Preb David Reginald. b 29. AKC54. **d** 55 **p** 56. C Hockerill *St Alb* 55-58; C Combe Down *B & W* 58-61; V Pill 61-70; V Wedmore 70-74; V Wedmore w Theale 74-78; RD Axbridge 77-89; P-in-c Blackford 77-78; V Wedmore w Theale and Blackford 78-95; Preb Wells Cathl from 85; Warden of Readers 85-91; rtd 95; Perm to Offic *B & W* from 95. *Whitelake Lodge, Lower Street, Pilton, Shepton Mallet, Somerset BA4 4DD*

MILLER, David Samuel. b 31. Lich Th Coll 62. **d** 63 **p** 64. C Leek St Edw *Lich* 63-66; C Blurton 66; C Southbourne St Kath *Win* 66-71; V E and W Worldham, Hartley Mauditt w Kingsley etc 71-76; TV Buckhurst Hill *Chelmsf* 76-80; V Elm Park St Nic Hornchurch 80-93; rtd 93; Chapl Torrevieja *Eur* 95-97. *8 Church Road, Lowestoft, Suffolk NR32 1TQ*

MILLER, Edward Jeffery. b 24. St Jo Coll Cam BA48 MA50. Wells Th Coll 48. **d** 50 **p** 51. C S Lyncombe *B & W* 50-53; India 54-67; P-in-c Wootton Courtenay *B & W* 68-74; R 74-83; P-in-c Timberscombe 68-74; V 74-83; P-in-c Selworthy 79-83; R Selworthy and Timberscombe and Wootton Courtenay 83-93; P-in-c Luccombe 86; R 86-93; rtd 93; Perm to Offic *B & W* 93-96. *Lodge Rocks Cottage, Old Cleeve, Minehead, Somerset TA24 6RD* Tel (01984) 41228

MILLER, Dr Ernest Charles. b 56. Franklin & Marshall Coll (USA) BA78 Univ of Michigan MA79 Keble Coll Ox DPhil90. Nashotah Ho MDiv82. **d** 82 **p** 83. USA 82-84 and from 96; Asst Chapl Keble Coll Ox 84-88; Warden Ho of SS Greg and Macrina 84-90; Lic to Offic *Ox* 87-91; P-in-c New Marston 91-96; Prof Hist and Ascetical Th Nashotah Ho Wisconsin from 96. *Bishopstead, W153 Oakwood Drive, Delafield, WI 53018, USA, or 2777 Mission Road, Nashotah, WI 53018, USA*

MILLER, Francis Rogers. b 54. Ex Univ BA86. St Steph Ho Ox 86. **d** 88 **p** 89. C Wednesfield *Lich* 88-93; P-in-c Caldmore from 93; C Walsall St Mary and All SS Palfrey from 93. *St Michael's Vicarage, St Michael's Street, Walsall WS1 3RQ* Tel (01922) 23445

MILLER, Geoffrey Edward. b 28. Leeds Univ BA56. Coll of Resurr Mirfield 53. **d** 57 **p** 58. C Birm St Aid Small Heath *Birm* 57-59; C Chiswick St Paul Grove Park *Lon* 59-61; C Barnsley St Pet *Wakef* 61-63; R Claypole *Linc* 63-76; P-in-c Westborough w Dry Doddington and Stubton 63-65; R 65-76; P-in-c Bierley *Bradf* 76-78; V 78-91; rtd 91; Chantry Priest Chpl St Mich & H So Walsingham from 91; Perm to Offic *Nor* from 91. *20 Cleaves Drive, Little Walsingham, Norfolk NR22 6EQ* Tel (01328) 820591

MILLER, Geoffrey Vincent. b 56. BEd. St Jo Coll Nottm. **d** 83 **p** 84. C Jarrow *Dur* 83-86; TV Billingham St Aid 86-92; Dioc Urban Development Officer from 91; Community Chapl Stockton-on-Tees 92-94; P-in-c Darlington St Cuth 94-96; V from 96. *26 Upsall Drive, Darlington, Co Durham DL3 8RB* Tel (01325) 358911

MILLER, The Ven George Charles Alexander. b 20. TCD BA45. CITC 46. **d** 46 **p** 47. C Wexford w Rathaspeck *C & O* 46-49; Asst Chapl Miss to Seamen Belf 49-51; Chapl Pernis Rotterdam Miss to Seamen *Eur* 51-55; I Billis w Ballyjamesduff *K, E & A* 55-57; I Knockbride w Shercock 57-65; I Urney w Denn and Derryheen 65-89; Preb Kilmore Cathl 77-87; Adn Kilmore 87-89; rtd 89. *Wavecrest, Blenacup, Cavan, Irish Republic* Tel Cavan (49) 61270

✠**MILLER, The Rt Revd Harold Creeth.** b 50. TCD BA73 MA78 Nottm Univ BA75. St Jo Coll Nottm 73. **d** 76 **p** 77 **c** 97. C Carrickfergus *Conn* 76-79; Dir Ext Studies St Jo Coll Nottm 79-84; Chapl QUB 84-89; I Carrigrohane Union *C, C & R* 89-97; Bp's Dom Chapl 91-97; Can Cork and Cloyne Cathls 94-96; Treas Cork Cathl 96-97; Preb Cork Cathl 96-97; Preb Tymothan St Patr Cathl Dublin from 96; Bp D & D from 97. *The See House, 32 Knockdene Park South, Belfast BT5 7AB* Tel (01232) 471973 Fax 650584

MILLER (née BLUNDEN), Mrs Jacqueline Ann. b 63. Leic Univ BA86 SS Coll Cam BA90. Ridley Hall Cam 88. **d** 91. Par Dn Bedford St Paul *St Alb* 91-94; C 94-95. *St Mary's Vicarage, Lansdowne Road, London N17 9XE* Tel 0181-808 6644

MILLER, James Ivimey. b 33. Trin Hall Cam BA55 MA59. Ridley Hall Cam 56. **d** 61 **p** 62. C Beccles St Mich *St E* 61-63; C

Blackpool St Jo *Blackb* 63-67; C Kirk Ella *York* 67-73; R Cockfield *St E* 73-78; rtd 78; Perm to Offic *St E* from 78. *3 Grosvenor Gardens, Bury St Edmunds, Suffolk IP33 2JS* Tel (01284) 762839

MILLER, John David. b 50. Nottm Univ BTh73 Lanc Univ CertEd74 Newc Univ MA93. Kelham Th Coll 68. **d** 74 **p** 75. C Horden *Dur* 74-79; C Billingham St Aid 79-80; TV 80-84; TR S Shields All SS from 84. *The Rectory, Tyne Terrace, South Shields, Tyne & Wear NE34 0NF* Tel 0191-456 1851

MILLER, John Douglas. b 24. FCA60. N Ord Course 74. **d** 77 **p** 78. C Prestbury *Ches* 77-80; V Ashton Hayes 80-87; rtd 87; Perm to Offic *Ex* from 87. *35 Branscombe Close, Colyford, Colyton, Devon EX13 6RF* Tel (01297) 553581

MILLER, John Forster. b 32. Ox NSM Course. **d** 83 **p** 84. NSM Patcham *Chich* 83-86; NSM Radlett *St Alb* 86-93; Perm to Offic from 93. *4 Craigweil Avenue, Radlett, Herts WD7 7EU* Tel (01923) 857148

MILLER, John Gareth. b 57. St Jo Coll Dur BA78. Ridley Hall Cam 79 Ven English Coll Rome 80. **d** 81 **p** 82. C Addiscombe St Mary *Cant* 81-84; TV Melbury *Sarum* 84-88; TR 88-91; V Leamington Priors All SS *Cov* 91-94. *13 Parr's Place, Hampton, Middx TW12 2NJ*

MILLER, John Selborne. b 32. RMN70 Lon Univ DBS68. S'wark Ord Course 64. **d** 71 **p** 72. C Kenton *Lon* 71-74; C Fulham St Etheldreda w St Clem 74-78; Asst at Convent of the Epiphany Truro 79-80; Hon C Pimlico St Sav 80-84; C Shirley *Birm* 84-86; rtd 86; Perm to Offic *Nor* from 86. *28 Knight Street, Walsingham, Norfolk NR22 6DA* Tel (01328) 820824

MILLER, Kenneth Leslie. b 50. Lanc Univ BEd74 Liv Univ BPhil94 FRSA. N Ord Course 78. **d** 80 **p** 81. NSM Formby St Pet *Liv* 80-87; Chapl St Marg High Sch from 86; NSM Anfield St Columba from 87. *9 Hampton Road, Formby, Liverpool L37 6EJ* Tel (01704) 831256

MILLER, Kim Hurst. b 49. Ex Univ PhD89. Canberra Coll of Min BTh82. **d** 82 **p** 83. Australia 82-86 and from 89; Perm to Offic *Ex* 86-89. *41 Warrawong Street, (PO Box 933), Kooringal, NSW, Australia 2650* Tel Wagga Wagga (69) 263361 or 217030

MILLER, Luke Jonathan. b 66. SS Coll Cam BA87 MA91. St Steph Ho Ox BA90. **d** 91 **p** 92. C Oxhey St Matt *St Alb* 91-94; C Tottenham St Mary *Lon* 94-95; V from 95. *St Mary's Vicarage, Lansdowne Road, London N17 9XE* Tel 0181-808 6644

MILLER, Martin Michael. b 55. St Jo Coll Dur BSc78. Trin Coll Bris 94. **d** 96 **p** 97. C Leamington Priors St Paul *Cov* from 96. *49 Wathen Road, Leamington Spa, Warks CV32 5UY* Tel (01926) 886687

MILLER, Dr Michael Daukes. b 46. MRCGP74 DRCOG Qu Coll Cam MA71 Lon Univ BCh70 MB71 DCH. Glouc Th Course 82. **d** 85 **p** 94. NSM Lydney w Aylburton *Glouc* 85-95; NSM Lydney from 95. *Highmead House, Blakeney, Glos GL15 4DY* Tel (01594) 516668

MILLER, Dr Patrick Figgis. b 33. Ch Coll Cam BA56 MA60 Surrey Univ PhD95. Cuddesdon Coll 56. **d** 58 **p** 59. C Portsea St Cuth *Portsm* 58-61; C Cambridge Gt St Mary w St Mich *Ely* 61-63; Hd Dept Man Gr Sch 63-69; Can Res and Lib S'wark Cathl *S'wark* 69-72; Dir of Studies Qu Mary's Coll Basingstoke 72-79; Prin Sunbury Coll 79-80; Prin Esher Coll from 81; Lic to Offic *Guildf* from 84. *31 Hare Lane, Claygate, Esher, Surrey KT10 9BT* Tel (01372) 467563

MILLER, Paul. b 49. Oak Hill Th Coll 71. **d** 74 **p** 75. C Upton *Ex* 74-77; C Farnborough *Guildf* 77-78; P-in-c Torquay St Luke *Ex* 78-81; V 81-86; V Green Street Green *Roch* 86-94; V Green Street Green and Pratts Bottom from 94; RD Orpington from 96. *The Vicarage, 46 Worlds End Lane, Orpington, Kent BR6 6AG* Tel (01689) 852905

MILLER, Paul Richard. b 37. K Coll Lon BSc60 AKC60. Linc Th Coll 60. **d** 62 **p** 63. C Sheff St Geo *Sheff* 62-65; C Bottesford *Linc* 65-67; Bp's Youth Chapl 67-69; C Corringham 67-69; Dioc Youth Officer *Ripon* 69-74; Hd Youth Nat Coun of Soc Services 74-79; P-in-c Battlesden and Pottesgrove *St Alb* 79-80; P-in-c Eversholt w Milton Bryan 79-80; P-in-c Woburn 79-80; V Woburn w Eversholt, Milton Bryan, Battlesden etc from 80. *The Vicarage, Park Street, Woburn, Milton Keynes MK17 9PG* Tel (01525) 290225

MILLER, Canon Paul William. b 18. Qu Coll Birm DipTh50. **d** 50 **p** 51. C Staveley *Derby* 50-53; C Matlock and Tansley 53-55; V Codnor 53-55; C Derby Cathl 64-66; Can Res 66-83; Chapl to The Queen 81-89; rtd 83; Perm to Offic *Derby* from 83. *15 Forester Street, Derby DE1 1PP* Tel (01332) 344773

MILLER, Peter Tennant. b 21. Keble Coll Ox BA47 MA63. Ripon Hall Ox 62. **d** 63 **p** 64. C Wigmore w Hempstead *Roch* 63-68; V Worksop St Paul *S'well* 68-73; P-in-c Nottingham St Cath 74-75; C Nottingham St Mary 75-77; R Edith Weston w N Luffenham and Lyndon w Manton *Pet* 77-86; rtd 86; Perm to Offic *Cov* 86-90. *Regency Cottage, 9 Cross Road, Leamington Spa, Warks CV32 5PD* Tel (01926) 314236

MILLER, Philip Harry. b 58. Leeds Univ BA79. Chich Th Coll 80. **d** 82 **p** 83. C Reddish *Man* 82-86; R Lower Broughton Ascension 86-94; P-in-c Cheetwood St Alb 91-94; P-in-c Langley and Parkfield from 95. *The Rectory, Wood Street, Middleton, Manchester M24 3GL* Tel 0161-643 5013

MILLER, Philip Howard. b 40. Tyndale Hall Bris 67. **d** 72 **p** 73. Argentina 72-73; C Rusholme H Trin *Man* 73-74; Paraguay 74-77; C Toxteth St Cypr w Ch Ch *Liv* 78-80; V Burscough Bridge 80-85; V Woodbridge St Jo *St E* 85-91; P-in-c Combs 91-92 and 93-96; Chapl Burrswood Cen for Divine Healing 92-93; V Yoxford and Peasenhall w Sibton *St E* from 96. *The Vicarage, High Street, Yoxford, Saxmundham, Suffolk IP17 3EU* Tel (01728) 668712

MILLER, Richard Bracebridge. b 45. Wycliffe Hall Ox 68. **d** 70 **p** 71. C Lee Gd Shep w St Pet *S'wark* 70-74; C Roehampton H Trin 74-77; C Earley St Pet *Ox* 77-80; V Aldermaston w Wasing and Brimpton 80-96; C Newbury from 96. *23 Harvest Green, Newbury, Berks RG14 6DN* Tel 0118-971 2281

MILLER, Robert George. b 15. Bris Univ BA37. Bible Churchmen's Coll 37. **d** 39 **p** 40. C W Streatham St Jas *S'wark* 39-42; C Weymouth St Jo *Sarum* 42-43; C Brompton H Trin *Lon* 43-44; V Holloway St Jas 44-47; V Upper Edmonton St Jas 47-79; Chapl N Middx Hosp 48-81; rtd 79; Perm to Offic *Lon* 80-89. *Carseldine Chateau's, Unit 35, 30 Graham Road, Carseldine, Queensland, Australia 4034* Tel Brisbane (7) 263-8114

MILLER, Robert Stephen. b 71. QUB BSc92. CITC BTh95. **d** 95 **p** 96. C Shankill *D & D* from 95. *Shankhill Parish Curatage, 136 Lough Road, Lurgan, Craigavon, Co Armagh BT66 6JL* Tel (01762) 325962

MILLER, Ronald Andrew John. b 46. LNSM course 96. **d** 96 **p** 97. NSM Heywood St Luke w All So *Man* from 96. *153 Rochdale Road East, Heywood, Lancs OL10 1QU* Tel (01706) 624326 Fax as telephone

MILLER, Ronald Anthony. b 41. CEng CPA MRAeS City Univ BSc63. S'wark Ord Course 69. **d** 72 **p** 80. NSM Crookham *Guildf* 72-73 and 80-85; NSM New Haw from 85. *Glen Anton, Horsley Road, Downside, Cobham, Surrey KT11 3NY* Tel (01932) 863394

MILLER, Rosamund Joy. *See* SEAL, Mrs Rosamund Joy

MILLER, Mrs Rosslyn Leslie. b 43. St Andr Univ MA65 Ox Univ DipEd66 Cam Univ DipRK69. **dss** 72 **d** 87. Dir of Studies Inst of Chr Studies 72; St Marylebone All SS *Lon* 72; Adult Educn Officer 73-78; Alford w Rigsby *Linc* 86-87; C 87-90; Dioc Dir of Readers from 90; Gen Preacher from 95. *120A Station Road, Waddington, Lincoln LN5 9QS* Tel (01522) 720819

MILLER, Roy. b 29. **d** 88 **p** 93. NSM Leic Cathl *Leic* 88-91; NSM Leic H Apostles from 91. *5 Bratmyr, Fleckney, Leicester LE8 0BJ* Tel 0116-240 2004

MILLER, Stephen Michael. b 63. NE Lon Poly BSc86 Nottm Univ BTh91. Linc Th Coll 88. **d** 91 **p** 92. C Dudley St Fran *Worc* 91-94; V Sedgley St Mary from 94. *St Mary's Vicarage, St Mary's Close, Dudley, W Midlands DY3 1LD* Tel (01902) 883310

MILLER, Stuart William. b 71. Univ of Wales (Cardiff) BA92. Trin Coll Bris BA94. **d** 97. C Fordingbridge *Win* from 97. *Hale Rectory, Woodgreen, Fordingbridge, Hants SP6 2AN* Tel (01725) 512307

MILLER, William David. b 45. Man Univ BA66. Linc Th Coll 69. **d** 71 **p** 72. C Newc St Geo *Newc* 71-74; C Corbridge w Halton 74-77; C N Gosforth 77-81; TV Whorlton 81-90; Chapl K Sch Tynemouth from 90. *7 Strawberry Terrace, Hazelrigg, Newcastle upon Tyne NE13 7AR* Tel 0191-236 5024 or 258 5995

MILLETT, Canon Francis Henry Walter. b 19. AKC48. **d** 49 **p** 50. C Plumstead St Nic *S'wark* 49-54; C Wimbledon 54-61; R Nor St Jo Timberhill w All SS *Nor* 61-75; V Nor St Jo Sepulchre 61-75; RD Nor E 70-81; TR Nor St Pet Parmentergate w St Jo 75-77; Hon Can Nor Cathl 77-86; V Nor St Giles 77-86; rtd 87; Perm to Offic *Nor* from 87. *203A Unthank Road, Norwich NR2 2PH* Tel (01603) 52641

MILLETT, Maxwell Roy (Max). b 45. Clare Coll Cam BA67. S Dios Minl Tr Scheme 92. **d** 95 **p** 96. NSM Southsea St Pet *Portsm* from 95. *32 Belmont Street, Southsea, Hants PO5 1ND* Tel (01705) 817216

MILLETT, William Hugh. b 21. AKC49. **d** 50 **p** 51. C Barbourne *Worc* 50-53; V Catshill 53-58; R Richard's Castle *Heref* 58-78; P-in-c Stoke Lacy, Moreton Jeffries w Much Cowarne etc 78-82; Perm to Offic *Worc* from 83; rtd 86; Perm to Offic *Heref* from 93. *151 Upper Welland Road, Malvern, Worcs WR14 4LB* Tel (01684) 567056

MILLGATE, Victor Frederick. b 44. St Mich Coll Llan 81. **d** 83 **p** 84. C Pembroke St Mary and St Mich *St D* 83-85; V Manobier and St Florence w Redberth from 85. *The Vicarage, Manorbier, Tenby SA70 7TN* Tel (01834) 871617

MILLICHAMP, Mrs Penelope Mary. b 39. CertEd60. WMMTC 82. **dss** 85 **d** 87 **p** 94. Wednesfield *Lich* 85-94; Par Dn 87-90; TD 90-94; Perm to Offic 94-95; NSM Wrockwardine Deanery from 95. *9 The Buck, Sheinton, Cressage, Shrewsbury SY5 6DJ* Tel (01952) 510403

MILLIER, Gordon. b 28. St Aid Birkenhead 63. **d** 65 **p** 66. C Congresbury *B & W* 65-69; P-in-c Badgworth w Biddisham 69-76; R Weare w Badgworth and Biddisham 76-84; R Pilton w Croscombe, N Wootton and Dinder 84-93; rtd 93; Perm to Offic *Ex* from 93. *28 Withy Close, Canal Hill, Tiverton, Devon EX16 4HZ* Tel (01884) 253128

MILLIGAN, William Edward. b 03. TCD BA25 MA29. CITC 28. **d** 28 **p** 29. C Belfast St Mary *Conn* 28-32; C Drumgath *D & D*

32-36; I 36-41; C Drumballyroney 32-36; I 36-41; C Clonduff 36; I 36-41; P-in-c Scarva 41-53; I Bright w Ballee and Killough 68-73; rtd 73. *2 Blackwood Court, Helen's Bay, Bangor, Co Down BT19 1TJ* Tel (01247) 852795

MILLIGAN, Canon William John (Barney). b 28. OBE95. Em Coll Cam BA49. Cuddesdon Coll 53. **d** 55 **p** 56. C Portsea N End St Mark *Portsm* 55-62; V New Eltham All SS *S'wark* 62-71; V Roehampton H Trin 71-79; Can Res St Alb 79-86; Chapl Strasbourg *Eur* 86-95; Angl Rep Eur Insts 90-95; rtd 95; Perm to Offic *S'wark* from 95. *29 Stirling Road, London SW9 9EF* Tel 0171-274 4827

MILLINER, Llewelyn Douglas. b 14. Univ of Wales BSc35. **d** 38 **p** 39. C Aberdare St Fagan *Llan* 38-41; C Wellingborough St Mary *Pet* 41-43; CF 43-63; Asst Master K Sch Worc 63-66; C-in-c Chelmsf St Luke CD *Chelmsf* 66-69; Dep Hd Master Widford Lodge Sch Chelmsf 69-80; Perm to Offic *Chelmsf* 69-80; rtd 80; Perm to Offic *Ex* from 80. *Fordings, Weare Giffard, Bideford, Devon EX39 4QS* Tel (01237) 473729

MILLING, David Horace. b 29. Or Coll Ox BA51 MA54 Cam Univ PhD73. Cuddesdon Coll 54. **d** 56 **p** 57. C Bris St Mary Redcliffe w Temple *Bris* 56-59; C Fishponds St Jo 59-62; India 62-69; Lect St D Coll Lamp 73-75; C Caversham *Ox* 77-81; C Mapledurham 77-81; C Caversham St Andr 81-86; TV Upper Kennet *Sarum* 86-88; rtd 88; Perm to Offic *Glouc* from 90. *10 The Maples, Cirencester, Glos GL7 1TQ* Tel (01285) 650400

MILLINGTON, Robert William Ernest. b 51. Sheff Univ BA73 St Jo Coll Dur DipTh75. **d** 76 **p** 77. C Ormskirk *Liv* 76-79; C Litherland St Paul Hatton Hill 79-81; V Bootle Ch Ch 81-88; Chapl K Edw Sch Witley from 88. *Queen's House, 3 Gurdon's Lane, Wormley, Godalming, Surrey GU8 5TF* Tel (01428) 684298

MILLINGTON, Stuart. b 45. Lich Th Coll 67. **d** 70 **p** 71. C Boulton *Derby* 70-73; C Moseley St Mary *Birm* 73-76; TV Staveley and Barrow Hill *Derby* 76-82; R Wingerworth from 82; RD Chesterfield 91-97. *The Rectory, Longedge Lane, Wingerworth, Chesterfield, Derbyshire S42 6PU* Tel (01246) 234242

MILLINS, Leslie Albert. b 20. St Paul's Grahamstown. **d** 53 **p** 54. S Rhodesia 53-60; C Kensal Green St Jo *Lon* 60-61; C Hampstead Garden Suburb 61-62; C Old St Pancras w Bedford New Town St Matt 62-69; V 69-76; V Edmonton St Alphege 76-89; rtd 89; Perm to Offic *Chich* from 90. *68 Parkstone Road, Hastings, E Sussex TN34 2NT*

MILLS, Alan Francis. b 29. Ch Coll Cam BA52 MA91. Linc Th Coll 52. **d** 54 **p** 55. C Hucknall Torkard *S'well* 54-58; C Bath Bathwick St Jo *B & W* 58-70; V Drayton 70-76; V Muchelney 70-76; V Alcombe from 76. *The Vicarage, Bircham Road, Alcombe, Minehead, Somerset TA24 6BE* Tel (01643) 703285

MILLS, Alexandra. b 56. Univ of Wales (Abth) BMus78 CertEd79. Ripon Coll Cuddesdon 88. **d** 90 **p** 94. Par Dn Earlsfield St Andr *S'wark* 90-94; C 94; C Kingston All SS w St Jo from 94. *2 Grove Lane, Kingston-upon-Thames, Surrey KT1 2SU* Tel 0181-546 9882

MILLS, Anthony James. b 55. Nottm Univ BA. Linc Th Coll. **d** 84 **p** 85. C Mexborough *Sheff* 84-86; C Howden TM *York* 86-89; V Fylingdales and Hawsker cum Stainsacre 89-95; V Scarborough St Sav w All SS from 95. *St Saviour's Vicarage, 1 Manor Road, Scarborough, N Yorkshire YO12 7RZ* Tel (01723) 360648

MILLS, David Bryn. b 49. Ox NSM Course. **d** 83 **p** 84. NSM Stantonbury *Ox* 83-87; NSM Stantonbury and Willen from 87. *3 Tuffnell Close, Willen, Milton Keynes MK15 9BL* Tel (01908) 605171

MILLS, David Francis. b 51. DipHE78. Oak Hill Th Coll 76. **d** 79 **p** 80. C Rodbourne Cheney *Bris* 79-82; C Wolverhampton St Matt *Lich* 82-85; CF 85-88; TV Braunstone *Leic* 88-95; Past Asst to Adn Leic 95-97; C Barkestone w Plungar, Redmile and Stathern from 97. *11 Dixon Drive, Leicester LE2 1RA* Tel 0116-270 6340

MILLS, Canon Geoffrey Charles Malcolm. b 33. Wycliffe Hall Ox 59. **d** 61 **p** 62. C Buckhurst Hill *Chelmsf* 61-65; C Ecclesall *Sheff* 65-69; V Endcliffe 69-78; R Whiston from 78; Hon Can Sheff Cathl from 96. *The Rectory, Whiston, Rotherham, S Yorkshire S60 4JA* Tel (01709) 364430

MILLS, Miss Glenys Christine. b 38. Open Univ BA81. Dalton Ho Bris DipTh64. **d** 87 **p** 94. Par Dn Clifton Ch Ch w Em *Bris* 87-94; C 94-95; P-in-c Gt w Lt Abington *Ely* from 95; Chapl Arthur Rank Hospice Cambridge from 95. *The Vicarage, 35 Church Lane, Little Abington, Cambridge CB1 6BQ* Tel (01223) 891350

MILLS, Gordon Derek. b 35. Lich Th Coll 60. **d** 63 **p** 64. C W Derby St Mary *Liv* 63-65; C Clifton w Glapton *S'well* 65-67; V N Wilford St Faith 67-72; V Farnsfield 72-82; P-in-c Kirklington w Hockerton 77-82; Asst Dir of Educn *Blackb* 82-86; P-in-c Brindle 82-86; V Gt Budworth *Ches* 86-88; P-in-c Appleton Thorn and Antrobus 87-88; V Gt Budworth and Antrobus 88-92; V Gt Budworth from 92. *The Vicarage, Great Budworth, Northwich, Cheshire CW9 6HF* Tel (01606) 891324

MILLS, Canon Hubert Cecil. b 44. TCD BA66 MA71. CITC 67. **d** 67 **p** 68. C Dublin Rathfarnham *D & G* 67-72; Min Can St Patr Cathl Dublin 69-92; Succ 72-92; Preb Rathmichael St Patr Cathl Dublin from 92; C Dublin St Steph and St Ann *D & G* 72-77; I Holmpatrick w Balbriggan and Kenure 77-86; I Killiney H Trin 86-93. *Holy Trinity Rectory, Killiney Road, Killiney, Co Dublin, Irish Republic* Tel Dublin (1) 285 2695

MILLS, Jack Herbert. b 14. Selw Coll Cam BA38 MA42. Cuddesdon Coll 39. **d** 40 **p** 41. C Camberwell St Geo *S'wark* 40-42; C Southfields St Barn 42-46; USPG 46-47; Chapl Hurstpierpoint Coll Hassocks 47-52; New Zealand 52-56, 59-61 and from 87; Australia 57-59 and 62-73; Hd Master St Wilfrid's Sch Ex 74-79; Chapl Community of St Wilfrid 74-79; Hon C Ewhurst *Chich* 79-81; Hon C Bodiam 79-81; Perm to Offic *Ex* 81-85; Perm to Offic *Chich* 85-87; rtd 87. *3 St Chad's Square, Selwyn Village, Point Chevalier, Auckland 2, New Zealand* Tel Auckland (9) 892243

MILLS, Jennifer Clare. *See* TOMLINSON, Mrs Jennifer Clare

MILLS, John Kettlewell. b 53. BA. Cranmer Hall Dur. **d** 84 **p** 85. C Ashton on Mersey St Mary *Ches* 84-87; TV Didsbury St Jas and Em *Man* from 87. *The Vicarage, 453 Parrswood Road, East Didsbury, Manchester M20 0NE* Tel 0161-445 1310

MILLS, Leslie. b 17. Open Univ BSc94 Reading Univ MA95. Wycliffe Hall Ox 68. **d** 68 **p** 69. C Basingstoke *Win* 68-77; C Basing 78-80; C York Town St Mich *Guildf* 80-84; rtd 84; Perm to Offic *Win* from 84; Perm to Offic *Guildf* from 85; Perm to Offic *Ox* from 86. *21 Mill Lane, Yateley, Hants GU46 7TE* Tel (01252) 870689

MILLS, Michael Henry. b 51. AKC73. St Aug Coll Cant. **d** 74 **p** 75. C Newton Aycliffe *Dur* 74-78; C Padgate *Liv* 78-79; TV 79-95; V Frodsham *Ches* from 95. *The Vicarage, Vicarage Lane, Frodsham, Warrington WA6 7DU* Tel (01928) 733378

MILLS, Pamela Ann. S Tr Scheme. **d** 97. NSM Hurstbourne Tarrant, Faccombe, Vernham Dean etc *Win* from 97. *Sunnyside, The Dene, Hurstbourne Tarrant, Andover, Hants SP11 0AS* Tel (01264) 736286

MILLS, Peter John. b 52. Sarum & Wells Th Coll 87. **d** 89 **p** 90. C Chatham St Wm *Roch* 89-92; V Perry Street 92-95; V E Malling from 95. *The Vicarage, 21 High Street, East Malling, Maidstone, Kent ME19 6AJ* Tel (01732) 843282

MILLS, Roger Conrad. b 58. Selw Coll Cam BA79 MA83. St Jo Coll Nottm DPS85. **d** 85 **p** 86. C Jesmond H Trin *Newc* 85-88; C Alnwick St Mich and St Paul 88-91; Chapl Newc Univ from 91; P-in-c Newc St Barn and St Jude 95-97. *The Chaplaincy, University of Newcastle, Newcastle upon Tyne NE1 7RU* Tel 0191-222 6341 Fax 261 1182 E-mail roger.mills@ncl.ac.uk

MILLS, Walter Charles. b 30. Oak Hill Th Coll 82. **d** 85 **p** 86. NSM Broomfield *Chelmsf* 85-88; C Pleshey 88-95; rtd 95; Perm to Offic *Chelmsf* from 95. *29 Mill Lane, Broomfield, Chelmsford CM1 7BQ* Tel (01245) 441117

MILLS-POWELL, Mark Oliver McLay. b 55. Edin Th Sem Virginia. **d** 83 **p** 84. C Huyton St Mich *Liv* 83-86; USA 86-95; P-in-c Basildon w Aldworth and Ashampstead *Ox* from 95. *The Vicarage, Upper Basildon, Reading RG8 8LS* Tel (01491) 671223

MILLSON, Capt Brian Douglas. b 53. Univ of W Ontario BA76 Huron Coll MDiv84. Westcott Ho Cam 82. **d** 83 **p** 84. C Walton-on-Thames *Guildf* 83-86; Canada from 86. *PO 239 Ralston, Alberta, Canada, TOJ 2NO* Tel Calgary (403) 544 3283 Fax 544 5054

MILLSON, Mrs Margaret Lily. b 41. CertEd61. EMMTC 83. **dss** 86 **d** 87 **p** 94. NSM Bottesford w Ashby *Linc* from 86. *65 Timberland, Bottesford, Scunthorpe, S Humberside DN16 3SH* Tel (01724) 865489

MILLWARD, Mark Anthony. b 61. Leeds Poly BSc. St Steph Ho Ox. **d** 86 **p** 87. C Sunderland Red Ho *Dur* 86-89; C Leic Ch Sav *Leic* 89-90; V Sunderland Pennywell St Thos *Dur* 90-96; Chapl City Hosps Sunderland NHS Trust from 96. *The Chaplain's Office, Sunderland District General Hospital, Kayll Road, Sunderland SR4 7TP* Tel 0191-565 6256

MILLWARD, Miss Pauline Freda. b 50. AMA74. N Ord Course 89. **d** 92 **p** 94. NSM Warley *Wakef* 92-95; P-in-c Halifax St Hilda from 95; Missr for Halifax Town Cen from 95. *8 Hill Park Mount, Sowerby Bridge, W Yorkshire HX6 3JB* Tel (01422) 823576

MILLWOOD, Stephen Grant. b 44. Sheff Tech Coll HNC66 Sheff City Coll of Educn CertEd77 Open Univ BA92. St Jo Coll Nottm DipThMin92. **d** 94 **p** 95. C Anston *Sheff* from 94. *20 St James Avenue, Anston, Sheffield S31 7DR* Tel (01909) 550579

MILLYARD, Alexander John. b 29. St Jo Coll Dur BA53. Qu Coll Birm 53. **d** 54 **p** 55. C Middlesbrough St Aid *York* 54-56; C Pocklington w Yapham-cum-Meltonby, Owsthorpe etc 56-58; C Millington w Gt Givendale 56-58; C Rickmansworth *St Alb* 58-61; R Wormley 61-65; Asst Chapl HM Pris Pentonville 65-67; Chapl HM Pris Leeds 67-69; Chapl HM Pris Ex 69-71; Chapl HM Pris Wandsworth 72-73; V Snibston *Leic* 73-75; V Leic All So 75-79; V Blakesley and Adstone *Pet* 79-89; R Blakesley w Adstone and Maidford etc 89-91; rtd 91; Perm to Offic *Chich* from 91. *Flat 6, Gainsborough House, Eaton Gardens, Hove, E Sussex BN3 3UA* Tel (01273) 728722

✠**MILMINE, The Rt Revd Douglas.** b 21. CBE83. St Pet Hall Ox BA46 MA46. Clifton Th Coll 47. **d** 47 **p** 48 **c** 73. C Ilfracombe SS Phil and Jas *Ex* 47-50; C Slough *Ox* 50-53; Chile 54-69; Adn N Chile, Bolivia and Peru 63-69; Hon Can Chile from 69; Area Sec SAMS 69-72; Bp Paraguay 73-85; rtd 86. *1C Clive Court, 24 Grand Parade, Eastbourne, E Sussex BN21 3DD* Tel (01323) 734159

MILMINE, Neil Edward Douglas. b 46. Kent Univ BSc70. Wycliffe Hall Ox 80. **d** 82 **p** 83. C Hailsham *Chich* 82-86; C Horsham 86; TV 86-93; V Patcham from 93. *The Vicarage, 12 Church Hill, Brighton BN1 8YE* Tel (01273) 552157

MILN, Dr Peter. b 43. MBIM Univ of Wales (Swansea) BA65 Nottm Univ MTh81 PhD89. EMMTC 76. **d** 79 **p** 80. NSM Uttoxeter w Bramshall *Lich* 79-85; CF (TAVR) from 82; Perm to Offic *Chelmsf* from 92. *41 Balance Street, Uttoxeter, Staffs ST14 8JQ* Tel (01889) 565110

MILNE, Alan. b 54. RMN SRN FETC. Cranmer Hall Dur 89. **d** 91 **p** 92. C Hartlepool St Luke *Dur* 91-94; P-in-c Dalton le Dale from 94; P-in-c Hawthorn from 94. *The Vicarage, Church Lane, Murton, Seaham, Co Durham SR7 9RD* Tel 0191-526 2410

MILNE, Miss Christine Helen. b 48. LTCL71 Lon Univ DipRS86. S'wark Ord Course 83. **dss** 86 **d** 87 **p** 90. S Lambeth St Steph *S'wark* 86-89; Par Dn 87-89; New Zealand from 89. *NGA Tawa School, Private Bag 1101, Marton, New Zealand* Tel Marton (6) 327 7955 or 327 6429 Fax 327 7954

MILNE, Glenn Alexander Roscoe. b 62. Or Coll Ox BA85 MA89. Westcott Ho Cam 87. **d** 89 **p** 90. C Hexham *Newc* 89-92; CF 92-95; I Castlepollard and Oldcastle w Loughcrew etc *M & K* from 95. *St Michael's Rectory, Castlepollard, Mullingar, Co Westmeath, Irish Republic* Tel Mullingar (44) 61123

MILNER, Darryl Vickers. b 43. DipTh66. St Chad's Coll Dur. **d** 66 **p** 67. C Oswestry H Trin *Lich* 66-69; S Africa 69-81; New Zealand from 81. *The Vicarage, 47 Church Street, Northcote, North Shore 1309, New Zealand* Tel Auckland (9) 480 7568

MILNER, David. b 38. St Aid Birkenhead 63. **d** 66 **p** 67. C Ulverston H Trin *Carl* 66-68; C Mickleover All SS *Derby* 68-71; C Mickleover St Jo 68-71; V 71-82; P-in-c Sandiacre 82-86; P-in-c Doveridge from 86; RD Longford 86-96; P-in-c Sudbury and Somersal Herbert from 92. *The Vicarage, Church Lane, Doveridge, Ashbourne, Derbyshire DE6 5NN* Tel (01889) 563420

MILNER, Eric. b 10. Mert Coll Ox BA33 MA37. Linc Th Coll 35. **d** 36 **p** 37. C Hemsworth *Wakef* 36-39; C Dewsbury All SS 39-40; C Beckenham St Jas *Roch* 40-42; C Chatham All SS 42-44; Chapl RNVR 44-46; Chapl RN 46-65; V Bentley *Sheff* 67-80; rtd 80; Perm to Offic *Wakef* from 86. *30 Hillcrest Avenue, Ossett, W Yorkshire WF5 9PP* Tel (01924) 271740

MILNER, Leslie. b 35. MBE93. Birm Univ BSc57 St Jo Coll Cam BA59. Wells Th Coll 61. **d** 63 **p** 64. C Yardley St Edburgha *Birm* 63-66; C Seacroft *Ripon* 66-71; Dir St Basil's Cen Deritend from 71; Lic to Offic *Birm* 71-86; Perm to Offic from 86. *St Basil's Centre, Heathmill Lane, Birmingham B9 4AX* Tel 0121-772 2483

✠**MILNER, The Rt Revd Ronald James.** b 27. Pemb Coll Cam BA49 MA52. Wycliffe Hall Ox 51. **d** 53 **p** 54 **c** 88. Succ Sheff Cathl *Sheff* 53-58; V Westwood *Cov* 58-64; V Fletchamstead 64-70; R Southampton St Mary w H Trin *Win* 70-72; P-in-c Southampton St Matt 70-72; Lic to Offic 72-73; TR Southampton (City Cen) 73-83; Hon Can Win Cathl 75-83; Adn Linc 83-88; Can and Preb Linc Cathl 83-88; Suff Bp Burnley *Blackb* 88-93; rtd 93; Asst Bp S'well from 94. *7 Crafts Way, Southwell, Notts NG25 0BL* Tel (01636) 816256

MILNER, William David. b 52. St Jo Coll Nottm DCM93. **d** 93 **p** 94. C Wollaton *S'well* 93-97; P-in-c Daybrook from 97. *St Paul's Vicarage, 241 Oxclose Lane, Nottingham NG5 6FB* Tel 0115-926 2686

MILNES, David Ian. b 45. Chich Th Coll 74. **d** 76 **p** 77. C Walthamstow St Sav *Chelmsf* 76-80; C Chingford SS Pet and Paul 80-83; P-in-c Gt Ilford St Alb 83-87; V from 87. *The Vicarage, 99 Albert Road, Ilford, Essex IG1 1HS* Tel 0181-478 2428

MILROY, Mrs Ethel Doreen. b 33. Bedf Coll Lon BSc54 Bris Univ PGCE69 Nottm Univ MEd79. N Ord Course 88. **d** 91 **p** 94. NSM Tideswell *Derby* 91-95; P-in-c Rowsley from 95. *The Vicarage, Rowsley, Matlock, Derbyshire DE4 2EA* Tel (01629) 733296

MILTON, Andrew John. b 54. BD. St Steph Ho Ox. **d** 83 **p** 84. C Highfield *Ox* 83-87; TV Banbury 87-95; P-in-c Thorney Abbey *Ely* from 95. *The Abbey Vicarage, The Green, Thorney, Peterborough PE6 0QD* Tel (01733) 270388

MILTON, Miss Angela Daphne. b 50. FILEx79. Oak Hill Th Coll 84. **d** 87 **p** 94. NSM Watford *St Alb* 87-97; C Stevenage St Mary Sheppall w Aston from 97. *31 Harefield, Bandley Hill, Stevenage, Herts SG2 9NG* Tel (01438) 749695

MILTON, Claudius James Barton. b 29. K Coll Lon BD52 AKC53. **d** 53 **p** 54. C Sudbury St Andr *Lon* 53-56; Asst Chapl Bedford Sch 57-65; Asst Master 57-65; Chapl Cranbrook Sch Kent 65-74; Asst Master and Housemaster 65-74; Chapl & Asst Master Clayesmore Sch Blandford 74-89; Clayesmore Prep Sch 74-89; rtd 89. *28 Oakwood Drive, Iwerne Minster, Blandford Forum, Dorset DT11 8QT* Tel (01747) 811792

MILTON, Derek Rees. b 45. Open Univ BA76 Lon Univ BD80. St Jo Sem Wonersh 63. **d** 68 **p** 69. In RC Ch 68-84; Hon C Luton Lewsey St Hugh *St Alb* 84-85; Hon C Houghton Regis 85-86; C 86-89; TV Brixham w Churston Ferrers and Kingswear *Ex* from 89. *All Saints' Vicarage, 16 Holwell Road, Brixham, Devon TQ5 9NE* Tel (01803) 855549

MILTON-THOMPSON, Dr David Gerald. b 17. OBE76. MRCS LRCP42 Em Coll Cam BA39 MA MB BChir49. Lon Coll of Div 62. **d** 63 **p** 64. CMS 49-81 and 85-88; Kenya 52-81; C Chadwell *Chelmsf* 81-82; Hon C 82-85; Uganda 85-88; rtd 88; Hon C Sevenoaks St Nic *Roch* from 88. *1 The Glebe, Oak Lane, Sevenoaks, Kent TN13 1NN* Tel (01732) 462977

MILTON-THOMPSON, Jonathan Patrick. b 51. Nottm Univ BA76. Oak Hill Th Coll 86. **d** 88 **p** 89. C Bispham *Blackb* 88-92; C Darfield *Sheff* 92; C-in-c Gt Houghton CD from 92. *16 High Street, Great Houghton, Barnsley, S Yorkshire S72 0AB* Tel (01226) 752320

MILVERTON, Frederic Jack. b 15. Lon Univ BSc37 Leeds Univ MEd40. Ripon Hall Ox 56. **d** 57 **p** 58. C Ecclesall *Sheff* 57-60; V Thurcroft 60-61; Lect Nottm Coll of Educn 61-67; Lect Weymouth Coll of Educn 67-76; Hd of Educn 70-76; Dean Educn Dorset Inst of HE 76-79; TV Oakdale St Geo *Sarum* 79-82; rtd 82. *Flat 4, Compass South, Rodwell Road, Weymouth, Dorset DT4 8QT* Tel (01305) 788930

MILVERTON, Mrs Ruth Erica. b 32. Open Univ BA78 Southn Univ MA82. Sarum Th Coll 83. **dss** 86 **d** 87 **p** 95. Weymouth H Trin *Sarum* 86-87; Hon Par Dn 87-95; NSM from 95. *4 Compass South, Rodwell Road, Weymouth, Dorset DT4 8QT* Tel (01305) 788930

MILVERTON of Lagos and Clifton, The Revd and Rt Hon Lord (Fraser Arthur Richard Richards). b 30. Bps' Coll Cheshunt. **d** 57 **p** 58. C Beckenham St Geo *Roch* 57-59; C Sevenoaks St Jo 59-60; C Gt Bookham *Guildf* 60-63; V Okewood 63-67; R Christian Malford w Sutton Benger etc *Bris* 67-93; Public Preacher 93-95; rtd 95. *7 Betjeman Road, Barton Park, Marlborough, Wilts SN8 1TL* Tel (01672) 86568

MILWARD, Terence George. b 23. Ripon Hall Ox 66. **d** 68 **p** 69. C Selly Oak St Mary *Birm* 68-70; C Edgbaston St Bart 70-75; TV Bournemouth St Pet w St Swithun, H Trin etc *Win* 75-81; R Smannell w Enham Alamein 81-88; rtd 88; Perm to Offic *Guildf* from 88. *Church House Flat, Church Lane, Witley, Godalming, Surrey GU8 5PN* Tel (01428) 685308

MINALL, Peter. b 26. Lon Univ BSc47. Bps' Coll Cheshunt 51. **d** 53 **p** 54. C Bishop's Stortford St Mich *St Alb* 53-57; C Luton w E Hyde 57-63; C Tuffley *Glouc* 63-65; Asst Youth Chapl 65-69; V Stroud 69-84; RD Bisley 78-84; P-in-c Barnwood 84-91; Chapl Coney Hill Hosp Glouc 86-91; Lic to Offic *Glouc* from 91; rtd 91. *Amberwood, Knapp Lane, Painswick, Stroud, Glos GL6 6YE* Tel (01452) 813730

MINAY, Francis Arthur Rodney. b 44. Edin Coll of Art DA65. Westcott Ho Cam 66. **d** 68 **p** 69. C Edenbridge *Roch* 68-73; C Bromley St Mark 73-75; V Tudeley w Capel 75-79; TV Littleham w Exmouth *Ex* 79-82; P-in-c Bolton Percy *York* from 82; Asst Chapl to Arts and Recreation in the NE from 82. *The Rectory, Bolton Percy, York YO5 7AL* Tel (01904) 744213

MINCHER, John Derek Bernard. b 31. **d** 60 **p** 61. OSB 54-80; Lic to Offic *Ox* 60-80; Perm to Offic *St E* 81-87; C Halesworth w Linstead, Chediston, Holton etc 87-90; P-in-c Worlingworth, Southolt, Tannington, Bedfield etc 90-91; R 91-96; rtd 96. *3 Bracken Row, Thurston, Bury St Edmunds, Suffolk IP31 3AT* Tel (01359) 231976

MINCHEW, Donald Patrick. b 48. Univ of Wales (Cardiff) BD76. St Mich Coll Llan 72. **d** 76 **p** 77. C Glouc St Aldate *Glouc* 76-80; P-in-c Sharpness CD 80-81; V Sharpness w Purton and Brookend 81-95; Miss to Seamen from 81; V Croydon St Mich w St Jas *S'wark* from 95. *St Michael's Vicarage, 39 Oakfield Road, Croydon CR0 2UX* Tel 0181-680 8413

MINCHIN, Anthony John. b 35. St Cath Coll Cam BA59 MA. Wells Th Coll 59. **d** 61 **p** 62. C Cheltenham St Pet *Glouc* 61-64; C Bushey *St Alb* 64-67; V Cheltenham St Mich *Glouc* 67-74; V Lower Cam 74-82; V Tuffley 82-92; R Huntley and Longhope from 92. *The Rectory, 56 Byford Road, Huntley, Glos GL19 3EL* Tel (01452) 831044

MINCHIN, Charles Scott. b 51. Trin Coll Cam BA72 MA75. Linc Th Coll 73. **d** 75 **p** 76. C Gt Wyrley *Lich* 75-78; TV Wilnecote 78-82; C Tamworth 82-84; C-in-c Glascote CD 84-88; R Brierley Hill 88-93; R Brierley Hill *Worc* from 93. *The Rectory, 2 Church Hill, Brierley Hill, W Midlands DY5 3PX* Tel (01384) 78146

MINCHIN, Canon George Reginald. b 05. TCD BA31 MA43. **d** 31 **p** 32. C Londonderry Ch Ch *D & R* 31-35; C Mevagh 35-46; C Camus-juxta-Bann 46-65; I 65-75; RD Limavady 65-75; Can Derry Cathl 70-75; rtd 75. *4 Fortview, Portballintrae, Bushmills, Co Antrim BT57 8TJ* Tel (01265) 731607

MINGINS, Canon Marion Elizabeth. b 52. Birm Univ BSocSc73 CQSW75. Cam DipRS78. **d** 87 **p** 94. CA from 79; NSM Battersea Park All SS *S'wark* 87-89; Sen Selection Sec ACCM 87-89; OHP from 89; Asst Dioc Dir of Ords and Voc Adv *St E* from 91; Chapl St E Cathl 91-93; Min Can 91-92; Hon Can St E Cathl 92-93; Can Res St E Cathl from 93; Chapl to The Queen from 96. *2 Abbey Precincts, The Churchyard, Bury St Edmunds, Suffolk IP33 1RS* Tel (01284) 753396

MINHINNICK, Leslie. b 18. Jes Coll Ox BA39 MA43. Wycliffe Hall Ox 40. **d** 41 **p** 42. C Briton Ferry *Llan* 41-43; C Canton St Jo 43-45; Tutor St Aid Birkenhead 45-50; Vice-Prin 50-51; V Over St Jo *Ches* 51-54; V Birkenhead St Mark 54-60; V Preston St Jo *Blackb* 60-61; V Chipping 61-66; V Lytham St Jo 66-81; rtd 81; Perm to Offic *Ban* from 81. *The Old School House, Cemaes, Anglesey LL67 0NG* Tel (01407) 710601

MINICH, Mason Faulconer. b 38. **d** 66 **p** 67. USA 66-71 and from 81; C Alverstoke *Portsm* 80; C Romford Ascension Collier Row

Chelmsf 80-81. *5055 Seminary Road, Apartment 1319, Alexandria, Virginia 22311, USA*

MINION, Arthur. b 65. TCD BTh92. CITC 89. **d** 92 **p** 93. C Bandon Union *C, C & R* 92-95; I Taunagh w Kilmactranny, Ballysumaghan etc *K, E & A* from 95. *The Rectory, Riverstown, Via Boyle, Co Sligo, Irish Republic* Tel Sligo (71) 65368

MINNS, David Andrew. b 59. St Jo Coll Nottm 95. **d** 97. C Burpham *Guildf* from 97. *8 Selbourne Road, Burpham, Guildford, Surrey GU4 7JP* Tel (01483) 456602

MINNS, John Alfred. b 38. Oak Hill Th Coll 63. **d** 68 **p** 69. C Cheadle Hulme St Andr *Ches* 68-72; C Hartford 72-74; V Wharton 74-85; V Halliwell St Paul *Man* 85-87; C Halliwell St Pet 87-91; rtd 91; Perm to Offic *Glouc* from 91. *39 Hambidge Lane, Lechlade, Glos GL7 3BJ* Tel (01367) 253549

MINNS, John Charles. b 42. EAMTC. **d** 85 **p** 86. NSM Heigham St Barn w St Bart *Nor* 85-91; NSM Nor St Geo Tombland from 91; Asst Chapl Norfolk & Nor Hosp from 92. *18 Thunder Lane, Thorpe St Andrew, Norwich NR7 0JW* Tel (01603) 37000

MINORS, Graham Glyndwr Cavil. b 44. Glouc Sch of Min. **d** 79 **p** 79. Hon C Lower Cam *Glouc* 79-83; C Leckhampton SS Phil and Jas w Cheltenham St Jas 83-89; V Cainscross w Selsley from 89; RD Stonehouse from 97. *The Vicarage, 58 Cashes Green Road, Stroud, Glos GL5 4RA* Tel (01453) 755148

MINSHALL, Douglas Arthur. b 24. EMMTC 78. **d** 81 **p** 82. NSM Worksop Priory *S'well* 81-85; NSM E Retford 85-87; C 87-88; NSM W Retford 85-87; C 87-88; P-in-c Clarborough w Hayton 88-93; rtd 93. *3 Avon Rise, Retford, Notts DN22 6QH* Tel (01777) 869872

MINSON, Roger Graham. b 41. Leeds Univ BA64 Bris Univ DSA69. Coll of Resurr Mirfield 64. **d** 66 **p** 67. C Horfield St Greg *Bris* 66-70; C Southmead 70-73; V Lawrence Weston 74-81; TV Knowle 81-93; V Knowle St Martin 93-95; V Fishponds St Mary from 95. *St Mary's Vicarage, Vicar's Close, Bristol BS16 3TH* Tel 0117-965 4462

MINTY, Kenneth Desmond. b 25. Ch Ch Ox BA48 MA51. Lich Th Coll 71 Qu Coll Birm 72. **d** 73 **p** 74. Asst Chapl Wrekin Coll Shropshire 73-84; Chapl 84-86; Hon C Lawley *Lich* 74-75; Hon C Cen Telford 75-81; Hon C Longdon-upon-Tern, Rodington, Uppington etc 81-89; V Ercall Magna 89-95; V Rowton 89-95; rtd 95; Perm to Offic *Lich* from 95. *9 Shawbirch Road, Telford TF5 0AD* Tel (01952) 244218

MINTY, Selwyn Francis. b 34. St D Coll Lamp 58. **d** 61 **p** 62. C Tonyrefail *Llan* 61-66; C Pontypridd St Cath 66-69; V Cilfynydd 69-84; V Crynant from 84. *The Vicarage, 35 Main Road, Crynant, Neath SA10 8NT* Tel (01639) 750226

MIR, Amene Rahman. b 58. Man Univ BA81 PhD93. Coll of Resurr Mirfield 81. **d** 83 **p** 84. C Walton St Mary *Liv* 83-87; Chapl Walton Hosp Liv 83-87; Perm to Offic *Man* 87-90; Asst Chapl Salford Mental Health Unit 90-94; Chapl Salford Mental Health Services NHS Trust 94-96; Chapl R Marsden NHS Trust Lon and Surrey from 96. *The Chaplain's Office, Royal Marsden NHS Trust, Downs Road, Sutton, Surrey SM2 5PT, or 66 Furzedown Road, Sutton, Surrey SM2 5QF* Tel 0181-642 6011 ext 3074 or 642 7395

MITCHAM, Andrew Mark. b 66. Kent Univ BA87 Leeds Univ BA90. Coll of Resurr Mirfield 88. **d** 91 **p** 92. C Downham Market w Bexwell *Ely* 91-94; Priest Shrine of Our Lady of Walsingham 94-96; V W Worthing St Jo *Chich* from 96. *St John's Vicarage, 15 Reigate Road, Worthing, W Sussex BN11 5NF* Tel (01903) 247340

MITCHELL, Canon Albert George. b 48. TCD BA. **d** 88 **p** 89. Bp's C Skreen w Kilmacshalgan and Dromard *T, K & A* from 88; Can Killala Cathl from 96. *Kilglass Glebe, Enniscrone, Co Sligo, Irish Republic* Tel Kilglass (96) 36258

MITCHELL, Allan. b 52. Kelham Th Coll 74 Linc Th Coll 78. **d** 78 **p** 79. C Kells *Carl* 78-81; C Upperby St Jo 81-83; V Pennington w Lindal and Marton 83-88; V Westf St Mary from 88. *St Mary's Vicarage, Salisbury Street, Workington, Cumbria CA14 3TR* Tel (01900) 603227

MITCHELL, Andrew Patrick (Paddy). b 37. Ripon Coll Cuddesdon 84 English Coll Valladolid 59. **d** 64 **p** 65. In RC Ch 64-85; C Woolwich St Mary w St Mich *S'wark* 85-87; V E Wickham 87-94; P-in-c Walsall St Andr *Lich* from 94. *119 Hollyhedge Lane, Walsall WS2 8PU* Tel (01922) 721658

MITCHELL, Cecil Robert. b 32. QUB BScEng54. CITC 65. **d** 65 **p** 66. C Belfast St Mary Magd *Conn* 65-68; C Belfast St Mark 68-69; Dioc Sec 70-74; Dioc Sec *D & D* 70-74; I Ballywalter 74-82; V Malew *S & M* 82-84; I Bright w Ballee and Killough *D & D* 84-89; I Killyleagh 89-94; rtd 94. *20 Innisfayle Crescent, Bangor, Co Down BT19 1DT* Tel (01247) 466167

MITCHELL, Christopher Allan (Chris). b 51. Newc Univ BA72. Oak Hill Th Coll 82. **d** 84 **p** 85. C Guisborough *York* 84-87; C Thornaby on Tees 87-88; TV 88-92; V Dent w Cowgill *Bradf* from 92. *The Vicarage, Dent, Sedbergh, Cumbria LA10 5QR* Tel (015396) 25226

MITCHELL, Christopher Ashley. b 69. Leeds Univ BA(Econ)91. Ridley Hall Cam CTM92. **d** 95 **p** 96. Min Can St As Cathl *St As* from 95. *13 Llys Clwyd, St Asaph LL17 0UA* Tel (01745) 582560

MITCHELL, Christopher Derek. b 61. Univ of Wales (Lamp) BA85 Leic Univ MA86 Qu Coll Cam BA88 MA92. Westcott Ho Cam 87. **d** 89 **p** 90. C Streetly *Lich* 89-92; C Brookfield St Mary *Lon* 92-96. *221 Moselle Avenue, London N22 6EY* Tel 0181-881 0692

MITCHELL, Canon David George. b 35. QUB BA56. Sarum Th Coll 59. **d** 61 **p** 62. C Westbury-on-Trym H Trin *Bris* 61-64; C Cricklade w Latton 64-68; V Fishponds St Jo 68-77; RD Stapleton 76-77; TR E Bris 77-87; Hon Can Bris Cathl from 87; R Syston 87-94; V Warmley 87-94; P-in-c Bitton 87-94; R Warmley, Syston and Bitton from 94; RD Bitton 87-93. *The Rectory, Church Avenue, Bristol BS15 5JJ* Tel 0117-967 3965

MITCHELL, Preb David Norman. b 35. Tyndale Hall Bris 64. **d** 67 **p** 68. C Marple All SS *Ches* 67-70; C St Helens St Helen *Liv* 70-72; V S Lambeth St Steph *S'wark* 72-78; P-in-c Brixton Road Ch Ch 73-75; SE Area Sec CPAS 78-81; R Uphill *B & W* 81-92; TR from 92; Chapl Weston-super-Mare Gen Hosp from 86; Preb Wells Cathl *B & W* from 90. *The Rectory, 3 Old Church Road, Uphill, Weston-super-Mare, Avon BS23 4UH* Tel (01934) 620156

MITCHELL, Edwin. b 44. St Jo Coll Nottm BTh74. **d** 74 **p** 75. C Worksop St Jo *S'well* 74-77; C Waltham Abbey *Chelmsf* 77-80; V Whiston *Liv* 80-91; R Wombwell *Sheff* from 91. *The Rectory, 1 Rectory Close, Wombwell, Barnsley, S Yorkshire S73 8EY* Tel (01226) 752166

MITCHELL, Eric Sidney. b 24. S Dios Minl Tr Scheme 77. **d** 80 **p** 81. NSM Portland All SS w St Pet *Sarum* 80-83; C 88-92; Bermuda 83-88; Chapl HM Pris The Verne from 91; rtd 92. *10 Underhedge Gardens, Portland, Dorset DT5 2DX* Tel (01305) 821059

MITCHELL, Frank. b 21. Ely Th Coll 49. **d** 51 **p** 52. C Leeds St Aid *Ripon* 51-54; V Bramham *York* 54-62; V Scarborough St Sav 62-73; V Scarborough St Sav w All SS 73-83; rtd 83; Perm to Offic *York* from 83. *6 Sitwell Street, Scarborough, N Yorkshire YO11 5EX* Tel (01723) 367948

MITCHELL, Canon Frank Leonard. b 14. St Cath Soc Ox BA39 MA47. Wycliffe Hall Ox 46. **d** 48 **p** 49. C Rainham *Roch* 48-50; V Borstal 50-56; V Meopham 56-65; RD Cobham 58-65; R Hayes 66-77; Hon Can Roch Cathl 76-79; C Speldhurst w Groombridge and Ashurst 77-79; rtd 79; Perm to Offic *Chich* from 80; Perm to Offic *Roch* 82-95. *10 Beechwood Close, Burwash, Etchingham, E Sussex TN19 7BS* Tel (01435) 882601

MITCHELL, Geoffrey. b 36. CEng66 FCIT92 FIMechE76 SS Coll Cam BA60 MA64. EMMTC 88. **d** 91 **p** 92. NSM Oaks in Charnwood and Copt Oak *Leic* 91-94; NSM Loughborough All SS w H Trin from 94. *36 Brick Kiln Lane, Shepshed, Loughborough, Leics LE12 9EL* Tel (01509) 502280

MITCHELL, Geoffrey Peter. b 30. Liv Univ BEng57 Man Univ MSc68. Wells Th Coll 57. **d** 59 **p** 60. C Bradford cum Beswick *Man* 59-61; R Man St Pet Oldham Road w St Jas 61-64; Lic to Offic 64-68; Hon C Unsworth 68-86; V Woolfold 86-95; rtd 95; Perm to Offic *Man* from 95. *14 Redfearn Wood, Rochdale, Lancs OL12 7GA* Tel (01706) 38180

MITCHELL, Canon George Alfred. b 23. TCD BA45 MA56. **d** 46 **p** 47. C Belfast St Matt *Conn* 46-48; C Ballymoney 48-51; C Belf Cathl Miss 51-52; I Broomhedge 52-58; I Carrickfergus 59-70; I Bangor St Comgall *D & D* 70-88; Can Belf Cathl 78-88; rtd 88. *2 Glendun Park, Bangor, Co Down BT20 4UX* Tel (01247) 460882

MITCHELL, Gordon Frank Henry. b 26. QFSM. FIFireE. Sarum & Wells Th Coll 74. **d** 77 **p** 78. NSM Alderbury and W Grimstead *Sarum* 77-91; NSM Alderbury Team 91-96. *Seefeld, Southampton Road, Whaddon, Salisbury SP5 3EB* Tel (01722) 710516

MITCHELL, Graham Bell. b 40. Otago Univ BA64 MA65 Worc Coll Ox BA73 MA76. St Chad's Coll Dur 66. **d** 68 **p** 69. C Bris St Agnes w St Simon *Bris* 68-71; C Bedminster St Mich 73-76; V Auckland St Pet *Dur* 76-78; Vice-Prin Chich Th Coll 78-83; C Brighton St Pet w Chpl Royal and St Jo *Chich* 83-86; P-in-c Scaynes Hill from 86. *The Vicarage, Scaynes Hill, Haywards Heath, W Sussex RH17 7PB* Tel (01444) 831265

MITCHELL, Canon Henry Gordon. b 20. St Chad's Coll Dur BA44 DipTh45 MA47. **d** 45 **p** 46. C Walton St Mary *Liv* 45-52; R Fulbeck *Linc* 52-72; RD Loveden 64-72; Can and Preb Linc Cathl 67-85; P-in-c Carlton Scroop w Normanton 69-72; V New Sleaford 72-85; rtd 85; Perm to Offic *Linc* from 85. *3 Lime Grove, Caythorpe, Grantham, Lincs NG32 3DH* Tel (01400) 73346

MITCHELL, Jolyon Peter. b 64. Selw Coll Cam BA88 MA90. St Jo Coll Dur MA93. **d** 93 **p** 94. NSM St Mary's Cathl *Edin* from 93; Lect Edin Univ from 93. *4 Bruntsfield Terrace, Edinburgh EH10 4EX* Tel 0131-229 8154

MITCHELL, Miss Josephine Dorothy (Jose). b 36. Dalton Ho Bris 65. **dss** 76 **d** 87 **p** 94. Hailsham *Chich* 75-85; Enfield St Jas *Lon* 85-87; Par Dn 87-94; C 94-96; rtd 96. *24 Benedictine Gate, Waltham Cross, Herts EN8 0XB*

MITCHELL, Kevin. b 49. Newc Univ BSc71 Ox Univ BA83. Ripon Coll Cuddesdon 81. **d** 83 **p** 84. C Cantril Farm *Liv* 83-86; Chapl N Middx Hosp 86-90; C Gt Cambridge Road St Jo and St Jas *Lon* 86-90; P-in-c Cricklewood St Pet 90-96; V Whetstone St Jo from 96. *St John's Vicarage, 1163 High Road, London N20 0PG* Tel 0181-445 4569

MITCHELL, Dr Leonard David. b 30. ACA56 FCA66. Wells Th Coll 60 Canadian Th Sem DMin94. **d** 61 **p** 62. C Hilborough w

Bodney *Nor* 61-64; C Oxborough w Foulden and Caldecote 61-64; C Cockley Cley w Gooderstone 61-64; C Gt and Lt Cressingham w Threxton 61-64; V Ernesettle *Ex* 64-67; Canada from 67; rtd 95. *8 Jane Street, PO Box 4101, Picton, Ontario, Canada, K0K 2T0* Tel Picton (613) 476 5203

MITCHELL, The Very Revd Patrick Reynolds. b 30. FSA81 Mert Coll Ox BA52 MA56. Wells Th Coll 52. **d** 54 **p** 55. C Mansfield St Mark *S'well* 54-57; Chapl Wells Th Coll 57-61; PV Wells Cathl *B & W* 57-61; V Milton *Portsm* 61-67; V Frome St Jo *B & W* 67-73; P-in-c Woodlands 67-73; Dir of Ords 70-74; Dean Wells 73-89; Dean of Windsor and Dom Chapl to The Queen from 89. *The Deanery, Windsor Castle, Windsor, Berks SL4 1NJ* Tel (01753) 865561 or 865538

MITCHELL, Peter Derek. b 30. Roch Th Coll 67. **d** 69 **p** 70. C Wargrave *Ox* 69-72; V Lund *Blackb* 72-80; V Badsey w Aldington and Wickhamford *Worc* 80-96; rtd 96. *Althaea, 29 Lavender Walk, Evesham, Worcs WR11 6LN*

MITCHELL, Richard John Anthony. b 64. St Martin's Coll Lanc BA85 PGCE86. Sarum & Wells Th Coll 88. **d** 91 **p** 92. C Kendal H Trin *Carl* 91-95; TV Kirkby Lonsdale from 95. *The Vicarage, Vicarage Lane, Kirkby Lonsdale, Cumbria LA6 2BA* Tel (01524) 272078

MITCHELL, Robert Hugh. b 53. Ripon Coll Cuddesdon. **d** 82 **p** 83. C E Dulwich St Jo *S'wark* 82-86; C Cambridge Gt St Mary w St Mich *Ely* 86-90; Chapl Girton Coll Cam 86-90; Asst Chapl Win Coll 90-91; Assoc Chapl Addenbrooke's Hosp Cam 91-93; Chapl Portsm Hosps NHS Trust 93-95; Chapl St Mary's Hosp Portsm 93-95; Chapl R Free Hampstead NHS Trust from 95. *The Chaplains' Office, The Royal Free Hospital, Pond Street, London NW3 2QG* Tel 0171-830 2742 or 794 0500

MITCHELL, Robert McFarlane. b 50. Man Univ BA72. Wycliffe Hall Ox 73. **d** 75 **p** 76. C Tonbridge SS Pet and Paul *Roch* 75-80; CF from 80. *MOD Chaplains (Army), Trenchard Lines, Upavon, Pewsey, Wilts SN9 6BE* Tel (01980) 615804 Fax 615800

MITCHELL, Roger Sulway. b 36. Chich Th Coll 70. **d** 71 **p** 71. C Sidcup St Jo *Roch* 71-74; C Pembury 74-76; Lic to Offic *Truro* 76-97; Chapl St Lawr Hosp Bodmin 76-96; Chapl Cornwall and Is of Scilly Mental Health Unit 88-96; Chapl Cornwall Healthcare Trust 96-97; TV Bodmin w Lanhydrock and Lanivet *Truro* from 97. *12 Beacon Road, Bodmin, Cornwall PL31 1AS* Tel (01208) 251300

MITCHELL, Sheila Rosemary. b 53. Chester Coll CertEd74 ADEd80. Nor Ord Course 93. **d** 96 **p** 97. NSM Plemstall w Guilden Sutton *Ches* from 96. *99 Barkhill Road, Vicar's Cross, Chester CH3 5JH* Tel (01244) 317601

MITCHELL, Stephen Andrew John. b 56. Ch Ch Coll Cant CertEd78 K Coll Lon AKC77 BD80 Lambeth STh90. Coll of Resurr Mirfield 80. **d** 82 **p** 83. C Chatham St Steph *Roch* 82-87; C Edenbridge 87-91; V from 91; P-in-c Crockham Hill H Trin from 91. *The Vicarage, Mill Hill, Edenbridge, Kent TN8 5DA* Tel (01732) 862258 Fax 864335

MITCHELL, Stephen John. b 51. Ex Univ BA73 Fitzw Coll Cam BA78 MA. Ridley Hall Cam 76. **d** 79 **p** 80. C Gt Malvern St Mary *Worc* 79-81; Prec Leic Cathl *Leic* 82-85; R Barrow upon Soar w Walton le Wolds from 85. *The Rectory, 27 Cotes Road, Barrow on Soar, Loughborough, Leics LE12 8JP* Tel (01509) 412471

MITCHELL, Steven. b 58. BTh. St Jo Coll Nottm. **d** 83 **p** 84. C Ovenden *Wakef* 83-87; V Gawthorpe and Chickenley Heath from 87. *The Vicarage, 73 Chickenley Lane, Dewsbury, W Yorkshire WF12 8QD* Tel (01924) 451547

MITCHELL, Dr Stuart <u>Ian</u>. b 50. Wadh Coll Ox BA71 DPhil74. S'wark Ord Course DipRS84. **d** 85 **p** 87. NSM Charlton St Luke w H Trin *S'wark* 85-86; NSM Kidbrooke 86-88; NSM Newbold w Dunston *Derby* 88-94; C 94-96; C Newbold w Dunston and Gt Barlow 96-97; P-in-c Matlock Bank from 97. *All Saints Vicarage, Smedley Street, Matlock, Derbyshire DE4 3JG* Tel (01629) 582235

MITCHELL, Tim. b 63. Trin Coll Bris DipHE95. **d** 97. C Cromer *Nor* from 97. *18 Vicarage Road, Cromer, Norfolk NR27 9DQ* Tel (01263) 514352

MITCHELL, Tom Good. b 21. K Coll (NS) STh62. **d** 63 **p** 64. Canada 63-81; V Misterton and W Stockwith *S'well* 81-87; rtd 87; Perm to Offic *Glouc* from 87. *Ashbury, Binyon Road, Winchcombe, Cheltenham, Glos GL54 5QQ* Tel (01242) 604279

MITCHELL, William Blanchard. b 26. Lon Univ DipTh54. St Aid Birkenhead 53. **d** 55 **p** 56. C Kendal H Trin *Carl* 55-59; C Dalton-in-Furness 59-60; V Nichol Forest 60-61; CF 61-77; V Nicholforest and Kirkandrews on Esk *Carl* 77-84; R Kirkby Thore w Temple Sowerby and Newbiggin 84-89; rtd 89; Perm to Offic *Carl* from 89. *Koi Hai, 23 Longlands Road, Carlisle CA3 9AD* Tel (01228) 42630

MITCHELL-INNES, Charles William. b 47. Pemb Coll Cam BA69 MA73. Sarum Th Coll 83. **d** 86 **p** 87. Asst Chapl Sherborne Sch 86-89; Chapl Milton Abbey Sch Dorset 90-96; Conduct Eton Coll from 96. *3 Savile House, Eton College, Windsor, Berks SL4 6DT* Tel (01753) 671004

MITCHELL-INNES, James Alexander. b 39. Ch Ch Ox BA64 MA66. Lon Coll of Div 65. **d** 67 **p** 68. C Cullompton *Ex* 67-71; Nigeria 71-75; P-in-c Puddletown w Athelhampton and Burleston *Sarum* 75-78; R Puddletown and Tolpuddle 78-82; V Win Ch Ch *Win* 82-92; V Titchfield *Portsm* from 92. *The Vicarage, 24 Castle Street, Titchfield, Fareham, Hants PO14 4DU* Tel (01329) 842324

MITCHINSON, Frank. b 37. AKC60. **d** 61 **p** 62. C Cross Heath *Lich* 61-64; C Forrabury w Minster and Trevalga *Truro* 64-68; C Harpenden St Nic *St Alb* 68-70; R Southwick *Chich* 70-83; V Billingshurst 83-88; V Preston from 88. *35 Preston Drove, Brighton BN1 6LA* Tel (01273) 555033

MITCHINSON, Canon Ronald (<u>Ron</u>). b 35. Westmr Coll Ox MA91. Linc Th Coll 66. **d** 68 **p** 69. C Heworth St Mary *Dur* 68-72; C Banbury *Ox* 72-73; TV 73-76; New Zealand 76-82; TR Banbury *Ox* 82-86; RD Deddington 84-86; Ind Chapl 86-92; Hon Can Ch Ch 90-92; TV Brayton *York* 92-96; Sen Ind Chapl Selby Coalfield 92-96; rtd 96. *6 St John's Crescent, York YO3 7QP*

MITFORD, Bertram William Jeremy (<u>Bill</u>). b 27. Wells Th Coll 62. **d** 64 **p** 65. C Hollinwood *Man* 64-67; C Atherton 67-68; C Frome St Jo *B & W* 68-71; V Cleeve 72-74; V Cleeve w Chelvey and Brockley 74-79; Chapl HM Pris Shepton Mallet 79-92; C Shepton Mallet *B & W* 79-84; C Shepton Mallet w Doulting 84-92; rtd 92. *2 Charlton Road, Shepton Mallet, Somerset BA4 5NY* Tel (01749) 342825

MITRA, Avijit. b 53. Keble Coll Ox BA76. Ox NSM Course 84. **d** 88 **p** 89. NSM Abingdon *Ox* 88-96; Asst Chapl Abingdon Sch 88-96; Chapl Ch Hosp Horsham from 96. *Christ's Hospital, Horsham, W Sussex RH13 7LP* Tel (01403) 266305

MITRA, Mrs Nicola Jane. b 54. St Hugh's Coll Ox BA76 PGCE77 MA81. Ox Min Course DipMin94. **d** 94 **p** 95. NSM Abingdon *Ox* 94-96; Chapl Ch Hosp Horsham from 96. *Christ's Hospital, Horsham, W Sussex RH13 7LP* Tel (01403) 266305

MITSON, Mrs Carol Mae. b 46. Oak Hill NSM Course 89. **d** 93 **p** 94. NSM Lawford *Chelmsf* from 93. *Drift Cottage, The Drift, Dedham, Colchester CO7 6AH* Tel (01206) 323116

MITSON, John Dane. b 29. Solicitor 56 SS Coll Cam MA53 LLM54. Oak Hill Th Coll 91 EAMTC 93. **d** 94 **p** 95. Dio Registrar and Legal Sec to Bp St E&I from 75; NSM Greenstead juxta Colchester *Chelmsf* from 94. *Drift Cottage, The Drift, Dedham, Colchester CO7 6AH* Tel (01206) 323116 Fax 230524

MITSON, Miss Joyce. b 37. Man Univ CertEd64. Trin Coll Bris DipHE79. **dss** 79 **d** 87 **p** 94. Wellington w Eyton *Lich* 79-85; Farnworth *Liv* 85-87; Par Dn 87-91; TD Bilston *Lich* 91-94; TV 94; Lich Local Min Adv 91-94; C W Bromwich St Jas from 94. *St Paul's Vicarage, 93 Bagnall Street, West Bromwich, W Midlands B70 0TS*

MITTON, Michael Simon. b 53. Ex Univ BA75. St Jo Coll Nottm 76. **d** 78 **p** 79. C High Wycombe *Ox* 78-82; C Kidderminster St Geo *Worc* 82; TV 82-89; Dir Angl Renewal Min from 89; Angl Renewal Min Adv *Ripon* 90-91. *30 Bromley Street, Derby DE22 1HJ* Tel (01332) 368062 or 200175 Fax 200185

MLEMETA, Kedmon Hezron. b 60. CertEd78. CA Tr Coll Nairobi 86. **d** 89 **p** 90. Tanzania 89-96; P-in-c Loughb Gd Shep *Leic* from 96. *21 Parklands Drive, Loughborough, Leics LE11 2SZ* Tel (01509) 211005

MNGOMEZULU, Sipho <u>Percy</u>. **d** 78 **p** 78. Swaziland 78-96; NSM Cricklewood St Gabr and St Mich *Lon* from 96. *15 Aylestone Avenue, London NW6 7AE* Tel 0181-459 3372

MOAT, Terry. b 61. Nottm Univ BTh92. Aston Tr Scheme 86 Linc Th Coll 88. **d** 92 **p** 93. C Caterham *S'wark* 92-96. *70 Spencer Road, Caterham, Surrey CR3 5LB* Tel (01883) 340882

MOATE, Gerard Grigglestone. b 54. BA. Oak Hill Th Coll 79. **d** 82 **p** 83. C Mildmay Grove St Jude and St Paul *Lon* 82-85; C Hampstead St Jo 85-88; P-in-c Pinxton *Derby* 88; V Charlesworth and Dinting Vale 88-95; V Dedham *Chelmsf* from 95. *The Vicarage, High Street, Dedham, Colchester CO7 6DE* Tel (01206) 322136

MOATE, Phillip. b 47. RGN70 Lon Univ DN73 RNT75 Leeds Univ CCouns94. N Ord Course 87. **d** 90 **p** 91. NSM Upper Holme Valley *Wakef* 90-92; NSM Almondbury Deanery 92-94; NSM Honley 94-95; P-in-c Roos and Garton in Holderness w Tunstall etc *York* from 95. *The Rectory, Rectory Road, Roos, Hull HU12 0LD* Tel (01964) 670384

MOATT, Richard Albert. b 54. K Coll Lon BD76 AKC76. Linc Th Coll 80. **d** 81 **p** 82. C Egremont and Haile *Carl* 81-85; V Addingham, Edenhall, Langwathby and Culgaith from 85. *The Vicarage, Langwathby, Penrith, Cumbria CA10 1LW* Tel (01768) 881212

MOBBERLEY, Keith John. b 56. BA. Westcott Ho Cam. **d** 84 **p** 85. C Coventry Caludon *Cov* 84-87; C Kenilworth St Nic 87-92; V Keresley and Coundon from 92. *The Vicarage, 34 Tamworth Road, Coventry CV6 2EL* Tel (01203) 332717

MOBBERLEY, Mrs Susan. b 57. Kent Univ BA79. Westcott Ho Cam 81. **dss** 84 **d** 90 **p** 94. Coventry Caludon *Cov* 84-87; Lic to Offic 87-92; NSM Keresley and Coundon from 92. *The Vicarage, 34 Tamworth Road, Coventry CV6 2EL* Tel (01203) 332717

MOBBS, Bernard Frederick. b 26. S'wark Ord Course 71. **d** 72 **p** 73. C Purley St Barn *S'wark* 72-74; Vice-Prin S'wark Ord Course 74-80; P-in-c Sydenham St Bart *S'wark* 80-87; V Dormansland 87-92; rtd 92; Perm to Offic *Chich* from 92. *Fair Havens, Fletching Street, Mayfield, E Sussex TN20 6TH* Tel (01435) 872910

MOBERLY, Richard Hamilton. b 30. Trin Hall Cam BA53 MA57. Cuddesdon Coll 53. **d** 55 **p** 56. C Walton St Mary *Liv* 55-59; C Kensington St Mary Abbots w St Geo *Lon* 59-63; N Rhodesia 63-64; Zambia 64-66; V Kennington Cross St Anselm *S'wark*

67-73; TV N Lambeth 74-80; Ind Chapl 80-95; rtd 95. *5 Atherfold Road, London SW9 9LL* Tel 0171-733 6754

MOBERLY, Robert Walter Lambert. b 52. New Coll Ox MA77 Selw Coll Cam MA80 Trin Coll Cam PhD81. Ridley Hall Cam 74. **d** 81 **p** 82. C Knowle *Birm* 81-85; Lect Dur Univ from 85; Perm to Offic *Dur* from 85. *8 Princes Street, Durham DH1 4RP* Tel 0191-386 4255 or 374 2067

MOBLEY, Ronald John. b 15. Worc Ord Coll. **d** 62 **p** 63. C Cropthorne w Charlton *Worc* 62-65; C Kingswood *S'wark* 65-68; V Eastleach w Southrop *Glouc* 68-73; V Newland w Redbrook 74-80; rtd 80; Hon C St Mary le Strand w St Clem Danes *Lon* 85-86. *35 Church Street, Eastbourne, E Sussex BN21 1HN*

MOCKFORD, John Frederick. b 28. Em Coll Cam BA52 MA56. Ridley Hall Cam 52. **d** 54 **p** 55. C Ardwick St Silas *Man* 54; C Harpurhey Ch Ch 54-57; V Bootle St Leon *Liv* 57-64; CMS 65-73; Uganda 66-73; Can Missr Kampala 72-73; V Bushbury *Lich* 73-77; TR 77-84; Preb Lich Cathl 81-84; Dir Miss and Past Studies Ridley Hall Cam 84-88; V Ipswich St Marg *St E* 88-93; rtd 93. *10 Castle Brooks, Framlingham, Woodbridge, Suffolk IP13 9RN* Tel (01728) 724193

MOCKFORD, Peter John. b 57. Nottm Univ BSc79 St Jo Coll Dur BA88. Cranmer Hall Dur 86. **d** 89 **p** 90. C Tamworth *Lich* 89-94; V Blurton from 94. *The Vicarage, School Lane, Stoke-on-Trent ST3 3DU* Tel (01782) 312163

MOESEL, Joseph Sams. b 65. Villanova Univ USA BA90 Ox Univ BTh93. Ripon Coll Cuddesdon DipMin95. **d** 95 **p** 96. C Twigworth, Down Hatherley, Norton, The Leigh etc *Glouc* from 95. *The Glebe House, Sandhurst Lane, Gloucester GL1 9NP* Tel (01452) 730447

MOFFAT, George. b 46. Edin Univ BD77 Open Univ BA87. Edin Th Coll 67. **d** 72 **p** 73. C Falkirk *Edin* 73-76; C Edin St Pet 76-81; Chapl Edin Univ 77-81; C Heston *Lon* 81-84; V S Elmsall *Wakef* 84-93; TR Manningham *Bradf* from 93. *The Rectory, 63 St Paul's Road, Manningham, Bradford, W Yorkshire BD8 7LS* Tel (01274) 487042

MOFFATT, Neil Thomas. b 46. Fitzw Coll Cam BA68 MA72. Qu Coll Birm 69. **d** 71 **p** 72. C Charlton St Luke w St Paul *S'wark* 71-74; C Walworth St Pet 74-75; C Walworth 75-77; V Dormansland 77-86; TR Padgate *Liv* 86-96; V Padgate from 96. *The Rectory, Station Road, Padgate, Warrington WA2 0PD* Tel (01925) 821555

MOFFETT, Mrs Marie-Louise. b 25. St Andr Univ MA46 Cam Univ DipRS76. **d** 87 **p** 94. St Andr Univ Angl Chapl Team 87-91; C St Andrews All SS *St And* from 91. *10 Queen's Gardens, St Andrews, Fife KY16 9TA* Tel (01334) 473678

MOFFITT, Mrs Vivien Louisa. b 37. LSE BSc59 DipPM60. Sarum & Wells Th Coll 90. **d** 91 **p** 94. NSM Chandler's Ford *Win* from 91. *13 Velmore Road, Eastleigh, Hants SO53 3HD* Tel (01703) 265327

MOGER, Peter John. b 64. Mert Coll Ox BA85 BMus86 MA89 St Jo Coll Dur BA93. Cranmer Hall Dur 89. **d** 93 **p** 94. C Whitby *York* 93-95; Prec, Sacr and Min Can Ely Cathl *Ely* from 95. *The Precentor's House, 32 High Street, Ely, Cambs CB7 4JU* Tel (01353) 660335 Fax 665658

MOGFORD, Canon Stanley Howard. b 13. St Pet Hall Ox BA35 DipTh36 MA39. Westcott Ho Cam 36. **d** 37 **p** 38. C Aberdare St Jo *Llan* 37-41; C Llan Cathl 41-48; V Cyfarthfa 48-54; V Pontypridd St Cath 54-63; V Llanblethian w Cowbridge 63-66; V Llanblethian w Cowbridge and Llandough etc 66-80; RD Llantwit Major and Cowbridge 69-80; Can Llan Cathl 71-80; rtd 80; Perm to Offic *Llan* from 80. *Fortis Green, 19 Plas Treoda, The Common, Whitchurch, Cardiff CF4 1PT* Tel (01222) 618839

MOGRIDGE, Christopher James. b 31. Culham Coll of Educn CertEd62 LCP70 FCollP86. St Steph Ho Ox 93. **d** 94 **p** 95. NSM Wellingborough St Andr *Pet* from 94. *April Cottage, Little Harrowden, Wellingborough, Northants NN9 5BB* Tel (01933) 678412

MOIR, Canon David William. b 38. St Aid Birkenhead 64. **d** 67 **p** 68. C Danbury *Chelmsf* 67-70; C Bollington St Jo *Ches* 70-72; V Sutton St Jas 72-81; V Prestbury 81-95; RD Macclesfield from 88; P-in-c Bosley and N Rode w Wincle and Wildboarclough from 95; Hon Can Ches Cathl from 96. *The Vicarage, Wincle, Macclesfield, Cheshire SK11 0QH* Tel (01260) 227234

MOIR, Nicholas Ian. b 61. G&C Coll Cam BA82 MA86 Ox Univ BA86. Wycliffe Hall Ox 84. **d** 87 **p** 88. C Enfield St Andr *Lon* 87-91; Bp's Dom Chapl *St Alb* 91-94; Chapl St Jo Coll Cam from 94. *St John's College, Cambridge CB2 1TP* Tel (01223) 338600

MOLD, Peter John. b 33. **d** 63 **p** 64. C Boston *Linc* 63-67; C Scarborough St Mary w Ch Ch, St Paul and St Thos *York* 67-68; Australia from 69. *Stone Grange, 29 Newcastle Street, York, W Australia 6302* Tel York (96) 411965

MOLE, Arthur Penton. b 10. Witwatersrand Univ BA30. Bps' Coll Cheshunt 33. **d** 35 **p** 36. C Pokesdown All SS *Win* 35-37; C Wolborough w Newton Abbot *Ex* 37-44; R Goldsborough *Ripon* 44-49; Dioc Dir of Educn *St Alb* 49-51; V Barnet Vale St Mark 51-59; RD Barnet 55-59; V Southbourne St Kath *Win* 59-71; R Old Alresford 71-76; P-in-c Brown and Chilton Candover w Northington etc 72-74; R 74-76; rtd 76; Perm to Offic *Worc* from 76. *15 Garden Styles, Pershore, Worcs WR10 1JW* Tel (01386) 554167

MOLE, David Eric Harton. b 33. Em Coll Cam BA54 MA58 PhD62. Ridley Hall Cam 55. **d** 59 **p** 59. C Selly Hill St Steph *Birm* 59-62; Tutor St Aid Birkenhead 62-63; Chapl Peterho Cam 63-69; Ghana 69-72; Lect Qu Coll Birm 72-76; Tutor USPG Coll of the Ascension Selly Oak 76-87; C Burton *Lich* 87-93; Chapl Burton Gen Hosp 87-93; Chapl Ostend w Knokke and Bruges *Eur* from 93. *Ganzestraat 20/2, B-8000 Brugge, Belgium* Tel Brugge (50) 347677

MOLE, Jennifer Vera. b 49. CertEd70. Qu Coll Birm 82. **d** 84. C Pontypool *Mon* 84-87; C Cyncoed 87-88; TD 88-96; C Caerleon from 96. *28 Roman Reach, Caerleon, Newport NP6 1SG*

MOLESWORTH, Canon Anthony Edward Nassau. b 23. Pemb Coll Cam BA45 MA48. Coll of Resurr Mirfield 45. **d** 46 **p** 47. C Blyth St Mary *Newc* 46-51; C High Elswick St Phil 51-52; Swaziland 52-68; Can 68-71; Can Zululand 63-68; R Huish Episcopi w Pitney *B & W* 71-78; P-in-c High Ham 76-78; TR Langport Area Chs 78-84; R Charlton Musgrove, Cucklington and Stoke Trister 84-90; RD Bruton 86-90; rtd 90; Perm to Offic *B & W* from 90. *3 Barrow Hill, Stourton Caundle, Sturminster Newton, Dorset DT10 2LD* Tel (01963) 362337

MOLL, David Henry. b 27. St Chad's Coll Dur 50. **d** 54 **p** 55. C Wallsend St Pet *Newc* 54-58; C Wymondham *Nor* 59-62; R Yaxham 62-68; R Welborne 62-68; R Gt w Lt Poringland and Howe 69-75; R Framingham Earl 79-92; rtd 92. *48 Sadler Road, Norwich NR6 6PQ* Tel (01603) 406992

MOLL, Randell Tabrum. b 41. Lon Univ BD65. Wycliffe Hall Ox 62. **d** 66 **p** 67. C Drypool St Columba w St Andr and St Pet *York* 66-70; Asst Chapl HM Pris Hull 66-70; Asst Master Hull Gr Sch 66-70; C Netherton *Liv* 70-74; C Sefton 70-72; Ind Chapl 70-74 and from 92; Belgium 75-76; P-in-c Brockmoor *Lich* 76-81; Team Ldr Black Country Urban Ind Miss 76-81; Dir Chilworth Home Services 81-84; Asst Master Bp Reindarp Sch Guildf 84-90; France and Iraq 91; Chapl Sedbergh Sch 92; Sen Chapl Miss in the Economy (Merseyside) from 92. *79 Moor Lane, Crosby, Liverpool L23 2SQ* Tel 0151-932 0507 or 709 5586 Fax 709 7596

MOLLAN, Patricia Ann Fairbank. b 44. QUB BSc67 PhD70 BD97. **d** 97. Aux Min *D & D* from 97. *Orchard Hill, 167 Bangor Road, Craigavad, Holywood, Co Down BT18 0EY* Tel (01232) 423529

MOLLAN, Raymond Alexander Boyce. b 43. MB BCh BAO MD FRCS DObstRCOG. **d** 97. Aux Min *D & D* from 97. *Orchard Hill, 167 Bangor Road, Craigavad, Holywood, Co Down BT18 0EY* Tel (01232) 423529 E-mail mollan@unite.co.uk

MOLLER, Canon George Brian. b 35. TCD BA60 MA64 Lon Univ BD84. **d** 61 **p** 62. C Belfast St Pet *Conn* 61-64; C Larne and Inver 64-68; P-in-c Rathcoole 68-69; I 69-86; I Belfast St Bart from 86; Chapl Stranmillis Coll of Educn Belf from 88; Preb Conn Cathl *Conn* 90-96; Treas Lisburn Ch Ch Cathl 96; Prec from 96. *St Bartholomew's Rectory, 16 Mount Pleasant, Belfast BT9 5DS* Tel (01232) 669995

MOLLOY, Mrs Heather. b 54. Bradf Univ BTech76. LNSM course 92. **d** 95 **p** 96. NSM Harwood *Man* from 95. *7 Fellside, Bolton BL2 4SH* Tel (01204) 520395

MOLLOY, Terrence Harold. b 36. **d** 71 **p** 72. New Zealand 71-81 and from 83; C Skegness and Winthorpe *Linc* 81-82. *190B Finlayson Avenue, Manurewa, Auckland 1702, New Zealand* Tel Auckland (9) 267 1455

MOLONY, Nicholas John. b 43. St Jo Coll Dur BA67 Birm Univ DipTh70 MA78. Qu Coll Birm 67. **d** 70 **p** 71. C Beaconsfield *Ox* 70-75; P-in-c Chesham Ch Ch 75-80; TV Gt Chesham 80-81; P-in-c Weston Turville 81-90; P-in-c Stoke Mandeville 87-89; P-in-c Gt Marlow 90-93; P-in-c Bisham 90-93; TR Gt Marlow w Marlow Bottom, Lt Marlow and Bisham from 93. *The Rectory, The Causeway, Marlow, Bucks SL7 2AA* Tel (01628) 482660

MONBERG, Ms Ulla Stefan. b 52. BA79. Westcott Ho Cam 88. **d** 90 **p** 94. C Westmr St Jas *Lon* 90-94; Dean Women's Min and Area Dir of Ords Cen Lon from 94; Dean Women's Min Kensington from 94; Sec Dioc Bd of Women Candidates for Ord from 94; C Paddington St Jo w St Mich from 96. *11 Ormonde Mansions, 106 Southampton Row, London WC1B 4BP* Tel 0171-242 7533

MONDS, Anthony John Beatty. b 53. Solicitor 77. LNSM course 96. **d** 97. NSM Queen Thorne *Sarum* from 97. *Holway Hill House, Corton Denham, Sherborne, Dorset DT9 4LW* Tel (01963) 220586

MONK, Mrs Mary. b 38. CertEd58. S'wark Ord Course 85. **d** 88 **p** 94. NSM Lee Gd Shep w St Pet *S'wark* from 88. *9 Horn Park Lane, London SE12 8UX* Tel 0181-318 5802

MONK, Nicholas John. b 32. Westcott Ho Cam 61. **d** 63 **p** 64. C Bris H Cross Inns Court *Bris* 63-67; C Stoke Bishop 67-69; V Swindon All SS 69-75; V Ashton Keynes w Leigh 75-87; P-in-c Minety w Oaksey 82-87; RD Malmesbury 85-88; V Ashton Keynes, Leigh and Minety 87-91; TR Swindon St Jo and St Andr 91-97; rtd 97. *The Riddings Cottage, Newcastle on Clun, Craven Arms, Shropshire SY7 8QT* Tel (01686) 670929

MONKS, Ian Kay. b 36. K Coll Lon BA60 Lon Inst of Educn PGCE61. Oak Hill NSM Course 90. **d** 93 **p** 94. NSM Woodford Bridge *Chelmsf* from 93. *46 Summit Drive, Woodford Green, Essex IG8 8QP* Tel 0181-550 2390

MONKS, John Stanley. b 12. AKC42. St D Coll Lamp 38. **d** 42 **p** 43. C Warrington St Elphin *Liv* 42-45; C Tynemouth Priory *Newc* 45-49; V Spittal 49-54; V Scotswood 54-66; V Blyth St Cuth 66-83; rtd 83. *56 West Dene Drive, North Shields, Tyne & Wear NE30 2SZ* Tel 0191-257 0157

MONKS, Roger James. b 39. G&C Coll Cam BA61. Coll of Resurr Mirfield 61. **d** 63 **p** 64. C Higham Ferrers *Pet* 63-66; C Cheshunt *St Alb* 68-70; Chapl Dartington Hall Sch 70-71. *18 Coleson Hill Road, Wrecclesham, Farnham, Surrey GU10 4QQ*

MONMOUTH, Archdeacon of. *See* WOODMAN, The Ven Peter Wilfred

MONMOUTH, Bishop of. *See* WILLIAMS, The Rt Revd Rowan Douglas

MONMOUTH, Dean of. *See* FENWICK, The Very Revd Richard David

MONROE, Canon James Allen. b 35. Stranmillis Coll TCert57. St Aid Birkenhead 63. **d** 64 **p** 65. C Belfast St Mich *Conn* 64-68; C Coleraine 68-71; I 77-86; I Ballynure and Ballyeaston 71-77; I Holywood *D & D* from 86; RD Holywood from 89; Can Belf Cathl from 91. *The Vicarage, 156 High Street, Holywood, Co Down BT18 9HT* Tel (01232) 422069 or 423622

MONTAGUE, Mrs Juliet. b 52. Nottm Univ BTh82. Linc Th Coll 78. **dss** 82 **d** 87 **p** 94. Gainsborough All SS *Linc* 82-86; Chapl Linc Cathl 86-92; Chapl Linc Colls of FE 86-92; D-in-c Whaplode Drove 92-94; P-in-c from 94; D-in-c Gedney Hill 92-94; P-in-c from 94. *The Vicarage, Whaplode Drove, Spalding, Lincs PE12 0TN* Tel (01406) 330392

MONTAGUE-YOUENS, Canon Hubert Edward. b 30. Ripon Hall Ox 55. **d** 58 **p** 59. C Redditch St Steph *Worc* 58-59; C Halesowen 59-62; V Kempsey 62-69; V Kidderminster St Geo 69-72; R Ribbesford w Bewdley and Dowles 72-81; RD Kidderminster 74-81; Hon Can Worc Cathl 78-81; TR Bridport *Sarum* 81-86; RD Lyme Bay 82-86; V Easebourne *Chich* 86-89; Chapl K Edw VII Hosp Midhurst 86-89; rtd 89; Perm to Offic *Glouc* 89-95; Perm to Offic *Worc* from 89; P-in-c Twyning *Glouc* from 96. *The Vicarage, Church End, Twyning, Tewkesbury, Glos GL20 6DA* Tel (01684) 292553

✠**MONTEFIORE, The Rt Revd Hugh William.** b 20. St Jo Coll Ox BA46 MA47 SS Coll Cam BD63 Aber Univ Hon DD77 Birm Univ Hon DD85. Westcott Ho Cam 48. **d** 49 **p** 50 **c** 70. C Newc St Geo *Newc* 49-51; Chapl and Tutor Westcott Ho Cam 51-53; Vice-Prin 53-54; Dean G&C Coll Cam 54-63; Asst Lect Th Cam Univ 56-59; Lect 59-63; Can Th Cov Cathl *Cov* 59-69; V Cambridge Gt St Mary w St Mich *Ely* 63-70; Hon Can Ely Cathl 69-70; Suff Bp Kingston *S'wark* 70-78; Bp Birm 78-87; rtd 87; Asst Bp S'wark from 87. *White Lodge, 23 Bellevue Road, London SW17 7EB* Tel 0181-672 6697

MONTEITH, David Robert Malvern. b 68. St Jo Coll Dur BSc89 Nottm Univ BTh92 MA93. St Jo Coll Nottm 90. **d** 93 **p** 94. C Kings Heath *Birm* 93-97; C St Martin-in-the-Fields *Lon* from 97. *6 St Martins Place, London WC2N 4JJ* Tel 0171-930 0089 Fax 839 5163

MONTGOMERIE, Alexander (Sandy). b 47. St Jo Coll Nottm CertCS94. **d** 94 **p** 96. NSM Irvine St Andr LEP *Glas* from 94; NSM Ardrossan from 94. *105 Sharphill Road, Saltcoats, Ayrshire KA21 5QU* Tel (01294) 465193

MONTGOMERIE, Andrew Simon. b 60. Keble Coll Ox BA82. Ridley Hall Cam 83. **d** 85 **p** 86. C Childwall All SS *Liv* 85-87; C Yardley St Edburgha *Birm* 87-90; TV Solihull 90-96; P-in-c Balsall Common 96; V from 96. *St Peter's House, Holly Lane, Balsall Common, Coventry CV7 7EA* Tel (01676) 532721

MONTGOMERY, Canon Anthony Alan. b 33. Trin Hall Cam BA56. Edin Th Coll 56. **d** 58 **p** 59. C Dumfries *Glas* 58-63; P-in-c Airdrie 63-66; R 66-68; Asst Chapl Gordonstoun Sch 68-93; Can St Andr Cathl Inverness *Mor* from 81; rtd 93. *Easter Hillside, Mosstowie, Elgin, Morayshire IV30 3XE* Tel (01343) 850282 Fax as telephone

MONTGOMERY, Charles George Greathead. b 08. AKC33. **d** 33 **p** 34. C Perry Street *Roch* 33-40; C-in-c St Gennys 42-44; V Poundstock *Truro* 44-45; rtd 75. *Jasmine Cottage, Ash Cross, Bradworthy, Holsworthy, Devon EX22 7SP*

MONTGOMERY, Ian David. b 44. St Andr Univ LLB66 FCA69. Wycliffe Hall Ox 71. **d** 75 **p** 76. C Fulham St Dionis Parson's Green *Lon* 75-78; USA from 78. *1142 Sewanee Road, Nashville, Tennessee, 37220 USA*

MONTGOMERY (née YOUATT), Mrs Jennifer Alison. b 49. St Aid Coll Dur BSc70 Homerton Coll Cam PGCE71. N Ord Course 89. **d** 92 **p** 94. NSM Ripon H Trin *Ripon* from 92. *Washington House, Littlethorpe, Ripon, N Yorkshire HG4 3LJ* Tel (01765) 605276

MONTGOMERY, Canon John Alexander. b 11. TCD BA34. **d** 35 **p** 36. C Clogh 35-37; C Belfast St Simon *Conn* 37-40; Lic to Offic *K, E & A* 40-45; C Drumshambo 45-50; I Taunagh w Kilmactranny, Ballysumaghan etc 50-54; RD Newtownforbes 67-80; I Ardagh w Kilcommick 67-80; Preb Elphin Cathl 78-80; rtd 80; Hon C Bathgate *Edin* 83-91; Hon C Linlithgow 83-91. *6 Watson Place, Armadale, Bathgate, West Lothian EH48 2NJ* Tel (01501) 731470

MONTGOMERY, Pembroke John Charles. b 24. Codrington Coll Barbados. **d** 53 **p** 55. St Vincent 55-73; Can Kingstown Cathl 63-73; P-in-c Derby St Jas *Derby* 73-74; V 74-90; rtd 90. *37 Church Street, Tetbury, Glos GL8 8JG* Tel (01666) 504817

MONTGOMERY, Miss Rachel. b 63. Reading Univ BA85. Wycliffe Hall Ox BTh94. **d** 94 **p** 95. C Tufnell Park St Geo and All SS *Lon* from 94. *35 Weatherbury House, Wedmore Street, London N19 4RB* Tel 0171-272 3057

MONTGOMERY, Stanley. b 18. St Cath Coll Cam BSc. Lich Th Coll. **d** 52 **p** 53. P-in-c Hitcham w Lt Finborough *St E* 93-95; Perm to Offic from 95. *34 Drovers Rise, Stanton, Bury St Edmunds, Suffolk IP31 2BW* Tel (01359) 250359

MONTGOMERY, Canon Thomas Charles Osborne. b 59. Edin Univ BD81. Edin Th Coll 77. **d** 82 **p** 83. C Glas St Mary *Glas* 82-85; C Dumfries 85-88; R Hamilton 88-96; Can St Mary's Cathl from 94; R Glas St Marg from 96. *St Margaret's Rectory, 22 Monreith Road, Glasgow G43 2NY* Tel 0141-632 3292 or 636 1131

MONTGOMERY, Timothy Robert (Tim). b 59. Hull Univ BA82 Cam Univ PGCE83. EAMTC 90. **d** 93 **p** 94. NSM Cambridge St Phil *Ely* from 93; Dir Romsey Mill Community Cen 93-94. *21 Coleridge Road, Cambridge CB1 3PH* Tel (01223) 248806 Fax 415855

MONTGOMERY, Archdeacon of. *See* PRITCHARD, The Ven Thomas William

MOODY, Aubrey Rowland. b 11. Coll of Resurr Mirfield 53. **d** 55 **p** 56. C Wanstead St Mary *Chelmsf* 55-57; V Feering from 57. *Feering Vicarage, Colchester, Essex CO5 9NL* Tel (01376) 570226

MOODY, Christopher John Everard (Chris). b 51. New Coll Ox BA72 Lon Univ MSc90. Cuddesdon Coll BA74. **d** 75 **p** 76. C Fulham All SS *Lon* 75-79; C Surbiton St Andr and St Mark *S'wark* 79-82; Chapl K Coll Lon 82-87; V S Lambeth St Anne and All SS *S'wark* 87-95; RD Lambeth 90-95; P-in-c Market Harborough *Leic* from 95; P-in-c Market Harborough Transfiguration from 95. *The Rectory, Rectory Lane, Market Harborough, Leics LE16 8AS* Tel (01858) 462926

MOODY, Colin John. b 36. Chich Th Coll 61. **d** 63 **p** 64. C Hove All SS *Chich* 63-69; C Dulwich St Barn *S'wark* 69-70; Perm to Offic *Bris* 70-71; Perm to Offic *Chich* 72-78 and from 90; Lic to Offic *Ely* 78-93. *11 Hewitts, Henfield, W Sussex BN5 9TD* Tel (01273) 495062

MOODY, Derek Frank. b 41. Univ of Wales BA62. Chich Th Coll 63. **d** 65 **p** 66. C Ellesmere Port *Ches* 65-69; C Lewisham St Jo Southend *S'wark* 69-73; TV Catford (Southend) and Downham 73-75; V Ham St Rich 75-83; V Catford St Laur 83-88; TV Brighton St Pet and St Nic w Chpl Royal *Chich* from 88. *5 Clifton Road, Brighton BN1 3HP* Tel (01273) 321399

MOODY, Preb George Henry. b 27. ACIS56 ARCA68 DipChD77. Cranmer Hall Dur 69. **d** 71 **p** 72. C Marske in Cleveland *York* 71-74; Chapl to the Deaf *Lich* 74-89; Preb Lich Cathl 83-89; rtd 89; Perm to Offic *York* from 90. *21 Priestcrofts, Marske-by-the-Sea, Redcar, Cleveland TS11 7HW* Tel (01642) 489660

MOODY, Ivor Robert. b 57. K Coll Lon BD AKC. Coll of Resurr Mirfield. **d** 82 **p** 83. C Leytonstone St Marg w St Columba *Chelmsf* 82-85; C Leigh-on-Sea St Marg 85-88; V Tilbury Docks 88-96; Chapl Anglia Poly Univ from 96. *4 Bishop Court Gardens, Chelmsford CM2 6AZ* Tel (01245) 261700 or 493131

MOODY, Canon John Kelvin. b 30. St Fran Coll Brisbane ThL55. **d** 56 **p** 57. Australia 56-61; C Earl's Court St Cuth w St Matthias *Lon* 61-64; Chapl Ankara *Eur* 64-69; Chapl Istanbul 64-66; Chapl Palma 69-75; Chapl Tangier 75-79; Can Gib Cathl 74-79; Hon Can from 79; Australia from 79; rtd 95. *1 Short Street, Watson's Bay, NSW, Australia 2030* Tel Sydney (2) 337 2871

MOOKERJI, Michael Manoje. b 45. Baring Union Coll Punjab BSc69. Ridley Hall Cam 83. **d** 85 **p** 86. C Heanor *Derby* 85-92; V Codnor and Loscoe 92-93; V Codnor from 93. *The Vicarage, Codnor, Ripley, Derbyshire DE5 9SN* Tel (01773) 742516

MOON, Arthur Thomas. b 22. ACP53 LCP56 Lon Univ DipTh66. Sarum Th Coll 65. **d** 66 **p** 67. C Fulwood Ch Ch *Blackb* 66-71; Hon C Bispham 71-80; C 80-87; rtd 87; Perm to Offic *Blackb* from 87. *15 Kirkstone Drive, Blackpool FY5 1QQ* Tel (01253) 853521

MOON, John Charles. b 23. Sarum Th Coll 49. **d** 51 **p** 52. C Bottesford *Linc* 51-54; C Habrough 54-55; V Immingham 55-61; V Weaste *Man* 61-67; V Spalding St Jo *Linc* 67-82; V Spalding St Jo w Deeping St Nicholas 82-86; rtd 86; Perm to Offic *Linc* from 87. *14 Harrox Road, Moulton, Spalding, Lincs PE12 6PR* Tel (01406) 370111

MOON, Philip Russell. b 56. Em Coll Cam BA78 MA81 Reading Univ PGCE79. Wycliffe Hall Ox BA82. **d** 85 **p** 86. C Crowborough *Chich* 85-87; Hd of CYFA (CPAS) 87-94; V Lowestoft Ch Ch *Nor* from 94. *The Vicarage, 16 Corton Road, Lowestoft, Suffolk NR32 4PL* Tel (01502) 572444

MOON, Thomas Arnold. b 24. Lon Univ BA51. Oak Hill Th Coll 49. **d** 52 **p** 53. C Fazakerley Em *Liv* 52-56; V Everton St Benedict 56-70; V Formby St Luke 70-95; rtd 95. *8 Harington Road, Formby, Liverpool L37 1NU* Tel (01704) 872249

MOONEY, Canon Paul Gerard. b 58.. **d** 84 **p** 85. In RC Ch 84-90; Korea 90-94; Miss to Seamen 90-94; Chapl Antwerp Seafarers' Cen *Eur* 94-97; Asst Chapl Antwerp St Boniface 94-97; C Galway w Kilcummin *T, K & A* from 97. *77 Knocknacarra Park, Galway, Irish Republic* Tel Galway (91) 522998

MOOR, David Drury. b 18. St Edm Hall Ox BA39 MA44. Wells Th Coll 46. **d** 48 **p** 49. C Tuffley *Glouc* 48-52; P-in-c Symondsbury *Sarum* 52-53; R 53-61; V Bournemouth St Andr *Win* 61-69; V Bournemouth St Mich 69-83; rtd 83; Perm to Offic *Sarum* from 83; Perm to Offic *Win* from 83. *93 Western Avenue, Bournemouth BH10 6HG* Tel (01202) 512455

MOOR, Simon Alan. b 65. Nottm Univ BTh93. Linc Th Coll 90. **d** 93 **p** 94. C Skegness and Winthorpe *Linc* 93-96; C Airedale w Fryston *Wakef* from 96. *31 Redhill Road, Castleford, W Yorkshire WF10 3AD* Tel (01977) 553122

MOORE, Albert William (Bill). b 47. Birm Poly FTC72. WMMTC 91. **d** 94 **p** 95. C Hobs Moat *Birm* from 94. *18 Newbold Close, Bentley Heath, Solihull, W Midlands B93 9BS* Tel (01564) 775145

MOORE, Andrew Jonathon. b 57. York Univ BA82. Wycliffe Hall Ox BA84 MA89. **d** 86 **p** 86. Australia 86-90; Asst Chapl Worc Coll Ox 91-94; Chapl Jes Coll Ox from 94. *Jesus College, Oxford OX1 3DW* Tel (01865) 279757 Fax 274215 E-mail andrew.moore@jesus.ox.ac.uk

MOORE, Anthony Harry. b 34. Westcott Ho Cam 88. **d** 90 **p** 91. C Eyke w Bromeswell, Rendlesham, Tunstall etc *St E* 90-93; V Aldeburgh w Hazlewood from 93. *The Vicarage, Church Walk, Aldeburgh, Suffolk IP15 5DU* Tel (01728) 452223

MOORE, Anthony Richmond (Tony). b 36. Clare Coll Cam BA59 MA63. Linc Th Coll 59. **d** 61 **p** 62. C Roehampton H Trin *S'wark* 61-66; C New Eltham All SS 66-70; PM Blackbird Leys CD *Ox* 70-81; Dioc Ecum Officer from 80; TV Dorchester 81-93; V Enstone and Heythrop from 93. *The Vicarage, Little Tew Road, Church Enstone, Chipping Norton, Oxon OX7 4NL* Tel (01608) 677319

MOORE, Ms Arlene. b 64. Dundee Univ BSc87 Aber Coll of Educn PGCE90. CITC BTh95. **d** 95 **p** 96. C Portadown St Mark *Arm* from 95. *115 Brownstown Road, Portadown, Co Armagh BT62 3PZ* Tel (01762) 335562

MOORE, Dr Arthur Lewis. b 33. Dur Univ BA58 PhD64. Cranmer Hall Dur DipTh59. **d** 62 **p** 63. C Stone *Roch* 62-66; C Clevedon St Andr *B & W* 66-68; Chapl Wycliffe Hall Ox 68-70; Vice-Prin 70-83; P-in-c Ampfield *Win* 83-84; V Hursley and Ampfield 84-92; TV Ewyas Harold w Dulas, Kenderchurch etc *Heref* 92-94; P-in-c from 94. *The Rectory, Ewyas Harold, Hereford HR2 0EY* Tel (01981) 240484

MOORE, Arthur Robert (Bob). b 15. Sarum Th Coll 62. **d** 63 **p** 64. C Calne and Blackland *Sarum* 63-67; V Steeple Ashton w Semington 67-79; V Keevil 72-79; Chapl Southwick w Boarhunt *Portsm* 79-91; rtd 84; Perm to Offic *Portsm* from 91. *1 High Street, Southwick, Fareham, Hants PO17 6EB* Tel (01705) 382113 Fax 370991

MOORE, Canon Bernard Geoffrey. b 27. New Coll Ox BA47 MA52. Ely Th Coll 49. **d** 51 **p** 52. C Chorley St Pet *Blackb* 51-54; Bp's Dom Chapl 54-55; C-in-c Blackpool St Mich CD 55-67; Chapl Victoria Hosp Blackpool 58-67; V Morecambe St Barn *Blackb* 67-81; R Standish 81-88; Hon Can Blackb Cathl 86-92; RD Chorley 86-92; V Charnock Richard 88-92; rtd 92; Perm to Offic *Ex* from 92. *29 Wiltshire Close, Exeter EX4 1LU* Tel (01392) 58686

MOORE, Bernard George. b 32. Qu Coll Birm 57. **d** 60 **p** 61. C Middlesbrough St Columba *York* 60-62; S Africa 62-70; Chapl RN 70-74; C Milton *Portsm* 74-76; New Zealand from 76. *45 Feasegate Street, Manurewa, South Auckland 1702, New Zealand* Tel Auckland (9) 267 6924

MOORE, Brian Philip. b 51. AKC72. St Aug Coll Cant 72. **d** 74 **p** 75. C Hatfield *St Alb* 74-78; C Radlett 78-81; V Eaton Bray w Edlesborough 81-92; RD Dunstable 85-90; V St Alb St Sav from 92. *St Saviour's Vicarage, 25 Sandpit Lane, St Albans, Herts AL1 4DF* Tel (01727) 851526

✠**MOORE, The Rt Revd Bruce Macgregor.** b 31. Univ of NZ BA55. Coll of Resurr Mirfield. **d** 57 **p** 58 **c** 92. C Blackpool St Steph *Blackb* 57-61; New Zealand from 61; Hon Can Auckland 78-96; Adn Manukau 81-90; Asst Bp Auckland from 92. *4 Lemonwood Place, Manurewa, Auckland 1702, New Zealand* Tel Auckland (9) 268 1805 Fax 268 1905 E-mail 10024.1126@compuserve.com

MOORE, Charles David (Charlie). b 59. Dundee Univ BSc82 BArch85 RIBA86. St Jo Coll Nottm DTS93 MA96. **d** 93 **p** 94. C Deane *Man* from 93. *281 Deane Church Lane, Bolton BL3 4ES* Tel (01204) 64313

MOORE, Preb Clive Granville. b 31. St Pet Hall Ox BA54 MA58. Wycliffe Hall Ox 54. **d** 55 **p** 56. C Newbarns w Hawcoat *Carl* 55-57; CF 57-61; Chapl Joyce Green Hosp Dartford 61-69; R Stone *Roch* 61-69; R Radstock *B & W* 69-71; P-in-c Writhlington 69-71; R Radstock w Writhlington 71-83; RD Midsomer Norton 81-83; R S Petherton w the Seavingtons 83-95; RD Crewkerne 83-92; RD Crewkerne and Ilminster 93; Preb Wells Cathl 90-95; rtd 95; Perm to Offic *B & W* from 95. *Mowries Stable, West Street, Somerton, Somerset TA11 6NA* Tel (01458) 274649

MOORE, Canon Colin Frederick. b 49. CITC 69. **d** 72 **p** 73. C Drumglass w Moygashel *Arm* 72-80; I Newtownhamilton w Ballymoyer and Belleek 80-87; I Newtownhamilton w Ballymoyer and Pomeroy etc 87-91; I Newtownhamilton w Ballymoyer and Belleck from 91; Hon V Choral Arm Cathl from 85; RD Mullabrack from 92; Preb Arm Cathl from 97. *71 Ballymoyer Road, Whitecross, Armagh BT60 2LA* Tel (01861) 507256

MOORE, David. b 36. Univ of Wales (Lamp) BA61 Magd Coll Cam BA63 MA68. Linc Th Coll 63. **d** 65 **p** 66. C Saltburn-by-the-Sea *York* 65-69; C Northallerton w Kirby Sigston 69-72; V Kirklevington from 72; V High and Low Worsall from 73; Chapl HM Det Cen Kirklevington 72-89; Chapl HM Young Offender Inst Kirklevington Grange from 89. *The Vicarage, Kirk Levington, Yarm, Cleveland TS15 9LQ* Tel (01642) 782439 Fax 790530

MOORE, David James Paton. b 60. Sheff Univ BEng82. Cranmer Hall Dur 88. **d** 91 **p** 92. C Pemberton St Mark Newtown *Liv* 91-94; C St Helens St Helen 94-97; V Canonbury St Steph *Lon* from 97. *St Stephen's Vicarage, 9 River Place, London N1 2DE* Tel 0171-226 7526

MOORE, David Leonard. b 51. **d** 80 **p** 82. Hon C Brixton St Matt *S'wark* 80-82; C 82-84; TV Bris St Agnes and St Simon w St Werburgh *Bris* 84-86; Perm to Offic 86-88; Perm to Offic *Blackb* from 88. *154 Victoria Road, Fulwood, Preston PR2 4NQ*

MOORE, Dr David Metcalfe. b 41. Hull Univ BA64 PhD69. Trin Coll Bris 76. **d** 78 **p** 79. C Marple All SS *Ches* 78-82; V Loudwater *Ox* 82-90; V Chilwell *S'well* 90-93; rtd 93. *10 Cromwell Avenue, Thame, Oxon OX9 3TD* Tel (01844) 217556

MOORE, David Roy. b 39. Clare Coll Cam BA61. Ripon Hall Ox 61. **d** 63 **p** 64. C Melton Mowbray w Thorpe Arnold *Leic* 63-66; Dep Dir The Samaritans 66-73; C St Steph Walbrook and St Swithun etc *Lon* 66-73; C Daybrook *S'well* 77-80; V 80-87; V Ham St Andr *S'wark* from 87. *The Vicarage, Ham Common, Richmond, Surrey TW10 5HG* Tel 0181-940 9017

MOORE, Dr Deborah Claire Patricia. b 62. Essex Univ BSc83 Liv Univ PhD88 SS Coll Cam BA89. Ridley Hall Cam 87. **d** 90 **p** 94. Par Dn Hale and Ashley *Ches* 90-94; C 94; C Prenton from 94. *91 Woodchurch Lane, Prenton, Birkenhead, Merseyside L42 9PL* Tel 0151-608 9793

MOORE, Canon Dennis Charles. b 19. Lon Univ BD46. Tyndale Hall Bris 39. **d** 43 **p** 44. C Broadwater St Mary *Chich* 43-47; Org Sec (E England) CPAS 47-51; V Eccleston St Luke *Liv* 51-55; V New Catton St Luke *Nor* 55-62; V Wellington w Eyton *Lich* 62-70; RD Wrockwardine 66-70; V Watford St Mary *St Alb* 70-73; P-in-c Watford St Jas 70-73; V Watford 73-84; RD Watford 75-81; Hon Can St Alb 80-84; rtd 84; Perm to Offic *Nor* from 84. *82 Greenways, Eaton, Norwich NR4 6HF* Tel (01603) 502492

MOORE, Donald John. b 31. Chich Th Coll 86. **d** 87 **p** 88. C Uckfield *Chich* 87-88; C Southwick 88-90; Bermuda from 90; Asst P St Geo 90-97; P-in-c St Dav 90-97; Chapl St Brendan's Psychiatric Hosp 92-97; rtd 97. *West Cedars, 5A Cedars Lane, Sandys MA 03, Bermuda* Tel Bermuda (1-441) 234 1804

MOORE, Douglas Gregory. b 49. Bris Univ BA71 CertEd72. Coll of Resurr Mirfield 87. **d** 89 **p** 90. C Hessle *York* 89-93; P-in-c Micklefield 93-94; P-in-c Micklefield w Aberford 94-95; V Aberford w Micklefield from 95. *The Vicarage, Great North Road, Micklefield, Leeds LS25 4AG* Tel 0113-286 2154

✠**MOORE, The Rt Revd Edward Francis Butler.** b 06. TCD BA28 MA40 PhD44 Hon DD59. **d** 30 **p** 31 **c** 59. C Bray *D & G* 30-32; Hon Clerical V Ch Ch Cathl Dublin 31-35; C Dublin Clontarf 32-34; I Castledermot w Kinneagh 34-40; I Greystones 40-58; RD Delgany 50-58; Can Ch Ch Cathl Dublin 51-58; Adn Glendalough 57-58; Bp K, E & A 59-81; rtd 81. *Drumlona, Sea Road, Kilcoole, Co Wicklow, Irish Republic* Tel Dublin (1) 287 6648

MOORE, Canon Edward James. b 32. TCD BA56 MA59. **d** 56 **p** 57. C Belfast St Luke *Conn* 56-59; CF 59-62; C Dunmurry *Conn* 62-64; P-in-c Kilmakee 64-70; I Belfast H Trin 70-80; I Jordanstown w Monkstown 80-91; I Jordanstown from 91; RD N Belfast from 88; Can Belf Cathl from 89. *120A Circular Road, Newtownabbey, Co Antrim BT37 0RH* Tel (01232) 862119

MOORE, Canon Fred. b 11. St Jo Coll Dur LTh42 BA44. St Aid Birkenhead 39. **d** 43 **p** 44. C Openshaw *Man* 43-45; C Westhoughton 45-47; C Thornham w Gravel Hole 47-49; V Tunstead 49-54; V Camerton, Seaton and W Seaton *Carl* 54-72; RD Maryport 67-70; Hon Can Carl Cathl 70-77; RD Solway 70-77; V Gt Broughton 72-77; rtd 77; Perm to Offic *Carl* from 77. *Flat 12, Firth House, Seaton, Workington, Cumbria CA14 1JD* Tel (01900) 62358

MOORE, Canon Henry James William. b 33. TCD BA55 MA70. **d** 56 **p** 57. C Mullabrack *Arm* 56-61; C Drumglass 61-63; I Clogherney 63-81; I Ballinderry w Tamlaght and Arboe from 81; Preb Arm Cathl from 90. *10 Brookmount Road, Coagh, Cookstown, Co Tyrone BT80 0BB* Tel (01648) 418255

✠**MOORE, The Rt Revd Henry Wylie.** b 23. Liv Univ BCom50 Leeds Univ MA72. Wycliffe Hall Ox 50. **d** 52 **p** 53 **c** 83. C Farnworth *Liv* 52-54; C Middleton *Man* 54-56; CMS 56-60; Iran 57-60; R Burnage St Marg *Man* 60-63; R Middleton 60-74; Home Sec CMS 74-80; Exec Sec CMS 80-83; Bp Cyprus and the Gulf 83-86; Gen Sec CMS 86-90; rtd 90; Asst Bp Dur 90-94; Perm to Offic *Heref* from 94. *Fern Hill Cottage, Hopesay, Craven Arms, Shropshire SY7 8HD* Tel (01588) 660248

MOORE, Preb Hugh Desmond. b 37. St Cath Soc Ox BA58 MA64. St Steph Ho Ox 58. **d** 61 **p** 62. C Kingston St Luke *S'wark* 61-68; Asst Chapl Lon Univ *Lon* 68-70; Chapl Edgware Gen Hosp from

70; V Hendon St Alphage *Lon* from 70; AD W Barnet 85-90; Preb St Paul's Cathl from 95. *The Vicarage, Montrose Avenue, Edgware, Middx HA8 0DN* Tel 0181-952 4611

MOORE, Ivan. MA BTh. **d** 90 **p** 91. C Knock *D & D* 90-93; I Taney *D & G* from 97. *Church Cottage, 21 Taney Road, Dundrum, Dublin 14, Irish Republic* Tel Dublin (1) 269 0736 or 298 5491

✠**MOORE, The Rt Revd James Edward.** b 33. TCD BA54 MA64. **d** 56 **p** 57 **c** 95. C Knock *D & D* 56-60; C Bangor St Comgall 60-62; P-in-c Belvoir 62-68; I Groomsport 68-75; I Dundela 75-95; Can Down Cathl 85-89; Treas 87-89; Adn Down 89-95; Chan Belf Cathl 89-95; Bp Conn from 95. *Bishop's House, 113 Upper Road, Greenisland, Carrickfergus, Co Antrim BT38 8RR* Tel (01232) 863165 Fax 364266

MOORE, James Frederick. b 12. Sheff Univ BSc35 MSc36. **d** 38 **p** 40. Br Honduras 38-54; Lic to Offic *Bradf* 55-84; rtd 77. *215 Bradford Road, Riddlesden, Keighley, W Yorkshire BD20 5JR* Tel (01535) 606094

MOORE, Canon James Kenneth. b 37. AKC62. St Boniface Warminster 62. **d** 63 **p** 64. C W Hartlepool St Oswald *Dur* 63-66; C-in-c Manor Park CD *Sheff* 66-76; TV Sheff Manor 76-78; R Frecheville and Hackenthorpe 78-87; V Bilham 87-91; V Sheff St Oswald from 91; Hon Can Sheff Cathl from 93. *St Oswald's Vicarage, 2 Bannerdale Road, Sheffield S7 2DL* Tel 0114-250 8226 Fax as telephone

MOORE, John. b 22. St Aid Birkenhead 54. **d** 57 **p** 58. C Glenavy w Tunny and Crumlin *Conn* 57-59; I Kingscourt w Drumconrath, Syddan and Moybologue *M & K* 60-63; C Carnmoney *Conn* 63-65; P-in-c Templepatrick w Donegore 65-68; I Templepatrick 68-85; rtd 85. *Cuthona, 67 Prospect Road, Portstewart, Co Londonderry BT55 7NQ* Tel (01265) 833905

MOORE, John. b 26. Univ of Wales (Lamp) BA51. Oak Hill Th Coll 51. **d** 53 **p** 54. C Illogan *Truro* 53-57; C Margate H Trin *Cant* 57-58; C Abingdon w Shippon *Ox* 58-67; V Retford *S'well* 67-73; R Aspenden and Layston w Buntingford *St Alb* 73-86; V Stanstead Abbots 86-91; rtd 91. *20 Radley Road, Abingdon, Oxon OX14 3PQ* Tel (01235) 532518

MOORE, John Arthur. b 33. Cuddesdon Coll 70. **d** 71 **p** 72. Hon C Gt Burstead *Chelmsf* 71-74; Chapl Barnard Castle Sch from 74. *Littlemoor, Mount Eff Lane, Barnard Castle, Co Durham DL12 8UW* Tel (01833) 38601

MOORE, Canon John Cecil. b 37. TCD BA61 MA67 BD69. CITC 62. **d** 62 **p** 63. C Belfast St Matt *Conn* 62-65; C Holywood *D & D* 65-70; I Ballyphilip w Ardquin 70-77; I Mt Merrion 77-79; I Donaghcloney w Waringstown from 79; Treas Dromore Cathl 90-93; Chan from 93. *54 Banbridge Road, Waringstown, Lurgan, Co Armagh BT66 7QD* Tel (01762) 881218

MOORE, John David (Dick). b 30. St Chad's Coll Dur BA54 DipTh55 DipEd56. **d** 56 **p** 57. C Wallsend St Pet *Newc* 56-60; C Leamington Priors All SS *Cov* 60-62; V Longford 62-75; P-in-c Nuneaton St Mary 75-77; V 77-83; V St Ives *Ely* from 83. *The Vicarage, Westwood Road, St Ives, Huntingdon, Cambs PE17 4DH* Tel (01480) 463254

MOORE, John Ernest. b 24. Oak Hill NSM Course. **d** 84 **p** 85. NSM Hornchurch H Cross *Chelmsf* 84-86; NSM S Woodham Ferrers 86-91; NSM Canvey Is 91-95; Perm to Offic from 95. *124 Beehive Lane, Chelmsford CM2 9SH* Tel (01245) 269026

MOORE, John Henry. b 35. Nottm Univ BMus56 CertEd57 MA61. EMMTC 87. **d** 90 **p** 91. NSM Gotham *S'well* 90-95; NSM Kingston and Ratcliffe-on-Soar 90-95; NSM Bunny w Bradmore 95-97; P-in-c from 97. *19 Hall Drive, Gotham, Nottingham NG11 0JT* Tel 0115-983 0670

MOORE, John Keith. b 26. Sarum & Wells Th Coll 78. **d** 81 **p** 82. NSM Guildf All SS *Guildf* 81-86; NSM Guildf H Trin w St Mary 86-94; Dean of Chapter 90-94; Perm to Offic from 94; Perm to Offic *Chich* from 94. *6 Oakhurst, Crossways Road, Grayshott, Hindhead, Surrey GU26 6JW* Tel (01428) 607174

MOORE, John Michael. b 48. Em Coll Cam BA70 MA73. Cuddesdon Coll 72. **d** 74 **p** 75. C Almondbury *Wakef* 74-78; TV Basingstoke *Win* 78-88; P-in-c Southampton St Alb 88-91; V Swaythling from 91. *St Alban's Vicarage, 357 Burgess Road, Southampton SO16 3BD* Tel (01703) 554231

MOORE, Canon John Richard. b 35. LTh59. St Jo Coll Nottm 56. **d** 59 **p** 60. C Northwood Em *Lon* 59-63; V Burton Dassett *Cov* 63-66; Youth Chapl 63-71; Dir Lindley Lodge Educn Trust Nuneaton 71-82; TR Kinson *Sarum* 82-88; Dir CPAS 88-96; Hon Can Cov Cathl *Cov* from 95; Internat Dir Intercon Ch Soc from 96. *c/o Intercontinental Church Society, 175 Tower Bridge Road, London SE1 2AQ* Tel 0171-407 4588 Fax 378 0541

MOORE, John Richard. b 45. Linc Th Coll 80. **d** 82 **p** 83. C Gt Grimsby St Mary and St Jas *Linc* 82-86; V Skirbeck Quarter 86-95; Miss to Seamen from 86; P-in-c Coningsby w Tattershall *Linc* from 95. *The Rectory, 22 High Street, Coningsby, Lincoln LN4 4RA* Tel (01526) 342223

MOORE, Leonard Richard. b 22. Leeds Univ BA47. Coll of Resurr Mirfield 47. **d** 49 **p** 50. C Hendon St Mary *Lon* 49-54; C Stevenage *St Alb* 54-60; V Bedford All SS 60-68; Lic to Offic 68-70; P-in-c Bedford H Trin 70-74; rtd 87; Hon C Cardington *St Alb* from 87. *22 Dart Road, Bedford MK41 7BT* Tel (01234) 357536

MOORE, Mrs Margaret Doreen. b 37. Westf Coll Lon BA58 CertEd59 BD63. Dalton Ho Bris 61. **dss** 85 **d** 87 **p** 94. Harold Hill St Paul *Chelmsf* 85-87; Hon Par Dn S Woodham Ferrers 87-91; C Canvey Is 91-95; TV Gt Baddow from 95. *124 Beehive Lane, Chelmsford CM2 9SH* Tel (01245) 269026

MOORE, Matthew Edward George. b 38. Oak Hill Th Coll 77. **d** 77 **p** 78. C Larne and Inver *Conn* 77-80; I Desertmartin w Termoneeny *D & R* 80-84; I Milltown *Arm* 84-96; I Culmore w Muff and Belmont *D & R* from 96; Dioc Warden for Min of Healing from 97. *The Rectory, Heathfield, Culmore Road, Londonderry BT48 8JD* Tel (01504) 352396 Fax as telephone

MOORE, Canon Mervyn. b 18. Leeds Univ BA40. Coll of Resurr Mirfield 40. **d** 42 **p** 43. C Middlesbrough St Martin *York* 42-45; C Helmsley 45-49; V Osbaldwick w Murton 49-54; S Africa from 54. *Canonsgarth, 11A Twelfth Avenue, Parktown North, 2193 South Africa* Tel Johannesburg (11) 298724

MOORE, Canon Michael Mervlyn Hamond. b 35. Pemb Coll Ox BA60 MA63. Wells Th Coll 60. **d** 62 **p** 63. C Bethnal Green St Matt *Lon* 62-66; Chapl Bucharest w Sofia and Belgrade *Eur* 66-67; Asst Gen Sec C of E Coun on Foreign Relns 67-70; Gen Sec 70-72; Abp's Asst Chapl on Foreign Relns *Cant* 72-82; Hon C Walworth St Pet *S'wark* 73-80; Hon Can Cant Cathl *Cant* 74-90; Chapl Chpl Royal Hampton Court Palace from 82; Dep P in O from 92. *Hampton Court Palace, West Molesey, Surrey KT8 9AU* Tel 0181-977 2762

MOORE, Norman Butler. b 25. St Jo Coll Dur BA50 DipTh52. **d** 52 **p** 53. C Aston St Jas *Birm* 52-55; V 57-59; C Gravesend St Jas *Roch* 55-57; PC Warley Woods *Birm* 59-64; Bp's Youth Chapl and Asst Dir of Educn *Worc* 65-66; V Lucton w Eyton *Heref* 66-69; V Hazelwell *Birm* 69-75; V Watford St Andr *St Alb* 75-94; rtd 94. *5 Vicarage Close, St Albans, Herts AL1 2PU* Tel (01727) 863219

MOORE, Dr Paul. b 59. Ball Coll Ox BA82 DPhil86. Wycliffe Hall Ox DipTh87. **d** 89 **p** 90. C Ox St Andr *Ox* 89-93; V Kildwick *Bradf* from 93. *The Vicarage, Kildwick, Keighley, W Yorkshire BD20 9BB* Tel (01535) 633307

MOORE, Peter. b 21. Leeds Univ BA47. Coll of Resurr Mirfield 46. **d** 48 **p** 49. C N Stoneham *Win* 48-51; C Portsea St Alb *Portsm* 51-53; V Tynemouth H Trin W Town *Newc* 53-58; V Thetford St Mary *Nor* 58-65; R Mundford w Lynford 65-76; P-in-c Ickburgh w Langford 65-76; P-in-c Cranwich 65-76; RD Thetford 69; V Whitley *Newc* 76-86; rtd 86; Perm to Offic *Newc* from 86. *31 Glebelands, Corbridge, Northd NE45 5DS* Tel (01434) 633207

MOORE, The Very Revd Peter Clement. b 24. OBE93. FSA Ch Ch Ox BA45 MA48 DPhil54. Cuddesdon Coll 45. **d** 47 **p** 48. Min Can Cant Cathl *Cant* 47-49; C Bladon w Woodstock *Ox* 49-51; Chapl New Coll Ox 49-51; V Alfrick w Lulsley *Worc* 52-59; V Pershore w Wick 59-67; RD Pershore 65-67; Can Res Ely Cathl *Ely* 67-73; Treas 69; Vice-Dean 71; Dean St Alb 73-93; rtd 93. *Elm Barn, Meadow Lane, Fulbrook, Burford, Oxon OX8 4BS* Tel (01993) 823220

MOORE, Raymond. b 47. QUB BSc70. **d** 87 **p** 88. NSM Belfast All SS *Conn* 87-95; NSM 95-96; NSM Kilmakee from 96. *17 Royal Lodge Avenue, Purdysburn, Belfast BT8 4YR* Tel (01232) 705481

MOORE, Canon Richard Noel. b 34. TCD BA56 MA60. **d** 57 **p** 58. C Derry Cathl *D & R* 57-60; I Clondehorkey 60-66; I Stranorlar w Meenglas and Kilteevogue 66-76; I Glendermott from 76; Can Derry Cathl from 89. *Glendermott Rectory, Altnagelvin, Londonderry BT47 2LS* Tel (01504) 343001

MOORE, Richard Norman Theobald. b 39. St Andr Univ BSc62 Lon Univ BD66. Clifton Th Coll. **d** 66 **p** 67. C Stowmarket *St E* 66-69; C New Humberstone *Leic* 69-72; P-in-c Leic Martyrs 73; V 73-84; Chapl Manor Hosp Epsom 84-94; Chapl Surrey Heartlands NHS Trust from 94. *72 Newton Wood Road, Ashtead, Surrey KT21 1NO, or St Ebba's Hospital, Hook Road, Epsom, Surrey KT19 8NL* Tel (01372) 272525 or 722212

MOORE, Robert Allen. b 32. Univ of the Pacific BA54 Boston Univ STB58 STM59. **d** 63 **p** 63. USA 63-80; V Farington *Blackb* 80-83; TV Preston St Jo 83-85; P-in-c Fleetwood 85-87; V Leyland St Jas 87-97; rtd 97. *19 Lea Road, Whittle-le-Woods, Chorley, Lancs PR16 7PF* Tel (01257) 265701

MOORE, Canon Robert Denholm. b 23. TCD BA45 Div Test46. **d** 46 **p** 47. C Londonderry Ch Ch *D & R* 46-49; C Dublin Clontarf *D & G* 49-53; I Clondehorkey *D & R* 53-60; RD Kilmacrenan W 59-60; I Clonleigh w Donaghmore 60-65; I Tamlaghtfinlagan w Myroe 65-92; Chapl HM Pris Magilligan 72-92; Can Derry Cathl *D & R* 80-92; rtd 92. *22 Tyler Road, Limavady, Co Londonderry BT49 0DP* Tel (01504) 768597

MOORE, Canon Robert George Chaffey. b 11. Kelham Th Coll 28. **d** 39 **p** 40. C Linc St Giles *Linc* 39-42; Chapl RAF 42-47; R Compton Abbas *Sarum* 49-73; Can and Preb Sarum Cathl 72-77; TV Shaston 73-77; rtd 77. *Fairfax House, 85 Castle Road, Salisbury SP1 3RW* Tel (01722) 332846

MOORE, Robin Alan. b 42. Portsm Coll of Tech DBS65 Lon Univ BA71 Garnett Coll Lon CertEd75 Open Univ AdDipEdMan87. S Dios Minl Tr Scheme 91. **d** 94 **p** 95. NSM Barcombe *Chich* from 94. *Yew Tree House, School Path, Barcombe, Lewes, E Sussex BN8 5DN* Tel (01273) 400747

MOORE, Robin Hugh. b 52. CertEd BEd QUB BD TCD DipTh. **d** 84 **p** 85. C Derryloran *Arm* 84-86; C Knock *D & D* 86-89; Bp's C Belfast St Steph w St Luke *Conn* 89-94; I 94-96; I

Whitehouse from 96. *283 Shore Road, Newtownabbey, Co Antrim BT37 9SR* Tel (01232) 851622

MOORE, The Very Revd Thomas Robert. b 38. TCD 65. Lambeth DipTh79 MA84. **d** 68 **p** 69. C Dublin Drumcondra w N Strand *D & G* 68-70; C Portadown St Columba *Arm* 70-72; I Kilskeery w Trillick *Clogh* 72-85; RD Kilskeery 81-86; Dioc Sec from 83; I Trory w Killadeas 85-95; Can Clogh Cathl 86-89; Preb 89-91; Preb Donaghmore St Patr Cathl Dublin 91-95; Dean Clogh from 95; I Clogh w Errigal Portclare from 95. *The Deanery, 10 Augher Road, Clogher, Co Tyrone BT76 0AD* Tel (01662) 548235 Fax as telephone

MOORE, Thomas Sydney (Tom). b 50. St Paul's Coll Grahamstown DipTh77. **d** 79 **p** 80. S Africa 79-96; C Bushey *St Alb* from 97. *Trinity House, Bushey Mill Lane, Bushey, Herts WD2 2AS* Tel (01923) 220565

MOORE, Mrs Wendy. b 44. Westcott Ho Cam CTM94. **d** 94 **p** 95. C Rotherham *Sheff* 94-97; V Laughton w Throapham from 97. *The Vicarage, 1 Church Corner, Laughton, Sheffield S31 7YB* Tel (01909) 562300

MOORE, William Henry. b 14. K Coll Lon 34. **d** 38 **p** 39. C Mill End *St Alb* 38-41; C Tring 41-44; C Gt Yarmouth *Nor* 44-46; New Zealand 46-52; R Houghton Conquest *St Alb* 52-56; Canada 56-59; R Filby w Thrigby *Nor* 60-62; P-in-c Mautby 60-62; Perm to Offic 62-71; Asst Master Mildenhall Sec Sch 68-73; Heartsease Sch Nor 73-75; C Mildenhall *St E* 71-73; rtd 79; Hon C Thorpe *Nor* from 88. *21 Green Court, Avenue Green, Norwich NR7 0DN* Tel (01603) 432758

MOORE, Canon William James Foster. b 26. TCD BA50. **d** 50 **p** 51. C Glenavy *Conn* 50-53; C Coleraine 53-57; I Rasharkin w Finvoy 57-66; I Broomhedge 66-83; I Dunluce 83-95; Can Belf Cathl 88-95; rtd 95. *2 Dunluce Park, Portballintrae, Bushmills, Co Antrim BT57 8YZ* Tel (01265) 732645

MOORE, Canon William Morris. b 33. QUB BSc55 TCD. **d** 61 **p** 62. C Belfast St Mich *Conn* 61-64; I 70-80; C Belfast All SS 64-70; I Ballynafeigh St Jude *D & D* from 80; Can Belf Cathl from 95. *10 Mornington, Annadale Avenue, Belfast BT7 3JS* Tel (01232) 491602

MOORE, William Thomas Sewell. b 21. MRCS LRCP MA. Westcott Ho Cam. **d** 82 **p** 83. Chapl Countess Mountbatten Ho Southn 84-90; Hon C Shedfield *Portsm* 84-86; Perm to Offic from 86; rtd 90. *Crossways, Blind Lane, Wickham, Fareham, Hants PO17 5HD* Tel (01329) 832119

MOORGAS, Geoffrey Gordon. b 30. Sarum & Wells Th Coll 80. **d** 81 **p** 82. C Brixton St Matt *S'wark* 81-84; C Clapham Old Town 84-87; C Clapham TM 87; Namibia 87-94; rtd 95. *St Silvan's House, Red Lane, Oxted, Surrey RH8 0RS* Tel (01883) 723452

MOORHEAD, Michael David. b 52. BSc BA. St Steph Ho Ox. **d** 83 **p** 84. C Kilburn St Aug w St Jo *Lon* 83-87; C Kenton 87-89; V Harlesden All So from 89; P-in-c Willesden St Matt from 92. *All Souls' Vicarage, 3 Station Road, London NW10 4UJ* Tel 0181-965 4988

MOORHOUSE, Christine Susan. b 49. K Coll Lon BD71. WMMTC. **dss** 86 **d** 87 **p** 94. NSM Stourbridge St Thos *Worc* from 86. *20 High Street, Stourbridge, W Midlands DY8 4NJ* Tel (01384) 395381

MOORHOUSE, Humphrey John. b 18. Oak Hill Th Coll 37. **d** 41 **p** 42. C Dalston St Mark w St Bart *Lon* 41-42; C Chadwell Heath *Chelmsf* 42-45; R Vange 45-83; rtd 83; Perm to Offic *Chelmsf* from 83. *12 Waverley Road, Benfleet, Essex SS7 4AZ* Tel (01268) 754952

MOORHOUSE, Llewellyn Owen. b 14. Ely Th Coll 63 St Deiniol's Hawarden. **d** 64 **p** 65. C Kirkby Stephen w Mallerstang *Carl* 64-66; C Barrow St Geo w St Luke 66-68; V Grayrigg 68-75; P-in-c Sawrey 75-80; rtd 80; Perm to Offic *Ban* from 80. *Regent House, 17 Church Street, Beaumaris LL58 8AB* Tel (01248) 810628

MOORHOUSE, Peter. b 42. Liv Univ BSc64 Hull Univ CertEd. Linc Th Coll 79. **d** 81 **p** 82. C Horsforth *Ripon* 81-85; R Ackworth *Wakef* 85-96; Dep Chapl HM Pris Leeds 96-97; Chapl HM Pris Stocken from 97. *HM Prison Stocken, Stocken Hall Road, Stretton, Oakham, Leics LE15 7RD* Tel (01780) 485100 Fax 410681

MOORSOM, Christopher Arthur Robert. b 55. Ox Univ BA. Sarum & Wells Th Coll 79. **d** 82 **p** 83. C Bradford-on-Avon *Sarum* 82-85; R Broad Town, Clyffe Pypard and Tockenham 85-89; V Banwell *B & W* 89-96; R Upper Stour *Sarum* from 96. *The Rectory, Zeals, Warminster, Wilts BA12 6PG* Tel (01747) 840221

MOORSOM, Robert Coverdale. b 23. ARCM48. Cuddesdon Coll 49. **d** 50 **p** 51. C Sedbergh w Killington *Bradf* 50-54; S Africa 54-64; V Bierley *Bradf* 65-71; C Wareham *Sarum* 71-80; TV Gillingham 80-83; R The Lulworths, Winfrith Newburgh and Chaldon 83-89; rtd 89. *4 Hodges Close, Poole, Dorset BH17 7QE* Tel (01202) 684897

MORALEE, Thomas Edward (Tony). b 33. S'wark Ord Course. **d** 82 **p** 83. NSM Wandsworth All SS *S'wark* 82-90; NSM Gt Bookham *Guildf* 91-92; Perm to Offic from 92. *71 Eastwick Park, Leatherhead, Surrey KT23 3NH* Tel (01372) 454433

MORAY, ROSS AND CAITHNESS, Bishop of. *See* MACGREGOR, The Rt Revd Gregor

MORAY, ROSS AND CAITHNESS, Dean of. *See* FORREST, The Very Revd Robin Whyte

MORCOM, Canon Anthony John. b 16. Clare Coll Cam BA38 MA42. Cuddesdon Coll 38. **d** 39 **p** 40. C Paddington St Mary Magd *Lon* 39-42; C Pimlico St Mary Graham Terrace 42-47; Bp's Chapl 47-55; Adn Middx 53-66; V St Marylebone St Cypr 55-66; V Cambridge St Mary Less *Ely* 66-73; RD Cambridge 71-73; Can Res Ely Cathl 74-83; rtd 84; Lic to Offic *Ely* from 84. *33 Porson Road, Cambridge CB2 2ET* Tel (01223) 62352

MORDECAI, Mrs Betty. b 27. Birm Univ BA48 Cam Univ CertEd49. Wycliffe Hall Ox 85. **dss** 86 **d** 87 **p** 94. Leamington Priors All SS *Cov* 86-87; Hon Par Dn 87-89; C Worc City St Paul and Old St Martin etc *Worc* 89-94; rtd 94. *8 Swains Crofts, Leamington Spa, Warks CV31 1YW* Tel (01926) 882001

MORDECAI, Thomas Huw. b 59. Bris Univ BA81 St Jo Coll Dur BA85. Cranmer Hall Dur 83. **d** 87 **p** 88. C Gillingham St Mary *Roch* 87-90; Chapl Warw Sch 90-96; Chapl Giggleswick Sch from 96. *Little Howsons, Giggleswick School, Settle, N Yorkshire BD24 0DE* Tel (01729) 823545 or 823241 Fax 824187

MORE, Canon Richard David Antrobus. b 48. St Jo Coll Dur BA70 DipTh71. Cranmer Hall Dur 70. **d** 72 **p** 73. C Macclesfield St Mich *Ches* 72-77; Chapl Lee Abbey 77-82; V Porchester *S'well* 82-96; RD Gedling 90-96; Bp's Dom Chapl *Chelmsf* from 96; Can Chelmsf Cathl from 96. *Willowdene, Maldon Road, Margaretting, Ingatestone, Essex CM4 9JW* Tel (01277) 352472

MORECROFT, Michael William. b 40. MIBiol Man Univ MEd. WMMTC. **d** 86 **p** 87. Hd Master Polesworth Sch Warks from 86; Hon C Wylde Green *Birm* 86-89; Hon C Castle Bromwich St Clem from 89. *St Clement's Vicarage, Lanchester Way, Birmingham B36 9JG* Tel 0121-747 4460

MORETON, Mark. b 39. Jes Coll Cam BA64 MA68. Westcott Ho Cam. **d** 65 **p** 66. C Portsea All SS *Portsm* 65-70; C St Martin-in-the-Fields *Lon* 70-72; Chapl Jes Coll Cam 72-77; R Stafford St Mary and St Chad *Lich* 77-79; P-in-c Stafford Ch Ch 77-79; P-in-c Marston w Whitgreave 77-79; TR Stafford 79-91; V W Bromwich All SS from 91. *All Saints' Vicarage, 90 Hall Green Road, West Bromwich, W Midlands B71 3LB* Tel 0121-588 2647

MORETON, Dr Michael Bernard. b 44. St Jo Coll Cam BA66 MA70 Ch Ch Ox BA66 MA69 DPhil69. St Steph Ho Ox 66. **d** 68 **p** 69. C Banstead *Guildf* 68-74; R Alburgh *Nor* 74-75; R Denton 74-75; R Middleton Cheney w Chacombe *Pet* 75-87. *Penny Royal, 19 Thorpe Road, Chacombe, Banbury, Oxon OX17 2JW* Tel (01295) 710631

MORETON, Preb Michael Joseph. b 17. Univ Coll Lon BA40 Ch Ch Ox BA47 MA53. Wells Th Coll 47. **d** 48 **p** 49. C Rowbarton *B & W* 48-52; C Ilfracombe H Trin *Ex* 52-59; Lect Th Ex Univ 57-86; R Ex St Mary Steps *Ex* 59-86; P-in-c 86-92; RD Christianity 83-89; Preb Ex Cathl 85-86; rtd 86; Perm to Offic *Ex* from 86. *3 Glenthorne Road, Duryard, Exeter EX4 4QU* Tel (01392) 438083

MORETON, Philip Norman Harley. b 28. Linc Th Coll. **d** 57 **p** 58. C Howden *York* 57-60; C Bottesford *Linc* 60-65; V Linc St Giles 65-70; V Bracebridge Heath 71-77; V Seasalter *Cant* 77-84; TV Whitstable 84-88; rtd 88; Perm to Offic *York* from 96. *The Cottage, 2 Broad Lane, Howden, Goole, N Humberside DN14 7DN* Tel (01430) 430552

MORETON, Rupert Robert James. b 66. TCD BA89. CITC BTh92. **d** 92 **p** 93. C Dublin Ch Ch Cathl Gp *D & G* 92-96; Asst Chapl Costa Blanca *Eur* from 96. *Buzon 3, La Cometa 18, 03729 Senija (Benisa), Spain* Tel Benidorm (65) 73 24 65

✠**MORGAN, The Rt Revd Alan Wyndham.** b 40. Univ of Wales (Lamp) BA62. St Mich Coll Llan 62. **d** 64 **p** 65 **c** 89. C Llangyfelach and Morriston *S & B* 64-69; C Swansea St Pet 69-72; C Cov E *Cov* 72-73; TV 73-83; Bp's Officer for Soc Resp 78-83; Adn Cov 83-89; Suff Bp Sherwood *S'well* from 89. *Sherwood House, High Oakham, Mansfield, Notts NG18 5AJ* Tel (01623) 657491 Fax 662526

MORGAN, Dr Alison Jean. b 59. Girton Coll Cam BA82 MA85 Darw Coll Cam PhD86. EMMTC 93. **d** 96 **p** 97. NSM Oadby *Leic* from 96. *29 Holmfield Road, Leicester LE2 1SE* Tel 0116-270 4986

MORGAN, Anthony Hogarth. b 42. St Josef Missiehuis Holland 60 St Jos RC Coll Lon 62. **d** 65 **p** 66. In RC Ch 66-93; NSM Handsworth Woodhouse *Sheff* 93-94; C Sheff Norwood St Leon 94-97; P-in-c Shiregreen St Hilda from 97. *St Hilda's House, 2 Firth Park Crescent, Sheffield S5 6HE* Tel 0114-243 6308

✠**MORGAN, The Rt Revd Barry Cennydd.** b 47. Lon Univ BA69 Selw Coll Cam BA72 MA74 Univ of Wales PhD86. Westcott Ho Cam 70. **d** 72 **p** 73 **c** 93. Chapl Bryn-y-Don Community Sch 72-75; C St Andrew's Major and Michaelston-le-Pit *Llan* 72-75; Ed Welsh Churchman 75-82; Lect Th Univ of Wales (Cardiff) 75-77; Chapl and Lect St Mich Coll Llan 75-77; Warden Ch Hostel Ban 77-84; Chapl and Lect Th Univ of Wales (Ban) 77-84; In-Service Tr Adv *Ban* 78-84; Dir of Ords 82-84; Can Ban Cathl 83-84; R Wrexham *St As* 84-86; Adn Meirionnydd *Ban* 86-93; R Criccieth w Treflys 86-93; Bp Ban from 93. *Tyr Esgob, Bangor LL57 2SS* Tel (01248) 362895 Fax 354866

MORGAN, Miss Beryl. b 30. **dss** 63 **d** 87 **p** 94. Rickerscote *Lich* 63-69; Hd Dss 70-87; Dioc Lay Min Adv 70-93; Willenhall H Trin 80-87; Par Dn 87-93; rtd 93; Hon C Penn *Lich* from 94. *11A*

Church Hill, Penn, Wolverhampton WV4 5NP Tel (01902) 337173

MORGAN, Brian. b 35. Lon Univ BA58. Wells Th Coll 59. **d** 61 **p** 62. C Withington St Chris *Man* 61-63; C Rochdale 63-65; Trinidad and Tobago 65-69; V Heywood St Jas *Man* 69-74; Miss to Seamen 74-80; Kenya 74-77; Chapl Pernis Miss to Seamen *Eur* 77-78; Antwerp 78-80; V Skerton St Chad *Blackb* 80-84; P-in-c Oswaldtwistle Immanuel 84-87; P-in-c Oswaldtwistle All SS 84-87; V Barrowford from 87. *The Vicarage, Wheatley Lane Road, Barrowford, Nelson, Lancs BB9 6QS* Tel (01282) 613206

MORGAN, Canon Christopher Heudebourck. b 47. Lon Univ DipTh70 Lanc Univ BA73 Heythrop Coll Lon MTh91. Kelham Th Coll 66. **d** 73 **p** 74. C Birstall *Leic* 73-76; Asst Chapl Brussels *Eur* 76-80; P-in-c Redditch St Geo *Worc* 80-81; TV Redditch, The Ridge 81-85; V Sonning *Ox* 85-96; Prin Berks Chr Tr Scheme 85-89; Dir Past Studies Ox Min Course 92-96; Dioc Officer for Min *Glouc* from 96; Dioc Can Res Glouc Cathl from 96. *9 College Green, Gloucester GL1 2LX* Tel (01452) 507002

MORGAN, Christopher John. b 46. Brasted Th Coll 68 Linc Th Coll 70. **d** 72 **p** 73. C Earley St Pet *Ox* 72-76; C Epsom St Martin *Guildf* 76-79; V Stoneleigh 79-83; Ind Chapl *York* 83-87; NACRO 87-91; V York St Hilda *York* 92-96; TV E Greenwich Ch Ch w St Andr and St Mich *S'wark* 96-97; TV E Greenwich from 97. *Christ Church Vicarage, 52 Earlswood Street, London SE10 9ES* Tel 0181-853 5950

MORGAN, David Farnon Charles. b 43. Leeds Univ BA68. Coll of Resurr Mirfield 68. **d** 70 **p** 71. C Swinton St Pet *Man* 70-73; C Langley All SS and Martyrs 73-75; R Salford St Clem w St Cypr Ordsall 75-76; R Salford Ordsall St Clem 76-86; V Adlington *Blackb* from 86. *St Paul's Vicarage, Railway Road, Adlington, Chorley, Lancs PR6 9QZ* Tel (01257) 480253

MORGAN, David Joseph (Joe). b 47. Bp Burgess Hall Lamp 66 St Deiniol's Hawarden 74. **d** 74 **p** 75. C Pembroke Dock *St D* 74-77; C Burry Port and Pwll 77-80; Miss to Seamen from 80; Sen Chapl and Sec Welsh Coun from 85. *25 Glanmor Park Road, Sketty, Swansea SA2 0QG* Tel (01792) 206637

MORGAN, David Watcyn. b 14. St D Coll Lamp. **d** 64 **p** 65. C Cardigan *St D* 64-69; R Herbrandston 69-70; R Herbrandston and St Ishmael w Hasguard 70-83; rtd 83. *31 Glenalla Road, Llanelli SA15 1EE* Tel (01554) 776572

MORGAN, Denis. b 36. Cuddesdon Coll 67. **d** 69 **p** 70. C Bush Hill Park St Steph *Lon* 69-72; C Stevenage St Nic *St Alb* 72-75; V Croxley Green St Oswald 75-85; V Shillington 85-95; rtd 95; Perm to Offic *Roch* from 95. *7 Fromandez Drive, Horsmonden, Tonbridge, Kent TN12 8LN* Tel (01892) 722388

MORGAN, Enid Morris Roberts. b 40. St Anne's Coll Ox BA61 Univ of Wales (Ban) MA73. United Th Coll Abth BD81. **d** 84 **p** 97. C Llanfihangel w Llanafan and Llanwnnws etc *St D* 84-86; D-in-c 86-93; Dir Bd of Miss Ch in Wales from 93. *The Church in Wales Centre, Woodland Place, Penarth CF64 2EX* Tel (01222) 708234 Fax 712413

MORGAN, Gareth Morison Kilby. b 33. Bris Univ BA56. Cuddesdon Coll 57 Bangalore Th Coll. **d** 61 **p** 62. C St Helier *S'wark* 61-65; Chapl Scargill Ho 65-70; Dir RE *Linc* 71-74; Dir of Educn *St E* 74-81; TR Hanley H Ev *Lich* 81-89; TR Cen Telford 89-92; Warden Glenfall Ho *Glouc* from 92. *Glenfall House, Harp Hill, Cheltenham, Glos GL54 4EP* Tel (01242) 583654 Fax 251314

MORGAN, Geoffrey. b 51. AKC72. St Aug Coll Cant 73. **d** 74 **p** 75. C Hulme Ascension *Man* 74-77; C Nantwich *Ches* 77-79; R Hatfield *St Alb* 79-86; Chapl S Beds HA 86-91; Chapl Luton and Dunstable Hosp 86-91; Chapl Cov Poly *Cov* 91-92; Chapl Cov Univ 92-95; rtd 95; Perm to Offic *Cov* from 95; Perm to Offic *Birm* from 96. *2 Guys Cliffe Terrace, Warwick CV34 4LP* Tel (01926) 401007

MORGAN, Glyn. b 21. Oak Hill Th Coll 73. **d** 76 **p** 77. Hon C Barton Seagrave w Warkton *Pet* from 76. *St Edmund's House, Warkton, Kettering, Northants NN15 5AB* Tel (01536) 520610

MORGAN, Glyn. b 33. Univ of Wales (Ban) BA55 MA69. Coll of Resurr Mirfield 55. **d** 57 **p** 58. C Dolgellau *Ban* 57-60; C Conway 60-63; V Corris 63-68; Hd of RE Friars' Sch Ban 69-70; Lic to Offic 70-71; Hd of RE Oswestry Boys' Modern Sch 70-74; Hd of RE Oswestry High Sch for Girls 74-79; Hon C Oswestry H Trin *Lich* 71-79; Hd of RE Fitzalan Sch Oswestry 79-88; Perm to Offic 79-84; Perm to Offic *St As* 84-88; V Meifod and Llangynyw from 88; RD Caereinion from 89. *The Vicarage, Meifod SY22 6DH* Tel (01938) 84231

MORGAN, Graham. b 47. S'wark Ord Course. **d** 83 **p** 84. NSM S Kensington St Steph *Lon* 83-90; NSM Hammersmith H Innocents from 90. *24 Charville Court, Charville Road, London W14 9JG* Tel 0171-381 3211

MORGAN, Canon Gwilym Owen. b 17. LSE BSc47. Westcott Ho Cam 46. **d** 48 **p** 49. C Bury St Mary *Man* 48-51; Chapl Salford R Hosp 51-71; R Salford St Phil *Man* 51-59; R Salford St Steph 54-59; R Salford St Phil w St Steph 59-71; RD Salford 57-71; Hon Can Man Cathl 62-71; Can Res 71-85; Sub-Dean 72-85; rtd 86; Perm to Offic *Man* from 86. *20 Lyndhurst Road, Didsbury Village, Manchester M20 0AA* Tel 0161-434 2732

MORGAN, Harold Evan. b 17. St D Coll Lamp BA38. **d** 40 **p** 41. C Oldbury *Birm* 40-42; C Northleach and Hampnett w Stowell and Yanworth *Glouc* 42-43; V Newcastle *Llan* 68-82; rtd 83; Perm to Offic *Llan* from 82. *28 Seaview Drive, Ogmore-by-Sea, Bridgend CF32 0PB* Tel (01656) 880467

MORGAN, Henry. b 45. Hertf Coll Ox BA68. Westcott Ho Cam 68. **d** 70 **p** 71. C Lee St Marg *S'wark* 70-73; C Newington St Paul 73-76; V Camberwell St Mich w All So w Em 76-84; V Kingswood 84-93; Perm to Offic from 93. *4 Glebe Gardens, New Malden, Surrey KT3 5RY* Tel 0181-942 4362

MORGAN, Ian David John. b 57. LTCL75 Hull Univ BA78. Ripon Coll Cuddesdon 80. **d** 83 **p** 84. C Heref H Trin *Heref* 83-86; C New Shoreham *Chich* 86-88; Researcher, Producer & Presenter BBC Local Radio 88-92; V Ipswich All Hallows *St E* 92-95; TR Ipswich St Mary at Stoke w St Pet from 95. *The Rectory, 74 Ancaster Road, Ipswich IP2 9AJ* Tel (01473) 601895

MORGAN, Ian Stephen. b 50. Open Univ BA88. Sarum & Wells Th Coll 86. **d** 88 **p** 89. C Baldock w Bygrave *St Alb* 88-91; C Rumburgh w S Elmham w the Ilketshalls *St E* 91-92; C S Elmham and Ilketshall 92-95; V Bungay H Trin w St Mary from 95. *The Vicarage, 3 Trinity Gardens, Bungay, Suffolk NR35 1HH* Tel (01986) 892110

MORGAN, James Geoffrey Selwyn. b 59. Ex Univ BA81 PGCE82 Dur Univ CCSk91. Cranmer Hall Dur 88. **d** 91 **p** 92. C Reading St Agnes w St Paul *Ox* 91-93; C Bromham w Oakley and Stagsden *St Alb* 94-95; Perm to Offic *Pet* from 95. *64 Kingsthorpe Grove, Northampton NN2 6NT*

MORGAN, John Aeron. b 15. St D Coll Lamp BA37. **d** 40 **p** 41. C Pen-bre *St D* 40-52; C Church Stretton *Heref* 52-62; R Harley w Kenley 62-73; P-in-c Hughley 65-73; V Pencarreg and Llanycrwys *St D* 73-86; rtd 86. *46 Penybryn, Cwmann, Lampeter SA48 8HG* Tel (01570) 422198

MORGAN, John Geoffrey Basil. b 21. Wells Th Coll 59. **d** 60 **p** 61. C Oakdale St Geo *Sarum* 60-64; C Talbot Village 64-67; C-in-c Ensbury St Thos CD 67-69; V Ensbury 69-82; C W Parley 82-86; rtd 86. *57 Selwood Caravan Park, Weymans Avenue, Bournemouth BH10 7JX* Tel (01202) 582327

MORGAN, John Roland. b 31. Birm Univ BA54. Bps' Coll Cheshunt 54. **d** 55 **p** 56. C Selly Oak St Mary *Birm* 55-57; C Yardley Wood 57-58; C Hamstead St Paul 58-61; V Smethwick St Chad 61-68; V Balsall Common 68-82; V N Leigh *Ox* 82-95; RD Woodstock 87-92; rtd 95; Perm to Offic *Ely* from 95. *Dyn Caryn, 2 Hayling Close, Godmanchester, Huntingdon, Cambs PE18 8XB* Tel (01480) 459522

MORGAN, John William Miller. b 34. Lon Univ BSc56. Wycliffe Hall Ox 61. **d** 63 **p** 64. C St Alb Ch Ch *St Alb* 63-68; V Luton St Matt High Town 68-79; V Mangotsfield *Bris* 79-90; P-in-c Stanton St Quintin, Hullavington, Grittleton etc 90-95; R Hullavington, Norton and Stanton St Quintin from 95. *The Rectory, 1 Rectory Close, Stanton St Quintin, Chippenham, Wilts SN14 6DE* Tel (01666) 837187 E-mail 100714.36@compuserve.com

MORGAN, Katharine. b 41. **d** 91 **p** 97. NSM Lougher *S & B* from 91. *68 Borough Road, Lougher, Swansea SA4 6RT*

MORGAN, Kathleen Irene. b 52. St Martin's Coll Lanc CertEd74. W of England Minl Tr Course 93. **d** 96. Hon C Barnwood *Glouc* from 96. *7 Popes Meade, Highnam, Gloucs GL2 8LH* Tel (01452) 520766

MORGAN, Kenneth James. b 14. Selw Coll Cam BA36 MA43. Wells Th Coll 36. **d** 38 **p** 39. C Moulsecoomb *Chich* 38-40; C Preston 40-41; Chapl RAFVR 41-47; Chapl Miss to Seamen 47; Lic to Offic *Dur* 47; Chapl Oslo Norway 47-51; V Blacklands Ch Ch *Chich* 51-58; V Weston St Jo *B & W* 58-66; V Shalford *Guildf* 66-84; rtd 84; Perm to Offic *Guildf* from 85. *Greenwood, The Close, Wonersh, Guildford, Surrey GU5 0PA* Tel (01483) 898791

MORGAN, Mark Anthony. b 58. LLB. Chich Th Coll. **d** 84 **p** 85. C Thorpe *Nor* 84-87; C Eaton 87-90; V Southtown 90-92; Perm to Offic from 92. *86 Yarmouth Road, Norwich NR7 0QZ* Tel (01603) 702186

MORGAN, Mark Steven Glyn. b 60. Essex Univ BSc83 RGN86. Ridley Hall Cam 95. **d** 97. C Herne Bay Ch Ch *Cant* from 97. *19 Central Avenue, Herne Bay, Kent CT6 8RX* Tel (01227) 360902

MORGAN, Martin Paul. b 46. St Steph Ho Ox 71. **d** 73 **p** 74. C Kettering St Mary *Pet* 73-76; C Fareham SS Pet and Paul *Portsm* 76-80; V Portsea Ascension 80-94; V Rottingdean *Chich* from 94. *The Vicarage, Steyning Road, Rottingdean, Brighton BN2 7GA* Tel (01273) 309216

MORGAN, Mervyn Thomas. b 24. Ch Coll Cam BA48 MA71. Chich Th Coll 79. **d** 80 **p** 81. NSM Lewes All SS, St Anne, St Mich and St Thos *Chich* 80-82; P-in-c Glynde, W Firle and Beddingham 82-84; V Burwash Weald 84-89; R Alphamstone w Lamarsh and Pebmarsh *Chelmsf* 89-92; rtd 92. *The Sergeant's House, High Street, Aldeburgh, Suffolk IP15 5AB* Tel (01728) 453636

MORGAN, Michael. b 32. Lon Univ BSc57 MSc67 PhD63. **d** 74 **p** 75. NSM Portsdown *Portsm* from 74. *1 Widley Road, Cosham, Portsmouth PO6 2DS* Tel (01705) 377442

MORGAN, Michael John. b 45. Nottm Univ BA66 MEd71. Linc Th Coll 80. **d** 82 **p** 83. C Bulkington *Cov* 82-83; C Bulkington w Shilton and Ansty 83-85; V Longford 85-89; R Norton *Sheff* from 89. *The Rectory, Norton, Sheffield S8 8JQ* Tel 0114-274 5066

MORGAN, Morley Roland. b 47. Univ of Wales (Lamp) BA76. St Steph Ho Ox 76. **d** 77 **p** 78. C Merthyr Dyfan *Llan* 77-78; C Llantrisant 78-80; TV Coventry Caludon *Cov* 80-86; Chapl N Man Gen Hosp 86-93; Chapl N Man Healthcare NHS Trust from 93. *North Manchester General Hospital, Delaunays Road, Crumpsall, Manchester M8 6RB* Tel 0161-795 4567 or 720 2990

MORGAN, Nicholas John. b 50. K Coll Lon BD71 AKC71 CertEd. St Aug Coll Cant 72. **d** 73 **p** 74. C Wythenshawe Wm Temple Ch *Man* 73-76; C Southam w Stockton *Cov* 76-79; V Brailes from 79; R Sutton under Brailes from 79; RD Shipston from 90. *The Vicarage, Brailes, Banbury, Oxon OX15 5HT* Tel (01608) 685230

MORGAN, Nicola. b 64. Nottm Univ BA86. Linc Th Coll BTh95. **d** 95 **p** 96. C Lillington *Cov* from 95. *34 Lime Avenue, Leamington Spa, Warks CV32 7DF* Tel (01926) 37710

MORGAN, Philip. b 51. Lon Univ BSc75 Univ of Wales (Cardiff) BD78. St Mich Coll Llan 75. **d** 78 **p** 79. C Swansea St Nic *S & B* 78-81; C Morriston 81-83; C Swansea St Mary w H Trin 83-84; USA from 84. *705 Sixth, Box 374, Howe, Indiana 46746, USA*

MORGAN, Canon Philip Brendan. b 35. G&C Coll Cam BA59 MA63. Wells Th Coll 59. **d** 61 **p** 62. C Paddington Ch Ch *Lon* 61-66; C Trunch w Swafield *Nor* 66-68; P-in-c Nor St Steph 68-72; Sacr Nor Cathl 72-74; Can Res and Sub-Dean St Alb *St Alb* 74-81; Hon Can St Alb 81-94; R Bushey 81-94; RD Aldenham 91-94; Can Res and Treas Win Cathl *Win* from 94. *8 The Close, Winchester, Hants SO23 9LS* Tel (01962) 854771

MORGAN, Canon Philip Reginald Strange. b 27. St D Coll Lamp BA51 Keble Coll Ox BA53 MA57. Wells Th Coll 57. **d** 57 **p** 58. C Fleur-de-Lis *Mon* 57-59; C Bassaleg 59-62; CF (TA) 62-74; V Dingestow and Wanastow *Mon* 62-65; V Dingestow and Penrhos 65-66; R Machen and Rudry 66-75; R Machen 75-76; V Caerleon 76-95; Can St Woolos Cathl 84-95; rtd 95. *4 Anthony Drive, Caerleon, Newport NP6 1DS* Tel (01633) 422238

MORGAN, Philip Richard Llewelyn. b 27. Wadh Coll Ox BA50 MA52. St Steph Ho Ox 53. **d** 55 **p** 56. C Warlingham w Chelsham and Farleigh *S'wark* 55-58; Chapl Haileybury Coll Herts 58-73; Hd Master Haileybury Jun Sch Berks 73-87; R The Deverills *Sarum* 87-94; rtd 94; Perm to Offic *Guildf* from 95. *6 Phillips Close, Headley, Bordon, Hants GU35 8LY* Tel (01428) 712194

MORGAN, Canon Reginald Graham. b 25. St D Coll Lamp BA46 LTh48. **d** 48 **p** 49. C Chirk *St As* 48-50; C Llangollen and Trevor 50-55; R Llanwyddelan w Manafon 55-66; V Rhuddlan 66-94; RD St As 78-94; Hon Can St As Cathl 83-89; Can from 89; rtd 94. *Manafon, Plot 64, The Fairlands, Rhuddlan, Rhyl LL18 2SR* Tel (01745) 591036

MORGAN, Reginald Graham Tharle. b 46. St Jo Coll Nottm LTh75. **d** 75 **p** 76. C Oadby *Leic* 76-79; S Africa from 80. *PO Box 112, Greytown, Natal, 3500 South Africa* Tel Greytown (334) 32192

MORGAN, Richard Mervyn. b 50. Wadh Coll Ox BA73 MA75 K Alfred's Coll Win PGCE74. **d** 92 **p** 93. CMS 85-94; Kenya 88-94; Perm to Offic *S'wark* 95-96; R Therfield w Kelshall *St Alb* from 96. *The Rectory, Church Lane, Therfield, Royston, Herts SG8 9QD* Tel (01763) 287364

MORGAN, Richard Thomas. b 70. Peterho Cam BA91. Wycliffe Hall Ox 94. **d** 96 **p** 97. C Bath Twerton-on-Avon *B & W* from 96. *42 High Street, Twerton On Avon, Bath BA2 1DB* Tel (01225) 427966

MORGAN, Robert Chowen. b 40. St Cath Coll Cam BA63 MA. St Chad's Coll Dur 64. **d** 66 **p** 67. C Lancaster St Mary *Blackb* 66-76; Lect Lanc Univ 67-76; Lect Th Ox Univ from 76; Fell and Acting Chapl Linacre Coll Ox from 76; P-in-c Sandford-on-Thames *Ox* from 87. *Lower Farm, Sandford-on-Thames, Oxford OX4 4YR* Tel (01865) 748848 Fax 271650

MORGAN, Canon Robert Harman. b 28. OBE94. Univ of Wales (Cardiff) BA55. Coll of Resurr Mirfield 55. **d** 57 **p** 58. C Penarth w Lavernock *Llan* 57-61; C Caerau w Ely 61-67; V Glan Ely 67-95; Hon Can Llan Cathl from 94; rtd 95; Perm to Offic *Llan* from 95. *Y Felin Wynt, St Davids, Haverfordwest SA62 6QS* Tel (01437) 720130

MORGAN, Robert Hugh. b 49. **d** 91 **p** 92. C Swansea St Pet *S & B* 91-94; V Oxwich w Penmaen and Nicholaston from 94. *The Rectory, Penmaen, Swansea SA3 2HH* Tel (01792) 371241

MORGAN, Roger. b 32. Bris Univ BA59. Tyndale Hall Bris 56. **d** 61 **p** 62. C Chitts Hill St Cuth *Lon* 61-64; R Kingham *Ox* 64-69; R Kingham and Daylesford 69-78; P-in-c Sarsden w Churchill 74-78; V W Hampstead St Cuth *Lon* 78-87; P-in-c Fyfield *Chelmsf* 87-89; R Fyfield and Moreton w Bobbingworth 90-93; P-in-c Willingale w Shellow and Berners Roding 88-93; R Fyfield, Moreton w Bobbingworth etc from 93. *The Rectory, Fyfield, Ongar, Essex CM5 0SD* Tel (01277) 899255

MORGAN, Roger William. b 40. Mert Coll Ox BA62 Cam Univ MA67. Ridley Hall Cam 80. **d** 81 **p** 82. NSM Cambridge St Paul *Ely* 81-84; V Corby St Columba *Pet* 84-90; V Leic H Trin w St Jo *Leic* from 90. *29 Holmfield Road, Leicester LE2 1SE* Tel 0116-270 4986

MORGAN, Canon Samuel. b 07. St D Coll Lamp BA32. **d** 32 **p** 33. C Llandysul *St D* 32-35; Argentina 35-42; V Llanwenog w Llanwnen *St D* 42-64; RD Lampeter 54-64; V Felin-foel 64-77; RD Kidwelly 72-77; Can St D Cathl 72-79; rtd 77. *10 Ty'r Fran Avenue, Llanelli SA15 3LP* Tel (01554) 772977

MORGAN, Simon John. b 58. Univ of Wales (Swansea) BA81 Univ of Wales (Cardiff) BD86 MA94. St Mich Coll Llan 83. **d** 86 **p** 87. C Penarth All SS *Llan* 86-87; C Port Talbot St Theodore 87-89; C Gelligaer 89-91; R Dowlais 91-96; Asst P Peacehaven *Chich* 96; Asst P Telscombe w Piddinghoe and Southease 96; P-in-c E Dean w Friston and Jevington from 96. *The Rectory, East Dean, Eastbourne, E Sussex BN20 0DL* Tel (01323) 423266

MORGAN, Steve Shelley. b 48. Univ of Wales DipTh70. St Mich Coll Llan 67. **d** 71 **p** 72. C Llan w Capel Llanilltern *Llan* 71-74; C Llanharan w Peterston-super-Montem 71-74; C Neath w Llantwit 74-77; TV Merthyr Tydfil and Cyfarthfa 77-91; V Merthyr Tydfil Ch Ch from 91; RD Merthyr Tydfil from 93. *Christchurch Vicarage, Heol S O Davies, Merthyr Tydfil CF48 1DR* Tel (01685) 371995

MORGAN, Thomas John Walford. b 16. Univ of Wales BA37. St D Coll Lamp 37. **d** 39 **p** 40. C Roath St Marg *Llan* 39-42; C Heavitree *Ex* 42-45; C Merton St Mary *S'wark* 45-50; CF 50-71; V Swallowfield *Ox* 71-81; rtd 81. *57 Felinfoel Road, Llanelli SA15 3JQ* Tel (01554) 752303

MORGAN, Verna Ireta. b 42. NE Ord Course. **d** 89 **p** 94. NSM Potternewton *Ripon* 89-92; Par Dn Longsight St Luke *Man* 92-94; C 94-95; P-in-c Gorton St Phil from 95. *St Philip's Rectory, Lavington Grove, Manchester M18 7RS* Tel 0161-231 2201

MORGAN, Canon William Charles Gerwyn. b 30. Univ of Wales (Lamp) BA52. St Mich Coll Llan 52. **d** 56 **p** 57. C Hubberston *St D* 56-62; V Ambleston w St Dogwells 62-68; Miss to Seamen 68-93; V Fishguard w Llanychar *St D* 68-85; V Fishguard w Llanychar and Pontfaen w Morfil etc 85-93; Can St D Cathl 85-93; Chan 91-93; rtd 93. *Wrth y Llan, Pontycleifion, Cardigan SA43 1DW* Tel (01239) 613943

MORGAN, William John. b 38. Selw Coll Cam BA62 MA66. Cuddesdon Coll 62. **d** 65 **p** 66. C Cardiff St Jo *Llan* 65-68; Asst Chapl Univ of Wales (Cardiff) 68-70; Perm to Offic *Lon* 70-73; C Albany Street Ch Ch 73-78; P-in-c E Acton St Dunstan 78-80; V E Acton St Dunstan w St Thos 80-95; V Isleworth All SS from 95; P-in-c St Margarets on Thames from 95. *All Saints' Vicarage, 63 Church Street, Isleworth, Middx TW7 6BE* Tel 0181-560 6662

MORGAN, William Stanley Timothy. b 41. Univ of Wales (Lamp) BA63. Wycliffe Hall Ox 63. **d** 66 **p** 67. C Aberystwyth St Mich *St D* 66-69; V Ambleston w St Dogwells 69-70; V Ambleston, St Dogwells, Walton E and Llysyfran 70-74; V Llan-non 74-80; V Lampeter 80-87; V Lampeter Pont Steffan w Silian from 87. *The Vicarage, Lampeter SA48 7EJ* Tel (01570) 422460

MORGAN-JONES, Christopher John (Chris). b 43. Bris Univ BA66 Chicago Univ MBA68 McMaster Univ Ontario MA69. Cuddesdon Coll 70. **d** 73 **p** 74. C Folkestone St Sav *Cant* 73-76; P-in-c Swalecliffe 76-82; V Addington 82-84; V Addington *S'wark* 85-92; RD Croydon Addington 85-90; V Maidstone All SS and St Phil w Tovil *Cant* from 92. *The Vicarage, Priory Road, Maidstone, Kent ME15 6NL* Tel (01622) 756002

MORGAN-JONES, Richard James. b 46. Em Coll Cam BA68. Ripon Hall Ox 73. **d** 75 **p** 76. C Bromley St Mark *Roch* 75-77; Perm to Offic 77-84. *15 Wendover Road, Bromley BR2 9JU*

MORGANS, Paul Hywel. b 61. LWCMD83. Chich Th Coll 86. **d** 90 **p** 91. C Johnston w Steynton *St D* 90-92; C Caerau w Ely *Llan* 92-95; V Pentre from 95. *The Vicarage, 7 Llewellyn Street, Pentre CF41 7BY* Tel (01443) 433651

MORISON, John Donald. b 34. ALCD60. **d** 61 **p** 62. C Rayleigh *Chelmsf* 61-64; C St Austell *Truro* 64-67; V Meltham Mills *Wakef* 67-71; Youth Chapl *Cov* 71-76; S Africa 76-82; Can Port Elizabeth 80-82; Bardsley Missr 82-86; Lic to Offic *S'wark* 82-86; Dioc Missr *Derby* from 86; V Quarndon from 86. *St Paul's Vicarage, 149 Church Road, Quarndon, Derby DE22 5JA* Tel (01332) 559333

MORLEY, Athelstan John. b 29. Linc Coll Ox BA52 MA56. Ridley Hall Cam. **d** 54 **p** 55. C Surbiton St Matt *S'wark* 54-57; Succ Chelmsf Cathl *Chelmsf* 57-60; R Mistley w Manningtree 60-69; R Hadleigh St Jas 69-94; rtd 94; Hon C Prittlewell *Chelmsf* from 94. *29 Tattersall Gardens, Leigh-on-Sea, Essex SS9 2QS* Tel (01702) 551494

MORLEY, Frank. b 15. Worc Ord Coll 63. **d** 65 **p** 66. C Melksham *Sarum* 65-68; V Overton w Fyfield and E Kennett 68-73; V Urchfont w Stert 74-81; rtd 81; Perm to Offic *Heref* 81-86; Perm to Offic *Worc* 86-91. *5 Barton Lodge, Station Road, Barton under Needwood, Burton-on-Trent, Staffs DE13 8DR* Tel (01283) 716304

MORLEY, Miss Gillian Dorothy. b 21. Greyladies Coll 49. **dss** 70 **d** 87. Lewisham St Swithun *S'wark* 70-82; Sturry w Fordwich and Westbere w Hersden *Cant* 82-87; Perm to Offic from 87. *28 Glen Iris Avenue, Canterbury, Kent CT2 8HP* Tel (01227) 459992

MORLEY, James Walter. b 58. Oak Hill Th Coll BA92 MA94. **d** 96 **p** 97. C Bispham *Blackb* from 96. *Church Villa, All Hallows Road, Blackpool FY2 0AY* Tel (01253) 53648

MORLEY, John. b 43. AKC67 St Deiniol's Hawarden 67. **d** 68 **p** 69. C Newbold on Avon *Cov* 69-73; C Solihull *Birm* 73-77; C-in-c Elmdon Heath CD 76-77; Chapl RAF 77-93; TR Wallingford w Crowmarsh Gifford etc *Ox* from 93; RD

Wallingford from 95. *The Rectory, 22 Castle Street, Wallingford, Oxon OX10 8DW* Tel (01491) 837280

MORLEY, Keith. b 44. St Chad's Coll Dur BA66 DipTh67 Open Univ BSc93. **d** 67 **p** 68. C S Yardley St Mich *Birm* 67-70; C Solihull 70-73; V Shaw Hill 73-77; P-in-c Burton Coggles *Linc* 77-79; P-in-c Boothby Pagnell 77-79; V Lenton w Ingoldsby 77-79; P-in-c Bassingthorpe w Bitchfield 77-79; R Ingoldsby 79-87; RD Beltisloe 84-87; P-in-c Old Dalby and Nether Broughton *Leic* 87-94; RD Framland 88-90. *11 Swallow Close, Quarrington, Sleaford, Lincs NG34 7UU*

MORLEY, Canon Leslie James. b 45. K Coll Lon BD67 AKC67 MTh68. **d** 69 **p** 70. C Birm St Pet *Birm* 69-72; C W Brompton St Mary *Lon* 72; C W Brompton St Mary w St Pet 73-74; Chapl Nottm Univ *S'well* 74-80; Dir of Post-Ord Tr 80-85; Can Res and Vice-Provost S'well Minster 80-85; Hon Can from 85; Chapl Blue Coat Sch Nottm 85-90; R Nottingham St Pet and St Jas *S'well* from 85; AD Nottingham Cen 90-93. *3 King Charles Street, Nottingham NG1 6GB* Tel 0115-947 4891

MORLEY, Peter. b 36. St Jo Coll Nottm 81. **d** 83 **p** 84. C Sheff St Jo *Sheff* 83-87; Chapl Shrewsbury Hosp Sheff 85-87; V Worsbrough Common 87-93; Chapl Mt Vernon Hosp Barnsley 87-93; R Harthill and Thorpe Salvin *Sheff* from 93. *The Rectory, 36 Union Street, Harthill, Sheffield S31 8YH* Tel (01909) 770279

MORLEY, Terence Martin Simon. b 49. SS Hild & Bede Coll Dur CertEd78. St Steph Ho Ox 71. **d** 74 **p** 75. C Kingston upon Hull St Alb *York* 74-76; C Middlesbrough All SS 76-77; Perm to Offic *Dur* 77-78; Hon C Worthing St Andr *Chich* 78-80; C Brighton Ch Ch 80-82; C Hove St Patr 80-82; C Ayr *Glas* 83-86; C Maybole 83-84; P-in-c Coatbridge 86-88; R 88-92; Perm to Offic 92-93; V Plymouth St Jas Ham *Ex* from 93. *St James's Vicarage, Ham Drive, Plymouth PL2 2NJ* Tel (01752) 362485

MORLEY, Trevor. b 39. MPS62 MRSH84 Man Univ BSc62. Ripon Hall Ox 65. **d** 67 **p** 68. C Compton Gifford *Ex* 67-70; Chapl Hammersmith Hosp Lon 70-83; Hon C N Hammersmith St Kath *Lon* 70-83; Chapl Univ Coll Hosp Lon 83-94; Chapl Univ Coll Lon Hosps NHS Trust from 94; Hon Chapl St Luke's Hosp for the Clergy from 89. *University College Hospital, Grafton Way, London WC1E 6AU* Tel 0171-387 9300

MORLEY-BUNKER, John Arthur. b 27. Wells Th Coll 67. **d** 68 **p** 69. C Horfield H Trin *Bris* 68-71; P-in-c Easton All Hallows 71-75; V 75-82; RD Bris City 74-79; V Horfield St Greg 82-93; rtd 93; Perm to Offic *Bris* from 93. *1 Knoll Court, Knoll Hill, Bristol BS9 1QX* Tel 0117-968 5837

MORLING, David Arthur. b 45. CertEd66 Open Univ BA78. S Dios Minl Tr Scheme 83. **d** 85 **p** 86. NSM Parklands St Wilfrid CD *Chich* from 85. *52 Worcester Road, Chichester, W Sussex PO19 4DZ* Tel (01243) 782281

MORPHET, George Thexton. b 12. ACT ThL47. **d** 38 **p** 39. Australia 38-62 and from 68; Miss to Seamen 53-77; rtd 77. *68 Spowers Street, Bribie Island, Queensland, Australia 4507* Tel Gold Coast (75) 408 1635

MORPHY, George David. b 49. Lon Univ BA Birm Univ BEd Warw Univ MA90. WMMTC. **d** 89 **p** 90. NSM Ribbesford w Bewdley and Dowles *Worc* from 89. *41 Hallow Road, Worcester WR2 6BX* Tel (01905) 422007

MORPHY, Michael John. b 43. Newc Univ BSc65 Dur Univ MSc66 QUB PhD73. Ripon Coll Cuddesdon 82. **d** 84 **p** 85. C Halifax *Wakef* 84-86; V Luddenden w Luddenden Foot 86-97; V Corbridge w Halton and Newton Hall *Newc* from 97. *The Vicarage, Greencroft Avenue, Corbridge, Northd NE45 5DW* Tel (01434) 632128

MORRELL, Geoffrey Bernard. b 45. AKC68. **d** 69 **p** 71. C W Leigh CD *Portsm* 69-76; V Shedfield from 76; RD Bishops Waltham 82-88. *The Vicarage, Church Road, Shedfield, Southampton SO32 2HY* Tel (01329) 832162

MORRELL, Mrs Jennifer Mary. b 49. N Ord Course 84. **d** 87 **p** 94. Par Dn Crewe All SS and St Paul *Ches* 87-90; Par Dn Padgate *Liv* 90-94; C 94-95; TV Kirkby from 95. *St Martins House, Peatwood Avenue, Kirkby, Liverpool L32 7PR* Tel 0151-546 2387

MORRELL, Nigel Paul. b 38. S'wark Ord Course 73. **d** 76 **p** 77. C Letchworth St Paul w Willian *St Alb* 76-85; V Farley Hill St Jo 85-95; RD Luton 90-94; V Cardington from 95. *The Vicarage, Cardington, Bedford MK44 3SS* Tel (01234) 838203

MORRELL, Paul Rodney. b 49. SRN70. SW Minl Tr Course 90. **d** 93 **p** 94. NSM Heavitree w Ex St Paul *Ex* from 93. *65 Quarry Park Road, Exeter EX2 5PD* Tel (01392) 431367

MORRELL, Robin Mark George. b 29. Cuddesdon Coll 58. **d** 60 **p** 61. C Petersfield w Sheet *Portsm* 60-63; C-in-c Stockwood CD *Bris* 63-71; Lic to Offic 71-72; R Honiton, Gittisham and Combe Raleigh *Ex* 72-78; Lay Tr Officer *S'wark* 78-81; Asst Chapl HM Pris Brixton 81-85; Past Counsellor from 85; Hon C Hatcham St Cath *S'wark* from 91; rtd 94. *46 Erlanger Road, London SE14 5TG* Tel 0171-252 9346

MORRELL, Mrs Susan Marjorie. b 46. Open Univ BA90. SEITE 93. **d** 96 **p** 97. NSM E Peckham and Nettlestead *Roch* from 96. *7 Pippin Road, East Peckham, Tonbridge, Kent TN12 5BT* Tel (01622) 871150

MORRIS, Alan Ralph Oakden. b 29. Roch Th Coll 59. **d** 61 **p** 62. C Riverhead *Roch* 61-62; C Roch St Pet w St Marg 62-66; C Wrotham 66-74; V Biggin Hill 74-82; R Kingsdown 82-88; V Seal St Pet 88-92; rtd 92; P-in-c Renhold *St Alb* 92-93; Perm to Offic *Roch* from 93. *46 Old Mill Close, Eynsford, Dartford DA4 0BN* Tel (01322) 863153

MORRIS, Albert George. b 15. Tyndale Hall Bris 47. **d** 48 **p** 49. C Dagenham *Chelmsf* 48-51; C Clacton St Paul 51-53; V Clapham Park All SS *S'wark* 53-58; R Beeston next Mileham *Nor* 58-61; Kenya 61-67; C Rowner *Portsm* 67; C-in-c Bridgemary CD 67-80; rtd 81; Perm to Offic *Portsm* from 82. *1 Ashcroft Court, Winton Road, Petersfield, Hants GU32 3HE* Tel (01730) 265190

MORRIS, Canon Alexander Dorner. b 23. Jes Coll Cam BA48 MA53. Linc Th Coll 49. **d** 51 **p** 52. C Wincobank *Sheff* 51-53; C Rotherham 53-54; C-in-c Manor Park CD 54-59; India 59-63; V Bexley St Mary *Roch* 63-71; V Leatherhead *Guildf* 71-89; RD Leatherhead 72-77; Hon Can Guildf Cathl 86-89; rtd 89. *9 Roses Cottages, West Street, Dorking, Surrey RH4 1QL* Tel (01306) 882485

MORRIS, Arthur Ronald. b 17. Jes Coll Ox BA38 MA42. St Steph Ho Ox 38. **d** 40 **p** 41. C Rhosddu *St As* 40-42; C Buckley 42-45; Tanganyika 46-51; N Rhodesia 51-55; V Sneinton St Alb *S'well* 55-59; V Sneinton St Steph 55-59; N Rhodesia 59-62; C Torquay St Martin Barton *Ex* 63-66; V Edmonton St Mich *Lon* 66-71; Australia from 71; rtd 82. *118 The Palms, Melody Court, Warana, Queensland, Australia 4575*

MORRIS, Bernard Lyn. b 28. St Aid Birkenhead 55. **d** 58 **p** 59. C-in-c Hartcliffe St Andr CD *Bris* 58-61; C Bishopston 61-63; R Ardwick St Thos *Man* 63-69; R Aylton w Pixley, Munsley and Putley *Heref* 69-79; P-in-c Tarrington w Stoke Edith 72-77; R 77-79; P-in-c Queen Camel, Marston Magna, W Camel, Rimpton etc *B & W* 79-80; R 80-87; R Queen Camel w W Camel, Corton Denham etc 87-95; rtd 95; Perm to Offic *B & W* from 95. *Canterbury Bells, Ansford Hill, Castle Cary, Somerset BA7 7JL* Tel (01963) 351154

MORRIS, Beti Elin. b 36. CertEd57. Sarum & Wells Th Coll 87. **d** 89 **p** 97. C Llangeitho and Blaenpennal w Betws Leucu etc *St D* 89-92; C-in-c Pencarreg and Llanycrwys 92-97; V from 97. *Hafdir, Llanwnen Road, Lampeter SA48 7JP* Tel (01570) 422385

MORRIS, Brian Michael Charles. b 32. S Dios Minl Tr Scheme 82. **d** 85 **p** 86. NSM Denmead *Portsm* 85-89; C S w N Hayling 89-96; P-in-c Shalfleet from 96. *The Vicarage, Warlands Lane, Shalfleet, Newport, Isle of Wight PO30 4NF* Tel (01983) 78238

MORRIS, Christopher John. b 45. K Coll Lon AKC67 BD68. **d** 68 **p** 69. C W Bromwich All SS *Lich* 68-72; C Porthill 72-74; Min Can Carl Cathl *Carl* 74-77; Ecum Liaison Officer BBC Radio Carl 74-77; Dioc Communications Officer *Carl* 77-83; V Thursby 77-83; Angl Adv Border TV from 82; V Upperby St Jo *Carl* 83-91; P-in-c Lanercost w Kirkcambeck and Walton from 91. *The Vicarage, Lanercost, Brampton, Cumbria CA8 2HQ* Tel (016977) 2478

MORRIS, Christopher Mangan. b 47. Chich Th Coll 71. **d** 73 **p** 74. C Athersley *Wakef* 73-76; C Kippax *Ripon* 76-78; TV Seacroft 78-81; V Oulton w Woodlesford 81-86; V Hawksworth Wood 86-93; V Rawdon *Bradf* from 93. *The Vicarage, Rawdon, Leeds LS19 6QQ* Tel 0113-250 3263

MORRIS, Prof Colin. b 28. FRHistS71 Qu Coll Ox BA48 MA53. Linc Th Coll 51. **d** 53 **p** 54. Chapl Pemb Coll Ox 53-69; Prof Medieval Hist Southn Univ from 69; Lic to Offic *Win* from 69. *53 Cobbett Road, Southampton SO18 1HJ* Tel (01703) 227258

MORRIS, Canon David Edmond. b 27. Univ of Wales (Cardiff) BA55. St D Coll Lamp 55. **d** 57 **p** 58. C Llanfihangel-ar-arth *St D* 57-59; C Ysbyty Ystwyth w Ystradmeurig 59-61; CF 61-81; QHC 78-93; V Penllergaer *S & B* 81-93; RD Llwchwr 86-93; Can Brecon Cathl 90-93; Hon Can from 93; rtd 93; Perm to Offic *St D* from 93. *21 Brynglas Crescent, Llangunnor, Carmarthen SA31 2HT*

MORRIS, David Freestone (Brother Augustine). b 05. Lon Univ 22. **d** 36 **p** 37. OSB from 24; C Taplow *Ox* 36-39; C Beaconsfield 41-43; Prior Nashdom Abbey 45-48; Abbot 48-74; Lic to Offic *Ox* from 54; rtd 74. *Elmore Abbey, Church Lane, Speen, Newbury, Berks RG13 1SA* Tel (01635) 33080

MORRIS, Preb David Meeson. b 35. Trin Coll Ox BA56 MA60. Chich Th Coll 57. **d** 60 **p** 61. C Westmr St Steph w St Jo *Lon* 60-65; Lib Pusey Ho 65-68; Chapl Wadh Coll Ox 67-68; C Sheff Norwood St Leon *Sheff* 68-69; Ind Chapl 68-72; C Brightside St Marg 69-72; R Adderley *Lich* 72-82; V Drayton in Hales 72-82; RD Tutbury 82-95; Chapl Burton Gen Hosp 82-90; P-in-c Burton St Modwen *Lich* 82; V Burton from 82; Preb Lich Cathl from 93; P-in-c Shobnall from 94. *The Vicarage, Rangemore Street, Burton-on-Trent, Staffs DE14 2ED* Tel (01283) 536235

MORRIS, David Michael. b 59. Ox Univ MA84. Sarum & Wells Th Coll 82. **d** 84 **p** 85. C Angell Town St Jo *S'wark* 84-87; C Mitcham SS Pet and Paul 87-90; V Llandygwydd and Cenarth w Cilrhedyn etc *St D* from 90. *The Vicarage, Llechryd, Cardigan SA43 2NE* Tel (01239) 682552

MORRIS, Canon David Pryce. b 39. Univ of Wales (Ban) DipTh62. Kelham Th Coll 55 St Mich Coll Llan 62. **d** 63 **p** 64. C Colwyn Bay *St As* 63-70; R St George 70-76; Dioc Children's Adv 75-87; V Bodelwyddan and St George 76-79; V Connah's Quay 79-95; St As Dioc Adult Lay Tr Team from 88; Ed St As Dioc News from 89; Dioc Info Officer from 90; V Shotton from 95; Hon Can St As Cathl from 96. *The Vicarage, Chester Road East, Shotton, Deeside CH5 1QD* Tel (01244) 812183

MORRIS, Dennis Gordon. b 41. ALCM58 DipTh67. St D Coll Lamp 64. **d** 67 **p** 68. C Neath w Llantwit *Llan* 67-92; V Troedrhiwgarth from 92. *Garth Vicarage, 72 Bridgend Road, Maesteg CF34 0NL* Tel (01656) 732441

MORRIS, Dr Edward. b 42. **d** 72 **p** 73. C Darlington H Trin *Dur* 72-75; Tutor St Steph Ho Ox 75-82; Sen Tutor 79-82; R Shadforth *Dur* 82-86; Chapl Hammersmith Hosp Lon 86-94; Chapl Qu Charlotte's Hosp Lon 86-94; Chapl Hammersmith Hosps NHS Trust from 94. *The Chaplain's Office, Hammersmith Hospital, Du Cane Road, London W12 0HS* Tel 0181-743 2030

MORRIS, Edward Andrew (Andy). b 57. St Jo Coll Nottm 90. **d** 96 **p** 97. C Conisbrough *Sheff* from 96. *130 Old Road, Conisbrough, Doncaster, S Yorkshire DN12 3LR* Tel (01709) 863525

MORRIS, Canon Edwin Alfred. b 32. Wells Th Coll 62. **d** 64 **p** 65. C Wood End *Cov* 64-66; Lic to Offic 66-68; Ind Chapl 68-85; P-in-c Churchover w Willey 74-85; RD Rugby 78-85; R City of Bris 85-97; Hon Can Bris Cathl 89-97; RD Bris City 91-94; rtd 97. *117 Lower Hillmorton Road, Rugby, Warks CV21 3TN* Tel (01788) 546980

MORRIS, Mrs Elizabeth Mary. b 22. Univ Coll Lon BSc50 DipRS82. S'wark Ord Course 82. **dss** 83 **d** 87 **p** 94. Purley St Mark Woodcote *S'wark* 83-87; Hon Par Dn Littleham w Exmouth *Ex* 87-94; Hon C from 94. *7 Strawberry Hill, Lympstone, Exmouth, Devon EX8 5JZ* Tel (01395) 265727

MORRIS, Canon Frank Leo. b 20. St Steph Ho Ox 50. **d** 53 **p** 54. C Bickley *Roch* 53-55; C Letchworth *St Alb* 55-61; V Wareside 61-65; R Wyddial 65-79; P-in-c 79-82; V Gt w Lt Hormead 65-79; RD Buntingford 68-75; V Gt w Lt Hormead, Anstey, Brent Pelham etc 79-82; V Hormead, Wyddial, Anstey, Brent Pelham etc 82-89; Hon Can St Alb 85-89; rtd 89. *9 Manland Avenue, Harpenden, Herts AL5 4RG* Tel (01582) 462348

MORRIS, Geoffrey David. b 43. Fitzw Coll Cam BA65 MA69 Westmr Coll Ox DipEd67. N Ord Course. **d** 82 **p** 83. C Man Clayton St Cross w St Paul *Man* 82-85; V Lower Kersal from 85. *St Aidan's Vicarage, Littleton Road, Salford M7 0TN* Tel 0161-792 3072

MORRIS, George Erskine. b 34. Codrington Coll Barbados Qu Coll Birm 60. **d** 62 **p** 63. C Kidderminster St Jo *Worc* 62-66; Canada from 66. *11203-68 Street NW, Edmonton, Alberta, Canada, T5B 1N6*

MORRIS, Graham Edwin. b 60. Sarum & Wells Th Coll 83. **d** 86 **p** 87. C Coalbrookdale, Iron-Bridge and Lt Wenlock *Heref* 86-90; TV Bilston *Lich* from 90. *8 Cumberland Road, Bilston, Wolverhampton WV14 6LT* Tel (01902) 497794

MORRIS, Canon Gwilym Alun. b 09. CBE64. Qu Coll Birm 38. **d** 39 **p** 40. C Linthorpe *York* 39-42; CF (EC) 42-46; Palestine 46-48; Min N Hull St Mich *York* 48-54; Bahrain 54-65; Hon Can Jerusalem 60-67; Adn E Arabia and the Gulf 62-65; Miss to Seamen 67-70; V Coxwold *York* 70-75; rtd 75; Perm to Offic *York* from 75; Hon Can Bahrain from 88. *c/o Buchannan and White, 23 Baxtergate, Whitby, N Yorkshire YO21 1BW* Tel (01947) 602131

MORRIS, Henry James. b 47. Lon Univ BSc69. Wycliffe Hall Ox MA. **d** 79 **p** 80. C Woodford Wells *Chelmsf* 79-82; C Gt Baddow 82-87; R Siddington w Preston *Glouc* from 87; RD Cirencester from 97. *The Rectory, Preston, Cirencester, Glos GL7 5PR* Tel (01285) 654187

MORRIS, Ian Henry. b 42. Sarum & Wells Th Coll 73. **d** 75 **p** 76. C Lawrence Weston *Bris* 75-78; C St Buryan, St Levan and Sennen *Truro* 78-81; P-in-c Lanteglos by Fowey 81-84; V 84-85; R Lanteglos by Camelford w Advent 85-95; RD Trigg Minor and Bodmin from 93; TR Probus, Ladock and Grampound w Creed and St Erme from 95. *The Sanctuary, Wagg Lane, Probus, Truro, Cornwall TR2 4JX* Tel (01726) 882746

MORRIS, Ian James Patrick. b 43. Dur Univ BA65. Westcott Ho Cam 67. **d** 69 **p** 70. C Wisbech SS Pet and Paul *Ely* 69-72; C Gaywood, Bawsey and Mintlyn *Nor* 72-76; Asst Chapl Basingstoke Distr Hosp 76-78; Chapl Meanwood Park Hosp Gp Leeds 78-88; Chapl Addenbrooke's Hosp Cam 88-94; Chapl Addenbrooke's NHS Trust Cam from 94. *Addenbrooke's Hospital, Hills Road, Cambridge CB2 2QQ* Tel (01223) 217769 or 245151

MORRIS, Ivor Leslie. b 50. Chich Th Coll 82. **d** 84 **p** 85. C Southend *Chelmsf* 84-87; C Somers Town St Mary *Lon* 87-90; P-in-c Chelmsf Ascension *Chelmsf* 90-96; V from 96; P-in-c Chelmsf All SS 92-96. *The Vicarage, 57 Maltese Road, Chelmsford CM1 2PD* Tel (01245) 353914

MORRIS, Miss Jane Elizabeth. b 50. York Univ BA71 CertEd72 MSc80. NE Ord Course CMinlStuds92. **d** 92 **p** 94. NSM York St Mich-le-Belfrey *York* 92-95; C Leeds St Geo *Ripon* from 95. *46 Vesper Lane, Leeds LS5 3NR* Tel 0113-274 2300

MORRIS, Dr Jeremy Nigel. b 60. Ball Coll Ox MA81 DPhil86 Clare Coll Cam BA92. Westcott Ho Cam CTM93. **d** 93 **p** 94. C Battersea St Mary *S'wark* 93-96; Dir Studies Westcott Ho Cam from 96. *1 Short Street, Cambridge CB1 1LB* Tel (01223) 352922

MORRIS, Canon John. b 25. Westcott Ho Cam. **d** 65 **p** 66. C St Alb St Mich *St Alb* 65-68; V Leverstock Green 68-80; TR Chambersbury (Hemel Hempstead) 80-82; V N Mymms 82-90; RD Hatfield 83-88; Hon Can St Alb 89-90; rtd 90; Perm to Offic *Nor* 92-94; P-in-c Barney, Fulmodeston w Croxton, Hindringham etc 94-95; Perm to Offic from 95. *Elba, Croxton Road, Fulmodeston, Fakenham, Norfolk NR21 0NJ* Tel (01328) 878685

MORRIS, John Derrick. b 18. MRCS43 LRCP43. Lon Coll of Div 62. **d** 64 **p** 65. C Cromer *Nor* 64-67; V Broadway *Worc* 67-71; Hon C St Leonards St Leon *Chich* 71-83; rtd 83; Perm to Offic *Chich* from 84. *Heather Bank, June Lane, Midhurst, W Sussex GU29 9EL* Tel (01730) 814084

MORRIS, Dr John Douglas (Johnny). b 37. Cam Univ BA58 Lon Inst of Educn PGCE60 Univ of E Africa MEd67 Ex Univ PhD87. S Dios Minl Tr Scheme 94. **d** 95 **p** 96. NSM Twyford and Owslebury and Morestead *Win* from 95. *Gifford House, St Giles Hill, Winchester, Hants SO23 0JH* Tel (01962) 869720

MORRIS, John Dudley. b 33. Ball Coll Ox BA57 DipTh59 MA61. Wycliffe Hall Ox 58. **d** 60 **p** 61. C Tonbridge SS Pet and Paul *Roch* 60-65; C Enfield Ch Ch Trent Park *Lon* 65-69; Chapl Elstree Sch Woolhampton 70-74; Hd Master Handcross Park Sch W Sussex 74-89; V Rudgwick *Chich* from 89; RD Horsham from 93. *The Vicarage, Rudgwick, Horsham, W Sussex RH12 3DD* Tel (01403) 822127

MORRIS, John Edgar. b 20. Keble Coll Ox BA42 MA50. Wycliffe Hall Ox 42. **d** 44 **p** 45. C Eccleston St Thos *Liv* 44-48; C Warrington H Trin 48-50; V Newton-le-Willows 50-57; R Wavertree H Trin 57-66; V Ainsdale 66-82; R Broadwell, Evenlode, Oddington and Adlestrop *Glouc* 82-88; rtd 89; Perm to Offic *Glouc* from 89. *29 Letch Hill Drive, Bourton-on-the-Water, Cheltenham, Glos GL54 2DQ* Tel (01451) 820571

MORRIS, John Owen. b 56. Nottm Univ BCom82. Linc Th Coll 79. **d** 82 **p** 83. C Morriston *S & B* 82-84; C Kingstone w Clehonger and Eaton Bishop *Heref* 84-87; P-in-c Lugwardine w Bartestree and Weston Beggard 87-92; Chapl RN from 92. *Royal Naval Chaplaincy Service, Room 203, Victory Building, HM Naval Base, Portsmouth PO1 3LS* Tel (01705) 727903 Fax 727112

MORRIS, Canon John Richard. b 23. Or Coll Ox BA48 MA52. Westcott Ho Cam 48. **d** 50 **p** 51. C Birm St Geo *Birm* 50-52; C Kings Norton 52-57; PC Longbridge 57-64; R Sanderstead All SS *S'wark* 64-70; Warden Caius Ho Miss 70-88; V Battersea St Mary 70-88; Hon Can S'wark Cathl 76-88; RD Battersea 76-81; Hon C Battersea St Mary-le-Park 76-79; Hon C Battersea Park All SS 84-88; rtd 88; Master Abp Holgate Hosp Hemsworth from 88. *Archbishop Holgate Hospital, Robin Lane, Hemsworth, Pontefract, W Yorkshire WF9 4PP* Tel (01977) 610434

MORRIS, Kenneth Owen. b 12. Univ of Wales BA34. St Mich Coll Llan 35. **d** 37 **p** 38. C Rhosymedre *St As* 37-46; CF 39-46; V Raveningham *Nor* 46-54; V Hales w Heckingham 48-54; R Benington *St Alb* 54-59; P-in-c Aston 54-59; V Aston w Benington 59-60; Lic to Offic 60-77; rtd 77. *20 Middle Mead, Hook, Basingstoke, Hants RG27 9NX* Tel (01256) 762228

MORRIS, Kevin John. b 63. Univ of Wales (Ban) BMus84. Westcott Ho Cam 85. **d** 88 **p** 89. C Roath St Marg *Llan* 88-91; C Holborn St Alb w Saffron Hill St Pet *Lon* 91-96; V Bedford Park from 96. *St Michael's Vicarage, Priory Gardens, London W4 1TT* Tel 0181-994 1380

MORRIS, Leslie Heber. b 26. Ox Univ MA47. Qu Coll Birm 83. **d** 84 **p** 93. NSM W Leigh *Portsm* 84-85; NSM Warblington and Emsworth from 93. *3 Park Crescent, Emsworth, Hants PO10 7NT* Tel (01243) 373389

MORRIS, Sister Lillian Rosina. b 29. **dss** 70 **d** 87. CSA from 68; Mother Superior 82-94; Sherston Magna w Easton Grey *Bris* 71-73; Notting Hill All SS w St Columb *Lon* 74-82. *St Andrew's House, 2 Tavistock Road, London W11 1BA* Tel 0171-229 2662

MORRIS, Ms Margaret Anne. b 61. Man Univ BA82 MA91. Nor Ord Course 94. **d** 96 **p** 97. C Bury St Pet *Man* from 96. *424 Manchester Road, Bury, Lancs BL9 9NS* Tel 0161-761 7605

MORRIS, Canon Margaret Jane. EMMTC 86. **d** 89 **p** 94. NSM Quorndon *Leic* 89-96; Chapl to People affected by AIDS/HIV from 94; NSM Loughborough All SS w H Trin from 96; Hon Can Leic Cathl from 97. *10 Toller Road, Quorn, Loughborough, Leics LE12 8AH* Tel (01509) 412092

MORRIS, Canon Martin Geoffrey Roger. b 41. Trin Coll Cam BA63 MA67. St D Coll Lamp 63. **d** 66 **p** 67. C Newport St Paul *Mon* 66-72; R Lamp Velfrey *St D* 72-74; R Lamp Velfrey and Llanddewi Velfrey from 74; RD St Clears from 83; Can St D Cathl from 92. *The Rectory, Lampeter Velfrey, Narberth SA67 8UH* Tel (01834) 831241

MORRIS, Ms Mary. b 27. Birm Univ BA49 CertEd50 MA56. **dss** 68 **d** 87 **p** 94. Kinver *Lich* 83-87; Hon Par Dn Kinver and Enville 87-94; Hon C from 94. *Lyndhurst, Dunsley Road, Kinver, Stourbridge, W Midlands DY7 6LN* Tel (01384) 877245

MORRIS, Michael Alan. b 46. Jes Coll Cam BA70 MA74. Coll of Resurr Mirfield 79. **d** 81 **p** 82. C Leamington Priors All SS *Cov* 81-83; C Milton *Portsm* 83-88; R Petworth *Chich* 88-90; R Egdean 88-90; Chapl St Pet Hosp Chertsey 90-95; Hon C Thorpe *Guildf* 90-95; P-in-c Harbledown *Cant* from 95; Chapl St Nic Hosp Cant from 95. *The Rectory, Summer Hill, Harbledown, Canterbury, Kent CT2 8NW* Tel (01227) 464117

MORRIS, Norman Foster Maxwell. b 46. Ex Univ BA68 MA72 Leic Univ PGCE69 K Coll Lon MTh85 Univ of Wales (Cardiff) MA91. S'wark Ord Course 75. **d** 78 **p** 79. C Hackbridge and N Beddington *S'wark* 78-81; Chapl Tonbridge Sch 81-85; Chapl

Mon Sch from 85; Lic to Offic *Mon* from 87; Asst Warden Jones Almshouses Mon from 89. *The Chaplain's House, The Burgage, Old Dixton Road, Monmouth NP5 3DP* Tel (01600) 713506

MORRIS, Paul David. b 56. St Jo Coll Nottm BTh79. **d** 80 **p** 81. C Billericay and Lt Burstead *Chelmsf* 80-84; C Luton Lewsey St Hugh *St Alb* 84-89; Bp's Adv on Evang *S'well* from 89. *39 Davies Road, Nottingham NG2 5JE* Tel 0115-981 1311

MORRIS, Peter. b 45. Leeds Univ CertEd66. Tyndale Hall Bris 68. **d** 71 **p** 72. C Southport SS Simon and Jude *Liv* 71-74; Min-in-c Ch Ch Netherley LEP 74-76; V Bryn 76-91; R Redenhall, Harleston, Wortwell and Needham *Nor* from 91. *The Rectory, 10 Swan Lane, Harleston, Norfolk IP20 9AN* Tel (01379) 852068

MORRIS, Canon Peter Arthur William. b 23. Bps' Coll Cheshunt 57. **d** 58 **p** 59. C Croxley Green All SS *St Alb* 58-62; V Sawbridgeworth 62-74; V S Gillingham *Roch* 74-79; Warden Pleshey Retreat Ho 79-85; P-in-c Pleshey *Chelmsf* 79-85; Hon Can Chelmsf Cathl 81-85; P-in-c Rumburgh w S Elmham w the Ilketshalls *St E* 85-89; rtd 89; Perm to Offic *St E* from 90. *The Cottage on the Common, Westleton, Saxmundham, Suffolk IP17 3AZ* Tel (01728) 73788

MORRIS, Canon Peter Michael Keighley. b 27. St Jo Coll Ox BA49 MA56. Westcott Ho Cam 51. **d** 54 **p** 55. C Bedwellty *Mon* 54-55; Lic to Offic *St D* 55-85; Lect Univ of Wales (Lamp) 55-69; Sen Lect 69-90; Dean Faculty of Th 77-81; Can St D Cathl 85-90; rtd 90; Can and Treas St D Cathl *St D* from 92. *Hafdir, Llanwnen Road, Lampeter SA48 7JP* Tel (01570) 422385

MORRIS, Philip Gregory. b 50. Leeds Univ BA71 MPhil74. Coll of Resurr Mirfield 71. **d** 73 **p** 74. C Aberdare St Jo *Llan* 74-77; C Neath w Llantwit 77-80; V Cymmer and Porth 80-88; Dioc Missr from 88; TV Llantwit Major from 88. *60 Ham Lane South, Llantwit Major CF6 9RN* Tel (01446) 793770 Fax as telephone

MORRIS, Raymond. b 48. Open Univ HND70 BA88. N Ord Course 80. **d** 83 **p** 84. C Tonge w Alkrington *Man* 83-86; R Blackley St Paul 86-91; V Heyside from 91. *St Mark's Vicarage, Heyside, Royton, Oldham OL2 6LS* Tel (01706) 844502

MORRIS, Raymond Arthur (Ray). b 42. Trin Coll Ox BA64 MA66 Lon Univ LLB71 CQSW72. Clifton Th Coll 66. **d** 67 **p** 91. C Greenstead juxta Colchester *Chelmsf* 67-68; Perm to Offic *York* 69-91; NSM Linthorpe from 91. *3 Medina Gardens, Middlesbrough, Cleveland TS5 8BN* Tel (01642) 593726

MORRIS, Raymond John Walton. b 08. OBE69. Em Coll Cam BA33 MA37. Lon Coll of Div 33. **d** 34 **p** 35. C E Twickenham St Steph *Lon* 34-37; C Bradf Cathl *Bradf* 37-40; V Plymouth Em *Ex* 40-45; V E Twickenham St Steph *Lon* 45-56; Chapl Br Emb Ch Paris *Eur* 56-69; RD France 56-69; V Brompton H Trin *Lon* 69-75; rtd 75. *12 St Edward's Court, Shaftesbury, Dorset SP7 8LZ* Tel (01747) 851950

MORRIS, Reginald Brian. b 31. St Mich Coll Llan 56. **d** 59 **p** 60. C St Jo in Bedwardine *Worc* 59-61; P-in-c Tolladine 61-62; CF 62-78; V Cheswardine *Lich* 78-84; V Hales 78-84; Perm to Offic 84-86; C Cen Telford 86-89; rtd 89; Perm to Offic *Heref* from 90. *Woodside Cottage, School Lane, Prees, Whitchurch, Shropshire SY13 2BU* Tel (01948) 840090

MORRIS, Richard Samuel. b 10. TCD BA35 MA39. Edgehill Th Coll Belf 31. **d** 58 **p** 59. C Belfast St Donard *D & D* 58-60; C Dundela 60-62; I Aghalee 62-64; I Magheradroll 64-69; I Kilsaran w Drumcar, Dunleer and Dunany *Arm* 69-75; rtd 75. *20 Kerrington Court, 119 Marlborough Park South, Belfast BT9 6HN* Tel (01232) 662261

MORRIS, Canon Robert John. b 45. Leeds Univ BA67. Coll of Resurr Mirfield 74. **d** 76 **p** 77. C Beeston Hill St Luke *Ripon* 76; C Holbeck 76-78; C Moseley St Mary *Birm* 78-83; P-in-c Handsworth St Jas 83-88; V from 88; P-in-c Handsworth St Mich 86-87; RD Handsworth from 92; Hon Can Birm Cathl from 97. *St James's Vicarage, Austin Road, Birmingham B21 8NU* Tel 0121-554 4151

MORRIS, Robert Lee. b 47. W Virginia Univ BA69. Gen Th Sem (NY) MDiv73. **d** 73 **p** 74. USA 73-74 and from 84; Community of Celebration 74-94; P-in-c Cumbrae (or Millport) *Arg* 75-76 and 79-84. *All Saints Church, 3577 McClure Avenue, Pittsburgh, Pennsylvania, USA*

MORRIS, Canon Robin Edward. b 32. St Jo Coll Ox BA55 MA60. Westcott Ho Cam 55. **d** 57 **p** 58. C Halliwell St Thos *Man* 57-61; V Castleton Moor 61-71; V Stalybridge 71-80; R Heswall *Ches* 80-97; Hon Can Ches Cathl 91-97; RD Wirral N 93-97; rtd 97. *122 Kiln Lane, Milnrow, Rochdale, Lancs OL16 3HA* Tel (01706) 42846

MORRIS, Roger Anthony Brett. b 68. ARCS89 Imp Coll Lon BSc89 Trin Coll Cam BA92. Ridley Hall Cam CTM93. **d** 93 **p** 94. C Northleach w Hampnett and Farmington *Glouc* 93-96; C Cold Aston w Notgrove and Turkdean 93-96; P-in-c Sevenhampton w Charlton Abbotts and Hawling etc from 96; P-in-c Dowdeswell and Andoversford w the Shiptons etc from 96. *The Rectory, Shipton Oliffe, Cheltenham, Glos GL54 4HU* Tel (01242) 820230

MORRIS, Stanley James. b 35. Keble Coll Ox BA58 MA63. Chich Th Coll 59. **d** 61 **p** 62. C Tunstall Ch Ch *Lich* 61-64; C W Bromwich All SS 64-67; V Wilnecote 67-88; V Alrewas from 88; V Wychnor from 88. *The Vicarage, Alrewas, Burton-on-Trent, Staffs DE13 7BT* Tel (01283) 790486

MORRIS, Stephen Bryan. b 54. Linc Th Coll 88. **d** 90 **p** 91. C Glouc St Geo w Whaddon *Glouc* 90-94; C Glouc St Mary de Crypt w St Jo and Ch Ch 94-95; C Glouc St Mary de Crypt w St Jo, Ch Ch etc from 95; Chapl to the Deaf from 94. *2 High View, Hempsted, Gloucester GL2 5LN* Tel (01452) 416178

MORRIS, Stephen Francis. b 52. St Jo Coll Nottm BTh79. **d** 79 **p** 80. C N Hinksey *Ox* 79-82; C Leic H Apostles *Leic* 82-85; TV Shenley and Loughton *Ox* 85-88; TV Watling Valley 88-95; V Chatham St Wm *Roch* from 95. *The Vicarage, 18 Marion Close, Chatham, Kent ME5 9QA* Tel (01634) 861975

MORRIS, The Very Revd Stuart Collard. b 43. AKC66. St Boniface Warminster 66. **d** 67 **p** 68. C Hanham *Bris* 67-71; C Whitchurch 71-74; P-in-c Wapley w Codrington and Dodington 74-77; P-in-c Westerleigh 74-77; P-in-c Holdgate w Tugford *Heref* 77-82; P-in-c Abdon w Clee St Margaret 77-82; R Diddlebury w Bouldon and Munslow 77-82; P-in-c Sotterley, Willingham, Shadingfield, Ellough etc *St E* 82-87; RD Beccles and S Elmham 83-94; P-in-c Westhall w Brampton and Stoven 86-88; P-in-c Flixton w Homersfield and S Elmham 86-92; Hon Can St E Cathl from 87; V Bungay H Trin w St Mary 87-94; P-in-c Hadleigh w Layham and Shelley 94-96; R Hadleigh from 96; Dean Bocking from 94; RD Hadleigh from 94. *The Deanery, Church Street, Hadleigh, Ipswich IP7 5DT* Tel (01473) 822218

MORRIS, Canon Thomas Gordon. b 25. CertEd48. St Mich Coll Llan 80. **d** 83 **p** 85. NSM Morriston *S & B* 83-86; C Caereithin 86-87; P-in-c 87-88; V 88-95; rtd 95; Hon Can Brecon Cathl *S & B* from 96. *5 The Close, Llangyfelach, Swansea SA5 7JL* Tel (01792) 793212

MORRIS, The Very Revd Timothy David. b 48. Lon Univ BSc69. Trin Coll Bris DipTh75. **d** 75 **p** 76. C Edin St Thos *Edin* 75-77; R Edin St Jas 77-83; R Troon *Glas* 83-85; R Galashiels *Edin* from 85; Dean Edin from 92. *The Rectory, Parsonage Road, Galashiels, Selkirkshire TD1 3HS* Tel (01896) 753118

MORRIS, Mrs Valerie Ruth. b 46. St Hugh's Coll Ox BA68 MA72. Qu Coll Birm 76. **dss** 78 **d** 87. Burton *Lich* 82-87; Par Dn 87-90; Hon Par Dn from 90. *The Vicarage, Rangemore Street, Burton-on-Trent, Staffs DE14 2ED* Tel (01283) 536235

MORRIS, William Humphrey Francis. b 29. Univ of Wales BA54 MA72 Birm Univ DipTh58 Trin Coll Cam BA62 MA66 Man Univ MEd76 Trin Coll Cam PhD75 Man Univ PhD80 Ox Univ DPhil85 DD88 FRAS84 FInstP92. Qu Coll Birm 56. **d** 58 **p** 59. C Prestbury *Ches* 58-60; C Neston 60-65; V Sandbach Heath 65-68; Lic to Offic from 69; rtd 84; Lic to Offic *Lich* from 93. *Stonyflats Farm, Smallwood, Sandbach, Cheshire CW11 2XH* Tel (01477) 500354

MORRIS, William James. b 23. St Deiniol's Hawarden 72. **d** 73 **p** 74. NSM Brecon Adnry 73-78; NSM Crickhowell w Cwmdu and Tretower *S & B* 78-93. *The School House, Cwmdu, Crickhowell NP8 1RU* Tel (01874) 730355

MORRIS, William Richard Price. b 23. FCollP82. Glouc Sch of Min. **d** 88 **p** 89. Hon C Bussage *Glouc* 88-90; Perm to Offic 90-91; Hon C France Lynch 91; Hon C Chalford and France Lynch 91-93; rtd 93; Perm to Offic *Glouc* from 93. *Langendum House, Burleigh View, Bussage, Stroud, Glos GL6 8DD* Tel (01453) 886382

MORRISON, Alexander Grant (Alex). b 37. St Fran Coll Brisbane ThL ACT St Columb's Hall Wangaratta. **d** 66 **p** 67. Australia 66-82; C Hayes St Mary *Lon* 83-84; R Black Notley *Chelmsf* from 84. *The Rectory, 71 Witham Road, Black Notley, Braintree, Essex CM7 8LJ* Tel (01376) 349619

MORRISON, Andrew Leslie. b 11. TD53. Pemb Coll Ox BA33 MA37. Westcott Ho Cam 33. **d** 35 **p** 36. C S Westoe *Dur* 35-38; V Castleside 38-42; CF (TA) 39-56; R Branston *Linc* 46-49; V Gateshead Ch Ch *Dur* 49-55; Chapl Bensham Hosp Gateshead 50-55; R Fenny Compton and Wormleighton *Cov* 55-64; RD Dassett Magna 59-64; V Bury and Houghton *Chich* 64-76; rtd 76; Perm to Offic *Chich* from 76. *14 Guildford Place, Chichester, W Sussex PO19 4DU* Tel (01243) 784310

MORRISON, Barbara Anne. b 29. St Andr Univ BSc50. **d** 95 **p** 96. NSM Eorrapaidh *Arg* from 95. *46 Upper Coll, Back, Lewis HS2 0LQ* Tel (01851) 820559 Fax as telephone

MORRISON, Barry John. b 44. Pemb Coll Cam BA66 MA70. ALCD69. **d** 69 **p** 70. C Stoke Bishop *Bris* 69-72; C Edgware *Lon* 72-76; Chapl Poly Cen Lon 76-83; Hon C Langham Place All So 76-83; P-in-c W Hampstead St Luke 83-88; V from 88; Chapl Westf Coll 84-92. *St Luke's Vicarage, 12 Kidderpore Avenue, London NW3 7SU* Tel 0171-794 2634

MORRISON, Iain Edward. b 36. St Steph Ho Ox 76. **d** 78 **p** 79. C Brighton St Aug and St Sav *Chich* 78-81; C Felpham w Middleton 81-83; P-in-c Barnham and Eastergate 83-85; R Aldingbourne, Barnham and Eastergate 85-91; V Jarvis Brook from 91. *The Vicarage, Tubwell Lane, Jarvis Brook, Crowborough, E Sussex TN6 3RH* Tel (01892) 652639

MORRISON, James Wilson Rennie (Jimmy). b 42. Aber Univ MA65. Linc Th Coll 76. **d** 78 **p** 79. C Whitley Ch Ch *Ox* 78-81; R Burghfield 81-87; CF 87-97; P-in-c Burghill *Heref* from 97; P-in-c Stretton Sugwas from 97. *The Vicarage, Burghill, Hereford HR4 7SG* Tel (01432) 760246

MORRISON, The Ven John Anthony. b 38. Jes Coll Cam BA60 MA64 Linc Coll Ox MA68. Chich Th Coll 61. **d** 64 **p** 65. C Birm St Pet *Birm* 64-68; C Ox St Mich *Ox* 68-71; Chapl Linc Coll Ox 68-74; C Ox St Mich w St Martin and All SS *Ox* 71-74; V Basildon 74-82; RD Bradfield 78-82; V Aylesbury 82-89; RD

Aylesbury 85-89; TR Aylesbury w Bierton and Hulcott 89-90; Adn Buckingham from 90; P-in-c Princes Risborough w Ilmer 96-97. *60 Wendover Road, Aylesbury, Bucks HP21 9LW* Tel (01296) 23269 Fax 397324

MORRISON, Richard James. b 55. Sarum & Wells Th Coll 87. **d** 89 **p** 90. C Boston *Linc* 89-93; P-in-c Digby from 93. *The Vicarage, 3 Beck Street, Digby, Lincoln LN4 3NE* Tel (01526) 321099

MORRISON, Robin Victor Adair. b 45. Nottm Univ BA67. Bucharest Th Inst 67 Ripon Hall Ox 68. **d** 70 **p** 71. C Hackney St Jo *Lon* 70-73; Chapl Newc Univ *Newc* 73-76; P-in-c Teversal *S'well* 76-78; Chapl Sutton Cen 76-78; Asst Hd Deans Community Sch Livingston *Edin* 78-80; R Edin St Columba 80-81; Chapl Birm Univ *Birm* 81-88; Prin Soc Resp Officer *Derby* 88-96; TV Southampton (City Cen) *Win* from 96. *22 Gordon Avenue, Southampton SO14 6WD* Tel (01703) 584301

MORRISON, Walter John Raymond (Ray). b 30. Jes Coll Cam BA55 MA58. Westcott Ho Cam 55. **d** 57 **p** 58. C Dalston St Mark w St Bart *Lon* 57-60; C Totteridge *St Alb* 60-63; V Letchworth St Paul 63-71; RD Hitchin 70-71; R Ludlow *Heref* 72-83; RD Ludlow 78-83; Preb Heref Cathl 78-83; P-in-c Ludlow, Ludford, Ashford Carbonell etc 80-83; Chapl St Thos Hosp Lon 83-86; Chapl Eastbourne Distr Gen Hosp 86-95; rtd 95. *190 Farleigh Road, Pershore, Worcs WR10 1LY* Tel (01386) 556542

MORRISON-WELLS, Canon John Frederick Pritchard. b 42. Univ of Wales (Lamp) BA65. Coll of Resurr Mirfield 65. **d** 67 **p** 68. C Bartley Green *Birm* 67-70; C Handsworth St Andr 70-73; V Perry Barr 73-80; RD Bordesley 80-90; V Birm St Aid Small Heath 80-92; P-in-c Small Heath St Greg 83-85 and 89-92; Hon Can Birm Cathl 83-92; P-in-c Bordesley St Oswald 91-92; V Ox St Giles and SS Phil and Jas w St Marg *Ox* 92-97; P-in-c Monk Bretton *Wakef* from 97. *St Paul's Vicarage, Monk Bretton, Barnsley, S Yorkshire S71 2HQ* Tel (01226) 203159

MORROW, David. b 63. NUU BSc86 TCD BTh89. CITC 86. **d** 89 **p** 90. C Portadown St Mark *Arm* 89-91; C Ballymena w Ballyclug *Conn* 91-94; I Tempo and Clabby *Clogh* from 94. *The Rectory, Clabby, Fivemiletown, Co Tyrone BT75 0RD* Tel (01365) 521697

MORROW, Canon Edward Sidney (Ed). b 34. Qu Coll Birm 73. **d** 74 **p** 75. Namibia 75-78 and 79-87 and 89-90; C Truro St Paul *Truro* 78-79; Chapl to Namibians in Eur 87-89; C W Hackney St Barn *Lon* 87-89; Hon Can Windhoek from 87; V Stamford Hill St Thos *Lon* from 90. *The Vicarage, 37 Clapton Common, London E5 9AA* Tel 0181-806 1463

MORROW, Canon Henry Hugh (Harry). b 26. TCD BA49 MA67 Flinders Univ Aus BSocAdmin76. TCD Div Sch Div Test49. **d** 49 **p** 50. C Dublin St Thos *D & G* 49-53; I Rathmolyon *M & K* 53-58; I Killoughter *K, E & A* 58-63; C Portadown St Columba *Arm* 63-65; I Ballinderry w Tamlaght 65-70; Australia from 70; Can Adelaide from 84. *5 Allendale Grove, Stony Fell, S Australia 5066* Tel Adelaide (8) 332 5890

MORROW, Joseph John. b 54. JP87. Edin Univ BD79. NY Th Sem DMin87 Edin Th Coll 76. **d** 79 **p** 80. Chapl St Paul's Cathl Dundee *Bre* 79-82; P-in-c Dundee St Martin 82-85; R 85-90; P-in-c Dundee St Jo from 85. *Braidwood, Strathmore Road, Glamis, Forfar, Angus DD8 1RX* Tel (01307) 840582 Fax 451424

MORSE, Mrs Elisabeth Ann. b 51. New Hall Cam MA73 Qu Eliz Coll Lon MSc74. S'wark Ord Course 91. **d** 94 **p** 95. C Wimbledon *S'wark* from 94. *9 Thornton Road, London SW19 4NE* Tel 0181-946 4494

MORSE, Harry Arthur Carminowe. b 59. St Jo Coll Dur BA81 SS Paul & Mary Coll Cheltenham PGCE85. Oak Hill Th Coll BA91. **d** 91 **p** 92. C Summerfield *Birm* 91-92; C Hamstead St Bernard 92-96; C Downend *Bris* from 96. *8 Farm Court, Bristol BS16 6DF* Tel 0117-956 0847

MORSHEAD, Ivo Francis Trelawny. b 27. ACA52 FCA63. Cuddesdon Coll 61. **d** 63 **p** 64. C Bris St Mary Redcliffe w Temple etc *Bris* 63-68; C Wimbledon *S'wark* 68-73; V Elham *Cant* 73-78; V Whitchurch *Ex* 78-91; rtd 91. *28 Edge Street, London W8 7PN* Tel 0171-727 5975

MORSON, Mrs Dorothy Mary. b 29. Linc Th Coll 71. **d** 87. Par Dn Cen Telford *Lich* 87-89; rtd 89; Perm to Offic *Lich* from 89. *Ashleigh, Hunter Street, Shrewsbury SY3 8QN* Tel (01743) 369225

MORSON, Mrs Eleanor. b 42. CA Tr Coll 63. **d** 95 **p** 96. CA from 65; NSM Kirkwall *Ab* from 96. *The Rectory, Dundas Crescent, Kirkwall, Orkney KW15 1JQ* Tel (01856) 872024

MORSON, John. b 41. **d** 88 **p** 92. NSM Eyemouth *Edin* 88-92; NSM Duns 88-89; CF 89-92; R Stromness *Ab* from 92; R Kirkwall from 92. *The Rectory, Dundas Crescent, Kirkwall, Orkney KW15 1JQ* Tel (01856) 872024

MORT, Alister. b 52. BSc BA. Oak Hill Th Coll. **d** 82 **p** 83. C Cheadle Hulme St Andr *Ches* 82-85; C Rodbourne Cheney *Bris* 86-87; TV 87-90; V New Milverton *Cov* from 90. *2 St Mark's Road, Leamington Spa, Warks CV32 6DL* Tel (01926) 421004

MORT, Ivan Laurence (Laurie). b 61. Nottm Univ BTh87. Linc Th Coll 84. **d** 87 **p** 88. C Aston cum Aughton and Ulley *Sheff* 87-90; C Greenstead juxta Colchester *Chelmsf* 90-94; Chapl Toulouse *Eur* from 94. *1 rue Pasteur, 31700 Cornebarrieu, Toulouse, France* Tel France (33) 61 85 17 67

MORT, Marian. **d** 97. NSM Swanmore St Barn *Portsm* from 97. *Rivendell, High Street, Shirrell Heath, Southampton SO32 2JN* Tel (01329) 832178

MORTER, Ian Charles. b 54. AKC77. Coll of Resurr Mirfield 77. **d** 78 **p** 79. C Colchester St Jas, All SS, St Nic and St Runwald *Chelmsf* 78-82; C Brixham w Churston Ferrers *Ex* 82-83; TV 84-86; TV Brixham w Churston Ferrers and Kingswear 86; TV Sidmouth, Woolbrook and Salcombe Regis 86-91; TV Sidmouth, Woolbrook, Salcombe Regis, Sidbury etc 91-95; P-in-c Exminster and Kenn from 95. *The Rectory, Milbury Lane, Exminster, Exeter EX6 8AD* Tel (01392) 824283

MORTIBOYS, John William. b 45. K Coll Lon BD69 AKC69. Sarum Th Coll 71. **d** 71 **p** 72. C Reading All SS *Ox* 71-95; Hon Assoc P Portsea St Alb *Portsm* from 97. *13 Oyster Street, Portsmouth PO1 2HZ* Tel (01705) 756676

MORTIMER, Anthony John. b 42. Sarum & Wells Th Coll 68. **d** 71 **p** 72. C Heref St Martin *Heref* 71-79; V Kingstone 79-85; P-in-c Clehonger 80-85; P-in-c Eaton Bishop 80-85; TR Pinhoe and Broadclyst *Ex* from 85. *The Rectory, 9 Church Hill, Pinhoe, Exeter EX4 9ER* Tel (01392) 67541

MORTIMER, Charles Philip. b 38. Linc Th Coll 68. **d** 70 **p** 71. C Penistone w Midhope *Wakef* 70-74; V Luddenden 74-77; P-in-c Luddenden Foot 74-77; Chapl RAF 77-91; Asst Chapl-in-Chief RAF 91-93; V Staincliffe *Wakef* from 93. *The Vicarage, Staincliffe Hall Road, Batley, W Yorkshire WF17 7QX* Tel (01924) 473343

MORTIMER, The Very Revd Hugh Sterling. b 23. TCD BA44 MA53. **d** 46 **p** 47. C Finaghy *Conn* 46-49; Dean's V Belf Cathl 49-53; V Choral Belf Cathl 53-55; I Tartaraghan *Arm* 55-61; Hon VC 57-85; I Magherafelt 61-66; I Arm St Mark 66-83; Can Arm Cathl 67-72; Treas 72-73; Chan 73-75; Prec 75-83; Dean Elphin and Ardagh *K, E & A* 83-91; I Sligo w Knocknarea and Rosses Pt 83-91; rtd 91; Perm to Offic *Conn* from 91. *95 Sharman Road, Belfast BT9 5HE* Tel (01232) 669184

MORTIMER, Jonathan Michael. b 60. Bris Univ BA83. Oak Hill Th Coll BA92. **d** 92 **p** 93. C Rugby St Matt *Cov* 92-96; C Southgate *Chich* from 96. *1 Wainwrights, Crawley, W Sussex RH10 6TA* Tel (01293) 551217

MORTIMER, Lawrence George. b 45. St Edm Hall Ox BA67 MA71 St Chad's Coll Dur DipTh68. **d** 70 **p** 71. C Rugby St Andr *Cov* 70-75; V Styvechale 75-89; Dioc Broadcasting Officer 80-89; Dioc Communications Officer 89-95; P-in-c Wootton Wawen from 95. *The Vicarage, Wootton Wawen, Solihull, W Midlands B95 6BD* Tel (01564) 792659 E-mail 101506.2364 @compuserve.com

MORTIMER, William Raymond. b 31. GradIEE58 AMIEE66. St Deiniol's Hawarden 68. **d** 69 **p** 70. C Flint *St As* 69-71; Lic to Offic 72-73; V Llanwddyn and Llanfihangel and Llwydiarth 73-85; RD Llanfyllin 83-84; R Llanrwst and Llanddoget and Capel Garmon 85-96; rtd 96. *1 Coed Masarn, Woodlands Estate, Abergele LL22 7EE*

MORTIMORE, David Jack. b 42. Master Mariner 69. St Mich Coll Llan. **d** 91 **p** 92. C Pembroke St Mary and St Mich *St D* 91-92; C Bargoed and Deri w Brithdir *Llan* 92-97. *6 Heol yr Gaer, The Knap, Barry CF62 6UH* Tel (01446) 421560

MORTIMORE, Robert Edward. b 39. Kelham Th Coll 61 Wells Th Coll 66. **d** 69 **p** 70. C Byfleet *Guildf* 69-72; New Zealand from 72. *25 St Judes Street, Avondale, Auckland 1007, New Zealand* Tel Auckland (9) 828 7520

MORTON, Alan McNeile. b 28. Lon Univ BD49 AKC51 MTh68 BA78. St Boniface Warminster. **d** 52 **p** 53. C Egham Hythe *Guildf* 52-55; Bp's Dom Chapl *St E* 55-58; Dioc Youth Officer 56-58; C Ipswich St Mary Stoke 58-59; V Ipswich St Fran 59-64; Perm to Offic *Ely* 68-69; Chapl Reading Sch 69-78 and 83-88; Hd Master St Sebastian's Sch Wokingham 78-83; rtd 93. *8 Blenheim Drive, Oxford OX2 8DG* Tel (01865) 56371

MORTON, Albert George. b 34. Saskatchewan Univ BA61 McGill Univ Montreal MA73. Em Coll Saskatoon 56. **d** 61 **p** 61. Canada 61-65; C Stanford-le-Hope *Chelmsf* 66-69; V Linc St Geo Swallowbeck *Linc* 69-82; R Lt Munden w Sacombe *St Alb* 82-89; R The Mundens w Sacombe 89-96; rtd 96. *10 Church Green, Bishop's Caundle, Sherborne, Dorset DT9 5NN* Tel (01963) 23383

MORTON, Andrew Edward. b 51. Lon Univ BA72 BD74 AKC74 Univ of Wales (Cardiff) MPhil93. St Aug Coll Cant 75. **d** 76 **p** 77. C Feltham *Lon* 76-79; C Pontlottyn w Fochriw *Llan* 79-81; V Ferndale w Maerdy 81-88; V Tylorstown w Ynyshir 88-93; Dir of Studies Llan Ord Course 91-93; R Llangybi and Coedypaen w Llanbadoc *Mon* from 93; Chapl Gwent Tertiary Coll from 93. *The Rectory, Parc Road, Llangybi, Usk NP5 1NL* Tel (01633) 450214

MORTON, Mrs Christine Mary. b 39. Linc Th Coll 78. **dss** 80 **d** 87 **p** 94. Ore *Chich* 80-84; Southwick 84-85; Winchmore Hill St Paul *Lon* 85-87; Par Dn 87-94; C from 94. *122 Bourne Hill, London N13 4BD* Tel 0181-886 3157

MORTON, Clive Frederick. b 47. Lon Univ BA70. St Jo Coll Dur 78. **d** 80 **p** 81. C Countesthorpe w Foston *Leic* 80-83; C Glen Parva and S Wigston 83-86; V Birm St Pet *Birm* from 86. *St Peter's Vicarage, 32 George Street West, Birmingham B18 7HF* Tel 0121-523 8000

MORTON, Howard Knyvett. b 30. St Jo Coll Cam BA51 MA67. Linc Th Coll 55. **d** 57 **p** 58. C Hatfield Hyde *St Alb* 57-60; Head RE Heaton Gr Sch Newc 60-66 and 72-75; CMS 66-72; Heworth Grange Sch Dur 75-83; Regional Org Oxfam 88-91; Grainger Gr Sch Newc 91-94; Lic to Offic *Newc* 73-93; Dioc World Development Officer 94-95; rtd 95; Perm to Offic *Dur* from 95. *6 Ryelea, Longhoughton, Alnwick, Northd NE66 3DE* Tel (01665) 577958

MORTON, Mrs Jenny. b 50. Bedf Coll Lon BA72 Leic Univ PGCE73. EMMTC 87. **d** 90 **p** 94. C New Mills *Derby* 90-94; Chapl Asst Nottm City Hosp NHS Trust from 94; Chapl Basford Hosp Nottm from 94. *56 Marshall Drive, Bramcote, Nottingham NG9 3LD* Tel 0115-939 5784

MORTON, John Francis Eric. b 17. Leeds Univ BA38. Coll of Resurr Mirfield 38. **d** 40 **p** 41. C Leeds St Wilfrid *Ripon* 40-43; C-in-c Hough End CD 43-46; CF (EC) 46-47; CF 47-55; V Hudswell w Downholme *Ripon* 55-60; P-in-c Marske 58-60; V Beeston Hill H Spirit 60-77; rtd 77. *1 Deanery Close, Minster Road, Ripon, N Yorkshire HG4 1LZ* Tel (01765) 701227

MORTON, Canon John Ivan. b 32. Linc Coll Ox BA55 MA59. Wells Th Coll. **d** 57 **p** 58. C Shrewsbury St Chad *Lich* 57-60; C Dunham Massey St Marg *Ches* 60-62; V Derby St Luke *Derby* 62-70; R W Kirby St Andr *Ches* 70-75; V Northampton St Matt *Pet* 75-96; RD Northn 79-88; Can Pet Cathl 82-96; rtd 96; Perm to Offic *Derby* from 96. *59 Dale Road, Spondon, Derby DE21 7DG* Tel (01332) 667906

MORTON, Mark Paul. b 58. Univ of Wales (Swansea) BA79. Ridley Hall Cam CTM92. **d** 92 **p** 93. C Daventry, Ashby St Ledgers, Braunston etc *Pet* 92-95; CF (TA) 93-95; CF from 95. *MOD Chaplains (Army), Trenchard Lines, Upavon, Pewsey, Wilts SN9 6BE* Tel (01980) 615804 Fax 615800

MORTON, Sister Rita. b 34. Wilson Carlile Coll. **dss** 85 **d** 87 **p** 94. CA from 76; Par Dn Harlow New Town w Lt Parndon *Chelmsf* 87-89; C Harold Hill St Geo 89-94; rtd 94; NSM Elm Park St Nic Hornchurch *Chelmsf* from 94. *16 Cheviot Road, Hornchurch, Essex RH11 1LP*

MORTON, Robert Hart (Bob). b 28. Moray Ord Course 91. **d** 94. Hon C St Andr Cathl Inverness *Mor* from 94. *75 Fairfield Road, Inverness IV3 5LJ* Tel (01463) 223525

MORTON, Rupert Neville. b 25. St Steph Ho Ox 51. **d** 54 **p** 55. C Aldershot St Mich *Guildf* 54-57; Prec Guildf Cathl 57-58; V Middlesbrough St Chad *York* 58-62; Chapl Carter Bequest Hosp Middlesb 58-62; V Bramley *Guildf* 62-79; V Grafham 62-79; RD Cranleigh 71-76; R Haslemere 79-91; rtd 91; Perm to Offic *Chich* from 91. *Rock House, Wormley, Godalming, Surrey GU8 5SN* Tel (01428) 682614

MORTON, Mrs Sheila. b 44. Leeds Univ DipTh92. Sarum & Wells Th Coll 79. **dss** 84 **d** 87 **p** 94. HM Forces Düsseldorf 84-86; Cov St Mary *Cov* 86-87; Par Dn 87-89; Par Dn Boston Spa *York* 89-92; Par Dn Flitwick *St Alb* 93-94; C from 94. *32 St Albans Close, Flitwick, Bedford MK45 1UA* Tel (01525) 718561

MORTON, Canon William Derek. b 28. Wells Th Coll 67. **d** 69 **p** 70. C Kibworth Beauchamp *Leic* 69-72; Ind Chapl *Nor* 72-93; Hon Can Nor Cathl 90-93; RD Nor E 90-93; rtd 93; Perm to Offic *Nor* from 93. *55 Cameron Green, Taverham, Norwich NR8 6UA* Tel (01603) 861240

MORTON, Canon William Wright. b 56. ALAM TCD BTh88 QUB DPhil96. **d** 88 **p** 89. C Drumachose *D & R* 88-91; I Conwal Union w Gartan from 91; Bp's Dom Chapl from 92; Can Raphoe Cathl from 94. *Conwal Rectory, Magherennan, Letterkenny, Co Donegal, Irish Republic* Tel Letterkenny (74) 22573

MOSEDALE, Hugh Alfred. b 14. AKC48. **d** 49 **p** 50. C W Derby St Mary *Liv* 49-52; C Lewisham St Mary *S'wark* 52-55; C Walton St Mary *Liv* 55-57; V Middleton Junction *Man* 57-61; R Boxworth *Ely* 61-96; R Elsworth w Knapwell 61-96; RD Bourn 72-81; rtd 96. *Flat 13, Botany Close, Crescent Road, New Barnet, Herts EN4 9RX* Tel 0181-441 2266

MOSELEY, Arthur William. b 27. Lich Th Coll. **d** 60 **p** 61. C Castle Church *Lich* 60-64; C Bloxwich 64-66; V Bradley St Martin 66-72; C Stoke upon Trent 73-74; V Brown Edge 74-85; V Criftins 85-93; V Dudleston 85-93; rtd 93. *Pentre Collen, 2 Cil-y-Coed, Ruabon, Wrexham LL14 4EN*

MOSELEY, David John Reading. b 30. Univ Coll Ox BA54 MA58. Wells Th Coll 54. **d** 56 **p** 57. C Farnworth and Kearsley *Man* 56-59; Trinidad and Tobago 59-63; V Bedminster St Paul *Bris* 63-75; TV Bedminster 75-78; V Kilmington w Shute *Ex* 78-95; P-in-c Stockland w Dalwood 90; rtd 95; Perm to Offic *Ex* from 95. *Wimpole, 1 King Street, Colyton, Devon EX13 6LD* Tel (01297) 553725

MOSELEY, Hugh Martin. b 47. St Jo Coll Dur BA70. Westcott Ho Cam 71. **d** 73 **p** 74. C Hythe *Cant* 73-77; P-in-c Eythorne w Waldershare 77-83; V Ringmer *Chich* from 83; RD Lewes and Seaford from 93. *The Vicarage, Ringmer, Lewes, E Sussex BN8 5LA* Tel (01273) 812243

MOSELEY, Roger Henry. b 38. Edin Th Coll 60. **d** 63 **p** 64. C Friern Barnet All SS *Lon* 63-66; C Grantham St Wulfram *Linc* 66-69; P-in-c Swaton w Spanby 69-73; P-in-c Horbling 69-73; V Soberton w Newtown *Portsm* 73-80; V Sarisbury from 80. *The Vicarage, 149 Bridge Road, Sarisbury Green, Southampton SO31 7EN* Tel (01489) 572207 Fax as telephone

MOSELING, Peter. b 48. WMMTC 92. **d** 95 **p** 96. C Daventry, Ashby St Ledgers, Braunston etc *Pet* from 95. *48 Trinity Close, Daventry, Northants NN11 4RN* Tel (01327) 78697

MOSES, The Very Revd Dr John Henry. b 38. Nottm Univ BA59 PhD65. Linc Th Coll 62. **d** 64 **p** 65. C Bedford St Andr *St Alb* 64-70; P-in-c Cov St Pet *Cov* 70-73; P-in-c Cov St Mark 71-73; TR Cov E 73-77; RD Cov E 73-77; Adn Southend *Chelmsf* 77-82; Provost Chelmsf 82-96; Chmn Coun of Cen for Th Study Essex Univ 87-96; Dean St Paul's *Lon* from 96. *The Deanery, 9 Amen Court, London EC4M 7BU* Tel 0171-236 2827 Fax 332 0298

MOSES, Leslie Alan. b 49. Hull Univ BA71 Edin Univ BD76. Edin Th Coll 73. **d** 76 **p** 77. C Edin Old St Paul *Edin* 76-79; R Leven *St And* 79-85; R Edin Old St Paul *Edin* 85-95; P-in-c Edin St Marg 86-92; V St Marylebone All SS *Lon* from 95. *All Saints' Vicarage, 7 Margaret Street, London W1N 8JQ* Tel 0171-636 1788 or 636 9961 Fax 436 4470

MOSFORD, Denzil Huw Erasmus. b 56. St D Coll Lamp DipTh77 AKC78 Sarum & Wells Th Coll 77. **d** 79 **p** 80. C Clydach *S & B* 79-82; V from 87; Jamaica 82-85; V Ystalyfera *S & B* 85-87; RD Cwmtawe from 93. *The Vicarage, 53 Bryntawe Road, Ynystawe, Swansea SA6 5AD* Tel (01792) 843202

MOSFORD, Denzil Joseph. b 28. **d** 86 **p** 87. C Manselton *S & B* 86-89; V Port Eynon w Rhosili and Llanddewi and Knelston from 89. *The Rectory, Port Eynon, Swansea SA3 1NL* Tel (01792) 390456

MOSLEY, Edward Peter. b 38. Clifton Th Coll 62. **d** 67 **p** 68. C Mirehouse *Carl* 67-69; C Newbarns w Hawcoat 69-72; R Aikton 72-77; R Orton St Giles 72-77; V Silloth 77-78; CF 78-94; Hon C Grantown-on-Spey *Mor* 94-95; Hon C Rothiemurchus 94-95. *Tigh-na-Drochaid, Nethy Bridge, Inverness-shire PH25 3DW* Tel (01479) 821666

MOSS, Barbara Penelope. b 46. Ox Univ BA66 MA70. EAMTC 95. **d** 97. NSM Leytonstone H Trin Harrow Green *Chelmsf* from 97. *36 Haroldstone Road, London E17 7AW* Tel 0181-521 0198

MOSS, The Very Revd Basil Stanley. b 18. Qu Coll Ox BA41 MA45. Linc Th Coll 42. **d** 43 **p** 44. C Leigh St Mary *Man* 43-45; Tutor Linc Th Coll 45-46; Sub-Warden 46-51; Tutor St Cath Cumberland Lodge 51-53; V Bris St Nath w St Kath *Bris* 53-60; Dioc Dir of Ords 56-66; Hon Can Bris Cathl 59-60 and 66-73; Can Res Bris Cathl 60-66; Chief Sec ACCM 66-73; Provost Birm 73-85; rtd 85; Perm to Offic *Worc* from 85; Perm to Offic *Birm* from 86. *25 Castle Grove, Stourbridge, W Midlands DY8 2HH* Tel (01384) 378799

MOSS, Christopher Ashley. b 52. Ex Univ BA73 York Univ DSA77 Southn Univ DASS78 CQSW78. Wycliffe Hall Ox 89. **d** 91 **p** 92. C Malvern H Trin and St Jas *Worc* 91-96; V Longdon, Castlemorton, Bushley, Queenhill etc from 96. *The Vicarage, Longdon, Tewkesbury, Glos GL20 6AT* Tel (01684) 81256

MOSS, David Glyn. b 62. St Anne's Coll Ox BA83 Em Coll Cam BA89. Westcott Ho Cam 87. **d** 90 **p** 91. C Halesowen *Worc* 90-93; Tutor St Steph Ho Ox from 93. *St Stephen's House, 16 Marston Street, Oxford OX4 1JX* Tel (01865) 247874

MOSS, David Sefton. b 59. MRPharmS81 Sunderland Poly BSc80. Ridley Hall Cam CTM93. **d** 93 **p** 94. C Highworth w Sevenhampton and Inglesham etc *Bris* 93-97; V Bedminster St Mich from 97. *St Michael's Vicarage, 153 St John's Lane, Bedminster, Bristol BS3 5AE* Tel 0117-977 6132

MOSS, Denis. b 32. St Jo Coll Auckland LTh83. **d** 74 **p** 75. New Zealand 74-92; Chapl Budapest *Eur* from 92. *Budenz Utca 4/B, Budapest 1021, Hungary*

MOSS, Harold George Edward. b 20. Glouc Th Course 79. **d** 80 **p** 81. NSM Cirencester *Glouc* 80-83; NSM Brimpsfield, Cranham, Elkstone and Syde 83-89; rtd 89; Perm to Offic *Glouc* from 89. *57 Queen Elizabeth Road, Cirencester, Glos GL7 1DH* Tel (01285) 652857

MOSS, Ivan Douglas Francis. b 24. Chich Th Coll. **d** 76 **p** 77. Hon C Crawley *Chich* 76-93; rtd 93; Perm to Offic *Chich* from 93. *14 Normanhurst Close, Three Bridges, Crawley, W Sussex RH10 1YL* Tel (01293) 522172

MOSS, James Wilfred. b 15. Oak Hill Th Coll 75. **d** 76 **p** 77. Hon C Frogmore *St Alb* 76-78 and 81-93; Hon C Watford St Luke 78-81; Perm to Offic from 93. *8A The Rise, Park Street, St Albans, Herts AL2 2NT* Tel (01727) 872467

MOSS, Preb Kenneth Charles. b 37. ARCS59 Lon Univ BSc59 DIC62 PhD62. **d** 66 **p** 67. Canada 66-73; Chapl Ex Univ *Ex* 73-83; V St Marychurch from 83; RD Ipplepen 87-93; Preb Ex Cathl from 92. *The Vicarage, Hampton Avenue, St Marychurch, Torquay TQ1 3LA* Tel (01803) 327661 or 329054

MOSS, The Ven Leonard Godfrey. b 32. K Coll Lon BD59 AKC59. **d** 60 **p** 61. C Putney St Marg *S'wark* 60-63; C Cheam 63-67; R Much Dewchurch w Llanwarne and Llandinabo *Heref* 67-72; Dioc Ecum Officer 69-83; V Marden w Amberley 72-80; V Marden w Amberley and Wisteston 80-84; P-in-c 92-94; Preb Heref Cathl from 79; Can Heref Cathl 84-91; Dioc Soc Resp Officer 84-91; Adn Heref from 91. *The Archdeacon's House, The Close, Hereford HR1 2NG* Tel (01432) 272873

MOSS, Mrs Nelva Elizabeth. b 44. Bp Grosseteste Coll TCert66 Sussex Univ BEd73. S Dios Minl Tr Scheme 90. **d** 93 **p** 94. NSM Bincombe w Broadwey, Upwey and Buckland Ripers *Sarum* 93-96; NSM Langtree *Ox* from 96. *The Vicarage, Crabtree*

Corner, Ipsden, Wallingford, Oxon OX10 6BN Tel (01491) 681129

MOSS, Peter Hextall. b 34. Clare Coll Cam BA59 MA62. Linc Th Coll 59. **d** 61 **p** 62. C Easington Colliery *Dur* 61-63; C Whickham 63-65; C-in-c Town End Farm CD 65-72; TV Mattishall *Nor* 72-75; P-in-c Welborne 75-84; P-in-c Mattishall w Mattishall Burgh 75-84; P-in-c Yaxham 80-84; TR Hempnall 84-89. *High House Cottage, Gunn Street, Foulsham, Dereham, Norfolk NR20 5RN* Tel (01362) 683823

MOSS, Peter John. b 41. K Coll Cam BA64 MA67. Westcott Ho Cam 63. **d** 84 **p** 85. Hon C Leighton Buzzard w Eggington, Hockliffe etc *St Alb* 84-93; NSM Luton St Sav from 93. *84 Regent Street, Leighton Buzzard, Beds LU7 8JZ* Tel (01525) 372904

MOSS, Stephen. b 51. Lon Univ BSc69. S'wark Ord Course. **d** 85 **p** 86. NSM Clapham Ch Ch and St Jo *S'wark* 85-87; NSM Clapham TM from 87. *59A Bromfelde Road, London SW4 6PP* Tel 0171-720 3152

MOSS, Victor Charles. b 25. Oak Hill Th Coll BD65. **d** 66 **p** 67. C Macclesfield St Mich *Ches* 66-68; C Belper *Derby* 69-71; V Chesterfield Ch Ch 71-93; rtd 93; Perm to Offic *Derby* from 93. *16 Nether Croft Road, Brimington, Chesterfield, Derbyshire S43 1QD* Tel (01246) 206260

MOSS, Wilfrid Maurice. b 10. St Jo Coll Dur LTh34 BA35 MA41. Tyndale Hall Bris 31. **d** 35 **p** 36. C Preston All SS *Blackb* 35-38; Min Buxton Trin Prop Chpl *Derby* 38-42; R Man Albert Memorial Ch *Man* 42-50; V Sidcup Ch Ch *Roch* 50-75; RD Sidcup 70-75; rtd 75; Perm to Offic *Ex* 75-85; Perm to Offic *B & W* from 85. *Stonehaven, 4 West View Close, Middlezoy, Bridgwater, Somerset TA7 0NP* Tel (01823) 698851

MOSSE, Mrs Barbara Ann. b 51. CertEd73 Open Univ BA77. CA Tr Coll IDC81 Lambeth STh83. **d** 90 **p** 95. NSM Southbourne w W Thorney *Chich* 90-93; Perm to Offic 93-95; Community Mental Health Chapl Fareham/Gosport from 94; NSM Purbrook *Portsm* from 95. *8 Long Copse Court, Long Copse Lane, Emsworth, Hants PO10 7UW* Tel (01243) 376155

MOSSMAN, Preb Donald Wyndham Cremer. b 13. OBE65. Lon Coll of Div LTh39. **d** 39 **p** 40. C Bethnal Green St Jas Less *Lon* 39-42; P-in-c Upper Chelsea St Simon 42-44; V 44-49; Chapl Amsterdam w Haarlem and Den Helder *Eur* 49-51; Chapl Zurich w St Gallen and Winterthur 55-64; RD Switzerland 55-64; RD Austria 55-63; Preb St Paul's Cathl *Lon* 60-86; P-in-c Hornsey Ch Ch 64-69; RD W Haringey 67-71; C Highgate St Mich 69-71; R St Jas Garlickhythe w St Mich Queenhithe etc 71-84; Hon C Warsaw *Eur* 77-84; Hon Can Brussels Cathl 81-84; rtd 84. *The Charterhouse, Charterhouse Square, London EC1M 6AN* Tel 0171-251 8002

MOSSOP, Henry Watson. b 08. Lich Th Coll 52. **d** 54 **p** 55. Lic to Offic *Pet* 54-55; C Eydon 55-57; C Moreton Pinkney 55-57; C Culworth 55-57; V Mears Ashby 57-59; R Hardwick 57-59; R Colby w Banningham and Tuttington *Nor* 59-66; V Twyford w Guist 66-73; rtd 73; Perm to Offic *Nor* 74-93 and from 95. *Crossing Cottage, Pond Lane, Antingham, North Walsham, Norfolk NR28 0NH* Tel (01692) 403561

MOSSOP, Patrick John (Pat). b 48. Solicitor St Jo Coll Cam MA LLB. Linc Th Coll BTh93. **d** 93 **p** 94. C Halstead St Andr w H Trin and Greenstead Green *Chelmsf* 93-97; Assoc Chapl Essex Univ from 97. *University of Essex, Wivenhoe Park, Colchester CO4 3SQ*

MOSSOP, Canon Robert Owen. b 09. Peterho Cam BA30 MA35. Westcott Ho Cam 32. **d** 33 **p** 34. C Earley St Pet *Ox* 33-40; Chapl RAF 40-46; R Ruan Lanihorne w Philleigh *Truro* 46-50; V Constantine 50-73; RD Kerrier 60-73; Hon Can Truro Cathl 69-84; rtd 73; Perm to Offic *Truro* from 84. *Westwood, Carnmenellis, Redruth, Cornwall TR16 6PB* Tel (01209) 860288

MOTE, Gregory Justin. b 60. Oak Hill Th Coll BA83. **d** 86 **p** 87. C W Ealing St Jo w St Jas *Lon* 86-90; C St Helen Bishopsgate w St Andr Undershaft etc 90-95; V Poulton Lancelyn H Trin *Ches* from 96. *6 Chorley Way, Wirral, Merseyside L63 9LS* Tel 0151-334 6780

MOTH, Miss Susan. b 44. Leic Univ BA65 K Coll Lon CertEd66. Linc Th Coll 83. **dss** 85 **d** 87 **p** 94. Churchdown St Jo *Glouc* 85-87; C 87-93; D-in-c The Rissingtons 93-94; P-in-c from 94. *The Rectory, Great Rissington, Cheltenham, Glos GL54 2LL* Tel (01451) 810611

MOTHERSDALE, Paul John. b 52. N Ord Course 94. **d** 97. C Kirkleatham *York* from 97. *44 Ayton Drive, Redcar, Cleveland TS10 4LR* Tel (01642) 490475 Mobile 0589-194647 Fax as telephone E-mail paul862@aol.com

MOTHERSOLE, John Robert. b 25. Chich Th Coll. **d** 84 **p** 85. NSM Hayes St Anselm *Lon* 84-93; NSM Hayes St Edm from 93. *116 Nestles Avenue, Hayes, Middx UB3 4QD* Tel 0181-848 0626

MOTT, Julian Ward. b 52. Loughb Univ BSc77. Ripon Coll Cuddesdon 78. **d** 81 **p** 82. C Aylestone *Leic* 81-84; C Gt Ilford St Mary *Chelmsf* 84-88; R Chevington w Hargrave and Whepstead w Brockley *St E* from 88. *The Rectory, Chevington, Bury St Edmunds, Suffolk IP29 5QL* Tel (01284) 850204

MOTT, Peter John. b 49. Ch Coll Cam BA70 MA75 Dundee Univ PhD73 Nottm Univ BA79. St Jo Coll Nottm 77. **d** 80 **p** 81. C Hull Newland St Jo *York* 80-83; C Selly Park St Steph and St Wulstan *Birm* 83-87; C Mosborough *Sheff* 87-92; R Colne St Bart *Blackb* from 92. *The Rectory, Albert Road, Colne, Lancs BB8 0AE* Tel (01282) 863479

MOTTERSHEAD, Derek. b 39. Open Univ BA74 BEd. Chich Th Coll 65. **d** 69 **p** 70. C Walthamstow St Barn and St Jas Gt *Chelmsf* 69-72; C Chelmsf All SS 72-77; P-in-c Cold Norton w Stow Maries 77-80; V Leytonstone St Andr 80-92; V Eastbourne St Sav and St Pet *Chich* from 92; Miss to Seamen from 92. *St Saviour's Vicarage, Spencer Road, Eastbourne, E Sussex BN21 4PA* Tel (01323) 722317

MOTTRAM, Andrew Peter. b 53. AKC77. Ripon Coll Cuddesdon 77. **d** 78 **p** 79. C E Bedfont *Lon* 78-81; C Hatfield *St Alb* 81-84; V Milton Ernest 84-91; V Thurleigh 84-91; P-in-c Heref All SS *Heref* from 91. *All Saints' Vicarage, 45 Venns Lane, Hereford HR1 1DE* Tel (01432) 266588 or 355088 Fax 344428

MOTYER, John Alexander. b 24. TCD BA46 MA51 BD51. Wycliffe Hall Ox 47. **d** 47 **p** 48. C Penn Fields *Lich* 47-50; C Bris H Trin *Bris* 51-54; Tutor Clifton Th Coll 51-54; Tutor Tyndale Hall Bris 52-54; Vice-Prin Clifton Th Coll 54-65; V W Hampstead St Luke *Lon* 65-70; Dep Prin Tyndale Hall Bris 70-71; Prin and Dean Trin Coll Bris 71-81; Min Westbourne Ch Ch Prop Chpl *Win* 81-89; rtd 89; Perm to Offic *Ex* from 90. *10 Littlefield, Bishopsteignton, Teignmouth, Devon TQ14 9SG* Tel (01626) 770986

MOTYER, Stephen. b 50. Pemb Coll Cam BA73 MA77 Bris Univ MLitt79. Trin Coll Bris 73. **d** 76 **p** 77. Lect Oak Hill Th Coll 76-83; C Braughing, Lt Hadham, Albury, Furneux Pelham etc *St Alb* 83-87; Perm to Offic from 87; Lect Lon Bible Coll from 87. *7 Hangar Ruding, Watford WD1 5BH* Tel 0181-386 6829

MOUGHTIN, Ross. b 48. St Cath Coll Cam BA70 St Jo Coll Dur BA75. **d** 76 **p** 77. C Litherland St Paul Hatton Hill *Liv* 76-79; C Heswall *Ches* 79-84; Chapl Edw Unit Rochdale Infirmary 83-92; V Thornham w Gravel Hole *Man* 84-92; V Aughton Ch Ch *Liv* from 92. *Christ Church Vicarage, 22 Long Lane, Aughton, Ormskirk, Lancs L39 5AT* Tel (01695) 422175

MOULD, Mrs Jacqueline. b 66. QUB BD88. **d** 91 **p** 92. C Belfast St Aid *Conn* 91-94; C Drumragh w Mountfield *D & R* 94-96; NSM Kinson *Sarum* from 97. *4 Home Road, Kinson, Bournemouth BT79 0JE* Tel (01202) 578355

MOULD, Jeremy James. b 63. Nottm Univ BA85. CITC 88. **d** 91 **p** 92. C Mossley *Conn* 91-94; C Drumragh w Mountfield *D & R* 94-96; C Kinson *Sarum* from 97. *4 Home Road, Kinson, Bournemouth BH11 9BN* Tel (01202) 578355

MOULDER, Kenneth. b 53. Lon Univ BEd75. Ridley Hall Cam 78. **d** 81 **p** 82. C Harold Wood *Chelmsf* 81-84; C Darfield *Sheff* 84-88; V Walkergate *Newc* 88-92; P-in-c Byker St Mark 90-92; V Byker St Mark and Walkergate St Oswald from 92. *St Oswald's Parsonage, Woodhead Road, Newcastle upon Tyne NE6 4RX* Tel 0191-263 6249

MOULE, Prof Charles Francis Digby. b 08. CBE85. FBA66 Em Coll Cam BA31 MA34 St Andr Univ Hon DD58 Cam Univ Hon DD88. Ridley Hall Cam 31. **d** 33 **p** 34. C Cambridge St Mark *Ely* 33-34; Tutor Ridley Hall Cam 33-34; C Rugby St Andr *Cov* 34-36; C Cambridge Gt St Mary w St Mich *Ely* 36-40; Vice-Prin Ridley Hall Cam 36-44; Dean Clare Coll Cam 44-51; Fell from 44; Select Preacher Cam Univ 42, 48 and 53; Select Preacher Ox Univ 54 and 73; Lect Div Cam Univ 47-51; Lady Marg Prof Div Cam Univ 51-76; Can Th Leic Cathl *Leic* 55-76; rtd 76; Perm to Offic *Chich* from 81. *1 King's Houses, Pevensey, E Sussex BN24 5JR* Tel (01323) 762436

MOULE, Kevin David. b 54. Coll of Resurr Mirfield 77. **d** 80 **p** 81. C E Finchley All SS *Lon* 80-84; C Notting Hill St Mich and Ch Ch 84-91; P-in-c Isleworth St Fran 91-94; P-in-c Walham Green St Jo w St Jas from 94. *The Vicarage, 40 Racton Road, London SW6 1LP* Tel 0171-385 3676 Fax 385 7634

MOULT, Jane Elizabeth Kate. b 61. Trin Coll Bris DipHE93. **d** 94 **p** 95. NSM St Jo in Bedwardine *Worc* 94-97; NSM Bilton *Cov* from 97. *St Mark's House, 51 Falstaff Drive, Bilton, Rugby, Warks CV22 6LJ* Tel (01788) 810761

MOULT, Simon Paul. b 66. Nene Coll Northampton DipChir88. Trin Coll Bris BA94. **d** 94 **p** 95. C St Jo in Bedwardine *Worc* 94-97; C Bilton *Cov* from 97. *St Mark's House, 51 Falstaff Drive, Bilton, Rugby, Warks CV22 6LJ* Tel (01788) 810761

MOULTON, Paul Oliver. b 43. BSc. N Ord Course 77. **d** 80 **p** 81. C Wilmslow *Ches* 80-85; V Knutsford St Cross 85-92; Chapl Mary Dendy Hosp Knutsford 86-92; V Gatley *Ches* from 92. *St James's Vicarage, 11 Northenden Road, Cheadle, Cheshire SK8 4EN* Tel 0161-428 4764

MOULTON, William Arthur. b 11. Man Univ Leic Univ MEd64. Wells Th Coll 47. **d** 48 **p** 49. Asst Chapl & Sen Lect Coll SS Mark & Jo Chelsea 48-62; Prin Lect Bp Grosseteste Coll Linc 62-76; Hon PV Linc Cathl *Linc* from 76. *Bungalow 7, Terrys Cross, Woodmancote, Henfield, W Sussex BN5 9SX* Tel (01273) 493091

MOUNCER, David Peter. b 65. Univ of Wales (Abth) BA86. Oak Hill Th Coll BA94. **d** 94 **p** 95. C Foord St Jo *Cant* from 94. *126 Lucy Avenue, Folkestone, Kent CT19 5TN* Tel (01303) 250280

MOUNSEY, William Lawrence Fraser. b 51. St Andr Univ BD75. Edin Th Coll 76. **d** 78 **p** 79. C Edin St Mark *Edin* 78-81; Chapl RAF from 81; R Dalmahoy *Edin* 90-96; Chapl Heriot-Watt Univ 90-96. *Chaplaincy Services (RAF), HQ, Personnel and Training*

Command, RAF Innsworth, Gloucester GL3 1EZ Tel (01452) 712612 ext 5164 Fax 510828

MOUNSTEPHEN, Philip Ian. b 59. Southn Univ BA80 Magd Coll Ox MA87. Wycliffe Hall Ox 85. **d** 88 **p** 89. C Gerrards Cross and Fulmer *Ox* 88-92; V W Streatham St Jas *S'wark* from 92. *St James' Vicarage, 236 Mitcham Lane, London SW16 6NT* Tel 0181-677 3947

MOUNT, Canon Judith Mary. b 35. Bedf Coll Lon BA56 Lon Univ CertEd57. Ripon Coll Cuddesdon 81. **dss** 83 **d** 87 **p** 94. Carterton *Ox* 83-85; Charlton on Otmoor and Oddington 85-87; Dioc Lay Min Adv and Asst Dir of Ords 86-89; Par Dn Islip w Charlton on Otmoor, Oddington, Noke etc 87-94; C 94-95; Assoc Dioc Dir Ords and Adv for Women in Ord Min 89-95; Hon Can Ch Ch 92-95; rtd 95; Hon C Shill Valley and Broadshire *Ox* from 95. *The Vicarage, Filkins, Lechlade, Glos GL7 3JQ* Tel (01367) 860460

MOUNTFORD, Brian Wakling. b 45. Newc Univ BA66 Cam Univ MA73 Ox Univ MA90. Westcott Ho Cam 66. **d** 68 **p** 69. C Westmr St Steph w St Jo *Lon* 68-69; C Paddington Ch Ch 69-73; Chapl SS Coll Cam 73-78; V Southgate Ch Ch *Lon* 78-86; V Ox St Mary V w St Cross and St Pet *Ox* from 86; Chapl St Hilda's Coll Ox from 89. *12 Mansfield Road, Oxford OX1 3TA* Tel (01865) 243806

MOUNTFORD, Ian David. b 65. St Jo Coll Nottm BTh93. **d** 96 **p** 97. C Chilwell *S'well* from 96. *29 Farm Road, Beeston, Nottingham NG9 5BZ* Tel 0115-922 5966

MOUNTFORD, John. b 55. Nottm Univ BEd77 Birm Univ MA80 Ex Univ MPhil86. Linc Th Coll 73. **d** 78 **p** 79. C Wombourne *Lich* 78-80; C Upper Gornal 80-82; C Paignton St Jo *Ex* 82-86; Papua New Guinea 86-87; Chapl Blue Coat Sch Birm 87-90; Perm to Offic *Birm* 88-90; Australia 91-94. *Address temp unknown*

MOUNTNEY, Frederick Hugh. b 14. St Chad's Coll Dur BA36 MA39. Lich Th Coll 36. **d** 37 **p** 38. C Beighton *Derby* 37-39; C Spondon 39-40; C Byker St Laur *Newc* 40-44; Backworth St Jo 44-48; V N Gosforth 48-51; R Lillingstone Dayrell w Lillingstone Lovell *Ox* 51-56; V Heref All SS *Heref* 56-75; Chapl Victoria Eye Hosp Heref 56-75; Dioc Ecum Officer 63-69; Chapl Bonn w Cologne *Eur* 75-79; rtd 79; Perm to Offic *Heref* 79-90; Perm to Offic *St E* and *Nor* from 82; Perm to Offic *Eur* from 90. *St Martin's, 44 London Road, Harleston, Norfolk IP20 9BW* Tel (01379) 853744

MOUNTNEY, John Michael. b 47. St Chad's Coll Dur BA69 MA84. Cuddesdon Coll 69. **d** 71 **p** 72. C Morpeth *Newc* 71-75; C Longbenton St Bart 75-77; Sub-Warden Community of All Hallows Ditchingham 77-83; R Blundeston w Flixton and Lound *Nor* 83-87; TR Nor St Pet Parmentergate w St Jo 87-93; Warden Julian Shrine 87-93; V Embleton w Rennington and Rock *Newc* from 93. *The Vicarage, Embleton, Alnwick, Northd NE66 3UW* Tel (01665) 576660

MOURANT, Julia Caroline. b 58. Sheff Univ BA79. St Jo Coll Nottm DPS84. **dss** 84 **d** 92 **p** 94. Cropwell Bishop w Colston Bassett, Granby etc *S'well* 84-86; Marple All SS *Ches* 86-89; Harlow St Mary and St Hugh w St Jo the Bapt *Chelmsf* 89-92; NSM from 92. *St Mary's Vicarage, 5 Staffords, Harlow, Essex CM17 0JR* Tel (01279) 450633

MOURANT, Sidney Eric. b 39. DipTh70. Oak Hill Th Coll BD73. **d** 89 **p** 90. C Oxton *Ches* 89-92; V Douglas St Thos *S & M* 92-96; I Rathkeale w Askeaton and Kilcornan *L & K* from 96. *The Rectory, Cragmore, Askeaton, Co Limerick, Irish Republic* Tel Limerick (61) 392783 Mobile 087-2399875 Fax as telephone

MOURANT, Stephen Philip Edward. b 54. Nottm Univ BTh83. St Jo Coll Nottm. **d** 83 **p** 84. C Cropwell Bishop w Colston Bassett, Granby etc *S'well* 83-86; C Marple All SS *Ches* 86-89; P-in-c Harlow St Mary and St Hugh w St Jo the Bapt *Chelmsf* 89-90; V from 90. *St Mary's Vicarage, 5 Staffords, Harlow, Essex CM17 0JR* Tel (01279) 450633

MOVERLEY, Ruth Elaine. b 55. K Alfred's Coll Win 73. Llan Dioc Tr Scheme 85. **d** 90 **p** 97. C Llangynwyd w Maesteg *Llan* 90-95; C Glan Ely from 95. *2 Deere Close, Ely, Cardiff CF5 4NU* Tel (01222) 592129

MOWAT, Geoffrey Scott. b 17. CCC Ox BA39 MA49. Ripon Hall Ox 58. **d** 59 **p** 60. C Clifton Ch Ch *Bris* 59-61; Lect and Chapl St Mary's Coll Cheltenham 61-64; V Coln St Aldwyn w Hatherop and Quenington *Glouc* 64-77; RD Fairford 74-77; Malaysia 77-83; rtd 83; Perm to Offic *B & W* 86-87; from 92; Min Bath St Mary Magd Holloway 87-92. *3 Chedworth Close, Bath BA2 7AF* Tel (01225) 833310

MOWBRAY, David. b 38. Fitzw Ho Cam BA60 MA64 Lon Univ BD62. Clifton Th Coll. **d** 63 **p** 64. C Northampton St Giles *Pet* 63-66; Lect Watford St Mary *St Alb* 66-70; V Broxbourne 70-77; R Broxbourne w Wormley 77-84; V Hertford All SS 84-91; V Darley Abbey *Derby* from 91; Asst Chapl Derby R Infirmary 91-94. *Darley Abbey Vicarage, 25 Church Lane, Derby DE22 1EX* Tel (01332) 553192

MOWBRAY, Derek David Whitfield. b 19. Lon Univ BD42 Dur Univ MLitt52 Sheff Univ PhD58 Leeds Univ PhD59. ALCD42. **d** 42 **p** 43. C Morden *S'wark* 42-45; Asst Master Parmiter's Foundn Sch Lon 48-50; Tutor All Nations Bible Coll Ox 50-52; C Doncaster St Geo *Sheff* 54-55; V Kettlewell w Conistone *Bradf* 55-60; V Wrangthorn *Ripon* 60-70; R Bris St Jo w St Mary-le-Port *Bris* 71-74; Perm to Offic 75-84; rtd 84. *Glenavon, Coleford Road, Tutshill, Chepstow NP6 7BU* Tel (01291) 626827

MOWER, Miss Marguerite Mary. b 36. Bris Univ BA57. Cant Sch of Min 90. **d** 93 **p** 94. NSM Eythorne and Elvington w Waldershare etc *Cant* from 93. *Meadow Bank, Eythorne Road, Shepherdswell, Dover, Kent CT15 7PN* Tel (01304) 830226

MOWFORTH, Mark. b 64. Reading Univ BSc86. Trin Coll Bris 93. **d** 96 **p** 97. C Buckingham w Radclive cum Chackmore *Ox* 96-97; C Buckingham from 97. *Church House, 5 Chandos Close, Buckingham MK18 1AW* Tel (01280) 812160

MOWLL, John William Rutley. b 42. Sarum Th Coll 63. **d** 66 **p** 67. C Oughtibridge *Sheff* 66-69; C Hill *Birm* 69-73; Ind Chapl *Worc* 73-78; V Upper Arley 73-78; P-in-c Upton Snodsbury and Broughton Hackett etc 78-81; R 81-83; V Boughton under Blean w Dunkirk *Cant* 83-89; V Boughton under Blean w Dunkirk and Hernhill from 89; RD Ospringe from 95. *The Vicarage, 101 The Street, Boughton-under-Blean, Faversham, Kent ME13 9BG* Tel (01227) 751410

MOXLEY, Cyril Edward. b 09. Ch Coll Cam BA32 MA37. Ely Th Coll 33. **d** 35 **p** 37. India 35-37; C Clerkenwell H Redeemer w St Phil *Lon* 37-41; Perm to Offic *Cant* 41-42; C Upper Norwood St Jo 42-44; Chapl RAFVR 44-50; R Charlton Adam w Charlton Mackrell *B & W* 50-52; Chapl RAF 52-65; Prin RAF Chapl Sch 60-64; Asst Chapl-in-Chief RAF Germany 64-65; V S Stoneham *Win* 65-74; rtd 74; Hon Chapl Win Cathl *Win* from 79. *19 Old Parsonage Court, Otterbourne, Winchester SO21 2EP* Tel (01962) 714936

MOXON, Canon Michael Anthony. b 42. Lon Univ BD78. Sarum Th Coll 67. **d** 70 **p** 71. C Kirkley *Nor* 70-74; Min Can St Paul's Cathl *Lon* 74-81; Sacr 77-81; Warden Coll of Min Canons 79-81; V Tewkesbury w Walton Cardiff *Glouc* 81-90; Chapl to The Queen from 86; Can Windsor from 90; Chapl Royal Chpl Windsor Gt Park from 90. *The Chaplain's Lodge, The Great Park, Windsor, Berks SL4 2HP* Tel (01784) 432434

MOXON, William James. b 25. Qu Coll Birm 68. **d** 69 **p** 70. C Letchworth St Paul *St Alb* 69-72; C-in-c N Brickhill CD 72-76; Chapl Puerto de la Cruz Tenerife *Eur* 76-78; Egypt 78-80; V Altrincham St Jo *Ches* 80-90; rtd 90. *75 Overn Avenue, Buckingham MK18 1LU* Tel (01280) 823132

MOY, Mrs Joy Patricia. b 35. Cant Sch of Min 87. **d** 90 **p** 94. NSM Cranbrook *Cant* from 90. *1 Dobells, Cranbrook, Kent TN17 3EL* Tel (01580) 713066

MOYNAGH, Dr David Kenneth. b 46. LRCP70 MRCS70 MRCGP76 Lon Univ MB, BS70. S Dios Minl Tr Scheme 88. **d** 91 **p** 92. NSM Ore *Chich* from 91. *Stalkhurst Farm, Ivyhouse Lane, Hastings, E Sussex TN35 4NN* Tel (01424) 751314

MOYNAGH, Michael Digby. b 50. Southn Univ BA73 Lon Univ MA74 Aus Nat Univ PhD78 Bris Univ MA85. Trin Coll Bris DipHE84. **d** 85 **p** 86. C Northwood Em *Lon* 85-89; P-in-c Wilton *B & W* 89-90; TR 90-96; Dir Cen for Third Millenium Studies St Jo Coll Nottm from 96. *St John's College, Bramcote, Nottingham NG9 3DS* Tel 0115-922 0991 Fax as telephone

MOYNAN, David George. b 53. DipTh. **d** 86 **p** 87. C Seagoe *D & D* 86-88; C Taney *D & G* 88-89; I Arklow w Inch and Kilbride 89-94; Miss to Seamen from 89; Dioc Stewardship Adv *D & G* from 92; I Kilternan from 94; Dioc Dir for Decade of Evang from 96. *The Rectory, Kilternan, Co Dublin, Irish Republic* Tel Dublin (1) 295 5603

MOYNAN, Canon William John. b 20. TCD BA44. **d** 44 **p** 45. C Chapelizod *D & G* 44-49; C Dublin Drumcondra w N Strand 49-56; Clerical V Ch Ch Cathl Dublin 52-56; I Portarlington w Cloneyhurke and Lea *M & K* 56-63; I Donabate w Lusk *D & G* 63-68; I Swords w Donabate and Killsallaghan 68-90; Can Ch Ch Cathl Dublin 83-90; Chapl Shelton Abbey Pris 89-90; rtd 90. *Briarwood, Ballycarnane, Tramore, Waterford, Irish Republic* Tel Waterford (51) 390199

MOYSE, Mrs Pauline Patricia. b 42. Ex Univ CertEd62. S Dios Minl Tr Scheme 88. **d** 91 **p** 94. Hon C Fleet *Guildf* 91-92; C from 93; Chapl Farnborough Coll of Tech from 96. *38 Oasthouse Drive, Ancell's Farm, Fleet, Aldershot, Hants GU13 8UL* Tel (01252) 629976

MPUNZI, Nduna Ananias. b 46. Birm Univ DPS79 Glas Univ LTh84. St Pet Coll Alice 69. **d** 71 **p** 72. S Africa 71-78; C Bilston *Lich* 84-86; TV 86-90; P-in-c Walsall St Mary and All SS Palfrey 90-96; P-in-c Caldmore 90-93; C 93-96; C Tettenhall Regis from 96. *Palfrey Vicarage, Dale Street, Walsall WS1 4AN* Tel (01922) 33451

MUDDIMAN, John Bernard. b 47. Keble Coll Ox BA67 MA72 DPhil76 Selw Coll Cam BA71 MA75. Westcott Ho Cam 69. **d** 72 **p** 73. Hon C Ox St Giles *Ox* 72-83; Chapl New Coll Ox 72-76; Tutor St Steph Ho Ox 76-83; Vice-Prin 80-83; Lect Th Nottm Univ 83-90; Fell Mansf Coll Ox from 90; Lic to Offic *Ox* from 90. *Mansfield College, Oxford OX1 3TF* Tel (01865) 270999

MUDGE, Frederick Alfred George. b 31. Leeds Univ BSc58 Univ of Wales BD67. St Mich Coll Llan 58. **d** 61 **p** 62. C Cwmavon *Llan* 61-64; PV Llan Cathl 64-70; R Llandough w Leckwith 70-88; V Penarth All SS 88-96; rtd 96. *Taffways, 6 Fairwater Road, Llandaff, Cardiff CF5 2LD*

MUDIE, Martin Bruce. b 54. Golds Coll Lon BA76. Sarum & Wells Th Coll CMinlEd92. **d** 92 **p** 93. C Bromley St Mark *Roch* 92-95; rtd 95. *164 Queen Anne Drive, Bromley BR2 0SF*

MUGAN, Miriam Ruth. b 56. RNMH77. Oak Hill Th Coll 93. **d** 96 **p** 97. NSM St Alb St Sav *St Alb* from 96. *137 Kings Road, London Colney, St Albans, Herts AL2 1ER* Tel (01727) 825971

MUGGLETON, Major George. b 25. Chich Th Coll 55. **d** 57 **p** 58. C Oldham St Mary *Man* 57-59; C Ashton St Mich 59-61; V Croydon H Trin *Cant* 61-68; R Stisted *Chelmsf* 68-69; P-in-c Pattiswick 68-69; P-in-c Bradwell 68-69; R Stisted w Bradwell and Pattiswick 69-87; rtd 87. *Curvalion House, Creech St Michael, Taunton, Somerset TA3 5QF* Tel (01823) 443842

MUGRIDGE, Mrs Gloria Janet. b 45. R Holloway Coll Lon BA66 Bedf Coll Lon DSocStuds67. S Dios Minl Tr Scheme 90. **d** 95 **p** 96. NSM Dorchester *Sarum* from 95; Asst Chapl Weymouth Coll from 95. *63 Syward Close, Dorchester, Dorset DT1 2AN* Tel (01305) 269203

MUIR, David Murray. b 49. Glas Univ MA70 Nottm Univ BA72. St Jo Coll Nottm 70. **d** 76 **p** 77. C Fulham St Mary N End *Lon* 76-80; C Aspley *S'well* 80; India 81-85; Dir Ext Studies St Jo Coll Nottm from 85; Perm to Offic *Derby* from 85. *St John's College, Chilwell Lane, Bramcote, Nottingham NG9 3DS* Tel 0115-925 1117 or 925 1114 Fax 922 0134 or 943 6438

MUIR, Canon David Trevor. b 49. TCD MA MLitt93. CITC. **d** 78 **p** 79. C Dublin Clontarf *D & G* 78-80; C Monkstown St Mary 80-83; I Kilternan 83-94; I Delgany from 94; Can Ch Ch Cathl Dublin from 95. *The Rectory, Delgany, Co Wicklow, Irish Republic* Tel Dublin (1) 287 4515

MUIR, John Johnston. b 20. Strathclyde Univ BSc81 ARCT51. St Jo Coll Nottm 83. **d** 85 **p** 87. Hon C Glas St Marg *Glas* 85-91; rtd 91; Perm to Offic *B & W* from 91. *265 Milton Road, Weston-super-Mare, Avon BS22 8JA* Tel (01934) 622036

MUIR, John William. b 38. Dur Univ BA59 Mansf Coll Ox MA65. Chich Th Coll 78. **d** 78 **p** 79. In Congr Ch (England & Wales) 62-70; In United Ch of Zambia 70-78; C Brighouse *Wakef* 78-80; V Northowram 80-87; V Sowerby from 87. *The Vicarage, Towngate, Sowerby, Sowerby Bridge, W Yorkshire HX6 1JJ* Tel (01422) 831036

MUKHERJEE (or MUKHOPADHYAY), Supriyo. b 42. Calcutta Univ BA70. Serampore Th Coll BD76 Bp's Coll Calcutta 70. **d** 75 **p** 76. India 75-91; C Crook *Dur* 91-92; V Nelson in Lt Marsden *Blackb* 92-95; Dioc Community Relns Officer *Cov* from 95; TV Cov E from 95. *St Barnabas' Vicarage, 55 St Paul's Road, Coventry CV6 5DE* Tel (01203) 688264

MULCOCK, Edward John. b 16. Leeds Univ BA37. Coll of Resurr Mirfield 37. **d** 39 **p** 40. C Long Eaton St Laur *Derby* 39-48; V Leeds St Hilda *Ripon* 48-55; V Roath St German *Llan* 55-60; Min S Kenton Annunciation CD *Lon* 61-66; V Fulham St Jo Walham Green 66-76; V Fulham St Jas Moore Park 69-76; V Walham Green St Jo w St Jas 76-83; rtd 84. *Flat 2, Gardens Court, 57 Parkstone Road, Poole, Dorset BH15 2NX* Tel (01202) 673162

MULHOLLAND, Nicholas Christopher John (Chris). b 44. Chich Th Coll 77. **d** 79 **p** 80. C Thornbury *Glouc* 79-83; R Boxwell, Leighterton, Didmarton, Oldbury etc from 83. *The Rectory, Leighterton, Tetbury, Glos GL8 8UW* Tel (01666) 890283

MULKERN, Richard Neville. b 39. S'wark Ord Course 88. **d** 91 **p** 92. NSM Leytonstone St Andr *Chelmsf* 91-93; Min Sec and Welfare Officer Miss to Seamen 91-93; Welfare Sec 93-94; Dir N Region from 94; Perm to Offic *Blackb* from 94; Perm to Offic *Bradf* from 95; NSM Oulton w Woodlesford *Ripon* from 96. *14 Northwood Park, Woodlesford, Leeds LS26 8PF* Tel 0113-282 1668 or 270 5578

MULLARD, George Edward. b 14. St D Coll Lamp BA38 Sarum Th Coll 38. **d** 39 **p** 40. C Hartland and Welcombe *Ex* 39-42; C Plymouth St Gabr 42-45; C Northam 45-48; V E Coker *B & W* 48-69; V E Coker w Sutton Bingham 69-79; rtd 79; Perm to Offic *B & W* from 79. *Alvington Cottage, Brympton, Yeovil, Somerset BA22 8TH* Tel (01935) 471752

MULLEN, Charles William. b 64. CITC BTh92. **d** 92 **p** 93. C Lecale Gp *D & D* 92-95; I Gorey w Kilnahue, Leskinfere and Ballycanew *C & O* from 95. *Christ Church Rectory, The Avenue, Gorey, Co Wexford, Irish Republic* Tel Gorey (55) 21383 Mobile 088-618878 Fax as telephone

MULLEN, Peter John. b 42. Liv Univ BA70. **d** 70 **p** 71. C Manston *Ripon* 70-72; C Stretford All SS *Man* 72-73; C Oldham St Mary w St Pet 73-74; Lic to Offic 74-77; V Tockwith and Bilton w Bickerton *York* 77-89. *16 Whin Road, Dringhouses, York YO2 2JZ*

MULLENGER, Canon Alan Edward Clement. b 15. Lon Univ BD64. Kelham Th Coll 35. **d** 40 **p** 41. SSM from 40; C Sheff Parson Cross St Cecilia *Sheff* 40-48; S Africa 48-56; Basutoland 56-61; Wycliffe Hall Ox 63-64; Perm to Offic *Ox* 63-64; Perm to Offic *Nor* 64-65; St Aug Coll Walsingham 64-65; Ghana 65-74; Hon Can Kumasi 73-74; Lesotho from 74; Hon Can Lesotho Cathl from 88. *PO Box 122, Roma 180, Lesotho* Tel Lesotho (266) 315079

MULLENGER, William. b 44. Linc Th Coll 68. **d** 69 **p** 70. C Clapham St Jo *S'wark* 69-73; C Hook 73-81; P-in-c Camberwell St Phil and St Mark 81-85; V Hackbridge and N Beddington 85-93; rtd 93; Perm to Offic *Roch* from 93. *30 Constance Crescent, Bromley BR2 7QJ*

MULLENS, John Langford. b 06. Selw Coll Cam BA28 MA52. Westcott Ho Cam 29. **d** 29 **p** 30. C Benwell St Jas *Newc* 29-36; C Hexham 36-39; V Delaval 39-54; R Farthinghoe w Thenford *Pet* 54-71; rtd 71; Perm to Offic *Roch* 72-95; Perm to Offic *Cant* and *Chich* from 72. *Brentwood Court, 29D Frant Road, Tunbridge Wells, Kent TN2 5JT* Tel (01892) 527770

MULLER, Vernon. b 40. Natal Univ BA61 St Chad's Coll Dur DipTh64. **d** 64 **p** 65. S Africa 64-76; Chapl Friern Hosp Lon 77-91; Chapl R Berks Hosp Reading 91-95; Chapl Battle Hosp Reading 91-95; Perm to Offic *Chelmsf* from 95. *8 Ruskin Road, Chelmsford CM2 6HN* Tel (01245) 345865

MULLER, Wolfgang Wilhelm Bernard Heinrich Paul. b 28. ALCD54. **d** 55 **p** 56. C Tonbridge SS Pet and Paul *Roch* 55-56; C Chatham St Steph 56-59; C-in-c Wigmore w Hempstead CD 59-65; V Wigmore w Hempstead 65-72; V S Gillingham 72-73; W Germany 73-90; Germany from 90; rtd 93. *Krokusweg 14, 34431 Marsberg 14, Germany*

MULLETT, John St Hilary. b 25. St Cath Coll Cam BA47 MA49. Linc Th Coll. **d** 50 **p** 51. C Tottenham All Hallows *Lon* 50-52; S Rhodesia 52-61; V Bollington St Jo *Ches* 61-69; V Oxton 69-77; R Ashwell *St Alb* 77-90; RD Buntingford 82-88; rtd 90; Fell St Cath Coll Cam from 90; Perm to Offic *Ely* from 90. *13 Church Lane, Madingley, Cambridge CB3 8AF* Tel (01954) 211670

MULLIGAN, Colin. b 42. **d** 96 **p** 97. NSM Neath w Llantwit *Llan* from 96. *12 Chestnut Road, Neath SA11 3PB*

MULLINEAUX, John. b 16. Man Univ BA38. Kelham Th Coll 38. **d** 41 **p** 42. C Bedminster St Jo *Bris* 41-44; CF 44-47; Min Can Blackb Cathl *Blackb* 47-50; V Brierfield 50-60; V Lancaster Ch Ch 60-67; V Caton w Littledale 67-81; rtd 81; Lic to Offic *Blackb* from 81. *10 Ashfield Avenue, Lancaster LA1 5DZ* Tel (01524) 36769

MULLINER, Denis Ratliffe. b 40. BNC Ox BA62 MA66. Linc Th Coll 70. **d** 72 **p** 73. C Sandhurst *Ox* 72-76; Chapl Bradfield Coll Berks from 76. *Great Oaks, Bradfield, Reading RG7 6AR* Tel 0118-974 4263

MULLINS, Joe. b 20. MC45. Trin Coll Ox BA49 MA59. Ridley Hall Cam 48. **d** 50 **p** 51. C Portman Square St Paul *Lon* 50-52; India 52-74; Australia from 74; rtd 86. *24 Bunny Street, Weston, ACT, Australia 2611* Tel Canberra (6) 288-9973

MULLINS, Malcolm David. b 42. St Edm Hall Ox BA63. St Steph Ho Ox 63. **d** 65 **p** 66. C Kirkby *Liv* 65-69; C Lamorbey H Redeemer *Roch* 69-75; C Solihull *Birm* 75-77; rtd 77. *PO Box 3127, London NW7 3SZ*

MULLINS, Mrs Margaret. b 49. Southn Univ CertEd70 K Alfred's Coll Win DSpEd87. Sarum & Wells Th Coll DCTM94. **d** 94 **p** 95. C Bishopstoke *Win* from 94. *5 Harding Lane, Fair Oak, Eastleigh, Hants SO50 8GL* Tel (01703) 601031

MULLINS, Peter Matthew. b 60. Ch Ch Ox BA82 MA86 Birm Univ DPS84 Irish Sch of Ecum MPhil90. Qu Coll Birm 82. **d** 84 **p** 85. C Caversham and Mapledurham *Ox* 84-88; Perm to Offic *D & G* 88-89; TV Old Brumby *Linc* 89-94; Clergy Tr Adv from 94; Gen Preacher from 95. *1 St Giles Avenue, Lincoln LN2 4PE* Tel (01522) 528199

MULLINS, Timothy Dougal. b 59. Dur Univ. Wycliffe Hall Ox 83. **d** 85 **p** 86. C Reading Greyfriars *Ox* 85-89; C Haughton le Skerne *Dur* 89-95; Chapl Eton Coll from 95. *2 Church Close, High Street, Eton, Windsor, Berks SL4 6AP* Tel (01753) 671373

MULLIS, Robert Owen (Bob). b 49. Bris Univ BA71 CertEd71 Birm Univ ACertEd91. St Mich Coll Llan DMinlStuds93. **d** 93 **p** 94. NSM Llangenni and Llanbedr Ystrad Yw w Patricio *S & B* from 93. *3 Pontfaen, Llanbedr, Crickhowell NP8 1SJ* Tel (01873) 811927

MULRAINE, Miss Margaret Haskell. b 24. Birm Univ BA45 DipEd46. Sarum Th Coll 83. **dss** 86 **d** 87 **p** 94. Wareham *Sarum* 86-87; Hon Par Dn 87-93; Perm to Offic from 93. *5 Trinity Close, Trinity Lane, Wareham, Dorset BH20 4LL* Tel (01929) 552523

MULRENAN, Richard John. b 12. ACA36 FCA60. Tyndale Hall Bris 37. **d** 46 **p** 48. BCMS Miss W China 38-50; C Bris St Phil and St Jacob w Em *Bris* 46; C Bucknall and Bagnall *Lich* 51-53; V Bayston Hill 53-57; V Branksome St Clem *Sarum* 57-66; V Braintree *Chelmsf* 66-77; Chapl Wm Julien Courtauld Hosp 66-77; rtd 77; P-in-c Glympton *Ox* 80-81; Perm to Offic from 81. *36 Emmbrook Court, Reading RG6 5TZ* Tel 0118-986 1453

MUMFORD, Dr David Bardwell. b 49. MRCPsych86 St Cath Coll Cam BA71 MA75 Bris Univ MB, ChB81 Edin Univ MPhil89. Bp's Coll Calcutta 71 Cuddesdon Coll 73. **d** 75. C Bris St Mary Redcliffe w Temple etc *Bris* 75-76; NSM 76-82; NSM Edin St Columba *Edin* 82-86; NSM Calverley *Bradf* 86-92; Perm to Offic *B & W* from 92. *14 Clifton Vale, Clifton, Bristol BS8 4PT* Tel 0117-927 2221

MUMFORD, David Christopher. b 47. Mert Coll Ox BA68 MA74 York Univ MSW CQSW81. Linc Th Coll 84. **d** 86 **p** 87. C Shiremoor *Newc* 86-89; C N Shields 89-91; V Byker St Ant from 91; RD Newc E 96-97. *St Anthony's Vicarage, Enslin Gardens, Newcastle upon Tyne NE6 3ST* Tel 0191-265 1605

MUMFORD, Grenville Alan. b 34. Richmond Th Coll DipTh. **d** 78 **p** 78. C Witham *Chelmsf* 78-81; C-in-c Gt Ilford St Marg CD 81-85; V Gt Ilford St Marg 85-87; P-in-c Everton and Mattersey w Clayworth *S'well* 87-89; R 89-96; RD Bawtry 93-96; rtd 96. *146 Audlem Road, Nantwich, Cheshire CW5 7EB* Tel (01777) 817364

MUMFORD, Canon Hugh Raymond. b 24. Oak Hill Th Coll 50. **d** 53 **p** 54. C Bethnal Green St Jas Less *Lon* 53-57; C Watford

St Mary *St Alb* 57-59; R Thetford St Pet w St Nic *Nor* 59-69; RD Thetford 68-69; V Nether Cerne *Sarum* 69-71; R Godmanstone 69-71; R Cerne Abbas w Upcerne 69-71; R Minterne Magna 69-71; V Cerne Abbas w Godmanstone and Minterne Magna 71-89; RD Dorchester 75-79; Can and Preb Sarum Cathl 77-89; rtd 89. *10 South Walks Road, Dorchester, Dorset DT1 1ED* Tel (01305) 264971

MUMFORD, John Alexander. b 52. St Andr Univ MTh75. Ridley Hall Cam 75. **d** 77 **p** 78. C Canford Magna *Sarum* 77-82; C Ches Square St Mich w St Phil *Lon* 82-85; USA 85-87; SW Lon Vineyard Chr Fellowship from 87. *572 Kingston Road, London SW20 8DR*

MUMFORD, Michael David. b 29. **d** 79 **p** 80. Chapl Lister Hosp Stevenage 79-83; C Royston *St Alb* 83-87; P-in-c Kelshall 83-88; P-in-c Therfield 83-88; C Barkway, Reed and Buckland w Barley 87-88; R Ewhurst *Chich* 88-94; R Bodiam 88-94; RD Rye 90-91; rtd 94; Perm to Offic *Chich* from 94. *6 Whydown Place, Bexhill-on-Sea, E Sussex TN39 4RA* Tel (01424) 845278

MUNBY, Philip James. b 52. Pemb Coll Ox BA75 MA80. St Jo Coll Nottm 76. **d** 78 **p** 79. C Gipsy Hill Ch Ch *S'wark* 78-82; C-in-c W Dulwich Em CD 82-88; V Barnsley St Geo *Wakef* from 88. *St George's Vicarage, 100 Dodworth Road, Barnsley, S Yorkshire S70 6HL* Tel (01226) 203870

MUNCEY, William. b 49. BA80. Oak Hill Th Coll. **d** 80 **p** 81. C Wandsworth St Mich *S'wark* 80-84; C Morden 84-88; TV from 88. *5 Willows Avenue, Morden, Surrey SM4 5SG* Tel 0181-646 2002

MUNCHIN, David Leighfield. b 67. Imp Coll Lon BSc88. Ripon Coll Cuddesdon 89. **d** 92 **p** 93. C Golders Green *Lon* 92-94; C Golders Green 94-96; Prec St Alb Abbey *St Alb* from 96. *Flat 1, The Deanery, Sumpter Yard, St Albans, Herts AL1 1BY* Tel (01727) 855321

MUNDEN, Alan Frederick. b 43. Nottm Univ BTh74 Birm Univ MLitt80 Dur Univ PhD87. St Jo Coll Nottm LTh74. **d** 74 **p** 75. C Cheltenham St Mary *Glouc* 74-76; C Cheltenham St Mary, St Matt, St Paul and H Trin 76; Hon C Jesmond Clayton Memorial *Newc* 76-80; C 80-83; V Cheylesmore *Cov* from 83. *Christ Church Vicarage, 11 Frankpledge Road, Coventry CV3 5GT* Tel (01203) 502770

MUNGAVIN, David Stewart. b 60. Stirling Univ BA80. Edin Th Coll 87. **d** 90 **p** 91. C Glas St Marg *Glas* 90-92; P-in-c Airdrie 92-96; R from 96; P-in-c Coatbridge 92-96; R from 96; P-in-c Gartcosh 92-96; R from 96. *24 Etive Drive, Airdrie, Lanarkshire ML6 9QQ* Tel (01236) 756550 Fax as telephone

MUNGAVIN, Canon Gerald Clarence. b 27. Edin Th Coll 51. **d** 54 **p** 55. C Dunfermline *St And* 54-55; C Glas Gd Shep *Glas* 55-57; CF 57-60; C Stanwix *Carl* 60-62; Chapl RAF 62-75; R Turriff *Ab* 75-81; R Cuminestown 75-81; R Banff 75-81; R Banchory 81-92; R Kincardine O'Neil 81-92; Can St Andr Cathl from 89; rtd 92. *Craigleith, Bowfield Road, Howwood, Johnstone, Renfrewshire PA9 1BS* Tel (01505) 702461

MUNN, Carole Christine. b 45. EMMTC 83. **d** 90 **p** 94. NSM Long Bennington w Foston *Linc* 90-95; NSM Saxonwell from 95; Asst Chapl HM Pris Linc from 96. *The Rectory, Claypole, Newark, Notts NG23 5BH* Tel (01636) 626224

MUNN, George. b 44. MM72. Linc Th Coll 85. **d** 87 **p** 88. C Boston *Linc* 87-90; R Claypole from 90. *The Rectory, Claypole, Newark, Notts NG23 5BH* Tel (01636) 626224

MUNN, Richard Probyn. b 45. Selw Coll Cam BA67 MA69. Cuddesdon Coll 67. **d** 69 **p** 70. C Cirencester *Glouc* 69-71; USPG 71-79; Zambia 71-79; Adn S Zambia 79; P-in-c Kings Stanley *Glouc* 80-83; R Lezant w Lawhitton and S Petherwin w Trewen *Truro* 84-92; Lesotho from 93. *PO Box 249, Leribe, Lesotho* Tel Lesotho (266) 400731

MUNNS, Stuart Millington. b 36. OBE77. MIDPM91 St Cath Coll Cam BA58 MA62. Cuddesdon Coll 58. **d** 60 **p** 61. C Allenton and Shelton Lock *Derby* 60-63; C Brampton St Thos 63-65; C-in-c Loundsley Green Ascension CD 65-66; Bp's Youth Chapl 66-72; Nat Dir of Community Industry 72-77; Hon C Hornsey Ch Ch *Lon* 72-77; Dioc Missr *Liv* 77-82; V Knowsley 77-82; P-in-c Stramshall *Lich* 82-88; V Uttoxeter w Bramshall 82-88; RD Uttoxeter 82-87; P-in-c Kingstone w Gratwich 84-88; P-in-c Marchington w Marchington Woodlands 84-88; P-in-c Checkley 86-88; Perm to Offic *B & W* 88-90; NSM Wells St Thos w Horrington 90-94; P-in-c Ditcheat w E Pennard and Pylle from 94. *The Rectory, Ditcheat, Shepton Mallet, Somerset BA4 6RE* Tel (01749) 860429 Fax as telephone

MUNRO, Basil Henry. b 40. Ripon Hall Ox 73. **d** 75 **p** 76. C N Mymms *St Alb* 75-78; C St Alb St Steph 78-80; V 80-87; R Aston-on-Trent and Weston-on-Trent *Derby* from 87; Chapl Aston Hall Hosp Derby from 87. *The Rectory, Rectory Gardens, Aston-on-Trent, Derby DE72 2AZ* Tel (01332) 792658

MUNRO, Donald Alexander. b 08. Clifton Th Coll. **d** 46 **p** 47. C Drumholm and Rossnowlagh *D & R* 46-48; C Chilvers Coton *Cov* 48-51; V Ansley 51-57; V Shapwick w Ashcott *B & W* 57-69; V Kilmington 69-83; rtd 84; Perm to Offic *B & W* 84-90. *182 Harepath Road, Seaton, Devon EX12 2HE* Tel (01297) 20567

MUNRO, Duncan John Studd. b 50. Magd Coll Ox BA72 MA76. Wycliffe Hall Ox 73. **d** 76 **p** 77. C Ecclesall *Sheff* 76-77; C Sheff St Barn and St Mary 78-80; Lic to Offic 80-95. *Poppyfields, Church Road, Crowle, Worcester WR7 4AT* Tel (01905) 381893

MUNRO, Robert Speight. b 63. Bris Univ BSc84 Man Univ PGCE87. All So Coll of Applied Th DipApTh86 Oak Hill Th Coll BA93. **d** 93 **p** 94. C Hartford *Ches* from 93. *The Rectory, Church Street, Davenham, Cheshire CW9 8NF* Tel (01606) 42450

MUNRO, Canon Terence George. b 34. Jes Coll Cam BA56 MA60. Linc Th Coll 59. **d** 61 **p** 62. C Far Headingley St Chad *Ripon* 61-64; Jamaica 64-70; R Methley w Mickletown *Ripon* 70-79; V Hunslet Moor St Pet and St Cuth 79-85; R Barwick in Elmet 85-93; V Woodhouse and Wrangthorn from 93; Dioc Ecum Officer from 93; Hon Can Ripon Cathl from 94. *St Mark's Vicarage, St Mark's Avenue, Leeds LS2 9BN* Tel 0113-245 4893 Fax as telephone

MUNT, Cyril. b 27. AKC52. **d** 53 **p** 54. C Ashford *Cant* 53-56; C Dorking w Ranmore *Guildf* 56-60; R Cheriton w Newington *Cant* 60-68; R Harbledown 68-83; R Porlock w Stoke Pero *B & W* 83-92; rtd 92; Perm to Offic *B & W* from 92. *Applegarth, 26 Hood Close, Glastonbury, Somerset BA6 8ES* Tel (01458) 831842

MUNT, Canon Donald James. b 20. ALCD53 St Jo Coll Nottm LTh74. **d** 53 **p** 54. C Purley Ch Ch *S'wark* 53-56; C Hatcham St Jas 56-61; V Oulton Broad *Nor* 61-69; V Deptford St Pet *S'wark* 69-76; R Litcham w Kempston w E and W Lexham *Nor* 76-83; P-in-c Mileham 81-83; P-in-c Beeston next Mileham 81-83; P-in-c Stanfield 81-83; R Litcham, Kempston, Lexham, Mileham, Beeston etc 84-87; RD Brisley and Elmham 85-87; Hon Can Nor Cathl 87-88; rtd 88; Perm to Offic *Nor* from 88. *7 Irwin Close, Reepham, Norwich NR10 4EQ* Tel (01603) 870618

MUNT, Mrs Linda Christine. b 55. NE Ord Course DipHE92. **d** 95 **p** 96. NSM Beverley St Nic *York* 95-96; C from 96. *11 Cherry Garth, Beverley, N Humberside HU17 0EP* Tel (01482) 869945

MUNT, Canon Neil. b 20. AKC43. Linc Th Coll 43. **d** 44 **p** 45. C St Helier *S'wark* 44-46; C Redhill St Matt 46-51; C Uckfield *Chich* 51-53; V Malden St Jas *S'wark* 53-62; V Godmanchester *Ely* 62-74; Hon Can Ely Cathl 74-86; V Ely 74-86; V Prickwillow 76-86; V Chettisham 76-86; RD Ely 82-86; rtd 86; Perm to Offic *Ely* from 86. *8A Wood Street, Doddington, March, Cambs PE15 0SA* Tel (01354) 740738

MURCH, Canon Robin Norman. b 37. Wells Th Coll. **d** 67 **p** 68. C Wisbech St Aug *Ely* 67-70; C Basingstoke *Win* 70-73; C Whitstable All SS *Cant* 73-76; V Queenborough from 76; Hon Can Cant Cathl from 96. *The Vicarage, North Road, Queenborough, Kent ME11 5ET* Tel (01795) 662648

MURDIN, Frank Laurence. b 11. Leeds Univ BA34. Coll of Resurr Mirfield 34. **d** 36 **p** 37. C Pet St Paul *Pet* 36-41; R Culworth 41-58; RD Culworth 50-58; V Moreton Pinkney 55-58; R Brampton Ash w Dingley 58-65; RD Weldon 64-65; V Greetham w Stretton and Clipsham 65-76; rtd 76. *48 Pinewood Close, Bourne, Lincs PE10 9RL* Tel (01778) 423696

MURDOCH, Alexander Edward Duncan. b 37. Oak Hill Th Coll 68. **d** 71 **p** 72. C Kensington St Helen w H Trin *Lon* 71-72; C Kensington St Barn 73-74; CF 74-78; C W Kirby St Bridget *Ches* 78-84; V N Shoebury *Chelmsf* 84-87; V W Poldens *B & W* 87-96; R Gayhurst w Ravenstone, Stoke Goldington etc *Ox* from 96. *The Rectory, Stoke Goldington, Newport Pagnell, Bucks MK16 8LL* Tel (01908) 55221

MURDOCH, David John. b 58. Birm Univ BSocSc81. Ripon Coll Cuddesdon 81. **d** 84 **p** 85. C Penwortham St Leon *Blackb* 84-87; C Wirksworth w Alderwasley, Carsington etc *Derby* 87-89; R Shirland 89-97; Dioc World Development Officer from 96; P-in-c New Mills from 97. *St George's Vicarage, Church Lane, New Mills, Stockport, Cheshire SK12 4NP* Tel (01663) 746301

MURFET, Edward David. b 36. Qu Coll Cam BA59 MA63. Chich Th Coll 59. **d** 61 **p** 62. C Croydon St Mich *Cant* 61-64; C Hunslet St Mary and Stourton *Ripon* 64-65; C Hackney Wick St Mary of Eton w St Aug *Lon* 65-69; Chapl Berne *Eur* 69-71; Chapl Naples 71-74; Chapl Rome 74-77; Lic to Offic *Bris* 78-81; Gen Sec CEMS 81-86; C Leeds St Pet *Ripon* 87-89; P-in-c 89-90; C Leeds City 91-93; Min Can Ripon Cathl from 93. *17 High St Agnesgate, Ripon, N Yorkshire HG4 1QR* Tel (01765) 602609

MURFET, Gwyn. b 44. Linc Th Coll 71. **d** 74 **p** 75. C Scalby w Ravenscar and Staintondale *York* 74-77; P-in-c S Milford 77-83; R 83-84; V Kirkby Ireleth *Carl* from 84. *The Vicarage, School Road, Kirkby-in-Furness, Cumbria LA17 7UQ* Tel (01229) 889256

MURGATROYD, Canon Eric. b 17. Open Univ BA77. Lich Th Coll 43. **d** 46 **p** 46. C Otley *Bradf* 46-49; C Skipton H Trin 49-51; V Grindleton 51-56; V Yeadon St Andr 56-66; V Cottingley 66-77; Hon Can Bradf Cathl 77-83; V Woodhall 77-83; rtd 83; Perm to Offic *Bradf* from 83. *34 Ferncliffe Drive, Baildon, Shipley, W Yorkshire BD17 5AQ* Tel (01274) 594072

MURIEL, Sister. *See* ARTHINGTON, Sister Muriel

MURPHIE, Andrew Graham. b 65. Reading Univ BA86. St Jo Coll Nottm BTh91 MA92. **d** 92 **p** 93. C Boulton *Derby* 92-96; C Marston on Dove w Scropton from 96. *The Vicarage, 28 Back Lane, Hilton, Derby DE65 5GJ* Tel (01283) 733433

MURPHY, Alexander Charles. b 28. St Edm Coll Ware 50. **d** 55 **p** 56. NSM Edin St Jas *Edin* 88-90; TV Edin St Mark 90-93; TV

Edin St Andr and St Aid 90-93; TV Edin St Marg 93-96; rtd 96. *29 Shadepark Drive, Dalkeith, Midlothian EH22 1DA* Tel 0131-660 1574

MURPHY, Andrew John. b 46. Edin Univ LLB67 MA68. **d** 95. NSM Aberdeen St Marg *Ab* from 95. *c/o St Margaret's Clergy House, Gallowgate, Aberdeen AB1 1EA* Tel (01324) 620822

MURPHY, Jack. b 27. N Ord Course 83. **d** 86 **p** 87. C Armley w New Wortley *Ripon* 86-90; C Hawksworth Wood 90-94; rtd 94; Perm to Offic *York* from 96. *70 Avocet Way, Bridlington, N Humberside YO15 3NT* Tel (01262) 609477

MURPHY, Dr James Royse. b 54. DRCOG80 MRCGP81 Bris Univ MB, ChB77. Glouc Sch of Min 89. **d** 92 **p** 94. NSM Glouc St Cath *Glouc* from 92. *31 Plock Court, Gloucester GL2 9DW* Tel (01452) 411772

MURPHY, Canon John Gervase Maurice Walker (Gerry). b 26. LVO87. TCD BA52 MA55. **d** 52 **p** 53. C Lurgan Ch Ch *D & D* 52-55; CF 55-73; Asst Chapl Gen 73-77; V Ranworth w Panxworth *Nor* 77-79; RD Blofield 79; Dom Chapl to The Queen 79-87; Chapl to The Queen from 87; R Sandringham w W Newton *Nor* 79-87; RD Heacham and Rising 85-87; Hon Can Nor Cathl 86-87; Chapl Intercon Ch Soc 87-91; Falkland Is 87-91; Miss to Seamen 87-91; rtd 91; Chapl St Pet-ad-Vincula at HM Tower of Lon 91-96; Dep P in O from 92; Extra Chapl to The Queen from 96. *Saffron Close, 17 Ringstead Road, Heacham, King's Lynn, Norfolk PE31 7JA* Tel (01485) 572351

MURPHY, Maurice Vincent. b 49. Van Mildert Coll Dur BSc70. **d** 85 **p** 86. NSM Malpas *Mon* 85-86; Perm to Offic *Man* 86-90; NSM Bolton Breightmet St Jas 90-94; NSM Rawtenstall St Mary from 94. *18 Higher Ridings, Bromley Cross, Bolton BL7 9HP*

MURPHY, Owen. b 52. Open Univ BA85. Chich Th Coll 92. **d** 94 **p** 95. C Oxhey St Matt *St Alb* 94-96; C Watford St Mich from 96. *57 Whippendell Road, Watford WD1 7LY* Tel (01923) 248739

MURPHY, Peter Frederick. b 40. AKC65. **d** 67 **p** 68. C Paddington St Jo w St Mich *Lon* 67-72; P-in-c Basingstoke *Win* 72-76; TV 76-81; V Hythe 81-92; V Lyndhurst and Emery Down from 92; P-in-c Copythorne and Minstead from 95. *The Vicarage, 5 Forest Gardens, Lyndhurst, Hants SO43 7AF* Tel (01703) 282154

MURPHY, Philip John Warwick. b 65. Kent Univ BA87 Southn Univ BTh93 SSC. Chich Th Coll 88. **d** 91 **p** 92. C Broadstone *Sarum* 91-94; C Teddington SS Pet and Paul and Fulwell *Lon* 94-96; V Leytonstone St Marg w St Columba *Chelmsf* from 96; P-in-c Leytonstone St Andr from 96. *St Margaret's Vicarage, 15 Woodhouse Road, London E11 3NG* Tel 0181-519 0813 Mobile 0973-132024 Fax as telephone E-mail fatherphilip @shrine.demon.co.uk

MURPHY, Ronald Frederick. b 38. **d** 84 **p** 85. P-in-c N Cerney w Bagendon *Glouc* 87-90. *70 Tattershall, Toot Hill, Swindon SN5 8BX* Tel (01793) 694870

MURPHY, William Albert. b 43. Lon Univ BD73 QUB MTh78. **d** 73 **p** 74. C Lisburn Ch Ch *Conn* 73-79; Supt & Chapl Ulster Inst for the Deaf from 79; Chapl HM Pris Maze from 82; Dioc Dir Ords *Conn* from 92. *Ulster Institute for the Deaf, 5-6 College Square North, Belfast BT1 6AR* Tel (01232) 321733 Fax 233868

MURRAY, Alan. b 37. Sarum Th Coll 62. **d** 64 **p** 65. C High Elswick St Phil *Newc* 64-68; C Seaton Hirst 68-74; V Seghill from 74. *The Vicarage, Seghill, Cramlington, Northd NE23 7EA* Tel 0191-237 1601

MURRAY, Alan. b 61. St Jo Coll Nottm BTh92. **d** 92 **p** 93. C Wombwell *Sheff* 92-95; C Mortomley St Sav High Green from 95. *161 Mortomley Lane, High Green, Sheffield S30 4HT* Tel 0114-284 6668

MURRAY, Mrs Christine Jean. b 57. Qu Coll Birm 93. **d** 95. C Milton *Win* from 95. *15 Conway Close, New Milton, Hants BH25 6HL* Tel (01425) 620409

MURRAY, Christopher James. b 49. Open Univ BA78. St Jo Coll Nottm 79. **d** 81 **p** 82. C Heatherlands St Jo *Sarum* 81-84; C Hamworthy 84-90; R Passenham *Pet* from 90. *The Rectory, Deanshanger, Milton Keynes MK19 6JP* Tel (01908) 262371

MURRAY, David McIlveen. b 36. ALCD61. **d** 61 **p** 62. C Mortlake w E Sheen *S'wark* 61-64; C Lyncombe *B & W* 64-67; C Horsham *Chich* 67-73; V Devonport St Bart *Ex* 73-79; R Chalfont St Peter *Ox* 79-95; RD Amersham 86-89; R Lower Windrush from 95. *The Rectory, Stanton Harcourt, Witney, Oxon OX8 1RP* Tel (01865) 880249

MURRAY, Gordon Stewart. b 33. Birkb Coll Lon BSc72. Ripon Coll Cuddesdon 76. **d** 78 **p** 79. C Kenilworth St Nic *Cov* 78-81; V Potterspury w Furtho and Yardley Gobion *Pet* 81-83; V Potterspury, Furtho, Yardley Gobion and Cosgrove 84; TV Wolvercote w Summertown *Ox* 84-90; P-in-c Walworth *S'wark* 90-95; TR Walworth St Pet from 95. *St Peter's Rectory, Liverpool Grove, London SE17 2HH* Tel 0171-703 3139

MURRAY, Ian Hargraves. b 48. Man Univ BSc71. St Jo Coll Nottm 79. **d** 81 **p** 82. C Erith St Paul *Roch* 81-84; C Willenhall H Trin *Lich* 84-87; TV 87-92; P-in-c Moxley from 92. *The Vicarage, 5 Sutton Road, Moxley, Wednesbury, W Midlands WS10 8SG* Tel (01902) 491807

MURRAY, Ian William. b 32. Lon Univ BA53 PGCE54. Oak Hill NSM Course 80. **d** 83 **p** 84. NSM Pinner *Lon* from 83. *4 Mansard Close, West End Lane, Pinner, Middx HA5 3FQ* Tel 0181-866 2984

MURRAY, Canon John Desmond. b 16. TCD BA38 MA46. CITC 39. **d** 39 **p** 40. C Dublin St Werburgh *D & G* 39-41; C Dublin Ch Ch Leeson Park 41-43; C Dublin Rathmines 43-49; Min Can St Patr Cathl Dublin 43-53; I Powerscourt *D & G* 49-53; Chapl RN 53-55; I Dalkey St Patr *D & G* 55-70; I Milltown 70-82; Hon Chapl to Abp Dublin 73-82; Can Ch Ch Cathl Dublin 79-82; rtd 82. *3 Adare Close, Killincarrig, Greystones, Co Wicklow, Irish Republic* Tel Dublin (1) 287 6359

MURRAY, John Douglas. b 16. Keble Coll Ox BA38 MA46. Bps' Coll Cheshunt 38. **d** 40 **p** 41. C Lowther w Askham *Carl* 40-41; C Barrow St Geo 41-43; CF 43-47; V Brigham *Carl* 47-50; Tutor St Pet Coll of Educn Birm 50-78; Lic to Offic *Birm* 50-79; P-in-c Streat w Westmeston *Chich* 79-86; rtd 81; Perm to Offic *Birm* from 87. *51 Walkers Way, South Bretton, Peterborough PE3 9AX*

MURRAY, The Ven John Grainger. b 45. CITC 67. **d** 70 **p** 71. C Carlow *C & O* 70-72; C Limerick St Mary *L & K* 72-77; I Rathdowney w Castlefleming, Donaghmore etc *C & O* from 77; Preb Leighlin Cathl 83-88; Chan 89-90; Prec 90-92; Preb Ossory Cathl 83-88; Chan 89-90; Prec 90-92; Adn Ossory and Leighlin from 92; Adn Cashel, Waterford and Lismore from 94. *The Rectory, Rathdowney, Portlaoise, Co Laois, Irish Republic* Tel Rathdowney (505) 46311 Fax 46540

MURRAY, John Louis. b 47. Keble Coll Ox BA67 MA69. **d** 82 **p** 83. Asst Chapl Strasbourg *Eur* from 82. *10 rue du General Gourard, 67000 Strasbourg, France* Tel France (33) 88 36 12 25

MURRAY, John Thomas. b 33. Edin Th Coll 63. **d** 66 **p** 67. C Golcar *Wakef* 66-69; Guyana 70-74; Perm to Offic *S'wark* 74-75; Perm to Offic *Lon* 75-79; Hon C Paddington St Mary Magd 79-82; Asst Chapl Athens w Kifissia *Eur* 82-83; Chapl Br Emb Ankara 83-85; R Johnstone *Glas* 86-91; Perm to Offic *Sheff* 91-96; Perm to Offic *Wakef* 91-96; Guyana from 96. *St Alban's Rectory, Belladrum, West Coast Berbice, Guyana*

MURRAY, Mrs Margaret Janice. b 46. Carl Dioc Tr Course. **dss** 86 **d** 87 **p** 94. Walney Is *Carl* 86-87; Hon Par Dn 87-89; Par Dn Carl H Trin and St Barn 89-94; C 94; Chapl Cumberland Infirmary 90-94; C Harraby *Carl* from 94; Chapl Garlands Hosp from 94; Chapl to the Deaf and Hard of Hearing *Carl* from 94. *398 London Road, Carlisle CA1 3ER* Tel (01228) 596427

MURRAY, Paul Ridsdale. b 55. BEd. St Steph Ho Ox. **d** 83 **p** 84. C Hartlepool St Oswald *Dur* 83-86; C S Shields All SS 86-88; V Sacriston and Kimblesworth 88-94; P-in-c Waterhouses from 94. *21 The Wynds, Esh Winning, Durham DH7 9DT* Tel 0191-373 4273

MURRAY, Mrs Ruth Elizabeth. b 55. Dur Univ BA77 Man Coll of Educn CertEd78. **d** 94 **p** 95. NSM Alloa *St And* from 94; Chapl Stirling Univ from 94. *2 Wallace Street, Alloa, Clackmannanshire FK10 3RZ* Tel (01259) 217432 or 724550 Fax 215113

MURRAY (née GOULD), Mrs Susan Judith. b 61. BSc83. St Jo Coll Nottm DTS90. **d** 91 **p** 94. Par Dn Stokesley *York* 91-94; CMS from 94; Perm to Offic *Birm* 94-95; Argentina from 95. *Mision Anglicana, Casilla 9, 3636 Ingeniero Juarez, Prov de Formosa, Argentina*

MURRAY, William Robert Craufurd. b 44. St Chad's Coll Dur BA66 DipTh68. **d** 68 **p** 69. C Workington St Mich *Carl* 68-71; C Harrogate St Wilfrid *Ripon* 71-74; P-in-c Sawley 74; V Winksley cum Grantley and Aldfield w Studley 74; R Fountains 74-81; New Zealand from 81; Can Christchurch Cathl (NZ) from 91. *St Barnabas's Vicarage, 7 Makora Street, Fendalton, Christchurch 4, New Zealand* Tel Christchurch (3) 351 7064 or 351 7392 Fax 351 6374

MURRAY-LESLIE, Adrian John Gervase. b 46. Lich Th Coll 67. **d** 69 **p** 70. C Sheff St Cuth *Sheff* 69-73; C Mosborough 73-75; C-in-c Mosborough CD 75-80; Warden Champion Ho Youth Cen Edale from 80; P-in-c Edale *Derby* from 80. *The Vicarage, Edale, Sheffield S30 2ZA* Tel (01433) 670254

MURRELL, Canon John Edmund. b 28. Westcott Ho Cam. **d** 66 **p** 67. C Ivychurch w Old Romney and Midley *Cant* 66-70; R Bardwell *St E* 70-75; Perm to Offic *Ely* 75-77; V Wenhaston w Thorington and Bramfield w Walpole *St E* 77-86; V Thorington w Wenhaston and Bramfield 86-92; P-in-c Walberswick w Blythburgh 86-92; V Thorington w Wenhaston, Bramfield etc 92-93; RD Halesworth 85-90; Hon Can St E Cathl 89-93; rtd 93. *Blyth Reach, The Street, Walberswick, Southwold, Suffolk IP18 6UN*

MURRIE, Clive Robert. b 44. Ripon Coll Cuddesdon. **d** 79 **p** 80. C Kenton Ascension *Newc* 79-80; C Prudhoe 80-83; V Burnopfield *Dur* 83-87; R Stella 87-91; V Coalpit Heath *Bris* 91-95; P-in-c Sittingbourne St Mich *Cant* from 95. *St Michael's Vicarage, Valenciennes Road, Sittingbourne, Kent ME10 1EN* Tel (01795) 472874

MURRIN, Robert Staddon (Bob). b 42. RMA 62 Reading Univ BA68 Birm Univ DPS93 Open Univ MA96. W of England Minl Tr Course 90 Birm Bible Inst DipRS92. **d** 93. NSM Peterchurch w Vowchurch, Turnastone and Dorstone *Heref* 93-95; NSM Tupsley w Hampton Bishop from 95; Chapl Kemp Hospice Kidderminster from 97. *Albion Cottage, Peterchurch, Hereford HR2 0RP* Tel (01981) 550467 Fax 550432

MURSELL, Alfred Gordon. b 49. ARCM74 BNC Ox BA70 MA73 BD87. Cuddesdon Coll 71. **d** 73 **p** 74. C Walton St Mary *Liv* 73-77; V E Dulwich St Jo *S'wark* 77-86; Tutor Sarum Th Coll 87-91; TR Stafford *Lich* from 91. *The Rectory, 32 Rowley Avenue, Stafford ST17 9AG* Tel (01785) 58511

MUSGRAVE, Canon James Robert Lord. b 20. MBE97. TCD BA43 MA51. **d** 44 **p** 45. C Belfast St Andr *Conn* 44-46; C Derriaghy 46-51; R Duneane w Ballyscullion 51-54; I Belfast St Steph 54-64; I Magheragall 64-85; Can Conn Cathl 82-85; Bp's C Killead w Gartree 87-95; rtd 95. *61 Crumlin Road, Aldergrove, Crumlin, Co Antrim BT29 4AQ* Tel (01849) 453532

MUSHEN, Canon Francis John. b 34. Birm Univ BA60. Ripon Hall Ox 60. **d** 62 **p** 63. C Foleshill St Laur *Cov* 62-65; C Halesowen *Worc* 65-69; V Stourbridge St Mich Norton 69-81; Hon Can Worc Cathl from 81; P-in-c Bromsgrove St Jo 81-87; V 87-92; R Kempsey and Severn Stoke w Croome d'Abitot from 92. *The Vicarage, Old Road South, Kempsey, Worcester WR5 3NJ* Tel (01905) 820202

MUSINDI, Philip. b 63. Bp Tucker Coll Mukono DipTh87 BD91 St Mich Coll Llan 91. **d** 87 **p** 90. Uganda 87-92; C Builth and Llanddewi'r Cwm w Llangynog etc *S & B* 92-94; C Newport St Teilo *Mon* 94-97; P-in-c Newport St Matt from 97. *St Matthew's Vicarage, 124 Caerleon Road, Newport NP9 7GS* Tel (01633) 262377

MUSK, Dr Bill Andrew. b 49. Ox Univ BA70 MA75 Univ of S Africa D Litt et Phil84 Lon Univ DipTh73. Fuller Th Sem California ThM80 Trin Coll Bris DipTh81. **d** 81 **p** 82. Egypt 81-86; CMS 88-89; TV Maghull *Liv* from 89. *St Peter's Vicarage, 1 St Peter's Row, Moorhey Road, Liverpool L31 5LU* Tel 0151-526 3434

MUSKETT, David John. b 63. Southn Univ BA85. Ripon Coll Cuddesdon 87. **d** 90 **p** 91. C Kempston Transfiguration *St Alb* 90-93; C Ampthill w Millbrook and Steppingley 93-96; V Milford *Guildf* from 96. *The Vicarage, Milford Heath Road, Godalming, Surrey GU8 5BX* Tel (01483) 414710

MUSPRATT, Oscar. b 06. Ridley Coll Melbourne ThL29. **d** 29 **p** 30. Australia 29-41; CF (EC) 41-45; V Penn *Ox* 45-89; rtd 90. *Kalorama, 81 Pontwillim, Brecon LD3 9BS* Tel (01874) 623277

MUSSON, David John. b 46. Open Univ BA86 Univ of Wales (Lamp) MPhil96. Linc Th Coll 70. **d** 73 **p** 74. C New Sleaford *Linc* 73-76; C Morton 76-80; P-in-c Thurlby 80-86; R Quarrington w Old Sleaford from 86; P-in-c Silk Willoughby 86-87; R from 87. *The Rectory, 77 Grantham Road, Quarrington, Sleaford, Lincs NG34 7NP* Tel (01529) 306776

MUSSON, Dr John Keith. b 39. CEng MIMechE Nottm Univ BSc61 PhD66. St As Minl Tr Course 85. **d** 88 **p** 89. Assoc Prin NE Wales Inst of HE from 80; NSM Holywell *St As* 88-93; C 93-95; R Caerwys and Bodfari from 95. *The Rectory, Pen y Cefn Road, Caerwys, Mold CH7 5AQ* Tel (01352) 720223

MUSSON, William John. b 58. UMIST BSc80. St Jo Coll Nottm 88. **d** 91 **p** 92. C Nantwich *Ches* 91-94; C Finchley Ch Ch *Lon* 94-97; V Lynchmere and Camelsdale *Chich* from 97. *The Vicarage, School Road, Camelsdale, Haslemere, Surrey GU27 3RN* Tel (01428) 642983

MUST, Albert Henry. b 27. Clifton Th Coll 61. **d** 63 **p** 64. C Becontree St Mary *Chelmsf* 63-68; V Highbury Vale St Jo *Lon* 68-78; V Highbury New Park St Aug 78-84; V Walthamstow St Jo *Chelmsf* 84-93; rtd 93; Perm to Offic *Cant* from 93. *24 Nightingale Avenue, Whitstable, Kent CT5 4TR* Tel (01227) 772160

MUST, Mrs Shirley Ann. b 35. St Mich Ho Ox 61. **dss** 82 **d** 87 **p** 94. Highbury New Park St Aug *Lon* 82-84; Walthamstow St Jo *Chelmsf* 84-87; Hon Par Dn 87-93; Perm to Offic *Cant* 93-94; Hon C Herne Bay Ch Ch from 94. *24 Nightingale Avenue, Whitstable, Kent CT5 4TR* Tel (01227) 772160

MUSTOE, Alan Andrew. b 52. Man Univ BA74. Qu Coll Birm DipTh77. **d** 78 **p** 79. C Chatham St Wm *Roch* 78-82; R Burham and Wouldham 82-88; Dioc Info Officer 83-88; V Strood St Nic w St Mary from 88. *The Vicarage, 3 Central Road, Strood, Rochester, Kent ME2 3HF* Tel (01634) 719052

MUSTON, David Alan. b 33. Nottm Univ BA60. Ridley Hall Cam 62. **d** 64 **p** 65. C Tankersley *Sheff* 64-67; C Goole 67-70; Asst Sec Ind Cttee of Gen Syn Bd for Soc Resp 70-76; Ind Chapl *Win* 77-79; V Leigh St Mary *Man* 79-83; R Otham w Langley *Cant* from 83. *The Rectory, Church Road, Otham, Maidstone, Kent ME15 8SB* Tel (01622) 861470 Fax 863644

MUSTON, James Arthur. b 48. Leic Univ CertRS91 Open Univ BA92. EMMTC 89. **d** 91 **p** 92. NSM Chaddesden St Mary *Derby* 91-95; C Gt Grimsby St Andr w St Luke and All SS *Linc* from 95. *August House, 18 Vivian Road, Grimsby, S Humberside DN32 8QF* Tel (01472) 200545

MUTCH, Miss Sylvia Edna. b 36. St Mich Ho Ox 57. **dss** 79 **d** 87 **p** 94. Clifton *York* 79-95; Par Dn 87-94; C 94-95; Chapl Clifton Hosp York 81-94; R Elvington w Sutton on Derwent and E Cottingwith *York* from 95. *The Rectory, Church Lane, Elvington, York YO4 5AD* Tel (01904) 608462

MWANGI, Capt Joel Waweru. b 59. Nairobi Univ CertRS84. CA Tr Coll Nairobi 81. **d** 93 **p** 94. Kenya 93-96; C Sheff St Mary Bramhall Lane *Sheff* from 96. *5 Colver Road, Sheffield S2 4UP* Tel 0114-255 5906

MYATT, Andrew William Gilchrist. b 62. Wycliffe Hall Ox 85. **d** 88 **p** 89. C Cogges *Ox* 88-91; C S Leigh 88-91; Vineyard Ministries from 91. *144A London Road, Oxford OX3 9ED* Tel (01865) 742131

MYATT, Edwin Henry. b 54. MA. Ripon Coll Cuddesdon. **d** 84 **p** 85. C W Bromwich St Fran *Lich* 84-88; C Sedgley All SS 88-93; V Trent Vale 93-94. *The Conifers, 5 Prestwick Road, Kingswinford, W Midlands ST4 6JY*

MYATT, Francis Eric (Fran). b 60. St Jo Coll Nottm LTh92. **d** 92 **p** 93. C W Derby St Luke *Liv* 92-95; TV Sutton from 95. *80 Waterdale Crescent, St Helens, Merseyside WA9 3PH* Tel (01744) 815158

MYATT, Philip Bryan. b 29. Wycliffe Hall Ox 54. **d** 57 **p** 58. C Fareham St Jo *Portsm* 57-61; C Westgate St Jas *Cant* 61-64; R Woodchester *Glouc* 64-70; R Bath Walcot *B & W* 70-91; R The Edge, Pitchcombe, Harescombe and Brookthorpe *Glouc* 91-94; rtd 94; Perm to Offic *Glouc* from 94. *West Cottage, Amberley, Glos GL5 5AL*

MYCOCK, Geoffrey John Arthur. b 22. Open Univ BA76. St Deiniol's Hawarden 76. **d** 77 **p** 78. Hon C Ches H Trin *Ches* 77-79; Bp's Dom Chapl 79-80; P-in-c Hargrave 79-80; V Sandbach Heath 80-82; Chapl and Lect St Deiniol's Lib Hawarden 82-85; V Holt *St As* 85-90; rtd 90; Perm to Offic *St As* from 90; Perm to Offic *Ches* from 91. *20 Eaton Close, Broughton, Chester CH4 0RF* Tel (01244) 531214

MYERS, Canon Arnold George. b 23. Keble Coll Ox BA44 DipTh46 MA48 TCD BA51. St Steph Ho Ox. **d** 47 **p** 48. C Harrington *Carl* 47-50; C Liv Our Lady and St Nic *Liv* 50-53; V Edge Hill St Dunstan 53-62; R W Derby St Mary 62-79; TR 79-84; RD W Derby 71-78; Hon Can Liv Cathl 74-84; rtd 84; Perm to Offic *Liv* from 84. *10 Surrey Drive, West Kirby, Wirral, Merseyside L48 2HP* Tel 0151-625 2250

MYERS, Duncan Frank. b 57. Warw Univ BSc. St Jo Coll Nottm. **d** 84 **p** 85. C Upton cum Chalvey *Ox* 84-86; C Farnborough *Guildf* 86-90; Chapl Nottm Poly *S'well* 90-92; Chapl Nottm Trent Univ 92-95; Sen Past Adv Nottm Trent Univ from 95. *3 Carisbrooke Drive, Nottingham NG3 5DS* Tel 0115-960 5447 or 941 8418

MYERS, Ms Gillian Mary. b 57. Warw Univ BSc78 Nottm Univ MA96. St Jo Coll Nottm 83. **d** 95 **p** 97. NSM Nottingham St Jude *S'well* 95-97; NSM Gedling from 97. *3 Carisbrooke Drive, Nottingham NG3 5DS* Tel 0115-960 5447

MYERS, John Bulmer. b 19. Worc Ord Coll 64. **d** 66 **p** 67. C Linthorpe *York* 66-68; NSM Huddersfield St Jo *Wakef* 74-76; C 76-79; V Cornholme 79-88; rtd 88; Perm to Offic *Wakef* from 88. *284 Burnley Road, Todmorden, Lancs OL14 8EW* Tel (01706) 812224

MYERS, Paul Henry. b 49. Liv Poly ALA72. Qu Coll Birm 74. **d** 77 **p** 78. C Baildon *Bradf* 77-80; C W Bromwich All SS *Lich* 80-83; Chapl RAF 83-86; V Milton *Lich* 87-92; C Baswich from 96. *21 Lansdowne Way, Stafford ST17 4RD* Tel (01785) 660835

MYERS, Peter John. b 60. St Jo Coll Dur BA81. Linc Th Coll CMM84. **d** 84 **p** 85. C Bulwell St Mary *S'well* 84-88; C Shrewsbury H Cross *Lich* 88-92; rtd 92. *7 Peace Cottages, Old Coleham, Shrewsbury SY3 7BD* Tel (01743) 360791

MYERS, Robert William John. b 57. Aus Nat Univ BSc80 Newc Univ Aus DipEd82. Trin Coll Bris DipHE95. **d** 95 **p** 96. C Addiscombe St Mary Magd w St Martin *S'wark* from 95. *68 Elgin Road, Croydon CR0 6XA* Tel 0181-654 6925

MYERSCOUGH, Robin Nigel. b 44. K Coll Lon BD69 Nottm Univ PGCE70. Coll of Resurr Mirfield 66. **d** 81 **p** 92. Hon C Diss *Nor* 81-84; Chapl Nor Sch 81-84; Hd Relig Studies Sedbergh Sch Cumbria 84-85; Chapl and Hd Relig Studies Dur Sch 85-92; Chapl Gresham's Sch Holt from 92. *10 Kelling Road, Holt, Norfolk NR25 6RT* Tel (01263) 713234

MYHILL, Christopher John. b 47. Oak Hill Th Coll DipHE79. **d** 79 **p** 80. C Stanford-le-Hope w Mucking *Chelmsf* 79-82; C Leyton St Luke 82-87; V Chatteris *Ely* from 87. *The Vicarage, Church Lane, Chatteris, Cambs PE16 6JA* Tel (01354) 692173

MYLES, Peter Rodney. b 42. K Coll Lon 61 St Aug Coll Cant 70. **d** 71 **p** 72. C Tideswell *Derby* 71-74; C W Brompton St Mary w St Pet *Lon* 74-79; P-in-c Notting Hill St Pet 79-82; Chapl to Bp Kensington 82-87; C Kensington St Mary Abbots w St Geo 82-92; P-in-c Isleworth St Jo from 92. *The Vicarage, St John's Road, Isleworth, Middx TW7 6NY* Tel 0181-560 4916

MYLNE, Denis Colin. b 31. Jordan Hill Coll Glas CYCW75. Kelham Th Coll 69. **d** 71. Perm to Offic *Glas* 74-84; Perm to Offic *Ab* 84-88; C Bedford All SS *St Alb* 88-91; C Harpenden St Jo 91-96; rtd 96. *Gracegarth, Ubbanford, Norham, Berwick-upon-Tweed TD15 2JZ* Tel (01289) 382187

MYNETT, Colin. b 25. Roch Th Coll 61. **d** 63 **p** 64. C Liskeard w St Keyne *Truro* 63-66; R Lifton *Ex* 66-71; R Kelly w Bradstone 66-71; TV Devonport St Aubyn 71-75; V Cinderford St Jo *Glouc* 75-84; P-in-c Cheltenham All SS 84-89; rtd 89. *5 Heron Close, Cheltenham, Glos GL51 6HA* Tel (01242) 523341

MYNETT, John Alan. b 37. CEng MIMechE67 Bris Univ BSc59 MSc61. N Ord Course 82. **d** 85 **p** 86. NSM Poynton *Ches* 85-90; NSM Macclesfield Team Par from 90. *46 Barber Street, Macclesfield, Cheshire SK11 7HT* Tel (01625) 614103

MYNORS, James Baskerville. b 49. Peterho Cam BA70 MA74. Ridley Hall Cam 70 St Jo Coll Nottm 77. **d** 78 **p** 80. Hon C Leic H Apostles *Leic* 78-79; C Virginia Water *Guildf* 79-83; C Patcham *Chich* 83-88; P-in-c Fowlmere *Ely* from 88; P-in-c Thriplow from 88; Sen Tutor E Anglian Minl Tr Course 88-90; Vice-Prin from 90. *The Rectory, Fowlmere, Royston, Herts SG8 7SU* Tel (01763) 208195

N

NADEN, Anthony Joshua. b 38. Jes Coll Ox BA62 MA64 SOAS Lon PhD73. Wycliffe Hall Ox 60. **d** 62 **p** 63. C Rowner *Portsm* 62-66; C Fisherton Anger *Sarum* 70-72; Ghana from 72. *PO Box 3, Walewale, NR Ghana*

NADERER, Gordon Kenneth Charles Maximilian. b 14. Wycliffe Hall Ox. **d** 44 **p** 45. C Chatham St Paul *Roch* 44-46; P-in-c Ashburnham w Penhurst *Chich* 55-58; R Rodmell w Southease 58-74; V Westham 74-83; rtd 83; Perm to Offic *Chich* from 83. *65 Church Lane, South Bersted, Bognor Regis, W Sussex PO22 9QA* Tel (01243) 866885

NADIN, Dennis Lloyd. b 37. St D Coll Lamp BA60 Man Univ MEd81. Ridley Hall Cam 63. **d** 64 **p** 65. C Childwall All SS *Liv* 64-67; C Seacroft *Ripon* 67-69; Project Officer Grubb Inst 69-70; Lect CA Tr Coll Blackheath 70-72; Community Educn Essex Co Coun 73-80; Public Preacher *Chelmsf* from 73. *The Hermitage, 201 Willowfield Road, Harlow, Essex CM18 6RZ* Tel (01279) 430176

NAGEL, Lawson Chase Joseph. b 49. ARHistS75 Univ of Michigan BA71 K Coll Lon PhD82. Sarum & Wells Th Coll. **d** 83 **p** 84. C Chiswick St Nic w St Mary *Lon* 83-86; Sec Gen Confraternity of the Blessed Sacrament from 85; C Horsham *Chich* 86; TV 86-91; OStJ from 89; V Aldwick *Chich* from 91. *The Vicarage, 25 Gossamer Lane, Aldwick, Bognor Regis, W Sussex PO21 3AT* Tel (01243) 262049

NAIDU, Michael Sriram. b 28. Univ of the South (USA) 81. Ridley Hall Cam 86. **d** 80 **p** 85. Acting Chapl Stuttgart *Eur* 85-91; Chapl Stuttgart from 91. *Kloster Kinchberg, 72172 Sulz am Neckar, Stuttgart, Germany* Tel Stuttgart (7454) 883136 or 883105

NAIRN, Frederick William. b 43. TCD 64. Luther NW Th Sem DMin88. **d** 67 **p** 68. C Larne and Inver *Conn* 67-70; Chapl RAF 70-74; P-in-c Harmston *Linc* 75-77; V 77-84; V Coleby 78-84; USA from 84. *4900 Nathan Lane, Plymouth, Minnesota 55442, USA*

NAIRN, Stuart Robert. b 51. K Coll Lon BD75 AKC75. St Aug Coll Cant 75. **d** 76 **p** 77. C E Dereham *Nor* 76-80; TV Hempnall 80-88; V Narborough w Narford from 88; V Pentney St Mary Magd w W Bilney from 88; RD Lynn from 91; P-in-c Castle Acre w Newton, Rougham and Southacre from 97. *The Vicarage, Narborough, King's Lynn, Norfolk PE32 1TE* Tel (01760) 338552

NAIRN-BRIGGS, The Very Revd George Peter. b 45. AKC69. St Aug Coll Cant 69. **d** 70 **p** 71. C Catford St Laur *S'wark* 70-73; C Raynes Park St Sav 73-75; V Salfords 75-81; V St Helier 81-87; Dioc Soc Resp Adv *Wakef* 87-97; Can Res Wakef Cathl 92-97; Provost Wakef from 97. *1 Cathedral Close, Margaret Street, Wakefield, W Yorkshire WF1 2DQ* Tel (01924) 372402 Fax 383842

NAISH, Timothy James Neville. b 57. St Jo Coll Ox BA80 MA88. WMMTC 86. **d** 87 **p** 88. CMS from 81; C Cov H Trin *Cov* 87; Zaire 88-91; Perm to Offic *Birm* 91-93; Uganda from 93. *Bishop Tucker Theological College, PO Box 4, Mukono, Uganda*

NAISMITH, Mrs Carol. b 37. St Andr Univ MA59. Edin Dioc NSM Course 85. **d** 90 **p** 94. NSM Edin Old St Paul *Edin* from 90; NSM Edin St Marg from 90. *38 Castle Avenue, Edinburgh EH12 7LB* Tel 0131-334 4486

✠**NALEDI, The Rt Revd Theophilus.** b 36. St Bede's Coll Umtata. **d** 59 **p** 60 **c** 87. S Africa 59-70; Rhodesia 70-72; Botswana 72-83; C Wimbledon *S'wark* 83-85; Botswana 85-87; Bp Matabeleland from 87. *PO Box 2422, Bulawayo, Zimbabwe*

NANCARROW, Mrs Rachel Mary. b 38. Cam Inst of Educn TCert59. EAMTC 87. **d** 90 **p** 94. NSM Girton *Ely* 90-95; P-in-c Foxton from 95. *The Vicarage, 7 West Hill Road, Foxton, Cambridge CB2 6SZ* Tel (01223) 870375

NANKIVELL, Christopher Robert Trevelyan. b 33. Jes Coll Ox BA55 MA63. Linc Th Coll 56. **d** 58 **p** 59. C Bloxwich *Lich* 58-60; C Stafford St Mary 60-64; P-in-c Malins Lee 64-72; Soc Welfare Sector Min to Milton Keynes Chr Coun 73-76; Lic to Offic *Ox* 73-76; Lect Qu Coll Birm 76-81; rtd 96. *77 Pereira Road, Birmingham B17 9JA*

NAPIER, Charles John Lenox. b 29. Univ Coll Ox BA52 MA57. Philosophical and Th Coll of Soc of Jes Louvain STL60. **d** 60 **p** 60. In RC Ch 60-63; C Illogan *Truro* 63-66; Tutor Lon Coll of Div 66-70; Tutor St Jo Coll Nottm 70-73; TV S Molton w Nymet St George *Ex* 73-75; TV S Molton, Nymet St George, High Bray etc 75-80; R Drewsteignton from 80; V Hittisleigh from 80; V Spreyton from 80. *The Rectory, Drewsteignton, Exeter EX6 6QW* Tel (01647) 281227

NAPIER, Graeme Stewart Patrick Columbanus. b 66. Magd Coll Ox MA MPhil LRSM. DipMin86 St Steph Ho Ox 93. **d** 95 **p** 96. C Inverness St Andr *Mor* from 95. *14 Scorguie Terrace, Inverness IV3 6SE* Tel (01463) 223559 Fax as telephone E-mail user@napier.dial.netmedia.co.uk

NAPIER, Lady Jennifer Beryl. b 39. S Dios Minl Tr Scheme 89. **d** 93 **p** 96. NSM Itchen Valley *Win* from 93. *Upper Chilland House, Martyr Worthy, Winchester, Hants SO21 1EB* Tel (01962) 779307 Fax as telephone

NAPLEY, David John. b 13. S'wark Ord Course 65. **d** 68 **p** 69. C Hurst Green *S'wark* 68-71; C Ham St Andr 71-74; TV Quidenham w Eccles and Snetterton *Nor* 74-77; P-in-c Earsham 77-79; R Earsham w Alburgh and Denton 79-83; rtd 83; Perm to Offic *Nor* 84-90; Perm to Offic *St E* 87-88. *Wainford House, 1 Saltgate, Beccles, Suffolk NR34 9AN* Tel (01502) 714975

NARUSAWA, Masaki Alec. b 53. K Coll Lon BD77 AKC77. Linc Th Coll 77. **d** 78 **p** 79. C Hendon St Alphage *Lon* 78-81; C Eastcote St Lawr 81-84; V Glodwick *Man* from 84. *St Mark's Vicarage, 1 Skipton Street, Oldham OL8 2JF* Tel 0161-624 4964

NASCIMENTO de JESUS, Anesia. b 62. Mogidas Cruces Univ 86. Porto Allegre Th Sem 91. **d** 91 **p** 93. Brazil 91-94; Lic to Offic *St Alb* 96-97; C Dinnington *Sheff* from 97. *32 Shakespeare Drive, Dinnington, Sheffield S31 7RP* Tel (01909) 563682

NASH, Alan Frederick. b 46. Sarum & Wells Th Coll 72. **d** 75 **p** 76. C Foley Park *Worc* 75-79; P-in-c Mildenhall *Sarum* 79-82; Wilts Adnry Youth Officer 79-82; TV N Wingfield, Pilsley and Tupton *Derby* 82-85. *33 Manvers Road, Sheffield S6 2PJ*

NASH, Brian John. b 54. St Jo Coll Dur BSc75. St Jo Coll Nottm 77. **d** 80 **p** 81. C Birm St Luke *Birm* 80-84; C Bucknall and Bagnall *Lich* 84; TV 84-92. *191 Selly Oak Road, Birmingham B30 1HU* Tel 0121-486 3169

NASH, David. b 25. K Coll Lon BD51 AKC51. **d** 52 **p** 53. C Buckhurst Hill *Chelmsf* 52-58; Min St Cedd CD Westcliff 58-66; R Rivenhall 66-83; P-in-c Boscastle w Davidstow *Truro* 83-85; TR 85-90; rtd 90; Perm to Offic *Truro* from 90. *9 Boscundle Avenue, Falmouth, Cornwall TR11 5BU*

NASH, Preb David John. b 41. Pemb Coll Ox BA64 MA70. Wells Th Coll 65. **d** 67 **p** 68. C Preston Ascension *Lon* 67-70; TV Hackney 70-75; TV Clifton *S'well* 76-82; V Winchmore Hill St Paul *Lon* from 82; AD Enfield 87-91; Preb St Paul's Cathl from 96. *St Paul's Vicarage, Church Hill, London N21 1JA* Tel 0181-886 3545

NASH, Mrs Ingrid. b 36. SRN57 RNT80 BEd78 CCouns89. S'wark Ord Course 91. **d** 94 **p** 95. NSM Eltham Park St Luke *S'wark* from 94; Chapl Bromley Hosps NHS Trust from 94. *13 Crookston Road, London SE9 1YH* Tel 0181-850 0750

NASH, James Alexander. b 56. Seale-Hayne Agric Coll HND79. St Jo Coll Nottm BA94. **d** 97. C Trunch *Nor* from 97. *The Rectory, Knapton Road, Trunch, North Walsham, Norfolk NR28 0QE* Tel (01263) 722799

NASH, Paul Alexander. b 20. Glouc Th Course 73. **d** 76 **p** 76. NSM Coleford w Staunton *Glouc* 76-88. *16 Orchard Road, Coombs Park, Coleford, Glos GL16 8AU* Tel (01594) 832758

NASH, Reginald Frank. b 15. **d** 66 **p** 67. C Glouc St Jas *Glouc* 66-69; P-in-c Sharpness 69-75; V Dymock w Donnington 75-77; R Dymock w Donnington and Kempley 77-80; rtd 80; Perm to Offic *Glouc* 80-94. *Holcombe Glen Cottage, Minchinhampton, Stroud, Glos GL6 9AJ* Tel (01453) 835635

NASH, Richard Edward. b 10. Westcott Ho Cam 54. **d** 56 **p** 57. C Weymouth H Trin *Sarum* 56-59; R Graffham w Woolavington *Chich* 59-65; P-in-c Lewes St Thos and All SS 65-68; V Eridge Green 68-72; R Winterborne Came *Sarum* 73-75; P-in-c Stinsford 73-75; rtd 75. *Manormead Nursing Home, Tilford Road, Hindhead, Surrey GU26 6RA* Tel (01428) 604780

NASH, Robin Louis. b 51. Open Univ BA87. Chich Th Coll 82. **d** 84 **p** 85. C Lymington *Win* 84-86; C Andover w Foxcott 86-90; R Kegworth *Leic* from 90. *The Rectory, 24 Nottingham Road, Kegworth, Derby DE74 2FH* Tel (01509) 672349 Fax as telephone Mobile (0378) 638989

NASH, The Ven Trevor Gifford. b 30. Clare Coll Cam BA53 MA57. Cuddesdon Coll 53. **d** 55 **p** 56. C Cheshunt *St Alb* 55-57; CF (TA) 56-61; C Kingston All SS *S'wark* 57-61; C Stevenage *St Alb* 61-63; V Leagrave 63-67; Dir Luton Samaritans 66-67; Chapl St Geo Hosp Lon 67-73; R Win St Lawr and St Maurice w St Swithun *Win* 73-82; Bp's Adv Min of Healing from 73; P-in-c Win H Trin 77-82; RD Win 75-82; Hon Can Win Cathl 80-95; Adn Basingstoke 82-90; Acorn Trust Exec Co-ord from 90; rtd 95. *The Corner Stone, 50B Hyde Street, Winchester, Hants SO23 7DY* Tel (01962) 861759

NASH, William Henry. b 31. Oak Hill Th Coll 58. **d** 61 **p** 62. C New Milverton *Cov* 61-64; C Toxteth Park St Philemon w St Silas *Liv* 64-67; V Bryn 67-76; NW Area Sec CPAS 76-82; V Penn Fields *Lich* from 82. *St Philip's Vicarage, Church Road, Bradmore, Wolverhampton WV3 7EN* Tel (01902) 341943

NASH, William Paul. b 48. St Mich Coll Llan 86. **d** 87 **p** 88. C Pembroke Dock *St D* 87-89; P-in-c Llawhaden w Bletherston and Llanycefn 89-90; V 90-92; P-in-c E Brixton St Jude *S'wark* 92-96; V from 96. *St Jude's Vicarage, Dulwich Road, London SE24 0PA* Tel 0171-274 3183

NASH, William Warren. b 09. TCD BA35 MA58. CITC 36. **d** 36 **p** 38. C Birkenhead St Mary w St Paul *Ches* 36; Lic to Offic *K, E & A* 37-38; C Portadown St Mark *Arm* 38-40; P-in-c Cooneen w Mullaghfad *Clogh* 40-44; P-in-c Drummully 44-51; I Aghadrumsee 51-74; rtd 74. *Strathmore, 45 Mulberry Green, Harlow, Essex CM17 0EY*

NASH-WILLIAMS, Piers le Sor Victor. b 35. Trin Hall Cam BA57 MA61. Cuddesdon Coll 59. **d** 61 **p** 62. C Milton *Win* 61-64; Asst Chapl Eton Coll 64-66; Perm to Offic *Chich* 66-68; C Furze Platt *Ox* 69-72; V Newbury St Geo Wash Common 72-73; TV Newbury 73-91; R Ascot Heath from 91. *The Rectory, Ascot Heath, Ascot, Berks SL5 8DQ* Tel (01344) 21200

NASON, David. b 44. ACA68 FCA78 Open Univ BA92. Ripon Coll Cuddesdon 84. **d** 86 **p** 87. C Banstead *Guildf* 86-89; PV Chich Cathl *Chich* from 89; Chapl Prebendal Sch Chich from 89. *1 St Richard's Walk, Canon Lane, Chichester, W Sussex PO19 1QA* Tel (01243) 775615

NATERS, Charles James Reginald. b 20. Selw Coll Cam BA45 MA47. Coll of Resurr Mirfield 46. **d** 47 **p** 48. C Ardwick St Benedict *Man* 47-52; SSJE from 54; S Africa 59-68; Lic to Offic *Ox* 69-76; Lic to Offic *Lon* 76-85 and from 88; Lic to Offic *Leic* 85-88; rtd 90; Superior Gen SSJE from 91. *St Edward's House, 22 Great College Street, London SW1P 3QA* Tel 0171-222 9234

NATHANAEL, Brother. *See* THOMPSON, Kenneth

NATHANAEL, Martin Moses. b 43. Lon Univ BEd73 K Coll Lon MTh77. Ripon Coll Cuddesdon 77. **d** 79 **p** 80. C Hampton All SS *Lon* 79-82; P-in-c Kensal Town St Thos w St Andr and St Phil 82-83; Hd Div Bp Stopford Sch Lon 83-91; TV Tring *St Alb* from 91. *The Vicarage, Watery Lane, Wilstone, Tring, Herts HP23 4PH* Tel (01442) 823008

NATHANIEL, Ivan Wasim. Punjab Univ MA65. Bp's Coll Calcutta 59. **d** 62 **p** 64. India 62-68; C Newland St Aug *York* 68-70; Hon C Crawley *Chich* from 70; Chapl H Trin Sch Crawley from 70; Hd of Relig Studies from 91. *13 Haywards, Crawley, W Sussex RH10 3TR*

NATTRASS, Michael Stuart. b 41. Man Univ BA62. Cuddesdon Coll 62. **d** 64 **p** 65. C Easington Colliery *Dur* 64-65; C Silksworth 65-68; Perm to Offic *S'well* 68-72; Lic to Offic *Dur* 72-76; Perm to Offic *Lon* 76-78; Hon C Pinner from 78. *81 Cecil Park, Pinner, Middx HA5 5HL* Tel 0181-866 0217

NAUDE, John Donald. Ridley Hall Cam. **d** 97. C Kettering Ch the King *Pet* from 97. *9 Churchill Way, Kettering, Northants NN15 5DP*

NAUMANN, Canon David Sydney. b 26. Ripon Hall Ox 54. **d** 55 **p** 56. C Herne Bay Ch Ch *Cant* 55-58; Asst Chapl United Sheff Hosps 58-60; V Reculver *Cant* 60-64; Dioc Youth Chapl 63-70; R Eastwell w Boughton Aluph 65-67; V Westwell 65-67; Warden St Gabr Retreat Ho Westgate 68-70; V Littlebourne 70-82; RD E Bridge 78-82; Hon Can Cant Cathl from 81; R Sandwich 82-91; RD Sandwich 85-90; rtd 91. *2 The Forrens, The Precincts, Canterbury, Kent CT1 2ER* Tel (01227) 458939

NAUNTON, Hugh Raymond. b 38. Whitelands Coll Lon CertEd69 Open Univ BA75. Bernard Gilpin Soc Dur 59 Chich Th Coll 60. **d** 63 **p** 64. C Stanground *Ely* 63-66; NSM Woolwich St Mary w H Trin *S'wark* 66-67; NSM Wandsworth St Anne 67-69 and 71-73; NSM Paddington St Sav *Lon* 69-71; NSM Cuddington *Guildf* 73-78; Hon C Cheam Common St Phil *S'wark* 79-95; C Cheam from 95. *49 Brocks Drive, Sutton, Surrey SM3 9UW* Tel 0181-641 1516

NAYLOR, Frank. b 36. Lon Univ BA58 Liv Univ MA63. NW Ord Course 75. **d** 75 **p** 76. NSM Eccleston Ch Ch *Liv* 75-92; Asst Dioc Chapl to the Deaf 92-94; Sen Chapl from 94. *27 Daresbury Road, Eccleston, St Helens, Merseyside WA10 5DR* Tel (01744) 57034

NAYLOR, Frederick. b 11. St Aug Coll Cant 34. **d** 38 **p** 39. C Dewsbury Moor *Wakef* 38-41; S Africa 41-51; V Cross Stone *Wakef* 51-53; V Paddock 53-60; V Bossall w Buttercrambe *York* 60-66; V Bishop Burton 66-77; rtd 78; Perm to Offic *York* from 78. *2 York Road, Bishop Burton, Beverley, N Humberside HU17 8QF* Tel (01964) 550226

NAYLOR, Ian Frederick. b 47. AKC70 Open Univ BA92. St Aug Coll Cant 70. **d** 71 **p** 72. C Camberwell St Giles *S'wark* 71-74; OSB 74-86; Chapl RN from 86. *Royal Naval Chaplaincy Service, Room 203, Victory Building, HM Naval Base, Portsmouth PO1 3LS* Tel (01705) 727903 Fax 727112

NAYLOR, James Barry. b 50. Lon Univ BSc71 St Benet's Hall Ox BA75. Wycliffe Hall Ox 72. **d** 76 **p** 76. C Catford (Southend) and Downham *S'wark* 76-79; TV 79-82; P-in-c Lewisham St Swithun 82-87; V E Dulwich St Jo 87-97; RD Dulwich 90-97; P-in-c Blythburgh w Reydon *St E* from 97. *The Rectory, 45 Wangford Road, Reydon, Southwold, Suffolk IP18 6PZ* Tel (01502) 722192

NAYLOR, Miss Jean. b 29. Linc Th Coll 77. **dss** 79 **d** 87. Charlton St Luke w H Trin *S'wark* 79-84; Crofton Park St Hilda w St Cypr 84-89; Par Dn 87-89; rtd 89; Perm to Offic *Wakef* from 89. *12 Winter Terrace, Barnsley, S Yorkshire S75 2ES* Tel (01226) 204767

NAYLOR, John Watson. b 26. Trin Hall Cam BA52 MA56. Ripon Hall Ox 64. **d** 66 **p** 67. C Newc St Andr *Newc* 66-69; C Otterburn w Elsdon and Horsley w Byrness 69-72; R Husborne Crawley w Ridgmont *St Alb* 72-76; Chapl Caldicott Sch Farnham Royal 76-80; P-in-c Chollerton w Thockrington *Newc* 80-82; R Chollerton w Birtley and Thockrington 82-91; rtd 91. *Abbeyfield House, Bellingham, Hexham, Northd NE48 2BS* Tel (01434) 220106

NAYLOR, Canon Peter Aubrey. b 33. Kelham Th Coll 54 Ely Th Coll 57. **d** 58 **p** 59. C Shepherd's Bush St Steph *Lon* 58-62; C Portsea N End St Mark *Portsm* 62-66; Chapl HM Borstal Portsm 64-66; V Foley Park *Worc* 66-74; V Maidstone All SS w St Phil and H Trin *Cant* 74-81; P-in-c Tovil 79-81; V Maidstone All SS and St Phil w Tovil 81-91; Hon Can Cant Cathl 79-93; RD Sutton 80-86; R Biddenden and Smarden 91-93; P-in-c Leic St Marg and All SS *Leic* 93-96; P-in-c Leic St Aug 93-96; TR The Abbey Leicester 96. *12 Oatfield Close, Cranbrook, Kent TN17 3NH* Tel (01580) 715756

NAYLOR, Peter Edward. b 30. Linc Th Coll 58. **d** 61 **p** 62. C S Beddington St Mich *S'wark* 61-64; V S Lambeth St Ann 64-77; V Nork *Guildf* 77-90; R Ecton *Pet* 90-97; Warden Ecton Ho from 90. *The Rectory, 23 West Street, Ecton, Northampton NN6 0QE* Tel (01604) 416322 or 406442 Fax 787052

NAYLOR, Peter Henry. b 41. MIMechE HND64. Chich Th Coll 64. **d** 67 **p** 68. C Filton *Bris* 67-70; C Brixham *Ex* 70-72; C Leckhampton St Pet *Glouc* 72-76; V Brockworth 76-94; P-in-c Gt Witcombe 91-94; RD Glouc N 91-94; P-in-c The Ampneys w Driffield and Poulton 94-95; R from 95. *The Rectory, Ampney Crucis, Cirencester, Glos GL7 5RY* Tel (01285) 851240

NAYLOR, Robert James. b 42. Liv Univ CQSW66. N Ord Course 74. **d** 77 **p** 78. C Aigburth *Liv* 77-80; Soc Resp Officer *Glouc* 80-85; Leonard Cheshire Foundn (Lon) 85-93. *The Stable Family Home Trust, The Stables, Bisterne, Ringwood, Hants BH24 3BN* Tel (01425) 478043

NAYLOR, Russell Stephen. b 45. Leeds Univ BA70 St Chad's Coll Dur DipTh72. Ho of Resurr Mirfield 64. **d** 72 **p** 73. C Chapel Allerton *Ripon* 72-75; Ind Chapl *Liv* 75-81; P-in-c Burtonwood 81-83; V from 83. *The Vicarage, Chapel Lane, Burtonwood, Warrington WA5 4PT* Tel (01925) 225371

NAYLOR, Stanley. b 29. NW Ord Course 76. **d** 79 **p** 80. NSM Girlington *Bradf* 79-80; C Tong 80-83; C Ingrow cum Hainworth 83-85; P-in-c Bradf St Clem 85-93; C Baildon 93-96; rtd 96. *6 Heaton Close, Baildon, Shipley, W Yorkshire BD17 5PL* Tel (01274) 593441

NAYLOR, Ms Vivien Frances Damaris (Liz). b 55. RGN86 DTM89 New Hall Cam BA78 MA82. Ripon Coll Cuddesdon DipMin93. **d** 93 **p** 94. C Northampton St Jas *Pet* 93-95; Chapl Asst Southn Univ Hosps NHS Trust from 95. *31 Winnington, Fareham, Hants PO15 6HP* Tel (01329) 239664

✠**NAZIR-ALI, The Rt Revd Dr Michael James.** b 49. Karachi Univ BA70 St Edm Hall Ox BLitt74 MLitt81 Fitzw Coll Cam MLitt76 ACT PhD83. Ridley Hall Cam 70. **d** 74 **p** 76 **c** 84. Tutorial Supervisor Th Cam Univ 74-76; C Cambridge H Sepulchre w All SS *Ely* 74-76; Pakistan 76-86; Sen Tutor Karachi Th Coll 76-81; Provost Lahore 81-84; Bp Raiwind 84-86; Asst to Abp Cant 86-89; Co-ord of Studies and Ed Lambeth Conf 86-89; Hon C Ox St Giles and SS Phil and Jas w St Marg *Ox* 86-89; Hon C Limpsfield and Titsey *S'wark* 89-94; Gen Sec CMS 89-94; Asst Bp S'wark 89-94; Can Th Leic Cathl *Leic* 92-94; Bp Roch from 94; Visiting Prof Th and Relig Studies Greenwich Univ from 96. *Bishopscourt, Rochester, Kent ME1 1TS* Tel (01634) 842721 Fax 831136

NDUMBU, Joel Mbithi Gideon. b 30. Clare Coll Cam DipTh68 BA73 MA77 ALBC64 TCert50. Ridley Hall Cam 65. **d** 68 **p** 69. C Chesterton St Andr *Ely* 68-71; C Cherry Hinton St Andr 73-75; Kenya from 75; rtd 96. *PO Box 454, Kitui, Kenya* Tel Kitui (141) 22441 or 22378

✠**NDUNGANE, The Most Revd Winston Hugh Njongonkulu.** b 41. K Coll Lon BD78 AKC78 MTh. St Pet Coll Alice 71. **d** 73 **p** 74 **c** 91. S Africa 73-75 and from 80; C Mitcham St Mark *S'wark* 75-76; C Hammersmith St Pet *Lon* 76-77; C Primrose Hill St Mary w Avenue Road St Paul 77-79; Prin St Bede's Th Coll Umtata 85-87; Prov Exec Officer 87-91; Bp Kimberley and Kuruman 91-96; Abp Cape Town from 96. *Bishopscourt, 16-20 Bishopscourt Drive, Claremont, 7700 South Africa* Tel Cape Town (21) 761-2531 Fax 761-4193

NEAL, Alan. b 27. Trin Coll Bris DipTh84. **d** 84 **p** 85. Hon C Broughty Ferry *Bre* 84-85; P-in-c Dundee St Ninian 85-86; R Annan *Glas* 86-94; R Lockerbie 86-94; rtd 94. *c/o Mr and Mrs Graham, 3 Vallance Drive, Lockerbie, Dumfriesshire DG11 2DU*

NEAL, Canon Anthony Terrence. b 42. BA CertEd. Chich Th Coll 65. **d** 68 **p** 69. C Cross Green St Sav and St Hilda *Ripon* 68-73; NSM Hawksworth Wood 73-78; Asst Chapl & Hd RE Abbey Grange High Sch Leeds 73-81; NSM Farnley 78-81; Dioc Adv in RE *Truro* 81-85; Children's Officer 85-87; Stewardship Adv 87-88; P-in-c St Erth 81-84; V 84-96; P-in-c Phillack w Gwithian and Gwinear 94-96; P-in-c Hayle 94-96; Hon Can Truro Cathl from 94; TR Godrevy from 96. *The Rectory, Forth an Tewennow, Phillack, Hayle, Cornwall TR27 4QE* Tel (01736) 753541

NEAL, Christopher Charles. b 47. St Pet Coll Ox BA69. Ridley Hall Cam 69. **d** 72 **p** 73. C Addiscombe St Mary *Cant* 72-76; C

Camberley St Paul *Guildf* 76-83; TV 83-86; V Thame w Towersey *Ox* from 86. *The Vicarage, Lashlake Lane, Thame, Oxon OX9 3AB* Tel (01844) 212225

NEAL, Miss Frances Mary. b 37. **d** 96. NSM Catford (Southend) and Downham *S'wark* from 96. *29 Ballamore Road, Downham, Bromley, Kent BR1 5LN* Tel 0181-698 6616

NEAL, Canon Geoffrey Martin. b 40. AKC63. **d** 64 **p** 65. C Wandsworth St Paul *S'wark* 64-66; USA 66-68; C Reigate St Mark *S'wark* 68-70; P-in-c Wandsworth St Faith 70-72; V 72-75; V Houghton Regis *St Alb* 75-95; Hon Can St Alb 93-95. *19 Rectory Close, Carlton, Bedford MK43 7JT*

NEAL, James Christian. b 62. Trin Coll Cam BA84 MA88. Coll of Resurr Mirfield 93. **d** 95 **p** 96. C Lt Stanmore St Lawr *Lon* from 95. *18 Milford Gardens, Edgware, Middx HA8 6EY* Tel 0181-951 3662

NEAL, John Edward. b 44. Nottm Univ BTh74. Linc Th Coll 70. **d** 74 **p** 75. C Lee St Marg *S'wark* 74-77; C Clapham St Jo 77; C Clapham Ch Ch and St Jo 77-81; P-in-c Eltham St Barn 81-83; V from 83; Sub-Dean Eltham 89-91; Sub-Dean Greenwich S 91-97; RD Greenwich S from 97. *St Barnabas Vicarage, 449 Rochester Way, London SE9 6PH* Tel 0181-856 8294

NEAL, Stephen Charles. b 44. MIMgt76 K Coll Lon BSc66. N Ord Course 90. **d** 93 **p** 94. C Walmsley *Man* 93-96; P-in-c Bolton St Matt w St Barn from 96. *St Matthew's Vicarage, Stowell Street, Bolton BL1 3RQ* Tel (01204) 522810

NEALE, Alan James Robert. b 52. LSE BSc(Econ)73 Ox Univ BA76 MA81. Wycliffe Hall Ox 74. **d** 77 **p** 78. C Plymouth St Andr w St Paul and St Geo *Ex* 77-80; C Portswood Ch Ch *Win* 80-82; V Stanstead Abbots *St Alb* 82-85; Asst Master Chelmsf Hall Sch Eastbourne 85-88; USA from 88. *28 Greenough Place, Newport, RI, 02840-2752 USA*

NEALE, David. b 50. Lanchester Poly BSc72. St Mich Coll Llan BD83. **d** 83 **p** 84. Min Can St Woolos Cathl *Mon* 83-87; Chapl St Woolos Hosp Newport 85-87; R Blaina and Nantyglo *Mon* 87-91; Video Production Officer Bd of Miss from 91. *Church in Wales Centre, Woodlands Place, Penarth CF64 2EX* Tel (01222) 705278 or 708234

NEALE, Geoffrey Arthur. b 41. Brasted Th Coll 61 St Aid Birkenhead 63. **d** 65 **p** 66. C Stoke *Cov* 65-68; C Fareham H Trin *Portsm* 68-71; TV 71-72; R Binstead 72-77; TR Bottesford w Ashby *Linc* 77-80; V Horncastle w Low Toynton 80-90; V Brigg 90-95; V Blockley w Aston Magna and Bourton on the Hill *Glouc* from 95; Local Min Officer from 95. *The Vicarage, Blockley, Moreton-in-Marsh, Glos GL56 9ES* Tel (01386) 700283

NEALE, Canon James Edward McKenzie (Eddie). b 38. Selw Coll Cam BA61. Clifton Th Coll 61. **d** 63 **p** 64. C Everton St Ambrose w St Tim *Liv* 63-72; Relig Adv BBC Radio Merseyside 72-76; V Bestwood St Matt *S'well* 76-86; Dioc Urban Officer 86-91; V Nottingham St Mary and St Cath from 91; Hon Can S'well Minster from 91. *St Mary's Vicarage, Standard Hill, Nottingham NG1 6GA* Tel 0115-947 2476

NEALE, Mrs Jan Celia. b 42. EMMTC CTPS92. **d** 92 **p** 94. C Gt and Lt Coates w Bradley *Linc* 92-96; TV from 96. *St Nicholas Vicarage, Great Coates Road, Great Coates, Grimsby, S Humberside DN37 9NS* Tel (01472) 882495

✠**NEALE, The Rt Revd John Robert Geoffrey.** b 26. AKC54 St Boniface Warminster 54. **d** 55 **p** 56 **c** 74. C St Helier *S'wark* 55-58; Chapl Ardingly Coll Haywards Heath 58-62; Recruitment Sec CACTM 63-66; ACCM 66-68; R Hascombe *Guildf* 68-74; Can Missr and Dir Post-Ord Tr 68-74; Hon Can Guildf Cathl 68-74; Adn Wilts *Sarum* 74-80; Suff Bp Ramsbury 74-81; Area Bp Ramsbury 81-88; Can and Preb Sarum Cathl 74-88; Sec Partnership for World Miss 89-91; Asst Bp S'wark 89-91; Asst Bp Lon 89-91; rtd 91; Asst Bp B & W from 91. *26 Prospect, Corsham, Wilts SN13 9AF* Tel (01249) 712557

NEALE, Martyn William. b 57. G&C Coll Cam BA78 MA82. Ripon Coll Cuddesdon 78. **d** 81 **p** 82. C Perry Hill St Geo *S'wark* 81-83; C Purley St Mark Woodcote 83-85; V Abbey Wood from 85. *The Vicarage, 1 Conference Road, London SE2 0YH* Tel 0181-311 0377

NEAUM, Canon David. b 12. Lich Th Coll 34. **d** 37 **p** 38. C Burton All SS *Lich* 37-39; C Cannock 39-43; R Kingstone w Gratwich 43-46; R Leigh 46-52; Tristan da Cunha 52-56; S Rhodesia 56-65; Rhodesia 65-80; Zimbabwe 80-81; St Helena 81-84; rtd 84; Australia from 84. *St John's Rectory, 225 Beechworth, Wodonga, Victoria, Australia 3690* Tel Albury (60) 242053

NEAVE, Garry Reginald. b 51. Leic Univ MA73 PGCE74. S'wark Ord Course DipRS DipPSE. **d** 82 **p** 83. Hon C Harlow St Mary Magd *Chelmsf* from 82; Chapl Harlow Tertiary Coll from 84; Hon C St Mary-at-Latton *Chelmsf* from 87. *35 Perry Springs, Harlow, Essex CM17 9DQ* Tel (01279) 435684

NEECH, Canon Alan Summons. b 15. Dur Univ LTh37. Tyndale Hall Bris 34. **d** 39 **p** 40. BCMS 39-81; India 39-66; Can Lucknow 64-66; Overseas Sec BCMS 64-66; Gen Sec 66-81; Hon Can Cen Tanganyika from 72; Hon C Slough *Ox* 75-81; rtd 80; RD Loddon *Nor* 85-90; Perm to Offic from 90. *The Gardens Cottage, Rockland St Mary, Norwich NR14 7HQ* Tel (01508) 538519

NEED, Philip Alan. b 54. AKC75. Chich Th Coll 76. **d** 77 **p** 78. C Clapham Ch Ch and St Jo *S'wark* 77-79; C Luton All SS w St Pet *St Alb* 80-83; V Harlow St Mary Magd *Chelmsf* 83-89; P-in-c Chaddesden St Phil *Derby* 89-91; Bp's Dom Chapl *Chelmsf* 91-96; R Bocking St Mary from 96; Dean Bocking from 96. *The Deanery, Deanery Hill, Braintree, Essex CM7 5SR* Tel (01376) 324887

NEEDHAM, Miss Patricia. b 32. **d** 87 **p** 94. Par Dn Warmsworth *Sheff* 87-89; Par Dn Norton Woodseats St Chad 89-92; Chapl Beauchief Abbey from 89; rtd 92. *14 Dalewood Drive, Sheffield S8 0EA* Tel 0114-236 2688

NEEDHAM, Brother Peter Douglas. b 56. Chich Th Coll 86. **d** 88 **p** 88. SSF from 80; C S Moor *Dur* 88-90; Chapl RN 91-93; Lic to Offic *Newc* 91-96; Lic to Offic *Lon* from 97. *110 Ellesmere Road, London NW10 1JS* Tel 0181-452 7285 Fax as telephone

NEEDLE, Paul Robert. b 45. Lon Univ DipTh70. Oak Hill Th Coll 67. **d** 70 **p** 71. C Gt Horton *Bradf* 70-74; C Pudsey St Lawr 74-77; Chapl St Luke's Hosp Bradf 78-80; Hon C Horton *Bradf* 78-80; NSM Irthlingborough *Pet* 87-90; NSM Gt w Lt Addington 90-94; NSM Gt w Lt Addington and Woodford from 94. *The Rectory, Woodford Road, Great Addington, Kettering, Northants NN14 4BS* Tel (01536) 78257

NEEDS, Dr Michael John. b 42. Open Univ BA82 Univ of Wales (Swansea) MSc84 PhD87. Wycliffe Hall Ox 91. **d** 93 **p** 94. C Aberystwyth *St D* 93-96; R Llanllwchaearn and Llanina from 96. *The Rectory, Llandysul Road, New Quay SA45 9RE* Tel (01545) 560059

NEELY, Canon William George. b 32. Lon Univ BD62 QUB PhD. **d** 56 **p** 57. C Cregagh *D & D* 56-62; C-in-c Mt Merrion 62-68; I 68-76; Dioc Missr (Down) 70-76; Can Down Cathl 74-76; I Kilcooley w Littleton, Crohane and Killenaule *C & O* 76-84; P-in-c Fertagh 79-84; I Keady w Armaghbreague and Derrynoose *Arm* from 84; Tutor for Aux Min (Arm) from 86; RD Tynan from 91; Preb Swords St Patr Cathl Dublin from 97. *31 Crossmore Road, Keady, Armagh BT60 3JY* Tel (01861) 531230

NEILL, Canon Erberto Mahon. b 16. TCD BA40 MA Div Test. **d** 39 **p** 40. I Castleknock w Mulhuddart, Clonsilla etc *D & G* 61-75; I Dublin Harold's Cross 77-81; I Boyle Union *K, E & A* 81-87; Preb Elphin Cathl 83-87; rtd 87. *2 The Court, Newtownpark House, Blackrock, Co Dublin, Irish Republic*

NEILL, The Very Revd Ivan Delacherois. b 12. CB63 OBE58 Knight Officer Order of Orange Nassau (w swords) 46. Jes Coll Cam BA35 MA38. Lon Coll of Div 35. **d** 36 **p** 37. C Fulham St Mary N End *Lon* 36-38; Hon C Hornsey Ch Ch 38-39; CF 39-66; Chapl Gen 60-66; QHC 60-62; Chapl to The Queen 62-66; Provost Sheff 66-74; Perm to Offic *Glouc* 74-86; rtd 77; Perm to Offic *S'wark* 86-94; Perm to Offic *Chich* from 94. *York House, 194 High Street, Uckfield, E Sussex TN22 1RD* Tel (01825) 766184

NEILL, James Purdon. b 41. Lon Univ DipTh63. Oak Hill Th Coll 60. **d** 64 **p** 65. C Kendal St Thos *Carl* 64-68; Chapl Park Hill Flats Sheff 68-71; P-in-c Mansfield St Jo *S'well* 71-77; V Nottingham St Ann w Em from 77. *St Ann's Vicarage, 17 Robin Hood Chase, Nottingham NG3 4EY* Tel 0115-950 5471

✠**NEILL, The Rt Revd John Robert Winder.** b 45. TCD BA66 MA69 Jes Coll Cam BA68 MA72. Ridley Hall Cam 67. **d** 69 **p** 70 **c** 86. C Glenageary *D & G* 69-71; Lect CITC 70-71 and 82-84; Dioc Registrar (Ossory, Ferns and Leighlin) *C & O* 71-74; Bp's V, Lib and Chapter Registrar Kilkenny Cathl 71-74; I Abbeystrewry *C, C & R* 74-78; I Dublin St Bart w Leeson Park *D & G* 78-84; Chapl Community of St Jo the Ev 78-84; Dean Waterford *C & O* 84-86; Prec Lismore Cathl 84-86; Adn Waterford 84-86; I Waterford w Killea, Drumcannon and Dunhill 84-86; Bp T, K & A 86-97; Bp C & O from 97. *The Palace, Kilkenny, Irish Republic* Tel Kilkenny (56) 21560 Fax 64399

NEILL, Richard Walter. b 67. Wadh Coll Ox BA89 Em Coll Cam BA92. Westcott Ho Cam CTM93. **d** 93 **p** 94. C Abbots Langley *St Alb* 93-97; C Wisley w Pyrford *Guildf* from 97. *33 Engliff Lane, Woking, Surrey GU22 8SU* Tel (01923) 400245

NEILL, Robert Chapman. b 51. Lon Univ BD82. CITC 77. **d** 77 **p** 78. C Lurgan Ch the Redeemer *D & D* 77-82; I Tullylish 82-88; I Mt Merrion from 88. *The Rectory, 122 Mount Merrion Avenue, Belfast BT6 0FS* Tel (01232) 644308

NEILL, Stephen Mahon. b 69. TCD BA91. CITC 91. **d** 93 **p** 94. C Monkstown *D & G* 93-95; Dom Chapl to Bp of Killaloe and Clonfert *L & K* from 95; C Limerick City from 95. *14 Springfield Drive, Dooradoyle, Limerick, Irish Republic* Tel Limerick (61) 302038 Mobile 087-235 5912 or 088-532822 Fax as telephone E-mail smneill@iol.ie

NEILL, The Ven William Barnet. b 30. TCD BA61. **d** 63 **p** 64. C Belfast St Clem *D & D* 63-66; C Dundonald 66-72; I Drumgath 72-80; I Drumgooland 76-80; I Mt Merrion 80-83; I Dromore Cathl from 83; Adn Dromore from 85. *Dromore Cathedral Rectory, 20 Church Street, Dromore, Co Down BT25 1AA* Tel (01846) 692275

NEILL, The Very Revd William Benjamin Alan. b 46. Open Univ BA76. CITC 68. **d** 71 **p** 72. C Dunmurry *Conn* 71-74; C Coleraine 75-77; C Dublin St Ann w St Steph *D & G* 77-78; I Convoy w Monellan and Donaghmore *D & R* 78-81; I Faughanvale 81-86; I Waterford w Killea, Drumcannon and Dunhill *C & O* from 86; Dean Waterford from 86; Prec Lismore Cathl from 86; Prec Cashel Cathl from 87; Preb Ossory and Leighlin Cathls from 96.

The Deanery, 41 Grange Park Road, Waterford, Irish Republic Tel Waterford (51) 74119 Fax as telephone

NELLIST, Canon Valerie Ann. b 48. SRN69 SCM71. St And Dioc Tr Course 87. **d** 90 **p** 94. NSM Dunfermline *St And* from 90; NSM W Fife Team Min from 90; Perth St Ninian from 97. *28 Glamis Gardens, Dalgety Bay, Dunfermline, Fife KY11 5TD* Tel (01383) 824066 Fax as telephone E-mail rnellist44@aol. com

NELMES, Mrs Christine. b 41. St Mary's Coll Cheltenham DipT63. S Dios Minl Tr Scheme 92. **d** 95 **p** 96. NSM Winscombe *B & W* from 95. *23 Sidcot Lane, Winscombe, Avon BS25 1LA* Tel (01934) 844300 Fax 842973

NELSON, Canon Allen James. b 29. CITC 53. **d** 55 **p** 56. C Glenageary *D & G* 55-57; C Dublin Clontarf 57-60; I Bailieborough w Mullagh *K, E & A* 60-75; P-in-c Knockbride 66-72; P-in-c Knockbride w Shercock 72-75; I Julianstown w Colpe *M & K* 75-81; I Julianstown and Colpe w Drogheda and Duleek from 81; Dioc Glebes Sec from 81; Can Meath from 84. *The Rectory, Eastham Road, Bettystown, Co Meath, Irish Republic* Tel Drogheda (41) 27345

NELSON, Christopher James. b 57. Preston Poly HNC80 Nottm Univ BTh88. Aston Tr Scheme 83 St Jo Coll Nottm 85. **d** 88 **p** 89. C Blackpool St Thos *Blackb* 88-90; C Altham w Clayton le Moors 90-92; V Knuzden from 92. *St Oswald's Vicarage, Bank Lane, Blackburn BB1 2AP* Tel (01254) 698321

NELSON, Frank. b 12. Jes Coll Ox BA35 MA40 Lon Univ BSc44. Ox NSM Course. **d** 78 **p** 78. NSM Sutton Courtenay w Appleford *Ox* 78-89; Lic to Offic from 89. *6 Tullis Close, Sutton Courtenay, Abingdon, Oxon OX14 4BD* Tel (01235) 848567

NELSON, Graham William. b 61. Birm Univ CYCW85. St Jo Coll Nottm BA91. **d** 91 **p** 92. C Pype Hayes *Birm* 91-93; C Lancaster St Mary *Blackb* from 94; Chapl HM Pris Lanc Castle from 94. *24 Milkingstile Lane, Lancaster LA1 5QB* Tel (01524) 382362

NELSON, Jane. b 42. **d** 94. Par Dn Muchalls *Bre* from 94; Asst Chapl Grampian Health Care from 93. *4 St Michael's Road, Newtonhill, Stonehaven, Kincardineshire AB3 2RW* Tel (01569) 730967

NELSON, Julie. b 52. St Aid Coll Dur BA73. SW Minl Tr Course 92. **d** 95 **p** 96. NSM Tavistock and Gulworthy *Ex* from 95. *21 Deer Park Road, Tavistock, Devon PL19 9HG* Tel (01822) 612736

NELSON, Kenneth Edmund. b 10. St Jo Coll Cam BA33 MA36. Qu Coll Birm 46. **d** 47 **p** 48. C Huddersfield St Pet *Wakef* 47-50; C Pocklington *York* 50-52; R Brotton Parva 52-58; V Sheriff Hutton 58-65; Aden 65-67; P-in-c Crayke w Brandsby and Yearsley 67-68; R 68-78; rtd 78; P-in-c Wold Newton *York* 78-81. *Flat 1, Holly Mount, 23B Ripon Road, Harrogate, N Yorkshire HG1 2JL* Tel (01423) 568460

NELSON, Mark Richard. b 61. Ushaw Coll Dur BA84. NE Ord Course 89. **d** 84 **p** 85. In RC Ch 84-89; C Birtley *Dur* 91-94; P-in-c Middlesbrough St Cuth *York* 94-96; Urban Development Officer from 94; C Middlesbrough St Oswald from 96. *95 Southwell Road, Middlesbrough, Cleveland TS5 6NG* Tel (01642) 820838

NELSON, Canon Michael. b 44. Lon Univ BD66. Coll of Resurr Mirfield 66. **d** 68 **p** 69. C Newbold w Dunston *Derby* 68-72; C N Gosforth *Newc* 72-77; V Seaton Hirst 77-83; V Blyth St Mary 83-93; P-in-c Horton 86-87; RD Bedlington 88-93; R Hexham from 93; Hon Can Newc Cathl from 94; Acting RD Hexham 96-97. *The Rectory, Eilansgate, Hexham, Northd NE46 3EW* Tel (01434) 603121

NELSON, Sister Norma Margaret. b 34. Liv Univ DASS77 CQSW77. CA Tr Coll IDC60. **d** 93 **p** 94. TD Kirkby *Liv* 93-94; TV 94-95; rtd 95; Perm to Offic *Liv* from 95. *15 Pateley Close, Kirkby, Liverpool L32 4UT* Tel 0151-545 0037

NELSON, Paul John. b 52. Nottm Univ BCombStuds84. Linc Th Coll 81. **d** 84 **p** 85. C Waltham Cross *St Alb* 84-87; C Sandridge 87-90; V from 90. *The Vicarage, 2 Anson Close, House Lane, Sandridge, St Albans, Herts AL4 9EN* Tel (01727) 866089

NELSON, Ralph Archbold. b 27. St Cuth Soc Dur BA50. Bps' Coll Cheshunt 50. **d** 52 **p** 53. C Penwortham St Mary *Blackb* 52-57; C Eglingham *Newc* 57-58; V Featherstone *Wakef* 58-80; V Kirkham *Blackb* 80-92; RD Kirkham 88-91; rtd 92; Perm to Offic *Blackb* from 92. *6 Blundell Lane, Penwortham, Preston PR1 0EA* Tel (01772) 742573

NELSON, Robert Gibson. b 34. ALCD61. **d** 61 **p** 62. C Isleworth St Mary *Lon* 61-64; C-in-c Reading St Barn CD *Ox* 64-69; Australia 69-72; V Guernsey St Jo *Win* 72-78; R Guernsey Ste Marie du Castel 78-86; V Guernsey St Matt 84-86; rtd 86. *Le Petit Feugre, Clos des Mielles, Castel, Guernsey, Channel Islands* Tel (01481) 52726

NELSON, Robert Towers. b 43. MSOSc Liv Coll of Tech BSc65. NW Ord Course 76. **d** 79 **p** 80. NSM Liv Our Lady and St Nic w St Anne *Liv* 79-83; NSM Liscard St Thos *Ches* 83-87; P-in-c from 87; Dioc Ind Missr from 87; Asst Sec SOSc from 89; Perm to Offic *Liv* from 89. *5 Sedbergh Road, Wallasey, Merseyside L44 2BR* Tel 0151-630 2830

NELSON, Roger Charles. b 44. ATII74 Newc Univ LLB66 Solicitor 69. Cant Sch of Min 88. **d** 91 **p** 92. NSM Deal St Leon and St Rich and Sholden *Cant* 91-96; NSM Gt Mongeham w Ripple and Sutton by Dover from 96; NSM Eastry and Northbourne w Tilmanstone etc from 96. *377 London Road, Deal, Kent CT14 9PS* Tel (01304) 366681

NELSON, Warren David. b 38. TCD BA67. **d** 68 **p** 69. C Belfast St Mich *Conn* 68-70; I Kilcooley w Littleton, Crohane, Killenaule etc *C & O* 70-76; Chapl Coalbrook Fellowship Hosp Ho Thurles 76-94; Perm to Offic (Cashel, Waterford and Lismore) 93-94; I Lurgan w Billis, Killinkere and Munterconnaught *K, E & A* from 94. *The Rectory, Virginia, Co Cavan, Irish Republic* Tel Cavan (49) 47389

NELSON, William. b 38. Oak Hill Th Coll 74. **d** 76 **p** 77. C Hensingham *Carl* 76-81; V Widnes St Paul *Liv* 81-89; R Higher Openshaw *Man* from 89; AD Ardwick from 96. *St Clement's Rectory, Ashton Old Road, Manchester M11 1HJ* Tel 0161-370 1538

NENER, Canon Thomas Paul Edgar. b 42. FRCSEd71 FRCS71 Liv Univ MB, ChB. Coll of Resurr Mirfield 78. **d** 80 **p** 81. C Warrington St Elphin *Liv* 80-83; V Haydock St Jas 83-95; V W Derby (or Tuebrook) St Jo from 95; Hon Can Liv Cathl from 95. *St John's Vicarage, Tuebrook, Liverpool L13 7EA* Tel 0151-228 2023

NENO, David Edward. b 62. SS Mark & Jo Coll Plymouth BA85. Ripon Coll Cuddesdon 85. **d** 88 **p** 89. C Chapel Allerton *Ripon* 88-91; C Acton St Mary *Lon* 91-94; V Kingsbury H Innocents from 94. *The Vicarage, 54 Roe Green, London NW9 0PJ* Tel 0181-204 7531

NESBITT, Charles Howard. b 09. St Jo Coll Dur LTh34 BA35. Bp Wilson Coll 31. **d** 35 **p** 36. C Liv St Chris Norris Green *Liv* 35-37; C Blackb St Matt *Blackb* 37-41; C Gt Harwood St Jo 41-46; V Wrightington 46-58; V Baxenden 58-68; V Stalmine 68-74; rtd 75. *Sunnyside Eventide Home, 75 South Oswald Road, Edinburgh EH9 2HH* Tel 0131-667 6831

NESBITT, Heather Hastings. b 48. S'wark Ord Course 88. **d** 90 **p** 94. Par Dn Camberwell St Luke *S'wark* 90-94; C Addiscombe St Mary Magd w St Martin from 94. *97 Stretton Road, Croydon CR0 6ET* Tel 0181-662 0282

NESBITT, Ronald. b 58. Sheff Univ LLB TCD DipTh85. CITC 82. **d** 85 **p** 86. C Ballymena w Ballyclug *Conn* 85-88; C Holywood *D & D* 88-90; I Helen's Bay 90-96; I Bangor Abbey from 96. *The Abbey Rectory, 5 Downshire Road, Bangor, Co Down BT20 3TW* Tel (01247) 460173

NESHAM, George Dove. b 20. ALCD50. Lon Coll of Div. **d** 50 **p** 51. C Harrington *Carl* 50-52; C Ferryhill *Dur* 52-55; V Stanley 55-62; V W Ardsley *Wakef* 62-77; V Ripponden 77-80; V Satley *Dur* 80-87; RD Stanhope 81-87; rtd 87. *29 Ettrick Road, Jarrow, Tyne & Wear NE32 5SL* Tel 0191-489 8071

✠**NESTOR, The Rt Revd Donald Patrick.** b 38. Ex Coll Ox BA63 MA66 Birm Univ DipTh65. Qu Coll Birm 63. **d** 65 **p** 66 **c** 79. C W Ardsley *Wakef* 65-68; C Forton *Lich* 68-72; Lesotho 72-79; Chapl Nat Univ 74-77; Warden Angl Sem Roma 74-79; Bp Lesotho 79-92; Asst Bp Blackb from 92; P-in-c Bretherton from 92. *The Rectory, 156 South Road, Bretherton, Preston PR5 7AH* Tel (01772) 600206 E-mail sjb@bafs.demon.co.uk

NETHERWAY, Diana Margaret. b 47. Bp Otter Coll CertHE94. **d** 96. NSM Northwood *Portsm* from 96; NSM Gurnard from 96. *106 Victoria Road, Cowes, Isle of Wight PO31 7HP* Tel (01983) 298505

NETHERWAY, Robert Sydney (Bob). b 37. Bp Otter Coll CertHE94. **d** 96. NSM Cowes St Faith *Portsm* from 96. *106 Victoria Road, Cowes, Isle of Wight PO31 7HP* Tel (01983) 298505

NETHERWOOD, Mrs Anne Christine. b 43. ARIBA68 Liv Univ BArch66 Lon Univ BD92. St Deiniol's Hawarden 88. **d** 91 **p** 94. NSM Ellesmere and Welsh Frankton *Lich* 91-94; C Dudleston 94-97; C Criftins 94-97; C Criftins w Dudleston and Welsh Frankton from 97. *The Vicarage, Criftins, Ellesmere, Shropshire SY12 9LN* Tel (01691) 75212

NEUDEGG, Mrs Joan Mary. b 36. Cant Sch of Min 81. **dss** 84 **d** 87 **p** 94. Chalk *Roch* 84-86; Hon C Dean Forest H Trin *Glouc* 87-90; Hon C Woolaston w Alvington 90-95; Hon C Woolaston w Alvington and Aylburton 95-96; rtd 96; Perm to Offic *Ex* from 96. *48 Marker Way, Honiton, Devon EX14 8EN* Tel (01404) 43957

NEUDEGG, Leslie. b 35. Lon Univ DipRS83 Open Univ BA84. S'wark Ord Course 77. **d** 80 **p** 81. Hon C Chalk *Roch* 80-86; Area Org CECS 86-89; P-in-c Woolaston w Alvington *Glouc* 89-95; R Woolaston w Alvington and Aylburton 95-96; rtd 96; Perm to Offic *Ex* from 96. *48 Marker Way, Honiton, Devon EX14 8EN* Tel (01404) 43957

NEVILL, James Michael. b 50. Cranmer Hall Dur 84. **d** 86 **p** 87. C Sowerby Bridge w Norland *Wakef* 86-91; CF 91-94; TV Broadwater St Mary *Chich* from 94. *80 Dominion Road, Worthing, W Sussex BN14 8JT* Tel (01903) 230759

NEVILL, Mavis Hetty. b 45. Westhill Coll Birm CertYS68 Sheff Poly DipEdMan85 Bradf and Ilkley Coll DipPSE85 Bradf Univ BEd95 Univ Coll Ches CertRE96. N Ord Course 92. **d** 95 **p** 96. NSM Mount Pellon *Wakef* from 95. *11 Lane Ends, Wheatley, Halifax, W Yorkshire HX2 8TW* Tel (01422) 362280

NEVILLE, Alfred John. b 21. K Coll Lon BA40. Sarum & Wells Th Coll. **d** 83 **p** 84. NSM Weston-super-Mare St Paul *B & W* 83-93; Perm to Offic from 93. *12 Woodford Court, 21 Clarence*

Road North, Weston-super-Mare, Avon BS23 4AW Tel (01934) 631176

NEVILLE, David Bruce. b 61. Ravensbourne Coll of Art & Design BA83. St Jo Coll Nottm LTh89. **d** 91 **p** 92. C Broxtowe *S'well* 91-94; C Attenborough 94-95. *29 Osbourne Street, Nottingham NG7 5LY*

NEVILLE, Canon Graham. b 22. CCC Cam BA47 MA49 CertEd Cam Univ BD94. Chich Th Coll 48. **d** 50 **p** 51. C Sutton in Ashfield St Mary *S'well* 50-53; Chapl Sheff Univ *Sheff* 53-58; R Culworth *Pet* 58-63; R Eydon 58-63; RD Culworth 62-63; Chapl Ch Ch Coll Cant 63-68; Chapl Sutton Valence Sch Kent 68-73; Six Preacher Cant Cathl *Cant* 69-78; Prin Lect Relig Studies Eastbourne Coll of Educn 73-80; Dir of Educn *Linc* 80-87; Can and Preb Linc Cathl 82-88; rtd 87; Perm to Offic *Linc* from 88. *16 Silverdale Avenue, Worcester WR5 1PY* Tel (01905) 360319

NEVILLE, Michael Robert John. b 56. Hatf Coll Dur BA80 Hughes Hall Cam PGCE81. Wycliffe Hall Ox 82. **d** 85 **p** 86. C E Twickenham St Steph *Lon* 85-88; Asst Dir Proclamation Trust 88-93; R Fordham *Chelmsf* from 93. *The Rectory, Wood Lane, Fordham Heath, Colchester CO3 5TR* Tel (01206) 240221

NEVIN, Alan Joseph. b 51. MIPM80 Univ Coll Galway BA72. Aux Course 92 St Deiniol's Hawarden CertRS94. **d** 92 **p** 93. Aux P Youghal Union *C, C & R* 92-94; NSM Waterford w Killea, Drumcannon and Dunhill *C & O* 94-95; C from 95. *34 Pheasant Walk, Collins Avenue, Waterford, Irish Republic* Tel Waterford (51) 857949 Fax as telephone

NEVIN, Ronald. b 32. DMin88. Wesley Coll Leeds Linc Th Coll 63. **d** 64 **p** 65. C Norton St Mary *Dur* 64-66; R Cockfield 66-70; USA from 70; rtd 95. *19879 Gator Creek Court, North Fort Myers, FL 33903, USA* Tel Fort Myers (941) 731 8843

NEW, David John. b 37. Lon Univ BSc58. Chich Th Coll 65. **d** 67 **p** 68. C Folkestone St Mary and St Eanswythe *Cant* 67-72; C Kings Heath *Birm* 72-74; V S Yardley St Mich 74-83; V Moseley St Agnes from 83. *St Agnes' Vicarage, 5 Colmore Crescent, Birmingham B13 9SJ* Tel 0121-449 0368

NEW, Derek. b 30. **d** 86 **p** 87. NSM Brondesbury St Anne w Kilburn H Trin *Lon* from 86. *20 Lynton Road, London NW6 6BL* Tel 0171-328 0187

NEW, Philip Harper. b 08. St Jo Coll Dur LTh32 BA33. St Aid Birkenhead 29. **d** 33 **p** 34. C Melton Mowbray w Burton Lazars, Freeby etc *Leic* 33-37; C Leic St Aug 37-38; R W Leake w Kingston-on-Soar and Ratcliffe-on-Soar *S'well* 38-47; CF 43-46; V Pleasley Hill *S'well* 47-53; R Kimberley 53-59; V Thurgarton w Hoveringham 59-69; R Beckingham 69-73; P-in-c Walkeringham 69-73; rtd 73; Perm to Offic *S'well* from 73. *Belvoir Vale Residential Home, Widmerpool, Keyworth, Nottingham NG12 5QL*

NEW, Canon Thomas Stephen. b 30. K Coll Cam BA52 MA56. Cuddesdon Coll 52. **d** 54 **p** 55. C Greenford H Cross *Lon* 54-55; C Old St Pancras w Bedford New Town St Matt 55-58; C Woodham *Guildf* 58-64; V Guildf All SS 64-72; V Banstead 72-93; RD Epsom 76-80; Hon Can Guildf Cathl 79-93; Sub-Chapl HM Pris Downview 88-93; rtd 93; Perm to Offic *Ex* from 94. *St Katharine's, North Street, Denbury, Newton Abbot, Devon TQ12 6DJ* Tel (01803) 813775

NEWALL, Arthur William. b 24. Univ of Wales (Lamp) BA49. Chich Th Coll 49. **d** 51 **p** 52. C Hulme St Phil *Man* 51-53; C Fallowfield 53-55; V Oldham St Barn 55-60; V Aspull *Liv* 60-68; R Foots Cray *Roch* 68-78; V Henlow *St Alb* 78-89; rtd 89; Perm to Offic *Liv* from 89. *38 Fairhaven Road, Southport, Merseyside PR9 9UH* Tel (01704) 26045

NEWALL, Richard Lucas. b 43. AKC66. **d** 66 **p** 67. C Roby *Liv* 66-69; C Douglas St Geo and St Barn *S & M* 69-71; Lic to Offic *Man* 72-75; C Ban St Mary *Ban* 75-77; R Newborough w Llangeinwen w Llangaffo etc from 77. *Newborough Rectory, Anglesey LL61 6RP* Tel (01248) 440285

NEWARK, Archdeacon of. *See* HAWTIN, The Ven David Christopher

NEWBON, Eric. b 23. Fitzw Ho Cam BA51 MA55. Ridley Hall Cam 51. **d** 53 **p** 54. C Garston *Liv* 53-57; V Bickershaw 57-65; V Southport All So 65-85; rtd 85; Perm to Offic *Ches* from 86. *33 Haymakers Way, Saughall, Chester CH1 6AR* Tel (01244) 880123

NEWBON, Kenneth. b 29. Wells Th Coll 67. **d** 69 **p** 70. C Church Stretton *Heref* 69-72; P-in-c Cressage w Sheinton 72-75; R Braunstone *Leic* 75-81; TR 81-84; P-in-c Eardisley w Bollingham and Willersley *Heref* 84-88; P-in-c Brilley w Michaelchurch on Arrow 84-88; P-in-c Whitney w Winforton 84-88; RD Kington and Weobley 87-95; R Eardisley w Bollingham, Willersley, Brilley etc 88-96; rtd 96. *Grace Dieu, Staunton-on-Wye, Hereford*

NEWBON, Michael Charles. b 59. Oak Hill Th Coll DipHE94. **d** 94 **p** 95. C Bedford St Jo and St Leon *St Alb* from 94. *53 Hillesdon Avenue, Elstow, Bedford MK42 9AJ* Tel (01234) 358307

NEWBURY, Canon Robert. b 22. St D Coll Lamp BA46. **d** 48 **p** 49. C Killay *S & B* 48-55; V Glascwm and Rhulen 55-63; V Manselton 63-84; V Manselton w Hafod 84-90; Hon Can Brecon Cathl from 85; rtd 91. *4 Cobham Close, Gorseinon, Swansea SA4 4FA* Tel (01792) 654848

NEWBY, Peter Gordon. b 23. **d** 64 **p** 65. C Leic St Phil *Leic* 64-69; R Lt Bowden St Nic 69-72; V Jersey Gouray St Martin *Win* 72-77; Chapl Jersey Gp of Hosps 78-80; R Much Birch w Lt Birch, Much Dewchurch etc *Heref* 80-88; rtd 89; Perm to Offic *Ex* from 90. *18 Woodfields, Seaton, Devon EX12 2UX* Tel (01297) 24562

NEWCASTLE, Bishop of. *See* WHARTON, The Rt Revd John Martin

NEWCASTLE, Provost of. *See* COULTON, The Very Revd Nicholas Guy

NEWCOMBE, John Adrian. b 61. Univ of Wales (Lamp) BA83 SS Paul & Mary Coll Cheltenham PGCE85. Ripon Coll Cuddesdon 90. **d** 92 **p** 93. C Stroud and Uplands w Slad *Glouc* 92-96; C Nailsworth from 96. *The Vicarage, Horsley, Stroud, Glos GL6 0PR* Tel (01453) 833814

NEWCOMBE, Kenneth Harry. b 27. Ridley Hall Cam 70. **d** 72 **p** 73. C Melton Mowbray w Thorpe Arnold *Leic* 72-78; P-in-c W Bridgford *S'well* 78-84; V Radcliffe-on-Trent 84-85; V Shelford 84-85; P-in-c Holme Pierrepont w Adbolton 84-85; R Radcliffe-on-Trent and Shelford etc from 85. *The Rectory, Radcliffe-on-Trent, Nottingham NG12 2FB* Tel 0115-933 2203

NEWCOMBE, Timothy James Grahame. b 47. AKC75. St Aug Coll Cant 75. **d** 76 **p** 77. C Heref St Martin *Heref* 76-79; C Hitchin *St Alb* 79-85; R Croft and Stoney Stanton *Leic* 85-91; P-in-c Launceston *Truro* 91-92; V Launceston from 92. *St Mary's Vicarage, Dunheved Road, Launceston, Cornwall PL15 9JE* Tel (01566) 772974

NEWCOME, Canon James William Scobie. b 53. Trin Coll Ox BA74 MA78 Selw Coll Cam BA77 MA81. Ridley Hall Cam 75. **d** 78 **p** 79. C Leavesden All SS *St Alb* 78-82; P-in-c Bar Hill LEP *Ely* 82-92; V Bar Hill 92-94; Tutor Ridley Hall Cam 83-88; P-in-c Dry Drayton *Ely* 89-94; RD N Stowe 93-94; Can Res Ches Cathl and Dioc Dir of Ords *Ches* from 94. *5 Abbey Street, Chester CH1 2JF* Tel (01244) 315532

NEWELL, Aubrey Francis Thomas. b 20. St D Coll Lamp BA43. **d** 45 **p** 46. C Rhosddu *St As* 45-49; C Llanwnog *Ban* 49-50; C Gabalfa *Llan* 50-53; C Gt Marlow *Ox* 53-57; R Lavendon w Cold Brayfield 57-62; V Gawcott and Hillesden 62-77; P-in-c Radclive 69-72; RD Buckingham 70-76 and 82-84; P-in-c Padbury w Adstock 72-77; V Lenborough 77-87; rtd 87. *5 Church View, Steeple Claydon, Buckingham MK18 2QR* Tel (01296) 738271

NEWELL, Christopher David. b 53. CCouns92. S'wark Ord Course DipRS87. **d** 87 **p** 88. C Stockwell St Mich *S'wark* 87-90; Asst Chapl R Lon Hosp (Whitechapel) 90-92; Asst Chapl R Lon Hosp (Mile End) 90-92; R Birch St Agnes *Man* 92-96; P-in-c Longsight St Jo w St Cypr 94-96; R Birch St Agnes w Longsight St Jo w St Cypr from 97. *St Agnes's Rectory, Slade Lane, Manchester M13 0GN* Tel 0161-224 2596

NEWELL, Dr Edmund John. b 61. Univ Coll Lon BSc83 Nuff Coll Ox DPhil88 MA89. Ox Min Course 89 Ripon Coll Cuddesdon 92. **d** 94 **p** 95. C Deddington w Barford, Clifton and Hempton *Ox* from 94. *Meadow View, Hempton Road, Barford St Michael, Banbury, Oxon OX15 0RZ* Tel (01869) 338988

NEWELL, Jack Ernest. b 26. CEng FIChemE ARCS BSc. Glouc Th Course 80. **d** 83 **p** 84. NSM Hempsted *Glouc* 83-95; Perm to Offic from 95. *Hempsted House, Hempsted, Gloucester GL2 6LW* Tel (01452) 523320

NEWELL, Kenneth Ernest. b 22. S Dios Minl Tr Scheme 77. **d** 79 **p** 80. NSM Lynton, Brendon, Countisbury, Lynmouth etc *Ex* 79-85; TR 85-89; RD Shirwell 84-89; rtd 89; Perm to Offic *Ex* from 89. *Mole End, Lydiate Lane, Lynton, Devon EX35 6HE*

NEWELL, Samuel James (Jim). b 28. TCD BA53 MA63. TCD Div Sch Div Test54. **d** 54 **p** 55. C Belfast St Mary *Conn* 54-57; C Derriaghy 57-60; C Reading St Mary V *Ox* 60-63; V Chesham Ch Ch 63-74; P-in-c Wraysbury 74-78; TV Riverside 78-94; rtd 94. *41 Redford Road, Windsor, Berks SL4 5ST* Tel (01753) 862300

NEWELL of Staffa, Gerald Frederick Watson. b 34. Sarum Th Coll 56. **d** 59 **p** 61. C Southampton SS Pet and Paul w All SS *Win* 59-61; C Overton w Laverstoke and Freefolk 61-63; CF (TA) 61-63; CF 63-66; R Spennithorne *Ripon* 66-68; R Finghall 66-68; R Hauxwell 66-68; Hon C Steyning *Chich* 74-78; Perm to Offic *Ex* 93-95; P-in-c Breamore *Win* from 95. *The Rectory, Breamore, Fordingbridge, Hants SP6 2BY* Tel (01725) 513098

NEWELL PRICE, Dr John Charles. b 29. MRCGP64 SS Coll Cam BA50 MB, ChB53. LNSM course 88. **d** 91 **p** 94. NSM Frensham *Guildf* from 91. *Dragon Lodge, Millbridge, Frensham, Farnham, Surrey GU10 3DQ* Tel (01252) 793317

NEWHAM, Jill. b 37. Oak Hill NSM Course. **d** 89 **p** 95. NSM W w E Mersea *Chelmsf* 89-91 and 95-97; NSM Peldon w Gt and Lt Wigborough 93-97; P-in-c Bildeston w Wattisham *St E* from 97. *Hitcham Rectory, Ipswich IP7 7NF* Tel (01449) 740350

NEWHOUSE, The Ven Robert John Darrell. b 11. Worc Coll Ox BA35 MA38. Cuddesdon Coll 35. **d** 36 **p** 37. C Pet St Jo *Pet* 36-40; C Cambridge St Giles w St Pet *Ely* 40-46; Chapl RNVR 41-46; R Ashwater *Ex* 46-56; RD Holsworthy 54-56; RD Aylesbeare 65-66; V Littleham w Exmouth 56-66; Adn Totnes 66-76; Can Res Ex Cathl 66-76; Treas 70-76; rtd 76; Perm to Offic *Ex* from 76. *Pound Cottage, Northlew, Okehampton, Devon EX20 3NN* Tel (01409) 221532

✠**NEWING, The Rt Revd Kenneth Albert.** b 23. Selw Coll Cam BA53 MA57. Coll of Resurr Mirfield 53. **d** 55 **p** 56 **c** 82. C Plymstock *Ex* 55-63; R Plympton St Maurice 63-82; RD Plympton 71-76; Preb Ex Cathl 75-82; Adn Plymouth 78-82; Suff Bp Plymouth 82-88; Lic to Offic *Ox* 88-93; OSB from 89; rtd

93. *Elmore Abbey, Church Lane, Newbury, Berks RG13 1SA* Tel (01635) 33080

NEWING, Dr Peter. b 33. Birm Univ CertEd55 Dur Univ BA63 Bris Univ BEd76 State Univ NY BSc85 EdD88 Cam Univ DipRS91 FRSA60 FSAScot59 ACP67 MCollP86 FCollP95 APhS63. Cranmer Hall Dur 63. **d** 65 **p** 66. C Blockley w Aston Magna *Glouc* 65-69; P-in-c Taynton 69-75; P-in-c Tibberton 69-75; R Brimpsfield w Elkstone and Syde 75-83; R Brimpsfield, Cranham, Elkstone and Syde 83-97; P-in-c Daglingworth w the Duntisbournes and Winstone 95-97; R Brimpsfield w Birdlip, Syde, Daglingworth, etc from 97. *The Rectory, Lower End, Daglingworth, Cirencester, Glos GL7 7AL* Tel (01285) 654561

NEWLAND, Mrs Patricia Frances. b 35. Edin Univ MA56 DipSoc57. EAMTC 96. **d** 97. NSM Duxford *Ely* from 97; NSM Hinxton from 97; NSM Ickleton from 97. *Ickleton Lodge, Ickleton, Saffron Walden, Essex CB10 1SH* Tel (01799) 530268 Fax 531146

NEWLANDS, Christopher William. b 57. Bris Univ BA79. Westcott Ho Cam 81. **d** 84 **p** 85. C Bishops Waltham *Portsm* 84-87; Hon C Upham 85-87; Prec, Sacr and Min Can Dur Cathl *Dur* 87-92; Chapl Bucharest w Sofia *Eur* 92-95; V Shrub End *Chelmsf* from 96. *All Saints' Vicarage, 270 Shrub End Road, Colchester CO3 4RL* Tel (01206) 574178

NEWLANDS, Prof George McLeod. b 41. Edin Univ MA63 Heidelberg Univ BD66 PhD70 Ch Coll Cam MA73. **d** 82 **p** 82. Lect Cam Univ 73-86; Lic to Offic *Ely* from 82; Fell and Dean Trin Hall Cam 82-86; Prof Div Glas Univ from 86; Perm to Offic *Glas* from 86. *8 Hills Avenue, Cambridge CB1 4XA, or The University, Glasgow G12 8QQ* Tel (01223) 248631 or 0141-339 8855

NEWLYN, Canon Edwin. b 39. AKC64. **d** 65 **p** 66. C Belgrave St Mich *Leic* 65-68; Miss to Seamen 68-81; Brazil 68-69; C Glas St Gabr *Glas* 69-73; S Africa 73-76; V Fylingdales *York* 81; P-in-c Hawsker 81; V Fylingdales and Hawsker cum Stainsacre 81-88; RD Whitby 85-92; P-in-c Goathland from 88; Can and Preb York Minster from 90. *The Vicarage, Goathland, Whitby, N Yorkshire YO22 5AN* Tel (01947) 896227 or 896239 Fax 896316

NEWMAN, Adrian. b 58. Bris Univ BSc80 DipHE85 MPhil89. Trin Coll Bris 82. **d** 85 **p** 86. C Forest Gate St Mark *Chelmsf* 85-89; V Hillsborough and Wadsley Bridge *Sheff* 89-96; RD Hallam 94-96; R Birm St Martin w Bordesley St Andr *Birm* from 96. *The Rectory, 37 Barlows Road, Birmingham B15 2PN* Tel 0121-454 0119

NEWMAN, Alan George. b 18. Lich Th Coll 41. **d** 44 **p** 45. C Twerton *B & W* 44-52; V Clandown 52-56; V Bradford-on-Avon Ch Ch *Sarum* 56-76; R Monkton Farleigh w S Wraxall 76-84; rtd 84; Perm to Offic *Sarum* from 84. *14 White Horse Road, Winsley, Bradford-on-Avon, Wilts BA15 2JZ* Tel (01225) 854119

NEWMAN, Alfred John Gordon. b 19. Qu Coll Birm 71. **d** 74 **p** 74. Hon C Hall Green St Pet *Birm* 74-84; Perm to Offic *St E* 84-96; Perm to Offic *Chich* from 96. *Flat 5, Southdown Court, Bell Banks Road, Hailsham, E Sussex BN27 2AT* Tel (01323) 441378

NEWMAN, Cecil Ernest. b 21. Bris Univ BA58 DipTh58. Roch Th Coll 61. **d** 62 **p** 63. C Tiverton St Pet *Ex* 62-64; C Wolborough w Newton Abbot 64-67; Lic to Offic *Roch* 67-86; Chapl Darenth Park Hosp Dartford 67-86; rtd 86; Perm to Offic *Roch* from 86. *27 Nursery Road, Meopham, Gravesend, Kent DA13 0LR* Tel (01474) 812955

NEWMAN, David Malcolm. b 54. FSAScot81 Aber Univ LTh BTh. St Steph Ho Ox 89. **d** 91 **p** 92. C St Mary-at-Latton *Chelmsf* 91-94; R Weeley and Lt Clacton from 94. *The Vicarage, 2 Holland Road, Little Clacton, Clacton-on-Sea, Essex CO16 9RS* Tel (01255) 860241

NEWMAN, David Maurice Frederick. b 54. Hertf Coll Ox BA75 MA79. St Jo Coll Nottm. **d** 79 **p** 80. C Orpington Ch Ch *Roch* 79-83; C Bushbury *Lich* 83-86; V Ockbrook *Derby* 86-97; TR Loughborough Em and St Mary in Charnwood *Leic* from 97. *The Rectory, 47 Forest Road, Loughborough, Leics LE11 3NW* Tel (01509) 263264

NEWMAN, Mrs Diana Joan. b 43. Sarum Th Coll 81. **dss** 84 **d** 87 **p** 94. Parkstone St Pet w Branksea and St Osmund *Sarum* 84-87; Hon Par Dn 87-94; Hon C 94-97; TV from 97. *62 Vale Road, Poole, Dorset BH14 9AU* Tel (01202) 745136

NEWMAN, Eric William. b 26. Vancouver Sch of Th STh65. **d** 56 **p** 57. Canada 56-67; Miss to Seamen 56-64 and 67-91; Chapl Victoria Docks Lon 67-68; Chapl Newport, Gwent 68-78; Chapl Tyne & Wear 78-91; rtd 91. *1 Sunnycroft, Portskewett, Chepstow NP6 4RY* Tel (01291) 420679

NEWMAN, Geoffrey Maurice. b 22. Ox NSM Course 77. **d** 80 **p** 81. NSM Binfield *Ox* 80-84; Chapl St Geo Sch Ascot 82-84; V Teynham *Cant* 84-87; rtd 87; Perm to Offic *Cant* from 87. *55 St Mildred's Road, Westgate-on-Sea, Kent CT8 8RJ* Tel (01843) 833837

NEWMAN, Graham Anthony. b 44. Ripon Coll Cuddesdon 79. **d** 81 **p** 82. C Walker *Newc* 81-84; C Whorlton 84-87; V Warkworth and Acklington 87-94; V Haltwhistle and Greenhead from 94; Chapl Northumberland HA from 94. *The Vicarage, Edens Lawn, Haltwhistle, Northd NE49 0AB* Tel (01434) 320215

NEWMAN, James Edwin Michael. b 59. Nottm Univ BA80 Ox Univ BA90. Wycliffe Hall Ox 88. **d** 91 **p** 92. C Bidston *Ches* 91-95; C Cheadle from 95. *4 Cuthbert Road, Cheadle, Cheshire SK8 2DT* Tel 0161-428 3983

NEWMAN, John Humphrey. b 17. ALCD49. **d** 49 **p** 50. C Hove Bp Hannington Memorial Ch *Chich* 49-52; V Welling *Roch* 52-64; V Penge St Jo 64-74; R Knockholt 74-82; rtd 82; Perm to Offic *Chich* from 82. *Stonegarth, Pett Level Road, Fairlight, Hastings, E Sussex TN35 4EA* Tel (01424) 812518

NEWMAN, Laurence Victor. b 23. Wells Th Coll. **d** 66 **p** 67. C Hythe *Cant* 66-69; C Milton *Win* 69-71; Asst Chapl HM Pris Wandsworth 71-72; Chapl HM Rem Cen Ashford 72-77; Chapl HM Pris Win 77-88; Chapl Las Palmas *Eur* 88-89; Chapl Algarve 89-91; rtd 91. *The Vicarage, Stockland, Honiton, Devon EX14 9EF*

NEWMAN, Michael Alan. b 40. Chich Th Coll 67. **d** 70 **p** 71. C Kilburn St Aug *Lon* 70-73; C St Geo-in-the-East St Mary 75-78; rtd 78. *April Cottage, Georges Lane, Storrington, Pulborough, W Sussex RH20 3JH* Tel (01903) 744354

NEWMAN, Michael John. b 50. Leic Univ BA72 MA75 Ex Coll Ox DipTh74. Cuddesdon Coll 73. **d** 75 **p** 76. C Tettenhall Regis *Lich* 75-79; C Uttoxeter w Bramshall 79-82; R Norton Canes 82-89; TR Rugeley from 89. *The Rectory, 20 Church Street, Rugeley, Staffs WS15 2AB* Tel (01889) 582149

NEWMAN, Paul Anthony. b 48. Lon Univ BSc70 Leeds Univ DipTh75. Coll of Resurr Mirfield 73. **d** 76 **p** 77. C Catford St Laur *S'wark* 76-81; TV Grays All SS *Chelmsf* 81-83; TV Lt Thurrock St Mary 81-83; W Ham Adnry Youth Chapl 83-87; P-in-c Forest Gate All SS 83-89; V 89-91; Dep Chapl HM Pris Wormwood Scrubs 91-92; Chapl HM Pris Downview from 92. *HM Prison Downview, Sutton Lane, Sutton, Surrey SM2 5PD* Tel 0181-770 7500 Fax 770 7673

NEWMAN, Richard David. b 38. BNC Ox BA60 MA63. Lich Th Coll 60. **d** 62 **p** 63. C E Grinstead St Swithun *Chich* 62-66; C Gt Grimsby St Jas *Linc* 66-69; C Gt Grimsby St Mary and St Jas 69-73; TV 73-74; V St Nicholas at Wade w Sarre *Cant* 74-75; P-in-c Chislet w Hoath 74-75; V St Nicholas at Wade w Sarre and Chislet w Hoath 75-81; V S Norwood H Innocents 81-84; V S Norwood H Innocents *S'wark* from 85. *Holy Innocents' Vicarage, 192A Selhurst Road, London SE25 6XX* Tel 0181-653 2063

NEWNHAM, Eric Robert. b 43. Sarum & Wells Th Coll 70. **d** 75 **p** 76. Hon C Blackheath Ascension *S'wark* from 75. *27 Morden Hill, London SE13 7NN* Tel 0181-692 6507 or 691 6559

NEWNS, Donald Frederick. b 07. St Aid Birkenhead 34. **d** 37 **p** 38. C Elton St Steph *Man* 37-39; C Nottingham St Andr *S'well* 39-40; C Mansfield St Jo 40-43; C Stoke upon Trent *Lich* 43-44; Chapl Stoke-on-Trent City Gen Hosp 43-44; Chapl Sheff R Infirmary and Hosp 45-49; V Eastwood *Sheff* 49-51; Dep Chapl HM Pris Wandsworth 52-53; Chapl HM Pris Parkhurst 53-59; R Litcham w Kempston *Nor* 59-61; P-in-c E w W Lexham *Nor* 59-61; R Litcham w Kempston w E and W Lexham 61-72; rtd 73. *Woodgate, 7 Albert Road North, Malvern, Worcs WR14 2PT*

NEWPORT, Derek James. b 39. Acadia Univ (NS) BA82 MEd84. Sarum & Wells Th Coll 74. **d** 76 **p** 77. C Tavistock and Gulworthy *Ex* 76-78; Canada 78-86; V Malborough w S Huish, W Alvington and Churchstow *Ex* 86-95; TR Widecombe-in-the-Moor, Leusdon, Princetown etc from 95. *The Rectory, Widecombe-in-the-Moor, Newton Abbot, Devon TQ13 7TB* Tel (01364) 621334

NEWPORT, Archdeacon of. *See* TYTE, The Ven Keith Arthur Edwin

NEWSOME, David Ellis. b 55. St Jo Coll Dur BA77. Westcott Ho Cam 80. **d** 82 **p** 83. C Finchley St Mary *Lon* 82-85; C Fulham All SS 85-87; Bp's Dom Chapl *Birm* 87-91; V Gravelly Hill from 91; P-in-c Stockland Green 93-96; RD Aston from 95. *All Saints' Vicarage, Broomfield Road, Birmingham B23 7QA* Tel 0121-373 0730

NEWSOME, John Keith. b 49. Mert Coll Ox BA73 MA76. Ripon Coll Cuddesdon 73. **d** 76 **p** 77. C Bywell St Pet *Newc* 76-78; C Berwick H Trin 78-82; Chapl Bonn w Cologne *Eur* 86-93; Chapl Hamburg from 93. *Beim Grünen Jager 16, 2000 Hamburg 36, Germany* Tel Hamburg (40) 439-2334

NEWSTEAD, Dominic Gerald. b 65. Wycliffe Hall Ox BTh95. **d** 95 **p** 96. C Windlesham *Guildf* from 95. *57 Poplar Avenue, Windlesham, Surrey GU20 6PW* Tel (01276) 453066

NEWSUM, Alfred Turner Paul. b 28. Coll of Resurr Mirfield 52. **d** 53 **p** 54. C Roath St German *Llan* 53-59; C Westmr St Matt *Lon* 59-60; C Washwood Heath *Birm* 60-68; P-in-c Small Heath St Greg 68-78; V Birm St Aid Small Heath 72-80; V Stockland Green 80-93; rtd 93; Perm to Offic *Llan* from 93. *Ty'r Offeiriad, 18 Almond Drive, Cardiff CF2 7HD*

NEWTH, Barry Wilfred. b 33. Bris Univ BA56. ALCD58. **d** 58 **p** 59. C Upton (Overchurch) *Ches* 58-62; C Kimberworth *Sheff* 62-63; V Clifton *Man* 63-72; V Radcliffe St Thos 72-74; V Radcliffe St Thos and St Jo 74-81; R Heaton Mersey 81-86; V Kirkby Malham *Bradf* 86-87; P-in-c Coniston Cold 86-87; V Kirkby-in-Malhamdale w Coniston Cold 87-97; rtd 97. *1 Higher Ridings, Bromley Cross, Bolton BL17 9HP*

NEWTH, Canon Frederick John. b 07. Keble Coll Ox BA28 MA35. Cuddesdon Coll 28. **d** 30 **p** 31. C York St Mary Bishophill Senior *York* 30-33; C Leckhampton St Pet *Glouc* 33-38; V Wotton

St Mary 38-48; P-in-c Glouc St Cath 42-46; V Tuffley 48-50; S Africa 50-83; Adn Heidelberg 57-61; Hon Can Johannesburg 68-83; rtd 68. *Lot 4, Beckmans Road, Tewantin, Queensland, Australia 4565* Tel Tewantin (74) 740200

NEWTON, Miss Ann. b 46. Trin Coll Bris 75. **d** 87 **p** 94. Par Dn Rothley *Leic* 87-91; Par Dn Becontree St Mary *Chelmsf* 91-94; C from 94. *19 Bosworth Road, Dagenham, Essex RM10 7NU* Tel 0181-593 6780

NEWTON, Barrie Arthur. b 38. Dur Univ BA61. Wells Th Coll 61. **d** 63 **p** 64. C Walton St Mary *Liv* 63-67; C N Lynn w St Marg and St Nic *Nor* 67-69; Chapl Asst The Lon Hosp (Whitechapel) 69-71; Chapl K Coll Hosp Lon 72-77; P-in-c Bishops Sutton w Stowey *B & W* 77-81; P-in-c Compton Martin w Ubley 79-81; P-in-c Bridgwater St Jo w Chedzoy 81-83; Chapl St Mary's Hosp Praed Street Lon 83-94; Chapl St Mary's NHS Trust Paddington from 94. *St Mary's Hospital, Praed Street, London W2 1NY* Tel 0171-725 6666 or 725 1508

NEWTON, Brian Karl. b 30. Keble Coll Ox BA55 MA59. Wells Th Coll 56. **d** 58 **p** 59. C Barrow St Geo *Carl* 58-61; Trinidad and Tobago 61-69 and 71-77; Gen Ed USPG 69-71; P-in-c Gt Coates *Linc* 77; TV Gt and Lt Coates w Bradley 78-88; V Burgh le Marsh 88-94; R Bratoft w Irby-in-the-Marsh 88-94; V Orby 88-94; R Welton-le-Marsh w Gunby 88-94; rtd 94; Perm to Offic *Linc* from 94. *27 Somersby Way, Boston, Lincs PE21 9PQ* Tel (01205) 362433

NEWTON, Canon Christopher Wynne. b 25. Trin Hall Cam BA46. Westcott Ho Cam 48. **d** 50 **p** 51. C Gateshead Ch Ch *Dur* 50-52; Canada 52-55; C Harrow Weald All SS *Lon* 55-58; V Radlett *St Alb* 58-66; RD St Alb 63-66; TR Hemel Hempstead 66-72; RD Milton Keynes *Ox* 72-77; TV Swan 78-84; RD Claydon 78-84; Dioc Ecum Officer 79-84; Hon Can Ch Ch 80-83; P-in-c Lt Gaddesden *St Alb* 84-86; rtd 86; Perm to Offic *St Alb* from 86. *24 Slade Court, Watling Street, Radlet, Herts WD7 7BT* Tel (01923) 859131

NEWTON, David Ernest. b 42. Sarum & Wells Th Coll 72. **d** 74 **p** 75. C Wigan All SS *Liv* 74-80; V Choral York Minster *York* 80-85; R Ampleforth w Oswaldkirk 85-86; P-in-c E Gilling 85-86; R Ampleforth and Oswaldkirk and Gilling E from 86; RD Helmsley from 94. *The Rectory, Ampleforth, York YO6 4DU* Tel (01439) 788264

NEWTON, Derek. b 50. Sunderland Poly HND72. NE Ord Course 89. **d** 92 **p** 93. NSM Houghton le Spring *Dur* 92-96; NSM Seaham w Seaham Harbour from 96. *Pinelodge, Warwick Drive, Houghton le Spring, Tyne & Wear DH5 8JR* Tel 0191-584 9169

NEWTON, George Peter Howgill. b 62. Pemb Coll Cam BA84 MA88. Oak Hill Th Coll BA93. **d** 93 **p** 94. C Blackpool St Thos *Blackb* from 93. *8 Collingwood Avenue, Blackpool FY3 8BZ* Tel (01253) 302679

NEWTON, Gerald Blamire. b 30. Lich Th Coll. **d** 69 **p** 70. C Leeds Halton St Wilfrid *Ripon* 69-73; C Gt Yarmouth *Nor* 73-74; P-in-c Cattistock w Chilfrome and Rampisham w Wraxall *Sarum* 74-77; V Coney Hill *Glouc* 77-79; V Bryneglwys and Llandegla *St As* 79-80; R Llandegla and Bryneglwys and Llanarmon-yn-Ial 80-86; P-in-c Burythorpe, Acklam and Leavening w Westow *York* 86-95; rtd 95; Perm to Offic *York* from 95. *9 Ropery Walk, Malton, N Yorkshire YO17 0JS* Tel (01653) 692084

NEWTON, Graham Hayden. b 47. AKC69. St Aug Coll Cant 70. **d** 70 **p** 71. C St Mary-at-Lambeth *S'wark* 70-73; TV Catford (Southend) and Downham 73-78; P-in-c Porthill *Lich* 78-79; TV Wolstanton 79-86; V Stevenage H Trin *St Alb* 86-96; TR Dunstable from 96; RD Dunstable from 96. *The Rectory, 8 Furness Avenue, Dunstable, Beds LU6 3BN* Tel (01582) 664467 or 477401

NEWTON, John. b 39. AKC65. **d** 66 **p** 67. C Whipton *Ex* 66-68; C Plympton St Mary 68-74; V Broadwoodwidger 74-81; R Kelly w Bradstone 74-81; R Lifton 74-81; Chapl All Hallows Sch Rousdon 81-94; Lic to Offic *Ex* 81-94. *Home Farm, Allhallows School, Rousdon, Lyme Regis, Dorset DT7 3RA* Tel (01297) 21606

NEWTON, John Richard. b 25. FBIM. St Jo Coll Dur 76 Cranmer Hall Dur. **d** 78 **p** 79. C Cottingham *York* 78-80; R Beeford w Frodingham and Foston 80-86; R Todwick *Sheff* 86-92; rtd 92; Perm to Offic *Linc* from 92. *Quiet Corner, 12 Pelham Close, Sudbrooke, Lincoln LN2 2SQ* Tel (01522) 595123

NEWTON, Canon Keith. b 52. K Coll Lon BD73 AKC73 Ch Ch Coll Cant PGCE75. St Aug Coll Cant 74. **d** 75 **p** 76. C Gt Ilford St Mary *Chelmsf* 75-78; TV Wimbledon *S'wark* 78-85; Malawi 85-91; Dean Blantyre 86-91; Can S Malawi from 86; P-in-c Knowle *Bris* 91-93; V Knowle H Nativity from 93; RD Brislington from 95; P-in-c Easton All Hallows from 97. *Holy Nativity Vicarage, 41 Lilymead Avenue, Bristol BS4 2BY* Tel 0117-977 4260

NEWTON, Louis Kalbfield. b 44. N Texas State Univ BA73. Westcott Ho Cam CTM93. **d** 93 **p** 94. C Walthamstow St Pet *Chelmsf* from 93. *1 Beech Court, Bisterne Avenue, London E17 3QX* Tel 0181-521 3333

NEWTON, Nigel Ernest Hartley. b 38. St Jo Coll Nottm CertCS87. **d** 89 **p** 90. Hon C Largs *Glas* 89-92; Asst Chapl Ashbourne Home Largs 89-92; P-in-c Eyemouth *Edin* 92-95; Chapl Miss to Seamen 92-95; P-in-c Challoch w Newton Stewart *Glas* from 95; Chapl Newton Stewart Hosp from 95; Chapl HM Pris Pennington from 96. *All Saints Rectory, Challoch, Newton Stuart, Wigtownshire DG8 6RB* Tel (01671) 402101

NEWTON, Miss Pauline Dorothy. b 48. Southn Univ BA70 PGCE71 MPhil79. Sarum Th Coll 79. **dss** 82 **d** 87 **p** 94. Bemerton *Sarum* 82-87; Hon Par Dn 87-94; C from 94; Perm to Offic *Worc* from 86; Dep Hd Malvern Girls' Coll from 86. *13 Highbury Avenue, Salisbury SP2 7EX* Tel (01722) 325707

NEWTON, Peter. b 35. Sarum & Wells Th Coll 74. **d** 77 **p** 78. Hon C Reading St Barn *Ox* 77-79; C Bracknell 79-83; TV 83-85; V Knowl Hill w Littlewick from 85. *St Peter's Vicarage, Knowl Hill, Reading RG10 9YD* Tel (01628) 822732

NEWTON, Peter. b 39. St Jo Coll Nottm 73. **d** 75 **p** 76. C Porchester *S'well* 75-79; R Wilford from 79. *The Rectory, Main Road, Wilford, Nottingham NG11 7AJ* Tel 0115-981 5661

NEWTON, Raymond David. b 43. K Coll Lon BSc65. Linc Th Coll 65. **d** 67 **p** 68. C Ipswich St Matt *St E* 67-71; C E w W Barkwith *Linc* 71-74; R Chelmondiston w Harkstead *St E* 74-78; R Chelmondiston w Harkstead and Shotley w Erwarton 78-91; R Chelmondiston and Erwarton w Harkstead from 91. *The Rectory, Chelmondiston, Ipswich IP9 1HY* Tel (01473) 780214

NEWTON, Richard. b 47. Lon Univ DipTh72. Trin Coll Bris 72. **d** 73 **p** 74. C Fareham St Jo *Portsm* 73-76; C Cheltenham St Mark *Glouc* 76-83; P-in-c Malvern St Andr *Worc* 83-95; TR Kingswood *Bris* from 95. *Holy Trinity Vicarage, High Street, Kingswood, Bristol BS15 4AD* Tel 0117-967 3627

NEWTON, Richard John Christopher. b 60. Bris Univ BSc81. Qu Coll Birm 85. **d** 88 **p** 89. C Bris Ch the Servant Stockwood *Bris* 88-92; C Dorking w Ranmore *Guildf* 92-96; P-in-c Hagley *Worc* from 96. *The Rectory, 6 Middlefield Lane, Hagley, Stourbridge, W Midlands DY9 0PX* Tel (01562) 882442

NEWTON, Robert Keith. b 61. Man Univ BA83. St Steph Ho Ox 86. **d** 89 **p** 90. C Ludlow *Heref* 89-91; Egypt from 92. *Flat 17, 15 Ahmed Sabri, Zamalek, Cairo, Egypt*

NEWTON, Canon William Ronald. b 12. Birm Univ BA43. Westcott Ho Cam 41. **d** 43 **p** 44. C Truro St Paul *Truro* 43-48; PV Truro Cathl 45-46; V Treslothan 48-52; V Moulsecoomb *Chich* 52-56; V Stanmer w Falmer and Moulsecoomb 56-63; V Truro St Paul *Truro* 63-73; Hon Can Truro Cathl 71-83; V Penzance St Mary w St Paul 73-82; rtd 82; Perm to Offic *Chich* from 83; Perm to Offic *Truro* from 83. *52 Rutland Court, New Church Road, Hove, E Sussex BN3 4BB* Tel (01273) 773422

NEY, The Ven Reginald Basil. b 22. OBE78. ARCM55. Lich Th Coll 41. **d** 45 **p** 46. C Gnosall *Lich* 45-47; Prec Gib Cathl *Eur* 47-54; Chapl Gib 47-54; Chapl St Bart Hosp Lon 54-56; Chapl Madrid *Eur* 56-87; Can Gib Cathl 62-87; Adn Gib 63-87; rtd 87. *Apartmento 24, Bloque A-3, Colonia Ducal, Playa de Gandia, Valencia, Spain*

NIAS, John Charles Somerset. b 18. Worc Coll Ox BA40 MA45 BD46. Wells Th Coll 40. **d** 41 **p** 42. C Portsea St Mary *Portsm* 41-44; Warden's Sec St Deiniol's Lib Hawarden 44-46; Chapl Heswall Nautical Sch 44-46; C Northolt Park St Barn *Lon* 46-47; R Blandford St Mary *Sarum* 47-54; V Bryanston 52-54; V Uttoxeter w Bramshall *Lich* 54-56; V Finstock and Fawler *Ox* 56-83; V Ramsden 56-83; Dir of Studies C of E Bd of Educn 61-63; Dir of Studies Cen Readers' Bd 63-73; rtd 83; Perm to Offic *Win* 83-95; Perm to Offic *Portsm* from 83; Perm to Offic *Chich* from 88. *29 Southleigh Road, Warblington, Havant, Hants PO9 2QG* Tel (01705) 453186

NIBLETT, David John Morton. b 24. Wells Th Coll 51. **d** 54 **p** 55. C Stepney St Dunstan and All SS *Lon* 54-59; V Syston *Leic* 59-65; V Barnstaple St Pet w H Trin *Ex* 65-75; V S Brent 75-90; rtd 90; Perm to Offic *B & W* from 90. *2 Beretun Orchard, Glastonbury, Somerset BA6 8AX* Tel (01458) 833101

NICE, John Edmund. b 51. Univ of Wales (Ban) BA73. Coll of Resurr Mirfield 74. **d** 76 **p** 77. C Oxton *Ches* 76-79; C Liscard St Mary w St Columba 79-82; V Latchford St Jas 82-92; R Holyhead w Rhoscolyn w Llanfair-yn-Neubwll *Ban* 92-95; R Holyhead from 95. *The Rectory, Newry Street, Holyhead, Anglesey LL65 1HS* Tel (01407) 763001

NICHOL, William David. b 58. Hull Univ BA84. Ridley Hall Cam 84. **d** 87 **p** 88. C Hull Newland St Jo *York* 87-90; C Kirk Ella 90-92; TV from 92. *2A Chestnut Avenue, Willerby, Hull HU10 6PA* Tel (01482) 658974

NICHOLAS, Canon Arnold Frederick. b 34. Jes Coll Cam BA58 MA62. Ely Th Coll 58. **d** 60 **p** 61. C Wisbech St Aug *Ely* 60-63; P-in-c Lt Massingham *Nor* 63-65; Youth Chapl 63-67; Chapl Bp Otter Coll Chich 67-70; R Westbourne *Chich* 70-76; V Stansted 70-76; Can and Preb Chich Cathl 76-82; RD Chich 76-80; P-in-c Chich St Pet 76-81; V Chich St Paul and St Bart 80-81; V Chich St Paul and St Pet 81-82; V Wisbech SS Pet and Paul *Ely* 82-90; RD Wisbech 82-90; V Fordham St Pet 90-95; P-in-c Kennett 90-95; Perm to Offic *Chich* from 97. *19 Roman Way, Fishbourne, Chichester, W Sussex PO19 3QN* Tel (01243) 781388

NICHOLAS, Brian Arthur. b 19. St Edm Hall Ox BA47 MA53. Wycliffe Hall Ox 62. **d** 64 **p** 65. C Gerrards Cross *Ox* 64-66; C Whitley Ch Ch 66-69; V Chudleigh Knighton *Ex* 69-76; V Ex St Mark 76-84; rtd 84; Perm to Offic *Ex* from 84. *Windyridge, 4 Little Johns Cross Hill, Exeter EX2 9PJ* Tel (01392) 219222

NICHOLAS, Ernest Milton. b 25. ACP50 Newc Univ DipAdEd69 Lanc Univ MA78. NE Ord Course 85. **d** 86 **p** 87. NSM Hexham

Newc from 86. *Hillside, Eilansgate, Hexham, Northd NE46 3EW* Tel (01434) 603609

NICHOLAS, Herbert Llewellyn. b 19. St D Coll Lamp 51. **d** 53 **p** 54. C Merthyr Tydfil *Llan* 53-65; V Pontypridd St Matt 65-89; rtd 89; Perm to Offic *Llan* from 89. *47 Meadow Crescent, Tonteg, Pontypridd CF38 1NL* Tel (01443) 206156

NICHOLAS, Malcolm Keith. b 46. FIBMS71 Open Univ BA79. S Dios Minl Tr Scheme 81. **d** 84 **p** 85. NSM Gatcombe *Portsm* 84-92; NSM Shorwell w Kingston 88-92; C Hartley Wintney, Elvetham, Winchfield etc *Win* 92-96; TV Grantham *Linc* from 96. *Harrowby Parsonage, Edinburgh Road, Grantham, Lincs NG31 9QR* Tel (01476) 564781

NICHOLAS, Maurice Lloyd. b 30. Kelham Th Coll 54. **d** 58 **p** 59. C Stepney St Dunstan and All SS *Lon* 58-60; C Sevenoaks St Jo *Roch* 60-65; Chapl RADD 65-75; C Northolt St Mary *Lon* 75-85; rtd 85; Hon C Upper Teddington SS Pet and Paul *Lon* 85-90; Hon C Teddington SS Pet and Paul and Fulwell from 90. *58 Elton Close, Hampton Wick, Kingston-upon-Thames, Surrey KT1 4EE* Tel 0181-977 9340

NICHOLAS, Paul James. b 51. Univ of Wales (Lamp) DipTh73 BA. Coll of Resurr Mirfield 73. **d** 74 **p** 75. C Llanelli *St D* 74-78; C Roath St Marg *Llan* 78-84; P-in-c Leic St Pet *Leic* 84-87; V Shard End *Birm* 87-96; rtd 96; Perm to Offic *Birm* from 96. *50 Delrene Road, Shirley, Solihull, W Midlands B90 9HJ* Tel 0121-745 7339

NICHOLL, Joseph Edward Chancellor. b 20. MC45. Qu Coll Cam BA46 MA48. Ridley Hall Cam. **d** 48 **p** 49. C Penge St Jo *Roch* 48-50; Chapl Sutton Valence Sch Kent 50-59; Asst Chapl Stowe Sch Bucks 59-60; Chapl 60-62; Asst Chapl 62-72; Chapl 72-75; P-in-c Stowe *Ox* 75-81; R Angmering *Chich* 82-85; rtd 85; Perm to Offic *Chich* from 86. *24 Rufus Close, Lewes, E Sussex BN7 1BG* Tel (01273) 479164

NICHOLLS, Alan Fryer. b 26. Univ Coll Ex BA50. Sarum Th Coll 50. **d** 52 **p** 53. C Wootton Bassett *Sarum* 52-55; C Chesterfield St Mary and All SS *Derby* 55-56; V Ringley *Man* 56-60; Chapl Prebendal Sch Chich 60-63; PV Chich Cathl *Chich* 60-63; V Selmeston w Alciston 63-65; Chapl Woodbridge Sch 65-66; Asst Chapl and Ho Master Woodbridge Sch Suffolk 66-86; TV Bruton and Distr *B & W* 86-92; rtd 92; Perm to Offic *B & W* from 92. *9 Southover, Wells, Somerset BA5 1UG* Tel (01749) 677513

NICHOLLS, Brian Albert. b 39. LBIPP LMPA. St Jo Coll Nottm CertCS84 WMMTC 90. **d** 93 **p** 94. NSM Oakham, Hambleton, Egleton, Braunston and Brooke *Pet* 93-96; R Edith Weston w N Luffenham and Lyndon w Manton from 96. *The Rectory, 8 Church Lane, Edith Weston, Oakham, Leics LE15 8EY* Tel (01780) 720931

✠**NICHOLLS, The Rt Revd John (Jack).** b 43. AKC66. **d** 67 **p** 68 **c** 90. C Salford St Clem Ordsall *Man* 67-69; C Langley All SS and Martyrs 69-72; V 72-78; Dir Past Th Coll of Resurr Mirfield 78-83; Lic to Offic *Wakef* 79-83; Can Res Man Cathl *Man* 83-90; Suff Bp Lancaster *Blackb* 90-97; Bp Sheff from 97. *Bishopscroft, Snaithing Lane, Sheffield S10 3LG* Tel 0114-230 2170 Fax 263 0110

NICHOLLS, John Gervase. b 15. Qu Coll Cam BA38 MA42. Lon Coll of Div 38. **d** 39 **p** 40. C E Twickenham St Steph *Lon* 39-43; Youth Chapl *S'wark* 43-45; V Summerstown 45-50; V Salisbury St Fran *Sarum* 50-57; S Africa 57-59; Kenya 59-63; V Herne Bay Ch Ch *Cant* 63-67; Cyprus 67-75; R Ipswich St Clem w H Trin *St E* 75-81; rtd 81; P-in-c Wilby w Brundish *St E* 81-84; Perm to Offic *Chich* 85-88; Perm to Offic *Nor* from 88. *17 Moorfield Road, Mattishall, Dereham, Norfolk NR20 3NZ* Tel (01362) 858501

NICHOLLS, Leonard Samuel. b 07. Ex Coll Ox BA29 MA34. Bps' Coll Cheshunt 30. **d** 32 **p** 33. C Headley All SS *Guildf* 32-34; C Pimlico St Gabr *Lon* 34-41; C Haslemere *Guildf* 41-49; R Monken Hadley *Lon* 49-54; C Bletchingley *S'wark* 54-60; C Isfield *Chich* 60-61; C Lt Horsted 60-61; C Uckfield 60-61; C Waldron 61-65; C Durrington 67-68; R Etwall w Egginton *Derby* 68-71; rtd 71. *Old Post House, Framfield, Uckfield, E Sussex TN22 5PN* Tel (01825) 890311

NICHOLLS, Mark Richard. b 60. LSE BSc82 Leeds Univ BA88. Coll of Resurr Mirfield 86. **d** 89 **p** 90. C Warrington St Elphin *Liv* 89-92; V Wigan St Andr 92-96; Zimbabwe from 96. *St Margaret's Rectory, 2 Greenfield Square, North End, Bulawayo, Zimbabwe* Tel Bulawayo (19) 63053

NICHOLLS, Mark Simon. b 57. Down Coll Cam MA79. Ripon Coll Cuddesdon 92. **d** 94 **p** 95. C Farnham *Guildf* from 94. *23 Hazell Road, Farnham, Surrey GU9 7BW* Tel (01252) 714521

NICHOLLS, Michael Stanley. b 34. AKC59. St Boniface Warminster 59. **d** 60 **p** 61. C Torquay St Martin Barton CD *Ex* 60-63; C E Grinstead St Mary *Chich* 63-66; C-in-c Salfords CD *S'wark* 66-68; V Salfords 68-75; V Tunbridge Wells St Barn *Roch* from 75. *The Vicarage, 31 Lansdowne Road, Tunbridge Wells, Kent TN1 2NQ* Tel (01892) 523609

NICHOLLS, Neil David Raymond. b 65. Univ Coll Lon BA86. Wycliffe Hall Ox BA90. **d** 91 **p** 92. C Westmr St Steph w St Jo *Lon* 91-94; C Islington St Mary 94-96; Chapl LSE from 96. *Flat 3, 80A Southampton Road, London WC1B 4BB* Tel 0171-831 9288

NICHOLLS, Roy Meacham. b 29. CEng MIMechE62. Glouc Sch of Min 85. **d** 88 **p** 89. NSM Pershore w Pinvin, Wick and Birlingham *Worc* 88-94; Perm to Offic from 94. *5 Paddock Close, Pershore, Worcs WR10 1HJ* Tel (01386) 553508

NICHOLLS, Stanley Charles. b 28. St Chad's Coll Dur BA53. Bps' Coll Cheshunt 53. **d** 54 **p** 55. C Middlesbrough St Thos *York* 54-59; C Hornsea and Goxhill 59-60; V Kingston upon Hull St Jo Newington 60-62; V Liverton 62-68; V Ruswarp w Sneaton 68-78; V Kirkby-in-Cleveland 78-88; rtd 88; Perm to Offic *York* from 88. *1 Brecks Close, Wigginton, York YO3 3TW* Tel (01904) 765114

NICHOLS, Albert Percival. b 18. Tyndale Hall Bris. **d** 57 **p** 57. Canada 57-59; C Attenborough w Bramcote *S'well* 59-60; P-in-c Chiselborough w W Chinnock *B & W* 60-70; R E Chinnock 60-77; R Middle Chinnock 60-70; R Middle w W Chinnock 70-78; RD Martock 75-78; P-in-c Norton sub Hamdon w Chiselborough 77-78; R Norton sub Hamdon, W Chinnock, Chiselborough etc 78-86; rtd 86; Perm to Offic *B & W* from 86; Perm to Offic *Sarum* from 86. *14 Manor Drive, Merriott, Somerset TA16 5NT* Tel (01460) 72734

NICHOLS, Dennis Harry. b 25. Kelham Th Coll 47. **d** 52 **p** 53. C Oakham *Pet* 52-55; C Kettering St Mary 55-57; P-in-c Spalding St Paul *Linc* 57-61; V Bury H Trin *Man* 61-81; V St Gluvias *Truro* 81-90; RD Carnmarth S 85-90; rtd 90; Perm to Offic *Truro* from 90. *11 Marlborough Crescent, Falmouth, Cornwall TR11 2RJ* Tel (01326) 312243

NICHOLS, Derek Edward. b 33. Lon Univ BD58 Monash Univ Aus DipEd82. Chich Th Coll 73. **d** 72 **p** 73. C S w N Hayling *Portsm* 73-75; Perm to Offic *Linc* 75-77; Australia from 80. *20 Mitchell Street, North Rothbury, Branxton, NSW, Australia 2335* Tel Cessnock (49) 383315

NICHOLS, Mark Steven. b 68. Lon Bible Coll BA94 Ridley Hall Cam CTM95. **d** 97. C Balham Hill Ascension *S'wark* from 97. *30 Canford Road, London SW11 6NZ* Tel 0181-675 8626 E-mail rev_mark@msn.com or 100043.1571@compuserve.com

NICHOLS, Canon Raymond Maurice. b 22. ALCD53. **d** 53 **p** 54. C Childwall All SS *Liv* 53-56; Kenya 56-64; Home Sec SPCK 64-71; Overseas Sec 67-73; Publisher 73-74; P-in-c Dorchester *Ox* 74-78; P-in-c Newington 77-78; TR Dorchester 78-87; V Warborough 78-87; rtd 87. *12 Abbey Court, Cerne Abbas, Dorchester, Dorset DT2 7JH* Tel (01300) 341456

NICHOLS, Robert Warren (Bob). b 54. **d** 96. NSM Headington Quarry *Ox* 96-97; C from 97. *32 York Road, Headington, Oxford OX3 8NW* Tel (01865) 433540

NICHOLSON, Brian Warburton. b 44. St Jo Coll Nottm 70 Lon Coll of Div ALCD73 LTh74. **d** 73 **p** 74. C Canford Magna *Sarum* 73-77; C E Twickenham St Steph *Lon* 77-80; V Colchester St Jo *Chelmsf* 80-96; R Church Oakley and Wootton St Lawrence *Win* from 96. *The Rectory, 9 The Drive, Oakley, Basingstoke, Hants RG23 7DA* Tel (01256) 780825

NICHOLSON, Miss Clare. b 46. RMN80 Keele Univ BA70 CertEd70 Lon Univ DN80. St Jo Coll Nottm DPS85. **dss** 85 **d** 87 **p** 94. Bletchley *Ox* 85-87; Par Dn 87-89; Par Dn Milton Keynes 89-90; Par Dn Prestwood and Gt Hampden 90-94; C from 94. *28 St Peter's Close, Prestwood, Great Missenden, Bucks HP16 9ET* Tel (01494) 866351

NICHOLSON, David. b 57. Sarum & Wells Th Coll 80. **d** 83 **p** 84. C Trevethin *Mon* 83-85; C Ebbw Vale 85-87; V Newport St Steph and H Trin 87-95; Hon Chapl Miss to Seamen from 87; V Abertillery w Cwmtillery w Six Bells *Mon* from 95. *The Vicarage, Church Street, Abertillery NP3 1DA* Tel (01495) 212246

NICHOLSON, Canon Donald. b 10. St Chad's Coll Dur BA32 DipTh34 MA35. **d** 33 **p** 34. C Darlington H Trin *Dur* 33-36; C S Kensington St Steph *Lon* 36-39; C Ruislip St Martin 39-43; C Beaconsfield *Ox* 43-46; P-Miss Beaconsfield St Mich CD 46-47; V Ox St Barn 47-55; Vice-Prin Edin Th Coll 56-64; Hon Chapl St Mary's Cathl *Edin* 56-64; Hon Can from 64; V Pimlico St Mary Graham Terrace *Lon* 64-71; Chapl Stacklands Retreat Ho W Kingsdown 71-75; Hon Chapl 75-80; rtd 75; Perm to Offic *Edin* from 75; Perm to Offic *Mor* from 80; Chapl St Marg Convent Aber from 80; Hon Can St Andr Cathl *Ab* from 84. *The Chaplaincy, St Margaret's Convent, 17 Spital, Aberdeen AB24 3HT* Tel (01224) 638407

NICHOLSON, Dorothy Ann. b 40. S'wark Ord Course 81. **dss** 84 **d** 87 **p** 94. Carshalton Beeches *S'wark* 84-87; Par Dn 87-88; Par Dn Brixton Road Ch Ch 88-89; C Malden St Jo 89-95; V Balham St Mary and St Jo from 95. *St Mary's Vicarage, 35 Elmsfield Road, London SW17 8AG* Tel 0181-673 1188

NICHOLSON, Dr Ernest Wilson. b 38. TCD BA60 MA64 Glas Univ PhD64 Cam Univ BD71 DD78. Westcott Ho Cam 69. **d** 69 **p** 70. Lect Div Cam Univ 67-79; Fell Chapl and Dir of Th Studies Pemb Coll Cam 69-79; Dean 73-79; Prof of Interpr of H Scripture Or Coll Ox 79-90; Provost from 90; Lic to Offic *Ox* from 84. *The Provost's Lodgings, Oriel College, Oxford OX1 4EW* Tel (01865) 276533

NICHOLSON, Gary. b 62. BA91. Cranmer Hall Dur 91 NE Ord Course DipHE95. **d** 95 **p** 96. NSM Whitworth w Spennymoor *Dur* 95-97; NSM Spennymoor, Whitworth and Merrington from 97. *14 Front Street, Helmington Row, Crook, Co Durham DL15 0RY* Tel (01388) 765266

NICHOLSON, Harold Sydney Leonard. b 35. Leic Univ HNC65 Garnett Coll Lon PGCE67 Open Univ BA77. S'wark Ord Course DipRS86 Oak Hill NSM Course 92. **d** 94 **p** 95. NSM

Stanwell *Lon* from 94. *7 Academy Court, Fordbridge Road, Sunbury-on-Thames, Middx TW16 6AN* Tel (01932) 787690

NICHOLSON, John Paul. b 57. Sarum Th Coll. **d** 82 **p** 83. C Kirkby *Liv* 82-85; TV Speke St Aid 85-95; Slough *Ox* 95; Ind Chapl from 95. *1 Ivy Crescent, Slough SL1 5DA* Tel (01753) 528131

NICHOLSON, Joseph. b 14. LRAM45 St Jo Coll Dur BA35 DipTh37 MA38. **d** 37 **p** 38. C Auckland St Pet *Dur* 37-39; C W Pelton 39-42; C Gainsborough All SS *Linc* 42-45; Asst Master Tettenhall Coll 45-50; Chapl Romsey Coll 50-53; Perm to Offic *Win* 50-53; V York St Thos *York* 55-58; V Healaugh w Wighill and Bilbrough 58-60; R Moresby *Carl* 60-63; V Eppleton *Dur* 63-69; Asst Master Penhill Secondary Sch Swindon 69-75; Perm to Offic *Bris* 69-75; Perm to Offic *Mon* 75-77; P-in-c Blaenavon w Capel Newydd 77-79; rtd 79. *52 Seacroft Road, Mablethorpe, Lincs LN12 2DJ* Tel (01507) 477574

NICHOLSON, Kevin Smith. b 47. CQSW76. Edin Th Coll 89. **d** 91 **p** 92. C Burntisland *St And* 91-94; C W Fife Team Min 91-94; P-in-c 94-95; R Kinross from 95. *St Paul's Rectory, 55 Muirs, Kinross KY13 7AU* Tel (01577) 862271

NICHOLSON, Nigel Patrick. b 46. Sarum & Wells Th Coll 72. **d** 75 **p** 76. C Farnham *Guildf* 75-78; C Worplesdon 78-81; P-in-c Compton 81-85; R Compton w Shackleford and Peper Harow 85-89; R Cranleigh from 89; RD Cranleigh from 95. *The Rectory, High Street, Cranleigh, Surrey GU6 8AS* Tel (01483) 273620

NICHOLSON, Miss Pamela Elizabeth. b 47. Ripon Coll Cuddesdon. **d** 92 **p** 94. C Balsall Heath St Paul *Birm* 92-95; V Smethwick St Matt w St Chad from 95. *1 St Matthew's Road, Smethwick, Warley, W Midlands B66 3TN* Tel 0121-558 1653

NICHOLSON, Canon Peter Charles. b 25. OBE92. Lambeth Hon MA89 Chich Th Coll 57. **d** 59 **p** 60. C Sawbridgeworth *St Alb* 59-62; Min Can, Prec and Sacr Pet Cathl *Pet* 62-67; V Wroxham w Hoveton *Nor* 67-74; V Lyme Regis *Sarum* 74-80; Gen Sec St Luke's Hosp for the Clergy 80-93; NSM Harlington *Lon* 80-87; Hon PV S'wark Cathl *S'wark* from 87; Can and Preb Chich Cathl *Chich* 89-93; rtd 93. *St Luke's Cottage, 13 Brearley Close, Uxbridge, Middx UB8 1JJ* Tel (01895) 233522

NICHOLSON, Peter Charles. b 44. Oak Hill Th Coll 74. **d** 76 **p** 77. C Croydon Ch Ch Broad Green *Cant* 76-80; C Gt Baddow *Chelmsf* 80-88; TV 88-96; V Westcliff St Mich from 96. *St Michael's Vicarage, 5 Mount Avenue, Westcliff-on-Sea, Essex SS0 8PS* Tel (01702) 78462

NICHOLSON, Rodney. b 45. Mert Coll Ox BA68 MA71. Ridley Hall Cam 69. **d** 72 **p** 73. C Colne St Bart *Blackb* 72-75; C Blackpool St Jo 75-78; V Ewood 78-90; V Clitheroe St Paul Low Moor from 90. *The Vicarage, St Paul's Street, Clitheroe, Lancs BB7 2LS* Tel (01200) 22418

NICHOLSON, Roland. b 40. Sarum & Wells Th Coll 72. **d** 74 **p** 75. C Morecambe St Barn *Blackb* 74-78; V Feniscliffe 78-90; V Sabden and Pendleton from 90. *St Nicholas's Vicarage, Westley Street, Sabden, Clitheroe, Lancs BB7 9EH* Tel (01282) 771384

NICHOLSON, Mrs Samantha (<u>Sam</u>). b 69. St Jo Coll York BA92. St Jo Coll Nottm MA95 LTh93. **d** 96 **p** 97. C Toxteth St Cypr w Ch Ch *Liv* from 96. *66 Fell Street, Liverpool L7 2QD* Tel 0151-263 3774

NICHOLSON, Trevor Parry. b 35. St Edm Hall Ox BA58 MA. Wycliffe Hall Ox 58. **d** 60 **p** 61. C Eastbourne Ch Ch *Chich* 60-63; C Ifield 63-67; Asst Youth Chapl *Win* 67-73; Chapl Shoreham Gr Sch 73-78; P-in-c Capel *Guildf* 78-85; V 85-90; Chapl Qu Anne's Sch Caversham from 90. *2 Henley Road, Caversham, Reading RG4 0DY* Tel 0118-947 4191 or 947 1582

NICHOLSON, Miss Velda Christine. b 44. CertEd65. Birm Bible Inst DipTh69 Cranmer Hall Dur 81. **dss** 82 **d** 87 **p** 94. Gt and Lt Driffield *York* 82-86; Newby 86-87; Par Dn 87-88; TD Cramlington *Newc* 88-94; TV 94-96; Perm to Offic from 96. *24 Glendale, Amble, Morpeth, Northd NE65 0RE* Tel (01665) 713796

NICHOLSON, William Surtees. b 15. Leeds Univ 36. Coll of Resurr Mirfield 39. **d** 41 **p** 42. C Wilmslow *Ches* 41-44; C Wallsend St Pet *Newc* 44-48; C-in-c Balkwell CD 48-61; V Ashington *Chich* 61-74; V Bamburgh and Lucker *Newc* 74-81; rtd 81. *Pepper Close Cottage, The Wynding, Bamburgh, Northd NE69 7DB* Tel (01668) 214437

NICKALLS, Frederick William (<u>Fred</u>). b 13. Oak Hill Th Coll 49. **d** 51 **p** 52. C Penge St Jo *Roch* 51-53; C-in-c Wollaton Park CD *S'well* 53-55; V Everton Em *Liv* 55-58; V Barnehurst *Roch* 58-67; R Nailsea H Trin *B & W* 67-78; rtd 78; Perm to Offic *St E* from 94. *34 Suffolk Place, Woodbridge, Suffolk IP12 1XB* Tel (01394) 380539

NICKLESS, Christopher John (<u>Chris</u>). b 58. Univ of Wales BA79. Coll of Resurr Mirfield 79. **d** 81 **p** 82. C Bassaleg *Mon* 81-85; TV Ebbw Vale 85-93; V Newport St Teilo from 93. *St Teilo's Vicarage, 1 Aberthaw Road, Newport NP9 9NS* Tel (01633) 273593

NICKLESS, Canon Victor George. b 08. Dur Univ BA34 LTh34. Lon Coll of Div 30. **d** 34 **p** 35. C Penge Lane H Trin *Roch* 34-37; C Bexley St Jo 37-41; CF (EC) 41-45; V Bexley St Jo *Roch* 45-50; TR Strood 50-63; R Wrotham 63-77; Hon Can Roch Cathl 70-77; RD Shoreham 75-77; rtd 77. *East Wing, Ford Place, Ford Lane, Wrotham Heath, Sevenoaks, Kent TN15 7SE* Tel (01732) 844172

NICKLIN, Ivor. b 41. FRSA68 BEd MTh73 PhD76 MA84. Wycliffe Hall Ox. **d** 84 **p** 85. NSM Weaverham *Ches* 84-89; P-in-c Kings Walden *St Alb* 89-91; P-in-c Offley w Lilley 89-91; V King's Walden and Offley w Lilley 91-93; V Basford *Lich* from 93. *211 Basford Park Road, Basford, Newcastle, Staffs S75 0PG* Tel (013967) 619045

NICKOLS-RAWLE, Peter John. b 44. St Luke's Coll Ex CertEd73. Sarum & Wells Th Coll 76. **d** 78 **p** 79. C Ex St Thos *Ex* 78-80; C Ex St Thos and Em 80; C Old Shoreham *Chich* 80-86; C New Shoreham 80-86; P-in-c Donnington 86-90; Chapl RAF 90-92; TV Ottery St Mary, Alfington, W Hill, Tipton etc *Ex* 92-97; P-in-c Breage w Germoe *Truro* from 97. *The Vicarage, Breage, Helston, Cornwall TR13 9PN* Tel (01326) 573449

NICOL, Ernest. b 25. S'wark Ord Course 71. **d** 74 **p** 75. NSM Hornsey Ch Ch *Lon* 74-75; NSM Hornsey St Geo 76-84; C Hendon Ch Ch 85-90; rtd 90; C Steeton *Bradf* 90-96; Asst Chapl Airedale Hosp Bradf 90-96. *75 Nightingale Lane, London N8 7RA* Tel 0181-341 5496

NICOLE, Bruce. b 54. ACIB. Wycliffe Hall Ox 89. **d** 91 **p** 92. C Headley All SS *Guildf* 91-95; V Camberley St Mich Yorktown from 95. *The Vicarage, 286 London Road, Camberley, Surrey GU15 3JP* Tel (01276) 23602

NICOLL, Alexander Charles Fiennes. b 34. Lon Univ DipTh66. Lon Coll of Div 66. **d** 68 **p** 69. C Trentham *Lich* 68-71; C Hednesford 72-74; P-in-c Quarnford 74-84; V Longnor 74-84; P-in-c Sheen 80-84; V Longnor, Quarnford and Sheen from 85; RD Alstonfield from 96. *The Vicarage, Longnor, Buxton, Derbyshire SK17 0PA* Tel (01298) 83316

NICOLL, Miss Angela Olive. b 50. Linc Th Coll 77. **dss** 79 **d** 87 **p** 94. Catford St Laur *S'wark* 79-83; Peckham St Jo w St Andr 83-87; Par Dn 87-88; Par Dn New Addington 88-94; C from 94. *78 Gascoigne Road, Croydon CR0 0NE* Tel (01689) 848123

NICOLL, George Lorimer. b 23. LNSM course 75. **d** 75. NSM Clydebank *Glas* from 75. *19 McKenzie Avenue, Clydebank, Dunbartonshire G81 2AT* Tel 0141-952 5116

NICOLSON, Paul Roderick. b 32. Cuddesdon Coll 65. **d** 67 **p** 68. C Farnham Royal *Ox* 67-70; Lic to Offic *St Alb* 70-82; C Hambleden Valley *Ox* from 82. *The Vicarage, Turville, Henley-on-Thames, Oxon RG9 6QU* Tel (01491) 638240

NIE, Miss Muriel Rose. b 29. St Mich Ho Ox IDC57. **d** 87 **p** 94. NSM Leyton All SS *Chelmsf* from 87. *2 Queens Court, Manor Road, London E10 7HP* Tel 0181-556 0457

NIELSEN, Ronald Marius Boniface. b 09. **d** 51 **p** 52. OSB from 46; Lic to Offic *Ox* from 51. *Elmore Abbey, Speen, Newbury, Berks RG13 1SA* Tel (01635) 33080

NIGHTINGALE, John Brodie. b 42. Pemb Coll Ox BA64 Bris Univ DSocStuds65 Qu Coll Cam BA67. Westcott Ho Cam 65. **d** 67 **p** 68. C Wythenshawe St Martin *Man* 67-70; Nigeria 70-76; P-in-c Amberley w N Stoke *Chich* 76-79; Adult Educn Adv 76-79; Asst Home Sec Gen Syn Bd for Miss and Unity 80-84; Miss Sec 84-87; P-in-c Wolverton w Norton Lindsey and Langley *Cov* 87-95; Dioc Miss Adv 87-95; V Rowley Regis *Birm* from 95. *St Giles' Vicarage, 192 Hanover Road, Rowley Regis, Warley, W Midlands B65 9EQ* Tel 0121-559 1251

NIGHTINGALE, Mrs Susan (<u>Sue</u>). b 44. Keele Univ BA66 DipSocSc66 Coll of Ripon & York St Jo CertCS85. S'wark Ord Course 90. **d** 93 **p** 94. NSM St Giles Cripplegate w St Bart Moor Lane etc *Lon* from 93. *31 Shakespeare Tower, London EC2Y 8DR* Tel 0171-638 5440

NIKKEL, Marc Randall. b 50. Fuller Th Sem California MDiv80 Gen Th Sem (NY) STM85. **d** 85 **p** 86. Sudan 81-87; Kenya 88; NSM Edin St Pet *Edin* 89-90; NSM Stoke Newington St Olave *Lon* 91-93. *430 Seven Sisters Road, London N4 2RE* Tel 0181-809 6860

NIMMO, Canon Alexander <u>Emsley</u>. b 53. Aber Univ BD76 Edin Univ MPhil83. Edin Th Coll 76. **d** 78 **p** 79. Prec St Andr Cathl Inverness *Mor* 78-81; P-in-c Stornoway *Arg* 81-83; R 84; R Edin St Mich and All SS *Edin* 84-90; Chapl HM Pris Saughton 87-90; R Aberdeen St Marg *Ab* from 90; Can St Andr Cathl from 96. *St Margaret's Rectory, Gallowgate, Aberdeen AB25 1EA* Tel (01224) 644969

NIND, Canon Anthony Lindsay. b 26. MBE86. Ball Coll Ox BA50 MA50. Cuddesdon Coll 50. **d** 52 **p** 53. C Southbroom *Sarum* 52-54; C Wareham w Arne 54-56; Hong Kong 56-61; R Langton Matravers *Sarum* 61-70; Brazil 70-75; Chapl Vienna *Eur* 75-80; Adn Switzerland 80-86; Chapl Zürich w St Gallen and Winterthur 80-86; Hon Can Brussels Cathl 81-89; Dean Gib 86-89; rtd 89. *Heusbergstrasse 15, 8614 Bertschikon, Switzerland*

NIND, Robert William Hampden. b 31. Ball Coll Ox BA54 MA60. Cuddesdon Coll 54. **d** 56 **p** 57. C Spalding *Linc* 56-60; Jamaica 60-67; P-in-c Battersea St Bart *S'wark* 67-70; V Brixton St Matt 70-82; Lic to Offic 82-84; Ind Chapl 84-89; Ind Chapl *Ox* 89-95; rtd 95. *19 Binswood Avenue, Headington, Oxford OX3 8NY* Tel (01865) 66604

NINEHAM, Prof Dennis Eric. b 21. Qu Coll Ox BA43 MA46 Cam Univ BD64 Birm Univ Hon DD72. Linc Th Coll 44. **d** 44 **p** 45. Asst Chapl Qu Coll Ox 44-46; Chapl 46-54; Prof Bibl and Hist Th K Coll Lon 54-58; Prof Div Lon Univ 58-64; Regius Prof Div Cam Univ 64-69; Warden Keble Coll Ox 69-79; Hon Can Bris Cathl *Bris* 80-86; Prof Th Bris Univ 80-86; rtd 86; Perm to Offic

Ox from 87. *4 Wootten Drive, Iffley Turn, Oxford OX4 4DS* Tel (01865) 715941

NINIS, The Ven Richard Betts. b 31. Linc Coll Ox BA53 MA62. Linc Th Coll 53. **d** 55 **p** 56. C Poplar All SS w St Frideswide *Lon* 55-62; V Heref St Martin *Heref* 62-71; V Upper and Lower Bullinghope w Grafton 68-71; R Dewsall w Callow 68-71; Dioc Missr 69-74; Preb Heref Cathl 70-74; Telford Planning Officer *Lich* 70-74; Can Res and Treas Lich Cathl from 74; Adn Stafford 74-80; Adn Lich from 80. *24 The Close, Lichfield, Staffs WS13 7LD* Tel (01543) 258813 Fax 419478

NISBETT, Canon Thomas Norman. b 25. OBE91. Codrington Coll Barbados. **d** 62 **p** 63. Barbados 62-64; Bermuda from 65; Hon Can Bermuda Cathl from 81; rtd 97. *2 Shelton Road, Pembroke HM 20, Bermuda* Tel Bermuda (1-441) 236-0537 Fax as telephone

NIXON, Mrs Annette Rose. b 37. K Coll Lon BD58 Newc Univ CertEd73. **d** 88 **p** 94. Dioc Youth Officer *Ox* 84-90; Par Dn Earley St Pet 88-93; Par Dn Olney w Emberton 93-94; C 94-96; P-in-c Worminghall w Ickford, Oakley and Shabbington from 96. *The Rectory, 32A The Avenue, Worminghall, Aylesbury, Bucks HP18 9LE* Tel (01844) 338839

NIXON, Canon Charles Hunter. b 07. Keble Coll Ox BA30 MA47. Dorchester Miss Coll 31. **d** 33 **p** 34. C Lon Docks St Pet w Wapping St Jo *Lon* 33-35; Chapl Dorchester Miss Coll 36-38; Vice-Prin 38-39; C Lon Docks St Pet w Wapping St Jo 39-47; CF 43-46; V Swanley St Mary *Roch* 47-64; R Woodston *Ely* 64-73; RD Yaxley 64-71; Hon Can Ely Cathl 70-78; R Coveney 73-78; rtd 78; Perm to Offic *Nor* from 78; Perm to Offic *Ely* from 78. *23 Cleeves Drive, Walsingham, Norfolk NR22 6EQ* Tel (01328) 820310

NIXON, David John. b 59. St Chad's Coll Dur BA81. St Steph Ho Ox 88. **d** 91 **p** 92. C Plymouth St Pet *Ex* 91-94; Chapl Ex Univ from 94. *29 Barnardo Road, Exeter, Devon EX2 4ND* Tel (01392) 420162 E-mail d.j.nixon@exeter.ac.uk

NIXON, Frances (Isobel). b 34. TCD BA62. **d** 94 **p** 95. NSM Rossory *Clogh* from 94. *63 Granshaugh Road, Enniskillen, Co Fermanagh BT92 2BL* Tel (01365) 348723

NIXON, John David. b 38. CEng70 MICE Leeds Univ BSc60. Linc Th Coll 76. **d** 78 **p** 79. C Rugby St Andr *Cov* 78-83; TV 83-86; TV Bicester w Bucknell, Caversfield and Launton *Ox* from 86. *The Vicarage, The Spinney, Launton, Bicester, Oxon OX6 0EP* Tel (01869) 252377

NIXON, Phillip Edward. b 48. Ch Ch Ox MA73 DPhil73 Trin Coll Cam BA80. Westcott Ho Cam 78. **d** 81 **p** 82. C Leeds Halton St Wilfrid *Ripon* 81-84; V Goring *Ox* 84; V Goring w S Stoke from 84; RD Henley from 94. *The Vicarage, Manor Road, Goring, Reading RG8 9DR* Tel (01491) 872196

NIXON, Canon Rosemary Ann. b 45. Bp Grosseteste Coll CertEd66 Dur Univ MA83 Edin Univ MTh95. Dalton Ho Bris IDC72 DipTh72 BD73. **d** 87 **p** 94. Tutor St Jo Coll w Cranmer Hall Dur 75-89; Dir St Jo Coll Ext Progr 82-89; NSM Chester le Street *Dur* 87-89; TD Gateshead 89-92; Dir Cranmer Hall Urban Studies Unit 89-92; Edin Th Coll from 92; Prin from 95; Can St Mary's Cathl *Edin* from 96. *The Theological Institute, 21 Inverleith Terrace, Edinburgh EH3 5NS* Tel 0131-343 2038 or 667 1433 Fax 315 3754

NIXSON, Peter. b 27. Ball Coll Ox BA51 MA59 Ex Univ PGCE67 DipEd72. Coll of Resurr Mirfield 51. **d** 53 **p** 54. C Babbacombe *Ex* 53-56; C Swindon New Town *Bris* 56-57; C Boyne Hill *Ox* 57-60; C-in-c Bayswater St Mary CD 60-66; Perm to Offic *Ex* 66-67 and 70-85; Perm to Offic *Lich* 67-69; Hd RE Oswestry Boys' High Sch 67-69; Hon C Oswestry H Trin 69-70; Sch Coun Tiverton 70-75; Newton Abbot 75-85; V Winkleigh *Ex* 85-92; R Ashreigney 85-92; R Broadwoodkelly 85-92; V Brushford 85-92; RD Chulmleigh 87-93; rtd 93; Perm to Offic *Ex* from 93. *34 Osney Crescent, Paignton, Devon TQ4 5EY* Tel (01803) 522698

NIXSON, Ms Rosemary Clare (Rosie). b 57. Westf Coll Lon BA79 Liv Univ MA80 MPhil82. Aston Tr Scheme 89 Trin Coll Bris BA94. **d** 94 **p** 95. C E Bris 94; C Bris St Andr Hartcliffe from 94. *404 Bishport Avenue, Hartcliffe, Bristol BS13 0HX* Tel 0117-978 4052

NOAKES, Mrs Dorothy. b 35. Derby Coll of Educn CertEd55 Ex Univ BEd85 BPhil(Ed)92. LNSM course 94. **d** 96 **p** 97. NSM Helston and Wendron *Truro* from 96. *6 Tenderah Road, Helston, Cornwall TR13 8NT* Tel (01326) 573239

✠**NOAKES, The Rt Revd George.** b 24. Univ of Wales (Abth) BA48 Univ of Wales Hon DD90. Wycliffe Hall Ox 49. **d** 50 **p** 52 **c** 82. C Lampeter *St D* 50-56; V Eglwyswrw and Meline 56-59; V Tregaron 59-67; V Cardiff Dewi Sant *Llan* 67-76; R Aberystwyth *St D* 76-80; Can St D Cathl 77-79; Adn Cardigan 79-82; V Llanychaearn w Llanddeiniol 80-82; Bp St D 82-91; Abp Wales 87-91; rtd 91. *Hafod-Lon, Rhydargaeau, Carmarthen SA32 7DT* Tel (01267) 253302

NOBBS, John Ernest. b 35. Tyndale Hall Bris 60. **d** 63 **p** 64. C Walthamstow St Mary *Chelmsf* 63-66; C Braintree 66-69; C Wakef St Andr and St Mary *Wakef* 69-71; C Tooting Graveney St Nic *S'wark* 71-74; C Woking St Pet *Guildf* 74-78; C Worthing St Geo *Chich* 78-88; C Rayleigh *Chelmsf* 88-94; rtd 94. *89 Panfield Lane, Braintree, Essex CM7 5RP* Tel (01376) 322901

NOBLE, Alexander Frederick Innes (Sandy). b 30. Selw Coll Cam BA53 MA58. Lon Coll of Div ALCD55. **d** 55 **p** 56. C Stratton St Margaret *Bris* 55-57; C Brislington St Luke 57-59; Chapl Pierrepont Sch Frensham 59-61; Asst Chapl Repton Sch Derby 61-63; Chapl 63-66; Chapl Blundell's Sch Tiverton 66-72; St Jo C of E Sch Cowley 73-77; Chapl Cranbrook Sch Kent 77-81; Chapl St Geo Sch Harpenden 81-90; Hon C Herriard w Winslade and Long Sutton etc *Win* 90-94; rtd 95; P-in-c Oare w Culbone *B & W* from 95. *The Rectory, Oare, Lynton, Devon EX35 6NX* Tel (01598) 741270

NOBLE, Canon Arthur. b 12. TCD BA35 MA38. TCD Div Sch Div Test. **d** 36 **p** 37. C Newtownards *D & D* 36-39; C Belfast St Mark *Conn* 39-41; C Lurgan Ch Ch *D & D* 41-44; I Rasharkin w Finvoy *Conn* 44-49; I Belfast St Aid 49-61; I Lisburn Ch Ch 61-82; Preb Conn Cathl 74-79; Prec 79-82; rtd 82. *38 King's Road, Belfast BT5 6JJL* Tel (01232) 282217

NOBLE, Christopher John Lancelot. b 58. Aston Tr Scheme 88 Oak Hill Th Coll DipHE90. **d** 90 **p** 91. C Tonbridge SS Pet and Paul *Roch* 90-95; P-in-c Stansted w Fairseat and Vigo from 95. *The Rectory, 9 The Coach Drive, Meopham, Gravesend, Kent DA13 0SZ* Tel (01732) 822494

NOBLE, David. b 37. S Dios Minl Tr Scheme 84. **d** 87 **p** 88. C Alverstoke *Portsm* 87-89; Australia from 90. *The Rectory, Hampton Street, Bridgetown, W Australia 6255* Tel Bridgetown (97) 611031

NOBLE, Mrs Eileen Joan. b 45. NE Ord Course 90. **d** 93 **p** 94. C Gosforth All SS *Newc* 93-96; C Cramlington 96-97; TV from 97. *1 Cateran Way, Cramlington, Northd NE23 6EX* Tel (01670) 714261

NOBLE, Francis Alick. b 10. Trin Coll Cam BA33 MA37. Linc Th Coll 33. **d** 36 **p** 37. C Barnsley St Edw *Wakef* 36-38; C Smawthorpe St Mich 38-40; C Shelton *Lich* 41-43; V Edensor 43-50; V Crofton St Paul *Roch* 50-67; R Guiseley *Bradf* 67-78; rtd 78; Perm to Offic *St As* from 78. *16 Aberconwy Parc, Prestatyn LL19 9HH* Tel (01745) 856820

NOBLE, Graham Edward. b 49. SS Paul & Mary Coll Cheltenham CertEd71 Open Univ BA74. EAMTC 85. **d** 88 **p** 89. C Kesgrave *St E* 88-90; P-in-c Gt and Lt Blakenham w Baylham and Nettlestead 90-95; P-in-c Debenham w Aspall and Kenton from 95. *The Vicarage, 34 Gracechurch Street, Debenham, Stowmarket, Suffolk IP14 6RE* Tel (01728) 860265

NOBLE, Paul Vincent. b 54. Leeds Univ BA75 PGCE76 Ox Univ BA81 MA85. St Steph Ho Ox 79. **d** 82 **p** 83. C Prestbury *Glouc* 82-85; P-in-c Avening w Cherington 85-90; V The Suttons w Tydd *Linc* from 90. *The Vicarage, Sutton St James, Spalding, Lincs PE12 0EE* Tel (01945) 85457

NOBLE, Peter Hirst. b 37. Lon Univ BD68 Leeds Univ MPhil72. Cranmer Hall Dur 65. **d** 68 **p** 69. C Honley *Wakef* 68-72; P-in-c Moss *Sheff* 72-81; V Askern 72-92; rtd 92. *40 Broome Close, Huntington, York YO3 9RH* Tel (01904) 766203

NOBLE, Philip David. b 46. Glas Univ BSc67 Edin Univ BD70. Edin Th Coll 67. **d** 70 **p** 71. C Edin Ch Ch *Edin* 70-72; Papua New Guinea 72-75; R Cambuslang *Glas* 76-83; R Uddingston 76-83; Ev Prestwick 83-85; R Prestwick from 85. *56 Ayr Road, Prestwick, Ayrshire KA9 1RR* Tel (01292) 477108

NOBLE, Robert. b 43. TCD BA66 BD73. **d** 68 **p** 69. C Holywood *D & D* 68-71; Chapl RAF from 71. *Chaplaincy Services (RAF), HQ, Personnel and Training Command, RAF Innsworth, Gloucester GL3 1EZ* Tel (01452) 712612 ext 5164 Fax 510828

NOBLETT, William Alexander. b 53. Southn Univ BTh78. Sarum & Wells Th Coll 74. **d** 78 **p** 79. C Sholing *Win* 78-80; I Ardamine w Kiltennel, Glascarrig etc *C & O* 80-82; Chapl RAF 82-84; V Middlesbrough St Thos *York* 84-87; Asst Chapl HM Pris Wakef 87-89; Chapl 89-92; Chapl HM Pris Nor 92-97; Chapl HM Pris Full Sutton from 97. *HM Prison, Full Sutton, York YO4 1PS* Tel (01759) 375100 Fax 371206 E-mail william.noblett@btinternet.com

NOCK, Peter Arthur. b 15. Keble Coll Ox BA36 MA42. Bps' Coll Cheshunt 37. **d** 39 **p** 40. C Gt Harwood St Bart *Blackb* 39-40; C Lancaster Priory Ch 40-45; V Over Wyresdale 45-50; V Darwen St Cuth 50-64; V Sparkhill St Jo *Birm* 64-71; RD Bordesley 67-71; V Maney 71-81; rtd 81; Perm to Offic *Carl* from 81. *West View, Dufton, Appleby, Cumbria CA16 6DB* Tel (017683) 51413

NOCK, Roland George William. b 62. St Andr Univ BSc84 BD89. Edin Th Coll 91. **d** 91 **p** 92. C Dunfermline *St And* 91-93; C W Fife Team Min 91-93; R Cupar 93-96; CF from 96. *MOD Chaplains (Army), Trenchard Lines, Upavon, Pewsey, Wilts SN9 6BE* Tel (01980) 615804 Fax 615800

NOCKELS, John Martin. b 46. Lich Th Coll Qu Coll Birm 73. **d** 73 **p** 74. C Eccleshill *Bradf* 73-76; C Fawley *Win* 76-78; V Southampton St Jude 78-84; R Tadley St Pet from 84. *The Rectory, The Green, Tadley, Basingstoke, Hants RG26 6PB* Tel (0118) 981 4860

NODDER, Jonathan James Colmore. b 37. Lon Univ DipTh64. Tyndale Hall Bris 63. **d** 65 **p** 66. C Bebington *Ches* 65-71; V Stockport St Mark 71-88; V Burton in Kendal *Carl* 88-90; V Burton and Holme from 90. *St James's Vicarage, Glebe Close, Burton-in-Kendal, Carnforth, Lancs LA6 1PL* Tel (01524) 781391

NODDER, Thomas Arthur (Brother Arnold). b 20. K Coll Lon 58. **d** 60 **p** 61. Brotherhood of the H Cross from 49; C Rotherhithe

St Mary w All SS *S'wark* 60-63; SSF from 63; Lic to Offic *Chelmsf* 63-66; C Plaistow St Andr 66-68; Lic to Offic *Newc* 69-70; Lic to Offic *Birm* 70-83; Perm to Offic from 90; Lic to Offic *Sarum* 83-89; rtd 90. *113 Gillott Road, Birmingham B16 0ET* Tel 0121-454 8302

NODDINGS, John Henry. b 39. Chich Th Coll 80. **d** 81 **p** 82. C Southborough St Pet w Ch Ch and St Matt *Roch* 81-83; C Prittlewell *Chelmsf* 83-86; V Clay Hill St Jo *Lon* 86-88; V Clay Hill St Jo and St Luke from 88; Chapl Chase Farm Hosp Enfield 88-94; Chapl Chase Farm Hosps NHS Trust Enfield from 94. *St Luke's Vicarage, 92 Browning Road, Enfield, Middx EN2 0HG* Tel 0181-363 6055

NOEL, Brother. *See* ALLEN, Noel Stephen

NOEL, Canon Frank Arthur. b 20. TCD BA44 MA49. CITC 45. **d** 45 **p** 46. C Aghalee *D & D* 45-48; C Portadown St Mark *Arm* 48-51; I Ballinderry w Tamlaght 51-59; I Tullaniskin w Clonoe 59-63; I Mullabrack w Kilcluney 63-75; RD Mullabrack 75-88; I Acton w Drumbanagher 75-88; Preb Arm Cathl 86-88; rtd 88; Lic to Offic *Arm* from 90. *31 Woodford Drive, Armagh BT60 7AY* Tel (01861) 527787

NOEL-COX, Edward Lovis. b 99. Bps' Coll Cheshunt 22. **d** 23 **p** 25. C Plaistow St Martin CD *Chelmsf* 23-24; C Latchingdon w Mundham 24-25; C Southend All SS 25-27; C Sandhurst *Ox* 27-29; C Minehead *B & W* 29-35; V Langport 35-42; C Reading St Mary V *Ox* 42-51; Chapl Qu Mary's Hosp Carshalton 51-64; rtd 64; Perm to Offic *Chich* 66-93. *1 Stirling Court, 20 Portarlington Road, Bournemouth BH4 8BY* Tel (01202) 765461

NOKES, Peter Warwick. b 48. Leic Univ BA71. Westcott Ho Cam 79. **d** 81 **p** 82. C Northfield *Birm* 81-84; C Ludlow *Heref* 84-87; P-in-c Writtle w Highwood *Chelmsf* 87-91; V 91-92; P-in-c Epping St Jo 92-95; P-in-c Coopersale 93-95; TR Epping Distr from 95. *The Vicarage, Hartland Road, Epping, Essex CM16 4PD* Tel (01992) 572906

NOKES, Robert Harvey. b 39. Keble Coll Ox BA61 MA65 Birm Univ DipTh63. Qu Coll Birm 61. **d** 63 **p** 64. C Totteridge *St Alb* 63-67; C Dunstable 67-73; V Langford 73-90; R Braughing w Furneux Pelham and Stocking Pelham from 90. *The Rectory, 7A Green End, Braughing, Ware, Herts SG11 2PG* Tel (01920) 822619

NOLAN, James Charles William. b 44. Chich Th Coll 75. **d** 77 **p** 78. C Crewe St Andr *Ches* 77-79; C Sale St Anne 79-83; R Holme Runcton w S Runcton and Wallington *Ely* from 83; V Tottenhill w Wormegay from 83; R Watlington from 83. *The Rectory, Downham Road, Watlington, King's Lynn, Norfolk PE33 0HS* Tel (01553) 810305

NOLAN, James Joseph. b 16. Cranmer Hall Dur. **d** 61 **p** 62. C Worksop St Jo *S'well* 61-63; V Edge Hill St Cath *Liv* 63-66; V Heworth w Peasholme St Cuth *York* 66-72; CPAS Staff 72-74; R Bridlington Priory *York* 74-82; rtd 82; Perm to Offic *York* from 82. *9 Vicarage Close, Seamer, Scarborough, N Yorkshire YO12 4QS* Tel (01723) 862443

NOLAN, Canon John. b 25. TCD BA51 MA55. CITC 51. **d** 51 **p** 52. C Carrickfergus *Conn* 51-53; Dean's V Belf Cathl 53-55; VC 55-79; Min Can 60-88; Can from 88; C Belfast Upper Falls *Conn* 79-92; RD Derriaghy 90-92; rtd 92. *Apartment 32, Mount Royal, Millisle Road, Donaghadee, Co Down BT21 0HY* Tel (01247) 882655

NOLAN, Marcus. b 54. Bris Univ BEd. Ridley Hall Cam. **d** 83 **p** 84. C Dagenham *Chelmsf* 83-86; C Finchley St Paul and St Luke *Lon* 86-90; V W Hampstead Trin from 90. *Holy Trinity Church Office, Finchley Road, London NW3 5HT* Tel 0171-435 0083 or 794 2975

NOLLAND, Dr John Leslie. b 47. New England Univ (NSW) BSc67 Clare Coll Cam PhD78. Moore Th Coll Sydney ThL70 BD71. **d** 71 **p** 72. Australia 71-78; Canada 78-86; Asst Prof NT Studies Regent Coll Vancouver 78-86; Tutor Trin Coll Bris from 86; Vice Prin from 91. *129 Reedley Road, Stoke Hill, Bristol BS9 1BE* Tel 0117-968 4053

NOLLER, Hilda Elizabeth Mary (Sister Elizabeth Mary). **d** 95. *St Denys Convent, Vicarage Street, Warminster, Wilts BA12 8JD* Tel (01985) 213020

NOON, Canon Edward Arthur. b 16. Selw Coll Cam BA38 MA42. Bps' Coll Cheshunt 38. **d** 40 **p** 41. C Kingston St Jo *S'wark* 40-43; C Dulwich St Barn 43-48; P-in-c S Wimbledon St Pet 48-50; V 50-55; V Mitcham St Mark 55-65; V Horley 65-77; RD Reigate 72-76; Hon Can S'wark Cathl 72-83; P-in-c Purley St Barn 77-83; rtd 83; Hon C Overbury w Teddington, Alstone etc *Worc* 83-86; Perm to Offic *Glouc* 86-95. *40 Shepherds Leaze, Wotton-under-Edge, Glos GL12 7LQ* Tel (01453) 844978

NORBURN, Christopher Richard (Chris). b 62. Cov Poly BSc85. Aston Tr Scheme 92 Ridley Hall Cam 94. **d** 96 **p** 97. C Exning St Martin w Landwade *St E* from 96. *3 Norfolk Avenue, Newmarket, Suffolk CB8 0DE* Tel (01638) 661120

NORBURN, The Very Revd Richard Evelyn Walter. b 21. Witwatersrand Univ BA44 TDip44. St Paul's Grahamstown 49. **d** 51 **p** 53. S Africa 51-62; C Croydon St Sav *Cant* 63-64; V Norbury St Phil 65-75; V Addington 75-81; Hon Can Cant Cathl 79-81; RD Croydon Addington 81; Dean Botswana 81-88; rtd 89. *Tebogong, 2 Rectory Cottages, Middleton, Saxmundham, Suffolk IP17 3NR* Tel (01728) 73721

NORBURN, Canon Richard Henry. b 32. MBE97. St Edm Hall Ox BA57 DipTh58. Wycliffe Hall Ox 57. **d** 59 **p** 59. C Sudbury St Greg and St Pet *St E* 59-65; Dioc Youth Officer 65-74; P-in-c Gt Livermere 74-81; R Ampton w Lt Livermere and Ingham 74-81; RD Thingoe 78-88; Hon Can St E Cathl from 81; R Ingham w Ampton and Gt and Lt Livermere 81-92; TV Blackbourne from 92. *The Rectory, Ingham, Bury St Edmunds, Suffolk IP31 1NS* Tel (01284) 728430

NORFIELD, David Jonathan. b 67. Humberside Univ BA89. Linc Th Coll 94 Westcott Ho Cam CTM95. **d** 97. C Halstead St Andr w H Trin and Greenstead Green *Chelmsf* from 97. *47 Tidings Hill, Halstead, Essex CO9 1BL* Tel (01787) 475528

NORFOLK, The Ven Edward Matheson. b 21. Leeds Univ BA44. Coll of Resurr Mirfield 41. **d** 46 **p** 47. C Greenford H Cross *Lon* 46-47; C S Mymms K Chas 47-50; C Bushey *St Alb* 50-53; PC Waltham Cross 53-59; V Welwyn Garden City 59-69; R Gt Berkhamsted 69-81; Hon Can St Alb 72-82; V Kings Langley 81-82; Adn St Alb 82-87; rtd 87; Perm to Offic *Ex* from 87. *5 Fairlawn Court, Sidmouth, Devon EX10 8UR* Tel (01395) 514222

NORFOLK, Archdeacon of. *See* HANDLEY, The Ven Anthony Michael

✠**NORGATE, The Rt Revd Cecil Richard.** b 21. St Chad's Coll Dur BA47 DipTh49. **d** 49 **p** 50 **c** 84. C Wallsend St Pet *Newc* 49-54; Tanganyika 54-64; Tanzania from 64; UMCA 54-57; V-Gen Masasi 77-84; Bp Masasi 84-92; rtd 92. *St Cyprian's College, Rondo, PO Box 212, Lindi, Tanzania*

NORGATE, Norman George. b 32. Qu Coll Cam BA55 MA58. Ridley Hall Cam. **d** 57 **p** 58. C Erith St Paul *Roch* 57-60; C E Twickenham St Steph *Lon* 60-63; V Bexleyheath St Pet *Roch* 63-71; V Woking St Mary *Guildf* 71-83; V Tunbridge Wells St Jas *Roch* 83-92; TR Tunbridge Wells St Jas w St Phil 92-97; rtd 97. *Crathie, 58 Sexton Meadows, Bury St Edmunds, Suffolk IP33 2SB* Tel (01284) 767363

NORKETT, Alan. b 45. Sarum & Wells Th Coll 85. **d** 87 **p** 88. C Shrewsbury St Giles w Sutton and Atcham *Lich* 87-90; V Mow Cop 90-94. *21 Bedford Road, Kidsgrove, Stoke-on-Trent ST7 1HQ*

NORMAN, Andrew Herbert. b 54. K Coll Lon BD77 AKC77 Lon Univ PhD88. St Steph Ho Ox 77. **d** 78 **p** 79. C Deal St Leon w Sholden *Cant* 78-81; C Maidstone All SS and St Phil w Tovil 81-84; V Tenterden St Mich 84-93; Chapl Benenden Hosp Kent 86-91; Dir of Post-Ord Tr *Cant* 91-93; R Guildf St Nic *Guildf* from 93. *The Rectory, 3 Flower Walk, Guildford, Surrey GU2 5EP* Tel (01483) 504895

NORMAN, Andrew Robert. b 63. Newc Poly DMS90 Univ Coll Ox BA84 Newc Poly AIL89 Selw Coll Cam BA94. Ridley Hall Cam CTM95 BA94. **d** 95 **p** 96. Asst Chapl Paris St Mich *Eur* from 95. *St Michael's Church, 5 rue d'Aguesseau, 75008 Paris, France* Tel France (33) 47 42 70 88 Fax (33) 47 42 70 11

NORMAN, Arthur Leslie Frayne. b 08. Sarum Th Coll 29. **d** 31 **p** 33. C Swansea St Jude *S & B* 31-37; C Swansea St Gabr 37-46; V Swansea St Jo 46-58; V Swansea Ch Ch 58-75; Chapl HM Pris Swansea 58-75; rtd 75. *4 Malvern Terrace, Brynmill, Swansea SA2 0BE* Tel (01792) 465310

NORMAN, Catherine. b 51. Nottm Univ BSc73 N Counties Coll Newc CertEd74. Linc Th Coll CMinlStuds95. **d** 95 **p** 96. C Scartho *Linc* from 95. *25 Waltham Road, Grimsby, S Humberside DN33 2LY* Tel (01472) 870373

NORMAN, Canon Edward Robert. b 38. FRHistS72 Selw Coll Cam BA61 PhD64 MA65 BD67 DD78. Linc Th Coll 65. **d** 65 **p** 71. Fell Jes Coll Cam 64-71; Lect Cam Univ 64-88; Lic to Offic *Ely* 65-95; Fell and Dean Peterho 71-88; Six Preacher Cant Cathl *Cant* 84-89; Chapl Ch Ch Coll Cant 88-95; Can Res and Treas York Minster *York* from 95. *3 Minster Court, York YO1 2JJ* Tel (01904) 625599

NORMAN, The Ven Garth. b 38. St Chad's Coll Dur BA62 DipTh63 MA68 Cam Inst of Educn PGCE68 UEA MEd84. **d** 63 **p** 64. C Wandsworth St Anne *S'wark* 63-66; C Trunch w Swafield *Nor* 66-71; R Gimingham 71-77; RD Repps 75-83; TR Trunch 77-83; Prin Chiltern Chr Tr Course *Ox* 83-87; C W Wycombe w Bledlow Ridge, Bradenham and Radnage 83-87; Dir of Tr *Roch* 88-94; Hon Can Roch Cathl from 91; Adn Bromley from 94. *6 Horton Way, Farningham, Kent DA4 0DQ* Tel (01322) 864522

NORMAN, Jillianne Elizabeth. b 59. DCR80. Ridley Hall Cam 85. **d** 88 **p** 94. Par Dn Fishponds St Jo *Bris* 88-92; Perm to Offic 92-94; Hon C Warmley, Syston and Bitton from 94. *74 Blackhorse Road, Mangotsfield, Bristol BS17 3AY* Tel 0117-956 1551

NORMAN, Canon John Ronald. b 15. GradIT Lon Univ BA40. Linc Th Coll 40. **d** 42 **p** 43. C Yarm *York* 42-43; C Stokesley 43-46; R Muchalls *Bre* 46-50; V Kirkby Ireleth *Carl* 50-55; R Greystoke 55-60; P-in-c Matterdale 56-60; Warden Greystoke Coll Carl 56-60; Chapl St Hilda's Priory and Sch Whitby 60-61; R Dunnington *York* 61-72; RD Bulmer 65-72; R Bolton Percy 72-82; Dioc Worship Adv 72-82; Can and Preb York Minster 77-92; rtd 82. *Iona, 5 Northfield Close, Pocklington, York YO4 2EG* Tel (01759) 303170

NORMAN, Linda Mary. b 48. Man Univ BSc69 CertEd70 St Jo Coll Dur BA82. **dss** 83 **d** 87. York St Mich-le-Belfrey *York* 83-88;

Par Dn 87-88; rtd 88. *23 Ainsty Avenue, Dringhouses, York YO2 2HH* Tel (01904) 706152

NORMAN, Michael Heugh. b 18. Qu Coll Cam BA48 Kent Univ MA. Westcott Ho Cam 48. **d** 50 **p** 51. C St Peter-in-Thanet *Cant* 50-52; S Africa from 52. *5 Rosedale Cottage, Lower Nursery Road, Rosebank, 7700 South Africa* Tel Cape Town (21) 685-3622

NORMAN, Michael John. b 59. Southn Univ LLB82. Wycliffe Hall Ox 82. **d** 85 **p** 86. C Woodley St Jo the Ev *Ox* 85-89; C Uphill *B & W* 89-92; TV from 92. *2 Westbury Crescent, Weston-super-Mare, Avon BS23 4RB* Tel (01934) 623195

NORMAN, Michael John (Mick). b 61. St Jo Coll Ox BSc83 Univ Coll Lon MSc84. Aston Tr Scheme 89 St Jo Coll Nottm 91. **d** 93 **p** 94. C Haughton le Skerne *Dur* from 93. *1 Aviemore Court, Darlington, Co Durham DL1 2TF* Tel (01325) 486382

NORMAN, Peter John. b 59. Chich Th Coll 84. **d** 87 **p** 88. C Farncombe *Guildf* 87-91; C Cockington *Ex* 91-94; V Winkleigh from 94; R Ashreigney from 94; R Broadwoodkelly from 94; V Brushford from 94. *The Vicarage, Torrington Road, Winkleigh, Devon EX19 8HR* Tel (01837) 83719

NORMAN, Richard Hudson. b 58. Louisiana State Univ BS84 MA88. NY Th Sem MDiv93 STM93. **d** 92 **p** 93. NSM Southgate St Andr *Lon* 92; USA 92-97; C Southgate St Andr *Lon* from 97. *10 The Woodlands, London N14 5RN* Tel 0181-368 3276

NORMAN, Roy Albert. b 23. **d** 65 **p** 66. C Brockworth *Glouc* 65-67; C Thornbury 67-70; P-in-c Woolaston w Alvington 70-80; R 80-88; rtd 88. *William Annett's Dwelling, Crossways, Ruardean, Glos GL17 9XB* Tel (01594) 542503

NORMAN, Canon William Beadon. b 26. Trin Coll Cam BA49 MA55. Ridley Hall Cam 52. **d** 52 **p** 53. C Beckenham St Jo *Roch* 52-54; Uganda 55-65; V Alne *York* 65-74; RD Warley *Birm* 74-79; V Blackheath 74-79; Hon Can Birm Cathl 78-91; TR Kings Norton 79-91; RD Kings Norton 82-87; Warden Dioc Readers Bd 84-91; rtd 91; Perm to Offic *S'wark* from 91; Perm to Offic *Lon* from 94; Preacher Lincoln's Inn from 94. *37 Cloudesdale Road, London SW17 8ET* Tel 0181-673 9134 Fax 675 6890

NORMAN, William John. b 08. St Andr Whittlesford. **d** 44 **p** 45. C Stoke next Guildf St Jo *Guildf* 44-47; Org Sec (Dios Newc and Dur) BFBS 47-50; R Ruan Lanihorne w Philleigh *Truro* 50-52; PC Gateshead St Edm *Dur* 52-54; Area Sec (Dios Chich, Guildf and Portsm) CMS 54-74; (Dios Lon and S'wark) 64-66; Reg Sec 56-74; R Buriton *Portsm* 74-79; rtd 79. *22 Middlehill Road, Colehill, Wimborne, Dorset BH21 2SD* Tel (01202) 884775

NORMAND, Stephen Joseph William. b 48. N Texas State Univ BSEd80. Sarum & Wells Th Coll 90. **d** 92 **p** 93. C Norton *St Alb* 92-94; C St Alb St Pet 95-97; Chapl Oaklands Coll 95-97; TV Horsham *Chich* from 97. *St Leonard's Vicarage, Cambridge Road, Horsham, W Sussex RH13 5ED* Tel (01403) 266903

NORMINGTON, Eric. b 16. S'wark Ord Course. **d** 63 **p** 64. C Coulsdon St Jo *S'wark* 63-66; C Bath Abbey w St Jas *B & W* 66-71; V Bath Weston All SS 71-78; P-in-c N Stoke 76-78; R Bath Weston All SS w N Stoke 78-81; RD Keynsham 75-76; rtd 81; Perm to Offic *Ex* from 81. *53 Higher Woolbrook Park, Sidmouth, Devon EX10 9ED* Tel (01395) 512016

NORRIS, Mrs Alison. b 55. St Andr Univ MTheol77 Dur Univ CertEd78. Cant Sch of Min. **dss** 82 **d** 87 **p** 94. Warlingham w Chelsham and Farleigh *S'wark* 83-85; Willingham *Ely* 85-87; Hon Par Dn 87-90; Hon Par Dn Worle *B & W* 90-94; NSM Milverton w Halse and Fitzhead from 94. *The Vicarage, Parsonage Lane, Milverton, Taunton, Somerset TA4 1LR* Tel (01823) 400305

NORRIS, Allan Edward. b 43. St Jo Coll Dur BA72 DipTh73. Cranmer Hall Dur 69. **d** 73 **p** 74. C Plumstead St Jo w St Jas and St Paul *S'wark* 73-78; C Battersea Park St Sav 78-82; C Battersea St Geo w St Andr 78-82; V Grain w Stoke *Roch* 82-92; V Sissinghurst w Frittenden *Cant* from 92. *The Rectory, Oakleaves, Frittenden, Cranbrook, Kent TN17 2DD* Tel (01580) 80275

NORRIS, Andrew David. b 54. CPsychol St Andr Univ BSc78 Lon Univ MPhil80. EAMTC 87. **d** 90 **p** 91. C Worle *B & W* 90-94; R Milverton w Halse and Fitzhead from 94. *The Vicarage, Parsonage Lane, Milverton, Taunton, Somerset TA4 1LR* Tel (01823) 400305

NORRIS, Andrew Peter. b 62. Aston Univ BSc83. St Jo Coll Nottm BA86 DPS87. **d** 87 **p** 88. C Mountsorrel Ch Ch and St Pet *Leic* 87-90; C Harborne Heath *Birm* 90-91; P-in-c Edgbaston St Germain 91-92; V from 92. *St Germain's Vicarage, 180 Portland Road, Birmingham B16 9TD* Tel 0121-429 3431

NORRIS, Barry John. b 46. Nottm Univ CQSW75 MTh86 Open Univ BA80. St Jo Sem Wonersh. **d** 70 **p** 71. In RC Ch 70-72; C Wisbech SS Pet and Paul *Ely* 76-78; TV E Ham w Upton Park St Alb *Chelmsf* 78-81; Chapl RAF 81-87; V N Tadley St Mary *Win* from 87. *St Mary's Vicarage, Bishopswood Road, Tadley, Basingstoke, Hants RG26 6HQ* Tel (0118) 981 4435

NORRIS, Clifford Joseph. b 29. Codrington Coll Barbados. **d** 61 **p** 68. Antigua 61-62; C Penton Street St Silas w All SS *Lon* 68-70; C Stepney St Dunstan and All SS 70-73; P-in-c Bethnal Green St Jas the Gt w St Jude 73-82; V Aveley and Purfleet *Chelmsf* from 82. *The Vicarage, Mill Road, Aveley, South Ockendon, Essex RM15 4SR* Tel (01708) 864865

NORRIS, Eric Richard. b 43. MICFM86. Bernard Gilpin Soc Dur 65 Ripon Hall Ox 66. **d** 69 **p** 70. C Huyton St Mich *Liv* 69-72; C Mexborough *Sheff* 72-74; V Dalton 74-78; Org Sec (Dio Carl) CECS 78-89; Area Appeals Manager N Co 89-93; Lic to Offic *Carl* 78-93; Lic to Offic *Dur* 89-93; TR Thirsk *York* from 93. *The Rectory, Thirsk, N Yorkshire YO7 1PR* Tel (01845) 523183

NORRIS, Mark. b 68. Brunel Univ BEng90. Oak Hill Th Coll DipHE92 BA93. **d** 93 **p** 94. C Roby *Liv* 93-97; C St Helens St Helen from 97. *75 King Edward Road, St Helens, Merseyside WA10 6LE* Tel (01744) 613122

NORTH, Albert. b 13. Lon Univ BA35. Sarum Th Coll 64. **d** 65 **p** 66. C Squirrels Heath *Chelmsf* 65-70; V Gt w Lt Saling 70-72; V St Osyth 72-81; rtd 81; Perm to Offic *Chelmsf* from 81; Perm to Offic *B & W* from 86. *18 Nelson House, Nelson Place West, Bath BA1 2BA* Tel (01225) 330896

NORTH, Barry Albert. b 46. **d** 82 **p** 83. C Brampton St Thos *Derby* 82-84; C Chesterfield St Aug 84-88; P-in-c Derby St Mark 88-91; R Coalbrookdale, Iron-Bridge and Lt Wenlock *Heref* 91-97; Ch and Community Worker (Manlake Deanery) *Linc* from 97. *43 Copse Road, Ashby, Scunthorpe DN16 3JA* Tel (01724) 276241

NORTH, David Roland. b 45. Lich Th Coll 70 Qu Coll Birm 72. **d** 73 **p** 74. C Salesbury *Blackb* 73-76; C Marton 76-79; V Penwortham St Leon 79-87; R Whittington St Jo *Lich* from 87; P-in-c W Felton from 96. *The Rectory, Whittington, Oswestry, Shropshire SY11 4DF* Tel (01691) 652222

NORTH, Philip John. b 66. York Univ BA88. St Steph Ho Ox BA91. **d** 92 **p** 93. C Sunderland Springwell w Thorney Close *Dur* 92-95; C Sunderland St Mary and St Pet 95-96; V Hartlepool H Trin from 96. *Holy Trinity Vicarage, Davison Drive, Hartlepool, Cleveland TS24 9BX* Tel (01429) 267618

NORTH, Preb Robert. b 54. Lon Univ BSc77. Ripon Coll Cuddesdon 78. **d** 81 **p** 82. C Leominster *Heref* 81-86; TV Heref St Martin w St Fran (S Wye TM) 86-92; TV Dewsall w Callow 86-92; TV Holme Lacy w Dinedor 86-92; TV Lt Dewchurch, Aconbury w Ballingham and Bolstone 86-92; TV Upper and Lower Bullinghope w Grafton 86-92; P-in-c Heref St Nic from 92; Dir of Ords from 92; Preb Heref Cathl from 94. *St Nicholas's Rectory, 76 Breinton Road, Hereford HR4 0JY* Tel (01432) 273810

NORTH, Canon Vernon Leslie. b 26. Bps' Coll Cheshunt 61. **d** 63 **p** 64. C N Holmwood *Guildf* 63-65; C Dunstable *St Alb* 65-68; V Stotfold 68-91; RD Shefford 79-91; Hon Can St Alb 89-92; R Stotfold and Radwell 91-92; rtd 92. *Hunters Moon, 10 High Street, Little Paxton, St Neots, Huntingdon, Cambs PE19 4HA* Tel (01480) 471146

NORTH WEST EUROPE, Archdeacon of. *See* ALLEN, The Ven Geoffrey Gordon

NORTHALL, Malcolm Walter. b 26. Cheshunt Coll Cam 59 Ely Th Coll 63. **d** 64 **p** 65. C Bromsgrove St Jo *Worc* 64-67; V Blockley w Aston Magna *Glouc* 67-82; P-in-c Churchdown 82; V 82-92; rtd 92; Perm to Offic *Ban* from 92. *5 Maethlon Close, Tywyn LL36 0BN* Tel (01654) 710123

NORTHAM, Cavell Herbert James Cavell. *See* CAVELL-NORTHAM, Canon Cavell Herbert James

NORTHAM, Mrs Susan Jillian (Jill). b 36. Oak Hill Th Coll DipHE87. **d** 89. NSM Enfield Ch Ch Trent Park *Lon* 89-91; Par Dn 91-94; C 94-97; rtd 97. *22 Crescent East, Barnet, Herts EN4 0EN* Tel 0181-449 4483

NORTHAMPTON, Archdeacon of. *See* CHAPMAN, The Ven Michael Robin

NORTHCOTT, Canon Geoffrey Stephen. b 21. Leeds Univ BA42. Coll of Resurr Mirfield 40. **d** 47 **p** 48. C Stockwell Green St Andr *S'wark* 47-54; C St Alb St Sav *St Alb* 54-57; P-in-c Luton St Sav 57-68; V 68-89; Hon Can St Alb 72-89; RD Luton 82-89; rtd 89; Perm to Offic *B & W* from 89. *8 Nelson House, Nelson Place West, Bath BA1 2BA* Tel (01225) 338296

NORTHCOTT, Dr Michael Stafford. b 55. St Chad's Coll Dur BA76 MA77 PhD. St Jo Coll Dur 80. **d** 81 **p** 82. C Chorlton-cum-Hardy St Clem *Man* 81-84; Malaysia 84-89; Lect Chr Ethics New Coll Edin Univ 89-91; NSM Edin Old St Paul *Edin* 89-91; NSM Edin St Jas 91-93; TV Edin St Marg from 93. *8 Dudley Gardens, Edinburgh EH6 4PY* Tel 0131-554 1651

NORTHCOTT, William Mark. b 36. Clifton Th Coll 61. **d** 64 **p** 65. C Walthamstow St Luke *Chelmsf* 64-68; C Idle H Trin *Bradf* 68-70; N Sec CMJ 70-79; V Withnell *Blackb* 79-90; P-in-c Glenrothes *St And* 90-91; Asst Dioc Supernumerary 90-91; Perm to Offic *Blackb* from 91; Perm to Offic *Liv* from 91. *30 The Laund, Leyland, Preston PR5 3XX* Tel (01772) 620331

NORTHFIELD, Stephen Richmond. b 55. Lon Univ BSc77 Southn Univ BTh84. Sarum & Wells Th Coll 79. **d** 82 **p** 83. C Colchester St Jas, All SS, St Nic and St Runwald *Chelmsf* 82-85; C Chelmsf All SS 85-89; V Ramsey w Lt Oakley and Wrabness 89-95; V Hatfield Peverel w Ulting from 95. *The Vicarage, Church Road, Hatfield Peverel, Chelmsford CM3 2LE* Tel (01245) 380958

NORTHING, Capt Ross. b 58. Wilson Carlile Coll DipEvang87 St Steph Ho Ox DipMin94. **d** 94 **p** 95. CA from 87; C Up Hatherley *Glouc* from 94; C Cheltenham St Steph 94-95; C Cheltenham Em w St Steph from 95. *28 Davallia Drive, Cheltenham, Glos GL51 5XB* Tel (01242) 863019

NORTHOLT, Archdeacon of. *See* BROADBENT, The Ven Peter Alan

NORTHOVER, Kevin Charles. b 57. Coll of Resurr Mirfield 89. **d** 91 **p** 92. C Kingston upon Hull St Alb *York* 91-94; V Moorends *Sheff* from 94. *The Vicarage, West Road, Moorends, Doncaster, S Yorkshire DN8 4LH* Tel (01405) 741758

NORTHRIDGE, Canon Herbert Aubrey Hamilton. b 16. TCD BA40 MA43. **d** 41 **p** 42. C Londonderry Ch Ch *D & R* 41-45; P-in-c Convoy 45-47; I Derg 50-81; Can Derry Cathl 72-81; rtd 81. *Goblusk, Ballinamallard, Co Fermanagh BT94 2LW* Tel (01365) 81676

NORTHUMBERLAND, Archdeacon of. *See* ELLIOTT, The Ven Peter

NORTHWOOD, Michael Alan. b 36. Lon Univ BSc60. Wells Th Coll 62. **d** 64 **p** 65. C Eastbourne St Mary *Chich* 64-66; C Sanderstead All SS *S'wark* 66-68; P-in-c Alton Barnes w Alton Priors etc *Sarum* 69-75; Lic to Offic 76-86; Perm to Offic *Ox* from 86. *Saratoga, Long Grove, Seer Green, Beaconsfield, Bucks HP9 2QH* Tel (01494) 671127

NORTON, Anthony Bernard. b 40. Man Univ BA62. Linc Th Coll 63. **d** 65 **p** 66. C Westbury-on-Trym H Trin *Bris* 65-68; C Bris St Agnes w St Simon 68-70; P-in-c Bris St Werburgh 70-72; TV Bris St Agnes and St Simon w St Werburgh 72-77; V Lakenham St Alb *Nor* 77-85; TV Trunch 85-93; TV Halesworth w Linstead, Chediston, Holton etc *St E* from 93. *The Vicarage, Spexhall, Halesworth, Suffolk IP19 0RQ* Tel (01986) 875453

NORTON, James Herbert Kitchener. b 37. Qu Coll Birm 78. **d** 81 **p** 82. NSM Donnington Wood *Lich* 81-83; C Matson *Glouc* 83-86; V New Mills *Derby* 86-96; RD Glossop 93-96; TR Buxton w Burbage and King Sterndale from 96. *The Rectory, 7 Lismore Park, Buxton, Derbyshire SK17 9AU* Tel (01298) 22151

NORTON, John Colin (Andrew). b 25. Magd Coll Ox BA50 MA54. Cuddesdon Coll 50. **d** 52 **p** 53. C Bris St Mary Redcliffe w Temple *Bris* 52-57; C Bitterne Park *Win* 57-61; C-in-c Bishopwearmouth St Mary V w St Pet CD *Dur* 63-68; V Clifton All SS w Tyndalls Park *Bris* 68-78; Hon Can Bris Cathl 77-80; V Clifton All SS w St Jo 78-80; V Penistone *Wakef* 80-83; CR from 85; rtd 95. *House of the Resurrection, Mirfield, W Yorkshire WF14 0BN* Tel (01924) 494318

NORTON, Leslie Miles. b 10. Sarum Th Coll 46. **d** 48 **p** 49. C Dulwich St Barn *S'wark* 48-52; C Cheam 52-55; V Dulwich Common St Pet 55-83; rtd 83; Perm to Offic *Bris* 83-90. *46 St Dennis Road, Malmesbury, Wilts SN16 9BH* Tel (01666) 824767

NORTON (or HARCOURT-NORTON), Michael Clive Harcourt. b 34. MACE84 Selw Coll Cam BA58 MA60 Univ of NSW MCom81. Union Th Sem (NY) STM69 Wells Th Coll 56. **d** 58 **p** 59. C Gt Ilford St Jo *Chelmsf* 58-62; Australia 62-68 and from 69; USA 68-69. *2 Ambrose Street, Hunters Hill, Sydney, NSW, Australia 2110* Tel Sydney (2) 817 2167 Fax 879 4051

NORTON, Michael James Murfin. b 42. Lich Th Coll 66. **d** 67 **p** 68. C W Bromwich St Fran *Lich* 67-70; C Wellington Ch Ch 70-72; C Norwood All SS *Cant* 72-76; V Elstow *St Alb* 76-82; Asst Chapl HM Pris Wakef 82-83; Chapl HM Pris Camp Hill 83-86; Chapl HM Pris Parkhurst 86-88; Chapl HM Pris Win 88-93; V Somborne w Ashley *Win* from 93. *The Vicarage, Winchester Road, Kings Somborne, Stockbridge, Hants SO20 6PF* Tel (01794) 388223

NORTON, Paul James. b 55. BA86. Oak Hill Th Coll 83. **d** 86 **p** 87. C Luton St Fran *St Alb* 86-89; C Bedworth *Cov* 89-95; TV Hitchin *St Alb* from 95. *St Mark's Vicarage, St Mark's Close, Hitchin, Herts SG5 1UR* Tel (01462) 434686

NORTON, Peter Eric Pepler. b 38. TCD BA61 G&C Coll Cam PhD64. St Jo Coll Dur 78. **d** 80 **p** 81. C Ulverston St Mary w H Trin *Carl* 80-83; P-in-c Warcop, Musgrave, Soulby and Crosby Garrett 83-84; R 84-90; OCF 83-90; V Appleby *Carl* from 90; R Ormside from 90. *The Vicarage, Appleby-in-Westmorland, Cumbria CA16 6QW* Tel (017683) 51461

NORTON, William Fullerton. b 23. Selw Coll Cam BA46 MA52. Wycliffe Hall Ox 46. **d** 48 **p** 49. C Leic H Apostles *Leic* 48-52; Singapore 52-54; Malaya 54-63; The Philippines 63-66; C Homerton St Luke *Lon* 67; C Tooting Graveney St Nic *S'wark* 68-71; V Hanley Road St Sav w St Paul *Lon* 71-89; rtd 89. *21 Peel Road, Brighton BN2 5ND* Tel (01273) 677332

NORWICH, Archdeacon of. *See* OFFER, The Ven Dr Clifford Jocelyn

NORWICH, Bishop of. *See* NOTT, The Rt Revd Peter John

NORWICH, Dean of. *See* PLATTEN, The Very Revd Stephen George

NORWOOD, Andrew David. b 65. Lon Bible Coll BA91 Cranmer Hall Dur DMS94. **d** 94 **p** 95. C Headingley *Ripon* from 94. *5 Derwentwater Grove, Leeds LS6 3EN* Tel 0113-275 8937

NORWOOD, David John. b 40. SS Paul & Mary Coll Cheltenham BEd82. Linc Th Coll 65. **d** 68 **p** 69. C Hitchin St Mary *St Alb* 68-71; Zambia 72-76; C Littlehampton St Jas *Chich* 76-77; P-in-c Chacewater *Truro* 77-79; Chapl R Cornwall Hosp Treliske 77-79; Head RE Red Maids Sch Bris 82-85; Appeals Organiser Children's Soc 86-94; P-in-c Clarkston *Glas* from 94. *St Aidan's Rectory, 8 Golf Road, Clarkston, Glasgow G76 7LZ* Tel 0141-571 8018

NORWOOD, Philip Geoffrey Frank. b 39. Em Coll Cam BA62 MA66. Cuddesdon Coll 63. **d** 65 **p** 66. C New Addington *Cant* 65-69; Abp's Dom Chapl 69-72; V Hollingbourne 72-78; P-in-c Wormshill 74-78; P-in-c Bredgar w Bicknor and Huckinge 74-78; P-in-c St Laurence in the Isle of Thanet 78-82; V 82-88; RD Thanet 86-88; V Spalding *Linc* from 88; RD Elloe W from 96. *The Parsonage, Church Street, Spalding, Lincs PE11 2PB* Tel (01775) 722772

NORWOOD, Timothy. b 70. Aber Univ BD94. Westcott Ho Cam 95. **d** 97. C Upton cum Chalvey *Ox* from 97. *134 Albert Street, Slough SL1 2AU* Tel (01753) 694083 Mobile 0402-809720

NOTLEY, Michael James. b 41. St Edm Hall Ox BA63 MA68 DipEd64. EMMTC 84. **d** 87 **p** 88. Hon C Oadby *Leic* 87-96; P-in-c Holbeach Marsh *Linc* from 96; P-in-c Lutton w Gedney Drove End, Dawsmere from 96. *The Vicarage, Marsh Road, Holbeach Hurn, Holbeach, Spalding, Lincs PE12 8JX* Tel (01406) 425816

NOTT, George Thomas Michael. b 34. Ex Coll Ox BA58 MA62 Birm Univ MEd88. Coll of Resurr Mirfield. **d** 60 **p** 61. C Solihull *Birm* 60-69; Min Can Worc Cathl *Worc* 69-77; Chapl K Sch Worc 69-77; P-in-c Worc St Nic *Worc* 77-84; P-in-c Worc St Andr and All SS w St Helen 82-84; Children's Officer 84-87; Droitwich Spa 87-89; V Broadheath, Crown East and Rushwick from 89; Chapl Worc Coll of HE 89-96; RD Martley and Worc W *Worc* from 96. *The Vicarage, Crown East Lane, Rushwick, Worcester WR2 5TU* Tel (01905) 428801

✠**NOTT, The Rt Revd Peter John.** b 33. Fitzw Ho Cam BA61 MA65. Westcott Ho Cam 58. **d** 61 **p** 62 **c** 77. C Harpenden St Nic *St Alb* 61-64; Chapl Fitzw Coll Cam 64-69; Fell 66-69; Chapl New Hall Cam 66-69; R Beaconsfield *Ox* 69-76; TR 76-77; Preb Wells Cathl *B & W* 77-85; Suff Bp Taunton 77-85; Bp Nor from 85. *The Bishop's House, Norwich NR3 1SB* Tel (01603) 629001 Fax 761613

NOTTAGE, Preb Terence John. b 36. Oak Hill Th Coll 62. **d** 65 **p** 66. C Finchley St Paul Long Lane *Lon* 65-68; C Edgware 68-72; V Harlesden St Mark 72-86; V Kensal Rise St Mark and St Martin 86; TR Plymouth Em w Efford *Ex* 86-92; P-in-c Laira 88-92; TR Plymouth Em, St Paul Efford and St Aug 93-96; Preb Ex Cathl from 96; Adv for Voc and Dioc Dir of Ords from 96. *2 West Avenue, Pennsylvania, Exeter EX4 4SD* Tel (01392) 214867 Fax 251229

NOTTINGHAM, Dr Birman. b 29. St Chad's Coll Dur BA53 MA56 MEd66 DipClinPs58 DipEd61 MBPsS66 Lanc Univ PhD75. Ely Th Coll 53. **d** 55 **p** 56. C Monkwearmouth Ven Bede *Dur* 55-58; Lic to Offic 58-70; P-in-c Newc St Cuth and All SS *Newc* 62-66; St Martin's Coll Lanc 66-94; Lic to Offic *Blackb* from 66; rtd 94. *33 Newlands Road, Lancaster LA1 4JE* Tel (01524) 66949

NOTTINGHAM, Archdeacon of. *See* OGILVIE, The Ven Gordon

NOURSE, John. b 22. St Jo Coll Cam BA43 MA47 ACertCM90. Wells Th Coll 48. **d** 49 **p** 51. C Bournemouth St Aug *Win* 49-51; Asst Master Hurstpierpoint Coll Hassocks 51-52; C Shere *Guildf* 52-57; C Eton w Boveney *Ox* 57-62; Min Can Windsor and Asst Master St Geo Choir Sch 57-67; Succ 61-67; V Amesbury *Sarum* 67-69; Offg Chapl RAF 67-69; Prec Cant Cathl *Cant* 69-73; V Charing w Lt Chart 73-83; V Charing w Charing Heath and Lt Chart 84-88; rtd 88; Perm to Offic *Ex* from 90. *High Meadow, Greenhill Avenue, Lympstone, Exmouth, Devon EX8 5HW* Tel (01395) 264480

NOWELL, John David. b 44. AKC67. **d** 68 **p** 69. C Lindley *Wakef* 68-70; C Lightcliffe 70-72; V Wyke *Bradf* 72-80; V Silsden 80-92; V Baildon from 92. *The Vicarage, Baildon, Shipley, W Yorkshire BD17 6BY* Tel (01274) 594941

NOY, Frederick William Vernon. b 47. Sarum Th Coll 67. **d** 71 **p** 72. C Swindon St Jo *Bris* 71-75; Chapl to the Deaf *Sarum* 75-80; P-in-c Stinsford, Winterborne Came w Whitcombe etc 76-80; Perm to Offic from 80. *54 Casterbridge Road, Dorchester, Dorset DT1 2AG* Tel (01305) 264269

NOYCE, Colin Martley. b 45. Brasted Th Coll 73 Ridley Hall Cam 74. **d** 76 **p** 77. C Cambridge St Jas *Ely* 76-78; Chapl RN 78-82; R Mistley w Manningtree *Chelmsf* 82-86; Miss to Seamen 86-90; Kenya 86-89; Trinidad and Tobago 89-90; V Four Marks *Win* from 90. *The Vicarage, 22 Lymington Bottom, Four Marks, Alton, Hants GU34 5AA* Tel (01420) 563344

NOYCE, Graham Peter. b 62. Bedf Coll Lon BSc84. Trin Coll Bris BA92. **d** 92 **p** 93. C Sketty *S & B* 92-94; C Swansea St Jas 94-96; C Kensal Rise St Mark and St Martin *Lon* from 96. *26 Ashburnham Road, London NW10 5SD* Tel 0181-960 6211

NOYES, Roger. b 39. Linc Th Coll 65. **d** 67 **p** 68. C Adel *Ripon* 67-70; Chapl Aldenham Sch Herts 70-74; V Aldborough w Boroughbridge and Roecliffe *Ripon* 74-89; Rural Min Adv 89-90. *Rose Cottage, Moor End, Nun Monkton, York YO5 8DY* Tel (01423) 330846

NUDDS, Douglas John. b 24. St Aid Birkenhead 48. **d** 51 **p** 52. C E Dereham w Hoe *Nor* 51-55; C Birstall *Leic* 55-58; V Bardon Hill 58-62; V Belgrave St Mich 62-68; Chapl Leic R Infirmary 68-72; High Royds Hosp Menston 72-79; V Bradf St Wilfrid Lidget Green *Bradf* 79-84; Lic to Offic *St Alb* 84-93; Chapl Shenley Hosp Radlett Herts 84-89; rtd 89; Perm to Offic *Nor* from 89. *Longview, Southgate Close, Wells-next-the-Sea, Norfolk NR23 1HG* Tel (01328) 711926

NUGENT, Canon Alan Hubert. b 42. Dur Univ BA65 MA78. Wycliffe Hall Ox 65 United Th Coll Bangalore DipTh66. **d** 67 **p** 68. C Mossley Hill St Matt and St Jas *Liv* 67-71; C Bridgnorth St Mary *Heref* 71-72; Chapl Dur Univ *Dur* 72-78; P-in-c Bishopwearmouth Ch Ch 78-85; P-in-c Brancepeth 85-94; Dioc Dir of Educn from 85; Hon Can Dur Cathl from 86. *20 Dickens Wynd, Durham DH1 3QY* Tel 0191-386 0473

NUGENT, David Richard. b 54. MInstPS84 Liv Poly BA87. Oak Hill Th Coll BA95. **d** 95 **p** 96. C Birkenhead St Jas w St Bede *Ches* from 95. *3 Buckingham Avenue, Birkenhead, Merseyside L43 8TD* Tel 0151-652 9180

NUGENT, Eric William. b 26. Bps' Coll Cheshunt 56. **d** 58 **p** 59. C Rochford *Chelmsf* 58-61; C Eastwood 61-62; C-in-c Eastwood St Dav CD 62-66; V Eastwood St Dav 66-79; P-in-c Weeley 79-81; V Lt Clacton 80-81; R Weeley and Lt Clacton 81-93; rtd 93; Perm to Offic *Chelmsf* from 93. *1 King's Court, King's Road, Dovercourt, Harwich, Essex CO12 4DS* Tel (01255) 552640

NUNN, Ms Alice Candida. b 52. Ripon Coll Cuddesdon 95. **d** 97. C Margate St Jo *Cant* from 97. *173 Ramsgate Road, Margate, Kent CT9 4EY* Tel (01843) 294621

NUNN, Andrew Peter. b 57. Leic Poly BA79 Leeds Univ BA82. Coll of Resurr Mirfield 80. **d** 83 **p** 84. C Manston *Ripon* 83-87; C Leeds Richmond Hill 87-91; Chapl Agnes Stewart C of E High Sch Leeds 87-95; V Leeds Richmond Hill *Ripon* 91-95; Personal Asst to Bp S'wark from 95. *70 Pollards Hill North, London SW16 4NY* Tel 0181-679 4908

NUNN, Geoffrey William John. b 24. St Jo Coll Dur BA51. **d** 52 **p** 53. C Upminster *Chelmsf* 52-58; V Dagenham St Martin 58-94; C 95; C Becontree S 95-96; rtd 97. *St Martin's Vicarage, Goresbrook Road, Dagenham, Essex RM9 6UX* Tel 0181-592 0967

NUNN, Peter. b 32. Kelham Th Coll 53. **d** 57 **p** 58. C Wigan St Geo *Liv* 57-60; C Warrington St Elphin 60-62; V Warrington St Pet 62-65; Chapl Winwick Hosp Warrington 65-90; rtd 90; Perm to Offic *Liv* from 90. *1 Rylands Street, Springfield, Wigan, Lancs WN6 7BL* Tel (01942) 35407

NUNN, Canon Peter Michael. b 38. Sarum Th Coll 64. **d** 66 **p** 67. C Hornsey St Geo *Lon* 66-71; C Cleator Moor w Cleator *Carl* 71-72; V Carl St Luke Morton 72-79; V Wotton St Mary *Glouc* from 79; Offg Chapl RAF from 80; RD Glouc City *Glouc* 88-94; Hon Can Glouc Cathl from 90. *Holy Trinity Vicarage, Church Road, Longlevens, Gloucester GL2 0AJ* Tel (01452) 524129

NUNN, Peter Rawling. b 51. Ox Univ BA73 Sheff Univ MSc74 BA85. Oak Hill Th Coll 82. **d** 85 **p** 86. C Bispham *Blackb* 85-87; C-in-c Anchorsholme 87-89; V from 89. *The Vicarage, 36 Valeway Avenue, Thornton Cleveleys, Lancs FY5 3RN* Tel (01253) 856646 E-mail peter.r.nunn@dial.pipex.com.

NUNN, Mrs Sheila Jean. b 43. Southn Univ DipT64. Sarum & Wells Th Coll DipMin94. **d** 94 **p** 95. C Caversham and Mapledurham *Ox* from 94. *25 Ilkley Road, Reading RG4 7BD* Tel 0118-947 2070

NUNN, Stephen Robert. b 64. St Jo Coll Nottm BTh92. **d** 92 **p** 93. C Hailsham *Chich* 92-95; C Hollington St Leon from 95. *158 Old Church Road, St Leonards-on-Sea, E Sussex TN38 9HD* Tel (01424) 852486

NUNNERLEY, William John Arthur. b 27. Univ of Wales (Lamp) BA54 St Chad's Coll Dur DipTh56. **d** 56 **p** 57. C Tredegar St Geo *Mon* 56-60; Chapl RN 60-81; QHC from 79; R Barnoldby le Beck *Linc* 81-92; R Waltham 81-92; rtd 92. *Juniper Cottage, 82B Lower Street, Merriott, Somerset TA16 5NW* Tel (01460) 76049

NUNNEY, Miss Sheila Frances. b 49. NNEB69 SRN74 RSCN74 SCM75 RCN STDip81. Oak Hill Th Coll BA92. **d** 92 **p** 94. C Swaffham *Nor* 92-96; Chapl Asst Norfolk and Nor Healthcare NHS Trust from 96. *Norfolk and Norwich Hospital, Brunswick Road, Norwich NR1 3SR* Tel (01603) 286286

NURSER, Canon John Shelley. b 29. Peterho Cam BA50 MA54 PhD58. Wells Th Coll 58. **d** 58 **p** 59. C Tankersley *Sheff* 58-61; Dean Trin Hall Cam 61-68; Australia 68-74; R Freckenham w Worlington *St E* 74-76; Can Res and Chan Linc Cathl *Linc* 76-92; Can and Preb Linc Cathl 92-94; P-in-c Shudy Camps *Ely* 92-94; rtd 94. *68 Friars Street, Sudbury, Suffolk CO10 6AG* Tel (01787) 378595

NURTON, Robert. b 44. Univ of Wales (Lamp) BA67. Ridley Hall Cam 67. **d** 69 **p** 70. C Bris St Andr Hartcliffe *Bris* 69-73; C Ipswich St Mary at Stoke w St Pet & St Mary Quay *St E* 73-77; Chapl RN from 77. *Royal Naval Chaplaincy Service, Room 203, Victory Building, HM Naval Base, Portsmouth PO1 3LS* Tel (01705) 727903 Fax 727112

NUTH, Stephen William. b 55. Nazarene Th Coll Man CertRS87 St Jo Coll Nottm LTh95. **d** 95 **p** 96. C Wadhurst *Chich* from 95; C Stonegate from 95. *The Vicarage, Stonegate, Wadhurst, E Sussex TN5 7EJ* Tel (01580) 200515

NUTTALL, George Herman. b 31. St Jo Coll Dur BA59 DipTh61. Cranmer Hall Dur 59. **d** 61 **p** 62. C Eccleshill *Bradf* 61-65; V Oldham St Barn *Man* 65-70; Area Sec (Dios Derby and Lich) CMS 70-81; V Derby St Aug *Derby* 81-84; Chapl Bournemouth and Poole Coll of FE *Sarum* 85-97; Chapl Dorset Inst of HE 85-90; Chapl Bournemouth Poly *Win* 90-92; Chapl Bournemouth Univ 92-97; rtd 97; Perm to Offic *Sarum* from 97. *22 Colletts Close, Corfe Castle, Wareham, Dorset BH20 5HG* Tel (01929) 480103

NUTTALL, The Ven Michael John Berkeley. b 36. AKC60. St Boniface Warminster 61. **d** 61 **p** 62. C Chapel Allerton *Ripon* 61-64; C Stanningley St Thos 64-68; V Leeds Gipton Epiphany 68-76; P-in-c Stainby w Gunby *Linc* 76-83; R N Witham 76-83; R S Witham 76-83; TV Bottesford w Ashby 83-88; I Adare w Kilpeacon and Croom *L & K* from 88; Adn Limerick from 92. *The Rectory, Adare, Co Limerick, Irish Republic* Tel Limerick (61) 396227 Fax as telephone

NUTTALL, Wilfrid. b 29. ACP59 Open Univ BA82. Chich Th Coll 82. **d** 84 **p** 85. C Accrington St Jo *Blackb* 84-86; C Darwen St Cuth w Tockholes St Steph 86-89; V Foulridge 89-92; rtd 92; Perm to Offic *Cant* from 92. *15 Hope Road, Deal, Kent CT14 7DG*

NYAHWA, Stanley Musa. b 33. Gweru Coll Zimbabwe TCert52 FRCS61 BBC Film Sch CFTV67 Ryerson Coll Toronto ACTVR71. Edin Th Coll 62. **d** 65 **p** 66. C Chapel Allerton *Ripon* 65-67; Zambia 68-74; Chapl Haarlem *Eur* 76-81 and 83-87; Zimbabwe 81-83; C Lewisham St Mary *S'wark* 90-92; Namibia 93-94; Kenya 94-95; C New Humberstone *Leic* 95-96; TV Leic Presentation from 96. *St Barnabas Vicarage, 32 St Barnabas Road, Leicester LE5 4BD* Tel 0116-276 6054 Fax as telephone

NYE, Canon David Charles. b 39. K Coll Lon BD65. **d** 63 **p** 64. C Charlton Kings St Mary *Glouc* 63-67; C Yeovil St Jo w Preston Plucknett *B & W* 67-70; V Lower Cam *Glouc* 70-74; Min Can Glouc Cathl 74-79; Dir of Ords 74-79; Prin Glouc Th Course 74-79; V Glouc St Mary de Lode and St Nic *Glouc* 74-76; V Maisemore 76-79; Chapl Grenville Coll Bideford 79-81; V Leckhampton SS Phil and Jas w Cheltenham St Jas *Glouc* 81-95; Hon Can Glouc Cathl from 88; RD Cheltenham 89-95; P-in-c Northleach w Hampnett and Farmington from 95; P-in-c Cold Aston w Notgrove and Turkdean from 95. *The Vicarage, Northleach, Cheltenham, Glos GL54 3HL* Tel (01451) 860293

NYE, The Ven Nathaniel Kemp (Niel). b 14. AKC36. Cuddesdon Coll 36. **d** 37 **p** 38. C St Helier *S'wark* 37-40; Chapl RAFVR 40-46; R Clapham H Trin *S'wark* 46-54; V St Helier 54-61; V Maidstone All SS w St Phil *Cant* 61-66; Hon Can Cant Cathl 61-79; RD Sutton 65-66; Tait Missr Cant 66-72; Warden Dioc Retreat Ho Westgate 70-72; Adn Maidstone 72-79; rtd 79. *Lees Cottage, Boughton Lees, Ashford, Kent TN25 4HX* Tel (01233) 626175

O

OADES, Michael Anthony John. b 45. Brasted Th Coll 69 Sarum & Wells Th Coll 71. **d** 73 **p** 74. C Eltham Park St Luke *S'wark* 73-78; C Coulsdon St Andr 78-81; P-in-c Merton St Jas 81-85; V 85-87; V Benhilton from 87. *All Saints' Vicarage, All Saints' Road, Sutton, Surrey SM1 3DA* Tel 0181-644 9070

OADES, Canon Peter Robert. b 24. Fitzw Ho Cam BA47 CertEd48 MA53. **d** 67 **p** 67. C Warblington and Emsworth *Portsm* 67-68; V Choral Sarum Cathl *Sarum* 68-74; Chapl Sarum Cathl Sch 68-74; P-in-c Sturminster Newton and Hinton St Mary *Sarum* 74-75; V 75-81; R Stock and Lydlinch 75-81; RD Blackmore Vale 78-81; V Woodford Valley 81-89; Can and Preb Sarum Cathl 85-89; rtd 89; Hon Chapl to the Deaf *Sarum* 82-92; Perm to Offic *Win* from 89; Perm to Offic *Sarum* from 89. *28 Mulberry Gardens, Fordingbridge, Hants SP6 1BP* Tel (01425) 657113

OAKE, Barry Richard. b 47. ARICS71. Ripon Coll Cuddesdon 83. **d** 85 **p** 86. C Wantage *Ox* 85-88; C Warlingham w Chelsham and Farleigh *S'wark* 88-91; R N w S Wootton *Nor* from 91. *The Rectory, Castle Rising Road, South Wootton, King's Lynn, Norfolk PE30 3JA* Tel (01553) 671381

OAKES, Graham. b 42. Leeds Univ DipTh68. Chich Th Coll 68. **d** 70 **p** 71. C Hulme Ascension *Man* 70-74; C Clifton All SS w Tyndalls Park *Bris* 74-76; P-in-c Chadderton St Mark *Man* 76-78; V 78-82; V King Cross *Wakef* 82-95; R Bath H Trin *B & W* from 95. *Holy Trinity Rectory, 9 Marlborough Lane, Bath BA1 2NQ* Tel (01225) 422311

OAKES, Miss Jennifer May. b 43. Trin Coll Bris DipHE80. **dss** 82 **d** 87 **p** 94. Wilnecote *Lich* 82-85; Stoneydelph St Martin CD 82-85; Bentley 85-87; Par Dn 87-89; NSM Hixon w Stowe-by-Chartley 89-93; Par Dn 93-94; Par Dn Fradswell, Gayton, Milwich and Weston 93-94; C Hixon w Stowe-by-Chartley from 94; C Fradswell, Gayton, Milwich and Weston from 94. *Church House, 10 Meadow Glade, Hixon, Stafford ST18 0NT* Tel (01889) 271068

OAKES, Jeremy Charles. b 51. ACA75 FCA81. Westcott Ho Cam 75. **d** 78 **p** 79. C Evington *Leic* 78-81; C Ringwood *Win* 81-84; P-in-c Thurnby Lodge *Leic* 84-89; TV Oakdale *Sarum* 89-95; P-in-c Canford Cliffs and Sandbanks from 95. *The Vicarage,*

14 Flaghead Road, Poole, Dorset BH13 7JW Tel (01202) 700341 Fax as telephone E-mail jeremy.oakes@virgin.net

OAKES, John Cyril. b 49. AKC71. St Aug Coll Cant 71. **d** 72 **p** 73. C Broseley w Benthall *Heref* 72-76; C Cannock *Lich* 76-79; TV 79-83; V Rough Hills from 83; P-in-c Wolverhampton St Steph from 94. *St Martin's Vicarage, Dixon Street, Wolverhampton WV2 2BG* Tel (01902) 341030

OAKES, Canon Leslie John. b 28. AKC53. **d** 54 **p** 55. C Bedford Leigh *Man* 54-58; C Walsall St Matt *Lich* 58-60; Chapl Selly Oak Hosp Birm 60-64; V Longbridge *Birm* 64-93; Hon Can Birm Cathl 84-93; rtd 93; Perm to Offic *Birm* from 93. *108 Hole Lane, Birmingham B31 2DF* Tel 0121-476 8514

OAKES, Melvin. b 36. Linc Th Coll 77. **d** 79 **p** 80. C Lt Ilford St Mich *Chelmsf* 79-82; V Highams Park All SS 82-96; rtd 96. *115 Richmond Avenue, London E4 9RR* Tel 0181-527 0457

OAKES, Robert. b 47. Ex & Truro NSM Scheme. **d** 82 **p** 83. NSM Probus, Ladock and Grampound w Creed and St Erme *Truro* 82-84; TV Bodmin w Lanhydrock and Lanivet 85-88; R S Hill w Callington from 88; P-in-c Linkinhorne 88-89; RD E Wivelshire from 95. *The Rectory, Liskeard Road, Callington, Cornwall PL17 7JD* Tel (01579) 383341

OAKHAM, Archdeacon of. *See* FERNYHOUGH, The Ven Bernard

OAKLEY, Barry Wyndham. b 32. TD72. SS Coll Cam BA53 MA57. Ridley Hall Cam 56. **d** 58 **p** 59. C Alverstoke *Portsm* 58-61; C Bermondsey St Mary w St Olave and St Jo *S'wark* 61-63; V Crofton *Portsm* 63-78; V Edmonton All SS *Lon* 78-82; P-in-c Edmonton St Mich 80-82; V Edmonton All SS w St Mich from 82. *All Saints' Vicarage, 43 All Saints' Close, London N9 9AT* Tel 0181-803 9199

OAKLEY, Hilary Robert Mark. b 53. Univ of Wales (Ban) BSc75 Ox Univ BA78. Ripon Coll Cuddesdon 76. **d** 79 **p** 80. C Birm St Pet *Birm* 79-82; C Cambridge Gt St Mary w St Mich *Ely* 82-86; Chapl Girton Coll Cam 82-86; Chapl Zürich w St Gallen and Winterthur *Eur* 86-88; NSM Lon 88-92; Perm to Offic *St Alb* from 92. *40 Kimberley Road, St Albans, Herts AL3 5PX* Tel (01272) 834072

OAKLEY, Jeremy Steven. b 52. Trin Coll Bris DipHE95. **d** 97. C Walsall *Lich* from 97. *164 Birmingham Road, Walsall WS1 2NJ* Tel (01922) 645445

OAKLEY, Mark David. b 68. K Coll Lon BD90 AKC90 FRSA96. St Steph Ho Ox 90. **d** 93 **p** 94. C St Jo Wood *Lon* 93-96; Bp's Chapl from 96; Dep P in O from 96. *The Old Deanery, Dean's Court, London EC4V 5AA* Tel 0171-222 8661 Fax 799 2629

OAKLEY, Peter Geoffrey. b 30. LSE BSc52 Cranfield Inst of Tech MSc81. Qu Coll Birm 56. **d** 58 **p** 59. C St Alb St Sav *St Alb* 58-63; R Maulden 63-73; Community Worker Soc Services Lambeth 73-74; Milton Keynes Development Corp 74-85; Culpeper Community Garden Islington 86-93; rtd 95. *6 Whitecroft, St Albans, Herts AL1 1UU* Tel (01727) 862135

OAKLEY, Richard John. b 46. AKC69 St Aug Coll Cant 69. **d** 70 **p** 71. C Wythenshawe Wm Temple Ch *Man* 70-75; V Ashton H Trin 75-80; CR 80-93; Lic to Offic *Lon* 88-93; V Cantley *Sheff* from 93. *St Wilfrid's Vicarage, 200 Cantley Lane, Doncaster, S Yorkshire DN4 6PA* Tel (01302) 535133

OAKLEY, Robert Paul. b 51. Sheff Univ BScTech72 PGCE74. St Jo Coll Nottm DipTh89. **d** 89 **p** 90. C Heatherlands St Jo *Sarum* 89-92; V Burton All SS w Ch Ch *Lich* from 92. *242 Blackpool Street, Burton-on-Trent, Staffs DE14 3AU* Tel (01283) 565134

OAKLEY, Robin Ian. b 37. Ripon Hall Ox 68. **d** 70 **p** 71. C Leighton Buzzard *St Alb* 70-73; C Watford St Mich 73-76; R Ickleford 76-80; R Ickleford w Holwell from 80. *The Rectory, 36 Turnpike Lane, Ickleford, Hitchin, Herts SG5 3XB* Tel (01462) 432925

OAKLEY, Susan Mary. *See* HENWOOD, Mrs Susan Mary

OAKLEY, Timothy Crispin (Tim). b 45. Qu Coll Cam BA66 MA70. St Jo Coll Nottm 73. **d** 76 **p** 77. C Bromley Common St Aug *Roch* 76-79; C Fairfield *Liv* 79-81; CMS 82-90; Kenya 82-90 and from 96; P-in-c Beaford, Roborough and St Giles in the Wood *Ex* 91-96; Chapl St Andr Sch Turi from 96. *St Andrew's Senior School, Turi, Private Bag, Molo, Kenya* Fax (363) 21061

OATES, Alan. b 32. S'wark Ord Course 79. **d** 80 **p** 81. NSM Rayleigh *Chelmsf* 80-87; TV Jarrow *Dur* 87-92; P-in-c Stella 92-95; R from 95. *The Rectory, Shibdon Road, Blaydon-on-Tyne, Tyne & Wear NE21 5AE* Tel 0191-414 2720

OATES, Austin Edwin. b 17. Worc Ord Coll. **d** 63 **p** 64. C Prestbury *Ches* 63-67; V Plemstall w Guilden Sutton 67-74; V Crowton 74-88; rtd 88; Perm to Offic *Ches* from 88. *31 Haleview Road, Helsby, Warrington WA6 9PH* Tel (01928) 723908

OATES, Douglas. **d** 97. NSM Balderstone *Man* from 97. *46 Queen's Gate Drive, Royton, Oldham OL2 5SD* Tel 0161-633 4459

OATES, Canon John. b 30. Kelham Th Coll 53. **d** 57 **p** 58. C Hackney Wick St Mary of Eton w St Aug *Lon* 57-60; Development Officer C of E Youth Coun 60-64; Sec C of E Coun Commonwealth Settlement 64-65; Gen Sec 65-72; Sec C of E Cttee on Migration & Internat Affairs 68-72; Hon Can Bunbury from 69; V Richmond St Mary *S'wark* 70-79; P-in-c Richmond St Jo 76-79; V Richmond St Mary w St Matthias and St Jo 79-84; RD Richmond and Barnes 79-84; R St Bride Fleet Street w Bridewell etc *Lon* from 84; AD The City from 97. *St Bride's Rectory, Fleet Street, London EC4Y 8AU* Tel 0171-353 1301 or 583 0239 Fax 583 4867

OATES, John Francis Titus. b 27. SSC Worc Coll Ox BA50 MA54. Qu Coll Birm 50. **d** 52 **p** 53. C Hunslet St Mary *Ripon* 52-56; Chapl RN 56-67; USA from 67; rtd 92. *Percival House, 78 Bayridge Road, Northport, Maine 04849, USA*

OATES, Michael Graham. b 62. Leic Poly BSc84. Aston Tr Scheme 87 Cranmer Hall Dur 89. **d** 92 **p** 93. C Enfield St Andr *Lon* 92-96; TV Oakdale *Sarum* from 96. *The Vicarage, 16 Rowbarrow Close, Poole, Dorset BH17 9EA* Tel (01202) 699807

OATEY, Canon Michael John. b 31. Chich Th Coll 57. **d** 60 **p** 61. C W Drayton *Lon* 60-66; V Chiswick St Mich 66-74; R St Sampson *Truro* from 74; V Tywardreath w Tregaminion from 74; Hon Can Truro Cathl from 88. *The Vicarage, Tywardreath, Par, Cornwall PL24 2PL* Tel (01726) 812998

OBAN, Provost of. *See* MACLEAN, The Very Revd Allan Murray

OBEE, Douglas Walter. b 18. Roch Th Coll 65. **d** 67 **p** 68. C Beckenham St Geo *Roch* 67-71; R Whitestone *Ex* 71-75; V Oldridge 72-75; P-in-c Harford 76-87; V Ivybridge 76-87; V Ivybridge w Harford 87; rtd 87; Perm to Offic *Ex* from 88. *16 Kerswill Road, Exeter EX4 1NY* Tel (01392) 439405

O'BENEY, Robin Mervyn. b 35. Ely Th Coll 61. **d** 64 **p** 65. C Liss *Portsm* 64-65; C Portsea St Cuth 65-68; Hon C Wymondham *Nor* 74-76; R Swainsthorpe w Newton Flotman 76-80; NSM Sparkenhoe Deanery *Leic* 87-90; V Billesdon and Skeffington 90-91; rtd 95. *Tigh Na Bochd, Bunessan, Isle of Mull PA67 6DH* Tel (01681) 700281

OBERST, Simon Julian. b 57. ACA83 Trin Coll Cam BA79 MA82. Wycliffe Hall Ox DipTh90. **d** 91 **p** 92. C S Croydon Em *S'wark* 91-95; V Chipping Campden w Ebrington *Glouc* from 95. *The Vicarage, Chipping Campden, Glos GL55 6HU* Tel (01386) 840671

OBIORA, Arthur Cuenyem. b 42. JP91. DipSM68. LNSM course 92. **d** 95 **p** 95. NSM Hatcham St Cath *S'wark* from 95. *15 Besson Street, London SE14 5AE* Tel 0171-732 1065

O'BRIEN, Andrew David. b 61. Nottm Univ BTh88. Linc Th Coll 85. **d** 88 **p** 89. C Clare w Poslingford *St E* 88-89; C Clare w Poslingford, Cavendish etc 89-91; V Belton All SS *Linc* 91-97; P-in-c Melbourn *Ely* from 97; P-in-c Meldreth from 97. *The Vicarage, Melbourn, Royston, Herts SG8 6DY* Tel (01763) 260295

O'BRIEN, Donogh Smith. b 34. St Pet Hall Ox BA56 MA60. Ripon Hall Ox 56. **d** 57 **p** 58. C Gt Sankey *Liv* 57-63; C Farnworth 63-66; Lic to Offic from 66; Asst Master Wade Deacon Gr Sch Widnes from 66. *Fourways, 178 Lunts Heath Road, Farnworth, Widnes, Cheshire WA8 9AZ* Tel 0151-424 0147

O'BRIEN, Elaine. b 55. **d** 97. AM Killyman *Arm* from 97. *40 Carrybarragh Road, Moneymore, Magherfelt, Co Londonderry* Tel (01648) 748104

O'BRIEN, George Edward. b 32. Clifton Th Coll 61. **d** 64 **p** 65. C Denton Holme *Carl* 64-68; V Castle Town *Lich* 68-88; Chapl St Geo Hosp Stafford 88-94; Chapl Kingsmead Hosp Stafford 88-94; Chapl Foundation NHS Trust Stafford from 94; rtd 92. *Abily, 185 Tixall Road, Stafford ST16 3XJ* Tel (01785) 44261

O'BRIEN, Canon James Henry. b 10. Bps' Coll Cheshunt 42. **d** 44 **p** 45. C Blackb St Jo *Blackb* 44-47; V Blackb St Aid 47-67; RD Darwen 64-75; V Darwen St Cuth 67-75; Hon Can Blackb Cathl 73-75; rtd 75; C Adlington *Blackb* 75-79; Lic to Offic from 79. *21 Suffolk Street, Blackburn BB2 4ES* Tel (01254) 264799

O'BRIEN, John. b 41. St Jo Coll Cam BA63 MA67. Ridley Hall Cam 63. **d** 65 **p** 66. C Wotton St Mary *Glouc* 65-69; Youth Chapl 67-69; Lect Coll of SS Paul and Mary Cheltenham 69-85; V Twigworth, Down Hatherley, Norton, The Leigh etc *Glouc* from 85; RD Glouc N from 94. *The Rectory, Twigworth, Gloucester GL2 9PQ* Tel (01452) 731483

O'BRIEN, Mary. *See* GUBBINS, Mrs Mary

O'BRIEN, Peter Thomas. b 35. **d** 61 **p** 62. Australia 61-63 and from 74; India 64-68 and 71-73; C Cheadle *Ches* 68-71. *Moore Theological College, Carillon Avenue, Newtown, NSW, Australia 2042* Tel Sydney (2) 519 2644 or 557 3072 Fax 550 5859

O'BRIEN, Shelagh Ann. *See* STACEY, Mrs Shelagh Ann

O'BYRNE, Francis Michael. b 12. Tyndale Hall Bris 41. **d** 44 **p** 45. C Eccleston St Luke *Liv* 44-46; C Dublin St Kevin *D & G* 46-47; P-in-c Banagher w Clochan, Clonmacnoise, Kinnitty etc *M & K* 47-54; P-in-c Athboy Union 54-56; I 56-81; Can Meath 76-81; rtd 81. *Birch Lea, Old Connaught Avenue, Bray, Co Wicklow, Irish Republic* Tel Dublin (1) 282 4429

OCKFORD, Paul Philip. b 46. St Chad's Coll Dur BA67. St Steph Ho Ox 68. **d** 70 **p** 71. C Streatham St Pet *S'wark* 70-74; C Cheam 74-77; P-in-c Eastrington *York* 77-79; TV Howden TM 80-83; R Sherburn and W and E Heslerton w Yedingham 83-92; V Bampton, Morebath, Clayhanger and Petton *Ex* from 92. *The Vicarage, Bampton, Tiverton, Devon EX16 9NG* Tel (01398) 331385

OCKWELL, Canon Herbert Grant. b 12. Kelham Th Coll 30. **d** 36 **p** 37. C Newington St Matt *S'wark* 36-40; CF (EC) 40-46; V Lambeth St Phil *S'wark* 46-52; V Surbiton St Andr 52-62; V Balham Hill Ascension 62-70; Hon Can S'wark Cathl 64-70; R Blendworth, Chalton and Idsworth *Portsm* 70-81; rtd 81; Perm to

Offic *Portsm* from 81; Perm to Offic *Chich* from 82. *72 Bowes Hill, Rowland's Castle, Hants PO9 6BS* Tel (01705) 412301

O'CONNELL, Miss Mary Joy. b 49. York Univ BA71 Leeds Univ CertEd74. Chich Th Coll 84. **dss** 86 **d** 87 **p** 94. Cinderhill *S'well* 86-87; Par Dn 87-94; C 94; P-in-c from 94. *The Vicarage, Nuthall Road, Nottingham NG8 6AD* Tel 0115-978 1514

O'CONNOR, Alfred Stanley. b 20. TCD BA43 MA60. **d** 43 **p** 44. C Belfast St Mich *Conn* 43-45; C Urney Union *K, E & A* 45-49; I Killesher 49-54; I Roscrea *L & K* 54-62; RD Ely O'Carroll 60-62; I Camlough w Killeavy *Arm* 62-65; I Drumglass 65-85; Can Arm Cathl 83-85; rtd 85. *25 West Street, Stewartstown, Dungannon, Co Tyrone BT71 5HT* Tel (01868) 738784

O'CONNOR, Canon Brian Michael McDougal. b 42. St Cath Coll Cam BA67 MA69. Cuddesdon Coll 67. **d** 69 **p** 70. C Headington *Ox* 69-71; Sec Dioc Past and Redundant Chs Uses Cttees 72-79; P-in-c Mert 72-76; V Rainham *Roch* from 79; RD Gillingham 81-88; Hon Can Roch Cathl from 89. *The Vicarage, 80 Broadview Avenue, Gillingham, Kent ME8 9DE* Tel (01634) 231538 Fax 233282 E-mail 100754.3272@compuserve.com

O'CONNOR, Canon Daniel. b 33. Univ Coll Dur BA54 MA67 St Andr Univ PhD81. Cuddesdon Coll 56. **d** 58 **p** 59. C Stockton St Pet *Dur* 58-62; C W Hartlepool St Aid 62-63; Cam Miss to Delhi 63-70; USPG 70-72; India 63-72; Chapl St Andr Univ *St And* 72-77; R Edin Gd Shep *Edin* 77-82; Prin Coll of the Ascension Selly Oak 82-90; Dir Scottish Chs Ho (Chs Together in Scotland) 90-93; Can Res Wakef Cathl *Wakef* 93-96; Bp's Adv on Inter-Faith Issues 93-96; rtd 96. *The Old Parsonage, Rotten Row, Elie, Fife KY9 1DY* Tel (01333) 330254

O'CONNOR, Edward Howard. b 32. AIMLS59 FRSH65. Linc Th Coll 81 Immanuel Coll Ibadan 76. **d** 77 **p** 79. Nigeria 77-81; P-in-c Newchurch *Portsm* 81-83; V 83-91; P-in-c Arreton 82-83; V 83-91; Chapl HM Pris Kingston (Portsm) from 91; rtd 92. *23 Arundel Road, Ryde, Isle of Wight PO33 1BW* Tel (01983) 617062

O'CONNOR, John Goodrich. b 34. Keble Coll Ox BA58 MA60. Lich Th Coll. **d** 61 **p** 62. C Blackpool St Steph *Blackb* 61-66; C Holbeck *Ripon* 66-68; C Hendon St Mary *Lon* 68-73; TV Thornaby on Tees *York* 73-79; TR 79-89; V Blyth St Cuth *Newc* 89-96; Chapl Wellesley Nautical Sch 89-96; V Feniscliffe *Blackb* from 96. *The Vicarage, St Francis Road, Feniscliffe, Blackburn BB2 2TZ* Tel (01254) 201757

O'CONNOR, Nigel George. b 25. TD66. Linc Th Coll 53. **d** 55 **p** 56. C S Ormsby w Ketsby, Calceby and Driby *Linc* 55-58; R Partney w Dalby 58-65; V Skendleby 59-65; R Ashby by Partney 59-65; CF (TA) 62-71; R Ivychurch w Old Romney and Midley *Cant* 65-74; V Brenzett w Snargate and Snave 65-74; R Newchurch 65-74; R St Mary in the Marsh 65-74; R Burmarsh 65-74; V Brookland w Fairfield 65-74; CF (R of O) 71-91; V S w N Hayling *Portsm* 74-85; V Corby Glen *Linc* 85-91; rtd 91. *Winterbourne House, Allington, Salisbury SP4 0BZ* Tel (01980) 611453

ODA-BURNS, John Macdonald. b 31. AKC56. **d** 57 **p** 58. C St Marychurch *Ex* 57-59; S Africa 59-64; Bahamas 64-67; USA from 67; rtd 96. *611 La Mesa Drive, Portola Valley, CA94028, USA* Tel San Francisco (415) 854-2831

ODDY, Canon Frederick Brian. b 29. Univ of Wales (Lamp) BA50. Linc Th Coll 50. **d** 52 **p** 53. C Preston Em *Blackb* 52-55; C St Annes 55-57; V Chorley St Jas 57-64; V Warton St Oswald 64-76; P-in-c Yealand Conyers 74-76; V Warton St Oswald w Yealand Conyers from 76; RD Tunstall 84-90; Hon Can Blackb Cathl from 89. *St Oswald's Vicarage, Warton, Carnforth, Lancs LA5 9PG* Tel (01524) 732946

ODLING-SMEE, Dr George William. b 35. FRCS68 K Coll Dur MB, BS59. **d** 77 **p** 78. NSM Belfast St Thos *Conn* 77-90; NSM Belfast St Geo from 90. *10 Deramore Park South, Belfast BT9 5JY* Tel (01232) 669275

ODLUM, Michael Julian. b 24. DFC45. St Mich Coll Llan 55. **d** 56 **p** 57. C Risca *Mon* 56-59; St Vincent 60-65; P-in-c Spaxton w Charlynch *B & W* 65-67; V Sampford Arundel 67-74; Asst Chapl HM Pris Wandsworth 74; Chapl HM Pris Standford Hill 74-81; Chapl HM Pris Leic 82-89; rtd 89; Perm to Offic *Leic* from 89. *67A Main Street, Kirby Muxloe, Leicester LE9 2AN*

O'DONNELL, Kevin George. b 57. Man Univ BA78 Didsbury Coll Man PGCE79. St Steph Ho Ox 86. **d** 88 **p** 89. C Tokyngton St Mich *Lon* 88-90; C Ascot Heath *Ox* 90-92; Perm to Offic from 94; Chapl Heathfield Sch Ascot from 96. *16 Maple Drive, Crowthorne, Berks RG45 6SL*

O'DONOVAN, Canon Oliver Michael Timothy. b 45. Ball Coll Ox BA68 MA71 DPhil75. Wycliffe Hall Ox 68. **d** 72 **p** 73. Tutor Wycliffe Hall Ox 72-77; Canada 77-82; Regius Prof Moral and Past Th Ox Univ from 82; Can Res Ch Ch *Ox* from 82. *Christ Church, Oxford OX1 1DP* Tel (01865) 276219

OEHRING, Anthony Charles. b 56. Sheff City Poly BA79 CQSW79. Ridley Hall Cam 86. **d** 88 **p** 89. C Gillingham *Sarum* 88-91; TV S Gillingham *Roch* from 91. *60 Parkwood Green, Gillingham, Kent ME8 9PP* Tel (01634) 235837

OEPPEN, John Gerard David. b 44. St D Coll Lamp DipTh67. **d** 67 **p** 68. C-in-c Cwmmer w Abercregan CD *Llan* 67-70; TV Glyncorrwg w Afan Vale and Cymmer Afan 70-71; C Whitchurch 71-74; V Aberavon H Trin 74-78; V Bargoed and Deri w Brithdir 78-86; R Barry All SS from 86. *The Rectory, 3 Park Road, Barry CF62 6NU* Tel (01446) 734629

OESTREICHER, Canon Paul. b 31. OM(Ger)95. Univ of NZ BA53 MA56 Cov Poly Hon DLitt91. Linc Th Coll 56. **d** 59 **p** 60. C Dalston H Trin w St Phil *Lon* 59-61; C S Mymms K Chas 61-68; Asst in Relig Broadcasting BBC 61-64; Assoc Sec Internat Affairs Dept BCC 64-69; V Blackheath Ascension *S'wark* 68-81; Dir of Tr 69-72; Hon Can S'wark Cathl 78-81; Lic to Offic 81-86; Asst Gen Sec BCC 81-86; Can Res Cov Cathl *Cov* from 86; Dir of Internat Min from 86; Humboldt Fell, Inst of Th, Free Univ of Berlin 92-93; Lic to Offic *Eur* 92-93. *20 Styvechale Avenue, Coventry CV5 6DX* Tel (01203) 673704 or 634531 Fax 631448

O'FERRALL, The Very Revd Basil Arthur. b 24. CB79. TCD BA48 MA65. TCD Div Sch Div Test48. **d** 48 **p** 49. C Coleraine *Conn* 48-51; Chapl RN 51-75; Chapl of the Fleet and Adn for the RN 75-80; QHC 75-80; Hon Can Gib Cathl *Eur* 77-80; Chapl to The Queen 80-85; V Ranworth w Panxworth and Woodbastwick *Nor* 80-85; Bp's Chapl Norfolk Broads 80-85; Hon Can Win Cathl *Win* 85-93; R Jersey St Helier 85-93; Dean Jersey 85-93; Pres Jersey Miss to Seamen 85-93; Angl Adv Channel TV 85-93; rtd 93; Perm to Offic *Chich* from 93. *The Stone House, Barrack Square, Winchelsea, E Sussex TN36 4EG* Tel (01797) 223458

OFFER, The Ven Clifford Jocelyn. b 43. Ex Univ BA67 FRSA97. Westcott Ho Cam 67. **d** 69 **p** 70. C Bromley SS Pet and Paul *Roch* 69-74; TV Southampton (City Cen) *Win* 74-83; TR Hitchin *St Alb* 83-94; Adn Nor from 94; Can Res Nor Cathl from 94. *26 The Close, Norwich NR1 4DZ* Tel (01603) 620375

OGDEN, Cyril Newton. b 12. AKC39. **d** 39 **p** 40. C Coulsdon St Andr *S'wark* 39-40; C Charlton St Luke w St Paul 40-42; Chapl RAFVR 42-46; Lic to Offic *S'wark* 48-60; P-in-c Holbeach Fen *Linc* 60-69; V 69-77; V Whaplode 60-77; rtd 77; Perm to Offic *Linc* 77-88; Perm to Offic *Glouc* 88-96. *1 Chapelside, Clapton Row, Bourton-on-the-Water, Cheltenham, Glos GL54 2DN* Tel (01451) 821440

OGDEN, Eric. b 34. NW Ord Course 73. **d** 76 **p** 77. NSM Lydgate St Anne *Man* 76-92; NSM St Anne Lydgate w Ch Ch Friezland from 92. *40 Burnedge Lane, Grasscroft, Oldham OL4 4EA* Tel (01457) 873661

OGDEN, Canon Eric Grayson. b 06. AKC32. St Steph Ho Ox 32. **d** 32 **p** 33. C Ealing Ch the Sav *Lon* 32-37; Chapl Chich Th Coll 37-40; CF (EC) 40-45; C Walton-on-Thames *Guildf* 45-48; V Fairwarp *Chich* 48-51; V Hastings All So 51-54; V Brighton St Mich 54-65; R Upper St Leonards St Jo 65-72; rtd 72; Chapl Costa del Sol E *Eur* 72-76; Chapl Malaga w Almunecar and Nerja 76-78; Hon C Worthing St Andr *Chich* from 79. *Fernbank, 25 Gratwicke Road, Worthing, W Sussex BN11 4BJ*

OGDEN, Harry. b 30. AKC57. **d** 58 **p** 59. C Hollinwood *Man* 58-60; C Langley St Aid CD 60-61; R Lightbowne 61-69; V Farnworth and Kearsley 69-72; V Oldham St Steph and All Martyrs 72-79; R Moss Side Ch Ch 79-95; rtd 95; Perm to Offic *Man* from 95. *16 Tysoe Gardens, Salford M3 6BL* Tel 0161-839 1761

OGILVIE, The Ven Gordon. b 42. Glas Univ MA64 Lon Univ BD67. ALCD66. **d** 67 **p** 68. C Ashtead *Guildf* 67-72; V New Barnet St Jas *St Alb* 72-80; Dir Past Studies Wycliffe Hall Ox 80-87; P-in-c Harlow New Town w Lt Parndon *Chelmsf* 87-89; R 89-94; TR Harlow Town Cen w Lt Parndon 94-96; Chapl Princess Alexandra Hosp Harlow 88-96; Hon Can Chelmsf Cathl *Chelmsf* 94-96; Adn Nottingham *S'well* from 96. *2B Spencer Avenue, Mapperley, Nottingham NG3 5SP* Tel 0115-967 0875

OGILVIE, Ian Douglas. b 37. Em Coll Cam BA59 MA63. Linc Th Coll 59. **d** 61 **p** 62. C Clapham H Trin *S'wark* 61-63; C Cambridge Gt St Mary w St Mich *Ely* 63-66; Chapl Sevenoaks Sch 66-77; Hon C Sevenoaks St Nic *Roch* 67-77; Chapl Malvern Coll 77-84; Hd Master St Geo Sch Harpenden 84-87; Lic to Offic *St Alb* 84-87; Bp's Dom Chapl 87-89; P-in-c Aldenham 87-91; Appeals Dir Mind 89-91; Fund Raising Dir Br Deaf Assn 91-94; NSM Tring *St Alb* 92-94; Perm to Offic from 94; Fund Raising Dir R Nat Miss to Deep Sea Fishermen from 94. *The White House, 19 Lower Icknield Way, Marsworth, Tring, Herts HP23 4LN* Tel (01296) 661479

OGLE, Ms Catherine. b 61. Leeds Univ BA82 MPhil85 Fitzw Coll Cam BA87. Westcott Ho Cam 85. **d** 88 **p** 94. C Middleton St Mary *Ripon* 88-91; Relig Progr Ed BBC Radio Leeds 91-95; NSM Leeds St Marg and All Hallows 91-95; P-in-c Woolley *Wakef* from 95. *The Vicarage, Church Street, Woolley, Wakefield, W Yorkshire WF4 2JU* Tel (01226) 382550

OGLESBY, Canon Leslie Ellis (Les). b 46. Univ Coll Ox BA69 MA73 City Univ MPhil73 Fitzw Coll Cam BA73 MA77. Ripon Coll Cuddesdon 77. **d** 78 **p** 79. C Stevenage St Mary Shephall *St Alb* 78-80; Dir St Alb Minl Tr Scheme 80-87; V Markyate Street *St Alb* 80-87; Dir Continuing Minl Educn 87-94; Hon Can St Alb from 93; TR Hitchin from 94. *The Rectory, 21 West Hill, Hitchin, Herts SG5 2HZ* Tel (01462) 434017 or 452758

OGLEY, John. b 40. Oak Hill Th Coll 62. **d** 65 **p** 66. C Ardsley *Sheff* 65-68; C Carlton-in-the-Willows *S'well* 68-71; P-in-c Tollerton 71-79; V Skegby 79-93; R Carlton-in-Lindrick from 93. *The Rectory, Carlton-in-Lindrick, Worksop, Notts S81 9EF* Tel (01909) 730222

O'GORMAN, Paul Anthony. b 46. Portsm Poly BSc79. Oak Hill Th Coll DipHE81. **d** 81 **p** 82. C Leyton St Mary w St Edw

Chelmsf 81-83; C Rayleigh 83-84; CF 84-87; R Northiam *Chich* 87-93; V Hastings Em and St Mary in the Castle from 93. *The Vicarage, Vicarage Road, Hastings, E Sussex TN34 3NA* Tel (01424) 421554

OGUGUO, Barnabas Ahuna. b 47. Rome Univ BA70 BD74 Glas Univ MTh84 PhD90 Strathclyde Univ PGCE93. **d** 73 **p** 74. Nigeria 73-93; RE Teacher Lenzie Academy *Glas* 93-96; Bearsden Academy from 96; Hon C Lenzie from 95. *4 Kennedy Path, Townhead, Glasgow G4 0PW* Tel 0141-552 2628 Fax as telephone

O'HANLON, Canon William Douglas. b 11. Peterho Cam BA32 MA37. Clifton Th Coll 32. **d** 37 **p** 38. C Heatherlands St Jo *Sarum* 37-39; Chapl RAFVR 39-46; R Langton Matravers *Sarum* 46-51; V Calne 51-62; P-in-c Heddington 53-62; V Calne and Blackland 62-69; Can and Preb Sarum Cathl 61-82; V Coombe Bissett w Homington 69-72; R Studland 72-82; rtd 82. *Crown Hill, 14 Bon Accord Road, Swanage, Dorset BH19 2DT* Tel (01929) 425416

OHS, Lt Comdr Douglas Fredrick. b 49. Saskatchewan Univ BA74. Em Coll Saskatoon LTh75. **d** 74 **p** 75. C Bridgwater St Mary w Chilton Trinity *B & W* 75-77; Canada from 77. *Chaplain (P), 17 Wing Winnipeg, PO Box 17000 STN Forces, Winnipeg, MB, Canada, R3J 3Y5* Tel Winnipeg (204) 833 2500 ext 5417 Fax 833 2565

OJI, Dr Erasmus Oluchukwu. b 43. LRCP70 MRCS70 FRCS76 Lon Univ BSc66. Oak Hill Th Coll 75. **d** 78 **p** 79. C Ealing Dean St Jo *Lon* 78-80; Nigeria 80-90; Asst Chapl Rotherham Distr Gen Hosp 90-91; Perm to Offic *Sheff* from 92. *369 Fulwood Road, Sheffield S10 3BS* Tel 0114-266 1360

OKE, Michael John. b 42. Ox Min Course 89. **d** 92 **p** 93. NSM Stratfield Mortimer *Ox* from 92. *Gladstone Cotage, 18 Windmill Road, Mortimer, Reading RG7 3RN* Tel 0118-933 2829

OKEKE, Canon Ken Sandy Edozie. b 41. Nigeria Univ BSc67. **d** 76 **p** 76. Nigeria 76-80 and 87-89; Chapl to Nigerians in UK and Irish Republic 80-87; Hon Can Kwara from 85; C Man Whitworth *Man* 89-95; Chapl Insts Higher Learning Man 89-95; CMS from 95; Perm to Offic *S'wark* from 96. *CMS, Pertnership House, 157 Waterloo Road, London SE1 8UU* Tel 0171-928 8681

OKELLO, Modicum. b 53. Nairobi Sch of Miss DipMiss82 Haggaih Inst of Chr Leadership DipCL86 Wycliffe Hall Ox 86 Trin Coll Bris BA90 St Paul's Coll Limuru DipTh78. **d** 78 **p** 79. Kenya 78-80; Uganda 80-86; NSM Goodmayes All SS *Chelmsf* 91-92; C Barking St Marg w St Patr 92-96; C Stratford St Jo and Ch Ch w Forest Gate St Jas from 96. *29 Maryland Park, London E15 1HB* Tel 0181-534 7503

OLANCZUK, Jonathan Paul Tadeusz. b 49. UEA CertRS95. EAMTC 94. **d** 96 **p** 97. C Haverhill w Withersfield, the Wrattings etc *St E* from 96. *12 Wratting Road, Haverhill, Suffolk CB9 0DD* Tel (01440) 702223 Fax as telephone

OLD, Arthur Anthony George (Tony). b 36. Clifton Th Coll 69. **d** 71 **p** 72. C Clitheroe St Jas *Blackb* 71-73; C Bispham 73-77; V Haslingden St Jo Stonefold 77-81; TV Lowestoft and Kirkley *Nor* 81-83; Chapl to the Deaf *Cant* from 83; P-in-c Hernhill 83-85; C Preston next Faversham, Goodnestone and Graveney from 85. *25 Dence Park, Herne Bay, Kent CT6 6BQ* Tel (01227) 360948

OLDALE, Harry. b 17. Bps' Coll Cheshunt 51. **d** 53 **p** 54. C Warmsworth w Edlington *Sheff* 53-56; C Woodlands 56-58; V Moorends 58-60; R Edgefield *Nor* 60-71; V Weybourne w Upper Sheringham 71-76; R Kelling w Salthouse 76-83; V Weybourne w Upper Sheringham 76-83; rtd 83; Perm to Offic *Nor* from 85. *St Stephen's, 24 Station Road, Holt, Norfolk NR25 6BS* Tel (01263) 713964

OLDEN, Canon Aidan Ronald Cuming. b 17. TCD BA38 MA41. CITC 39. **d** 40 **p** 41. C Newry St Mary *D & D* 40-41; Dean's V Belf Cathl 41-42; Succ St Patr Cathl Dublin 42-47; I Kingscourt *M & K* 47-60; Can Meath 58-92; I Kells w Balrathboyne, Moynalty etc 60-92; Preb Tipper St Patr Cathl Dublin 64-92; RD Clonard and Trim *M & K* 67-92; rtd 92. *Balreask New, Navan, Co Meath, Irish Republic* Tel Navan (46) 27874

OLDFIELD, Roger Fielden. b 45. Qu Coll Cam BA67 MA71 City of Lon Poly DMS69 Lon Univ BD75. Trin Coll Bris 75. **d** 75 **p** 76. C Halliwell St Pet *Man* 75-80; V from 80; AD Bolton from 93. *St Peter's Vicarage, 1 Sefton Road, Harpers Lane, Bolton BL1 6HT* Tel (01204) 849412 Fax 849440

OLDHAM, Canon Arthur Charles Godolphin. b 05. AKC33. **d** 33 **p** 34. C Witley *Guildf* 33-36; V Brockham Green *S'wark* 36-43; R Merrow *Guildf* 43-50; RD Guildf 49-50; V Godalming 50-62; RD Godalming 57-62; Hon Can Guildf Cathl 59-61; Dir of Ords 58-71; Asst Dioc Dir of Ords 71-73; Can Res Guildf Cathl 61-71; rtd 71; Perm to Offic *Guildf* 81-92. *The Lawn, Holybourne, Alton, Hants GU34 4ER* Tel (01420) 544293

OLDHAM, Charles Harry. b 14. St D Coll Lamp BA48. **d** 48 **p** 49. C Atherton *Man* 48-53; V Rochdale St Alb 53-59; P-in-c Goff's Oak St Jas *St Alb* 59-68; V 68-79; rtd 79; Hon C Bishopstrow and Boreham *Sarum* 81-92. *94 Prestbury Drive, Warminster, Wilts BA12 9LE* Tel (01985) 213678

OLDHAM, Dale Raymond. b 40. NZ Coll of Pharmacy MPS63 Cant Univ (NZ) MA87. Ridley Hall Cam 64. **d** 67 **p** 68. C Woking St Mary *Guildf* 67-70; New Zealand 71-73 and from 81; CMS 74-81; Tanzania 74-81. *6 Emmett Street, Christchurch 8001, New Zealand* Tel Christchurch (3) 385 6282 or 385 2027

OLDHAM, Canon John. b 19. Kelham Th Coll 38. **d** 44 **p** 45. C Staveley *Derby* 44-48 and 54-57; S Rhodesia 48-53; V Somercotes *Derby* 57-64; V Derby St Bart 64-72; V Buxton 72-74; TR Buxton w Burbage and King Sterndale 74-84; Hon Can Derby Cathl 79-85; rtd 84; Perm to Offic *Derby* from 84. *Rose Cottage, Holt Lane, Lea, Matlock, Derbyshire DE4 5GQ* Tel (01629) 534469

OLDLAND, Dr Hubert Charles (Peter). b 29. ARCS53 FRIC62 FRACI67 Imp Coll Lon BSc53 PhD56 DIC56. Ridley Coll Melbourne ThL85. **d** 83 **p** 84. Australia from 83; rtd 94. *5 Abbott Street, North Balwyn, Victoria, Australia 3104* Tel Melbourne (3) 9857 8768

OLDNALL, Frederick Herbert. b 16. Ripon Hall Ox 56. **d** 57 **p** 58. C Radford *Cov* 57-59; C Stratford-on-Avon 59-62; V Rosliston w Coton in the Elms *Derby* 62-83; rtd 83; Perm to Offic *Cov* from 93. *19 Keeling Road, Kenilworth, Coventry, Warks CV8 2JP* Tel (01926) 52417

OLDROYD, Preb Colin Mitchell. b 30. Down Coll Cam BA54 MA60. Wells Th Coll 60. **d** 61 **p** 62. C Elton All SS *Man* 61-63; C Ex St Dav *Ex* 63-66; P-in-c Neen Sollars w Milson *Heref* 66-78; P-in-c Coreley w Doddington 66-78; R Cleobury Mortimer w Hopton Wafers 66-78; RD Ludlow 75-78; P-in-c Eastnor 78-81; R Ledbury 78-81; RD Ledbury 78-81; Chapl Ledbury Cottage Hosp Heref 79-95; R Ledbury w Eastnor *Heref* 81-95; Preb Heref Cathl 84-95; P-in-c Lt Marcle 85-95; rtd 95; Perm to Offic *Heref* from 96. *2 Hampton Manor Close, Hereford HR1 1TG* Tel (01432) 340569

OLDROYD, David Christopher Leslie. b 42. FRICS. S Dios Minl Tr Scheme. **d** 85 **p** 86. NSM Four Marks *Win* 85-90; rtd 90. *Hill House, Spring Lane, Farnham, Surrey GU9 0JD* Tel (01252) 737586

OLDROYD, James Healey. b 08. Worc Ord Coll. **d** 55 **p** 56. C Kidderminster St Mary and All SS, Trimpley etc *Worc* 55-57; C Tardebigge 57-61; V Worc St Mark 61-75; rtd 75; Perm to Offic *Worc* from 75. *7 Magnolia Close, Worcester WR5 3SJ* Tel (01905) 355603

OLDROYD, Trevor. b 33. Hatf Coll Dur BA55 Lon Univ BD60. Wycliffe Hall Ox 60. **d** 61 **p** 62. C Barnes St Mary *S'wark* 61-65; C Wimbledon 65-68; W Germany 68-73; Chapl Dudley Sch 73-80; Asst Chapl Wellington Coll Berks 80-82; P-in-c Rendcomb *Glouc* 82-86; Chapl Rendcomb Coll 82-86; Chapl Wrekin Coll Shropshire 86-90; V Deptford St Jo w H Trin *S'wark* 91-94; rtd 94. *3 Dolphin Court, Northbrook Road, Swanage, Dorset BH19 1QJ* Tel (01929) 427954

OLHAUSEN, William John. b 37. TCD BA60 MA63. Ridley Hall Cam 60. **d** 62 **p** 63. C Grassendale *Liv* 62-66; Asst Chapl Dur Univ *Dur* 66-70; Lect Dur Univ 66-70; V Hazlemere *Ox* 70-89; RD Wycombe 78-83; Perm to Offic 89-93. *7 The Brae, Groomsport, Co Down BT19 6JG* Tel (01247) 464454

OLIVE, Dan. b 29. ARIBA54. Sarum & Wells Th Coll 79. **d** 82 **p** 83. NSM Wells St Cuth w Wookey Hole *B & W* 82-85; C Yatton Moor 86-88; R Mells w Buckland Dinham, Elm, Whatley etc 88-97; RD Frome 93-97; rtd 97. *Roseleigh, Woodcombe, Minehead, Somerset TA24 8SA* Tel (01643) 702218

OLIVER, Arthur Norman. b 16. Worc Ord Coll 63. **d** 65 **p** 66. C Willingdon *Chich* 65-69; C W Worthing St Jo 69-71; R Etchingham 71-85; V Hurst Green 72-85; rtd 85; Perm to Offic *Ely* 86-89; Perm to Offic *Chich* from 89. *1 April Place, Buckhurst Road, Bexhill-on-Sea, E Sussex TN40 1UE* Tel (01424) 219838

OLIVER, Bernard John. b 31. CEng65 MIMechE. S'wark Ord Course 75. **d** 78 **p** 79. NSM Chipping Ongar *Chelmsf* 78-81; C Waltham Abbey 81-85; C High Ongar w Norton Mandeville 85-87; C Somerton w Compton Dundon, the Charltons etc *B & W* 87-88; rtd 96. *1 Orchard Way, Mosterton, Beaminster, Dorset DT8 3LT* Tel (01308) 868037

OLIVER, Canon Beverley Stephen. b 29. Lich Th Coll 58. **d** 60 **p** 61. S Africa 61-96; Adn of the Ordinary 80-96; Lect and Preacher Newland Almshouses from 96. *The Lecturer's House, Almshouse Road, Newland, Coleford, Glos GL16 8NL* Tel (01594) 832441

OLIVER, Canon David Ryland. b 34. Univ of Wales (Lamp) BA56 St Cath Coll Ox BA58 MA62. Wycliffe Hall Ox 56. **d** 58 **p** 59. C Carmarthen St Pet *St D* 58-61; C Llangyfelach and Morriston *S & B* 61-63; R Aberedw w Llandeilo Graban etc 63-66; R Llanbadarn Fawr, Llandegley and Llanfihangel etc 66-67; Lic to Offic *Llan* 68-70; Lic to Offic *Ban* 70-73; V Nefyn w Pistyll w Tudweiliog w Llandudwen etc 73-74; V Abercraf and Callwen *S & B* 74-77; V Llangyfelach 77-79; R Llanllwchaearn and Llanina *St D* 79-83; V Cwmaman 83-94; Can St D Cathl from 90; RD Dyffryn Aman 93-94; V Cynwyl Gaeo w Llansawel and Talley from 94. *The Vicarage, Talley, Llandeilo SA19 7YP* Tel (01558) 685229

OLIVER, Graham Frank. b 42. St Barn Coll Adelaide. **d** 68 **p** 69. Australia 68-86; C Ealing Ch the Sav *Lon* 86-93; Perm to Offic 94-97; Asst Chapl Ypres St George *Eur* from 97. *Haiglaan 12, 8900 Ypres, Belgium* Tel Ypres (57) 21 56 85

OLIVER, John Andrew George. b 28. OBE83. St Jo Coll Dur BA53 DipTh55. **d** 55 **p** 56. C Bermondsey St Mary w St Olave and St Jo *S'wark* 55-58; C Dulwich St Barn 58-61; Chapl RN 61-83; QHC 79-83; R Guisborough *York* 83-89; Chapl and Tutor Whittington Coll Felbridge 89-93; rtd 93; Perm to Offic *Carl* from 93. *Allandale, Thacka Lane, Penrith, Cumbria CA11 9HX* Tel (01768) 892096

OLIVER, The Ven John Graham Wyand. b 47. Ridley Hall Cam 76. **d** 78 **p** 79. C Shortlands *Roch* 78-81; C Hammersmith St Paul *Lon* 81-85; Zambia from 85; Adn S Zambia from 89. *USPG, Partnership House, 157 Waterloo Road, London SE1 8XA* Tel 0171-928 8681 Fax 928 2371

✠**OLIVER, The Rt Revd John Keith.** b 35. G&C Coll Cam BA59 MA63 MLitt65. Westcott Ho Cam. **d** 64 **p** 65 **c** 90. C Hilborough w Bodney *Nor* 64-68; Chapl Eton Coll 68-72; R S Molton w Nymet St George *Ex* 73-75; P-in-c Filleigh w E Buckland 73-75; P-in-c Warkleigh w Satterleigh and Chittlehamholt 73-75; P-in-c High Bray w Charles 73-75; RD S Molton 74-80; TR S Molton, Nymet St George, High Bray etc 75-82; P-in-c N Molton w Twitchen 77-79; TR Cen Ex 82-85; Adn Sherborne *Sarum* 85-90; P-in-c W Stafford w Frome Billet 85-90; Can Res Sarum Cathl 85-90; Bp Heref from 90. *Bishop's House, The Palace, Hereford HR4 9BN* Tel (01432) 271355 Fax 343047

OLIVER, The Ven John Michael. b 39. Univ of Wales (Lamp) BA62. Ripon Hall Ox 62. **d** 64 **p** 65. C High Harrogate St Pet *Ripon* 64-67; C Bramley 67-72; V Low Harrogate St Mary 72-78; V Beeston 78-92; RD Armley 86-92; Hon Can Ripon Cathl from 87; Adn Leeds from 92. *Archdeacon's Lodge, 2 Halcyon Hill, Leeds LS7 3PU* Tel 0113-269 0594 Fax as telephone

OLIVER, John Rodney. b 31. BA Lon Univ MTh73. Bps' Coll Cheshunt 54. **d** 56 **p** 57. C Much Hadham *St Alb* 56-57; Australia from 73. *17 Hale Street, East Kew, Victoria, Australia 3102* Tel Melbourne (3) 9859 8593 Fax 9819 7033

OLIVER, Mrs Judith Anne. b 54. WMMTC. **d** 96 **p** 97. C Old Swinford Stourbridge *Worc* from 96. *6 Gladstone Drive, Wollaston, Stourbridge, W Midlands DY8 3PF* Tel (01384) 372847

OLIVER, Canon Paul Robert. b 41. Lon Univ DipTh65. Tyndale Hall Bris 63. **d** 66 **p** 67. C Virginia Water *Guildf* 66-70; Scripture Union (E Region) 70-74; TV Thetford *Nor* 75-83; V Earlham St Anne from 83; RD Nor S from 94; Hon Can Nor Cathl from 96. *The Vicarage, Bluebell Road, Norwich NR4 7LP* Tel (01603) 52922

OLIVER, Philip Maule. b 38. Birm Univ LLB59. Wells Th Coll 62. **d** 64 **p** 65. C Chesterton *Lich* 64-67; C Tettenhall Wood 67-71; V Milton 71-78; V Ixworth and Bardwell *St E* 78-92; P-in-c Honington w Sapiston and Troston 81-92; TR Blackbourne from 92; RD Ixworth 85-94. *The Vicarage, Ixworth, Bury St Edmunds, Suffolk IP31 2HE* Tel (01359) 30311

OLIVER, Mrs Philippa Mary Olive (Penny). b 30. R Holloway Coll Lon BA52. Cant Sch of Min 89. **d** 92 **p** 95. NSM Eythorne and Elvington w Waldershare etc *Cant* from 92. *34 Milner Road, Elvington, Dover, Kent CT15 4EL* Tel (01304) 831166

OLIVER, Roland John. b 29. Ex Univ TCert54. Lich Th Coll. **d** 59 **p** 60. C Sedgley All SS *Lich* 59-62; V Weston Rhyn 62-77; V Lt Aston 77-94; rtd 94. *1 Perivale Close, Radbrook, Shrewsbury SY3 6DH*

OLIVER, Canon Stephen John. b 48. AKC69. St Aug Coll Cant 70. **d** 71 **p** 72. C Clifton w Glapton *S'well* 71-75; P-in-c Newark Ch Ch 75-79; R Plumtree 79-85; Sen Producer BBC Relig Broadcasting Dept Lon 85-87; Chief Producer 87-91; Perm to Offic *Pet* 87-91; TR Leeds City *Ripon* 91-97; Can Res and Prec St Paul's Cathl *Lon* from 97. *3 Amen Court, London EC4M 7BU* Tel 0171-236 4532

OLIVER, Canon Terence Maule. b 07. Univ Coll Dur BA32. Linc Th Coll 31. **d** 36 **p** 37. C Mansfield St Mark *S'well* 36-37; C-in-c Mansfield St Aidan CD 37-47; CF 47-51; Singapore 51-66; V Shilbottle *Newc* 66-76; rtd 76; Lic to Offic *Newc* from 76; Hon Can Kuala Lumpur from 87. *Restharrow, Longhorsley, Morpeth, Northd NE65 8SY* Tel (01670) 788253

OLIVER, Canon Thomas Gordon. b 48. Nottm Univ BTh72 LTh74 DipAdEd80. St Jo Coll Nottm 68 ALCD72. **d** 72 **p** 73. C Thorpe Edge *Bradf* 72-76; C Woodthorpe *S'well* 76-80; V Huthwaite 80-85; Dir Past Studies St Jo Coll Nottm 85-94; Dir of Tr *Roch* from 94; Hon Can Roch Cathl from 95. *18 King's Avenue, Rochester, Kent ME1 3DS* Tel (01634) 841232 or 830333 Fax 829463

OLIVER, Ms Wendy Louise. b 54. Aston Tr Scheme 93 Oak Hill Th Coll DipHE94. **d** 96 **p** 97. C Walmsley *Man* from 96. *38 Queen's Avenue, Bromley Cross, Bolton, Lancs BL7 9BL* Tel (01204) 303080 Fax as telephone

OLIVEY, Hugh Charles Tony. b 35. St Mich Coll Llan 77. **d** 79 **p** 80. C St Winnow *Truro* 79-81; C Lanhydrock 81-82; C Lostwithiel 81-82; C Lanivet 81-82; P-in-c 82-83; TV Bodmin w Lanhydrock and Lanivet 84-89; P-in-c St Neot 89-90; P-in-c Warleggan 89-90; R St Neot and Warleggan from 90. *The Vicarage, St Neot, Liskeard, Cornwall PL14 6NG* Tel (01579) 20472

OLIVIER, Bertrand Maurice Daniel. b 62. BA84. S'wark Ord Course 93. **d** 96. C Walworth St Jo *S'wark* from 96. *16 Larcom Street, London SE17 1NQ* Tel 0171-703 1043 or 703 4375

OLLIER, Canon Timothy John Douglas. b 44. Trin Hall Cam BA66 MA69. Cuddesdon Coll 66. **d** 68 **p** 69. C Silksworth *Dur* 68-71; C St Marylebone w H Trin *Lon* 71-74; C Winlaton *Dur* 74-77; V Bishopton w Gt Stainton 77-88; R Redmarshall 77-88; P-in-c Grindon and Stillington 83-88; RD Barnard Castle from 88; V Gainford from 88; R Winston from 88; Hon Can Dur Cathl from 94. *The Vicarage, Gainford, Darlington, Co Durham DL2 3DS* Tel (01325) 730261

OLLIFF, Rowland. b 61. Coll of Resurr Mirfield CPS95. **d** 95 **p** 96. C Bickleigh (Roborough) and Shaugh Prior *Ex* from 95. *47 The Heathers, Roborough, Plymouth PL6 7QS* Tel (01752) 777168

O'LOUGHLIN, Gordon Raymond. b 32. Linc Coll Ox BA56 MA60. Wells Th Coll 56. **d** 58 **p** 59. C Bournemouth St Fran *Win* 58-62; C Tunbridge Wells St Barn *Roch* 62-65; Chapl Roch Th Coll 65-67; Sub-Warden 67-69; V Kingston upon Hull St Alb *York* 69-78; Dir of Post-Ord Tr 77-82; Can and Preb York Minster 78-81; TV York All SS Pavement w St Crux and St Martin etc 78-82; V Bromley St Andr *Roch* 82-87; P-in-c Brighton St Paul *Chich* 87-94; V from 94. *St Paul's Parsonage, 9 Russell Place, Brighton BN1 2RG* Tel (01273) 739639

O'LOUGHLIN, Dr Michael Wilfred Bryan. b 23. Ch Coll Cam BA47 MA58 PhD64. **d** 81 **p** 82. NSM Linton *Ely* from 81; Chapl Addenbrooke's Hosp Cam 84-88; NSM Shudy Camps 84-96; NSM Castle Camps 84-96; Chmn Dioc Bd Soc Resp from 88. *Ditches Close, 42 The Grip, Linton, Cambridge CB1 6NR* Tel (01223) 891357

OLSEN, Arthur Barry. b 37. Univ of NZ BA61. Melbourne Coll of Div BD73 ACT ThL64. **d** 64 **p** 64. New Zealand 64-81; C Hersham *Guildf* 81-84; P-in-c Botleys and Lyne 84-95; V from 95; P-in-c Long Cross 84-95; V from 95. *The Vicarage, Lyne Lane, Lyne, Chertsey, Surrey KT16 0AJ* Tel (01932) 874405

OLUKANMI, Miss Stella Grace Oluwafunmilayo Olanrewaju. b 57. St Jo Coll Nottm BTh95 LTh92. **d** 96 **p** 97. C Gt Ilford St Jo *Chelmsf* from 96. *73 Ladysmith Avenue, Newbury Park, Essex IG2 7AX*

OLUMIDE, Oluseye Abiola Abisogun Okikiade ('Seye). b 42. Westhill Coll Birm CertCEd66 Bradf Univ BA89 MSc92. Clifton Th Coll 68. **d** 71 **p** 72. C Halliwell St Pet *Man* 71-72; C Collyhurst St Oswald and St Cath 71; C Salford St Phil w St Steph 72; P-in-c Wood Green St Mich *Lon* 73; C Stanmer w Falmer and Moulsecoomb *Chich* 73-76; C Hulme Ascension *Man* 76-77; Chapl Asst N Man Gen Hosp 77-80; Chapl St Bernard's Hosp Southall 80-86; Chapl Bradf R Infirmary 86-96; Chapl Lynfield Mt Hosp Bradf 86-96; Chapl St Luke's Hosp Bradf 86-96; Chapl Parkside Community NHS Trust Lon from 96. *Chaplain's Office, St Charles Community Hospital, Exmoor Street, London W10 6DZ* Tel 0181-962 4370, 969 2488 or 743 3951 Mobile 0468-753874

OLYOTT, The Ven Leonard Eric (Len). b 26. Lon Univ BA50. Westcott Ho Cam 50. **d** 52 **p** 53. C Camberwell St Geo *S'wark* 52-55; C Hatfield *St Alb* 55-60; V Chipperfield St Paul 60-68; V Crewkerne *B & W* 68-71; R Crewkerne w Wayford 71-77; RD Crewkerne 72-77; Preb Wells Cathl 76-92; Adn Taunton 77-92; rtd 92; Perm to Offic *B & W* from 92. *5 Greendale, Ilminster, Somerset TA19 0EB* Tel (01460) 55062

O'MALLEY, Brian Denis Brendan. b 40. Oscott Coll (RC) Coll of Resurr Mirfield 82. **d** 77 **p** 83. In RC Ch 77-81; Warden St Greg Retreat Rhandirmwyn *St D* 81-82; Lic to Offic 82-83; Chapl and Min Can St D Cathl 83-85; V Wiston w Ambleston, St Dogwells, Walton E etc 85-89; V Wiston w Clarbeston and Walton E 89; R Walton W w Talbenny and Haroldston W from 89. *All Saints' Rectory, Walton West, Haverfordwest SA62 3UB* Tel (01437) 781279

OMAN, Brian Malcolm. b 14. Qu Coll Cam BA36 MA46. Chich Th Coll 36. **d** 37 **p** 38. C Gorton Our Lady and St Thos *Man* 37-40; OGS from 39; Perm to Offic *Ox* 40-42; Chapl St Mary's Abbey W Malling 42-46; C Tunbridge Wells St Barn *Roch* 46-55; V Cardiff St Mary *Llan* 55-62; R Greenford H Cross *Lon* 62-74; V Kings Sutton *Pet* 74-88; rtd 88; Perm to Offic *Pet* from 88. *The Old Post Office, Church Street, Sulgrave, Banbury, Oxon OX17 2RP* Tel (01295) 768317

O'NEILL, Christopher John. b 53. ALAM LGSM MSAPP Worc Coll Ox BA75 MA80 CertEd91 CCouns91 DipTHPsych91. Ripon Coll Cuddesdon 77. **d** 78 **p** 79. Asst Chapl Rugby Sch 78-80; Chapl Charterhouse Godalming from 81. *14 Chapelfields, Charterhouse Road, Godalming, Surrey GU7 2BF* Tel (01483) 414437

O'NEILL, Edward Daniel (Eddie). b 42. Man Univ BA62 Bradf Univ MSc76. N Ord Course 89. **d** 92 **p** 93. NSM Prenton *Ches* from 92. *Holmhurst, 24 Column Road, West Kirby, Wirral, Merseyside L48 8AX* Tel 0161-625 7704

O'NEILL, Canon Gary. b 57. K Coll Lon BD79 AKC79. Westcott Ho Cam 80. **d** 81 **p** 82. C Oldham *Man* 81-84; C Birch w Fallowfield 84-87; R Moston St Chad 87-97; Can Res Birm Cathl *Birm* from 97. *119 Selly Park Road, Birmingham B29 7HY* Tel 0121-472 0146

O'NEILL, Irene. *See* CARTER, Mrs Irene

ONIONS, Martin Giles. b 63. TC. Chich Th Coll 85. **d** 88 **p** 89. C Eastbourne St Mary *Chich* 88-91; C-in-c The Hydneye CD 91-96; V The Hydneye from 96. *St Peter's House, The Hydneye, Eastbourne, E Sussex BN22 9BY* Tel (01323) 504392

ONSLOW, Sister Denzil Octavia. b 19. CertRK58. **dss** 61 **d** 87 **p** 94. CSA from 56; Novice Guardian 68-73 and 90-94; R Foundn of St Kath in Ratcliffe 73-79; Notting Hill St Jo and St Pet *Lon* 80-87; Hon Par Dn 87-94; Hon C from 94; rtd 96. *St Andrew's House, 2 Tavistock Road, London W11 1BA* Tel 0171-229 2662

ONUNWA, The Ven Udobata Rufus. b 47. Nigeria Univ BA78 MA81 PhD85. Trin Coll Nigeria DipTh74. **d** 74 **p** 75. Nigeria 74-96; Perm to Offic *Birm* from 96. *14 Bowood End, New Hall, Sutton Coldfield, W Midlands B76 1LU* Tel 0121-311 1542

ORAM, Canon Geoffrey William James. b 14. Em Coll Cam BA37 MA40. Ridley Hall Cam 36. **d** 38 **p** 39. C Tooting Graveney St Nic *S'wark* 38-40; C Rugby St Andr *Cov* 40-41; V Ipswich St Thos *St E* 41-49; R E Bergholt 49-64; Bp's Chapl 54-67; Hon Can St E Cathl 59-80; RD Samford 59-64; V Aldeburgh w Hazlewood 64-80; rtd 80; Perm to Offic *St E* 80-81 and from 86; P-in-c Ipswich St Mich 81-86. *Pantiles, Spring Meadow, Hillfarm Road, Playford, Ipswich IP6 9ED* Tel (01473) 622566

ORAM, John Ernest Donald. b 34. Open Univ BA74. Tyndale Hall Bris. **d** 61 **p** 62. C Cheetham Hill *Man* 61-64; C Gt Baddow *Chelmsf* 64-67; V Blackb St Barn *Blackb* 67-72; Bp's Chapl for Soc Resp *Sheff* 72-86; Chapl Psychotherapist 79-86; Perm to Offic from 86. *12 Montgomery Road, Sheffield S7 1LQ* Tel 0114-258 2332 or 268 2883

✠ORAM, The Rt Revd Kenneth Cyril. b 19. Lon Univ BA39 AKC41. Linc Th Coll 42. **d** 42 **p** 43 **c** 74. C Cranbrook *Cant* 42-45; S Africa 46-87; Adn Bechuanaland 53-60; Dean Kimberley 60-64; Dean and Adn Grahamstown 64-74; Bp 74-87; Asst Bp Lich from 87; rtd 93. *10 Sandringham Road, Stafford ST17 0AA* Tel (01785) 53974

ORAM, Roland Martin David. b 45. ARCM70 Trin Coll Cam BA68. Cranmer Hall Dur DipTh78. **d** 78 **p** 79. C Aspley *S'well* 78-81; Chapl Alleyn's Sch Dulwich 81-88; Chapl Versailles w Grandchamp and Chevry *Eur* 88-92; Chapl Denstone Coll Uttoxeter from 92. *Denstone College, Uttoxeter, Staffs ST14 5HN* Tel (01889) 590484 or 590372 Fax 591295

ORAM, Stephen John. b 58. **d** 84 **p** 85. C Kidderminster St Jo *Worc* 84-88; Chapl RAF 88-92; P-in-c Brislington St Anne *Bris* 92-97; V Cricklade w Latton from 97. *3 Ockwells, Cricklade, Wilts SN6 6ED* Tel (01793) 750300

ORCHARD, Canon George Richard. b 41. Ex Coll Ox BA62 BA64 MA66. Ripon Hall Ox 62. **d** 65 **p** 66. C Greenhill St Pet *Derby* 65-70; Member Ecum Team Min Sinfin Moor 70-78; V Sinfin Moor 76-78; TR Dronfield 78-86; Can Res Derby Cathl 86-92; Hon Can Derby Cathl from 92; P-in-c Baslow 92-93; P-in-c Curbar and Stoney Middleton 92-93; V Baslow w Curbar and Stoney Middleton from 93. *The Vicarage, Curbar Lane, Calver, Sheffield S30 1YF* Tel (01433) 630387

ORCHARD, Harry Frank. b 23. Roch Th Coll. **d** 63 **p** 64. C Sturminster Newton *Sarum* 63-65; Argentina 65-67; V Preston *Sarum* 67-71; R Teffont Evias and Teffont Magna 71-73; V Dinton 71-73; C Fovant w Compton Chamberlayne etc 76-78; Lic to Offic 78-80 and from 82; RD Chalke 80-82; rtd 88. *Flat 7 Harnleigh Green, 80 Harnham Road, Salisbury SP2 8JN* Tel (01722) 324912

ORCHARD, Nigel John. b 56. CertEd78. St Steph Ho Ox 82. **d** 85 **p** 86. C Tottenham St Paul *Lon* 85-89; C Is of Dogs Ch Ch and St Jo w St Luke 89-90; TV 90-92; P-in-c Southall Ch Redeemer from 92. *Christ The Redeemer Vicarage, 299 Allenby Road, Southall, Middx UB1 2HE* Tel 0181-578 2711

ORCHARD, Mrs Tryphena Jane. b 35. Westf Coll Lon BA57. S'wark Ord Course 87. **d** 92 **p** 94. NSM Shaston *Sarum* from 92. *Old Cann Rectory, Salisbury Road, Shaftesbury, Dorset SP7 8ER* Tel (01747) 855228 Fax as telephone

ORCHIN, Robert Andrew. b 71. K Coll Lon BD92. Ripon Coll Cuddesdon DipMin95. **d** 95 **p** 96. C Leigh Park *Portsm* from 95; C Warren Park St Clare from 96. *13 Riders Lane, Havant, Hants PO9 4QS* Tel (01705) 475746

O'REILLY, Clare Maria. *See* KING, Clare Maria

O'REILLY, Ms Eileen Catherine. b 47. TCD BTh95. **d** 96 **p** 97. C Annagh w Drumgoon, Ashfield etc *K, E & A* from 96. *The Rectory, Cootehill, Co Cavan, Irish Republic* Tel Cavan (49) 52004 Fax 56321 E-mail priest@iol.ie

O'REILLY, Philip Jonathon. b 66. ARICS Portsm Poly BSc87 Kent Univ MA97. Westcott Ho Cam CTMin93. **d** 93 **p** 94. C Selsdon St Jo w St Fran *S'wark* 93-96; TV Staveley and Barrow Hill *Derby* from 96. *The Vicarage, 30 Cedar Street, Hollingwood, Chesterfield, Derbyshire S43 2LE* Tel (01246) 472175

ORFORD, Barry Antony. b 49. St Steph Ho Ox 71. **d** 73 **p** 74. C Monmouth *Mon* 73-77; V Choral St As Cathl *St As* 77-81; C St As and Tremeirchion 77-81; CR from 83. *House of the Resurrection, Mirfield, W Yorkshire WF14 0BN* Tel (01924) 494318

ORFORD, Keith John. b 40. FCIT. EMMTC 76. **d** 79 **p** 80. NSM Matlock Bank *Derby* from 79. *27 Lums Hill Rise, Matlock, Derbyshire DE4 3FX* Tel (01629) 55349

ORLAND, Canon Ernest George. b 28. Lich Th Coll 61. **d** 62 **p** 63. C Northampton St Mich *Pet* 62-65; R Gayton w Tiffield 65-69; R Corby SS Pet and Andr 69-72; TR Corby SS Pet and Andr w Gt and Lt Oakley 72-81; RD Corby 79-81; Can Pet Cathl 79-93; V Pet All SS 81-93; rtd 93; Perm to Offic *Pet* from 93; Perm to Offic *Linc* from 95. *43 Godsey Lane, Market Deeping, Peterborough PE6 8HY* Tel (01778) 380724

ORME, John. b 29. Sarum Th Coll 58. **d** 60 **p** 61. C Heald Green St Cath *Ches* 60-64; C Ellesmere Port 64-67; Chapl Harperbury Hosp Radlett 67-73; P-in-c Luton All SS w St Pet *St Alb* 73-79; V 79-87; V Oxhey St Matt 87-96; rtd 97. *1 Alzey Gardens, Harpenden, Herts AL5 5SZ* Tel (01582) 761931

ORME, Stewart. b 22. Leeds Univ BA49 Open Univ BA75. St Steph Ho Ox 50. **d** 52 **p** 53. C Leatherhead *Guildf* 52-57; C-in-c Lightwater CD 57-59; R Albury w St Martha 59-87; rtd 87. *The Spinney, Hawksfold Lane, Fernhurst, Haslemere, Surrey GU27 3NT* Tel (01428) 654789

ORME, Sydney. b 27. Oak Hill Th Coll 54. **d** 58 **p** 59. C Halliwell St Pet *Man* 58-61; V Friarmere 61-73; V Knypersley *Lich* 73-92; rtd 92; Perm to Offic *Ches* from 92. *10 Elworth Road, Sandbach, Cheshire CW11 9HQ* Tel (01270) 759233

ORMEROD, Henry Lawrence. b 35. Pemb Coll Cam BA58 MA63. Qu Coll Birm DipTh59. **d** 60 **p** 61. C Chigwell *Chelmsf* 60-64; C Thundersley 64-68; C Canvey Is 68-72; V Stanground *Ely* 72-77; TR Stanground and Farcet 77-81; TR Swindon St Jo and St Andr *Bris* 81-90; TR N Wingfield, Clay Cross and Pilsley *Derby* from 90. *The Rectory, St Lawrence Road, North Wingfield, Chesterfield, Derbyshire S42 5HX* Tel (01246) 851181

ORMISTON, Albert Edward. b 26. AMCT46. Oak Hill Th Coll 53. **d** 56 **p** 57. C Worksop St Jo *S'well* 56-58; P-in-c Everton St Polycarp *Liv* 58-59; V 59-63; Org Sec SAMS 63-67; Perm to Offic *Bradf* 63-67; Perm to Offic *Carl* 63-67; Perm to Offic *Ches* 63-67; Perm to Offic *Liv* 63-67; Perm to Offic *Man* 63-67; Lic Preacher *Blackb* 63-67; R Gateacre *Liv* 67-73; V Tonbridge St Steph *Roch* 73-86; V Dent w Cowgill *Bradf* 86-91; rtd 91; Perm to Offic *Ches* from 91. *29 Bollin Drive, Congleton, Cheshire CW12 3RR* Tel (01260) 276828

ORMROD, Paul William. b 57. Liv Univ BA80. Westcott Ho Cam 80. **d** 83 **p** 84. C Prescot *Liv* 83-86; TV Padgate 86-95; V Formby St Pet from 95. *St Peter's Vicarage, Cricket Path, Formby, Liverpool L37 7DP* Tel (01704) 873369

ORMSBY, Diana Clare. b 21. CertEd41. Sarum & Wells Th Coll 77 Gilmore Course 78. **dss** 80 **d** 87 **p** 94. Lydford, Brent Tor, Bridestowe and Sourton *Ex* 80-87; Hon C Lydford and Brent Tor 87-96; Hon C Peter Tavy, Mary Tavy, Lydford and Brent Tor from 96. *Lipscliffe, Coryton, Okehampton, Devon EX20 4AB* Tel (01822) 860344

ORMSBY, Robert Daly. b 22. CCC Ox BA42 MA48. Sarum & Wells Th Coll 77. **d** 78 **p** 79. Hon C Lydford and Brent Tor *Ex* 78-96; Hon C Peter Tavy, Mary Tavy, Lydford and Brent Tor from 96. *Lipscliffe, Coryton, Okehampton, Devon EX20 4AB* Tel (01822) 860344

ORMSTON, Derek. b 43. Univ of Wales (Lamp) DipTh67. **d** 67 **p** 68. C Ogley Hay *Lich* 67-70; C Tettenhall Regis 70-74; P-in-c Leek All SS 74-79; TV Leek and Meerbrook 79-83; Youth Chapl *Bris* 83-87; R Brinkworth w Dauntsey from 87; Chapl New Coll Swindon from 87. *The Rectory, Brinkworth, Chippenham, Wilts SN15 5AS* Tel (01666) 510207

ORMSTON, Richard Jeremy. b 61. Southlands Coll Lon BA83. Oak Hill Th Coll BA87. **d** 87 **p** 88. C Rodbourne Cheney *Bris* 87-91; R Collingtree w Courteenhall and Milton Malsor *Pet* from 91; RD Wootton from 96. *The Rectory, Barn Corner, Collingtree, Northampton NN4 0NF* Tel (01604) 761895

O'ROURKE, Brian Joseph Gerard. b 58. TCD BA82 HDipEd83. CITC 89. **d** 92 **p** 93. Chapl Glendalough Sch 90-96; C Newcastle w Newtownmountkennedy and Calary *D & G* 92-96; Bp's C from 96. *The Vicarage, Newcastle, Greystones, Co Wicklow, Irish Republic, or Windyridge, 102 Glebemount, Wicklow, Irish Republic* Tel Wicklow (404) 281 9300 or Dublin (1) 281 1596 Fax Dublin (1) 281 1596

ORPIN, Mrs Gillian. b 32. SRN53. Oak Hill Th Coll 82. **d** 87 **p** 95. Par Dn Passenham *Pet* 87-92; rtd 92; NSM Oban St Jo *Arg* 92-95; Dioc Chapl from 95. *Gual Reidh, Taynuilt, Argyll PA35 1JQ* Tel (01866) 822281

ORR, Andrew Dermot Harman. b 66. Sheff Univ BSc89. CITC BTh92. **d** 92 **p** 93. C Ballymacash *Conn* 92-95; I Castlecomer w Colliery Ch, Mothel and Bilbo *C & O* from 95; Dioc Registrar (Ossory, Ferns and Leighlin) from 96. *The Rectory, Castlecomer, Co Kilkenny, or St Canice's Library, Kilkenny, Co Kilkenny, Irish Republic* Tel Kilkenny (56) 41677 or 61910 Fax 41677 or 51813

ORR, David Cecil. b 33. TCD BA56 MA68. **d** 57 **p** 58. C Drumragh *D & R* 57-60; I Convoy 60-70; RD Raphoe 66-70; I Maghera 70-80; I Drumragh w Mountfield 80-84; Dean Derry 84-97; I Templemore 84-97; Miss to Seamen 84-97; rtd 97. *Deanfield Lodge, 33 Deanfield, Londonderry BT47 1HY* Tel (01504) 348183

ORTON, Richard. b 33. Keble Coll Ox BA56 MA60 Leeds Univ. Lich Th Coll 60. **d** 61 **p** 64. C Penistone w Midhope *Wakef* 61-62; Hon C Meltham 62-69; Hon C Horsforth *Ripon* 69-72; C Far Headingley St Chad 72-75; V Hellifield *Bradf* 75-80; RD Bowland 78-80; R Hutton *Chelmsf* 80-87; R Wallasey St Hilary *Ches* from 87; Dioc Ecum Officer from 92; RD Wallasey from 96. *St Hilary's Rectory, Church Hill, Wallasey, Merseyside L45 3NH* Tel 0151-638 4771

OSBORN, Miss Anne. b 40. Reading Univ BA62 MA64 Lon Univ PGCE67. Oak Hill NSM Course 87. **d** 92. Chapl Lon Univ *Lon* 92-94; Chapl Lon Guildhall Univ 94-96; Chapl Univ Westmr 94-95; Assoc Tutor N Thames Minl Tr Course from 97. *8 Beaufort House, Talbot Road, London N15 4DR* Tel 0181-801 0115

OSBORN, David Ronald. b 42. Bris Univ BA66 Leeds Univ CertEd77 Bath Univ MEd80. Clifton Th Coll 62. **d** 66 **p** 67. C Farndon *S'well* 66-69; P-in-c W Bridgford 69-72; Asst Dioc Dir Educn *Carl* 72-77; P-in-c Kirkandrews-on-Eden w Beaumont and Grinsdale 72-77; Hd RE and Chapl Dauntsey's Sch Devizes 77-83; USA 83; V Southbroom *Sarum* 83-86; Consultant to Lay Tr Schemes *Ox* 86; Hd RE Bexhill High Sch 86-90; TV Langtree 93-95; TR from 95. *The Rectory, Checkendon, Reading RG8 0QS* Tel (01491) 680252 Fax 682191

OSBORN, David Thomas. b 58. PGCE80 K Coll Lon BD79 AKC79. Linc Th Coll 82. **d** 83 **p** 84. C Bearsted w Thurnham *Cant* 83-86; Chapl RAF 86-90; R Bassingham *Linc* 90-91; V Aubourn w Haddington 90-91; V Carlton-le-Moorland w Stapleford 90-91; R Thurlby w Norton Disney 90-91; Chapl RAF from 91. *Chaplaincy Services (RAF), HQ, Personnel and Training Command, RAF Innsworth, Gloucester GL3 1EZ* Tel (01452) 712612 ext 5164 Fax 510828

OSBORN, Mrs Diana Marian. b 52. R Holloway Coll Lon BSc74 Birm Univ PGCE75. NE Ord Course 81. **dss** 84 **d** 87 **p** 94. Malden St Jo *S'wark* 84-89; Par Dn 87-89; Par Dn Brampton *Ely* 89-92; Par Dn Richmond H Trin and Ch Ch *S'wark* 92-93; Chapl Ridley Hall Cam 94-96; C Milton *Ely* 95-96; Chapl Milton Children's Hospice from 96. *30 Chestnut Close, Brampton, Huntingdon, Cambs PE18 8TP* Tel (01480) 411389

OSBORN, Preb John Geoffrey Rowland. b 33. Jes Coll Cam BA55 MA59. Wells Th Coll 63. **d** 65 **p** 66. C Easthampstead *Ox* 65-68; Lic to Offic *Blackb* 68-70; Brunei 70-75; Asst Dir RE *Blackb* 75-77; V Tockholes 75-77; Dir RE *B & W* 77-83; Dir and Sec Lon Dioc Bd for Schs *Lon* 83-95; Preb St Paul's Cathl 86-95; rtd 96. *4 Musson Close, Abingdon, Oxon OX14 5RE* Tel (01235) 528701

OSBORN, Maurice. b 25. Univ of Wales BA50. Wycliffe Hall Ox 55. **d** 55 **p** 56. C E Wickham *S'wark* 55-57; Chapl Dauntsey's Sch Devizes 57-72; Asst Master 58-78; P-in-c Bishop's Lavington *Sarum* 79-83; P-in-c Lt Cheverell 82-83; P-in-c W Lavington and the Cheverells 83-90; rtd 90. *Greensand Cottage, West Lavington, Devizes, Wilts SN10 4LB* Tel (01380) 813244

OSBORN, Peter George. b 14. Sydney Univ BA35. Cuddesdon Coll 61. **d** 63 **p** 64. C Forton *Portsm* 63-66; Australia 66-68 and from 75; Chapl Abingdon Sch 68-73; P-in-c Hawley H Trin *Guildf* 74-75; rtd 79. *Unit 8, 33 Buxton Street, North Adelaide, Australia 5006* Tel Adelaide (8) 239 0959

OSBORNE, Alexander Deas. b 34. Liv Univ BSc54 PhD57. Oak Hill NSM Course 78. **d** 81 **p** 82. NSM Redbourn *St Alb* from 81. *19 Rickyard Meadow, Redbourn, St Albans, Herts AL3 7HT* Tel (01582) 793749

OSBORNE, Canon Anthony Russell. b 47. Sarum & Wells Th Coll 77. **d** 79 **p** 80. C Heref St Martin *Heref* 79-81; TV 82-86; TV Hanley H Ev *Lich* 86-92; Dioc Soc Resp Officer *Heref* from 92; Can Heref Cathl from 92. *1 Carter Grove, Hereford HR1 1NT* Tel (01432) 265465 or 355248

OSBORNE, Arthur Frederick. b 09. K Coll Lon BD44 AKC44. K Coll Lon 28. **d** 33 **p** 34. C Beaconsfield *Ox* 33-35; C Tottenham St Benet Fink *Lon* 35-36; C E Barnet *St Alb* 36-38; V Lindsell *Chelmsf* 38-44; V Barnet Vale St Mark *St Alb* 44-51; RD Barnet 48-51; Sen Lect and Chapl Sarum Dioc Tr Coll 51-56; V Bradford-on-Avon *Sarum* 56-65; Chapl and Prin Lect Kirkby Fields Coll of Educn 65-72; Chapl Northn Coll of Educn 72-75; rtd 75. *1 Braham Court, 11 Nuns Close, Hitchin, Herts SG5 1EP* Tel (01462) 433976

OSBORNE, Canon Brian Charles. b 38. St Andr Univ MA61 Lon Univ DipTh80. Clifton Th Coll 61. **d** 63 **p** 64. C Skirbeck H Trin *Linc* 63-68; V from 80; P-in-c New Clee 68-71; V 71-75; V Derby St Aug *Derby* 75-80; Chapl Pilgrim Hosp Boston 84-88; RD Holland E *Linc* 85-95; Can and Preb Linc Cathl from 92; Chapl to The Queen from 97. *Holy Trinity Vicarage, 64 Spilsby Road, Boston, Lincs PE21 9NS* Tel (01205) 363657

OSBORNE, Christopher Hazell (Chris). b 60. Aston Tr Scheme 89 Sarum & Wells Th Coll DCM93. **d** 93 **p** 94. C Paignton St Jo *Ex* 93-96; C Hooe 96-97; TV Plymstock and Hooe from 97. *The Vicarage, St Johns Drive, Plymouth PL9 9SD* Tel (01752) 403076

OSBORNE, David Champernowne. b 61. Coll of Resurr Mirfield 90. **d** 93 **p** 94. C W Leigh *Portsm* 93-96; TV Malvern Link w Cowleigh *Worc* from 96. *165 Leigh Sinton Road, Malvern, Worcs WR14 1LB* Tel (01886) 832463

OSBORNE, David Robert. b 50. Birm Univ BSc71 MEd86 Nottm Univ DipTh72 Bris Univ PGCE73. St Jo Coll Dur 78. **d** 80 **p** 81. C Penkridge w Stretton *Lich* 80-85; R Longdon-upon-Tern, Rodington, Uppington etc 85-94; R Pilton w Croscombe, N Wootton and Dinder *B & W* from 94. *The Rectory, High Meadows, Pilton, Shepton Mallet, Somerset BA4 4DX* Tel (01225) 317535

OSBORNE, David Victor. b 36. Dur Univ BA59. Cranmer Hall Dur DipTh62. **d** 62 **p** 63. C Kennington Cross St Anselm *S'wark* 62-66; C Sandal St Helen *Wakef* 66-67; R Ancoats *Man* 67-73; V Claremont H Angels 73-80; R Breedon cum Isley Walton and Worthington *Leic* 80-87; V Beaumont Leys 87-92; V Billesdon and Skeffington from 92. *The Vicarage, Gaulby Road, Billesdon, Leicester LE7 9AG* Tel (0116) 259 6321

OSBORNE, Derek James. b 32. Tyndale Hall Bris 53. **d** 57 **p** 58. C Weymouth St Mary *Sarum* 57-60; C Southgate *Chich* 60-63; V Croydon Ch Ch Broad Green *Cant* 63-71; V Cromer *Nor* 71-83; P-in-c Gresham w Bessingham 71-83; Hon Can Nor Cathl 77-83; V Northwood Em *Lon* 83-94; Chapl Lee Abbey 94-97; rtd 97. *Lee Abbey, Lynton, Devon EX35 6JJ* Tel (01598) 752621 Fax 752619

OSBORNE, Graham Daking. b 51. City Univ ACII74 FCII77. Cuddesdon Coll 94. **d** 96 **p** 97. C Cirencester *Glouc* from 96. *54 Alexander Drive, Cirencester, Glos GL7 1UH* Tel (01285) 643231

OSBORNE, Hayward John. b 48. New Coll Ox BA70 MA73. Westcott Ho Cam 71. **d** 73 **p** 74. C Bromley SS Pet and Paul *Roch* 73-77; C Halesowen *Worc* 77-80; TV 80-83; TR Worc St Barn w Ch Ch 83-88; V Moseley St Mary *Birm* from 88; RD Moseley from 94. *St Mary's Vicarage, 18 Oxford Road, Birmingham B13 9EH* Tel 0121-449 1459 or 449 2243

OSBORNE, Jonathan Lloyd. b 62. Ripon Coll Cuddesdon 95. **d** 97. C Mill End and Heronsgate w W Hyde *St Alb* from 97. *St Thomas House, 46 Chalfont Road, Rickmansworth, Herts WD3 2TB* Tel (01923) 771022

OSBORNE, Canon June. b 53. Man Univ BA74. St Jo Coll Nottm. **dss** 80 **d** 87 **p** 94. Birm St Martin *Birm* 80-84; Old Ford St Paul and St Mark *Lon* 84-95; Par Dn Old Ford St Paul w St Steph and St Mark 87-94; P-in-c Old Ford St Paul and St Mark 94-95; Can Res and Treas Sarum Cathl *Sarum* from 95; Bp's Dom Chapl from 95. *Loders, 23 The Close, Salisbury SP1 2EH* Tel (01722) 322172

OSBORNE, Malcolm Eric (Max). b 64. EN(G)87 RMN92. St Jo Coll Nottm 94. **d** 96 **p** 97. C Walton *St E* from 96. *27 Treetops, Felixstowe, Suffolk IP11 9ER* Tel (01394) 282654

OSBORNE, Mark William. b 67. Univ of Wales BA89. Coll of Resurr Mirfield CPT94. **d** 94 **p** 95. C Goldthorpe w Hickleton *Sheff* from 94. *Church House, West Street, Goldthorpe, Rotherham, S Yorkshire S63 9JU* Tel (01709) 881468

OSBORNE, Ralph. b 38. Kent Univ DipTh80. Bernard Gilpin Soc Dur 62 Clifton Th Coll 63. **d** 66 **p** 67. C Harpurhey Ch Ch *Man* 66-68; C Chorlton on Medlock St Sav 68-71; C Wilmington *Roch* 71-74; V St Mary Cray and St Paul's Cray 74-85; P-in-c Bath St Steph *B & W* 85-88; P-in-c Charlcombe 86-88; R Charlcombe w Bath St Steph from 88. *St Stephen's Rectory, Richmond Place, Lansdown, Bath BA1 5PZ* Tel (01225) 317535

OSBORNE, Canon Robin Orbell. b 29. Leeds Univ BA54. Coll of Resurr Mirfield 52. **d** 54 **p** 55. C Wellingborough All Hallows *Pet* 54-58; C Oxhey St Matt *St Alb* 60-61; V Woburn 61-65; V Battlesden and Pottesgrove 61-65; V Cheshunt 65-82; RD Cheshunt 70-81; Hon Can St Alb 76-82; V Penzance St Mary w St Paul *Truro* 82-88; Can Res and Treas Truro Cathl 88-94; Perm to Offic *B & W* from 94; rtd 94. *7 The Judge's Lodgings, 19 New Street, Wells, Somerset BA5 2LD* Tel (01749) 672326

OSBOURNE, David John. b 56. Linc Th Coll 78. **d** 79 **p** 80. C Houghton le Spring *Dur* 79-82; C Spalding St Jo *Linc* 82-83; C Spalding St Jo w Deeping St Nicholas 83-84; V Swineshead 84-94; RD Holland W 86-92; P-in-c Boultham from 94. *The Rectory, 2A St Helen's Avenue, Lincoln LN6 7RA* Tel (01522) 682026

OSBOURNE, Steven John. b 59. St Jo Coll Nottm 92. **d** 94 **p** 95. C Bushbury *Lich* from 94. *11 Wistwood Hayes, Wolverhampton WV10 8QU* Tel (01902) 784907

OSGERBY, Dr John Martin. b 34. Sheff Univ BSc56 PhD59. Linc Th Coll 75. **d** 77 **p** 78. C Rotherham *Sheff* 77-80; C-in-c W Bessacarr CD 80-84; V W Bessacarr 84-87; Warden of Readers from 86; R Fishlake w Sykehouse, Kirk Bramwith, Fenwick etc from 87; RD Snaith and Hatfield from 93. *The Vicarage, Fishlake, Doncaster, S Yorkshire DN7 5JW* Tel (01302) 841396

OSGOOD, Graham Dean. b 39. Lon Univ BSc62. ALCD71 St Jo Coll Nottm 71. **d** 71 **p** 72. C Bebington *Ches* 71-76; V Gee Cross from 76. *The Vicarage, Higham Lane, Hyde, Cheshire SK14 5LX* Tel 0161-368 2337

OSGOOD, Sylvia Joy. **d** 97. NSM Bredbury St Mark *Ches* from 97. *The Vicarage, 16 Higham Lane, Hyde, Cheshire SK14 5LX* Tel 0161-368 2337

OSMAN, David Thomas. b 49. Bradf Univ BTech72. Trin Coll Bris 75. **d** 78 **p** 79. C Stranton *Dur* 78-81; C Denton Holme *Carl* 81-84; V Preston on Tees *Dur* from 84. *The Vicarage, Quarry Road, Eaglescliffe, Stockton-on-Tees, Cleveland TS16 9BD* Tel (01642) 780516

OSMAN, Ernest. b 35. St Aid Birkenhead 61. **d** 64 **p** 65. C Heaton Ch Ch *Man* 64-68; V Farnworth St Pet 68-77; V St Martin's *Lich* 77-85; V Endon w Stanley from 85. *The Vicarage, Leek Road, Endon, Stoke-on-Trent ST9 9BH* Tel (01782) 502166

OSMAN, Stephen William. b 53. Matlock Coll of Educn CertEd74 Teesside Poly CQSW80. St Jo Coll Dur 88. **d** 90 **p** 91. C Newbarns w Hawcoat *Carl* 90-93; TV Marfleet *York* from 93. *St Phillip's House, 107 Amethyst Road, Hull HU9 4JG* Tel (01482) 762087

OSMASTON, Miss Amiel Mary Ellinor. b 51. Ex Univ BA73 St Jo Coll Dur BA84. St Jo Coll Nottm DPS77 Cranmer Hall Dur 82. **dss** 84 **d** 87 **p** 94. Chester le Street *Dur* 84-87; Par Dn 87-88; Dir Miss and Past Studies Ridley Hall Cam 89-96; Field Officer Tr *Ches* from 96. *7 Earlsway, Curzon Park, Chester CH4 8AX* Tel (01244) 679311

OSMOND, David Methuen. b 38. Qu Coll Birm 75. **d** 77 **p** 78. C Yardley St Edburgha *Birm* 77-80; V Withall 80-89; R W Coker w Hardington Mandeville, E Chinnock etc *B & W* 89-95; Perm to Offic from 96. *4 Barrows Court, Weston Street, East Chinnock, Yeovil, Somerset BA22 9EJ* Tel (01935) 864185

OSMOND, Mrs Heather Christine. b 44. ABSM64 ARCM65 Birm Poly CertEd65. Qu Coll Birm 83. **dss** 84 **d** 87. Brandwood *Birm* 84-85; Withall 85-89; Par Dn 87-89; Perm to Offic *B & W* from 89. *4 Barrows Court, Weston Street, Esat Chinnock, Yeovil, Somerset BA22 9EJ* Tel (01935) 864185

OSMOND, Oliver Robert. b 44. Ch Coll Cam BA66 MA70. Cuddesdon Coll 66 Trin Coll Toronto STB69. **d** 69 **p** 70. Canada 69-81; V Mill Hill Jo Keble Ch *Lon* from 81. *John Keble Vicarage, 142 Deans Lane, Edgware, Middx HA8 9NT* Tel 0181-959 1312

OSSORY AND LEIGHLIN, Archdeacon of. *See* MURRAY, The Ven John Grainger

OSSORY, Dean of. *See* LYNAS, The Very Revd Norman Noel

O'SULLIVAN, Mrs Hazel. b 50. S Dios Minl Tr Scheme 91. **d** 94 **p** 95. C Cove St Jo *Guildf* from 94. *1 Mariners Drive, Farnborough, Hants GU14 8DA* Tel (01252) 544127

OSWALD, John Edward Guy. b 39. Qu Coll Cam BA63 MA67. Ridley Hall Cam. **d** 68 **p** 69. C Chippenham St Paul w Langley Burrell *Bris* 68-72; C Hengrove 72-75; P-in-c Hardenhuish 75-79; P-in-c Kington 75-79; TV Chippenham St Paul w Hardenhuish etc 79-82; P-in-c Gt w Lt Somerford and Seagry 82-86; P-in-c Corston w Rodbourne 84-86; R Gt Somerford, Lt Somerford, Seagry, Corston etc from 86. *The Rectory, Frog Lane, Great Somerford, Chippenham, Wilts SN15 5JA* Tel (01249) 720220

OSWALD, Ronald William. b 17. TCD BA38 MA53 BD57 BA59. TCD Div Sch. **d** 55 **p** 56. C Dublin St Geo *D & G* 55-58; C Taunton St Jas *B & W* 58-60; CMJ 60-67; Tunisia 60-67; V Castle Hedingham *Chelmsf* 67-80; R Panfield 80-87; rtd 87; Perm to Offic *B & W* from 87. *1 Abbey Cottages, Galhampton, Yeovil, Somerset BA22 7AQ* Tel (01963) 50623

OSWIN, Frank Anthony (Tony). b 43. Chich Th Coll 69. **d** 71 **p** 72. C Radford *Cov* 71-74; C Shrub End *Chelmsf* 74-76; V Layer-de-la-Haye 76-80; V Eastwood St Dav 80-93; TR Withycombe Raleigh *Ex* from 93. *The Rectory, 74 Withycombe Village Road, Exmouth, Devon EX8 3AE* Tel (01395) 264182

OTTAWAY, Bernard Wyndham. b 15. Keble Coll Ox BA38 MA43. Cuddesdon Coll 38. **d** 39 **p** 40. C Victoria Docks St Luke *Chelmsf* 39-40; C Southend St Alb 40-43; C Upminster 43-47; V Becontree St Pet 47-55; R Loughton St Jo 55-71; R Birdbrook w Sturmer 71-76; P-in-c Ashen w Ridgewell 74-76; R Ridgewell w Ashen, Birdbrook and Sturmer 76-81; P-in-c Farnham 81-85; rtd 85; Perm to Offic *Guildf* 86-89; Perm to Offic *Chelmsf* from 89. *7 Upper Grange Road, Beccles, Suffolk NR34 9NU* Tel (01502) 716721

OTTAWAY, Michael John. b 17. Mert Coll Ox BA40 MA44. Cuddesdon Coll 40. **d** 41 **p** 42. C Leytonstone St Marg *Chelmsf* 41-45; C Kettering SS Pet and Paul *Pet* 45-48; C Kibworth Beauchamp *Leic* 48-49; V Wolvercote *Ox* 49-76; TV Wolvercote w Summertown 76-83; rtd 83; Perm to Offic *Chich* from 84. *3 Lower Drive, Seaford, E Sussex BN25 3AR* Tel (01323) 899179

OTTER, Anthony Frank. b 32. Kelham Th Coll 54. **d** 59 **p** 60. C Bethnal Green St Jo w St Simon *Lon* 59-63; C Aylesbury *Ox* 63-68; V Hanslope w Castlethorpe 68-77; P-in-c N w S Moreton 77-79; P-in-c Aston Tirrold w Aston Upthorpe 77-79; R S w N Moreton, Aston Tirrold and Aston Upthorpe from 79. *The Rectory, South Moreton, Didcot, Oxon OX11 9AF* Tel (01235) 812042

OTTERWELL, Anthony David. b 40. **d** 89 **p** 90. NSM Brighton Resurr *Chich* 89-97; Perm to Offic from 97. *11 Welesmere Road, Rottingdean, Brighton BN2 7DN* Tel (01273) 301339

OTTEWELL, Dr David. b 42. Sheff Univ BSc65 Leic Univ PhD69. N Ord Course 90. **d** 93 **p** 94. NSM Barnby Dun *Sheff* 93-97; P-in-c Finningley w Auckley *S'well* from 97. *The Rectory, Rectory Lane, Finningley, Doncaster, S Yorkshire DN9 3DA* Tel (01302) 770240

OTTEY, Canon John Leonard. b 34. AKC60 Nottm Univ BA70. **d** 61 **p** 62. C Grantham St Wulfram *Linc* 61-64; R Keyworth *S'well* 70-85; P-in-c Stanton-on-the-Wolds 71-85; P-in-c E Retford 85-87; V from 87; P-in-c W Retford 85-87; R from 87; Hon Can S'well Minster from 93. *The Rectory, Rectory Road, Retford, Notts DN22 7AY* Tel (01777) 703116

OTTLEY, David Ronald. b 57. Lanc Univ BA78. Sarum & Wells Th Coll 79. **d** 81 **p** 82. C Urmston *Man* 81-85; Lect Bolton St Pet 85-87; P-in-c Halliwell St Thos 87-88; V Bolton St Thos from 88. *St Thomas's Vicarage, Cloister Street, Bolton BL1 3HA* Tel (01204) 841731

OTTLEY, Ronald. b 28. St Deiniol's Hawarden 81. **d** 83 **p** 84. Hon C Prestbury *Ches* from 83. *The Beeches, 4 Salisbury Place, Tytherington, Macclesfield, Cheshire SK10 2HP* Tel (01625) 432649

OTTO, Francis James Reeve. b 42. New Coll Ox BA64 BA68 Ex Univ 82. St Steph Ho Ox 66 Wells Th Coll 68. **d** 69 **p** 70. C St Stephen by Saltash *Truro* 69-72; C Newquay 72-73; V Lanteglos by Fowey 73-79; V St Goran w St Mich Caerhays 79-82; Chapl St Mary's Hall Brighton 82-88; Chapl Reading Sch 88-90; Teacher The Abbey Sch Reading 91-93; Chapl Lic Victuallers' Sch Ascot 93-94; Lic to Offic *Ox* 89-95; C Boyne Hill 95; P-in-c Cocking, Bepton and W Lavington *Chich* from 95. *The Rectory, Mill Lane, Cocking, Midhurst, W Sussex GU29 0HJ* Tel (01730) 817340

OTTOSSON, Krister Alexander. b 39. Lon Univ BSc61. Wycliffe Hall Ox 62 Ch Div Sch of the Pacific (USA) MDiv65. **d** 65 **p** 66. C Chester le Street *Dur* 65-68; NW Area Sec Chr Educn Movement 68-71; Educn Sec BCC 71-76; Adv in Lay Tr *Dur* 76-81; Adult Educn Officer Gen Syn Bd of Educn 81-82; City Cen Chapl *Newc* from 82; Perm to Offic *Dur* from 82. *71 Longdean Park, Chester le Street, Co Durham DH3 4DG* Tel 0191-388 9622

OUGH, John Christopher. b 51. Lon Univ CertEd Open Univ BA. SW Minl Tr Course 91. **d** 94 **p** 95. C Plymouth Em, St Paul Efford and St Aug *Ex* from 94. *27 Efford Crescent, Plymouth PL3 6NH* Tel (01752) 786250

OULD, Julian Charles. b 57. MHCIMA77. Coll of Resurr Mirfield 80. **d** 83 **p** 84. C Hebburn St Cuth *Dur* 83-86; C Pet H Spirit Bretton *Pet* 86-90; R Peakirk w Glinton 90-95; R Peakirk w Glinton and Northborough 95-96; TR Is of Scilly *Truro* from 96. *The Chaplaincy, Church Road, St Mary's, Isles of Scilly TR21 0NA* Tel (01720) 423128

OULESS, John Michael. b 22. AKC49. Ridley Hall Cam 49. **d** 50 **p** 51. C Dallington *Pet* 50-55; C Evesham *Worc* 55-56; R Halewood *Liv* 56-62; V Southwick w Glapthorn *Pet* 62-71; Chapl Glapthorn Road Hosp Oundle 63-71; R Cogenhoe *Pet* 71-89; R Whiston 71-89; rtd 89. *2 Clos du Roncherez, St Brelade, Jersey, Channel Islands JE3 8FG* Tel (01534) 44916

OUTEN (née BAILEY), Mrs Joyce Mary Josephine. b 33. St Gabr Coll Lon CertEd69 DipRS83. S'wark Ord Course 80. **dss** 83 **d** 87 **p** 94. Par Dn Woolwich St Mary w St Mich *S'wark* 87-89; Par Dn Rusthall *Roch* 89-94; C 94-97; rtd 97. *10 Foxgrove Road, Whitstable, Kent CT5 1PB* Tel (01227) 273643

OUTHWAITE, Stephen Anthony (Tony). b 35. Wells Th Coll 62. **d** 64 **p** 65. C Bitterne Park *Win* 64-67; C-in-c N Tadley CD 67-71; R Milton 71-93; RD Christchurch 82-90; V Win St Cross w St Faith from 93; Master St Cross Hosp from 93. *The Master's Lodge, St Cross Hospital, Winchester, Hants SO23 9SD* Tel (01962) 852888

OUTRAM, David Michael. b 42. Univ of Wales (Ban) BA77 BD79. Coll of Resurr Mirfield 79. **d** 80 **p** 81. C Llandegfan and Beaumaris w Llanfaes w Penmon etc *Ban* 80-82; Chapl Prebendal Sch Chich 82-86; PV Chich Cathl *Chich* 82-86; Asst Chapl Wellington Coll Berks 86-89; Hd Div from 87; Chapl from 89. *7 Chaucer Road, Wellington Chase, Crowthorne, Berks RG45 7QN* Tel (01344) 778373 or 772262

OVENDEN, John Anthony. b 45. Open Univ BA80 BA93 K Coll Lon MA96. Sarum & Wells Th Coll 71. **d** 74 **p** 75. C Handsworth *Sheff* 74-77; C Isfield *Chich* 77-80; C Uckfield 77-80; P-in-c Stuntney *Ely* 80-85; Min Can, Prec and Sacr Ely Cathl 80-85; V Primrose Hill St Mary w Avenue Road St Paul *Lon* from 85; Dir English Hymnal Co from 93. *St Mary's Vicarage, 44 King Henry's Road, London NW3 3RP* Tel 0171-722 3062 or 722 3238

OVENDEN, Richard Reginald. b 1900. Sarum Th Coll 24. **d** 27 **p** 28. C Mere w W Knoyle *Sarum* 27-30; C Milford *Win* 30-36; V Stourpaine *Sarum* 36-54; V Iwerne Stepleton 36-53; R Durweston 53-54; V W Alvington *Ex* 54-69; rtd 69. *St Clare, 12 Rodney Road, Backwell, Bristol BS19 3HW* Tel (01275) 833161

OVEREND, Alan. b 53. Sheff Univ BA75. Oak Hill Th Coll 84. **d** 86 **p** 87. C Aughton St Mich *Liv* 86-89; P-in-c Eccleston Park 89-92; V from 92. *St James's Vicarage, 159A St Helen's Road, Prescot, Merseyside L34 2QB* Tel 0151-426 6421

OVEREND, Barry Malcolm. b 49. K Coll Lon BD71 AKC71 DipMin88. St Aug Coll Cant 71. **d** 72 **p** 73. C Nailsworth *Glouc* 72-74; C High Harrogate Ch Ch *Ripon* 75-78; V Collingham w Harewood 78-87; V Far Headingley St Chad from 87. *St Chad's Vicarage, Otley Road, Leeds LS16 5JT* Tel 0113-275 2224 or 274 4322

OVEREND, Paul. b 66. Coll of Ripon & York St Jo BA88. Coll of Resurr Mirfield 88. **d** 93 **p** 94. C Cayton w Eastfield *York* 93-96; Asst Chapl Univ of Wales (Cardiff) *Llan* 96; Sen Chapl from 97. *University Anglican Chaplaincy, 61 Park Place, Cardiff CF1 3AT* Tel (01222) 232550 E-mail xmiswg@cardiff.ac.uk

OVERINGTON, David Vernon. b 34. W Aus Advanced Ed Coll DipRE90. ALCD60. **d** 60 **p** 61. C Penge Ch Ch w H Trin *Roch* 60-62; C Lenton *S'well* 62-65; P-in-c Brackenfield w Wessington *Derby* 65-71; P-in-c Cubley w Marston Montgomery 71-76; Australia from 76; Can Bunbury 84-85. *52 Pangbourne Street, Wembley, W Australia 6014* Tel Perth (9) 387 2287 or 387 2487

OVERTHROW, Royston John (Roy). b 45. Southn Univ BTh94. Portsm Dioc Tr Course 84. **d** 85. NSM Portsm Cathl *Portsm* 85-91; Perm to Offic 91-94; Dn to Bp Sarum from 94. *11 Burford Road, Salisbury SP2 8AN* Tel (01722) 338146

OVERTON, Charles Henry. b 51. CCC Ox BA74 MA77 Fitzw Coll Cam PGCE75 BA79 MA85. Ridley Hall Cam 77. **d** 80 **p** 81. C Tonbridge SS Pet and Paul *Roch* 80-84; Lic to Offic *Cant* 84-87; Asst Chapl St Lawr Coll Ramsgate 84-87; P-in-c Aythorpe w High and Leaden Roding *Chelmsf* 88-95; P-in-c Hughenden *Ox* from 95. *The Vicarage, Valley Road, Hughenden Valley, High Wycombe, Bucks HP14 4PF* Tel (01494) 563439

OVERTON, David Malcolm. b 52. Chich Th Coll. **d** 84 **p** 85. C Ches H Trin *Ches* 84-86; C Woodchurch 86-88; C Coppenhall 88-91; C Croydon St Jo *S'wark* 91-94; C-in-c 91-94. *90 Cambridge Road, Teddington, Middx TW11 8DJ* Tel 0181-977 1294

OVERTON, Keith Charles. b 28. EAMTC 78. **d** 81 **p** 82. NSM Duxford *Ely* 81-84; NSM Whittlesford 84-88; P-in-c 88-94; P-in-c Pampisford 88-90; Perm to Offic *Bris* from 94. *86 Pittsfield, Cricklade, Swindon SN6 6AW* Tel (01793) 750321

OVERTON, Thomas Vincent Edersheim. b 34. New Coll Ox BA58 DipTh59 MA61. Wycliffe Hall Ox 58. **d** 60 **p** 61. C W Hampstead Trin *Lon* 60-63; C Leeds St Geo *Ripon* 63-67; Perm to Offic *Lon* 68-71; Thailand 71-78; R Knossington and Cold Overton *Leic* 78-81; V Owston and Withcote 78-81; R Bedford St Jo and St Leon *St Alb* 81-90; Perm to Offic *B & W* 90-91; V Leigh *Roch* from 91. *The Vicarage, Leigh, Tonbridge, Kent TN11 8QJ* Tel (01732) 833022

OVERTON BENGE, Angela Margaret. b 46. EAMTC 94. **d** 97. NSM Moulsham St Jo *Chelmsf* from 97. *133 Pines Road, Chelmsford CM1 2EZ* Tel (01245) 495027

OVERY, Arthur William. b 19. JP. Nor Ord Course 73. **d** 76 **p** 77. NSM Lowestoft St Marg *Nor* 76-78; NSM Lowestoft and Kirkley 79-89; Perm to Offic from 89. *The Hollies, Warren Road, Lowestoft, Suffolk NR32 4QD* Tel (01502) 561289

OVEY, Michael John. b 58. Ball Coll Ox BA81 BCL82. Ridley Hall Cam 88. **d** 91 **p** 92. C Crowborough *Chich* 91-95; Australia from 95. *39 King Street, Newtown, NSW, Australia 2042* Tel Hobart (2) 519 2644

OWEN, Bryan Philip. b 47. Keswick Hall Coll CertEd70. Cant Sch of Min 83. **d** 86 **p** 87. NSM Deal St Geo *Cant* 86-87; C Herne 87-89; R Clarkston *Glas* 89-93; Warden Scottish Chs Ho (Chs Together in Scotland) 93-96; V Cuddington *Guildf* from 96. *St Mary's Vicarage, St Mary's Road, Worcester Park, Surrey KT4 7JL* Tel 0181-337 4026 Fax 337 6680

OWEN, Christine Rose. b 62. Univ of Wales (Ban) BA83 PGCE84. Qu Coll Birm 86. **d** 88 **p** 94. C Ynyscynhaearn w Penmorfa and Porthmadog *Ban* 88-90; Chapl Lon Univ *Lon* 90-96; Hon C St Marylebone w H Trin 94-96; Prec Worc Cathl *Worc* from 96. *5A College Yard, Worcester WR1 2LA* Tel (01905) 723617

OWEN, Canon Cledwyn. b 15. Univ of Wales BA36. Dorchester Miss Coll 36. **d** 38 **p** 39. C Llanwnog *Ban* 38-40; C Llandudno 40-47; R Henllan *St As* 47-57; V Llanfair Caereinion w Llanllugan 57-67; R Newtown w Llanllwchaiarn w Aberhafesp 67-74; Can Cursal St As Cathl 69-76; V Llangollen w Trevor and Llantysilio 74-82; Chan St As Cathl 76-82; rtd 82; Perm to Offic *Lich* from 83; Perm to Offic *Heref* from 95. *14 Green Lane, Bayston Hill, Shrewsbury SY3 0NS* Tel (01743) 873506

OWEN, Dafydd Gwyn. b 62. St Steph Ho Ox 95. **d** 97. C Whitchurch *Bris* from 97. *127 Bristol Road, Whitchurch, Bristol BS14 0PU* Tel (01275) 834992

OWEN, Canon David William. b 31. Down Coll Cam BA55 MA58. Linc Th Coll 55. **d** 57 **p** 58. C Salford St Phil w St Steph *Man* 57-61; C Grantham St Wulfram *Linc* 61-65; V Messingham 65-70; V Spilsby w Hundleby 70-77; R Aswardby w Sausthorpe 71-77; R Langton w Sutterby 71-77; R Halton Holgate 73-77; P-in-c Firsby w Gt Steeping 75-77; P-in-c Lt Steeping 75-77; TR Louth 77-92; Chapl Louth Co Hosp 77-92; RD Louthesk *Linc* 82-89; Can and Preb Linc Cathl 85-92; TR Swan *Ox* 92-97; RD Claydon 94-96. *19 Stephen Road, Headington, Oxford OX3 9AY* Tel (01865) 766585

OWEN, Derek Malden. b 29. Oak Hill Th Coll 74. **d** 76 **p** 77. C Eastbourne H Trin *Chich* 76-78; C Walthamstow St Mary w St Steph *Chelmsf* 78-81; R Ditcheat w E Pennard and Pylle *B & W* 81-83; Warden Shaftesbury Housing Assn 86-94; rtd 94; Hon C Fairlight, Guestling and Pett *Chich* 94-97. *3 Forge Road, Southborough, Tunbridge Wells, Kent TN4 0EU*

OWEN, Edgar. b 26. WMMTC. **d** 82 **p** 83. NSM Garretts Green *Birm* 82-88; NSM Stechford 88-94; rtd 94; Perm to Offic *Birm* from 94. *Flat 1, 41 Averill Road, Birmingham B26 2EG* Tel 0121-783 5603

✠**OWEN, The Rt Revd Edwin.** b 10. TCD BA32 MA41. **d** 34 **p** 35 **c** 72. C Glenageary *D & G* 34-36; C Dublin Ch Ch Leeson Park 36-38; Min Can St Patr Cathl Dub 35-36; Chan V 36-38; Succ 38-42; I Birr w Eglish *L & K* 42-57; RD Lower Ormond 46-57; Can Killaloe Cathl 54-57; Dean Killaloe 57-72; Dioc Sec (Killaloe etc) 57-72; RD Upper O'Mullod and Traderry 57-60; RD Kilfenora and Corkovasker 60-72; Bp Killaloe 72-76; Bp L & K 76-81; rtd 81. *4 Cypress, Hazeldene, Anglesea Road, Donnybrook, Dublin 4, Irish Republic* Tel Dublin (1) 660 8260

OWEN, Emyr. b 69. Lancs Poly BSc91. Westcott Ho Cam BA94 CTM95. **d** 95 **p** 96. C Llanbeblig w Caernarfon and Betws Garmon etc *Ban* 95-96; C Llanberis w Llanrug from 96. *Flat 2, The Rectory, Llanberis, Caernarvon LL55 4TF* Tel (01286) 872053

OWEN, Eric Cyril Hammersley. b 46. Liv Univ LLB68 Barrister 69. St As Minl Tr Course 95. **d** 97. NSM Gresford *St As* from 97. *Thistle Patch, 28 Wynnstay Lane, Marford, Wrexham LL12 8LG* Tel (01978) 856495 Fax 854830

OWEN, Ethelston John Charles. b 20. St D Coll Lamp BA42. **d** 48 **p** 49. C Gresford *St As* 48-50; C Abergele 50-55; R Llanfynydd 55-58; Chapl Mersey Miss to Seamen 58-60; V Clehonger *Heref* 60-80; R Eaton Bishop 60-80; rtd 80; Perm to Offic *Heref* from 81. *3 Yew Tree Close, Kingstone, Hereford HR2 9HG* Tel (01981) 250785

✠**OWEN, The Rt Revd Eugene.** b 33. Singapore Teaching Coll DipT52. Trin Coll Bris DipTh85. **d** 90 **p** 90 **c** 92. Serving in Philippine Independent Catholic and Episc Churches from 90. *38 Haddo House, Haddo Street, London SE10 9SG* Tel 0181-858 9269 Fax as telephone

OWEN, Geoffrey Neill. b 55. Chich Th Coll. **d** 85 **p** 86. C Streatham St Pet *S'wark* 85-89; C Battersea Ch Ch and St Steph 89-91; TV Surbiton St Andr and St Mark from 91. *St Andrew's Vicarage, 1 The Mall, Surbiton, Surrey KT6 4EH* Tel 0181-399 6806

OWEN, Gerald. b 16. St D Coll Lamp BA49. **d** 50 **p** 51. C Minera *St As* 50-54; V Foxt w Whiston *Lich* 54-57; V Shrewsbury St Mich 57-63; V Wednesbury St Bart 64-83; rtd 83. *35 Troon Place, Wordsley, Stourbridge, W Midlands DY8 5EN* Tel (01384) 294952

OWEN, Gordon Campbell. b 41. FRMetS65 MRAeS66 Univ of Wales (Ban) BD76 PGCE77. Ban Ord Course 79. **d** 81 **p** 82. Hd RE Eirias High Sch Colwyn Bay 77-88; Chapl RAFVR from 81; Asst P Ban Cathl *Ban* 82-88; Chapl St Kath Coll and Liv Inst of HE 88-91; Dioc Liaison Officer for RE *Liv* 88-91; V Llanfair-is-gaer and Llanddeiniolen *Ban* 91-97; Educn Officer 91-97; Lic to Offic from 97. *The Shieling, Penrhosgarnedd, Bangor LL57 2NH*

OWEN, Graham Anthony. b 54. Birm Univ BA77. Trin Coll Bris DipHE94. **d** 94 **p** 95. C Wiveliscombe w Chipstable, Huish Champflower etc *B & W* from 94. *29 Lion d'Angers, Wiveliscombe, Taunton, Somerset TA4 2PN* Tel (01984) 624164

OWEN, Graham Wynne. b 46. GTCL67 FTCL70 Lon Inst of Educn MA81. Cant Sch of Min 90. **d** 93 **p** 94. C Eltham H Trin *S'wark* from 93. *25 Parkhill Road, Sidcup, Kent DA15 7NJ* Tel 0181-300 8079 or 859 6274

OWEN, Harry Dennis. b 47. Oak Hill Th Coll 73. **d** 76 **p** 77. C Fulham Ch Ch *Lon* 76-81; V Byker St Mark *Newc* 81-89; V Plumstead All SS *S'wark* from 89. *All Saints' Vicarage, 106 Herbert Road, London SE18 3PU* Tel 0181-854 2995

OWEN, James Thomas. b 48. Linc Th Coll 77. **d** 80 **p** 81. C Palmers Green St Jo *Lon* 80-84; C Timperley *Ches* 84-87; C Bramhall 87-92; V Latchford St Jas from 92; RD Gt Budworth from 96. *St James's Vicarage, Manx Road, Warrington WA4 6AJ* Tel (01925) 631893

OWEN, John Edward. b 52. Middx Poly BA75. Sarum & Wells Th Coll BTh81. **d** 81 **p** 82. C S Ashford Ch Ch *Cant* 81-85; TV Bemerton *Sarum* 85-91; V St Leonards and St Ives *Win* 91-95; R N Stoneham from 95. *The Rectory, 62 Glen Eyre Road, Southampton S02 3NL* Tel (01703) 768123

OWEN, Keith Robert. b 57. Warw Univ BA Ox Univ BA MA85 Hull Univ MA(Ed)89. St Steph Ho Ox 79. **d** 82 **p** 83. C Headingley *Ripon* 82-85; Chapl Grimsby Colls of H&FE 85-90; Chapl for Educn *Linc* 85-90; P-in-c Linc St Botolph by Bargate 90-95; Chapl to Caring Agencies Linc City Cen 90-95; V Steeton *Bradf* from 95; Chapl Airedale Gen Hosp from 95. *The Vicarage, 2 Halsteads Way, Steeton, Keighley, W Yorkshire BD20 6SN* Tel (01535) 652004

OWEN, Kenneth Phillip. b 56. Liv Univ BA77 PGCE78. N Ord Course 92. **d** 95 **p** 96. C Heswall *Ches* from 95. *The Croft, Croftsway, Heswall, Wirral, Merseyside L60 9JP* Tel 0151-342 4841

OWEN, Lionel Edward Joseph. b 19. S'wark Ord Course 66. **d** 69 **p** 70. C Hythe *Cant* 69-73; C Deal St Leon 73-75; V Teynham 75-84; RD Ospringe 80-84; rtd 84; Perm to Offic *Cant* from 84. *Green Hayes, London Road, Hythe, Kent CT21 4JH* Tel (01303) 267642

OWEN, Preb Noah. b 10. St D Coll Lamp BA34. **d** 34 **p** 35. C Winford *B & W* 34-40; C Wellow 40-44; CF 44-47; V Dulverton *B & W* 47-64; R Chew Stoke 64-73; RD Chew Magna 71-77; R Chew Stoke w Nempnett Thrubwell 73-77; R Norton Malreward 67-77; rtd 77; Perm to Offic *B & W* 79-80; Preb Wells Cathl 76-77 and from 80. *West Grove, Crewkerne, Somerset TA18 7ES* Tel (01460) 74023

OWEN, Owen Thomas. b 19. Liv Univ 37 Lanc Univ MA77. St Chad's Coll Dur DipTh45. **d** 45 **p** 46. C Easington Colliery *Dur* 45-48; Chapl and Tutor St Jo Coll York 48-51; PC Hedgefield *Dur* 51-56; R Dur St Mary le Bow w St Mary the Less 56-60; Chapl Dur Univ 56-60; R Clifton w Glapton *S'well* 60-62; Chapl and Sen Lect Nottm Coll of HE 60-62; Sen Lect Liv Coll of HE 62-65; Prin 65-84; rtd 84. *1 Oakwood Road, Halewood, Liverpool L26 1XD* Tel 0151-486 8672

OWEN, Peter Russell. b 35. St Mich Coll Llan DipTh63. **d** 63 **p** 64. C Wrexham *St As* 63-64; C Connah's Quay 64-65; Asst Chapl Miss to Seamen 66-69; P-in-c Upper Norwood All SS w St Marg *Cant* 69-72; C Hawarden *St As* 72-75; V Cilcain and Nannerch 75-79; R Cilcain and Nannerch and Rhyd-y-mwyn 79-83; V Brymbo and Bwlchgwyn 83-87; R Llangynhafal and Llanbedr Dyffryn Clwyd from 87. *The Rectory, Llanbedr Dyffryn Clwyd, Ruthin, Clwyd LS15 1UP* Tel (01824) 704051

OWEN, Phillip Clifford. b 42. G&C Coll Cam BA65 MA69. Ridley Hall Cam 71. **d** 73 **p** 74. C Stowmarket *St E* 73-76; C Headley All SS *Guildf* 76-81; TV 81-89; P-in-c Clifton-on-Teme, Lower Sapey and the Shelsleys *Worc* from 89; Dioc Ecum Officer from 89. *The*

Rectory, Clifton-on-Teme, Worcester WR6 6DJ Tel (01886) 812483

OWEN, Raymond Philip. b 37. Man Univ BScTech60 AMCT60 Teesside Poly DMS83. Chich Th Coll 65. **d** 67 **p** 68. C Elland *Wakef* 67-70; C Lindley 70-73; V Bradshaw 73-80; Ind Chapl *Dur* 80-91; TR Hanley H Ev *Lich* from 91. *The Rectory, 35 Harding Road, Stoke-on-Trent ST1 3BQ* Tel (01782) 266031

OWEN, Richard Ellis. b 12. Clifton Th Coll 48. **d** 50 **p** 51. C Littleover *Derby* 50-53; C Whitchurch *Lich* 53-55; R Elkstone w Syde and Winstone *Glouc* 55-61; V Badminton w Acton Turville 61-71; V Kemble w Poole Keynes 71-73; R Pebworth w Dorsington 73-83; rtd 83; Perm to Offic *Glouc* 83-94. *40 Ballards Close, Mickleton, Chipping Campden, Glos GL55 6TN* Tel (01386) 438755

OWEN, Canon Richard Llewelyn. b 27. Univ of Wales (Lamp) BA51. St Mich Coll Llan 51. **d** 53 **p** 54. C Holyhead w Rhoscolyn w Llanfair-yn-Neubwll *Ban* 53-57; C Porthmadog 57-59; R Llanfechell w Bodewryd, Rhosbeirio etc 59-67; Youth Chapl 66-67; V Penrhyndeudraeth and Llanfrothen 67-77; R Llangefni w Tregaean and Llangristiolus etc 77-89; Can Ban Cathl 82-93; Treas 86-93; Can Missr and V Bangor Cathl Par 89-93; RD Arfon 92-93; rtd 93; Hon Can Ban Cathl *Ban* from 93; Lic to Offic from 93. *Bodowen, Great Ormes Road, Llandudno LL30 2BW* Tel (01492) 872765

OWEN, Richard Matthew. b 49. Sheff Univ BA70 Leeds Univ CertEd73. N Ord Course 84. **d** 87 **p** 88. NSM Chorlton-cum-Hardy St Werburgh *Man* 87-89; C N Reddish 89-91; Perm to Offic *York* 91-96; NSM York St Olave w St Giles from 96. *9 Albion Street, Skeldergate, York YO1 1HJ* Tel (01904) 679989

OWEN, Robert David Glyn. b 06. Bps' Coll Cheshunt 37. **d** 39 **p** 40. C Cerrigydrudion and Llanfihangel Glyn Myfyr etc *St As* 39; P-in-c Llannefydd 46-50; V Capel Garmon 50-54; C Norton 54-58; R Grindon *Lich* 58-63; V Butterton 58-63; V Burslem St Paul 63-67; rtd 67. *18 Bromley College, High Street, Bromley BR1 1PE* Tel 0181-460 2570

OWEN, Robert Glynne. b 33. St Mich Coll Llan 56. **d** 58 **p** 59. C Machynlleth and Llanwrin *Ban* 58-62; C Llanbeblig w Caernarfon 62-65; V Carno and Trefeglwys 65-69; Hon C Dorking w Ranmore *Guildf* 69-75; Perm to Offic *St As* 75-94; V Broughton from 94. *The Vicarage, Bryn y Gaer Road, Pentre, Broughton, Wrexham LL11 6AT* Tel (01978) 756210

OWEN, Robert Lee. b 56. Univ of Wales (Cardiff) BD79. Qu Coll Birm 79. **d** 81 **p** 82. C Holywell *St As* 81-84; Perm to Offic *Birm* 85-87; Chapl Blue Coat Sch Birm 85-87; Chapl St Elphin's Sch Matlock 87-94; Chapl Qu Marg Sch York from 94. *Queen Margaret's School, Escrick Park, Escrick, York YO4 6EU* Tel (01904) 728261

OWEN, Ronald Alfred. b 44. Sarum & Wells Th Coll 80. **d** 81 **p** 82. C Wotton St Mary *Glouc* 81-83; CF from 83; Perm to Offic *S'wark* 94-97. *MOD Chaplains (Army), Trenchard Lines, Upavon, Pewsey, Wilts SN9 6BE* Tel (01980) 615804 Fax 615800

OWEN, Roy Meredith. b 21. Univ of Wales BA43. St Mich Coll Llan 43. **d** 45 **p** 46. C Roath St Martin *Llan* 45-47; C Penarth w Lavernock 47-51; C Merthyr Dyfan 51-56; V Llangeinor 56-62; V Pontyclun w Talygarn 62-75; C Cadoxton-juxta-Barry 82-85; rtd 85; Perm to Offic *Llan* 86-88. *20 Mary Street, Llandaff North, Cardiff CF4 2JQ* Tel (01222) 569427

OWEN, Canon Stanley Alfred George. b 17. Worc Ord Coll 57. **d** 59 **p** 60. C Bickenhill w Elmdon *Birm* 59-60; R 60-86; rtd 86; Perm to Offic *Birm* from 86; Chmn and Sec Assn Ch Fellowships from 88. *Bickenhill House, 154 Lode Lane, Solihull, W Midlands B91 2HP* Tel 0121-704 9281

OWEN, Mrs Susan Margaret. b 38. St Andr Univ MA61 Univ of Wales (Swansea) MPhil91 Univ of Wales (Ban) BD93. Qu Coll Birm 94. **d** 95 **p** 96. NSM Shrewsbury St Geo *Lich* from 95. *21 Brookside, Bicton, Shrewsbury SY3 8EP* Tel (01743) 850174

OWEN, William. b 05. OBE. Lon Univ BD55. Tyndale Hall Bris 27. **d** 30 **p** 31. BCMS 30-37; CMS 37-53; Kenya 54-81; rtd 81; Perm to Offic *Cant* 81-94. *51 Bridge Down, Bridge, Canterbury, Kent CT4 5BA* Tel (01227) 830625

OWEN, William David. b 17. Univ of Wales BA39. Wycliffe Hall Ox 40. **d** 41 **p** 42. C Fishguard *St D* 41-45; C Old Swinford *Worc* 45-49; C-in-c Astwood Bank and Crabbs Cross CD 49-50; V Astwood Bank w Crabbs Cross 50-63; V Claines St Jo 63-94; rtd 94. *Ball Mill Bunglow, Main Road, Hallow, Worcester WR2 6LS* Tel (01905) 640385

OWEN-JONES, Peter Charles. b 57. Ridley Hall Cam 92. **d** 94 **p** 95. C Leverington *Ely* 94-97; C Wisbech St Mary 94-97; R Haslingfield w Harlton and Gt and Lt Eversden from 97. *The Rectory, Broad Lane, Haslingfield, Cambridge CB3 7JF* Tel (01223) 870285

OWEN-JONES, Peter John. b 47. CEng84 MIMechE84 MBIM87 FPWI90 RMCS BScEng68. EMMTC 85. **d** 88 **p** 89. NSM Holbrook and Lt Eaton *Derby* from 88. *6 Station Road, Little Eaton, Derby DE21 5DN* Tel (01332) 831423

OWENS, Mrs Ann Lindsay. b 47. St Hild Coll Dur CertEd68 Man Univ BA94. N Ord Course 92. **d** 95 **p** 96. Chapl St Jas Sch Farnworth 94-97; NSM New Bury *Man* 95-97; C Heywood St Luke w All So from 97. *173 Rochdale Road East, Heywood, Lancs OL10 1QU* Tel (01706) 626008

OWENS, Christopher Lee. b 42. Coll of Ripon & York St Jo 61 Lon Inst of Educn TCert. Linc Th Coll 66. **d** 69 **p** 70. C Dalston H Trin w St Phil *Lon* 69-72; C Portsea N End St Mark *Portsm* 72-81; TV E Ham w Upton Park St Alb *Chelmsf* 81-92; C Is of Dogs Ch Ch and St Jo w St Luke *Lon* from 92. *St Luke's House, Strafford Street, London E14 8LT* Tel 0171-515 9888

OWENS, Philip Roger. b 47. Univ of Wales (Ban) DipTh70. Wells Th Coll 71. **d** 71 **p** 72. C Colwyn Bay *St As* 71-74; C Wrexham 74-77; TV 77-80; P-in-c Yoxford *St E* 80-85; Asst Stewardship and Resources Adv 80-85; R Ban Monachorum and Worthenbury *St As* from 85; Dioc Stewardship Officer from 89; RD Ban Isycoed from 92. *The Rectory, 8 Ludlow Road, Bangor-on-Dee, Wrexham LL13 0JG* Tel (01978) 780608

OWENS, Canon Rodney Stones. b 19. Lon Univ BA53. Bps' Coll Cheshunt 48. **d** 50 **p** 51. C Darenth *Roch* 50-51; C Wokingham All SS *Ox* 51-55; R Gt Livermere w Troston *St E* 55-59; P-in-c Ampton and Lt Livermere 55-59; V Ipswich St Aug 59-65; Perm to Offic 65-74; Asst Master Ipswich Sch 65-74; R Coddenham 74-75; R Gosbeck 74-75; P-in-c Hemingstone w Henley 74-75; R Coddenham w Gosbeck and Hemingstone w Henley 75-84; RD Bosmere 78-84; Hon Can St E Cathl 81-84; rtd 84; Perm to Offic *St E* from 85. *10 Warren Lane, Martlesham Heath, Ipswich IP5 3SH* Tel (01473) 623411

OWENS, Stephen Graham Frank. b 49. Ch Coll Cam BA71 CertEd72 MA75. Qu Coll Birm 73. **d** 75 **p** 76. C Stourbridge St Mich Norton *Worc* 75-80; Tanzania 80-88; V Dudley Wood *Worc* from 88. *The Vicarage, 57 Lantern Road, Dudley, W Midlands DY2 0DL* Tel (01384) 569018

OWERS, Ian Humphrey. b 46. Em Coll Cam BA68 MA72. Westcott Ho Cam 71. **d** 73 **p** 74. C Champion Hill St Sav *S'wark* 73-77; V Peckham St Sav 77-82; P-in-c E Greenwich Ch Ch w St Andr and St Mich 82-83; V 83-94; P-in-c Westcombe Park St Geo 85-94; RD Greenwich 92-94. *3 Prestwood House, Drummond Road, London SE16 4BX* Tel 0171-237 9608

OWST, Clifford Samuel. b 09. FCII34. Linc Th Coll 77. **d** 77 **p** 78. Hon C Mablethorpe w Stain *Linc* 77-78; Hon C Mablethorpe w Trusthorpe 78-83; New Zealand from 83. *1/1062 Beraih Road, Torbay, Auckland 1310, New Zealand* Tel Auckland (9) 473 8599

OXBROW, Mark. b 51. Reading Univ BSc72 Fitzw Ho Cam BA75 MA79. Ridley Hall Cam 73. **d** 76 **p** 77. C Luton Ch Ch *Roch* 76-80; TV Newc Epiphany *Newc* 80-88; Chapl Newc Mental Health Unit 80-88; Regional Sec Eur CMS from 88; Communication Resources Sec CMS from 94. *10 Nettleden Avenue, Wembley, Middx HA9 6DP, or CMS, Partnership House, 157 Waterloo Road, London SE1 8UU* Tel 0181-900 2485 or 0171-928 8681 Fax 0171-401 3215

OXENFORTH, Colin Bryan. b 45. St Chad's Coll Dur BA67 DipTh69. **d** 69 **p** 70. C Bromley St Andr *Roch* 69-72; C Nunhead St Antony *S'wark* 72-76; V Toxteth St Marg *Liv* 76-89; V Brixton St Matt *S'wark* from 89. *The Vicarage, 5 St Matthew's Road, London SW2 1ND* Tel 0171-274 3553

OXFORD (Christ Church), Dean of. *See* DRURY, The Very Revd John Henry

OXFORD, Archdeacon of. *See* WESTON, The Ven Frank Valentine

OXFORD, Bishop of. *See* HARRIES, The Rt Revd Richard Douglas

OXLEY, Cecil Robert. b 23. TEng72. Coll of Resurr Mirfield 84. **d** 84 **p** 85. NSM Derby St Luke *Derby* 84-92; rtd 92; Perm to Offic *Derby* from 92. *8 Top Farm Court, Highfield Road, Kilburn, Belper, Derbyshire DE56 0PU* Tel (01332) 781079

OXLEY, Christopher Robert. b 51. Sheff Univ BA73 PGCE74 Ox Univ BA78 MA83. Wycliffe Hall Ox 76. **d** 79 **p** 80. C Greasbrough *Sheff* 79-82; C Doncaster St Leon and St Jude 82-84; Asst Chapl Brussels *Eur* 84-87; V Humberstone *Leic* 87-93; V Beaumont Leys from 93. *The Vicarage, 10 Parkside Close, Leicester LE4 1EP* Tel 0116-235 2667

OXLEY, David William. b 63. TCD BA85 BTh89. CITC 85. **d** 89 **p** 90. C Dublin Ch Ch Cathl Gp *D & G* 89-92; Clerical V Ch Ch Cathl Dublin 90-92; I Templebreedy w Tracton and Nohoval *C, C & R* 92-96; Min Can Cork Cathl 95-96; I Tullow w Shillelagh, Aghold and Mullinacuff *C & O* from 96. *The Rectory, Tullow, Co Carlow, Irish Republic* Tel Carlow (503) 51481

OXLEY, Martin Neil. b 65. Birm Univ BA86 Edin Univ BD95. Edin Th Coll CECM95. **d** 95 **p** 96. C Glas St Mary *Glas* 95-97; C Glas St Matt 95-97; C Clydebank 95-97; P-in-c Glas St Matt from 97; Dir Studies Edin Th Coll from 97. *St Mary's House, 42 Hillhead Street, Glasgow G12 8PZ* Tel 0141-339 8904

OXLEY, Mrs Paula Jane. b 51. Sheff Univ BA74 PGCE75. EMMTC 90. **d** 93 **p** 94. NSM Birstall and Wanlip *Leic* 93-95; NSM Beaumont Leys 95-96; C from 96. *The Vicarage, 10 Parkside Close, Leicester LE4 1EP* Tel 0116-235 2667

OYET, Canon Julius Isotuk. b 39. Concordia Coll (USA) MA79. Immanuel Coll Ibadan DipTh70. **d** 70 **p** 72. Nigeria 70-90 and from 96; Hon Can Ondo from 88; Miss Partner CMS from 91; C Warblington and Emsworth *Portsm* 91-95; C Kirkby *Liv* 95-96. *c/o The Rt Revd the Bishop of Akure, Bishopscourt, Alagbaka GRA, PO Box 1622, Akure, Nigeria*

P

PACEY, Edgar Prentice. b 29. Edin Univ MA50. Edin Th Coll 52. **d** 54 **p** 55. C Motherwell *Glas* 54-56; C Glas St Mary 56-61; R Coatbridge 61-70; Perm to Offic 70-77; Hon C Glas St Martin 77-83; P-in-c Rothesay *Arg* 83-93; R Tighnabruaich 91-93; Perm to Offic *Glas* from 91; rtd 93; Perm to Offic *Arg* from 93. *Dunstan, 16 Broomfield Drive, Dunoon, Argyll PA23 7LJ*

PACEY, Graham John. b 52. Leeds Univ CertEd74 Open Univ BA81 Teesside Poly ADEd85. NE Ord Course 90. **d** 93 **p** 94. C Kirkleatham *York* 93-96; V Middlesbrough St Agnes from 96. *The Vicarage, 1 Broughton Avenue, Middlesbrough, Cleveland TS4 3PX* Tel (01642) 316144

PACEY, Michael John. **d** 96 **p** 97. NSM Tamworth *Lich* from 96. *1 Benson View, Tamworth, Staffs B79 8TD* Tel (01827) 65879

PACKER, Prof James Innell. b 26. CCC Ox BA48 MA52 DPhil55. Wycliffe Hall Ox 49. **d** 52 **p** 53. C Harborne Heath *Birm* 52-54; Lect Tyndale Hall Bris 55-61; Lib Latimer Ho Ox 61-62; Warden 62-69; Prin Tyndale Hall Bris 70-72; Assoc Prin Trin Coll Bris 72-79; Prof Hist Th Regent Coll Vancouver 79-89; Prof Th from 89; rtd 91. *6017 Holland Street, Vancouver, Canada, V6N 2B2*

✠**PACKER, The Rt Revd John Richard.** b 46. Keble Coll Ox BA67 MA. Ripon Hall Ox 67. **d** 70 **p** 71. C St Helier *S'wark* 70-73; Chapl Abingdon St Nic *Ox* 73-77; Tutor Ripon Hall Ox 73-75; Tutor Ripon Coll Cuddesdon 75-77; V Wath-upon-Dearne w Adwick-upon-Dearne *Sheff* 77-86; RD Wath 83-86; TR Sheff Manor 86-91; RD Attercliffe 90-91; Adn W Cumberland *Carl* 91-96; Suff Bp Warrington *Liv* from 96. *34 Central Avenue, Eccleston Park, Prescot, Merseyside L34 2QP* Tel 0151-708 9480

PACKER, Canon John William. b 18. K Coll Lon BA40 AKC40 BD41 MTh48. **d** 41 **p** 42. C Attenborough w Bramcote *S'well* 41-44; Asst Master Lanc Gr Sch 44-49; Lect RE Leeds Univ 50-53; Hd Master Canon Slade Gr Sch Bolton 53-77; Lic to Offic *Man* 53-77; Hon Can Man Cathl 75-78; rtd 77; Perm to Offic *Cant* from 78. *Netherbury, Meadow Close, Bridge, Canterbury, Kent CT4 5AT* Tel (01227) 830364

PACKER, Peter Aelred. b 48. St Jo Coll Dur BA70 St Chad's Coll Dur PhD79 Warw Univ Postgraduate Certificate in Group Psychotherapy 94 Ven English Coll Rome 95. **d** 96 **p** 97. SSM from 93; Lic to Offic *S'wark* from 96; Hon C S Lambeth St Anne and All SS from 96. *Elmore Abbey, Church Lane, Speen, Newbury, Berks RG14 1SA* Tel (01635) 33080

PACKER, Roger Ernest John. b 37. ARCO59 Pemb Coll Cam BA60 MA64. Cuddesdon Coll 60. **d** 62 **p** 63. C Chippenham St Andr w Tytherton Lucas *Bris* 62-65; C Caversham *Ox* 65-70; R Sandhurst 70-91; V Bridgwater St Mary, Chilton Trinity and Durleigh *B & W* from 91; RD Bridgwater from 94. *The Vicarage, 7 Durleigh Road, Bridgwater, Somerset TA6 7HU* Tel (01278) 422437 or 424972

PACKHAM, Ms Elizabeth Daisy. b 33. Golds Coll Lon BSc54 CertEd55. N Ord Course. **dss** 83 **d** 87 **p** 94. Fairfield *Derby* 83-84; Buxton w Burbage and King Sterndale 84-87; Par Dn 87-94; C 94-95; P-in-c Chinley w Buxworth from 95. *The Vicarage, Buxworth, Stockport, Cheshire SK12 7NH* Tel (01663) 732243

PADDICK, Graham. b 47. S'wark Ord Course. **d** 89 **p** 90. C St Helier *S'wark* 89-93; P-in-c Thornton Heath St Paul 93-96; V from 96. *The Vicarage, 1 Norbury Avenue, Thornton Heath, Surrey CR7 8AH* Tel 0181-653 2762

PADDISON, Michael David William. b 41. Oak Hill Th Coll 75. **d** 77 **p** 78. C Gt Warley Ch Ch *Chelmsf* 77-80; C Rayleigh 80-83; R Scole, Brockdish, Billingford, Thorpe Abbots etc *Nor* 83-95; RD Redenhall 89-95; R Reepham, Hackford w Whitwell, Kerdiston etc from 95. *The Rectory, Station Road, Reepham, Norwich NR10 4LJ* Tel (01603) 870220

PADDOCK, Canon Gerald Alfred. b 39. Oak Hill Th Coll 66. **d** 69 **p** 70. C Whitehall Park St Andr Hornsey Lane *Lon* 69-73; C Edgware 73-76; P-in-c Ab Kettleby w Wartnaby and Holwell *Leic* 76-81; Dioc Missr 80-87; Hon Can Leic Cathl from 80; V Oaks in Charnwood and Copt Oak from 81; Police Liaison Officer from 81; Dioc Voc Officer from 81. *The Vicarage, Oaks Road, Oaks-in-Charnwood, Loughborough, Leics LE12 9YD* Tel (01509) 503246

PADDOCK, John Allan Barnes. b 51. Liv Univ BA74 MA91 Man Univ PGCE75 Ox Univ BA77 MA81 FRSA94. St Steph Ho Ox 75. **d** 80 **p** 81. C Matson *Glouc* 80-82; Asst Chapl Madrid *Eur* 82-83; Chapl R Gr Sch Lanc 83-86; Chapl RAF 86-91; Offg Chapl RAF 92-94; Chapl St Olave's Gr Sch Orpington 91-94; Perm to Offic *Blackb* from 94; Perm to Offic *Roch* from 97; Chapl R Russell Sch Croydon from 97. *The Royal Russell School, Coombe Lane, Croydon CR9 5BY* Tel 0181-657 4433 Fax 657 9555

PADGET, William Thomas. b 19. **d** 77 **p** 78. NSM Rodbourne Cheney *Bris* 77-90; rtd 90; Perm to Offic *Bris* from 90. *39 George Tweed Gardens, Ramleaze Drive, Swindon SN5 9PX* Tel (01793) 723789

PAGAN, Canon Keith Vivian. b 37. St Jo Coll Dur BA60 MA66. Chich Th Coll 60. **d** 62 **p** 63. C Clacton St Jas *Chelmsf* 62-64; C Wymondham *Nor* 64-70; P-in-c Guestwick 70-80; P-in-c Kettlestone 70-79; V Hindolveston 70-80; R Islay *Arg* from 80; R Campbeltown from 80; Miss to Seamen from 80; Can St Jo Cathl Oban *Arg* from 85; Can Cumbrae from 85. *Mariefield, Southend, Campbeltown, Argyll PA28 6RW* Tel (01586) 830310

PAGE, Canon Alan George. b 24. Em Coll Cam BA48 MA52. Wycliffe Hall Ox 49. **d** 51 **p** 52. C Islington St Andr w St Thos and St Matthias *Lon* 51-53; Kenya 53-71; Hon Can Mt Kenya 71-75; Hon Can Mt Kenya S 75-84; C S Lyncombe *B & W* 71-72; R Freshford w Limpley Stoke 72-76; R Freshford, Limpley Stoke and Hinton Charterhouse 76-84; Can Mt Kenya Cen from 84; C Fulham St Mary N End *Lon* 87-89; rtd 89; Perm to Offic *B & W* from 89. *45 Ashley Avenue, Bath BA1 3DS* Tel (01225) 310532

PAGE, Alan Richard Benjamin. b 38. Univ of Wales (Lamp) BA60 BSc. St Mich Coll Llan 60. **d** 62 **p** 63. C Cardiff St Andr and St Teilo *Llan* 62-64; C Newport St Julian *Mon* 64-67; C Hoxton H Trin w St Mary *Lon* 67-69; C Winchmore Hill H Trin 69-71; V Camden Town St Mich w All SS and St Thos from 71. *St Michael's Vicarage, 1 Bartholomew Road, London NW5 2AH* Tel 0171-485 1256

PAGE, Arthur Henry. b 21. Open Univ BA79. Sarum & Wells Th Coll. **d** 82 **p** 82. NSM Gtr Corsham *Bris* 82-87; Perm to Offic *Dur* 88; NSM Shadforth 89-91; rtd 91; Perm to Offic *Dur* from 91. *9 Foxton Way, High Shincliffe, Durham DH1 2PJ* Tel 0191-386 2141

PAGE, David. b 48. Bris Univ BA70 Leic Univ MA74 Southn Univ PGCE74 Nottm Univ DipTh82. St Jo Coll Nottm 81. **d** 83 **p** 84. C Morden *S'wark* 83-86; V Wimbledon St Luke 86-91; P-in-c Clapham Common St Barn 91-92; V from 92. *St Barnabas' Vicarage, 12 Lavender Gardens, London SW11 1DL* Tel 0171-223 5953

PAGE, David James. b 62. Liv Univ BSc83 Qu Coll Ox DPhil87. Trin Coll Bris BA93 MA95. **d** 96 **p** 97. C Knutsford St Jo and Toft *Ches* from 96. *92 Grove Park, Knutsford, Cheshire WA16 8QB* Tel (01565) 632894

✠**PAGE, The Rt Revd Dennis Fountain.** b 19. G&C Coll Cam BA41 MA45. Linc Th Coll 41. **d** 43 **p** 44 **c** 75. C Rugby St Andr *Cov* 43-49; R Weeting *Ely* 49-65; R Hockwold w Wilton 49-65; RD Feltwell 53-65; Hon Can Ely Cathl 63-65 and 68-75; V Yaxley 65-75; Adn Huntingdon 65-75; Suff Bp Lancaster *Blackb* 75-85; rtd 85; Perm to Offic *St E* from 85. *Larkrise, Hartest, Bury St Edmunds, Suffolk IP29 4ES* Tel (01284) 830694

PAGE, Mrs Dorothy Jean. b 29. Portsm Poly CertEd50. Ox NSM Course 84. **d** 87 **p** 94. NSM Wantage Downs *Ox* from 87. *11 North Street, Marcham, Abingdon, Oxon OX13 6NG* Tel (01865) 391462

PAGE, Ian George. b 62. Ex Univ BSc84 York Univ PGCE85. Edin Th Coll 87. **d** 90 **p** 91. C Blackpool St Steph *Blackb* 90-92; Perm to Offic *Ex* from 92. *31 Winston Park, South Molton, Devon EX36 3AY* Tel (01769) 572895

PAGE, Mrs Irene May. b 38. Birm Univ BA58. NE Ord Course 85. **d** 87 **p** 94. Par Dn Cockfield *Dur* 87-90; Par Dn Waterloo St Jo w St Andr *S'wark* 90-94; C 94-95; R Woolwich St Thos from 95. *The New Rectory, Maryon Road, London SE7 8DJ* Tel 0181-855 1718

PAGE, John Jeremy. b 56. Keble Coll Ox BA79 MA83 Edin Univ BD86. Edin Th Coll 83. **d** 86 **p** 87. C Wetherby *Ripon* 86-89; TV Wrexham *St As* 89-92; Chapl Hymers Coll Hull from 92. *46 Sunny Bank, Hull HU3 1LQ* Tel (01482) 43555

PAGE, John Laurance Howard. b 40. ALCD. **d** 65 **p** 66. C Spitalfields Ch Ch w All SS *Lon* 65-69; C Win Ch Ch *Win* 69-72; C Ringwood 72-76; V Lockerley and E Dean w E and W Tytherley 76-89; RD Romsey 85-89; V Lord's Hill from 89. *1 Tangmere Drive, Southampton SO16 8GY* Tel (01703) 731182

PAGE, Canon Michael John. b 42. K Coll Lon BD66 AKC66. **d** 67 **p** 68. C Rawmarsh w Parkgate *Sheff* 67-72; C-in-c Gleadless Valley CD 72-74; TR Gleadless Valley 74-77; V Lechlade *Glouc* 77-86; RD Fairford 81-86; V Winchcombe, Gretton, Sudeley Manor etc from 86; Hon Can Glouc Cathl from 91; RD Winchcombe from 94. *The Vicarage, Langley Road, Winchcombe, Cheltenham, Glos GL54 5QP* Tel (01242) 602368

PAGE, Owen Richard. b 53. FIBMS83 Trent Poly HNC77 Derby Coll of Educn DMS85. Linc Th Coll 89. **d** 91 **p** 92. C Gt Bookham *Guildf* 91-94; V Kings Heath *Pet* from 94. *The Vicarage, Church Green, Northampton NN5 7LS* Tel (01604) 407074

PAGE, Canon Richard Dennis. b 23. G&C Coll Cam BA48 MA50. Ridley Hall Cam 48. **d** 50 **p** 51. C Ecclesfield *Sheff* 50-52; Chapl St Lawr Coll Ramsgate 52-58; Chapl Dean Close Sch Cheltenham 58-60 and 62-64; Chapl Netherton Tr Sch Morpeth 60-62; V Ecclesfield *Sheff* 64-71; RD Ecclesfield 66-71; P-in-c Holkham w Egmere and Waterden *Nor* 71-78; R Wells next the Sea 71-78; RD Burnham and Walsingham 72-78; V Hemsby 78-83; P-in-c Brooke w Kirstead 83-85; P-in-c Mundham w Seething 83-85; P-in-c Thwaite 83-85; R Brooke, Kirstead, Mundham w Seething and Thwaite 85-89; Hon Can Nor Cathl 87-89; rtd 90; Perm to Offic *Nor* from 90. *The Greyhound, Back Street, Reepham, Norfolk NR10 4SJ* Tel (01603) 870886

PAGE, Robert William Charles. b 67. St Steph Ho Ox 90. **d** 93 **p** 94. C Hockerill *St Alb* 93-95; C Kilburn St Aug w St Jo *Lon* from 95.

122 Dibdin House, Maida Vale, London W9 1QG Tel 0171-328 9301

PAGE, Teehan Dawson. b 61. Ch Ch Ox BA83 MA87. St Steph Ho Ox 91. **d** 93 **p** 94. C Surbiton St Andr and St Mark *S'wark* 93-96; Chapl Reed's Sch Cobham from 96. *Clover, Reed's School, Sandy Lane, Cobham, Surrey KT11 2BL* Tel (01932) 869006

PAGE, Thomas William. b 57. Sarum & Wells Th Coll 84. **d** 87 **p** 88. C Caterham *S'wark* 87-91; C Cheam 91-95; P-in-c Cranham *Chelmsf* from 95. *All Saints House, 51 Courtney Gardens, Upminster, Essex RM14 1DM* Tel (01708) 228200

PAGE, Canon Trevor Melvyn. b 41. Dur Univ BA63 Fitzw Coll Cam BA67 MA72. Westcott Ho Cam 64. **d** 67 **p** 68. C Millhouses H Trin *Sheff* 67-69; Chapl Sheff Univ 69-74; V Doncaster Intake 74-82; Dioc Dir of In-Service Tr 82-95; Dioc Dir of Ords and Post-Ord Tr from 82; Can Res Sheff Cathl from 82. *393 Fulwood Road, Sheffield S10 3GE* Tel 0114-230 5707

PAGE, William George. b 42. Linc Th Coll 83. **d** 85 **p** 86. C Boston *Linc* 85-89; V Sibsey w Frithville from 89; RD Holland E from 95. *The Vicarage, Sibsey, Boston, Lincs PE22 0RT* Tel (01205) 750305

PAGE-CHESTNEY, Michael William. b 47. Linc Th Coll 80. **d** 82 **p** 83. C Barton upon Humber *Linc* 82-85; TV Gt Grimsby St Mary and St Jas 85-91; V E Stockwith 91-96; V Blyton w Pilham 91-93; V Laughton w Wildsworth 91-93; V Corringham and Blyton Gp from 93. *The Vicarage, Church Lane, Blyton, Gainsborough, Lincs DN21 3JZ* Tel (01427) 628216

PAGE-CHESTNEY, Mrs Susan Valerie. b 49. EMMTC DipTh86. **dss** 86 **d** 87 **p** 94. NSM Gt Grimsby St Mary and St Jas *Linc* 86-91; NSM Blyton w Pilham 91-93; NSM Laughton w Wildsworth 91-93; NSM Corringham and Blyton Gp from 93. *The Vicarage, Church Lane, Blyton, Gainsborough, Lincs DN21 3JZ* Tel (01427) 628216

PAGE-CLARK, Howard David. b 53. Fitzw Coll Cam MA77. LNSM course 96. **d** 97. NSM Lytchett Minster *Sarum* from 97. *Sparrows Nest, East Holton Farm, Holton Heath, Poole, Dorset BH16 6JN* Tel (01202) 632540 Fax 632532

PAGE-TURNER, Edward Gregory Ambrose Wilford. b 31. Qu Coll Birm 57. **d** 60 **p** 61. C Helmsley *York* 60-64; C Kensington St Phil Earl's Court *Lon* 64-67; C Walton-on-Thames *Guildf* 67-70; V Seend *Sarum* 70-71; V Seend and Bulkington 71-79; R Bladon w Woodstock *Ox* 79-87; P-in-c Begbroke 80-86; P-in-c Shipton-on-Cherwell 80-86; P-in-c Hampton Gay 80-85; RD Woodstock 84-87; P-in-c Wootton by Woodstock 85-87; R Patterdale *Carl* 87-89; R Askerswell, Loders and Powerstock *Sarum* from 89; RD Lyme Bay from 92; RD Beaminster from 94. *The Vicarage, Loders, Bridport, Dorset DT6 3SA* Tel (01308) 427175

PAGET, Alfred Ivor. b 24. St Aid Birkenhead 56. **d** 59 **p** 60. C Hoylake *Ches* 59-62; Hong Kong 62-63; Australia 63-64; C Hyde St Geo *Ches* 64-66; R Gt and Lt Henny w Middleton *Chelmsf* 66-74; C Gt Holland 74-79; V Holland-on-Sea 79-92; rtd 92; Perm to Offic *S'wark* from 92. *94 Wellfield Road, London SW16 2BP* Tel 0181-769 3394

PAGET, David Rolf. b 54. Worc Coll Ox BA78. St Steph Ho Ox BA80. **d** 81 **p** 82. C Sheerness H Trin w St Paul *Cant* 81-84; C E Bedfont *Lon* 84-88; P-in-c Fulham St Andr Fulham Fields 88-89; V from 89. *St Andrew's Vicarage, 10 St Andrew's Road, London W14 9SX* Tel 0171-385 5578

PAGET, Richard Campbell. b 54. Collingwood Coll Dur BA76 Rob Coll Cam BA87. Ridley Hall Cam 85. **d** 88 **p** 89. C Gipsy Hill Ch Ch *S'wark* 88-92; R Chatham St Mary w St Jo *Roch* from 92. *The Rectory, 65 Maidstone Road, Chatham, Kent ME4 6DP* Tel (01634) 843632

PAGET, Robert James Innes. b 35. AKC59. **d** 60 **p** 61. C Attenborough w Bramcote *S'well* 60-63; C Cheltenham St Mark *Glouc* 63-72; P-in-c Pilsley *Derby* 72-73; TV N Wingfield, Pilsley and Tupton 73-89; R Pinxton 89-97; P-in-c Ambergate and Heage from 97. *The Vicarage, 65 Derby Road, Ambergate, Belper, Derbyshire DE56 2GD* Tel (01773) 852613

PAGET-WILKES, The Ven Michael Jocelyn James. b 41. NDA64. ALCD69. **d** 69 **p** 70. C Wandsworth All SS *S'wark* 69-74; V Hatcham St Jas 74-82; V Rugby St Matt *Cov* 82-90; Adn Warwick from 90. *10 Northumberland Road, Leamington Spa, Warks CV32 6HA* Tel (01926) 313337 or 674328

PAGETT, Andrew Stephen. b 45. Bris & Glouc Tr Course. **d** 82 **p** 83. NSM Swindon New Town *Bris* from 82. *93 Lansdown Road, Swindon SN1 3ND* Tel (01793) 539283

PAICE, Michael Antony. b 35. Kelham Th Coll 55. **d** 60 **p** 61. C Skegby *S'well* 60-62; C Carlton 62-66; V Misterton and W Stockwith 66-81; P-in-c Littleton on Severn w Elberton *Bris* 81-83; V Olveston 81-83; Deputation Appeals Org CECS 83-89; R Sutton St Nicholas w Sutton St Michael *Heref* 89-96; R Withington w Westhide 89-96; rtd 96. *Frankhurst, Sutton St Nicholas, Hereford HR1 3BN* Tel (01432) 880253

PAICE, William Henry. b 08. Worc Ord Coll. **d** 57 **p** 58. C Dudley St Aug Holly Hall *Worc* 57-59; C Redditch St Steph 59-62; C-in-c Hayling St Pet CD *Portsm* 62-68; C-in-c Gurnard All SS CD 68-73; rtd 73. *Garden House, The Laurels, Church Street, Shelfanger, Diss, Norfolk IP22 2DG* Tel (01379) 651128

PAIN, Canon David Clinton. b 36. K Coll Lon 56. **d** 64 **p** 64. Benin 64-67; Ghana 67-86; Hon Can Accra 80-86; V Kemp Town St Mary *Chich* 86-93; Chapl St Mary's Hall Brighton from 88; V Billingshurst *Chich* from 93. *The Vicarage, East Street, Billingshurst, W Sussex RH14 9PY* Tel (01403) 782332

PAIN, Lawrence Percy Bernard. b 11. Lon Univ BA32. Wells Th Coll 48. **d** 49 **p** 50. C Cranleigh *Guildf* 49-52; V Frimley Green 52-63; TR Cove St Jo 63-70; RD Aldershot 65-69; V Rowledge 70-81; rtd 81; Perm to Offic *Portsm* from 89. *c/o D M Pain Esq, Wold Cottage, Winchester Road, Lower Upham, Southampton SO32 1HA*

PAIN, Michael Broughton George. b 37. Dur Univ BA61. Wycliffe Hall Ox 61. **d** 63 **p** 64. C Downend *Bris* 63-67; C Swindon Ch Ch 67-70; V Alveston 70-78; V Guildf Ch Ch *Guildf* 78-90; TR Melksham *Sarum* from 90; Chapl Melksham Hosp from 90. *The Rectory, Canon Square, Melksham, Wilts SN12 6LX* Tel (01225) 703262

PAIN, Richard Edward. b 56. Bris Univ BA79 Univ of Wales (Cardiff) BD84. St Mich Coll Llan 81. **d** 84 **p** 85. C Caldicot *Mon* 84-86; P-in-c Cwmtillery 86-88; V 88-91; V Six Bells 88-91; V Risca from 91. *The Vicarage, 1 Gelli Crescent, Risca, Newport NP1 6QG* Tel (01633) 612307

PAINE, Alasdair David Maconnell. b 60. Trin Coll Cam BA82 MA86 MSc84. Wycliffe Hall Ox 94. **d** 96 **p** 97. C Ex St Leon w H Trin *Ex* from 96. *27 Barnardo Road, Exeter EX2 4ND* Tel (01392) 277540

PAINE, Dr David Stevens. b 24. St Jo Coll Cam MB47 BChir47 MA52. Ridley Hall Cam 52. **d** 54 **p** 55. C Rowner *Portsm* 54-56; C Freshwater 56-59; V S Cerney w Cerney Wick *Glouc* 59-64. *42 Newton Road, Cambridge CB1 5EF* Tel (01223) 353300

PAINE, Peter Stanley. b 46. K Coll Lon BD69 AKC69. Linc Th Coll DipMin89 Cuddesdon Coll 69. **d** 71 **p** 72. C Leeds St Aid *Ripon* 71-74; C Harrogate St Wilfrid 74-78; V Beeston Hill H Spirit 78-82; TV Seacroft 82-90; V Martham w Repps w Bastwick *Nor* 90-94; V Martham and Repps with Bastwick, Thurne etc from 94. *The Vicarage, Martham, Great Yarmouth, Norfolk NR29 4PR* Tel (01493) 740240

PAINE, William Barry. b 58. TCD DipTh84. CITC. **d** 84 **p** 85. C Glendermott *D & R* 84-86; C Lurgan St Jo *D & D* 86-88; I Kilbarron w Rossnowlagh and Drumholm *D & R* 88-91; CF from 91. *MOD Chaplains (Army), Trenchard Lines, Upavon, Pewsey, Wilts SN9 6BE* Tel (01980) 615804

PAINE DAVEY, Nathan Paul. b 64. Barrister-at-Law 88 Birm Poly LLB86. St Steph Ho Ox 89. **d** 92 **p** 93. C Palmers Green St Jo *Lon* 92-95; C Kentish Town St Silas from 95; C Haverstock Hill H Trin w Kentish Town St Barn from 95. *30A Hadley Street, London NW1 8SS* Tel 0171-482 1170

PAINTER, Canon David Scott. b 44. LTCL65 Worc Coll Ox BA68 MA72. Cuddesdon Coll 68. **d** 70 **p** 71. C Plymouth St Andr *Ex* 70-73; Chapl Plymouth Poly 71-73; C St Marylebone All SS *Lon* 73-76; Abp's Dom Chapl *Cant* 76-80; Dir of Ords 76-80; V Roehampton H Trin *S'wark* 80-91; PV Westmr Abbey 81-91; RD Wandsworth *S'wark* 85-90; Perm to Offic 91; Can Res and Treas S'wark Cathl from 91; Dioc Dir of Ords from 91. *22 Rochelle Close, London SW11 2RX* Tel 0181-871 1118 or 0171-403 8686

PAINTER, John. b 25. Selw Coll Cam BA48 MA53. Ripon Hall Ox 48. **d** 50 **p** 51. C Stoke Newington St Mary *Lon* 50-55; C Woodside Park St Barn 55-56; C Llangiwg *S & B* 56-59; C-in-c Swansea St Jo 59-60; R Chipstable w Raddington *B & W* 61-64; V Audenshaw St Steph *Man* 64-66; V Sandown Ch Ch *Portsm* 66-72; R Keinton Mandeville *B & W* 72-77; P-in-c Lydford-on-Fosse 76-77; R Keinton Mandeville w Lydford on Fosse 77-90; RD Cary 81-90; RD Bruton 82-85; rtd 90; Perm to Offic *B & W* from 90. *2 Juniper Gardens, Gillingham, Dorset SP8 4RF* Tel (01747) 823818

PAIRMAN, David Drummond. b 47. GGSM CertEd. Chich Th Coll 82. **d** 84 **p** 85. C Cowes St Mary *Portsm* 84-87; C Marshwood Vale *Sarum* 87-90; C Hawkchurch 87-90; C Marshwood Vale TM 90-95; rtd 95. *Achilles, Old Pinn Lane, Exeter EX1 3RF* Tel (01392) 464488

PAISEY, Gerald Herbert John. b 31. Wm Booth Memorial Coll 51 Lon Univ CertRS60 Leic Univ CertEd62 Nottm Univ DipRE68 DipAdEd70 MPhil77 Lanc Univ MA78 K Coll Lon PhD91. St Alb Minl Tr Scheme 80. **d** 88 **p** 90. NSM Montrose *Bre* 88-90; NSM Inverbervie 88-90; NSM Stonehaven from 90; NSM Catterline from 90. *20 St Michael's Way, Newtonhill, Stonehaven, Kincardineshire AB3 2GS* Tel (01567) 730322

PAISEY, Jeremy Mark. b 58. Aber Univ LLB81 Solicitor 83. Coates Hall Edin 92. **d** 94 **p** 95. C Turriff *Ab* 94-97; C Buckie 94-97; C Banff 94-97; C Cuminestown 94-97; C Portsoy 94-97; P-in-c Buckie from 97; P-in-c Portsoy from 97. *All Saints House, Cluny Square, Buckie, Banffshire AB56 1HA* Tel (01542) 832312

PAISH, Miss Muriel Dorothy. b 21. Birm Univ CertEd41. Glouc Sch of Min. **dss** 85 **d** 87 **p** 94. Uley w Owlpen and Nympsfield *Glouc* 85-96; Hon C 87-96; Perm to Offic from 97. *5 Woodstock Terrace, Uley, Dursley, Glos GL11 5SW* Tel (01453) 860429

PAISLEY, James. b 05. Edin Th Coll 27. **d** 29 **p** 30. C Dalton-in-Furness *Carl* 29-31; Borneo 31-42; Australia 42-45; V Compton *Ox* 47-70; V Hampstead Norris 47-70; rtd 70; Perm to Offic *Ex* from 70. *15 Wilton Way, Abbotskerswell, Newton Abbot, Devon TQ12 5PG* Tel (01626) 53728

PAISLEY, Ronald Gordon. b 15. Clifton Th Coll 50. **d** 52 **p** 53. C Upper Holloway St Pet *Lon* 52-55; V Newchapel *Lich* 55-60; V Becontree St Alb *Chelmsf* 60-73; V Toxteth Park St Clem *Liv*

73-80; rtd 80; Perm to Offic *Carl* from 86. *Glen Rosa, Station Road, Brampton, Cumbria CA8 1EX* Tel (016977) 3022

PAISLEY, Samuel Robinson (Robin). b 51. Man Univ BSc72. Edin Th Coll BD91. **d** 91 **p** 92. C St Mary's Cathl *Glas* 91-95; P-in-c Bishopbriggs from 95; Chapl Stobhill NHS Trust from 95. *St James's Rectory, 9 Meadowburn, Bishopbriggs, Glasgow G64 3HA* Tel 0141-772 4514

PAKENHAM, Charles Wilfrid. b 18. Trin Coll Ox BA40 MA52. Wycliffe Hall Ox 40. **d** 41 **p** 42. C Sutton *Liv* 41-44; CMS 44-49; Nigeria 44-49; C Cheltenham St Mary *Glouc* 49-52; V Litherland Ch Ch *Liv* 52-84; rtd 84; P-in-c W Woodhay w Enborne, Hampstead Marshall etc *Ox* 91-92. *15 Cook Road, Albourne, Marlborough, Wilts SN8 2EG* Tel (01672) 40531

PAKENHAM, Stephen Walter. b 29. Qu Coll Cam BA57 MA61. Linc Th Coll 57. **d** 59 **p** 60. C Handsworth St Jas *Birm* 59-61; C Handsworth St Andr 61-64; V Donnington *Chich* 64-75; V Appledram 64-75; V Durrington 75-81; V St Mary Bourne and Woodcott *Win* 81-88; rtd 88; Perm to Offic *Ex* from 88. *The Malthouse, Frogmore, Kingsbridge, Devon TQ7 2PG* Tel (01548) 531703

PALIN, John Edward. b 47. Univ of Wales (Cardiff) DipTh70 DPS71 Open Univ BA83 Leeds Univ MA89. St Mich Coll Llan 67. **d** 71 **p** 72. C Staveley *Derby* 71-74; C Nottingham St Mary *S'well* 75-77; P-in-c Thistleton 77-79; V Greetham w Stretton and Clipsham *Pet* 77-79; V Greetham and Thistleton w Stretton and Clipsham 79-83; TR Staveley and Barrow Hill *Derby* 83-87; Chapl R Hallamshire Hosp Sheff 87-88; Perm to Offic *Sheff* 88-90; C Bramley *Ripon* 90-91; TV 91-93; Chapl Doncaster Health Care NHS Trust from 93. *Tickhill Road Hospital, Tickhill Road, Doncaster, S Yorkshire DN4 8QL* Tel (01302) 853241

PALIN, Roy. b 34. Man Univ BA56. Ripon Hall Ox 65. **d** 67 **p** 68. C Ilkeston St Mary *Derby* 67-70; C Wollaton *S'well* 70-71; V Harby w Swinethorpe 71-79; V Thorney w Wigsley and Broadholme 71-79; P-in-c N Clifton 75-79; R Harby w Thorney and N and S Clifton 79-80; V Tuxford 80-81; P-in-c Laxton 80-81; P-in-c Markham Clinton 80-81; P-in-c Weston 80-81; V Tuxford w Weston and Markham Clinton 81-90; R Nuthall from 90. *The Rectory, 24 Watnall Road, Nuthall, Nottingham NG16 1DU* Tel 0115-938 4987

PALK, Mrs Deirdre Elizabeth Pauline. b 41. AIL77 Reading Univ BA63 City of Lon Poly DipBS74 DipRS84. S'wark Ord Course 81. **dss** 84 **d** 87. Wanstead H Trin Hermon Hill *Chelmsf* 84-87; Hon Par Dn from 87; Hon Par Dn Walthamstow St Pet from 88. *3 Ashdon Close, Woodford Green, Essex IG8 0EF* Tel 0181-505 3547

PALLANT, Canon Roger Frank. b 35. Trin Coll Cam BA57 MA61. Wells Th Coll 57. **d** 59 **p** 60. C Stafford St Mary *Lich* 59-62; C Ipswich St Mary le Tower *St E* 62-65; Dioc Youth Chapl 62-65; Dev Officer C of E Youth Coun 65-70; Hon C Putney St Mary *S'wark* 66-71; Org Sec New Syn Gp 70-71; R Hintlesham w Chattisham *St E* 71-80; V Ipswich All Hallows 80-88; Hon Can St E Cathl from 85; P-in-c Sproughton w Burstall from 88; Dioc Officer for LNSM from 88; RD Samford from 93. *The Rectory, Glebe Close, Sproughton, Ipswich IP8 3BQ* Tel (01473) 241078

PALLETT, Ian Nigel. b 59. Leeds Univ BA80. Linc Th Coll 81. **d** 84 **p** 85. C Halesowen *Worc* 84-88; C Mansfield Woodhouse *S'well* 88-91; R Morton and Stonebroom *Derby* from 91. *The Vicarage, 14 High Street, Stonebroom, Alfreton, Derbyshire DE55 6JY* Tel (01773) 872353

PALMER, Alister Gordon. b 46. Univ of Tasmania BA73 DipEd74. Trin Coll Bris 78 Ridley Hall Cam 80. **d** 80 **p** 81. C Patchway *Bris* 80-83; C Bushbury *Lich* 83-86; V Wednesfield Heath 86-93; NSM independent Ch Community work from 93. *31 Lea Road, Penn Fields, Wolverhampton WV3 0LU* Tel (01902) 710415

PALMER, Angus Douglas. b 40. St Chad's Coll Dur BA62 DipTh63. **d** 63 **p** 64. C Wallsend St Pet *Newc* 63-66; C Newc H Cross 66-69; C Bottesford *Linc* 69-70; R Penicuik *Edin* 70-83; R W Linton 77-83. *6 Hackworth Gardens, Wylam, Northd NE41 8EJ* Tel (01661) 853786

PALMER, Bernard Joseph. b 20. St Cath Soc Ox BA49 MA64. Worc Ord Coll 64. **d** 66 **p** 67. C St Stephen by Saltash *Truro* 66-69; R Harvington *Worc* 69-78; V Stoulton w Drakes Broughton and Pirton 78-85; rtd 85; Perm to Offic *Ex* 85-95; Perm to Offic *Truro* from 95. *Belvedere, Treloyhan Park Road, St Ives, Cornwall TR26 2AH* Tel (01736) 796846

PALMER, David Michael. b 53. QUB BA95. CITC 95. **d** 97. C Glenageary *D & G* from 97. *10 Silchester Park, Dun Laoghaire, Co Dublin, Irish Republic* Tel Dublin (1) 280 7543 E-mail palmerdm@tcd.ie

PALMER, David Philip. b 50. Sarum & Wells Th Coll. **d** 84 **p** 85. C St Ives *Ely* 84-86; C Luton All SS w St Pet *St Alb* 86-88; V Stocksbridge *Sheff* 88-97; P-in-c Seaton Hirst *Newc* from 97. *The Vicarage, Newbiggin Road, Ashington, Northd NE63 0TQ* Tel (01670) 813218

PALMER, David Roderick. b 34. St Jo Coll Dur BA56 Birm Univ DipTh58 Trin Coll Ox. Qu Coll Birm 56. **d** 60 **p** 61. C Loughton St Jo *Chelmsf* 60-63; C Pimlico St Gabr *Lon* 63-64; Miss to Seamen 64-67; CF 67-74; Chapl Luxembourg *Eur* 74-80; P-in-c Exton and Winsford and Cutcombe w Luxborough *B & W* 80-82; P-in-c Wrington w Butcombe 82-84; Dep Dir of Tr Inst Wednesbury St Jas *Lich* 84-86; C Gt Wyrley 86-89; V Wilshamstead and Houghton Conquest *St Alb* from 90. *The Vicarage, Wilshamstead, Bedford MK45 3EU* Tel (01234) 740423

PALMER, Canon Derek George. b 28. Selw Coll Cam BA50 MA54. Wells Th Coll 50. **d** 52 **p** 53. C Stapleton *Bris* 52-54; C Bishopston 54-58; C-in-c Hartcliffe St Andr CD 58-62; V Bris St Andr Hartcliffe 62-68; V Swindon Ch Ch 68-76; Hon Can Bris Cathl 74-76; Adn Roch 77-83; Can Res Roch Cathl 77-83; Hon Can 83-87; Home Sec Gen Syn Bd for Miss and Unity 83-87; TR Dronfield *Derby* 87-90; TR Dronfield w Holmesfield 90-95; Chapl to The Queen from 90; Hon Can Derby Cathl *Derby* 92-95; rtd 95. *124 Bath Road, Banbury, Oxon OX16 0TR* Tel (01295) 268201

PALMER, Derek James. b 54. Man Univ BA77. Qu Coll Birm 77. **d** 79 **p** 80. C Leek *Lich* 79-83; CF 83-92; USA 92-95; C S Ockendon *Chelmsf* from 95; C Belhus Park from 95. *The Rectory, 18 North Road, South Ockendon, Essex RM15 6QJ* Tel (01708) 853349

PALMER, Edward Wilton. b 31. K Coll Cam BA55 Cam Univ MA60. EAMTC 96. **d** 97. NSM Helmdon w Stuchbury and Radstone etc *Pet* from 97. *Vine Cottage, 8 Broad Street, Syresham, Brackley, Northants NN13 5HS* Tel (01280) 850252

PALMER, Miss Elizabeth Anne. b 46. Reading Univ BA68 Nottm Univ PGCE69 MEd78. St Jo Coll Nottm DTS91. **d** 91 **p** 94. C Scartho *Linc* 91-96; P-in-c Ilkeston St Jo *Derby* from 96. *The Vicarage, 41 St John's Road, Ilkeston, Derbyshire DE7 5PA* Tel 0115-932 5446

PALMER, Preb Francis Harvey. b 30. Jes Coll Cam BA52 MA56. Wycliffe Hall Ox 53. **d** 55 **p** 56. C Knotty Ash St Jo *Liv* 55-57; C Southgate *Chich* 58-60; Chapl Fitzw Ho Cam 60-64; V Cambridge H Trin *Ely* 64-71; Chapl to Cam Pastorate 64-71; Prin Ridley Hall Cam 71-72; R Worplesdon *Guildf* 72-80; Bp's Ecum Officer 74-80; P-in-c Blymhill w Weston-under-Lizard *Lich* 80-82; Dioc Missr and Sec to Bd for Miss and Unity 80-90; Preb Lich Cathl 86-89; TV Walsall 87-90; rtd 90; Perm to Offic *Lich* from 90; Perm to Offic *Heref* from 93. *The Old Vicarage, Claverley, Wolverhampton WV5 7DT* Tel (01746) 710746

PALMER, Graham. b 31. Em Coll Cam BA53 MA57. Qu Coll Birm 56. **d** 58 **p** 59. C Camberwell St Giles *S'wark* 58-61; C Kilburn St Aug *Lon* 61-67; P-in-c Fulham St Alb 67-73; V 73-92; V Fulham St Alb w St Aug from 92. *St Alban's Vicarage, 4 Margravine Road, London W6 8HJ* Tel 0171-385 0724

PALMER, Hugh. b 50. Pemb Coll Cam BA72 MA76. Ridley Hall Cam 73. **d** 76 **p** 77. C Heigham H Trin *Nor* 76-80; Bp's Chapl for Tr and Miss 80-84; C St Helen Bishopsgate w St Andr Undershaft etc *Lon* 85-95; C Fulwood *Sheff* from 95. *1 Silver Birch Avenue, Sheffield S10 3TA* Tel 0114-263 0926

PALMER, Hugh Maurice Webber. b 28. Magd Coll Cam BA51 MA55. Cuddesdon Coll 51. **d** 53 **p** 54. C Bitterne Park *Win* 53-57; N Rhodesia 57-62; V Owslebury w Morestead *Win* 62-65; Rhodesia 65-70; C Headbourne Worthy *Win* 70-71; P-in-c Stratton Strawless *Nor* 72-77; R Hainford 72-77; R Haynford w Stratton Strawless 77-80; Chapl HM Pris Stafford 80-82; Chapl HM Pris Standford Hill 82-89; Sub-Chapl HM Pris Nor 89-91; rtd 91. *2B Millfield Road, North Walsham, Norfolk NR29 0EB* Tel (01692) 403664

PALMER, Ian Stanley. b 50. K Coll Lon BD71. Cranmer Hall Dur 73. **d** 75 **p** 76. C Huyton St Mich *Liv* 75-78; Chapl Dur Univ *Dur* 78-83; V Collierley w Annfield Plain 83-90; Australia from 90. *114A Ntaba Road, Belmont North, NSW, Australia 2280* Tel Newcastle (49) 454573 Fax 454788 E-mail ian.palmer@accnet.net.au

PALMER, Mrs Jacqueline Merrill. b 60. Leeds Univ BA82. Cranmer Hall Dur 83. **dss** 85 **d** 87. Asst Chapl Hull Univ *York* 85-87. *60 Magnolia Road, Southampton SO19 7LH* Tel (01703) 432591

PALMER, John Richard Henry. b 29. AKC52. **d** 53 **p** 54. C Englefield Green *Guildf* 53-57; P-in-c Brewarrina Australia 57-62; C Wareham w Arne *Sarum* 62-63; PC Derby St Jo *Derby* 63-66; Chapl Holloway Sanatorium Virginia Water 66-70; Chapl Brookwood Hosp Woking 70-94; rtd 94; Perm to Offic *Truro* from 94. *Lightning Ridge, Pentreath Road, The Lizard, Helston, Cornwall TR12 7NY* Tel (01326) 290654

PALMER, John Russell. b 25. Birm Univ BSc46. Cuddesdon Coll 70. **d** 71 **p** 72. C Weeke *Win* 71-76; V Four Marks 76-90; rtd 90. *33 Montague Road, Bournemouth BH5 2EW* Tel (01202) 426536

PALMER, Malcolm Leonard. b 46. Sarum & Wells Th Coll. **d** 82 **p** 83. C Cannock *Lich* 82-85; Chapl RAF 85-89; Asst Chapl HM Pris Dur 89-90; Chapl HM Young Offender Inst Hewell Grange 90-93; Chapl HM Rem Cen Brockhill 90-93; Chapl HM Pris Blakenhurst from 93. *HM Prison Blakenhurst, Hewell Grange, Redditch, Worcester B97 6QS* Tel (01527) 543348 Fax 546382

PALMER, Marion Denise. b 42. SRN64 SCM66 Open Univ BA82. Linc Th Coll 84. **dss** 86 **d** 87 **p** 94. Poplar *Lon* 86-90; Par Dn 87-90; Par Dn Gillingham St Mary *Roch* 90-94; C 94-96; C Farnborough from 96. *Church House, Leamington Avenue, Orpington, Kent BR6 9BQ* Tel (01689) 852843

PALMER, Canon Maureen Florence. b 38. Qu Eliz Coll Lon BSc60 PhD64 DipRS79. Ripon Coll Cuddesdon DipTh84. **dss** 85 **d** 87

p 94. Tupsley *Heref* 85-87; C 87-88; Par Dn Talbot Village *Sarum* 88-91; Chapl Birm Cathl *Birm* 91-96; Can Res Guildf Cathl *Guildf* from 96. *2 Cathedral Close, Guildford, Surrey GU2 5TL* Tel (01483) 560329

PALMER, Michael Christopher. b 43. AKC67. **d** 68 **p** 69. C Easthampstead *Ox* 68-71; Miss to Seamen 71-73; Hong Kong 73; Lic to Offic *Ox* 76-79; Lic to Offic *Truro* 79-83; Dioc Soc Resp Adv from 83; Bp's Dom Chapl 85-87; V Devoran from 87. *The Vicarage, Devoran, Truro, Cornwall TR3 6PA* Tel (01872) 863116

PALMER, Norman Ernest. b 28. Lon Univ DipTh56 BD59. Roch Th Coll 66. **d** 67 **p** 67. C Chipping Norton *Ox* 67-69; V Bozeat w Easton Maudit *Pet* 69-90; rtd 90; Perm to Offic *Chich* from 90. *4 St Augustine's Close, Bexhill-on-Sea, E Sussex TN39 3AZ* Tel (01424) 218573

PALMER, Canon Peter Malcolm. b 31. Chich Th Coll 56. **d** 59 **p** 60. C Leighton Buzzard *St Alb* 59-63; C Apsley End 63-65; C Hitchin H Sav 65-69; R Ickleford 69-76; V Oxhey St Matt 76-86; V Kensworth, Studham and Whipsnade 86-96; Hon Can St Alb 94-96; rtd 97. *4 Sefton Close, St Albans, Herts AL1 4PF* Tel (01727) 835215

PALMER, Peter Parsons. b 27. **d** 59 **p** 61. SSJE from 59; Canada 59-79; Perm to Offic *Leic* 80-86; Perm to Offic *Lon* 86-94; Lic to Offic from 94. *SSJE Priory, 228 Iffley Road, Oxford OX4 1SE* Tel (01865) 242227

PALMER, Philip Edward Hitchen. b 35. St Jo Coll Cam MA61 DipAdEd74. Ridley Hall Cam 61 EAMTC 87. **d** 90 **p** 91. NSM Gt Oakley w Wix *Chelmsf* 90-96; NSM Gt Oakley w Wix and Wrabness from 96. *Glebe House, Great Oakley, Harwich, Essex CO12 5BJ* Tel (01255) 880737

PALMER, Robert William. b 28. DMS. Wells Th Coll 63. **d** 65 **p** 66. C Earlsdon *Cov* 65-69; P-in-c Cov St Mark 69-71; Chapl Cov and Warks Hosp 69-71; Hon C Binley *Cov* 72-76; V Sheff St Paul Wordsworth Avenue *Sheff* 76-84; V Deepcar 84-93; rtd 93; Perm to Offic *Sheff* from 93. *Moorlands, 26 Coal Pit Lane, Stocksbridge, Sheffield S30 5AW*

PALMER, Canon Stephen Charles. b 47. Oak Hill Th Coll 71. **d** 74 **p** 75. C Crofton *Portsm* 74-77; Bp's Dom Chapl 77-80; Chapl RNR from 78; R Brighstone and Brooke w Mottistone *Portsm* 80-91; P-in-c Shorwell w Kingston 82-86; RD W Wight 87-91; Hon Can Portsm Cathl from 91; Falkland Is 91-96; V Portsdown *Portsm* from 96. *Portsdown Vicarage, Portsdown Hill Road, Cosham, Portsmouth PO6 1BE* Tel (01705) 375360

PALMER, Steven Roy. b 51. Birm Univ BSc71. WMMTC 91. **d** 94 **p** 95. C Sheldon *Birm* 94-97; P-in-c Duddeston w Nechells from 97. *St Matthew's Vicarage, Duddeston Manor Road, Birmingham B7 4QD* Tel 0121-359 6965

PALMER, Canon Terence Henry James (Terry). b 34. St Edm Hall Ox BA65 MA69. St D Coll Lamp BA55 LTh57. **d** 57 **p** 58. C Griffithstown *Mon* 57-60; Min Can and C St D Cathl *St D* 60-63; Perm to Offic *Ox* 63-65; Perm to Offic *B & W* 63-65; C Monmouth *Mon* 65-69; C-in-c St Hilary Greenway CD 69-72; R Roggiett w Llanfihangel Roggiett 72-80; R Portskewett and Roggiett w Llanfihangel Rogiet from 80; RD Netherwent from 89; Dir NSM Studies from 91; Can St Woolos Cathl from 96. *The Rectory, 19 Main Road, Portskewett, Newport NP6 4SG* Tel (01291) 420313

PALMER, William Frederick. b 15. Kelham Th Coll 33. **d** 40 **p** 41. C St Helier *S'wark* 40-41; C Earlsfield St Jo 41-44; C Burnham *Ox* 44-49; R Langley Marish 49-68; R Chalfont St Giles 68-73; V Mill Hill St Mich *Lon* 73-81; rtd 81; Perm to Offic *St Alb* from 81. *22 The Sycamores, Baldock, Herts SG7 5BJ* Tel (01462) 892456

PALMER-PALMER-FFYNCHE, Barry Marshall. b 23. Hertf Coll Ox BA47 MA48. Westcott Ho Cam 47. **d** 49 **p** 50. C Alrewas *Lich* 49-52; C Wychnor 49-52; C Birchington w Acol *Cant* 52-56; R Harrietsham 56-66; Chapl Westmr Hosp Lon 66-73; V Chipping Sodbury and Old Sodbury *Glouc* 73-88; rtd 88; Perm to Offic *Glouc* from 89; Perm to Offic *Bris* from 89; Perm to Offic *Lon* from 90. *Finch's Folly, Home Farm Stables, 45 Hay Street, Marshfield, Chippenham, Wilts SN14 8PF* Tel (01225) 891096

PAMMENT, Canon Gordon Charles. b 31. TCD BA54. Linc Th Coll 56. **d** 58 **p** 60. C Hemel Hempstead *St Alb* 58-63; C Gedney Drove End *Linc* 63-65; I Macroom Union *C, C & R* 65-72; I Rathcormac Union 72-78; I Fermoy Union 78-91; Preb Ross Cathl 89-91; Preb Cork Cathl 89-91; rtd 91. *5 Langford Place, Co Cork, Irish Republic*

PAMPLIN, Dr Richard Lawrence. b 46. Lon Univ BScEng68 Dur Univ BA75. NY Th Sem DMin85 Wycliffe Hall Ox 75. **d** 77 **p** 78. C Greenside *Dur* 77-80; C Sheff St Barn and St Mary *Sheff* 80-84; R Wombwell 84-90; P-in-c Madeley *Heref* 90-91; TR from 91. *St Michael's Vicarage, Church Street, Madeley, Telford, Shropshire TF7 5BN* Tel (01952) 585718

PANG, Wing-On. b 43. BA67 Lon Univ MA70. Oak Hill Th Coll DipHE87. **d** 87 **p** 88. C Pennycross *Ex* 87-91; TV Mildenhall *St E* 91-96; Hong Kong from 96. *St Andrew's Church, 138 Nathan Road, Tsim Sha Tsui, Kowloon, Hong Kong* Tel Hong Kong (00852) 2367 1478 Fax 2367 6562 E-mail standrew@hk.super.net

PANGBOURNE, John Godfrey. b 36. Ridley Hall Cam 82. **d** 84 **p** 85. C Ashtead *Guildf* 84-88; V Ore Ch Ch *Chich* from 88. *Christ Church Vicarage, 76 Canute Road, Ore, Hastings, E Sussex TN35 5HT* Tel (01424) 421439

PANKHURST, Donald Araunah. b 28. Qu Coll Birm DipTh64. **d** 64 **p** 65. C Pemberton St Jo *Liv* 64-68; V Aspull 68-76; R Newchurch 76-88; R Winwick 88-94; rtd 94; Perm to Offic *Carl* from 94. *4 St Mary's Park, Windermere, Cumbria LA23 1AY* Tel (01539) 446390

PANNETT, Philip Anthony. b 36. MPS59 AKC63. **d** 64 **p** 65. C Stanmer w Falmer and Moulsecoomb *Chich* 64-68; C Hangleton 68-72; Teacher Bodiam Manor Sch 74-76; Perm to Offic from 76. *1 Fitzjohn Road, Lewes, E Sussex BN7 1PP* Tel (01273) 472804

PANTER, Canon Noel. b 09. Ex Coll Ox BA31 DipTh32 MA35. Wycliffe Hall Ox 31. **d** 33 **p** 34. C Kidderminster St Geo *Worc* 33-36; C Dudley St Fran 36-41; R Churchill w Blakedown 41-68; RD Kidderminster 63-68; Hon Can Worc Cathl 66-77; V Gt Malvern Ch Ch 68-77; rtd 77; Perm to Offic *Heref* from 78; Perm to Offic *Glouc* 79-93. *2 Park View, Oatleys Road, Ledbury, Herefordshire HR8 2BN* Tel (01531) 632789

PANTER, Richard James Graham. b 48. Oak Hill Th Coll 73. **d** 76 **p** 77. C Rusholme H Trin *Man* 76-80; C Toxteth St Cypr w Ch Ch *Liv* 80-85; V Clubmoor 85-96; P-in-c Litherland St Jo and St Jas from 96. *St John and St James Vicarage, 2A Monfa Road, Bootle, Merseyside L20 6BQ* Tel 0151-922 3758

PANTER MARSHALL, Mrs Susan Lesley. b 49. Portsm Poly BSc72 Grad LI84. S Dios Minl Tr Scheme 88. **d** 91 **p** 94. NSM Southover *Chich* 91-95; C Iford w Kingston and Rodmell from 95. *30 South Way, Lewes, E Sussex BN7 1LY* Tel (01273) 474670

PANTON, Alan Edward. b 45. K Coll Lon BD67 AKC67. **d** 68 **p** 69. C Eltham St Jo *S'wark* 68-73; C Horley 73-78; V Dallington *Pet* from 78. *The Vicarage, The Barton's Close, Dallington, Northampton NN5 7HQ* Tel (01604) 751478

PANTRY, John Richard. b 46. Oak Hill NSM Course DipTh93. **d** 93 **p** 94. NSM Alresford *Chelmsf* from 93. *2 Conifers Close, Alresford, Colchester CO7 8AW* Tel (01206) 824257

PAPANTONIOU, Ms Frances Caroline (Fran). b 52. S Dios Minl Tr Scheme 89. **d** 92 **p** 94. Par Dn Harrow Weald All SS *Lon* 92-94; C 94-95; C Preston Ascension from 95. *159 Kenton Lane, Harrow, Middx HA3 8TL* Tel 0181-907 0771

PAPE, Timothy Vernon Francis (Tim). b 39. Lon Univ BSc63. Wells Th Coll 63. **d** 65 **p** 66. C Pershore w Wick *Worc* 65-69; Perm to Offic *Bris* 69-73; Hon C Southbroom *Sarum* from 75; Hd Master Chirton Primary Sch Wilts from 81. *Mallards, Chirton, Devizes, Wilts SN10 3QX* Tel (01380) 840593

PAPWORTH, John. b 21. Lon Univ BSc(Econ). **d** 75 **p** 76. Zambia 76-81; Hon C Paddington St Sav *Lon* 81-83; Hon C St Marylebone St Mark Hamilton Terrace 85-97. *24 Abercorn Place, London NW8 9XP* Tel 0171-286 4366

PAPWORTH, Miss Shirley Marjorie. b 33. CA Tr Coll. **d** 88 **p** 94. Par Dn Hornchurch H Cross *Chelmsf* 88-93; rtd 93; NSM Hornchurch St Andr *Chelmsf* from 94. *4 Gosport Drive, Hornchurch, Essex RM12 6NU* Tel (01708) 524348

PARADISE, Bryan John. b 49. Southn Univ BSc Lon Bible Coll BA. Cranmer Hall Dur. **d** 82 **p** 83. C High Harrogate Ch Ch *Ripon* 82-86; Dioc Adult Educn Officer *Guildf* from 86; P-in-c Dunsfold 86-90; R 90-93; R E Horsley from 93. *The Rectory, Ockham Road South, East Horsley, Leatherhead, Surrey KT24 6RL* Tel (01483) 282359

PARE, Stephen Charles. b 53. Sussex Univ BEd75. St Mich Coll Llan DipTh80. **d** 80 **p** 81. C Cardiff St Jo *Llan* 80-83; P-in-c Marcross w Monknash and Wick 83; TV Llantwit Major 83-91; V Penmark w Porthkerry from 91. *The Vicarage, 6 Milburn Close, Rhoose, Barry CF62 3EJ* Tel (01446) 711713

PARFITT, Anthony Colin (Tony). b 44. Ox Univ Inst of Educn CertEd66 Open Univ BA71 Plymouth Poly MPhil84. SW Minl Tr Course 93. **d** 96 **p** 97. NSM Langport Area Chs *B & W* from 96. *Croftswood, Ducks Hill, Langport, Somerset TA10 9EN* Tel (01458) 252848 Fax as telephone

PARFITT, Brian John. b 49. Ex Coll Ox BA71 MA76. Wycliffe Hall Ox 71. **d** 74 **p** 75. C Newport St Mark *Mon* 74-78; R Blaina 78-83; R Blaina and Nantyglo 83-86; Chapl Blaina and Distr Hosp Gwent 83-86; Consultant W Midlands and Wales CPAS 86-95; V Magor w Redwick and Undy *Mon* from 95; Perm to Offic *Ban* from 95. *The Vicarage, Magor, Newport NP6 3BZ* Tel (01633) 880266

PARFITT, David George. b 65. De Montfort Univ Leic BA87 DipArch90. Wycliffe Hall Ox BTh92. **d** 95 **p** 96. C Malpas *Mon* from 95. *4 Aspen Way, Malpas, Newport NP9 6LB* Tel (01633) 821362

PARFITT, Graeme Stanley. b 36. Qu Coll Birm 77. **d** 79 **p** 80. C Fishponds St Jo *Bris* 79-82; V Southmead 82-91; V Stockwell St Mich *S'wark* from 91. *St Michael's Vicarage, 78 Stockwell Park Road, London SW9 0DA* Tel 0171-274 6357

PARFITT, John Arthur. b 49. St Jo Coll Nottm BTh81. **d** 81 **p** 82. C Radcliffe-on-Trent *S'well* 81-84; C Chilwell 84-86; V Awsworth w Cossall 86-91; Perm to Offic from 91. *133 Parkside, Nottingham NG8 2NL* Tel 0115-928 1907

PARFITT, Preb John Hubert. b 29. Birm Univ DipTh66 Southn Univ MA72 BPhil. Qu Coll Birm 78. **d** 80 **p** 81. C Fladbury, Wyre Piddle and Moor *Worc* 80-82; C Malvern Link w Cowleigh 82; V Hanley Castle, Hanley Swan and Welland 82-83; Dir RE *B & W*

84-93; Preb Wells Cathl 85-93; rtd 93; Perm to Offic *B & W* from 93; Master Hugh Sexey's Hosp Bruton from 95. *The Master's House, Sexey's Hospital, High Street, Bruton, Somerset BA10 0AS* Tel (01749) 813369

PARFITT, Canon Keith John. b 44. K Coll Lon BD68 AKC68. St Aug Coll Cant 69. **d** 70 **p** 71. C Kettering St Andr *Pet* 70-74; Asst Soc and Ind Adv *Portsm* 74-89; RD Alverstoke 79-86; C-in-c Bridgemary CD 81-82; V Bridgemary 82-89; Dioc UPA Officer *Blackb* 89-97; Can Res Blackb Cathl 94-97; Dir Is of Wight Rural Community Coun from 97. *Downsview, Farriers Way, Shorwell, Isle of Wight PO30 3JP* Tel (01983) 740434

PARGETER, Canon Muriel Elizabeth. b 28. St Mich Ho Ox 53. **dss** 82 **d** 87 **p** 95. Hd Dss *Roch* 82-87; Dioc Dir of Ords 87-90; Hon Can Roch Cathl 87-90; rtd 90; NSM Worthing Ch the King *Chich* from 95. *63 Pavilion Road, Worthing, W Sussex BN45 7EE* Tel (01903) 214476

PARISH, George Richard. b 33. ACIB60 Qu Coll Cam BA56 MA60. S'wark Ord Course 85. **d** 88 **p** 89. NSM Sunninghill *Ox* 88-96; P-in-c Withyham St Mich *Chich* from 96. *The Rectory, Withyham, Hartfield, E Sussex TH7 4BA* Tel (01892) 770241

PARISH, Nicholas Anthony. b 58. Oak Hill Th Coll BA84 Ridley Hall Cam 84. **d** 86 **p** 87. C Eltham H Trin *S'wark* 86-89; C Barnes St Mary 89-91; V Streatham St Paul 91-96; Ind Chapl *Ox* from 96. *4 Micheldever Way, Bracknell, Berks RG12 3XX* Tel (01344) 50651

PARISH, Stephen Richard. b 49. Oak Hill Th Coll DipTh77. **d** 77 **p** 78. C Chadderton Ch Ch *Man* 77-81; C Chell *Lich* 81-82; TV 82-88; V Warrington St Ann *Liv* from 88. *St Ann's Vicarage, 1A Fitzherbert Street, Warrington WA2 7QG* Tel (01925) 631781

PARK, Ernest Winston. b 10. St Paul's Cheltenham CertEd31. Moray Ord Course 89. **d** 92. C Poolewe *Mor* 92-95; rtd 95; Perm to Offic *B & W* from 95. *Sunnydene, 8 Morris Lane, Bathford, Bath BA1 7PP* Tel (01225) 859638

PARK, Tarjei Erling Alan. b 64. W Lon Inst of HE BA88 Lanc Univ MA89 Pemb Coll Ox DPhil96. Ripon Coll Cuddesdon DipMin94. **d** 94 **p** 95. C Lancaster St Mary *Blackb* from 94. *25 Bishopdale Road, Lancaster LA1 5NF* Tel (01524) 844672

PARK, Canon Trevor. b 38. Lon Univ BA64 Open Univ PhD90. Lambeth STh81 Linc Th Coll 64. **d** 66 **p** 67. C Crosthwaite Kendal *Carl* 66-68; Asst Chapl Solihull Sch 69-71; Chapl St Bees Sch Cumbria 71-77; V St Bees *Carl* 71-77; V Dalton-in-Furness 77-84; V Natland 84-97; Hon Can Carl Cathl from 86; RD Kendal 89-94; Ch Commr 93-97; Chapl Oslo w Bergen, Trondheim and Stavanger *Eur* from 97. *Harald Hårfagresgate 2, 0363 Oslo, Norway* Tel Oslo (2) 2692214

PARKE, W/Cdr Edmund George. b 14. JP71. TCD BA37 MA47. **d** 38 **p** 39. C Newcastle w Butterton *Lich* 38-42; Chapl RAF 42-69; Chapl Soc Work Dept Dundee Corp 69-75; Tayside Regional Coun 75-79; rtd 79; Perm to Offic *St And* from 79; Perm to Offic *Bre* from 79. *9 Netherlea Place, Newport-on-Tay, Fife DD6 8NW* Tel (01382) 542048

PARKE, Simon Frederick Fenning. b 57. MA. Wycliffe Hall Ox. **d** 84 **p** 85. C Isleworth St Jo *Lon* 84-87; C St Marylebone All So w SS Pet and Jo 87-88; C Langham Place All So 88-93; V Tufnell Park St Geo and All SS from 93; P-in-c W Holloway St Luke from 96. *The Vicarage, 72 Crayford Road, London N7 0ND* Tel 0171-609 1645 or 387 1360

PARKER, Alfred. b 20. Man Univ BA47. Wycliffe Hall Ox 47. **d** 49 **p** 50. C Droylsden St Mary *Man* 49-53; C New Bury 53-54; P-in-c Bolton St Bart 54-56; V 56-61; P-in-c Gt Lever 59-61; R 61-65; V Belmont 65-87; rtd 87. *21 Edgeley Road, Whitchurch, Shropshire SY13 1EU*

PARKER, Angus Michael Macdonald. b 53. Bris Univ BSc74. St Jo Coll Nottm DipTh81 DPS83. **d** 83 **p** 84. C Northampton St Giles *Pet* 83-86; C Attenborough *S'well* 86-96; V Pennycross *Ex* from 96. *St Pancras Vicarage, 66 Glentor Road, Plymouth PL3 5TR* Tel (01752) 774332

PARKER, Mrs Ann Jacqueline. b 41. Dur Inst of Educn TCert63 Sunderland Poly TCert65 Open Univ BA82. W of England Minl Tr Course 91. **d** 95 **p** 96. NSM Pilning w Compton Greenfield *Bris* from 95. *Wyngarth, Easter Compton, Bristol BS12 3RA* Tel (01454) 632329

PARKER, Arthur Townley. b 14. Worc Ord Coll 59. **d** 61 **p** 62. C Barbourne *Worc* 61-63; S Africa 63-64; V Rock w Heightington *Worc* 64-68; C W Wycombe *Ox* 68-70; C Watford St Jo *St Alb* 70-71; C Martin w Thornton *Linc* 73-75; Chapl Hostel of God Clapham 71-73; Asst Chapl HM Pris Wandsworth 71-73; rtd 74; Perm to Offic *Blackb* from 87. *30 Langdale Road, Morecambe, Lancs LA4 5XA* Tel (01524) 419183

PARKER, Mrs Carole Maureen. b 45. N Ord Course. **d** 87 **p** 95. NSM Coalville and Bardon Hill *Leic* 87-90; Perm to Offic 90-95; NSM Thorpe Acre w Dishley 95-96; P-in-c Packington w Normanton-le-Heath from 96. *The Vicarage, Mill Street, Packington, Ashby de la Zouch, Leics LE65 1WL* Tel (01530) 412215

PARKER, David Arthur. b 48. Lon Univ DipTh71. Kelham Th Coll. **d** 71 **p** 72. C Newc Ch Ch *Newc* 71-74; C Hendon *Dur* 74-79; C-in-c Southwick St Cuth CD 79-84; V Sunderland Red Ho 84-88; rtd 88; Perm to Offic *Ex* from 88. *Sisters of Charity, St Elizabeth House, Longbrook Street, Plymouth PL7 3NL* Tel (01752) 336112

PARKER, Dr David Charles. b 53. St Andr Univ MTh75 Em Coll Cam DipTh76 Univ of Leiden DTh90. Ridley Hall Cam 75. **d** 77 **p** 78. C Hendon St Paul Mill Hill *Lon* 77-80; C Bladon w Woodstock *Ox* 80-85; C-in-c Shipton-on-Cherwell 80-85; C-in-c Begbroke 80-85; C-in-c Hampton Gay 80-85; Perm to Offic *Birm* 85-89; Lic to Offic from 89; Lect Qu Coll Birm 85-93; Sen Angl Tutor 89-93; Lect Birm Univ from 93. *Department of Theology, PO Box 363, Birmingham University, Birmingham B15 2TT* Tel 0121-414 3344

PARKER, David John. b 33. St Chad's Coll Dur BA55 Hull Univ MA85. Linc Th Coll 57. **d** 59 **p** 60. C Tynemouth Ch Ch *Newc* 59-60; C Ponteland 60-63; C Byker St Mich 63-64; C-in-c Byker St Martin CD 64-69; V Whorlton 69-73; TR 73-80; Ind Chapl *Linc* 80-84; Master Newc St Thos Prop Chpl *Newc* 84-89; Lic Preacher *Man* from 90; Exec Officer Dioc Bd Ch and Soc from 90; Hon Can Man Cathl from 97. *43 Acresfield Road, Salford M6 7GE* Tel 0161-737 6891 or 832 5253

PARKER, David Louis. b 47. Lon Univ LLB70 Ox Univ MA82. Wycliffe Hall Ox BA79. **d** 80 **p** 81. C Broadwater St Mary *Chich* 80-84; TR Ifield from 84. *The Vicarage, Ifield, Crawley, W Sussex RH11 0NN* Tel (01293) 520843

PARKER, David William. b 21. SEN CQSW MBASW. Glouc Th Course 77 Sarum & Wells Th Coll 81. **d** 81 **p** 81. Chapl HM Pris Leyhill 81-84; NSM Cromhall w Tortworth *Glouc* 81-83; NSM Wickwar w Rangeworthy 83-87; Perm to Offic from 88. *22 Durham Road, Charfield, Wotton-under-Edge, Glos GL12 8TH* Tel (01454) 260253

PARKER, Dennis. b 22. Tyndale Hall Bris 63. **d** 64 **p** 65. C Polegate *Chich* 64-68; C-in-c Reading St Mary Castle Street Prop Chpl *Ox* 68-70; R Newdigate *Guildf* 70-87; rtd 87; Perm to Offic *Guildf* from 87. *Cleve House, Flint Hill, Dorking, Surrey RH4 2LL* Tel (01306) 889458

PARKER, George Jeffrey. b 24. LCP69. Cuddesdon Coll 70. **d** 70 **p** 71. Hd Master St Nic Sch Codsall 70-76; Hon C Codsall *Lich* 70-76; Hon C Lapley w Wheaton Aston 76-80; Lic to Offic 80-82; R Hepworth *St E* 82-86; P-in-c Hinderclay w Wattisfield 82-86; P-in-c Thelnetham 82-86; R Hepworth, Hinderclay, Wattisfield and Thelnetham 86-89; rtd 89; Perm to Offic *Lich* from 90. *Cranham, 42 Sheringham Covert, Beaconside, Staffs ST16 3YL* Tel (01785) 58223

PARKER, George William. b 29. BS53 BD57 Lon Univ PGCE67. K Coll (NS) 49. **d** 53 **p** 54. Canada 53-59 and 68-71 and 78-93; C W Hackney St Barn *Lon* 59-61; V Haggerston St Mary w St Chad 61-68; C Portsea N End St Mark *Portsm* 72-75; V Darlington St Jo *Dur* 75-78; rtd 91. *Spider Cottage, RR3 Newport, Nova Scotia, Canada, B0N 2A0*

PARKER, Hugh James. b 30. ACP55 TCD MA57 NUU DASE74. **d** 63 **p** 64. Lic to Offic *Conn* 63-70; Dioc C 70-96; Hd Master Larne High Sch 81-92; rtd 96. *29 Ransevyn Drive, Whitehead, Carrickfergus, Co Antrim BT38 8NW* Tel (01960) 378106

PARKER, John Bristo. b 26. Edin Th Coll 61. **d** 64 **p** 65. C Barrow St Jo *Carl* 64-68; V Sledmere *York* 68-74; R Cowlam 68-74; P-in-c Wetwang 69-74; V Sledmere and Wetwang w Cowlan 74-79; V Kirkby Ireleth *Carl* 79-83; V Rillington w Scampston, Wintringham etc *York* 83-87; R Bishop Wilton w Full Sutton, Kirby Underdale etc 87-91; rtd 91; Perm to Offic *York* from 91. *East Lodge, Sledmere, Driffield, N Humberside YO25 0XQ* Tel (01377) 86325

PARKER, Preb Joseph French. b 09. St Chad's Coll Dur BA37 DipTh38 MA40. **d** 38 **p** 39. C Warrington St Elphin *Liv* 38-40; C Shrewsbury St Mary *Lich* 40-42; C Wolverhampton St Pet 42-46; V Kingswinford St Mary 46-51; V Toxteth Park St Agnes *Liv* 51-60; RD W Bromwich *Lich* 61-76; V W Bromwich All SS 61-76; RD W Bromwich 61-76; Preb Lich Cathl 67-76; rtd 76; Perm to Offic *Carl* 77-93. *36 Glebe Farm Court, Up Hatherley, Cheltenham, Glos GL51 5EB* Tel (01242) 863273

PARKER, Julian Roderick. b 57. Essex Univ BA80. Sarum & Wells Th Coll DipMin93. **d** 93 **p** 94. C Gillingham *Sarum* 93-97; V N Bradley, Southwick and Heywood from 97. *The Vicarage, 62 Church Lane, North Bradley, Trowbridge, Wilts BA14 0TA* Tel (01225) 752635

PARKER, Miss Margaret. b 27. Lightfoot Ho Dur 54. **dss** 60 **d** 87 **p** 94. Ryhope *Dur* 60-61; Monkwearmouth St Andr 61-79; Adv for Accredited Lay Min 74-87; Adv for Accredited Lay Min *Newc* 79-87; Newc St Geo 79-87; C 87; Tutor Cranmer Hall Dur 87-92; Hon Dn Dur Cathl *Dur* 92-94; Min Can from 94; Chapl St Mary's Coll Dur from 95. *53 Devonshire Road, Durham DH1 2BJ* Tel 0191-386 3233

PARKER, Margaret Grace. *See* TORDOFF, Mrs Margaret Grace

PARKER, Matthew John. b 63. Man Univ BA85 SS Coll Cam BA88. Ridley Hall Cam 85. **d** 88 **p** 89. C Twickenham St Mary *Lon* 88-91; C Stockport St Geo *Ches* 91-93; Chapl Stockport Gr Sch from 91; P-in-c Stockport St Mark *Ches* 93-94; TV Stockport SW from 94. *St Mark's Vicarage, 66 Berlin Road, Stockport, Cheshire SK3 9QS* Tel 0161-480 5896

PARKER, Michael Alan. b 70. St Jo Coll Dur BA91. CITC BTh93. **d** 96 **p** 97. C Dundela *D & D* from 96. *29 Marmount Park, Belfast BT4 2GR* Tel (01232) 768786

PARKER, Canon Michael John. b 54. Cam Coll of Art and Tech BA76 Lon Univ BD85. Trin Coll Bris 82. **d** 85 **p** 86. C Leic H Trin w St Jo *Leic* 85-88; P-in-c Edin Clermiston Em *Edin* 88-90; Chapl

Edin St Thos from 90; Can St Mary's Cathl from 94. *16 Belgrave Road, Edinburgh EH12 6NF* Tel 0131-334 1309 Fax as telephone E-mail mjps + thoms@aol.com

PARKER, Michael John. b 57. BSc. Wycliffe Hall Ox 80. **d** 83 **p** 84. C Heigham H Trin *Nor* 83-86; C Muswell Hill St Jas w St Matt *Lon* 86-90; R Bedford St Jo and St Leon *St Alb* from 90. *St John's Rectory, 36 St John's Street, Bedford MK42 0DH* Tel (01234) 354818

PARKER, Nigel Howard. b 69. St Jo Coll Dur BSc90 CITC BTh94. **d** 97. C Holywood *D & D* from 97. *20 Princess Gardens, Holywood, Co Down BT18 0PN* Tel (01232) 423622

PARKER, Peter Edward. b 32. FRSA Edin Univ MA55 Lon Univ PGCE56. Sarum & Wells Th Coll 73. **d** 74 **p** 75. C Kirkby Lonsdale w Mansergh *Carl* 74-76; C Kingston St Jo *S'wark* 76; C Kingston All SS w St Jo 76-80; Chapl S Bank Poly 80-85; Ind Chapl *Chelmsf* 85-90; Chapl Chelmsf Cathl 85-90; R Mistley w Manningtree and Bradfield 90-97; rtd 97. *2 Waterside, Ely, Cambs CB7 4AZ* Tel (01353) 669932

PARKER, Philip Vernon. b 60. Birm Univ BSc82 PGCE83. Wycliffe Hall Ox BA89. **d** 90 **p** 91. C Walkergate *Newc* 90-92; C Byker St Mark and Walkergate St Oswald 92-93; Chapl Shiplake Coll Henley 93-96; Chapl Milton Abbey Sch Dorset 96-97; C Lindfield *Chich* from 97. *32 Noah's Ark Lane, Lindfield, W Sussex RH16 2LT* Tel (01444) 482989

PARKER, Ramon Lewis (Brother Raphael). b 36. Kelham Th Coll 56. **d** 61 **p** 62. C Tonge Moor *Man* 61-64; C Clerkenwell H Redeemer w St Phil *Lon* 64-65; V Prestwich St Hilda *Man* 65-71; SSF from 71; Chapl Univ of Wales (Lamp) *St D* 81-86; Lic to Offic *Sarum* from 87; rtd 97. *c/o Brother Samuel SSF, The Friary, Hilfield, Dorchester, Dorset DT2 7BE* Tel (01300) 341345 Fax 241293

PARKER, Richard Bryan. b 64. Sheff Poly BA87. Coll of Resurr Mirfield 92. **d** 95 **p** 96. C Norton *Sheff* from 95. *6 Hazlebarrow Close, Sheffield S8 8AL* Tel 0114-237 6273

PARKER, Richard Frederick. b 36. Oak Hill Th Coll 72. **d** 74 **p** 75. C Wootton *St Alb* 74-76; C Hove Bp Hannington Memorial Ch *Chich* 76-81; R Northwood *Portsm* 81-88; V W Cowes H Trin 81-88; V Aldershot H Trin *Guildf* from 88. *2 Cranmore Lane, Aldershot, Hants GU11 3AS* Tel (01252) 20618

PARKER, Robert Lawrence (Bob). b 34. ALCD59. **d** 59 **p** 60. C Chippenham St Paul *Bris* 59-61; C Swindon Ch Ch 61-63; New Zealand 63-71; P-in-c Over Stowey w Aisholt *B & W* 71-73; V Nether Stowey 71-73; V Nether Stowey w Over Stowey 73-93; RD Quantock 87-93; V Pitminster w Corfe from 93. *The Vicarage, Pitminster, Taunton, Somerset TA3 3AZ* Tel (01823) 421232

PARKER, Robert William. b 18. Linc Th Coll 81. **d** 81 **p** 82. NSM Mablethorpe w Trusthorpe *Linc* 81-83; NSM Alford w Rigsby 83-86; NSM Alberbury w Cardeston *Heref* 87-90; NSM Ford 87-90; rtd 90; Perm to Offic *Linc* from 90. *17 The Glade, Sandilands, Sutton-on-Sea, Lincs SN12 2RZ* Tel (01507) 442572

PARKER, Roger Thomas Donaldson. b 55. Simon Frazer Univ BC BA80 Univ of Wales (Cardiff) LLB84 Univ Coll Lon LLM85. Coll of Resurr Mirfield CPT95. **d** 95 **p** 96. C Swinton and Pendlebury *Man* from 95. *St Matthew's House, 46 Townsend Road, Swinton, Manchester M27 6SH* Tel 0161-794 1808

PARKER, Roland John Graham. b 48. AKC72 Hull Univ BA(Ed)83. St Aug Coll Cant 71. **d** 74 **p** 75. C Linc St Faith and St Martin w St Pet *Linc* 74-78; V Appleby 78-84; Ind Chapl 78-84; V N Kelsey 84-92; V Cadney 84-92; P-in-c Waddington from 92. *The Rectory, Waddington, Lincoln LN5 9RS* Tel (01522) 720323

PARKER, Russell Edward. b 48. Lon Univ DipTh77 Man Univ BA80 Nottm Univ MTh82. St Jo Coll Nottm 80. **d** 81 **p** 82. C Walmsley *Man* 81-85; V Coalville and Bardon Hill *Leic* 85-90; Acorn Chr Healing Trust from 90; Perm to Offic *Leic* from 90. *The Vicarage, Mill Street, Packington, Ashby de la Zouch, Leics LE65 1WL* Tel (01530) 412215

PARKER, Thomas Henry Louis. b 16. Em Coll Cam BA38 MA42 BD50 DD61. Lon Coll of Div 38. **d** 39 **p** 40. C Chesham St Mary *Ox* 39-42; C Cambridge St Phil *Ely* 42-43; C Cambridge St Andr Less 43-45; C Luddesdowne *Roch* 45-48; V Brothertoft *Linc* 48-55; R Lt Ponton w Stroxton 55-59; R Lt Ponton 59-61; R Gt Ponton 58-61; V Oakington *Ely* 61-71; Lect Dur Univ 71-81; rtd 81. *72 Windsor Road, Cambridge CB4 3JN* Tel (01223) 312215

PARKER, Thomas Richard (Tom). b 52. Imp Coll Lon BScEng73 Keele Univ MEd83. Cranmer Hall Dur CTM94. **d** 94 **p** 95. C Chadkirk *Ches* from 94. *29 Urwick Road, Romiley, Stockport, Cheshire SK6 3JS* Tel 0161-494 0547

PARKER, Timothy Percy. b 58. Man Univ BA. St Jo Coll Nottm DipTh. **d** 85 **p** 86. C Pitsmoor Ch Ch *Sheff* 85-87; C Kimberworth 87-89; C Brightside w Wincobank 89-91; C Upper Armley *Ripon* 91-95; TV Billingham St Aid *Dur* from 95. *17 Shadforth Drive, Billingham, Cleveland TS23 3PW* Tel (01642) 561870

PARKER, William Albert Stuart. b 26. Wells Th Coll 68. **d** 70 **p** 71. C Bartley Green *Birm* 70-72; C Sutton Coldfield H Trin 72-75; V Allens Cross 75-82; V Lydbrook *Glouc* 82-88; V Holbeach Marsh *Linc* 88-93; rtd 93; Perm to Offic *York* from 96. *78 Wold Road, Pocklington, York YO4 2QG* Tel (01759) 304032

PARKER, William Joseph. b 10. Man Univ BA37. Ridley Hall Cam 35. **d** 37 **p** 38. C Man Albert Memorial Ch *Man* 37-40; CF 40-46; V Burton H Trin *Lich* 46-54; V Sheff St Jo *Sheff* 54-66; R Barnburgh 66-77; rtd 77; Perm to Offic *St As* from 78; Perm to Offic *Ban* from 78. *23 Victoria Park, Colwyn Bay LL29 7AX* Tel (01492) 532057

PARKES, Kevin. b 62. Trent Poly BA84. Sarum & Wells Th Coll BTh90. **d** 88 **p** 89. C Wandsworth St Anne *S'wark* 88-92; USPG 92-95; Trinidad and Tobago 93-95; Kingston Area Miss Team *S'wark* from 95. *30 Gorringe Park Avenue, Mitcham, Surrey CR4 2DG* Tel 0181-685 0772

PARKES, Robert Stephen. b 12. Selw Coll Cam BA35 MA40. Linc Th Coll 37. **d** 38 **p** 39. C Eastleigh *Win* 38-48; Bp's Youth Chapl *St Alb* 49-54; Lic Preacher 49-50; V Offley 50-54; V Tilehurst St Geo *Ox* 54-65; R Pangbourne 65-77; rtd 78; Perm to Offic *Win* from 78. *22 Arle Close, Alresford, Hants SO24 9BG* Tel (01962) 734109

PARKHILL, Alan John. b 43. TCD BA66. CITC 68. **d** 67 **p** 68. C Knockbreda *D & D* 67-70; Asst Warden Elswick Lodge Newc 71-72; C Bangor St Comgall 73-78; Bp's C Kilmore 78-82; I Kilmore w Inch 82-86; I Clonfeacle w Derrygortreavy *Arm* from 86. *4 Clonfeacle Road, Benburb, Dungannon, Co Tyrone BT71 7LQ* Tel (01861) 548239

PARKIN, George David. b 37. Cranmer Hall Dur BA60 DipTh62. **d** 62 **p** 63. C Balderstone *Man* 62-65; C Tunstead 65-67; C Gateshead Fell *Dur* 69-73; Nigeria 74-76; V Walton Breck *Liv* 80-92; V Rawtenstall St Mary *Man* from 92. *2 Melia Close, Rawtenstall, Rossendale, Lancs BB4 6RQ* Tel (01706) 215585

PARKIN, John Edmund. b 44. Open Univ BA73. St Jo Coll Nottm 83. **d** 85 **p** 86. C Aberavon *Llan* 85-90; R Eglwysilan from 90. *The Rectory, Brynhafod Road, Abertridwr, Caerphilly CF83 4BH* Tel (01222) 830220

PARKIN, John Francis. b 40. Linc Th Coll 65. **d** 68 **p** 69. C Cullercoats St Geo *Newc* 68-72; C Stony Stratford *Ox* 72-73; TV Lt Coates *Linc* 73-76; Perm to Offic 88-93; NSM Horncastle w Low Toynton from 93; NSM High Toynton from 93. *The Firs, 68 Louth Road, Horncastle, Lincs LN9 5LJ* Tel (01507) 523208

PARKIN, Trevor Kinross. b 37. Cranmer Hall Dur 63. **d** 66 **p** 67. C Kingston upon Hull St Martin *York* 66-69; C Reading St Jo *Ox* 69-73; Ind Chapl *Lon* 73-80; Hon C Langham Place All So 73-80; Ind Chapl *Ely* 80-82; V Maidenhead St Andr and St Mary *Ox* from 82. *St Mary's Vicarage, 14 Juniper Drive, Maidenhead, Berks SL6 8RE* Tel (01628) 24908

PARKINSON, Andrew. b 56. Keble Coll Ox BA77 MA80. Westcott Ho Cam 78. **d** 80 **p** 81. C S Shore H Trin *Blackb* 80-85; V Lea 85-94; V Longton from 94. *Longton Vicarage, Birchwood Avenue, Hutton, Preston PR4 5EE* Tel (01772) 612179

PARKINSON, Arthur Norman. b 09. TCD BA32. **d** 33 **p** 34. C Arm St Patr *Arm* 33-36; C Portadown St Mark 36-38; P-in-c Mullavilly 38-40; I 40-46; I Grange 46-52; I Kilmore St Aid w Diamond 52-63; I Acton w Drumbanagher 63-75; Treas Arm Cathl 65-72; Chan 72-73; Prec 73-75; rtd 75. *34 Old Rectory Park, Portadown, Craigavon, Co Armagh BT62 3QH* Tel (01762) 336491

PARKINSON, Miss Brenda. b 40. Lancs Poly CQSW. Dalton Ho Bris 65. **dss** 74 **d** 87 **p** 94. Ribbleton *Blackb* 75-80; Ingol 82-87; Par Dn 87-88; Par Dn Ashton-on-Ribble St Mich 88-91; Par Dn Ashton-on-Ribble St Mich w Preston St Mark 91-92; Par Dn Gt Marsden 92-94; C from 94. *11 Hallam Crescent, Nelson, Lancs BB9 9PD* Tel (01282) 615819

PARKINSON, David Thomas. b 42. Linc Th Coll 77. **d** 79 **p** 80. C Yate New Town *Bris* 79-82; TV Keynsham *B & W* 82-88; R Bleadon from 88. *The Rectory, Coronation Road, Bleadon, Weston-super-Mare, Avon BS24 0PG* Tel (01934) 812297

PARKINSON, Derek Leslie. b 29. Ripon Hall Ox 64. **d** 66 **p** 67. C Guildf Ch Ch *Guildf* 66-69; P-in-c Preston St Sav *Blackb* 69-74; P-in-c Preston St Jas 69-74; P-in-c Fontmell Magna *Sarum* 74-81; P-in-c Ashmore 74-81; P-in-c Kingswood w Alderley and Hillesley *Glouc* 81-82; R 82-94; rtd 94. *The Old Manse, Ludgate Hill, Wotton-under-Edge, Glos GL12 7JJ*

PARKINSON, Edward James. b 19. TCD BA50 MA54 Div Test51. **d** 51 **p** 52. C Belfast St Mary *Conn* 51-53; C Lancaster St Mary *Blackb* 53-55; CF (TA) 54; R Limehouse St Anne *Lon* 55-60; V Hampton St Mary 60-69; Lic to Offic *Newc* 74-80; Master of the Charterhouse Hull 80-95; AD Cen and N Hull *York* 87-89; rtd 95; Perm to Offic *B & W* from 95. *100 High Street, Weston, Bath BA1 4DQ* Tel (01225) 425463

PARKINSON, Francis Wilson (Frank). b 37. DCouns88 Open Univ BA79. Bernard Gilpin Soc Dur 58 St Aid Birkenhead DipTh62. **d** 62 **p** 63. C Monkwearmouth St Andr *Dur* 62-64; C Speke All SS *Liv* 64-67; CF 67-93; Perm to Offic *Ox* from 93. *9 Priory Mead, Longcot, Faringdon, Oxon SN7 7TJ* Tel (01793) 784406

PARKINSON, George Stanley. b 20. St Jo Coll Dur BA47 DipTh48. **d** 48 **p** 49. C Widnes St Paul *Liv* 48-51; C Bradf Cathl Par *Bradf* 51-55; V Greengates 55-58; V Pennington *Man* 58-71; V Eccles St Mary 71-80; V Churt *Guildf* 80-90; RD Farnham 82-88; rtd 90. *12 Bevere Court, Bevere, Worcester WR3 7RE* Tel (01905) 457106

PARKINSON, Ian Richard. b 58. Univ Coll Dur BA79 Lon Univ BD84. Wycliffe Hall Ox 80. **d** 83 **p** 84. C Hull Newland St Jo *York* 83-86; C Linthorpe 86-92; V Saltburn-by-the-Sea from 92.

The Vicarage, Greta Street, Saltburn-by-the-Sea, Cleveland TS12 1LS Tel (01287) 622007

PARKINSON, The Very Revd John Fearnley. b 30. MBE90. ALCD54. **d** 55 **p** 56. C Plymouth St Andr *Ex* 55-59; Metrop Sec USCL 59-62; Relig Adv Westward TV 62-81; V Devonport St Budeaux 62-66; CF (TA) 63-77; V Kenton *Ex* 66-75; R Kenton w Mamhead 75-79; R Kenton w Mamhead and Powderham 79-83; Preb Ex Cathl 75-83; Relig Adv SW TV 82-83; Provost St Chris Cathl Bahrain 83-89; CMS 90-95; Hon Chapl Br Emb Israel 90-95; Dean Jerusalem 90-93; rtd 95; Perm to Offic *Ex* from 95. *6 Priory Gardens, Dawlish, Devon EX7 9JN* Tel (01626) 862415

PARKINSON, John Reginald. b 32. Qu Coll Birm 79. **d** 81 **p** 82. NSM Catshill *Worc* 81-85; C Knightwick w Doddenham, Broadwas and Cotheridge 85-88; C Martley and Wichenford 85-88; P-in-c Berrow w Pendock and Eldersfield 88-89; R Berrow w Pendock, Eldersfield, Hollybush etc from 89; RD Upton 95-97. *The Vicarage, Berrow, Malvern, Worcs WR13 6JN* Tel (01684) 833237

PARKINSON, Joseph Greenwood. b 10. Tyndale Hall Bris 30. **d** 34 **p** 36. C Tipton St Martin *Lich* 34-36; C Nottingham St Sav *S'well* 36-37; C St Alb St Paul *St Alb* 37-38; Asst Chapl Hill End Mental Hosp 37-38; R Elton 38-46; V Thornton *Leic* 49-51; R Burslem St Jo *Lich* 51-56; CF 55-58; V Onecote cum Bradnop *Lich* 58-75; rtd 75. *18 Alder Road, Market Drayton, Shropshire TF9 3HZ*

PARKINSON, Nicholas John (Nick). b 46. FCCA75 Cranfield Inst of Tech MBA85. St Alb Minl Tr Scheme 92. **d** 95 **p** 96. NSM Woburn Sands *St Alb* from 95. *Thornbank House, 7 Church Road, Woburn Sands, Milton Keynes MK17 8TE* Tel (01908) 583397

PARKINSON, Peter. b 23. Roch Th Coll 61. **d** 63 **p** 64. C Linc St Mary-le-Wigford w St Martin *Linc* 63-65; C Skegness 65-68; V Newton-on-Trent 68-73; R Kettlethorpe 68-73; V Grainthorpe w Conisholme 74-83; V Marshchapel 74-83; R N Coates 74-83; V Bicker 83-88; rtd 88. *11 Waltham Road, Doddington Park, Lincoln LN6 0SD* Tel (01522) 680604

PARKINSON, Raymond Neville. b 21. Bris Univ BA53. Tyndale Hall Bris 50. **d** 54 **p** 55. C Hove Bp Hannington Memorial Ch *Chich* 54-57; C Reading St Jo *Ox* 57-59; R Folke w Long Burton, N Wootton and Haydon *Sarum* 59-69; V Ashby-de-la-Zouch H Trin *Leic* 69-79; V Swannington St Geo and Coleorton 79-87; rtd 87; Perm to Offic *Leic* 87-88; Perm to Offic *Linc* from 88. *45 Kipling Drive, Mablethorpe, Lincs LN12 2RF* Tel (01507) 441140

PARKINSON, Simon George Denis. b 39. Univ of Wales (Lamp) BA66. Westcott Ho Cam 65. **d** 67 **p** 68. C Rothwell *Ripon* 67-70; Chapl RAF 70-73; C Leeds St Pet *Ripon* 74-75; V Horbury Junction *Wakef* 76-83; V Hanging Heaton 83-92; P-in-c Upper Hopton 92; V Eastthorpe and Upper Hopton from 92. *The Vicarage, 4 Hopton Hall Lane, Mirfield, W Yorkshire WF14 8EL* Tel (01924) 493569

PARKINSON, Thomas Alan. b 40. St Jo Coll York CertEd61 DipTh62. NW Ord Course 75. **d** 78 **p** 79. NSM Sheff Parson Cross St Cecilia *Sheff* 78-82; NSM Goldthorpe w Hickleton 82-90; C Cantley from 90; Dioc RE Adv from 93. *10 Manse Close, Cantley, Doncaster, S Yorkshire DN4 6QX* Tel (01302) 539783

PARKINSON, Vivian Leslie (Viv). b 54. St Luke's Coll Ex CertEd76 Brighton Poly BEd87. St Jo Coll Nottm 92. **d** 94 **p** 95. C Cowbridge *Llan* from 94. *3 Leoline Close, Cowbridge CF71 7BU*

PARLETT, Gordon Alec. b 14. Oak Hill Th Coll 46. **d** 49 **p** 50. C Roch St Marg *Roch* 49-51; C S Norwood St Mark *Cant* 51-56; R Buckland in Dover 56-72; Hon Chapl Miss to Seamen 58-72; Chapl Buckland Hosp Dover 59-72; V Loose *Cant* 72-87; rtd 87; Perm to Offic *Cant* from 89; Perm to Offic *Chich* from 89. *St Giles's Parsonage, Bodiam, Robertsbridge, E Sussex TN32 5UJ* Tel (01580) 830793

PARMENTER, Mrs Deirdre Joy. b 45. EAMTC 91. **d** 94 **p** 95. C Ipswich St Aug *St E* 94-97; P-in-c Haughley w Wetherden from 97. *The Vicarage, The Folly, Haughley, Stowmarket, Suffolk IP14 3MS* Tel (01449) 771647 Mobile 0421-587634

PARNELL, Bryan Donald. b 38. Chich Th Coll 66. **d** 69 **p** 70. C Lewisham St Jo Southend *S'wark* 69-72; Australia from 72. *9 Dinwoodie Avenue, Clarence Gardens, S Australia 5039* Tel Whyalla (8) 293 3027 Fax 351 0282

PARNELL-HOPKINSON, Clive. b 46. Sarum & Wells Th Coll 75. **d** 78 **p** 79. C Maldon All SS w St Pet *Chelmsf* 78-81; C Chandler's Ford *Win* 81-84; Chapl RAF from 84; Perm to Offic *Llan* from 84. *Chaplaincy Services (RAF), HQ, Personnel and Training Command, RAF Innsworth, Gloucester GL3 1EZ* Tel (01452) 712612 ext 5164 Fax 510828

PARR, Frank. b 35. Nottm Univ BCombStuds82 Lanc Univ MA86. Linc Th Coll 79. **d** 82 **p** 83. C Padiham *Blackb* 82-85; P-in-c Accrington St Andr 85-88; V Oswaldtwistle Immanuel and All SS 88-96; V Tunstall w Melling and Leck from 96. *The New Vicarage, Church Lane, Tunstall, Carnforth, Lancs LA6 2QN* Tel (01524) 274376

PARR, George. b 12. MC45. St Jo Coll Dur BA37. **d** 38 **p** 39. C Walton Breck *Liv* 38-40; CF 40-46; Hon CF 46; Org Sec (Dios Liv, Man and S & M) CMS 46-49; V Southport St Paul *Liv* 49-54; V Douglas St Thos *S & M* 54-59; V Ripon H Trin *Ripon* 59-78; rtd 78. *22 South Grange Road, Ripon, N Yorkshire HG4 2NH* Tel (01765) 604163

PARR, Canon James Edwin Cecil. b 20. TCD BA42 MA47. **d** 43 **p** 44. C Lisburn Ch Ch *Conn* 43-48; CF 48-50; C Whitehouse *Conn* 50-52; P-in-c Cloughfern 52-59; I 59-82; Can Conn Cathl 80-82; rtd 82. *Cloughfern Cottage, 26B Feumore Road, Ballinderry Upper, Lisburn, Co Antrim BT28 2LH* Tel (01846) 651851

PARR, Dr John. b 53. St Edm Hall Ox BA74 MA87 Lon Univ BD79 Sheff Univ PhD90. Trin Coll Bris 75. **d** 79 **p** 80. C Gt Crosby St Luke *Liv* 79-82; C Walton St Mary 82-84; V Ince St Mary 84-87; Tutor and Lect Ridley Hall Cam 87-95; Chapl 87-93; Dir Studies 93-95; P-in-c Harston w Hauxton *Ely* from 95. *The Vicarage, Church Street, Harston, Cambridge CB2 5NP* Tel (01223) 872496

PARRATT, Dennis. b 53. St Steph Ho Ox. **d** 84 **p** 85. C Cainscross w Selsley *Glouc* 84-88; C Old Shoreham *Chich* 88-91; C New Shoreham 88-91. *17 Colvill Avenue, Shoreham-by-Sea, W Sussex BN43 5WN* Tel (01273) 464528

PARRETT, Mrs Rosalind Virginia. b 43. Cant Sch of Min 84. **d** 87 **p** 94. NSM Selling w Throwley, Sheldwich w Badlesmere etc *Cant* 87-91; Asst Chapl Cant Hosp 87-91; Par Dn Stantonbury and Willen *Ox* 91-94; TV 94-96; P-in-c Owlsmoor from 96. *The Vicarage, 107 Owlsmoor Road, Owlsmoor, Camberley, Surrey GU15 4SS* Tel (01344) 780110 or 771286

PARRETT, Simon Christopher. b 60. Sarum & Wells Th Coll. **d** 87 **p** 88. C Ifield *Chich* 87-91; Chapl to the Deaf *Sarum* 91-94; NSM Bournemouth H Epiphany *Win* 94-96; Asst Chapl Poole Hosp NHS Trust from 96. *90 Wareham Road, Lytchett Matravers, Poole, Dorset BH16 6DT* Tel (01202) 622477

PARRETT, Stanley Frederick Donald. b 24. **d** 78 **p** 79. NSM Whitchurch w Ganarew *Heref* 78-83; C Goodrich w Welsh Bicknor and Marstow 83-86; C Walford w Bishopswood 83-86; R Pembridge w Moorcourt, Shobdon, Staunton etc 86-89; rtd 89. *4 Manley Lane, Pembridge, Leominster, Herefordshire HR6 9EE*

PARRISH, Robert Carey. b 57. St Steph Ho Ox 89. **d** 91 **p** 92. C Abington *Pet* 91-94; C Leckhampton SS Phil and Jas w Cheltenham St Jas *Glouc* from 94. *72 Salisbury Avenue, Cheltenham, Glos GL51 5DH* Tel (01242) 517057

PARROTT, David Wesley. b 58. Oak Hill Th Coll BA. **d** 84 **p** 85. C Thundersley *Chelmsf* 84-87; C Rainham 87-89; P-in-c Heydon w Gt and Lt Chishill 89-90; P-in-c Elmdon w Wendon Lofts and Strethall 89-90; P-in-c Chrishall 89-90; R Heydon, Gt and Lt Chishill, Chrishall etc 91-96; R Rayleigh from 96. *The Rectory, Hockley Road, Rayleigh, Essex SS6 8BA* Tel (01268) 742151

PARROTT, George. b 37. Leeds Univ BA61. Bps' Coll Cheshunt 61. **d** 63 **p** 64. C Lower Mitton *Worc* 63-65; C-in-c Fairfield St Rich CD 65-68; Zambia 68-70; C Cleethorpes *Linc* 70-75; R Withern 75-80; P-in-c Gayton le Marsh 76-80; P-in-c Strubby 76-80; P-in-c Authorpe 76-80; P-in-c Belleau w Aby and Claythorpe 76-80; P-in-c N and S Reston 76-80; P-in-c Swaby w S Thoresby 76-80; R Withern 80-90; V Reston 80-90; V Messingham 90-93; P-in-c Fincham *Ely* from 95; P-in-c Marham from 95; P-in-c Shouldham from 95; P-in-c Shouldham Thorpe from 95. *The Rectory, High Street, Fincham, Downham Market, Norfolk PE33 9EL* Tel (01366) 347491

PARROTT, Canon Gerald Arthur. b 32. St Cath Coll Cam BA56 MA60. Chich Th Coll. **d** 58 **p** 59. C Ashington *Newc* 58-61; C Brighton St Pet *Chich* 61-63; V Leeds St Wilfrid *Ripon* 63-68; R Lewisham St Jo Southend *S'wark* 69-73; TR Catford (Southend) and Downham 73-77; RD E Lewisham 75-77; Can Res and Prec S'wark Cathl 77-88; TR Wimbledon 88-95; rtd 95; Perm to Offic *Chich* from 95. *10 Palings Way, Fernhurst, Haslemere, Surrey GU27 3HJ*

PARROTT, Martin William. b 57. Keele Univ BA79 Lon Univ PGCE80. Ripon Coll Cuddesdon 82. **d** 85 **p** 86. C Birchfield *Birm* 85-88; Chapl Lon Univ *Lon* 88-93; P-in-c Univ Ch Ch the K Lon 90-93; V Hebden Bridge *Wakef* from 93. *St James's Vicarage, Church Lane, Hebden Bridge, W Yorkshire HX7 6DL* Tel (01422) 842138

PARRY, Canon Bryan Horace. b 33. St Mich Coll Llan 65. **d** 67 **p** 68. C Holyhead w Rhoscolyn w Llanfair-yn-Neubwll *Ban* 67-71; TV 71-73; P-in-c Small Heath St Greg *Birm* 73-78; V 78-80; V Perry Barr 80-94; RD Handsworth 83-91; P-in-c Kingstanding St Luke 86-92; Hon Can Birm Cathl 87-94; rtd 94; Perm to Offic *Nor* from 94. *St Seiriol, Old Crown Yard, Walsingham, Norfolk NR22 6BU* Tel (01328) 820019

PARRY, Brychan Vaughan. b 13. Univ of Wales DipTh37. St Andr Coll Pampisford 41. **d** 42 **p** 42. C Bedminster St Paul *Bris* 42-44; CF (EC) 44-46; V Greenbank *Bris* 46-53; CF 53-69; V Gt Barton *St E* 69-78; rtd 78. *64 Cuckmere Road, Seaford, E Sussex BN25 4DJ* Tel (01323) 898273

PARRY, David Allan. b 62. Bris Univ BSc83 Univ of Wales (Cardiff) CQSW88 DASS88. Trin Coll Bris DipHE94. **d** 94 **p** 95. C Withywood *Bris* from 94. *74 Gatehouse Avenue, Withywood, Bristol BS13 9AE* Tel 0117-964 2668

PARRY, David Thomas Newton. b 45. Selw Coll Cam BA67 MA71. Lambeth STh76 Cuddesdon Coll 67. **d** 69 **p** 70. C Oldham St Mary w St Pet *Man* 69-73; C Baguley 73-74; Tutor Sarum &

Wells Th Coll 74-78; V Westleigh St Pet *Man* 78-88; TR E Farnworth and Kearsley 88-97; TR Chambersbury (Hemel Hempstead) *St Alb* from 97. *The Rectory, 14 Pancake Lane, Hemel Hempstead, Herts HP2 4NB* Tel (01442) 64860

PARRY, Denis. b 34. Sarum & Wells Th Coll 83. **d** 85 **p** 86. C Hubberston w Herbrandston and Hasguard etc *St D* 85-89; P-in-c Herbrandston and Hasguard w St Ishmael's 89-90; R from 90. *The Rectory, Herbrandston, Milford Haven SA73 3SJ* Tel (01646) 693263

PARRY, Canon Dennis John. b 38. Univ of Wales (Lamp) BA60. St Mich Coll Llan 60. **d** 62 **p** 63. C Caerphilly *Llan* 62-64; C Aberdare St Fagan 64-67; Canada 67-69; R Gelligaer *Llan* 69-75; V Llanwnnog and Caersws w Carno *Ban* 75-89; V Llanidloes w Llangurig from 89; RD Arwystli from 89; Hon Can Ban Cathl from 90. *The Vicarage, Llanidloes SY18 6HZ* Tel (01686) 412370 Fax as telephone

PARRY, Derek Nugent Goulding. b 32. Ely Th Coll 60. **d** 63 **p** 64. C Fareham SS Pet and Paul *Portsm* 63-67; C Portsea N End St Mark 67-74; P-in-c Piddletrenthide w Plush, Alton Pancras etc *Sarum* 74-92; rtd 92. *Farthing Cottage, 12 Fordington Green, Dorchester, Dorset DT1 1LU* Tel (01305) 269794

PARRY, John Gareth. b 61. Univ of Wales (Abth) BA83 Univ of Wales (Ban) PGCE84. Westcott Ho Cam 94. **d** 96 **p** 97. C Holyhead *Ban* from 96. *Ty Sant Elbod, 3 Harbour View, Holyhead LL65 2HL* Tel (01407) 764780

PARRY, John Idris. b 16. St D Coll Lamp BA37. **d** 52 **p** 53. Sudan 52-61; Area Sec (Dios Dur and Newc) CMS 61-66; V Kirkwhelpington *Newc* 66-68; Warden CMS Fellowship Ho Foxbury 68-74; V Langton Green *Roch* 74-81; rtd 81. *Abbeyfield House, 39 East Parade, Rhyl LL18 3AN* Tel (01745) 332890

PARRY, John Seth. b 22. Tyndale Hall Bris 40 and 47. **d** 48 **p** 49. C St Helens St Mark *Liv* 48-52; C Bilton *Ripon* 52-55; R Clitheroe St Jas *Blackb* 55-60; V Chaddesden St Mary *Derby* 60-76; V Ravenhead *Liv* 76-87; rtd 87. *22 Thingwall Lane, Liverpool L14 7NX* Tel 0151-228 6832

PARRY, Keith Melville. b 31. ARICS65 Lon Univ DipRS83. S'wark Ord Course 80. **d** 83 **p** 84. NSM Bexley St Jo *Roch* 83-88; C Orpington All SS 88-96; rtd 96; Perm to Offic *Roch* from 96. *5 Greenside, Bexley, Kent DA5 3PA*

PARRY, Canon Kenneth Charles. b 34. Ripon Hall Ox 56. **d** 58 **p** 59. C Stoke *Cov* 58-61; Chapl RN 61-65; V Cradley *Worc* 65-70; V Gt Malvern H Trin 70-83; RD Malvern 74-83; Hon Can Worc Cathl 80-83; V Budleigh Salterton *Ex* 83-91; Can Res Ex Cathl from 91. *6 The Close, Exeter EX1 1EZ* Tel (01392) 272498

PARRY, Ms Manon Ceridwen. b 69. Wales Poly BA90 Selw Coll Cam BA93. Ridley Hall Cam CTM94. **d** 94 **p** 97. C Llandudno *Ban* from 94. *66 Rhuddlan Avenue, Llandudno LL30 1LN* Tel (01492) 871502

PARRY, Marilyn Marie. b 46. W Coll Ohio BA68 Man Univ MA77. Episc Th Sch Cam Mass BA68 Gilmore Ho 76. **dss** 79 **d** 87 **p** 94. Westleigh St Pet *Man* 79-85; Chapl Asst N Man Gen Hosp 85-90; Tutor N Ord Course 90-97; Lic Preacher *Man* 90-94; Hon C E Farnworth and Kearsley 94-97. *The Rectory, 14 Pancake Lane, Hemel Hempstead, Herts HP2 4NB* Tel (01442) 64860

PARRY, Nicholas John Sinclair. b 56. Sarum & Wells Th Coll 82. **d** 85 **p** 86. C Hendon St Mary *Lon* 85-87; C Verwood *Sarum* 87-90; TV Witney *Ox* 90-96; V Costessey *Nor* from 96. *The Vicarage, Folgate Lane, Costessey, Norwich NR8 5DP* Tel (01603) 742818

PARRY, Mrs Olwen Margaret. b 45. Cardiff Coll of Educn CertEd67. Llan Dioc Tr Scheme 88. **d** 92 **p** 97. NSM Newcastle *Llan* from 92. *17 Wernlys Road, Pen-y-Fai, Bridgend CF31 4NS* Tel (01656) 721860

PARRY, Richard Nigel. b 56. Univ of Wales (Cardiff) BD86. St Mich Coll Llan 82. **d** 86 **p** 87. C Holywell *St As* 86-89; V from 96; V Berse and Southsea 89-96. *The Vicarage, Fron Park Road, Holywell CH8 7UT* Tel (01352) 710010

PARRY, Miss Violet Margaret. b 30. Selly Oak Coll 53. **dss** 82 **d** 87. W Kilburn St Luke w St Simon and St Jude *Lon* 82-83; St Marylebone St Mary 83-86; Stamford All SS w St Jo *Linc* 86-87; C 87-90; rtd 90; Perm to Offic *Linc* from 90. *4 Torkington Gardens, Stamford, Lincs PE9 2EW* Tel (01780) 52831

PARRY, William Daniel. b 09. St Chad's Coll Dur BA31 DipTh32 MA34. **d** 32 **p** 33. C Towyn *St As* 32-36; C Dwygyfylchi *Ban* 36-38; C Llanaber 38-45; V Arthog 45-48; V Llandinam 48-72; V Llandinam w Trefeglwys w Penstrowed 72-78; RD Arwystli 53-73; Can Ban Cathl 60-70; Chan 70-78; rtd 78; Lic to Offic *Ban* from 78; Perm to Offic *St D* from 78. *14 Cae Mawr, Penrhyncoch, Aberystwyth SY23 3EJ* Tel (01970) 828118

PARRY CHIVERS, Stanley. b 06. St Paul's Coll Burgh 25. **d** 29 **p** 30. Australia 29-33; Hon C Teddington St Alb *Lon* 33-34; C Battersea St Bart *S'wark* 34-35; C Yeadon St Andr *Bradf* 35-36; R Fiddington *B & W* 36-42; V Compton Bishop 42-47; CF (EC) 40-46; Hon CF 46; V Brondesbury St Laur *Lon* 47-71; rtd 71; Perm to Offic *Ex* 71-73 and 74-91; P-in-c Barnstaple St Mary 73-74. *c/o Mrs W I Lim, 1 Hobart Cottages, Great Hampden, Great Missenden, Bucks HP16 9RQ* Tel (01494) 488625

PARRY-JENNINGS, Christopher William. b 34. Lon Coll of Div 57. **d** 60 **p** 62. C Claughton cum Grange *Ches* 60-63; C Folkestone H Trin w Ch Ch *Cant* 63-67; New Zealand from 67. *22 Ambleside Drive, Christchurch 8005, New Zealand* Tel Christchurch (3) 348 5633 Fax 358 9304

PARRY JONES, Leonard. b 29. Univ of Wales (Ban) BA52. St Mich Coll Llan 52. **d** 54 **p** 55. C Newtown w Llanllwchaiarn w Aberhafesp *St As* 54-58; C Abergele 58-60; V Pennant, Hirnant and Llangynog 60-65; V Llanynys w Llanychan 65-71; V Brynymaen w Trofarth 71-94; RD Rhos 77-94; rtd 94. *The Cottage, Kerry, Newtown SY16 4NU* Tel (01686) 670822

PARSELL, Howard Vivian. b 60. Univ of Wales (Lamp) BA87 Univ of Wales (Swansea) PGCE88. St Mich Coll Llan DPT93. **d** 94 **p** 95. C Builth and Llanddewi'r Cwm w Llangynog etc *S & B* 94-96; C Swansea St Thos and Kilvey from 96. *55 Ysgol Street, Port Tennant, Swansea SA1 8LG* Tel (01792) 470521

PARSELLE, Stephen Paul. b 53. LTh. St Jo Coll Nottm. **d** 82 **p** 83. C Boscombe St Jo *Win* 82-86; CF from 86. *MOD Chaplains (Army), Trenchard Lines, Upavon, Pewsey, Wilts SN9 6BE* Tel (01980) 615804 Fax 615800

PARSLOW, The Ven John Henry. b 18. MBE74. Qu Coll Birm 47. **d** 50 **p** 51. C Ribbesford w Bewdley and Dowles *Worc* 50-53; P-in-c Ronkswood CD 53-58; V Worc H Trin 58-60; Malawi from 60; Adn Shire Highlands from 69; Can S Malawi from 83; rtd 84. *PO Box 30642, Chichiri, Blantyre 3, Malawi* Tel Malawi (265) 640489

PARSONAGE, Robert Hugh. b 55. Nottm Trent Univ BSc78. Trin Coll Bris 95. **d** 97. C Chell *Lich* from 97. *2 Silverstone Crescent, Stoke-on-Trent ST6 6XA* Tel (01782) 834479

PARSONAGE, Robert Leslie. b 20. St Aid Birkenhead 43. **d** 46 **p** 47. C Farnworth *Liv* 46-47; C Bowdon *Ches* 47-51; V Everton St Geo *Liv* 51-52; CF 52-74; V Bayswater *Lon* 74-83; Perm to Offic 83-88; Preacher Newland Almshouses Glos 88-96; rtd 83; Perm to Offic *Glouc* from 96. *36 St Mary's Square, Gloucester GL1 2QT* Tel (01452) 309459

PARSONS, Andrew David. b 53. UEA BA74 Fitzw Coll Cam BA77 MA81. Westcott Ho Cam 75. **d** 78 **p** 79. C Hellesdon *Nor* 78-82; C Eaton 82-85; P-in-c Burnham Thorpe w Burnham Overy 85-87; R Burnham Sutton w Burnham Ulph etc 85-87; R Burnham Gp of Par 87-93; P-in-c Wroxham w Hoveton and Belaugh 93; R from 93. *The Vicarage, Church Lane, Wroxham, Norwich NR12 8SH* Tel (01603) 782678

PARSONS, Andrew Philip. b 50. RIBA80 Aston Univ BSc76 DipArch76. St Jo Coll Nottm DipThMin95. **d** 95 **p** 96. C Langdon Hills *Chelmsf* from 95. *4 Little Berry Lane, Langdon Hills, Basildon, Essex SS16 6TL* Tel (01268) 418275

PARSONS, Arthur. b 45. St Jo Coll Nottm LTh. **d** 75 **p** 76. C Cuddington *Guildf* 75-78; C Liskeard w St Keyne and St Pinnock *Truro* 78-81; P-in-c Ludgvan 81-83; R from 83; Chapl Falmouth Fire Brigade from 91; P-in-c Perranuthnoe from 93. *The Rectory, Ludgvan, Penzance, Cornwall TR20 8EZ* Tel (01736) 740784

PARSONS, Arthur Gordon Boyd (Father Bob). b 20. TD50. SSC MIPM47. Ripon Hall Ox BA54. **d** 56 **p** 57. C Doncaster St Mary *Sheff* 56-58; V N Wilford St Faith *S'well* 58-60; R W w E Allington and Sedgebrook *Linc* 60-66; P-in-c Woolsthorpe 60-64; R 64-66; V Grantham St Anne 66-69; Offg Chapl RAF 65-74; V Friskney *Linc* 69-74; R Tansor w Cotterstock and Fotheringhay *Pet* 74-76; V Forest Town *S'well* 76-78; V Sutton cum Lound 78-85; rtd 85; P-in-c Sampford Courtenay w Honeychurch *Ex* 85-87; P-in-c Exbourne w Jacobstowe 85-87; Hon C Holsworthy w Hollacombe and Milton Damerel 87-88; Hon C Bude Haven *Truro* 88-89; Hon C Stratton and Launcells 89-95; Perm to Offic *Linc* 95-96; Perm to Offic *B & W* from 96. *9 Thornash Close, Monkton Heathfield, Taunton, Somerset TA2 8PQ* Tel (01823) 413209

PARSONS, Bernard. b 26. Ely Th Coll 60. **d** 62 **p** 63. C Bourne *Linc* 62-64; V W Pinchbeck 64-71; V Sutton Bridge 71-83; R Coningsby w Tattershall 83-93; rtd 93; Perm to Offic *Linc* from 93. *2 St Peter's Drive, Woodhall Spa, Lincs LN10 6SY* Tel (01526) 353027

PARSONS, Christopher James Hutton. b 54. Univ of Wales (Ban) BA75 Birm Univ DipTh78. Qu Coll Birm. **d** 79 **p** 80. C Crowthorne *Ox* 79-83; V Tilehurst St Cath 83-88; P-in-c Wrentham w Benacre, Covehithe, Frostenden etc *St E* 89-91; R 91-94. *35 Tufton Gardens, West Molesey, Surrey KT8 1TD*

PARSONS, David. b 37. Qu Coll Cam BA61. Ridley Hall Cam. **d** 62 **p** 63. C Ormskirk *Liv* 62-65; C Beccles St Mich *St E* 65-68; V Woodbridge St Jo 68-73; Chapl Edgarley Hall Sch Glastonbury 73-78; Asst Master Bruton Sch for Girls from 78; Chapl Bruton Sch for Girls from 86. *13 Ivythorn Road, Street, Somerset BA16 0TE* Tel (01458) 46110

PARSONS, David Norman. b 39. FCIB83. Trin Coll Bris 92. **d** 94 **p** 95. NSM Swindon Dorcan *Bris* from 94. *7 Sedgebrook, Swindon SN3 6EY* Tel (01793) 642077

PARSONS, Desmond John. b 25. Coll of Resurr Mirfield 65. **d** 66 **p** 67. C Purley St Mark Woodcote *S'wark* 66-70; V W Dulwich All SS and Em 71-83; R Limpsfield and Titsey 83-95; rtd 95; Perm to Offic *S'wark* from 96; Perm to Offic *Guildf* from 96. *Priors House, The Court, Croft Lane, Crondall, Farnham, Surrey GU10 5QF* Tel (01252) 851137

PARSONS, Geoffrey Fairbanks. b 35. Trin Coll Cam BA58 MA68. Ridley Hall Cam 59. **d** 61 **p** 62. C Over St Chad *Ches* 61-64; C Heswall 64-69; V Congleton St Steph 69-75; V Weaverham

75-94; P-in-c Backford and Capenhurst from 94. *The Vicarage, Grove Road, Mollington, Chester CH2 4DG* Tel (01244) 851071

PARSONS, George Edward. b 35. St D Coll Lamp BA60 Ripon Hall Ox 60. **d** 62 **p** 63. C Leominster *Heref* 62-66; NSM Bromfield 67-72; NSM Culmington w Onibury 67-72; NSM Stanton Lacy 67-72; NSM Ludlow 72-77; P-in-c Caynham 77-79; NSM Bishop's Cleeve *Glouc* 79-91; Sub-Chapl HM Pris Glouc 88-91; P-in-c Hasfield w Tirley and Ashleworth from 91; P-in-c Maisemore from 91. *Ballalona, 1 Goodrich Hill, Ashleworth, Gloucester GL19 4JD* Tel (01242) 700659

PARSONS, George Horace Norman. b 19. S'wark Ord Course 65. **d** 68 **p** 69. C Hatcham St Cath *S'wark* 68-72; C Horley 72-76; P-in-c S Wimbledon All SS 76-78; P-in-c Caterham 78-81; C 82-84; Chapl St Lawr Hosp Caterham 82-84; rtd 85; Perm to Offic *S'wark* from 85. *8 Russell Road, Mitcham, Surrey CR4 2YS* Tel 0181-646 4386

PARSONS, Gilbert Harvey. b 20. St Pet Hall Ox BA46 MA46. Cuddesdon Coll 48. **d** 50 **p** 51. C Clapham St Pet *S'wark* 50-51; C Charlton St Luke w St Paul 51-56; V Stokenchurch and PC Cadmore End 56-61; V Stokenchurch and Cadmore End *Ox* 61-72; P-in-c Radnage 65-68; P-in-c Ibstone w Fingest 65-72; RD Aston 66-72; V Burford w Fulbrook 72-74; V Burford w Fulbrook and Taynton 74-85; rtd 85. *Windrush, 23 Highlands Way, Whiteparish, Salisbury SP5 2SZ* Tel (01794) 884832

PARSONS, Jeffrey Michael Langdon. b 41. MACE87 Univ of Wales (Lamp) BA72. St Jo Coll Morpeth ThL62. **d** 66 **p** 68. Australia 66-68 and from 78; C Cardigan and Mwnt and Y Ferwig *St D* 69-70; C Buckhurst Hill *Chelmsf* 70-71; Chapl Bancroft's Sch Woodford Green 72-75; R Lambourne w Abridge and Stapleford Abbotts *Chelmsf* 75-78; Foundn Chapl St Pet Colleg Girls' Sch Adelaide 78-80; Dean and R St D Cathl Hobart 80-83; Foundn Chapl St Mich Colleg Girls' Sch Hobart 83-86; Chapl Cranbrook Sch Sydney 87-91; Dep Hd Master 92-96; OStJ from 81; KStJ from 95. *58 Adelaide Street, Woollahra, NSW, Australia 2025* Tel Sydney (2) 389 5184 Fax 327 7619

PARSONS, Dr Jennifer Anne (Jeni). b 53. Univ of Wales (Lamp) BA76 MA78 Jes Coll Cam PhD90. Westcott Ho Cam CTM94. **d** 94 **p** 95. C Halesowen *Worc* from 94. *Alton House, 30 Tenterfields, Halesowen, W Midlands B63 3LH* Tel 0121-550 2278

PARSONS, John Banham. b 43. Selw Coll Cam BA65 MA68. Ridley Hall Cam 65. **d** 67 **p** 68. C Downend *Bris* 67-71; Public Preacher Withywood LEP 71-77; P-in-c Hengrove 77-78; V 78-85; V Letchworth St Paul w Willian *St Alb* 85-94; P-in-c Barking St Marg w St Patr *Chelmsf* from 94. *The Rectory, 166 Longbridge Road, Barking, Essex IG11 8SS* Tel 0181-594 2932

PARSONS, John Christopher. b 27. Keble Coll Ox BA52 MA56 CQSW77. St Steph Ho Ox 52. **d** 54 **p** 55. C Chingford SS Pet and Paul *Chelmsf* 54-57; Chapl RN 57-59; R Ingham w Sutton *Nor* 59-65; C Lowestoft St Marg 66-69; Lic to Offic *Chelmsf* 69-71; Chapl RADD Essex Area 69-71; Chapl to the Deaf 71-85; Lic to Offic *Truro* 71-74; Perm to Offic *Ex* 73-74; P-in-c Godolphin *Truro* 74-80; P-in-c St Enoder 80-92; rtd 92; Perm to Offic *Cant* from 92. *78 Poplar Drive, Greenhill, Herne Bay, Kent CT6 7QA* Tel (01227) 741516

PARSONS, Laurie. b 19. Keble Coll Ox BA41. Wells Th Coll 41. **d** 43 **p** 44. C Westwood *Cov* 43-49; C-in-c Galley Common Stockingford CD 49-57; V Priors Marston 57-69; V Radford Semele 70-83; V Radford Semele and Ufton 83-84; rtd 84; Perm to Offic *Cov* from 84; Perm to Offic *Pet* from 84. *86 Bull Baulk, Middleton Cheney, Banbury, Oxon OX17 2SR* Tel (01295) 711829

PARSONS, Mrs Margaret Anne. b 31. Sheff Poly CQSW77. EMMTC 73. **dss** 77 **d** 87 **p** 94. Dronfield *Derby* 77-87; Par Dn 87-89; Par Dn Tidworth, Ludgershall and Faberstown *Sarum* 89-94; C 94-95; P-in-c Wold-Marsh Gp *Linc* from 95. *The Rectory, Church Lane, Withern, Alford, Lincs LN13 0NG* Tel (01507) 450814

PARSONS, Canon Marlene Beatrice. b 43. Wilson Carlile Coll. **dss** 76 **d** 87 **p** 94. Coulsdon St Jo *S'wark* 76-79; Hill *Birm* 79-86; Dioc Lay Min Adv 80-90; Vice Prin W Midl Minl Tr Course 86-90; Hon Can Birm Cathl from 89; Dioc Dir of Ords from 90; Dean of Women from 90. *257 Gillott Road, Birmingham B16 0RX* Tel 0121-454 3974

PARSONS, Miss Mary Elizabeth. b 43. Wilson Carlile Coll 65. **dss** 78 **d** 87 **p** 94. Chapl Asst Chu Hosp Ox 78-89; Chapl 89-93; rtd 93. *21 Woodlands Road, Oxford OX3 7RU* Tel (01865) 63909

PARSONS, Dr Michael William Semper. b 47. St Cath Coll Ox BA69 MA74 DPhil74 Selw Coll Cam BA77 MA81. Ridley Hall Cam 75. **d** 78 **p** 79. C Edmonton All SS *Lon* 78-81; SPCK Research Fell Dur Univ 81-84; Hon Th Lect 84-85; SPCK Fell N of England Inst for Chr Educn 84-85; Lic to Offic *Dur* 81-85; P-in-c Derby St Aug *Derby* 85-95; TR Walbrook Epiphany 95-96; Dioc Voc Adv 86-96; P-in-c Hempsted *Glouc* from 96; Dir of Ords from 96. *The Rectory, Rectory Lane, Hempsted, Gloucester GL2 5LW* Tel (01452) 524550

PARSONS, Canon Robert Martin. b 43. Qu Coll Cam BA65 MA69. ALCD68. **d** 68 **p** 69. C Chapeltown *Sheff* 68-71; C Sheff St Jo 71-75; V Swadlincote *Derby* 75-91; RD Repton 81-91; P-in-c Gresley 82-86; R Etwall w Egginton 91-93; Can Res Derby Cathl from 93. *22 Kedleston Road, Derby DE22 1GU* Tel (01332) 385552

PARSONS, Roger John. b 37. Sarum Th Coll 62. **d** 65 **p** 66. C Bitterne Park *Win* 65-69; C Clerkenwell H Redeemer w St Phil *Lon* 69-72; C Willesden St Andr 72-76; C St Laurence in the Isle of Thanet *Cant* 76-81; Chapl Luton and Dunstable Hosp 81-86; Chapl St Mary's Hosp Luton 81-86; C Luton All SS w St Pet *St Alb* 81-86; Trustee St Benedict's Trust from 85; TV E Dereham *Nor* 86-88; TV E Dereham and Scarning 89; Perm to Offic 89-93. *16 Cremer Street, Sheringham, Norfolk NR26 8DZ* Tel (01263) 825849

PARSONS, Stephen Christopher. b 45. Keble Coll Ox BA67 MA72 BLitt78. Cuddesdon Coll 68. **d** 70 **p** 71. C Whitstable All SS *Cant* 70-71; C Croydon St Sav 71-74; Perm to Offic *Ox* 74-76; C St Laurence in the Isle of Thanet *Cant* 76-79; V Lugwardine w Bartestree and Weston Beggard *Heref* 79-87; V Lechlade *Glouc* from 87. *The Vicarage, Sherbourne Street, Lechlade, Glos GL7 3AH* Tel (01367) 252262

PARSONS, Stephen Drury. b 54. Qu Mary Coll Lon BSc76 CCC Cam MSc79. Westcott Ho Cam 79. **d** 82 **p** 83. C Stretford All SS *Man* 82-85; C Newton Heath All SS 85-86; V Ashton St Jas 86-90. *8 Ripponden Street, Oldham OL1 4JG*

PARSONS, William George. b 20. Em Coll Cam BA47 MA50. Wells Th Coll 49. **d** 51 **p** 52. C Bedminster Down *Bris* 51-54; C Bishopston 54-58; C-in-c Lawrence Weston CD 58-63; V Lawrence Weston 63; Australia 63-68; V Warmley *Bris* 68-71; P-in-c Syston 68-71; Lic to Offic 71-76; P-in-c Luckington w Alderton 76-80; C N Stoneham *Win* 80-84; Chapl St Cross Hosp Win 84-87; rtd 85; Perm to Offic *Win* 86-96. *c/o J W Parsons Esq, 105 Woolsbridge Road, Ashley Heath, Ringwood, Hants BH24 2LZ* Tel (01425) 474829

PARTINGTON, The Ven Brian Harold. b 36. St Aid Birkenhead 60. **d** 63 **p** 64. C Barlow Moor *Man* 63-66; C Deane 66-68; V Patrick *S & M* 68-96; Bp's Youth Chapl 68-77; RD Peel 76-96; P-in-c German St Jo 77-78; V 78-96; P-in-c Foxdale 77-78; V 78-96; Can St German's Cathl from 85; Adn Man from 96; V Douglas St Geo and St Barn from 96. *St George's Vicarage, 16 Devonshire Road, Douglas, Isle of Man IM2 3QY* Tel (01624) 675430 Fax 616136

PARTINGTON, Fred. b 31. Lon Univ BSc53. Ridley Hall Cam 59. **d** 61 **p** 62. C Bootle St Matt *Liv* 61-63; C Cove St Jo *Guildf* 63-67; rtd 96. *9 Qua Fen Common, Soham, Ely, Cambs CB7 5DQ* Tel (01353) 721631

PARTINGTON, Kenneth. b 41. Lanc Univ MA86. Ripon Hall Ox. **d** 70 **p** 71. C Atherton *Man* 70-72; C Kippax *Ripon* 72-75; V Cartmel Fell *Carl* 75-95; V Crosthwaite Kendal 75-95; V Witherslack 75-95; V Winster 78-95. *The Old Cottage, Lindeth, Windermere, Cumbria LA23 3NH* Tel (01539) 447174

PARTINGTON, Kevin. b 51. Huddersfield Poly BA73. St Jo Coll Nottm DCM93. **d** 93 **p** 94. C Salterhebble All SS *Wakef* 93-96; V Pontefract All SS from 96. *Grenton, South Baileygate, Pontefract, W Yorkshire WF8 2JL* Tel (01977) 794912

PARTINGTON, Peter John. b 57. Peterho Cam MA. St Jo Coll Nottm 79. **d** 81 **p** 82. C Cov H Trin *Cov* 81-85; C Woking St Jo *Guildf* 85-87; C from 94; R Busbridge 87-94; Dir of Ords from 94. *13 Heath Drive, Brookwood, Woking, Surrey GU24 0HG* Tel (01483) 799284

PARTRIDGE, Anthony John. b 38. Univ of Wales (Lamp) BA61 Linacre Ho Ox BA63 K Coll Lon PhD77. St Steph Ho Ox 61. **d** 64 **p** 65. C Sydenham All SS *S'wark* 64-67; Hon C 68-74; Lic to Offic from 74; Prin Lect Thames Poly 75-92; Greenwich Univ from 92. *40 Upwood Road, London SE12 8AN, or University of Greenwich, Wellington Street, London SE18 6PF* Tel 0181-318 9901 or 854 2030

PARTRIDGE, Canon David John Fabian. b 36. Ball Coll Ox BA60 MA. Westcott Ho Cam 60. **d** 62 **p** 63. C Halliwell St Thos *Man* 62-65; C St Martin-in-the-Fields *Lon* 65-69; R Warblington and Emsworth *Portsm* from 69; Hon Can Portsm Cathl from 84. *The Rectory, 20 Church Path, Emsworth, Hants PO10 7DP* Tel (01243) 372428

PARTRIDGE, Ian Starr. b 36. Linc Th Coll 87. **d** 89 **p** 90. C Barton upon Humber *Linc* 89-92; P-in-c Barkwith Gp 92-97; R from 97. *Barkwith Rectory, East Barkwith, Lincoln LN3 5RY* Tel (01673) 858291

PARTRIDGE, Miss Margaret Edith. b 35. Birm Univ DipTh68. Gilmore Ho 63. **dss** 85 **d** 87 **p** 94. Amblecote *Worc* 85-87; Par Dn 87-89; C Borehamwood *St Alb* 89-94; TV from 94. *All Saints Vicarage, 94 Shenley Road, Borehamwood, Herts WD6 1ED* Tel 0181-953 2554

PARTRIDGE, Martin David Waud. b 38. Ox NSM Course 86. **d** 89 **p** 90. NSM Wargrave *Ox* 89-97; NSM Schorne from 97. *The Rectory, Church Street, Quainton, Aylesbury, Bucks HP21 4AP* Tel (01296) 655237

PARTRIDGE, Michael John. b 61. St Edm Hall Ox BA83 MA89 St Jo Coll Dur BA86. Cranmer Hall Dur 84. **d** 87 **p** 88. C Amington *Birm* 87-90; C Sutton Coldfield H Trin 90-93; P-in-c W Exe *Ex* from 93; RD Tiverton from 96. *St Paul's Vicarage, Bakers Hill, Tiverton, Devon EX16 5NE* Tel (01884) 255705

PARTRIDGE, Ronald Malcolm (Ron). b 49. Lon Univ DipTh73 DAC94. Bris Bapt Coll LTh74 Cuddesdon Coll 74. **d** 75 **p** 76. C Bris St Andr Hartcliffe *Bris* 75-78; C E Bris 78-82; V Easton All

Hallows 82-85; TV Brighton St Pet w Chpl Royal and St Jo *Chich* 85-86; TV Brighton St Pet and St Nic w Chpl Royal 86-88; C-in-c Bermondsey St Hugh CD *S'wark* 88-90; Asst Chapl Gt Ormond Street Hosp for Sick Children Lon 91-94; Asst Chapl Gt Ormond Street Hosp for Children NHS Trust 94-97. *Address temp unknown*

PARTRIDGE, Ronald William (Ron). b 42. Shimer Coll Illinois BA64. Cant Sch of Min 93. **d** 96. NSM Upchurch w Lower Halstow *Cant* from 96. *4 The Green, Lower Halstow, Sittingbourne, Kent ME9 7DT* Tel (01795) 842007 Fax as telephone

PARTRIDGE, Canon Timothy Reeve. b 39. Lon Univ BSc60 AKC60. Wells Th Coll 60. **d** 62 **p** 63. C Glouc St Cath *Glouc* 62-65; C Sutton St Nicholas *Linc* 65-74; R Bugbrooke *Pet* 74-95; P-in-c Kislingbury w Rothersthorpe 95; R Bugbrooke w Rothersthorpe from 95; RD Daventry 81-88; Can Pet Cathl from 83. *The Rectory, Church Lane, Bugbrooke, Northampton NN7 3PB* Tel (01604) 830373

PASCHAL, Brother. *See* WORTON, David Reginald

PASKETT, Ms Margaret Anne. b 45. York Univ BSc81 Leeds Univ MEd83. NE Ord Course 84. **d** 87 **p** 94. Par Dn Marske in Cleveland *York* 87-91; C 92-96; Dioc Adv for Diaconal Mins 92-96; P-in-c Hemingbrough from 96. *The Vicarage, Hemingbrough, Selby, N Yorkshire YO8 7QG* Tel (01757) 638528

PASKINS, David James. b 52. Univ of Wales (Lamp) BA73 Trin Hall Cam BA76 MA81. Westcott Ho Cam 74. **d** 77 **p** 78. C St Peter-in-Thanet *Cant* 77-80; C Swanage *Sarum* 80-82; R Waldron *Chich* 82-92; R Bere Ferrers *Ex* 92-96; V Lockerley and E Dean w E and W Tytherley *Win* from 96. *The Vicarage, The Street, Lockerley, Romsey, Hants SO51 0JF* Tel (01794) 340635

PASSANT, Keith. b 39. St Jo Coll Dur BA62 CertEd70. St Alb Minl Tr Scheme 77. **d** 87 **p** 88. C Hatfield Hyde *St Alb* 87-93; rtd 93. *26 Monk's Rise, Welwyn Garden City, Herts AL8 7NF* Tel (01707) 332869

PASTERFIELD, Canon Dunstan Patrick. b 17. Clare Coll Cam BA49 MA53. Cuddesdon Coll 49. **d** 51 **p** 51. C Dennington *St E* 51-53; Canada from 53; Hon Can Calgary 78-82. *Box 212, Arcola, Saskatchewan, Canada, S0C 0G0* Tel Saskatchewan (306) 455-2785 Fax 455-2210

✠**PASTERFIELD, The Rt Revd Philip John.** b 20. Trin Hall Cam BA49 MA53. Cuddesdon Coll 49. **d** 51 **p** 52 **c** 74. C Streatham St Leon *S'wark* 51-54; Chapl K Edw VII Hosp Midhurst 54-60; V W Lavington *Chich* 54-60; R Woolbeding 55-60; V Oxton *Ches* 60-68; RD Birkenhead 66-68; Can Res St Alb 68-74; RD St Alb 71-74; Suff Bp Crediton *Ex* 74-84; rtd 84; Asst Bp Ex from 84. *2 Brixton Court, Brixton, Plymouth PL8 2AH* Tel (01752) 880817

PATCH, Simon John. b 63. Aus Nat Univ BA87. Chich Th Coll BTh95. **d** 95 **p** 96. C Ifield *Chich* from 95. *2 Lychgate Cottage, Ifield Street, Ifield, Crawley, W Sussex RH11 0NN* Tel (01293) 515373

PATCHELL, Miss Gwendoline Rosa (Wendy). b 49. Golds Coll Lon BA69 TCert70. Trin Coll Bris DipHE92. **d** 92 **p** 94. C Ashton on Mersey St Mary *Ches* from 92. *12 Willoughby Close, Sale, Cheshire M33 1PJ* Tel 0161-962 5204

PATCHING, Colin John. b 47. Linc Th Coll 84. **d** 86 **p** 87. C Farnley *Ripon* 86-89; C Didcot St Pet *Ox* 89-92; P-in-c Steventon w Milton from 92. *The Vicarage, 73 Field Gardens, Steventon, Abingdon, Oxon OX11 6TF* Tel (01235) 831243

PATE, Barry Emile Charles. b 50. NE Lon Poly BA80 CQSW80. S'wark Ord Course 85. **d** 88 **p** 89. NSM E Dulwich St Jo *S'wark* 88-92; C Farnborough *Roch* 92-94; C Broxbourne w Wormley *St Alb* from 94. *St Laurence's House, 11 Wharf Road, Broxbourne, Herts EN10 6HU* Tel (01992) 442356

PATEL, Miss Urmila Devi. b 59. Essex Univ BSc82. Chich Th Coll 90. **d** 92 **p** 94. Par Dn Leek and Meerbrook *Lich* 92-94; C 94-97; TV Hackney Marsh *Lon* from 97. *All Souls Vicarage, Overbury Street, London E5 0AJ* Tel 0181-986 5076

PATEMAN, Donald Herbert. b 15. ALCD48. **d** 48 **p** 49. C Bethnal Green St Jas Less *Lon* 48-51; Hon Sec Soc for Relief of Distress 52-66; C Bromley All Hallows 54-56; V Dalston St Mark w St Bart from 56. *St Mark's Vicarage, Sandringham Road, London E8 2LL* Tel 0171-254 4741

PATEMAN, Edward Brian. b 29. Leeds Univ BA51. Qu Coll Birm 51. **d** 53 **p** 54. C Stockton St Pet *Dur* 53-57; Lect Bolton St Pet 57-58; V Coxhoe 58-65; V Dalton le Dale 65-93; RD Houghton 72-75; R Hawthorn 88-93; rtd 93. *27 Atherton Drive, Houghton le Spring, Tyne & Wear DH4 6TA* Tel 0191-385 3168

PATEN, Richard Alfred. b 32. CEng MICE61 Ch Coll Cam BA56 MA60. Ripon Hall Ox 61. **d** 63 **p** 64. C Oadby *Leic* 63-67; C Pet St Mark *Pet* 67-71; Chapl Community Relns 71-93; Bp's Dioc Chapl 73-85; Perm to Offic from 93. *198 Lincoln Road, Peterborough PE1 2NQ* Tel (01733) 66288

PATERNOSTER, Canon Michael Cosgrove. b 35. Pemb Coll Cam BA59 MA63. Cuddesdon Coll 59. **d** 61 **p** 62. C Surbiton St Andr *S'wark* 61-63; Chapl Qu Coll Dundee 63-68; Dioc Supernumerary *Bre* 63-68; Chapl Dundee Univ 67-68; Sec Fellowship of SS Alb and Sergius 68-71; R Dollar *St And* 71-75; R Stonehaven *Bre* 75-90; Hon Can St Paul's Cathl Dundee from 81; R Aberdeen St Jas *Ab* from 90. *31 Gladstone Place, Aberdeen AB10 6UX* Tel (01224) 322631

PATERSON, David. b 33. Ch Ch Ox BA55 MA58. Linc Th Coll 56. **d** 58 **p** 59. C Kidderminster St Mary *Worc* 58-60; C Wolverhampton St Geo *Lich* 60-64; V Loughborough St Pet *Leic* from 64. *St Peter's Vicarage, 129 Ashby Road, Loughborough, Leics LE11 3AB* Tel (01509) 263047

PATERSON, Douglas Monro. b 30. Em Coll Cam BA54 MA57. Tyndale Hall Bris 55. **d** 57 **p** 58. C Walcot *B & W* 57-60; C Portman Square St Paul *Lon* 60-62; Lect Oak Hill Th Coll 60-62; C-in-c Hampstead St Jo Downshire Hill Prop Chpl *Lon* 62-65; Lect All Nations Chr Coll Ware 62-65; Rwanda 67-73; C Edin St Thos *Edin* 73-75; Lect Northumbria Bible Coll 73-94; Perm to Offic *Edin* 75-94; Lic to Offic *Newc* 76-94; rtd 94. *3 Penn Mead, Church Road, Penn, High Wycombe, Bucks HP10 8NY* Tel (01494) 812496

PATERSON, Geoffrey Gordon. b 45. Cant Univ (NZ) LTh69. **d** 69 **p** 70. New Zealand 69-74 and from 80; P-in-c Astwood Bank w Crabbs Cross *Worc* 78-80. *19 Ridder Place, Christchurch 8003, New Zealand* Tel Christchurch (3) 322 7787 or 365 3211

PATERSON, Gordon Ronald (Ron). b 16. MBE57. Ripon Hall Ox 58. **d** 59 **p** 60. C Warblington and Emsworth *Portsm* 59-62; V Swanmore St Barn 62-85; RD Bishops Waltham 79-82; rtd 85; Perm to Offic *Win* 85-95; Perm to Offic *Portsm* from 85. *28 Eastways, Bishops Waltham, Southampton SO32 1EX* Tel (01489) 895671

PATERSON, James Beresford. b 21. DSC42. St Andr Univ MPhil85 FRSA93. Westcott Ho Cam 59. **d** 61 **p** 62. C Woodbridge St Mary *St E* 61-64; R Broughty Ferry *Bre* 64-72; Dioc Supernumerary 72-75; Sec Scottish Ch Action for World Development 72-79; P-in-c Glencarse 76-84; Dioc Sec 79-84; Hon Can St Paul's Cathl Dundee 79-89; rtd 84; Perm to Offic *Bre* from 84. *67 Ipswich Road, Woodbridge, Suffolk IP12 4BT* Tel (01394) 383512

PATERSON, Mrs Jennifer Ann. b 49. Brooklands Tech Coll 69. S Dios Minl Tr Scheme 85. **d** 88. C Hale *Guildf* 88-92; Perm to Offic 94-95; NSM Seale, Puttenham and Wanborough from 95. *4 St George's Close, Badshot Lea, Farnham, Surrey GU9 9LZ* Tel (01252) 316775

PATERSON, The Very Revd John Thomas Farquhar. b 38. TCD BA61 MA64 BD71. CITC 63. **d** 63 **p** 64. C Drumglass *Arm* 63-65; C Dublin St Bart *D & G* 66-68; Min Can St Patr Cathl Dublin 67-83; Asst Dean of Residence TCD 68-72; C-in-c Dublin St Mark *D & G* 68-71; I Dublin St Bart w Leeson Park 72-78; Dean Kildare *M & K* 78-89; I Kildare w Kilmeague and Curragh 78-89; Lect Past Liturgy CITC 85-91; Hon Sec Gen Syn 85-91; Dean Ch Ch Cathl Dublin *D & G* from 89; I Dublin Ch Ch Cathl Gp from 89; Dio Radio Officer 91-94. *The Deanery, St Werburgh Street, Dublin 8, Irish Republic* Tel Dublin (1) 478 1797 or 677 8099 Fax 475 3442

PATERSON, Rex Douglas Trevor. b 27. AKC54. **d** 55 **p** 56. C Maidenhead St Luke *Ox* 55-58; C Littlehampton St Mary *Chich* 58-62; V Woodingdean 62-73; V Ferring 73-94; rtd 94; Perm to Offic *Chich* from 94. *4 Clapham Close, Clapham, Worthing, W Sussex BN13 3XA* Tel (01906) 74396

PATERSON, Robert Mar Erskine. b 49. St Jo Coll Dur BA71 DipTh72 MA82. **d** 72 **p** 73. C Harpurhey St Steph *Man* 72-73; C Sketty *S & B* 73-78; V Llangattock and Llangyndir 78-83; V Gabalfa *Llan* 83-94; R Cowbridge from 94. *The Vicarage, 85 Broadway, Llanblethian, Cowbridge CF71 7EY* Tel (01446) 775597 or 772302

PATERSON, Robin Fergus. b 32. Moore Th Coll Sydney 83. **d** 87 **p** 89. Singapore 87-88; NSM Crieff *St And* 88-92; NSM Comrie 88-92; R Dunkeld from 93; R Strathtay from 93. *St Mary's Rectory, St Mary's Road, Birnham, Dunkeld, Perthshire PH8 0BJ* Tel (01350) 727329

PATERSON, Robin Lennox Andrew. b 43. N Ord Course 84. **d** 87 **p** 88. C Manston *Ripon* 87-91; P-in-c Leeds All So 91-95; V from 95. *All Souls' Vicarage, Blackman Lane, Leeds LS2 9EY* Tel 0113-245 3078

PATERSON, Stuart Maxwell. b 37. Kelham Th Coll 57 Lich Th Coll 58. **d** 60 **p** 61. C Ilkeston St Mary *Derby* 60-64; V Somercotes 64-70; R Wingerworth 70-73; P-in-c Hawick *Edin* 92-95; R from 95. *St Cuthbert's Rectory, Rectory Close, Hawick, Roxburghshire TD9 0ET* Tel (01450) 372043

PATERSON, Mrs Susan Ann. b 57. St Hilda's Coll Ox MA84. EMMTC DTPS95. **d** 95 **p** 96. Hon C Evington *Leic* from 95. *82 Pine Tree Avenue, Leicester LE5 1AL* Tel 0116-276 0422

PATEY, The Very Revd Edward Henry. b 15. Liv Univ Hon LLD80. **d** 39 **p** 40. C Colchester St Mary V *Chelmsf* 39-42; C Bishopwearmouth St Mich *Dur* 42-50; Youth Chapl 46-50; V Oldland *Bris* 50-52; Youth Sec BCC 52-56; Asst Gen Sec 56-58; Can Res Cov Cathl *Cov* 58-64; Select Preacher Ox Univ 61; Dean Liv 64-82; rtd 82; Perm to Offic *Bris* from 82. *139 High Street, Malmesbury, Wilts SN16 9AL* Tel (01666) 822482

PATIENT, Peter Leslie. b 39. Chich Th Coll 63. **d** 66 **p** 67. C Headington *Ox* 66-69; C Stroud *Glouc* 69-72; C Welwyn *St Alb* 72-75. *28 Young's Rise, Welwyn Garden City, Herts AL8 6RU* Tel (01707) 328830

PATIENT, Terence Ian. b 35. Open Univ BA83. LNSM course 94. **d** 96. NSM Old Catton *Nor* from 96. *8 Players Way, Old Catton, Norwich NR6 7AU* Tel (01603) 427899

PATON, George Hemsell. b 23. Wadh Coll Ox MA49. Oak Hill Th Coll 50. **d** 52 **p** 53. C Earlham St Anne *Nor* 52-54; C Darfield *Sheff* 54-56; Area Sec (Dio Ely) CMS 56-62; Area Sec (Dios St E & I and Nor) CMS 56-66; P-in-c Kemp Town St Mark *Chich* 66-67; V Kemp Town St Mark and St Matt 67-71; R Ripe w Chalvington 71-76; R Laughton w Ripe and Chalvington 77-78; V Iford w Kingston and Rodmell 78-90; rtd 90; Perm to Offic *Chich* from 90. *77 Springett Avenue, Ringmer, Lewes, E Sussex BN8 5QT* Tel (01273) 812754

PATON, Canon Ian James. b 57. Jes Coll Cam MA78 PGCE79. Westcott Ho Cam MA81. **d** 82 **p** 83. C Whitley Ch Ch *Ox* 82-84; Bp's Dom Chapl 84-86; Chapl Wadh Coll Ox 86-90; C Ox St Mary V w St Cross and St Pet *Ox* 86-90; Can and Vice-Provost St Mary's Cathl Edin 90-94; R Edin St Mary 90-94; R Haddington from 94; R Dunbar from 94. *The Rectory, Church Street, Haddington, East Lothian EH41 3EX* Tel (01620) 822203

PATON, John David Marshall. b 47. Barrister 70. St Steph Ho Ox 81. **d** 83 **p** 84. C Bethnal Green St Matt *Lon* 83-84; C Bethnal Green St Matt w St Jas the Gt 84-86; P-in-c St Geo-in-the-East St Mary 86-89; V 89-92; AD Tower Hamlets 92-96; Dir Post-Ord Tr from 92; P-in-c Bethnal Green St Barn 92-96; P-in-c St Vedast w St Mich-le-Querne etc from 97. *St Vedast's Rectory, 4 Foster Lane, London EC2V 6HH* Tel 0171-606 3998 Fax as telephone

PATON, John William Scholar. b 52. Mert Coll Ox MA95. St Steph Ho Ox 93. **d** 95 **p** 96. C Sherborne w Castleton and Lillington *Sarum* from 95. *Askwith House, 1 Quarr Drive, Sherborne, Dorset DT9 4HZ* Tel (01935) 814277

PATON, The Ven Michael John Macdonald. b 22. Magd Coll Ox BA49 MA54. Linc Th Coll 52. **d** 54 **p** 55. C Gosforth All SS *Newc* 54-57; V Norton Woodseats St Chad *Sheff* 57-67; Sen Chapl Sheff United Hosps 67-70; Chapl Weston Park Hosp Sheff 70-78; V Sheff St Mark Broomhall *Sheff* 70-78; Adn Sheff 78-87; Can Res Sheff Cathl 78-87; rtd 88; Perm to Offic *Sheff* from 88. *947 Abbeydale Road, Sheffield S7 2QD* Tel 0114-236 6148

PATON-WILLIAMS, David Graham. b 58. Warw Univ BA81 Trin Coll Ox DipTh82 Selw Coll Cam BA86 MA90. Ridley Hall Cam 84. **d** 87 **p** 88. C S Westoe *Dur* 87-90; C Newton Aycliffe 90-91; TV 91-93; Chapl Univ Coll of Ripon and York St Jo from 93; Min Can Ripon Cathl *Ripon* from 93. *5 Crescent Parade, Ripon, N Yorkshire HG4 2JE* Tel (01765) 607346

PATRICIA, Sister. *See* PERKINS, Sister Patricia Doris

PATRICK, Hugh Joseph. b 37. TCD BA62 MA66. **d** 63 **p** 64. C Dromore Cathl *D & D* 63-66; C Lurgan Ch Ch 66-70; C Rothwell *Ripon* 70-73; V Thurnscoe St Hilda *Sheff* 73-78; V Wales from 78; P-in-c Thorpe Salvin 78-82; RD Laughton from 93. *The Vicarage, Manor Road, Wales, Sheffield S31 8PD* Tel (01909) 771111

PATRICK, John Andrew. b 62. St Jo Coll Dur BA84. Ripon Coll Cuddesdon 87. **d** 89 **p** 90. C Frankby w Greasby *Ches* 89-92; C Boston *Linc* 92-95; P-in-c Graffoe Gp from 95. *The Vicarage, Wellingore, Lincoln LN5 0JF* Tel (01522) 810246

PATRICK, John Peter. b 23. AKC. **d** 52 **p** 53. C S Westoe *Dur* 52-55; C Woodhouse *Wakef* 55-58; C Batley All SS 58-59; V Upperthong 59-75; V Slaithwaite w E Scammonden 75-80; V Donington *Linc* 80-92; rtd 92; Perm to Offic *Linc* from 92. *Little Paddock, 140 Main Road, Hundleby, Spilsby, Lincs PE23 5NQ* Tel (01790) 52304

PATRICK, Peter Charles. b 64. Leeds Univ BA86 Fitzw Coll Cam BA91. Ridley Hall Cam 89. **d** 92 **p** 93. C Barton upon Humber *Linc* 92-96; TV Gt Grimsby St Mary and St Jas from 96. *62A Brighowgate, Grimsby, S Humberside DN32 0QW* Tel (01472) 250877

PATSTON, Raymond Sidney Richard. b 26. Kelham Th Coll 47. **d** 51 **p** 52. C Hammersmith H Innocents *Lon* 51-53; C Acton Green St Pet 53-56; Area Sec E Counties UMCA 56-62; C Chesterton St Luke *Ely* 56-59; R Downham Market w Bexwell 61-71; V Clee *Linc* 71-97; rtd 97. *75 Littlefield Lane, Grimsby, S Humberside DN34 4NU* Tel (01472) 349788

PATTEN (née STARNS), Mrs Helen Edna. b 43. St Hilda's Coll Ox BA65 Lon Univ CertEd70 DipTh75. Trin Coll Bris 73 Oak Hill Th Coll 81. **dss** 82 **d** 87 **p** 94. Tunbridge Wells St Jo *Roch* 82-86; Patcham *Chich* 86-91; Par Dn 87-91; Par Dn Eckington w Handley and Ridgeway *Derby* 91-94; C 94-95; TV from 95. *The Vicarage, 1 Aintree Avenue, Eckington, Sheffield S31 9JA* Tel (01246) 436673

PATTEN, John. b 27. Qu Coll Birm 74. **d** 76 **p** 77. NSM Armitage *Lich* 76-79; NSM Lich St Mary w St Mich 79-96; NSM Lich St Mich w St Mary and Wall from 96. *31 Trent Valley Road, Lichfield, Staffs WS13 6EZ* Tel (01543) 268245

PATTENDEN, Henry Albert. b 11. Lich Th Coll 53. **d** 54 **p** 55. C Rugeley *Lich* 54-57; C-in-c Rickerscote CD 57-62; V Rickerscote 62-66; R Leighton w Eaton Constantine 66-67; V Etruria 67-72; C Widley w Wymering *Portsm* 72-73; rtd 76. *5 Compton Close, Lichfield Road, Stafford ST17 4PW* Tel (01785) 247355

PATTERSON, Alfred Percy. **d** 85 **p** 87. NSM Aghalee *D & D* 85-91; C Gilford 91-93; Bp's C 93-95; I from 95. *The Vicarage, 18 Scarva Road, Gilford, Craigavon, Co Armagh BT63 6BG* Tel (01762) 831130

PATTERSON, Andrew John. b 56. Master Mariner 85 Riversdale Coll OND76. Qu Coll Birm 85. **d** 88 **p** 89. C Newc St Phil and St Aug *Newc* 88-92; Chapl Hunter's Moor Hosp 91-92; Asst Chapl R Victoria Infirmary Newc 92-96; V Whitley *Newc* from 96; Chapl Hexham Gen Hosp from 96. *Whitley Vicarage, Hexham, Northd NE46 2LA* Tel (01434) 673379

PATTERSON, Anthony. b 43. Moore Th Coll Sydney BTh82. **d** 83 **p** 83. Australia 83-91; C Darfield *Sheff* 91-94; TR Marfleet *York* from 94. *St George's Rectory, 33 Carden Avenue, Hull HU9 4RT* Tel (01482) 791291

PATTERSON, Charles David Gilliat. b 40. Lon Univ DipTh74. Oak Hill Th Coll 71. **d** 74 **p** 75. C Brompton H Trin *Lon* 74-77; C Spring Grove St Mary 77-80; V Bures *St E* 80-92; R Bath Weston St Jo w Kelston *B & W* from 92. *The Rectory, 8 Ashley Avenue, Bath BA1 3DR* Tel (01225) 427206

PATTERSON, Colin Hugh. b 52. CertEd75 St Pet Coll Ox MA77 Univ of Wales (Cardiff) MPhil90. Trin Coll Bris DipHE86. **d** 87 **p** 88. C Blackb Sav *Blackb* 87-90; C Haughton le Skerne *Dur* 90-93; Adult Educn Adv from 93. *24 Monks Crescent, Durham DH1 1HD* Tel 0191-386 1691

PATTERSON, Colin Peter Matthew. b 62. Newc Poly HND82 BA84. St Steph Ho Ox 92. **d** 94 **p** 95. C Cullercoats St Geo *Newc* 94-97; Shrine P Shrine of Our Lady of Walsingham from 97. *The College, Walsingham, Norfolk NR22 6EE* Tel (01328) 820850

PATTERSON, Mrs Diane Rosemary. b 46. WMMTC 88. **d** 91 **p** 94. C Hill *Birm* 91-95; Perm to Offic 95-96; C Shottery St Andr *Cov* from 96. *134 Justins Avenue, Stratford-upon-Avon, Warks CV37 0DA* Tel (01789) 293754

PATTERSON, Hugh John. b 38. Southn Univ MPhil76. AKC63. **d** 64 **p** 65. C Epsom St Martin *Guildf* 64-65; Chapl Ewell Coll 65-68; Asst Chapl and Lect Bp Otter Coll Chich 68-71; Lect Dudley Coll of Educn 71-77; Lect Wolv Poly 77-92; Wolv Univ from 92; Chapl Wolv Univ *Lich* from 89; Hon C Morville w Aston Eyre *Heref* from 82; Hon C Upton Cressett w Monk Hopton from 82; Hon C Acton Round from 82. *6 Victoria Road, Bridgnorth, Shropshire WV16 4LA* Tel (01746) 765298

PATTERSON, Ian Francis Riddell. b 31. TCD BA55. **d** 55 **p** 56. C Belfast St Mary *Conn* 55-59; C Finaghy 59-63; I Craigs w Dunaghy and Killagan 63-66; Belfast Trin Coll Miss 66-68; I Belfast H Redeemer 68-80; I Kilroot 80-90; I Kilroot and Templecorran 90-92; I Donagh w Tyholland and Errigal Truagh *Clogh* from 92. *The Rectory, Glaslough, Co Monaghan, Irish Republic* Tel Monaghan (47) 88277

PATTERSON, Jennifer Mary. *See* TAYLOR, Sister Jennifer Mary

PATTERSON, John. b 27. MBIM76 Regent St Poly Lon DMS58. Bps' Coll Cheshunt 60. **d** 61 **p** 62. C Maidenhead St Luke *Ox* 61-65; Chapl RAF 65-72; V Ashton St Jas *Man* 72-78; USA 78-90; R Somercotes and Grainthorpe w Conisholme *Linc* 90-92; rtd 92; Perm to Offic *Linc* from 92. *9 Simpson Close, Barrow-upon-Humber, S Humberside DN19 7BL* Tel (01469) 30867

PATTERSON, Canon John Norton (Jack). b 39. TCD BA64 MA68. **d** 65 **p** 66. C Belfast St Paul *Conn* 65-68; C Larne and Inver 68-72; I Ballintoy w Rathlin and Dunseverick from 72; Miss to Seamen from 72; Can Belf Cathl from 97. *The Rectory, 2 Ballinlea Road, Ballintoy, Ballycastle, Co Antrim BT54 6NQ* Tel (01265) 762411

PATTERSON, Marjorie Jean. *See* BROWN, Mrs Marjorie Jean

PATTERSON, Norman John. b 47. Peterho Cam BA69. Lon Coll of Div ALCD DPS St Jo Coll Nottm 70. **d** 73 **p** 74. C Everton St Ambrose w St Tim *Liv* 73-74; C Everton St Pet 74-78; TV 79-84; C Aigburth 84-92; Dioc Adv Past Care and Counselling from 84; V Gt Crosby All SS from 92. *All Saints' Vicarage, 17 Moor Coppice, Crosby, Liverpool L23 2XJ* Tel 0151-924 6436

PATTERSON, Patric Douglas MacRae. b 51. Wycliffe Hall Ox 73. **d** 76 **p** 77. C Bebington *Ches* 76-79; Canada from 79. *The Rectory, PO Box 10, Milford, Ontario, Canada, K0K 2P0*

PATTERSON, Philip Fredrick. b 50. Ulster Univ BSc QUB BD. **d** 82 **p** 83. C Lurgan Ch the Redeemer *D & D* 82-86; I Carrowdore w Millisle 86-89; I Knockbreda from 89. *Knockbreda Rectory, 69 Church Road, Knockbreda, Belfast BT8 4AN* Tel (01232) 641493

PATTERSON, Susan Margaret. b 48. Otago Univ BA71 BD89 PhD92. Knox Coll Dunedin 84. **d** 88 **p** 89. New Zealand 88-91 and 92-97; C Dunedin St Martin 88-91; Tutor Otago Univ and Knox Coll 89-91; USA 91-92; Assoc P Hawke's Bay 92-96; Lect Trin Coll Bris from 97. *12 Ridgehill, Henleaze, Bristol BS9 4SB* Tel 0117-962 1047 Fax as telephone

PATTERSON, Trevor Harold. b 60. QUB BA82 Stranmillis Coll PGCE83. Trin Coll Bris DipHE93. **d** 93 **p** 94. C Ashtead *Guildf* from 93. *17 Loraine Gardens, Ashtead, Surrey KT21 1PD* Tel (01372) 273819

PATTERSON, William Alfred. b 54. Wycliffe Hall Ox 77. **d** 79 **p** 80. C Partington and Carrington *Ches* 79-81; Canada from 81. *Appartment 106, 1680 Richardson Avenue, Victoria, British Columbia, Canada, V8S 1R4*

PATTERSON, Canon William James. b 30. CBE91. Ball Coll Ox BA53 MA57. Ely Th Coll 53. **d** 55 **p** 56. C Newc St Jo *Newc* 55-58; Trinidad and Tobago 58-65; R Esher *Guildf* 65-72; RD Emly 68-72; R Downham *Ely* 72-80; P-in-c Coveney 78-80; Adn Wisbech 79-84; V Wisbech St Mary 80-84; Dean Ely 84-90; V

Everton w Tetworth 90-93; V Abbotsley 90-93; V Waresley 90-93; Hon Can Ely Cathl 90-93; rtd 93; Perm to Offic *Glouc* from 93. *1 Watledge Close, Tewkesbury, Glos GL20 5RJ*

PATTINSON, Sir William Derek. b 30. Kt90. Qu Coll Ox BA52 MA56. St Deiniol's Hawarden 90. **d** 91 **p** 92. NSM Pimlico St Gabr *Lon* from 91. *4 Strutton Court, Great Peter Street, London SW1P 2HH* Tel 0171-222 6307

PATTISON, Anthony. b 50. MRPharmS73 Heriot-Watt Univ BSc72. Sarum & Wells Th Coll 85. **d** 87 **p** 88. C Cullercoats St Geo *Newc* 87-89; Ind Chapl from 89; C Cramlington 89-91; TV from 91. *24 Lindsey Close, Beaconhill Glade, Cramlington, Northd NE23 8EJ* Tel (01670) 715464

PATTISON, George Linsley. b 50. Edin Univ MA72 BD77 Dur Univ PhD. Edin Th Coll 74. **d** 77 **p** 78. C Benwell St Jas *Newc* 77-80; P-in-c Kimblesworth *Dur* 80-83; R Badwell Ash w Gt Ashfield, Stowlangtoft etc *St E* 83-91; Dean of Chapl K Coll Cam from 91. *King's College, Cambridge CB2 1ST* Tel (01223) 350411 Fax 331315

PATTISON, Stephen Bewley. b 53. Selw Coll Cam BA76. Edin Th Coll 76. **d** 78 **p** 80. C Gosforth All SS *Newc* 78-79; NSM St Nic Hosp Newc 78-82; Hon C Newc St Thos Prop Chpl *Newc* 80-82; Chapl Edin Th Coll 82-83; Lect Past Studies Birm Univ 83-88; Perm to Offic *Birm* 83-86 and from 87; Hon C Moseley St Mary 86-87. *11A Salisbury Road, Moseley, Birmingham B13 8JS* Tel 0121-449 3023

PATTMAN, Andrew. b 53. Didsbury Coll Man BEd75. Westcott Ho Cam CTM95. **d** 95 **p** 96. C Washington *Dur* from 95. *40 Waskerley Road, Washington, Tyne & Wear NE38 8EP* Tel 0191-415 5524

PATTON, The Ven Desmond Hilton. b 12. TCD BA35. **d** 36 **p** 37. C Killermogh *C & O* 36-38; C Wexford 38-40; I Mothel 40-41; I Aghade w Ardoyne 41-51; I Clonenagh w Roskelton 51-59; I Ballyfin 58-59; I Carlow w Urglin and Staplestown 59-77; Preb Leighlin Cathl 60-71; Preb Ossory Cathl 60-62; Adn Ossory and Leighlin 62-76; rtd 76; Chapl Mageough Home *D & G* 78-88. *Littleholme, Delgany, Co Wicklow, Irish Republic* Tel Dublin (1) 287 5207

PATTON, Eugene Smith. b 19. BS41 MEd71 MSLS76. Virginia Th Sem MDiv61. **d** 61 **p** 62. USA 61-92 and from 94; NSM Monasterevan w Nurney and Rathdaire *M & K* 92-93. *PO Box 767, Morgantown, PA 19543, USA*

PAUL, Brother. *See* SINGLETON, Ernest George

PAUL, Ian Benjamin. **d** 96 **p** 97. C Longfleet *Sarum* from 96. *44 Kingston Road, Poole, Dorset BH15 2LS* Tel (01202) 680087

PAUL, Canon John Douglas. b 28. Edin Univ MA52. Ely Th Coll 52. **d** 54 **p** 55. C Portsea Ascension *Portsm* 54-56; Nyasaland 56-60; Portuguese E Africa 60-70; Adn Metangula 65-70; R Castle Douglas *Glas* 70-75; R Edin St Mark *Edin* 75-80; R Elgin w Lossiemouth *Mor* 80-92; Syn Clerk 89-91; Hon Can St Andr Cathl Inverness from 89; Dean Mor 91-92; rtd 92. *2 The Avenue, Gifford, Haddington, East Lothian EH41 4QX* Tel (01620) 810547

PAUL, John Matthew. b 61. K Coll Lon BA82 Fitzw Coll Cam BA88 MA92. Westcott Ho Cam 86. **d** 89 **p** 90. C Writtle w Highwood *Chelmsf* 89-94; Min Can and Chapl St Paul's Cathl *Lon* 94-96; Min Can and Sacr St Paul's Cathl from 96. *7A Amen Court, London EC4M 7BU* Tel 0171-248 6151

PAUL, John Wilfred. b 30. St Jo Coll Morpeth LTh52 BA82. **d** 51 **p** 52. Australia 51-57; C Mitcham Ascension *S'wark* 57-59; V Clapham St Jo 59-65; CF (TA) 60-67; V Balham St Mary *S'wark* 66-85; V Balham St Mary and St Jo 85-86; R St Andr-by-the-Wardrobe w St Ann, Blackfriars *Lon* from 86; R St Jas Garlickhythe w St Mich Queenhithe etc from 86. *St Andrew's House, St Andrew's Hill, London EC4V 5DE* Tel 0171-248 7546 Fax 329 3632

PAUL, Naunihal Chand (Nihal). b 40. Allahabad Univ MA. Bangalore Th Coll BD. **d** 69 **p** 70. India 70-74; C Urmston *Man* 75-77; P-in-c Farnworth St Pet 77-80; TV E Farnworth and Kearsley 80-83; TV Laindon St Martin and St Nic w Nevendon *Chelmsf* 83-90; R Laindon w Dunton from 90. *38 Claremont Road, Laindon, Basildon, Essex SS15 5PZ* Tel (01268) 411190

PAUL, Roger Philip. b 53. Clare Coll Cam BA74 CertEd76 MA88. Westcott Ho Cam 78. **d** 81 **p** 82. C Coventry Caludon *Cov* 81-85; R Warmington w Shotteswell and Radway w Ratley from 85. *The Rectory, Warmington, Banbury, Oxon OX17 1BT* Tel (0129589) 213

PAUL, Simon Nicholas. b 56. Hull Univ BA81 PGCE82. Trin Coll Bris BA95. **d** 95 **p** 96. C Cranleigh *Guildf* from 95. *22 Orchard Gardens, Cranleigh, Surrey GU6 7LG* Tel (01483) 272573

PAVEY, Mrs Angela Mary. b 55. Hull Univ BA77 Nottm Univ BCombStuds84. Linc Th Coll 81. **dss** 84 **d** 87 **p** 94. Linc St Faith and St Martin w St Pet *Linc* 84-86; Chapl Boston Coll of FE 87-95; Asst Min Officer *Linc* 89-95; Dioc Dir of Ords from 94; C Birchwood from 95. *St Luke's Vicarage, Jasmine Road, Lincoln LN6 0YR* Tel (01522) 683507

PAVEY, Gordon Sidney Alfred. b 19. Lon Univ BD47 Leeds Univ MEd58. Chich Th Coll 40. **d** 42 **p** 43. C S Mymms K Chas *Lon* 42-44; C Bedford Park 44-48; C Taunton H Trin *B & W* 48-50; Area Sec (N Midl) UMCA 50-54; V Huddersfield St Thos *Wakef* 54-64; Youth Chapl 54-57; Lic to Offic *Blackb* 64-68; Lic to Offic *Bris* 68-95; Prin Lect Th Bris Poly 77-92; Prin Lect Th Univ of the W of England, Bris from 92; rtd 84. *2 Carey's Close, Clevedon, Avon BS21 6BA* Tel (01275) 872623

PAVEY, John Bertram. b 51. Keele Univ BA73 Hull Univ PGCE74. Linc Th Coll 81. **d** 83 **p** 84. C Boultham *Linc* 83-86; R Fishtoft 86-95; P-in-c Birchwood from 95. *St Luke's Vicarage, Jasmin Road, Lincoln LN6 0YR* Tel (01522) 683507

PAVEY, Michael Trevor. b 32. Lon Univ BA80 Bris Univ MPhil92. ALCD59. **d** 59 **p** 60. C Nor St Pet Mancroft *Nor* 59-61; C N Walsham w Antingham 61-63; Chapl RAF 63-83; R Mark w Allerton *B & W* from 83. *The Rectory, Vicarage Lane, Mark, Highbridge, Somerset TA9 4NN* Tel (01278) 641258 Fax as telephone

PAVLIBEYI, Andrew Christos. b 53. Trent Poly CertEd76. Oak Hill Th Coll BA88 Wycliffe Hall Ox 84. **d** 86 **p** 87. C Finchley Ch Ch *Lon* 86-89; Chapl Lon Univ 89-92; V S Hampstead St Sav 92-93; P-in-c from 93. *St Saviour's Vicarage, 30 Eton Villas, London NW3 4SQ* Tel 0171-722 4621

PAWSEY, Jack Edward. b 35. Trin Coll Ox BA59 MA65. Westcott Ho Cam 64. **d** 66 **p** 67. Sec Coun Soc Aid *S'wark* 66-75; Race Relns Worker 75-78; Acting Sec Coun Soc Aid 78-82; Perm to Offic 84-86; Hon C Camberwell St Geo from 86. *20 Addington Square, London SE5 7JZ* Tel 0171-701 2769 or 735 5871

PAWSON, Preb John Walker. b 38. Kelham Th Coll 58. **d** 63 **p** 64. C N Hull St Mich *York* 63-67; C Lower Gornal *Lich* 67-70; V Tipton St Jo 70-78; V Meir Heath from 78; RD Stoke from 88; Preb Lich Cathl from 93. *St Francis's Vicarage, Meir Heath, Stoke-on-Trent ST3 7LH* Tel (01782) 393189

PAXON, Robin Michael Cuninghame. b 46. St Jo Coll Dur BA69. Westcott Ho Cam 69. **d** 71 **p** 72. C Croydon St Pet S End *Cant* 71-77; C Saffron Walden w Wendens Ambo and Littlebury *Chelmsf* 77-80; P-in-c Plaistow St Mary 80-83; TV Plaistow 83-89; TV Dovercourt and Parkeston 90-95; rtd 95. *20 Park Road, Harwich, Essex CO12 3BJ*

PAXTON, John Ernest. b 49. Ex Univ BA71. Westcott Ho Cam 74. **d** 74 **p** 75. C Redditch St Steph *Worc* 74-77; UAE 77-81; C Bolton St Pet *Man* 81-91; Ind Missr 81-91; TV Southampton (City Cen) *Win* 91-96; R S'wark Ch Ch *S'wark* from 96; Sen Chapl S Lon Ind Miss from 96. *Christ Church Rectory, 49 Colombo Street, London SE1 8DP* Tel 0171-633 9979

PAY, Norman John. b 50. St Jo Coll Dur BA72 DipTh73. Cranmer Hall Dur. **d** 74 **p** 75. C S Moor *Dur* 74-78; C Rawmarsh w Parkgate *Sheff* 78-80; C-in-c New Cantley CD 80-82; V New Cantley 82-89; V Doncaster St Leon and St Jude from 89; Asst Clergy In-Service Tr Officer from 90. *St Leonard's Vicarage, Barnsley Road, Doncaster, S Yorkshire DN5 8QE* Tel (01302) 784858

PAYN, Peter Richard. b 33. Moore Th Coll Sydney LTh59. **d** 60 **p** 60. Australia 60-79; C Blackb Ch Ch w St Matt *Blackb* 79-81; V Lowestoft Ch Ch *Nor* 81-92; P-in-c Tunbridge Wells St Pet *Roch* 92-96; V from 96. *St Peter's Vicarage, Bayhall Road, Tunbridge Wells, Kent TN2 4TP* Tel (01892) 530384

PAYNE, Alan Frank. b 19. Bps' Coll Cheshunt 63. **d** 65 **p** 66. C Horsforth *Ripon* 65-69; V Oulton w Woodlesford 69-80; V Thurgoland *Wakef* 80-82; rtd 82; Perm to Offic *Wakef* from 82. *602 King Lane, Alwoodley Park, Leeds LS17 7AN* Tel 0113-266 0221

PAYNE, Arthur Edwin. b 37. K Alfred's Coll Win CertEd59 Ban Coll DipRE60 Univ of Wales (Swansea) ACertEd68. St Mich Coll Llan 86. **d** 87 **p** 88. C Swansea St Gabr *S & B* 87-90; Chapl Univ of Wales (Swansea) 89-90; V Brynmawr 90-91; TV Wickford and Runwell *Chelmsf* 91-94; Chapl Runwell Hosp Essex 91-94; P-in-c Wraxall *B & W* 94-95; Perm to Offic 95-97; V Rhymney *Mon* from 97. *The Vicarage, Lawn Terrace, Rhymney NP2 5LL* Tel (01685) 840500

PAYNE, Canon Charles Thomas Leonard. b 11. Kelham Th Coll 29. **d** 34 **p** 35. C Lewisham St Jo Southend *S'wark* 34-39; C Malden St Jo 39-42; V Streatham Ch Ch 42-79; Chapl CA Hostel Streatham 48-79; RD Streatham *S'wark* 73-79; Hon Can S'wark Cathl 75-79; rtd 79; Perm to Offic *St E* from 79. *6 Cedar Walk, Acton, Sudbury, Suffolk CO10 0UN* Tel (01787) 376812

PAYNE, Cyril Douglas. b 16. Sarum Th Coll 46. **d** 49 **p** 50. C Corby St Columba *Pet* 49-51; C Wellingborough All Hallows 51-54; V Stourpaine *Sarum* 54-59; R Durweston 54-59; R Edith Weston w Normanton *Pet* 59-63; V Wellingborough All SS 63-82; rtd 82; Perm to Offic *Cant* from 82. *32 London Road, Canterbury, Kent CT2 8LN* Tel (01227) 765694

PAYNE, Cyril Gordon. b 26. Bris Univ BA53. Linc Th Coll 53. **d** 55 **p** 56. C Southall H Trin *Lon* 55-58; C Christchurch *Win* 58-63; V Otterbourne 63-75; V Milford 75-90; rtd 90. *11 Oaklands, Lymington, Hants SO41 3TH* Tel (01590) 671274

PAYNE, David Charles. b 62. Univ of Wales (Abth) BLib84. St Jo Coll Nottm MA95. **d** 95 **p** 96. C Horncastle w Low Toynton *Linc* from 95. *St Mary's House, 6 Park Road, Horncastle, Lincs LN9 5EF* Tel (01507) 524564

PAYNE, David James. b 31. Clare Coll Cam BA54 MA61. Wycliffe Hall Ox 60. **d** 62 **p** 63. C Gt Faringdon w Lt Coxwell *Ox* 62-63; C Guildf Ch Ch *Guildf* 63-66; R Shackleford 66-73; R Peper Harow 66-73; R Odell *St Alb* 73-78; V Pavenham 73-78; Warden Home of Divine Healing Crowhurst 78-84; R Wraxall *B & W* 84-92; rtd 92; Perm to Offic *Glouc* from 92. *Langet End, Upper Up, South Cerney, Cirencester, Gloucester GL7 5US* Tel (01285) 860677

PAYNE, David Ronald. b 49. DMS77 Open Univ BA87. St Mich Coll Llan. **d** 90 **p** 91. C Oystermouth *S & B* 90-93; V Penllergaer from 93. *The Vicarage, 16 Swansea Road, Penllergaer, Swansea SA4 1AQ* Tel (01792) 862603

PAYNE, Canon Denis Alfred. b 22. Or Coll Ox BA50 MA53. Wells Th Coll 50. **d** 51 **p** 52. C Sheff St Geo and St Steph *Sheff* 51-55; Uganda 55-67; Min Sec ACCM 67-69; Sen Selection Sec 69-73; Dir Post-Ord Tr and Further Tr for Clergy *St E* 73-84; Dioc Dir of Ords 73-87; Can Res St E Cathl 73-89; rtd 89; Perm to Offic *St E* from 90. *The Crooked House, Brussels Green, Darsham, Saxmundham, Suffolk IP17 3RN* Tel (01728) 77705

PAYNE, Francis Michael Ambrose. b 18. Keble Coll Ox BA39 MA43. Ely Th Coll 39. **d** 41 **p** 42. C Leic St Pet *Leic* 41-45; C Upton cum Chalvey *Ox* 45-48; V Long Clawson *Leic* 48-53; V Shepshed 53-58; V Ashby-de-la-Zouch St Helen 58-62; R Henley *Ox* 63-78; RD Henley 73-78; R Ecton *Pet* 78-83; rtd 83; Perm to Offic *Nor* from 83. *The Monastery, Happisburgh, Norwich NR12 0AB* Tel (01692) 650076

PAYNE, Frederick Gates (Eric). b 19. Jes Coll Cam BA40 MA43. Lon Coll of Div 40. **d** 42 **p** 43. C Walcot *B & W* 42-45; CF (EC) 45-48; Ethiopia 48-67; SW Org Sec CMJ 68-85; rtd 84; Perm to Offic *B & W* from 85. *83 Penn Lea Road, Bath BA1 3RQ* Tel (01225) 423092

PAYNE, James John Henry (Jim). b 26. MBE69. St Pet Hall Ox BA53 MA59. Tyndale Hall Bris 48 Linc Th Coll 53. **d** 53 **p** 54. Chapl Supt Mersey Miss to Seamen 53-55; C Stoneycroft All SS *Liv* 55-57; Nigeria 57-88; Hon Can Lagos 71-88; rtd 88; Perm to Offic *Ox* 88-93; Hon C Uffington, Shellingford, Woolstone and Baulking from 93. *1 Timberyard Cottages, Shellingford, Faringdon, Oxon SN7 7QA* Tel (01367) 710274

PAYNE, John. b 58. Glas Univ BSc80 Edin Univ BD84. Edin Th Coll 81. **d** 90 **p** 90. C Dur St Nic *Dur* 90-94; Australia from 94. *321 Canterbury Road, Forest Hill, Victoria, Australia 3131* Tel Melbourne (3) 9878 1831

PAYNE, John Charles. b 04. St Aid Birkenhead 50. **d** 51 **p** 52. C Stanwix *Carl* 51-53; C Dalton-in-Furness 53-55; V Glodwick Ch Ch *Man* 55-62; V Preston St Sav *Blackb* 62-69; rtd 69. *84 Ackworth Road, Pontefract, W Yorkshire WF8 4NG*

PAYNE, John Percival. b 49. Nottm Univ BA70. Cuddesdon Coll 70. **d** 72 **p** 73. C Tilehurst St Mich *Ox* 72-76; C Cross Green St Sav and St Hilda *Ripon* 76-79; Chapl St Hilda's Priory Sneaton, Whitby 79-83; V Leeds Belle Is St Jo and St Barn *Ripon* 83-88; Chapl St Hilda's Sch Whitby 88-97; R Loftus and Carlin How w Skinningrove *York* from 97. *The New Rectory, St Hilda's Place, Loftus, Saltburn-by-the-Sea, Cleveland TS13 4JY* Tel (01287) 640738

PAYNE, John Rogan. b 44. Episc Th Coll São Paulo. **d** 78 **p** 79. Brazil 78-86; C Ilkley All SS *Bradf* 86-88; R Elvington w Sutton on Derwent and E Cottingwith *York* 88-94. *Manor Farm House, East Flotmanby Road, Filey, N Yorkshire YO14 0HX* Tel (01723) 513969

PAYNE, Canon Joseph Marshall. b 17. TCD BA38 MA52. **d** 40 **p** 41. C Belfast St Aid *Conn* 40-43; C Ballynafeigh St Jude *D & D* 43-44; Chapl RAF 44-65; Asst Chapl-in-Chief RAF 65-72; QHC 70-72; V Malew *S & M* 72-82; RD Castletown 77-82; Can St German's Cathl 78-84; Treas 80-84; rtd 82; Perm to Offic *S & M* from 84. *Ard-ny-Shee, 3 Viking Close, Ballakillowey, Colby, Isle of Man IM9 4BH* Tel (01624) 832039

PAYNE, Kenneth Alan. b 45. Pemb Coll Ox BA68 MA71. Qu Coll Birm 71. **d** 74 **p** 74. Hon C Perry Barr *Birm* 74-78; Hon C Ruislip Manor St Paul *Lon* 78-79; C Hawksworth Wood *Ripon* 79-84; R Stanningley St Thos 84-94; TR Kippax w Allerton Bywater from 94; RD Whitkirk from 95. *The Rectory, Kippax, Leeds LS25 7HF* Tel 0113-286 2710

PAYNE, Leonard John. b 49. St Jo Coll Nottm DipThMin95. **d** 95 **p** 96. C Trimley *St E* from 95. *3 Black Barns, Trimley, Ipswich IP10 0XT* Tel (01394) 274015

PAYNE, Leonard Vivian. b 20. St D Coll Lamp BA42 Lich Th Coll 42. **d** 44 **p** 46. C Whitchurch *Llan* 44-50; C Weston-super-Mare St Paul *B & W* 50-55; V Bedminster St Paul *Bris* 55-62; V Weston-super-Mare St Paul *B & W* 62-81; rtd 81. *23 Downs View, Aberthin, Cowbridge CF7 7HF* Tel (01446) 775130

PAYNE, Mark James Townsend. b 69. Van Mildert Coll Dur BA90. Ridley Hall Cam CTM94. **d** 94 **p** 95. C Angmering *Chich* from 94. *Vestry Cottage, Arundel Road, Angmering, Littlehampton, W Sussex BN16 4JR* Tel (01903) 776529

PAYNE, Michael Frederick. b 49. NE Surrey Coll of Tech HND72. St Jo Coll Nottm 81. **d** 83 **p** 84. C Hyson Green *S'well* 83-86; P-in-c Peckham St Mary Magd *S'wark* 86-90; V from 90. *St Mary's Vicarage, 22 St Mary's Road, London SE15 2DW* Tel 0171-639 4596

PAYNE, Mrs Penelope Kenward (Pennie). b 42. LGSM64 SEN75. Bp Otter Coll. **d** 94. NSM Portsea N End St Mark *Portsm* from 94. *35 Saltmarsh Lane, Hayling Island, Hants PO11 0JT* Tel (01705) 465259

PAYNE, Ralfe Dudley. b 22. Lon Univ BA50. Qu Coll Birm 50. **d** 52 **p** 53. C Tettenhall Wood *Lich* 52-57; C Tamworth 57-60; V Gayton w Fradswell 60-63; V Brockmoor 63-75; C Kinver 76-79; R Himley 79-89; V Swindon 79-89; rtd 89; Perm to Offic *Lich* from 89. *Highfield, Dunsley, Kinver, Stourbridge, W Midlands DY7 6LY* Tel (01384) 873612

PAYNE, Richard Derek. b 29. K Coll Lon 51. **d** 55 **p** 56. C Stevenage *St Alb* 55-58; C Clayton w Keymer *Chich* 58-60; C-in-c Coldean CD 60-63; R Telscombe w Piddinghoe 63-75; R Telscombe w Piddinghoe and Southease 75-76; Chapl Holmewood Ho Sch Tunbridge Wells 76-78; Perm to Offic *Chich* 78-93; Perm to Offic *Cant* from 79; Org Sec (SE England) CECS 78-93; rtd 93; Chapl Lanzarote *Eur* 94-95; P-in-c Barlavington, Burton w Coates, Sutton and Bignor *Chich* from 96. *The Rectory, Sutton, Pulborough, W Sussex RH20 1PW* Tel (01798) 869220

PAYNE, Robert Christian. b 42. St Mich Coll Llan DipTh65. **d** 65 **p** 66. C Charlton Kings St Mary *Glouc* 65-69; C Waltham Cross *St Alb* 69-71; V Falfield *Glouc* 71-72; P-in-c Rockhampton 71-72; V Falfield w Rockhampton 72-76; Chapl HM Det Cen Eastwood Park 71-76; Chapl HM Youth Cust Cen Everthorpe 76-79; Chapl HM Youth Cust Cen Glen Parva 79-85; Pris Service Chapl Tr Officer 85-88; Chapl HM Pris Swinfen Hall 85-88; Asst Chapl Gen of Pris (SW) 88-90; Asst Chapl Gen of Pris from 90. *HM Prison Service Chaplaincy, PO Box 349, Stafford ST16 3DL* Tel (01785) 213456 Fax 227734

PAYNE, Robert Harold Vincent (Bob). b 44. St Jo Coll Nottm 77. **d** 79 **p** 80. C Didsbury St Jas *Man* 79-80; C Didsbury St Jas and Em 80-83; V Southchurch Ch Ch *Chelmsf* 83-90; P-in-c Charles w Plymouth St Matthias *Ex* 90-94; Warden Lee Abbey from 94. *Garden Lodge, Lee Abbey, Lynton, Devon EX35 6JJ* Tel (01598) 52621 Fax 52619

PAYNE, Robert Sandon. b 48. ARICS72 Reading Univ BSc69. Ripon Coll Cuddesdon 77. **d** 80 **p** 81. C Bridgnorth, Tasley, Astley Abbotts and Oldbury *Heref* 80-83; P-in-c Wistanstow 83-92; P-in-c Acton Scott 86-92; P-in-c Dorrington 92-94; P-in-c Leebotwood w Longnor 92-94; P-in-c Smethcott w Woolstaston 92-94; P-in-c Stapleton 92-94; R Dorrington w Leebotwood, Longnor, Stapleton etc from 94. *The Rectory, Dorrington, Shrewsbury SY5 7JL* Tel (01743) 718578

PAYNE, Victor John. b 45. Open Univ BA81 MBTI94 DipPs96. St Mich Coll Llan DipTh69 DPS70. **d** 70 **p** 71. C Ystrad Mynach *Llan* 70-72; C Whitchurch 72-75; CF (TA) 74-75; CF 75-93; V Talgarth and Llanelieu *S & B* 85-87; Chapl Mid-Wales Hosp 85-87; C Bassaleg *Mon* 93-96; TV from 96. *St John's Vicarage, 25 Wern Terr, Rogerstone, Newport NP1 9FG* Tel (01633) 893357

PAYNE, Walter Richard Stanley. b 29. FRSC64 Lon Univ BSc54 PhD63 DipRS78. S'wark Ord Course 75. **d** 78 **p** 79. NSM Lamorbey H Trin *Roch* 78-85; Perm to Offic from 85. *120 Hurst Road, Sidcup, Kent DA15 9AF* Tel 0181-302 0267

PAYNE, Warwick Martin. b 26. AKC51. **d** 52 **p** 53. C Mansfield St Pet *S'well* 52-56; Gambia 56-58; C Winlaton *Dur* 59-62; S Africa from 63; rtd 97. *Braehead House, Auburn Road, 7700 Kenilworth, Cape, South Africa*

PAYNE COOK, John Andrew Somerset. b 43. St Pet Coll Ox BA65 MA. Coll of Resurr Mirfield 65. **d** 68 **p** 69. C St Mary-at-Latton *Chelmsf* 68-71; C Gt Berkhamsted *St Alb* 71-76; C-in-c N Brickhill CD 76-82; V N Brickhill and Putnoe 83-85; TR Tring from 85; RD Berkhamsted from 92. *The Rectory, Church Yard, Tring, Herts HP23 5AE* Tel (01442) 822170

PAYNTER, Stephen Denis. b 59. Bath Univ BSc82 CertEd82. Trin Coll Bris BA89. **d** 89 **p** 90. C Nailsea Ch Ch *B & W* 89-92; C Farnborough *Guildf* 92-97; TV N Farnborough from 97. *The Parsonage, 45 Sand Hill, Farnborough, Hants GU14 8ER* Tel (01252) 543789

PAYNTON, Paul Alexander. b 42. Hull Univ DipMin88. Linc Th Coll 72. **d** 74 **p** 75. C Uppingham w Ayston *Pet* 74-77; P-in-c Market Overton w Thistleton 77-79; R Teigh w Whissendine 77-79; R Teigh w Whissendine and Market Overton 79-95; V Irchester from 95. *The Vicarage, 19 Station Road, Irchester, Wellingborough, Northants NN9 7EH* Tel (01933) 312674

PAYTON, Canon Arthur Edward. b 16. Lambeth MA81. **d** 39 **p** 41. Brotherhood of St Paul from 36; St Kitts-Nevis 39-42; C Bedminster Down *Bris* 42-44; OCF 43-45; Org Sec Br Empire Leprosy Relief Assoc 44-49; P-in-c Toxteth Park St Jo and St Thos *Liv* 49-50; V 50-56; R Gt and Lt Wigborough w Salcot Virley *Chelmsf* 56-64; V Highwood 64-66; Hon C Feering 66-69; Hon C Kelvedon 69-82; Managing Dir Inter Ch Travel 54-82; Hon Can Gib Cathl *Eur* 73-84; rtd 81; P-in-c Wickmere w Lt Barningham and Itteringham *Nor* 84-88; Perm to Offic from 88. *The Grange, Sandy Lane, West Runton, Cromer, Norfolk NR27 9LT* Tel (01263) 837400

PAYTON, John Vear. b 36. Bps' Coll Cheshunt 60. **d** 63 **p** 64. C Hatfield Hyde *St Alb* 63-72; V Farley Hill St Jo 72-84; Counsellor (Inner Healing) 84-91. *41 Trowbridge Gardens, Luton LU2 7JY* Tel (01582) 450612

PEACE, Brian. b 38. St Jo Coll Nottm DCM92. **d** 92 **p** 93. C Huddersfield H Trin *Wakef* 92-95; R Cheswardine, Childs Ercall, Hales, Hinstock etc *Lich* from 95. *The Vicarage, Cheswardine, Market Drayton, Shropshire TF9 2RS* Tel (01630) 661204

PEACE, Geoffrey. b 23. S'wark Ord Course. **d** 68 **p** 69. NSM Ashford St Hilda CD *Lon* 68-73; NSM Ashford St Hilda 73-80; C Spilsby w Hundleby *Linc* 80-83; C Sandhurst *Ox* 83-85; V Owlsmoor 85-88; rtd 88. *9 Barley Mow Close, Winchfield, Basingstoke, Hants RG27 8ZZ*

PEACH, Malcolm Thompson. b 31. St Chad's Coll Dur BA56. Sarum Th Coll 56. **d** 58 **p** 59. C Beamish *Dur* 58-61; Chapl Dur Univ 61-65; NE England Sec SCM 61-65; C-in-c Stockton St Mark CD *Dur* 65-72; P-in-c Bishopwearmouth St Nic 72-81; V 81-85; V S Shields St Hilda w St Thos 85-95; Hon Chapl Miss to Seamen 85-95; P-in-c S Shields St Aid w St Steph *Dur* 92-95; rtd 95; Perm to Offic *Dur* from 95. *116 Mount Road, Sunderland SR4 7QD* Tel 0191-522 6216

PEACHELL, David John. b 45. Oak Hill Th Coll 85. **d** 86 **p** 87. C Prescot *Liv* 86-89; CF from 89. *MOD Chaplains (Army), Trenchard Lines, Upavon, Pewsey, Wilts SN9 6BE* Tel (01980) 615804 Fax 615800

PEACOCK, David. b 39. Liv Univ BA61 Lanc Univ MA71 FRSA95. Westcott Ho Cam 84. **d** 84 **p** 85. Prin Lect St Martin's Coll Lanc 84-85; Hon C Lancaster St Mary *Blackb* 84-85; Prin Whitelands Coll *S'wark* from 85; Hon C Roehampton H Trin 85-92; Hon C Putney St Mary from 92. *Whitelands College, West Hill, London SW15 3SN* Tel 0181-392 3501 or 788 4195

PEACOCK, David Christopher. b 57. York Univ BA78 DPhil83. Wycliffe Hall Ox 89. **d** 91 **p** 92. C Old Brumby *Linc* 91-95; TV Bottesford w Ashby from 95. *St Peter's Vicarage, Old School Lane, Bottesford, Scunthorpe, S Humberside DN16 3RD* Tel (01724) 840616

PEACOCK, John. b 35. ALCD60. **d** 60 **p** 61. C Addiscombe St Mary *Cant* 60-62; C Felixstowe St Jo *St E* 62-65; Chapl RAF 65-70; Australia from 71. *4, 15 Westminster Drive, Castle Hill, NSW, Australia 2154* Tel Sydney (2) 894 9995 or 634 0705

PEACOCK, Thomas Edward. b 35. Dur Univ BSc55 PhD58. **d** 64 **p** 65. C S'wark St Sav w All Hallows *S'wark* 64-67; Australia 67-68 and from 70; C Jarrow *Dur* 68-69. *9 Bergamot Street, Bald Hills, Queensland, Australia 4036* Tel Brisbane (7) 3261 1711

PEACOCK, William John. b 15. Worc Ord Coll 65. **d** 67 **p** 68. C Dudley St Fran *Worc* 67-69; C Netherton St Andr 69-74; R Ebbw Vale *Mon* 74-78; V Caerwent w Dinham and Llanfair Discoed 78-83; rtd 83; Perm to Offic *Chich* from 87. *2 Dickens Way, Eastbourne, E Sussex BN23 7TG* Tel (01323) 763897

PEACOCKE, Canon Arthur Robert. b 24. MBE93. Ex Coll Ox BA45 BSc47 MA48 DPhil48 DSc62 DD82 Birm Univ DipTh60 BD71. **d** 71 **p** 71. Fell and Tutor St Pet Hall Ox 65-73; Dean Clare Coll Cam 73-84; Lic to Offic *Ely* 73-85; Lic to Offic *Ox* from 85; Dir Ian Ramsey Cen Ox 85-88; Warden SOSc from 87; Hon Chapl Ch Ch Ox from 88; Hon Can Ch Ch from 94. *55 St John's Street, Oxford OX1 2LQ, or Exeter College, Oxford OX1 3DP* Tel (01865) 512041

PEAD, Charles Henry. b 31. **d** 87 **p** 88. NSM Llanfrechfa and Llanddewi Fach w Llandegveth *Mon* 87-92; NSM Mamhilad and Llanfihangel Pontymoile 92-95. *Jasmine, Caerleon Road, Llanfrechfa, Cwmbran NP44 8DQ* Tel (01633) 482685

PEAKE, Charles Clifford. b 17. St Jo Coll Ox BA38 Leeds Univ MA88. Qu Coll Birm 38. **d** 40 **p** 41. C Shipley St Paul *Bradf* 40-42; C Ilkley All SS 43; C Pudsey St Lawr 47-49; V Wyke 49-56; V Bellerby *Ripon* 56-68; V Leyburn 56-68; V Starbeck 68-78; R Farnham w Scotton and Staveley and Copgrove 78-82; rtd 82. *8 Burke Street, Harrogate, N Yorkshire HG1 4NR* Tel (01423) 522265

PEAKE, Robert Ernest. b 27. Univ Coll Lon BSc51 FSS. Coll of Resurr Mirfield 83. **d** 85 **p** 86. C Linslade *Ox* 85-88; TV Gt Chesham 88-89; rtd 89; Hon C Princes Risborough w Ilmer *Ox* from 93. *Butley Cottage, Chestnut Way, Longwick, Princes Risborough, Bucks HP27 9SD* Tel (01844) 344952

PEAKE, The Ven Simon Jeremy Brinsley. b 30. Worc Coll Ox BA54 MA56. St Steph Ho Ox 53. **d** 57 **p** 58. C Eastbourne St Andr *Chich* 57-60; S Africa 60-69; Zambia 69-77; Chapl Athens w Kifissia *Eur* 77-87; Chapl Vienna w Budapest and Prague 87-91; Chapl Vienna w Budapest 91-93; Chapl Vienna from 93; Hon Can Malta Cathl 87-92; Can Malta Cathl from 92; Adn E Adnry from 95. *Thugutstrasse 2/12, 1020 Vienna 2, Austria* Tel Vienna (1) 720-7973 or 712-9193 Fax 714-7824

PEAL, Jacqueline (Jacquie). b 46. MCSP70. Cant Sch of Min 88. **d** 91 **p** 94. NSM Bexley St Jo *Roch* from 91; NSM Crayford 91-94; C from 94. *St John's Vicarage, 29 Park Hill Road, Bexley, Kent DA5 1HX* Tel (01322) 521786

PEAL, John Arthur. b 46. K Coll Lon BD70 AKC. **d** 71 **p** 72. C Portsea All SS w St Jo Rudmore *Portsm* 71-74; C Westbury *Sarum* 71-77; V Borstal *Roch* 77-82; Chapl HM Pris Cookham Wood 78-82; Chapl Erith and Distr Hosp from 82; V Erith Ch Ch *Roch* 82-91; P-in-c Erith St Jo 86-91; V Bexley St Jo from 91. *St John's Vicarage, 29 Park Hill Road, Bexley, Kent DA5 1HX* Tel (01322) 521786

PEAL, William John. b 26. K Coll Lon BSc47 AKC PhD52. St Jo Coll Nottm 79. **d** 80 **p** 81. C Coalville and Bardon Hill *Leic* 80-83; TV Melton Mowbray w Thorpe Arnold 83-86; TV Melton Gt Framland 86-90; rtd 90; Perm to Offic *Lich* from 91. *20 Conway Road, Knypersley, Stoke-on-Trent ST8 7AL* Tel (01782) 513580

PEARCE, Adrian Francis. b 55. S Dios Minl Tr Scheme 92. **d** 95 **p** 96. NSM Jersey St Jas *Win* from 95; NSM Jersey St Luke from 95. *24 Richelieu Park, Tower Road, St Helier, Jersey, Channel Islands JE2 3HT* Tel (01534) 873115

PEARCE, Andrew John. b 66. Ex Univ BA89 Homerton Coll Cam PGCE93. St Mich Coll Llan DPT94. **d** 96 **p** 97. C Llansamlet *S & B* from 96. *The Parsonage, 456 Birchgrove Road, Birchgrove, Swansea SA7 9NR* Tel (01792) 817300

PEARCE, Mrs Angela Elizabeth. b 36. K Coll Lon BSc58 CertEd59 BD79 AKC79. **dss** 79 **d** 87. Chapl Raines Sch 79-87; Homerton St Barn w St Paul *Lon* 79-85; Upper Chelsea St Simon 85-89; Hon Par Dn 87-89; Hon Par Dn Limehouse from 89-97. *50 Crown Street, Bury St Edmunds, Suffolk IP33 1QX*

PEARCE, Canon Brian Edward. b 39. Kelham Th Coll 59. **d** 64 **p** 65. C Smethwick St Matt *Birm* 64-68; C Kings Norton 68-72; TV 73-80; TR Swindon Dorcan *Bris* 80-91; Min Withywood CD 91-94; RD Bedminster from 92; V Withywood from 94; Hon Can Bris Cathl from 97. *Withywood Church House, 63 Turtlegate Avenue, Bristol BS13 8NN* Tel 0117-964 7763

PEARCE, Clive. b 40. Univ of Wales (Lamp) BA63. St Steph Ho Ox 63. **d** 65 **p** 66. C Acton Green St Pet *Lon* 65-67; C Eastcote St Lawr 67-73; V Hatch End St Anselm from 73. *The Vicarage, 50 Cedar Drive, Pinner, Middx HA5 4DE* Tel 0181-428 4111

PEARCE, Colin James. b 51. Trin Coll Bris DipTh96. **d** 96. C Kingswood *Bris* from 96. *1 Downend Road, Kingswood, Bristol BS15 1RT* Tel 0117-967 6122

PEARCE, Canon Denis William Wilfrid. b 25. Bps' Coll Cheshunt 55. **d** 58 **p** 59. C Lt Ilford St Mich *Chelmsf* 58-62; C Leytonstone St Jo 62-65; C-in-c Leytonstone St Aug CD 65-74; V Leytonstone H Trin Harrow Green 65-81; P-in-c Leyton St Luke 78-81; R Capel w Lt Wenham *St E* 81-86; P-in-c Lavenham 86-89; R 89-93; RD Lavenham 87-93; Hon Can St E Cathl 90-93; rtd 93; Clergy Retirement Officer *St E* from 93. *74 Hintlesham Drive, Felixstowe, Suffolk IP11 8YL* Tel (01394) 279189

PEARCE, Desmond. b 30. Univ of Wales (Abth) BA52. EMMTC 85. **d** 88 **p** 89. NSM Chellaston *Derby* 88-90; NSM Walsall St Gabr Fulbrook *Lich* 90; C Stoke Lacy, Moreton Jeffries w Much Cowarne etc *Heref* from 91. *Shalom, Ullingswick, Hereford HR1 3JG* Tel (01432) 820385

PEARCE, Preb Eustace Kenneth Victor. b 13. FRAI64 Univ Coll Lon BSc65 St Pet Coll Ox DipAnth64 Florida State Univ (USA) DEd91. ALCD37. **d** 37 **p** 38. C Toxteth Park St Clem *Liv* 37-40; R Sutton 40-42; C Fordington *Sarum* 42-44; V Camberwell All SS *S'wark* 44-50; R Bucknall and Bagnall *Lich* 50-71; CF (TA) 66-81; Preb Lich Cathl *Lich* 67-81; V Audley 71-81; rtd 81; Chief Exec Evidence for Truth Broadcasting Assn from 83; Perm to Offic *Ches* from 83; Perm to Offic *Lich* 83-95; Perm to Offic *Chich* from 83. *15 Kinnersley Avenue, Kidsgrove, Stoke-on-Trent ST7 1AP, or 13 Lismore Road, Eastbourne, E Sussex BN21 3AY, or EFT Institute, PO Box 255, Stoke-on-Trent ST8 YY* Tel (01782) 773325 or (01323) 725231 or (01782) 642000 Fax (01323) 649240 or (01782) 641121

PEARCE, Canon Frank. b 31. St Aid Birkenhead. **d** 57 **p** 58. C Worksop Priory *S'well* 57-61; P-in-c W Retford 61-62; R 62-70; R Kettering SS Pet and Paul *Pet* 70-94; Chapl Kettering Gen and St Mary's Hosps 70-94; Can Pet Cathl *Pet* 78-94; rtd 94. *Sherwood Lodge, 36 Queen Eleanor Road, Geddington, Kettering, Northants NN14 1AY* Tel (01536) 742334

PEARCE, Canon Gerald Nettleton. b 25. St Jo Coll Dur BA49 DipTh51. **d** 51 **p** 52. C Bury St Edmunds St Mary *St E* 51-54; C Attenborough w Bramcote and Chilwell *S'well* 54-56; V Selston 56-61; R Wilford 61-73; RD Bingham 73-84; P-in-c Holme Pierrepont w Adbolton 73-84; V Radcliffe-on-Trent 73-84; V Shelford 73-84; Hon Can S'well Minster 77-84; R Sigglesthorne and Rise w Nunkeeling and Bewholme *York* 84-91; RD N Holderness 86-90; Perm to Offic from 91; rtd 91; Dioc Rtd Clergy and Widows Officer from 91. *Sutherland Bridge, Cropton, Pickering, N Yorkshire YO18 8EU* Tel (01751) 417420

PEARCE, Mrs Janet Elizabeth. b 49. Somerville Coll Ox BA72 MA76 CertEd74. N Ord Course 85. **d** 88 **p** 94. Par Dn Helsby and Dunham-on-the-Hill *Ches* 88-94; C 94-96; C Norley and Crowton from 96; C Kingsley from 96. *St John's House, Pike Lane, Kingsley, Warrington WA6 8EH* Tel (01928) 788386

PEARCE, Preb John Frederick Dilke. b 32. Ex Coll Ox BA55 MA59. Westcott Ho Cam. **d** 57 **p** 58. C Dalston St Mark w St Bart *Lon* 57-60; C Chelsea Ch Ch 60-63; R Lower Homerton St Paul 63-81; Preb St Paul's Cathl from 70; P-in-c Clapton Park All So 72-77; V 77-84; RD Hackney 74-79; R Homerton St Barn w St Paul 81-85; TR Hackney Marsh 85; P-in-c Upper Chelsea St Simon 85-89; AD Chelsea 88-89; R Limehouse from 89. *50 Crown Street, Bury St Edmunds, Suffolk IP33 1QX*

PEARCE, Jonathan. b 55. St Jo Coll Nottm BTh85. **d** 85 **p** 86. C Gt Chesham *Ox* 85-89; C Newport Pagnell w Lathbury and Moulsoe 89-93; TV Waltham H Cross *Chelmsf* from 93. *The Vicarage, Church Road, High Beach, Loughton, Essex IG10 4AJ* Tel 0181-508 1791

PEARCE, Kenneth Jack. b 25. CIPFA. Linc Th Coll 62. **d** 63 **p** 64. C Wootton Bassett *Sarum* 63-66; C Broad Town 63-66; P-in-c Derby St Andr *Derby* 66-68; V Derby St Mark 68-87; rtd 87. *117 Oaks Cross, Stevenage, Herts SG2 8LT* Tel (01438) 317385

PEARCE, Michael Hawkins. b 29. Sarum Th Coll 61. **d** 62 **p** 63. C Bedminster St Aldhelm *Bris* 62-65; C Bishopston 65-68; R Jacobstow w Warbstow *Truro* 68-74; V Treneglos 68-74; V St Teath 74-94; rtd 94; Perm to Offic *Truro* from 94. *32 Trenant*

Road, Tywardreath, Par, Cornwall PL24 1QJ Tel (01726) 813658

PEARCE, Neville John Lewis. b 33. CBIM88 Leeds Univ LLB53 LLM54. Trin Coll Bris 90. **d** 91 **p** 92. NSM Bath Walcot *B & W* 91-93; P-in-c Swainswick w Langridge and Woolley 93; NSM Bath St Sav w Swainswick and Woolley from 93. *Penshurst, Weston Lane, Bath BA1 4AB* Tel (01225) 426925

PEARCE, Reginald Frederic George. b 15. St Aug Coll Cant 38. **d** 40 **p** 41. C Bury St Mark *Man* 40-42; S Africa 42-57 and 58-68; Brazil 57-58; V Laneast w St Clether *Truro* 68-76; V Tresmere 70-76; V Laneast w St Clether and Tresmere 76-78; P-in-c St Erth 78-80; rtd 80; Perm to Offic *Truro* from 80. *Braehead House, Auburn Road, Kenilworth, 7700 South Africa* Tel Cape Town (21) 797-1917

PEARCE, Robert John. b 47. GLCM LLCM72 Birm Univ PGCE73. Ripon Coll Cuddesdon 79. **d** 82 **p** 83. C Broseley w Benthall *Heref* 82-83; C Kington w Huntington, Old Radnor, Kinnerton etc 83-85; R Westbury 85-94; R Yockleton 85-94; V Gt Wollaston 85-94; V Gwersyllt *St As* from 94. *The Vicarage, Old Mold Road, Gwersyllt, Wrexham LL11 4SB* Tel (01978) 756391

PEARCE, Trevor John. b 27. FSR57. Roch Th Coll 65. **d** 67 **p** 68. C Cheriton Street *Cant* 67-69; C Willesborough w Hinxhill 69-73; V Devonport St Barn *Ex* 73-79; Chapl N Devon Distr Hosp Barnstaple 79-83; V Derby St Andr w St Osmund *Derby* 83-84; Chapl Derbyshire R Infirmary 83-92; Lic to Offic *Derby* from 84; rtd 92. *4 Morrell Wood Drive, Westfields, Belper, Derbyshire DE56 0JD* Tel (01773) 828450

PEARCEY, Canon Paul Alan Cyril. b 37. St Jo Coll Dur BA59. Cranmer Hall Dur DipTh61. **d** 61 **p** 62. C Deane *Man* 61-65; Chapl Red Bank Schs 65-67; C-in-c Blackley White Moss St Mark CD *Man* 67-73; R Cwmbach Llechryd and Llanelwedd w Llanfaredd *S & B* 73-79; V Llanelwedd w Llanfaredd w Llansantffraed etc from 79; RD Builth from 84; Hon Can Brecon Cathl from 97. *The Rectory, Llanelwedd, Builth Wells LD2 3TY* Tel (01982) 553701

PEARCY, Vernon Charles. b 23. K Coll Lon BD56 AKC56. **d** 56 **p** 57. C St Helier *S'wark* 56-59; C Westmr St Jas *Lon* 59-61; Chapl St Geo Sch Harpenden 61-62; C Sutton St Nic *S'wark* 62-63; C Croydon St Pet S End *Cant* 63-67; C Belmont *S'wark* 68-70; C Wimbledon 70-76; C S w N Hayling *Portsm* 76-77; R Warbleton and Bodle Street Green *Chich* 78-83; C Cleethorpes *Linc* 83-86; rtd 88. *20 Springfield Crescent, Poole, Dorset BH14 0LL* Tel (01202) 743782

PEARE, Canon Oliver Arthur Patrick. b 17. TCD BA43 MA55. CITC 46. **d** 46 **p** 47. C Clonmel *C & O* 46-52; I Tallow w Kilwatermoy 52-55; I Youghal *C, C & R* 55-59; I Youghall w Killeagh 59-63; I Abbeystrewry 63-66; I Kinsale Union 66-87; Treas Cork Cathl 84-87; Preb Tymothan St Patr Cathl Dublin 84-87; rtd 87. *High Copse, Compass Hill, Kinsale, Co Cork, Irish Republic* Tel Cork (21) 774191

PEARKES, Nicholas Robin Clement. b 49. Ex Univ BA. Linc Th Coll. **d** 82 **p** 83. C Plymstock *Ex* 82-85; P-in-c Weston Mill 85-86; TV Devonport St Boniface and St Phil from 86. *The Vicarage, Bridwell Lane North, Plymouth PL5 1AN* Tel (01752) 362060

PEARMAIN, Andrew Neil. b 55. K Coll Lon BD79 AKC79. Ridley Hall Cam 79. **d** 81 **p** 82. C Cranleigh *Guildf* 81-84; P-in-c Frimley 85-86; C 86-87; Chapl Frimley Park Hosp 87. *35 Cavendish Road, Bournemouth BH1 1QZ* Tel (01202) 553395

PEARMAIN, Canon Brian Albert John. b 34. Lon Univ BD68. Roch Th Coll 63. **d** 66 **p** 67. C Shirley St Jo *Cant* 66-69; C Selsdon St Jo w St Fran 69-73; P-in-c Louth H Trin *Linc* 73-75; TV Louth 75-79; R Scartho 79-97; RD Grimsby and Cleethorpes 89-94; Can and Preb Linc Cathl 94-97; rtd 97. *665 Finchley Road, London NW2 2HN* Tel 0410-510355 (Mobile)

PEARSE, Andrew George. b 46. Wycliffe Hall Ox 71. **d** 74 **p** 75. C Homerton St Luke *Lon* 74-77; C Chadderton Em *Man* 77-81; R Collyhurst 81-89; Area Sec (NE and E Midl) SAMS from 89; Perm to Offic *Dur* from 89; Perm to Offic *Linc* from 91. *9 Troutsdale Avenue, Rawcliffe, York YO3 6TR* Tel (01904) 655881

PEARSE, Percy George Hedley. b 13. Univ Coll Dur LTh35 BA36 MA39. ALCD35. **d** 36 **p** 37. C Kidbrooke St Jas *S'wark* 36-38; C Kingston Hill St Paul 38-40; Chapl Kingston Hosp Surrey 40-41; C Leeds St Geo *Ripon* 41-44; C Gt Ilford St Clem *Chelmsf* 44-48; R Stanford-le-Hope 48-59; R Doddinghurst 59-72; R Stondon Massey 59-72; R Debden 72-77; RD Saffron Walden 74-78; rtd 78; Perm to Offic *Win* 78-92. *3 Chalfont Avenue, Christchurch, Dorset BH23 2SB* Tel (01202) 482914

PEARSE, Ronald Thomas Hennessy. b 26. AKC52. **d** 53 **p** 54. C Leic St Pet *Leic* 53-55; C Hanwell St Thos *Lon* 55-58; R Asfordby *Leic* 58-84; P-in-c Scalford w Wycombe and Chadwell 75-76; R Thurcaston 84-89; rtd 89; Perm to Offic *Leic* from 89. *15 Burton Street, Loughborough, Leics LE11 2DT* Tel (01509) 215478

PEARSON, Andrew George Campbell. b 41. Qu Coll Ox BA63 BA66. Wycliffe Hall Ox 63. **d** 71 **p** 72. C Gillingham St Mark *Roch* 71-72; C Billingshurst *Chich* 72-77; C Ches Square St Mich w St Phil *Lon* 77-82; Co-ord Busoga Trust from 82; P-in-c St Marg Pattens *Lon* from 90. *15 Chadwin Road, London E13 8ND, or 2 Elizabeth Street, London SW1W 9RB* Tel 0171-476 6730 or 623 6630

PEARSON, Andrew John. b 59. Humberside Coll of Educn HND83. Westcott Ho Cam 86. **d** 89 **p** 90. C Knaresborough *Ripon* 89-92; C Wetherby 92-94; P-in-c Hunslet Moor St Pet and St Cuth 94-96; V from 96. *St Peter's Vicarage, 139 Dewsbury Road, Leeds LS11 5NW* Tel 0113-277 2464

PEARSON, Brian. b 29. LTCL53 Lon Inst of Educn CertEd54. Sarum & Wells Th Coll 71. **d** 73 **p** 74. C Rainham *Roch* 73-77; Chapl Asst Pembury Hosp Tunbridge Wells 77-80; C Pembury *Roch* 77-80; V Gravesend St Aid from 80; Chapl Gravesend and N Kent Hosp 81-83. *The Vicarage, St Gregory's Crescent, Gravesend, Kent DA12 4JL* Tel (01474) 352500

PEARSON, Canon Brian Robert. b 35. Leeds Univ BA59. Coll of Resurr Mirfield 59. **d** 61 **p** 62. C Chesterfield St Mary and All SS *Derby* 61-66; P-in-c Derby St Jo 66-72; P-in-c Derby St Anne 66-72; R Thorpe *Nor* 72-90; Hon Can Nor Cathl 85-90; RD Nor E 86-90; V Harrogate St Wilfrid *Ripon* from 90. *St Wilfrid's Vicarage, 51B Kent Road, Harrogate, N Yorkshire HG1 2EU* Tel (01423) 503259

PEARSON, Canon Brian William. b 49. CEng MBCS FHSM Brighton Poly BSc71 City Univ MSc80. S'wark Ord Course and Clapham Ord Scheme 76. **d** 79 **p** 80. Hon C Plumstead All SS *S'wark* 79-81; Perm to Offic *Chich* 81-83; Hon C Broadwater St Mary 83-88; Bp's Research and Dioc Communications Officer *B & W* 88-90; Dioc Missr 91; Abp's Officer for Miss and Evang and Tait Missr *Cant* 91-97; Abp's Dioc Chapl 91-97; Hon Can Cant Cathl 92-97; Dir CPAS from 97. *CPAS, Athena Drive, Tatchbrook Park, Warwick CV34 6NG* Tel (01926) 334242 Fax 337613 E-mail bpearson@cpas.org.uk

PEARSON, Christian David John (Brother Christian). b 42. Open Univ BA76 CCC Cam BA79 MA83. AKC65. **d** 66 **p** 67. C Pallion *Dur* 66-68; C Peterlee 68-71; SSF from 71; Lic to Offic *Sarum* 71-73; Tanzania 74-75; Lic to Offic *Ely* 75-90; Asst Chapl Keble Coll Ox 82-83; Chapl St Cath Coll Cam 83-86; Chapl Down Coll Cam 86-90; Lic to Offic *Lon* from 90; Dep Warden and Chapl Lon Ho Trust 90-93; Dep Warden and Chapl Lon Goodenough Trust 93-95. *Holy Trinity House, Orsett Terrace, London W2 6AH* Tel 0171-723 9735 or 351 8437 Fax 351 8578

PEARSON, Christopher Ian. b 65. Thames Poly BA91 K Coll Lon MA96. Coll of Resurr Mirfield CPS93. **d** 93 **p** 94. C Newington St Mary *S'wark* 93-95; C Streatham St Pet 95-97; V Kennington Park St Agnes from 97. *The Vicarage, 37 St Agnes Place, London SE11 4BB* Tel 0171-735 3860 E-mail chrispsdircon.co.uk

PEARSON, Christopher John. b 49. GRSM LRAM ARCM. Oak Hill NSM Course 81. **d** 84 **p** 85. NSM Barton Seagrave w Warkton *Pet* 84-86; C Kettering St Andr 86-88; V Nassington w Yarwell and Woodnewton 88-91; V Pet St Mark from 91. *St Mark's Vicarage, 82 Lincoln Road, Peterborough PE1 2SN* Tel (01733) 54516

PEARSON, David. b 57. Man Poly BA78. Trin Coll Bris 85. **d** 88 **p** 89. C Shawbury *Lich* 88-91; C Morton 88-91; C Stanton on Hine Heath 88-91; R Mattishall w Mattishall Burgh, Welborne etc *Nor* from 91. *The Vicarage, Back Lane, Mattishall, Dereham, Norfolk NR20 3PU* Tel (01362) 850243

PEARSON, Edgar. b 13. Tyndale Hall Bris 37. **d** 41 **p** 42. C Handforth *Ches* 41; Burma 42; India 42-47; Hon CF 47; Chile 50-55; Australia 55-65; R Dallinghoo and Pettistree *St E* 65-83; P-in-c Bredfield w Boulge 74-86; rtd 83; P-in-c Dallinghoo and Pettistree *St E* 83-86. *Maendy House, Penrhos, Raglan NP5 2LQ* Tel (01600) 85398

PEARSON, Fergus Tom. b 58. Middx Poly BA81. Oak Hill Th Coll DipHE92. **d** 92 **p** 93. C Mildmay Grove St Jude and St Paul *Lon* 92-95; Australia from 96. *Address temp unknown*

PEARSON, Geoffrey Charles (Geoff). b 49. ARCS BSc. Oak Hill Th Coll. **d** 82 **p** 83. C Foord St Jo *Cant* 82-86; V Ramsgate St Luke 86-93; Chapl to People at Work in Cam *Ely* from 93. *31 Thornton Close, Girton, Cambridge CB3 0NF* Tel (01223) 276657

PEARSON, Geoffrey Seagrave. b 51. St Jo Coll Dur BA72 DipTh73. Cranmer Hall Dur 72. **d** 74 **p** 75. C Kirkheaton *Wakef* 74-77; C-in-c Blackb Redeemer *Blackb* 77-82; V 82-85; Asst Home Sec Gen Syn Bd for Miss and Unity 85-89; Hon C Forty Hill Jes Ch *Lon* 85-89; Exec Sec BCC Evang Cttee 86-89; V Roby *Liv* from 89. *The Vicarage, 11 Church Road, Liverpool L36 9TL* Tel 0151-489 1438

PEARSON, George Michael. b 31. FCA FBCS MIMC. Coll of Resurr Mirfield 89 Qu Coll Birm 86. **d** 88 **p** 90. NSM Solihull *Birm* 88-95; Perm to Offic from 95. *The Parsonage, 67A Hampton Lane, Solihull, W Midlands B91 2QD* Tel 0121-705 0288

PEARSON, Harold (Brother Geoffrey). b 21. Ch Coll Cam BA43 MA46. Chich Th Coll 43. **d** 45 **p** 46. C Weymouth H Trin *Sarum* 45-48; SSF from 48; P-in-c Plaistow St Andr *Chelmsf* 53-57; Chapl Denstone Coll Uttoxeter 58; Papua New Guinea 59-70; Min Gen SSF 70-85; Australia 67-70; Hon Can Win Cathl *Win* 81-86; Zimbabwe from 86; rtd 91. *St Augustine's Mission, PO Penhalonga, Zimbabwe*

PEARSON, Henry Gervis. b 47. Mansf Coll Ox BA72 MA76. St Jo Coll Nottm 72. **d** 74 **p** 75. C Southgate *Chich* 74-76; TV 76-82; V Debenham w Aspall and Kenton *St E* 82-91; Chapl to Suffolk

Fire Service 88-91; RD Loes 89-91; TR Marlborough *Sarum* from 91; Chapl Savernake Hosp Marlborough from 91; RD Marlborough *Sarum* from 94. *The Rectory, 1 Rawlingswell Lane, Marlborough, Wilts SN8 1AU* Tel (01672) 512357

PEARSON, Ian. b 49. Liv Univ BA71 DAA72. S'wark Ord Course 79. **d** 82 **p** 83. Hon C Lavender Hill Ascension *S'wark* 82-84; Archivist USPG 82-85; Archivist Nat Soc 85-91; Lic to Offic *Lon* 84-86 and 88-90; Hon C Westmr St Matt 86-88; Perm to Offic *S'wark* 85-90; Perm to Offic *St Alb* 90-91; C Chesterfield St Mary and All SS *Derby* 91-95; R Bengeo *St Alb* from 95. *The Rectory, Byde Street, Hertford SG14 3BS* Tel (01992) 504997

PEARSON, Canon James Stuart. b 28. St Jo Coll Dur BA57. Cranmer Hall Dur 57. **d** 58 **p** 59. C Halifax St Jo Bapt *Wakef* 58-63; V Alverthorpe 63-70; V Knottingley 70-78; Dioc Soc Resp Adv 78-87; V Woolley 78-94; Chapl Bretton Hall Coll of Educn 87-94; Hon Can Wakef Cathl 89-94; RD Chevet 93-94; rtd 94; Perm to Offic *York* from 96. *21 Orrin Close, York YO2 2RA* Tel (01904)708521

PEARSON, James William (Jim). b 20. FCA59. Qu Coll Birm 75. **d** 78 **p** 79. NSM Beoley *Worc* 78-90; Perm to Offic from 90. *Ringwood, Rowney Green, Alvechurch, Birmingham B48 7QE* Tel (01527) 66952

PEARSON, John Nigel. b 45. CA Tr Coll IDC75 EMMTC 78. **d** 81 **p** 82. C Stapenhill w Cauldwell *Derby* 81-83; V Measham *Leic* from 83. *The Vicarage, High Street, Measham, Swadlincote, Derbyshire DE12 7HZ* Tel (01530) 270354

PEARSON, Kevin. b 54. Leeds Univ BA75 Edin Univ BD79. Edin Th Coll 76. **d** 79 **p** 80. C Horden *Dur* 79-81; Chapl Leeds Univ *Ripon* 81-87; R Edin St Salvador *Edin* 87-93; Chapl Napier Poly 88-92; Chapl Napier Univ 92-94; Dioc Dir of Ords 90-95; Prov Dir of Ords from 91; Assoc R Edin Old St Paul 93-94; P-in-c Linlithgow 94-95; R Edin St Mich and All SS from 95. *203 Gilmore Place, Edinburgh EH3 9PN* Tel 0131-229 6368

PEARSON, Mrs Lindsey Carole. b 61. Cov Poly BA85 CQSW85. Westcott Ho Cam 86. **d** 89 **p** 94. Par Dn High Harrogate St Pet *Ripon* 89-93; Par Dn Moor Allerton 93-94; C 94-96; TV Seacroft from 96. *St Peter's Vicarage, 139 Dewsbury Road, Leeds LS11 5NW* Tel 0113-277 2464

PEARSON, Michael John. b 53. Southn Univ BTh78. Sarum Th Coll 74. **d** 78 **p** 79. C Paignton St Jo *Ex* 78-82; TV Ilfracombe, Lee, W Down, Woolacombe and Bittadon 82-85; TV Ilfracombe, Lee, Woolacombe, Bittadon etc 85-86; TV Barnstaple from 86; Chapl N Devon Distr Hosp Barnstaple 86-96. *The Rectory, Sowden Lane, Barnstaple, Devon EX32 8BU* Tel (01271) 73837

PEARSON, Peter. b 09. Tyndale Hall Bris 32. **d** 35 **p** 36. C Tipton St Matt *Lich* 35-37; C Cobridge 37-40; V Buildwas 40-45; V Fremington *Ex* 45-74; rtd 75; P-in-c Nymet Rowland w Coldridge *Ex* 75-77; P-in-c Chawleigh w Cheldon 77-78; Lic to Offic from 78. *41 Barum Court, Litchdon Street, Barnstaple, Devon EX32 8QL* Tel (01271) 73525

PEARSON, Mrs Priscilla Dawn. b 45. Oak Hill Th Coll BA90. **d** 90 **p** 94. Par Dn Stanford-le-Hope w Mucking *Chelmsf* 90-94; C 94; C Colchester St Jo 94-96. *3 Northfield Gardens, Colchester CO4 4TL*

PEARSON, Raymond Joseph. b 44. AKC71. St Aug Coll Cant 71. **d** 72 **p** 73. C Wetherby *Ripon* 72-75; C Goring-by-Sea *Chich* 75-77; C Bramley *Ripon* 77-82; V Patrick Brompton and Hunton 82-94; V Crakehall 82-94; V Hornby 82-94; World Miss Officer from 88; RD Wensley 92-94; V Bardsey from 94. *The Vicarage, Wood Acre Lane, Bardsey, Leeds LS17 9DG* Tel (01937) 572243

PEARSON, Robert James Stephen. b 52. Cov Poly BA74. St Steph Ho Ox 85. **d** 87 **p** 88. C Stoke Newington St Mary *Lon* 87-90; C Haggerston All SS from 90. *All Saint's Vicarage, Livermere Road, London E8 4EZ* Tel 0171-254 0436

PEARSON, Robert Lyon (Bob). b 57. St Jo Coll Nottm DCM92. **d** 92 **p** 93. C Netherton *Liv* 92-96; V Woolston from 96. *The Vicarage, 20 Warren Lane, Woolston, Warrington WA1 4ES* Tel (01925) 813083

PEARSON, Roderick Percy. b 21. Linc Th Coll 74. **d** 75 **p** 76. C Darlington St Cuth w St Hilda *Dur* 75-80; V Bishop Middleham 80-91; rtd 91. *The Lever Flat, Christ's Hospital in Sherburn, Sherburn House, Durham DH1 2SE* Tel 0191-372 1753

PEARSON, Preb Roy Barthram. b 35. K Coll Lon 56. **d** 60 **p** 61. C Brookfield St Mary *Lon* 60-64; C St Marylebone St Cypr 64-70; V Tottenham All Hallows from 70; AD E Haringey from 95; Preb St Paul's Cathl from 96. *The Priory, Church Lane, London N17 7AA* Tel 0181-808 2470

PEARSON, Stephen. **d** 43 **p** 44. C Ribchester w Stidd *Blackb* 43; Canada 43-47; C Rayleigh *Chelmsf* 47-49; C Newburn *Newc* 49-51; V Chilcompton *B & W* 51-54; V Bolton St Matt *Man* 54-57; V Goodshaw 57-61; R Brome w Oakley *St E* 61-69; R Luddington w Hemington and Thurning *Pet* 69-77; P-in-c Clapton 69-77; rtd 77. *Address excluded by request*

PEARSON-MILES, David. b 37. St Jo Coll Nottm 74. **d** 76 **p** 77. C Hazlemere *Ox* 76-79; R Waddesdon w Over Winchendon and Fleet Marston 79-82; CF 82-92; P-in-c Barcombe *Chich* 92-94; R from 94. *The Rectory, The Grange, Barcombe, Lewes, E Sussex BN8 5AT* Tel (01273) 400260

PEART, John Graham. b 36. Bps' Coll Cheshunt 65. **d** 68 **p** 69. C Cheshunt *St Alb* 68-70; C St Alb St Pet 70-73; R Hunsdon 73-76; R Widford 73-76; Ind Chapl 76-82; Chapl St Geo Hosp and Distr Gen Hosp Stafford 82-87; Qu Eliz Hosp and Bensham Hosp Gateshead 87-89; Garlands Hosp 89-94; P-in-c Cotehill and Cumwhinton *Carl* 89-94; V Irthington, Crosby-on-Eden and Scaleby from 94. *The Vicarage, Irthington, Carlisle CA6 4NJ* Tel (016977) 2379

PEASTON, Canon Monroe. b 14. BNC Ox BA36 MA43 Lon Univ BD48. Union Th Sem (NY) PhD64 Montreal Dioc Th Coll Hon DD75 Wycliffe Hall Ox 36. **d** 38 **p** 39. C St Helens St Helen *Liv* 38-40; C Claughton St Mich *Ches* 40-43; Org Sec (Dios Bradf, Blackb and Carl) CMS 43-45; Chapl Wrekin Coll Wellington 45-48; New Zealand 48-64; Hon Can Christchurch 61-64; Canada 64-84; Hon Can Montreal from 66; rtd 84; USA from 84. *Address temp unknown*

PEAT, David James. b 62. Leeds Univ BA84. Cranmer Hall Dur 86. **d** 89 **p** 90. C Wetherby *Ripon* 89-92; C Beeston 92-95; Chapl St Lawr Coll Ramsgate from 95. *St Lawrence College, College Road, Ramsgate, Kent CT11 7AE* Tel (01843) 582084 or 587666

PEAT, Dr David William. b 37. Clare Coll Cam BA59 PhD63. Westcott Ho Cam 72. **d** 75 **p** 76. C Chesterton St Andr *Ely* 75-77; Chapl Univ Coll of Ripon and York St Jo 77-83; V E Ardsley *Wakef* 83-87; Prin Willesden Min Tr Scheme 87-94; NSM Headingley *Ripon* from 94; Research Lect Leeds Univ from 94. *12 North Grange Mews, Headingley, Leeds LS6 2EW* Tel 0113-275 3179

PEAT, The Ven Lawrence Joseph (Lawrie). b 28. Linc Th Coll 55. **d** 58 **p** 59. C Bramley *Ripon* 58-61; V 65-73; R Heaton Norris All SS *Man* 61-65; P-in-c Southend St Erkenwald *Chelmsf* 73-74; TR Southend St Jo w St Mark, All SS w St Fran etc 74-79; V Skelsmergh w Selside and Longsleddale *Carl* 79-86; RD Kendal 84-89; TV Kirkby Lonsdale 86-89; Hon Can Carl Cathl 88-95; Adn Westmorland and Furness 89-95; rtd 95; Perm to Offic *Carl* from 95. *17 Railway Terrace, Lindal, Ulverston, Cumbria LA12 0LQ* Tel (01229) 468069

PEATFIELD, Canon Alfred Charles Henry. b 22. New Coll Ox BA48 MA48. Ripon Hall Ox 48. **d** 51 **p** 52. C Hackney St Jo *Lon* 51-54; V Battersea St Paul *S'wark* 54-56; Malaya 56-63; Malaysia 63-70; Adn N Malaya 64-70; V Hornchurch St Andr *Chelmsf* 70-92; RD Havering 76-80; Hon Can Chelmsf Cathl 80-92; rtd 92; Perm to Offic *Chelmsf* from 92. *10 Tyne Close, Upminster, Essex RM14 1QB* Tel (01708) 220598

PEATMAN (née HUGHES), Mrs Debbie Ann. b 62. SS Hild & Bede Coll Dur BA83 St Jo Coll Dur BA89. Cranmer Hall Dur 87. **d** 90 **p** 94. C Edin Old St Paul *Edin* 90-91; NSM Greasley *S'well* 92-94; NSM Whitley *Cov* from 94. *St James's Vicarage, 171 Abbey Road, Coventry CV3 4BG* Tel (01203) 301617

PEATMAN, Michael Robert. b 61. Keble Coll Ox BA85 MA89 St Jo Coll Dur BA89. Cranmer Hall Dur 87. **d** 90 **p** 91. C Greasley *S'well* 90-94; P-in-c Whitley *Cov* from 94; Dio Stewardship Adv from 94. *St James's Vicarage, 171 Abbey Road, Coventry CV3 4BG* Tel (01203) 301617

PEBERDY (née GARNETT), Mrs Alyson Susan. b 48. Trevelyan Coll Dur BA69 Reading Univ MA75 St Ant Coll Ox DipSocAnth77. Ox Min Course 95. **d** 96. C New Windsor *Ox* from 96. *36A Alexandra Road, Windsor, Berks SL4 1HR* Tel (01753) 858114

PECK, David George. b 11. Jes Coll Cam BA32 MA48 Linc Coll Ox MA51. St Steph Ho Ox 32. **d** 34 **p** 35. C Richmond St Jo *S'wark* 34-37; C Wimbledon 37-39; C Wanstead H Trin Hermon Hill *Chelmsf* 39-41; Ind Chr Fellowship SW Area Dir 41-43; V Lt Bedwyn *Sarum* 43-51; Perm to Offic *Ox* 51-53; R Stratton Audley w Godington 53-59; Chapl Cokethorpe Sch Oxon 59-63; R Shellingford 63-83; rtd 83. *The Barn House, Chapel Road, Stanford in the Vale, Faringdon, Oxon SN7 8LE* Tel (01367) 710511

PECK, David Warner. b 66. BA88 Selw Coll Cam BA94. Westcott Ho Cam CTM95. **d** 95 **p** 96. C Weybridge *Guildf* from 95. *87 Greenlands Road, Weybridge, Surrey KT13 8PS* Tel (01932) 846398

PECK, Trevor Paul Owen. b 47. Lich Th Coll 69. **d** 72 **p** 73. C Hatfield *Sheff* 72-74; C Swinton 75-77; TV Gt Grimsby St Mary and St Jas *Linc* 77-81; P-in-c Glentworth 81-86; P-in-c Hemswell w Harpswell 81-86; V Burgh le Marsh 86-87; R Bratoft w Irby-in-the-Marsh 86-87. *Address temp unknown*

PECKETT, Desmonde Claude Brown. b 19. Ex & Truro NSM Scheme. **d** 77 **p** 78. NSM Charlestown *Truro* from 77. *Smugglers, Porthpean, St Austell, Cornwall PL26 6AY* Tel (01726) 72768

PECKHAM, Richard Graham. b 51. Sarum & Wells Th Coll 84. **d** 86 **p** 87. C Bishop's Cleeve *Glouc* 86-89; TV Ilfracombe, Lee, Woolacombe, Bittadon etc *Ex* 89-96; TV Sidmouth, Woolbrook, Salcombe Regis, Sidbury etc from 96. *St Francis' Vicarage, Woolbrook Road, Sidmouth, Devon EX10 9XH* Tel (01395) 514522

PEDDER, Brian. b 38. Carl Dioc Tr Inst 88. **d** 91 **p** 92. NSM Wigton *Carl* 91-93; C Cleator Moor w Cleator 93-96; P-in-c Grayrigg, Old Hutton and New Hutton from 96. *The Vicarage, Grayrigg, Kendal, Cumbria LA8 9BU* Tel (01539) 824272

PEDLAR, John Glanville. b 43. Ex Univ BA68. St Steph Ho Ox 68. **d** 70 **p** 71. C Tavistock and Gulworthy *Ex* 70-73; Prec Portsm Cathl *Portsm* 74-77; Prec St Alb Abbey *St Alb* 77-81; V Redbourn from 81; PV Westmr Abbey from 87. *The Vicarage,*

Church End, Redbourn, St Albans, Herts AL3 7DU Tel (01582) 793122

PEDLEY, Miss Betty. b 49. ALCM78 Leeds Univ BEd71 Ripon Coll of Educn CertEd70 Coll of Preceptors DSpEd81. N Ord Course 85. **d** 88. Par Dn Sowerby *Wakef* 88-92; Par Educn Adv from 92; Youth Chapl from 92. *27 Pye Nest Grove, Halifax, W Yorkshire HX2 7JY* Tel (01422) 346007

PEDLEY, Canon Geoffrey Stephen. b 40. Qu Coll Cam BA64 MA67. Cuddesdon Coll 64. **d** 66 **p** 67. C Liv Our Lady and St Nic *Liv* 66-69; C Cov H Trin *Cov* 69-71; Zambia 71-77; P-in-c Stockton H Trin *Dur* 77-83; V Stockton St Pet 77-88; Chapl to The Queen from 84; R Whickham *Dur* 88-93; Can Res Dur Cathl from 93. *6A The College, Durham DH1 3EQ* Tel 0191-384 5489

PEDLEY, Nicholas Charles (Nick). b 48. DipSocWork75 CQSW75. Qu Coll Birm 88. **d** 90 **p** 91. C Stafford St Jo and Tixall w Ingestre *Lich* 90-93; C Kingswinford St Mary *Worc* 93-96; TV 96-97; C Cheswardine, Childs Ercall, Hales, Hinstock etc *Lich* from 97; Chapl HM Young Offender Inst Stoke Heath from 97. *The Vicarage, 5A Village Road, Childs Ercall, Market Drayton, Shropshire TF9 2BZ*

PEDLOW, Henry Noel. b 37. QUB BA59. **d** 61 **p** 62. C Belfast St Phil *Conn* 61-66; C Belfast St Nic 66-70; I Eglantine 70-82; I Kilkeel *D & D* 82-89; I Belfast St Donard from 89. *St Donard's Rectory, 421 Beersbridge Road, Belfast BT5 5DU* Tel (01232) 652321

PEEBLES, Alexander Paterson. b 21. Westcott Ho Cam 62. **d** 63 **p** 64. C Hatfield *St Alb* 63-65; C Marsh Gibbon *Ox* 66-67; C Grendon Underwood w Edgcott 66-67; C Preston Bissett, Chetwode and Barton Hartshorn 66-67; C Twyford (Bucks) 66-67; P-in-c Grendon Underwood w Edgcott 67-73; P-in-c Twyford (Bucks) 67-73; P-in-c Marsh Gibbon 67-73; P-in-c Preston Bissett, Chetwode and Barton Hartshorn 67-73; RD Claydon 71-73; R Glenrothes *St And* 73-81; Can St Ninian's Cathl Perth 78-82; Dioc Supernumerary 81-82; P-in-c Bathgate *Edin* 82-87; P-in-c Linlithgow 82-87; rtd 86; P-in-c Newburgh *St And* from 88. *The Studio, 5 Hillside Place, Newport-on-Tay, Fife DD6 8DH* Tel (01382) 542530

PEEBLES, David Thomas. b 64. Bris Univ BA85 St Chad's Coll Dur PGCE86 Man Univ MA94. Coll of Resurr Mirfield CPT90. **d** 90 **p** 91. C Crewe St Andr *Ches* 90-93; Lect and Asst Dir Studies Mirfield 93-95; Chapl Qu Mary and Westf Coll *Lon* from 95. *24 Sidney Square, London E1 2EY* Tel 0171-775 3179 or 791 1973

PEEK, John Richard. b 51. Bris Univ BSc72 Nottm Univ BA75. St Jo Coll Nottm DPS76. **d** 76 **p** 77. C Hebburn St Jo *Dur* 76-78; C Dunston 78-81; R Armthorpe *Sheff* 81-86; RE Teacher K Edw VI Sch Southn 87-88; Chapl and Hd RE Casterton Sch Cumbria 89; Teacher Furze Platt Comp Sch Berks 89-90; Perm to Offic *Portsm* 90-96; Chapl Bearwood Coll Wokingham from 96. *Bearwood College, Wokingham, Berks RG41 5BG* Tel 0118-1978 6915

PEEK, Roland Denys. b 17. Sarum Th Coll 69. **d** 70 **p** 71. C Ex St Matt *Ex* 70-74; R Moretonhampstead 74-78; R Moretonhampstead, N Bovey and Manaton 78-84; rtd 84. *6 The Oaks, St Mary's Park, Bovey Tracey, Newton Abbott, Devon TQ13 9XQ* Tel (01626) 834565

PEEL, Basil Headley. b 26. TCD BA52 MA55. Wells Th Coll 52. **d** 54 **p** 55. C Oswestry St Oswald *Lich* 54-59; C Leek St Edw 59-62; V Chesterton 62-68; V Willenhall H Trin 68-79; V Longsdon 79-92; P-in-c Rushton 84-92; P-in-c Horton 84-92; rtd 92. *Tyn-y-ddol, Penybontfawr, Oswestry, Shropshire SY10 0PB* Tel (01691) 74551

PEEL, Mrs Christine Mary. b 44. Whitelands Coll Lon CertEd66. Portsm Dioc Tr Course. **d** 90. NSM Sheet *Portsm* from 90. *7 Crundles, Herne Farm, Petersfield, Hants GU31 4PJ* Tel (01730) 266926

PEEL, David Charles. b 41. AKC75. St Aug Coll Cant 75. **d** 76 **p** 77. C Tynemouth Cullercoats St Paul *Newc* 76-79; C Tynemouth St Jo 79-84; Ldr Cedarwood Project 84-88 and from 91; Warden Communicare Ho 89-91; Min Killingworth 89-91. *3 Elmfield Grove, Gosforth, Newcastle upon Tyne NE3 4XA* Tel 0191-285 1484

PEEL, Derrick. b 50. Open Univ BA82. Linc Th Coll 75. **d** 78 **p** 79. C Otley *Bradf* 78-82; V Shelf 82-94; P-in-c Buttershaw St Aid 89-94; TR Shelf St Mich w Buttershaw St Aid 94-95; V E Crompton *Man* from 95. *East Crompton Vicarage, Salts Street, Shaw, Oldham OL2 7TE* Tel (01706) 847454

PEEL, John Bruce. b 30. TCD BA54 MA68. Wells Th Coll 69. **d** 70 **p** 71. C Wilmslow *Ches* 70-75; V Weston 75-83; V Henbury 83-95; Chapl Parkside Hosp Ches 83-95; rtd 95; Perm to Offic *Ches* from 95. *Winneba, 29 Hungerford Terrace, Crewe CW1 1HF* Tel (01270) 587464

PEEL, Michael Jerome. b 31. Bris Univ BA55 MLitt73 St Cath Soc Ox DipTh59 Man Univ BD65 K Coll Lon PhD88 FRSA94. Wycliffe Hall Ox 57. **d** 59 **p** 60. C Stretford St Matt *Man* 59-61; C Chorlton upon Medlock 61-62; Chapl Man Univ 61-62; C Chorlton-cum-Hardy St Clem 62-65; V Chirbury *Heref* 65-68; P-in-c Marton 65-68; R Iver Heath *Ox* 68-87; V Linslade 87-95; rtd 95; Warden Coll of St Barn Lingfield from 95; Perm to Offic *Chich* from 95; Perm to Offic *Roch* from 95. *The Lodge, College of St Barnabas, Blackberry Lane, Lingfield, Surrey RH7 6NJ* Tel (01342) 870366 or 870260 Fax 870193

PEELING, Mrs Pamela Mary Alberta. b 44. Oak Hill Th Coll 83. **dss** 86 **d** 87 **p** 94. NSM Moulsham St Luke *Chelmsf* 86-88; NSM N Springfield 88-95; C Basildon St Martin from 95. *7 Botelers, Basildon, Essex SS16 5SE* Tel (01268) 413376

PEERS, John Edward. b 39. Bps' Coll Cheshunt 60. **d** 63 **p** 64. C Crayford *Roch* 63-67; C Beckenham St Jas 67-69; C Winlaton *Dur* 69-72; P-in-c Silksworth 72-81; R Lt Bowden St Nic *Leic* 81-86; P-in-c Lt Bowden St Hugh 83-86; RD Gartree I 84-88; R Market Harborough Transfiguration 86-88; V Skipton Ch Ch *Bradf* from 88. *Christ Church Vicarage, Carleton Road, Skipton, N Yorkshire BD23 2BE* Tel (01756) 793612

PEERS, Michael John. b 65. SS Paul & Mary Coll Cheltenham BA86. Ripon Coll Cuddesdon 88. **d** 91 **p** 92. C Birstall and Wanlip *Leic* 91-94; C Leic St Marg and All SS 94-96; TV The Abbey Leicester from 96. *St Margaret's Vicarage, 46 Brading Road, Leicester LE3 9BG* Tel 0116-262 7362

PEERS, Richard Charles. b 65. K Alfred's Coll Win BEd88. Chich Th Coll BTh93. **d** 93 **p** 94. C Grangetown *York* 93-95; C Portsea St Mary *Portsm* from 95. *2 Glebe Flats, Nutfield Place, Portsmouth PO1 4JF* Tel (01705) 826892

PEET, Derek Edwin. b 26. Sheff Univ BA51 DipEd Lon Univ DipTh57. Qu Coll Birm 66. **d** 67 **p** 68. C Hebden Bridge *Wakef* 67-70; V Darton 70-79; TR Gleadless Valley *Sheff* 79-85; V Kirk Hallam *Derby* 85-96; rtd 96. *44 Parkways Grove, Woodlesford, Leeds LS26 8TP* Tel 0113-282 3079

PEET, John Christopher. b 56. Or Coll Ox BA80 MA83 Clare Coll Cam BA82 MA87. Ridley Hall Cam 80. **d** 83 **p** 84. C Menston w Woodhead *Bradf* 83-86; C Prenton *Ches* 86-89; V Harden and Wilsden *Bradf* 89-97; V Cononley w Bradley from 97. *The Vicarage, 3 Meadow Close, Cononley, Keighley, W Yorkshire BD20 8LZ* Tel (01535) 634369

PEET, John Michael. b 44. AKC67. **d** 68 **p** 72. C Battersea St Pet *S'wark* 68-69; C Sutton St Nic 69-74; C Perry Hill St Geo 74-78; TV Stepney St Dunstan and All SS *Lon* 78-81; P-in-c Stamford Hill St Bart 81-86; V 87-89; P-in-c Mile End Old Town H Trin 89-90; P-in-c Bromley All Hallows 89-90; TR Bow H Trin and All Hallows from 90. *Holy Trinity Vicarage, 28 Coborn Street, London E3 2AB* Tel 0181-980 2074

PEGG, Brian Peter Richard (Bill). b 30. Ox NSM Course 77 Sarum & Wells Th Coll 82. **d** 83 **p** 84. C Furze Platt *Ox* 83-85; V Ashbury, Compton Beauchamp and Longcot w Fernham 85-94; Chapl Malaga *Eur* 94-97; rtd 97. *21-2D Paseo de Reding, Malaga 29016, Spain* Tel Malaga (52) 219396 Fax 227218

PEGG, Gerald Francis. b 37. FCII69 Birkb Coll Lon DipRS91. S'wark Ord Course 88. **d** 91 **p** 92. NSM Belmont *S'wark* 91-95; NSM Winchelsea and Icklesham *Chich* from 95. *Pilgrim's End, Manor Close, Icklesham, Winchelsea, E Sussex TN36 4BT* Tel (01424) 814735

PEGLER, Frederic Arthur. b 19. Selw Coll Cam BA46 MA48. Qu Coll Birm 46. **d** 47 **p** 48. C Crawley *Chich* 47-49; C Rickmansworth *St Alb* 49-50; V Sark *Win* 50-52; PV S'well Minster *S'well* 52-55; Canada 55-84; rtd 84; Perm to Offic *St Alb* 84-85. *206-1149 Rockland Avenue, Victoria, British Columbia, Canada, V8V 4T5*

PEIRCE, John. b 35. Worc Coll Ox BA59 MA64 Kent Univ MA96. Wycliffe Hall Ox 59. **d** 61 **p** 62. C Brompton H Trin *Lon* 61-64; C Wareham w Arne *Sarum* 64-68; V Sturminster Newton and Hinton St Mary 68-74; V Kingswood *Bris* 74-79; Dir Coun Chr Care *Ex* 79-89; Public Preacher 89-92; NSM Hackney *Lon* 90-94; NSM St Botolph Aldgate w H Trin Minories from 94; Co-ord Ch Action on Disability from 90; Perm to Offic *Ex* from 92. *91 Mildenhall Road, London E5 0RY, or Rushford Forge, Narrowbridge, Chagford, Newton Abbot TQ13 8DA* Tel 0181-985 3150 or (01647) 433650

PEIRCE, Canon John Martin. b 36. Jes Coll Cam BA59 MA65. Westcott Ho Cam 65. **d** 66 **p** 67. C Croydon *Cant* 66-70; C Fareham H Trin *Portsm* 70-71; TV 71-76; TR Langley Marish *Ox* 76-85; RD Burnham 78-82; Dir of Ords from 85; Dir of Post-Ord Tr from 85; Can Res Ch Ch from 87. *70 Yarnells Hill, Oxford OX2 9BG* Tel (01865) 721330

PELHAM, John. b 36. New Coll Ox BA61 MA65. **d** 79 **p** 80. NSM Balerno *Edin* 79-91; Hon C W Linton 91-94; Hon C Penicuik 91-94; Dioc Supernumerary from 94. *2 Horsburgh Bank, Balerno, Midlothian EH14 7DA* Tel 0131-449 3934

PELL, Charles Andrew. b 54. Leeds Univ CertEd77. Aston Tr Scheme 87 St Jo Coll Nottm 87. **d** 89 **p** 90. C Mottram in Longdendale w Woodhead *Ches* 89-90; C Handforth 90-93; P-in-c Walton Breck *Liv* 93-94; V 94-96; P-in-c Glyndyfrdwy and Llansantfraid Glyn Dyfrdwy *St As* from 96. *The Vicarage, Glyndyfrdwy, Corwen LL21 9HG* Tel (01490) 83201

PELLANT, Walter Reginald Guy. b 14. OBE79. AKC42. Cuddesdon Coll 42. **d** 43 **p** 44. C Newington St Paul *S'wark* 43-45; C Kennington St Jo 45-48; Chapl RAF 48-69; Asst Chapl-in-Chief RAF 69-71; QHC from 70; Chapl Geneva *Eur* 71-80; rtd 80. *3 Fountain Court, 13 The Avenue, Poole, Dorset BH13 6EZ* Tel (01202) 768521

PELLEY, John Lawless. b 34. Oak Hill Th Coll 67. **d** 69 **p** 70. C Fareham St Jo *Portsm* 69-72; C Frogmore *St Alb* 72-76; V

Standon 76-96; RD Bishop's Stortford 91-95; rtd 96. *7 Home Close, Histon, Cambridge CB4 4JL* Tel (01223) 234636

PELLY, Raymond Blake. b 38. Worc Coll Ox BA61 MA69 Geneva Univ DTh71. Linc Th Coll. **d** 63 **p** 64. C Gosforth All SS *Newc* 63-65. *28 Collingwood Street, Freeman's Bay, Auckland 1, New Zealand* Tel Auckland (9) 764923

PELTON, Ian Simpson. b 30. Keble Coll Ox 50. Sarum Th Coll 55. **d** 57 **p** 58. C Crook *Dur* 57-61; C Harton 61-65; V Coxhoe 65-95; rtd 95. *49 Buckinghamshire Road, Belmont, Durham DH1 2BE* Tel 0191-386 2273

PELTOR, Lawrence Frank. b 08. Keble Coll Ox BA33 MA37. Linc Th Coll 33. **d** 34 **p** 35. C Linc St Nic w St Jo Newport *Linc* 34-37; C Middlesbrough St Paul *York* 37-39; C Whitby 39-40; CF 40-45; V Spittlegate *Linc* 46-55; Chapl Hill View Hosp Grantham 46-55; V Thirkleby w Kilburn and Bagby *York* 55-60; Hon CF 45; R Willey w Barrow *Heref* 60-72; C Wybunbury *Ches* 72-73; rtd 73; Perm to Offic *Heref* from 73. *5 Cliff Gardens, Cliff Road, Bridgnorth, Shropshire WV16 4EZ* Tel (01746) 763173

PELZ, Werner. b 21. Lon Univ BA49. Linc Th Coll 50. **d** 51 **p** 52. C Birch St Jas *Man* 51-54; C-in-c Lostock CD 54-63; rtd 86. *183 Badger Creek Road, Healesville, Victoria, Australia 3777*

PEMBERTON, Anthony Thomas Christie (Chris). b 57. BA. Cranmer Hall Dur 82. **d** 84 **p** 85. C Maidstone St Luke *Cant* 84-88; Chapl Ox Pastorate from 88. *14 Walton Street, Oxford OX1 2HG* Tel (01865) 244713

PEMBERTON, Mrs Carolyn Mary (Carrie). b 55. St Hilda's Coll Ox BA78 Cam Univ PGCE81 Leeds Univ MA92. Cranmer Hall Dur 83 NE Ord Course 84. **dss** 86 **d** 87 **p** 94. NSM Leeds St Geo *Ripon* 86-87; Miss Partner CMS 87-91; Dir Women's Studies Angl Th Inst Zaire 87-91; Perm to Offic *Pet* 92-94; NSM Bourn and Kingston w Caxton and Longstowe *Ely* from 94. *The Rectory, 2 Short Street, Bourn, Cambridge CB3 7SG* Tel (01954) 719728

PEMBERTON, Crispin Mark Rugman. b 59. St Andr Univ MTh83. St Steph Ho Ox 84. **d** 86 **p** 87. C Acton St Alb w All SS *Lon* 86-88; C Acton Green 88-90; C Leckhampton SS Phil and Jas w Cheltenham St Jas *Glouc* 90-93; V Tuffley 93-97; RE Teacher Cheltenham Coll Jun Sch from 97. *14 Ewlin Road, Cheltenham, Glos GL53 7PB* Tel (01242) 583217

PEMBERTON, David Charles. b 35. K Coll Lon 57. **d** 61 **p** 62. C Pokesdown St Jas *Win* 61-65; C W Derby St Mary *Liv* 65-67; C-in-c Cantril Farm St Jude CD 67-71; V Cantril Farm 71-74; V Devonport St Boniface *Ex* 75-83; V Stanwell *Lon* from 83; AD Spelthorne from 92. *The Vicarage, 1 Lord Knyvett Close, Staines, Middx TW19 7PQ* Tel (01784) 252044

PEMBERTON, Jeremy Charles Baring. b 56. Mert Coll Ox MA77 Fitzw Ho Cam BA80 Leeds Univ MA92. Ridley Hall Cam 78. **d** 81 **p** 82. C Stranton *Dur* 81-84; C Leeds St Geo *Ripon* 84-87; CMS Miss Partner and Dir Angl Th Inst Zaire 87-91; V Irchester *Pet* 92-94; P-in-c Bourn and Kingston w Caxton and Longstowe *Ely* 94; R from 94. *The Rectory, 2 Short Street, Bourn, Cambridge CB3 7SG* Tel (01954) 719728

PEMBERTON, Canon Wilfred Austin. b 14. Lon Univ BA39 AKC41 BD42 Nottm Univ PhD52. **d** 41 **p** 42. C Colchester St Giles *Chelmsf* 41-43; P-in-c 43-46; PC Stonebroom *Derby* 46-51; Asst Dioc Insp of Schs 48-51; Chapl Morton Hosp Derby 49-51; R Breaston *Derby* 51-61; R Wilne and Draycott w Breaston 61-91; Chapl Draycott Hosp Derby 62-72; Hon Can Derby Cathl *Derby* 80-91; rtd 91; Perm to Offic *Derby* from 91; Perm to Offic *Leic* from 93. *19 Cordwell Close, Castle Donnington, Derby DE74 2JL* Tel (01332) 853392

PEMBERY, Gerald Marcus. b 29. Glouc Sch of Min 89. **d** 90 **p** 91. NSM Bream *Glouc* 90-97; rtd 97 *Kings Wood, The Tufts, Bream, Lydney, Glos GL15 6HW* Tel (01594) 562750

PENBERTHY (formerly LEGG), Ms Joanna Susan. b 60. Newnham Coll Cam BA81 MA85. St Jo Coll Nottm DipTh82 MTh84 St Jo Coll Dur 83. **dss** 84 **d** 87 **p** 97. Haughton le Skerne *Dur* 84-85; Llanishen and Lisvane *Llan* 85-87; NSM 87-89; NSM Llanwddyn and Llanfihangel and Llwydiarth *St As* 89-93; NSM Llansadwrn w Llanwrda and Manordeilo *St D* 93-95; Officer Div for Par Development Ch in Wales from 95. *The Church in Wales Centre, Woodland Place, Penarth CF64 2EX* Tel (01222) 708234

PENDLEBURY, Stephen Thomas. b 50. ACA78 Southn Univ BSc73. Ridley Hall Cam 86. **d** 88 **p** 89. C Birkenhead St Jas w St Bede *Ches* 88-91; V from 91. *St James Vicarage, 56 Tollemache Road, Birkenhead, Merseyside L43 8SZ* Tel 0151-652 1016

PENDLETON, David Julian. b 24. K Coll Lon BD54 AKC54. **d** 54 **p** 55. C Shard End *Birm* 54-59; C Northfield 59-65; C-in-c Shenley Green CD 65-70; V Shenley Green 70-89; rtd 89. *258 Mulberry Road, Birmingham B30 1ST* Tel 0121-475 4874

PENDLETON, John Thomas. b 12. Dorchester Miss Coll 39. **d** 41 **p** 42. C Padiham *Blackb* 41-44; V Cornholme *Wakef* 44-49; V Slaithwaite w E Scammonden 49-61; P-in-c Cleckheaton St Luke 61-62; V 62-77; rtd 77; Perm to Offic *Wakef* from 77. *25 Meadow Close, Robertown, Liversedge, W Yorkshire WF15 7QE* Tel (01924) 405255

PENDLETON, Mervyn Boulton. b 13. SS Coll Cam BA35 MA42. Chich Th Coll 35. **d** 37 **p** 38. C Hastings All So *Chich* 37-39; C Upper Beeding 39-42; C Bramber w Botolphs 39-42; C W Tarring 42-44; C Rusthall *Roch* 44-45; R Brington *Pet* 45-52; V Wollaston and Strixton 52-60; Chapl St Steph Coll Broadstairs 60-62; Chapl Ringwood Gr Sch Bournemouth 65-68; Warden Whittington Coll Almshouses Felbridge 68-69; C Yateley *Win* 69-71; R Kimpton w Thruxton w Fyfield 71-78; rtd 78. *20 Owers Way, West Wittering, Chichester, W Sussex PO20 8HA*

PENDORF, Canon James Gordon. b 45. Drew Univ New Jersey BA67. Episc Th Sch Cam Mass BD71. **d** 71 **p** 71. USA 71-76; V Colne H Trin *Blackb* 76-80; Sen Dioc Stewardship Adv *Chelmsf* 80-83; Dioc Sec *Birm* 83-95; Hon Can Birm Cathl from 90; P-in-c Highgate 95-97; V from 97; Dioc Stewardship Adv 95-97; RD Birm City from 96. *120 Stanhope Street, Birmingham B12 0XB* Tel 0121-440 4605 or 427 5141 Fax 428 1114

PENFOLD, Brian Robert. b 54. Lon Univ BSc75 Bris Univ PGCE77. Oak Hill Th Coll BA84. **d** 84 **p** 85. C Norwood St Luke *S'wark* 84-88; C Rayleigh *Chelmsf* 88-92; V New Barnet St Jas *St Alb* from 92. *The Vicarage, 11 Park Road, Barnet, Herts EN4 9QA* Tel 0181-449 4043

PENFOLD, Colin Richard. b 52. St Pet Coll Ox BA74 MA78. Ridley Hall Cam 81. **d** 84 **p** 85. C Buckhurst Hill *Chelmsf* 84-87; C Greenside *Dur* 87-90; V Cononley w Bradley *Bradf* 90-97; P-in-c Shipley St Paul and Frizinghall from 97. *The Rectory, 47 Kirkgate, Shipley, W Yorkshire BD18 3EH* Tel (01274) 583652

PENFOLD, Dr Susan Irene Winn. b 52. York Univ BA73 Bris Univ PhD77 Selw Coll Cam BA83 MA87. Ridley Hall Cam 81. **dss** 84 **d** 87 **p** 94. Buckhurst Hill *Chelmsf* 84-87; Hon C Greenside *Dur* 87-90; Hon C Cononley w Bradley *Bradf* 90-97; Assoc Dioc Dir of Ords from 96; Hon C Shipley St Paul and Frizinghall from 97. *The Rectory, 47 Kirkgate, Shipley, W Yorkshire BD18 3EH* Tel (01274) 583652

PENGELLEY, Peter John. b 22. Sarum & Wells Th Coll 72. **d** 74 **p** 75. C Midsomer Norton *B & W* 74-78; R Stogursey w Fiddington 78-88; Ind Chapl 80-88; rtd 88; Perm to Offic *B & W* from 89. *Rosslyn Cottage, Roadwater, Watchet, Somerset TA23 0RB* Tel (01984) 40798

PENGELLY, Geoffrey. b 50. Oak Hill Th Coll 86. **d** 88 **p** 89. C Redruth w Lanner and Treleigh *Truro* 88-91; TV Bolventor 91-92; V Egloskerry, N Petherwin, Tremaine and Tresmere from 92. *The Vicarage, Egloskerry, Launceston, Cornwall PL15 8RX* Tel (01566) 785365

PENMAN, John Bain. b 67. Aber Univ BD89 New Coll Edin MTh93 SSC96. Edin Th Coll CECM93. **d** 93 **p** 94. C Glas St Ninian *Glas* 93-96; C Ealing Ch the Sav *Lon* from 96. *The Clergy House, The Grove, London W5 5DX* Tel 0181-840 6603

PENMAN, Miss Margaret Heather. b 50. St Martin's Coll Lanc CertEd71 Lanc Univ DipEd82 DipRE87 FRSA95. Carl Dioc Tr Inst 90. **d** 93 **p** 94. Headteacher Hesketh w Becconsall All SS C of E Sch from 85; NSM Lostock Hall *Blackb* 93-95; NSM Leyland St Jas from 95. *9 Oakfield Drive, Leyland, Preston PR5 3XE* Tel (01772) 435927 or 812630 Fax 814721

PENMAN, Robert George (Bob). b 42. St Jo Coll Auckland LTh66. **d** 65 **p** 66. New Zealand 65-73; C Alverstoke *Portsm* 73-74; CF 74-77; C Bridgwater St Mary w Chilton Trinity *B & W* 77-80; P-in-c Haselbury Plucknett w N Perrott 80-81; P-in-c Misterton 80-81; V Haselbury Plucknett, Misterton and N Perrott 81-89; P-in-c Appleton *Ox* from 89; P-in-c Besselsleigh w Dry Sandford from 89. *The Rectory, Oaksmere, Appleton, Abingdon, Oxon OX13 5JS* Tel (01865) 862458

PENN, Canon Arthur William. b 22. Man Univ BA49. Wycliffe Hall Ox 49. **d** 51 **p** 52. C Bowdon *Ches* 51-53; C Alston w Garrigill *Newc* 53-56; V Kirkdale *York* 56-67; V Brampton *Carl* 67-83; RD Brampton 74-83; P-in-c Gilsland w Nether Denton 75-81; Hon Can Carl Cathl 78-88; P-in-c Gilsland 81-83; V Rockcliffe and Blackford 83-88; rtd 88; Perm to Offic *Carl* from 88. *1 Well Lane, Warton, Carnforth, Lancs LA5 9QZ* Tel (01524) 733079

PENN, Barry Edwin. b 46. Univ of Wales (Swansea) BA72. St Jo Coll Nottm 77. **d** 79 **p** 80. C New Barnet St Jas *St Alb* 79-83; TV Preston St Jo *Blackb* 83-92; V Patchway *Bris* from 92. *St Chad's Vicarage, Southsea Road, Patchway, Bristol BS12 5DP* Tel 0117-969 2935 or 979 3978

PENN, Christopher Francis. b 34. ACII63. Wells Th Coll 68. **d** 70 **p** 71. C Andover w Foxcott *Win* 70-72; C Odiham w S Warnborough 72-75; C Keynsham w Queen Charlton *B & W* 75; C Keynsham 75-76; TV 76-82; R Chilcompton w Downside and Stratton on the Fosse 82-87; RD Midsomer Norton 84-86; V Bathford 87-90; V Avonmouth St Andr *Bris* 90-96; Ind Chapl 90-96; rtd 96; Perm to Offic *B & W* from 96; Perm to Offic *Bris* from 96. *53 Caernarvon Road, Keynsham, Bristol BS18 2PF* Tel 0117-986 2367

PENN, Clive Llewellyn. b 12. Oak Hill Th Coll 47. **d** 48 **p** 49. C Deptford St Luke *S'wark* 48-50; C Guernsey St Sampson *Win* 50-54; Australia 55-65; V Jersey Gouray St Martin *Win* 66-71; Lic to Offic 71-86; rtd 77. *Unit 21, 4 Gorge Road, Campbell Town, Adelaide, S Australia 5074*

PENNAL, David Bernard. b 37. Ripon Hall Ox 64. **d** 67 **p** 68. C Moseley St Mary *Birm* 67-71; C Bridgwater St Mary w Chilton Trinity *B & W* 71-73; P-in-c Hilton w Cheselbourne and Melcombe Horsey *Sarum* 73-76; R Milton Abbas, Hilton w Cheselbourne etc 76-78; P-in-c Spetisbury w Charlton Marshall 78-88; R Spetisbury w Charlton Marshall etc from 89. *The*

Rectory, Spetisbury, Blandford Forum, Dorset DT11 9DF Tel (01258) 453153

PENNANT, Dr David Falconer. b 51. Trin Coll Cam MA73. Trin Coll Bris BD84 PhD88. **d** 86 **p** 87. C Bramcote *S'well* 86-88; C Woking St Jo *Guildf* 88-93; Dir of Music St Andr Prep Sch Woking from 93. *30 Oriental Road, Woking, Surrey GU22 7AW* Tel (01483) 768005

PENNANT, Philip Vivian Rogers. b 14. TD69. Trin Coll Cam BA47 MA48. St Mich Coll Llan 48. **d** 49 **p** 50. C Cherry Hinton St Jo *Ely* 49-52; I Strathmore (Calgary) Canada 52-56; V Blyth *S'well* 56-65; P-in-c Scofton w Osberton 56-61; V 61-65; R Sutton Bonington 65-79; P-in-c Adisham *Cant* 79-84; P-in-c Goodnestone H Cross w Chillenden and Knowlton 79-84; rtd 84. *2 Manor Close, Bradford Abbas, Sherborne, Dorset DT9 6RN* Tel (01935) 423059

PENNELL (née COFFIN), Ms Pamela. b 45. EAMTC 94. **d** 97. NSM Moulsham St Luke *Chelmsf* from 97. *33 Birch Lane, Stock, Ingatestone, Essex CM4 9NA* Tel (01277) 841270

PENNEY, David Richard John. b 39. Dur Univ BA63 DipTh65. Cranmer Hall Dur 63. **d** 67 **p** 68. C Chilvers Coton w Astley *Cov* 67-70; C Styvechale 70-72; P-in-c Shilton w Ansty 72-77; P-in-c Withybrook 74-77; R Easington w Liverton *York* 77-85; Soc Resp Adv *Sarum* 85-93; Perm to Offic *Blackb* from 93. *8 William Street, Colne, Lancs BB8 0HH* Tel (01282) 870076 Fax as telephone

PENNEY, John Edward. b 12. St Jo Coll Dur LTh33 BA34 MA37. Clifton Th Coll 30. **d** 35 **p** 36. C S Harrow St Paul *Lon* 35-36; C Northampton St Mich *Pet* 36-38; C Shere *Guildf* 38-43; V S Harrow St Paul *Lon* 43-51; V Wisborough Green *Chich* 51-77; rtd 77; Perm to Offic *Ex* from 77. *28 Oakleigh Road, Exmouth, Devon EX8 2LN* Tel (01395) 264863

PENNEY, William Affleck. b 41. MBIM75 FRSA91. K Coll Lon BD63 AKC63 St Boniface Warminster 65. **d** 66 **p** 67. C Chatham St Steph *Roch* 66-70; Ind Chapl 70-77; P-in-c Bredhurst 70-72; Hon C S Gillingham 72-74; Hon C Eynsford w Farningham and Lullingstone 74-77; Bp's Dom Chapl 74-88; Hon Ind Chapl 77-88; Hon C Balham St Mary and St Jo *S'wark* 89-91; Perm to Offic *St Alb* 91-94; Hon C Bushey from 94. *Michael Hall House, Aldenham Road, Elstree, Borehamwood, Herts WD6 3BT* Tel 0181-207 5745

PENNICEARD, Clifford Ashley. b 42. Monash Univ Aus BA65 Linacre Coll Ox BA67. St Steph Ho Ox 65. **d** 68 **p** 69. C S Leamington St Jo *Cov* 68-71; Australia from 71. *Laureston Park Stud, RMB 2150, Euroa, Victoria, Australia 3666* Tel Victoria (57) 903217

PENNINGTON, Frederick William. b 11. K Coll Lon. **d** 55 **p** 56. C Tiverton St Pet *Ex* 55-58; R Bradford 58-66; R Thornbury 58-66; V N Molton w Twitchen 66-77; P-in-c Molland 68-77; rtd 77; Lic to Offic *Ex* from 77. *Sunset Cottage, 103 West Street, Hartland, Bideford, Devon EX39 6BQ* Tel (01237) 441206

PENNINGTON, John Kenneth. b 27. Man Univ LLB48. Linc Th Coll 51. **d** 52 **p** 53. C Wavertree H Trin *Liv* 52-56; C Rotherham *Sheff* 56-59; India 59-63; V Nelson St Phil *Blackb* 64-66; Area Sec USPG (Dios Derby, Leic and S'well) 66-71; (Dios Derby and Sheff) 71-75; C Nottingham St Mary *S'well* 75-78; C Nottingham St Mary and St Cath 78-92; rtd 93. *3 St Jude's Avenue, Nottingham NG3 5FG* Tel 0115-962 3420

PENNINGTON, John Michael. b 32. IEng AMIEE MIHEEM Em Coll Cam BA54 MA58. Wells Th Coll 58. **d** 60 **p** 61. C Stockport St Geo *Ches* 60-64; V Congleton St Steph 64-68; Chapl Nor Sch 68-70; V Hattersley *Ches* 70-72; C-in-c Upton Priory CD 72-75; V Upton Priory 75-79; Perm to Offic *Newc* 83-87; V Tynemouth St Jo 87-94; P-in-c Cambois 94-97; Chapl Northumberland HA from 94; Wansbeck and Ashington Hosps from 94; rtd 97. *297 Wingrove Road North, Fenham, Newcastle upon Tyne NE4 9EE* Tel 0191-274 5281

PENNY, Diana Eleanor. b 51. Open Univ BA87. Nor Ord Course 87. **d** 89 **p** 94. NSM Gillingham w Geldeston, Stockton, Ellingham etc *Nor* 89-93; NSM Upton St Leonards *Glouc* 93-97; NSM Stiffkey and Cockthorpe w Morston, Langham etc *Nor* from 97. *The Vicarage, Holt Road, Langham, Holt, Norfolk NR25 7BX* Tel (01328) 830246

PENNY, Edwin John. b 43. Leeds Univ BA64. Coll of Resurr Mirfield 64. **d** 66 **p** 67. C Acocks Green *Birm* 66-69; C Wombourne *Lich* 69-71; C Wednesbury St Paul Wood Green 71-74; V Kingshurst *Birm* 74-79; Chapl All Hallows Convent Norfolk 79-82; Hon Chapl Overgate Hospice Yorkshire 82-84; Hon C Raveningham *Nor* 84-90; All Hallows Hosp Nor Past Team 90-93; P-in-c Upton St Leonards *Glouc* 93-97; Dioc Communications Officer 93-97; P-in-c Stiffkey and Cockthorpe w Morston, Langham etc *Nor* from 97. *The Vicarage, Holt Road, Langham, Holt, Norfolk NR25 7BX* Tel (01328) 830246

PENNY, Michael John. b 36. Linc Th Coll 78. **d** 80 **p** 81. C Knighton St Mary Magd *Leic* 80-83; TV Leic Resurr 83-85; V Blackfordby 85-95; V Blackfordby and Woodville from 95; RD Akeley W 88-93. *11 Vicarage Close, Blackfordby, Swadlincote, Derbyshire DE11 8AZ* Tel (01524) 219445

PENNY, Wilfred Joseph. b 05. K Coll Lon 29. **d** 32 **p** 33. C Hackney St Jo *Lon* 32-38; Lon Dioc Home Missr Staines Ch Ch 38-51; Min 51-57; V Compton Dundon *B & W* 57-62; R Winford 62-73; rtd 73. *Dunloe Residential Home, 17 Jesmond Road, Clevedon, Avon BS21 7RZ* Tel (01275) 873744

PENRITH, Suffragan Bishop of. *See* GARRARD, The Rt Revd Richard

PENTLAND, Raymond Jackson. b 57. Open Univ BA90. St Jo Coll Nottm DPS88. **d** 88 **p** 89. C Nottingham St Jude *S'well* 88-90; Chapl RAF Coll Cranwell from 90. *Chaplaincy Services (RAF), HQ, Personnel and Training Command, RAF Innsworth, Gloucester GL3 1EZ* Tel (01452) 712612 ext 5164 Fax 510828

PENTREATH, Canon Harvey. b 29. Wells Th Coll 54. **d** 57 **p** 58. C Bris St Ambrose Whitehall *Bris* 57-60; C Leatherhead *Guildf* 60-63; C Haslemere 63-65; R Elstead 65-72; V Cuddington 73-80; Hon Can Guildf Cathl 80; V Helston *Truro* 80-85; RD Kerrier 84-86; TR Helston and Wendron 85-92; Hon Can Truro Cathl 88-92; rtd 93; Perm to Offic *Truro* from 93. *Penmarr, 15 Penarwyn Crescent, Heamoor, Penzance, Cornwall TR18 3JU* Tel (01736) 60133

PEOPLES, James Scott. b 59. TCD BA DipTh HDipEd90. **d** 85 **p** 86. C Carlow w Urglin and Staplestown *C & O* 85-90; Chapl Kilkenny Coll 90-91; I Portarlington w Cloneyhurke and Lea *M & K* from 91; Dioc Youth Officer (Kildare) from 92. *The Rectory, Portarlington, Co Laois, Irish Republic* Tel Portarlington (502) 43063

PEPPER, David Reginald. b 50. Lon Bible Coll DipCK86. St Alb Minl Tr Scheme 89. **d** 92 **p** 93. NSM Cheshunt *St Alb* from 92. *93 Rowan Drive, Broxbourne, Herts EN10 6HQ* Tel (01992) 463735

PEPPER, Leonard Edwin. b 44. Ex Univ BA71. Ripon Hall Ox 71. **d** 73 **p** 74. C Cottingham *York* 73-76; C Kingshurst *Birm* 76-79; Dir Past Studies St Steph Ho Ox 80-89; TV Aylesbury w Bierton and Hulcott *Ox* 89-91; TV High Wycombe 91-96; rtd 96. *19 Gardiner Street, Oxford OX3 7AW* Tel (01865) 66191

PEPPIATT, Martin Guy. b 33. Trin Coll Ox BA57 MA60. Wycliffe Hall Ox 57. **d** 59 **p** 60. C St Marylebone All So w SS Pet and Jo *Lon* 59-63; Kenya 65-69; V E Twickenham St Steph *Lon* 69-96; rtd 96. *Pipers Cottage, East End, North Leigh, Witney, Oxon OX8 6PZ* Tel (01993) 883001

PEPPIATT, Quintin Brian Duncombe. b 63. Ex Univ BSc85 St Luke's Coll Ex PGCE86. Ripon Coll Cuddesdon 89 Ch Div Sch of the Pacific (USA) 90. **d** 92 **p** 93. C Gt Ilford St Clem and St Marg *Chelmsf* 92-95; TV E Ham w Upton Park St Alb from 95. *1 Norman Road, London E6 4HN* Tel 0181-471 8751

PERCIVAL, Brian Sydney. b 37. Univ of Wales (Ban) BA61. N Ord Course 81. **d** 84 **p** 85. NSM Norbury *Ches* 84-88; P-in-c Werneth from 88. *The Vicarage, Compstall, Stockport, Cheshire SK6 5HU* Tel 0161-427 1259

PERCIVAL, Geoffrey. b 46. Ridley Hall Cam 73. **d** 76 **p** 77. C Eccleshill *Bradf* 76-79; C Otley 79-82; V Windhill from 82. *The Vicarage, 300 Leeds Road, Windhill, Shipley, W Yorkshire BD18 1EZ* Tel (01274) 581502

PERCIVAL, James Edward Charles. b 50. C&G69. N Ord Course 92. **d** 95 **p** 96. C Broughton *Blackb* from 95. *25 Northway, Fulwood, Preston PR2 9TP* Tel (01772) 713880

PERCIVAL, Joanna Vera. b 52. Univ of San Francisco BA87. Ch Div Sch of Pacific MDiv94. **d** 94 **p** 94. USA 94-95; NSM Ockham w Hatchford *Guildf* 95-96; C Cobham from 96. *The Flat, Church Gate House, Downside Bridge Road, Cobham, Surrey KT11 3EJ* Tel (01932) 860837

PERCIVAL, Martin Eric. b 45. Lon Univ BSc66 Linacre Coll Ox BA70 MA74. Wycliffe Hall Ox 67. **d** 70 **p** 71. C Anfield St Marg *Liv* 70-73; C Witney *Ox* 73-74; TV Bottesford w Ashby *Linc* 74-76; TV Grantham 76-80; R Coningsby w Tattershall 80-82; P-in-c Coleford w Holcombe *B & W* 82-83; V 83-84; Chapl Rossall Sch Fleetwood 84-88; Chapl Woodbridge Sch from 88. *27 Haughgate Close, Woodbridge, Suffolk IP12 1LQ* Tel (01394) 383997

PERCIVAL, Richard Thomas. b 33. Edin Coll of Art DipTP67 ARICS59 MRTPI67 FRICS71. Edin Dioc NSM Course 79. **d** 91. S Africa 91-94; NSM Edin St Ninian *Edin* from 94. *2/1 Fettes Rise, Edinburgh EH4 1QH* Tel 0131-552 5271

PERCIVAL, Robert Standring. b 27. Sheff Univ BA55 Aston Univ DCouns83. Qu Coll Birm 57. **d** 59 **p** 60. C Lightbowne *Man* 59-62; C Prestwich St Marg 62-63; V Pendlebury St Aug 63-68; Lect Glos Coll of Arts and Tech 68-93; NSM Glouc St Mary de Crypt w St Jo and Ch Ch *Glouc* 68-82; Perm to Offic from 82; rtd 92. *5 Firwood Drive, Gloucester GL4 0AB* Tel (01452) 522739

PERCY, Brian. b 34. LNSM course 91. **d** 93 **p** 94. NSM Walton *St E* from 93. *16 Lynwood Avenue, Felixstowe, Suffolk IP11 9HS* Tel (01394) 286782

PERCY, Donald. b 45. Kelham Th Coll 66. **d** 71 **p** 72. C Hendon St Ignatius *Dur* 71-75; C Gorton Our Lady and St Thos *Man* 75-77; C Middlesbrough St Thos *York* 77-82; Guyana 82-86; P-in-c S Moor *Dur* 86-90; V 90-95. *8 Ritson Street, Stanley, Co Durham DH9 0NH*

PERCY, Mrs Emma Margaret. b 63. Jes Coll Cam BA85 MA89 St Jo Coll Dur BA89. Cranmer Hall Dur 87. **d** 90 **p** 94. C Bedford St Andr *St Alb* 90-91; Par Dn 91-94; C 94; Chapl Anglia Poly Univ *Ely* 94-97; P-in-c Millhouses H Trin *Sheff* from 97. *Holy Trinity Vicarage, 80 Millhouses Lane, Sheffield S7 2HB* Tel 0114-236 2838

PERCY, Gordon Reid. b 46. St Jo Coll Dur BA68 DipTh70. Cranmer Hall Dur 69. **d** 71 **p** 72. C Flixton St Jo *Man* 71-76; C Charlesworth *Derby* 76-77; P-in-c 77-87; P-in-c Dinting Vale 80-87; V Long Eaton St Jo from 87; RD Ilkeston from 92. *St John's Vicarage, 59 Trowell Grove, Long Eaton, Nottingham NG10 4AY* Tel 0115-973 4819

PERCY, Canon Martyn William. b 62. Bris Univ BA84 K Coll Lon PhD92 St Jo Coll Dur CCSk90. Cranmer Hall Dur 88. **d** 90 **p** 91. C Bedford St Andr *St Alb* 90-94; Lect Bedf Coll De Montfort Univ Leic 92-94; Chapl Ch Coll Cam 94-97; Dir Th and Relig Studies 94-97; Dir Th and Relig Studies SS Coll Cam 95-97; Dir Linc Th Inst from 97; Lect Relig and Soc Sheff Univ *Sheff* from 97; Hon Can Sheff Cathl from 97; Hon C Millhouses H Trin from 97. *The Lincoln Theological Institute, 36 Wilkinson Street, Sheffield S10 2GB* Tel 0114-222 6399 E-mail m.percy@sheffield.ac.uk

PERDUE, Ernon Cope Todd. b 30. TCD BA52 BD56 MEd73 UCD DipPsych76 MPsychSc80. TCD Div Sch 53. **d** 54 **p** 55. C Dublin Drumcondra w N Strand *D & G* 54-58; C Dublin Booterstown w Carysfort 58-60; Dean of Res TCD 60-68; C-in-c Dublin St Mark *D & G* 66-68; C-in-c Dublin St Steph 68-69; I Rathmichael 69-76; Careers Counsellor Wicklow Voc Sch 76-82; I Limerick *L & K* 82-87; Can Limerick Cathl 82-87; Dean Killaloe, Kilfenora and Clonfert 87-95; I Killaloe w Stradbally 87-95; rtd 95. *6 Corbally Park, Westbrook Glen, Dublin 24, Irish Republic* Tel Dublin (1) 462 1379

✠**PERDUE, The Rt Revd Richard Gordon.** b 10. TCD BA31 MA38 BD38. **d** 33 **p** 34 **c** 54. C Dublin Drumcondra w N Strand *D & G* 33-36; C Dublin Rathmines 36-40; I Castledermot w Kinneagh 40-43; I Roscrea *L & K* 43-54; Adn Killaloe and Kilfenora 51-54; Bp Killaloe, Kilfenora, Clonfert and Kilmacduagh 54-57; Bp C, C & R 57-78; rtd 78. *Hadlow 4RD, Timaru, South Island, New Zealand* Tel Timaru (68) 60250

PERERA, George Anthony. b 51. Edin Univ BD74. Linc Th Coll 74. **d** 76 **p** 77. Chapl Mabel Fletcher Tech Coll Liv 76-79; C Wavertree H Trin *Liv* 76-79; TV Maghull 79-94; Chapl Park Lane Hosp Maghull 79-89; Asst Chapl Ashworth Hosp from 89; V Hunts Cross *Liv* from 94. *The Vicarage, 7 Kingsmead Drive, Liverpool L25 0NG* Tel 0151-486 1220

PERHAM, Canon Michael Francis. b 47. Keble Coll Ox BA74 MA78. Cuddesdon Coll 74. **d** 76 **p** 77. C Addington *Cant* 76-81; Sec C of E Doctrine Commn 79-84; Bp's Dom Chapl *Win* 81-84; TR Oakdale *Sarum* 84-92; Prec and Can Res Nor Cathl *Nor* from 92. *27 The Close, Norwich NR1 4DZ* Tel (01603) 219484 Fax 766032

PERKES, Brian Robert Keith. b 46. St Andr Univ BSc68 Liv Univ DipOR72. Nor Ord Course 91. **d** 94 **p** 95. NSM Witton *Ches* from 94. *20 Broad Acre, Comberbach, Northwich, Cheshire CW9 6QD* Tel (01606) 891784

PERKIN, David Arthur. b 30. Pemb Coll Ox BA54 MA58. Linc Th Coll 54. **d** 56 **p** 57. C St Jo Wood *Lon* 56-61; Chapl Loughb Univ *Leic* 61-84; V Paddington St Jas *Lon* 84-92; rtd 92. *14 Englewood Road, London SW12 9NZ*

PERKIN, Jonathan Guy. b 52. Westmr Coll Ox BEd76. Trin Coll Bris 89. **d** 91 **p** 92. C Cullompton *Ex* 91-96; C Ashtead *Guildf* from 96. *Redlands, Ottways Lane, Ashtead, Surrey KT21 2PB* Tel (01372) 276091

PERKIN, Paul John Stanley. b 50. Ch Ch Ox BA71 MA75 CertEd. Wycliffe Hall Ox 78. **d** 80 **p** 81. C Gillingham St Mark *Roch* 80-84; C Brompton H Trin w Onslow Square St Paul *Lon* 84-87; P-in-c Battersea Rise St Mark *S'wark* 87-92; V from 92. *St Mark's Vicarage, 7 Elsynge Road, London SW18 2HW* Tel 0181-874 6023

PERKINS, Alban Leslie Tate. b 08. Kelham Th Coll 28. **d** 34 **p** 35. SSM from 33; C Nottingham St Geo w St Jo *S'well* 34-37 and 68-72; S Africa 37-67 and 76-80; Can Bloemfontein Cathl 52-67; Lesotho 72-76; Perm to Offic *Man* 81-86; Perm to Offic *Blackb* from 86. *Willen Priory, Milton Keynes MK15 9AA* Tel (01908) 663749

PERKINS, Colin Blackmore. b 35. FCII65. Lon Coll of Div 68. **d** 70 **p** 71. C Hyson Green *S'well* 70-73; V Clarborough w Hayton 73-79; P-in-c Cropwell Bishop 79-84; P-in-c Colston Bassett 79-84; P-in-c Granby w Elton 79-84; P-in-c Langar 79-84; V Tithby w Cropwell Butler 79-84; R Cropwell Bishop w Colston Bassett, Granby etc 84-94; P-in-c Sutton Bonington w Normanton-on-Soar from 94. *19A Park Lane, Sutton Bonington, Loughborough, Leics LE12 5NQ* Tel (01509) 672236

PERKINS, David. b 51. Sarum & Wells Th Coll. **d** 87 **p** 88. C New Mills *Derby* 87-90; V Marlpool 90-95; P-in-c Turnditch from 95; Min in charge Belper Ch Ch and Milford from 95; Chapl Babington Hosp Belper from 95; RD Duffield *Derby* from 97. *Christ Church Vicarage, Bridge Street, Belper, Derbyshire DE56 1BA* Tel (01773) 824974

PERKINS, David John Elmslie. b 45. ATII75 Dur Univ BA66 DipTh68. Cranmer Hall Dur. **d** 69 **p** 70. C Wadsley *Sheff* 69-71; C Shortlands *Roch* 71-73; Perm to Offic *Lon* 76-78; Perm to Offic *B & W* 78-80; Lic to Offic 80-95. *Rainbow's End, Montacute Road, Stoke-sub-Hamdon, Somerset TA14 6UQ* Tel (01935) 823314

PERKINS, Canon Eric William. b 08. Leeds Univ BA29. Coll of Resurr Mirfield 26. **d** 31 **p** 32. C Newington St Paul *S'wark* 31-33; C Washwood Heath *Birm* 34-35; C Fenny Stratford *Ox* 35-38; C Reading St Mary V 38-44; V Boyne Hill 44-56; R Upton cum Chalvey 56-76; Hon Can Ch Ch 62-79; RD Burnham 69-74; Sub Warden Community St Jo Bapt Clewer from 70; rtd 76; C Burnham w Dropmore, Hitcham and Taplow *Ox* 83-84; C Farnham Royal w Hedgerley 84-85. *Flat 22, Stuart Court, High Street, Kibworth, Leicester LE8 0LE* Tel 0116-279 6349

PERKINS, Miss Julia Margaret. b 49. Linc Th Coll 85. **d** 87 **p** 94. Par Dn Owton Manor *Dur* 87-89; Par Dn Leam Lane 89-94; C 94; P-in-c Stockton St Chad 94-96; V from 96. *The Vicarage, Ragpath Lane, Stockton-on-Tees, Cleveland TS19 9JN* Tel (01642) 674737

PERKINS, Malcolm Bryan. b 20. SS Coll Cam BA41 MA45. Wycliffe Hall Ox 41. **d** 43 **p** 44. C Rainham *Roch* 43-47; C Bexley St Jo 47-50; P-in-c Chalk 50-51; V 51-56; V Borstal 56-61; Chapl St Bart Hosp Roch 59-74; P-in-c Strood St Mary *Roch* 61-65; R Wouldham 65-73; Chapl Medway Hosp Gillingham 65-67; Toc H Staff Padre (SE Region) 73-85; Hon C Roch 74-85; rtd 85; Perm to Offic *Roch* from 85; Perm to Offic *Cant* from 85. *Roke Cottage, 3 Belgrave Terrace, Laddingford, Maidstone, Kent ME18 6BP* Tel (01622) 871774

PERKINS, Sister Patricia Doris. b 29. Gilmore Ho 60. **dss** 73 **d** 87. CSA from 71; Sherston Magna w Easton Grey *Bris* 73-75; Cant St Martin and St Paul *Cant* 76-78; Kilburn St Aug w St Jo *Lon* 80-84; Abbey Ho Malmesbury 84-87; Hon Par Dn Bayswater 87-94; Chapl St Mary's Hosp Praed Street Lon 88-89; Chapl St Chas Hosp Ladbroke Grove 88-89; rtd 89; Dean of Women's Min *Lon* from 89; Dioc Dir of Ords 90-94; Hon Par Dn St Olave Hart Street w All Hallows Staining etc from 94. *St Andrew's House, 2 Tavistock Road, London W11 1BA* Tel 0171-229 2662

PERKINSON, Neil Donald. b 46. Wycliffe Hall Ox 84. **d** 85 **p** 86. C Workington St Jo *Carl* 85-88; TV Cockermouth w Embleton and Wythop 88-93; TV St Laur in Thanet *Cant* from 93. *St Mary's House, 1 Sandwich Road, Cliffsend, Ramsgate, Kent CT12 5HX* Tel (01843) 597123

PERKINTON, Keith Glyn. b 61. Humberside Poly BA83 Leeds Univ BA92. Coll of Resurr Mirfield CPT93. **d** 93 **p** 94. C Knowle H Nativity *Bris* 93-97; TV Brighton Resurr *Chich* from 97. *St Luke's Vicarage, Queen's Park Terrace, Brighton BN2 2YA* Tel (01273) 603946

PERKS, David Leonard Irving. b 38. Sussex Univ MA76 Avery Hill Coll TCert61. S Dios Minl Tr Scheme 84. **d** 87 **p** 88. NSM Lewes All SS, St Anne, St Mich and St Thos *Chich* 87-91; Chapl HM Pris Lewes 91-94; NSM Lewes & Seaford RD 94-96; C Peacehaven *Chich* from 96; C Telscombe w Piddinghoe and Southease from 96. *45 Fitzjohn Road, Lewes, E Sussex BN7 1PR* Tel (01273) 478719

PERKS, Edgar Harold Martin. b 31. Open Univ BA87. Glouc Sch of Min 85. **d** 88 **p** 89. NSM Bromfield *Heref* 88-89; NSM Culmington w Onibury 88-89; NSM Stanton Lacy 88-89; NSM Culmington w Onibury, Bromfield etc from 90. *The Oaklands, Bromfield Road, Ludlow, Shropshire SY8 1DW* Tel (01584) 875525

PERMAN, George Hayward. b 01. Tyndale Hall Bris 31. **d** 34 **p** 35. C Burnage St Marg *Man* 34-37; C Southborough St Pet *Roch* 37-38; C St Andr Holborn *Lon* 38-39; V Clerkenwell St Pet 39-53; RD Finsbury and Holborn 47-53; V Ealing St Mary 53-68; RD Ealing 54-60; rtd 68; Perm to Offic *Chich* from 80. *Koinonia, 4 Winchester Road, Worthing, W Sussex BN11 4DJ*

PERRENS, Eric George. b 16. Sheff Univ BA38. Lich Th Coll 38. **d** 40 **p** 41. C Stockport St Matt *Ches* 40-44; C Ecclesfield *Sheff* 45-47; Min New Edlington 47-51; V Mortomley St Sav 51-60; V Thorpe Salvin 60-69; V Rawcliffe 69-77; R Bradfield 77-82; rtd 82. *1A Greenhead Lane, Chapeltown, Sheffield S30 4TN* Tel 0114-240 2895

PERRENS, Everard George. b 15. St Cath Coll Cam BA37 MA42. Linc Th Coll 40. **d** 42 **p** 43. C Rugby St Andr *Cov* 42-44; CF 44-47; CMS 47-65; Uganda 47-65; Chapl St Marg Sch Bushey 65-74; Hon C Earlsdon *Cov* 75-79; C Allesley Park 79-80; rtd 80; Hon C Earlsdon *Cov* 80-83; Perm to Offic from 83. *4 Regency Drive, Kenilworth, Warks CV8 1JE* Tel (01926) 55779

PERRETT, David Thomas. b 48. Cranmer Hall Dur 80. **d** 82 **p** 83. C Stapleford *S'well* 82-86; V Ollerton 86-87; P-in-c Boughton 86-87; V Ollerton w Boughton 87-93; V Winklebury *Win* from 93. *The Vicarage, Willoughby Way, Basingstoke, Hants RG23 8BD* Tel (01256) 23941

PERRICONE, Vincent James. b 50. Connecticut Univ BA74. **d** 89 **p** 90. In RC Ch 89-94; C Glas St Mary *Glas* 94-95; P-in-c Knightswood H Cross Miss from 95; P-in-c Glas All SS from 95. *2 Skaterigg Drive, Burlington Gate, Glasgow G13 1SR* Tel 0141-959 3730

PERRINS, Harold. b 21. Kelham Th Coll 38. **d** 44 **p** 45. C Fenton *Lich* 44-49; C Talke 49-53; R Armitage 53-61; V Lapley w Wheaton Aston 61-65; V Priorslee 65-69; V Edingale 69-77; R Harlaston 69-77; V Shobnall 77-86; rtd 86; Perm to Offic *Lich* from 86. *20 Meadow Rise, Barton under Needwood, Burton-on-Trent DE13 8DT* Tel (01283) 713515

PERRINS, Lesley. b 53. St Hugh's Coll Ox BA74 S Bank Poly DCG75. S Dios Minl Tr Scheme CECM93. **d** 93 **p** 95. NSM Stoneleigh *Guildf* 93-94; NSM Haxby w Wigginton *York* from

94. *Galtres Cottage, 21 The Village, Wigginton, York YO3 3PL* Tel (01904) 762809

PERRIS, Anthony. b 48. Univ of Wales (Abth) BSc69 Selw Coll Cam BA76 MA79. Ridley Hall Cam 74. **d** 77 **p** 78. C Sandal St Helen *Wakef* 77-80; C Plymouth St Andr w St Paul and St Geo *Ex* 80-87; TV Yeovil *B & W* 87-88; V Preston Plucknett from 88. *St James's Vicarage, 1 Old School House, Yeovil, Somerset BA21 3UB* Tel (01935) 29398

PERRIS, John Martin. b 44. Liv Univ BSc66 Bris Univ DipTh70. Trin Coll Bris 69. **d** 72 **p** 73. C Sevenoaks St Nic *Roch* 72-76; C Bebington *Ches* 76-79; V Redland *Bris* 79-97; RD Horfield 91-97; R Barton Seagrave w Warkton *Pet* from 97. *The Rectory, Barton Seagrave, Kettering, Northants NN15 6SR* Tel (01536) 513629 or 414052

PERROTT, John Alastair Croome. b 36. Univ of NZ LLB60. Clifton Th Coll 62. **d** 64 **p** 65. C Tunbridge Wells St Pet *Roch* 64-67; C Stanford-le-Hope *Chelmsf* 67-78; R Elmswell *St E* from 78. *The Rectory, Elmswell, Bury St Edmunds, Suffolk IP30 9DY* Tel (01359) 40512

PERROTT, Canon Joseph John. b 19. **d** 64 **p** 65. C Dublin St Geo *D & G* 64-71; C Dublin Drumcondra 71-72; I Drimoleague Union *C, C & R* 72-75; RD Cork City 74-80; I Mallow Union 75-78; I Ballydehob w Aghadown 78-93; Can Cloyne Cathl 85-93; Preb Cork Cathl 85-93; rtd 93. *6 Kingston College, Mitchelstown, Co Cork, Irish Republic* Tel Mitchelstown (25) 84882

PERRY, Andrew Nicholas. b 62. Westmr Coll Ox BA86. Trin Coll Bris MA91. **d** 91 **p** 92. C Bath Weston All SS w N Stoke *B & W* 91-93; C Bath Weston All SS w N Stoke and Langridge 93-95; P-in-c Longfleet *Sarum* from 95. *The Vicarage, 32 Alverton Avenue, Poole, Dorset BH15 2QG* Tel (01202) 723359

PERRY, Andrew William. b 44. R Agric Coll Cirencester NDA65 MRAC65 ADFM66. WMMTC 91. **d** 94 **p** 95. NSM Redmarley D'Abitot, Bromesberrow w Pauntley etc *Glouc* from 94. *Rye Cottage, Broomsgreen, Dymock, Glos GL18 2DP* Tel (01531) 890489 Fax 632552

PERRY, Anthony Henry. b 54. Leic Univ BA76. Aston Tr Scheme 89 Linc Th Coll CMinlStuds93. **d** 93 **p** 94. C Bartley Green *Birm* 93-97; V Bearwood from 97. *St Mary's Vicarage, 27 Poplar Avenue, Birmingham B17 8EG* Tel 0121-429 2165

PERRY, Anthony Robert. b 21. Kelham Th Coll 48. **d** 52 **p** 53. SSM from 52; C Sheff Parson Cross St Cecilia *Sheff* 52-56; S Africa 56-59 and 70-88; Lesotho 59-70; Chapl Chich Th Coll 88-90; Willen Priory 90-92; rtd 91. *St Anthony's Priory, Claypath, Durham DH1 1QT* Tel 0191-384 3747

PERRY, Canon Colin Charles. b 16. K Coll Cam BA38 MA42. Westcott Ho Cam 39. **d** 40 **p** 41. C Champion Hill St Sav *S'wark* 40-42; C Redhill St Jo 42-44; Ghana 45-56; V Aldbourne *Sarum* 56-64; V Baydon 57-64; PC Salisbury St Fran Sarum 64-69; V 69-71; V Preston 71-81; RD Weymouth 75-79; Can and Preb Sarum Cathl 77-82; TR Preston w Sutton Poyntz and Osmington w Poxwell 81-82; rtd 82. *6 The Ridgeway, Corfe Mullen, Wimborne, Dorset BH21 3HS* Tel (01202) 697298

PERRY, David William. b 42. St Chad's Coll Dur BA64 DipTh66. **d** 66 **p** 67. C Middleton St Mary *Ripon* 66-69; C Bedale 69-71; C Marton-in-Cleveland *York* 71-75; V Skirlaugh w Long Riston from 75; N Humberside Ecum Officer from 75. *The Vicarage, Skirlaugh, Hull HU11 5HE* Tel (01964) 562259

PERRY, Edward John. b 35. AKC62. **d** 63 **p** 64. C Honicknowle *Ex* 63-65; C Ashburton w Buckland-in-the-Moor 65-70; V Cornwood 70-92; Asst Dir of Educn 71-92; Chapl Moorhaven Hosp 91-93; V Ermington and Ugborough *Ex* from 92. *The Vicarage, Lutterburn Street, Ugborough, Ivybridge, Devon PL21 0NG* Tel (01752) 896957

PERRY, Mrs Joanna Teresa. b 60. BA. Trin Coll Bris. **d** 96. C Thornbury *Glouc* from 96. *16 Finch Close, Thornbury, Bristol BS12 1TD* Tel (01454) 417056

PERRY, John. b 09. TD60. PhD50. **d** 32 **p** 33. C Edin Ch Ch *Edin* 32-35; C Edin St Jas 35-38; P-in-c Bathgate 38-39; CF (R of O) 39-48; CF (TA) 48-59; R Kemnay *Ab* 46-49; R Turriff 49-53; R Newport-on-Tay *St And* 53-65; Can St Ninian's Cathl Perth 61-77; R Comrie 65-77; rtd 77. *29 Balhousie Street, Perth PH1 5HJ* Tel (01738) 26594

✠**PERRY, The Rt Revd John Freeman.** b 35. Lon Coll of Div ALCD59 LTh74 MPhil86. **d** 59 **p** 60 **c** 89. C Woking Ch Ch *Guildf* 59-62; C Chorleywood Ch Ch *St Alb* 62; Min Chorleywood St Andr CD 63-66; V Chorleywood St Andr 66-77; RD Rickmansworth 72-77; Warden Lee Abbey 77-89; RD Shirwell *Ex* 80-84; Suff Bp Southampton *Win* 89-96; Bp Chelmsf from 96. *Bishopscourt, Margaretting, Ingatestone, Essex CM4 0HD* Tel (01277) 352001 Fax 355374

PERRY, John Neville. b 20. Leeds Univ BA41. Coll of Resurr Mirfield 41. **d** 43 **p** 44. C Poplar All SS w St Frideswide *Lon* 43-50; V De Beauvoir Town St Pet 50-63; V Feltham 63-75; RD Hounslow 67-75; Adn Middx 75-82; R Orlestone w Snave and Ruckinge w Warehorne *Cant* 82-86; rtd 86; Perm to Offic *Chich* from 90. *73 Elizabeth Crescent, East Grinstead, W Sussex RH19 3JG* Tel (01342) 315446

PERRY, John Walton Beauchamp. b 43. Ex Coll Ox BA64 Sussex Univ MA67. EAMTC 82 Westcott Ho Cam 84. **d** 85 **p** 86. C Shrewsbury St Chad w St Mary *Lich* 85-89; V Batheaston w St Cath *B & W* from 89. *The Vicarage, 34 Northend, Batheaston, Bath BA1 7ES* Tel (01225) 858192

PERRY, Jonathan Robert. b 55. St Jo Coll Nottm DipTh. **d** 82 **p** 83. C Filey *York* 82-84; C Rayleigh *Chelmsf* 84-88; Asst Chapl St Geo Hosp Linc 88-90; Chapl Qu Eliz Hosp Gateshead 90-94; Chapl Gateshead Hosps NHS Trust from 94. *The Chaplain's Office, Queen Elizabeth Hospital, Gateshead, Tyne & Wear NE9 4SX* Tel 0191-487 8989

PERRY, Mrs Lynne Janice. b 48. **d** 90 **p** 97. NSM Llanfair Mathafarn Eithaf w Llanbedrgoch *Ban* 90-97; C Ban from 97. *1 Alotan Crescent, Penrhosgarnedd, Bangor LL57 2NG* Tel (01248) 355911

PERRY, Martin Herbert. b 43. Cranmer Hall Dur 66. **d** 70 **p** 71. C Millfield St Mark *Dur* 70-74; C Haughton le Skerne 74-77; V Darlington St Matt 77-79; V Darlington St Matt and St Luke 79-84; TR Oldland *Bris* 84-91; V from 91. *Oldland Vicarage, 39 Sunnyvale Drive, Longwell Green, Bristol BS15 6YQ* Tel 0117-932 7178

PERRY, Martyn. b 57. S Wales Bapt Coll DipTh85 DPS86 Coll of Resurr Mirfield 89. **d** 90 **p** 91. In Bapt Ch 85-89; C Hornsey St Mary w St Geo *Lon* 90-93; V Pontlottyn w Fochriw *Llan* from 93. *St Tyfaelog's Vicarage, 9 Picton Street, Pontlottyn, Bargoed CF81 9PT* Tel (01685) 841322

PERRY, Canon Michael Charles. b 33. Trin Coll Cam BA55 MA59. Westcott Ho Cam 56. **d** 58 **p** 59. C Baswich *Lich* 58-60; Chapl Ripon Hall Ox 61-63; Chief Asst Home Publishing SPCK 63-70; Can Res Dur Cathl *Dur* from 70; Adn Dur 70-93; Bp's Sen Chapl from 93. *7 The College, Durham DH1 3EQ* Tel 0191-386 1891 Fax (01388) 605264

PERRY, The Very Revd Robert Anthony. b 21. Leeds Univ BA47. Coll of Resurr Mirfield 47. **d** 49 **p** 50. C Middlesbrough St Jo the Ev *York* 49-54; Sarawak 54-66 and 76-79; Provost Kuching 60-66; R Hasfield w Tirley *Glouc* 66-69; Asst Chapl HM Pris Man 69; Chapl HM Pris Gartree 70-73; P-in-c Mottingham St Edw *S'wark* 73-75; P-in-c Presteigne w Discoed *Heref* 80-83; R Presteigne w Discoed, Kinsham and Lingen 83-86; rtd 86; Perm to Offic *Heref* 87-93; Chapl Laslett's *Worc* 91-92; P-in-c Ryhall w Essendine *Pet* 94-95; P-in-c Ryhall w Essendine and Carlby 95-96; Perm to Offic *Linc* from 95. *15 Northwick Road, Ketton, Stamford, Lincs PE9 3SB* Tel (01780) 721827

PERRY, Roy John. b 28. Chich Th Coll 71. **d** 72 **p** 73. Hon C Yeovil H Trin *B & W* 72-76; C 76-77; Perm to Offic from 77; TV Withycombe Raleigh *Ex* 77-84; TR Ex St Thos and Em 84; TV Sampford Peverell, Uplowman, Holcombe Rogus etc 86-93; P-in-c Halberton 87-88; rtd 93; Perm to Offic *Ex* from 93. *Tri-Stones, West End, Kingsbury Episcopi, Martock, Somerset TA12 6AY* Tel (01935) 823064

PERRY, Timothy Richard (Tim). b 64. Trin Coll Bris BA93. **d** 93 **p** 95. C Abingdon *Ox* 93-97. *33 Mattock Way, Abingdon, Oxon OX14 2PQ* Tel (01235) 555083

PERRY, Valerie Evelyn. b 39. Southn Univ CertEd59 Lon Univ DipRS85. S'wark Ord Course 82. **dss** 85 **d** 87 **p** 94. Romford St Edw *Chelmsf* 85-87; NSM 87-89; Par Dn 89-91; Asst Chapl Middx Hosp Lon 92-94; Chapl S Kent Hosps NHS Trust from 94. *William Harvey Hospital, Kennington Road, Willesborough, Ashford, Kent TN24 0LY* Tel Ashford (01233) 633331

PERRY, William Francis Pitfield. b 61. MA. Ripon Coll Cuddesdon. **d** 96 **p** 97. C Brockworth *Glouc* from 96. *54 Abbotswood Road, Brockworth, Gloucester GL3 4HZ* Tel (01452) 862075

PERRY-GORE, Canon Walter Keith. b 34. Univ of Wales (Lamp) BA59. Westcott Ho Cam 60. **d** 61 **p** 62. C St Austell *Truro* 61-64; R H Innocents Barbados 64-71; Canada from 71; R New Carlisle 71-74; R N Hatley 74-96; rtd 96. *1115 Rue Massawippi, PO Box 540, North Hatley, Quebec, Canada, J0B 2C0* Tel Sherbrooke (819) 842 4665 Fax 842 2176

PERRYMAN, David Francis. b 42. Brunel Univ BSc64. Oak Hill Th Coll 74. **d** 76 **p** 77. C Margate H Trin *Cant* 76-80; R Ardingly *Chich* 80-90; V Bath St Luke *B & W* from 90; RD Bath from 96. *St Luke's Vicarage, Hatfield Road, Bath BA2 2BD* Tel (01225) 311904 Fax 400975 E-mail dperdper@aol

PERRYMAN, Graham Frederick. b 56. Southn Univ BA78 Reading Univ PGCE80. Aston Tr Scheme 90 Trin Coll Bris DipHE94. **d** 94 **p** 95. C Hamworthy *Sarum* from 94. *35 Inglesham Way, Hamworthy, Poole, Dorset BH15 4PA* Tel (01202) 678702

PERRYMAN, James Edward (Jim). b 56. Lon Bible Coll BA85 Oak Hill Th Coll 86. **d** 88 **p** 89. C Gidea Park *Chelmsf* 88-91; C Becontree St Mary 91-94; Chapl Lyon *Eur* from 94. *38 Chemin de Taffignon, 69110 Ste-Foy-les-Lyon, France* Tel France (33) 78 59 67 06 Fax 72 39 09 31

PERRYMAN, John Frederick Charles. b 49. Mert Coll Ox BA71 MA74. Ridley Hall Cam 72. **d** 74 **p** 75. C Shortlands *Roch* 74-78; Asst Chapl St Geo Hosp Lon 78-82; Chapl Withington Hosp Man 83-94; Chapl S Man Univ Hosps NHS Trust from 94. *Withington Hospital, Nell Lane, Manchester M20 8LR, or 24 Alan Road, Withington, Manchester M20 9WG* Tel 0161-445 8111 or 445 4769

PERSSON, Matthew Stephen. b 60. Dundee Univ BSc82. Wycliffe Hall Ox 88. **d** 91 **p** 92. C Bath Twerton-on-Avon *B & W* 91-94; C Shepton Mallet w Doulting from 94; Chapl HM Pris Shepton

Mallet from 94. *Ham Manor, Bowlish, Shepton Mallet, Somerset BA4 5JR*

✠**PERSSON, The Rt Revd William Michael Dermot.** b 27. Or Coll Ox BA51 MA55. Wycliffe Hall Ox 51. **d** 53 **p** 54 **c** 82. C S Croydon Em *Cant* 53-55; C Tunbridge Wells St Jo *Roch* 55-58; V S Mimms Ch Ch *Lon* 58-67; R Bebington *Ches* 67-79; V Knutsford St Jo and Toft 79-82; Suff Bp Doncaster *Sheff* 82-92; rtd 93. *Ryalls Cottage, Burton Street, Marnhull, Sturminster Newton, Dorset DT10 1PS* Tel (01258) 820452

PERTH, Provost of. *See* FRANZ, The Very Revd Kevin Gerhard

PESCOD, John Gordon. b 44. Leeds Univ BSc70. Qu Coll Birm DipTh71. **d** 72 **p** 73. C Camberwell St Geo *S'wark* 72-75; Chapl R Philanthropic Soc Sch Redhill 75-80; P-in-c Nunney w Wanstrow and Cloford *B & W* 80-84; R Nunney and Witham Friary, Marston Bigot etc 84-87; R Milverton w Halse and Fitzhead 87-93; V Frome St Jo and St Mary from 93; V Woodlands from 93; RD Frome from 97. *The Vicarage, Vicarage Street, Frome, Somerset BA11 1PU* Tel (01373) 462325

PESKETT, Canon Osmond Fletcher. b 12. Dur Univ LTh44. Tyndale Hall Bris. **d** 37 **p** 38. China 38-43 and 45-50; C Felixstowe SS Pet and Paul *St E* 45; V Chadderton Ch Ch *Man* 51-55; V Tonbridge St Steph *Roch* 55-65; Tanzania 65-68; Chan Morogoro 65-68; Hon Can Morogoro from 68; V St Keverne *Truro* 68-77; rtd 77; Perm to Offic *Ex* from 91. *Gairloch, Hensleigh Drive, St Leonards, Exeter EX2 4NZ* Tel (01392) 214387

PESKETT, Richard Howard. b 42. Selw Coll Cam BA64 MA67. Ridley Hall Cam 64. **d** 68 **p** 69. C Jesmond H Trin *Newc* 68-71; Singapore 71-91; Lect Trin Coll Bris from 91. *Trinity College, Stoke Hill, Bristol BS9 1JP* Tel 0117-968 2803

PESKETT, Timothy Lewis (Tim). b 64. St Kath Coll Liv BA86. Chich Th Coll BTh90. **d** 90 **p** 91. C Verwood *Sarum* 90-91; C Southsea H Spirit *Portsm* 91-95; TV Burgess Hill St Jo w St Edw *Chich* from 95. *St Edward's House, 7 Dunstall Avenue, Burgess Hill, W Sussex RH15 8PJ* Tel (01444) 241300

PESTELL, Robert Carlyle. b 54. Aston Tr Scheme 89 Linc Th Coll 91. **d** 93 **p** 94. C Matson *Glouc* 93-97; P-in-c Charfield from 97. *The Rectory, 36 Wotton Road, Charfield, Wotton-under-Edge, Glos GL12 8TG* Tel (01454) 260489

PETCH, Douglas Rodger. b 57. Nottm Univ BSc79. All Nations Chr Coll Cam DipRS81 St Jo Coll Nottm MTS95. **d** 94 **p** 94. Nigeria 94-96; C Pendleton *Man* from 96. *14 Eccles Old Road, Pendleton, Salford M6 7AF* Tel 0161-736 0945

PETER, Brother. *See* ROUNDHILL, Stanley Peter

PETER, Christopher (Javed). b 51. BA75. Qu Coll Birm 94. **d** 96 **p** 97. C Darwen St Pet w Hoddlesden *Blackb* from 96. *44 Minster Crescent, Darwen, Lancs BB3 3PY* Tel (01254) 703796

PETER DOUGLAS, Brother. *See* NEEDHAM, Brother Peter Douglas

PETERBOROUGH, Bishop of. *See* CUNDY, The Rt Revd Ian Patrick Martyn

PETERBOROUGH, Dean of. *See* BUNKER, The Very Revd Michael

PETERKEN, Canon Peter Donald. b 28. K Coll Lon BD51 AKC51. **d** 52 **p** 53. C Swanley St Mary *Roch* 52-55 and 62-65; C Is of Dogs Ch Ch and St Jo w St Luke *Lon* 55-57; R S Perrott w Mosterton and Chedington *Sarum* 57-59; Br Guiana 59-62; R Killamarsh *Derby* 65-70; V Derby St Luke 70-90; RD Derby N 79-90; Hon Can Derby Cathl 85-95; R Matlock 90-95; rtd 95; Perm to Offic *Derby* from 95. *64 Brayfield Road, Littleover, Derby DE23 6GT* Tel (01332) 766285

PETERS, Carl Richard. b 62. Ripon Coll Cuddesdon 95. **d** 97. C Coventry Caludon *Cov* from 97. *111 Momus Boulevard, Coventry CV2 5NB* Tel (01203) 457727

PETERS, Christopher Lind. b 56. Oak Hill Th Coll. **d** 82 **p** 83. C Knockbreda *D & D* 82-84; C Lisburn Ch Ch Cathl *Conn* 84-87; I Kilmocomogue Union *C, C & R* 87-93; P-in-c Beara 92-93; I Killiney H Trin *D & G* from 93. *Killiney Rectory, 21 Killiney Avenue, Killiney, Co Dublin, Irish Republic* Tel Dublin (1) 285 6180

PETERS, Canon Cyril John (Bill). b 19. Fitzw Ho Cam BA42 MA45. Chich Th Coll 40. **d** 42 **p** 43. C Brighton St Mich *Chich* 42-45 and 47-50; CF (EC) 45-47; Hon CF from 47; Chapl Brighton Coll 50-69; R Uckfield *Chich* 69-96; R Isfield 69-96; R Lt Horsted 69-96; RD Uckfield 73-96; Can and Preb Chich Cathl 81-89; rtd 96; Perm to Offic *Chich* from 96. *Canon's Lodge, 9 Calvert Road, Uckfield, E Sussex TN22 2DB* Tel (01825) 766397

PETERS, David Lewis. b 38. Ch Ch Ox BA62 MA66. Westcott Ho Cam 63. **d** 65 **p** 66. C Oldham St Mary w St Pet *Man* 65-69; C Stand 70-74; P-in-c Hillock 70-74; V 74-82; V Haslingden w Haslingden Grane *Blackb* 82-88; rtd 88; Perm to Offic *Man* from 88; Perm to Offic *Blackb* from 88. *2 Mount Terrace, Earnshaw Road, Bacup, Lancs OL13 9BP*

PETERS, Geoffrey John. b 51. MInstC(Glas) BCom BSc MDiv. Gujranwala Th Sem 90 Oak Hill Th Coll 85. **d** 87 **p** 88. C Forest Gate St Sav w W Ham St Matt *Chelmsf* 87-90; C Wembley St Jo *Lon* 90-92; TV Manningham *Bradf* from 92. *St Luke's Vicarage, 1 Selborne Grove, Manningham, Bradford, W Yorkshire BD9 4NL* Tel (01274) 541110

PETERS, John Peter Thomas. b 63. Keble Coll Ox BL85. Wycliffe Hall Ox BA91. **d** 95 **p** 96. C Brompton H Trin w Onslow Square St Paul *Lon* from 95. *130A Swaby Road, London SW18 3QY* Tel 0181-946 7533

PETERS, John Thomas. b 58. Connecticut Univ BA80 LTh. St Jo Coll Nottm 84. **d** 87 **p** 88. C Virginia Water *Guildf* 87-93; USA from 93. *710 NW 20th Avenue 202, Grand Rapids, Minnesota 55744, USA*

PETERS, Canon Kenneth (Ken). b 54. Univ of Wales (Cardiff) DipTh77 Tokyo Univ MBA88. St Mich Coll Llan 74. **d** 77 **p** 78. C Mountain Ash *Llan* 77-80; Asst Chapl Mersey Miss to Seamen 80-82; Perm to Offic *Ches* 80-82; Chapl Miss to Seamen from 82; Japan 82-89; Hon Can Kobe from 85; Chapl Supt Mersey Miss to Seamen 89-93; Justice and Welfare Sec from 94. *St Michael Paternoster Royal, College Hill, London EC4R 2RL* Tel 0171-248 5202 Fax 248 4761

PETERS, Canon Michael. b 41. Chich Th Coll 75. **d** 77 **p** 78. C Redruth *Truro* 77-79; TV 79-80; TV Redruth w Lanner 80-82; R St Mawgan w St Ervan and St Eval 82-86; Chapl HM Pris Liv 86-87; Chapl HM Pris Bris from 87; Perm to Offic *B & W* from 87; Hon Can Bris Cathl *Bris* from 96. *The Chaplain's Office, HM Prison, Cambridge Road, Bristol BS7 8PS* Tel 0117-942 6661 Fax 924 4228

PETERS, Robert David. b 54. BA76. Oak Hill Th Coll 78. **d** 79 **p** 80. C Hyde St Geo *Ches* 79-83; C Hartford 83-86; V Lindow 86-96; V Throop *Win* from 96. *St Paul's Vicarage, Chesildene Avenue, Bournemouth BH8 0AZ* Tel (01202) 531064

PETERS, Stephen Eric. b 45. Westcott Ho Cam 74. **d** 77 **p** 78. C Wanstead St Mary *Chelmsf* 77-79; C Leigh-on-Sea St Marg 79-81; P-in-c Purleigh 81-82; P-in-c Cold Norton w Stow Maries 81-82; R Purleigh, Cold Norton and Stow Maries 83-84; V Bedford Park *Lon* 84-87; Perm to Offic *Ex* 87-88; TR Totnes and Berry Pomeroy 88-90; Chapl Ex Sch 91-93; Chapl St Marg Sch Ex 91-93; Lic to Offic *Ex* from 91. *20 South Street, Totnes, Devon TQ9 5DZ* Tel (01803) 867199

PETERSEN, Miss Jennifer Elizabeth (Jenny). b 55. Aus Nat Univ BA78. Moore Th Coll Sydney BTh82 Wycliffe Hall Ox 92. **dss** 85 **d** 94 **p** 95. Australia 85-94; C Elloughton and Brough w Brantingham *York* 94-96; C Ealing St Mary *Lon* from 96; Chapl Thames Valley Univ from 96. *16 Gerrards Court, South Ealing Road, London W5 4QB* Tel 0181-579 1591

PETERSON, Dennis. b 25. Oak Hill Th Coll 51. **d** 54 **p** 55. C Leyton All SS *Chelmsf* 54-56; C Leeds St Geo *Ripon* 56-58; V E Brixton St Jude *S'wark* 58-91; rtd 91; Perm to Offic *Chelmsf* from 91. *79 Cavendish Gardens, Westcliff-on-Sea, Essex SS0 9XP* Tel (01702) 334400

PETERSON, Paul. b 67. Trin Coll Bris 94. **d** 97. C Burney Lane *Birm* from 97. *136 Burney Lane, Ward End, Birmingham B8 2AF*

PETFIELD, Bruce le Gay. b 34. FHA. NE Ord Course 76. **d** 79 **p** 80. NSM Morpeth *Newc* 79-86; C Knaresborough *Ripon* 86-87; V Flamborough *York* 87-94; V Bempton 87-94; rtd 94; Perm to Offic *York* from 94. *36 Maple Road, Bridlington, N Humberside YO16 5TE*

PETIT, Andrew Michael. b 53. Solicitor Cam Univ MA. Trin Coll Bris DipHE82. **d** 83 **p** 84. C Stoughton *Guildf* 83-87; C Shirley *Win* 87-92; V Cholsey *Ox* from 92. *The Vicarage, Church Road, Cholsey, Wallingford, Oxon OX10 9PP* Tel (01491) 651216

PETITT, Michael David. b 53. BCombStuds. Linc Th Coll 79. **d** 82 **p** 83. C Arnold *S'well* 82-86; Asst Chapl HM Youth Cust Cen Glen Parva 86-87; V Blaby *Leic* 87-94; V Leagrave *St Alb* from 94. *St Luke's Vicarage, High Street, Leagrave, Luton LU4 9JY* Tel (01582) 572737

PETRICHER, Georges Herbert Philippe. b 53. St Paul's Coll Mauritius. **d** 84 **p** 85. Mauritius 83-85; Hon C Tooting All SS *S'wark* 85-87; C Kings Heath *Birm* 87-90; C Hamstead St Paul 90-93; C Stechford 93-96; Perm to Offic from 96. *174 Perrywood Road, Great Barr, Birmingham B42 2BH*

PETRIE, Alistair Philip. b 50. Lon Univ DipTh76. Fuller Th Sem California DMin91 Oak Hill Th Coll 76. **d** 76 **p** 77. C Eston *York* 76-79; P-in-c Prestwick *Glas* 79-81; R 81-82; Canada from 82. *2042 Haidey Terrace, Saanichton, British Columbia, Canada V8M 1M8* Tel Saanichton (250) 652 5025 Fax 652 8033

PETRIE, Ian Robert (Eric). b 53. Avery Hill Coll PGCE84. Oak Hill Th Coll BA83 Qu Coll Birm 93. **d** 95 **p** 96. C Sedgley All SS *Worc* from 95. *13 The Priory, Sedgley, Dudley, W Midlands DY3 3UB* Tel (01902) 664625

PETT, Douglas Ellory. b 24. Lon Univ BD46 BD48 AKC48 PhD74. K Coll Lon 48. **d** 49 **p** 50. C Prittlewell St Mary *Chelmsf* 49-54; C Glouc St Mary de Lode and St Nic *Glouc* 54-58; Min Can Glouc Cathl 54-58; Lic to Offic *Nor* 54-58; C Ches Square St Mich w St Phil *Lon* 58-61; V Gulval *Truro* 61-66; Chapl St Mary's Hosp Praed Street Lon 66-83; rtd 83. *23 Polsue Way, Tresillian, Truro, Cornwall TR2 4BE* Tel (01872) 520573

PETTENGELL, Ernest Terence. b 43. K Coll Lon. **d** 69 **p** 70. C Chesham St Mary *Ox* 69-72; C Farnborough *Guildf* 72-75; Asst Master K Alfred Sch Burnham-on-Sea 75-78; C Bishop's Cleeve *Glouc* 78-80; Chapl Westonbirt Sch 80-85; P-in-c Shipton Moyne w Westonbirt and Lasborough *Glouc* 80-85; V Berkeley w Wick, Breadstone and Newport 85-92; TV Weston-super-Mare Cen Par *B & W* 92-95; P-in-c Weston super Mare Em from 96.

5 Walliscote Road, Weston-super-Mare, Avon BS23 1XE Tel (01934) 621046

PETTERSEN, Dr Alvyn Lorang. b 51. TCD BA73 Dur Univ BA75 PhD81. Sarum & Wells Th Coll 78. **d** 81 **p** 82. Chapl Clare Coll Cam 81-85; Lic to Offic *Ely* 81-85; Fell and Chapl Ex Coll Ox 85-92; Research Fell Linc Coll Ox 92-93; Lic to Offic *Ox* 85-93; V Frensham *Guildf* from 93. *The Vicarage, Frensham, Farnham, Surrey GU10 3DT* Tel (01252) 792137

PETTET, Christopher Farley (Chris). b 54. Ox Univ BEd78. St Jo Coll Nottm 87. **d** 90 **p** 91. C Luton St Mary *St Alb* 90-93; C Fawley *Win* 93-97; P-in-c Amport, Grateley, Monxton and Quarley from 97. *The Vicarage, Amport, Andover, Hants SP11 8BE* Tel (01264) 772950

PETTIFER, Bryan George Ernest. b 32. Qu Coll Cam BA55 MA59 MEd. Wm Temple Coll Rugby 56 Ridley Hall Cam 57. **d** 59 **p** 60. C Attercliffe w Carbrook *Sheff* 59-61; C Ecclesall 61-65; Chapl City of Bath Tech Coll 65-74; Adult Educn Officer *Bris* 75-80; Dir Past Th Sarum & Wells Th Coll 80-85; Can Res St Alb 85-92; Prin St Alb Minl Tr Scheme 85-92; Prin Ox Area Chr Tr Scheme *Ox* 92-94; Perm to Offic from 94; Min and Deployment Officer/ Selection Sec ABM from 94. *23 Botley Road, Oxford OX2 0BL* Tel (01865) 727444

PETTIFER, John Barrie. b 38. Linc Th Coll 63. **d** 65 **p** 66. C Stretford St Matt *Man* 65-67; C Stand 67-71; V Littleborough from 71. *The Vicarage, Deardon Street, Littleborough, Lancs OL15 9DZ* Tel (01706) 378334

PETTIFOR, David Thomas. b 42. Ripon Coll Cuddesdon 78. **d** 81 **p** 82. C Binley *Cov* 81-84; P-in-c Wood End 84-88; V 88-92; V Finham from 92. *St Martin's Vicarage, 136 Green Lane South, Coventry CV3 6EA* Tel (01203) 418330

PETTIGREW, Miss Claire Gabrielle. b 23. St Mich Ho Ox 55. **dss** 77 **d** 87 **p** 95. Nor Heartsease St Fran *Nor* 77-81; Heigham H Trin 81-87; Dioc Lay Min Adv 83-87; Assoc Dioc Dir of Ords 87-89; rtd 89; Lic to Offic *Nor* from 89. *41 Home Colne House, London Road, Cromer, Norfolk NR27 9EF* Tel (01263) 515215

PETTIGREW, Canon Stanley. b 27. TCD BA49 MA62. **d** 50 **p** 51. C Newcastle *D & D* 50-53; C Dublin Clontarf *D & G* 53-57; I Derralossary 57-62; Miss to Seamen 62-92; I Wicklow w Killiskey *D & G* 62-92; RD Delgany 85-92; Can Ch Ch Cathl Dublin 87-92; rtd 92. *Corr Riase, Ballarney South, Wicklow, Irish Republic* Tel Wicklow (404) 69755

PETTINGELL, Hubert (Hugh). b 32. ACA54 FCA65 AKC58. **d** 59 **p** 60. C Mansfield St Pet *S'well* 59-61; CMS 61-66; Iran 61-66; C Wellington w W Buckland and Nynehead *B & W* 67-68; Warden Student Movement Ho Lon 68-69; R Holywell w Needingworth *Ely* 69-71; Dir Finance WCC 80-96; Perm to Offic *Eur* from 94. *Chemin du Pommier 22, 1218 Le Grand Saconnex, Geneva, Switzerland* Tel Geneva (22) 798-8586

PETTIT, Arthur George Lifton. b 08. Jes Coll Ox BA31 MA35. St D Coll Lamp BA29 St Steph Ho Ox 32. **d** 32 **p** 33. C Llanelli *St D* 32-38; V Rosemarket 38-48; R Bosherston w St Twynells 48-50; R Remenham *Ox* 50-73; rtd 73. *324 Cowley Mansions, Mortlake High Street, London SW14* Tel 0181-876 8671

PETTITT, Donald. b 09. Bps' Coll Cheshunt 57. **d** 57 **p** 58. C Thetford St Mary *Nor* 57; P-in-c Cranwich w Didlington and Colveston 57-62; R Ickburgh w Langford 58-62; R Ashby w Thurton, Claxton and Carleton 62-69; V Worstead w Westwick and Sloley 69-78; rtd 78; Perm to Offic *Nor* from 79. *15 Arbor Road, Cromer, Norfolk NR27 9DW* Tel (01263) 512539

PETTITT, Maurice. b 13. Clare Coll Cam BA35 MA57 MusBac37. Lich Th Coll 56. **d** 57 **p** 58. Asst Chapl Wellingborough Sch 57-62; R Rounton w Welbury *York* 62-69; V Riccall 69-78; RD Escrick 73-78; rtd 78; Perm to Offic *York* from 78. *Holbeck House, Low Street, Lastingham, York YO6 6TJ* Tel (01751) 417517

PETTITT, Mervyn Francis. b 39. Qu Coll Birm DipTh66. **d** 66 **p** 67. C Colchester St Jas, All SS, St Nic and St Runwald *Chelmsf* 66-69; C Loughton St Jo 69-72; R Downham w S Hanningfield 72-82; P-in-c W w S Hanningfield 77-78; C Leigh-on-Sea St Marg 82-85; rtd 85. *60 Suffolk Avenue, Leigh-on-Sea, Essex SS9 3HF* Tel (01702) 72202

PETTITT, Robin Adrian. b 50. MRTPI79 Newc Univ BA77. St Steph Ho Ox 81. **d** 83 **p** 84. C Warrington St Elphin *Liv* 83-87; C Torrisholme *Blackb* 87-93; P-in-c Charnock Richard from 93; Dioc Par Development Officer from 93. *The Vicarage, Church Lane, Charnock Richard, Chorley, Lancs PR7 5NA* Tel (01257) 791385

PETTITT, Canon Simon. b 50. Nottm Univ BTh74 CertEd. Kelham Th Coll 70. **d** 75 **p** 76. C Penistone *Wakef* 75-78; Dioc Youth Officer 78-80; Dioc Schs Officer *St E* 80-86; P-in-c Hintlesham w Chattisham 80-86; V Bury St Edmunds St Jo 86-93; RD Thingoe 88-92; Dioc Communications Officer from 93; Hon Can St E Cathl from 93. *3 Crown Street, Bury St Edmunds, Suffolk IP33 1QX* Tel (01284) 753866 Fax as telephone

PETTY, Brian. b 34. Man Univ BA90 Melbourne Univ DipRE. St Aid Birkenhead 59. **d** 62 **p** 63. C Meole Brace *Lich* 62-65; Chapl RAF 65-69; Australia 70-75; P-in-c Kimbolton w Middleton-on-the-Hill *Heref* 76-79; P-in-c Pudleston-cum-Whyle w Hatfield, Docklow etc 76-79; P-in-c Haddenham *Ely* 79-80; V 80-84; V Fairfield *Derby* 84-90; Chapl St Geo Sch Ascot 90-93; TR Sampford Peverell, Uplowman, Holcombe Rogus etc *Ex* from 93; RD Cullompton from 95. *The Rectory, Blackdown View, Sampford Peverell, Tiverton, Devon EX16 7BP* Tel (01884) 821879

PETTY, The Very Revd John Fitzmaurice. b 35. Trin Hall Cam BA59 MA65. Cuddesdon Coll 64. **d** 66 **p** 67. C Sheff St Cuth *Sheff* 66-69; C St Helier *S'wark* 69-75; V Hurst *Man* 75-88; AD Ashton-under-Lyne 83-87; Hon Can Man Cathl 86-88; Provost Cov from 88. *Provost's Lodge, Priory Row, Coventry CV1 5ES* Tel (01203) 227597 Fax 631448

PETTY, Capt Stuart. b 56. Wilson Carlile Coll DipEvang85 Chich Th Coll 91. **d** 93 **p** 94. CA from 88; C W Bromwich St Andr w Ch Ch *Lich* 93-96; Asst Chapl Walsall Hosps NHS Trust from 96. *The Chaplain's Office, Manor Hospital, Moat Road, Walsall WS2 9PS* Tel (01922) 721172

PETZER, Garth Stephen. St Paul's Coll Grahamstown. **d** 88 **p** 91. S Africa 88-95; Chapl RN from 96. *Royal Naval Chaplaincy Service, Room 203, Victory Building, HM Naval Base, Portsmouth PO1 3LS* Tel (01705) 727903 Fax 727112

PETZSCH, Diana Frances Louise. b 54. BA73 MA74 MLitt79 CertEd81. **d** 96. C Perth St Jo *St And* from 96. *Reids House, Glenalmond College, Perth PH1 3RY* Tel (01738) 880214

PETZSCH, Hugo Max David. b 57. Edin Univ MA79 BD83 PhD95. Edin Th Coll 80. **d** 83 **p** 84. C Dollar *St And* 83-86; New Zealand 86-90; Chapl Glenalmond Coll *St And* from 91; P-in-c Alyth, Blairgowrie and Coupar Angus 90-91. *Glenalmond College, Glenalmond, Perth PH1 3RY* Tel (01738) 880202 or 880214

PEVERELL, Paul Harrison. b 57. Ripon Coll Cuddesdon. **d** 82 **p** 83. C Cottingham *York* 82-85; V Middlesbrough St Martin 85-93; V Gt Ayton w Easby and Newton in Cleveland from 93. *The Vicarage, Low Green, Great Ayton, Middlesbrough, Cleveland TS9 6NN* Tel (01642) 722333

PEYTON, Nigel. b 51. JP. Edin Univ MA73 BD76. Union Th Sem (NY) STM77 Edin Th Coll 73. **d** 76 **p** 77. Chapl St Paul's Cathl Dundee *Bre* 76-82; Dioc Youth Chapl 76-85; Chapl Invergowrie 79-82; P-in-c 82-85; P-in-c Nottingham All SS *S'well* 85; V 86-91; Chapl Bluecoat Sch Nottm 90-92; P-in-c Lambley from 91; Dioc Min Development Adv from 91. *The Rectory, Lambley, Nottingham NG4 4QP* Tel (0115) 931 3531 or (01636) 814331 Fax (01636) 815084

PEYTON JONES, Donald Lewis. b 14. DSC42. K Coll Lon 59. **d** 61 **p** 62. C Withycombe Raleigh *Ex* 61-62; V Salcombe Regis 62-72; C-in-c Lundy Is 73-78; V Appledore 73-78; rtd 79; Chapl Miss to Seamen from 79; Lic to Offic *Ex* from 79. *Fort Cottage, Cawsand, Torpoint, Cornwall PL10 1PA* Tel (01752) 822382 or 223865

PEYTON JONES, Mrs Dorothy Helen. b 58. LMH Ox BA79 MPhil80. Trin Coll Bris DipTh86. **dss** 86 **d** 87 **p** 94. W Holloway St Luke *Lon* 86-87; Par Dn 87-89; C Glas St Oswald *Glas* 89-92; NSM Knightswood H Cross Miss from 92. *144 Garscadden Road, Glasgow G15 6PR* Tel 0141-944 8491

PHARAOH, Douglas William. b 18. MSHAA56. Worc Ord Coll 68. **d** 69 **p** 70. C Gt Malvern Ch Ch *Worc* 69-71; Area Sec Leprosy Miss 71-72; P-in-c Gateshead St Cuth *Dur* 72-73; V New Seaham 73-76; P-in-c Wymeswold *Leic* 76-78; V Wymeswold and Prestwold w Hoton 78-80; P-in-c Grandborough w Willoughby and Flecknoe *Cov* 80-81; V 81-83; rtd 83; Perm to Offic *Cov* from 83. *5 Margetts Close, Kenilworth, Warks CV8 1EN* Tel (01926) 53807

PHAROAH, Donald James. b 05. AKC27. **d** 28 **p** 29. C Sevenoaks St Jo *Roch* 28-32; C Lamorbey H Trin 32-33; C Deal St Andr *Cant* 33-39; V Cant St Greg 39-57; Chapl St Jo Hosp Cant 39-57; RD Cant 51-57; V Headcorn 57-71; rtd 71; Perm to Offic *Roch* 71-94. *5 Springshaw Close, Sevenoaks, Kent TN13 2QE* Tel (01732) 456542

PHEELY, William Rattray. b 35. EN(M)88. Edin Th Coll 57. **d** 60 **p** 61. C Glas St Mary *Glas* 60-63; C Salisbury St Martin *Sarum* 63-66; Guyana 66-82; V Bordesley St Oswald *Birm* 82-86; Perm to Offic from 86. *Flat 23, Frogmoor House, 571 Hob Moor Road, Birmingham B25 8XD* Tel 0121-783 1970

PHEIFFER, John Leslie. b 18. Wells Th Coll. **d** 67 **p** 68. C Northwood Hills St Edm *Lon* 67-69; Chapl Twickenham Prep Sch 69-71; C Chobham w Valley End *Guildf* 71-76; C Highcliffe w Hinton Admiral *Win* 77-79; V Portswood St Denys 79-85; rtd 86. *4 Haywards Close, Felpham, Bognor Regis, W Sussex PO22 8HF* Tel (01243) 828985

PHELAN, Thomas Sylvester Patrick. b 36. Leic Univ DSocStuds62 Southn Univ DASS79 CQSW79. Chich Th Coll DipTh94. **d** 94 **p** 95. C Somers Town St Mary *Lon* 94-96; C St Pancras H Cross w St Jude and St Pet from 96. *2A Camden Terrace, London NW1 9BP* Tel 0171-267 8704

PHELPS, Canon Arthur Charles. b 26. St Cath Coll Cam BA50 MA55. Ridley Hall Cam 51. **d** 53 **p** 54. C Kirkdale St Lawr *Liv* 53-56; C Rainham *Chelmsf* 56-60; Min Collier Row St Jas CD 60-65; V Collier Row St Jas 65-75; R Thorpe Morieux w Preston and Brettenham *St E* 75-84; R Rattlesden w Thorpe Morieux and Brettenham 84-90; Hon Can St E Cathl 89-90; rtd 90; Perm to Offic *Truro* from 90. *Newland, Sandy Lane, Harlyn Bay, Padstow, Cornwall PL28 8SD* Tel (01841) 520697

PHELPS, Ian James. b 29. Oak Hill Th Coll 53. **d** 56 **p** 57. C Peckham St Mary *S'wark* 56-59; R Gaddesby w S Croxton *Leic* 59-67; R Beeby 59-67; Asst Dioc Youth Chapl and Rural Youth Adv 65-67; CF (TA) 60-67; CF (R of O) 67-84; Youth Chapl *Leic* 67-85; Dioc Adult Educn Officer 85-91; Past Asst to Adn Leic 91-94; rtd 94; Perm to Offic *Leic* from 94. *Farrier's Cottage, 1 Weir Lane, Houghton on the Hill, Leicester LE7 9GR* Tel 0116-241 6599

PHELPS, Ian Ronald. b 28. FLS58 Lon Univ BSc53 PhD57. Chich Th Coll 57. **d** 59 **p** 60. C Brighton Gd Shep Preston *Chich* 59-61; C Sullington 62-64; C Storrington 62-64; R Newtimber w Pyecombe 64-68; V Brighton St Luke 68-74; TV Brighton Resurr 74-76; V Peacehaven 76-94; rtd 94; Perm to Offic *Chich* from 94. *2 Kingston Green, Seaford, E Sussex BN25 4NB* Tel (01323) 899511

PHILBRICK, Gary James. b 57. Southn Univ BA78 K Alfred's Coll Win CertEd79 ACertCM84 Edin Univ BD86. Edin Th Coll 83. **d** 86 **p** 87. C Southampton Maybush St Pet *Win* 86-90; R Fawley from 90. *The Rectory, 1 Sheringham Close, Southampton SO45 1SQ* Tel (01703) 893552

PHILIP, Peter Wells. b 35. Ridley Hall Cam 64. **d** 67 **p** 68. C Tollington Park St Mark w St Anne *Lon* 67-70; C Battersea St Pet *S'wark* 70-72; Hon C Kennington St Mark 72-73; New Zealand 73-92 and from 94; C Finchley Ch Ch *Lon* 92-93. *The Vicarage, 8 Vincent Place, Dinsdale, Hamilton, New Zealand* Tel Hamilton (7) 847 6053 or 846 6910

PHILIPSON, John Wharton. b 05. St Jo Coll York 24. St Deiniol's Hawarden 66. **d** 66 **p** 67. Asst Dioc Dir of Educn *Newc* from 66; Hon C Gosforth St Nic 66-79. *Scarborough Court, Alexandra Way, Cramlington, Northd NE23 6ED* Tel (01670) 713633

PHILLIPS, Andrew Graham. b 58. Ex Univ BSc79. Chich Th Coll 84. **d** 87 **p** 88. C Frankby w Greasby *Ches* 87-89; C Liv St Chris Norris Green *Liv* 89-92; CF 92-97. *Address temp unknown*

PHILLIPS, Canon Anthony Charles Julian. b 36. Lon Univ BD63 AKC63 G&C Coll Cam PhD67 St Jo Coll Ox MA75 DPhil80. Coll of Resurr Mirfield 66. **d** 66 **p** 67. C-in-c Chesterton Gd Shep CD *Ely* 66-69; Fell Dean and Chapl Trin Hall Cam 69-74; Chapl St Jo Coll Ox 75-85; Hd Master K Sch Cant 85-96; Hon Can Cant Cathl *Cant* 86-96; Can Th Truro Cathl *Truro* from 86. *10 St Peter's Hill, Flushing, Falmouth, Cornwall TR11 5TP* Tel (01326) 377217

PHILLIPS, Mrs Audrey Katherine. b 32. Lorain Coll Ohio BS73. Ox Min Course 88. **d** 91 **p** 94. NSM Princes Risborough w Ilmer *Ox* from 91. *1 The Chestnuts, Kirtlington, Kidlington, Oxon OX5 3UB* Tel (01869) 50194

PHILLIPS, Benjamin Lambert Meyrick (Ben). b 64. K Coll Cam BA86 MA90. Ridley Hall Cam 87. **d** 90 **p** 91. C Wareham *Sarum* 90-94; C Chipping Barnet w Arkley *St Alb* 94-96; V Bodicote *Ox* from 96. *The Vicarage, Wykham Lane, Bodicote, Banbury, Oxon OX15 4BW* Tel (01295) 270174

PHILLIPS, Brian Edward Dorian William. b 36. Bris Univ BA58. Ripon Hall Ox 58. **d** 60 **p** 61. C Ross *Heref* 60-64; Chapl RAF 64-68; Hon C Fringford w Hethe and Newton Purcell *Ox* 68-73; Chapl Howell's Sch Denbigh 73-76; C Cleobury Mortimer w Hopton Wafers *Heref* 76-80; V Dixton from 80. *The Vicarage, 38 Hillcrest Road, Wyesham, Monmouth NP5 3LH* Tel (01600) 712565

PHILLIPS, Canon Brian Robert. b 31. Clare Coll Cam BA53 MA57. Linc Th Coll 54. **d** 56 **p** 57. C Tuffley *Glouc* 56-59; C Southgate Ch Ch *Lon* 59-62; R Luckington w Alderton *Bris* 62-69; V Highworth w Sevenhampton and Inglesham etc 69-84; Hon Can Bris Cathl 84-90; P-in-c Long Newnton 84-87; P-in-c Crudwell w Ashley 84-87; R Ashley, Crudwell, Hankerton, Long Newnton etc 87-90; rtd 90; Perm to Offic *Portsm* from 90. *Hannington, Hospital Road, Shirrell Heath, Southampton SO32 2JR* Tel (01329) 834547

PHILLIPS, The Very Revd Christopher John. b 46. **d** 79 **p** 80. Hong Kong from 79; Chapl Hong Kong Cathl 83-87; Dean Hong Kong from 88. *c/o St John's Cathedral, Garden Road, Hong Kong* Tel Hong Kong (852) 523-4157 Fax 521-7830

PHILLIPS, David Arthur. b 36. S Dios Minl Tr Scheme 90. **d** 94 **p** 95. NSM Canford Magna *Sarum* from 94. *32 Lynwood Drive, Merley, Wimborne, Dorset BH21 1UG* Tel (01202) 880262

PHILLIPS, David Elwyn. b 17. St D Coll Lamp 62. **d** 64 **p** 65. C Ferndale *Llan* 64-68; C Port Talbot St Theodore 68-70; V Abercanaid 70-87; rtd 87; Perm to Offic *Llan* from 87. *Carmel, 13 Tyleri Gardens, Abertillery NP3 1EZ*

PHILLIPS, David Keith. b 61. New Coll Ox MA90. St Jo Coll Dur BA90. **d** 91 **p** 92. C Denton Holme *Carl* 91-94; C Chadderton Ch Ch *Man* from 94. *23 Lindale Avenue, Chadderton, Oldham OL9 9DW* Tel 0161-624 0278 E-mail dphillipssa@cix.compulink.co.uk

PHILLIPS, Duncan Laybourne. b 08. Wycliffe Hall Ox 45. **d** 47 **p** 48. C Keighley *Bradf* 47-51; V Morval *Truro* 51-57; Chapl HM Pris Wandsworth 57-66; Albany 66-69; P-in-c Eye, Croft w Yarpole and Lucton *Heref* 69-73; R 73-81; rtd 81; Perm to Offic *Heref* 81-96. *The Old Parsonage, Eye, Leominster, Herefordshire HR6 0DP* Tel (01568) 613513

PHILLIPS, Edward Leigh. b 12. St Edm Hall Ox BA34 MA47. Wycliffe Hall Ox 33. **d** 35 **p** 36. Asst Chapl Dean Close Sch Cheltenham 35-37; C Highfield *Ox* 37-38; C-in-c Patcham Chr the K CD *Chich* 39-41; CF (EC) 41-46; R Ide Hill *Roch* 46-49; V Moulsecoomb *Chich* 49-52; V Kingston w Iford 52-75; V Iford w Kingston and Rodmell 75-78; RD Lewes 65-77; rtd 78; Perm to Offic *Glouc* from 78. *35 Woodland Green, Upton St Leonards, Gloucester GL4 8BD* Tel (01452) 619894

PHILLIPS, Mrs Elizabeth Beryl. b 34. **d** 94 **p** 95. C N Farnborough *Guildf* from 94. *19 Fleming Close, Farnborough, Hants GU14 8BT* Tel (01252) 546093

PHILLIPS, Canon Frederick Wallace (Ferdie). b 12. MC43. Univ of Wales BA34. St Mich Coll Llan 34. **d** 36 **p** 37. C Fochriw w Deri *Llan* 36-38; C Roath St Marg 38-40; CF 40-46; C Epsom Common Ch Ch *Guildf* 46-47; R Harrietsham *Cant* 47-56; V Faversham 56-64; V Margate St Jo 64-74; Hon Can Cant Cathl 66-84; R Smarden 74-82; R Biddenden 80-82; rtd 82; Perm to Offic *Cant* from 84; Almoner Cant Cathl 85-93; Retirement Officer from 93. *15A The Precincts, Canterbury, Kent CT1 2EL* Tel (01227) 450891

PHILLIPS, Geoff Clarke. b 50. SW Minl Tr Course 94. **d** 96. NSM Georgeham *Ex* from 96. *Bridge Cottage, 2 St Mary's Road, Croyde, Braunton, Devon EX33 1PE* Tel (01271) 890589

PHILLIPS, Canon Geoffrey John. b 23. BNC Ox BA47 MA56. Ridley Hall Cam 54. **d** 56 **p** 57. C Kettering St Andr *Pet* 56-59; C Tideswell *Derby* 59-62; Ceylon 62-65; R Gillingham w Geldeston and Stockton *Nor* 65-70; V Eaton 70-81; RD Nor S 71-81; Hon Can Nor Cathl 78-81; Chapl Vienna w Budapest and Prague *Eur* 81-87; rtd 87; Perm to Offic *Nor* from 87. *Mere Farmhouse, White Heath Road, Bergh Apton, Norwich NR15 1AY* Tel (01508) 480656

PHILLIPS, Gwilym Caswallon Howell. b 07. Brothers of St Paul Barfield 30. **d** 32 **p** 33. New Zealand 32-38; Chapl Buckingham Coll Harrow 38-39; Hon C Roos w Tunstall *York* 39-40; C Charlton Kings H Apostles *Glouc* 41-44; C Bromsgrove All SS *Worc* 44-45; C Luton St Sav *St Alb* 45-48; V Stotfold 48-61; V Evenley *Pet* 61-72; rtd 72. *1 The Glebe, Flore, Northampton NN7 4LX* Tel (01327) 40423

PHILLIPS, Horace George. b 38. Man Univ BA60 Birm Univ DipTh62 MEd84. Qu Coll Birm 60. **d** 62 **p** 63. C Wotton St Mary *Glouc* 62-65; C Standish w Hardwicke and Haresfield 65-68; C-in-c Watermoor Holy Trin 68-74; V Churchdown St Jo 74-79; P-in-c Beckford w Ashton under Hill 79-85; P-in-c Overbury w Alstone, Teddington and Lt Washbourne *Worc* 84-85; V Overbury w Teddington, Alstone etc 85-88; P-in-c Peopleton and White Ladies Aston etc 88-94; Dioc Sch Officer from 88; R Peopleton and White Ladies Aston w Churchill etc from 94. *The Rectory, Peopleton, Pershore, Worcs WR10 2EE* Tel (01905) 840243 Fax 612302

PHILLIPS, Ivor Lynn. b 44. Leeds Univ BA70. Cuddesdon Coll 69. **d** 71 **p** 72. C Bedlinog *Llan* 71-73; C Roath St Marg 73-77; TV Wolverhampton All SS *Lich* 77-78; TV Wolverhampton 78-81; Chapl Charing Cross Hosp Lon 81-91; Chapl Milan w Genoa and Lugano *Eur* 91-94; C Hampstead St Jo *Lon* from 95. *3 Holly Bush Vale, London NW3 6TX* Tel 0171-433 1115

PHILLIPS, Mrs Janet Elizabeth. b 37. Bp Grosseteste Coll CertEd57. EMMTC 81. **dss** 84 **d** 87 **p** 94. Wisbech St Aug *Ely* 84-86; Cambridge St Jas 86-87; Par Dn 87-91; Par Dn Wisbech SS Pet and Paul 91-94; C from 94. *St Peters Lodge, Love Lane, Wisbech, Cambs PE13 1HP* Tel (01945) 476149

PHILLIPS, Jeffery Llewellyn. b 32. Sarum & Wells Th Coll. **d** 87 **p** 88. C Ringwood *Win* 87-90; V Somborne w Ashley 90-93; rtd 93. *Queen's Acre, 3 Solent Avenue, Lymington, Hants SO41 3SD* Tel (01590) 673955

PHILLIPS, John David. b 29. G&C Coll Cam BA50 MA54 CertEd69. SW Minl Tr Course 85. **d** 87 **p** 88. NSM St Martin w E and W Looe *Truro* 87-88; NSM St Merryn 88-94; rtd 94; Perm to Offic *Truro* from 94. *The Vicarage, St Merryn, Padstow, Cornwall PL28 8ND* Tel (01841) 520379

PHILLIPS, John Eldon. b 50. Univ of Wales (Cardiff) BEd85 MEd92. St Mich Coll Llan. **d** 90 **p** 91. NSM Merthyr Cynog and Dyffryn Honddu etc *S & B* 90-94; Lic to Offic *St D* from 94; NSM Ystradgynlais *S & B* from 95; Chapl Trin Coll Carmarthen from 95. *Heddfan, 105 Tawe Park, Ystradgynlais, Swansea SA9 1GU* Tel (01639) 849237 or (01267) 237971 Mobile 0850-273070 Fax (01267) 230933

PHILLIPS, John Reginald. b 64. St Steph Ho Ox BTh93. **d** 96 **p** 97. C Bognor *Chich* from 96. *44 Southdown Road, Bognor Regis, W Sussex PO21 2JP* Tel (01243) 860617

PHILLIPS, John William Burbridge. b 39. Dur Univ BSc60 Lon Univ BD68. Tyndale Hall Bris 65. **d** 68 **p** 69. C Barton Seagrave *Pet* 68-71; C Northampton All SS w St Kath 71-75; R Irthlingborough 75-88; V Weedon Lois w Plumpton and Moreton Pinkney etc 88-95; rtd 95; Perm to Offic *Pet* from 95. *Finca Morito 8, 12579 Alcoceber, Castellon, Spain*

PHILLIPS, Joseph Benedict. b 11. **d** 37 **p** 38. In RC Ch 37-43; C St Mary-at-Lambeth *S'wark* 47-50; C Woking St Jo *Guildf* 50-53; V Burton in Kendal *Carl* 53-59; V Bradf St Andr *Bradf* 59-66; rtd 76. *100 Ruskin Avenue, Lincoln LN2 4BT* Tel (01522) 534411

PHILLIPS, Judith Mary. b 46. Reading Univ BA67 Cardiff Coll of Educn PGCE86. St Mich Coll Llan 93. **d** 95 **p** 97. Lect Neath Coll from 84; NSM Clydach *S & B* from 95. *Gwalia, Felindre, Swansea SA5 7PQ* Tel (01792) 772523

PHILLIPS, Canon Kenneth John. b 37. Coll of Resurr Mirfield 67. **d** 67 **p** 68. C Blackb St Jas *Blackb* 67-69; C-in-c Lea CD 70-80; V Lea 80-84; P-in-c Priors Hardwick, Priors Marston and Wormleighton *Cov* from 85; RD Southam 89-95; Hon Can Cov Cathl from 94. *The Vicarage, Priors Marston, Rugby, Warks CV23 8RT* Tel (01327) 60053

PHILLIPS, Lamont Wellington Sanderson. b 33. S'wark Ord Course 73. **d** 76 **p** 78. NSM Tottenham St Paul *Lon* 76-83; P-in-c Upper Clapton St Matt 83-88; V from 88. *St Matthew's Vicarage, 20 Moresby Road, London E5 9LF* Tel 0181-806 2430

PHILLIPS, Canon Martin Nicholas. b 32. Em Coll Cam BA57 MA61. Linc Th Coll 57. **d** 59 **p** 60. C Stocking Farm CD *Leic* 59-63; V Sheff Gillcar St Silas *Sheff* 63-71; V Birstall *Leic* 72-82; R Wanlip 72-82; V Birstall and Wanlip 82-88; TR Loughborough Em and St Mary in Charnwood 88-96; Hon Can Leic Cathl 90-96; rtd 96; Perm to Offic *Leic* from 96. *Foxhollow, 40A Lodge Close, Barrow On Soar, Loughborough, Leics LE12 8ZL*

PHILLIPS, Michael John. b 54. Trent Poly BA77. Sarum & Wells Th Coll 78. **d** 81 **p** 82. C Killay *S & B* 81-83; C Treboeth 83-85; Hong Kong 85-89; Japan 89-91; TR Is of Scilly *Truro* 91-95; R Cwmbran *Mon* from 95. *The Rectory, Clomendy Road, Cwmbran NP44 3LS* Tel (01633) 484880

PHILLIPS, Michael Thomas. b 46. CQSW81. Linc Th Coll 89. **d** 90 **p** 91. C Hyson Green *S'well* 90-91; C Basford w Hyson Green 91-93; Chapl HM Pris Gartree from 93. *HM Prison Gartree, Gallow Field Road, Market Harborough, Leics LE16 7RP* Tel (01858) 410234 Fax 410808

PHILLIPS, Mrs Patricia. b 45. Glouc Sch of Min 83. **dss** 86 **d** 87 **p** 94. Newent and Gorsley w Cliffords Mesne *Glouc* 86-95; C 87-95; P-in-c Childswyckham w Aston Somerville, Buckland etc from 95. *New Vicarage, Buckland Road, Childswickham, Broadway, Worcs WR12 7HH* Tel (01386) 853824

PHILLIPS, Patrick Noble Stowell. b 22. Edin Univ MA50 CertEd63. ALCD52. **d** 52 **p** 53. Niger 52-55; C Mossley Hill St Matt and St Jas *Liv* 55-57; Canada 57-60; Benin 60-63; R Moresby *Carl* 63-66; Canada 66-71; R Arthuret *Carl* 71-88; rtd 88. *14 Gipsy Lane, Reading RG6 7HB* Tel 0118-926 4654

PHILLIPS, Miss Pauline. b 54. LNSM course 96. **d** 96 **p** 97. NSM Mossley *Man* from 96. *38 Lorne Street, Mossley, Ashton-under-Lyne, Lancs OL5 0HQ* Tel (01457) 832363

PHILLIPS, Percy Graham. b 26. St Aid Birkenhead 46. **d** 51 **p** 52. C Wallasey St Hilary *Ches* 51-54; C Thrybergh *Sheff* 54-58; C Guernsey St Michel du Valle *Win* 58-60; V Heytesbury w Tytherington and Knook *Sarum* 60-65; V Stonebridge St Mich *Lon* 65-70; R Vernham Dean w Linkenholt *Win* 70-78; C Farnham *Guildf* 78-82; TV Cove St Jo 82-89; rtd 89. *22 Charts Close, Cranleigh, Surrey GU6 8BH*

PHILLIPS, Peter. b 26. Oak Hill Th Coll 63. **d** 65 **p** 66. C Eastbourne All SS *Chich* 65-69; C St Alb St Paul *St Alb* 69-73; V Riseley w Bletsoe 73-84; R Arley *Cov* 84-91; rtd 91; Perm to Offic *B & W* from 91. *Milford House, 10 Albert Road, Clevedon, Avon BS21 7RP* Tel (01275) 875801

PHILLIPS, Peter Miles Lucas. b 44. Reading Univ BA66 QUB DipEd69 Univ of Wales (Cardiff) MEd89. St Mich Coll Llan 89. **d** 92 **p** 93. Dep Hd Teacher Dynevor Sch 82-96; NSM Llangyfelach *S & B* 92-96; Dep Chapl HM Pris Liv from 96. *HM Prison, 68 Hornby Road, Liverpool L9 3DF* Tel 0151-525 5971 Fax 525 0813

PHILLIPS, Raymond Arthur. b 29. K Coll Lon 49. **d** 53 **p** 54. C Stepney St Aug w St Phil *Lon* 53-56; N Rhodesia 56-64; Zambia 64-68; V Stoke Newington St Faith, St Matthias and All SS *Lon* 68-73; Trinidad and Tobago 73-80; V Hillingdon All SS *Lon* 80-94; AD Hillingdon 93-94; Chapl St Cross Hosp Win from 94; rtd 94. *The Chaplain's Lodge, Hospital of St Cross, St Cross, Winchester, Hants SO23 9SD* Tel (01962) 853525

PHILLIPS, Robin Michael. b 33. AKC58. **d** 59 **p** 60. C Hanwell St Mellitus *Lon* 59-61; C St Margarets on Thames 61-64; C Hangleton *Chich* 64-68; V Mellor *Derby* 68-95; RD Glossop 89-93; rtd 95; Hon C Bridekirk *Carl* 95-96. *87 George Lane, Bredbury, Stockport, Cheshire SK6 1DH*

PHILLIPS, Stephen. b 38. QUB BA60. Linc Th Coll 60. **d** 62 **p** 63. C Waddington *Linc* 62-65; C Gt Grimsby St Jas 65-72; V Kirmington 72-97; V Limber Magna w Brocklesby 73-97; RD Yarborough from 92; V Brocklesby Park from 97. *The Vicarage, Great Limber, Grimsby, S Humberside DN37 8JN* Tel (01469) 560641

PHILLIPS, Thomas Wynford. b 15. Univ of Wales BA37 BD40. St Mich Coll Llan. **d** 43 **p** 44. C Shotton *St As* 43-46; C Rhyl 46-50; C Hall Green Ascension *Birm* 50-52; R Shustoke 52-55; P-in-c Maxstoke 52-55; V Clay Cross *Derby* 55-68; R Upton Magna *Lich* 68-73; V Withington 68-73; R Roche *Truro* 73-80; R Withiel 73-80; RD St Austell 76-80; rtd 80; Perm to Offic *Truro* from 80. *Brynawelon, Wheal Quoit Avenue, St Agnes, Cornwall TR5 0SJ* Tel (01872) 552862

PHILLIPS-SMITH, Edward Charles. b 50. AKC71. **d** 73 **p** 74. C Wolverhampton *Lich* 73-76; Chapl St Pet Colleg Sch Wolv 77-87; Hon C Wolverhampton *Lich* 78-87; V Stevenage St Pet Broadwater *St Alb* 87-89; Chapl Millfield Jun Sch Somerset 89-95; Lic to Offic *Ox* from 95. *The Flat, Parkhill, 218 Chobham Road, Sunningdale, Ascot, Berks SL5 0HY*

PHILLIPSON, Christopher Quintin. b 14. Ch Coll Cam BA36 MA40. Ridley Hall Cam 36. **d** 38 **p** 39. C Turnham Green Ch Ch *Lon* 38-40; C Stamford Hill St Ann 40-44; CMS Miss India 44-54; V Southbourne *Chich* 54-62; R W Thorney 56-62; R Ardingly 62-70; V Aldingbourne 70-81; rtd 81; Perm to Offic *Chich* from 82. *91 Little Breach, Chichester, W Sussex PO19 4TZ* Tel (01243) 785557

PHILLIPSON-MASTERS, Miss Susan Patricia. b 52. FIST76 ACP80 Sussex Univ CertEd73 K Alfred's Coll Win BEd81. Trin Coll Bris DipHE88. **d** 89 **p** 95. C Saltford w Corston and Newton St Loe *B & W* 89-94; C Uphill 94-97; C Nailsea Ch Ch w Tickenham from 97. *32 Southfield Road, Nailsea, Bristol BS19 1JB* Tel (01275) 855789

PHILLPOT, Donald John. b 27. St Jo Coll Dur BA53 DipTh55. **d** 55 **p** 56. C Southmead *Bris* 55-60; C Brislington St Luke 60-63; R Stapleton *Heref* 63-68; V Dorrington 63-68; P-in-c Astley Abbotts 68-78; R Bridgnorth w Tasley 68-78; V Lillington *Cov* 78-92; rtd 92; Perm to Offic *Glouc* from 92. *22 Williams Orchard, Highnam, Gloucester GL2 8EL* Tel (01452) 386844

PHILP (née NOBLE), Mrs Ann Carol. b 42. Sarum Dioc Tr Coll CertEd63 Southn Univ MA(Ed)89 MIPD. S Dios Minl Tr Scheme. **d** 95 **p** 96. Chapl Sarum Cathl *Sarum* from 95; Dir Sarum Chr Centre from 95. *55 The Close, Salisbury SP1 2EL* Tel (01722) 323554 Fax as telephone

PHILPOTT, Barbara May. *See* WILKINSON, Mrs Barbara May

PHILPOTT, Canon John David. b 43. Leic Univ BA64. Trin Coll Bris 69. **d** 72 **p** 73. C Knutsford St Jo *Ches* 72-75; C Toft 72-75; C Bickenhill w Elmdon *Birm* 75-79; V Birm St Luke 79-91; RD Birm City 83-88; Hon Can Birm Cathl 89-91; V Chilvers Coton w Astley *Cov* from 91; RD Nuneaton from 95; Hon Can Cov Cathl from 96. *Chilvers Coton Vicarage, Coventry Road, Nuneaton, Warks CV11 4NJ* Tel (01203) 383010

PHILPOTT, John Wilfred. b 44. K Coll Lon BD67 AKC67. **d** 68 **p** 69. C Norbury St Steph *Cant* 68-71; C Addiscombe St Mildred 71-75; V Whitfield w Guston from 75. *The Vicarage, 45 Bewsbury Cross Lane, Whitfield, Dover CT16 3EZ* Tel (01304) 820314

PHILPOTT, Ronald (Ron). b 38. IPFA69. Cranmer Hall Dur 88. **d** 89 **p** 90. NSM S Ossett *Wakef* 89-93; R Clitheroe St Jas *Blackb* from 93. *The Rectory, Woone Lane, Clitheroe, Lancs BB7 1BJ* Tel (01200) 23608

PHILPOTT, Preb Samuel. b 41. Kelham Th Coll 60. **d** 65 **p** 66. C Swindon New Town *Bris* 65-70; C Torquay St Martin Barton *Ex* 70-73; TV Withycombe Raleigh 73-76; V Shaldon 76-78; P-in-c Plymouth St Pet 78-80; V from 80; RD Plymouth Devonport 86-93 and from 95; Preb Ex Cathl from 91. *St Peter's Vicarage, 23 Wyndham Square, Plymouth PL1 5EG* Tel (01752) 662110

PHILPS, Mark Seymour. b 51. Worc Coll Ox BA73 MA78 Lon Univ MA75 Nottm Univ BA79. St Jo Coll Nottm 77. **d** 80 **p** 81. C Chadwell Heath *Chelmsf* 80-83; C Woodford Wells 83-87; V Tipton St Matt *Lich* from 87. *St Matthew's Vicarage, Dudley Road, Tipton, W Midlands DY4 8DJ* Tel 0121-557 1929

PHILSON, James Alexander Summers (Hamish). b 20. Edin Th Coll 48. **d** 51 **p** 52. C Falkirk *Edin* 51-53; R Dunblane *St And* 53-62; Australia from 62; rtd 85. *38 Allenswood Road, Greenwood, W Australia 6024* Tel Perth (9) 447 9523

PHIPPS, David John. b 46. Bris Univ BSc68 Ex Univ PhD94. Trin Coll Bris 75. **d** 78 **p** 79. C Madron w Morvah *Truro* 78-80; C Kenilworth St Jo *Cov* 80-83; TV Barnstaple, Goodleigh and Landkey *Ex* 83-84; TV Barnstaple 85-95; I Abercraf w Callwen w Capel Coelbren *S & B* from 95. *The Vicarage, Heol Tawe, Abercrave, Swansea SA9 1TJ* Tel (01639) 730640

PHIPPS, John Maclean. b 14. Em Coll Cam BA38 MA50. Cuddesdon Coll 38. **d** 39 **p** 40. C Banbury *Ox* 39-41; P-in-c Cambois *Newc* 41-46; C Newport Pagnell *Ox* 47-53; V Speenhamland 53-71; V Buckland 72-79; V Littleworth 72-79; R Pusey 72-79; rtd 79; Perm to Offic *Chich* 84-93; Perm to Offic *St Alb* from 93. *10 The Limes, Linden Road, Bedford MK40 2UX* Tel (01234) 365137

✠**PHIPPS, The Rt Revd Simon Wilton.** b 21. MC45. Trin Coll Cam BA48 MA53. Westcott Ho Cam 48. **d** 50 **p** 51 **c** 68. C Huddersfield St Pet *Wakef* 50-53; Chapl Trin Coll Cam 53-58; Ind Chapl *Cov* 58-68; C Cov Cathl 58-68; Hon Can Cov Cathl 65-68; Suff Bp Horsham *Chich* 68-75; Bp Linc 75-86; rtd 86; Asst Bp Chich from 86; Asst Bp S'wark from 86. *Sarsens, Shipley, Horsham, W Sussex RH13 8PX* Tel (01403) 741354

PHIZACKERLEY, The Ven Gerald Robert. b 29. Univ Coll Ox BA52 MA56. Wells Th Coll 52. **d** 54 **p** 55. C Carl St Barn *Carl* 54-57; Chapl Abingdon Sch 57-64; R Gaywood, Bawsey and Mintlyn *Nor* 64-78; RD Lynn 68-78; Hon Can Nor Cathl 75-78; Hon Can Derby Cathl *Derby* 78-96; P-in-c Ashford w Sheldon 78-91; Adn Chesterfield 78-96; rtd 96; Perm to Offic *Derby* from 96. *Archway Cottage, Hall Road, Leamington Spa, Warks CV32 5RA* Tel (01926) 332740

PHYPERS, David John. b 39. Leic Univ BA60 CertEd61 Lon Univ BD65. Linc Th Coll 76. **d** 78 **p** 79. NSM Normanton *Derby* 78-80; NSM Sinfin 80-87; Lic to Offic 87-88; P-in-c Denby from 88; P-in-c Horsley Woodhouse from 88. *103 Church Street, Denby Village, Ripley, Derbyshire DE5 8PH* Tel (01332) 780730

PIACHAUD, Preb Francois Allen. b 12. Lon Univ BA32 BD35 Selw Coll Cam BA37 MA41. Westcott Ho Cam 37. **d** 37 **p** 38. C Walkergate *Newc* 37-40; C Edin St Jo *Edin* 40-44; V Wrangthorn *Ripon* 44-51; V Chelsea Ch Ch *Lon* 51-86; Preb St Paul's Cathl 61-86; RD Chelsea 74-77; rtd 86; Perm to Offic *Ox* 86-96. *8 Linden Avenue, Maidenhead, Berks SL6 6HB* Tel (01628) 20866

PICK, David. b 44. Linc Th Coll 85. **d** 87 **p** 88. C Howden TM *York* 87-90; P-in-c Sledmere and Cowlam w Fridaythorpe, Fimer etc 90-91; V 91-96; rtd 96; Perm to Offic *York* from 96. *Westwood Close, 16 North Street, Nafferton, Driffield, N Humberside YO25 0JW* Tel (01377) 240360

PICK, William Harry. b 23. Open Univ BA77. St Aid Birkenhead 51. **d** 54 **p** 55. C Wigan St Geo *Liv* 54-57; V Newton-le-Willows 57-67; V Stoneycroft All SS 67-79; R N Meols 79-88; rtd 88; Perm to Offic *Liv* from 88. *8 Morley Road, Southport, Merseyside PR9 9JS* Tel (01704) 541428

PICKARD, Canon Frank Eustace. b 31. Lon Univ BSc52 St Cath Soc Ox BA56 MA63. St Steph Ho Ox. **d** 57 **p** 58. C Haydock St Jas *Liv* 57-59; C Davenham *Ches* 59-60; Asst Master St Dunstan's Sch Lon 60-63; Min Can Pet Cathl *Pet* 63-72; P-in-c Newborough 67-68; V 68-72; R Isham w Pytchley 72-76; R Abington 76-96; Can Pet Cathl from 86; rtd 97; P-in-c Weedon Lois w Plumpton and Moreton Pinkney etc *Pet* from 97. *Weedon Lois Vicarage, Towcester, Northamptonshire NN12 8PN* Tel (01327) 860278

PICKARD, Ronald William. b 16. ALCD39. **d** 39 **p** 40. C Drypool St Columba *York* 39-41; Chapl RN 41-51; Maracaibo Ch Venezuela 51-62; Lima Ch of the Gd Shep Peru 62-69; Hon Can Chile 65-70; Chapl Br Emb Ankara *Eur* 70-71; rtd 81. *23 Tower Gardens, Deep Lane, Crediton, Devon EX17 2BQ* Tel (01363) 774234

PICKARD, Stephen Kim. b 52. Newc Univ Aus BCom Dur Univ PhD. Melbourne Coll of Div BD St Jo Coll Morpeth 77. **d** 80 **p** 80. Australia 80-82 and from 91; C Dur St Cuth *Dur* 82-84; Chapl Van Mildert Coll Dur 84-90; Chapl Trev Coll Dur 84-90. *14 Williams Road, North Rocks, NSW Australia 2151* Tel Sydney (2) 871 6558 or 683 3655 Fax 683 6617

PICKARD, William Priestley. b 31. MIPM72. Clifton Th Coll 56. **d** 59 **p** 60. C Upper Tulse Hill St Matthias *S'wark* 59-63; Asst Warden Shaftesbury Crusade Bris from 64; rtd 96. *2 Edingworth Mansions, 2 Atlantic Road South, Weston-super-Mare, Avon BS23 2DE* Tel (01934) 628994

PICKEN, David Anthony. b 63. Lon Univ BA84 Kent Univ PGCE85 Nottm Univ MA96. Linc Th Coll 87. **d** 90 **p** 91. C Worth *Chich* 90-93; TV Wordsley *Worc* 93-97; TR from 97. *The Rectory, 13 Dunsley Drive, Wordsley, Stourbridge, W Midlands DY8 8RA* Tel (01384) 277215

PICKEN, James Hugh. b 51. Victoria Univ (BC) BMus75 ARCT73. Ripon Coll Cuddesdon BA79. **d** 80 **p** 81. C Jarrow *Dur* 80-83; SSF 83-93; Perm to Offic *Sarum* 86-92; Guardian Alnmouth Friary 92-94; Lic to Offic *Newc* 92-94; Canada from 94. *929-4th Street NW, Calgary, Alberta, Canada T2N 1P4* Tel Calgary (403) 270 9661

PICKEN, William Middlewood Martin. b 06. SS Coll Cam BA28 MA32. Westcott Ho Cam 29. **d** 30 **p** 31. C Elland *Wakef* 30-34; C Truro St Mary *Truro* 34-37; PV Truro Cathl 34-37; Hon PV Truro Cathl from 37; R St Martin by Looe 37-71; rtd 71. *2 Stratton Terrace, Falmouth, Cornwall TR11 2SY*

PICKERING, David Colville. b 41. Kelham Th Coll 61. **d** 66 **p** 67. C Chaddesden St Phil *Derby* 66-70; C New Mills 70-72; C Buxton 72-74; V Chesterfield St Aug 74-90; R Whittington from 90. *The Rectory, 84 Church Street North, Chesterfield, Derbyshire S41 9QW* Tel (01246) 450651

PICKERING, The Ven Fred. b 19. St Pet Hall Ox BA41 MA45. St Aid Birkenhead 41. **d** 43 **p** 44. C Leyland St Andr *Blackb* 43-46; C Islington St Mary *Lon* 46-48; NE Area Sec CPAS 48-51; V Burton All SS *Lich* 51-56; V Carl St Jo *Carl* 56-63; V Chitts Hill St Cuth *Lon* 63-74; RD E Haringey 68-73; Adn Hampstead 74-84; rtd 84; Perm to Offic *Pet* 84-93; Perm to Offic *Ex* 94-96. *16 The Close, Easton on the Hill, Stamford, Lincs PE9 3NA* Tel (01780) 481318

PICKERING, Geoffrey Craig (Geoff). b 40. Newc Coll of Arts NDD61 Leic Coll of Art and Design ATD62 Leic Univ CertEd62. S Dios Minl Tr Scheme 90. **d** 93 **p** 94. C Horsham *Chich* from 93. *St Leonard's Vicarage, Cambridge Road, Horsham, W Sussex RH13 5ED* Tel (01403) 266903

PICKERING, John Alexander. b 41. TCD BA63 MA66. CITC 65. **d** 65 **p** 66. C Magheralin *D & D* 65-67; C-in-c Outeragh *K, E & A* 67-68; I 68-71; Deputation Sec Hibernian Bible Soc 71-74; C-in-c Drumgoon and Ashfield 74-80; I Keady w Armaghbreague and Derrynoose *Arm* 80-83; I Drumcree from 83. *Drumcree Rectory, 78 Drumcree Road, Portadown, Craigavon, Co Armagh BT62 1PE* Tel (01762) 333711

PICKERING, John David. b 38. **d** 86 **p** 86. NSM Ellon *Ab* 86-88; NSM Cruden Bay 86-88; Ind Chapl *Dur* 88-97; TV Jarrow 91-97; P-in-c Newton Hall from 97. *31 York Crescent, Newton Hall, Durham DH1 5PT* Tel 0191-386 8049

PICKERING, John Michael Staunton. b 34. Sarum & Wells Th Coll 71. **d** 72 **p** 73. C Gaywood, Bawsey and Mintlyn *Nor* 72-77; P-in-c Foulsham 77-81; R Foulsham w Hindolveston and Guestwick 81-88; P-in-c Bacton w Edingthorpe w Witton and Ridlington from 88. *The Vicarage, Church Road, Bacton, Norwich NR12 0JP* Tel (01692) 650375

PICKERING, John Roger. b 28. Fitzw Ho Cam BA52 MA56. Linc Th Coll 62. **d** 63 **p** 66. C Haxby w Wigginton *York* 63-64; CF 66-69; C Folkestone H Trin w Ch Ch *Cant* 71-73; P-in-c Buckland Newton *Sarum* 73-77; P-in-c Wootton Glanville and Holnest 73-77; P-in-c Osmington w Poxwell 77-80; C Eston w Normanby *York* 83-84; P-in-c Swine 84-90; rtd 90. *The Bull Pens, Treworder Farm, Ruan Minor, Helston, Cornwall TR12 7JL* Tel (01326) 290908

PICKERING, Malcolm. b 37. Sarum Th Coll 65. **d** 68 **p** 69. C Milton *Portsm* 68-70; C Stanmer w Falmer and Moulsecoomb *Chich* 70-75; Chapl Brighton Coll of Educn 71-75; V Hooe *Chich* 75-80; R Ninfield 75-80; V Ventnor H Trin *Portsm* 80-88; V Ventnor St Cath 80-88; Chapl St Cath Sch Ventnor 87-88; V Marton *Blackb* 88-97; P-in-c Badingham w Bruisyard, Cransford and Dennington *St E* from 97. *The Rectory, 5 Orchard Rise, Badingham, Woodbridge, Suffolk IP13 8LN* Tel (01728) 638784

PICKERING, Mark Penrhyn. b 36. Liv Univ BA59 St Cath Coll Ox BA62 MA67. Wycliffe Hall Ox 60. **d** 63 **p** 64. C Claughton cum Grange *Ches* 63-67; C Newland St Jo *York* 67-72; TV Marfleet 72-76; V Kingston upon Hull St Nic 76-85; V Elloughton and Brough w Brantingham 85-88; Chapl R Hull Hosps NHS Trust from 88. *Hull Royal Infirmary, Anlaby Road, Hull HU3 2JZ, or 8 The Pickerings, North Ferriby, N Humberside HU14 3DW* Tel (01482) 328541 or 634892

PICKERING, Stephen Philip. b 52. St Jo Coll York CertEd75. Coll of Resurr Mirfield 77. **d** 79 **p** 80. C Wallsend St Luke *Newc* 79-82; Chapl RN 82-92; C-in-c Ryecroft St Nic CD *Sheff* 92-97; V Ryecroft St Nic from 97. *St Nicolas' House, Kilnhurst Road, Rawmarsh, Rotherham, S Yorkshire S62 5NG* Tel (01709) 522596

PICKERING, Thomas. b 07. Ch Coll Cam BA28 MA32. Ely Th Coll 30. **d** 30 **p** 31. C Leic St Mary *Leic* 30-35; C Leic St Geo 35-46; Lic to Offic 46-81; Perm to Offic from 81. *10 Park Hill Drive, Leicester LE2 8HR* Tel 0116-283 1242

PICKERING, William Stuart Frederick. b 22. K Coll Lon BD49 AKC49 PhD58 Manitoba Univ Hon DCL81. **d** 50 **p** 51. C Frodingham *Linc* 50-53; Lic to Offic Guildf & Linc 55-56; Tutor K Coll Lon 55-56; Canada 56-66; Lic to Offic *Newc* 66-87; rtd 87; Perm to Offic *Ely* from 87. *1 Brookfield Road, Coton, Cambridge CB3 7PT* Tel (01954) 210525

PICKETT, Brian Laurence. b 48. Reading Univ BA70. Qu Coll Birm BA73 MA77 Ripon Coll Cuddesdon. **d** 88 **p** 88. C Highcliffe w Hinton Admiral *Win* 88-91; P-in-c Colbury from 91. *The Vicarage, Deerleap Lane, Southampton SO40 7EH* Tel (01703) 292132

PICKETT, Mrs Joanna Elizabeth. b 53. Leic Univ BA74 MA80. Wycliffe Hall Ox 87. **d** 89 **p** 94. Chapl Southn Univ *Win* 89-94; C N Stoneham 94-95. *The Vicarage, Deerleap Lane, Southampton SO40 7EH* Tel (01703) 292132

PICKETT, Mark William Leslie. b 60. Westhill Coll Birm BEd84. Trin Coll Bris DipHE95. **d** 95 **p** 96. C Hellesdon *Nor* from 95. *7 Chapel Court, Norwich NR6 5NU* Tel (01603) 405360

PICKETT, Peter Leslie. b 28. MRCS Lon Univ LDS. S Dios Minl Tr Scheme 83. **d** 86 **p** 87. NSM Eastbourne H Trin *Chich* 86-88; P-in-c Danehill 88-93; rtd 93; Perm to Offic *Chich* from 93. *33 Pashley Road, Eastbourne, E Sussex BN20 8DY* Tel (01323) 731709

PICKLES, Harold. b 13. Sarum Th Coll 34. **d** 36 **p** 37. C Wirksworth w Carsington *Derby* 36-39; C Chesterfield St Mary and All SS 39-42; P-in-c Bolsover 42-45; C Burbage 45-46; V Beighton 46-57; V Edwinstowe w Carburton *S'well* 57-78; rtd 78; NSM Bishop's Stortford St Mich *St Alb* 78-84; Perm to Offic *Ripon* 84-93. *3 Old Deanery Close, Minster Road, Ripon, N Yorkshire HG4 1LZ* Tel (01765) 604375

PICKLES, Mark Andrew. b 62. Edin Univ BA83. Cranmer Hall Dur 85. **d** 88 **p** 89. C Rock Ferry *Ches* 88-91; C Hartford 91-93; V Wharton from 93. *The Vicarage, 165 Crook Lane, Winsford, Cheshire CW7 3DR* Tel (01606) 593215

PICKSTONE, Charles Faulkner. b 55. BNC Ox BA77 MA81 Leeds Univ BA80. Coll of Resurr Mirfield 78. **d** 81 **p** 82. C Birkenhead Priory *Ches* 81-84; Chapl Paris St Geo *Eur* 84; C Camberwell St Giles w St Matt *S'wark* 84-89; V Catford St Laur from 89; Asst RD E Lewisham from 92. *St Laurence's Vicarage, 31 Bromley Road, London SE6 2TS* Tel 0181-698 9706

PICKTHORN, Canon Charles Howard. b 25. Linc Coll Ox BA48 MA52. Sarum Th Coll 48. **d** 50 **p** 51. C High Harrogate Ch Ch *Ripon* 50-54; C Cheam *S'wark* 54-60; R Bourton-on-the-Water w Clapton *Glouc* 60-91; Chapl RAF 60-76; RD Stow *Glouc* 67-90; P-in-c Gt Rissington 68-81; Hon Can Glouc Cathl 77-91; rtd 91; Perm to Offic *Glouc* from 91. *267 Prestbury Road, Prestbury, Cheltenham, Glos GL52 2EX* Tel (01242) 521447

PICKUP, Harold. b 17. St Pet Hall Ox BA39 MA46. Ridley Hall Cam 46. **d** 47 **p** 48. C Middleton *Man* 47-50; V Gravesend St Mary *Roch* 51-57; Australia from 57; rtd 82. *69 Haig Street, Mowbray Heights, Tasmania, Australia 7248* Tel Launceston (03) 262820

PICTON, Arthur David. b 39. Ch Ch Ox BA62 MA67. Chich Th Coll. **d** 65 **p** 66. C Hulme St Phil *Man* 65-67; C Swinton St Pet

67-71; R Stretford St Pet 71-79; P-in-c Knights Enham *Win* 79-86; R 86-89; V Basing from 89; RD Basingstoke from 93; Hon Can Win Cathl from 96. *The Vicarage, Church Lane, Old Basing, Basingstoke, Hants RG24 0DJ* Tel (01256) 473762

PIDOUX, Ian George. b 32. Univ Coll Ox BA55 MA60. Coll of Resurr Mirfield 54. **d** 57 **p** 58. C Middlesbrough All SS *York* 57-60; C Haggerston St Aug w St Steph *Lon* 60-62; C Aylesford *Roch* 80-81; TV Rye *Chich* 81-84; P-in-c Bridgwater St Jo *B & W* 84-86; V from 86; Chapl Bridgwater Hosp from 91. *St John's Vicarage, Blake Place, Bridgwater, Somerset TA6 5AU* Tel (01278) 422540

PIDSLEY, Preb Christopher Thomas. b 36. ALCD61. **d** 61 **p** 62. C Enfield Ch Ch Trent Park *Lon* 61-66; C Rainham *Chelmsf* 66-70; V Chudleigh *Ex* from 70; RD Moreton 86-91; Preb Ex Cathl from 92. *The Vicarage, Chudleigh, Newton Abbot, Devon TQ13 0JF* Tel (01626) 853241

PIERCE, Alan. b 46. St Mark & St Jo Coll Lon TCert68 Southlands Coll Lon BEd75 K Coll Lon MA85. Lon Bible Coll DipTh72 N Ord Course 89. **d** 92 **p** 93. NSM Bolton St Thos *Man* from 92. *3 Astley Road, Bolton BL2 4BR* Tel (01204) 300071

PIERCE, The Ven Anthony Edward. b 41. Univ of Wales (Swansea) BA63 Linacre Coll Ox BA65 MA71. Ripon Hall Ox 63. **d** 65 **p** 66. C Swansea St Pet *S & B* 65-67; C Swansea St Mary and H Trin 67-74; Chapl Univ of Wales (Swansea) 71-74; V Llwynderw 74-92; P-in-c Swansea St Barn 92-96; Dioc Dir of Educn from 93; Can Brecon Cathl from 93; Adn Gower from 95; V Swansea St Mary w H Trin from 96. *St Mary's Vicarage, 7 Eden Avenue, Uplands, Swansea SA2 0PS* Tel (01792) 298616

PIERCE, Brian William. b 42. St Steph Ho Ox 86. **d** 88 **p** 89. C Cudworth *Wakef* 88-93; TV Manningham *Bradf* from 93. *The Vicarage, 16 Wood Street, Bradford, W Yorkshire BD8 8HY* Tel (01274) 730726

PIERCE, Bruce Andrew. b 58. TCD BBS80 BTh89. CITC 86. **d** 89 **p** 90. C Raheny w Coolock *D & G* 89-92; C Taney 92-93; I Lucan w Leixlip from 93. *The Rectory, 5 Uppercross, Ballyowen Lane, Ballydowd, Lucan, Co Dublin, Irish Republic* Tel Dublin (1) 624 9147

PIERCE, Canon Claude Anthony (Tony). b 19. OBE46. Magd Coll Cam BA47 MA49 BD53. Ely Th Coll 47. **d** 48 **p** 49. C Chesterfield St Mary and All SS *Derby* 48-51; Chapl Magd Coll Cam 51-56; Lect Th Magd Coll Cam 54; Australia from 56; Hon Can Perth 64-66; Can Perth 66-85; rtd 85. *61 Hawkestone Street, Cottesloe, W Australia 6011* Tel Perth (9) 383 2719

PIERCE, Jeffrey Hyam. b 29. FBIM80 Chelsea Coll Lon BSc51. Ox NSM Course 86. **d** 88 **p** 89. NSM Gt Missenden w Ballinger and Lt Hampden *Ox* 88-93; NSM Penn from 93. *The Well House, Lee Common, Great Missenden, Bucks HP16 9JX* Tel (01494) 837477

PIERCE, Jonathan Douglas Marshall. b 70. UCD BA91. CITC BTh96. **d** 96 **p** 97. C Knockbreda *D & D* from 96. *8 Newtown Park, Belfast BT8 4LH* Tel (01232) 702271

PIERCE, Stephen Barry. b 60. Birm Univ BA81 MA82. Cranmer Hall Dur. **d** 85 **p** 86. C Huyton St Mich *Liv* 85-89; V Walton Breck Ch Ch from 89. *Christ Church Vicarage, 157 Hartnup Street, Liverpool L5 1UW* Tel 0151-263 2518

PIERCE, Thomas David Benjamin. b 67. Ulster Univ BA88. Oak Hill Th Coll DipHE92 BA94. **d** 94 **p** 95. C Cromer *Nor* 94-97; C Belfast St Donard *D & D* from 97. *21 Orangefield Drive, Belfast BT5 6DN* Tel (01232) 651216

PIERCE, William Johnston. b 32. N Ord Course. **d** 89 **p** 90. NSM Gt Crosby St Luke *Liv* from 89. *1 Forton Lodge, Blundellsands Road East, Liverpool L23 8SA* Tel 0151-924 2400

PIERPOINT, Canon David Alfred. b 56. **d** 86 **p** 88. NSM Athboy w Ballivor and Killallon *M & K* 86-88; NSM Killiney Ballybrack *D & G* 88-89; NSM Narraghmore w Timolin, Castledermot and Kinneagh 89-91; Chan V St Patr Cathl Dublin 90-96; C Dublin St Patr Cathl Gp *D & G* 92-95; I Dublin Ch Ch Cathl Gp from 95; Can Ch Ch Cathl Dublin from 95. *All Saints' Vicarage, 30 Phibsborough Road, Dublin 7, Irish Republic* Tel Dublin (1) 830 4601 Mobile 087-630402

PIERSSENE, Jeremy Anthony Rupert. b 31. CCC Cam BA55 MA. Ridley Hall Cam 56. **d** 58 **p** 59. C Enfield Ch Ch Trent Park *Lon* 58-61; Travelling Sec Scripture Union 61-69; Chapl Rugby Sch 69-76; R Windlesham *Guildf* 76-96; RD Surrey Heath 84-90; rtd 96. *12 Portway, Warminster, Wilts BA12 8QD* Tel (01985) 216764

PIGGOTT, Andrew John. b 51. Qu Mary Coll Lon BSc(Econ)72. St Jo Coll Nottm 83. **d** 86 **p** 87. C Dorridge *Birm* 86-89; TV Kidderminster St Geo *Worc* 89-94; V Biddulph *Lich* from 94. *The Vicarage, Congleton Road, Biddulph, Stoke-on-Trent ST8 7RG* Tel (01782) 513247

PIGGOTT, Clive. b 47. St Luke's Coll Ex CertEd69. LNSM course 93. **d** 96. NSM Malden St Jas *S'wark* from 96. *84 Manor Drive North, New Malden, Surrey KT3 5PA* Tel 0181-337 0801

PIGGOTT, Raymond George. b 16. Leeds Univ BA38. Coll of Resurr Mirfield 38. **d** 40 **p** 41. C Leic St Mark *Leic* 40-42; C Munster Square St Mary Magd *Lon* 42-47; Chapl RN 47-53; C Felixstowe St Jo *St E* 53-54; V Barney w Thursford *Nor* 54-56; V Ilkley St Marg *Bradf* 56-65; V Roughey *Chich* 65-80; P-in-c Lynch w Iping Marsh 80-83; rtd 83; Perm to Offic *Chich* from 85. *Flat 3, Bramwell Lodge, Terry's Cross, Woodmancote, Henfield, W Sussex BN5 9SX* Tel (01273) 493749

PIGOTT, Graham John. b 44. Kingston Coll of Art NDD64 Lon Univ DipTh71 BD73 Nottm Univ MPhil84. St Jo Coll Nottm DPS81. **d** 81 **p** 82. C Beeston *S'well* 81-84; P-in-c W Bridgford 84-88; V Wilford Hill from 88. *The Parsonage, Boundary Road, West Bridgford, Notts NG2 7BD* Tel 0115-923 3492

PIGOTT, Canon John Drummond. b 26. TCD Div Test50 BA50 MA56. **d** 51 **p** 52. C Belfast St Phil *Conn* 51-54; C Jordanstown 54-56; Chapl RAF 56-59; R Upper Clatford w Goodworth Clatford *Win* 59-65; V Warley Woods *Birm* 65-74; RD Warley 72-74; V Boldmere 74-97; Hon Can Birm Cathl 81-97; RD Sutton Coldfield 88-93; rtd 97. *Clatford House, 41 Farriers Green, Monkton Heathfield, Taunton, Somerset TA2 8PP* Tel (01823) 413552

PIGOTT, Nicholas John Capel. b 48. Qu Coll Birm 75. **d** 78 **p** 79. C Belmont *Dur* 78-79; C Folkestone St Sav *Cant* 79-82; C Birm St Geo *Birm* 82-85; V Stevenage St Hugh and St Jo *St Alb* 85-91; TV Totnes and Berry Pomeroy *Ex* 91; TV Totnes, Bridgetown and Berry Pomeroy etc from 91. *St John's Vicarage, Crosspark, Totnes, Devon TQ9 5BQ* Tel (01803) 867961

PIGREM, Terence John (Tim). b 39. Oak Hill Th Coll 66. **d** 69 **p** 70. C Islington St Andr w St Thos and St Matthias *Lon* 69-73; C Barking St Marg w St Patr *Chelmsf* 73-75; TV 75-76; C W Holloway St Luke *Lon* 76-79; V 79-95; P-in-c Abbess Roding, Beauchamp Roding and White Roding *Chelmsf* 95-96; R Leaden Roding and Abbess Roding etc from 96; RD Dunmow from 97. *The Rectory, Stortford Road, Leaden Roding, Dunmow, Essex CM6 1QZ* Tel (01279) 876313

PIKE, David Frank. b 35. CEng MIMechE BA Lon Univ TCert. S Dios Minl Tr Scheme 82. **d** 85 **p** 86. NSM Lancing w Coombes *Chich* 85-88; R Albourne w Sayers Common and Twineham 88-94; V Wisborough Green from 94. *The Vicarage, Wisborough Green, Billingshurst, W Sussex RH14 0DZ* Tel (01403) 700339

PIKE, Eric Sydney. b 13. Lon Univ BSc52 Lon Inst of Educn DipRE67. S'wark Ord Course 78. **d** 79 **p** 80. NSM Wimbledon Em Ridgway Prop Chpl *S'wark* 79-84; NSM Iford *Win* 84-85; Perm to Offic 85-95. *31 Seaward Avenue, Bournemouth BH6 3SJ* Tel (01202) 432398

PIKE, George Richard. b 38. BSc. WMMTC 79. **d** 82 **p** 83. NSM Edgbaston St Bart *Birm* 82-89; NSM S Yardley St Mich from 89. *131 Charlbury Crescent, Birmingham B26 2LW* Tel 0121-783 2818 Fax as telephone

PIKE, Horace Douglas. b 13. AKC48. **d** 48 **p** 49. C Todmorden *Wakef* 48-52; P-in-c Lundwood 52-55; V Gawber 55-59; V Baildon *Bradf* 59-71; R Burnsall 72-78; rtd 78; P-in-c Birdsall w Langton *York* 81-86. *18 Southfield Close, Rufforth, York YO2 3RE* Tel (01904) 738418

PIKE, Canon James. b 22. TCD. **d** 68 **p** 69. C Clooney *D & R* 68-72; I Ardstraw 72-76; I Ardstraw w Baronscourt 76-86; I Ardstraw w Baronscourt, Badoney Lower etc 76-92; Can Derry Cathl 90-92; rtd 92. *19 Knockgreenan Avenue, Omagh, Co Tyrone BT79 0EB* Tel (01662) 249007 Fax 251382

PIKE, Paul Alfred. b 38. Wycliffe Hall Ox. **d** 84 **p** 85. C Penn Fields *Lich* 84-89; OMF Internat from 89; Japan from 89. *c/o OMF, Belmont, The Vine, Sevenoaks, Kent TN13 3TZ* Tel (01732) 450747 Fax 456164

PIKE, Peter John. b 53. Southn Univ BTh. Sarum & Wells Th Coll 81. **d** 84 **p** 85. C Broughton *Blackb* 84-88; V Woodplumpton 88-93; Asst Dir of Ords and Voc Adv 89-93; P-in-c Barnacre w Calder Vale from 93; Carl Dioc Tr Course from 93. *The Vicarage, Delph Lane, Barnacre, Garstang, Preston PR3 1GL* Tel (01995) 602117

PIKE, Robert James. b 47. Kelham Th Coll 66. **d** 70 **p** 71. C Cov St Pet *Cov* 70-74; C Bilton 74-76; P-in-c Southall St Geo *Lon* 76-81; V S Harrow St Paul 81-86; C Hillingdon St Jo 86-88; Chapl Hillingdon Hosp & Mt Vernon Hosp Uxbridge 88-90; Perm to Offic from 91. *6 Salt Hill Close, Uxbridge, Middx UB8 1PZ* Tel (01895) 235212

PIKE, Canon Roger Walter. b 31. Roch Th Coll 65. **d** 67 **p** 68. C Wokingham St Paul *Ox* 67-70; C Whitley Ch Ch 70-76; C-in-c California CD 76-80; V Cowes St Faith *Portsm* 80-94; Hon Can Portsm Cathl 92-94; rtd 94; Perm to Offic *Truro* from 94. *45 Conway Road, Falmouth, Cornwall TR11 4LA* Tel (01326) 315901

PIKE, Timothy David. b 68. Collingwood Coll Dur BA90 Leeds Univ BA94. Coll of Resurr Mirfield 92. **d** 95 **p** 96. C Owton Manor *Dur* from 95. *40 Wisbech Close, Hartlepool, Cleveland TS25 2LW* Tel (01429) 871522

PILDITCH, Miss Patricia Desiree. b 21. **dss** 82 **d** 87 **p** 94. Barnstaple *Ex* 82-87; Hon Par Dn 87-94; Hon C from 94; Asst Chapl N Devon Distr Hosp Barnstaple from 82. *4 The Mews, Bydown, Swimbridge, Barnstaple, Devon EX32 0QB* Tel (01271) 830770

PILGRIM, Colin Mark. b 56. BA77 Geneva Univ CES84. Westcott Ho Cam 81. **d** 84 **p** 85. C Chorlton-cum-Hardy St Clem *Man* 84-87; C Whitchurch *Bris* 87-89; V Bedminster Down 89-95; Dioc Youth Officer from 95; Hon C Stoke Bishop from 96. *4 Glenbrook, Glen Drive, Bristol BS9 1SB* Tel 0117-968 5833

PILGRIM, Donald Eric. b 55. Cant Univ (NZ) BA80. St Jo Coll (NZ) 81. **d** 81 **p** 82. New Zealand 81-85 and from 86; C Southampton Maybush St Pet *Win* 85-86. *212 Hoon Hay Road, Christchurch, New Zealand* Tel Christchurch (3) 338 4277 Fax as telephone

PILGRIM, Ms Judith Mary. b 44. Westcott Ho Cam 88. **d** 90 **p** 94. C Probus, Ladock and Grampound w Creed and St Erme *Truro* 90-94; Par Dn Nottingham All SS *S'well* 94; C 94-97; Asst Chapl to the Deaf from 94; C Nottingham All SS from 94. *4 Birkland Avenue, Peel Street, Nottingham NG1 4GT* Tel 0115-941 0369

PILKINGTON, Miss Anne. b 57. Aston Tr Scheme 88 N Ord Course 90. **d** 93 **p** 94. C Wythenshawe Wm Temple Ch *Man* 93-96; P-in-c from 96. *William Temple Vicarage, Robinswood Road, Manchester M22 6BU* Tel 0161-437 3194

PILKINGTON, Charles George Willink. b 21. Trin Coll Cam BA42 MA64. Westcott Ho Cam. **d** 63 **p** 64. C Pendleton St Thos *Man* 63-65; C Brindle Heath 63-65; C Chorlton-cum-Hardy St Clem 65-68; R Withington St Chris 68-88; rtd 88; Perm to Offic *Man* from 88. *32 Rathen Road, Withington, Manchester M20 9GH* Tel 0161-434 5365

PILKINGTON, Canon Christopher Frost. b 23. Trin Coll Cam BA50 MA60. Ridley Hall Cam 50. **d** 52 **p** 53. C St Jo in Bedwardine *Worc* 52-55; V Worc St Mark 55-60; V Bromsgrove St Jo 60-68; R Bris St Steph w St Nic and St Leon *Bris* 68-81; P-in-c 81-82; Hon Can Bris Cathl 79-82; Hon Chapl Cancer Help Cen Bris 82-89; Lic to Offic from 82; rtd 89. *North Lawn, Ston Easton, Bath BA3 4DG* Tel (01761) 241472

PILKINGTON, Edward Russell. b 39. ALCD65. **d** 65 **p** 66. C Eccleshill *Bradf* 65-68; C Billericay St Mary *Chelmsf* 68-72; V New Thundersley 72-78; R Theydon Garnon 78-82; V Gidea Park from 82. *St Michael's Vicarage, Main Road, Romford RM2 5EL* Tel (01708) 741084

PILKINGTON, John Rowan. b 32. Magd Coll Cam BA55 MA59. Ridley Hall Cam 57. **d** 59 **p** 60. C Ashtead *Guildf* 59-61; C Wimbledon *S'wark* 62-65; R Newhaven *Chich* 65-75; R Farlington *Portsm* 75-89; V Darlington St Mark w St Paul *Dur* 89-97; rtd 97. *38 Main Road, Emsworth, Hants PO10 8AU* Tel (01243) 375830

PILKINGTON, Timothy William. b 54. Nottm Univ BA85. Linc Th Coll 82. **d** 85 **p** 86. C Newquay *Truro* 85-88; C Cockington *Ex* 88-91; R St John w Millbrook *Truro* from 91. *The Vicarage, Millbrook, Torpoint, Cornwall PL10 1BW* Tel (01752) 822264

PILKINGTON of Oxenford, Revd Canon Lord (Peter). b 33. Jes Coll Cam BA55 MA59. Westcott Ho Cam 58. **d** 59 **p** 60. C Bakewell *Derby* 59-62; Chapl Eton Coll 62-75; Hd Master K Sch Cant 75-85; Hon Can Cant Cathl *Cant* 75-90; High Master St Paul's Sch Barnes 86-92; Chmn Broadcasting Complaints Commn from 92; Hon C Pimlico St Mary Graham Terrace *Lon* from 92. *The Presbytery, 30 Bourne Street, London SW1W 8JS, or Oxenford House, Ilminster, Somerset TA19 0PP* Tel (01460) 52813 Fax (01460) 55280

✠**PILLAR, The Rt Revd Kenneth Harold.** b 24. Qu Coll Cam BA48 MA53. Ridley Hall Cam 48. **d** 50 **p** 51 **c** 82. C Childwall All SS *Liv* 50-53; Chapl Lee Abbey 53-57; V New Beckenham St Paul *Roch* 57-62; V Cant St Mary Bredin *Cant* 62-65; Warden Lee Abbey 65-70; V Waltham Abbey *Chelmsf* 70-82; RD Chigwell 76-78; RD Epping Forest 78-82; Suff Bp Hertford *St Alb* 82-89; rtd 89; Asst Bp Sheff from 89. *75 Dobcroft Road, Sheffield S7 2LS* Tel 0114-236 7902

PILLAR, Kenneth James. b 50. St Jo Coll Nottm 70. **d** 74 **p** 75. C Wilmington *Roch* 74-79; CF 79-87 and from 89; R Curry Rivel w Fivehead and Swell *B & W* 87-89. *MOD Chaplains (Army), Trenchard Lines, Upavon, Pewsey, Wilts SN9 6BE* Tel (01980) 615804 Fax 615800

PILLING, Neville. b 32. ACMA60 FCCA81 CertEd71. Is of Man Tr Inst 88. **d** 92 **p** 93. NSM Douglas St Matt *S & M* from 92. *Morwenna, Athol Park, Port Erin, Isle of Man IM9 6ES* Tel (01624) 832382

PIMENTEL, Peter Eric. b 55. BA. Ridley Hall Cam. **d** 82 **p** 83. C Gt Ilford St Andr *Chelmsf* 82-85; Chapl Basingstoke Distr Hosp 85-88; TV Grays Thurrock 88-96; P-in-c Barton *Portsm* from 96; Dioc Ecum Officer from 96. *St Paul's Vicarage, Barton Road, Newport, Isle of Wight PO30 2HZ* Tel (01983) 522075

PIMM, Robert John. b 57. ACIB82 Bris Univ BA78. Trin Coll Bris ADMT94. **d** 94 **p** 95. C Long Benton *Newc* from 94. *5 Ravenswood Close, Forest Hall, Newcastle upon Tyne NE12 9LU* Tel 0191-270 2011

PIMPERTON, Raymond Swindale. b 12. Linc Th Coll 77. **d** 77 **p** 78. Hon C Holbeach *Linc* 77-83; rtd 83; Perm to Offic *Linc* 83-92. *6 Chestnut Avenue, Holbeach, Spalding, Lincs PE12 7NE* Tel (01406) 22458

PINCHES, Donald Antony. b 32. Pemb Coll Cam BA55 MA60 Linacre Coll Ox BA67. Wycliffe Hall Ox 64. **d** 67 **p** 68. C Aylesbury *Ox* 67-71; C Compton Gifford *Ex* 71-74; TV Lydford, Brent Tor, Bridestowe and Sourton 74-77; V Shiphay Collaton from 77. *St John's Vicarage, 83 Cadewell Lane, Torquay TQ2 7HP* Tel (01803) 613361

PINDER, The Ven Charles. b 21. AKC49. **d** 50 **p** 51. C Raynes Park St Sav *S'wark* 50-53; V Hatcham Park All SS 53-60; C-in-c CCC Miss Camberwell 58-60; V Catford St Laur 60-73; Sub-Dean S Lewisham 68-73; Boro Dean Lambeth 73-86; Adn Lambeth 86-88; rtd 88; Perm to Offic *Chich* from 91. *22 Somerstown, Chichester, W Sussex PO19 4AG* Tel (01243) 779708

PINDER, John Ridout. b 43. Peterho Cam BA65 MA69. Cuddesdon Coll 65. **d** 73 **p** 74. C Leavesden All SS *St Alb* 73-76; Gen Sec Melanesian Miss 77-89; P-in-c Harpsden w Bolney *Ox* 82-89; R Farlington *Portsm* from 89; RD Portsm from 96. *The Rectory, 27 Farlington Avenue, Cosham, Portsmouth PO6 1DF* Tel (01705) 375145

PINDER-PACKARD, John. b 47. Lon Univ BSc. N Ord Course 81. **d** 84 **p** 85. NSM Mosborough *Sheff* 84-85; C Norton 85-88; V New Whittington *Derby* from 88; Chapl Whittington Hall Hosp from 88. *The Vicarage, 121 Handley Road, New Whittington, Chesterfield, Derbyshire S43 2EF* Tel (01246) 455830

PINE, David Michael. b 41. Lich Th Coll 68. **d** 71 **p** 72. C Northam *Ex* 71-74; R Toft w Caldecote and Childerley *Ely* 74-80; R Hardwick 74-80; V Ipswich St Andr *St E* 80-84; P-in-c Hazelbury Bryan w Stoke Wake etc *Sarum* 84-91; R Hazelbury Bryan and the Hillside Par 91-93; V Steep and Froxfield w Privett *Portsm* from 93. *The Vicarage, Church Road, Steep, Petersfield, Hants GU32 2DF* Tel (01730) 264282

PINES, Dr Christopher Derek (Chris). b 65. Lon Univ MB, BS89. Oak Hill Th Coll DipHE93 BA93. **d** 93 **p** 94. C Heref St Pet w St Owen and St Jas *Heref* from 93. *6 Ledbury Road, Hereford HR1 2SY* Tel (01432) 354197

PINFIELD, Leslie Arthur. b 57. Birm Univ BMus79 Univ Coll Lon DipLib90. St Steph Ho Ox DipMin94. **d** 94 **p** 95. C Bath Bathwick *B & W* from 94. *64 St Johns Road, Bath BA2 6PT* Tel (01225) 466375

PINK, Canon David. b 34. Qu Coll Cam BA58 MA62. Linc Th Coll 58. **d** 60 **p** 61. C Lt Ilford St Mich *Chelmsf* 60-63; Lect Boston 63-65; V Kirton in Holland *Linc* 65-71; V Spittlegate 71-77; Ecum Officer Lincs and S Humberside 77-85; Can and Preb Linc Cathl from 77; P-in-c Canwick 77-87; R Washingborough w Heighington 87-88; R Washingborough w Heighington and Canwick 88-90; rtd 90; Perm to Offic *Linc* from 90. *The Old School, Swarby, Sleaford, Lincs NG34 8TG* Tel (01529) 5403

PINKERTON, Ms Patricia Edith. b 38. California Univ BA72 MA75 BTh80. Ch Div Sch of the Pacific (USA). **d** 81 **p** 82. USA 81-88; C Coleford w Staunton *Glouc* 88-92; D-in-c St Briavels w Hewelsfield 92-94; P-in-c from 94. *The Vicarage, St Anne's Close, St Briavels, Lydney, Glos GL15 6UE* Tel (01594) 530345

PINNER, John Philip. b 37. K Coll Lon BA59. Westcott Ho Cam 69. **d** 71 **p** 72. C Dover St Mary *Cant* 71-74; Chapl Felsted Sch Essex 74-83; New Zealand from 81. *159 West Street, Greytown, New Zealand* Tel Masterton (6) 304 8301 or 378 8377 Fax 304 8301

PINNER, Canon Terence Malcolm William (Terry). b 35. Southn Univ MA89. AKC59. **d** 60 **p** 61. C Eltham St Barn *S'wark* 60-64; S Africa 64-67 and 69-74; USPG 67-69; Sec for Home Affairs Conf of Br Miss Socs 74-76; P-in-c Hinstock *Lich* 76-79; Adult Educn Officer 76-79; Adult RE Officer 79-83; Chapl Southn Univ *Win* 83-88; Tutor S Dios Minl Tr Scheme 88-92; Dioc Dir of Ords *Win* from 88; Hon Can Win Cathl from 92; P-in-c Old Alresford and Bighton from 93. *The Rectory, Kiln Lane, Old Alresford, Alresford, Hants SO24 9DY* Tel (01962) 732780

PINNINGTON, Ms Suzanne Jane. b 66. Trevelyan Coll Dur BA89. St Steph Ho Ox 95. **d** 97. C Oakham, Hambleton, Egleton, Braunston and Brooke *Pet* from 97. *45 Trent Road, Oakham, Leics LE15 6HE* Tel (01572) 756086

PINNOCK, Geoffrey Gilbert. b 16. K Coll Lon 47. **d** 50 **p** 51. C Paddington St Mich w All SS *Lon* 50-52; S Africa 52-57; Perm to Offic *Lon* 57-66; Acting Chapl Nat Hosp Qu Square Lon 60; St Steph Hosp Chelsea 61-62; Asst Chapl Univ Coll Hosp Lon 62-66; USA 66-72; Perm to Offic *Lon* 72-73; Perm to Offic *S'wark* 73-74; C Battersea St Phil w St Bart 74-75; P-in-c Boconnoc w Bradoc *Truro* 75-81; rtd 81. *11 Drove Acre Road, Oxford OX4 3DF* Tel (01865) 247355

PINNOCK, Martyn Elliott. b 47. Dartmouth RN Coll 65. Linc Th Coll CMinlStuds93. **d** 93 **p** 94. C Fordingbridge *Win* 93-97; V St Minver *Truro* from 97. *The Vicarage, St Minver, Wadebridge, Cornwall PL27 6QH* Tel (01208) 862398 E-mail 100015.1154@compuserve.com

PINSENT, Ewen Macpherson. b 30. Edin Th Coll 67. **d** 69 **p** 70. C Holt *Nor* 69-72; R Kelso *Edin* 72-82; R Blendworth w Chalton w Idsworth etc *Portsm* 82-90; R Blendworth w Chalton w Idsworth 90-92; rtd 92. *The Cross House, Child Okeford, Blandford Forum, Dorset DT11 8ED* Tel (01258) 860803

PIPE-WOLFERSTAN, Clare Rachel. b 54. Bris Univ BA75. Bris Sch of Min 84. **d** 88 **p** 94. NSM Bris St Mary Redcliffe w Temple etc *Bris* 88-96; Hon C E Bris from 96. *14 Acramans Road, Bristol BS3 1DQ* Tel 0117-966 3430

PIPER, Andrew. b 58. Magd Coll Ox BA79 MA83. Chich Th Coll 80. **d** 83 **p** 84. C Eastbourne St Mary *Chich* 83-88; TV Lewes All SS, St Anne, St Mich and St Thos 88-93; TR Worth from 93. *The Rectory, Church Road, Worth, Crawley, W Sussex RH10 7RT* Tel (01293) 882229 Fax 883079

PIPER, Clifford John. b 53. Aber Univ CSS88. Moray Ord Course 91. **d** 93 **p** 94. C Invergordon St Ninian *Mor* 93-96; NSM Tain from 96. *Charis, Kingsway Avenue, Tain, Ross-shire IV19 1NJ* Tel (01862) 893152

PIPER, Gary Quentin David. b 42. Nottm Coll of Educn TCert65 Maria Grey Coll Lon DipEd71. Oak Hill Th Coll 75. **d** 78 **p** 79. Hon C Fulham St Matt *Lon* 78-85; V from 85; AD Hammersmith 86-92. *St Matthew's Vicarage, 2 Clancarty Road, London SW6 3AB* Tel 0171-731 3272

PIPER, Graham. b 58. Chich Th Coll BTh91. **d** 91 **p** 92. C Horsham *Chich* 91-94; TV Haywards Heath St Wilfrid from 94. *The Vicarage, 1 Sandy Vale, Haywards Heath, W Sussex RH16 4JH* Tel (01444) 450173

PIPER, John Howard. b 09. St Chad's Coll Dur BA31. **d** 32 **p** 34. Asst Chapl Denstone Coll Uttoxeter 32-34; C Knowle H Nativity *Bris* 34-41; C Sidmouth St Nic *Ex* 41-44; Chapl RAFVR 44-46; C Cov St Mark *Cov* 46-49; C Paignton St Jo *Ex* 49-55; C Devonport St Budeaux 55-57; V Whitleigh 57-68; R Rearsby w Ratcliffe on the Wreake *Leic* 68-78; P-in-c Thrussington 77-78; R Rearsby w Ratcliffe-on-the-Wreake etc 78-82; rtd 82; Perm to Offic *Leic* from 82. *52 Avenue Road, Queniborough, Leicester LE7 3FA* Tel 0116-260 6605

PIPER, Kenneth John. b 29. St Luke's Coll Ex TCert53 Leeds Univ DipEd67. S Dios Minl Tr Scheme 79. **d** 82 **p** 83. NSM Bradford w Oake, Hillfarrance and Heathfield *B & W* 82-87; Chapl to Norway and Scandinavia Lay Tr Officer *Eur* 87-89; R Durrington *Sarum* 90-94; rtd 94; NSM Antony w Sheviock *Truro* from 94. *The Rectory, Sheviock, Torpoint, Cornwall PL11 3EH* Tel (01503) 30477

PIPER, Canon Leonard Arthur. b 08. Clifton Th Coll 32. **d** 35 **p** 36. C Spitalfields Ch Ch w All SS *Lon* 35-37; C Darlington St Cuth *Dur* 37-39; R Hurworth 39-73; Offg Chapl RAF 40-87; R Dinsdale w Sockburn *Dur* 61-73; Hon Can Dur Cathl 70-73; rtd 73. *Bridge Cottage, Over Dinsdale, Darlington, Co Durham DL2 1PW* Tel (01325) 332864

PIPPEN, Brian Roy. b 50. St D Coll Lamp DipTh73. **d** 73 **p** 74. C Maindee *Mon* 73-77; TV Cwmbran 77-84; V Newport Ch Ch 84-90; R Pontypool from 90. *The Vicarage, Trevethin, Pontypool NP4 8JF* Tel (01495) 762228

PIRET, Dr Michael John. b 57. State Univ NY BA79 Univ of Michigan MA80 PhD91 Mert Coll Ox MLitt89. Edin Th Coll 90. **d** 92 **p** 93. C St Andr Cathl Inverness *Mor* 92-94; Dean of Div and Chapl Magd Coll Ox from 94. *Magdalen College, Oxford OX1 4AU* Tel (01865) 276027

PIRRIE, Stephen Robin. b 56. Kent Univ BA79 Barrister 80 Cam Univ MA83. EAMTC 94. **d** 97. C King's Lynn St Marg w St Nic *Nor* from 97. *29 Goodwins Road, King's Lynn, Norfolk PE30 5QX* Tel 0850-827701 (Mobile)

PITCHER, Canon David John. b 33. Ely Th Coll 55. **d** 58 **p** 59. C Kingswinford St Mary *Lich* 58-61; C Kirkby *Liv* 61-66; R Ingham w Sutton *Nor* 66-72; V Lakenham St Jo 72-76; R Framlingham w Saxtead *St E* 76-91; RD Loes 82-89; Hon Can St E Cathl from 85; R Woodbridge St Mary from 91. *St Mary's Rectory, Church Street, Woodbridge, Suffolk IP12 1DR* Tel (01394) 382155

PITCHER, Robert Philip (Bob). b 47. Westhill Coll Birm DipEd70. Trin Coll Bris DipHE92. **d** 92 **p** 93. C Llansamlet *S & B* 92-96; V Caereithin from 96. *The Vicarage, 64 Cheriton Crescent, Portmead, Swansea SA5 5LA* Tel (01792) 583646

PITCHER, Ronald Charles Frederick. b 21. AKC50. **d** 51 **p** 52. C Burnage St Marg *Man* 51-53; C Heywood St Jas 53-55; C Newall Green CD 55-61; V Newall Green 61-73; Chapl Wythenshawe Hosp Man 64-73; C-in-c Danesholme CD *Pet* 73-81; V Estover *Ex* 81-91; rtd 91. *18 East Wyld Road, Weymouth, Dorset DT4 0RP* Tel (01305) 771916

PITCHFORD, Herbert John. b 34. Dur Univ BA60. Ridley Hall Cam 60. **d** 62 **p** 63. C Heref St Martin *Heref* 62-68; R Much Birch w Lt Birch 68-78; P-in-c Much Dewchurch w Llanwarne and Llandinabo 73-78; R Much Birch w Lt Birch, Much Dewchurch etc 78-80; V Grange Park St Pet *Lon* 80-91; V Wylde Green *Birm* from 91. *Emmanuel Vicarage, 17 Greenhill Road, Sutton Coldfield, W Midlands B72 1DS* Tel 0121-373 8348

PITE, Sheila Reinhardt. *See* STEVENSON, Mrs Sheila Reinhardt

PITHERS, Canon Brian Hoyle. b 34. Chich Th Coll 63. **d** 66 **p** 67. C Wisbech SS Pet and Paul *Ely* 66-70; V Fenstanton 70-75; V Hilton 70-75; V Habergham Eaves St Matt *Blackb* 75-85; P-in-c Habergham Eaves H Trin 78-85; V Burnley (Habergham Eaves) St Matt w H Trin 85-86; TR Ribbleton 86-92; V Torrisholme from 92; Hon Can Blackb Cathl from 97. *The Ascension Vicarage, 63 Michaelson Avenue, Morecambe, Lancs LA4 6SF* Tel (01524) 413144 Fax as telephone

PITMAN, Clifford George. b 19. St D Coll Lamp BA48. **d** 49 **p** 50. C Llangynwyd w Maesteg *Llan* 49-52; C Caerphilly 52-54; C Llanharan w Peterston-super-Montem 54-59; R Neath w Llantwit and Tonna 59-60; V Tonna 60-85; rtd 85; Perm to Offic *Llan* from 85. *7 Mackworth Drive, Neath SA11 2BR* Tel (01639) 630262

PITT, Beatrice Anne. b 50. CertEd DipHE. Trin Coll Bris 80. **d** 82 **p** 97. C Rhyl w St Ann *St As* 82-85; CMS 87-92; Zaire 88-92; NSM Penycae *St As* from 92. *St Thomas's Vicarage, Church Street, Penycae, Wrexham LL14 2RL* Tel (01978) 840878

PITT, George. b 52. QUB BD79. CITC 81. **d** 81 **p** 82. C Belfast St Mary *Conn* 81-86; C Hawarden *St As* 87; CMS 87-92; Zaire 88-92; V Penycae *St As* from 92. *St Thomas's Vicarage, Church Street, Penycae, Wrexham LL14 2RL* Tel (01978) 840878

PITT, Miss Karen Lesley Finella. b 62. Lon Univ BA84. Chich Th Coll BTh94. **d** 94 **p** 95. C Walton-on-the-Hill *Liv* from 94. *The Rectory Flat, Walton Rectory, Walton, Liverpool L4 6TJ* Tel 0151-523 0683

PITT, Robert Edgar. b 37. Chich Th Coll 70. **d** 73 **p** 74. C Knowle *Bris* 73-77; C Wells St Cuth w Coxley and Wookey Hole *B & W* 77-81; TV Wellington and Distr 81-94; V Burnham from 94. *The Vicarage, Rectory Road, Burnham-on-Sea, Somerset TA8 2BZ* Tel (01278) 782991

PITT, Canon Trevor. b 45. Hull Univ BA66 MA69 Open Univ DipEd91. Linc Th Coll 68 Union Th Sem (NY) STM70. **d** 70 **p** 71. C Sheff St Geo *Sheff* 70-74; TV Gleadless Valley 74-78; TR 78-79; P-in-c Elham *Cant* 79-82; V Elham w Denton and Wootton 82-91; Vice-Prin Cant Sch of Min 81-91; Six Preacher Cant Cathl *Cant* 85-91; Prin NE Ord Course *Newc* from 91; Hon Can Newc Cathl from 91. *Rose Cottage, The Causeway, Wolsingham, Bishop Auckland, Co Durham DL13 3AZ, or Carter House, Pelaw Leaze Lane, Durham DH1 1TB* Tel (01388) 527467 or 0191-384 8317 Fax 0191-384 7529

PITTIS, Stephen Charles. b 52. Oak Hill Th Coll DipTh75. **d** 76 **p** 77. C Win Ch Ch *Win* 76-79; Chapl Bournemouth and Poole Coll of FE *Sarum* 79-84; V Woking St Paul *Guildf* from 84. *St Paul's Vicarage, Pembroke Road, Woking, Surrey GU22 7ED* Tel (01483) 772081

PITTS, Miss Evadne Ione (Eve). b 50. Qu Coll Birm. **d** 89 **p** 94. C Bartley Green *Birm* 89-93; TD Kings Norton 93-94; TV from 94. *195 Monyhull Hall Road, Birmingham B30 3QN* Tel 0121-458 3483

PITTS, The Very Revd Michael James. b 44. Worc Coll Ox BA67. Qu Coll Birm 67. **d** 69 **p** 70. C-in-c Pennywell St Thos and Grindon St Oswald CD *Dur* 69-72; C Darlington H Trin 72-74; Chapl Dunkerque w Lille Arras etc Miss to Seamen *Eur* 74-79; V Tudhoe *Dur* 79-81; Chapl Helsinki w Moscow *Eur* 81-85; Chapl Stockholm 85-88; Hon Can Brussels Cathl 87-88; Canada from 88; Hon Chapl Miss to Seamen from 88; Dean and R Ch Ch Cathl Montreal from 91. *414 Rosyln Avenue, Westmount, PQ, Canada, H3Y 2T5*

PITYANA, Nyameko Barney. b 45. BA BD. Ripon Coll Cuddesdon. **d** 82 **p** 83. C Woughton *Ox* 82-85; V Highters Heath *Birm* 85-88; Dir Progr to Combat Racism WCC 89-92; Perm to Offic *Ox* from 92. *51 Derwent Avenue, Gladstone Park, Didcot, Oxon OX11 7RF*

PIX, Stephen James. b 42. Ex Coll Ox BA64 DipTh65 MA68 Univ of Wales (Cardiff) LLM97. Clifton Th Coll 66. **d** 68 **p** 69. C St Helens St Helen *Liv* 68-71; Lic to Offic *S'wark* 71-76; Hon C Wallington H Trin 76-84; V Osmotherley w E Harlsey and Ingleby Arncliffe *York* 84-89; V Ox St Mich w St Martin and All SS *Ox* from 89. *The Vicarage, 24 St Michael's Street, Oxford OX1 2EB* Tel (01865) 242444 or 240940

PIZZEY, Lawrence Roger. b 42. Dur Univ BA64. Westcott Ho Cam 65. **d** 67 **p** 68. C Bramford *St E* 67-71; Tutor Woodbridge Abbey 71-77; Asst Chapl Woodbridge Sch 71-77; P-in-c Flempton w Hengrave and Lackford *St E* 77-85; R Culford, W Stow and Wordwell 77-85; P-in-c Acton w Gt Waldingfield 85-89; V 89-95; P-in-c Sudbury and Chilton from 95; RD Sudbury from 96. *The Rectory, Christopher Lane, Sudbury, Suffolk CO10 6AS* Tel (01787) 372611

PLACE, Donald Lee. b 37. **d** 74. C Stainton-in-Cleveland *York* 79-81; TV Loughton St Jo *Chelmsf* 81-83; Chapl Worc R Infirmary and Hosps 83-85; rtd 95. *PO Box 500113, Marathon, Florida 33050, USA*

PLACE, Rodger Goodson. b 37. St Chad's Coll Dur BA60 DipTh62. **d** 62 **p** 63. C Pontesbury I and II *Heref* 62-65; C Heref St Martin 65-68; V Ditton Priors 68-75; R Neenton 68-75; P-in-c Aston Botterell w Wheathill and Loughton 69-75; P-in-c Burwarton w N Cleobury 69-75; P-in-c Dacre *Ripon* 75; P-in-c Dacre w Hartwith 75-76; V 76-82; V Wyther Ven Bede 82-92; P-in-c Roundhay St Jo 92-97; V from 97. *St John's Vicarage, Oakwood Grove, Leeds LS8 2PA* Tel 0113-265 8583

PLACE, Thomas Richard (Tom). b 59. Ridley Hall Cam CTMin93. **d** 93 **p** 94. C Huyton St Geo *Liv* 93-97; CF from 97. *MOD Chaplains (Army), Trenchard Lines, Upavon, Pewsey, Wilts SN9 6BE* Tel (01980) 615804 Fax 615800

PLAISTER, Keith Robin. b 43. K Coll Lon BD65 AKC65. **d** 66 **p** 67. C Laindon w Basildon *Chelmsf* 66-71; V Gt Wakering 71-78; P-in-c Foulness 78; V Gt Wakering w Foulness 78-90; C Witham from 91. *57 Powers Hall End, Witham, Essex CM8 2NH* Tel (01376) 519017

PLAISTOWE, The Ven Ronald Percy Frank. b 11. St Jo Coll Dur LTh34 BA35. Clifton Th Coll. **d** 35 **p** 36. C Bris St Ambrose Whitehall *Bris* 35-39; C St Alb Westbury Park Clifton 39-42; PC Cleeve *B & W* 42-48; New Zealand from 48; Adn Timaru 53-63; Adn Sumner 63-68; Adn Christchurch 68-71. *165 Main Road, Christchurch 8008, New Zealand* Tel Christchurch (3) 384 9632

PLANT, Mrs Edith Winifred Irene (Ewith). b 31. Liv Univ BEd71. Cranmer Hall Dur 81. **dss** 83 **d** 87. Countesthorpe w Foston *Leic* 83-86; Loughborough All SS and H Trin 86-90; Par Dn 87-90; Par Dn Thurnby Lodge 90-91; rtd 91; Perm to Offic *Leic* 91-96. *Craighall Cottage, 26 South Road, Ellon, Aberdeenshire AB41 9NP* Tel (01358) 723628

PLANT, John Frederick. b 61. Man Univ BA82 Birm Univ DPS. Qu Coll Birm 83. **d** 85 **p** 86. C Kersal Moor *Man* 85-88; Chapl Aston Univ *Birm* 88-94; TR Market Bosworth, Cadeby w Sutton Cheney etc *Leic* from 94. *The Rectory, Park Street, Market Bosworth, Nuneaton, Warks CV13 0LL* Tel (01455) 290239

PLANT, Richard. b 41. Open Univ BSc93. Qu Coll Birm 88. **d** 90 **p** 91. C Skelmersdale St Paul *Liv* 90-93; R Golborne from 93. *The Rectory, Church Street, Golborne, Warrington WA3 3TH* Tel (01942) 728305

PLANT, Richard George Nicholas. b 45. Man Univ BA67. Coll of Resurr Mirfield 68. **d** 71 **p** 72. C Cleckheaton St Jo *Wakef* 71-74; P-in-c Adel *Ripon* 74-78; V Ireland Wood 78-82; V Armley w New Wortley 82-92; R Garforth from 92. *The Rectory, Church Lane, Garforth, Leeds LS25 1NR* Tel 0113-286 3737

PLANT, Robert David. b 28. Birm Univ BSc49. St Deiniol's Hawarden 74. **d** 76 **p** 80. NSM Llandrillo-yn-Rhos *St As* 76-79; NSM St Nicholas at Wade w Sarre and Chislet w Hoath *Cant* from 79. *4 Sandalwood Drive, St Nicholas-at-Wade, Birchington, Kent CT7 0PE* Tel (01843) 847276

PLASTOW, Graham Henry George. b 40. St Jo Coll Nottm 68. **d** 71 **p** 72. C St Marylebone w H Trin *Lon* 71-74; C Marlborough *Sarum* 74-77; P-in-c N Shoebury *Chelmsf* 77-83; Chapl St Jo Hosp Chelmsf 83-88; P-in-c E Hanningfield *Chelmsf* 83-91; P-in-c W Hanningfield 87-89; V Enfield St Mich *Lon* from 91. *The Vicarage, Gordon Hill, Enfield, Middx EN2 0QP* Tel 0181-363 2483

PLATT, Andrew Martin Robert. b 41. Oak Hill Th Coll 74. **d** 76 **p** 77. C St Alb St Paul *St Alb* 76-79; V Gazeley w Dalham and Moulton *St E* 79-85; RD Mildenhall 84-86; V Gazeley w Dalham, Moulton and Kentford 85-86; P-in-c Saxmundham 86-89; R 89-97; P-in-c Sudbury w Ballingdon and Brundon from 97. *All Saints' Vicarage, Church Street, Sudbury, Suffolk CO10 6BL* Tel (01787) 372400

PLATT, Harold Geoffrey. b 27. Down Coll Cam BA50 MA52. Ridley Hall Cam 51. **d** 53 **p** 54. C Cambridge St Paul *Ely* 53-56; C-in-c Cam St Martin CD 56-57; R Lower Broughton St Clem *Man* 57-66; P-in-c Salford St Matthias w St Simon 62-66; Lic to Offic 66-76; Lic to Offic *Worc* 76-82; Hon C Belbroughton 83-86; Hon C Belbroughton w Fairfield and Clent 86-90; NSM Hagley 87-90; rtd 90; Co-ord for Decade of Evang 90-95; Perm to Offic *Nor* from 95. *Brecklands Cottage, Brecklands Green, North Pickenham, Swaffham, Norfolk PE37 8LG* Tel (01760) 441581

PLATT, John Dendy. b 24. Magd Coll Cam BA49 MA55. Wells Th Coll 50. **d** 52 **p** 53. C Headley All SS *Guildf* 52-56; C Haslemere 56-58; R Skelton w Hutton-in-the-Forest *Carl* 59-71; rtd 89. *17 Primula Drive, Norwich NR4 7LZ* Tel (01603) 504272

PLATT, Dr John Emerson. b 36. Pemb Coll Ox BA59 MA65 DPhil77 Hull Univ MTh72. Cuddesdon Coll 59. **d** 61 **p** 62. C Adlington *Blackb* 61-64; C Sutton St Mich *York* 64-68; C Ox St Giles *Ox* 68-71; Asst Chapl Pemb Coll Ox 68-69; Chapl from 69. *Pembroke College, Oxford OX1 1DW* Tel (01865) 276426

PLATT, Mrs Katherine Mary (Kitty). b 29. ARIBA51 Sheff Univ BA51. Westcott Ho Cam 76. **dss** 79 **d** 87. Chesterton Gd Shep *Ely* 78-84; Whitton St Aug *Lon* 84-86; Dean of Women's Min 86-94; Hampton St Mary 86-94; Par Dn 87-94; rtd 94; Perm to Offic *Ches* from 94. *56 Mereheath Park, Knutsford, Cheshire WA16 6AU* Tel (01656) 651192

PLATT, Michael Robert. b 39. SS Coll Cam MA60 Nottm Univ PGCE61. Cuddesdon Coll 62. **d** 64. C Far Headingley St Chad *Ripon* 64-65; Asst Teacher Belmont Coll Barnstaple 65-68; Qu Coll Taunton from 68; Ho Master 72-83. *8 Court Hill, Taunton, Somerset TA1 4SX* Tel (01823) 270687

PLATT, William David. b 31. St Chad's Coll Dur BA54. Coll of Resurr Mirfield 54. **d** 56 **p** 57. C Bethnal Green St Jo w St Simon *Lon* 56-60; C Pinner 60-65; V N Hammersmith St Kath 65-72; V Woodham *Guildf* 72-88; Chapl Community of St Mary V Wantage 88-96; rtd 96; NSM Blewbury, Hagbourne and Upton *Ox* from 96. *St Andrew's House, 1 Saxons Way, Didcot, Oxon OX11 9RA* Tel (01235) 814729

PLATTEN, The Very Revd Stephen George. b 47. Lon Univ BEd72 Trin Coll Ox DipTh74. Cuddesdon Coll 72. **d** 75 **p** 76. C Headington *Ox* 75-78; Chapl and Tutor Linc Th Coll 78-83; Can Res Portms Cathl and Dir of Ords *Portsm* 83-89; Abp's Sec for Ecum Affairs *Cant* 90-95; Hon Can Cant Cathl 90-95; Dean Nor from 95. *The Deanery, Cathedral Close, Norwich NR1 4EG* Tel (01603) 218308 Fax 613309

PLATTS, Mrs Hilary Anne Norrie. b 60. SRN81 K Coll Lon BD85 AKC85. Ripon Coll Cuddesdon 86. **d** 88 **p** 94. C Moulsham St Jo *Chelmsf* 88-90; Chapl Reading Univ *Ox* from 90; C Calcot 90-92. *St Nicolas' Vicarage, 53 Sutcliffe Avenue, Reading RG6 7JN* Tel 0118-966 3563

PLATTS, Timothy Caradoc (Tim). b 61. LMH Ox BA83 MA88 St Cross Coll Ox DPhil88. Ripon Coll Cuddesdon 87. **d** 89 **p** 90. C Whitley Ch Ch *Ox* 89-95; P-in-c Earley St Nic from 95. *St Nicolas' Vicarage, 53 Sutcliffe Avenue, Reading RG6 7JN* Tel 0118-966 3563

PLAXTON, Edmund John Swithun. b 36. AKC60. **d** 61 **p** 62. C Crofton Park St Hilda w St Cypr *S'wark* 61-65; C Coulsdon St Jo 65-69; V Forest Hill St Paul 69-80; V Belmont 80-93; V Lingfield and Crowhurst from 93. *The Vicarage, Vicarage Road, Lingfield, Surrey RH7 6HA* Tel (01342) 832021

PLAYER, Leslie Mark. b 65. Ridley Hall Cam CTM95. **d** 95 **p** 96. C Belper *Derby* from 95. *St Swithun's House, Holbrook Road, Belper, Derbyshire DE56 1PA* Tel (01773) 825026

PLEDGER, Miss Alison Frances. b 56. Univ of Wales (Cardiff) BA79 K Alfred's Coll Win PGCE80. Linc Th Coll 89. **d** 91 **p** 94. Par Dn Soham *Ely* 91-94; C Ely 94-96; C Rusthall *Roch* from 97. *6 Ashley Gardens, Rusthall, Tunbridge Wells, Kent TN4 8TY* Tel (01892) 512587

PLIMLEY, Canon William (Bill). b 17. St Aid Birkenhead 50. **d** 52 **p** 53. C Norbury *Ches* 52-55; V Laisterdyke *Bradf* 55-83; Hon Can Bradf Cathl 67-83; rtd 83; Perm to Offic *Bradf* from 83. *465 Bradford Road, Pudsey, W Yorkshire LS28 8ED* Tel (01274) 664862

PLIMMER, Wayne Robert. b 64. St Chad's Coll Dur BA85. St Steph Ho Ox 86. **d** 88 **p** 89. C Cockerton *Dur* 88-91; C Poulton-le-Fylde *Blackb* 91-93; V Darton *Wakef* from 93. *The Vicarage, 6 Jacob's Hall Court, Darton, Barnsley, S Yorkshire S75 5LY* Tel (01226) 384596

PLOWMAN, Richard Robert Bindon. b 38. Solicitor 61. Ridley Hall Cam 76. **d** 78 **p** 79. C Combe Down w Monkton Combe *B & W* 78-81; C Combe Down w Monkton Combe and S Stoke 81-83; V Coxley, Henton and Wookey from 83; RD Shepton Mallet from 95. *The Vicarage, Vicarage Lane, Wookey, Wells, Somerset BA5 1JT* Tel (01749) 677244 Fax as telephone

PLUCK, Richard. b 60. Southn Univ BTh90. Aston Tr Scheme 84 Sarum & Wells Th Coll 86. **d** 90 **p** 91. C Harpenden St Nic *St Alb* 90-94; CF from 94. *MOD Chaplains (Army), Trenchard Lines, Upavon, Pewsey, Wilts SN9 6BE* Tel (01980) 615804 Fax 615800

PLUMB, Gordon Alan. b 42. Leeds Univ BA. Sarum & Wells Th Coll. **d** 82 **p** 83. C Biggleswade *St Alb* 82-86; TV Grantham *Linc* 86-95; P-in-c Saxby All Saints from 95; P-in-c Bonby from 95; P-in-c Horkstow from 95; P-in-c S Ferriby from 95; P-in-c Worlaby from 95. *The Rectory, 1 Church Street, Saxby-All-Saints, Brigg, S Humberside DN20 0QE* Tel (01652) 618747

PLUMLEY, Prof Jack Martin. b 10. St Jo Coll Dur BA32 MLitt39 K Coll Cam MA50. **d** 33 **p** 34. C Homerton St Luke *Lon* 33-35; C Enfield St Andr 35-37; C Kingsway H Trin and St Jo Drury Lane 37-40; C Holborn St Geo w H Trin 40-41; V Hoxton Ch Ch 41-45; V Tottenham St Paul 45-47; R Milton *Ely* 47-57; Select Preacher Cam Univ 55 and 59; Prof Egyptology Cam Univ 57-77; Fell Selw Coll Cam from 57; Perm to Offic *Ely* 67-80 and from 80; P-in-c Longstowe 80; Chapl Pemb Coll Cam 81-82; Acting Dean 81-82; rtd 94. *13 Lyndewode Road, Cambridge CB1 2HL* Tel (01223) 350328

PLUMLEY, Paul Jonathan. b 42. St Jo Coll Nottm 71. **d** 74 **p** 75. C Mile Cross *Nor* 74-77; P-in-c Wickham Skeith *St E* 77-79; P-in-c Stoke Ash, Thwaite and Wetheringsett 77-79; Assoc Min Woodbridge St Jo 80-81; Chapl RAF 81-86; Perm to Offic *Roch* 86-95; R Hever, Four Elms and Mark Beech from 95. *The Rectory, Hever, Edenbridge, Kent TN8 7LH* Tel (01732) 862249 Fax as telephone

PLUMMER, Mrs Deborah Ann. b 49. St Hugh's Coll Ox BA71 MA75. St Alb Minl Tr Scheme 82. **dss** 85 **d** 87 **p** 94. Ickenham *Lon* 85-87; Par Dn 87-88; C Northolt St Mary 88-92; Chapl Lee Abbey 92-95; Lic to Offic *Ex* 92-95; P-in-c Kintbury w Avington *Ox* from 95. *The Vicarage, 3 Elizabeth Gardens, Kintbury, Newbury, Berks RG17 9TB* Tel (01488) 658243

PLUMMER, Frances. b 36. **dss** 82 **d** 87 **p** 94. NSM Salfords *S'wark* from 87. *50 Park View Road, Salfords, Redhill RH6 7HU* Tel (01293) 785852

PLUMMER, Miss June Alice. b 29. Bris Univ BA50 CertEd51. Sarum & Wells Th Coll 89. **d** 89 **p** 94. NSM Hanham *Bris* 89-97; rtd 97. *11 Glenwood Drive, Oldland Common, Bristol BS15 6RZ* Tel 0117-949 8667

PLUMPTON, Paul. b 50. Keble Coll Ox BA72 MA76. St Steph Ho Ox 72. **d** 74 **p** 75. C Tonge Moor *Man* 74-76; C Atherton 76-79; V Oldham St Jas from 79. *The Vicarage, Yates Street, Oldham OL1 4AR* Tel 0161-633 4441

PLUMPTRE, John Basil. b 25. Pemb Coll Cam BA49 MA54 CertEd52. Launde Abbey 75. **d** 75 **p** 76. C Leic St Pet *Leic* 75-80; C Stanford on Soar *S'well* 81-90; C Rempstone 81-90; C Costock 81-90; C E Leake 81-90; rtd 91; Perm to Offic *Leic* from 92. *14 Outwoods Road, Loughborough, Leics LE11 3LT* Tel (01509) 215452

PLUNKETT, Michael Edward. b 38. Leeds Univ BSc61. Ely Th Coll 61. **d** 63 **p** 64. C Kirkby *Liv* 63-68; Lect Stockton-on-Tees 68-72; Lic to Offic *Dur* 72-73; TV Stockton 73-75; V Cantril Farm *Liv* 75-81; Soc Resp Officer 81-89; V Melling 81-91; TR Speke St Aid from 91. *The Rectory, Parade Crescent, Speke, Liverpool L24 2SH* Tel 0151-486 1521

PLUNKETT, Pelham Stanley. b 12. TCD BA36 MA39. **d** 59 **p** 59. C Tonbridge SS Pet and Paul *Roch* 59-62; C Hildenborough 62-63; V 63-68; Lect Poole *Sarum* 68-69; V Mile Cross *Nor* 69-81; rtd 81; Hon C Hordle *Win* 81-86; Hon C Eastbourne All SS *Chich* from 86. *Flat 3, 11 Grassington Road, Eastbourne, E Sussex BN20 7BJ* Tel (01323) 648193

PLUNKETT, Peter William. b 30. Oak Hill Th Coll. **d** 61 **p** 62. C Fazakerley Em *Liv* 61-64; C St Helens St Mark 64-68; V Kirkdale St Paul N Shore 68-79; P-in-c Bootle St Mary w St Jo 77-79; V Bootle St Mary w St Paul 79-81; V Goose Green 81-89;

V W Derby St Jas from 89. *St James's Vicarage, Mill Lane, Liverpool L12 7LQ* Tel 0151-256 8693

PLYMOUTH, Archdeacon of. *See* ELLIS, The Ven Robin Gareth

PLYMOUTH, Suffragan Bishop of. *See* GARTON, The Rt Revd John Henry

PNEMATICATOS, Nicholas Peter Anthony. b 59. N Lon Univ BA92 Lon Univ MA93. Ripon Coll Cuddesdon DipMin95. **d** 95 **p** 96. C Yeovil St Mich *B & W* from 95; Chapl Yeovil Coll 95-96. *220 Goldcroft, Yeovil, Somerset BA21 4DA* Tel (01935) 25621

POARCH, Canon John Chilton. b 30. Bris Univ BA54. Ridley Hall Cam 54. **d** 56 **p** 57. C Swindon Ch Ch *Bris* 56-59; C Corsham 59-61; Seychelles 61-63; V Brislington St Cuth *Bris* 63-69; Adn Seychelles 69-72; V Warmley *Bris* 72-86; R Syston 72-86; RD Bitton 79-85; P-in-c Bitton 80-86; Hon Can Bris Cathl 82-95; P-in-c Langley Fitzurse 86-94; Dioc Dir of Ords 86-94; Dir Ord Tr 94-95; P-in-c Draycot Cerne 87-94; rtd 95; Perm to Offic *Bris* from 95. *86 Stanshaws Close, Bradley Stoke, Bristol BS12 9AF* Tel (01454) 619053

POCOCK, Frank Lovell. b 08. OBE59. Em Coll Cam BA32 MA36. Ridley Hall Cam 33. **d** 33 **p** 34. Chapl Newton Coll Newton Abbot 34-36; Chapl RN 36-63; V Martin *Sarum* 63-67; R Ringwould w Oxney *Cant* 67-77; P-in-c Kingsdown 74-77; rtd 77; Perm to Offic *Cant* from 78. *60 Liverpool Road, Walmer, Deal, Kent CT14 7LG* Tel (01304) 372314

POCOCK, Mrs Gillian Margaret. b 35. Nottm Univ BA57. Cranmer Hall Dur 82. **dss** 83 **d** 87 **p** 94. Bearpark *Dur* 83-88; Hon Par Dn 87-88; Par Dn S Hetton w Haswell 88; Chapl St Aid Coll Dur 89-92; Par Dn Esh *Dur* 90-92; P-in-c from 92. *11 Cooke's Wood, Broompark, Durham DH7 7RL* Tel 0191-386 1140 or 386 5011

POCOCK, Lynn Elizabeth. b 48. Coll of Wooster Ohio BA69 CertEd71 Birm Univ DipTh75. Qu Coll Birm 73. **dss** 82 **d** 87 **p** 94. Gleadless *Sheff* 82-85; Thorpe Hesley 85-87; Par Dn 87-92; NSM Ribbesford w Bewdley and Dowles *Worc* from 92. *The Rectory, 57 Park Lane, Bewdley, Worcs DY12 2HA* Tel (01299) 402275

POCOCK, Canon Nigel John. b 47. Lon Univ BSc68 Birm Univ MA83. Lambeth STh78 Oak Hill Th Coll 69. **d** 72 **p** 73. C Tunbridge Wells St Jas *Roch* 72-75; C Heatherlands St Jo *Sarum* 75-78; V Leic St Chris *Leic* 78-83; R Camborne *Truro* from 83; RD Carnmarth N 91-96; Hon Can Truro Cathl from 92. *The Rectory, Rectory Gardens, Camborne, Cornwall TR14 7DN* Tel (01209) 613020

PODGER, Richard Philip Champeney. b 38. K Coll Cam BA61 MA66. Cuddesdon Coll 62. **d** 64 **p** 65. C Doncaster St Geo *Sheff* 64-68; C Orpington All SS *Roch* 68-74; W Germany 76-88; Chapl Kassel *Eur* 83-88; TV Whitstable *Cant* 88-94; Perm to Offic from 95. *3 Alcroft Grange, Tyler Hill, Canterbury, Kent CT2 9NN* Tel (01227) 464038

POGMORE, Edward Clement. b 52. Sarum & Wells Th Coll 76. **d** 79 **p** 80. C Calne and Blackland *Sarum* 79-82; TV Oakdale 82-89; Min Creekmoor LEP 82-89; Chapl Geo Eliot Hosp Nuneaton 89-94; Chapl Nuneaton Hosps 89-94; Chapl Geo Eliot Hosp NHS Trust Nuneaton from 94; Perm to Offic *Leic* from 91. *George Eliot Hospital, College Street, Nuneaton, Warks CV10 7DJ* Tel (01203) 865281 or 351351

POIL, Canon Ronald Wickens (Ron). b 30. AKC56. **d** 57 **p** 58. C Willesborough *Cant* 57-60; Chapl RAF 60-76; P-in-c Edith Weston w Normanton *Pet* 65-67; V Southbourne *Chich* 76-80; P-in-c W Thorney 76-80; RD Westbourne 78-91; V Southbourne w W Thorney 80-96; Can and Preb Chich Cathl 90-96; rtd 96. *33 Mays Lane, Stubbington, Fareham, Hants PO14 2EW*

POINTS, John David. b 43. Qu Coll Birm 78. **d** 80 **p** 81. C Wednesbury St Paul Wood Green *Lich* 80-85; V from 93; V Sedgley St Mary 85-93. *The Vicarage, Wood Green Road, Wednesbury, W Midlands WS10 9QT* Tel 0121-556 0687

POLASHEK, Miss Stella Christine. b 44. Leic Poly MA85. EMMTC 92. **d** 95 **p** 96. NSM The Appleby Gp *Leic* from 95. *7 Hillside, Appleby Magna, Swadlincote, Derbyshire DE12 7AB* Tel (01530) 272707

POLE, David John. b 46. Bath Academy of Art BA72. Trin Coll Bris 84. **d** 86 **p** 87. C Bris St Mary Redcliffe w Temple etc *Bris* 86-90; V Alveston from 90. *The Vicarage, Gloucester Road, Alveston, Bristol BS12 2QT* Tel (01454) 414810 E-mail 100574.2504@compuserve.com

POLE, Francis John Michael. b 42. FRSA MBIM CQSW AMInstTA. St Jo Sem Wonersh 62. **d** 67 **p** 68. In RC Ch 67-75; NSM Walthamstow St Pet *Chelmsf* 75; NSM Penge Lane H Trin *Roch* 76-77; NSM Shirley St Jo *Cant* 77-79; Assoc Chapl The Hague *Eur* 79-83; V Norbury St Steph and Thornton Heath *Cant* 83-84; V Norbury St Steph and Thornton Heath *S'wark* from 85. *St Stephen's Vicarage, Warwick Road, Thornton Heath, Surrey CR7 7NH* Tel 0181-684 3820 Fax 683 0201

POLHILL, Arthur John Henry. b 20. Sarum Th Coll 65. **d** 67 **p** 68. C Tormohun *Ex* 67-71; V Tipton w Venn Ottery 71-87; rtd 87. *8 Case Gardens, Seaton, Devon EX12 2AP* Tel (01297) 625823

POLHILL, Mrs Christine. b 46. Nottm Coll of Educn CertEd67. St Alb Minl Tr Scheme 81. **dss** 84 **d** 87 **p** 94. St Alb St Mary Marshalswick *St Alb* 84-87; Hon Par Dn 87-94; NSM Cottered w Broadfield and Throcking 94-96; P-in-c from 96. *The Rectory, Warren Lane, Cottered, Buntingford, Herts SG9 9QA* Tel (01763) 281218

POLITT, Robert William. b 47. ARCM LGSM68. Oak Hill Th Coll 73. **d** 76 **p** 77. C Bexleyheath St Pet *Roch* 76-82; TV Southgate *Chich* 82-90; Chapl N Foreland Lodge Sch Basingstoke from 90. *Cottage, North Foreland Lodge School, Sherfield-on-Loddon, Basingstoke, Hants RG27 0HU* Tel (01256) 880051

POLKINGHORNE, Dr John Charlton. b 30. FRS74 Trin Coll Cam BA52 PhD55 MA56 ScD74. Westcott Ho Cam 79. **d** 81 **p** 82. NSM Chesterton St Andr *Ely* 81-82; C Bedminster St Mich *Bris* 82-84; V Blean *Cant* 84-86; Dean Trin Hall Cam 86-89; Pres Qu Coll Cam 89-96; Can Th Liv Cathl *Liv* from 94; rtd 95; Six Preacher Cant Cathl *Cant* from 96. *74 Hurst Park Avenue, Cambridge CB4 2AF* Tel (01223) 360743

POLL, Martin George. b 61. Kent Univ BA83. Ripon Coll Cuddesdon 84. **d** 87 **p** 88. C Mill Hill Jo Keble Ch *Lon* 87-90; Chapl RN from 90. *Royal Naval Chaplaincy Service, Room 203, Victory Building, HM Naval Base, Portsmouth PO1 3LS* Tel (01705) 727903 Fax 727112

POLLAK, Canon Peter Henry. b 18. Worc Ord Coll 67. **d** 69 **p** 70. C Claines St Jo *Worc* 69-73; R Grimley w Holt 73-88; RD Martley and Worc W 84-88; Hon Can Worc Cathl 85-88; rtd 88. *2 Tweenways, Main Road, Kempsey, Worcester WR5 3JY* Tel (01905) 820351

POLLARD, Mrs Christine Beryl. b 45. DCR DNM. N Ord Course 86. **d** 89 **p** 94. Par Dn Ingrow cum Hainworth *Bradf* 89-94; C Nuneaton St Nic *Cov* from 94. *113 St Nicolas Park Drive, Nuneaton, Warks CV11 6EF* Tel (01203) 375830

POLLARD, Canon Clifford Francis. b 20. AKC49. **d** 50 **p** 51. C Leominster *Heref* 50-53; C Luton St Mary *St Alb* 53-56; V Stopsley 56-60; Chapl Toc H (Kent and Sussex) 60-64; R Mersham *Cant* 64-68; Asst Dir of Educn 68-69; Dir of Educn 69-87; Hon Can Cant Cathl 72-87; rtd 87. *6 Lady Wootton's Green, Canterbury, Kent CT1 1NG* Tel (01227) 761674

POLLARD, David. b 55. LSE BSc77. Trin Coll Bris DipHE80. **d** 80 **p** 81. Canada 81-84; C-in-c Hillsfield and Monkspath LEP *Birm* 85-89; BCMS 89-93; Crosslinks 93-95; Spain 89-94; V Doncaster St Jas *Sheff* from 95. *The Vicarage, 54 Littlemoor Lane, Doncaster, S Yorkshire DN4 0LB* Tel (01302) 365544

POLLARD, David John Athey. b 44. ACP74 Culham Coll Ox CertEd69. St Jo Coll Nottm LTh88. **d** 88 **p** 89. C Illogan *Truro* 88-91; R Roche and Withiel 91-95; TV Maidstone St Martin *Cant* from 95; C Parkwood CD from 95. *Church House, Wallis Avenue, Maidstone, Kent ME15 9JJ* Tel (01622) 764170

POLLARD, David Stanley. b 49. Lon Univ BD80 AKC80 Bradf Univ MA. **d** 80 **p** 81. CGA 78-89; C Manningham St Mary and Bradf St Mich *Bradf* 80-83; P-in-c 83-84; TV Manningham 84-85; C 86-87; Lic to Offic 85-89; P-in-c Sidlesham *Chich* 89-94; Chapl Chich Coll of Tech 90-94; R Petworth *Chich* from 94; RD Petworth from 95. *The Rectory, Petworth, W Sussex GU28 0DB* Tel (01798) 342505 Fax as telephone

POLLARD, Eric John. b 43. Chich Th Coll 83. **d** 85 **p** 86. C Brighton St Matthias *Chich* 85-90; C E Grinstead St Swithun 90-96; C Hove from 96. *83 Davigdor Road, Hove, E Sussex BN3 1RA* Tel (01273) 733971

POLLARD, James Adrian Hunter. b 48. St Jo Coll Nottm BTh78. **d** 78 **p** 79. C Much Woolton *Liv* 78-81; CMS 81-84; V Toxteth Park Ch Ch *Liv* 85-90; CF from 90; Perm to Offic *S'wark* 92-94. *MOD Chaplains (Army), Trenchard Lines, Upavon, Pewsey, Wilts SN9 6BE* Tel (01980) 615804 Fax 615800

POLLARD, John Edward Ralph. b 40. ALCD68. **d** 67 **p** 68. C Ollerton *S'well* 67-71; C Walton H Trin *Ox* 71-74; P-in-c Cuddington w Dinton 74-77; V Haddenham 74-77; V Kingsey 75-77; V Haddenham w Cuddington and Kingsey 77-85; RD Aylesbury 80-85; V Haddenham w Cuddington, Kingsey etc 85-87; V Furze Platt 87-96; rtd 97. *St Andrews, 116 Catalina Drive, Poole, Dorset BH15 1TQ*

POLLARD, Noel Stewart. b 28. Sydney Univ BA51 BD56 Ch Ch Ox BA58 MA63. **d** 53 **p** 53. Australia 53-56 and 61-72; Chapl Ch Ch Ox 57-58; C Cambridge St Sepulchre *Ely* 58-61; Lect St Jo Coll Nottm 72-88; Lect Nottm Univ 72-88; Vice-Prin Ridley Hall Cam 88-93; rtd 93. *193 Huntingdon Road, Cambridge CB3 0DL* Tel (01223) 276328

POLLARD, Mrs Patricia Julie. b 46. Cant Sch of Min 94. **d** 96. NSM Eastling w Ospringe and Stalisfield w Otterden *Cant* from 96. *5 Priory Row, Faversham, Kent ME13 7EG* Tel (01795) 535407

POLLARD, Roger Frederick. b 32. Sheff Univ BSc52 K Coll Lon PGCE55 Lanc Univ MA78. Linc Th Coll 56. **d** 58 **p** 59. C Catford St Laur *S'wark* 58-63; Ghana 63-66; C Fulford *York* 66-67; C Camberwell St Geo *S'wark* 67; Asst Master Roch Valley Sch Milnrow 68-69; S Craven Sch Cross Hills 69-91; rtd 91; Perm to Offic *Bradf* 69-93; Perm to Offic *B & W* from 93. *Little Garth, Rectory Lane, Dowlish Wake, Ilminster, Somerset TA19 0NX* Tel (01460) 52594

POLLARD, Vaughan. b 59. Aston Tr Scheme 90 Trin Coll Bris DipHE92. **d** 92 **p** 93. C Nailsea H Trin *B & W* 92-95; C Acomb St Steph *York* from 95. *36 Fellbrook Avenue, Acomb, York YO25 5PS* Tel (01904) 793240

POLLINGER, Mrs Judith. b 41. Ex Univ TCert78 BEd79. SW Minl Tr Course 92. **d** 95 **p** 96. NSM St Endellion w Port

Isaac and St Kew *Truro* from 95. *Hillows House, St Teath, Bodmin, Cornwall PL30 3JJ* Tel (01840) 212604

POLLIT, Preb Michael. b 30. Worc Coll Ox BA54 MA58. Wells Th Coll 54. **d** 56 **p** 57. C Cannock *Lich* 56-59; C Codsall 59-62; V W Bromwich St Pet 62-67; R Norton in the Moors 67-76; RD Leek 72-76; V Shrewsbury St Chad 76-87; V Shrewsbury St Chad w St Mary 87-95; Preb Lich Cathl 81-95; P-in-c Shrewsbury St Alkmund 91-95; rtd 95; Perm to Offic *Heref* from 96. *Pentreheyling House, Churchstoke, Montgomery SY15 6HU* Tel (01588) 620273

POLLIT, Ruth Mary. *See* LILLINGTON, Mrs Ruth Mary

POLLITT, Graham Anthony. b 48. BA79. Oak Hill Th Coll 76. **d** 79 **p** 80. C Rusholme H Trin *Man* 79-82; TV Southgate *Chich* 82-83; C Burgess Hill St Andr 83-86; Chapl St Martin's Coll of Educn *Blackb* 86-90; Chapl Cheltenham and Glouc Coll of HE from 90. *3 The Lanes, Leckhampton, Cheltenham, Glos GL53 0PU* Tel (01242) 260291

POLLOCK, Christopher John. b 62. TCD BTh89. CITC 86. **d** 89 **p** 90. C Agherton *Conn* 89-91; C Ballymoney w Finvoy and Rasharkin 91-93; I Derryvolgie from 93. *53 Kennedy Drive, Belsize Road, Lisburn, Co Antrim BT27 4JA* Tel (01846) 663707

POLLOCK, Duncan James Morrison. b 54. QGM. Linc Th Coll BCombStuds. **d** 83 **p** 84. C Folkestone St Mary and St Eanswythe *Cant* 83-85; CF from 85. *MOD Chaplains (Army), Trenchard Lines, Upavon, Pewsey, Wilts SN9 6BE* Tel (01980) 615804 Fax 615800

POLLOCK, Hugh Gillespie. b 36. Oak Hill Th Coll 61. **d** 64 **p** 65. C Maidstone St Luke *Cant* 64-68; C Washfield *Ex* 68-71; C Washfield, Stoodleigh, Withleigh etc 71-73; Chapl Lee Abbey 73-76; V Dersingham *Nor* 76-80; P-in-c Anmer 79-80; P-in-c Shernbourne 79-80; R Dersingham w Anmer and Shernborne 80-89; RD Heacham and Rising 87-89; C Barnstaple *Ex* 89-94; P-in-c Atherington and High Bickington 94-96; P-in-c Burrington 94-96; TV Newton Tracey, Horwood, Alverdiscott etc from 96. *The Rectory, High Bickington, Umberleigh, Devon EX37 9BB* Tel (01769) 60283

POLLOCK, James Colin Graeme. b 53. St Chad's Coll Dur BA76. Ripon Coll Cuddesdon 77. **d** 78 **p** 79. C Hartlepool St Oswald *Dur* 78-81; C Hartlepool St Aid 81-84; V Dawdon from 84. *The Vicarage, Melbury Street, Seaham, Co Durham SR7 7NF* Tel 0191-581 2317

POLLOCK, Jennifer Susan. b 51. Liv Univ BA72 PGCE73. Glouc Sch of Min 89. **d** 92 **p** 94. NSM Leominster *Heref* 92-97; P-in-c Eardisley w Bollingham, Willersley, Brilley etc from 97. *Church House, Church Road, Eardisley, Hereford HR3 6NN* Tel (01544) 327440

POLLOCK, John Charles. b 23. Trin Coll Cam BA46 MA48. Ridley Hall Cam 49. **d** 51 **p** 52. C Portman Square St Paul *Lon* 51-53; Ed The Churchman 53-58; R Horsington *B & W* 53-58; Perm to Offic *Ex* from 61; rtd 88. *Rose Ash House, South Molton, Devon EX36 4RB* Tel (01769) 550403

POLLOCK, Neil Thomas. b 38. Lon Univ DipTh68. Bernard Gilpin Soc Dur 63 Lich Th Coll 64. **d** 67 **p** 68. C Lt Stanmore St Lawr *Lon* 67-72; C-in-c Uxbridge St Marg 72-81; R Norwood St Mary 81-86; TR Ridgeway *Sarum* 86-95; P-in-c Chickerell w Fleet from 95. *The Rectory, East Street, Chickerell, Weymouth, Dorset DT3 4DS* Tel (01305) 784915

POLOMSKI, Elias Robert Michael. b 42. **d** 85 **p** 86. In RC Ch 85-90; C Headington Quarry *Ox* 91-94; Chapl St Alb Abbey *St Alb* 94-97; Chapl St Alb Sch 94-97; P-in-c Streatley w Moulsford *Ox* from 97. *The Vicarage, Streatley, Reading RG8 9HX* Tel (01491) 872191

POMEROY, Michael James. b 26. Sarum Th Coll 64. **d** 66 **p** 67. C Broadstone *Sarum* 66-69; Co Chapl ACF 69-89; Hon CF from 89; P-in-c Ibberton w Belchalwell and Woolland *Sarum* 69-72; R 72-73; R Okeford Fitzpaine, Ibberton, Belchalwell etc 73-90; rtd 90. *Brandon, Wavering Lane, Gillingham, Dorset SP8 4NR* Tel (01747) 822498

POMERY, David John. b 45. SS Mark & Jo Coll Chelsea CertEd67. Chich Th Coll 75. **d** 77 **p** 78. C Coseley Ch Ch *Lich* 77-79; C Stocksbridge *Sheff* 79-81; V Bentley 81-87; Radlett Prep Sch from 87. *Radlett Preparatory School, Kendall Hall, Radlett, Herts WD7 9HW* Tel (01923) 856812

POMFRET, Albert. b 23. Univ of Wales (Cardiff) BSc57 Lon Univ MA69. Oak Hill NSM Course 72. **d** 75 **p** 76. NSM Dartford Ch Ch *Roch* 75-80; Perm to Offic 80-92; Perm to Offic *Ex* from 92. *9 St Margaret's Court, Exe Street, Topsham, Exeter EX3 0JA* Tel (01392) 873404

POND, Geraldine Phyllis. b 53. SRN74. St Jo Coll Nottm MA97. **d** 97. C Ancaster Wilsford Gp *Linc* from 97. *Holy Cross House, Old Lincoln Road, Caythorpe, Grantham, Lincs NG32 3DF* Tel (01400) 273350

POND, Nigel Peter Hamilton. b 40. AKC65. **d** 66 **p** 67. C E Dereham w Hoe *Nor* 66-69; C Chapl RN 69-85; TR Woughton *Ox* 85-93; Chapl Milton Keynes Gen Hosp 85-94; Chapl Milton Keynes Gen NHS Trust from 94; RD Milton Keynes *Ox* 90-93; R Olney w Emberton 93-97; R Olney from 97. *Olney Rectory, 9 Orchard Rise, Olney, Bucks MK46 5HB* Tel (01234) 713308

✠**PONNIAH, The Rt Revd Jacob Samuel.** b 22. Bihar Univ MA59. Western Th Sem Michigan MTh64 Madras Chr Coll BA48 United Th Coll Bangalore 48. **d** 52 **p** 53 **c** 78. India 53-90 and from 91; Bp Vellore 78-87; Dioc Missr *Linc* 90-91; P-in-c Fulletby w Greetham and Ashby Puerorum 90-91; P-in-c Hameringham w Scrafield and Winceby 90-91; P-in-c High Toynton 90-91; P-in-c Mareham on the Hill 90-91; P-in-c Belchford 90-91; Miss Partner CMS from 91. *Address temp unknown*

PONSONBY, Simon Charles Reuben. b 66. MLitt96. Trin Coll Bris BA94. **d** 95 **p** 96. C Thorpe Edge *Bradf* from 95. *146 Rowantree Drive, Bradford, W Yorkshire BD10 8DH* Tel (01274) 615330

PONT, Gordon John Harper. b 35. Glas Univ BSc56 BD65. Edin Th Coll 56. **d** 59 **p** 60. C Dunfermline *St And* 59-62; C Motherwell *Glas* 62-65; R Largs 65-68; Dioc Supernumerary *Bre* 68-71; Chapl Dundee Univ 68-73; R Dundee St Luke 71-74; NSM Dundee St Paul from 74; Hon Chapl St Paul's Cathl Dundee from 74; Dioc Sec from 96. *5 Westpark Road, Dundee DD2 1NU* Tel (01382) 669883

PONTEFRACT, Archdeacon of. *See* ROBINSON, The Ven Anthony William

PONTEFRACT, Suffragan Bishop of. *See* FINNEY, The Rt Revd John Thornley

PONTER, Dr John Arthur. b 37. Univ of Wales (Abth) BA61 Linacre Coll Ox BA63 MA68 UEA PhD81. Wycliffe Hall Ox 61. **d** 63 **p** 64. C Gidea Park *Chelmsf* 63-67; C-in-c Colchester St Anne CD 67-69; V Colchester St Anne 69-72; Chapl UEA *Nor* 72-78; Chapl Chelmsf Cathl *Chelmsf* 78-79; Chapl Chelmsf Cathl Cen 78-84; V Moulsham St Jo 79-85; Lic to Offic *Man* 85-92; Dir Man Chr Inst and Chr Leadership Course 85-92; Educn Officer N Federation for Tr in Min 85-92; TR Stantonbury and Willen *Ox* from 92. *The Rectory, The Green, Great Linford, Milton Keynes MK14 5BD* Tel (01908) 605892

PONTIN, Colin Henry. b 37. Trin Coll Bris. **d** 83 **p** 84. C Downend *Bris* 83-86; C Riverside *Ox* 86-88; V Eton w Eton Wick and Boveney 88-90; TV Riverside 91-95; V Churt *Guildf* from 95. *The Vicarage, Old Kiln Lane, Churt, Farnham, Surrey GU10 2HX* Tel (01428) 713368

POOBALAN, Isaac Munuswamy. b 62. Chr Med Coll RN84 New Coll Edin BD94. Edin Th Coll 91. **d** 94 **p** 95. C Edin St Pet *Edin* from 94. *10 Hope Park Crescent, Edinburgh EH8 9NA* Tel 0131-668 1541

POODHUN, Canon Lambert David. b 30. Natal Univ BA53. Edin Th Coll 54. **d** 56 **p** 57. S Africa 56-76; Adn Durban 75-76; C Upton cum Chalvey *Ox* 77-80; Chapl Kingston Hosp Surrey 80-81; Chapl Tooting Bec Hosp Lon 81-84; Chapl Hurstwood Park Hosp Haywards Heath from 84; Chapl St Fran Hosp Haywards Heath 84-94; Chapl Mid Sussex NHS Trust from 94; Can and Preb Chich Cathl *Chich* from 93; rtd 95. *8 Nursery Close, Haywards Heath, W Sussex RH16 1HP, or The Princess Royal Hospital, Lewes Road, Haywards Heath, W Sussex RH16 4EX* Tel (01444) 452571 or 441881

POOLE, Clifford George. b 36. Keble Coll Ox BA61 MA65. S'wark Ord Course 83. **d** 86 **p** 87. C W Dulwich All SS and Em *S'wark* 86-90; Chapl Luxembourg *Eur* from 90. *89 rue de Mühlenbach, L-2168 Luxembourg* Tel Luxembourg (352) 439593 Fax as telephone

POOLE, Denis Tom. b 19. St Jo Coll Dur 39. St Aid Birkenhead 41. **d** 43 **p** 44. C Toxteth Park St Silas *Liv* 43-45; C Kirkdale St Lawr 45-48; Chapl Mariners' Ch Glouc 48-51; Chapl Glouc R Infirmary 48-51; V Lambeth St Andr w St Thos *S'wark* 51-54; V New Ferry *Ches* 54-63; V Biddulph *Lich* 64-85; Chapl Biddulph Grange Hosp Staffs 64-85; rtd 85; Perm to Offic *Win* from 85. *14 Curlew Drive, Hythe, Southampton SO45 3GA* Tel (01703) 846497

POOLE, Mrs Denise June. b 49. Leic Univ BSc70 Bradf and Ilkley Coll DipAE85. N Ord Course 90. **d** 93 **p** 94. C Horton *Bradf* 93-97; C Bradf St Oswald Chapel Green 93-97; Chapl Bradf Hosps NHS Trust from 97. *4 Crestville Close, Clayton, Bradford, W Yorkshire BD14 6DZ* Tel (01274) 816547

POOLE, Edward John. b 53. Hull Univ BA81. St Steph Ho Ox 81. **d** 83 **p** 84. C Stevenage St Andr and St Geo *St Alb* 83-86; Madagascar 86-88; V Weston *St Alb* 88-96; P-in-c Ardeley 88-96; P-in-c Cottered w Broadfield and Throcking 94-96; Chapl Bucharest w Sofia *Eur* from 96. *Church of the Resurrection, Str Xenopol 2, Bucharest, Romania* Tel Bucharest (1) 615-1392 or 210-2937 Fax 111634

POOLE, Frederick Harold. b 14. Clifton Th Coll 54. **d** 56 **p** 56. C Bucknall and Bagnall *Lich* 56-60; R Chorlton on Medlock St Steph *Man* 60-68; rtd 79. *43 Albion Street, Wallasey, Merseyside L45 9LE* Tel 0151-638 8952

POOLE, Helen Margaret. b 39. **d** 94 **p** 95. NSM Ludgvan *Truro* from 94. *Underhill Farmhouse, St Levan, Penzance, Cornwall TR19 6JS* Tel (01736) 810842

POOLE, Miss Joan Wendy. b 37. Sarum Dioc Teacher Tr Coll CertEd57 Dalton Ho Bris DipTh66 Trin Coll Bris 86. **d** 87 **p** 94. Par Dn Longfleet *Sarum* 87-89; Par Dn Hamworthy 89-94; C 94-97; rtd 97. *35 Borley Road, Creekmoor, Poole, Dorset BH17 7DT*

POOLE, John. b 19. Peterho Cam MA44. St Alb Minl Tr Scheme 77. **d** 80 **p** 81. NSM Bedford St Andr *St Alb* 80-87; NSM Elstow 87-92; Perm to Offic from 92. *35 Falcon Avenue, Bedford MK41 7DY* Tel (01234) 262208

POOLE, John Denys Barlow. b 33. Qu Coll Cam BA57 MA61. Cuddesdon Coll 57. **d** 59 **p** 60. CF 57-72; C Leagrave *St Alb*

59-62; C Raynes Park St Sav *S'wark* 62-65; C Apsley End *St Alb* 65-72; R W Wickham St Jo *Cant* 73-84; V W Wickham St Jo *S'wark* from 85. *The Rectory, 30 Coney Hill Road, West Wickham, Kent BR4 9BX* Tel 0181-462 4001

POOLE, Martin Bryce. b 59. Reading Univ BSc80 Nottm Univ DipTh82 DipAct85. St Jo Coll Nottm DPS84. **d** 87 **p** 88. NSM Tulse Hill H Trin and St Matthias *S'wark* from 87. *117 Casewick Road, London SE27 0UP* Tel 0181-761 3190

POOLE, Martin Ronald. b 59. Aston Univ BSc81 Leeds Univ BA86. Coll of Resurr Mirfield 84. **d** 87 **p** 88. C Sheff St Cath Richmond Road *Sheff* 87-90; C W Hampstead St Jas *Lon* 90-94; V Colindale St Matthias from 94. *St Matthias' Vicarage, Rushgrove Avenue, London NW9 6QY* Tel 0181-205 8783

POOLE, Peter William. b 35. St Pet Hall Ox BA59 MA63. Wells Th Coll 59. **d** 61 **p** 62. C Cheriton Street *Cant* 61-64; C Birchington w Acol 64-67; V Newington 67-73; P-in-c Lower Halstow 72-73; V Bearsted 73-76; V Lane End w Cadmore End *Ox* 84-89; R Chalfont St Giles from 89. *The Rectory, 2 Deanway, Chalfont St Giles, Bucks HP8 4JH* Tel (01494) 872097

POOLE, Roy John. b 26. Lon Univ BD54. St Jo Coll Lon LTh54. **d** 54 **p** 55. C Benwell St Aid *Newc* 54-57; Australia 57-61; R Bradford cum Beswick *Man* 61-66; Area Sec Chr Aid Dept BCC 66-68; Regional Supervisor (S and E England) Chr Aid 68-74; Australia from 74; rtd 91. *3/362 Mill Point Road, Perth, W Australia 6151*

POOLE, Stanley Burke-Roche. b 09. K Coll Lon BA31 MA34. Qu Coll Birm 36. **d** 38 **p** 39. C Edgbaston St Germain *Birm* 38-39; Lect Qu Coll Birm 38-39; K Sch Cant 39-64; Asst Chapl 39-48 and 55-64; Lect St Aug Coll Cant 49-50 and 52-53; V Littlebourne *Cant* 48-70; rtd 74. *13 Chaucer Court, New Dover Road, Canterbury, Kent CT1 3AU* Tel (01227) 451586

POOLE, Stuart. b 33. CEng65 FIEE85 Loughb Coll of Educn DLC55 Lon Univ BScEng55 Man Univ MSc76. **d** 91 **p** 92. NSM Cheadle *Ches* from 91. *1 Dene House, Green Pastures, Stockport, Cheshire SK4 3RB* Tel 0161-432 6426

POOLEY, Peter Owen. b 32. Kelham Th Coll 54. **d** 58 **p** 59. C Paddington St Mary Magd *Lon* 58-62; R Rockland St Mary w Hellington *Nor* 62-67; Asst Master Thos Lethaby Sch 67-70; St Phil Gr Sch Edgbaston 70-74; Lordswood Gr Sch 74-80; Hon C Edgbaston St Geo *Birm* 77-80; R Elton *Ely* from 80; P-in-c Stibbington from 80; P-in-c Water Newton from 80. *The Rectory, Elton, Peterborough PE8 6SA* Tel (01832) 280222

POOLMAN, Alfred John. b 46. K Coll Lon BD69 AKC69 Sheff Univ DipPs83. St Aug Coll Cant 69. **d** 70 **p** 71. C Headingley *Ripon* 70-74; C Moor Allerton 75-78; C Monk Bretton *Wakef* 78-80; C Athersley 80; V Copley 80-90; Chapl Halifax Gen Hosp 80-90; R Llanfynydd *St As* from 90. *The Rectory, Llanfynydd, Wrexham LL11 5HH* Tel (01978) 762304

POOLTON, Martin Ronald. b 60. Kingston Poly BSc81 Salford Univ MSc83 Bp Grosseteste Coll PGCE85 FRGS81. Cuddesdon Coll DipMin95. **d** 97. C Penzance St Mary w St Paul *Truro* from 97. *2 Clarence Place, Penzance, Cornwall TR18 2QA* Tel (01736) 363229

POPE, Charles Guy. b 48. AKC70. St Aug Coll Cant 70. **d** 71 **p** 72. C Southgate Ch Ch *Lon* 71-74; C N St Pancras All Hallows 74-77; C Hampstead St Steph 74-77; V New Southgate St Paul 77-86; V Brookfield St Mary from 86; P-in-c Brookfield St Anne, Highgate Rise from 88; AD S Camden (Holborn and St Pancras) from 95. *St Mary's Vicarage, 85 Dartmouth Park Road, London NW5 1SL* Tel 0171-267 5941

POPE, Colin. b 51. Brasted Place Coll 74. Linc Th Coll 75. **d** 78 **p** 79. C W Derby Gd Shep *Liv* 78-81; C-in-c Westbrook St Phil CD 81-82; V Westbrook St Phil 82-87; V Orrell 87-96; Chapl Billinge Hosp Wigan 87-96; V Southport Em *Liv* from 96. *Emmanuel Vicarage, 12 Allerton Road, Southport, Merseyside PR9 9NJ* Tel (01704) 532743

POPE, Daniel Legh (Dan). b 23. Cuddesdon Coll 67. **d** 68 **p** 69. C Llanelli *St D* 68-71; V Radley *Ox* 71-88; Miss to Seamen 88-92; Cyprus 88-92; rtd 92; P-in-c Shipley *Chich* from 92. *Shipley Vicarage, Horsham, W Sussex RH13 8PH* Tel (01403) 741238

POPE, David Allan. b 20. Or Coll Ox BA45 MA72. Ely Th Coll 45. **d** 47 **p** 48. C Folkestone St Mary and St Eanswythe *Cant* 47-51; V Tovil 51-54; R E Horsley *Guildf* 54-63; R Ivychurch w Old Romney and Midley *Cant* 63-65; P-in-c Brenzett w Snargate and Snave 64-65; P-in-c Newchurch 64-65; P-in-c St Mary in the Marsh 64-65; P-in-c Burmarsh 64-65; R Broadstairs 65-73; P-in-c Berwick *Chich* 73-76; P-in-c Arlington 73-75; P-in-c Selmeston w Alciston 74-76; R Berwick w Selmeston and Alciston 76; P-in-c Rusper 76-79; R Colsterworth *Linc* 79-81; P-in-c Ingworth 81-85; P-in-c Alby w Thwaite *Nor* 81-85; P-in-c Erpingham w Calthorpe 81-85; P-in-c Aldborough w Thurgarton 83-85; rtd 85; Perm to Offic *Nor* from 85. *Brickfield Farm, Stibbard, Fakenham, Norfolk NR21 0EE*

POPE, Donald Keith. b 35. Sarum & Wells Th Coll 81. **d** 76 **p** 77. Hon C Caerleon *Mon* 76-82; C 82-83; V Pontypool 83-86; R Grosmont and Skenfrith and Llangattock etc from 86; RD Abergavenny from 93. *The Rectory, Grosmont, Abergavenny NP7 8LW* Tel (01981) 240587

POPE, Michael John. b 37. Sarum Th Coll 62. **d** 65 **p** 66. C Broseley w Benthall *Heref* 65-68; C Shrewsbury St Giles *Lich* 68-71; P-in-c Shrewsbury St Geo 71-75; V 75-79; V Gnosall from 79; RD Eccleshall from 92. *The Vicarage, Gnosall, Stafford ST20 0ER* Tel (01785) 822213

POPE, Michael Ronald. b 41. Bps' Coll Cheshunt 65. **d** 68 **p** 69. C Lyonsdown H Trin *St Alb* 68-72; C Seaford w Sutton *Chich* 72-76; R Hurstpierpoint 76-80. *Isle of Wight Cheshire Home, Popham Road, Shanklin, Isle of Wight PO37 6RG* Tel (01983) 862193

POPE, The Very Revd Robert William. b 16. OBE70. Dur Univ LTh40. St Aug Coll Cant 35. **d** 39 **p** 40. C Milton next Gravesend H Trin *Roch* 39-41; C Guildf St Nic *Guildf* 42-43; C Shere 43-44; Chapl RN 44-71; V Whitchurch w Tufton and Litchfield *Win* 71-77; Dean Gib *Eur* 77-82; rtd 82; Min Prov Third Order Soc of St Fran 85-87; Min Gen 87-90. *5 Wreath Green, Tatworth, Chard, Somerset TA20 2SN* Tel (01460) 220987

POPE, Rodney John. b 22. St D Coll Lamp BA48 BD67 MA71. **d** 49 **p** 50. C Bredbury St Mark *Ches* 49-52; C W Kirby St Bridget 52-53; V Egremont St Jo 53-62; V Eastham 62-72; V Gt w Lt Saling *Chelmsf* 72-87; rtd 87; Perm to Offic *B & W* from 89. *4 Abbey Close, Curry Rivel, Langport, Somerset TA10 0EL* Tel (01458) 250808

POPEJOY, Wilfred. b 28. St Jo Coll Nottm 88. **d** 88. Hon C Donisthorpe and Moira w Stretton-en-le-Field *Leic* from 88. *79 Donisthorpe Lane, Moira, Swadlincote, Derbyshire DE12 6BB* Tel (01283) 760476

POPP, Miss Julia Alice Gisela. b 45. Univ of BC BA71. St Jo Coll Nottm 78. **dss** 81 **d** 87 **p** 94. Woking St Mary *Guildf* 81-83; Hornsey Rise St Mary w St Steph *Lon* 83-87; Par Dn Hornsey Rise Whitehall Park Team 87-91; Par Dn Sutton St Nic *S'wark* 91-94; C from 94; Missr Sutton Town Cen from 91. *14 Strathearn Road, Sutton, Surrey SM1 2RS* Tel 0181-643 6712

POPPLE, The Ven Dennis. b 31. Vancouver Sch of Th LTh72 San Francisco Th Sem DMin89 St Aid Birkenhead 59. **d** 62 **p** 63. C Walkden Moor *Man* 62-65; Canada from 65; Admin Adn 87-96; rtd 96. *8580 General Currie Road, Suite 113, Richmond, British Columbia, Canada, V6Y 3V5*

POPPLEWELL, Andrew Frederick. b 53. St Jo Coll Dur BA75. Wycliffe Hall Ox 76. **d** 78 **p** 79. C Clifton *York* 78-81; C Lich St Chad *Lich* 82-84; V Laisterdyke *Bradf* from 84. *The Vicarage, Parsonage Road, Laisterdyke, Bradford, W Yorkshire BD4 8PY* Tel (01274) 664565

PORTEOUS, Canon Eric John. b 34. AKC58. **d** 59 **p** 60. C Wandsworth St Paul *S'wark* 59-62; C Leeds St Pet *Ripon* 62-66; V Wortley de Leeds 66-72; RD Armley 70-72; R Woolwich St Mary w H Trin *S'wark* 72-77; Sub-Dean Woolwich 74-77; P-in-c Woolwich St Mich 75-77; R Woolwich St Mary w St Mich 77-79; Chapl Whipps Cross Hosp Lon 79-96; Lic to Offic *Chelmsf* 79-86; Hon Can Chelmsf Cathl 86-96; rtd 96; Perm to Offic *Chelmsf* from 96. *128 Grove Hill, London E18 2HZ* Tel 0181-530 5660

PORTEOUS, Michael Stanley. b 35. S'wark Ord Course 70. **d** 73 **p** 74. C Barnes St Mich *S'wark* 73-76; Chapl Greycoat Hosp Sch 76-78; C Brighton Annunciation *Chich* 78-80; Chapl Ch Hosp Horsham 80-85; TV Moulsecoomb *Chich* 85-88; R W Blatchington from 88. *St Peter's Rectory, 23 Windmill Close, Hove, E Sussex BN3 7LJ* Tel (01273) 732459

PORTER, Anthony. b 52. Hertf Coll Ox BA74 MA78 Fitzw Ho Cam BA76 MA80. Ridley Hall Cam 74. **d** 77 **p** 78. C Edgware *Lon* 77-80; C Haughton St Mary *Man* 80-83; P-in-c Bacup Ch Ch 83-87; V 87-91; R Rusholme H Trin from 91. *Holy Trinity Rectory, Platt Lane, Manchester M14 5NF* Tel 0161-224 1123 or 248 8005

PORTER, Arthur William. b 29. St Deiniol's Hawarden 70. **d** 70 **p** 71. C Ruislip St Martin *Lon* 70-80; V Kingsbury H Innocents 80-94; rtd 94. *24 Belle Vue Road, Salisbury SP1 3YG* Tel (01722) 331314

PORTER, Barbara Judith. *See* JEAPES, Mrs Barbara Judith

PORTER, Brian John Henry. b 33. SW Minl Tr Course 78. **d** 81 **p** 82. NSM Plymouth St Andr w St Paul and St Geo *Ex* 81-85; NSM Perm to Offic 85-87; NSM Devonport St Barn 87-90; C Brampton St Thos *Derby* 90-95; Asst Chapl Amsterdam w Den Helder and Heiloo *Eur* 95-97; rtd 97. *32 Brookside Glen, Chesterfield, Derbyshire S40 3PF* Tel (01246) 566346

PORTER, Brian Meredith. b 39. MACE Monash Univ Aus BA66 Trin Coll Cam BA75 MA79 New England Univ (NSW) BLitt79. Cuddesdon Coll 66. **d** 68 **p** 69. C Richmond H Trin *S'wark* 68-69; Australia 69-73 and from 75; Perm to Offic *Ely* 73-75. *4 Fairholm Grove, Camberwell, Victoria, Australia 3124* Tel Melbourne (3) 9882 8740 Fax 9882 4137

PORTER, Damian Michael. b 66. Linc Th Coll BTh92. **d** 92 **p** 93. C Pelsall *Lich* 92-96; V Greenlands *Blackb* from 96. *St Anne's House, Salmesbury Avenue, Blackpool FY2 0PR* Tel (01253) 353900

PORTER, David Anthony (Tony). b 34. Wycliffe Hall Ox 73. **d** 75 **p** 76. C Watford St Luke *St Alb* 75-78; C Worting *Win* 78-81; V Snettisham *Nor* 81-82; P-in-c Ingoldisthorpe 81-82; C Fring 81-82; R Snettisham w Ingoldisthorpe and Fring 82-84; Chapl Asst Colchester Gen Hosp 87-88; Chapl Maidstone Hosp 88-94; Chapl Mid Kent Healthcare NHS Trust from 94. *Maidstone Hospital, Hermitage Lane, Maidstone, Kent ME16 9QQ, or 10 Belmont Close, Maidstone, Kent ME16 9DY* Tel (01622) 729000 or 720851

PORTER, David Michael. b 37. Coll of Ripon & York St Jo BA88. Ely Th Coll 61. **d** 64 **p** 65. C Clun w Chapel Lawn *Heref* 64-67; C Scarborough St Mary w Ch Ch, St Paul and St Thos *York* 67-69; C Fulford 69-71; V Strensall 71-78; Chapl Claypenny and St Monica's Hosps 78-91; V Easingwold w Raskelfe *York* 78-91; TR York All SS Pavement w St Crux and St Martin etc from 91. *All Saints' Rectory, 52 St Andrewgate, York YO1 2BZ* Tel (01904) 631116

PORTER, David Michael. b 46. Nottm Univ BMedSci80 BM82 BS82. EMMTC 94. **d** 97. NSM Edwinstowe w Carburton *S'well* from 97. *Gorsethorpe Cottage, Edwinstowe, Notts NG21 9HJ* Tel (01623) 844657

PORTER, Dennis Percy. b 26. K Coll Lon BSc47 AKC49 Birm Univ DipTh58. **d** 72 **p** 73. NSM Ecclesall *Sheff* 72-79; Perm to Offic from 79; Chapl Whirlow Grange Conf Cen Sheff from 79. *75 Marsh House Road, Sheffield S11 9SQ* Tel 0114-236 2058

PORTER, John Dudley Dowell. b 33. St Edm Hall Ox BA60 MA61. Qu Coll Birm 57. **d** 59 **p** 60. C Londonderry *Birm* 59-62; C Tettenhall Regis *Lich* 62-65; Chapl RAF 65-69; V Wombourne *Lich* 69-75; V Rickerscote 75-81; P-in-c Chapel Chorlton 81-85; P-in-c Maer 81-85; P-in-c Whitmore 81-85; R Chapel Chorlton, Maer and Whitmore 85-92; TR Wednesfield from 92. *The Rectory, 9 Vicarage Road, Wednesfield, Wolverhampton WV11 1SB* Tel (01902) 731462 Fax (01902) 725560

PORTER, Canon Prof Joshua Roy. b 21. Mert Coll Ox BA42 MA47. St Steph Ho Ox 42. **d** 45 **p** 46. C Portsea St Mary *Portsm* 45-47; Bp's Dom Chapl *Chich* 47-49; Chapl and Lect Or Coll Ox 49-62; Tutor Or Coll Ox 50-62; Lect Th Ox Univ 50-62; Prof Th Ex Univ 62-86; Can and Preb Chich Cathl *Chich* 65-88; Wiccamical Preb Chich Cathl from 88; rtd 86; Lic to Offic *Lon* from 87. *36 Theberton Street, London N1 0QX* Tel 0171-354 5861

PORTER, Miss Joy Dove. b 50. Lon Univ PGCE83 Ex Univ CPS86. Lon Bible Coll BA81 Wycliffe Hall Ox 89. **d** 91 **p** 94. Par Dn Chalgrove w Berrick Salome *Ox* 91-92; Par Dn Chipping Norton 92-94; C 94-95; Hong Kong from 96. *Missions to Seamen, The Mariners' Club, 11 Middle Road, Kowloon, Hong Kong*

PORTER, Kenneth Wilfred. b 27. St Aid Birkenhead 58. **d** 61 **p** 62. C Queensbury *Bradf* 61-63; C Oldham St Paul *Man* 63-65; V Wardle 65-91; Chapl Birch Hill Hosp 84-91; rtd 91; Perm to Offic *Man* from 91. *27 Polegate Drive, Leigh, Lancs WN7 5TB* Tel (01942) 526184

PORTER, Matthew James. b 69. Nottm Univ BA90. Wycliffe Hall Ox BTh93. **d** 96 **p** 97. C Dore *Sheff* from 96. *21 Causeway Head Road, Sheffield S17 3DR* Tel 0114-262 0385

PORTER, Michael Edward. b 44. Trin Coll Bris 75. **d** 77 **p** 78. C Corby St Columba *Pet* 77-81; C Rainham *Chelmsf* 81-82; TV 82-92; TV Rainham w Wennington 92; P-in-c S Hornchurch St Jo and St Matt 92-95; V Anerley *Roch* from 95. *The Vicarage, 234 Anerley Road, London SE20 8TJ* Tel 0181-778 4800

PORTER, William Albert. b 28. Univ of NZ BA51 MA52. Coll of Resurr Mirfield 53. **d** 55 **p** 56. C Perry Barr *Birm* 55-58; New Zealand 59-62; Fiji 62-67; Can and Prec H Trin Cathl Suva 65-67; C Wimbledon *S'wark* 68; Asst Chapl HM Pris Liv 69-70; Chapl 79-87; Chapl HM Pris Brixton 70-74; Chapl HM Pris Long Lartin 74-79; Chapl HM Pris Nottm 87-90; P-in-c Sneinton St Matthias *S'well* 90-93; rtd 94. *33 Valley Road, Banbury, Oxon OX16 9BH* Tel (01295) 261892

PORTER, William George Ernest. b 17. Ripon Hall Ox 60. **d** 60 **p** 61. C Brinsley w Underwood *S'well* 60-62; C-in-c Broxtowe CD 62-63; V Broxtowe 63-67; V Brinsley w Underwood 67-82; rtd 82; Perm to Offic *S'well* from 82. *6 Ringwood Avenue, Mansfield, Notts NG18 4DA* Tel (01623) 21656

PORTER-PRYCE, Ms Julia Frances. b 57. Man Univ BA78 Leic Univ MPhil94. NTMTC 93. **d** 96 **p** 97. C Stoke Newington Common St Mich *Lon* from 96. *99A Grosvenor Avenue, London N5 2NL* Tel 0171-359 5347

PORTEUS, Canon Alan Cruddas. b 12. St Chad's Coll Dur BA32 DipTh34. **d** 35 **p** 36. C Haxby *York* 35-37; C Tynemouth H Trin W Town *Newc* 37-40; C Sighill 40-47; PC Ridgeway *Derby* 47-52; V St Oswald in Lee w Bingfield *Newc* 52-60; V Ponteland 60-77; RD Newc W 64-74; Hon Can Newc Cathl 72-79; P-in-c Blanchland w Hunstanworth 77-79; rtd 79. *14 Wembley Avenue, Whitley Bay, Tyne & Wear NE25 8TE* Tel 0191-251 1895

PORTEUS, James Michael. b 31. Worc Coll Ox BA55 MA58. Cuddesdon Coll. **d** 57 **p** 58. C Fleetwood *Blackb* 57-60; C Ox St Mary V *Ox* 60-62; Staff Sec SCM Ox 60-62; USA 62-69 and 86-91; Chapl Lon Univ *Lon* 69-74; V Hampstead Garden Suburb 74-86; Min Livingston LEP *Edin* 91-96; rtd 96; P-in-c Portree *Arg* from 96. *The Rectory, Somerled Square, Portree, Isle of Skye IV51 9EH* Tel (01478) 613135

PORTEUS, Robert John Norman. b 50. TCD BA72. CITC 75. **d** 75 **p** 76. C Portadown St Mark *Arm* 75-79; I Ardtrea w Desertcreat 79-83; I Annaghmore from 83. *54 Moss Road, Portadown, Co Armagh BT62 1NB* Tel (01762) 851555

PORTHOUSE, Canon John Clive. b 32. Lon Univ BD58. Tyndale Hall Bris 55 Oak Hill Th Coll 58. **d** 60 **p** 61. C Leyton All SS *Chelmsf* 60-62; C Kendal St Thos *Carl* 62-64; V Flimby 64-68; V Sidcup St Andr *Roch* 68-74; V Beckenham St Jo 74-86; RD Beckenham 80-86; V Southborough St Pet w Ch Ch and St Matt 86-96; TR 96-97; Hon Can Roch Cathl 96-97; rtd 97. *148 Stairbank Road, Kendal, Cumbria LA9 5BE* Tel (01892) 528534

PORTHOUSE, Roger Gordon Hargreaves. b 39. Tyndale Hall Bris 66. **d** 69 **p** 70. C Wellington w Eyton *Lich* 69-71; C Cheadle *Ches* 71-75; R Frettenham w Stanninghall *Nor* 75-81; R Spixworth w Crostwick 75-81; V Hailsham *Chich* from 81; RD Dallington from 96. *St Mary's Vicarage, Vicarage Road, Hailsham, E Sussex BN27 1BL* Tel (01323) 842381

PORTSMOUTH, Archdeacon of. *See* KNOWLES, The Ven Graeme Paul

PORTSMOUTH, Bishop of. *See* STEVENSON, The Rt Revd Kenneth William

PORTSMOUTH, Provost of. *See* YORKE, The Very Revd Michael Leslie

PORTWOOD, Prof Derek. b 31. Keele Univ MA69 PhD79. Lon Coll of Div ALCD57. **d** 57 **p** 58. C Laisterdyke *Bradf* 57-60; C-in-c Westlands St Andr CD *Lich* 60-66; V Westlands St Andr 66-69; rtd 96. *51 River Lane, Cambridge CB5 8HP* Tel (01223) 311044 Fax as telephone

POSKITT, Mark Sylvester. b 63. Loughb Univ BSc84. St Jo Coll Nottm MA95. **d** 97. C Brigg, Wrawby and Cadney cum Howsham *Linc* from 97. *5 Winston Way, Brigg, S Humberside DN20 8UA* Tel (01652) 655609

POST, David Charles William. b 39. Jes Coll Cam BA61 MA65. Oak Hill Th Coll 61. **d** 63 **p** 64. C Orpington Ch Ch *Roch* 63-66; C Fulwood *Sheff* 66-68; V Lathom *Liv* 68-75; V Poughill *Truro* 75-78; V Braddan *S & M* 78-79; Dioc Missr 78-79; P-in-c Santan 78; V 78-79; V Sherburn in Elmet *York* 79-91; P-in-c Kirk Fenton 84-85; V Thornthwaite cum Braithwaite and Newlands *Carl* 91-93; R Wheldrake w Thorganby *York* from 93. *The Rectory, Church Lane, Wheldrake, York YO4 6AW* Tel (01904) 448230

POST, Oswald Julian. b 48. Derby Lonsdale Coll BEd79. EMMTC. **d** 84 **p** 85. Travelling Sec Rwanda Miss 79-89; Hon C Hulland, Atlow, Bradley and Hognaston *Derby* 84-89; V Wormhill, Peak Forest w Peak Dale and Dove Holes from 89. *The Parsonage, The Hallsteads, Dove Holes, Buxton, Derbyshire SK17 8BJ* Tel (01298) 813344

POSTILL, John Edward. b 35. Oak Hill Th Coll 64. **d** 67 **p** 68. C Southgate *Chich* 67-70; C Bowling St Jo *Bradf* 70-74; TV Winfarthing w Shelfanger *Nor* 74-79; R Slaugham *Chich* from 79. *The Rectory, Handcross, Haywards Heath, W Sussex RH17 6BU* Tel (01444) 400221

POSTILL, Richard Halliday. b 37. Hull Univ BSc59. Westcott Ho Cam 66. **d** 68 **p** 69. C Wylde Green *Birm* 68-72; C Kingswinford St Mary *Lich* 72-76; V Yardley Wood *Birm* 76-86; V Acocks Green from 86; RD Yardley from 93. *The Vicarage, 34 Dudley Park Road, Acocks Green, Birmingham B27 6QR* Tel 0121-706 9764

POSTLES, Donald. b 29. MPS51 Birm Univ DipTh59 MA65. Qu Coll Birm 56. **d** 59 **p** 60. C Southport H Trin *Liv* 59-62; C Prescot 62-63; V Wigan St Steph 63-71; V Farnworth 71-84; V Mossley Hill St Barn 84-92; rtd 93. *43 The Broadway, Abergele LL22 7DD* Tel (01745) 826165

POSTLETHWAITE, Alan James. b 38. Dur Univ BA60. Linc Th Coll 60. **d** 62 **p** 63. C Cottingham *York* 62-65; C Cockermouth All SS w Ch Ch *Carl* 65-68; V Seascale 68-77; P-in-c Irton w Drigg 75-77; V Whitehaven 77-84; TR Kidderminster St Mary and All SS w Trimpley etc *Worc* 84-97; RD Kidderminster 91-95; rtd 97. *Long Coppice, Trimpley Lane, Shatterford, Bewdley, Worcs DY12 1RF*

POTHEN, Simon John. b 60. Westmr Coll Ox BA86. Ripon Coll Cuddesdon 86. **d** 88 **p** 89. C Southgate Ch Ch *Lon* 88-91; C Tottenham St Mary 91-93; TV Gt Grimsby St Mary and St Jas *Linc* 93-96; R Friern Barnet St Jas *Lon* from 96. *The Rectory, 147 Friern Barnet Lane, London N20 0NP* Tel 0181-445 7844

POTIPHER, John Malcolm Barry. b 42. St Alb Minl Tr Scheme 79. **d** 82 **p** 83. Chapl Herts Fire Brigade 82-91; NSM Chambersbury (Hemel Hempstead) *St Alb* 82-84; NSM Hemel Hempstead 84-86; NSM Digswell and Panshanger 86-92; P-in-c Pirton 92-95; rtd 95. *66 Peartree Lane, Welwyn Garden City, Herts AL7 3UH*

POTTER, Charles Elmer. b 42. Georgetown Univ (USA) BS65 Valparaiso Univ JD73. Wycliffe Coll Toronto MDiv81. **d** 81 **p** 82. C Southport Ch Ch *Liv* 81-84; Chapl Lee Abbey 84-87; Australia 87-93; P-in-c Aldingham and Dendron and Rampside *Carl* 93-96; P-in-c Aldingham, Dendron, Rampside and Urswick from 96. *The New Rectory, Aldingham, Ulverston, Cumbria LA12 9RT* Tel (01229) 869305

POTTER, Christopher Nicholas Lynden. b 49. Leeds Univ BA71. St As Minl Tr Course 90. **d** 93 **p** 94. C Flint *St As* 93-96; V Llanfair, Derwen, Llanelidan and Efenechtyd from 96. *The Vicarage, Llanfair Dyffryn Clwyd, Ruthin LL15 2SA*

POTTER, Clive Geoffrey. b 55. Aston Tr Scheme 88 Sarum & Wells Th Coll 90. **d** 92 **p** 93. C Epsom Common Ch Ch *Guildf* 92-97; TV Westborough from 97. *St Francis Vicarage, Beckingham Road, Guildford, Surrey GU2 6BU* Tel (01483) 504228

POTTER, Colin Michael. b 53. Lanc Univ BA74 Birm Univ DipTh82. Qu Coll Birm 80. **d** 83 **p** 84. C Middlewich w Byley *Ches* 83-87; TV Ches Team from 87. *St Thomas of Canterbury*

Vicarage, 33 Abbott's Grange, Liverpool Road, Chester CH2 1AJ Tel (01244) 371612

POTTER, Frank Higton. b 23. CEng MICE55 FIWSc70 Man Univ BScTech49 AMCT49. Sarum & Wells Th Coll 89. **d** 89 **p** 90. Lic to Offic *St E* 89-92; R Badwell Ash w Gt Ashfield, Stowlangtoft etc 92-94; P-in-c 94-96; rtd 96. *Iceni, Workhouse Green, Little Cornard, Sudbury, Suffolk CO10 0NZ* Tel (01787) 228158

POTTER, George Koszelski St John (John). b 22. ARCM45 Em Coll Cam BA43 MA47 St Cath Coll Ox DipTh53. Wycliffe Hall Ox 51. **d** 53 **p** 54. C Chelsea St Luke *Lon* 53-56; V Rochdale St Aid *Man* 56-62; V Riverhead *Roch* 62-68; P-in-c Dunton Green 67-68; Hd of RE Harris C of E High Sch Rugby 68-76; Hd of RE Rock Valley Sch Rochdale 76-77; V Langcliffe w Stainforth *Bradf* 77-84; P-in-c Horton-in-Ribblesdale 80-84; V Langcliffe w Stainforth and Horton 85-87; rtd 87; Perm to Offic *Bradf* from 87. *Bridge Cottage, Station Road, Clapham, Lancaster LA2 8DP* Tel (015242) 51628

POTTER, Harry Drummond. b 54. Em Coll Cam BA76 MA79 MPhil81. Westcott Ho Cam 79. **d** 81 **p** 82. C Deptford St Paul *S'wark* 81-84; Chapl Selw Coll Cam 84-87; Chapl Newnham Coll Cam 84-87; Chapl HM Pris Wormwood Scrubs 87-88; Chapl HM Young Offender Inst Aylesbury 88-93; NSM Camberwell St Giles w St Matt *S'wark* from 93. *64 Courtlands Anenue, London SE12 8JA*

POTTER, Canon James David. b 35. AKC66. **d** 67 **p** 68. C Longbridge *Birm* 67-70; Lic to Offic 71-73; V N Harborne 73-78; V Smethwick H Trin w St Alb 78-83; V Blurton *Lich* 83-90; V Dordon *Birm* from 90; RD Polesworth 91-96; Hon Can Birm Cathl from 96. *St Leonard's Vicarage, Watling Street, Dordon, Tamworth, Staffs B78 1TE* Tel (01827) 892294

POTTER, John Dennis. b 39. Ealing Tech Coll. S Dios Minl Tr Scheme 92. **d** 94 **p** 95. NSM Box w Hazlebury and Ditteridge *Bris* from 94. *6 Fuller Road, Bath BA1 7BB* Tel (01225) 316656

POTTER, John Ellis. b 45. Sarum & Wells Th Coll 82. **d** 84 **p** 85. C Wootton Bassett *Sarum* 84-88; TV Swindon New Town *Bris* 88-96; V Milber *Ex* from 96. *St Luke's Vicarage, 10 Laburnum Road, Newton Abbot, Devon TQ12 4LQ* Tel (01626) 65837

POTTER, Canon John Henry. b 26. Lon Univ BA50. Oak Hill Th Coll 50. **d** 52 **p** 53. C Islington St Mary *Lon* 52-55; C Kinson *Sarum* 55-58; V Upper Holloway St Jo *Lon* 58-65; R Illogan *Truro* 65-69; P-in-c Ilfracombe SS Phil and Jas *Ex* 69-72; V 72-76; R Poole *Sarum* 76-87; RD Poole 80-85; Can and Preb Sarum Cathl 83-91; P-in-c Charmouth and Catherston Leweston 87-91; rtd 91. *3 Millhams Close, Bournemouth BH10 7LW* Tel (01202) 580269

POTTER, John Michael. b 28. ALCD56. **d** 56 **p** 57. C Addiscombe St Mary *Cant* 56-60; V Kettlewell w Conistone *Bradf* 60-79; P-in-c Arncliffe w Halton Gill 75-78; P-in-c Hubberholme 78-79; V Kettlewell w Conistone and Hubberholme 79-82; R Somersham w Flowton and Offton w Willisham *St E* 82-93; rtd 93; Perm to Offic *Bradf* from 93. *61 Hurrs Road, Skipton, N Yorkshire BD23 2JX* Tel (01756) 797009

POTTER, Keith Clement. b 39. Leeds Univ CSocStuds78 Bradf Univ MA81. Chich Th Coll 62. **d** 64 **p** 65. C Doncaster Ch Ch *Sheff* 64-68; C Tong *Bradf* 68-70; V Bradf St Columba w St Andr 70-79; V Yeadon St Andr from 79. *St Andrew's Vicarage, Haw Lane, Yeadon, Leeds LS19 7XQ* Tel 0113-250 3989

POTTER, Kenneth Benjamin. Lon Univ BA. NE Ord Course. **d** 87 **p** 88. NSM Ryton w Hedgefield *Dur* 87-95; NSM Harby w Thorney and N and S Clifton *S'well* from 95. *The Rectory, South Clifton, Newark, Notts NG25 7AA* Tel (01522) 778258

POTTER, Mrs Linda. b 47. Cranmer Hall Dur 92. **d** 94 **p** 95. C Shildon w Eldon *Dur* from 94. *4 Eldon Bank, Eldon, Bishop Auckland, Co Durham DL14 8DX* Tel (01388) 772397

POTTER, Malcolm Emmerson. b 48. Bedf Coll Lon BSc70. St Jo Coll Nottm DPS75. **d** 75 **p** 76. C Upton (Overchurch) *Ches* 76-78; CPAS Staff 78-84; Development Officer St Jo Coll Nottm 84-86; P-in-c Wellington, All SS w Eyton *Lich* 86-95; V from 95. *All Saints' Vicarage, 35 Crescent Road, Wellington, Telford, Shropshire TF1 3DW* Tel (01952) 641251

POTTER, Peter Maxwell. b 46. Univ of Wales (Swansea) BA69 Univ of BC MA71. Sarum & Wells Th Coll 83. **d** 85 **p** 86. C Bradford-on-Avon *Sarum* 85-88; C Harnham 88-91; P-in-c N Bradley, Southwick and Heywood 91-96; V Sale St Anne *Ches* from 96. *St Anne's Vicarage, Church Road, Sale, Cheshire M33 3HB* Tel 0161-973 4145

POTTER, Phillip. b 54. Stirling Univ BA75. Trin Coll Bris 82. **d** 84 **p** 85. C Yateley *Win* 84-88; V Haydock St Mark *Liv* from 88. *St Mark's Vicarage, 2 Stanley Bank Road, Haydock, St Helens, Merseyside WA11 0UW* Tel (01744) 23957

POTTER, Richard Antony. b 36. K Coll Cam BA60 MA64. Ridley Hall Cam 60. **d** 62 **p** 63. C Luton w E Hyde *St Alb* 62-72; V Lyonsdown H Trin 72-85; R Broxbourne w Wormley from 85. *The Vicarage, Churchfields, Broxbourne, Herts EN10 7AU* Tel (01992) 462382

POTTER, Stephen Michael. b 55. Oak Hill Th Coll 93. **d** 95 **p** 96. C Chesterfield H Trin and Ch Ch *Derby* from 95. *31 Newbold Road, Chesterfield, Derbyshire S41 7PG* Tel (01246) 232048

POTTER, Timothy John (Tim). b 49. Bris Univ BSc71. Oak Hill Th Coll 73. **d** 76 **p** 77. C Wallington H Trin *S'wark* 76-79; C Hampreston *Sarum* 79-81; TV Stratton St Margaret w S Marston etc *Bris* 81-87; P-in-c Hatfield Heath *Chelmsf* 87-89; P-in-c Sheering 87-89; R Hatfield Heath and Sheering from 90. *The Vicarage, Broomfields, Hatfield Heath, Bishop's Stortford, Herts CM22 7EA* Tel (01279) 730288

POTTIER, Ronald William. b 36. S'wark Ord Course 73. **d** 76 **p** 77. NSM Lower Sydenham St Mich *S'wark* from 76. *12 Neiderwald Road, London SE26 4AD* Tel 0181-699 4375

POTTS, Canon Hugh Cuthbert Miller. b 07. Linc Coll Ox BA29 MA41. St Steph Ho Ox 37. **d** 37 **p** 38. C Cirencester *Glouc* 37-44; V Chepstow St Arvan's w Penterry *Mon* 44-49; R Eastington and Frocester *Glouc* 49-52; R Stow on the Wold 52-61; P-in-c Evenlode 52-61; RD Stow 59-61; V Glouc St Cath 61-80; Hon Can Glouc Cathl 69-90; rtd 80. *c/o Maes y Brenin, Feidr Brenin, Newport SA42 0RZ* Tel (01239) 820653

POTTS, James. b 30. K Coll Lon BD56 AKC56. **d** 57 **p** 58. C Brighouse *Wakef* 57-59; Tanganyika 59-64; Tanzania 64-71; C-in-c Athersley and New Lodge CD *Wakef* 71-73; V Athersley 73-77; V Madeley *Lich* 77-85; V Baswich 85-93; RD Stafford 88-95; rtd 93. *2 Chebsey Drive, Stafford ST16 1ST*

POTTS, William Gilbert. b 17. Bps' Coll Cheshunt 46. **d** 49 **p** 50. C Fenton *Lich* 49-52; C W Bromwich St Andr 52-53; C Ashbourne w Mapleton and Clifton *Derby* 53-57; V Beighton *Sheff* 57-64; V Winshill *Derby* 64-82; rtd 82; Perm to Offic *Derby* from 82. *28 Roydon Close, Mickleover, Derby DE3 5PN* Tel (01332) 516328

POULARD, Christopher. b 39. FCA. Ridley Hall Cam 82. **d** 84 **p** 85. C N Walsham w Antingham *Nor* 84-86; C Oulton Broad 86-90; TV Raveningham 90-94; R The Raveningham Gp from 94. *The Rectory, Rectory Road, Haddiscoe, Norwich NR14 6PG* Tel (01502) 677774

POULTER, Canon Alan John. b 39. St Aid Birkenhead 64. **d** 67 **p** 68. C Heswall *Ches* 67-72; V Bredbury St Mark 72-78; V Oxton 78-97; RD Birkenhead 93-97; Hon Can Ches Cathl from 96; TR Ches Team from 97. *6 Elizabeth Crescent, Chester CH4 7AZ* Tel (01244) 683585 Fax 674246

POULTER, Joseph William. b 40. Dur Univ BA61 BA66 DipTh67. Cranmer Hall Dur 66. **d** 67 **p** 68. C Harlow New Town w Lt Parndon *Chelmsf* 67-71; C Washington *Dur* 71-77; Producer Metro Radio from 75; C-in-c Town End Farm CD 77-83; V Sunderland Town End Farm from 83. *Town End Farm House, Bootle Street, Sunderland SR5 4EY* Tel 0191-536 3823

POULTNEY, Wilfred Howard. b 25. Qu Coll Birm 71. **d** 73 **p** 74. NSM S Leamington St Jo *Cov* 73-85; NSM Holbrooks 85-95; NSM Walsall St Gabr Fulbrook *Lich* from 95. *28 Walstead Road, Walsall WS5 4LX* Tel (01922) 21673

POULTON, Arthur Leslie. b 28. K Coll Lon BA53 AKC53 BD60 Leic Univ MA85. Tyndale Hall Bris 53. **d** 55 **p** 56. C New Catton St Luke *Nor* 55-56; C Earlham St Anne 56-58; C Chorleywood Ch Ch *St Alb* 58-61; R E Barnet 61-64; Ches Coll of FE 64-87; Chapl 64-84; Sen Lect 66-87; P-in-c Gt Canfield *Chelmsf* 87-94; Dir of Studies Course in Chr Studies 87-94; rtd 94. *Chaldon, Great Mollington, Chester CH1 6LG* Tel (01244) 851338

POULTON, Ian Peter. b 60. Lon Univ BSc(Econ)83 TCD DipTh86 Open Univ BA94. **d** 86 **p** 87. C Newtownards *D & D* 86-89; I Bright w Ballee and Killough 89-96; Relig Adv Downtown Commercial Radio 91-96; I Larne and Inver *Conn* from 96. *The Rectory, Lower Cairncastle Road, Larne, Co Antrim BT40 1PQ* Tel (01574) 272788 Fax as telephone E-mail 106522.740@compuserve.com

POULTON, Katharine Margaret. b 61. Man Univ BA83 TCD DipTh87. **d** 87. C Bangor St Comgall *D & D* 87-91; C Seagoe 91-96; C Kilwaughter w Cairncastle and Craigy Hill *Conn* from 96. *The Rectory, Lower Cairncastle Road, Larne, Co Antrim BT40 1PQ* Tel (01574) 272788 Fax as telephone

POUNCE, Alan Gerald. b 34. Lon Univ BSc55 Dip Counselling. Wycliffe Hall Ox 57. **d** 59 **p** 60. C Wednesfield Heath *Lich* 59-61; C Heref St Pet w St Owen *Heref* 61-63; R Gt w Lt Dunham *Nor* 63-69; Asst Master Windsor Boys' Sch 69-94; Perm to Offic *Ox* from 69; rtd 94. *38 Longdown Road, Sandhurst, Berks GU47 8QG* Tel (01344) 772870

POUNCEY, Canon Cosmo Gabriel Rivers. b 11. Qu Coll Cam BA32 MA36. Cuddesdon Coll 33. **d** 34 **p** 35. C Kennington St Jo *S'wark* 34-44; Sec Ch Educn League 43-46; V Woodham *Guildf* 46-63; Hon Can Guildf Cathl 62-63; V Tewkesbury w Walton Cardiff *Glouc* 63-81; P-in-c Tredington w Stoke Orchard and Hardwicke 63-81; RD Tewkesbury 68-81; Hon Can Glouc Cathl 72-81; P-in-c Deerhurst w Apperley 74-80; Perm to Offic from 81; rtd 81; Perm to Offic *Worc* 81-93; Perm to Offic *Sarum* from 93. *Church Walk, Littlebredy, Dorchester, Dorset DT2 9HG* Tel (01308) 482356

POUND, Canon Keith Salisbury. b 33. St Cath Coll Cam BA54 MA58. Cuddesdon Coll 55. **d** 57 **p** 58. C St Helier *S'wark* 57-61; Tr Officer Hollowford Tr & Conf Cen Sheff 61-64; Warden 64-67; V S'wark H Trin 68-74; P-in-c Newington St Matt 68-74; V S'wark H Trin w St Matt 74-78; RD S'wark and Newington 73-78; TR Thamesmead 78-86; Sub-Dean Woolwich 84-86; RD Greenwich 85-86; Hon Can S'wark Cathl 85-86; Chapl Gen of Pris 86-93; Chapl to The Queen from 88; Chapl HM Pris Grendon and Spring Hill from 93. *1 Park Road, Grendon Underwood, Aylesbury, Bucks HP18 0TD* Tel (01296) 770494 Fax 770756

POUNDE, Nigel. b 46. Edin Univ MA69. Cranmer Hall Dur DipTh71. **d** 72 **p** 73. C Southsea St Simon *Portsm* 72-75; C Clayton w Keymer *Chich* 75-79; Malaysia 80-86; TV Wolverhampton *Lich* 87-97; Dioc Inter-Faith Officer 92-97; Care Services Co-ord HIV Network from 97. *15 Courtland Avenue, Coventry CV6 1GU* Tel (01203) 599987 Fax as telephone

POUNTAIN, Eric Gordon. b 24. Sarum Th Coll 65. **d** 66 **p** 67. C New Bury *Man* 66-76; Lic to Offic *Blackb* 76-80; Chapl Lancs (Preston) Poly 80-81; P-in-c Preston St Mark 80-81; V Salesbury 81-86; rtd 86. *116 Harewood Road, Rishton, Blackburn BB1 4DZ* Tel (01254) 888091

POVALL, Charles Herbert. b 18. Man Univ MEd71. St Deiniol's Hawarden 75. **d** 76 **p** 77. C Norbury *Ches* 76-83; rtd 83; Perm to Offic *Ches* from 83. *3 Magda Road, Stockport, Cheshire SK2 7LX* Tel 0161-483 6713

POVEY, John Michael. b 44. St Jo Coll Nottm BTh76. **d** 76 **p** 77. USA from 76. *67 East, Pittsfield, Massachusetts 01201, USA*

POVEY, Canon Kenneth Vincent. b 40. AKC62. **d** 63 **p** 64. C Crewe Ch Ch *Ches* 63-66; C Neston 66-69; C Kensington St Mary Abbots w St Geo *Lon* 69-72; R Ches H Trin *Ches* 72-81; Chapl Copenhagen w Aarhus *Eur* 81-86; R Gawsworth *Ches* from 86; Hon Can Ches Cathl from 92. *The Rectory, Gawsworth, Macclesfield, Cheshire SK11 9RJ* Tel (01260) 223201

POVEY, Dr William Peter. b 36. JP85. MRCS61 LRCP61 FFPHM79 FRIPHH DObstRCOG HonFChS Liv Univ DPH68 Man Univ MSc82. N Ord Course 90. **d** 93 **p** 94. NSM Latchford Ch Ch *Ches* from 93; Dioc HIV/AIDS Adv and Drug Liaison Officer from 93. *The Gables, 153 Chester Road, Grappenhall, Warrington WA4 2SB* Tel (01925) 265530

POW, Miss Joyce. b 29. RGN55 SCM57 RSCN60 RNT73. St Jo Coll Nottm CertCS88. **d** 88 **p** 94. Hon Par Dn Largs *Glas* 88-94; Hon C from 94. *15 Shuma Court, Skelmorlie, Ayrshire PA17 5EJ* Tel (01475) 520289

POWE, David James Hector. b 50. Brighton Poly CertMS86. Wycliffe Hall Ox 88. **d** 90 **p** 91. C Ventnor St Cath *Portsm* 90-92; Chapl HM Pris Belmarsh 93-94; Chapl HM Pris Lewes from 94. *HM Prison Lewes, Brighton Road, Lewes, E Sussex BN7 1EA* Tel (01273) 477331 Fax 483042

POWE, Eric James. b 23. Univ of Wales (Lamp) BA50 BD61. St Steph Ho Ox 50. **d** 52 **p** 53. C Ramsgate H Trin *Cant* 52-54; C Buckland in Dover 54-57; CF 57-73; R Broadstairs *Cant* 73-94; rtd 94; Perm to Offic *Cant* from 94. *34 Palm Bay Avenue, Cliftonville, Margate, Kent CT9 3DF* Tel (01843) 294673

POWE, Roger Wayne. b 46. Lon Univ BEd70 MA78. S'wark Ord Course 73. **d** 76 **p** 77. NSM Surbiton St Andr *S'wark* 76-77; NSM Surbiton St Andr and St Mark 77-79; Asst Chapl Giggleswick Sch 79-80; C St Marylebone All SS *Lon* 80-81; Asst Chapl Hurstpierpoint Coll Hassocks 81-90. *10/50 Kings Road, Brighton BN1 2PJ* Tel (01273) 726398

POWELL, Anthony James. b 51. Sarum & Wells Th Coll 78. **d** 79 **p** 80. C Larkfield *Roch* 79-83; C Leybourne 79-83; V Borough Green from 83. *The Vicarage, 24 Maidstone Road, Borough Green, Sevenoaks, Kent TN15 8BD* Tel (01732) 882447 Fax as telephone

POWELL, Christopher John. b 71. K Coll Lon BA94 AKC94. Coll of Resurr Mirfield 95. **d** 97. C Botley *Portsm* from 97. *1 Rectory Court, Botley, Southampton SO30 2SJ* Tel (01489) 787715

POWELL, Colin Arthur. b 32. Hatf Coll Dur BA53. Oak Hill Th Coll 56. **d** 58 **p** 59. C Leyland St Andr *Blackb* 58-61; C Lancaster St Thos 61-64; C Tranmere St Cath *Ches* 64-65; R Cheetham Hill *Man* 65-81; TV Oldham 81-86; TV Rochdale from 86; Chapl Birch Hill Hosp from 94. *Good Shepherd Vicarage, 160 Entwisle Road, Rochdale, Lancs OL16 2JJ* Tel (01706) 40130

POWELL, Mrs Diane. b 41. SW Minl Tr Course 85. **d** 88 **p** 94. Hon C St Merryn *Truro* 88-92; D-in-c Gerrans w St Antony in Roseland 92-94; P-in-c from 94. *The Rectory, Gerrans, Portscatho, Truro, Cornwall TR2 5EB* Tel (01872) 580277

POWELL, Dudley John. b 44. Tyndale Hall Bris 65. **d** 69 **p** 70. C Blackb Sav *Blackb* 69-71; C Rodbourne Cheney *Bris* 71-74; P-in-c Kingsdown 74-79; V 79-80; V Stoke Gifford 80-90; TR 90-91; Albania 91-94; Perm to Offic *Bris* from 94. *20 Queens Field, Stratton, Swindon SN2 6SX*

POWELL, Canon Eleanor Ann. b 55. Gwent Coll Newport CertEd76 Univ of Wales BA82. Qu Coll Birm 82. **d** 83 **p** 94. C Caereithin *S & B* 83-86; C Bishopston 86-88; Dioc Children's Officer *Glouc* 88-94; Hon Can Glouc Cathl from 94; P-in-c The Edge, Pitchcombe, Harescombe and Brookthorpe from 94; Dioc Adv for Women's Min from 94. *The Rectory, Edge, Stroud, Glos GL6 6PF* Tel (01452) 812319

POWELL, Francis David Claude. b 09. Leeds Univ BA31. Coll of Resurr Mirfield 31. **d** 33 **p** 34. C Tunbridge Wells St Barn *Roch* 33-36; C Pimlico St Mary Graham Terrace *Lon* 36-42; Chapl RNVR 42-45; Tanganyika 45-64; Tanzania 64-65; Br Honduras 66-69; Dean Belize 66-69; V Hammersmith St Matt *Lon* 70-75; rtd 75; Perm to Offic *Ox* 75-88; Perm to Offic *St Alb* from 75. *St Martha's Lodge, Park Road, Tring, Herts HP23 6BP* Tel (01442) 823041

POWELL, Preb Frank. b 29. AKC52. **d** 53 **p** 54. C Stockingford *Cov* 53-56; C Netherton St Andr *Worc* 56-60; P-in-c W Bromwich St Jo *Lich* 60-66; C W Bromwich Gd Shep w St Jo 60-66; V 66-69; V Bilston St Leon 69-76; P-in-c Hanbury 76-82; V Hanbury w Newborough 83-86; V Basford 86-92; Preb Lich Cathl 87-92; rtd 92; Perm to Offic *Ches* from 92. *17 Thorley Grove, Wistaston, Crewe CW2 8BA* Tel (01270) 650513

POWELL, Gary Charles. b 62. UWIST BSc84. Coll of Resurr Mirfield 92. **d** 95 **p** 96. C Roath St Marg *Llan* from 95. *St Anne's House, 3 Snipe Street, Roath, Cardiff CF2 3RB* Tel (01222) 493940

POWELL, Geoffrey Peter. b 25. Chich Th Coll 54. **d** 56 **p** 57. C Bris St Agnes w St Simon *Bris* 56-58; C Sherston Magna w Easton Grey 58-62; V Wanborough 62-75; R Lyddington w Wanborough 75-80; V St Cleer *Truro* 80-90; rtd 91; Perm to Offic *Bris* from 91; Perm to Offic *Truro* from 91. *The Old Bakery, Oare, Marlborough, Wilts SN8 4JQ* Tel (01672) 62627

POWELL, John. b 44. St Luke's Coll Ex CertEd66. Glouc Sch of Min 81. **d** 84 **p** 85. NSM Stroud and Uplands w Slad *Glouc* 84-89; Chapl Eliz Coll Guernsey 89-92; C Llandudno *Ban* 92-93; TV 94-96; V Dwygyfylchi from 96. *The Vicarage, Church Road, Penmaenmawr LL34 6BN* Tel (01492) 623300

POWELL, John Keith Lytton. b 52. Warden Worshipful Company of Cooks. E Sussex Agric Coll OND. S Dios Minl Tr Scheme 91. **d** 94 **p** 95. NSM Bridgwater H Trin *B & W* from 94. *Postridge Farm, Spaxton, Bridgwater, Somerset TA5 1BN* Tel (01278) 671328

POWELL, John Reginald. b 36. Nottm Univ BA59 PGCE71 St Cath Coll Ox DipPSA60. Ripon Hall Ox 59. **d** 61 **p** 62. C Thornhill *Wakef* 61-64; C Hebden Bridge 61-64; P-in-c Halifax St Aug 64-67; Hon C Lancaster Ch Ch *Blackb* 67-69; V Holland Fen *Linc* 69-73; Perm to Offic *York* 73-84; Chapl K Sch Ely 77-84; V Skerton St Chad *Blackb* 84-89; V Ashton-on-Ribble St Andr from 89; RD Preston from 92. *The Vicarage, 240 Tulketh Road, Ashton-on-Ribble, Preston PR2 1ES* Tel (01772) 726848

POWELL, Miss Katherine (Kate). b 56. Sydney Univ BSocStuds79. Wycliffe Hall Ox 84. **dss** 86 **d** 87 **p** 94. Broadwater St Mary *Chich* 86-87; Par Dn 87-91; Asst Chapl Ch Hosp Horsham 91-96; Australia from 96. *The Glennie School, Herries Street, Toowoomba, Queensland 4350, Australia* Tel Toowoomba (76) 324488

POWELL, Kelvin. b 49. Wycliffe Hall Ox 71. **d** 74 **p** 75. C Prescot *Liv* 74-77; C Ainsdale 77-79; V Bickershaw 79-85; R Hesketh w Becconsall *Blackb* from 85. *All Saints' Rectory, Silverdale, Hesketh Bank, Preston PR4 6RZ* Tel (01772) 814798

POWELL, Llewellyn. b 28. Glouc Th Course 67. **d** 70 **p** 71. C Quinton *Glouc* 70-73; P-in-c 74-76; V Church Honeybourne w Cow Honeybourne 76-83; R Pebworth w Dorsington and Honeybourne 83-87; rtd 87; Perm to Offic *St D* from 87. *Bodathro Bungalow, Llangynin, St Clears, Carmarthen SA33 4LD* Tel (01994) 448301

POWELL, Dr Mark. b 57. Bath Univ BSc78 PhD81. Ripon Coll Cuddesdon BA84 MA88. **d** 85 **p** 86. C Evesham *Worc* 85-88; V Exhall *Cov* 88-96; V Leavesden All SS *St Alb* from 96. *All Saints' Vicarage, Horseshoe Lane, Garston, Watford WD2 7HJ* Tel (01923) 672375

POWELL, Ralph Dover. b 49. ARMCM70. Chich Th Coll 71. **d** 74 **p** 75. C Coppenhall *Ches* 74-77; C Heref H Trin *Heref* 77-80; V Crewe St Barn *Ches* from 80. *St Barnabas' Vicarage, West Street, Crewe CW1 3AX* Tel (01270) 212418

POWELL, Raymond Leslie. b 35. AKC61. **d** 62 **p** 63. C Hendon St Mary *Lon* 62-67; C Huntingdon All SS w St Jo *Ely* 67-75; V Huntingdon St Barn 75-79; P-in-c Sawston 79-81; V from 81; P-in-c Babraham from 85; RD Shelford 89-94. *The Vicarage, Church Lane, Sawston, Cambridge CB2 4JR* Tel (01223) 832248

POWELL, Richard Michael Wheler. b 19. St Edm Hall Ox BA45. Wells Th Coll 47. **d** 49 **p** 50. C Hale *Ches* 49-52; V Crowle *Worc* 52-56; V Kempsey 57-62; R Tarporley *Ches* 62-72; P-in-c Lt Budworth 69-70; R Overton w Laverstoke and Freefolk *Win* 73-81; P-in-c Damerham *Sarum* 81-84; P-in-c Martin 81-84; rtd 84; Perm to Offic *B & W* 85-94; Perm to Offic *Ex* from 94. *38 Pine Park Road, Honiton, Devon EX14 8HR* Tel (01404) 43429

POWELL, Richard Penry. b 15. Dur Univ LTh38. St Aid Birkenhead 34. **d** 38 **p** 39. C Brierley Hill *Lich* 38-42; C Derby St Chad *Derby* 42-45; C Uttoxeter w Bramshall *Lich* 45-47; V Alton 47-60; V Bradley-in-the-Moors 48-60; R Drayton Bassett 60-64; Min Canwell CD 60-64; V Wrockwardine 64-80; V Uppington 64-80; rtd 80; Perm to Offic *Lich* from 80. *34 Herbert Avenue, Wellington, Telford, Shropshire TF1 2BS* Tel (01952) 242528

POWELL, Robert John (Rob). b 65. Trin Coll Bris DipHE91 BA92. **d** 92 **p** 93. C Biggin Hill *Roch* 92-95; C Edgware *Lon* from 95. *St Peters Parsonage, Stonegrove, Edgware, Middx HA8 8AB* Tel 0181-958 5791

POWELL, Roger Roy. b 68. Thames Poly BSc91. Ripon Coll Cuddesdon BTh94. **d** 94 **p** 95. C Leic St Jas *Leic* from 94. *Ashman House, 1 Dixon Drive, Leicester LE2 1RA* Tel 0116-270 0340

POWELL, Samuel John. b 21. Qu Coll Ox BA53 MA57. **d** 47 **p** 48. Lic to Offic *Ox* 47-53 and 56-58; C Pontnewynydd *Mon* 53-55; C Ashchurch *Glouc* 55-56; Brazil from 58. *Caixa Postal 161, Campos do Jordao, Sao Paulo, Brazil*

POWELL, Stuart William. b 58. K Coll Lon BD80 AKC80. Ripon Coll Cuddesdon 86. **d** 88 **p** 89. C Horden *Dur* 88-90; C Northolt

Park St Barn *Lon* 90-93; V Castle Vale St Cuth *Birm* from 93. *St Cuthbert's Vicarage, Reed Square, Birmingham B35 7PS* Tel 0121-747 4041

POWELL, William Michael. b 33. Bps' Coll Cheshunt 58. **d** 61 **p** 62. C Golders Green St Mich *Lon* 61-64; C Hatcham St Cath *S'wark* 64-67; C Woodham *Guildf* 67-72; V Guildf All SS 72-84; RD Guildf 78-84; TR Headley All SS 84-89; V Addlestone from 89. *The Vicarage, 140 Church Road, Addlestone, Surrey KT15 1SJ* Tel (01932) 842879

POWER, Alan Edward. b 26. Worc Coll Ox BA50 MA53. Lich Th Coll. **d** 57 **p** 58. C Summerfield *Birm* 57-60; C Oldbury 60-63; V Short Heath from 63. *St Margaret's Vicarage, Somerset Road, Birmingham B23 6NQ* Tel 0121-373 6989

POWER, David Michael. b 56. BA81 BEd. Oak Hill Th Coll. **d** 81 **p** 82. C Warblington and Emsworth *Portsm* 81-84; C-in-c Hartplain CD 84-88; V Hartplain 88-91; Adv in Evang 91-97; V Portsea St Cuth from 97. *St Cuthbert's Vicarage, 2 Lichfield Road, Portsmouth PO3 6DE* Tel (01705) 827071 Fax as telephone

POWER, Canon Ivor Jonathan. b 43. Lambeth STh87 CITC 66. **d** 69 **p** 70. C Dromore Cathl *D & D* 69-71; C Enniscorthy *C & O* 71-74; I Youghal *C, C & R* 74-78; I Youghal Union 78-81; I Athlone w Benown, Kiltoom and Forgney *M & K* from 81; RD Clonmacnoise from 86; Can Meath from 87; Dir of Ords (Meath) 91-97. *The Rectory, Bonavalley, Athlone, Co Westmeath, Irish Republic* Tel Athlone (902) 78350 Fax 76720

POWER, James Edward. b 58. Nottm Univ BSc81 Leeds Univ BA85. Coll of Resurr Mirfield 83. **d** 86 **p** 87. C Cadoxton-juxta-Barry *Llan* 86-89; Chapl Harrow Sch from 89; Perm to Offic *Lon* from 89. *35 West Street, Harrow, Middx HA1 3EG* Tel 0181-869 1234

POWER, Mrs Jeanette. b 57. Oak Hill Th Coll BA81. **dss** 82 **d** 87 **p** 94. Warblington and Emsworth *Portsm* 82-84; Hartplain CD 84-87; Hon C Hartplain 87-91; Community Mental Health Chapl Havant and Petersfield from 91; NSM Wickham 93-97; NSM Portsea St Cuth from 97. *St Cuthbert's Vicarage, 2 Lichfield Road, Portsmouth PO3 6DE* Tel (01705) 827071 Fax as telephone

POWIS, Michael Ralph (Mike). b 63. St Jo Coll Nottm BTh95. **d** 95 **p** 96. C Dibden *Win* from 95. *2 Corsai Drive, Dibden Purlieu, Southampton SO45 5UF* Tel (01703) 844376

POWLES, Charles Anthony. b 39. EAMTC. **d** 88 **p** 89. Hon C Hemsby *Nor* from 88. *Mairin, Ormesby Road, Hemsby, Great Yarmouth, Norfolk NR29 4LA* Tel (01493) 732493

POWLES, Michael Charles. b 34. Reading Univ BSc56. Qu Coll Birm DipTh60. **d** 60 **p** 61. C Goodmayes All SS *Chelmsf* 60-65; C Surbiton St Matt *S'wark* 65-78; Lic to Offic from 79. *Spring Cottage, 3 Rushett Close, Long Ditton, Surrey KT7 0UR* Tel 0181-398 9654

POWLEY, Robert Mallinson. b 39. Fitzw Coll Cam MA65 DPS68 DipSocWork69. Ridley Hall Cam 61. **d** 63 **p** 64. C Bermondsey St Mary w St Olave, St Jo etc *S'wark* 63-67; C Moseley St Anne *Birm* 67-69; Lic to Offic *Man* 72-77; Hon C Walshaw Ch Ch 77-88; V Prestwich St Gabr 88-94; Bp's Dom Chapl 88-94; P-in-c Hargrave *Ches* from 94; Exec Officer BSR from 94. *The Vicarage, Hargrave, Chester CH3 7RN* Tel (01829) 781378

POWNALL, Lydia Margaret. *See* HURLE, Mrs Lydia Margaret

POWNE, Peter Rebbeck Lamb. b 23. Sarum & Wells Th Coll 80. **d** 83 **p** 84. C Calne and Blackland *Sarum* 83-86; V Netheravon w Fittleton and Enford 86-93; rtd 93. *2 Oak Lane, Fighelden, Salisbury SP4 8JS* Tel (01980) 670326

POWNEY, Derek John. b 40. Univ Coll Ox BA62 MA66. EAMTC 90. **d** 93 **p** 94. C Tilbury Docks *Chelmsf* 93-96; Perm to Offic from 96. *1 Eastview Drive, Rayleigh, Essex SS6 9NY* Tel (01268) 780622

POYNER, Maurice John. b 20. St Deiniol's Hawarden. **d** 83 **p** 84. Hon C Humberstone *Leic* 83-90; Perm to Offic from 90. *127 Colchester Road, Leicester LE5 2DJ* Tel 0116-276 8372

POYNTING, Charles Robert Macvicar. b 23. Hertf Coll Ox BA48 MA48. Wells Th Coll 48. **d** 50 **p** 51. C Gt Bookham *Guildf* 50-52; C Epsom Common Ch Ch 52-55; V Ashton H Trin *Man* 55-62; V Belfield 62-82; V Digby *Linc* 82-92; rtd 92. *Digby Cottage, Noke, Oxford OX3 9TX* Tel (01865) 842794

✠**POYNTZ, The Rt Revd Samuel Greenfield.** b 26. TCD BA48 MA51 BD53 PhD60 Ulster Univ Hon DLitt95. TCD Div Sch Div Test50. **d** 50 **p** 51 **c** 78. C Dublin St Geo *D & G* 50-52; C Bray 52-55; C Dublin St Michan w St Paul 55-59; Sec and Sch Insp Ch Educn Soc for Ireland 56-75; I Dublin St Steph 59-67; I Dublin St Ann 67-70; I Dublin St Ann w St Steph 70-78; Adn Dublin 74-78; Bp C, C & R 78-87; Bp Conn 87-95; rtd 95. *10 Harmony Hill, Lisburn, Co Antrim BT27 4EP* Tel (01846) 679013

PRAGNELL, John William. b 39. Lon Univ BD65. Lambeth STh87 LTh88. **d** 65 **p** 66. C Bitterne *Win* 65-68; C Hatfield Hyde *St Alb* 68-73; Kuwait 73-75; Chapl Leavesden Hosp and Abbots Langley Hosp 75-88; Chapl Watford Gen Hosp 86-88; V St Alb St Steph *St Alb* 88-95; RD St Alb 91-95; P-in-c Copythorne and Minstead *Win* from 95; Dio Ecum Officer from 95. *The Vicarage, Pine Ridge, Romsey Road, Cadnam, Southampton SO40 2NN* Tel (01703) 814769

PRAGNELL, Michael John. b 40. CChem MRSC FIQA81 MSOSc88 MA PhD. Ox NSM Course 81. **d** 84 **p** 85. NSM High Wycombe *Ox* from 84. *28 Carver Hill Road, High Wycombe, Bucks HP11 2UA* Tel (01494) 533056

PRAILL, David William. b 57. FRGS90 York Univ BA79. Cranmer Hall Dur 81. **d** 82 **p** 83. C Digswell and Panshanger *St Alb* 82-84; CMS 84-89; Course Dir St Geo Coll Jerusalem 85-89; Dir McCabe Educn Trust 90-91; Dir St Luke's Hospice Harrow and Wembley from 91; Perm to Offic *S'wark* from 91; Perm to Offic *Lon* from 94. *1A St Ann's Crescent, London SW18 2ND* Tel 0181-870 3694

PRANCE, Robert Penrose. b 47. Southn Univ DipTh. Sarum & Wells Th Coll 69. **d** 72 **p** 73. C Gillingham and Fifehead Magdalen *Sarum* 72-76; P-in-c Edmondsham 76-80; P-in-c Woodlands 76-80; P-in-c Wimborne St Giles 76-80; P-in-c Cranborne 77-80; R Cranborne w Boveridge, Edmondsham etc 80-83; Chapl Sherborne Sch 83-93; V Stoke Gabriel and Collaton *Ex* from 93; Dep PV Ex Cathl from 95. *The Vicarage, Stoke Gabriel, Totnes, Devon TQ9 6QX* Tel (01803) 782358

PRASADAM, Goruganthula Samuel Narayanamurthy (Sam). b 34. Andhra Univ India BA57. Bangalore Th Coll BD65 Union Th Sem (NY) STM68. **d** 62 **p** 65. India 62-74; C Llanbeblig w Caernarfon and Betws Garmon etc *Ban* 75-76; C Norbury *Ches* 77-78; V Aberaman and Abercwmboi *Llan* 78-83; N Sec CMS 83-87; V Luton All SS w St Pet *St Alb* 87-96. *St Silas's Vicarage, 103 Heathfield Road, Birmingham B19 1HE* Tel 0121-523 5645

PRASADAM, Jemima. b 38. BD61 BA87. Cranmer Hall Dur 86. **d** 87 **p** 94. Miss Partner CMS from 87; Par Dn Luton All SS w St Pet *St Alb* 87-94; C 94-96; P-in-c Lozells St Paul and St Silas *Birm* from 96. *St Silas's Vicarage, 103 Heathfield Road, Birmingham B19 1HE* Tel 0121-523 5645

PRATT, Basil David. b 38. Ripon Hall Ox 64. **d** 67 **p** 68. C Lewisham St Jo Southend *S'wark* 67-68; C Caterham Valley 68-70; CF 70-93. *St Michael's, Bankend Road, Dumfries DE1 4AL* Tel (01387) 267933

PRATT, Christine Fiona. b 60. Reading Univ BSc81. Ox Min Course 88. **d** 91 **p** 94. NSM Earley St Pet *Ox* 91-95; NSM Reading St Luke w St Bart from 95. *Flat 1, 59 Christchurch Road, Reading RG2 7BD* Tel 0118-986 9570

PRATT, Edward Andrew (Ted). b 39. Clare Coll Cam BA61 MA65. Clifton Th Coll 63. **d** 66 **p** 67. C Southall Green St Jo *Lon* 66-69; C Drypool St Columba w St Andr and St Pet *York* 69-71; P-in-c Radbourne *Derby* 71-74; R Kirk Langley 71-78; V Mackworth All SS 71-78; V Southsea St Simon *Portsm* 78-97; rtd 97. *7 Bay Close, Swanage, Dorset BH19 1RE*

PRATT, Mrs Janet Margaret. b 40. Herts Coll BEd78. St Alb Minl Tr Scheme 78. **dss** 81 **d** 87 **p** 94. High Wych and Gilston w Eastwick *St Alb* 81-87; Hon Par Dn 87-89; Par Dn Histon *Ely* 89-94; C from 94; Par Dn Impington 89-94; C from 94. *The Vicarage, 60 Impington Lane, Impington, Cambridge CB4 4NJ* Tel (01223) 232826

PRATT, John Anthony. b 38. Selw Coll Cam BA61 MA65. Qu Coll Birm DipTh66. **d** 66 **p** 67. C Harrow Weald All SS *Lon* 66-69; C St Pancras w St Jas and Ch Ch 69-74; C Saffron Walden *Chelmsf* 74-75; TV Saffron Walden w Wendens Ambo and Littlebury 75-79; V St Mary-at-Latton 79-88; Chapl Princess Alexandra Hosp Harlow 82-88; RD Harlow *Chelmsf* 83-88; R Tolleshunt Knights w Tiptree and Gt Braxted from 88. *The Rectory, Rectory Road, Tiptree, Colchester CO5 0SX* Tel (01621) 815260

PRATT, Kenneth George. b 21. EAMTC 81. **d** 84 **p** 85. NSM March St Jo *Ely* 84-87; Chapl Doddington Community Hosp from 86; P-in-c Doddington w Benwick *Ely* 87-94; rtd 94; Perm to Offic *Ely* from 94. *2 Windsor Drive, March, Cambs PE15 8DF* Tel (01354) 658814

PRATT, Michael. *See* HARRIS, Michael

PRATT, Richard David. b 55. Linc Coll Ox BA77 MA81 Nottm Univ BCombStuds84. Linc Th Coll 81. **d** 84 **p** 85. C Wellingborough All Hallows *Pet* 84-87; TV Kingsthorpe w Northn St Dav 87-92; V Northampton St Benedict 92-97; P-in-c Carl St Cuth w St Mary *Carl* from 97; Dioc Communications Officer from 97. *St Cuthbert's Vicarage, West Walls, Carlisle CA3 8UF* Tel (01228) 21982

PRATT, Samuel Charles. b 40. Oak Hill Th Coll 69. **d** 71 **p** 72. C Upper Holloway St Jo *Lon* 71-73; C Bucknall and Bagnall *Lich* 73-76; V Liv St Mich *Liv* 76-80; Chapl R Liv Hosp 80-94; Chapl R Liv Univ Hosp NHS Trust from 94. *23 Caithness Road, Liverpool L8 9SJ, or Royal Liverpool Hospital, Prescot Street, Liverpool L7 8XP* Tel 0151-427 4997 or 706 2000

PRATT, Canon William Ralph (Will). b 47. Keble Coll Ox BA69 MA73. Linc Th Coll 70. **d** 72 **p** 73. C Ifield *Chich* 72-78; TV 78; C Brighton St Pet w Chpl Royal 79-80; C Brighton St Pet w Chpl Royal and St Jo 80-83; P-in-c Hove St Jo 83-87; Dioc Communications Officer from 87; Can and Preb Chich Cathl from 90. *23 Wilbury Avenue, Hove, E Sussex BN3 6HS* Tel (01273) 748756 Fax 821810

PRAVISANI, Roberto Luigi. b 62. Pordenone Tech Inst 82. SA Internat Tr Coll 90 Coll of Resurr Mirfield BA96. **d** 96. C Adel *Ripon* 96-97; C Ashton H Trin *Man* from 97. *2A Hutton Avenue, Ashton under Lyne, Lancs OL6 6QY* Tel 0161-330 8521

PREBBLE, The Ven Albert Ernest. b 08. Univ of NZ BA31 MA32 St Jo Coll Auckland 32. **d** 32 **p** 33. New Zealand 32-63; Adn Waimate 44-49; Adn Manukau 49-56; V Gen and Adn Auckland 56-63; Perm to Offic *Pet* from 59; V Greenhill St Jo *Lon* 63-72;

rtd 73. *23 Glebe Rise, Kings Sutton, Banbury, Oxon OX17 3PH* Tel (01295) 811993

PREECE, Barry Leslie. b 48. Lich Th Coll 68. **d** 71 **p** 72. C Ewell *Guildf* 71-74; C York Town St Mich 75-77; P-in-c Ripley 77-81; Chapl HM Det Cen Send 77-81; V Cuddington *Guildf* 81-88; V Cobham from 88. *The Vicarage, St Andrew's Walk, Cobham, Surrey KT11 3EQ* Tel (01932) 862109

PREECE, Colin George. b 51. Bernard Gilpin Soc Dur 71 Chich Th Coll 72. **d** 75 **p** 76. C Upper Gornal *Lich* 75-78; C Wednesbury St Paul Wood Green 78-81; V Oxley 81-89; V Kennington *Cant* from 89; RD E Charing from 92. *The Vicarage, 212 Faversham Road, Kennington, Ashford, Kent TN24 9AF* Tel (01233) 620500

PREECE, Joseph. b 23. Univ of Wales (Ban) BA50 Univ of Wales (Swansea) DipSocSc51 LSE CertCC52 Lon Univ DBRS72. NW Ord Course 73. **d** 73 **p** 74. C Claughton cum Grange *Ches* 73-74; C Barnston 74-75; R Aldford and Bruera 75-80; V Wincle and Wildboarclough 80-82; P-in-c Cleeton w Silvington *Heref* 82-86; P-in-c Farlow 82-86; V Stottesdon 82-86; R Stottesdon w Farlow, Cleeton and Silvington 86-88; rtd 88; Perm to Offic *Heref* from 91. *Lingholm, Woodhall Drive, Hanwood, Shrewsbury SY5 8JU* Tel (01743) 860946

PREECE, Mark Richard. b 61. St Paul's Cheltenham BA85. Linc Th Coll 85. **d** 87 **p** 88. C Coity w Nolton *Llan* 87-89; C Penarth w Lavernock 89-92; R Ewenny w St Brides Major from 92. *The Vicarage, Southerndown Road, St Brides Major, Bridgend CF32 0SD* Tel (01656) 880108

PREECE, Ronald Alexander (Ron). b 29. Lon Univ BD56. ALCD55. **d** 56 **p** 57. C Rusholme H Trin *Man* 56-59; Teacher Kidbrooke Sch Lon 59-60; Brazil 60-63; Perm to Offic *Cant* 63-70; Teacher Abp's Sch Cant 64-70; OMF 70-94; SW Regional Dir 76-94; Perm to Offic *Bris* 76-94; rtd 94. *5 Tonford Lane, Canterbury CT1 3XU* Tel (01227) 471061

PRENTICE, Brian. b 40. St Jo Coll Nottm 81. **d** 83 **p** 84. C W Bromwich All SS *Lich* 83-86; C Tettenhall Wood 86-89; TV 89-90; V Essington from 90. *The Vicarage, Wolverhampton Road, Essington, Wolverhampton WV11 2BX* Tel (01922) 478540

PRENTICE, Michael Charles. b 35. Bps' Coll Cheshunt 59. **d** 62 **p** 63. C Lon Docks St Pet w Wapping St Jo *Lon* 62-66; C Cranford 66-70; C Bethnal Green St Jas the Gt w St Jude 70-71; C Walsingham and Houghton *Nor* 71-73; C Southall Ch Redeemer *Lon* 73; V Acton Vale St Thos 73-78; P-in-c Stow Bardolph w Wimbotsham and Stow Bridge *Ely* 78-80; R Woodford *Pet* 80-94. *Doric Cottage, 1 Low Road, Wretton, King's Lynn, Norfolk PE33 9QN* Tel (01366) 500210

PRENTICE, Walter Gordon. b 07. Nor Ord Course 73. **d** 75 **p** 76. C Swanton Morley w Worthing *Nor* 75-77; P-in-c Scarning w Wendling 77-78; rtd 78; Perm to Offic *Nor* 78-80; Perm to Offic *St E* 80-88; Hon C Cherry Hinton St Andr *Ely* from 88. *13 St Andrew's Glebe, Cherry Hinton, Cambridge CB1 3JS* Tel (01223) 215285

PRENTIS, Calvert Clayton. b 62. St Jo Coll Nottm DipTh95. **d** 97. C Wood End *Cov* from 97. *189 Deedmore Road, Wood End, Coventry CV2 1ER*

PRENTIS, Richard Hugh. b 36. Ch Coll Cam BA60 MA64. Sarum Th Coll 69. **d** 71 **p** 72. C Bath Bathwick St Mary *B & W* 71-76; Bp's Dom Chapl *Lich* 76-80; PV Lich Cathl 76-80; V Longton St Mary and St Chad 80-84; V Shifnal 84-94; P-in-c Badger 84-85; P-in-c Ryton 84-85; P-in-c Beckbury 84-85; rtd 94. *23B The Close, Lichfield, Staffs WS13 7LD* Tel (01543) 411234

PRESCOTT, Canon Anthony John. b 34. AKC59. **d** 60 **p** 61. C Swindon New Town *Bris* 60-66; P-in-c Birm St Aid Small Heath *Birm* 66-68; V 68-71; Hon C Washwood Heath 72-95; Asst Sec ACS 71-73; Gen Sec 73-95; Hon Can St Woolos Cathl *Mon* from 83; rtd 95. *58 rue Albert Vincon, Certe, 44570 Trignac, Loire Atlantique, France* Tel France (33) 40 45 92 17 Fax 40 45 92 18

PRESCOTT, Thomas Robert. b 41. St Mich Coll Llan DPT95. **d** 95 **p** 96. C Abertillery w Cwmtillery w Six Bells *Mon* from 95. *St Paul's Vicarage, Church Lane, Cwmtillery, Abertillery NP3 1PS* Tel (01495) 212364

PRESCOTT, William Allan. b 57. ACIS87. Sarum & Wells Th Coll DCM93. **d** 93 **p** 94. C Horsell *Guildf* from 93. *6 Waldens Park Road, Woking, Surrey GU21 4RN* Tel (01483) 715440

PRESS, Richard James. b 45. Southn Univ CertEd67. Sarum & Wells Th Coll CMinlStuds92. **d** 92 **p** 93. C Bradford-on-Avon *Sarum* 92-95; P-in-c Rowde and Poulshot from 95. *The Rectory, Cock Road, Rowde, Devizes, Wilts SN10 2PN* Tel (01380) 724413

PRESSWELL, John Lawrence Rowley. b 28. Southn Univ BEd79. AKC51. **d** 52 **p** 53. C Surbiton St Andr *S'wark* 52-55; C Battersea Park All SS 55-57; C Horley 57-61; Chapl Univ Coll of Ripon and York St Jo 61-62; V Wandsworth St Faith *S'wark* 62-69; V Battersea St Bart 69-71; P-in-c Newtown St Luke *Win* 71-73; C Lymington 73-79; Chapl Crookham Court Sch Newbury 79-81; Chapl Stanbridge Earls Sch Romsey 81-82; C Doncaster St Geo *Sheff* 82-85; V Edlington 85-86; C Handsworth 86-88; C Rotherham 88-90; rtd 90; Perm to Offic *Linc* from 92. *The Cottage, Todds Lane, Burton-upon-Stather, Scunthorpe, S Humberside DN15 9DG* Tel (01724) 721266

PREST, Canon Walter. b 09. St Chad's Coll Dur BA33 DipTh34 MA36. **d** 34 **p** 35. C Millom H Trin *Carl* 34-35; Min Can Carl Cathl 35-39; C Cantley w Limpenhoe and Southwood *Nor* 39-42; V Weasenham 42-45; V Bude Haven *Truro* 45-69; RD Stratton 48-63; Hon Can Truro Cathl 61-82; Preb St Endellion 70-81; R St Endellion 70-81; rtd 81; Perm to Offic *Truro* from 82. *College of St Barnabas, Blackberry Lane, Lingfield, Surrey RH7 6NJ* Tel (01342) 870612

PRESTNEY, Mrs Patricia Christine Margaret (Pat). b 49. Oak Hill Th Coll 84. **d** 87 **p** 94. NSM Lawford *Chelmsf* 87-95; Perm to Offic *St E* 91-95; Chapl Benenden Sch Kent from 95. *Benenden School, Benenden, Cranbrook, Kent TN17 4AA* Tel (01580) 240592

PRESTON, David Francis. b 50. BNC Ox BA72 MA78. St Steph Ho Ox 72. **d** 74 **p** 75. C Beckenham St Jas *Roch* 74-79; C Hockley *Chelmsf* 81-83; C Lamorbey H Redeemer *Roch* 83-89; V Gillingham St Barn from 89. *1 St Barnabas's Close, Oxford Road, Gillingham, Kent ME7 4BU* Tel (01634) 851010

PRESTON, Donald George. b 30. St Alb Minl Tr Scheme 77. **d** 80 **p** 81. NSM Elstow *St Alb* 80-87; NSM Goldington from 87. *106 Putnoe Street, Bedford MK41 8HJ* Tel (01234) 367313

PRESTON, Preb Frederick Arnold. MBE53. Leeds Univ BA42. Coll of Resurr Mirfield 42. **d** 44 **p** 45. C Greenford H Cross *Lon* 44-51; CF 51-61; R W Hackney St Barn *Lon* from 61; Preb St Paul's Cathl from 75. *The Rectory, 306 Amhurst Road, London N16 7UE* Tel 0171-254 3235

PRESTON, Frederick John. b 32. MBE72. Oak Hill Th Coll 54 St Jo Coll Northwood LTh67. **d** 57 **p** 58. C Hove Bp Hannington Memorial Ch *Chich* 57-59; C-in-c Knaphill *Guildf* 60-62; CF 62-69; V Otterton *Ex* 69-71; CF 71-79; NSM 79-84; Chapl Intercon Ch Soc 84-89; rtd 89; Perm to Offic *Nor* from 96. *92 Charles Close, Wroxham, Norwich NR12 8TT*

PRESTON, James Martin. b 31. Trin Coll Cam MA55 Ch Ch Ox MA57. Virginia Th Sem 57 S'wark Ord Course 87. **d** 88 **p** 88. NSM Blackheath Ascension *S'wark* from 88. *14A Church Terrace, London SE13 5BT* Tel 0181-318 3089

PRESTON, John. b 26. St Aid Birkenhead 58. **d** 52 **p** 52. In RC Ch 50-57; C Chadderton Ch Ch *Man* 58-59; C Didsbury Ch Ch 59-63; R Cheetham St Jo 63-96; rtd 96. *Edelweiss, 31 Rectory Road, Crumpsall, Manchester M8 5EA 7* Tel 0161-740 2533

PRESTON, John Baker. b 23. Lon Univ BA49. Oak Hill Th Coll 46. **d** 51 **p** 52. C Fazakerley Em *Liv* 51-55; C Eastbourne H Trin *Chich* 55-57; V Blackheath St Jo *S'wark* 57-65; Perm to Offic *Cant* 69-91; rtd 88. *43 Wedgwood Drive, Poole, Dorset BH14 8ES*

PRESTON, Dr John Michael. b 40. K Coll Lon BD63 AKC63 Lon Univ BA81 Southn Univ PhD91. St Boniface Warminster. **d** 65 **p** 66. C Heston *Lon* 65-67; C Northolt St Mary 67-72; Trinidad and Tobago 72-74; P-in-c Aveley *Chelmsf* 74-78; V 78-82; C Eastleigh *Win* 82-84; C-in-c Boyatt Wood CD 84-87; V W End from 87. *The Vicarage, Elizabeth Close, West End, Southampton SO3 3BU* Tel (01703) 472180

PRESTON, Mrs Junko Monica. b 38. Aoyama Gakuin Tokyo BA. **d** 92 **p** 93. C St Paul's Cathl Wellington from 92. *12A Hobson Street, Thorndon, Wellington, New Zealand* Tel Wellington (4) 473 1902

PRESTON, Leonard Arthur. b 09. Leeds Univ BA32 DipEd48. Coll of Resurr Mirfield 34. **d** 34 **p** 35. C Egremont St Columba *Ches* 34-36; Chapl Laleham Abbey 56-76; rtd 76; Perm to Offic *Cant* from 64. *Underhill, Mountain Street, Chilham, Canterbury, Kent CT4 8DG* Tel (01227) 730266

PRESTON, Maurice. b 25. Lon Univ DipTh69 BD77. St Aid Birkenhead. **d** 57 **p** 58. C Stapleford *S'well* 57-59; C Wombwell *Sheff* 59-62; V Thorpe Hesley 62-84; V Rawcliffe 84-89; rtd 89. *19 Erw Goch, Abergele LL22 9AQ* Tel (01745) 826952

PRESTON, Michael Christopher. b 47. Hatf Coll Dur BA68. Ripon Coll Cuddesdon 75. **d** 78 **p** 79. C Epsom St Martin *Guildf* 78-82; C Guildf H Trin w St Mary 82-86; V Epsom St Barn from 86. *St Barnabas' Vicarage, Hook Road, Epsom, Surrey KT19 8TU* Tel (01372) 722874

PRESTON, Canon Percival Kenneth. b 16. Ch Ch Ox BA38 MA48. Cuddesdon Coll 38. **d** 40 **p** 45. C Jersey St Helier *Win* 40-46; C Ox SS Phil and Jas *Ox* 46-48; C Westbury-on-Trym H Trin *Bris* 48-50; Min Lawrence Weston CD 50-55; V Horfield St Greg 55-81; Hon Can Bris Cathl 74-82; RD Horfield 76-81; rtd 81; Perm to Offic *Bris* from 82; Perm to Offic *Glouc* from 83. *56 Gloucester Road, Rudgeway, Bristol BS12 2RT* Tel (01454) 612794

PRESTON, Reuben James. b 65. York Univ BSc86 MEng87. Westcott Ho Cam 88. **d** 91 **p** 92. C Weoley Castle *Birm* 91-94; TV Malvern Link w Cowleigh *Worc* 94-96; Perm to Offic *Birm* from 96. *56 Eva Road, Winson Green, Birmingham B18 4NQ* Tel 0121-523 3888

PRESTON, Canon Ronald Haydn. b 13. Lon Univ BSc(Econ)35 St Cath Soc Ox BA40 MA44 DD83. Ripon Hall Ox 38. **d** 40 **p** 41. C Sheff St Jo *Sheff* 40-43; Study Sec SCM 43-48; Warden St Anselm Hall Man 48-63; Lect Chr Ethics Man Univ 49-70; C Man Victoria Park *Man* 50-57; Can Res Man Cathl 57-71; Sub-Dean 70-71; Hon Can 71-80; Select Preacher Cam Univ 63; Select Preacher Ox Univ 76 and 80; Prof of Soc and Past Th Man Univ 70-80; rtd 80; Perm to Offic *Man* from 80. *161 Old Hall Lane, Manchester M14 6HJ* Tel 0161-225 3291

PRESTON, Miss Rosemary Muriel. b 23. St Mich Ho Ox DipTh. **dss** 80 **d** 87. Burundi 80-85; NSM Buckland Monachorum *Ex*

87-92; Perm to Offic from 92. *Fresh Springs, 3 Buckland Court, Crapstone, Yelverton, Devon PL20 7UE* Tel (01822) 854037

PRESTON, Thomas Leonard. b 27. Tyndale Hall Bris. **d** 64 **p** 65. C Moss Side St Jas *Man* 64-66; C Urmston 66-68; V Thornham w Gravel Hole 68-76; Chapl to the Deaf *Chich* 76-80; TV York All SS Pavement w St Crux and St Martin etc *York* 80-93; Chapl to the Deaf 80-93; rtd 93; Perm to Offic *Man* from 93. *31 The Green, Royle Fields, Rochdale, Lancs* Tel (01706) 358797

PRESTON, William. b 25. St Cath Coll Cam BA46 MA50 Reading Univ MSc79. Oak Hill Th Coll 48. **d** 50 **p** 51. C Hyson Green *S'well* 50-52; C Lenton 52-55; Kenya 55-62; Bethany Sch Goudhurst 62-69; Cranbrook Sch Kent 69-90; Perm to Offic *Cant* from 64; Perm to Offic *Roch* from 66; rtd 90. *29 Orchard Way, Horsmonden, Tonbridge, Kent TN12 8LA* Tel (01892) 722616

PRESTON-THOMAS, Canon Colin Barnabas Rashleigh. b 28. K Coll Lon 48 Edin Th Coll 51. **d** 53 **p** 54. C Edin St Dav *Edin* 53-54; Chapl St Ninian's Cathl Perth *St And* 54-55; Prec St Ninian's Cathl Perth 55-60; Chapl HM Pris Perth 55-60; P-in-c Inverkeithing *St And* 60; R 61-72; P-in-c Rosyth 60; R 61-72; Syn Clerk 68-93; Can St Ninian's Cathl Perth 68-93; R Forfar 72-82; Dioc Sec 80-90; R Kilmaveonaig 82-93; R Pitlochry 82-93; rtd 93; Hon Can St Ninian's Cathl Perth *St And* from 93. *14 Muirend Grove, Perth PH1 1JW* Tel (01738) 627807

PRESTWOOD, Ms Jayne Marie. b 64. Man Univ BA86. Linc Th Coll DipMin93 MA94. **d** 94 **p** 95. C Reddish *Man* from 94. *2 Rowsley Grove, Stockport, Cheshire SK5 7AH* Tel 0161-443 1949

PREVETT, Mark Norman. b 59. Univ of Wales (Cardiff) BD88. St Mich Coll Llan 85. **d** 88 **p** 89. C Brynmawr *S & B* 88-90; C Bassaleg *Mon* 90-92; R Blaina and Nantyglo from 92. *The Rectory, Station Road, Blaina NP3 3BW* Tel (01495) 290079

PREVITE, The Ven Anthony Michael Allen. b 41. TCD DipTh88. CITC 85. **d** 88 **p** 89. C Galway w Kilcummin *T, K & A* 88-91; I Omey w Ballynakill, Errislannan and Roundstone 91-93; RD Tuam from 92; Dean Tuam 93-96; I Tuam w Cong and Aasleagh 93-96; Adn Tuam from 96; Can Tuam Cathl from 96; I Omey w Ballynakill, Errislannan and Roundstone from 96. *The Rectory, Church Hill, Clifden, Co Galway, Irish Republic* Tel Clifden (95) 21147 Fax as telephone

PREWER, Dennis. b 30. Kelham Th Coll 50. **d** 54 **p** 55. C Stockport St Thos *Ches* 54-58; C Gt Grimsby St Mary and St Jas *Linc* 58-62; V Gt Harwood St Jo *Blackb* 62-64; V Scarcliffe *Derby* 64-70; Org Sec CECS 70-92; Dios Liv, Ban and St As 70-78; Dio Man 78-92; Lic to Offic *Ches* from 70; Perm to Offic *Man* from 78; rtd 92. *19 Alan Drive, Marple, Stockport, Cheshire SK6 6LN* Tel 0161-427 2827

PRICE, Alec John. b 32. Solicitor 58 Univ of Wales (Abth) LLB55. St Deiniol's Hawarden 77. **d** 79 **p** 80. Hon C St As *St As* 79-80; V Choral St As Cathl 79-83; Hon C St As and Tremeirchion 80-83; R Cilcain and Nannerch and Rhyd-y-mwyn 84-88; Min Can and PV Bre Cathl *S & B* 88-90; Perm to Offic *Lich* 90-91; C Shrewsbury St Chad w St Mary 91-96; Chapl Shrewsbury Town Cen 91-96; rtd 96. *Lindenhurst, Green Acre Road, Copthorne, Shrewsbury SY3 8LR* Tel (01743) 245013

PRICE, Miss Alison Jane. b 63. NNEB84. Aston Tr Scheme 91 Westcott Ho Cam CTM95. **d** 95 **p** 96. C Upper Norwood All SS *S'wark* from 95. *51 Chevening Road, London SE19 3TD* Tel 0181-768 0269

PRICE, Alun Huw. b 47. St D Coll Lamp DipTh70. **d** 70 **p** 71. C Carmarthen St Dav *St D* 70-73; V Betws Ifan 73-77; CF from 77. *MOD Chaplains (Army), Trenchard Lines, Upavon, Pewsey, Wilts SN9 6BE* Tel (01980) 615804 Fax 615800

PRICE, Anthony Ronald (Tony). b 49. Linc Coll Ox BA71 MA83 St Jo Coll Dur BA78. **d** 79 **p** 80. C St Alb St Paul *St Alb* 79-81; C Wootton 81-85; C Lydiard Millicent w Lydiard Tregoz *Bris* 85-86; TV The Lydiards 86-91; V Marston *Ox* 91-95; V Marston w Elsfield from 95; RD Cowley from 97. *The Vicarage, Marston, Oxford OX3 0PR* Tel (01865) 247034

PRICE, The Ven Cecil Johnston. b 25. ARCM TCD BA48 MA52. CITC 49. **d** 50 **p** 51. C Tralee *L & K* 50-53; C Cork St Ann w St Luke Shandon *C, C & R* 53-56; I Desertserges 56-58; I Limerick St Mich *L & K* 58-67; Can Limerick Cathl 63-67; I Bandon *C, C & R* 67-69; I Delgany *D & G* 69-94; Adn Glendalough 89-94; rtd 94. *31 Bellvue Park, Greystones, Co Wicklow, Irish Republic* Tel Dublin (1) 287 6805

PRICE, Mrs Christine Janice. b 45. Sarum & Wells Th Coll 83. **dss** 86 **d** 87 **p** 94. Roxbourne St Andr *Lon* 86-87; NSM 87-90; NSM Roxeth Ch Ch and Harrow St Pet 90-93; NSM Roxeth 93-94; C 94-96; C Costessey *Nor* from 96. *St Helen's House, Gurney Road, New Costessey, Norwich NR5 0HH* Tel (01603) 744285

PRICE, Canon Clive Stanley. b 42. ALCD69. **d** 69 **p** 70. C Chenies and Lt Chalfont *Ox* 69-75; R Upper Stour *Sarum* 75-79; C-in-c Panshanger CD *St Alb* 79-82; TV Digswell and Panshanger 82-86; P-in-c St Oswald in Lee w Bingfield *Newc* from 86; Dioc Ecum Officer from 86; Hon Can Newc Cathl from 97. *St Oswald's Vicarage, Wall, Hexham, Northd NE46 4DU* Tel (01434) 681354

PRICE, David. b 27. Wycliffe Hall Ox 61. **d** 63 **p** 64. C Bucknall and Bagnall *Lich* 63-67; C Abingdon w Shippon *Ox* 67-76; Israel 76-84; V S Kensington St Luke *Lon* 84-92; P-in-c S Kensington St Jude 88-92; rtd 92; Hon C Hordle *Win* from 92. *Church Cottage, Sway Road, Tiptoe, Lymington, Hants SO41 6FR* Tel (01425) 616670

PRICE, David Gareth Michael. b 64. Ex Univ BA86 Kent Univ MA87 FSS. Wycliffe Hall Ox BTh94. **d** 97. C Godalming *Guildf* from 97. *13 Lammas Road, Godalming, Surrey GU7 1YL* Tel (01483) 424756

PRICE, Canon David Rea. b 39. St Aid Birkenhead 61. **d** 63 **p** 64. C Green Street Green *Roch* 63-66; C Gillingham St Mary 66-69; C New Windsor St Jo *Ox* 69-72; V Winkfield 72-80; RD Bracknell 78-86; V Sunningdale 80-86; TR Wimborne Minster and Holt *Sarum* 86-96; R Wimborne Minster from 96; Chapl Wimborne Hosp from 86; RD Wimborne from 88; Can and Preb Sarum Cathl from 92. *The Rectory, 17 King Street, Wimborne, Dorset BH21 1DZ* Tel (01202) 882340

PRICE, Canon David Trevor William. b 43. Keble Coll Ox BA65 MA69 MEHS FRHistS79 FSA95. Sarum & Wells Th Coll 72. **d** 72 **p** 73. Lect Univ of Wales (Lamp) *St D* 70-87; Sen Lect 87-97; Chapl 79-80; Dean of Chpl 90-91; Dioc Archivist from 82; P-in-c Betws Bledrws 86-97; Hon Can St D Cathl 90-92 and from 92; V Cydweli and Llandyfaelog from 97. *The Vicarage, Vicarage Lane, Kidwelly SA17 4SY* Tel (01554) 890295

PRICE, Dawson. b 31. OBE. Peterho Cam BA52. Oak Hill NSM Course 88. **d** 91 **p** 92. NSM Harpenden St Nic *St Alb* from 91. *1 Rye Close, Harpenden, Herts AL5 4LD* Tel (01582) 460380

PRICE, Canon Derek William. b 27. St Pet Hall Ox BA51 MA55. Qu Coll Birm 51. **d** 53 **p** 54. C St Marylebone St Mark Hamilton Terrace *Lon* 53-57; C Stevenage *St Alb* 57-63; Jamaica 63-67; R Bridgham and Roudham *Nor* 67-80; R E w W Harling 69-80; Hon Can Nor Cathl 75-92; RD Thetford and Rockland 76-86; P-in-c Kilverstone 80-87; P-in-c Croxton 80-87; TR Thetford 80-87; R Castle Acre w Newton, Rougham and Southacre 87-92; rtd 92; Perm to Offic *Nor* from 92. *Fourways, King's Road, Dereham, Norfolk NE19 2AG* Tel (01362) 691660

PRICE, Chan Desmond. b 23. St D Coll Lamp BA50. **d** 51 **p** 52. C Llwynypia *Llan* 51-52; C Ystradyfodwg 52-54; C Watford Ch Ch *St Alb* 54-56; Chapl RAF 56-68; R Dinas and Llanllawer *St D* 68-72; V Llandeilo Fawr w Llandyfeisant 72-79; V Llandeilo and Taliaris 79-91; Can St D Cathl 83-91; Chan 89-91; RD Llangadog and Llandeilo 90-91; rtd 91; Hon Can St D Cathl *St D* from 91. *24 Diana Road, Llandeilo SA19 6RS* Tel (01558) 824039

PRICE, Canon Edward Glyn. b 35. Univ of Wales (Lamp) BA55. Ch Div Sch of the Pacific (USA) BD58. **d** 58 **p** 59. C Denbigh *St As* 58-65; V Llanasa 65-76; V Buckley 76-91; Dioc RE Adv from 77; RD Mold 86-91; Can St As Cathl from 87; Preb and Sacr from 95; V Llandrillo-yn-Rhos from 91. *Llandrillo Vicarage, 36 Llandudno Road, Colwyn Bay LL28 4UD* Tel (01492) 548878

PRICE, Canon Eric. b 14. Bps' Coll Cheshunt 42. **d** 44 **p** 45. C Wednesbury St Paul Wood Green *Lich* 44-47; C W Bromwich St Andr 47-48; Chapl Harborne Colleg Sch 48-56; V Ashford Carbonell w Ashford Bowdler *Heref* 56-61; P-in-c Brimfield 60-61; V Handsworth St Mich *Birm* 61-84; rtd 85; Perm to Offic *Birm* from 85. *11 Brosil Avenue, Birmingham B20 1LB* Tel 0121-523 0414

PRICE, Frank Watkin. b 22. ALCM37 Univ of Wales (Lamp) BA45. St Mich Coll Llan 45. **d** 47 **p** 48. C Cwmaman *St D* 47-50; C Llanelli 50-52; Chapl RAF 52-68; Hd Master Amman Valley Lower Sch 68-85; R St Nicholas w Bonvilston and St George-super-Ely *Llan* 85-92; rtd 92; Perm to Offic *Llan* 92-94; Perm to Offic *St D* from 92. *105 Gwscwm Road, Burry Port SA16 0YU* Tel (01554) 834048

PRICE, Frederick Leslie. b 30. Oak Hill Th Coll 59. **d** 61 **p** 62. C Hougham in Dover Ch Ch *Cant* 61-64; R Plumbland and Gilcrux *Carl* 64-95; rtd 95. *1 Beech Hill, Oughterside, Aspatria, Carlisle CA5 2QA*

PRICE, Geoffrey David. b 46. NDA NCA. Oak Hill Th Coll DipHE. **d** 83 **p** 84. C Gt Baddow *Chelmsf* 83-86; C Hampreston *Sarum* 86-88; TV 88-93; P-in-c Drayton in Hales *Lich* from 93; P-in-c Adderley 93-97; P-in-c Moreton Say 93-97. *St Mary's Vicarage, Market Drayton, Shropshire TF9 1AQ* Tel (01630) 652527

PRICE, Gerald Andrew. b 31. NE Ord Course. **d** 84 **p** 85. C Monkseaton St Mary *Newc* 84-87; V Cowgate 87-94; C Beltingham w Henshaw 94-96; C Haydon Bridge 94-96; rtd 96. *24 Hallstile Bank, Hexham, Northd NE46 3PQ* Tel (01434) 603374

PRICE, The Very Revd Hilary Martin Connop. b 12. Qu Coll Cam BA33 MA37. Ridley Hall Cam 34. **d** 36 **p** 37. C Hersham *Guildf* 36-40; C Portsm Cathl *Portsm* 40-41; C Cambridge H Trin *Ely* 41-46; Chapl RAFVR 43-46; V Bishopwearmouth St Gabr *Dur* 46-56; R Newcastle w Butterton *Lich* 56-67; RD Newcastle 56-67; Preb Lich Cathl 64-67; Provost Chelmsf 67-77; rtd 77. *98 St James's Street, Shaftesbury, Dorset SP7 8HF* Tel (01747) 52118

PRICE, John Francis. b 32. Qu Coll Cam BA54 MA. Ridley Hall Cam 54. **d** 56 **p** 57. C Leic H Apostles *Leic* 56-60; V Forest Gate St Mark *Chelmsf* 60-71; V Harold Hill St Geo 72-79; R Loughton St Mary 79-83; TR Loughton St Mary and St Mich 83-88; R Kirby-le-Soken w Gt Holland 88-92; rtd 92. *97 Kings*

Parade, Holland-on-Sea, Clacton-on-Sea, Essex CO15 5JH Tel (01255) 813202

PRICE, John Joseph. b 44. Ridley Hall Cam 89. **d** 92 **p** 93. C Glenfield *Leic* 92-97; Relig Affairs Adv BBC Radio Leics 93-97; Midl Regional Co-ord Crosslinks from 97; Perm to Offic *Birm, Derby, St E, Lich, Nor* and *S'well* from 97. *Copper Beeches, 59A Peterborough Road, Castor, Peterborough PE5 7AL* Tel (01733) 380025

PRICE, Canon John Lowry Augustine. b 13. Mercer Ho Melbourne TDip69. AKC39. **d** 39 **p** 40. C Luton St Andr *St Alb* 39-42; C St Alb St Sav 46-48; Australia from 48; Can Ballarat 60-62; rtd 65. *88 Carrington Street, Macedon, Victoria, Australia 3440* Tel Macedon (54) 261941

PRICE, John Newman. b 32. St Alb Minl Tr Scheme 80. **d** 83 **p** 84. NSM Bedford St Pet w St Cuth *St Alb* 83-88; C Lt Berkhamsted and Bayford, Essendon etc 88-92; P-in-c Benington w Walkern from 92. *The Rectory, Bockings, Walkern, Stevenage, Herts SG2 7PB* Tel (01438) 861322

PRICE, Canon John Richard. b 34. Mert Coll Ox BA58 MA62. Westcott Ho Cam 58. **d** 60 **p** 61. C Man St Aid *Man* 60-63; C Bramley *Ripon* 63-67; V Leeds All Hallows w St Simon 67-74; P-in-c Wrangthorn 73-74; V Claughton cum Grange *Ches* 74-78; V Mottram in Longdendale w Woodhead 78-88; RD Mottram 79-88; Hon Can Ches Cathl from 86; R Nantwich from 88. *The Rectory, Nantwich, Cheshire CW5 5RQ* Tel (01270) 625268

PRICE, Joseph Roderick (<u>Rod</u>). b 45. St Mich Coll Llan 71. **d** 75 **p** 76. C Fleur-de-Lis *Mon* 75-79; CF from 79. *MOD Chaplains (Army), Trenchard Lines, Upavon, Pewsey, Wilts SN9 6BE* Tel (01980) 615804 Fax 615800

PRICE, Lawrence Robert. b 43. LICeram71 N Staffs Poly CertCT66 MDCT74. St Jo Coll Dur 76. **d** 78 **p** 79. C Harlescott *Lich* 78-80; C Cheddleton 80-83; P-in-c Calton 83-84; P-in-c Cauldon 83-84; P-in-c Grindon 83-84; P-in-c Waterfall 83-84; R Calton, Cauldon, Grindon and Waterfall 85-88; rtd 88; P-in-c Kingsley *Lich* from 95. *The Rectory, Kingsley, Stoke-on-Trent ST10 2BA* Tel (01538) 754754

PRICE, Mari Josephine. b 43. St Hugh's Coll Ox BA65 Ox Univ MA69 DipEd66. Llan Dioc Tr Scheme 93. **d** 97. NSM Lisvane *Llan* from 97. *23 Ty Draw Road, Roath, Cardiff CF2 5HB* Tel (01222) 456757 or 0850-019883 (Mobile)

PRICE, Martin Randall Connop. b 45. Lon Univ BSc71 Fitzw Coll Cam BA75 MA79. Ridley Hall Cam 73. **d** 76 **p** 77. C Keynsham *B & W* 76-79; Ind Chapl *Sheff* 79-83; V Wortley 79-83; R Hook Norton w Gt Rollright, Swerford etc *Ox* 83-91; V Shiplake w Dunsden from 91. *The Vicarage, Shiplake, Henley-on-Thames, Oxon RG9 4BS* Tel (0118) 940 1306

PRICE, Michael Graham. b 62. Ex Coll Ox BA84. Linc Th Coll 84. **d** 86 **p** 87. C Salford St Phil w St Steph *Man* 86-90; R Man Gd Shep 90-95; V Netherton St Andr *Worc* from 95. *The Vicarage, Highbridge Road, Netherton, Dudley, W Midlands DY2 0HT* Tel (01384) 253118

PRICE, Canon Norman Havelock. b 28. Univ of Wales (Lamp) BA52. St Mich Coll Llan 52. **d** 54 **p** 55. C Maindee *Mon* 54-58; V Llantilio Crossenny and Llanfihangel Ystern etc 58-64; V Mon St Thos-over-Monnow 64-65; V Mon St Thos-over-Monnow and Wonastow 65-71; V Overmonnow w Wonastow and Michel Troy 71-93; RD Mon 84-93; Can St Woolos Cathl 91-93; rtd 93; Hon Can St Woolos Cathl *Mon* from 93. *Escholl, Llanellen Road, Llanfoist, Abergavenny NP7 9NF* Tel (01873) 854749

PRICE, Canon Peter Bryan. b 44. Oak Hill Th Coll 72. **d** 74 **p** 75. C Portsdown *Portsm* 74-78; Chapl Scargill Ho 78-80; P-in-c Addiscombe St Mary *Cant* 80-81; V 81-84; V Addiscombe St Mary *S'wark* 85-88; Can Res and Chan S'wark Cathl 88-91; Perm to Offic from 92; Gen Sec USPG from 92. *14 Oakwood Road, London SW20 0PW or, USPG, Partnership House, 147 Waterloo Road, London SE1 8XA* Tel 0181-946 3814 or 0171-928 8681 Fax 0171-928 2371

PRICE, Peter Charles. b 27. Vancouver Sch of Th DipTh61. **d** 61 **p** 62. Canada 61-66; C St Mary-at-Latton *Chelmsf* 66-68; C Bearsted *Cant* 68-74; TV Ebbw Vale *Mon* 74-77; V Llanfihangel Crucorney w Oldcastle etc 77-87; St Helena 87-90; V Llanishen w Trellech Grange and Llanfihangel etc *Mon* 90-94; rtd 94; Perm to Offic *Heref* from 95. *1 Kynaston, Much Marcle, Ledbury, Herefordshire HR8 2PD* Tel (01531) 670687

PRICE, Philip. b 24. Tyndale Hall Bris 50. **d** 55 **p** 56. Kenya 55-75; R Gt Horkesley *Chelmsf* 75-89; rtd 89; Perm to Offic *Chelmsf* from 89. *229 Meadgate Avenue, Great Baddow, Chelmsford CM2 7NJ* Tel (01245) 251499

PRICE, Raymond Francklin. b 30. Wycliffe Hall Ox 61. **d** 62 **p** 63. C Bilston St Leon *Lich* 62-67; C Keighley *Bradf* 67-70; V Mangotsfield *Bris* 70-79; Ind Chapl *Birm* 79-86; C Birm St Martin 84-85; C Birm St Martin w Bordesley St Andr 85-86; V Edgbaston St Aug from 86. *St Augustine's Vicarage, 44 Vernon Road, Birmingham B16 9SH* Tel 0121-454 0127

PRICE, Dr Roland Kendrick. b 41. Cam Univ MA64 Essex Univ PhD69. St Alb and Ox Min Course CBTS95. **d** 95 **p** 96. NSM Cholsey *Ox* 95-97. *Bentinckstraat 129, 2582 ST, Den Haag, The Netherlands*

PRICE, Roy Ernest. b 13. AKC38. **d** 38 **p** 39. C Ilminster w Whitelackington *B & W* 38-40; CF (EC) 40-47; CF 47-59; V S Stoke w Woodcote *Ox* 59-79; rtd 79; Perm to Offic *Win* from 82. *74A London Road, Whitchurch, Hants RG28 7LY* Tel (01256) 892581

PRICE, Stanley George. b 32. FRICS69. Trin Coll Bris 84. **d** 85 **p** 86. C Newport w Longford and Chetwynd *Lich* 85-88; V Ipstones w Berkhamsytch and Onecote w Bradnop from 88. *The Vicarage, Ipstones, Stoke-on-Trent ST10 2LF* Tel (01538) 266313

PRICE, Timothy Fry. b 51. NE Lon Poly CQSW. St Jo Coll Nottm 85. **d** 87 **p** 88. C Church Stretton *Heref* 87-91; V Sinfin *Derby* from 91. *St Stephen's Vicarage, 311 Sinfin Lane, Sinfin, Derby DE24 9GP* Tel (01332) 760186

PRICE, Victor John. b 35. Oak Hill Th Coll 62. **d** 65 **p** 66. C Rainham *Chelmsf* 65-70; V Dover St Martin *Cant* 70-78; V Madeley *Heref* 78-90; P-in-c Derby St Pet and Ch Ch w H Trin *Derby* 90-91; V 91-96; P-in-c Smalley from 96; P-in-c Morley from 96. *The Vicarage, 80 Main Road, Smalley, Ilkeston, Derbyshire DE7 6EF* Tel (01332) 880380

PRICE, William Haydn (<u>Dai</u>). b 20. Sarum & Wells Th Coll 77. **d** 80 **p** 81. NSM Alverstoke *Portsm* 80-85; rtd 85; Perm to Offic *Portsm* from 85. *15 Amersham Close, Alverstoke, Gosport, Hants PO12 2RU* Tel (01705) 580965

PRICE, William <u>Norman</u>. b 52. GRNCM73. N Ord Course 86. **d** 89 **p** 90. C Lower Broughton Ascension *Man* 89-91; Min Can and Succ St E Cathl *St E* 92-96; Prec 94-96; V Par *Truro* from 96. *The Vicarage, 42 Vicarage Road, Tywardreath, Par, Cornwall PL24 2PH* Tel (01726) 812775 Fax as telephone E-mail frnorman@compuserve.com

PRICE-ROBERTS, Mervyn. b 29. Trin Coll Carmarthen TCert51 Univ of Wales DipRE52 BEd79. St Mich Coll Llan 89 Ban Ord Course 84. **d** 87 **p** 88. NSM Caerhun w Llangelynin w Llanbedr-y-Cennin *Ban* 87-89; V Llandygai w Tregarth from 89. *St Ann's Vicarage, Bethesda, Bangor LL57 4AX* Tel (01248) 600357

PRICHARD, Canon Thomas John. b 16. FRHistS82 Keele Univ PhD81 Univ of Wales (Ban) BA38 MA72. Chich Th Coll 38. **d** 39 **p** 40. C Blaenau Ffestiniog *Ban* 39-41; C Machynlleth *Llan* 41-42; C Llanfabon 42-44; C Ystradyfodwg 44-50; V Dinas w Penygraig 50-69; RD Rhondda 64-84; Can Llan Cathl 66-84; R Neath w Llantwit 69-84; rtd 84. *Tros-yr-Afon, Llangwnnadl, Pwllheli LL53 8NS* Tel (01758) 612832

PRIDAY, Gerald Nelson. b 35. Glouc Th Course. **d** 85 **p** 88. NSM Eardisland *Heref* 85-91; NSM Aymestrey and Leinthall Earles w Wigmore etc 85-91; NSM Kingsland 85-91; NSM Eye, Croft w Yarpole and Lucton 91-94; NSM Heref All SS 94-96; NSM Letton w Staunton, Byford, Mansel Gamage etc from 96. *St Mary's House, Staunton-on-Wye, Herefordshire HR4 7LT* Tel (01981) 500181

PRIDDIN, Mrs Maureen Anne. b 46. Leeds Univ BA67 Nottm Univ DipEd68. EMMTC 82. **dss** 85 **d** 87 **p** 94. Mickleover St Jo *Derby* 85-87; Hon Par Dn 87; C from 90; Dioc World Development Officer 87-90. *7 Portland Close, Mickleover, Derby DE3 5BR* Tel (01332) 513672

✠**PRIDDIS, The Rt Revd Anthony Martin.** b 48. CCC Cam BA69 MA73 New Coll Ox DipTh71 MA75. Cuddesdon Coll 69. **d** 72 **p** 73 **c** 96. C New Addington *Cant* 72-75; Chapl Ch Ch Ox 75-80; Lic to Offic *Ox* 76-80; TV High Wycombe 80-86; P-in-c Amersham 86-90; R 90-96; RD Amersham 92-96; Hon Can Ch Ch 95-96; Suff Bp Warw *Cov* from 96. *Warwick House, 139 Kenilworth Road, Coventry CV4 7AF* Tel (01203) 416200 Fax 415254

PRIDEAUX, Humphrey Grevile. b 36. CCC Ox BA60 MA63 Birm Univ CertEd66 Lon Univ DipEd73 Open Univ BA87. Linc Th Coll 59. **d** 61 **p** 62. C Northampton St Matt *Pet* 61-62; C Milton *Portsm* 62-65; Perm to Offic *Birm* 65-66; Hd of RE Qu Mary's Gr Sch Walsall 66-69; Lic to Offic *Lich* 66-69; Lect St Martin's Coll Lanc 69-80; Lic to Offic *Blackb* 69-80; Perm to Offic *Portsm* 80-86; Hon C Fareham H Trin 86-90; Hon C Bishops Waltham 90-94; NSM P-in-c W Meon and Warnford from 94. *The Rectory, Doctors Lane, West Meon, Petersfield, Hants GU32 1LR* Tel (01730) 829226

PRIDGEON, Paul Garth Walsingham. b 45. Sussex Univ BA69 CertEd. Glouc Sch of Min 87. **d** 87 **p** 88. NSM Cirencester *Glouc* 87-97; NSM Cold Aston w Notgrove and Turkdean from 97; NSM Northleach w Hampnett and Farmington from 97. *4 Abbey Way, Cirencester, Glos GL7 2DT* Tel (01285) 656860

PRIDHAM, Peter Arthur George Drake. b 16. Ely Th Coll 62. **d** 64 **p** 65. C Benwell St Aid *Newc* 64-67; C Berwick H Trin 67-71; V Sleekburn 71-76; P-in-c Otterburn w Elsdon and Horsley w Byrness 76-80; TV Bellingham/Otterburn Gp 80-84; rtd 84. *5 Hospital Close, Greatham, Hartlepool, Cleveland TS25 2HS* Tel (01429) 870582

PRIDIE, William Raleigh (<u>Will</u>). b 49. ACP82 FCollP83 Bris Univ BEd72 DipMan82. **d** 93 **p** 94. C Kingstone w Clehonger, Eaton Bishop etc *Heref* 93-96; P-in-c Kimbolton w Hamnish and Middleton-on-the-Hill from 96; P-in-c Bockleton w Leysters from 96; Continuing Min Educn Officer from 96. *The New Vicarage, Kimbolton, Leominster, Herefordshire HR6 0EJ* Tel (01568) 615295

PRIDMORE, John Stuart. b 36. Nottm Univ BA62 MA67. Ridley Hall Cam 62. **d** 65 **p** 66. C Camborne *Truro* 65-67; Tutor Ridley Hall Cam 67-68; Chapl 68-71; Asst Chapl K Edw Sch Witley 71-75; Chapl 75-86; Tanzania 86-88; Angl Chapl Hengrave Hall

Cen 88-89; C St Martin-in-the-Fields *Lon* 89-95; TR Hackney from 95. *The Rectory, 356 Mare Street, London E8 1HR* Tel 0181-985 5374

PRIEST, Richard Mark. b 63. Oak Hill Th Coll BA90. **d** 90 **p** 91. C Okehampton w Inwardleigh *Ex* 90-94; C Okehampton w Inwardleigh, Bratton Clovelly etc 94; CF from 94. *MOD Chaplains (Army), Trenchard Lines, Upavon, Pewsey, Wilts SN9 6BE* Tel (01980) 615804 Fax 615800

PRIESTLEY, Canon Alan Charles. b 41. Lon Univ BD69. Kelham Th Coll 64 Wm Temple Coll Rugby 65. **d** 65 **p** 66. C Edgbaston St Aug *Birm* 65-68; C Chelmsley Wood 68-72; TV 72-76; V Hazelwell from 76; Dioc Communications Officer from 83; Bp's Press Officer from 85; Hon Can Birm Cathl from 87. *The Vicarage, 316 Vicarage Road, Birmingham B14 7NH* Tel 0121-444 4469 Fax 444 8184

PRIESTLEY, John Christopher. b 39. Trin Coll Ox BA60. Wells Th Coll 61. **d** 68 **p** 69. C Habergham All SS *Blackb* 68-70; C Padiham 70-75; V Colne Ch Ch from 75; Chapl to The Queen from 90; RD Pendle *Blackb* 91-96. *The Vicarage, Keighley Road, Colne, Lancs BB8 7HF* Tel (01282) 863511

PRIESTLEY, Rosemary Jane. b 67. **d** 96 **p** 97. C Scotforth *Blackb* from 96. *10 Lawnswood Avenue, Scotforth, Lancs LA1 4NZ* Tel (01524) 65717

PRIESTLY, Thomas Herbert (Tom). b 67. Ulster Univ BA91. CITC BTh94. **d** 94 **p** 95. C Ballymena w Ballyclug *Conn* from 94. *6 Rockgrove Brae, Ballymena, Co Antrim BT43 5HY* Tel (01266) 42805

PRIESTNALL, Reginald Hayward. b 22. Jes Coll Cam BA44 MA47. Ridley Hall Cam 44. **d** 45 **p** 46. C Streatham Immanuel *S'wark* 45-48; C Barking St Marg *Chelmsf* 48-51; R Bonsall *Derby* 51-53; P-in-c Mackworth St Fran 53-54; V 54-67; Chapl Kingsway Hosp Derby 61-67; V Rockingham w Caldecote *Pet* 67-71; V Northampton St Mich 71-77; V Ketton 77-89; RD Barnack 86-89; rtd 89. *Lavender Cottage, 486 Earlham Road, Norwich NR4 7HP*

PRIESTNER, Hugh. b 45. Nottm Univ BTh75. Linc Th Coll 71. **d** 75 **p** 76. C Seaton Hirst *Newc* 75-78; C Longbenton St Bart 78-81; P-in-c Glendale Gp 81-82; TV 83-88; Chapl Stafford Distr Gen Hosp 88-91; Chapl Stafford Distr Infirmary 88-91. *Address temp unknown*

PRIESTNER, James Arthur. b 14. Leeds Univ BA39. Coll of Resurr Mirfield 39. **d** 41 **p** 42. C Wigston Magna *Leic* 41-44; CF (EC) 44-47; Hon CF 47; C Amersham *Ox* 47-51; V Lt Lever *Man* 51-60; V Benwell St Aid *Newc* 60-70; V Longhoughton w Howick 70-79; rtd 79. *16 Eastfield Avenue, Monkseaton, Whitley Bay, Tyne & Wear NE25 8LT* Tel 0191-252 9518

PRIGG, Patrick John. b 53. K Coll Lon BD82. Sarum & Wells Th Coll 89. **d** 92 **p** 93. C Wavertree St Mary *Liv* 92-96; Chapl Sandown Coll 92-96; P-in-c Glem Valley United Benefice *St E* from 96. *The Rectory, Glemsford, Sudbury, Suffolk CO10 7RF* Tel (01787) 282164

PRIME, Geoffrey Daniel. b 12. Lich Th Coll 32. **d** 35 **p** 36. C Uttoxeter w Bramshall *Lich* 35-42; P-in-c Newborough w Ch Ch on Needwood 42-43; V Pattingham 43-55; V Longstone *Derby* 55-62; Org Sec (Dios Derby, Linc, Sheff & S'well) CECS 62-65; Perm to Offic *Derby* from 62; rtd 77. *Westside Mill Farm, Hulme End, Buxton, Derbyshire SK17 0EY* Tel (01298) 84461

PRIMROSE, David Edward Snodgrass. b 55. Univ of Wales (Cardiff) DipSocWork78 St Jo Coll Cam MA80. Trin Coll Bris BA92. **d** 87 **p** 92. Pakistan 87-89; C Glouc St Paul *Glouc* 92-96; R Badgeworth, Shurdington and Witcombe w Bentham from 96. *The Rectory, Shurdington, Cheltenham, Glos GL51 5TQ* Tel (01242) 862241

PRINCE (née RUMBLE), Mrs Alison Merle. b 49. Surrey Univ BSc71. Trin Coll Bris BA89. **d** 89 **p** 94. Par Dn Willesden Green St Gabr *Lon* 89-91; Par Dn Cricklewood St Gabr and St Mich 92; Par Dn Herne Hill *S'wark* 92-94; C 94-95; Chapl Greenwich Healthcare NHS Trust 95-96; TV Sanderstead All SS *S'wark* from 97. *4 Mitchley Avenue, Purley, Surrey CR8 1EA* Tel 0181-660 8123

PRINCE (née GRIFFITHS), Caroline Heidi Ann. b 66. Ex Univ BA88. Linc Th Coll CMM90. **d** 90 **p** 97. Chapl St Woolos Cathl *Mon* 90-94; C Newport St Woolos 90-94; C Abergavenny Deanery 94-96; TV Cwmbran from 96. *St Peter's Vicarage, 30 Longhouse Grove, Henllys, Cwmbran NP44 6HQ* Tel (01633) 867613

PRINCE, Dennis Alan Ford. b 18. AKC48. **d** 48 **p** 49. C Prittlewell St Mary *Chelmsf* 48-50; Hon C Prittlewell St Steph CD 50-54; V Golcar *Wakef* 54-60; R Slinfold *Chich* 60-73; R Sedlescombe w Whatlington 73-88; rtd 88. *7 Windmill Close, Clanfield, Waterlooville, Hants PO8 0NA* Tel (01705) 596675

PRINCE, Helena. b 23. Lightfoot Ho Dur. **dss** 66 **d** 87 **p** 94. W Derby St Mary *Liv* 65-85; rtd 85; Perm to Offic *Liv* from 85. *5 Dominic Close, Liverpool L16 1JZ* Tel 0151-722 0263

PRING, Althon Kerrigan (Kerry). b 34. AKC58. **d** 59 **p** 60. C Limehouse St Anne *Lon* 59-61; C Lt Stanmore St Lawr 61-64; C Langley Marish *Ox* 64-68; P-in-c Radnage 68-72; P-in-c Ravenstone w Weston Underwood 72-75; P-in-c Stoke Goldington w Gayhurst 72-75; R Gayhurst w Ravenstone, Stoke Goldington etc 75-85; P-in-c 85-86; RD Newport 78-80; TV Woughton 86-90; P-in-c Nash w Thornton, Beachampton and Thornborough 90-94; R 94-96; rtd 96. *Firtree Cottage, 17 High Street, Stoke Goldington, Newport Pagnell, Bucks MK16 8NP* Tel (01908) 551343

PRINGLE, The Ven Cecil Thomas. b 43. TCD BA65. CITC 66. **d** 66 **p** 67. C Belfast St Donard *D & D* 66-69; I Cleenish *Clogh* 69-80; I Mullaghdun 78-80; I Rossory from 80; Preb Clogh Cathl 86-89; Adn Clogh from 89. *Rossory Rectory, Derryhonnelly Road, Enniskillen, Co Fermanagh BT74 7JE* Tel (01365) 322874

PRINGLE, Graeme Lindsley. b 59. St Cath Coll Cam BA81 MA85. St Jo Coll Nottm DTS94. **d** 94 **p** 95. C Binley *Cov* from 94. *57 Princethorpe Way, Coventry CV3 2HG* Tel (01203) 636335

PRINGLE, Miss Janyce Mary. b 32. ARCM53 LRAM54 Ex Univ DipAdEd70 MPhil85. SW Minl Tr Course 83. **dss** 86 **d** 87 **p** 94. Torquay St Matthias, St Mark and H Trin *Ex* 86-87; Hon Par Dn 87-94; Hon C from 94; Chapl Asst Torbay Hosp Torquay 86-94; Chapl Asst S Devon Healthcare NHS Trust from 94. *Pendower, Wheatridge Lane, Torquay TQ2 6RA* Tel (01803) 607136

PRINGLE, John Richard. b 55. Lon Univ AKC76 CertEd77 Open Univ BA84. Chich Th Coll 78. **d** 78 **p** 79. C Northampton St Matt *Pet* 78-81; C Delaval *Newc* 81-84; V Newsham from 84; RD Bedlington from 93. *St Bede's Vicarage, Newcastle Road, Newsham, Blyth, Northd NE24 4AS* Tel (01670) 352391

PRINGLE, Thomas Andrew (Tom). b 36. FRMetS MRIN. Cant Sch of Min 85 Edin Th Coll 89. **d** 89 **p** 91. NSM Is of Arran *Arg* from 89; Hon Chapl Miss to Seamen from 89. *8 Torr-Righe, Shiskine, Brodick, Isle of Arran KA27 8HD* Tel (01770) 860222

PRINS, Canon Stanley Vernon. b 30. TD76. Dur Univ BSc54 MA69. Ripon Hall Ox 56. **d** 58 **p** 59. C Benwell St Jas *Newc* 58-61; Asst Chapl Newc Univ 61-65; CF (TA) from 64; C-in-c Whorlton H Nativity Chpl Ho Estate *Newc* 65-72; TV Whorlton 73-76; V Humshaugh 76-83; P-in-c Simonburn 82-83; P-in-c Wark 82-83; RD Bellingham 83-93; R Humshaugh w Simonburn and Wark 83-96; Hon Can Newc Cathl 88-96; rtd 96. *Woodside Cottage, Scrogwood, Bardon Mill, Hexham, Northd NE47 7AA* Tel (01434) 344876

PRINT, Norman George. b 38. Cuddesdon Coll 64. **d** 66 **p** 67. C Banbury *Ox* 66-69; C Whitley Ch Ch 69-75; P-in-c Shiplake 75-77; V Shiplake w Dunsden 77-90; R Balcombe *Chich* from 90. *The Rectory, Balcombe, Haywards Heath, W Sussex RH17 6PA* Tel (01444) 811249

PRIOR, The Ven Christopher. b 12. CB68. Keble Coll Ox BA37 MA41. Cuddesdon Coll 37. **d** 38 **p** 39. C Hornsea and Goxhill *York* 38-41; Chapl RN 41-69; Chapl of the Fleet and Adn for the RN 66-69; QHC 66-69; Adn Portsm 69-77; rtd 77. *Ponies End, West Melbury, Shaftesbury, Dorset SP7 0LY* Tel (01747) 811239

PRIOR, David Clement Lyndon. b 40. Trin Coll Ox BA63 MA66. Ridley Hall Cam 65. **d** 67 **p** 68. C Reigate St Mary *S'wark* 67-72; S Africa 72-79; Can Cape Town 76-79; C Ox St Aldate w H Trin *Ox* 79-82; C Ox St Aldate w St Matt 82-84; USA 84-85; V Ches Square St Mich w St Phil *Lon* 85-95; P-in-c Mayfair Ch Ch from 85; Public Preacher from 95; P-in-c St Botolph without Aldersgate from 97. *21 Portman Close, London W1H 9HL* Tel 0171-935 3477

PRIOR, Ian Graham. b 44. Lon Univ BSc(Econ)71. Oak Hill Th Coll DipHE80. **d** 80 **p** 81. C Luton Ch Ch *Roch* 80-83; TV Southgate *Chich* 83-93; V Burgess Hill St Andr from 93. *St Andrew's Vicarage, 2 Cants Lane, Burgess Hill, W Sussex RH15 0LG* Tel (01444) 232023

PRIOR, Ian Roger Lyndon. b 46. St Jo Coll Dur BA68. Lon Coll of Div 68. **d** 70 **p** 71. C S Croydon Em *Cant* 70-73; Perm to Offic *S'wark* 73-85; Dir Overseas Personnel TEAR Fund 73-79; Dep Dir 79-83; Fin and Admin Dir CARE Trust and CARE Campaigns 85-92; NSM New Malden and Coombe *S'wark* from 85; Dir Careforce from 92. *39 Cambridge Avenue, New Malden, Surrey KT3 4LD* Tel 0181-949 0912 or 543 8671 Fax 540 0113

PRIOR, James Murray. b 39. Edin Univ BCom64. St And Dioc Tr Course 85. **d** 90 **p** 91. NSM Kirriemuir *St And* from 90; NSM Forfar from 90. *Horniehaugh, Glenquiech, Forfar, Angus DD8 3UG* Tel (01575) 540420

PRIOR, John Gilman Leathes. b 15. Qu Coll Cam BA37 MA41. Ridley Hall Cam 37. **d** 39 **p** 40. C Ipswich St Marg *St E* 39-41; CF 41-46; V Springfield H Trin *Chelmsf* 46-49; V Guildf Ch Ch *Guildf* 49-63; V Camberley St Paul 63-74; V Crondall 75-77; V Crondall and Ewshot 77-80; rtd 80; Perm to Offic *Win* from 80; Perm to Offic *Guildf* from 82; Perm to Offic *Portsm* from 84. *River Cottage, Station Road, Bentley, Farnham, Surrey GU10 5JY* Tel (01420) 23413

PRIOR, Preb John Miskin. b 27. Lon Univ BSc(Econ)48. Westcott Ho Cam 49. **d** 51 **p** 52. C Bedminster St Fran *Bris* 51-55; C Sherston Magna w Easton Grey 55-57; C Yatton Keynell 57-61; C Castle Combe 57-61; C Biddestone w Slaughterford 57-61; V Bishopstone w Hinton Parva 61-66; V Marshfield w Cold Ashton 66-82; P-in-c Tormarton w W Littleton 68-82; RD Bitton 73-79; R Trull w Angersleigh *B & W* 82-91; RD Taunton 84-90; Preb Wells Cathl 90-91; Chapl Huggens' Coll Northfleet 91-97; rtd 92. *7 St Margarets Street, Rochester, Kent ME1 1TU* Tel (01634) 846422

PRIOR, Canon Kenneth Francis William. b 26. St Jo Coll Dur BA49. Oak Hill Th Coll 46. **d** 49 **p** 50. C S Mimms Ch Ch *Lon* 49-52; C Eastbourne H Trin *Chich* 52-53; V Onslow Square St Paul *Lon* 53-65; V Hove Bp Hannington Memorial Ch *Chich* 65-70; R Sevenoaks St Nic *Roch* 70-87; Hon Can Roch Cathl 82-87; C-in-c Hampstead St Jo Downshire Hill Prop Chpl *Lon* 87-90; rtd 89; Perm to Offic *Chelmsf* from 89. *41 Osidge Lane, London N14 5JL* Tel 0181-368 4586

PRIOR, Canon Kenneth George William. b 17. Bris Univ BA39. Bible Churchmen's Coll 35. **d** 40 **p** 41. C Toxteth Park St Clem *Liv* 40-43; C Edge Hill St Cypr 43-45; C Garston 45-48; V Plymouth St Jude *Ex* 48-55; V Longfleet *Sarum* 55-82; Chapl Poole Gen Hosp 55-76; RD Poole *Sarum* 75-80; Can and Preb Sarum Cathl 77-82; rtd 82. *Flat 5, 61 Dorchester Road, Weymouth, Dorset DT4 7JX* Tel (01305) 766253

PRIOR, Nigel John. b 56. Bris Univ BA78. Westcott Ho Cam 79. **d** 81 **p** 82. C Langley All SS and Martyrs *Man* 81-82; C Langley and Parkfield 82-84; C Bury St Jo w St Mark 84-87; R Man Clayton St Cross w St Paul from 87. *The Rectory, 54 Clayton Hall Road, Manchester M11 4WH* Tel 0161-223 0766

PRIOR, Stephen Kenneth. b 55. Rhode Is Coll (USA) BA78. Wycliffe Hall Ox 79. **d** 82 **p** 83. C Aberavon *Llan* 82-85; P-in-c New Radnor and Llanfihangel Nantmelan etc *S & B* 85-86; V 86-90; V Llansamlet 90-94; P-in-c Chester le Street *Dur* 94-96; R from 96. *The Rectory, Lindisfarne Avenue, Chester le Street, Co Durham DH3 3PT* Tel 0191-388 4027

PRIORY, Barry Edwin. b 44. FCIS Open Univ BA81. Qu Coll Birm 84. **d** 86 **p** 87. C Boldmere *Birm* 86-89; C Somerton w Compton Dundon, the Charltons etc *B & W* 89-93; R Porlock w Stoke Pero from 93; RD Exmoor from 97. *The Rectory, Parsons Street, Porlock, Minehead, Somerset TA24 8QL* Tel (01643) 863172

PRISTON, David Leslie. b 28. Lon Bible Coll 49 Oak Hill Th Coll 66. **d** 66 **p** 67. C Heref St Pet w St Owen *Heref* 66-71; R Beeby *Leic* 72-88; R Gaddesby w S Croxton 72-88; R S Croxton Gp 88-93; rtd 93. *20 Central Avenue, Chilwell, Nottingham NG9 4DU* Tel 0115-922 7643

PRITCHARD, Antony Robin. b 53. Van Mildert Coll Dur BSc74 SS Paul & Mary Coll Cheltenham CertEd75. St Jo Coll Nottm DipTh82 DPS84. **d** 84 **p** 85. C Desborough *Pet* 84-87; C Rushden w Newton Bromswold 87-91; R Oulton St Mich *Nor* from 91. *The Rectory, Christmas Lane, Oulton, Lowestoft, Suffolk NR32 3JX* Tel (01502) 565722

PRITCHARD, Brian James Pallister. b 27. CCC Cam BA51 MA66. Westcott Ho Cam 51. **d** 53 **p** 54. C Attercliffe w Carbrook *Sheff* 53-58; V New Bentley 58-60; Chapl Park Hill Flats Sheff 60-67; P-in-c Sheff St Swithun *Sheff* 67-72; V Welton *Linc* 72-92; RD Lawres 86-92; rtd 92; Perm to Offic *Derby* from 92. *Bridgeways, Milford Lane, Bakewell, Derbyshire DE45 1DX* Tel (01629) 813553

PRITCHARD, Colin Ivor. b 44. Lon Inst of Educn TCert65. Chich Th Coll 66. **d** 69 **p** 70. C Kettering St Mary *Pet* 69-72; Chapl Clayesmore Sch Blandford 72-74; Asst Chapl Ellesmere Coll Shropshire 74-77; C Duston *Pet* 77-80; V Wellingborough St Andr 80-89; R Sedlescombe w Whatlington *Chich* from 89. *The Rectory, Church Hill, Sedlescombe, Battle, E Sussex TN33 0QP* Tel (01424) 870233

PRITCHARD, Colin Wentworth. b 38. K Coll Lon St Boniface Warminster 59. **d** 63 **p** 64. C Putney St Marg *S'wark* 63-67; C Brixton St Matt 67-70; C Milton *Portsm* 70-74; V Mitcham St Mark *S'wark* 74-82; R Long Ditton 82-94; V Earlsfield St Andr from 94. *22 St Andrew's Court, London SW18 3QF* Tel 0181-946 4214

PRITCHARD, David Paul. b 47. FRCO LTCL BA. Wycliffe Hall Ox 80. **d** 82 **p** 83. C Kidlington *Ox* 82-84; P-in-c Marcham w Garford 84-85; V 86-96; RD Abingdon 91-96; R Henley on Thames w Remenham from 96. *The Rectory, Hart Street, Henley-on-Thames, Oxon RG9 2AU* Tel (01491) 577340

PRITCHARD, Donald Oliver. b 22. Qu Coll Birm 73. **d** 75 **p** 76. Hon C Dunchurch *Cov* 75-83; P-in-c Mells w Buckland Dinham, Elm, Whatley etc *B & W* 83-84; R 84-88; rtd 88; Perm to Offic *Truro* from 88. *Moonrakers, Pengelly, Callington, Cornwall PL17 7DZ* Tel (01579) 84329

PRITCHARD, The Ven John Lawrence. b 48. St Pet Coll Ox BA70 DipTh70 MA73 Dur Univ MLitt93. Ridley Hall Cam 70. **d** 72 **p** 73. C Birm St Martin *Birm* 72-76; Asst Dir RE *B & W* 76-80; Youth Chapl 76-80; P-in-c Wilton 80-88; Dir Past Studies Cranmer Hall Dur 89-93; Warden 93-96; Adn Cant and Can Res Cant Cathl *Cant* from 96. *Chillenden Chambers, 29 The Precincts, Canterbury, Kent CT1 2EP* Tel (01227) 463036 Fax 785209

PRITCHARD, Miss Kathryn Anne. b 60. St Cath Coll Ox MA Bradf Univ DIT. St Jo Coll Dur. **d** 87. Par Dn Addiscombe St Mary *S'wark* 87-90; CPAS Staff 90-92; Perm to Offic *Cov* 92-95. *Address temp unknown*

PRITCHARD, Kenneth John. b 30. Liv Univ BEng51. NW Ord Course 72. **d** 74 **p** 75. C Ches Team *Ches* 74-78; Miss to Seamen 78-84; V Runcorn St Jo Weston *Ches* 78-84; V Gt Meols from 84. *St John's Vicarage, Birkenhead Road, Meols, South Wirral L47 0LF* Tel 0151-632 1661

PRITCHARD, Malcolm John. b 55. Bradf Univ BA85 CQSW85. St Jo Coll Nottm 86. **d** 88 **p** 89. C Peckham St Mary Magd *S'wark* 88-93; V Luton St Matt High Town *St Alb* from 93. *St Matthew's Vicarage, Wenlock Street, Luton LU2 0NQ* Tel (01582) 32320

PRITCHARD, Michael Owen. b 49. Trin Coll Carmarthen CertEd71. St Mich Coll Llan 71. **d** 73 **p** 74. C Conwy w Gyffin *Ban* 73-76; TV Dolgellau w Llanfachreth and Brithdir etc 76-78; Dioc Children's Officer 77-86; V Bettws y Coed and Capel Curig 78-83; CF (TAVR) from 79; V Betws-y-Coed and Capel Curig w Penmachno etc *Ban* 83-86; Chapl Claybury Hosp Woodford Bridge 86-96; Chapl Team Leader Forest Healthcare NHS Trust Lon from 96. *Dept of Spiritual and Religious Care, Whipps Cross Hospital, Leytonstone, London E11 1NR, or 50 Harpenden Road, London E12 5HN* Tel 0181-535 6819 or 989 3813

PRITCHARD, Canon Neil Lawrence. b 15. St Jo Coll Dur BA39 MA45. **d** 39 **p** 40. C Harpurhey Ch Ch *Man* 39-40; C Stretford St Matt 40-44; R Salford St Clem Ordsall 44-50; Prin CA Tr Coll Reading 50-52; Lon 52-53; Lic to Offic *Ox* 50-52; Lic to Offic *Lon* 52-58; Dep Chief Sec CA 53-58; V S Shore H Trin *Blackb* 58-73; Bp's Dom Chapl 61-66; Exchange R St Paul's Greenville N Carolina USA 65-66; Hon Can Blackb Cathl 66-81; Dir of Ords 73-82; V Salesbury 73-80; Bp's Dom Chapl 78-83; rtd 80; Lic to Offic *Blackb* 83-93. *Sayers, Holmfield, High Street, Lyndhurst, Hants SO43 7BH* Tel (01703) 283020

PRITCHARD, Mrs Norma Kathleen. b 32. Birm Univ BA53 CertEd54. EMMTC 81. **dss** 84 **d** 87 **p** 94. Derby St Alkmund and St Werburgh *Derby* 84-90; Par Dn 87-90; Par Dn Derby St Andr w St Osmund 90-94; C 94-96; Assoc Min Alvaston from 96. *44 Evans Avenue, Allestree, Derby DE22 2EN* Tel (01332) 557702

PRITCHARD, Dr Peter Benson. b 30. FPhS60 LCP68 Univ of Wales (Lamp) BA51 St Cath Coll Ox DipTh57 Lon Univ PGCE68 DipEd70 Liv Univ MEd74 PhD81. Ripon Hall Ox 55. **d** 58 **p** 59. C Wavertree H Trin *Liv* 58-60; C Sefton 60-61; C-in-c Thornton CD 61-64; Chapl Liv Coll Boys' Sch 64-70; Hon C Wavertree St Bridget 70-89; Lect CF Mott Coll of Educn 70-76; Sen Lect Liv Coll of HE 76-83; Liv Poly 83-87; Perm to Offic 90-96; Perm to Offic *Ches* from 90; Chapl St Jo Hospice Wirral from 93; Tutor Open Univ 90-95; rtd 95. *68 Gleggside, West Kirby, Wirral, Merseyside L48 6EA* Tel 0151-625 8093

PRITCHARD, Peter Humphrey. b 47. Univ of Wales (Ban) BA70 Liv Univ PGCE73 Birm Univ DipTh87. Qu Coll Birm 85. **d** 87 **p** 88. C Llanbeblig w Caernarfon and Betws Garmon etc *Ban* 87-90; R Llanberis w Llanrug 90-94; R Llanfaethlu w Llanfwrog and Llanrhuddlad etc from 94. *The Rectory, 7 Tynlon Estate, Llanrhyddlad, Holyhead LL65 4HT* Tel (01407) 730251

PRITCHARD, Thomas. b 14. Ch Ch Ox BA37 MA40. Westcott Ho Cam 37. **d** 38 **p** 39. C Rugby St Andr *Cov* 38-45; Mauritius 45-49; V Ipswich All Hallows *St E* 49-61; Hon Can St E Cathl 58-61; V Ex St Dav *Ex* 62-81; rtd 81; Perm to Offic *Ex* from 81. *3 Mill Cottages, Exton, Exeter EX3 0PH* Tel (01392) 873018

PRITCHARD, The Ven Thomas William. b 33. Keele Univ BA55 DipEd55. St Mich Coll Llan 55. **d** 57 **p** 58. C Holywell *St As* 57-61; C Ruabon 61-63; V 77-87; R Pontfadog 63-71; R Llanferres, Nercwys and Eryrys 71-77; Dioc Archivist from 76; Can St As Cathl from 84; RD Llangollen 86-87; Adn Montgomery from 87; V Berriew and Manafon from 87. *The Vicarage, Berriew, Welshpool SY21 8PL* Tel (01686) 640223

PRITT, Stephen. b 06. AKC31. **d** 31 **p** 32. C Witton *Blackb* 31-34; C St Annes 34-37; PC Ennerdale *Carl* 37-40; V Amblecote *Worc* 40-45; V Wolverley 46-48; V Warrington H Trin *Liv* 48-55; V Thornham w Titchwell *Nor* 55-58; Clerical Org Sec (Dios Cant, Chich, Roch and Win) CECS 58-60; R Helhoughton w Raynham *Nor* 60-80; rtd 80; Perm to Offic *Glouc* 80-93. *23 Addiscombe Road, Weston-super-Mare, Avon BS23 4LT* Tel (01934) 622795

PRIVETT, Peter John. b 48. Qu Coll Birm 75. **d** 78 **p** 79. C Moseley St Agnes *Birm* 78-81; V Kingsbury 81-87; P-in-c Dilwyn and Stretford *Heref* 87-90; Dioc Children's Adv from 87; TV Leominster from 90. *165 Bargates, Leominster, Herefordshire HR6 8QT* Tel (01568) 613176

PROBART, Raymond. b 21. Sarum Th Coll 49. **d** 51 **p** 52. C Padiham *Blackb* 51-54; C Burnley St Pet 54-56; V Heyhouses 56-60; V Douglas 60-88; rtd 88; Perm to Offic *B & W* from 88. *76 Waterside Way, Radstock, Bath BA3 3YQ* Tel (01761) 433908

PROBERT, Christopher John Dixon. b 54. Univ of Wales (Cardiff) DipTh77 DPS78 Univ of Wales BTh95. St Mich Coll Llan 74. **d** 78 **p** 79. C Aberdare St Fagan *Llan* 78-79; C Cadoxton-juxta-Barry 79-81; R Llanfynydd *St As* 81-84; V Gosberton Clough and Quadring *Linc* 84-86; TV Coventry Caludon *Cov* 86-88; V Llanrhian w Llanhywel and Llanrheithan *St D* 88-91; V Tregaron w Ystrad Meurig and Strata Florida 91-93; Chapl Tregaron Hosp 91-93; Tutor St D NSM Course 89-93; V Betws-y-Coed and Capel Curig w Penmachno etc *Ban* from 93. *The Vicarage, Betws-y-Coed LL24 0AD* Tel (01690) 710313 Fax as telephone

PROBERT, Edward Cleasby. b 58. St Cath Coll Cam BA80 MA84. Ripon Coll Cuddesdon BA84. **d** 85 **p** 86. C Esher *Guildf* 85-89; V Earlsfield St Andr *S'wark* 89-94; V Belmont from 94.

The Vicarage, Belmont Rise, Sutton, Surrey SM2 6EA Tel 0181-642 2363

PROBETS, Canon Desmond. b 26. AKC50. **d** 51 **p** 52. C Finsbury St Clem *Lon* 51-52; C Kenton 52-62; Solomon Is 62-72; Dean Honiara Cathl 69-72; V Timperley *Ches* 72-92; RD Bowdon 77-87; Hon Can Ches Cathl 82-92; rtd 92; Perm to Offic *Wakef* from 92. *24 Shelley Close, Penistone, Sheffield S30 6GT* Tel (01226) 766402

PROCTER, Andrew David. b 52. St Jo Coll Ox BA74 MA BA86. Trin Coll Bris 74. **d** 77 **p** 78. C Barnoldswick w Bracewell *Bradf* 77-80; P-in-c Kelbrook 80-82; V 82-87; V Heaton St Barn 87-93; V Swanley St Paul *Roch* from 93. *The Vicarage, Rowhill Road, Swanley, Kent BR8 7RL* Tel (01322) 662320

PROCTER, Robert Hendy. b 31. Trin Hall Cam BA54 MA. Edin Dioc NSM Course 88. **d** 93 **p** 94. NSM Edin Ch Ch *Edin* from 93. *2 Braid Avenue, Edinburgh EH10 6DR* Tel 0131-447 1140

PROCTOR, The Ven Jesse Heighton. b 08. Lon Univ BA29 MA32. St Andr Whittlesford 34. **d** 35 **p** 36. C Whittlesford *Ely* 35-38; C Leic St Phil *Leic* 38-39; V Glen Parva and S Wigston 39-46; Prec Cov Cathl *Cov* 46-58; Hon Can Cov Cathl 47-54; Can Th 54-59; Chapl Gulson Road Hosp Cov 53-58; Adn Warwick *Cov* 58-74; rtd 74; Perm to Offic *Heref* from 75. *Dilkusha, 22 Bank Crescent, Ledbury, Herefordshire HR8 1AA* Tel (01531) 632241

PROCTOR, Kenneth Noel. b 33. St Aid Birkenhead 61. **d** 63 **p** 64. C Oldham St Paul *Man* 63-66; C Davyhulme St Mary 66-69; V Norden w Ashworth from 69. *The Vicarage, Heap Road, Rochdale, Lancs OL12 7SN* Tel (01706) 41001

PROCTOR, Michael John (Mike). b 59. Longlands Coll of FE C&G78 BTEC NC81. Cranmer Hall Dur CTMin93. **d** 93 **p** 94. C Leatherhead *Guildf* from 93. *58 Kingscroft Road, Leatherhead, Surrey KT22 7BU* Tel (01372) 379954

PROCTOR, Canon Michael Thomas. b 41. Ch Ch Ox BA65 MA67. Westcott Ho Cam 63. **d** 65 **p** 66. C Monkseaton St Mary *Newc* 65-69; Pakistan 69-72; C Willington *Newc* 72-77; TV Willington Team 77-79; Ed Sec Nat Soc 79-84; P-in-c Roxwell *Chelmsf* 79-84; Dir of Miss and Unity 85-94; Bp's Ecum Officer from 85; Hon Can Chelmsf Cathl from 85; P-in-c Gt Waltham w Ford End from 94. *The Vicarage, Great Waltham, Chelmsford CM3 1AR* Tel (01245) 360334

PROCTOR, Canon Noel. b 30. MBE93. St Aid Birkenhead 62. **d** 64 **p** 65. C Haughton le Skerne *Dur* 64-67; R Byers Green 67-70; Chapl HM Pris Eastchurch 70-74; Chapl HM Pris Dartmoor 74-79; Chapl HM Pris Man 79-95; Hon Can Man Cathl *Man* from 91; rtd 95; Lic to Offic *Man* from 95. *222 Moor Lane, Salford M7 3QH* Tel 0161-792 1284

PROCTOR, Mrs Susan Katherine. b 44. **d** 89 **p** 94. Par Dn Beighton *Sheff* 89-91; Par Dn Aston cum Aughton and Ulley 91-93; Par Dn Aston cum Aughton w Swallownest, Todwick etc 93-94; TV 94-96; R Dinnington from 96. *The Rectory, 217 Nursery Road, Dinnington, Sheffield S31 7QU* Tel (01909) 562335

PROFIT, David Hollingworth. b 17. Man Univ BA38. Cuddesdon Coll 40. **d** 41 **p** 42. C Kings Heath *Birm* 41-43; S Africa from 43. *Braehead House, Auburn Road, Kenilworth, 7700 South Africa* Tel Cape Town (21) 762-6041

PROPHET, Canon John Roy Henderson. b 10. Dur Univ LTh48 BA49. ALCD34. **d** 34 **p** 35. C Low Leyton *Chelmsf* 34-37; C Canvey Is 37-38; P-in-c Walthamstow St Andr 38-39; V 39-44; V Jesmond H Trin *Newc* 44-48; V Fenham St Jas and St Basil 48-61; V Blaby *Leic* 61-73; Hon Can Leic Cathl 70-80; R Church Langton w Thorpe Langton and Tur Langton 73-80; rtd 80; Perm to Offic *Leic* from 80; Perm to Offic *Pet* from 80. *29 Glebe Way, Oakham, Leics LE15 6LX* Tel (01572) 755852

PROSSER, Canon David George. b 33. Univ of Wales (Lamp) BA55. Coll of Resurr Mirfield 55 St Mich Coll Llan 59. **d** 60 **p** 61. C Caerphilly *Llan* 60-64; C Moordown *Win* 64-65; Chapl RN 65-81; V Morecambe St Barn *Blackb* 81-85; V Lt Paxton *Ely* 85-86; V Diddington 85-86; R Southoe w Hail Weston 85-86; Chapl Hamburg w Kiel *Eur* 86-93; Miss to Seamen 86-93; Hon Can Brussels Cathl *Eur* 91-95; Can Brussels Cathl 95-96; Chapl Copenhagen w Aarhus 93-96; rtd 96. *35 Kingsmead Avenue, Fareham, Hants PO14 2NN* Tel (01329) 665084

PROSSER, Malcolm George. b 22. Univ of Wales (Lamp) BA44. St Mich Coll Llan 44. **d** 45 **p** 46. C Llantwit Fadre *Llan* 45-49; C Roath St Marg 49-58; V Trealaw 58-66; V High Littleton *B & W* 66-87; rtd 87. *141 Westway, Broadstone, Dorset BH18 9LQ* Tel (01202) 694280

PROSSER, Rhys. b 51. BA74 Bris Univ CertEd75 Southn Univ BTh83 Hull Univ MA93. Sarum & Wells Th Coll 77. **d** 80 **p** 81. C Wimbledon *S'wark* 80-83; C St Helier 83-88; TV Gt and Lt Coates w Bradley *Linc* 88-95; P-in-c Saxilby Gp from 95. *The Rectory, 1 Westcroft Drive, Saxilby, Lincoln LN1 2PT* Tel (01522) 702427

PROSSER, Richard Hugh Keble. b 31. Trin Coll Cam BA53 MA57 Leeds Univ PGCE63. Cuddesdon Coll 55. **d** 57 **p** 58. C Wigan All SS *Liv* 57-60; CR 62-87; S Rhodesia 64-65; Rhodesia 65-80; Zimbabwe 80-90; TR Pocklington Team *York* 90; R Pocklington and Owsthorpe and Kilnwick Percy etc from 90. *The Vicarage, 29 The Balk, Pocklington, York YO4 2QQ* Tel (01759) 302133

PROSSER, Stephanie. b 42. Linc Th Coll 94. **d** 96. NSM Linc St Nic w St Jo Newport *Linc* from 96. *The Rectory, 1 Westcroft Drive, Saxilby, Lincoln LN1 2PT* Tel (01522) 702427

PROTHERO, Brian Douglas. b 52. St Andr Univ MTh75 Dundee Univ CertEd77. Linc Th Coll 84. **d** 86 **p** 87. C Thornbury *Glouc* 86-89; V Goodrington *Ex* from 89. *Goodrington Vicarage, 16 Cliff Park Avenue, Paignton, Devon TQ4 6LT* Tel (01803) 556476

PROTHERO, Cecil Charles. b 15. Lon Univ BSc(Econ)47 Bris Univ MEd74. **d** 68 **p** 69. C Ex St Mary Arches *Ex* 68-70; Chapl St Luke's Coll Ex 70-78; Dep PV Ex Cathl *Ex* from 78. *La Petite Grange, Grange Le Bourg 73, Salles de Villefagnan, Russec, France 16700*

PROTHERO, David John. b 43. St Pet Coll Ox BA66 MA70. St Steph Ho Ox 68. **d** 70 **p** 71. C Kirkby *Liv* 70-72; C St Marychurch *Ex* 72-74; V Marldon 74-83; Chapl HM Pris Channings Wood 78-83; V Torquay St Martin Barton *Ex* 83-91; P-in-c Bath Bathwick *B & W* 91-93; R from 93. *The Rectory, Sham Castle Lane, Bath BA2 6JL* Tel (01225) 460052

PROTHERO, John Martin. b 32. Oak Hill Th Coll 64. **d** 66 **p** 67. C Tipton St Martin *Lich* 66-69; C Wednesfield Heath 69-72; Distr Sec BFBS 72-85; Lic to Offic *S'well* 73-86; Hon C Gedling 73; V Willoughby-on-the-Wolds w Wysall and Widmerpool from 86. *The Rectory, Keyworth Road, Wysall, Nottingham NG12 5QQ* Tel (01509) 880269

PROTHEROE, Rhys Illtyd. b 50. St D Coll Lamp DipTh74. **d** 74 **p** 75. C Pen-bre *St D* 74-76; C Carmarthen St Dav 76-78; V Llanegwad 78-79; V Llanegwad w Llanfynydd 79-82; V Gors-las 82-95; RD Dyffryn Aman 94-95; V Llan-llwch w Llangain and Llangynog from 95. *The Vicarage, Llan-llwch, Carmarthen SA31 3RN* Tel (01267) 236805

PROTHEROE, Canon Robin Philip. b 33. St Chad's Coll Dur BA54 DipTh56 MA60 Nottm Univ MPhil75 Ox Univ DipEd62. **d** 57 **p** 58. C Roath St Marg *Llan* 57-60; Asst Chapl Culham Coll Abingdon 60-64; Perm to Offic *S'well* 64-66; Lic to Offic 66-84; P-in-c Barton in Fabis 70-73; P-in-c Thrumpton 70-73; Dir of Educn *Bris* from 84; Hon Can Bris Cathl from 85; Selector for ACCM 88-91; ABM from 91; Bp's Insp of Th Colls from 88. *29 Barley Croft, Bristol BS9 3TG* Tel 0117-968 3245 or 921 4411

PROUD, Andrew John. b 54. K Coll Lon BD79 AKC79. Linc Th Coll 79. **d** 80 **p** 81. C Stansted Mountfitchet *Chelmsf* 80-83; TV Borehamwood *St Alb* 83-90; C Hatfield 90-92; R E Barnet from 92. *The Rectory, 136 Church Hill Road, Barnet, Herts EN4 8XD* Tel 0181-368 3840 or 361 7524

PROUD, Clyde Douglas. b 09. St Aid Birkenhead 35. **d** 37 **p** 38. C Wakef St Andr *Wakef* 37-39; C Wallington H Trin *S'wark* 39-43; R Postwick *Nor* 43-62; Chapl St Andr Hosp Thorpe 43-63; Chapl Cane Hill Hosp Coulsdon 62-69; V Withernwick *York* 69-72; R Rise 69-72; C Bankfoot *Bradf* 72-79; rtd 74. *Beechwood Nursing Home, Esplanade Road, Scarborough, N Yorkshire YO11 2DB* Tel (01723) 374260

PROUD, David John. b 56. Leeds Univ BA77 Dur Univ CertEd78. Ridley Hall Cam 85. **d** 88 **p** 89. C Lindfield *Chich* 88-91; TV Horsham 91-97; V Ware Ch Ch *St Alb* from 97. *The Vicarage, 15 Hanbury Close, Ware, Herts SG12 7BZ* Tel (01920) 463165

PROUDMAN, Canon Colin Leslie John. b 34. K Coll Lon BD60 MTh63. Wells Th Coll 60. **d** 61 **p** 62. C Radlett *St Alb* 61-64; Canada from 64; Hon Can Toronto from 86; Dean Div Toronto Div Coll 90-92; rtd 97. *1802, 77 Maitland Place, Toronto, Ontario, Canada M4Y 2V6* Tel Toronto (416) 923 4235

PROUT, David William. b 47. FRSA Leeds Univ DipEd. St Steph Ho Ox 71. **d** 74 **p** 75. C Hanworth All SS *Lon* 74-77; Chapl Westmr City Sch 77-78; Hon C Pimlico St Pet w Westmr Ch Ch *Lon* 77-78; Chapl Roch Cathl *Roch* 78-81; C St Alb Abbey *St Alb* 81-82; Chapl St Hilda's Priory Sneaton, Whitby 82-89; P-in-c Aislaby and Ruswarp *York* 89-97; P-in-c Eastbourne St Elisabeth *Chich* from 97. *The Vicarage, 266 Victoria Drive, Eastbourne, E Sussex BN20 8QX* Tel (01323) 720068

PROUT, Hubert Douglas. b 18. St D Coll Lamp BA38. **d** 41 **p** 42. C Low Leyton *Chelmsf* 41-44; CF 44-47; C Wanstead St Mary *Chelmsf* 47-50; Perm to Offic *Llan* 52-56; C Wirksworth w Carsington *Derby* 56-58; C Idridgehay 56-58; V Kirk Hallam 58-84; rtd 84; Perm to Offic *Llan* from 85. *9 Caldy Close, Porthcawl CF36 3QL* Tel (01656) 786479

PROUT, Mrs Joan. b 42. Gipsy Hill Coll of Educn TCert63. LNSM course 95. **d** 97. NSM Whitton *Sarum* from 97. *22 Ermin Close, Baydon, Marlborough, Wilts SN8 2JQ* Tel (01672) 540465

PROVOST, Ian Keith. b 47. CA Tr Coll IDC73 Ridley Hall Cam CTMin93. **d** 93 **p** 94. C Verwood *Sarum* 93-97; P-in-c Redlynch and Morgan's Vale from 97. *Redlynch Vicarage, Vicarage Road, Lover, Salisbury SP5 2PE* Tel (01725) 510439

PROWSE, Mrs Barbara Bridgette Christmas. b 41. R Holloway Coll Lon BA62. **d** 91 **p** 94. C Kingsthorpe w Northn St Dav *Pet* 91-97; V Northampton St Jas from 97. *St James's Vicarage, Vicarage Road, Northampton NN5 7AX* Tel (01604) 751164

PRUDOM, William Haigh. b 26. STh79 APhS81 Hull Univ MPhil88. St D Coll Lamp 60. **d** 62 **p** 63. C Aylesford *Roch* 62-63; C Margate St Jo *Cant* 63-66; V Long Preston *Bradf* 66-73; C Darlington St Cuth *Dur* 73-75; V Ticehurst *Chich* 75-79; P-in-c Flimwell 78-79; V Ticehurst and Flimwell 79-81; R Spennithorne w Finghall and Hauxwell *Ripon* 81-91; rtd 91. *9 Sydall's Way, Catterick Village, Richmond, N Yorkshire DL10 7ND* Tel (01748) 818604

PRUEN, Edward Binney. b 56. K Coll Lon BD77 AKC77. St Jo Coll Nottm 78. **d** 79 **p** 80. C Kidderminster St Mary *Worc* 79-82; C Woking St Jo *Guildf* 82-84; Chapl Asst R Marsden Hosp Lon and Surrey 84-86; C Stapleford *S'well* 86-88; Min Winklebury CD *Win* 88; V Winklebury 88-93; Chapl Ld Mayor Treloar Coll Alton from 93. *2 St Joseph's Cottage, Upper Froyle, Alton, Hants GU34 4JY* Tel (01420) 23893

PRUEN, Hugh Barrington. b 18. AKC50. **d** 50 **p** 51. C Westmr St Steph w St Jo *Lon* 50-53; R Didmarton w Oldbury-on-the-Hill and Sopworth *Glouc* 53-56; V Ches St Jo *Ches* 56-64; R Skegness *Linc* 64-71; V Heckington w Howell 71-79; R Ashley w Weston by Welland and Sutton Bassett *Pet* 79-83; rtd 83; Perm to Offic *Linc* from 83. *Ashleigh, Church Road, Old Bolingbroke, Spilsby, Lincs PE23 4HF* Tel (01790) 763504

PRUEN, Hugh George. b 30. Worc Coll Ox BA53 MA62 Lambeth STh94 Southn Univ MTh96. Ely Th Coll 55. **d** 58 **p** 59. C Eastover *B & W* 58-63; Canada 63-66; P-in-c Selsey *Chich* 66-75; P-in-c Belbroughton *Worc* 75-82; V S w N Bersted *Chich* 82-92; rtd 92; Perm to Offic *Chich* from 92. *Ashmead, Fontwell Avenue, Eastergate, Chichester, W Sussex PO20 6RU* Tel (01243) 544641

PRYCE, Donald Keith. b 35. Man Univ BSc. Linc Th Coll 69. **d** 71 **p** 72. C Heywood St Jas *Man* 71-74; P-in-c 74-75; V 75-86; R Ladybarn from 86; Chapl S Man Coll from 87. *St Chad's Rectory, 1 St Chad's Road, Withington, Manchester M20 9WH* Tel 0161-445 1185

PRYCE, Robin Mark. b 60. Sussex Univ BA82 Cam Univ MA94. Westcott Ho Cam 84 United Th Coll Bangalore 85. **d** 87 **p** 88. C W Bromwich All SS *Lich* 87-90; Chapl and Fell CCC Cam from 90; Tutor from 92; Dean of Chpl from 96. *Corpus Christi College, Cambridge CB2 1RH* Tel (01223) 338002 or 338000

PRYCE, William Robert. b 28. MBE91. **d** 79 **p** 80. NSM Leverstock Green *St Alb* 79-80; Perm to Offic *Sheff* 80-84; NSM Sheff St Barn and St Mary 84-90; NSM Alveley and Quatt *Heref* 91-93; Perm to Offic from 93. *28 Crooks Cross, Alveley, Bridgnorth, Shropshire WV15 6LS* Tel (01746) 780588

PRYER, Miss Frances Margaret. b 24. Gilmore Ho 59. **dss** 69 **d** 87. Hornchurch St Andr *Chelmsf* 66-83; rtd 84; Hon Par Dn Leigh-on-Sea St Aid *Chelmsf* 87-93; Perm to Offic from 93. *131 Howard Road, Upminster, Essex RM14 2UQ* Tel (01708) 640451

PRYKE, Dr Edward John. b 20. K Coll Lon BD51 AKC51 St Cath Coll Ox BA53 MA57 BLitt63 Lon Univ PhD71. Wycliffe Hall Ox 51. **d** 53 **p** 54. C Ross *Heref* 53-56; Chapl Brasted Place Coll Westerham 56-60; Asst Chapl and Sen Lect Coll SS Mark and Jo Chelsea 62-73; Coll of SS Mark & Jo Plymouth 74-76; P-in-c S Pool w Chivelstone *Ex* 74-75; R E Portlemouth 74-76; P-in-c Gt Paxton *Ely* 76-78; V 78-84; P-in-c 85; P-in-c Offord D'Arcy w Offord Cluny 76-78; R 78-84; P-in-c 85; rtd 85; Co-ord BRF (Dio Glos) from 90. *3 Limber Hill, Wyman's Brook, Cheltenham, Glos GL50 4RJ* Tel (01242) 244629

PRYKE, Jonathan Justin Speaight. b 59. Trin Coll Cam BA80 MA85. Trin Coll Bris BD85. **d** 85 **p** 86. C Corby St Columba *Pet* 85-88; C Jesmond Clayton Memorial *Newc* from 88. *15 Lily Avenue, Jesmond, Newcastle upon Tyne NE2 2SQ* Tel 0191-281 9854

PRYOR, Derek John. b 29. Lon Univ DipTh57 BD63 Birm Univ MEd74. Linc Th Coll 79 Chich Th Coll 79. **d** 80 **p** 81. Hon C Youlgreave *Derby* 80-82; Hon C Stanton-in-Peak 80-82; Hon C Ingham w Cammeringham w Fillingham *Linc* 82-87 and from 92; Chapl Bp Grosseteste Coll Linc 83-84; Dioc Schs Officer *Linc* 87-92; rtd 92. *Walnut Cottage, Chapel Lane, Fillingham, Gainsborough, Lincs DN21 5BP* Tel (01427) 668276

PRYOR, William Lister Archibald. b 39. Trin Coll Cam BA67 MA69. Ox NSM Course 72. **d** 75 **p** 90. NSM Summertown *Ox* 75-76; NSM Wolvercote w Summertown from 76; Perm to Offic *Nor* from 93. *Elm Tree Cottage, Summerfields Road, Oxford OX2 7EH* Tel (01865) 515102

PRYS, Deiniol. b 53. Univ of Wales (Ban) DipTh82 Univ of Wales (Cardiff) DPS83. St Mich Coll Llan 82. **d** 83 **p** 84. C Llanbeblig w Caernarfon and Betws Garmon etc *Ban* 83-86; TV Amlwch 86-88; V Llanerch-y-medd 89-92; R Llansadwrn w Llanddona and Llaniestyn etc from 92. *The Rectory, Llansadwrn, Porthaethwy, Ynys Mon LL59 5SL* Tel (01248) 810534

PRYSE, Hugh Henry David. b 58. St Chad's Coll Dur BA81 SS Coll Cam PGCE82 K Coll Lon MA96. St Steph Ho Ox 94. **d** 96 **p** 97. C Branksome St Aldhelm *Sarum* from 96. *105A Winston Avenue, Branksome, Poole, Dorset BH12 1AB* Tel (01202) 386388

PRYSOR-JONES, John Glynne. b 47. CQSW73 Liv Univ DipSocWork73 Birm Univ DPS80 Heythrop Coll Lon MA94. Westcott Ho Cam 88. **d** 90 **p** 91. C Mitcham St Mark *S'wark* 90-93; V Dudley St Fran *Worc* from 93. *The Vicarage, 50 Laurel Road, Dudley, W Midlands DY1 3EZ* Tel (01384) 253123

PRYTHERCH, David. b 30. Down Coll Cam BA54 MA58 Lon Univ CertEd68 DipAdEd71. Coll of Resurr Mirfield 54. **d** 56 **p** 57. C Blackpool St Steph *Blackb* 56-61; R Matson *Glouc* 61-65; Chapl St Elphin's Sch Matlock 65-85; V Thornton-le-Fylde *Blackb* 85-94; RD Poulton 91-94; rtd 94. *8A Dunraven Road, West Kirby, Wirral, Merseyside L48 4DS*

PUCKRIN, Christopher. b 47. Oak Hill Th Coll. **d** 82 **p** 83. C Heworth *York* 82-84; C Sherburn in Elmet 84-85; P-in-c Kirkby Wharfe 85-86; P-in-c Kirk Fenton 85-86; V Kirk Fenton w Kirkby Wharfe and Ulleskelfe 86-87; C York St Mich-le-Belfrey 87-94; P-in-c Barnstaple *Ex* from 94. *Holy Trinity Vicarage, Victoria Road, Barnstaple, Devon EX32 9HP* Tel (01271) 44321

PUDDEFOOT, John Charles. b 52. St Pet Coll Ox BA74 Edin Univ BD78. Edin Th Coll 76. **d** 78 **p** 79. C Darlington H Trin *Dur* 78-81; Ind Chapl *Chich* 81-84; Asst Master Eton Coll from 84, Hd Mathematics from 92; Lic to Offic *Ox* from 85. *Eton College, Windsor, Berks SL4 6DB* Tel (01753) 671320

PUDDY, Kenneth Wilfred. b 15. Hatf Coll Dur BA36 DipTh38. St Aug Coll Cant 37. **d** 39 **p** 39. C Weston-super-Mare Em *B & W* 39-41; C Yeovil St Jo w Preston Plucknett 41-46; V Meare 46-55; V Kingsbury Episcopi w E Lambrook 55-89; RD Ilminster 59-71; rtd 90; Perm to Offic *Eur* from 90. *La Rambaudie, La Chapelle Gresignac, 24320 Verteillac, France* Tel France (33) 53 91 04 07

PUDGE, Mark Samuel. b 67. K Coll Lon BD90 AKC90. Ripon Coll Cuddesdon DipMin93. **d** 93 **p** 94. C Thorpe Bay *Chelmsf* 93-96; TV Wickford and Runwell from 97. *8 Friern Walk, Wickford, Essex SS12 0HZ*

PUGH, Canon David. b 22. Univ of Wales (Abth) BA48. St D Coll Lamp 48. **d** 50 **p** 51. C Llanllwchaiarn *St D* 50-57; R Bangor Teifi w Henllan 57-70; R Bangor Teifi w Henllan and Llanfairorllwyn 70-81; RD Emlyn 73-91; R Bangor Teifi w Henllan and Llanfairorllwyn etc 81-91; Can St D Cathl 88-92; rtd 92; Hon Can St D Cathl *St D* from 92. *2 Bro Dewi, Henllan, Llandyssul, Dyfed SA44 5PL* Tel (01559) 370619

PUGH, Ernest William. b 16. AKC41. **d** 41 **p** 42. C Knotty Ash H Spirit *Liv* 41-44; C W Derby St Mary 44-56; Ch Ch Ox 56-58; Asst Master Giggleswick Sch 59; Hd of Div Ormskirk Gr Sch 59-81; Hon C Liv St Steph w St Cath *Liv* 59-73; P-in-c 73-81; rtd 81; Hon C W Derby (or Tuebrook) St Jo *Liv* 81-89; Perm to Offic from 89. *The Cottage, 54 Derwent Road, Liverpool L13 6QR* Tel 0151-228 4022

PUGH, Frank William. b 19. Roch Th Coll 62. **d** 64 **p** 65. C Oatlands *Guildf* 64-67; V Hilton w Cheselbourne and Melcombe Horsey *Sarum* 67; R Fordington 70-73; TV Dorchester 73-78; R Stalbridge 78-89; rtd 89; Perm to Offic *B & W* 89-95. *3 Rose Cottages, Balsam Lane, Wincanton, Somerset BA9 9HZ* Tel (01963) 34100

PUGH, Harry. b 48. K Coll Lon BD70 AKC71 Lanc Univ MA89. **d** 72 **p** 73. C Milnrow *Man* 72-75; P-in-c Rochdale Gd Shep 75-78; TV Rochdale 78-79; Perm to Offic *Liv* 79-82; C Darwen St Cuth *Blackb* 82-85; C Darwen St Cuth w Tockholes St Steph 85-86; V Burnley St Steph 86-93; R Hoole from 93. *The Rectory, 69 Liverpool Old Road, Much Hoole, Preston PR4 4GA* Tel (01227) 612267

PUGH, Ronald Keith. b 32. Jes Coll Ox BA54 MA57 DPhil57. Ripon Hall Ox 56. **d** 59 **p** 60. C Bournemouth St Mich *Win* 59-61; Asst Chapl Bryanston Sch Dorset 61-66; Chapl Cranleigh Sch Surrey 66-68; Lic to Offic *Win* from 68; Lect K Alfred Coll Winchester 68-97; Sec & Treas Win & Portsm Dioc Clerical Registry from 97. *Church House, 9 The Close, Winchester, Hants SO23 9LS* Tel (01962) 844644

PUGH, Stephen Gregory. Southn Univ BEd77. Linc Th Coll 85. **d** 87 **p** 88. C Harpenden St Nic *St Alb* 87-90; C Stevenage All SS Pin Green 90-93; R Stotfold and Radwell from 93. *The Vicarage, Church Road, Stotfold, Hitchin, Herts SG5 4NE* Tel (01462) 730218

PUGH, Miss Wendy Kathleen. b 48. Newnham Coll Cam BA69 MA75. Trin Coll Bris DipTh95. **d** 95 **p** 96. C Hailsham *Chich* from 95. *19 St Wilfrid's Green, Hailsham, E Sussex BN27 1DR* Tel (01323) 442132

PUGH, William Bryan. b 34. Man Univ. Ridley Hall Cam 59. **d** 61 **p** 62. C Oseney Crescent St Luke w Camden Square St Paul *Lon* 61-64; C N Wembley St Cuth 64-67; CF 67-88; QHC from 85; Chapl Heathfield Sch Ascot from 88. *3 College Close, Camberley, Surrey GU15 4JU* Tel (01276) 28799

PUGMIRE, Alan. b 37. Lon Univ DipTh63. Tyndale Hall Bris 61. **d** 64 **p** 65. C Islington St Steph w St Bart and St Matt *Lon* 64-66; C St Helens St Mark *Liv* 66-71; R Stretford St Bride *Man* 71-82; R Burnage St Marg from 82; AD Heaton from 88. *St Margaret's Rectory, 250 Burnage Lane, Manchester M19 1FL* Tel 0161-432 1844

PUGSLEY, Anthony John. b 39. ACIB. Oak Hill Th Coll 89. **d** 90 **p** 91. C Chadwell *Chelmsf* 90-94; P-in-c Gt Warley Ch Ch from 94. *Christ Church Vicarage, 79 Mount Crescent, Brentwood CM14 5DD* Tel (01277) 220428

PULESTON, Mervyn Pedley. b 35. K Coll Lon BD60 AKC60. **d** 61 **p** 62. C Gt Marlow *Ox* 61-65; C-in-c Blackbird Leys CD 65-70; V Kidlington 70-85; TR Kidlington w Hampton Poyle 85-86; Chapl Geneva *Eur* 86-92; TV Dorchester *Ox* from 92. *The Vicarage, Clifton Hampden, Abingdon, Oxon OX14 3EE* Tel (01865) 407784

PULFORD, Christopher. b 59. Pemb Coll Ox BA81 MA87. Trin Coll Bris. **d** 84 **p** 85. C Parr *Liv* 84-87; Chapl Berkhamsted Colleg Sch Herts 87-92. *131 High Street, Berkhamsted, Herts HP4 2DJ* Tel (01442) 873008

PULFORD, John Shirley Walter. b 31. Jes Coll Cam BA55 MA59 Lon Univ DipC&G79. Cuddesdon Coll 55. **d** 57 **p** 58. C Blackpool St Steph *Blackb* 57-60; N Rhodesia 60-63; V Newington St Paul *S'wark* 63-68; C Seacroft *Ripon* 68-70; Chapl HM Pris Liv 70-72; Chapl HM Pris Linc 72-73; Student Counsellor Linc Colls of Art and Tech 73-79; Cam Univ Counselling Service 79-96; Dir 82-96; rtd 96. *St John's House, 36 West Road, Bury St Edmunds, Suffolk IP33 3EJ* Tel (01284) 752721 Fax 752414

PULFORD, Canon Stephen Ian. b 25. Clifton Th Coll 53. **d** 56 **p** 57. C Heref St Jas *Heref* 56-58; R Coberley w Cowley *Glouc* 58-94; P-in-c Colesborne 75-94; Hon Can Glouc Cathl 84-94; RD Cirencester 88-89; rtd 94. *16 Bafford Grove, Charlton Kings, Cheltenham, Glos GL53 9JE* Tel (01242) 524261

PULLAN, Ben John. b 43. MSc. **d** 77 **p** 78. NSM Westbury-on-Trym St Alb *Bris* 77-91; NSM Henleaze from 91. *52 Druid Stoke Avenue, Bristol BS9 1DQ* Tel 0117-968 2697

PULLAN, Lionel Stephen. b 37. ARCO58 FIST77 Keble Coll Ox BA58 MA62. Cuddesdon Coll 58. **d** 60 **p** 61. C Tranmere St Paul *Ches* 60-63; C Higher Bebington 63-64; Perm to Offic 64-70; Hon C Luton St Chris Round Green *St Alb* 70-72; Hon C Hitchin H Sav 72-73; Hon C Welwyn 73-75; Hon C Welwyn w Ayot St Peter 75-78; Hon C Kimpton w Ayot St Lawrence 78-82; Hon C Stevenage St Andr and St Geo 82-85; Deputation Appeals Org CECS 85-90; Perm to Offic *St Alb* 85-89; Public Preacher 89-90; V Sundon from 90. *St Mary's Vicarage, 1 Selina Close, Sundon, Luton LU3 3AW* Tel (01582) 583076 or 573236

PULLAN, Mrs Pauline Margaret. b 32. N Ord Course 79. **dss** 82 **d** 87 **p** 94. Stockport St Sav *Ches* 82-83; Wilmslow 83-87; Par Dn 87-92; NSM 92-94; Sub-Chapl HM Pris Styal 89-92; rtd 92; NSM Altrincham St Jo *Ches* from 94. *12 Acacia Avenue, Wilmslow, Cheshire SK9 6AX* Tel (01625) 525865

PULLEN, James Stephen. b 43. Lon Univ BSc64 Linacre Coll Ox BA68. St Steph Ho Ox 66. **d** 68 **p** 69. C Chorlton-cum-Hardy St Clem *Man* 68-72; C Doncaster St Leon and St Jude *Sheff* 72-73; Chapl St Olave's and St Sav Schs Orpington 73-75; Chapl Haileybury Coll Herts from 75; Perm to Offic *St Alb* from 75. *Edmonstone House, Haileybury College, Hertford SG13 7NU* Tel (01992) 463384

PULLEN, Roger Christopher. b 43. Lon Univ BSc65 PGCE90. Wells Th Coll 65. **d** 67 **p** 68. C S w N Hayling *Portsm* 67-69; C Farlington 69-73; V Farington *Blackb* 73-80; V Chorley All SS 80-83; V Kingsley *Ches* 83-92; R Cilcain and Nannerch and Rhyd-y-mwyn *St As* from 92. *The Rectory, 9 Pen y Coed, Nannerch, Mold CH7 5RS* Tel (01352) 741367

PULLEN, Timothy John Tim. b 61. BNC Ox BA84. Cranmer Hall Dur 93. **d** 96 **p** 97. C Allesley *Cov* from 96. *1 Halifax Close, Allesley, Coventry CV5 9NZ* Tel (01203) 404518

PULLIN, Andrew Eric. b 47. Linc Th Coll 71. **d** 73 **p** 74. C Pershore w Wick *Worc* 73-75; C Pershore w Pinvin, Wick and Birlingham 75-77; TV Droitwich 77-80; V Woburn Sands *St Alb* 80-85; Perm to Offic *B & W* 85-95. *85 Weymouth Road, Frome, Somerset BA11 1HJ* Tel (01373) 472170

PULLIN, Arthur. b 18. St Jo Coll Dur LTh39 BA40 MA45. ALCD39. **d** 41 **p** 42. Asst Chapl Kingham Hill Sch Oxon 41-43; C Penge St Jo *Roch* 43-45; Chapl St Lawr Coll Ramsgate 45-50; Chapl Ch Hosp Horsham 50-64; V Midhurst *Chich* 65-85; R Woolbeding 65-85; RD Midhurst 81-85; rtd 85; Perm to Offic *Chich* from 85. *38 Carters Way, Wisborough Green, W Sussex RH14 0BY* Tel (01403) 700566

PULLIN, Christopher. b 56. St Chad's Coll Dur BA77. Ripon Coll Cuddesdon 79. **d** 80 **p** 81. C Tooting All SS *S'wark* 80-85; V New Eltham All SS 85-92; V St Jo in Bedwardine *Worc* from 92. *St John's Vicarage, 143 Malvern Road, Worcester WR2 4LN* Tel (01905) 422327

PULLIN, Peter. MA MSc CEng. Trin Coll Bris. **d** 88 **p** 89. NSM Rugby St Andr *Cov* 88-90; NSM Aylesbeare, Rockbeare, Farringdon etc *Ex* from 90. *Applegarth, 5 Minchin Orchard, Aylesbeare, Exeter EX5 2BY* Tel (01395) 232877

PULLINGER, Mrs Catherine Ann (Cathy). b 54. York Univ BA76. Oak Hill Th Coll DipHE93. **d** 93 **p** 97. NSM Luton St Paul *St Alb* from 93. *45 Manton Drive, Luton LU2 7DJ* Tel (01582) 38362

PULLINGER, Ian Austin. b 61. Oak Hill Th Coll. **d** 96 **p** 97. C Weston *Win* from 96. *194 Weston Lane, Southampton SO19 9HL* Tel (01703) 444316

PULMAN, Edgar James. b 17. Selw Coll Cam BA48 MA53. ALCD50. **d** 50 **p** 51. C Lee Gd Shep *S'wark* 50-52; C Stoke sub Hamdon *B & W* 52-53; V 53-58; C Norton sub Hamdon 52-53; R 53-58; Singapore 58-62; V Finchley H Trin *Lon* 63-76; C Norton sub Hamdon, W Chinnock, Chiselborough etc *B & W* 77-78; Lic to Offic from 79; rtd 82. *5 Manor House, Norton-sub-Hamdon, Stoke-sub-Hamdon, Somerset TA14 6SJ* Tel (01935) 881521

PULMAN, John. b 34. Nottm Univ CTPS81. EMMTC 78. **d** 81 **p** 82. NSM Mansfield St Pet *S'well* 81-83; C Mansfield Woodhouse 83-86; V Flintham from 86; R Car Colston w Screveton from 86; Chapl HM Young Offender Inst Whatton 87-90; Chapl HM Pris Whatton from 90. *The Vicarage, Woods Lane, Flintham, Newark, Notts NG23 5LR* Tel (01636) 525750 or (01949) 850511 Fax (01949) 850124

PUMPHREY, Norman John Albert. b 21. Nor Ord Course 76. **d** 77 **p** 78. NSM Aylsham *Nor* 77-94; Chapl St Mich Hosp Aylsham from 88; Perm to Offic *Nor* from 94. *12 Buxton Road, Aylsham, Norwich NR11 6JD* Tel (01263) 733207

PUNSHON, Ms Carol Mary. b 59. Liv Inst of Educn BEd83. Ridley Hall Cam CTM94. **d** 94 **p** 95. C Bushey *St Alb* 94-97; C Watford Ch Ch from 97. *77 Northfield Gardens, Watford WD2 4RF* Tel (01923) 225411

PUNSHON, George Wilson. b 30. Ripon Hall Ox 71. **d** 73 **p** 74. C Knighton St Mary Magd *Leic* 73-76; V Donisthorpe and Moira w Stretton-en-le-Field 76-82; V Gt Bowden w Welham 82-83; R Gt Bowden w Welham, Glooston and Cranoe 83-86; Zimbabwe 87-89; rtd 93; Perm to Offic *Pet* from 96. *5 Richardson Way, Raunds, Wellingborough, Northants NN9 6RH* Tel (01933) 460977

PUNSHON, Canon Keith. b 48. JP. Jes Coll Cam BA69 MA73 Birm Univ DipTh73 MA77. Qu Coll Birm 71. **d** 73 **p** 74. C Yardley St Edburgha *Birm* 73-76; Chapl Eton Coll 76-79; V Hill *Birm* 79-86; CF (TA) from 79; V S Yardley St Mich *Birm* 86-96; Can Res Ripon Cathl *Ripon* from 96. *St Peter's House, Minster Close, Ripon, N Yorkshire HG4 4QJ* Tel (01765) 604108

PURCELL, Canon William Ernest. b 09. Univ of Wales BA34 Keble Coll Ox BA36 MA43. Qu Coll Birm 36. **d** 37 **p** 38. C Ingrow cum Hainworth *Bradf* 37-40; C Dover St Mary *Cant* 40-43; V Maidstone St Pet 43-47; R Allington 43-47; V Sutton Valence w E Sutton 47-54; Chapl HM Borstal Inst E Sutton Park 49-54; Relig Broadcasting Org Midl Region 54-66; Can Th Cov Cathl *Cov* 59-66; Can Res Worc Cathl *Worc* 66-76; rtd 76; Perm to Offic *Ox* 83-95; Perm to Offic *Ely* from 95. *Flat 3, Gretton Court, Girton, Cambridge CB3 0QN* Tel (01223) 277234

PURCHAS, Canon Catherine Patience Ann. b 39. St Mary's Coll Dur BA61. St Alb Minl Tr Scheme 77. **dss** 80 **d** 87 **p** 94. RE Resource Cen 80-81; Relig Broadcasting Chiltern Radio 81-87; Wheathampstead *St Alb* 81-87; Hon Par Dn 87-94; Hon C from 94; Relig Broadcasting Beds Radio from 88; Bp's Officer for Women from 93; Bp's Officer for NSM and Asst Dir of Ords from 93; Hon Can St Alb from 96. *The Rectory, Church Street, Wheathampstead, St Albans, Herts AL4 8LR* Tel (01582) 833144 or 834285 Fax 834285

PURCHAS, Thomas. b 35. Qu Coll Birm 59. **d** 62 **p** 63. C Hatfield *St Alb* 62-71; R Blunham 71-78; P-in-c Tempsford w Lt Barford 71-78; R Blunham w Tempsford and Lt Barford 78-80; R Wheathampstead from 80; RD Wheathampstead from 92. *The Rectory, Church Street, Wheathampstead, St Albans, Herts AL4 8LR* Tel (01582) 833144 or 843285 Fax 834285

PURDIE, Dr Anthony Watson. b 08. FRCOG51 FRCSGlas65 FRCPGlas68 Glas Univ MB, ChB31 K Coll Lon BD76 AKC76. **d** 76 **p** 77. NSM Waltham Abbey *Chelmsf* 76-77; NSM Goodmayes St Paul 77-80; Perm to Offic *Ex* from 82. *Shearwater, Pope's Lane, Colyford, Colyton, Devon EX13 6QR* Tel (01297) 553206

PURDY, John David. b 44. Leeds Univ BA65 DipTh74 MPhil76. Coll of Resurr Mirfield 72. **d** 75 **p** 76. C Marske in Cleveland *York* 75-78; C Marton-in-Cleveland 78-80; V Newby 80-87; V Kirkleatham 87-95; V Kirkbymoorside w Gillamoor, Farndale etc from 95. *The Vicarage, Kirkbymoorside, York YO6 6AZ* Tel (01751) 31452

PURSER, Alan Gordon. b 51. Leic Univ BSc73. Wycliffe Hall Ox 74. **d** 77 **p** 78. C Beckenham Ch Ch *Roch* 77-81; TV Barking St Marg w St Patr *Chelmsf* 81-84; S Africa 84-88; C Enfield Ch Ch Trent Park *Lon* from 88; Proclamation Trust from 88. *The Parsonage, 34 Crescent East, Hadley Wood, Herts EN4 0EN* Tel 0181-449 2572

PURVEY-TYRER, Neil. b 66. Leeds Univ BA87 MA88. Westcott Ho Cam 88. **d** 90 **p** 91. C Denbigh and Nantglyn *St As* 90-92; Chapl Asst Basingstoke Distr Hosp 92-95; TV Cannock *Lich* from 95. *St Aidan's Vicarage, Albert Street, Cannock, Staffs WS11 2JD* Tel (01543) 505674

PURVIS, Canon Colin. b 19. Kelham Th Coll 37. **d** 44 **p** 45. C Hebburn St Cuth *Dur* 44-47; C Sunderland 47-50; C Darlington St Cuth 50-53; C-in-c Bishopwearmouth St Mary V w St Pet CD 53-62; V Heworth St Mary 62-76; RD Gateshead 69-76; R Egglescliffe 76-84; Hon Can Dur Cathl 83-92; rtd 84; Perm to Offic *Newc* from 84; Perm to Offic *Ripon* from 84. *15 Milbank Court, Darlington, Co Durham DL3 9PF* Tel (01325) 355711

PURVIS, Stephen. b 48. AKC70. **d** 71 **p** 72. C Peterlee *Dur* 71-75; Dioc Recruitment Officer 75-79; V Stevenage All SS Pin Green *St Alb* 79-88; TR Borehamwood from 88; RD Aldenham from 94. *Holy Cross Vicarage, 1 Warren Grove, Borehamwood, Herts WD6 2QU* Tel 0181-953 2183

PUSEY, Ian John. b 39. Sarum Th Coll 69. **d** 71 **p** 72. C Waltham Abbey *Chelmsf* 71-75; TV Stantonbury *Ox* 75-80; P-in-c Bletchley 80-84; R from 84; RD Milton Keynes from 96. *The Rectory, 75 Church Green Road, Bletchley, Milton Keynes MK3 6BY* Tel (01908) 373357

PUTMAN, Nina Maude Elaine. b 20. **dss** 75 **d** 87 **p** 94. New Malden and Coombe *S'wark* 75-87; NSM 87-92; rtd 80; Perm to Offic *S'wark* from 92. *57 Alric Avenue, New Malden, Surrey KT3 4JL* Tel 0181-949 6042

PYATT, Noel Watson. b 34. AKC57. **d** 58 **p** 59. C Prenton *Ches* 58-61; C Cheadle Hulme All SS 61-63; P-in-c Hattersley 63-66; V

66-70; V Ches St Paul from 70. *St Paul's Vicarage, 10 Sandy Lane, Chester CH3 5UL* Tel (01244) 351377

PYBURN, Canon Alan. b 29. G&C Coll Cam BA51 MA55. Westcott Ho Cam 53. **d** 55 **p** 56. C Barnard Castle *Dur* 55-57; Chapl G&C Coll Cam 57-60; V Dallington *Pet* 60-72; V Ox St Giles *Ox* 72-79; P-in-c Remenham 79-94; R Henley 79-94; RD Henley 84-94; Hon Can Ch Ch 90-95; R Henley on Thames w Remenham 94-95; rtd 95. *Pippin Cottage, Well Hill, Finstock, Chipping Norton, Oxon OX7 3BU* Tel (01993) 868651

PYBUS, Antony Frederick. b 54. Birm Univ BA77. St Jo Coll Dur 78. **d** 81 **p** 82. C Ches H Trin *Ches* 81-84; C W Hampstead St Jas *Lon* 84-89; V Alexandra Park St Andr 89-93; V Alexandra Park from 93. *The Vicarage, 34 Alexandra Park Road, London N10 2AB* Tel 0181-444 6898 Fax 442 1736

PYE, Alexander Frederick. b 61. St Mich Coll Llan DipPTh95. **d** 95 **p** 96. C Griffithstown *Mon* from 95. *82 Greenhill Road, Sebastopol, Pontypool NP4 5BQ* Tel (01495) 763962

PYE, Canon Allan Stephen. b 56. Univ of Wales (Lamp) BA78 Lanc Univ MA85 MPhil87. Westcott Ho Cam 79. **d** 81 **p** 82. C Scotforth *Blackb* 81-85; C Oswaldtwistle All SS 85-87; Chapl Wrightington Hosp 87-91; V Wrightington *Blackb* 87-91; P-in-c Hayton St Mary *Carl* 91-93; V Hayton w Cumwhitton from 93; RD Brampton from 96; Hon Can Carl Cathl from 97. *The Vicarage, Hayton, Carlisle CA4 9HR* Tel (01228) 70248

PYE, Gay Elizabeth. **d** 96 **p** 96. NSM Castle Church *Lich* from 96; Asst Chapl HM Pris Stafford from 96. *Castle Church Vicarage, Castle Bank, Stafford ST16 1DJ* Tel (01785) 223673

PYE, James Timothy. b 58. Oak Hill Th Coll BA90. **d** 90 **p** 91. C Normanton *Derby* 90-94; R Talke *Lich* from 94. *The Rectory, Crown Bank, Talke, Stoke-on-Trent ST7 1PU* Tel (01782) 782348

PYE, Joseph Terence Hardwidge. b 41. ARICS64. Trin Coll Bris 70. **d** 73 **p** 74. C Blackb Ch Ch *Blackb* 73-76; OMF 77-90; Korea 77-90; V Castle Church *Lich* from 90. *Castle Church Vicarage, Castle Bank, Stafford ST16 1DJ* Tel (01785) 223673

PYKE, Alan. b 37. Trin Coll Bris BA87. **d** 87 **p** 88. CA 58-87; C Ipswich St Mary at Stoke w St Pet *St E* 87-90; R Creeting St Mary, Creeting St Peter etc from 90. *The Rectory, Forward Green, Stowmarket, Suffolk IP14 5EF* Tel (01449) 711347

PYKE, Barry John. b 62. FGS84 Qu Mary Coll Lon BSc84 Southn Univ BTh94. Sarum & Wells Th Coll BTh91. **d** 94 **p** 95. C Bengeworth *Worc* 94-96; C Worc City St Paul and Old St Martin etc from 96. *35 Lobelia Close, Worcester WR5 3RR*

PYKE, Richard Ernest. b 50. Sarum & Wells Th Coll. **d** 82 **p** 83. C Bushey *St Alb* 82-85; C Gt Berkhamsted 85-89; V St Alb St Mary Marshalswick from 89. *The Vicarage, 1 Sherwood Avenue, St Albans, Herts AL4 9QA* Tel (01727) 851544

PYKE, Thomas Fortune (Tom). b 62. St Chad's Coll Dur BA85 Fitzw Coll Cam BA88. Ridley Hall Cam 86. **d** 89 **p** 90. C Hitchin *St Alb* 89-94; Chapl Aston Univ *Birm* from 94. *27 Worlds End Road, Handsworth Wood, Birmingham B20 2NP* Tel 0121-507 0247 or 359 3621 Fax 359 4240 E-mail t.f.pyke@aston.ac.uk

PYLE, John Alan. b 31. Qu Coll Birm. **d** 69 **p** 70. C Fenham St Jas and St Basil *Newc* 69-72; C Monkseaton St Pet 72-74; C Morpeth 74-78; R Bothal 78-83; TV Willington Team 83-91; R Chollerton w Birtley and Thockrington 91-97; rtd 97. *37 Ullswater Drive, Killingworth, Newcastle upon Tyne NE12 0GX* Tel 0191-268 6044

PYM, David Pitfield. b 45. Nottm Univ BA65 Ex Coll Ox DPhil68. Ripon Hall Ox 66. **d** 68 **p** 69. C Nottingham St Mary *S'well* 68-72; Chapl RN 72-76 and 79-84; Chapl Worksop Coll Notts 76-79; R Avon Dassett w Farnborough and Fenny Compton *Cov* from 84. *The Rectory, Avon Dassett, Leamington Spa, Warks CV33 0AR* Tel (01295) 690305

PYM, Francis Victor. b 24. ARIBA52 DipArch52. St Jo Coll Dur 74. **d** 76 **p** 77. C Keighley *Bradf* 76-79; Chapl Bethany Fellowship 79-87; Dir Joshua Chr Trust from 88; Research Asst Ho of Lords from 89; Dir Gp Apologetics Initiative from 92. *Bolney House, Bolney, Haywards Heath, W Sussex RH17 5QR* Tel (01444) 881877

PYM, Gordon Sydney. b 19. Worc Ord Coll 59. **d** 61 **p** 62. C Highweek *Ex* 61-63; C Plymouth Em 63-66; V Kilnhurst *Sheff* 66-69; V Owston 69-72; V Hensall 72-75; rtd 75; Perm to Offic *Sheff* from 75. *6 Greno Road, Swinton, Mexborough, S Yorkshire S64 8RP* Tel (01709) 586884

PYNE, Robert Leslie. b 51. Lanchester Poly BA72 Leeds Univ DipTh78. Coll of Resurr Mirfield 76. **d** 79 **p** 80. C Clifton All SS w St Jo *Bris* 79-81; Bp's Dom Chapl *Ox* 81-84; TV High Wycombe 84-90; Chapl RN from 90. *Royal Naval Chaplaincy Service, Room 203, Victory Building, HM Naval Base, Portsmouth PO1 3LS* Tel (01705) 727903 Fax 727112

PYNN, Catherine. b 45. Reading Univ BSc67. St Alb and Ox Min Course 93. **d** 96 **p** 97. NSM Caversham and Mapledurham *Ox* from 96. *42 Geoffreyson Road, Caversham, Reading RG4 7HS* Tel 0118-947 6065 or 0410-442946 (mobile)

✠**PYTCHES, The Rt Revd George Edward David.** b 31. Bris Univ BA54 Nottm Univ MPhil84. Tyndale Hall Bris 51. **d** 55 **p** 56 **c** 70. C Ox St Ebbe *Ox* 55-58; C Wallington H Trin *S'wark* 58-59; Chile 59-77; Suff Bp Valparaiso 70-72; Bp Chile, Bolivia and Peru 72-77; V Chorleywood St Andr *St Alb* 77-96; rtd 96. *Red Tiles, Homefield Road, Chorleywood, Rickmansworth, Herts WD3 5QJ* Tel (01923) 283763

PYTCHES, Preb Dr Peter Norman Lambert. b 32. Lon Univ BD57 Bris Univ MLitt67 Southn Univ PhD81. Lambeth STh74 Tyndale Hall Bris 53. **d** 57 **p** 58. C Heatherlands St Jo *Sarum* 57-61; C Cromer *Nor* 61-63; V Plymouth St Jude *Ex* 63-71; V Heatherlands St Jo *Sarum* 71-76; Dir Past Tr Oak Hill Th Coll 76-81; V Finchley Ch Ch *Lon* 81-91; AD Cen Barnet 86-91; V Forty Hill Jes Ch from 91; Preb St Paul's Cathl from 92. *The Vicarage, Forty Hill, Enfield, Middx EN2 9EU* Tel 0181-363 1935

Q

QUANCE, John David. b 42. Kelham Th Coll 61. **d** 67 **p** 68. C Southgate Ch Ch *Lon* 67-70; C Norbury St Phil *Cant* 70-73; Asst Chapl Middx Hosp Lon 73-80; R Failsworth St Jo *Man* 80-95; Australia 84-85; P-in-c Healey *Man* from 95. *Healey Vicarage, Gandy Lane, Rochdale, Lancs OL12 6EF* Tel (01706) 350808

QUARMBY, David John. b 43. St Jo Coll Dur BA64 Lon Univ CertEd70 Man Univ MEd89. Ridley Hall Cam 65. **d** 67 **p** 68. C Bournville *Birm* 67-71; V Erdington St Chad 71-73; Lic to Offic *Blackb* 73-83; Perm to Offic *Man* 83-90; C Oldham St Paul from 90; Counsellor Huddersfield Poly 90-92; Huddersfield Univ from 92. *30 College Avenue, Oldham OL8 4DS* Tel 0161-626 2771

QUARRELL, John Beck. b 39. Hull Coll of Educn CertEd59. Chich Th Coll 67. **d** 70 **p** 71. C Horbury *Wakef* 70-71; C Sowerby 71-73; V Brotherton 74-80; Chapl Pontefract Gen Hosp 78-80; Staincliffe Hosp Wakef 82-88; V Staincliffe *Wakef* 80-88; R Farndon w Thorpe, Hawton and Cotham *S'well* from 89. *The Rectory, 3 Marsh Lane, Farndon, Newark, Notts NG24 3SS* Tel (01636) 705048

QUARTON, Robert Edward. b 43. EMMTC 84. **d** 87 **p** 88. C Gresley *Derby* 87-88; C Clay Cross 88-90; C N Wingfield, Clay Cross and Pilsley 90-91; R Darley from 91. *The Rectory, 15 Hall Rise, Darley Dale, Matlock, Derbyshire DE4 2FW* Tel (01629) 734257

QUASH, Jonathan Ben. b 68. Peterho Cam BA90 MA94. Westcott Ho Cam 91. **d** 95 **p** 96. NSM Cambridge St Mary Less *Ely* 95-96; Asst Chapl Peterho Cam 95-96; Chapl Fitzw Coll Cam from 96; Tutor Wesley Ho Cam from 96. *Fitzwilliam College, Cambridge CB3 0DG* Tel (01223) 332013 or 741037 E-mail jbq1000@cam.ac.uk

✠**QUASHIE, The Rt Revd Kobina Adduah.** b 34. ACIS60 Univ of Ghana LLB71 LLM74 DipTh80. **d** 78 **p** 78 **c** 92. Ghana 78-80 and from 92; Chapl Middx Hosp Lon 80; Funding Officer USPG 80-92; Hon Can Kumasi from 86; Hon Can Koforidua from 86; Hon Can Accra from 87; Bp Cape Coast from 92. *Bishopscourt, PO Box A233, Adiadel Estates, Cape Coast, Ghana*

QUENNELL, Brian Michael. b 19. **d** 74 **p** 75. C Oakham w Hambleton and Egleton *Pet* 74-78; V Denford w Ringstead 78-87; rtd 87; Perm to Offic *Pet* from 87. *3 Crispin Cottages, Baker Street, Walgrave, Northampton NN6 9QL* Tel (01604) 781022

QUICK, Roger Aelfred Melvin Tricquet. b 55. Leeds Univ BA79 PGCE81. Coll of Resurr Mirfield BA94. **d** 96 **p** 97. C Chapel Allerton *Ripon* from 96. *21 Carr Manor Grove, Leeds LS17 5AH*

QUIGLEY, John Molesworth. b 21. BNC Ox BA43 MA47. Wycliffe Hall Ox 43. **d** 44 **p** 45. C Wembley St Jo *Lon* 44-46; Hon C Ellesmere Port *Ches* 75; Hon C Bromborough 75-77 and 80-82; Hon C Prenton 77-80; Hon C Wallasey St Hilary 82-84; rtd 84; Perm to Offic *Bradf* from 85. *Flat 3, Ashbrook, 4 Grove Road, Ilkley, W Yorkshire LS29 9PE* Tel (01943) 609380

QUILL, John Stephen. b 51. Nottm Univ DipTh78. Linc Th Coll 76. **d** 79 **p** 80. C Sawbridgeworth *St Alb* 79-81; C Watford Ch Ch 81-85; Dioc Soc Services Adv *Worc* 85-90; Adv to Bd of Soc Resp 90-95. *77 Northfield Gardens, Bushey, Watford WD2 4RF* Tel (01923) 225411

QUILL, Canon Walter Paterson. b 35. **d** 60 **p** 61. C Glendermott *D & R* 60-63; I Kilbarron 63-66; I Kilcronaghan w Ballynascreen 66-81; I Derg w Termonamongan from 81; RD Strabane from 87; Can Derry Cathl from 89; RD Newtownstewart and Omagh from 90; Preb Howth St Patr Cathl Dublin from 94. *13 Strabane Road, Castlederg, Co Tyrone BT81 7HZ* Tel (01662) 671362

QUILLIAM, Miss Anne Eleanor Scott. b 31. Bedf Coll Lon BA54 CertEd55. Dalton Ho Bris 59. **d** 87. Par Dn Toxteth St Philemon w St Gabr and St Cleopas *Liv* 87-92; rtd 92; Perm to Offic *S & M* from 92. *13 Raad ny Gabbil, Ballalough, Castletown, Isle of Man IM9 1HH* Tel (01624) 822357

QUIN, Eric Arthur. b 22. Magd Coll Cam BA46 MA48 Lon Univ BD56. Bps' Coll Cheshunt 46. **d** 48 **p** 49. C Luton St Andr *St Alb* 48-50; C Barnoldswick w Bracewell *Bradf* 50-52; PC Bradf St Sav

52-57; P-in-c Gt w Lt Wymondley *St Alb* 57-58; P-in-c St Ippolyts 57-58; V 58-70; RD Hitchin 68-70; V Haynes 70-87; rtd 87; Perm to Offic *Ches* from 87. *Annabel's Cottage, The Lydiate, Wirral, Merseyside L60 8PR* Tel 0151-342 8650

QUIN, John James Neil. b 31. Ox Univ MA DipEd53. Qu Coll Birm 61. **d** 63 **p** 64. C Cannock *Lich* 63-68; V Sneyd Green 68-78; V Stafford St Paul Forebridge 78-90; TV Tettenhall Regis from 90. *Church Cottage, Church Road, Tettenhall, Wolverhampton WV6 9AJ* Tel (01902) 751941

QUIN, The Ven Thomas Rothwell. b 15. OBE80. TCD BA39 MA49. **d** 39 **p** 40. C Ballymacarrett St Patr *D & D* 39-41; Chapl RAFVR 41-46; Chapl RAF 46-70; Asst Chapl-in-Chief RAF 63-70; Prin RAF Chapl Sch 66-70; QHC 67-70; Chapl Zurich w St Gallen and Winterthur *Eur* 70-80; Adn Switzerland 79-80; rtd 80; Perm to Offic *Sarum* from 80. *New Rushford, Walnut Close, Sutton Veny, Warminster, Wilts BA12 7BS* Tel (01985) 40794

QUINE, Christopher Andrew. b 38. St Aid Birkenhead 61. **d** 64 **p** 65. C Hunts Cross *Liv* 64-67; C Farnworth 67-71; C-in-c Widnes St Jo 67-71; V Clubmoor 71-78; V Formby H Trin from 78. *Holy Trinity Vicarage, 2A Brows Lane, Formby, Liverpool L37 3HZ* Tel (01704) 873642

QUINE, David Anthony. b 28. Qu Coll Cam BA52 MA59. Ridley Hall Cam 53. **d** 55 **p** 56. C Beckenham Ch Ch *Roch* 55-59; C Normanton *Derby* 59-60; V Low Elswick *Newc* 60-66; V Houghton *Carl* 66-68; Lic to Offic *York* 68-71; Chapl Monkton Combe Sch Bath 71-85; rtd 85; Perm to Offic *Carl* from 85. *Briar Cragg, Gale Rigg, Ambleside, Cumbria LA22 0AZ* Tel (01539) 433563

QUINE, Canon Dr Ernest Kendrick Leigh. b 21. St Jo Coll Dur BA50 MA55 DipTh51 Nottm Univ DPhil68. **d** 51 **p** 52. C Grassendale *Liv* 51-52; C Shrewsbury St Alkmund *Lich* 52-54; C-in-c Park Estate St Chris CD *Leic* 54-61; V Belgrave St Pet 61-93; Hon Can Leic Cathl 67-93; rtd 93; Perm to Offic *Leic* from 93. *63 Somerset Drive, Glenfield, Leicester LE3 8QW* Tel 0116-232 1994

✠QUINLAN, The Rt Revd Alan Geoffrey. b 33. Kelham Th Coll 54. **d** 58 **p** 59 **c** 88. C Bedford Leigh *Man* 58-61; S Africa from 61; Suff Bp Cen Region from 88. *Bishop's House, 79 Kildare Road, Newlands, 7700 South Africa* Tel Cape Town (21) 642444

QUINN, Arthur Hamilton Riddel. b 37. TCD BA60 MA64 BD67. **d** 61 **p** 62. C Belfast H Trin *Conn* 61-63; C Belfast St Mary Magd 63-64; Chapl Hull Univ *York* 64-69; Chapl Keele Univ *Lich* 69-74; P-in-c Keele 72-74; V Shirley St Jo *Cant* 74-84; V Shirley St Jo *S'wark* from 85; RD Croydon Addington from 95. *The Vicarage, 49 Shirley Church Road, Croydon CR0 5EF* Tel 0181-654 1013

QUINN, Cecil Hugh. b 24. Oak Hill Th Coll 74. **d** 76 **p** 77. C Bedford St Jo and St Leon *St Alb* 76-79; Deputation Sec Irish Ch Miss 79-89; I Rathmullan w Tyrella *D & D* 80-96; rtd 96. *15 Pemberton Park, Downpatrick, Co Down BT30 6DJ* Tel (01396) 616741

QUINN, Derek John. b 55. TCD BTh88. **d** 88 **p** 89. C Mossley *Conn* 88-91; I Cappagh w Lislimnaghan *D & R* from 91. *Erganagh Rectory, 1 Erganagh Road, Cappagh, Omagh, Co Tyrone BT79 7SX* Tel (01662) 242572

QUINN, Dr Eugene Frederick. b 35. **d** 74 **p** 75. Chapl Warsaw *Eur* 94-95; USA from 95. *5702 Kirkside Drive, Chevy Chase, MD 20815-7116, USA*

QUINN, George Bruce. b 23. **d** 82 **p** 83. NSM Douglas St Ninian *S & M* from 82. *85 Port-e-Chee Avenue, Douglas, Isle of Man IM2 5EZ* Tel (01624) 674080

QUINN, Mrs Helen Elizabeth. b 46. Keswick Hall Coll CertEd67. EAMTC 92. **d** 95 **p** 96. Hon C Old Catton *Nor* 95-96. *Address temp unknown*

QUINN, Dr John James. b 46. TCD BA70 PhD76. St Jo Coll Nottm DipTh80. **d** 81 **p** 82. C Gorleston St Andr *Nor* 81-84; R Belton 84-90; R Burgh Castle 84-90; R Belton and Burgh Castle from 90. *The Rectory, Belton, Great Yarmouth, Norfolk NR31 9JQ* Tel (01493) 780210

QUINN, Kenneth Norman. b 40. QUB BSc62 CEng MICE. CITC 80. **d** 85 **p** 86. NSM Seapatrick *D & D* 85-91; Lic to Offic from 91. *4 Knollwood, Seapatrick, Banbridge, Co Down BT32 4PE* Tel (01820) 623515

QUINN, Marjorie. **d** 94 **p** 97. NSM Hawarden *St As* from 94. *21 Hawarden Way, Mancot, Deeside CH5 2EL* Tel (01244) 531639

QUINNELL, Peter Francis. b 48. St Steph Ho Ox DipMin95. **d** 95 **p** 96. C Tewkesbury w Walton Cardiff *Glouc* from 95. *83 York Road, Tewkesbury, Glos GL20 5HB* Tel (01684) 294756

QUINNEY, Canon William Elliott. b 33. Linc Th Coll 62. **d** 64 **p** 65. C Coalville *Leic* 64-68; P-in-c Ibstock 68-69; R Nailstone w Carlton 69-79; R Nailstone and Carlton w Shackerstone from 79; Hon Can Leic Cathl from 97. *The Rectory, Rectory Lane, Nailstone, Nuneaton, Warks CV13 0QQ* Tel (01530) 260281

QUINT, Mrs Patricia Mary. b 51. Milton Keynes Coll of Ed CertEd76 Open Univ BA77. St Alb Minl Tr Scheme 90. **d** 93 **p** 94. C Hertford St Andr *St Alb* 93-96; C Bromham w Oakley and Stagsden from 96. *St Mary's House, 65 Lincroft, Oakley, Bedford MK43 7SS* Tel (01234) 826153

R

RABIN, Peter David. b 62. Southlands Coll Lon BA86. Aston Tr Scheme 88 Ripon Coll Cuddesdon BTh93. **d** 93 **p** 94. C Hornsey St Mary w St Geo *Lon* 93-97; V Cricklewood St Pet from 97. *St Peter's Vicarage, 5 Farm Avenue, London NW2 2EG* Tel 0181-450 9043

RABJOHNS, Alan. b 40. Leeds Univ BA62. Coll of Resurr Mirfield 62. **d** 64 **p** 65. C Ashington *Newc* 64-67; C Upton cum Chalvey *Ox* 67-76; V Roath St Sav *Llan* from 76. *St Saviour's Vicarage, 115 Splott Road, Cardiff CF2 2BY* Tel (01222) 461203

RABLEN, Antony Ford. b 52. St Jo Coll Nottm. **d** 82 **p** 83. C Clifton *York* 82-85; TV Marfleet 85-92; P-in-c Welton w Melton from 92. *St Helen's Vicarage, Welton, Brough, N Humberside HU15 1ND* Tel (01482) 666677

RABY, Canon Alfred Charles. b 04. St Jo Coll Ox BA27 MA30. Wells Th Coll 27. **d** 28 **p** 29. C Lambeth *S'wark* 28-33; C Raynes Park St Sav 33-36; V Shooters Hill Ch Ch 36-39; V Purley St Mark Woodcote 39-54; V Clapham Ch Ch 54-74; Hon Can S'wark Cathl 57-75; R Clapham H Trin 54-75; RD Clapham and Brixton 63-74; rtd 75; Perm to Offic *St E* from 75. *134B Southgate Street, Bury St Edmunds, Suffolk IP33 2AF* Tel (01284) 703487

RABY, Malcolm Ernest. b 47. St Jo Coll York BEd73. N Ord Course 81. **d** 84 **p** 85. NSM Chadkirk *Ches* 84-88; Consultant E England CPAS 88-94; Perm to Offic *Linc* from 92; C Ely 94-96; TV Ely from 96. *44 Bentham Way, Ely, Cambs CB6 1BS* Tel (01353) 644964

RACE, Alan. b 51. Bradf Univ BTech73 Ox Univ DipTh75 Birm Univ MA82. Ripon Coll Cuddesdon 73. **d** 76 **p** 77. C Tupsley *Heref* 76-79; Asst Chapl Kent Univ *Cant* 79-84; Dir Studies S'wark Ord Course 84-94; R Aylestone St Andr w St Jas *Leic* from 94. *The Rectory, Old Church Street, Leicester LE2 8ND* Tel 0116-283 2458

RACE, Christopher Keith. b 43. St Paul's Grahamstown DipTh78. **d** 78 **p** 80. S Africa 78-86; V Tanworth St Patr Salter Street *Birm* 86-96; P-in-c Rothiemurchus *Mor* from 96. *The Rectory, Inverdruie, Rothiemurchus, Aviemore, Inverness-shire PH22 1QH* Tel (01479) 811433

RACTLIFFE, Dudley John. b 38. Man Univ BA62 Birm Univ DPS69. Ridley Hall Cam 63. **d** 66 **p** 67. C Radford *Cov* 66-68; C Haslemere *Guildf* 69-73; V Perry Beeches *Birm* 73-78; V Worle *B & W* 78-88; Dioc Ecum Officer 88-93; R Dowlishwake w Kingstone, Chillington etc 88-93; TR Swanage and Studland *Sarum* from 93. *The Rectory, 12 Church Hill, Swanage, Dorset BH19 1HU* Tel (01929) 422916

RADCLIFF, Henry Robert Moshe. b 30. Moore Th Coll Sydney ThL57. **d** 60 **p** 61. C Walthamstow St Andr *Chelmsf* 60-61; C Romford Gd Shep Collier Row 61-62; Australia 62-64; C Becontree St Mary *Chelmsf* 64-66; C St Luke in the City *Liv* 66-70; CMJ 67-80; rtd 95. *27 Melville street, Glasgow G41 2JL* Tel 0141-423 2002

RADCLIFFE, Canon Albert Edward. b 34. Lon Univ BD63. St Aid Birkenhead Ch Div Sch of the Pacific (USA) 61. **d** 62 **p** 63. C Knotty Ash St Jo *Liv* 62-64; C Blundellsands St Nic 64-66; Israel 66-69; V Tonge w Alkrington *Man* 69-77; R Ashton St Mich 77-91; AD Ashton-under-Lyne 87-91; Can Res Man Cathl from 91. *46 Shrewsbury Road, Prestwich, Manchester M25 8EQ* Tel 0161-798 0459 or 833 2220 Fax 839 6226

RADCLIFFE, David Jeffrey. b 52. Linc Th Coll 77. **d** 79 **p** 80. C Poulton-le-Fylde *Blackb* 79-84; V Ingol 84-88; R Lowther and Askham *Carl* 88-96; R Lowther and Askham and Clifton and Brougham from 96. *The Rectory, Lilac House, Lowther, Penrith, Cumbria CA10 2HH* Tel (01931) 712277

RADCLIFFE, Eileen Rose (Rosie). b 54. Carl Dioc Tr Inst 92. **d** 95 **p** 96. NSM Gt Salkeld w Lazonby *Carl* from 95. *The Rectory, Lilac House, Lowther, Penrith, Cumbria CA10 2HH* Tel (01931) 712277

RADCLIFFE, James Warner. b 23. FICE66 FRTPI66 Liv Univ BEng43 MEng46. Cranmer Hall Dur 76. **d** 78 **p** 79. C Penrith *Carl* 78-79; C Penrith w Newton Reigny 79-81; P-in-c Barton w Pooley Bridge 81-83; P-in-c Martindale 83; V Barton, Pooley Bridge and Martindale 83-86; Perm to Offic from 86; rtd 88. *Sunny Vale, Church View, Heversham, Milnthorpe, Cumbria LA7 7EN* Tel (015395) 63572

RADCLIFFE, Mrs Rosemary. b 45. SW Minl Tr Course 87. **d** 90 **p** 94. NSM Devoran *Truro* 90-93; D-in-c N Newton w St Michaelchurch, Thurloxton etc *B & W* 93-94; P-in-c from 94; Chapl to the Deaf 93-96. *The Rectory, Thurloxton, Taunton, Somerset TA2 8RH* Tel (01823) 412479

RADFORD, Canon Andrew John (Andy). b 44. Trin Coll Bris 72. **d** 74 **p** 75. C Shirehampton *Bris* 74-78; C Henleaze 78-80; Producer Relig Progr BBC Radio Bris 74-80; V Bath St Barn w Englishcombe *B & W* 80-85; Dioc Communications Officer *Glouc* 85-93; Producer Relig Progr Severn Sound Radio 85-93; Hon Can Glouc Cathl from 91; Development and Tr Officer Ch Ho Westmr from 93. *11 Foley Rise, Hartpury, Gloucester GL19 3DW* Tel (01452) 700055

RADFORD, Leslie. b 24. Lon Univ DipTh75. LNSM course. **d** 85 **p** 86. NSM Scotter w E Ferry *Linc* 85-94. *1 Carr Villas, Laughton, Gainsborough, Lincs DN21 3QF* Tel (01427) 628265

RADLEY, Peter. b 31. Bps' Coll Cheshunt 60. **d** 62 **p** 63. C Lillington *Cov* 62-63; C Nuneaton St Nic 63-67; P-in-c Skillington *Linc* 67-68; V Waltham *Ox* 68-95; rtd 95; NSM N Ockendon *Chelmsf* from 95. *1 School House, Church Lane, North Ockendon, Upminster, Essex RM14 3QA* Tel (01708) 224347

RADLEY, Stephen Gavin. b 62. K Coll Lon BSc83 AKC83. Cranmer Hall Dur BA87 St Jo Coll Dur 85. **d** 89 **p** 90. C Darlington St Matt and St Luke *Dur* 89-92; P-in-c Chilton 92-96; P-in-c Marley Hill from 96. *Grange House, Streetgate, Sunniside, Newcastle upon Tyne NE16 5LQ* Tel 0191-488 8487

RADLEY, Stephen John. b 68. Lancs Coll of Agric NDA89. St Jo Coll Nottm BTh93. **d** 96 **p** 97. C Boulton *Derby* from 96. *14 Courtland Drive, Alvaston, Derby DE24 0GS* Tel (01332) 756466

RAFFAY, Julian Paul. b 60. Stirling Univ BSc84. Cranmer Hall Dur BA89. **d** 90 **p** 91. C Adel *Ripon* 90-93; C Leeds Halton St Wilfrid 93-95; Asst Chapl S Derbys Mental Health NHS Trust from 95. *Kingsway Hospital, Kingsway, Derby DE22 3LZ, or 101 Sunnyhill Avenue, Sunnyhill, Derby DE23 7JS* Tel (01332) 362221 or 763712

RAGAN, Mrs Jennifer Mary. b 39. Linc Th Coll 71. **dss** 80 **d** 87 **p** 94. Hackney *Lon* 80-84; Hornchurch St Andr *Chelmsf* 84-87; Par Dn 87-88; Par Dn Ingrave St Steph CD 88-90; Par Dn Gt Parndon 90-94; C from 94. *14 Deer Park, Harlow, Essex CM19 4LD* Tel (01279) 431133

RAGBOURNE, Miss Pamela Mary. b 27. CertEd47. Dalton Ho Bris 53. **dss** 76 **d** 87 **p** 94. CPAS Staff 68-79; Tottenham St Jo *Lon* 79-81; Gt Cambridge Road St Jo and St Jas 82-84; Camberley St Paul *Guildf* 84-86; rtd 87; Perm to Offic *Glouc* 87-93; NSM Winchcombe, Gretton, Sudeley Manor etc from 93. *14 Crispin Close, Winchcombe, Cheltenham, Glos GL54 5JY* Tel (01242) 603469

RAHI, Hakim Banta Singh. b 36. Union Bibl Sem Yavatmal BD71. **d** 74 **p** 74. India 74-83; In URC 83-88; Perm to Offic *Birm* 88-93; Ecum Evang Asian Community 88-93. *3 Hobson Close, Norton Street, Birmingham B18 5RH* Tel 0121-554 2144

RAHILLY, Philip James. b 54. Univ of Wales (Cardiff) BD86. Wycliffe Hall Ox 86. **d** 88 **p** 89. C Knightwick w Doddenham, Broadwas and Cotheridge *Worc* 88; C Martley and Wichenford, Knightwick etc 89-91; C Worc St Barn w Ch Ch 91-92; TV Kidderminster St Mary and All SS w Trimpley etc 92-95; P-in-c Childe Okeford, Okeford Fitzpaine, Manston etc *Sarum* from 95. *The Rectory, Childe Okeford, Blandford Forum, Dorset DT11 8DX* Tel (01258) 860547

RAI, Mrs Mary Anne. b 61. La Sainte Union Coll BTh83 PGCE84. Trin Coll Bris DipTh85. **dss** 86 **d** 87. Bury St Edmunds St Mary *St E* 86-89; Par Dn 87-89; Perm to Offic 90-93; Perm to Offic *Cov* from 94. *331A Anstey Road, Coventry CV2 3FN* Tel (01203) 612534

RAIKES, Canon Myles Kenneth. b 23. New Coll Ox BA47 MA51. Wells Th Coll 47. **d** 49 **p** 50. C Chelmsf Cathl *Chelmsf* 49-51; C Stratford St Jo 51-53; P-in-c Hockerill *St Alb* 53-55; V 55-63; Chapl Herts and Essex Hosp Bp's Stortford 56-63; V Bushey Heath *St Alb* 63-70; R Digswell 70-77; Hon Can St Alb 76-77; P-in-c Meare *B & W* 77-81; P-in-c W Coker 82-83; Dioc Ecum Officer 84-88; C Ilminster w Whitelackington 84-85; C S Petherton w the Seavingtons 85-87; rtd 88; Perm to Offic *B & W* from 88. *7 West Street, South Petherton, Somerset TA13 5DQ* Tel (01460) 241056

RAIKES, Peter. b 37. St Mich Coll Llan 78. **d** 80 **p** 81. C Roath St Marg *Llan* 80-82; V Resolven 82-86; V Resolven w Tonna 86-92; RD Neath from 89; V Skewen from 92. *Skewen Vicarage, Hill Road, Neath Abbey SA10 7NP* Tel (01792) 814116

RAIKES, Robert Laybourne. b 32. Wells Th Coll 59. **d** 61 **p** 62. C Poplar All SS w St Frideswide *Lon* 61-66; C Grendon Underwood w Edgcott *Ox* 66-68; C Swan 68-71; V Whitchurch Canonicorum and Wootton Fitzpaine *Sarum* 71-75; V Whitchurch Canonicorum w Wooton Fitzpaine etc 75-81; P-in-c Branksome St Aldhelm 81-82; V 82-91; V Pitminster w Corfe *B & W* 91-92; rtd 92; Chapl Madeira *Eur* 93-95; Perm to Offic *Glouc* from 95. *Old School House, Hasfield, Gloucester GL19 4LJ* Tel (01452) 780201

RAILTON, John Robert Henry. b 45. FCIB79 Reading Univ BSc68. S Dios Minl Tr Scheme 82. **d** 85 **p** 86. NSM Wickham *Portsm* 85-89; C Bridgemary 89-90; V 90-96; TR Ridgeway *Sarum* from 96. *The Rectory, 3 Butts Road, Chiseldon, Swindon SN4 0NN* Tel (01793) 740369

RAINBOW, Preb Gerald Anton Hayward. b 15. St Edm Hall Ox BA38 MA41. Linc Th Coll 38. **d** 39 **p** 40. C Monkwearmouth St Andr *Dur* 39-43; Chapl RAFVR 43-47; V Claverley *Heref* 47-57; V Leominster 57-80; RD Leominster 60-80; Preb Heref Cathl 67-95; P-in-c Eyton 69-80; rtd 80; Perm to Offic *Heref* from 89. *65 King's Acre Road, Hereford HR4 0QL* Tel (01432) 266718

RAINBOW, Henry David. b 10. Ripon Hall Ox 64. **d** 65 **p** 66. C Reading St Luke *Ox* 65-67; Chapl HM Pris Cardiff 67-71; Chapl HM Pris Pentonville 71-74; Chapl HM Pris Cant 74-78; rtd 78; Perm to Offic *Cant* 79-89; Perm to Offic *Ex* from 89. *1 Upton Hill Road, Brixham, Devon TQ5 9QR* Tel (01803) 854611

RAINE, Alan. b 49. MIPD93. NE Ord Course DipHE95. **d** 95 **p** 96. NSM Jarrow *Dur* from 95. *49 Brixham Crescent, Jarrow, Tyne & Wear NE32 3SL* Tel 0191-489 3042

RAINE, Patrick John Wallace. b 21. DFC. Sarum & Wells Th Coll 72. **d** 74 **p** 75. C Chandler's Ford *Win* 74-76; R Highclere and Ashmansworth w Crux Easton 76-84; R Copythorne and Minstead 84-87; rtd 87; P-in-c Breamore *Win* 91-95. *Little Cottage, 26 Cholderton, Salisbury SP4 0DN* Tel (01725) 513098

RAINE, Stephen James. b 49. Lanchester Poly DipAD69 Sheff Poly BA80. N Ord Course 85. **d** 86 **p** 87. C Cottingham *York* 86-90; V Dunscroft Ch Ch *Sheff* 90-92; V Dunscroft St Edwin 92-96; V Kettering St Mary *Pet* from 96. *The Vicarage, 175 Avondale Road, Kettering, Northants NN16 8PN*

RAINER, John Charles. b 54. Ex Univ BA76 DipTh78 CertEd78. St Jo Coll Nottm 86. **d** 88 **p** 89. C Fletchamstead *Cov* 88-94; V Leic H Apostles *Leic* from 94. *Holy Apostles' Vicarage, 281 Fosse Road South, Leicester LE3 1AE* Tel 0116-282 4336

RAINES, Mrs Gisela Rolanda. b 58. Groningen Univ Kandidaats80. K Coll Lon BD83. **dss** 84 **d** 87 **p** 94. Charlton St Luke w H Trin *S'wark* 84-87; Par Dn 87; Chapl Imp Coll *Lon* 87-91; Hon C Birch w Fallowfield *Man* 94-95; P-in-c Withington St Chris from 95. *197 Old Hall Lane, Manchester M14 6HJ* Tel 0161-224 6643

RAINES, William Guy (Bill). b 46. Lon Univ BSc69 MSc70 Ox Univ BA80. Ripon Coll Cuddesdon 78. **d** 81 **p** 82. C W Drayton *Lon* 81-84; C Charlton St Luke w H Trin *S'wark* 84-87; Chapl K Coll Lon 87-94; Chapl Imp Coll 91-94; P-in-c Birch w Fallowfield *Man* 94-95; R from 95. *197 Old Hall Lane, Manchester M14 6HJ* Tel 0161-224 1310

RAINEY, Graeme Norman. b 66. Van Mildert Coll Dur BA88. Ridley Hall Cam CTMin93. **d** 93 **p** 94. C Maltby *Sheff* 93-96; Chapl Reading Univ *Ox* from 96. *30 Shinfield Road, Reading RG2 7BW* Tel 0118-987 1495

RAINFORD, Robert Graham. b 55. Lanc Univ CertEd76 BEd77. St Steph Ho Ox 81. **d** 83 **p** 84. C Burnley St Cath w St Alb and St Paul *Blackb* 83-86; C-in-c Hawes Side St Chris CD 86-89; V Hawes Side from 89. *The Vicarage, Hawes Side Lane, Blackpool FY4 5AH* Tel (01253) 697937

RAINSBERRY, Edward John. b 24. TCD BA48 MA58. TCD Div Sch Div Test49. **d** 49 **p** 50. C Abbeystrewry Union *C, C & R* 49-52; Chapl RAF 52-58; V Long Compton *Cov* 58-84; R Whichford 58-84; V Long Compton, Whichford and Barton-on-the-Heath 84-95; rtd 95; Perm to Offic *Ox* from 95; Perm to Offic *Pet* from 95. *12 Portway Gardens, Aynho, Banbury, Oxon OX17 3AR* Tel (01869) 810417

RAINSBURY, Mark James. b 56. NE Lon Poly BA79. Oak Hill Th Coll BA87. **d** 88 **p** 89. C Tonbridge St Steph *Roch* 88-95; C Hampreston *Sarum* 95-97; TV from 97. *3 Dudsbury Road, Ferndown, Dorset BH22 8RA* Tel (01202) 876552

RAINSFORD, Peter John. b 31. FCP72. Qu Coll Birm 75. **d** 77 **p** 78. Hon C Lich St Chad *Lich* 77-81; C 82; C Coseley Ch Ch 82-84; V Wednesbury St Bart 84-91; Chapl Sandwell Distr Gen Hosp 89-91; rtd 91; Perm to Offic *Lich* 91-97. *157 Broadway, Walsall, W Midlands WS1 3HD* Tel (01922) 24526

RAISTRICK, Dr Brian. b 38. St Paul's Cheltenham TCert60 Ex Univ ADEd68 Newc Univ MEd76 UEA PhD86. Westcott Ho Cam 92. **d** 93 **p** 94. C Haverhill w Withersfield, the Wrattings etc *St E* 93-95; P-in-c Horringer cum Ickworth from 95. *The Rectory, Manor Lane, Horringer, Bury St Edmunds, Suffolk IP29 5PY* Tel (01284) 735206

RAITH, Robert. b 31. Edin Univ MA61. Coll of Resurr Mirfield 57. **d** 59 **p** 60. C Edin St Jas *Edin* 59-61; P-in-c 76-77; Asst Prov Youth Org 61-65; C Dalmahoy 61-65; C Edin St Mark 66-76; Dioc Supernumerary 77-78; P-in-c Edin St Luke 78-79; Perm to Offic from 79; Pilsdon Community 87-90. *62 Rodwell Road, Weymouth, Dorset DT4 8QU* Tel (01305) 781386

RAITT, Derek. b 41. K Coll Lon BD63 AKC63. **d** 64 **p** 65. C Blackb St Jas *Blackb* 64-67; C Burnley St Pet 67-69; V Foulridge 69-74; V Euxton 74-91; V Penwortham St Mary from 91. *St Mary's Vicarage, Cop Lane, Penwortham, Preston PR1 0SR* Tel (01772) 743143

RAJKOVIC, Dr Michael. b 52. Sheff Univ BMet74 MMet75 PhD79. St Jo Coll Nottm MA95. **d** 95 **p** 96. C Harrow Weald All SS *Lon* from 95. *17 Windsor Road, Harrow Weald, Harrow, Middx HA3 5PT* Tel 0181-930 1649

RAKE, David John. b 47. Nottm Univ BA68 PhD73. Wycliffe Hall Ox DipTh73. **d** 74 **p** 75. C Radcliffe-on-Trent *S'well* 74-77; P-in-c Upwell St Pet *Ely* 77-79; P-in-c Outwell 77-79; Chapl Warw Univ *Cov* 79-86; V Kenilworth St Nic from 86. *The Vicarage, 7 Elmbank Road, Kenilworth, Warks CV8 1AL* Tel (01926) 54367

RALPH, Brian Charles. b 66. St Steph Ho Ox 89. **d** 92 **p** 93. C Yeovil St Mich *B & W* 92-95; C Shoreditch St Leon and Hoxton St Jo *Lon* 95; TV St Jo on Bethnal Green from 95. *60 Cephas Avenue, London E1 4AR* Tel 0171-423 9273

RALPH, Charles. b 15. TCD BA47 MA58. **d** 47 **p** 48. C Kilmegan *D & D* 47-49; C Drumcree *Arm* 49-50; I Arboe 50-51; C Arm St Mark 51-53; I Durrus *C, C & R* 53-54; I Kilcooley *C & O* 54-58; V Toxteth Park St Cleopas *Liv* 58-62; I Kilscoran *C & O*

62-64; R Fordley w Middleton *St E* 64-81; R Theberton 64-81; rtd 82; Perm to Offic *St E* from 82; TV Raveningham *Nor* 82; P-in-c Rossinver *K, E & A* 85-86. *5 Gayfer Avenue, Kesgrave, Ipswich IP5 7PZ* Tel (01473) 622154

RALPH, Nicholas Robert (Nick). b 63. Lanc Univ BSc85. Westcott Ho Cam BA91 CTM92. **d** 92 **p** 93. C Fareham H Trin *Portsm* 92-95; C Portsea St Cuth 95-96; V Hayling Is St Andr from 96; V N Hayling from 96. *27 Seaview Road, Hayling Island, Hants PO11 9PD* Tel (01705) 461980

RALPH, Dr Richard Gale. b 51. Pemb Coll Ox BA73 MA78 DPhil78. S Dios Minl Tr Scheme 84. **d** 87 **p** 88. NSM St Leonards Ch Ch and St Mary *Chich* from 87; NSM St Pancras H Cross w St Jude and St Pet *Lon* 87-94; Prin Westmr Coll Ox from 96. *Westminster College, Harcourt Hill, Oxford OX2 9AT, or St Alban, 11 The Mount, St Leonards-on-Sea, E Sussex TN38 0HR* Tel (01865) 247644 or (01424) 422722

RALPHS, John Eric. b 26. MBAP66 St Cath Coll Ox BA52 MA56. Wycliffe Hall Ox 53. **d** 53 **p** 54. C Wolvercote *Ox* 53-55; Chapl Asst Radcliffe Infirmary Ox 54-62; Lic to Offic *Ox* 55-66; Chapl Dragon Sch Ox 55-68; Asst Chapl HM Pris Ox 58-61; Jun Chapl Mert Coll Ox 59-62; Chapl St Hugh's Coll Ox 62-67; Priest-Psychotherapist from 68; Lic to Offic *Ox* from 83; rtd 91. *209 Woodstock Road, Oxford OX2 7AB* Tel (01865) 515550

RALPHS, Robert Brian. b 31. Qu Coll Birm 75. **d** 78 **p** 79. Hon C Wednesbury St Jo *Lich* 78-80; Hon C Wednesbury St Paul Wood Green 80-81; Perm to Offic 81-96; C W Bromwich Gd Shep w St Jo 96. *204 Bromford Lane, West Bromwich, W Midlands B70 7HX* Tel 0121-553 0119

RALPHS, Sharon Ann. *See* SIMPSON, Mrs Sharon Ann

RAMELL, John Edwin. b 25. Bris Univ BA55. Tyndale Hall Bris. **d** 56 **p** 57. C New Milverton *Cov* 56-60; V Wombridge *Lich* 60-70; TR Chell 70-82; V Congleton St Pet *Ches* 82-90; rtd 90. *10 Newland Close, Eynsham, Witney, Oxon OX8 1LE* Tel (01865) 880180

RAMM, Canon Norwyn MacDonald. b 24. Linc Coll Ox BA60 MA64. St Pet Coll Jamaica 49. **d** 51 **p** 52. Jamaica 51-57; C Ox St Mich *Ox* 57-61; V 61-71; P-in-c Ox All SS w St Martin 61-71; V Ox St Mich w St Martin and All SS 71-88; Chapl HM Pris Ox 75-88; Hon Can Ch Ch *Ox* 85-88; Chapl to The Queen from 85; rtd 88. *Fairlawn, Church Lane, Harwell, Didcot, Oxon OX11 0EZ* Tel (01235) 835454

RAMON, Brother. *See* LLOYD, Raymond David

RAMPTON, Paul Michael. b 47. St Jo Coll Dur BA69 DipTh70 MA73 K Coll Lon PhD85. Wycliffe Hall Ox 72. **d** 73 **p** 74. C Folkestone H Trin w Ch Ch *Cant* 73-77; P-in-c Kingsdown 77-79; P-in-c Ringwould w Oxney 77-79; R Ringwould w Kingsdown 79-83; V Maidstone St Paul 83-88; V Maidstone St Martin 88-95; V Steyning *Chich* from 95; R Ashurst from 95. *St Andrew's Vicarage, Steyning, W Sussex BN44 3YL* Tel (01903) 813256

RAMPTON, Canon Valerie Edith. b 41. Nottm Univ BSc63 MSc66 BA79. Gilmore Course 78. **dss** 82 **d** 87 **p** 94. Sneinton St Chris w St Phil *S'well* 80-87; Par Dn 87-88; Par Dn Stapleford 88-93; Dioc Adv on Women in Min 90-93; D-in-c Kneesall w Laxton and Wellow 93-94; V from 94; Hon Can S'well Minster from 97. *The Vicarage, 19 Baulk Lane, Kneesall, Newark, Notts NG22 0AA* Tel (01623) 835820

RAMSARAN (or COOPER), Dr Susan Mira. b 49. K Coll Lon BA70 Univ Coll Lon MA72 PhD78. Ripon Coll Cuddesdon BA92. **d** 93 **p** 94. C Selling w Throwley, Sheldwich w Badlesmere etc *Cant* 93-97; P-in-c Plaxtol *Roch* from 97; P-in-c Shipbourne from 97. *The Rectory, Plaxtol, Sevenoaks, Kent TN15 0QG* Tel (01732) 810319

RAMSAY, Canon Alan Burnett. b 34. AKC62. **d** 63 **p** 64. C Clapham H Trin *S'wark* 63-67; C Warlingham w Chelsham and Farleigh 67-71; P-in-c Stockwell St Mich 71-78; V Lingfield 78-85; P-in-c Crowhurst 83-85; V Lingfield and Crowhurst 85-92; RD Godstone 88-92; V Mitcham St Mark from 92; Hon Can S'wark Cathl from 93. *St Mark's Vicarage, Locks Lane, Mitcham, Surrey CR4 2JX* Tel 0181-648 2397

RAMSAY, Carl Anthoney St Aubyn. b 55. WMMTC 88. **d** 90 **p** 91. C Wednesfield Heath *Lich* 90-94; V Willenhall St Anne from 94. *St Anne's Vicarage, Ann Street, Willenhall, W Midlands WV13 1EN* Tel (01902) 66516

RAMSAY, Christopher. b 68. St Jo Coll Dur BA90. Wycliffe Hall Ox BTh94. **d** 97. C Cricklewood St Gabr and St Mich *Lon* from 97. *31 Olive Road, London NW2 6TY* Tel 0181-450 8707

RAMSAY, Eric Nicholson. b 29. **d** 94 **p** 95. C Forfar *St And* from 94; C Kirriemuir from 94. *4 Beechwood Place, Kirriemuir, Angus DD8 5DZ* Tel (01575) 572029

RAMSAY, James Anthony. b 52. MA. **d** 86 **p** 87. C Olney w Emberton *Ox* 86-89; V Blackbird Leys from 89. *Church House, 1 Cuddesdon Way, Oxford OX4 5JH* Tel (01865) 778728

RAMSAY, Kenneth William. b 18. ALCD48. **d** 52 **p** 53. C Southall Green St Jo *Lon* 52-57; Asst Chapl Lee Abbey 57-60; Perm to Offic *Portsm* 69-80; Perm to Offic *Sarum* 77-87; rtd 87; Hon C Burstow *S'wark* from 87. *14 Woodside Crescent, Smallfield, Horley, Surrey RH6 9ND* Tel (01342) 843561

RAMSAY, Kerry. b 59. Heythrop Coll Lon MA94. Westcott Ho Cam CTM92. **d** 94 **p** 96. S Africa 95-96; C Dulwich St Barn *S'wark* 96; C Charlton St Luke w H Trin from 96. *73 Elliscombe Road, London SE7 7PF* Tel 0181-858 4336

RAMSAY, Max Roy MacGregor. b 34. Ball Coll Ox MA58. Qu Coll Birm 82. **d** 84 **p** 85. C Hale *Ches* 84-86; C Nantwich 87; V Haslington w Crewe Green 87-91; P-in-c Dunham Massey St Marg 92-93; P-in-c Dunham Massey St Mark 92-93; P-in-c Dunham Massey St Marg and St Mark 93-95; rtd 95; Perm to Offic *Ches* from 95. *6 Comber Way, Knutsford, Cheshire WA16 9BT* Tel (01565) 632362

RAMSBOTTOM, Mrs Julie Frances. b 54. Trevelyan Coll Dur BA76. S'wark Ord Course 88. **d** 91 **p** 94. Par Dn Bray and Braywood *Ox* 91-94; C 94-97; R W Woodhay w Enborne, Hampstead Marshall etc from 97. *The Rectory, Enborne, Newbury, Berks RG20 0HD* Tel (01635) 34427

RAMSBURY, Area Bishop of. *See* VAUGHAN, The Rt Revd Peter St George

RAMSDEN, Canon Arthur Stuart. b 34. Kelham Th Coll 56. **d** 61 **p** 62. C Featherstone *Wakef* 61-63; C Barnsley St Pet 63-67; V Charlestown 67-70; V Middlestown 70-77; V Purston cum S Featherstone from 77; Hon Can Wakef Cathl from 95. *The Vicarage, Victoria Street, Featherstone, Pontefract, W Yorkshire WF7 5EZ* Tel (01977) 792288

RAMSDEN, Peter Stockton. b 51. Univ Coll Lon BSc74 Leeds Univ DipTh76 MA92. Coll of Resurr Mirfield 74. **d** 77 **p** 78. C Houghton le Spring *Dur* 77-80; C S Shields All SS 80-83; Papua New Guinea 83-90 and 93-96; P-in-c Micklefield *York* 90-93; V Long Benton *Newc* from 96. *The Vicarage, 3 Station Road, Benton, Newcastle upon Tyne NE12 8AN* Tel 0191-266 2015

RAMSDEN, Raymond Leslie. b 49. Open Univ BA86. **d** 78 **p** 79. C Greenhill St Jo *Lon* 78-85; C Staines St Mary and St Pet 85-90; V Hounslow St Steph from 90. *St Stephen's Vicarage, Parkside Road, Hounslow TW3 2BP* Tel 0181-570 3056

RAMSEY-HARDY, Stuart John Andrew. b 46. St Jo Coll Dur BA69. Wycliffe Hall Ox 69. **d** 74 **p** 75. C Stoke Newington St Mary *Lon* 74-77; C Hersham *Guildf* 78-79; Hon C Thames Ditton 79-83. *23 New Row, London WC2N 4LA* Tel 0171-836 2217

RAMSHAW, Marcus John. b 71. St Andr Univ MTheol93 York Univ MA94. Cranmer Hall Dur DipMin94. **d** 96 **p** 97. C Hythe *Cant* from 96. *2 Palmarsh Avenue, Hythe, Kent CT21 6NT* Tel (01303) 261699

RANCE, Miss Eleanor Jane. b 72. K Coll Lon BA93 AKC93. Cranmer Hall Dur DMS94. **d** 96 **p** 97. C Barnes St Mary *S'wark* from 96. *52 Boileau Road, London SW13 9BL* Tel 0181-748 8328

RANDALL, Colin Antony. b 57. SS Paul & Mary Coll Cheltenham BEd78 Bris Univ DipHE82 Lon Univ BD84. Trin Coll Bris 80. **d** 84 **p** 85. C Denton Holme *Carl* 84-87; C Brampton RD 87-90; R Hanborough and Freeland *Ox* from 90. *The Rectory, Swan Lane, Long Hanborough, Witney, Oxon OX8 8BT* Tel (01993) 881270 E-mail carandall@argonet.co.uk

RANDALL, Colin Michael Sebastian. b 50. Aston Univ BSc72. Qu Coll Birm 72. **d** 75 **p** 76. C Tonge w Alkrington *Man* 75-78; C Elton All SS 78-82; P-in-c Bridgwater H Trin *B & W* 82-86; V 86-90; V Bishops Hull from 90. *The Vicarage, Bishops Hull, Taunton, Somerset TA1 5EB* Tel (01823) 333032

RANDALL, Canon Edmund Lawrence. b 20. CCC Cam BA40 MA47. Wells Th Coll 47. **d** 49 **p** 50. C Bournemouth St Luke *Win* 49-52; Fell and Lect Selw Coll Cam 52-57; Chapl 53-57; Prin Ely Th Coll 57-59; Can Res Ely Cathl *Ely* 57-59; Australia from 60; Hon Can Wangaratta from 89. *44 Mackay Street, Wangaratta, Victoria, Australia 3677* Tel Wangaratta (57) 219007

RANDALL, Elizabeth. b 55. RGN75 SCM81. EAMTC 94. **d** 97. C Loddon, Sisland w Hales and Heckingham *Nor* from 97. *The Rectory, Rectory Lane, Chedgrave, Norwich NR14 6NE* Tel (01508) 520535

RANDALL, Gareth John. b 49. Southn Univ BA72 PGCE73 ACP80. Oak Hill NSM Course 90. **d** 93 **p** 94. Dir of Studies Dame Alice Owen's Sch Potters Bar 84-95; Dir of Personnel from 95; NSM S Mymms K Chas *St Alb* from 93. *196 Barnet Road, Potters Bar, Herts EN6 2SE* Tel (01707) 651958 or 643441

RANDALL, Ian Neville. b 39. Or Coll Ox BA62 MA65. St Steph Ho Ox 62. **d** 65 **p** 66. C Perivale *Lon* 65-68; C Fulham St Jo Walham Green 68-73; C Cowley St Jas *Ox* 73-79; TV 79-82; V Didcot St Pet 82-93; P-in-c Clewer St Andr from 93. *Clewer Rectory, 16 Parsonage Lane, Windsor, Berks SL4 5EN* Tel (01753) 865185

RANDALL, James Anthony. b 36. ACIB69 Kent Univ DipTh80. Ridley Hall Cam 68. **d** 70 **p** 71. C Rusthall *Roch* 70-74; V Shorne 74-79; V Bexleyheath Ch Ch 79-89; R Stone from 89. *The Rectory, Church Road, Stone, Greenhithe, Kent DA9 9BE* Tel (01322) 842076

RANDALL, Canon John Terence. b 29. St Cath Coll Cam BA52 MA59. Ely Th Coll 52. **d** 54 **p** 55. C Luton Ch Ch *St Alb* 54; C Dunstable 54-57; C Ely 57-60; C March St Jo 60-62; Area Sec (S Midl) UMCA 62-64; Area Sec (Dios Birm and Cov) USPG 65-76; P-in-c Avon Dassett w Farnborough *Cov* 76-78; P-in-c Fenny Compton 76-78; R Avon Dassett w Farnborough and Fenny Compton 78-84; V New Bilton 84-94; RD Rugby 89-94; Hon Can Cov Cathl 93-94; rtd 94; Perm to Offic *Pet* from 94; Perm to Offic *Leic* from 96. *52 Cymbeline Way, Rugby, Warks CV22 6LA* Tel (01788) 816659

RANDALL, Julian Adrian. b 45. Open Univ BA78 Stirling Univ MSc94 MIPD. St Jo Sem Wonersh 68. **d** 70 **p** 71. Asst P Mortlake w E Sheen *S'wark* 71-72; Asst P Welling 72-74; Asst P Tunbridge Wells H Trin w Ch Ch *Roch* 74-79; NSM Dunfermline *St And* from 96. *36 Copper Beech Wynd, Cairneyhill, Dunfermline, Fife KY12 8UP* Tel (01383) 881195 Fax 880748 E-mail pauline_r @msn.com

RANDALL, Kelvin John. b 49. JP. K Coll Lon BD71 AKC71 PGCE72. St Jo Coll Nottm DPS73. **d** 74 **p** 75. C Peckham St Mary Magd *S'wark* 74-78; C Portsdown *Portsm* 78-81; C-in-c Crookhorn Ch Cen CD 81-82; R Bedhampton 82-90; RD Havant 87-89; P-in-c Bournemouth St Jo w St Mich *Win* 90-94; V from 94; Chapl Talbot Heath Sch Bournemouth from 90. *The Vicarage, 13 Durley Chine Road South, Bournemouth BH2 5JT* Tel (01202) 761962

RANDALL, Mrs Lynda Lorraine. b 44. Sarum & Wells Th Coll 89. **d** 91 **p** 94. Par Dn Chesterton St Andr *Ely* 91-94; C 94-95; C Linton 95-96; TV Linton from 96. *Castle and Shudy Camps Vicarage, Park Lane, Castle Camps, Cambridge CB1 6SU* Tel (01799) 584803

RANDALL, Miss Marian Sally. b 49. Trin Coll Bris 75. **dss** 80 **d** 87 **p** 94. Peckham St Mary Magd *S'wark* 80-83; Sutton Ch Ch 83-87; Par Dn 87-94; C from 94. *14A Christchurch Park, Sutton, Surrey SM2 5TN* Tel 0181-661 7130

RANDALL, Martin Trevor. b 51. St Jo Coll Dur BA74. Trin Coll Bris 74. **d** 77 **p** 78. C Ashton on Mersey St Mary *Ches* 77-80; C Everton St Sav w St Cuth *Liv* 80-82; V W Derby Gd Shep 82-91; P-in-c Toxteth Park Ch Ch 91-94; P-in-c Toxteth Park St Bede 91-94; V Toxteth Park Ch Ch w St Bede 95-97; Chapl HM Pris Altcourse from 97. *HM Prison Altcourse, Higher Lane, Liverpool L9 7AG* Tel 0151-525 1462 Fax 525 1192

RANDALL, Samuel Paul. b 59. Leeds Univ MA90. Ridley Hall Cam 84. **d** 87 **p** 88. C Kingston upon Hull St Nic *York* 87-89; CF 89-93; TV Bramley *Ripon* 93-96; Dioc Ecum Officer *Dur* from 97. *The Rectory, Witton Gilbert, Durham DH7 6ST*

RANDELL, David Peter. b 48. Trin Coll Bris BA88. **d** 92 **p** 93. C Wells St Cuth w Wookey Hole *B & W* 92-95; TV Wellington and Distr from 95. *22 Dyers Close, West Buckland, Wellington, Somerset TA21 9JU* Tel (01823) 664925

RANDELL, John Harrison. b 35. Lon Univ BD62. Chich Th Coll 77. **d** 78 **p** 78. C Ribbleton *Blackb* 78-82; V Barton from 82. *St Lawrence's Vicarage, 786 Garstang Road, Barton, Preston PR3 5AA* Tel (01772) 862020

RANDELL, Phillip John. b 45. Lon Univ DipTh68 BD73 CertEd. Linc Th Coll 67. **d** 68 **p** 69. C Henbury *Bris* 68-71; C Summertown *Ox* 71-73; C Liskeard w St Keyne *Truro* 73-75; Chapl Coll of St Mark and St Jo Plymouth *Ex* 75-79; Tanzania 80-82; R Alvescot w Black Bourton, Shilton, Holwell etc *Ox* 82-87; R St Gennys, Jacobstow w Warbstow and Treneglos *Truro* 87-97; rtd 97. *Marnays, Higher Tristram, Polzeath, Wadebridge, Cornwall PL27 6TF*

RANDLE, Canon Howard Stanley. b 12. St Jo Coll Dur LTh34 BA35. St Aid Birkenhead 30. **d** 35 **p** 36. C Gt Horton *Bradf* 35-38; C New Brighton St Jas *Ches* 38-41; CF (EC) 41-45; R Mobberley *Ches* 46-80; RD Knutsford 65-80; Hon Can Ches Cathl 69-80; rtd 80; Perm to Offic *Ches* from 80. *7 Carlisle Close, Mobberley, Knutsford, Cheshire WA16 7HD* Tel (01565) 873483

RANGER, Keith Brian. b 34. Down Coll Cam BA58 MA63. Glas NSM Course 58. **d** 81 **p** 82. OMF Internat from 81; Ethnic Min Co-ord from 90; Hong Kong 81-89; Perm to Offic *Ches* from 89; Perm to Offic *Man* from 93. *28 Charter Road, Altrincham, Cheshire WA15 9RL* Tel 0161-941 5268

RANKEN, Michael David. b 28. Man Univ BScTech49. S'wark Ord Course 76. **d** 79 **p** 80. Hon C Epsom St Martin *Guildf* from 79. *9 Alexandra Road, Epsom, Surrey KT17 4BH* Tel (01372) 724823

RANKIN, John Cooper. b 24. Glas Univ MA44 Lon Univ BD53. Edin Th Coll 48. **d** 50 **p** 51. C Dundee St Mary Magd *Bre* 50-52; Chapl R Merchant Navy Sch Bearwood 53-60; Min Can Bris Cathl *Bris* 60-66; Lic to Offic *Lich* 66-69; Prin Lect Bp Otter Coll Chich 69-84; rtd 84. *28 Worcester Road, Chichester, W Sussex PO19 4DW* Tel (01243) 789467

RANKIN, Stephen Brian. b 65. Salford Univ BSc88. Trin Coll Bris 95. **d** 97. C Ashton on Mersey St Mary *Ches* from 97. *109 Ascot Avenue, Sale, Cheshire CH33 4GT* Tel 0161-976 1693

RANKIN, William <u>John</u> Alexander. b 45. Van Mildert Coll Dur BA68 Fitzw Coll Cam BA73 MA77. Westcott Ho Cam 71. **d** 74 **p** 75. C St Jo Wood *Lon* 74-78; Chapl Clifton Coll Bris 78-86; P-in-c The Claydons *Ox* 86-91; R 91-93; R Clare w Poslingford, Cavendish etc *St E* from 93. *Durham House Vicarage, Cavendish Road, Clare, Sudbury, Suffolk CO10 8PJ* Tel (01787) 278501

RANKINE, Christopher Barry. b 66. Portsm Poly BA88. Linc Th Coll BTh93. **d** 93 **p** 95. C Farlington *Portsm* 93-96; C Alverstoke from 96. *32 Privett Place, Gosport, Hants PO12 3SQ* Tel (01705) 581999

RANN, Preb Harry Harvey. b 18. Sarum Th Coll 47. **d** 50 **p** 51. C Victoria Docks Ascension *Chelmsf* 50-52; C Christchurch *Win* 52-56; C Mill Hill Jo Keble Ch *Lon* 56-57; V Woolfold *Man* 57-62; Dean's Chapl and PV Ex Cathl *Ex* 62-77; Sacr 65-77; Succ 73-77; V Colyton 77-84; R Colyton and Southleigh 84-86; RD Honiton 84-86; Preb Ex Cathl 84-87; TR Colyton, Southleigh, Offwell, Widworthy etc 86-87; rtd 87; Perm to Offic *Ex* from 87. *4 Scattor View, Bridford, Exeter EX6 7JF* Tel (01647) 52741

RANSOM, Nigel Lester. b 60. Leeds Univ BA81. Wycliffe Hall Ox 83 SE Asia Sch of Th MTh83. **d** 85 **p** 86. C Gidea Park *Chelmsf* 85-88; C Widford 88-91; V Eastwood from 91. *The Vicarage, Eastwoodbury Lane, Southend-on-Sea SS2 6UH* Tel (01702) 525272

RANSOME, Arthur. b 21. St Jo Coll Nottm 71. **d** 72 **p** 72. Israel 72-76; C Virginia Water *Guildf* 76-79; P-in-c Peper Harow 79-82; P-in-c Shackleford 79-82; P-in-c Seale 82-89; rtd 89; Perm to Offic *Truro* from 89. *St Gwendron, Rock Road, Rock, Wadebridge, Cornwall PL27 6NP* Tel (01208) 862825

RANSON, Arthur Frankland. b 50. St Jo Coll Dur BA73. Wycliffe Hall Ox 73. **d** 75 **p** 76. C Bare *Blackb* 75-78; C Scotforth 78-81; V Leyland St Ambrose from 81; RD Leyland from 96. *St Ambrose Vicarage, 61 Moss Lane, Leyland, Preston PR5 2SH* Tel (01772) 462204

RANSON, George Sidney. b 28. Open Univ BA78. NE Ord Course 85. **d** 86 **p** 87. NSM Acomb H Redeemer *York* 86-88; C Warton St Oswald w Yealand Conyers *Blackb* 88-90; V Pilling 90-95; rtd 95; Perm to Offic *Blackb* from 95. *18 Cotswold Road, Lytham St Annes, Lancs FY8 4NN*

RANSON, Terence William James (<u>Terry</u>). b 42. AFAIM91 AKC64 MTh87 STM88. St Boniface Warminster 64. **d** 65 **p** 66. C Walton St Mary *Liv* 65-69; C Ipswich St Mary le Tower *St E* 69-71; Chapl Mersey Miss to Seamen 71-74; V N Keyham *Ex* 74-79; Australia 79-91; Sen Chapl and State Sec Fremantle Miss to Seamen 79-91; V N Mymms *St Alb* from 91. *The Vicarage, North Mymms Park, Hatfield, Herts AL9 7TN* Tel (01727) 822062

RANYARD, Michael Taylor. b 43. Nottm Univ BTh74. Linc Th Coll 71. **d** 74 **p** 75. C Sutton in Ashfield St Mary *S'well* 74-76; Hon C Lewisham St Mary *S'wark* 76-77; C Rushmere *St E* 77-79; R Hopton, Market Weston, Barningham etc 79-83; Chr Educn and Resources Adv *Dur* 83-93; Prin Adv to Dioc Bd of Educn *Blackb* from 93. *17 Beardwood Park, Blackburn BB2 7BW* Tel (01254) 676281

RAPHAEL, Brother. *See* PARKER, Ramon Lewis

RAPHAEL, The Ven Timothy John. b 29. Leeds Univ BA53. Coll of Resurr Mirfield. **d** 55 **p** 56. C Westmr St Steph w St Jo *Lon* 55-60; V Welling *S'wark* 60-63; New Zealand 63-72; Dean Dunedin 65-72; V St Jo Wood *Lon* 72-83; AD Westmr St Marylebone 82-83; Adn Middx 83-96; rtd 96. *121 Hales Road, Cheltenham, Glos GL50 6ST*

RAPHOE, Archdeacon of. *See* HARTE, The Ven Matthew Scott

RAPHOE, Dean of. *See* WHITE, The Very Revd Stephen Ross

RAPKIN, Kevern. b 39. Univ of Wales (Lamp) BA62. Lich Th Coll 63. **d** 65 **p** 66. C Hanley w Hope *Lich* 65-68; C Woodchurch *Ches* 68-70; C Abbots Langley *St Alb* 70-73; Australia from 73. *The Rectory, 195 Lesmurdie Road, Lesmurdie, W Australia 6076* Tel Perth (9) 291 9300

RAPLEY, Frederick Arthur. b 27. Roch Th Coll 67. **d** 69 **p** 70. C Tenterden St Mildred w Smallhythe *Cant* 69-75; P-in-c Sittingbourne H Trin w Bobbing 75-85; V 85-89; rtd 89; Hon C Luton St Andr *St Alb* 89-92; Perm to Offic from 92. *99 Bedford Road, Letchworth, Herts SG6 4DU* Tel (01462) 670626

RAPLEY, Mrs Joy Naomi. b 41. CertEd63 Open Univ BA73. Sarum & Wells Th Coll 87. **d** 89 **p** 94. Par Dn Welwyn Garden City *St Alb* 89-92; Chapl S Beds Community Healthcare Trust from 92; C Wilbury *St Alb* 94-95. *99 Bedford Road, Letchworth, Herts SG6 4DU, or Fairfield Hospital, Stotfold, Hitchin, Herts SG6 4AA* Tel (01462) 670626 or 730123

RAPSEY, Peter Nigel. b 46. K Coll Lon BD68 AKC68. St Boniface Warminster. **d** 69 **p** 70. C Walton-on-Thames *Guildf* 69-73; C Fleet 73-77; P-in-c The Collingbournes and Everleigh *Sarum* 77-79; TV Wexcombe 79-84; R Wokingham St Paul *Ox* 84-93; Chapl Warminster Sch 93-96; V Frome Ch Ch *B & W* from 96. *Christ Church Vicarage, 73 Weymouth Road, Frome, Somerset BA11 1HJ* Tel (01373) 473249

RASHBROOK, Alan Victor. b 42. S'wark Ord Course. **d** 75 **p** 76. Hon C Woking St Mary *Guildf* 75-83. *Hope Cottage, Robin Hood Lane, Sutton Green, Guildford, Surrey GU4 7QG* Tel (01483) 762760

RASON, Frederick George. b 26. Qu Coll Birm 68. **d** 69 **p** 70. C Weymouth H Trin *Sarum* 69-72; P-in-c Yatesbury 72-73; P-in-c Cherhill 72-73; R Oldbury 73-76; R W Parley 76-91; rtd 91. *4 Knoll Gardens, St Ives, Ringwood, Hants BH24 2LW* Tel (01425) 475761

RASTALL, Preb Thomas <u>Eric</u>. b 19. St Aid Birkenhead 62. **d** 63 **p** 64. C Leek St Luke *Lich* 64-67; V Brown Edge 67-74; P-in-c Croxden 74-78; V Denstone 74-81; P-in-c Ellastone 78-81; V Denstone w Ellastone and Stanton 81-91; RD Uttoxeter 87-91; Preb Lich Cathl 89-91; rtd 91. *21 Hammerton Way, Wellesbourne, Warwick CV35 9NS* Tel (01789) 842422

RATCHFORD, William Joseph. b 52. St Meinrad Coll (USA) BA74. St Meinrad Sch of Th (USA) MDiv79. **d** 78 **p** 79. In RC Ch 78-86; USA 78-90; NSM St Martin-in-the-Fields *Lon* from 90. *6 St Martin's Place, London WC2N 4JH* Tel 0171-930 0089

RATCLIFF, The Ven David William. b 37. K Coll Lon DipAdEd82. Edin Th Coll 59. **d** 62 **p** 63. C Croydon St Aug *Cant* 62-65; C Selsdon St Jo w St Fran 65-69; V Milton Regis

St Mary 69-75; Hon Min Can Cant Cathl 75-91; Asst Dir of Educn 75-91; Dioc Adv in Adult Educn and Lay Tr 75-91; Hon Pres Protestant Assn for Adult Educn in Eur 82-88; Chapl Frankfurt-am-Main *Eur* from 91; Adn Scandinavia from 96. *Sebastian-Rinz Strasse 22, D-60323 Frankfurt, Germany* Tel Frankfurt (69) 550184 or 550186 Fax 550184 E-mail david.ratcliff.parti@ecunet.org

RATCLIFFE, Michael David. b 43. Lon Univ BSc65 Southn Univ PGCE67 Lon Univ BA75 Dur Univ DipTh77 Lanc Univ MA84. Cranmer Hall Dur 75. **d** 77 **p** 78. C Blackpool St Thos *Blackb* 77-81; V Oswaldtwistle St Paul from 81. *St Paul's Vicarage, 71 Union Road, Oswaldtwistle, Accrington, Lancs BB5 3DD* Tel (01254) 231038

RATCLIFFE, Peter William Lewis. b 30. Birm Univ BSc55 Lon Univ BD58. Tyndale Hall Bris 55. **d** 58 **p** 59. C Cambridge St Andr Less *Ely* 58-61; R Wistow 61-74; R Bury 61-74; V Rainham *Chelmsf* 74-85; R Wennington 75-85; V Heacham *Nor* 85-87; P-in-c Sedgeford w Southmere 85-87; V Heacham and Sedgeford 87-95; rtd 95; Perm to Offic *Nor* from 95. *22 Birchfield Gardens, Mulbarton, Norwich NR14 8BT* Tel (01508) 570511

RATHBAND, Kenneth William. b 60. Edin Univ BD86. Edin Th Coll 82. **d** 86 **p** 87. NSM Dundee St Paul *Bre* 86-88; TV Dundee St Martin 88-89; NSM Edin SS Phil and Jas *Edin* 90-91; R Alyth *St And* from 91; R Blairgowrie from 91; R Coupar Angus from 91. *Carnach, Back Road, Bridge of Cally, Blairgowrie, Perthshire PH10 7JL* Tel (01250) 886224 or 874583

RATHBONE, Paul. b 36. BNC Ox BA58 MA62. Wycliffe Hall Ox 58. **d** 60 **p** 61. C Carl St Jo *Carl* 60-63; C Heworth w Peasholme St Cuth *York* 63-68; V Thorganby w Skipwith and N Duffield 68-83; V Acaster Malbis from 83; V Bishopthorpe from 83. *The Vicarage, 48 Church Lane, Bishopthorpe, York YO2 1QG* Tel (01904) 706476

RATHBONE, Royston George (Roy). b 27. Leeds Univ CertEd78. St D Coll Lamp 58. **d** 60 **p** 61. C Risca *Mon* 60-63; C Newport St Mark 63-65; CF (TAVR) 64-73; V Ebbw Vale St Jo *Mon* 65-69; Chapl HM Pris Coldingley 69-73; Chapl HM Pris Linc 73-77; Chapl HM Pris Man 77-79; Chapl HM Borstal Everthorpe 79-85; Chapl HM Pris Lindholme 85-89; Chapl HM Pris Everthorpe 89-92; rtd 92. *6 Jobson's Road, South Cave, Brough, N Humberside HU15 2HN* Tel (01430) 423254

RATINGS, Canon John William. b 37. St Pet Coll Ox BA62 MA71. Cuddesdon Coll 62. **d** 64 **p** 65. C Langley All SS and Martyrs *Man* 64-68; C Easthampstead *Ox* 68-71; V Wargrave from 71; RD Sonning from 88; Hon Can Ch Ch from 97. *The Vicarage, Wargrave, Reading RG10 8EU* Tel 0118-940 2202 Fax 940 1470

RATLEDGE, Canon Ernest David. b 11. Man Univ BA32 MA33 BD52. Bps' Coll Cheshunt 33. **d** 34 **p** 35. C E Crompton *Man* 34-36; C Whalley Range St Marg 36-42; Chapl RAFVR 42-46; R Moston St Jo *Man* 46-52; R Chorlton-cum-Hardy St Clem 52-67; R Prestwich St Mary 67-78; RD Stretford 55-67; RD Radcliffe and Prestwich 67-78; Hon Can Man Cathl 62-78; rtd 78. *c/o Mrs J Cooper, Meadow Cottage, 7/9 Ayot Green, Ayot St Peter, Welwyn, Herts AL6 9AB* Tel (01707) 335075

RATTENBERRY, Christopher James (Chris). b 59. Solicitor York Univ BA80. St Jo Coll Nottm DTS93. **d** 93 **p** 94. C Porchester *S'well* from 93. *127A Digby Avenue, Nottingham NG3 6DT* Tel 0115-987 7553

✠**RATTERAY, The Rt Revd Alexander Ewen.** b 42. Codrington Coll Barbados 61. **d** 65 **p** 66 **c** 96. C S Kirkby *Wakef* 66-68; C Sowerby St Geo 68-71; V Airedale w Fryston 71-80; Bermuda from 80; Adn Bermuda 94-96; Bp Bermuda from 96. *Bishop's Lodge, PO Box HM 769, Hamilton HM CX, Bermuda* Tel Bermuda (1-441) 292-2967 or 292-6987 Fax 296-0592 or 292-5421

RATTIGAN, Paul Damian. b 61. Reading Univ BSc87 Sussex Univ PGCE88. Qu Coll Birm DipTh95. **d** 95 **p** 96. C Parr *Liv* from 95. *83 Malvern Road, St Helens, Merseyside WA9 2EZ* Tel (01744) 759803

RAVALDE, Canon Geoffrey Paul. b 54. Barrister 78 St Cuth Soc Dur BA76 SS Coll Cam BA86 MA90 Lon Univ MTh91. Westcott Ho Cam 84. **d** 87 **p** 88. C Spalding *Linc* 87-91; P-in-c Wigton *Carl* 91-92; V from 92; RD Carl from 95; Hon Can Carl Cathl from 96. *The Vicarage, Longthwaite Road, Wigton, Cumbria CA7 9JR* Tel (016973) 42337

RAVEN, Barry. b 48. Sarum & Wells Th Coll 69. **d** 72 **p** 73. C Henbury *Bris* 72-76; P-in-c S Marston w Stanton Fitzwarren 76-78; TV Stratton St Margaret w S Marston etc 78-80; P-in-c Coalpit Heath 80-84; V 84-91; R Ashley, Crudwell, Hankerton, Long Newnton etc from 91. *The Rectory, 1 Days Court, Crudwell, Malmesbury, Wilts SN16 9HG* Tel (01666) 577118

RAVEN, Charles Frank. b 58. ACIB84 Magd Coll Ox BA80 MA86 St Jo Coll Dur BA87. Cranmer Hall Dur 85. **d** 88 **p** 89. C Heckmondwike *Wakef* 88-92; TV Kidderminster St Jo and H Innocents *Worc* from 92. *St John's Vicarage, 33 Lea Bank Avenue, Kidderminster, Worcs DY11 6PA* Tel (01562) 822649

RAVEN, Thomas Denys Milville. b 22. Lon Coll of Div 65. **d** 66 **p** 67. C Bradfield *Ox* 66-71; V Otterton *Ex* 71-74; V Tidebrook *Chich* 74-85; V Wadhurst 74-85; P-in-c Tasburgh *Nor* 85-87; P-in-c Tharston 85-87; P-in-c Forncett St Mary w St Pet 85-87; P-in-c Flordon 85-87; R Tasburgh w Tharston, Forncett and Flordon 87-89; rtd 89; Perm to Offic *St E* from 90. *Barfield, Church View, Holton, Halesworth, Suffolk IP19 8PB* Tel (01986) 875185

RAVENS, David Arthur Stanley. b 30. Jes Coll Ox BA53 MA61 Lon Univ BD63. Wells Th Coll 61. **d** 63 **p** 64. C Seacroft *Ripon* 63-70; TV 70-73; Sir Wm Borcase's Sch Marlow 73-87; rtd 95. *44 Arthursdale Grange, Scholes, Leeds LS15 4AW* Tel 0113-273 6648

RAVENSCROFT, The Ven Raymond Lockwood. b 31. Leeds Univ BA53. Coll of Resurr Mirfield 54. **d** 55 **p** 56. S Africa 55-57; S Rhodesia 57-59; Bechuanaland 59-62; C St Ives *Truro* 62-64; V Falmouth All SS 64-68; V St Stephens by Launceston 68-73; P-in-c Launceston St Thos 68-73; V Launceston St Steph w St Thos 73-74; TR Probus, Ladock and Grampound w Creed and St Erme 74-88; RD Powder 77-81; Hon Can Truro Cathl 82-88; P-in-c St Erme 84-85; Adn Cornwall and Can Lib Truro Cathl 88-96; rtd 96; Perm to Offic *Truro* from 96. *Bosvran House, 5 Trelinnoe Close, South Petherwin, Launceston, Cornwall PL15 7JX* Tel (01566) 773746

RAVENSDALE, Jonathan Christopher (Jon). b 56. Aston Tr Scheme 90 Chich Th Coll DipTh94. **d** 94 **p** 95. C Leytonstone St Marg w St Columba *Chelmsf* from 94. *St Andrew's Vicarage, 7 Forest Glade, London E11 1LU* Tel 0181-989 0942

RAVENSDALE, Canon Victor Andrew Joseph. b 14. OBE73. Golds Coll Lon. CMS Tr Coll Blackheath 48 Makerere Coll Kampala 64. **d** 66 **p** 67. Uganda 66-73; Prin Buloba Coll Kampala 66-69; Chapl Kampala and Entebbe 70-73; R Stilton w Denton and Caldecote *Ely* 73-77; R Folksworth w Morborne 74-77; Chapl Lisbon *Eur* 77-84; Can Gib Cathl 81-85; rtd 84; Asst Chapl Lisbon *Eur* 84-85; Perm to Offic *Cant* from 85. *96 Church Path, Deal, Kent CT14 9TJ* Tel (01304) 360523

✠**RAWCLIFFE, The Rt Revd Derek Alec.** b 21. OBE71. Leeds Univ BA42. Coll of Resurr Mirfield 42. **d** 44 **p** 45 **c** 74. C Claines St Geo *Worc* 44-47; Solomon Is 47-58; New Hebrides 58-80; Adn S Melanesia 59-74; Asst Bp Melanesia 74-75; Bp New Hebrides 75-80; Bp Glas 81-91; rtd 91; Asst Bp Ripon 91-96; Lic to Offic from 91. *7 Dorset Avenue, Leeds LS8 3RA*

RAWDON-MOGG, Timothy David. b 45. St Jo Coll Dur BA76. Cuddesdon Coll 75. **d** 77 **p** 78. C Wotton St Mary *Glouc* 77-80; C Ascot Heath *Ox* 80-82; V Woodford Halse w Eydon *Pet* 82-88; V Shrivenham w Watchfield and Bourton *Ox* from 88. *St Andrew's Vicarage, Shrivenham, Swindon SN6 8AN* Tel (01793) 782243

RAWE, Alan Charles George. b 29. ALCD56. **d** 56 **p** 57. C W Kilburn St Luke w St Simon and St Jude *Lon* 56-59; Lect Watford St Mary *St Alb* 59-61; R Ore *Chich* 61-69; R Moreton *Ches* 69-80; V Coppull *Blackb* 80-83; Miss to Seamen 83-94; Felixstowe Seafarers' Cen 88-94; rtd 94; Perm to Offic *Blackb* from 94. *15 Starfield Close, Lytham St Annes, Lancs FY8 4QA* Tel (01253) 733647

RAWLING, Miss Jane Elizabeth. b 51. Birm Univ BSc73 St Jo Coll York CertEd75. St Jo Coll Nottm LTh84. **dss** 84 **d** 87 **p** 94. Southsea St Jude *Portsm* 84-87; C 87-88; C St Paul's Cray St Barn *Roch* 88-91; Hon C from 91; SE Regional Co-ord BCMS Crosslinks from 91; Perm to Offic *S'wark* from 92; Perm to Offic *Cant* from 95; Perm to Offic *Chelmsf* from 95; Perm to Offic *Chich* from 95; Perm to Offic *Guildf* from 95. *50 Batchwood Green, Orpington, Kent BR5 2NF* Tel (01689) 871467

RAWLING, Stephen Charles. b 43. Man Univ BSc64 Bris Univ MSc71 DipTh73. Sarum & Wells Th Coll 71. **d** 73 **p** 74. C Bris St Andr Hartcliffe *Bris* 73-76; C Westlands St Andr *Lich* 76-78; R Darlaston St Lawr 78-90; TR Bloxwich from 90. *All Saints' Vicarage, 3 Elmore Row, Bloxwich, Walsall WS3 2HR* Tel (01922) 476598

RAWLINGS, Miss Brenda Susan. b 48. Sussex Univ CertEd69 DipHE81. Oak Hill Th Coll 85. **d** 87 **p** 94. Par Dn Green Street Green *Roch* 87-90; Par Dn Collier Row St Jas and Havering-atte-Bower *Chelmsf* 90-94; C 94; C Greenstead juxta Colchester from 94. *6 Patmore Road, Colchester CO4 3PN* Tel (01206) 864131

RAWLINGS, John Dunstan Richard. b 25. Oak Hill Th Coll 62. **d** 64 **p** 65. C Farnborough *Guildf* 64-66; C Wisley w Pyrford 66-68; Chapl R Aircraft Establishment Farnborough 69-80; Hon C Camberley St Paul 76-80; C 80; P-in-c Strethall *Chelmsf* 80-81; P-in-c Elmdon and Wendon Lofts 80-81; V Elmdon w Wendon Lofts and Strethall 81-88; rtd 88. *49 Ailesbury Way, Burbage, Marlborough, Wilts SN8 3TD* Tel (01672) 810805

RAWLINGS, John Edmund Frank. b 47. AKC69. St Aug Coll Cant 69. **d** 70 **p** 71. C Rainham *Roch* 70-73; C Tattenham Corner and Burgh Heath *Guildf* 73-76; Chapl RN 76-92; V Tavistock and Gulworthy *Ex* from 92. *The Vicarage, 5A Plymouth Road, Tavistock, Devon PL19 8AU* Tel (01822) 612162

RAWLINGS, Philip John. b 53. St Jo Coll Nottm BTh83. **d** 83 **p** 84. C Blackley St Andr *Man* 83-87; C Halliwell St Pet 87-93; R Stretford St Bride from 93. *St Bride's Rectory, 29 Shrewsbury Street, Old Trafford, Manchester M16 9AP* Tel 0161-226 6064

RAWLINS, Geoffrey Ernest Francis. b 30. **d** 56 **p** 57. C St Marylebone All So w SS Pet and Jo *Lon* 56-66; Hon C 66-67; USA 67-95; rtd 95. *Flat 2, 60 Elm Park Road, London SW3 6AU* Tel 0171-352 4076

RAWLINSON, Curwen. b 32. MBE73. Leeds Univ CertEd55 Man Univ DipEd56 Open Univ BA80. Sarum Th Coll 59. **d** 61 **p** 62. C Wigan St Mich *Liv* 61-63; CF 63-78; Dep Asst Chapl Gen 78-80;

Asst Chapl Gen 80-85; QHC from 83; R Uley w Owlpen and Nympsfield *Glouc* from 85; RD Dursley 89-96. *The Rectory, Uley, Dursley, Glos GL11 5SN* Tel (01453) 860249

RAWLINSON, Dr John. b 47. Guy's Hosp Medical Sch BSc67 MB, BS71. EAMTC 89. **d** 92 **p** 93. NSM Tilbrook *Ely* from 92; NSM Covington from 92; NSM Catworth Magna from 92; NSM Keyston and Bythorn from 92. *The Malt House, 42 Stonely, Huntingdon, Cambs PE18 0EH* Tel (01480) 860263

RAWLINSON, Rowland. b 20. Liv Univ DipAdEd68 Open Univ BA74. St Deiniol's Hawarden 79. **d** 80 **p** 81. Hon C Barnston *Ches* 80-82; C 82-85; rtd 85; Hon C Higher Bebington *Ches* from 85. *18 Winston Grove, Wirral, Merseyside L46 0PQ* Tel 0151-677 5641

RAWSON, Christopher Derek. b 39. Ox Min Course CBTS95. **d** 95 **p** 96. NSM Shill Valley and Broadshire *Ox* from 95. *Little May, Broadwell, Lechlade, Glos GL7 3QS* Tel (01367) 860255

RAWSON, Michael Graeme. b 62. York Univ BA84 Ox Univ BA88. St Steph Ho Ox 86. **d** 89 **p** 90. C Brighouse St Martin *Wakef* 89-92; C Brighouse and Clifton 92-93; V Gomersal from 93. *The Vicarage, 404 Spen Lane, Gomersal, Cleckheaton, W Yorkshire BD19 4LS* Tel (01274) 872131

RAY, Mrs Joanna Zorina. b 55. AIMLS78 K Coll Lon BSc77 Garnett Coll Lon PGCE80 Lon Inst of Educn MA92. S'wark Ord Course 84. **d** 87 **p** 94. NSM Carshalton *S'wark* 87-91; NSM Sutton New Town St Barn 91-93; NSM Knighton St Mary Magd *Leic* 93-94; Par Dn Leic H Spirit 94; C from 94; Chapl to the Deaf from 94. *58 Kingsmead Road, Knighton, Leicester LE2 3YD* Tel 0116-270 5439

RAY, John Mead. b 28. OBE79. St Andr Univ MA50 DipEd51. CMS Tr Coll Chislehurst 60. **d** 70 **p** 71. Miss Partner CMS 70-95; C Sparkhill St Jo *Birm* 87-90; C Sparkbrook Em 87-90; C Sparkhill w Greet and Sparkbrook 90; Deanery Missr 90-95; rtd 95; Perm to Offic *Birm* from 95. *190 Sarehole Road, Birmingham B28 8EF* Tel 0121-777 6143

RAY, Robin John. b 44. Sarum & Wells Th Coll 72. **d** 74 **p** 75. C Bourne Valley *Sarum* 74-78; P-in-c Dilton Marsh 78-82; V 82-87; V Taunton Lyngford *B & W* 87-93; R Exford, Exmoor, Hawkridge and Withypool from 93; Rural Affairs Officer from 93; ACORA Link Officer from 93. *The Rectory, Exford, Minehead, Somerset TA24 7LX* Tel (0164383) 586

RAYBOULD, Norman William. b 18. Lich Th Coll 51. **d** 54 **p** 55. C Bloxwich *Lich* 54-57; C Tettenhall Wood 57-60; C Stoke upon Trent 60-61; P-in-c Hanley H Ev 61-67; V St Martin's 67-76; V Sheriffhales w Woodcote 76-83; rtd 83; Perm to Offic *Lich* from 83. *Borrowdale, St Martin's Road, Gobowen, Oswestry, Shropshire SY11 3PH* Tel (01691) 652621

RAYFIELD, Dr Lee Stephen. b 55. Southn Univ BSc78 Lon Univ PhD81 SOSc95. Ridley Hall Cam CTMin93. **d** 93 **p** 94. C Woodford Wells *Chelmsf* from 93. *8 Firs Walk, Woodford Green, Essex IG8 0TD* Tel 0181-505 0660

RAYMENT-PICKARD, Hugh Douglas John. b 61. Kent Univ BA84 Em Coll Cam BA87. Westcott Ho Cam 85. **d** 88 **p** 89. C St Jo on Bethnal Green *Lon* 88-91; C Hackney 91-92; TV 92-95; V Notting Dale St Clem w St Mark and St Jas from 95. *St Clement's House, 95 Sirdar Road, London W11 4EQ* Tel 0171-727 5450

RAYMER, Dr Victoria Elizabeth. b 46. Wellesley Coll (USA) BA68 Harvard Univ MA69 JD78 PhD81. St Steph Ho Ox MA91 Qu Coll Birm DPS89. **d** 89 **p** 94. Par Dn Bushey *St Alb* 89-94; C 94; C Eaton Socon from 94. *53 Shakespeare Road, Eaton Socon, St Neots, Huntingdon, Cambs PE19 3HG* Tel (01480) 214980

RAYNER, David. b 49. Trin Hall Cam BA72 MA75. Westcott Ho Cam 75. **d** 78 **p** 79. C Chorlton-cum-Hardy St Clem *Man* 78-81; C Cambridge Gt St Mary w St Mich *Ely* 81-84; Warden Trin Coll Cen Camberwell 84-88; V Camberwell St Geo *S'wark* 84-88; Warden Bp Mascall Cen *Heref* 89-90; V Smethwick H Trin w St Alb *Birm* 90-92; P-in-c W Smethwick 90-92; P-in-c Smethwick SS Steph and Mich 92-95; V Smethwick Resurr from 92; RD Warley 93-97. *The Vicarage, 69 South Road, Smethwick, Warley, W Midlands B67 7BP* Tel 0121-558 0373

RAYNER, Canon George Charles. b 26. Bps' Coll Cheshunt 50. **d** 52 **p** 53. C Rowbarton *B & W* 52-56; V Taunton H Trin 56-63; Chapl Taunton and Somerset Hosp 60-63; V Lower Sandown St Jo *Portsm* 63-69; R Wootton 69-89; Hon Can Portsm Cathl 84-89; rtd 89; Perm to Offic *B & W* from 89. *Grianan, 23 Hood Close, Glastonbury, Somerset BA6 8ES* Tel (01458) 833795

RAYNER (formerly SPIERS), Jennifer Christine. b 44. NTMTC 94. **d** 97. NSM Southend *Chelmsf* from 97. *1A Princes Street, Southend-on-Sea, Essex SS1 1QA* Tel (01702) 393057

RAYNER, Paul Anthony George. b 39. Dur Univ BA60 Lon Univ BD68 Cape Town Univ MA79. Lon Coll of Div 65. **d** 68 **p** 69. C Crookes St Thos *Sheff* 68-72; S Africa 72-79; P-in-c S Shoebury *Chelmsf* 80-84; R 84-97; V Loughton St Mich from 97. *St Michael's House, Roding Road, Loughton, Essex IG10 3EJ* Tel 0181-508 1489

RAYNER, Richard Noel. b 24. Lon Univ BD51. Oak Hill Th Coll 50. **d** 52 **p** 53. C Plymouth St Jude *Ex* 52-55; V Walthamstow St Luke *Chelmsf* 55-61; V Romford Gd Shep Collier Row 61-65; V Slough *Ox* 65-72; V Heworth w Peasholme St Cuth *York* 72-75; V Heworth 75-81; V Okehampton w Inwardleigh *Ex* 81-89; RD Okehampton 87-89; rtd 89; Perm to Offic *Ex* from 90; Perm to Offic *B & W* from 90. *Redlands, 5 Ladymeade, Ilminster, Somerset TA19 0EA* Tel (01460) 52491

RAYNER, Stewart Leslie. b 39. St Jo Coll Dur BA61 DipTh66 MA73. Cranmer Hall Dur. **d** 67 **p** 68. C Whiston *Sheff* 67-70; C Doncaster St Geo 70-74; Chapl Doncaster R Infirmary 70-74; R Adwick-le-Street *Sheff* 74-85; V Totley 85-91; Asst Chapl Pastures Hosp Derby 91-94; Asst Chapl Kingsway Hosp Derby 91-94; Asst Chapl S Derby Mental Health Services 91-94; P-in-c Etwall w Egginton *Derby* from 94; RD Longford from 96. *The Rectory, 1 Rectory Court, Main Street, Etwall, Derby DE65 6LP* Tel (01283) 732349

RAYNES, Andrew. b 60. R Holloway Coll Lon BA83. Wycliffe Hall Ox DipMin95. **d** 95 **p** 96. C Crowborough *Chich* from 95. *2 Woodland Way, Crowborough, E Sussex TN6 3BG* Tel (01892) 662909

RAYNOR, Duncan Hope. b 58. Ex Coll Ox MA80 MA82 Birm Univ PGCE88. Qu Coll Birm 82. **d** 84 **p** 85. C Kings Heath *Birm* 84-87; Perm to Offic from 87; Hd of RE Alderbrook Sch Solihull 88-94; Chapl K Edw Sch Birm from 94. *134 Addison Road, Birmingham B14 7EP* Tel 0121-443 2147

RAYNOR, Michael. b 53. Lanc Univ BA74 MSc75. Ripon Coll Cuddesdon BA84. **d** 85 **p** 86. C Gt Crosby St Faith *Liv* 85-88; V Warrington St Barn 88-97; V Orford St Andr from 97. *St Andrew's Vicarage, Poplars Avenue, Orford, Warrington WA2 9UE* Tel (01925) 631903

RAYNOR-SMITH, Charles Alfred Walter. b 12. Sarum Th Coll. **d** 55 **p** 56. C Oakdale St Geo *Sarum* 55-58; C Swanage 58-62; V Colehill 62-81; rtd 81. *19 Tatnam Road, Poole, Dorset BH15 2OW* Tel (01202) 681996

RAZEY, Miss Florence Hannah. b 12. St Andr Ho Portsm 38. **dss** 43 **d** 87. Elson *Portsm* 47-54; Testwood *Win* 54-56; Weston-super-Mare St Andr Bournville *B & W* 56-58; Portsea St Mary *Portsm* 58-61; Alverstoke 61-67; Goole *Sheff* 67-69; Nether Hoyland St Pet 69-72; rtd 72; Elson *Portsm* 72-92; Hon C 87-92; Perm to Offic from 92. *Tamar, 10 Beech Grove, Alverstoke, Gosport, Hants PO12 2EJ* Tel (01705) 523799

RAZZALL, Charles Humphrey. b 55. Worc Coll Ox BA76 Qu Coll Cam BA78 Worc Coll Ox MA81. Westcott Ho Cam 76. **d** 79 **p** 80. C Catford (Southend) and Downham *S'wark* 79-83; V Crofton Park St Hilda w St Cypr 83-87; UPA Field Officer from 87; TV Oldham *Man* from 87; AD Oldham from 93. *Holy Trinity Vicarage, 46 Godson Street, Oldham OL1 2DB* Tel 0161-627 1640

READ, Andrew Gordon. b 40. ARICS63 Nottm Univ BA69. Cuddesdon Coll 70. **d** 70 **p** 71. C E Retford *S'well* 70-72; C Woodthorpe 72-76; P-in-c Newark St Leon 76-78; Perm to Offic *Roch* from 79. *13 Clevedon Road, London SE20 7QQ* Tel 0181-778 9545

READ, Charles William. b 60. Man Univ BA81 Man Poly CertEd82. St Jo Coll Nottm 86. **d** 88 **p** 89. C Oldham *Man* 88-90; C Urmston 90-94; P-in-c Broughton St Jas w St Clem and St Matthias 94-96; TV Broughton from 96. *St James's Rectory, Great Cheetham Street East, Higher Broughton, Salford M7 0UH* Tel 0161-792 1208

READ, Christopher Holditch. b 19. Qu Coll Birm 50. **d** 53 **p** 54. C Portishead *B & W* 53-56; C Walton on Trent, Coton in the Elms and Rosliston *Derby* 56-58; R Bonsall 58-63; V Cromford 58-63; R Grangemouth *Edin* 63-72; V Parwich w Alsop en le Dale *Derby* 72-87; P-in-c Fenny Bentley, Thorpe and Tissington 77; rtd 87; Perm to Offic *Mor* 88-89. *c/o 55 Power Street, Hawthorn, Victoria, Australia 3122*

READ, Geoffrey Philip. b 61. Bris Univ LLB82. Wycliffe Hall Ox 85. **d** 88 **p** 89. C Dorking St Paul *Guildf* 88-92; TV Westborough 92-97; TR from 97. *St Clare's Vicarage, Cabell Road, Guildford, Surrey GU2 6JW* Tel (01483) 503348

READ, Ian. b 34. Selw Coll Cam BA57. Linc Th Coll 57. **d** 59 **p** 60. C Shard End *Birm* 59-63; Mozambique 64-76; Dean Maciene 71-76; P-in-c Edgbaston St Germain *Birm* 76-80; V Worc St Wulstan *Worc* 80-92; R Stoulton w Drake's Broughton and Pirton etc from 92. *The Rectory, Worcester Road, Drakes Broughton, Pershore, Worcs WR10 2AQ* Tel (01905) 840528

READ, Jack. b 19. Qu Coll Birm 67. **d** 68 **p** 69. C Tong *Bradf* 68-70; C Baildon 70-72; V Queensbury 72-86; rtd 86; Perm to Offic *Bradf* from 86. *7 Silver Birch Grove, Wyke, Bradford, W Yorkshire BD12 9ET* Tel (01274) 670737

READ, James Arthur. b 51. Nottm Coll of Educn BEd74. EMMTC 84. **d** 87 **p** 88. C Weoley Castle *Birm* 87-91; C W Smethwick 91-92; C Smethwick Resurrection 92; TV Atherton *Man* 92-97; P-in-c Facit from 97. *The Vicarage, Market Street, Whitworth, Rochdale, Lancs OL12 8LU* Tel (01706) 853931

READ, John. b 33. Worc Coll Ox BA56 MA60. Chich Th Coll 56. **d** 58 **p** 59. C Babbacombe *Ex* 58-60; C Heavitree 60-63; V Swimbridge 63-69; V Ex St Matt 69-80; P-in-c Ex St Sidwell 79-80; R Ex St Sidwell and St Matt 80-83; Chapl Warneford Hosp Leamington Spa 83-89; Chapl S Warks Hosps 83-89; Chapl Dur and Ches le Street Hosps 89-95; Chapl Dryburn Hosp 89-95; rtd 95; NSM Tamworth *Lich* from 95. *The Parsonage, Church Drive, Hopwas, Tamworth, Staffs B78 3AL* Tel (01827) 54599

READ, John Hanson. b 17. St Jo Coll Ox BA49 MA53. Qu Coll Birm 49. **d** 50 **p** 51. C Eastbourne St Mary *Chich* 50-53; C

Horsham 53-57; V Brighton St Wilfrid 57-61; R Beddington *S'wark* 61-78; RD Sutton 65-70; P-in-c Guestling *Chich* 78; P-in-c Pett 78; R Guestling and Pett 78-83; rtd 83; Perm to Offic *Chich* from 84; RD Rye 89-90. *6 Oast House Road, Icklesham, Winchelsea, E Sussex TN36 4BN* Tel (01424) 814440

READ, John Samuel. b 33. Fitzw Ho Cam BA56. Clifton Th Coll 62. **d** 64 **p** 65. C Sneinton St Chris w St Phil *S'well* 64-67; C Huyton St Geo *Liv* 67-70; Lic to Offic *Blackb* 70-72; V Moldgreen *Wakef* 72-84; V Rawtenstall St Mary *Man* 84-91; Chapl Rossendale Gen Hosp 84-91; R Earsham w Alburgh and Denton *Nor* from 91; P-in-c Ditchingham, Hedenham and Broome from 94. *The Rectory, Earsham, Bungay, Suffolk NR35 2TF* Tel (01986) 892147

READ, Nicholas John (Nick). b 59. Keble Coll Ox BA81 MSc82 MA85. Ox Min Course 92. **d** 95 **p** 96. NSM Charlbury w Shorthampton *Ox* from 95. *54 The Green, Charlbury, Oxford OX7 3QB* Tel (01608) 811374

READ, Robert Edgar. b 47. Kelham Th Coll 66. **d** 70 **p** 71. C Harton Colliery *Dur* 70-75; C Wilmslow *Ches* 76-80; V Gatley 80-92; V Offerton from 92. *St Alban's Vicarage, Offerton Lane, Stockport, Cheshire SK2 5AG* Tel 0161-480 3773

READ, Victor. b 29. Lon Univ BD58. ALCD57. **d** 58 **p** 59. C Wimbledon *S'wark* 58-61; C Lt Marlow *Ox* 61-64; V Wootton *Linc* 64-67; R Croxton 64-67; V Ulceby 64-67; V Linc St Pet in Eastgate w St Marg 67-73; V W Wimbledon Ch Ch *S'wark* 73-94; rtd 94; Perm to Offic *Pet* from 94. *27 Nightingale Drive, Towcester, Northants NN12 6RA* Tel (01327) 352027

READE, The Ven Nicholas Stewart. b 46. Leeds Univ BA70 DipTh72. Coll of Resurr Mirfield 70. **d** 73 **p** 74. C Coseley St Chad *Lich* 73-75; C Codsall 75-78; V Upper Gornal 78-82; V Mayfield *Chich* 82-88; RD Dallington 82-88; V Eastbourne St Mary from 88; RD Eastbourne 88-97; Can and Preb Chich Cathl from 90; Min The Hydneye CD 91-93; Adn Lewes and Hastings from 97. *The Vicarage, 2 Glebe Close, Eastbourne, E Sussex BN20 8AW* Tel (01323) 720420

READE, Richard Barton. b 66. Wolv Poly BA88. Ripon Coll Cuddesdon BA91. **d** 92 **p** 93. C Wilnecote *Lich* 92-96; C Penkridge Team from 96. *31 Saxon Road, Penkridge, Stafford ST19 5EP*

READER, John. b 53. Trin Coll Ox BA75 MA79 Man Univ DSPT83 MPhil87. Ripon Coll Cuddesdon 76. **d** 78 **p** 79. C Ely 78-80; C Baguley *Man* 80-83; TV Kirkby Lonsdale *Carl* 83-86; V Lydbury N *Heref* 86-89; P-in-c Hopesay w Edgton 86-89; R Lydbury N w Hopesay and Edgton 89-90; Tutor Glouc Sch for Min 86-88; Vice-Prin 88-90; Dir Past Th Sarum & Wells Th Coll 90-92; P-in-c Elmley Lovett w Hampton Lovett and Elmbridge etc *Worc* from 92; Assoc Tr and Educn Officer from 92. *The Rectory, Elmley Lovett, Droitwich, Worcs WR9 0PU* Tel (01299) 251798

READER, Dr Trevor Alan John. b 46. Lon Univ BSc68 MSc70 Portsm Poly PhD72. S Dios Minl Tr Scheme 83. **d** 86 **p** 87. C Alverstoke *Portsm* 86-89; P-in-c Hook w Warsash 89-95; V from 95. *The Vicarage, 112 Osborne Road, Warsash, Southampton SO3 6GH* Tel (01489) 572324

READER-MOORE, Anthony. b 43. Kent Univ BA80 Hull Univ MA83. Linc Th Coll. **d** 82 **p** 83. C Addiscombe St Mildred *Cant* 82-84; C Addiscombe St Mildred *S'wark* 85-86; R N Wheatley, W Burton, Bole, Saundby, Sturton etc *S'well* 86-93; Rural Officer 89-93; P-in-c Alford w Rigsby *Linc* 93-97; P-in-c Bilsby w Farlesthorpe 93-97; P-in-c Hannah cum Hagnaby w Markby 93-97; P-in-c Well 93-97; P-in-c Maltby 93-94; P-in-c Saleby w Beesby 93-94; P-in-c Saleby w Beesby and Maltby 95-97; V Alford w Rigsby from 97; V Bilsby w Farlesthorpe from 97; R Hannah cum Hagnaby w Markby from 97; R Saleby w Beesby and Maltby from 97; R Well from 97. *The Vicarage, 15 Bilsby Road, Alford, Lincs LN13 9EW* Tel (01507) 462448

READING, Canon Laurence John. b 14. DSC44. Lon Univ BD39 AKC39. **d** 39 **p** 40. C Prittlewell *Chelmsf* 39-42; Chapl RNVR 42-46; C-in-c Prittlewell St Pet CD 46-60; V Shrub End *Chelmsf* 60-64; Tr Officer Bd of Educn Adult Cttee 64; Sec 65-72; Can Heref Cathl *Heref* 72-82; rtd 82; Perm to Offic *Chelmsf* from 82. *11 Wakelin Way, Witham, Essex CM8 2TX* Tel (01376) 513251

READING, Miss Sian Jacqueline Mary. b 64. Westcott Ho Cam CTM95. **d** 95 **p** 96. C Northampton St Alb *Pet* from 95. *12 Oulton Rise, Northampton NN3 1EW* Tel (01604) 492965

READING, Area Bishop of. *See* WALKER, The Rt Revd Edward William Murray

REAGON, Darrol Franklin. b 46. Univ of Wales (Cardiff) DipTh76. St Mich Coll Llan 74. **d** 76 **p** 77. C Llandrillo-yn-Rhos *St As* 76-78; C Hawarden 78-81; V Northwich St Luke and H Trin *Ches* 81-85; V Moulton *Linc* 85-91; V Scunthorpe Resurr 91-92; P-in-c Branston 92-94; R Branston w Nocton and Potterhanworth from 94. *The Rectory, Branston, Lincoln LN4 1NN* Tel (01522) 791296

REAKES-WILLIAMS, Gordon Martin. b 63. St Cath Coll Cam BA86 MA89. St Jo Coll Dur BA90. **d** 91 **p** 92. C Harold Wood *Chelmsf* 91-94; Chapl Leipzig *Eur* from 95. *Hardenbergstrasse 44A, 04275 Leipzig, Germany* Tel Leipzig (341) 302-7951 Mobile (0)177-240 4207 Fax (341) 309-0631 E-mail earwig@t-online.de

REALE, Mrs Kathleen. b 38. Carl Dioc Tr Course 83. **dss** 86 **d** 87 **p** 94. Dalston *Carl* 86-87; Par Dn 87-90; Par Dn Westward, Rosley-w-Woodside and Welton 87-90; Par Dn Thursby 89-90; D-in-c Gt Salkeld w Lazonby 90-94; P-in-c from 94. *The Rectory, Lazonby, Penrith, Cumbria CA10 1BL* Tel (01768) 898750

REANEY, Christopher Thomas. b 60. Univ of Wales (Lamp) BA82. St Mich Coll Llan DipTh85. **d** 85 **p** 86. C Maindee *Mon* 85-87; C Griffithstown 88-89; V Treherbert w Treorchy *Llan* from 89. *The Vicarage, 58 Miskin Street, Treherbert, Treorchy CF42 5LR* Tel (01443) 772241

REANEY, Joseph Silvester. b 13. Selw Coll Cam BA35 MA42. Wells Th Coll 36. **d** 37 **p** 38. C Lewisham St Jo Southend *S'wark* 37-40; C Bellingham St Dunstan 40-42; Chapl RAFVR 42-46; V Gt Barr *Lich* from 47. *Great Barr Vicarage, Chapel Lane, Birmingham B43 7BD* Tel 0121-357 1390

REARDON, Bernard Morris Garvin. b 13. Keble Coll Ox BA35 MA38. Ripon Hall Ox 35. **d** 37 **p** 38. C Saffron Walden *Chelmsf* 37-38; C Shenfield 38-40; P-in-c 40-41; CF (EC) 41-46; V Hornchurch H Cross *Chelmsf* 46-47; R Kelly w Bradstone *Ex* 47-59; R Parham and Wiggonholt w Greatham *Chich* 59-63; Sen Lect, Reader, and Hd Relig Studies Newc Univ 63-78; rtd 78. *2 The Grove, Benton, Newcastle upon Tyne NE12 9PE* Tel 0191-266 1574

REARDON, Canon Martin Alan. b 32. OBE97. Selw Coll Cam BA54 MA58. Cuddesdon Coll 56. **d** 58 **p** 59. C Rugby St Andr *Cov* 58-62; C Wicker w Neepsend *Sheff* 62-65; Lic to Offic 65-71; Sub-Warden Linc Th Coll 71-78; Gen Sec Gen Syn Bd for Miss and Unity 78-89; Can and Preb Linc Cathl *Linc* 79-89; Perm to Offic *Chich* 81-89; R Plumpton w E Chiltington 89-90; Gen Sec Chs Together in England from 90; Perm to Offic *S'wark* from 95. *Churches Together in England, Interchurch House, 35-41 Lower Marsh, London SE1 7RL* Tel 0171-620 4444 Fax 928 5771

REASON, Jack. b 28. St Alb Minl Tr Scheme 77. **d** 80 **p** 81. NSM Luton Lewsey St Hugh *St Alb* 80-85; C Bideford *Ex* 85-88; R Northlew w Ashbury 88-93; R Bratton Clovelly w Germansweek 88-93; rtd 93; Perm to Offic *Ex* from 94. *5 Merryfield Road, Bideford, Devon EX39 4BX* Tel (01237) 472150

REAST, Eileen Joan. *See* BANGAY, Mrs Eileen Joan

REAVIL, Michael Edward. b 51. Qu Coll Birm 89. **d** 91 **p** 92. C Cofton Hackett w Barnt Green *Birm* 91-94; C Stevenage St Mary Sheppall w Aston *St Alb* 94-97; P-in-c Lt Leigh and Lower Whitley *Ches* from 97; P-in-c Antrobus from 97; P-in-c Aston by Sutton from 97. *The Vicarage, Street Lane, Lower Whitley, Warrington WA4 3EN* Tel (01925) 730850

RECORD, Canon John. b 47. St Chad's Coll Dur BA71. Westcott Ho Cam 71. **d** 73 **p** 74. C Paddington St Jo w St Mich *Lon* 73-75; C Witney *Ox* 75-78; P-in-c Lt Compton and Chastleton 78-80; R Lt Compton w Chastleton, Cornwell etc 80-83; V Hawkhurst *Cant* from 83; RD W Charing 89-95; Hon Can Cant Cathl from 96. *The Vicarage, Hawkhurst, Kent TN18 4QB* Tel (01580) 753397

RECORD, Sister Marion Eva. b 25. MRCS50 LRCP50 Leeds Univ FFARCS57 Lon Univ BD79. **dss** 78 **d** 87 **p** 94. OHP from 72; Chapl Hull Univ *York* 72-78; Chapl York Univ 78-80; Lic to Offic 80-95; Perm to Offic from 95; rtd 96. *St Hilda's Priory, Sneaton Castle, Whitby, N Yorkshire YO21 3QN* Tel (01947) 602079

REDDING, Roger Charles. b 45. Chich Th Coll 87. **d** 89 **p** 90. C Yeovil St Mich *B & W* 89-93; P-in-c Salisbury St Mark *Sarum* 93-94; Lic to Offic 94-96; TV Chalke Valley W from 96. *The Vicarage, Ebbesbourne Wake, Salisbury SP5 5JL* Tel (01722) 780408

REDDINGTON, Gerald Alfred. b 34. Lon Univ DipRS79. S'wark Ord Course 76. **d** 79 **p** 79. NSM St Vedast w St Mich-le-Querne etc *Lon* 79-85; Dir Past Support Gp Scheme 83-86; Hon C St Marylebone All SS 85-90; Perm to Offic *Portsm* from 88; V Ealing St Barn *Lon* from 90. *St Barnabas' Vicarage, 66 Woodfield Road, London W5 1SH* Tel 0181-998 0826

REDFEARN, James Jonathan. b 62. Newc Univ BA83 PGCE89. Cranmer Hall Dur CTMin95. **d** 95 **p** 96. C Kidsgrove *Lich* from 95. *42 Lamb Street, Kidsgrove, Stoke-on-Trent ST7 4AL* Tel (01782) 782793

REDFEARN, John William Holmes. Sheff Univ BA30 MA31 DipEd31. **d** 33 **p** 34. C Bishopwearmouth St Mich *Dur* 33-35; Asst Master Bede Coll Sch Sunderland 31-45; Chapl Berkhamsted Colleg Sch Herts 45-55; Chapl Haberdashers' Aske's Sch Elstree 56-72; Perm to Offic *Lon* 61-76; rtd 72. *184 Cardiff Road, Llandaff, Cardiff CF5 2AD* Tel (01222) 567692

REDFEARN, Michael. b 42. Open Univ BA78 Hull Univ MA84 BA86. St Aid Birkenhead 64. **d** 68 **p** 69. C Bury St Pet *Man* 68-71; C Swinton St Pet 71-74; Ind Chapl *Bris* 74-81; Ind Chapl *York* 81-86; St Alb Minl Tr Scheme 86-93; V Southill *St Alb* 86-93; Asst Chapl HM Pris Wandsworth 94; Chapl HM Young Offender Inst and Rem Cen Feltham from 94; Lic to Offic *Lon* from 94. *HM YOI and Remand Centre, Bedfont Road, Feltham, Middx TW13 4ND* Tel 0181-890 0061

REDFEARN, Ms Tracy Anne. b 66. Heythrop Coll Lon BD88. Ripon Coll Cuddesdon 91. **d** 93 **p** 94. C Haslemere *Guildf* 93-97; TV Gt Grimsby St Mary and St Jas *Linc* from 97. *St Mark's*

Vicarage, 2A Winchester Road, Grimsby, S Humberside DN33 1EW Tel (01472) 750818

REDFERN, Canon Alastair Llewellyn John. b 48. Trin Coll Cam BA74 Ch Ch Ox MA74. Qu Coll Birm 75. **d** 76 **p** 77. C Tettenhall Regis *Lich* 76-79; Tutor Ripon Coll Cuddesdon 79-87; Hon C Cuddesdon *Ox* 83-87; Can Res Bris Cathl *Bris* from 87; Dioc Dir Tr from 91. *Bristol Cathedral, College Green, Bristol BS1 5TJ* Tel 0117-942 1039

REDFERN, Paul. b 48. Ulster Univ BA88. CITC BTh94. **d** 94 **p** 95. C Belfast St Aid *Conn* 94-97; I Belfast St Mark from 97. *St Mark's Rectory, 119 Ligoniel Road, Belfast BT14 8DN* Tel (01232) 713151

REDGERS, Brian. b 42. Dur Univ BA65. Westcott Ho Cam 65. **d** 67 **p** 68. C Rushmere *St E* 67-73; Lic to Offic from 73. *44 Belvedere Road, Ipswich IP4 4AB*

REDGRAVE, Cecil Goulden. b 14. Oak Hill Th Coll 37. **d** 41 **p** 42. C Higher Openshaw *Man* 41-43; C Ashton St Jas 43-44; C Chadderton Ch Ch 44-46; V Thornton *Leic* 46-49; V Fairlight *Chich* 49-60; V New Milverton *Cov* 60-76; R Tredington and Darlingscott w Newbold on Stour 76-83; rtd 83; Perm to Offic *Cov* from 83. *30 Elmdene Road, Kenilworth, Warks CV8 2BX* Tel (01926) 857118

REDGRAVE, Miss Christine Howick. b 50. AIAT73. Trin Coll Bris 75. **dss** 78 **d** 87 **p** 94. Watford *St Alb* 78-83; Maidenhead St Andr and St Mary *Ox* 83-85; Bracknell 85-87; Par Dn 87-94; TV 94-96; Asst Dir of Ords from 95; P-in-c Woolhampton w Midgham and Beenham Valance from 96. *Design House, Birds Lane, Midgham, Reading RG7 5RY* Tel (0118) 971 2264

REDGRAVE, Ronald Oliver. b 18. Ox NSM Course. **d** 83 **p** 84. NSM Boyne Hill *Ox* 83-85; Perm to Offic *St E* 85-86; P-in-c Alderton w Ramsholt and Bawdsey 86-88; rtd 88. *3 Micheldever Way, Bracknell, Berks RG12 0XX* Tel (01344) 409067

REDGRAVE, Miss Susan Frances. b 55. CQSW75. St Deiniol's Hawarden 89. **d** 90 **p** 94. NSM Leic Resurr *Leic* 90; Par Dn De Beauvoir Town St Pet *Lon* 90-94; C 94-95; C Evington *Leic* 95-96; C Leic St Phil 95-96. *Address excluded by request*

REDHEAD, Edward. b 30. St Deiniol's Hawarden 60. **d** 63 **p** 64. C Mottram in Longdendale w Woodhead *Ches* 63-67; V Rivington *Man* 67-72; V Bloxwich *Lich* 72-75; Hon C Lich St Chad 82-84; P-in-c Bromfield w Waverton *Carl* 84-85; V 85-90; P-in-c W Newton 84-85; V 85-90; R Harrington 90-93; rtd 93. *Tigh-na-Mara, 2-3 Caroy, Struan, Isle of Skye IV56 8FQ* Tel (01470) 572338

REDHOUSE, Mark David. b 67. BTEC NC86. Oak Hill Th Coll BA94. **d** 94 **p** 95. C Fulham St Mary N End *Lon* 94-96; C Hove Bp Hannington Memorial Ch *Chich* from 96. *43 Hogarth Road, Hove, E Sussex BN3 5RH* Tel (01273) 725642

REDKNAP, Clive Douglas. b 53. Trin Coll Bris BA95. **d** 95 **p** 96. C Patcham *Chich* from 95. *70 Overhill Drive, Brighton BN1 8WJ* Tel (01273) 554791

REDMAN, Canon Arthur Thomas. b 28. Dur Univ BA52 DSA PGCE. Ridley Hall Cam 62. **d** 63 **p** 64. C Heaton St Barn *Bradf* 63-66; C Hitchin St Mary *St Alb* 66-70; PM 72-75; Perm to Offic *Nor* 70-72; V Swanwick and Pentrich *Derby* 75-80; Warden of Readers 78-97; Dir Bp's Cert 78-88; V Allestree 80-96; P-in-c Morley 82-85; Hon Can Derby Cathl 86-96; RD Duffield 88-96; rtd 96; Hon C Bretby w Newton Solney *Derby* from 96. *9 Ludgate Walk, Mackworth, Derby DE22 4HQ* Tel (01332) 521733

REDMAN, Canon Douglas Stuart Raymond. b 35. MCIOB64. Roch Th Coll 66. **d** 68 **p** 69. C Shortlands *Roch* 68-71; V from 80; R Kingsdown 71-76; R Chatham St Mary w St Jo 76-80; RD Beckenham from 90; Hon Can Roch Cathl from 93. *The Vicarage, 37 Kingswood Road, Bromley BR2 0HG* Tel 0181-460 4989

REDPATH, Stewart Rosbotham. b 11. TCD BA39. CITC 39. **d** 39 **p** 40. C Shankill *D & D* 39-41; C Drumcree *Arm* 41-43; I Kildress 43-46; I Camlough w Killeavy 47-62; I Loughgall 62-80; rtd 80. *22 Rosemount Park, Armagh BT60 1AX* Tel (01861) 522698

REDRUP, Canon Robert John. b 38. Leeds Univ BA65. Oak Hill Th Coll 65. **d** 69 **p** 70. C Maidenhead St Andr and St Mary *Ox* 69-74; C St Keverne *Truro* 74-78; P-in-c Kea 78-80; V from 80; P-in-c Highertown and Baldhu 80-84; Hon Can Truro Cathl from 96. *The Vicarage, Kea, Truro, Cornwall TR3 6AE* Tel (01872) 72850

REDVERS HARRIS, Jonathan Francis. b 60. Solicitor 87 Southn Univ LLB81 Univ of Wales (Cardiff) LLM94. Ridley Hall Cam 87. **d** 90 **p** 91. C Enfield St Jas *Lon* 90-93; PV Llan Cathl *Llan* 93-96; Succ 94-96; V Houghton Regis *St Alb* from 96. *The Vicarage, Bedford Road, Houghton Regis, Dunstable, Beds LU5 5DJ* Tel (01582) 867593

REDWOOD, Canon David Leigh. b 32. Glas Univ DipSocWork78. Edin Th Coll 57. **d** 59 **p** 60. C Stirling *Edin* 59-61; C Glas Ch Ch *Glas* 61-64; P-in-c Glas Ascension 64-66; R 66-69; R Hamilton 69-74; R Callander *St And* 74-76; Hon C 76-78; R Lochearnhead 74-76; R Killin 74-76; Hon C Doune 76-78; Hon C Aberfoyle 78-85; R Dunfermline 85-97; TR W Fife Team Min 85-97; Can St Ninian's Cathl Perth 90-97; rtd 97. *8 Strathmore Avenue, Dunblane, Perthshire FK15 9HX* Tel (01786) 825493

REECE, Gp Capt Arthur. b 13. DSO44 OBE54 DFC42 AFC43. St Deiniol's Hawarden 77. **d** 79 **p** 80. Hon C Lache cum Saltney *Ches* 79-80; V Tilstone Fearnall and Wettenhall 80-90; rtd 90. *Tawelfan, Bryan Goodman, Ruthin LL15 1EL* Tel (01824) 702968

✠REECE, The Rt Revd David. b 13. G&C Coll Cam BA34 MA38. St Mich Coll Llan 35. **d** 36 **p** 37 **c** 77. C Aberystwyth St Mich *St D* 36-41; C Llanelli 41-49; V Pembroke St Mary and St Mich 49-56; V Port Talbot St Theodore *Llan* 56-71; RD Margam 66-71; Can Llan Cathl 69-71; Adn Margam 71-81; Asst Bp Llan 77-83; rtd 83. *16 Preswylfa Court, Merthyr Mawr Road, Bridgend CF31 3NX* Tel (01656) 653115

REECE, Donald Malcolm Hayden. b 36. CCC Cam BA58 MA62. Cuddesdon Coll 58. **d** 60 **p** 61. C Latchford St Jas *Ches* 60-63; C Matlock and Tansley *Derby* 63-67; C-in-c Hackenthorpe Ch Ch CD 67-70; Rhodesia 70-73; V Leic St Pet *Leic* 74-82; V Putney St Marg *S'wark* 82-91; Home Sec Coun for Chr Unity from 92; Perm to Offic 93-94; Hon C Wandsworth St Anne 94-97; V Shepherd's Bush St Steph w St Thos *Lon* from 97. *St Stephen's Vicarage, Coverdale Road, London W12 8JJ* Tel 0181-743 3166 Fax 0171-799 2714

REECE, Paul Michael. b 60. Southn Univ BA81. Coll of Resurr Mirfield 83. **d** 85 **p** 86. C Borehamwood *St Alb* 85-89; C Potters Bar 89-92; R Lt Stanmore St Lawr *Lon* from 92; Chapl R Nat Orthopaedic Hosp from 93; AD Harrow *Lon* from 97. *Whitchurch Rectory, St Lawrence Close, Edgware, Middx HA8 6RB* Tel 0181-952 0019

REED, Alan Ronald. b 44. Sarum Th Coll 66. **d** 68 **p** 70. C Ifield *Chich* 68-71; C Perivale *Lon* 71-72; C Ruislip St Martin 72-75; C Burgess Hill St Jo *Chich* 76-78; V Shoreham Beach 78-80; V Roughey 80-97; P-in-c Rusper 84-86; V Hove St Barn and St Agnes from 97. *St Barnabas' Vicarage, 88 Sackville Road, Hove, E Sussex BN3 3HE* Tel (01273) 732427

REED, Allan Norman. b 31. Keble Coll Ox BA55 MA59 Didsbury Coll Man CertEd72. Wycliffe Hall Ox 55. **d** 57 **p** 58. C Beverley Minster *York* 57-60; C Marfleet 60-64; R S Levenshulme *Man* 64-71; Lic Preacher 71-95; rtd 92. *21 Lyons Road, Richmond, N Yorkshire DL10 4UA* Tel (01748) 825767

REED, Ms Annette Susan. b 54. Birm Univ BA76 Univ of Wales (Cardiff) CQSW78. Qu Coll Birm 84. **d** 87 **p** 94. C Churchover w Willey *Cov* 89-92; C Clifton upon Dunsmore and Newton 89-92; C Walsgrave on Sowe 92-95; C Cov E 92-95; C Burbage w Aston Flamville *Leic* from 95; C Hinckley St Mary from 95. *46 Salisbury Road, Burbage, Hinckley, Leics LE10 2AR* Tel (01455) 616226

REED, Brian. b 43. Bris Univ BSc65 Nottm Univ DipTh76. Linc Th Coll 73. **d** 76 **p** 77. C S Ashford Ch Ch *Cant* 76-78; C Spring Park 78-83; V Barming Heath from 83. *St Andrew's Vicarage, 416 Tonbridge Road, Maidstone, Kent ME16 9LW* Tel (01622) 726245

REED, Bruce Douglas. b 20. Fitzw Ho Cam BA52 MA56 Lambeth Hon MLitt90. Moore Th Coll Sydney LTh45. **d** 46 **p** 46. Australia 46-49; Chapl Fitzw Ho Cam 50-54; C Cambridge St Paul *Ely* 53-54; Chmn Grubb Inst from 69; rtd 85. *The Grubb Institute, Cloudesley Street, London N1 0HU* Tel 0171-278 8061 Fax 278 0728

REED, Christopher John. b 42. Selw Coll Cam BA64 MA68 Dur Univ DipTh66. Cranmer Hall Dur 64. **d** 67 **p** 68. C Gt Ilford St Andr *Chelmsf* 67-70; P-in-c Bordesley St Andr *Birm* 70-72; V 72-80; V Crofton St Paul *Roch* from 80. *St Paul's Vicarage, 2 Oakwood Road, Orpington, Kent BR6 8JH* Tel (01689) 852939

REED, Colin Bryher. b 58. York Univ BA80 RGN86. Ridley Hall Cam CTM95. **d** 95 **p** 96. C Grays North *Chelmsf* from 95. *141 Southend Road, Grays, Essex RM17 5NP* Tel (01375) 377249

REED, Colin Charles Gilmour. b 40. LCP75 FCP86 St Luke's Coll Ex TCert63 Lon Univ DipTh69. Tyndale Hall Brisbane 67. **d** 69 **p** 70. C Weston-super-Mare Ch Ch *B & W* 69-71; Kenya 71-79; Australia from 80. *St Andrew's Hall, 190 The Avenue, Parkville, Victoria, Australia 3052* Tel Melbourne (3) 9388 1663 Fax 9387 1372

REED, Canon Douglas Victor. b 19. AKC41 Middlebury Coll (USA) Hon DD51. St Steph Ho Ox 41. **d** 42 **p** 43. C Poplar St Sav w St Gabr and St Steph *Lon* 42-44; C Bedford St Paul *St Alb* 44-45; Asst Org Sec SPCK 46-47; V Belvedere St Aug *Roch* 47-52; V Chislehurst Annunciation 52-85; Hon Can Roch Cathl 81-85; rtd 85; Perm to Offic *Roch* 85-94. *6 Crown Lane, Chislehurst, Kent BR7 5PL* Tel 0181-467-3360

REED, Duncan Esmond Bousfield. b 51. AKC74 Ch Ch Coll Cant PGCE75. St Aug Coll Cant 76. **d** 76 **p** 77. C Houghton le Spring *Dur* 76-79; C Stockton St Pet 79-83; V Darlington St Mark w St Paul 83-88; V Benfieldside 88-93; P-in-c Whickham 93-95; R from 95. *The Rectory, Church Chare, Whickham, Newcastle upon Tyne NE16 4SH* Tel 0191-488 7397

REED, Mrs Elizabeth Christine. b 43. Lon Bible Coll BD65. W of England Minl Tr Course 95. **d** 97. NSM Ledbury w Eastnor *Heref* from 97. *The Old Barn, Perrystone Hill, Ross-on-Wye, Herefordshire HR9 7QX* Tel (01989) 780439

REED, Ethel Patricia Ivy. *See* WESTBROOK, Mrs Ethel Patricia Ivy

REED, Geoffrey Martin. b 51. Univ of Wales (Cardiff) BA73. C Hill Th Coll 73. **d** 76 **p** 77. C Swansea St Nic *S & B* 76-7 Sketty 78-84; V Glasbury and Llowes 84-86; V Glasbur

Llowes w Clyro and Betws from 86. *St Peter's Vicarage, Glasbury, Hereford HR3 5NU* Tel (01497) 847657

REED, Jack. b 23. Bris Univ BA49 Lon Univ BD51. Tyndale Hall Bris. **d** 51 **p** 52. C Crookes St Thos *Sheff* 51-54; C Cheltenham St Mark *Glouc* 54-56; R Bickenhill w Elmdon *Birm* 56-60; V Sparkbrook Ch Ch 60-66; V Drypool St Columba w St Andr and St Pet *York* 66-80; TR Drypool 80-83; P-in-c Thwing 83-85; P-in-c Rudston w Boynton and Kilham 83-85; V 85-87; Perm to Offic from 87; rtd 88. *32 Dower Rise, Swanland, North Ferriby, N Humberside HU14 3QT* Tel (01482) 632649

REED, John Peter Cyril. b 51. BD78 AKC78. Ripon Coll Cuddesdon 78. **d** 79 **p** 80. C Croydon *Cant* 79-82; Prec St Alb Abbey *St Alb* 82-86; R Timsbury and Priston *B & W* 86-93; Chapl Rural Affairs Bath Adnry 87-93; P-in-c Ilminster w Whitelackington 93-94; TR Ilminster and District from 94. *The Rectory, Court Barton, Ilminster, Somerset TA19 0DU* Tel (01460) 52610

REED, Capt John William. b 57. Sussex Univ BSc79 Ch Ch Coll Cant DipHE93. N Ord Course 95. **d** 97. C Padgate *Liv* from 97. *18 West View, Padgate, Warrington WA2 0NX* Tel (01925) 837124

REED, Matthew Colin. b 50. Edin Univ BD82. Edin Th Coll 72. **d** 84 **p** 85. C Edin St Pet *Edin* 84-87; P-in-c Linlithgow 87-94; P-in-c Bathgate 87-91; Chapl HM Pris Polmont from 91; R Motherwell *Glas* from 94; R Wishaw from 94. *The Rectory, 14 Crawford Street, Motherwell, Lanarkshire ML1 3AD* Tel (01698) 262634

REED, Matthew Graham. b 68. Nottm Univ BEng89 Ox Univ MA97. Ripon Coll Cuddesdon BA92. **d** 93 **p** 94. C Oxton *Ches* 93-97; TV Gt Marlow w Marlow Bottom, Lt Marlow and Bisham *Ox* from 97. *165 Marlow Bottom Road, Marlow, Bucks SL7 3PL* Tel (01628) 472816 Fax as telephone

REED, Neil Andrew. b 62. St Chad's Coll Dur BA84. Coll of Resurr Mirfield. **d** 87 **p** 88. C Bishopwearmouth Ch Ch *Dur* 87-89; C Sunderland Springwell w Thorney Close 89-93; TV E Darlington 93-94. *42 Croft Avenue, Sunderland SR4 7DP* Tel 0191-567 0755

REED, Mrs Pamela Kathleen. b 38. EMMTC. **dss** 84 **d** 87 **p** 94. Cambridge Ascension *Ely* 84-87; Par Dn 87-88; Par Dn Cherry Hinton St Andr 88-90; C 91-95; C Teversham 91-95; V Chesterton St Geo from 95. *St George's Vicarage, 8 Chesterfield Road, Cambridge CB4 1LN* Tel (01223) 423374

REED, Richard David. b 32. Trin Coll Carmarthen. **d** 91 **p** 92. NSM Dale and St Brides w Marloes *St D* 91-96; P-in-c Blisland w St Breward *Truro* from 96. *c/o Mrs C Hartley, Lavethan, Blisland, Bodmin, Cornwall PL30 4QG*

REED, Robert Chase. b 47. Boston Univ BSc70 TCD HDipEd72. **d** 87 **p** 88. Aux Min Taney *D & G* from 87; Res Hd Master Wesley Coll Dub from 87; Succ St Patr Cathl Dublin 93-97; Treas St Patr Cathl Dublin from 96. *Embury House, Wesley College, Dublin 16, Irish Republic* Tel Dublin (1) 269 3150 Fax as telephone E-mail bobreed@indigo.ie

REED, Roger William. b 39. Wycliffe Hall Ox 65. **d** 68 **p** 69. C Portsea St Cuth *Portsm* 68-71; C Enfield St Jas *Lon* 71-74; P-in-c Becontree St Thos *Chelmsf* 74-78; R Debden and Wimbish w Thunderley 78-93; RD Saffron Walden 82-91; P-in-c Blendworth w Chalton w Idsworth *Portsm* from 93. *The Rectory, Blendworth, Horndean, Portsmouth PO8 0AB* Tel (01705) 592174

REED, Simon John. b 63. Trin Coll Ox BA86 MA90. Wycliffe Hall Ox BA90. **d** 91 **p** 92. C Walton H Trin *Ox* 91-96; P-in-c Hanger Hill Ascension and W Twyford St Mary *Lon* from 96. *The Ascension Vicarage, Beaufort Road, London W5 3EB* Tel 0181-566 9920

REED, William Harvey. b 47. K Coll Lon BD69 AKC69. St Aug Coll Cant 69. **d** 70 **p** 71. C Stockton St Mark CD *Dur* 70-72; C Billingham St Cuth 72-76; C S Westoe 76-79; V Chilton Moor 79-87; R Hutton *Chelmsf* 87-95; V Hullbridge from 95. *The Vicarage, 93 Ferry Road, Hockley, Essex SS5 6EL* Tel (01702) 232017

REEDE, The Very Revd Samuel William. b 24. TCD BA48 MA52 BD55. CITC 50. **d** 50 **p** 51. C Waterford Ch Ch *C & O* 50-54; C Cregagh *D & D* 54-59; Hd S Ch Miss Ballymacarrett 59-67; Chapl Stranmillis Coll Belf 64-68; Can Raphoe Cathl *D & R* 67-92; I Raphoe w Raymochy 67-68; I Raphoe w Raymochy and Clonleigh 68-92; Dean Raphoe 80-92; rtd 92. *Rooskey, Newtowncunningham, Co Donegal, Irish Republic* Tel Letterkenny (74) 56426

REES, Anthony John. b 49. St Jo Coll Dur BA72 DipTh73 MA77 Man Univ MEd89. **d** 74 **p** 75. C Smethwick St Matt w St Chad *Birm* 74-77; C Bolton St Pet *Man* 77-80; R Cheetham St Mark [illegible] 88; V Mottram in Longdendale w Woodhead *Ches* 88-93; V [illegible]m in Longdendale from 93. *The Vicarage, 29 Ashworth [illegible]m, Hyde, Cheshire SK14 6NT* Tel (01457) 762268

[illegible] McGill Univ Montreal BA74 St Andr Univ [illegible]al Dioc Th Coll 76. **d** 80 **p** 81. Canada [illegible]*lb* from 85; Chapl Bedford Sch 85-92; Hd [illegible]ch from 92. *Pemberley House, 17 Park [illegible]K40 2LF* Tel (01234) 355999

[illegible]**yn.** b 18. Univ of Wales BA38. Lon Coll of Div [illegible]althamstow St Luke *Chelmsf* 41-43; C Birm Bp [illegible]6; V W Bromwich St Paul Golds Hill *Lich* 46-52;

V Handforth *Ches* 52-60; V St Alb Ch Ch *St Alb* 60-84; rtd 84; C Weobley w Sarnesfield and Norton Canon *Heref* 84-91; Perm to Offic from 92. *2 Nelson Cottage, Bridge Sollars, Hereford HR4 7JN* Tel (01981) 590296

REES, Christopher John. b 40. Dur Univ BA62. Ridley Hall Cam 62. **d** 64 **p** 65. C Wilmslow *Ches* 64-70; C Birkenhead St Pet w St Matt 70-75; V Lostock Gralam 75-83; R Davenham 83-96; P-in-c Aldford and Bruera from 96. *The Rectory, Middle Lane, Aldford, Chester CH3 6JA* Tel (01244) 620281

REES, David Aylwin. b 14. Univ of Wales (Lamp) BA46. **d** 47 **p** 48. C Eglwysnewydd *St D* 47-50; C Pembroke St Mary and St Mich 50-53; V Spittal and Treffgarne 53-75; V Dale 75-77; V Dale and St Brides w Marloes 78-84; rtd 84. *Cartrefle, North Road, Aberystwyth SY23 2EE* Tel (01970) 615745

REES, David Elwyn. b 37. Univ of Wales (Swansea) BA60. Ripon Hall Ox 63. **d** 65 **p** 66. C Swansea St Thos and Kilvey *S & B* 65-69; V 81-87; C Sketty 69-73; V Clyro w Bettws, Llowes and Glasbury All SS 73-80; V Hay w Llanigon and Capel-y-Ffin from 87. *The Beeches, Newport Street, Hay-on-Wye, Hereford HR3 5BG* Tel (01497) 820612

REES, Canon David Frederick. b 21. SS Coll Cam BA48 MA52. Sarum Th Coll 48. **d** 50 **p** 51. C Blackb St Luke *Blackb* 50-53; C St Annes 53-55; V Choral York Minster *York* 55-62; V Penwortham St Mary *Blackb* 62-90; RD Leyland 70-84; Hon Can Blackb Cathl 79-90; rtd 90; Perm to Offic *Blackb* from 91. *4 Queensdale Close, Walton-le-Dale, Preston PR5 4JU* Tel (01772) 259010

REES, David Grenfell. b 18. St D Coll Lamp BA40 Qu Coll Birm. **d** 43 **p** 44. C Llangeinor *Llan* 43-47; C Cadoxton-juxta-Barry 47-53; C St Andrews Major 53-60; V Dyffryn 60-84; rtd 84; Perm to Offic *Llan* from 84. *10 Tyn-yr-Heol Road, Bryncoch, Neath SA10 7EA* Tel (01639) 644488

REES, Canon David Philip Dunn Hugh. b 38. Jes Coll Ox BA60 MA64 Ox Univ DipEd67. Westcott Ho Cam 62. **d** 64 **p** 65. C Salford St Phil w St Steph *Man* 64-66; Perm to Offic *St As* 66-67; Perm to Offic *Derby* 67-74; Chapl St Marg C of E High Sch Aigburth Liv 74-83; V Meliden and Gwaenysgor *St As* from 84; Dioc Adv for Schs from 85; Warden of Readers from 89; Warden of Ords from 91; Hon Can St As Cathl 93-95; Can Cursal from 95; Chan from 96. *The Vicarage, Meliden, Prestatyn LL19 8HN* Tel (01745) 856220

REES, David Richard. b 60. St Mich Coll Llan DipTh84. **d** 84 **p** 85. C Llanstadwel *St D* 84-86; C Carmarthen St Dav 86-91; V Llanrhian w Llanhywel and Carnhedryn etc from 91. *The Vicarage, Llanrhian, Haverfordwest SA62 5BG* Tel (01348) 831354

REES, Ms Diane Eluned. b 61. Univ of Wales (Ban) BSc82 Em Coll Cam PGCE83 Univ of Wales (Swansea) MEd87 CPsychol AFBPsS. St Jo Coll Nottm BTh93 MA93. **d** 96. C Hall Green St Pet *Birm* from 96. *4 Etwall Road, Hall Green, Birmingham B28 0LE* Tel 0121-778 4375

REES, Eric Vernon. b 19. St Jo Coll Dur BA41 MA44. St Andr Pampisford 43. **d** 43 **p** 44. C Tollington Park St Mark *Lon* 43-51; C Edmonton All SS 51-66; C N St Pancras All Hallows 66-68; C-in-c Enfield St Giles CD 68-80; C Edmonton All SS 80-82; C Edmonton All SS w St Mich 82-90; rtd 90. *45 Monmouth Road, London N9 0JB* Tel 0181-807 4329

REES, Gruffydd Nicholas. b 23. Univ of Wales (Lamp) BA46. Wycliffe Hall Ox 46. **d** 48 **p** 49. C Fishguard *St D* 48-51; C Betws w Ammanford 51-53; C Carmarthen St Dav 53-57; C Epsom St Martin *Guildf* 57-62; V Llanbister and Llanbadarn Fynydd w Llananno *S & B* 62-75; V New Radnor and Llanfihangel Nantmelan etc 75-84; V Llangenni and Llanbedr Ystrad Yw w Patricio 84-88; rtd 88. *Trefilan, 26 Lakeside Avenue, Llandrindod Wells LD1 5NT* Tel (01597) 825451

✠**REES, The Rt Revd John Ivor.** b 26. Univ of Wales (Abth) BA50. Westcott Ho Cam 50. **d** 52 **p** 53 **c** 88. C Fishguard w Llanychar *St D* 52-55; C Llangathen w Llanfihangel Cilfargen 55-57; P-in-c Uzmaston and Boulston 57-59; V Slebech and Uzmaston w Boulston 59-65; V Llangollen and Trevor *St As* 65-74; RD Llangollen 70-74; R Wrexham 74-76; Can St As Cathl 75-76; Dean Ban 76-88; V Ban Cathl Par 79-88; Asst Bp St D 88-91; Adn St D 88-91; Bp St D 91-95; Sub-Prelate OStJ from 93; rtd 95. *Llys Dewi, 45 Clover Park, Uzmaston Road, Haverfordwest SA61 1UE* Tel (01437) 764846

REES, John Martin Rawlins Gore. b 30. St D Coll Lamp BA53. **d** 55 **p** 57. C Mold *St As* 55-56; C Broughton 56-59; C Newtown 59-61; V Penycae 61-73; V Northop 73-83; V Bickerton w Bickley *Ches* 83-91; Lic to Offic from 91; rtd 95. *Hafod, 9 High Park, Gwernaffield, Mold CH7 5EE* Tel (01352) 740412

REES, John Philip Walford. b 41. St D Coll Lamp BA62 Linacre Coll Ox BA64 MA69 Univ of Wales (Cardiff) BD73. Wycliffe Hall Ox 62. **d** 64 **p** 65. C Reading St Jo *Ox* 64-67; V Patrick *S & M* 67-68; C Pontypool *Mon* 68-70; Area Sec (Dios Glouc, Heref and Worc) CMS 70-75; V Bream *Glouc* 75-91; Team Ldr Ichthus Chr Fellowship 91-96; R Glyncorrwg w Afan Vale and Cymmer Afan *Llan* from 96. *The Vicarage, 17 School Road, Cymmer, Port Talbot SA13 3EG*

REES, The Ven John Wynford Joshua. b 24. Univ of Wales (Lamp) BA52. **d** 53 **p** 54. C Aberystwyth *St D* 53-60; V Llanyre w Llanfihangel Helygen, Llanwrthwl etc *S & B* 60-71; R Llanyre w

Llanfihangel Helygen and Diserth 71-87; V Llanllyr-yn-Rhos w Llanfihangel Helygen 87-94; RD Maelienydd 74-87; Hon Can Brecon Cathl 77-79; Can Res 79-94; Treas 83-87; Adn Brecon 87-94; rtd 94. *Denebrook, Ithan Road, Llandrindod Wells LD1 6AS* Tel (01597) 823573

REES, Canon Judith Margaret (Judy). b 39. Southn Univ BTh89. **dss** 86 **d** 87 **p** 94. Sanderstead All SS *S'wark* 86-87; Par Dn 87; Dir Cottesloe Chr Tr Progr *Ox* from 89; Par Dn Gt Horwood 89-91; Par Dn Winslow w Gt Horwood and Addington 91-94; C from 94; RD Claydon from 96; Hon Can Ch Ch from 97. *15 Weston Road, Great Horwood, Milton Keynes MK17 0QR* Tel (01296) 713603

✠**REES, The Rt Revd Leslie Lloyd.** b 19. Kelham Th Coll 36. **d** 42 **p** 43 **c** 80. C Roath St Sav *Llan* 42-45; Asst Chapl HM Pris Cardiff 42-45; Chapl HM Pris Dur 45-48; V Princetown *Ex* 48-55; Chapl HM Pris Dartmoor 48-55; Chapl HM Pris Win 55-62; Chapl Gen of Pris 62-80; Hon Can Cant Cathl *Cant* 66-80; Chapl to The Queen 71-80; Suff Bp Shrewsbury *Lich* 80-86; rtd 86; Asst Bp Win from 87. *Kingfisher Lodge, 20 Arle Gardens, Alresford, Hants SO24 9BA* Tel (01962) 734619

REES, Michael Lloyd. b 51. St D Coll Lamp DipTh74. **d** 74 **p** 75. C Cardigan and Mwnt and Y Ferwig *St D* 74-77; Min Can St D Cathl 77-81; TV Aberystwyth 81-83; Dioc Children's Adv 83-92; V Pen-boyr 83-88; V Henfynyw w Aberaeron and Llanddewi Aberarth from 88; RD Glyn Aeron from 95. *The Vicarage, Panteg Road, Aberaeron SA46 0EP* Tel (01545) 570433

REES, Percival Antony Everard. b 35. Pemb Coll Ox BA56 MA59. Clifton Th Coll 58. **d** 60 **p** 61. C Heatherlands St Jo *Sarum* 60-65 and 69-70; India 65-69; V W Hampstead St Luke *Lon* 70-82; Lect Oak Hill Th Coll 82-86; V Enfield Ch Ch Trent Park *Lon* from 87. *Christ Church Vicarage, Chalk Lane, Barnet, Herts EN4 9JQ* Tel 0181-441 1230 or 449 0556

REES, Peter Frederick Ransom. b 18. Lon Univ BA47. Linc Th Coll 47. **d** 49 **p** 50. C Leigh St Mary *Man* 49-52; C Bedford Leigh 52-53; V Laneside *Blackb* 53-83; rtd 83; Lic to Offic *Blackb* from 84. *11 Rydal Road, Morecambe, Lancs LA3 1DT* Tel (01524) 424482

REES, Canon Richard John Edward Williams. b 36. Univ of Wales (Lamp) BA58. St Mich Coll Llan 58. **d** 60 **p** 61. C St Issells *St D* 60-64; C Llanedy 64-67; V Whitchurch w Solva and St Elvis 67-77; RD Dewisland and Fishguard from 73; V Whitchurch w Solva and St Elvis w Brawdy etc from 77; Can St D Cathl from 87. *The Vicarage, Whitchurch, Solva, Haverfordwest SA62 6UD* Tel (01437) 721281

REES, Canon Richard Michael. b 35. St Pet Hall Ox BA57 MA61. Tyndale Hall Bris 57. **d** 59 **p** 60. C Crowborough *Chich* 59-62; C Clifton Ch Ch w Em *Bris* 62-64; V Clevedon Ch Ch *B & W* 64-72; V Cambridge H Trin *Ely* 72-84; Lic to Offic *S'wark* 84-90; Chief Sec CA 84-90; Can Res Ches Cathl *Ches* from 90; Dioc Missr from 90. *5 Abbey Green, Chester CH1 2JH* Tel (01244) 347500

REES, Canon Sidney. b 12. St D Coll Lamp BA34 St Mich Coll Llan 35. **d** 37 **p** 38. C Llandeilo Fawr w Llandyfeisant *St D* 37-40; C Pembrey w Burry Port 40-47; V St Ishmael's w Llan-saint and Ferryside 47-65; RD Kidwelly 64-65; V Whitland and Kiffig 65-79; Can St D Cathl 77-79; rtd 79. *10 Morfa Lane, Carmarthen SA31 3AS* Tel (01267) 235757

REES, Vivian John Howard. b 51. Southn Univ LLB72 Ox Univ BA79 MA84 Leeds Univ MPhil84. Wycliffe Hall Ox 76. **d** 79 **p** 80. C Moor Allerton *Ripon* 79-82; Sierra Leone 82-86; Lic to Offic *Ox* from 86; Dep Dioc Reg from 90. *Oxford Diocesan Registry, 16 Beaumont Street, Oxford OX1 2LZ* Tel (01865) 241974 Fax 726274 E-mail johnrees@mailbox.rmplc.co.uk

REES, William David Cledwyn. b 25. FRGS54 Qu Coll Cam BA49 DipEd50 MA52 Univ of Wales MA75 PhD81. St Deiniol's Hawarden 63. **d** 65 **p** 66. Hon C Rhyl w St Ann *St As* 65-72; Chapl and Lect St Mary's Coll Ban 72-77; Lic to Offic *Ban* 72-77; Lect Univ of Wales (Ban) from 77; Chapl Univ of Wales (Ban) *Ban* 77-84; Sec Dioc Schs Cttee 84-86. *Anwylfa, Fron Park Avenue, Llanfairfechan LL33 0AS* Tel (01248) 680054

REES, Canon William Elfyn. b 17. St D Coll Lamp BA37 Wycliffe Hall Ox 38. **d** 40 **p** 45. C Richmond *Ripon* 40-41; C Leeds St Geo 45-46; C Warblington and Emsworth *Portsm* 46-50; R Blendworth, Chalton and Idsworth 50-62; R Alverstoke 62-82; rtd 82. *28 Church Close, Llangynidr, Crickhowell NP8 1NY* Tel (01874) 730125

REESE, Preb John David. b 49. Cuddesdon Coll 73. **d** 76 **p** 77. C Kidderminster St Mary *Worc* 76-81; Malaysia 81-85; V Bishop's Castle w Mainstone *Heref* 85-91; RD Clun Forest 87-91; V Tupsley 91-93; P-in-c Hampton Bishop and Mordiford w Dormington 91-93; V Tupsley w Hampton Bishop from 93; RD Heref City from 96; Preb Heref Cathl from 96. *The Vicarage, 107 Church Road, Hereford HR1 1RT* Tel (01432) 274490

REEVE, Canon Brian Charles. b 36. Lon Univ BSc57 BD60. Tyndale Hall Bris 58. **d** 61 **p** 62. C Eccleston St Luke *Liv* 61-63; C Upton (Overchurch) *Ches* 63-65; C Pemberton St Mark Newtown *Liv* 65-68; V Macclesfield Ch Ch *Ches* 68-74; V Stone Ch Ch *Lich* 74-84; RD Trentham 77-84; V Hoole *Ches* 84-94; Chapl Ches City Hosp 84-91; P-in-c Alderley *Ches* from 94; Hon Can Ches Cathl from 94. *St Mary's Rectory, Nether Alderley, Macclesfield, Cheshire SK10 4TW* Tel (01625) 583134

REEVE, David Michael. b 44. St Cath Coll Cam BA67 MA71. Coll of Resurr Mirfield 68. **d** 70 **p** 71. C Willingdon *Chich* 70-73; C Hove All SS 73-76; C Moulsecoomb 76-80; R Singleton 80-90; V E Dean 80-90; V W Dean 80-90; R Hurstpierpoint from 90. *The Rectory, 21 Cuckfield Road, Hurstpierpoint, Hassocks, W Sussex BN6 9RP* Tel (01273) 832203

REEVE, John Richard. b 65. Southn Univ BA86 La Sainte Union Coll PGCE88. Ripon Coll Cuddesdon 95. **d** 97. C Hale *Guildf* from 97. *195 Eton Place, Sandy Hill, Farnham, Surrey GU9 0EG* Tel (01252) 713826

REEVE, Kenneth John (Ken). b 42. Sarum & Wells Th Coll DCM93. **d** 93 **p** 94. C Thorpe St Matt *Nor* 93-96; P-in-c S Lynn from 96. *The Rectory, 33 Goodwins Road, King's Lynn, Norfolk PE30 5QX* Tel (01553) 771779

REEVE, Kenneth Robert. b 23. St Cath Coll Ox BA49 MA53. Sarum Th Coll 64. **d** 68 **p** 69. Hon C Farleigh Hungerford w Tellisford *B & W* 68-71; Hon C Norton St Philip 72-74; Hon C Hinton Charterhouse 72-74; Seychelles 74-76; Perm to Offic *B & W* from 77; Perm to Offic *Chich* 78-82. *Sundial, Hill Close, Wincanton, Somerset BA9 9NF* Tel (01963) 33369

REEVE, Richard Malcolm. b 64. Reading Univ BSc85. Trin Coll Bris BA92. **d** 92 **p** 93. C Northolt St Mary *Lon* 92-95; C Acton Green from 95. *276 Osborne Road, London W3 8SR* Tel 0181-993 3237

REEVE, Dr Richard Noel. b 29. MB, ChB. St Deiniol's Hawarden. **d** 84 **p** 85. Hon C Norton *Ches* 84-85; C Filey *York* 85-87; TV Brayton 87-90; rtd 90; Perm to Offic *Man* 90-93; Res Min Bicton, Montford w Shrawardine and Fitz *Lich* from 97. *The Rectory, 15 Brookside, Bicton, Shrewsbury SY3 8ED* Tel (01785) 813796

REEVE, Preb Roger Patrick. b 42. Fitzw Coll Cam BA65 MA68. Coll of Resurr Mirfield. **d** 67 **p** 68. C Barnstaple St Pet w H Trin *Ex* 67-74; V Ernesettle 74-78; V Braunton from 78; RD Barnstaple 85-93; Preb Ex Cathl from 92. *The Vicarage, Church Street, Braunton, Devon EX33 2EL* Tel (01271) 813367

REEVE, Canon Ronald Ernest. b 22. St Pet Hall Ox BA48 MA52 BD54 Ox Univ DPhil76. Wycliffe Hall Ox 48. **d** 50 **p** 51. C Bexleyheath Ch Ch *Roch* 50-52; V New Hythe 52-54; Canada 54-59 and from 63; Vice-Prin Cranmer Hall Dur 60-63; Prof K Coll NS 63-68; Prof Bp's Univ Lennoxville & Can Quebec Cathl 68-88; rtd 88. *1145 Wintergreen Crescent, Kingston, Ontario, Canada K7P 2G5* Tel Kingston (613) 634 1479

REEVES, Christopher. b 30. Nottm Univ BA53. Wells Th Coll 53. **d** 55 **p** 56. C Rowbarton *B & W* 55-59; C Cant St Greg *Cant* 59-61; Chapl Schiedam Miss to Seamen *Eur* 61-67; V Barkingside H Trin *Chelmsf* 67-97; rtd 97. *3 Albany Close, Goonown St Agnes, Cornwall TR5 0XE*

REEVES, David Eric. b 46. Sarum Th Coll 68. **d** 71 **p** 72. C Guildf H Trin w St Mary *Guildf* 71-74; C Warmsworth *Sheff* 74-78; V Herringthorpe 78-90; V Cleveleys *Blackb* from 90; RD Poulton from 94. *The Vicarage, Rough Lea Road, Thornton Cleveleys, Lancs FY5 1DP* Tel (01253) 852153

REEVES, Donald St John. b 34. Qu Coll Cam BA57 MA61. Cuddesdon Coll 62. **d** 63 **p** 64. C Maidstone All SS w St Phil *Cant* 63-65; Bp's Dom Chapl *S'wark* 65-68; V St Helier 69-80; R Westmr St Jas *Lon* from 80. *St James's Rectory, 197 Piccadilly, London W1V 9LF* Tel 0171-734 4511

REEVES, Elizabeth Anne. *See* THOMAS, Mrs Elizabeth Anne

REEVES, Gillian Patricia. b 46. S'wark Ord Course 87. **d** 90 **p** 94. Par Dn Shirley St Geo *S'wark* 90-94; C 94-96; C Caterham from 96. *The Parsonage, 43 Banstead Road, Caterham, Surrey CR3 5QG* Tel (01883) 342422

REEVES, Graham. b 65. Chich Th Coll BTh94. **d** 94 **p** 95. C Cardiff St Mary and St Steph w St Dyfrig etc *Llan* 94-95; C Roath St Marg from 95. *St Philip's House, Cairnmuir Road, Tremorfa, Cardiff CF2 2RU* Tel (01222) 460600

REEVES, James Lacey (Jim). b 23. FCIS58. S'wark Ord Course 60. **d** 74 **p** 75. NSM Wisborough Green *Chich* 74-81; C Horsham 81-83; R W Chiltington 83-92; rtd 93. *4 Borough House, North Street, Midhurst, W Sussex GU29 9DX* Tel (01730) 815122

REEVES, John Graham. b 44. Kelham Th Coll 64. **d** 69 **p** 71. C Aston cum Aughton *Sheff* 69-71; C Ribbleton *Blackb* 72-74; C Cleveleys 74-75; P-in-c Huncoat 75-77; V 77-82; V Knuzden 82-92; V Sandylands from 92. *St John's Vicarage, 2 St John's Avenue, Morecambe, Lancs LA3 1EU* Tel (01524) 411299

REEVES, Kenneth Gordon. b 32. K Coll Lon BD53 AKC53 CertEd54. Ripon Coll Cuddesdon 86. **d** 87 **p** 88. NSM Dorchester *Ox* 87-89; V Deddington w Barford, Clifton and Hempton from 89. *The Vicarage, Earls Lane, Deddington, Banbury, Oxon OX15 0TJ* Tel (01869) 338329

REEVES, Kenneth William. b 38. TCD 67 NUI DipSocSc76. **d** 69 **p** 70. C Killowen *D & R* 69-70; I Ardara 70-76; TV Quidenham *Nor* 76-81; V Swaffham 81-86; Chapl Nor Coll of Educn 86-91; P-in-c Lakenham St Alb *Nor* 86-91; rtd 92; Perm to Offic *Nor* from 92. *15 Morris Close, Stoke Holy Cross, Norwich NR14 8LL* Tel (01508) 494583

REEVES, Nicholas John Harding. b 44. ALCD69. **d** 69 **p** 70. ' Upton (Overchurch) *Ches* 69-72; C Woodlands *Sheff* 72- C-in-c Cranham Park CD *Chelmsf* 74-79; V Cranham 79-88; R Aldridge *Lich* from 88. *The Rectory, 14 The ' Aldridge, Walsall WS9 8NH* Tel (01922) 52414

✠**REEVES, The Rt Revd Paul Alfred.** b 32. GCMG85 GCVO86. Univ of NZ BA55 MA56 St Pet Hall Ox BA61 MA65 Ox Univ Hon DCL85 Wellington Univ (NZ) Hon LLD89 Gen Th Sem NY Hon DD92. St Jo Coll Auckland LTh58. **d** 58 **p** 60 **c** 71. New Zealand 58-59 and from 64; C Ox St Mary V *Ox* 59-61; C Kirkley *Nor* 61-63; C Lewisham St Mary *S'wark* 63-64; Bp Waiapu 71-79; Bp Auckland 79-85; Abp New Zealand 80-85; Gov Gen NZ 85-90; KStJ from 86; ACC Rep at United Nations 91-93; Asst Bp New York 91-93; Dean Te Rau Kahikatea Th Coll Auckland 94-95. *16E Cathedral Place, Parnell, Auckland, New Zealand* Tel Auckland (9) 302 2913 or 373 7599 ext 4754 Fax 308 2312 E-mail p.reeves@auckland.ac.nz

REGAN, Brian. b 46. MBIM80. WMMTC 88. **d** 91 **p** 92. C Cov St Jo *Cov* 91-94; FSJ from 93; V Tile Hill *Cov* from 94. *St Oswald's Vicarage, 228 Jardine Crescent, Coventry CV4 9PL* Tel (01203) 465072

REGAN, Philip. b 49. Qu Mary Coll Lon BSc MSc. Wycliffe Hall Ox 81. **d** 83 **p** 84. Hon C Scotforth *Blackb* 83-89; P-in-c Combe St Nicholas w Wambrook *B & W* from 89; P-in-c Whitestaunton from 89. *The Vicarage, Combe St Nicholas, Chard, Somerset TA20 3NJ* Tel (01460) 62121

REGINALD, Brother. *See* BOX, Reginald Gilbert

REGLAR, Canon Gerald John. b 11. Melbourne Univ BA Ox Univ MA48. Kelham Th Coll 34. **d** 37 **p** 38. C Cowley St Jo *Ox* 37-40; Australia from 40. *13 Binnowie Street, Ingle Farm, S Australia 5098* Tel Adelaide (8) 263 8473

REID, Amanda Joy. *See* MARRIOTT, Mrs Amanda Joy

REID, Andrew John. b 47. Birm Univ BEd70 Man Univ MEd76 Lon Univ DipRS88. S'wark Ord Course 88. **d** 88 **p** 89. NSM Westerham *Roch* 88-90; Chapl Abp Tenison's Gr Sch Kennington from 90. *Archbishop Tenison's School, 55 Kennington Oval, London SE11 5SR* Tel 0171-435 3771 or 435 6126

REID, Canon Colin Guthrie. b 30. **d** 56 **p** 57. C Kendal St Thos *Carl* 56-59; C Crosthwaite Keswick 59-60; R Caldbeck w Castle Sowerby 60-76; RD Wigton 69-70; P-in-c Sebergham 75-76; R Caldbeck, Castle Sowerby and Sebergham 76-93; Hon Can Carl Cathl 88-93; rtd 93; Perm to Offic *Carl* from 93. *Mellbreak, Longthwaite Road, Wigton, Cumbria CA7 9JR* Tel (016973) 45625

REID, Donald. b 58. Glas Univ LLB79 Pemb Coll Ox MPhil81 Edin Univ BD85. Edin Th Coll 82. **d** 85 **p** 86. C Greenock *Glas* 85-88; C Baillieston 88-91; R 91-95; C Glas St Serf 87-91; R 91-95; Chapl Glas Univ from 89; Chapl Glas Caledonian Univ from 95; Chapl Strathclyde Univ from 95. *212 Wilton Street, Glasgow G20 6BL* Tel 0141-946 1145

REID, The Very Revd Douglas William John. b 34. Edin Th Coll 60. **d** 63 **p** 64. C Ayr *Glas* 63-68; R Glas St Jas 68-73; R Glas St Ninian from 73; Syn Clerk from 79; Can St Mary's Cathl from 79; Dean Glas 87-96. *32 Glencairn Drive, Glasgow G41 4PW* Tel 0141-423 1247

✠**REID, The Rt Revd Gavin Hunter.** b 34. K Coll Lon BA56. Oak Hill Th Coll 58. **d** 60 **p** 61 **c** 92. C E Ham St Paul *Chelmsf* 60-63; C Rainham 63-66; Publications Sec CPAS 66-71; Hon C St Paul's Cray St Barn *Roch* 68-71; Ed Sec USCL 71-74; Hon C Woking St Jo *Guildf* 72-92; Sec for Evang CPAS 74-92; Consultant Missr CPAS and BMU Adv 90-92; Suff Bp Maidstone *Cant* from 92; Six Preacher Cant Cathl 92-97. *Bishop's House, Pett Lane, Charing, Ashford, Kent TN27 0DL* Tel (01233) 712950 Fax 713543

REID, Herbert Alan. b 31. AKC55. **d** 56 **p** 57. C Penwortham St Mary *Blackb* 56-59; C-in-c Penwortham St Leon CD 59-63; V Brierfield 63-72; V Warton St Paul 72-79; V Read in Whalley from 79. *The Vicarage, George Lane, Read, Burnley, Lancs BB12 7RQ* Tel (01282) 771361

REID, Hugh Gamble. b 33. Roch Th Coll 63. **d** 64 **p** 64. C Martin w Thornton *Linc* 64-66; Bp's Youth Chapl 66-69; C Alford w Rigsby 66-69; Chapl HM Borstal Everthorpe 69-71; Chapl HM Pris Dur 71-74; Chapl HM Pris Wakef 74-77; V Northowram *Wakef* 77-79; Chapl HM Pris Coldingley 79-81; Chapl HM Rem Cen Risley 81-85; Chapl HM Pris Holloway 85-88; C Guilden Morden *Ely* 88-89; C Shingay Gp of Par 90; R Upwell Ch Ch 90-93; R Welney 90-93; rtd 93; Perm to Offic *Ely* from 93. *Banff, 23 Northwold, Ely, Cambs CB6 1BG* Tel (01353) 663924

REID, Canon Ian Davison. b 37. Liv Univ BA61 MA63. Clifton Th Coll 63. **d** 65 **p** 66. C Edge Hill St Cath *Liv* 65-68; C Heworth *York* 68-76; V Linthorpe from 76; Can and Preb York Minster from 90. *5 Park Road South, Middlesbrough, Cleveland TS5 6LD* Tel (01642) 817306

REID, James. b 46. Strathclyde Univ BSc69. WMMTC 88. **d** 91 … C Attleborough *Cov* 91-95; V Walsall Pleck and Bescot *Lich* … *St John's Vicarage, Vicarage Terrace, Walsall* …l (01922) 31989

…30. Qu Coll Cam BA53 MA72. St Mich Coll …ntwit Major and St Donat's *Llan* 80-83; …, V Laleston w Tythegston 84; V Laleston …thyr Mawr 84-88; V Roath St Marg from … *Waterloo Road, Cardiff CF2 5AD* Tel

…**nas.** b 45. Oak Hill Th Coll 66. **d** 70 **p** 71. C …*y* 70-73; C Leyland St Andr *Blackb* 73-78; V Halliwell St Luke *Man* 78-95; V Southport Ch Ch *Liv* from 95. *The Vicarage, 12 Gloucester Road, Southport, Merseyside PR8 2AU* Tel (01704) 565120

REID, Canon William Frederick (Eric). b 22. OBE88. TCD BA45 MA53. **d** 46 **p** 47. C Belfast Ardoyne *Conn* 46-49; C Finaghy 49-52; C Dublin Donnybrook *D & G* 52-54; I Carbury *M & K* 54-59; Dep Dir The Samaritans 59-67; C St Steph Walbrook and St Swithun etc *Lon* 59-67; Chapl Netherne Hosp Coulsdon 67-76; C-in-c Netherne St Luke CD *S'wark* 67-76; Lic to Offic from 76; Sec and Dir Tr Gen Syn Hosp Chapl Coun 76-87; Hon Can Newc Cathl *Newc* 79-88; rtd 88. *65 Lagham Park, South Godstone, Godstone, Surrey RH9 8EP* Tel (01342) 893312

REID, The Ven William Gordon. b 43. Edin Univ MA63 Keble Coll Ox BA66 MA72. Edin Th Coll 63 Cuddesdon Coll 66. **d** 67 **p** 68. C Edin St Salvador *Edin* 67-69; Chapl and Tutor Sarum Th Coll 69-72; R Edin St Mich and All SS *Edin* 72-84; Provost St Andr Cathl Inverness *Mor* 84-87; Chapl Ankara *Eur* 87-89; Chapl Stockholm w Gavle and Vasteras 89-92; V Gen to Bp Eur from 92; Can Gib Cathl from 92; Adn in Eur from 96; P-in-c St Mich Cornhill w St Pet le Poer etc *Lon* from 97. *4 The Courtyard, Barnsbury Terrace, London N1 1JH* Tel 0171-607 3834 or 976 8001 Fax 976 8002 E-mail 100642.731@compuserve.com

REIGATE, Archdeacon of. *See* BADDELEY, The Ven Martin James

REILLY, Frederick James. b 29. CITC 70. **d** 73 **p** 74. C Agherton *Conn* 73-75; C Ballymena 75-82; I Ballyscullion *D & R* from 82. *The Rectory, 8 Ballynease Road, Bellaghy, Co Londonderry BT45 8JD* Tel (01648) 386214

REILLY, Thomas Gerard (Gerry). b 38. **d** 64 **p** 64. In RC Ch 64-73; Hon C Clapton Park All So *Lon* 73-76; Hon C Haggerston All SS 76-78; Hon C Walthamstow St Sav *Chelmsf* 79-85; P-in-c Forest Gate Em w Upton Cross 85-89; V 89-92; V Chaddesden St Phil *Derby* from 92; RD Derby N from 95. *St Philip's Vicarage, Taddington Road, Chaddesden, Derby DE21 4JU* Tel (01332) 673428

REILY, Paul Alan. b 59. UEA BA81. St Jo Coll Nottm DTS91 MA92. **d** 92 **p** 93. C Westcliff St Mich *Chelmsf* 92-96; P-in-c Barkingside St Cedd from 96. *10 Marston Road, Ilford, Essex IG5 0LY* Tel 0181-551 3406

REINDORP, David Peter Edington. b 52. Trin Coll Cam BA82 MA86 CQSW DASS. Westcott Ho Cam 79. **d** 83 **p** 84. C Chesterton Gd Shep *Ely* 83-85; C Hitchin *St Alb* 85-88; V Waterbeach *Ely* from 88; R Landbeach from 88; OCF from 88; RD Quy *Ely* from 94. *The Vicarage, 8 Chapel Street, Waterbeach, Cambridge CB5 9HR* Tel (01223) 860353

REINDORP, Michael Christopher Julian. b 44. Trin Coll Cam BA67 MA70. Cuddesdon Coll 67 United Th Coll Bangalore 68. **d** 69 **p** 70. C Poplar *Lon* 69-74; V Chatham St Wm *Roch* 74-84; R Stantonbury *Ox* 84-87; TR Stantonbury and Willen 87-92; P-in-c Richmond St Mary w St Matthias and St Jo *S'wark* 92-95; TR from 96. *The Vicarage, Ormond Road, Richmond, Surrey TW10 6TH* Tel 0181-940 0362

REISS, Michael Jonathan. b 58. FIBiol90 Trin Coll Cam BA78 MA82 PhD82 PGCE83. EAMTC 87. **d** 90 **p** 91. NSM Comberton *Ely* from 90. *7 Barrons Way, Comberton, Cambridge CB3 7EQ* Tel (01223) 262958

REISS, Peter Henry. b 62. Hertf Coll Ox BA85 MA91 Natal Univ MA95. Trin Coll Bris DipHE90 St Jo Coll Nottm 95. **d** 95 **p** 96. C Sherwood *S'well* from 95. *56 Edwinstowe Drive, Nottingham NG5 3EP* Tel 0115-962 0899

REISS, The Ven Robert Paul. b 43. Trin Coll Cam BA67 MA71. Westcott Ho Cam 67. **d** 69 **p** 70. C St Jo Wood *Lon* 69-73; Bangladesh 73; Chapl Trin Coll Cam 73-78; Selection Sec ACCM 78-85; Sen Selection Sec 83; TR Grantham *Linc* 86-96; RD Grantham 92-96; Adn Surrey *Guildf* from 96. *The Archdeacon's House, New Road, Wormley, Godalming, Surrey GU8 5SU* Tel (01428) 682563

REITH, Ivor Stuart Weston. b 16. Ridley Hall Cam 65. **d** 66 **p** 67. C Eastbourne H Trin *Chich* 66-69; R Angmering 69-81; rtd 81; Perm to Offic *Chich* from 84. *8 Windmill Close, Hove, E Sussex BN3 7LJ* Tel (01273) 733187

REITH, Robert Michael. b 55. Oak Hill Th Coll BA83. **d** 83 **p** 84. C Kendal St Thos *Carl* 83-87; C Leyland St Andr *Blackb* 87-92; V Leyland St Jo 92-94; TR Dagenham *Chelmsf* from 94. *The Vicarage, Church Lane, Dagenham, Essex RM10 9UL* Tel 0181-592 1339

REMPEY, Philip Roland. b 19. Glouc Th Course 74. **d** 76 **p** 76. NSM Charlton Kings St Mary *Glouc* 76-88; Perm to Offic from 88. *87 Ravensgate Road, Charlton Kings, Cheltenham, Glos GL53 8NS* Tel (01242) 519313

RENDALL, Canon John Albert. b 43. Hull Univ BTh84 MA89. Ripon Hall Ox 65. **d** 68 **p** 69. C Southsea St Simon *Portsm* 68-71; C Wallington H Trin *S'wark* 71-77; P-in-c Rufforth w Moor Monkton and Hessay *York* 77-79; R from 79; P-in-c Long Marston 77-79; R from 79; RD New Ainsty from 85; Can and Preb York Minster from 94. *The Vicarage, Rufforth, York YO2 3QB* Tel (01904) 738262

RENDALL, Richard John. b 54. Solicitor 78 Wadh Coll Ox BA76 LLB76 MA92. Wycliffe Hall Ox 90. **d** 92 **p** 93. C Heswall *Ches* from 92. *15 Castle Drive, Heswall, Wirral, Merseyside L60 4RY* Tel 0151-342 1598

RENFREY, Edward Donald John-Baptist. b 53. DipTh. St Barn Coll Adelaide 75. **d** 76 **p** 77. Australia 76-84; Chapl RN from 84. *Royal Naval Chaplaincy Service, Room 203, Victory Building, HM Naval Base, Portsmouth PO1 3LS* Tel (01705) 727903 Fax 727112

RENISON, Gary James. b 62. SS Hild & Bede Coll Dur BA83. Ridley Hall Cam 84. **d** 86 **p** 87. C Stapenhill w Cauldwell *Derby* 86-89; C Cheadle Hulme St Andr *Ches* 89-92; Min Cheadle Hulme Em CD 92-95; P-in-c Bar Hill *Ely* from 95. *108 Stonefield, Bar Hill, Cambridge CB3 8TE* Tel (01954) 781629

RENNARD, Edward Lionel. b 51. Nottm Univ BTh80. Linc Th Coll 76. **d** 80 **p** 81. C Old Brumby *Linc* 80-82; C-in-c Gt Grimsby St Matt Fairfield CD 82-86; V Fairfield St Matt 86-88; V Hykeham 88-91; TR from 91. *The Rectory, Mill Lane, North Hykeham, Lincoln LN6 9PA* Tel (01522) 681168 E-mail edward.r2@ukonline.co.uk

RENNARD, Margaret Rose. b 49. CertEd75. Linc Th Coll 76. **d** 87 **p** 94. C Fairfield St Matt *Linc* 87-88; C Hykeham from 88; Chapl HM Pris Morton Hall from 91. *The Rectory, Mill Lane, North Hykeham, Lincoln LN6 9PA* Tel (01522) 681168 Fax 868068

RENNIE, Iain Hugh. b 43. Ripon Coll Cuddesdon 88. **d** 90 **p** 91. C Poulton-le-Sands w Morecambe St Laur *Blackb* 90-94; V Hornby w Claughton from 94. *The Vicarage, Main Street, Hornby, Lancaster LA2 8JY* Tel (015242) 221238

RENNIE, Paul Antony. b 58. Heriot-Watt Univ BSc82 Edin Univ LTh. **d** 87 **p** 88. C Nairn *Mor* 87-90; C Forres 87-90; C Edin St Pet *Edin* 90-92; Dep Chapl HM Pris Leeds 92; Chapl HM Young Offender Inst Hindley 93-95; Chapl HM Pris Liv from 95. *HM Prison, 68 Hornby Road, Liverpool L9 3DF* Tel 0151-525 5971 Fax 525 0813

RENNISON, Walter Patrick. b 18. MBE52. TCD BA40 MA45. **d** 42 **p** 43. C Ballymacarrett St Martin *D & D* 42-45; CF 45-73; V Milland *Chich* 73-87; rtd 87; Perm to Offic *Guildf* from 87. *14 Heathfield Court, Fleet, Hants GU13 8DX* Tel (01252) 615358

RENOUF, Peter Mark. b 30. Down Coll Cam BA55 MA59 Cam Univ DipEd56. Ridley Hall Cam. **d** 58 **p** 59. C Rainham *Chelmsf* 58-61; Asst Chapl Wellington Coll Berks 61-63; Chapl 63-69; V Eastbourne All SS *Chich* 69-78; R Farnborough *Guildf* 78-84; C Welford w Wickham and Gt Shefford *Ox* 85-86; C Welford w Wickham and Gt Shefford, Boxford etc 86-89; P-in-c Beedon and Peasemore w W Ilsley and Farnborough 89-97. *The Vicarage, Beedon, Newbury, Berks RG16 8SW* Tel (01635) 281244

RENOUF, Canon Robert Wilson. b 28. Niagara Univ BSc51 Pacific State Univ PhD77. Claremont Sch of Th DMin81 Lambeth STh86 Selly Oak Coll CMM86 Gen Th Sem (NY) MDiv54. **d** 54 **p** 55. USA 54-56 and 58-82 and from 91; Nicaragua 56-58 and 82-85; Fell and Tutor Coll of the Ascension Selly Oak 85-86; Hon PV S'wark Cathl *S'wark* 86-91; Miss Personnel Sec USPG 86-88; Adv Decade of Evang ACC 89-91. *4502 North Caminito de la Puerta, Tuscon, Arizona 85718, USA*

RENOWDEN, The Very Revd Charles Raymond. b 23. Univ of Wales (Lamp) BA44 Selw Coll Cam BA49 MA53. Ridley Hall Cam 50. **d** 51 **p** 52. C Hubberston *St D* 51-55; Lect St D Coll Lamp 55-67; Sen Lect 67-71; Dean and Lib St As Cathl *St As* 71-92; P-in-c Cefn 71-88; V St As 71-80; V St As and Tremeirchion 80-92; rtd 92. *17 Llys Idris, St Asaph LL17 0AJ* Tel (01745) 584591

RENOWDEN, The Ven Glyndwr Rhys. b 29. CB87. St D Coll Lamp BA49 LTh52. **d** 52 **p** 53. C Tenby and Gumfreston *St D* 52-55; C Chepstow *Mon* 55-58; Chapl RAF 58-75; Asst Chapl-in-Chief RAF 75-83; Chapl-in-Chief RAF 83-88; QHC from 80; Can and Preb Linc Cathl *Linc* 83-88; P-in-c Llanfallteg w Clunderwen and Castell Dwyran *St D* from 89. *Red Cedars, Kenystyle, Penally, Tenby SA70 7PH* Tel (01834) 842673

RENSHAW, Anthony. b 40. McGill Univ Montreal LTh87 DipMin87. Montreal Dioc Th Coll 83. **d** 87 **p** 88. Canada 87-90; P-in-c Ainsdale *Liv* 90-91; V from 91. *The Vicarage, 708 Liverpool Road, Southport, Merseyside PR8 3QE* Tel (01704) 577760

RENSHAW, David William. b 59. Oak Hill Th Coll BA85. **d** 85 **p** 86. C Shawbury *Lich* 85-88; V Childs Ercall 88-92; R Stoke upon Tern 88-92; V Stoneleigh *Guildf* 92-97; RD Epsom 95-97; Chapl St Catherine's Hospice Scarborough from 97; Chapl Scarborough Hosps from 97. *185 Dean Road, Scarborough, N Yorkshire YO12 7JH* Tel (01723) 371107

RENSHAW, Peter Selwyn Kay. b 29. Keble Coll Ox BA52 MA64. St Steph Ho Ox 52. **d** 64 **p** 65. Lic to Offic *Ox* 64-66; Chapl RN 66-70; Chapl Athens St Paul and Br Emb *Eur* 71-74; Gothenburg 74-75; Chapl RN Sch Haslemere 75-81; Costa Blanca *Eur* 81-82; R Ewelme *Ox* 83-85; R Ewelme, Brightwell Baldwin, Cuxham w Easington 85-92; rtd 92. *Lovedays House, Painswick, Stroud, Glos GL6 6QB* Tel (01452) 812811

RENSHAW, Timothy John. **d** 97. C Calverton *S'well* from 97; C Epperstone from 97; C Gonalston from 97; C Oxton from 97. *52 St Michael's Avenue, Gedling, Nottingham NG4 3NN* Tel 0115-952 6428

RENWICK, Colin. b 30. St Aid Birkenhead. **d** 59 **p** 60. C Drypool St Columba w St Andr and St Pet *York* 59-62; C Wigan St Cath *Liv* 62-64; Min Thornton CD 64-77; V Thornton 77-97; RD Bootle 83-89; rtd 97. *27 Briar Drive, Heswall, Wirral L60 5RN*

RENYARD, Christopher. b 52. Open Univ BA87. Coll of Resurr Mirfield 81. **d** 84 **p** 85. C Heckmondwike *Wakef* 84-88; C Harpenden St Nic *St Alb* 88-95; Asst Chapl Salisbury Healthcare NHS Trust from 95. *Salisbury District Hospital, Salisbury SP2 8BJ* Tel (01722) 336262

RENYARD, Paul Holmwood. b 42. K Coll Lon BD65 AKC65. **d** 66 **p** 67. C Croydon St Aug *Cant* 66-69; C Farnham *Guildf* 69-72; V Capel 72-78; Asst Dir RE 72-78; Asst Dir RE *Roch* 78-83; Hon C Roch 78-83; V Holdenhurst *Win* 83-95; V Pennington from 95. *The Vicarage, 29 Ramley Road, Pennington, Lymington, Hants SO41 8LH* Tel (01590) 672646

REPATH, George David. b 43. Univ of Wales (Lamp) DipTh68. **d** 68 **p** 69. C Cardiff St Jo *Llan* 68-73; C Gt Stanmore *Lon* 73-77; V Stratfield Mortimer *Ox* 77-85; RD Bradfield 82-85; P-in-c Mortimer W End w Padworth 83-85; V Bray and Braywood from 85. *The Vicarage, Bray, Maidenhead, Berks SL6 2AB* Tel (01628) 21527

REPATH, John Richard. b 48. Univ of Wales (Cardiff) DipTh75. St Mich Coll Llan 72. **d** 75 **p** 76. C Canton St Jo *Llan* 75-79; C Burghclere w Newtown and Ecchinswell w Sydmonton *Win* 80-83; R Bewcastle and Stapleton *Carl* 83-88; P-in-c Kirklinton w Hethersgill and Scaleby 86-88; R Bewcastle, Stapleton and Kirklinton etc from 88. *The Rectory, Stapleton, Carlisle CA6 6LD* Tel (01697) 748660

REPTON, Suffragan Bishop of. *See* RICHMOND, The Rt Revd Francis Henry Arthur

RESTALL, Gerald Dalton. b 22. K Coll Lon BD50 AKC50. **d** 51 **p** 52. C Grays Thurrock *Chelmsf* 51-55; C-in-c Rush Green St Aug CD 55-58; Youth Chapl 58-62; CF (TA) 58-69; V Becontree St Elisabeth *Chelmsf* 62-71; P-in-c Becontree St Geo 62-65; CF (R of O) 69-77; R & V Reading St Mary *Ox* 72-77; R & V Reading St Mary w St Laur 77-88; rtd 88; Perm to Offic *Heref* from 91. *20 Sudbury Avenue, Hereford HR1 1YB* Tel (01432) 279194

RESTALL, Miss Susan Roberta (Sue). b 45. SRD. Sarum & Wells Th Coll 79. **dss** 82 **d** 87 **p** 94. Dorchester *Sarum* 82-84; Portland All SS w St Pet 84-87; Par Dn 87; TD Yate New Town *Bris* 87-94; TV 94-95; Chapl Birmingham Heartlands and Solihull NHS Trust from 95. *Birmingham Heartlands Hospital, Bordesley Green East, Birmingham B9 5SS* Tel 0121-766 6611 Fax 773 6897

REUSS, John Christopher Edward. b 1900. Lon Coll of Div 36. **d** 38 **p** 39. C Sydenham H Trin *S'wark* 38-39; Chapl RAF 39-45; R Longhope *Glouc* 45-46; Canada 46-48 and from 52; USA 48-52. *Address temp unknown*

REVELEY, James Stewart. b 69. Golds Coll Lon BMus92 Univ of the Pacific 95. Ripon Coll Cuddesdon BA93. **d** 96 **p** 97. C Goldington *St Alb* from 96. *1 Atholl Walk, Goldington, Bedford MK41 0BG* Tel (01234) 212973

REVELL, Patrick Walter Millard. b 32. Wells Th Coll 65. **d** 67 **p** 68. C Leic St Jas *Leic* 67-74; V Quorndon 74-82; TR Camelot Par *B & W* 82-90; RD Cary 90-96; RD Bruton 90-96; V Castle Cary w Ansford from 90. *The Vicarage, Church Street, Castle Cary, Somerset BA7 7EJ* Tel (01963) 351615

REVETT, Canon Graham Francis. b 40. AKC63. **d** 64 **p** 65. C Pennywell St Thos and Grindon St Oswald CD *Dur* 64-68; C Hartlepool St Aid 68-71; V Shiney Row 71-80; V Herrington 73-80; RD Houghton 76-80; TR Cullercoats St Geo *Newc* 80-97; RD Tynemouth 87-92; Hon Can Newc Cathl from 94; R Bolam w Whalton and Hartburn w Meldon from 97; V Nether Witton from 97. *The Rectory, Whalton, Morpeth, Northd NE61 3UX* Tel (01670) 775360

REX, James Maxwell. b 29. TD66. CEng59 FICE73. Trin Coll Bris 88. **d** 89 **p** 90. NSM Stoke Bishop *Bris* 89-91; Hon C Ashburnham w Penhurst *Chich* 92-93; P-in-c Danehill from 93. *The Vicarage, Danehill, Haywards Heath, W Sussex RH17 7ER* Tel (01825) 790269

REX, Keith Leslie Herbert. b 30. K Coll Lon 53. **d** 55 **p** 56. C Shepton Mallet *B & W* 55-58; C Cheshunt *St Alb* 58-60; V Weston-super-Mare St Andr Bournville *B & W* 60-67; R Charlton Adam w Charlton Mackrell 67-69; rtd 90. *68 Wellington Court, Weymouth, Dorset DT4 8UE*

REYNISH, David Stuart. b 52. Nottm Univ BEd75. Linc Th Coll 72. **d** 77 **p** 78. C Boston *Linc* 77-80; C Chalfont St Peter *Ox* 80-84; V Thursby *Carl* 84-88; R Iver Heath *Ox* from 88. *The Rectory, 2 Pinewood Close, Iver Heath, Iver, Bucks SL0 0QS* Tel (01753) 654470

REYNOLDS, Alan Martin. b 53. Sarum & Wells Th Coll 73. **d** 77 **p** 78. C Glan Ely *Llan* 77-84; V Pontyclun w Talygarn 84-97. *22 Osborn Square, Cardiff CF1 8BG* Tel (01222) 239344

REYNOLDS, Alan Thomas William. b 43. Lon Univ BSc64. Linc Th Coll 64. **d** 66 **p** 67. C Leic St Pet *Leic* 66-70; C Huntington *York* 70-72; Jamaica 72-76; V Stechford *Birm* 76-83; P-in-c Hampton in Arden 83-86; V 87-93; Chapl E Birm Hosp 86-88; Chapl Parkway Hosp Solihull 88-93; V Moseley St Anne *Birm* from 93. *The Vicarage, 15 Park Hill, Birmingham B13 8DU* Tel 0121-449 1071

REYNOLDS, Alfred Stanley. b 18. Birm Univ BSc39 Open Univ BA88. St Deiniol's Hawarden 69. **d** 70 **p** 71. Hon C Illogan *Truro* 70-85; Hon C Trowbridge St Thos and W Ashton *Sarum* from

85. *42 Cloford Close, Trowbridge, Wilts BA14 9DH* Tel (01225) 763542

REYNOLDS, Mrs Angela Heather. b 44. Wye Coll Lon BSc66 Birm Univ CertEd67. EAMTC 94. **d** 97. Hon C Barnham Broom *Nor* from 97. *3 Mattishall Road, Brandon Parva, Norwich NR9 4DH* Tel (01603) 759368

REYNOLDS, David Hammerton. b 39. St Jo Coll Dur BA62. Qu Coll Birm DipTh63. **d** 65 **p** 66. C N Ormesby *York* 65-68; C Hessle 68-71; V Sherburn in Elmet 71-79; V Fulford 79-87; Resp for Clergy In-Service Tr York Area 82-87; C Egloskerry *Truro* 87; TV Bolventor 87-90; TR Brayton *York* from 90. *The Rectory, Doncaster Road, Brayton, Selby, N Yorkshire YO8 9HE* Tel (01757) 704707

REYNOLDS, David James. b 48. St Jo Coll Dur BA72 DipTh73 Lanc Univ MA85. Cranmer Hall Dur 69. **d** 73 **p** 74. C Formby H Trin *Liv* 73-77; P-in-c Widnes St Paul 77-80; V Southport St Paul 80-87; P-in-c Mawdesley *Blackb* 87-91; R from 91; Chapl Derian Ho Children's Hospice from 93. *Mawdesley Rectory, Green Lane, Ormskirk, Lancs L40 3TH* Tel (01704) 822203

REYNOLDS, Derrick Wilfrid. b 15. St Paul's Grahamstown LTh. **d** 49 **p** 50. S Africa 49-61; V Sparkwell *Ex* 62-73; V Ilsington 73-86; rtd 86; Perm to Offic *Ex* from 86. *White Gates, 7 West Buckeridge Road, Teignmouth, Devon TQ14 8NF* Tel (01626) 772165

REYNOLDS, Gordon. b 42. Sarum & Wells Th Coll 71. **d** 72 **p** 73. C Tunstall *Lich* 72-74; Zambia 75-88; C Southmead *Bris* 88-90; SSF from 90. *The Friary, Hilfield, Dorchester, Dorset DT2 7BE* Tel (01300) 341345

REYNOLDS, Canon John Lionel. b 34. JP. Chich Th Coll 58. **d** 61 **p** 62. C Whitkirk *Ripon* 61-64; C Tong *Bradf* 64-68; V Chisledon and Draycot Foliatt *Sarum* 68-74; RD Marlborough 74-76; TR Ridgeway 74-76; V Calne and Blackland 76-89; RD Calne 77-84; Can and Preb Sarum Cathl from 80; V Woodford Valley from 89. *The Vicarage, Middle Woodford, Salisbury SP4 6NR* Tel (01722) 782310

REYNOLDS, John Stewart. b 19. FSA81 St Edm Hall Ox BA42 MA45 BLitt50. Ridley Hall Cam 42. **d** 44 **p** 45. C Ox St Clem *Ox* 44-46; C-in-c Ox All SS w St Martin 46-49; R Easton-on-the-Hill *Pet* 49-56; R Besselsleigh w Dry Sandford *Ox* 56-85; Lect Wycliffe Hall Ox 71-78; rtd 85; Perm to Offic *Ox* from 85. *Linden Lodge, 59 St Mary's Road, Oxford OX4 1PZ* Tel (01865) 727386

REYNOLDS, Paul Andrew. b 57. BA86. Trin Coll Bris 83. **d** 86 **p** 87. C Reading St Jo *Ox* 86-90; C Dorridge *Birm* 90-95; TV Riverside *Ox* from 95. *The Vicarage, 69A Eton Wick Road, Windsor, Berks SL4 6NE* Tel (01753) 852268

REYNOLDS, Paul Frederick. b 56. Lon Bible Coll DRBS78 St Jo Coll Nottm DipMM92. **d** 92 **p** 93. C Hyde St Geo *Ches* 92-96; P-in-c Delamere from 96. *The Rectory, Delamere, Northwich, Cheshire CW8 2HS* Tel (01606) 882184

REYNOLDS, Philip Delamere. b 53. Leeds Univ CertEd74 Nottm Univ BCombStuds82. Linc Th Coll 79. **d** 82 **p** 83. C Huddersfield St Jo *Wakef* 82-85; C Barkisland w W Scammonden 85-87; P-in-c Skelmanthorpe from 87. *St Aidan's Vicarage, Radcliffe Street, Skelmanthorpe, Huddersfield HD8 9AF* Tel (01484) 863232

REYNOLDS, Raymond Ernest. b 29. Nottm Univ MPhil89. Lambeth STh84 CA Tr Coll 50 Chich Th Coll 58. **d** 60 **p** 61. C Leeds St Marg *Ripon* 60-62; C Beeston *S'well* 62-64; R Farnley *Ripon* 64-76; R Higham-on-the-Hill w Fenny Drayton *Leic* 76-81; R Higham-on-the-Hill w Fenny Drayton and Witherley 81-90; V Sutton *Ely* 90-94; R Witcham w Mepal 90-94; rtd 94; C Nantwich *Ches* 94-96; Perm to Offic from 96. *4 St Alban's Drive, Nantwich, Cheshire CW5 7DW* Tel (01270) 623534

REYNOLDS, Richard Michael. b 42. St Steph Ho Ox 65. **d** 67 **p** 68. C Kidderminster St Mary *Worc* 67-70; Guyana 70-73; TV N Creedy *Ex* 73-80; R Holsworthy w Hollacombe 80-86; R Holsworthy w Hollacombe and Milton Damerel from 86. *The Rectory, Holsworthy, Devon EX22 6BH* Tel (01409) 253435

REYNOLDS, Roderick Bredon (Rory). b 58. Man Univ BA80. Ripon Coll Cuddesdon DipMin95. **d** 95 **p** 96. C Hitchin *St Alb* from 95. *67 Whitehill Road, Hitchin, Herts SG4 9HP* Tel (01462) 438859

REYNOLDS, Canon Stanley Kenneth. b 14. Bps' Coll Cheshunt 47. **d** 50 **p** 51. C Derby St Andr *Derby* 50-57; PC Stonebroom 57-64; V Chaddesden St Phil 64-70; V Greenhill St Pet 70-74; V Greenhill *Sheff* 74-81; P-in-c Burghwallis w Skelbrooke 81-89; Hon Can Sheff Cathl 83-89; rtd 89; Perm to Offic *Nor* from 89. *4 Burton Close, Diss, Norfolk IP22 3YJ* Tel (01379) 650562

RHAM, Canon John Theodore. b 27. Magd Coll Cam BA50 MA65. Sarum Th Coll 50. **d** 52 **p** 53. C Harborne St Pet *Birm* 52-54; C Coleshill 54-56; C Falmouth K Chas *Truro* 56-59; R St Ewe 59-68; RD St Austell 65-68; V Budock 68-93; RD Carnmarth S 77-84; Hon Can Truro Cathl 80-93; rtd 93; France from 94. *Villa Budoc, 36 Route de Bernis, Langlade, 30980 Gard, France*

RHODES, Adrian Michael. b 48. K Coll Lon BD71 AKC71 DPST76. Qu Coll Birm 71. **d** 72 **p** 73. C Bury St Jo *Man* 73-75; Chapl N Man Gen Hosp 75-77; C Crumpsall *Man* 75-77; Chapl Walsall Manor and Bloxwich Hosps 77-83; Chapl Walsall Gen Hosp 81-83; Chapl Man R Infirmary 83-94; Chapl St Mary's Hosp Man 83-94; Chapl Man R Eye Hosp 83-94; Chapl Cen Man Healthcare NHS Trust from 94. *Manchester Royal Infirmary, Oxford Road, Manchester M13 9WL* Tel 0161-224 1739 or 276 4726/276 1234

RHODES, Anthony John. b 27. Mert Coll Ox BA50 MA53 DipTh53. St Steph Ho Ox 52. **d** 54 **p** 55. C Northampton St Alb *Pet* 54-57; C Oakham 57-60; P-in-c S Queensferry *Edin* 60-74; V Mitcham St Olave *S'wark* 74-81; V Owston *Linc* 81-92; V W Butterwick 81-92; rtd 92. *1 Trentside, Owston Ferry, Doncaster, S Yorkshire DN9 1RS* Tel (0142772) 237

RHODES, Arthur. b 31. Dur Univ BA58. Cranmer Hall Dur 57. **d** 59 **p** 60. C Kirkdale St Lawr *Liv* 59-61; C Litherland St Phil 61-64; V St Helens St Matt Thatto Heath 64-67; V Samlesbury *Blackb* 67-79; NSM Broughton from 79. *88 Deborah Avenue, Fulwood, Preston PR2 9HU* Tel (01772) 712212

RHODES, Benjamin (Ben). b 71. Portsm Univ BSc93. Westcott Ho Cam CTM94. **d** 97. C Upminster *Chelmsf* from 97. *6 Gaynes Park Road, Upminster, Essex RM4 2HH* Tel (01708) 226004 E-mail benrhodes@br.u-net.com

RHODES, David. b 34. St Chad's Coll Dur BA60. **d** 61 **p** 62. C Dudley St Jo *Worc* 61-64; C-in-c Stourbridge St Mich Norton CD 64-68; V Astwood Bank w Crabbs Cross 69-78; Dioc Ecum Officer 73-78; TR Hackney *Lon* 78-88; R St Giles Cripplegate w St Bart Moor Lane etc from 88. *The Rectory, 4 The Postern, Wood Street, London EC2Y 8BJ* Tel 0171-606 3630

RHODES, David George. b 45. Univ of Wales (Abth) BA66. Trin Coll Bris 83. **d** 85 **p** 86. C Brinsworth w Catcliffe *Sheff* 85-89; V Mortomley St Sav 89-90; V Mortomley St Sav High Green from 90. *The Vicarage, Mortomley Lane, High Green, Sheffield S30 4HS* Tel 0114-284 8231

RHODES, David Grant. b 43. Ex Univ BA66 Leeds Univ DipAdEd75. Sarum & Wells Th Coll 69. **d** 72 **p** 73. C Mirfield *Wakef* 72-75; V Batley St Thos 75-80; Dioc Adult Educn Officer 76-80; Hon C Huddersfield St Jo 85-86; Dir BRF 86-87; V Roberttown *Wakef* 87-94; Project Worker 'Faith in Leeds' from 94; NSM Potternewton *Ripon* from 95. *111 Potternewton Lane, Leeds LS7 3LW* Tel 0113-262 7247

RHODES, Duncan. b 35. Leeds Univ BSc56. Local Minl Tr Course 90. **d** 93 **p** 94. NSM Saddleworth *Man* from 93. *Folden Cottage, 21 Spurn Lane, Diggle, Oldham OL3 5QP* Tel (01457) 872399

RHODES, Canon Geoffrey David. b 34. Birm Univ BSc55. Ridley Hall Cam 68. **d** 70 **p** 71. C Sedbergh *Bradf* 70-74; P-in-c Howgill w Firbank 73-76; P-in-c Killington 73-76; C Sedbergh, Cautley and Garsdale 74-76; R Carleton-in-Craven 76-78; P-in-c Lothersdale 76-78; R Carleton and Lothersdale 78-85; V Giggleswick and Rathmell w Wigglesworth from 85; Hon Can Bradf Cathl from 91; RD Bowland from 96. *The Vicarage, Bankwell Road, Giggleswick, Settle, N Yorkshire BD24 0AP* Tel (01729) 822425

RHODES, Heather. b 32. **d** 88. Par Dn Purley St Mark Woodcote *S'wark* 89-94; C from 94. *24 Highfield Road, Purley, Surrey CR8 2JG* Tel 0181-660 1486

RHODES, Canon John Lovell. b 33. MBE81. Lon Univ BD59. St Aid Birkenhead 55. **d** 59 **p** 60. C Bradf St Clem *Bradf* 59-61; C Heeley *Sheff* 61-66; Ind Chapl *Linc* 66-81; Sen Ind Chapl from 81; RD Grimsby and Cleethorpes 76-83; Can and Preb Linc Cathl from 77; Chapl Franklin Coll from 92. *19 Augusta Close, Grimsby, S Humberside DN34 4TQ* Tel (01472) 343167

RHODES, Lois Christine. b 34. Lon Univ BSc61. Glouc Sch of Min 84. **d** 87 **p** 94. NSM Weobley w Sarnesfield and Norton Canon *Heref* 87-92; NSM Letton w Staunton, Byford, Mansel Gamage etc 87-92; Asst Chapl Heref Hosps NHS Trust from 93. *Bellbrook, Bell Square, Weobley, Hereford HR4 8SE* Tel (01544) 318410

RHODES, Matthew Ivan. b 66. Bris Univ BA89. Qu Coll Birm BD93. **d** 94 **p** 95. C Willenhall H Trin *Lich* from 94. *13 Wesley Road, Willenhall, W Midlands WV12 5QT* Tel (01922) 405242

RHODES, Peter Stuart. b 26. ACP67. Coll of Resurr Mirfield 77. **d** 78 **p** 79. NSM Newbold w Dunston *Derby* 78-96; NSM Newbold w Dunston and Gt Barlow from 96. *42 Westbrook Drive, Chesterfield, Derbyshire S40 3PQ* Tel (01246) 566628

RHODES, Robert George (Bob). b 41. Man Univ BSc62. Ripon Hall Ox DipTh73. **d** 74 **p** 75. C Banbury *Ox* 74-77; TV Banbury 77-81; P-in-c Long Horsley *Newc* 81-86; Adult Educn Adv 81-86; R Wolverton *Ox* from 86. *The Rectory, Aylesbury Street, Wolverton, Milton Keynes MK12 5HY* Tel (01908) 312501

RHODES, Canon Trevor Martin. b 38. Kelham Th Coll 59 Qu Coll Birm 70. **d** 71 **p** 71. C Bordesley St Oswald *Birm* 71-73; Chapl St Basil's Ch Cen Birm 72-73; C Padiham *Blackb* 73-76; P-in-c Preston St Oswald 76-78; Chapl HM Borstal Hindley 78-80; V Blackhill *Dur* 80-83; V Cowgate *Newc* 83-87; Hon Can Koforidua from 86; V Wesham *Blackb* 87-90; V Danby *York* 90-96; P-in-c Bishopwearmouth Gd Shep *Dur* 96-97. *The Beacon, Goathland, Whitby, N Yorkshire YO22 5AN*

RHODES-WRIGLEY, James. b 35. AKC59. **d** 60 **p** 61. C S Harrow St Paul *Lon* 60-66; V Hendon Ch Ch 66-71; V Northolt Park St Barn 71-92; rtd 92; Hon C Whyke w Rumboldswhyke and Portfield *Chich* from 96. *4 Gordon Avenue, Donnington, Chichester, W Sussex PO19 2QY* Tel (01243) 781664

RHYDDERCH, David Huw. b 48. Univ of Wales (Cardiff) DipTh73. St Mich Coll Llan 70. **d** 73 **p** 74. C Gelligaer *Llan* 73-76; C Penarth All SS 76-78; V Resolven 78-81; V Ystrad Rhondda w Ynyscynon 81-93; RD Rhondda 89-93; R

St Andrew's Major and Michaelston-le-Pit from 93. *The Rectory, Lettons Way, Dinas Powys CF64 4BY* Tel (01222) 512555

RHYS, Canon David Edwin. b 37. Peterho Cam BA61 MA65 Lon Univ BA74. St Steph Ho Ox. **d** 63 **p** 64. C Tividale *Lich* 63-65; C Eltham St Jo *S'wark* 65-72; Hon C 75-82; Chapl and Warden LMH Settlement 72-75; P-in-c Woolwich St Mary w St Mich 82-83; R 83-95; RD Greenwich 86-90; Sub-Dean Woolwich 86-87; Hon Can S'wark Cathl 90-97; TV Catford (Southend) and Downham 95-97; rtd 97; NSM Catford (Southend) and Downham *S'wark* from 97. *233 Bellingham Road, London SE6 1EH* Tel 0181-695 6376

RICE, Brian Keith. b 32. Peterho Cam BA55 MA59. Seabury-Western Th Sem BD57 STM67 MDiv79 Linc Th Coll. **d** 57 **p** 58. C Winchmore Hill St Paul *Lon* 57-60; C Derby St Werburgh *Derby* 60-63; C Mackworth St Fran 63-66; Chapl Kingsway Hosp Derby 63-66; Educn Sec USPG 66-72; Dir of Educn *Birm* 72-84; Chapl St Chad's Hosp Birm 77-84; Soc Resp Officer *Dur* from 84. *39 Darlington Road, Hartburn, Stockton-on-Tees, Cleveland TS18 5ET* Tel (01642) 582241

RICE, Brian Thomas. b 46. Univ of Wales (Cardiff) BD77. St Mich Coll Llan 75. **d** 77 **p** 78. C Llanelli *St D* 77-79; P-in-c Llandygwydd and Cenarth w Cilrhedyn 79-80; V 80-83; V Llandingat w Myddfai from 83; RD Llangadog and Llandeilo from 91. *The Vicarage, Towy Avenue, Llandovery SA20 0EH* Tel (01550) 720524

RICE, David. b 57. Nottm Univ BA79. Ripon Coll Cuddesdon 80. **d** 82 **p** 83. C Cirencester *Glouc* 82-86; R Theale and Englefield *Ox* from 86. *The Rectory, Theale, Reading RG7 5AS* Tel 0118-930 2759

RICE, Franklin Arthur. b 20. FRICS49. St Alb Minl Tr Scheme 77. **d** 80 **p** 81. NSM Hoddesdon *St Alb* 80-84; Perm to Offic *Guildf* from 85. *1 Oatlands Court, St Mary's Road, Weybridge, Surrey KT13 9QE* Tel (01932) 846462

RICE, John Leslie Hale. b 38. FBIM GIMechE Lon Univ BScEng60 BD68. EMMTC 73. **d** 76 **p** 77. NSM Allestree St Nic *Derby* 76-91; NSM Ind Specialist from 90. *14 Gisborne Crescent, Allestree, Derby DE22 2FL* Tel (01332) 557222

RICE-OXLEY, John Richard. b 44. Keble Coll Ox BA66 MA69 Dur Univ MA85. Lon Coll of Div 68. **d** 70 **p** 71. C Eastwood *S'well* 70-73; Youth Adv CMS 73-78; V Mansfield St Jo *S'well* 78-82; P-in-c Thornley *Dur* 82-85; P-in-c Darlington St Matt and St Luke 85-87; V from 87. *32 Skeldale Grove, Darlington, Co Durham DL3 0GW* Tel (01325) 463412

RICH, Brian John. b 49. Reading Univ BSc70. Guildf Dioc Min Course 94. **d** 97. NSM Stoke Hill *Guildf* from 97. *Roewen, 1 Trentham Crescent, Old Woking, Surrey GU22 9EW* Tel (01483) 829541

RICH, Canon Christopher Robin. b 49. LSE MSc(Econ)95. Sarum & Wells Th Coll 72. **d** 74 **p** 75. C Sholing *Win* 74-76; C Southampton Maybush St Pet 76-79; R Fawley 79-90; Dir Soc Resp from 90; Hon Can Win Cathl from 96. *15 Shelley Close, Winchester, Hants SO22 5AS* Tel (01962) 620065 Fax 841814

RICH, Harold Reginald. b 22. LNSM course. **d** 79 **p** 80. NSM St Austell *Truro* 79-87; rtd 87; Perm to Offic *Truro* from 87. *106 Eastbourne Road, St Austell, Cornwell PL25 4SS* Tel (01726) 75600

RICH, Nicholas Philip. b 49. St Cuth Soc Dur BA74 PGCE75 Coll of Ripon & York St Jo CertEd83. Linc Th Coll 86. **d** 88 **p** 89. C W Acklam *York* 88-91; Chapl St Geo Sch Harpenden 91-95; Lic to Offic *St Alb* 91-95; rtd 95. *2 Linwood Road, Harpenden, Herts AL5 1RR* Tel (01582) 760920

RICH, Paul Michael. b 36. OBE87. Sarum Th Coll 62. **d** 65 **p** 66. C Woodbridge St Mary *St E* 65-68; C W Wycombe *Ox* 68-70; CF 70-88; Lic to Offic *S & B* 88-90; V Crondall and Ewshot *Guildf* from 91. *The Vicarage, Farm Lane, Crondall, Farnham, Surrey GU10 5QE* Tel (01252) 850379

RICH, Peter Geoffrey. b 45. Oak Hill Th Coll 74. **d** 77 **p** 78. C Blackheath St Jo *S'wark* 77-80; C Surbiton St Matt 80-87; V St Alb St Luke *St Alb* from 87. *St Luke's Vicarage, Cellbarnes Lane, St Albans, Herts AL1 5QJ* Tel (01727) 865399

RICH, Thomas. b 52. St Jo Coll Nottm 86. **d** 88 **p** 89. C Netherton *Liv* 88-91; P-in-c Bootle Ch Ch 91-93; V from 93. *Christ Church Vicarage, 1 Breeze Hill, Bootle, Merseyside L20 9EY* Tel 0151-525 2565

RICHARD, David Thomas. b 16. St D Coll Lamp BA39. **d** 40 **p** 41. C Llandeilo Fawr *St D* 40-43; C Llanstadwel 43-45; C Cardigan 45-54; R Bangor Teifi w Henllan 54-57; PC Runcorn H Trin *Ches* 57-58; R Stoney Stanton *Leic* 58-62; V Darlaston St Geo *Lich* 62-70; V Mostyn *St As* 70-86; rtd 86; Perm to Offic *St D* from 86. *Ael-y-Bryn, New Quay SA45 9SE* Tel (01545) 560745

RICHARDS, Alan Grenville. b 41. Kelham Th Coll 64. **d** 69 **p** 70. C Northolt St Mary *Lon* 69-75; V Fatfield *Dur* 75-84; V Beighton *Sheff* 84-91; V Endcliffe 91-94; Deputation Appeals Org Children's Soc from 94; Perm to Offic *Chich* from 94. *11 Priors Close, Upper Beeding, Steyning, W Sussex BN44 3HT* Tel (01903) 879733

RICHARDS, Albert George Granston. b 06. Lon Univ BSc30. Wycliffe Hall Ox 54. **d** 55 **p** 60. Hon C Watford *St Alb* 55-67; Hon C St Alb St Pet 67-69; V Offley w Lilley 69-74; RD Hurst *Chich* 75-80; P-in-c Poynings 80-82; P-in-c Edburton 80-82; rtd 82; Perm to Offic *Chich* from 82. *3 Clerks Acre, Hassocks, W Sussex BN6 8UY* Tel (01273) 844203

RICHARDS, Andrew David Thomas. b 55. St Jo Coll Dur BA76 FRSA96. St Steph Ho Ox 76. **d** 78 **p** 79. C Shirley *Birm* 78-80; C Cowley St Jo *Ox* 80-82; Perm to Offic *Win* 84-88; Perm to Offic *Sarum* 88-92; NSM Hazelbury Bryan and the Hillside Par 92-94; Chapl Rossall Sch Fleetwood from 94. *2 Newell Court, Rossall School, Fleetwood, Lancs FY7 8JW* Tel (01253) 776564 or 874657

RICHARDS, Anthony Francis. b 26. Edin Univ BA45 Wadh Coll Ox BA51 MA54. Ridley Hall Cam 50. **d** 52 **p** 53. C Finchley Ch Ch *Lon* 52-55; C Maidenhead St Andr and St Mary *Ox* 55-59; Lect All Nations Chr Coll Ware 58-59; V High Wycombe Ch Ch *Ox* 59-63; P-in-c 63-66; V Terriers 63-73; USA 70-71; V Cinderford St Steph w Littledean *Glouc* 73-80; V Clacton St Paul *Chelmsf* 80-93; New Zealand 88-89; rtd 93. *Mont, 58230 Ouroux en-Morvan, Montsauche, France* Tel France (33) 86 78 24 44

RICHARDS, Mrs April Deborah. b 42. Man Univ BSc63. S Dios Minl Tr Scheme 82. **dss** 85 **d** 87 **p** 94. Catherington and Clanfield *Portsm* 85-87; C 87-89; C E Meon 89-95; C Langrish 89-95; Chapl St Mary's Hosp Portsm 92-93; Chapl Portsm Hosps NHS Trust 93-95; P-in-c Blackmoor *Portsm* from 95. *The Vicarage, Blackmoor, Liss, Hants GU33 6BN* Tel (01420) 473548

RICHARDS, Barbara May. b 53. Sarum & Wells Th Coll. **d** 88. Chapl Princess Marg Hosp Swindon 88-96; Lect Reading Univ *Ox* from 96. *46 Broomfield Road, Tilehurst, Reading RG30 6AZ* Tel (0118) 942 8915

RICHARDS, Basil Ernest. b 18. Lich Th Coll 51. **d** 53 **p** 54. C Kidderminster St Mary *Worc* 53-55; C Northfield *Birm* 55-56; Hon C Gt Malvern Ch Ch *Worc* 78-84; Perm to Offic from 84; Chapl Laslett's Almshouses 84-88; rtd 88. *42 Viscount Cobham Court, Pickersleigh Road, Malvern, Worcs WR14 2RJ* Tel (01684) 565441

RICHARDS, Brian. b 39. Open Univ BA78. Nor Ord Course 65 St Deiniol's Hawarden 94. **d** 94 **p** 94. C St Mellons and Michaelston-y-Fedw *Mon* 94-96; P-in-c Michaelston-y-Fedw from 96. *The Rectory, Michaelston-y-Fedw, Cardiff CF3 9XS* Tel (01222) 680414

RICHARDS, Brian Gordon. b 21. Sarum & Wells Th Coll 71. **d** 73 **p** 74. C Milton *Win* 73-78; P-in-c Hook w Greywell 78-83; R Hook 83-88; rtd 88; Perm to Offic *B & W* from 88. *Grenville Cottage, Main Road, Bourton, Gillingham, Dorset SP8 5ES* Tel (01747) 840514

RICHARDS, Charles Dennis Vincent. b 37. AKC61. **d** 62 **p** 63. Chapl St Ninian's Cathl Perth *St And* 62-64; C Pimlico St Mary Graham Terrace *Lon* 64-66; C St Marylebone Ch Ch w St Barn 66-68; C Wood Green St Mich 68-69; C-in-c S Kenton Annunciation CD 69-77; P-in-c Wembley Park St Aug 70-73; Hon C Paddington St Jo w St Mich from 76. *48A Kendal Street, London W2 2BP* Tel 0171-262 5633

RICHARDS, Charles Edmund Nicholas. b 42. Trin Coll Cam BA64 MA68. Westcott Ho Cam 64. **d** 66 **p** 67. C Rugby St Andr *Cov* 66-72; TV Basingstoke *Win* 72-77; R Rotherhithe St Mary w All SS *S'wark* from 77; RD Bermondsey 81-91. *The Rectory, 72 St Marychurch Street, London SE16 4JE* Tel 0171-231 2465

RICHARDS, Dr Christopher Mordaunt. b 40. New Coll Ox BA63 MA72 Bris Univ MB, ChB72. Cuddesdon Coll 63. **d** 65 **p** 81. C Bris St Mary Redcliffe w Temple etc *Bris* 65-66; Perm to Offic 66-72; Hon C Keynsham *B & W* 81-90; Perm to Offic 90-93. *4 St Ronans Avenue, Bristol BS6 6EP* Tel 0117-974 4062

RICHARDS, Daniel James (Dan). b 40. St D Coll Lamp DipTh66. **d** 66 **p** 67. C Kingswinford H Trin *Lich* 66-69; C Banbury *Ox* 69-71; C Aylesbury 71-73; C-in-c Stoke Poges St Jo Manor Park CD 73-78; R W Slough 78-80; R Ilchester w Northover, Limington, Yeovilton etc *B & W* 80-90; RD Ilchester 81-91; RD Martock 89-91; TR Bruton and Distr 90-97; R Axbridge w Shipham and Rowberrow from 97. *The Rectory, Cheddar Road, Axbridge, Somerset BS26 2DL* Tel (01934) 732261

RICHARDS, David. b 30. Bris Univ BA52. St Mich Coll Llan 52. **d** 54 **p** 55. C Llangynwyd w Maesteg *Llan* 54-56; Iran 57-61 and 62-66; C Skewen *Llan* 61-62; V Cwmbach 66-76; Warden of Ords 71-77; R Coity w Nolton 76-96; Can Llan Cathl 88-96; rtd 96. *Inglewood, 5 Hopewell Close, Bulwark, Chepstow NP6 5ST*

RICHARDS, David Arnold. b 56. Wycliffe Hall Ox 76. **d** 81 **p** 82. C Skewen *Llan* 81-84; C Barking St Marg w St Patr *Chelmsf* 84-85; TV 85-90; Chapl Barking Hosp 87-88; P-in-c Stratford St Jo and Ch Ch w Forest Gate St Jas *Chelmsf* 90-97; V from 97. *Stratford Vicarage, Deanery Road, London E15 4LP* Tel 0181-534 8388

RICHARDS, David Gareth. b 60. Hull Univ BA83 Birm Univ DipTh91. Qu Coll Birm 89. **d** 92 **p** 93. C Knowle *Birm* 92-96; Assoc R Edin St Paul and St Geo *Edin* from 96. *11 East Fettes Avenue, Edinburgh EH4 1DN* Tel 0131-332 3904 or 556 1355 Fax 556 0492 E-mail compuserve106070.1301

RICHARDS, Dennis. b 48. St Mich Coll Llan 95. **d** 97. C Cwmbran *Mon* from 97. *13 Melbourne Court, Green Meadow, Cwmbran NP44 3AR* Tel (01633) 871051

RICHARDS, Edwin Thomas. Leeds Univ BA41. St D Coll Lamp 46. **d** 48 **p** 49. C Llangynwyd w Maesteg *Llan* 48-50; S Africa 50-86; R Llanganten, Llanafan Fawr, Llangammarch etc *S & B*

86-89; rtd 89. *St John's Church, PO Box 62, Fort Beaufort, 5720 South Africa*

RICHARDS, Canon Eric. b 36. TD86. Ely Th Coll 62. **d** 63 **p** 64. C Fen Ditton *Ely* 63-65; C Woodston 65-68; Ceylon 68-71; Miss to Seamen 71-73; R Roos w Tunstall *York* 73-74; P-in-c Garton w Grimston and Hilston 73-74; R Roos and Garton in Holderness w Tunstall etc 74-79; CF (TAVR) 73-79; CF (TA) 79-89; Sen CF (TA) 89-92; V Wykeham and Hutton Buscel *York* from 79; RD Pickering 80-94; Abp's Adv on Rural Affairs from 83; Can and Preb York Minster from 92. *The Vicar's House, Hutton Buscel, Scarborough, N Yorkshire YO13 9LL* Tel (01723) 862945 Fax 862916

RICHARDS, Harold John Thomas. b 16. St D Coll Lamp BA39 St Mich Coll Llan 45. **d** 47 **p** 48. C Fochriw w Deri *Llan* 47-50; C Pontnewynydd *Mon* 50-53; C Panteg w Llanddewi Fach 53-56; V Garndiffaith 56-69; R Goetre 69-82; rtd 82. *48 Longhouse Barn, Goetre, Pontypool NP4 0BD* Tel (01873) 880744

RICHARDS, Canon Iorwerth. b 20. Univ of Wales (Lamp) BA41. K Coll Lon 41. **d** 43 **p** 44. C Swansea St Mary *S & B* 43-53; P-in-c Llanddewi Ystradenni 53-55; V Llanddewi Ystradenni and Abbey Cwmhir 55-60; R Penmaen w Nicholaston 60-71; RD Gower 71-88; V Oxwich w Penmaen and Nicholaston 71-89; Hon Can Brecon Cathl 83-85; Can Brecon Cathl 85-89; rtd 89; Perm to Offic *St D* from 89. *17 Carrick Avenue, Llanelli SA15 3JZ* Tel (01554) 770729

RICHARDS, Canon Irving St Clair. b 40. Coll of Resurr Mirfield 72. **d** 74 **p** 75. C Wigston Magna *Leic* 74-78; P-in-c N Evington from 78; Hon Can Leic Cathl from 97; Bp's Officer for Race and Community Relns from 94. *The Vicarage, 214 East Park Road, Leicester LE5 5FD* Tel 0116-273 6752

RICHARDS, James Harcourt. b 30. Oak Hill Th Coll. **d** 63 **p** 64. C Liv Ch Ch Norris Green *Liv* 63-66; C Fazakerley Em 66-68; P-in-c Edge Hill St Cath 68-73; V St Helens St Matt Thatto Heath 73-87; R Feltwell *Ely* 87-92; rtd 92; Perm to Offic *Nor* from 93. *Pantiles, Church Terrace, Aylsham, Norfolk NR11 6EU* Tel (01263) 733468

RICHARDS, James Johnston. b 59. Solicitor 84 MLawSoc84 Dur Univ MA97. Lon Bible Coll BA90 Cranmer Hall Dur 90. **d** 92 **p** 93. C Harrow Trin St Mich *Lon* 92-95; C Kendal H Trin *Carl* from 95. *7 Wattsfield Road, Kendal, Cumbria LA9 5JH* Tel (01539) 729572

RICHARDS, Mrs Jane Valerie. b 43. Westf Coll Lon BA64 Birm Univ CertEd65. S Dios Minl Tr Scheme 84. **d** 87 **p** 94. NSM Locks Heath *Portsm* 87-90; Asst Chapl Qu Alexandra Hosp Portsm 90-92; Chapl Portsm Hosps NHS Trust 92-95; Asst to RD Fareham *Portsm* 95-96; C Locks Heath 95-96; Chapl Southn Univ Hosps NHS Trust from 96. *16 Lodge Road, Locks Heath, Southampton SO31 6QY* Tel (01489) 573891

RICHARDS, John. b 20. FSA70 Univ of Wales (Lamp) BA40 Keble Coll Ox BA42 MA46 BLitt48. Westcott Ho Cam 43. **d** 43 **p** 44. C Chirk *St As* 43-44; CF 44-45; C Bollington St Jo *Ches* 46-50; V Macclesfield St Pet 50-56; Lect Macclesfield Coll of FE 53-56; V New Brighton All SS 56-67; CF (TA) 62-86; Master Wellington Sch Somerset 67-82; V Hoylake *Ches* 67-86; rtd 86; Perm to Offic *Ches* from 86. *Ithaca, 56 Cleveley Road, Meols, South Wirral L47 8XR* Tel 0151-632 5135

✠**RICHARDS, The Rt Revd John.** b 33. SS Coll Cam BA55 MA59. Ely Th Coll 57. **d** 59 **p** 60 **c** 94. C Ex St Thos *Ex* 59-64; R Holsworthy w Cookbury 64-74; R Hollacombe 64-74; RD Holsworthy 70-74; V Heavitree 74-77; TR Heavitree w Ex St Paul 78-81; RD Christianity 78-81; Adn Ex and Can Res Ex Cathl 81-94; Suff Bp Ebbsfleet (PEV) *Cant* from 94; Asst Bp B & W from 96. *The Rectory, Church Leigh, Stoke-on-Trent ST10 4PT* Tel (01889) 502366

RICHARDS, Preb John Francis. b 37. Dur Univ BA61. Wells Th Coll 61. **d** 63 **p** 64. C Sherwood *S'well* 63-67; C Bishopwearmouth St Mich *Dur* 67-69; C Egg Buckland *Ex* 69-75; V Plymouth St Jas Ham 75-83; V Plympton St Mary from 83; RD Plymouth Moorside 88-93 and from 96; Preb Ex Cathl from 91. *St Mary's Vicarage, 58 Plymbridge Road, Plympton, Plymouth PL7 4QG* Tel (01752) 336157

RICHARDS, John George. b 48. Qu Coll Birm 87. **d** 89 **p** 90. C Acocks Green *Birm* 89-92; TV Shirley 92-96; P-in-c Yardley Wood from 96. *Christ Church Vicarage, School Road, Yardley Wood, Birmingham B14 4EP* Tel (0121) 436 7726

RICHARDS, John Henry. b 34. CCC Cam BA57 MA75. St Mich Coll Llan BD77. **d** 77 **p** 78. C Llangynwyd w Maesteg *Llan* 77-79; C Cardiff St Jo 79-82; Asst Chapl Univ of Wales (Cardiff) 79-82; V Penmark w Porthkerry 82-83; R Stackpole Elidor w St Petrox *St D* 83-85; R St Petrox w Stackpole Elidor and Bosherston etc from 85. *The Rectory, Stackpole, Pembroke SA71 5BZ* Tel (01646) 672472

RICHARDS, John Michael. b 53. Coll of Ripon & York St Jo TCert76 Open Univ BA81. Cranmer Hall Dur CTMin93. **d** 93 **p** 94. C Wath-upon-Dearne *Sheff* 93-95; R Warmsworth from 95. *The Rectory, 187 Warmsworth Road, Doncaster, S Yorkshire DN4 0TW* Tel (01302) 853324

RICHARDS, John Stanley. b 39. St Jo Coll Dur BA60. Ridley Hall Cam 61. **d** 64 **p** 65. C Fordingbridge w Ibsley *Win* 64-67; CF (TA) 64-68; C Bitterne Park *Win* 67-68; C Pokesdown All SS 68-70; Fell Qu Coll Birm 70-71; C Chesterton St Andr *Ely* 71-73; Asst Chapl Canford Sch Wimborne 73-77; Assoc Dir Fountain Trust 77-80; Perm to Offic *Guildf* 77-81; Dir Renewal Servicing from 81; NSM New Haw *Guildf* 81-84. *Renewal Servicing, PO Box 17, Shepperton, Middx TW17 8NU*

RICHARDS, John William. b 29. Southn Univ BSc55. Sarum & Wells Th Coll 78. **d** 81 **p** 82. NSM Woking St Mary *Guildf* 81-85; C Addlestone 85-87; C S Gillingham *Roch* 87-89; Hon C W Byfleet *Guildf* 91-95; rtd 94. *16 Normandy Way, Poundbury Whitfield, Dorchester, Dorset DT1 2PP* Tel (01305) 251529

RICHARDS, Jonathan Berry Hillacre. b 52. DipHE86. Oak Hill Th Coll 84. **d** 86 **p** 87. C Okehampton w Inwardleigh *Ex* 86-89; C Bratton Fleming 89; TV Shirwell, Loxhore, Kentisbury, Arlington, etc 90-92; TR 92-96; P-in-c Shebbear, Buckland Filleigh, Sheepwash etc 96-97. *Address temp unknown*

RICHARDS, Julian. b 25. Wycliffe Hall Ox 71. **d** 73 **p** 74. C Hessle *York* 73-76; P-in-c Rowley 76-82; Chapl HM Pris Hull 79-82; P-in-c Boldre *Win* 82-83; P-in-c Boldre w S Baddesley 83; V 83-93; rtd 93; RD Alton *Win* from 93. *Manor End, Worldham Hill, East Worldham, Alton, Hants GU34 3AX* Tel (01420) 86894

RICHARDS, Keith David. b 50. Didsbury Coll of Educn CertEd72. S'wark Ord Course 79. **d** 82 **p** 83. NSM Walworth *S'wark* 82-85; Chapl Derbyshire Coll of HE 85-87; V Rottingdean *Chich* 87-93; TR Crawley 93-97; V Arundel w Tortington and S Stoke from 97. *21 Nineveh Shipyard, River Road, Arundel, W Sussex BN18 9SU* Tel (01903) 885209

RICHARDS, Kelvin. b 58. Univ of Wales (Abth) BSc80 MA88. Ripon Coll Cuddesdon BA82. **d** 83 **p** 84. C Killay *S & B* 83-86; C Morriston 86-89; V Llangattock and Llangyndir from 89. *The Rectory, Llangattock, Crickhowell NP8 1PH* Tel (01873) 810270

RICHARDS, Kendrick Steven William. b 55. DMS81 Nottm Univ BTh87. St Jo Coll Nottm 84. **d** 87 **p** 88. C Belper *Derby* 87-91; V Ilkeston St Jo 91-95; rtd 95; Perm to Offic *Derby* from 95. *30 Newstead Road North, Shipley View, Ilkeston, Derbyshire DE7 8UB*

RICHARDS, Llewelyn. b 15. St Deiniol's Hawarden 73. **d** 75 **p** 76. NSM Corwen and Llangar *St As* 75-85; Past Care Gwyddelwern 78-85; rtd 85. *120 Maesyfallen, Corwen LL21 9AD* Tel (01490) 412195

RICHARDS, Mrs Mary Edith. b 33. SW Minl Tr Course 85. **d** 87 **p** 94. NSM Kea *Truro* 87-88; Asst Chapl Bris Poly *Bris* 88-91; C E Clevedon and Walton w Weston w Clapton *B & W* 91-96; rtd 96; Hon C Probus, Ladock and Grampound w Creed and St Erme *Truro* from 97; Mental Health Chapl Cornwall Healthcare Trust from 97. *62 Midway Drive, Uplands Park, Truro, Cornwall TR1 1NQ* Tel (01872) 77556

RICHARDS, Norman John. b 47. BSc. Ridley Hall Cam. **d** 83 **p** 84. C Luton St Fran *St Alb* 83-86; R Aspenden and Layston w Buntingford 86-95; P-in-c Westmill 94-95; R Aspenden, Buntingford and Westmill from 95. *The Vicarage, Vicarage Road, Buntingford, Herts SG9 9BH* Tel (01763) 271552

RICHARDS, Peter Garth. b 30. Lon Univ BA51 Ex Univ PGCE72. St Chad's Coll Dur DipTh55. **d** 55 **p** 56. C Manston *Ripon* 55-57; C Adel 57-62; V Holbeck St Matt 62-66; C Clyst St George *Ex* 66-75; TV Clyst St George, Aylesbeare, Clyst Honiton etc 75-81; rtd 92. *6 Cutlers Rough Close, Birmingham B31 1LX* Tel 0121-477 9308

RICHARDS, Robert Graham. b 42. St Jo Coll Nottm LTh. **d** 80 **p** 81. C Radipole and Melcombe Regis *Sarum* 80-83; TV Billericay and Lt Burstead *Chelmsf* 84-91; UK Dir CMJ 91-95; Lic to Offic *St Alb* from 92; Chief Exec Nat Bibl Heritage Cen Ltd Trust from 95. *22 Dove Park, Chorleywood, Rickmansworth, Herts WD3 5NY* Tel (01923) 285878 Fax as telephone

RICHARDS, Ronald Jervis. b 16. St D Coll Lamp BA37 St Mich Coll Llan 38. **d** 39 **p** 40. C Minera *St As* 39-43; Chapl RAF 43-71; R Quendon w Rickling *Chelmsf* 71-75; V Dedham 75-83; rtd 83. *2 Hollies Road, St Stephens, Launceston, Cornwall PL15 8HB* Tel (01566) 776296

RICHARDS, Shaun. b 62. St Steph Ho Ox DipMin95. **d** 97. C Willesden Green St Andr and St Fran of Assisi *Lon* from 97. *150 Ellesmere Road, Gladstone Park, London NW10 1JT* Tel 0181-452 3999

RICHARDS, Simon Granston. b 47. Nottm Univ BTh72. St Jo Coll Nottm 68 ALCD72. **d** 72 **p** 73. C Waltham Abbey *Chelmsf* 72-77; TV Basildon St Martin w H Cross and Laindon etc 77-80; V Grayshott *Guildf* 80-88; V Eccleston Ch Ch *Liv* 88-92; V Berkeley w Wick, Breadstone and Newport *Glouc* from 92; RD Dursley from 96. *The Vicarage, Church Lane, Berkeley, Glos GL13 9BH* Tel (01453) 810294

RICHARDS, Canon Thomas John Wynzie. b 25. St D Coll Lamp BA49. **d** 51 **p** 52. C Llandybie *St D* 51-53; V 71-87; C Llandegai *Ban* 53-56; R Llanymawddwy 56-57; Chapl Nat Nautical Sch Portishead 57-71; RD Dyffryn Aman *St D* 78-85; Can St D Cathl 83-92; Treas St D Cathl 89-92; V Pencarreg and Llanycrwys 87-92; rtd 92. *Maes Teifi, Cwmann, Lampeter SA48 8DT* Tel (01570) 423354

RICHARDS, William Antony. b 28. Ex Coll Ox BA52 MA56. St Steph Ho Ox 52. **d** 54 **p** 55. C Fenton *Lich* 54-55; C Kingswinford St Mary 55-60; V Meir 60-64; R Warmington w Shotteswell *Cov* 64-75; RD Dassett Magna 70-74; Org Sec (Dios

Cov, Leic and Pet) CECS 75-81; V Bidford-on-Avon *Cov* 81-92; rtd 92. *4 Harbour Close, Bidford-on-Avon, Alcester, Warks B50 4EW* Tel (01789) 772699

RICHARDS, Canon William Hughes. b 37. St D Coll Lamp BA58. **d** 60 **p** 61. C Llandysul *St D* 60-63; C Llanelli 63-65; V Llanddewi Brefi w Llanbadarn Odwyn 65-73; V Pen-bre 73-83; V Llangynnwr and Cwmffrwd 83-88; V Cardigan and Mwnt and Y Ferwig from 88; Can St D Cathl from 89. *The Vicarage, Napier Gardens, Cardigan SA43 1EG* Tel (01239) 612722

RICHARDS, Canon William Neal (Bill). b 38. ALCD63. **d** 63 **p** 64. C Otley *Bradf* 63-65; C Leamington Priors St Mary *Cov* 65-67; CMS 67-69; Kenya 69-74; Asst Provost and Can Res Nairobi Cathl 70-74; V Gt Malvern St Mary *Worc* 74-86; Chapl Kidderminster Health Distr 86-91; RD Kidderminster *Worc* 89-91; R Martley and Wichenford, Knightwick etc from 91. *The Rectory, Martley, Worcester WR6 6QA* Tel (01886) 888664

RICHARDSON, Andrew John. b 44. Ex Univ CertEd69. Trin Coll Bris. **d** 82 **p** 83. Kenya 82-87; Chapl Brentwood Sch Essex 88; Chapl Scarborough Coll from 88. *Scarborough College, Filey Road, Scarborough, N Yorkshire YO11 3BA* Tel (01723) 360620

RICHARDSON, Canon Charles. b 13. AKC35. Linc Th Coll 35. **d** 36 **p** 37. C Eltham St Barn *S'wark* 36-40; C St Helier 40-45; Chapl RNVR 45-47; Min Mitcham Ascension CD *S'wark* 47-53; PC 53-54; R Rawmarsh *Sheff* 54-60; R Rawmarsh w Parkgate 60-76; RD Rotherham 74-76; Hon Can Sheff Cathl 75-80; R Harthill 76-80; rtd 80; Perm to Offic *Sheff* from 81. *41 Nether Green Road, Sheffield S11 7EH* Tel 0114-230 4699

RICHARDSON, Charles Leslie Joseph. b 54. St Jo Coll Dur BA76. Coll of Resurr Mirfield 76. **d** 79 **p** 80. C Folkestone St Mary and St Eanswythe *Cant* 79-83; C Maidstone St Martin 83-86; Selection Sec and Voc Adv ACCM 86-91; PV Westmr Abbey 87-91; R Hastings St Clem and All SS *Chich* from 91; RD Hastings from 92. *Old Town Rectory, 106 High Street, Hastings, E Sussex TN34 3ES* Tel (01424) 422023

RICHARDSON, Clive John. b 57. Trin Coll Bris BA82 Oak Hill Th Coll DipHE83. **d** 83 **p** 84. C Woking St Pet *Guildf* 83-86; C Worplesdon 86-90; V Rowledge from 90. *The Vicarage, Church Lane, Rowledge, Farnham, Surrey GU10 4EN* Tel (01252) 792402

RICHARDSON, David Anthony. b 41. Kelham Th Coll 57. **d** 66 **p** 67. C Tong *Bradf* 66-68; C Richmond St Mary *S'wark* 68-71; C Sanderstead All SS 71-74; TV 74-78; R Beddington 78-92; V Dormansland from 92; RD Godstone from 95. *The Vicarage, The Platt, Dormansland, Lingfield, Surrey RH7 6QU* Tel (01342) 832391

RICHARDSON, David Gwynne. b 39. AMIMinE. K Coll Lon 60. **d** 64 **p** 65. C Birtley *Dur* 64-67; Bp's Soc and Ind Adv 67-77; TV Brayton *York* 78-92; Ind Chapl 78-92; Chapl IMinE from 85; R Monk Fryston and S Milford from 92; RD Selby from 93. *The Rectory, Main Street, Hillam, Leeds LS25 5HH* Tel (01977) 682357

RICHARDSON, David John. b 50. MA LLB. S'wark Ord Course. **d** 85 **p** 86. NSM S Croydon Em *S'wark* from 85. *20 Hurst View Road, South Croydon, Surrey CR2 7AG* Tel 0181-688 4947 or 688 6676

RICHARDSON, The Very Revd David John Leyburn. b 46. Queensland Univ BA69. St Barn Coll Adelaide ACT ThL70 Melbourne Coll of Div BD75. **d** 70 **p** 71. Australia 70-75 and from 79; Dean Adelaide from 89; C Cambridge Gt St Mary w St Mich *Ely* 76-79. *26 Wakefield Street, Kent Town, Australia 5067* Tel Adelaide (8) 267 4551 or 332 7713 Fax 239 2010

RICHARDSON, Preb Douglas Stanley. b 23. Bps' Coll Cheshunt 55. **d** 57 **p** 58. C Hampton St Mary *Lon* 57-61; V W Twyford 61-69; V Notting Hill St Pet 69-78; V Staines St Pet 78-83; P-in-c Staines St Mary 81-83; V Staines St Mary and St Pet 83-92; AD Spelthorne 83-92; Preb St Paul's Cathl 92; rtd 92. *22 Rooks Down Road, Badgers Farm, Winchester, Hants SO22 4LT* Tel (01962) 863687

RICHARDSON, Edward John. b 39. **d** 65 **p** 66. C Chessington *Guildf* 65-70; V Stoneleigh 75-79; Perm to Offic *S'wark* 92-94; Hon C Kingston All SS w St Jo from 94. *3 Westways, Stoneleigh, Epsom, Surrey KT19 0PH* Tel 0181-393 3648

RICHARDSON, Canon Eric Hatherley Humphrey. b 12. Qu Coll Ox BA35. Westcott Ho Cam 35. **d** 36 **p** 37. C Stoke Newington St Mary *Lon* 36-39; S Africa from 39. *PO Box 2289, Kramerview, 2060 South Africa* Tel Johannesburg (11) 787-7813

RICHARDSON, Geoffrey Stewart. b 47. St Jo Coll Ox BA69 MA73. St Steph Ho Ox 70. **d** 72 **p** 73. C Roxbourne St Andr *Lon* 72-75; C Woodford St Barn *Chelmsf* 75-80; V Goodmayes St Paul 80-87; R Stow in Lindsey *Linc* 87-92; P-in-c Coates 87-92; P-in-c Willingham 87-92; R Stow Gp from 92; RD Corringham from 93. *The Rectory, Stow in Lindsey, Lincoln LN1 2DF* Tel (01427) 788251

RICHARDSON, Gerald. b 24. Chich Th Coll 54. **d** 56 **p** 57. C Northolt St Mary *Lon* 56-59; C Caversham *Ox* 59-63; V Snibston *Leic* 63-67; V Smethwick St Steph *Birm* 67-72; R Aylestone Park *Leic* 72-85; Perm to Offic from 85; rtd 89. *St Eanswythe, 55 Stonesby Avenue, Leicester LE2 6TX* Tel 0116-283 0561

RICHARDSON, Harold. b 22. Worc Ord Coll 62. **d** 64 **p** 65. C Carl St Barn *Carl* 64-66; V Rockcliffe 66-74; rtd 87. *21 St Catherine's Place, Edinburgh EH9 1NU* Tel 0131-667 8040

RICHARDSON, Canon Jack Cyril. b 11. Leeds Univ BSc36. Coll of Resurr Mirfield 35. **d** 35 **p** 36. C Mottingham St Andr *S'wark* 35-38; S Africa 38-45; CF 40-45; C Farnham Royal *Ox* 45-53; V S Stoneham *Win* 53-65; R Upper Clatford w Goodworth Clatford 65-77; RD Andover 67-75; Hon Can Win Cathl 73-77; rtd 77; Perm to Offic *St Alb* from 78. *Robin Cottage, The Street, Braughing, Ware, Herts SG11 2QR* Tel (01920) 822020

RICHARDSON, James Aidan. b 28. St Chad's Coll Dur BA51 DipTh54. **d** 54 **p** 55. C Ferryhill *Dur* 54-56; C Stirling *Edin* 56-58; P-in-c Bo'ness 58-64; P-in-c Linlithgow 58-64; V Linthwaite *Wakef* 64-79; RD Blackmoorfoot 77-79; V Clifton 79-92; P-in-c Hartshead 83-88; rtd 92. *10B Brooke Street, Cleckheaton, W Yorkshire BD19 3RY* Tel (01274) 874587

RICHARDSON, James Arthur. b 19. MC44. ARICS53 Lon Univ BSc51. Ridley Hall Cam 60. **d** 62 **p** 62. C Wandsworth All SS *S'wark* 62-65; V Streatham Park St Alb 65-87; rtd 87; Perm to Offic *Chich* from 87. *18 Cranden Road, Eastbourne, E Sussex BN20 8LW* Tel (01323) 737711

RICHARDSON, James Horner. b 19. Ch Coll Cam BA42 MA45. Ridley Hall Cam 41. **d** 43 **p** 44. C Normanton *Derby* 43-47; C Far Headingley St Chad *Ripon* 47-48; C High Harrogate St Pet 48-50; CF 50-53; Hon CF from 53; V Chadderton Em *Man* 53-59; V Huyton St Mich *Liv* 59-70; V Ormskirk 70-80; V Giggleswick *Bradf* 80-82; P-in-c Rathmell 80-82; V Giggleswick and Rathmell w Wigglesworth 82-84; rtd 84; Hon Chapl Spennithorne Hall *Ripon* from 84; Hon C Aysgarth and Bolton cum Redmire from 84. *25 Longdale Avenue, Settle, N Yorkshire BD24 9BB* Tel (01729) 823793

RICHARDSON, Canon James John (Jim). b 41. FRSA91 Hull Univ BA63 Sheff Univ DipEd64. Cuddesdon Coll 66. **d** 69 **p** 70. C Wolverhampton St Pet *Lich* 69-72; P-in-c Hanley All SS 72-75; R Nantwich *Ches* 75-82; Hon Can Ripon Cathl *Ripon* 82-88; V Leeds St Pet 82-88; Exec Dir Coun of Chrs and Jews 88-92; Lic to Offic *Pet* 88-93; P-in-c Brington w Whilton and Norton 93-96; P-in-c Church Brampton, Chapel Brampton, Harleston etc 94-96; TR Bournemouth St Pet w St Swithun, H Trin etc *Win* from 96. *St Peter's Rectory, 18 Wimborne Road, Bournemouth BH2 6NT* Tel (01202) 554058

RICHARDSON, John. b 41. Qu Coll Birm 69. **d** 72 **p** 73. C Ormskirk *Liv* 72-74; C Doncaster St Geo *Sheff* 74-77; R Hemsworth *Wakef* 77-79; V Penallt *Mon* 79-85; R Amotherby w Appleton and Barton-le-Street *York* 85-89; P-in-c Hovingham 86-89; C 89; P-in-c Slingsby 86-89; TR Street TM 89-90; R Skelton w Shipton and Newton on Ouse 90-93; V Alsager St Mary *Ches* 93-96; V Grangetown *York* from 96. *The Vicarage, Clynes Road, Grangetown, Middlesbrough, Cleveland TS6 7LY* Tel (01642) 453704

RICHARDSON, John. b 47. Linc Th Coll 78. **d** 80 **p** 81. C Keighley St Andr *Bradf* 80-83; V Hugglescote w Donington *Leic* 83-84; V Hugglescote w Donington-le-Heath and Ellistown 84-86; TR Hugglescote w Donington, Ellistown and Snibston 86-97; RD Akeley S 87-96; R Hallaton w Horninghold, Allexton, Tugby etc from 97. *The Rectory, Churchgate, Hallaton, Market Harborough, Leics LE16 8TY* Tel (01858) 555363

RICHARDSON, John. b 55. Lon Univ BEd BD. St Steph Ho Ox. **d** 83 **p** 84. C Thornbury *Glouc* 83-86; C Sheff Parson Cross St Cecilia *Sheff* 86-87; C Clacton St Jas *Chelmsf* 87-90; R Gt Tey and Wakes Colne w Chappel from 90. *The Rectory, Brook Road, Great Tey, Colchester CO6 1JF* Tel (01206) 211481

RICHARDSON, John Aubrey. b 33. NE Ord Course 90. **d** 93 **p** 94. NSM Warkworth and Acklington *Newc* from 93. *Harvest Lodge, 27 Acklington Village, Morpeth, Northd NE65 9BL* Tel (01670) 760761

RICHARDSON, John Hedley. b 45. Leeds Univ BA72. Qu Coll Birm 72. **d** 74 **p** 75. C Chaddesden St Phil *Derby* 74-76; Perm to Offic 76-86; TV Old Brampton and Loundsley Green 86-91; R Caston w Griston, Merton, Thompson etc *Nor* 91-95; RD Breckland from 94; P-in-c Hockham w Shropham Gp of Par 94-95; R Caston, Griston, Merton, Thompson etc from 95. *The Rectory, The Street, Caston, Attleborough, Norfolk NR17 1DD* Tel (01953) 483222

✠**RICHARDSON, The Rt Revd John Henry.** b 37. Trin Hall Cam BA61 MA65. Cuddesdon Coll 61. **d** 63 **p** 64 **c** 94. C Stevenage *St Alb* 63-66; C Eastbourne St Mary *Chich* 66-68; V Chipperfield St Paul *St Alb* 68-75; V Rickmansworth 75-86; RD Rickmansworth 77-86; V Bishop's Stortford St Mich 86-94; Hon Can St Alb 87-94; Suff Bp Bedford from 94. *168 Kimbolton Road, Bedford MK41 8DN* Tel (01234) 357551 Fax 218134

RICHARDSON, John Humphrey. b 33. Dur Univ BA57. Chich Th Coll 57. **d** 59 **p** 60. C Bexhill St Barn *Chich* 59-61; C Stanmer w Falmer and Moulsecoomb 61-64; C Ifield 64-70; R Earnley and E Wittering 70-79; V Stamford All SS w St Pet *Linc* 79-81; R Stamford St Jo w St Clem 79-81; RD Aveland and Ness w Stamford 80-87; V Stamford All SS w St Jo 81-92; P-in-c Metheringham w Blankney 92-94; V Metheringham w Blankney and Dunston from 94. *The Vicarage, 38 Drury Street, Metheringham, Lincoln LN4 3EZ* Tel (01526) 321115

RICHARDSON, Canon John Malcolm. b 39. Glas Univ MA60 BD63. Andover Newton Th Coll STM65 Edin Th Coll 84. **d** 84 **p** 85. C Edin Old St Paul *Edin* 84-86; R Leven *St And* 86-90; R Newport-on-Tay 90-96; R Tayport 90-96; Can St Ninian's Cathl

Perth from 93; R Forfar from 96. *The Rectory, 24 St James's Road, Forfar, Angus DD8 1LG* Tel (01307) 463440

RICHARDSON, John Peter. b 50. Keele Univ BA72. St Jo Coll Nottm 73. **d** 76 **p** 77. C Birm St Paul *Birm* 76-79; C Blackheath 79-81; P-in-c Sparkbrook Ch Ch 81-83; Chapl NE Lon Poly *Chelmsf* 83-92; Chapl E Lon Univ from 92; Hon C Stratford St Jo and Ch Ch w Forest Gate St Jas from 83. *4 Matthew's Park Avenue, London E15 4AE* Tel 0181-536 0230 or 590 7722

RICHARDSON, The Very Revd John Stephen. b 50. Southn Univ BA71. St Jo Coll Nottm 72. **d** 74 **p** 75. C Bramcote *S'well* 74-77; C Radipole and Melcombe Regis *Sarum* 77-80; P-in-c Stinsford, Winterborne Came w Whitcombe etc 80-83; Asst Dioc Missr 80-83; V Nailsea Ch Ch *B & W* 83-90; Adv on Evang 86-90; Provost Bradf from 90. *The Provost's House, Cathedral Close, Bradford BD1 4EG* Tel (01274) 732023 Fax 722898

RICHARDSON, Prof John Stuart. b 46. Trin Coll Ox BA68 MA71 DPhil73. **d** 79 **p** 80. NSM St Andrews St Andr *St And* 79-87; Chapl St Andr Univ 80-87; Prof Classics Edin Univ from 87; TV Edin St Columba *Edin* from 87. *29 Merchiston Avenue, Edinburgh EH10 4PH* Tel 0131-228 3094

RICHARDSON, John Thandule. b 49. Bradf and Ilkley Coll Cert Youth & Community Work 78 BSc80. Carl and Blackb Tr Inst 94. **d** 97. NSM Lea *Blackb* from 97. *65 Lower Bank Road, Fulwood, Preston PR2 8NU* Tel (01772) 787689

RICHARDSON, John William. b 56. Bp Otter Coll BA85 Chich Th Coll 85. **d** 87 **p** 88. C E Preston w Kingston *Chich* 87-89; C Goring-by-Sea 89-90; TV Aldrington 91-92; V Sompting from 92. *The Vicarage, West Street, Sompting, Lancing, W Sussex BN15 0AX* Tel (01903) 234511

RICHARDSON, Joseph Edmund. b 27. St Chad's Coll Dur BA49. Sarum Th Coll 51. **d** 52 **p** 53. C Far Headingley St Chad *Ripon* 52-56; C Hoylake *Ches* 56-58; R Halton *Ox* 58-65; R Davenham *Ches* 65-76; V Sale St Anne 76-84; R Delamere 84-88; rtd 88; Perm to Offic *Ex* from 94. *10 Glenthorne Road, Exeter EX4 4QU* Tel (01392) 438539

RICHARDSON, Laurence Leigh. b 71. Trin Coll Carmarthen BA92 PGCE93 Univ of Wales (Cardiff) BTh97. St Mich Coll Llan DipTh94. **d** 97. C Carmarthen St Pet *St D* from 97. *St Peter's Clergy House, 10A The Parade, Carmarthen SA31 1LY* Tel (01267) 237303

RICHARDSON, Maurice. b 12. **d** 66 **p** 67. C Hawksworth w Scarrington *S'well* 66-69; V Lowdham 69-77; rtd 77; Perm to Offic *S'well* from 77; Perm to Offic *Leic* from 82. *Old Orchard, Granby, Nottingham NG13 9PR* Tel (01949) 50860

RICHARDSON, Neil. b 46. Southn Univ BTh83. Sarum & Wells Th Coll 71. **d** 74 **p** 75. C Oldham St Mary w St Pet *Man* 74-77; C-in-c Holts CD 77-82; R Greenford H Cross *Lon* from 82. *The Rectory, Oldfield Lane, Greenford, Middx UB6 9JS* Tel 0181-578 1543

RICHARDSON, Paul. b 58. Univ of Wales (Cardiff) BSc80. Ridley Hall Cam 81. **d** 84 **p** 85. C Stanwix *Carl* 84-87; Ind Chapl 87-89; Staff Priest Dalton-in-Furness 87-89; V Marton Moss *Blackb* 89-95; P-in-c Prestwich St Gabr *Man* from 95; Bp's Dom Chapl from 95. *St Gabriel's Vicarage, 8 Bishops Road, Prestwich, Manchester M25 0HT* Tel 0161-773 8839 or 792 2096

RICHARDSON, Ronald Eric (<u>Ron</u>). b 48. York Univ CertEd Leeds Univ BEd. N Ord Course. **d** 82 **p** 83. NSM Wakef St Andr and St Mary *Wakef* 82-83; C 83-90; NSM S Ossett 90-95; Perm to Offic from 95. *37 Stanley Road, Wakefield, W Yorkshire WF1 4NA* Tel (01924) 381047

RICHARDSON, Miss Susan. b 58. Cranmer Hall Dur. **d** 87 **p** 94. Par Dn Stokesley *York* 87-91; Par Dn Beverley St Nic 91-94; P-in-c Cloughton 94-97; Tr Officer E Riding Adnry from 94; V Cloughton and Burniston w Ravenscar etc from 97. *The Vicarage, Mill Lane, Cloughton, Scarborough, N Yorkshire YO13 0AB* Tel (01723) 870270

RICHARDSON, Canon William. b 11. Qu Coll Ox BA34 MA37 BD52. Ripon Hall Ox 35. **d** 36 **p** 37. C Bilston St Leon *Lich* 36-37; C Wem 37-39; Tutor Ripon Hall Ox 39-43; Chapl 40-43; Asst Master Stamford Sch 43-48; P-in-c Stamford Baron *Linc* 43-46; R Careby w Holywell and Aunby 46-48; Asst Chapl Oundle Sch 48-51; Chapl Malvern Coll 51-52; V Whitgift w Adlingfleet *Sheff* 52-59; Lect Th Hull Univ *York* 54-72; R Routh 59-61; V Wawne 59-61; Select Preacher Cam Univ 61; V Sutton St Jas *York* 61-71; P-in-c Wawne 61-69; V 69-71; TR Sutton St Jas and Wawne 71-78; Can and Preb York Minster 70-87; rtd 78. *Manormead Nursing Home, Tilford Road, Hindhead, Surrey GU26 6RA* Tel (01428) 604780

RICHBOROUGH, Suffragan Bishop of (Provincial Episcopal Visitor). *See* BARNES, The Rt Revd Edwin Ronald

RICHENS, Canon Geoffrey Roger. b 23. ALCD52. **d** 52 **p** 53. C St Helens St Helen *Liv* 52-56; V Widnes St Mary 56-80; V Skelmersdale St Paul 80-93; Hon Can Liv Cathl 89-93; rtd 93; Perm to Offic *Liv* from 93. *43 West View, Parbold, Wigan, Lancs WN8 7NT* Tel (01257) 463143

RICHERBY, Glynn. b 51. K Coll Lon BD73 AKC73. St Aug Coll Cant 73. **d** 74 **p** 75. C Weston Favell *Pet* 74-78; Prec Leic Cathl *Leic* 78-81; V Glen Parva and S Wigston 81-93; Dir Post Ord Tr 86-95; V Leic St Jas from 93; Dir of Continuing Minl Educn from 95. *St James the Greater Vicarage, 216 London Road, Leicester LE2 1NE* Tel 0116-254 4113

RICHES, Prof John Kenneth. b 39. CCC Cam BA61 MA65. Kirchliche Hochschule Th Coll Berlin 61 Westcott Ho Cam 62. **d** 65 **p** 66. C Costessey *Nor* 65-68; Chapl and Fell SS Coll Cam 68-72; Lect Glas Univ 72-86; Sen Lect 86-91; Prof Div and Bibl Criticism Glas Univ from 91; Chmn Balmore Trust from 80; Lic to Offic *Glas* from 85. *Viewfield, Balmore, Torrance, Glasgow G64 4AE* Tel (01360) 620254

✠**RICHES, The Rt Revd Kenneth.** b 08. CCC Cam BA31 MA35. Gen Th Sem (NY) Hon STD56 Lambeth DD57 Cuddesdon Coll 32. **d** 32 **p** 33 **c** 52. C Portsea St Mary *Portsm* 32-35; C E Dulwich St Jo *S'wark* 35-36; Chapl SS Coll Cam 36-42; Lic to Offic *Bradf* 36-44; R Bredfield w Boulge *St E* 42-44; Prin Cuddesdon Coll 44-52; V Cuddesdon *Ox* 44-52; Hon Can Portsm Cathl *Portsm* 50-52; Suff Bp Dorchester *Ox* 52-56; Adn Ox and Can Res Ch Ch 52-56; Bp Linc 56-74; rtd 74; Perm to Offic *St E* from 74. *Little Dingle, Dunwich, Saxmundham, Suffolk IP17 3EA* Tel (01728) 648316

RICHES, Malcolm Leslie. b 46. St Jo Coll Nottm DipThMin94. **d** 94 **p** 95. C Swaythling *Win* from 94. *12 Willis Road, Swaythling, Southampton SO16 2NT* Tel (01703) 586002

RICHEY, Canon Robert Samuel Payne. b 23. TCD BA46. **d** 48 **p** 49. C Moy *Arm* 48-50; I Killinagh w Kiltyclogher *K, E & A* 50-60; I Killinagh w Kiltyclogher and Innismagrath 60-72; I Killinagh w Kiltyclogher, Killargue etc 72-91; I Killinagh w Kiltyclogher and Innismagrath from 91; Sec Dioc Bd Educn from 64; Dioc Sec (Kilmore) from 72; Dioc Info Officer (Kilmore) from 81; Preb Kilmore Cathl from 80; Preb Mulhuddart St Patr Cathl Dublin from 94. *Killinagh Rectory, Blacklion, Sligo, Irish Republic* Tel Manorhamilton (72) 53010 Fax as telephone

RICHMOND, Arnold. b 19. Sarum & Wells Th Coll 77. **d** 80 **p** 81. NSM Axminster *Ex* 80-83; Dep PV Ex Cathl from 83; NSM Axminster, Chardstock, Combe Pyne and Rousdon 83-86; NSM Colyton, Southleigh, Offwell, Widworthy etc from 86. *New House Farm, Combpyne Road, Musbury, Axminster, Devon EX13 6SS* Tel (01297) 553501

✠**RICHMOND, The Rt Revd Francis <u>Henry</u> Arthur.** b 36. TCD BA59 MA66 Strasbourg Univ BTh60 Linacre Coll Ox MLitt64. Wycliffe Hall Ox 60. **d** 63 **p** 64 **c** 86. C Woodlands *Sheff* 63-66; Chapl Sheff Cathl 66-69; V Sheff St Geo 69-77; Chapl Sheff Univ 74-77; Warden Linc Th Coll 77-86; Can and Preb Linc Cathl *Linc* 77-86; Suff Bp Repton *Derby* from 86; Hon Can Derby Cathl from 86. *Repton House, Lea, Matlock, Derbyshire DE4 5JP* Tel (01629) 534644 Fax 534003

RICHMOND, Gordon Hazlewood. b 33. Launde Abbey 77. **d** 79 **p** 80. C Leic St Paul *Leic* 79-81; C Shepshed 81-84; V Ryhall w Essendine *Pet* 84-91; RD Barnack 89-91; V Gretton w Rockingham from 91. *The Vicarage, Station Road, Gretton, Corby, Northants NN17 3BU* Tel (01536) 770237

RICHMOND, Patrick Henry. b 69. Ball Coll Ox BA90 Green Coll Ox DPhil94 MA94. Wycliffe Hall Ox BA96. **d** 97. C Leic Martyrs *Leic* from 97. *62 Ashleigh Road, Leicester LE3 0FB* Tel 0116-254 1341

RICHMOND, Peter James. b 54. Writtle Agric Coll HND76 Ex Univ PGCE95. St Jo Coll Nottm LTh80. **d** 80 **p** 81. C Ogley Hay *Lich* 80-83; C Trentham 83-85; P-in-c Wolverhampton St Jo 85-89; P-in-c Loppington w Newtown 89-93; P-in-c Edstaston 89-93; Perm to Offic *Ex* 94-95; P-in-c Weston Zoyland w Chedzoy *B & W* from 95. *The Vicarage, Church Lane, Westonzoyland, Bridgwater, Somerset TA7 0EP* Tel (01278) 691743

RICHMOND, Archdeacon of. *See* GOOD, The Ven Kenneth Roy

RICKETTS, Allan Fenn. b 46. Open Univ BA76. Cranmer Hall Dur 68. **d** 71 **p** 72. C Rowley Regis *Birm* 71-72; C The Quinton 72-74; C Brierley Hill *Lich* 74-77; TV Chelmsley Wood *Birm* 77-82; TV Ross w Brampton Abbotts, Bridstow and Peterstow *Heref* 82-88; R Linton w Upton Bishop and Aston Ingham 88-96. *13 Falaise Close, Ross-on-Wye, Herefordshire HR9 5UT* Tel (01989) 565077

RICKETTS, Graham Victor. b 67. Leic Univ BSc89. Chich Th Coll 89. **d** 92 **p** 93. C Brighton St Geo w St Anne and St Mark *Chich* 92-95; C Worth 95-96; TV from 96. *3 Mayflower Close, Maidenbower, Crawley, W Sussex RH10 4WH* Tel (01293) 884309

RICKETTS, Canon Kathleen Mary (<u>Kate</u>). b 39. Southlands Coll Lon TCert59 Univ of W Aus BA79. Westcott Ho Cam 81. **dss** 83 **d** 87 **p** 94. All Hallows by the Tower etc *Lon* 83-87; C 87-88; C Hall Green Ascension *Birm* 88-91; Chapl Birm Children's Hosp 91-94; Chapl Birm Children's Hosp NHS Trust from 94; Hon Can Birm Cathl *Birm* from 96. *28 Glaisdale Road, Birmingham B28 8PX, or Birmingham Children's Hospital, Birmingham B16 8NT* Tel 0121-778 6233 or 454 4851

RICKETTS, Peter William. b 28. DLC53. St Alb Minl Tr Scheme 76. **d** 79 **p** 80. NSM Hertford All SS *St Alb* 79-86; R Blunham w Tempsford and Lt Barford 86-93; rtd 93. *277 Hillgrounds Road, Kempston, Bedford MK42 8TH* Tel (01234) 841635

RICKMAN, Peter Alan. b 68. Ripon Coll Cuddesdon BTh94. **d** 97. C Bitterne Park *Win* from 97. *24 Lacon Close, Southampton SO18 1JA* Tel (01703) 584640 Mobile 0585-799280 Fax as telephone E-mail peter.rickman@virgin.net

RIDDEL, Canon Robert John. b 37. CITC. **d** 68 **p** 69. C Derryloran *Arm* 68-74; I Keady w Armaghbreague and Derrynoose 74-80; I Mullaghdun *Clogh* 80-84; I Cleenish 80-84; I Fivemiletown from 84; RD Clogh from 85; Can Clogh Cathl from 91; Preb Donaghmore St Patr Cathl Dublin from 95. *The Rectory, 160 Ballagh Road, Fivemiletown, Co Tyrone BT75 0QP* Tel (01365) 521030

RIDDELL, Morris Stroyan. b 34. Lon Univ DipTh59 BD69. Tyndale Hall Bris 57. **d** 60 **p** 60. S Africa 60-63; V N Grimston w Wharram Percy and Wharram-le-Street *York* 63-67; V Kirby Grindalythe 63-67; P-in-c Weaverthorpe w Helperthorpe and Luttons 65-67; P-in-c Settrington 65-67; P-in-c Wintringham 65-67; P-in-c Thorpe Bassett 65-67; R Bris St Jo w St Mary-le-Port *Bris* 67-70; Dir Bris Samaritans 67-70; Chapl HM Pris Long Lartin 71-74; Brixton 74-78; Chapl Cane Hill Hosp Coulsdon 78-85; Chapl HM Rem Cen Latchmere Ho 85-89; rtd 95. *1 Orchard Way, Pinelands 7405, Cape Town, South Africa* Fax 0944 171 233 1763

RIDDELSDELL, Canon John Creffield. b 23. Selw Coll Cam BA47 MA52 Lon Univ BD70. Ridley Hall Cam 47. **d** 49 **p** 50. C Kilburn St Mary *Lon* 49-52; Kenya 52-77; V Gt Ilford St Andr *Chelmsf* 77-88; rtd 88; Perm to Offic *Chelmsf* from 88. *Waverley, Mill Lane, Walton on the Naze, Essex CO14 8PE* Tel (01255) 850213

RIDDING, George. b 24. Or Coll Ox BA50 MA57. Wells Th Coll 60. **d** 61 **p** 62. C Countess Wear *Ex* 61-62; Chapl Ex Sch 62-64; India 64-68; Hd Master W Buckland Sch Barnstaple 68-78; USPG 78-82; P-in-c Broadhembury w Payhembury *Ex* 82-83; P-in-c Plymtree 82-83; R Broadhembury, Payhembury and Plymtree 83-89; rtd 89. *Cherwell, Higher Blandford Road, Shaftesbury, Dorset SP7 8DA* Tel (01747) 851390

RIDDING, William Thomas. b 54. Southn Univ BTh. Sarum & Wells Th Coll 80. **d** 83 **p** 84. C Verwood *Sarum* 83-86; TV Gillingham from 86; RD Blackmore Vale from 95. *The Vicarage, Kington Magna, Gillingham, Dorset SP8 5EW* Tel (01747) 838494

RIDDLE, Kenneth Wilkinson. b 20. St Cath Soc Ox BA42 MA46. Ripon Hall Ox 42. **d** 43 **p** 44. C Lowestoft St Marg *Nor* 43-47; C Luton St Mary *St Alb* 47-49; V Sundon w Streatley 49-52; R Pakefield *Nor* 52-59; V Nor St Pet Mancroft 59-60; R E w W Harling 60-65; P-in-c Bridgham and Roudham 60-61; R 61-65; R Lowestoft St Marg 65-68; rtd 85. *The Old Post Office, East Lyng, Taunton, Somerset TA3 5AU* Tel (01823) 698427

RIDEOUT, Canon Gordon Trevor. b 38. BA87 Westmr Coll Ox MTh96. Lon Coll of Div 58. **d** 62 **p** 63. C Southgate *Chich* 62-65; Chapl Dr Barnardo's Barkingside & Woodford Br 65-67; CF 67-73; V Nutley *Chich* 73-79; V Eastbourne All SS from 79; Chapl Moira Ho Sch E Sussex from 79; Chapl Brighton Poly *Chich* 80-92; Chapl Brighton Univ from 92; Can and Preb Chich Cathl from 90; RD Eastbourne from 97. *All Saints' Vicarage, Grange Road, Eastbourne, E Sussex BN21 4HE* Tel (01323) 410033

RIDER, Andrew. b 62. RMN85 Nottm Univ BTh90 K Coll Lon MA96. Aston Tr Scheme 85 St Jo Coll Nottm 87. **d** 90 **p** 91. C Luton Ch Ch *Roch* 90-93; C w resp for Clubhouse Langham Place All So *Lon* from 93. *25 Fitzroy Street, London W1P 5AF* Tel 0171-580 3745 or 387 1360 Fax 387 2593 E-mail club_house@compuserve.com

RIDER, Canon Dennis William Austin. b 34. Lon Univ DipTh61. St Aid Birkenhead 58. **d** 61 **p** 62. C Derby St Aug *Derby* 61-64; C Sutton *Liv* 64-67; R Stiffkey w Morston, Langham Episcopi etc *Nor* 67-71; V Buxton w Oxnead 71-79; R Lammas w Lt Hautbois 72-79; R Gaywood, Bawsey and Mintlyn 79-91; RD Lynn 89-91; Hon Can Nor Cathl from 90; R E Dereham and Scarning from 91; RD Hingham and Mitford from 95. *The Vicarage, 1 Vicarage Meadows, Dereham, Norfolk NR19 1TW* Tel (01362) 693143

RIDER, Geoffrey Malcolm. b 29. Selw Coll Cam BA53 MA56 Lon Inst of Educn PGCE68. Coll of Resurr Mirfield 53. **d** 55 **p** 56. C S Elmsall *Wakef* 55-60; C Barnsley St Mary 60-63; V Cleckheaton St Jo 63-67; Public Preacher *S'wark* 67-92; rtd 92; S Africa 92-95; Perm to Offic *S'wark* from 95. *6 Kenwyn Road, London SW20 8TR* Tel 0181-946 5735

RIDER, Neil Wilding. b 35. St Jo Coll Dur BA59 DipTh61. Cranmer Hall Dur 59. **d** 62 **p** 63. C Blackb St Barn *Blackb* 62-64; C Chadderton Em *Man* 64-69; C Deane 69-72; V Coldhurst 72-75; Perm to Offic *Ely* 76-78; C Didsbury Ch Ch *Man* 78-80; Perm to Offic *St D* from 80. *Caergrawnt, Cwmann, Lampeter SA48 8EL* Tel (01570) 422921

RIDGE, Aubrey. b 25. Oak Hill Th Coll 67. **d** 68 **p** 69. C Gorleston St Andr *Nor* 68-70; C Hamworthy *Sarum* 70-75; P-in-c Pitsea *Chelmsf* 75-78; R 78-81; P-in-c Stoke Ash, Thwaite and Wetheringsett *St E* 81-85; P-in-c Bedingfield and Thorndon w Rishangles 81-85; P-in-c Thorndon w Rishangles, Stoke Ash, Thwaite etc 85-86; P-in-c Risby w Gt and Lt Saxham and Westley 86-90; rtd 90; Perm to Offic *Sarum* 90-93; Hon C Milford *Win* from 93. *5 Oak Tree Court, Whitby Road, Milford on Sea, Lymington, Hants SO41 0UJ* Tel (01590) 643504

RIDGE, Haydn Stanley. b 24. Univ of Wales (Lamp) BA51 Bris Univ CertEd52. Qu Coll Birm 56. **d** 56 **p** 57. C Blackheath *Birm* 56-60; Div Master Guernsey Gr Sch 60-75; Perm to Offic *Win* 60-62; Hon C Guernsey St Steph from 62; Dep Hd Master St Peter Port Sch 75-80; Hd Master St Sampson Sch 75-87; rtd 91. *St David, Les Cherfs, Castel, Guernsey, Channel Islands GY5 7HG* Tel (01481) 56209

RIDGEWAY, David. b 59. St Chad's Coll Dur BSc80 Cam Univ CertEd81. Ripon Coll Cuddesdon 84. **d** 87 **p** 88. C Kempston Transfiguration *St Alb* 87-90; C Radlett 90-95; P-in-c Heath and Reach from 95. *The Vicarage, 2 Reach Lane, Heath and Reach, Leighton Buzzard, Beds LU7 0AL* Tel (01525) 237633

RIDGEWELL, Miss Mary Jean. b 54. Dur Univ BA76 PGCE77. Ridley Hall Cam 89. **d** 91 **p** 94. Par Dn Trowbridge St Jas *Sarum* 91-94; C 94-95; Chapl Lee Abbey 95-96; NSM Bradford Peverell, Stratton, Frampton etc *Sarum* from 96. *4 Church Hill View, Sydling, Dorchester, Dorset DT2 9SY*

RIDGWAY, David. b 28. Trin Hall Cam BA54 MA58. Westcott Ho Cam 54. **d** 56 **p** 57. C Milton *Portsm* 56-59; CF 59-63; R Gosforth *Carl* 63-70; V Walney Is 70-76; P-in-c Irthington 76-78; P-in-c Crosby-on-Eden 77-78; V Irthington, Crosby-on-Eden and Scaleby 79-93; rtd 93. *11 Woodleigh, Walton, Brampton, Cumbria CA8 2DS* Tel (016977) 3252

RIDGWAY, Mrs Janet Elizabeth Knight. b 40. St Alb Minl Tr Scheme. **dss** 86 **d** 87 **p** 94. Tring *St Alb* 86-87; Hon Par Dn 87-94; Hon C from 94. *Barleycombe, Trooper Road, Aldbury, Tring, Herts HP23 4RW* Tel (01442) 851303

RIDGWAY, Canon Maurice Hill. b 18. FSA BA. St D Coll Lamp BA40 Westcott Ho Cam 40. **d** 41 **p** 42. C Grappenhall *Ches* 41-44; C Hale 44-49; V Bunbury 49-62; V Bowdon 62-83; Hon Can Ches Cathl 66-83; rtd 83; Perm to Offic *Ches* from 83; Perm to Offic *St As* from 83; Perm to Offic *Lich* from 84. *Milkwood Cottage, Rhydycroesau, Oswestry, Shropshire SY10 7PS* Tel (01691) 655330

RIDING, Pauline Alison. *See* BICKNELL, Mrs Pauline Alison

RIDLEY, Alfred Forbes. b 34. Bps' Coll Cheshunt 62. **d** 65 **p** 66. C Prittlewell St Mary *Chelmsf* 65-69; R Paulerspury *Pet* 69-73; P-in-c Wicken 71-73; V W Haddon w Winwick 73-83; RD Brixworth 80-83; R Guernsey St Philippe de Torteval *Win* 83-92; R Guernsey St Pierre du Bois 83-92; R Blakesley w Adstone and Maidford etc *Pet* from 92. *The Vicarage, Blakesley, Towcester, Northants NN12 8RF* Tel (01327) 860507

RIDLEY, Andrew Roy. b 55. St Pet Coll Ox BA77. Ripon Coll Cuddesdon 78. **d** 79 **p** 80. C Bollington St Jo *Ches* 79-83; V Runcorn St Mich 83-94; Dioc Chapl to MU from 92; RD Frodsham from 94; V Helsby and Dunham-on-the-Hill from 94; P-in-c Alvanley from 94. *St Paul's Vicarage, Vicarage Lane, Helsby, Warrington WA6 9AB* Tel (01928) 722151 Fax as telephone

RIDLEY, David Gerhard (Vic). b 60. Southn Univ BSc82 Bath Univ PGCE83. Qu Coll Birm 91. **d** 93 **p** 94. C Faversham *Cant* 93-97; Min Folkestone St Mary and St Eanswythe from 97. *6 Copthall Gardens, Folkestone, Kent CT20 1HF* Tel (01303) 245807

RIDLEY, Derek. b 40. Newc Univ BSc74. Cranmer Hall Dur 75. **d** 78 **p** 79. C Upperby St Jo *Carl* 78-81; C Penrith w Newton Reigny 81; C Penrith w Newton Reigny and Plumpton Wall 81-82; TV 82-86; V Cadishead *Man* from 86. *St Mary's Vicarage, Penry Avenue, Cadishead, Manchester M30 5AF* Tel 0161-775 2171

RIDLEY, Jay. b 41. Birm Univ BA63. St Steph Ho Ox 63. **d** 65 **p** 66. C Woodford St Mary *Chelmsf* 65-67; C Prittlewell St Mary 67-70; C-in-c Dunscroft CD *Sheff* 70-75; Chapl HM Pris Wormwood Scrubs 75-77; Chapl HM Rem Cen Ashford 77-84; Chapl HM Young Offender Inst Feltham 84-91; Chapl HM Pris Ashwell from 91. *HM Prison Ashwell, Oakham, Leics LE15 7LS* Tel (01572) 756075 Fax 724460

RIDLEY, Canon Laurence Roy. b 19. St Pet Hall Ox BA41 MA45. Wycliffe Hall Ox 41. **d** 42 **p** 43. C Everton St Sav *Liv* 42-44; C Roby 44-51; C Reading St Mary V *Ox* 51-57; V Middlewich *Ches* 57-69; RD Middlewich 66-69; V Higher Bebington 69-90; RD Wirral N 79-89; Hon Can Ches Cathl 80-90; rtd 90; Perm to Offic *Ches* from 90. *6 Newtons Lane, Winterley, Sandbach, Cheshire CW11 9NL* Tel (01270) 505929

RIDLEY, Mrs Lesley. b 46. Cranmer Hall Dur 75. **dss** 78 **d** 87 **p** 94. Upperby St Jo *Carl* 78-81; Penrith w Newton Reigny and Plumpton Wall 81-86; Cadishead *Man* 86-87; Par Dn 87-94; C from 94. *St Mary's Vicarage, Penry Avenue, Cadishead, Manchester M30 5AF* Tel 0161-775 2171

RIDLEY, Michael Edward. b 37. Ex Univ MA90. AKC62. **d** 63 **p** 64. C Chapel Allerton *Ripon* 63-67; C Epsom St Martin *Guildf* 67-70; C Claxby w Normanby-le-Wold etc *Linc* 70-72; V Leake 72-75; R Harlaxton w Wyville and Hungerton 75-80; R Stroxton 76-80; Dioc Stewardship Adv *Portsm* 80-86; P-in-c Rowlands Castle 80-82; C Blendworth w Chalton w Idsworth etc 83-86; TV N Creedy *Ex* 86-90; R W Downland *Sarum* from 90; RD Chalke from 92. *The Rectory, 97 Mill End, Damerham, Fordingbridge, Hants SP6 3HU* Tel (01725) 518642

RIDLEY, Michael Laurence. b 59. BA81. Ripon Coll Cuddesdon 81. **d** 83 **p** 84. C Bollington St Jo *Ches* 83-88; V Thelwall 88-95; V Weaverham from 95. *The Vicarage, Weaverham, Northwich, Cheshire CW8 3NJ* Tel (01606) 852110

RIDLEY, Peter John. b 39. Keble Coll Ox BA61. Tyndale Hall Bris 61. **d** 63 **p** 64. C Clifton Ch Ch w Em *Bris* 63-67; C Lambeth St Andr w St Thos *S'wark* 67-69; V W Hampstead St Cuth *Lon* 69-77; V Eynsham *Ox* 77-85; RD Woodstock 82-84; V

Nicholforest and Kirkandrews on Esk *Carl* 85-96; P-in-c E Knoyle, Semley and Sedgehill *Sarum* from 96. *The Rectory, Semley, Shaftesbury, Dorset SP7 9AU* Tel (01747) 830362

RIDLEY, Simon. b 33. Magd Coll Ox BA54 MA58 BD66. Linc Th Coll 54. **d** 57 **p** 58. C St Jo Wood *Lon* 57-60; Abp's Dom Chapl *Cant* 60-61; V N Wootton *B & W* 61-66; Lect Wells Th Coll 61-65; Hong Kong 66-70; TR Basingstoke *Win* 70-73; rtd 96; Perm to Offic *Cant* from 96. *Oxney House, The Street, Wittersham, Tenterden, Kent TN30 7ED* Tel (01797) 270215

RIDLEY, Stephen James. b 57. St Pet Coll Ox MA83. Ripon Coll Cuddesdon 80. **d** 82 **p** 83. C Heald Green St Cath *Ches* 82-85; Chapl Ches Coll 85-90; Dioc Press Officer 85-90; Chapl Birkenhead Sch Merseyside 90-96; Lic to Offic *Ches* 90-96; Chapl Barnard Castle Sch from 96. *3 Old Courts, Barnard Castle School, Newgate, Barnard Castle, Co Durham DL12 8UN* Tel (01833) 690222

RIDLEY, Stewart Gordon. b 47. AKC72. St Aug Coll Cant 72. **d** 73 **p** 74. C Armley w New Wortley *Ripon* 73-77; C Hawksworth Wood 77-79; C Rothwell w Lofthouse 79-81; R Whitwood *Wakef* 81-87; R Ingoldmells w Addlethorpe *Linc* 87-92; RD Calcewaithe and Candleshoe 89-92; V Settle *Bradf* from 92; Dioc Chapl MU from 93. *The Vicarage, Townhead Way, Settle, N Yorkshire BD24 9JB* Tel (01729) 822288

RIDOUT, Canon Christopher John. b 33. K Coll Lon BD57 AKC57 MA92. **d** 58 **p** 59. C Roxeth Ch Ch *Lon* 58-62; CMS 62-63; Kenya 63-75; C Gt Malvern St Mary *Worc* 75-79; R Bredon w Bredon's Norton from 79; RD Pershore 91-97; Hon Can Worc Cathl from 92. *The Rectory, Bredon, Tewkesbury, Glos GL20 7LT* Tel (01684) 772237

✠**RIDSDALE, The Rt Revd Philip Bullen.** b 15. Trin Coll Cam BA37 MA45. Ridley Hall Cam 45. **d** 47 **p** 48 **c** 72. C St Helens St Helen *Liv* 47-49; Uganda 49-64; Adn Ruwenzori 61-64; Hon Can Ruwenzori from 63; R Bramfield w Stapleford *St Alb* 64-66; P-in-c Waterford 64-66; R Bramfield w Stapleford and Waterford 66-72; RD Hertford 70-72; Bp Boga-Zaire 72-80; rtd 81; Perm to Offic *Ely* from 81. *3 Pemberton Terrace, Cambridge CB2 1JA* Tel (01223) 62690

RIDYARD, Preb John Gordon. b 33. St Aid Birkenhead 59. **d** 62 **p** 63. C Lancaster St Mary *Blackb* 62-65; C Bushbury *Lich* 65-68; V Darlaston All SS 68-76; TV Wolverhampton St Mark 76-78; TV Wolverhampton 78-82; Preb Lich Cathl from 82; V Bishopswood 82-89; V Brewood 82-89; RD Penkridge 83-89; R Newcastle w Butterton from 89. *The Rectory, Seabridge Road, Newcastle-under-Lyme, Staffs ST5 2HS* Tel (01782) 616397

RIDYARD, Malcolm Charles. b 32. St D Coll Lamp BA54 Wycliffe Hall Ox 54. **d** 56 **p** 57. C Widnes St Paul *Liv* 56-59; C Ashton-in-Makerfield St Thos 59-61; India 62-71; Area Sec (Dios B & W, Bris and Sarum) CMS 71-80; P-in-c Church Coniston *Carl* 80-87; P-in-c Torver 80-87; R Bootle, Corney, Whicham and Whitbeck from 87. *The Rectory, Bootle, Millom, Cumbria LA19 5TH* Tel (01229) 718223

RIEM, Roland Gerardus Anthony. b 60. St Chad's Coll Dur BSc82 Kent Univ PhD86. St Jo Coll Nottm DipTh87 DPS89. **d** 89 **p** 90. C Deal St Leon and St Rich and Sholden *Cant* 89-92; Sen Chapl Nottm Univ *S'well* from 92. *3 Wortley Close, University Park, Nottingham NG7 2RD* Tel 0115-951 3927 or 951 3374

RIESS, Trevor William. b 54. Down Coll Cam MA76 CertEd77. St Jo Coll Nottm 84. **d** 86 **p** 87. C Stainforth *Sheff* 86-88; Chapl St Jas Choir Sch Grimsby 89; C Lowestoft and Kirkley *Nor* 89-90; TV 90-94; TV Lowestoft St Marg 94-95; Lothingland Hosp 90-95; V Gorleston St Mary *Nor* from 95. *The Vicarage, 41 Nuffield Crescent, Gorleston, Great Yarmouth, Norfolk NR31 7LL* Tel (01493) 661741

RIGBY, Francis Michael. b 29. Glouc Sch of Min. **d** 90 **p** 91. NSM Alvescot w Black Bourton, Shilton, Holwell etc *Ox* 90-92; P-in-c Gt w Lt Tew 92-95; P-in-c Bishop's Frome w Castle Frome and Fromes Hill *Heref* from 96; P-in-c Acton Beauchamp and Evesbatch from 96. *The Vicarage, Bishops Frome, Worcester WR6 5AR* Tel (01885) 490204

RIGBY, Harold. b 34. Nottm Univ BA56 Man Poly DipEd77. Ripon Hall Ox BA58 MA62. **d** 58 **p** 59. C Barlow Moor *Man* 58-61; C Bury St Jo 61-64; C-in-c Lostock CD 64-76; C Davyhulme St Mary 76; Hon C 76-79; Lic Preacher from 79; Perm to Offic *Ches* from 79. *17 Atwood Road, Manchester M20 0TA* Tel 0161-445 7454

RIGBY, John Basil. b 19. Sarum Th Coll 46. **d** 48 **p** 49. C Horsforth *Ripon* 48-50; C Baldock w Bygrave and Clothall *St Alb* 50-53; V Rye Park St Cuth 53-61; V Boreham Wood All SS 61-72; V Sandbach *Ches* 72-83; rtd 83; Perm to Offic *Ches* from 83. *6 West Way, Sandbach, Cheshire CW11 9LQ* Tel (01270) 763615

RIGBY, Joseph. b 37. Open Univ BA72. Ox NSM Course. **d** 78 **p** 79. NSM Earley St Pet *Ox* 78-80; C Penzance St Mary w St Paul *Truro* 80-82; V Mevagissey 82-83; P-in-c St Ewe 83; R Mevagissey and St Ewe 83-90; rtd 90; Perm to Offic *Truro* from 90. *5 The Close, Upland Crescent, Truro, Cornwall TR1 1LX* Tel (01872) 40440

RIGBY, Michael John. b 52. MA MSc. Ridley Hall Cam. **d** 82 **p** 83. C Reading St Jo *Ox* 82-86; C Wallington H Trin *S'wark* 86-92; Pastor Foundns Chr Fellowship Trust Ch from 92. *14 Dinorben Court, Woodcote Road, Wallington, Surrey SM6 0PZ* Tel 0181-647 8649

RIGBY, William. b 51. Leic Univ BSc(Econ)72 Newc Poly BSc82. Cranmer Hall Dur 86. **d** 88 **p** 89. C Morpeth *Newc* 88-92; R St John Lee from 92; Chapl to the Deaf from 92. *St John Lee Rectory, Hexham, Northd NE46 4PE* Tel (01434) 602220

RIGG, Arthur Neville. b 17. Lanc Univ MA69. St Aid Birkenhead 49. **d** 51 **p** 52. C Walkden Moor *Man* 51-54; C Whalley Range St Marg 54-55; V Allhallows *Carl* 55-62; V Egton w Newland 62-70; V Kirkby Stephen 70-80; rtd 81. *Nab Barn, South Dyke, Penrith, Cumbria CA11 9LL* Tel (01768) 898762

RIGGS, Marcus John Ralph. b 55. Brighton Poly BA78 Southn Univ BTh82. Chich Th Coll 79. **d** 82 **p** 83. C St Leonards Ch Ch and St Mary *Chich* 82-85; C Eastbourne St Andr 85-86; C Brighton St Mich 86-88; Asst Dir Dioc Bd of Soc Resp 88-93; Lic to Offic from 93; rtd 96. *32 Bennett Road, Brighton BN2 5JL* Tel (01273) 601016

RIGGS, Sidney James. b 39. Bps' Coll Cheshunt 62. **d** 63 **p** 64. C S'wark St Geo *S'wark* 63-66; C Plymouth Crownhill Ascension *Ex* 66-69; Asst Youth Chapl *Glouc* 69-71; Hon Min Can Glouc Cathl 71-74; Min Can Glouc Cathl 74-76; V Glouc St Mary de Lode and St Nic 76-92; R Rodborough from 92; RD Stonehouse 94-96. *The Rectory, Walkley Hill, Rodborough, Stroud, Glos GL5 3TX* Tel (01453) 764399

RIGHTON, Sidney Lawrence. b 13. Bps' Coll Cheshunt 46. **d** 48 **p** 49. C Cannock *Lich* 48-50; V Linthwaite *Wakef* 50-57; V Outwood 58-67; V Dewsbury Moor 67-76; V Darrington w Wentbridge 76-79; rtd 79. *Flat 2, Hereford Court, Hereford Road, Harrogate, N Yorkshire HG1 2PX* Tel (01423) 507128

RILEY, John Graeme. b 55. St Jo Coll Dur BA78. Trin Coll Bris 79. **d** 81 **p** 82. C Hensingham *Carl* 81-84; C Preston St Cuth *Blackb* 84-87; V Blackb Ch Ch w St Matt from 87; Chapl Qu Park Hosp Blackb 87-94. *The Vicarage, Brandy House Brow, Blackburn BB2 3EY* Tel (01254) 56292

RILEY, Preb John Martin. b 37. St D Coll Lamp BA62 DipTh63. **d** 63 **p** 64. C Conwy w Gyffin *Ban* 63-68; P-in-c Llanfachraeth 68-70; TV Dolgellau, Llanfachreth, Brithdir etc 70-72; V Beddgelert 72-78; Dioc Youth Chapl 72-78; V Towyn 78-82; V Tywyn w Aberdyfi 82-95; V Llanegryn w Aberdyfi w Tywyn from 95; RD Ystumaner from 87; Can Ban Cathl 90-97; Preb from 97. *The Vicarage, Tywyn LL36 9DD* Tel (01654) 710295 Fax as telephone

RILEY, The Very Revd Kenneth Joseph (Ken). b 40. Univ of Wales BA61 Linacre Ho Ox BA64. Wycliffe Hall Ox 61. **d** 64 **p** 65. C Fazakerley Em *Liv* 64-66; Chapl Brasted Place Coll Westerham 66-69; Chapl Oundle Sch 69-74; Chapl Liv Cathl *Liv* 74-75; Chapl Liv Univ 74-93; V Mossley Hill St Matt and St Jas 75-83; RD Childwall 82-83; Can Res Liv Cathl 83-93; Treas 83-87; Prec 87-93; Dean Man from 93. *The Deanery, 44 Shrewsbury Road, Prestwich, Manchester M25 8GQ* Tel 0161-773 2959 or 833 2220 Fax 839 6226

RILEY, Mrs Lesley Anne. b 54. Totley Thornbridge Coll TCert75. Trin Coll Bris DipHE81. **dss** 81 **d** 87. Hensingham *Carl* 81-84; Preston St Cuth *Blackb* 84-87; Hon Par Dn Blackb Ch Ch w St Matt from 87; Asst Dir of Ords from 96. *The Vicarage, Brandy House Brow, Blackburn BB2 3EY* Tel (01254) 256292

RILEY, Martin Shaw. b 47. Selw Coll Cam BA71 Cam Univ CertEd72 MA75. Sarum & Wells Th Coll 85. **d** 87 **p** 88. C Tuffley *Glouc* 87-91; Hon Min Can Glouc Cathl from 88; P-in-c Barnwood 91-94; V from 94. *The Vicarage, 27A Barnwood Avenue, Gloucester GL4 3AB* Tel (01452) 613760

RILEY, Michael Charles. b 57. Ball Coll Ox BA79 MA83 Ex Univ CertEd80. Edin Th Coll 84. **d** 86 **p** 87. C Newc St Geo *Newc* 86-89; C Chiswick St Nic w St Mary *Lon* 89-90; V Chiswick St Paul Grove Park from 90. *St Paul's Vicarage, 64 Grove Park Road, London W4 3SB* Tel 0181-994 2163

RILEY, Patrick John. b 39. Leeds Univ BA62. Coll of Resurr Mirfield 62. **d** 64 **p** 65. C Rowbarton *B & W* 64-72; P-in-c Farleigh Hungerford w Tellisford 72-73; P-in-c Rode, Rode Hill and Woolverton 72-73; R Rode Major 73-85; RD Frome 78-85; V Glastonbury w Meare, W Pennard and Godney from 85; Preb Wells Cathl from 90. *The Vicarage, 17 Lambrook Street, Glastonbury, Somerset BA6 8BY* Tel (01458) 832362

RILEY, Peter Arthur. b 23. Kelham Th Coll 40. **d** 51 **p** 52. C Aston cum Aughton *Sheff* 51-53; C Doncaster Ch Ch 53-55; Trinidad and Tobago 55-59; C-in-c Leic St Chad CD *Leic* 59-62; Jamaica 62-77; V Abertillery *Mon* 77-83; R Panteg 83-88; rtd 88; Hon C Dartmouth *Ex* from 88. *6 Church Field, Dartmouth, Devon TQ6 9HH* Tel (01803) 835309

RILEY, Reuben Cecil. b 17. St Pet Hall Ox BA39 MA43. Wycliffe Hall Ox. **d** 50 **p** 51. C Hartlebury *Worc* 50-52; Chapl Embley Park Sch Romsey 52-68; Hd Master 56-68; V Blackb St Luke *Blackb* 68-71; V Tunstall 71-90; P-in-c Leck 84-90; rtd 90; Perm to Offic *Blackb* from 90. *4 Harling Bank, Kirkby Lonsdale, Carnforth, Lancs LA6 2DJ* Tel (01524) 271000

RILEY, Sidney David. b 43. Birm Univ BA. Ridley Hall Cam 69. **d** 71 **p** 72. C Herne Bay Ch Ch *Cant* 71-74; C Croydon St Sav 74-77; C-in-c Aylesham CD 77; P-in-c Aylesham 77-78; V 78-82; V Tudeley w Capel *Roch* from 82; Asst Chapl Pembury Hosp 83-86. *2 Bridge Court, Morley, Leeds LS27 0BD* Tel 0113-238 1037

RILEY, Canon William. b 24. St Aid Birkenhead 48. **d** 51 **p** 52. C Edge Hill St Dunstan *Liv* 51-53; C Halsall 53-57; V Prestolee

Man 57-62; P-in-c Ringley 60-62; R Tarleton *Blackb* 62-92; RD Leyland 84-89; Hon Can Blackb Cathl 90-92; rtd 92; Perm to Offic *Blackb* from 92. *114 Liverpool Road, Hutton, Preston PR4 5SL* Tel (01772) 614267

RIMELL, Gilbert William. b 22. Llan Dioc Tr Scheme 76. **d** 81 **p** 82. NSM Laleston w Tythegston and Merthyr Mawr *Llan* 81-94; rtd 94; Perm to Offic *Llan* from 94. *75 Bryntirion Hill, Bridgend CF31 4BY* Tel (01656) 658002

RIMMER, Andrew Malcolm. b 62. Magd Coll Cam BA84 MA88. Wycliffe Hall Ox 86. **d** 88 **p** 89. C Romford Gd Shep Collier Row *Chelmsf* 88-92; C Hazlemere *Ox* from 92. *Church House, George's Hill, Widmer End, High Wycombe, Bucks HP15 6BH* Tel (01494) 713848

RIMMER, Anthony Robert Walters (Tony). b 41. Hull Univ BA63. Coll of Resurr Mirfield 64. **d** 66 **p** 67. C Leeds All SS *Ripon* 66-69; C Kippax 69-72; C Preston St Jo *Blackb* 72-76; TV 76-83; P-in-c Glasson Ch Ch 83-86; Chapl Dunkerque Miss to Seamen *Eur* from 86. *130 rue de l'Ecole Maternelle, 59140 Dunkerque, France* Tel France (33) 28 59 04 36 Fax as telephone

RIMMER, David Henry. b 36. Ex Coll Ox BA60 MA65. Linc Th Coll 62. **d** 64 **p** 65. C Liv Our Lady and St Nic *Liv* 64-66; C Daybrook *S'well* 66-69; Chapl St Mary's Cathl *Edin* 69-71; R Kirkcaldy *St And* 71-78; R Haddington *Edin* 78-83; R Dunbar 79-83; R Edin Gd Shep from 83. *9 Upper Coltbridge Terrace, Edinburgh EH12 6AD* Tel 0131-337 2698

RIMMER, John Clive. b 25. Oak Hill Th Coll 63. **d** 65 **p** 66. C Earlestown *Liv* 65-69; C-in-c Dallam CD 69-74; V Southport SS Simon and Jude 74-83; V Westhead 83-90; Chapl Ormskirk Hosp Liv 84-90; rtd 90; Perm to Offic *Liv* from 90. *14 Hurlston Drive, Ormskirk, Lancs L39 1LD* Tel (01695) 570838

RIMMER, Paul Nathanael. b 25. Jes Coll Ox BA48 MA50. Wycliffe Hall Ox 48. **d** 50 **p** 51. C Douglas St Thos *S & M* 50-52; C Windermere St Martin *Carl* 52-55; India 55-59; V Marston *Ox* 59-90; RD Cowley 69-73; rtd 90. *32 Ulfgar Road, Wolvercote, Oxford OX2 8AZ* Tel (01865) 352567

RIMMER, Peter Anthony. b 39. St As Minl Tr Course 90. **d** 96 **p** 97. C Abergele *St As* from 96. *8 Bryntirion Terrace, Abergele, Conwy LL22 7BG* Tel (01745) 833222

RIMMER, Roy Malcolm. b 31. Fitzw Ho Cam BA58 MA62. Tyndale Hall Bris 54. **d** 59 **p** 60. C Ox St Clem *Ox* 59-62; The Navigators 62-70; Oslo St Edm *Eur* 62-64; Public Preacher *S'wark* 64-66; Perm to Offic *Ox* 66-70; C Portman Square St Paul *Lon* 70-75; R Rougham *St E* 75-87; P-in-c Rushbrooke 78-87; P-in-c Beyton and Hessett 86-87; V Newmarket All SS 87-93; rtd 93. *Ramsey House, 3 Oakfield Place, Old Station Road, Newmarket, Suffolk CB8 8GA* Tel (01638) 660852

RIMMINGTON, Dr Gerald Thorneycroft. b 30. FCP66 Lon Univ BSc56 PhD64 Leic Univ MA59 Nottm Univ MEd72 PhD75. **d** 76 **p** 78. Canada 76-79; Lic to Offic *Leic* 79-80; R Paston *Pet* 81-86; V Cosby *Leic* 86-90; Dir of Continuing Minl Educn 87-90; R Barwell w Potters Marston and Stapleton 90-95; rtd 95; Perm to Offic *Leic* from 95. *7 Beechings Close, Countesthorpe, Leicester LE8 5PA* Tel 0116-277 7155

RINGER, Philip James (Phil). b 47. Ox Min Course 88. **d** 91 **p** 92. NSM Chalfont St Peter *Ox* 91-95; TV Combe Martin, Berrynarbor, Lynton, Brendon etc *Ex* from 96. *The Rectory, 20 Lee Road, Lynton, Devon EX35 6BP* Tel (01598) 753251

RINGLAND, Tom Laurence. b 61. SS Hild & Bede Coll Dur BSc83. Trin Coll Bris BA89. **d** 89 **p** 90. C Southgate *Chich* 89-92; C Polegate 92-96; P-in-c Coalville and Bardon Hill *Leic* from 96. *Christ Church Vicarage, London Road, Coalville, Leics LE67 3JA* Tel (01530) 838287

RINGROSE, Brian Sefton. b 31. Clare Coll Cam BA54 MA58. Tyndale Hall Bris 56. **d** 58 **p** 59. C Ox St Ebbe *Ox* 58-60; C Erith St Paul *Roch* 60-61; India 61-75; P-in-c Ox St Matt *Ox* 75-78; Interserve (Scotland) 78-96; Perm to Offic *Glas* 78-96; rtd 96. *1 Napier Road, Edinburgh EH10 5BE* Tel 0131-447 2012

RINGROSE, Canon Hedley Sidney. b 42. Open Univ BA79. Sarum Th Coll 65. **d** 68 **p** 69. C Bishopston *Bris* 68-71; C Easthampstead *Ox* 71-75; V Glouc St Geo w Whaddon *Glouc* 75-88; RD Glouc City 83-88; Hon Can Glouc Cathl from 86; V Cirencester from 88; RD Cirencester 89-97. *Cirencester Vicarage, 1 Dollar Street, Cirencester, Glos GL7 2AJ* Tel (01285) 653142

RIOCH, Mrs Wenda Jean. b 35. Sarum & Wells Th Coll 84. **d** 87 **p** 94. Par Dn Basingstoke *Win* 87-91; Par Dn Catshill and Dodford *Worc* 91-94; C from 94. *27 Greendale Close, Catshill, Bromsgrove, Worcs B61 0LR* Tel (01527) 835708

RIPLEY, Preb Geoffrey Alan. b 39. Dur Univ BA62. St Aid Birkenhead. **d** 64 **p** 65. C E Herrington *Dur* 64-67; Hon C Hodge Hill CD *Birm* 68-70; Youth Chapl *Liv* 70-75; Chapl Liv Cathl 70-78; Bp's Dom Chapl 75-78; V Wavertree St Bridget 78-87; Lay Tr Adv *B & W* 87-95; Dioc Chapl MU from 92; R S Petherton w the Seavingtons from 95; Preb Wells Cathl from 97. *The Rectory, Hele Lane, South Petherton, Somerset TA13 5DY* Tel (01460) 240377

RIPON, Bishop of. *See* YOUNG, The Rt Revd David Nigel de Lorentz

RIPON, Dean of. *See* METHUEN, The Very Revd John Alan Robert

RIPPINGALE, Denis Michael. b 29. Leeds Univ BA52. Coll of Resurr Mirfield 52. **d** 54 **p** 55. C S Kirkby *Wakef* 54-58; C King Cross 58-60; C Derby St Thos *Derby* 60-63; V Altofts *Wakef* 63-71; V S Elmsall 71-84; V Marsden 84-92; rtd 92. *61 Viking Road, Bridlington, N Humberside YO16 5PW* Tel (01262) 601838

RISBY, John. b 40. Lon Univ DipTh66. Lambeth STh82 Oak Hill Th Coll 64. **d** 67 **p** 68. C Fulham Ch Ch *Lon* 67-68; C Ealing St Mary 68-70; C Chitts Hill St Cuth 70-73; C Hove Bp Hannington Memorial Ch *Chich* 73-76; V Islington St Jude Mildmay Park *Lon* 76-82; P-in-c Islington St Paul Ball's Pond 78-82; V Mildmay Grove St Jude and St Paul 82-84; R Hunsdon w Widford and Wareside *St Alb* from 84; RD Hertford 91-96; RD Hertford and Ware from 96. *The Rectory, Acorn Street, Hunsdon, Ware, Herts SG12 8PB* Tel (01920) 870171

RISDON, John Alexander. b 42. Lon Univ DipTh66. Clifton Th Coll 66. **d** 68 **p** 69. C Ealing Dean St Jo *Lon* 68-72; C Heref St Pet w St Owen *Heref* 72-74; Ord Cand Sec CPAS 74-77; Hon C Bromley Ch Ch *Roch* 74-77; TV Cheltenham St Mary, St Matt, St Paul and H Trin *Glouc* 77-86; R Stapleton *Bris* from 86. *The Rectory, 21 Park Road, Bristol BS16 1AZ* Tel 0117-958 3858

RISING, Sidney Frederick. b 28. EMMTC 73. **d** 76 **p** 77. NSM W Bridgford *S'well* 76-79; C 79-82; V Whatton w Aslockton, Hawksworth, Scarrington etc 82-87; Chapl HM Det Cen Whatton 82-87; Chapl Notts Police 87-93; Rural Officer *S'well* 87-89; P-in-c Perlethorpe 88-90; P-in-c Norton Cuckney 89-90; P-in-c Staunton w Flawborough 90-93; P-in-c Kilvington 90-93; rtd 93. *3 Pelham Close, Newark, Notts NG24 4XL* Tel (01636) 72293

RITCHIE, Brian Albert. b 34. Open Univ BA80 Birm Univ MA84. Qu Coll Birm 60. **d** 63 **p** 64. C S Leamington St Jo *Cov* 63-67; C-in-c Canley CD 67-70; Perm to Offic 71-80; Hon C Cov H Trin 82-88; R Hatton w Haseley, Rowington w Lowsonford etc 88-97; rtd 97. *10 Margetts Close, Kenilworth, Warks CV8 1EN*

RITCHIE, Canon David Caldwell. b 20. Ex Coll Ox BA42 MA46. Wells Th Coll 45. **d** 47 **p** 48. C Poplar All SS w St Frideswide *Lon* 47-52; P-in-c W Brompton St Mary 52-54; V 54-60; V Norton *St Alb* 60-65; V Pinner *Lon* 65-73; P-in-c Bradford-on-Avon *Sarum* 73-75; V 75-81; RD Bradford 80-84; Can and Preb Sarum Cathl 81-85; V Winsley 81-84; Custos St Jo Hosp Heytesbury 84-85; rtd 85; Hon Can Papua New Guinea from 85. *5 Berkshire Road, Salisbury SP2 8NY* Tel (01722) 321338

RITCHIE, David John Rose. b 48. St Jo Coll Dur BA72 DipTh74. **d** 74 **p** 75. C Harold Wood *Chelmsf* 74-79; TV Ipsley *Worc* 79-84; Chapl Vevey w Chateau d'Oex and Villars *Eur* 84-93; V Stoke Bishop *Bris* from 93. *The Vicarage, Mariner's Drive, Bristol BS9 1QJ* Tel 0117-968 1858

RITCHIE, David Philip. b 60. Hatf Coll Dur BA85. Wycliffe Hall Ox 85. **d** 87 **p** 88. C Chadwell *Chelmsf* 87-90; C Waltham H Cross 90-94; TV Becontree W from 94. *St Thomas' Vicarage, 187 Burnside Road, Dagenham, Essex RM8 2JN* Tel 0181-590 6190

RITCHIE, Miss Jean. b 30. Lon Univ CertEd51 DipCD71. Trin Coll Bris DipTh79. **dss** 79 **d** 87 **p** 94. Ox St Ebbe w H Trin and St Pet *Ox* 79-87; Par Dn 87-91; rtd 91; Perm to Offic *B & W* 91-94 and from 96; NSM Clevedon St Andr and Ch Ch 94-96. *63 Holland Road, Clevedon, Avon BS21 7YJ* Tel (01275) 871762

RITCHIE, John Young Wylie. b 45. Aber Univ MA69 Univ of Wales (Cardiff) BD76. St Mich Coll Llan 73. **d** 76 **p** 77. C Trevethin *Mon* 76-78; C Cwmbran 78-81; TV 81-82; C Ind Chapl *York* 82-91; P-in-c Micklefield 82-88; P-in-c Aislaby and Ruswarp 88-89; C Scalby w Ravenscar and Staintondale 89-91; C Shelf *Bradf* 91-94; C Shelf St Mich w Buttershaw St Aid 94-97; V Owston *Sheff* from 97. *The Vicarage, 11 Crabgate Lane, Skellow, Doncaster, S Yorkshire DN6 8LE* Tel (01302) 337101

RITCHIE, Samuel (Sam). b 31. Lon Coll of Div 65. **d** 67 **p** 68. C Westlands St Andr *Lich* 67-70; V Springfield H Trin *Chelmsf* 70-82; Chapl HM Pris Chelmsf 70-82; Chapl HM Pris Brixton 82-84; Chapl HM Pris Hull 84-86; Sen Chapl HM Prison Wymott 86-95; NW Area Chapl Co-ord 86-95; rtd 95; P-in-c Helmingham w Framsden and Pettaugh w Winston *St E* from 96. *The Rectory, The Street, Framsden, Stowmarket, Suffolk IP14 6HG* Tel (01473) 890561

RITCHIE, William James. b 62. TCD MA DipTh. **d** 86 **p** 87. C Enniscorthy w Clone, Clonmore, Monart etc *C & O* 86-89; Egypt 89-91; Bp's C Kells Union *C & O* 91-92; I Kells w Balrathboyne, Moynalty etc *M & K* from 92; Warden of Readers 93-97. *The Rectory, Kells, Co Meath, Irish Republic* Tel Ceanannus Mor (46) 40151 Fax as telephone

RITSON, Arthur William David. b 35. AKC58. **d** 59 **p** 60. C Bishopwearmouth St Mich *Dur* 59-63; Chapl RN 63-67; C Sudbury St Greg and St Pet *St E* 67-69; R Lt Hallingbury *Chelmsf* 69-83; P-in-c Broomfield from 83. *The Vicarage, Butlers Close, Broomfield, Chelmsford CM1 5BE* Tel (01245) 440318

RITSON, Canon Gerald Richard Stanley (Bill). b 35. CCC Cam BA59 MA63. Linc Th Coll 59. **d** 61 **p** 62. C Harpenden St Jo *St Alb* 61-65; C Goldington 65-69; R Clifton 69-76; Sec to Dioc Past Cttee 76-87; P-in-c Aldenham 76-87; Hon Can St Alb 80-87; Can Res St Alb from 87. *2 Sumpter Yard, St Albans, Herts AL1 1BY* Tel (01727) 861744

RIVERS, Arthur. b 20. Oak Hill Th Coll 52. **d** 53 **p** 54. C Wigan St Cath *Liv* 53-56; V Parr Mt 56-60; V Burscough Bridge 60-79; V Holmesfield *Derby* 79-86; rtd 86; Hon C Warton St Oswald w

Yealand Conyers *Blackb* 86-88; Perm to Offic from 88; Perm to Offic *Carl* from 88. *Holmlea, Hale, Milnthorpe, Cumbria LA7 7BL* Tel (015395) 63588

RIVERS, David John. b 51. St Jo Coll Nottm. **d** 84 **p** 85. C Woodthorpe *S'well* 84-88; C Hyson Green St Paul w St Steph 88; Asst Chapl Colchester Gen Hosp 89-91; Chapl United Leeds Teaching Hosps NHS Trust from 91. *Leeds General Infirmary, St George Street, Leeds LS1 3EX* Tel 0113-292 3527 or 292 2914

RIVERS, John Arthur. b 21. EAMTC 79. **d** 81 **p** 82. NSM Blakeney w Cley, Wiveton, Glandford etc *Nor* 81-86; Hon C Cromer 86-87; Perm to Offic from 87. *28 Compit Hills, Cromer, Norfolk NR27 9LJ* Tel (01263) 513051

RIVETT, Dr Andrew George. b 52. LRCP76 MRCS76 Lon Univ MB, BS76. Oak Hill Th Coll 85. **d** 87 **p** 88. C Stanford-le-Hope w Mucking *Chelmsf* 87-90; C Slough *Ox* 90-93; TV Totton *Win* from 93. *The Vicarage, Netley Marsh, Woodlands, Southampton S04 2GX* Tel (01703) 862124

RIVETT, Leonard Stanley. b 23. MSSCLE82 MYPS90 St Jo Coll Dur BA47 DipTh49 York Univ CLHist88. **d** 49 **p** 50. C Chorlton-cum-Hardy St Clem *Man* 49-53; C-in-c Wythenshawe Wm Temple Ch CD 53-57; Area Chapl Toc H (E and W Yorkshire) 57-62; V Norton juxta Malton *York* 62-74; Warden Wydale Hall 74-83; R Elvington w Sutton on Derwent and E Cottingwith 83-88; rtd 88; Perm to Offic *York* from 88; Offg Chapl RAF from 90. *47 Ryecroft Avenue, York YO2 2SD* Tel (01904) 705364

RIVETT, Peter John. b 42. St Jo Coll Dur BA71 DipTh72. Cranmer Hall Dur. **d** 72 **p** 73. C Newland St Jo *York* 72-76; TV Marfleet 76-82; V Oxhey All SS *St Alb* 82-93; TR Swanborough *Sarum* from 93. *The Rectory, Church Road, Woodborough, Pewsey, Wilts SN9 5PH* Tel (01672) 851746

RIVETT-CARNAC, Canon Sir Thomas Nicholas, Bt. b 27. Westcott Ho Cam. **d** 63 **p** 64. C Rotherhithe H Trin *S'wark* 63-68; C Brompton H Trin *Lon* 68-72; P-in-c Kennington St Mark *S'wark* 72-87; V 87-89; RD Lambeth 79-83; Hon Can S'wark Cathl 80-89; rtd 89; Perm to Offic *Chich* from 89. *1 The Stable, Ashburnham Place, Battle, E Sussex TN33 9NF* Tel (01424) 892910

RIVIERE, Jonathan Byam Valentine. b 54. Cuddesdon Coll. **d** 83 **p** 84. C Wymondham *Nor* 83-88; TV Quidenham 88-94; P-in-c Somerleyton w Ashby, Fritton and Herringfleet 94; R Somerleyton, Ashby, Fritton, Herringfleet etc from 95. *The Rectory, The Street, Somerleyton, Lowestoft, Suffolk NR32 5PT* Tel (01502) 731885

RIVIERE, Mrs Tanagra June (Tana). b 41. S Dios Minl Tr Scheme 88. **d** 91. NSM Medstead cum Wield *Win* 91-94; NSM Bishop's Sutton and Ropley and W Tisted 94-96. *The Vicarage, Lyeway Lane, Ropley, Alresford, Hants SO24 0DW* Tel (01962) 772205

RIX, Patrick George. b 30. Magd Coll Ox BA54 DipEd55 MA57. Ridley Hall Cam 58. **d** 60 **p** 61. C Dur St Nic *Dur* 60-62; Asst Chapl Wrekin Coll Shropshire 62-70; Asst Chapl Gresham's Sch Holt 70-80; Chapl Bloxham Sch 80-86; rtd 86; P-in-c Swanton Abbott w Skeyton *Nor* 89; Perm to Offic from 89. *5 Rye Close, North Walsham, Norfolk NR28 9EY* Tel (01692) 402649

ROACH, Charles Alan. b 08. SS Coll Cam BA33 MA37. Westcott Ho Cam 33. **d** 35 **p** 36. C Boston *Linc* 35-40; Lect 38-40; Iraq 40-46; P-in-c Goldington *St Alb* 46-47; V W Dulwich Em *S'wark* 47-51; Adn Seychelles and Sub Dean St Paul's Pro-Cathl 51-55; V Croydon St Sav *Cant* 55-62; Chapl R Masonic Hosp Lon 62-66; St Mich Mt 66-75; Perm to Offic *Truro* from 66; rtd 75. *Trehoward, Green Lane West, Marazion, Cornwall TR17 0HH* Tel (01736) 710514

ROACH, Kenneth Thomas. b 43. St Andr Univ BD69 Fitzw Coll Cam BA71 MA76. Westcott Ho Cam 69. **d** 71 **p** 72. C Glas St Marg *Glas* 71-73; CF 73-76; R Johnstone *Glas* 76-85; R Bearsden 85-96; TR from 96; CF (TA) from 86. *34 Roman Road, Bearsden, Glasgow G61 2SQ* Tel 0141-942 0386

ROAKE, Anthony Richard (Tony). b 52. Keble Coll Ox BA75 MA80. Wycliffe Hall Ox 75. **d** 77 **p** 78. C Clifton *S'well* 77-80; V Lapley w Wheaton Aston *Lich* 80-86; V Bournemouth St Andr *Win* from 86. *St Andrew's Vicarage, 53 Bennett Road, Bournemouth BH8 8QQ* Tel (01202) 396022

ROAN, Canon William Forster. b 21. St Chad's Coll Dur BA47 DipTh49. **d** 49 **p** 50. C Barrow St Jas *Carl* 49-52; C-in-c Westf St Mary CD 52-58; V Westf St Mary 58-61; R Greystoke 61-69; V Workington St Jo 70-86; Hon Can Carl Cathl 72-86; RD Solway 77-84; rtd 86; Perm to Offic *Carl* from 86. *41 Chiswick Street, Carlisle CA1 1HJ* Tel (01228) 21756

ROBB, Ian Archibald. b 48. K Coll Lon 68. **d** 72 **p** 73. C E Ham w Upton Park *Chelmsf* 72-74; C Leckhampton SS Phil and Jas w Cheltenham St Jas *Glouc* 74-79; P-in-c Cheltenham St Mich 79-90; V Lower Cam w Coaley from 90. *St Bartholomew's Vicarage, 99 Fairmead, Lower Cam, Dursley, Glos GL11 5JR* Tel (01453) 542679

ROBB, Robert Hammond Neill. b 46. Open Univ BA89 Man Univ 66. St Deiniol's Hawarden 87. **d** 87 **p** 88. C Lache cum Saltney *Ches* 87-89; V Norley and Crowton from 89; P-in-c Kingsley from 95. *The Vicarage, Crowton, Northwich, Cheshire CW8 2RQ* Tel (01928) 788310

ROBBINS, Angela Mary. *See* WEAVER, Ms Angela Mary

ROBBINS, David Ronald Walter. b 47. Sarum & Wells Th Coll 85. **d** 87 **p** 88. C Meir Heath *Lich* 87-89; C Collier Row St Jas and Havering-atte-Bower *Chelmsf* 89-93; C Tamworth *Lich* from 93. *The Parsonage, Masefield Drive, Tamworth, Staffs B79 8JB* Tel (01827) 64918

ROBBINS, Peter Tyndall. b 25. Magd Coll Ox BA46 DipTh47 MA51. Westcott Ho Cam 48. **d** 50 **p** 51. C Bury St Paul *Man* 50-53; C Swinton St Pet 53-55; V Prestwich St Hilda 55-59; V Lower Halstow *Cant* 59-63; V Charing w Lt Chart 63-73; V Basing *Win* 73-83; V Kingsclere 83-90; rtd 90; Perm to Offic *Birm* from 91; Asst RD Tamworth *Lich* 91-95; Perm to Offic from 95. *73 Summerfield Road, Tamworth, Staffs B77 3PJ* Tel (01827) 60805

ROBBINS, Richard Harry. b 14. Lon Univ BD47 Keble Coll Ox DipTh50. ALCD41. **d** 41 **p** 42. C Enfield St Geo *Lon* 41-44; Chile 63-86; rtd 86. *61 Richmond Wood Road, Bournemouth BH8 9DQ* Tel (01202) 512247

ROBBINS, Stephen. b 53. K Coll Lon BD74 AKC74. St Aug Coll Cant 75. **d** 76 **p** 77. C Tudhoe Grange *Dur* 76-80; C-in-c Harlow Green CD 80-84; V Gateshead Harlow Green 84-87; CF from 87. *MOD Chaplains (Army), Trenchard Lines, Upavon, Pewsey, Wilts SN9 6BE* Tel (01980) 615804 Fax 615800

ROBBINS, Walter. b 35. **d** 72 **p** 73. Argentina 73-82; Adn N Argentina 80-82; C Southborough St Pet w Ch Ch and St Matt *Roch* 82-86; V Sidcup St Andr 86-95; V Grain w Stoke from 95. *The Parsonage, High Street, Isle of Grain, Rochester, Kent ME3 0BS* Tel (01634) 270263

ROBBINS-COLE, Adrian Peter. b 62. LSE BSc(Econ)84. Ch Div Sch of the Pacific (USA) 90 Ripon Coll Cuddesdon BA92. **d** 93 **p** 94. C S Dulwich St Steph *S'wark* 93-97; V Motspur Park from 97. *The Vicarage, 2 Douglas Avenue, New Malden, Surrey KT3 6HT* Tel 0181-942 3117

ROBBINS-COLE, Ms Sarah Jane. b 68. Vermont Univ BA90. Ch Div Sch of the Pacific (USA) 92 Ripon Coll Cuddesdon BA95. **d** 95 **p** 96. C W Dulwich All SS *S'wark* from 95. *20 Drake Court, Tylney Avenue, London SE19 1LW* Tel 0181-670 6513

ROBERT, Brother. *See* ATWELL, Brother Robert Ronald

ROBERT HUGH, Brother. *See* KING-SMITH, Philip Hugh

ROBERTS, Alan Moss. b 39. CEng68 MIMechE68 MIMarE68. St Jo Coll Nottm 77. **d** 79 **p** 80. C Bromsgrove St Jo *Worc* 79-83; C Edgbaston St Germain *Birm* 83-89; R Broadhembury, Payhembury and Plymtree *Ex* from 89. *The Rectory, Broadhembury, Honiton, Devon EX14 0LT* Tel (01404) 841240

ROBERTS, Andrew Alexander (Andy). b 49. Open Univ BA75. Bp Otter Coll CertEd70 Sarum & Wells Th Coll 76. **d** 80 **p** 81. NSM Dorchester *Sarum* 80-85; C Swanage and Studland 85-87; TV 87-94; TR Bridgnorth, Tasley, Astley Abbotts, Oldbury etc *Heref* from 94. *The Rectory, 16 East Castle Street, Bridgnorth, Shropshire WV16 4AL* Tel (01746) 763256

ROBERTS, Anne Judith. b 44. CertEd65 DipEd78 Open Univ BA82 DCouns91. S Dios Minl Tr Scheme 86. **d** 89 **p** 94. Hon Par Dn S Kensington H Trin w All SS *Lon* 89-92; NSM Barnes St Mich *S'wark* from 92. *5 Avenue Gardens, London SW14 8PB* Tel 0181-878 5642

ROBERTS, Mrs Anne Marie. b 55. WMMTC. **d** 96 **p** 97. NSM Meole Brace *Lich* from 96. *The Vicarage, Meole Brace, Shrewsbury SY3 9EZ* Tel (01743) 231744

ROBERTS, Arthur Frederick. b 09. K Coll Lon 38. **d** 39 **p** 40. C Bris St Agnes w St Simon *Bris* 39-41; C Bris St Mary Redcliffe w Temple 42 and 45-46; P-in-c 43-44; V Clifton All SS 46-49; V Horsford *Nor* 49-58; R Felthorpe w Haveringland 49-57; V Horsham St Faith w Newton St Faith 57-58; R Blakeney w Lt Langham 58-62; RD Walsingham 59-62; R Shipdham 62-75; rtd 75; Perm to Offic *Nor* from 75. *Moatside, Page's Lane, Saham Toney, Thetford, Norfolk IP25 7HJ* Tel (01953) 882405

ROBERTS, Bernard John. b 21. Ox NSM Course 79. **d** 82 **p** 83. NSM Wendover *Ox* from 82. *19 The Paddocks, Wendover, Aylesbury, Bucks HP22 6HE* Tel (01296) 623445

ROBERTS, Bryan Richard. b 55. Univ of Wales (Cardiff) DipTh78 BD80. St Mich Coll Llan 78. **d** 80 **p** 81. C Finham *Cov* 80-83; Asst Youth Officer *Nor* 83-86; R N and S Creake w Waterden 86-91; P-in-c E w N and W Barsham 86-91; Chapl Epsom Coll from 91. *3 Heron Court, 53 Alexandra Road, Epsom, Surrey KT17 4HU* Tel (01372) 743016

ROBERTS, Charles Richard Meyrick. b 53. Huddersfield Poly ARCM75 BA75. St Paul's Grahamstown DipTh91. **d** 92 **p** 92. S Africa 92-94; C Bath Abbey w St Jas *B & W* from 94. *48 Devonshire Buildings, Bath BA2 4SU* Tel (01225) 422506

ROBERTS, Christopher Michael. b 39. CCSk93 Man Univ DipAE79. Qu Coll Birm 62. **d** 64 **p** 65. C Milton next Gravesend Ch Ch *Roch* 64-68; C Thirsk w S Kilvington *York* 68-69; V Castleton *Derby* 69-75; TV Buxton w Burbage and King Sterndale 75-79; Perm to Offic 84-87; NSM Marple All SS *Ches* 87-90; Asst Chapl Rainhill Hosp Liv 90-91; Asst Chapl St Helens Hosp Liv 90-91; Chapl Asst Whiston Co Hosp Prescot 90-91; Chapl R United Hosp Bath 91-94; Chapl R United Hosp Bath NHS Trust from 94. *The Chaplain's Office, Royal United Hospital, Combe Park, Bath BA1 3NG* Tel (01225) 428331

ROBERTS, Colin Edward. b 50. Sarum & Wells Th Coll. **d** 83 **p** 84. C Harton *Dur* 83; C S Shields All SS 83-85; C Thamesmead *S'wark* 85-87; TV 87-89; C Streatham St Pet 89-90 and 92;

Zimbabwe 90-92; V Earlsfield St Jo *S'wark* from 92. *St John's Vicarage, 40 Atheldene Road, London SW18 3BW* Tel 0181-874 2837

ROBERTS, Cyril. b 41. St Deiniol's Hawarden. **d** 84 **p** 85. C Maltby *Sheff* 84-86; TR Gt Snaith from 86. *The Rectory, Pontefract Road, Snaith, Goole, N Humberside DN14 9JS* Tel (01405) 860866

ROBERTS, David. b 44. Ex Univ BA65. St Steph Ho Ox 65. **d** 67 **p** 68. C Southwick St Columba *Dur* 67-72; C-in-c Southwick St Cuth CD 72-79; R Alyth *St And* 79-84; R Blairgowrie 79-84; R Coupar Angus 79-84; P-in-c Taunton St Jo *B & W* from 84; Chapl Somerset Coll of Arts and Tech from 84. *17 Henley Road, Taunton, Somerset TA1 5BW* Tel (01823) 284176

ROBERTS, David Alan. b 38. Open Univ BA82. Ripon Hall Ox 71. **d** 73 **p** 74. C W Bridgford *S'well* 73-77; V Awsworth w Cossall 77-82; V Oxclose *Dur* 82-94; P-in-c New Seaham from 94. *The Vicarage, 269 Station Road, Seaham, Co Durham SR7 0BH* Tel 0191-581 3270

ROBERTS, David Donald. b 21. TD69. Univ of Wales BA42. St Mich Coll Llan 42. **d** 44 **p** 45. C Johnston w Steynton *St D* 44-45; C Cardigan 45-48; C Holmer w Huntington *Heref* 48-53; V Ditton St Mich *Liv* 53-59; CF (TA) 55-91; V Newton in Makerfield St Pet *Liv* 59-70; V Birkdale St Jas 70-91; rtd 91. *The Annexe, Ellensmead, Stondon Road, Ongar, Essex CM5 9BU*

ROBERTS, Preb David Henry. b 38. St Chad's Coll Dur BA60. Qu Coll Birm DipTh62. **d** 62 **p** 63. C Stonehouse *Glouc* 62-65; C Hemsworth *Wakef* 65-69; V Newsome 69-76; R Pontesbury I and II *Heref* from 76; RD Pontesbury 83-93; Preb Heref Cathl from 85. *The Deanery, Pontesbury, Shrewsbury SY5 0PS* Tel (01743) 790316

ROBERTS, Canon David John. b 36. Man Univ BSc58. St D Coll Lamp 65. **d** 67 **p** 68. C Rhosllannerchrugog *St As* 67-70; R Cerrigydrudion w Llanfihangel G M, Llangwm etc 70-75; R Llanrwst and Llanddoget 75-77; R Llanrwst and Llanddoget and Capel Garmon 77-84; RD Llanrwst 77-84; V Abergele from 84; RD Rhos from 94; Hon Can St As Cathl 95-96; Can Cursal St As Cathl from 96. *The Vicarage, Rhuddlan Road, Abergele LL22 7HH* Tel (01745) 833132

ROBERTS, Dewi. b 57. LWCMD77 Cyncoed Coll CertEd78. St Mich Coll Llan DipTh84. **d** 84 **p** 85. C Clydach *S & B* 84-88; V Glantawe 88-94; V Lougher from 94. *The Rectory, 109 Glebe Road, Lougher, Swansea SA4 6SR* Tel (01792) 891958

ROBERTS, Dewi James Llewelyn. b 63. United Th Coll Abth 83. **d** 96 **p** 97. C Llandudno *Ban* from 96. *The Parsonage, 9 Morfa Road, West Shore, Llandudno LL30 2BS* Tel (01492) 860070

ROBERTS, Dilwyn Carey. b 38. St Deiniol's Hawarden 74. **d** 76 **p** 77. C Glanadda *Ban* 76-77; TV Amlwch, Rhosybol, Llandyfrydog etc 77-81; V Llanllechid 81-85; V Caerhun w Llangelynin 85-87; V Caerhun w Llangelynin w Llanbedr-y-Cennin 87-92; rtd 93. *67 St Georges Drive, Conwy LL31 9PR*

ROBERTS, Donald James (Don). b 26. Sarum & Wells Th Coll 83. **d** 86 **p** 87. NSM Corfe Castle, Church Knowle, Kimmeridge etc *Sarum* 86-88; C Broadstone 88-91; rtd 91; NSM Corfe Castle, Church Knowle, Kimmeridge etc *Sarum* 91-95; Perm to Offic from 95. *14 Colletts Close, Corfe Castle, Wareham, Dorset BH20 5HG* Tel (01929) 480900

ROBERTS, Canon Edward Eric. b 11. St Aug Coll Cant 34. **d** 61 **p** 62. C Nottingham St Mary *S'well* 61-65; Dir of Educn 61-68; Hon Can S'well Minster 65-68; Can Res and Vice-Provost S'well Minster 69-79; Bp's Dom Chapl 69-79; rtd 80; Perm to Offic *S'well* 84-95. *Queen Elizabeth Court, Clarence Drive, Craig-y-Don, Llandudno, Gwynedd LW30 1TR*

ROBERTS, Edward Henry. b 06. Man Univ BA33 BD36. Ridley Hall Cam 64. **d** 65 **p** 66. C Gt Clacton *Chelmsf* 65-67; R High Laver w Magdalen Laver 67-77; P-in-c Moreton w Lt Laver 73-77; rtd 77; Perm to Offic *Chelmsf* from 77. *154 High Street, Ongar, Essex CM5 9JJ* Tel (01277) 363066

✠**ROBERTS, The Rt Revd Edward James Keymer.** b 08. CCC Cam BA30 MA35 Hon DD65. Cuddesdon Coll 30. **d** 31 **p** 32 **c** 56. C St Marylebone All SS *Lon* 31-35; Vice-Prin Cuddesdon Coll 35-39; Hon Can Portsm Cathl *Portsm* 47-49; R Brading w Yaverland 49-52; Adn Is of Wight 49-52; Adn Portsm 52-56; Suff Bp Malmesbury *Bris* 56-62; Suff Bp Kensington *Lon* 62-64; Bp Ely 64-77; rtd 77; Asst Bp Portsm from 77. *The House on the Marsh, Quay Lane, Brading, Sandown, Isle of Wight PO36 0BD* Tel (01983) 407434

ROBERTS, Edward John Walford. b 31. Trin Coll Carmarthen CertEd. St D Dioc Tr Course. **d** 79 **p** 80. NSM Burry Port and Pwll *St D* from 79. *St Mary's Parsonage, Llwynygog, Cwm, Burry Port SA16 0YR* Tel (01554) 833652

ROBERTS, Canon Edward Owen (Ed). b 38. K Coll Lon BD63 AKC63. **d** 64 **p** 65. C Auckland St Andr and St Anne *Dur* 64-67; C Cheltenham St Paul *Glouc* 67-68; Asst Master Colne Valley High Sch Linthwaite 69-71; V Meltham Mills *Wakef* 71-75; R Emley 75-88; RD Kirkburton 80-88; V Huddersfield H Trin from 88; RD Huddersfield from 89; Hon Can Wakef Cathl from 92. *Holy Trinity Vicarage, 132 Trinity Street, Huddersfield HD1 4DT* Tel (01484) 422998

ROBERTS, Canon Elwyn. b 25. Univ of Wales (Ban) DipTh54. St Mich Coll Llan 54. **d** 55 **p** 56. C Llanfairfechan *Ban* 55-61; V Capel Curig 61-69; V Glanogwen 69-88; Hon Can Ban Cathl 84-90; R Llansadwrn w Llanddona and Llaniestyn etc 88-91; rtd 91; Lic to Offic *Ban* from 91. *Llain Delyn, 10 Cae'r Delyn, Bodffordd, Anglesey LL77 7EJ* Tel (01248) 750407

ROBERTS, The Ven Elwyn. b 31. Univ of Wales (Ban) BA52 Keble Coll Ox BA54 MA59. St Mich Coll Llan 54. **d** 55 **p** 56. C Glanadda *Ban* 55-57; V 66-71; Lib and Lect St Mich Coll Llan 57-66; Dir Post-Ord Tr *Ban* 70-90; R Llandudno 71-83; Can Ban Cathl 77-78; Chan Ban Cathl 78-83; Adn Meirionnydd 83-86; R Criccieth w Treflys 83-86; Adn Ban from 86. *Deiniol, 31 Trefonwys, Bangor LL57 2HU* Tel (01248) 355515

ROBERTS, Eric. b 40. Ban Ord Course 90 St Mich Coll Llan 92. **d** 93 **p** 94. Min Can Ban Cathl *Ban* 93-97; R Llanllyfni from 97. *The Rectory, 2 Mor Awel, Penygroes, Caernarfon LL54 6RA* Tel (01286) 881124

ROBERTS, Frederick Henry. b 22. CPsychol89 AFBPsS Univ of Wales (Ban) BA49 Lon Univ MA60 PhD68. Wycliffe Hall Ox. **d** 51 **p** 52. C Kirkby *Liv* 51-53; C Woodford Wells *Chelmsf* 53-56; V Hatfield Heath 56-62; Dir St Giles' Cen Camberwell 63-66; Chapl Maudsley Hosp Lon 64-75; Perm to Offic *Chelmsf* 76-89; rtd 91. *27 Portugal Street, Cambridge CB5 8AW* Tel (01223) 323522

ROBERTS, Geoffrey Thomas. b 12. ARCM33. Worc Ord Coll 64. **d** 65 **p** 66. C Stamford All SS w St Pet *Linc* 65-67; V Edenham 67-79; P-in-c Witham on the Hill 76-79; rtd 79; Perm to Offic *Linc* 79-89. *West Flat, The Riding School, Grimsthorpe, Bourne, Lincs PE10 0LY* Tel (01778) 591240

ROBERTS, George Nelson. b 24. Cranmer Hall Dur 83. **d** 84 **p** 85. C Netherton *Liv* 84-86; V Carr Mill 86-91; rtd 91; Perm to Offic *Ches* from 91. *58 Church Road, Saughall, Chester CH1 6EP* Tel (01244) 880761

ROBERTS, Gordon Branford. b 11. **d** 83 **p** 83. NSM Prestonville St Luke *Chich* from 83. *Flat 42, Tongdean Court, London Road, Brighton BN1 6YL* Tel (01273) 558172

ROBERTS, Graham Miles. b 59. Open Univ BA95. Trin Coll Bris DipHE92. **d** 92 **p** 93. C Charles w Plymouth St Matthias *Ex* 92-96; Chapl Plymouth Univ 92-94; TV Liskeard, St Keyne, St Pinnock, Morval etc *Truro* from 96. *The Parsonage, Tremeddan Lane, Liskeard, Cornwall PL14 3DS* Tel (01579) 346236

ROBERTS, Canon Henry Edward (Ted). b 28. Oak Hill Th Coll 53. **d** 56 **p** 57. C Edgware *Lon* 56-58; C Bedworth *Cov* 58-61; V Bethnal Green St Jas Less *Lon* 61-73; V Old Ford St Mark Victoria Park 61-73; V Bethnal Green St Jas Less w Victoria Park 73-78; RD Tower Hamlets 76-78; Can Res Bradf Cathl *Bradf* 78-82; Dioc Dir Soc Resp 78-82; V Bermondsey St Jas w Ch Ch *S'wark* 82-90; P-in-c Bermondsey St Anne 82-90; Hon Can S'wark Cathl 90-93; Gen Adv for Inner City Min 90-93; rtd 93. *12 Bromeswell Road, Ipswich IP4 3AS* Tel (01473) 288956

ROBERTS, Hughie Graham. b 28. St Mich Coll Llan 57. **d** 60 **p** 62. C Pontlottyn *Llan* 60-62; C Roath St German 62; C Ystrad Mynach 62-63; C Tonge w Alkrington *Man* 63-65; Chapl RN 65-69; V Goldcliffe and Whiston and Nash *Mon* 69-73; V Garndiffaith 73-78; V Monkton *St D* 78-82; V Llansteffan and Llan-y-bri etc 82-91; rtd 91. *2 Parc-y-Ffordd, Johnstown, Carmarthen SA31 3HD* Tel (01267) 238848

ROBERTS, James Arthur. b 34. Lon Univ BSc56. Bps' Coll Cheshunt 58. **d** 60 **p** 61. C Upper Holloway St Steph *Lon* 60-62; C March St Jo *Ely* 62-65; V Coldham 65-70; V Friday Bridge 65-70; PC Ridgeway *Derby* 70-72; P-in-c Gleadless *Sheff* 72-74; TR 74-79; P-in-c Catfield *Nor* 79-82; P-in-c Ingham w Sutton 79-82; R Aldwincle w Thorpe Achurch, Pilton, Wadenhoe etc *Pet* 82-91; R Barby w Kilsby 91-96; RD Daventry 92-96; rtd 96. *29 Whiteacres, Whittlesey, Peterborough PE7 1XR* Tel (01733) 351602

ROBERTS, James Michael Bradley. b 18. Wycliffe Hall Ox 53. **d** 55 **p** 56. C St Mary Cray and St Paul's Cray *Roch* 55-62; V Clerkenwell St Jas and St Jo w St Pet *Lon* 62-88; rtd 88. *6 Bromley College, London Road, Bromley BR1 1PE* Tel 0181-460 3455

ROBERTS, Miss Janet Lynne. b 56. Trin Coll Bris 76. **dss** 82 **d** 87 **p** 94. Dagenham *Chelmsf* 82-86; Huyton St Mich *Liv* 86-87; Par Dn 87-91; C Aughton Ch Ch from 91. *25 Peet Avenue, Ormskirk, Lancs L39 4SH* Tel (01695) 577958

ROBERTS, Mrs Jasmine Cynthia. b 46. Cant Sch of Min 88. **d** 91. NSM Sandwich *Cant* from 91. *The Rectory, Knightrider Street, Sandwich, Kent CT13 9ER* Tel (01304) 613138

ROBERTS, Jeffrey David. b 25. St Cath Coll Cam BA46 MA50 Lon Univ BSc58. **d** 65 **p** 66. Hd Master Adams' Gr Sch Newport Shropshire 59-73; Hd Master St Geo Sch Gravesend 74-82. *Corner House, Keyston, Huntingdon, Cambs PE18 0RD* Tel (018014) 254

ROBERTS, John Anthony Duckworth. b 43. K Coll Lon BD65 AKC65. St Boniface Warminster 65. **d** 66 **p** 67. C Wythenshawe Wm Temple Ch CD *Man* 66-69; C Bradford-on-Avon *Sarum* 69-72; Chapl Dauntsey's Sch Devizes 72-73; CF 73-77; P-in-c Verwood *Sarum* 77-81; V 81-86; V Clitheroe St Mary *Blackb* 86-97; Bermuda from 97. *St Paul's Church, PO Box PG 290, Paget, PGBX, Bermuda*

ROBERTS, John Arthur. b 37. CEng68 MIEE68 Man Univ BScTech59. Cranmer Hall Dur DipTh71. **d** 71 **p** 72. C Wellington w Eyton *Lich* 71-75; P-in-c Newton Flowery Field

Ches 75-80; V Dunham Massey St Marg 80-91; Chapl Countess of Ches Hosp NHS Trust from 91; Chapl W Cheshire NHS Trust from 94; Lic to Offic *Ches* from 91. *500 Overpool Road, Whitby, South Wirral L66 2JJ* Tel 0151-356 5458

ROBERTS, John Charles. b 50. Nottm Univ BA71 Univ of the W of England, Bris DLLP93. Westcott Ho Cam BA73. **d** 73 **p** 74. C Newark St Mary *S'well* 73-77; Chapl RAF 77-93; Lic to Offic *Bris* 93-95. *15 Foxbrook, Wootton Bassett, Swindon SN4 8QD* Tel (01793) 851518

ROBERTS, John Charles Welch. b 39. UMIST BSc60. Oak Hill NSM Course 91 SW Minl Tr Course 92. **d** 94 **p** 95. NSM Washfield, Stoodleigh, Withleigh etc *Ex* from 94. *East Sidborough, Loxbeare, Tiverton, Devon EX16 8DA* Tel (01884) 256302 Fax as telephone

ROBERTS, John David. b 08. MBE. St D Coll Lamp BA33. **d** 33 **p** 34. C Eglwysilan *Llan* 33-37; C Ffestiniog w Blaenau Ffestiniog *Ban* 37-41; C Maentwrog w Trawsfynydd 37-41; V Llanfihangel-y-Pennant 41-45; R Penegoes and Darowen 45-51; C Ipswich St Clem *St E* 51-52; R Worlingham 52-62; Chapl Miss to Seamen from 62; rtd 73. *17 Arwenack Avenue, Falmouth, Cornwall TR11 3JW* Tel (01326) 312415

ROBERTS, John Edward Meyrick. b 20. TD. Cam Univ CertEd73 ACP78 Keble Coll Ox BA80 MA80 Westmr Coll Ox Dip Chr Studies 95. Nor Ord Course 76. **d** 80 **p** 81. NSM Mundford w Lynford *Nor* 80-83; P-in-c W Wratting *Ely* 83-88; P-in-c Weston Colville 83-88; rtd 88; Hon C Clun w Bettws-y-Crwyn and Newcastle *Heref* from 89. *Ford House, Clun, Craven Arms, Shropshire SY7 8LD* Tel (01588) 640784

ROBERTS, John Hugh. b 42. K Alfred's Coll Win CertEd72 Open Univ BA75. Wells Th Coll 65. **d** 67 **p** 68. C Wareham w Arne *Sarum* 67-70; C Twyford *Win* 70-72; Asst Teacher Rawlins Sch Leics 72-74; V Nassington w Yarwell *Pet* 74-77; Asst Teacher Sponne Sch Towcester 78-92; P-in-c Helmdon w Stuchbury and Radstone etc from 93; RD Brackley from 94. *Pimlico House, Pimlico, Brackley, Northants NN13 5TN* Tel (01280) 850378

ROBERTS, John Mark Arnott. b 54. K Coll Lon AKC75 CertEd76. Chich Th Coll 77. **d** 77 **p** 78. C Ashford *Cant* 77-82; V St Mary's Bay w St Mary-in-the-Marsh etc 82-91; R Sandwich from 91. *The Rectory, Knightrider Street, Sandwich, Kent CT13 9ER* Tel (01304) 613138

ROBERTS, Canon John Victor. b 34. St Edm Hall Ox BA58 MA62. Tyndale Hall Bris 58. **d** 60 **p** 61. C Southport Ch Ch *Liv* 60-62; C Pemberton St Mark Newtown 62-65; V Blackb Sav *Blackb* 65-71; Chapl Blackb and Lancs R Infirmary and Park Lee Hosp 65-71; V Parr *Liv* 71-73; TR 73-80; R Much Woolton from 80; RD Childwall 84-89; AD Liv S from 89; Hon Can Liv Cathl from 95. *The Rectory, 67 Church Road, Liverpool L25 6DA* Tel 0151-428 1853

ROBERTS, John Victor. b 40. GIPE61. Qu Coll Birm 83. **d** 85 **p** 86. C Ludlow *Heref* 85-89 and 92-93; P-in-c Coreley w Doddington 89-92; P-in-c Knowbury 89-92; TV Ludlow, Ludford, Ashford Carbonell etc from 93. *St Mary's Vicarage, Ashford Carbonell, Ludlow, Shropshire SY8 4DA* Tel (01584) 831352

ROBERTS, John William. b 09. ALCD38. **d** 38 **p** 39. C Kirkdale St Lawr *Liv* 38-40; N Sec CMJ 40-44; V Toxteth Park St Bede *Liv* 44-48; R Ulverston H Trin *Carl* 48-54; CF (TA) 49-60; V Widnes St Paul *Liv* 54-60; R Grappenhall *Ches* 60-74; rtd 74. *11 Oakley Road, Morecambe, Lancs LA3 1NR* Tel (01524) 414234

ROBERTS, Jonathan George Alfred. b 60. Lon Univ BD. Qu Coll Birm. **d** 84 **p** 85. C Shepshed *Leic* 84-86; C Braunstone 86-87; Dioc Youth Adv *Dur* 88-92; Nat Youth Officer Gen Syn Bd of Educn 92-94; P-in-c Washington *Dur* 94-95; R from 95. *The Rectory, The Avenue, Washington, Tyne & Wear NE38 7LE* Tel 0191-416 3957

ROBERTS, Joseph Aelwyn. b 18. Univ of Wales (Lamp) BA40. St Mich Coll Llan 41. **d** 42 **p** 43. C Llanllyfni *Ban* 42-44; Min Can Ban Cathl 44-52; V Llandegai 52-88; Dioc Dir for Soc Work 73-88; rtd 88; Lic to Offic *Ban* from 88. *The Vicarage, Llandegai, Bangor LL57 4LA* Tel (01248) 353711

ROBERTS, Keith Mervyn. b 55. LGSM78 St Pet Coll Birm CertEd76. Qu Coll Birm 89. **d** 91 **p** 92. C Hall Green St Pet *Birm* 91-95; TV Warwick *Cov* from 95; Relig Affairs Correspondent BBC Radio Cov & Warw from 95. *184 Myton Road, Warwick CV34 6PS*

ROBERTS, Canon Kenneth William Alfred. b 26. Roch Th Coll 63. **d** 65 **p** 66. C Waterlooville *Portsm* 65-67; C Honicknowle *Ex* 67-68; C Christchurch *Win* 68-69; C Shiphay Collaton *Ex* 70-71; CF 71-74; R Bassingham *Linc* 74-75; V Carlton-le-Moorland w Stapleford 74-75; R Thurlby w Norton Disney 74-75; V Aubourn w Haddington 74-75; Chapl R Hosp Sch Holbrook 75-78; P-in-c Copdock w Washbrook and Belstead *St E* 78-79; P-in-c Brandeston w Kettleburgh 79-82; Chapl Brandeston Hall Sch 79-84; Chapl Lisbon *Eur* 84-86; Can and Chan Malta Cathl 86-89; R Wimbotsham w Stow Bardolph and Stow Bridge etc *Ely* 89-91; rtd 91. *7 Borley Crescent, Tudor Mill, Elmswell, Bury St Edmunds, Suffolk IP30 9UG* Tel (01359) 41881

ROBERTS, Kevin Thomas. b 55. Qu Coll Cam BA78 MA82 Nottm Univ BA82. St Jo Coll Nottm 80. **d** 83 **p** 84. C Beverley Minster *York* 83-86; C Woodley St Jo the Ev *Ox* 86-91; V Meole Brace *Lich* from 91. *The Vicarage, Meole Brace, Shrewsbury SY3 9EZ* Tel (01743) 231744

ROBERTS, Laurence James. b 51. AMGAS86 Sussex Univ BEd73. Sarum & Wells Th Coll 75. **d** 78 **p** 79. C Rotherhithe St Mary w All SS *S'wark* 78-81; Ind Chapl 81-84; Hon Priest Nunhead St Silas 82-84; TV Plaistow *Chelmsf* 84-89; Chapl Newham Gen Hosp and Plaistow Hosp 84-90; Tutor Community Nursing Services 89-90; Tutor Westmr Past Foundn from 90; Perm to Offic *Chelmsf* from 90. *40 Boleyn Road, London E7 9QE* Tel 0181-472 2430

ROBERTS, Malcolm Kay. b 54. Jes Coll Ox BA76 MA82. Ripon Coll Cuddesdon 84. **d** 87 **p** 88. C Frodingham *Linc* 87-91; R Fiskerton w Reepham from 91. *The Rectory, Reepham Road, Fiskerton, Lincoln LN3 4EZ* Tel (01522) 750577

ROBERTS, Martin Vincent. b 53. LRAM72 Birm Univ BA76 MA77 PhD82. Ripon Coll Cuddesdon 76. **d** 78 **p** 79. C Perry Barr *Birm* 78-81; Sen Chapl and Lect W Sussex Inst of HE 81-86; Leic Poly *Leic* 86-92; Sen Chapl De Montfort Univ 92-95; TV Leic H Spirit 86-89; TR 89-95; V Baswich *Lich* from 95. *The Vicarage, 97 Baswich Lane, Stafford ST17 0BN* Tel (01785) 51057

ROBERTS, Matthew Garnant. b 13. St D Coll Lamp BA37. **d** 37 **p** 38. C St Brides Minor *Llan* 37-39; C Iford *Win* 39-43; C Bournemouth St Alb 43-46; Chapl RAF 47-68; P-in-c Hinton Ampner w Bramdean *Win* 68-70; R 70-74; R Hinton Ampner w Bramdean and Kilmeston 74-78; rtd 78; Lic to Offic *B & W* 79-96. *The Granary, Quaperlake Street, Bruton, Somerset BA10 0NA* Tel (01749) 812545

ROBERTS, Michael. b 46. Sarum Th Coll 86. **d** 88 **p** 89. C Reading St Matt *Ox* 88-91; NSM Douglas St Geo and St Barn *S & M* 91-93; V Malew from 93. *Malew Vicarage, St Mark's Road, Ballasalla, Isle of Man IM9 3FF* Tel (01624) 822469

ROBERTS, Michael Brian. b 46. Or Coll Ox BA68 MA72 St Jo Coll Dur BA73 DipTh74. Cranmer Hall Dur 71. **d** 74 **p** 75. C St Helens St Helen *Liv* 74-76; C Goose Green 76-78; C Blundellsands St Nic 78-80; V Fazakerley St Nath 80-87; V Chirk *St As* from 87. *The Vicarage, Trevor Road, Chirk, Wrexham LL14 5HD* Tel (01691) 778519

ROBERTS, Michael Graham Vernon. b 43. Keble Coll Ox BA65. Cuddesdon Coll 65 Ch Div Sch of the Pacific (USA) MDiv67. **d** 67 **p** 68. C Littleham w Exmouth *Ex* 67-70; Chapl Clare Coll Cam 70-74; V Bromley St Mark *Roch* 74-79; Tutor Qu Coll Birm 79-85; TR High Wycombe *Ox* 85-90; Vice-Prin Westcott Ho Cam 90-93; Prin from 93. *Westcott House, Jesus Lane, Cambridge CB5 8BP* Tel (01223) 350074 or 64680

ROBERTS, Myrfyn Wyn. b 35. Univ of Wales (Ban) BA57 BMus60 Lon Univ DipRS77. S'wark Ord Course 74. **d** 76 **p** 77. C Stepney St Dunstan and All SS *Lon* 76-79; R Crofton *Wakef* 79-85; Chapl HM Pris Dur 85-87; Chapl HM Rem Cen Ashford 87-88; Chapl HM Young Offender Inst Dover 88-92; Chapl HM Pris Albany 92-95; V Llanpumsaint w Llanllawddog *St D* 95-96. *Llan-yr-Afon, Earlsfield Stud, St Nicholas, Cardiff CF5 6TY* Tel (01446) 761077

ROBERTS, Nicholas John. b 47. Lon Univ BD70 AKC70 MTh78 Surrey Univ MSc93. St Aug Coll Cant 70. **d** 71 **p** 72. C Tividale *Lich* 71-74; C St Pancras H Cross w St Jude and St Pet *Lon* 74-76; C Camberwell St Giles *S'wark* 76-78; Chapl Ch Coll Cam 78-82; V Kingstanding St Luke *Birm* 82-85; Chapl St Chas Hosp Ladbroke Grove 85-96; Chapl Princess Louise Hosp Lon 85-96; Chapl Paddington Community Hosp 85-96; Chapl Cen Middx Hosp NHS Trust from 96. *Chaplains' Office, Central Middlesex Hospital, Acton Lane, London NW10 7NS* Tel 0181-965 5733

ROBERTS, Patricia. **d** 96. NSM Buckhurst Hill *Chelmsf* from 96. *Glebe House, High Road, Buckhurst Hill, Essex IG9 5RX* Tel 0181-504 6652

ROBERTS, Paul Carlton. b 57. Worc Coll Ox BA78 MA86 CertEd. St Jo Coll Nottm 84. **d** 87 **p** 88. C Hazlemere *Ox* 87-91; C Woodley St Jo the Ev 91-92; TV Woodley from 92. *St James's Vicarage, 35 Highgate Road, Reading RG5 3ND* Tel 0118-969 6197 Fax as telephone

ROBERTS, Paul John. b 60. Man Univ BA82 Man Poly PGCE83 Man Univ PhD91. St Jo Coll Nottm 83. **d** 85 **p** 86. C Burnage St Marg *Man* 85-88; Tutor Trin Coll Bris from 88. *13 Henleaze Avenue, Bristol BS9 4EU, or Trinity College, Stoke Hill, Bristol BS9 1JP* Tel 0117-962 3535 or 968 2803 E-mail paul.roberts@bristol.ac.uk

ROBERTS, Peter. b 40. NW Ord Course 71. **d** 74 **p** 75. C Stockport St Geo *Ches* 74-77; V Bickerton 77-78; V Bickerton w Bickley 78-83; R Alderley 83-94; rtd 94. *8C Cliff Road, Bridgnorth, Shropshire WV16 4EY*

ROBERTS, Peter Francis. b 59. N Illinois Univ BSc81 Leeds Univ BA87. Coll of Resurr Mirfield 85. **d** 88 **p** 89. C Leeds All So *Ripon* 88-92; Asst Dioc Youth Chapl 91-92; USPG 92-94; Belize 92-94; V Collingham w Harewood *Ripon* from 95. *The Vicarage, Church Lane, Collingham, Wetherby, W Yorkshire LS22 5AU* Tel (01937) 573975

ROBERTS, Peter Gwilym. b 42. N Ord Course 78. **d** 81 **p** 82. NSM Seaforth *Liv* 81-83; TV Kirkby 83-88; Dioc Adv on UPA 88-91; P-in-c Southport H Trin 91-94; S Africa from 94. *St Matthias Anglican Church, PO Box 231, Welkom 9460, S Africa*

ROBERTS, Peter Reece. b 43. Chich Th Coll 73. **d** 75 **p** 76. C Cadoxton-juxta-Barry *Llan* 75-79; C Brixham w Churston Ferrers *Ex* 79-81; C Bexhill St Pet *Chich* 81-84; R Heene from

84; RD Worthing 89-97. *Heene Rectory, 4 Lansdowne Road, Worthing, W Sussex BN11 4LY* Tel (01903) 202312

ROBERTS, Philip Alan. b 59. Chich Th Coll 85. **d** 88 **p** 89. C Friern Barnet St Jas *Lon* 88-93; C Farnham Royal w Hedgerley *Ox* from 93. *7 Rectory Close, Farnham Royal, Slough SL2 3BG* Tel (01753) 644293

ROBERTS, Philip Anthony. b 50. St Jo Coll Dur BA73. Wycliffe Hall Ox 75. **d** 77 **p** 78. C Roby *Liv* 77-79; C Ainsdale 79-80; C Pershore w Pinvin, Wick and Birlingham *Worc* 80-83; Chapl Asst Radcliffe Infirmary Ox 83-88; John Radcliffe and Littlemore Hosps Ox 83-88; Chapl R Victoria and Bournemouth Gen Hosps 88-91; Chapl Heref Co Hosp 91-94; Chapl Heref Hosps NHS Trust from 94. *The County Hospital, Union Walk, Hereford HR1 2ER* Tel (01432) 355444

ROBERTS, Philip John. b 20. **d** 74 **p** 75. NSM Downend *Bris* 74-90; Perm to Offic from 90. *Windrush, 190A Overndale Road, Bristol BS16 2RH* Tel 0117-956 8753

ROBERTS, Canon Phillip. b 21. Sarum Th Coll 55. **d** 57 **p** 58. C Salisbury St Mich *Sarum* 57-60; Australia 60-63; V Westbury *Sarum* 63-73; TR Dorchester 73-80; Can and Preb Sarum Cathl 75-87; R Upper Chelsea H Trin w St Jude *Lon* 80-87; rtd 87; V of Close Sarum Cathl *Sarum* 89-95. *112 Harnham Road, Salisbury SP2 8JW* Tel (01722) 323291

ROBERTS, The Ven Raymond Harcourt. b 31. CB84. St Edm Hall Ox BA54 MA58. St Mich Coll Llan 54. **d** 56 **p** 57. C Bassaleg *Mon* 56-59; Chapl RNR 57-59; Chapl RN 59-84; Chapl of the Fleet and Adn for the RN 80-84; QHC 80-84; Hon Can Gib Cathl *Eur* 80-84; Gen Sec JMECA 85-89; C Hale *Guildf* 85-89; Hon Chapl Llan Cathl *Llan* 90-95; Lic to Offic from 95. *8 Baynton Close, Llandaff, Cardiff CF5 2NZ* Tel (01222) 578044

ROBERTS, Richard. b 23. Univ of Wales BA48. St Mich Coll Llan 48. **d** 50 **p** 51. C Pwllheli *Ban* 50-53; C Llangelynnin 53-57; V Llanwnog w Penstrowed 57-68; R Llanrwst and Llanddoget *St As* 68-75; RD Llanrwst 73-75; V Llandrillo-yn-Rhos 75-90; rtd 91; Perm to Offic *Ban* from 91. *2 Bryn Ithel, Abergele LL22 8QB* Tel (01745) 826353

ROBERTS, Canon Richard Stephanus Jacob (Steph). b 28. TCD BA51 MA57. TCD Div Sch Div Test51. **d** 51 **p** 52. C Orangefield *D & D* 51-54; Miss to Seamen 51-94; Portuguese E Africa 51-65; Ceylon 65-68; Chapl Miss to Seamen Dublin 68-72; Chapl Miss to Seamen Southn 72-94; Sen Chapl Ch on the High Seas 72-94; Hon Can Win Cathl *Win* 82-94; rtd 94. *25 Bassett Crescent West, Southampton SO16 7EB* Tel (01703) 790734

ROBERTS, Ronald Barry. b 40. S Dios Minl Tr Scheme 80. **d** 83 **p** 85. NSM Wedmore w Theale and Blackford *B & W* 83-85; C Odd Rode *Ches* 85-87; V Eaton and Hulme Walfield from 87. *The Vicarage, Hulme Walfield, Congleton, Cheshire CW12 2JG* Tel (01260) 279863

ROBERTS, Mrs Rosanne Elizabeth. b 51. Glouc Sch of Min 85. **d** 88 **p** 94. NSM Charlton Kings St Mary *Glouc* 88-93; C Leckhampton SS Phil and Jas w Cheltenham St Jas 93-96; R Ashchurch from 96. *The Rectory, Ashchurch, Tewkesbury, Glos GL20 8JZ* Tel (01684) 293729

ROBERTS, Stephen Bradley. b 66. K Coll Lon BD90 Wycliffe Hall Ox 89. **d** 91 **p** 92. C W Hampstead St Jas *Lon* 91-94; TV Uxbridge from 94. *St Margaret's Vicarage, 72 Harefield Road, Uxbridge, Middx UB8 1PL* Tel (01895) 270759

ROBERTS, Stephen John. b 58. BD. Westcott Ho Cam. **d** 83 **p** 84. C Riverhead w Dunton Green *Roch* 83-86; C St Martin-in-the-Fields *Lon* 86-89; Warden Trin Coll Cen Camberwell from 89; V Camberwell St Geo *S'wark* from 89. *St George's Vicarage, 115 Wells Way, London SE5 7SZ* Tel 0171-703 2895

ROBERTS, Miss Susan Emma. b 60. La Sainte Union Coll BTh93. St Steph Ho Ox DipMin94. **d** 96 **p** 97. C Petersfield *Portsm* from 96. *42 Heath Road, Petersfield, Hants GU31 4EH* Tel (01730) 263190

ROBERTS, Sydney Neville Hayes. b 19. K Coll Lon 38. Cuddesdon Coll 45. **d** 47 **p** 48. C Aylesbury *Ox* 47-52; CF 52-69; R Theale w N Street *Ox* 69-76; R Theale and Englefield 76-85; rtd 85. *34 Stonebridge Road, Steventon, Abingdon, Oxon OX13 6AU* Tel (01235) 834777

ROBERTS, Mrs Sylvia Ann. b 40. Stockwell Coll Lon TCert60. S Dios Minl Tr Scheme 81. **dss** 84 **d** 87 **p** 94. Crookhorn *Portsm* 84-88; Hon Par Dn Bedhampton 88-89; Par Dn Southampton (City Cen) *Win* 89-91; TD 91-94; TV 94-96; V Merton St Jo *S'wark* from 96. *St John's Vicarage, High Path, London SW19 2JY* Tel 0181-542 3283

ROBERTS, Tegid. b 47. **d** 87 **p** 88. Lic to Offic *Ban* 87-93; NSM Llandinorwig w Penisa'r-waen from 93. *Arwel, Llanrug, Caernarfon LL55 3BA* Tel (01286) 870760

ROBERTS, Terry Harvie. b 45. Sarum & Wells Th Coll 87. **d** 89 **p** 90. C Weymouth H Trin *Sarum* 89-93; TV Basingstoke *Win* from 93. *45 Beaconsfield Road, Basingstoke, Hants RG21 3DG* Tel (01256) 464616

ROBERTS, Canon Thomas Ewart. b 17. VRD65. Liv Univ BA41. St Aid Birkenhead 39. **d** 41 **p** 42. C Bowdon *Ches* 41-44; V Dunham Massey St Marg 47-52; Chapl RNVR 44-47 and 53-58; Chapl RNR 58-67; Ind Chapl *S'wark* 52-55; C-in-c Woolwich H Trin CD 52-55; Chapl R Arsenal Woolwich 52-55; PC Selsdon *Cant* 55-59; V Dover St Mary 59-71; RD Dover 59-71; Hon Can Cant Cathl 67-71; V Chesterfield St Mary and All SS *Derby* 71-75; Hon Can Cant Cathl *Cant* 81-84; V Tenterden St Mildred w Smallhythe 75-82; RD W Charing 81-82; rtd 82; Asst Chapl Kent and Cant Hosp 82-91; Perm to Offic *Cant* from 84. *2 Lesley Avenue, Canterbury, Kent CT1 3LF* Tel (01227) 451072

ROBERTS, Tudor Vaughan. b 58. Newc Univ BA81. All Nations Chr Coll 91 Trin Coll Bris BA94. **d** 96. C Buckhurst Hill *Chelmsf* from 96. *Glebe House, High Road, Buckhurst Hill, Essex IG9 5RX* Tel 0181-504 6652

ROBERTS, Vaughan Edward. b 65. Selw Coll Cam BA88 MA91. Wycliffe Hall Ox 89. **d** 91 **p** 92. C Ox St Ebbe w H Trin and St Pet *Ox* 91-95; Student Pastor from 95. *St Ebbe's Flat, 1 Roger Bacon Lane, Oxford OX1 1QE* Tel (01865) 248365

ROBERTS, Vaughan Simon. b 59. Univ of Wales (Ban) BA80. McCormick Th Sem Chicago MA82 Westcott Ho Cam 83. **d** 85 **p** 86. C Bourne *Guildf* 85-89; Chapl Phyllis Tuckwell Hospice Farnham 88-89; Chapl Bath Univ *B & W* 89-96; NSM Bath Ch Ch Prop Chpl 90-96; P-in-c 92-96; P-in-c Chewton Mendip w Ston Easton, Litton etc from 96. *The Rectory, Lower Street, Chewton Mendip, Bath BA3 4PD* Tel (01761) 241644 Fax as telephone E-mail vaughanroberts@compuserve.com

ROBERTS, Vincent Akintunde. b 55. Kingston Poly BA(Econ)81. S'wark Ord Course. **d** 91 **p** 92. Hon C Brixton Road Ch Ch *S'wark* 91-96; C Mitcham St Barn from 96. *7 Graham Road, Mitcham, Surrey CR4 2HB* Tel 0181-648 3284

ROBERTS, Vivian Phillip. b 35. Univ of Wales BD78. St D Coll Lamp 57. **d** 60 **p** 61. C Cwmaman *St D* 60-64; R Puncheston, Lt Newcastle and Castle Bythe 64-72; V Brynamman 72-77; V Brynaman w Cwmllynfell 77-83; V Pen-bre from 83. *The Vicarage, Ar-y-Bryn, Pen-bre, Burry Port SA16 0AJ* Tel (01554) 832403

ROBERTS, Wallace Lionel. b 31. Univ of Wales (Lamp) BA58. St D Coll Lamp 55. **d** 59 **p** 60. C Astley Bridge *Man* 59-61; Asst Master Stand Gr Sch 61-66; Hon C Stand 61-66; Hon CF Aden 66-67; Lect Stockport Tech Coll 67-70; Hon C Heaton Moor *Man* 67-70; Chapl Qu Sch Rheindahlen 70-76; Hon CF 70-76; Swaziland 76-85; Chapl Oporto *Eur* 86-89; Chapl Hordle Ho Sch Milford-on-Sea 89-90; C Portishead *B & W* 91-96; rtd 96; Perm to Offic *B & W* from 96. *44 Hallett's Way, Portishead, Bristol BS20 9BT* Tel (01275) 817484

ROBERTS, William James (Jim). b 55. Hughes Hall Cam PGCE78. Lon Bible Coll BA77 NE Ord Course 92. **d** 94 **p** 95. NSM York St Mich-le-Belfrey *York* from 94. *12 Bishop's Way, York YO1 5JG* Tel (01904) 413479

ROBERTS, Wynne. b 61. Univ of Wales (Ban) DipTh85. Ridley Hall Cam 85. **d** 87 **p** 88. C Ban Cathl Par *Ban* 87-90; Min Can Ban Cathl 87-90; V Ynyscynhaearn w Penmorfa and Porthmadog 90-94; TV Ban from 94. *St Peter's Vicarage, Penrhosgarnedd, Bangor LL57 2NN* Tel (01248) 352388 Pager (01893) 910102

ROBERTSHAW, John Sean. b 66. Cranmer Hall Dur 90. **d** 93 **p** 94. C Morley St Pet w Churwell *Wakef* 93-96; TV Upper Holme Valley from 96. *The Vicarage, Kirkroyds Lane, New Mill, Huddersfield HD7 7LS* Tel (01484) 683375

ROBERTSHAW, Jonothan Kempster Pickard Sykes. b 41. AKC65. **d** 66 **p** 67. C Perranzabuloe *Truro* 66-69; Miss to Seamen 69-76; Hong Kong 69-72; Namibia 73-76; TV Probus, Ladock and Grampound w Creed and St Erme *Truro* 76-79; TV N Hill w Altarnon, Bolventor and Lewannick 79-80; P-in-c Lansallos 80-84; R 84-96; P-in-c Talland 80-84; V 84-96; V Madron from 96. *The Vicarage, Madron, Penzance, Cornwall TR20 8SW* Tel (01736) 60992

ROBERTSON, Agnes Muriel Hodgson. b 20. Edin Univ MA41. Edin Th Coll. **d** 91 **p** 94. NSM Lochgelly *St And* 91-92; Par Dn Glenrothes 92-94; C from 94; C Leven from 94; C Lochgelly from 94. *35 Queen Margaret Drive, Glenrothes, Fife KY7 4HR* Tel (01592) 610899

ROBERTSON, Brian Ainsley. b 50. Warw Univ BSc72. St Jo Coll Nottm DTS94. **d** 94 **p** 95. C Leic Martyrs *Leic* from 94. *62 Ashleigh Road, Leicester LE3 0FB* Tel 0116-254 1341

ROBERTSON, Charles Peter. b 57. Linc Th Coll 94 Aston Tr Scheme 92. **d** 96 **p** 97. C Holbeach *Linc* from 96. *33 Spalding Road, Holbeach, Spalding, Lincs PE12 7HG* Tel (01406) 490310

ROBERTSON, David John. b 54. Sheff Univ BA76. Ridley Hall Cam 77. **d** 79 **p** 80. C Downend *Bris* 79-83; C Yate New Town 83-85; TV 85-87; TV High Wycombe *Ox* 87-97; RD Wycombe 91-97; V Ovenden *Wakef* from 97; P-in-c Halifax All So from 97. *2 Bracewell Drive, Wheatley, Halifax, W Yorkshire HX3 5BT* Tel (01422) 354153

ROBERTSON, Denis Ayre. b 33. Edin Dioc NSM Course 90. **d** 92 **p** 93. NSM Dalmahoy *Edin* 92-95; NSM Forfar *St And* from 95. *38 McCulloch Drive, Arbroath Road, Forfar, Angus DD8 2EB* Tel (01307) 466269

ROBERTSON, Canon Donald Keith. b 07. St D Coll Lamp BA36. **d** 36 **p** 37. C Wednesfield St Thos *Lich* 36-40; C Petersfield w Sheet *Portsm* 40-43; V Walsall Pleck and Bescot *Lich* 44-48; R Lich St Chad 48-52; R Cannock 52-60; RD Rugeley 54-60; Preb Lich Cathl 59-60; Can Res Lich Cathl 60-76; Dir Post-Ord Tr 61-76; rtd 76; Perm to Offic *Carl* 77-93. *c/o A M Robertson Esq, 11 Church Road, Winford, Bristol BS18 8EW* Tel (01275) 472115

ROBERTSON, Edward Macallan. b 28. Aber Univ MA49 Qu Coll Ox BLitt51. Coll of Resurr Mirfield 53. **d** 55 **p** 56. C Swindon

New Town *Bris* 55-60; C Hawick *Edin* 60-69; R Alloa *St And* 70-73; Lic to Offic *Edin* 74-78; P-in-c Bathgate 78-82; P-in-c Linlithgow 78-82; Hon C Strathtay *St And* 82-90; P-in-c Auchterarder 90-93; P-in-c Muthill 90-93; rtd 93. *65 Smithfield Crescent, Blairgowrie, Perthshire PH10 6UE* Tel (01250) 874427

ROBERTSON, Ernest Ian. b 22. Bede Coll Dur BA49. Wycliffe Hall Ox 49. **d** 51 **p** 52. C Jarrow St Paul *Dur* 51-54; C Sedgefield 54-56; V Eighton Banks 56-60; Chapl Shotley Bridge Gen Hosp 60-81; V Benfieldside *Dur* 60-87; Chapl HM Det Cen Medomsley 61-87; rtd 87. *Flat 11, Thornley House, Sherburn House Hospital, Durham DH1 2SE* Tel 0191-372 1992

ROBERTSON, George Edward. b 14. Rhodes Univ BA35 MA35 Stellenbosch Univ MA48. Wells Th Coll 52. **d** 53 **p** 61. C Wells St Cuth *B & W* 53-54; S Africa 54-73 and 74-79; C Fort Beaufort 54-59; C Plumstead 59-64; C Pinelands 64-66; C Goodwood 66-73; Australia 73-74; Lic to Offic Dio Cape Town 74-79; rtd 79; Perm to Offic *Chich* 79-91. *c/o Mr P J Kean, Methodist Annexe, PO Box 106, Simonstown, 7995 South Africa*

ROBERTSON, Ian Hugh. b 44. LGSM64 ARCM65 Makerere Univ Kampala DipTh83 Lanc Univ MA91. St Mark's Dar-es-Salaam 80. **d** 83 **p** 83. SSF 73-82; Zimbabwe 83-87; TV Barrow St Geo w St Luke *Carl* 87-90; V Reigate St Mark *S'wark* from 90. *St Mark's Vicarage, 8 Alma Road, Reigate, Surrey RH2 0DA* Tel (01737) 210639 or 210785

ROBERTSON, James Alexander. b 46. Sarum & Wells Th Coll 72. **d** 75 **p** 76. C Monkseaton St Pet *Newc* 75-78; C Prudhoe 78-79; TV Brayton *York* 79-84; V Redcar 84-93; V Selby Abbey 93-96; V Monkseaton St Pet *Newc* from 96. *St Peter's Vicarage, 6 Elmwood Road, Whitley Bay, Tyne & Wear NE25 8EX* Tel 0191-252 1991

ROBERTSON, Canon James Smith. b 17. OBE84. Glas Univ MA38. Edin Th Coll 38. **d** 40 **p** 41. C Edin St Martin *Edin* 40-41; C Edin St Salvador 41-45; Zambia 45-65; Warden St Mark's Tr Coll Mapanza 50-55; Warden Chalimbana Tr Coll 55-65; Hon Can Zambia 66-70; Hon Can Lusaka from 71; Lect St Bede Coll Dur 65-68; Sec for Ch Colls of Educn Gen Syn Bd of Educn 68-73; Sec USPG 73-83; Chapl to The Queen 80-88; rtd 83; Perm to Offic *Lon* 83-93 and from 96; Perm to Offic *S'wark* 83-95. *Flat 8, 26 Medway Street, London SW1P 2BD*

ROBERTSON, John Charles. b 61. St Pet Coll Ox BA81 Trin Coll Cam BA89. Ridley Hall Cam 87. **d** 90 **p** 91. C Kenilworth St Jo *Cov* 90-94; Chapl York Univ *York* from 94. *Bede House, Heslington, York YO1 5EE* Tel (01904) 413925

ROBERTSON, Mrs Priscilla Biddulph. b 25. St And Dioc Tr Course 87. **d** 90 **p** 94. C St Andrews St Andr *St And* from 90. *8 Balrymonth Court, St Andrews, Fife KY16 8XT* Tel (01334) 474976

ROBERTSON, Scott. b 64. Edin Univ BD90. Edin Th Coll 86. **d** 90 **p** 91. C Glas Gd Shep and Ascension *Glas* 90-92; P-in-c 92-97; P-in-c Ardrossan from 97; P-in-c Irvine St Andr LEP from 97; P-in-c Dalry from 97. *31 Milgarholm Avenue, Irvine, Ayrshire KA12 0EL* Tel (01294) 278341 Fax as telephone E-mail revscottrobertson@msn.com

ROBERTSON, Stephen Andrew. b 60. Strathclyde Univ BSc82. Trin Coll Bris DTS92. **d** 92 **p** 93. C Vange *Chelmsf* 92-96; V Creeksea w Althorne, Latchingdon and N Fambridge from 96. *The Vicarage, Fambridge Road, Althorne, Chelmsford CM3 6BZ* Tel (01621) 740250

ROBERTSON, Stuart Lang. b 40. Glas Univ MA63 Nottm Univ DipTh74. St Jo Coll Nottm 72. **d** 75 **p** 76. C Litherland St Jo and St Jas *Liv* 75-78; C Edin St Thos *Edin* 78-81; Chapl Edin Univ 81-83; C Edin St Pet 81-83; R Edin St Jas 83-91; Miss to Seamen 83-91; Russia from 91; BCMS 91-93; Crosslinks from 93; Chapl St Petersburg *Eur* 93-95. *c/o Crosslinks, 251 Lewisham Way, London SE4 1XF* Tel 0181-691 6111

ROBERTSON, Thomas John. b 15. Univ of Wales BA38 Lon Univ DipTh64 DipEd66. St Steph Ho Ox 38. **d** 40 **p** 41. C Welshpool *St As* 40-42; C Shotton 42-45; C Colwyn Bay 45-48; V Choral St As Cathl 48-49; R Newmarket 49-53; V Woolfold *Man* 53-57; V Bury St Thos 57-61; Hd of RE Bramhall Gr Sch 61-74; Lic to Offic 61-74; V Taddington and Chelmorton *Derby* 74-80; rtd 80; Perm to Offic *Derby* 80-87; Perm to Offic *Ches* 80-95; Perm to Offic *Man* 80-95. *The Coach House, Halstead Hall, Halstead, Sevenoaks, Kent TN14 7DH*

ROBERTSON-GLASGOW, John Nigel. b 13. Cuddesdon Coll 46. **d** 47 **p** 48. C Banbury *Ox* 47-50; R Chipping Warden w Edgcote *Pet* 50-79; R Chipping Warden w Edgcote and Aston le Walls 79; RD Culworth 63-70; rtd 79; Perm to Offic *Nor* from 80. *Room 7, Abbeyfield House, 134 Norwich Road, Fakenham, Norfolk NR21 8LF*

ROBIN, John Bryan Carteret. b 22. Trin Coll Ox BA48 MA55. Cuddesdon Coll 49. **d** 77 **p** 78. Chapl Rishworth Sch Ripponden 77-81; Australia from 82; rtd 94. *8 Heron Court, Point Lonsdale, Victoria, Australia 3225* Tel Geelong (52) 584432

ROBIN, Peter Philip King. b 23. Trin Coll Cam BA48 MA81. Cuddesdon Coll 49. **d** 51 **p** 52. C Bethnal Green St Matt *Lon* 51-54; Papua New Guinea 54-75; R Elsing w Bylaugh *Nor* 76-85; R Lyng w Sparham 76-85; P-in-c Holme Cultram St Mary *Carl* 85-88; rtd 88; Perm to Offic *Carl* from 88. *191 Brampton Road, Carlisle CA3 9AX* Tel (01228) 45293

ROBINS, Christopher Charles. b 41. St Mich Coll Llan 66. **d** 68 **p** 69. C Bideford *Ex* 68-71; C Dawlish 71-74; V Laira 74-81; P-in-c E Allington 81; P-in-c Dodbrooke 81-83; P-in-c Churchstow w Kingsbridge 81-83; R Kingsbridge and Dodbrooke from 83. *The Rectory, Church Street, Kingsbridge, Devon TQ7 1NW* Tel (01548) 856231

ROBINS, Douglas Geoffrey. b 45. Open Univ BA90. Ex & Truro NSM Scheme. **d** 81 **p** 83. NSM Kenwyn *Truro* 81-84; Lic to Offic from 84. *4 Enys Road, Truro, Cornwall TR1 3TE* Tel (01872) 77469

ROBINS, Henry Temple. b 02. Qu Coll Cam BA24 MA29. Cuddesdon Coll 24. **d** 25 **p** 27. C Drayton in Hales *Lich* 25-29; C Smethwick Old Ch *Birm* 29-34; C Holmfirth *Wakef* 34-38; V Cross Roads cum Lees *Bradf* 38-43; V S Milton *Ex* 43-55; RD Woodleigh 54-55; R Whimple 55-72; rtd 73; Perm to Offic *Ex* 73-89. *Woodhayes, 36-40 St Leonard's Road, Exeter EX2 4LR* Tel (01392) 422539

ROBINS, Ian Donald Hall. b 28. K Coll Lon BD51 AKC51 Lanc Univ MA74. **d** 52 **p** 53. C St Annes *Blackb* 52-55; C Clitheroe St Mary 55-57; V Trawden 57-67; Hd of RE St Chris C of E Sch Accrington 67-76; P-in-c Hugill *Carl* 76-82; Asst Adv for Educn 76-82; Chapl St Martin's Coll of Educn *Blackb* 82-86; V St Annes St Marg 86-91; rtd 91; Perm to Offic *Blackb* from 91. *20 Painter Wood, Billington, Blackburn BB7 9JD* Tel (01254) 824930

ROBINS, Mrs Mary Katherine. b 34. FRGS Bris Univ BSc55 CertEd56. St Alb Minl Tr Scheme. **dss** 84 **d** 87 **p** 94. N Mymms *St Alb* 84-87; Hon Par Dn 87-92; NSM Northaw from 92. *15 Bluebridge Road, Brookmans Park, Hatfield, Herts AL9 7UW* Tel (01707) 656670

ROBINS, Roger Philip. b 44. AKC68. **d** 69 **p** 70. C Farncombe *Guildf* 69-73; C Aldershot St Mich 73-79; V New Haw 79-89; RD Runnymede 83-88; Chapl Merrist Wood Coll of Agric and Horticulture from 88; R Worplesdon *Guildf* from 89. *The Rectory, Perry Hill, Worplesdon, Guildford, Surrey GU3 3RB* Tel (01483) 234616

ROBINS, Ms Wendy Sheridan. b 56. Lanc Univ BA77. EAMTC DipTh93. **d** 93 **p** 94. Dir of Communications and Resources *S'wark* from 92; NSM Walthamstow St Pet *Chelmsf* from 93. *17 Hillcrest Road, London E17 4AP, or Trinity House, 4 Chapel Court, Borough High Street, London SE1 1HW* Tel 0181-523 0016 or 0171-403 8686 Fax 0171-403 4770

ROBINSON, Alan Booker. b 27. Keble Coll Ox BA51 MA56. Sarum Th Coll 51. **d** 53 **p** 54. C Leeds All So *Ripon* 53-56; C Ilkley St Marg *Bradf* 57-59; V Carlton *Wakef* 59-66; V Hooe *Ex* 66-95; RD Plympton 81-82; RD Plymouth Sutton 86-91; rtd 95; Perm to Offic *Ripon* from 95. *1 Charlton Court, Knaresborough, N Yorkshire HG5 0BZ* Tel (01423) 860884

ROBINSON, Albert. b 15. Roch Th Coll 60. **d** 61 **p** 62. C Limpsfield and Titsey *S'wark* 61-64; R Grimston w Congham *Nor* 64-73; P-in-c Roydon All SS 64-73; V Gt w Lt Plumstead 73-81; rtd 81; Perm to Offic *Glouc* 81-91. *63 Marleyfield Way, Churchdown, Gloucester GL3 1JW* Tel (01452) 855178

ROBINSON, Andrew Nesbitt. b 43. AKC67. **d** 68 **p** 69. C Balsall Heath St Paul *Birm* 68-71; C Westmr St Steph w St Jo *Lon* 71-75; Chapl Sussex Univ *Chich* from 75; Chapl Brighton Poly 75-92; Chapl Brighton Univ 92-93; P-in-c Stanmer w Falmer from 80. *St Laurence House, Park Street, Brighton BN1 9PG* Tel (01273) 606928 or 606755

ROBINSON, Andrew Stephen. b 49. Lanc Univ BA71 Worc Coll of Educn PGCE72 Glam Univ DipEdMan82. St Mich Coll Llan 90 DipTh93. **d** 95 **p** 96. NSM Llangattock and Llangyndir *S & B* from 95. *17 Pencommin, Llangynidr, Crickhowell NP8 1LT* Tel (01874) 730034

ROBINSON, The Ven Anthony William. b 56. CertEd. Sarum & Wells Th Coll. **d** 82 **p** 83. C Tottenham St Paul *Lon* 82-85; TV Leic Resurr *Leic* 85-89; TR Leic Resurr 89-97; RD Christianity N 92-97; P-in-c Belgrave St Pet 94-95; Hon Can Leic Cathl 94-97; Adn Pontefract *Wakef* from 97. *10 Arden Court, Horbury, Wakefield, W Yorkshire WF4 5AH* Tel (01924) 276797 Fax 261095

ROBINSON, Arthur Robert Basil. b 32. ACP67 St Jo Coll Dur BA56 Bradf Univ MA84. Wycliffe Hall Ox 56. **d** 58 **p** 59. C Pemberton St Mark Newtown *Liv* 58-62; CF 62-65; Asst Master Colne Valley High Sch Linthwaite 65-69; Asst Chapl HM Pris Man 69; Chapl HM Borstal Roch 69-74; Peru 74-77; V Golcar *Wakef* 77-83; rtd 94. *Morangie, 2A Brecksfield, Skelton, York YO3 6YD* Tel (01904) 470558

ROBINSON, Arthur William. b 35. Dur Univ BSc60. Clifton Th Coll 60. **d** 62 **p** 63. C Ox St Clem *Ox* 62-65; Chile 65-77; V Hoxton St Jo w Ch Ch *Lon* 78-88; TV Gateacre *Liv* from 88. *Christ Church House, 44 Brownbill Bank, Liverpool L27 7AE* Tel 0151-487 7759

ROBINSON, Canon Brian. b 39. St Aid Birkenhead 62. **d** 64 **p** 65. C Knotty Ash St Jo *Liv* 64-68; C Sutton 68-72; V Hunts Cross 72-79; V Livesey *Blackb* 79-88; V Burscough Bridge *Liv* 88-95; P-in-c Widnes St Mary from 95; AD Widnes from 95; Hon Can Liv Cathl from 96. *St Mary's Vicarage, St Mary's Road, Widnes, Cheshire WA8 0DN* Tel 0151-424 4233

ROBINSON, Brian John Watson. b 33. St Cath Coll Cam BA56 MA60. Westcott Ho Cam 57. **d** 58 **p** 59. C Whitworth w

Spennymoor *Dur* 58-62; India 62-66; P-in-c Preston St Steph *Blackb* 66-72; V Ashton-on-Ribble St Andr 72-79; Lic to Offic 79-82; V Preston St Jude w St Paul 82-97; Chapl Preston Hosp N Shields 83-94; Chapl N Tyneside Healthcare NHS Trust 94-97; rtd 97. *50 Green Acres, Fulwood, Preston PR2 7DB*

ROBINSON, Canon Bryan. b 32. Fitzw Ho Cam BA56. Ely Th Coll 56. **d** 58 **p** 59. C Fleetwood *Blackb* 58-65; V Burnley St Andr 65-74; V Burnley St Marg 65-74; V Burnley St Andr w St Marg 74-97; RD Burnley 85-91; P-in-c Burnley St Jas 92-97; Hon Can Blackb Cathl 94-97; rtd 97. *50 Fountains Avenue, Simonstone, Burnley, Lancs BB12 7PY* Tel (01282) 776518

ROBINSON, Cedric Henry. b 17. K Coll Lon. **d** 58 **p** 59. C Kings Heath *Birm* 58-62; V Shaw Hill 62-67; V Norton w Whittington *Worc* 67-79; P-in-c Hanbury 79-84; R W Bowbrook 84-87; rtd 87. *7 Mortlake Drive, Martley, Worcester WR6 6QU* Tel (01886) 888628

ROBINSON, Christopher Gordon. b 49. Ridley Hall Cam. **d** 82 **p** 83. C Stanton *St E* 82-85; C Lawshall 85-86; C Lawshall w Shimplingthorne and Alpheton 86; P-in-c 86-89; TV Oakdale *Sarum* from 89. *The Vicarage, 25 Nuthatch Close, Poole, Dorset BH17 7XR* Tel (01202) 602441

ROBINSON, Daffyd Charles. b 48. Qu Coll Birm 77. **d** 80 **p** 85. C Abington *Pet* 80-82; C Immingham *Linc* 85-90; R Willoughby from 90. *The Rectory, Station Road, Willoughby, Alford, Lincs LN13 9NA* Tel (01507) 462045

ROBINSON, David. b 42. Sarum & Wells Th Coll. **d** 82 **p** 83. C Billingham St Cuth *Dur* 82-86; V Longwood *Wakef* 86-94; C Athersley 94-97; P-in-c Brotherton from 97. *St Andrew's Vicarage, 5 Pontefract Road, Knottingley, W Yorkshire WF11 8PN* Tel (01977) 672772

ROBINSON, Canon David Hugh. b 47. Linc Th Coll 76. **d** 79 **p** 80. C Bulkington *Cov* 79-82; P-in-c Whitley 82-87; Chapl Walsgrave Hosp Cov 87-94; Chapl Walsgrave Hosp NHS Trust Cov from 94; Hon Can Cov Cathl *Cov* from 92. *Walsgrave General Hospital, Clifford Bridge Road, Walsgrave on Sowe, Coventry CV2 2DX* Tel (01203) 538950 or 622683

ROBINSON, David Mark. b 55. Univ Coll Dur BSc76 Leic Univ MA80 CQSW80. Cranmer Hall Dur 86. **d** 88 **p** 89. C Shipley St Pet *Bradf* 88-92; P-in-c Ingrow cum Hainworth 92-97; V Bramhope *Ripon* from 97. *The Vicarage, 26 Leeds Road, Bramhope, Leeds LS16 9BQ* Tel 0113-284 2543

ROBINSON, David Michael Wood. b 28. Glas Univ BSc50 Lon Univ BD54. **d** 57 **p** 57. C Erith St Jo *Roch* 57-58; Japan 58-71; R Holton and Waterperry *Ox* 71-88; RD Aston and Cuddesdon 88-92; R Holton and Waterperry w Albury and Waterstock 88-94; Chapl Ox Poly 90-92; Chapl Ox Brookes Univ 92-94; rtd 94. *72 Divinity Road, Oxford OX4 1LJ* Tel (01865) 245466

ROBINSON, Capt Denis Hugh. b 53. SS Mark & Jo Coll Plymouth CertEd75. Sarum & Wells Th Coll 88. **d** 91 **p** 92. NSM Bisley and W End *Guildf* from 91; Asst Chapl Gordon's Sch Woking from 91. *Ashleigh, Bagshot Road, West End, Woking, Surrey GU24 9PX* Tel (01276) 857535 Fax (01276) 855335

ROBINSON, Denis Winston. b 42. QUB BSc68. CITC. **d** 88 **p** 89. NSM Mullavilly *Arm* 88-92; NSM Arm St Mark w Aghavilly 92-95; C Portadown St Mark from 95. *4 Killycomaine Drive, Portadown, Craigavon, Co Armagh BT63 5JJ* Tel (01762) 335813

ROBINSON, Derek Charles. b 43. S'wark Ord Course 91. **d** 94 **p** 95. NSM Abbey Wood *S'wark* from 94. *19 Siverdale Road, Bexleyheath, Kent DA7 5AB* Tel (01322) 523870

ROBINSON, Douglas. b 48. Nottm Univ BEd70 Lon Univ BD74. Trin Coll Bris 71 Union Th Sem Virginia MA75. **d** 75 **p** 76. C Southport Ch Ch *Liv* 75-78; V Clubmoor 78-85; Chapl Epsom Coll 85-88; Chapl Dauntsey's Sch Devizes 89-95; Germany from 95. *Espensteigstrasse 18, Espensteig, 67661 Kaiserslautern, Germany*

ROBINSON, Dugald Clifford. b 23. Qu Coll Birm 69. **d** 70 **p** 71. C Stratford-on-Avon w Bishopton *Cov* 70-74; V Allesley Park 74-86; rtd 86; Perm to Offic *Cov* from 86. *5 Wedgewoods, 34 Beechwood Avenue, Coventry CV5 6QG* Tel (01203) 679617

ROBINSON, Ernest Yeomans. b 03. **d** 56 **p** 57. C Dublin St Jas *D & G* 56-59; I Dromod *L & K* 59-64; I Kilscoran w Carn, Tacumshin, Killinick etc *C & O* 64-68; V Hensall *Sheff* 68-72; I Kilmoe Union *C, C & R* 76-78; rtd 78. *Ilen Lodge, Rath, Baltimore, Skibereen, Co Cork, Irish Republic* Tel Skibbereen (28) 20152

ROBINSON, Geoffrey. b 28. Hartley Victoria Coll 49 Ely Th Coll 52. **d** 53 **p** 54. C Prenton *Ches* 53-58; V Gt Saughall 58-95; rtd 95; Perm to Offic *Ches* from 95. *Lochaber, 20 Aspen Grove, Saughall, Chester CH1 6AL* Tel (01244) 880485

ROBINSON, George. b 27. MIMechE HNC59. Oak Hill Th Coll 59. **d** 61 **p** 62. C Branksome St Clem *Sarum* 61-64; Australia from 64. *24 Abingdon Road, Roseville, NSW, Australia 2069* Tel Roseville (2) 416 4330

ROBINSON, Mrs Gillian Dawn. b 69. Edin Univ BD91. Trin Coll Bris 94. **d** 96 **p** 97. C Totton *Win* from 96. *7 Briardene Court, Totton, Southampton SO4 3WD* Tel (01703) 663267

ROBINSON, Canon Gordon Victor Michael. b 18. Keble Coll Ox BA40 MA46. Cuddesdon Coll 40. **d** 41 **p** 42. C Coppenhall *Ches* 41-47; C Warsop *S'well* 47-48; R Coppenhall *Ches* 48-55; V Ellesmere Port 55-71; Hon Can Ches Cathl 62-83; TR Ellesmere Port 71-73; R Tarporley 73-76; TR Birkenhead Priory 76-82; Exec Officer Bd for Soc Resp 82-83; rtd 83; Perm to Offic *Ches* from 83. *69 Marian Drive, Great Boughton, Chester CH3 5RY* Tel (01244) 315828

ROBINSON, Hugh Stanley. b 21. AKC47. **d** 47 **p** 48. C Tilehurst St Geo *Ox* 47-50; CF 50-53; C Farnham Royal *Ox* 53-59; V Wheatley 59-67; V Chiddingly *Chich* 67-83; V Laughton 67-76; Asst Chapl HM Pris Northeye 83-86; rtd 86; Perm to Offic *Lich* from 86. *2 Brook Drive, Wem, Shrewsbury SY4 5HQ* Tel (01939) 234683

ROBINSON, Ian. b 57. Nottm Univ BTh87. Linc Th Coll 84. **d** 87 **p** 88. C Bottesford w Ashby *Linc* 87-90; TV 90-95; P-in-c Caistor w Clixby from 95; P-in-c Grasby from 95; P-in-c Searby w Owmby from 95. *The Vicarage, 1 Cromwell View, Caistor, Lincoln LN7 6OH* Tel (01472) 851339

ROBINSON, Ian Cameron. b 19. OBE72. Em Coll Cam BA40 MA44. Linc Th Coll 71. **d** 72 **p** 73. C Ipswich St Aug *St E* 72-74; V Darsham 74-84; V Westleton w Dunwich 74-84; RD Saxmundham 79-83; rtd 84; Perm to Offic *St E* from 84. *Corner House, Rectory Street, Halesworth, Suffolk IP19 8BS* Tel (01986) 873573

ROBINSON, James. b 23. Ridley Hall Cam 70. **d** 72 **p** 73. C Mixenden CD *Wakef* 72-73; C Carlton-in-Lindrick *S'well* 73-74; C Tuxford 75-77; C Selston 77-85; P-in-c Shireoaks 85-93; rtd 93. *15 Walnut Avenue, Shireoaks, Worksop, Notts S81 8PQ* Tel (01909) 483045

ROBINSON, Mrs Jane Hippisley. b 41. Somerville Coll Ox MA66 K Coll Lon PGCE. S Dios Minl Tr Scheme 88. **d** 91. NSM Ealing St Pet Mt Park *Lon* 91-96; NSM N Acton St Gabr from 96. *60 Madeley Road, London W5 2LU* Tel 0181-991 0206

ROBINSON, Mrs Janet. b 34. Milton Keynes Coll of Ed CertEd77 Open Univ BA78. WMMTC 89. **d** 92 **p** 94. NSM Roade and Ashton w Hartwell *Pet* 92-94; NSM Potterspury, Furtho, Yardley Gobion and Cosgrove from 94. *73 Eastfield Crescent, Yardley Gobion, Towcester, Northants NN12 7TT* Tel (01908) 542331

ROBINSON, John Francis Napier (Frank). b 42. St Edm Hall Ox BA64 MA68 Lon Univ DipTh68. Clifton Th Coll 65. **d** 68 **p** 69. C Southport Ch Ch *Liv* 68-71; C Coleraine *Conn* 71-74; Deputation Sec (Ireland) BCMS 74-76; TV Marfleet *York* 76-81; V Yeadon St Jo *Bradf* 81-95; V Rounds Green *Birm* from 95. *The Vicarage, Shelsley Avenue, Oldbury, Warley, W Midlands B69 1BG* Tel 0121-552 2822

ROBINSON, John Howard. b 52. Stockport Tech Coll C&G82 Jo Dalton Coll Man HNC84. St Jo Coll Nottm DCM92. **d** 92 **p** 93. C Meole Brace *Lich* 92-96; R Baschurch and Weston Lullingfield w Hordley from 96. *The Rectory, Baschurch, Shrewsbury SY4 2EB* Tel (01939) 260305

ROBINSON, The Ven John Kenneth. b 36. K Coll Lon BD61 AKC61. **d** 62 **p** 63. C Poulton-le-Fylde *Blackb* 62-65; C Lancaster St Mary 65-66; Chapl HM Pris Lanc 65-66; Singapore 66-68; V Colne H Trin *Blackb* 68-71; USPG 71-74; Grenada 71-74; V Skerton St Luke *Blackb* 74-81; Area Sec (E Anglia) USPG 81-91; Min Can St E Cathl *St E* 82-91; Chapl Gtr Lisbon *Eur* from 91; Adn Gib from 94; Can Gib Cathl from 94. *Rua da Ginjeira, Lote 5, Alcoitao, 2765 Estoril, Portugal* Tel Lisbon (1) 469-2303 Fax as telephone

ROBINSON, John Leonard William. b 23. Lon Univ BA50. Bps' Coll Cheshunt 50. **d** 52 **p** 53. C Victoria Docks Ascension *Chelmsf* 52-55; C Kilburn St Aug *Lon* 55-63; C Westmr St Jas 63-81; V Compton, the Mardens, Stoughton and Racton *Chich* 81-93; V Stansted 85-93; rtd 93. *19 Greenhill Park, Barnet, Herts EN5 1HQ* Tel 0181-449 3984

ROBINSON, John Michael. b 57. K Coll Lon BD79 AKC79. St Steph Ho Ox 81. **d** 81 **p** 82. C Plymouth St Pet *Ex* 81-84; C Sheff Parson Cross St Cecilia *Sheff* 84-87; V Thurcroft 87-88; Chapl St Jas Univ Hosp Leeds 89-91; Hon C Dalton *Sheff* 91-92; C 92-95; P-in-c Devonport St Bart *Ex* from 95; P-in-c Devonport St Mark Ford from 95. *St Bartholomew's Vicarage, 13 Outland Road, Plymouth PL2 3BZ* Tel (01752) 562623

ROBINSON, Jonathan William Murrell. b 42. Sarum Th Coll 65. **d** 68 **p** 69. C Tooting All SS *S'wark* 68-71; C Bourne *Guildf* 71-76; Dir Grail Trust Chr Community Cen Burtle *B & W* 78-82; Hon C Willesden Green St Gabr *Lon* 78-82; V Stoke St Gregory w Burrowbridge and Lyng *B & W* 82-90; Dir Grail Retreat Cen 90-92; NSM Aymestrey and Leinthall Earles w Wigmore etc *Heref* 92-96; NSM Kingsland w Eardisland, Aymestrey etc from 97. *The Rectory, Wigmore, Leominster, Herefordshire HR6 9UW* Tel (01568) 86272

ROBINSON, Canon Joseph. b 27. K Coll Lon BD51 AKC51 MTh58 FKC73. **d** 52 **p** 53. C Tottenham All Hallows *Lon* 52-55; Min Can St Paul's Cathl 55-68; Lect K Coll Lon 59-68; Can Res Cant Cathl *Cant* 68-80; Lib 68-73; Treas 72-80; Master of The Temple from 81. *The Master's House, Temple, London EC4 7BB* Tel 0171-353 8559

ROBINSON, Keith. b 48. Lon Univ BA75 BD77 AKC77. Westcott Ho Cam 77. **d** 78 **p** 79. C Bow w Bromley St Leon *Lon* 78-81; C Leighton Buzzard w Eggington, Hockliffe etc *St Alb* 81-88; PV Westmr Abbey 82-90; V Bulkington w Shilton and Ansty *Cov* 88-95; P-in-c Salisbury St Martin *Sarum* from 95; P-in-c

Laverstock from 95. *The Rectory, Tollgate Road, Salisbury SP1 2JJ* Tel (01722) 335895

ROBINSON, Kenneth Borwell. b 37. Lon Univ BA62. Ridley Hall Cam 68. **d** 70 **p** 71. C Walthamstow St Jo *Chelmsf* 70-74; P-in-c Becontree St Alb 74-78; P-in-c Heybridge w Langford 78-84; C Horley *S'wark* 84; TV from 84. *St Francis's House, 84 Balcombe Road, Horley, Surrey RH6 9AY* Tel (01293) 776322

ROBINSON, Leslie. b 31. St Aid Birkenhead 56. **d** 59 **p** 60. C Hugglescote w Donington *Leic* 59-61; C Greenside *Dur* 61-63; C-in-c New Cantley CD *Sheff* 63-66; V Choral Heref Cathl *Heref* 66-67; R Easton-on-the-Hill *Pet* 67-69; Hon Min Can Pet Cathl 68-69; C Weston-super-Mare St Jo *B & W* 69-70; V Winkleigh *Ex* 70-72; V Thorpe Acre w Dishley *Leic* 72-78; V Cloughton *York* 78-79; V Hedon w Paull 79-81; V Bywell St Pet *Newc* 81-86; V Wymeswold and Prestwold w Hoton *Leic* 86-97; rtd 97. *19 Ambleside Close, Loughborough, Leics LE11 3SH* Tel (01509) 263790

ROBINSON, Miss Margaret. b 32. S'wark Ord Course 83. **dss** 86 **d** 87 **p** 94. Finsbury St Clem w St Barn and St Matt *Lon* 86-87; Par Dn St Giles Cripplegate w St Bart Moor Lane etc 87-94; C 94-95; rtd 95. *8 Morley College, The Close, Winchester, Hants SO23 9LF* Tel (01962) 869834

ROBINSON, Michael John. b 45. Nottm Univ BA66. Linc Th Coll 78. **d** 79 **p** 80. C Aston cum Aughton *Sheff* 79-80; C Rotherham 80-82; TV Howden TM *York* 82-86; V Heywood St Jas *Man* 86-92; V Astley 92; R Blackley St Paul 92-97; V Hale and Ashley *Ches* from 97. *St Peter's Vicarage, 1 Harrop Road, Hale, Altrincham, Cheshire WA15 9BU* Tel 0161-928 4182

ROBINSON, Dr Neal Sydney. b 48. Worc Coll Ox BA70 MA75 Birm Univ PhD77. Qu Coll Birm 74. **d** 76 **p** 77. C Folkestone St Sav *Cant* 76-79; Chapl Bradf Univ *Bradf* 79-87; Perm to Offic *Glouc* 87-93; Lect Coll of SS Mary and Paul Cheltenham 87-88; Sen Lect 88-90; Sen Lect Cheltenham & Glouc Coll of HE 90-92; Lect Leeds Univ from 92; C Potternewton *Ripon* from 92. *44 Sholebroke Avenue, Leeds LS7 3HB* Tel 0113-262 3024

ROBINSON, The Ven Neil. b 29. St Jo Coll Dur BA52 DipTh54. **d** 54 **p** 55. C Kingston upon Hull H Trin *York* 54-58; V Glen Parva and S Wigston *Leic* 58-68; Hon Can Leic Cathl 68-83; RD Sparkenhoe I 69-83; R Market Bosworth w Shenton 69-83; Can Res Worc Cathl *Worc* 83-87; Adn Suffolk *St E* 87-94; rtd 94. *Skell Green, 32 Mallorie Park Drive, Ripon, N Yorkshire HG4 2QF* Tel (01765) 603075

ROBINSON, Norman Leslie. b 50. Liv Univ BSc71. Lon Bible Coll BA78 Wycliffe Hall Ox 78. **d** 80 **p** 81. C Bebington *Ches* 80-83; C St Helens St Helen *Liv* 83-90; P-in-c Westward, Rosley-w-Woodside and Welton *Carl* from 90. *The Vicarage, Rosley, Wigton, Cumbria CA7 8AU* Tel (016973) 43723

ROBINSON, Paul Leslie. b 46. Dur Univ BA67 Nottm Univ DipTh73. Linc Th Coll 71. **d** 74 **p** 75. C Poynton *Ches* 74-76; C Prenton 76-78; V Seacombe 78-88; V Stalybridge St Paul from 88. *St Paul's Vicarage, Huddersfield Road, Stalybridge, Cheshire SK15 2PT* Tel 0161-338 2514

ROBINSON, Paul Leslie. b 65. St Steph Ho Ox 95. **d** 97. C Upholland *Liv* from 97. *8 Beacon View Drive, Upholland, Skelmersdale, Lancs WN8 0HL* Tel (01695) 622181

ROBINSON, Peter. b 42. Univ of Wales (Lamp) BA63 DipEd64 Univ of Wales (Cardiff) BD71. N Ord Course 78. **d** 81 **p** 82. NSM Rochdale *Man* 81-83; C Rochdale 83-86; V Shore 86-91; Chapl for Readers from 90. *131 Starkey Street, Heywood, Lancs OL10 4JH* Tel (01706) 367557

ROBINSON, Peter Charles. b 53. Open Univ BA83. Oak Hill Th Coll 85. **d** 87 **p** 88. C Nottingham St Ann w Em *S'well* 87-89; C Worksop St Anne 89-92; V S Ramsey St Paul *S & M* from 92. *St Paul's Vicarage, Walpole Drive, Ramsey, Isle of Man IM8 1NA* Tel (01624) 812275

ROBINSON, Peter Edward Barron. b 40. Sarum & Wells Th Coll 76. **d** 78 **p** 79. C Petersfield w Sheet *Portsm* 78-82; R Bentworth and Shalden and Lasham *Win* 82-88; R W Horsley *Guildf* from 88. *The Rectory, 80 East Lane, West Horsley, Leatherhead, Surrey KT24 6LQ* Tel (01483) 282173

ROBINSON, Peter John Alan. b 61. St Jo Coll Cam BA83. St Jo Coll Dur BA92. **d** 95 **p** 96. C N Shields *Newc* from 95. *24 Cleveland Road, North Shields, Tyne & Wear NE29 0NG* Tel 0191-258 0554

ROBINSON, Peter McCall. b 24. Worc Coll Ox BA48 MA50. Wells Th Coll 48. **d** 50 **p** 51. S Africa 50-54; C Stoke Poges *Ox* 55-57; S Africa 57-71; V Payhembury *Ex* 71-79; R Cheriton w Tichborne and Beauworth *Win* 79-81; S Africa 81-82; V Marystowe, Coryton, Stowford, Lewtrenchard etc *Ex* 82-85; V Blackawton and Stoke Fleming 85-88; rtd 88; Perm to Offic *Ex* from 89. *8 Malden Road, Sidmouth, Devon EX10 9LS* Tel (01395) 514494

ROBINSON, Philip. b 38. JP79. MIPM74. S Dios Minl Tr Scheme 88. **d** 91 **p** 92. NSM Ickenham *Lon* 91-95; P-in-c from 95. *St Giles's Rectory, 38 Swakeleys Road, Ickenham, Uxbridge, Middx UB10 8BE* Tel (01895) 622970 Mobile 0956-570176 Fax as telephone E-mail stgilesickenham@compuserve.com

ROBINSON, Raymonde Robin. b 43. St Jo Coll Dur BA66. Chich Th Coll 67. **d** 70 **p** 71. C Ealing St Barn *Lon* 70-72; C Pinner 72-75; C Clerkenwell H Redeemer w St Phil 75-80; TV Kingsthorpe w Northn St Dav *Pet* 80-89; R Letchworth *St Alb* 89-95; V Noel Park St Mark *Lon* from 95. *St Mark's Vicarage, Ashley Crescent, London N22 6LJ* Tel 0181-888 3442

ROBINSON, Richard Hugh. b 35. St Jo Coll Cam BA58 MA62. Ridley Hall Cam 58. **d** 60 **p** 81. C Cheadle Hulme St Andr *Ches* 60-62; Hon C Alvanley 62-64; Perm to Offic *York* 64-80; Hon C Elloughton and Brough w Brantingham 80-86; C 86-87; Ext Dir CMJ 87-88; NSM Appleby *Carl* 91-93; Perm to Offic from 93. *Sledmere Cottage, The Green, North Newbald, York YO4 3SA*

ROBINSON, Canon Richard Malcolm. b 20. Ex Coll Ox BA42 DipTh43 MA46. Wycliffe Hall Ox 42. **d** 44 **p** 45. C Bedminster St Paul *Bris* 44-45; C Brinkworth 45-48; Youth Adv CMS 48-52; V Manningham St Luke *Bradf* 52-56; V Shipley St Pet 56-64; R Edin Ch Ch *Edin* 64-76; V Dent w Cowgill *Bradf* 76-85; RD Ewecross 80-85; Hon Can Bradf Cathl 83-85; rtd 85; Perm to Offic *Bradf* from 85. *Hollinwood, 15 Raikeswood Road, Skipton, N Yorkshire BD23 1NB* Tel (01756) 791577

ROBINSON, Canon Roger George. b 24. Qu Coll Cam BA46 MA50. Ridley Hall Cam 46. **d** 48 **p** 49. C Gorleston St Andr *Nor* 48-51; C Drypool St Andr and St Pet *York* 51-54; P-in-c Kingston upon Hull St Aid Southcoates 54-55; V 55-60; V Clifton 60-70; Chapl Clifton Hosp York 61-70; V Far Headingley St Chad *Ripon* 70-81; RD Headingley 72-81; Hon Can Ripon Cathl 81; R Drayton w Felthorpe *Nor* 81-91; rtd 91. *24 St Matthew's Walk, Leeds LS7 3PS* Tel 0113-269 6307

ROBINSON, Ronald Frederick (Ron). b 46. Brasted Place Coll 72. Oak Hill Th Coll 74. **d** 76 **p** 77. C Pennington *Man* 76-77; C Bedhampton *Portsm* 77-79; C Portsea N End St Mark 79-82; V 90-92; R Rowner 82-90; rtd 93; P-in-c Coldwaltham and Hardham *Chich* from 96; P-in-c Bury and Houghton from 96. *The Vicarage, Church Lane, Coldwaltham, Pulborough, W Sussex RH20 1LW* Tel (01798) 872146

ROBINSON, Roy David. b 35. AKC59. **d** 60 **p** 61. C Acocks Green *Birm* 60-62; C Shirley 62-65; C Haslemere *Guildf* 65-70; R Headley w Box Hill 70-85; V Hinchley Wood from 85. *The Vicarage, 98 Manor Road, Esher, Surrey KT10 0AE* Tel 0181-398 4443

ROBINSON, Simon John. b 51. Edin Univ MA72 DSA73 PhD89 Ox Univ BA77. Wycliffe Hall Ox 75. **d** 78 **p** 79. C Haughton le Skerne *Dur* 78-81; Chapl Asst N Tees Hosp Stockton-on-Tees 81-83; C Norton St Mary *Dur* 81-83; Chapl Heriot-Watt Univ *Edin* 83-90; R Dalmahoy 83-90; Chapl Leeds Univ *Ripon* from 90; P-in-c Leeds Em from 90. *14 Parkside Green, Leeds LS6 4NY* Tel 0113-274 6297 or 233 5070

ROBINSON, Stuart. b 39. N Ord Course. **d** 87 **p** 88. C Hull St Martin w Transfiguration *York* 87-90; P-in-c Preston and Sproatley in Holderness 90-91; R from 91. *The Rectory, Staithes Road, Preston, Hull HU12 8TB* Tel (01482) 898375

ROBINSON, Canon Thomas Fisher. b 20. St Jo Coll Dur BA49. **d** 50 **p** 51. C Pendlebury St Jo *Man* 50-54; C Davyhulme St Mary 54-56; V Litherland St Andr *Liv* 56-62; V Wigan St Cath 62-67; V Garston 67-88; Hon Can Liv Cathl 85-88; rtd 88; Perm to Offic *Liv* from 88. *208 Mather Avenue, Liverpool L18 9TG* Tel 0151-475 7870

ROBINSON, Thomas Hugh. b 34. CBE89. TCD BA55 MA71. **d** 57 **p** 58. C Belfast St Clem *D & D* 57-60; Kenya 61-64; I Youghal *C, C & R* 64-66; CF 66-89; Dep Chapl Gen 86-89; TR Cleethorpes *Linc* from 90. *The Rectory, 42 Queens Parade, Cleethorpes, S Humberside DN35 0DG* Tel (01472) 693234

ROBINSON, Thomas Irven. b 10. TCD BA34 MA45. **d** 34 **p** 35. C Maidstone St Paul *Cant* 34-36; C Cliftonville 36-39; Chapl RAFVR 39-45; C All Hallows Barking *Lon* 45-46; Chapl RAF 46-62; V Hilmarton and Highway *Sarum* 62-67; Bahrain 67-69; Dhahran 69-71; P-in-c Stourpaine, Durweston and Bryanston *Sarum* 71-77; rtd 77; Perm to Offic *Ox* 77-88. *c/o Mrs B A Oatey, Green Gates, Terrace Road North, Binfield, Berkshire RG42 5JG* Tel (01344) 486728

ROBINSON, Timothy James. b 59. Middx Poly BA84. St Steph Ho Ox 88. **d** 91 **p** 92. C W Acklam *York* 91-95; P-in-c N Ormesby 95-96; V from 96. *The Vicarage, James Street, North Ormesby, Middlesbrough, Cleveland TS3 6LD* Tel (01642) 225272

ROBINSON, Virgil Austin Anderson. b 38. Univ of SW Louisiana BS62. St Steph Ho Ox 77. **d** 79 **p** 80. NSM Bicester w Bucknell, Caversfield and Launton *Ox* 79-82; USA from 82. *1527 Chapel Court, Northbrook, Illinois 60062, USA*

ROBINSON, The Ven William David. b 31. Univ Coll Dur BA54 DipTh58 MA62. Cranmer Hall Dur. **d** 58 **p** 59. C Standish *Blackb* 58-61; C Lancaster St Mary 61-63; V Blackb St Jas 63-73; P-in-c Shireshead 73-86; Hon Can Blackb Cathl 75-96; Adn Blackb 86-96; V Balderstone 86-87; rtd 96; Perm to Offic *Blackb* from 96. *21 Westbourne Road, Warton, Carnforth, Lancs LA5 9NP* Tel (01524) 720591

ROBINSON, William Pitchford. b 50. Nottm Univ BTh75. Kelham Th Coll 71. **d** 75 **p** 76. C Bow w Bromley St Leon *Lon* 75-79; Hon C Barkingside St Geo *Chelmsf* 79-82; Chapl Claybury Hosp Woodford Bridge 79-85; Hon C Barkingside St Fran *Chelmsf* 82-85; Australia from 86. *5 Comet Street, Mandurah, W Australia 6210* Tel Perth (9) 581 1301

ROBLIN, The Ven Graham Henry. b 37. OBE83. AKC61. St Boniface Warminster 60. **d** 62 **p** 63. C St Helier *S'wark* 62-66; CF 66-81; Dep Asst Chapl Gen 81-83; Warden RAChD Cen Bagshot 83-85; Asst Chapl Gen (BOAR) 86-89; Dep Chapl

Gen 89-93; Adn for the Army 90-93; QHC from 87; R Bere Regis and Affpuddle w Turnerspuddle *Sarum* from 93. *The Vicarage, Bere Regis, Wareham, Dorset BH20 7HQ* Tel (01929) 471262

ROBOTHAM, The Ven Eric William. b 07. Ex Coll Ox BA30 BTh32 MA35. Wycliffe Hall Ox 30. **d** 32 **p** 33. C Chadwell Heath *Chelmsf* 32-34; C Leytonstone St Jo 35-37; Chapl RAF 37-46; R W w E Putford *Ex* 46-49; P-in-c Swimbridge 49-52; Australia from 53; Adn Goldfields 56-60; rtd 77. *38 North Street, Bassendean, W Australia 6054* Tel Perth (9) 279 8393

ROBOTTOM, David Leonard Douglas. b 40. Qu Coll Birm 80 Sarum & Wells Th Coll 81. **d** 83 **p** 84. C Uppingham w Ayston and Wardley w Belton *Pet* 83-87; TV Sidmouth, Woolbrook and Salcombe Regis *Ex* 87-91; TV Sidmouth, Woolbrook, Salcombe Regis, Sidbury etc 91-95; R Bradninch and Clyst Hydon from 95. *The Rectory, 27 West End Road, Bradninch, Exeter EX5 4QS* Tel (01392) 881264

ROBSON, Angus William. b 13. Kelham Th Coll 32. **d** 38 **p** 39. C Regent Square St Pet *Lon* 38-40; C Mill End *St Alb* 40-45; CF 43-45; P-in-c Luton St Pet 45; Perm to Offic *St Alb* 45-46; V Sark *Win* 46-50; V Jersey St Jas 50-75; Chapl HM Pris Jersey 60-75; rtd 78. *Flat 1, La Petite Carrière, Wellington Road, St Helier, Jersey, Channel Islands JE2 4RJ* Tel (01534) 31656

ROBSON, Featherstone. b 30. Southn Univ CertEd52 Nottm Univ DipEd74. Oak Hill Th Coll 55. **d** 58 **p** 59. C Illogan *Truro* 58-60; Chapl Bedstone Sch Shropshire 60-61; Teacher Larkmead Sch Abingdon 68-71; Teacher Dorking Gr Sch 71-76; Ho Master Scarisbrook Hall Sch Ormskirk 77-78; Chapl Dean Close Jr Sch Cheltenham 78-79; Asst Chapl K Edw Sch Witley 79-81; Deputation Sec for England, Irish Ch Miss 82-86; Perm to Offic *Ox* from 86; rtd 86. *71 Springfield Drive, Abingdon, Oxon OX14 1JF* Tel (01235) 533421

ROBSON, George. b 34. AKC58. **d** 59 **p** 60. C Chorley St Geo *Blackb* 59-62; Chapl RAF 62-87; R Raithby *Linc* from 87; R Lt Steeping from 87; V Spilsby w Hundleby from 87; R Aswardby w Sausthorpe from 87; R Langton w Sutterby from 87; R Halton Holgate from 87; R Firsby w Gt Steeping from 87. *The Vicarage, 1 Church Street, Spilsby, Lincs PE23 5DU* Tel (01790) 52526

ROBSON, Gilbert Alan. b 30. St Pet Hall Ox BA53 MA57. Linc Th Coll 56. **d** 57 **p** 58. C Chatham St Mary w St Jo *Roch* 57-59; Sub Warden Roch Th Coll 59-62; Min Can Roch Cathl *Roch* 59-62; Bp's Dom Chapl 61-64; Chapl Roch Th Coll 62-64; R Wouldham *Roch* 62-64; Chapl Nor Coll of Educn 65-68; Sen Lect in Div 68-72; V Shotwick *Ches* 72-74; Dir of Ords 72-74; Bp's Dom Chapl 72-74; Hd of Div Eton Coll Windsor 74-89; R Wrotham *Roch* 89-95; rtd 95; Perm to Offic *Nor* from 95. *3 Staden Park, Trimingham, Norwich NR11 8HX* Tel (01263) 834887

ROBSON, Preb Ian Leonard. b 32. Bps' Coll Cheshunt 61. **d** 63 **p** 64. C Croxley Green All SS *St Alb* 63-65; C Harpenden St Nic 65-68; V Redbourn 68-72; V Ashford St Matt *Lon* 72-77; V Kensington St Mary Abbots w St Geo from 77; AD Kensington from 94; Preb St Paul's Cathl from 96. *St Mary Abbots Vicarage, Vicarage Gate, London W8 4HN* Tel 0171-937 6032 or 937 9490 Fax 938 4317

ROBSON, Irwin. b 20. **d** 63 **p** 64. C Longbenton St Bart *Newc* 63-69; C-in-c Byker St Martin CD 69-74; V Willington 74-76; TR Willington Team 76-83; V Ulgham 83-87; V Widdrington 83-87; rtd 88; Perm to Offic *Newc* from 88. *8 Brinkburn Place, Amble, Morpeth, Northd NE65 0BJ* Tel (01665) 710765

ROBSON, James Edward. b 65. Pemb Coll Ox BA88. Wycliffe Hall Ox 91. **d** 94. C Enfield Ch Ch Trent Park *Lon* from 94. *2 Chalk Lane, Barnet, Herts EN4 9JQ* Tel 0181-449 4042

ROBSON, John Phillips. b 32. St Edm Hall Ox. AKC58. **d** 59 **p** 60. C Huddersfield St Pet and St Paul *Wakef* 59-62; Asst Chapl Ch Hosp Horsham 62-65; Chapl 65-80; Chapl Wellington Coll Berks 80-89; Lic to Offic *Ox* 80-89; Chapl to RVO and Qu Chpl of the Savoy from 89; Chapl to The Queen from 93; rtd 97. *The Queen's Chapel of the Savoy, Savoy Hill, Strand, London WC2R 0DA* Tel 0171-836 7221 or 379 8088 Fax 836 3098

ROBSON, Mrs Margery June. b 44. Darlington Tr Coll CertEd65. St Steph Ho Ox DIM94. **d** 94 **p** 95. C Tuffley *Glouc* from 94. *18 Tuffley Lane, Gloucester GL4 0DT* Tel (01452) 423104

ROBSON, Martin Douglas. b 62. St Andr Univ MTh85 Cam Univ PGCE88 Edin Univ MTh94. Edin Th Coll 93. **d** 94 **p** 95. C Perth St Ninian *St And* from 94. *28B Balhousie Street, Perth PH1 5HJ* Tel (01738) 622140

ROBSON, Michael Douglas. b 62. St Andr Univ MTheol85 Qu Coll Cam PGCE88 Edin Univ MTh93. Edin Th Coll CECM94. **d** 94 **p** 95. NSM Perth St Ninian *St And* from 94. *286 Balhouse Street, Perth PH1 5HJ* Tel (01738) 622140

ROBSON, Mrs Patricia Anne. b 40. CertEd60. SW Minl Tr Course 85. **d** 87 **p** 94. Dioc Youth Officer *Truro* 87-92; Hon C Paul 87-92; Hon C Kenwyn St Geo 88-92; C-in-c St Enoder 92; D-in-c 93-94; P-in-c from 94. *St Enoder Rectory, Summercourt, Newquay, Cornwall TR8 5DF* Tel (01726) 860724 or 74242

ROBSON, Paul Coutt. b 37. Leeds Univ BA60. Coll of Resurr Mirfield 63. **d** 64 **p** 65. C Stokesay *Heref* 64-66; S Africa 66-69; Chapl HM Pris Man 70-71; Chapl HM Borstal Feltham 71-74; Chapl HM Borstal Hollesley 74-78; Chapl HM Pris Grendon and Spring Hill 79-87; Chapl HM Pris Nor 87-92; Chapl HM Pris Brinsford from 92. *Pilgrims, Henley Common, Church Stretton, Shropshire SY6 6RS* Tel (01694) 781221 or (01902) 791118 Fax (01902) 790889

ROBSON, Peter Cole. b 45. Clare Coll Cam BA66 MA70 Or Coll Ox BLitt69 MLitt70. Coll of Resurr Mirfield 70. **d** 71 **p** 72. C Gt Grimsby St Mary and St Jas *Linc* 71-73; Chapl BNC Ox 73-76; R Timsbury *B & W* 76-79; P-in-c Blanchland w Hunstanworth *Newc* 80-83; rtd 87. *13 Homer Terrace, Durham DH1 4JT*

ROBSON, Stephen Thomas. b 54. Chich Th Coll 84. **d** 86 **p** 87. C Newc St Fran *Newc* 86-89; C Gateshead St Cuth w St Paul *Dur* 89-91; TV Stanley 91-96; V Sugley *Newc* from 96. *Sugley Vicarage, Lemington, Newcastle upon Tyne NE15 8RD* Tel 0191-267 4633

ROBSON, William (Bill). b 34. FCIS66 FCCA80. Sarum & Wells Th Coll 77. **d** 79 **p** 80. C Lymington *Win* 79-81; CF 81-93; V Barton Stacey and Bullington etc *Win* from 93. *The Rectory, Longparish, Andover, Hants SP11 6PG* Tel (01264) 720215

ROBUS, Keith Adrian. b 59. Chich Th Coll 85. **d** 88 **p** 89. C Greenhill St Jo *Lon* 88-92; C Willesden St Matt from 92. *St Matthew's Vicarage, St Mary's Road, London NW10 4AU* Tel 0181-965 3748 Fax as telephone

ROBY, Richard James (Dick). b 33. Imp Coll Lon BSc54 Lon Inst of Educn PGCE55. St Alb Minl Tr Scheme 82. **d** 85 **p** 86. NSM Bushey *St Alb* 85-92; NSM Wootton from 92. *35 Sir Malcolm Stewart Homes, Stewartby, Bedford MK43 9LS* Tel (01234) 767979

ROCHDALE, Archdeacon of. *See* DALBY, The Ven Dr John Mark Meredith

ROCHE, Barry Robert Francis. b 40. Lon Univ BD66 Dur Univ DipTh67 DipApTh92 Ox Univ MTh93. Clifton Th Coll 63. **d** 68 **p** 69. C Beckenham Ch Ch *Roch* 68-72; C Chester le Street *Dur* 72-74; C-in-c N Bletchley CD *Ox* 74-78; R Luton Ch Ch *Roch* 78-92; Chapl All SS Hosp Chatham 78-92; TR Glascote and Stonydelph *Lich* from 92; RD Tamworth from 95. *20 Melmerby, Stonydelph, Tamworth, Staffs B77 4LP* Tel (01827) 331163

ROCHE, Harold John. b 24. Ripon Hall Ox 54. **d** 54 **p** 55. C Southport St Phil *Liv* 54-57; V Wigan St Steph 57-63; R Sutcombe *Ex* from 63; R W w E Putford 64-71; V Putford from 71; P-in-c Bradworthy 71-72; RD Holsworthy 80-94. *The Rectory, Sutcombe, Holsworthy, Devon EX22 7PU* Tel (01409) 241298

ROCHESTER, Thomas Robson. b 33. NE Ord Course 85. **d** 90 **p** 91. NSM Glendale Gp *Newc* from 90. *Yearle House, Wooler, Northd NE71 6RB* Tel (01668) 81314

ROCHESTER, Archdeacon of. *See* WARREN, The Ven Norman Leonard

ROCHESTER, Bishop of. *See* NAZIR-ALI, The Rt Revd Dr Michael James

ROCHESTER, Dean of. *See* SHOTTER, The Very Revd Edward Frank

ROCK, Mrs Jean. b 37. Gilmore Course 76. **dss** 79 **d** 87 **p** 97. Douglas St Matt *S & M* 79-81; Marown 81-83; Chapl Asst Oswestry and Distr Hosp 83-87; Oswestry St Oswald *Lich* 83-90; Par Dn 87-90; C-in-c Pont Robert and Pont Dolanog *St As* 90-97; R from 97; rtd 97. *Ty'r Eglwys, Pont Robert, Meifod SY22 6HY* Tel (01938) 500454

ROCKALL, Miss Valerie Jane. b 42. City of Cov Coll CertEd63. St Alb Minl Tr Scheme 78. **dss** 81 **d** 87 **p** 94. Asst Hd Wigginton Sch Tring 73-90; Boxmoor St Jo *St Alb* 81-87; NSM Hemel Hempstead 87-90; Par Dn Ampthill w Millbrook and Steppingley 90-93; TD Southampton (City Cen) *Win* 93-94; TV from 94. *2 Merchant's Walk, Southampton SO14 2AS* Tel (01703) 211106

RODDA, William Reginald. b 09. Clifton Th Coll 35. **d** 36 **p** 37. C Ox St Matt *Ox* 36-39; C Thame 39-42; P-in-c Towersey w Aston Sandford 39-42; Chapl RAFVR 42-46; R Caundle Bishop w Caundle Marsh *Sarum* 46-53; V Broadwindsor w Burstock 53-59; R Corfe Mullen 59-66; V Salisbury St Mich 66-70; R Leigh w Batcombe 71-73; rtd 74. *2 Cuthburga Road, Wimborne, Dorset BH21 1LH* Tel (01202) 883285

RODEN, Cyril John. b 20. EAMTC 79. **d** 81 **p** 82. NSM Clenchwarton *Ely* 81-89; rtd 89; Perm to Offic *Ely* from 89; Perm to Offic *Nor* from 89. *52 Jubilee Bank, Clenchwarton, King's Lynn, Norfolk PE34 4BW* Tel (01553) 773826

RODEN, John Michael. b 37. St Jo Coll York CertEd64 Open Univ BA82. Ripon Hall Ox 71. **d** 73 **p** 74. C Saltburn-by-the-Sea *York* 73-77; Chapl St Pet Sch York 77-82; Warden Marrick Priory *Ripon* 83; Hon C Appleton Roebuck w Acaster Selby *York* 84-85; P-in-c from 86; Youth Officer from 86; Sen Ind Chapl Selby Coalfield from 96. *All Saints' Vicarage, Appleton Roebuck, York YO5 7DG* Tel (01904) 744327

RODEN, Michael Adrian Holland. b 60. Ripon Coll Cuddesdon 82. **d** 85 **p** 86. C S Lambeth St Anne and All SS *S'wark* 85-88; C Wandsworth St Paul 88-90; C Ox St Mary V w St Cross and St Pet *Ox* 90-94; Chapl Wadh Coll Ox 90-94; R Steeple Aston w N Aston and Tackley *Ox* from 94. *The Rectory, Fir Lane, Steeple Aston, Bicester, Oxon OX5 3SF* Tel (01869) 347793

RODERICK, Bertram David. b 22. S'wark Ord Course 63. **d** 66 **p** 67. C Surbiton St Matt *S'wark* 66-69; C Horley 69-72; V Sutton New Town St Barn 73-82; R Burstow 82-89; rtd 89; Perm to Offic *Chich* from 90. *April Cottage, 2 Church Lane, Henfield, W Sussex BN5 9NY* Tel (01273) 493797

RODERICK, Philip David. b 49. Univ of Wales (Swansea) BA70 Univ of Wales (Abth) BD77 Lon Univ CertEd71.. Linc Th Coll 80. **d** 80 **p** 81. C Llanfair-is-gaer and Llanddeiniolen *Ban* 80-82; TV Holyhead w Rhoscolyn w Llanfair-yn-Neubwll 82-84; Chapl and Lect Th Univ of Wales (Ban) 84-88; Warden Angl Chapl Cen 84-88; Prin Bucks Chr Tr Scheme *Ox* 88-94; Dir Chiltern Chr Tr Progr 88-94; Dir Quiet Garden Trust from 92; V Amersham on the Hill *Ox* from 96. *The Vicarage, 70 Sycamore Road, Amersham, Bucks HP6 5DR* Tel (01494) 727553 Fax as telephone

RODFORD, Brian George. b 50. Hatf Poly BEd84. **d** 79 **p** 80. Hon C St Alb St Steph *St Alb* 79-85; Chapl St Mary's Sch 81-90; Sen Teacher 83-90; Hon C Hendon St Mary *Lon* 85-90; Hon C Golders Green 85-90; Hon C Winchmore Hill H Trin 90-95; V Ponders End St Matt from 95. *The Vicarage, Church Road, Enfield, Middx EN3 4NT* Tel 0181-443 2255

✠**RODGER, The Rt Revd Patrick Campbell.** b 20. Ch Ch Ox BA43 MA47. Westcott Ho Cam 47. **d** 49 **p** 50 **c** 70. C Edin St Jo *Edin* 49-51; Chapl Edin Univ 51-55; C Woodside Park St Barn *Lon* 55-58; Study Sec SCM 55-58; R Kilmacolm *Glas* 58-61; R Bridge of Weir 58-61; Exec Sec of Faith & Order Dept WCC 61-66; R Edin St Mary *Edin* 66-70; Vice-Provost St Mary's Cathl 66-67; Provost 67-70; Bp Man 70-78; Bp Ox 78-86; rtd 86; Asst Bp *Edin* from 86. *12 Warrender Park Terrace, Edinburgh EH9 1EG* Tel 0131-229 5075

RODGER, Canon Raymond. b 39. Westmr Coll Ox DipApTh91 MTh93. Bps' Coll Cheshunt 62. **d** 63 **p** 64. C Frodingham *Linc* 63-66; Asst Chapl St Geo Hosp Lon 66-69; C Waltham *Linc* 69-73; V Nocton 73-86; P-in-c Potter Hanworth 74-86; P-in-c Dunston 77-86; RD Graffoe 81-92; Can and Preb Linc Cathl from 85; V Nocton w Dunston and Potterhanworth 86-92; Bp's Dom Chapl from 92; Gen Preacher from 92. *Bishop's House, Eastgate, Lincoln LN2 1QQ* Tel (01522) 534701 Fax 511095

RODGERS, Canon Cyril George Hooper. b 20. Qu Coll Birm 50. **d** 52 **p** 53. C Bishop's Cleeve *Glouc* 52-56; V Nailsworth 56-61; Chapl Longford's Approved Sch Minchinhampton 56-57; CF (TA) 58-62; R Upwell Ch Ch *Ely* 61-66; CF (TA - R of O) 62-87; V Wiggenhall St Germans and Islington *Ely* 66-76; RD Lynn Marshland 68-76; R Woolpit *St E* 76-84; RD Lavenham 78-87; Hon Can St E Cathl 84-87; R Woolpit w Drinkstone 84-87; rtd 87. *Fox Farm, Wetherden, Stowmarket, Suffolk IP14 3NE* Tel (01359) 40364

RODGERS, David. b 26. Sarum Th Coll 63. **d** 65 **p** 66. C Combe Down *B & W* 65-68; V Leigh Woods 68-76; R Wellow w Foxcote and Shoscombe 76-79; C Wells St Cuth w Coxley and Wookey Hole 79-82; P-in-c Wookey w Henton 79-82; V Ercall Magna *Lich* 82-89; V Rowton 82-89; RD Wrockwardine 84-88; rtd 89. *7 Bishop Crescent, Shepton Mallet, Somerset BA4 5XX*

RODGERS, Frank. b 27. Linc Th Coll 69. **d** 71 **p** 72. C Alford w Rigsby *Linc* 71-75; P-in-c Quadring 75-80; P-in-c Gosberton Clough 75-80; V Gosberton Clough and Quadring 80; R S Kelsey 80-84; P-in-c Usselby 80-84; P-in-c Kirkby w Kingerby 80-84; P-in-c N Owersby w Thornton le Moor 80-84; R S Kelsey Gp 84-86; V Cranwell 86-92; R Leasingham 86-92; rtd 92; Perm to Offic *Linc* from 92. *1 Manor Road, Quarrington, Sleaford, Lincs NG34 8UJ*

RODGERS, Preb Frank Ernest. b 46. Tyndale Hall Bris 68. **d** 71 **p** 72. C Madeley *Heref* 71-74; C Littleover *Derby* 74-77; V Clodock and Longtown w Craswell and Llanveyno *Heref* 77-79; P-in-c St Margaret's w Michaelchurch Eskley and Newton 77-79; V Clodock and Longtown w Craswall, Llanveynoe etc from 79; RD Abbeydore 90-96; Preb Heref Cathl from 96. *The Vicarage, Longtown, Hereford HR2 0LD* Tel (01873) 87289

RODGERS, Canon John Terence Roche. b 28. TCD BA53 MA57. Bps' Coll Cheshunt. **d** 57 **p** 58. C Templecorran *Conn* 57-60; C Derriaghy 60-61; C Antrim All SS 61-64; I Belfast St Steph 64-79; I Dunmurry 79-94; RD Derriaghy 92-93; Can Belf Cathl from 92; rtd 94. *8 Aberdelghy Park, Lambeg, Lisburn, Co Antrim BT27 4QF* Tel (01846) 660430

RODGERS, Dr Richard Thomas Boycott. b 47. FRCS81 Lon Univ MB BS70. St Jo Coll Nottm DipTh77. **d** 77 **p** 78. C Littleover *Derby* 77-80; C Birm St Martin w Bordesley St Andr *Birm* 89-90; Lect from 89; Perm to Offic from 90. *63 Meadow Brook Road, Birmingham B31 1ND* Tel 0121-476 0789

RODHAM, Morris. b 59. Hatf Coll Dur BA81 St Jo Coll Dur PGCE85 Bris Univ MA93. Trin Coll Bris DipHE92. **d** 93 **p** 94. C New Milverton *Cov* 93-97; V Leamington Priors St Mary from 97. *The Vicarage, 28 St Mary's Road, Leamington Spa, Warks CV31 1JP* Tel (01926) 425927

RODLEY, Ian Tony. b 48. Qu Coll Birm 77. **d** 80 **p** 81. Dioc Children's Adv *Bradf* 80-85; C Baildon 80-85; V Bradf St Wilfrid Lidget Green 85-90; Chapl to the Deaf 88-90; V Otley from 90. *The Vicarage, Otley, W Yorkshire LS21 3HR* Tel (01943) 462240

RODRIGUEZ-VEGLIO, Francis Bonny. b 33. Sarum Th Coll 62. **d** 64 **p** 65. C Alnwick St Paul *Newc* 64-68; V Horton w Piddington *Pet* 68-79; P-in-c Preston Deanery 68-79; Chapl ACF 75-82; TV Is of Scilly *Truro* 79-82; Hon Chapl Miss to Seamen 79-82; Perm to Offic *Pet* 86-88; C Leic Ch Sav *Leic* 88-91; V Kirkwhelpington, Kirkharle, Kirkheaton and Cambo *Newc* 91-95; Perm to Offic *Pet* from 95. *Gemacq Cottage, 14 Daventry Road, Norton, Daventry, Northants NN11 5ND* Tel (01327) 72030

RODWELL, Barry John. b 39. Birm Univ CertEd59 Cam Univ DipAdEd77. Ridley Hall Cam 67. **d** 70 **p** 71. C Sudbury St Greg and St Pet *St E* 70-73; Hd RE Hedingham Sch 73-80; R Sible Hedingham *Chelmsf* 80-85; RE Adv 85-93; V Gt Burstead from 93. *The Vicarage, 111 Church Street, Billericay, Essex CM11 2TR* Tel (01277) 625947

RODWELL, John Stanley. b 46. Leeds Univ BSc68 Ox Univ DipTh73 Southn Univ PhD74. Cuddesdon Coll 71. **d** 74 **p** 75. Hon C Horfield H Trin *Bris* 74-75; Hon C Skerton St Luke *Blackb* 75-77; Lic to Offic from 77. *7 Derwent Road, Lancaster LA1 3ES* Tel (01524) 62726

ROE, Mrs Caroline Ruth. b 57. Birm Univ BA80. Wycliffe Hall Ox 81. **dss** 84 **d** 87 **p** 96. Olveston *Bris* 84-87; Par Dn 87; NSM Alveley and Quatt *Heref* 87-94; Bp's Voc Officer 90-94; Hon C Loughborough Em and St Mary in Charnwood *Leic* from 97. *4 John's Lee Close, Loughborough, Leics LE11 3LH* Tel (01509) 260217

ROE, Frank Ronald. b 31. Brasted Th Coll Westcott Ho Cam 55. **d** 57 **p** 58. C S w N Hayling *Portsm* 57-61; Hong Kong 61-77; Sen Chapl St Jo Cathl 61-66; Asst Chapl 77; Sen Chapl Miss to Seamen 66-69; Australia from 77; Hon Chapl Miss to Seamen from 77; rtd 96. *PO Box 810, Esperance, W Australia 6450* Tel Kalgoorlie (90) 713661 or 712772

ROE, Canon Dr Joseph Thorley. b 22. AKC49 DipAdEd Hull Univ PhD90. K Coll Lon 46. **d** 50 **p** 51. C Methley *Ripon* 50-53; C Richmond 53-55; V Leeds Gipton Epiphany 55-60; C of E Youth Coun Tr Officer 60-64; Sec Youth Dept BCC 64-67; Prin Lect Bretton Hall Coll Wakef 67-74; Sec for Miss and Unity *Ripon* 74-78; Dioc Missr and Bp's Dom Chapl 75-78; Can Res Carl Cathl *Carl* 78-82; Dioc Dir of Tr 78-82; Dioc Adult Educn Officer *Wakef* 82-88; Hon Can Wakef Cathl 83-88; Dir of Educn 85-88; rtd 88; Perm to Offic *Wakef* from 88. *29 Milnthorpe Drive, Wakefield, W Yorkshire WF2 7HU* Tel (01924) 256938

ROE, Peter Harold. b 37. K Coll Lon BD62 AKC62. **d** 63 **p** 64. C Knowle St Barn *Bris* 63-65; C Leckhampton St Pet *Glouc* 65-68; V Shaw Hill *Birm* 68-73; V Hobs Moat 73-90; V Packwood w Hockley Heath from 90. *The Vicarage, Nuthurst Lane, Hockley Heath, Solihull, W Midlands B94 5RP* Tel (01564) 783121

ROE, Robert Henry. b 22. LCP57. Westcott Ho Cam 72. **d** 74 **p** 75. Hd Master St Mary's Primary Sch Saffron Walden 74-83; NSM Saffron Walden w Wendens Ambo *Chelmsf* 74-75; NSM Saffron Walden w Wendens Ambo and Littlebury 75-87; NSM Blakeney w Cley, Wiveton, Glandford etc *Nor* from 87. *Larchmount, High Street, Cley, Holt, Norfolk NR25 7RG* Tel (01263) 740369

ROE, Robin. b 28. CBE MC68. TCD BA52 MA55. **d** 53 **p** 54. C Dublin Sandford *D & G* 53-55; CF 55-81; QHC 77-81; R Merrow *Guildf* 81-89; rtd 89; Perm to Offic *Guildf* from 89. *Lansdowne, 6 Mitchells Close, Shalford, Guildford, Surrey GU4 8HY* Tel (01483) 63852

✠**ROE, The Rt Revd William Gordon.** b 32. Jes Coll Ox BA55 MA57 DipTh57 DPhil62. St Steph Ho Ox 56. **d** 58 **p** 59 **c** 80. C Bournemouth St Pet *Win* 58-61; C Abingdon w Shippon *Ox* 61-69; Vice-Prin St Chad's Coll Dur 69-74; V Dur St Oswald *Dur* 74-80; RD Dur 74-80; Hon Can Dur Cathl 79-80; Suff Bp Huntingdon *Ely* 80-97; Can Res Ely Cathl 80-89; Hon Can Ely Cathl 89-97; rtd 97. *8 Eldon Road, Bournemouth BH9 2RT* Tel (01202) 535127

ROEMMELE, Michael Patrick. b 49. TCD BA72 MA76. **d** 73 **p** 74. C Portadown St Columba *Arm* 73-77; C Drumachose *D & R* 77-80; Bahrain 79-83; Cyprus 79-83; Chapl RAF from 83. *Chaplaincy Services (RAF), HQ, Personnel and Training Command, RAF Innsworth, Gloucester GL3 1EZ* Tel (01452) 712612 ext 5164 Fax 510828

ROESCHLAUB, Robert Friedrich. b 39. Purdue Univ BSc63. Berkeley Div Sch MDiv66. **d** 66 **p** 66. USA 66-77; Hon C Tilehurst St Cath *Ox* 78-79; Hon C Tilehurst St Mich 79-82; P-in-c Millom H Trin w Thwaites *Carl* 82-85; P-in-c Millom 85-89; R Dunstall w Rangemore and Tatenhill *Lich* 89-93; rtd 94. *20 Pannatt Hill, Millom, Cumbria LA18 5DB*

ROFF, Andrew Martin. b 42. Bede Coll Dur BSc65. Westcott Ho Cam 65. **d** 70 **p** 71. C Ches St Mary *Ches* 70-73; Min Can Blackb Cathl *Blackb* 73-76; P-in-c Blackb St Jo 74-75; V Longton 76-81; Chapl Trin Coll Glenalmond 82-83; R Allendale w Whitfield *Newc* 83-92; V Gosforth St Nic from 92. *The Vicarage, 17 Rectory Road, Gosforth, Newcastle upon Tyne NE3 1XR* Tel 0191-285 1326

ROFF, John Michael. b 47. St Chad's Coll Dur BSc69. Westcott Ho Cam 70. **d** 72 **p** 73. C Lancaster St Mary *Blackb* 72-75; C Dronfield *Derby* 75-76; TV 76-80; TR N Wingfield, Pilsley and Tupton 80-85; V Ilkeston St Mary 85-90; V Stockport St Geo *Ches* 90-94; Dioc Ecum Officer from 92; TR Stockport SW from 94; RD Stockport from 95. *St George's Vicarage, 28 Buxton Road, Stockport, Cheshire SK2 6NU* Tel 0161-480 2453

ROGAN, Canon John. b 28. St Jo Coll Dur BA49 MA51 DipTh54 Open Univ BPhil81. **d** 54 **p** 55. C Ashton St Mich *Man* 54-57; C Sheff Sharrow *Sheff* 57-61; Ind Chapl 57-61; Sec C of E Ind Cttee 61-66; V Leigh St Mary *Man* 66-78; RD Leigh 71-78; Hon Can Man Cathl 75-78; Provost St Paul's Cathl Dundee *Bre* 78-83; R Dundee St Paul 78-83; Soc Resp Adv *Bris* 83-93; Can Res Bris

Cathl 83-93; rtd 93; Perm to Offic *Bris* from 93. *84 Concorde Drive, Bristol BS10 6PX* Tel 0117-950 5803

ROGERS, Alan Chad John. b 33. Selw Coll Cam BA56 MA60. Bps' Coll Cheshunt 58. **d** 60 **p** 61. C Sudbury St Andr *Lon* 60-62; Mauritius 62-66; V Edmonton St Alphege *Lon* 66-71; V Enfield St Geo 71-95. *Barren Cott, 25 Front Green, Hempton, Fakenham, Norfolk NR21 7LG* Tel (01328) 862814

ROGERS, Canon Alan David. b 24. K Coll Cam BA47 MA50. Cuddesdon Coll 50. **d** 52 **p** 53. C Saffron Walden *Chelmsf* 52-54; C Walthamstow St Mich 54-57; Madagascar 57-66; Qu Coll Birm 66-67; Lect Div Weymouth Coll 67-73; Lic to Offic *Sarum* from 69; Hd of Relig and Th Depts Dorset Inst of Educn 73-82; Hon Can Antananarivo from 84; rtd 89. *4 Fossett Way, Weymouth, Dorset DT4 9HD* Tel (01305) 779942

✠**ROGERS, The Rt Revd Alan Francis Bright.** b 07. Lambeth MA59 Bps' Coll Cheshunt 28. **d** 30 **p** 31 **c** 59. C Shepherd's Bush St Steph *Lon* 30-32; C Twickenham Common H Trin 32-34; Mauritius 34-49; Adn 46-49; Bp 59-66; Hon Can St Jas Cathl 44-59; V Twickenham St Mary *Lon* 49-54; Hon C from 85; V Hampstead St Jo 54-59; RD Hampstead 55-59; Suff Bp Fulham 66-70; Suff Bp Edmonton 70-75; rtd 75; Asst Bp Pet 75-84; P-in-c Wappenham w Abthorpe and Slapton 77-80; C Abthorpe w Slapton 81-83; Asst Bp Lon from 85. *20 River Way, Twickenham TW2 5JP* Tel 0181-894 2031

ROGERS, Brian Robert. b 36. Open Univ BA80. St Jo Coll Nottm 70. **d** 72 **p** 73. C Ealing St Mary *Lon* 72-74; C Greenside *Dur* 74-75; Lic to Offic 75-85; Perm to Offic *Lich* 85-95; rtd 97. *71 Alderney Avenue, Poole, Dorset BH12 4LF* Tel (01202) 772103

ROGERS, Brian Victor. b 50. Trin Coll Bris 75. **d** 78 **p** 79. C Plumstead St Jo w St Jas and St Paul *S'wark* 78-83; P-in-c Gayton *Nor* 83-85; P-in-c Gayton Thorpe w E Walton 83-85; P-in-c Westacre 83-85; P-in-c Ashwicken w Leziate 83-85; R Gayton Gp of Par 85-91; R Rackheath and Salhouse 91-96; P-in-c Warmington, Tansor, Cotterstock and Fotheringhay *Pet* from 96. *The Vicarage, Warmington, Peterborough PE8 6TE* Tel (01832) 280263

ROGERS, Cecil George. b 05. St D Coll Lamp BA28. **d** 28 **p** 29. C Sutton New Town St Barn *S'wark* 28-30; C Bournemouth St Mich *Win* 31-37; V Collingbourne Kingston *Sarum* 37-40; R Okeford Fitzpaine 40-43; R W Horsley *Guildf* 43-53; rtd 53; Perm to Offic *Lon* 82-91. *Sutton Manor, Sutton Scotney, Winchester, Hants SO21 3JX* Tel (01962) 760188

ROGERS, Charles Murray. b 17. Qu Coll Cam BA38 MA40 Lon Univ DipEd43. Westcott Ho Cam 38. **d** 40 **p** 41. C Plymouth St Andr *Ex* 40-42; Perm to Offic *Ely* 42; CMS 43-71; India 46-71; Jerusalem 71-80; Hong Kong 80-89; rtd 82; Canada from 89. *Box 683, 103 Brant Street, Deseronto, Ontario, Canada, K0K 1X0*

ROGERS, Christopher Antony. b 47. N Ord Course 79. **d** 81 **p** 82. C Chesterfield St Aug *Derby* 81-84; C Chaddesden St Phil 84-86; R Whitwell 86-95; V W Burnley *Blackb* from 95. *All Saints Vicarage, Padiham Road, Burnley, Lancs BB12 6PA* Tel (01282) 775629

ROGERS, Christopher John. b 47. Bp Lonsdale Coll CertEd Nottm Univ DipEd. EMMTC. **d** 84 **p** 85. NSM Ockbrook *Derby* 84-91; P-in-c Risby w Gt and Lt Saxham and Westley *St E* 91; R from 91. *The Rectory, Risby, Bury St Edmunds, Suffolk IP28 6RQ* Tel (01284) 810416

ROGERS, Clive William. b 62. Selw Coll Cam BA83 MA87 MEng93 Southn Univ BTh90. Chich Th Coll 87. **d** 90 **p** 91. C Leic St Aid *Leic* 90-93; P-in-c Ryhall w Essendine *Pet* 93-94. *13 St John's Street, Duxford, Cambridge CB2 4RA*

ROGERS, Cyril David. b 55. Birm Univ BA76 BTh. Sarum & Wells Th Coll 80. **d** 83 **p** 84. C Leagrave *St Alb* 83-87; TV Langtree *Ox* from 87. *The Vicarage, Reading Road, Woodcote, Reading RG8 0QZ* Tel (01491) 680979

ROGERS, David. b 48. Univ of Wales (Ban) BA69. Westcott Ho Cam 70. **d** 72 **p** 73. C Rainbow Hill St Barn *Worc* 72-75; C Tolladine 72-75; C Astwood Bank w Crabbs Cross 75-79; V Cradley 79-90; V Beoley from 90. *The Vicarage, Church Hill, Beoley, Redditch, Worcs B98 9AR* Tel (01527) 63976

ROGERS, David Alan. b 55. MCIT82 City of Lon Poly BA77. Linc Th Coll 88. **d** 90 **p** 91. C Kingston upon Hull St Nic *York* 90-93; P-in-c Kingston upon Hull St Mary 93-96; N Humberside Ind Chapl from 93. *1023 Anlaby Road, Hull HU4 7PN* Tel (01482) 503286

ROGERS, The Ven David Arthur. b 21. Ch Coll Cam BA47 MA52. Ridley Hall Cam 47. **d** 49 **p** 50. C Stockport St Geo *Ches* 49-53; R Levenshulme St Pet *Man* 53-59; P-in-c Cautley w Dowbiggin *Bradf* 59-60; P-in-c Garsdale 59-60; V Sedbergh 59-74; RD Sedbergh 59-73; V Garsdale 60-74; V Cautley w Dowbiggin 60-74; Hon Can Bradf Cathl 67-77; P-in-c Firbank, Howgill and Killington 73-77; RD Ewecross 73-77; V Sedbergh, Cautley and Garsdale 74-79; Adn Craven 77-86; rtd 86; Lic to Offic *Bradf* from 86; Perm to Offic *Blackb* from 87; Perm to Offic *Carl* from 89. *Borrens Farm, Leck, Carnforth, Lancs LA6 2JG* Tel (015242) 71616

ROGERS, David Barrie. b 46. S Dios Minl Tr Scheme 89. **d** 93. NSM Old Alresford and Bighton *Win* 93-96; Warden Dioc Retreat Ho (Holland Ho) Cropthorne *Worc* from 96. *The Den, Kennel Corner, Cropthorne, Pershore, Worcs WR10 3ND* Tel (01386) 860330

ROGERS, David Martyn. b 56. Univ of Wales (Lamp) BA77 K Coll Lon BD79 AKC79 St Kath Coll Liv DipEd86 Liv Univ BPhil94. Chich Th Coll 79. **d** 80 **p** 81. C Hockerill *St Alb* 80-85; Perm to Offic *St As* 85-87; C W Hampstead St Jas *Lon* 87; C Kilburn St Mary 87-90; V New Longton *Blackb* from 90; Chapl to Lancs Constabulary from 90. *All Saints' Vicarage, Station Road, New Longton, Preston PR4 4LN* Tel (01772) 613347

ROGERS, Canon Donovan Charles Edgar. b 08. Clifton Th Coll 32. **d** 35 **p** 36. C Leyton Em *Chelmsf* 35-37; C N Woolwich 37-38; Chapl RAF 38-41; CF 41-46; S Africa from 47. *The Cottage, Beach Road, Noordhoek, 7985 South Africa* Tel Cape Town (21) 891117

ROGERS, Edward Lyon Beresford Cheselden. b 22. VRD65. Keble Coll Ox BA48 MA51. Wells Th Coll 48. **d** 49 **p** 50. C Hinckley St Mary *Leic* 49-52; C Knighton St Mary Magd 52-54; Chapl RNVR 53-58; V Knighton St Mich *Leic* 54-59; Chapl RNR 58-74; R Old Street St Luke w St Mary Charterhouse etc *Lon* 59-66; R St Giles Cripplegate w St Bart Moor Lane etc 66-87; rtd 87; Perm to Offic *Chelmsf* from 87. *Windy Ridge, Wethersfield Road, Finchingfield, Braintree, Essex CM7 4NS* Tel (01371) 810741

ROGERS, Henry Richard. b 04. Trin Coll Cam BA26 MA30. Westcott Ho Cam 25. **d** 27 **p** 28. C Camberwell St Geo *S'wark* 27-30; Bp's Dom Chapl 30-32; V Nunhead St Antony 32-35; C Elgin H Trin *Mor* 35-37; Chapl Gordonstoun Sch 35-37; C Melksham *Sarum* 38-40; CF (EC) 40-45; Ind Adv to Bp Bris 62-63; R Liddington *Bris* 63-68; Preb Lyddington from 65; rtd 69. *Ellary, Achahoish, Lochgilphead, Argyll PA31 8PA* Tel (01880) 770301

ROGERS, The Very Revd John. b 34. Univ of Wales (Lamp) BA55 Or Coll Ox BA58 MA61. St Steph Ho Ox 57. **d** 59 **p** 60. C Roath St Martin *Llan* 59-63; Br Guiana 63-66; Guyana 66-71; V Caldicot *Mon* 71-77; V Monmouth 77-84; RD Mon 81-84; R Ebbw Vale 84-93; RD Blaenau Gwent 86-93; Can St Woolos Cathl 88-93; Dean Llan from 93; V Llan w Capel Llanilltern from 93. *The Deanery, The Cathedral Green, Llandaff, Cardiff CF5 2YF* Tel (01222) 561545 or 564554

ROGERS, John Robin. b 36. St Alb Minl Tr Scheme 78. **d** 81 **p** 82. NSM Digswell and Panshanger *St Alb* 81-84; C Welwyn w Ayot St Peter 85-92; R Wilden w Colmworth and Ravensden from 92. *The Rectory, Wilden, Bedford MK44 2PB* Tel (01234) 771434

ROGERS, John William Trevor. b 28. Qu Coll Birm. **d** 85 **p** 86. NSM Dunchurch *Cov* from 85. *15 Hillyard Road, Southam, Leamington Spa, Warks CV33 0LD* Tel (01926) 813469

ROGERS, Keith Frederick. b 10. Keble Coll Ox BA33 MA37. Chich Th Coll 34. **d** 36 **p** 37. C Milton *Win* 36-41; C Alton St Lawr 41-43; C Charlton Kings St Mary *Glouc* 43-46; R Taynton 46-54; V Tibberton 46-54; R Rodborough 54-61; V Methwold *Ely* 61-64; V Chalford *Glouc* 64-70; R Chilthorne Domer, Yeovil Marsh and Thorne Coffin *B & W* 71-75; rtd 75. *35 All Saints Terrace, Cheltenham, Glos GL52 6UA* Tel (01242) 581117

ROGERS, Canon Kenneth (Ken). b 33. Cuddesdon Coll 68. **d** 69 **p** 70. C Perranzabuloe *Truro* 69-71; C Truro St Paul 71-74; P-in-c Kenwyn St Geo 74-87; RD Powder 81-88; Hon Can Truro Cathl from 87; TR Bodmin w Lanhydrock and Lanivet from 87; RD Trigg Minor and Bodmin 89-93. *The Rectory, Bodmin, Cornwall PL31 2AB* Tel (01208) 73867

ROGERS, Llewelyn. Univ of Wales (Lamp) BA59. St Mich Coll Llan. **d** 61 **p** 62. C Holywell *St As* 61-64; C Hawarden 64-70; R Bodfari 70-73; V Rhosymedre 73-77; V Llansantffraid-ym-Mechain 77-83; V Llansantffraid-ym-Mechain and Llanfechain from 83; RD Llanfyllin 84-88. *The Vicarage, Llansantffraid SY22 6TZ* Tel (01691) 828244

ROGERS, Malcolm Dawson. b 63. SS Hild & Bede Coll Dur BA84 Selw Coll Cam BA88. Ridley Hall Cam 86. **d** 89 **p** 90. C Ipswich St Jo *St E* 89-93; CMS 93-95; Russia 93-95; C Holloway St Mary Magd *Lon* from 95. *59 Bride Street, London N7 8RN* Tel 0171-607 2984

ROGERS, Malcolm Kenneth. b 72. Liv Inst of Educn BA93. St Jo Coll Nottm MA95 LTh96. **d** 96 **p** 97. C W Derby St Luke *Liv* from 96. *66 Baycliff Road, West Derby, Liverpool L12 6QX* Tel 0151-228 5455

ROGERS, Mark James. b 64. Univ of Wales (Lamp) BA. Qu Coll Birm. **d** 89 **p** 90. C Dudley St Aug Holly Hall *Worc* 89-93; C Worc St Barn w Ch Ch 93-94; TV 94-97; Belize from 97. *USPG, Partnership House, 157 Waterloo Road, London SE1 8XA* Tel 0171-928 8681

ROGERS, Martin Brian. b 53. LNSM course 89. **d** 92 **p** 93. NSM Collyhurst *Man* from 92. *8 Greenford Road, Crumpsall, Manchester M8 7NW* Tel 0161-740 4614

ROGERS, Martin Stephen. b 28. St Edm Hall Ox BA50 MA54. Cuddesdon Coll 50. **d** 52 **p** 53. C Reading St Mary V *Ox* 52-54; C Buxton *Derby* 54-57; Australia 58-64; Lect Cuddesdon Coll 65-73; Chapl Littlemore Hosp Ox 65-74; Dept of Educn Cam Univ 73-76; Chapl Univ Coll of Ripon and York St Jo 76-93; Postgraduate Medical Educn Adv Leeds Univ 90-93; rtd 93. *Freshwater, 4 Marles Close, Awliscombe, Honiton, Devon EX14 0GA* Tel (01404) 44296

ROGERS, Maurice George Walden. b 23. AKC51. **d** 52 **p** 53. C Bedford All SS *St Alb* 52-56; C Southfields St Barn *S'wark* 56-58; C Chingford SS Pet and Paul *Chelmsf* 58-61; V Gt Ilford St Luke 61-72; V Woodford St Barn 72-89; rtd 89; Perm to Offic *Chelmsf* from 89. *The Coach House, 13 Bodorgan Road, Bournemouth BH2 6NQ* Tel (01202) 291034

ROGERS, Michael Ernest. b 34. Sarum & Wells Th Coll 83. **d** 85 **p** 86. C Roehampton H Trin *S'wark* 85-88; V Ryhill *Wakef* 88-94; V S Elmsall from 94. *The Vicarage, Doncaster Road, South Elmsall, Pontefract, W Yorkshire WF9 2HS* Tel (01977) 642861

ROGERS, Michael Hugh Walton. b 52. K Coll Lon BD73 AKC73. St Aug Coll Cant 74. **d** 75 **p** 76. C Eastbourne St Andr *Chich* 75-78; C Uppingham w Ayston *Pet* 78-82; V Eye 82-90; R Cottesmore and Barrow w Ashwell and Burley from 90; RD Rutland from 95. *The Rectory, Cottesmore, Oakham, Leics LE15 7DJ* Tel (01572) 812202

ROGERS, Canon Noel Desmond. b 26. TD71. Univ of Wales (Lamp) BA51. **d** 53 **p** 54. C Rhyl w St Ann *St As* 53-58; V Everton St Geo *Liv* 58-64; CF (TA) 59-75; R Newton in Makerfield Em *Liv* 64-74; V Rostherne w Bollington *Ches* from 74; CF (R of O) 75-81; RD Knutsford *Ches* 85-96; Hon Can Ches Cathl from 87. *The Vicarage, Rostherne, Knutsford, Cheshire WA16 6RY* Tel (01565) 830595

ROGERS, Mrs Pamela Rose. b 46. Keswick Hall Coll CertEd68. S Dios Minl Tr Scheme 92. **d** 95 **p** 96. NSM Axbridge w Shipham and Rowberrow *B & W* from 95. *28 Beech Road, Shipham, Winscombe, Avon BS25 1SB* Tel (01934) 842685

ROGERS, Mrs Patricia Anne. b 54. Lon Univ BD. Trin Coll Bris. **d** 87 **p** 94. Hon C Gayton Gp of Par *Nor* 87-91; Hon C Rackheath and Salhouse 91-96; Chapl to the Deaf 91-96; Chapl to the Deaf *Pet* from 96. *The Vicarage, Warmington, Peterborough PE8 6TE* Tel (01832) 280263

ROGERS, Percival Hallewell. b 12. MBE45. St Edm Hall Ox BA35 MA46. Bps' Coll Cheshunt. **d** 46 **p** 47. Chapl Haileybury Coll Herts 52-54; Hd Master Portora R Sch Enniskillen 54-73; Chapl Gresham's Sch Holt 74-75; USA 76-80; Warden Lay Readers and Ords *Clogh* 81-84; C Sandford-on-Thames *Ox* 85-87; rtd 87; Perm to Offic *Ox* from 87. *7 Eyot Place, Oxford OX4 1SA* Tel (01865) 244976

ROGERS, Philip John. b 52. Univ of Wales CertEd74 Nottm Univ BTh79. St Jo Coll Nottm 76. **d** 79 **p** 80. C Stretford St Bride *Man* 79-84; P-in-c Plumstead St Jo w St Jas and St Paul *S'wark* 84-85; V from 85. *St John's Vicarage, 176 Griffin Road, London SE18 7QA* Tel 0181-855 1827

ROGERS, Richard Anthony. b 46. Ex Coll Ox BA69 Birm Univ DipTh70. Qu Coll Birm 70. **d** 71 **p** 72. C Shirley *Birm* 71-74; Chapl Solihull Sch 74-78; Hon C Cotteridge *Birm* 78-84; Hon C Hill 84-93; Head RE Kings Norton Sch from 93. *48 Jordan Road, Sutton Coldfield, W Midlands B75 5AB* Tel 0121-308 0310

ROGERS, Richard Jonathan. b 64. Trin Coll Bris BTh96. **d** 96 **p** 97. C Carterton *Ox* from 96. *8 Alderley Close, Carterton, Oxon OX18 3QP* Tel (01993) 845116

ROGERS, Robert. b 42. Bernard Gilpin Soc Dur 66 St Aid Birkenhead 67 Ridley Hall Cam 69. **d** 70 **p** 71. C Childwall St Dav *Liv* 70-73; C Huntington *York* 73-76; TR Brayton 76-89; RD Selby 84-89; V New Malton from 89. *The Vicarage, 17 The Mount, Malton, York YO17 0ND* Tel (01653) 692089

ROGERS, Robert Charles. b 55. St Pet Coll Birm CertEd77. St Jo Coll Nottm 87. **d** 89 **p** 90. C Wellesbourne *Cov* 89-93; R Bourton w Frankton and Stretton on Dunsmore etc from 93. *The Rectory, Frankton, Rugby, Warks CV23 9PB* Tel (01926) 632805

ROGERS, Ronald James. b 31. Bris Univ BA56 St Cath Soc Ox BA58 MA65. Wycliffe Hall Ox 56. **d** 58 **p** 59. C Gt Yarmouth *Nor* 58-62; C Newington St Mary *S'wark* 67-69; C Liv Our Lady and St Nic w St Anne *Liv* 78-83; C Pimlico St Pet w Westmr Ch Ch *Lon* 83-85; Chapl Westmr City Sch 85-87; P-in-c Pimlico St Sav *Lon* 87-96; Chapl Izmir (Smyrna) w Bornova *Eur* from 96; rtd 96. *Alsanak St John and Bornova St Mary, PK 1005, Izmir, Turkey* Tel Izmir (232) 463-7263

ROGERS, Ms Sally Jean. b 54. Univ of Wales (Lamp) BA77 Nottm Univ BTh87. Linc Th Coll 84. **d** 87 **p** 94. Par Dn Bris St Mary Redcliffe w Temple etc *Bris* 87-90; Par Dn Greenford H Cross *Lon* 90-94; C 94-96; TV Hemel Hempstead *St Alb* from 96. *St Mary's Vicarage, 51 Walnut Grove, Hemel Hempstead, Herts HP2 4AP* Tel (01442) 256708

ROGERS, Thomas More Fitzgerald. b 13. **d** 62 **p** 63. C Cant St Dunstan w H Cross *Cant* 62-64; Chapl Rochdale Distr Adult Deaf and Dumb Soc 64-65; Chapl RADD W Ham 65-70; Chapl to the Deaf *Guildf* 69-72; Chapl to the Deaf *Cant* 72-77; rtd 77. *15 Saunders Lane, Mayford, Woking, Surrey GU22 0NN* Tel (01483) 770029

ROGERS, William Arthur (Bill). b 41. Lon Univ BA64 CertEd. Chich Th Coll 79. **d** 81 **p** 82. C Chandler's Ford *Win* 81-84; R Bentley and Binsted 84-94; P-in-c The Lulworths, Winfrith Newburgh and Chaldon *Sarum* from 94. *The Rectory, West Road, West Lulworth, Wareham, Dorset BH20 5RY* Tel (01929) 400550

✠**ROGERSON, The Rt Revd Barry.** b 36. Leeds Univ BA60 Bris Univ Hon LLD93. Wells Th Coll 60. **d** 62 **p** 63 **c** 79. C S Shields St Hilda w St Thos *Dur* 62-65; C Bishopwearmouth St Nic 65-67; Lect Lich Th Coll 67-71; Vice-Prin 71-72; Lect Sarum & Wells Th Coll 72-74; V Wednesfield St Thos *Lich* 75-79; TR Wednesfield 79; Suff Bp Wolverhampton 79-85; Bp Bris from 85. *Bishop's House, Clifton Hill, Bristol BS8 1BW* Tel 0117-973 0222 Fax 923 9670

ROGERSON, Colin Scott. b 30. St Andr Univ MA55. Edin Th Coll. **d** 57 **p** 58. C Byker St Ant *Newc* 57-59; C Newc St Geo 59-63; C Wooler 63-67; V Tynemouth St Aug 67-75; C Dur St Marg *Dur* 75-88; P-in-c Hebburn St Jo 88-95; rtd 95; Perm to Offic *Dur* from 95. *6 Edlingham Road, Durham DH1 5YS* Tel 0191-386 1956

ROGERSON, David George. b 38. St Chad's Coll Dur BA60 DipTh63 Newc Univ DipEd67. **d** 63 **p** 64. C Wallsend St Luke *Newc* 63-67; C Delaval 67-70; V Long Benton St Mary 70-81; V N Sunderland from 81; Warden Seahouses Dioc Hostel from 81; Miss to Seamen from 81. *The Vicarage, South Lane, North Sunderland, Seahouses, Northd NE68 7TU* Tel (01665) 720202

ROGERSON, Derek Russell. b 23. Lon Univ BA51. Sarum Th Coll 51. **d** 53 **p** 54. C Balham Hill Ascension *S'wark* 53-56; C Mottingham St Andr 56-60; R Sapcote *Leic* 60-64; R Harpurhey St Steph *Man* 64-70; V Rochdale Gd Shep 70-74; Asst Chapl HM Pris Man 74-76; Chapl HM Pris Kirkham 76-83; Chapl HM Pris Haverigg 84-88; rtd 88; Perm to Offic *Carl* from 88. *26 Market Street, Millom, Cumbria LA18 4AH* Tel (01229) 775261

ROGERSON, Ian Matthew. b 45. Bede Coll Dur CertEd67 Open Univ BA76. Oak Hill Th Coll DipHE81. **d** 83 **p** 84. C Haughton St Mary *Man* 83-86; V Ramsbottom St Andr from 86; AD Bury from 96. *St Andrew's Vicarage, 2 Henwick Hall Avenue, Ramsbottom, Bury, Lancs BL0 9YH* Tel (01706) 826482 Fax as telephone

ROGERSON, Canon Prof John William. b 35. Man Univ BD61 DD75 Linacre Ho Ox BA63 MA67. Ripon Hall Ox 61. **d** 64 **p** 66. C Dur St Oswald *Dur* 64-67; Lect Th Dur Univ 64-75; Sen Lect 75-79; Lic to Offic *Dur* 67-79; Lic to Offic *Sheff* from 79; Prof Bibl Studies Sheff Univ from 79; Hon Can Sheff Cathl *Sheff* 82-95. *60 Marlborough Road, Sheffield S10 1DB* Tel 0114-268 1426

ROLAND, Andrew Osborne. b 45. Mert Coll Ox BA66 DPM69. Cranmer Hall Dur BA84. **d** 84 **p** 85. C Streatham St Leon *S'wark* 84-87; C Kingston All SS w St Jo 87-94; P-in-c Hackbridge and N Beddington from 94. *All Saints' Vicarage, New Road, Mitcham, Surrey CR4 4JL* Tel 0181-648 3650

ROLFE, Charles Edward. b 34. Wells Th Coll 68. **d** 70 **p** 71. C Bath Twerton-on-Avon *B & W* 70-79; TV Wellington and Distr 79-85; P-in-c Frome Ch Ch 85-89; V 89-94; Chapl Victoria Hosp Frome 85-94; Chapl St Adhelm's Hosp Frome 88-94; rtd 94; NSM Fordingbridge *Win* from 95; NSM Hale w S Charford from 95. *14 Ashford Close, Fordingbridge, Hants SP6 1DH* Tel (01425) 652684

ROLFE, Joseph William. b 37. Qu Coll Birm 78. **d** 81 **p** 82. NSM Tredington and Darlingscott w Newbold on Stour *Cov* 81-91; NSM Brailes from 91; NSM Sutton under Brailes from 91; NSM Shipston Deanery from 91. *35 Manor Lane, Shipston-on-Stour, Warks CV36 4EF* Tel (01608) 661737

ROLFE, Paul Douglas. b 46. MIBC90. N Ord Course 90. **d** 93 **p** 94. C Urmston *Man* 93-96; V Lawton Moor from 96. *The Vicarage, Orton Road, Manchester M23 0LH* Tel 0161-998 2461

ROLL, Sir James William Cecil, Bt. b 12. Chich Th Coll 34. **d** 37 **p** 38. C Bethnal Green St Jas the Gt w St Jude *Lon* 37-40; C Victoria Docks St Matt *Chelmsf* 40-44; C E Ham St Mary 44-58; V Becontree St Jo 58-83; rtd 83; Perm to Offic *Chelmsf* from 83. *82 Leighcliff Road, Leigh-on-Sea, Essex SS9 1DN*

ROLLETT, Robert Henry. b 39. Leeds Univ BA61 Leic Univ CertEd62. Linc Th Coll 77. **d** 79 **p** 80. C Littleport *Ely* 79-82; P-in-c Manea 82-83; V 83-85; P-in-c Wimblington 82-83; R 83-85; V Thorney Abbey 85-93; P-in-c The Ramseys and Upwood 93-94; TR from 94. *The Rectory, Hollow Lane, Ramsey, Huntingdon, Cambs PE17 1DE* Tel (01487) 813271

ROLLINSON, Frederick Mark (Fred). b 24. **d** 71 **p** 72. C Bow w Bromley St Leon *Lon* 71-76; NSM Bethnal Green St Barn from 76. *11 Vivian Road, London E3 5RE* Tel 0181-980 3568 or 981 6511

ROLLINSON, Canon John Knighton. b 14. FRCO34 Sheff Univ BMus36 AKC48. **d** 49 **p** 50. C Ilkeston St Mary *Derby* 49-53; C Wirksworth w Carsington 53-55; PC Dethick, Lea and Holloway 55-64; R Whittington 64-81; Chapl Whittington Hall Hosp 64-82; P-in-c New Whittington 78-81; rtd 81; Perm to Offic *Derby* from 81. *75 Yew Tree Drive, Somersall, Chesterfield, Derbyshire S40 3NB* Tel (01246) 568647

ROLLS, Peter. b 40. HNC Leeds Inst of Educn CertEd. N Ord Course. **d** 83 **p** 84. NSM Meltham *Wakef* from 83. *14 Heather Road, Meltham, Huddersfield HD7 3EY* Tel (01484) 850389

ROLPH, Pauline Gladys. b 30. SRN51 SCM53 HVCert65. Oak Hill Th Coll 88. **d** 90 **p** 94. Hon C Chingford St Anne *Chelmsf* 90-96; rtd 96. *1 Black Lawn, Gillingham, Dorset SP8 4SD* Tel (01747) 822502 Fax as telephone

ROLPH, Reginald Lewis George. b 29. Open Univ BA74. Bps' Coll Cheshunt 55. **d** 58 **p** 59. C Perivale *Lon* 58-61; C Wokingham St Paul *Ox* 61-63; C Letchworth *St Alb* 63-78; Perm to Offic from 78; rtd 93. *22 Souberie Avenue, Letchworth, Herts SG6 3JA* Tel (01462) 684596

ROLSTON, Cyril Willis Matthias. b 29. CITC 66. **d** 68 **p** 69. C Portadown St Mark *Arm* 68-71; I Loughgilly w Clare 71-81; Dir of Ords from 72; I Moy w Charlemont 81-96; Preb Arm Cathl 92-96; rtd 96. *19 Lower Parklands, Dungannon, Co Tyrone BT71 7JN*

ROLSTON, John Ormsby. b 28. TCD BA51 MA59 BD63. CITC 51. **d** 51 **p** 52. C Belfast St Mary Magd *Conn* 51-55; C Knock *D & D* 55-59; P-in-c Gilnahirk 59-63; I 63-66; I Belfast St Jas *Conn* 66-79; I Belfast St Jas w St Silas 79-96; RD N Belfast 71-88; Can Belf Cathl 82-96; Prec Belf Cathl 88-96; Adn Conn 88-96; rtd 96; Dioc C *Conn* from 96. *5 Springburn Park, Lisburn, Co Antrim BT27 5QZ* Tel (01846) 678932

ROLTON, Patrick Hugh. b 49. Sarum & Wells Th Coll 72. **d** 74 **p** 75. C Roch 74-79; C Edenbridge 79-81; R N Cray w Ruxley from 81. *St James's Rectory, 2 St James Way, Sidcup, Kent DA14 5ER* Tel 0181-300 1655

ROM, Hugh. b 22. S'wark Ord Course 77. **d** 80 **p** 81. NSM Ealing Ascension Hanger Hill *Lon* 80-82; P-in-c St Kath Cree 82-89; Perm to Offic from 90. *187 Linden Court, Brunswick Road, London W5 1AL* Tel 0181-998 5588

ROM, Norman Charles. b 24. S'wark Ord Course 63. **d** 66 **p** 67. C Leatherhead *Guildf* 66-71; Chapl HM Pris Cant 71-74; Chapl HM Pris Pentonville 74-85; Chapl HM Pris Stocken 85-87; P-in-c Empingham *Pet* 85-87; R Empingham and Exton w Horn w Whitwell 87-94; rtd 94; Perm to Offic *Pet* from 94. *11 Dundee Drive, Stamford, Lincs PE9 2TR* Tel (01780) 482051

ROMANES, William. b 11. Magd Coll Cam BA35 MA39. Ripon Hall Ox 35. **d** 36 **p** 37. C Erdington St Barn *Birm* 36-40; P-in-c Water Orton 40-45; Dioc Chapl and P-in-c Hockley St Sav 45-49; R Newton Regis w Seckington 49-52; V Sparkbrook Em 52-64; R Bp Latimer Memorial Ch 64-71; R Ringsfield w Redisham *St E* 71-76; rtd 76; Hon C Bordesley St Benedict *Birm* 76-93; Perm to Offic from 93. *10 Shireland Close, Birmingham B20 1AN* Tel 0121-523 7572

ROMANIS, Adam John Aidan. b 57. Pemb Coll Ox BA78 MA83. Westcott Ho Cam 81. **d** 84 **p** 85. C Northfield *Birm* 84-88; TV Seaton Hirst *Newc* 88-93; V Newc Ch Ch w St Ann from 93. *The Vicarage, 11 Gibson Street, Newcastle upon Tyne NE1 6PY* Tel 0191-232 0516

RONAYNE, Peter Henry. b 34. FCA68. Oak Hill Th Coll 64. **d** 66 **p** 67. C Chesham St Mary *Ox* 66-69; C Worthing H Trin *Chich* 69-74; V Shoreditch St Leon w St Mich *Lon* 74-82; P-in-c Norwood St Luke *S'wark* 82-85; V 85-94; V W Norwood St Luke from 94; RD Streatham 87-91. *The Vicarage, 6 Chatsworth Way, London SE27 9HR* Tel 0181-670 2706 or 761 0068

RONCHETTI, Quentin Marcus. b 56. Ripon Coll Cuddesdon 79. **d** 80 **p** 81. C Eastbourne St Mary *Chich* 80-83; C Moulsecoomb 83-85; TV 85-90; V Findon Valley 90-97; V Shoreham Beach from 97. *The Vicarage, West Beach, Shoreham-by-Sea, W Sussex BN43 5LF* Tel (01273) 453768

RONE, The Ven James (Jim). b 35. St Steph Ho Ox 79. **d** 80 **p** 81. C Stony Stratford *Ox* 80-82; P-in-c Fordham St Pet *Ely* 82-83; V 83-89; P-in-c Kennett 82-83; R 83-89; Can Res Ely Cathl 89-95; Treas 92-95; Adn Wisbech from 95; Hon Can Ely Cathl from 95. *Archdeacon's House, 24 Cromwell Road, Ely, Cambs CB6 1AS* Tel (01353) 662909 Fax 662056

ROOKE, George William Emmanuel. b 12. Lon Univ BA33 BD34 AKC34. **d** 35 **p** 36. C Milton next Gravesend w Denton *Roch* 35-38; C Walsall St Matt *Lich* 38-44; V Lt Drayton 44-54; R Ladybarn *Man* 54-66; R Worc St Martin-in-the-Cornmarket *Worc* 66-77; P-in-c Worc St Paul 67-74; rtd 77; Perm to Offic *Heref* from 77. *106 Church Road, Hereford HR1 1RT* Tel (01432) 266915

ROOKE, Henry John Warburton. b 10. Ch Ch Ox BA32 MA45. Wycliffe Hall Ox 34. **d** 35 **p** 36. C Hayes *Roch* 35-40; CF (EC) 40-46; C Edgbaston St Geo *Birm* 48-51; V Weobley w Sarnesfield *Heref* 51-69; RD Weobley 64-67; rtd 69. *Flat 22, Manormead, Tilford Road, Hindhead, Surrey GU26 6RA* Tel (01428) 605082

ROOKE, James Templeman (Jim). b 43. Saltley Tr Coll Birm CertEd65. EMMTC CTPS82. **d** 84 **p** 85. NSM Bassingham *Linc* 84-94; NSM Hykeham 89-94; P-in-c Borrowdale *Carl* from 94; Chapl HM Pris Morton Hall 94; Chapl Keswick Sch from 94. *The Vicarage, Borrowdale, Keswick, Cumbria CA12 5XQ* Tel (017687) 77238

ROOKE, John George Michael. b 47. St Jo Coll Dur BA72 DipTh74. Cranmer Hall Dur 71. **d** 74 **p** 75. C Skelmersdale St Paul *Liv* 74-78; TV Speke St Aid 78-81; Ind Chapl 81-85; V Knotty Ash St Jo from 85. *St John's Vicarage, Thomas Lane, Liverpool L14 5NR* Tel 0151-228 2396

ROOKE, Patrick William. b 55. Open Univ BA85. Sarum & Wells Th Coll 75. **d** 78 **p** 79. C Mossley *Conn* 78-81; C Ballywillan 81-83; I Craigs w Dunaghy and Killagan 83-88; I Ballymore *Arm* 88-94; Asst Prov and Dioc Registrar 92-94; Hon V Choral Arm Cathl 93-94; I Agherton *Conn* from 94. *The Rectory, 59 Strand Road, Portstewart, Co Derry BT55 7LU* Tel (01265) 832538

ROOKWOOD, Colin John. b 40. TCD BA64 MA68 Lon Univ PGCE67 DipTh69. Clifton Th Coll 67. **d** 70 **p** 71. C Eccleston Ch Ch *Liv* 70-75; V Penge St Jo *Roch* 75-82; V Childwall All SS *Liv* 82-91; Chapl Bethany Sch Goudhurst from 91. *Providence Cottage, South Curtisden Green, Goudhurst, Cranbrook, Kent TN17 1LD* Tel (01580) 211579

ROOM, Canon Frederick John. b 24. St Jo Coll Ox BA49 MA53. Wells Th Coll 49. **d** 51 **p** 52. C Bradford cum Beswick *Man* 51-54; C Halliwell St Marg 54-56; C Farnham Royal *Ox* 56-58; C-in-c Farnham Royal S CD 58-70; TV Thetford *Nor* 70-89; Sen Ind Missr 75-89; Hon Can Nor Cathl 77-89; rtd 89; Perm to Offic *Nor* from 89. *61 Beechwood Drive, Thorpe St Andrew, Norwich NR7 0LN* Tel (01603) 35877

ROOMS, Nigel James. b 60. CEng86 MIChemE86 Leeds Univ BSc81. St Jo Coll Nottm DipTh89. **d** 90 **p** 91. C Chell *Lich* 90-94; Tanzania from 94. *St Margaret's Church, PO Box 306, Moshi, Tanzania*

ROONEY, The Ven James. b 31. TCD BA58. **d** 58 **p** 59. C Belfast St Matt *Conn* 58-60; I 74-82; C Coleraine 60-61; I Ballintoy 61-66; P-in-c Rathlin 62-66; I Craigs w Dunaghy and Killagan 67-74; RD M Belfast 80-82; I Cloughfern 82-93; Can Belf Cathl from 90; I Skerry w Rathcavan and Newtowncrommelin *Conn* from 93; Adn Dalriada from 96. *The Rectory, Raceview Road, Broughshane, Ballymena, Co Antrim BT42 4JL* Tel (01266) 861215

ROOSE-EVANS, James Humphrey. b 27. St Benet's Hall Ox BA52 MA56. **d** 81 **p** 81. Lic to Offic *Heref* 81-89; Perm to Offic *Lon* from 89. *71 Belsize Park Gardens, London NW3 4JP*

ROOSE FRANCIS, Leslie. *See* FRANCIS, Leslie

ROOT, Canon Howard Eugene. b 26. Univ of S California BA45 St Cath Soc Ox BA51 Magd Coll Cam MA53 Magd Coll Ox MA70. Ripon Hall Ox 49. **d** 53 **p** 54. C Trumpington *Ely* 53; Asst Lect Div Cam Univ 53-57; Lect 57-66; Fell and Chapl Em Coll Cam 54-56; Fell and Dean 56-66; Wilde Lect Ox Univ 57-60; Angl Observer Second Vatican Coun 63-65; Prof Th Southn Univ 66-81; Hon Chapl Win Cathl *Win* 66-67; Can Th 67-80; Chmn Abp's Commn on Marriage 68-71; Consultant Lambeth Confs 68 and 88; Jt Ed Journal of Th Studies 69-74; Pope Adrian VI Prof Univ of Louvain 79; St Aug Can Cant Cathl *Cant* 80-91; Dir Angl Cen Rome 81-91; Abp Cant's Counsellor on Vatican Affairs 81-91; Visiting Prof Pontifical Gregorian Univ Rome 84-91; Preceptor Malling Abbey from 93. *26 St Swithun Street, Winchester, Hants SO23 9HU* Tel (01962) 862982

ROOT, John Brereton. b 41. Lon Univ BA64 Em Coll Cam BA66 MA. Ridley Hall Cam 64. **d** 68 **p** 69. C Harlesden St Mark *Lon* 68-73; C Lower Homerton St Paul 73-76; Chapl Ridley Hall Cam 76; Vice-Prin 76-79; V Alperton *Lon* from 79; AD Brent from 95. *The Vicarage, 34 Stanley Avenue, Wembley, Middx HA0 4JB* Tel 0181-902 1729

ROOTES, William Brian. b 44. Edin Th Coll. **d** 91. NSM Auchterarder *St And* from 91; NSM Muthill from 91. *Belhie Aberuthven, Auchterarder, Perthshire PH3 1EH* Tel (01764) 663259

ROPER, David John. b 53. St Steph Ho Ox DipMin95. **d** 95 **p** 96. C Hunstanton St Mary w Ringstead Parva etc *Nor* from 95. *The Rectory, Broad Lane, Brancaster, King's Lynn, Norfolk PE31 8AH* Tel (01485) 210268

ROPER, Canon Timothy Hamilton. b 34. Qu Coll Cam BA57 MA61. Sarum Th Coll 57. **d** 59 **p** 60. C Kingsthorpe *Pet* 59-62; C Kirkby *Liv* 62-65; Chapl Rossall Sch Fleetwood 65-84; R Arthingworth, Harrington w Oxendon and E Farndon *Pet* from 84; RD Brixworth 89-94; Can Pet Cathl from 94. *The Rectory, 35 Main Street, Great Oxendon, Market Harborough, Leics LE16 8NE* Tel (01858) 462052

ROPER, Preb William Lionel. b 17. Leeds Univ BA39. Coll of Resurr Mirfield 39. **d** 41 **p** 42. C S Molton w Nymet St George *Ex* 41-43; C Devonport St Aubyn 43-47; P-in-c 47-51; C Devonport St Jo 43-47; P-in-c 47-51; V Exwick 51-61; R S Molton w Nymet St George 61-71; R High Bray w Charles 61-71; RD S Molton 68-72; V Paignton St Jo 72-82; Preb Ex Cathl 77-82; rtd 82; Perm to Offic *Ex* from 89. *12 Exeter Gate, South Molton, Devon EX36 4AN* Tel (01769) 572147

ROSAMOND, Derek William. b 49. Linc Th Coll 87. **d** 89 **p** 90. C Coventry Caludon *Cov* 89-93; Northd Ind Miss *Dur* 93-96; TV Sunderland from 96. *21 Thornhill Terrace, Sunderland SR2 7JL* Tel 0191-567 3040

ROSCAMP, Alan Nicholas Harrison. b 12. Dur Univ LTh37 BA39 MA42. St Aid Birkenhead 32. **d** 36 **p** 37. C Latchford Ch Ch *Ches* 36-38; C Tarvin 39-44; P-in-c Bowdon 44-45; V Macclesfield St Paul 45-51; V Wadhurst *Chich* 51-63; V Tidebrook 52-63; Perm to Offic *Cant* from 63; rtd 78. *Horton Green, Ruckinge, Ashford, Kent TN26 2PF* Tel (01233) 732491

ROSCOE, David John. b 64. UEA BA87 Selw Coll Cam BA93. Aston Tr Scheme 89 Westcott Ho Cam CTM94. **d** 94 **p** 95. C Ditton St Mich *Liv* from 94. *24 Crown Avenue, Widnes, Cheshire WA8 8AT* Tel 0151-423 5134

ROSE, Andrew David. b 45. BA81. Oak Hill Th Coll 78. **d** 81 **p** 82. C Northwood Em *Lon* 81-86; V Iver *Ox* 86-95; R Frinton *Chelmsf* from 95. *The Rectory, 22 Queens Road, Frinton-on-Sea, Essex CO13 9BL* Tel (01255) 674664

ROSE, Anthony James. b 47. Trin Coll Bris BD72. **d** 73 **p** 74. C Halliwell St Pet *Man* 73-76; CF 76-94; R Colchester Ch Ch w St Mary V *Chelmsf* from 94. *The Rectory, 21 Cambridge Road, Colchester CO3 3NS* Tel (01206) 560175

ROSE, Anthony John. b 53. Birm Univ BA79 DipHE86. Trin Coll Bris 84. **d** 86 **p** 87. C The Quinton *Birm* 86-90; R Abbas and Templecombe w Horsington *B & W* from 90. *The Rectory, 8 Church Hill, Templecombe, Somerset BA8 0HG* Tel (01963) 370302

ROSE, Canon Barry Ernest. b 35. Chich Th Coll 58. **d** 61 **p** 62. C Forest Gate St Edm *Chelmsf* 61-64; Antigua 64-66; Dominica 66-69; V St Mary-at-Latton *Chelmsf* 69-79; V Stansted Mountfitchet 79-88; V Halstead St Andr w H Trin and Greenstead Green from 88; RD Halstead and Coggeshall 91-95; RD Hinckford from 95; Hon Can Chelmsf Cathl from 96. *The Vicarage, Parsonage Street, Halstead, Essex CO9 2LD* Tel (01787) 472171

ROSE, Bernard Frederick. b 47. LNSM course. **d** 91 **p** 92. NSM Ipswich St Thos *St E* from 91. *84 Chesterfield Drive, Ipswich IP1 6DN* Tel (01473) 462390

ROSE, Miss Geraldine Susan. b 47. Trin Coll Bris DipTh76 BD78. **dss** 78 **d** 87 **p** 94. Tonbridge St Steph *Roch* 78-80; Littleover *Derby* 80-87; Par Dn 87-88; Par Dn Wombwell *Sheff* 88-94; C 94-96; rtd 96. *5 Wheatcroft, Conisbrough, Doncaster, S Yorkshire DN12 2BL* Tel (01709) 867761

ROSE, Glyn Clee. b 16. Jes Coll Ox BA39 MA42. Bps' Coll Cheshunt 49. **d** 51 **p** 52. C De Beauvoir Town St Pet *Lon* 51-54; C Newtown St Luke *Win* 54-58; SPCK Port Chapl Southampton 58-66; Miss to Seamen 66-73; R Millbrook *Win* 73-81; rtd 81; Perm to Offic *Win* from 81. *11 Collins Lane, Hursley, Winchester, Hants SO21 2JX* Tel (01962) 775403

ROSE, Canon Gordon Henry. b 23. St Cath Soc Ox BA48 MA53. Wells Th Coll 49. **d** 50 **p** 51. C Bournemouth St Andr *Win* 50-55; R Bishopstoke 55-92; Hon Can Win Cathl 82-92; rtd 92. *44 Westbury Court, Hedge End, Southampton SO30 0HN* Tel (01489) 781309

ROSE, Ingrid Elizabeth. b 57. Univ of Wales (Abth) BA78 DipEd79. St D Coll Lamp 84. **d** 87. NSM Ysbyty Cynfyn w Llantrisant and Eglwys Newydd *St D* 87-90 and 92-95. *Ystwyth Villa, Pontrhydygroes, Ystrad Meurig SY25 6DF*

ROSE, John Clement Wansey. b 46. New Coll Ox BA71 MA72. Ripon Hall Ox 70. **d** 72 **p** 73. C Harborne St Pet *Birm* 72-76; TV Kings Norton 76-81; V Maney from 81. *The Vicarage, Maney Hill Road, Sutton Coldfield, W Midlands B72 1JJ* Tel 0121-354 2426

ROSE, Dr Judith Anne. b 36. Newnham Coll Cam BA57 MA65 Ox Univ DipTh87 K Coll Lon PhD91. Ripon Coll Cuddesdon 86. **d** 87 **p** 94. Par Dn Kettering All SS *Pet* 87-92; P-in-c Aldwincle w Thorpe Achurch, Pilton, Wadenhoe etc from 92. *The Rectory, Aldwincle, Kettering, Northants NN14 3EP* Tel (01832) 720613

ROSE, The Ven Kathleen Judith. b 37. Lon Univ DipTh66. Lon Bible Coll BD73 St Mich Ho Ox 64. **dss** 76 **d** 87 **p** 94. Leeds St Geo *Ripon* 76-81; Bradf Cathl *Bradf* 81-85; S Gillingham *Roch* 85-87; Par Dn 87-90; RD Gillingham 88-90; Bp's Dom Chapl 90-95; Asst Dir of Ords 90-95; Hon Can Roch Cathl from 93; Acting Adn Tonbridge 95-96; Adn Tonbridge from 96. *3 The Ridings, Tunbridge Wells, Kent TN2 4RU* Tel (01892) 520660 Fax as telephone

ROSE, Lionel Stafford. b 38. MBE93. Wells Th Coll 69. **d** 71 **p** 72. C Minchinhampton *Glouc* 71-73; C Thornbury 73-75; R Ruardean 75-80; V Whiteshill 80-84; CF 84-93; Chapl HM Pris Kirkham 93-95; Chapl HM Pris Wymott from 95. *Chaplain's Office, HM Prison Wymott, Ulnes Walton, Leyland, Preston PR3 3LW* Tel (01772) 421461

ROSE, Mrs Lynda Kathryn. b 51. Called to the Bar (Gray's Inn) 81 Ex Univ BA73 Ox Univ BA86. Wycliffe Hall Ox 86. **d** 87 **p** 94. C Highfield *Ox* 87-88; C Ox St Clem 89-93; Dir Anastasis Ministries from 93; NSM Ambrosden w Mert and Piddington from 94. *95 Staunton Road, Oxford OX3 7TR* Tel (01865) 68774

ROSE, Canon Paul Rosamond. b 32. Trin Hall Cam BA56 MA60. Westcott Ho Cam 57. **d** 59 **p** 60. C Wandsworth St Anne *S'wark* 59-61; C Tormohun *Ex* 61-64; S Rhodesia 64-65; Rhodesia 65-67; Min Can, Prec and Sacr Pet Cathl *Pet* 67-72; V Paddington St Jo w St Mich *Lon* 72-79; PV Westmr Abbey 74-79; Min Can and Prec Cant Cathl *Cant* 79-84; V Rothwell w Orton *Pet* 84-87; R Rothwell w Orton, Rushton w Glendon and Pipewell from 87; Can Pet Cathl from 94. *The Vicarage, Squire's Hill, Rothwell, Kettering, Northants NN14 2BQ* Tel (01536) 710268

ROSE, Peter Charles. b 30. St Aug Coll Cant 70. **d** 72 **p** 73. C St Martin-in-the-Fields *Lon* 72-76; C St Buryan, St Levan and Sennen *Truro* 76-78; V Feock 78-82; TV Gt Grimsby St Mary and St Jas *Linc* 82-84; rtd 84. *25 Quai du Hable, 76200 Dieppe, France* Tel France (33) 35 84 51 06

ROSE, Robert Alec Lewis (Bob). b 41. Man Univ BSc64. Wycliffe Hall Ox 85. **d** 87 **p** 88. C Vange *Chelmsf* 87-91; C Langdon Hills 91-94; P-in-c Bentley Common from 94; P-in-c Kelvedon Hatch from 94; P-in-c Navestock from 94. *The Vicarage, 6 Applegate, Pilgrims Hatch, Brentwood, Essex CM14 5PL* Tel (01277) 372200

ROSE, Roy. b 11. Worc Ord Coll 63. **d** 64 **p** 64. C Hykeham *Linc* 64-68; R Hale 68-77; V Helpringham 68-77; P-in-c Scredington 73-77; rtd 77; Perm to Offic *Linc* from 77. *72 Lincoln Road, Ruskington, Sleaford, Lincs NG34 9AP* Tel (01526) 832669

ROSE, Miss Susan Mary. b 36. Lon Univ DipTh70 TCert56. Dalton Ho Bris 68 Trin Coll Bris 74. **dss** 81 **d** 87 **p** 94. Brinsworth w Catcliffe *Sheff* 75-77; Scargill Ho 77-83; Netherthorpe *Sheff* 83-87; Tutor Trin Coll Bris 87-96; V Normanton *Wakef* from 96. *The Vicarage, High Street, Normanton, W Yorkshire WF6 1NR* Tel (01924) 898169

ROSE, Westmoreland Charles Edward. b 32. St Jo Coll Nottm 85. **d** 87 **p** 88. C Fairfield *Derby* 87-90; V Linton and Castle Gresley from 90. *The Vicarage, 40 Main Street, Linton, Swadlincote, Derbyshire DE12 6PZ* Tel (01283) 761441

ROSE-CASEMORE, Claire Pamela. b 63. St Paul's Cheltenham BA84 St Luke's Coll Ex PGCE85. Ridley Hall Cam MA98. **d** 97. Par Dn Kingsthorpe w Northn St Dav *Pet* from 97. *22 Tollgate Close, Kingsthorpe, Northampton NN2 6RP* Tel (01604) 553794

ROSE-CASEMORE, John. b 27. Chich Th Coll. **d** 55 **p** 56. C Epsom Common Ch Ch *Guildf* 55-58; C Hednesford *Lich* 58-60; V Dawley 60-65; R Puttenham and Wanborough *Guildf* 65-72; R Frimley 72-83; RD Surrey Heath 76-81; R Ludgershall and Faberstown *Sarum* 83-86; R Tidworth, Ludgershall and Faberstown 86-92; rtd 92; Perm to Offic *Ex* from 93. *2 Churchtown Cottages, Cornwood, Ivybridge, Devon PL21 0QJ* Tel (01755) 37786

ROSE-CASEMORE, Miss Penelope Jane. b 56. Bris Univ CertEd77 BEd78. Westcott Ho Cam DipRS82. **dss** 85 **d** 87 **p** 94. Waterloo St Jo w St Andr *S'wark* 85-87; Par Dn 87-88; Asst Chapl Gt Ormond Street Hosp for Sick Children Lon 88-90; Par Dn Balham St Mary and St Jo *S'wark* 90-94; C 94-96; Par Dn Upper Tooting H Trin 90-94; C 94-96; TV Clapham TM from 96. *Christchurch Vicarage, 39 Union Grove, London SW8 2QT* Tel 0171-720 0827

ROSEWEIR, Clifford John. b 43. Glas Univ MA64 Kingston Poly DipPM81 MIPD81. S'wark Ord Course 83. **d** 84 **p** 85. NSM Redhill H Trin *S'wark* 84-89; P-in-c Croydon St Martin 89-92; Perm to Offic 92-93; Hon C Wallington H Trin 93-94; V Croydon Ch Ch from 94. *Christ Church Vicarage, 34 Longley Road, Croydon CR0 3LH* Tel 0181-665 1277 Fax as telephone

ROSHEUVEL, Canon Siegfried Winslow Patrick. b 39. Lon Univ BA86. Codrington Coll Barbados 64. **d** 68 **p** 68. Guyana 68-75; C Worksop Priory *S'well* 75-78; Area Sec (Dios Chelmsf and St Alb) USPG 78-89; (Dio Lon) 78-92; Chapl HM Pris Wandsworth 92-93; Chapl HM Pris Rudgate 93-96; Chapl HM Pris Thorp Arch 93-96; Can Cape Coast from 94; Chapl HM Pris Brixton from 96. *HM Prison Brixton, PO Box 369, Jebb Avenue, London SW2 5XF* Tel 0181-674 9811 Fax 674 6128

ROSIER, The Rt Revd Stanley Bruce. b 28. Univ of W Aus BSc48 Ox Univ MA56. Melbourne Coll of Div DipRE63 Westcott Ho Cam 53. **d** 54 **p** 55 **c** 67. C Eccleshall *Lich* 54-57; Australia from 57; Can Perth 66-67; Adn Northam 67; Bp Willochra 70-87; rtd 94. *5A Fowler's Road, Glenunga, S Australia 5064* Tel Adelaide (8) 379 5213

ROSKELLY, James Hereward Emmanuel. b 57. BSc ACSM80. Cranmer Hall Dur 83. **d** 86 **p** 87. C Dunster, Carhampton and Withycombe w Rodhuish *B & W* 86-90; C Ealing St Mary *Lon* 90-93; Chapl R Marsden Hosp Lon and Surrey 93-95; CF from 95. *MOD Chaplains (Army), Trenchard Lines, Upavon, Pewsey, Wilts SN9 6BE* Tel (01980) 615804 Fax 615800

ROSKILLY, Dr John Noel. b 33. DRCOG60 MRCGP68 Man Univ MB, ChB58. St Deiniol's Hawarden 74. **d** 75 **p** 76. NSM Bramhall *Ches* 75-86; V Capesthorne w Siddington and Marton 86-91; Dioc Dir of Counselling 84-93; Bp's Officer for NSM 87-93; NSM Macclesfield St Paul 92-93; rtd 93; Perm to Offic *Ches* from 93. *North View, Hawkins Lane, Rainow, Macclesfield, Cheshire SK10 5TL* Tel (01625) 501014

ROSKROW, Neil. b 27. FSMC50 FBCO80. St Alb Minl Tr Scheme 82. **d** 85 **p** 86. NSM Digswell and Panshanger *St Alb* 85-90; P-in-c Gt Gaddesden 90-95; P-in-c Lt Gaddesden 92-95; rtd 96. *Treunnard, 64 New Road, Welwyn, Herts AL6 0AN*

ROSKROW, Mrs Pamela Mary. b 25. St Alb Minl Tr Scheme. **dss** 85 **d** 87 **p** 94. Digswell and Panshanger *St Alb* 85-90; Hon Par Dn 87-90; Hon Par Dn Gt Gaddesden 90-94; Hon C 94-95; Hon Par Dn Lt Gaddesden 92-94; Hon C 94-95. *Treunnard, 64 New Road, Welwyn, Herts AL6 0AN*

ROSOMAN, Richard John. b 59. Ripon Coll Cuddesdon 90. **d** 92 **p** 93. C Cradley *Worc* 92-96; C Coseley from 96; Ind Chapl from 96. *12 Ribbesford Crescent, Coseley, Bilston, W Midlands WV14 8XU* Tel (01902) 493600

ROSS, Alastair Alexander. b 54. CCC Ox BA75. St Jo Coll Nottm 76. **d** 79 **p** 80. C Huyton St Mich *Liv* 79-82; C-in-c Halewood St Mary CD 82-83; TV Halewood 83-87; V Netherton 87-94; Hon Can Liv Cathl 91-94; V Halifax *Wakef* from 94; RD Halifax from 95. *The Vicarage, Kensington Road, Halifax, W Yorkshire HX3 0BQ* Tel (01422) 365477

ROSS, Anthony McPherson (Tony). b 38. OBE. Univ of Wales (Lamp) BA60 Lon Univ BD63. St Mich Coll Llan 60. **d** 61 **p** 62. C Gabalfa *Llan* 61-65; Chapl RN 65-93; Hon Chapl to The Queen 89-93; P-in-c Coln St Aldwyns, Hatherop, Quenington etc *Glouc* 93-95; V from 95; RD Fairford from 96. *The Vicarage, Coln St Aldwyns, Cirencester, Glos GL7 5AG* Tel (01285) 750013

ROSS, David Alexander (Alex). b 46. Lon Univ DipTh73. Oak Hill Th Coll 73. **d** 75 **p** 76. C Northwood Em *Lon* 75-80; R Eastrop *Win* 80-86; V Hove Bp Hannington Memorial Ch *Chich* 86-93; V

Muswell Hill St Jas w St Matt *Lon* from 93. *St James's Vicarage, 2 St James's Lane, London N10 3DB* Tel 0181-883 6277

ROSS, Preb Duncan Gilbert. b 48. Lon Univ BSc70. Westcott Ho Cam 75. **d** 78 **p** 79. C Stepney St Dunstan and All SS *Lon* 78-84; V Hackney Wick St Mary of Eton w St Aug 84-95; Preb St Paul's Cathl from 95; P-in-c Bow Common from 95. *St Paul's Vicarage, Leopold Street, London E3 4LA* Tel 0171-987 4941

ROSS, Frederic Ian. b 34. Man Univ BSc56. Westcott Ho Cam 58 Episc Th Sem Mass DipTh61. **d** 62 **p** 63. C Oldham *Man* 62-65; Sec Th Colls Dept SCM 65-69; Teacher Man Gr Sch 69-84; Lic to Offic *Man* 69-84; V Shrewsbury H Cross *Lich* from 84. *131 Underdale Road, Shrewsbury SY2 5EG* Tel (01743) 248859

ROSS, Canon Frederick. b 36. Qu Coll Birm. **d** 64 **p** 65. C Hessle *York* 64-68; V Marlpool *Derby* 68-73; P-in-c Norbury w Snelston 73-74; R 74-81; P-in-c Clifton 73-74; V 74-81; RD Ashbourne 78-81; V Melbourne from 81; RD Melbourne 81-86 and 91-96; Hon Can Derby Cathl from 92. *The Vicarage, Church Square, Melbourne, Derby DE7 1EN* Tel (01332) 862347

ROSS, Henry Ernest. b 40. NW Ord Course 70. **d** 73 **p** 74. NSM Litherland St Phil *Liv* 73-75; C Newton-le-Willows 75-77; P-in-c Walton St Luke 77-79; V from 79; RD Walton 84-89. *46 Somerset Drive, Ainsdale, Southport, Merseyside PR8 3SN* Tel (01704) 571287

ROSS, John. b 41. Wells Th Coll 66. **d** 69 **p** 70. C Newc St Gabr *Newc* 69-71; C Prudhoe 71-75; Hon C Shotley 75-87; Hon C Whittonstall 75-87; P-in-c Wallsend St Pet from 93. *St Peter's Rectory, Canterbury Avenue, Wallsend, Tyne & Wear NE28 6PY* Tel 0191-262 3852

ROSS, John Colin. b 50. Oak Hill Th Coll 84. **d** 86 **p** 87. C Stowmarket *St E* 86-89; C Wakef St Andr and St Mary *Wakef* 89-91; R Gt and Lt Whelnetham w Bradfield St George *St E* 91-94; V Newmarket All SS from 94. *The Vicarage, 17 Cardigan Street, Newmarket, Suffolk CB8 8HZ* Tel (01638) 662514

ROSS, Malcolm Hargrave. b 37. Dur Univ BSc58. Westcott Ho Cam 63. **d** 64 **p** 65. C Armley St Bart *Ripon* 64-67; USPG 67-71; Trinidad and Tobago 67-71; V New Rossington *Sheff* 71-75; Bp's Missr in E Lon 75-82; P-in-c Haggerston All SS 75-82; V Bedford Leigh *Man* 82-85; Area Sec (Dios Bris and Glouc) USPG 85-90; Bp's Officer for Miss and Evang *Bris* 90-94; P-in-c Lacock w Bowden Hill 90-94; V Sherston Magna, Easton Grey, Luckington etc from 94. *The Vicarage, Green Lane, Sherston, Malmesbury, Wilts SN16 0NP* Tel (01666) 840209

ROSS, Oliver Charles Milligan. b 58. Lon Univ BA80 St Edm Ho Cam BA85. Ridley Hall Cam 84. **d** 87 **p** 88. C Preston St Cuth *Blackb* 87-90; C Paddington St Jo w St Mich *Lon* 90-95; V Hounslow H Trin w St Paul from 95. *The Vicarage, 66 Lampton Road, Hounslow TW3 4JD* Tel 0181-570 3066

ROSS, Canon Raymond John. b 28. Trin Coll Cam BA52 MA57. St Steph Ho Ox 52. **d** 54 **p** 55. C Clifton All SS *Bris* 54-58; C Solihull *Birm* 58-66; C-in-c Hobs Moat CD 66-67; V Hobs Moat 67-72; R Newbold w Dunston *Derby* 72-95; RD Chesterfield 78-91; Hon Can Derby Cathl 86-95; rtd 96; Perm to Offic *Derby* from 96. *Threeways, Bridge Hill, Belper, Derbyshire DE56 2BY* Tel (01773) 825876

ROSS, Vernon. b 57. RGN86 Portsm Poly BSc79. Trin Coll Bris DipHE91. **d** 91 **p** 92. C Fareham St Jo *Portsm* 91-94; P-in-c Witheridge, Thelbridge, Creacombe, Meshaw etc *Ex* from 94. *The Vicarage, Witheridge, Tiverton, Devon EX16 8AE* Tel (01884) 860768

ROSS, Dean of. *See* HENDERSON, The Very Revd Richard Crosbie Aitken

ROSSDALE, David Douglas James. b 53. Westmr Coll Ox DipApTh90 MA91. K Coll Lon 72 Chich Th Coll 80. **d** 81 **p** 82. C Upminster *Chelmsf* 81-86; V Moulsham St Luke 86-90; V Cookham *Ox* from 90; RD Maidenhead from 94. *The Vicarage, Church Gate, Cookham, Maidenhead, Berks SL6 9SP* Tel (01628) 523969 or 529661

ROSSETER, Miss Susan Mary. b 46. Man Univ BA67 Edin Univ DASS71. St Jo Coll Nottm LTh84. **d** 87 **p** 94. Par Dn Bromley Common St Aug *Roch* 87-88; C Pudsey St Lawr and St Paul *Bradf* 88-95; C Haughton le Skerne *Dur* from 95. *2 Tayside, Darlington, Co Durham DL1 3QT* Tel (01325) 357455

ROSSITER, Donald William Frank. b 30. **d** 80 **p** 81. NSM Abergavenny St Mary w Llanwenarth Citra *Mon* 80-96; NSM Govilon w Llanfoist w Llanelen from 96. *10 Meadow Lane, Abergavenny NP7 7AY* Tel (01873) 855648

ROSSITER, Raymond Stephen David. b 22. St Deiniol's Hawarden 75. **d** 76 **p** 77. NSM Sale St Anne *Ches* 76-90; Perm to Offic from 90; rtd 91. *75 Temple Road, Sale, Cheshire M33 2FQ* Tel 0161-962 3240

ROSTRON, Derek. b 34. St Mich Coll Llan 65. **d** 67 **p** 68. C Morecambe St Barn *Blackb* 67-70; C Ribbleton 70-72; V Chorley All SS 72-79; C Woodchurch *Ches* 79-80; V Audlem from 80; RD Nantwich from 87. *St James's Vicarage, 66 Heathfield Road, Audlem, Crewe CW3 0HG* Tel (01270) 811543 Fax as telephone

ROTHERHAM, Eric. b 36. Clifton Th Coll 63. **d** 67 **p** 68. C Gt Crosby St Luke *Liv* 67-69; C Sutton 69-71; V Warrington St Paul 72-79; Lic to Offic 79-80; Perm to Offic from 80; Perm to Offic *Ches* from 80. *7 Paul Street, Warrington WA2 7LE* Tel (01925) 633048

ROTHERY, Cecil Ivor. b 24. St Jo Coll Winnipeg 50. **d** 53 **p** 54. Canada 53-72; C Gainsborough All SS *Linc* 72-74; R Fleet 74-79; P-in-c Wrawby 79-80; C Glanford Bridge 79-80; rtd 80; Perm to Offic *S'well* 80-83; Perm to Offic *Sheff* 83-93. *129 Queen Street, Retford, Notts DN22 7DA* Tel (01777) 701551

ROTHERY, Robert Frederick (Fred). b 34. Lon Coll of Div 67. **d** 69 **p** 70. C Burscough Bridge *Liv* 69-72; C Chipping Campden *Glouc* 72-75; P-in-c Didmarton w Oldbury-on-the-Hill and Sopworth 75-77; R Boxwell, Leighterton, Didmarton, Oldbury etc 77-83; R Stow on the Wold from 83; RD Stow from 90. *The Rectory, Stow on the Wold, Cheltenham, Glos GL54 1AA* Tel (01451) 830607

ROTHWELL, Bryan. b 60. St Edm Hall Ox BA81 MA85. Trin Coll Bris. **d** 85 **p** 86. C Carl St Jo *Carl* 85-88; C Ulverston St Mary w H Trin 88-90; P-in-c Preston St Mary *Blackb* 90-96; P-in-c St Johns-in-the-Vale w Wythburn *Carl* from 96; Warden Dioc Youth Cen from 96. *The Rectory, Threlkeld, Keswick, Cumbria CA12 4RT* Tel (01768) 772542

ROTHWELL, Edwin John. b 53. Lanc Univ BA74 PhD79. Sarum & Wells Th Coll 88. **d** 90 **p** 91. C Malvern Link w Cowleigh *Worc* 90-94; R Bowbrook N from 94. *The Rectory, Droitwich Road, Hanbury, Bromsgrove, Worcs B60 4DB* Tel (01527) 821826

ROTHWELL, Canon Eric. b 12. Man Univ BA35. Lich Th Coll 35. **d** 37 **p** 38. C Padiham *Blackb* 37-41; P-in-c Burnley St Cath 41-42; C Blackpool St Mary 42-47; V Warton St Oswald 47-63; RD Tunstall 55-63; Hon Can Blackb Cathl 61-77; R Chorley St Laur 63-77; rtd 77; Perm to Offic *Carl* from 77; Perm to Offic *Blackb* from 79. *1 Town End Meadow, Cartmel, Grange-over-Sands, Cumbria LA11 6QG* Tel (01539) 536574

ROTHWELL, Harold. b 34. AKC58. K Coll Lon St Boniface Warminster. **d** 59 **p** 60. C Old Brumby *Linc* 59-62; P-in-c Sheff St Steph w St Phil and St Ann *Sheff* 62-64; V Caistor w Holton le Moor and Clixby *Linc* 67-77; Chapl Caistor Hosp 67-77; Org Sec (Dios Ex and B & W) CECS 77-81; P-in-c Deeping Fen *Linc* 78-81; C Boston 86-88; C Spilsby w Hundleby 88-91; C Bracebridge Heath 91-94; rtd 94; Perm to Offic *Linc* from 94. *47 Ridgeway, Nettleham, Lincoln LN2 2TL* Tel (01522) 751610

ROTHWELL, Michael John Hereward. b 46. Chich Th Coll 74. **d** 78 **p** 79. C Chelmsf All SS *Chelmsf* 78-82; C Clacton St Jas 82-85; V Thorpe *Guildf* from 85. *The Vicarage, Church Approach, Coldharbour Lane, Thorpe, Egham, Surrey TW20 8TQ* Tel (01932) 565986

ROTHWELL-JACKSON, Christopher Patrick. b 32. St Cath Soc Ox BA58 MA61 Bris Univ PGCE66. St Steph Ho Ox 55. **d** 59 **p** 60. C E Clevedon All SS *B & W* 59-62; C Midsomer Norton 62-65; Asst Teacher St Pet Primary Sch Portishead 65-67; Clevedon Primary Sch 67-72; Dep Hd 72-75; Lic to Offic from 69; Hd Master Bp Pursglove Sch Tideswell 75-89; Lic to Offic *Derby* 76-89; Perm to Offic *Ex* from 95; rtd 89. *Rosedale, Hookway, Crediton, Devon EX17 3PU* Tel (01363) 772039

ROUCH, David Vaughan. b 36. Oak Hill Th Coll 67. **d** 69 **p** 70. C Denton Holme *Carl* 69-74; V Litherland St Jo and St Jas *Liv* 74-95; V Pemberton St Mark Newtown from 95. *The Vicarage, Victoria Street, Wigan, Lancs WN5 9BN* Tel (01942) 43611 E-mail drouch@jennyr.win-uk.net

ROULSTON, Dr Joseph Ernest. b 52. MIBiol77 FRSC86 BNC Ox BA74 MA78 Lon Univ PhD81. Edin Dioc NSM Course 83. **d** 86 **p** 87. C Edin St Hilda *Edin* 86-88; C Edin St Fillan 86-88; NSM Edin St Mich and All SS from 88; Dioc Supernumerary Chapl from 96. *16 Summerside Street, Edinburgh EH6 4NU* Tel 0131-554 6382 or 536 2703 Fax 536 2758 E-mail j.e.roulston@ed.ac.uk

ROUND, Keith Leonard. b 49. Sarum & Wells Th Coll 88. **d** 90 **p** 91. C Meir *Lich* 90-95; V Burslem St Werburgh from 95. *The Presbytery, Haywood Road, Stoke-on-Trent ST6 7AH* Tel (01782) 87582

ROUND, Malcolm John Harrison. b 56. Lon Univ BSc77 BA81. Oak Hill Th Coll. **d** 81 **p** 82. C Guildf St Sav w Stoke-next-Guildford *Guildf* 81-85; C Hawkwell *Chelmsf* 85-88; R Balerno *Edin* from 88. *53 Marchbank Drive, Balerno, Midlothian EH14 7ER* Tel 0131-449 4127

ROUNDHILL, Andrew (John). b 65. CCC Cam BA87. Ripon Coll Cuddesdon BTh93. **d** 93 **p** 94. C Lancaster Ch Ch w St Jo and St Anne *Blackb* from 93. *36 Ambleside Road, Lancaster LA1 3HT* Tel (01524) 849186 E-mail gt56@dial.pipex.com

ROUNDHILL, Canon Jack. b 22. TCD BA44 MA47 BD47. **d** 45 **p** 46. C Greenhill St Jo *Lon* 45-49; Dean of Res QUB 49-51; Min Can Belf Cathl 49-51; Sec SCM (Ireland) 49-51; V S Harrow St Paul *Lon* 52-58; V Heston 58-63; V Dorking w Ranmore *Guildf* 63-76; RD Dorking 70-75; Hon Can Guildf Cathl 76-89; R Cranleigh 76-89; rtd 89; Perm to Offic *Bris* 89-93; Perm to Offic *Sarum* from 89; Perm to Offic *Ox* 89-96; Chapl Hawtrey's Sch Marlborough from 93. *2 River Park, Marlborough, Wilts SN8 1NH* Tel (01672) 516312

ROUNDHILL, Stanley Peter. b 14. Chich Th Coll 46. **d** 49 **p** 50. Community of Our Lady and St John from 39; Lic to Offic *Win* from 50; rtd 84. *Alton Abbey, Abbey Road, Beech, Alton, Hants GU34 4AP* Tel (01420) 562145 or 563575 Fax 561691

ROUNDS, Canon Philip Rigby. b 21. Wells Th Coll 49. **d** 52 **p** 53. C Weymouth H Trin *Sarum* 52-56; V Laverstock 56-67; R Wyke Regis 67-89; Can and Preb Sarum Cathl 77-89; rtd 89. *8 Rodwell*

Lodge, Rodwell Road, Weymouth, Dorset DT4 8QT Tel (01305) 781373

ROUNDTREE, The Ven Samuel William. b 19. TCD BA42 MA54. CITC 43. **d** 43 **p** 44. C Waterford Ch Ch *C & O* 44-47; I Tallow w Kilwatermoy 47-51; I Kiltegan w Stratford (and Rathvilly from 60) 51-62; Treas Leighlin Cathl 62-78; RD Maryborough 62-82; Preb Ossory Cathl 62-78; I Dunleckney 62-82; Chan Ossory and Leighlin Cathls 78-80; Prec 80-82; I New w Old Ross, Whitechurch, Fethard etc 82-88; Adn Ferns 86-88; rtd 88. *7 Bellevue Cottages, Delgany, Greystones, Co Wicklow, Irish Republic* Tel Dublin (1) 287 4428

ROUNTREE, Canon Richard Benjamin. b 52. NUI BA73. CITC 76. **d** 76 **p** 77. C Orangefield *D & D* 76-80; C Dublin Zion Ch *D & G* 80-83; I Dalkey St Patr 83-97; Dioc Dir Decade of Evang 90-96; Can Ch Ch Cathl Dublin from 92; I Powerscourt w Kilbride and Annacrevy from 97. *Powerscourt Rectory, Enniskerry, Bray, Co Wicklow, Irish Republic* Tel Dublin (1) 286 3534 Fax as telephone

ROUSE, Graham. b 58. Sheff City Coll of Educn CertEd79 Leic Univ DipEd84. Cranmer Hall Dur 90. **d** 92 **p** 93. C Longridge *Blackb* 92-96; P-in-c Fairhaven from 96. *Fairhaven Vicarage, 83 Clifton Drive, Lytham St Annes, Lancs FY8 1BZ* Tel (01253) 734562

ROUTH, Mrs Eileen Rosemary. b 41. Cant Sch of Min 82. **dss** 85 **d** 87 **p** 94. Folkestone St Sav *Cant* 85-90; Par Dn 87-90; Par Dn Woodnesborough w Worth and Staple 90-91; D-in-c 91-94; V 94-96; V Maidstone St Martin from 96. *St Martin's Vicarage, Northumberland Road, Maidstone, Kent ME15 7LP* Tel (01622) 676282

ROUTH, William John. b 60. Magd Coll Ox BA81 MA92. Ripon Coll Cuddesdon 93. **d** 95 **p** 96. C Longton *Blackb* from 95. *66 Franklands, Longton, Preston PR4 5WD* Tel (01772) 615473

ROW, Mrs Pamela Anne. b 54. Open Univ BA86 MA92 Homerton Coll Cam BEd75. N Ord Course 94. **d** 96 **p** 97. NSM Neston *Ches* from 96. *9 Ashtree Close, Little Neston, S Wirral L64 9QS* Tel 0151-336 3797

ROWBERRY, Christopher Michael. b 58. Plymouth Univ CQSW85. Qu Coll Birm 94. **d** 96 **p** 97. C Lytchett Minster *Sarum* from 96. *15 Guest Road, Upton, Poole, Dorset BH16 5LQ* Tel (01202) 623637 Fax as telephone E-mail 100410.1035 @compuserve.com

ROWBERRY, Michael James. b 46. Sussex Univ BA74. Edin Th Coll 85. **d** 87 **p** 92. C Wolvercote w Summertown *Ox* 87-88; NSM Cov St Fran N Radford *Cov* from 91. *93 Kingston Road, Coventry CV5 6LQ* Tel (01203) 677915

ROWCROFT, Kenneth George Caulfeild. b 19. Sarum Th Coll 48. **d** 50 **p** 51. C Bradford-on-Avon *Sarum* 50-53; C Broadstone 53-55; C Lyme Regis 55-64; R Hawkchurch w Fishpond 64-74; V Monkton Wyld 67-74; rtd 75. *Colway Rise, Colway Lane, Lyme Regis, Dorset DT7 3HE* Tel (01297) 443349

ROWDON, John Michael Hooker. b 27. Witwatersrand Univ BA52. Ridley Hall Cam 52. **d** 54 **p** 55. C Broadwater St Mary *Chich* 54-56; C Streatham Immanuel w St Anselm *S'wark* 56-59; Nigeria 60-62; C All Hallows Lon Wall *Lon* 62-66; Warden Toc H Tower Hill 64-66; Australia from 66; rtd 92. *PO Box 1111, Subiaco, W Australia 6008* Tel Perth (9) 382 1648

ROWE, Andrew Gidleigh Bruce. b 37. AKC62. St Boniface Warminster. **d** 63 **p** 64. C Midsomer Norton *B & W* 63-68; Chapl RN 68-84; Hon C Winkfield and Cranbourne *Ox* 84-86; Chapl Heathfield Sch 84-86; TV Wellington and Distr *B & W* 86-95; R Chewton Mendip w Ston Easton, Litton etc 95-96; Perm to Offic *Ex* from 96. *2 Springfield Park, Cheriton Bishop, Exeter EX6 6JN* Tel (01647) 24043

ROWE, Andrew Robert (Andy). b 64. Westmr Coll Ox BA85 PGCE86. Ridley Hall Cam CTM95. **d** 95 **p** 96. C Broadheath *Ches* from 95. *21 Woodheys Drive, Sale, Cheshire M33 4JB* Tel 0161-973 5274

ROWE, Canon Antony Silvester Buckingham. b 26. St Jo Coll Dur 53. **d** 55 **p** 56. C Holbrooks *Cov* 55-59; V Cov St Mary 59-83; RD Cov S 72-82; Hon Can Cov Cathl 76-92; R Harbury and Ladbroke 83-92; rtd 92; Perm to Offic *Cov* from 92; Perm to Offic *Glouc* 92-95. *3 Cotswold Edge, Mickleton, Chipping Campden, Glos GL55 6TR* Tel (01386) 438622

ROWE, Arthur John. b 35. TCD 73. **d** 76 **p** 77. C Bangor Abbey *D & D* 76-78; I Kilbarron *D & R* 78-79; I Kilbarron w Rossnowlagh 79-82; P-in-c Hockering *Nor* 82-85; P-in-c Honingham w E Tuddenham 82-85; P-in-c N Tuddenham 82-85; R Hockwold w Wilton *Ely* 85-95; R Weeting 85-95; rtd 95. *Orchard Villa, Back Lane, Castle Acre, King's Lynn, Norfolk PE32 2AR* Tel (01760) 755170

ROWE, Bryan. b 50. Carl Dioc Tr Course 87. **d** 90 **p** 91. C Kells *Carl* 90-93; P-in-c Aspatria w Hayton from 93. *The Vicarage, King Street, Aspatria, Carlisle CA5 3AL* Tel (016973) 20398

ROWE, Cecil Leonard. b 16. AKC48. **d** 48 **p** 49. C Southwick *Chich* 48-51; C Seaford w Sutton 51-54; C Aldwick 54-55; C Uckfield 55-59; V Ashley Green *Ox* 59-62; V Charlton All Saints *Sarum* 62-68; R Girvan *Glas* 68-72; R Stratford St Mary *St E* 72-83; P-in-c Higham 72-83; rtd 83. *15 Bristol Road, Colchester CO1 2YU* Tel (01206) 866411

ROWE, Mrs Christine Elizabeth. b 55. Southn Univ BEd77. Ripon Hall Ox 83. **dss** 86 **d** 87 **p** 94. Denham *Ox* 86-87; Par Dn 87-89; Par Dn Aylesbury 89; Par Dn Aylesbury w Bierton and Hulcott 89-93; NSM Caversham St Jo from 93. *The Vicarage, St John's Road, Caversham, Reading RG4 0AN* Tel 0118-947 1814

ROWE, David Brian. b 58. Trin Coll Bris DipHE82. **d** 83 **p** 84. C Radipole and Melcombe Regis *Sarum* 83-86; C Cranham Park *Chelmsf* 86-88; Assoc Min and Par Missr Eastrop *Win* 88-92; P-in-c Arborfield w Barkham *Ox* from 92. *The Rectory, Church Lane, Arborfield, Reading RG2 9HZ* Tel (0118) 976 0285

ROWE, Geoffrey Lewis. b 44. Univ of Wales (Lamp) BA. Ripon Coll Cuddesdon 80. **d** 82 **p** 83. C Milber *Ex* 82-84; TV Withycombe Raleigh 84-90; R Clyst St Mary, Clyst St George etc from 90. *The Rectory, 40 Clyst Valley Road, Clyst St Mary, Exeter EX5 1DD* Tel (01392) 874363

ROWE, Miss Joan Patricia. b 54. Trin Coll Bris BA87. **d** 88 **p** 94. C Radstock w Writhlington *B & W* 88-92; C Nailsea H Trin 92-96; P-in-c Shapwick w Ashcott and Burtle from 96. *The Vicarage, Vicarage Lane, Shapwick, Bridgwater, Somerset TA7 9LR* Tel (01458) 210260

ROWE, John Goring. b 23. McGill Univ Montreal BA48 BD51 Selw Coll Cam BA53. Montreal Dioc Th Coll LTh51. **d** 51 **p** 52. Canada 51; C Trumpington *Ely* 51-53; Hon C Bow Common *Lon* 53-84; rtd 88. *10 Cordelia Street, London E14 6DZ* Tel 0171-515 4681

ROWE, John Nigel. b 24. Ball Coll Ox MA52 BD53 Leeds Univ PhD82. Ely Th Coll 49. **d** 54 **p** 55. C Gt Grimsby St Jas *Linc* 54-57; C Ches St Jo *Ches* 57-58; Hon C Birch St Jas *Man* 58-59; C Gorton St Jas 59-60; V Newchurch-in-Pendle *Blackb* 60-80; V Denholme Gate *Bradf* 80-89; rtd 89. *12 Begwyns Bluff, Clyro, Hereford HR3 5SR* Tel (01497) 820086

ROWE, Peter Farquharson. b 19. Selw Coll Cam BA41. Westcott Ho Cam 41. **d** 43 **p** 44. C Putney St Mary *S'wark* 43-47; C Lewisham St Jo Southend 47-54; V Mitcham Ascension 54-65; V Eltham Park St Luke 65-77; V Ravensthorpe w E Haddon and Holdenby *Pet* 77-84; rtd 84; Perm to Offic *Ex* 84-89; Perm to Offic *Sarum* 89-92; Perm to Offic *Win* from 92. *28 Gordon Avenue, Winchester, Hants SO23 0QQ* Tel (01962) 869806

ROWE, Philip William. b 57. Southn Univ BSc78. Lambeth STh86 Trin Coll Bris 82. **d** 85 **p** 86. C Tooting Graveney St Nic *S'wark* 85-89; V Abbots Leigh w Leigh Woods *Bris* 89-96; V Almondsbury from 96; P-in-c Littleton on Severn w Elberton from 96. *The Vicarage, Almondsbury, Bristol BS12 4DS* Tel (01454) 613223

ROWE, Richard Nigel. b 41. St Pet Coll Saltley DipEd64. St Steph Ho Ox 67. **d** 70 **p** 71. C Acton Green St Pet *Lon* 70-74; C Leigh St Clem *Chelmsf* 74-80; V Leytonstone St Marg w St Columba 80-89; RD Waltham Forest 86-89; V Thaxted from 89. *The Vicarage, Watling Lane, Thaxted, Essex CM6 2QY* Tel (01371) 830221

ROWE, Samuel Ernest Allen. b 16. TCD BA39 MA44. **d** 40 **p** 41. C Wexford w Rathaspeck *C & O* 40-43; CF 43-68; I Newtownfertullagh *M & K* 68-72; I Monart w Ballycarney and Templescobin *C & O* 72-83; rtd 83. *Chestnut Lodge, Bloomfield, Enniscorthy, Co Wexford, Irish Republic* Tel Enniscorthy (54) 33171

ROWE, Canon Stanley Hamilton. b 18. St Pet Hall Ox BA48 MA52. ALCD50. **d** 50 **p** 51. C Leyton St Paul *Chelmsf* 50-52; CMS Nigeria 52-65; P-in-c Becontree St Cedd *Chelmsf* 65-67; Hd of RE Jo Hampden Sch High Wycombe 67-83; Perm to Offic *Ox* 67-84 and from 86; rtd 83; Hon P-in-c Aston Rowant w Crowell *Ox* 84-86; Hon Can Oke-Osun from 94. *37 Greenwood Avenue, Chinnor, Oxon OX9 4HW* Tel (01844) 351278

ROWE, Stephen Mark Buckingham. b 59. SS Mark & Jo Coll Plymouth BA81. Ripon Coll Cuddesdon 83. **d** 86 **p** 87. C Denham *Ox* 86-89; C Aylesbury 89; C Aylesbury w Bierton and Hulcott 89-90; TV 90-93; V Caversham St Jo from 93. *The Vicarage, St John's Road, Caversham, Reading RG4 0AN* Tel 0118-947 1814

ROWE, William Alfred. b 11. Open Univ BA72. Bps' Coll Cheshunt 50. **d** 52 **p** 53. C Ipswich St Marg *St E* 52-54; V Walsham le Willows 54-57; R Boyton w Capel 57-62; P-in-c Bawdsey 57-60; V Ermington *Ex* 62-72; R Bratton Clovelly w Germansweek 72-76; rtd 76; Lic to Offic *Ex* from 76. *Pendennis, 64 Dartmouth Road, Paignton, Devon TQ4 5AW* Tel (01803) 556124

ROWELL, Alan. b 50. Lon Univ BSc71 AKC71. Trin Coll Bris DipTh75. **d** 75 **p** 76. C W Hampstead St Cuth *Lon* 75-78; C Camborne *Truro* 78-81; V Pendeen w Morvah from 81. *The Vicarage, Pendeen, Penzance, Cornwall TR19 7SE* Tel (01736) 788777

✠**ROWELL, The Rt Revd Douglas Geoffrey.** b 43. CCC Cam BA64 MA68 PhD68 Keble Coll Ox DD97. Cuddesdon Coll. **d** 68 **p** 69 **c** 94. Lic to Offic *Ox* 68-94; Asst Chapl New Coll Ox 68-72; Chapl Keble Coll Ox 72-94; Wiccamical Preb Chich Cathl *Chich* 81-94; Suff Bp Basingstoke *Win* from 94. *Bishopswood End, Kingswood Rise, Four Marks, Alton, Hants GU34 5BD* Tel (01420) 562925 Fax 561251

ROWELL, Frank. b 22. Chich Th Coll 50. **d** 52 **p** 53. C Ipswich All SS *St E* 52-56; R Earl Stonham 56-65; R Otley 65-83; R Clopton 65-83; R Clopton w Otley, Swilland and Ashbocking 83-88; rtd 88; Perm to Offic *St E* from 90. *37 Riverview, Melton, Woodbridge, Suffolk IP12 1QU* Tel (01394) 385449

ROWELL, William Kevin. b 51. Reading Univ BSc71. Linc Th Coll 78. **d** 80 **p** 81. C Cannock *Lich* 80-83; Ind Chapl 83-86; C Ketley and Oakengates 83-86; R Norton in the Moors 86-93; RD Leek 92-93; P-in-c Minsterley *Heref* from 93; P-in-c Habberley from 93. *The Vicarage, Minsterley, Shrewsbury SY5 0AA* Tel (01743) 791213

ROWETT, David Peter. b 55. Univ Coll Dur BA76. Ripon Coll Cuddesdon 82. **d** 84 **p** 85. C Yeovil *B & W* 84-88; C Yeovil St Mich 88-89; V Fairfield St Matt *Linc* from 89. *St Matthew's Vicarage, Thirlmere Avenue, Grimsby, S Humberside DN33 3EA* Tel (01472) 821183

ROWETT, Mrs Margaret Pettigrew Coupar. b 33. Sarum & Wells Th Coll 84. **dss** 86 **d** 87 **p** 95. Widley w Wymering *Portsm* 86-88; C 87-88; Par Dn Plympton St Mary *Ex* 88-91; rtd 91; NSM St Mewan *Truro* from 94. *Epiphany Cottage, 9 Socotra Drive, Trewoon, St Austell, Cornwall PL25 5SQ* Tel (01726) 71450

ROWETT, Brig William Berkeley. b 09. ADipR58 Lon Univ BA61. Westcott Ho Cam 62. **d** 62 **p** 63. C St Martin-in-the-Fields *Lon* 62-66; Chapl Scilly Is and V St Mary's *Truro* 66-71; V Madron w Morvah 71-80; rtd 80; Perm to Offic *Guildf* from 80; Perm to Offic *Lon* from 81; Perm to Offic *S'wark* from 81. *Three Ducks, 30 The Island, Thames Ditton, Surrey KT7 0SQ* Tel 0181-398 7196

ROWLAND, Barry William. b 59. St Jo Coll Nottm DipThMin95 BA95. **d** 95 **p** 96. C Welling *Roch* from 95. *52 Clifton Road, Welling, Kent DA16 1QD* Tel 0181-304 4179

ROWLAND, Prof Christopher Charles. b 47. Ch Coll Cam BA69 MA73 PhD75. Ridley Hall Cam 72. **d** 75 **p** 76. Hon C Benwell St Jas *Newc* 75-78; Hon C Gosforth All SS 78-79; Dean Jes Coll Cam 79-91; Lic to Offic *Ely* from 79; Prof of Exegesis of H Scripture Ox Univ from 91. *Queen's College, Oxford OX1 4AW* Tel (01865) 279121

ROWLAND, Ms Dawn Jeannette. b 38. RSCN61 RGN63. S'wark Ord Course. **dss** 84 **d** 87 **p** 94. Par Dn Croydon H Sav *S'wark* 84-89; NSM Riddlesdown from 89. *9 Hartley Hill, Purley, Surrey CR8 4EP* Tel 0181-660 6270

ROWLAND, Derek John. b 47. St Jo Coll Nottm 84. **d** 86 **p** 87. C Porchester *S'well* 86-89; V Fairfield *Liv* 89-96; V Buckfastleigh w Dean Prior *Ex* from 96. *The Vicarage, Glebelands, Buckfastleigh, Devon TQ11 0BH* Tel (01364) 644228

ROWLAND, Derrick Edward. b 31. Univ of Wales (Lamp) BA55 St Cath Soc Ox BA57. Wycliffe Hall Ox. **d** 57 **p** 58. C Reading St Jo *Ox* 57-61; V Smethwick St Matt *Birm* 61-67; V Turnditch *Derby* 67-74; Dir of Educn 74-83; Lic to Offic 83-85; Adult Educn Officer Gen Syn Bd of Educn 85-89; rtd 96. *Hill Top, Eardisley, Hereford HR3 6LX*

ROWLAND, Eric Edward James. b 35. Leeds Univ BA62. Coll of Resurr Mirfield 61. **d** 63 **p** 64. C S Kirkby *Wakef* 63-65; C Headingley *Ripon* 65-70; V Osmondthorpe St Phil 70-79; R Sandy *St Alb* from 79; RD Biggleswade 85-94. *The Rectory, Sandy, Beds SG19 1AQ* Tel (01767) 680512

ROWLAND, Geoffrey Watson. b 17. **d** 55 **p** 56. BCMS 55-65; Burma 55-65; C Blackheath Park St Mich *S'wark* 65-71; V W Bromwich St Paul Golds Hill *Lich* 71-76; Chapl Community Relns *Lon* 77-83; C Southall Green St Jo 83; rtd 83; Perm to Offic *Lon* from 83. *3 Amber Court, Longford Avenue, Southall, Middx UB1 3QR* Tel 0181-574 3442

ROWLAND, Robert William. b 51. Birm Univ BA72 Univ of Wales (Cardiff) DPS73. St Mich Coll Llan 72. **d** 74 **p** 75. C Connah's Quay *St As* 74; C Shotton 74-76; C Llanrhos 76-81; V Dyserth and Trelawnyd and Cwm from 81; RD St As from 94. *The Vicarage, Dyserth, Rhyl LL18 6DB* Tel (01745) 570750

ROWLANDS, The Very Revd Daniel John. b 25. Pemb Coll Cam BA49 MA54. Bps' Coll Cheshunt 49. **d** 51 **p** 52. C Woodford St Mary *Chelmsf* 51-53; Miss to Seamen 53-75; Asst Chapl Rotterdam 53-55; Port Chapl Dar-es-Salaam 55-61; Chapl The Tees 62-69; V Wilton *York* 63-69; Asst Gen Sec Miss to Seamen Paternoster R 69-75; R Woodbridge St Mary *St E* 75-82; Dean Gib *Eur* 82-86; Perm to Offic *St D* 86-88; P-in-c Llangrannog and Llandysiliogogo 88-92; RD Glyn Aeron 89-95; rtd 95. *Glyn Coed, Clos Dolwen, Aberporth, Cardigan SA43 2DE* Tel (01239) 811042 Fax as telephone

ROWLANDS, Edward. b 18. DipFL90. Kelham Th Coll 37. **d** 44 **p** 44. C Upholland *Liv* 44-47; C Leigh St Mary *Man* 47-49; V Anfield SS Simon and Jude *Liv* 49-52; Area Sec USPG (Dios York, Ripon, Bradf, Wakef) 52-58; V Winshill *Derby* 58-64; V Pemberton St Jo *Liv* 64-75; V Haigh 75-83; rtd 83; Perm to Offic *Liv* from 83; Asst Chapl Billinge Hosp Wigan 83-93. *24 Hallbridge Gardens, Up Holland, Skelmersdale, Lancs WN8 0ER* Tel (01695) 624362

ROWLANDS, Canon Emyr Wyn. b 42. Univ of Wales (Ban) DipTh70. St Mich Coll Llan 69. **d** 70 **p** 71. C Holyhead w Rhoscolyn *Ban* 70-74; V Bodedern w Llechgynfarwy and Llechylched etc 74-88; R Machynlleth and Llanwrin 88-97; R Machynlleth w Llanwrin and Penegoes from 97; RD Cyfeiliog and Mawddwy from 96; Can Ban Cathl from 97. *The Rectory, Newtown Road, Machynlleth SY20 8HE* Tel (01654) 702261

ROWLANDS, Forrest John. b 25. LSE BSc(Econ)51. Chich Th Coll 54. **d** 56 **p** 57. C Hove St Phil *Chich* 56-58; C Haywards Heath St Wilfrid 58-62; R Kingston by Sea 62-74; rtd 90. *14 Hazel Close, Thorpe Marriott, Norwich NR8 6YE* Tel (01603) 261704

ROWLANDS, Gareth Richard. b 70. Univ of Wales BA93. St Steph Ho Ox BTh93. **d** 96 **p** 97. C Shotton *St As* from 96. *St Andrew's House, Sealand Avenue, Garden City, Deeside CH5 2HL*

ROWLANDS, Graeme Charles. b 53. K Coll Lon BD74 AKC74. St Aug Coll Cant 75. **d** 76 **p** 77. C Higham Ferrers w Chelveston *Pet* 76-79; C Gorton Our Lady and St Thos *Man* 79-81; C Reading H Trin *Ox* 81-89; P-in-c Kentish Town St Silas *Lon* 89-92; V from 92; P-in-c Haverstock Hill H Trin w Kentish Town St Barn from 93. *St Silas's House, 11 St Silas's Place, London NW5 3QP* Tel 0171-485 3727

ROWLANDS, Canon John Henry Lewis. b 47. Univ of Wales (Lamp) BA68 Magd Coll Cam BA70 MA74 Dur Univ MLitt86. Westcott Ho Cam 70. **d** 72 **p** 73. C Aberystwyth *St D* 72-76; Chapl Univ of Wales (Lamp) 76-79; Youth Chapl 76-79; Dir Academic Studies St Mich Coll Llan 79-84; Sub-Warden 84-88; Warden 88-97; Lect Univ of Wales (Cardiff) *Llan* 79-97; Asst Dean 81-83; Dean 83-97; Dean of Div Univ of Wales 91-94; Dir of Ords 85-88; Hon Can Llan Cathl from 90; V Whitchurch from 97; Chapl Whitchurch Hosp Cardiff from 97. *The Vicarage, 6 Penlline Road, Cardiff CF4 2AD* Tel (01222) 626072

ROWLANDS, Canon Joseph Haydn. b 36. Univ of Wales (Lamp) BA61 DipTh63. **d** 63 **p** 64. C Llanfairisgaer *Ban* 63-68; R Maentwrog w Trawsfynydd 68-75; V Henfynyw w Aberaeron and Llanddewi Aberarth *St D* 75-80; R Trefdraeth *Ban* 80-84; V Llandysul *St D* from 84; Hon Can St D Cathl 88-90; Can St D Cathl from 90; RD Emlyn from 92. *The Vicarage, Well Street, Llandyssul SA44 4DR* Tel (01559) 362277

ROWLANDS, Kenneth Albert. b 41. MA DipAE. NW Ord Course 70. **d** 73 **p** 74. NSM Hoylake *Ches* 73-80; NSM Oxton 80-82; Perm to Offic from 82; C Stoneycroft All SS *Liv* 92-94; V Mossley Hill St Barn from 94. *St Barnabas's Vicarage, 1 Carsdale Road, Mossley Hill, Liverpool L18 1LZ* Tel 0151-733 1432

ROWLANDS, Mark. b 56. Cranmer Hall Dur 86. **d** 88 **p** 89. C Hattersley *Ches* 88-90; C Offerton 91-94; V Baddiley and Wrenbury w Burleydam from 94. *The Vicarage, The Green, Wrenbury, Nantwich, Cheshire CW5 8EY* Tel (01270) 780398

ROWLANDS, Michael Huw. b 62. Birm Univ BA85 Univ of Wales (Cardiff) BD88. St Mich Coll Llan 85. **d** 88 **p** 89. C Penarth All SS *Llan* 88-91; V Martletwy w Lawrenny and Minwear etc *St D* from 91. *St John's Rectory, Templeton, Narberth SA67 8XX* Tel (01834) 861412

ROWLANDS, Richard. b 34. St Mich Coll Llan 59. **d** 62 **p** 63. C Towyn *Ban* 62-65; C Dwygyfylchi 65-69; V Carno and Trefeglwys 69-71; CF 71-83. *Rhyd Casadog, Ty'n Lon Po, Holyhead LL65 3AQ* Tel (01407) 720843

ROWLANDS, Robert. b 31. Roch Th Coll. **d** 68 **p** 69. C Hooton *Ches* 68-71; V Stretton 71-88; P-in-c Appleton Thorn and Antrobus 87-88; V Stretton and Appleton Thorn from 88. *The Vicarage, Stretton, Warrington WA4 4NT* Tel (01925) 673276

ROWLANDSON, Gary Clyde. b 50. Lon Univ CertEd72 BA85. Oak Hill Th Coll 82. **d** 85 **p** 86. C Muswell Hill St Jas w St Matt *Lon* 85-89; C Northwood Em 89-93; R Chesham Bois *Ox* from 93. *The Rectory, Glebe Way, Chesham Bois, Amersham, Bucks HP6 5ND* Tel (01494) 726139

ROWLEY, Christopher Francis Elmes. b 48. St Jo Coll Dur BA70 St Luke's Coll Ex PGCE71. St Steph Ho Ox 76. **d** 78 **p** 79. C Parkstone St Pet w Branksea and St Osmund *Sarum* 78-81; TV 82-85; P-in-c Chard Gd Shep Furnham *B & W* 85-89; P-in-c Dowlishwake w Chaffcombe, Knowle St Giles etc 88-89; R Chard Furnham w Chaffcombe, Knowle St Giles etc 89-91; V Stoke St Gregory w Burrowbridge and Lyng from 91. *The Vicarage, Stoke St Gregory, Taunton, Somerset TA3 6EG* Tel (01823) 490247

ROWLEY, David Michael. b 39. N Ord Course 87. **d** 90 **p** 91. C Stainland *Wakef* 90-93; V Hayfield *Derby* from 93; RD Glossop from 96. *The Vicarage, 7 Station Road, Birch Vale, High Peak, Derbyshire SK22 1BP* Tel (01663) 743350 Fax as telephone

ROWLEY, Edward Patrick. b 29. Dur Univ BSc52. Coll of Resurr Mirfield 55. **d** 57 **p** 58. C Kirby Moorside w Gillamoor *York* 57-59; C Huntington 59-61; Malaya 61-63; Malaysia 63-65; R Ampleforth w Oswaldkirk *York* 65-73; Chapl Yorkshire Res Sch for Deaf Doncaster 74-84; R Finningley *S'well* 84-85; P-in-c Elkesley w Bothamsall 87-91; P-in-c Gamston w Eaton and W Drayton 88-91; rtd 91. *116 Lincoln Road, Tuxford, Newark, Notts NG22 0HS* Tel (01777) 871524

ROWLING, Mrs Catherine. b 55. Man Poly BEd77. Westcott Ho Cam 83 NE Ord Course 85. **dss** 86 **d** 87 **p** 94. Gt Ayton w Easby and Newton in Cleveland *York* 86-89; Par Dn 87-89; Chapl Teesside Poly 89-92; Chapl Teesside Univ 92-96; Dioc Adv for Diaconal Mins from 96. *The Vicarage, Ingleby Greenhow, Middlesbrough, Cleveland TS9 6LL* Tel (01642) 723947

ROWLING, Richard Francis. b 56. BA. Westcott Ho Cam. **d** 84 **p** 85. C Stokesley *York* 84-87; C Stainton-in-Cleveland 87-90; V New Marske 90-96; V Wilton 92-96; P-in-c Ingleby Greenhow w Bilsdale Priory, Kildale etc from 96. *The Vicarage, Ingleby Greenhow, Middlesbrough, Cleveland TS9 6LL* Tel (01642) 723947

ROWNTREE, Peter. b 47. St D Coll Lamp BA68 Univ of Wales (Cardiff) MA70. St Steph Ho Ox 70. **d** 72 **p** 73. C Stanwell *Lon* 72-75; C Northolt St Mary 75-79; Chapl Ealing Gen Hosp 79-83 and 87-94; Chapl Ealing Hosp NHS Trust from 94; Chapl W Lon Health Care NHS Trust from 94; Chapl Cherry Knowle Hosp Sunderland 83-87; Chapl Ryhope Hosp Sunderland 83-87. *Ealing Hospital, Uxbridge Road, Southall, Middx UB1 3HW* Tel 0181-967 5130 or 574 2444

ROWSELL, Canon John Bishop. b 25. Jes Coll Cam BA49 MA55. Ely Th Coll 49. **d** 51 **p** 52. C Hackney Wick St Mary of Eton w St Aug *Lon* 51-55; C Is of Dogs Ch Ch and St Jo w St Luke 55-56; C Reading St Mary V *Ox* 56-59; V Hightown *Wakef* 59-69; R Harlton *Ely* 69-81; V Haslingfield 69-81; V Methwold 81-95; RD Feltwell 81-95; R Northwold 82-95; Hon Can Ely Cathl 84-95; rtd 95; P-in-c Hockwold w Wilton *Ely* from 95; P-in-c Weeting from 95. *The Rectory, Hockwold, Thetford, Norfolk IP26 4JG* Tel (01842) 828271

ROWSON, Frank. b 40. CEng67 MIStructE67. Sarum & Wells Th Coll 87. **d** 90 **p** 91. NSM Ore Ch Ch *Chich* from 90. *149 Priory Road, Hastings, E Sussex TN34 3JD* Tel (01424) 439802

ROWSTON, Geoffrey. b 34. Sarum Th Coll 59. **d** 62 **p** 63. C Ashburton w Buckland-in-the-Moor *Ex* 62-65; C Basingstoke *Win* 65-68; V Netley 68-78; V W End 78-87; R Alderbury and W Grimstead *Sarum* 87-91; P-in-c Whiteparish 89-91; TR Alderbury Team from 91. *The Rectory, 5 The Copse, Alderbury, Salisbury SP5 3BL* Tel (01722) 710229

✠**ROWTHORN, The Rt Revd Jeffery William.** b 34. Societas Liturgica MNAAL MHSA MHSGBI Ch Coll Cam BA57 MA62 Or Coll Ox BLitt72. Berkeley Div Sch DD87 Cuddesdon Coll 61 Union Th Sem (NY) BD61. **d** 62 **p** 63 **c** 87. C Woolwich St Mary w H Trin *S'wark* 62-65; R Garsington *Ox* 65-68; USA 68-93; Chapl and Dean Union Th Sem NY 68-73; Assoc Prof Past Th Yale and Berkeley Div Schs 73-87; Suff Bp Connecticut 87-93; Bp in Charge Convocation of American Chs in Eur from 94; Asst Bp Eur from 95. *c/o 23 Avenue George V, 75008 Paris, France* Tel France (33) 47 20 17 92 or 47 20 64 44 Fax 47 23 95 30

✠**ROXBURGH, The Rt Revd James William.** b 21. St Cath Coll Cam BA42 MA46. Wycliffe Hall Ox 42. **d** 44 **p** 45 **c** 83. C Folkestone H Trin w Ch Ch *Cant* 44-47; C Handsworth St Mary *Birm* 47-50; V Bootle St Matt *Liv* 50-56; V Drypool St Columba w St Andr and St Pet *York* 56-65; V Barking St Marg *Chelmsf* 65-73; P-in-c Barking St Patr 65-73; Hon Can Chelmsf Cathl 72-77; V Barking St Marg w St Patr 73-75; TR 75-77; Adn Colchester 77-83; Suff Bp Barking 83-84; Area Bp Barking 84-90; rtd 90; Asst Bp Liv from 91. *53 Preston Road, Southport, Merseyside PR9 9EE* Tel (01704) 542927

ROXBY, Gordon George. b 39. Lon Univ BSc61. Coll of Resurr Mirfield 61. **d** 63 **p** 64. C Fleetwood *Blackb* 63-66; C Kirkham 66-68; V Runcorn St Jo Weston *Ches* 68-78; R Moston St Chad *Man* 78-86; V Bury St Pet from 86; AD Bury 86-96; Hon Can Man Cathl from 97. *St Peter's Vicarage, St Peter's Road, Bury, Lancs BL9 9QZ* Tel 0161-764 1187

ROY, David Brian. b 25. MIA ARIBA Leeds Coll of Art DipArch50. **d** 88 **p** 89. Hon C Burrough Hill Pars *Leic* 88-90; Hon C Framland Deanery 88 and 90-91; TV Melton Gt Framland 91-93; TV Melton Mowbray 93-95; rtd 95; Perm to Offic *Leic* from 95. *16 Somerby Road, Pickwell, Melton Mowbray, Leics LE14 2RA* Tel (01664) 77775

ROYALL, Preb Arthur Robert. b 19. Lambeth MA Qu Coll Birm 51. **d** 53 **p** 54. C Ashford St Matt *Lon* 53-56; V Heap Bridge *Man* 56-59; V Whitton St Aug *Lon* 59-64; P-in-c Bromley St Mich 64-71; R Poplar All SS w St Frideswide 64-71; RD Poplar 65-66; P-in-c Poplar St Sav w St Gabr and St Steph 68-71; RD Tower Hamlets 68-76; R Poplar 71-73; P-in-c Mile End Old Town H Trin 73-76; P-in-c Bethnal Green St Barn 73-75; Preb St Paul's Cathl 73-86; R Bow w Bromley St Leon 73-76; Clergy Appts Adv 76-85; Perm to Offic *Nor* from 77; Perm to Offic *Ely* from 78; rtd 86; Perm to Offic *Lon* 86-91. *Carmelite House, 10 Pit Lane, Swaffham, Norfolk PE37 7DA* Tel (01760) 723300

ROYCROFT, James Gordon Benjamin. b 26. CITC. **d** 56 **p** 57. C Belfast St Aid *Conn* 56-58; C Crossmolina *T, K & A* 58-63; ICM Sec (N England) 63-67; I Drung w Castleterra *K, E & A* 67-83; I Larah and Lavey 67-83; I Drumkeeran w Templecarne and Muckross *Clogh* 83-91; rtd 91. *Boa Island, Kesh, Enniskillen, Co Fermanagh BT93 1TE*

ROYDEN, Charles. b 60. Wycliffe Hall Ox BA86. **d** 87 **p** 88. C Bidston *Ches* 87-91; V N Brickhill and Putnoe *St Alb* 91-92; V Bedf St Mark from 93. *The Vicarage, Calder Rise, North Brickhill, Bedford MK41 7UY* Tel (01234) 358699 or 342613

ROYDEN, Eric Ramsay. b 29. St Deiniol's Hawarden 75. **d** 77 **p** 78. Hon C Tranmere St Paul w St Luke *Ches* 77-81; C Eastham 81; V New Brighton All SS 81-95; P-in-c 95-97; rtd 95. *14 Kinglass Road, Bebington, Wirral, Merseyside L63 9AJ*

ROYDEN, Ross Eric. b 55. Nottm Univ MTh82. Lon Bible Coll BA77 Wycliffe Hall Ox 79. **d** 81 **p** 82. C Moreton *Ches* 81-84; Chapl Bedf Coll of HE *St Alb* 84-93; R Banchory *Ab* from 93; R Kincardine O'Neil from 93. *The Rectory, High Street, Banchory, Kincardineshire AB31 3TB* Tel (01330) 822783

ROYDS, John Caress. b 20. Qu Coll Cam BA47 MA52. **d** 74 **p** 75. C Kettering St Andr *Pet* 74-76; P-in-c Loddington w Cransley 76; R 76-81; Dir of Educn 76-81; V Northampton St Jas 81-85; CMS 85-86; Pakistan 85-86; rtd 87. *16B Donaldson Road, Salisbury SP1 3AD* Tel (01722) 332293

ROYLANCE, Mrs Margaret. b 47. CertEd68. Cant Sch of Min 92. **d** 96. NSM Tenterden St Mildred w Smallhythe *Cant* from 96; Chapl Ch Ch High Sch Ashford from 96. *5 Southgate Road, Tenterden, Kent TN30 7BS* Tel (01580) 762332

ROYLE, Antony Kevan. b 50. FIA76 Lon Univ BSc71. Trin Coll Bris 76. **d** 79 **p** 80. C Chell *Lich* 79-82; C Leyland St Andr *Blackb* 82-86; V Blackb Sav 86-95; Chapl Blackb R Infirmary & Park Lee Hosp 86-95; Chapl E Lancs Hospice 86-95; TR Walton H Trin *Ox* from 95. *The Rectory, 42 Redwood Drive, Walton Road, Aylesbury, Bucks HP21 7TN* Tel (01296) 394834

ROYLE, Michael Arthur. b 38. Univ of Wales (Ban) BSc61 Lon Univ DipTh63. St Jo Coll Nottm 81. **d** 82 **p** 83. C Boulton *Derby* 82-85; C Belper 85-87; P-in-c Smalley 87-95; P-in-c Morley 87-95; RD Heanor 89-94; V Charlesworth and Dinting Vale from 95. *The Vicarage, Marple Road, Charlesworth, Broadbottom, Hyde, Cheshire SK14 6DA* Tel (01457) 852440 or 868740

ROYLE, Canon Peter Sydney George. b 34. K Coll Lon BD57 AKC57. **d** 58 **p** 59. C St Helier *S'wark* 58-62; Australia 62-68; P-in-c Sydenham St Phil *S'wark* 69-72; V Leigh Park *Portsm* 72-85; RD Havant 77-82; V S w N Hayling 85-96; V S Hayling 96-97; Hon Can Portsm Cathl 95-97; rtd 97. *Fairbank, 74 Newton Road, Bishopsteignton, Devon TQ14 9PP* Tel (01626) 779252

ROYLE, Canon Roger Michael. b 39. AKC61 Lambeth Hon MA90. **d** 62 **p** 63. C Portsea St Mary *Portsm* 62-65; C St Helier *S'wark* 65-68; Succ S'wark Cathl 68-71; Warden Eton Coll Dorney Par Project *Ox* 71-74; Conduct Eton Coll 74-79; Lic to Offic *S'wark* 79-90; Chapl Ld Mayor Treloar Coll Alton 90-92; Hon C Froyle and Holybourne *Win* 90-92; Hon Can and Chapl S'wark Cathl *S'wark* from 93. *c/o Southwark Cathedral, Montague Close, London SE1 9DA* Tel 0171-407 3708 Fax 430 6085

ROYLE, Canon Stanley Michael. b 43. K Coll Lon BD69 AKC69 Man Univ MA75. St Aug Coll Cant 71. **d** 72 **p** 73. C Timperley *Ches* 72-76; Perm to Offic 76-81; R Milton Abbas, Hilton w Cheselbourne etc *Sarum* 81-86; Dir of Ords from 86; Adv on Continuing Minl Educn from 86; Can and Preb Sarum Cathl from 89. *Three Firs, Blandford Road, Sturminster Marshall, Wimborne, Dorset BH21 4AF* Tel (01258) 857326

ROYSTON-BALL, Peter. b 38. St Mich Coll Llan 61. **d** 65 **p** 66. C Dartford St Alb *Roch* 65-67; C Chislehurst Annunciation 67-69; C St Marylebone Ch Ch w St Paul *Lon* 69-75; Hon C New Windsor *Ox* 75-78; Perm to Offic *S'wark* 75-88; C Leic St Eliz Nether Hall *Leic* 88-94; V Belvedere St Aug *Roch* from 94. *The Vicarage, St Augustine's Road, Belvedere, Kent DA17 5HH* Tel 0181-311 6307

RUCK, John. b 47. Bris Univ BSc68. Selly Oak Coll DipRE87 All Nations Chr Coll 77. **d** 80 **p** 83. Indonesia 80-86 and 87-91; Perm to Offic *Birm* 86-87 and from 91. *94 Gristhorpe Road, Birmingham B29 7SL* Tel 0121-472 7460

RUDD, Canon Charles Robert Jordeson. b 34. TCD BA56 MA65 BD65. **d** 57 **p** 58. C Lurgan Redeemer *D & D* 57-61; C Lisburn Ch Ch Cathl *Conn* 61-62; C Willowfield *D & D* 62-66; I Drumgooland w Kilcoo 66-75; I Moira 75-95; Can Belf Cathl 90-95; I Magherally w Annaclone *D & D* from 95. *Magherally Rectory, 46 Kilmacrew Road, Banbridge, Co Down BT32 4EP* Tel (01820) 623655

RUDD, Colin Richard. b 41. AKC64. **d** 65 **p** 66. C N Stoneham *Win* 65-70; V Rotherwick, Hook and Greywell 70-74; R Hook w Greywell 74-78; Toc H 78-89; Lic to Offic *Ox* 83-89; V Buckland from 89; V Littleworth from 89; R Pusey from 89; RD Vale of White Horse from 96. *The Vicarage, Buckland, Faringdon, Oxon SN7 8QN* Tel (01367) 87618

RUDD, Canon Julian Douglas Raymond. b 19. Leeds Univ BA40. Coll of Resurr Mirfield 40. **d** 42 **p** 43. C Bury St Edmunds St Jo *St E* 42-46; C Holborn St Alb w Saffron Hill St Pet *Lon* 46-49; V Bournemouth St Fran *Win* 49-60; RD Bournemouth 56-60; R Old Alresford 60-70; RD Alresford 60-70; Hon Can Win Cathl 62-70; V Warwick St Mary *Cov* 70-76; V Warwick St Mary w St Nic 76-83; Hon Can Cov Cathl 76-84; TR Warwick 83-84; RD Warwick 77-79; rtd 84. *East Close, Church Walk, Penny Street, Sturminster Newton, Dorset DT10 1DF* Tel (01258) 73283

RUDD, Robert Arthur (Bob). b 33. ALCD60. **d** 60 **p** 61. C Blackb Sav *Blackb* 60-63; C Huyton St Geo *Liv* 63-65; V Bickershaw 65-72; Asst Chapl HM Pris Liv 72-73; Chapl HM Pris Birm 73-78; Chapl HM Pris Parkhurst 78-86; Chapl HM Pris Camp Hill 86-92; Chapl St Mary's Hosp Newport 92-95; rtd 95. *The Elms, 13 Horsebridge Hill, Newport, Isle of Wight PO30 5TJ* Tel (01983) 524415

RUDDLE, Canon Donald Arthur (Don). b 31. Linc Th Coll 64. **d** 66 **p** 67. C Kettering SS Pet and Paul *Pet* 66-70; V Earlham St Anne *Nor* 70-79; V E Malling *Roch* 79-95; RD Malling 84-93; Hon Can Roch Cathl 88-95; Chapl Boulogne w Calais *Eur* 95-97; rtd 97. *16 rue du Calvaire, Enquine-les-Mines, 62145 Pas de Calais, France* Tel France (33) 21 93 69 46

RUDDOCK, Brian John. b 45. Dur Univ BA66 Nottm Univ MEd91. Westcott Ho Cam 67. **d** 69 **p** 70. C Ross *Heref* 69-72; C Kettering SS Pet and Paul *Pet* 72-75; P-in-c Colchester St Steph *Chelmsf* 75-77; TR Colchester St Leon, St Mary Magd and St Steph 77-84; R March St Pet *Ely* 84-89; R March St Mary

84-89; RD March 87-89; Dioc Unemployment Officer *Sheff* 89-94. *36 Sandygate, Wath-upon-Dearne, Rotherham, S Yorkshire S63 7LW* Tel (01709) 873254 or 698583 Fax 698016

RUDDOCK, Canon Charles Cecil. b 28. TCD DBS. TCD Div Sch. **d** 57 **p** 58. C Belfast St Mary *Conn* 57-59; C Carnmoney 59-61; C Belfast St Aid 61-63; I Kiltegan w Rathvilly *C & O* 63-69; C Newtownards *D & D* 69-72; Australia 72-83; I Mallow Union *C, C & R* 83-89; I Fenagh w Myshall, Aghade and Ardoyne *C & O* 89-95; Preb Ossory and Leighlin Cathls 92-95; rtd 95; Perm to Offic *Glouc* from 95. *2 Osborne Terrace, London Road, Thrupp, Stroud, Glos GL5 2BJ* Tel (01453) 731697

RUDDOCK, Edgar Chapman. b 48. St Jo Coll Dur BA70 DipTh73 MA76. **d** 74 **p** 75. C Birm St Geo *Birm* 74-78; R 78-83; Swaziland 83-91; TR Stoke-upon-Trent *Lich* from 91. *The Rectory, St Peter's Close, Stoke-on-Trent ST4 1LP* Tel (01782) 45287

RUDDOCK, Kenneth Edward. b 30. TCD BA52 QUB MTh79. CITC 53 Div Test. **d** 53 **p** 54. C Ballymena *Conn* 53-56; C Belfast St Thos 56-60; I Tomregan w Drumlane *K, E & A* 60-68; I Belfast St Luke *Conn* 68-80; Miss to Seamen 80-96; I Whitehead w Islandmagee *Conn* 80-96; Can Lisburn Cathl 90-96; RD Carrickfergus 90-94; Dioc Info Officer from 90; Chan Conn Cathl from 96. *24 Fourtowns Manor, Ahoghill, Ballymena, Co Antrim BT42 1RS* Tel (01266) 878966

RUDDOCK, Leonard William. b 58. CITC 91. **d** 94 **p** 95. NSM Roscrea w Kyle, Bourney and Corbally *L & K* from 94. *Short Corville, Roscrea, Co Tipperary, Irish Republic* Tel Roscrea (505) 22034

RUDDOCK, Canon Norman Trevor. b 35. TCD BA57 MA60 HDipEd62. TCD Div Sch 58. **d** 58 **p** 59. C Belfast St Steph *Conn* 58-60; C Dublin Ch Ch Leeson Park *D & G* 60-63; Perm to Offic 63-73; USA 70-72; I Killanne *C & O* 73-81; I Castlepollard and Oldcastle w Loughcrew etc *M & K* 84-93; Can Meath 92-93; I Wexford w Ardcolm and Killurin *C & O* from 93; Treas Ferns Cathl from 96. *The Rectory, Park, Wexford, Irish Republic* Tel Wexford (53) 43013

RUDDOCK, Canon Reginald Bruce. b 55. AGSM77. Chich Th Coll. **d** 83 **p** 84. C Felpham w Middleton *Chich* 83-86; C Portsea St Mary *Portsm* 86-88; P-in-c Barnes St Mich *S'wark* 88-95; Dir Angl Cen Rome from 95; Hon Can American Cathl Paris from 96. *The Anglican Centre, Palazzo Doria, via del Corso 303, 00186 Rome, Italy* Tel Rome (6) 678-0302 Fax 678-0675

RUDDY, Canon Denys Henry. b 22. Jes Coll Ox BA48 MA53. Linc Th Coll 48. **d** 50 **p** 51. C Petersfield w Sheet *Portsm* 50-53; C Gt Grimsby St Jas *Linc* 53-58; R Longworth and Hinton Waldrist *Ox* 58-77; RD Vale of White Horse 68-75; Warden of Readers 70-87; Chapl Abingdon St Nic 77-87; Hon Can Ch Ch 79-87; RD Abingdon 79-80; rtd 87; Perm to Offic *Ox* from 87; Perm to Offic *Pet* from 87. *32 Coberley Close, Downhead Park, Milton Keynes MK15 9BJ* Tel (01908) 604719

RUDIGER, David John. b 42. MIMgt91. Ox Min Course CBTS94. **d** 94 **p** 95. NSM Woughton *Ox* from 94. *32 Forest Rise, Eaglestone, Milton Keynes MK6 5EU* Tel (01908) 679691

RUDKIN, Simon David. b 51. Bradf Univ BA74 K Coll Lon BD77 AKC77. Coll of Resurr Mirfield 77. **d** 78 **p** 79. C Flixton St Mich *Man* 78-81; C Atherton 81-84; V Lever Bridge 84-91; P-in-c Pennington w Lindal and Marton *Carl* 91-96; P-in-c Pennington and Lindal w Marton and Bardsea from 96. *The Vicarage, Main Road, Swarthmoor, Ulverston, Cumbria LA12 0SE* Tel (01229) 583174

RUDLAND, Patrick Ivor. b 20. ACP62 Lon Univ CertEd62. Tyndale Hall Bris 56. **d** 59 **p** 60. C Tunbridge Wells St Jas *Roch* 59-62; Lic to Offic 62-66; Hon C Sevenoaks St Nic 66-69; Hon C Tonbridge SS Pet and Paul 69-85; Hon C Shipbourne 85-88; Perm to Offic from 88. *Flat 4, 12 Dry Hill Road, Tonbridge, Kent TN9 1LX* Tel (01732) 351694

RUDMAN, David Walter Thomas. b 48. Lon Univ DipTh70 BD72. Oak Hill Th Coll 68. **d** 72 **p** 73. C Plymouth St Jude *Ex* 72-75; C Radipole *Sarum* 76-77; Warden of St Geo Ho Braunton from 77; R Georgeham *Ex* from 88; Dioc Adv in Adult Tr from 97. *The Rectory, Newberry Road, Georgeham, Braunton, Devon EX33 1JS* Tel (01271) 890809

RUDMAN, Thomas Peter William. b 22. Oak Hill Th Coll 60. **d** 62 **p** 63. C St Paul's Cray St Barn CD *Roch* 62-65; C Morden *S'wark* 65-67; V Lowestoft Ch Ch *Nor* 67-73; V Stapenhill w Cauldwell *Derby* 73-81; V Sutton le Marsh *Linc* 81-87; RD Calcewaithe and Candleshoe 85-87; rtd 87; Perm to Offic *Win* 87-96; Perm to Offic *Ex* from 96. *28 Gracey Court, Woodland Road, Broadclyst, Exeter EX5 3LP* Tel (01392) 466436

RUEHORN, Eric Arthur. b 33. St Aid Birkenhead 58. **d** 61 **p** 62. C Harpurhey Ch Ch *Man* 61-65; V Roughtown 65-74; V Hawkshaw Lane from 74. *St Mary's Vicarage, Bolton Road, Hawkshaw, Bury, Lancs BL8 4JN* Tel (01204) 882955

RUFF, Brian Chisholm. b 36. FCA70 Lon Univ BD66. Oak Hill Th Coll 63. **d** 67 **p** 68. C Cheadle *Ches* 67-71; Educn and Youth Sec CPAS 72-76; V New Milverton *Cov* 76-90; Min Westbourne Ch Ch CD *Win* from 90. *43 Branksome Dene Road, Bournemouth BH4 8JW* Tel (01202) 762164

RUFF, Michael Ronald. b 49. K Coll Lon BD72 AKC72. St Aug Coll Cant 72. **d** 73 **p** 74. C Old Shoreham *Chich* 73-76; Chapl Ellesmere Coll Shropshire 77-81; Chapl Grenville Coll Bideford 81-87; Chapl Stamford Sch from 87; Perm to Offic *Linc* from 87. *12 Redcot Gardens, Stamford, Lincs PE9 1DL* Tel (01780) 66567

RUFFLE, Preb John Leslie. b 43. ALCD66. **d** 66 **p** 67. C Eastwood *S'well* 66-70; C Keynsham w Queen Charlton *B & W* 70-75; P-in-c Weston-super-Mare Em 75; TV Weston-super-Mare Cen Par 75-84; V Yatton Moor 84-91; TR from 91; Preb Wells Cathl from 97. *The Rectory, 1 Well Lane, Yatton, Bristol BS19 4HT* Tel (01934) 832184

RUFFLE, Leslie Norman. b 12. Tyndale Hall Bris 49. **d** 50 **p** 51. C Eastwood *S'well* 50-51; C Bucknall and Bagnall *Lich* 51-52; R Collyhurst *Man* 52-54; V Sneinton St Chris *S'well* 54-59; R Heanton Punchardon *Ex* 59-70; R Chawleigh w Cheldon 70-77; R Eggesford 70-77; rtd 77; Perm to Offic *Ex* from 86. *1 Eden Croft, Kenilworth, Warks CV8 2BG*

RUFFLE, Peter Cousins. b 19. Lon Univ BD42. ALCD42. **d** 42 **p** 43. C Highbury Ch Ch *Lon* 42-46; India 46-52; Youth Adv CMS 52-57; Hon C Bromley St Jo *Roch* 54-57; V Walton Breck *Liv* 57-60; V Aigburth 60-66; Prin CA Wilson Carlile Coll of Evang 66-74; Can Res Blackb Cathl *Blackb* 74-78; V Meole Brace *Lich* 78-85; rtd 85; Perm to Offic *Win* from 85; Perm to Offic *Portsm* from 85. *84 Queen's Crescent, Stubbington, Fareham, Hants PO14 2QQ* Tel (01329) 314870

RUFLI, Alan John. b 63. TCD BA89. **d** 91 **p** 92. C Donaghcloney w Waringstown *D & D* 91-94; C Knock 94-95; I Rathcoole *Conn* from 95. *Rathcoole Rectory, 3 Strathmore Park North, Belfast BT15 5HQ* Tel (01232) 370471 or 853251 Mobile 01802-182486 E-mail rufrev@aol.com

RUGG, Andrew Philip. b 47. Kent Univ BA82. Sarum & Wells Th Coll 83. **d** 85 **p** 86. C Harlesden All So *Lon* 85-90; TV Benwell Team *Newc* from 90. *56 Dunholme Road, Newcastle upon Tyne NE4 6XE* Tel 0191-273 5356

✠**RUMALSHAH, The Rt Revd Munawar Kenneth (Mano).** b 41. Punjab Univ BSc60 Serampore Coll BD65 Karachi Univ MA68 Cam Univ PGCE86. Bp's Coll Calcutta DipTh65. **d** 65 **p** 66 **c** 94. Pakistan 65-69 and from 89; C H Trin Cathl Karachi 65-69; C Roundhay St Edm *Ripon* 70-73; Area Sec (Dios Ripon and York) CMS 73-78; Asst Home Sec York Prov 73-78; Educn Sec BCC 78-81; P-in-c Southall St Geo *Lon* 81-88; USPG from 89; Bp Peshawar from 94. *Diocesan Centre, 1 Sir Syed Road, Peshawar 25000, Pakistan* Tel Peshawar (521) 276519 Fax 277499

RUMBALL, Preb Frank Thomas. b 43. Sarum & Wells Th Coll 72. **d** 74 **p** 75. C Bromyard *Heref* 74-78; TV Ewyas Harold w Dulas 78-79; TV Ewyas Harold w Dulas, Kenderchurch etc 79-81; C Minsterley 81-82; P-in-c Eye, Croft w Yarpole and Lucton 82-91; R Condover w Frodesley, Acton Burnell etc from 91; Preb Heref Cathl from 97. *The Vicarage, Condover, Shrewsbury SY5 7AA* Tel (01743) 872251

RUMBALL, Dr William Michael. b 41. Surrey Univ BSc63 Birm Univ PhD66 BA75 MIM66 MINucE73. Wycliffe Hall Ox 78. **d** 80 **p** 81. C S Molton, Nymet St George, High Bray etc *Ex* 80-83; V S Hetton w Haswell *Dur* 83-90; V S Wingfield and Wessington *Derby* from 90. *The Vicarage, South Wingfield, Alfreton, Derbyshire DE55 7LJ* Tel (01773) 832484

RUMBLE, Alison Merle. *See* PRINCE, Mrs Alison Merle

RUMBOLD, Bernard John. b 43. **d** 73 **p** 75. Papua New Guinea 73-76; C Gt Burstead *Chelmsf* 76-77; Chapl RAF 77-93; Chapl HM Pris Featherstone 93-95; C Wordsley *Worc* 95-96; TV from 96; Chapl Dudley Gp of Hosps NHS Trust from 96. *St Paul's House, Hawbush Road, Brierley Hill, W Midlands DY5 3NL*

RUMBOLD, Graham Charles. b 44. Open Univ BA79. S Dios Minl Tr Scheme 76. **d** 79 **p** 80. NSM Widley w Wymering *Portsm* 79-82; Chapl Cynthia Spencer Unit Manfield Hosp from 82; Lic to Offic *Pet* from 82; NSM Weston Favell from 93. *3 Calstock Close, Northampton NN3 3BA* Tel (01604) 27389

RUMENS, Canon John Henry. b 21. AKC49. **d** 50 **p** 51. C Wareham w Arne *Sarum* 50-54; V Alderholt 54-59; R Salisbury St Edm 59-72; RD Salisbury 69-72; Can and Preb Sarum Cathl 72-85; R Trowbridge H Trin 72-79; P-in-c Sturminster Marshall 79-83; V 83-85; rtd 85. *20 Constable Way, Salisbury SP2 8LN* Tel (01722) 334716

RUMENS, Ms Katharine Mary. b 53. UEA BEd76. Westcott Ho Cam 90. **d** 92 **p** 94. Par Dn E Ham w Upton Park St Alb *Chelmsf* 92-94; C 94-95; C Waterloo St Jo w St Andr *S'wark* from 95. *1 Cranfield Row, Gerridge Street, London SE1 7QN* Tel 0171-928 2259

RUMING, Canon Gordon William. b 27. Kelham Th Coll 45. **d** 52 **p** 53. C Baildon *Bradf* 52-55; C Prestbury *Glouc* 55-60; C Penzance St Mary *Truro* 60-61; R Calstock 61-92; Hon Can Truro Cathl 79-92; RD E Wivelshire 85-91; rtd 92; Perm to Offic *Truro* from 92. *3 Derry Avenue, Plymouth PL4 6BH* Tel (01752) 661986

RUMSEY, Andrew Paul. b 68. Reading Univ BA89. Ridley Hall Cam 94. **d** 97. C Harrow Trin St Mich *Lon* from 97. *2 Earls Crescent, Harrow, Middx HA1 1XN* Tel 0181-863 2803

RUMSEY, Ian Mark. b 58. Van Mildert Coll Dur BSc79 St Jo Coll Dur BA89. Cranmer Hall Dur 87. **d** 90 **p** 91. C Dalston *Carl* 90-94; C Wreay 92-94; TV Cockermouth w Embleton and Wythop from 94. *The Vicarage, 14 Harrot Hill, Cockermouth, Cumbria CA13 0BL* Tel (01900) 824383

RUMSEY, Thomas Philip. b 14. Selw Coll Cam BA37 MA41. St Aug Coll Cant 33. **d** 38 **p** 39. C Camberwell St Geo *S'wark* 38-40; SPG Miss Dio Dornakal (India) 40-50; C Strood St Nic *Roch* 50-52; V Stratfield Mortimer *Ox* 52-70; V Skelsmergh w Selside and Longsleddale *Carl* 70-79; rtd 79; Perm to Offic *Carl* from 79. *Heversham House, Heversham, Milnthorpe, Cumbria LA7 7ER* Tel (015395) 63634

✠**RUNCIE of Cuddesdon, The Rt Revd and Rt Hon Lord (Robert Alexander Kennedy).** b 21. MC45 PC80. BNC Ox BA48 MA48 Hon DD80 Cam Univ Hon DD81 Univ of the South (USA) Hon DD81 Keele Univ Hon DLitt81 Liv Univ Hon DLitt83 Herts Univ Hon DLitt92 FKC81. W Indies United Th Coll Hon DCL84 Trin Coll Toronto Hon DD86 Westcott Ho Cam 48. **d** 50 **p** 51 **c** 70. C Gosforth All SS *Newc* 50-52; Chapl Westcott Ho Cam 53-54; Vice-Prin 54-56; Dean Trin Hall Cam 56-60; V Cuddesdon *Ox* 60-70; Prin Cuddesdon Coll 60-70; Can and Preb Linc Cathl *Linc* 69-70; Bp St Alb 70-80; Abp Cant 80-91; Hon Fell BNC Ox from 78; rtd 91; Asst Bp St Alb from 91. *26A Jennings Road, St Albans, Herts AL1 4PD* Tel (01727) 848021

RUNCORN, David Charles. b 54. BA77 Ox Poly DipPsych88. St Jo Coll Nottm 77. **d** 79 **p** 80. C Wealdstone H Trin *Lon* 79-82; Chapl Lee Abbey 82-89; C Ealing St Steph Castle Hill *Lon* 89-90; V 90-96; Dir Past and Evang Studies Trin Coll Bris from 96. *15 Cranleigh Gardens, Bristol BS9 1HD* Tel 0117-968 2028 or 968 2803

RUNCORN, Canon Dennis Brookes. b 22. Ch Coll Cam BA47 MA52. Ridley Hall Cam 47. **d** 49 **p** 50. C Ashtead *Guildf* 49-53; Hong Kong 54-62; Prin CMS Tr Coll Chislehurst 62-67; V Shortlands *Roch* 67-80; RD Beckenham 73-80; Hon Can Roch Cathl 78-87; V Shorne 80-87; rtd 87; Perm to Offic *Derby* from 87. *14 Hollowood Avenue, Littleover, Derby DE23 6JD* Tel (01332) 765859

RUNDLE, Mrs Beryl Rosemary. b 28. Bris Univ BA49 CertEd50. S Dios Minl Tr Scheme 83. **dss** 86 **d** 87. Tangmere *Chich* 86-87; Hon Par Dn 87-92; Boxgrove 86-87; Hon Par Dn 87-92; Hon Par Dn Eastbourne St Sav and St Pet from 92. *2 College Court, Spencer Road, Eastbourne, E Sussex BN21 4PE* Tel (01323) 417433

RUNDLE, Nicholas John. b 59. Southn Univ BA80. St Steph Ho Ox. **d** 84 **p** 85. C E Preston w Kingston *Chich* 84-87; Chapl RAF 87-91; Australia from 91. *7 Charles Sturt Avenue, Grange, S Australia 5022* Tel Adelaide (8) 356 8119

RUNDLE, Penelope Anne. b 36. St Hugh's Coll Ox MA59 Lon Univ DAA64. S Dios Minl Tr Scheme 85. **d** 88 **p** 94. Hon Par Dn Mere w W Knoyle and Maiden Bradley *Sarum* 88-91; Hon Par Dn Upper Stour 91-94; Hon C from 94. *2 The Common, Kilmington, Warminster, Wilts BA12 6QY* Tel (01985) 844610

RUPP, Ernest Walter. b 25. Westmr Coll Lon CertEd55. St Jo Coll Nottm 84. **d** 85 **p** 86. NSM Leic Ascension *Leic* 85-89; Chapl Glenfield Hosp Leic 86-89; R Barkestone w Plungar, Redmile and Stathern *Leic* 89-94; rtd 94; Perm to Offic *Leic* from 94. *4 Laura Davies Close, Melton Mowbray, Leics LE13 1EG* Tel (01664) 500748

RUSCHMEYER, Henry Cassell. b 44. Union Coll NY BA66 Bank St Coll of Ed NY MEd73 NY Univ MA88. Gen Th Sem (NY) MD78. **d** 78 **p** 79. USA 78-89; NSM Wilton Place St Paul *Lon* 89-96. *2115 Brookhaven Drive, Sarasota, Florida, 34239 USA*

RUSCOE, John. b 12. Man Univ BA35. Lich Th Coll 35. **d** 37 **p** 38. C Weaste *Man* 37; C Wardleworth St Mary 37-39; P-in-c 39-42; CF 42-47; V Penwerris *Truro* 47-57; R Redruth 57-70; R Mawnan 70-84; rtd 84; Perm to Offic *Truro* from 84. *34 Tregenver Road, Falmouth, Cornwall TR11 2QW* Tel (01326) 315300

RUSCOE, Canon John Ernest. b 32. Dur Univ BA57. Qu Coll Birm 57. **d** 59 **p** 60. C Jarrow St Paul *Dur* 59-63; C Whitburn 63-65; V S Hylton from 65; Hon Can Dur Cathl from 85. *The Vicarage, South Hylton, Sunderland SR4 0QB* Tel 0191-534 2325

RUSHER, James Victor Francis. b 28. RMA. Ridley Hall Cam 58. **d** 60 **p** 61. C Kensington St Helen w H Trin *Lon* 60-63; C Edgbaston St Bart *Birm* 63-66; V Summerfield 66-71; V Knowle 71-82; Perm to Offic 82-93; Chapl Parkway Hosp Solihull 85-93; rtd 93. *4 Froxmere Close, Solihull, W Midlands B91 3XG* Tel 0121-705 4514

RUSHFORD, Harold Tilney. b 08. Qu Coll Birm 55. **d** 56 **p** 57. C Monkwearmouth All SS *Dur* 56-59; V Dawdon 59-83; rtd 84. *Dalden, 18 Windsor Drive, Houghton le Spring, Tyne & Wear DH5 8JS* Tel 0191-584 9682

RUSHFORTH, Colin Stephen. b 53. Chich Th Coll 74. **d** 77 **p** 78. C Moulsecoomb *Chich* 77-79; C Rumboldswyke 79-81; C Whyke w Rumboldswhyke and Portfield 81-82; V Friskney *Linc* 82-84; P-in-c Thorpe St Peter 82-84; TV Leic H Spirit *Leic* 84-87; Chapl Leic R Infirmary 87-94; Chapl Leic R Infirmary NHS Trust from 94. *Leicester Royal Infirmary, Infirmary Square, Leicester LE1 5WW* Tel 0116-254 1414 or 258 5487

RUSHFORTH, Richard Hamblin. b 40. Keble Coll Ox BA62 MA71. Chich Th Coll 62. **d** 64 **p** 65. C St Leonards Ch Ch *Chich* 64-79; Org Sec Fellowship of St Nic 79-81; V Portslade St Nic and St Andr from 81; Min Portslade Gd Shep CD 88-89. *The Vicarage, South Street, Portslade, Brighton BN41 2LE* Tel (01273) 418090

RUSHTON, James David. b 39. Dur Univ BA61. Cranmer Hall Dur DipTh64. **d** 64 **p** 65. C Upper Armley *Ripon* 64-67; C Blackpool Ch Ch *Blackb* 67-70; V Preston St Cuth 70-79; V Denton Holme *Carl* 79-96; P-in-c Preston All SS *Blackb* from 96. *All Saints' Vicarage, 94 Watling Street Road, Fulwood, Preston PR2 4BP* Tel (01772) 700672

RUSHTON, Ms Janet Maureen (Jan). b 46. Keele Univ BA68 Leic Univ PGCE69. Wycliffe Hall Ox BTh94. **d** 94 **p** 95. C Harrow St Mary *Lon* from 94. *The Flat, 6 Crown Street, Harrow, Middx HA2 0HR* Tel 0181-864 7050

RUSHTON, Malcolm Leslie. b 47. Bris Univ BSc69 Birm Univ PhD72 Fitzw Coll Cam BA74. Ridley Hall Cam 72. **d** 75 **p** 76. C Cullompton *Ex* 75-79; Chapl Univ Coll *Lon* 79-87; Chapl R Veterinary Coll Lon 87-90; Chapl R Free Medical Sch 87-90. *191A Kentish Town Road, London NW5 2AE* Tel 0171-482 4077

RUSHTON, Philip William. b 38. Open Univ BA87. Clifton Th Coll 62. **d** 65 **p** 66. C Brixton St Paul *S'wark* 65-67; C Aldridge *Lich* 67-69; C Bushbury 69-71; Chapl Nat Nautical Sch Portishead 71-72; Chapl RAF 72-79; P-in-c Bolton on Swale *Ripon* 79-87; P-in-c The Cowtons 80-82; V 82-89; CF (TA) from 88; R Litcham, Kempston, Lexham, Mileham, Beeston etc *Nor* 89-95; P-in-c Tittleshall w Godwick 93-95; R Litcham w Kempston, E and W Lexham, Mileham etc 95-96; P-in-c Scole, Brockdish, Billingford, Thorpe Abbots etc from 96. *The Rectory, Scole, Diss, Norfolk IP21 4DY* Tel (01379) 740250

RUSHTON, Mrs Susan Elizabeth. b 44. Univ of Wales (Cardiff) BA65. Bris Sch of Min 83. **dss** 86 **d** 87 **p** 94. Westbury-on-Trym H Trin *Bris* 86-91; Hon Par Dn 87-91; C Wotton St Mary *Glouc* 91-94; Chapl United Bris Healthcare NHS Trust from 94; P-in-c Frampton Cotterell *Bris* from 94. *The Rectory, Rectory Road, Frampton Cotterell, Bristol BS17 2BP* Tel (01454) 772112

RUSHTON, Mrs Valerie Elizabeth Wendy. b 40. Birm Univ BSocSc62 DPS87. WMMTC 86. **d** 89 **p** 94. C Nuneaton St Nic *Cov* 89-93; C Stockingford 93-96; TV Watling Valley *Ox* from 96. *The Rectory, Pitchers Lane, Loughton, Milton Keynes MK5 8AU* Tel (01908) 666253

RUSK, Canon Frederick John. b 28. QUB BA50. **d** 53 **p** 54. C Ballymoney *Conn* 53-56; C Belfast St Nic 56-59; I Broomhedge 59-65; RE Insp 64-66; I Belfast St Simon 65-78; I Ballymena w Ballyclug 78-88; I Belfast St Nic from 88; Preb Conn Cathl 84-86; Treas 86-90; Prec 90; Chan Conn Cathl from 90; Dean Conn from 95. *15 Harberton Park, Belfast BT9 6TW* Tel (01232) 667753

RUSK, Michael Frederick. b 58. Cam Univ BA MA. Westcott Ho Cam 81. **d** 84 **p** 85. C Altrincham St Geo *Ches* 84-87; Chapl Collingwood and Grey Coll *Dur* 87-90; C-in-c Neville's Cross St Jo CD from 90. *St John's Vicarage, The Avenue, Durham DH1 4DX* Tel 0191-384 4260

RUSS, Timothy John (Tim). b 41. AKC64. Sarum Th Coll 66. **d** 66 **p** 67. C Walthamstow St Pet *Chelmsf* 66-70; C Epping St Jo 70-73; C Stepney St Dunstan and All SS *Lon* 73-75; Youth Officer 75-79; Tutor YMCA Nat Coll Walthamstow 79-84; Hon C St Botolph Aldgate w H Trin Minories *Lon* 82-89; Selection Sec ACCM 84-89; Dir St Marylebone Healing and Counselling Cen 89-92; Gen Sec Inst of Religion and Medicine 89-92; Hon C Hoxton St Anne w St Columba *Lon* 90-92; P-in-c St Dennis *Truro* from 92; Par Development Adv from 92. *The Rectory, Carne Hill, St Dennis, St Austell, Cornwall PL26 8AZ* Tel (01726) 822317

RUSSELL, Adrian Camper. b 45. Chich Th Coll 79. **d** 81 **p** 82. C Marton *Blackb* 81-84; C Haslemere *Guildf* 84-85; V Hartlepool H Trin *Dur* 85-89; P-in-c Cornforth 89-94; R Auchterarder *St And* from 94; R Muthill from 94. *St Kessog's Rectory, High Street, Auchterarder, Perthshire PH3 1AD* Tel (01764) 662525 Fax as telephone

✠**RUSSELL, The Rt Revd Anthony John.** b 43. St Chad's Coll Dur BA65 Trin Coll Ox DPhil71. Cuddesdon Coll 65. **d** 70 **p** 71 **c** 88. C Hilborough w Bodney *Nor* 70-73; P-in-c Preston-on-Stour w Whitchurch *Cov* 73-76; P-in-c Atherstone on Stour 73-76; V Preston on Stour and Whitchurch w Atherstone 77-88; Can Th Cov Cathl 77-88; Chapl Arthur Rank Cen 73-82; Dir 83-88; Chapl to The Queen 83-88; Area Bp Dorchester *Ox* from 88. *Holmby House, Sibford Ferris, Banbury, Oxon OX15 5RG*

RUSSELL, Brian Kenneth. b 50. Trin Hall Cam BA73 MA76 Birm Univ MA77 PhD83. Cuddesdon Coll 74. **d** 76 **p** 77. C Redhill St Matt *S'wark* 76-79; Dir of Studies NE Ord Course 79-83; P-in-c Merrington *Dur* 79-83; Dir of Studies and Lect Linc Th Coll 83-86; Perm to Offic *S'wark* 86-93; Selection Sec and Sec Cttee for Th Educn ACCM 86-91; Selection Sec ABM 91-93; Bp's Dir for Min *Birm* from 93. *43 Cartland Road, Birmingham B30 2SD* Tel 0121-444 7641 or 427 5141 Fax 428 1114

RUSSELL, Brian Robert. b 61. QUB BA TCD DipTh85. **d** 85 **p** 86. C Dublin Drumcondra w N Strand *D & G* 85-87; C Carrickfergus *Conn* 87-90; I Kilmegan w Maghera *D & D* 90-96; I Bailieborough w Knockbride, Shercock and Mullagh *K, E & A* from 96. *The Rectory, Bailieborough, Co Cavan, Irish Republic* Tel Dundalk (42) 65436

RUSSELL, Christopher Ian. b 68. St Jo Coll Dur BA91. Ridley Hall Cam 93. **d** 96 **p** 97. C Deptford St Jo w H Trin *S'wark* from 96. *3 Orchard Hill, London SE13 7QZ* Tel 0181-694 8400

RUSSELL, David John. b 57. Sarum & Wells Th Coll BTh94. **d** 94 **p** 95. C Glouc St Geo w Whaddon *Glouc* from 94. *3 Rylands, Gloucester GL4 0QA* Tel (01452) 500716

RUSSELL, David Robert. b 43. Brasted Th Coll 66 Sarum Th Coll 68. **d** 70 **p** 71. C Leintwardine *Heref* 70-73; C Bridgnorth w Tasley 73-75; Australia from 75. *239 Orrong Road, Carlisle, W Australia 6101* Tel Adelaide (8) 9470 5861

RUSSELL, Canon Derek John. b 30. St Pet Hall Ox BA54 MA58. Qu Coll Birm 54. **d** 56 **p** 57. C Boxley *Cant* 56-59; C Whitstable All SS 59-63; Chapl HM Pris Wormwood Scrubs 63-65 and 71-89; Chapl HM Pris Stafford 65-69; Pentonville 70; SE Regional Chapl 74-81; Chapl HM Rem Cen Latchmere Ho 74-77; Asst Chapl Gen of Pris 81-83; Dep 83-90; Hon Can Cant Cathl *Cant* 86-90; rtd 90; Perm to Offic *Cant* from 90. *25 Pier Avenue, Whitstable, Kent CT5 2HQ* Tel (01227) 276654

RUSSELL, Ms Elizabeth Marilyn Vivia (Liz). b 50. LRAM70 GRSM72. Westcott Ho Cam 95. **d** 97. C Alton St Lawr *Win* from 97. *13 Walnut Close, Alton, Hants GU34 2BA* Tel (01420) 542288

RUSSELL, Eric. b 19. Dur Univ LTh42 BA48 MA53 Man Univ BD52 Nottm Univ MPhil87. Oak Hill Th Coll 38. **d** 42 **p** 43. C Rusholme H Trin *Man* 42-45; C Cheadle *Ches* 45-47; C Bispham *Blackb* 47-49; Org Sec NW Area CPAS 49-52; V Litherland St Jo and St Jas *Liv* 52-57; Asst Master Broadway Sch Cheadle 59-61; Div Master Wilmslow Gr Sch 61-64; Sen Lect Relig Educn W Midl Tr Coll Walsall 64-67; Hd of Relig Studies Sheff Coll of Educn 67-78; Lic to Offic *Sheff* 67-78; Lect Liv Bible Coll 78-88; rtd 88; Perm to Offic *Liv* from 88. *16A St Paul's Street, Southport, Merseyside PR8 1LZ* Tel (01704) 534797

RUSSELL, Eric Watson. b 39. FCA73. Clifton Th Coll 66. **d** 69 **p** 70. C Kinson *Sarum* 69-73; C Peckham St Mary Magd *S'wark* 73-77; TV Barking St Marg w St Patr *Chelmsf* 77-82; V Lozells St Paul and St Silas *Birm* 82-95; RD Aston 89-94; P-in-c Barston from 95; C Knowle from 95. *20 Slater Road, Bentley Heath, Solihull, W Midlands B93 8AG* Tel (01564) 776864

RUSSELL, The Ven Harold Ian Lyle. b 34. Lon Coll of Div ALCD59 BD60. **d** 60 **p** 61. C Iver *Ox* 60-63; C Fulwood *Sheff* 63-67; V Chapeltown 67-75; RD Tankersley 73-75; V Nottingham St Jude *S'well* 75-89; Hon Can S'well Minster 88-89; Adn Cov from 89. *9 Armorial Road, Coventry CV3 6GH* Tel (01203) 417750

RUSSELL, Herbert Mark. b 12. Dur Univ LTh38. Trin Coll Bris 35. **d** 38 **p** 39. C Hougham in Dover Ch Ch *Cant* 38-40; C Dagenham *Chelmsf* 40-42; PC Gt Yarmouth St Geo *Nor* 42-45; V Hougham in Dover Ch Ch *Cant* 45-51; V Whitehall Park St Andr Hornsey Lane *Lon* 51-56; Chapl Whittington Hosp Lon 52-56; Warden Mabledon Conf Cen 56-67; V Danehill *Chich* 67-77; rtd 77; Hon C Glynde, W Firle and Beddingham *Chich* 77-80; Perm to Offic 80-96. *Pelham House, London Road, Cuckfield, Haywards Heath, W Sussex RH17 5EU* Tel (01444) 417954

RUSSELL, Mrs Isabel. b 31. Lightfoot Ho Dur 58. **dss** 71 **d** 87 **p** 94. Gt Barr *Lich* 71-74; E Farleigh and Coxheath *Roch* 75-84; Ogwell and Denbury *Ex* 85-87; Hon Par Dn 87-91; Sub-Chapl HM Pris Dartmoor from 89; rtd 91; Perm to Offic *Ex* from 91. *Church Cottage, Manaton Green, Newton Abbot, Devon TQ13 9UJ*

RUSSELL, Mrs Janet Mary. b 53. Univ of Wales BSc74 BArch76. Ox Min Course 91. **d** 94 **p** 95. C Watlington w Pyrton and Shirburn *Ox* 94-97; C Icknield from 97. *Timbers, Pyrton, Watlington, Oxford OX9 5AP* Tel (01491) 613022

RUSSELL, Canon John Arthur. b 29. AKC62. **d** 63 **p** 64. C Fareham H Trin *Portsm* 63-67; R Greatham w Empshott 67-79; V Ham St Andr *S'wark* 79-87; P-in-c Battersea St Luke 87-92; V 92-96; Hon Can S'wark Cathl 95-96; rtd 97. *23 Vicarage Street, Frome, Somerset BA11 1PU* Tel (01373) 472226

RUSSELL, John Bruce. b 56. Ripon Coll Cuddesdon DipMin95. **d** 95 **p** 96. C Newport Pagnell w Lathbury and Moulsoe *Ox* from 95. *3 Castle Meadow Close, Newport Pagnell, Bucks MK16 9EJ* Tel (01908) 613161

RUSSELL, John Graham. b 35. G&C Coll Cam BA58 MA62. Westcott Ho Cam 59. **d** 61 **p** 62. C Durleigh *B & W* 61-66; C Bridgwater St Mary w Chilton Trinity 61-66; C Far Headingley St Chad *Ripon* 66-72; P-in-c Leeds St Matt Lt London 72-79; V Rowley Regis *Birm* 79-84; V Hall Green Ascension 84-95; Deanery Priest Warley Deanery from 95. *1 Stapylton Avenue, Harborne, Birmingham B17 0BA* Tel 0121-426 4529

RUSSELL, Canon Jonathan Vincent Harman. b 43. K Coll Lon 68. **d** 69 **p** 70. C Addington *Cant* 69-73; C Buckland in Dover w Buckland Valley 73-76; P-in-c Selling 76-85; P-in-c Throwley w Stalisfield and Otterden 79-85; R Selling w Throwley, Sheldwich w Badlesmere etc 85-95; Hon Min Can Cant Cathl 83-94; Hon Can Cant Cathl from 94; RD Ospringe 90-95; P-in-c Elham w Denton and Wootton from 95. *The Vicarage, Elham, Canterbury, Kent CT4 6TT* Tel (01303) 840219

RUSSELL, Jonathan Wingate (Jon). b 55. BSc BA DMS DIM. St Jo Coll Nottm 81. **d** 84 **p** 85. C Southsea St Jude *Portsm* 84-87; P-in-c Shorwell w Kingston 87-92; V from 92; P-in-c Gatcombe 87-92; R from 92; P-in-c Chale 89-92; R from 92; RD W Wight from 96. *The Vicarage, 5 Northcourt Close, Shorwell, Newport, Isle of Wight PO30 3LD* Tel (01983) 741044

RUSSELL, Lloyd George Winkler. b 19. Hatf Coll Dur LTh45 BA49. **d** 45 **p** 46. Jamaica 45-48 and 50-52 and 82-85; Perm to Offic *Dur* 48-50; Perm to Offic *Lon* 53-58; Perm to Offic *S'wark* 53-59; Perm to Offic *Roch* 58-81 and from 85; rtd 85; Perm to Offic *S'wark* from 85. *39 Pembroke Road, Bromley BR1 2RT* Tel 0181-460 1498

RUSSELL, Martin Christopher. b 48. St Jo Coll Dur BA70. Coll of Resurr Mirfield 72. **d** 74 **p** 75. C Huddersfield St Pet and St Paul *Wakef* 74-75; C Huddersfield St Pet 75-77; Trinidad and Tobago 78-85; V S Crosland *Wakef* from 85; P-in-c Helme from 85. *The Vicarage, Church Lane, South Crosland, Huddersfield HD4 7DB* Tel (01484) 661080

RUSSELL, Michael John. b 38. Clifton Th Coll 68. **d** 68 **p** 69. C Cranham Park CD *Chelmsf* 68-70; C Bucknall and Bagnall *Lich* 70-77; P-in-c Tintwistle *Ches* 77-79; V 79-86; New Zealand from 86. *201 Cambridge Avenue, Ashurst, New Zealand* Tel Ashurst (6) 326 8543

RUSSELL, Neil. b 47. Nottm Univ CPS81 Ox Univ DipApTh95. EMMTC 78. **d** 81 **p** 82. NSM Wyberton *Linc* 81-84; C 84-85; V Frampton 85-93; Agric Chapl and Countryside Officer 88-93; P-in-c Stamford All SS w St Jo 93-97; V from 97. *All Saints' Vicarage, Casterton Road, Stamford, Lincs PE9 2YL* Tel (01780) 756942

RUSSELL, Mrs Noreen Margaret. b 39. Man Univ BA60 Lon Univ PGCE61 BD66. WMMTC 90. **d** 91 **p** 94. NSM Swynnerton and Tittensor *Lich* from 91. *40 Old Road, Barlaston, Stoke-on-Trent ST12 9EQ* Tel (01785) 817780

RUSSELL, Canon Norman Atkinson. b 43. Chu Coll Cam BA65 MA69 Lon Univ BD70. Lon Coll of Div 67. **d** 70 **p** 71. C Clifton Ch Ch w Em *Bris* 70-74; C Enfield Ch Ch Trent Park *Lon* 74-77; R Harwell w Chilton *Ox* 77-84; P-in-c Gerrards Cross 84-88; P-in-c Fulmer 85-88; R Gerrards Cross and Fulmer from 88; Hon Can Ch Ch from 95; RD Amersham from 96. *The Rectory, Oxford Road, Gerrards Cross, Bucks SL9 7DJ* Tel (01753) 883301 Fax 892177

RUSSELL, Miss Pamela. b 34. SRN SCM. Coll of Resurr Mirfield 85. **dss** 86 **d** 87. Barnburgh w Melton on the Hill *Sheff* 86-93; Hon Par Dn 87-93; Chapl Asst Grimsby Distr Gen Hosp 93-94; Asst Chapl Grimsby Health NHS Trust from 94. *Grimsby District General Hospital, Scartho Road, Grimsby, S Humberside DN33 2BA* Tel (01472) 874111

RUSSELL, Paul Selwyn. b 38. ALCD61. **d** 61 **p** 62. C Gillingham St Mark *Roch* 61-64; SAMS 64-84; Chile, Peru and Bolivia 64-84; V Brinsworth w Catcliffe *Sheff* 84-91; R Brinklow *Cov* from 91; R Harborough Magna from 91; V Monks Kirby w Pailton and Stretton-under-Fosse from 91. *The Rectory, 31 Coventry Road, Brinklow, Rugby, Warks CV23 0NE* Tel (01788) 832274 E-mail 101576.370@compuserve.com

RUSSELL, Philip John Seymour. b 1900. Wells Th Coll 22. **d** 23 **p** 24. C Whitby *York* 23-27; C Lansdown *B & W* 27-30; V Liverton *York* 30-34; V Lythe 34-45; V Bishopthorpe 45-55; V Acaster Malbis 45-55; Hon Chapl to Abp York 47-55; RD Ainsty 50-55; V N Elmham w Billingford *Nor* 55-58; Sec Dioc Reorganization Cttee 58-67; Sec DBP 59-67; Warden of Readers 61-67; Lic to Offic 58-67; rtd 67; Perm to Offic *Glas* from 68. *High Portling, Dalbeattie, Kirkcudbrightshire DG5 4PZ* Tel (01556) 630359

RUSSELL, Ralph Geoffrey Major. b 19. St Aug Coll Cant 47 Sarum Th Coll 48. **d** 50 **p** 51. C Redruth *Truro* 50-55; C Hayes St Mary *Lon* 55-56; C W Wycombe *Ox* 56-62; V New Bradwell w Stantonbury 62-73; P-in-c Gt Linford w Willen and Gt and Lt Woolstone 62-64; P-in-c Linslade 74-75; V 75-87; rtd 87; Perm to Offic *Ox* from 87; Perm to Offic *Pet* from 89. *60 Cheneys Walk, Bletchley, Milton Keynes MK3 6JY* Tel (01908) 641998

RUSSELL, Richard Alexander. b 44. Univ of Wales (Abth) BA65 McMaster Univ Ontario MA67 Bris Univ MA73 PGCE74 MEd76. Trin Coll Bris DipHE81. **d** 82 **p** 83. C Hartlepool St Paul *Dur* 82-85; P-in-c Bath Widcombe *B & W* 85-88; V from 88. *Widcombe Vicarage, 65 Prior Park Road, Bath BA2 4NL* Tel (01225) 310580

RUSSELL, Roger Geoffrey. b 47. Worc Coll Ox BA69 MA73. Cuddesdon Coll 70. **d** 72 **p** 73. C Anlaby Common St Mark *York* 72-75; C Wilton Place St Paul *Lon* 75-86; R Lancing w Coombes *Chich* from 86; RD Worthing from 97. *The Vicarage, 63 Manor Road, Lancing, W Sussex BN15 0EY* Tel (01903) 753212

RUSSELL, William Douglas. b 16. LCP72 Open Univ BA73. Worc Ord Coll 57. **d** 59 **p** 60. C Farlington *Portsm* 59-61; V Stanton Drew *B & W* 61-82; rtd 82; Perm to Offic *B & W* from 82. *42 Keward Avenue, Wells, Somerset BA5 1TS* Tel (01749) 677203

RUSSELL, William Warren. b 52. QUB BSocSc74. CITC 74. **d** 77 **p** 78. C Agherton *Conn* 77-79; C Lisburn Ch Ch Cathl 79-83; I Magheradroll *D & D* from 83; RD Dromore from 93. *18 Church Road, Ballynahinch, Co Down BT24 8LP* Tel (01238) 562289

RUSSELL-SMITH, Miss Joy Dorothea. b 29. St Anne's Coll Ox BA52 MA55 K Coll Lon BD67. Ridley Hall Cam 83. **dss** 85 **d** 87 **p** 94. Witney *Ox* 85-87; Par Dn 87-88; NSM Saffron Walden w Wendens Ambo and Littlebury *Chelmsf* 88-95; rtd 92; NSM Heydon, Gt and Lt Chishill, Chrishall etc *Chelmsf* from 96. *1 The Meadow, Littlebury Green, Saffron Walden, Essex CB11 4XE* Tel (01763) 838856 or (01799) 525303

RUSSELL-SMITH, Mark Raymond. b 46. New Coll Edin MTh91. St Jo Coll Dur BA71 Cranmer Hall Dur DipTh72. **d** 72 **p** 73. C Upton (Overchurch) *Ches* 72-75; C Deane *Man* 75-77; UCCF Travelling Sec 77-80; Lic to Offic *York* 78-81; BCMS 81-92; Kenya 81-92; P-in-c Slaidburn *Bradf* from 92; P-in-c Long Preston w Tosside from 97. *The Rectory, Slaidburn, Clitheroe, Lancs BB7 3ER* Tel (01200) 446238

✠**RUSTON, The Rt Revd John Harry Gerald.** b 29. SS Coll Cam BA52 MA56. Ely Th Coll 52. **d** 54 **p** 55 **c** 83. C Leic St Andr *Leic* 54-57; OGS from 55; Tutor Cuddesdon Coll 57-61; C Cuddesdon *Ox* 57-61; S Africa 62-91; Suff Bp Pretoria 83-91; Bp St Helena from 91. *Bishopsholme, PO Box 62, St Helena* Tel St Helena (290) 4471

RUTHERFORD, Anthony Richard (Tony). b 37. Culham Coll Ox TCert62 Lon Univ DipAdEd68 Sussex Univ MA77. S'wark Ord Course 83. **d** 86 **p** 87. Hon C Tunbridge Wells St Luke *Roch* 86-88; C Bromley SS Pet and Paul 88-90; V Wragby *Linc* 90-94; Asst Min Officer 90-94; V Penge Lane H Trin *Roch* from 94. *Holy Trinity Vicarage, 64 Lennard Road, London SE20 7LX* Tel 0181-778 7258 Fax as telephone

RUTHERFORD, Arthur Ernest. b 26. Saltley Tr Coll Birm CertEd53 Loughb Coll of Educn DipEd54. Sarum & Wells Th Coll 91. **d** 92 **p** 93. NSM Lilliput *Sarum* 92-96. *Kirinyaga, 8 Jennings Road, Poole, Dorset BH14 8RY* Tel (01202) 748777

RUTHERFORD, Daniel Fergus Peter. b 65. Hatf Coll Dur BA86 CertEd87. Ridley Hall Cam 88. **d** 90 **p** 91. C Harold Wood *Chelmsf* 90-94; C Hove Bp Hannington Memorial Ch *Chich* from 94. *47 Nevill Avenue, Hove, E Sussex BN3 7NB* Tel (01273) 739144

RUTHERFORD, David Lesslie Calderwood. b 29. Master Mariner 55 Open Univ BA76. LNSM course 89. **d** 91 **p** 92. Dioc Moderator for Reader Tr *St E* 90-95; NSM Acton w Gt Waldingfield from 91. *18 Gotsfield Close, Acton, Sudbury, Suffolk CO10 0AS* Tel (01787) 374169

RUTHERFORD, Graeme Stanley. b 43. Cranmer Hall Dur BA77 MA78 ACT 66. **d** 66 **p** 67. Australia 66-73 and from 77; C Holborn St Geo w H Trin and St Bart *Lon* 73-74; C Dur St Nic *Dur* 74-77. *552 Burke Road, Camberwell, Victoria, Australia 3124* Tel Melbourne (3) 9882 4851 Fax 9882 0086

RUTHERFORD, Ian William. b 46. Univ of Wales (Lamp) BA68. Cuddesdon Coll 68. **d** 70 **p** 71. C Gosforth All SS *Newc* 70-72; C Prestbury *Glouc* 73-76; Chapl RN 76-93; TV Redruth w Lanner and Treleigh *Truro* 93-94; V Paulsgrove *Portsm* from 94. *St Michael's Vicarage, Hempsted Road, Portsmouth PO6 4AS* Tel (01705) 375912

RUTHERFORD, Janet Elizabeth. b 37. S'wark Ord Course 86. **d** 89. NSM Plaistow St Mary *Roch* 89-90; NSM Linc St Botolph by Bargate *Linc* 91-94. *Holy Trinity Vicarage, 64 Lennard Road, London SE20 7LX* Tel 0181-778 7258

RUTHERFORD, Canon John Allarton Edge. b 10. SS Coll Cam BA32 MA36. Westcott Ho Cam 32. **d** 33 **p** 34. C Portsm Cathl *Portsm* 33-40; Chapl St Jo Coll York 40-42; Chapl Abp Holgate's Gr Sch 40-42; Chapl RAFVR 42-46; Chapl Charterhouse Godalming 46-70; V Walsham le Willows *St E* 70-83; P-in-c 83-85; Hon Can St E Cathl 82-85; rtd 84; Perm to Offic *St E* from 85. *Jalla Halli, Hinderclay, Diss, Norfolk IP22 1HN* Tel (01379) 898948

RUTHERFORD, Canon John Bilton. b 23. Qu Coll Birm 49. **d** 52 **p** 53. C Newc H Cross *Newc* 52-57; C Longbenton St Bart 57-60; V High Elswick St Phil 60-66; V Walker 66-74; V Benwell St Jas 74-81; Hon Can Newc Cathl 80-90; V Lesbury w Alnmouth 81-90; RD Alnwick 86-89; rtd 90. *68 Worcester Way, Woodlands Park, Wideopen, Newcastle upon Tyne NE4 5JE* Tel 0191-236 4785

RUTHERFORD, Peter George. b 34. Nor Ord Course 73. **d** 76 **p** 77. NSM New Catton Ch Ch *Nor* 76-79; NSM Eaton 79-80; NSM Nor St Steph 81-92; Perm to Offic 92-94; P-in-c Earlham St Mary from 94. *126 Colman Road, Norwich NR4 7AA* Tel (01603) 457629

RUTHERFORD, Peter Marshall. b 57. St Andr Univ MTheol81 Ulster Univ MA96. CITC 83. **d** 83 **p** 84. C Stormont *D & D* 83-85; CF from 85. *c/o MOD (Army), Bagshot Park, Bagshot, Surrey GU18 5PL* Tel (01276) 471717 Fax 412834

RUTLEDGE, Canon Christopher John Francis. b 44. Lon Univ BSc67 Clare Coll Cam PGCTh70 Lon Inst of Educn FETC80 Univ of Wales MPhil94. Sarum Th Coll 67. **d** 70 **p** 71. C Birm St Pet *Birm* 70-73; C Calne and Blackland *Sarum* 73-76; P-in-c Derry Hill 76-78; V 78-81; P-in-c Talbot Village 81-82; V from 82; Can and Preb Sarum Cathl from 95. *The Vicarage, 20 Alton Road, Bournemouth BH10 4AE* Tel (01202) 529349

RUTLEDGE, Francis George. b 62. DipTh Ulster Poly BA83 TCD BTh90. **d** 86 **p** 87. C Holywood *D & D* 86-89; C Willowfield 89-91; I Kilmakee *Conn* from 91. *Kilmakee Rectory, 60 Killeaton Park, Dunmurry, Belfast BT17 9HE* Tel (01232) 610505

RUTT, Canon Denis Frederic John. b 17. Kelham Th Coll 34. **d** 41 **p** 42. C Luton Ch Ch *St Alb* 41-46; R Yaxham *Nor* 54-61; R Welborne 54-61; R Kirkley 61-71; RD Lothingland 65-71; R N Lynn w St Marg and St Nic 71-76; Can Res and Prec Lich Cathl *Lich* 76-83; rtd 83; Perm to Offic *Bradf* from 83. *1 Grovenor Terrace, Otley, W Yorkshire LS21 1HJ* Tel (01943) 464586

RUTT-FIELD, Benjamin John. b 48. Chich Th Coll. **d** 90 **p** 91. C Wickford and Runwell *Chelmsf* 90-94; V Goodmayes St Paul from 94. *St Paul's Vicarage, 20 Eastwood Road, Ilford, Essex IG3 8XA* Tel 0181-590 6596

RUTTER, Canon Allen Edward Henry (Claude). b 28. Qu Coll Cam BA52 Cam Univ DipAgr53 Qu Coll Cam MA56. Cranmer Hall Dur DipTh58. **d** 59 **p** 60. C Bath Abbey w St Jas *B & W* 59-60; C E Dereham w Hoe *Nor* 60-64; R Cawston 64-69; Chapl Cawston Coll 64-69; P-in-c Felthorpe w Haveringland 64-69; S Africa 69-73; P-in-c Over and Nether Compton, Trent etc *Sarum* 73-80; RD Sherborne 77-87; P-in-c Oborne w Poyntington 79-80; P-in-c Queen Thorne 80-96; Can and Preb Sarum Cathl 86-96; rtd 96. *Home Farm, Chilson, South Chard, Somerset TA20 2NX* Tel (01460) 221368

RUTTER, John Edmund Charles. b 53. Qu Coll Cam MA76. All Nations Chr Coll DipMiss82 St Jo Coll Nottm MA93. **d** 93 **p** 94. C Penge St Jo *Roch* 93-97; P-in-c Bangor Primacy *D & D* from 97. *4 Glendowan Road, Bangor, Co Down BT19 7SP* Tel (01247) 457057

RUTTER, Martin Charles. b 54. Wolv Poly BSc75 Southn Univ BTh81. Sarum & Wells Th Coll 76. **d** 79 **p** 80. C Cannock *Lich* 79-82; C Uttoxeter w Bramshall 82-86; V W Bromwich St Jas from 86; P-in-c W Bromwich St Paul Golds Hill from 89; RD W Bromwich from 94. *St James's Vicarage, 151A Hill Top, West Bromwich, W Midlands B70 0SB* Tel 0121-556 0805

RYALL, John Francis Robert. b 30. New Coll Ox BA52 MA57. Westcott Ho Cam 52. **d** 54 **p** 55. C Petersfield w Sheet *Portsm* 54-56; C Portsea St Mary 56-62; C Warblington and Emsworth 62-65; C Freshwater 65-67; R Frating w Thorrington *Chelmsf* 67-73; R Gt Yeldham 74-76; P-in-c Lt Yeldham 75-76; R Gt w Lt Yeldham 76-80; P-in-c Thorley *Portsm* 80-82; P-in-c Shalfleet 80-82; V 82-95; V Calbourne w Newtown 82-95; rtd 95; Perm to Offic *Portsm* from 95. *Weald House, Main Road, Wellow, Yarmouth, Isle of Wight PO41 0SZ* Tel (01983) 760783

RYALL, Michael Richard. b 36. TCD BA58 MA65 HDipEd66. TCD Div Sch Div Test58. **d** 58 **p** 59. C Dublin St Geo *D & G* 58-62; CF 62-65 and 68-90; CF (TAVR) 67-68; C Dublin Rathmines *D & G* 65-66; Dungannon Sec Sch 66-68; R Yardley Hastings, Denton and Grendon etc *Pet* 90-96; R Yardley Hastings, Denton and Grendon etc from 96. *The Rectory, Castle Ashby Road, Yardley Hastings, Northampton NN7 1EL* Tel (01604) 696223

RYAN, David Peter. b 64. Aston Univ BSc86. Linc Th Coll BTh94. **d** 94 **p** 95. C Horsforth *Ripon* 94-97; C Bedale from 97. *The Rectory, Thornton Watlass, Ripon, N Yorkshire HG4 4AH* Tel (01677) 422737

RYAN, Graham William Robert (Gregg). b 51. CITC 90 St Jo Coll Nottm CertCS93. **d** 93 **p** 94. NSM Clonsast w Rathangan, Thomastown etc *M & K* 93-97; Dioc Communications Officer 96-97; Press Officer from 97; Dioc C from 97. *Millicent Hall, Millicent South, Sallins, Naas, Co Kildare, Irish Republic* Tel Sallins (45) 879464 Fax as telephone

RYAN, James Francis. b 47. Surrey Univ BSc. Trin Coll Bris DipHE St Jo Coll Nottm. **d** 83 **p** 84. C Littleover *Derby* 83-86; C Chipping Sodbury and Old Sodbury *Glouc* 86-89; V Pype Hayes *Birm* from 89. *St Mary's Vicarage, 1162 Tyburn Road, Birmingham B24 0TB* Tel 0121-373 3534

RYAN, Roger John. b 47. Lon Bible Coll BA79 Oak Hill Th Coll 79. **d** 80 **p** 81. C Luton St Fran *St Alb* 80-83; R Laceby *Linc* 83-88; V Summerstown *S'wark* from 88. *St Mary's Vicarage, 46 Wimbledon Road, London SW17 0UQ* Tel 0181-946 9853

RYAN, Stephen John. b 49. Univ of Wales (Swansea) BA70 Bris Univ DipTh73. Sarum & Wells Th Coll 70. **d** 73 **p** 74. C Llantrisant *Llan* 73-77; V Treherbert w Treorchy 77-89; Youth Chapl 80-85; RD Rhondda 84-89; V Aberdare St Fagan from 89; RD Aberdare from 97. *St Fagan's Vicarage, Trecynon, Aberdare CF44 8LL* Tel (01685) 881435

RYCROFT, Stanley. b 30. Bris Univ MEd81 Open Univ BA84. Sarum Th Coll 56. **d** 59 **p** 60. C Earley St Bart *Ox* 59-62; Chapl Whittlebury Sch Towcester 62-63; C Christchurch *Win* 63-67; Chapl Durlston Court Sch Barton on Sea 67-71; Chapl Millfield Jun Sch Somerset 71-75; Chapl Wellington Sch Somerset 75-83; V Silksworth *Dur* 84-95; rtd 95; Perm to Offic *Linc* from 95. *5 Park Road, Allington, Grantham, Lincs NG32 2EB* Tel (01400) 281516

RYDER, Derek Michael. b 36. St Cath Coll Cam BA60 MA64. Tyndale Hall Bris 61. **d** 63 **p** 64. C Hampreston *Sarum* 63-66; Asst Chapl Brentwood Sch Essex 66-72; Chapl Ipswich Sch 72-77; Home Sec CMJ 77-87; TR Wexcombe *Sarum* from 87; RD Pewsey from 89. *The Vicarage, Shalbourne, Marlborough, Wilts SN8 3QH* Tel (01672) 870421

RYDER, John Merrick. b 55. Natal Univ BA75 BA77. St Pet Coll Natal 81. **d** 82 **p** 83. S Africa 84-88; St Helena 88-91; C Havant *Portsm* 91-95; P-in-c Godshill from 95. *The Vicarage, Church Hill, Godshill, Ventnor, Isle of Wight PO38 3HY* Tel (01983) 840895

RYDER, Canon Lisle Robert Dudley. b 43. Selw Coll Cam BA68 MA72 Birm Univ DPS76. Sarum Th Coll 69. **d** 71 **p** 72. C Lowestoft St Marg *Nor* 71-75; Chapl Asst Oxon Area HA 76-79; C Littlehampton St Jas *Chich* 79-85; C Wick 79-85; C Littlehampton St Mary 79-85; Chapl Worc R Infirmary 85-94;

Chapl Worc R Infirmary NHS Trust from 94; Hon Can Worc Cathl *Worc* from 89. *1 Holywell Hill, Worcester WR2 5NZ, or Worcester Royal Infirmary, Castle Street, Worcester WR1 3AS* Tel (01905) 763333

RYDINGS, Donald. b 33. Jes Coll Ox BA57 MA61. Linc Th Coll 57. **d** 59 **p** 60. C Poulton-le-Fylde *Blackb* 59-62; C Ox St Mary V *Ox* 62-66; Staff Sec SCM Ox 62-66; C-in-c Bourne End St Mark CD 66-74; R Hedsor and Bourne End 74-76; P-in-c Gt Missenden w Ballinger and Lt Hampden 76-93; RD Wendover 79-89; V Gt Missenden w Ballinger and Lt Hampden from 93. *The Vicarage, 2 Walnut Close, Great Missenden, Bucks HP16 9AA* Tel (01494) 862470

RYE, David Ralph. b 33. AKC59. **d** 60 **p** 61. C Rushmere *St E* 60-64; C Barnham Broom w Kimberley, Bixton etc *Nor* 64-76; TV Barnham Broom 76-82; TR 82-95; P-in-c Reymerston w Cranworth, Letton, Southburgh etc 85-95; rtd 95; Perm to Offic *Nor* from 95. *5A Yarmouth Road, Norwich NR7 0EA*

RYECART, John Reginald. b 07. AKC32. St Steph Ho Ox 32. **d** 33 **p** 34. C Newark St Leon *S'well* 33-35; C Sevenoaks St Jo *Roch* 35-41; Chapl RAFVR 41-46; V Leek Wootton *Cov* 47-49; R Honiley 49-53; PC Wroxall 49-53; Israel 53-60; V Gt Sampford w Hempstead *Chelmsf* 60-74; rtd 74; Perm to Offic *Chelmsf* from 74. *100 Fronks Road, Dovercourt, Essex CO12 3RY* Tel (01255) 507370

RYELAND, John. b 58. K Coll Lon BD80 AKC80. Linc Th Coll 80. **d** 81 **p** 82. C Enfield St Jas *Lon* 81-84; C Coulsdon St Andr *S'wark* 84-87; C-in-c Ingrave St Steph CD *Chelmsf* from 87. *St Stephen's House, St Stephen's Crescent, Ingrave, Essex CM13 2AT* Tel (01277) 214623

RYLAND, Colin William. b 16. TD52. MRCVS. St Steph Ho Ox 61. **d** 62 **p** 63. C Plymstock *Ex* 62-66; R Church w Chapel Brampton *Pet* 66-73; V Wellingborough St Barn 73-83; rtd 83; Perm to Offic *Dur* from 83; Chapl St Chad's Coll from 94. *13 St John's Road, Durham DH1 4NU* Tel 0191-386 9638

RYLANDS, Mrs Amanda Craig. b 52. CertEd75. All Nations Chr Coll DipMiss82 Trin Coll Bris DipHE85. **dss** 85 **d** 87 **p** 94. Chippenham St Andr w Tytherton Lucas *Bris* 85-87; Par Dn Stockport St Geo *Ches* 87-91; Par Dn Acton and Worleston, Church Minshull etc 91-94; C from 94; Dio Adv for Min Among Children 95-97. *St Mary's Vicarage, Chester Road, Acton, Nantwich, Cheshire CW5 8LG* Tel (01270) 628864

RYLANDS, Mark James. b 61. SS Hild & Bede Coll Dur BA83. Trin Coll Bris BA87. **d** 87 **p** 88. C Stockport St Geo *Ches* 87-91; V Acton and Worleston, Church Minshull etc from 91. *St Mary's Vicarage, Chester Road, Acton, Nantwich, Cheshire CW5 8LG* Tel (01270) 628864

RYLANDS, Canon Thomas Michael. b 18. CCC Cam BA39 MA46. Wells Th Coll. **d** 47 **p** 48. C Nantwich *Ches* 47-51; R Malpas and Threapwood 68-85; RD Malpas 70-84; Hon Can Ches Cathl 72-85; rtd 85; Perm to Offic *Ches* from 85. *Haughton Thorn, Tarporley, Cheshire CW6 9RN* Tel (01829) 260215

RYLE, Denis Maurice. b 16. OBE70. St Aid Birkenhead 35. **d** 39 **p** 40. C Parr *Liv* 39-42; C Widnes St Paul 42-44; C Much Woolton 44-45; CF 45-58; Sen CF 58-65; Dep Asst Chapl Gen 65-73; P-in-c Latimer w Flaunden *Ox* 73-85; rtd 85; Perm to Offic *York* from 90. *5 Church Close, Wheldrake, York YO4 6DP* Tel (01904) 898124

RYLEY, Canon Patrick Macpherson. b 30. Pemb Coll Ox BA54 Lon Univ BD56. Clifton Th Coll 54. **d** 56 **p** 57. C Ox St Clem *Ox* 56-59; Burma 60-66; Kenya 68-75; V Lynn St Jo *Nor* 76-92; V King's Lynn St Jo the Ev 92-95; RD Lynn 78-83; Hon Can Nor Cathl 90-95; rtd 95; Perm to Offic *Bradf* from 95. *106 Little Lane, Ilkley, W Yorkshire LS29 8JJ* Tel (01943) 817026

RYLEY, Timothy Patrick (<u>Tim</u>). b 64. Man Univ BA86. St Jo Coll Nottm DTS92 MA93. **d** 93 **p** 94. C Pendlebury St Jo *Man* 93-97; P-in-c Norris Bank from 97. *St Martin's Rectory, 110 Crescent Park, Stockport, Cheshire SK4 2JE* Tel 0161-432 3537

RYMER, David John Talbot. b 37. Chich Th Coll 63. **d** 66 **p** 67. C Tuffley *Glouc* 66-69; Rhodesia 69-79; P-in-c S Kensington St Jude *Lon* 79-82; V 82-88; P-in-c Ambergate *Derby* 88-91; P-in-c Heage 88-91; P-in-c Ambergate and Heage 91; R 91-96; P-in-c Willington from 96; P-in-c Findern from 96. *The Vicarage, 66 The Castleway, Willington, Derby DE6 6BU* Tel (01283) 702203

RYRIE, Alexander Crawford. b 30. Edin Univ MA52 BD55 Glas Univ MLitt75. Union Th Sem (NY) STM56. **d** 83 **p** 83. Hon C Edin St Mary *Edin* 83-85; R Jedburgh 85-95; rtd 95. *Boisils, Bowden, Melrose, Roxburghshire TD6 0ST* Tel (01835) 823226

RYRIE, Mrs Isabel. b 31. ABPsS73 CPsychol88 Edin Univ MA51 Glas Univ MEd70. Moray Ho Edin DipRE52. **d** 89 **p** 94. Bp's Dn *Edin* 89-91; NSM Edin St Mary from 91. *Boisils, Bowden, Melrose, Roxburghshire TD6 0ST* Tel (01835) 823226

S

SABAN, Ronald Graham Street. b 28. Bps' Coll Cheshunt 60. **d** 62 **p** 63. C Maidstone St Martin *Cant* 62-66; C Croydon St Sav 66; rtd 94. *34 Kingsway, Caversham Park Village, Reading RG4 0RA* Tel 0118-947 9454

SABELL, Michael Harold. b 42. Open Univ BA78 Surrey Univ MSc. Sarum & Wells Th Coll 77. **d** 80 **p** 81. NSM Shirley *Win* 80-82; NSM Finham *Cov* 82-85; Chapl to the Deaf *Win* 81-82; *Cov* 82-85; *Sheff* 85-89; *Lich* 89-96; *St Alb* from 96; P-in-c Gt and Lt Wymondley w Graveley and Chivesfield from 96. *5 Arch Road, Great Wymondley, Hitchin, Herts SG4 7EP* Tel (01438) 729219

SABOURIN, Robert. b 21. TCD. **d** 52 **p** 53. C Wembley St Jo *Lon* 52-54; C Guernsey St Sampson *Win* 54-57; V Guernsey St Matt 57-60; Public Preacher 60-80; Perm to Offic 80-86; rtd 86; Chapl Rouen and Le Havre *Eur* 86-87; Chapl Menton 87-90; Lic to Offic from 90. *Anchorage, 21 rue du 11 Novembre, 27690 Lery, France*

SADDINGTON, Peter David. b 42. Cranmer Hall Dur. **d** 84 **p** 85. C Tudhoe Grange *Dur* 84-86; C Monkwearmouth St Andr 86-88; V Burnopfield 88-94; P-in-c Greenside 94-96; V from 96. *The Vicarage, Greenside, Ryton, Tyne & Wear NE40 4AA* Tel 0191-413 8281

SADGROVE, The Very Revd Michael. b 50. Ball Coll Ox BA71 MA75. Trin Coll Bris 72. **d** 75 **p** 76. Lic to Offic *Ox* 75-77; Tutor Sarum & Wells Th Coll 77-82; Vice-Prin 80-82; V Alnwick St Mich and St Paul *Newc* 82-87; Can Res and Prec Cov Cathl 87-95; Vice-Provost 87-95; Provost Sheff from 95. *Provost's Lodge, 22 Hallam Gate Road, Sheffield S10 5BS* Tel 0114-266 2373 Fax 278 0244

SADLER, Preb Anthony Graham. b 36. Qu Coll Ox BA60 MA64. Lich Th Coll 60. **d** 62 **p** 63. C Burton St Chad *Lich* 62-65; V Rangemore 65-72; V Dunstall 65-72; V Abbots Bromley 72-79; V Pelsall 79-90; RD Walsall 82-90; Preb Lich Cathl from 87; P-in-c Uttoxeter w Bramshall 90-97; P-in-c Stramshall 90-97; P-in-c Kingstone w Gratwich 90-97; P-in-c Checkley 90-97; P-in-c Marchington w Marchington Woodlands 90-97; P-in-c Leigh 93-97; TR Uttoxeter Area from 97. *The Vicarage, 12 Orchard Close, Uttoxeter, Staffs ST14 7DZ* Tel (01889) 563651

SADLER, John Ernest. b 45. Nottm Univ BTh78. Linc Th Coll 74. **d** 78 **p** 79. C Brampton St Thos *Derby* 78-81; TV Coventry Caludon *Cov* 81-85; P-in-c High Elswick St Phil *Newc* 85; P-in-c Newc St Aug 85; V Newc St Phil and St Aug 86-94; P-in-c Newc Epiphany from 94. *12 Shannon Court, Newcastle upon Tyne NE3 2XF* Tel 0191-286 4050

SADLER, Michael Stuart. b 57. Wycliffe Hall Ox 78. **d** 81 **p** 82. C Henfynyw w Aberaeron and Llanddewi Aberarth *St D* 81-88; V Llanddewi Rhydderch w Llangattock-juxta-Usk etc *Mon* 88-90; V Llanddewi Rhydderch and Llangattock etc from 90. *The Vicarage, Llanddewi Rhydderch, Abergavenny NP7 9TS* Tel (01873) 840373

SAGAR, Brian. b 39. Sarum & Wells Th Coll 78. **d** 80 **p** 81. C Radcliffe St Thos and St Jo *Man* 80-82; P-in-c Charlestown 82-85; R Gt Lever 85-89; Chapl Cov Ch Housing Assn *Cov* 89-92; V Wing w Grove *Ox* from 92. *The Vicarage, 27B Aylesbury Road, Wing, Leighton Buzzard, Beds LU7 0PD* Tel (01296) 688496

SAGE, Andrew George. b 58. Chich Th Coll 83. **d** 85 **p** 86. C Rawmarsh w Parkgate *Sheff* 85-87; C Fareham SS Pet and Paul *Portsm* 87-89; C Southsea H Spirit 89-91; P-in-c Nuthurst *Chich* 91-93; R 93-95; V Hangleton from 95. *The Vicarage, 127 Hangleton Way, Hove, E Sussex BN3 8ER* Tel (01273) 419409

SAGE, Canon Jesse. b 35. Trin Hall Cam BA61 MA65. Chich Th Coll 61. **d** 63 **p** 64. C Feltham *Lon* 63-67; S Africa 67-72; R Abbas and Temple Combe *B & W* 72-75; R Abbas and Templecombe w Horsington 76-77; Chapl Agric and Rural Soc in Kent *Cant* 78-95; Hon Can Cant Cathl 90-95; S Africa from 96. *The Rectory, PO Box 431, 30 Smith Street, Gonubie, 5256 South Africa* Tel East London (431) 403086 Fax as telephone

SAGE, John Arthur. b 32. MInstP Lon Univ BSc54. St Alb Minl Tr Scheme 78. **d** 81 **p** 82. NSM Stevenage St Mary Shephall *St Alb* 81-86; NSM Stevenage St Mary Sheppall w Aston 86-87; C St Peter-in-Thanet *Cant* from 87. *St Andrew's House, 29 Reading Street, Broadstairs, Kent CT10 3AZ* Tel (01843) 868923

SAGOVSKY, Dr Nicholas. b 47. CCC Ox BA69 St Edm Ho Cam PhD81. St Jo Coll Nottm BA73. **d** 74 **p** 75. C Newc St Gabr *Newc* 74-77; C Cambridge Gt St Mary w St Mich *Ely* 81; Vice-Prin Edin Th Coll 82-86; Dean of Chpl Clare Coll Cam from 86. *5 St Andrews Road, Cambridge CB2 1DH* Tel (01223) 460115

✠**SAINSBURY, The Rt Revd Roger Frederick.** b 36. Jes Coll Cam BA58 MA62. Clifton Th Coll. **d** 60 **p** 61 **c** 91. C Spitalfields Ch Ch w All SS *Lon* 60-63; Missr Shrewsbury Ho Everton 63-74; P-in-c Everton St Ambrose w St Tim *Liv* 67-74; Warden Mayflower Family Cen Canning Town *Chelmsf* 74-81; P-in-c Victoria Docks St Luke 78-81; V Walsall *Lich* 81-87; TR 87-88; Adn W Ham *Chelmsf* 88-91; Area Bp Barking from 91. *Barking Lodge,*

110 Capel Road, London E7 0JS, or Bishop's Office, 1B Cranbrook House, 61 Cranbrook Road, Ilford, Essex IG1 4PG Tel 0181-478 2456 or 514 6044 Fax 514 6049

SAINT, Arthur James Maxwell. b 10. St Jo Coll Ox BA31 MA35. Cuddesdon Coll 34. **d** 35 **p** 36. C Stoke upon Trent *Lich* 35-37; Hd Master St Thos Sch Kuching Sarawak 37-41; C Shrewsbury St Mary 42-43; V Shawbury 43-48; V Cheltenham St Steph *Glouc* 48-60; Chapl Guy's Hosp Lon 60-65; V Ox SS Phil and Jas *Ox* 65-76; rtd 76. *65 Ramsay Road, Oxford OX3 8AY* Tel (01865) 761241

SAINT, David Gerald. b 45. Sarum & Wells Th Coll 72. **d** 75 **p** 76. C Wellingborough All Hallows *Pet* 75-79; R Kislingbury w Rothersthorpe 79-83; V Kings Heath 83-85; Relig Progr Producer BBC Radio Northn from 85; Perm to Offic *Pet* from 86. *49 Colwyn Road, Northampton NN1 3PZ* Tel (01604) 239100

ST ALBANS, Archdeacon of. *See* DAVIES, The Ven Philip Bertram

ST ALBANS, Bishop of. *See* HERBERT, The Rt Revd Christopher William

ST ALBANS, Dean of. *See* LEWIS, The Very Revd Christopher Andrew

ST ANDREWS, DUNKELD AND DUNBLANE, Bishop of. *See* HENLEY, The Rt Revd Michael Harry George

ST ANDREWS, DUNKELD AND DUNBLANE, Dean of. *See* WATT, The Very Revd Alfred Ian

ST ASAPH, Archdeacon of. *See* DAVIES, The Ven John Stewart

ST ASAPH, Bishop of. *See* JONES, The Most Revd Alwyn Rice

ST ASAPH, Dean of. *See* GOULSTONE, The Very Revd Thomas Richard Kerry

ST DAVIDS, Archdeacon of. *See* DAVIES, The Ven Graham James

ST DAVIDS, Bishop of. *See* JONES, The Rt Revd David Huw

ST DAVIDS, Dean of. *See* EVANS, The Very Revd John Wyn

ST EDMUNDSBURY AND IPSWICH, Bishop of. *See* LEWIS, The Rt Revd John Hubert Richard

ST EDMUNDSBURY AND IPSWICH, Provost of. *See* ATWELL, The Very Revd James Edgar

ST GERMANS, Suffragan Bishop of. *See* JAMES, The Rt Revd Graham Richard

ST JOHN-CHANNELL, Michael Alister Morrell. b 53. Bris Univ BEd76. Ripon Coll Cuddesdon 76. **d** 78 **p** 79. C Portsea St Mary *Portsm* 78-81; PV Linc Cathl *Linc* 82-85; P-in-c Linc St Mary-le-Wigford w St Benedict etc 82-85; R Cranford *Lon* 85-92; V Staines St Mary and St Pet from 92. *St Peter's Vicarage, 14 Thames Side, Staines, Middx TW18 2HA* Tel (01784) 453039 or 469155

ST JOHN NICOLLE, Michael George. b 29. St Jo Coll Dur BA52 DipEd. **d** 70 **p** 71. C Lt Bowden St Nic *Leic* 70; C Knighton St Jo 71-74; R Desford 74-81; R Tarrant Valley *Sarum* 81-85; R Jersey St Jo *Win* 85-94; rtd 94. *Les Noyers, Les Chenoles, St John, Jersey JE3 4FB* Tel (01534) 865276

SAKER, Sidney William. b 08. Dur Univ 32. ALCD35. **d** 35 **p** 36. C Islington St Andr *Lon* 35-38; C Bermondsey St Mary w St Olave and St Jo *S'wark* 38-39; C-in-c Reading St Mary Castle Street Prop Chpl *Ox* 39-46; Midl Area Sec BCMS 46-73; Org Sec (Midl) BCMS 46-73; Org Sec (W Area) SAMS 53-63; S Area Sec SAMS 63-64; Metrop Area Sec CCCS 64-65; Asst Sec 65-71; Area Sec (SW Lon) Leprosy Miss 71-73; Perm to Offic *Leic* from 46; rtd 73. *397 Uppingham Road, Leicester LE5 4DP* Tel 0116-276 0855

SALENIUS, Richard Mark. b 57. K Coll Lon BD79 AKC79. Linc Th Coll 79. **d** 80 **p** 81. C St Marylebone w H Trin *Lon* 80-84; C Sale St Anne *Ches* 84-87; V Macclesfield St Jo 87-96; V Brightlingsea *Chelmsf* from 96. *The Vicarage, Richard Avenue, Brightlingsea, Colchester CO7 0LP* Tel (01206) 302407

SALES, Patrick David. b 43. K Coll Lon AKC68 BD74. **d** 69 **p** 70. C Maidstone All SS w St Phil *Cant* 69-72; C Chart next Sutton Valence 72-74; C Birchington w Acol 75-77; V Boughton under Blean w Dunkirk 77-83; Hon Min Can Cant Cathl from 83; V Herne from 83; RD Reculver 86-92. *The Vicarage, Herne, Herne Bay, Kent CT6 7HE* Tel (01227) 374328

SALISBURY, Miss Anne Ruth. b 37. Bible Churchmen's Coll. **d** 87 **p** 94. C Harrow Trin St Mich *Lon* from 87. *1A Headstone Drive, Harrow, Middx HA3 5QX* Tel 0181-427 1129 or 863 6131

SALISBURY, George Malcolm Owen. b 11. Bp's Coll Calcutta 40. **d** 43 **p** 44. India 43-49; C St Alb St Pet *St Alb* 49-61; V Markyate Street 61-68; R Shenley 68-81; rtd 81; Chapl St Alb City Hosp 81-87. *33 Elizabeth Court, Jersey Farm, St Albans, Herts AL4 9JB* Tel (01727) 834568

SALISBURY, Harold Gareth. b 21. St Pet Hall Ox BA42 MA46. Wycliffe Hall Ox 42. **d** 44 **p** 45. C Pet St Mark *Pet* 44-46; India 47-63; V Duddo *Newc* 63-70; V Norham 63-70; V Norham and Duddo 70-78; V Snaith *Sheff* 78-86; P-in-c Cowick 78-86; TR Gt Snaith 86; rtd 86; Perm to Offic *Pet* from 87. *33 Nightingale Drive, Towcester, Northants NN12 6RA* Tel (01327) 353674

SALISBURY, John Forbes. b 16. St Jo Coll Dur 46. **d** 50 **p** 51. C Gt Malvern Ch Ch *Worc* 50-53; C Dudley St Jo 53-57; V Manningham St Luke *Bradf* 57-62; V Riddlesden 62-67; V Tosside 67-79; Lic to Offic 80-84; rtd 81; Perm to Offic *Bradf* from 84. *14 Victoria Mill, Belmont Wharf, Skipton, N Yorkshire BD23 1RL* Tel (01756) 701411

SALISBURY, Peter Brian Christopher. b 58. MBCS85 UMIST BSc80. Sarum & Wells Th Coll BTh92. **d** 92 **p** 93. C Stanmore *Win* 92-95; V Chilworth w N Baddesley from 95. *The Vicarage, 33 Crescent Road, North Baddesley, Southampton SO5 9HU* Tel (01703) 732393

SALISBURY, Roger John. b 44. Lon Univ BD67. Lon Coll of Div 66. **d** 68 **p** 69. C Harold Wood *Chelmsf* 68-73; V Dorking St Paul *Guildf* 73-82; R Rusholme H Trin *Man* 82-90; TR Gt Chesham *Ox* from 90. *The Rectory, Church Street, Chesham, Bucks HP5 1HY* Tel (01494) 783629

SALISBURY, Canon Tobias (Toby). b 33. Em Coll Cam BA60. Ripon Hall Ox 60. **d** 62 **p** 63. C Putney St Mary *S'wark* 62-65; C Churchdown St Jo *Glouc* 65-67; V Urchfont w Stert *Sarum* 67-73; R Burton Bradstock w Shipton Gorge and Chilcombe 73-79; P-in-c Long Bredy w Lt Bredy and Kingston Russell 75-79; TR Bride Valley 79-86; V Gt and Lt Bedwyn and Savernake Forest from 86; Can and Preb Sarum Cathl from 92. *The Vicarage, Church Street, Great Bedwyn, Marlborough, Wilts SN8 3PF* Tel (01672) 870779

SALISBURY, Archdeacon of. *See* HOPKINSON, The Ven Barnabas John

SALISBURY, Bishop of. *See* STANCLIFFE, The Rt Revd David Staffurth

SALISBURY, Dean of. *See* WATSON, The Very Revd Derek Richard

SALMON, Andrew Ian. b 61. St Jo Coll Nottm BTh88. **d** 88 **p** 89. C Collyhurst *Man* 88-92; P-in-c Pendleton St Ambrose 92-95; TV Pendleton from 95. *St Ambrose's Vicarage, 92 Fitzwarren Street, Pendleton, Salford M6 5RS* Tel 0161-745 7608

SALMON, Andrew Meredith Bryant. b 30. Jes Coll Cam BA54 MA58. Ridley Hall Cam 54. **d** 56 **p** 57. C Enfield Ch Ch Trent Park *Lon* 56-58; Chapl Monkton Combe Sch Bath 58-71; Chapl Milton Abbey Sch Dorset 71-89; TV Bride Valley *Sarum* 89-96; rtd 97. *1 Barnhill Road, Ridge, Wareham, Dorset BH20 5BD* Tel (01929) 554039

SALMON, Anthony James Heygate. b 30. CCC Ox BA53 DipTh54 MA57. Cuddesdon Coll 54. **d** 56 **p** 57. C S Norwood St Mark *Cant* 56-59; S Africa 59-69; Chapl USPG Coll of the Ascension Selly Oak 69-74; P-in-c Frinsted 74-78; R Harrietsham *Cant* 74-85; P-in-c Ulcombe 81-85; V Chobham w Valley End *Guildf* 85-95; rtd 95. *24 Elmwood, Welwyn Garden City, Herts AL8 6LE*

SALMON, Bernard Bryant. b 24. Trin Hall Cam BA50 MA54. Wells Th Coll 50. **d** 52 **p** 53. C Stockton St Pet *Dur* 52-55; C Longbenton St Bart *Newc* 55-58; R Cramlington 58-71; V Winscombe *B & W* 71-91; RD Locking 78-86; rtd 91; Perm to Offic *B & W* from 91. *Scaddens House, Scaddens Lane, Rodney Stoke, Cheddar, Somerset BS27 3UR* Tel (01749) 870194

SALMON, Mrs Constance Hazel. b 25. R Holloway Coll Lon BSc46. Lon Bible Coll 66 Gilmore Course 71. **dss** 80 **d** 87 **p** 96. Sidcup St Andr *Roch* 80-88; NSM 87-88; Perm to Offic 88-96; NSM Eynsford w Farningham and Lullingstone from 96. *43 Old Mill Close, Eynsford, Dartford DA4 0BN* Tel (01322) 866034

SALMON, Mrs Margaret. b 37. Leeds Univ BA59 CertEd60. SW Minl Tr Course 85. **d** 88 **p** 94. NSM Yelverton, Meavy, Sheepstor and Walkhampton *Ex* from 88. *Hinnies, Leg-o-Mutton Corner, Yelverton, Devon PL20 6DJ* Tel (01822) 853310

SALMON, Richard Harold. b 35. Fitzw Ho Cam BA57. Clifton Th Coll 57. **d** 59 **p** 60. C Blackheath Park St Mich *S'wark* 59-62; C St Alb St Paul *St Alb* 62-64; OMF 64-66; Malaysia 66-75; P-in-c March St Wendreda *Ely* 75-76; R 76-85; V Congresbury w Puxton and Hewish St Ann *B & W* from 85. *The Vicarage, Station Road, Congresbury, Bristol BS19 5DX* Tel (01934) 833126

SALMON, The Very Revd Thomas Noel Desmond Cornwall. b 13. TCD BA35 BD42 MA49. CITC 36. **d** 37 **p** 38. C Bangor St Comgall *D & D* 37-40; C Belfast St Jas *Conn* 40-41; C Larne and Inver 42-44; Clerical V Ch Ch Cathl Dublin *D & G* 44-45; Lect TCD 45-89; I Dublin Rathfarnham *D & G* 45-50; Hon Clerical V Ch Ch Cathl Dublin 45-63; I Tullow 50-62; I Dublin St Ann 62-67; Preb Dunlavin St Patr Cathl Dublin 63-67; Dean Ch Ch Cathl Dublin *D & G* 67-89; I Dublin Ch Ch Cathl 76-89; rtd 89. *3 Glenageary Terrace, Dun Laoghaire, Co Dublin, Irish Republic* Tel Dublin (1) 280 0101

SALMON, William John. b 50. Lon Univ BSc72. St Jo Coll Dur 77. **d** 79 **p** 80. C Summerstown *S'wark* 79-81; C Hampreston *Sarum* 81-86; V Sundon *St Alb* 86-90; Dep Chapl HM Young Offender Inst Glen Parva 90-91; Chapl HM Pris Whitemoor 91-95; Chapl HM Pris Blundeston from 95. *The Chaplain's Office, HM Prison Blundeston, Lowestoft, Suffolk NR32 5BG* Tel (01502) 730591 Fax 730138

SALONIA, Ivan. b 38. CQSW78 Open Univ BA81 N Lon Poly MA85. Milan Th Coll (RC). **d** 63 **p** 64. In RC Ch (Hong Kong) 64-73; Hon C Woolwich St Thos *S'wark* 89-91; C Greenwich St Alfege w St Pet and St Paul 91-93; C Kidbrooke 93-95; TV from 95. *48 Crookston Road, London SE9 1YB* Tel 0181-850 0529 or 319 3874

SALOP, Archdeacon of. *See* FROST, The Ven George

SALSBURY, Harry. b 31. Lon Univ TCert62. **d** 60 **p** 61. In RC Ch 60-82; NSM Bexhill St Pet *Chich* 83-84; Chapl Brighton Coll Jun Sch 84-93; C Eastbourne St Mary *Chich* 93-94; Perm to Offic from 94. *39 Croxden Way, Eastbourne, E Sussex BN22 0TZ* Tel (01323) 507091

SALT, Canon David Christopher. b 37. Univ of Wales (Lamp) BA59. Sarum Th Coll 59. **d** 61 **p** 62. C Kidderminster St Mary *Worc* 61-66; Ind Chapl 66-72; R Knightwick w Doddenham, Broadwas and Cotheridge 72-82; Chapl Worc Coll of HE 72-82; V Redditch St Steph from 82; P-in-c Tardebigge 84-88; RD Bromsgrove from 91; Hon Can Worc Cathl from 92. *St Stephen's Vicarage, 248 Birchfield Road, Redditch, Worcs B97 4LZ* Tel (01527) 541738

SALT, David Thomas Whitehorn. b 32. K Coll Lon AKC56 BD57. **d** 57 **p** 58. New Hebrides 57-63; Solomon Is 63-66; C Hawley H Trin *Guildf* 66-68; V Shelf *Bradf* 68-73; R Checkendon *Ox* 73-81; RD Henley 78-84; TR Langtree 81-84; Chapl Hungerford Hosp 84-89; V Hungerford and Denford *Ox* 84-89; P-in-c Harpsden w Bolney 89-95; Gen Sec Melanesian Miss 89-95; rtd 95. *Willow Cottage, 239 East Grafton, Marlborough, Wilts SN8 3DP* Tel (01672) 810049

SALT, The Very Revd John William. b 41. Kelham Th Coll 61. **d** 66 **p** 67. C Barrow St Matt *Carl* 66-70; S Africa from 70; Adn S Zululand and Dean Eshowe Cath from 89. *PO Box 207, Eshowe, 3815 South Africa* Tel Eshowe (354) 41215 E-mail jwsogs @iafrica.com

SALT, Leslie. b 29. Linc Th Coll 68. **d** 69 **p** 69. C Alford w Rigsby *Linc* 69-75; V Torksey 75-94; R Kettlethorpe 77-94; V Marton 77-94; V Newton-on-Trent 77-94; rtd 94; Perm to Offic *Linc* from 94. *2 Holdenby Close, Lincoln LN2 4TQ*

SALTER, Arthur Thomas John. b 34. TD88. AKC60. **d** 61 **p** 62. C Ealing St Pet Mt Park *Lon* 61-65; C Shepherd's Bush St Steph w St Thos 65-66; C Holborn St Alb w Saffron Hill St Pet 66-70; P-in-c Barnsbury St Clem 70-77; P-in-c Islington St Mich 70-77; V Pentonville St Silas w All SS and St Jas from 70; CF (TAVR) from 75; Gen Sec Angl and E Chs Assn from 76; Chmn from 90; P-in-c St Dunstan in the West *Lon* from 79. *The Vicarage, 87 Richmond Avenue, London N1 0LX* Tel 0171-607 2865 or 405 1929

SALTER, Canon George Alfred. b 25. TCD BA47 MA. CITC 49. **d** 49 **p** 50. C Rathdowney *C & O* 49-51; C Cork St Luke *C, C & R* 51-53; I Fermoy Union 53-55; I Cork St Luke w St Ann 55-73; Preb Ross Cathl 69-88; Preb Cork Cathl 69-88; Treas 88-94; I Cork St Luke Union 73-94; Preb Tymothan St Patr Cathl Dublin 88-94; rtd 94. *Mount Vernon House, 66 Wellington Road, Cork, Irish Republic* Tel Cork (21) 506844

SALTER, Mrs Janet Elizabeth (Jan). b 48. Leeds Univ CertEd69. SW Minl Tr Course 92. **d** 95. C Coleshill *Birm* 95-97. *6 Maple Close, St Columb, Cornwall TR9 6SL*

SALTER, John Frank. b 37. Dur Univ BA62 DipTh64. Cranmer Hall Dur 62. **d** 64 **p** 65. C Bridlington Priory *York* 64-67; Travelling Sec IVF 67-70; V Stoughton *Guildf* from 70; RD Guildf 89-94. *The Vicarage, 3 Shepherd's Lane, Guildford, Surrey GU2 6SJ* Tel (01483) 61603

SALTER, John Leslie. b 51. AKC76. Coll of Resurr Mirfield 77. **d** 78 **p** 79. C Tottenham St Paul *Lon* 78-82; P-in-c Castle Vale *Birm* 82-83; TV Curdworth w Castle Vale 83-90; V Castle Vale St Cuth 90-92; V Wantage *Ox* from 93. *The Vicarage, The Cloisters, Wantage, Oxon OX12 8AQ* Tel (01235) 762214

SALTER, Nigel Christopher Murray. b 46. Loughb Univ BTech. Ripon Coll Cuddesdon 79. **d** 81 **p** 82. C Glouc St Aldate *Glouc* 81-84; C Solihull *Birm* 84-88; V Highters Heath 88-97; Asst Chapl Greenwich Healthcare NHS Trust from 97. *Greenwich District Hospital, Vanburgh Road, London SE10 9HE* Tel 0181-312 6248

SALTER, Richard. b 24. Edin Th Coll 46. **d** 48 **p** 49. C Dundee St Salvador *Bre* 48-51; C Watford St Andr *St Alb* 51-54; C Oxhey St Matt 54-58; V Roberttown *Wakef* 58-62; V Watford St Jo *St Alb* from 62. *St John's Vicarage, 9 Monmouth Road, Watford WD1 1QW* Tel (01923) 236174

SALTER, Roger John. b 45. Trin Coll Bris 75. **d** 79 **p** 80. C Bedminster St Mich *Bris* 79-82; C Swindon Ch Ch 82-84; V Bedminster Down 84-89; P-in-c Northwood *Portsm* 89-93; P-in-c W Cowes H Trin 89-92; V Cowes H Trin and St Mary 92-94; USA from 94. *1300 Panorama Drive, Vestavia Hills, Alabama 35216, USA* Tel Birmingham (205) 823-7967

SALTER, Samuel. b 22. St Edm Hall Ox BA49 MA53. St Steph Ho Ox 49. **d** 50 **p** 51. C Brighton St Wilfrid *Chich* 50-53; C Felpham w Middleton 53-56; V Barkston w Syston *Linc* 56-59; R Coningsby 59-65; Chapl RAF 59-65; Chapl Cheltenham Coll 65-81; TV Grantham *Linc* 81-87; rtd 87; Perm to Offic *Linc* from 87. *6 Gladstone Terrace, Grantham, Lincs NG31 8BW* Tel (01476) 560249

SALWAY, Canon Donald Macleay. b 31. St Pet Hall Ox BA54 MA59. Oak Hill Th Coll 54. **d** 56 **p** 57. C Holloway St Mary w St Jas *Lon* 56-67; V Cambridge St Phil *Ely* 67-81; V Mile Cross *Nor* 81-96; RD Nor N 89-95; Hon Can Nor Cathl 91-96; rtd 96; Perm to Offic *B & W* from 96. *Lype House, Long Road, Langport, Somerset TA10 9LD* Tel (01458) 241623

SAMBELL, David John. b 31. St Aid Birkenhead 60. **d** 63 **p** 64. C Sutton St Geo *Ches* 63-67; C Alsager St Mary 67-71; V Crewe St Pet 71-81; V Upton Priory from 81. *The Vicarage, Church Way, Macclesfield, Cheshire SK10 3HT* Tel (01625) 827761

SAMMAN, Peter Bryan. b 27. TCD BA53. Coll of Resurr Mirfield 53. **d** 55 **p** 56. C Adlington *Blackb* 55-57; C Church Kirk 57-60; V Briercliffe 60-67; V Lancaster Ch Ch 67-74; V Lostock Hall 74-85; V Morecambe St Barn 85-91; rtd 91; Perm to Offic *Blackb* from 91. *14 Wentworth Crescent, Morecambe, Lancs LA3 3NX* Tel (01524) 425208

SAMME, Raymond Charles (Ray). b 50. Trent Poly MIBiol80. Oak Hill Th Coll 85. **d** 87 **p** 88. C Holmer w Huntington *Heref* 87-90; C Derby St Alkmund and St Werburgh *Derby* 90-93; V Romford Gd Shep Collier Row *Chelmsf* from 93. *Good Shepherd Vicarage, 97 Collier Row Lane, Romford RM5 3BA* Tel (01708) 745626

SAMMONS, John Trevor. b 22. Birm Univ BA48. Ripon Hall Ox. **d** 50 **p** 51. C The Quinton *Birm* 50-55; V Birm St Luke 55-70; Chapl Birm Skin Hosp 56-70; P-in-c Nomans Heath *Lich* 70-82; R Newton Regis w Seckington and Shuttington *Birm* 70-86; rtd 87; Perm to Offic *Birm* from 87. *39 Kurtus, Dosthill, Tamworth, Staffs B77 1NX* Tel (01827) 283875

SAMPFORD, John Alfred. b 36. Lich Th Coll 58. **d** 61 **p** 62. C Lambeth St Phil *S'wark* 61-65; C Beddington 65-69; V Hampstead Ch Ch *Lon* 69-79; V Enfield Chase St Mary from 79. *St Mary Magdalene Vicarage, 30 The Ridgeway, Enfield, Middx EN2 8QH* Tel 0181-363 1875

SAMPSON, Brian Andrew. b 39. **d** 94 **p** 95. C Glem Valley United Benefice *St E* 94-96; C Pentlow, Foxearth, Liston and Borley *Chelmsf* 96-97; P-in-c from 97. *The Rectory, The Street, Foxearth, Sudbury, Suffolk CO10 7JG* Tel (01787) 313132

SAMPSON, Clive. b 38. St Jo Coll Cam BA61 MA64. Ridley Hall Cam 63. **d** 65 **p** 66. C Tunbridge Wells St Jo *Roch* 65-69; Travelling Sec Scripture Union 69-79; V Maidstone St Luke *Cant* 79-94. *25 Townsend Drive, St Albans, Herts AL3 5RF* Tel (01727) 850282

SAMPSON, Desmond William John. b 25. FRICS60. Roch Th Coll 63. **d** 65 **p** 66. C Hythe *Cant* 65-70; V Alkham w Capel le Ferne and Hougham 70-76; V Wingham w Elmstone and Preston w Stourmouth 76-86; RD E Bridge 81-86; C Hythe 86-91; rtd 91; Perm to Offic *Cant* from 91. *25 Albert Road, Hythe, Kent CT21 6BP* Tel (01303) 268457

SAMPSON, Jeremy John Egerton. b 23. Dur Univ BSc45. Wells Th Coll 46. **d** 48 **p** 49. C Longbenton St Bart *Newc* 48-51; Singapore 51-62; V Killingworth *Newc* 62-76; V Consett *Dur* 76-90; RD Lanchester 80-85; rtd 90; Perm to Offic *Dur* from 90. *6 Kilkenny Road, Guisborough, Cleveland TS14 7LE* Tel (01287) 632734

SAMPSON, Canon Terence Harold Morris. b 41. ACA64 FCA75. Bps' Coll Cheshunt 64. **d** 67 **p** 68. C Penrith St Andr *Carl* 67-72; V Carl St Barn 72-80; TR Carl H Trin and St Barn 80-84; Chapl Cumberland Infirmary 83-84; R Workington St Mich *Carl* from 84; Hon Can Carl Cathl from 89; RD Solway 90-95. *St Michael's Rectory, Dora Crescent, Workington, Cumbria CA14 2EZ* Tel (01900) 602311

SAMS, David Stevenson. b 27. Hertf Coll Ox BA50 MA54 Man Univ DipAE78. Wycliffe Hall Ox 50. **d** 52 **p** 53. C Kersal Moor *Man* 52-55; C Benchill 55-57; V Dixon Green 57-61; TR Didsbury St Jas and Em 61-69; Lic Preacher 69-79; Welfare Officer Stockport Tech Coll 69-79; Perm to Offic *Chelmsf* 79-92; Sen Tutor Colchester Inst 79-91; rtd 91; Perm to Offic *Chelmsf* from 91. *26 Beaconsfield Road, Clacton-on-Sea, Essex CO15 6BU* Tel (01255) 432295

SAMS, Michael Charles. b 34. Ox NSM Course 81. **d** 84 **p** 85. NSM Abingdon *Ox* from 84. *13 Hound Close, Abingdon, Oxon OX14 2LU* Tel (01235) 529084

SAMUEL, Brother. *See* DOUBLE, Canon Richard Sydney

SAMUEL, Canon James Louis (Jim). b 30. Birm Poly CQSW72 Open Univ BA77. Sarum Th Coll 59. **d** 61 **p** 62. C Dursley *Glouc* 61-63; C Matson 63-65; C Leckhampton SS Phil and Jas 65-66; C Blakenall Heath *Lich* 67-69; P-in-c Dudley St Aug Holly Hall *Worc* 81-86; V 86-94; RD Dudley 87-93; Hon Can Worc Cathl 88-94; rtd 94; Perm to Offic *Worc* 94-96; C Kidderminster St Mary and All SS w Trimpley etc from 96. *44 Broadwaters Drive, Kidderminster, Worcs DY10 2RY* Tel (01562) 68533

SAMUEL, Stuart. b 48. AKC70. St Aug Coll Cant 70. **d** 71 **p** 72. C Golcar *Wakef* 71-77; V Brampton St Mark *Derby* 77-79; P-in-c Hathern *Leic* 79-83; R Hathern, Long Whatton and Diseworth 83-90; R Hathern, Long Whatton and Diseworth w Belton etc 90-97; RD Akeley E 92-96; P-in-c Waltham on the Wolds, Stonesby, Saxby etc from 97; P-in-c Wymondham w Edmondthorpe, Buckminster etc from 97; P-in-c High Framland Parishes from 97. *Waltham Rectory, 23 Melton Road, Waltham on the Wolds, Melton Mowbray, Leics LE14 4AJ* Tel (01664) 464564

SAMUEL, Theophilus (Theo). b 34. BScTech59. Oak Hill Th Coll 70. **d** 72 **p** 73. C Slough *Ox* 72-73; Chapl Community Relns 73-78; Chapl Brunel Univ *Lon* 78-85; V W Drayton from 85. *The Vicarage, 191 Station Road, West Drayton, Middx UB7 7NQ* Tel (01895) 442194 Fax as telephone

SAMUELS, Mrs Ann Elizabeth. b 51. Birm Univ BA73 CertEd74. Trin Coll Bris 85. **d** 87 **p** 94. Par Dn Moreton *Ches* 87-91; Par Dn Halton 91-94; C from 94; Bp's Adv for Women in Min 94-96; Asst Dir of Ords from 96. *The Vicarage, Halton, Runcorn, Cheshire WA7 2BE* Tel (01928) 563636

SAMUELS, Canon Christopher William John. b 42. AKC66. **d** 67 **p** 68. C Kirkholt *Man* 67-72; C-in-c Houghton Regis St Thos CD *St Alb* 72-76; R Tarporley *Ches* 76-83; R Ches St Mary from 83;

RD Ches from 95; Hon Can Ches Cathl from 97. *The Rectory, St Mary-without-the-Walls, Chester CH4 7HL* Tel (01244) 671202

SAMUELS, Raymond John. b 49. Qu Mary Coll Lon BSc73 Essex Univ CertEd74. Trin Coll Bris 85. **d** 87 **p** 88. C Moreton *Ches* 87-91; V Halton from 91. *The Vicarage, Halton, Runcorn, Cheshire WA7 2BE* Tel (01928) 563636

SAMUELS, Mrs Sheila Mary. b 57. St Andr Univ MA79 Wolfs Coll Ox MLitt82 CertEd83. Trin Coll Bris BA89. **d** 89 **p** 94. C Skirbeck H Trin *Linc* 89-96. *43 Spilsby Road, Boston, Lincs PE21 9NX* Tel (01205) 368721

SAMWAYS, Denis Robert. b 37. Leeds Univ BA62. Coll of Resurr Mirfield 62. **d** 64 **p** 65. C Clun w Chapel Lawn *Heref* 64-69; C Pocklington w Yapham-cum-Meltonby, Owsthorpe etc *York* 69-71; C Millington w Gt Givendale 69-71; R Hinderwell w Roxby 71-76; Hon C 80-91; Hon C Loftus 76-80; V Boosbeck w Moorsholm 91-95; R Kirby Misperton w Normanby, Edston and Salton from 95. *The Rectory, Normanby, Sinnington, York YO6 6RH* Tel (01751) 31288

SAMWAYS, John Feverel. b 44. BA DipTh. Trin Coll Bris 81. **d** 83 **p** 84. C Patcham *Chich* 83-86; C Ox St Aldate w St Matt *Ox* 86-94; R Ox St Matt from 95. *The Vicarage, Marlborough Road, Oxford OX1 4LW* Tel (01865) 243434

SANDAY, Robert Ward. b 55. Sarum & Wells Th Coll 89. **d** 91 **p** 92. C Swindon Ch Ch *Bris* 91-94; R Lyddington and Wanborough and Bishopstone etc from 94. *The Vicarage, 19 Church Road, Wanborough, Swindon SN4 0BZ* Tel (01793) 790242

SANDBERG, Peter John. b 37. Lon Univ LLB59. Lon Coll of Div 67. **d** 69 **p** 70. C Hailsham *Chich* 69-72; C Billericay St Mary *Chelmsf* 72-77; TV Billericay and Lt Burstead 77-83; R Thundersley from 83; RD Hadleigh from 90. *St Peter's Rectory, 390 Church Road, Thundersley, Benfleet, Essex SS7 3HG* Tel (01268) 792235

SANDELLS-REES, Mrs Kathy Louise. b 68. Abth Coll of FE DipBBSS87 Univ of Wales (Cardiff) DipTh90. Qu Coll Birm DipTh92. **d** 92 **p** 97. C Holyhead w Rhoscolyn w Llanfair-yn-Neubwll *Ban* 92-94; C Ban 94-95; Chapl Gwynedd Hosp Ban from 94; P-in-c Ban from 95. *1 Belmont Road, Bangor LL57 2LL* Tel (01248) 353405 or 384384

SANDEMAN, Arthur Alastair Malcolm. b 14. Chich Th Coll 37. **d** 39 **p** 40. St Vincent 39-40; Canada 40-43; C Cranford *Lon* 43-46; C Swanage *Sarum* 46-49; C Croydon Woodside *Cant* 49-51; C S Kensington St Steph *Lon* 51-52; Hon C Kensington St Mary Abbots w St Geo 52-54; R Wick *Mor* 54-56; V Brinksway *Ches* 56-60; V Cressing *Chelmsf* 61-75; rtd 75; Perm to Offic *Ex* from 75. *20 Orient Road, Paignton, Devon TQ3 2PB* Tel (01803) 521385

SANDERS, Allan Cameron Ebblewhite. b 34. CCC Ox MA59 Univ of E Africa MEd69. Ox NSM Course 82. **d** 85 **p** 86. Hd Master Reading Blue Coat Sch from 74; Hon C Sonning *Ox* from 85. *Headmaster's House, Reading Blue Coat School, Reading RG4 0SU* Tel 0118-969 3200

SANDERS, Colin Anthony Wakefield. b 26. Wadh Coll Ox MA55. Ox NSM Course 89. **d** 90 **p** 91. NSM Eynsham and Cassington *Ox* 90-95; NSM Bladon w Woodstock from 95. *Little Firs, 41 Bladon Road, Woodstock, Oxon OX20 1QD* Tel (01993) 813357

SANDERS, Graham Laughton. b 32. Kelham Th Coll 52. **d** 56 **p** 57. C Glouc St Paul *Glouc* 56-60; India 61-68; V Heaton St Martin *Bradf* 68-76; V Gt Waltham *Chelmsf* 76-79; Sec Dioc Liturg Cttee 78-87; P-in-c Ford End 79; V Gt Waltham w Ford End 79-87; TR Guiseley w Esholt *Bradf* 87-94; Perm to Offic from 95; rtd 97. *4 Marlborough Road, Shipley, W Yorkshire BD18 3NX* Tel (01274) 587896

SANDERS, Henry William. b 36. **d** 62 **p** 64. C Nottingham St Ann *S'well* 62-65; C Dagenham *Chelmsf* 65-67; C W Thurrock 67-73; C W Ham 73-78. *20 Vale Road, London E7 8BJ*

SANDERS, Herbert. b 21. Clifton Th Coll 51. **d** 53 **p** 54. C Laisterdyke *Bradf* 53-56; C Bingley All SS 56-59; V Oxenhope 59-66; Lic to Offic *Linc* 66-81 and from 95; rtd 81. *The Vicarage, Low Toynton, Horncastle, Lincs LN9 6JU* Tel (01507) 523410

SANDERS, Mrs Hilary Clare. b 57. Hull Univ BA79 UEA CertEd81. EAMTC 83. **dss** 85 **d** 87 **p** 94. Haverhill w Withersfield, the Wrattings etc *St E* 85-87; Hon Par Dn Melton 87-94; Hon C from 94; Dioc Schs Officer from 88. *The Rectory, Station Road, Woodbridge, Suffolk IP12 1PX* Tel (01394) 380279

SANDERS, James Alexander. b 29. **d** 65 **p** 66. Australia 65-78; C Enfield St Jas *Lon* 78-81; rtd 94. *81 Queen Street, Woollahra, NSW 2025, Australia*

SANDERS, Mark. b 57. Hull Univ BA79 Cam Univ BA82. Westcott Ho Cam 80. **d** 83 **p** 84. C Haverhill w Withersfield, the Wrattings etc *St E* 83-87; P-in-c Melton 87-91; R from 91. *The Rectory, Station Road, Melton, Woodbridge, Suffolk IP12 1PX* Tel (01394) 380279

SANDERS, Michael Barry. b 45. Fitzw Coll Cam BA67 MA71 Lon Univ BD71. St Jo Coll Nottm 68 Lon Coll of Div. **d** 71 **p** 72. C Ashtead *Guildf* 71-74; Chapl St Jo Coll Cam 75-79; V Dorridge *Birm* 79-89; TR Walsall *Lich* from 89. *The Vicarage, 48 Jesson Road, Walsall WS1 3AX* Tel (01922) 24012

SANDERS, Nigel Wilding. b 29. Mert Coll Ox MA55. Ox Min Course 91. **d** 92 **p** 93. NSM Maidenhead St Andr and St Mary *Ox* from 92. *Fieldway, Worcester Road, Cookham, Maidenhead, Berks SL6 9JG* Tel (01628) 521516

SANDERS, Mrs Nora Irene. b 29. Lon Univ BA50 CertEd51. WMMTC 74. **dss** 78 **d** 87 **p** 94. Dorridge *Birm* 78-87; Par Dn 87-90; rtd 90; Hon C Tanworth *Birm* 94-96; Perm to Offic from 96. *8 Cransley Grove, Solihull, W Midlands B91 3ZA* Tel 0121-705 2391

SANDERS, Roderick David Scott. b 58. Southn Univ BA80 CertEd81. Cranmer Hall Dur 85. **d** 88 **p** 89. C Luton St Mary *St Alb* 88-93; P-in-c Clovelly *Ex* 93-94; P-in-c Woolfardisworthy and Buck Mills 93-94; TV Parkham, Alwington, Buckland Brewer etc from 94. *The Rectory, Old Market Drive, Woolsery, Bideford, Devon EX39 5QF* Tel (01237) 431571

SANDERS, Mrs Susan Rachel (Susie). b 61. St Mary's Coll Dur BA83. Cranmer Hall Dur 85. **d** 88 **p** 94. Par Dn Luton St Mary *St Alb* 88-93; Perm to Offic *Ex* 93-94; NSM Parkham, Alwington, Buckland Brewer etc from 94. *The Rectory, Old Market Drive, Woolsery, Bideford, Devon EX39 5QF* Tel (01237) 431571

SANDERS, Mrs Wendy Elizabeth. b 49. Carl Dioc Tr Course 87. **d** 90 **p** 94. NSM Bampton w Mardale *Carl* 90-92; C Walney Is 92-94; C Stanwix from 94. *45 Knowe Park Avenue, Carlisle CA3 9EL* Tel (01228) 21528 or 511430

SANDERS, William John. b 48. Liv Inst of Educn BA80. Wycliffe Hall Ox 81. **d** 83 **p** 84. C Netherton *Liv* 83-87; P-in-c Wavertree St Bridget 87-97; V Wavertree St Bridget and St Thos from 97. *St Bridget's Vicarage, 93 Salisbury Road, Wavertree, Liverpool L15 2HU* Tel 0151-733 1117

SANDERSON, Colin James. b 54. SEN SRN. St Mich Coll Llan 85. **d** 87 **p** 88. C Merthyr Dyfan *Llan* 87-90; C Cadoxton-juxta-Barry 90-91; V Llangeinor from 91. *The Vicarage, Corbett Street, Ogmore Vale, Bridgend CF32 7AA* Tel (01656) 842565

SANDERSON, Canon Daniel. b 40. AKC66. **d** 67 **p** 68. C Upperby St Jo *Carl* 67-72; V Addingham 72-75; V Ireleth w Askam from 75; RD Furness from 94; Hon Can Carl Cathl from 95. *St Peter's Vicarage, Duke Street, Askham-in-Furness, Cumbria LA16 7AD* Tel (01229) 462647

SANDERSON, Canon Gillian. b 47. Cranmer Hall Dur 80. **dss** 82 **d** 87 **p** 94. Allesley *Cov* 82-86; Warwick 86-87; C 87-94; TV from 94; Hon Can Cov Cathl from 94. *The Vicarage, 25 Sutherland Close, Warwick CV34 5UJ* Tel (01926) 492097

SANDERSON, Harold. b 26. St Aid Birkenhead. **d** 61 **p** 62. C Pemberton St Mark Newtown *Liv* 61-64; V Warrington St Ann 64-73; P-in-c Warrington St Pet 70-73; V Orrell 73-79; V Scarisbrick 79-91; rtd 91; Perm to Offic *Liv* from 91. *29 Green Lane, Ormskirk, Lancs L39 1ND* Tel (01695) 571421

SANDERSON, The Very Revd Peter Oliver. b 29. St Chad's Coll Dur BA52 DipTh54. **d** 54 **p** 55. C Houghton le Spring *Dur* 54-59; Jamaica 59-63; Chapl RAF 63-67; P-in-c Winksley cum Grantley and Aldfield w Studley *Ripon* 67-68; V 68-74; V Leeds St Aid 74-84; Can St Paul's Cathl Dundee *Bre* 84-91; Provost St Paul's Cathl Dundee 84-91; R Dundee St Paul 84-91; USA from 91; rtd 94. *805 Meadow Lane, Storm Lake, Iowa 50588-2756, USA* Tel Storm Lake (712) 732-7189

SANDERSON, Peter Richard Fallowfield. b 18. St Cath Soc Ox BA41 MA46. Chich Th Coll 41. **d** 42 **p** 44. C Bishops Hull St Jo *B & W* 42-48; C Ox St Paul *Ox* 48-49; Perm to Offic *Ex* 49-55; V Poundstock *Truro* 56-74; P-in-c Hove St Patr *Chich* 74-79; P-in-c Buxted St Mary 79-82; P-in-c Hadlow Down 79-82; P-in-c Buxted and Hadlow Down 82-83; rtd 83; Perm to Offic *Chich* from 83. *Nova Scotia, 48 Parklands Road, Hassocks, W Sussex BN6 8JZ* Tel (01273) 843117

SANDERSON, Scott. b 42. Oak Hill Th Coll DipHE. **d** 82 **p** 83. C Galleywood Common *Chelmsf* 82-88; P-in-c Newport w Widdington 88-92; V Newport from 92. *The Vicarage, Newport, Saffron Walden, Essex CB11 2RB* Tel (01799) 540339

SANDES, Denis Lindsay. BTh. **d** 89 **p** 90. C Bandon Union *C, C & R* 89-92; I Kells Union *C & O* from 92. *The Priory, Kells, Co Kilkenny, Irish Republic* Tel Kilkenny (56) 28367

SANDFORD, Jack. b 11. Ripon Hall Ox. **d** 60 **p** 61. C Eastwood *Chelmsf* 60-63; V Mayland 63-66; V Steeple 63-66; V Barkingside St Laur 67-77; rtd 77; Perm to Offic *Chelmsf* from 77. *15 Lyndhurst Road, Holland-on-Sea, Clacton-on-Sea, Essex CO15 5HT* Tel (01255) 815294

SANDFORD, Nicholas Robert. b 63. Kent Univ BA84 Univ of Wales (Cardiff) BD87. St Mich Coll Llan 84. **d** 87 **p** 88. C Neath w Llantwit *Llan* 87-90; C Cardiff St Jo 90-94; R Cilybebyll from 94; Chapl HM Pris Swansea from 95. *The Rectory, 7 Cwmnantllyd Road, Gellinudd, Pontardawe, Swansea SA8 3DT* Tel (01792) 862118

SANDFORD, Paul Richard. b 47. Em Coll Cam BA69 MA73. Wycliffe Hall Ox 72. **d** 75 **p** 76. C Upper Holloway St Pet *Lon* 75-77; C Finchley St Paul Long Lane 77-81; Ind Chapl *Newc* 81-88; TV Cramlington 81-88; TV Dronfield *Derby* 88-90; TV Dronfield w Holmesfield from 90. *St Philip's Vicarage, 43 Firthwood Road, Dronfield, Sheffield S18 6BW* Tel (01246) 413893

SANDFORD of Banbury, The Revd and Rt Hon Lord (John Cyril Edmondson). b 20. DSC43. Dartmouth RN Coll. Westcott Ho

Cam 56. **d** 58 **p** 60. C Harpenden St Nic *St Alb* 58-63; Perm to Offic from 63; Chapl for Miss and Ecum St Alb 63-66; Chmn Redundant Chs Cttee Ch Commrs 82-88; rtd 85. *27 Ashley Gardens, Ambrosden Avenue, London SW1P 1QD* Tel 0171-834 5722

SANDHAM, Stephen McCourt. b 41. K Coll Lon BD65 AKC65. **d** 66 **p** 67. C Stockton St Pet *Dur* 66-69; C Bishopwearmouth Gd Shep 69-71; C Bishopwearmouth St Mich w St Hilda 71-75; V Darlington St Mark w St Paul 75-82; P-in-c Sunderland St Chad 82-87; R Shincliffe from 87. *The Rectory, Shincliffe, Durham DH1 2NJ* Tel 0191-386 2142

SANDOM, Miss Carolyn Elizabeth (Carrie). b 63. Homerton Coll Cam BEd85. Wycliffe Hall Ox BTh93. **d** 94. C St Helen Bishopsgate w St Andr Undershaft etc *Lon* 94-96; C Cambridge H Sepulchre *Ely* from 96. *12 Eden Street, Cambridge CB1 1EL* Tel (01223) 578016

SANDS, Colin Robert. b 38. JP84. Chester Coll CertEd64. N Ord Course 82. **d** 85 **p** 86. Hd Master Magull Primary Sch from 80; NSM Bootle Ch Ch *Liv* 85-94; NSM Maghull from 94. *16 Strafford Drive, Bootle, Merseyside L20 9JW* Tel 0151-525 8709

SANDS, Frederick William. b 25. St Deiniol's Hawarden 86. **d** 87 **p** 88. Chapl Asst Leic Gen Hosp 87-89; Chapl 89-95; rtd 95; Perm to Offic *Leic* from 95. *Gwendolen Road, Leicester LE5 4PW* Tel 0116-249 0490

SANDS, Nigel Colin. b 39. Dur Univ BA64 MA68. Oak Hill Th Coll 65. **d** 67 **p** 68. C Skelmersdale St Paul *Liv* 67-71; C Childwall All SS 71-72; V Wavertree St Bridget 72-78; P-in-c Welford w Wickham and Gt Shefford *Ox* 78-86; P-in-c Boxford w Stockcross and Speen 84-86; R Welford w Wickham and Gt Shefford, Boxford etc from 86. *The Rectory, Wickham, Newbury, Berks RG16 8HD* Tel (01488) 608244

SANDS, William James (Bill). b 55. St Jo Coll Nottm LTh83. **d** 83 **p** 84. C St Mary-at-Latton *Chelmsf* 83-86; Zimbabwe 86-87 and from 92; C-in-c Barkingside St Cedd *Chelmsf* 87-89; C Woodford St Mary w St Phil and St Jas 87-89; P-in-c Elmsett w Aldham *St E* 89-92; P-in-c Kersey w Lindsey 89-92. *The Rectory, St Mary's Church, PO Esigodini, Zimbabwe* Tel Esigodini (88) 263

SANGER, Reginald Stephen John. b 15. Wycliffe Hall Ox. **d** 57 **p** 58. C New Beckenham St Paul *Roch* 57-60; Youth Chapl 57-62; Warden Dioc Conf Ho and Youth Cen 60-62; V Lee St Mildred *S'wark* 62-83; rtd 83; Perm to Offic *Chich* from 87. *62 Quantock Road, Durrington, Worthing, W Sussex BN13 2HQ* Tel (01903) 692905

SANGSTER, Andrew. b 45. K Coll Lon BD67 AKC67 BA71 MA84 Lon Inst of Educn MPhil93. St Boniface Warminster. **d** 69 **p** 70. C Aylesford *Roch* 69-72; C Shirley *Win* 73-76; V Woolston 76-79; Prov Youth Chapl Ch in Wales 79-82; New Zealand 82-89; Chapl Eton Coll 89-92; Hd Master St Edm Sch Hindhead from 92; Perm to Offic *Guildf* from 92. *St Edmund's School, Hindhead, Surrey GU26 6BH* Tel (01428) 604808

SANKEY, Julian. b 52. Qu Coll Ox BA74 MA79. St Jo Coll Nottm 84. **d** 86 **p** 87. C New Barnet St Jas *St Alb* 86-89; C Mansfield St Pet *S'well* 89-94; Chapl St Luke's Hospice Sheff from 94. *St Lukes Hospice, Little Common Lane, Sheffield S11 9NE, or 2 Woodvale Road, Sheffield S10 3EX* Tel 0114-236 9911

SANKEY, Terence Arthur Melville (Terry). b 51. CertTS. Trin Coll Bris 87. **d** 89 **p** 90. C Chalke Valley W *Sarum* 89-93; NSM Chalke Deanery from 93. *Rookhaye Farmhouse, Bower Chalke, Salisbury SP5 5BT* Tel (01722) 780774

SANSBURY, Christopher John. b 34. Peterho Cam BA57 MA. Westcott Ho Cam 58. **d** 59 **p** 60. C Portsea N End St Mark *Portsm* 59-63; C Weeke *Win* 63-71; V N Eling St Mary 71-78; R Long Melford *St E* from 78. *The Rectory, Long Melford, Sudbury, Suffolk CO10 9DL* Tel (01787) 310845

SANSOM, John Reginald. b 40. St Jo Coll Nottm 73. **d** 75 **p** 76. C Ipswich St Marg *St E* 75-79; P-in-c Emneth *Ely* 79-85; P-in-c Hartford 85-86; TV Huntingdon 86-91; R Sawtry 91-97; R Sawtry and Glatton from 97. *The Rectory, Sawtry, Huntingdon, Cambs PE17 5TD* Tel (01487) 830215

SANSOM, Canon Michael Charles. b 44. Bris Univ BA66 St Jo Coll Dur PhD74. Cranmer Hall Dur 68. **d** 72 **p** 73. C Ecclesall *Sheff* 72-76; Lic to Offic *Ely* 76-88; Dir of Studies Ridley Hall Cam 76-88; Vice-Prin 79-88; Dir of Ords *St Alb* from 88; Can Res St Alb from 88. *4D Harpenden Road, St Albans, Herts AL3 5AB* Tel (01727) 833777

SANSOM, Robert Arthur. b 29. BA. St Aid Birkenhead 60. **d** 62 **p** 63. C Sutton in Ashfield St Mary *S'well* 62-65; V Holbrooke *Derby* 65-70; Canada from 70. *2254 Amherst Avenue, Sidney, British Columbia, Canada, V8L 2G7*

SANSOME, Geoffrey Hubert. b 29. Man Univ BA53. Qu Coll Birm DipTh62. **d** 62 **p** 63. C Prenton *Ches* 62-68; P-in-c Liscard St Thos 68-72; V Kingsley 72-83; V Wybunbury w Doddington 83-91; V Marbury from 91. *The Vicarage, Marbury, Whitchurch, Shropshire SY13 4LN* Tel (01948) 663758

SANSUM, Canon David Henry. b 31. Bris Univ BA52 MA63. St Aid Birkenhead 54. **d** 56 **p** 57. C Henleaze *Bris* 56-59; C Stratton St Margaret 59-60; C Stoke Bishop 60-64; V Stechford *Birm* 64-76; V Ashbourne w Mapleton *Derby* from 76; V Ashbourne St Jo from 81; RD Ashbourne from 91; Hon Can Derby Cathl from 95. *The Vicarage, Belle Vue Road, Ashbourne, Derbyshire DE6 1AT* Tel (01335) 343129

✠**SANTER, The Rt Revd Mark.** b 36. Qu Coll Cam BA60 MA64. Westcott Ho Cam. **d** 63 **p** 64 **c** 81. Tutor Cuddesdon Coll 63-67; C Cuddesdon *Ox* 63-67; Fell and Dean Clare Coll Cam 67-72; Tutor 68-72; Prin Westcott Ho Cam 73-81; Hon Can Win Cathl *Win* 78-81; Area Bp Kensington *Lon* 81-87; Bp Birm from 87. *Bishop's Croft, Old Church Road, Birmingham B17 0BG* Tel 0121-427 1163 Fax 426 1322

SANTRAM, Philip James. b 27. MA Delhi Univ BSc48 Serampore Univ BD53. Bp's Coll Calcutta 49. **d** 52 **p** 54. India 52-66; Ethiopia 66-68; C Horton *Bradf* 68-71; C Whitley Ch Ch *Ox* 71-72; P Missr St Mary Magd Conv Tilehurst 72-76; V Tilehurst St Mary 76-78; Canada from 78; rtd 92. *3544 Boulevard du Souvenir, Chomedey, Laval, Quebec, Canada, H7V 1X2*

SAPSFORD, John Garnet. b 38. **d** 76 **p** 76. C Whiteshill *Glouc* 76-81; Australia from 81. *PO Box 884, Croydon, Victoria, Australia 3136* Tel Melbourne (3) 9723 6739

SARALIS, Preb Christopher Herbert (Chris). b 34. Univ of Wales BA54 St Cath Coll Ox BA56 MA60. Wycliffe Hall Ox. **d** 57 **p** 58. C Abergavenny St Mary w Llanwenarth Citra *Mon* 57-61; C Bridgwater St Mary w Chilton Trinity *B & W* 61-65; V Berrow 65-72; RD Burnham 72-76; R Berrow and Breane 72-76; V Minehead 76-92; RD Exmoor 80-86; Preb Wells Cathl 84-92; V Bovey Tracey SS Pet, Paul and Thos w Hennock *Ex* from 92. *The Vicarage, Coombe Cross, Bovey Tracey, Newton Abbot, Devon TQ13 9EP* Tel (01626) 833813

SARAPUK, Susan. b 59. Lon Univ BA80 Univ of Wales PGCE81. St Mich Coll Llan DPS90. **d** 90 **p** 97. C Morriston *S & B* 90-94; C Swansea St Pet 94-97; P-in-c Llangyfelach from 97. *The Vicarage, 64 Heol Pentrefelin, Morriston, Swansea SA6 6BY* Tel (01792) 774120

SARGAN, Miss Phyllis Elsie. b 24. TCert44 Lon Univ DSocStuds67. Gilmore Ho IDC51. **d** 88 **p** 94. Hon C Bawtry w Austerfield and Misson *S'well* from 88; rtd 90. *Pilgrim House, 1 Highfield Road, Bawtry, Doncaster, S Yorkshire DN10 6QN* Tel (01302) 710587

SARGANT, Canon John Raymond. b 38. CCC Cam BA61 MA70. Westcott Ho Cam 64 Harvard Div Sch 66. **d** 67 **p** 68. C Croydon *Cant* 67-72; Zambia 72-75; P-in-c Bradford-on-Avon Ch Ch *Sarum* 76-81; V 81-90; TV Marlborough from 90; Adv on Inter-Faith Relns from 90; Can and Preb Sarum Cathl from 92. *Preshute Vicarage, 7 Golding Avenue, Marlborough, Wilts SN8 1TH* Tel (01672) 513408

✠**SARGEANT, The Rt Revd Frank Pilkington.** b 32. St Jo Coll Dur BA55 DipTh58 Nottm Univ DipAdEd73. Cranmer Hall Dur 57. **d** 58 **p** 59 **c** 84. C Gainsborough All SS *Linc* 58-62; C Gt Grimsby St Jas 62-66; V Hykeham 66-73; Dir In-Service Tr and Adult Educn *Bradf* 73-84; Can Res Bradf Cathl 73-77; Adn Bradf 77-84; Suff Bp Stockport *Ches* 84-94; Bp at Lambeth (Hd of Staff) *Cant* from 94. *2nd Floor Flat, Queen's Stairs, Lambeth Palace, London SE1 7JU* Tel 0171-928 8282 Fax 261 9836

SARGEANT, George Henry. b 19. Bps' Coll Cheshunt 60. **d** 62 **p** 63. C Woodbridge St Jo *St E* 62-64; C Ipswich St Thos 64-68; C-in-c Gt w Lt Wratting 69-70; R 70-77; C-in-c Barnardiston 69-70; R 71-77; rtd 84. *1 Belgrave Gardens, Dereham, Norfolk NR19 1PZ* Tel (01362) 693020

SARGEANT, Kenneth Stanley. b 19. Lon Coll of Div 68. **d** 70 **p** 71. C E Ham St Paul *Chelmsf* 70-73; C Southborough St Pet w Ch Ch and St Matt *Roch* 73-77; Chapl Joyce Green Hosp Dartford 77-88; R Greenhithe St Mary *Roch* 77-88; rtd 88; Perm to Offic *Chich* from 88. *2 Westfield Close, Polegate, E Sussex BN26 6EF* Tel (01323) 488153

SARGEANTSON, Kenneth William. b 30. **d** 90 **p** 91. NSM The Marshland *Sheff* 90-93; NSM Goole from 93. *St Mary's Church House, Swinefleet Road, Goole, N Humberside DN14 5TN* Tel (01405) 761749

SARGENT, Charles Edward. b 68. K Coll Lon BD89 Leeds Univ. Coll of Resurr Mirfield 94. **d** 96 **p** 97. C Notting Dale St Clem w St Mark and St Jas *Lon* from 96. *176 Holland Road, London W14 8AH* Tel 0171-603 8453

SARGENT, David Gareth. b 63. Sheff Univ BA85. Cranmer Hall Dur BA93. **d** 96 **p** 97. C Norbury *Ches* from 96. *27 Davenport Road, Hazel Grove, Stockport, Cheshire SK7 4HA* Tel 0161-483 6922

SARGENT, John Philip Hugh. b 34. Or Coll Ox BA55 MA63. Chich Th Coll 55. **d** 57 **p** 58. C Kington w Huntington *Heref* 57-59; C Bridgnorth St Mary 59-63; C Leighton Buzzard *St Alb* 63-64; PC Stonebroom *Derby* 64-73; Chapl Southn Gen Hosp 74-95. *Flat 2, 352 Winchester Road, Southampton SO16 6TW*

SARGENT, Preb Richard Henry. b 24. Man Univ BA50. Ridley Hall Cam 50. **d** 52 **p** 53. C Rusholme H Trin *Man* 52-54; C Cheadle *Ches* 54-59; V Cheadle Hulme St Andr 59-67; V Bushbury *Lich* 67-73; V Castle Church 73-89; RD Stafford 81-88; Preb Lich Cathl 87-89; rtd 89. *6 Kingcup Road, Stafford ST17 9JQ* Tel (01785) 223582

SARGISSON, Conrad Ralph. b 24. Keble Coll Ox BA46 MA50. Wells Th Coll 48. **d** 50 **p** 51. C Charlton Kings St Mary *Glouc* 50-53; C Prestbury 53-55; V St Briavels 55-58; V Lanteglos by Fowey *Truro* 58-62; V Penzance St Mary 62-73; RD Penwith 72-73; V Westbury-on-Trym H Trin *Bris* 73-79; P-in-c Blisland w

St Breward *Truro* 79-83; V Mylor w Flushing 83-91; P-in-c St Hilary w Perranuthnoe 93-96; rtd 96; Perm to Offic *Truro* from 96. *Cassacawn Farmhouse, Blisland, Bodmin, Cornwall PL30 4JU* Tel (01208) 850371

SARKIES, Col John Walter Robert Courtney. b 12. MRCS36 LRCP36 DOMS48. Cuddesdon Coll 57. **d** 59 **p** 60. C Bearsted *Cant* 59-61; S Africa 61-67; Mauritius 67-69; Hon C Douglas St Matt *S & M* from 69; Perm to Offic from 94. *2 Westminster Terrace, Douglas, Isle of Man IM1 4ED* Tel (01624) 674835

SARMEZEY, George Arpad. b 61. Qu Mary Coll Lon BA83 Golds Coll Lon PGCE86. Westcott Ho Cam CTM92. **d** 92 **p** 93. C Eastville St Anne w St Mark and St Thos *Bris* 92-94; C Stratton St Margaret w S Marston etc 94-97; Asst Chapl Northn Gen Hosp NHS Trust from 97. *16 Milton Street, Kingsley, Northampton NN2 7JF* Tel (01604) 235773

SASADA, Benjamin John. b 33. MA. EAMTC. **d** 82 **p** 83. NSM Dickleburgh, Langmere, Shimpling, Thelveton etc *Nor* 82-88; Perm to Offic *St E* from 84; NSM Diss *Nor* from 88. *The Grange, Walcott Green, Diss, Norfolk IP22 3SS* Tel (01379) 642174

SASSER, Col Howell Crawford. b 37. Maryland Univ BA72 Geo Mason Univ Virginia MA74 Westmr Coll Ox MTh97. Washington Dioc Course 75. **d** 77 **p** 78. USA 77; W Germany 77-80; Somalia 80-92; Chapl Montreux w Gstaad *Eur* 92-97; Chapl Oporto from 97. *rua do Campo Alegre 640-5DTO, 4100 Porto, Portugal* Tel Porto (2) 609 1006 E-mail 40021.2511@compuserve.com

SATTERFORD, Douglas Leigh. b 18. DSC42. Ripon Hall Ox 59. **d** 60 **p** 61. C Sanderstead All SS *S'wark* 60-65; V Lyminster *Chich* 65-85; V Poling 66-85; rtd 85; Perm to Offic *Chich* 85-90; Perm to Offic *St E* from 90. *24 Wheatfields, Whatfield, Ipswich IP7 6RB*

SATTERLY, Gerald Albert. b 34. Lon Univ BA56 Ex Univ Hon BA. Wycliffe Hall Ox 58. **d** 60 **p** 61. C Southborough St Pet *Roch* 60-63; C S Lyncombe *B & W* 63-66; V Sheff St Barn *Sheff* 66-69; R Adwick-le-Street 69-73; V Awre and Blakeney *Glouc* 73-82; P-in-c Newnham 80-82; V Newnham w Awre and Blakeney 82-90; R Instow *Ex* from 90; V Westleigh from 90. *The Rectory, Quay Lane, Instow, Bideford, Devon EX39 4JR* Tel (01271) 860346

✠**SATTERTHWAITE, The Rt Revd John Richard.** b 25. CMG91. Leeds Univ BA46. Coll of Resurr Mirfield 48. **d** 50 **p** 51 **c** 70. C Carl St Barn *Carl* 50-53; C Carl St Aid and Ch Ch 53-55; Asst Gen Sec C of E Coun on Foreign Relns 55-59; C St Mich Paternoster Royal *Lon* 55-59; P-in-c 59-65; Gen Sec C of E Coun on Foreign Relns 59-70; V St Dunstan in the West *Lon* 59-70; Hon Can Cant Cathl *Cant* 63-70; Gen Sec Abp's Commn on RC Relns 65-70; Suff Bp Fulham *Lon* 70-80; Bp Gib 70-80; Bp Eur 80-93; Dean Malta 70-93; rtd 93; Hon Asst Bp Carl from 94. *25 Spencer House, St Paul's Square, Carlisle CA1 1DG* Tel (01228) 594055

SAUL, Norman Stanley. b 30. St Aid Birkenhead 51. **d** 54 **p** 55. C S Shore H Trin *Blackb* 54-57; C Poulton-le-Fylde 57-59; PC Freckleton 59-66; V Blackb St Luke 66-68; V Barton 68-72; V Foxdale *S & M* 72-77; V Maughold 77-90; CF (ACF) 80-86; rtd 90; Perm to Offic *Blackb* from 90. *15 Croft Meadow, Bamber Bridge, Preston PR5 8HX* Tel (01772) 314475

SAUNDERS, Andrew Vivian. b 44. Leeds Univ BA65. Coll of Resurr Mirfield 66. **d** 68 **p** 69. C Goodmayes St Paul *Chelmsf* 68-71; C Horfield H Trin *Bris* 71-75; C Oldland 75-77; Ind Chapl *B & W* 77-80; P-in-c Buckland Dinham w Elm, Orchardleigh etc 77-78; P-in-c Buckland Dinham 78-80; V Westfield 80-90; R Clutton w Cameley from 90. *The Rectory, Main Road, Temple Cloud, Bristol BS18 5DA* Tel (01761) 552296

SAUNDERS, Brian Gerald. b 28. Pemb Coll Cam BA49 MA53. Cuddesdon Coll 63. **d** 66 **p** 67. NSM Gt Berkhamsted *St Alb* 66-87; P-in-c Lt Gaddesden 87-92; rtd 92; Perm to Offic *Ox* 92-94; Perm to Offic *St Alb* from 92; Perm to Offic *Pet* from 95. *73 Drayton Road, Newton Longville, Milton Keynes MK17 0BH* Tel (01908) 641876

SAUNDERS, Bruce Alexander. b 47. St Cath Coll Cam BA68 MA72 Ox Univ DipTh70. Cuddesdon Coll 68. **d** 71 **p** 72. C Westbury-on-Trym H Trin *Bris* 71-74; Hon C Clifton St Paul 74-78; Asst Chapl Bris Univ 74-78; TV Fareham H Trin *Portsm* 78-84; TR Mortlake w E Sheen *S'wark* from 84; RD Richmond and Barnes 89-94. *The Rectory, 170 Sheen Lane, London SW14 8LZ* Tel 0181-876 4816

SAUNDERS, David. b 28. Keble Coll Ox BA50 DipTh51 MA59. Cuddesdon Coll 51. **d** 53 **p** 54. C Mexborough *Sheff* 53-56; C Sheff St Cuth 56-60; V New Bentley 60-67; V Grimsby All SS *Linc* 67-78; V Caistor w Clixby 78-88; P-in-c Grasby 78-94; Chapl Caistor Hosp 78-94; P-in-c Searby w Owmby *Linc* 79-94; V Dunholme 88-92; P-in-c Welton and Dunholme w Scothern 92-94; rtd 94; Perm to Offic *Linc* from 94. *2 Oundle Close, Washingborough, Lincoln LN4 1DR* Tel (01522) 793164

SAUNDERS, David Anthony. b 48. Trin Coll Bris 76. **d** 78 **p** 79. C Bath Walcot *B & W* 78-80; Asst Dir RE 80-83; Youth Chapl 80-83; C Long Ashton 83-84; V Bath St Bart 84-90; Offg Chapl RN 84-90; V Cullompton *Ex* 90-97; R Kentisbeare w Blackborough 90-97; USA from 97. *Address temp unknown*

SAUNDERS, Edward George Humphrey. b 23. St Jo Coll Cam BA48 MA50. Ridley Hall Cam. **d** 50 **p** 51. C Ox St Ebbe *Ox* 50-52; Cand Sec CPAS 52-54; Clerical Asst Sec 54-58; V Finchley Ch Ch *Lon* 58-64; V Chipping Campden *Glouc* 64-69; P-in-c Ebrington 66-69; Lic to Offic *Leic* 69-71; V Ches Square St Mich w St Phil *Lon* 71-84; P-in-c Mayfair Ch Ch 80-84; Hon C Ox St Andr *Ox* 84-90; rtd 88. *The Hensol, Shire Lane, Chorleywood, Rickmansworth, Herts WD3 5NH* Tel (01923) 284816

SAUNDERS, George Arthur. b 18. Kelham Th Coll 35. **d** 41 **p** 42. C Eltham St Barn *S'wark* 41-42; C Camberwell St Giles 42-45; P-in-c Camberwell Em 46-52; V 52-57; V Plumstead Ascension 57-82; rtd 82; Perm to Offic *B & W* from 82. *69 Estuary Park, Combwich, Bridgwater, Somerset TA5 2RF* Tel (01278) 653091

SAUNDERS, Graham Howard. b 53. Hatf Poly BSc77. Trin Coll Bris BA86. **d** 86 **p** 87. C Birm St Martin w Bordesley St Andr *Birm* 86-89; C Olton 89-96; TV Bedminster *Bris* from 96. *St Paul's Vicarage, 2 Southville Road, Bristol BS3 1DG* Tel 0117-923 1092

SAUNDERS, Guy. b 27. AKC51. **d** 52 **p** 53. C Highgate St Mich *Lon* 52-55; C Hurstpierpoint *Chich* 55-59; V Aldingbourne 59-65; V Whitehawk 65-69; P-in-c Burton w Coates 69-81; P-in-c Up Waltham 69-81; P-in-c Duncton 69-81; P-in-c Bolney 81-83; V 83-91; rtd 91; Hon C Zeal Monachorum *Ex* from 92. *The Rectory, Zeal Monachorum, Crediton, Devon EX17 6DG* Tel (01363) 82342

SAUNDERS, John Barry. b 40. Chich Th Coll. **d** 83 **p** 84. C St Breoke *Truro* 83-84; C St Breoke and Egloshayle 84-87; V Treverbyn 87-96; RD St Austell 91-96; V Perranzabuloe from 96. *The Vicarage, Station Road, Perranporth, Cornwall TR6 0DD* Tel (01872) 573375

SAUNDERS, Canon John Michael. b 40. Brasted Th Coll 66 Clifton Th Coll 68. **d** 70 **p** 71. C Homerton St Luke *Lon* 70-74; SAMS from 74; Brazil 74-91; P-in-c Horsmonden *Roch* from 91; Area Sec (SE England) SAMS from 91. *The Rectory, Goudhurst Road, Horsmonden, Tonbridge, Kent TN12 8JU* Tel (01892) 722521

SAUNDERS, Kenneth John. b 35. Linc Th Coll 73. **d** 75 **p** 76. C Boultham *Linc* 75-79; V Swinderby 79-87; V Cherry Willingham w Greetwell 87-95; P-in-c S Kelsey Gp from 95; P-in-c N Kelsey from 95. *The Vicarage, Grange Lane, North Kelsey, Lincoln LN7 6EH* Tel (01652) 678205

SAUNDERS, Malcolm Walter Mackenzie. b 34. Em Coll Cam BA58 MA62. Wycliffe Hall Ox 58. **d** 60 **p** 61. C Northampton St Giles *Pet* 60-63; C Northampton St Alb 63-66; V Corby St Columba 66-84; Nat Dir Evang Explosion 84-91; Lic to Offic *Pet* 84-91; V Ketton 91-92; R Ketton w Tinwell from 92. *The Vicarage, 4 Edmonds Drive, Ketton, Stamford, Lincs PE9 3TH* Tel (01780) 720228

SAUNDERS, Mrs Margaret Rose. b 49. Newnham Coll Cam BA71 St Jo Coll York CertEd72. St Alb Minl Tr Scheme 85. **d** 88 **p** 94. Hon Par Dn Gt Berkhamsted *St Alb* 88-90; Hon Chapl Asst Gt Ormond St Hosp Lon 88-90; Asst Chapl Aylesbury Vale HA Priority Care Unit 90-92; Asst Chapl Stoke Mandeville Hosp 90-92; Chapl St Jo Hosp Aylesbury 90-92; Chapl Milton Keynes Gen Hosp 92-94; Chapl Milton Keynes Gen NHS Trust from 94; Chapl Milton Keynes Community NHS Trust from 94. *Milton Keynes General Hospital, Standing Way, Milton Keynes MK6 5LD* Tel (01908) 660033/641876

SAUNDERS, Martin Paul. b 54. K Coll Lon BD76 AKC76. Westcott Ho Cam 77. **d** 78 **p** 79. C Seaton Hirst *Newc* 78-81; Hong Kong 81; C Egglescliffe *Dur* 81-82; Chapl to Arts and Recreation 81-84; C Jarrow 82-84; TV 84-88; V Southwick St Columba 88-94; Perm to Offic from 94. *65 Deckham Terrace, Gateshead, Tyne & Wear NE5 3UY* Tel 0191-477 2853

SAUNDERS, Michael. b 35. AKC61. **d** 61 **p** 62. C Leigh Park *Portsm* 61-66; V Weston *Guildf* 66-73; C St Alb Abbey *St Alb* 73-76; P-in-c Eversholt w Milton Bryan 76-79; C 79-80; P-in-c Old Alresford *Win* 80; R Old Alresford and Bighton 80-82; Perm to Offic 82-95; Perm to Offic *Portsm* from 83; rtd 95. *11 Perins Close, Alresford, Hants SO24 9QL* Tel (01962) 733496

SAUNDERS, Dr Michael. b 38. Lon Univ MB, BS FRCP FRCPEd MSOSc. NE Ord Course 82. **d** 84 **p** 85. Lic to Offic *York* 84-92; Tutor NE Ord Course 84-93; NSM Stokesley *York* 92-93; C Ripon Cathl *Ripon* 93-95; Perm to Offic *York* from 93; NSM Gt and Lt Ouseburn w Marton-cum-Grafton *Ripon* from 95; Tutor NE Ord Course from 95. *9 Park Street, Ripon, N Yorkshire HG4 2AX* Tel (01765) 606425

SAUNDERS, Michael Walter (Mike). b 58. CChem MRSC84 Grey Coll Dur BSc79. Wycliffe Hall Ox 86. **d** 89 **p** 90. C Deane *Man* 89-93; TV Eccles 93-96; TV Eccles from 96. *St Andrew's Vicarage, 11 Abbey Grove, Eccles, Manchester M30 9QN* Tel 0161-707 1742

SAUNDERS, Reginald Frederick. b 15. LNSM course 76. **d** 79 **p** 80. NSM Perth St Ninian *St And* from 79; NSM Stanley from 79. *31 Muirend Road, Perth PH1 1JU* Tel (01738) 626217

SAUNDERS, Canon Richard Charles Hebblethwaite. b 17. Qu Coll Ox BA40 DipTh41 MA42. Westcott Ho Cam 41. **d** 42 **p** 43. C Darnall H Trin *Sheff* 42-45; India 46-49; V Thornton-le-Street w Thornton-le-Moor etc *York* 49-52; V Eastwood *Sheff* 52-62; V Bris St Ambrose Whitehall *Bris* 62-75; P-in-c Easton All Hallows 65-68; TR E Bris 75-77; P-in-c Colerne 77-82; P-in-c N Wraxall 77-82; RD Chippenham 80-82; Hon Can Bris Cathl 82; rtd 82; Hon C Honiton, Gittisham, Combe Raleigh, Monkton etc *Ex* from 85. *St Michael's Cottage, Gittisham, Honiton, Devon EX14 0AH* Tel (01404) 850634

SAUNDERS, Richard George (Dick). b 54. BNC Ox BA76 MA81. St Jo Coll Nottm 82. **d** 85 **p** 86. C Barrow St Mark *Carl* 85-89; C Cranham Park *Chelmsf* 89-97; TV Kinson *Sarum* from 97. *St Philip's Vicarage, 41 Moore Avenue, Kinson, Bournemouth BH11 8AT* Tel (01202) 581135

SAUNDERS, Ronald. b 37. ACP67 St Pet Coll Birm CertEd62 CertRE62 Columbia Univ MA82 PhD87. Sarum Th Coll 69. **d** 68 **p** 70. Malawi 68-72; C Kensington St Mary Abbots w St Geo *Lon* 72-73; C Bournemouth St Fran *Win* 73-75; Canada 75-81; C Gt Marlow *Ox* 81-82; Area Org Leprosy Miss 82-85; V Penycae *St As* 85-87; TV Wrexham 87-89; NSM Dio Ox 90-91; Chapl Morden Coll Blackheath 91-97; Master Wyggeston's Hosp Leics from 97. *The Master's House, Wyggeston's Hospital, Hinckley Road, Leicester LE3 0UX* Tel 0116-254 8682

SAUNDERS, Ms Wendy Jennifer. b 49. S'wark Ord Course 86. **d** 95 **p** 96. Bp's Adv for Urban Min and Leadership *S'wark* 90-91; C Thamesmead from 95. *22 St Katherines Road, Erith, Kent DA18 4DS* Tel 0181-310 6412 Mobile 0802-603754 Fax as telephone

SAUNT, James Peter Robert. b 36. Chich Th Coll 73. **d** 75 **p** 76. C Portland All SS w St Pet *Sarum* 75-78; P-in-c Bratton 78-81; V 81-94; Chapl HM Young Offender Inst Erlestoke Ho 81-94; P-in-c Oldbury *Sarum* from 94. *The Rectory, Heddington, Calne, Wilts SN11 0PR* Tel (01380) 850411 Fax 818663

SAUSBY, John Michael. b 39. AKC. **d** 63 **p** 64. C Crosland Moor *Wakef* 63-65; C Halifax St Jo Bapt 65-67; V Birkby 67-77; V Holmfirth 77-89; TR Upper Holme Valley from 89. *The Vicarage, 2 Rosegarth Avenue, Newmill Road, Holmfirth, Huddersfield HD7 2TE* Tel (01484) 683285

SAVAGE, Andrew Michael. b 67. Wye Coll Lon BSc89 Cranfield Inst of Tech MSc91. Wycliffe Hall Ox 93. **d** 96 **p** 97. C Ecclesall *Sheff* from 96. *48 Renshaw Road, Eccleshall, Sheffield S11 7PD* Tel 0114-266 2313

SAVAGE, Christopher Marius. b 46. Bps' Coll Cheshunt Qu Coll Birm 68. **d** 70 **p** 71. C Battersea St Luke *S'wark* 70-75; TV Newbury *Ox* 75-80; R Lich St Mary w St Mich *Lich* 80-85; V Chessington *Guildf* 85-91; Ind Chapl *Win* from 91; Chapl Basingstoke Coll of Tech from 91. *15 Camwood Close, Basingstoke, Hants RG21 3BL* Tel (01256) 469219

SAVAGE, Mrs Hilary Linda. b 48. RGN71 RM86. WMMTC 89. **d** 92 **p** 94. C Quinton Road W St Boniface *Birm* 92-96; P-in-c Edgbaston SS Mary and Ambrose from 96. *St Ambrose Vicarage, 15 Raglan Road, Birmingham B5 7RA* Tel 0121-440 2196

SAVAGE, John. **d** 97. C Falmouth K Chas *Truro* from 97. *21 Avenue Road, Falmouth, Cornwall TR11 3RP* Tel (01326) 314176

SAVAGE, Jonathan Mark. b 57. Kingston Poly BSc79 MSc89 Roehampton Inst PGCE80. Ridley Hall Cam 94. **d** 96 **p** 97. C Ely from 96. *25 John Anmer Close, Ely, Cambs CB6 1DT* Tel (01353) 667568

SAVAGE, Leslie Walter. b 15. Cranmer Hall Dur 63. **d** 65 **p** 66. C Stanwix *Carl* 65-69; V Bolton w Cliburn 69-74; V Holme-in-Cliviger *Blackb* 74-81; rtd 81; Perm to Offic *Chich* from 81. *42 Wilton Road, Bexhill-on-Sea, E Sussex TN40 1HX* Tel (01424) 223829

SAVAGE, Mark David John. b 55. Birm Univ BA76 Dur Univ BA82 Newc Univ MLitt83. Cranmer Hall Dur 80. **d** 83 **p** 84. C Newc St Gabr *Newc* 83-86; Adult Educn Adv 86-94; V Bedlington from 94. *The Vicarage, 21 Church Lane, Bedlington, Northd NE22 5EL* Tel (01670) 829220

SAVAGE, Michael Atkinson. b 33. St Pet Hall Ox BA57 MA61. Tyndale Hall Bris 57. **d** 59 **p** 60. C Rugby St Matt *Cov* 59-62; C Welling *Roch* 62-66; V Bowling St Steph *Bradf* 66-73; V Ben Rhydding 73-92; RD Otley 87-92; TR Quidenham *Nor* 92-97; V Quidenham Gp from 97. *The Rectory, Church Street, Banham, Norwich NR16 2HN* Tel (01953) 887562

SAVAGE, Paul James. b 58. Liv Univ BA81. Wycliffe Hall Ox 88. **d** 91 **p** 92. C Litherland St Phil *Liv* 91-94; CMS from 94. *Church Mission Society, Partnership House, 157 Waterloo Road, London SE1 8UU* Tel 0171-928 8681 Fax 401 3215

SAVIDGE, Dr Graham John. b 47. Univ of Wales (Ban) BSc69 PhD78. CITC 89. **d** 92 **p** 94. Lic to Offic *D & D* from 92; NSM Down Cathl from 94. *7 Cedar Grove, Ardglass, Downpatrick, Co Down BT30 7UE* Tel (01396) 841501

SAVIGEAR, Miss Elfrida Beatrice. b 49. Wye Coll Lon BSc71 Edin Univ DipAE72 Bath Univ MSc85 Lambeth STh94. Trin Coll Bris DTS90 Ridley Hall Cam 91. **d** 93 **p** 94. C Ross w Brampton Abbotts, Bridstow, Peterstow etc *Heref* 93-97; P-in-c Butlers Marston and the Pillertons w Ettington *Cov* from 97; P-in-c Alderminster and Halford from 97. *The Vicarage, Ettington, Stratford-upon-Avon, Warks CV37 7SH* Tel (01789) 740225

SAVILE, Canon Ian Keith Wrey. b 26. Trin Hall Cam BA50 MA54. Ridley Hall Cam 51. **d** 53 **p** 54. C Bootle St Matt *Liv* 53-56; C Birkdale St Jo 56-57; V Barrow St Mark *Carl* 57-64; V Wandsworth All SS *S'wark* 64-74; RD Wandsworth 69-74; V S'well H Trin *S'well* 74-80; Bp's Adv on Evang 74-80; V Canford Magna *Sarum* 80-88; TR 88; RD Wimborne 85-88; Can and Preb Sarum Cathl 86-88; Patr Sec CPAS 88-93; Perm to Offic *Cov* 88-93; rtd 93. *Corner Cottage, West Street, Winterbourne Stickland, Blandford Forum, Dorset DT11 0NT* Tel (01258) 880459

SAVILL, David. b 27. TD69 and Bar 75. Em Coll Cam BA49 MA52. Ridley Hall Cam 50. **d** 52 **p** 53. Chapl St E Cathl *St E* 52-54; C St Martin-in-the-Fields *Lon* 54-57; V Sunbury 57-67; V Heston 67-73; Hon C Mettingham w Ilketshall St John *St E* 73-79; Hon C Mettingham 79-80; Chapl Felixstowe Coll 80-90; rtd 90; Perm to Offic *B & W* from 90. *Sancroft, 210 Park View, Crewkerne, Somerset TA18 8JL* Tel (01460) 77298

SAVILLE, Andrew. b 66. Worc Coll Ox BA88. Wycliffe Hall Ox DipTh. **d** 95 **p** 96. C Tonbridge SS Pet and Paul *Roch* from 95. *12 Salisbury Road, Tonbridge, Kent TN10 4PB* Tel (01732) 357205

SAVILLE, David James. b 39. Ch Ch Ox BA60 MA64. Clifton Th Coll 61. **d** 63 **p** 64. C Darfield *Sheff* 63-66; C St Leonards St Leon *Chich* 66-68; Cand Sec CPAS 69-74; V Taunton St Jas *B & W* 74-80; RD Taunton N 78-80; V Chorleywood Ch Ch *St Alb* 80-90; RD Rickmansworth 86-90; Dioc Adv for Evang *Lon* from 91. *9 Twyford Avenue, London N2 9NU* Tel 0181-442 1442

SAVILLE, Edward Andrew. b 47. Leeds Univ CertEd70 Open Univ BA75. Carl Dioc Tr Inst. **d** 90 **p** 91. C Accrington St Jo w Huncoat *Blackb* 90-93; C Standish 93-95; V Brierfield from 95. *The Vicarage, 22 Reedley Road, Reedley, Burnley, Lancs BB10 2LU* Tel (01282) 613235 E-mail 100553.1707 @compuserve.com

SAVILLE, George Edward. b 15. **d** 42 **p** 43. C Longton St Mary and St Chad *Lich* 42-44; C Carlton *S'well* 44-46; C Lambeth St Mary the Less *S'wark* 46-49; C Barnes St Mich 49-50; C Charlton St Luke w St Paul 50-52; V New Charlton H Trin 52-56; V Ilkeston H Trin *Derby* 56-63; rtd 80. *Fernecumbe House, Kings Coughton, Alcester, Warks B49 5QD* Tel (01789) 762960

SAVILLE, Jeremy David. b 35. Or Coll Ox BA59 MA62. Chich Th Coll 58. **d** 60 **p** 61. C Tynemouth Cullercoats St Paul *Newc* 60-63; C Hexham 63-65; Lic to Offic *Ox* 65-68; Chapl Cuddesdon Coll 65-68; R Holt *Nor* 68-73; P-in-c Kelling w Salthouse 68-71; R Edgefield 71-73; R Hoe 73-78; R E Dereham w Hoe 73-80; V E Dereham 80-81; R Scarning w Wendling 78-81; R Beckenham St Geo *Roch* 81-89; Hon Can Roch Cathl 86-89; R Ashdon w Hadstock *Chelmsf* from 89; RD Saffron Walden from 97. *The Rectory, Ashdon, Saffron Walden, Essex CB10 2HP* Tel (01799) 584897

SAVILLE, Mrs Margaret. b 46. SW Minl Tr Course 93. **d** 94 **p** 95. C Over St Chad *Ches* from 94. *St Chad's House, 9 Heaton Square, Winsford, Cheshire CW7 1EB* Tel (01606) 553989

SAVILLE-DEANE, Marcus. b 58. Imp Coll Lon BSc80. Wycliffe Hall Ox 83. **d** 87 **p** 88. C Spring Grove St Mary *Lon* 87-92. *c/o The Bishop of Kensington, 19 Campden Hill Square, London W8 7JY* Tel 0171-727 9818 Fax 229 3651

SAWARD, Canon Michael John. b 32. Bris Univ BA55. Tyndale Hall Bris. **d** 56 **p** 57. C Croydon Ch Ch Broad Green *Cant* 56-59; C Edgware *Lon* 59-64; Sec Liv Coun of Chs 64-67; Radio and TV Officer CIO 67-72; Hon C Beckenham St Jo *Roch* 70-72; V Fulham St Matt *Lon* 72-78; V Ealing St Mary 78-91; AD Ealing E 79-84; P-in-c Ealing St Paul 86-89; Preb St Paul's Cathl 85-91; Can Res and Treas St Paul's Cathl from 91. *6 Amen Court, London EC4M 7BU* Tel 0171-248 8572 Fax as telephone

SAWLE, Martin. b 49. Solicitor 74 Dundee Univ LLB70. N Ord Course 87. **d** 90 **p** 91. NSM Longton *Blackb* 90-92; P-in-c Hoghton from 92. *The Vicarage, Chapel Lane, Hoghton, Preston PR5 0RY* Tel (01254) 852529

SAWLE, Ralph Burford. b 14. Lich Th Coll 34. **d** 37 **p** 38. C Sawley *Derby* 37-40; C Walthamstow St Barn *Chelmsf* 40-43; P-in-c Hanley All SS *Lich* 43-46; V Hanford 46-52; V Malins Lee 52-57; V Ocker Hill 57-61; V Werrington *Truro* 61-72; RD Trigg Major 66-72; V St Giles on the Heath w Virginstow 68-72; V St Neot 72-79; rtd 79; Perm to Offic *Win* from 79. *32 Cavendish Close, Romsey, Hants SO51 7HT* Tel (01794) 516132

SAWREY, Harold. b 14. Edin Th Coll 58. **d** 60 **p** 61. C Kirkby Stephen w Mallerstang *Carl* 60-63; R Orton All SS 63-80; P-in-c Tebay 77-80; rtd 80; Perm to Offic *Carl* 81-93. *Room 8, Abbeyfield Residential Home, 78 Beech Road, Halton, Lancaster LA2 6QH* Tel (01524) 812131

SAWYER, Andrew William. b 49. AKC71 St Aug Coll Cant 71. **d** 72 **p** 73. C Farnham *Guildf* 72-75; C Dawlish *Ex* 75-78; R Colkirk w Oxwick, Whissonsett and Horningtoft *Nor* 78-82; R Colkirk w Oxwick w Pattesley, Whissonsett etc 82-90; V Hungerford and Denford *Ox* from 90. *The Vicarage, Parsonage Lane, Hungerford, Berks RG17 0JB* Tel (01488) 682844

SAWYER, Derek Claude. b 33. ALCD58. **d** 58 **p** 59. C Kirby Muxloe *Leic* 58-60; C Braunstone 60-65; Mauritius 65-68; V Knighton St Mich *Leic* 68-82; Chapl Kifissia *Eur* 82; Lic to Offic *Glouc* 85-87; V Glouc St Aldate from 87. *St Aldate's Vicarage, Finlay Road, Gloucester GL4 6TN* Tel (01452) 523906

SAWYERS, Thomas Adam Barton. b 21. Edgehill Th Coll Belf 58. **d** 61 **p** 62. C Drumragh *D & R* 61-63; I Tamlaght O'Crilly 63-69; I Lissan *Arm* 69-82; rtd 82. *Lynwood, 82 Coleraine Road, Portrush, Co Antrim BT56 8HN* Tel (01265) 823441

✠**SAXBEE, The Rt Revd John Charles.** b 46. Bris Univ BA68. Cranmer Hall Dur DipTh69 PhD74. **d** 72 **p** 73 **c** 94. C Compton

Gifford *Ex* 72-77; P-in-c Weston Mill 77-80; V 80-81; TV Cen Ex 81-87; Jt Dir SW Min Tr Course 81-92; Preb Ex Cathl 88-92; Adn Ludlow *Heref* from 92; Preb Heref Cathl from 92; P-in-c Wistanstow 92-94; P-in-c Acton Scott 92-94; Suff Bp Ludlow from 94. *Bishop's House, Corvedale Road, Halford, Craven Arms, Shropshire SY7 9BT* Tel (01588) 673571 Fax 673585

SAXBY, Harold. b 11. St Chad's Coll Dur BA37 MA40. **d** 38 **p** 39. C Lewisham St Jo Southend *S'wark* 38-41; P-in-c Hartlepool H Trin *Dur* 41-45; V Williton *B & W* 45-52; Chapl Williton Hosp for Aged 47-52; V Highbridge 52-61; V Cockerton *Dur* 61-64; R Jarrow St Paul 64-76; P-in-c Jarrow St Pet 64-69; P-in-c Jarrow St Mark 64-68; rtd 76; Hon C Wrington w Butcombe *B & W* 79-84; Perm to Offic *Chich* from 84. *Terrys Cross House, Woodmancote, Henfield, W Sussex BN5 9SX* Tel (01273) 494648

SAXBY, Martin Peter. b 52. St Jo Coll Dur BA77 DipTh78. Cranmer Hall Dur 74. **d** 78 **p** 79. C Peckham St Mary Magd *S'wark* 78-81; C Ramsey *Ely* 81-84; P-in-c Yaxham *Nor* 84-89; P-in-c Welborne 84-89; P-in-c Mattishall w Mattishall Burgh 84-89; R Mattishall w Mattishall Burgh, Welborne etc 89-90; V Rugby St Matt *Cov* from 90. *St Matthew's Vicarage, 7 Vicarage Road, Rugby, Warks CV22 7AJ* Tel (01788) 330879 E-mail 100744.2274@compuserve.com

SAXON, Miss Doreen Harold Graham. b 29. Qu Coll Birm 77. **dss** 80 **d** 87 **p** 94. Wolverhampton *Lich* 86-87; Par Dn 87-89; rtd 89. *20 Chequerfield Drive, Penn Fields, Wolverhampton WV3 7DH* Tel (01902) 342432

SAXON, Canon Eric. b 14. Man Univ BA35 Hon MA80 Lon Univ BD40. ALCD40. **d** 40 **p** 41. C Droylsden St Mary *Man* 40-44; C Davyhulme Ch Ch 44; Hon C Heaton Norris Ch Ch 44-47; BBC Relig Broadcasting Org (N of England) 44-51; Hon C Man St Ann 47-51; R 51-82; Chapl to The Queen 67-84; OStJ from 73; rtd 82; Perm to Offic *Man* from 82; Perm to Offic *Ches* from 83. *27 Padstow Drive, Bramhall, Stockport, Cheshire SK7 2HU* Tel 0161-439 7233

SAXTON, James. b 54. Lanc Univ BEd77 Hull Univ MEd85. Linc Th Coll 84. **d** 86 **p** 87. C Moor Allerton *Ripon* 86-90; C Knaresborough 90-92; TV Seacroft 92-95; V Ireland Wood from 95. *St Paul's Vicarage, Raynel Drive, Leeds LS16 6BS* Tel 0113-267 2907

✠**SAY, The Rt Revd Richard David.** b 14. KCVO88. Ch Coll Cam BA38 MA41 Kent Univ Hon DCL87. Lambeth DD61 Ridley Hall Cam 38. **d** 39 **p** 40 **c** 61. C Croydon *Cant* 39-43; C St Martin-in-the-Fields *Lon* 43-50; Asst Sec C of E Youth Coun 42-44; Gen Sec 44-47; Gen Sec BCC 47-55; R Hatfield *St Alb* 55-61; Hon Can St Alb 57-61; Bp Roch 61-88; ChStJ from 61; High Almoner 70-88; rtd 88; Asst Bp Cant from 88. *23 Chequers Park, Wye, Ashford, Kent TN25 5BB* Tel (01233) 812720

SAYER, Derek John. b 32. St Steph Ho Ox 55. **d** 58 **p** 58. C Tottenham All Hallows *Lon* 58-61; C Letchworth *St Alb* 61-63; Chapl RADD 63-64 and 66-82; C Lancing St Mich *Chich* 64-66; C Dorking w Ranmore *Guildf* 89-92; V Holmwood 92-95; Perm to Offic from 95. *24 Chalkpit Lane, Dorking, Surrey RH4 1ER* Tel (01306) 882610

SAYER, Harold John. b 15. CCC Cam BA36. **d** 67 **p** 68. C Churchdown St Jo *Glouc* 67-71; C-in-c Wapley w Codrington and Dodington *Bris* 71-73; R Highnam w Lassington and Rudford *Glouc* 73-81; rtd 81; Perm to Offic *Glouc* 81-91; Perm to Offic *Ox* 83-96. *27 Woolstrop Way, Quedgeley, Gloucester GL2 6NL* Tel (01452) 502091

SAYER, Canon William Anthony John (Bill). b 37. St Mich Coll Llan 60. **d** 64 **p** 65. C Gorleston St Andr *Nor* 64-67; P-in-c Witton w Ridlington 67-71; P-in-c Honing w Crostwight 67-71; V Bacton w Edingthorpe 67-71; CF 71-84; Miss to Seamen from 84; R Holkham w Egmere w Warham, Wells and Wighton *Nor* from 84; RD Burnham and Walsingham 87-92; Hon Can Nor Cathl from 97. *The Rectory, Wells-next-the-Sea, Norfolk NR23 1JB* Tel (01328) 710107

SAYERS, Guy Anthony. b 10. Ex Coll Ox BA35 MA37. Ely Th Coll 34. **d** 36 **p** 37. C Vauxhall St Pet *S'wark* 36-41; CF (EC) 41-46; CF (TA) 49-65; C Kilburn St Aug *Lon* 46-50; V Doncaster Ch Ch *Sheff* 50-58; V Kettering St Mary *Pet* 58-68; R Empingham 68-81; rtd 81; Perm to Offic *Pet* 82-93. *5 Gracey Court, Woodland Road, Broadclyst, Exeter EX5 3LP* Tel (01392) 460721

SAYERS, Simon Philip. b 59. Cam Univ MA81. Oak Hill Th Coll 83. **d** 85 **p** 86. C Alperton *Lon* 85-89; C Hornsey Rise Whitehall Park Team 89-90; TV 90-96; Min Panshanger CD *St Alb* from 96. *The Vicarage, 69 Hardings, Welwyn Garden City, Herts AL7 2HA* Tel (01707) 333272

SAYLE, Philip David. b 61. St Jo Coll Nottm DipThMin94. **d** 94 **p** 95. C Helston and Wendron *Truro* from 94. *Wendron Vicarage, Wendron, Helston, Cornwall TR13 0EA* Tel (01326) 572169

SAYWELL, Philip. b 33. Linc Th Coll 57. **d** 60 **p** 61. C Stepney St Dunstan and All SS *Lon* 60-63; C Calstock *Truro* 63-66; V Lanteglos by Fowey 66-73; Iran 73-77; R Cockley Cley w Gooderstone *Nor* 78-81; V Didlington 78-81; R Gt and Lt Cressingham w Threxton 78-81; R Hilborough w Bodney 78-81; R Oxborough w Foulden and Caldecote 78-81; UAE 81-84; Perm to Offic *Chich* 84-88; Nat Co-ord (UK) SOMA 85-88; rtd 93. *Little Ashott, Exford, Minehead, Somerset TA24 7NG* Tel (0164383) 619

SCAIFE, Andrew. b 50. Ex Coll Ox BA73 MA76. Wycliffe Hall Ox. **d** 77 **p** 78. C Everton St Geo *Liv* 77-81; P-in-c Liv St Mich 81; TV St Luke in the City 81-86; V Litherland St Phil 86-96; Chapl Wirral Hosp NHS Trust from 96. *Arrowe Park Hospital, Upton, Wirral, Merseyside L49 5PE* Tel 0151-678 5111

SCALES, Barbara Marion. b 24. S'wark Ord Course. **dss** 82 **d** 87 **p** 94. St Helier *S'wark* 82-87; Hon Par Dn 87-89; Chapl Asst St Helier Hosp Carshalton 82-88; NSM Cheam Common St Phil *S'wark* 89-95; rtd 95; Perm to Offic *S'wark* from 95. *51 Tonfield Road, Sutton, Surrey SM3 9JP* Tel 0181-644 3712

SCAMMELL, Frank. b 56. Cam Univ MA. St Jo Coll Nottm BA83. **d** 82 **p** 83. C Stapenhill w Cauldwell *Derby* 82-86; TV Swanage and Studland *Sarum* 86-92; Min Southgate LEP *St E* from 92. *1A Mayfield Road, Bury St Edmunds, Suffolk IP33 2TJ* Tel (01284) 767693

SCAMMELL, John Richard Lyn. b 18. TD50. Bris Univ LLB45. Wycliffe Hall Ox 46. **d** 48 **p** 49. C Bishopston *Bris* 48-50; C Stoke Bishop 50-52; RAChD 53-73; P-in-c Bicknoller *B & W* 73-78; P-in-c Crowcombe 75-78; R Bicknoller w Crowcombe and Sampford Brett 78-81; Perm to Offic 81-93; rtd 83; Perm to Offic *Guildf* from 84. *4 Pine Ridge Drive, Lower Bourne, Farnham, Surrey GU10 3JW* Tel (01252) 713100

SCANDINAVIA AND GERMANY, Archdeacon of. *See* RATCLIFF, The Ven David William

SCANLON, Geoffrey Edward Leyshon. b 44. Coll of Resurr Mirfield. **d** 76 **p** 77. C Beamish *Dur* 76-79; C-in-c Bishopwearmouth St Mary V w St Pet CD 79-81; USA from 81. *1226 North Vermilion, Danville, Illinois 61832, USA* Tel Illinois (217) 442-1677

SCANTLEBURY, James Stanley. b 48. St Jo Coll Dur BA69 Heythrop Coll Lon MTh80. Westcott Ho Cam 70. **d** 72 **p** 73. C Upperby St Jo *Carl* 72-75; C Guildf H Trin w St Mary *Guildf* 75-77; Order of St Aug 77-86; Chapl Austin Friars Sch Carl 80-86; Chapl Mayfield Coll E Sussex 86-88; Chapl H Trin Sen Sch Halifax 88-90; NSM Ripponden *Wakef* 88-90; V Torpenhow *Carl* 91-94; V Allhallows 91-94; V Falmouth All SS *Truro* from 94. *All Saints' Vicarage, 72 Dracaena Avenue, Falmouth, Cornwall TR11 2EN* Tel (01326) 314141

SCARBOROUGH, John Richard Derek. b 32. Lon Univ BA54. Cuddesdon Coll. **d** 69 **p** 70. C Fulbeck *Linc* 69-72; C Bassingham 73-74; Lic to Offic 74-76 and 78-93; R Boothby Graffoe 76-77; R Navenby 76-77; V Wellingore w Temple Bruer 76-77; V Graffoe 77-78; NSM Bassingham from 93; NSM Aubourn w Haddington from 93; NSM Carlton-le-Moorland w Stapleford from 93; NSM Thurlby w Norton Disney from 93. *Hales Cottage, 47 High Street, Navenby, Lincoln LN5 0DZ* Tel (01522) 811031

SCARGILL, Christopher Morris. b 57. UEA BA79 York Univ MA81 Leeds Univ CertEd81 Nottm Univ BTh89. Linc Th Coll 86. **d** 89 **p** 90. C Desborough *Pet* 89-92; C Buxton w Burbage and King Sterndale *Derby* 92-93; TV from 93. *17 Lismore Road, Buxton, Derbyshire SK17 9AN* Tel (01298) 22433

SCARTH, John Robert. b 34. Leeds Univ BSc55 CertEd St Jo Coll Dur DipTh65. Cranmer Hall Dur 63. **d** 65 **p** 66. C Dewsbury All SS *Wakef* 65-68; V Shepley 68-72; Asst Master Kingston-upon-Hull Gr Sch 72-78; St Mary's C of E Sch Hendon 78-81; V Ossett cum Gawthorpe 81-88; R Tarrington w Stoke Edith, Aylton, Pixley etc *Heref* 88-96; rtd 96; Perm to Offic *Wakef* from 96. *44 Gagewell Drive, Horbury, Wakefield, W Yorkshire WF4 6BS* Tel (01924) 272055

SCARTH, Maurice John. b 31. MInstPS. St Deiniol's Hawarden 81. **d** 83 **p** 84. C Llandrillo-yn-Rhos *St As* 83-87; V Rhosymedre 87-91; V Kerry and Llanmerewig and Dolfor 91-93; rtd 93. *23 Penrhyn Beach East, Penrhyn Bay, Llandudno LL30 3NU* Tel (01492) 547906

SCATTERGOOD, William Henry. b 26. **d** 56 **p** 57. Australia 56-84; V Lonan *S & M* 84-92; V Laxey 84-92; rtd 92; Perm to Offic *Chich* from 92. *5 Sandgate Close, Seaford, E Sussex BN25 3LL* Tel (01323) 492203

SCEATS, Preb David Douglas. b 46. Ch Coll Cam BA68 MA72 Bris Univ MA71. Clifton Th Coll 68. **d** 71 **p** 72. C Cambridge St Paul *Ely* 71-74; Lect Trin Coll Bris 74-83; V Shenstone *Lich* 83-86; Dioc Tr Officer 86-91; P-in-c Colton 86-90; Dioc Dir of Local Min Development from 91; Warden of Readers from 91; C Lich St Chad from 94; Preb Lich Cathl from 96. *Diocesan Local Ministry Office, St Mary's House, The Close, Lichfield, Staffs WS13 7LD* Tel (01543) 414551

SCHAEFER, Carl Richard. b 67. Coll of Resurr Mirfield CPS94. **d** 94 **p** 95. C Ribbleton *Blackb* from 94. *43 Grange Place, Preston PR2 6QT* Tel (01772) 702960

SCHARF, Ulrich Eduard Erich Julian. b 35. Melbourne Univ BA59 MA67 Linacre Coll Ox BA67 MA72 Lon Univ PhD81. Ripon Hall Ox 65. **d** 67 **p** 68. C Hackney St Jo *Lon* 68-71; Lic to Offic 71-75; Bp Stepney's Chapl 71-75; P-in-c Shadwell St Paul w Ratcliffe St Jas 75-90; R St Geo-in-the-East w St Paul 79-86; P-in-c W Ham *Chelmsf* 90-95; V from 95. *The Vicarage, Devenay Road, London E15 4AZ* Tel 0181-519 0955

SCHEMANOFF, Mrs Natasha Anne. b 50. **d** 96 **p** 97. C Freshford, Limpley Stoke and Hinton Charterhouse *B & W* from 96. *Bathford Vicarage, Ostlings Lane, Bath BA1 7RW* Tel (01225) 859575

SCHIBILD, Nigel Edmund David. b 47. Oak Hill Th Coll BA81. **d** 81 **p** 82. C Eccleston Ch Ch *Liv* 81-85; P-in-c Sydenham H Trin *S'wark* 85-87; V 87-91; Chapl Mildmay Miss Hosp from 91. *Mildmay Mission Hospital, Hackney Road, London E2 7NA* Tel 0171-739 2331

SCHIFF, Canon Leonard Maro. b 08. Ex Coll Ox BA29 MA34. Westcott Ho Cam 32. **d** 32 **p** 33. C Leeds Ch Ch and St Jo and St Barn Holbeck *Ripon* 32-33; Vice-Prin Qu Coll Birm 33-35; Asst Chapl 34-35; C Barnsbury St Clem *Lon* 35-37; USPG 38-41; India 38-43; V Whitworth w Spennymoor *Dur* 43-47; Warden Internat Centre Sheff 47-49; India 49-59; Lic to Offic *Cant* 59-65; Prin Coll of the Ascension Selly Oak 65-69; Chapl to Overseas Peoples *Birm* 69-75; Hon Can Birm Cathl 69-75; Chapl Aston Univ 72-75; rtd 75; Perm to Offic *Carl* from 77. *Gracey Court, Woodland Road, Broadclyst, Exeter EX5 3LP* Tel (01392) 468163

SCHILD, John. b 38. ALCD64. **d** 64 **p** 65. C Cheltenham Ch Ch *Glouc* 64-67; Area Sec (Dios Sheff and S'well) CMS 67-73; Area Sec (Dios Chelmsf and St Alb) CMS 73-76; V Lt Heath *St Alb* 76-88; R Bedford St Pet w St Cuth 88-94; P-in-c King's Walden and Offley w Lilley from 94. *The Vicarage, Church Road, Kings Walden, Hitchen, Herts SG4 8LX* Tel (01438) 871278 E-mail john@schild.demon.co.uk

SCHLEGER, Ms Maria Francesca. b 57. LSE BA78 SS Coll Cam BA84 MA89. Westcott Ho Cam 82. **dss** 85 **d** 87 **p** 94. De Beauvoir Town St Pet *Lon* 85-87; Par Dn 87-90; D-in-c Bromley All Hallows 90; TD Bow H Trin and All Hallows 90-94; Dean of Women's Min (Stepney Area) 90-94; TV Bow H Trin and All Hallows 94; Perm to Offic *Birm* from 94. *The Vicarage, 69 South Road, Smethwick, Warley, W Midlands B67 7BP* Tel 0121-558 0373

SCHOFIELD, Andrew Thomas. b 47. K Coll Lon BD70 AKC71 PGCE72. St Aug Coll Cant 70. **d** 81 **p** 82. C Whittlesey *Ely* 81-84; C Ramsey 84-87; P-in-c Ellington 87-94; P-in-c Grafham 87-94; P-in-c Spaldwick w Barham and Woolley 87-94; P-in-c Easton 87-94; P-in-c March St Jo 94; R from 94. *St John's Rectory, Station Road, March, Cambs PE15 8NG* Tel (01354) 53525

SCHOFIELD, David. b 43. Linc Th Coll 74. **d** 75 **p** 76. C Gainsborough All SS *Linc* 75-78; R Bolingbroke w Hareby 78-79; P-in-c Hagnaby 78-79; P-in-c Hagworthingham w Asgarby and Lusby 78-79; P-in-c Mavis Enderby w Raithby 78-79; P-in-c E Kirkby w Miningsby 78-79; R Bolingbroke 79-81; C-in-c Stamford Ch Ch CD 81-90; V Crowle from 90. *The Vicarage, Crowle, Scunthorpe, S Humberside DN17 4LE* Tel (01724) 710268

SCHOFIELD, Edward Denis. b 20. **d** 61 **p** 62. C Addiscombe St Mildred *Cant* 61-63; P-in-c Croydon St Jas 63-64; V 64-66; V Boughton under Blean 66-75; P-in-c Dunkirk 73-75; V Boughton under Blean w Dunkirk 75-76; V Sandgate St Paul 76-85; rtd 85. *53 Haydons Park, Honiton, Devon EX14 8TA* Tel (01404) 42584

SCHOFIELD, Canon John Martin. b 47. Selw Coll Cam BA69 MA73. St Steph Ho Ox 70. **d** 72 **p** 73. C Palmers Green St Jo *Lon* 72-75; C Friern Barnet St Jas 75-80; V Luton St Aug Limbury *St Alb* 80-89; V Biddenham 89-94; Dir Continuing Minl Educn 89-94; Dir Minl Tr *Guildf* from 94; Can Res Guildf Cathl from 95. *4 Cathedral Close, Guildford, Surrey GU2 5TL* Tel (01483) 577713 or 571826

SCHOFIELD, John Verity. b 29. Jes Coll Ox BA52 DipTh53 MA56. Cuddesdon Coll 53. **d** 55 **p** 56. C Cirencester *Glouc* 55-59; R Stella *Dur* 59-67; Kenya 67-69; Asst Chapl St Paul's Sch Barnes 69-70; Chapl 71-80; Australia 81-83; Gen Sec Friends of Elderly & Gentlefolk's Help 83-94; rtd 94. *Bishops Barn, Foots Hill, Cann, Shaftesbury, Dorset SP7 0BW* Tel (01747) 853852

SCHOFIELD, Nigel Timothy. b 54. FRCO Dur Univ BA76 Nottm Univ BCombStuds83. Linc Th Coll 80. **d** 83 **p** 84. C Cheshunt *St Alb* 83-86; TV Colyton, Southleigh, Offwell, Widworthy etc *Ex* 86-94; V Seaton from 94. *The Vicarage, Colyford Road, Seaton, Devon EX12 2DF* Tel (01297) 20391

SCHOFIELD, Richard Wyndham. b 09. Or Coll Ox BA32 MA38. St Steph Ho Ox 32 Ripon Hall Ox 36. **d** 37 **p** 38. C Taunton St Mary *B & W* 37-39; Perm to Offic *Derby* 39-40; C Stanford in the Vale w Goosey *Ox* 40-45; C Haydock St Jas *Liv* 45-46; C Newcastle w Butterton *Lich* 48-52; C Paddington St Steph w St Luke *Lon* 52-58; R Grundisburgh w Burgh *St E* 58-82; rtd 82; Perm to Offic *St E* from 82. *5 Constable Road, Ipswich IP4 2UN* Tel (01473) 256340

SCHOFIELD, Preb Rodney. b 44. St Jo Coll Cam BA64 MA67 St Pet Hall Ox BA70 MA73. St Steph Ho Ox 68. **d** 71 **p** 72. C Northampton St Mary *Pet* 71-76; V Irchester 76-84; Lesotho 84-86; R W Monkton *B & W* from 86; Asst Dir of Ords 87-89; Dir of Ords from 89; Preb Wells Cathl from 90. *The Rectory, West Monkton, Taunton, Somerset TA2 8QT* Tel (01823) 412226

SCHOLEFIELD, John. b 27. Leeds Univ BSc50. Wells Th Coll 51. **d** 53 **p** 54. C Ossett cum Gawthorpe *Wakef* 53-56; C Hebden Bridge 56-58; V Sowerby St Geo 58-64; V Darton 64-70; V Stoke Gabriel *Ex* 70-84; P-in-c Collaton St Mary 82-84; V Stoke Gabriel and Collaton 84-92; rtd 92; Perm to Offic *Ex* from 92. *25 Droridge, Dartington, Totnes, Devon TQ9 6JQ* Tel (01803) 863192

SCHOLER, Douglas William. b 23. Chich Th Coll 47. **d** 50 **p** 51. C Bishops Hull St Jo *B & W* 50-58; V Bridgwater H Trin 58-69; V W Pennard w W Bradley 70-81; P-in-c Bleadon 81-82; R 82-87; rtd 87; Perm to Offic *B & W* from 87. *Rose Cottage, Middle Road, Cossington, Bridgwater, Somerset TA7 8LH* Tel (01278) 722778

SCHOLEY, Donald. b 38. Leeds Univ CertEd60. Lich Th Coll 69. **d** 72 **p** 73. C Blaby *Leic* 72-75; TV Daventry w Norton *Pet* 75-78; R Wootton w Quinton and Preston Deanery from 78. *The Rectory, Water Lane, Wootton, Northampton NN4 0LG* Tel (01604) 761891

SCHOLFIELD, Peter. b 35. Sarum Th Coll 64. **d** 66 **p** 67. C S Kirkby *Wakef* 66-69; P-in-c Carlton 69-90; rtd 90; Perm to Offic *Wakef* from 90. *31 Springhill Avenue, Crofton, Wakefield, W Yorkshire WF1 1HA* Tel (01924) 863430

SCHOLLAR, Mrs Pamela Mary. b 39. Southn Univ DipEd80. S Dios Minl Tr Scheme 89. **d** 92 **p** 94. NSM Bournemouth St Andr *Win* 92-94; NSM Pokesdown St Jas from 94. *22 Bethia Road, Bournemouth BH8 9BD* Tel (01202) 397925

SCHOLZ, Terence Brinsley. b 44. **d** 97. NSM St Annes *Blackb* from 97. *5 Bracken Drive, Freckleton, Preston PR4 1TH* Tel (01772) 632966

SCHOOLING, Bruce James. b 47. Rhodes Univ BA73. St Paul's Grahamstown 76. **d** 76 **p** 77. S Africa 76-86; C Wanstead St Mary *Chelmsf* 87-90; V Leigh-on-Sea St Jas from 90. *St James's Vicarage, 103 Blenheim Chase, Leigh-on-Sea, Essex SS9 3BY* Tel (01702) 471786 Fax as telephone E-mail b.schooling@btinternet.com

SCHORAH, Michael James (Mike). b 63. Keble Coll Ox BA89 MA91. Trin Coll Bris BA95. **d** 95 **p** 96. C Cheltenham St Mary, St Matt, St Paul and H Trin *Glouc* from 95. *18 Eldon Road, Cheltenham, Glos GL52 6TU* Tel (01242) 528567 Fax 519520 E-mail mschorah@aol.com

SCHRAM, Dr Ralph. b 27. Down Coll Cam BA49 MA MB BChir55 St Thos Hosp Lon MD67. Oak Hill NSM Course 84. **d** 87 **p** 88. NSM Croydon Ch Ch *S'wark* 87-93; Perm to Offic *Portsm* from 93. *Nile Cottage, Colwell Road, Freshwater, Isle of Wight PO40 9NB* Tel (01983) 754865

SCHRODER, Edward Amos. b 41. **d** 67 **p** 68. C St Marylebone All So w SS Pet and Jo *Lon* 67-71; USA from 72. *510 Belknap, San Antonio, Texas 78212, USA*

SCHULD DE VERNY, Dietrich Gustave. *See* DE VERNY, David Dietrich

SCHUNEMANN, Bernhard George. b 61. LRAM83 K Coll Lon BD86 AKC86. Ripon Coll Cuddesdon 88. **d** 90 **p** 91. C Kirkby *Liv* 90-93; C St Martin-in-the-Fields *Lon* 93-97; Chapl Br Sch of Osteopathy 93-97; P-in-c Littlemore *Ox* from 97. *The Vicarage, St Nicholas' Road, Oxford OX4 4PP* Tel (01865) 749939

SCHWABACHER, Kurt Frederick. b 12. Chich Th Coll 36. **d** 39 **p** 40. C Plumstead St Mark *S'wark* 39-44; C Catford St Laur 44-51; P-in-c Forest Hill St Paul 51-63; V 63-68; Perm to Offic *Roch* 68-95; rtd 77. *1 Raleigh Court, 21A The Avenue, Beckenham, Kent BR3 2DL* Tel 0181-650 8670

SCHWIER, Peter Andrew. b 52. **d** 91 **p** 92. NSM Fressingfield, Mendham, Metfield, Weybread etc *St E* from 91. *Valley Farm, Metfield, Harleston, Norfolk IP20 0JZ* Tel (01379) 384517

SCLATER, John Edward. b 46. Nottm Univ BA68 St Edm Hall Ox CertEd71. Cuddesdon Coll 69. **d** 71 **p** 72. C Bris St Mary Redcliffe w Temple etc *Bris* 71-75; Chapl Bede Ho Staplehurst 75-79; Chapl Warw Sch 79; P-in-c Offchurch *Cov* 79-80; Belgium 81-89; Willen Priory 89-91; C Linslade *Ox* 91-94; P-in-c Hedsor and Bourne End from 94. *The Rectory, 1 Wharf Lane, Bourne End, Bucks SL8 5RS* Tel (01628) 523046

SCOBIE, Dr Geoffrey Edward Winsor (Geoff). b 39. Bris Univ BSc62 MSc68 Birm Univ MA70 Glas Univ PhD78 FRSA96 AFBPsS. Tyndale Hall Bris 62. **d** 65 **p** 66. C Summerfield *Birm* 65-66; C Moseley St Anne 66-67; Lect Psychology Glas Univ from 67; Hon C Glas St Silas *Glas* 70-83; P-in-c 83-84; Hon R 84-85; TR 85-86; Team Chapl 86-88; Hon Asst Team Chapl from 88. *3 Norfolk Crescent, Bishopbriggs, Glasgow G64 3BA* Tel 0141-722 2907

SCOONES, Roger Philip. b 48. DipTh. Trin Coll Bris. **d** 82 **p** 83. C Childwall All SS *Liv* 82-85; Bradf Cathl *Bradf* 85-90; V Congleton St Pet *Ches* 90-96; P-in-c Congleton St Steph 94-96; R Stockport St Mary from 96. *St Mary's Rectory, Gorsey Mount Street, Stockport, Cheshire SK1 4DU* Tel 0161-429 6564

SCORER, John Robson. b 47. Westcott Ho Cam 73. **d** 75 **p** 76. C Silksworth *Dur* 75-78; C Newton Aycliffe 78-82; V Sherburn 82-83; V Sherburn w Pittington 83-89; P-in-c Croxdale 89-93; Chapl Dur Constabulary from 89. *1 Vicarage Close, Howden le Wear, Crook, Co Durham DL15 8RB* Tel (01388) 764938

SCOTLAND, Nigel Adrian Douglas. b 42. McGill Univ Montreal MA71 Aber Univ PhD75 CertEd75 Bris Univ MLitt. Gordon-Conwell Th Sem MDiv70 Lon Coll of Div ALCD66 LTh74. **d** 66 **p** 67. C Harold Wood *Chelmsf* 66-69; USA 69-70; Canada 70-72; Lic to Offic *Ab* 72-75; Chapl and Lect St Mary's Coll Cheltenham 75-79; Sen Lect 77-79; Chapl and Sen Lect Coll of SS Paul and Mary 79-84; NSM Cheltenham St Mark *Glouc* 85-92; Field Chair Relig Studies Cheltenham and Glouc Coll of HE from 89; Prin Lect Cheltenham and Glouc Coll of HE from 96; Perm to Offic *Glouc* from 92. *23 School Road, Charlton Kings, Cheltenham, Glos GL53 8BG* Tel (01242) 529167

SCOTLAND, Primus of the Episcopal Church in. *See* HOLLOWAY, The Most Revd Richard Frederick

SCOTT, Prof Adam. b 47. TD78. Ch Ch Ox BA68 MA72 City Univ MSc79 Barrister 72 FRSA95 CEng81 MIEE81 FIEE94. S'wark Ord Course 73. **d** 75 **p** 76. MSE Blackheath Park St Mich *S'wark* from 75; Dean for MSE, Woolwich from 90; Prof Fell St Andr Univ *St And* from 96; Perm to Offic from 96. *19 Blackheath Park, London SE3 9RW, or St Katharine's West, The Scores, St Andrews, Fife KY16 9AT* Tel 0181-852 3286 or (01334) 462871 Fax 0181-852 6247 or (01334) 426872

SCOTT, Alfred Thomas. b 19. St Steph Ho Ox 78. **d** 81 **p** 82. NSM S Ascot *Ox* 81-85; NSM Bridport *Sarum* 85-89; Perm to Offic 89-90; rtd 90; Perm to Offic *Truro* from 90. *22 Castle Hill Court, Cross Lane, Bodmin, Cornwall PL31 2LE*

SCOTT, Preb Allan George. b 39. Man Univ BA61. Coll of Resurr Mirfield 61. **d** 63 **p** 64. C Bradford cum Beswick *Man* 63-66; P-in-c 66-72; Hon C Bramhall *Ches* 72-74; Hon C Tottenham St Jo *Lon* 74-76; Hon C Bush Hill Park St Steph 76-79; R Stoke Newington St Mary from 79; Preb St Paul's Cathl from 91; P-in-c Brownswood Park 95-97. *The Rectory, Stoke Newington Church Street, London N16 9ES* Tel 0171-254 6072

SCOTT, Andrew Charles Graham. b 28. Mert Coll Ox BA57 MA. Wells Th Coll 57. **d** 59 **p** 60. C Rugby St Andr *Cov* 59-64; Chapl RN 64-68; C Prenton *Ches* 68-71; V Tow Law *Dur* 71-81; RD Stanhope 77-81; V Bampton w Clanfield *Ox* 81-95; rtd 95; Perm to Offic *Ex* from 95. *99 Speedwell, Plymouth PL6 5SZ* Tel (01752) 773570

SCOTT, Barrie. b 63. Birm Univ BA85 Golds Coll Lon PGCE86. St Steph Ho Ox 93. **d** 95 **p** 96. C Tilehurst St Mich *Ox* from 95. *Tilston Lodge, New Lane Hill, Reading RG3 4JN* Tel 0118-941 1487

SCOTT, Basil John Morley. b 34. Qu Coll Cam BA59 Banaras Hindu Univ MA65. Ridley Hall Cam 58. **d** 60 **p** 61. C Woking St Pet *Guildf* 60-63; India 63-83; TR Kirby Muxloe *Leic* 83-89; Asian Outreach Worker (Leic Martyrs) 89-95; Derby Asian Chr Min Project *Derby* from 95. *11 Harrington Street, Derby DE23 8PE* Tel Derby (01332) 772360

SCOTT, Brian. b 35. CCC Ox BA58. Coll of Resurr Mirfield 59. **d** 61 **p** 65. C Carl St Aid and Ch Ch *Carl* 61-62; Asst Master Hutton Gr Sch 63-65; Perm to Offic *Leic* 65-67; Lic to Offic 67-70; P-in-c Theddingworth 71-78; V Lubenham 71-78; Asst Chapl Oundle Sch 78-83; R Barrowden and Wakerley w S Luffenham *Pet* from 83. *The Rectory, Barrowden, Oakham, Leics LE15 8ED* Tel (01572) 87248

SCOTT, Charles Geoffrey. b 32. St Jo Coll Cam BA54 MA58. Cuddesdon Coll 56. **d** 58 **p** 59. C Brighouse *Wakef* 58-61; C Bathwick w Woolley *B & W* 61-64; V Frome Ch Ch 64-78; R Winchelsea *Chich* 78-93; R Winchelsea and Icklesham 93-95; rtd 95; Perm to Offic *Chich* from 95. *Hickstead, Main Street, Iden, Rye, E Sussex TN31 7PT* Tel (01797) 280096

SCOTT, Christopher John Fairfax. b 45. Magd Coll Cam BA67 MA71. Westcott Ho Cam 68. **d** 70 **p** 71. C Nor St Pet Mancroft *Nor* 70-73; Chapl Magd Coll Cam 73-79; V Hampstead Ch Ch *Lon* 79-94. *49 St Barnabas Road, Cambridge CB1 2BX* Tel (01223) 359421

SCOTT, Christopher Michael. b 44. SS Coll Cam BA66 MA70. Cuddesdon Coll 66. **d** 68 **p** 69. C New Addington *Cant* 68-73; C Westmr St Steph w St Jo *Lon* 73-78; V Enfield St Mich 78-81; V Effingham w Lt Bookham *Guildf* 81-87; R Esher from 87; RD Emly 91-96. *The Rectory, 4 Esher Place Avenue, Esher, Surrey KT10 8PY* Tel (01372) 462611

SCOTT, Christopher Stuart (Chris). b 48. Surrey Univ BA92. Sarum & Wells Th Coll 79. **d** 81 **p** 82. C Enfield Chase St Mary *Lon* 81-82; C Coalbrookdale, Iron-Bridge and Lt Wenlock *Heref* 82-86; P-in-c Breinton 86-89; Chapl Hickey's Almshouses Richmond from 89; Lic to Offic *S'wark* from 89. *164 Sheen Road, Richmond, Surrey TW9 1XD* Tel 0181-940 6560

SCOTT, Claude John. b 37. Qu Mary Coll Lon BSc60 PhD64 Lon Inst of Educn PGCE61 FRSA94. EAMTC 88. **d** 91 **p** 92. NSM Heigham H Trin *Nor* from 91. *17 Lime Tree Road, Norwich NR2 2NQ* Tel (01603) 55686

SCOTT, Clifford Wentworth. b 04. Lon Univ BSc25. Ridley Hall Cam 25. **d** 27 **p** 28. C Toxteth Park Ch Ch *Liv* 27-29; P-in-c Clifton St Jas *Sheff* 29-32; P-in-c Thurcroft 32-35; V Sheff St Bart 35-41; CF 41-46; V Ardsley *Sheff* 46-56; R N Kilworth *Leic* 56-64; R Sapcote 64-72; rtd 72. *4 Egerton Road, Padstow, Cornwall PL28 8DJ* Tel (01841) 532649

SCOTT, Colin. b 32. Dur Univ BA54. Coll of Resurr Mirfield 58. **d** 60 **p** 61. C Wallsend St Pet *Newc* 60-64; C Seaton Hirst 64-68; C Longbenton St Bart 68-70; V Benwell St Aid 70-77; V Sleekburn 77-89; P-in-c Cambois 77-88; V Longhoughton w Howick 89-96; rtd 96. *3 Bank Top, Chillingham, Alnwick, Northd NE66 5NG* Tel (01668) 215499

✠**SCOTT, The Rt Revd Colin John Fraser.** b 33. Qu Coll Cam BA56 MA60. Ridley Hall Cam 56. **d** 58 **p** 59 **c** 84. C Clapham Common St Barn *S'wark* 58-61; C Hatcham St Jas 61-64; V Kennington St Mark 64-71; RD Lambeth 68-71; Vice-Chmn Dioc Past Cttee 71-77; Hon Can S'wark Cathl 73-84; TR Sanderstead All SS 77-84; Suff Bp Hulme *Man* from 84; Chmn CCC from 94. *1 Raynham Avenue, Didsbury, Manchester M20 0BW* Tel 0161-445 5922 Fax 448 9687

SCOTT, Cuthbert Le Messurier. b 13. Wells Th Coll 60. **d** 61 **p** 62. C Highgate St Mich *Lon* 61-64; V Paddington St Jo w St Mich 64-72; V Shamley Green *Guildf* 72-83; rtd 83; Perm to Offic *Chich* 84-95; Chapl St Dunstans 88-95. *Flat 30, Manormead, Tilford Road, Hindhead, Surrey GU26 6RA*

SCOTT, David. b 40. Rhodes Univ BA63. St Paul's Grahamstown LTh65. **d** 65 **p** 66. S Africa 65-91; TV Cheltenham St Mark *Glouc* 92-96; R Swanscombe *Roch* from 96. *The Rectory, Swanscombe Street, Swanscombe, Kent DA10 0JZ* Tel (01322) 843160

SCOTT, David Lloyd Thomas. b 31. FCA Jes Coll Cam BA76 MA80. Ridley Hall Cam 73. **d** 76 **p** 77. C Swindon Ch Ch *Bris* 76-79; R Ripple *Worc* 79-82; V Broadheath, Crown East and Rushwick 82-88; V Lenton *S'well* 88-93; rtd 93; Perm to Offic *Derby* from 93. *6 Chandres Court, Allestree, Derby DE22 2FA* Tel (01332) 551445

SCOTT, David Victor. b 47. St Chad's Coll Dur BA69. Cuddesdon Coll 69. **d** 71 **p** 72. C St Mary-at-Latton *Chelmsf* 71-73; Chapl Haberdashers' Aske's Sch Elstree 73-80; V Torpenhow *Carl* 80-91; V Allhallows 80-91; R Win St Lawr and St Maurice w St Swithun *Win* from 91; Warden Sch of Spirituality Win from 91. *The Rectory, Colebrook Street, Winchester, Hants SO23 9LH* Tel (01962) 868056

SCOTT, Edgar. b 12. Linc Th Coll 76. **d** 76 **p** 76. Hon C Wombwell *Sheff* 76-90; rtd 90; Perm to Offic *Sheff* 90-93. *17 Wood Walk, Wombwell, Barnsley, S Yorkshire S73 0LZ* Tel (01226) 753020

SCOTT, Canon Eric Walter. b 16. St Jo Coll Cam BA38 MA43. Ridley Hall Cam 38. **d** 40 **p** 41. C Reading St Jo *Ox* 40-43; C Cambridge H Trin *Ely* 43-45; C-in-c Tilehurst St Mary CD *Ox* 45-49; V Brimpton w Wasing 49-53; Canada 53-87 and 89-90; Perm to Offic *Nor* 87-89; Perm to Offic *Ely* from 89. *4 Allen Court, Hauxton Road, Trumpington, Cambridge CB2 2LU* Tel (01223) 841015

SCOTT, Gary James. b 61. Edin Univ BD87. Edin Th Coll 85. **d** 87 **p** 88. C Edin St Cuth *Edin* 87-90; R Peebles 90-92; P-in-c Innerleithen 92-96; R Penicuik from 96; R W Linton from 96. *The Rectory, 23 Broomhill Road, Penicuik, Midlothian EH26 9EE* Tel (01968) 672862

SCOTT, Canon Gordon. b 30. Man Univ BA51. St Jo Coll Dur 51. **d** 53 **p** 54. C Monkwearmouth St Andr *Dur* 53-55; C Stranton 55-56; C Chester le Street 56-59; V Marley Hill 59-62; Chapl Forest Sch Snaresbrook 62-66; Chapl Dunrobin Sch Sutherland 66-72; Chapl Pocklington Sch York 72-74; V Barton w Pooley Bridge *Carl* 74-80; RD Penrith 79-82; P-in-c Lazonby 80; R Gt Salkeld w Lazonby 80-90; Hon Can Carl Cathl 83-94; P-in-c Patterdale 90-94; rtd 94; Perm to Offic *Carl* from 94. *48 Lakeland Park, Keswick, Cumbria CA12 4AT* Tel (017687) 75862

SCOTT, Harold James. b 05. Dur Univ LTh30 Jes Coll Cam 61. St Aug Coll Cant 27. **d** 30 **p** 31. C Kings Heath *Birm* 30-33; Barbados 33-40; P-in-c Allens Cross *Birm* 40-45; V Bourn *Ely* 45-50; R Kingston 45-50; Asst Dir Educn 45-50; RD Bourn 47-50; V Walpole St Andrew 50-61; V Swavesey 61-71; rtd 71; Perm to Offic *Ely* from 71. *Flat 14, Stuart Court, High Street, Kibworth, Leicester LE8 0LE* Tel 0116-279 6351

SCOTT, Mrs Helen Ruth. b 59. St Thos Hosp Lon SRN81 R Shrewsbury Hosp RM85. S'wark Ord Course DipRS92. **d** 92 **p** 94. NSM Richmond St Mary w St Matthias and St Jo *S'wark* from 92. *164 Sheen Road, Richmond, Surrey TW9 1XD* Tel 0181-940 6560

SCOTT, Ian. b 45. MBChA87 MSSCh87. Qu Coll Birm 92. **d** 94 **p** 95. C Cropthorne w Charlton *Worc* from 94. *The Vicarage, Cropthorne, Pershore, Worcs WR10 3NB* Tel (01386) 860279

SCOTT, Mrs Inez Margaret Gillette. b 26. St Alb Minl Tr Scheme 76. **dss** 79 **d** 87 **p** 94. Preston w Sutton Poyntz and Osmington w Poxwell *Sarum* 83-86; Dorchester 86-87; Par Dn 87-88; NSM 88-96; rtd 88. *14 Came View Road, Dorchester, Dorset DT1 2AE* Tel (01305) 267547

SCOTT, James Alexander Gilchrist (Jim). b 32. Linc Coll Ox BA56 DipTh57 MA60. Wycliffe Hall Ox 56. **d** 58 **p** 59. C Shipley St Paul *Bradf* 58-61; Abp's Dom Chapl *York* 61-65; Brazil 65-68; V Grassendale *Liv* 68-77; V Thorp Arch *York* 77; P-in-c Walton 77; V Thorp Arch w Walton 77-89; Chapl HM Pris Rudgate 77-82; Askham Grange 82-87; RD Tadcaster 78-86; V Kirk Ella 89-92; TR from 92. *The Vicarage, 2 School Lane, Kirk Ella, Hull HU10 7NR* Tel (01482) 653040

SCOTT, James William. b 39. S Dios Minl Tr Scheme 84. **d** 88 **p** 89. NSM Bremhill w Foxham and Hilmarton *Sarum* 88-94; NSM Derry Hill w Bremhill and Foxham from 94. *14 Bremhill, Calne, Wilts SN11 9LA* Tel (01249) 813114

SCOTT, Mrs Janice Beasant. b 44. MCSP66 Middx Hosp Physiotherapy Sch DipTP70. EAMTC 89. **d** 92 **p** 94. NSM Fakenham w Alethorpe *Nor* 92-95; C Eaton from 95. *347 Unthank Road, Eaton, Norwich NR4 7QG* Tel (01603) 461020 E-mail revjan@dial.pipex.com

SCOTT, John. b 54. QUB BD79. CITC 80. **d** 81 **p** 82. C Willowfield *D & D* 81-83; C Newtownards 83-85; I Kilskeery w Trillick *Clogh* 85-90; Lic to Offic *D & D* 90-96; I Bright w Ballee and Killough from 96. *Bright Rectory, 126 Killough Road, Downpatrick, Co Down BT30 8LL* Tel (01396) 842041

SCOTT, John. b 54. Heriot-Watt Univ BA76. Coll of Resurr Mirfield BA97. **d** 97. C Bethnal Green St Matt w St Jas the Gt *Lon* from 97. *The Rectory, Hereford Street, London E2 6EX* E-mail jscott@demon.co.uk

SCOTT, John David. b 52. St Jo Coll Ox BA74 MA78 Leeds Univ BA78. Coll of Resurr Mirfield 76. **d** 78 **p** 79. C Oundle *Pet* 78-81; C Dalston H Trin w St Phil *Lon* 81-85; V Ponders End St Matt 85-91; Chapl Bede Ho Staplehurst from 91. *Bede House, Goudhurst Road, Staplehurst, Tonbridge, Kent TN12 0HQ* Tel (01580) 891995

SCOTT, John Eric. b 16. FSA St Cath Coll Ox BA38 MA42. Ripon Hall Ox 39. **d** 40 **p** 41. C Heworth St Alb *Dur* 40-43; C Gateshead St Mary 43-45; Chapl and Sacr Ch Ch *Ox* 45-47; Ho Master Forest Sch Snaresbrook 55-81; P-in-c St Mich Cornhill w St Pet le Poer etc *Lon* 81-85; rtd 85. *17 Harman Avenue, Woodford Green, Essex IG8 9DS* Tel 0181-505 7093

SCOTT, Preb John Gilbert Mortimer. b 25. St Edm Hall Ox BA49 MA52. Bps' Coll Cheshunt. **d** 51 **p** 52. C Ex St Thos *Ex* 51-54; C Wolborough w Newton Abbot 54-58; V Clawton 58-66; R Tetcott w Luffincott 58-66; RD Holsworthy 65-66; V Newton St Cyres 66-84; RD Cadbury 81-84; Preb Ex Cathl from 84; P-in-c Bampton 84; P-in-c Clayhanger 84; P-in-c Petton 84; V Bampton, Morebath, Clayhanger and Petton 84-91; rtd 91. *Trelake, Bridgetown Hill, Totnes, Devon TQ9 5BA* Tel (01803) 867754

SCOTT, John Harold. b 46. Univ of Wales (Cardiff) BSc69. St Steph Ho Ox 69. **d** 72 **p** 73. C Skewen *Llan* 72-74; C Port Talbot St Theodore 74-77; P-in-c Bedlinog 77-78; V 78-85; R Penderyn w Ystradfellte and Pontneathvaughan *S & B* from 85. *The Vicarage, Ystradfellte, Aberdare CF44 9JE* Tel (01639) 720405

SCOTT, John Peter. b 47. Open Univ BA80. Lambeth STh81 K Coll Lon 69 St Aug Coll Cant 74. **d** 75 **p** 76. C Dartford St Alb *Roch* 75-78; C-in-c Goring-by-Sea *Chich* 78-81; Chapl Wells and Meare Manor Hosps 81-86; CF (TAVR) 82-90; Chapl Pangbourne Coll 86-90; Min Reigate St Phil CD *S'wark* 90-92; P-in-c Reigate St Phil from 92; Chapl St Bede's Ecum Sch Reigate from 90. *The Parsonage, 102A Nutley Lane, Reigate, Surrey RH2 9HA* Tel (01737) 244542

SCOTT, Keith Brounton de Salve. b 55. QUB BD. DipTh. **d** 83 **p** 84. C Belfast St Matt *Conn* 83-87; I Ardclinis and Tickmacrevan w Layde and Cushendun from 87. *76 Largy Road, Carnlough, Ballymena, Co Antrim BT44 0JJ* Tel (01574) 885618

SCOTT, Kenneth James (Ken). b 46. Bris Univ BA68. Trin Coll Bris 71. **d** 73 **p** 74. C Illogan *Truro* 73-76; C Camberley St Paul *Guildf* 76-81; R Bradford Peverell, Stratton, Frampton etc *Sarum* from 81; RD Dorchester from 95. *The Rectory, Church Lane, Frampton, Dorchester, Dorset DT2 9NL* Tel (01300) 320429

SCOTT, Dr Kevin Francis. b 51. GRSC Peterho Cam MA Mert Coll Ox DPhil76. Wycliffe Hall Ox. **d** 83 **p** 84. C Ox St Ebbe w H Trin and St Pet *Ox* 83-86; P-in-c Prestonpans *Edin* 86-93; R Musselburgh 86-93; R Edin SS Phil and Jas from 93. *The Rectory, 5 Wardie Road, Edinburgh EH5 3QE* Tel 0131-552 4300

SCOTT, Kevin Peter. b 43. Reigate Coll of Art DipAD73. Coll of Resurr Mirfield CPT93. **d** 93 **p** 94. C Rushall *Lich* 93-97; P-in-c Goldenhill from 97. *St John's Vicarage, Drummond Street, Stoke-on-Trent ST6 5RF* Tel (01782) 782736

SCOTT, Kevin Willard. b 53. Westhill Coll Birm CYCW77 Open Univ BA96. Linc Th Coll CMinlStuds92. **d** 92 **p** 93. C Walton-on-Thames *Guildf* from 92. *1 Egmont Road, Walton-on-Thames, Surrey KT12 2NW* Tel (01932) 229621

SCOTT, Lester Desmond Donald. NUI BA89. CITC BTh92. **d** 92 **p** 93. C Kilmore w Ballintemple, Kildallon etc *K, E & A* 92-95; I Fenagh w Myshall, Aghade and Ardoyne *C & O* from 95. *The Glebe House, Ballon, Carlow, Irish Republic* Tel Carlow (503) 59367 Mobile 088-504322 Fax as telephone

SCOTT, Canon Malcolm Kenneth Merrett. b 30. ACA53 FCA64. Clifton Th Coll 56. **d** 58 **p** 59. C Highbury Ch Ch *Lon* 58-60; CMS 60-61; Uganda 61-74; V Sunnyside w Bourne End *St Alb* 74-90; V Clapham 90-95; rtd 95. *10 The Ring, Little Haywood, Stafford ST18 0TP* Tel (01889) 881464

SCOTT, Michael Bernard Campion. b 29. Or Coll Ox BA52 MA56 DTh. Edin Th Coll 52. **d** 54 **p** 55. C Kirkcaldy *St And* 54-58; C Hitchin H Sav *St Alb* 58-61; Antigua 61-66; C Reading St Mary V *Ox* 66-72; C-in-c Reading St Mark CD 72-76; C-in-c Orton Malborne CD *Ely* 76-91; Chapl Glouc Cen for Mentally Handicapped Orton 77-91; rtd 91. *13 Mill Street, Puddletown, Dorchester, Dorset DT2 8SQ* Tel (01305) 848030

SCOTT, Patrick Henry Fowlis. b 25. Jes Coll Cam BA51 MA55. Wells Th Coll 51. **d** 53 **p** 54. C Milton next Gravesend w Denton *Roch* 53-54; V New Hythe 54-57; CF 57-70; Dep Asst Chapl Gen 70-71 and 74-80; Sen CF 72-74; P-in-c Fridaythorpe w Fimber and Thixendale *York* 80-83; P-in-c Sledmere and Wetwang w Cowlan 80-83; V Sledmere and Cowlam w Fridaythorpe, Fimer etc 84-90; rtd 90; Perm to Offic *York* from 90. *3 Appleby Glade, Haxby, York YO3 3YW* Tel (01904) 769258

SCOTT, Peter Crawford. b 35. Ch Ch Ox BA56 MA61. Cuddesdon Coll 60. **d** 62 **p** 63. C Broseley w Benthall *Heref* 62-66; P-in-c Hughenden *Ox* 66-71; C Hykeham *Linc* 71-73; P-in-c Stottesdon *Heref* 73-76; Australia from 76. *Christ Church Rectory, 30 High Street, Macarthur, Victoria, Australia 3286* Tel Macarthur (55) 761022

SCOTT, Peter James Douglas Sefton. b 59. Edin Univ BD83. Edin Th Coll 81. **d** 83 **p** 84. C Helensburgh *Glas* 83-86; C-in-c Glas St Oswald 86-89; R 89-91; Chapl RN from 91. *Royal Naval Chaplaincy Service, Room 203, Victory Building, HM Naval Base, Portsmouth PO1 3LS* Tel (01705) 727903 Fax 727112

SCOTT, Peter Lindsay. b 29. Keble Coll Ox BA54 MA58. Linc Th Coll 54. **d** 56 **p** 57. C Weston-super-Mare St Sav *B & W* 56-59; C Knowle H Nativity *Bris* 59-61; P-in-c Glas St Pet *Glas* 61-63; V Heap Bridge *Man* 63-73; V Rochdale St Geo w St Alb 73-86; R Droylsden St Andr 86-94; rtd 94; Perm to Offic *Man* from 94. *2 Chancel Place, Rochdale, Lancs OL16 1FB* Tel (01706) 523270

SCOTT, Simon James. b 65. Ch Ch Ox BA87 MA91. Wycliffe Hall Ox 88. **d** 91 **p** 92. C Cheadle All Hallows *Ches* 91-95; Scripture Union from 95. *59F Lake Street, Oxford OX1 4RR* Tel (01865) 723318 Fax as telephone

SCOTT, Terence. b 56. QUB BSc77. CITC 77. **d** 80 **p** 81. C Ballymena *Conn* 80-83; C Antrim All SS 83-85; P-in-c Connor w Antrim St Patr 85-88; I Magherafelt *Arm* from 88; Hon V Choral Arm Cathl from 95. *St Swithin's Rectory, 1 Churchwell Lane, Magherafelt, Co Londonderry BT45 6AL* Tel (01648) 32365

SCOTT, Mrs Theresa Anne. b 53. Bris Univ BSc75 Lon Univ PGCE76. Ox Min Course 89. **d** 92 **p** 94. NSM Wickham Bishops w Lt Braxted *Chelmsf* 92-93; NSM Drayton St Pet (Berks) *Ox* from 94; NSM Convenor (Berks Adnry) from 97. *The Driftway, Sutton Wick Lane, Drayton, Oxon OX14 4HJ* Tel (01235) 533714

SCOTT, Timothy Charles Nairne (Tim). b 61. Ex Univ BA83. Westcott Ho Cam 84. **d** 87 **p** 88. C Romford St Edw *Chelmsf* 87-89; Community Priest 89-94; P-in-c Leytonstone H Trin Harrow Green 94-97; V from 97. *The Vicarage, 4 Holloway Road, London E11 4LD* Tel 0181-539 7760

SCOTT, Vernon Malcolm. b 30. TCD BA57 MA60. TCD Div Sch Div Test56 Ridley Hall Cam 58. **d** 58 **p** 59. C Limehouse St Anne *Lon* 58-62; C N St Pancras All Hallows 62-66; V Enfield St Mich 66-77; R Tansor w Cotterstock and Fotheringhay *Pet* 77-81; R Barby w Onley 81-83; V Kilsby 81-83; R Barby w Kilsby 83-90; R Coxford Gp *Nor* 90-94; P-in-c South Raynham, E w W Raynham, Helhoughton, etc 94-96; R E and W Rudham, Houghton-next-Harpley etc 95-96; rtd 96; Perm to Offic *Nor* from 96. *5 Wells Road, Walsingham, Norfolk NR22 6DL* Tel (01328) 820151

SCOTT, Walter David Craig. b 22. Selw Coll Cam BA49 MA53. Sarum Th Coll 49. **d** 51 **p** 52. C Shildon *Dur* 51-55; Min Cleadon Park St Cuth CD 55-67; V Cleadon Park 67-71; V Bulkington *Cov* 72-83; RD Bedworth 76-79; V Bulkington w Shilton and Ansty 83-87; rtd 87; Perm to Offic *Cov* from 87. *8 Osprey Close, Nuneaton, Warks CV11 6TF* Tel (01203) 345561

SCOTT, William. b 20. MBE97. Coll of Resurr Mirfield. **d** 60 **p** 61. C Wolborough w Newton Abbot *Ex* 60-63; Chapl St Cath Sch Bramley 63-66; Chapl Sch of St Mary and St Anne Abbots Bromley 72-76; Perm to Offic *Cant* 79-90; Chapl Boulogne-sur-Mer w Calais and Lille *Eur* 90-93; Chapl Lille from 93. *Christ Church, rue Watteau, 59000 Lille, France*

SCOTT, William John. b 46. TCD BA70. CITC. **d** 71 **p** 72. C Bangor St Comgall *D & D* 71-74; C Holywood 74-80; I Carnalea 80-90; I Seapatrick from 90. *The Rectory, 63 Lurgan Road, Banbridge, Co Down BT32 4LY* Tel (01820) 622612

SCOTT, William Sievwright. b 46. Edin Th Coll 67. **d** 70 **p** 71. C Glas St Ninian *Glas* 70-73; C Bridgwater St Fran *B & W* 73-77; R Shepton Beauchamp w Barrington, Stocklinch etc 77-81; P-in-c Cossington 82-84; P-in-c Woolavington 82-84; Chapl Community of All Hallows Ditchingham 84-91; V Pimlico St Mary Graham Terrace *Lon* from 91. *St Mary's Presbytery, 30 Bourne Street, London SW1W 8JJ* Tel 0171-730 2423

SCOTT-DEMPSTER, Canon Colin Thomas. b 37. Em Coll Cam BA65 MA68. Cuddesdon Coll 64. **d** 66 **p** 67. C Caversham *Ox* 66-69; Chapl Coll of SS Mark and Jo Chelsea 69-73; V Chieveley w Winterbourne and Oare *Ox* from 73; RD Newbury from 77; Hon Can Ch Ch from 90. *Chieveley Vicarage, Newbury, Berks RG16 8UT* Tel (01635) 248341

SCOTT-HAMBLEN, Shane. b 66. Webster Univ (USA) BMus89 St Thos Aquinas Univ Rome STB94 MA96 STL96 St Louis Univ 90. **d** 94 **p** 95. C Staines St Mary and St Pet *Lon* from 97. *Peterhouse, St Peter's Close, Laleham Road, Staines, Middx TW18 2ED* Tel (01784) 450861 E-mail saintpeters @saintpeters.demon.co.uk

✠**SCOTT-JOYNT, The Rt Revd Michael Charles.** b 43. K Coll Cam BA65 MA68. Cuddesdon Coll 65. **d** 67 **p** 68 **c** 87. C Cuddesdon *Ox* 67-70; Tutor Cuddesdon Coll 67-71; Chapl 71-72; TV Newbury St Nic *Ox* 72-75; P-in-c Bicester 75-79; P-in-c Caversfield 75-79; P-in-c Bucknell 76-79; TR Bicester w Bucknell, Caversfield and Launton 79-81; RD Bicester and Islip 76-81; Can Res St Alb 82-87; Dir of Ords and Post-Ord Tr 82-87; Suff Bp Stafford *Lich* 87-92; Area Bp Stafford 92-95; Bp Win from 95. *Wolvesey Palace, Winchester SO23 9ND* Tel (01962) 854050 Fax 842376

SCOTT-OLDFIELD, Ivor Erroll Lindsay. b 21. Univ Coll Dur BA49. Sarum Th Coll 49. **d** 51 **p** 52. C Trowbridge St Jas *Sarum* 51-54; C Haggerston St Paul *Lon* 54-58; V Enfield SS Pet and Paul 58-61; V Kentish Town St Benet and All SS 61-68; Dir Gen RADD 68-87; rtd 87. *11E Prior Bolton Street, London N1 2NX*

SCOTT-THOMPSON, Ian Mackenzie. b 57. Ch Ch Ox BA78. St Jo Coll Nottm BA82. **d** 83 **p** 84. C Hartley Wintney, Elvetham, Winchfield etc *Win* 83-85; C Bitterne 85-89; V Iford from 89.

St Saviour's Vicarage, Holdenhurst Avenue, Bournemouth BH7 6RB Tel (01202) 425978

SCRACE, David Peter. b 46. Sarum & Wells Th Coll 79. **d** 81 **p** 82. C Abbots Langley *St Alb* 81-85; TV Chippenham St Paul w Hardenhuish etc *Bris* 85-91; P-in-c Harnham *Sarum* from 91; RD Salisbury from 93. *The Vicarage, Old Blandford Road, Harnham, Salisbury SP2 8DQ* Tel (01722) 333564

SCRAGG, Michael John. b 39. **d** 74 **p** 75. C Chesterton Gd Shep *Ely* 77-79; Australia from 79. *PO Box 389, Morphet Vale, S Australia 5162, or 8 Pultney Road, Reynella, S Australia 5161* Tel Adelaide (8) 322 3329

SCREECH, Prof Michael. b 26. l'Ordre national du Merite 83 l'Ordre national de la Legion d'Honneur 93. FBA81 FRSL87 Univ Coll Lon BA50 DLitt82 Birm Univ DLitt59 All So Coll Ox MA84 DLitt90 Ex Univ Hon DLitt93. Ox Min Course 92. **d** 93 **p** 94. Fell Univ Coll Lon from 82; NSM Ox St Giles and SS Phil and Jas w St Marg *Ox* from 93. *5 Swanston Field, Whitchurch, Reading RG8 7HP* Tel (0118) 984 2513

SCREECH, Royden. b 53. K Coll Lon BD74 AKC74. St Aug Coll Cant 75. **d** 76 **p** 77. C Hatcham St Cath *S'wark* 76-80; V Nunhead St Antony 80-87; P-in-c Nunhead St Silas 82-87; RD Camberwell 83-87; V New Addington 87-94; Perm to Offic from 95; Selection Sec ABM from 94. *6 Brooklyn Grove, London SE25 4NJ, or Church House, Great Smith Street, London SW1P 3NZ* Tel 0181-656 8965 or 0171-222 9022 Fax 799 2714

SCRINE, Ralph. b 19. Bris Univ BA40 Fitzw Ho Cam BA46 MA60 Lon Univ MPhil81. Westcott Ho Cam 45. **d** 46 **p** 47. C Moorfields *Bris* 46-51; P-in-c Biddestone w Slaughterford 51-52; P-in-c Lockleaze CD 52-60; V St Jas Less 60-65; Chapl Eliz Coll Guernsey 60-65; Lect Div Ch Ch Coll Cant 65-68; Chapl Ch Ch Coll Cant 68-75; Sen Lect Ch Ch Coll Cant 68-84; rtd 84; Perm to Offic *Cant* from 84. *Little Henny, Stone Street, Petham, Canterbury, Kent CT4 5PP* Tel (01227) 700725

✠**SCRIVEN, The Rt Revd Henry William.** b 51. Sheff Univ BA72. St Jo Coll Nottm DPS75. **d** 75 **p** 76 **c** 95. C Wealdstone H Trin *Lon* 75-79; SAMS (Argentina) 79-82; USA 82-83; SAMS (Spain) 84-90; Chapl Madrid w Bilbao *Eur* 90-95; Suff Bp Eur from 95; Dean Brussels 95-97; Dir of Ords from 97. *23 Carlton Road, Redhill RH1 2BY* Tel (01737) 766617 E-mail 100642.731@compuserve.com

SCRIVEN, Hugh Alexander. b 59. Trin Coll Cam BA80. Cranmer Hall Dur 81. **d** 84 **p** 85. C Pudsey St Lawr and St Paul *Bradf* 84-87; C Madeley *Heref* 87-91; TV from 91; Assoc RD Telford Severn Gorge from 96. *Sutton Hill Vicarage, 1 Spencer Drive, Sutton Hill, Telford, Shropshire TF7 4JY* Tel (01952) 680004

SCRIVEN, Paul Michael. b 51. Bris Univ BSc72 Lon Univ CertEd74. S Dios Minl Tr Scheme 84. **d** 87 **p** 88. NSM Redmarley D'Abitot, Bromesberrow w Pauntley etc *Glouc* 87-90; Lic to Offic *Heref* 90-95; Lic to Offic *Mon* 94-95; V Dingestow and Llangovan w Penyclawdd etc from 95; Perm to Offic *Heref* from 96. *The Vicarage, Dingestow, Monmouth NP5 4DY* Tel (01600) 83206

SCRIVENER, Robert Allan. b 54. Nottm Univ BEd78. Linc Th Coll 79. **d** 80 **p** 81. C Sherwood *S'well* 80-83; C Burghclere w Newtown and Ecchinswell w Sydmonton *Win* 83-86; TV Hemel Hempstead *St Alb* 86-93; V Kingston upon Hull St Nic *York* from 93. *St Nicholas' Vicarage, 898 Hessle High Road, Hull HU4 6SA* Tel (01482) 507944

SCRIVENS, Ernest. b 25. Lon Univ DipTh53. Wycliffe Hall Ox. **d** 62 **p** 63. C Chesham St Mary *Ox* 62-64; CF (S Rhodesia) 64-67; Jamaica 67-68; R Ardington w E Lockinge *Ox* 68-69; Miss to Seamen W Australia 69-79; V Yeadon St Jo *Bradf* 79-80; Australia from 81; rtd 88. *19 Gretna Street, Mansfield, Queensland, 4122 Australia* Tel Brisbane (7) 3395 1015

SCRUBY, The Ven Ronald Victor. b 19. Trin Hall Cam BA48 MA52. Cuddesdon Coll 48. **d** 50 **p** 51. Chapl K Edw VII Hosp Midhurst 50-53; C Rogate *Chich* 50-53; V Eastney *Portsm* 58-65; RD Portsm 60-65; Adn Is of Wight 65-77; Adn Portsm 77-85; rtd 85; Perm to Offic *Chich* 85-94; Perm to Offic *Portsm* from 85. *Church House, Rogate, Petersfield, Hants GU31 5EA* Tel (01730) 821784

SCUFFHAM, Canon Frank Leslie. b 30. AKC56 DSRS68. **d** 57 **p** 58. C Kettering SS Pet and Paul *Pet* 57-59; Ind Chapl *Sheff* 60-61; Ind Chapl *Pet* 61-95; Can Pet Cathl 72-95; RD Corby 76-79; P-in-c Stoke Albany w Wilbarston 79; R 79-95; rtd 95. *The Orchard, Earlsford Road, Mellis, Eye, Suffolk IP23 8EA* Tel (01379) 783378

SCULLY, Kevin John. b 55. NIDA BDA96. St Steph Ho Ox 91. **d** 93 **p** 94. C Stoke Newington St Mary *Lon* 93-97; C Stepney St Dunstan and All SS from 97; Dir of Ords from 97; Voc Adv from 97. *6 Arbour Square, London E1 0SH* Tel 0171-791 0330

SCUTTER, Canon James Edward. b 36. AKC59 St Boniface Warminster 59. **d** 60 **p** 61. C Tilbury Docks *Chelmsf* 60-63; S Rhodesia 63-65; Rhodesia 65-70; New Zealand from 80; Hon Can Wellington from 87. *7 Kotare Place, Burnham, New Zealand* Tel Christchurch (3) 347 6831 or 363 0169

SEABROOK, Alan Geoffrey. b 43. ALCD65. **d** 66 **p** 67. C Bethnal Green St Jas Less *Lon* 66-70; C Madeley *Heref* 70-73; V Girlington *Bradf* 74-80; P-in-c Abdon w Clee St Margaret *Heref* 80-83; R Bitterley 80-83; P-in-c Cold Weston 80-83; P-in-c Hopton Cangeford 80-83; P-in-c Stoke St Milburgh w Heath 80-83; R Bitterley w Middleton, Stoke St Milborough etc from 83. *The Rectory, Bitterley, Ludlow, Shropshire SY8 3HJ* Tel (01584) 890239

SEABROOK, Geoffrey Barry. b 45. Open Univ BA77 DipEd Lon Univ MA(Ed)84. Chich Th Coll 66. **d** 69 **p** 70. C Tottenham All Hallows *Lon* 69-72; C Winchmore Hill H Trin 72-74; V Hornsey St Geo 74-82; P-in-c Hornsey St Mary 80-82; R Hornsey St Mary w St Geo from 82; P-in-c Hornsey H Innocents 84-92; AD W Haringey from 95. *Hornsey Rectory, 140 Cranley Gardens, London N10 3AH* Tel 0181-883 6846

SEABROOK, Richard Anthony. b 68. Southn Univ BTh92. Chich Th Coll 92. **d** 92 **p** 93. C Cottingham *York* 92-94; C Hawley H Trin *Guildf* from 94. *All Saints' Parsonage, 295 Fernhill Road, Farnborough, Hants GU14 9EW* Tel (01276) 34241 Mobile 0973-341275 Fax as telephone E-mail fatherseabrook@incense.demon.co.uk

SEAFORD, The Very Revd John Nicholas. b 39. Dur Univ BA67 DipTh68. St Chad's Coll Dur 68. **d** 68 **p** 69. C Bush Hill Park St Mark *Lon* 68-71; C Stanmore *Win* 71-73; V N Baddesley 73-76; V Chilworth w N Baddesley 76-78; V Highcliffe w Hinton Admiral 78-93; RD Christchurch 90-93; Hon Can Win Cathl from 93; Dean Jersey from 93; R Jersey St Helier from 93. *The Deanery, St Helier, Jersey, Channel Islands JE2 4TB* Tel (01534) 20001 Fax 617488

SEAGER, Roland Douglas. b 08. St Boniface Warminster 32. **d** 33 **p** 34. C Wardleworth St Mary *Man* 33-36; Tanganyika 37-38; Zanzibar 38-39; C Sneinton St Steph *S'well* 39-41; P-in-c Olney *Ox* 41-43; V Barlby *York* 43-48; S Africa 48-59; N Midl Area Sec SPG 59-64; V Kirkby Woodhouse *S'well* 64-71; P-in-c Nottingham St Cath 71-73; rtd 74; Perm to Offic *S'well* from 74. *22 Willow Road, Nottingham NG4 3BH*

SEAL, Edward Hugh. b 10. ARCM31 Lon Univ BMus36. Wells Th Coll 46. **d** 48 **p** 49. C Midsomer Norton *B & W* 48-50; V Churt *Guildf* 50-57; V Pemberton St Jo *Liv* 57-63; R Poulton-le-Sands *Blackb* 63-78; rtd 78; Lic to Offic *Blackb* from 79. *3 Fern Bank, Scotforth, Lancaster LA1 4TT* Tel (01524) 67078

SEAL, Nicholas Peter. b 57. Ex Univ BA. Linc Th Coll 81. **d** 83 **p** 84. C Wareham *Sarum* 83-87; Chapl K Alfred Coll *Win* 87-91; V Stanmore from 91. *St Luke's Vicarage, Mildmay Street, Stanmore, Winchester, Hants SO22 4BX* Tel (01962) 865240

SEAL, Philip Trevor. b 32. AKC55. **d** 56 **p** 57. C Godalming *Guildf* 56-60; C Tamworth *Lich* 60-61; R Lich St Chad 61-73; Chapl HM Youth Cust Cen Swinfen Hall 66-73; R Shere *Guildf* 74-88; RD Cranleigh 76-81; V Abbotsbury, Portesham and Langton Herring *Sarum* 88-97; rtd 97. *2 Moorlane Cottages, Poltimore, Exeter EX4 0AQ*

SEAL, Ronald Frederick. b 28. CA Tr Coll 50 Lich Th Coll 59. **d** 61 **p** 62. C Bedhampton *Portsm* 61-65; R N and S Kilworth *Leic* 65-71; R Barwell w Potters Marston and Stapleton 71-80; P-in-c Upper Stour *Sarum* 80-83; R Upper Stour 84-90; RD Heytesbury 87-89; Bermuda 90-92; Miss to Seamen 90-92; rtd 92. *8 Briar Close, Wyke, Gillingham, Dorset SP8 4SS* Tel (01747) 825462

SEAL (née MILLER), Mrs Rosamund Joy. b 56. Lon Univ BSc77 Whitelands Coll Lon PGCE80. EMMTC CTPS92. **d** 94 **p** 96. NSM Grantham *Linc* 94-96; C Stamford All SS w St Jo from 96. *Church House, 26 Hazel Grove, Stamford, Lincs PE9 2HJ* Tel (01780) 51676

SEAL, William Christopher Houston. b 50. Occidental Coll (USA) BA72. Ch Div Sch of the Pacific (USA) MDiv81. **d** 81 **p** 82. USA 81-88 and from 94; R Etton w Helpston *Pet* 88-94. *The Rectory, 171 Grove Street, Nevada City, California 95959, USA*

SEAL, William George. b 27. Lon Univ DipTh71. Oak Hill Th Coll 67. **d** 70 **p** 71. C Plumstead St Jo w St Jas and St Paul *S'wark* 70-73; C Camberwell All SS 73-80; V Luton St Matt High Town *St Alb* 80-92; rtd 93. *1A Barnfield Avenue, Luton LU2 7AS* Tel (01582) 576939

SEALE, William Arthur. b 62. NUI BA84 TCD DipTh87. **d** 87 **p** 88. C Drumragh w Mountfield *D & R* 87-90; I Drumgath w Drumgooland and Clonduff *D & D* from 90. *The Rectory, 29 Cross Road, Hilltown, Newry, Co Down BT34 5TF* Tel (01820) 630304

SEALY, Daniel O'Neill. b 21. Oak Hill Th Coll 62. **d** 64 **p** 65. C Walcot *B & W* 64-67; Chapl RN 67-73; Nigeria 73-79; Libya 79-82; Tunisia 82-86; rtd 86; I Kilgariffe Union *C, C & R* 87-92. *Swanhill, Culver Street, Newent, Glos GL18 1JA*

SEALY, Canon Gordon William Hugh. b 27. Leeds Univ BA53 MA64. Coll of Resurr Mirfield 53. **d** 55 **p** 56. C Greenford H Cross *Lon* 55-58; Br Honduras 58-68; R Tarrant Gunville, Tarrant Hinton etc *Sarum* 68-74; V Leic St Paul *Leic* 74-96; Hon Can Leic Cathl 86-96; rtd 96. *12 Kingfisher Court, West Bay, Bridport, Dorset DT6 4HQ*

SEALY, Stephen. b 52. K Coll Lon BD86 AKC86. Linc Th Coll 86. **d** 88 **p** 89. C Botley *Portsm* 88-91; Prec Cant Cathl *Cant* 91-96; Hon Min Can Cant Cathl 91-96; V Pembury *Roch* from 96. *The Vicarage, 4 Hastings Road, Pembury, Tunbridge Wells, Kent TN2 4PD* Tel (01892) 824761

SEAMAN, Canon Arthur Roland Mostyn. b 32. TCD BA55 DipEd56 Div Test56 MA58. Westcott Ho Cam 58. **d** 58 **p** 59. C Blackley St Pet *Man* 58-61; C Sanderstead All SS *S'wark* 61-62; V Heywood St Luke *Man* 62-70; Dir of Educn 70-85; Hon Can

Man Cathl 74-95; R Chorlton-cum-Hardy St Werburgh 85-95; rtd 95. *10 The Haven, Beadnell, Chathill, Northd NE67 5AW*

SEAMAN, Canon Brian Edward. b 35. Dur Univ BA59. Cranmer Hall Dur. **d** 61 **p** 62. C Burnage St Marg *Man* 61-65; Chapl Mayflower Family Cen Canning Town *Chelmsf* 65-75; V High Elswick St Paul *Newc* 75-96; Hon Can Newc Cathl from 82; TV Glendale Gp from 96. *Church House, 2 Queens Road, Wooler, Northd NE71 6DR* Tel (01668) 281468

SEAMAN, Christopher Robert. b 34. Solicitor 62 St Jo Coll Ox BA58 MA74. Ox Min Course 92 St Alb and Ox Min Course 94. **d** 95 **p** 96. NSM Watlington w Pyrton and Shirburn *Ox* 95-97; NSM Icknield from 97. *6 Chaucer Court, Ewelme, Wallingford, Oxon OX10 6HW* Tel (01491) 834157

SEAMAN, Paul Robert. b 61. Bp Grosseteste Coll BEd82. Chich Th Coll 83. **d** 86 **p** 87. C Tilehurst St Mich *Ox* 86-91; TV Moulsecoomb *Chich* 91-95; R Whyke w Rumboldswhyke and Portfield from 95. *St George's Rectory, 199 Whyke Road, Chichester, W Sussex PO19 4HQ* Tel (01243) 782535

SEAMAN, Robert John. b 44. ACP DipEd. EAMTC. **d** 84 **p** 85. NSM Downham Market w Bexwell *Ely* 84-90; V Southea w Murrow and Parson Drove 90-97; V Guyhirn w Ring's End 90-97; V Newnham w Awre and Blakeney *Glouc* from 97. *The Vicarage, Unlawater Lane, Newnham, Glos GL14 1BL* Tel (01594) 516648

SEAMER, Stephen James George. b 50. AKC73. Ridley Hall Cam 74. **d** 75 **p** 76. C Rustington *Chich* 75-78; C Bulwell St Jo *S'well* 78-79; P-in-c Camber and E Guldeford *Chich* 79-80; TV Rye 80-83; V Knowle *Birm* 83-87; Assoc Chapl Brussels Cathl *Eur* 87-88; P-in-c Tervuren from 88; P-in-c Liege from 90; Chapl Tervuren and P-in-c Liege from 94. *Smisstraat 63, 3080 Vossem Turvuren, Belgium* Tel Brussels (2) 767-3435 or 767-3021 Fax 767 3435

SEAR, Peter Lionel. b 49. Ex Univ BA72. Linc Th Coll 72. **d** 74 **p** 75. C Sheldon *Birm* 74-77; C Caversham *Ox* 77-81; C Caversham and Mapledurham 81-85; TR Thatcham from 85. *The Rectory, 17 Church Gate, Thatcham, Berks RG19 3PN* Tel (01635) 862616

SEAR, Terence Frank (Terry). b 39. LDSRCSEng62 Univ Coll Lon BDS63. Portsm Dioc Tr Course 88. **d** 89. NSM Ryde H Trin *Portsm* from 89; NSM Swanmore St Mich w Havenstreet 89-92; NSM Swanmore St Mich and All Angels from 92. *Glebe Cottage, Wray Street, Ryde, Isle of Wight PO33 3ED* Tel (01983) 615856

SEARLE, Charles Peter. b 20. Selw Coll Cam BA48 MA53. Ridley Hall Cam. **d** 50 **p** 51. C Becontree St Mary *Chelmsf* 50-53; P-in-c Bedford St Jo *St Alb* 53-56; R 56-60; V Weston-super-Mare Ch Ch *B & W* 60-70; V Woking Ch Ch *Guildf* 70-85; rtd 85; Perm to Offic *Ex* from 85. *Old Chimes, 14 Gravel Walk, Cullompton, Devon EX15 1DA* Tel (01884) 33386

SEARLE, Capt Francis Robert. b 52. IDC74. CA Tr Coll 72 St Steph Ho Ox 88. **d** 90 **p** 91. CA from 72; C Lancing w Coombes *Chich* 90-93; V Hampden Park from 93. *The Vicarage, 60 Brassey Avenue, Eastbourne, E Sussex BN22 9QH* Tel (01323) 503166

SEARLE, Canon Hugh Douglas. b 35. St Cath Coll Cam BA59 MA63 Cranfield Inst of Tech MSc85. Oak Hill Th Coll 59. **d** 61 **p** 62. C Islington H Trin Cloudesley Square *Lon* 61-64; Chapl HM Pris Lewes 64-65; Chapl HM Borstal Roch 65-69; Chapl HM Youth Cust Cen Hollesley Bay Colony 70-74; Chapl HM Pris Parkhurst 74-78; P-in-c Barton *Ely* 78-84; V from 84; P-in-c Coton 78-84; R from 84; RD Bourn 81-94; Hon Can Ely Cathl from 97. *The Vicarage, Barton, Cambridge CB3 7BG* Tel (01223) 262218

SEARLE, Ms Jacqueline Ann (Jackie). b 60. Whitelands Coll Lon BEd82. Trin Coll Bris DipHE92. **d** 92 **p** 94. Par Dn Roxeth Ch Ch and Harrow St Pet *Lon* 92-93; Par Dn Roxeth 93-94; C Ealing St Steph Castle Hill 94-96; Lect Trin Coll Bris from 96. *15 Cranleigh Gardens, Bristol BS9 1HD* Tel 0117-968 2028 or 968 2803

SEARLE, Dr John Francis. b 42. FRCA70 FRSM84 Lon Univ MB, BS66. SW Minl Tr Course 92. **d** 95 **p** 96. NSM Ex St Leon w H Trin *Ex* from 95. *8 Thornton Hill, Exeter EX4 4NS* Tel (01392) 432153

SEARLE, Michael Stanley. b 38. HNC60. AMIQ63. N Ord Course 93. **d** 95 **p** 96. NSM Hoole *Ches* from 95. *48 Green Lane, Vicars Cross, Chester CH3 5LB* Tel (01244) 347828 Fax as telephone

SEARLE, Michael Westran. b 47. Leeds Univ LLB68 Nottm Univ DipTh69. Cuddesdon Coll 69. **d** 71 **p** 72. C Norton St Mary *Dur* 71-74; C Westbury-on-Trym H Trin *Bris* 74-77; V Bedminster Down 77-84; V Bris Ch the Servant Stockwood 84-88; Dir of Tr *York* from 88. *Cavalino, Back Lane, Allerthorpe, York YO4 4RP* Tel (01759) 302544

SEARLE, Philip Robert. b 67. Westcott Ho Cam. **d** 95 **p** 96. C Plymstock *Ex* 95-97; C Plymstock and Hooe from 97. *19 Long Park Close, Plymstock, Plymouth PL9 9JR* Tel (01752) 407788

SEARLE, Ralph Alan. b 57. Cam Univ MA. Coll of Resurr Mirfield 81. **d** 83 **p** 84. C Cockerton *Dur* 83-86; C S Shields All SS 86-88; TV 88-96; C Worksop Priory *S'well* 96-97; Assoc P Paignton St Jo *Ex* from 97. *St Boniface House, Belfield Road, Paignton, Devon TQ3 3UZ* Tel (01803) 556612

SEARLE-BARNES, Albert Victor. b 28. Sheff Univ BA48 Lon Univ BD53. ALCD53. **d** 53 **p** 54. C Iver *Ox* 53-55; C Attenborough w Bramcote *S'well* 55-59; C Bramcote 55-59; R Cratfield w Heveningham and Ubbeston *St E* 59-64; R Wick w Doynton *Bris* 64-70; Perm to Offic 70-72; V Downend 73-78; V Market Rasen *Linc* 78-86; R Linwood 79-86; V Legsby 79-86; R Green's Norton w Bradden *Pet* 86-88; V Hambledon *Portsm* 88-92; rtd 92; Perm to Offic *Glouc* from 92. *32 Oakland Avenue, Prestbury Road, Cheltenham, Glos GL52 3EP* Tel (01242) 227425

SEARLE-BARNES, Belinda Rosemary. b 51. ARCM72 GRSM73 Bris Univ 93 Lon Univ DipPTh90 MA91 Southn Univ DipMin93. Sarum Th Coll 93. **d** 96. NSM Pimperne, Stourpaine, Durweston and Bryanston *Sarum* from 96. *High Corrie, Letton Close, Pimperne, Blandford, Dorset DT11 7SS* Tel (01258) 451782

SEARS, Derek Lynford. b 25. St Jo Coll Cam BA49 MA53. Wycliffe Hall Ox 49. **d** 51 **p** 52. C Blackb St Steph *Blackb* 51-53; C Preston St Paul 53-56; V Burnley St Jas 56-62; Jamaica 62-66; V Freckleton *Blackb* 66-74; Jamaica 74-78; V Ashton-on-Ribble St Mich *Blackb* 78-90; P-in-c Preston St Mark 82-90; rtd 90; Perm to Offic *Blackb* from 90. *61 Greencroft, Penwortham, Preston PR1 9LB* Tel (01772) 740190

SEARS, Frank. b 29. Wycliffe Hall Ox 62. **d** 64 **p** 65. C Ashtead *Guildf* 64-72; V Finchley St Luke *Lon* 72-82; P-in-c Finchley St Paul Long Lane 76-82; TR Whitton *Sarum* 82-90; P-in-c Trowbridge St Thos and W Ashton from 91; Chapl St Jo Hosp Trowbridge from 95; Chapl Trowbridge Community Hosp from 95. *St Thomas's Vicarage, York Buildings, Trowbridge, Wilts BA14 8SF* Tel (01225) 754826

SEARS, Dr Jeanette. b 59. Man Univ BA80 PhD84 Lon Univ PGCE85. Wycliffe Hall Ox DPS. **d** 92 **p** 94. NSM Ox St Aldate w St Matt *Ox* 92-94; NSM Ox St Aldate from 95. *2 Fairacres Road, Oxford OX4 1TE* Tel (01865) 249305

SEARS, Michael Antony. b 50. Birm Univ BSc71 PGCE72. Linc Th Coll 78. **d** 80 **p** 81. C Willenhall H Trin *Lich* 80-83; C Caldmore 83-84; P-in-c 84-86; V 86-89; Abp Ilsley RC Sch Birm from 89; Perm to Offic *Birm* from 94. *131 Lowlands Avenue, Streetley, Sutton Coldfield, W Midlands B74 3RE* Tel 0121-353 8739

SEATON, Canon James Bradbury. b 29. Ch Coll Cam BA53 MA57. Westcott Ho Cam 53. **d** 55 **p** 56. C Derby St Werburgh *Derby* 55-58; C Darlington St Cuth *Dur* 58-64; V Preston on Tees 64-72; TV Stockton H Trin 72-73; TV Cen Stockton 73-75; R Anstey *Leic* 75-89; RD Sparkenhoe III 81-89; Hon Can Leic Cathl 87-94; R Market Harborough Transfiguration 89-94; rtd 94; Perm to Offic *Glouc* from 94. *Wayside, Sheep Street, Chipping Campden, Glos GL55 6DW* Tel (01386) 841753

SEBER, Derek Morgan. b 43. Man Univ CertRS79 Man Poly CTUS83 MA87 Man Metrop Univ MPhil96. Oak Hill Th Coll 71. **d** 73 **p** 74. C Collyhurst *Man* 73-76; C Radcliffe St Thos and St Jo 76-77; Ind Missr 77-89; P-in-c Hulme St Geo 77-83; Hon C Moss Side St Jas w St Clem 83-96; Project Officer Linking Up 89-96; Lic Preacher 90-96; P-in-c Cheetham St Jo from 97. *56 Allness Road, Whalley Range, Manchester M16 8HW* Tel 0161-861 0360

SECCOMBE, Marcus John. b 34. Oak Hill Th Coll 60. **d** 63 **p** 64. C Woodthorpe *S'well* 63-67; C Doncaster St Mary *Sheff* 67-72; V Owston 72-90; R Rossington from 90. *The Rectory, Sheep Bridge Lane, Rossington, Doncaster, S Yorkshire DN11 0EZ* Tel (01302) 867597

SECKER, Brian. b 34. Qu Coll Birm 62. **d** 65 **p** 66. C Goldthorpe *Sheff* 65-68; V New Bentley 68-75; P-in-c Pet St Barn *Pet* 75-80; V Pet St Paul from 75. *St Paul's Vicarage, Peterborough PE1 2PA* Tel (01733) 343746

SECOMBE, Preb Frederick Thomas. b 18. St D Coll Lamp BA40 St Mich Coll Llan 40. **d** 42 **p** 43. C Swansea St Mark *S & B* 42-44; C Knighton 44-46; C Machen *Mon* 46-49; C Newport St Woolos 49-52; Chapl St Woolos Hosp Newport 49-52; V Llanarth w Clytha, Llansantffraed and Bryngwyn *Mon* 52-54; R Machen and Rudry 54-59; V Swansea St Pet *S & B* 59-69; R Hanwell St Mary *Lon* 69-83; AD Ealing W 78-82; Preb St Paul's Cathl 81-83; rtd 83. *30 Westville Road, Penylan, Cardiff CF2 5AG* Tel (01222) 483978

SECRETAN, Ms Jenny Ruth. b 54. St Aid Coll Dur BA76 Ex Univ PGCE77 Nottm Univ DipTh82. Linc Th Coll 81 Cranmer Hall Dur 83. **dss** 84 **d** 87 **p** 94. Asst Chapl Newc Poly *Newc* 84-86; Sunderland St Chad *Dur* 84-86; Bordesley St Oswald *Birm* 86-87; Par Dn 87-91; Assoc Soc Resp Officer *Dur* from 92. *14 Southwood Gardens, Kenton, Newcastle upon Tyne NE3 3BU*

SEDDON, Ernest Geoffrey. b 26. ARIBA51 Man Univ DipArch50 DipTh83 MA85. St Deiniol's Hawarden 80. **d** 80 **p** 81. C Dunham Massey St Marg *Ches* 80-83; P-in-c Warburton 82-87; P-in-c Dunham Massey St Mark 85-86; V 86-92; rtd 92; Perm to Offic *Ches* from 92. *Maes Mawr Farm, Crefnant Road, Trefriw LL27 0JZ* Tel (01492) 642107

SEDDON, Philip James. b 45. Jes Coll Cam BA68 MA71. Ridley Hall Cam 67. **d** 70 **p** 71. C Tonge w Alkrington *Man* 70-74; Nigeria 74-78; Lect St Jo Coll Nottm 78-79; Lic to Offic *Ely* 79-85; Chapl Magd Coll Cam 79-85; Lect Bibl Studies Selly Oak

Colls from 86; Lic to Offic *Birm* from 87. *Central House, Selly Oak Colleges, Birmingham B29 6QT* Tel 0121-472 4231

SEDEN, Martin Roy. b 47. Man Univ MSc Salford Univ PhD. EMMTC. **d** 82 **p** 83. NSM Knighton St Mary Magd *Leic* from 82; Chapl De Montfort Univ from 89. *139 Shanklin Drive, Leicester LE2 3QG* Tel 0116-270 2128 E-mail const@dmu.ac.uk

SEDGLEY, Mrs Jean. b 41. Whitelands Coll Lon CertEd63. S Dios Minl Tr Scheme 92. **d** 95 **p** 96. NSM Haywards Heath St Wilfrid *Chich* from 95. *25 Pasture Hill Road, Haywards Heath, W Sussex RH16 1LY* Tel (01444) 413974

SEDGLEY, Canon Timothy John. b 42. St Jo Coll Ox BA63 DipTh64 MA68. Westcott Ho Cam 64. **d** 66 **p** 67. C Nor St Pet Mancroft *Nor* 66-70; V Costessey 70-79; RD Nor N 75-79; V Walton-on-Thames *Guildf* from 79; Hon Can Guildf Cathl from 86; RD Emly 86-91. *The Vicarage, 53 Ashley Park Avenue, Walton-on-Thames, Surrey KT12 1EV* Tel (01932) 227184

SEDGMORE, Evan. b 09. St D Coll Lamp 47. **d** 50 **p** 51. C Neath w Llantwit *Llan* 50-54; C Garw Valley w Blaengarw 54-59; V Fochriw w Deri 59-71; V Llanbradach 71-76; rtd 76; Perm to Offic *Llan* from 76. *52 Hookland Road, Porthcawl CF36 5SG* Tel (01656) 718991

SEDGWICK, Jonathan Maurice William. b 63. BNC Ox BA85 MA89 Leeds Univ BA88. Coll of Resurr Mirfield 86. **d** 89 **p** 90. C Chich St Paul and St Pet *Chich* 89-91; Dean of Div and Chapl Magd Coll Ox 91-94; Perm to Offic *S'wark* from 97. *91 Landells Road, London SE22 9PH* Tel 0181-299 2384

SEDGWICK, Peter Humphrey. b 48. Trin Hall Cam BA70 Dur Univ PhD83. Westcott Ho Cam 71. **d** 74 **p** 75. C Stepney St Dunstan and All SS *Lon* 74-77; P-in-c Pittington *Dur* 77-79; Lect Th Birm Univ 79-82; Hon C The Lickey *Birm* 79-82; Th Consultant for NE Ecum Gp *Dur* 82-88; Abp's Adv on Ind Issues *York* 88-94; Lect Th Hull Univ 88-94; Vice-Prin Westcott Ho Cam 94-96; Asst Sec Gen Syn Bd for Soc Resp from 96; NSM Pet St Barn *Pet* from 96. *19 Danes Close, Peterborough PE1 5LJ, or Church House, Great Smith Street, London SW1P 3NZ* Tel (01733) 53526 or 0171-340 0307 Fax 0171-233 2576

SEED, Richard Edward. b 55. UNISA BTh86 Westmr Coll Ox MEd. Kalk Bay Bible Inst S Africa DipTh79. **d** 80 **p** 81. S Africa 80-85 and 87-89; Zimbabwe 85-87; Asst Chapl Kingham Hill Sch 89-90; C Beckenham Ch Ch *Roch* 90-95; Chapl Dusseldorf *Eur* from 96. *Mulvany House, Rotterdamerstrasse 135, 40474 Dusseldorf, Germany* Tel Dusseldorf (211) 452759 Fax 454 2216

SEED, Richard Murray Crosland. b 49. Leeds Univ MA91. Edin Th Coll 69. **d** 72 **p** 73. C Skipton Ch Ch *Bradf* 72-75; C Baildon 75-77; Chapl HM Det Cen Kidlington 77-80; TV Kidlington *Ox* 77-80; V Boston Spa *York* from 80; P-in-c Newton Kyme 84-85; P-in-c Clifford from 89; Chapl Martin House Hospice for Children Boston Spa from 85. *The Vicarage, Boston Spa, Wetherby, W Yorkshire LS23 5EA* Tel (01937) 842454 or 844402

SEELEY, Martin Alan. b 54. Jes Coll Cam BA76 MA79. Ripon Coll Cuddesdon 76 Union Th Sem (NY) STM78. **d** 78 **p** 79. C Bottesford w Ashby *Linc* 78-80; USA 80-90; Selection Sec ABM 90-96; Sec for Continuing Minl Educn 90-96; V Is of Dogs Ch Ch and St Jo w St Luke *Lon* from 96. *Christ Church Vicarage, Manchester Road, London E14 3BN* Tel 0171-987 1915

SEGAL, Michael Bertram. b 20. Lon Univ BA44. Cuddesdon Coll 46. **d** 48 **p** 49. C Lewisham St Jo Southend *S'wark* 48-53; C Coulsdon St Andr 53-61; V S Wimbledon St Pet 61-71; V Crofton Park St Hilda w St Cypr 72-82; P-in-c Grendon w Castle Ashby *Pet* 82-85; V Gt Doddington 82-85; rtd 85; Perm to Offic *Cant* from 85. *9 Glebe Gardens, Lenham, Maidstone, Kent ME17 2QA* Tel (01622) 858033

SEIGNIOR, James Frederick. b 97. TD46. Univ Coll Lon ALA28. St Deiniol's Hawarden 45. **d** 46 **p** 47. C Hawarden *St As* 46-49; V Bruera *Ches* 49-69; rtd 69; Australia 69-79; Perm to Offic *Glouc* 79-80; Perm to Offic *Guildf* 80-94. *College of St Barnabas, Blackberry Lane, Lingfield, Surrey RH7 6NJ*

SELBY, Miss Carole Janis. b 50. Chelsea Coll Lon CertEd71 Sussex Univ BEd72. Westcott Ho Cam CTM95. **d** 95 **p** 96. C Worc St Barn w Ch Ch *Worc* from 95. *22 Salters Close, Worcester WR4 9XT* Tel (01905) 456504

✠**SELBY, The Rt Revd Peter Stephen Maurice.** b 41. St Jo Coll Ox BA64 MA67 K Coll Lon PhD75. Episc Th Sch Cam Mass BD66 Bps' Coll Cheshunt 66. **d** 66 **p** 67 **c** 84. C Queensbury All SS *Lon* 66-69; C Limpsfield and Titsey *S'wark* 69-77; Assoc Dir of Tr 69-73; Vice-Prin S'wark Ord Course 70-72; Asst Dioc Missr *S'wark* 73-77; Dioc Missr *Newc* 77-84; Can Res Newc Cathl 77-84; Suff Bp Kingston *S'wark* 84-91; Area Bp Kingston 91-92; Pres Modern Churchpeople's Union from 91; Wm Leech Professorial Fell Dur Univ 92-97; Asst Bp Dur 92-97; Asst Bp Newc 92-97; Bp Worc from 97. *The Bishop's House, Hartlebury Castle, Kidderminster, Worcs DY11 7XX* Tel (01299) 250214 Fax 250027

SELBY, Canon Sydney Arthur. b 17. K Coll Lon 41. **d** 48 **p** 49. C Menston w Woodhead *Bradf* 48-53; V Kildwick 53-74; RD S Craven 73-74; Hon Can Bradf Cathl 73-82; V Gisburn 74-82; RD Bowland 80-81; rtd 82; Perm to Offic *Bradf* from 82. *Clough Cottage, Clough Lane, Simonstone, Burnley, Lancs BB12 7HW* Tel (01282) 773108

SELBY, Suffragan Bishop of. *See* TAYLOR, The Rt Revd Humphrey Vincent

SELF, David Christopher. b 41. Toronto Univ BSc62 MA64 K Coll Lon BD68 AKC68. **d** 69 **p** 70. C Tupsley *Heref* 69-73; Chapl Dur Univ *Dur* 73-78; TV Southampton (City Cen) *Win* 78-84; TR Dunstable *St Alb* 84-95; RD Dunstable 90-91; TR Bris St Paul's *Bris* from 95. *St Paul's Rectory, 131 Ashley Road, Bristol BS6 5NU* Tel 0117-955 0150

SELF, John Andrew. b 47. Pershore Coll of Horticulture Worcs CANP68. Trin Coll Bris 74 CMS Tr Coll Crowther Hall 76. **d** 81 **p** 83. CMS 77-91; Pakistan 77-91; AV Bath Weston All SS w N Stoke *B & W* 91-92; V Sparkhill w Greet and Sparkbrook *Birm* from 92. *St John's Vicarage, 15 Phipson Road, Birmingham B11 4JE* Tel 0121-449 2760

SELF, Peter Allen. b 41. S Dios Minl Tr Scheme 84. **d** 87 **p** 87. NSM Wilton *B & W* 87-91; NSM Taunton Lyngford from 91. *20 Dyers Close, West Buckland, Wellington, Somerset TA21 9JU* Tel (01823) 663408

SELFE, John Ronald. b 41. EMMTC 85. **d** 95 **p** 96. NSM Mid Marsh Gp *Linc* from 95. *Bookend, 236 Eastgate, Louth, Lincs LN11 8DA* Tel (01507) 603809

SELL, Noel Lightfoot. b 15. St Cath Coll Cam BA38 MA44. Wycliffe Hall Ox. **d** 41 **p** 42. C W Ham All SS *Chelmsf* 41-43; C Radlett *St Alb* 43-46; Chapl Shenley Hosp Radlett Herts 46-51; R Hotham *York* 51-54; V Sheff Abbeydale St Pet *Sheff* 54-64; V Kingston St Mary *B & W* 64-77; V Broomfield 64-77; rtd 77. *32 Saxon Way, Saffron Walden, Essex CB11 4EG* Tel (01799) 526165

SELLARS, Charles Harold. b 18. Leeds Univ BA40. Coll of Resurr Mirfield 37. **d** 42 **p** 44. C Clee *Linc* 42-46; Chapl Barnard Castle Sch 47-49; Chapl RAF 49-52; Chapl Solihull Sch 52-56; CF 56-61; Chapl Qu Sch Rheindahlen Germany *Eur* 61-70; V Hampton St Mary *Lon* 70-78; R Nuthurst *Chich* 78-83; P-in-c Lynch w Iping Marsh 83-86; rtd 86; Perm to Offic *Chich* from 87. *50 Rushams Road, Horsham, W Sussex RH12 2NZ* Tel (01403) 260641

SELLER, James Stoddart. b 16. TD64. St Jo Coll Dur LTh45. Tyndale Hall Bris 40. **d** 44 **p** 45. C Cambridge St Andr Less *Ely* 44-47; C Holborn St Geo w H Trin *Lon* 47-48; C Whitby *York* 48-50; V Ravenscar 51-53; V Sledmere 53-60; P-in-c Huttons Ambo 57-60; R Burnby 60-89; R Londesborough 60-89; R Nunburnholme 60-89; P-in-c Shiptonthorpe w Hayton 78-89; rtd 89; Perm to Offic *York* from 89. *7 Wilton Road, Hornsea, N Humberside HU18 1QU* Tel (01964) 533160

SELLER, Dr Mary Joan. b 40. Qu Mary Coll Lon BSc61 Lon Univ PhD64 DSc82. S'wark Ord Course. **d** 91 **p** 94. NSM Hurst Green *S'wark* from 91. *11 Home Park, Oxted, Surrey RH8 0JS* Tel (01883) 715675

SELLERS, Anthony. b 48. Southn Univ BSc71 PhD76. Wycliffe Hall Ox 84. **d** 86 **p** 87. C Luton St Mary *St Alb* 86-90; V Luton St Paul from 90. *37A Arthur Street, Luton LU1 3SG* Tel (01582) 481796

SELLERS, George William. b 35. N Ord Course. **d** 89 **p** 90. NSM Rothwell *Ripon* from 89. *16 Thornegrove, Rothwell, Leeds LS26 0HP* Tel 0113-282 3522

SELLERS, Robert. b 58. Coll of Resurr Mirfield 90. **d** 92 **p** 93. C Wotton St Mary *Glouc* 92-95; TV Redruth w Lanner and Treleigh *Truro* from 95. *Pencoys Vicarage, Four Lanes, Redruth, Cornwall TR16 6LR* Tel (01209) 215035

SELLERS, Warren John. b 43. Bp Otter Coll Chich TCert73 W Sussex Inst of HE DipAdEd88. K Coll Lon 63 Sarum Th Coll 65. **d** 68 **p** 69. C Guildf H Trin w St Mary *Guildf* 68-72; Hon C Chich St Paul and St Pet *Chich* 72-73; C Epping St Jo *Chelmsf* 73-76; Hon C Pulborough *Chich* 76-90; Hon C Fleet *Guildf* 90-92; Teacher 73-89; Waltham Abbey St Lawr and H Cross Schs Essex 73-76; Pulborough St Mary, Easeboure & Bp Tuffnell Schs 76-89; Hd Teacher St Pet Jun Sch Farnborough 90-92; TV Upper Kennet *Sarum* 92-95; TR from 95. *The Vicarage, Broad Hinton, Swindon SN4 9PA* Tel (01793) 731310

SELLEY, Paul Edward Henry. b 47. Bris Univ BEd70. Sarum Th Coll 93. **d** 96. C Swindon Dorcan *Bris* from 96. *18 Larksfield, Covingham, Swindon, Wilts SN3 4AD* Tel (01793) 520139 Fax as telephone

SELLGREN, Eric Alfred. b 33. AKC61. **d** 62 **p** 63. C Ditton St Mich *Liv* 62-66; V Hindley Green 66-72; V Southport St Paul 72-80; Warden Barn Fellowship Winterborne Whitchurch 80-86; V The Iwernes, Sutton Waldron and Fontmell Magna *Sarum* from 86. *The Vicarage, Iwerne Minster, Blandford Forum, Dorset DT11 8NF* Tel (01747) 811291

SELLIX, Martin Gordon. b 45. Ridley Hall Cam 74. **d** 76 **p** 77. C Crofton St Paul *Roch* 76-80; Ind Chapl *Chelmsf* 80-94; R Rayne 80-86; V Blackmore and Stondon Massey 86-94; RD Ongar 89-94; TR Liskeard, St Keyne, St Pinnock, Morval etc *Truro* from 94. *The Rectory, Church Street, Liskeard, Cornwall PL14 3AQ* Tel (01579) 342178

SELLORS, The Very Revd Michael Harry. b 36. K Coll Lon 60 St Boniface Warminster 61. **d** 61 **p** 62. C Willesden St Mary *Lon* 61-64; C Aldershot St Mich *Guildf* 64-67; V Hale 67-84; P-in-c E w W Beckham *Nor* 84-85; P-in-c Bodham 84-85; V Weybourne w

Upper Sheringham 84-85; R Kelling w Salthouse 84-85; R Weybourne Gp 85-91; V Hunstanton St Edm w Ringstead 91-97; Dean Jerusalem from 97. *St George's Cathedral, PO Box 19018, Jerusalem 91190* Tel (2) 628 3261 Fax 627 6401

SELMAN, Cyril Allen. b 25. Wycliffe Hall Ox 64. **d** 65 **p** 65. C Thame *Ox* 65-69; V Beedon 69-87; R Peasemore 69-87; rtd 88; Perm to Offic *Ban* from 88. *10 Griffin Terrace, Penrhyndeudraeth LL48 6LR*

SELMAN, Michael Richard. b 47. Sussex Univ BA68 Bris Univ MA70. Coll of Resurr Mirfield 71. **d** 73 **p** 74. C Hove All SS *Chich* 73-74; C Horfield H Trin *Bris* 74-78; P-in-c Landkey *Ex* 78-79; C Barnstaple and Goodleigh 78-79; TV Barnstaple, Goodleigh and Landkey 79-82; TR 82-84; RD Barnstaple 83-85; P-in-c Sticklepath 83-85; TR Barnstaple 85; TR Cen Ex from 85. *The Rectory, 3 Spicer Road, Exeter EX1 1SX* Tel (01392) 272450

SELMES, Brian. b 48. Nottm Univ BTh74. Linc Th Coll 70. **d** 74 **p** 75. C Padgate *Liv* 74-77; C Sydenham St Bart *S'wark* 77-80; Chapl Darlington Memorial Hosp 80-94; Chapl Darlington Memorial Hosp NHS Trust from 94; Chapl Aycliffe Hosp Darlington from 80. *Memorial Hospital, Hollyhead Road, Darlington, Co Durham DL3 6HX* Tel (01325) 359688 or 380100

SELVEY, Canon John Brian. b 33. Dur Univ BA54. Cuddesdon Coll 56. **d** 58 **p** 59. C Lancaster St Mary *Blackb* 58-61; C Blackb Cathl 61-65; Cathl Chapl 64-65; V Foulridge 65-69; V Walton-le-Dale 69-82; V Cleveleys 82-89; Hon Can Bloemfontein Cathl from 88; V Slyne w Hest *Blackb* from 89; Hon Can Blackb Cathl from 93. *The Vicarage, Summerfield Drive, Slyne, Lancaster LA2 6AQ* Tel (01524) 822128

SELWOOD, Michael. b 40. Oak Hill Th Coll DipHE90 BA91. **d** 91 **p** 92. Canada 91-95; P-in-c Sherborne, Windrush, the Barringtons etc *Glouc* from 95. *The New Vicarage, Windrush, Burford, Oxon OX18 4TS* Tel (01451) 844276

SELWOOD, Robin. b 37. ALCD61. **d** 61 **p** 62. C Lenton *S'well* 61-63; C Norbury *Ches* 63-66; V Newton Flowery Field 66-75; V Kelsall 75-89; V Sale St Paul from 89. *St Paul's Vicarage, 15 Springfield Road, Sale, Cheshire M33 1XG* Tel 0161-973 1042

SELWOOD, Timothy John. b 45. Lon Univ LLB66. Sarum Th Coll. **d** 83 **p** 84. NSM Colbury *Win* 83-85; NSM Copythorne and Minstead 85-90. *Forest Cottage, Seamans Lane, Minstead, Lyndhurst, Hants SO43 7FT* Tel (01703) 812873

SELWYN, David Gordon. b 38. MEHS Clare Coll Cam BA62 MA66 New Coll Ox MA66. Ripon Hall Ox 62. **d** 64 **p** 65. C Ecclesall *Sheff* 64-65; Asst Chapl New Coll Ox 65-68; Lect Univ of Wales (Lamp) *St D* from 68; Perm to Offic from 68. *19 Penbryn, Lampeter SA48 7EU* Tel (01570) 422748

SEMEONOFF, Canon Jean Mary Agnes. b 36. BSc56 Leic Univ CertEd57. EMMTC 84. **d** 87 **p** 94. Par Dn Leic H Spirit *Leic* 87 and 89-94; Chapl to the Deaf *Derby* 87-89; Chapl to the Deaf *Leic* 89-93; Hon Can Leic Cathl 92-94; rtd 94; Chapl Women's Min from 94; NSM Leic St Anne *Leic* from 94. *107 Letchworth Road, Leicester LE3 6FN* Tel 0116-285 8854

SEMEONOFF, Dr Robert. b 40. Edin Univ PhD67 BSc62. EMMTC 81. **d** 84 **p** 85. NSM Leic H Spirit *Leic* 84-88 and 89-97; NSM Loughb Gd Shep 88-89; Asst Chapl Leic Univ 89-94; Min for Special Past Duties from 94. *107 Letchworth Road, Leicester LE3 6FN* Tel 0116-285 8854

SEMPER, The Very Revd Colin Douglas. b 38. Keble Coll Ox BA62. Westcott Ho Cam 61. **d** 63 **p** 64. C Guildf H Trin w St Mary *Guildf* 63-67; Sec ACCM 67-69; Producer Relig Broadcasting Dept BBC 69-75; Overseas Relig Broadcasting Org BBC 75-79; Hd of Relig Progr BBC Radio 79-82; Hon Can Guildf Cathl *Guildf* 80-82; Provost Cov 82-87; Can and Treas Westmr Abbey 87-97; Steward 87-90; rtd 97. *8 Thames Mews, Poole, Dorset BH15 1JY*

SEMPLE, Dr Henry Michael. b 40. CMath FIMA FIMgt FRSA K Coll Lon BSc62 Birkb Coll Lon PhD67. S Dios Minl Tr Scheme. **d** 87 **p** 88. NSM Steyning *Chich* 87-91; Perm to Offic *Guildf* 87-91; Perm to Offic *Linc* 92-93; NSM Linc Cathl from 93. *15 Minster Yard, Lincoln LN2 1PW* Tel (01522) 535938

SEMPLE, Patrick William. b 45. Sussex Univ BA66 Bris Univ DipTh70. Sarum & Wells Th Coll 68. **d** 72 **p** 73. C Paddington Ch Ch *Lon* 72-75; Ind Chapl *Nor* 75-79; P-in-c Woodbastwick 76-79; V Kensington St Barn *Lon* 79-83; V Coleford w Staunton *Glouc* from 83; P-in-c Forest of Dean Ch Ch w English Bicknor 84-89. *The Vicarage, 40 Boxbush Road, Coleford, Glos GL16 8DN* Tel (01594) 833379

SEMPLE, Studdert Patrick. b 39. TCD BA66. CITC 67. **d** 67 **p** 68. C Orangefield *D & D* 67-70; I Stradbally *C & O* 71-82; Ch of Ireland Adult Educn Officer 82-88; I Donoughmore and Donard w Dunlavin *D & G* 88-96; Bp's C Dublin St Geo and St Thos from 96. *49 Richmond Park, Monkstown, Co Dublin, Irish Republic* Tel Dublin (1) 230 1712 Mobile 087-476526

SENIOR, Brian Stephen. b 55. Brighton Coll of Educn CertEd76. Oak Hill Th Coll DipHE93. **d** 93 **p** 94. C Hildenborough *Roch* from 93. *112 Tunbridge Road, Hildenborough, Tonbridge, Kent TN11 9EL* Tel (01732) 832638

SENIOR, David John. b 47. Oak Hill Th Coll. **d** 82 **p** 83. C Market Harborough *Leic* 82-85; TV Marfleet *York* 85-91; R Desford and Peckleton w Tooley *Leic* 91-96; P-in-c Hall Green Ascension *Birm* from 96. *The Vicarage, 592 Fox Hollies Road, Birmingham B28 9DX* Tel 0121-777 3689

SENIOR, George. b 36. Open Univ BA83. EMMTC 82. **d** 86 **p** 87. NSM Spratton *Pet* 86-90; NSM Cottesbrooke w Gt Creaton and Thornby 86-90; C Darwen St Pet w Hoddlesden *Blackb* 90-92; V Foulridge from 92. *The Vicarage, Skipton Road, Foulridge, Colne, Lancs BB8 7NP* Tel (01282) 865491

SENIOR, John Peter. b 23. Lon Univ BSc48. Edin Th Coll 63. **d** 65 **p** 66. C Marton *Blackb* 65-68; C Heysham 68-71; V Blackpool St Mich 71-79; V Heddon-on-the-Wall *Newc* 79-88; rtd 88; Perm to Offic *Wakef* from 88. *56 Thorpe Lane, Huddersfield HD5 8TA* Tel (01484) 530466

SENIOR, Patrick Nicolas Adam. b 63. Univ of Wales (Ban) BA86. Trin Coll Bris BA94. **d** 94 **p** 95. C Derringham Bank *York* from 94. *176 Willerby Road, Hull HU5 5JW* Tel (01482) 53299

✠**SENTAMU, The Rt Revd John Mugabi.** b 47. MA DD. **d** 79 **p** 79. Chapl HM Rem Cen Latchmere Ho 79-82; C Ham St Andr *S'wark* 79-82; C Herne Hill St Paul 82-83; P-in-c Tulse Hill H Trin 83-84; V Upper Tulse Hill St Matthias 83-84; V Tulse Hill H Trin and St Matthias 85-96; P-in-c Brixton Hill St Sav 87-89; Hon Can S'wark Cathl 93-96; Area Bp Stepney *Lon* from 96. *63 Coborn Road, London E3 2DB* Tel 0181-981 2323 Fax 981 8015

SENTANCE, Cecil Leslie. b 23. Lon Univ BSc58. S'wark Ord Course 64. **d** 67 **p** 68. C Finchley St Mary *Lon* 67-73; V Friern Barnet St Pet le Poer 73-75; V Feltham 75-82; Bursar Chich Th Coll and Custos St Mary's Hosp 82-86; rtd 86. *Bryn Gosal, Eglwysbach, Colwyn Bay LL28 5UN* Tel (01492) 650768

SEPPALA, Christopher James. b 59. St Jo Coll Dur BA82. Chich Th Coll 83. **d** 85 **p** 86. C Whitstable *Cant* 85-88; C S Ashford Ch Ch 88-91. *9 Newton Road, Whitstable, Kent CT5 2JD* Tel (01227) 266411

SERJEANT, Frederick James. b 28. Lon Inst of Educn BEd77. AKC53 St Boniface Warminster 53. **d** 54 **p** 55. C Leytonstone St Marg w St Columba *Chelmsf* 54-58; C Parkstone St Pet w Branksea *Sarum* 58-59; V Reigate St Luke S Park *S'wark* 59-65; V Battersea St Pet 65-71; C-in-c Battersea St Paul 67-71; V W Mersea *Chelmsf* 71-73; P-in-c E Mersea 71-73; R W w E Mersea 73-75; rtd 93. *5 Bothen Drive, Bridport, Dorset DT6 4DJ* Tel (01308) 420573

SERJEANT, John Frederick. b 33. K Coll Lon 52. **d** 56 **p** 57. C Over St Chad *Ches* 56-59; C-in-c Brinnington St Luke CD 59-63; V Brinnington 63-69; V Gatley 69-79; TV Halesworth w Linstead and Chediston *St E* 79-80; TV Halesworth w Linstead, Chediston, Holton etc 80-82; C Chesterfield St Mary and All SS *Derby* 82-88; Chapl Chesterfield R Hosp 82-88; Chapl Chesterfield and N Derbyshire R Hosp 88-95; rtd 95. *188 Queen Victoria Road, New Tupton, Chesterfield, Derbyshire S42 6DW* Tel (01246) 863395

SEROCOLD, Ralph Edward Pearce. b 16. ERD54. Trin Coll Cam BA38 MA45. Bps' Coll Cheshunt 57. **d** 58 **p** 59. C St E Cathl Distr *St E* 58-61; V Long Sutton *B & W* 61-69; Chapl Ld Wandsworth Coll Basingstoke 61-69; RD Odiham *Win* 65-69; R N Stoneham 69-75; V Hamble le Rice 75-82; rtd 82; Perm to Offic *Portsm* 82-96. *99 Vinery Road, Cambridge CB1 3DW* Tel (01223) 215186

SERTIN, John Francis. b 22. Fitzw Ho Cam BA50 MA54. Tyndale Hall Bris. **d** 45 **p** 46. C Sidcup Ch Ch *Roch* 45-47; Chapl Fitzw Ho Cam 47-50; C-in-c St Paul's Cray St Barn CD *Roch* 50-59; V Chitts Hill St Cuth *Lon* 59-62; Sec Ch Soc 62-67; P-in-c Woburn Square Ch Ch *Lon* 67-77; R Holborn St Geo w H Trin and St Bart 67-80; R Donyatt w Horton, Broadway and Ashill *B & W* 80-92; rtd 92; Perm to Offic *B & W* from 92. *9 Lower Vellow, Williton, Taunton, Somerset TA4 4LS* Tel (01984) 561141

SERTIN, Canon Peter Frank. b 27. Fitzw Ho Cam BA50 MA55. Ridley Hall Cam 50. **d** 52 **p** 53. C Beckenham Ch Ch *Roch* 52-55; Chapl K Edw Sch Witley 55-62; V Woking St Paul *Guildf* 62-69; V Chorleywood Ch Ch *St Alb* 69-80; Chapl Paris St Mich *Eur* 80-85; Adn N France 84-85; R Hambledon *Guildf* 85-89; TR Canford Magna *Sarum* 89-94; rtd 94; Perm to Offic *Portsm* from 94; Perm to Offic *Chich* from 94. *1 Kiln Field, Station Road, Liss, Hampshire GU33 7SW* Tel (01730) 894482

SERVANT, Ms Alma Joan. b 51. Nottm Univ BA76 DipLib79. Westcott Ho Cam 83. **dss** 85 **d** 87 **p** 94. Ordsall *S'well* 85-88; Par Dn 87-88; Par Dn Man Whitworth *Man* 88-94; TV 94-96; Chapl Man Poly 88-92; Chapl Man Metrop Univ 92-96; P-in-c Heaton Norris St Thos from 96. *St Thomas's Rectory, 6 Heaton Moor Road, Stockport, Cheshire SK4 4NS* Tel 0161-432 1912

SERVANTE, Kenneth Edward. b 29. AKC55. **d** 56 **p** 57. C Chaddesden St Phil *Derby* 56-58; C Brampton St Thos 58-61; C Whitfield 61-63; V Derby St Paul 63-70; V Elmton 70-81; P-in-c Winster 81-82; P-in-c Elton 81-82; R S Darley, Elton and Winster 82-94; rtd 94; Perm to Offic *Derby* from 94. *14 Ashes Avenue, Hulland Ward, Derby DE6 3FT* Tel (01335) 370561

SESSFORD, Alan. b 34. Bps' Coll Cheshunt 65. **d** 66 **p** 67. C Highcliffe w Hinton Admiral *Win* 66-69; C Minehead *B & W* 70; C Chandler's Ford *Win* 70-73; V Burton and Sopley from 73; RD Christchurch from 93. *The Vicarage, Preston Lane, Burton, Christchurch, Dorset BH23 7JU* Tel (01202) 484471

SETTERFIELD, Nicholas Manley. b 63. Colchester Inst of Educn BA89. St Steph Ho Ox 89. **d** 92 **p** 93. C Prestbury *Glouc* 92-96; R

Letchworth *St Alb* from 96. *The Rectory, 39 South View, Letchworth, Herts SG6 3JJ* Tel (01462) 684822

SETTIMBA, John Henry. b 52. Nairobi Univ BSc78 Leeds Univ MA91. Pan Africa Chr Coll BA78. **d** 78 **p** 80. Kenya 78-81; Uganda 81-85; C Allerton *Bradf* 86-87; C W Ham *Chelmsf* 87-91; C-in-c Forest Gate All SS 91-94; P-in-c 94-96; TV Hackney *Lon* from 96. *St James House, 59A Kenninghall Road, London E5 8BS* Tel 0181-985 1804

SEVILLE, Christopher John. b 57. Trin Hall Cam MA80. Coll of Resurr Mirfield 87. **d** 89 **p** 90. C Knowle *Bris* 89-93; CR from 93. *House of the Resurrection, Mirfield, W Yorkshire WF14 0BN* Tel (01924) 494318

SEWARD, Jolyon Frantom. b 57. Univ of Wales (Cardiff) BA81. Chich Th Coll 83. **d** 86 **p** 87. C Llanblethian w Cowbridge and Llandough etc *Llan* 86-88; C Newton Nottage 88-93; V Penyfai w Tondu from 93. *The Vicarage, Pen y Fai, Bridgend CF31 4LS* Tel (01656) 652849

SEWELL, Andrew William. b 61. Nottm Univ BSc83. St Jo Coll Nottm DTS93. **d** 93 **p** 94. C Adel *Ripon* 93-96; C Far Headingley St Chad from 96. *64 Becketts Park Crescent, Leeds LS6 3PF* Tel 0113-274 3636

SEWELL, Miss Elizabeth Jill. b 56. Reading Univ BSc77. Trin Coll Bris 95. **d** 97. C Rothley *Leic* from 97. *105 Balmoral Road, Mountsorrel, Loughborough, Leics LE12 7EL* Tel 0116-230 3199

SEWELL, John. b 10. MBE46. Tyndale Hall Bris 60. **d** 61 **p** 62. C Dagenham *Chelmsf* 61-63; C Lt Burstead 63-69; Chapl New Lodge Billericay 64-69; R Yelvertoft w Clay Coton and Lilbourne *Pet* 69-74; rtd 75. *Flat 4, 7 Chatsworth Gardens, Eastbourne, E Sussex BN20 7JP* Tel (01323) 640980

SEWELL, John Andrew Clarkson (Andy). b 58. Aston Tr Scheme 93 Ripon Coll Cuddesdon 95. **d** 97. C Horsham *Chich* from 97. *18 Queensway, Horsham, W Sussex RH13 5AY* Tel (01403) 252986 or 0402-209984

SEWELL, Dr John Barratt (Barry). b 39. DRCOG66 St Bart Hosp Medical Coll MB, BS63. Ridley Hall Cam CTM92. **d** 92 **p** 93. C Ulverston St Mary w H Trin *Carl* 92-94; Asst Chapl R Cornwall Hosps NHS Trust from 94. *Trelisk Hospital, Truro, Cornwall TR1 3LJ, or Cleswyth, Creegbrawse, St Day, Redruth, Cornwall TR16 5QR* Tel (01872) 74242 or (01209) 821696

SEWELL, Jonathan William. b 60. Lanc Univ BA82 BTh86. Linc Th Coll 83. **d** 86 **p** 87. C Ilkeston St Mary *Derby* 86-89; C Enfield Chase St Mary *Lon* 89-92; Dioc Youth Officer *Win* from 92. *Diocesan Youth Officer, Church House, 9 The Close, Winchester, Hants SO23 9LS* Tel Winchester (01962) 844644 Fax 841815

SEWELL, Robin Warwick. b 42. Trin Coll Bris. **d** 82 **p** 83. C Hinckley H Trin *Leic* 82-85; C Broadwater St Mary *Chich* 85-89; Chapl Barcelona *Eur* from 89. *Calle San Juan de la Salle 41, Horacio 38, 08022 Barcelona, Spain* Tel Barcelona (3) 417-8867 Fax 212-8433

SEWELL, Miss Sarah Frances. b 61. Wycliffe Hall Ox 87. **d** 91 **p** 94. C Binley *Cov* 91-94; Asst Chapl Derriford Hosp Plymouth 94-96; Chapl Stoke Mandeville Hosp NHS Trust from 96. *Stoke Mandeville Hospital, Mandeville Road, Aylesbury, Bucks HP20 8AL* Tel (01296) 315000 or 316677

SEXTON, Canon Michael Bowers. b 28. SS Coll Cam BA52 MA56. Wells Th Coll 52. **d** 54 **p** 55. C Miles Platting St Luke *Man* 54-57; C Bradford cum Beswick 57-58; C-in-c Oldham St Chad Limeside CD 58-62; R Filby w Thrigby w Mautby *Nor* 62-72; P-in-c Runham 67-72; P-in-c Stokesby w Herringby 68-72; R Hethersett w Canteloff 72-85; V Ketteringham 73-84; RD Humbleyard 81-86; Hon Can Nor Cathl 85-93; R Hethersett w Canteloff w Lt and Gt Melton 85-86; V Hunstanton St Mary w Ringstead Parva, Holme etc 86-93; rtd 94; Perm to Offic *Nor* from 94. *3 Forge Close, Poringland, Norwich NR14 7SZ* Tel (01508) 493885

SEYMOUR, Anthony Nicholas. b 39. QUB BA61. **d** 96 **p** 97. Community of Our Lady and St John from 86. *Alton Abbey, Abbey Road, Beech, Alton, Hants GU34 4AP* Tel (01420) 562145 or 563575 Fax 561691

SEYMOUR, David. b 43. Kelham Th Coll 60. **d** 68 **p** 69. C Cowley St Jas *Ox* 68-73; TV Lynton, Brendon, Countisbury, Lynmouth etc *Ex* 73-77; C-in-c Luton (Princes Park) CD *Roch* 78-79; V Rosherville 79-90; rtd 90. *4 Swinburne Drive, Lowry Hill, Carlisle CA3 0PY* Tel (01228) 818246

SEYMOUR, David Raymond Russell. b 56. Keble Coll Ox BA79 MA88. St Steph Ho Ox 79. **d** 81 **p** 82. C Tilehurst St Mich *Ox* 81-85; TV Parkstone St Pet w Branksea and St Osmund *Sarum* 85-91; V Bradford-on-Avon Ch Ch from 91. *Christ Church Vicarage, 3D Mount Pleasant, Bradford-on-Avon, Wilts BA15 1SJ* Tel (01225) 867656

SEYMOUR, Canon John Charles. b 30. Oak Hill Th Coll 51 and 55 Wycliffe Coll Toronto 54. **d** 57 **p** 58. C Islington St Andr w St Thos and St Matthias *Lon* 57-60; C Worthing St Geo *Chich* 60-63; V Thornton *Leic* 63-70; R Kirby Muxloe 70-81; TR 81-83; Hon Can Leic Cathl 82-93; RD Sparkenhoe I 83-88; R Market Bosworth w Shenton 83-87; TR Market Bosworth, Cadeby w Sutton Cheney etc 87-93; RD Sparkenhoe W 89-92; rtd 93. *7 Merton Close, Broughton Astley, Leicester LE9 6QP* Tel (01455) 282525

SEYMOUR, Ralph. b 05. Cuddesdon Coll 73. **d** 73 **p** 73. Hon C Tring *St Alb* 73-80; Perm to Offic 80-96. *6 Regal Court, Tring, Herts HP23 4PT* Tel (01442) 822223

SEYMOUR-WHITELEY, Richard Dudley. b 59. Leic Poly BSc80. Linc Th Coll 82. **d** 85 **p** 86. C Bushey *St Alb* 85-89; C Stevenage St Mary Sheppall w Aston 89-93; P-in-c Blunham w Tempsford and Lt Barford from 93. *The Rectory, Park Lane, Blunham, Bedford MK44 3NJ* Tel (01767) 40298

SHACKELL, Daniel William. b 42. LNSM course 92. **d** 95 **p** 96. NSM Streatham St Leon *S'wark* from 95. *194 Crowborough Road, London SW17 9QF* Tel 0181-767 4517

SHACKELL, Kenneth Norman. b 26. S'wark Ord Course. **d** 69 **p** 70. NSM Greenwich St Alfege w St Pet and St Paul *S'wark* 69-95; Perm to Offic *Sarum* from 95. *17 Portman Drive, Child Okeford, Blandford Forum, Dorset DT11 8HU* Tel (01258) 861583

SHACKERLEY, Capt Albert Paul. b 56. Birkb Coll Lon DipRS86 DipTh89 Chich Tech Coll CCouns93 K Coll Lon MA97. CA Tr Coll DipEvang83 Chich Th Coll DMinlTh93. **d** 93 **p** 94. C Harlesden All So *Lon* 93-96; P-in-c Chelmsf All SS *Chelmsf* from 96. *All Saints' Vicarage, 76A Kings Road, Chelmsford CM1 4HP* Tel (01245) 352005

SHACKLADY, Mrs Thelma. b 38. Liv Univ BA60. St Alb Minl Tr Scheme 89. **d** 92 **p** 94. NSM Luton St Andr *St Alb* 92-96; NSM Luton All SS w St Pet from 96. *31 Fairford Avenue, Luton LU2 7ER* Tel (01582) 23252 or 31901

SHACKLETON, Canon Alan. b 31. Sheff Univ BA53. Wells Th Coll 54. **d** 56 **p** 57. C Ladybarn *Man* 56-58; C Bolton St Pet 58-61; V Middleton Junction 61-70; V Heywood St Luke 70-84; AD Rochdale 82-92; Hon Can Man Cathl 84-97; V Heywood St Luke w All So 85-86; TV Rochdale 86-91; TR 91-97; rtd 97. *28 Taunton Avenue, Rochdale, Lancs OL11 5LD* Tel (01706) 45335 E-mail alan@g34shack.demon.co.uk

SHACKLETON, Ian Roderick. b 40. St Fran Coll Brisbane 69 ACT ThL71. **d** 72 **p** 72. Australia 72-78; C Birch St Agnes *Man* 79-80; P-in-c Newton Heath St Wilfrid and St Anne 80-87; NSM W Derby (or Tuebrook) St Jo *Liv* 87-90; C 90-94; P-in-c Southport St Luke from 94; Asst Chapl HM Pris Liv from 94. *The Clergy House, 71 Hawkshead Street, Southport, Merseyside PR9 9BT* Tel (01704) 538703

SHACKLOCK, David Peter Riley. b 36. CCC Cam BA60 MA64. Ridley Hall Cam 60. **d** 62 **p** 63. C Park Estate St Chris CD *Leic* 62-66; CF 66-71; R Northiam *Chich* 71-80; V Fulham St Mary N End *Lon* 80-87; V Redhill H Trin *S'wark* from 87. *Holy Trinity Vicarage, 2 Carlton Road, Redhill RH1 2BX* Tel (01737) 766604

SHAFEE, Kenneth Harold. b 30. ALA64. Ex & Truro NSM Scheme 78. **d** 81 **p** 82. NSM Littleham w Exmouth *Ex* 81-85; Custos St Jo Hosp Heytesbury 85-89; NSM Lydford, Brent Tor, Bridestowe and Sourton *Ex* 89-90; rtd 90; Perm to Offic *Ex* from 90. *The Firs, Exeter Road, Dawlish, Devon EX7 0LX* Tel (01626) 888326

SHAHZAD, Sulaiman. b 60. BA. Oak Hill Th Coll BA93. **d** 96 **p** 97. C Winchmore Hill St Paul *Lon* from 96. *St Paul's Lodge, 58 Church Hill, London N21 1JA* Tel 0181-882 3298

SHAIL, Canon William Frederick. b 15. Kelham Th Coll. **d** 41 **p** 42. C Deptford St Paul *S'wark* 41-44; C Lewisham St Mary 44-47; C Christchurch *Win* 47-52; R N Stoneham 52-68; V Bournemouth St Alb 68-78; V Burley Ville 78-84; rtd 84; Perm to Offic *Win* from 84. *19 Halton Close, Bransgore, Christchurch, Dorset BH23 8HZ* Tel (01425) 673064

SHAKESPEARE, Daniel. b 19. EAMTC 79. **d** 81 **p** 82. NSM Hethersett w Canteloff *Nor* 81-85; NSM Hethersett w Canteloff w Lt and Gt Melton 85-89; Perm to Offic from 89. *23 Central Crescent, Hethersett, Norwich NR9 3EP* Tel (01603) 810727

SHAKESPEARE, Dr Steven. b 68. CCC Cam BA89 PhD94. Westcott Ho Cam 93. **d** 96 **p** 97. C Cambridge St Jas *Ely* from 96. *130 Hulatt Road, Cambridge CB1 4TH* Tel (01223) 210602

SHALLCROSS, Canon Martin Anthony. b 37. FRICS70. Sarum & Wells Th Coll 75. **d** 78 **p** 79. NSM Landford w Plaitford *Sarum* 78-81; NSM Bramshaw 78-81; NSM Tisbury from 81; Can and Preb Sarum Cathl from 93. *Wallmead Farm, Tisbury, Salisbury SP3 6RB* Tel (01747) 870208

SHAMBROOK, Roger William. b 46. Sarum & Wells Th Coll 78. **d** 83 **p** 84. OSP 76-82; C Southbourne St Kath *Win* 83-86; TV Bridport *Sarum* from 86; Chapl Bridport Hosp from 86. *The Vicarage, Parsonage Road, Bridport, Dorset DT6 5ET* Tel (01308) 423458

SHAND, Dr Brian Martin. b 53. Univ Coll Lon BA76 PhD82. St Steph Ho Ox 85. **d** 87 **p** 88. C Uxbridge St Marg *Lon* 87-88; C Uxbridge 88-90; C Worplesdon *Guildf* 90-94; Relig Affairs Producer BBC Radio Surrey 90-94; V Weston from 94. *All Saints' Vicarage, 1 Chestnut Avenue, Esher, Surrey KT10 8JL* Tel 0181-398 1849

SHAND, John. b 06. Aber Univ MA27. Edin Th Coll 32. **d** 34 **p** 35. C Edin St Martin *Edin* 34-41; Lic to Offic *Ox* 43-44; Chapl St Andr Home Joppa and C Old St Paul 44-45; P-in-c Kemnay *Ab* 45-46; P-in-c Aberdeen St Ninian 46-49; S Africa 49-59; R Buckie *Ab* 69-71; rtd 71. *7 Albany Court, Dennyduff Road, Fraserburgh, Aberdeenshire AB43 5NG* Tel (01346) 27948

SHANKS, Robert Andrew Gulval. b 54. Ball Coll Ox BA75 G&C Coll Cam BA79. Westcott Ho Cam 77. **d** 80 **p** 81. C Potternewton

Ripon 80-83; C Stanningley St Thos 84-87. *52 Newton Court, Leeds LS8 2PH* Tel 0113-248 5011

SHANNON, Brian James. b 35. St Chad's Coll Dur BA59 DipTh61. **d** 61 **p** 62. C Palmers Green St Jo *Lon* 61-65; C Kenton 65-70; V Roxbourne St Andr 70-81; V Thorpe-le-Soken *Chelmsf* 81-91; V Gt Wakering w Foulness from 91. *The Vicarage, 2 New Road, Great Wakering, Southend-on-Sea SS3 0AH* Tel (01702) 219226

SHANNON, Canon Francis Thomas. b 16. TCD BA39 MA. CITC. **d** 39 **p** 40. C Rathdowney *C & O* 39-41; I Mothel 41-51; I Aghade w Ardoyne 51-61; I Carnew w Kilrush 61-91; RD Wexford 68-91; Preb Ferns Cathl 71-91; Treas 80-81; Chan 81-85; Prec 85-91; rtd 91. *16 Clonattin, Gorey, Co Wexford, Irish Republic* Tel Gorey (55) 22284

SHANNON, The Ven Malcolm James Douglas. b 49. TCD BA72 MA75. CITC 75. **d** 75 **p** 76. C Clooney *D & R* 75-78; I Kilcolman w Kiltallagh, Killorglin, Knockane etc *L & K* from 78; Adn Ardfert and Aghadoe from 88; Treas Limerick Cathl from 88; Dir of Ords from 91. *Kilcolman Rectory, Miltown, Killarney, Co Kerry, Irish Republic* Tel Tralee (66) 67302 Mobile 088-539906 Fax as telephone

SHANNON, Canon Trevor Haslam. b 33. Selw Coll Cam BA57 MA61 Lon Univ BD69. Westcott Ho Cam 57. **d** 59 **p** 60. C Moss Side Ch Ch *Man* 59-62; V Woolfold 62-66; Chapl Forest Sch Snaresbrook 66-80 and 87-88; V Gt Ilford St Marg *Chelmsf* 88-90; TR Gt Ilford St Clem and St Marg 90-96; V from 96; RD Redbridge from 90; Hon Can Chelmsf Cathl from 93. *The Vicarage, 70 Brisbane Road, Ilford, Essex IG1 4SL* Tel 0181-554 7542

SHAPLAND, David Edward. b 26. Cuddesdon Coll 51. **d** 53 **p** 54. C Cranbrook *Cant* 53-55; Chapl St Cath Coll Cam 55-61; R Fittleworth *Chich* 62-65; Warden Bede Ho Staplehurst 65-69; Warden Llanerchwen Trust 70-91; Lic to Offic *S & B* 70-79; Perm to Offic *Chich* 79-91; rtd 91. *The Long Barn, Peagham Barton, St Giles, Torrington, Devon EX38 7HZ* Tel (01805) 624640

SHARE, David James. b 30. Sarum Th Coll 56. **d** 58 **p** 59. C Whipton *Ex* 58-63; Min Tiverton St Andr Statutory Distr 63-69; RD Tiverton 67-74; V Tiverton St Andr 69-79; P-in-c Ex St Thos 79-80; TR Ex St Thos and Em 80-83; V Woodbury 83-95; rtd 95; Perm to Offic *Ex* from 95. *57 Coombeshead Road, Newton Abbot, Devon TQ12 1PZ* Tel (01626) 62516

SHARLAND, Canon Charles Thomas. b 08. Wycliffe Hall Ox 45. **d** 45 **p** 46. Sudan 45-53; V Toxteth Park St Bede *Liv* 53-61; R Heigham H Trin *Nor* 61-75; Hon Can Nor Cathl 73-85; rtd 75; Perm to Offic *Nor* from 75. *35 Cromwell House, Cecil Road, Norwich NR1 2QL* Tel (01603) 626817

SHARLAND, Mrs Marilyn. b 40. City of Birm Coll CertEd61. Oak Hill Th Coll 84. **dss** 86 **d** 87 **p** 94. Barkingside St Laur *Chelmsf* 86-87; Hon Par Dn 87-88; Hon Par Dn Hucclecote *Glouc* 88-89; C Coney Hill from 89. *58 Bullfinch Road, Gloucester GL4 8LX* Tel (01452) 416788

SHARMAN, Herbert Leslie John. b 27. St Aid Birkenhead 60. **d** 62 **p** 63. C Stanwix *Carl* 62-66; C Brandon and Santon Downham *St E* 66-87; Perm to Offic from 87; rtd 92. *18 Princes Close, Brandon, Suffolk IP27 0LH* Tel (01842) 811163

SHARMAN, Hilary John. b 32. Leeds Univ BA58. Coll of Resurr Mirfield 58. **d** 60 **p** 61. C Hertford St Andr *St Alb* 60-64; C Harpenden St Nic 64-72; V High Cross from 72; V Thundridge from 72. *7 Ducketts Wood, Thundridge, Ware, Herts SG12 0SR* Tel (01920) 465561

SHARP, Alfred James Frederick. b 30. Oak Hill Th Coll 62. **d** 64 **p** 65. C Hanley Road St Sav w St Paul *Lon* 64-68; P-in-c Leverton *Linc* 68-84; Chapl Pilgrim Hosp Boston 76-84; P-in-c Benington w Leverton *Linc* 84; V Ch Broughton w Boylestone amd Sutton on the Hill *Derby* 84-89; R Ch Broughton w Barton Blount, Boylestone etc 89-94; rtd 94. *14 Edgefield, Weston, Spalding, Lincs PE12 6RQ* Tel (01406) 370376

SHARP, Andrew Timothy. b 58. K Alfred's Coll Win BA79. Wycliffe Hall Ox 82. **d** 85 **p** 86. C Scarborough St Mary w Ch Ch and H Apostles *York* 85-89; C Luton St Fran *St Alb* 89-90; V from 90. *The Vicarage, 145 Hollybush Road, Luton LU2 9HQ* Tel (01582) 28030

SHARP, Bernard Harold. b 40. Linc Th Coll 64. **d** 67 **p** 68. C Newton Aycliffe *Dur* 67-69; C Leam Lane CD 69-71; Malawi 72-75; P-in-c Blakenall Heath *Lich* 75-77; TV Gateshead *Dur* 77-79; C Warmsworth *Sheff* 84; C Caerau w Ely *Llan* 85-92; V Cwmbach from 92. *The Vicarage, Bridge Road, Cwmbach, Aberdare CF44 0LS* Tel (01685) 878674

SHARP, Brian Phillip. b 48. Cant Sch of Min 85. **d** 88 **p** 89. C S Ashford Ch Ch *Cant* 88-92; C St Laur in Thanet 92-96; V Margate St Jo from 96. *The Vicarage, 24 St Peter's Road, Margate, Kent CT9 1TH* Tel (01843) 230766

SHARP, Canon David Malcolm. b 33. Hertf Coll Ox BA56 MA59. Cuddesdon Coll 56. **d** 58 **p** 59. C Bris St Mary Redcliffe w Temple *Bris* 58-65; V Henleaze 65-75; V Nor St Pet Mancroft *Nor* 75-82; R Nor St Pet Mancroft w St Jo Maddermarket from 82; Hon Can Nor Cathl from 86; Dioc Eur Contact from 91. *The Chantry, Chantry Road, Norwich NR2 1QZ* Tel (01603) 610443 or 627816

SHARP, Mrs Janice Anne. b 54. Aston Tr Scheme 91 Nor Ord Course 93. **d** 96 **p** 97. C Skipton H Trin *Bradf* from 96. *7 Princes Drive, Skipton, N Yorkshire BD23 1HN* Tel (01756) 701063

SHARP, Nicholas Leonard (Nick). b 64. Grey Coll Dur BA85. St Jo Coll Nottm DTS94 MA95. **d** 95 **p** 96. C Oakwood St Thos *Lon* from 95. *22 Curthwaite Gardens, Enfield, Middx EN2 7LN* Tel 0181-363 4396

SHARP, Canon Reuben Thomas George (Tom). b 27. ALCD57. **d** 57 **p** 58. C Pudsey St Lawr *Bradf* 57-60; V Cononley w Bradley 60-63; Dioc Youth Chapl 60-63; Dioc Youth Officer *Wakef* 63-68; V Dewsbury All SS 68-84; RD Dewsbury 68-90; Hon Can Wakef Cathl 76-97; TR Dewsbury 84-90; V Cawthorne 90-97; rtd 97. *1 St Barnabas Drive, Littleborough, Lancs OL15 8EJ*

SHARP, Preb Robert. b 36. FLCM58. St Aid Birkenhead 64. **d** 67 **p** 68. C Shipley St Paul *Bradf* 67-70; C-in-c Thwaites Brow CD 70-74; V Thwaites Brow 74-77; P-in-c Alberbury w Cardeston *Heref* 77-78; V 78-87; V Ford 77-87; V Claverley w Tuckhill 87-97; RD Bridgnorth 89-96; Preb Heref Cathl 91-97; rtd 97. *62 Biddulph Way, Ledbury, Herefordshire HR8 2HN* Tel (01531) 631972

SHARPE, Canon Alan Brian. b 39. Lich Th Coll 64. **d** 67 **p** 68. C Croydon Woodside *Cant* 67-70; C Portsea St Mary *Portsm* 70-75; V Sheerness H Trin w St Paul *Cant* 75-83; V Hove St Patr w Ch Ch and St Andr *Chich* 83-90; V Hove St Patr from 90; Can and Preb Chich Cathl from 93. *St Patrick's Vicarage, 30 Cambridge Road, Hove, E Sussex BN3 1DF* Tel (01273) 733151

SHARPE, Bruce Warrington. b 41. JP88. DMS(Ed)85 MIMgt85. Ely Th Coll 62 St Steph Ho Ox 64. **d** 65 **p** 66. C Streatham St Pet *S'wark* 65-67; St Lucia 67-68; Hon C Leic St Matt and St Geo *Leic* 68-69; Hon C Catford St Laur *S'wark* 69-70; Hon C Deptford St Paul 70-75; Hon C Lamorbey H Redeemer *Roch* 76-83; Perm to Offic 83-88; Hon C Sidcup St Andr from 88. *72 Faraday Avenue, Sidcup, Kent DA14 4JF* Tel 0181-300 0695

SHARPE, Cecil Frederick. b 23. Edin Th Coll 52. **d** 54 **p** 55. C Falkirk *Edin* 54-56; C Kings Norton *Birm* 56-58; V Withall 58-80; Perm to Offic from 80; rtd 88. *35 Shirley Park Road, Shirley, Solihull, W Midlands B90 2BZ* Tel 0121-745 6905

SHARPE, David Francis. b 32. Ex Coll Ox BA56 MA59. St Steph Ho Ox 57. **d** 60 **p** 61. C Hunslet St Mary and Stourton *Ripon* 60-63; C Notting Hill St Jo *Lon* 63-68; V Haggerston St Mary w St Chad 68-78; P-in-c Haggerston St Aug w St Steph 73-78; V Haggerston St Chad 78-83; V Mill Hill St Mich from 83. *St Michael's Vicarage, 9 Flower Lane, London NW7 2JA* Tel 0181-959 1449

SHARPE, Derek Martin Brereton (Pip). b 29. Birkb Coll Lon BA60. NE Ord Course 90. **d** 90 **p** 91. NSM Scarborough St Luke *York* 90-92; Asst Chapl Scarborough Distr Hosp 90-92; P-in-c Sherburn and W and E Heslerton w Yedingham from 92. *Low Farm House, Allerston, Pickering, N Yorkshire YO18 7PG* Tel (01723) 859271

SHARPE, Gerard John. b 23. Westcott Ho Cam. **d** 64 **p** 65. C Thetford St Cuth w H Trin *Nor* 64-70; V Holme *Ely* 70-76; R Conington 70-76; R Glatton 74-93; V Holme w Conington 76-93; RD Yaxley 82-88; rtd 93; Perm to Offic *Ely* from 93. *24 St Margaret's Road, Girton, Cambridge CB3 0LT* Tel (01223) 574246

SHARPE, Miss Joan Valerie. b 33. EMMTC 73. **dss** 84 **d** 88 **p** 94. Hon Par Dn Warsop *S'well* 88-94; Hon C from 94. *1 Forest Court, Eakring Road, Mansfield, Notts NG18 3DP* Tel (01623) 631505

SHARPE, John Brebber (Brother Mark). b 14. **d** 85. CSWG from 82; Lic to Offic *Chich* from 85. *The Monastery, 23 Cambridge Road, Hove, E Sussex BN3 1DE* Tel (01273) 726698

SHARPE, John Edward. b 50. Dur Univ BSc72 St Jo Coll Dur DipTh75. **d** 76 **p** 77. C Woodford Wells *Chelmsf* 76-79; C Ealing St Mary *Lon* 79-83; Min Walsall St Martin *Lich* 83-87; TV Walsall 87-96; R Glenfield *Leic* from 96. *The Rectory, Main Street, Glenfield, Leicester LE3 8DG* Tel 0116-287 1604

SHARPE, Canon John Leslie. b 33. MInstGA89 Birm Univ DPS72 Open Univ BA75. Kelham Th Coll 54. **d** 58 **p** 59. C Charlton St Luke w St Paul *S'wark* 58-61; Papua New Guinea 62-70; Adn N Distr 68-70; P-in-c Southampton SS Pet and Paul w All SS *Win* 71-73; TV Southampton (City Cen) 73-75; Chapl SW Hants Psychiatric Services 75-93; Chapl Knowle Hosp Fareham 75-93; Hon Can Portsm Cathl *Portsm* 86-93; rtd 93. *Clare Cottage, 23 West Dean, Salisbury SP5 1JB* Tel (01742) 340028

SHARPE, Canon Kenneth William (Ken). b 40. Univ of Wales (Lamp) BA61. Sarum Th Coll 61. **d** 63 **p** 64. C Hubberston *St D* 63-71; TV Cwmbran *Mon* 71-74; Dioc Children's Adv 72-82; Dioc Youth Chapl 74-82; V Dingestow and Llangovan w Penyclawdd and Tregaer 74-82; V Newport St Mark from 82; Chapl Alltyryn Hosp Gwent from 83; RD Newport *Mon* from 93; Can St Woolos Cathl from 94. *The Vicarage, 7 Goldtops, Newport NP9 4PH* Tel (01633) 263321

SHARPE, Mrs Margaret Theresa (Maggie). b 48. Man Univ BEd70 Dur Univ DipTh74. Cranmer Hall Dur 72 WMMTC 90. **d** 91 **p** 94. C W Bromwich H Trin *Lich* 91-96; Asst Chapl Glenfield Hosp NHS Trust Leic from 96. *The Rectory, Main Street, Glenfield, Leicester LE3 8DG, or Chaplain's Dept, Glenfield Hospital, Groby Road, Leicester LE3 9QP* Tel 0116-287 1604 or 287 1471

SHARPE, Miss Mary. b 31. CQSW71. Dalton Ho Bris 58. **dss** 78 **d** 87 **p** 94. Upton (Overchurch) *Ches* 78-83; Harlescott *Lich* 83-84; New Brighton All SS *Ches* 85-89; Par Dn 87-89; rtd 89. *13 Manor Close, Neston, South Wirral L64 6TE*

SHARPE, Mrs Mary Primrose. b 22. Coll of St Matthias Bris CertEd. Gilmore Ho CertRK51 DC51 CMS Tr Coll Chislehurst. **dss** 81 **d** 87. Coley *Wakef* 81-87; Hon Par Dn 87-89; rtd 89; Perm to Offic *Bradf* from 89. *54 Bradford Road, Menston, Ilkley, W Yorkshire LS29 6BX* Tel (01943) 877710

SHARPE, Richard Gordon. b 48. Birm Univ BA69. St Jo Coll Nottm BA74. **d** 75 **p** 76. C Hinckley H Trin *Leic* 75-78; C Kingston upon Hull H Trin *York* 78-85; Chapl Marston Green Hosp Birm 85-88; Chapl Chelmsley Hosp Birm 86-88; TV Chelmsley Wood *Birm* 85-88; P-in-c Dosthill 88-93; V from 93. *The Vicarage, Dosthill, Tamworth, Staffs B77 1LU* Tel (01827) 281349

SHARPE, Canon Roger. b 35. TCD BA60 MA63. Qu Coll Birm 60. **d** 62 **p** 63. C Stockton H Trin *Dur* 62-64; C Oakdale St Geo *Sarum* 64-68; V Redlynch and Morgan's Vale 68-86; RD Alderbury 82-86; V Warminster St Denys 86-88; R Upton Scudamore 86-88; V Horningsham 86-88; R Warminster St Denys, Upton Scudamore etc 88-95; Can and Preb Sarum Cathl from 89; RD Heytesbury 89-95; Chmn Dioc Assn for Deaf from 91; P-in-c Corsley 92-95; TR Cley Hill Warminster from 95. *The Rectory, 5 Church Street, Warminster, Wilts BA12 8PG* Tel (01985) 213456

SHARPE, Tony Ernest Charles. EAMTC. **d** 93 **p** 94. NSM Leigh-on-Sea St Jas *Chelmsf* 93-96; NSM Thorpe Bay from 96. *39 Grange Road, Leigh-on-Sea, Essex SS9 2HT* Tel (01702) 79949

SHARPLES, Canon Alfred Cyril. b 09. Man Univ BA33. Linc Th Coll 33. **d** 35 **p** 36. C Rochdale *Man* 35-39; C Ashton St Mich 39-42; R Cheetham St Mark 42-46; V Tonge w Alkrington 46-51; V Hope St Jas 51-76; Hon Can Man Cathl 74-76; rtd 76; Perm to Offic *Ches* from 77; Perm to Offic *Man* from 77. *30 Greenbank Drive, Bollington, Macclesfield, Cheshire SK10 5LW* Tel 0161-207 5073

SHARPLES, David. b 41. Linc Th Coll 71. **d** 73 **p** 74. C Reddish *Man* 73-75; C Prestwich St Mary 76-78; V Ashton St Jas 78-86; V Hope St Jas from 86. *Hope Vicarage, Vicarage Close, Pendleton, Salford M6 8EJ* Tel 0161-789 3303

SHARPLES, David. b 58. Lon Univ BD81 AKC81. Coll of Resurr Mirfield. **d** 82 **p** 83. C Prestwich St Mary *Man* 82-87; V Royton St Anne from 87; AD Tandle from 94. *St Anne's Vicarage, St Anne's Avenue, Royton, Oldham OL2 5AD* Tel 0161-624 2249 Fax as telephone

SHARPLES, Dr Derek. b 35. SS Paul & Mary Coll Cheltenham CertEd57 Liv Univ DipEd63 Man Univ MEd66 Bath Univ PhD72 Open Univ BA79 FCollP86. WMMTC 83. **d** 86 **p** 87. NSM Malvern H Trin and St Jas *Worc* 86-90; C St Jo in Bedwardine 90-92; R Belbroughton w Fairfield and Clent from 92. *The Rectory, Bradford Lane, Belbroughton, Stourbridge, W Midlands DY9 9TF* Tel (01562) 730531

SHARPLES, John Charles. b 29. St Jo Coll York TCert48 Lon Univ BSc55. St Deiniol's Hawarden 87. **d** 87 **p** 88. Hon C Wigan St Mich *Liv* 87-89; P-in-c New Springs from 89. *New Springs Vicarage, 7 Lealholme Avenue, Wigan, Lancs WN2 1EH* Tel (01942) 43071

SHARPLES, Ms Susan Margaret (Sue). b 58. SRN82 Worc Coll of Educn BA89. WMMTC 91. **d** 94 **p** 95. NSM Worc SE *Worc* 94-95; C from 95. *Hazelwood, 24 Albert Road, Worcester WR5 1EB* Tel (01905) 356656

SHARPLEY, The Ven Roger Ernest Dion. b 28. Ch Ch Ox BA52 MA56. St Steph Ho Ox 52. **d** 54 **p** 55. C Southwick St Columba *Dur* 54-60; V Middlesbrough All SS *York* 60-81; P-in-c Middlesbrough St Hilda w St Pet 64-72; RD Middlesbrough 70-81; Can and Preb York Minster 74-81; P-in-c Middlesbrough St Aid 79; V 79-81; V St Andr Holborn *Lon* 81-92; Adn Hackney 81-92; rtd 92; Perm to Offic *Dur* from 92. *2 Hill Meadows, High Shincliffe, Durham DH1 2PE* Tel 0191-386 1908

SHARPUS-JONES, Trevor. b 20. TD66. St And Dioc Tr Course 83. **d** 87 **p** 88. NSM St Andrews St Andr *St And* 87-89; P-in-c Elie and Earlsferry 89-90; P-in-c Pittenweem 89-90; NSM Leven 90-92; Chapl Monte Carlo *Eur* 93-95; C Leven *St And* from 95; C St Andrews St Andr from 95. *Etta Bank, 40 Leven Road, Lundin Links, Leven, Fife KY8 6AH* Tel (01333) 320510

SHAW, Alan. b 24. Man Univ BSc44 MSc48 PhD51. Ely Th Coll 55. **d** 57 **p** 58. C Orford St Marg *Liv* 57-59; C Bury St Mary *Man* 59-61; Perm to Offic *Liv* 61-71; V Beckermet St Jo *Carl* 71-76; V Lt Leigh and Lower Whitley *Ches* 76-80; V Latchford Ch Ch 80-91; rtd 91; Perm to Offic *Ches* from 91; Perm to Offic *Liv* from 91. *7 Gainsborough Road, Warrington WA4 6DA* Tel (01925) 240133

SHAW, Alan Taylor. b 52. Sarum & Wells Th Coll 88. **d** 90 **p** 91. C Beeston *Ripon* 90-93; C Stanningley St Thos 93-96; TV Seacroft from 96. *St Luke's Vicarage, Stanks Lane North, Leeds LS14 5AS* Tel 0113-273 1302

SHAW, Alan Walter. b 41. MIEI TCD BA63 BAI63 Chu Coll Cam MSc66. **d** 94 **p** 95. NSM Drumcliffe w Kilnasoolagh *L & K* 94-97; NSM Kenmare w Sneem, Waterville etc from 97. *St Patrick's Rectory, Kenmare, Co Kerry, Irish Republic* Tel Killarney (64) 41121 Fax as telephone

SHAW, Canon Alexander Martin. b 44. AKC67. **d** 68 **p** 69. C Glas St Oswald *Glas* 68-70; C Edin Old St Paul *Edin* 70-75; Chapl K Coll Cam 75-77; C St Marylebone All SS *Lon* 77-78; R Dunoon *Arg* 78-81; Succ Ex Cathl *Ex* 81-83; Dioc Miss and Ecum Officer 83-89; TV Cen Ex 83-87; Can Res St E Cathl *St E* from 89; Prec from 96. *1 Abbey Precincts, Bury St Edmunds, Suffolk IP33 1RS* Tel (01284) 761982

SHAW, Andrew Jonathan. b 50. Leeds Univ CertEd72 Open Univ BA81. Wycliffe Hall Ox 85. **d** 87 **p** 88. C Witton w Brundall and Braydeston *Nor* 87-89; C Postwick 87-89; C Brundall w Braydeston and Postwick 89-90; C Grayswood *Guildf* 90-91; P-in-c from 91; Chapl RN Sch Haslemere from 90. *Church House, Church Close, Grayswood, Haslemere, Surrey GU27 2DB* Tel (01428) 656504

SHAW, Ms Anne Lesley (Annie). b 50. Linc Th Coll 77. **dss** 80 **d** 87 **p** 94. Camberwell St Luke *S'wark* 80-85; Chapl Asst Lon Hosp (Whitechapel) 85-90; Chapl Lewisham Hosp 90-94; Chapl Lewisham Hosp NHS Trust from 94; Chapl Hither Green Hosp from 90. *The Chaplain's Office, Lewisham Hospital, High Street, London SE13 6LH* Tel 0181-690 4311 or 333 3000

SHAW, Dr Anne Patricia Leslie. b 39. MRCS LRCP63 MB, BS63 DA68. Qu Coll Birm 79. **dss** 81 **d** 87 **p** 94. Pinner *Lon* 81-84; Rickmansworth *St Alb* 84-87; NSM from 87. *37 Sandy Lodge Road, Moor Park, Rickmansworth, Herts WD3 1LP* Tel (01923) 827663

SHAW, Anthony Keeble. b 36. K Alfred's Coll Win CertEd60. SW Minl Tr Course 78. **d** 81 **p** 82. NSM E Teignmouth *Ex* 81-83; NSM Highweek and Teigngrace 83-87; C Southbourne St Kath *Win* 87-89; Teaching 89-96; Perm to Offic *Lon* 93-96; P-in-c Winthorpe *S'well* from 96; P-in-c Langford w Holme from 96; Dioc Chief Insp of Schs from 96. *The Rectory, The Spinney, Newark, Notts NG24 2NT* Tel (01636) 704985

SHAW, Colin Clement Gordon. b 39. RMN60 TNC62 DPS72. Linc Th Coll 65. **d** 67 **p** 68. C Tettenhall Regis *Lich* 67-70; C Tile Cross *Birm* 70-72; V Edstaston *Lich* 72-75; V Whixall 72-75; Chapl Stoke Mandeville Hosp and St Jo Hosp 75-90; Manor Ho Hosp and Tindal Gen Hosp Aylesbury 75-90; R Bledlow w Saunderton and Horsenden *Ox* 90-96; rtd 96. *5 Wyre Close, Haddenham, Aylesbury, Bucks HP17 8AU* Tel (01844) 344762

SHAW, Colin Martin. b 21. Oak Hill Th Coll 68. **d** 69 **p** 70. C Halliwell St Pet *Man* 69-72; V Tonge Fold 72-78; V Gresley *Derby* 78-82; V Gt Marsden *Blackb* 82-87; rtd 87; Perm to Offic *Ely* from 87. *Holborn Close, Huntingdon, Cambs PE17 3AJ* Tel (01487) 822246

SHAW, David George. b 40. Lon Univ BD64. Tyndale Hall Bris 58. **d** 65 **p** 66. C Kirkdale St Lawr *Liv* 65-68; C Bebington *Ches* 68-70; V Swadlincote *Derby* 70-75; R Eyam from 75. *The Rectory, Eyam, Sheffield S30 1QH* Tel (01433) 630821

SHAW, David Michael. b 61. Univ Coll Dur BA83. Trin Coll Bris DipHE93. **d** 93 **p** 94. C Wotton-under-Edge w Ozleworth and N Nibley *Glouc* from 93. *39 Parklands, Wotton-under-Edge, Glos GL12 7LT* Tel (01453) 843945

SHAW, David Parlane. b 32. CITC. **d** 69 **p** 70. Bp's C Lower w Upper Langfield *D & R* 69-75; R Chedburgh w Depden and Rede *St E* 75-78; R Chedburgh w Depden, Rede and Hawkedon 79-82; R Desford *Leic* 82-83; R Desford and Peckleton w Tooley 84-91; P-in-c Ramsden Crays w Ramsden Bellhouse *Chelmsf* 91-95; rtd 95; Perm to Offic *Leic* from 95. *9 Hambleton Close, Leicester Forest East, Leicester LE3 3NA* Tel 0116-239 5591

SHAW, David Thomas. b 45. Open Univ BA78. WMMTC 87. **d** 90 **p** 91. C Sheldon *Birm* 90-93; TR Chelmsley Wood from 93. *The Rectory, Pike Drive, Birmingham B37 7US* Tel 0121-770 5155 or 770 1511

SHAW, Denis. b 26. Westcott Ho Cam. **d** 59 **p** 60. C Bethnal Green St Matt *Lon* 59-63; R Newton Heath St Wilfrid *Man* 63-71; R Clewer St Andr *Ox* 71-92; rtd 92. *The Coach House Cottage, Bedford Place, Bridport, Dorset DT6 3QL* Tel (01308) 421700

SHAW, Denis Alfred Arthur. b 24. Wells Th Coll 64. **d** 65 **p** 66. C Redditch St Steph *Worc* 65-70; R Addingham *Bradf* 70-92; rtd 92; Perm to Offic *Bradf* from 92. *67 Crowther Avenue, Calverley, Pudsey, W Yorkshire LS28 5SA* Tel (01274) 611746

SHAW, Ernest Ronald. b 16. K Coll Lon BA38. Chich Th Coll 72. **d** 72 **p** 73. Chapl Cov Cathl *Cov* 72-78; Perm to Offic *Sarum* 79-80; C Semley and Sedgehill 80-85; rtd 85. *Fairmead, Church Hill, Stour Row, Shaftesbury, Dorset SP7 0QW* Tel (01747) 838350

SHAW, Mrs Felicity Mary. b 46. UEA BSc67 MSc68 Liv Inst of Educn DipRE87. N Ord Course 88. **d** 91 **p** 94. Par Dn Benchill *Man* 91-94; C 94-95; TV E Farnworth and Kearsley from 95. *The Vicarage, 195 Harrowby Street, Farnworth, Bolton BL4 9QU* Tel (01204) 572455

SHAW, Frederick Hugh. b 16. CChem MRSC Dur Univ BSc49 MSc66. EMMTC 73. **d** 76 **p** 77. Hon C Wingerworth *Derby* 76-96; Perm to Offic from 96. *1 Frances Drive, Wingerworth, Chesterfield, Derbyshire S42 6SJ* Tel (01246) 278321

SHAW, Gary Robert. b 59. **d** 85 **p** 86. C Dundonald *D & D* 85-87; I Tullaniskin w Clonoe *Arm* 87-94; Bp's C Stoneyford *Conn* from 94; Chapl R Vic Hosps Belf from 94. *62 Stoneyford Road, Stoneyford, Lisburn, Co Antrim BT28 3SP* Tel (01846) 648300

SHAW, Canon Geoffrey Norman. b 26. Jes Coll Ox MA50. Wycliffe Hall Ox 49. **d** 51 **p** 52. C Rushden *Pet* 51-54; C Woking Ch Ch *Guildf* 54-59; V Woking St Paul 59-62; R St Leonards St Leon *Chich* 62-68; Lic to Offic *Sheff* 68-72; Vice-Prin and Lect Oak Hill Th Coll 72-79; Prin Wycliffe Hall Ox 79-88; Hon Can Ch Ch *Ox* 86-88; rtd 88; Lic to Offic *Nor* 88-91. *15A West Street, Kingham, Chipping Norton, Oxon OX7 6YF* Tel (01608) 658006

SHAW, Gerald Oliver. b 32. K Coll Lon 56. **d** 60 **p** 61. C Burnley St Cuth *Blackb* 60-62; C Heysham 62-65; C-in-c Oswaldtwistle All SS CD 65-66; V Oswaldtwistle All SS 66-69; Chapl Leavesden Hosp Abbots Langley 69-75; Chapl Broadmoor Hosp Crowthorne 75-88; C Easthampstead *Ox* 88-92; P-in-c Beech Hill, Grazeley and Spencers Wood from 92. *The Vicarage, 11 Clares Green Road, Spencers Wood, Reading RG7 1DY* Tel 0118-988 3215

SHAW, Graham. b 44. Worc Coll Ox BA65. Cuddesdon Coll. **d** 69 **p** 70. C Esher *Guildf* 69-73; R Winford *B & W* 73-78; Chapl Ex Coll Ox 78-85; R Farnborough *Roch* 88-95. *7 The Barnyard, Ebbisham Lane, Tadworth, Surrey KT20 7UW* Tel (01737) 812398

SHAW, Grahame David. b 44. Lich Th Coll 65. **d** 68 **p** 69. C Grange St Andr *Ches* 68-73; TV E Runcorn w Halton 73-74; TV Thamesmead *S'wark* 74-79; V Newington St Paul from 79; S'wark Adnry Ecum Officer from 90; RD S'wark and Newington from 96. *The Vicarage, Lorrimore Square, London SE17 3QU* Tel 0171-735 2947 or 735 8815

SHAW, Mrs Irene. b 45. Gilmore Course 80 NE Ord Course 82. **dss** 83 **d** 87 **p** 94. Elloughton and Brough w Brantingham *York* 83-86; Westborough *Guildf* 86-87; C 87-88; C Shottermill 88-91; C Lamorbey H Redeemer *Roch* 91-97; V Belvedere All SS from 97. *All Saints' Vicarage, Nuxley Road, Belvedere, Kent DA17 5JE* Tel (01322) 432169

SHAW, Jack Firth. b 11. Dorchester Miss Coll 35. **d** 38 **p** 39. C Bolsover *Derby* 38-41; C Walthamstow St Sav *Chelmsf* 41-42; Dir (W Midl) ICF and C Bridgtown St Paul 42-45; PC Barrowhill *Derby* 46-50; Chapl St Aug Hosp Cant 50-52; V Maidstone H Trin *Cant* 52-57; Chapl Springfield Hosp Lon 57-59 and 61-64; V Brabourne w Monks Horton and Smeeth *Cant* 59-61; V Merton St Jo *S'wark* 64-76; rtd 77; Perm to Offic *Cant* 79-92. *3 Worcester Drive, Langland, Swansea SA3 4HL* Tel (01792) 368516

SHAW, James Alan. b 20. Keble Coll Ox BA42 MA47. Linc Th Coll 42. **d** 44 **p** 45. C Egremont *Carl* 44-49; C Redditch St Steph *Worc* 49-50; C Wakef Cathl *Wakef* 50-54; Sacr Wakef Cathl 50-54; Asst Master Qu Eliz Gr Sch 54-56; V N Bradley, Southwick and Heywood *Sarum* 56-65; R Flax Bourton *B & W* 65-80; V Barrow Gurney 77-80; Chapl and Lect St Deiniol's Lib Hawarden 80-81; rtd 81; Perm to Offic *Ban* 82-89; Perm to Offic *Mor* from 90. *Ceol na Mara, 25 Dalchalm, Brora, Sutherland KW9 6LP* Tel (01408) 21058

SHAW, Mrs Janet Elaine. b 53. EMMTC 94. **d** 97. C Cleveleys *Blackb* from 97. *58 Stockdove Way, Thornton Cleveleys, Lancs FY5 2AR* Tel (01253) 827744

SHAW, John. b 20. K Coll Lon 57. **d** 59 **p** 60. C Monkseaton St Mary *Newc* 59-62; C Benwell St Jas 62-63; V Burnley St Cuth *Blackb* 63-74; V Goosnargh w Whittingham 74-85; RD Garstang 79-85; rtd 85; Perm to Offic *Newc* from 85. *9 Villiers Road, Woodthorpe, Nottingham NG5 4FB* Tel 0115-960 5108

SHAW, John Reginald Derek. b 32. Sarum Th Coll 57. **d** 59 **p** 60. C Thornbury *Bradf* 59-61; C Tong 62-63; C Clifford *York* 63-65; V Bramham from 65. *The Vicarage, Vicarage Lane, Bramham, Wetherby, W Yorkshire LS23 6QG* Tel (01937) 843631

SHAW, John Richard Astley. b 24. St Jo Coll Dur 46. ACT ThL53. **d** 51 **p** 53. Australia 51-55; C Braunstone *Leic* 55-57; R Rearsby w Ratcliffe on the Wreake 57-65; R Guernsey St Marguerite de la Foret *Win* 65-90; rtd 90. *St Antony, Clos de Cornus, St Martin's, Guernsey, Channel Islands* Tel (01481) 37097

SHAW, Kenneth James. b 36. St Jo Coll Nottm 85 Edin Th Coll 88. **d** 87 **p** 89. NSM Troon *Glas* 87-89; C Glas St Mary 89-90; R Lenzie from 90. *The Rectory, 1A Beech Road, Lenzie, Glasgow G66 4HN* Tel 0141-776 4149

SHAW, Michael Howard. b 38. Leeds Univ BSc61. Linc Th Coll 64. **d** 66 **p** 67. C W Hartlepool St Paul *Dur* 66-68; Asst Master Stockbridge Co Sec Sch 68; Totton Coll 69; Gravesend Boys' Gr Sch 70-72; Maidstone Gr Sch from 72; Perm to Offic *Roch* from 82. *2 Bredgar Close, Maidstone, Kent ME14 5NG* Tel (01622) 673415

SHAW, Neil Graham. b 61. St Jo Coll Nottm LTh89. **d** 91 **p** 92. C Leamington Priors St Paul *Cov* 91-95; TV Bestwood *S'well* from 95. *St Matthews Vicarage, Padstow Road, Bestwood, Nottingham NG5 5GH* Tel 0115-927 6107

SHAW, Norman. b 33. Cranmer Hall Dur. **d** 82 **p** 83. C Beamish *Dur* 82-84; P-in-c Craghead 84-88; V Cleadon from 88. *The Vicarage, 5 Sunderland Road, Sunderland SR6 7UR* Tel 0191-536 7147

SHAW, Peter Haslewood. b 17. Pemb Coll Cam BA39 MA65. Worc Ord Coll 65. **d** 67 **p** 68. C S Kensington St Jude *Lon* 67-69; V Alderney *Win* 69-78; V Disley *Ches* 78-82; rtd 82; Chapl Athens w Kifissia, Patras and Corfu *Eur* 82-85; Hon C Las Palmas 84-85; Hon C Breamore *Win* 85-89. *Manor Cottage, Church Road, Greatworth, Banbury, Oxon OX17 2DU* Tel (01295) 712102

SHAW, Ralph. b 38. Man Univ MEd70. Sarum & Wells Th Coll 78. **d** 80 **p** 81. C Consett *Dur* 80-84; P-in-c Tanfield 84-88; V from 88. *The Vicarage, Tanfield, Stanley, Co Durham DH9 9PX* Tel (01207) 232750

SHAW, Ralph Michael. b 45. DipAdEd. Lich Th Coll 68. **d** 70 **p** 71. C Dewsbury All SS *Wakef* 70-75; TV Redcar w Kirkleatham *York* 75-76; Dioc Youth Officer *St Alb* 76-91; Lic to Offic from 91; Chief Exec Jo Grooms Assn for the Disabled from 91. *Welwyn, 18 Wyton Road, Welwyn Garden City, Herts AL7 2PF* Tel (01707) 321813 Fax 0181-809 1754

SHAW, Richard Tom. b 42. AKC69. St Aug Coll Cant 69. **d** 70 **p** 71. C Dunston St Nic *Dur* 70-73; C Maidstone All SS w St Phil and H Trin *Cant* 73-75; Chapl RN 75-79; V Barrow-on-Humber *Linc* 79-83; V Linc St Faith and St Martin w St Pet 83-91; V Clun w Bettws-y-Crwyn and Newcastle *Heref* from 91; RD Clun Forest from 94. *The Vicarage, Vicarage Road, Clun, Craven Arms, Shropshire SY7 8JG* Tel (01588) 640809

SHAW, Robert Christopher. b 34. Man Univ BA BD. Union Th Sem (NY) STM. **d** 82 **p** 83. C Sharlston *Wakef* 82-83; C Scissett St Aug 83-85; R Cumberworth w Denby Dale 85-90; P-in-c Denby 85-90; R Bolton w Ireby and Uldale *Carl* 90-95; rtd 95. *Stonecroft, Sproxton, York YO6 5EF* Tel (01439) 770178

SHAW, Robert William. b 46. Lon Univ BD69. St Aug Coll Cant 69. **d** 70 **p** 71. C Hunslet St Mary and Stourton *Ripon* 70-71; C Hunslet St Mary 71-74; C Hawksworth Wood 74-76; R Stanningley St Thos 76-84; V Potternewton 84-94; V Manston from 94. *Manston Vicarage, Church Lane, Leeds LS15 8JB* Tel 0113-260 0348 or 264 5530

SHAW, Roderick Kenneth. b 37. MBIM77. Moray Ord Course 88. **d** 92 **p** 95. Hon C Grantown-on-Spey *Mor* 92-96; Hon C Rothiemurchus from 92. *The Cottage, Balliefurth, Grantown-on-Spey, Morayshire PH26 3NH* Tel (01479) 821496

SHAW, Ronald Forbes. b 16. FRICS55 RIBA47. S'wark Ord Course 67. **d** 70 **p** 71. C Belmont *S'wark* 70-73; P-in-c Lower Sydenham St Mich 73-83; rtd 83; Hon C Surbiton St Matt *S'wark* 83-88; Hon C Kingswood from 88. *6 St Andrews Close, Reigate, Surrey RH2 7JF* Tel (01737) 246290

SHAW, Mrs Rosemary Alice. b 44. CertEd65 DipTh75 CQSW78. S'wark Ord Course 87. **d** 89 **p** 94. Par Dn Walworth *S'wark* 89-92; Par Dn E Dulwich St Jo 92-95; NSM 95-96; Eileen Kerr Mental Health Fellow Maudsley Hosp 95-96; Chapl King's Healthcare NHS Trust from 96. *King's College Hospital, London SE5 9PJ* Tel 0171-346 3522

SHAYLER-WEBB, Peter. b 57. Bath Univ BSc81 BArch83. Ripon Coll Cuddesdon 93. **d** 95 **p** 96. C Bedford St Paul *St Alb* from 95. *54 The Grove, Bedford MK40 3JN* Tel (01234) 218563

SHEA, Guy Roland John. b 33. Trin Coll Connecticut BA55 Ch Ch Ox BA58 MA62. Coll of Resurr Mirfield 60. **d** 60 **p** 61. C Kennington St Jo *S'wark* 60-63 and 75-77; C N Audley Street St Mark *Lon* 63-67; C Hammersmith St Sav 67-70; P-in-c Gunnersbury St Jas 70-75; Perm to Offic 77-82; Hon C Fulham St Alb 82-92; Hon C Fulham St Alb w St Aug from 92. *c/o St Alban's Vicarage, 4 Margravine Road, London W6 8HJ* Tel 0171-385 0724

SHEAD, John Frederick Henry. b 38. ACP74 FCP81. Westcott Ho Cam 72. **d** 74 **p** 75. Hd Master Thaxted Co Primary Sch 70-85; Hon C Thaxted *Chelmsf* 74-85; C Saffron Walden w Wendens Ambo and Littlebury 86-88; P-in-c Wethersfield w Shalford 88-96; P-in-c Finchingfield and Cornish Hall End 94-96; RD Braintree from 95; V Finchingfield and Cornish Hall End etc from 96. *The Vicarage, Finchingfield, Braintree, Essex CM7 4JR* Tel (01371) 810309

SHEARCROFT, Sister Elizabeth Marion. b 57. **d** 94 **p** 95. NSM Margate H Trin *Cant* from 94; Chapl Thanet Healthcare NHS Trust from 94. *Queen Elizabeth the Queen Mother Hospital, St Peter's Road, Margate, Kent CT9 4AN* Tel (01843) 290826 or 225544

SHEARD, Andrew Frank. b 60. York Univ BA81. St Jo Coll Nottm 92. **d** 94 **p** 95. C Uxbridge *Lon* 94-96; TV from 96. *St Andrew's Vicarage, The Greenway, Uxbridge, Middx UB8 2PJ* Tel (01895) 237853

SHEARD, Ernest. b 29. Linc Th Coll 73. **d** 74 **p** 75. Hon C Birstall *Leic* 74-82; Hon C Birstall and Wanlip 82-84; Asst Chapl Loughb Univ and Colls 75-90; Lic to Offic *Leic* from 90. *21 Orchard Road, Birstall, Leicester LE4 4GD* Tel 0116-267 3901

SHEARD, Gillian Freda. *See* COOKE, Ms Gillian Freda

SHEARD, Dr Michael Rowland. b 42. K Coll Lon BA Man Univ PhD. **d** 95 **p** 95. *68 Sneyd Lane, Essington, Wolverhampton WV11 2DH* Tel (01922) 475915

SHEARD, Neil Jeremy. b 58. Chich Th Coll. **d** 84 **p** 85. C Gelligaer *Llan* 84-86; C Caerphilly 86-90; V Treboeth *S & B* from 90. *St Alban's Vicarage, Heol Fach, Treboeth, Swansea SA5 9DE* Tel (01792) 771332

SHEARER, The Very Revd John. b 26. OBE94. TCD BA48 MA53 BD53. **d** 50 **p** 51. C Magheralin w Dollingstown *D & D* 50-52; C Ballymacarrett St Patr 52-59; I Magheradroll 59-64; I Seagoe 64-85; Adn Dromore 70-85; I Belfast St Anne *Conn* from 85;

Dean Belf from 85. *The Deanery, 5 Deramore Drive, Belfast BT9 5JQ* Tel (01232) 660980 or 328332 Fax 238855

SHEARER, John Frank. b 35. Ex Univ BSc60. Tyndale Hall Bris 62. **d** 63 **p** 64. C Blackheath St Jo *S'wark* 63-67; R Nuff *Ox* from 67. *The Rectory, Nuffield, Henley-on-Thames, Oxon RG9 5SN* Tel (01491) 641305

SHEARING, Michael James. b 39. Lanc Univ BA71. Linc Th Coll. **d** 66 **p** 67. Hon C Hartlepool St Paul *Dur* 66-76; Asst Master Dyke Ho Comp Sch Hartlepool 76-87; C Houghton le Spring 87; P-in-c Wheatley Hill 87-95; V Bishopwearmouth St Nic 95-97; R Cockfield from 97; V Lynesack from 97. *The Rectory, Cockfield, Bishop Auckland, Co Durham DL13 5AA* Tel (01388) 718447

SHEARLOCK, The Very Revd David John. b 32. FRSA91 Birm Univ BA55. Westcott Ho Cam 56. **d** 57 **p** 58. C Guisborough *York* 57-60; C Christchurch *Win* 60-64; V Kingsclere 64-71; V Romsey 71-82; Dioc Dir of Ords 77-82; Hon Can Win Cathl 78-82; Dean Truro from 82; R Truro St Mary from 82; Chapl Cornwall Fire Brigade from 91. *The Deanery, Lemon Street, Truro, Cornwall TR1 2PE* Tel (01872) 72661 or 76782 Fax 77788

SHEARMAN, Michael Alan. b 22. Down Coll Cam BA44 MA48. Coll of Resurr Mirfield 46. **d** 48 **p** 49. C Bounds Green *Lon* 48-53; C Wembley Park St Aug 53-58; V Enfield St Luke 58-87; rtd 87; Perm to Offic *Nor* from 87. *18 Thompson Avenue, Holt, Norfolk NR25 6EN* Tel (01263) 713072

SHEARS, Canon Michael George Frederick. b 33. Pemb Coll Cam BA57 MA68. St Steph Ho Ox 57. **d** 59 **p** 60. C Grantham St Wulfram *Linc* 59-68; R Waltham 68-80; R Barnoldby le Beck 74-80; RD Haverstoe 78-80; V Soham *Ely* from 80; RD Fordham 83-95; Hon Can Ely Cathl from 94. *The Vicarage, Soham, Ely, Cambs CB7 5DU* Tel (01353) 720423

SHEARWOOD, Alexander George Dobbie. b 21. New Coll Ox BA48. Wells Th Coll 49. **d** 50 **p** 51. C Walworth St Jo *S'wark* 50-52; C Kennington Cross St Anselm 52-57; Asst Chapl Beecholme Residential Sch 57-59; C Nork *Guildf* 57-59; R Wickenby w Friesthorpe *Linc* 59-81; R Lissington w Holton cum Beckering 60-81; R Snelland w Snarford 63-81; R Wickenby Gp 82; Perm to Offic *Truro* from 82; rtd 86. *Trelowen, 3 Old Road, Boscastle, Cornwall PL35 0AJ* Tel (01840) 250663

SHEASBY, Adrian. b 29. Open Univ BA89. St Aid Birkenhead 54. **d** 57 **p** 58. C Foleshill St Paul *Cov* 57-60; C Pet St Jo *Pet* 60-65; V Maxey w Northborough 65-94; rtd 94; Perm to Offic *Linc* from 94; Perm to Offic *Pet* from 94. *26 Beech Close, Market Deeping, Peterborough PE6 8LL* Tel (01778) 347581

SHEDDEN, Mrs Valerie. b 56. Ripon Coll of Educn CertEd77. Cranmer Hall Dur 81. **dss** 84 **d** 87 **p** 94. Tudhoe Grange *Dur* 84-85; Whitworth w Spennymoor 85-87; Par Dn 87-91; Par Dn E Darlington 91-94; TV 94; P-in-c Bishop Middleham from 94; Dioc RE Adv from 94. *1 Broad Oaks, Bishop Middleham, Ferryhill, Co Durham DL17 9BW* Tel (01740) 654591

SHEEHY, Jeremy Patrick. b 56. Magd Coll Ox BA78 MA81 New Coll Ox DPhil90. St Steph Ho Ox 78. **d** 81 **p** 82. C Erdington St Barn *Birm* 81-83; C Small Heath St Greg 83-84; Dean Div, Fell and Chapl New Coll Ox 84-90; V Leytonstone St Marg w St Columba *Chelmsf* 90-96; P-in-c Leytonstone St Andr 93-96; Prin St Steph Ho Ox from 96. *St Stephen's House, 16 Marston Street, Oxford OX4 1JX* Tel (01865) 247874 Fax 794338

SHEEKEY, Raymond Arthur. b 23. Chich Th Coll 51. **d** 53 **p** 54. C Ramsgate St Geo *Cant* 53-56; C Birchington w Acol 56-61; V Brabourne w Smeeth 61-79; RD N Lympne 75-78; Chapl Lenham Hosp 79-88; R Lenham w Boughton Malherbe 79-88; rtd 88; Perm to Offic *Bris* from 88. *Rosewell Cottage, Leighterton, Tetbury, Glos GL8 8UJ* Tel (01666) 890268

SHEEN, Canon John Harold. b 32. Qu Coll Cam BA54 MA58. Cuddesdon Coll 56. **d** 58 **p** 59. C Stepney St Dunstan and All SS *Lon* 58-62; V Tottenham St Jo 62-68; V Wood Green St Mich 68-78; P-in-c Southgate St Mich 77-78; R Bride *S & M* 78-97; Chapl Ramsey Cottage Hosp from 80; V Lezayre St Olave Ramsey from 80; RD Ramsey from 88; Can St German's Cathl from 91; Dir of Ords from 93. *The Rectory, Kirk Bride, Ramsey, Isle of Man IM7 4AT* Tel (01624) 880351

SHEEN, Canon Victor Alfred. b 17. Tyndale Hall Bris 47. **d** 49 **p** 50. Uganda 49-56; C Cheltenham St Mark *Glouc* 56-58; V W Streatham St Jas *S'wark* 58-65; V Clapham St Jas 65-86; RD Clapham and Brixton 75-82 and 85-86; Hon Can S'wark Cathl 80-86; rtd 86; Perm to Offic *Chich* from 86. *10 Porters Way, Polegate, E Sussex BN26 6AP* Tel (01323) 487487

SHEERAN, Canon Ernest William. b 17. St Aid Birkenhead 47. **d** 50 **p** 51. C Aspley *S'well* 50-52; C W Bridgford 52-55; V Edwalton 55-86; RD Bingham S 68-86; Hon Can S'well Minster 72-86; rtd 86; Perm to Offic *S'well* from 86. *Brodick, 20 Taunton Road, Nottingham NG2 6EW* Tel 0115-923 1895

SHEFFIELD, Michael Julian (Mike). b 53. Brentwood Coll of Educn CertEd. Sarum & Wells Th Coll 76. **d** 79 **p** 80. C Locks Heath *Portsm* 79-83; C Waterlooville 83; C Ryde All SS 83-86; P-in-c Ryde H Trin 86-92; V 92-96; P-in-c Swanmore St Mich w Havenstreet 86-92; V Swanmore St Mich and All Angels 92-96; V W Leigh from 96. *St Alban's Vicarage, Martin Road, Havant, Hants PO9 5ET* Tel (01705) 451751 Fax as telephone

SHEFFIELD, Archdeacon of. *See* LOWE, The Ven Stephen Richard

SHEFFIELD, Bishop of. *See* NICHOLLS, The Rt Revd John

SHEFFIELD, Provost of. *See* SADGROVE, The Very Revd Michael

SHEGOG, Preb Eric Marshall. b 37. Lon Univ DipTh60 City Univ MA88 FRSA92. Lich Th Coll 64. **d** 65 **p** 66. C Benhilton *S'wark* 65-68; Asst Youth Adv 68-70; V Abbey Wood 70-76; Chapl Sunderland Town Cen 76-83; C Bishopwearmouth St Mich w St Hilda *Dur* 76-83; Hd Relig Broadcasting IBA 84-90; Perm to Offic *Lon* 85-90; Perm to Offic *St Alb* 85-89; Hon C Harpenden St Nic 89-97; Dir Communications for C of E 90-97; Dioc Communications Officer *Lon* from 97; Preb St Paul's Cathl from 97. *73A Gloucester Place, London W1H 3PF* Tel 0171-487 4814

SHEILD, Canon Edward Oscar. b 10. Univ of NZ LLB33 Qu Coll Ox BA36 MA40 BD82. **d** 36 **p** 37. C Fallowfield *Man* 36-39; New Zealand 39-46; Tutor Cuddesdon Coll 46-49; Lic to Offic *Ox* 46-58; Lic Preacher *Man* 49-58; Dioc Miss 49-58; Hon Can Man Cathl 54-58; Dean Singapore 58-64; V Chapel Allerton *Ripon* 64-75; rtd 75; Perm to Offic *Carl* from 75; P-in-c Coldstream *Edin* 77-79. *Midtown Cottage, Askham, Penrith, Cumbria CA10 2PF* Tel (01931) 712427

SHELDON, John Gordon. b 22. Trin Coll Cam BA43 MA44. Ridley Hall Cam 43. **d** 45 **p** 46. C Morden *S'wark* 45-49; Cand Sec CPAS 49-51; V Beckenham St Jo *Roch* 51-57; V Worthing St Geo *Chich* 57-62; V Lindfield 62-80; P-in-c Cowden *Roch* 80-81; R Cowden w Hammerwood *Chich* 81-87; rtd 87; Perm to Offic *B & W* from 87. *Portland Cottage, Thornhill, Stalbridge, Sturminster Newton, Dorset DT10 2SJ* Tel (01963) 362469

SHELDON, Jonathan Mark Robin. b 59. Cam Univ MA83. Ridley Hall Cam 81. **d** 83 **p** 84. C Dulwich St Barn *S'wark* 83-86; C Worle *B & W* 86-88; V Chesterton St Andr *Ely* 88-97. *13 Grove Road, Rushden, Northants NN10 0JX* Tel (01933) 317268

SHELLEY, Derrick Sydney David. b 38. Lon Univ LLB60 AKC65. Linc Th Coll. **d** 68 **p** 69. C Weybridge *Guildf* 68-72; Chapl Red Bank Schs 72-77; Lic to Offic *Blackb* 80-97; NSM Lytham St Cuth 80-97; rtd 97. *Penwiel Cocks, Perranporth, Truro, Cornwall PL26 0AT*

SHELLEY, George. b 18. Qu Coll Birm 56. **d** 57 **p** 58. C Boscombe St Andr *Win* 57-60; Oxfam 60-67; Miss to Seamen 67-71; R Gt Ringstead *Nor* 71-77; P-in-c Sedgeford w Southmere 71-77; P-in-c Gateshead St Jas *Dur* 77-78; R 78-82; rtd 82; Perm to Offic *Nor* from 82. *18 Burnt Hills, Cromer, Norfolk NR27 9LW* Tel (01263) 512957

SHELLEY, Robin Arthur. b 34. CEng MIMechE. St Jo Coll Nottm 85. **d** 87 **p** 88. C Countesthorpe w Foston *Leic* 87-90; V Enderby w Lubbesthorpe and Thurlaston from 90. *The Rectory, 16A Desford Road, Thurlaston, Leicester LE9 7TE* Tel (01445) 888488

SHELLOCK, Norman Stanley. b 15. ATCL53 Dur Univ LTh38. St Aug Coll Cant 34. **d** 38 **p** 39. C Biscot *St Alb* 38-41; Br Guiana 41-59; Area Sec (Dios Ely and St E) USPG 59-80; rtd 80; Perm to Offic *Nor* from 80; Perm to Offic *St E* from 81; Perm to Offic *Ely* from 81. *24 Runnymede Green, Bury St Edmunds, Suffolk IP33 2LH* Tel (01284) 703506

SHELLS, Canon Charles Harry. b 15. St Chad's Coll Dur BA38 MA43. **d** 39 **p** 40. C Almondbury *Wakef* 39-42; C Camberwell St Geo *S'wark* 42-47; V Newington St Paul 47-54; V Wandsworth St Anne 54-65; RD Wandsworth 63-65; R Trunch w Swafield *Nor* 65-71; R Bradfield 65-71; P-in-c Gimingham 65-71; P-in-c Trimingham 65-71; P-in-c Antingham w Thorpe Market 65-71; P-in-c Felmingham 65-68; P-in-c Suffield 65-68; P-in-c Gunton St Pet 65-71; RD Tunstead 65-68; Can Res Bris Cathl *Bris* 71-81; rtd 81; Lic to Offic *B & W* from 81; Lic to Offic *Sarum* from 81; Perm to Offic *Bris* from 81. *13 Dod Lane, Glastonbury, Somerset BA6 8BZ* Tel (01458) 832052

SHELTON, Ian Robert. b 52. BEd74 Lon Univ MA79. Ripon Coll Cuddesdon BA81 MA90. **d** 82 **p** 83. C Wath-upon-Dearne w Adwick-upon-Dearne *Sheff* 82-86; TV Grantham *Linc* 86-93; P-in-c Waltham from 93; P-in-c Barnoldby le Beck from 93. *The Rectory, 95 High Street, Waltham, Grimsby, S Humberside DN37 0PN* Tel (01472) 822172

SHENTON, Brian. b 43. Chich Th Coll 73. **d** 75 **p** 76. C Mill Hill Jo Keble Ch *Lon* 75-78; C New Windsor *Ox* 78-81; TV 81-82; P-in-c Cherbury 82-83; V Calcot 83-89; R Reading St Mary w St Laur from 89; RD Reading from 95; P-in-c Reading St Matt from 96. *39 Downshire Square, Reading RG1 6NH* Tel 0118-957 1738 or 957 1057

SHENTON, David. b 57. Aston Tr Scheme 91 Ripon Coll Cuddesdon DipMin95. **d** 95 **p** 96. C Thurmaston *Leic* from 95. *118 Dovedale Road, Thurmaston, Leicester LE4 8ND* Tel 0116-269 5440

SHEPHARD, Brian Edward. b 34. Magd Coll Cam BA56 MA60 Ox Univ DipPSA60 CertEd71 HDipRE71. Wycliffe Hall Ox 58. **d** 60 **p** 61. C Wigan St Cath *Liv* 60-62; C Kidderminster St Geo *Worc* 62-65; Lect CA Tr Coll Blackheath 65-70; Lect Hamilton Coll of Educn 70-77; Perm to Offic *Glas* 70-77; Chapl Buchan Sch Castletown 77-88; Lic to Offic *S & M* 77-88; Lic to Offic *S'wark* 88-89; Tutor CA Wilson Carlile Coll of Evang 88-89; C Andreas St Jude *S & M* 89-91; C Jurby 89-91; V Lezayre from 91. *The Vicarage, Lezayre, Ramsey, Isle of Man IM7 2AN* Tel (01624) 812500

SHEPHEARD-WALWYN, John. b 16. Or Coll Ox BA38 MA44. Wells Th Coll 38. **d** 40 **p** 42. C Roch St Pet w St Marg *Roch* 41-44; C Lamorbey H Redeemer 44-49; C Edenbridge 49-56; V Rosherville 56-61; R Horwood *Ex* 61-78; V Westleigh 61-78; P-in-c Harberton w Harbertonford 78-82; rtd 82; Perm to Offic *Bris* from 82. *12 Luccombe Hill, Bristol BS6 6SN* Tel 0117-973 1261

SHEPHERD, Anthony Michael. b 50. Em Coll Cam BA72 MA76. Westcott Ho Cam 72. **d** 74 **p** 75. C Folkestone St Mary and St Eanswythe *Cant* 74-79; Bp's Dom Chapl *Ripon* 79-87; Dioc Communications Officer 79-87; V High Harrogate St Pet from 87. *St Peter's Vicarage, 13 Beech Grove, Harrogate, N Yorkshire HG2 0ET* Tel (01423) 500901

SHEPHERD, Christopher Francis Pleydell. b 44. St Steph Ho Ox 68. **d** 69 **p** 70. C Milber *Ex* 69-72; C Ex St Thos 72-74; TV Ilfracombe, Lee and W Down 74-78; TV Ilfracombe, Lee, W Down, Woolacombe and Bittadon 78-80; P-in-c Tregony w St Cuby and Cornelly *Truro* 80-83; R 83-96. *The Rectory, Tregony, Truro, Cornwall TR2 5SE* Tel (01872) 530507

SHEPHERD, David. b 42. St Jo Coll Dur BA65 MA68 MLitt76. Edin Th Coll 66. **d** 68 **p** 69. Chapl St Paul's Cathl Dundee *Bre* 68-79; Chapl Dundee Univ 73-79; R Dundee St Mary Magd from 79. *14 Albany Terrace, Dundee DD3 6HR* Tel (01382) 223510

SHEPHERD, David Mark. b 59. Reading Univ BA81 Nottm Univ BTh86. Linc Th Coll 83. **d** 86 **p** 87. C Wilmslow *Ches* 86-89; C Bromborough 89-92; V Leasowe from 92. *St Chad's Vicarage, 123 Reeds Lane, Wirral, Merseyside L46 1QT* Tel 0151-677 6550

SHEPHERD, Ernest John Heatley. b 27. TCD BA48 BD53. **d** 50 **p** 51. C Belfast St Mary Magd *Conn* 50-54; I Whitehouse 54-96; Can Conn Cathl 86-90; Co-ord Aux Min 87-96; Treas Conn Cathl 90; Prec Conn Cathl 90-96; rtd 96. *15 Downshire Gardens, Carrickfergus, Co Antrim BT38 7LW* Tel (01960) 362243

SHEPHERD, Miss Jayne Elizabeth. b 57. Reading Univ BA78. Cranmer Hall Dur 79. **dss** 82 **d** 87 **p** 94. Wombourne *Lich* 82-85; Harlescott 85-87; Par Dn 87-90; Chapl Asst Qu Medical Cen Nottm Univ Hosp NHS Trust 90-97; Asst Chapl Nottm Healthcare NHS Trust 90-97; Chapl Pet Hosps NHS Trust from 97. *Peterborough District Hospital, Thorpe Road, Peterborough PE3 6DA* Tel (01733) 874000

SHEPHERD, Mrs Joan Francis Fleming. b 45. RGN66. **dss** 84 **d** 86 **p** 94. NSM Ellon *Ab* from 84; NSM Cruden Bay from 84; Bp's Chapl for Tr and Educn from 95. *8 Ythan Court, Ellon, Aberdeenshire AB41 9BL* Tel (01358) 723241

SHEPHERD, John Donald. b 33. Cranmer Hall Dur BA59 DipTh61. **d** 61 **p** 62. C Dewsbury All SS *Wakef* 61-63; C Chapelthorpe 63-66; V Stainland 66-70; Dioc Youth Chapl *Truro* 70-74; V Newquay 74-84; RD Pydar 81-84; Chapl Borocourt Mental Handicap Hosp 84-95; TR Langtree *Ox* 84-95. *21 Sparkham Close, Shrewsbury SY3 6BX* Tel (01743) 244453

SHEPHERD, The Very Revd John Harley. b 42. Melbourne Univ BA66 ThL68 Cam Univ PhD80. Union Th Sem (NY) MSacMus72. **d** 67 **p** 68. Australia 67-70 and from 88; C Stretford St Matt *Man* 71; USA 72-77; C Cherry Hinton St Andr *Ely* 78-80; Chapl Ch Ch Ox 80-88; Chapl Univ W Australia 88-90; Dean Perth from 90. *The Deanery, 50 Mount Street, Perth, W Australia 6000* Tel Perth (9) 322 7265 or 325 5766 Fax 221 4289

SHEPHERD, John Martin. b 68. St Jo Coll Cam BA90. Oak Hill Th Coll BA93. **d** 96 **p** 97. C Rusholme H Trin *Man* from 96. *2 The Grange, Manchester M14 5NY* Tel 0161-256 3718

SHEPHERD, John Michael. b 42. BNC Ox BA63 MA72. Coll of Resurr Mirfield 64. **d** 66 **p** 67. C Clapham H Spirit *S'wark* 66-69; C Kingston All SS 69-72; V Upper Tooting H Trin 73-80; V Wandsworth St Paul 80-90; P-in-c Mitcham SS Pet and Paul 90-92; V from 92; RD Merton from 96. *21 Church Road, Mitcham, Surrey CR4 3BE* Tel 0181-648 1566

SHEPHERD, John William. b 20. S'wark Ord Course 67. **d** 70 **p** 71. C Leighton Buzzard *St Alb* 70-77; P-in-c Studham w Whipsnade 77-80; V 80-82; P-in-c Kensworth 82; V Kensworth, Studham and Whipsnade 82-86; rtd 86; Asst Chapl Costa Blanca *Eur* 86-89. *24 Church Road, Studham, Dunstable, Beds LU6 2QA* Tel (01582) 872298

SHEPHERD, Keith Frederick. b 42. EMMTC 86. **d** 89 **p** 90. Hon C Stocking Farm *Leic* 89-94; P-in-c Church Langton w Tur Langton, Thorpe Langton etc from 94. *The Rectory, Stonton Road, Church Langton, Market Harborough, Leics LE16 7SZ* Tel (01858) 545740

SHEPHERD, Peter James. b 38. Dur Univ BA64. Ridley Hall Cam 64. **d** 66 **p** 67. C Luton Ch Ch *Roch* 66-70; C Belvedere All SS 70-71; C Wisley w Pyrford *Guildf* 71-75; V Thorney Abbey *Ely* 75-85; V Yaxley 85-93; RD Yaxley 88-92; P-in-c Feltwell 93-95; rtd 96. *51 Middlefield Road, Sawtry, Huntingdon, Cambs PE17 5SH* Tel (01487) 834084

SHEPHERD, Peter William. b 48. DASE Reading Univ BA71 Lon Univ BD80 Brighton Poly MPhil87 Lanc Univ MA94. Chich Th Coll 77. **d** 80 **p** 81. NSM Eastbourne St Sav and St Pet *Chich* 80-83; Hd Master Wm Temple Sch Preston 83-88; NSM Clitheroe St Mary *Blackb* from 83; Hd Master Canon Slade Sch Bolton from 89; Perm to Offic *Man* from 89. *Homestead, Eastham Street, Clitheroe, Lancs BB7 2HY* Tel (01200) 25053

SHEPHERD, Thomas. b 52. SRN74 Man Univ BA79 Didsbury Coll Man PGCE83. N Ord Course 92. **d** 95 **p** 96. C Baguley *Man* from 95. *39 Dalebrook Road, Sale, Cheshire M33 3LD* Tel 0161-905 1219

SHEPHERD, Timothy Roy. b 34. Selw Coll Cam BA58. Linc Th Coll 62. **d** 64 **p** 65. C Selly Oak St Mary *Birm* 64-67; C Stockland Green 67-72; V Perry Common 72-76; V Holton-le-Clay *Linc* 76-84; V Habrough Gp 84-93; P-in-c Uffington 93-95; R Uffington Gp from 95. *The Rectory, 67 Main Road, Uffington, Stamford, Lincs PE9 4SN* Tel (01780) 481786

✠**SHEPPARD, The Rt Revd David Stuart.** b 29. Trin Hall Cam BA53 MA56. Ridley Hall Cam 53. **d** 55 **p** 56 **c** 69. C Islington St Mary *Lon* 55-58; Chapl and Warden Mayflower Family Cen Canning Town *Chelmsf* 58-69; Suff Bp Woolwich *S'wark* 69-75; Bp Liv 75-97; rtd 97. *11 Melloncroft Drive, West Kirby, Wirral, Merseyside L48 2JA*

SHEPPARD, Ian Arthur Lough. b 33. Sarum & Wells Th Coll 71. **d** 74 **p** 75. C Bishop's Cleeve *Glouc* 74-77; Chapl RAF 77-81; V Gosberton *Linc* 81-87; V Leven Valley *Carl* 87-90; Deputation and Gen Appeals Org Children's Soc from 90; Perm to Offic *Dur* from 95. *57 Seymour Grove, Eaglescliffe, Stockton-on-Tees, Cleveland TS16 0LE* Tel (01642) 790777

SHEPPARD, Martin. b 37. Hertf Coll Ox BA61 MA65. Chich Th Coll 63. **d** 65 **p** 66. C N Hull St Mich *York* 65-68; C Hove St Jo *Chich* 68-71; V Heathfield St Rich 71-77; V New Shoreham 77-94; V Old Shoreham 77-94; TR Rye from 94; RD Rye from 95. *St Mary's Rectory, Gungarden, Rye, E Sussex TN31 7HH* Tel (01797) 222430

SHEPPARD, Norman George. b 32. Wolv Teacher Tr Coll CertEd73. St D Coll Lamp 57. **d** 59 **p** 60. C Burry Port and Pwll *St D* 59-64; SAMS 64-68; Chile 64-68; C Madeley *Heref* 68-69; Asst Master Madeley Court Sch 73-75; Gilbert Inglefield Sch Leighton Buzzard 75-80; USPG 80-81; Argentina from 80; rtd 95. *Santa Rosa 1650, Vincente Lopez, Province of Buenos Aires, Argentina* Tel Buenos Aires (1) 797-9748

SHEPPARD, Stanley Gorton. b 18. St Jo Coll Dur 46. **d** 62 **p** 63. C Leic St Mark *Leic* 62-65; R Cole Orton 65-75; V Ashby Folville and Twyford w Thorpe Satchville 75-88; rtd 88; Perm to Offic *Ex* from 89. *1 Peak Coach House, Cotmaton Road, Sidmouth, Devon EX10 8SY* Tel (01395) 516124

SHEPTON, Robert Leonard McIntyre (Bob). b 35. Jes Coll Cam BA58 MA61. Oak Hill Th Coll 59. **d** 61 **p** 62. C Weymouth St Jo *Sarum* 61-63; Boys' Ldr Cam Univ Miss Bermondsey 63-66; Warden Ox-Kilburn Club 66-69; Chapl St D Coll Llandudno 69-77; Chief Instructor Carnoch Outdoor Cen 77-80; Chapl Kingham Hill Sch Oxon 80-92; rtd 92. *Innisfree, Appin, Argyll PA38 4DA* Tel (01631) 730437

SHERBORNE, Archdeacon of. *See* WHEATLEY, The Ven Paul Charles

SHERBORNE, Area Bishop of. *See* KIRKHAM, The Rt Revd John Dudley Galtrey

SHERGOLD, William Frank. b 19. St Chad's Coll Dur BA40 MA47. Coll of Resurr Mirfield 40. **d** 42 **p** 43. C Poplar All SS w St Frideswide *Lon* 42-49; V Hanworth All SS 49-58; V Hackney Wick St Mary of Eton w St Aug 59-64; V Paddington St Mary 64-69; V Charlton-by-Dover St Bart *Cant* 69-72; P-in-c Charlton-by-Dover SS Pet and Paul 70-72; R Charlton-in-Dover 72-78; R Tunstall 78-83; rtd 84; TV Poplar *Lon* 84; Hon C 84-92; Perm to Offic *Chich* from 92. *6 College Gardens, Brighton BN2 1HP* Tel (01273) 696174

SHERIDAN, Mrs Deborah Jane. b 47. ALA73 Kent Univ BA69. WMMTC 90. **d** 93 **p** 94. NSM Lich St Chad *Lich* from 93. *45 High Grange, Lichfield, Staffs WS13 7DU* Tel (01543) 264363

SHERIDAN, Peter. b 37. Saltley Tr Coll Birm CertEd59 Leic Poly BEd82. N Ord Course 89. **d** 92 **p** 93. NSM Braunstone *Leic* 92-95; NSM Ratby w Groby from 95; NSM Newtown Linford from 95. *The Vicarage, 554 Bradgate Road, Newtown Linford, Leicester LE6 0HB* Tel (01530) 242955

SHERIFF (née WORRALL), Mrs Suzanne. b 63. Trin Coll Bris BA86. **d** 87 **p** 94. Par Dn Kingston upon Hull St Nic *York* 87-91; Par Dn Kingston upon Hull St Aid Southcoates 91-94; C 94-96; TV Marfleet from 96. *256 Annandale Road, Greatfield Estate, Hull HU9 4JY* Tel (01482) 799100

SHERLEY-PRICE, Lionel Digby (Leo). b 11. SS Coll Cam BA32 MA36. Chich Th Coll 33. **d** 34 **p** 35. C Ryde All SS *Portsm* 34-36; Chapl RN 36-63; R Thurlestone *Ex* 63-69; RD Woodleigh 65-69; V Dawlish 69-74; R Manaton 74-78; R N Bovey 74-78; rtd 78; RD Moreton *Ex* 80-83; Lic to Offic from 83. *7 High Close, Bovey Tracey, Newton Abbot, Devon TQ13 9EX* Tel (01626) 833448

SHERLOCK, Charles Patrick. b 51. New Coll Ox BA73 MA76. Ripon Coll Cuddesdon 75. **d** 77 **p** 78. C Ashtead *Guildf* 77-81; Ethiopia 81-82; Chapl Belgrade w Zagreb *Eur* 82-84; USPG (Ethiopia) 84-91; R Dollar *St And* from 91. *St James's Rectory, 12 Harviestoun Road, Dollar, Clackmannanshire FK14 7HF* Tel (01259) 742494

SHERLOCK, Canon Desmond. b 31. K Coll Lon BD60 AKC60. **d** 61 **p** 62. C Mitcham Ascension *S'wark* 61-64; C Reigate St Luke S Park 64-67; V Aldersbrook *Chelmsf* 67-77; RD

Redbridge 74-77; TR Witham from 77; Can Chelmsf Cathl from 93. *The Vicarage, 7 Chipping Dell, Witham, Essex CM8 2JX* Tel (01376) 512056

SHERLOCK, Ewart Templeman. b 03. AKC31. **d** 30 **p** 31. C Fulham St Etheldreda *Lon* 30-33; C Paddington H Trin w St Paul 34-36; C Hampstead St Steph 36-43; C Stevenage St Nic *St Alb* 43-44; V Stowe *Lich* 44-47; R Croft w Yarpole *Heref* 47-48; V Treverbyn *Truro* 48-51; CF 51-56; R Risby *St E* 56-60; V Dorney *Ox* 60-70; rtd 71. *11 Fairview Road, Taplow, Maidenhead, Berks SL6 0NQ* Tel (01628) 604226

SHERLOCK, Thomas Alfred. b 40. Aux Course 87. **d** 90 **p** 91. NSM Kilmallock w Kilflynn, Kilfinane, Knockaney etc *L & K* 90-94; C Templemore w Thurles and Kilfithmone *C & O* from 95. *The Rectory, Roscrea Road, Templemore, Co Tipperary, Irish Republic* Tel Templemore (504) 31175 Fax as telephone

SHERRATT, David Arthur. b 60. Univ of Wales (Lamp) BA82 Leeds Univ BA91. Coll of Resurr Mirfield CPT92. **d** 92 **p** 93. C St Jo on Bethnal Green *Lon* 92-95; C W Hampstead St Jas from 95. *2 St James House, 2 Sherriff Road, London NW6 2AP* Tel 0171-372 6441

SHERRING, Patrick. b 55. Trent Park Coll of Educn BEd78 CertEd77 Lon Inst of Educn DipPSE88. Ridley Hall Cam CTM95. **d** 97. C Leyton St Mary w St Edw and St Luke *Chelmsf* from 97. *27 Crawley Road, London E10 6RG* Tel 0181-556 5325

SHERSBY, Brian Alfred. b 41. Clifton Th Coll 68. **d** 71 **p** 72. C Stoughton *Guildf* 71-74; C Heref St Pet w St Owen *Heref* 75-79; V Earlham St Mary *Nor* 79-91; R Murston w Bapchild and Tonge *Cant* from 91. *Bapchild Rectory, School Lane, Sittingbourne, Kent ME9 9NL* Tel (01795) 472929

SHERWIN, David Royston. b 56. HNC. St Jo Coll Nottm 84. **d** 89 **p** 90. C Conisbrough *Sheff* 89-95; V Wheatley Park from 95; Dioc Adv for Evang from 95. *The Vicarage, 278 Thorne Road, Doncaster, S Yorkshire DN2 5AJ* Tel (01302) 326041

SHERWIN, Mrs Jane. b 41. Kingston Coll of Art DipAD61. Sarum Th Coll 93. **d** 96 **p** 97. NSM Brightling, Dallington, Mountfield etc *Chich* from 96. *Holly Tree Cottage, Hollingrove Hill, Brightling, Robertsbridge, E Sussex TN32 5HU* Tel (01424) 838540 Fax 773682

SHERWIN, Miss Margaret Miriam. b 32. **dss** 83 **d** 87 **p** 94. Holborn St Alb w Saffron Hill St Pet *Lon* 83-87; Par Dn 87-88; Par Dn Highgate St Mich 88-93; rtd 93; NSM Purbrook *Portsm* from 93. *16 Lombard Court, Lombard Street, Portsmouth PO1 2HU* Tel (01705) 838429

SHERWOOD, David James. b 45. Solicitor 69 Univ of Wales (Cardiff) LLM94. St Steph Ho Ox 81. **d** 83 **p** 84. C Westbury-on-Trym H Trin *Bris* 83-85; C Corringham *Chelmsf* 85-87; V Hullbridge 87-94; V Kenton *Lon* from 94. *St Mary's Vicarage, 3 St Leonard's Avenue, Harrow, Middx HA3 8EJ* Tel 0181-907 2914

SHERWOOD, Denys Charles. b 20. Lon Univ BA49. Oak Hill Th Coll. **d** 51 **p** 52. C Hornsey Rise St Mary *Lon* 51-54; C Dagenham *Chelmsf* 54-56; V Bedminster St Luke w St Silas *Bris* 56-63; Org Sec (SE Area) CPAS 63-67; V Lenton Abbey *S'well* 67-77; V Basford *Lich* 77-85; rtd 85; Perm to Offic *S'well* from 85. *5 Larch Crescent, Eastwood, Nottingham NG16 3RB* Tel (01773) 760922

SHERWOOD, Gordon Frederick. b 29. Sarum & Wells Th Coll 77. **d** 80 **p** 81. Hon C Weeke *Win* 80-82; C Kirk Ella *York* 82-85; P-in-c Burstwick w Thorngumbald 85-87; V 87-90; R Kirby Misperton w Normanby, Edston and Salton 90-94; rtd 94; Perm to Offic *Cant* from 95. *76 Bysing Wood Road, Faversham, Kent ME13 7RH* Tel (01795) 535934

SHERWOOD, Canon Ian Walter Lawrence. b 57. TCD BA80 DipTh82. **d** 82 **p** 84. C Dublin St Patr Cathl Gp *D & G* 82-83; Chapl Billinge Hosp Wigan 83-86; C Orrell *Liv* 83-86; Chapl Bucharest w Sofia *Eur* 86-89; Chapl Istanbul w Moda from 89; Can Malta Cathl from 97. *c/o Foreign and Commonwealth Office (Istanbul), King Charles Street, London SW1A 2AH* Tel Istanbul (1) 244-4228

SHERWOOD, Kenneth Henry. b 37. CITC 90. **d** 93 **p** 94. NSM Malahide w Balgriffin *D & G* 93-96; NSM Castleknock and Mulhuddart, w Clonsilla 96-97; NSM Leighlin w Grange Sylvae, Shankill etc *C & O* from 97. *St Laserian's Deanery, Old Leighlin, Co Carlow, Irish Republic* Tel Carlow (503) 21411

SHERWOOD, Nigel John Wesley. b 58. DipTh. CITC 86. **d** 86 **p** 87. C Kilmore w Ballintemple, Kildallon etc *K, E & A* 86-88; I Tullow w Shillelagh, Aghold and Mullinacuff *C & O* 88-95; I Arklow w Inch and Kilbride *D & G* from 95. *The Rectory, Arklow, Co Wicklow, Irish Republic* Tel Arklow (402) 32439

SHERWOOD, Suffragan Bishop of. *See* MORGAN, The Rt Revd Alan Wyndham

SHEWAN, Alistair Boyd. b 44. Open Univ BA83. Edin Th Coll 63. **d** 67 **p** 68. Prec St Andr Cathl Inverness *Mor* 67-69; C Shepherd's Bush St Steph w St Thos *Lon* 70-72; Hon C Edin St Mich and All SS *Edin* 73-75; Perm to Offic 75-81; Hon C Edin Old St Paul 81-86; NSM Edin St Columba 87-91; Asst Dioc Supernumerary from 91. *3 Castle Wynd North, Edinburgh EH1 2NQ* Tel 0131-225 6537

SHEWAN, James William. b 36. Sarum Th Coll 61. **d** 63 **p** 64. C Rainbow Hill St Barn *Worc* 63-64; C Newton Aycliffe *Dur* 64-66; C Harton 66-69; V S Moor 69-72; CF 72-77; CF(V) from 81; P-in-c Benwell St Aid *Newc* 77-79; V Longhoughton w Howick 79-88; V Spittal from 88; V Scremerston from 88; RD Norham from 96. *St John's Vicarage, 129 Main Street, Spittal, Berwick-upon-Tweed TD15 1RP* Tel (01289) 307342

SHEWELL, Edward Charles Beaudon. b 12. St Pet Hall Ox BA36 MA46. Ridley Hall Cam 36. **d** 37 **p** 38. C Plymouth St Andr *Ex* 37-41; P-in-c Devonport St Jo 41-42; C Torwood St Mark 42-44; Chapl RNVR 44-47; C Wimbledon St Luke *S'wark* 47-51; C Cheam 51-54; V Berry Pomeroy *Ex* 54-77; RD Totnes 63-66; R Lt Hempston 69-77; rtd 77; Hon C Tetcott w Luffincott *Ex* 77-81; Hon C Clawton 77-81. *Flat 43, The Courtyard, Auchlochan House, Lesmahagow, Lanark ML11 0JS*

SHIELD, Ian Thomas. b 32. Hertf Coll Ox BA56 MA60 BLitt60. Westcott Ho Cam 59. **d** 61 **p** 62. C Shipley St Paul *Bradf* 61-64; Tutor Lich Th Coll 64-71; Chapl 67-71; V Dunston w Coppenhall *Lich* 71-79; TV Wolverhampton 79-86; rtd 87; Perm to Offic *Lich* 87-96. *13 Duke Street, Penn Fields, Wolverhampton WV3 7DT* Tel (01902) 337037

SHIELDS, Canon Michael Penton. b 30. Bps' Coll Cheshunt. **d** 64 **p** 65. C Kingsbury St Andr *Lon* 64-67; C Friern Barnet All SS 67-69; V Colindale St Matthias 69-76; V Sevenoaks St Jo *Roch* 76-95; RD Sevenoaks 84-95; Chapl Sevenoaks Hosp 78-94; Chapl St Mich Sch Otford 90-95; Hon Can Roch Cathl *Roch* 94-95; rtd 95; Hon PV Roch Cathl *Roch* from 96. *Flat 14, Bromley College, London Road, Bromley BR1 1PE* Tel 0181-464 7906

SHIELS, Donald Allan Patterson. b 15. Selw Coll Cam BA38 MA42. Wycliffe Hall Ox 38. **d** 39 **p** 40. C Taunton St Mary *B & W* 39-42; C Bermondsey St Mary w St Olave and St Jo *S'wark* 42-45; C Redhill St Jo 45-47; V Brownswood Park *Lon* 47-62; V Stoke Gifford *Bris* 62-80; rtd 80; Perm to Offic *Glouc* from 80. *5 Down Hatherley Lane, Gloucester GL2 9PT* Tel (01452) 730367

SHILL, Kenneth Leslie. b 49. Leic Univ BA70 Lon Univ BD73 Cam Univ DipTh77. Ridley Hall Cam 75. **d** 77 **p** 78. C Harborne Heath *Birm* 77-83; V Mansfield St Jo *S'well* 83-93; Bp's Adv on Healing 89-93; Chapl Amsterdam w Heiloo *Eur* 93-95; TR Bath Twerton-on-Avon *B & W* from 95. *The Rectory, Watery Lane, Bath BA2 1RL* Tel (01225) 421438

SHILLAKER, Mrs Christine Frances. b 39. Lon Univ DipTh61. Gilmore Ho 74. **dss** 86 **d** 87 **p** 94. Colchester St Leon, St Mary Magd and St Steph *Chelmsf* 86-89; Par Dn 87-89; Par Dn Colchester, New Town and The Hythe 89-94; C 94-96; P-in-c Ramsey w Lt Oakley and Wrabness from 96. *The Vicarage, Ramsey Road, Ramsey, Harwich, Essex CO12 5EU* Tel (01255) 880291

SHILLAKER, John. b 34. K Coll Lon BD60 AKC60. **d** 61 **p** 62. C Bush Hill Park St Mark *Lon* 61-65; C Milton *Win* 65-69; C-in-c Moulsham St Luke CD *Chelmsf* 69-78; V Moulsham St Luke 78-85; P-in-c Colchester St Leon, St Mary Magd and St Steph 85-86; R 86-89; R Colchester, New Town and The Hythe 89-96; rtd 96. *The Vicarage, Ramsey Road, Ramsey, Harwich, Essex CO12 5EU* Tel (01255) 880291

SHILLING, Ms Audrey Violet. b 26. Dur Univ BA69. CA Tr Coll 51 Cranmer Hall Dur 66. **d** 87 **p** 94. CA from 53; NSM Gillingham H Trin *Roch* 87-93; NSM Rainham from 94. *13 Motney Hill Road, Gillingham, Kent ME8 7TZ* Tel (01634) 233654

SHILLINGFORD, Brian. b 39. Lich Th Coll 65. **d** 68 **p** 69. C Lewisham St Swithun *S'wark* 68-71; C Godstone 71-75; TV Croydon *Cant* 75-81; TV N Creedy *Ex* 81-93; TR from 93. *The Rectory, Morchard Bishop, Crediton, Devon EX17 6PJ* Tel (01363) 877221

SHILSON-THOMAS, Mrs Annabel Margaret. b 60. Jes Coll Ox BA82. Westcott Ho Cam 87. **d** 89. Par Dn Sydenham St Bart *S'wark* 89-93; Journalist CAFOD from 95. *21 Burney Avenue, Surbiton, Surrey KT5 8DF* Tel 0181-339 9479

SHILSON-THOMAS, Hugh David. b 64. Ex Coll Ox BA86. Westcott Ho Cam 87. **d** 89 **p** 90. C Sydenham All SS *S'wark* 89-92; C Lower Sydenham St Mich 89-92; Ecum Chapl Kingston Univ from 93. *21 Burney Avenue, Surbiton, Surrey KT5 8DF* Tel 0181-547 7311 or 339 9479 Fax 547 7029 E-mail h.shilson-thomas@kingston.ac.uk

SHILVOCK, Geoffrey. b 47. Univ of Wales (Lamp) BA69. Sarum Th Coll 70. **d** 72 **p** 73. C Kidderminster St Mary *Worc* 72-78; P-in-c Gt Malvern Ch Ch 78-85; V Wolverley and Cookley from 85; RD Kidderminster from 95. *The Vicarage, Wolverley, Kidderminster, Worcs DY11 5XD* Tel (01562) 851133

SHILVOCK, Kelvin David. b 50. MHCIMA71 Birm Coll of Food OND69. Qu Coll Birm 91. **d** 93 **p** 94. C Kidderminster St Jo and H Innocents *Worc* from 93. *59 Stretton Road, Kidderminster, Worcs DY11 6NQ* Tel (01562) 754194

SHIMWELL, Robert John. b 46. ARCM65. Lon Bible Coll DipTh68 Trin Coll Bris 75. **d** 78 **p** 79. C Richmond H Trin *S'wark* 78-79; C Cullompton *Ex* 79-81; C Kentisbeare w Blackborough 79-81; V S Cave and Ellerker w Broomfleet *York* 81-87; Chapl Lee Abbey 87-88; R Glas St Silas *Glas* 88-94; V Upton (Overchurch) *Ches* from 94; RD Wirral N from 97. *The Vicarage, 20 Church Road, Upton, Wirral, Merseyside L49 6JZ* Tel 0151-677 4810 or 677 1186 Fax 606 1935

SHINER, Michael Joseph. b 21. Chich Th Coll 51. **d** 53 **p** 54. C Weymouth H Trin *Sarum* 53-56; V Stanbridge w Tilsworth

St Alb 56-63; V Powerstock w W Milton, Witherstone and N Poorton *Sarum* 67-73; V Knutsford St Cross *Ches* 73-75; Area Sec Age Concern Cornwall 75-86; Co Org W Sussex 80-86; rtd 86. *55 Tennyson Drive, Malvern, Worcs WR14 2UL* Tel (01684) 563269

SHINN, William Raymond. b 22. Sarum & Wells Th Coll 71. **d** 73 **p** 74. C Letchworth St Paul *St Alb* 73-75; C Dunstable 76-78; TV 78-80; V Luton St Chris Round Green 80-88; rtd 88. *31 Coleridge Close, Hitchin, Herts SG4 0QX* Tel (01462) 450899

SHIPLEY, Miss Marjorie. b 17. Gilmore Ho 67. **dss** 72 **d** 87 **p** 94. Acomb St Steph *York* 72-78; rtd 78; Perm to Offic *York* 78-84; from 95; NSM Scarborough St Martin 84-95. *43 Hartford Court, 33 Filey Road, Scarborough, N Yorkshire YO11 2TP* Tel (01723) 353150

SHIPLEY, Stephen Edwin Burnham. b 52. Univ Coll Dur BA74. Westcott Ho Cam 85. **d** 87 **p** 88. C Ipswich St Marg *St E* 87-90; P-in-c Stuntney *Ely* 90-95; Min Can, Prec and Sacr Ely Cathl 90-95; Producer Worship Progr BBC Relig Broadcasting from 95; Lic to Offic *Derby* from 96. *21 Devonshire Road, Buxton, Derbyshire SK17 6RZ* Tel (01298) 78383 or 0161-244 3292 Fax 0161-244 3290 E-mail stephen.shipley@bbc.co.uk

SHIPP, Mrs Patricia Susan. b 54. Univ of Wales BA76. St Paul's Grahamstown 77 Linc Th Coll 81. **d** 83 **p** 94. C Cyncoed *Mon* 83-87; Par Dn Lawrence Weston *Bris* 89-91; Par Dn Henbury 91-94; D-in-c Longwell Green 94; P-in-c from 94; Hon Can Bris Cathl from 97. *The Vicarage, 85 Bath Road, Longwell Green, Bristol BS15 6DF* Tel 0117-983 3373

SHIPSIDES, Brian Kenneth. b 56. Reading Univ BA. Westcott Ho Cam 79. **d** 82 **p** 83. C Bramley *Ripon* 82-85; C Notting Dale St Clem w St Mark and St Jas *Lon* 85-90; Chapl N Lon Poly 90-92; Chapl N Lon Univ 92-97; P-in-c Forest Gate All SS and St Edm *Chelmsf* from 97. *St Edmund's Church Flat, 464 Katherine Road, London E7 8NP*

SHIPTON, Andrew James. b 60. Leeds Univ BA82. Cranmer Hall Dur 83. **d** 85 **p** 86. C Fishponds St Jo *Bris* 85-88; C Gosforth All SS *Newc* 88-91; V Long Benton St Mary 91-96; Chapl Univ of Northumbria at Newc from 96. *282 Wingrove Road North, Newcastle upon Tyne NE4 9EE* Tel 0191-274 9761

SHIPTON, Miss Linda Anne. b 60. Avery Hill Coll DipHE84. Westcott Ho Cam 84. **dss** 86 **d** 87 **p** 94. Borehamwood *St Alb* 86-89; Par Dn 87-89; Par Dn Sheff St Cuth *Sheff* 89-90; Chapl Asst N Gen Hosp Sheff 89-90; Chapl 90-96; Chapl Qu Mary's NHS Trust Sidcup from 96. *Queen Mary's Hospital, Frognal Avenue, Sidcup, Kent DA14 6LT* Tel 0181-302 2678

SHIPTON (née WILSON), Mrs Marjorie Jayne. b 59. Hull Univ BA80 K Alfred's Coll Win PGCE81. St Jo Coll Dur 85. **dss** 86 **d** 87 **p** 94. Ormesby *York* 86-87; Par Dn 87-89; Chapl Asst Newc Gen Hosp 89-91; Chapl 91-95; Dep Hd Chapl R Victoria Infirmary and Assoc Hosps NHS Trust from 95; NSM Whorlton *Newc* 94-97. *Newcastle General Hospital, Westgate Road, Newcastle upon Tyne NE4 6BE* Tel 0191-273 8811

SHIRE, William Stanley. b 17. TCD BA39 MA43. **d** 40 **p** 41. C Dundalk *Arm* 40-43; C Portadown St Mark 43-45; P-in-c Mullaglass 45-51; I 51-57; C Attenborough w Bramcote and Chilwell *S'well* 57-58; V Lowdham 58-66; R Pilton w Wardenhoe and Stoke Doyle *Pet* 67-70; R Aldwincle w Thorpe Achurch, Pilton, Wadenhoe etc 70-82; rtd 82; Lic to Offic *Pet* 82-85; Perm to Offic from 85. *96 Glapthorne Road, Oundle, Peterborough PE8 4PS* Tel (01832) 272125

SHIRES, Alan William. b 36. Lon Univ BA60. Oak Hill Th Coll 57. **d** 61 **p** 62. C York St Paul *York* 61-64; C Southgate *Chich* 64-67; V Doncaster St Mary *Sheff* 67-75; Perm to Offic *Portsm* 75-96; Student Counsellor Portsm Poly 75-88; Hd Student Services Portsm Poly 88-96; rtd 96. *15 Broomfield Road, Admaston, Wellington, Shropshire TF5 0AR*

SHIRESS, Canon David Henry Faithfull. b 27. St Cath Coll Cam BA49 MA53. Ridley Hall Cam 51. **d** 53 **p** 54. C Southport Ch Ch *Liv* 53-55; C St Helens St Mark 55-58; V Shrewsbury St Julian *Lich* 58-67; V Blackheath Park St Mich *S'wark* 67-93; Sub-Dean Greenwich 81-90; RD Greenwich 90-91; Hon Can S'wark Cathl 89-93; rtd 93. *35 Rempstone Road, Wimborne, Dorset BH21 1SS* Tel (01202) 887845

SHIRLEY, Timothy Francis. b 25. Univ Coll Ox BA49 MA49. Qu Coll Birm 49. **d** 51 **p** 52. C Pimlico St Gabr *Lon* 51-56; C-in-c Hayes St Edm CD 56-65; V Fulham St Etheldreda 65-68; V Fulham St Etheldreda w St Clem 68-90; rtd 90. *70 St Dunstan's Cresent, Worcester WR5 2AQ* Tel (01905) 353930

SHIRLEY, Valerie Joy. b 42. LNSM course 93. **d** 96. Hon C Sydenham H Trin *S'wark* from 96. *Flat 9, Faircroft, 5 Westwood Hill, London SE26 6BG* Tel 0181-778 2551

SHIRRAS, The Ven Edward Scott (Eddie). b 37. St Andr Univ BSc61. Clifton Th Coll 61. **d** 63 **p** 64. C Surbiton Hill Ch Ch *S'wark* 63-66; C Jesmond Clayton Memorial *Newc* 66-68; Youth Sec CPAS 68-71; Publications Sec 71-74; Asst Gen Sec 74-75; Hon C Wallington H Trin *S'wark* 69-75; V Roxeth Ch Ch *Lon* 75-82; V Roxeth Ch Ch and Harrow St Pet 82-85; AD Harrow 82-85; Adn Northolt 85-92; V Win Ch Ch *Win* from 92. *Christ Church Vicarage, Sleepers Hill, Winchester, Hants SO22 4ND* Tel (01962) 862414

SHIRRAS, Ms Rachel Joan. b 66. Univ of Wales (Abth) BSc88. St Jo Coll Nottm 88. **d** 91 **p** 94. Par Dn Ockbrook *Derby* 91-94; C Bris St Matt and St Nath *Bris* 94-97; V Beckton St Mark *Chelmsf* from 97. *15 Greenwich Crescent, London E6 4TU* Tel 0171-476 0618

SHOLL, Preb Ernest Redfern. b 09. AKC33. **d** 33 **p** 34. C Camberwell St Mark *S'wark* 33-34; C Camberwell St Luke 34-38; Lic to Offic *Cant* 38; Perm to Offic *B & W* 39-44; R Holford w Dodington 44-53; RD Quantoxhead 53-68; V Stogursey 53-74; V Stockland Bristol 55-70; Preb Wells Cathl 57-74; P-in-c Fiddington 60-64; R 64-74; rtd 74. *Langdale, Kirtlebridge, Lockerbie, Dumfriesshire DG11 3LT* Tel (01461) 500659

SHONE, John Terence. b 35. Selw Coll Cam BA58 MA64 Newc Univ MA92. Linc Th Coll 58. **d** 60 **p** 61. C St Pancras w St Jas and Ch Ch *Lon* 60-62; Chapl Aber Univ *Ab* 62-68; Chapl St Andr Cathl 62-65; V Gt Grimsby St Andr and St Luke *Linc* 68-69; Chapl Stirling Univ *St And* 69-80; R Bridge of Allan 69-86; P-in-c Alloa 77-85; Can St Ninian's Cathl Perth 80-89; P-in-c Dollar 81-86; Dean St Andr 82-89; Research and Development Officer 86-89; Dioc Supernumerary 86-89; TV Cullercoats St Geo *Newc* from 89. *St Hilda's Vicarage, Preston Gate, North Shields, Tyne & Wear NE29 9QB* Tel 0191-257 6595

SHONE, Raymond. b 21. St Jo Coll Dur BA47 MA54 Brighton Poly DCouns81. Linc Th Coll 48. **d** 48 **p** 49. C Penn *Lich* 48-50; C Warblington and Emsworth *Portsm* 50-58; R Monks Risborough *Ox* 58-61; Chapl and Lect Bp Otter Coll Chich 61-66; Perm to Offic *Chich* from 66; Sen Lect Eastbourne Coll of Educn 66-76; E Sussex Coll of HE 76-79; Brighton Poly 79-80; Counsellor W Sussex Inst of HE 83-87; rtd 87. *28 Hawthorn Close, Chichester, W Sussex PO19 3DZ* Tel (01243) 774543

SHONE, Robert Alan. b 16. Qu Coll Cam BA38 MA42. St Steph Ho Ox 39. **d** 39 **p** 40. C W Derby Gd Shep *Liv* 39-41; C Wigan All SS 41-42; C Birch St Jas *Man* 42-45; C Wardleworth St Mary 45-47; R Withington St Chris 47-56; V Morley St Paul *Wakef* 56-63; V Wardleworth St Mary *Man* 63-73; V Wardleworth St Jas 66-73; V Wardleworth St Mary w St Jas 73-81; rtd 81; Perm to Offic *Man* from 81. *172 Bar Terrace, Market Street, Whitworth, Rochdale, Lancs OL12 8TB* Tel (01706) 344405

SHONE, Miss Ursula Ruth. b 34. Lon Univ DBRS59 Stirling Univ BA75 Open Univ BPhil88. **dss** 81 **d** 86 **p** 94. Bridge of Allan *St And* 81-85; Lochgelly 85-87; Chapl Cov Cathl *Cov* 87-90; Ind Chapl 87-90; Par Dn Ainsdale *Liv* 90-94; Dioc Science Adv from 90; C Ainsdale 94-96; C Childwall St Dav from 96. *27 Score Lane, Liverpool L16 6AN* Tel 0151-722 2451

SHOOTER, Ms Susan. b 58. Nottm Univ BA81 PGCE82. St Jo Coll Nottm MA94. **d** 96. C Dartford H Trin *Roch* 96-97; C Crayford from 97. *68 Priory Road, Dartford DA1 2BS* Tel (01322) 278655

SHORROCK, John Musgrave. b 29. TCD BA54 MA58. Bps' Coll Cheshunt 54. **d** 56 **p** 57. C Fleetwood *Blackb* 56-59; C Lancaster St Mary 59-61; C-in-c Blackpool St Wilfred CD 61-65; V Blackpool St Wilfrid 65-67; Min Can and Sacr Cant Cathl *Cant* 67-70; V Chorley St Geo *Blackb* 71-78; P-in-c Bredgar w Bicknor and Huckinge *Cant* 78-82; P-in-c Frinsted w Wormshill and Milstead 78-82; R Bredgar w Bicknor and Frinsted w Wormshill etc 82-92; rtd 92; Perm to Offic *Cant* from 92; Clergy Widows Officer Cant Adnry from 97. *Bradgate, School Lane, Bekesbourne, Canterbury, Kent CT4 5ER* Tel (01227) 832133

SHORT, Brian Frederick. b 29. St Jo Coll Nottm 70. **d** 72 **p** 73. C Walton *St E* 72-75; P-in-c Barking w Darmsden and Gt Bricett 75-78; P-in-c Ringshall w Battisford and Lt Finborough 75-78; TV Nor St Pet Parmentergate w St Jo *Nor* 78-88; R Winfarthing w Shelfanger w Burston w Gissing etc 88-90; rtd 90; Perm to Offic *Nor* from 92. *31 Nursery Gardens, Blofield, Norwich NR13 4JE* Tel (01603) 712396

SHORT, Ms Clare. b 50. Leic Univ BA72 St Mary's Coll Twickenham PGCE73. All Nations Chr Coll CDRS81 S Dios Minl Tr Scheme 89. **d** 92 **p** 94. NSM Horsham *Chich* from 92. *19 York Close, Southwater, Horsham, W Sussex RH13 7XJ* Tel (01403) 730880

SHORT, Eileen. b 45. **d** 96 **p** 97. NSM Castleton Moor *Man* from 96. *2 Netherwood Road, Northenden, Manchester M22 4BQ*

SHORT, Canon John Sinclair. b 33. Oak Hill Th Coll 64. **d** 66 **p** 67. C Islington St Mary *Lon* 66-70; V Becontree St Mary *Chelmsf* 70-76; V New Malden and Coombe *S'wark* 76-90; RD Kingston 79-84; Hon Can S'wark Cathl 83-90; P-in-c Peldon w Gt and Lt Wigborough *Chelmsf* 90-93; rtd 93; Perm to Offic *S'wark* from 93. *22 Chart Lane, Reigate, Surrey RH1 7BP* Tel (01737) 245244

SHORT, John Timothy. b 43. Lon Univ DipTh67. Kelham Th Coll 63. **d** 68 **p** 69. C St Marylebone Ch Ch w St Barn *Lon* 68-70; C Southgate Ch Ch 70-72; P-in-c Mosser *Carl* 72-78; Dioc Youth Officer 72-78; R Heyford w Stowe Nine Churches *Pet* 78-87; V Northampton St Jas 87-96; RD Wootton 88-96; TR Kingsthorpe w Northn St Dav from 96. *The Rectory, 16 Green End, Kingsthorpe, Northampton NN2 6RD* Tel (01604) 717133

SHORT, Kenneth Arthur. b 33. Tyndale Hall Bris 64. **d** 67 **p** 68. C E Twickenham St Steph *Lon* 67-71; C Paddock Wood *Roch* 71-74; SE Area Sec BCMS 74-82; Hon C Sidcup Ch Ch 74-82; V Tollington Park St Mark w St Anne *Lon* 82-86; V Holloway St Mark w Em 86-89; R Alfold and Loxwood *Guildf* from 89. *The*

Rectory, Loxwood, Billingshurst, W Sussex RH14 0RG Tel (01403) 752320

SHORT, Martin Peter. b 54. Peterho Cam BA77 MA81. Wycliffe Hall Ox 77. **d** 79 **p** 80. C Shipley St Pet *Bradf* 79-82; C Becontree St Mary *Chelmsf* 82-86; V Bolton St Jas w St Chrys *Bradf* 86-92; Dioc Communications Officer from 92; C Otley from 92. *30 Newall Hall Park, Otley, W Yorkshire LS21 2RD* Tel (01943) 465071 Fax 467269

SHORT, Martin Ronald. b 57. Crewe & Alsager Coll CertEd78 Leic Univ BEd85. St Jo Coll Nottm DTS93. **d** 93 **p** 94. C Frankby w Greasby *Ches* from 93. *5 Flail Close, Greasby, South Wirral L49 2RN* Tel 0151-605 0735

SHORT, Canon Michael John. b 38. Univ of Wales (Lamp) BA59. Sarum Th Coll 59. **d** 61 **p** 62. C Swansea St Nic *S & B* 61-64; C Oystermouth 64-69; V Merthyr Vale w Aberfan *Llan* 69-82; RD Merthyr Tydfil 76-82; R Caerphilly from 82; RD Caerphilly from 83; Can Llan Cathl from 89. *The Rectory, 2 St Martin's Road, Caerphilly CF83 1EJ* Tel (01222) 882992

SHORT, Neil Robert. b 58. Loughb Univ BSc81 St Jo Coll Dur BA86. Cranmer Hall Dur 83. **d** 86 **p** 87. C Whitfield *Derby* 86-90; C Bradf St Aug Undercliffe *Bradf* 90-96; V Burscough Bridge *Liv* from 96. *St John's Vicarage, 253 Liverpool Road South, Ormskirk, Lancs L40 7TD* Tel (01704) 893205

SHORT, Robert Leslie. b 48. Em Coll Cam BA70 MA76. Wycliffe Hall Ox 87. **d** 92 **p** 92. Mexico 92-93; Chapl Repton Sch Derby from 93. *Repton School, Repton, Derby DE65 6FH* Tel (01283) 813640

SHORT, Vincent Charles. b 57. Oak Hill Th Coll DipHE95. **d** 97. C Chatham St Phil and St Jas *Roch* from 97. *3A Kit Hill Avenue, Walderslade, Chatham, Kent ME5 9ET* Tel (01634) 864348

SHORTEN, Richard Deering. b 08. Qu Coll Cam BA30 MA48. Westcott Ho Cam 30. **d** 32 **p** 33. C Leeds St Wilfrid *Ripon* 32-35; I Hunslet St Silas 35-38; V Kirkby Wharfe *York* 38-56; Chapl RAFVR 41-48; V Preshute *Sarum* 56-75; Asst Chapl Marlborough Coll 56-75; RD Marlborough *Sarum* 64-75; rtd 75. *Throg Cottage, Preshute Lane, Marlborough, Wilts SN8 4HQ* Tel (01672) 512447

SHORTER, Robert Edward. b 48. Ripon Coll Cuddesdon 89. **d** 91 **p** 92. C Braunton *Ex* 91-94; C Bishopsnympton, Rose Ash, Mariansleigh etc 94-96; TV from 96. *The Vicarage, Molland, South Molton, Devon EX36 3NG* Tel (01769) 550551

SHORTHOUSE, Raymond Trevor. b 34. DipAdEd. Ridley Hall Cam 68. **d** 70 **p** 71. C Gt Ilford St Andr *Chelmsf* 70-73; C Ludlow *Heref* 73-75; P-in-c Cressage w Sheinton 76-80; P-in-c Harley w Kenley 76-80; P-in-c Denby *Derby* 80-84; Adult Educn Officer 80-85; RD Heanor 83-84; V Chellaston 84-88; P-in-c Breadsall from 88; Dioc Dir of Studies 88-96. *Breadsall Rectory, Derby DE21 5LL* Tel (01332) 831352

SHORTT, Canon Noel Christopher. b 36. Open Univ BA76 Ulster Univ MA DipContEd DPhil91. Bps' Coll Cheshunt 63. **d** 63 **p** 64. C Belfast St Mary *Conn* 63-66; C Agherton 66-68; Chapl RAF 68-69; I Duneane w Ballyscullion *Conn* 69-79; I Belfast St Steph w St Luke 79-89; RD M Belfast 82-86 and 88-89; I Ballyrashane w Kildollagh from 89; Can Belfast St Anne from 96. *9 Sandelwood Avenue, Coleraine, Co Londonderry BT52 1JW* Tel (01265) 43061

SHOTLANDER, Lionel George. b 27. Cant Univ (NZ) BA49 MA51. **d** 51 **p** 52. New Zealand 51-58 and 60-74; C Southsea St Pet *Portsm* 58-60; V Curdridge 74-85; R Durley 79-85; V Twyford and Owslebury and Morestead *Win* 85-91; rtd 91. *Cambria, High Street, Shirrell Heath, Southampton SO32 2JN* Tel (01329) 832353

SHOTTER, The Very Revd Edward Frank. b 33. Univ of Wales (Lamp) BA58. St Steph Ho Ox 58. **d** 60 **p** 61. C Plymouth St Pet *Ex* 60-62; Inter-Colleg Sec SCM (Lon) 62-66; Perm to Offic *Lon* 62-69; Dir Lon Medical Gp 63-89; Chapl Lon Univ Medical Students *Lon* 69-89; Dir Inst of Medical Ethics 74-89; Preb St Paul's Cathl *Lon* 77-89; Dean Roch from 89. *The Deanery, Rochester, Kent ME1 1TG* Tel (01634) 844023 or 843366 Fax 410410

SHOULER, Simon Frederic. b 54. ARICS77 Pemb Coll Cam MA79. EMMTC 82. **d** 85 **p** 86. NSM Asfordby *Leic* 85-92; Perm to Offic from 92. *Tower Cottage, Wartnaby, Melton Mowbray, Leics LE14 3HU* Tel (01664) 822698

SHREEVE, The Ven David Herbert. b 34. St Pet Hall Ox BA57 MA61. Ridley Hall Cam 57. **d** 59 **p** 60. C Plymouth St Andr *Ex* 59-64; V Bermondsey St Anne *S'wark* 64-71; V Eccleshill *Bradf* 71-84; RD Calverley 78-84; Hon Can Bradf Cathl 83-84; Adn Bradf from 84. *11 The Rowans, Baildon, Shipley, W Yorkshire BD17 5DB* Tel (01274) 583735 Fax 586184

SHREWSBURY, Preb Michael Buller. b 30. St Jo Coll Dur BA54. Linc Th Coll 54. **d** 56 **p** 57. C Salford St Phil w St Steph *Man* 56-60; Chapl RN 60-63; Chapl HM Pris Pentonville 64-67; Bermuda 67-70; V Dalston H Trin w St Phil *Lon* 70-86; AD Hackney 79-84; Preb St Paul's Cathl 86-92; R Stepney St Dunstan and All SS 86-92; rtd 92; Perm to Offic *Lon* from 92. *Flat 1, 150 Wapping High Street, London E1 9XG* Tel 0171-480 5479

SHREWSBURY, Area Bishop of. *See* HALLATT, The Rt Revd David Marrison

SHRIMPTON, Canon Aner Clive. b 14. Lon Univ BD39. ALCD39. **d** 39 **p** 40. C Ore Ch Ch *Chich* 39-41; C Battle 42-46; P-in-c S Patcham 46-52; V Ruddington *S'well* 52-84; Hon Can S'well Minster 78-84; rtd 84; Perm to Offic *S'well* from 84. *36 Brookview Drive, Keyworth, Nottingham NG12 5JN* Tel 0115-937 2795

SHRIMPTON, George Roderick. b 33. Selw Coll Cam BA56 MA60. Linc Th Coll 56. **d** 58 **p** 59. C Bilston St Leon *Lich* 58-63; C High Wycombe All SS *Ox* 63-67; V Dalton *Sheff* 67-74; V Milborne Port w Goathill *B & W* 74-90; P-in-c Barkston and Hough Gp *Linc* 90; R from 90; RD Loveden from 93. *The Parsonage, The Drift, Syston, Grantham, Lincs NG32 2BY* Tel (01400) 50381

SHRIMPTON, Mrs Sheila Nan. b 32. Qu Mary Coll Lon BA54 LSE CSocStuds55. St Chris Coll Blackheath 57. **dss** 83 **d** 87 **p** 94. Lic to Offic *B & W* 83-90; NSM Barkston and Hough Gp *Linc* 90-97; Asst Local Min Officer 90-97; C Brant Broughton and Beckingham from 97. *The Parsonage, The Drift, Syston, Grantham, Lincs NG32 2BY* Tel (01400) 50381

SHRINE, Robert Gerald (Bob). b 44. Birm Univ BA65 Univ of Zambia PGCE70 Lanc Univ MA74 Open Univ BA80. St Jo Coll Nottm 95. **d** 97. C Blackpool St Thos *Blackb* from 97. *3 Caledonian Avenue, Blackpool FY3 8RB* Tel (01253) 395504

SHRISUNDER, David Shripat. b 29. Osmania Univ Hyderabad BA52 Serampore Univ BD59 Shivaji Univ Kolhapur MA69. Bp's Coll Calcutta 54. **d** 57 **p** 58. India 57-71, 72-75, 77-79 and 88-90; C Batley All SS *Wakef* 71-72; C Skegness *Linc* 75-77; C Derringham Bank *York* 80-81; TV Grays Thurrock *Chelmsf* 81-85; R Uddingston *Glas* 85-88; R Cambuslang 85-88; P-in-c Sinfin Moor *Derby* 90-94; rtd 94; Perm to Offic *Wakef* from 94. *8 Jessamine Street, Dewsbury, W Yorkshire WF13 3HY* Tel (01924) 496127

SHRIVES, Austen Geoffrey. b 28. Lon Univ BD68 MTh77. S'wark Ord Course. **d** 64 **p** 65. C Lower Sydenham St Mich *S'wark* 64-68; Miss to Seamen 68-74; V Epsom St Martin *Guildf* 74-84; V York Town St Mich 84-87; R Churchstanton, Buckland St Mary and Otterford *B & W* 87-93; rtd 93. *16 Watling Street, Ross-on-Wye, Herefordshire HR9 5UF*

SHUCKSMITH, John Barry. b 37. Lon Univ DipTh68 Hull Univ DipTh84 FRSA87. Oak Hill Th Coll. **d** 68 **p** 69. C Tooting Graveney St Nic *S'wark* 68-70; S Africa 74-76; P-in-c Liv Ch Ch Norris Green *Liv* 82-86; Chapl RN 86-91; R Broughton *Linc* 91-94. *3 Fourth Avenue, Portsmouth PO6 3HX* Tel (01705) 375100

SHUFFLEBOTHAM, Alastair Vincent. b 32. Nottm Univ CSocSc57. Lich Th Coll 63. **d** 65 **p** 66. C W Kirby St Bridget *Ches* 65-69; V Tranmere St Paul 69-71; V Tranmere St Paul w St Luke 71-78; V Neston from 78. *The Vicarage, Neston, South Wirral L64 9TZ* Tel 0151-336 4544

SHUKMAN, Dr Ann Margaret. b 31. Girton Coll Cam BA53 MA58 LMH Ox DPhil74. WMMTC 80. **dss** 84 **d** 92 **p** 94. Steeple Aston w N Aston and Tackley *Ox* 84-96; NSM 92-96; rtd 96; Perm to Offic *Ox* from 96. *Old School House, Tackley, Kidlington, Oxon OX5 3AH* Tel (01869) 331761

SHUTT, Anthony John. b 57. Brunel Univ BSc79 DipHE89. Trin Coll Bris 87. **d** 89 **p** 90. C Epsom St Martin *Guildf* 89-95; P-in-c Send from 95. *St Mary's Vicarage, Vicarage Lane, Send, Woking, Surrey GU23 7JN* Tel (01483) 222193

SHUTT, Laurence John. b 42. MPS64 MRPharmS88. St Steph Ho Ox 87 Llan Dioc Tr Scheme 80. **d** 84 **p** 85. NSM Whitchurch *Llan* 84-87; C Llanishen and Lisvane 88-90; Chapl RNR from 89; V Middlestown *Wakef* from 90. *The Vicarage, 19 Wood Mount, Overton, Wakefield, W Yorkshire WF4 4SB* Tel (01924) 276159

SHUTT, Nicholas Stephen. b 58. Qu Mary Coll Lon LLB80 Solicitor 83. SW Minl Tr Course 91. **d** 94 **p** 95. NSM Yelverton, Meavy, Sheepstor and Walkhampton *Ex* from 94. *12 Blackbrook Close, Walkhampton, Yelverton, Devon PL20 6JF* Tel (01822) 854653

SHUTT, Rowland James Heath. b 11. St Chad's Coll Dur BA33 PhD36 MA36. **d** 35 **p** 36. Jun Fell St Chad's Coll Dur 35-36; Fell 36-39; C Farnham Royal *Ox* 39-45; R Rampisham w Wraxall *Sarum* 45-47; R Shaston 47-53; Tutor Sarum Th Coll 47-53; R Cadeleigh *Ex* 53-57; Chapl Ex Univ 54-63; R Ex St Martin, St Steph, St Laur etc 57-64; Warden Worc Ord Coll 64-69; Hon Min Can Worc Cathl *Worc* 64-78; Lect Worc Coll of Educn 59-76; rtd 77. *7 Greenhill, Bath Road, Worcester WR5 2AT* Tel (01905) 355410

SHUTTLEWORTH, Claude Tone. b 16. Solicitor 48 St Cath Coll Cam BA38 MA54. Edin Th Coll 55. **d** 57 **p** 58. C Carl H Trin and St Barn *Carl* 57-61; R Lamplugh w Ennerdale 61-65; rtd 81. *31 Thorntrees Drive, Thornhill, Egremont, Cumbria CA22 2SU* Tel (01946) 820014

SIBBALD, Olwyn. *See* MARLOW, Mrs Olwyn Eileen

SIBLEY, Jonathan Paul Eddolls. b 55. Newc Univ BA77. Westcott Ho Cam 78 Ripon Coll Cuddesdon 85. **d** 87 **p** 88. C Waltham Cross *St Alb* 87-90; C Chalfont St Peter *Ox* 90-96; P-in-c Sulhamstead Abbots and Bannister w Ufton Nervet from 96. *The Rectory, Ufton Nervet, Reading RG7 4DH* Tel 0118-983 2328 Fax as telephone

SIBLEY, Peter Linsey. b 40. Selw Coll Cam BA61 MA63 DipHE. Oak Hill Th Coll 79. **d** 81 **p** 82. C Crofton *Portsm* 81-84; TV

Cheltenham St Mark *Glouc* 84-93; P-in-c Tewkesbury H Trin 93-96; V from 96; RD Tewkesbury from 97. *Holy Trinity Vicarage, 49 Barton Street, Tewkesbury, Glos GL20 5PU* Tel (01684) 293233

SIBSON, Edward John. b 39. Brasted Th Coll 61 St Aid Birkenhead 63. **d** 65 **p** 66. C Gt Parndon *Chelmsf* 65-69; C Saffron Walden 69-72; P-in-c Colchester St Leon 72-77; Ind Chapl 72-80; TV Colchester St Leon, St Mary Magd and St Steph 77-80; V Layer-de-la-Haye 80-90; R Chipping Ongar w Shelley from 90; RD Ongar from 94. *The Rectory, Shakletons, Ongar, Essex CM5 9AT* Tel (01277) 362173

SIBSON, Robert Francis. b 46. Leeds Univ CertEd68. Sarum & Wells Th Coll 78. **d** 80 **p** 81. C Watford St Mich *St Alb* 80-83; TV Digswell and Panshanger 83-90; V Biggleswade from 90; RD Biggleswade from 96. *The Vicarage, Shortmead Street, Biggleswade, Beds SG18 0AT* Tel (01767) 312243

SICHEL, Stephen Mackenzie. b 59. RGN85 RMN87 UEA BA80 Birm Univ MA95. Ripon Coll Cuddesdon 87. **d** 90 **p** 91. C Tettenhall Regis *Lich* 90-95; C Camberwell St Giles w St Matt *S'wark* from 95. *St Matthew's House, 77 Coldharbour Lane, London SE5 9NS* Tel 0171-274 3778

SIDAWAY, Canon Geoffrey Harold. b 42. Kelham Th Coll 61. **d** 66 **p** 67. C Beighton *Derby* 66-70; C Chesterfield St Mary and All SS 70-72; P-in-c Derby St Bart 72-74; V 74-77; V Maidstone St Martin *Cant* 77-86; V Bearsted w Thurnham from 86; RD Sutton from 92; Hon Can Cant Cathl from 94. *The Vicarage, Church Lane, Bearsted, Maidstone, Kent ME14 4EF* Tel (01622) 737135 Fax as telephone

SIDDALL, Arthur. b 43. Lanc Univ MA81 DMS90 Surrey Univ PGCE94 MIMgt96. Lon Coll of Div ALCD67 LTh74. **d** 67 **p** 68. C Formby H Trin *Liv* 67-70; C Childwall All SS 70-72; CMS 72-77; Bangladesh 74-77; V Clitheroe St Paul Low Moor *Blackb* 77-82; V Blackb St Gabr 82-90; Dep Gen Sec Miss to Seamen 90-93; Perm to Offic *Lon* 90-93; Hon C Leatherhead *Guildf* 93-96; Perm to Offic 94-96; V Chipping and Whitewell *Blackb* from 96. *The Vicarage, Garstang Road, Chipping, Preston PR3 2QH* Tel (01995) 61252

SIDDLE, Michael Edward. b 33. Dur Univ BA54. St Aid Birkenhead 55. **d** 57 **p** 58. C Fazakerley Em *Liv* 57-59; C Farnworth 59-62; V Swadlincote *Derby* 62-70; Distr Sec (Northd and Dur) BFBS 70-72; Yorkshire 72-82; V Bamber Bridge St Aid *Blackb* 82-87; V Horsforth *Ripon* from 87. *St Margaret's Vicarage, Church Lane, Horsforth, Leeds LS18 5LA* Tel 0113-258 2481

SIDEBOTHAM, Canon Stephen Francis. b 35. Qu Coll Cam BA58 MA80. Linc Th Coll 58. **d** 60 **p** 61. C Bitterne Park *Win* 60-64; Hong Kong 64-83; Dean Hong Kong 76-83; Chapl Gravesend and N Kent Hosp 83-94; R Gravesend St Geo *Roch* 83-94; RD Gravesend 91-94; P-in-c Rosherville 91-94; Acorn Chr Healing Trust from 94. *Whitehill Chase, High Street, Bordon, Hants GU35 0AP* Tel (01420) 472779

SIDEBOTTOM, Andrew John. b 54. FRCO75 FTCL76 LRAM75 Univ of Wales (Abth) BMus76 St Martin's Coll Lanc PGCE78. Sarum & Wells Th Coll 79. **d** 81 **p** 82. C Tenby w Gumfreston *St D* 81-84; C Llanelli 84-86; V Monkton 86-91; V Fairfield *Derby* 91-96; P-in-c Barlborough from 96. *The Rectory, Church Street, Barlborough, Chesterfield, Derbyshire S43 4EP* Tel (01246) 810401

SIDEBOTTOM, George. b 16. TCD 43. **d** 49 **p** 50. C Drumholm and Rossnowlagh *D & R* 49-52; C Maghera 52-53; C Ches St Mary *Ches* 53-56; I Achill w Dugort, Castlebar and Turlough *T, K & A* 56-60; V Felmersham *St Alb* 60-81; w Bletsoe 62-79; R Bletsoe 60-62; rtd 81; Perm to Offic *St Alb* from 81. *11 Cody Road, Clapham, Bedford MK41 6ED* Tel (01234) 356189

SIDES, Canon James Robert. b 37. TCD BA66. CITC 68. **d** 67 **p** 68. C Belfast St Clem *D & D* 67-70; C Antrim All SS *Conn* 70-73; I Tomregan w Drumlane *K, E & A* 73-80; I Killesher 80-97; Preb Kilmore Cathl from 89; I Kildrumferton w Ballymachugh and Ballyjamesduff from 97. *Kildrumferton Rectory, Crosserlough PO, Co Cavan, Irish Republic* Tel Cavan (49) 36211

SILCOCK, Donald John. b 30. AKC59. **d** 60 **p** 61. C Hackney St Jo *Lon* 60-63; C-in-c Plumstead Wm Temple Ch Abbey Wood CD *S'wark* 63-68; C Felpham w Middleton *Chich* 68-74; R Ightham *Roch* 74-84; R Cliffe at Hoo w Cooling 84-92; RD Strood 85-91; rtd 92; Perm to Offic *Chich* from 92. *Puck's House, 26 Ancton Way, Elmer Sands, Middleton-on-Sea, Bognor Regis, W Sussex PO22 6JN* Tel (01243) 582589

SILK, Ian Geoffrey. b 60. Pemb Coll Cam BA81 MA85. Trin Coll Bris BA89. **d** 89 **p** 90. C Linc St Giles *Linc* 89-93; P-in-c Linc St Geo Swallowbeck from 93. *St George's Vicarage, Eastbrook Road, Lincoln LN6 7EW* Tel (01522) 683394

SILK, John Arthur. b 52. Selw Coll Cam BA73 MA77 K Coll Lon MTh80. Westcott Ho Cam 75. **d** 77 **p** 78. C Banstead *Guildf* 77-80; C Dorking w Ranmore 80-84; R Ringwould w Kingsdown *Cant* 84-95; V Thames Ditton *Guildf* from 95. *The Vicarage, Summer Road, Thames Ditton, Surrey KT7 0QQ* Tel 0181-398 3446

✠**SILK, The Rt Revd Robert David.** b 36. Ex Univ BA58. St Steph Ho Ox 58. **d** 59 **p** 60 **c** 94. C Gillingham St Barn *Roch* 59-62; C Lamorbey H Redeemer 63-69; R Swanscombe SS Pet and Paul 69-71; P-in-c Swanscombe All SS 69-71; R Swanscombe 71-75; R Beckenham St Geo 75-80; Adn Leic 80-94; TR Leic H Spirit 82-88; Australia from 94; Bp Ballarat from 94. *Bishopscourt, 454 Wendouree Parade, Ballarat, Victoria, Australia 3350* Tel Ballarat (53) 311183 Fax 382782

SILKSTONE, Harry William James. b 21. St D Coll Lamp BA48. **d** 49 **p** 50. C Dowlais *Llan* 49-51; C Aberdare St Fagan 51-53; C Southall H Trin *Lon* 53-56; V Stratford New Town St Paul *Chelmsf* 56-63; R Debden 63-72; V Bocking St Pet 72-78; R Gt Hallingbury 78-86; rtd 86; Perm to Offic *B & W* 86-93. *4 Mortimer Place, Clare, Sudbury, Suffolk CO10 8QP*

SILKSTONE, Thomas William. b 27. St Edm Hall Ox BA51 MA55 BD67. Wycliffe Hall Ox 51. **d** 53 **p** 54. C Aston SS Pet and Paul *Birm* 53-56; Div Master Merchant Taylors' Sch Crosby 56-62; Lect K Alfred's Coll Win 62-65; Sen Lect 65-75; Prin Lect 75-85; Lic to Offic *Win* 62-85; Perm to Offic *Truro* from 82; rtd 92. *Trevalyon, Lansallos, Looe, Cornwall PL13 2PX* Tel (01503) 72110

SILLER, James Robert William. b 44. Pemb Coll Ox BA65 MA70 Qu Coll Cam 69. Westcott Ho Cam 67. **d** 70 **p** 71. C Spring Grove St Mary *Lon* 70-73; C Leeds St Pet *Ripon* 73-77; P-in-c Quarry Hill 73-77; V Gilling and Kirkby Ravensworth 77-82; P-in-c Melsonby 77-82; R Farnley 82-94; V Potternewton from 94. *St Martin's Vicarage, 2A St Martin's View, Leeds LS7 3LB* Tel 0113-262 4271

SILLETT, Angela Veronica Isabel. *See* BERNERS-WILSON, Mrs Angela Veronica Isabel

SILLEY, Michael John. b 48. Ripon Coll Cuddesdon 82. **d** 84 **p** 85. C Frodingham *Linc* 84-87; V Ingham w Cammeringham w Fillingham 87-96; R Aisthorpe w Scampton w Thorpe le Fallows etc 87-96; RD Lawres 92-96; P-in-c N w S Carlton 93-96; P-in-c Brigg 96-97; V Brigg, Wrawby and Cadney cum Howsham from 97. *The Vicarage, 10 Glanford Road, Brigg, S Humberside DN20 8DJ* Tel (01652) 653989

SILLIS, Andrew Keith. b 66. Wolv Poly BSc87. Aston Tr Scheme 91 Westcott Ho Cam 93. **d** 96 **p** 97. C Boyne Hill *Ox* from 96. *St Paul's House, 3 Church Close, Maidenhead, Berks SL6 4HE*

SILLIS, Eric Keith. b 41. NW Ord Course 75. **d** 78 **p** 79. C Blackpool St Steph *Blackb* 78-82; V Huncoat 82-86; V Blackpool St Wilfrid 86-95; V Fleetwood St Dav from 95. *St David's Vicarage, 211 Broadway, Fleetwood, Lancs FY7 8AZ* Tel (01253) 779725

SILLIS, Graham William. b 46. S'wark Ord Course 73. **d** 76 **p** 77. C Palmers Green St Jo *Lon* 76-79; C Dawlish *Ex* 79-81; V Ipswich St Thos *St E* 81-87; V Babbacombe *Ex* 87-95. *8 Waterloo Road, Torquay TQ1 3AY* Tel (01803) 291005

SILLITOE, Pauline Ann. b 42. ACP71 FCP82 CertEd69 Birm Poly DipEd80. Qu Coll Birm 82. **dss** 85 **d** 87 **p** 94. Kingshurst *Birm* 85-86; Castle Bromwich St Clem 86-87; NSM from 87; Chapl Chelmsley Hosp Birm from 92. *The Vicarage, Lanchester Way, Birmingham B36 9JG* Tel 0121-747 4460

SILLITOE, William John. b 37. Lich Th Coll 67. **d** 69 **p** 70. C Ettingshall *Lich* 69-71; C March St Jo *Ely* 72-74; P-in-c Kennett 74-77; V Fordham St Pet 74-77; V Castle Bromwich St Clem *Birm* from 77. *The Vicarage, Lanchester Way, Birmingham B36 9JG* Tel 0121-747 4460

SILLS, Peter Michael. b 41. Barrister 76 Nottm Univ BA63 LLM68. S'wark Ord Course 78. **d** 81 **p** 82. C W Wimbledon Ch Ch *S'wark* 81-85; P-in-c Barnes H Trin 85-93; Wandsworth Adnry Ecum Officer 90-93; V Purley St Mark Woodcote from 93. *St Mark's Vicarage, 22 Peaks Hill, Purley, Surrey CR8 3JE* Tel 0181-660 7204

SILVERSIDES, Mark. b 51. Lon Univ BD73. St Jo Coll Nottm 74. **d** 76 **p** 77. C Hornchurch St Andr *Chelmsf* 76-80; P-in-c Becontree St Thos 80-85; TR Becontree W 85-86; CPAS Staff 86-92; Freelance Chr Video and Resources Producer from 92; Perm to Offic *Dur* from 93. *15 Glenhurst Drive, Whickham, Newcastle upon Tyne NE5 1FE* Tel 0191-488 1937

SILVERTHORN, Alan. b 37. St Mich Coll Llan 62. **d** 65 **p** 66. C Machen and Rudry *Mon* 65-71; V New Tredegar 71-83; V Llanfrechfa and Llanddewi Fach w Llandegveth from 83. *The Vicarage, Llanfrechfa, Cwmbran NP44 8DQ* Tel (01633) 482343

SILVESTER, David. b 59. Qu Mary Coll Lon BSc80 Nottm Univ BCombStuds85. Linc Th Coll 82. **d** 85 **p** 86. C Walthamstow St Mary w St Steph *Chelmsf* 85-90; TV Barking St Marg w St Patr 90-96; V Mildmay Grove St Jude and St Paul *Lon* from 96. *The Vicarage, 71 Marquess Road, London N1 2PT* Tel 0171-226 5924

SILVESTER, Stephen David. b 59. Chu Coll Cam BA80 MA83 Man Univ PGCE82. St Jo Coll Nottm 88. **d** 91 **p** 92. C Nottingham St Jude *S'well* 91-96; V Gamston and Bridgford from 96. *10 Scafell Close, West Bridgford, Nottingham NG2 6RJ* Tel 0115-982 5993

SIM, David Hayward. b 29. Qu Coll Birm 57. **d** 59 **p** 60. C Foleshill St Laur *Cov* 59-62; C Kenilworth St Nic 62-64; V Devonport St Aubyn *Ex* 64-69; V Frampton *Linc* 69-74; V Gainsborough St Geo 74-82; V Sturminster Newton and Hinton St Mary *Sarum* 82-89; R Stock and Lydlinch 82-89; Dorchester 89-94; Chapl HM Pris Dorchester 89-94; rtd 95. *12 Eldridge Close, Dorchester, Dorset DT1 2JS* Tel (01305) 269262

SIMCOCK, Canon Michael Pennington. b 27. Qu Coll Cam BA50 MA52. Bps' Coll Cheshunt 50. **d** 52 **p** 53. C Andover w Foxcott

Win 52-55; C Eastleigh 55-57; Min Tadley St Mary CD 57-67; V Altarnon and Bolventor *Truro* 67-70; V Treleigh 70-87; RD Carnmarth N 75-91; Hon Can Truro Cathl 82-92; R Redruth w Lanner 87-88; TR Redruth w Lanner and Treleigh 88-92; rtd 92; Perm to Offic *Truro* from 92. *1C Straton Place, Falmouth, Cornwall TR11 2ST*

SIMISTER, Charles Arnold. b 19. MM44. Edin Th Coll 49. **d** 52 **p** 53. C Glas Ch Ch *Glas* 52-57; C Worsley *Man* 57-60; V Downton *Sarum* 60-63; CF 63-84; R Kircudbright *Glas* 63-84; R Gatehouse of Fleet 63-84; rtd 84; Perm to Offic *Glas* from 84. *98 High Street, Kirkcudbright DG6 4TX* Tel (01557) 330747

SIMISTER, Norman Harold. b 39. Bris Univ BSc60. LNSM course 91. **d** 93 **p** 94. NSM Wainford *St E* from 93. *Romaine, 1 School Road, Ringsfield, Beccles, Suffolk NR34 8NZ* Tel (01502) 715549

SIMMONDS, David Brian. b 38. Selw Coll Cam BA62 MA66. Ridley Hall Cam. **d** 65 **p** 66. C Newcastle w Butterton *Lich* 65-69; V Branston 69-97; RD Tutbury 95-97; V Branston w Tatenhill from 97. *The Vicarage, Church Road, Branston, Burton-on-Trent, Staffs DE14 3ER* Tel (01283) 568926

SIMMONDS, Edward Alan. b 32. St Edm Hall Ox MA60. Ripon Coll Cuddesdon 88. **d** 89 **p** 90. NSM Ox St Mich w St Martin and All SS *Ox* 89-92; NSM Ox St Mary V w St Cross and St Pet 92-94; Chapl Lugano *Eur* from 94. *13 via al Nido, 6900 Lugano-Besso, Switzerland* Tel Lugano (91) 581038

SIMMONDS, John. b 24. Sheff Univ BA50. Ridley Hall Cam 50. **d** 52 **p** 53. C Portsdown *Portsm* 52-55; C-in-c Fareham St Jo Ev CD 55-65; V W Streatham St Jas *S'wark* 65-73; V Congresbury *B & W* 73-75; P-in-c Puxton w Hewish St Ann and Wick St Lawrence 73-75; V Congresbury w Puxton and Hewish St Ann 75-84; Warden Home of Divine Healing Crowhurst 84-89; rtd 89. *Beach Villa, 14 The Beach, Clevedon, Avon BS21 7QU* Tel (01275) 342295

SIMMONDS, Paul Andrew Howard. b 50. Nottm Univ BSc73 Lon Univ DipTh78. Trin Coll Bris 75. **d** 78 **p** 79. C Leic H Trin w St Jo *Leic* 78-82; SW Regional Co-ord CPAS 83-86; Hd Adult Tr and Resources CPAS 86-95; C Wolston and Church Lawford *Cov* from 89; Dioc Miss Adv from 95. *31 John Simpson Close, Wolston, Coventry CV8 3HX* Tel (01203) 543188 E-mail 101765.3550@compuserve.com

SIMMONDS, Canon Paul Richard. b 38. AKC63. **d** 64 **p** 65. C Newington St Mary *S'wark* 64-67; C Cheam 68-73; P-in-c Stockwell Green St Andr 73-87; V from 87; Hon Can S'wark Cathl from 97. *St Andrew's Vicarage, Moat Place, London SW9 0TA* Tel 0171-274 7531

SIMMONDS, Robert John. Ripon Coll Cuddesdon Aston Tr Scheme. **d** 96 **p** 97. C Southampton Thornhill St Chris *Win* from 96. *22 Lydgate Green, Thornhill, Southampton SO19 6LP* Tel (01703) 406351

SIMMONDS, Robert William (Bob). b 52. Nottm Univ BTh77 Birm Poly DCG79. Linc Th Coll 72. **d** 80 **p** 81. C Roehampton H Trin *S'wark* 80-83; TV Hemel Hempstead *St Alb* 83-90; V S Woodham Ferrers *Chelmsf* 90-94; rtd 94. *14 Hardy Street, Maidstone, Kent ME14 2SH* Tel (01622) 681129

SIMMONDS, William Hugh Cyril. b 08. Lon Univ DipOAS47. St Jo Hall Highbury. **d** 37 **p** 38. China 30-51; P-in-c Sinfin *Derby* 52-54; V Wolverhampton St Jude *Lich* 54-67; V S Malling *Chich* 67-78; rtd 78; Perm to Offic *Roch* from 96. *5 Cornford Court, Cornford Lane, Pembury, Tunbridge Wells, Kent TN2 4QX* Tel (01892) 824196

SIMMONS, Barry Jeremy. b 32. Leeds Univ BA54 MA62. Ridley Hall Cam 61. **d** 63 **p** 64. C Buttershaw St Aid *Bradf* 63-65; Jamaica 65-68; V Earby *Bradf* 68-73; Hong Kong 73-74; Bahrain 75-79; Chapl Luxembourg *Eur* 80-91; V Shoreham *Roch* from 91. *The Vicarage, Shoreham, Sevenoaks, Kent TN14 7SA* Tel (01959) 522363

SIMMONS, Bernard Peter. b 26. CA Tr Coll 48 S'wark Ord Course 86. **d** 88 **p** 88. C Chatham St Wm *Roch* 88-91; rtd 91; P-in-c Underriver *Roch* 91-95; P-in-c Seal St Lawr 91-95; Perm to Offic *Pet* from 95. *5 Sycamore Drive, Desborough, Kettering, Northants NN14 2YH* Tel (01536) 763302

SIMMONS, Canon Brian Dudley. b 35. Master Mariner. St Steph Ho Ox 62. **d** 64 **p** 65. C Bournemouth St Pet *Win* 64-67; Miss to Seamen 67-71; Hon C Milton next Gravesend w Denton *Roch* 67-70; Hon C Gravesend St Geo 70-71; V Lamorbey H Trin 71-90; R Hever w Mark Beech 90-93; P-in-c Four Elms 90-93; R Hever, Four Elms and Mark Beech 93-94; Hon Can Roch Cathl from 91; V Langton Green from 94. *The Vicarage, The Green, Langton Green, Tunbridge Wells, Kent TN3 0JB* Tel (01892) 862072

SIMMONS, Christopher John. b 49. Mert Coll Ox MA77. NE Ord Course 88. **d** 90 **p** 91. C Kirkleatham *York* 90-93; P-in-c Barlby 93-95; V Barlby w Riccall from 95. *The Vicarage, York Road, Barlby, Selby, N Yorkshire YO8 7JP* Tel (01757) 702384

SIMMONS, Eric. b 30. Leeds Univ BA51. Coll of Resurr Mirfield 51. **d** 53 **p** 54. C Chesterton St Luke *Ely* 53-57; Chapl Keele Univ *Lich* 57-61; Lic to Offic *Wakef* 63-65 and 67-95; CR from 63; Lic to Offic *Ripon* 65-67; Warden Hostel of the Resurr Leeds 66-67; Superior CR 74-87. *Royal Foundation of St Katharine, 2 Butcher Row, London E14 8DS* Tel 0171-790 3540

SIMMONS, Gary David. b 59. Trin Coll Bris BA86. **d** 87 **p** 88. C Ecclesfield *Sheff* 87-90; Min Stapenhill Immanuel CD *Derby* 90-96; V Stapenhill Immanuel from 97. *Immanuel Vicarage, 150 Hawthorn Crescent, Burton-on-Trent, Staffs DE15 9QW* Tel (01283) 563959

SIMMONS, Godfrey John. b 39. Open Univ BA77. Edin Th Coll 77. **d** 74 **p** 74. Dioc Supernumerary *St And* 74-75 and 80-81; C Strathtay 75-77; C Dunkeld 75-77; C Bridge of Allan 77-80; C Alloa 77-80; Chapl Stirling Univ 79-80; Chapl HM Pris Perth 80-85; Min Crieff *St And* 80-81; R 81-85; Min Muthill 80-81; R 81-85; Min Comrie 80-81; R 81-85; R Stromness *Ab* 85-89; R Kirkwall 85-91; Miss to Seamen from 85; Hon Chapl (Scotland) 85-90; Hon Area Chapl (Scotland) 90-94; R Longside *Ab* 91-94; R Old Deer 91-94; R Peterhead 91-92; R Strichen 91-94; Chapl HM Pris Peterhead 91-94; Chapl Supt Mersey Miss to Seamen from 94; Perm to Offic *Ches* from 94. *Colonsay House, 20 Crosby Road South, Liverpool L22 1RQ* Tel 0151-920 3253 Fax 928 0244

SIMMONS, Miss Joan Yvonne. b 14. Gilmore Ho 57. **dss** 61 **d** 87. Harringay St Paul *Lon* 61-63; Belsize Park 63-69; Adult Educn Officer 69-78; rtd 78; Perm to Offic *Chich* from 87. *12 Whittington College, London Road, East Grinstead, W Sussex RH19 2QU* Tel (01342) 312781

SIMMONS, John. b 53. Carl Dioc Tr Course 82. **d** 85 **p** 86. C Wotton St Mary *Glouc* 85-88; P-in-c Amberley 88-92; R Burton Latimer *Pet* from 92; RD Kettering from 94. *The Rectory, Preston Court, Burton Latimer, Kettering, Northants NN15 5LR* Tel (01536) 722959 Fax as telephone

SIMMONS, John Graham. b 54. Westf Coll Lon BSc75 Man Univ PGCE76 CertRE81. N Ord Course 89. **d** 92 **p** 93. C Thame w Towersey *Ox* 92-97; R Heydon, Gt and Lt Chishill, Chrishall etc *Chelmsf* from 97. *1 Hall Lane, Great Chishill, Royston, Herts SG8 8SG* Tel (01763) 838703

SIMMONS, John Harold. b 46. FCCA. Sarum & Wells Th Coll 86. **d** 89 **p** 90. NSM The Iwernes, Sutton Waldron and Fontmell Magna *Sarum* from 89. *Fourways, Iwerne Courteney, Blandford Forum, Dorset DT11 8QL* Tel (01258) 860515

SIMMONS, Canon Maurice Samuel. b 27. St Chad's Coll Dur BA50 DipTh52. **d** 52 **p** 53. C S Shields St Hilda *Dur* 52-58; Youth Chapl 56-60; R Croxdale 58-81; Soc and Ind Adv to Bp Dur 61-70; Gen Sec Soc Resp Gp 70-75; Hon Can Dur Cathl from 71; Sec Dioc Bd for Miss and Unity 75-82; V Norton St Mary 81-92; RD Stockton 85-92; rtd 92. *11 Roecliffe Grove, Stockton-on-Tees, Cleveland TS19 8JU* Tel (01642) 618880

SIMMONS, Norman. b 11. Wycliffe Hall Ox 49. **d** 49 **p** 50. C Rotherham *Sheff* 49-53; V Doncaster St Leon and St Jude 53-74; R Burghwallis w Skelbrooke 74-81; rtd 81; Perm to Offic *York* from 90. *21 Norseway, Stamford Bridge, York YO4 1DR* Tel (01759) 72298

SIMMONS, Raymond Agar. b 35. Linc Th Coll 69. **d** 71 **p** 72. C Hartlepool St Luke *Dur* 71-74; P-in-c Purleigh *Chelmsf* 74-81; Ind Chapl 74-81; P-in-c Cold Norton w Stow Maries 81; Chapl Rampton Hosp Retford 81-97; rtd 97. *13 Caenby Road, Cleethorpes, S Humberside DN35 0JT*

SIMMONS, Richard Andrew Cartwright. b 46. Trin Coll Bris 73. **d** 75 **p** 76. C Worting *Win* 75-80; R Six Pilgrims *B & W* 80-92; R Bincombe w Broadwey, Upwey and Buckland Ripers *Sarum* from 92. *The Rectory, 526 Littlemoor Road, Weymouth, Dorset DT3 5PA* Tel (01305) 812542

SIMMS, Ernest Desmond Ross. b 25. TCD BA48 MA51 BD51. **d** 51 **p** 52. C Ballymena *Conn* 51-53; C Belfast St Mary 53-55; C Carnmoney 55-62; CF 62-81; R Cheriton w Tichborne and Beauworth *Win* 81-90; RD Alresford 84-90; rtd 90. *11 Buttermere Gardens, Alresford, Hants SO24 9NN* Tel (01962) 735526

SIMMS, William Michael (Bill). b 41. DMA66 ACIS70 MIPM75 Open Univ BA87. NE Ord Course 84. **d** 87 **p** 88. NSM Croft *Ripon* 87; C 88; NSM Middleton Tyas and Melsonby 87; C 88; C Headingley 88-90; C Richmond w Hudswell 90-93; C-in-c Downholme and Marske 90-93; V Hawes and Hardraw from 93. *The Vicarage, Hawes, N Yorkshire DL8 3NP* Tel (01969) 667553

SIMON, Brother. *See* BROOK, Peter Geoffrey

SIMON, David Sidney. b 49. CDipAF76 Univ of Wales (Abth) BSc(Econ)70 Hull Univ MA83. NE Ord Course 84. **d** 87 **p** 88. NSM Beverley St Mary *York* 87-94; NSM Beverley Deanery from 94; Lect Humberside Coll of HE 87-90; Humberside Poly 90-92; Humberside Univ *York* 92-96; Lincs and Humberside Univ from 96. *8 Melrose Park, Beverley, N Humberside HU17 8JL* Tel (01482) 862855

SIMON, Frederick Fairbanks. b 42. Ripon Coll Cuddesdon 74. **d** 77 **p** 78. C Cheddleton *Lich* 77-79; C Woodley St Jo the Ev *Ox* 79-82; V Spencer's Wood 82-85; P-in-c Steventon w Milton 85-87; Chapl Grenville Coll Bideford 87-95; rtd 96; Perm to Offic *Ex* from 96. *The Chimes, 18 Fore Street, Moretonhampstead, Newton Abbot, Devon TQ13 8LL* Tel (01647) 440979

SIMON, Haydn Henry England. b 56. Llan Dioc Tr Scheme 92 St Mich Coll Llan 97. **d** 96 **p** 97. NSM Penydarren *Llan* 96-97; C Caerphilly from 97. *71 Barlett Street, Caerphilly CF83 1JT* Tel (01222) 882695

SIMON, Oliver. b 45. Dur Univ BA67 Sussex Univ MA68 Ox Univ DipTh71 Man Univ CertRS89 Sheff Univ MMinTheol94. Cuddesdon Coll 69. **d** 71 **p** 72. C Kidlington *Ox* 71-74; C Bracknell 74-78; V Frodsham *Ches* 78-88; R Easthampstead *Ox* from 88. *The Rectory, Easthampstead, Bracknell, Berks RG12 7ER* Tel (01344) 423253 or 425205 Fax 641609 E-mail 100661.130@compuserve.com

SIMONS, Miss Christine. b 40. RGN62 RM64 RHV69. St Jo Coll Nottm 82. **dss** 84 **d** 87 **p** 94. Claygate *Guildf* 84-87; C Camberley St Paul 87-93; NSM from 93. *70 Inglewood Avenue, Camberley, Surrey GU15 1RS* Tel (01276) 684702

SIMONS, Preb John Trevor. b 34. Lon Univ BD67. ALCD66. **d** 67 **p** 68. C Becontree St Mary *Chelmsf* 67-71; V Cranham Park 71-78; P-in-c Nailsea H Trin *B & W* 78-83; R 83-97; Sen Asst P from 97; Preb Wells Cathl from 90. *3 Wedmore Road, Nailsea, Bristol BS19 2PZ* Tel (01225) 790320

SIMONS, Mark Anselm. b 38. ARCM62. Oak Hill Th Coll 62. **d** 65 **p** 66. C Nottingham St Ann *S'well* 65-68; C N Ferriby *York* 68-75; P-in-c Sherburn 75-78; V Gt and Lt Driffield 78-93; Perm to Offic from 93. *7 Royal Crescent, Scarborough, N Yorkshire YO11 2RN* Tel (01723) 378056

SIMONS, William Angus. b 18. Keble Coll Ox BA39 MA47. Cuddesdon Coll 40. **d** 41 **p** 42. C Poplar All SS w St Frideswide *Lon* 41-44 and 47-48; RAChD 44-47; C Is of Dogs Ch Ch and St Jo w St Luke *Lon* 48-54; V Fulham St Jas Moore Park 54-62; Ind Chapl Worc and Lon 62-65; Chapl Hammersmith Hosp Lon 65-68; St Edm Hosp 68-88; Northn Gen Hosp 68-72; Lic to Offic *Pet* 68-72 and from 81; P-in-c Northampton St Lawr 72-76; C Northampton H Sepulchre w St Andr and St Lawr 76-81; Northants Past Coun Service from 76; Founder Dir 76-84; Supervisor from 84; rtd 84. *54 Park Avenue North, Northampton NN3 2JE* Tel (01604) 713767

SIMONSON, Canon Juergen Werner Dietrich. b 24. Lon Univ BD52. ALCD52. **d** 52 **p** 53. C W Kilburn St Luke w St Simon and St Jude *Lon* 52-56; Nigeria 57-63; Chapl CMS Tr Coll Chislehurst 64-65; Vice-Prin 65-67; Prin CMS Tr Coll Chislehurst 67-69; V Putney St Marg *S'wark* 69-81; RD Wandsworth 74-81; Hon Can S'wark Cathl 75-90; R Barnes St Mary 81-90; rtd 90. *Elm Cottage, Horseshoe Lane, Ibthorpe, Andover, Hants SP11 0BY* Tel (01264) 76381

SIMPER, Miss Rachel Dawn. b 67. K Coll Lon BD89. Westcott Ho Cam CTM92. **d** 92 **p** 94. Par Dn Clitheroe St Mary *Blackb* 92-94; C 94-95; C Nor St Pet Mancroft w St Jo Maddermarket *Nor* from 95. *63 Recreation Road, Norwich NR2 3PA* Tel (01603) 51878

SIMPER, Terence Ernest. b 27. Qu Coll Birm 53. **d** 56 **p** 57. C Fishponds St Mary *Bris* 56-59; C Shirehampton 59-61; C-in-c Chippenham St Pet CD 61-69; Australia 69-75; P-in-c Bris Lockleaze St Mary Magd w St Fran *Bris* 76-79; P-in-c Brislington St Anne 79-84; P-in-c St Dominic *Truro* 84-87; P-in-c St Mellion w Pillaton 84-87; P-in-c Landulph 84-87; R St Dominic, Landulph and St Mellion w Pillaton 87-90; rtd 90. *21 St Anne's Drive, Oldland Common, Bristol BS15 6RD* Tel 0117-932 2514

SIMPKIN, Mrs Doris Lily. b 30. EMMTC 79. **dss** 82 **d** 87 **p** 94. Mugginton and Kedleston *Derby* 82-87; NSM 87-94; Perm to Offic from 94. *71 Wheeldon Avenue, Derby DE22 1HP* Tel (01332) 343830

SIMPKIN, Paul. b 29. EMMTC. **d** 82 **p** 83. NSM Mugginton and Kedleston *Derby* 82-92; Lic to Offic from 92. *71 Wheeldon Avenue, Derby DE22 1HP* Tel (01332) 343830

SIMPKINS, Frank Charles. b 19. Oak Hill Th Coll 72. **d** 75 **p** 76. C Harrow Weald St Mich *Lon* 75-78; Hon C 81-84; P-in-c Dollis Hill St Paul 78-80; Chapl Northwick Park Hosp Harrow 81-83; Hon C Harrow Trin St Mich *Lon* 84-94; Perm to Offic from 94. *7 Milne Field, Pinner, Middx HA5 4DP* Tel 0181-428 2477

SIMPKINS, Canon Lionel Frank. b 46. UEA BSc68. Lambeth STh77 St Jo Coll Nottm ALCD72 LTh74. **d** 73 **p** 74. C Leic H Apostles *Leic* 73-77; C Bushbury *Lich* 77-80; V Sudbury w Ballingdon and Brundon *St E* 80-96; Chapl Sudbury Hosps 80-96; RD Sudbury 88-96; Hon Can St E Cathl from 94; V Ipswich St Aug from 96. *St Augustine's Vicarage, 2 Bucklesham Road, Ipswich IP3 8TJ* Tel (01473) 728654

SIMPSON, Alexander (Alex). b 31. Oak Hill Th Coll 74. **d** 76 **p** 77. Hon C Lower Homerton St Paul *Lon* 76-81; Hon C Homerton St Barn w St Paul 81-85; TV Hackney Marsh 85-87; V Kensington St Helen w H Trin from 87. *St Helen's Vicarage, St Helen's Gardens, London W10 6LP* Tel 0181-969 1520

SIMPSON, Andrew. b 48. Liv Univ BEng69. Sarum Th Coll 83. **d** 86 **p** 87. NSM Canford Magna *Sarum* from 86. *17 Sopwith Crescent, Wimborne, Dorset BH21 1SH* Tel (01202) 883996

SIMPSON, Athol. b 20. Lich Th Coll 41. **d** 44 **p** 45. C Gosforth All SS *Newc* 44-48; C Benwell St Jas 48-52; V Mickley 52-57; R Man St Pet Oldham Road w St Jas *Man* 57-60; C Gosforth All SS *Newc* 60-63; P-in-c Kenton Ascension 60-63; V Amble 63-90; rtd 90. *63 Briardene Crescent, Gosforth, Newcastle upon Tyne NE3 4RX*

SIMPSON, Dr Charles Michael. b 38. St Cath Coll Cam MA64 Campion Hall Ox MA65 K Coll Lon PhD71 Heythrop Coll Lon STL69. **d** 68 **p** 69. Lect Th Lon Univ 72-84; Chapl Prince of Peace Community Greenwich 85-87; Retreat Dir St Beuno's Clwyd 87-91; P-in-c Selkirk *Edin* 91-94; P-in-c Offchurch *Cov* 94-96; Warden Offa Retreat Ho and Dioc Spirituality Adv from 94. *The Vicarage, Offchurch, Leamington Spa, Warks CV33 9AL* Tel (01926) 424401 Fax 330350

SIMPSON, David John. b 61. Univ Coll Dur BA85. Sarum & Wells Th Coll 89. **d** 91 **p** 92. C Selby Abbey *York* 91-94; C Romsey *Win* from 94. *15 Mount Temple, Romsey, Hants SO51 5UW* Tel (01794) 523840

SIMPSON, Derek John. b 59. Oak Hill Th Coll BA89. **d** 89 **p** 90. C Alperton *Lon* 89-95; TR Brentford from 95. *3 The Butts, Brentford, Middx TW8 8BJ*

SIMPSON, Derrick. b 27. NW Ord Course 72. **d** 75 **p** 76. C Disley *Ches* 75-79; C Stockport St Geo 79-81; R Wistaston 81-90; Chapl Barony Hosp Nantwich 81-89; V Newton in Mottram *Ches* 90-93; rtd 93; Perm to Offic *Ches* from 93. *60 Dane Bank Avenue, Crewe CW2 8AD*

SIMPSON, Mrs Elizabeth Ann. b 59. Lon Bible Coll BA80 Trin Coll Bris 84. **dss** 86 **d** 97. Thornbury *Glouc* 86-87; Beckenham Ch Ch *Roch* 87-90; Heydon, Gt and Lt Chishill, Chrishall etc *Chelmsf* 90-93; Shirwell, Loxhore, Kentisbury, Arlington, etc *Ex* 93-97; NSM from 97. *The Rectory, Shirwell, Barnstaple, Devon EX31 4JR* Tel (01271) 850436

SIMPSON, Dr Geoffrey Sedgwick. b 32. Hamilton Coll (NY) BA54 Wisconsin Univ MA Pemb Coll Cam PhD70. Gen Th Sem (NY) STB57. **d** 57 **p** 57. USA 57-77; Chapl Birm Univ *Birm* 77-80; V Shoreham *Roch* 80-90; TR Street TM *York* from 90. *The Rectory, Barton-le-Street, Malton, N Yorkshire YO17 0PL* Tel (01653) 628376

SIMPSON, George William. b 18. Ox NSM Course. **d** 76 **p** 77. NSM Didcot *Ox* 76-87; C Swan 87-89; rtd 89; Perm to Offic *Ex* 90-95. *21 Crescent Gardens, Ivybridge, Plymouth PL21 0BS* Tel (01752) 894425

SIMPSON, Mrs Georgina (Georgie). b 46. Westmr Coll Ox BTh93 Birm Univ MA95. St Alb and Ox Min Course 95. **d** 97. NSM Littlemore *Ox* from 97. *85 Church Road, Sandford-on-Thames, Oxford OX4 4YA* Tel (01865) 775160

SIMPSON, Godfrey Lionel. b 42. Sarum Th Coll 63. **d** 66 **p** 67. C Leintwardine *Heref* 66-70; C Leominster 70-73; P-in-c Whitbourne 73-79; V Barlaston *Lich* from 79; RD Trentham from 85. *The Vicarage, Barlaston, Stoke-on-Trent ST12 9AB* Tel (01782) 372452

SIMPSON, Herbert. b 20. Carl Dioc Tr Course. **d** 82 **p** 83. NSM Barrow St Aid *Carl* 82; NSM Barrow St Jo 82-90; rtd 90; Perm to Offic *Carl* from 90. *3 Glenridding Drive, Barrow-in-Furness, Cumbria LA14 4PE* Tel (01229) 823707

SIMPSON, The Very Revd John Arthur. b 33. Keble Coll Ox BA56 MA60. Clifton Th Coll 56. **d** 58 **p** 59. C Low Leyton *Chelmsf* 58-59; C Orpington Ch Ch *Roch* 59-62; Tutor Oak Hill Th Coll 62-72; V Ridge *St Alb* 72-79; P-in-c 79-81; Dir of Ords and Post-Ord Tr 75-81; Hon Can St Alb 77-79; Can Res St Alb 79-81; Adn Cant and Can Res Cant Cathl *Cant* 81-86; Dean Cant from 86. *The Deanery, The Precincts, Canterbury, Kent CT1 2EH* Tel (01227) 765983 or 762862

SIMPSON, John Bernard. b 40. ACP66 St Paul's Cheltenham CertEd62 Ox Univ MTh95. **d** 93 **p** 93. In URC 63-93; Asst to RD Lothingland *Nor* 93-94; C Hopton w Corton 93-94; P-in-c from 94. *The Vicarage, 51 The Street, Corton, Lowestoft, Suffolk NR32 5HT* Tel (01502) 730977 Fax 731272

SIMPSON, Canon John Lawrence. b 33. ARCM60 SS Coll Cam BA55 MA59. Wells Th Coll 63. **d** 65 **p** 66. Chapl Win Cathl *Win* 65-66; C Win St Bart 65-69; Chapl Repton Sch Derby 69-71; Hd of RE Helston Sch 71-78; Lic to Offic *Truro* 71-78; P-in-c Curry Rivel *B & W* 79-80; R Curry Rivel w Fivehead and Swell 80-86; V Tunbridge Wells K Chas *Roch* 86-89; Can Res Bris Cathl *Bris* from 89. *55 Salisbury Road, Bristol BS6 7AS* Tel 0117-942 1452

SIMPSON, John Peter. b 39. ALCD66. **d** 66 **p** 67. C Woodside *Ripon* 66-69; C Burnage St Marg *Man* 69-72; V Rochdale Deeplish St Luke 72-80; R Lamplugh w Ennerdale *Carl* from 80. *The Rectory, Vicarage Lane, Ennerdale, Cleator, Cumbria CA23 3BE* Tel (01946) 861310

SIMPSON, John Raymond. b 41. MASCH87 NSW Sch of Hypnotic Sciences DipCH87 Univ of S Aus GradDipEd92. Chich Th Coll 65. **d** 67 **p** 68. C Scarborough St Martin *York* 67-71; C Grangetown 71-72; Bermuda 72-75; C Lewisham St Mary *S'wark* 76; Australia from 76. *Chaplaincy House, 306 ABW, RAAF Base Pearce, Bullsbrook, W Australia 6084* Tel Perth (9) 571 7252 Fax 571 7278

SIMPSON, John Raymond. b 55. Oak Hill Th Coll 88. **d** 90 **p** 91. C Immingham *Linc* 90-94; TV The Ramseys and Upwood *Ely* from 94. *The Vicarage, Thatchers Close, Upwood, Huntingdon, Cambs PE17 1PN* Tel (01487) 814473

SIMPSON, Mrs June Hall. b 31. LRAM59 Sheff Univ BEd74. EMMTC 83. **dss** 86 **d** 87 **p** 94. Hon Par Dn Carlton-in-Lindrick *S'well* 87-94; Hon C from 94. *57 Arundel Drive, Carlton-in-Lindrick, Worksop, Notts S81 9DL* Tel (01909) 730665

SIMPSON, Lars Henrik. b 66. Lanc Univ BA91. Chich Th Coll 92 St Steph Ho Ox BTh94. **d** 96 **p** 97. C Blackpool St Mich *Blackb* from 96. *14 Adstone Avenue, Blackpool FY3 7PD* Tel (01253) 398636 Fax as telephone

SIMPSON, Miss Margery Patricia. b 36. SRN57 SCM59. Oak Hill Th Coll BA86. **dss** 86 **d** 87 **p** 94. Rodbourne Cheney *Bris* 86-87;

Par Dn 87-90; Par Dn Warmley 90-94; C Warmley, Syston and Bitton 94-95; TV Yate New Town 95-96; rtd 97. *12 Hunter Close, Colehill, Wimborne, Dorset BH21 2TZ* Tel (01202) 842059

SIMPSON, Patrick Verrent. b 26. Fitzw Ho Cam BA49 MA54 Lon Univ PGCE70. Ridley Hall Cam 49. **d** 51 **p** 52. C Redhill St Jo *S'wark* 51-54; C Handsworth St Mary *Birm* 54-55; R Stifford *Chelmsf* 55-59; Chapl St Aid Birkenhead 59-62; V Green Street Green *Roch* 62-67; Lect Brasted Place Coll 62-67; Lect Rachel McMillan Coll of Educn 66-67; W Germany 67-71; Chapl Northfleet Girl's Sch 71-81; Hon C Meopham w Nurstead *Roch* 72-81; P-in-c Weare Giffard w Landcross *Ex* 81-82; P-in-c Littleham 81-82; P-in-c Monkleigh 81-82; R Landcross, Littleham, Monkleigh etc 82-86; P-in-c Bovey Tracey SS Pet and Paul 86-91; Chapl Bovey Tracey Hosp 86-91; Chapl Hawkmoor Hosp 86-87; rtd 91; Perm to Offic *Carl* from 91. *10 Vicarage Close, Burton-in-Kendal, Carnforth, Lancs LA6 1NP* Tel (01524) 782386

SIMPSON, Peter. b 28. Trin Hall Cam BA56 MA60. **d** 57 **p** 58. C Kemp Town St Mark *Chich* 57-60, C Walthamstow St Pet *Chelmsf* 60-64; V Chingford St Anne 64-75; P-in-c Widdington 75; Perm to Offic *Win* 76-79; Chapl Princess Eliz Hosp Guernsey 77-79; R Guernsey St Michel du Valle *Win* 79-91; V Sark 91-95; rtd 95. *The Chantry, Route de Portinfer, Vale, Guernsey, Channel Islands GY6 8LY* Tel (01481) 55784

SIMPSON, Canon Peter Wynn. b 32. Birm Univ BA53. Ripon Hall Ox 55. **d** 57 **p** 58. C Leamington Priors H Trin *Cov* 57-60; C Croydon *Cant* 60-63; V Foleshill St Laur *Cov* 63-70; V Radford 70-79; RD Cov N 76-79; V Finham 79-91; RD Cov S 82-88; Hon Can Cov Cathl 83-91; rtd 91. *Faith Cottage, 118 Main Street, Wolston, Coventry CV8 3HP* Tel (01203) 418330

SIMPSON, Philip Alexander. b 54. Keele Univ BA79 CQSW79. CMS Tr Coll Selly Oak 85. **d** 89. CMS from 85; Pakistan from 85. *42 H/6 Pechs, Karachi 75400, Pakistan* Tel Karachi (21) 438332 or 515180 Fax 455-4278 or 568-0236

SIMPSON, Raymond James. b 40. Lon Coll of Div ALCD63 LTh74. **d** 64 **p** 65. C Longton St Jas *Lich* 64-68; C Upper Tooting H Trin *S'wark* 68-71; BFBS Distr Sec E Anglia 71-77; C-in-c Bowthorpe CD *Nor* 78-84; V Bowthorpe 84-96; Perm to Offic *Newc* from 96; Guardian Community of Aidan and Hilda from 96. *Lindisfarne Retreat, Marygate, Holy Island, Berwick-upon-Tweed TD15 2SD* Tel (01289) 389320

SIMPSON, Richard Lee (Rick). b 66. Keble Coll Ox BA88 MPhil91 Westmr Coll Ox PGCE89. Wycliffe Hall Ox DipMin93. **d** 93 **p** 94. C Newc St Gabr *Newc* 93-97; P-in-c Jesmond H Trin from 97; P-in-c Newc St Barn and St Jude from 97. *Holy Trinity Vicarage, 63 Roseberry Crescent, Jesmond, Newcastle upon Tyne NE2 1EX* Tel 0191-281 1663

SIMPSON, Robert Charles. b 46. Ridley Hall Cam. **d** 85 **p** 86. C Eastwood *S'well* 85-88; V Yardley St Cypr Hay Mill *Birm* 88-93; P-in-c Newent and Gorsley w Cliffords Mesne *Glouc* 93-95; R from 95. *The Rectory, 43 Court Road, Newent, Glos GL18 1SD* Tel (01531) 820248

SIMPSON, Robert David. b 61. Fitzw Coll Cam BA83 MA87 Bris Univ MLitt94. Trin Coll Bris DipHE87. **d** 87 **p** 88. C Beckenham Ch Ch *Roch* 87-90; C Heydon w Gt and Lt Chishill *Chelmsf* 90; C Chrishall 90; C Elmdon w Wendon Lofts and Strethall 90; C Heydon, Gt and Lt Chishill, Chrishall etc 91-93; TV Shirwell, Loxhore, Kentisbury, Arlington, etc *Ex* from 93. *The Rectory, Shirwell, Barnstaple, Devon EX31 4JR* Tel (01271) 850436

SIMPSON, Robert Theodore (Theo). b 34. Linc Coll Ox BA58 MA61 K Coll Lon PhD71 UNISA DTEd83 MEd85. Chich Th Coll 58. **d** 60 **p** 61. C Ellesmere Port *Ches* 60-63; CR 63-66; S Africa 68-88; Prin St Pet Coll 72-75; Pres Federal Th Sem 73-75; Sen Lect Th Swaziland Univ 83-87; Assoc Prof Th 87-88; Chapl and Lect Coll of SS Mark and Jo Plymouth 88-90; Tutor Simon of Cyrene Th Inst 90-92; Perm to Offic *S'wark* 91-92; P-in-c Shadwell St Paul w Ratcliffe St Jas *Lon* from 92. *The Vicarage, 298 The Highway, London E1 9DH* Tel 0171-488 4633

SIMPSON, Roger Westgarth. b 51. Lon Univ BSc72. St Jo Coll Nottm 77. **d** 79 **p** 80. C St Marylebone All So w SS Pet and Jo *Lon* 79-85; R Edin St Paul and St Geo *Edin* 85-95; Canada from 95. *1440 West 12th Avenue, Vancouver, Canada, V6H 1M8*

SIMPSON, The Ven Samuel. b 26. TCD BA55 MA69 Div Test56. **d** 56 **p** 57. C Coleraine *Conn* 56-60; I Donagh w Cloncha and Clonmany *D & R* 60-64; I Ballyscullion 64-81; RD Maghera and Kilrea 75-89; Can Derry Cathl from 78; I Errigal w Garvagh 81-96; Adn Derry 89-96; rtd 96. *53 Magheramenagh Drive, Atlantic Road, Portrush, Co Antrim BT56 8SP* Tel (01265) 824292

SIMPSON (née RALPHS), Mrs Sharon Ann. b 55. St Mary's Coll Dur BA77. Cranmer Hall Dur 81. **dss** 83 **d** 87 **p** 94. Caverswall *Lich* 83-87; Par Dn 87-89; Asst Dioc Officer for Minl Tr *St As* 90-91; NSM Selkirk *Edin* 91-94; C Offchurch *Cov* 94-96; Warden Offa Retreat Ho and Dioc Spirituality Adv from 94. *The Vicarage, Offchurch, Leamington Spa, Warks CV33 9AL* Tel (01926) 424401 Fax 330350

SIMPSON, Thomas Eric. b 31. St Chad's Coll Dur BA55. Ely Th Coll 55. **d** 57 **p** 58. C Jarrow St Paul *Dur* 57-61; C Bishopwearmouth St Mary V w St Pet CD 61-63; V Chopwell 63-92; Chapl Norman Riding Hosp Tyne & Wear 79-83; Chapl Shotley Bridge Gen Hosp 83-90; rtd 92. *58 Tanmeads, Nettlesworth, Chester le Street, Co Durham DH2 3PY* Tel 0191-371 9814

SIMPSON, William Michael. b 45. Leeds Univ BA66. St Jo Coll Nottm 75. **d** 77 **p** 78. C Desborough *Pet* 77-80; P-in-c Arthingworth w Kelmarsh and Harrington 79-80; Hong Kong 80-85 and from 92; P-in-c Beetham and Milnthorpe *Carl* 85-92. *Christ Church Vicarage, 2 Derby Road, Kowloon Tong, Kowloon, Hong Kong* Tel Hong Kong (852) 2338 4433 Fax 2338 8422

SIMPSON, William Thomas. b 10. St Chad's Coll Dur BA35 DipTh36 MA38. **d** 36 **p** 37. C Portsea St Cuth *Portsm* 36-46; V Kennington Park St Agnes *S'wark* 46-49; V Sheff St Matt *Sheff* 49-59; R Week St Mary *Truro* 59-81; R Whitstone 62-81; rtd 81; Perm to Offic *Truro* from 81. *Waverley, Under Road, Gunnislake, Cornwall PL18 9JL* Tel (01822) 833396

SIMPSON, William Vaughan. b 16. Worc Ord Coll 55. **d** 57 **p** 58. C Charlton Kings St Mary *Glouc* 57-60; R Willersey w Saintbury 60-73; RD Campden 70-73; P-in-c Cherington 74-76; V Clearwell 76-79; Perm to Offic 79-91; rtd 81. *62 Fruitlands, Malvern, Worcs WR14 4XA* Tel (01684) 567009

SIMS, Bernard David. b 40. LRSC65 MIWEM68 Bris Coll DipTech Chem63 Bath Univ BSc66. Ox Min Course 91. **d** 94 **p** 95. NSM Beedon and Peasemore w W Ilsley and Farnborough *Ox* from 94. *58 Berkeley Road, Newbury, Berks RG14 5JG* Tel (01635) 47991

SIMS, Christopher Sidney. b 49. Wycliffe Hall Ox 74. **d** 77 **p** 78. C Walmley *Birm* 77-80; V Yardley St Cypr Hay Mill 80-88; V Stanwix *Carl* 88-96; RD Carl 89-95; Hon Can Carl Cathl 91-95; P-in-c Bassenthwaite, Isel and Setmurthy from 96; P-in-c Bolton w Ireby and Uldale from 96; P-in-c Allhallows from 96; P-in-c Torpenhow from 96. *The Vicarage, Torpenhow, Carlisle CA5 1HT* Tel (01697) 371295

SIMS, David John. b 18. Handsworth Coll Birm 44 St Aug Coll Cant 59. **d** 56 **p** 56. In Meth Ch 47-56; W Indies 47-63; V Haxey *Linc* 63-73; USA 73-83; rtd 83; Perm to Offic *Chich* from 87. *Bungalow 6, Terry's Cross, Brighton Road, Henfield, W Sussex BN5 9SX* Tel (01273) 493487

SIMS, James Henry. b 35. St Jo Coll Nottm. **d** 89 **p** 91. NSM Bangor Abbey *D & D* 89-93; C Holywood 93; Bp's C Kilbroney from 93; RD Kilbroney from 95. *The Vicarage, 15 Kilbroney Road, Rostrevor, Newry, Co Down BT34 3BH* Tel (01693) 738293

SIMS, Keith George. b 29. LNSM course 92. **d** 95 **p** 96. NSM Forest Hill St Aug *S'wark* from 95. *68 Forest Hill Road, London SE22 0RS* Tel 0181-693 7225

SIMS, Peter George Russell. b 36. Univ of Wales (Swansea) BA57. St Mich Coll Llan 63. **d** 65 **p** 66. C Brecon w Battle *S & B* 65-72; Min Can Brecon Cathl 65-72; V Llanfrynach and Cantref w Llanhamlach from 72. *The Rectory, Llanfrynach, Brecon LD3 7AJ* Tel (01874) 86667

SIMS, Sidney. b 20. Wycliffe Hall Ox. **d** 64 **p** 65. C Attenborough w Bramcote *S'well* 64-67; V Ramsey St Mary's w Ponds Bridge *Ely* 67-70; V Cambridge St Matt 70-85; Algeria 85-86; rtd 86; Perm to Offic *Nor* from 86. *66 Morston Road, Blakeney, Norfolk NR25 7BE* Tel (01263) 740184

SINCLAIR, Andrew John McTaggart. b 58. Ex Univ BA80. Westcott Ho Cam 81. **d** 84 **p** 85. C Aston cum Aughton and Ulley *Sheff* 84-87; C Rotherham 87-88; TV Edin Old St Paul *Edin* 88-93; Hon Angl Chapl Edin Univ and Moray Ho Coll 89-93; TV Dunstable *St Alb* from 93. *The Priory Vicarage, 20 Friars Walk, Dunstable, Beds LU6 3JA* Tel (01582) 600972 or 696725 E-mail a.and.j.sinclair@dial.pipex.com

SINCLAIR, Arthur Alfred. b 46. **d** 87 **p** 89. Hon C St Andr Cathl Inverness *Mor* 87-92; C from 93; Chapl Asst Inverness Hosp 87-89; Dioc Chapl 87-89; NSM Culloden St Mary-in-the-Fields 89-92; P-in-c from 93; Edin Th Coll 92-93; P-in-c Inverness St Jo *Mor* from 93; Chapl Raigmore Hosp Inverness from 93. *St John's Rectory, Southside Road, Inverness IV2 3BG* Tel (01463) 716288

SINCLAIR, Charles Horace. b 19. Keble Coll Ox BA40 MA44. Linc Th Coll 41. **d** 42 **p** 43. C Upper Norwood St Jo *Cant* 42-45; Chapl K Coll Auckland 46-50; Asst Chapl Haileybury Coll Herts 51; Hd Master Prebendal Sch Chich 51-53; PV Chich Cathl *Chich* 51-53; Chapl and Sen Tutor Brookland Hall Welshpool 53-57; Hd Master St Aid Sch Denby Dale 57-64; Perm to Offic *Wakef* 58-64; rtd 84; Perm to Offic *Cant* from 84. *Oakstead, 93 Harbour Way, Folkestone, Kent CT20 1NB* Tel (01303) 250882

SINCLAIR, Colin. b 30. **d** 84 **p** 85. NSM Ramoan w Ballycastle and Culfeightrin *Conn* 84-92. *4 Bushfoot Cottages, Portballintrae, Bushmills, Co Antrim BT57 8RN* Tel (012657) 31551

SINCLAIR, Gordon Keith. b 52. MA. Cranmer Hall Dur. **d** 84 **p** 85. C Summerfield *Birm* 84-88; V Aston SS Pet and Paul from 88. *Aston Vicarage, Sycamore Road, Birmingham B6 5UH* Tel 0121-327 5856

SINCLAIR, Canon Jane Elizabeth Margaret. b 56. St Hugh's Coll Ox BA78 MA80 Nottm Univ BA82. St Jo Coll Nottm 80. **dss** 83 **d** 87 **p** 94. Herne Hill St Paul *S'wark* 83-86; Chapl and Lect St Jo Coll Nottm 86-93; Can Res Sheff Cathl *Sheff* from 93. *62 Kingfield Road, Sheffield S11 9AU* Tel 0114-255 7782 or 275 3434

SINCLAIR, John Robert. b 58. Oak Hill Th Coll DipHE92. **d** 92 **p** 93. C Ponteland *Newc* 92-96; V Long Benton St Mary from 96. *St Mary's House, Blackfriars Way, Newcastle upon Tyne NE12 8ST* Tel 0191-266 2326

✠**SINCLAIR, The Most Revd Maurice Walter.** b 37. Nottm Univ BSc59 Leic Univ PGCE60. Tyndale Hall Bris 62. **d** 64 **p** 65 **c** 90. C Boscombe St Jo *Win* 64-67; SAMS from 67; Personnel Sec 79-83; Asst Gen Sec 83-84; Prin Crowther Hall CMS Tr Coll Selly Oak 84-90; Perm to Offic *Birm* 84-90; Bp N Argentina from 90; Primate of S Cone from 95. *Iglesia Anglicana, Casilla 187, 4400 Salta, Argentina* Tel Salta (87) 310167

SINCLAIR, Michael David Bradley. b 42. N Ord Course Coll of Resurr Mirfield. **d** 97. NSM Settrington w N Grimston, Birdsall w Langton *York* from 97. *24 St Saviourgate, York YO1 2NN* Tel (01904) 632554

SINCLAIR, Nigel Craig. b 65. Teesside Poly BA87. St Jo Coll Dur BA93. **d** 94 **p** 95. C Marton-in-Cleveland *York* 94-97; TV Thirsk from 97. *The Vicarage, Carlton Miniott, Thirsk, N Yorkshire YO7 4NJ* Tel (01845) 522003

SINCLAIR, Peter. b 44. Oak Hill Th Coll 86. **d** 88 **p** 89. C Darlington H Trin *Dur* 88-91; C-in-c Bishop Auckland Woodhouse Close CD from 91. *18 Watling Road, Bishop Auckland, Co Durham DL14 6RP* Tel (01388) 604086

SINCLAIR, Robert Charles. b 28. Liv Univ LLB49 QUB LLM69 PhD82. Ely Th Coll 58. **d** 60 **p** 61. C Glenavy *Conn* 60-63; Chapl RN 63-67; C Cregagh *D & D* 67-68; Perm to Offic *Conn* from 69. *Juniper Cottage, 11A Glen Road, Glenavy, Crumlin, Co Antrim BT29 4LT* Tel (01849) 453126

SINCLAIR, Robert Michael. b 41. CQSW81. Edin Th Coll 63. **d** 66 **p** 67. C Dunfermline *St And* 66-68; C Edin Old St Paul *Edin* 68-72; P-in-c Edin St Dav 72-77; Hon Dioc Supernumerary from 77. *121/19 Comiston Drive, Edinburgh EH10 5QU* Tel 0131-447 5068

SINDALL, Mrs Christine Ann. b 42. ALA69. EAMTC 84. **d** 87 **p** 94. NSM Sutton *Ely* 87-89; C Cambridge Ascension 89-94; TV 94-96; R Cheveley from 96; R Ashley w Silverley from 96; V Kirtling from 96; V Wood Ditton w Saxon Street from 96. *The Rectory, 130 High Street, Cheveley, Newmarket, Suffolk CB8 9DG* Tel (01638) 730770

SINFIELD, George Edward. b 16. EMMTC 73. **d** 76 **p** 77. NSM Radcliffe-on-Trent *S'well* 76-79; NSM St Oswald in Lee w Bingfield *Newc* 79-86; rtd 86; Perm to Offic *S'well* from 86; Perm to Offic *Linc* from 89. *The Herons, Calverton Close, Beeston, Nottingham NG9 6EY* Tel (01636) 892766

SINGH, Balwant. b 32. BA60. Saharanpur Th Coll 50. **d** 53 **p** 58. India 53-67 and 71-73; Hon C Handsworth St Jas *Birm* 67-71; Hon C N Hinksey *Ox* 73-80; Lic to Offic 80-81; Hon C S Hinksey from 82. *9 Jersey Road, Oxford OX4 4RT* Tel (01865) 717277

SINGH, Vivian Soorat. b 30. Trin Coll Cam BA MA53. Westcott Ho Cam 54. **d** 55 **p** 56. C Yardley Wood *Birm* 55-57; C Birm St Paul 57-59; Asst Master Framlingham Coll Suffolk 59-72; Chapl 60-72; Chapl Wymondham Coll 72-75; Dep Hd Litcham High Sch 75-88; rtd 88; Perm to Offic *Nor* from 88. *Manor Cottage, Wendling Road, Longham, Dereham, Norfolk NR12 2RD* Tel (01362) 687382

SINGLETON, Mrs Editha Mary. b 27. WMMTC 85. **dss** 84 **d** 87 **p** 94. Lich St Chad *Lich* 84-90; Hon Par Dn 87-90; Hon Par Dn Beaulieu and Exbury and E Boldre *Win* 90-94; Hon C from 94. *The Peregrine, The Lane, Fawley, Southampton SO45 1EY* Tel (01703) 894364

SINGLETON, Ernest George (Paul). b 15. St Aug Coll Cant 38. **d** 41 **p** 42. C Portsea N End St Mark *Portsm* 41-46; C Hendon St Mary *Lon* 46-48; CR 48-68; Lic to Offic *Wakef* 49-51; Lic to Offic *Lon* 52-56; S Africa 56-60; Prior St Teilo's Priory Cardiff 61-68; Perm to Offic *Lon* 68-91 and 93-95; rtd 80; Hon C Twickenham St Mary *Lon* 91-93. *Suite 268, Postnet X31, Saxonwold 2132, Johannesburg, South Africa* Tel Johannesburg (11) 880 2982 Fax 442 4732

SINGLETON, James Richard. b 56. CEng85 RN Eng Coll Plymouth BSc79 RN Coll Greenwich DipNuc81. Ripon Coll Cuddesdon 90. **d** 92 **p** 93. C Bourne *Guildf* 92-96; TV Wimborne Minster and Holt *Sarum* 96; P-in-c Horton and Chalbury 96; V Horton, Chalbury, Hinton Martel and Holt St Jas 96-97; P-in-c from 97. *The Rectory, Hinton Martel, Wimborne, Dorset BH21 7HD* Tel (01258) 840256

SINGLETON, Kenneth Miller (Ken). b 58. Oak Hill Th Coll DipHE91. **d** 91 **p** 92. C Grove *Ox* 91-95; P-in-c Ashbury, Compton Beauchamp and Longcot w Fernham from 95. *The Vicarage, Ashbury, Swindon SN6 8LN* Tel (01793) 710231

SINNAMON, Canon William Desmond. b 43. TCD BA65. CITC 66. **d** 66 **p** 67. C Seapatrick *D & D* 66-70; C Arm St Mark *Arm* 70-74; V Choral Arm Cathl 73-74; I Ballinderry 75-80; I Dublin St Patr Cathl Gp *D & G* 80-83; Preb Tipperkevin St Patr Cathl Dublin 80-83; I Taney *D & G* from 83; RD Taney from 91; Can Ch Ch Cathl Dublin from 91; Treas St Patr Cathl Dublin 91-96; Chan from 96. *Taney Rectory, 6 Stoney Road, Dundrum, Dublin 14, Irish Republic* Tel Dublin (1) 298 4497 or 298 5491

SINNICKSON, Charles. b 21. Princeton Univ BA44. Cuddesdon Coll 60. **d** 63 **p** 64. C Soho St Anne w St Thos and St Pet *Lon* 63-67; C Chelsea St Luke 67-72; Hon C S Kensington St Jude 72-81; NSM Upper Chelsea St Simon 81-86; NSM S Kensington St Aug 86-90; rtd 90; Perm to Offic *Lon* from 90. *4 Cranley Mansion, 160 Gloucester Road, London SW7 4QF* Tel 0171-373 2767

SINTON, Bernard. b 43. Leic Univ BSc66. Sarum & Wells Th Coll 87. **d** 90 **p** 91. NSM Horsham *Chich* from 90. *Kinsale, 28 Kennedy Road, Horsham, W Sussex RH13 5DA* Tel (01403) 262991

SINTON, Vera May. b 43. Somerville Coll Ox BA65 MA Bris Univ CertEd66. Trin Coll Bris DipHE81. **dss** 81 **d** 87 **p** 94. Broxbourne w Wormley *St Alb* 81-87; Hon Par Dn 87; Tutor All Nations Chr Coll 81-87; Chapl St Hilda's Coll Ox 87-90; Tutor Wycliffe Hall Ox from 87. *22 Norham Gardens, Oxford OX2 6QD* Tel (01865) 274212 (work)

SIRMAN, Allan George. b 34. Lon Univ BA58. Oak Hill Th Coll 55. **d** 59 **p** 60. C Uphill *B & W* 59-61; C Morden *S'wark* 61-65; R Chadwell *Chelmsf* 65-75; V Wandsworth All SS *S'wark* 75-95; rtd 95. *Marydale, Kingsley Drive, St Alkeldas Road, Middleham, Leyburn, N Yorkshire DL8 4PW* Tel (01969) 624582

SIRR, The Very Revd John Maurice Glover. b 42. TCD BA63. CITC 65. **d** 65 **p** 66. C Belfast St Mary *Conn* 65-68; C Finaghy 68-69; I Drumcliffe w Lissadell and Munninane *K, E & A* 69-87; RD S Elphin 75-87; Preb Elphin Cathl 81-87; Dean Limerick and Ardfert *L & K* from 87; I Limerick City from 87; Chapl Limerick Pris from 87. *The Deanery, 7 Kilbane, Castletroy, Limerick, Irish Republic* Tel Limerick (61) 338697 Mobile 086-2541121 Fax as telephone

SISSON, Trevor. b 54. St Jo Coll Dur 76 St Jo Coll Nottm LTh94. **d** 79 **p** 80. C Rainworth *S'well* 79-83; C Worksop Priory 83-85; R Bilborough w Strelley 85-94; P-in-c Keyworth from 94; P-in-c Stanton-on-the-Wolds from 94; RD Bingham S from 95; P-in-c Bunny w Bradmore 95-97. *The Rectory, Nottingham Road, Keyworth, Nottingham NG12 5ED* Tel 0115-937 2017

SITCH, Keith Frank. b 40. Ex Univ BA63. S'wark Ord Course 72. **d** 75 **p** 76. NSM Romford St Edw *Chelmsf* 75-78; NSM Kidbrooke *S'wark* from 78. *92 Kidbrooke Park Road, London SE3 0DX* Tel 0181-856 3843

SITSHEBO, Wilson Timothy. b 52. UNISA BTh82 MTh93. St Bede's Coll Umtata DipTh77. **d** 79 **p** 80. Zimbabwe 80-96; Tutor Coll of the Ascension Selly Oak from 96; Lic to Offic *Birm* from 96. *United College of the Ascension, Weoley Park Road, Birmingham B29 6RD* Tel 0121-415 4778 Fax 472 4320

SIVITER, Cecil Isaac Hill. b 11. Trin Coll Bris 36. **d** 41 **p** 42. C Ealing St Paul *Lon* 41-43; C Frogmore *St Alb* 43-46; R Pettaugh and Winston *St E* 46-48; R Markfield *Leic* 48-55; Chapl Markfield Sanatorium 48-55; V Old Ford St Mark Victoria Park *Lon* 55-60; V Pott Shrigley *Ches* 60-74; V Alsager Ch Ch 74-79; rtd 79; Perm to Offic *Ches* from 79. *193 South Parade, West Kirby, Wirral, Merseyside L48 3HX* Tel 0151-625 6676

SIVITER, Hugh Basil. b 21. St Pet Hall Ox MA47. Wycliffe Hall Ox 46. **d** 48 **p** 49. C Gt Yarmouth *Nor* 48-52; V Birkdale St Pet *Liv* 52-59; R Gateacre 59-66; V Knotty Ash St Jo 66-84; rtd 85. *2 Heol Bodran, Abergele LL22 7UW* Tel (01745) 824860

SIZER, Stephen Robert. b 53. Sussex Univ BA DipHE Ox Univ MTh94. Trin Coll Bris 80. **d** 83 **p** 84. C St Leonards St Leon *Chich* 83-86; C Guildf St Sav w Stoke-next-Guildford *Guildf* 86-89; R Stoke-next-Guildf 89-97; V Virginia Water from 97. *Christ Church Vicarage, Christ Church Road, Virginia Water, Surrey GU25 4LD* Tel (01344) 842374

SKEET, Edward Kenneth Walter (Ted). b 27. Southn Univ BEd70. Chich Th Coll 78. **d** 81 **p** 82. Hon C Denmead *Portsm* 81-85; Perm to Offic from 85. *76 Whichers Gate Road, Rowland's Castle, Hants PO9 6BB* Tel (01705) 412084

SKEET, Hedley Ernest Burt. b 24. Lon Univ DipRE. Sarum & Wells Th Coll. **d** 84 **p** 85. Hon C Frimley *Guildf* from 84. *42 Denton Way, Frimley, Camberley, Surrey GU16 5UQ* Tel (01276) 27742

SKELDING, Donald Brian. b 23. Trin Coll Cam BA47 MA52. Cuddesdon Coll. **d** 50 **p** 51. C Sedgley All SS *Lich* 50-54; C W Bromwich All SS 54-56; V Tong 56-61; V Walton St Jo *Liv* 61-65; V Southport St Paul 65-72; R Norton Canes *Lich* 72-81; R Hinstock and Sambrook 81-84; rtd 84; C Alderbury Team *Sarum* 91-94; Perm to Offic from 94. *7 The Old Alms Houses, Church Road, Farley, Salisbury SP5 1AH* Tel (01722) 712414

SKELDING, Mrs Hazel Betty. b 25. LGSM66 CertEd45. Gilmore Course 80. **dss** 83 **d** 87 **p** 94. Hinstock and Sambrook *Lich* 83-84; Asst Children's Adv RE 86-91; Hon Par Dn Alderbury Team *Sarum* 91-94; C 94-96; rtd 96. *7 The Old Alms Houses, Church Road, Farley, Salisbury SP5 1AH* Tel (01722) 712414

SKELTON, Beresford. b 52. St Chad's Coll Dur BA74 SSC. Chich Th Coll 74. **d** 76 **p** 77. C Byker St Ant *Newc* 76-80; Chapl Asst Newc Gen Hosp 80-81; C Newc St Jo *Newc* 80-82; Chapl Asst Freeman Hosp Newc 81-82; V Cresswell and Lynemouth *Newc* 82-88; P-in-c Millfield St Mary *Dur* 88-93; V from 93. *St Mary Magdalene's Vicarage, Wilson Street, Sunderland SR4 6HJ* Tel 0191-565 6318 Fax as telephone

SKELTON, Dennis Michael. b 33. K Coll Lon BSc55. NE Ord Course 76. **d** 79 **p** 80. NSM Pennywell St Thos and Grindon St Oswald CD *Dur* 79-84; V Heatherycleugh from 84; V St John in Weardale from 84; V Westgate from 84. *Heatherycleugh Vicarage, Cowshill, Bishop Auckland, Co Durham DL13 1DA* Tel (01388) 537260

SKELTON, Frank Seymour. b 20. DFC and Bar 44 DSO and Bar 45. Trin Hall Cam BA48 MA52. Ridley Hall Cam 48. **d** 50 **p** 51. C Ormskirk *Liv* 50-52; Chapl Clare Coll Cam 52-59; R Bermondsey St Mary w St Olave, St Jo etc *S'wark* 59-69; P-in-c Bermondsey St Luke 59-65; RD Bermondsey 65-69; Dir Lambeth Endowed Charities 69-85; Lic to Offic 69-85; rtd 85. *Flat B, 36 Champion Hill, London SE5 8AP* Tel 0171-737 2187

SKELTON, Canon Henry John Nugent. b 13. Linc Th Coll 37. **d** 40 **p** 41. C Grantham St Wulfram *Linc* 40-43; Chapl RAFVR 43-47; V Heckington w Howell *Linc* 47-56; V Holbeach 56-73; RD Elloe E 68-73; Can and Preb Linc Cathl 70-73; rtd 78; Perm to Offic *St D* from 78. *Upton Castle, Cosheston, Pembroke Dock SA72 4SE* Tel (01646) 682435

✠**SKELTON, The Rt Revd Kenneth John Fraser.** b 18. CBE72. CCC Cam BA40 MA44. Wells Th Coll 40. **d** 41 **p** 42 **c** 62. C Normanton *Derby* 41-43; C Bakewell 43-45; C Bolsover 45-46; PV Wells Cathl *B & W* 46-50; Lect Wells Th Coll 46-50; V Howe Bridge *Man* 50-55; R Walton St Mary *Liv* 55-62; Bp Matabeleland 62-70; Asst Bp Dur 70-75; R Bishopwearmouth St Mich w St Hilda 70-75; RD Wearmouth 70-75; Bp Lich 75-84; rtd 84; Asst Bp Derby from 84; Asst Bp Sheff from 84. *65 Crescent Road, Sheffield S7 1HN* Tel 0114-255 1260

SKELTON, Melvyn Nicholas. b 38. St Pet Coll Ox BA61 MA65 Selw Coll Cam BA63 MA68. Ridley Hall Cam 62. **d** 64 **p** 65. C St Marychurch *Ex* 64-66; C Bury St Edmunds St Mary *St E* 66-69; Hon C 69-78; Lic to Offic from 78. *22A The Street, Moulton, Newmarket, Suffolk CB8 8RZ* Tel (01638) 750563

SKELTON, Pamela Dora. b 38. Hull Coll of Educn DipEd58. Edin Th Coll 80. **dss** 78 **d** 86 **p** 94. Edin St Barn *Edin* 78-86; D-in-c 86-90; Dioc Youth Chapl 83-90; Min Edin Ch Ch from 91. *112 St Alban's Road, Edinburgh EH9 2PG* Tel 0131-667 1280

SKEMP, Canon Stephen Rowland. b 12. Wadh Coll Ox BA34 MA62. Cuddesdon Coll 34. **d** 35 **p** 36. C W Hendon St Jo *Lon* 35-39; S Africa 39-46; R Publow w Pensford, Compton Dando and Chelwood *B & W* 47-50; V Hornsea and Goxhill *York* 50-62; V Atwick w Nunkeeling and Bewholme 50-62; RD N Holderness 52-62; R Gt Stanmore *Lon* 62-71; Chapl Br Emb Ankara *Eur* 71-74; Adn Aegean 71-77; Chapl Athens St Paul 74-77; rtd 77; Can Malta Cathl *Eur* from 80; Perm to Offic *Ox* 83-96. *Orchard Bank, Goose Green, Deddington, Oxford OX15 0SZ* Tel (01869) 38487

SKEOCH, Canon David Windsor. b 37. Ch Ch Ox BA58 MA62. Westcott Ho Cam 73. **d** 74 **p** 75. NSM Pimlico St Mary Graham Terrace *Lon* 74-79; Bp's Dom Chapl *Truro* 79-81; Bp's Chapl *Lon* 81-83; V Pimlico St Gabr from 83; Can The Murray from 92. *St Gabriel's Vicarage, 30 Warwick Square, London SW1V 2AD* Tel 0171-834 7520 or 834 2136

SKEPPER, Robert. b 25. **d** 67 **p** 68. C Loughborough All SS *Leic* 67-71; R Shelthorpe Gd Shep 71-80; V Loughb Gd Shep 80-82; rtd 90. *69 Ings Garth, Pickering, N Yorkshire YO18 8DA*

SKETCHLEY, Edward Sydney. b 20. Qu Coll Birm. **d** 49 **p** 50. C Bakewell *Derby* 49-53; PC Ridgeway 53-57; PC Abbey Dale 57-65; V Walsgrave on Sowe *Cov* 65-73; V Hound *Win* 73-90; rtd 90. *55 Terminus Terrace, Southampton SO14 3FE* Tel (01703) 233249

SKIDMORE, Mrs Sheila Ivy. b 36. **d** 87 **p** 94. Hon Par Dn Leic Resurr *Leic* 87-91; Par Dn Clarendon Park St Jo w Knighton St Mich 91-94; TV from 94. *St Michael and All Angels Vicarage, 12 Scott Street, Leicester LE2 6DW* Tel 0116-270 0964

SKIDMORE, Walton Sudbury. b 09. Leeds Univ BA32. Coll of Resurr Mirfield 28. **d** 34 **p** 35. C Long Eaton St Jo *Derby* 34-37; Chapl RN 37-64; rtd 64; Perm to Offic *Sarum* 64-71; Perm to Offic *Glouc* 73-75; Perm to Offic *Ex* 75-79. *Granby Court, Granby Road, Harrogate, N Yorkshire HG1 4SR*

SKILLEN, John Clifford Tainish. b 50. NUU BA72 MA82 QUB DipEd73 TCD BTh89. CITC 86. **d** 89 **p** 90. C Bangor Abbey *D & D* 89-92; I Kilwarlin Upper w Kilwarlin Lower 92-96; I Finaghy *Conn* from 96. *St Polycarp's Rectory, 104 Upper Lisburn Road, Finaghy, Belfast BT10 0BB* Tel (01232) 629764

SKILLINGS, Martyn Paul. b 46. St Chad's Coll Dur BA68. Linc Th Coll 68. **d** 70 **p** 71. C Stanley *Liv* 70-72; C Warrington St Elphin 72-75; Ind Chapl 75-76; V Surfleet *Linc* 88-92; V Burton St Chad *Lich* from 92. *The Vicarage, 113 Hunter Street, Burton-on-Trent, Staffs DE14 2SS* Tel (01283) 564044

SKILTON, Christopher John (Chris). b 55. Magd Coll Cam BA76 MA80. Wycliffe Hall Ox 77. **d** 80 **p** 81. C Ealing St Mary *Lon* 80-84; C New Borough and Leigh *Sarum* 84-88; TV Gt Baddow *Chelmsf* 88-95; TR Sanderstead All SS *S'wark* from 95. *The Rectory, 1 Addington Road, South Croydon, Surrey CR2 8RE* Tel 0181-657 1366

SKILTON, Joseph Laurence. b 41. Univ of Wales TCert64 Univ of Wales (Cardiff) DipTh70 Murdoch Univ Aus BA89. St Mich Coll Llan. **d** 70 **p** 71. C Bicester *Ox* 71-73; C Shrewsbury St Chad *Lich* 73-76; V W Bromwich St Phil 76-80; Australia from 80. *Address temp unknown*

✠**SKINNER, The Rt Revd Brian Antony.** b 39. Reading Univ BSc60. Tyndale Hall Bris 66. **d** 67 **p** 68 **c** 77. C Woking St Pet *Guildf* 67-70; Chile 70-86; Adn Valparaiso 76-77; Suff Bp Valparaiso 77-86; C Chorleywood St Andr *St Alb* 87-96; V Iver *Ox* from 96. *The Vicarage, Widecroft Road, Iver, Bucks SL0 9QD* Tel (01753) 653131

SKINNER, David Malcolm. b 26. CCC Cam BA55 MA59. Wells Th Coll 55. **d** 57 **p** 58. C Bris Lockleaze St Mary Magd w St Fran *Bris* 57-60; Sec C of E Radio and TV Coun 60-64; Sec Abps' Radio and TV Coun 64-67; V Ston Easton w Farrington Gurney *B & W* 67-70; rtd 70. *Glasha, Cromane, Killorglin, Co Kerry, Irish Republic* Tel Tralee (66) 69149

SKINNER, Graeme John. b 57. Southn Univ BSc79. Trin Coll Bris BA. **d** 86 **p** 87. C Bebington *Ches* 86-90; V Ashton on Mersey St Mary from 90. *St Mary's Vicarage, 20 Beeston Road, Sale, Cheshire M33 5AG* Tel 0161-973 5118 Fax 973 3227

SKINNER, Mrs Jane Mary. b 59. Leeds Univ BA81. Cranmer Hall Dur 82. **dss** 84 **d** 87 **p** 94. Chatham St Phil and St Jas *Roch* 84-87; Hon Par Dn 87; Hon Par Dn Torver *Carl* 87-91; Hon Par Dn Church Coniston 87-91; NSM Dalton-in-Furness from 91; Chapl HM Pris Haverigg from 92. *The Vicarage, Market Place, Dalton-in-Furness, Cumbria LA15 8RZ* Tel (01229) 462526

SKINNER, Mrs Jean. b 47. RN68 RM70. NE Ord Course 93. **d** 96 **p** 97. NSM Ch the King in the Dio of Newc from 96. *32 Easedale Avenue, Melton Park, Newcastle upon Tyne NE3 5TB* Tel 0191-236 3474

SKINNER, Preb John Cedric. b 30. Bris Univ BA55 Lon Univ DipTh57. Tyndale Hall Bris 55. **d** 57 **p** 58. C St Leonard *Ex* 57-62; Univ Sec IVF 62-68; V Guildf St Sav *Guildf* 68-76; R Stoke next Guildf St Jo 74-76; R Guildf St Sav w Stoke-next-Guildford 76-84; R Ex St Leon w H Trin *Ex* from 84; Preb Ex Cathl from 92. *St Leonard's Rectory, 27 St Leonard's Road, Exeter EX2 4LA* Tel (01392) 55681

SKINNER, John Richard. b 45. N Ord Course 84. **d** 87 **p** 88. C Allerton *Liv* 87-90; C Huyton St Mich 90-97; P-in-c Fairfield from 97. *St John's Vicarage, 19 Lockerby Road, Liverpool L7 0HG* Tel 0151-263 4001

SKINNER, John Timothy. b 55. Linc Th Coll 79. **d** 81 **p** 82. C Newton Aycliffe *Dur* 81-82; Perm to Offic *Newc* from 95. *Northumbrian Community, Nether Springs, Hetton Hall, Chatton, Alnwick, Northd NE66 5SD*

SKINNER, Leonard Harold. b 36. K Coll Lon BD62 AKC62. **d** 63 **p** 64. C Hackney Wick St Mary of Eton w St Aug *Lon* 63-66; C Palmers Green St Jo 66-70; V Grange Park St Pet 70-80; TV Hanley H Ev *Lich* 80-86; Chapl Sunderland Poly *Dur* 86-92; Chapl Sunderland Univ 92-93; P-in-c Hebburn St Oswald from 93. *St Oswald's Vicarage, St Oswald's Road, Hebburn, Tyne & Wear NE31 1HR* Tel 0191-483 2082

SKINNER, Maurice Wainwright. b 30. FRSC70 St Jo Coll Ox BA53 MA59. Ox NSM Course. **d** 86 **p** 87. NSM Furze Platt *Ox* from 86; NSM Hurley and Stubbings from 94. *5 Clarefield Close, Maidenhead, Berks SL6 5DR* Tel (01628) 24875

SKINNER, Michael Thomas. b 39. Open Univ BA88 MA90. S'wark Ord Course 73. **d** 78 **p** 79. NSM Orpington St Andr *Roch* 78-82; NSM Orpington All SS from 82; Asst Bps Officer for Hon Clergy from 91. *80 Spur Road, Orpington, Kent BR6 0QN* Tel (01689) 825322

SKINNER, Raymond Frederick (Ray). b 45. St Jo Coll Dur BA67 Dur Univ MA93. Cranmer Hall Dur. **d** 70 **p** 71. C High Elswick St Paul *Newc* 70-76; V Newbottle *Dur* 76-87; Ind Chapl 81-87; RD Houghton 84-87; Oman 87-90; TR Morden *S'wark* from 90; Asst RD Merton from 91. *The Rectory, London Road, Morden, Surrey SM4 5QT* Tel 0181-648 3920 or 658 0012

SKINNER, Stephen John. b 52. AIA Bris Univ BSc St Jo Coll Dur BA Dur Univ MLitt. Cranmer Hall Dur. **d** 83 **p** 84. C Chatham St Phil and St Jas *Roch* 83-87; P-in-c Torver *Carl* 87-90; P-in-c Church Coniston 87-90; V 90-91; R Torver 90-91; V Dalton-in-Furness from 91. *The Vicarage, Market Place, Dalton-in-Furness, Cumbria LA15 8RZ* Tel (01229) 462526

SKIPPER, Joseph Allen. b 17. Selly Oak Coll 45 Lich Th Coll 58. **d** 59 **p** 60. C Halesowen *Worc* 59-61; C Wareham w Arne *Sarum* 61-64; R Bishopstrow and Boreham 64-72; R Fleet *Linc* 72-74; V Sutterton 74-78; P-in-c Wigtoft 77-78; V Sutterton and Wigtoft 78-83; rtd 83; P-in-c Tidworth *Sarum* 83-86; C Tidworth, Ludgershall and Faberstown 86-88. *c/o Mr B E Gardiner, Flat 10, 6 Glendinning Avenue, Weymouth, Dorset DT4 7QF*

SKIPPER, Mrs Joyce Evelyn. b 27. Cam Univ CertEd71. Gilmore Ho 73. **dss** 75 **d** 87 **p** 94. Cranham *Chelmsf* 75-87; Hon Par Dn 87-90; NSM Upminster 90-94; NSM N Ockendon from 94. *53 Tawny Avenue, Upminster, Essex RM14 2EP* Tel (01708) 225703

SKIPPER, Kenneth Graham. b 34. St Aid Birkenhead 65. **d** 68 **p** 69. C Newland St Aug *York* 68-71; C Newby 71-74; V Dormanstown 74-78; C-in-c Mappleton w Goxhill 78; C-in-c Withernwick 78; V Aldbrough w Cowden Parva 78; V Aldbrough, Mappleton w Goxhill and Withernwick 79-89; R Londesborough 89-96; R Burnby 90-96; R Nunburnholme and Warter 90-96; V Shiptonthorpe w Hayton 90-96; rtd 96. *18 Elber Crescent, Bowmore, Isle of Islay PA43 7HU* Tel (01496) 810321

SKIPPER, Canon Lawrence Rainald. b 17. St Pet Hall Ox BA39 MA43. Wycliffe Hall Ox 39. **d** 41 **p** 41. C Aldershot H Trin *Guildf* 41-44; C Paignton Ch Ch *Ex* 44-48; V Paignton St Paul Preston 48-50; Chapl Trent Coll Nottm 50-56; Lic to Offic *Derby* 51-56; V Claughton cum Grange *Ches* 56-65; R Christleton 65-72; RD Ches 69-78; R Eccleston and Pulford 72-82; Hon Can Ches Cathl 74-82; rtd 82; Perm to Offic *Ches* from 82. *10 Westminster Terrace, Chester CH4 7LF* Tel (01244) 683178

SKIPPON, Kevin John. b 54. St Steph Ho Ox 78. **d** 81 **p** 82. C Gt Yarmouth *Nor* 81-84; C Kingstanding St Luke *Birm* 84-86; V Smethwick SS Steph and Mich 86-92; Chapl Derbyshire R Infirmary 92-94; Chapl Derbyshire R Infirmary NHS Trust from 94. *Derbyshire Royal Infirmary, London Road, Derby DE1 2QY* Tel (01332) 347141

SKIPWITH, Osmund Humberston. b 06. New Coll Ox BA28 MA33. Cuddesdon Coll 29. **d** 30 **p** 31. C Leic St Pet *Leic* 30-35; Zanzibar 35-41; CF (EC) 41-47; CF 47-54; R Maperton *B & W* 54-66; P-in-c 66-71; R N Cheriton 54-66; P-in-c 66-71; RD Cary 60-71; P-in-c Compton Pauncefoot w Blackford 63-71; P-in-c Yarlington 63-71; Preb Wells Cathl 64-74; R N Cadbury 66-71; C Worle 71-74; rtd 74. *23 Heathdene Manor, Langley Road, Watford WD1 3PZ*

SKLIROS, Michael Peter. b 33. Clare Coll Cam BA57 MA62. Ridley Hall Cam 57. **d** 59 **p** 60. C Hornchurch St Andr *Chelmsf* 59-61; Asst Chapl Denstone Coll Uttoxeter 61-65; Chapl RAF 65-77; P-in-c Stowmarket *St E* 77-78; Lic to Offic 78-85; C Gt Finborough w Onehouse and Harleston 85-91; P-in-c 91; R Gt and Lt Bealings w Playford and Culpho 91-96; rtd 96. *17 Bury Hill Close, Melton, Woodbridge, Suffolk IP12 1LE* Tel (01394) 388104

SKUCE, David. b 56. NUU BSc79 QUB PGCE80 TCD BTh89. CITC 87. **d** 89 **p** 90. C Templemore *D & R* 89-92; I Kilbarron w Rossnowlagh and Drumholm from 92; Bp's Dom Chapl from 94. *The Rectory, Ballintra, Co Donegal, Irish Republic* Tel Ballintra (73) 34025

SLACK, Canon Ellis Edward. b 23. Birm Univ BA51 MA53. Qu Coll Birm 51. **d** 53 **p** 53. C Leeds Halton St Wilfrid *Ripon* 53-56; R Stanningley St Thos 57-64; V N Dulwich St Faith *S'wark* 64-72; V Bethnal Green St Jo w St Simon *Lon* 72-78; V Bethnal Green St Jo w St Bart 78-79; Can Res Portsm Cathl *Portsm* 79-83; V Woodplumpton *Blackb* 83-88; Dir of Post-Ord Tr 83-88; rtd 88; Perm to Offic *York* from 88. *6 Parkfield, Stillington, York YO6 1JW* Tel (01347) 810104

SLACK, Michael. b 53. RGN83 St Jo Coll Dur BA74 Lon Univ PGCE79 Newc Poly DPSN86. St Steph Ho Ox 74. **d** 76 **p** 77. C Wolverhampton St Steph *Lich* 76-77; NSM Bywell St Pet *Newc* 89-93; TV Cullercoats St Geo from 93. *St Aidan's Vicarage, 29 Billy Mill Lane, North Shields, Tyne & Wear NE29 8BZ* Tel 0191-257 3616

SLADDEN, Duncan Julius Edward. b 25. K Coll Cam BA50 MA51. Cuddesdon Coll 51. **d** 53 **p** 54. C Huddersfield St Pet *Wakef* 53-55; C Reading St Mary V *Ox* 55-61; R Largs *Glas* 61-65; P-in-c Stevenage *St Alb* 65-70; R Johnstone *Glas* 70-76; Prayer Gp Adv Scottish Chs Renewal 76-81; Sec Scottish Episc Renewal Fellowship 81-84; R E Kilbride 85-90; rtd 90. *17 Bruce Avenue, Dunblane, Perthshire FK15 9JB* Tel (01786) 825520

SLADDEN, Canon John Cyril. b 20. Mert Coll Ox BA42 MA46 BD66. Wycliffe Hall Ox 46. **d** 48 **p** 49. C Oswestry St Oswald *Lich* 48-51; Tutor St Aid Birkenhead 51-53; R Todwick *Sheff* 53-59; V Nether Peover *Ches* 59-86; RD Knutsford 80-85; Hon Can Ches Cathl 80-86; rtd 86. *Rossa, Penmon, Beaumaris LL58 8SN* Tel (01248) 490207

SLADDEN, John David. b 49. RN Eng Coll Plymouth BSc74 St Edm Coll Cam MA86. Ridley Hall Cam. **d** 83 **p** 84. C St Bees *Carl* 83-85; Perm to Offic *Lich* 85-87; Miss Co-ord Down to Earth Evangelistic Trust 85-87; V Doncaster St Jas *Sheff* 87-94. *30 Curlew Avenue, Chatteris, Cambs PE16 6PL* Tel (01354) 694097

SLADE, Canon Adrian Barrie. b 47. K Alfred's Coll Win DipEd68. St Jo Coll Nottm BTh73 ALCD72. **d** 73 **p** 74. C Streatham Immanuel w St Anselm *S'wark* 73-76; C Chipping Barnet *St Alb* 76-78; C Chipping Barnet w Arkley 78-80; V Sundon 80-85; Soc Resp Officer *Glouc* from 86; Hon Can Glouc Cathl from 91. *38 Sydenham Villas Road, Cheltenham, Glos GL52 6DZ* Tel (01242) 242672

SLADE, Alfred Laurence. b 12. ACII. Roch Th Coll 67. **d** 69 **p** 70. Hon C Cliftonville *Cant* 69-71; Hon C Westgate St Jas 71-75; Perm to Offic *Sarum* 75-81; Perm to Offic *Cant* 81-93. *21 McKinlay Court, The Parade, Minnis Bay, Birchington, Kent CT7 9QG* Tel (01843) 46882

SLADE, Herbert Edwin William. b 12. Lon Univ BA33. Dorchester Miss Coll 34. **d** 35 **p** 36. C Tuffley *Glouc* 35-39; SSJE from 39; Lic to Offic *Chich* 71-82; rtd 82. *The Anchorhold, 35 Paddockhall Road, Haywards Heath, W Sussex RH16 1HN* Tel Haywards Heath (01444) 452468

SLADE, Michael John Mike. b 55. Trin Coll Bris 94. **d** 96 **p** 97. C Blagdon w Compton Martin and Ubley *B & W* from 96. *2 The Score, Blagdon, Bristol BS18 6SH* E-mail 106517.431 @compuserve.com

SLADE, Canon William Clifford. b 24. St Jo Coll Dur BA47 DipTh49 MA53. **d** 49 **p** 50. C Northallerton w Deighton and Romanby *York* 49-52; C Eston 52-54; V Anlaby Common St Mark 54-60; V Brompton w Snainton 60-67; R Stokesley 67-71; V Felixkirk w Boltby 71-82; V Kirby Knowle 71-82; Can and Preb York Minster 79-86; C Topcliffe w Dalton and Dishforth 82-86; Abp's Adv for Spiritual Direction 82-86; Perm to Offic from 86; rtd 86. *Bede House, Beck Lane, South Kilvington, Thirsk, N Yorkshire YO7 2NL* Tel (01845) 522915

SLADEN, Philip. b 50. Fitzw Coll Cam BA71 MA75 DipTh. Ripon Hall Ox 72. **d** 75 **p** 76. C Bushey Heath *St Alb* 75-78; Chapl RAF from 78. *Chaplaincy Services (RAF), HQ, Personnel and Training Command, RAF Innsworth, Gloucester GL3 1EZ* Tel (01452) 712612 ext 5164 Fax 510828

SLADER, William Basil. b 16. Sarum Th Coll 55. **d** 57 **p** 58. C Overton w Laverstoke and Freefolk *Win* 57-60; R Copythorne and Minstead 60-70; V St Mary Bourne and Woodcott 70-81; rtd 81; Perm to Offic *Win* 81-88; Perm to Offic *Ely* from 81. *8 Crauden Gardens, Ely, Cambs CB7 4PR* Tel (01353) 666410

SLATER, Mrs Ann. b 46. Somerville Coll Ox BA67 MA71. WMMTC 92. **d** 95 **p** 96. C Northampton St Benedict *Pet* from 95. *44 Barn Owl Close, Northampton NN4 0AU* Tel (01604) 761878

SLATER, Edward Ian. b 31. EMMTC 81. **d** 84 **p** 85. NSM Cherry Willingham w Greetwell *Linc* 84-86; C Cleethorpes 86-88; TV 88-92; P-in-c Bassingham 92-96; P-in-c Aubourn w Haddington 92-96; P-in-c Thurlby w Norton Disney 92-96; P-in-c Carlton-le-Moorland w Stapleford 92-96; rtd 96; Perm to Offic *Linc* from 96. *Westcot, Scothern Road, Nettleham, Lincoln LN2 2TX*

SLATER, James Richard David. b 61. BA83 TCD BTh89. CITC 86. **d** 89 **p** 90. C Clooney w Strathfoyle *D & R* 89-93; I Aghadowey w Kilrea from 93. *Kilrea Rectory, 2 Moneygran Road, Kilrea, Co Londonderry BT51 5SJ* Tel (01266) 540257

SLATER, John. b 45. K Coll Lon BA67 AKC67 Fitzw Coll Cam BA69 MA73. Westcott Ho Cam 67 Union Th Sem (NY) STM70. **d** 70 **p** 71. C St Marylebone All SS *Lon* 70-77; V Paddington St Sav 77-83; Dir Post-Ord Tr from 82; V St Jo Wood from 83; AD Westmr St Marylebone from 92. *St John's House, St John's Wood High Street, London NW8 7NE* Tel 0171-722 4378

SLATER, John Albert. b 25. Lon Univ BA52. Oak Hill Th Coll 47. **d** 52 **p** 53. C Everton Em *Liv* 52-55; V Kirkdale St Paul N Shore 55-61; V Bacup St Sav *Man* 61-70; V Blackpool St Thos *Blackb* 70-84; rtd 84; Lic to Offic *Blackb* from 84. *18 Church Road, Thornton Cleveleys, Lancs FY5 2TZ* Tel (01253) 853330

SLATER, John Allen. b 20. St Aid Birkenhead 60. **d** 62 **p** 63. C Bridlington Quay Ch Ch *York* 62-65; V Welton w Melton 65-82; P-in-c Burstwick w Thorngumbald 82-84; rtd 85; Perm to Offic *York* from 85. *103 Burden Road, Beverley, N Humberside HU17 9LN* Tel (01482) 867825

SLATER, John Ralph. b 38. Kent Univ BA90. Linc Th Coll 71. **d** 73 **p** 74. C S Hackney St Mich w Haggerston St Paul *Lon* 73-74; C Leytonstone St Marg w St Columba *Chelmsf* 74-77; C Whitstable All SS w St Pet *Cant* 77-80; V Gt Ilford St Alb *Chelmsf* 80-83; V Clipstone *S'well* 83-87; rtd 87. *117 Canterbury Road, Westgate, Kent CT8 8NW* Tel (01227) 792154

SLATER, Mark Andrew. b 56. ARCS79 Imp Coll Lon BSc79. Ridley Hall Cam 87. **d** 89 **p** 90. C Northampton St Giles *Pet* 89-92; C Stopsley *St Alb* 92-93; C-in-c Bushmead CD from 93. *73 Hawkfields, Bushmead, Luton LU2 7NW* Tel (01582) 487327

SLATER, Paul John. b 58. CCC Ox MA83 Dur Univ BA83. Cranmer Hall Dur 81. **d** 84 **p** 85. C Keighley St Andr *Bradf* 84-88; Dir Dioc Foundn Course 88-93; P-in-c Cullingworth 88-93; Bp's Personal Exec Asst 93-95; R Haworth from 95. *The Rectory, Haworth, Keighley, W Yorkshire BD22 8EN* Tel (01535) 642169 Fax 544831

SLATER, Canon Philip David. b 27. K Coll Lon 58. **d** 60 **p** 61. C Havant *Portsm* 60-67; C Leigh Park 68-69; Hants Co RE Adv 69-74; Gosport and Fareham RE Adv 74-82; Hon C Bishops Waltham 76-82; V Bulford, Figheldean and Milston *Sarum* 82-93; RD Avon 85-95; Can and Preb Sarum Cathl 91-95; V Avon Valley 93-95; V of Close Sarum Cathl from 95; rtd 95. *102 Coombe Road, Salisbury SP2 8BD* Tel (01722) 332529

SLATER, Robert Adrian. b 48. St Jo Coll Nottm 76. **d** 79 **p** 80. C Bedworth *Cov* 79-82; TV Billericay and Lt Burstead *Chelmsf* 82-88; V Rounds Green *Birm* 88-94. *11 Lewis Road, Birmingham B30 2SU* Tel 0121-443 3646

SLATER, Thomas Ernest (Tom). b 37. Chelsea Coll Lon TCert60 Lon Univ BD71 NE Lon Poly DipG&C88. ALCD66. **d** 67 **p** 68. C Bootle Ch Ch *Liv* 67-72; C Stapleford *S'well* 72-75; Supt Tower Hamlets Miss 75-77; Hon C Stepney St Pet w St Benet *Lon* 78-79; Asst Chapl The Lon Hosp (Whitechapel) 79-83; Chapl 83-89; NSM Poplar *Lon* 89-92; Perm to Offic from 92. *11 Elgin House, Cordelia Street, London E14 6EG* Tel 0171-987 4504

SLATER, Victoria Ruth. b 59. Hertf Coll Ox BA82 MA87 Selw Coll Cam BA89. Westcott Ho Cam 86. **d** 89 **p** 94. Chapl Asst Man R Infirmary 89-94; Chapl Ox Radcliffe Hosp NHS Trust from 94; Chapl St Michael Sobell Ho Hospice from 94. *Churchill Hospital, Old Road, Headington, Oxford OX3 7LJ* Tel (01865) 741841 or 226090

SLATER, William Edward. b 51. Bolton Inst of Tech HNC77. Aston Tr Scheme 85 Oak Hill Th Coll 87. **d** 89 **p** 90. C Balderstone *Man* 89-94; V Newchapel *Lich* from 94. *The Vicarage, 32 Pennyfield Road, Newchapel, Stoke-on-Trent ST7 4PN* Tel (01782) 782837

SLATOR, Edward Douglas Humphreys. b 18. TCD BA41 MA47 Hull Univ BPhil75. **d** 43 **p** 44. C Taney *D & G* 43-46; Chapl St Columba's Coll Dub 46-60; I Killea *C & O* 60-73; C Taney *D & G* 74-80; P-in-c Rathmolyon w Castlerickard, Rathcore and Agher *M & K* 80-87; rtd 87. *31 St John's, Park Avenue, Dublin 4, Irish Republic* Tel Dublin (1) 283 9395

SLATOR, Canon William Thompson Howard. b 09. TCD BA31 MA34. **d** 33 **p** 34. C Ballywillan *Conn* 33-35; P-in-c Mullaghdun *Clogh* 35-38; I Boyle w Aghanagh *K, E & A* 38-52; I Clonbroney w Killoe 52-66; RD Edgeworthstown 58-66; I Kiltoghart 66-81; Preb Elphin Cathl 66-81; RD Fenagh 67-81; rtd 81. *Bayside, 5 Haddington Terrace, Dun Laoghaire, Dublin, Irish Republic*

SLATTERY, Maurice Michael. b 43. Southlands Coll Lon TCert73 BEd74. S'wark Ord Course 91. **d** 94. NSM Malden St Jas *S'wark* 94-97; NSM Niton *Portsm* from 97; NSM St Lawrence from 97; NSM Whitwell from 97. *The Vicarage, Ashknowle Lane, Whitwell, Ventnor, Isle of Wight PO38 2PP* Tel (01983) 731096

SLAUGHTER, Clive Patrick. b 36. St Paul's Grahamstown DipTh78. **d** 77 **p** 78. S Africa 77-87; R Thorley w Bishop's Stortford H Trin *St Alb* 87-90; R Thorley from 90; RD Bishop's Stortford from 96. *The Rectory, Viceron's Place, Thorley, Bishop's Stortford, Herts CM23 4EL* Tel (01279) 654955

SLAUGHTER, Canon Maurice Basil. b 20. Leeds Univ BA42. Coll of Resurr Mirfield 42. **d** 44 **p** 45. C Kingswinford St Mary *Lich* 44-46; C Roch St Nic w St Clem *Roch* 46-47; C Luton Ch Ch *St Alb* 47-50; V Birm St Marg Ladywood *Birm* 50-52; V Newsome *Wakef* 52-60; V Queensbury *Bradf* 60-63; V Skipton Ch Ch 63-78; Hon Can Bradf Cathl 67-85; RD Skipton 73-82; P-in-c Bolton Abbey 78-85; P-in-c Rylstone 78-85; P-in-c Arncliffe w Halton Gill 79-82; rtd 85; Perm to Offic *Bradf* from 85; Perm to Offic *Wakef* from 85. *Hewitt Gate, Threshfield, Skipton, N Yorkshire BD23 5HB* Tel (01756) 752158

SLEDGE, The Ven Richard Kitson. b 30. Peterho Cam BA52 MA57. Ridley Hall Cam 52. **d** 54 **p** 55. C Compton Gifford *Ex* 54-57; C Ex St Martin, St Steph, St Laur etc 57-63; V Dronfield *Derby* 63-76; TR 76-78; RD Chesterfield 72-78; Adn Huntingdon *Ely* 78-96; R Hemingford Abbots 78-89; Hon Can Ely Cathl from 78; rtd 96; Bp's Dom Chapl *Ely* from 96. *7 Budge Close, Brampton, Huntingdon, Cambs PE18 8PL* Tel (01480) 380284

SLEDGE, Timothy Charles Kitson. b 64. Coll of Ripon & York St Jo BA87 York Univ MA88. Trin Coll Bris DipHE95 ADUT95. **d** 95 **p** 96. C Huddersfield St Thos *Wakef* from 95. *8 Longroyd Place, Huddersfield HD1 4RP* Tel (01484) 430681

SLEE, The Very Revd Colin Bruce. b 45. K Coll Lon BD69 AKC69. St Aug Coll Cant 69. **d** 70 **p** 71. C Nor Heartsease St Fran *Nor* 70-73; C Cambridge Gt St Mary w St Mich *Ely* 73-76; Chapl Girton Coll Cam 73-76; Tutor and Chapl K Coll Lon 76-82; Sub-Dean from 82; Can Res St Alb 82-94; Provost S'wark from 94. *The Provost's Lodging, 51 Bankside, London SE1 9JE* Tel 0171-928 6414 E-mail cathedra@dswark.org.uk

SLEE, John Graham. b 51. Brunel Univ BTech73. Oak Hill Th Coll 85. **d** 87 **p** 88. C St Columb Minor and St Colan *Truro* 87-91; R St Mawgan w St Ervan and St Eval from 91; RD Pydar from 93. *The Rectory, St Mawgan, Newquay, Cornwall TR8 4EZ* Tel (01637) 860358 E-mail johns@slee.avel.co.uk

SLEGG, John Edward. b 36. St Pet Coll Ox BA62 MA66. Ridley Hall Cam 62. **d** 64 **p** 65. C Perranzabuloe *Truro* 64-66; CF 66-86; P-in-c Poling *Chich* 86-89; V from 89; P-in-c Lyminster 86-89; V from 89. *The Vicarage, 3 Middle Paddock, Lyminster, Littlehampton, W Sussex BN17 7QH* Tel (01903) 882152

SLEIGHT, Gordon Frederick. b 47. AKC69. St Aug Coll Cant 69. **d** 70 **p** 71. C Boston *Linc* 70-74; P-in-c Louth St Mich 74-75; P-in-c Stewton 75; TV Louth 75-81; V Crosby 81-95; P-in-c Nettleham 95-97; V from 97. *The Vicarage, 2 Vicarage Lane, Nettleham, Lincoln LN2 2RH* Tel (01522) 754752

SLIM, David Albert. b 49. Westhill Coll Birm CertEd72. Linc Th Coll CMinlStuds90. **d** 90 **p** 91. C Walmley *Birm* 90-93; R Marchwiel and Isycoed *St As* from 93. *Marchwiel Rectory, Overton Road, Marchwiel, Wrexham LL13 0TE* Tel (01978) 780640

SLIPPER, Dr Charles Callan. b 55. Lanc Univ BA77 PhD84. S Dios Minl Tr Scheme 91. **d** 93 **p** 94. Focolare Movement from 77; NSM N Acton St Gabr *Lon* 93-96; Lic to Offic from 96. *57 Twyford Avenue, London W3 9PZ* Tel 0181-992 7666 Fax 993 6944

SLIPPER, Robert James. b 64. St Jo Coll Cam BA87 MA91. Wycliffe Hall Ox BA92. **d** 92 **p** 93. C Southgate *Chich* 92-95; C Stoughton *Guildf* from 95. *12 Grange Close, Guildford GU2 6QJ* Tel (01483) 573154

SLOANE, Isaac Reuben. b 16. TCD BA41 MA60. **d** 42 **p** 43. C Kinawley w H Trin *K, E & A* 42-44; I Gleneely w Culdaff *D & R* 44-54; I Ardstraw w Baronscourt, Badoney Lower etc 54-76; I Drumclamph w Drumquin 76-78; rtd 78. *40 Rawdon Place, Moira, Craigavon, Co Armagh BT67 0NX* Tel (01846) 611547

SLOGGETT, Donald George. b 49. Trin Coll Bris 81. **d** 83 **p** 84. C Horfield H Trin *Bris* 83-86; C Highworth w Sevenhampton and Inglesham etc 86-88; P-in-c Upavon w Rushall *Sarum* 88-90; R Uphavon w Rushall and Charlton from 90. *The Vicarage, 5A Vicarage Lane, Upavon, Pewsey, Wilts SN9 6AA* Tel (01980) 630248

SLOUGH, Colin Richard. b 40. AKC66. Ripon Hall Ox. **d** 68 **p** 69. Hon C Birm St Luke *Birm* 68-69; Hd of RE Lea-Mason Sch 68-69; P-in-c Portsea St Geo *Portsm* 70-72; Hon Chapl Portsm Cathl 70-72; RE Adv *Ox* 72-75; Lect Cudham Coll 72-75; Dep Hd Master St Luke's Sch Southsea 75-80; P-in-c Sandown Ch Ch *Portsm* 80; V 80-87; P-in-c Lower Sandown St Jo 80; V 80-87; Chapl Birm Poly *Birm* 87-91; Perm to Offic 91-92; rtd 91; Perm to Offic *Guildf* from 91. *2 South Hill, Godalming, Surrey GU7 1JT* Tel (01483) 416539

SLOW, Leslie John. b 47. Liv Univ BSc68 MSc69. N Ord Course 77. **d** 80 **p** 81. NSM Gt Horton *Bradf* from 80. *25 Grasleigh Way, Bradford, W Yorkshire BD15 9BE* Tel (01274) 491808

SLUMAN, Richard Geoffrey Davies. b 34. St Jo Coll Ox BA68 MA68. Sarum Th Coll 68. **d** 70 **p** 71. C Gt Yarmouth *Nor* 70-73; V Churchdown *Glouc* 73-82; P-in-c Blockley w Aston Magna 82-83; V Blockley w Aston Magna and Bourton on the Hill 83-94; rtd 94. *21 Manor Farm Road, Tredington, Shipston-on-Stour, Warks CV36 4NZ* Tel (01608) 662317

SLY, Canon Christopher John. b 34. Selw Coll Cam BA58 MA62. Wycliffe Hall Ox. **d** 60 **p** 61. C Buckhurst Hill *Chelmsf* 60-64; V Berechurch 64-75; V Southend St Sav Westcliff 75-87; R Wickham Bishops w Lt Braxted from 87; RD Witham from 87; Hon Can Chelmsf Cathl from 93. *The Rectory, 1 Church Road, Wickham Bishops, Witham, Essex CM8 3LA* Tel (01621) 891360

SLY, Canon Harold Kenneth. b 15. Kelham Th Coll 34. **d** 38 **p** 39. C Wigston Magna *Leic* 38-41; C Dudley St Edm *Worc* 41-43; C Redditch St Steph 43-49; V Worc St Swithun 49-57; V Hampton in Arden *Birm* 57-83; rtd 83; Perm to Offic *Worc* 83-91; Chapl Convent of the H Name Malvern 83-90; Perm to Offic *Birm* from 95. *28 Holifast Road, Sutton Coldfield, W Midlands B72 1AP* Tel 0121-384 6570

SLYFIELD, John David. b 32. TD67. Roch Th Coll 66. **d** 68 **p** 69. C St Mary in the Marsh *Cant* 68-71; P-in-c Steeple Claydon *Ox* 71-76; P-in-c Middle w E Claydon 71-76; RD Claydon 73-78; R The Claydons 76-78; V S Westoe *Dur* 78-82; V Tideswell *Derby* 82-92; RD Buxton 84-91; rtd 92; Perm to Offic *Derby* from 92. *Stile Close, Taddington, Buxton, Derbyshire SK17 9TP* Tel (01298) 85507

SMAIL, Richard Charles. b 57. CCC Ox BA80 MA83. Ox Min Course 90. **d** 93 **p** 95. NSM Keble Coll Ox 93-96; Chapl Fell and Lect BNC Ox from 97. *Brasenose College, Oxford OX1 4AJ* Tel (01865) 277833 Fax 277514

SMAIL, Canon Thomas Allan. b 28. Glas Univ MA49 Edin Univ BD52. **d** 79 **p** 79. Hon C E Twickenham St Steph *Lon* 79; Vice-Prin St Jo Coll Nottm 80-85; TR Sanderstead All SS *S'wark* 85-94; Hon Can S'wark Cathl 91-94; rtd 94; Perm to Offic *S'wark* from 94. *36B Alexandra Road, Croydon CR0 6EU* Tel 0181-656 9683

SMAILES, Robert Anthony. b 44. Linc Th Coll 79 DipMin88. **d** 81 **p** 82. C Stokesley *York* 81-83; V Lythe 83-85; P-in-c Ugthorpe 83-85; V Lythe w Ugthorpe 85-88; V Saltburn-by-the-Sea 88-92; V Ormesby from 92. *The Vicarage, 54 Church Lane, Ormesby, Middlesbrough, Cleveland TS7 9AU* Tel (01642) 314445

SMALE, Frederick Ronald (Fred). b 37. K Coll Lon BD60 AKC60. **d** 61 **p** 62. C Bearsted *Cant* 61-64; C Fishponds St Mary *Bris* 64-69; V Hartlip *Cant* 69-71; P-in-c Stockbury w Bicknor and Huckinge 69-71; V Hartlip w Stockbury 71-75; R River 75-85; V Birchington w Acol and Minnis Bay from 85. *All Saints' Vicarage, 15 Minnis Road, Birchington, Kent CT7 9SE* Tel (01843) 841117

SMALL, David Binney. b 39. Brasted Th Coll 61 Westcott Ho Cam 63. **d** 65 **p** 66. C Milton *Portsm* 65-69; CF 69-92; R Wickwar w Rangeworthy *Glouc* from 92; RD Hawkesbury from 94. *The Rectory, High Street, Wickwar, Wotton-under-Edge, Glos GL12 8NP* Tel (01454) 294267

SMALL, Gordon Frederick. b 41. St Jo Coll Nottm 77. **d** 79 **p** 80. C Belper *Derby* 79-84; NSM Matlock Bath 90-91; C Ripley 91-93; TV Bucknall and Bagnall *Lich* from 93. *The Vicarage, Dawlish Drive, Stoke-on-Trent ST2 0ET* Tel (01782) 260876

SMALL, Marcus Jonathan. b 67. Univ of Wales (Ban) BD94. Ripon Coll Cuddesdon 94. **d** 96. C Moseley St Mary *Birm* from 96. *4 Woodrough Drive, Moseley, Birmingham B13 9EP* Tel 0121-449 1336

SMALLDON, Keith. b 48. Open Univ BA76 Newc Univ MA94. St Mich Coll Llan DipTh71. **d** 71 **p** 72. C Cwmbran *Mon* 71-73; C Chepstow 73-75; Dioc Youth Adv *Bradf* 75-79; P-in-c Woolfold *Man* 82-85; Dioc Youth and Community Officer 82-90; P-in-c Thursby *Carl* 90-94; Dir of Clergy Tr 90-94; TR Daventry, Ashby St Ledgers, Braunston etc *Pet* from 94. *The Rectory, Golding Close, Daventry, Northants NN11 5PN* Tel (01327) 702638

SMALLEY, Mrs Kathleen. b 23. Linc Th Coll 81. **dss** 84 **d** 87 **p** 94. Leominster *Heref* 84-85; Bridgnorth, Tasley, Astley Abbotts, Oldbury etc 85-96; Hon C 87-96; Perm to Offic from 96. *8A Cliff Road, Bridgnorth, Shropshire WV16 4EY* Tel (01746) 766202

SMALLEY, The Very Revd Stephen Stewart. b 31. Jes Coll Cam BA55 MA58 PhD79. Eden Th Sem (USA) BD57 Ridley Hall Cam. **d** 58 **p** 59. C Portman Square St Paul *Lon* 58-60; Chapl Peterho Cam 60-63; Dean 62-63; Nigeria 63-69; Lect Th Man Univ 70-77; Can Res and Prec Cov Cathl *Cov* 77-87; Vice-Provost 86-87; Dean Ches from 87. *The Deanery, 7 Abbey Street, Chester CH1 2JF* Tel (01244) 351380 or 324756

SMALLMAN, Miss Margaret Anne. b 43. Hull Univ BSc64 Bris Univ CertEd65. St Jo Coll Nottm DipTh82. **dss** 83 **d** 87 **p** 94. Bromsgrove St Jo *Worc* 83-87; Par Dn 87-88; Par Dn Stoke Prior, Wychbold and Upton Warren 88-90; TD Tettenhall Wood *Lich* 91-94; TV from 94. *21 Tintagel Close, Perton, Wolverhampton WV6 7RG* Tel (01902) 750232

SMALLWOOD, Simon Laurence. b 58. St Jo Coll Dur BSc80. Cranmer Hall Dur 89. **d** 92 **p** 93. C Stapenhill w Cauldwell *Derby* 92-96; TV Dagenham *Chelmsf* from 96. *86 Rogers Road, Dagenham, Essex RM10 8JX* Tel 0181-593 2760

SMART, Barry Anthony Ignatius. b 57. Lanc Univ BEd79. St Steph Ho Ox 85. **d** 88 **p** 89. C Wantage *Ox* 88-91; C Abingdon 91-93; TV 93-95; C Princes Risborough w Ilmer 95-97; C Kingstanding St Luke *Birm* from 97. *79 Hawthorne Road, Kingstanding, Birmingham B44 8QT* Tel 0121-386 4168

SMART, Mrs Carol. b 45. SSF SRN67. S Dios Minl Tr Scheme 89. **d** 92 **p** 94. Chapl St Mary's Hosp Newport from 92; NSM Shorwell w Kingston *Portsm* from 92. *20 Sydney Close, Shide, Newport, Isle of Wight PO30 1YG* Tel (01983) 526242

SMART, Clifford Edward James. b 28. Kelham Th Coll 48. **d** 53 **p** 54. C Blackb St Pet *Blackb* 53-56; Korea 56-65; C Birm St Aid Small Heath *Birm* 65-66; Korea 66-93; rtd 93. *6430 Telegraph Road, St Louis, MO 63129-4934, USA* Tel St Louis (314) 846-5927

SMART, Harry Gavin. b 67. St D Coll Lamp BA90 Selw Coll Cam DipTh92. Westcott Ho Cam CTM94. **d** 94 **p** 95. C Thirsk *York* 94-97; C Sheff Norwood St Leon *Sheff* from 97. *29 Piper Road, Sheffield S5 7HZ* Tel 0114-242 6875

SMART, Canon Haydn Christopher. b 38. Wells Th Coll 66. **d** 69 **p** 70. C Hillmorton *Cov* 69-72; C Duston *Pet* 72-75; V Woodford Halse 75-79; V Woodford Halse w Eydon 79-82; V Wellingborough All SS 82-92; RD Wellingborough 87-92; V Longthorpe from 92; Can Pet Cathl from 92; RD Pet from 96. *The Vicarage, 315 Thorpe Road, Longthorpe, Peterborough PE3 6LU* Tel (01733) 263016

SMART, Mrs Hilary Jean. b 42. SOAS Lon BA63 CSocSc64 DASS67. EMMTC 85. **d** 88 **p** 94. Par Dn Walsall Pleck and Bescot *Lich* 88-94; C 94; TV Sheff Manor *Sheff* from 94; Bp's Ecum Officer from 94. *William Temple Vicarage, 195 Harborough Avenue, Sheffield S2 1QT* Tel 0114-239 8202

SMART, John Francis. b 36. Keble Coll Ox BA59 MA69. Cuddesdon Coll 59. **d** 61 **p** 66. C Cannock *Lich* 61-63; Hon C Gt Wyrley 63-66; C Wednesfield St Thos 66-70; V Brereton 70-85; R E Clevedon and Walton w Weston w Clapton *B & W* from 85. *The Rectory, All Saints' Lane, Clevedon, Avon BS21 6AU* Tel (01275) 873257

SMART, Richard Henry. b 22. St Jo Coll Dur 46 Clifton Th Coll 48. **d** 52 **p** 53. C Leeds St Geo *Ripon* 52-54; Kenya 54-56; C New Addington *Cant* 56-59; V Awsworth w Cossall *S'well* 59-63; BFBS Distr Sec E Anglia 63-70; Bp's Ecum Adv *Ely* 70-81; Dioc Missr 70-74; P-in-c Dry Drayton 74-81; Min Bar Hill LEP 74-81; P-in-c Madingley 80-81; V Sandylands *Blackb* 81-92; rtd 92; Perm to Offic *Blackb* from 92. *35 St Oswald Street, Bowerham, Lancaster LA1 3AS* Tel (01524) 65335

SMART, Richard Henry. b 23. Lon Univ BA51. Oak Hill Th Coll. **d** 53 **p** 54. C Bedworth *Cov* 53-56; C New Malden and Coombe *S'wark* 56-59; V Hanley Road St Sav w St Paul *Lon* 59-71; V Plumstead All SS *S'wark* 71-88; rtd 88; Perm to Offic *Chich* from 88. *2 Annington Road, Eastbourne, E Sussex BN22 8NG* Tel (01323) 726850

SMART, Canon Sydney. b 15. TCD BA37 MA43. **d** 39 **p** 40. C Belfast St Mich *Conn* 39-42; P-in-c Belfast St Barn 42-46; I 46-60; I Belfast All SS 60-83; Can Belf Cathl 76-83; rtd 83. *43 Norwood Avenue, Belfast BT4 2EF* Tel (01232) 653932

SMEATON, Malcolm John. b 56. BSc(Econ). Coll of Resurr Mirfield 79. **d** 83 **p** 84. C Tynemouth Ch Ch w H Trin *Newc* 83-84; C Long Benton 85-90; V Byker St Martin 90-95; Chapl HM Young Offender Inst Hindley from 95. *HM Prison Hindley, Gibson Street, Bickershaw, Wigan, Lancs WN2 5TH* Tel (01942) 866255 Fax 867442

SMEATON, Canon William Brian Alexander. b 37. CITC 69. **d** 71 **p** 72. C Belfast St Luke *Conn* 71-81; I Tullyaughnish w Kilmacrennan and Killygarvan *D & R* from 81; Bp's Dom Chapl from 87; Can Raphoe Cathl from 88; RD Kilmacrenan E and W from 90; Dioc Radio Officer from 90. *The Rectory, Ramelton, Letterkenny, Co Donegal, Irish Republic* Tel Ramelton (74) 51013

SMEDLEY, Paul Mark. b 59. Bris Univ BA80 Lanc Univ MA81. S Dios Minl Tr Scheme 89. **d** 92 **p** 93. NSM Acton St Mary *Lon* from 92. *12 Baldwyn Gardens, London W3 6HH* Tel 0181-993 5527

SMETHURST, David Alan. b 36. Lon Univ BD60 Man Univ MPhil84. Tyndale Hall Bris 57. **d** 61 **p** 62. C Burnage St Marg *Man* 61-63; P-in-c Whalley Range St Marg 63-65; R Haughton St Mary 65-74; R Ulverston St Mary w H Trin *Carl* 74-87; Dean Hong Kong 87; Dir Acorn Chr Healing Trust Resource Cen 88-93; V Epsom St Martin *Guildf* from 93; RD Epsom from 97. *The Vicarage, 35 Burgh Heath Road, Epsom, Surrey KT17 4LP* Tel (01372) 743336

SMETHURST, Gordon James. b 33. CEng FIStructE. N Ord Course 79. **d** 82 **p** 83. NSM Halliwell St Marg *Man* 82-87; NSM Bradshaw 87-88; Asst Chapl Bolton R Infirmary 88-95; Asst Chapl Bolton Gen Hosp 88-95; NSM Westhoughton and Wingates from 95. *91 Albert Road West, Bolton BL1 5ED* Tel (01204) 842561

SMETHURST, Gordon McIntyre. b 40. Man Univ BA62 BD69. **d** 70 **p** 71. C Sandal St Helen *Wakef* 70-72; P-in-c Smawthorpe St Mich 72-75; P-in-c Whitwood 74-75; Asst Master Goole Gr Sch 75-84; Hon C Howden *York* 77-79; Hon C Howden TM 80-84; Perm to Offic from 94. *20 Broadacre Park, Brough, N Humberside HU15 1LT* Tel (01482) 665525

SMETHURST, Leslie Beckett. b 22. CEng. NW Ord Course 72. **d** 75 **p** 76. C Baguley *Man* 75-78; TV Droylsden St Mary 78-81; V Droylsden St Martin 81-86; rtd 87; Perm to Offic *Blackb* from 87. *27 Calf Croft Place, Lytham St Annes, Lancs FY8 4PU* Tel (01253) 733159

SMILLIE, Linda Barbara. b 46. Oak Hill Th Coll DipHE87. **d** 87 **p** 94. Par Dn Holloway St Mary w St Jas *Lon* 87-88; Par Dn Holloway St Mary Magd 88-90; Chapl W End Stores 90-91; C Holloway St Mark w Em 90-91; Hon C Islington St Mary 92-94; C-in-c Southall Em CD from 95. *37 Dormers Wells Lane, Southall, Middx UB1 3HX* Tel 0181-843 9556

SMITH, Alan. b 38. Tyndale Hall Bris 63. **d** 65 **p** 66. C New Milverton *Cov* 65-68; C Cheadle *Ches* 68-71; V Handforth 71-78; Asst Chapl HM Pris Styal 75-78; Chapl HM Pris Wormwood Scrubs 78-79; Chapl HM Borstal Wellingborough 79-83; R Rushden w Newton Bromswold *Pet* 83-96; Chapl Rushden Sanatorium from 83; V Wollaston and Strixton *Pet* from 96. *The Vicarage, 81 Irchester Road, Wollaston, Wellingborough, Northants NN9 7RW* Tel (01933) 664256

SMITH, Alan Gregory Clayton. b 57. Birm Univ BA78 MA79. Wycliffe Hall Ox 79. **d** 81 **p** 82. C Pudsey St Lawr *Bradf* 81-82; C Pudsey St Lawr and St Paul 82-84; Chapl Lee Abbey 84-90; TV Walsall *Lich* from 90; Dioc Missr from 90. *14 Gorway Gardens, Walsall WS1 3BJ* Tel (01922) 26010

SMITH, Alan Leonard. b 51. Madeley Coll of Educn CertEd72. Trin Coll Bris DipTh95. **d** 95 **p** 96. C Taunton St Mary *B & W* from 95. *3 Woodrush Close, Taunton, Somerset TA1 3XB* Tel (01823) 289185

SMITH, Alan Pearce Carlton. b 20. Trin Hall Cam BA40 MA45 LLB46. Westcott Ho Cam 76. **d** 78 **p** 79. Hon C Cherry Hinton St Jo *Ely* 78-82; P-in-c Madingley 82-83; P-in-c Dry Drayton 82-83; P-in-c Swaffham Bulbeck 84-88; Perm to Offic from 88. *38 Alpha Road, Cambridge CB4 3DG* Tel (01223) 358124

SMITH, Alan Thomas. b 35. BA DipEd. Ridley Hall Cam 82. **d** 84 **p** 85. C Bedworth *Cov* 84-89; R Carlton Colville w Mutford and Rushmere *Nor* 89-97; rtd 97. *Elderberry Cottage, Dennington, Woodbridge, Suffolk IP13 8JF*

SMITH, Alec John. b 29. AKC53. **d** 54 **p** 55. C Charlton Kings St Mary *Glouc* 54-56; C-in-c Findon Valley CD *Chich* 56-57; V Viney Hill *Glouc* 57-65; V Churchdown St Jo 65-66; V Bishop's Cannings *Sarum* 66-69; CF 69-88; V Douglas St Thos *S & M* 88-92; rtd 92; Perm to Offic *S & M* from 92. *Church Barn, Church Road, Lonan, Isle of Man IM4 7JX* Tel (01624) 861325

SMITH, Alexander Montgomery. b 36. TCD BA59 MA64 BD65. TCD Div Sch Div Test60. **d** 61 **p** 62. C Knock *D & D* 61-64; C Belfast St Thos *Conn* 64-66; Lect St Kath Coll Liv 66-69; Sen Lect from 69; Asst Chapl St Kath Coll *Liv* 66-69; Chapl 69-80; NSM Allerton from 80. *15 Glenathol Road, Liverpool L18 3JS* Tel 0151-475 3310

SMITH, Alfred Lawrence. b 23. FCP84 Open Univ BA72 Birm Univ DipEd73. EMMTC 82. **d** 85 **p** 86. NSM Ashover *Derby* 85-86; NSM Ashover and Brackenfield 86-95; Perm to Offic from 95. *Cotton House Farm, Amber Lane, Ashover, Chesterfield, Derbyshire S45 0DZ* Tel (01246) 590265

SMITH, Andrew John. b 37. Leeds Univ BA61. Coll of Resurr Mirfield 61. **d** 63 **p** 64. C W Hackney St Barn *Lon* 63-65; Dir and Chapl Northorpe Hall Trust Yorkshire 65-72; Warden Ox Ho Bethnal Green 72-78; Dir and Chapl The Target Trust 78-86; P-in-c Gt Staughton *Ely* 86-88; Norfolk DTI Educn Adv 88-91; Perm to Offic *Ex* 92-96; C Widecombe-in-the-Moor, Leusdon, Princetown etc from 96. *6 Beacon Cottages, Buckland-in-the-Moor, Ashburton, Newton Abbot, Devon TQ13 7HL* Tel (01364) 652654

SMITH, Andrew John. b 46. ACGI Lon Univ BScEng67 DIC PhD71 Trin Coll Ox DipTh74 Bath Univ MEd88. Coll of Resurr Mirfield 74. **d** 76 **p** 77. C Swindon New Town *Bris* 76-78; C Southmead 78-79; Perm to Offic from 79. *15 Dyrham Close, Bristol BS9 4TF* Tel 0117-942 8594

SMITH, Andrew John. b 59. Birm Univ BSc80 PhD81. WMMTC 89. **d** 91 **p** 92. C Lower Mitton *Worc* 91-92; C Stourport and Wilden 92-95; TV Redditch, The Ridge from 95. *The Vicarage, St George's Road, Redditch, Worcs B98 8EE* Tel (01527) 63017

SMITH, Andrew Perry Langton. b 56. Sheff City Poly BSc79 Imp Coll Lon MSc80. Trin Coll Bris 89. **d** 91 **p** 92. C Littleover *Derby* 91-95; TV Walsall *Lich* from 95; Ind Chapl Black Country Urban Ind Miss from 95. *21 Buchanan Road, Walsall WS4 2EW*

SMITH, Mrs Anita Elisabeth. b 57. Westhill Coll Birm BEd79. Trin Coll Bris DipHE88 ADPS88. **d** 88 **p** 94. Par Dn Bermondsey St Anne *S'wark* 88-92; Par Dn Brockley Hill St Sav 92-94; C 94-95. *St Saviour's Vicarage, 5 Lowther Hill, London SE23 1PZ* Tel 0181-690 2499

SMITH, Ann Veronica. b 38. Doncaster Coll of Educn DipEd. Edin Dioc NSM Course 88. **d** 95 **p** 96. NSM S Queensferry *Edin* from 95. *16 Mannerston, Linlithgow, W Lothian EH49 7ND* Tel (01506) 834361

SMITH, Anthony Adam Dalziel. b 42. Qu Coll Birm 65. **d** 68 **p** 69. C Peterlee *Dur* 68-71; C Tilehurst St Mich *Ox* 71-76; V Wootton

(Boars Hill) 76-88; R Brightwalton w Catmore, Leckhampstead etc from 88. *The Rectory, Chaddleworth, Newbury, Berks RG20 7EW* Tel (01488) 638566

SMITH, Anthony Charles. b 43. Sarum & Wells Th Coll 90. **d** 92 **p** 93. C Dartford H Trin *Roch* 92-95; V Northfleet from 95. *The Vicarage, The Hill, Northfleet, Gravesend, Kent DA11 9EU* Tel (01474) 566400

SMITH, Anthony Cyril (Tony). b 40. K Coll Lon 65. **d** 69 **p** 70. C Crewkerne *B & W* 69-74; TV Hemel Hempstead *St Alb* 74-76; Asst Chapl K Coll Taunton 76-80; Chapl from 80. *40 South Road, Taunton, Somerset TA1 3DY* Tel (01823) 272251

SMITH, Anthony Grahame (Tony). b 29. ALCD54. **d** 54 **p** 55. C Stratford New Town St Paul *Chelmsf* 54-56; C Woodford Wells 56-58; Canada 58-60; Hon C Gt Ilford St Andr *Chelmsf* 60-62; V Chelmsf St Andr 62-69; R Mistley w Manningtree 69-81; RD Harwich 75-81; R Fordham 81-92; rtd 92. *Lockholme, North Walsham Road, Bacton, Norwich NR12 0LN* Tel (01692) 651224

SMITH, Anthony James. b 57. ACA Sheff Univ BA. Ridley Hall Cam 83. **d** 86 **p** 87. C Woking St Pet *Guildf* 86-90; C Reigate St Mary *S'wark* 90-94; CMS from 94; Kenya from 94. *PO Box 40360, Nairobi, Kenya*

SMITH, The Ven Anthony Michael Percival. b 24. G&C Coll Cam BA48 MA53. Westcott Ho Cam 48. **d** 50 **p** 51. C Leamington Priors H Trin *Cov* 50-53; Abp's Dom Chapl *Cant* 53-57; Chapl Norwood and Distr Hosp 57-66; V Norwood All SS 57-66; V Yeovil St Jo w Preston Plucknett *B & W* 66-72; RD Merston 68-72; Preb Wells Cathl 70-72; V Addiscombe St Mildred *Cant* 72-79; Adn Maidstone 79-89; Dir of Ords 80-89; Hon Can Cant Cathl 80-89; rtd 89; Perm to Offic *Cant* from 89; Perm to Offic *Chich* 89-91 and from 93; RD Rye 91-93. *The Garden House, Horseshoe Lane, Beckley, Rye, E Sussex TN31 6RZ* Tel (01797) 260514

SMITH, The Ven Arthur Cyril. b 09. VRD55. Sheff Univ BA34 MA50. St Jo Coll Manitoba 29 Westcott Ho Cam 33. **d** 34 **p** 35. C Keighley *Bradf* 34-37; C Hatfield *St Alb* 37-41; Chapl RNVR 40-46; R S Ormsby w Ketsby, Calceby and Driby *Linc* 46-60; P-in-c Harrington w Brinkhill 50-52; R 52-60; P-in-c Somersby w Bag Enderby 50-52; R 52-60; P-in-c Tetford and Salmonby 51-52; R 52-60; R Oxcombe 58-60; R Ruckland w Farforth and Maidenwell 58-60; P-in-c Worlaby 58-60; Adn Linc 60-76; Can and Preb Linc Cathl 60-77; R Algarkirk 60-76; RD Holland W 65-69; rtd 77. *28 London Court, London Road, Headington, Oxford OX3 7SL* Tel (01865) 744788

SMITH, Miss Audrey. b 47. S'wark Ord Course 89. **d** 92 **p** 94. NSM Croydon St Aug *S'wark* from 92. *19 Queen Street, Croydon CR0 1SY* Tel 0181-681 7005

SMITH, Mrs Audrey Isabel. b 20. Lon Univ. Qu Coll Birm IDC79. **dss** 84 **d** 87 **p** 94. NSM Kingston All SS w St Jo *S'wark* 87-95. *31 Copes Gardens, Truro, Cornwall TR1 3SN* Tel (01872) 261813

SMITH, Austin John Denyer. b 40. Worc Coll Ox BA62. Cuddesdon Coll 64. **d** 66 **p** 67. C Shepherd's Bush St Steph w St Thos *Lon* 66-69; C W Drayton 69-72; Chapl Sussex Univ *Chich* 72-79; V Caddington *St Alb* from 79. *The Vicarage, Collings Wells Close, Caddington, Luton LU1 4BG* Tel (01582) 31692

SMITH, Mrs Barbara Jean. b 39. Bris Univ BA62. S'wark Ord Course 83. **dss** 86 **d** 87 **p** 94. Chislehurst St Nic *Roch* 86-87; Hon Par Dn 87-90; Hon C Wrecclesham *Guildf* 90-94; NSM Herriard w Winslade and Long Sutton etc *Win* from 94. *The Parsonage, Gaston Lane, South Warnborough, Hants RG25 1RH* Tel (01256) 862843

SMITH, Mrs Barbara Mary. b 47. Doncaster Coll of Educn CertEd68. St Jo Coll Dur 82. **dss** 85 **d** 87 **p** 94. Beverley St Nic *York* 85-87; Par Dn 87; NSM S'wark H Trin w St Matt *S'wark* 89-90; Ind Chapl Teesside *York* 91-95; Hon C Middlesbrough St Chad 94-95; Chapl Anglia Poly Univ *Ely* 96-97; Perm to Offic *St Alb* from 96. *29 Wintringham Road, St Neots, Huntingdon, Cambs PE19 1NX* Tel (01480) 350920

SMITH, Barry. b 41. Univ of Wales (Lamp) BA62 Fitzw Ho Cam BA64 MA68 Man Univ MPhil91. Ridley Hall Cam. **d** 65 **p** 66. C Rhyl w St Ann *St As* 65-70; Chapl Scargill Ho 70-72; C Flint *St As* 72-74; V Broughton 74-86; Dioc Ecum Officer 82-95; RD Wrexham 82-86; R Wrexham 86-95; Can Cursal St As Cathl 86-95; Chan St As Cathl 95; Perm to Offic *S'wark* from 97. *74 Lillian Road, London SW13 9JF* Tel 0181-748 5169

SMITH, Brian. b 44. Westmr Coll Ox MTh95. Sarum & Wells Th Coll 71. **d** 74 **p** 75. C Pennywell St Thos and Grindon St Oswald CD *Dur* 74-77; Chapl RAF 77-95; P-in-c Keswick St Jo *Carl* 95-96; V from 96. *St John's Vicarage, Ambleside Road, Keswick, Cumbria CA12 4DD* Tel (01768) 772130

✠**SMITH, The Rt Revd Brian Arthur.** b 43. Edin Univ MA66 Fitzw Coll Cam BA68 MA72 Jes Coll Cam MLitt73. Westcott Ho Cam 66. **d** 72 **p** 73 **c** 93. Tutor and Lib Cuddesdon Coll 72-75; Dir of Studies 75-78; C Cuddesdon *Ox* 76-79; Sen Tutor Ripon Coll Cuddesdon 78-79; Dir Tr *Wakef* 79-87; P-in-c Halifax St Jo 79-85; Hon Can Wakef Cathl 81-87; Adn Craven *Bradf* 87-93; Suff Bp Tonbridge *Roch* from 93. *Bishop's Lodge, 48 St Botolph's Road, Sevenoaks, Kent TN13 3AG* Tel (01732) 456070 Fax 741449

SMITH, Brian Godfrey. b 24. Chich Th Coll 63. **d** 65 **p** 66. C Newc H Cross *Newc* 65-68; C Redcar *York* 68-72; C Kirkleatham 68-72; V Wortley de Leeds *Ripon* 72-76; Chapl Costa del Sol E *Eur* 76-82; Chapl Estoril 82-84; V Worfield *Heref* 84-89; rtd 89; Perm to Offic *Heref* from 92. *2 Pineway, Lodge Farm, Bridgnorth, Shropshire WV15 5DT* Tel (01746) 764088

SMITH, The Ven Brian John. b 33. Sarum Th Coll 62. **d** 65 **p** 66. C Whitstable All SS *Cant* 65-69; V Woodford w Wilsford *Sarum* 69-74; P-in-c Durnford 74; V Woodford Valley 74-76; V Mere w W Knoyle and Maiden Bradley 76-80; RD Heytesbury 78-80; Adn Wilts from 80; Can and Preb Sarum Cathl from 80; V Bishop's Cannings, All Cannings etc 80-83; Adv Chr Giving 83-90; Dioc Stewardship Adv 84-90; TV Redhorn from 90; RD Calne from 96. *The Vicarage, 57 The Street, Chirton, Devizes, Wilts SN10 3QS* Tel (01380) 840271

SMITH, Brian Michael. b 42. Kelham Th Coll 69. **d** 69 **p** 70. C Somers Town St Mary *Lon* 70-74; C Stamford Hill St Jo 74-75; C Stamford Hill St Bart 75-84; P-in-c Edmonton St Pet w St Martin 84-92; V from 92. *The Vicarage, St Peter's Road, London N9 8JP* Tel 0181-807 2974 Fax 345 6110

SMITH, Mrs Bridget Mary. b 46. Bp Otter Coll CertEd67 S Dios Minl Tr Scheme 88. **d** 91 **p** 94. C Pet H Spirit Bretton *Pet* 91-95; P-in-c Silverstone and Abthorpe w Slapton from 95. *The Vicarage, High Street, Silverstone, Towcester, Northants NN12 8US* Tel (01327) 857996

SMITH, Canon Charles. b 11. St Jo Coll Dur BA39 MA42. **d** 39 **p** 40. C Dur St Mary le Bow w St Mary the Less *Dur* 39-45; Chapl, Tutor and Burser St Jo Coll Dur 39-45; V Grindon *Dur* 46-48; V Heatherycleugh 48-83; V St John in Weardale 57-83; V Westgate 57-83; RD Stanhope 72-77; Hon Can Dur Cathl 79-83; rtd 83; Perm to Offic *York* from 93. *Rutson House, Nunnington, York YO6 5UR* Tel (01439) 748204

SMITH, Charles Frederick. b 18. St Aid Birkenhead 54. **d** 56 **p** 58. C Stanwix *Carl* 56-58; C Hoddesdon *St Alb* 58-60; R Everleigh *Sarum* 60-74; V Burneside *Carl* 74-79; Perm to Offic *Chich* from 80; rtd 83. *7 Manor Road, Seaford, E Sussex BN25 4NL* Tel (01323) 890433

SMITH, Charles Henry Neville. b 31. Nottm Univ BA52 MA65. Sarum Th Coll 55. **d** 57 **p** 58. C Thirsk w S Kilvington *York* 57-60; C Linthorpe 60-61; V Danby 61-66; Chapl United Cam Hosps 66-76; Chapl Lanc Moor Hosp 76-84; Hon Can Blackb Cathl *Blackb* 81-84; Asst Sec Gen Syn Hosp Chapl Coun 84-88; Hon C Lee St Marg *S'wark* 84-88; Chapl Guy's Hosp Lon 88-96; rtd 96; Hon PV S'wark Cathl *S'wark* from 96; Perm to Offic from 96. *57 Belmont Park, London SE13 5BW* Tel 0181-318 9993

SMITH, Charles Rycroft (Ryc). b 46. Sarum & Wells Th Coll 76. **d** 78 **p** 79. C Heref St Martin *Heref* 78-81; C Southampton Maybush St Pet *Win* 81-83; R The Candover Valley from 83; RD Alresford from 90. *The Rectory, Alresford Road, Preston Candover, Basingstoke, Hants RG25 2EE* Tel (01256) 389245

SMITH, Charles Septimus. b 23. Bris & Glouc Tr Course. **d** 79 **p** 80. NSM Bris St Agnes and St Simon w St Werburgh *Bris* 79-86; C 86-87; C Bris St Paul's 87-89; rtd 89. *353 Queen Street South, Mississauga, Ontario, Canada, L5M1 M3*

SMITH, Christine. **d** 97. C Salterhebble All SS *Wakef* from 97. *315 Skircoat Green Road, Halifax, W Yorkshire HX3 0NA*

SMITH, Christine Lydia. *See* CARTER, Mrs Christine Lydia

SMITH, Christopher Blake Walters. b 63. Univ of Wales (Cardiff) BMus84 BD88 LLM95. St Mich Coll Llan 85. **d** 88 **p** 89. C Aberdare St Jo *Llan* 88-93; V Tongwynlais from 93; Dioc Dir Post-Ord Tr from 95. *The Vicarage, 1 Merthyr Road, Tongwynlais, Cardiff CF4 7LE* Tel (01222) 810437

SMITH, Christopher Francis. b 46. K Coll Lon BD68 AKC68. St Aug Coll Cant 69. **d** 70 **p** 71. C Norwood All SS *Cant* 70-72; Asst Chapl Marlborough Coll 72-76; C Deal St Leon w Sholden *Cant* 77-81; P-in-c Benenden 81-83; V from 83. *The Vicarage, Benenden, Cranbrook, Kent TN17 4DL* Tel (01580) 240658

SMITH, Christopher Matthew. b 67. New Coll Ox BA89 MA93 Homerton Coll Cam PGCE90. St Steph Ho Ox BA94. **d** 95 **p** 96. C Wantage *Ox* from 95. *5 Barnards Way, Wantage, Oxon OX12 7EA* Tel (01235) 763309

SMITH, Canon Christopher Milne. b 44. Selw Coll Cam BA66. Cuddesdon Coll 67. **d** 69 **p** 70. C Liv Our Lady and St Nic *Liv* 69-74; TV Kirkby 74-81; R Walton St Mary 81-91; Can Res Sheff Cathl *Sheff* from 91; Bp's Adv on the Paranormal from 97. *9 Stumperlowe Hall Road, Sheffield S10 3QR* Tel 0114-230 4181 or 275 3434

SMITH, Clarice Mary. b 25. St Mich Coll Llan 76. **dss** 77 **d** 80. Llangiwg *S & B* 77-80; C Llwynderw 80-84; C Newton St Pet 84-88; rtd 88. *33 Sherringham Drive, Newton, Swansea SA3 4UG* Tel (01792) 367984

SMITH, Clifford. b 31. Lon Univ DipTh60. St Aid Birkenhead 59. **d** 61 **p** 62. C Limehouse St Anne *Lon* 61-63; C Ashtead *Guildf* 63-66; R Bromley All Hallows *Lon* 66-76; V Hillsborough and Wadsley Bridge *Sheff* 76-89; V Stainforth 89-96; rtd 96. *33 King Street Lane, Winnersh, Wokingham, Berks RG41 5AX* Tel 0118-978 9453

SMITH, Clive Leslie. b 50. Leeds Univ BA72 Ch Coll Liv PGCE73 K Coll Lon PGDHE96. Coll of Resurr Mirfield 75. **d** 77 **p** 78. C Goldington *St Alb* 77-81; C Cheshunt 81-84; V Watford St Pet 84-89; Chapl Leavesden Hosp Abbots Langley 89-94; Chapl

St Albans and Hemel Hempstead NHS Trust from 94. *Hemel Hempstead General Hospital, Hillfield Road, Hemel Hempstead, Herts HP2 4AD* Tel (01442) 213141 *or 34 Tanners Hill, Abbots Langley, Herts WD5 0LT* Tel (01923) 677977

SMITH, Colin Graham. b 59. Hatf Poly BA82 CQSW82. Trin Coll Bris BA88. **d** 88 **p** 89. C Bermondsey St Jas w Ch Ch *S'wark* 88-92; V Brockley Hill St Sav from 92. *St Saviour's Vicarage, 5 Lowther Hill, London SE23 1PZ* Tel 0181-690 2499

SMITH, Colin Ian McNaughton. b 28. St Jo Coll Dur BA53. **d** 55 **p** 56. C Consett *Dur* 55-59; Miss to Seamen 59-60; Sudan 60-63; C Wilton *York* 63-67; V Weaverthorpe w Helperthorpe and Luttons 67-76; P-in-c Kirby Grindalythe 74-76; RD Buckrose 75-76; V Weaverthorpe w Helperthorpe, Luttons Ambo etc 76-91; rtd 91; Perm to Offic *York* from 91. *Aynsley House, East Lutton, Malton, N Yorkshire YO17 8TG* Tel (01944) 738539

SMITH, Colin Richard. b 53. Liv Poly BA80 Liv Univ MTD83. Oak Hill Th Coll 84. **d** 86 **p** 87. C Ormskirk *Liv* 86-89; V Wigan St Cath 89-94; C St Helens St Helen from 94. *211A Dentons Green Lane, St Helens, Merseyside WA10 6RU* Tel (01744) 453681

SMITH, Craig Philip. b 61. Huddersfield Poly HND82 Sheff City Poly BA86. St Jo Coll Nottm DTS92 DipMM93. **d** 93 **p** 94. C Bramley and Ravenfield *Sheff* 93-95; C Bramley and Ravenfield w Hooton Roberts etc 95-97; C Rainham w Wennington *Chelmsf* from 97. *Mardyke Parsonage, 8A Frederick Road, Rainham, Essex RM13 8NT* Tel (01708) 552752

SMITH, Darren John Anthony. b 62. Nottm Univ BCombStuds84. Linc Th Coll 84. **d** 86 **p** 87. C Leic Ascension *Leic* 86-90; C Curdworth w Castle Vale *Birm* 90; C Castle Vale St Cuth 90-91; C Kingstanding St Luke 91-92; P-in-c 92-93; V from 93. *St Luke's Clergy House, 49 Caversham Road, Kingstanding, Birmingham B44 0LW* Tel 0121-354 3281

SMITH, David Charles Stuart. Oak Hill Th Coll 61. **d** 61 **p** 62. Australia from 61; from 90; C Luton Lewsey St Hugh *St Alb* 90. *8/28 Tivoli Place, South Yarra, Victoria, Australia 3141* Tel Melbourne (3) 9820 2729

SMITH, David Earling. b 35. AKC60. **d** 61 **p** 62. C Knebworth *St Alb* 61-63; C Chipping Barnet 64-66; C S Ormsby w Ketsby, Calceby and Driby *Linc* 66-69; R Claxby w Normanby-le-Wold 69-74; R Nettleton 69-74; R S Kelsey 69-74; R N Owersby w Thornton le Moor 69-74; R Stainton-le-Vale w Kirmond le Mire 69-74; V Ancaster 74-79; Warden and Chapl St Anne Bedehouses Linc 79-89; C Linc Minster Gp 79-89; rtd 89; Perm to Offic *Linc* from 90. *17 Egerton Road, Lincoln LN2 4PJ* Tel (01522) 510336

SMITH, David Graham. b 08. MBE46. Wadh Coll Ox BA31 MA34. Cuddesdon Coll 31. **d** 32 **p** 33. C Wimbledon *S'wark* 32-37; C Camberwell St Geo 37-39; P-in-c Cheam 39; CF 39-45; P-in-c Merton St Jas *S'wark* 45-48; V S Wimbledon H Trin 48-59; R Woldingham 59-76; rtd 76; Perm to Offic *B & W* from 86. *St Mary's, Whitegate Road, Minehead, Somerset TA24 5SP* Tel (01643) 702036

✠**SMITH, The Rt Revd David James.** b 35. AKC58. **d** 59 **p** 60 **c** 87. C Gosforth All SS *Newc* 59-62; C Newc St Fran 62-64; C Longbenton St Bart 64-68; V Longhirst 68-75; V Monkseaton St Mary 75-82; RD Tynemouth 80-82; Hon Can Newc Cathl 81-87; Adn Lindisfarne 81-87; V Felton 82-83; Suff Bp Maidstone *Cant* 87-92; Bp HM Forces 90-92; Bp Bradf from 92. *Bishopscroft, Ashwell Road, Heaton, Bradford, W Yorkshire BD9 4AU* Tel (01274) 545414 Fax 544831

SMITH, Canon David John. b 32. Lon Univ BA76 MSc79. Lon Coll of Div 68. **d** 70 **p** 71. C Clerkenwell St Jas and St Jo w St Pet *Lon* 70-73; P-in-c Penge St Paul *Roch* 74-78; V 78-89; RD Beckenham 86-89; Chapl Bromley and Sheppard's Colls from 90; Perm to Offic *S'wark* from 90; Dioc Clergy Widows and Retirement Officer *Roch* from 90; Hon Can Roch Cathl from 95. *The Chaplain's House, Bromley College, London Road, Bromley BR1 1PE* Tel 0181-460 4712

SMITH, David John. b 42. Oak Hill Th Coll 75. **d** 77 **p** 78. C New Milverton *Cov* 77-81; V Hartshill 81-86; V Attleborough 86-95; AD Nuneaton 93-95; N Regional Co-ord Crosslinks from 95. *4 Kentsford Drive, Radcliffe, Manchester M26 3XX* Tel (01204) 707534 Fax as telephone E-mail clinksn@mighty-micro.co.uk

SMITH, David John Parker. *See* EVANS, David Victor

SMITH, David Leonard. b 37. St Alb Minl Tr Scheme 84. **d** 91 **p** 92. NSM Potton w Sutton and Cockayne Hatley *St Alb* from 91. *11 Judith Gardens, Potton, Sandy, Beds SG19 2RJ* Tel (01767) 260583

SMITH, David Roland Mark. b 46. ACP78 FRSA87 SSC88 Dur Univ BA68. Edin Th Coll 68. **d** 70 **p** 71. C Southwick St Columba *Dur* 70-74 and 81-82; Asst Chapl Univ of Wales (Cardiff) *Llan* 74-76; Hon C E Bris 76-78; Hon C Filton 78-79; Min Leam Lane CD *Dur* 80-81; V Leam Lane 81; Chapl Sunderland Poly 81-86; Co-ord Chapl Service 81-86; Chapl Birm Univ *Birm* 86-95; Perm to Offic *Cov* 88-95; Chapl Heathrow Airport *Lon* from 95; Perm to Offic *Ox* from 95. *12 Cherry Orchard, West Drayton, Middx UB7 7JR* Tel (01895) 447904 Mobile 037-887 6695 Fax (01895) 447904 or 0181-745 4261 E-mail frdavid@clara.net

SMITH, David Sidney Mark. b 54. Bris Univ BEd76. Ripon Coll Cuddesdon 77. **d** 79 **p** 80. C Wotton-under-Edge w Ozleworth and N Nibley *Glouc* 79-83; TV Malvern Link w Cowleigh *Worc* 83-93; Relig Affairs Producer BBC Heref and Worc 90-93; V Clevedon St Jo *B & W* from 93. *St John's Vicarage, 1 St John's Road, Clevedon, Avon BS21 7TG* Tel (01275) 872410

SMITH, David Stanley. b 41. Ox NSM Course. **d** 84 **p** 85. NSM Burghfield *Ox* 84-86; NSM Stratfield Mortimer 86-88; NSM Mortimer W End w Padworth 86-88; C St Breoke and Egloshayle *Truro* 88-93; V Penwerris from 93. *Penwerris Vicarage, 12 Stratton Terrace, Falmouth, Cornwall TR11 2SY* Tel (01326) 314263

SMITH, David Watson. b 31. Sarum Th Coll 63. **d** 65 **p** 66. C W Wimbledon Ch Ch *S'wark* 65-69; C Cheam 69-74; V Haslington *Ches* 74-83; V Haslington w Crewe Green 83-87; V Daresbury from 87. *The Vicarage, Daresbury, Warrington WA4 4AE* Tel (01925) 740348

SMITH, David William. b 46. Sarum Th Coll 70. **d** 72 **p** 73. C Stokesley *York* 72-75; C Edin St Mich and All SS *Edin* 75-77; R Galashiels 77-85; R Yarm *York* from 85. *The Rectory, 6 Westgate, Yarm, Cleveland TS15 9BU* Tel (01642) 781115

SMITH, Mrs Decia Jane. b 47. ALAM66. WMMTC 92. **d** 95 **p** 96. C Edgbaston St Germain *Birm* from 95. *74 Lordswood Road, Birmingham B17 9BY* Tel 0121-427 5526

SMITH, Denis Richard. b 53. St Jo Coll Nottm 83. **d** 85 **p** 86. C Hersham *Guildf* 85-88; C Thatcham *Ox* 88-91; V Shefford *St Alb* from 91. *The Vicarage, 9 The Hollies, Shefford, Beds SG17 5BX* Tel (01462) 811100

SMITH, Dennis Austin. b 50. Lanc Univ BA71 Liv Univ PGCE72. NW Ord Course 74. **d** 77 **p** 78. NSM Gt Crosby St Faith *Liv* 77-83; Hon C from 83; NSM Seaforth 77-83; Asst Chapl Merchant Taylors' Sch Crosby 79-83; Chapl from 83. *16 Fir Road, Liverpool L22 4QL* Tel 0151-928 5065

SMITH, Dennis Peter. b 35. Qu Coll Birm 83. **d** 85 **p** 86. C Sedgley All SS *Lich* 85-89; C Penkridge w Stretton 89-90; TV Penkridge Team 90-93; V Ketley and Oakengates from 93; RD Telford from 96; RD Telford Severn Gorge *Heref* from 96. *Holy Trinity Vicarage, Holyhead Road, Oakengates, Telford, Shropshire TF2 6BN* Tel (01952) 612926

SMITH, Derek Arthur. b 38. Chich Th Coll 63. **d** 66 **p** 67. C Cheadle *Lich* 66-70; C Blakenall Heath 70-72; P-in-c 76-77; TR 77-86; V Knutton 72-76; R Lich St Mary w St Mich 86-96; P-in-c Wall 90-96; R Lich St Mich w St Mary and Wall from 96. *St Michael's Rectory, St Michael Road, Lichfield, Staffs WS13 6SN* Tel (01543) 262420

SMITH, Derek Arthur Byott. b 26. Hull Univ MA89. S Dios Minl Tr Scheme 78. **d** 81 **p** 82. NSM Wimborne Minster and Holt *Sarum* 81-83; C Northampton St Alb *Pet* 83-85; Ind Chapl *York* 85-89; P-in-c Kingston upon Hull St Mary 88-89; P-in-c Newington w Dairycoates 89-93; rtd 93; Perm to Offic *York* from 93. *107 Cardigan Road, Bridlington, N Humberside YO15 3LP* Tel (01262) 678852

SMITH, Derek Arthur Douglas. b 26. Dur Univ BA51. Qu Coll Birm 58. **d** 60 **p** 61. C Evesham *Worc* 60-63; C Bollington St Jo *Ches* 63-68; V Thelwall 68-78; V Whitegate w Lt Budworth 78-92; rtd 92; Perm to Offic *Ches* from 92. *10 Newtons Crescent, Winterley, Sandbach, Cheshire CW11 9NS* Tel (01270) 589130

SMITH, Derek Graham. b 52. St Cath Coll Cam BA74 MA77. Westcott Ho Cam 74. **d** 76 **p** 77. C Weymouth H Trin *Sarum* 76-79; P-in-c Bradpole 79; TV Bridport 79-84; R Monkton Farleigh, S Wraxall and Winsley from 84. *The Rectory, 6 Millbourn Close, Winsley, Bradford-on-Avon, Wilts BA15 2NN* Tel (01225) 722230

SMITH, Donald Edgar. b 56. Oak Hill Th Coll 89. **d** 91 **p** 92. C Holloway St Mark w Em *Lon* 91-92; C Tollington 92-95; TV W Ealing St Jo w St Jas from 95. *23A Culmington Road, London W13 9NJ* Tel 0181-566 3459 Fax 566 3507

SMITH, The Ven Donald John. b 26. Univ of Wales LLM. Clifton Th Coll 50. **d** 53 **p** 54. C Edgware *Lon* 53-56; C Ipswich St Marg *St E* 56-58; V Hornsey Rise St Mary *Lon* 58-62; R Whitton and Thurleston w Akenham *St E* 62-75; Hon Can St E Cathl 73-91; R Rickinghall 75-76; P-in-c Redgrave w Botesdale and Wortham 75-76; Adn Suffolk 75-84; R Redgrave cum Botesdale w Rickinghall 76-78; Adn Sudbury 84-91; rtd 91; Perm to Offic *Glouc* from 91. *St Peter's Cottage, Stretton-on-Fosse, Moreton-in-Marsh, Glos GL56 9SE* Tel (01608) 662790

✠**SMITH, The Rt Revd Donald Westwood.** b 28. Edin Th Coll 54 St D Coll Lamp 50. **d** 54 **p** 55 **c** 90. Asst Dioc Supernumerary *Ab* 54-55; Chapl St Andr Cathl 55-56; Canada 56-57; R Longside *Ab* 57-65; Mauritius 65-85; P-in-c St Geo-in-the-East St Mary *Lon* 85-86; Seychelles 86-87; Madagascar from 87; Bp Toamasina from 90; rtd 96. *Eveche Anglican, BP 5, Toamasina 501, Madagascar* Tel Madagascar (261) 532163

SMITH, Douglas David Frederick. b 28. Lon Univ BD53. ALCD53. **d** 53 **p** 54. C Fulham Ch Ch *Lon* 53-57; C Heatherlands St Jo *Sarum* 57-61; V Hyson Green *S'well* 61-66; Lic to Offic *York* 66-69; NE Area Sec CPAS 66-69; R Higher Openshaw *Man* 69-80; R Church w Chapel Brampton *Pet* 80-81; R Church and Chapel Brampton w Harlestone 81-86; Perm to Offic *Ox* from 86; rtd 89. *1 Maybush Walk, Olney, Bucks MK46 5NA* Tel (01234) 712256

SMITH, Ms Elizabeth. b 46. Liv Inst of Educn CertEd67 Heythrop Coll Lon BD76 Lon Univ MPhil84. Westcott Ho Cam CTM92. **d** 92 **p** 94. Par Dn Moulsham St Jo *Chelmsf* 92-94; C 94-96; V

Westcliff St Andr from 96. *St Andrew's Vicarage, 65 Electric Avenue, Westcliff-on-Sea, Essex SS0 9NN* Tel (01702) 342868

SMITH (née HOWSE), Mrs Elizabeth Ann (Beth). b 39. Bath Academy of Art CertEd60 Warw Univ BEd85 Westhill Coll Birm DipRE88. WMMTC 91. **d** 94 **p** 95. C Fletchamstead *Cov* from 94. *20 Hathaway Road, Coventry CV4 9HW* Tel (01203) 473197

SMITH, Miss Elizabeth Jane (Liz). b 50. Birm Univ BA72 DCG73. Trin Coll Bris 88. **d** 90 **p** 95. C Lowestoft and Kirkley *Nor* 90-94; TV Rugby St Andr *Cov* from 94. *63A Lower Hillmorton Road, Rugby, Warks CV21 3TQ*

SMITH, Elizabeth Marion (Beth). b 52. ACA76 FCA82. Carl Dioc Tr Inst 91. **d** 94 **p** 95. C Appleby *Carl* from 94. *10 Castle View Road, Appleby-in-Westmorland, Cumbria CA16 6HH* Tel (01768) 352786

SMITH, Elvyn Garston. b 09. St Pet Hall Ox BA36 MA40. Wycliffe Hall Ox 36. **d** 37 **p** 38. C Ealing Dean St Jo *Lon* 37-40; Org Sec (SW Distr) CPAS 40-45; R Chesterfield H Trin *Derby* 45-55; Chapl Scarsdale Hosp 45-55; V Patcham *Chich* 55-75; RD Preston 73-75; rtd 75; Perm to Offic *Chich* from 75. *45 Sheridan Road, Worthing, W Sussex BN14 8EU* Tel (01903) 208611

SMITH, Eric Frederick. b 19. Lon Univ BA40 BD42. ALCD42. **d** 42 **p** 43. C Talbot Village *Sarum* 42-44; C S'wark St Jude *S'wark* 44-48; P-in-c Mottingham St Edward LD 48-56; V Lee Gd Shep w St Pet 56-67; Sub-Dean Lewisham 61-67; R Long Ditton 67-81; V Deal St Geo *Cant* 81-85; RD Sandwich 82-85; rtd 85; Perm to Offic *Cant* from 85; Chapl Cant Sch of Min 88-94; Chapl SEITE from 94. *Beach Cottage, 179 Beach Street, Deal, Kent CT14 6LE* Tel (01304) 367648

SMITH, Ernest John. b 24. ARICS49. Oak Hill Th Coll 59. **d** 61 **p** 62. C Low Leyton *Chelmsf* 61-64; C Hove Bp Hannington Memorial Ch *Chich* 64-72; V W Hampstead Trin *Lon* 72-89; rtd 90; Perm to Offic *Chelmsf* from 90. *11 Oziers, Elsenham, Bishop's Stortford, Herts CM22 6LS* Tel (01279) 816872

SMITH, Esmond Ernest Carrington. b 22. Mert Coll Ox BA43 MA47. Westcott Ho Cam 46. **d** 46 **p** 47. V E Crompton *Man* 51-57; V Ripley *Derby* 57-65; V Aston SS Pet and Paul *Birm* 65-75; RD Aston 71-75; Asst Master Stainiforth Sch Thetford 75-78; Perm to Offic *St E* from 78; rtd 87. *The Saltings, Broad Street, Orford, Suffolk IP12 2NQ* Tel (01394) 405234

SMITH, Eustace. b 20. St Pet Hall Ox BA43 MA46. Wycliffe Hall Ox 43. **d** 46 **p** 46. C Tiverton St Pet *Ex* 46-47; C Lenton *S'well* 47-49; C Aston SS Pet and Paul *Birm* 49-53; V Bermondsey St Anne *S'wark* 53-59; V Buckminster w Sewstern *Leic* 59-74; V Buckminster w Sewstern, Sproxton and Coston 74-82; R Algarkirk *Linc* 82-88; V Fosdyke 82-88; rtd 89; Perm to Offic *Leic* from 89. *32 Wordsworth Way, Measham, Swadlincote, Derbyshire DE12 7ER* Tel (01530) 273765

SMITH, Father Luke. *See* SMITH, Philip Sydney Bellman

SMITH, Dr Felicity Ann. b 40. Bris Univ MB, ChB63. Qu Coll Birm. **dss** 86 **d** 87 **p** 94. NSM Dioc Bd for Soc Resp *Cov* from 86. *14 Oakwood Grove, Warwick CV34 5TD* Tel (01926) 492452

SMITH, Francis Armand. b 10. Sarum Th Coll 59. **d** 61 **p** 62. C Marlborough *Sarum* 61-63; V Upavon w Rushall 63-76; rtd 76; Perm to Offic *S'wark* from 76; Perm to Offic *Roch* 77-93; Perm to Offic *Chich* 78-93. *15 High Street, Cowden, Edenbridge, Kent TN8 5AB* Tel (01342) 850484

SMITH, Francis James Prall. b 22. Nor Ord Course 73. **d** 76 **p** 77. NSM Gunthorpe w Bale *Nor* 76-82; NSM Friston *St E* 82-86; NSM Knodishall w Buxlow 82-86; NSM Aldringham w Thorpe, Knodishall w Buxlow etc 86-89; rtd 89; Perm to Offic *St E* from 90. *6 Bluebell Way, Worlingham, Beccles, Suffolk NR34 7BT* Tel (01502) 711528

SMITH, Francis Malcolm (Frank). b 44. FBIM AIB69 Open Univ BA82. EAMTC 90. **d** 93 **p** 94. NSM Prittlewell *Chelmsf* from 93. *43 Burlescoombe Road, Southend-on-Sea SS1 3QE* Tel (01702) 586680 Fax 586293

SMITH, Frank. b 39. Nottm Univ CertEd65 Open Univ BA76. Paton Congr Coll Nottm 61 Cuddesdon Coll 69. **d** 69 **p** 70. In Congr Ch 65-69; C Davyhulme St Mary *Man* 69-72; PC Peak Forest and Wormhill *Derby* 72-78; R W Hallam and Mapperley 78-85; V Henleaze *Bris* from 85; RD Clifton from 93. *St Peter's Vicarage, 17 The Drive, Bristol BS9 4LD* Tel 0117-962 0636 or 962 3196

SMITH, Frank John. b 55. SS Mark & Jo Coll Chelsea BA85 Ex Univ MPhil96. Chich Th Coll CMT93. **d** 93 **p** 94. C Solihull *Birm* from 93. *17 Church Hill Close, Solihull, W Midlands B91 3JB* Tel 0121-705 8923

SMITH, Gary Russell. b 56. Southn Univ BTh94. Cuddesdon Coll 94. **d** 96 **p** 97. C Southampton Maybush St Pet *Win* from 96. *All Saints House, 60 Brookwood Road, Maybush, Southampton SO16 9AT* Tel (01703) 781909

SMITH, Canon Geoffrey. b 45. Bernard Gilpin Soc Dur 65 Sarum Th Coll 66. **d** 69 **p** 70. C Hatfield *Sheff* 69-71; C Bolton St Pet *Man* 71-74; V Lt Hulton 74-78; P-in-c Newc St Andr *Newc* 78-87; Soc Resp Adv 78-87; Hon Can Newc Cathl 84-87; Public Preacher *Birm* 87-93; Dir Cen for Applied Chr Studies 87-91; Team Ldr Home Office Birm Drug Prevention Unit 91-93; C Brampton and Farlam and Castle Carrock w Cumrew *Carl* 93-96; ACUPA Link Officer 94-96; Can Res Bradf Cathl *Bradf* from 96. *3 Cathedral Close, Bradford, W Yorkshire BD1 4EG* Tel (01274) 727806 Fax 722898

SMITH, Canon Geoffrey Cobley. b 30. Bps' Coll Cheshunt 63. **d** 65 **p** 66. C Hockerill *St Alb* 65-68; C Evesham *Worc* 68-72; V Walberswick w Blythburgh *St E* 72-85; RD Halesworth 81-85; R Newmarket St Mary w Exning St Agnes from 85; RD Mildenhall from 86; Hon Can St E Cathl from 87. *The Rectory, 5A Fitzroy Street, Newmarket, Suffolk CB8 0JW* Tel (01638) 662448

SMITH, Geoffrey Keith. b 37. Lon Coll of Div 57. **d** 60 **p** 61. C Leek St Luke *Lich* 60-63; C Trentham 63-66; V Lilleshall 66-84; P-in-c Sheriffhales w Woodcote 83-84; V Lilleshall and Sheriffhales 84-87; P-in-c Haughton 87-91; R Derrington, Haughton and Ranton from 91; RD Stafford from 95. *The Rectory, Haughton, Stafford ST18 9HU* Tel (01785) 780181

SMITH, Geoffrey Raymond. b 49. AKC71. St Aug Coll Cant 71. **d** 72 **p** 73. C Hendon St Alphage *Lon* 72-75; C Notting Hill St Mich and Ch Ch 75-78; P-in-c Isleworth St Fran 78-83; P-in-c Chipping Ongar *Chelmsf* 83-84; R 84-86; R Shelley 84-86; R Chipping Ongar w Shelley 86-89; RD Ongar 88-89; P-in-c Harlow St Mary Magd 89-90; V from 90. *The Vicarage, Harlow Common, Harlow, Essex CM17 9ND* Tel (01279) 422681

SMITH, George Ælbert. b 15. Sarum & Wells Th Coll 77. **d** 80 **p** 81. NSM Milton Abbot w Dunterton *Ex* 80-81; Hon C 80-81; NSM Milton Abbot, Dunterton, Lamerton etc 81-83; Perm to Offic 83-86; NSM Colyton, Southleigh, Offwell, Widworthy etc from 86. *St Mary's, Church Street, Colyton, Devon EX13 6JY* Tel (01297) 552089

SMITH, Canon George Robert Henry. b 24. Chich Th Coll 49. **d** 52 **p** 53. C Glouc St Steph *Glouc* 52-56; V Dean Forest St Paul 56-65; P-in-c Clearwell 60-62; V Tuffley 65-82; Hon Can Glouc Cathl 81-94; R Leckhampton St Pet 82-94; rtd 94; NSM Westcote w Icomb and Bledington *Glouc* from 95. *The Vicarage, Chapel Street, Bledington, Chipping Norton, Oxon OX7 6UR* Tel (01608) 658102

SMITH, Gerald. b 36. Sarum Th Coll 61. **d** 63 **p** 64. C Menston w Woodhead *Bradf* 63-66; Chapl RAF 66-70; C Hoylake *Ches* 70-72; R Inverurie *Ab* 72-74; R Kemnay 72-74; TV Hucknall Torkard *S'well* 74-75; Falkland Is 75-78; V Luddenden w Luddenden Foot *Wakef* 79-86; V Scopwick Gp *Linc* 86-94; P-in-c Leasingham 94-96; rtd 96; Perm to Offic *Ex* from 96. *Ivy House, Woolsery, Bideford, Devon EX39 5QS* Tel (01237) 431298

SMITH, Preb Gilbert. b 14. Lon Univ BD64. Lambeth STh57 K Coll Lon 39. **d** 40 **p** 41. C Brierley Hill *Lich* 40-42; CF 42-50; R Wrockwardine Wood *Lich* 51-58; V Codsall 58-83; RD Penkridge 72-82; Preb Lich Cathl 82-88; rtd 83; P-in-c Blymhill w Weston-under-Lizard *Lich* 83-88; Perm to Offic from 89. *14 Malthouse Lane, Bradley, Stafford ST18 9DU* Tel (01785) 780365

SMITH, Mrs Gillian Angela (Gill). b 39. RGN60 RM62. All Nations Chr Coll IDC65. **d** 94 **p** 95. NSM Haydock St Mark *Liv* 94-96. *1 Courtland Avenue, Cambridge CB1 4AT* Tel (01223) 247410

SMITH (née SPARK), Mrs Gloria Elizabeth. b 36. St Mary's Coll Dur BTh58 DipEd59. NE Ord Course 93. **d** 96 **p** 97. NSM Gosforth All SS *Newc* from 96. *1 Columba Walk, Newcastle upon Tyne NE3 1AY* Tel 0191-284 5120

SMITH, Godfrey Declan Burfield. b 42. TCD BA64 MA67 PGCE65. Irish Sch of Ecum DipEcum82 Sarum Th Coll. **d** 69 **p** 70. Zambia 70-75; Perm to Offic *D & G* from 81; S Regional Sec (Ireland) CMS from 81; Overseas Sec 87-97; Miss Personnel Sec from 97. *Overseas House, 3 Belgrave Road, Rathmines, Dublin 6, Irish Republic* Tel Dublin (1) 497 0931 or 280 7452 Fax 497 0939 or 280 7452 E-mail declan@cmsi.iol.ie

SMITH, Graeme Richard. b 65. Leeds Univ BA87. Qu Coll Birm 87. **d** 89 **p** 90. C Daventry *Pet* 90-92; C Daventry, Ashby St Ledgers, Braunston etc 92; Perm to Offic *Birm* from 92. *51 Weoley Avenue, Birmingham B29 6PP* Tel 0121-472 4178

SMITH, Graham Charles Morell. b 47. St Chad's Coll Dur BA74. Westcott Ho Cam 74. **d** 76 **p** 77. C Tooting All SS *S'wark* 76-80; TV Thamesmead 80-87; TR Kidlington w Hampton Poyle *Ox* from 87; RD Ox 89-95. *St Mary's Rectory, 19 Mill Street, Kidlington, Oxon OX5 2EE* Tel (01865) 372230 Fax 378014

SMITH, Graham David Noel. b 37. Oak Hill Th Coll 72. **d** 73 **p** 74. C Southborough St Pet w Ch Ch and St Matt *Roch* 73-76; C Bedworth *Cov* 76-79; C Coventry Caludon 79; R Treeton *Sheff* 79-84; V Riddlesden *Bradf* 84-96; RD S Craven 91-96; rtd 96. *7 Rosebank, Burley-in-Wharfedale, Ilkley, W Yorkshire LS29 7PQ* Tel (01943) 864754

SMITH, Canon Graham Francis. b 27. Leic Univ DSocStuds51 Lon Univ BD57. Wells Th Coll 51. **d** 54 **p** 55. C Howe Bridge *Man* 54-57; C Hatfield Hyde *St Alb* 57-63; V Angell Town St Jo *S'wark* 63-73; V Wandsworth St Anne 73-85; P-in-c Wandsworth St Faith 75-78; RD Wandsworth 81-85; Hon Can S'wark Cathl 82-92; Mert Deanery Missr 85-92; rtd 92. *The Haven, 9 High Street, Syresham, Brackley, Northants NN13 5HL* Tel (01280) 850421

SMITH, Graham John. b 31. SSC. **d** 75 **p** 76. Hon C Devonport St Mark Ford *Ex* 75-81; Hon C Plympton St Maurice 81-90; V Ernesettle from 90. *St Aidan's Vicarage, 122 Rochford Crescent, Plymouth PL5 2QD* Tel (01752) 364374

SMITH, Graham John. b 60. RN Coll Dartmouth 79 RN Eng Coll Plymouth BScEng84. Trin Coll Bris DipHE87 BA90. **d** 90 **p** 91. C

Herne *Cant* 90-93; Chapl RN 93-96; C Henfield w Shermanbury and Woodmancote *Chich* from 96. *Glebe House, 41 Furners Mead, Henfield, W Sussex BN5 9JA* Tel (01273) 494421 Fax 494421 E-mail compuserve 100712,2642

SMITH, Grahame Clarence. b 32. Lich Th Coll 58. **d** 60 **p** 61. C New Sleaford *Linc* 60-63; R Tydd 63-76; V Barholm w Stowe 76-81; V Tallington 76-81; R Uffington 76-81; P-in-c W Deeping 76-77; R 77-81; R Uffington 81-92; rtd 92; Perm to Offic *Linc* from 92. *Keeper's Cottage, Careby Road, Aunby, Stamford, Lincs PE9 4EG* Tel (01780) 66386

SMITH, Gregory James. *See* CLIFTON-SMITH, Gregory James

SMITH, Canon Guy Howard. b 33. Man Univ BA54. Coll of Resurr Mirfield 60. **d** 62 **p** 63. C Oswestry H Trin *Lich* 62-66; Malaysia 66-69; V Willenhall St Anne *Lich* 69-79; P-in-c Willenhall St Steph 75-79; Malawi 79-82; Adn Lilongwe Lake Malawi 80-82; V Tettenhall Wood *Lich* 82-89; TR 89-91; TR Kidderminster St Jo and H Innocents *Worc* from 91. *The Vicarage, 9 Sutton Park Road, Kidderminster, Worcs DY11 6LE* Tel (01562) 822186 Fax as telephone

SMITH, Harold. b 20. Qu Coll Birm 77. **d** 80 **p** 81. NSM Gravelly Hill *Birm* 80-85; NSM Duddeston w Nechells 85-93; Perm to Offic from 93. *37 Dovey Tower, Duddeston Manor Road, Birmingham B7 4LE* Tel 0121-359 0568

SMITH, Harvey Jefferson. b 19. AMCT39 FIEE38 FIMechE52 FIPlantE67 ACIArb78. St Alb Minl Tr Scheme 81. **d** 88. Hon C Hemel Hempstead *St Alb* 88-92; Perm to Offic 92-95. *43 Garland Close, Hemel Hempstead, Herts HP2 5HU* Tel (01442) 66377

SMITH, Sister Hazel Ferguson Waide. b 33. Univ Coll Lon BA55. **dss** 64 **d** 87. CSA 58-77; St Etheldreda's Children's Home Bedf 64-85; Bedford St Paul *St Alb* 85-92; Par Dn 87-92; rtd 92; Perm to Offic *St Alb* 92-95; Perm to Offic *Ox* 93-95. *Paddock House, 6 Linford Lane, Willen, Milton Keynes MK15 9DL* Tel (01908) 661554 or (0589) 654881

SMITH, Henry Neville. b 25. Chich Th Coll 53. **d** 54 **p** 55. C Oldham St Mary *Man* 54-56; C Mitcham St Olave *S'wark* 57-59; Succ Leic Cathl *Leic* 59-60; Chapl St Jas Hosp Balham 60-63; V Ivinghoe w Pitstone *Ox* 63-73; Chapl Qu Anne's Sch Caversham 73-90; rtd 90; Perm to Offic *Chich* from 90. *12 Poulner Close, Bognor Regis, W Sussex PO22 8HN* Tel (01243) 822716

SMITH, Henry Robert. b 41. Lanchester Poly BSc66. Qu Coll Birm 75. **d** 78 **p** 79. Hon C Hillmorton *Cov* 78-81; Lic to Offic *S'well* 81-85; Hon C Radcliffe-on-Trent and Shelford etc 85-89; C Sutton in Ashfield St Mary 89-92; P-in-c Forest Town from 92. *The Vicarage, Old Mill Lane, Forest Town, Mansfield, Notts NG19 0EP* Tel (01623) 21120

SMITH, Howard Alan. b 46. DCouns81 St Jo Coll Dur BA73 DipTh74. **d** 74 **p** 75. C Brighton St Matthias *Chich* 74-77; C Henfield 77-78; C Henfield w Shermanbury and Woodmancote 78-80; R Northiam 80-87; Chapl St Ebba's Hosp Epsom 87-94; Chapl Qu Mary's Hosp Carshalton 87-94; Chapl Merton and Sutton Community NHS Trust from 94. *Merton and Sutton Community Trust, Damson Way, Orchard Hill, Carshalton, Surrey SM5 4NR* Tel 0181-770 8000

SMITH, Howard Gilbert. b 48. Leeds Univ BA69. St Steph Ho Ox BA71 MA75 Ridley Hall Cam 72. **d** 73 **p** 74. C Wallsend St Luke *Newc* 73-76; C Farnworth and Kearsley *Man* 76-77; P-in-c Farnworth All SS 77-78; TV E Farnworth and Kearsley 78-82; V Belfield 82-93; V Leesfield from 93. *St Thomas's Vicarage, Wild Street, Lees, Oldham OL4 5AD* Tel 0161-624 3731

SMITH, Ian. b 62. Hull Univ BA83. Oak Hill Th Coll DipHE87 BA88. **d** 88 **p** 89. C W Hampstead St Luke *Lon* 88-90; C Woking St Pet *Guildf* 90-95; V Leyland St Jo *Blackb* from 95. *St John's Vicarage, Leyland Lane, Leyland, Preston PR5 3HB* Tel (01772) 621646

SMITH, Ian Charles. b 39. Lich Th Coll 65. **d** 68 **p** 69. C Kingshurst *Birm* 68-72; Chapl RAF 72-83; Chapl Winterton Hosp Sedgefield 83-91; Asst Chapl HM Pris Wakef 91-92; Chapl HM Pris Haverigg from 92. *HM Prison, Haverigg, Millom, Cumbria LA18 4NA* Tel (01229) 772131 Fax 772561

SMITH, Canon Ian Walker. b 29. Leeds Univ BA52. Coll of Resurr Mirfield 52. **d** 54 **p** 55. C Moulsecoomb *Chich* 54-61; Chapl K Sch Cant 61-62; C Crawley *Chich* 62-79; TV 79-81; R Clenchwarton *Ely* 81-94; RD Lynn Marshland 84-94; Hon Can Ely Cathl 88-94; Perm to Offic *Nor* from 88; rtd 94. *27 Jubilee Drive, Dersingham, King's Lynn, Norfolk PE31 6YA* Tel (01485) 540203

SMITH, James. b 26. NE Ord Course 76. **d** 79 **p** 80. NSM Seaton Hirst *Newc* 79-82; NSM Cresswell and Lynemouth 82-88; NSM Cambois 88-93; rtd 93. *140 Pont Street, Ashington, Northd NE63 0PX* Tel (01670) 816557

SMITH, James Edward. b 30. Chich Th Coll 57. **d** 58 **p** 59. C Ellesmere Port *Ches* 58-61; C W Bromwich All SS *Lich* 61-63; Chapl RN 63-65; V Walton St Jo *Liv* 65-71; V Anfield St Columba 71-79; V Altcar 79-92; rtd 92; Perm to Offic *Linc* from 93. *272 Skellingthorpe Road, Lincoln LN6 0EU* Tel (01522) 696865

SMITH, James Harold (Jim). b 31. Ch Coll Tasmania ThL61. **d** 61 **p** 61. Australia 61-63 and 66-85 and 92-94; Canada 64-65; Chapl St Chris Hospice Lon 86-87; Asst Chapl Brook Gen Hosp Lon 87-92; Asst Chapl Greenwich Distr Hosp Lon 87-92; Perm to Offic *S'wark* from 94. *15 Couthurst Road, London SE3 8TN* Tel 0181-858 4692

SMITH, James Henry. b 32. St Aid Birkenhead. **d** 65 **p** 66. C Wigan St Cath *Liv* 65-68; V Parkfield in Middleton *Man* 68-77; V Bolton Breightmet St Jas 77-97; rtd 97. *Flat 4, 14A Cropton Road, Formby, Merseyside L37 4AD* Tel (01704) 833682

SMITH, James William. b 47. SRN69 RMN70 MRIPHH69 MRSH92 Lambeth STh90 Sussex Coll of Tech MA95. Chich Th Coll 78. **d** 80 **p** 80. C Kenwyn *Truro* 80-82; C Haslemere *Guildf* 82-84; TV Honiton, Gittisham, Combe Raleigh, Monkton etc *Ex* 84-91; Chapl R Marsden Hosp Lon and Surrey 91-95; Perm to Offic *S'wark* 91-95; rtd 95. *22 Thrift Close, Stalbridge, Sturminster Newton, Dorset DT10 2LE* Tel (01963) 362445

SMITH, Jeffery Donald Morris. b 23. **d** 53 **p** 54. S Rhodesia 53-61; R Old Deer *Ab* 61-63; R Fraserburgh 63-68; S Africa 68-73; P-in-c Bintree w Themelthorpe *Nor* 73-76; V Twyford w Guist 73-76; R Twyford w Guist and Bintry w Themelthorpe 76-80; RD Sparham 79-81; R Twyford w Guist w Bintry w Themelthorpe etc 81; TR Hempnall 81-84; R Catfield 84-89; R Ingham w Sutton 84-89; rtd 89; Perm to Offic *Nor* from 89. *27 Dale Road, East Dereham, Norfolk NR19 2DD* Tel (01362) 697022

SMITH, Jeffry Bradford. b 56. BA82. Ch Div Sch of the Pacific (USA) MDiv85 Ripon Coll Cuddesdon. **d** 86 **p** 87. C Frimley *Guildf* 87-91; R E and W Clandon from 91; Chapl HM Pris Send 94-96. *The Rectory, The Street, West Clandon, Guildford, Surrey GU4 7RG* Tel (01483) 222573

SMITH, Mrs Jennifer Pamela (Jenny). b 63. Girton Coll Cam BA85 MA88. Oak Hill Th Coll BA91. **d** 91 **p** 94. C Rawdon *Bradf* 91-93; Chapl Bradf Cathl 93-96; P-in-c Kelbrook from 96. *The Vicarage, Vicarage Road, Kelbrook, Colne, Lancs BB8 6TQ* Tel (01282) 841607

SMITH, Jeremy Victor. b 60. Keble Coll Ox BA82. Chich Th Coll 83. **d** 85 **p** 86. C Alton St Lawr *Win* 85-88; C W Hampstead St Jas *Lon* 88-93; V St Geo-in-the-East St Mary 93-97. *St Mary's Vicarage, Johnson Street, London E1 0AQ* Tel 0171-790 0973

SMITH, Jesse Lee. b 70. Man Univ BA93. Linc Th Coll DipMM94 Westcott Ho Cam MA95. **d** 96 **p** 97. C Gomersal *Wakef* from 96. *St Mary's House, 25 Shirley Avenue, Cleckheaton, W Yorkshire BD19 4NA* Tel (01274) 873502

SMITH, John Alec. b 37. Lon Coll of Div ALCD62 BD63. **d** 63 **p** 64. C Cromer *Nor* 63-66; C Barking St Marg *Chelmsf* 66-69; V Attercliffe *Sheff* 69-75; P-in-c Sheff St Barn 76-78; V Sheff St Barn and St Mary 78-89; Ind Chapl 78-89; RD Ecclesall 80-85; TR Chippenham St Paul w Hardenhuish etc *Bris* from 89; V Kington from 89. *St Paul's Rectory, 9 Greenway Park, Chippenham, Wilts SN15 1QG* Tel (01249) 653839

SMITH, John Bartlett. b 50. AIPM St Chad's Coll Dur BA73 Lanchester Poly DipIR80. Cuddesdon Coll 73. **d** 76 **p** 77. C Heref St Martin *Heref* 76-86; NSM Isleworth St Mary *Lon* 86-89; NSM Millom *Carl* 89-92; NSM Balham St Mary and St Jo *S'wark* from 92. *101 Gosberton Road, London SW12 8LG* Tel 0181-675 1743

SMITH, John David Elliott. b 39. Dur Univ BA61. Cranmer Hall Dur 61. **d** 64 **p** 65. C Stratford-on-Avon w Bishopton *Cov* 64-70; P-in-c Tredington 70-76; P-in-c Newbold on Avon 76-81; V 81-89; P-in-c Arlington, Folkington and Wilmington *Chich* from 89. *The Vicarage, The Street, Wilmington, Polegate, E Sussex BN26 5SW* Tel (01323) 870268

SMITH, Dr John Denmead. b 44. Ox Univ BA65 MA69 DPhil71. Coll of Resurr Mirfield 72. **d** 75 **p** 76. Asst Chapl Win Coll from 75. *11 Kingsgate Street, Winchester, Hants SO23 9PD* Tel (01962) 861820

SMITH, Canon John Douglas. b 20. Roch Th Coll 63. **d** 65 **p** 66. C Byfleet *Guildf* 65-69; C Hersham 69-72; V Churt 72-80; V Cobham 80-88; RD Leatherhead 83-88; Hon Can Guildf Cathl 85-88; rtd 88. *77 Home Park, Oxted, Surrey RH8 0JT* Tel (01883) 714861

SMITH, John Eckersley. b 26. Univ of Wales (Lamp). St Aug Coll Cant Wycliffe Hall Ox 53. **d** 55 **p** 56. C Heywood St Jas *Man* 55-57; C Atherton 57-59; R Gorton All SS 59-65; C Northenden 73-75; V Charlestown 75-82; Perm to Offic from 85; rtd 91. *19 Arthur Street, Swinton, Manchester M27 3HP* Tel 0161-793 7707

SMITH, John Ernest. b 52. St Andr Univ MTh77. Wycliffe Hall Ox 78. **d** 79 **p** 80. C Bermondsey St Mary w St Olave, St Jo etc *S'wark* 79-87; P-in-c Whyteleafe from 87; RD Caterham from 96. *8 Whyteleafe Hill, Whyteleafe, Surrey CR3 0AA*

SMITH, John Graham. b 32. **d** 78 **p** 79. NSM Hordle *Win* from 78. *3 Marryat Road, New Milton, Hants BH25 5LW* Tel (01425) 615701

SMITH, John Lawrence. b 43. Birm Univ BSc65. Linc Th Coll 67. **d** 70 **p** 71. C Frodingham *Linc* 70-75; TV Gt Grimsby St Mary and St Jas 75-83; V Wolverhampton St Andr *Lich* from 83. *St Andrew's Vicarage, 66 Albert Road, Wolverhampton WV6 0AF* Tel (01902) 712935

SMITH, John Leslie. b 44. Trin Coll Cam BA65 MA71. Ripon Coll Cuddesdon 79. **d** 81 **p** 82. C Ollerton *S'well* 81-84; P-in-c Farndon 84-88; P-in-c Thorpe 84-88; P-in-c Langford w Holme 88-95; P-in-c Winthorpe 88-95; Dioc Chief Insp Ch Schs 88-95; Dir of Educn *Pet* from 95; P-in-c Cottingham w E Carlton from 97. *The Rectory, Cottingham, Market Harborough, Leics LE16 8GX*

SMITH, John Macdonald. b 29. Ch Coll Cam BA52 MA56. Wells Th Coll 56. **d** 58 **p** 59. C Westbury-on-Trym H Trin *Bris* 58-60; C

Reading St Giles *Ox* 60-63; V Kidmore End 63-82; rtd 82. *38 Main Road, Norton, Evesham, Worcs WR11 4TL* Tel (01386) 870918

SMITH, John Malcolm. b 36. ACIB60. N Ord Course 81. **d** 84 **p** 85. NSM Bury St Pet *Man* from 84. *46 Ajax Drive, Bury, Lancs BL9 8EF* Tel 0161-766 8378

SMITH, John Oswald Salkeld. b 32. Oak Hill Th Coll 57. **d** 60 **p** 61. C Peckham St Mary Magd *S'wark* 61-63; C Rodbourne Cheney *Bris* 63-67; V Bradf St Aug Undercliffe *Bradf* 67-74; P-in-c Hammersmith St Simon *Lon* 74-76; V Chelsea St Jo w St Andr from 76. *St Andrew's Vicarage, 43 Park Walk, London SW10 0AU* Tel 0171-352 1675

SMITH, Canon John Reginald. b 15. MBE97. TCD BA39 MA42. Wycliffe Hall Ox 40. **d** 41 **p** 42. C Heaton Norris Ch Ch *Man* 41-44; C Stretford St Matt 44-47; R Stretford All SS 47-49; V Radcliffe St Thos 49-59; R Sutton *Liv* 59-66; RD Bury *Man* 66-86; R Bury St Mary from 66; Hon Can Man Cathl from 72. *St Mary's Rectory, Bury, Lancs BL9 0JR* Tel 0161-764 2452

SMITH, John Roger. b 36. Dur Univ BA59. Tyndale Hall Bris 59. **d** 61 **p** 62. C Chaddesden St Mary *Derby* 61-63; C Gresley 63-66; V Burton Ch Ch *Lich* 66-76; V Doncaster St Mary *Sheff* 76-92; R Barnburgh w Melton on the Hill 92-94; R Barnburgh w Melton on the Hill etc from 94. *The Rectory, Barnburgh, Doncaster, S Yorkshire DN5 7ET* Tel (01709) 892598

SMITH, Canon John Stewart. b 18. St Cath Soc Ox BA42 MA46. Ripon Hall Ox 42. **d** 43 **p** 44. C Oldbury *Birm* 43-46; C Hengrove *Bris* 46-49; C-in-c Patchway CD 49-58; V Shirehampton 58-72; V Westbury-on-Trym St Alb 72-83; RD Clifton 73-79; Hon Can Bris Cathl 77-84; rtd 83; Chapl Hortham Hosp 83-93; Chapl Phoenix NHS Trust 93-94; Perm to Offic *Bris* from 84. *48A Downs Park West, Bristol BS6 7QL* Tel 0117-962 9208

SMITH, John Thomas. b 29. Shuttleworth Agric Coll NDA55 Keele Univ DASE72 Wolv Poly MPhil81 PhD87. WMMTC 87. **d** 91 **p** 92. NSM Drayton in Hales *Lich* from 91. *Red Bank House, Market Drayton, Shropshire TF9 1AY* Tel (01630) 652302

SMITH, John Thompson. b 30. Wycliffe Hall Ox 64. **d** 66 **p** 67. C Walsall *Lich* 66-69; V Stoke Prior *Worc* 69-75; Asst Gen Sec Red Triangle Club 75-85; R Tendring and Lt Bentley w Beaumont cum Moze *Chelmsf* 85-89; R Fairstead w Terling and White Notley etc 89-92; Chapl Heath Hosp Tendring 85-92; rtd 92; Perm to Offic *B & W* from 92. *1 Harvey Close, Weston-super-Mare, Avon BS22 0DW* Tel (01934) 514256

SMITH, John Trevor. b 47. GGSM. Coll of Resurr Mirfield 74. **d** 77 **p** 78. C Loughton St Jo *Chelmsf* 77-80; C Ruislip St Martin *Lon* 80-84; P-in-c Southall Ch Redeemer 84-91; V Kingsbury St Andr from 91. *St Andrew's Vicarage, 28 Old Church Lane, London NW9 8RZ* Tel 0181-205 7447

SMITH, Jonathan Paul. b 60. Univ of Wales (Lamp) BA81. Wycliffe Hall Ox 82. **d** 84 **p** 85. C Baglan *Llan* 84-88; C Gabalfa 88-90; V Llanganten and Llangammarch and Llanfechan etc *S & B* from 90; Dioc Missr from 95. *The Rectory, Maes y Glas, Llangammarch Wells LD4 4EE* Tel (01591) 2482

SMITH, Jonathan Peter. b 55. K Coll Lon BD77 AKC77 Cam Univ PGCE78. Westcott Ho Cam 79. **d** 80 **p** 81. C Gosforth All SS *Newc* 80-82; C Waltham Abbey *Chelmsf* 82-85; Chapl City Univ *Lon* 85-88; R Harrold and Carlton w Chellington *St Alb* 88-97; Chapl Beds Police from 90; V Harpenden St Jo from 97. *St John's Vicarage, 5 St John's Road, Harpenden, Herts AL5 1DJ* Tel (01582) 712776

SMITH, Julian. b 48. K Coll Lon 70. Linc Th Coll 71. **d** 73 **p** 74. C Taunton Lyngford *B & W* 73-76; TV Wellington and Distr 76-81; R Axbridge w Shipham and Rowberrow 81-96; Chapl St Jo Hosp Axbridge from 84; V Taunton St Andr *B & W* from 96. *118 Kingston Road, Taunton, Somerset TA2 7SR* Tel (01823) 332544

SMITH, Julian William. b 64. Liv Univ BSc85. Trin Coll Carmarthen BA93. **d** 93 **p** 94. C Henfynyw w Aberaeron and Llanddewi Aberarth *St D* from 93. *Hillcrest, Vicarage Hill, Aberaeron SA46 0DY* Tel (01545) 570792

SMITH, Keith. b 46. ACIB. S Dios Minl Tr Scheme 85. **d** 87 **p** 88. NSM W Worthing St Jo *Chich* 87-94; NSM Maybridge 94-96; C Durrington from 96. *20 Trent Road, Worthing, W Sussex BN12 4EL* Tel (01903) 505850

SMITH, Kenneth Robert. b 48. K Coll Lon BD75 AKC75. St Aug Coll Cant 75. **d** 76 **p** 77. C Birtley *Dur* 76-80; V Lamesley 80-90; R Whitburn from 90. *The Rectory, 51 Front Street, Whitburn, Sunderland SR6 7JD* Tel 0191-529 2232

SMITH, Kenneth Victor George. b 37. Lon Univ BD62. ALCD61. **d** 62 **p** 63. Hon C Bromley Common St Aug *Roch* 62-66; Hon C Streatham Immanuel w St Anselm *S'wark* 66-68; Perm to Offic 68-78; Hon C Sanderstead All SS 78-91; Chapl Whitgift Sch and Ho Croydon from 78; Hon C Croydon St Jo from 91. *Bridle Ways, Haling Grove, Croydon CR2 6DQ* Tel 0181-680 4460

SMITH, Kevin. b 66. Westmr Coll Ox BA89. Chich Th Coll 90. **d** 92 **p** 93. C Worksop Priory *S'well* 92-96; V New Cantley *Sheff* from 96. *St Hugh's House, Levet Road, Cantley, Doncaster, S Yorkshire DN4 6JQ* Tel (01302) 535739

SMITH, Canon Laurence Kenneth Powell. b 17. Lon Coll of Div ALCD41 LTh74. **d** 41 **p** 42. C Streatham Vale H Redeemer *S'wark* 41-44; C Surbiton St Matt 44-51; V Southampton St Matt *Win* 51-57; V Iford 57-72; R Stockbridge and Houghton 72-85; RD Romsey 79-85; Hon Can Win Cathl 82-85; rtd 85; Perm to Offic *Win* from 85. *8 Riverside Gardens, Romsey, Hants SO51 8HN* Tel (01794) 518262

SMITH, Laurence Sidney. b 37. Sarum & Wells Th Coll 70. **d** 73 **p** 74. C Surbiton St Matt *S'wark* 73-76; C Horley 76-81; V W Ewell *Guildf* 81-90; V W Byfleet from 90. *The Vicarage, 5 Dartnell Avenue, West Byfleet, Surrey KT14 6PJ* Tel (01932) 345270

SMITH, Lawrence Paul. b 51. Southn Univ BTh81. Chich Th Coll 76. **d** 79 **p** 80. C Margate St Jo *Cant* 79-84; R Eythorne w Waldershare 84-87; P-in-c Sibertswold w Coldred 85-87; R Eythorne and Elvington w Waldershare etc 87-97; Par Development Officer (Kensington Episc Area) *Lon* from 97. *3 Roman Close, London W3 8HE*

SMITH, Canon Lewis Shand. b 52. Aber Univ MA74 Edin Univ BD78. Edin Th Coll 74. **d** 77 **p** 78. C Wishaw *Glas* 77-79; P-in-c 79-80; C Motherwell 77-79; P-in-c 79-80; R Lerwick *Ab* from 80; R Burravoe from 80; Miss to Seamen from 80; Can St Andr Cathl *Ab* from 93. *1 Greenrig, Lerwick, Isle of Shetland ZE1 0AW* Tel (01595) 693862

SMITH, Miss Lorna Cassandra. b 43. Open Univ BA76. Cant Sch of Min 82. **dss** 86 **d** 87 **p** 94. Birchington w Acol and Minnis Bay *Cant* 86-87; Par Dn 87-92; C Addlestone *Guildf* 92-97; V Englefield Green from 97. *The Vicarage, 21 Willow Walk, Englefield Green, Egham, Surrey TW20 0DQ* Tel (01784) 432553 Fax as telephone

SMITH, Mrs Lorna Rosalind. b 53. Oak Hill NSM Course 89. **d** 92 **p** 94. NSM Squirrels Heath *Chelmsf* 92-94; NSM Stanford-le-Hope w Mucking from 94. *24 Martin's Close, Stanford-le-Hope, Essex SS17 8AB* Tel (01375) 642439/672271

SMITH, Mrs Margaret Elizabeth. b 46. Bretton Hall Coll CertEd67. N Ord Course 85. **d** 88 **p** 94. Hon Par Dn Battyeford *Wakef* 88-91; Hon C Mirfield 89-91; Chapl HM Pris New Hall 90-95; D-in-c Flockton cum Denby Grange *Wakef* 91-94; P-in-c 94-96; V Scholes from 96. *The Vicarage, Scholes Lane, Scholes, Cleckheaton, W Yorkshire BD19 6PA* Tel (01274) 873024

SMITH, Mark Gordon Robert Davenport. b 56. St Jo Coll Dur BA77. Ridley Hall Cam 78. **d** 80 **p** 81. C Sheff St Jo *Sheff* 80-83; C Brightside w Wincobank 83-86; V Kimberworth Park 86-91; Perm to Offic from 91; Consultant NE England CPAS from 91; Perm to Offic *Dur* from 95. *78 Storrs Hill Road, Ossett, Wakefield, W Yorkshire WF5 0DA* Tel (01924) 270497

SMITH, Mark Graham. b 63. Ex Univ BA86 Qu Coll Cam DipTh89. Westcott Ho Cam 87. **d** 90 **p** 91. C Cottingham *York* 90-92; C Guisborough 92-94; Chapl St Martin's Coll *Blackb* from 94. *St Martin's College, Bowerham Road, Lancaster LA1 3JD* Tel (01524) 63446

SMITH, Mark Richard Samuel. b 63. UMIST BSc84. Cranmer Hall Dur 86. **d** 89 **p** 90. C Kersal Moor *Man* 89-93; C Halliwell St Pet from 93. *St Andrew's House, 29 Tattersall Avenue, Bolton BL1 5TE* Tel (01204) 849432

SMITH, Martin David. b 52. LTCL Hull Univ BA75. Cuddesdon Coll 75. **d** 78 **p** 79. C Brentwood St Thos *Chelmsf* 78-80; C Reading St Giles *Ox* 80-91; R Colkirk w Oxwick w Pattesley, Whissonsett etc *Nor* 91-95; P-in-c Gt and Lt Ryburgh w Gateley and Testerton 94-95; P-in-c Hempton and Pudding Norton 94-95; P-in-c Nor St Pet Parmentergate w St Jo from 95. *The Rectory, 10 Stepping Lane, Norwich NR1 1PE* Tel (01603) 622509

SMITH, Martin John. b 59. Qu Coll Birm 86. **d** 89 **p** 90. C Grays Thurrock *Chelmsf* 89-92; C Warley Woods *Birm* 92-94; V Stocking Farm *Leic* from 94. *The Vicarage, 97 Halifax Drive, Stocking Farm, Leicester LE4 2DP* Tel 0116-235 3206

SMITH, Martin Lee. b 47. Worc Coll Ox BA68. Cuddesdon Coll 68. **d** 70 **p** 71. C Digswell *St Alb* 70-71; C Cheshunt 71-73; Perm to Offic *Ox* 74-80; USA from 81. *Society of St John the Evangelist, 980 Memorial Drive, Cambridge, MA 02138, USA* Tel Boston (617) 876 3037 Fax 876 5210

SMITH, Canon Martin William. b 40. K Coll Lon BD63 AKC63. **d** 64 **p** 65. C Ashford St Hilda CD *Lon* 64-67; Malaysia 67-71; V Lakenham St Mark *Nor* 72-85; V N Walsham w Antingham from 85; P-in-c Neatishead, Barton Turf and Irstead from 94; RD Tunstead 91-96; RD St Benet from 96; Hon Can Nor Cathl from 93. *The Vicarage, 28A Yarmouth Road, North Walsham, Norfolk NR28 9AT* Tel (01692) 406380

SMITH, Martyn. b 52. CertEd73. Oak Hill Th Coll BA81. **d** 81 **p** 82. C Halliwell St Pet *Man* 81-86; V Cambridge St Martin *Ely* 86-89; Vineyard Chr Fellowship from 89. *6 Lambeth Close, Horwich, Bolton BL6 6DQ* Tel (01204) 669529

SMITH, Maurice Jeffrey. b 18. Bps' Coll Cheshunt 56. **d** 56 **p** 57. C Muswell Hill St Jas *Lon* 56-58; V Springfield H Trin *Chelmsf* 58-70; Chapl HM Pris Chelmsf 65-70; R Wickham Bishops *Chelmsf* 70-86; RD Witham 76-86; rtd 86; Perm to Offic *Ex* from 88; Perm to Offic *Chelmsf* from 88. *88 Valley Way, Exmouth, Devon EX8 4RL* Tel (01395) 278524

SMITH, Merrick Thomas Jack. b 37. CEng65 MCIBSE65 Glos Coll of Arts & Tech ONC57. Oak Hill NSM Course 90. **d** 92 **p** 93. NSM Isleworth St Mary *Lon* 92-94; Perm to Offic *Birm* 94-96; P-in-c Warfield *Ox* from 96. *34 Horatio Avenue, Warfield, Bracknell, Berks RG42 3TX* Tel (01344) 412339

SMITH, Mervyn Gilbert Morris. b 18. Ripon Hall Ox 56. **d** 58 **p** 59. C Strood St Nic *Roch* 58-61; V Burham 61-67; V Rosherville 67-79; R Horsmonden 79-86; Chapl HM Det Cen Blantyre Ho 82-86; rtd 86; Perm to Offic *Portsm* from 86. *9 Golden Ridge, Freshwater, Isle of Wight PO40 9LE* Tel (01983) 754857

SMITH, Michael. b 54. Matlock Coll of Educn CertEd76 Nottm Univ BEd77. Ridley Hall Cam 87. **d** 89 **p** 90. C Ilkeston St Mary *Derby* 89-92; TV Wirksworth from 92; RD Wirksworth from 97. *The Vicarage, Brassington, Derby DE4 4DA* Tel (01629) 540281

SMITH, Michael Anthony. b 47. Univ of Wales (Abth) MA73. **d** 78 **p** 79. NSM Llandingat w Llanfair and Myddfai 78-82; Chapl Llandovery Coll 81-82; Chapl Pocklington Sch York from 82. *Hosmer Lodge, 35 Percy Road, Pocklington, York YO4 2LZ* Tel (01759) 304543 or 303125

SMITH, Michael David. b 57. BA80. St Steph Ho Ox 81. **d** 83 **p** 84. C Beaconsfield *Ox* 83-87; V Wing w Grove 87-92; R Farnham Royal w Hedgerley from 92. *The Rectory, Victoria Road, Farnham Royal, Slough SL2 3NJ* Tel (01753) 643233

SMITH, Michael George. b 33. Univ Coll Ox BA57 MA61 BD65. St Steph Ho Ox 57. **d** 60 **p** 61. C Ex St Thos *Ex* 60-63; C Ox St Mary V *Ox* 63-65; USA 65-70; Chapl Qu Marg Sch Escrick Park 70-74; Chapl Pocklington Sch York 74-82; V Ex St Dav *Ex* 82-91; R Silverton 91-95; R Butterleigh 91-95; Perm to Offic from 95. *1 Station Road, Ide, Exeter EX2 9RP* Tel (01392) 496523

SMITH, Michael Ian Antony. b 69. Warw Univ BSc91. Oak Hill Th Coll BA95. **d** 95 **p** 96. C Cheadle *Ches* from 95. *1 Warren Avenue, Cheadle, Cheshire SK8 1NB* Tel 0161-428 3001

SMITH, Michael James. b 47. AKC69. St Aug Coll Cant 70. **d** 71 **p** 72. C Corby St Columba *Pet* 71-78; V Collierley *Dur* 78-80; CPAS Evang from 83. *6 Blind Lane, Chester le Street, Co Durham DH3 4AG* Tel 0191-388 1977

SMITH, Michael John. b 47. Lon Univ DipTh71. Kelham Th Coll 65. **d** 71 **p** 72. C Cov St Mary *Cov* 71-75; Chapl RN 75-90; CF 90-95; V Lynch w Iping Marsh and Milland *Chich* from 95. *The Rectory, Fernhurst Road, Milland, Liphook, Hants GU30 7LU* Tel (01428) 741285

SMITH, Michael Keith John (Mike). b 66. Thames Poly BSc88. Linc Th Coll BTh95. **d** 95 **p** 96. C Birch St Agnes *Man* 95-96; C Longsight St Jo w St Cypr 95-96; C Birch St Agnes w Longsight St Jo w St Cypr from 97. *St John's Rectory, St John's Road, Longsight, Manchester M13 0WU* Tel 0161-224 2744

SMITH, Michael Raymond. b 36. ARCM56 ARCO56 Qu Coll Cam BA59 MA63. Cuddesdon Coll 64. **d** 65 **p** 66. C Redcar *York* 65-70; V Dormanstown 70-73; Prec Worc Cathl *Worc* 73-77; TR Worc St Barn w Ch Ch 77-83; RD Worc E 79-83; V Eskdale, Irton, Muncaster and Waberthwaite *Carl* 83-87; Chapl Uppingham Sch Leics 87-93; Lic to Offic *Pet* 88-93; P-in-c Stoke Lacy, Moreton Jeffries w Much Cowarne etc *Heref* from 93; Dioc Schs Officer from 97. *The Rectory, Stoke Lacy, Bromyard, Herefordshire HR7 4HH* Tel (01885) 490251

SMITH, Michael Richard Guy. b 55. Man Univ BA77. Ripon Coll Cuddesdon 88. **d** 90 **p** 91. C Wallasey St Hilary *Ches* 90-93; C Howden TM *York* 93-94; TV from 94. *The Vicarage, Pontington Road, Eastrington, Goole, N Humberside DN14 7QE* Tel (01430) 410282

SMITH, Michael Robin. b 34. ACIB58. Sarum Th Coll. **d** 62 **p** 63. C Perry Hill St Geo *S'wark* 62-65; C Streatham St Leon 65-68; NSM E Brixton St Jude 68-70; Brixton Chr Counselling Min 70-79; Wandsworth Ch Inst 80-91. *8 Turret House, Limmer Lane, Felpham, Bognor Regis, W Sussex PO22 7EN* Tel (01243) 864339

SMITH, Neil Reginald. b 47. Qu Coll Birm 70. **d** 72 **p** 73. C Horton *Bradf* 72-75; C New Mills *Derby* 76-79; Perm to Offic *Ches* from 79; Lic to Offic *Derby* from 79; Chapl Community of the K of Love Whaley Bridge from 79. *Whaley Hall, Reservoir Road, Whaley Bridge, Stockport, Cheshire SK12 7BL* Tel (01663) 32495

SMITH, Nicholas Victor. b 54. St Jo Coll Dur BA76. St Steph Ho Ox 76. **d** 78 **p** 85. C Saltley *Birm* 78-79; C St Marylebone Ch Ch *Lon* 84-87; C Barnsley St Mary *Wakef* 87-90; Perm to Offic *Birm* 93-96. *4 Cypress Square, Acocks Green, Birmingham B27 6NJ*

SMITH, Norman. b 22. Coll of Resurr Mirfield 85. **d** 85 **p** 86. Hon C Greenhill *Sheff* 85-89; rtd 89; Hon C Blackpool St Mary *Blackb* from 89. *21 Cairn Court, 167 Squires Gate Lane, Blackpool FY4 2QQ* Tel (01253) 401498

SMITH, Norman George. b 27. K Coll Lon BD52 AKC52. **d** 53 **p** 54. C Pennington *Man* 53-56; C Chorlton-cum-Hardy St Clem 56-57; V Heywood St Jas 57-63; R Bedhampton *Portsm* 63-81; V Win St Bart *Win* 81-92; RD Win 84-89; rtd 92. *40 Goring Field, Winchester, Hants SO22 5NH* Tel (01962) 852882

SMITH, Norman Jordan. b 30. Sarum Th Coll 57. **d** 60 **p** 61. C Dean Forest St Paul *Glouc* 60-61; C Clearwell 60-61; C W Tarring *Chich* 61-65; Australia 65-68; V Chidham *Chich* 68-94; rtd 95. *Potters Paradise, 82 Church Road, Hayling Island, Hants PO11 0NX*

SMITH, Mrs Olwen. b 44. Birm Univ BA66 DPS68. Selly Oak Coll 67. **d** 87 **p** 94. Ind Chapl Black Country Urban Ind Miss *Lich* from 84; TV Wolverhampton from 94. *66 Albert Road, Wolverhampton WV6 0AF* Tel (01902) 712935

SMITH, Miss Pamela Frances (Pam). b 44. St Mary's Coll Cheltenham TCert65. W of England Minl Tr Course 91. **d** 94 **p** 95. NSM Badgeworth w Shurdington *Glouc* 94-95; NSM Badgeworth, Shurdington and Witcombe w Bentham from 95. *The Tynings, 38 Ansdell Drive, Brockworth, Gloucester GL3 4BU* Tel (01452) 610805

SMITH, Paul Aidan. b 59. Birm Univ BA82. Wycliffe Hall Ox 82. **d** 85 **p** 86. C Selly Park St Steph and St Wulstan *Birm* 85-88; C Kensal Rise St Mark and St Martin *Lon* 88-91; V Water Eaton *Ox* from 91. *The Vicarage, 38 Mill Road, Bletchley, Milton Keynes MK2 2LD* Tel (01908) 374585 E-mail smith8013@aol.com

SMITH, Paul Andrew. b 55. St Chad's Coll Dur BA76. Chich Th Coll 78. **d** 80 **p** 81. C Habergham Eaves St Matt *Blackb* 80-83; C Ribbleton 83-86; V Rishton from 86; RD Whalley from 95. *The Vicarage, Somerset Road, Rishton, Blackburn BB1 4BP* Tel (01254) 886191

SMITH, Preb Paul Gregory. b 39. Ex Univ BA61. St Steph Ho Ox 61. **d** 63 **p** 64. C Walthamstow St Mich *Chelmsf* 63-66; C Devonport St Mark Ford *Ex* 66-69; C Hemel Hempstead *St Alb* 69-71; TV 71-83; R Bideford *Ex* 83-96; Chapl Bideford and Torridge Hosps 83-96; Preb Ex Cathl *Ex* from 95; TR Bideford, Northam, Westward Ho!, Appledore etc 96; P-in-c Ex St Jas from 96. *St James's Rectory, 4 Rosebank Crescent, Exeter EX4 6EJ* Tel (01392) 55871

SMITH, Paul Raymond. b 60. Sheff Univ BA81. Qu Coll Birm 82. **d** 85 **p** 86. C Frecheville and Hackenthorpe *Sheff* 85-88; C Rawmarsh w Parkgate 88-89; TV Staveley and Barrow Hill *Derby* 89-93. *55 Ladbrooke Crescent, Basford, Nottingham NG6 0GL*

SMITH, Mrs Pauline Frances. b 37. Bris Univ BA58 Lon Univ CertEd59. Sarum & Wells Th Coll 87. **d** 90 **p** 94. C Cobham *Guildf* 90-96; P-in-c Lower Wylye and Till Valley *Sarum* from 96. *The Rectory, Wishford, Salisbury SP2 2PQ* Tel (01722) 790363

SMITH, Peter. b 36. Keele Univ BA60. Cuddesdon Coll 73. **d** 75 **p** 76. C Shrewsbury St Chad *Lich* 75-80; V Burton St Chad 80-90; P-in-c Berwick w Selmeston and Alciston *Chich* 90-91; R from 91. *The Parsonage, Berwick, Polegate, E Sussex BN26 6SR* Tel (01323) 870512

SMITH, Peter. b 49. Ex Univ BSc69 PGCE73. Carl Dioc Tr Course. **d** 82 **p** 83. NSM Kendal H Trin *Carl* from 82. *55 Empson Road, Kendal, Cumbria LA9 5PR* Tel (01539) 721467

SMITH, Peter Albert. b 26. Keble Coll Ox BA51 MA55. Wells Th Coll 51. **d** 53 **p** 54. C Leeds City *Ripon* 53-55; C Kingswinford H Trin *Lich* 55-59; Chapl Lich Th Coll 59-62; Vice-Prin 62-67; Bp's Chapl to Students *Bradf* 67-73; V Madeley *Lich* 73-77; rtd 81; Lic to Offic *Glouc* 81-89. *8 Newport Road, Whitchurch, Shropshire SY13 1QE*

SMITH, Peter Alexander. *See* GRAYSMITH, Peter Alexander

SMITH, Peter Anson Stewart. b 16. AKC37. **d** 39 **p** 40. C Norwood St Luke *S'wark* 39-41; C S Ossett *Wakef* 41-44; C-in-c Broadfield CD *St Alb* 44-49; V Leavesden All SS 49-73; V Greenhill St Jo *Lon* 73-81; Selection Sec ACCM 75-81; rtd 81; Perm to Offic *Chich* 81-83; P-in-c Brighton St Matthias 83-84; P-in-c Brighton St Pet w Chpl Royal and St Jo 85; P-in-c Brighton St Mich 85-86; P-in-c Moulsecoomb 86-87; TV 88-89; P-in-c Preston 87-88; P-in-c Brighton St Aug and St Sav 89-91; P-in-c Hove St Andr Old Ch 92; P-in-c Ovingdean 95-96. *3 West Drive, Brighton BN2 2GD* Tel (01273) 605042

SMITH, Peter Denis Frank. b 52. Local Minl Tr Course. **d** 81 **p** 83. NSM Camberwell St Mich w All So w Em *S'wark* 81-94; NSM Croydon St Jo from 95. *57 Alton Road, Croydon CR0 4LZ* Tel 0181-760 9656

SMITH, Peter Francis Chasen. b 28. Leeds Univ BA54. Coll of Resurr Mirfield 54. **d** 56 **p** 57. C E Dulwich St Clem *S'wark* 56-59; C Sutton St Nic 59-62; C-in-c Wrangbrook w N Elmsall CD *Wakef* 62-68; Chapl St Aid Sch Harrogate 68-85; P-in-c Lower Nidderdale *Ripon* 85-93; rtd 93; Perm to Offic *York* from 95. *Clematis Cottage, Main Street, Kilburn, York YO6 4AH* Tel (01347) 868394

SMITH, Peter Howard. b 55. St Andr Univ MTh78. Trin Coll Bris 78. **d** 79 **p** 80. C Handforth *Ches* 79-82; C Eccleston St Luke *Liv* 82-85; V Leyton St Paul *Chelmsf* 85-91; V Darwen St Barn *Blackb* from 91. *St Barnabas' Vicarage, 68 Park Road, Darwen, Lancs BB3 2LD* Tel (01254) 702732

SMITH, Peter Howard. b 57. St Jo Coll Dur BSc78 Selw Coll Cam BA82 MA85. Ridley Hall Cam 80. **d** 83 **p** 84. C Welling *Roch* 83-87; C Hubberston w Herbrandston and Hasguard etc *St D* 87-89; C Hubbertson 89-91; V Canley *Cov* from 91. *St Stephen's Vicarage, 47 Glebe Close, Coventry CV4 8DJ* Tel (01203) 421685

SMITH, Peter James. b 23. K Coll Lon 49. **d** 53 **p** 54. C Atherton *Man* 53-55; C Wokingham All SS *Ox* 55-56; C Doncaster St Geo *Sheff* 56-59; V Whitgift w Adlingfleet 59-62; Chapl Highcroft Hosp Birm 62-71; C Wolborough w Newton Abbot *Ex* 71-74; C Furze Platt *Ox* 74-78; Travelling Sec Ch Coun for Health and Healing 78-81; P-in-c Bisham *Ox* 82-90; rtd 90; NSM Hindhead *Guildf* 90-96; Perm to Offic from 96. *4 Copse Close, Liss, Hants GU33 7EW* Tel (01730) 894099

SMITH, Peter Michael. b 28. Open Univ BA75. K Coll Lon 52. **d** 56 **p** 57. C Pokesdown St Jas *Win* 56-59; C Weeke 59-63; V Hutton Roof *Carl* 63-69; V Barrow St Aid 69-72; V Preston Patrick 72-93; rtd 93; Chapl to the Deaf and Hard of Hearing

Carl from 93; Perm to Offic from 93. *7 Green Road, Kendal, Cumbria LA9 4QR* Tel (01539) 726741 or (0973) 224289

SMITH, Peter William. b 31. Glouc Th Course 74. **d** 77 **p** 77. C Coleford w Staunton *Glouc* 77; Hon C 77-87; P-in-c Alderton w Gt Washbourne 87-94; R Alderton, Gt Washbourne, Dumbleton etc from 94. *The Rectory, Alderton, Tewkesbury, Glos GL20 8NR* Tel (01242) 620238

SMITH, Philip Hathway. b 66. St Andr Univ MTh88. Coll of Resurr Mirfield 90. **d** 92 **p** 93. C Shrewsbury St Giles w Sutton and Atcham *Lich* 92-94; C Clayton from 94. *Church House, 285 Clayton Road, Newcastle, Staffs ST5 3EU*

SMITH, Philip James. b 32. St Alb Minl Tr Scheme. **d** 82 **p** 83. NSM Radlett *St Alb* 82-85; C 85-89; V Codicote from 89; RD Hatfield from 95. *The Vicarage, 4 Bury Lane, Codicote, Hitchin, Herts SG4 8XT* Tel (01438) 820266

SMITH, Philip James. b 60. ACGI82 Imp Coll Lon BScEng82 Fitzw Coll Cam BA94. Ridley Hall Cam CTM95. **d** 95 **p** 96. C Aldborough w Boroughbridge and Roecliffe *Ripon* from 95. *Rollinson House, Ladywell Road, Boroughbridge, York YO5 9AX* Tel (01423) 324747

SMITH, Philip Lloyd Cyril. b 22. Ch Coll Cam BA47 MA49. Wycliffe Hall Ox 47. **d** 49 **p** 50. C St Helens St Helen *Liv* 49-52; C Woking St Jo *Guildf* 52-56; R Burslem St Jo *Lich* 56-83; P-in-c Burslem St Paul 82-83; R Burslem 83-86; rtd 86; Perm to Offic *Sheff* from 86. *7 Melfort Glen, Sheffield S10 5SU* Tel 0114-230 4238

SMITH, Philip Sydney Bellman (Luke). b 11. St Cath Soc Ox BA35 DipTh36 MA46. St Steph Ho Ox 35. **d** 37 **p** 38. C Highworth w Sevenhampton and Inglesham etc *Bris* 37-39; C Storrington *Chich* 39-42; Chapl RNVR 43-46; C Banbury *Ox* 47-48; CR from 51; S Africa 52-62; rtd 81. *House of the Resurrection, Mirfield, W Yorkshire WF14 0BN* Tel (01924) 494318

SMITH, Raymond Charles William (Ray). b 56. K Coll Lon BD78 AKC78. Coll of Resurr Mirfield 79. **d** 80 **p** 81. C Iffley *Ox* 80-83; C Wallingford w Crowmarsh Gifford etc 83-86; V Tilehurst St Mary 86-96; TR Haywards Heath St Wilfrid *Chich* from 96. *The Rectory, St Wilfrid's Way, Haywards Heath, W Sussex RH16 3QH* Tel (01444) 413300

SMITH, Canon Raymond Douglas. b 31. TCD BA53 MA56 BD56. **d** 54 **p** 55. C Belfast St Mich *Conn* 54-56; C Ballymacarrett St Patr *D & D* 56-58; CMS Tr Coll Chislehurst 58-60; Kenya (CMS) 60-71; Asst Gen Sec (Hibernian) CMS 71-74; Gen Sec CMS 74-86; CMS Ireland 76-86; Hon Can N Maseno from 78; I Powerscourt w Kilbride and Annacrevy *D & G* 86-96; Can Ch Ch Cathl Dublin from 94. *Glencarrig Lodge, Kindlestown Upper, Delgany, Co Wicklow, Irish Republic* Tel Dublin (1) 287 3229

SMITH, Raymond Frederick. b 28. Lon Univ BSc51 Leeds Univ MA65. Oak Hill Th Coll 51. **d** 53 **p** 54. C Toxteth Park St Philemon *Liv* 53-56; C Halliwell St Pet *Man* 56-58; V Denton *Bradf* 58-66; V Weston 58-66; V Normanton *Wakef* 66-81; RD Chevet 73-81; R Moreton *Ches* 81-90; rtd 90. *Peniarth Uchaf, Meifod SY22 6DS* Tel (01938) 84366

SMITH, Raymond George Richard. b 38. Univ of Wales (Ban) BSc61 MSc65. WMMTC 91. **d** 94 **p** 95. NSM Edgmond w Kynnersley and Preston Wealdmoors *Lich* 94-97; Chapl Princess R Hosp NHS Trust Telford from 95. *10 Chetwynd Road, Edgmond, Newport, Shropshire TF10 8HJ* Tel (01952) 813346

SMITH, Raymond Horace David (Ray). b 30. Sir John Cass Coll Lon FIBMS61. Lon Coll of Div 64. **d** 67 **p** 68. C Shoreditch St Leon *Lon* 67-70; SAMS 71-73; Chile 71-80; P-in-c Castle Hedingham *Chelmsf* 80-83; P-in-c Cambridge St Phil *Ely* 83-86; V 86-91; Chapl Ibiza *Eur* 91-94; C Lowton St Mary *Liv* 94-96; rtd 96. *1 Courtland Avenue, Cambridge CB1 4AT* Tel (01223) 247410

SMITH, Richard. b 47. St D Coll Lamp DipTh75. **d** 75 **p** 76. C Aberavon *Llan* 75-78; Ind Chapl 78-81; TV Bournemouth St Pet w St Swithun, H Trin etc *Win* 81-85; Chapl Colchester Gen Hosp 85-94; Chapl Severalls Hosp Colchester 85-94; Sen Chapl Essex Rivers Healthcare NHS Trust from 94. *Colchester General Hospital, Turner Road, Colchester CO4 3JL* Tel (01206) 832513

SMITH, Richard Geoffrey. b 46. St Jo Coll Dur BA68 MA69. St Steph Ho Ox BA74 MA78. **d** 75 **p** 76. C Brentwood St Thos *Chelmsf* 75-78; C Corringham 78-81; R Shepton Beauchamp w Barrington, Stocklinch etc *B & W* 81-83; TV Redditch, The Ridge *Worc* 85-89; R Teme Valley N from 89. *The Rectory, Lindridge, Tenbury Wells, Worcs WR15 8JQ* Tel (01584) 881331

SMITH, Richard Harwood. b 34. Sarum Th Coll 57. **d** 59 **p** 60. C Kington w Huntington *Heref* 59-62; Br Guiana 62-66; Guyana 66-69; C Broseley w Benthall *Heref* 69-70; Lic to Offic 70-76; USPG Area Sec (Dios Heref and Worc) 70-76; R Wigmore Abbey 76-84; V Eye w Braiseworth and Yaxley *St E* 84-96; P-in-c Bedingfield 84-96; P-in-c Occold 84-96; rtd 96. *33 Broad Street, Leominster, Herefordshire HR6 8DD* Tel (01568) 610676

SMITH, Richard Ian. b 46. Jes Coll Ox BA69 MA80. Ripon Hall Ox 69. **d** 70 **p** 71. C Eston *York* 70-76; TV E Ham w Upton Park St Alb *Chelmsf* 76-80; R Crook *Dur* 80-86; V Stanley 80-86; V Billingham St Cuth from 86; RD Stockton from 92. *St Cuthbert's Vicarage, Church Road, Billingham, Cleveland TS23 1BW* Tel (01642) 553236

SMITH, Richard Keith. b 44. Harper Adams Agric Coll NDA69. St Jo Coll Nottm. **d** 84 **p** 85. C Wirksworth w Alderwasley, Carsington etc *Derby* 84-87; R Hulland, Atlow, Bradley and Hognaston 87-96; V Long Compton, Whichford and Barton-on-the-Heath *Cov* from 96; P-in-c Wolford w Burmington from 97; P-in-c Cherington w Stourton from 97; P-in-c Barcheston from 97. *The Vicarage, Broad Street, Long Compton, Shipston-on-Stour, Warks CV36 5JH* Tel (01608) 684207

SMITH, Richard Michael. b 52. Lon Univ BA74. EAMTC 79. **d** 82 **p** 83. NSM Cambridge Ascension *Ely* 82-84; C Rainham *Roch* 84-88; V Southborough St Thos 88-96; P-in-c Lake *Portsm* from 96; P-in-c Shanklin St Sav from 96. *The Vicarage, Lake, Sandown, Isle of Wight PO36 9JT* Tel (01983) 405666

SMITH, Robert Harold. b 23. Lon Univ BA49. Oak Hill Th Coll 46. **d** 50 **p** 51. C Nottingham St Ann *S'well* 50-52; C-in-c Elburton CD *Ex* 52-57; V Lowestoft Ch Ch *Nor* 57-67; R Upton *Ex* 67-80; P-in-c Fersfield *Nor* 80-81; P-in-c N w S Lopham 80-81; R Bressingham 80-81; R Bressingham w N and S Lopham and Fersfield 81-87; rtd 87; Perm to Offic *Nor* from 87. *22 St Walstan's Road, Taverham, Norwich NR8 6NG* Tel (01603) 861285

✠**SMITH, The Rt Revd Robin Jonathan Norman.** b 36. Worc Coll Ox BA60 MA64. Ridley Hall Cam 60. **d** 62 **p** 63 **c** 90. C Barking St Marg *Chelmsf* 62-67; Chapl Lee Abbey 67-72; V Chesham St Mary *Ox* 72-80; RD Amersham 79-82; TR Gt Chesham 80-90; Hon Can Ch Ch 88-90; Suff Bp Hertford *St Alb* from 90. *Hertford House, Abbey Mill Lane, St Albans, Herts AL3 4HE* Tel (01727) 866420 Fax 811426

SMITH, Rodney Frederic Brittain. b 38. Jes Coll Cam BA61 MA64. St Steph Ho Ox 87. **d** 88 **p** 89. NSM Rainworth *S'well* 88-89; C Basford St Aid 89-91; C Sneinton St Cypr 91-94; P-in-c Sneinton St Matthias 94-96; V from 96. *St Matthias Vicarage, Woodhouse Street, Sneinton, Nottingham NG3 2FG* Tel 0115-950 2750

SMITH, Rodney John Boughton. b 19. AKC41. Sarum Th Coll 41. **d** 42 **p** 43. C Frome St Jo *B & W* 42-44; C Eastbourne St Andr *Chich* 45-48; C Belvedere St Aug *Roch* 48-49; C Horsham *Chich* 49-55; V Kings Bromley *Lich* 55-60; V Porthill 60-68; V E Meon *Portsm* 68-84; V Langrish 76-84; rtd 84; Perm to Offic *Ex* from 84. *3 Barton Orchard, Tipton St John, Sidmouth, Devon EX10 0AN* Tel (01404) 814673

SMITH, Roger Douglas St John. b 12. TD56 w clasp 62. Selw Coll Cam BA37 MA41 Jes Coll Ox BA39 MA43 Man Univ BD51. Ripon Hall Ox 37. **d** 39 **p** 40. C Kersal Moor *Man* 39-42; CF (EC) 42-46; Hon CF 46; CF (TA) 48-62; Dep Asst Chapl Gen (TA) 59-62; R Lower Crumpsall *Man* 46-48; V Crawshawbooth 48-53; V Astley Bridge 53-63; R Darley w S Darley *Derby* 63-77; Asst Chapl OStJ from 71; rtd 77. *28 Ffordd Penrhwylfa, Prestatyn LL19 8AG* Tel (01745) 857307

SMITH, Roger Owen. b 50. FRGS Univ of Wales (Abth) BA72 St Chad's Coll Dur CertEd73. S'wark Ord Course 84. **d** 87 **p** 88. NSM Nunhead St Antony w St Silas *S'wark* 87-91; NSM Forest Hill St Aug from 91; NSM Crofton Park St Hilda w St Cypr from 91; NSM Brockley Hill St Sav from 91. *32 Mundania Road, London SE22 0NW* Tel 0181-693 4882

SMITH, Roger Stuart. b 41. Chich Th Coll 65. **d** 66 **p** 67. C Garforth *Ripon* 66-70; C Cockley Cley w Gooderstone *Nor* 70-73; C Gt and Lt Cressingham w Threxton 70-73; C Didlington 70-73; C Hilborough w Bodney 70-73; C Oxborough w Foulden and Caldecote 70-73; TV 73-78; V Mendham w Metfield and Withersdale *St E* 78-89; P-in-c Fressingfield w Weybread 86-89; R Fressingfield, Mendham, Metfield, Weybread etc 90-91; RD Hoxne 86-91; R Kelsale-cum-Carlton, Middleton-cum-Fordley etc from 91; RD Saxmundham from 96. *The Rectory, Middleton, Saxmundham, Suffolk IP17 3NR* Tel (01728) 73421

SMITH, Ronald. b 26. ALCD56. **d** 56 **p** 57. C Gravesend St Jas *Roch* 56-59; C-in-c Istead Rise CD 59-79; V Istead Rise 79-93; rtd 93; Perm to Offic *Roch* from 93. *114 Maidstone Road, Rochester, Kent ME1 3DT* Tel (01834) 829183

SMITH, Ronald Deric. b 21. Lon Univ BA46. Bps' Coll Cheshunt 59. **d** 61 **p** 62. C Crayford *Roch* 61-67; USA 67-68; C W Malling w Offham *Roch* 68-71; V Slade Green 71-78; V Bromley Common St Luke 78-91; rtd 91; Perm to Offic *S'wark* from 91; Perm to Offic *Roch* from 91. *5 Bromley College, London Road, Bromley BR1 1PE* Tel 0181-464 0212

SMITH, Ronald Eric (Ron). b 43. EMMTC CTPS93. **d** 93 **p** 94. NSM Wingerworth *Derby* from 93. *21 Windsor Drive, Wingerworth, Chesterfield, Derbyshire S42 6TG* Tel (01246) 279004

SMITH, Ronald James. b 36. Linc Th Coll 73. **d** 75 **p** 76. C Bilborough St Jo *S'well* 75-78; P-in-c Colwick 78-81; R 81-85; P-in-c Netherfield 78-81; V 81-85; C Worksop Priory 85-90; TV Langley and Parkfield *Man* 90-95; P-in-c Barton w Peel Green from 95. *St Michael's Vicarage, 684 Liverpool Road, Eccles, Manchester M30 7LP* Tel 0161-789 3751

SMITH, Ronald William. b 16. ACIS40 FCIS61 Open Univ BA85. Worc Ord Coll 63. **d** 65 **p** 66. C Colwall *Heref* 65-68; V Stretton Grandison and Ashperton w Canon Frome 68-71; P-in-c Yarkhill 68-71; V Stretton Grandison w Ashperton, Canon Frome etc 71-81; rtd 81; Perm to Offic *Heref* from 82. *17 Knapp Close, Ledbury, Herefordshire HR8 1AW* Tel (01531) 634620

SMITH, Ronald William. b 45. St Jo Coll York CertEd67. Chich Th Coll 70. **d** 73 **p** 74. C Scarborough St Martin *York* 73-76; C Stainton-in-Cleveland 76-80; V Coatham 80-89; V Brookfield from 89. *Brookfield Vicarage, 89 Low Lane, Brookfield, Middlesbrough, Cleveland TS5 8EF* Tel (01642) 592136

SMITH, The Very Revd Rowan Quentin. b 43. AKC66. **d** 67 **p** 68. C Matroosfontein 67-69; C Bonteheuwel 70; C Plumstead All SS 71-72; P-in-c Grassy Park 72-77; CR from 80; Chapl St Martin's Sch Rosettenville 80-88; Chapl Cape Town Univ 88-90; Prov Exec Officer 90-96; Can of Prov 93-96; Can Pastor St Geo Cathl 96; Dean Cape Town from 96. *The Deanery, 29 Upper Orange Street, Oranjezicht, 8001 South Africa* Tel Cape Town (21) 452609 or 233371 Fax 238466

SMITH, Preb Roy Leonard. b 36. Clifton Th Coll 63. **d** 66 **p** 67. C Clapham St Jas *S'wark* 66-70; C Kennington St Mark 70-74; C-in-c Southall Em CD *Lon* 74-83; V Stonebridge St Mich from 83; Preb St Paul's Cathl from 96. *St Michael's Vicarage, Hillside, London NW10 8LB* Tel 0181-965 7443

SMITH, Royston. b 55. EMMTC 87. **d** 90 **p** 91. NSM Shirland *Derby* 90-94; NSM Ashover and Brackenfield from 95. *Kirkdale Cottage, Greenfield Lane, Milltown, Ashover, Chesterfield, Derbyshire S45 0HA* Tel (01246) 590975

SMITH, Royston Burleigh. b 26. St Deiniol's Hawarden 76. **d** 79 **p** 80. C Prestatyn *St As* 79-83; V Kerry and Llanmerewig 83-90; C Rhyl w St Ann 90-91; rtd 91. *18 Garth Clarendon, Kinmel Bay, Rhyl LL18 5DZ*

SMITH, Mrs Shirley Ann. b 46. RSCN68 RM82 RGN84 RHV86 Univ of Wales PGDipPastTh94. Sarum & Wells Th Coll 89. **d** 93 **p** 94. Par Dn Totton *Win* 93-94; C 94-96; Chapl Portsm Hosps NHS Trust from 96. *Queen Alexandra Hospital, Cosham, Portsmouth PO6 3LY* Tel (01705) 286000

SMITH, Canon Stanley. b 10. St D Coll Lamp BA35 LTh. **d** 35 **p** 36. C Beamish *Dur* 35-37; Miss to Seamen 37-38 and 49-54; S Africa 38-49; Canada from 54. *Apartment 304, 2710 Lonsdale Avenue, Vancouver, Canada, V7N 3J1*

SMITH, Stephen. b 53. Leeds Poly CQSW78. Sarum & Wells Th Coll 87. **d** 89 **p** 90. C Redcar *York* 89-92; C Leeds St Aid *Ripon* 92-96; R Lanteglos by Camelford w Advent *Truro* from 96. *The Rectory, Trefrew, Camelford, Cornwall PL32 9TR* Tel (01840) 212286

SMITH, Stephen <u>John</u>. b 46. Kelham Th Coll 65. **d** 69 **p** 70. C Warsop *S'well* 69-73; C Heaton Ch Ch *Man* 73-75; V Bolton St Bede 75-78; R Bilborough w Strelley *S'well* 78-84; R E Leake 84-92; P-in-c Costock 84-92; P-in-c Rempstone 84-92; P-in-c Stanford on Soar 84-92; R E and W Leake, Stanford-on-Soar, Rempstone etc from 92; RD Bingham W from 92. *The Rectory, 3 Bateman Road, East Leake, Loughborough, Leics LE12 6LN* Tel (01509) 852228

SMITH, Stephen John. b 55. Lon Univ BD80. Trin Coll Bris 77. **d** 81 **p** 82. C Fulham St Matt *Lon* 81-86; C Stoke Gifford *Bris* 86-90; TV from 90. *The Vicarage, Mautravers Close, Bradley Stoke, Bristol BS12 8ED* Tel 0117-931 2222

SMITH, Stephen John Stanyon. b 49. Sussex Univ BA81 Birm Univ MSocSc83. Westcott Ho Cam 83. **d** 85 **p** 86. C Four Oaks *Birm* 85-89; USA from 89. *23 Lynwood Place, New Haven, Connecticut 06511, USA*

SMITH, Stephen Thomas. b 55. Westcott Ho Cam 95. **d** 97. C Kempston Transfiguration *St Alb* from 97. *16 Rosedale Way, Kempston, Beds MK42 8JE*

SMITH, Steven Barnes. b 60. Cov Poly BA83 Leeds Univ BA86. Coll of Resurr Mirfield 84. **d** 87 **p** 88. C Darlington St Mark w St Paul *Dur* 87-89; C Prescot *Liv* 89-91; V Hindley Green 91-96; Asst Chapl Havering Hosps NHS Trust from 96. *Oldchurch Hospital, Oldchurch Road, Romford RM7 0BE* Tel (01708) 746090

SMITH, Steven Gerald Crosland. b 48. Linc Th Coll 82. **d** 84 **p** 85. Chapl St Jo Sch Tiffield 84-87; C Towcester w Easton Neston *Pet* 84-87; P-in-c Kings Heath 87-89; V 89-93; TV N Creedy *Ex* from 93. *The Vicarage, Cheriton Fitzpaine, Crediton, Devon EX17 4JB* Tel (01363) 866352

SMITH, Susan (<u>Sue</u>). **d** 96. NSM Burnham w Dropmore, Hitcham and Taplow *Ox* from 96. *Copperdell, 17A Green Lane, Burnham, Slough SL1 8DZ* Tel (01628) 603974

SMITH, Sydney John. b 21. Univ of Wales (Lamp) BA48. **d** 49 **p** 50. C Scarborough St Mary *York* 49-53; V Middlesbrough St Paul 53-59; V Scarborough St Luke 59-86; rtd 86; Perm to Offic *York* from 86. *309 Scalby Road, Scarborough, N Yorkshire YO12 6TF* Tel (01723) 378736

SMITH, Terence. b 38. Lon Univ DipTh69 Brunel Univ BSc79 Cranfield Inst of Tech MSc80. Tyndale Hall Bris 67. **d** 69 **p** 70. C Cheylesmore *Cov* 69-71; C Leamington Priors St Paul 71-74; V Halliwell St Paul *Man* 74-75; Lect Uxbridge Coll 80-86; R Medstead cum Wield *Win* from 86. *The Rectory, Trinity Hill, Medstead, Alton, Hants GU34 5LT* Tel (01420) 562050

SMITH, Terrence Gordon. b 34. TD83. MCSP58 SRN60. St Mich Coll Llan 68. **d** 70 **p** 71. C Gelligaer *Llan* 70-73; CF (TA) from 72; C Aberavon *Llan* 73-75; V Pontlottyn w Fochriw 75-77; V Kenfig Hill 77-84; V Dyffryn from 84. *The Vicarage, Dyffryn, Bryncoch, Neath SA10 7AZ* Tel (01792) 814237

SMITH, Thomas Robert Selwyn. b 12. Bps' Coll Cheshunt 35. **d** 37 **p** 38. C Workington St Mich *Carl* 37-40; C Wilton Place St Paul *Lon* 40-41; C Cheshunt *St Alb* 41-44; V Dalston *Carl* 44-55; V Box *Bris* 55-92; rtd 93; Perm to Offic *Bris* from 93. *Woodland View, Devizes Road, Box, Corsham, Wilts SN14 9EB* Tel (01225) 742405

SMITH, Thomas <u>Roger</u>. b 48. Cant Sch of Min 77. **d** 80 **p** 81. NSM Folkestone St Sav *Cant* 80-82; NSM Lyminge w Paddlesworth, Stanford w Postling etc 82-85; Chapl Cant Sch of Min 82-91; R Biddenden and Smarden *Cant* 86-91; TR Totnes, Bridgetown and Berry Pomeroy etc *Ex* 91-96; P-in-c Haslingden w Grane and Stonefold *Blackb* from 96. *St James's Vicarage, Church Lane, Haslingden, Rossendale, Lancs BB4 5QZ* Tel (01706) 215533

SMITH, Timothy Brian. b 62. Brisbane Coll BA(Theol)92. **d** 92 **p** 92. Australia 92-94 and from 96; C Heald Green St Cath *Ches* 94-96. *PO Box 98, Evans Head, New South Wales, Australia 2473* Tel Grafton (066) 825232 or 825226

SMITH, Tony. b 23. Roch Th Coll 62. **d** 64 **p** 65. Chapl TS Arethusa 64-67; C Frindsbury *Roch* 64-67; V Hadlow 67-78; R Wrotham 78-89; RD Shoreham 80-89; rtd 89; Perm to Offic *Roch* from 89. *25 Wye Road, Borough Green, Sevenoaks, Kent TN15 8DX* Tel (01732) 885884

SMITH, Trevor Andrew. b 60. St Jo Coll Dur BA86. Cranmer Hall Dur 83. **d** 87 **p** 88. C Guisborough *York* 87-90; C Northallerton w Kirby Sigston 90-95; P-in-c Middleton w Newton, Levisham and Lockton 95; R Middleton, Newton and Sinnington from 95. *St Andrew's House, 15 Carr Lane, Middleton, Pickering, N Yorkshire YO18 8PU* Tel (01751) 474858

SMITH, Trevor Bernard. b 33. Culham Coll of Educn CertEd70 Ox Poly BEd82. Oak Hill Th Coll 61. **d** 64 **p** 65. C Bispham *Blackb* 64-66; C Chesham St Mary *Ox* 66-68; Perm to Offic 90-94; rtd 96. *235 Whitecross, Wootton, Abingdon, Oxon OX13 6BW* Tel (01235) 521692

SMITH, Vernon Hemingway. b 33. St Alb Minl Tr Scheme 83. **d** 86 **p** 87. NSM Leighton Buzzard w Eggington, Hockliffe etc *St Alb* from 86. *41 Orion Way, Leighton Buzzard, Beds LU7 8XJ* Tel (01525) 377391

SMITH, Walter. b 37. Westcott Ho Cam 67. **d** 69 **p** 70. C N Hull St Mich *York* 69-72; C Whitby 72-74; V Newington w Dairycoates 74-77; P-in-c Skipton Bridge 77-78; P-in-c Baldersby 77-78; TV Thirsk 77-88; P-in-c Topcliffe w Dalton and Dishforth 82-87; V Lythe w Ugthorpe from 88. *The Vicarage, Lythe, Whitby, N Yorkshire YO21 3RL* Tel (01947) 893479

SMITH, Miss Wendy Hamlyn. b 41. ALA70 Open Univ BA85. Ridley Hall Cam 85. **d** 87 **p** 94. C Stroud H Trin *Glouc* 87-90 and 91-92; Australia 90-91; TD Stoke-upon-Trent *Lich* 92-94; TV from 94. *St Paul's House, 235 Wheildon Road, Fenton, Stoke-on-Trent ST4 4JT* Tel (01782) 44800

SMITH, William Carrington. b 16. Selw Coll Cam BA40 MA44. S'wark Ord Course 63. **d** 66 **p** 67. NSM Nunhead St Antony *S'wark* 66-83; rtd 83; Perm to Offic *Roch* from 83. *5 Reed Street, Cliffe, Rochester, Kent ME3 7UN* Tel (01634) 221898

SMITH, William Joseph Thomas. b 20. Chich Th Coll 54. **d** 55 **p** 56. C Laindon w Basildon *Chelmsf* 56-61; R Stifford 61-65; V Boreham 65-90; rtd 90; Perm to Offic *Chelmsf* from 90. *7 Trelawn, Church Road, Boreham, Chelmsford CM3 3EF* Tel (01245) 466930

SMITH, William Manton. b 64. Univ of Wales (Abth) LLB85 St Jo Coll Dur PGCE90. United Th Coll Abth BD89 St Jo Coll Nottm 91. **d** 93 **p** 94. C Coventry Caludon *Cov* 93-97; V Exhall from 97. *Exhall Vicarage, Ash Green, Coventry CV7 9AA* Tel (01203) 362997

SMITH, William <u>Melvyn</u>. b 47. K Coll Lon BD69 AKC69 PGCE70. St Aug Coll Cant 71. **d** 71 **p** 72. C Kingswinford H Trin *Lich* 71-73; Hon C Coseley Ch Ch 73-74; C Wednesbury St Paul Wood Green 75-78; V Coseley St Chad 78-91; RD Himley 83-93; RD Himley *Worc* 93-96; TR Wordsley *Lich* 91-93; TR Wordsley *Worc* 93-96; Stewardship and Resources Officer from 97. *330 Hagley Road, Pedmore, Stourbridge, W Midlands DY9 0RD* Tel (01562) 720404

SMITH-CAMERON, Canon Ivor Gill. b 29. Madras Univ BA50 MA52. Coll of Resurr Mirfield. **d** 54 **p** 55. C Rumboldswyke *Chich* 54-58; Chapl Imp Coll *Lon* 58-72; Dioc Missr *S'wark* 72-92; Can Res S'wark Cathl 72-94; C Battersea Park All SS 92-94; Hon C 94-96; Hon C Battersea Fields from 96; Co-ord All Asian Chr Consultation 92-93; rtd 94; Chapl to The Queen from 95. *100 Prince of Wales Drive, London SW11 4BN* Tel 0171-622 3809

SMITHAM (née HARVEY-COOK), Mrs Elizabeth <u>Ann</u>. b 62. St D Coll Lamp BA90 St Mich Coll Llan DPS91. **d** 92 **p** 97. C Llangiwg *S & B* 92-94; C Morriston from 94. *2 Monmouth Place, Parc Gwernfadog, Morriston, Swansea SA6 6RF* Tel (01792) 791397

✠**SMITHSON, The Rt Revd Alan.** b 36. Qu Coll Ox BA62 MA68. Qu Coll Birm DipTh64. **d** 64 **p** 65 **c** 90. C Skipton Ch Ch *Bradf* 64-68; C Ox St Mary V w St Cross and St Pet *Ox* 68-72; Chapl Qu Coll Ox 69-72; Chapl Reading Univ *Ox* 72-77; V Bracknell 77-83; TR 83-84; Can Res Carl Cathl *Carl* 84-90; Dir of Tr Inst 84-90; Dioc Dir of Tr 85-90; Suff Bp Jarrow *Dur* from 90. *The Old Vicarage, Hallgarth, Pittington, Co Durham DH6 1AB* Tel 0191-372 0225 Fax 372 2326

SMITHSON, Michael John. b 47. FRGS Newc Univ BA68 Lon Univ BD79 Dur Univ PGCE. Trin Coll Bris 76. **d** 79 **p** 80. C S

Mimms Ch Ch *Lon* 79-81; Support and Public Relations Sec UCCF 82-84; R Frating w Thorrington *Chelmsf* 84-88; V Portsea St Luke *Portsm* from 88. *St Luke's Vicarage, 19 Greetham Street, Southsea, Hants PO5 4LH* Tel (01705) 826073 Fax as telephone

SMITHURST, Jonathan Peter. b 54. EMMTC DTPS94. **d** 94 **p** 95. NSM Bramcote *S'well* from 94. *46 Sandy Lane, Beeston, Nottingham NG9 3GS* Tel 0115-925 7302

SMITS, Eric. b 29. **d** 61 **p** 62. C Thornaby on Tees St Paul *York* 61-66; R Brotton Parva from 66. *The Rectory, Brotton, Saltburn-by-the-Sea, Cleveland TS12 2PJ* Tel (01287) 676275

SMOUT, Canon Michael John. b 37. St Pet Coll Ox BA61 MA75 DipTh62 Lon Univ BD64. Lon Coll of Div 62. **d** 64 **p** 65. C Toxteth Park St Philemon w St Silas *Liv* 64-69; C Everton St Sav 69-70; Missr E Everton Gp of Chs 70-74; V Everton St Sav w St Cuth 74-79; R Aughton St Mich from 79; RD Ormskirk 82-89; AD from 89; Hon Can Liv Cathl from 92. *The Rectory, 10 Church Lane, Ormskirk, Lancs L39 6SB* Tel (01695) 423204

SMURTHWAITE, William. b 25. Edin Th Coll 54. **d** 57 **p** 58. C S Shields St Simon *Dur* 57-59; Miss to Seamen 59-72; Nigeria 59-63; Barbados 63-65; Lic to Offic *Linc* 65-72; R Ladybank *St And* 73-90; R Cupar 73-90; rtd 90. *10 Park View, Balmullo, St Andrews, Fife KY16 0DN* Tel (01334) 870639

SMYTH, Anthony Irwin. b 40. TCD BA63 MA66. Clifton Th Coll 64. **d** 66 **p** 67. C Worthing St Geo *Chich* 66-69; Chile 70-75; C Woodley St Jo the Ev *Ox* 76-80; V St Leonards St Ethelburga *Chich* 80-93; R Stopham and Fittleworth from 93. *The Rectory, Fittleworth, Pulborough, W Sussex RH20 1JG* Tel (01798) 865455 Fax as telephone

SMYTH, Francis George. b 20. Ridley Hall Cam 64. **d** 65 **p** 66. C Ormskirk *Liv* 65-70; V Bicton *Lich* 70-90; Chapl HM Pris Shrewsbury 71-90; rtd 90; Perm to Offic *Lich* from 90. *41 Sutton Road, Shrewsbury SY8 6DL* Tel (01743) 360030

SMYTH, Gordon William. b 47. Open Univ BA. St Jo Coll Nottm 81. **d** 83 **p** 84. C St Keverne *Truro* 83-86; V Landrake w St Erney and Botus Fleming 86-95; RD E Wivelshire 94-95; V Highertown and Baldhu from 95. *All Saints' Vicarage, Highertown, Truro, Cornwall TR1 3LD* Tel (01872) 261944 E-mail smyth @btinternet.com

SMYTH, Canon Kenneth James. b 44. TCD BA67 MA72. **d** 68 **p** 69. C Bangor Abbey *D & D* 68-71; C Holywood 71-74; I Gilnahirk 74-82; I Newtownards w Movilla Abbey 82-89; I Newtownards from 89; Preb Wicklow St Patr Cathl Dublin from 93. *36 Belfast Road, Newtownards, Co Down BT23 4TT* Tel (01247) 812527

SMYTH, Robert Andrew Laine (Brother Anselm). b 30. Trin Coll Cam BA53 MA59 Lon Univ PGCE60 DipEd65. **d** 79 **p** 80. SSF from 53; Min Prov Eur Prov SSF 79-91; Lic to Offic *Linc* 84-92; P-in-c Cambridge St Benedict *Ely* 92-93; V from 93. *St Francis House, 15 Botolph Lane, Cambridge CB2 3RD* Tel (01223) 321576

SMYTH, Trevor Cecil. b 45. Chich Th Coll 66. **d** 69 **p** 70. C Cookridge H Trin *Ripon* 69-73; C Middleton St Mary 73-75; C Felpham w Middleton *Chich* 75-78; P-in-c Wellington Ch Ch *Lich* 78-80; V 80-86; P-in-c W Wittering *Chich* 86; R W Wittering and Birdham w Itchenor 86-94. *5 Marshall Avenue, Bognor Regis, W Sussex PO21 2TH*

SMYTHE, Mrs Angela Mary. b 53. St Jo Coll Nottm 85. **d** 87 **p** 94. Par Dn Forest Town *S'well* 87-90; D-in-c Pleasley Hill 90-94; V from 94. *The Vicarage, Pleasley Hill, Mansfield, Notts NG19 7SZ*

SMYTHE, Harry Reynolds. b 23. Sydney Univ BA45 St Pet Hall Ox BA48 MA51 Ch Ch Ox DPhil51. Moore Th Coll Sydney 43 ACT ThL45. **d** 51 **p** 53. C Tavistock and Gulworthy *Ex* 51-52; C Ex St Mary Arches 53; Australia 54-70 and 81-83; Dir Angl Cen Rome 70-81; Lib Pusey Ho 83-91; Dir of Studies 91-94; Lic to Offic *Ox* 83-94; rtd 91. *57A Palace Street, Canterbury, Kent CT1 2DY* Tel (01227) 450685

SMYTHE, Canon Ronald Ingoldsby Meade. b 25. Qu Coll Ox BA46 MA48. Ely Th Coll 51. **d** 54 **p** 55. C Wanstead St Mary *Chelmsf* 54-56; C-in-c Belhus Park CD 56-59; Min Belhus Park ED 59-62; V Hatfield Heath 62-78; Hon C Writtle 78-81; Hon C Writtle w Highwood 81-85; P-in-c Whatfield w Semer, Nedging and Naughton *St E* 85-89; Dir Ipswich Concern Counselling Cen from 85; Dioc Adv for Counselling 85-89; Dioc Adv for Counselling and Past Care from 89; rtd 90; Hon Can St E Cathl *St E* from 93. *94 Wangford Road, Reydon, Southwold, Suffolk IP18 6NY* Tel (01502) 723413

SNAITH, Bryan Charles. b 33. Univ of Wales BSc55. St Mich Coll Llan 61. **d** 61 **p** 62. C Bargoed w Brithdir *Llan* 61-62; C Llanishen and Lisvane 62-71; Ind Chapl *Dur* 71-76; Ind Chapl *Worc* 76-81; P-in-c Stone 76-81; C Chaddesley Corbett 77-81; Ind Chapl *Chelmsf* from 81; TV Colchester St Leon, St Mary Magd and St Steph 81-86. *2 Colvin Close, Colchester CO3 4BS* Tel (01206) 767793

SNAPE, Sqn Ldr Bernard Reginald Roy. b 08. OBE56. Sarum Th Coll 69. **d** 69 **p** 70. C W Leigh *Portsm* 69-71; V Arreton 71-75; rtd 75. *23 Shady Bower Close, Salisbury SP1 2RQ* Tel (01722) 328645

SNAPE, Harry. b 21. Qu Coll Birm 76. **d** 78 **p** 79. NSM Highters Heath *Birm* 78-82; NSM Stirchley 82-84; TV Corby SS Pet and Andr w Gt and Lt Oakley *Pet* 84-89; rtd 89; Perm to Offic *Chich* from 89. *34 Outerwyke Road, Felpham, Bognor Regis, W Sussex PO22 8HX* Tel (01243) 863985

SNASDELL, Antony John. b 39. St Chad's Coll Dur BA63 DipTh65. **d** 65 **p** 66. C Boston *Linc* 65-70; Hon C Worksop Priory *S'well* 71-82; P-in-c Gt Massingham *Nor* 82-84; P-in-c Harpley 82-84; P-in-c Lt Massingham 82-84; R Gt and Lt Massingham and Harpley 84-91; R Thorpe from 91. *The Rectory, 56A Thunder Lane, Norwich NR7 0JW* Tel (01603) 33578

SNEARY, Michael William. b 38. Brentwood Coll of Educn CertEd71 Open Univ BA79. Ely Th Coll 61. **d** 64 **p** 65. C Loughton St Jo *Chelmsf* 64-67; Youth Chapl 67-70; Hon C Ingrave 70-71; Teacher Harold Hill Gr Sch Essex 71-74; Ivybridge Sch 74-76; Coombe Dean Sch Plymouth from 76. *The Lodge, Lower Port View, Saltash, Cornwall PL12 4BY*

SNEATH, Canon Sidney Dennis. b 23. Leeds Univ BA50. Bps' Coll Cheshunt 50. **d** 52 **p** 53. C Nuneaton St Mary *Cov* 52-59; C-in-c Galley Common Stockingford CD 59-68; V Camp Hill w Galley Common from 68; Hon Can Cov Cathl from 80. *The Vicarage, Cedar Road, Nuneaton, Warks CV10 9DL* Tel (01203) 392523

SNEDKER, Walter Frank. b 22. MBE. Bp Sumiu Takatsu Th Coll Brazil 78. **d** 80 **p** 81. Brazil from 80; rtd 93. *Caixa Postal 25, 11001 970, Santos SP, Brazil* Tel Santos (132) 372325

SNELGAR, Canon Douglas John. b 17. DSC45. Trin Hall Cam BA48 MA53. Westcott Ho Cam 48. **d** 50 **p** 51. C Fareham SS Pet and Paul *Portsm* 50-53; C Ventnor St Cath 53-57; C Ventnor H Trin 53-57; V Steep 57-92; P-in-c Froxfield w Privett 88-92; Hon Can Portsm Cathl 85-92; rtd 92; Perm to Offic *Chich* from 92. *37 South Acre, South Harting, Petersfield, Hants GU31 5LL* Tel (01730) 825142

✠**SNELGROVE, The Rt Revd Donald George.** b 25. TD72. Qu Coll Cam BA48 MA53. Ridley Hall Cam. **d** 50 **p** 51 **c** 81. C Oakwood St Thos *Lon* 50-53; C Hatch End St Anselm 53-56; V Dronfield *Derby* 56-62; CF (TA) 60-73; V Hessle *York* 63-70; RD Hull 67-70 and 81-90; Can and Preb York Minster 69-81; Adn E Riding 70-81; R Cherry Burton 70-78; Suff Bp Hull 81-94; rtd 94; Asst Bp Linc from 95. *Kingston House, 8 Park View, Barton-upon-Humber, S Humberside DN18 6AX*

SNELL, Mrs Brigitte. b 43. BA85. EAMTC 86. **d** 89 **p** 94. NSM Cambridge Gt St Mary w St Mich *Ely* 89-91; Par Dn Cambridge St Jas 91-94; C 94-95; V Sutton from 95; R Witcham w Mepal from 95. *The Vicarage, 7 Church Lane, Sutton, Ely, Cambs CB6 2RQ* Tel (01353) 778645

SNELL, Colin. b 53. Trin Coll Bris 94. **d** 96 **p** 97. C Martock w Ash *B & W* from 96. *3 Chestnut Road, Martock, Somerset TA12 6DP* Tel (01935) 824732

SNELL, James Osborne. b 13. Selw Coll Cam BA35 MA39. Ely Th Coll 35. **d** 36 **p** 37. C Summertown *Ox* 36-38; C Fenny Stratford 38-43; C Rugeley *Lich* 43-47; V Dawley Parva 47-52; V New Bradwell w Stantonbury *Ox* 52-61; P-in-c Gt Linford 55-61; R Charlton-in-Dover *Cant* 61-69; R Ramsgate H Trin 69-78; rtd 79; Perm to Offic *Cant* from 79. *3 Glebe Close, St Margarets-at-Cliffe, Dover, Kent CT15 6AF* Tel (01304) 852210

SNELL, William Graham Brooking. b 14. Lon Coll of Div 36. **d** 39 **p** 40. C Burton Ch Ch *Lich* 39-41; C Rushden St Pet 41-46; C Ealing St Paul *Lon* 46-48; C Cheltenham St Mark *Glouc* 48-51; V Beckford w Ashton under Hill 51-54; V Everton St Polycarp *Liv* 54-57; R Ashby w Oby, Thurne and Clippesby *Nor* 57-79; rtd 79; Perm to Offic *Nor* 79-96. *17 Burgh Park, Tower Road Fleggburgh, Great Yarmouth, Norfolk NR29 3DW* Tel (01493) 369776

SNELLGROVE, Martin Kenneth. b 54. City Univ BSc77 CEng80 MICE84. Aston Tr Scheme 85 Ridley Hall Cam 87. **d** 89 **p** 90. C Four Oaks *Birm* 89-92; TV Wrexham *St As* from 92. *The Vicarage, 160 Borras Road, Wrexham LL13 9ER* Tel (01978) 350202

SNELLING, Brian. b 40. Oak Hill Th Coll DipTh68. **d** 69 **p** 70. C Slough *Ox* 69-72; C Hoole *Ches* 72-76; V Millbrook 76-80; V Homerton St Luke *Lon* 80-90; R Marks Tey w Aldham and Lt Tey *Chelmsf* from 90. *The Rectory, Church Lane, Marks Tey, Colchester CO6 1LW* Tel (01206) 210396

SNELSON, William Thomas (Bill). b 45. Ex Coll Ox BA67 Fitzw Coll Cam BA69 MA75. Westcott Ho Cam 67. **d** 69 **p** 70. C Godalming *Guildf* 69-72; C Leeds St Pet *Ripon* 72-75; V Chapel Allerton 75-81; V Bardsey 81-93; Dioc Ecum Officer 86-93; W Yorkshire Ecum Officer *Bradf* 93-97; Gen Sec Chs Together in England from 97. *Inter-Church House, 35-41 Lower Marsh, London SE1 7RL, or 16 Oak Close, Harlington, Beds LU5 6PP* Tel 0171-620 4444 or (01525) 877115 Fax (01525) 877119

SNOOK, Mrs Margaret Ann. b 41. S Dios Minl Tr Scheme. **d** 91 **p** 94. NSM Keynsham *B & W* from 91. *32 Hurn Lane, Keynsham, Bristol BS18 1RS* Tel 0117-986 3439

SNOOK, Walter Currie. *See* CURRIE, Walter

SNOW, Campbell Martin Spencer. b 35. JP. Roch Th Coll 65. **d** 67 **p** 68. C Dover St Mary *Cant* 67-72; C Birchington w Acol 72-74; V Reculver 74-80; P-in-c New Addington 80-81; V 81-84; V New Addington *S'wark* 85-87; CF (ACF) 84-87; CF (TA) 87-92; P-in-c Caterham Valley *S'wark* from 87. *Caterham Valley Vicarage, 51 Crescent Road, Caterham, Surrey CR3 6LH* Tel (01883) 343188

SNOW, Canon Edward Brian. b 22. CITC. **d** 65 **p** 66. C Cork H Trin w St Paul, St Pet and St Mary *C, C & R* 65-67; C Dun Laoghaire

D & G 67-72; Hon Clerical V Ch Ch Cathl Dublin 69-72; I Rathkeale *L & K* 72-77; I Kilmallock w Kilflynn, Kilfinane, Knockaney etc 77-94; Adn Limerick 81-92; Chapter Clerk Limerick, Killaloe and Clonfert 92-94; RD Limerick 92-94; rtd 94. *Balladik, 9 St Catherine's Road, Glenageary, Co Dublin, Irish Republic* Tel Dublin (1) 284 6004

SNOW, Frank. b 31. Lon Univ BD57. **d** 83 **p** 84. Hon C Tweedmouth *Newc* 83-86; Hon C Berwick H Trin 86-89; Hon C Berwick St Mary 86-89; Hon C Berwick H Trin and St Mary 89-90; R Gt Smeaton w Appleton Wiske and Birkby etc *Ripon* 90-97; rtd 97. *Meadow View, 3 Swinburn Road, Masham, Ripon, N Yorkshire HG4 4HU* Tel (01765) 689858

SNOW, Glyn Francis. b 53. Dur Univ BA74 CertEd. St Steph Ho Ox 76. **d** 78 **p** 79. C Pontnewynydd *Mon* 78-82; TV Ebbw Vale 82-91. *25 William Street, Cwmfelinfach, Ynysddu, Newport NP1 7GY* Tel (01495) 201354

SNOW, Martyn James. b 68. Sheff Univ BSc89. Wycliffe Hall Ox BTh95. **d** 95 **p** 96. C Brinsworth w Catcliffe and Treeton *Sheff* from 95. *18 St George's Drive, Brinsworth, Rotherham, S Yorkshire S60 5NG* Tel (01709) 261677

SNOW, Miss Patricia Margaret. b 21. Dub Bible Coll 45 St Mich Ho Ox 51. **dss** 72 **d** 87 **p** 96. W Ham *Chelmsf* 72-78; Acomb St Steph *York* 78-83; rtd 83; NSM Northfleet *Roch* from 96. *29 Huggens' College, College Road, Northfleet, Gravesend, Kent DA11 9DL* Tel (01474) 352963

SNOW, Peter David. b 37. St Jo Coll Cam BA62 MA66. Ridley Hall Cam 62. **d** 64 **p** 65. C Kingshurst *Birm* 64-66; USA from 67. *927 36th Avenue, Seattle, Washington 98122, USA*

SNOW, Peter Normington. b 23. St Jo Coll Ox BA48 MA52. Ely Th Coll 48. **d** 50 **p** 51. C Lower Gornal *Lich* 50-52; C Solihull *Birm* 52-56; V Emscote *Cov* 56-89; RD Warwick 67-77; rtd 89. *3 Park Lane, Harbury, Leamington Spa, Warks CV33 9HX* Tel (01926) 612410

SNOW, Richard John. b 57. Bris Univ BSc80. **d** 90 **p** 91. C Preston Plucknett *B & W* 90-95; TV Stratton St Margaret w S Marston etc *Bris* from 95. *The Vicarage, South Marston, Swindon SN3 4SR* Tel (01793) 827021

SNOWBALL, Michael Sydney. b 44. Dur Univ BA70 MA72 St Jo Coll Dur DipTh72. **d** 72 **p** 73. C Stockton St Pet *Dur* 72-75; C Dunston St Nic 75-77; C Dunston 77-78; C Darlington St Jo 78-81; V Chilton 81-91; V Brompton w Deighton *York* from 91. *The Vicarage, Brompton, Northallerton, N Yorkshire DL6 2QA* Tel (01609) 772436

SNOWDEN, Miss Alice Isabel Glass. b 55. Lanc Univ BA77 Humberside Coll of Educn PGCE84. Ripon Coll Cuddesdon 91. **d** 94 **p** 95. C Mirfield *Wakef* from 94. *16 Towngate Grove, Mirfield, W Yorkshire WF14 9JF* Tel (01924) 495288

SNOWSELL, Raymond Ernest Elijah. b 15. Wycliffe Hall Ox 67. **d** 68 **p** 69. C Leic St Pet *Leic* 68-71; V Oaks (Charnwood Forest) 71-79; V Oaks in Charnwood and Copt Oak 79-80; rtd 80; Perm to Offic *B & W* from 81. *Charnwood, Castle Street, Keinton Mandeville, Somerton, Somerset TA11 6DX* Tel (01458) 223225

SNUGGS, David Sidney. b 49. Keble Coll Ox BA71 PGCE72 MA75. S Dios Minl Tr Scheme 89. **d** 92 **p** 93. C Bitterne *Win* 92-96; V Fair Oak from 96. *The Vicarage, Fair Oak Court, Fair Oak, Eastleigh, Hants SO5 7BG* Tel (01703) 692238

SOADY, Mark. b 60. RMN84 Univ of Wales BTh. St Mich Coll Llan 96. **d** 96 **p** 97. C Tenby *St D* from 96. *21 Clicketts Court, Tenby SA70 8DT* Tel 0589-184765 (Mobile)

SOAR, Arthur Leslie. b 20. ACII. Linc Th Coll 82. **d** 83 **p** 84. NSM Chilham *Cant* 83-86; NSM Crundale w Godmersham 86-90; NSM Elmsted w Hastingleigh 86-90; rtd 90; Perm to Offic *Cant* from 90. *9 Northdowns Close, Old Wives Lees, Canterbury, Kent CT4 8BP* Tel (01227) 730205

SOAR, Martin William. b 54. Wye Coll Lon BSc78. Wycliffe Hall Ox 86. **d** 88 **p** 89. C Henfynyw w Aberaeron and Llanddewi Aberarth *St D* 88-91; C Hubbertson 91-93; P-in-c Low Harrogate St Mary *Ripon* 93-95; V from 95. *St Mary's Vicarage, 22 Harlow Oval, Harrogate, N Yorkshire HG2 0DS* Tel (01423) 502614

SODOR AND MAN, Bishop of. *See* JONES, The Rt Revd Noel Debroy

SOGA, Hector Ian. b 47. Glas Univ MA70 BMus78 Selw Coll Cam BA72 MA76. St And NSM Tr Scheme 87. **d** 88 **p** 89. NSM Dollar *St And* from 88. *2 Harviestoun Road, Dollar, Clackmannanshire FK14 7HF* Tel (01259) 743169

SOKOLOWSKI (née MAHON), Mrs Stephanie Mary. b 56. Liv Univ BSc80 SRN80. S'wark Ord Course 91. **d** 94 **p** 95. C Warlingham w Chelsham and Farleigh *S'wark* from 94. *12 Marston Drive, Warlingham, Surrey CR6 9SY* Tel (01883) 565896

SOLOMON, Arthur Creagh. b 33. ACT LTh Ch Coll Hobart. **d** 62 **p** 63. Australia 62-67; C Addiscombe St Mildred *Cant* 67-68; Chapl Pierrepont Sch Frensham 69-72; R Clifton Campville w Chilcote *Lich* 72-95; P-in-c Thorpe Constantine 83-95; R Clifton Campville w Edingale 95. *Aufenthalt, 18 Valley Road, Overseal, Swadlincote, Derbyshire DE12 6NL* Tel (01283) 762226

SOLOMON, Gerald Tankerville Norris. b 12. Lon Univ BA36. Sarum Th Coll 37. **d** 39 **p** 40. C Broadstone *Sarum* 39-42; CF 42-63; R Corsley *Sarum* 63-78; rtd 78. *The Old Forge, Hindon, Salisbury SP3 6DR* Tel (01747) 89255

SOMERS-EDGAR, Carl John. b 46. Otago Univ BA69. St Steph Ho Ox 72. **d** 75 **p** 76. C Northwood H Trin *Lon* 75-79; C St Marylebone All SS 79-82; V Liscard St Mary w St Columba *Ches* 82-85; New Zealand from 85. *St Peter's Vicarage, 57 Baker Street, Caversham, Dunedin, New Zealand* Tel Christchurch (3) 455 3961

SOMERS HESLAM, Peter. b 63. Hull Univ BA89 Keble Coll Ox DPhil94 Trin Coll Cam BA96. Ridley Hall Cam CTM93. **d** 96. C Huntingdon *Ely* from 96. *83 Wertheim Way, Huntingdon, Cambs PE18 6UH* Tel (01480) 434388

SOMERVELL, Mrs Katherine Mary. b 30. Edin Univ CQSW51. WMMTC 86. **d** 88 **p** 94. Par Dn Caldmore *Lich* 88-92; Par Dn Wilnecote 92-94; C 94-95; NSM Loppington w Newtown from 95; rtd 95. *The Vicarage, Loppington, Shrewsbury SY4 5ST* Tel (01939) 233388

SOMERVILLE, John William Kenneth. b 38. St D Coll Lamp 60. **d** 63 **p** 64. C Rhosllannerchrugog *St As* 63-67; C Llangystennin 67-70; V Gorsedd 70-77; V Gorsedd w Brynford and Ysgeifiog from 77; RD Holywell from 96. *The Vicarage, The Village, Gorsedd, Holywell CH8 8QZ* Tel (01352) 711675

SOMMERVILLE, Prof Robert Gardner. b 27. Glas Univ MB50 ChB50 MD60 FRCPGlas67 Lon Univ FRCPath68. **d** 96 **p** 96. NSM Blairgowrie *St And* from 96; NSM Coupar Angus from 96; NSM Alyth from 96. *Monkmyre, Myreriggs Road, Coupar Angus, Blairgowrie, Perthshire PH13 9HS* Tel (01828) 627131 Fax as telephone E-mail rgsommer@netcomuk.co.uk

SONG, James. b 32. Lon Coll of Div 57. **d** 60 **p** 61. C Virginia Water *Guildf* 60-63; C Portman Square St Paul *Lon* 63-66; V Matlock Bath *Derby* 66-76; V Woking St Jo *Guildf* 76-94; RD Woking 87-92; rtd 94; Perm to Offic *Guildf* from 94. *Ash House, Churt, Farnham, Surrey GU10 2NU* Tel (01428) 714493

SOOSAINAYAGAM, Xavier. b 50. S'wark Ord Course 89 St Paul's Sem Trichy BTh77 Sri Lanka Nat Sem BPh73. **d** 76 **p** 77. In RC Ch 76-89; C Streatham St Leon *S'wark* 89-94; C Merton St Jas 94-97; V Croydon H Sav from 97. *10 Cheltenham Gardens, Stanley Road, Thornton Heath, Surrey CR0 3QA2* Tel 0181-664 8975

SOPER, Brian Malcolm. b 31. Lon Univ BSc53 Mansf Coll Ox DipTh56. Ripon Hall Ox 63. **d** 63 **p** 64. C Platt *Roch* 63-64; Chapl K Sch Roch 64-72; Chapl Repton Sch Derby 72-75; Chapl Bennett Memorial Sch Tunbridge Wells 75-84; Perm to Offic *Cant* 70-87; Perm to Offic *Chich* from 87. *The Croft, Point Hill, Rye, E Sussex TN31 7NP* Tel (01797) 222897

SOPER, Jonathan Alexander James. b 64. Univ Coll Dur BA85. Wycliffe Hall Ox 94. **d** 96 **p** 97. C Bath Weston All SS w N Stoke and Langridge *B & W* from 96. *23 Lucklands Road, Weston, Bath BA1 4AX* Tel (01225) 421417

SORENSEN, Ms Anna Katrine Elizabeth. b 58. Man Univ BA82. Ripon Coll Cuddesdon 83. **d** 87 **p** 94. Par Dn Ashton H Trin *Man* 87-88; Asst Chapl St Felix Sch Southwold 89-90; Chapl from 90; Hon Par Dn Reydon *St E* 89-92; Hon Par Dn Blythburgh w Reydon 92-94; Hon C from 94. *The Rectory, Moll's Lane, Brampton, Beccles, Suffolk NR34 8DB* Tel (01502) 575859

SOULSBY, Canon Michael. b 36. Dur Univ BSc57. Westcott Ho Cam 61. **d** 62 **p** 63. C Selly Oak St Mary *Birm* 62-66; C Kings Norton 66-72; TV 73-76; TR Sutton *Liv* 76-88; RD Prescot 84-88; P-in-c Orton Longueville *Ely* 88-96; RD Yaxley from 92; TR The Ortons, Alwalton and Chesterton from 96; Hon Can Ely Cathl from 94. *The Rectory, Orton Longueville, Peterborough PE2 7DN* Tel (01733) 371071

SOUPER, Patrick Charles. b 28. K Coll Lon BD55 AKC55. **d** 57 **p** 58. Chapl Derby City Hosp 57-62; Chapl Derby Cathl *Derby* 57-62; Asst Chapl Lon Univ *Lon* 62-64; C St Marylebone w H Trin 64-65; Chapl St Paul's Sch Barnes 65-70; Lect in Educn Southn Univ 70-93; Lic to Offic *Win* 70-93; rtd 93. *Villa Galini, Prines, 74100 Rethymnon, Crete, Greece* Tel Rethymnon (831) 31521

SOURBUT, Philip John. b 57. Cam Univ BA MA. Cranmer Hall Dur BA. **d** 85 **p** 86. C Springfield All SS *Chelmsf* 85-88; C Roxeth Ch Ch and Harrow St Pet *Lon* 88-91; P-in-c Bath St Sav *B & W* 91-93; R Bath St Sav w Swainswick and Woolley from 93. *St Saviour's Rectory, Claremont Road, Bath BA1 6LX* Tel (01225) 311637

SOUTER, William Ewen Logan. b 66. Em Coll Cam BA88 Univ Coll Lon PhD93. Trin Coll Bris BA94 MA97. **d** 97. C Harborne Heath *Birm* from 97. *55 Albert Road, Harborne, Birmingham B17 0AP* Tel 0121-426 2548 Mobile 0589-612861 E-mail 106314.2624@compuserve.com

SOUTH, Mrs Gillian. b 51. NE Ord Course 87. **d** 90 **p** 94. C Rothbury *Newc* 90-93; C Morpeth from 93. *23 Green Acres, Morpeth, Northd NE61 2AD* Tel (01670) 511662

SOUTH, Canon Thomas Horsman (Tom). b 06. Qu Coll Ox BA31 MA35. Cuddesdon Coll 31. **d** 32 **p** 33. C Banbury *Ox* 32-34; Warden St Anselm Hall Manchester 34-39; V Adderbury w Milton 39-47; R Amersham 47-62; V Coleshill 47-62; Chapl Amersham Hosp 47-62; V Latimer w Flaunden *Ox* 62-73; RD Amersham 65-70; Hon Can Ch Ch 66-73; rtd 73. *c/o The Red House, 34 Alexandra Road, Hemel Hempstead, Hertfordshire HP2 5BS* Tel (01442) 246665

SOUTHALL, Colin Edward. b 36. Lich Th Coll 63. **d** 65 **p** 82. C Wylde Green *Birm* 65-67; Perm to Offic 68-73; Perm to Offic *Pet*

73-81; Hon C Linc St Faith and St Martin w St Pet *Linc* 82-85; Hon C Gt Glen, Stretton Magna and Wistow etc *Leic* 85-93; Chapl Asst Leic R Infirmary 93-96; Hon C Fleckney and Kilby *Leic* from 96. *1 Spinney View, Great Glen, Leicester LE8 9EP* Tel 0116-259 2959

SOUTHAMPTON, Suffragan Bishop of. *See* GLEDHILL, The Rt Revd Jonathan Michael

SOUTHEND, Archdeacon of. *See* JENNINGS, The Ven David Willfred Michael

SOUTHERN, Humphrey Ivo John. b 60. Ch Ch Ox BA82 MA86. Ripon Coll Cuddesdon 83. **d** 86 **p** 87. C Rainham *Roch* 86-90; C Walton St Mary *Liv* 90-92; C Walton-on-the-Hill 92; V Hale *Guildf* 92-96; TR from 96; Dioc Ecum Officer from 92. *The Vicarage, 25 Upper Hale Road, Farnham, Surrey GU9 0NX* Tel (01252) 716469

SOUTHERN, John Abbott. b 27. Leeds Univ BA47. Coll of Resurr Mirfield. **d** 51 **p** 52. C Leigh St Mary *Man* 51-55; C Gt Grimsby St Jas *Linc* 55-58; V Oldham St Jas *Man* 58-60; V Haigh *Liv* 60-75; V Pemberton St Jo from 75. *The Vicarage, 148 Orrell Road, Orrell, Wigan, Lancs WN5 8HJ* Tel (01942) 222237

SOUTHERN, Paul Ralph. b 48. Oak Hill Th Coll DipHE. **d** 87 **p** 88. C Chadwell Heath *Chelmsf* 87-91; P-in-c Tolleshunt D'Arcy w Tolleshunt Major from 91. *8 Vicarage Close, Tolleshunt D'Arcy, Maldon, Essex CM9 8UG* Tel (01621) 860521

SOUTHERTON, Miss Kathryn Ruth. b 66. Univ of Wales (Lamp) BA88. Sarum & Wells Th Coll 90. **d** 92 **p** 97. C Connah's Quay *St As* 92-97; R Halkyn w Caerfallwch w Rhesycae from 97. *The New Rectory, Halkyn, Holywell CH8 8BU* Tel (01352) 781297

SOUTHERTON, Canon Peter Clive. b 38. Univ of Wales (Lamp) BA59. Qu Coll Birm DipTh60. **d** 61 **p** 62. C Llandrillo-yn-Rhos *St As* 61-68; Bermuda 68-71; V Esclusham *St As* 72-82; V Prestatyn from 82; Hon Can St As Cathl from 96. *The Vicarage, 109 High Street, Prestatyn LL19 9AR* Tel (01745) 853780

SOUTHEY, George Rubidge. b 34. St Mich Coll Llan 84. **d** 86 **p** 87. C Hessle *York* 86-89; P-in-c Scarborough St Columba 89-92; V from 92. *160 Dean Road, Scarborough, N Yorkshire YO12 7JH* Tel (01723) 375070

SOUTHGATE, Geoffrey Trevor Stanley. b 28. AKC56. **d** 57 **p** 58. C Tonge Moor *Man* 57-60; C Lon Docks St Pet w Wapping St Jo *Lon* 60-62; V Upper Clapton St Matt 62-67; V Fleetwood *Blackb* 68-85; R Cov St Jo *Cov* 85-95; rtd 95. *1 Margetts Close, Kenilworth, Warks CV8 1EN* Tel (01926) 56651

SOUTHGATE, Dr Graham. b 63. GIBiol85 Bris Poly HDipABiol83 NE Surrey Coll of Tech PhD89. Ripon Coll Cuddesdon BTh93. **d** 93 **p** 94. C Tisbury *Sarum* 93-97; TV Chalke Valley W from 97. *The Vicarage, Nunton, Salisbury SP5 4HP* Tel (01722) 330628

SOUTHGATE, The Very Revd John Eliot. b 26. St Jo Coll Dur BA53 DipTh55. **d** 55 **p** 56. C Glen Parva and S Wigston *Leic* 55-59; C Lee Gd Shep w St Pet *S'wark* 59-62; V Plumstead St Mark 62-66; R Charlton St Luke w St Paul 66-72; Boro Dean Greenwich 69-72; Hon Can S'wark Cathl 70-72; Can and Preb York Minster *York* 72-84; V Harome 72-77; Adn Cleveland 74-84; Dean York 84-94; Chmn Assn of English Cathls 90-94; rtd 94; Perm to Offic *Nor* from 94. *39 Churchfields, Hethersett, Norfolk NR9 3PH* Tel (01603) 812116

SOUTHWARD, Douglas Ambrose. b 32. St Jo Coll Nottm LTh74 ALCD57. **d** 57 **p** 58. C Otley *Bradf* 57-61; C Sedbergh 61-63; C Cautley w Dowbiggin 61-63; C Garsdale 61-63; PV Lich Cathl *Lich* 63-65; V Hope *Derby* 65-72; V Crosby Ravensworth *Carl* 72-82; V Bolton 74-82; Sec Dioc Past and Redundant Chs Uses Cttees 78-82; RD Appleby 78-82; Hon Can Carl Cathl 81-95; R Asby 81-82; V Hawkshead and Low Wray w Sawrey from 82; P-in-c Windermere St Jo 84-89; RD Windermere 84-89; P-in-c Colton w Satterthwaite and Rusland 94-95. *The Vicarage, Hawkshead, Ambleside, Cumbria LA22 0PD* Tel (015394) 36301

SOUTHWARD, James Fisher. b 57. St Martin's Coll Lanc BEd80. Chich Th Coll 83. **d** 86 **p** 87. C Woodford St Barn *Chelmsf* 86-89; TV Crawley *Chich* 89-95; V Higham and Merston *Roch* from 95. *The Vicarage, Hermitage Road, Higham, Rochester, Kent ME3 7NE* Tel (01634) 717360

SOUTHWARK, Archdeacon of. *See* BARTLES-SMITH, The Ven Douglas Leslie

SOUTHWARK, Bishop of. *See* WILLIAMSON, The Rt Revd Robert Kerr

SOUTHWARK, Provost of. *See* SLEE, The Very Revd Colin Bruce

SOUTHWELL, Peter John Mackenzie. b 43. New Coll Ox BA64 MA68. Wycliffe Hall Ox 66. **d** 67 **p** 68. Lect Sheff Univ 67-70; C Crookes St Thos *Sheff* 67-70; Sen Tutor Wycliffe Hall Ox from 70; Chapl Qu Coll Ox from 82. *Queen's College, Oxford OX1 4AW* Tel (01865) 279143 or 53829 Fax 274215

SOUTHWELL, The Ven Roy. b 14. AKC42. **d** 42 **p** 43. C Wigan St Mich *Liv* 42-44; C Kennington St Jo *S'wark* 44-48; V Ixworth *St E* 48-51; P-in-c Ixworth Thorpe 48-51; V Bury St Edmunds St Jo 51-56; R Bucklesham w Brightwell and Foxhall 56-59; Dir RE 59-68; Hon Can St E Cathl 59-68; V Hendon St Mary *Lon* 68-71; Adn Northolt 70-80; rtd 80; Warden Community of All Hallows Ditchingham 83-89; Lic to Offic *Nor* 83-89; Perm to Offic from 89. *397 Sprowton Road, Norwich NR3 4HY* Tel (01603) 405977

SOUTHWELL-SANDER, Canon Peter George. b 41. G&C Coll Cam BA64 MA67. Westcott Ho Cam 63. **d** 65 **p** 66. C Maidstone All SS w St Phil *Cant* 65-68; C Cambridge Gt St Mary w St Mich *Ely* 68-71; Chapl Girton Coll Cam 69-73; V Clapham St Paul *S'wark* 73-77; V Merton St Mary 77-84; P-in-c Merton St Jo 77-79; Dir of Min *Chelmsf* 85-94; Can Res Chelmsf Cathl 85-94; Public Preacher 94-96; Perm to Offic from 96; UK Adv Chicago Th Seminaries' DMin in Preaching from 95; USA from 96. *Hollybush House, Hadley Green Road, Barnet, Herts EN5 5PR, or 5298 North Riffle Way, Boise, ID 83703, USA* Tel 0181-440 8365 or (208) 853-2581 Fax 0181-440 8365 or (208) 853-4840

SOUTHWELL, Bishop of. *See* HARRIS, The Rt Revd Patrick Burnet

SOUTHWELL, Provost of. *See* LEANING, The Very Revd David

SOUTHWOOD, Robert Alfred. b 31. Sarum & Wells Th Coll 72. **d** 74 **p** 75. C Christchurch *Win* 74-76; C Fordingbridge w Ibsley 76-79; P-in-c Ernesettle *Ex* 79-80; V 80-83; R Stoke-in-Teignhead w Combe-in-Teignhead etc from 83. *The Rectory, Stoke-in-Teignhead, Newton Abbot, Devon TQ12 4QB* Tel (01626) 873493 E-mail southw@premier.co.uk

SOUTTAR, Preb Edward Herbert. b 16. Bps' Coll Cheshunt 38. **d** 46 **p** 47. C Plymouth St Pet *Ex* 46-52; V Lynton and Brendon 52-64; V Sidmouth St Nic 65-73; TR Sidmouth, Woolbrook, Salcombe Regis etc 73-81; Preb Ex Cathl 72-85; rtd 81; Perm to Offic *Ex* from 85. *20 Fosseway Close, Axminster, Devon EX13 5LW* Tel (01297) 34382

SOWDON, Henry Lewis Malcolm. b 37. TCD BA. Bps' Coll Cheshunt. **d** 64 **p** 65. C Newport w Longford *Lich* 64-66; C Caverswall 66-69; Chapl Clayesmore Sch Blandford 69-72; Hon C Hornsey Ch Ch *Lon* 72-80; Chapl Gordon's Sch Woking 80-86; TV Hodge Hill *Birm* 86-91; Perm to Offic from 91. *157 Heathfield Road, Birmingham B19 1JD* Tel 0121-515 3557

SOWERBUTTS, Alan. b 49. Sheff Univ BSc70 PhD73 Qu Coll Cam BA75 MA79. Westcott Ho Cam 74. **d** 76 **p** 77. C Salesbury *Blackb* 76-80; V Lower Darwen St Jas 80-84; V Musbury 84-93; P-in-c Brindle from 93; Sec Dioc Adv Cttee for the Care of Chs from 93. *The Rectory, Sandy Lane, Brindle, Chorley, Lancs PR6 8JN* Tel (01254) 854130

SOWERBY, Geoffrey Nigel Rake. b 35. St Aid Birkenhead 56. **d** 60 **p** 61. C Armley St Bart *Ripon* 60-63; Min Can Ripon Cathl 63-65; V Thornthwaite w Thruscross and Darley 65-69; V Leeds All SS 69-73; V Leyburn w Bellerby 73-81; R Edin Old St Paul *Edin* 81-86; V Hawes and Hardraw *Ripon* 86-92; Dioc Adv in Deliverance Min 91-92; rtd 92; Perm to Offic *Dur* from 92. *6 Wycar Terrace, Bedale, N Yorkshire DL8 2AG* Tel (01677) 425860

SOWERBY, Mark Crispin Rake. b 63. K Coll Lon BD85 AKC85 Lanc Univ MA94. Coll of Resurr Mirfield 85. **d** 87 **p** 88. C Knaresborough *Ripon* 87-90; C Darwen St Cuth w Tockholes St Steph *Blackb* 90-92; V Accrington St Mary 92-97; Chapl St Chris High Sch Accrington 92-97; Chapl Victoria Hosp Accrington 93-97; Asst Dir of Ords *Blackb* 93-97; Voc Officer and Selection Sec ABM from 97. *17 Tarbert Road, London SE22 8QB, or Church House, Great Smith Street, London SW1P 3NZ* Tel 0171-340 0234 or 0181-299 2865

SOWTER, Dr Colin Victor. b 35. Ball Coll Ox MA59 DPhil60. Oak Hill NSM Course 88. **d** 91 **p** 92. NSM Cranleigh *Guildf* 91-93; NSM Wonersh from 93. *Hollycroft, Grantley Avenue, Wonersh Park, Guildford, Surrey GU5 0QN* Tel (01483) 892094

SOX, Harold David. b 36. N Carolina Univ BA58. NY Th Sem MDiv61. **d** 61 **p** 61. USA 61-74; Hon C Richmond St Mary *S'wark* 74-79; Hon C Richmond St Mary w St Matthias and St Jo 79-82; Hon C Kensington St Mary Abbots w St Geo *Lon* 82-84 and 89-93; Perm to Offic 84-89; Hon C Beedon and Peasemore w W Ilsley and Farnborough *Ox* 93-94; Perm to Offic 93-97. *20 The Vineyard, Richmond, Surrey TW10 6AN* Tel 0181-940 0094

SPACKMAN, The Ven Peter John. b 37. Southn Univ BSc60. Westcott Ho Cam 65. **d** 66 **p** 67. C Boxmoor St Jo *St Alb* 66-69; C Alnwick St Paul *Newc* 69-72; Jamaica 72-74; Canada 74-95; Adn Gaspe 88-95; Perm to Offic *Ex* from 95. *4 Underwood Close, Dawlish, Devon EX7 9RY* Tel (01626) 862695

SPAFFORD, The Very Revd Christopher Garnett Howsin. b 24. St Jo Coll Ox BA48 MA54. Wells Th Coll 48. **d** 50 **p** 51. C Brighouse *Wakef* 50-53; C Huddersfield St Pet 53-55; V Hebden Bridge 55-61; R Thornhill 61-69; V Shrewsbury St Chad *Lich* 69-76; V Newc St Nic *Newc* 76-89; Provost Newc 76-89; rtd 89; Perm to Offic *Heref* from 93. *Low Moor, Elm Close, Leominster, Herefordshire HR6 8JX* Tel (01568) 614395

SPAIGHT, Robert George. b 45. Ridley Hall Cam. **d** 84 **p** 85. C St Columb Minor and St Colan *Truro* 84-87; C Worksop St Jo *S'well* 87-89; V Barlings *Linc* from 89. *The Vicarage, Station Road, Langworth, Lincoln LN3 5BB* Tel (01522) 754233

SPALDING, Wilfrid Frank. b 20. Sarum Th Coll. **d** 57 **p** 58. C Clitheroe St Mary *Blackb* 57-60; V Accrington St Paul 60-68; R Hoole 69-85; rtd 85; Perm to Offic *Blackb* from 85. *5 Park Walk, Fulwood, Preston PR2 4PA* Tel (01772) 774663

SPANNER, Douglas Clement. b 16. Lon Univ BSc46 PhD51 DSc72. LNSM course. **d** 73 **p** 75. Hon C Ealing St Mary *Lon* 73-78; Hon C Eynsham *Ox* 79-83; Hon C Grove 83-86; Lic to

Offic from 86. *Ivy Cottage, Main Street, Grove, Wantage, Oxon OX12 7JY* Tel (01235) 766845

SPANNER, Handley James. b 51. Lanchester Poly BSc73 BA. Oak Hill Th Coll 82. **d** 85 **p** 86. C Cov H Trin *Cov* 85-89; V Rye Park St Cuth *St Alb* from 89. *St Cuthbert's Vicarage, Ogard Road, Hoddesdon, Herts EN11 0NU* Tel (01992) 463168

SPARHAM, Canon Anthony George. b 41. St Jo Coll Dur BA69 DipTh. Cranmer Hall Dur 66. **d** 71 **p** 72. C Bourne *Linc* 71-74; TV Tong *Bradf* 74-76; V Windhill 76-81; Dir of Educn *St E* 82-85; V Goostrey *Ches* from 85; Dir Lay Tr 85-90; Jt Dir Lay Tr from 90; Hon Can Ches Cathl from 94. *c/o Mrs M Bramham, Diocesan House, Raymond Street, Chester CH1 4PN*

SPARKES, Colin Anthony. b 37. MIEE Surrey Univ MSc68 Bath Univ MEd83. Ox NSM Course 78. **d** 81 **p** 82. NSM Shrivenham w Watchfield and Bourton *Ox* 81-84; NSM Shellingford 84-91; R Hawkinge w Acrise and Swingfield *Cant* from 91. *The Rectory, 78 Canterbury Road, Hawkinge, Folkestone, Kent CT18 7BP* Tel (01303) 892369

SPARKES, Donald James Henry. b 33. Oak Hill Th Coll DipTh59. **d** 59 **p** 60. C Southall Green St Jo *Lon* 59-63; P-in-c Pitsmoor *Sheff* 63-70; V 70-73; P-in-c Wicker w Neepsend 70-73; V Pitsmoor w Wicker 73-79; V Pitsmoor w Ellesmere 79-86; V Pitsmoor Ch Ch 86-96; rtd 96; Perm to Offic *Derby* from 96. *8 Grosvenor Mansions, Broad Walk, Buxton, Derbyshire SK17 6JH* Tel (01298) 25134

SPARKS, Christopher Thomas. b 29. Lanc Univ PGCE69 Birm Univ 81. St D Coll Lamp BA53 Lich Th Coll 53. **d** 55 **p** 56. C Macclesfield St Mich *Ches* 55-59; C W Kirby St Bridget 59-61; V Altrincham St Jo 61-68; Lic to Offic *Blackb* 68-79; C Lancaster St Mary 79-83; Chapl HM Pris Lanc 83-84; Perm to Offic *Blackb* from 84; rtd 94. *The Hollies, Littlefell Lane, Lancaster LA2 0RG* Tel (01524) 60292

SPARKS, Herbert Francis. b 23. AKC49. **d** 50 **p** 51. C Middlesbrough St Oswald *York* 50-53; C Whitby 53-58; C Newington St Mary *S'wark* 58-59; V Middlesbrough St Paul *York* 59-64; Chapl HM Pris Leyhill 64-69; Chapl HM Pris Leic 69-74; Chapl HM Pris Kirkham 74-76; Chapl HM Pris Liv 76-79; Chapl HM Pris Long Lartin 79-84; rtd 84; Perm to Offic *York* from 84. *21 Chestnut Avenue, Withernsea, N Humberside HU19 2PG* Tel (01964) 614183

SPARKS, Ian. b 59. Lanc Univ BSc(Econ)81. Cranmer Hall Dur 94. **d** 96 **p** 97. C Bowdon *Ches* from 96. *Kilgowan, Vicarage Lane, Bowdon, Altrincham, Cheshire WA14 3AS* Tel 0161-928 2716

SPARLING, Harold William. b 19. ARCM53 Lon Univ BD40 AKC40. Bps' Coll Cheshunt 40. **d** 41 **p** 43. C S Norwood St Mark *Cant* 41-43; C-in-c Bradfield *Chelmsf* 43-46; R Langham 46-54; Min Can and Succ St Paul's Cathl *Lon* 54-56; R Cranham *Chelmsf* 56-60; R Upper Hardres w Stelling *Cant* 60-78; Teacher Ashford Sch Kent 75-80; Perm to Offic *St E* from 81; rtd 84. *89 Langton Green, Eye, Suffolk IP23 7SH* Tel (01379) 870073

SPARROW, Michael Kenneth. St Jo Coll Dur BA74. Coll of Resurr Mirfield 74. **d** 75 **p** 76. C N Hinksey *Ox* 75-78; C Portsea St Mary *Portsm* 78-85; V Midsomer Norton w Clandown *B & W* 85-93; Chapl Schiedam Miss to Seamen *Eur* from 93. *Jan Steenstraat 69, 3117 TC Schiedam, The Netherlands* Tel Schiedam (10) 427-0063

SPEAK, Geoffrey Lowrey. b 24. OBE70. Selw Coll Cam BA49 MA53. Ridley Hall Cam 49. **d** 51 **p** 52. C Sandal St Helen *Wakef* 51-54; Hong Kong 54-85; rtd 91. *Murren, Watery Lane, Donhead St Mary, Shaftesbury, Dorset SP7 9DP* Tel (01747) 828613

SPEAKMAN, Joseph Frederick. b 26. NW Ord Course 75. **d** 78 **p** 79. NSM Wallasey St Hilary *Ches* 78; C 79-82; V Marthall w Over Peover 82-91; rtd 91; Perm to Offic *Ches* from 91. *10 Aberford Avenue, Wallasey, Merseyside L45 8PX* Tel 0151-637 0109

SPEAR, Andrew James Michael. b 60. Dur Univ BA81. Ridley Hall Cam 83. **d** 86 **p** 87. C Haughton le Skerne *Dur* 86-90; C Eastbourne H Trin *Chich* 90-95; C Patcham from 95. *32 Fairview Rise, Brighton BN1 5GL* Tel (01273) 503926

SPEAR, Miss Jennifer Jane. b 53. Westhill Coll Birm BEd76. Trin Coll Bris DipHE84. **dss** 84 **d** 87 **p** 95. Reading St Jo *Ox* 84-90; Par Dn 87-90; Hon Par Dn Devonport St Barn *Ex* 90-91; Hon Par Dn Devonport St Mich 90-91; Par Dn Plymstock 91-94; C 94-97; TV Plymstock and Hooe from 97. *63 Plymstock Road, Plymstock, Plymouth PL9 7NX* Tel (01752) 405202

SPEAR, John Cory. b 33. Open Univ BA87. Ridley Hall Cam 68. **d** 70 **p** 71. C Gerrards Cross *Ox* 70-73; TV Washfield, Stoodleigh, Withleigh etc *Ex* 73-79; R Instow 79-90; V Westleigh 79-90; RD Hartland 82-89; V Pilton w Ashford from 90. *The Vicarage, 4 Northfield Lane, Pilton West, Barnstaple, Devon EX31 1QB* Tel (01271) 45958

SPEAR, Sylvia Grace. b 36. St Chris Coll Blackheath 60. **dss** 76 **d** 87 **p** 94. S Wimbledon H Trin and St Pet *S'wark* 76-80; Lee Gd Shep w St Pet 80-95; Par Dn 87-94; C 94-95; rtd 95; Perm to Offic *Nor* from 95. *19 Grovelands, Ingoldisthorpe, King's Lynn, Norfolk PE31 6PG* Tel (01485) 543469

SPEARS, Reginald Robert Derek. b 48. Trin Coll Ox BA72 MA75. Cuddesdon Coll 72. **d** 75 **p** 76. C Hampton All SS *Lon* 75-79; C Caversham *Ox* 79-81; C Caversham and Mapledurham 81-84; V Reading St Matt 84-94; V Earley St Pet from 94. *St Peter's Vicarage, 129 Whiteknights Road, Reading RG6 2BB* Tel 0118-926 2009

SPECK, Preb Peter William. b 42. Univ of Wales BSc64 Birm Univ BA66 DPS67 MA71. Qu Coll Birm 64. **d** 67 **p** 68. C Rhosddu *St As* 67-71; C Wrexham 71-72; Asst Chapl United Sheff Hosps 72-73; Chapl N Gen Hosp Sheff 73-79; Chapl R Free Hosp Lon 79-95; Hon Sen Lect Sch of Med 87-95; Preb St Paul's Cathl *Lon* 92-95; Chapl Southn Univ Hosps NHS Trust from 95. *The Chaplain's Office, Southampton General Hospital, Tremona Road, Southampton SO16 6YD* Tel (01703) 796745 or 777222

SPECK, Raymond George. b 39. Oak Hill Th Coll 64. **d** 67 **p** 68. C Stretford St Bride *Man* 67-70; C Roxeth Ch Ch *Lon* 70-74; V Woodbridge St Jo *St E* 74-85; R Jersey St Ouen w St Geo *Win* from 85. *The Rectory, St Ouen, Jersey, Channel Islands JE3 2GG* Tel (01534) 481800

SPEDDING, Geoffrey Osmond. b 46. Hull Univ BA67 Fitzw Coll Cam BA69 MA BD. **d** 70 **p** 71. C Bradf Cathl *Bradf* 70-73; C Sutton St Jas and Wawne *York* 73-76; TV Preston St Jo *Blackb* 76-82; TV Yate New Town *Bris* 82-87; TR Bestwood *S'well* 87-94; V Ravenshead from 94. *The Vicarage, 55 Sheepwalk Lane, Ravenshead, Nottingham NG15 9FD* Tel (01636) 892317

SPEDDING, William Granville. b 39. Lon Univ BD60. Tyndale Hall Bris 57. **d** 62 **p** 63. C Man Albert Memorial Ch *Man* 62-65; Co-ord Humanities Hayward Sch Bolton 65-93; Perm to Offic 65-67; Hon C New Bury 67-79; Hon C Bolton St Paul w Em 79-86; NSM Pennington from 86. *26 Milverton Close, Lostock, Bolton BL6 4RR* Tel (01204) 841248

SPEEDY, Canon Darrel Craven. b 35. St Chad's Coll Dur BA57. Wells Th Coll 57. **d** 59 **p** 60. C Frodingham *Linc* 59-63; V Heckington w Howell 63-71; V Barton upon Humber 71-79; R Tain *Mor* 79-85; Dioc Sec 82-85; Can St Andr Cathl Inverness 83-85; Syn Clerk 83-85; R Whaley Bridge *Ches* from 85; RD Chadkirk 88-95; Hon Can Ches Cathl from 96. *St James's Rectory, Taxal Road, Whaley Bridge, High Peak, Derbyshire SK23 7DY* Tel (01663) 732696

SPEERS, Canon Samuel Hall. b 46. TCD BA70 MA75. Cuddesdon Coll 70. **d** 73 **p** 74. C Boreham Wood All SS *St Alb* 73-76; Madagascar 76-88; Hon Can Antananarivo from 85; R S Lafford *Linc* from 88; RD Lafford from 96. *The Rectory, West Street, Folkingham, Sleaford, Lincs NG34 0SN* Tel (01529) 497391

SPENCE, Brian Robin. b 39. St Chad's Coll Dur BA61 DipTh63. **d** 63 **p** 64. C Weston *Guildf* 63-67; Lesotho 67-68; C Chobham w Valley End *Guildf* 68-71; C Gt Yarmouth *Nor* 71-74; V Warnham *Chich* 74-81; V E Grinstead St Mary 81-86; V Crowthorne *Ox* from 86. *The Vicarage, 56 Duke's Ride, Crowthorne, Berks RG11 6NY* Tel (01344) 772413

SPENCE, James Knox (Jim). b 30. Worc Coll Ox BA55 MA58. Ridley Hall Cam. **d** 57 **p** 58. C W Hampstead Trin *Lon* 57-60; C Ox St Ebbe w St Pet *Ox* 61-64; Cand Sec CPAS 64-68; V Reading Greyfriars *Ox* 68-78; C St Helen Bishopsgate w St Martin Outwich *Lon* 78-80; C St Helen Bishopsgate w St Andr Undershaft etc 80-82; P-in-c Gt Baddow *Chelmsf* 82-86; V 86-88; TR 88-95; rtd 95. *15 High Street, Wallingford, Oxon OX10 0BP* Tel (01491) 826814

SPENCE, James Timothy. b 35. St Jo Coll Cam BA59 MA63. Wycliffe Hall Ox 59. **d** 61 **p** 62. C Stoke *Cov* 61-64; C Cambridge H Trin *Ely* 64-67; R Tarrington w Stoke Edith *Heref* 67-72; Dioc Youth Officer 67-72; Lic to Offic *Win* 72-75; R Falstone *Newc* 75-80; TV Bellingham/Otterburn Gp 80-82; Dioc Ecum Adv 82-87; V Dinnington 82-87; V Shap w Swindale *Carl* 87-93; P-in-c Bowness from 93; P-in-c Kirkbride w Newton Arlosh from 93. *The Rectory, Church Road, Kirkbride, Carlisle CA5 5HY* Tel (016973) 51256

SPENCE, Canon John Edis. b 24. St Edm Hall Ox BA46 MA48. Westcott Ho Cam 47. **d** 48 **p** 49. C Newland St Jo *York* 48-50; Australia 50-54; C Uckfield *Chich* 54-55; Chapl RN 55-59 and 60-65; V Thornton-le-Street w Thornton-le-Moor etc *York* 59-60; Chapl RNR from 65; V St Germans *Truro* 65-73; V Tideford 65-73; P-in-c Sheviock 69-70; Perm to Offic 73-76; Dioc Chapl to Bp 76-78; C Newlyn St Newlyn 76-78; Chapl for Maintenance of the Min 78-87; Stewardship Adv 80-87; Hon Can Truro Cathl 84-89; Bp's Dom Chapl 87-89; P-in-c St Allen 87-89; rtd 89; Lic to Offic *Truro* 89-95; Perm to Offic *Ex* from 91. *26 Kerries Road, South Brent, Devon TQ10 9DA* Tel (01364) 72578

SPENCE, Philip Arthur. b 39. Lon Univ BD71 Open Univ BA76. Hartley Victoria Coll DipTh67 Westcott Ho Cam 78. **d** 78 **p** 79. In Meth Ch 67-78; C Walthamstow St Pet *Chelmsf* 78-80; Dioc Adv on Evang 80-87; Dep Dir Dept of Miss (Evang Division) 80-85; P-in-c Greensted 80-86; Bp's Adv on Tourism 81-87; Asst Dir of Miss and Unity 85-87; R Greensted-juxta-Ongar w Stanford Rivers 86-87; V Cambridge St Mark *Ely* 87-95; Chapl Wolfs Coll Cam 87-95; Relig Adv Anglia TV 91-95; V Pet St Jo *Pet* from 95. *7 Minster Precincts, Peterborough PE1 1XS* Tel (01733) 64899

SPENCE, Dr Susan Karen. b 65. Leeds Univ BSc86 Liv Univ PhD89. Wycliffe Hall Ox BA95 DipMin96. **d** 96 **p** 97. C Caverswall and Weston Coyney w Dilhorne *Lich* from 96. *30 Firbank Place, Stoke-on-Trent ST3 5RU* Tel (01782) 334500

SPENCE, The Very Revd Walter Cyril. b 19. TCD BA40 MA43 BD43. **d** 42 **p** 43. C Maghera *D & R* 43-48; C Roscommon *K, E & A* 48-50; I Ballysumaghan w Killery 50-55; I Tubbercurry w Kilmactigue *T, K & A* 55-60; I Achonry w Tubbercurry and Killoran 60-66; Can Achonry Cathl 62-66; Dean Tuam 66-81; I Tuam 66-81; Dioc Registrar 66-85; Preb Kilmactalway St Patr Cathl Dublin 67-85; I Kilmoremoy w Castleconnor, Easkey, Kilglass etc *T, K & A* 81-85; rtd 85. *Beth Shalom, 1 Gracefield Avenue, Dublin 5, Irish Republic*

SPENCELEY, Malcolm. b 40. St Jo Coll Dur 78. **d** 80 **p** 81. C Redcar *York* 80-85; V Middlesbrough Ascension 85-93; V Newby from 93. *The Vicarage, 77 Green Lane, Scarborough, N Yorkshire YO12 6HT* Tel (01723) 363205

SPENCER, Anthony Wade. b 50. AIQS78 Birm Poly HNC74 Wolv Poly MCIOB76. Ridley Hall Cam CTM94. **d** 94 **p** 95. C Bury St Edmunds St Geo *St E* 94-96; Perm to Offic 96-97; C Rougham, Beyton w Hessett and Rushbrooke from 97. *Bethesda, Church Road, Beyton, Bury St Edmunds, Suffolk IP30 9AL* Tel (01359) 270831

SPENCER, Christopher Graham (Chris). b 61. Magd Coll Cam BA83 MA87 Bath Univ MSc84. St Jo Coll Nottm DTS93. **d** 93 **p** 94. C Ore *Chich* from 93. *Church House, 311 The Ridge, Hastings, E Sussex TN34 2RA* Tel (01424) 754501

SPENCER, David William. b 43. EAMTC 80. **d** 81 **p** 82. NSM Wisbech St Aug *Ely* 81-84; C Whittlesey 84-86; R Upwell Ch Ch 86-90; R March St Pet from 90; R March St Mary from 90. *St Peter's Rectory, High Street, March, Cambs PE15 9JR* Tel (01354) 52297

SPENCER, Geoffrey. b 50. ALCM76 Nottm Univ CertEd78 ACertCM79 Open Univ BA84. Linc Th Coll 85. **d** 87 **p** 88. C Skegness and Winthorpe *Linc* 87-90; V Heckington 90-93; P-in-c Bottesford and Muston *Leic* from 93; P-in-c Harby, Long Clawson and Hose from 94; P-in-c Barkestone w Plungar, Redmile and Stathern from 94; RD Framland from 97. *The Rectory, 4 Rutland Lane, Bottesford, Nottingham NG13 0BX* Tel (01949) 42335

SPENCER, George. b 56. Cam Univ BA77 MA83. Coll of Resurr Mirfield 80. **d** 83 **p** 84. C Edin Old St Paul *Edin* 83-85; P-in-c Edin St Ninian 85-92; Chapl Asst St Helen's and Knowsley Hosps Trust from 92. *Chapel House, Whiston Hospital, Warrington Road, Prescot, Merseyside L35 5DR* Tel 0151-430 1657 or 426 1600

SPENCER, Gilbert Hugh. b 43. Lon Univ BD67. ALCD66. **d** 67 **p** 68. C Bexleyheath Ch Ch *Roch* 67-73; C Bexley St Jo 73-76; P-in-c Bromley St Jo 76-78; V 78-81; R Chatham St Mary w St Jo 81-91; V Minster in Sheppey *Cant* from 91; Chapl Sheppey Gen Hosp from 91; RD Sittingbourne *Cant* from 94. *The Vicarage, Vicarage Road, Minster-in-Sheppey, Sheerness, Kent ME12 2HE* Tel (01795) 873185

SPENCER, Gordon Charles Craig. b 13. Oak Hill Th Coll 35. **d** 38 **p** 39. C Attenborough w Bramcote *S'well* 38-41; C Heanor *Derby* 41-45; P-in-c Eastwood *S'well* 45-46; R W Hallam *Derby* 46-66; PC Mapperley 51-66; RD Ilkeston 62-66; V Bathampton *B & W* 66-81; Chapl R Sch Bath 72-81; rtd 81; P-in-c Ditteridge *Bris* 81-86; Perm to Offic *B & W* from 86; Perm to Offic *Bris* from 86. *26 Elm Grove, Bath BA1 7AZ* Tel (01225) 316570

SPENCER, Graham Lewis. b 48. St Jo Coll Nottm 80. **d** 82 **p** 83. C Leic St Anne *Leic* 82-85; P-in-c Frisby-on-the-Wreake w Kirby Bellars 85-86; TV Melton Gt Framland 86-93; V Upper Wreake from 93. *The Vicarage, 2 Carrfields Lane, Frisby on the Wreake, Melton Mowbray, Leics LE14 2NT* Tel (01664) 434878

SPENCER, John Edward. b 36. Bris Univ BA60. Tyndale Hall Bris 60. **d** 61 **p** 62. C St Helens St Mark *Liv* 61-64; Japan 65-70; Area Sec (Dios Leic and Pet) CMS 70-71; Warden and Chapl Rikkyo Japanese Sch Rudgwick 71-73; Hd Master and Chapl Pennthorpe Sch Rudgwick 74-96; NSM Rudgwick *Chich* 95-96; rtd 96; Perm to Offic *Chich* from 96; Perm to Offic *Guildf* from 96. *105 Poplar Way, Midhurst, W Sussex GU29 9TD* Tel (01730) 816312

SPENCER, John Leslie. b 09. St Cath Soc Ox BA30 MA34. St Aid Birkenhead 31. **d** 32 **p** 33. C Wimbledon St Luke *S'wark* 32-34; C Leic H Apostles *Leic* 34-37; Org Sec SAMS 37-43; R Peckleton *Leic* 39-43; Chapl RAF 40-43; Sec SAMS (Metrop Area) 43-48; V Stoughton *Guildf* 48-53; V Wimbledon St Luke *S'wark* 53-65; R Silverhill St Matt *Chich* 65-69; V Bramfield and Walpole *St E* 69-74; rtd 74; Perm to Offic *Chich* 80-91. *Flat 7, Capel Court, The Burgage, Prestbury, Cheltenham, Glos GL52 3EL* Tel (01242) 577516

SPENCER, Norman Ernest. b 07. FCIS70. **d** 74 **p** 75. NSM Olveston *Bris* 74-82; Perm to Offic from 82. *26 Park Crescent, Bristol BS16 1NZ* Tel 0117-956 8873

SPENCER, Peter Cecil. b 30. Lich Th Coll 58. **d** 61 **p** 62. C Alton St Lawr *Win* 61-63; C Bournemouth St Luke 63-66; C W End 67-70; C Reading St Mary V *Ox* 70-72; C-in-c Reading St Matt CD 72-76; V Reading St Matt 76-78; TV Sidmouth, Woolbrook and Salcombe Regis *Ex* 78-86; R Birch w Layer Breton and Layer Marney *Chelmsf* 86-96; rtd 96. *26 Ferndale Road, Lichfield, Staffs WS13 7DJ*

SPENCER, Peter Roy. b 40. CertEd. Sarum & Wells Th Coll 72. **d** 74 **p** 75. C Northampton St Alb *Pet* 74-77; TV Cov E *Cov* 77-90; V Erdington St Barn *Birm* from 90. *The Vicarage, 26 Church Road, Birmingham B24 9AX* Tel 0121-373 0884 or 350 9945

SPENCER, Richard Dennis. b 50. Imp Coll Lon BSc71. NTMTC 93. **d** 96 **p** 97. C Leek and Meerbrook *Lich* from 96. *Old Timbers, 5 Stockwell Street, Leek, Staffs ST13 6DH* Tel (01538) 383590

SPENCER, Richard Hugh. b 62. Univ of Wales (Cardiff) LLB84 BD88. St Mich Coll Llan 85. **d** 88 **p** 89. C Barry All SS *Llan* 88-90; Asst Chapl Univ of Wales (Cardiff) 90-92; Lect from 92; Tutor St Mich Coll Llan from 92. *St Michael's College, 54 Cardiff Road, Llandaff, Cardiff CF5 2YF* Tel (01222) 563379

SPENCER, Richard William Edward. b 33. WMMTC 78. **d** 81 **p** 82. NSM The Lickey *Birm* 81-83; Area Sec (Warks and W Midl) Chr Aid 83-93; Perm to Offic *Birm* 84-91 and from 95; Lic to Offic 91-95; Perm to Offic *Cov* from 85. *104 Witherford Way, Birmingham B29 4AW* Tel 0121-624 5344

SPENCER, Robert. b 48. St Jo Coll Nottm CertCS93. **d** 93 **p** 94. NSM Ellon *Ab* from 93; NSM Cruden Bay from 93. *12 Riverview Place, Ellon, Aberdeenshire AB41 9NW* Tel (01358) 723193

SPENCER, Roy Primett. b 26. Oak Hill Th Coll 50. **d** 53 **p** 54. C Bedford St Pet *St Alb* 53-55; C Luton Ch Ch 55-58; C Nottingham St Mary *S'well* 58-60; V Middlestown *Wakef* 60-61; Chapl Crumpsall Hosp Man 61-66; R Fleet *Linc* 66-69; V Accrington St Paul *Blackb* 69-78; V Woodplumpton 78-83; Chapl Preston Hosp N Shields 83-91; P-in-c Preston St Luke *Blackb* 83-89; P-in-c Preston St Luke and St Oswald 89-90; rtd 91; Perm to Offic *Blackb* from 91. *5 Hollywood Avenue, Penwortham, Preston PR1 9AS* Tel (01772) 743783

SPENCER, Dr Stephen Christopher. b 60. Ball Coll Ox BA82 DPhil90. Edin Th Coll 88. **d** 90 **p** 91. C Harlesden All So *Lon* 90-93; Zimbabwe from 93. *St James's Mission, PO Box 23, Nyamandhlovu, Zimbabwe* Tel Nyamandhlovu (87) 23419

SPENCER, Stephen Nigel Howard. b 53. Pemb Coll Ox BA75 Jes Coll Cam PGCE76. Trin Coll Bris 80. **d** 82 **p** 83. C Partington and Carrington *Ches* 82-85; C Brunswick *Man* 85-88; Chapl UEA *Nor* 88-92; rtd 92; Perm to Offic *Nor* from 92. *43 College Lane, Norwich NR4 6TW* Tel (01603) 506815

SPENCER, Mrs Susan. b 47. EMMTC 87. **d** 90 **p** 94. Par Dn Cotgrave *S'well* 90-94; C from 94. *Church House, 35 East Acres, Cotgrave, Notts NG12 3JP* Tel 0115-989 3478 Mobile 0850-469354

SPENCER-THOMAS, Owen Robert. b 40. Lon Univ BSc(Soc)70 LGSM96. Westcott Ho Cam 70. **d** 72 **p** 73. C S Kensington St Luke *Lon* 72-76; Lect Relig Studies S Kensington Inst 74-76; Dir Lon Chs Radio Workshop & Relig Producer BBC 76-78; Relig Producer Anglia TV 78-95; Lic to Offic *Lon* 76-86; Perm to Offic *Ely* 85-87; Perm to Offic *Lon* 86-87; Perm to Offic *Pet* from 86; NSM Cambridge Ascension *Ely* from 87; Chapl St Jo Coll Sch Cam from 93; Chapl St Bede's Sch Cam *Ely* from 97. *52 Windsor Road, Cambridge CB4 3JN* Tel (01223) 358446

SPENDLOVE, Mrs Lindsay Kate. b 55. Man Univ LLB77 Essex Univ BA88. EAMTC 89. **d** 92 **p** 94. NSM Lexden *Chelmsf* 92-94; NSM Colchester Ch Ch w St Mary V 94-96; NSM Pleshey from 97. *Stables, 4 Lexden Road, Colchester CO3 3NE* Tel (01206) 560495

SPERRING, Clive Michael. b 43. Oak Hill Th Coll 71. **d** 75 **p** 76. C Hawkwell *Chelmsf* 75-78; C-in-c Gt Baddow 78-82; New Zealand from 82. *49 Te Arawa Street, Orakei, Auckland 5, New Zealand* Tel Auckland (9) 528 4400 or 521 0296

SPICER, David John. b 49. Lon Univ BEd71. Linc Th Coll 76. **d** 78 **p** 79. C Upminster *Chelmsf* 78-80; C Mosborough *Sheff* 80-82; V Frisby-on-the-Wreake w Kirby Bellars *Leic* 82-84; Hon C Gt Ilford St Luke *Chelmsf* 85-88; C Cleethorpes *Linc* 88-90; C-in-c Stamford Ch Ch CD 90-92; V Stamford Ch Ch 92-96; P-in-c Cowbit 96-97; V Cowbit from 97. *The Vicarage, 2 Small Drove, Weston, Spalding, Lincs PE12 6HS* Tel (01406) 370152

SPICER, David John. b 52. Sussex Univ BA76 Lon Univ MTh78. Westcott Ho Cam 77. **d** 79 **p** 80. C E Dulwich St Jo *S'wark* 79-82; C Richmond St Mary w St Matthias and St Jo 82-87; V Lewisham St Swithun 87-91; Chapl Community of All Hallows Ditchingham from 91. *St Edmund's House, All Hallows Convent, Ditchingham, Bungay, Suffolk NR35 2DZ* Tel (01986) 892139

SPICER, Leigh Edwin. b 56. Sarum & Wells Th Coll 78. **d** 81 **p** 82. C Harborne St Pet *Birm* 81-83; C Bloxwich *Lich* 83-87; Chapl RAF from 87. *Chaplaincy Services (RAF), HQ, Personnel and Training Command, RAF Innsworth, Gloucester GL3 1EZ* Tel (01452) 712612 ext 5164 Fax 510828

SPICER, Nicolas. b 61. Univ of Wales (Lamp) BA84. Coll of Resurr Mirfield 84. **d** 86 **p** 87. C Westbury-on-Trym H Trin *Bris* 86-89; C Willesden Green St Andr and St Fran of Assisi *Lon* 89-93; Chapl Asst Charing Cross Hosp Lon 93-94; Asst Chapl Hammersmith Hosps NHS Trust from 94. *The Chaplaincy, Charing Cross Hospital, Fulham Palace Road, London W6 8RF* Tel 0181-846 1041 Fax 846 1111

SPIERS, The Ven Graeme Hendry Gordon. b 25. ALCD52. **d** 52 **p** 53. C Addiscombe St Mary *Cant* 52-56; Succ Bradf Cathl *Bradf* 56-58; V Speke All SS *Liv* 58-66; V Aigburth 66-80; RD Childwall 75-79; Hon Can Liv Cathl 77-91; Adn Liv 80-91; rtd 91; Perm to Offic *Liv* from 91. *19 Barkfield Lane, Formby, Merseyside L37 1LY* Tel (01704) 872902

SPIERS, Peter Hendry. b 61. St Jo Coll Dur BA82. Ridley Hall Cam 83. **d** 86 **p** 87. C W Derby St Luke *Liv* 86-90; TV Everton

St Pet 90-95; V Everton St Geo from 95. *St George's Vicarage, Northumberland Terrace, Liverpool L5 3QG* Tel 0151-263 1945

SPIKIN, Simon John Overington. b 48. Linc Th Coll 70. **d** 75 **p** 76. C Sawbridgeworth *St Alb* 75-79; C Odiham w S Warnborough and Long Sutton *Win* 79-81; R Dickleburgh w Thelveton w Frenze and Shimpling *Nor* 81-82; P-in-c Rushall 81-82; R Dickleburgh, Langmere, Shimpling, Thelveton etc 82-95; rtd 96. *Marley Court, Kingston, Canterbury, Kent CT4 6JH* Tel (01227) 832405

SPILLER, David Roger. b 44. St Jo Coll Dur BA70 Fitzw Coll Cam BA72 MA76 Nottm Univ DipAdEd80. Ridley Hall Cam 70. **d** 73 **p** 74. C Bradf Cathl *Bradf* 73-77; C Stratford-on-Avon w Bishopton *Cov* 77-80; Chapl Geo Eliot Hosp Nuneaton 80-90; V Chilvers Coton w Astley *Cov* 80-90; RD Nuneaton 84-90; Prin Aston Tr Scheme from 90; Lic to Offic *Birm* from 90. *Christ Church, Church Square, Oldbury, W Midlands B69 4DY* Tel 0121-544 2227

SPILLER, Edward William. b 32. Cranmer Hall Dur. **d** 82 **p** 83. C Kirkleatham *York* 82-85; R The Thorntons and The Otteringtons from 85. *The Vicarage, Thornton le Moor, Northallerton, N Yorkshire DL7 9DT* Tel (01609) 774232

SPILMAN, Derrick Geoffrey. b 27. Roch Th Coll. **d** 63 **p** 64. C Dover St Mary *Cant* 63-67; CF 67-71; Canada from 71. *5398 Walter Place, Burnaby, British Columbia, Canada V5G 4K2*

SPILSBURY, Stephen Ronald Paul. b 39. Nottm Univ BSc69 MPhil72. Linc Th Coll 71. **d** 64 **p** 65. In RC Ch 64-71; C Cricklade w Latton *Bris* 72-75; P-in-c Swindon All SS 76-81; V Lawrence Weston 81-95; RD Westbury and Severnside 89-91. *10 Woodside Grove, Bristol BS10 7RF* Tel 0117-959 1079

SPINDLER, Miss Jane Diana. b 54. Southn Univ BA75 CertEd76. Wycliffe Hall Ox 87. **d** 89 **p** 94. Par Dn Bishopsworth *Bris* 89-93; Par Dn Brislington St Luke 93-94; C 94; rtd 95; Perm to Offic *Bris* from 95. *143 Highridge Road, Bishopsworth, Bristol BS13 8HT* Tel 0117-935 8137

SPINK, Canon George Arthur Peter. b 26. Oak Hill Th Coll 54. **d** 56 **p** 57. C Thurnby w Stoughton *Leic* 56-58; C-in-c Thurnby Lodge CD 58-59; Chapl Bonn w Cologne *Eur* 59-62; Chapl Vienna w Budapest and Prague 62-68; Chapl Cov Cathl *Cov* 68-70; Can Res Cov Cathl 70-77; Warden The Dorothy Kerin Trust Burrswood 77-81; Prior Omega Order from 80; Lic to Offic *Roch* 80-86; Lic to Offic *B & W* 86-95; rtd 89. *The Priory, Winford Manor, Winford, Bristol BS18 8DW* Tel (01275) 472262 Fax 472065

SPINKS, Dr Bryan Douglas. b 48. FRHistS85 St Chad's Coll Dur BA70 DipTh71 BD79 K Coll Lon MTh72 Dur Univ DD88. **d** 75 **p** 76. C Witham *Chelmsf* 75-78; C Clacton St Jas 78-79; Lic to Offic *Ely* from 80; Chapl Chu Coll Cam from 80; Affiliated Lect Div Cam Univ from 82; Perm to Offic *St Alb* from 84. *97 Shakespeare Road, Eaton Socon, St Neots, Huntingdon, Cambs PE19 3HT* Tel (01480) 476790 Fax as telephone

SPINKS, Christopher George (Chris). b 53. Brighton Poly HND80. Oak Hill Th Coll BA88. **d** 88 **p** 89. C Hove Bp Hannington Memorial Ch *Chich* 88-92; Travelling Sec UCCF 92-95; Lic to Offic *Chich* from 92; Itinerant Min from 95. *35 St Heliers Avenue, Hove, E Sussex BN3 5RE* Tel (01273) 730027

SPINKS, John Frederick. b 40. Westmr Coll Ox MTh97. Oak Hill Th Coll 79. **d** 82 **p** 83. NSM Roxbourne St Andr *Lon* 82-89; C Northwood H Trin 89-93; P-in-c Greenhill St Jo 93-96; V from 96. *St John's Vicarage, 11 Flambard Road, Harrow, Middx HA1 2NB* Tel 0181-907 7956 or 863 3690

SPINNEY, Giles Martin. b 16. Ch Coll Cam BA39 MA43. Wycliffe Hall Ox 39. **d** 41 **p** 42. C Oakwood St Thos *Lon* 41-46; V Roxeth Ch Ch 46-50; R Kersal Moor *Man* 50-54; R Brixton Deverill *Sarum* 54-72; R Kingston Deverill w Monkton Deverill 55-72; R The Deverills 72-81; rtd 81. *17 Chancery Lane, Warminster, Wilts BA12 9JS* Tel (01985) 214813

SPITTLE, Robin. b 57. St Jo Coll Nottm 84. **d** 86 **p** 87. C Ipswich St Fran *St E* 86-91; Min Shotley St Mary CD 91-92; R Shotley from 92. *The Vicarage, 2 Gate Farm Road, Shotley, Ipswich IP9 1QH* Tel (01473) 788166

SPIVEY, Colin. b 35. ACII61 Ex Univ DSA68. Oak Hill Th Coll 74. **d** 76 **p** 77. C Egham *Guildf* 76-79; C Edgware *Lon* 79-83; R Haworth *Bradf* 83-95; V Thorpe Edge from 95. *The Vicarage, Northwood Crescent, Bradford, W Yorkshire BD10 9HX* Tel (01274) 613246

SPIVEY, Canon Peter. b 19. Edin Th Coll 46. **d** 48 **p** 49. C Dewsbury Moor *Wakef* 48-50; C Mirfield 50-53; R Whitwood Mere 53-61; V Meltham 61-85; RD Blackmoorfoot 79-85; Hon Can Wakef Cathl 81-85; rtd 85; Perm to Offic *Wakef* from 85. *3 Follett Avenue, Huddersfield HD4 5LW* Tel (01484) 654674

SPIVEY, Ronald. b 28. ACMA MInstAM. EMMTC 83. **d** 86 **p** 87. NSM Sutton St Mary *Linc* from 86. *5 Lancaster Drive, Long Sutton, Spalding, Lincs PE12 9BD* Tel (01406) 362084

SPOKES, Keith John. b 29. EAMTC. **d** 84 **p** 85. NSM Bury St Edmunds St Mary *St E* 84-89; P-in-c Helmingham w Framsden and Pettaugh w Winston 89-92; rtd 93. *16 Croft Rise, Bury St Edmunds, Suffolk IP33 2PY* Tel (01284) 706742

SPONG, Terence John. b 32. CLJ. Roch Th Coll 63. **d** 66 **p** 67. C Forton *Portsm* 66-68; Rhodesia 68-80; Zimbabwe 80-84; R Christow, Ashton, Trusham and Bridford *Ex* 84-86; Chapl Puerto de la Cruz Tenerife *Eur* 86-93; Miss to Seamen 86-93; rtd 93; Perm to Offic *Win* from 93; Chapl Christchurch Hosp from 97. *14B Stuart Road, Highcliffe, Christchurch, Dorset BH23 5JS* Tel (01425) 277833

SPOONER, Anthony Patrick David (Tony). b 45. Univ Coll of Rhodesia Univ Coll of Nyasaland BA68 Nottm Univ DipTh72. Linc Th Coll 71. **d** 74 **p** 75. C Glynde, W Firle and Beddingham *Chich* 74-77; Rhodesia 77-80; Zimbabwe 80-86; P-in-c Clacton St Jas *Chelmsf* 86-90; V from 90. *St James's Vicarage, 44 Wash Lane, Clacton-on-Sea, Essex CO15 1DA* Tel (01255) 422007

SPOOR, Norman Leslie. b 15. BSc PhD DipTh. Ripon Coll Cuddesdon. **d** 83 **p** 83. NSM Steventon w Milton *Ox* 88-90; NSM Abingdon 90-92; Perm to Offic 92-96. *4 Ladygrove Paddock, Drayton Road, Abingdon, Oxon OX14 5HT* Tel (01235) 528750

SPOTTISWOODE, Anthony Derek. b 25. Solicitor 50 Pemb Coll Cam BA47 MA86. Sarum & Wells Th Coll 85. **d** 86 **p** 87. C Hampstead St Jo *Lon* 86-94; rtd 95. *Flat 2, 26 Belsize Lane, London NW3 5AB* Tel 0171-435 6756

SPRACKLING, Frederick Phillips. b 16. Bible Churchmen's Coll 37. **d** 40 **p** 41. C Spitalfields Ch Ch w All SS *Lon* 40-46; R Botus Fleming *Truro* 46-49; V Islington All SS *Lon* 49-57; V Stamford Brook 57-81; rtd 81. *1 Tyrrell Square, Mitcham, Surrey CR4 3SD* Tel 0181-687 1614

SPRATLEY, Deryck Edward. b 30. BSc. Oak Hill Th Coll 62. **d** 64 **p** 65. C Ramsgate St Luke *Cant* 64-67; C W Holloway St Dav *Lon* 67-73; V Upper Holloway St Pet 73-79; V Upper Holloway St Pet w St Jo 79-82; P-in-c Dagenham *Chelmsf* 82-88; P-in-c Becontree St Geo 84-88; TR Dagenham 88-93; rtd 93; Perm to Offic *Chelmsf* from 93. *35 Upper Second Avenue, Frinton-on-Sea, Essex CO13 9LP* Tel (01255) 851216

SPRATT, Laurence Herbert. b 28. Linc Th Coll 76. **d** 78 **p** 79. C Mexborough *Sheff* 78-80; R Wrentham w Benacre, Covehithe, Frostenden etc *St E* 80-88; Perm to Offic *Arg* 89-90; P-in-c Inveraray 90-91; Perm to Offic from 91; rtd 93. *Inver, Minard, Inveraray, Argyll PA32 8YB* Tel (01546) 886276

SPRATT, Robert Percival (Bob). b 31. MRSH83. Carl Dioc Tr Inst 84. **d** 87 **p** 88. NSM Kendal St Thos *Carl* 87-89; Chapl HM Pris Preston 89-95; Perm to Offic *Blackb* from 95. *c/o Christian Literature Society, 35 Market Place, Kendal, Lancs LA9 4TP* Tel (01539) 720475

SPRAY, Canon Charles Alan Francis Thomas. b 27. ARSM51 Lon Univ BScEng51. Ridley Hall Cam 57. **d** 59 **p** 60. C Chich St Pancras and St Jo *Chich* 59-63; V Shipley 63-69; R Ore 70-85; V Burgess Hill St Andr 85-93; Can and Preb Chich Cathl 88-93; rtd 93; Perm to Offic *Chich* from 93. *6 Silverdale Road, Burgess Hill, W Sussex RH15 0EF* Tel (01444) 232149

SPRAY, John William. b 29. Sarum & Wells Th Coll 71. **d** 73 **p** 74. C Clayton *Lich* 73-77; V Hartshill 77-82; P-in-c Aston 82-83; P-in-c Stone St Mich 82-83; P-in-c Stone St Mich w Aston St Sav 83-84; R 84-90; rtd 90. *2 Belvoir Avenue, Trentham, Stoke-on-Trent ST4 8SY* Tel (01782) 644959

SPRAY, Richard Alan. b 43. **d** 88 **p** 89. NSM Cotgrave *S'well* 88-96; P-in-c Kingston and Ratcliffe-on-Soar from 96; P-in-c Thrumpton from 96; P-in-c Barton in Fabis from 96. *The Rectory, Church Lane, Barton in Fablis, Nottingham NG11 0AG* Tel 0115-983 0252

SPREAD, John Henry Seymour. b 14. MC46. Lon Univ BA37. Chich Th Coll 38. **d** 39 **p** 41. C Portsea St Steph *Portsm* 39-42; C W Hyde St Thos *St Alb* 42-44; CF 44-47; C Letchworth St Paul *St Alb* 47-49; V Ridgmont 49-53; V Sundon w Streatley 53-79; rtd 79; Hon C Gt w Lt Hormead, Anstey, Brent Pelham etc *St Alb* 79-89; Hon C Much Hadham 89-91; Perm to Offic from 91. *1 Old Red Lion, Much Hadham, Herts SG10 6DD* Tel (01279) 843140

SPRENT, Michael Francis (Brother Giles). b 34. Ex Coll Ox BA58 MA62. Kelham Th Coll 58. **d** 61 **p** 62. C Plaistow St Andr *Chelmsf* 61-63; SSF from 61; Papua New Guinea 65-69; Hilfield Friary 69-74 and 77-78; Alnmouth Friary 74-76; Harbledown Friary 78-82; Sweden 76-77; TV High Stoy *Sarum* 77-78; Solomon Is from 83. *La Verna Friary, Hautambu, PO Box 519, Honiara, Solomon Islands*

SPRIGGS, Harold. b 99. Dorchester Miss Coll 29. **d** 31 **p** 32. C Wednesbury St Paul Wood Green *Lich* 31-34; Australia 34-39; R Kingsley *Lich* 39-47; Chapl Garvald Sch Peeblesshire 47-48; C Edin Old St Paul *Edin* 48; V Shobnall *Lich* 48-60; V Mountfield *Chich* 60-85; V Netherfield 60-85; rtd 85; Perm to Offic *Chich* from 85. *2 Church Cottages, Mountfield, Robertsbridge, E Sussex TN32 5JS* Tel (01580) 880261

SPRIGGS, John David Robert. b 36. BNC Ox BA58 MA63. S'wark Ord Course 73. **d** 75 **p** 76. Lic to Offic *Ox* from 75; Chapl Pangbourne Coll from 95. *St Vincent, Bere Court Road, Pangbourne, Reading RG8 8JY* Tel 0118-984 4933

SPRINGATE, Paul Albert Edward. b 48. Oak Hill Th Coll 81. **d** 83 **p** 84. C Pennycross *Ex* 83-87; P-in-c Cossington and Seagrave *Leic* 87; TV Sileby, Cossington and Seagrave 87-96; Chapl and Warden Harnhill Healing Cen from 96. *Harnhill Christian Healing Centre, Cirencester, Glos GL7 5PX* Tel (01285) 850283 Fax 850 519

SPRINGBETT, John Howard. b 47. Pemb Coll Cam BA70 MA74. Ridley Hall Cam 70. **d** 72 **p** 73. C Ulverston St Mary w H Trin *Carl* 72-76; V Dewsbury Moor *Wakef* 76-84; V Hoddesdon *St Alb* from 84; RD Cheshunt from 94. *The Vicarage, 11 Amwell Street, Hoddesdon, Herts EN11 8TS* Tel (01992) 462127

SPRINGETT, Robert Wilfred. b 62. Nottm Univ BTh89. Linc Th Coll 86. **d** 89 **p** 90. C Colchester St Jas, All SS, St Nic and St Runwald *Chelmsf* 89-92; C Basildon St Martin w Nevendon 92-94; P-in-c Belhus Park from 94; P-in-c S Ockendon from 94. *The Vicarage, 121 Foyle Drive, South Ockendon, Essex RM15 5HF* Tel (01708) 853246

SPRINGETT, Simon Paul. b 56. Warw Univ LLB78. Wycliffe Hall Ox 78. **d** 81 **p** 82. C Harlow St Mary and St Hugh w St Jo the Bapt *Chelmsf* 81-84; C Gt Clacton 84-86; R Rayne 86-91; Chapl RN from 91. *Royal Naval Chaplaincy Service, Room 203, Victory Building, HM Naval Base, Portsmouth PO1 3LS* Tel (01705) 727903 Fax 727112

SPRINGFORD, Patrick Francis Alexander. b 45. Wycliffe Hall Ox 71. **d** 74 **p** 75. C Finchley Ch Ch *Lon* 74-79; CF from 79. *MOD Chaplains (Army), Trenchard Lines, Upavon, Pewsey, Wilts SN9 6BE* Tel (01980) 615804 Fax 615800

SPRINGHAM, Desmond John. b 32. Bris Univ BA56. Oak Hill Th Coll 56. **d** 58 **p** 59. C St Alb St Paul *St Alb* 58-61; C Reading St Jo *Ox* 61-66; R Worting *Win* 66-80; V Jersey St Andr 80-97; rtd 97. *19 Balmoral Crescent, Fordington Fields, Dorchester, Dorset DT1 2BN* Tel (01534) 34975

SPRINGTHORPE, David Frederick. b 47. Open Univ BA. AKC72. **d** 73 **p** 74. C Dartford St Alb *Roch* 73-77; C Biggin Hill 77-80; R Ash 80-89; R Ridley 80-89; R Eynsford w Farningham and Lullingstone 89-94; V Barnehurst from 94. *The Vicarage, 93 Pelham Road, Barnehurst, Bexleyheath, Kent DA7 4LY* Tel (01322) 523344

SPROSTON, Bernard Melvin. b 37. St Jo Coll Dur 77. **d** 79 **p** 80. C Westlands St Andr *Lich* 79-82; P-in-c Heage *Derby* 82-87; V Heath from 87. *The Vicarage, Main Street, Heath, Chesterfield, Derbyshire S44 5RX* Tel (01246) 850339

SPROULE, Gerald Norman. b 26. TCD DBS60. **d** 60 **p** 61. C Monaghan *Clogh* 60-62; I Cleenish 62-68; I Magheracross 68-73; Admin Sec (Ireland) BCMS 73-79; I Belfast St Aid *Conn* 79-86; I Magherally w Annaclone *D & D* 86-94; rtd 94. *4 Hilden Park, Lisburn, Co Antrim BT27 4UG* Tel (01846) 601528

SPURGEON, Michael Paul. b 53. MIEx. Linc Th Coll 83. **d** 85 **p** 86. C Lillington *Cov* 85-89; C Min Can Ripon Cathl *Ripon* 89-95; R Lower Nidderdale from 95. *Lower Nidderdale Rectory, Old Church Green, Kirk Hammerton, York YO5 8DL* Tel (01423) 331142

SPURIN, Canon Richard Mark. b 28. Peterho Cam BA52 MA60. Wycliffe Hall Ox 54. **d** 55 **p** 56. C Foleshill St Laur *Cov* 55-58; C Atherstone 58-60; CMS 60-61; Kenya 61-73; C-in-c Ewell St Paul Howell Hill CD *Guildf* 73-82; V Netherton *Liv* 82-86; V Brandwood *Birm* 86-91; C Padiham *Blackb* 91-93; Hon Can Nambale Cathl Kenya from 92; rtd 93; Perm to Offic *Blackb* from 93. *93 Westbourne Avenue South, Burnley, Lancs BB11 4QZ* Tel (01282) 421402

SPURR, Andrew. b 58. St Jo Coll Dur BA80. Ripon Coll Cuddesdon 80 Roch Div Sch (USA) 84 Qu Coll Birm 92. **d** 93 **p** 94. C Rainham *Roch* 93-96; C Stansted Mountfitchet *Chelmsf* 96; C Stansted Mountfitchet w Birchanger and Farnham from 97. *43 Gilbey Crescent, Stansted, Essex CM24 8DT*

SPURR, Roger Colin. b 29. Linc Th Coll. **d** 82 **p** 83. C Street w Walton *B & W* 82-85; R Stogumber w Nettlecombe and Monksilver 85-95; rtd 95. *15 Abbey Gate, Morpeth, Northd NE61 2XL* Tel (01670) 514561

SPURRELL, John Mark. b 34. FSA87 CCC Ox BA57 DipTh58 MA61. Linc Th Coll 58. **d** 60 **p** 61. C Tilbury Docks *Chelmsf* 60-65; C Boston *Linc* 65-76; R Stow in Lindsey 76-85; P-in-c Willingham 76-85; P-in-c Coates 76-85; P-in-c Brightwell w Sotwell *Ox* 85-97; rtd 97. *10 The Liberty, Wells, Somerset BA5 2SU* Tel (01749) 678966

SPURRIER, Richard Patrick Montague. b 25. Bris Univ BA59. Wycliffe Hall Ox 59. **d** 61 **p** 62. C S Lyncombe *B & W* 61-63; C Weston St Jo 63-64; rtd 90. *48 Longford Road, Melksham, Wilts SN12 6AU* Tel (01225) 707419

SQUAREY, Canon Gerald Stephen Miles. b 36. Lich Th Coll 59. **d** 62 **p** 63. C Poplar All SS w St Frideswide *Lon* 62-64; C Heston 64-67; V Bradford Abbas w Clifton Maybank *Sarum* 67-74; P-in-c Corfe Castle 74-79; R 79-84; R Steeple w Tyneham, Church Knowle and Kimmeridge 79-84; R Corfe Castle, Church Knowle, Kimmeridge etc 84-90; P-in-c Pimperne 90-91; P-in-c Stourpaine, Durweston and Bryanston 90-91; R Pimperne, Stourpaine, Durweston and Bryanston from 91; RD Milton and Blandford from 91; Can and Preb Sarum Cathl from 92. *The Vicarage, Shaston Road, Stourpaine, Blandford Forum, Dorset DT11 8TA* Tel (01258) 480580

SQUIRE, Clenyg. b 31. TCert53. Cuddesdon Coll 89. **d** 90 **p** 91. NSM Hale and Ashley *Ches* 90-93; P-in-c Kingsley 93-95; Perm to Offic *Man* from 95; Perm to Offic *Ches* from 95. *10 Higher Downs, Altrincham, Cheshire WA14 2QL* Tel 0161-928 3346

SQUIRE, David George Mitchell. b 31. Worc Coll Ox BA54 MA58. Qu Coll Birm DipTh66. **d** 67 **p** 68. C Dursley *Glouc* 67-70; V Cam 71-77; Org Sec (Dios Birm, Heref, Lich and Worc) CECS 77-88; Perm to Offic *Heref* from 81; rtd 88. *Ty Gwyn, Dihewyd, Lampeter SA48 7PP* Tel (01570) 470260

SQUIRE, Geoffrey Frank. b 36. Ex & Truro NSM Scheme. **d** 83 **p** 84. NSM Barnstaple, Goodleigh and Landkey *Ex* 83-85; NSM Barnstaple from 85. *Little Cross, Northleigh Hill, Goodleigh, Barnstaple, Devon EX32 7NR* Tel (01271) 44935

SQUIRE, Humphrey Edward. b 29. St Chad's Coll Dur BA55. Coll of Resurr Mirfield. **d** 57 **p** 58. C Newbold w Dunston *Derby* 57-59; C Thorpe *Nor* 59-61; Zanzibar 61-63; C Whittington *Derby* 63-64; R Drayton *Nor* 64-75; Chapl Dover Coll 75-83; TV Wareham *Sarum* 83-94; rtd 94. *La Retraite, Burbidge Close, Lytchett Matravers, Poole, Dorset BH16 6EG* Tel (01929) 552756

SQUIRE, Preb John Brinsmead. b 16. St Edm Hall Ox BA38 MA43. Linc Th Coll 38. **d** 40 **p** 40. C Knowle *Bris* 40-41; C Bath Bathwick *B & W* 41-45 and 48-51; C Walsall St Andr *Lich* 45-46; C Lower Gornal 47-48; V Bridgwater H Trin *B & W* 51-57; V Taunton St Andr 57-81; Preb Wells Cathl from 77; rtd 81. *Xanadu, 1 St Mary Street, Nether Stowey, Bridgwater, Somerset TA5 1LJ* Tel (01278) 732957

SQUIRES, John Wallace Howden. b 45. Sydney Univ BA67 Lon Univ BD75. Moore Th Coll Sydney ThL74. **d** 76 **p** 76. Australia 76-78 and from 80; C Luton St Mary *St Alb* 78-79. *37 Arabella Street, Longueville, Sydney, NSW, Australia 2066* Tel Sydney (2) 427-2666 Fax 418 9920

SQUIRES, Malcolm. b 46. St Chad's Coll Dur BA72. Cuddesdon Coll 72. **d** 74 **p** 75. C Headingley *Ripon* 74-77; C Stanningley St Thos 77-80; V Bradshaw *Wakef* 80-85; V Ripponden 85-89; V Barkisland w W Scammonden 85-89; V Mirfield 89-96; R Wrexham *St As* from 96. *The Rectory, 7 Westminster Drive, Wrexham LL12 7AT* Tel (01978) 263905

SSERUNKUMA, Michael Wilberforce. b 54. Trin Coll Bris DipHE88 BA90 Bp Tucker Coll Mukono 77. **d** 77 **p** 78. Uganda 77-87; C Gabalfa *Llan* 90-94; TV Cyncoed *Mon* 94-95; R Canton St Jo *Llan* from 95. *The Rectory, 3A Romilly Road, Cardiff CF1 1FH* Tel (01222) 229683

STABLES, Courtley Greenwood. b 13. Keble Coll Ox BA49 MA54. St Steph Ho Ox 48. **d** 50 **p** 51. C Watlington *Ox* 50-51; C Bracknell 51-55; Br Honduras 55-57; C Guildf H Trin w St Mary *Guildf* 57-61; Chapl Bedford Modern Sch 61-63; Sen Lect Coll of All SS Tottenham 63-72; Chmn Coun of Ch Schs Co 68-87; C St Andr Undershaft w St Mary Axe *Lon* 64-72; Hon C Uckfield *Chich* from 72; rtd 78. *Abotslare, Pound Green, Buxted, E Sussex TN22 4JZ* Tel (01825) 732467

STABLES, Miss Katharine Ruth. b 45. DipInstHSM70 R Holloway Coll Lon BA67. WMMTC 90. **d** 93 **p** 94. NSM Knutton *Lich* from 93; NSM Silverdale and Alsagers Bank 93-96; Soc Resp Officer from 96. *19 Kennet Close, Newcastle, Staffs ST5 4ER* Tel (01782) 633430

STACEY, Dr Helen Norman. Edin Univ MB, ChB45 PhD49. S'wark Ord Course 82. **dss** 83 **d** 87 **p** 94. Notting Hill St Jo and St Pet *Lon* 83-85; Upper Kennet *Sarum* 85-87; Hon Par Dn 87-93; Perm to Offic from 93. *Greystones House, Green Street, Avebury, Marlborough, Wilts SN8 1RE* Tel (01672) 539289

STACEY, Nicolas David. b 27. St Edm Hall Ox BA51 MA55. Cuddesdon Coll 51. **d** 53 **p** 54. C Portsea N End St Mark *Portsm* 53-58; Bp's Dom Chapl *Birm* 58-59; R Woolwich St Mary w H Trin *S'wark* 59-68; Boro Dean Greenwich 65-68; Dep Dir Oxfam 68-70; Perm to Offic *Ox* 68-71; P-in-c Selling *Cant* 76-78; Perm to Offic 79-84 and from 90; Six Preacher Cant Cathl 84-90; rtd 92. *The Old Vicarage, Selling, Faversham, Kent ME13 9RD* Tel (01227) 752833

STACEY (née O'BRIEN), Mrs Shelagh Ann. b 55. RGN83 Bedf Coll Lon BSc77. N Ord Course 89. **d** 92 **p** 94. Par Dn S Elmsall *Wakef* 92-94; C 94-95; C Carleton 95-97; P-in-c from 97; C E Hardwick 95-97; P-in-c from 97. *The Vicarage, 10 East Close, Pontefract, W Yorkshire WF8 3NS* Tel (01977) 702478

STACEY, Timothy Andrew (Tim). b 58. Imp Coll Lon BSc79 York Univ PGCE83. St Jo Coll Nottm DTS94. **d** 94 **p** 95. C Chorleywood Ch Ch *St Alb* from 94. *19 Highfield Way, Rickmansworth, Herts WD3 2PP* Tel (01923) 777966

STACEY, Canon Victor George. b 44. NUI BA69 QUB MTh. CITC 72. **d** 72 **p** 73. C Derriaghy *Conn* 72-76; C Knock *D & D* 76-79; I Ballymacarrett St Martin 79-86; I Dublin Santry w Glasnevin *D & G* 86-95; Bp's Dom Chapl from 90; RD Fingal 90-95; I Dun Laoghaire from 95; Prov and Dioc Registrar from 95; Preb Maynooth St Patr Cathl Dublin from 97. *Christ Church Vicarage, 2 Park Road, Dun Laoghaire, Co Dublin, Irish Republic* Tel Dublin (1) 280 9537

STACKPOLE, Robert Aaron. b 59. Williams Coll Mass BA82 Or Coll Ox MLitt88. St Steph Ho Ox 88. **d** 90 **p** 91. C Kettering SS Pet and Paul *Pet* 90-93; Canada from 93. *c/o Mrs Alice Stackpole, 378 Syasset-Woodbury Road, Woodbury, New York 11797, USA*

STAFF, Mrs Jean. b 44. CertEd64. EMMTC 81. **dss** 84 **d** 87 **p** 94. Old Brumby *Linc* 84-87; C 87-88; C Gainsborough St Geo 88-91; D-in-c 91-94; P-in-c 94-96; P-in-c Haxey from 96; P-in-c Owston from 96. *The Vicarage, Church Street, Haxey, Doncaster DN9 2HY* Tel (01427) 752351

STAFF, Miss Susan. b 59. Leeds Univ BA82. Ridley Hall Cam 88. **d** 90 **p** 94. Par Dn Mickleover All SS *Derby* 90-93; Par Dn Chatham St Wm *Roch* 93-94; C 94-97; TV Walton Milton Keynes *Ox* from 97. *The Rectory, Broughton, Milton Keynes MK10 9AA* Tel (01908) 667846

STAFFORD, David George. b 45. Qu Coll Birm 75. **d** 77 **p** 78. C Chesterfield St Aug *Derby* 77-80; C Ranmoor *Sheff* 80-83; V

Bolton-upon-Dearne from 83. *The Vicarage, 41 Station Road, Bolton-on-Dearne, Rotherham, S Yorkshire S63 8AA* Tel (01709) 893163

STAFFORD, Canon John Ingham Henry. b 31. TCD BA52 MA58. **d** 53 **p** 55. C Clonallon *D & D* 53-56; C Belfast Malone St Jo *Conn* 56-59; Australia 59-64; Min Can Down Cathl *D & D* 64-68; Hd of S Ch Miss Ballymacarrett 68-73; I Bright w Killough 73-83; C Bangor Primacy 83-92; Can Down Cathl 90-92; I Urney w Sion Mills *D & R* from 92. *112 Melmount Road, Sion Mills, Strabane, Co Tyrone BT82 9PY* Tel (01662) 658020

STAFFORD-WHITTAKER, William Paul. b 69. Chich Th Coll DipTh94. **d** 94 **p** 95. C Brighton Resurr *Chich* from 94. *St Martin's House, 6 Edinburgh Road, Brighton BN2 3HY* Tel (01273) 620232

STAFFORD, Area Bishop of. *See* HILL, The Rt Revd Christopher John

STAGG, Charles Roy. b 18. G&C Coll Cam BA45 MA47. Ripon Hall Ox 47. **d** 48 **p** 49. Chapl Dur Sch 48-54; C The Lickey *Birm* 54-55; Uganda 55-58; Chapl Aldenham Sch Herts 59-64; Kenya 64-80; Perm to Offic *Glouc* from 81. *Wyck Cottage, Childswickham, Broadway, Worcs WR12 7HF* Tel (01386) 853229

STAGG, Jeremy Michael. b 47. Leeds Univ BSc69 Fontainebleau MBA77. Sarum & Wells Th Coll 90. **d** 92 **p** 93. C Basing *Win* 92-96; P-in-c Barton, Pooley Bridge and Martindale *Carl* from 96; Hon CMS Rep from 96. *The Vicarage, Pooley Bridge, Penrith, Cumbria CA10 2LT* Tel (01768) 486220

STAGG, Michael Hubert. b 39. St Chad's Coll Dur 58. **d** 63 **p** 64. C Weston-super-Mare St Sav *B & W* 63-66; P-in-c Fosdyke *Linc* 66-71; R Brompton Regis w Upton and Skilgate *B & W* 71-78; P-in-c Kidderminster St Jo *Worc* 78-80; P-in-c Cannington *B & W* 80-84; R Cannington, Otterhampton, Combwich and Stockland 84-87; Dioc Communications Officer *Nor* 88-93; Bp's Chapl 88-93; R Sprowston w Beeston from 93; RD Nor N from 95. *The Vicarage, 2 Wroxham Road, Norwich NR7 8TZ* Tel (01603) 426492

STAINER, Richard Bruce. b 62. Linc Th Coll 92. **d** 94 **p** 95. C N Walsham w Antingham *Nor* from 94. *35 Kimberley Road, North Walsham, Norfolk NR28 9DZ* Tel (01692) 404755

STAINES, Edward Noel. b 26. Trin Coll Ox MA52 MSc85. Chich Th Coll 51 57. **d** 57 **p** 58. C Eastbourne St Mary *Chich* 57-61; V Amberley w N Stoke 61-70; V Forest Row 70-75; R Ashurst 70-75; V Bexhill St Aug 75-79; TR Ovingdean w Rottingdean and Woodingdean 79-85; V Rottingdean 85-86; Perm to Offic *Worc* from 86; Perm to Offic *Glouc* 86-88; Chapl Gtr Lisbon *Eur* 88-90; Chapl Marseille 90; rtd 90. *White House, Harpley Road, Defford, Worcester WR8 9BL* Tel (01386) 750817

STAINES, Michael John. b 28. Trin Coll Ox BA52 MA56. Wells Th Coll 62. **d** 64 **p** 65. C Southwick *Chich* 64-67; TV Harling Gp *Nor* 67-73; PM S Chilterns Gp *Ox* 74-75; R W Wycombe w Bledlow Ridge, Bradenham and Radnage 76-93; RD Wycombe 83-87; rtd 93; Perm to Offic *Heref* from 93. *Upper Town Cottage, Berrington, Tenbury Wells, Worcs WR15 8TH* Tel (01584) 811533

STALEY, John Colin George. b 44. Hull Univ MA83. Wycliffe Hall Ox 68. **d** 71 **p** 72. C Tinsley *Sheff* 71-73; C Slaithwaite w E Scammonden *Wakef* 73-75; V Wakef St Andr and St Mary 75-80; Warden Scargill Ho 80-82; P-in-c Macclesfield St Pet *Ches* 82-85; TV Macclesfield Team Par from 85; Dioc Ind Missr from 87; Sen Ind Chapl from 91. *261 Oxford Road, Macclesfield, Cheshire SK11 8JY* Tel (01625) 423851

STALKER, William John. b 49. N Ord Course 89. **d** 91 **p** 92. C Formby H Trin *Liv* 91-94; V Stoneycroft All SS from 94. *All Saints' Vicarage, West Oak Hill Park, Liverpool L13 4BW* Tel 0151-228 3581

STALLARD, Canon Frederick Hugh. b 11. Pemb Coll Cam BA33 MA37. Cuddesdon Coll 33. **d** 34 **p** 35. C Northampton St Matt *Pet* 34-40; CF (EC) 40-45; V Pet All SS *Pet* 46-81; RD Pet 52-68; Can Pet Cathl 57-81; rtd 81; Perm to Offic *Ely* from 81. *3 Friday Bridge Road, Elm, Wisbech, Cambs PE14 0AR* Tel (01945) 860812

STALLARD, John Charles. b 34. Selw Coll Cam BA58 MA62. Ripon Hall Ox 62. **d** 64 **p** 65. C Hall Green Ascension *Birm* 64-66; C Sutton Coldfield H Trin 66-68; C-in-c Brandwood CD 68-71; Chapl Dame Allan's Schs Newc 71-74; V Warley Woods *Birm* 75-84; TR Droitwich *Worc* 84-87; P-in-c Dodderhill 84-87; TR Droitwich Spa 87-94; V Pensnett from 94. *The Vicarage, Vicarage Lane, Pensnett, Brierley Hill, W Midlands DY5 4JH* Tel (01384) 262666

STALLARD, Ms Mary Kathleen Rose. b 67. Selw Coll Cam BA88 Lon Inst of Educn PGCE90. Qu Coll Birm 91. **d** 93 **p** 97. C Newport St Matt *Mon* 93-96; P-in-c Ysbyty Cynfyn w Llantrisant and Eglwys Newydd *St D* 96-97; V from 97. *The Vicarage, Ysbyty Cynfyn, Ponterwyd, Aberystwyth SY23 3JR* Tel (01970) 890663

STALLEY, Brian Anthony. b 38. Oak Hill Th Coll 60. **d** 63 **p** 64. C Summerstown *S'wark* 63-70; Surrey BFBS Sec 70-73; Manager Action Cen BFBS 73-76; R Branston *Linc* 76-91; rtd 91; Perm to Offic *Linc* from 91. *6 Sunningdale Grove, Washingborough, Lincoln LN4 1SP* Tel (01522) 794164 Fax as telephone

STAMFORD, Brian. b 37. **d** 91 **p** 92. CMS 88-95; Uganda 88-95; P-in-c North Hill and Lewannick *Truro* from 95. *The Rectory, North Hill, Launceston, Cornwall PL15 7PQ* Tel (01566) 782806

STAMP, Andrew Nicholas. b 44. Ex Univ BA67. Sarum Th Coll 67. **d** 69 **p** 70. C S Beddington St Mich *S'wark* 69-73; Tutor Sarum & Wells Th Coll 73-76; Chapl RN 76-81; C-in-c W Leigh CD *Portsm* 81-82; V W Leigh 82-87; R Botley 87-95; V Curdridge 94-95; R Durley 94-95; P-in-c Compton, the Mardens, Stoughton and Racton *Chich* from 95; Tutor Bp Otter Coll Chich from 95. *The Vicarage, Compton, Chichester, W Sussex PO18 9HD* Tel (01705) 631252

STAMP, Harold William Tremlett. b 08. St Aug Coll Cant 30. **d** 35 **p** 36. C Tilbury Docks *Chelmsf* 35-37; C Colyton *Ex* 37-39; Min Burnt Ho Lane CD 39-43; V Kilmington 43-49; R Hemyock w Culm Davy and Clayhidon 49-58; V Trull *B & W* 58-61; R Newton Ferrers w Revelstoke *Ex* 61-69; R Farway w Northleigh and Southleigh 69-72; V Branscombe 72-76; rtd 76; Hon C Nymet Rowland w Coldridge *Ex* 77-81; Lic to Offic 81-96. *5 Bramwell Lodge, Brighton Road, Woodmancote, Henfield, W Sussex BN5 9SX*

STAMP, Ian Jack. b 47. Aston Tr Scheme 82 N Ord Course 83. **d** 86 **p** 87. C Tonge w Alkrington *Man* 86-89; V Heywood St Marg from 89; P-in-c Heywood St Luke w All So from 96. *St Margaret's Vicarage, Heys Lane, Heywood, Lancs OL10 3RD* Tel (01706) 368053

STAMP, Philip Andrew. b 53. Linc Th Coll 86. **d** 88 **p** 89. C Barton w Peel Green *Man* 88-91; R Blackley H Trin from 91. *Holy Trinity Rectory, Goodman Street, Manchester M9 1FE* Tel 0161-205 2879

STAMP, Richard Mark. b 36. St Chad's Coll Dur BA60 DipTh62. **d** 62 **p** 63. Australia 62-69 and from 72; C Greenhill St Jo *Lon* 69-72. *69 Sullivan Street, Inglewood, Victoria, Australia 3517* Tel Inglewood (54) 383055

STAMPS, Dennis Lee. b 55. Biola Univ (USA) BA78 Dur Univ PhD95. Trin Evang Div Sch (USA) MDiv83 MA87 Westcott Ho Cam 90. **d** 92 **p** 93. C Moseley St Mary *Birm* 92-96; Dir WMMTC from 96. *73 Farquhar Road, Edgbaston, Birmingham B15 2QP, or WMMTC, Somerset Road, Edgbaston B15 2QH* Tel 0121-452 2607 or 452 2604

✠**STANAGE, The Rt Revd Thomas Shaun.** b 32. Pemb Coll Ox BA56 MA60 Nashotah Ho Wisconsin Hon DD86. Cuddesdon Coll 56. **d** 58 **p** 59 **c** 78. C Gt Crosby St Faith *Liv* 58-61; Min Orford St Andr CD 61-63; V Orford St Andr 63-70; S Africa from 70; Dean Kimberley 75-78; Suff Bp Johannesburg 78-82; Bp Bloemfontein 82-97; rtd 97. *Address temp unknown*

STANBRIDGE, The Ven Leslie Cyril. b 20. St Jo Coll Dur BA47 DipTh49 MA54. **d** 49 **p** 50. C Erith St Jo *Roch* 49-51; Tutor St Jo Coll Dur 51-55; Chapl 52-55; V Kingston upon Hull St Martin *York* 55-64; R Cottingham 64-72; Can and Preb York Minster from 68; Succ Canonicorum from 88; RD Hull 70-72; Adn York 72-88; rtd 88. *1 Deangate, York YO1 2JB* Tel (01904) 621174

✠**STANCLIFFE, The Rt Revd David Staffurth.** b 42. Trin Coll Ox BA65 MA68. Cuddesdon Coll 65. **d** 67 **p** 68 **c** 93. C Armley St Bart *Ripon* 67-70; Chapl Clifton Coll Bris 70-77; Dir of Ords *Portsm* 77-82; Can Res Portsm Cathl 77-82; Provost Portsm 82-93; Bp Sarum from 93. *South Canonry, 71 The Close, Salisbury SP1 2ER* Tel (01722) 334031 Fax 413112 E-mail 101324.1053@compuserve.com

STANDEN, Mark Jonathan. b 63. LMH Ox BA85 Barrister 86. Ridley Hall Cam BA94 CTM95. **d** 95 **p** 96. C Sevenoaks St Nic *Roch* from 95. *40 South Park, Sevenoaks, Kent TN13 1EJ* Tel (01732) 454221

STANDEN McDOUGAL, Canon John Anthony Phelps. b 33. AKC58. **d** 59 **p** 60. C Ipswich St Marg *St E* 59-63; C Bury St Edmunds St Mary 63-65; C Wadhurst *Chich* 65-70; C Tidebrook 65-70; R Tollard Royal w Farnham *Sarum* 70-81; P-in-c Gussage St Michael and Gussage All Saints 71-76; R 76-81; RD Milton and Blandford 81-86; R Tollard Royal w Farnham, Gussage St Michael etc 82-86; Can and Preb Sarum Cathl 86-94; TR Bride Valley 86-94; rtd 94. *Silverbridge Cottage, North Chideock, Bridport, Dorset DT6 6LG* Tel (01297) 489408

STANDING, Victor. b 44. FRCO67 Lon Univ BMus66 Ox Univ DipTh77 Clare Coll Cam CertEd68. Ripon Coll Cuddesdon 75. **d** 78 **p** 79. C Wimborne Minster *Sarum* 78-80; TV Wimborne Minster and Holt 80-83; R Ex St Sidwell and St Matt *Ex* 83-94; Dep PV Ex Cathl from 83; Chapl R Devon and Ex Hosp 83-94; Chapl W of England Eye Infirmary Ex 83-94; P-in-c Tedburn St Mary, Whitestone, Oldridge etc *Ex* 94-96; P-in-c Dunsford and Doddiscombsleigh 95-96; P-in-c Cheriton Bishop 95-96; R Tedburn St Mary, Whitestone, Oldridge etc from 96; RD Kenn from 97. *The Rectory, Church Lane, Whitestone, Exeter EX4 2JT* Tel (01392) 811406

STANDISH, Derrick Edgar. b 41. Univ of Wales (Lamp) BA67. Wycliffe Hall Ox 68. **d** 68 **p** 69. C Brynmawr *S & B* 68-69; C Morriston 69-74; V Merthyr Cynog and Dyffryn Honddu 74-76; R Llanwenarth Ultra *Mon* 76-83; V Abersychan and Garndiffaith 83-91. *7 Intermediate Road, Brynmawr NP3 4SF* Tel (01495) 312183

STANDLEY, Robert Henry. b 21. Lon Univ BD42. Linc Th Coll 42. **d** 44 **p** 45. C Gt Grimsby St Jas *Linc* 44-51; V Morton 51-59; V E Stockwith 52-59; Solomon Is 59-64; V Coleby *Linc* 65-74; V

Harmston 65-74; V Skirbeck Quarter 74-86; RD Holland E 80-85; rtd 86; Perm to Offic *Linc* from 86. *9 Grammar School Road, Brigg, S Humberside DN20 8AA* Tel (01652) 652020

STANDRING, Rupert Benjamin Charles. b 68. Pemb Coll Ox BA90. Ridley Hall Cam BA94 CTM95. **d** 95 **p** 96. C Bromley Ch Ch *Roch* from 95. *68 Warren Road, Bromley BR1 4BS* Tel 0181-460 1174

STANES, The Ven Ian Thomas. b 39. Sheff Univ BSc62 Linacre Coll Ox BA65 MA69. Wycliffe Hall Ox 63. **d** 65 **p** 66. C Leic H Apostles *Leic* 65-69; V Broom Leys 69-76; Warden Marrick Priory *Ripon* 76-82; Officer Miss, Min & Evang (Willesden Episc Area) *Lon* 82-92; Continuing Minl Educn Officer 82-92; Preb St Paul's Cathl 89-92; Adn Loughborough *Leic* from 92. *The Archdeaconry, 21 Church Road, Glenfield, Leicester LE3 8DP* Tel 0116-231 1632 Fax 232 1593

STANESBY, Canon Derek Malcolm. b 31. Leeds Univ BA56 Man Univ MEd75 PhD84 FRSA93. Coll of Resurr Mirfield 56. **d** 58 **p** 59. C Lakenham St Jo *Nor* 58-60; C Welling *S'wark* 60-62; V Bury St Mark *Man* 62-67; R Ladybarn 67-85; Can and Steward Windsor from 85. *4 The Cloisters, Windsor Castle, Windsor, Berks SL4 1NJ* Tel (01753) 864142

STANIFORD, Mrs Doris Gwendoline. b 43. Gilmore Course IDC79. **dss** 80 **d** 87 **p** 94. Hangleton *Chich* 80-82; Durrington 82-87; Par Dn 87-89; Chich Th Coll 83-89; C Crawley 89-97; Chapl Crawley Gen Hosp 89-97; Chapl St Catherine's Hospice Crawley 92-97; Dioc Voc Adv *Chich* 92-97; C Southwick from 97; Asst Dir of Ords from 97. *Church House, 1 Church House Close, Downsway, Southwick, W Sussex BN42 4WQ* Tel (01273) 594084

STANLEY, Arthur Patrick. b 32. TCD BA54 Div Test55 MA64. **d** 55 **p** 56. C Waterford H Trin *C & O* 55-57; CF 58-74; Dep Asst Chapl Gen 74-83; USA from 84; rtd 94. *RR1, Box 212, Stanton, Iowa 51573, USA* Tel Stanton (712) 829 2467

STANLEY, Baden Thomas. b 68. TCD BA91. CITC BTh94. **d** 94 **p** 95. C Seapatrick *D & D* from 94. *16 Bannview Heights, Banbridge, Co Down BT32 4LZ* Tel (01820) 628303

STANLEY, Bernard Leslie. b 32. Ox Poly ONC63. Ox NSM Course 75. **d** 76 **p** 77. NSM Thame w Towersey *Ox* 76-84; Asst Chapl Jo Radcliffe Hosp Ox 91-93; NSM Long Crendon w Chearsley and Nether Winchendon 92-93; Perm to Offic *Ex* from 94. *Christmas Cottage, 24 Church Street, Kingsteignton, Newton Abbot, Devon TQ12 3BQ* Tel (01626) 51043

STANLEY, Eric William. b 22. TCD BA45 MA58. **d** 45 **p** 46. C Carlow *C & O* 45-48; P-in-c Seirkieran 48-53 and 54-66; P-in-c Aghancon w Kilcoleman *L & K* 48-53 and 54-66; I Bourney w Dunkerrin 53; Can Killaloe Cathl 65-89; I Nenagh 66-89; Chan Killaloe Cathl 72-79; Adn Killaloe, Kilfenora, Clonfert etc 79-89; Preb Taney St Patr Cathl Dublin 81-89; rtd 89. *Cuanbeg, Ballycotton, Midleton, Co Cork, Irish Republic* Tel Midleton (21) 646076

STANLEY, Canon John Alexander. b 31. Tyndale Hall Bris DipTh56. **d** 56 **p** 57. C Preston All SS *Blackb* 56-60; C St Helens St Mark *Liv* 60-63; V Everton St Cuth 63-70; P-in-c Everton St Sav 69-70; V Everton St Sav w St Cuth 70-74; V Huyton St Mich from 74; Hon Can Liv Cathl from 87; AD Huyton from 89; Chapl to The Queen from 93. *The Vicarage, Huyton, Liverpool L36 7SA* Tel 0151-449 3900 Fax 480 6002

STANLEY, Joseph. b 12. Chich Th Coll 37. **d** 39 **p** 40. C Canvey Is *Chelmsf* 39-41; C Romford Ascension Collier Row 41-44; Chapl RNVR 44-46; P-in-c Walthamstow St Pet *Chelmsf* 47-51; V Swaffham *Nor* 51-60; rtd 77. *c/o Mrs M Stanley, 3 Coopers Cottages, Upper Dicker, Hailsham, E Sussex BN27 3QE*

STANLEY, Robert John. b 27. TCD BA50 MA54. **d** 50 **p** 51. C Belfast Trin Coll Miss *Conn* 50-52; C Belfast St Matt 52-54; I Tamlaghtard w Aghanloo *D & R* 54-60; I Donagheady 60-63; CF 63-79; V Prittlewell St Steph *Chelmsf* 79-92; rtd 92; Perm to Offic *Chelmsf* from 92. *281 Prittlewell Chase, Westcliff-on-Sea, Essex SS0 0PL* Tel (01702) 344204

STANLEY, Simon Richard. b 44. Wells Th Coll 66. **d** 69 **p** 70. C Foleshill St Laur *Cov* 69-71; C Hessle *York* 71-75; P-in-c Flamborough 75-80; R Dunnington 80-92; P-in-c York St Barn from 92. *St Barnabas's Vicarage, Jubilee Terrace, Leeman Road, York YO2 4YZ* Tel (01904) 654214

STANLEY-SMITH, James (Jim). b 29. Hatf Coll Dur BA54 DipEd55. S Dios Minl Tr Scheme 81. **d** 84 **p** 85. C Bournemouth St Jo w St Mich *Win* 84-87; R Hale w S Charford 87-94; rtd 94. *10 Rownhams Way, Rownhams, Southampton SO16 8AE* Tel (01703) 732529

STANNARD, Miss Beryl Elizabeth. b 36. SRN62 SCM64. Oak Hill Th Coll BA92. **d** 92 **p** 94. Par Dn Streatham Park St Alb *S'wark* 92-94; C 94-96; C Gerrards Cross and Fulmer *Ox* from 96. *24 Fulmer Drive, Gerrards Cross, Bucks SL9 7HJ* Tel (01753) 887587

STANNARD, Brian. b 46. MICE71 MIStructE71. Cranmer Hall Dur 86. **d** 88 **p** 89. C Burnage St Marg *Man* 88-91; V Walmersley from 91. *The Vicarage, 14 Springside Road, Bury, Lancs BL9 5JE* Tel 0161-797 9273

STANNARD, The Ven Colin Percy. b 24. TD66. Selw Coll Cam BA47 MA49. Linc Th Coll 47. **d** 49 **p** 50. C St E Cathl *St E* 49-52; C-in-c Nunsthorpe CD *Linc* 52-55; CF (TA) 53-67; V Barrow St Jas *Carl* 55-64; V Upperby St Jo 64-70; R Gosforth 70-75; RD Calder 70-75; P-in-c Natland 75-76; V 76-84; RD Kendal 75-84; Hon Can Carl Cathl 75-84; Can Res Carl Cathl 84-93; Adn Carl 84-93; rtd 93. *51 Longlands Road, Carlisle CA3 9AE* Tel (01228) 38584

STANNARD, Harold Frederick David. b 12. AKC37. **d** 37 **p** 38. C St Columb Major *Truro* 37-43; Chapl RAFVR 43-46; R Dunsby w Dowsby *Linc* 46-48; R W Quantoxhead *B & W* 48-77; rtd 77. *Little Orchard, Bosinver Lane, Polgooth, St Austell, Cornwall PL26 7BA* Tel (01726) 68712

STANNARD, Canon Peter Graville. b 59. Univ of Wales (Abth) BSc(Econ)81 Ox Univ MA86 BA85. St Steph Ho Ox 83. **d** 86 **p** 87. C Worksop Priory *S'well* 86-89; Ghana 89-96; Hon Can Koforidua from 93; TR Shelf St Mich w Buttershaw St Aid *Bradf* from 96. *The Rectory, 80 Carr House Road, Shelf, Halifax, W Yorkshire HX3 7RJ* Tel (01274) 677413 Fax 691886

STANSBURY, Alan David. b 29. Ridley Hall Cam 59. **d** 61 **p** 62. C Kennington St Mark *S'wark* 61-63; S Africa from 63. *PO Box 15, Aliwal North, 5530 South Africa* Tel Aliwal North (551) 2281

STANTON, Miss Barbara. b 51. DipNCTD77 Whitelands Coll Lon TCert72 Lon Univ BD86. WMMTC 89. **d** 92 **p** 94. NSM Hinckley St Mary *Leic* from 92. *25 Atterton Lane, Witherley, Atherstone, Warks CV9 3LP* Tel (01827) 717875

STANTON, David John. b 60. FSAScot89 St Andr Univ MTheol82. Ripon Coll Cuddesdon 83. **d** 85 **p** 86. C Beckenham St Geo *Roch* 85-88; Asst Chapl Shrewsbury Sch 88-90; Hon C Shrewsbury All SS w St Mich *Lich* 88-90; P-in-c Abbotskerswell *Ex* 90-94; Chapl Plymouth Univ 92-97; P-in-c Bovey Tracey St John, Chudleigh Knighton etc from 94. *St John's Vicarage, Newton Road, Bovey Tracey, Newton Abbot, Devon TQ13 9BD* Tel (01626) 833451

STANTON, Gregory John. b 47. Sarum & Wells Th Coll 84. **d** 86 **p** 87. C Willenhall H Trin *Lich* 86-89; C Plympton St Mary *Ex* 89-91; V Milton Abbot, Dunterton, Lamerton etc from 91. *The Vicarage, Milton Abbot, Tavistock, Devon PL19 0NZ* Tel (01822) 87384

STANTON, John Maurice. b 18. Univ Coll Ox BA45 MA45. Wycliffe Hall Ox 51. **d** 52 **p** 53. C Tonbridge SS Pet and Paul *Roch* 52-54; Hd Master Blundell's Sch 59-71; Public Preacher *Ex* 71-72; C Ex St Matt 72-73; R Chesham Bois *Ox* 73-83; rtd 83; Perm to Offic *Ox* from 83. *37 St Andrew's Road, Oxford OX3 9DL* Tel (01865) 765206

STANTON, Ronald Geoffrey. b 14. Leeds Univ BA48. Wells Th Coll. **d** 50 **p** 51. C Earlsdon *Cov* 50-53; C Cov H Trin 53-58; V Willenhall 58-61; V Wellesbourne 61-72; R Walton D'Eiville 61-72; V Finham 72-79; rtd 79; Perm to Offic *Cov* from 79. *8 Margetts Close, Kenilworth, Warks CV8 1EN* Tel (01926) 511036

STANTON, Thomas Hugh (Timothy). b 17. Trin Coll Cam BA38 MA45. Coll of Resurr Mirfield 46. **d** 47 **p** 48. C Camberwell St Geo *S'wark* 47-49; CR from 52; S Africa 54-87; rtd 87. *Community of the Resurrection, Mirfield, W Yorkshire WF14 0BN* Tel (01924) 494318

STANTON-HYDE, Mrs Marjorie Elizabeth. b 37. TCert58. Cranmer Hall Dur 86. **d** 88 **p** 94. Par Dn Elmley Lovett w Hampton Lovett and Elmbridge etc *Worc* 88-91; Par Dn Wilden 88-91; Par Dn Hartlebury 88-91; D-in-c 91-94; R 94; P-in-c from 94. *Church Rise, The Village, Hartlebury, Kidderminster, Worcs DY11 7TE* Tel (01299) 251535

STANTON-SARINGER, Maurice Charles. b 49. Bris Univ BSc71 PGCE72 Fitzw Coll Cam BA77 MA81. Ridley Hall Cam 75. **d** 78 **p** 79. C Gerrards Cross *Ox* 78-80; C Bletchley 80-83; Lic to Offic 83-91; Chapl Stowe Sch Bucks 83-91; R Sherington w Chicheley, N Crawley, Astwood etc *Ox* from 91; RD Newport from 95. *The Rectory, School Lane, Sherington, Newport Pagnell, Bucks MK16 9NF* Tel (01908) 610521

STANWAY, Peter David. b 48. K Coll Lon BD71. St Aug Coll Cant 72. **d** 73 **p** 74. C Maidstone All SS w St Phil and H Trin *Cant* 73-77; Canada 77-84; C Waterlooville *Portsm* 84-87; R Laughton w Ripe and Chalvington *Chich* 87-90; Chapl Witney Community Hosp 90-91; C Wheatley w Forest Hill and Stanton St John *Ox* 91-92; C Cowley St Jas from 93. *Benson Cottage, Beauchamp Lane, Cowley, Oxford OX4 3LF* Tel (01865) 778821

STAPLEFORD, Robin Duncan. b 62. St Jo Coll Nottm DipMin94 Aston Tr Scheme 92. **d** 96 **p** 97. C Evington *Leic* from 96. *14 Fallowfield Road, Evington, Leicester LE5 6LQ* Tel 0116-241 2833

STAPLES, David. b 35. Jes Coll Ox BA59 MA63 BD75. Linc Th Coll 59. **d** 61 **p** 62. C Kettering St Andr *Pet* 61-64; C Doncaster St Geo *Sheff* 64-66; Youth Chapl 66-71; V Mexborough 71-83; Chapl Montagu Hosp Mexborough 71-83; RD Wath *Sheff* 77-83; Hon Can Sheff Cathl 80-83; V W Haddon w Winwick *Pet* 83-88; RD Brixworth 83-89; V W Haddon w Winwick and Ravensthorpe from 88; ACUPA Link Officer from 90. *The Vicarage, 4 West End, West Haddon, Northampton NN6 7AY* Tel (01788) 510207

STAPLES, Canon Edward Eric. b 10. OBE73 CBE77. Chich Th Coll 46. **d** 48 **p** 49. C Wallington H Trin *S'wark* 48-51; Bp's Dom Chapl *Portsm* 51-55; V Shedfield 55-66; Chapl Helsinki w Moscow *Eur* 66-80; Chapl to The Queen 73-80; rtd 80; Perm to Offic *B & W* 81-86. *The Old Farmhouse, 13 Oxford Street, Ramsbury, Marlborough, Wilts SN8 2PG* Tel (01672) 521118

STAPLES, John Michael. **d** 97. C Tisbury *Sarum* from 97. *7 Church Street Close, Tisbury, Wilts SP3 6QY* Tel (01747) 870790

STAPLES, John Wedgwood. b 42. Hertf Coll Ox BA64 MA. Wycliffe Hall Ox 64. **d** 66 **p** 67. C Yardley St Edburgha *Birm* 66-69; C Knowle 69-74; R Barcombe *Chich* 74-81; V Old Windsor *Ox* 81-96; P-in-c Pangbourne w Tidmarsh and Sulham from 96. *The Rectory, St James's Close, Pangbourne, Reading RG8 7AP* Tel (0118) 984 2928

STAPLES, Peter. b 35. Jes Coll Ox BA59. Ripon Hall Ox 59. **d** 62 **p** 63. C Fairfield *Derby* 62-63; C Dore 63-66; C Wilne and Draycott w Breaston 66-71; The Netherlands from 72; Asst Chapl Utrecht w Arnhem, Zwolle, Amersfoort etc *Eur* from 94. *Doldersweg 39C, 3712 BR Huis Ter Heide, Utrecht, The Netherlands* Tel Utrecht (3404) 31928

STAPLES, Peter Brian. b 38. Bps' Coll Cheshunt 66. **d** 68 **p** 69. C Birkdale St Jas *Liv* 68-71; C Sevenoaks St Jo *Roch* 71-74; V Treslothan *Truro* 74-80; V Truro St Paul and St Clem from 80. *The Vicarage, 41 Tregolls Road, Truro, Cornwall TR1 1LE* Tel (01872) 72576

STAPLES, Terence Malcolm. b 43. Trin Coll Bris BA95. **d** 95 **p** 96. C Bath St Sav w Swainswick and Woolley *B & W* from 95. *40 Fairfield Avenue, Bath BA1 6NH* Tel (01225) 311598

STAPLETON, The Very Revd Henry Edward Champneys. b 32. FSA74 Pemb Coll Cam BA54 MA58. Ely Th Coll 54. **d** 56 **p** 57. C York St Olave w St Giles *York* 56-59; C Pocklington w Yapham-cum-Meltonby, Owsthorpe etc 59-61; R Seaton Ross w Everingham and Bielby and Harswell 61-67; RD Weighton 66-67; R Skelton by York 67-75; V Wroxham w Hoveton *Nor* 75-81; P-in-c Belaugh 76-81; Can Res and Prec Roch Cathl *Roch* 81-88; Dean Carl from 88. *The Deanery, Carlisle CA3 8TZ* Tel (01228) 23335

STAPLETON, Canon Kenneth Hargrave. b 11. St Pet Hall Ox BA38 MA42. Wells Th Coll 38. **d** 39 **p** 40. C Armley St Bart *Ripon* 39-43; P-in-c Bramley 43-45; CF 46-47; V Holbeck St Edw *Ripon* 47-62; V New Wortley St Jo 52-57; V Leeds Halton St Wilfrid 62-78; Hon Can Ripon Cathl 74-78; rtd 78; Perm to Offic *Ripon* 78-93; Perm to Offic *Wakef* from 90. *29 St Paul's Road, Mirfield, W Yorkshire WF14 8AY* Tel (01924) 491746

STAPLETON, Leonard Charles. b 37. Chich Th Coll 75. **d** 77 **p** 78. C Crayford *Roch* 77-81; C Lamorbey H Redeemer 81-83; V Belvedere St Aug 83-89; V Beckenham St Jas from 89. *The Vicarage, St James Avenue, Beckenham, Kent BR3 4HF* Tel 0181-650 0420

STAPLETON, Robert Michael Vorley (Bob). b 25. ALCD51. **d** 51 **p** 52. C Plymouth St Andr *Ex* 51-56; Chapl RN 56-60; C Surbiton St Matt *S'wark* 60-64; R Chenies and Lt Chalfont *Ox* 64-87; P-in-c Latimer w Flaunden 86-87; R Chenies and Lt Chalfont, Latimer and Flaunden 87-92; rtd 92. *Woodside, Swannaton Road, Dartmouth, Devon TQ6 9RL* Tel (01803) 832972

STAPLETON, Robert Vauvelle. b 47. Dur Univ BA70. Cranmer Hall Dur DipTh71. **d** 71 **p** 72. C Moreton *Ches* 71-73; C Monkwearmouth All SS *Dur* 73-76; C Stranton 76-79; P-in-c Kelloe 79-86; V New Shildon 86-96; R Stoke Albany w Wilbarston and Ashley etc *Pet* from 96. *The Rectory, Stoke Albany, Market Harborough, Leics LE16 8PZ* Tel (01858) 535213

STARBUCK, Francis Tony. b 36. Kelham Th Coll 57. **d** 61 **p** 62. C Mansfield St Mark *S'well* 61-64; C Didcot *Ox* 67-71; C-in-c California CD 71-75; R Barkham 74-75; V Hagbourne 75-82; V Maidenhead St Luke 82-87; New Zealand from 87. *The Vicarage, 45 North Road, Clevedon, New Zealand* Tel Clevedon (9) 292 8763

STARES, Brian Maurice William. b 44. St Deiniol's Hawarden 74. **d** 74 **p** 75. C Risca *Mon* 74-77; V Newport St Steph and H Trin 77-87; V Fleur-de-Lis 87-92; Asst Chapl HM Pris Belmarsh 92-93; Chapl HM Young Offender Inst Dover from 93. *HM Young Offender Institution, The Citadel, Western Heights, Dover, Kent CT17 9DR* Tel (01304) 203848 or 201869 Fax 215165

STARES, Mrs Olive Beryl. b 33. Sarum Th Coll 83. **dss** 86 **d** 87 **p** 94. Crofton *Portsm* 86-87; Hon C from 87. *62 Mancroft Avenue, Hill Head, Fareham, Hants PO14 2DD* Tel (01329) 668540

STARK, Mrs Beverley Ann. b 52. Bp Otter Coll CertEd73 EMMTC CTPS92. **d** 92 **p** 94. Par Dn Bulwell St Jo *S'well* 92-94; C 94-97; TV Bestwood from 97. *Emmanuel Vicarage, 10 Church View Close, Arnold, Nottingham NG5 9QP* Tel 0115-920 8879

STARK, John Jordan. b 40. Hull Univ BA62 St Chad's Coll Dur DipTh64. **d** 64 **p** 65. C Buxton *Derby* 64-67; C Wolborough w Newton Abbot *Ex* 67-74; R Belstone 74-79; P-in-c Plymouth St Gabr 79-80; V from 80. *The Vicarage, 1 Peverell Terrace, Plymouth PL3 4JJ* Tel (01752) 663938

STARK, Margaret Alison. b 46. Univ of Wales BA70 BA71. St Mich Coll Llan DPS90. **d** 90 **p** 97. C Llanishen and Lisvane *Llan* 90-93; C Llanishen 93-94; C Aberavon from 94. *77 Victoria Road, Port Talbot SA12 6QQ* Tel (01639) 892306

STARK, Michael. b 35. Dur Univ BSc56 SEN58. Chich Th Coll 58. **d** 60 **p** 61. C Middlesbrough St Paul *York* 60-64; C S Bank 64-66; R Skelton in Cleveland 66-74; P-in-c Upleatham 66-67; R 67-74; Asst Chapl HM Pris Wormwood Scrubs 74-76; Asst Chapl HM Pris Liv 75-76; Chapl HM Pris Featherstone 76-83; Chapl HM Pris Ex 83-89; Chapl HM Pris Leic 89-97; rtd 97. *28 St Peters Road, Highfields, Leicester LE2 1DA*

STARKEY, Gerald Dennis. b 34. Qu Coll Birm 79. **d** 82 **p** 83. C Wilnecote *Lich* 82-86; Min Stoke-upon-Trent 86-90; P-in-c W Bromwich St Pet from 90. *The Vicarage, Oldbury Road, West Bromwich, W Midlands B70 9DP* Tel 0121-525 5147

STARKEY, John Douglas. b 23. St Chad's Coll Dur BA47 DipTh48. **d** 48 **p** 49. C Horninglow *Lich* 48-52; C Lower Gornal 52-55; C-in-c W Bromwich Ascension CD 55-57; V Coseley Ch Ch 57-66; V Freehay 66-84; P-in-c Oakamoor w Cotton 78-84; R Dunstall w Rangemore and Tatenhill 84-88; rtd 88; Perm to Offic *Lich* from 88; Perm to Offic *Derby* from 88. *34 Park Crescent, Doveridge, Ashbourne, Derbyshire DE6 5NE* Tel (01889) 566384

STARKEY, Michael Stuart (Mike). b 63. LMH Ox BA85 Nottm Univ BTh92 MA93. St Jo Coll Nottm 90. **d** 93 **p** 94. C Ealing St Mary *Lon* 93-95; C Brownswood Park 95-97; P-in-c from 97. *St John's Vicarage, 2A Gloucester Drive, London N4 2LW* Tel 0181-211 0729

STARKEY, Simon Mark. b 36. Liv Univ BA78. Clifton Th Coll. **d** 66 **p** 67. C Ox St Ebbe w St Pet *Ox* 66-72; Community Chapl CPAS Kirkdale 72-77; TV Toxteth Park St Bede *Liv* 77-78; P-in-c 78-80; V 80-90; RD Toxteth 81-89; Chapl Ches Coll *Ches* 90-96; TV St Luke in the City *Liv* from 96. *31 Mount Street, Liverpool L1 9HD* Tel 0151-709 2788

STARKEY, Susan Anne (Sue). b 52. St Jo Coll Nottm DipTh95. **d** 97. C Watford St Luke *St Alb* from 97. *St Luke's Church Office, Devereux Drive, Watford WD1 3DD* Tel (01923) 231205

STARNES, Peter Henry. b 19. LTCL74 St Jo Coll Cam BA42 MA47 Ch Ch Coll Cant PGCE72. Linc Th Coll 42. **d** 44 **p** 45. C Gillingham *Sarum* 44-50; C St Peter-in-Thanet *Cant* 50-52; CF 52-55; Hon CF from 55; R Hothfield *Cant* 56-60; V Westwell 56-65; R Eastwell w Boughton Aluph 60-65; rtd 84. *Whitebeams, High Halden, Ashford, Kent TN26 3LY* Tel (01233) 850245

STARNS, Helen Edna. *See* PATTEN, Mrs Helen Edna

STARR, John Michael. b 50. Southn Univ. Sarum & Wells Th Coll 71. **d** 74 **p** 75. C Basingstoke *Win* 74-78; C Southampton Maybush St Pet 78-79; C Milton 79-83; V Lupset *Wakef* 83-90; V Kennington St Mark *S'wark* from 90. *St Mark's Vicarage, Kennington Oval, London SE11 5SW* Tel 0171-735 1801

STARR, Dr Michael Reginald. b 41. MICE71 Bris Univ BSc63 PhD66. Ox NSM Course 83. **d** 86 **p** 87. NSM Gt Faringdon w Lt Coxwell *Ox* from 86. *23 Gloucester Street, Faringdon, Oxon SN7 7JA* Tel (01367) 240686

STARR, Michael Richard. b 43. Sarum Th Coll 65. **d** 68 **p** 69. C Plymouth St Pet *Ex* 68-72; C Blackpool St Paul *Blackb* 72-74; V Burnley St Cuth 74-79; C Eastbourne St Mary *Chich* 79-84; P-in-c Eastbourne Ch Ch 84-87; V 87-88; R Guernsey Ste Marie du Castel *Win* from 88; V Guernsey St Matt from 94. *Castel Rectory, rue de la Lande, Castel, Guernsey GY5 7EJ* Tel (01481) 56793

STARTIN, Geoffrey Neil. b 56. Essex Univ BA81 Ch Ch Ox MSc84 Westmr Coll Ox CertEd85. St Steph Ho Ox 86. **d** 88 **p** 89. C Coseley Ch Ch *Lich* 88-90; C Wellingborough All Hallows *Pet* 90-92; Asst Chapl HM Pris Wormwood Scrubs 92-93; C Newton Nottage *Llan* 93-96; P-in-c Lydd *Cant* from 96. *All Saints' Rectory, Park Street, Lydd, Romney Marsh, Kent TN29 9AY* Tel (01797) 320345

STARTIN, Nicola Gail. b 57. K Coll Lon LLB79. St Steph Ho Ox 88. **d** 90 **p** 96. C Wellingborough All SS *Pet* 90-92; NSM Pyle w Kenfig *Llan* 94-95; Asst Chapl Mid Kent Healthcare NHS Trust from 95. *Chaplain's Office, Maidstone Hospital, Hermitage Lane, Maidstone, Kent ME16 9QQ* Tel (01622) 729000

STARTUP, Stephen Paul. b 53. CEng MIMechE MBIM Nottm Univ BSc76. Oak Hill Th Coll DTPS92. **d** 92 **p** 93. C Oakwood St Thos *Lon* 92-95; V Grange Park St Pet from 95. *St Peter's Vicarage, Langham Gardens, London N21 1DJ* Tel 0181-360 2294

STATHAM, Brian Edward. b 55. K Coll Lon MA AKC76. St Steph Ho Ox 77. **d** 78 **p** 79. C Ches H Trin *Ches* 78-81; C Birkenhead Priory 81-82; TV 82-86; V Newton 86-91; SSF 91-94; TV Horsham *Chich* from 95; Chapl Horsham Gen Hosp from 95. *Trinity House, Blunts Way, Horsham, W Sussex RH12 2BL* Tel (01403) 265401

STATHAM, John Francis. b 31. Kelham Th Coll 51. **d** 56 **p** 57. C Ilkeston St Mary *Derby* 56-58; C New Mills 58-59; V 69-81; C Newbold w Dunston 59-62; PC Ridgeway 62-69; RD Glossop 78-81; R Matlock 81-89; R Killamarsh 89-93; rtd 93; Perm to Offic *Derby* from 93. *33 Ackford Drive, The Meadows, Worksop, Notts S80 1YG* Tel (01909) 476031

STATON, Preb Geoffrey. b 40. Wells Th Coll 64. **d** 66 **p** 67. C Wednesfield St Thos *Lich* 66-69; C Cannock 69-72; V Cheddleton 72-82; RD Leek 77-82; V Harlescott 82-90; Preb Lich Cathl from 87; TR Penkridge Team from 90. *The Rectory, Penkridge, Stafford ST19 5DN* Tel (01785) 712378

STAUNTON, Richard Steedman. b 25. Wadh Coll Ox BA49 MA50 BSc51. Cuddesdon Coll 63. **d** 64 **p** 65. C Wyken *Cov* 64-68; V Tile Hill 68-76; V Hillmorton 76-90; rtd 90; Perm to Offic *Ban* from 90. *2 Tan-y-fron, Corris Uchaf, Machynlleth SY20 9BN* Tel (01654) 761466

STAVELEY, Dennis Frank. b 21. Open Univ BA75. S'wark Ord Course 77. **d** 80 **p** 81. C Danbury *Chelmsf* 80-84; P-in-c Lt Hallingbury 84-91; P-in-c Gt Hallingbury 86-91; R Gt Hallingbury and Lt Hallingbury 91; rtd 91. *99 Mumford Road, West Bergholt, Colchester CO6 3BN* Tel (01206) 240965

STAVELEY-WADHAM, Robert Andrew. b 43. ACII. Ridley Hall Cam 79. **d** 81 **p** 82. C Saffron Walden w Wendens Ambo and Littlebury *Chelmsf* 81-84; P-in-c Austrey *Birm* 84-87; P-in-c Warton 84-87; Perm to Offic *Chich* from 87; Perm to Offic *Ely* from 88. *2 Little Bognor Cottages, Fittleworth, Pulborough, W Sussex RH20 1JT* Tel (01798) 865668

STEAD, Andrew Michael. b 63. BA84. Coll of Resurr Mirfield 84. **d** 87 **p** 88. C Wellingborough All Hallows *Pet* 87-90; Chapl St Alb Abbey *St Alb* 90-94; Chapl Aldenham Sch Herts from 94. *Chaplain's Lodge, Aldenham School, Aldenham Road, Elstree, Borehamwood, Herts WD6 3AJ* Tel (01923) 853360 Fax 854410

STEAD, Canon George Christopher. b 13. FBA80 K Coll Cam BA35 MA38 LittD78 New Coll Ox BA35 Keble Coll Ox MA49. Cuddesdon Coll 38. **d** 38 **p** 41. Perm to Offic *Newc* 38-39; Fell K Coll Cam 38-48; Prof Fell K Coll Cam 71-80; Asst Master Eton Coll 40-44; Fell and Chapl Keble Coll Ox 49-71; Select Preacher Ox Univ 58-59 and 61; Ely Prof Div Cam Univ 71-80; Can Res Ely Cathl *Ely* 71-80; rtd 80; Perm to Offic *Ely* from 81. *13 Station Road, Haddenham, Ely, Cambs CB6 3XD* Tel (01353) 740575

STEAD, Philip John. b 60. Sheff Univ LLB82 City of Lon Poly ACII85. Linc Th Coll CMinlStuds95. **d** 95 **p** 96. C Warsop *S'well* from 95. *Churchside Cottage, Church Warsop, Mansfield, Notts NG20 0SF* Tel (01623) 847687

STEAD, Timothy James (Tim). b 60. Ex Univ BSc82. St Steph Ho Ox DipMin95. **d** 95 **p** 97. C Broseley w Benthall, Jackfield, Linley etc *Heref* from 95. *3 Blakeway Close, Broseley, Shropshire TF12 5SS* Tel (01952) 882153

STEADMAN, Fred. b 11. Univ Coll Ox BA34 MA65. **d** 65 **p** 66. C Timperley *Ches* 65-69; V Willaston 69-79; P-in-c Capenhurst 71-79; Perm to Offic from 79. *24 Glan Aber Park, Chester CH4 8LF* Tel (01244) 682989

STEADMAN, Norman Neil. b 39. QUB BSc61 TCD Div Test63. **d** 63 **p** 64. C Newtownards *D & D* 63-65; C Belfast Whiterock *Conn* 65-67; Asst Dean of Res QUB 67-71; Perm to Offic *St Alb* 71-73; Dioc Youth Officer 73-76; P-in-c Hitchin H Sav 76; TV Hitchin 77-84; V Brampton *Carl* 84-93; R Brampton and Farlam and Castle Carrock w Cumrew from 93. *St Martin's Vicarage, Main Street, Brampton, Cumbria CA8 1SH* Tel (016977) 2486

STEADMAN-ALLEN, Miss Barbara. b 53. ARCM83 Trent Park Coll of Educn CertEd74 Birm Univ BMus77. Cranmer Hall Dur 88. **d** 90 **p** 94. C Chessington *Guildf* 90-94; C Chertsey from 94. *4 North Grove, Chertsey, Surrey KT16 9DU* Tel (01932) 567944

STEADY, Miss Vilda May. b 51. Linc Th Coll 87. **d** 89 **p** 94. Par Dn Cannock *Lich* 89-91; Par Dn Hammerwich 91-94; C 94-95; Asst Chapl Eastbourne Hosps NHS Trust 95-97; Chapl Luton and Dunstable Hosp NHS Trust from 97. *Luton and Dunstable Hospital, Lewsey Road, Luton, Beds LU4 0DT* Tel (01582) 497370

STEAR, Michael Peter Hutchinson (Mike). b 47. Golds Coll Lon TCert68. Wycliffe Hall Ox 71. **d** 74 **p** 75. C Streatham Vale H Redeemer *S'wark* 74-77; C Ramsgate St Luke *Cant* 77-82; V Ramsgate St Mark 82-83; Min Jersey St Paul Prop Chpl *Win* 83-94; TR Radipole and Melcombe Regis *Sarum* from 94; Chapl Weymouth Coll from 94. *The Rectory, 27 Carlton Avenue South, Weymouth, Dorset DT4 7PL* Tel (01305) 785553

STEAR, Mrs Patricia Ann. b 38. Birm Univ BSc60. LNSM course 96. **d** 97. NSM Bradford Peverell, Stratton, Frampton etc *Sarum* from 97. *Westwood House, Bradford Peverell, Dorchester, Dorset DT2 9SE* Tel (01305) 889227 Fax 889 718

STEARE, Peter Douglas. b 27. S Dios Minl Tr Scheme. **d** 84 **p** 85. NSM Upton cum Chalvey *Ox* 84-86; Perm to Offic *Bris* 86-88; Hon C Kington 88-90; NSM Tetbury w Beverston *Glouc* 94-95; rtd 95. *Kensell, Hayes Road, Nailsworth, Glos GL6 0EB* Tel (01453) 833776

STEARN, Peter Reginald. b 38. ARCM. Linc Th Coll 75. **d** 77 **p** 78. C St Alb St Pet *St Alb* 77-79; C Bushey 79-82; V Kings Langley from 82. *The Vicarage, The Glebe, Kings Langley, Herts WD4 9HY* Tel (01923) 262939

STEBBING, Michael Langdale (Nicolas). b 46. Univ of Zimbabwe BA68 Univ of S Africa MTh86. Coll of Resurr Mirfield. **d** 74 **p** 75. C Borrowdale *Carl* 74-76; Rhodesia 76-79; S Africa 79-86; CR from 80. *House of the Resurrection, Mirfield, W Yorkshire WF14 0BN* Tel (01924) 494318

STEDMAN, Preb Michael Sydney. b 34. ARICS58. Clifton Th Coll 62. **d** 65 **p** 66. C Lindfield *Chich* 65-68; C Gt Baddow *Chelmsf* 68-73; TV Ashby w Thurton, Claxton and Carleton *Nor* 73-75; P-in-c 75-85; TV Rockland St Mary w Hellington 73-75; P-in-c 75-85; TV Framingham Pigot 73-75; P-in-c 75-85; TV Bramerton w Surlingham 73-75; P-in-c 75-85; TV Bergh Apton w Yelverton 73-75; P-in-c 75-85; RD Loddon 78-85; R Church Stretton *Heref* from 85; RD Condover 88-96; Preb Heref Cathl from 94. *The Rectory, Carding Mill Valley, Church Stretton, Shropshire SY6 6JF* Tel (01694) 722585

STEDMAN, Robert Alfred. b 24. Qu Coll Birm 50. **d** 52 **p** 53. C Portchester *Portsm* 52-55; V Brighton St Anne *Chich* 55-61; V Salehurst 61-76; R Newhaven 76-90; rtd 90; Perm to Offic *Chich* from 90. *12 Lady Wootton's Green, Canterbury, Kent CT1 1NG*

STEED, Herbert Edward. b 23. St Jo Coll Dur BA51 DipTh52. **d** 52 **p** 53. C Stoneycroft All SS *Liv* 52-55; C Folkestone H Trin w Ch Ch *Cant* 55-57; V Croydon St Jas 57-63; V Strood St Fran *Roch* 63-64; R E Barnet *St Alb* 65-91; rtd 91; Perm to Offic *Guildf* from 91. *1 Harrier Close, Cranleigh, Surrey GU6 7BS* Tel (01483) 278151

STEEL, David Pitcaithley. b 22. St Andr Univ MA70 Dundee Univ DipEd DipRE71 Jordan Hill Coll Glas HDipRE74 Harley Univ DD82. **d** 83. NSM Laurencekirk *Bre* from 83; NSM Drumtochty from 84; NSM Fasque 84-91; NSM Drumlithie 84-91. *Churchlands, 29 Arduthie Road, Stonehaven, Kincardineshire AB3 2EH* Tel (01569) 65341

STEEL, Graham Reginald. b 51. Cam Univ MA. Trin Coll Bris 80. **d** 83 **p** 84. C Gt Parndon *Chelmsf* 83-86; C Barking St Marg w St Patr 86-89; P-in-c Westcliff St Cedd 89-96; P-in-c Prittlewell St Pet 92-96; Chapl Southend Gen Hosp 89-92; V Prittlewell w Westcliff *Chelmsf* from 96. *122 Mendip Crescent, Westcliff-on-Sea, Essex SS0 0HN* Tel (01702) 525126

STEEL, Leslie Frederick. Univ of NZ LTh65. St Jo Coll Auckland 57. **d** 59 **p** 60. New Zealand 59-91; Chapl Lausanne *Eur* 91-97. *Fief-de-Chapitre 8, CH 1213 Petit Lancy, Lausanne, Switzerland* Tel Geneva (22) 793-5633 Fax as telephone

STEEL, Norman William. b 53. Sarum & Wells Th Coll 85. **d** 87 **p** 88. C S Woodham Ferrers *Chelmsf* 87-91; V Woolavington w Cossington and Bawdrip *B & W* from 91. *The Rectory, Woolavington, Bridgwater, Somerset TA7 8DX* Tel (01278) 683408

STEEL, Richard John. b 57. Dur Univ BA79 Cam Univ MA86. Ridley Hall Cam 81. **d** 84 **p** 85. C Hull Newland St Jo *York* 84-87; Relig Broadcasting Officer *Derby* 88-92; Dioc Communications Officer *Blackb* 92-97; Communication Dir CMS from 97. *CMS, Partnership House, 157 Waterloo Road, London SE1 8UU* Tel 0171-928 8681

STEEL, Thomas Molyneux. b 39. Man Univ BA61 Ox Univ DipPSA62. Ripon Hall Ox 61. **d** 63 **p** 64. C Newc H Cross *Newc* 63-66; P-in-c Man St Aid *Man* 66-71; R Failsworth St Jo 71-79; P-in-c Farnham Royal *Ox* 79-81; P-in-c Hedgerley 80-81; R Farnham Royal w Hedgerley 81-91; V Prescot *Liv* from 91. *The Vicarage, Prescot, Merseyside L34 1LA* Tel 0151-426 6719

STEELE, Charles Edward Ernest. b 24. Cuddesdon Coll 72. **d** 74 **p** 75. C Rubery *Birm* 74-77; P-in-c Shaw Hill 77-79; V 79-82; C Curdworth 82-83; C Curdworth w Castle Vale 83-85; rtd 85; Perm to Offic *Birm* from 85. *3 Dominic Drive, Middleton Hall Road, Birmingham B30 1DW* Tel 0121-451 3372

STEELE, David Robert. b 29. Peterho Cam BA53 MA57. Oak Hill Th Coll 53. **d** 56 **p** 57. C Portman Square St Paul *Lon* 56-59; C Sevenoaks St Nic *Roch* 59-62; Kenya 63-65; Lic to Offic *Lon* 65-83; Chapl Steward's Trust Lon 65-72; Jt Gen Sec Intercon Ch Soc 72-81; Dir 2 Tim 2 Trust from 82; Perm to Offic *Lon* 83-91; Perm to Offic *Win* from 83; rtd 94. *Worthy Park Grove, Abbots Worthy, Winchester, Hants SO21 1AN* Tel (01962) 882082

STEELE, Derek James. b 53. **d** 97. Aux Min Ballywillan *Conn* from 97. *106 Mountsandel Road, Coleraine, Co Londonderry BT52 1TY* Tel (01265) 51633

STEELE, Gerald Robert. b 25. St D Coll Lamp BA49. **d** 51 **p** 52. C Glyntaff *Llan* 51-63; V Llangeinor 63-73; R Cadoxton-juxta-Barry 73-91; Chapl Barry Community Hosp 73-91; Miss to Seamen 73-91; rtd 91; Perm to Offic *Llan* from 91. *74 Redbrink Crescent, Barry CF62 5TU* Tel (01446) 373554

STEELE, Gordon John. b 55. Kent Univ BA76 Worc Coll Ox BA82 MA87. Coll of Resurr Mirfield 82. **d** 84 **p** 85. C Greenhill St Jo *Lon* 84-88; C Uxbridge St Andr w St Jo 88; C Uxbridge 88; TV 88-94; V Northampton St Alb *Pet* from 94. *St Alban's Vicarage, Broadmead Avenue, Northampton NN3 2RA* Tel (01604) 407074

STEELE, John Thomas Robson. b 02. Qu Coll Ox BA24. **d** 32 **p** 33. C Manningham St Paul *Bradf* 32-34; C Wensley *Ripon* 34-37; C Leyburn 34-37; C Yardley St Cypr Hay Mill *Birm* 37-39; V Hardrow and St Jo w Lunds *Ripon* 39-46; V Askrigg w Stallingbusk 46-53; R Kirkandrews-on-Esk *Carl* 53-70; rtd 70; Lic to Offic *Carl* 70-93. *Croftfield Residential Home, Croftfield Annexe, Cotehill, Carlisle CA4 9TB* Tel (01228) 560316

STEELE, Keith Atkinson. b 28. CEng MIMechE. Oak Hill Th Coll 80. **d** 81 **p** 82. Hon C Westoning w Tingrith *St Alb* 81-87; Hon C Chalgrave 87-88; P-in-c from 88; RD Dunstable 91-96. *Mariner's Lodge, Church Road, Westoning, Bedford MK45 5JW* Tel (01525) 714111

STEELE, Peter Gerald (Pete). b 44. Bournemouth Tech Coll BSc67 Essex Univ MSc69. Sarum & Wells Th Coll DipTh93. **d** 93 **p** 94. C Beaminster Area *Sarum* 93-97; P-in-c Aldermaston w Wasing and Brimpton *Ox* from 97. *The Vicarage, Aldermaston, Reading RG7 4LX* Tel 0118-971 2281

STEELE, Terence. b 54. Linc Th Coll 85. **d** 87 **p** 88. C New Sleaford *Linc* 87-90; V Cowbit 90-95; P-in-c Burgh le Marsh 95-97; P-in-c Orby 95-97; P-in-c Bratoft w Irby-in-the-Marsh 95-97; P-in-c Welton-le-Marsh w Gunby 95-97; V Burgh le Marsh from 97; R Bratoft w Irby-in-the-Marsh from 97; V Orby from 97; R Welton-le-Marsh w Gunby from 97. *The Vicarage, 41 Chapman Avenue, Burgh, Skegness, Lincs PE24 5LY* Tel (01754) 810216

STEELE-PERKINS, Richard De Courcy. b 36. Clifton Th Coll 61. **d** 64 **p** 65. C Stoke Damerel *Ex* 64-65; C Washfield 65-68; P-in-c Wimbledon *S'wark* 68-70; Chapl Lambeth Hosp 70-74; Asst Chapl St Thos Hosp Lon 70-74; P-in-c Tawstock *Ex* 74-75; R 75-81; P-in-c Sticklepath 74-75; R 75-81; V Buckfastleigh w Dean Prior 81-91; TR Camelot Par *B & W* 91-94; Asst Chapl R Surrey County and St Luke's Hosps NHS Trust from 94; Asst Chapl Heathlands Mental Health Trust Surrey from 94. *Royal Surrey County Hospital, Egerton Road, Guildford, Surrey GU2 5XX* Tel (01483) 571122

STEEN, Dr Jane Elizabeth. b 64. Newnham Coll Cam BA88 MA90 PhD92. Westcott Ho Cam 93. **d** 96 **p** 97. C Chipping Barnet w Arkley *St Alb* from 96. *13 Cedar Lawn Avenue, Chipping Barnet, Herts EN5 2LW* Tel 0181-449 4797

STEER, Martin Leslie. b 41. Dur Univ BA65. Oak Hill Th Coll 65. **d** 67 **p** 68. C Rayleigh *Chelmsf* 67-70; CF 70-76; Past Care, Guidance & Counselling Univ of Wales 76-77; Teacher and Lib Intake High Sch Leeds 77-88; NSM Roundhay St Edm *Ripon* 83-85; NSM Moor Allerton 85-88; Chapl HM Young Offender Inst Portland 88-96; Chapl HM Pris Parkhurst from 96. *HM Prison Parkhurst, Newport, Isle of Wight PO30 5NX* Tel (01983) 523855 Fax 524861

STEINBERG, Eric Reed (Joseph). b 65. Trin Coll Bris BA94. **d** 94 **p** 95. C Chigwell and Chigwell Row *Chelmsf* from 94. *St Winifred's Vicarage, Manor Road, Chigwell, Essex IG7 5PS* Tel 0181-500 4608 Fax 500 2805

STEINER, Eduard Samuel Ted. b 52. Liv Univ MB, ChB74 DCH76. EMMTC 93. **d** 96. NSM Ravenshead *S'well* from 96. *La Corbiere, Cauldwell Drive, Mansfield, Notts NG18 4SL* Tel (01623) 653615

STELL, Peter Donald. b 50. MInstM BAC Acc MAPCC Leeds Univ 74. Sarum & Wells Th Coll 78. **d** 81 **p** 82. C Rothwell w Lofthouse *Ripon* 81-85; TV Brayton *York* 85-87; Chapl Asst Leybourne Grange Hosp W Malling 87-88; Chapl Asst Kent, Sussex and Pembury Hosps Tunbridge Wells 87-88; C Spalding St Jo w Deeping St Nicholas *Linc* 88-93; Chapl S Lincs HA Mental Handicap Unit 90-93; Chapl HM Pris Liv 93-94; Chapl HM Pris Wayland from 94. *HM Prison, Wayland, Griston, Thetford, Norfolk IP25 6RL* Tel (01953) 884103 Fax 885775

STENHOUSE, Joan Frances Fleming. b 45. **dss** 84 **d** 86 **p** 94. Ellon *Ab* 84-86; NSM from 86; Cruden Bay 84-86; NSM from 86. *8 Ythan Court, Ellon, Aberdeenshire AB41 9BL* Tel (01358) 723241

STEPHANIE, Sister. *See* STEPPAT, Ida Margaret Agnes Stefan

STEPHEN, Canon Kenneth George. b 47. Strathclyde Univ BA69 Edin Univ BD72. Edin Th Coll 69. **d** 72 **p** 73. C Ayr *Glas* 72-75; R Renfrew 75-80; R Motherwell 80-93; R Wishaw 80-93; Can St Mary's Cathl from 87; Syn Clerk from 87; R Kilmarnock from 93. *The Parsonage, 1 Dundonald Road, Kilmarnock, Ayrshire KA1 1EQ* Tel (01563) 523577

STEPHENI, Frederick William. b 28. TD73. FSAScot81 FRSA82 Cranfield Inst of Tech MSc82. Lambeth STh83 Qu Coll Birm 54. **d** 55 **p** 56. C Arnold *S'well* 55-57; P-in-c 57-58; P-in-c Hucknall Torkard 58-59; Chapl Stoke-on-Trent City Gen Hosp 59-62; Chapl N Staffs R Infirmary Stoke-on-Trent 59-62; CF (TA) 60-88; Chapl K Coll Hosp Lon 62-63; R Cotgrave *S'well* 63-76; V Owthorpe 63-76; Chapl Addenbrooke's Hosp Cam 76-88; Lic to Offic *Ely* from 76; rtd 88. *Thatchers, 13 Tunwells Lane, Great Shelford, Cambridge CB2 5LJ* Tel (01223) 842914

STEPHENS, Canon Archibald John. b 15. Selw Coll Cam BA37 MA44. Wells Th Coll 46. **d** 47 **p** 48. C Gt Malvern St Mary *Worc* 47-50; Nigeria 50-68 and 70-71; Hon Can Ondo 57-71; Hon Can Owerri from 71; C Swindon Ch Ch *Bris* 68-70; C-in-c Ash Vale CD *Guildf* 71-72; V Ash Vale 72-77; P-in-c Thursley 77-82; rtd 82; Perm to Offic *Guildf* from 85. *Fernhill, 12 Vicarage Lane, Farnham, Surrey GU9 8HN* Tel (01252) 722514

STEPHENS, Charles Herbert. b 18. Lon Univ BA41 AKC42. **d** 42 **p** 43. C Chell *Lich* 42-44; Asst Chapl Denstone Coll Uttoxeter 44-45; Asst Master Nottm High Sch 45-78; Perm to Offic *S'well* from 73; rtd 83. *96 Grassington Road, Nottingham NG8 3PE* Tel 0115-929 1586

STEPHENS, Francis William. b 21. ARCA50. S'wark Ord Course 68. **d** 70 **p** 71. C Primrose Hill St Mary w Avenue Road St Paul *Lon* 70-92; Perm to Offic from 92; Ed Ch Pulpit Year Book from 81. *14 St Edmund's Close, London NW8 7QS* Tel 0171-722 7931

STEPHENS, Geoffrey Elford. b 19. St Jo Coll Dur BA41 MA58. Ripon Hall Ox 41. **d** 43 **p** 44. C Werneth *Man* 43-45; C Whalley Range St Marg 45-46; C Douglas *Blackb* 46-53; CF (TA) 48-54; V Whitechapel *Blackb* 53-55; CF (TA - R of O) 54-68; V Preston Ch Ch *Blackb* 55-58; R Mawdesley 60-86; CF (R of O) 68-74; rtd 86; Perm to Offic *Liv* from 86; Perm to Offic *Blackb* from 86. *19 Cambridge Avenue, Southport, Merseyside PR9 9SA* Tel (01704) 212385

STEPHENS, Harold William Barrow. b 47. Lon Univ BEd. S Dios Minl Tr Scheme 80. **d** 82 **p** 83. NSM Heytesbury and Sutton Veny *Sarum* 82-83; NSM Bishopstrow and Boreham 83-91; Lic to Offic Heytesbury Deanery from 91; Dep Hd Master Westwood St Thos Sch Salisbury from 91. *14 Prestbury Drive, Warminster, Wilts BA12 9LB* Tel (01985) 217776 E-mail harold.stephens @ukonline.co.uk

STEPHENS, Horace Alfred Patrick. b 14. MRCVS49. **d** 77 **p** 78. NSM Dingle w Killiney and Kilgobbin *L & K* 77-94; NSM Tralee w Ballymacelligott, Kilnaughtin etc from 94. *Magharabeg, Castlegregory, Tralee, Co Kerry, Irish Republic* Tel Tralee (66) 39159 Fax as telephone

STEPHENS, James Charles. b 62. DipAnChem. **d** 91 **p** 92. C Kilcolman w Kiltallagh, Killorglin, Knockane etc *L & K* from 91. *Kilderry, Miltown, Co Kerry, Irish Republic* Tel Tralee (66) 67735

STEPHENS, Mrs Jean. b 46. St As Minl Tr Course. **d** 89 **p** 97. NSM Gwernaffield and Llanferres *St As* from 89. *Noddfa, Pen-y-Fron Road, Pantymwyn, Mold CH7 5EF* Tel (01352) 740037

STEPHENS, John James Frederick. b 10. QUB BA34. Lon Coll of Div 34. **d** 37 **p** 38. C Stambermill *Worc* 37-40; CF (EC) 40-46; C Seapatrick H Trin *D & D* 46-47; C Wollaston *Worc* 47-48; R The Shelsleys 48-51; V Broadheath 51-82; rtd 82; Perm to Offic *Worc* from 82. *Jerred Cottage, Church Lane, Lower Broadheath, Worcester WR2 6QY* Tel (01905) 640224

STEPHENS, John Michael. b 29. ARICS52. Lich Th Coll 62. **d** 64 **p** 65. C Birchington w Acol *Cant* 64-70; V Tovil 70-79; V Brabourne w Smeeth 79-94; RD N Lympne 87-94; rtd 94; Perm to Offic *York* from 94. *Southacre, Kirby Mills, Kirkbymoorside, York YO6 6NR* Tel (01751) 432766

STEPHENS, Miss Mary. b 26. Reading Univ BA50 BEd51. Linc Th Coll. **d** 87 **p** 94. NSM Gt Grimsby St Mary and St Jas *Linc* 86-91; C 91-92; TD 92-94; TV 94-96; rtd 96; Perm to Offic *Linc* from 96. *33 Amesbury Avenue, Grimsby, S Humberside DN33 3HT*

STEPHENS, Paul. b 53. AGSM73 Newton Park Coll Bath PGCE74. Trin Coll Bris DipHE93. **d** 93 **p** 94. C S Molton w Nymet St George, High Bray etc *Ex* 93-97; R Norton Fitzwarren *B & W* from 97. *The Rectory, Rectory Road, Norton Fitzwarren, Taunton, Somerset TA2 6SE* Tel (01823) 272570

STEPHENS, Peter John. b 42. Or Coll Ox BA64 MA67. Clifton Th Coll 63. **d** 68 **p** 68. C Lenton *S'well* 68-71; C Brixton Hill St Sav *S'wark* 71-73; P-in-c 73-82; TV Barnham Broom *Nor* 82-89; V Gorleston St Mary 89-94; RD Flegg (Gt Yarmouth) 92-94; P-in-c High Oak from 94; RD Humbleyard from 95; C Hingham w Wood Rising w Scoulton from 96. *The Rectory, Deopham Road, Morley St Botolph, Wymondham, Norfolk NR18 9DA* Tel (01953) 606332

STEPHENS, Preb Peter Stanley. b 33. ALCD59. **d** 59 **p** 60. C Paignton St Paul Preston *Ex* 59-64; V Buckland Monachorum 64-74; RD Tavistock 70-74; V Compton Gifford 74-85; RD Plymouth Sutton 83-86; Preb Ex Cathl from 84; TR Plymouth Em w Efford 85-86; R Thurlestone w S Milton from 86. *The Rectory, Thurlestone, Kingsbridge, Devon TQ7 3NJ* Tel (01548) 560232

STEPHENS, Richard William. b 37. Dur Univ BSc62 DipTh64. Cranmer Hall Dur 62. **d** 64 **p** 65. C Hensingham *Carl* 64-67; C Norbury *Ches* 67-71; R Elworth and Warmingham 71-79; V Bootle St Matt *Liv* 79-89; P-in-c Litherland St Andr 79-83; P-in-c Failsworth H Trin *Man* 89-93; R from 93. *Holy Trinity Rectory, 103 Oldham Road, Failsworth, Manchester M35 0BH* Tel 0161-682 7901

STEPHENS, Ronald John. b 13. Sarum Th Coll 56. **d** 57 **p** 58. C Calne *Sarum* 57-61; V Stanstead Abbots *St Alb* 61-82; rtd 82; Perm to Offic *Nor* from 82. *63 Beechlands Park, Southrepps, Norwich NR11 8NT* Tel (01263) 834893

STEPHENS, Simon Edward. b 41. Qu Coll Birm DPS68 PhD80 Bps' Coll Cheshunt 63. **d** 67 **p** 68. C Cov St Mark *Cov* 67-71; C Lillington 71-76; C-in-c Canley CD 76-79; V Canley 79-80; Chapl RN 80-97; Asst Chapl Menorca *Eur* from 97. *Address temp unknown*

STEPHENS-HODGE, Lionel Edmund Howard. b 14. Selw Coll Cam BA36 MA40. Ridley Hall Cam 36. **d** 38 **p** 39. C Kingston upon Hull H Trin *York* 38-40; C Heworth H Trin 40-41; P-in-c Bulmer 41-43; R 43-44; Chapl Trin Coll Cam 44-45; Lib Tyndale Ho Cam 44-45; R Hatch Beauchamp w Beercrocombe *B & W* 45-51; R Glas St Silas *Glas* 51-54; V Rosedale *York* 54-56; Lect Lon Coll of Div 56-64; R Brindle *Blackb* 64-74; rtd 74; Lic Preacher *Blackb* 74-79; Perm to Offic *Ex* from 79. *1 Gracey Court, Woodland Road, Broadclyst, Exeter EX5 3LP* Tel (01392) 469005

STEPHENS-WILKINSON, Patricia Ann. b 45. Univ of Wales (Cardiff) BA66 CQSW80 MSc(Econ)91. Bp Burgess Hall Lamp CPS69. **dss** 69 **d** 89. Aberystwyth *St D* 69-71; Lic to Offic *Carl* 71-74; Perm to Offic *Mon* 74-89; NSM Machen 89-93. *Address temp unknown*

STEPHENSON, David John. b 65. Bris Univ BSc(Soc)87 Dur Univ BA91. Cranmer Hall Dur DMinlStuds92. **d** 92 **p** 93. C Whickham *Dur* 92-94; C Sunderland Pennywell St Thos 94-97; V Stockton St Jo from 97. *St John the Baptist Vicarage, 168 Durham Road, Stockton-on-Tees, Cleveland TS19 0DZ* Tel (01642) 274119

STEPHENSON, Canon Eric George. b 41. Bede Coll Dur CertEd63. Qu Coll Birm DipTh65. **d** 66 **p** 67. C Wakef St Jo *Wakef* 66-69; C Seaham w Seaham Harbour *Dur* 69-73; C Cockerton 73-75; Lic to Offic 75-85; V E Boldon from 85; RD Jarrow from 92; Hon Can Dur Cathl from 93. *The Vicarage,*

2 Ashleigh Villas, East Boldon, Tyne & Wear NE36 0LA Tel 0191-536 2557

STEPHENSON, Ian Clarke. b 24. Lon Univ DipTh69. Tyndale Hall Bris 52. **d** 56 **p** 57. C Bedworth *Cov* 56-58; C Edgware *Lon* 58-65; R Biddulph Moor *Lich* 65-70; Hon C Biddulph 70-88; Hon C Burslem 85-88; New Zealand from 87; rtd 89. *5 Arthur Terrace, Balclutha, Otago, New Zealand* Tel Christchurch (3) 418 2657

STEPHENSON, John Joseph. b 35. St Jo Coll Dur BA74. Qu Coll Birm 75. **d** 76 **p** 77. C Whitworth w Spennymoor *Dur* 76-79; V Eppleton 79-96; rtd 96; Perm to Offic *Dur* from 96. *29 Launceston Drive, Sunderland SR3 3QB* Tel 0191-528 2144

STEPHENSON, Martin Woodard. b 55. St Cath Coll Cam BA77 MA82. Westcott Ho Cam 78. **d** 81 **p** 82. C Eastleigh *Win* 81-85; C Ferryhill *Dur* 85-87; Asst Dir of Ords 87-89; Chapl St Chad's Coll 87-89; TR Clarendon Park St Jo w Knighton St Mich *Leic* from 89. *The Rectory, 9 Springfield Road, Leicester LE2 3BB* Tel 0116-270 6097

STEPHENSON, Nicolas William. b 22. Ely Th Coll 60. **d** 62 **p** 63. C S Westoe *Dur* 62-65; CR from 68; Hon C Westgate Common *Wakef* 74-75; Lic to Offic 75-87; Asst Chapl HM Pris Wakef 84-87; rtd 87. *24 Nicholson Court, 25 Fitzroy Drive, Leeds LS8 4AB* Tel 0113-248 5166

STEPHENSON, Robert. b 36. St Chad's Coll Dur BA58 DipTh60. **d** 60 **p** 61. C Whickham *Dur* 60-63; C Gateshead St Mary 63-65; PC Low Team 65-67; R Stella 67-74; V Comberton *Ely* from 74; RD Bourn from 94. *The Vicarage, Comberton, Cambridge CB3 7ED* Tel (01223) 262793

STEPHENSON, Canon Robert Ommanney. b 09. St Cath Coll Cam BA32 MA36. Cuddesdon Coll 32. **d** 33 **p** 34. C W End *Win* 33-37; C Tonge Moor *Man* 37-41; V Horton *Newc* 41-47; V Bitterne Park *Win* 47-70; Hon Can Win Cathl 67-79; R E Woodhay and Woolton Hill 70-79; RD Whitchurch 72-79; rtd 79; Perm to Offic *B & W* 79-97. *Fairlawn, Witcombe Lane, Ash, Martock, Somerset TA12 6AH* Tel (01935) 824330

STEPHENSON, Simon George. b 44. St Jo Coll Dur BA67. Trin Coll Bris 74. **d** 76 **p** 77. C Hildenborough *Roch* 76-82; C Bishopsworth *Bris* 82-85; C-in-c Withywood CD 85-90; TV Wreningham *Nor* from 90; P-in-c Tasburgh w Tharston, Forncett and Flordon from 94. *The Vicarage, 16 The Fields, Tacolneston, Norwich NR16 1DG* Tel (01953) 788227

STEPNEY, Area Bishop of. *See* SENTAMU, The Rt Revd John Mugabi

STEPPAT, Ida Margaret Agnes Stefan (Sister Stephanie). **d** 95. *St Denys Convent, Vicarage Street, Warminster, Wilts BA12 8JD* Tel (01985) 214824

STERLING, Anne. *See* HASELHURST, Mrs Anne

STERLING, John Haddon. b 40. Pemb Coll Cam BA62 MA66. Cuddesdon Coll 63. **d** 65 **p** 66. S Africa 65-70; Chapl Bris Cathl *Bris* 71-74; Member Dioc Soc and Ind Team 71-74; Ind Chapl *Linc* 74-87; Ind Chapl *Ripon* 87-92; TV Hanley H Ev *Lich* 92-97; Min in Ind 92-97; P-in-c Hixon w Stowe-by-Chartley from 97; P-in-c Fradswell, Gayton, Milwich and Weston from 97. *The Vicarage, Weston, Stafford ST18 0HX*

STERRY, Christopher. b 54. K Coll Lon BD77 AKC77. Episc Sem Austin Texas CSpSt78 St Jo Coll Nottm DPS80. **d** 80 **p** 81. C Huddersfield St Jo *Wakef* 80-84; V Middlestown 84-89; Chapl and Tutor N Ord Course 89-94; Lect Ches Coll 93-94; Lic to Offic *Man* 89-92; NSM Padgate *Liv* 92-94; Chapl Whalley Abbey from 94; Bp's Dom Chapl *Blackb* from 94. *Whaley Lodge, Whalley Abbey, Whalley, Blackburn BB7 9SS* Tel (01254) 824679 or 248234 E-mail bishop.blackburn@dial.pipex.com.

STERRY, Timothy John (Tim). b 34. Or Coll Ox BA58 MA62 DipTh60. Wycliffe Hall Ox 58. **d** 60 **p** 61. C Cromer *Nor* 60-64; Chapl Oundle Sch 64-72; Chapl Cheam Sch Newbury 72-75; Hd Master Temple Grove Sch E Sussex 75-80; Team Ldr Scripture Union Independent Schs from 81; Perm to Offic *S'wark* from 81. *1 The Close, Chart Lane, Reigate, Surrey RH2 7BN* Tel (01737) 244370 Fax 0171-782 0014

STEVEN, David Bowring. b 38. AKC64. **d** 64 **p** 65. C Grantham St Wulfram *Linc* 64-68; S Africa 68-75; C Bramley *Ripon* 76-77; V Sutton Valence w E Sutton and Chart Sutton *Cant* 77-82; P-in-c Littlebourne 82-86; V Mansfield Woodhouse *S'well* from 86. *The Vicarage, 7 Butt Lane, Mansfield Woodhouse, Mansfield, Notts NG19 9JS* Tel (01623) 21875

STEVEN, James Henry Stevenson. b 62. CCC Cam MA87 St Jo Coll Dur BA87. Cranmer Hall Dur 84. **d** 87 **p** 88. C Welling *Roch* 87-91; C Bournemouth St Jo w St Mich *Win* 91-94; TV Bournemouth St Pet w St Swithun, H Trin etc from 94; Chapl Bournemouth and Poole Coll of FE from 94. *1 Gervis Road, Bournemouth BH1 3ED* Tel (01202) 291289

STEVENETTE, John Maclachlan. b 30. St Pet Coll Ox MA60. Ripon Hall Ox 60. **d** 61 **p** 62. C Newhaven *Chich* 61-66; V Lynch w Iping Marsh 66-74; R Birdham w W Itchenor 74-78; R Byfleet *Guildf* 78-86; V Whittlesey *Ely* 86-90; TR Whittlesey and Pondersbridge 91; R Itchen Valley *Win* from 91. *Itchen Valley Rectory, Chillandham Lane, Martyr Worthy, Winchester, Hants SO21 1AS* Tel (01962) 779832

STEVENETTE, Simon Melville. b 62. Hull Univ BA83. Wycliffe Hall Ox 84. **d** 87 **p** 88. C Carterton *Ox* 87-90; C Keynsham *B & W* 90-91; TV from 91; Chapl Keynsham Hosp Bris from 92. *9 Chelmer Grove, Keynsham, Bristol BS18 1QA* Tel 0117-986 6390

STEVENS, Alan Robert. b 55. Warw Univ BA77. St Jo Coll Nottm 87. **d** 89 **p** 90. C Ex St Leon w H Trin *Ex* 89-92; TV Rugby St Andr *Cov* from 92. *St Michael's House, 43 Bowfell, Brownsover, Rugby, Warks CV21 1JF* Tel (01788) 573696

STEVENS, Andrew Graham. b 54. BEd MA. Coll of Resurr Mirfield. **d** 83 **p** 84. C Leigh Park *Portsm* 83-87; TV Brighton Resurr *Chich* 87-94; V Plumstead St Nic *S'wark* from 94. *St Nicholas's Vicarage, 64 Purrett Road, London SE18 1JP* Tel 0181-854 0461

STEVENS, Anne Helen. b 61. Warw Univ BA82 Fitzw Coll Cam BA90 MA94. Ridley Hall Cam 88. **d** 91 **p** 94. Par Dn E Greenwich Ch Ch w St Andr and St Mich *S'wark* 91-94; Chapl Trin Coll Cam from 94. *7 Green Street, Cambridge CB2 3JU* Tel (01223) 32810 or 338400 Fax 338564

STEVENS, Anthony Harold. b 46. CEng71 MIStructE71 FIStructE87 MICE75 FICE92 S Bank Univ ONC65 HNC67. St Mich Coll Llan DipPTh95. **d** 95 **p** 96. C Cardiff St Jo *Llan* from 95. *41 Colum Road, Cardiff CF1 3EE* Tel (01222) 224036 or (0589) 819025

STEVENS, Arthur Edward Geary. b 14. Lon Coll of Div 34. **d** 37 **p** 38. C Woodside Park St Barn *Lon* 37-40; C W Hampstead St Luke 40-41; C Herne Hill Road St Sav *S'wark* 41-42; V W Hampstead St Cuth *Lon* 42-46; V S'well H Trin *S'well* 46-50; V Sheff St Jo *Sheff* 50-54; V Guernsey H Trin *Win* 54-67; Chapl Castel Hosp Guernsey 60-67; Chapl HM Pris Guernsey 61-67; V Bitterne *Win* 67-72; V Duffield *Derby* 72-94; rtd 94. *Flat 2, 3 Avenue Road, Duffield, Belper, Derbyshire DE56 4DW* Tel (01332) 842924

STEVENS, Brian Henry. b 28. Oak Hill Th Coll. **d** 69 **p** 70. C Chadwell *Chelmsf* 69-75; V Penge Ch Ch w H Trin *Roch* 75-85; V St Mary Cray and St Paul's Cray 85-93; rtd 93; Perm to Offic *Cant* from 93. *53 Middle Deal Road, Deal, Kent CT14 9RG*

STEVENS, Brian Henry. b 45. Open Univ BA80. S Dios Minl Tr Scheme 81. **d** 84 **p** 85. NSM S Malling *Chich* 84-86; C Langney 86-87; TV Wolverton *Ox* 87-88; V Welford w Sibbertoft and Marston Trussell *Pet* 88-91; V Hardingstone and Horton and Piddington from 91. *The Vicarage, 29 Back Lane, Hardingstone, Northants NN4 6BY* Tel (01604) 760110

STEVENS, Cyril David Richard. b 25. NZ Bd of Th Studies LTh66. **d** 59 **p** 60. New Zealand 59-65 and 67-68; V Playford w Culpho and Tuddenham St Martin *St E* 65-67; R Rendham w Sweffling and Cransford 69-73; RD Saxmundham 72-74; R Rendham w Sweffling 73-95; rtd 95. *Meadow Cottage, Low Road, Marlesford, Woodbridge, Suffolk IP13 0AW* Tel (01728) 746013

STEVENS, David Charles. b 31. Keble Coll Ox BA55 DipTh56 MA59. Wycliffe Hall Ox 55. **d** 57 **p** 58. C Plymouth St Andr *Ex* 57-60; S Rhodesia 61-65; Rhodesia 65-66; Asst Chapl Bryanston Sch Dorset 66-70; Chapl 70-73; P-in-c Shilling Okeford *Sarum* 73-76; Lic to Offic *Chelmsf* 76-86; Chapl Chigwell Sch Essex 76-86; R Tarrant Valley *Sarum* 86-94; rtd 94. *Bumble Cottage, 3 Yondover, Loders, Bridport, Dorset DT6 4NW* Tel (01308) 421025

STEVENS, David John. b 45. Bris Univ BA67 Lon Univ DipTh69. Clifton Th Coll. **d** 70 **p** 71. C Ex St Leon w H Trin *Ex* 70-75; P-in-c Lt Burstead *Chelmsf* 75-77; TV Billericay and Lt Burstead 77-81; P-in-c Illogan *Truro* 81-83; R St Illogan 83-96; RD Carnmarth N 96; V Highworth w Sevenhampton and Inglesham etc *Bris* from 96. *The Vicarage, 10 Stonefield Drive, Highworth, Swindon SN6 7DA* Tel (01793) 765554

STEVENS, Canon David Johnson (Brother David Stephen). b 13. St Cath Soc Ox BA51 MA55. Wycliffe Hall Ox 49. **d** 52 **p** 53. C Wigan St Cath *Liv* 52-54; P-in-c Litherland St Paul Hatton Hill 54-57; Ind Chapl 57-77; V Warrington St Paul 61-70; Guardian of Franciscan Ho Liv 70-77; Hon Can Liv Cathl 71-78; SSF from 77; Lic to Offic *Newc* from 79; rtd 83. *The Friary, Alnmouth, Alnwick, Northd NE66 3NJ* Tel (01665) 830213

STEVENS, David Leonard. b 28. St Edm Hall Ox BA51 MA57. Cuddesdon Coll 60. **d** 62 **p** 63. C Old Brumby *Linc* 62-67; Chapl St Alb Sch Chorley 67-71; V Linc St Faith and St Martin w St Pet *Linc* 72-83; C Wolborough w Newton Abbot *Ex* 83-87; P-in-c 87-94; rtd 94. *Yew Tree Cottage, Sticklepath, Okehampton, Devon EX20 2NW* Tel (01837) 840098

STEVENS, Douglas George. b 47. Lon Univ BA69. Westcott Ho Cam 69. **d** 72 **p** 73. C Portsea St Geo CD *Portsm* 72-75; C Portsea N End St Mark 75-79; Chapl NE Lon Poly *Chelmsf* 79-83; C-in-c Orton Goldhay CD *Ely* 83-87; V Elm 87-91; V Coldham 87-91; V Friday Bridge 87-91; R Woodston from 91; P-in-c Fletton from 94. *The Rectory, 183A London Road, Peterborough PE2 9DS* Tel (01733) 62786

STEVENS, Frank Hayman. b 11. Univ Coll Ox BA32 MA38. Linc Th Coll 64. **d** 65 **p** 66. C Burnham *B & W* 65-68; V Kenn 68-69; P-in-c Kingston Seymour 68-69; R Kenn w Kingston Seymour 69-74; P-in-c Cossington 74-76; rtd 76; Perm to Offic *B & W* from 76. *14 Eastgate Gardens, Taunton, Somerset TA1 1RD* Tel (01823) 270436

STEVENS, Frederick Crichton (Fred). b 42. K Coll Lon BD78 AKC78. St Steph Ho Ox 78. **d** 79 **p** 80. C Newquay *Truro* 79-81; C St Martin-in-the-Fields *Lon* 81-85; P-in-c Soho St Anne w

St Thos and St Pet 85-96; R from 96. *55 Dean Street, London W1V 5HH* Tel 0171-437 5244

STEVENS, James Anthony. b 47. Worc Coll Ox MA69. Trin Coll Bris 78. **d** 80 **p** 81. C Heref St Pet w St Owen and St Jas *Heref* 80-84; C Lowestoft and Kirkley *Nor* 84-85; TV 85-89; V Dorridge *Birm* from 89. *The Vicarage, 6 Manor Road, Dorridge, Solihull, W Midlands B93 8DX* Tel (01564) 772472 or 775652

STEVENS, John David Andrew. b 44. Wycliffe Hall Ox. **d** 68 **p** 69. C Standish *Blackb* 68-71; C Stonehouse *Glouc* 71-76; P-in-c Closworth *B & W* 76-77; P-in-c Barwick 76-77; TV Yeovil 77-80; R Chewton Mendip w Ston Easton, Litton etc 80-94; R Quantoxhead from 94; RD Quantock from 95. *The New Rectory, Kilve, Bridgwater, Somerset TA5 1DZ* Tel (01278) 741501

STEVENS, Martin Leonard. b 35. St Jo Coll Dur BA60 MA72. Oak Hill Th Coll 60. **d** 62 **p** 63. C Low Elswick *Newc* 62-65; C S Croydon Em *Cant* 65-69; Hon C 69-74; S England Dep Sec Irish Ch Miss 69-74; V Felling *Dur* 74-86; NSM Ches Square St Mich w St Phil *Lon* 92-96; rtd 95. *5 Cotter Close, Kentisbeare, Cullompton, Devon EX15 2DJ* Tel (01884) 266741

STEVENS, Michael John. b 37. St Cath Coll Cam BA63. Coll of Resurr Mirfield 63. **d** 65 **p** 66. C Poplar All SS w St Frideswide *Lon* 65-71; Asst Chapl The Lon Hosp (Whitechapel) 71-74; Chapl St Thos Hosp Lon 75-96; Hospitaller St Bart Hosp Lon from 96. *St Bartholomew's Hospital, West Smithfield, London EC1A 7BE, or 2 Walcot Square, London SE11 4TZ* Tel 0171-601 8066 or 735 7362

STEVENS, Neville. b 21. Clare Coll Cam BA52 MA54 Or Coll Ox DipTh54. Wycliffe Hall Ox 52. **d** 54 **p** 55. C Bishopsworth *Bris* 54-56; Chapl Leeds Gr Sch 56-84; Perm to Offic *Wakef* from 71; Perm to Offic *Ripon* from 85. *6 Hill Top Green, West Ardsley, Tingley, Wakefield, W Yorkshire WF3 1HS* Tel 0113-253 8038

STEVENS, Peter David. b 36. ARICS. Oak Hill Th Coll DipHE81. **d** 81 **p** 82. C Branksome St Clem *Sarum* 81-87; R Moreton and Woodsford w Tincleton from 87. *The Rectory, Moreton, Dorchester, Dorset DT2 8RH* Tel (01929) 462466

STEVENS, Philip Terence. b 55. MBIM Man Univ BSc76 Lon Univ BD81 St Jo Coll Dur MA86. Cranmer Hall Dur 81. **d** 83 **p** 84. C Withington St Paul *Man* 83-86; C Middleton 86-88; V Saddleworth 88-92; V Sheff St Paul Wordsworth Avenue *Sheff* 93-96; TR Sheff Manor from 96. *The Vicarage, Cary Road, Sheffield S2 1JP* Tel 0114-239 8360 or 253 0518

STEVENS, Canon Ralph. b 11. Selw Coll Cam BA36 MA40. Qu Coll Birm 36. **d** 38 **p** 39. C E Retford *S'well* 38-40; Hon C Harringay St Paul *Lon* 40-41; C Finchley St Mary 41-43; P-in-c Tottenham Ch Ch W Green 43-46; V Becontree St Thos *Chelmsf* 46-49; R Lambourne 49-65; R Colchester St Mary V 65-77; R Colchester Ch Ch w St Mary V 77-79; Hon Can Chelmsf Cathl 71-79; rtd 79; Perm to Offic *Chelmsf* from 79; Perm to Offic *St E* from 79. *9 York Road, Southwold, Suffolk IP18 6AN* Tel (01502) 723705

STEVENS, Canon Ralph Samuel Osborn. b 13. Birm Univ BSc34 St Cath Soc Ox BA36 MA41. Ripon Hall Ox 34. **d** 36 **p** 37. C Aston SS Pet and Paul *Birm* 36-45; P-in-c Birm St Paul 45-50; V 50-83; RD Cen Birmingham 46-58; RD Birm City 58-73; Hon Chapl to Bp 48-83; Hon Can Birm Cathl 52-83; Ind Chapl 54-78; Chapl to The Queen 67-83; rtd 83; Perm to Offic *Birm* from 84. *10 Harrison's Green, Birmingham B15 3LH* Tel 0121-454 3089

STEVENS, Richard William. b 36. AKC59. **d** 60 **p** 61. C Greenhill St Jo *Lon* 60-63; Chapl RAF 63-79; CF from 79; rtd 91. *The Old Vicarage, Stockbury, Sittingbourne, Kent ME9 7UN* Tel (01795) 844891

STEVENS, Robin George. b 43. Leic Univ BA65. Cuddesdon Coll 74. **d** 74 **p** 75. C Hemel Hempstead *St Alb* 74-77; Chapl K Coll Sch Wimbledon from 77. *329 Wimbledon Park Road, London SW19 6NS* Tel 0181-788 1501 or 947 9311

STEVENS, Miss Sylvia Joyce. b 41. Qu Mary Coll Lon BA63 Bris Univ CertEd64 St Jo Coll Dur BA77 DipTh78. Cranmer Hall Dur 75. **dss** 78 **d** 87 **p** 94. Chapl Trent (Nottm) Poly *S'well* 78-92; Chapl Nottm Trent Univ 92-93; Continuing Minl Educn Officer *Bris* 93-95; Tutor Trin Coll Bris 93-95; Hon C Chippenham St Pet *Bris* 93-95; C 95-97. *17 Linden Court, Hollin Lane, Leeds LS16 5NB* Tel 0113-275 5498

STEVENS, Thomas Walter. b 33. Bps' Coll Cheshunt. **d** 65 **p** 66. C Newc St Matt w St Mary *Newc* 65-69; C Wallsend St Luke 69-70; C Cranford *Lon* 70-87; C Fulwell St Mich and St Geo 87-90; C Teddington SS Pet and Paul and Fulwell 90-91; rtd 92; Perm to Offic *S'wark* from 92. *23A Samos Road, London SE20 7UQ*

✠**STEVENS, The Rt Revd Timothy John.** b 46. Selw Coll Cam BA68 MA72 DipTh. Ripon Coll Cuddesdon 75. **d** 76 **p** 77 **c** 95. C E Ham w Upton Park St Alb *Chelmsf* 76-80; TR Canvey Is 80-88; Dep Dir Cathl Cen for Research and Tr 82-84; Bp's Urban Officer 87-91; Hon Can Chelmsf Cathl 87-91; Adn W Ham 91-95; Suff Bp Dunwich *St E* from 95. *The Old Vicarage, Stowupland, Stowmarket IP14 4BQ* Tel (01449) 678234 Fax 771148

STEVENSON, Alastair Rice. b 42. Open Univ BA78. Ripon Coll Cuddesdon 78. **d** 80 **p** 81. C Bexhill St Pet *Chich* 80-82; C Brighton St Matthias 82-84; C Swindon Ch Ch *Bris* 84-87; Bp's Soc and Ind Adv 87-97; P-in-c Swindon All SS w St Barn from 97. *The Vicarage, Southbrook Street, Swindon SN2 1HF* Tel (01793) 612385

STEVENSON, Andrew James. b 63. SW Minl Tr Course. **d** 97. NSM Highertown and Baldhu *Truro* from 97. *88 Carne View Road, Truro, Cornwall TR2 4TR* Tel (01726) 883549

STEVENSON, Bernard Norman. b 57. Kent Univ BA78 Fitzw Coll Cam BA81 MA86. Ridley Hall Cam. **d** 82 **p** 83. C Mortlake w E Sheen *S'wark* 82-84; C Kensal Rise St Martin *Lon* 84-88; C Headstone St Geo 88-90; V Worfield *Heref* 90-95; R Hutton *B & W* from 95. *The Rectory, Church Lane, Hutton, Weston-super-Mare, Avon BS24 9SL* Tel (01934) 812366

STEVENSON, Brian. b 34. JP66. NW Ord Course 76. **d** 79 **p** 80. C Padiham *Blackb* 79-82; V Clitheroe St Paul Low Moor 82-89; V Blackb St Silas from 89. *St Silas' Vicarage, Preston New Road, Blackburn BB2 6PS* Tel (01254) 671293

STEVENSON, Christopher James. b 43. TCD BA65 MA73 Em Coll Cam BA69 MA73. Westcott Ho Cam 68. **d** 70 **p** 71. C Newc H Cross *Newc* 70-72; C Arm St Mark *Arm* 72-73; C Dublin Crumlin *D & G* 73-76; Hon Clerical V Ch Ch Cathl Dublin 75-76; C-in-c Appley Bridge All SS CD *Blackb* 76-82; P-in-c Appley Bridge 82-91; Bp's C Clooonclare w Killasnett, Lurganboy and Drumlease *K, E & A* from 92. *The Rectory, Manorhamilton, Co Leitrim, Irish Republic* Tel Manorhamilton (72) 55041

STEVENSON, David Andrew. b 60. Trin Coll Bris BA92. **d** 92 **p** 93. C Nottingham St Sav *S'well* 92-96; P-in-c Darlaston All SS *Lich* from 96; Ind Chapl Black Country Urban Ind Miss from 96. *All Saints' Vicarage, Walsall Road, Wednesbury, W Midlands WS10 9SQ* Tel 0121-568 6618

STEVENSON, Derick Neville. b 36. Open Univ BA76. Ridley Hall Cam 79. **d** 80 **p** 81. C Bonchurch *Portsm* 80-84; C-in-c Crookhorn Ch Cen CD 84-87; R Norton Fitzwarren *B & W* 87-96; P-in-c N Hartismere *St E* from 96. *The Rectory, Oakley, Diss, Norfolk IP21 4AU* Tel (01379) 740322

STEVENSON, Donald Macdonald (Don). b 48. Lon Univ BSc(Econ)70 Leeds Univ MA72 Univ of Wales (Abth) PGCE73 Warw Univ MEd78. Oak Hill Th Coll BA88. **d** 88 **p** 89. C Gt Malvern St Mary *Worc* 88-92; Chapl Bedford Sch from 92; Sen Chapl from 96. *Bedford School, De Parys Avenue, Bedford MK40 2TU* Tel (01234) 353493 or 406763

STEVENSON, Frank Beaumont. b 39. MInstGA(Lon) Duke Univ (USA) BA61. Episc Th Sch Harvard MDiv64. **d** 64 **p** 64. USA 64-66; Zambia 66-68; Lect Th Ox Univ from 68; Bp's Tr Officer *Ox* 69-70; Chapl Keble Coll Ox 71-72; Chapl Isis Gp Hosps 73-75; Chapl Littlemore Hosp Ox from 75; Officer for Continuing Minl Educn from 90. *Littlemore Hospital, Littlemore, Oxford OX4 4XN, or The School House, Stanton St John, Oxford OX33 1ET* Tel (01865) 778911 or 351635

STEVENSON, Gerald Ernest. b 35. S'wark Ord Course 80. **d** 83 **p** 84. NSM Eltham Park St Luke *S'wark* 83-88; Asst Chapl HM Pris Wormwood Scrubs from 88; Perm to Offic *S'wark* from 88. *106 Grangehill Road, London SE9 1SE* Tel 0181-850 2748 Fax 749 5655

STEVENSON, John. b 39. Glas Univ MA64 Jordan Hill Coll Glas TCert65. St Jo Coll Nottm 87. **d** 87 **p** 88. NSM Moffat *Glas* 87-92; P-in-c Eastriggs 92-95; P-in-c Gretna 92-95; P-in-c Langholm 92-95; Israel from 95. *Address temp unknown*

STEVENSON, John Charles. b 22. St Jo Coll Dur LTh48. Oak Hill Th Coll 45. **d** 49 **p** 50. C Davyhulme St Mary *Man* 49-51; C Thornham w Gravel Hole 51-54; V Steeple Claydon *Ox* 54-58; R Salford Stowell Memorial *Man* 58-64; RD Claydon *Ox* 58; V Bolton St Bede *Man* 64-75; Asst Chapl HM Pris Wandsworth 75-77; Chapl HM Pris Linc 77-80; R Fiskerton *Linc* 80-87; rtd 87; Perm to Offic *Blackb* from 87. *15 The Coppice, Redwood Park, Beaufort Road, Morecambe, Lancs LA4 6TY* Tel (01524) 423653

STEVENSON, John William. b 44. Salford Univ BSc66 E Warks Coll DipMan73 Univ of S Africa BTh89. St Paul's Grahamstown DipTh86. **d** 87 **p** 87. S Africa 87-93; V Broom Leys *Leic* from 93. *St David's Vicarage, 7 Greenhill Road, Coalville, Leics LE67 4RL* Tel (01530) 836262

✠**STEVENSON, The Rt Revd Kenneth William.** b 49. FRHistS90 Edin Univ MA70 Southn Univ PhD75 Man Univ DD87. Sarum & Wells Th Coll 70. **d** 73 **p** 74 **c** 95. C Grantham w Manthorpe *Linc* 73-76; C Boston 76-80; Chapl Man Univ *Man* 80-86; TV Man Whitworth 80-82; TR 82-86; Lect Man Univ 80-86; R Guildf H Trin w St Mary *Guildf* 86-95; Bp Portsm from 95. *Bishop's Grove, 26 Osborn Road, Fareham, Hants PO16 7DQ* Tel (01329) 280247 Fax 231538

STEVENSON, Leslie Thomas Clayton. b 59. TCD BA DipTh MPhil. **d** 83 **p** 84. C Dundela *D & D* 83-87; I Kilmore w Inch 87-92; I Donaghadee from 92. *3 The Trees, New Road, Donaghadee, Co Down BT21 0EJ* Tel (01247) 882594

STEVENSON, Lorna. b 43. Moray Ho Edin DipEd65. **dss** 85 **d** 86. NSM Dundee St Luke *Bre* from 85. *39 Charleston Drive, Dundee DD2 2HF* Tel (01382) 66631

STEVENSON, Michael Richard Nevin. b 52. Univ Coll Lon MA77. CITC DipTh86. **d** 86 **p** 87. C Clooney w Strathfoyle *D & R* 86-89; CF from 89. *MOD Chaplains (Army), Trenchard Lines, Upavon, Pewsey, Wilts SN9 6BE* Tel (01980) 615804 Fax 615800

STEVENSON, The Ven Richard Clayton. b 22. TCD BA48 MA56. CITC 48. **d** 48 **p** 49. C Belfast St Mary Magd *Conn* 48-51; C Bangor St Comgall *D & D* 51-54; I Comber 54-60; I Belfast St Barn *Conn* 60-70; I Belfast St Nic 70-88; Adn Conn 79-88; rtd 88. *42 Malone Heights, Belfast BT9 5PG* Tel (01232) 615006

STEVENSON, Robert Brian. b 40. QUB BA61 Qu Coll Cam BA67 MA71 Pemb Coll Ox BA69 BD76 MA76 Birm Univ PhD70. Cuddesdon Coll 69. **d** 70 **p** 71. C Lewisham St Jo Southend *S'wark* 70-73; C Catford (Southend) and Downham 73-74; Lect and Dir Past Studies Chich Th Coll 74-81; Acting Vice-Prin 80-81; V W Malling w Offham *Roch* from 81; RD Malling from 93. *The Vicarage, 138 High Street, West Malling, Kent ME19 6NE* Tel (01732) 842245

STEVENSON, Canon Ronald. b 17. Leeds Univ BA38. Coll of Resurr Mirfield 38. **d** 40 **p** 41. C Pontefract All SS *Wakef* 40-44; C-in-c Lundwood CD 44-47; Area Sec Miss to Seamen 47-49; Perm to Offic Linc, Ches, Man, Blackb, Carl 49-65; Leic, Derby and Pet 49-65; Chapl Lanc Moor Hosp 49-65; Chapl N Lancs and S Westmorland Hosps 65-75; Hon Can Blackb Cathl *Blackb* 71-75. *28 Slyne Road, Torrisholme, Morecambe, Lancs LA4 6PA* Tel (01524) 410957

STEVENSON (née PITE), Mrs Sheila Reinhardt. b 60. St Jo Coll Dur BA82. Oak Hill Th Coll BA88. **d** 88 **p** 94. Par Dn Derby St Aug *Derby* 88-92; C Brampton St Thos 92-95; Perm to Offic *St Alb* 95-96; P-in-c The Stodden Churches from 96. *Stodden Rectory, Upper Dean, Huntingdon, Cambs PE18 0ND* Tel (01234) 708531

STEVENSON, Trevor Donald. b 59. TCD Div Sch BTh. **d** 91 **p** 92. C Magheralin w Dollingstown *D & D* 91-95; CMS from 95; Uganda from 95. *Church Mission Society, Partnership House, 157 Waterloo Road, London SE1 8UU* Tel 0171-928 8681 Fax 401 3215

STEVENTON, Mrs June Lesley. b 61. Aston Tr Scheme 86 Sarum & Wells Th Coll BTh91. **d** 91 **p** 94. Par Dn Chatham St Steph *Roch* 91-94; C 94-96; Perm to Offic *York* from 96; Perm to Offic *Liv* from 97. *158 Birleywood, Skelmersdale, Lancs WN8 9BX* Tel (01695) 728091 Fax as telephone

STEVENTON, Kenneth. b 59. Cuddesdon Coll 94. **d** 96 **p** 97. C Spalding *Linc* from 96. *The Chantry, 7 Church Street, Spalding, Lincs PE11 2PB* Tel (01775) 722631

STEVINSON, Harold John Hardy. b 34. Selw Coll Cam BA57 MA61. Qu Coll Birm. **d** 59 **p** 60. C Bris St Mary Redcliffe w Temple *Bris* 59-63; C Caversham *Ox* 63-73; Soc Resp Officer *Dur* 74-82; Sec Dioc Bd for Miss and Unity 82-88; P-in-c Croxdale 82-88; P-in-c Leamington Hastings and Birdingbury *Cov* 88-96; rtd 96. *8 Greenways, Winchcombe, Cheltenham, Glos GL54 5LG* Tel (01242) 602195

STEVINSON, Josephine Mary (Jo). b 25. STh56. Cranmer Hall Dur 86. **dss** 86 **d** 87 **p** 94. Croxdale *Dur* 86-87; Lic to Offic 87-88; Lic to Offic *Cov* 88-96; NSM Leamington Hastings and Birdingbury 94-96; rtd 96; Perm to Offic *Glouc* from 96. *8 Greenways, Winchcombe, Cheltenham, Glos GL54 5LG* Tel (01242) 602195

STEWARD, Mrs Linda Christine. b 46. NE Lon Poly CQSW82. S'wark Ord Course 85. **d** 88 **p** 94. NSM E Ham w Upton Park St Alb *Chelmsf* 88-90; Chapl Newham Gen Hosp 90-94; Chapl Newham Healthcare NHS Trust Lon from 93; NSM Plaistow *Chelmsf* 94-96; NSM Plaistow and N Canning Town from 96. *Newham General Hospital, Glen Road, London E13 8RU, or 131 Windsor Road, London E7 0RA* Tel 0171-363 8053 or 0181-552 8877

STEWARDSON, Ian Joseph. b 28. Ex Coll Ox BA52 DipTh54 MA56. Wycliffe Hall Ox 52. **d** 54 **p** 55. C Farnworth *Liv* 54-57; C Mossley Hill St Matt and St Jas 57-60; V New Barnet St Jas *St Alb* 60-72; R Potton w Sutton and Cockayne Hatley 73-82; R Cottered w Broadfield and Throcking 82-94; rtd 94. *77 Burford Road, Witney, Oxon OX8 5DR* Tel (01993) 704076

STEWART, Alan Valentine. b 47. **d** 97. C Mullingar, Portnashangan, Moyliscar, Kilbixy etc *M & K* from 97. *Baltrasna, Ashbourne, Co Meath, Irish Republic* Tel Dublin (1) 835 0997

STEWART, Canon Alexander Butler. b 25. **d** 58 **p** 59. C Holywood *D & D* 58-61; Portuguese E Africa 61-64; I Donagh *D & R* 64-65; I Helen's Bay *D & D* 65-72; I Donegal w Killymard, Lough Eske and Laghey *D & R* 72-90; Can Raphoe Cathl 81-90; rtd 90; Lic to Offic *D & D* from 90. *31 Upper Ballygelagh Road, Ardkeen, Newtownards, Co Down BT22 1JG* Tel (01247) 738601

STEWART, Miss Betty. b 25. S'wark Ord Course 91. **d** 93 **p** 94. NSM Wandsworth Common St Mary *S'wark* from 93. *71 Ormond Drive, Hampton, Middx TW12 2TL* Tel 0181-979 6047

STEWART, Brian. b 59. BTh. **d** 91 **p** 92. C Ballywillan *Conn* 91-94; I Belfast St Geo from 94; Bp's Dom Chapl from 94. *St George's Rectory, 28 Myrtlefield Park, Belfast BT9 6NF* Tel (01232) 667134 or 231275

STEWART, Canon Charles. b 55. St Jo Coll Cam BA77 CertEd79 MA81. Wycliffe Hall Ox 85. **d** 87 **p** 88. C Bowdon *Ches* 87-90; C Bath Abbey w St Jas *B & W* 90-94; Can Res, Prec and Sacr Win Cathl *Win* from 94. *5 The Close, Winchester, Hants SO23 9LS* Tel (01962) 856236

STEWART, Ian Guild. b 43. Edin Th Coll 89. **d** 84 **p** 85. NSM Dundee St Mary Magd *Bre* 84-87; NSM Dundee St Jo 87-90; C 90-92; NSM Dundee St Martin 87-90; C 90-92; R Montrose from 92; P-in-c Inverbervie from 92. *The Rectory, 17 Panmure Place, Montrose, Angus DD10 8ER* Tel (01674) 672652

STEWART, James. b 32. **d** 69 **p** 70. C Belfast St Donard *D & D* 69-72; C Dundonald 72-74; I Rathmullan w Tyrella 74-80; I Belfast St Clem 80-97; I Moy w Charlemont *Arm* from 97. *St James' Rectory, 37 The Square, Moy, Dungannon, Co Tyrone BT71 7SG* Tel (01868) 784312

STEWART, James Patrick. b 55. Keele Univ BA77 Birm Univ MA78. Ridley Hall Cam 86. **d** 88 **p** 89. C Boulton *Derby* 88-91; C Cove St Jo *Guildf* 91-92; TV from 92. *Fircroft, 21 St John's Road, Farnborough, Hants GU14 9RL* Tel (01252) 543502

STEWART, Mrs Janet Margaret. b 41. CertEd62 DipRK70. Cranmer Hall Dur 67. **d** 87 **p** 94. Hon Par Dn Oulton Broad *Nor* 87-94; Hon C 94-97; Asst Chapl Lowestoft Hosp 94-97; Perm to Offic *B & W* from 97. *Sherford Farm House, Sherford, Taunton, Somerset TA1 3RF* Tel (01823) 288759 Fax 257085

STEWART, John. b 39. Oak Hill Th Coll 75. **d** 77 **p** 78. C Accrington Ch Ch *Blackb* 77-79; TV Darwen St Pet w Hoddlesden 79-86; R Coppull St Jo from 86. *St John's Vicarage, Darlington Street, Coppull, Chorley, Lancs PR7 5AB* Tel (01257) 791258

STEWART, Canon John Roberton. b 29. Sarum Th Coll 63. **d** 65 **p** 66. C Gillingham *Sarum* 65-70; R Langton Matravers 70-84; RD Purbeck 82-89; Can and Preb Sarum Cathl 83-90; R Kingston, Langton Matravers and Worth Matravers 84-90; Can Res Sarum Cathl 90-95; Treas 90-95; rtd 95. *Priestlands Lodge, Priestlands, Sherborne, Dorset DT9 4HN* Tel (01935) 817680

STEWART, John Vernon. b 36. BNC Ox BA57 MA66. Coll of Ressur Halki 59. **d** 61 **p** 62. Ghana 61-64; Madagascar 64-66; V Balsall Heath St Paul *Birm* 66-70; R Sibford *Ox* 70-75; R Northolt St Mary *Lon* 75-82; rtd 82; Hon Member Abp Cant's Research Staff 85-89. *2 Kirkland Hill, Wigtown, Newton Stewart, Wigtownshire DG8 9JB*

STEWART, John Wesley. b 52. QUB BD76 TCD 76. **d** 77 **p** 78. C Seagoe *D & D* 77-79; C Lisburn Ch Ch *Conn* 79-85; I Ballybay w Mucknoe and Clontibret *Clogh* 85-90; I Derryvullen S w Garvary from 90; RD Enniskillen 91-95; Bp Dom Chapl from 95. *The Rectory, Tullyharney, Enniskillen, Co Fermanagh BT74 4PR* Tel (01365) 387236 Fax as telephone

STEWART, Kim Deborah. *See* MATHERS, Mrs Kim Deborah

STEWART, Malcolm James. b 44. TD78. Solicitor 79 York Univ BA66 K Coll Lon MA68 Lon Inst of Educn PGCE69. NE Ord Course 89. **d** 93 **p** 94. NSM Upper Nidderdale *Ripon* 93-95; C Fountains Gp from 95. *1 Hazel Close, Grewelthorpe, Ripon, N Yorkshire HG4 3BL* Tel (01765) 658160

STEWART, The Very Revd Maurice Evan. b 29. TCD BA50 MA53 BD67 QUB PhD75. **d** 52 **p** 53. C Belfast St Jas *Conn* 52-55; Chapl Bps' Coll Cheshunt 55-58; Hd of Trin Coll Miss Belf 58-61; I Newcastle *D & D* 61-69; Lect CITC 69-91; Vice-Prin 80-91; Lect Div TCD 72-91; Chan St Patr Cathl Dublin 80-89; Prec 89-91; Dean St Patr Cathl Dublin from 91; I Dublin St Patr Cathl Gp *D & G* from 91. *The Deanery, Upper Kevin Street, Dublin 8, Irish Republic* Tel Dublin (1) 454 3428 or 453 9472 Fax 454 6374

STEWART, Maxwell Neville Gabriel. b 33. Hertf Coll Ox BA58. Wycliffe Hall Ox DipTh59. **d** 60 **p** 61. C Perry Beeches *Birm* 60-62; Chapl Rosenberg Coll St Gallen 62-64; Perm to Offic *Chelmsf* 64-70; Warden Leics Poly 70-92; De Montfort Univ Leic 92-93; Hon C Leic St Mary *Leic* 74-79; Perm to Offic from 79. *25 Sidney Court, Norwich Road, Leicester LE4 0LR*

STEWART, Michael. b 65. St Jo Coll Nottm LTh89. **d** 89 **p** 90. C Ealing St Paul *Lon* 89-93; P-in-c N Wembley St Cuth from 93. *St Cuthbert's Vicarage, 214 Carlton Avenue West, Wembley, Middx HA0 3QY* Tel 0181-904 7657

STEWART, Norman Andrew. b 32. Edin Th Coll 54. **d** 58 **p** 59. C Glas Ch Ch *Glas* 58-59; C Paisley H Trin 59-60; C Glas St Marg 60-62; C Kingsthorpe *Pet* 62-64; Belize from 70. *St Mary's Rectory, PO Box 246, Belize City, Belize*

STEWART, Raymond John. b 55. TCD BA79 MA82. CITC 74 Div Test77. **d** 79 **p** 80. C Clooney *D & R* 79-82; I Dunfanaghy 82-87; I Gweedore Union 85-87; Dioc Youth Adv 83-87; I Castledawson from 87; RD Maghera and Kilrea from 89; Ed D & R Dioc News 89-93. *12 Station Road, Castledawson, Magherafelt, Co Londonderry BT45 8AZ* Tel (01648) 468235

STEWART, Canon Robert Stevenson. b 15. TCD BA38. **d** 39 **p** 40. C Dublin Ch Ch Leeson Park *D & G* 39-43; C Belfast St Donard *D & D* 43-45; I Ahoghill *Conn* 45-59; I Ballymoney 59-82; Preb Conn Cathl 78-82; rtd 82. *7 Willan Drive, Portrush, Co Antrim BT56 8PU* Tel (01265) 824336

✠**STEWART, The Rt Revd William Allen.** b 43. Trin Coll Cam BA65 MA69. Cranmer Hall Dur DipTh68. **d** 68 **p** 69 **c** 97. C Ecclesall *Sheff* 68-72; C Cheltenham St Mary *Glouc* 72-74; V Glouc St Jas 74-80; P-in-c Glouc All SS 78-80; R Upton *Ex* 80-85; V Oulton Broad *Nor* 85-97; RD Lothingland 92-97; Hon Can Nor Cathl 94-97; Suff Bp Taunton *B & W* from 97. *Sherford Farm House, Sherford, Taunton, Somerset TA1 3RF* Tel (01823) 288759 Fax 257085

STEWART, William James. BA DipTh. **d** 83 **p** 84. C Glenageary *D & G* 83-86; Rostrevor Renewal Cen 86-87; I Naas w Kill and

Rathmore *M & K* 87-93; Min Dublin Ch Ch Cathl Gp *D & G* from 93; CORE (St Werburgh Ch) from 93; Chapl Rotunda Hosp from 94; Chapl Dub Coll of Catering from 94. *96 Lower Drumcondra Road, Dublin 9, Irish Republic* Tel Dublin (1) 830 0935

STEWART, William Jones. b 32. Trin Hall Cam BA55 MA59 Cam Univ CertEd56. Edin Th Coll 67. **d** 69 **p** 69. Chapl St Ninian's Cathl Perth *St And* 69-71; Bp's Dom Chapl *Ox* 71-75; V Lambourn 75-90; V Lambourn from 90; P-in-c Lambourne Woodlands 83-90; P-in-c Eastbury and E Garston from 83. *Lambourn Vicarage, Newbury, Berks RG16 7PD* Tel (01488) 71546

STEWART-DARLING, Dr Fiona Lesley. b 58. Kingston Poly GRSC79 Lon Univ PhD82. Trin Coll Bris BA91. **d** 91 **p** 94. C Cirencester *Glouc* 91-94; Chapl Cheltenham and Glouc Coll of HE 94-97; Chapl Portsm Univ *Portsm* from 97. *15 Grays Court, Portsmouth PO1 2PN*

STEWART ELLENS, Gordon Frederick. *See* ELLENS, Dr Gordon Frederick Stewart

STEWART-SMITH, Canon David Cree. b 13. K Coll Cam BA39 MA42. Cuddesdon Coll 40. **d** 41 **p** 42. C Northampton St Matt *Pet* 41-43; C Cheltenham St Steph *Glouc* 43-44; V Choral York Minster *York* 44-49; Sub-Chanter 48-49; Chapl Qu Marg Sch York 45-49; V Shadwell *Ripon* 49-52; Warden Brasted Place Coll Westerham 52-63; Dean Jerusalem 64-67; Hon Can Roch Cathl *Roch* 67-69 and 76-78; Adn Bromley 68-69; Adn Roch 69-76; Can Res Roch Cathl 69-76; Home Sec JEM 76-78; rtd 78; Perm to Offic *Glouc* from 86. *16 Capel Court, Prestbury, Cheltenham, Glos GL52 3EL* Tel (01242) 510972

STEWART-SYKES, Alistair Charles. b 60. St Andr Univ MA83 Birm Univ PhD92. Qu Coll Birm 86. **d** 89 **p** 90. C Stevenage St Andr and St Geo *St Alb* 89-92; C Castle Vale St Cuth *Birm* 92-93; Barbados 93-96; Assoc Min Hanley H Ev *Lich* from 97. *St Matthew's Vicarage, 19 Widecombe Road, Birches Head, Hanley, Stoke-on-Trent ST1 6SL* Tel (01782) 267243 Fax as telephone

STEWART-SYKES, Teresa Melanie. b 64. Bris Univ BA85. Qu Coll Birm 87. **d** 89. Par Dn Stevenage St Andr and St Geo *St Alb* 89-92; NSM Castle Vale St Cuth *Birm* 92-93; Barbados 93-96. *St Matthew's Vicarage, 19 Widecombe Road, Birches Head, Hanley, Stoke-on-Trent ST1 6SL* Tel (01782) 267243 Fax as telephone

STEYNOR, Victor Albert. b 15. Southn Univ DipEd62. S'wark Ord Course 68. **d** 71 **p** 72. C Bognor *Chich* 71-75; P-in-c Kenton and Ashfield w Thorpe *St E* 75-81; P-in-c Aspall 75-81; V Debenham 75-81; V Debenham w Aspall and Kenton 81-82; rtd 82; Perm to Offic *St E* from 82. *74 Elmhurst Drive, Ipswich IP3 0PB* Tel (01473) 728922

STIBBE, Dr Mark William Godfrey. b 60. Trin Coll Cam BA83 MA86 Nottm Univ PhD88. St Jo Coll Nottm 83. **d** 86 **p** 87. C Stapleford *S'well* 86-90; C Crookes St Thos *Sheff* 90-93; Lect Sheff Univ 90-97; V Grenoside 93-97; V Chorleywood St Andr *St Alb* from 97. *St Andrew's Vicarage, 37 Quickley Lane, Chorleywood, Rickmansworth, Herts WD3 5AE* Tel (01923) 282391

STICKLAND, Geoffrey John Brett. b 42. St D Coll Lamp DipTh66. **d** 66 **p** 67. C Aberavon H Trin *Llan* 66-69; C Llanrumney *Mon* 69-72; C Tetbury w Beverston *Glouc* 72-75; V Hardwicke 75-82; R Hardwicke, Quedgeley and Elmore w Longney from 82. *The Rectory, School Lane, Quedgeley, Gloucester GL2 6PN* Tel (01452) 720411

STIDOLPH, Robert Anthony. b 54. GBSM ARCM FRSA92. St Steph Ho Ox 77. **d** 80 **p** 80. C Hove All SS *Chich* 80-84; TV Brighton Resurr 84-87; Chapl Cheltenham Coll 87-94; Sen Chapl and Hd Relig Studies Wellington Coll from 94. *Wellington College, Crowthorne, Berks RG45 7PU* Tel (01344) 751193 or 772262

STIEVENARD, Alphonse Etienne Arthur. b 13. Selw Coll Cam BA36 MA40. Lon Coll of Div 36. **d** 37 **p** 38. C Northwood Em *Lon* 37-40; P-in-c Southborough St Pet *Roch* 40-44; V Leyton Ch Ch *Chelmsf* 44-51; V Jersey Millbrook St Matt *Win* 51-78; rtd 78. *Le Ruisselet, Mont Rossignol, St Ouen, Jersey, Channel Islands JE3 2LN* Tel (01534) 481215

STIFF, Derrick Malcolm. b 40. Lich Th Coll 69. **d** 72 **p** 73. C Cov St Geo *Cov* 72-75; R Benhall w Sternfield *St E* 75-79; P-in-c Snape w Friston 75-79; V Cartmel *Carl* 79-87; R Sudbury and Chilton *St E* 87-94; Min Can St E Cathl from 90; P-in-c Lavenham 94-95; P-in-c Preston 94-95; R Lavenham w Preston from 95; RD Lavenham from 95. *The Rectory, Lavenham, Sudbury, Suffolk CO10 9SA* Tel (01787) 247244

STILEMAN, William Mark Charles. b 63. Selw Coll Cam BA85 MA89 PGCE86. Wycliffe Hall Ox DipTh89. **d** 91 **p** 92. C Ox St Andr *Ox* 91-95; C Gt Chesham 95; TV from 95. *14A Manor Way, Chesham, Bucks HP5 3BG* Tel (01494) 784372

STILL, Colin Charles. b 35. Selw Coll Cam BA67 MA71. Cranmer Hall Dur DipTh68 United Th Sem Dayton STM69. **d** 69 **p** 70. C Drypool St Columba w St Andr and St Pet *York* 69-72; Abp's Dom Chapl 72-75; Recruitment Sec ACCM 76-80; P-in-c Ockham w Hatchford *Guildf* 76-80; R 80-90; Can Missr and Ecum Officer 80-90; Perm to Offic *Chich* from 92; rtd 96. *Flat 9, 16 Lewes Crescent, Brighton BN2 1GB* Tel (01273) 686014

STILL, Jonathan Trevor Lloyd. b 59. Ex Univ BA81 Qu Coll Cam BA84 MA88. Westcott Ho Cam 82. **d** 85 **p** 86. C Weymouth H Trin *Sarum* 85-88; Chapl for Agric *Heref* 88-93; V N Petherton w Northmoor Green *B & W* from 93. *The Dower House, North Petherton, Bridgwater, Somerset TA6 6SE* Tel (01278) 662429

STILL, Kenneth Donald. b 37. St Aid Birkenhead 64. **d** 67 **p** 95. C Ainsdale *Liv* 67-68; C Kirkby 68-69; C Sutton from 96. *316 Reginald Road, St Helens, Merseyside WA9 4HS* Tel (01744) 812380

STILLMAN, Roger John. b 47. St Steph Ho Ox 81. **d** 83 **p** 84. C St Helier *S'wark* 83-88; P-in-c Falinge *Man* 88; TV Rochdale 88-94; P-in-c Wokingham St Paul *Ox* from 94; Chapl Wokingham Hosp from 95. *St Paul's Rectory, Holt Lane, Wokingham, Berks RG11 1ED* Tel (0118) 978 0629

STILLWELL, Wayne Anthony. b 68. Greenwich Univ BA91. Oak Hill Th Coll 94. **d** 96 **p** 97. C Necton, Holme Hale w N and S Pickenham *Nor* from 96. *21 Chantry Lane, Necton, Swaffham, Norfolk PE37 8ES* Tel (01760) 722694

STILWELL, Malcolm Thomas. b 54. Coll of Resurr Mirfield 83. **d** 86 **p** 87. C Workington St Mich *Carl* 86-90; P-in-c Flimby 90-93; Perm to Offic 93-95; NSM Westf St Mary from 95. *18 Moorfield Avenue, Workington, Cumbria CA14 4HJ* Tel (01900) 66757

STIMPSON, Graham George. b 40. Lon Univ MB BS65 DPM. Cuddesdon Coll 69. **d** 70 **p** 71. NSM Bris St Mary Redcliffe w Temple etc *Bris* from 70. *12 Challoner Court, Bristol BS1 4RG* Tel 0117-926 0802

STIMPSON, Nigel Leslie. b 60. St Martin's Coll Lanc BA92. Coll of Resurr Mirfield CPT94. **d** 94 **p** 95. C Heyhouses on Sea *Blackb* 94-96; C Torrisholme from 96. *St Martin's House, Braddon Close, Morecambe, Lancs LA4 4UE* Tel (01524) 422249

STINSON, William Gordon. b 29. Lon Univ BSc50. Ely Th Coll 51. **d** 52 **p** 53. C Kingston upon Hull St Alb *York* 52-56; Br Guiana 56-61; V E and W Ravendale w Hatcliffe *Linc* 61-67; R Beelsby 61-67; P-in-c Ashby w Fenby and Brigsley 62-66; R 66-67; V New Cleethorpes 67-76; RD Grimsby and Cleethorpes 73-76; P-in-c Dovercourt *Chelmsf* 76-83; TR Dovercourt and Parkeston 83-91; RD Harwich 87-91; V Gosfield 91-95; rtd 95; Perm to Offic *Chelmsf* from 95. *14 The Columbines, Melford Road, Cavendish, Sudbury, Suffolk CO10 8AB* Tel (01787) 281381

STIRK, Peter Francis. b 24. Linc Coll Ox BA49 MA53. Qu Coll Birm 49. **d** 50 **p** 51. C Beeston *Ripon* 50-68; P-in-c Kirby-on-the-Moor 68-71; V 71-81; P-in-c Cundall 73-81; V Kirby-on-the-Moor, Cundall w Norton-le-Clay etc 81-90; rtd 90. *Devonshire Cottage, Marton le Moor, Ripon, N Yorkshire HG4 5AT* Tel (01423) 322330

STIRLING, Mrs Christina Dorita (Tina). b 48. Lon Univ BEd73. Wycliffe Hall Ox 87. **d** 89 **p** 94. Par Dn Thame w Towersey *Ox* 89-94; C from 94. *22 Stuart Way, Thame, Oxon OX9 3WP* Tel (01844) 216508

STIRRUP, Roger. b 34. St Cath Coll Cam BA58 MA62. Linc Th Coll 58. **d** 60 **p** 61. C Selly Oak St Mary *Birm* 60-63; C Battersea St Mary *S'wark* 63-65; Chapl St Andr Univ *St And* 65-68; Chapl Nottm High Sch 68-80; Asst Chapl Rugby Sch 80-85; V Fordingbridge *Win* 85-92; TR Ross w Brampton Abbotts, Bridstow and Peterstow *Heref* 92-93; TR Ross w Brampton Abbotts, Bridstow, Peterstow etc from 93; P-in-c Linton w Upton Bishop and Aston Ingham from 97. *The Rectory, Church Street, Ross-on-Wye, Herefordshire HR9 5HN* Tel (01989) 562175

STOBART, Mrs Judith Audrey. b 43. St Hugh's Coll Ox BA65 MA71 Lon Univ CertEd71 DipEd72. St Alb Minl Tr Scheme 82. **dss** 85 **d** 87 **p** 94. Hatfield *St Alb* 85-87; Par Dn Hatfield Hyde 87-91; NSM Welwyn Garden City 91-92; Par Dn 92-94; C 94-95; Perm to Offic 95-97; C Hatfield from 97. *St Michael's House, 31 Homestead Road, Hatfield, Herts AL10 0QJ* Tel (01707) 882276

STOCK, Lionel Crispian. b 58. ACMA85 ACIS94. Linc Th Coll BTh94. **d** 94 **p** 95. C Preston w Sutton Poyntz and Osmington w Poxwell *Sarum* from 94. *7 Wyke Oliver Close, Preston, Weymouth, Dorset DT3 6DR* Tel (01305) 835021

STOCK, Miss Ruth Vaughan. b 51. Birkb Coll Lon BA79 MA85. Wycliffe Hall Ox 91. **d** 93 **p** 94. Par Dn Toxteth St Philemon w St Gabr and St Cleopas *Liv* 93-94; C 94-97; TV from 97. *St Gabriel's Vicarage, 2 Steble Street, Liverpool L8 6QH* Tel 0151-708 7751

STOCK, Victor Andrew. b 44. AKC68 FRSA95. **d** 69 **p** 70. C Pinner *Lon* 69-73; Chapl Lon Univ 73-79; R Friern Barnet St Jas 79-86; R St Mary le Bow w St Pancras Soper Lane etc from 86; P-in-c St Mary Aldermary from 87. *The Rector's Lodgings, Cheapside, London EC2V 6AU* Tel 0171-248 5139

STOCK, Canon William Nigel. b 50. Dur Univ BA72 Ox Univ DipTh75. Ripon Coll Cuddesdon 75. **d** 76 **p** 77. C Stockton St Pet *Dur* 76-79; Papua New Guinea 79-84; V Shiremoor *Newc* 85-91; TR N Shields from 91; RD Tynemouth from 92; Hon Can Newc Cathl from 97. *The Vicarage, 26 Cleveland Road, North Shields, Tyne & Wear NE29 0NG* Tel 0191-257 1721

STOCK-HESKETH, Jonathan Philip. b 49. St Chad's Coll Dur BA Cam Univ CertEd Nottm Univ MTh PhD93. St Steph Ho Ox. **d** 83 **p** 84. C Leic St Phil *Leic* 83-86; C Loughborough Em 86-89; Lect Nottm Univ from 95. *Theology Department,*

Nottingham University, Nottingham NG7 2RD Tel 0115-951 5886

STOCKBRIDGE, Alan Carmichael. b 33. MBE89. Keble Coll Ox BA55 MA62. Wycliffe Hall Ox 66. **d** 68 **p** 69. CF 68-78 and 82-92; Chapl Reading Sch 78-82; R Harrietsham w Ulcombe *Cant* from 92. *The Rectory, Church Road, Harrietsham, Maidstone, Kent ME17 1AP* Tel (01622) 859466

STOCKBRIDGE, Nelson William. b 35. Trin Th Coll Auckland 61. **d** 84 **p** 85. New Zealand 85-86; C Shildon w Eldon *Dur* 87; C Norton St Mary 87-88; C Cottingham *York* 88-91; V Aldbrough, Mappleton w Goxhill and Withernwick 91-96; C Baildon *Bradf* from 96. *93 Hoyle Court Road, Baildon, Shipley, W Yorkshire BD17 6EL* Tel (01274) 594790

STOCKER, David William George. b 37. Bris Univ BA58 CertEd. Qu Coll Birm 59. **d** 60 **p** 61. C Sparkhill St Jo *Birm* 60-64; C Keighley *Bradf* 64-66; V Grenoside *Sheff* 66-83; V Sandbach *Ches* from 83. *The Vicarage, 15 Offley Road, Sandbach, Cheshire CW11 9AY* Tel (01270) 762379

STOCKER, Rachael Ann. *See* KNAPP, Mrs Rachael Ann

STOCKITT, Robin Philip. b 56. Liv Univ BA77 Crewe & Alsager Coll PGCE78 Open Univ Diploma in Special Needs 90. Ridley Hall Cam CTM95. **d** 97. C Billing *Pet* from 97. *80 Worcester Close, Little Billing, Northampton NN3 9GD* Tel (01604) 787163

STOCKLEY, Mrs Alexandra Madeleine Reuss. b 43. Cranmer Hall Dur 80 Carl Dioc Tr Inst. **dss** 84 **d** 87 **p** 94. Upperby St Jo *Carl* 84-87; Par Dn 87-89; D-in-c Grayrigg, Old Hutton and New Hutton 90-94; P-in-c 94-95; P-in-c Levens from 95. *The Vicarage, Vicarage Road, Levens, Kendal, Cumbria LA8 8PY* Tel (015395) 60233

STOCKLEY, Michael Ian. b 41. Lon Coll of Div 66. **d** 69 **p** 70. C St Helens St Mark *Liv* 69-74; C Fazakerley Em 74; TV 74-82; V Ince Ch Ch 82-92; V Birkdale St Pet from 92. *St Peter's Vicarage, 2 St Peter's Road, Southport, Merseyside PR8 4BY* Tel (01704) 68448

STOCKLEY, Roland. b 23. St Jo Coll Dur BA47 DipTh49. **d** 49 **p** 50. C Rainbow Hill St Barn *Worc* 49-52; CF 52-57; V Broadwaters *Worc* 57-66; V Himbleton w Huddington 66-68; R Pedmore 68-88; rtd 88; Perm to Offic *Lich* from 90. *64 Hyperion Road, Stourbridge, W Midlands DY7 6SB* Tel (01384) 393463

STOCKPORT, Suffragan Bishop of. *See* TURNER, The Rt Revd Geoffrey Martin

STOCKS, John Cedric Hawkesworth. b 13. Em Coll Cam BA37 MA40. Westcott Ho Cam 39. **d** 40 **p** 41. C Barnsley St Geo *Wakef* 40-43; C Crosland Moor 43-45; C Whitby *York* 45-46; C Guiseley *Bradf* 46-49; V Beckermet St Bridget *Carl* 49-52; V Ponsonby 49-52; Chapl Pelham Ho Sch 49-52; V Fewston *Bradf* 52-55; R Bentham St Jo 55-57; R Whitestone *Ex* 57-60; V Oldridge 57-60; V Ellerton Priory w Aughton and E Cottingwith *York* 60-65; V Sheriff Hutton 65-80; rtd 80. *2 Brookfield Garth, Hampsthwaite, Harrogate, N Yorkshire HG3 2EB* Tel (01423) 771039

STOCKTON, Dr Ian George. b 49. Selw Coll Cam BA72 MA76 Hull Univ PhD90. St Jo Coll Nottm CertEd74. **d** 75 **p** 76. C Chell *Lich* 75-78; C Trentham 78-80; R Dalbeattie *Glas* 80-84; P-in-c Scotton w Northorpe *Linc* 84-88; Asst Local Min Officer 84-88; Local Min Officer and LNSM Course Prin from 88. *105 Nettleham Road, Lincoln LN2 1RU* Tel (01522) 524428 or 542121

STOCKTON, Wilfred. b 32. Roch Th Coll 63. **d** 65 **p** 66. C Shirebrook *Derby* 65-67; C Boulton 67-69; V Ault Hucknall 69-73; R Pinxton 73-83; P-in-c Riddings 83-85; P-in-c Ironville 83-85; V Ladybrook *S'well* from 85. *St Mary's Vicarage, Bancroft Lane, Mansfield, Notts NG18 5LZ* Tel (01623) 21709

STOCKWELL, John Nicholas. b 49. Trin Coll Bris 80. **d** 82 **p** 83. C Flixton St Jo *Man* 82-86; V Accrington Ch Ch *Blackb* 86-90; R Chulmleigh *Ex* 90-93; R Chawleigh w Cheldon 90-93; R Wembworthy w Eggesford 90-93; P-in-c Burwash Weald *Chich* 93-97. *Address temp unknown*

STODDART, Dr David Easton. b 36. MIMechE66 CEng66 FIMgt72 FIQA76 HND57 K Coll Dur BSc60 PhD66. W of England Minl Tr Course 92. **d** 95 **p** 96. NSM Stroud H Trin *Glouc* from 95. *Dunelm, Pinfarthings, Amberley, Stroud, Glos GL5 5JJ* Tel (01453) 833028

STOKE-ON-TRENT, Archdeacon of. *Vacant*

STOKER, Andrew. b 64. Coll of Ripon & York St Jo BA86. Coll of Resurr Mirfield 87. **d** 90 **p** 91. C Horton *Newc* 90-92; C Clifford *York* 92-96; P-in-c Cawood from 96; P-in-c Ryther from 96; P-in-c Wistow from 96. *Cawood Vicarage, Selby, N Yorkshire YO8 0TB* Tel (01757) 268273

STOKER, Howard Charles. b 62. Linc Th Coll BTh93. **d** 93 **p** 94. C Hessle *York* 93-96; C Richmond w Hudswell *Ripon* from 96; C Downholme and Marske from 96. *1 Wathcote Place, Richmond, N Yorkshire DL10 7SR* Tel (01748) 826260

STOKER, Mrs Joanna Mary (Jo). b 57. Leic Univ BA79 Nottm Univ BCombStuds83. Linc Th Coll 80. **dss** 83 **d** 87 **p** 94. Greenford H Cross *Lon* 83-87; Par Dn 87-89; Par Dn Farnham Royal w Hedgerley *Ox* 89-92; Par Dn Seer Green and Jordans 92-94; D-in-c 94; P-in-c 94-97; TV Stantonbury and Willen from 97. *The Vicarage, 29 Bradwell Road, Bradville, Milton Keynes MK13 7AX* Tel (01908) 314224

STOKES, Canon Albert Edward. b 21. TCD BA43 MA46 BD46. CITC 43. **d** 46 **p** 47. Lect Ch of Ireland Coll of Educn Dub 49-79; I Powerscourt w Kilbride and Annacrevy *D & G* 56-86; Ch Ch Cathl Dublin 70-86; rtd 86. *Cotehele, The Riverwalk, Ashford, Wicklow, Irish Republic* Tel Wicklow (404) 40360

STOKES, Canon Andrew John. b 38. G&C Coll Cam BA60 MA64. Ripon Hall Ox 60. **d** 62 **p** 63. C Northampton All SS w St Kath *Pet* 62-65; C Endcliffe *Sheff* 65-68; Ind Missr 65-68; Sen Ind Chapl 69-74; P-in-c Bridport *Sarum* 75-79; TR Bridport 79-80; V Holbeach Marsh *Linc* 82-88; Bp's Dom Chapl from 88; Can Res and Prec Linc Cathl from 92. *The Precentory, 16 Minster Yard, Lincoln LN2 1PX* Tel (01522) 523644

STOKES, David Lewis. b 49. Keble Coll Ox BA74. Westcott Ho Cam 73. **d** 75 **p** 76. C Romford St Edw *Chelmsf* 76-78; USA from 78. *114 George Street, Providence, Rhode Island 02906-1189, USA*

STOKES, Donald Roy (Don). b 30. K Coll Lon BD79 AKC79. **d** 80 **p** 81. C St Geo-in-the-East w St Paul *Lon* 80-84; Ind Chapl 84-95; rtd 95. *Rose Cottage, 9 Tors Road, Lynmouth, Devon EX35 6ET*

STOKES, George Smithson Garbutt. b 13. Leeds Univ BA35. Coll of Resurr Mirfield 35. **d** 37 **p** 38. C S Shields St Fran *Dur* 37-39; C Summertown *Ox* 39-41; P-in-c Amport w Monxton *Win* 68-69; P-in-c Grateley cum Quarley 68-69; V Amport, Grateley and Quarley 69-74; V Sonning *Ox* 74-85; rtd 85; Perm to Offic *Ox* 85-94. *Myrtle Cottage, Sheep Street, Charlbury, Chipping Norton, Oxon OX7 3RR* Tel (01608) 811207

STOKES, Leonard Peter Norton. b 21. Jes Coll Cam BA43 MA47. Westcott Ho Cam 44. **d** 45 **p** 46. C Portsea St Mary *Portsm* 45-48; Chapl Jes Coll Cam 48-50; C St Marylebone w H Trin *Lon* 50-51; C Leverstock Green *St Alb* 51-59; C-in-c Hemel Hempstead St Barn CD 51-59; Chapl Newton Abbot Hosp 59-86; Chapl Forde Park Sch 59-86; R Wolborough w Newton Abbot *Ex* 59-86; rtd 86; Perm to Offic *Ex* from 86. *67 Conway Road, Paignton, Devon TQ4 5LH* Tel (01803) 529764

STOKES, Miss Mary Patricia. b 39. St Hilda's Coll Ox BA62 MA66 Lanc Univ MA80 Bris Univ CertEd63. EMMTC 78. **d** 87 **p** 94. Par Dn Pheasey *Lich* 87-93; C Walton-on-Thames *Guildf* from 93. *50 Misty's Field, Walton-on-Thames, Surrey KT12 2BG* Tel (01932) 248945

STOKES, Michael John. b 34. Lich Th Coll 63. **d** 65 **p** 66. C Worplesdon *Guildf* 65-68; Chapl RAF 68-84; Asst Chapl-in-Chief RAF 84-89; QHC 88-95; V Chesterton w Middleton Stoney and Wendlebury *Ox* 89-95; RD Bicester and Islip 92-95; Cyprus from 95. *PO Box 171, Girne, Mersin, Turkey* Tel Kyrenia (357-8) 54329

STOKES, Peter. b 31. Qu Coll Birm 68. **d** 69 **p** 70. C Norton *St Alb* 69-77; V Harlington 77-85; P-in-c Chalgrave 80-85; V Luton St Andr 85-94; Asst RD Luton 89-94; rtd 94; Perm to Offic *Ex* from 94. *Chinook, 27 Croft Road, Ipplepen, Newton Abbot, Devon TQ12 5ST* Tel (01803) 813664

STOKES, Canon Richard Spencer. b 29. TCD 66. **d** 68 **p** 69. C Lisburn Ch Ch Cathl *Conn* 68-71; C Dublin St Geo and St Thos *D & G* 71-75; C Dublin Rathfarnham 75-79; I Blessington w Kilbride, Ballymore Eustace etc 79-94; RD Ballymore and Salmon Leap 87-94; Can Ch Ch Cathl Dublin 92-94; rtd 94. *Camlagh, Church Road, Greystones, Co Wicklow, Irish Republic* Tel Dublin (1) 287 4147

STOKES, Roger Sidney. b 47. Clare Coll Cam BA68 MA72. Sarum & Wells Th Coll 69. **d** 72 **p** 73. C Keighley *Bradf* 72-74; C Bolton St Jas w St Chrys 74-78; V Hightown *Wakef* 78-85; Dep Chapl HM Pris Wakef 85-87; Chapl HM Pris Full Sutton 87-89; Perm to Offic *Wakef* 92-95; P-in-c Carlinghow from 95. *The Vicarage, 8A Amber Street, Batley, W Yorkshire WF17 8HH* Tel (01924) 472576

STOKES, Simon Colin. b 62. Nene Coll Northampton BSc83. Ridley Hall Cam CTM92. **d** 92 **p** 93. C New Catton Ch Ch *Nor* 92-96; P-in-c King's Lynn St Jo the Ev from 96. *St John's Vicarage, Blackfriars Road, King's Lynn, Norfolk PE30 1NT* Tel (01553) 773034

STOKES, Terence Harold. b 46. Man Univ DSPT84 Open Univ BA89. Sarum & Wells Th Coll 71. **d** 73 **p** 74. C Blakenall Heath *Lich* 73-75; C Walsall Wood 75-78; C Northampton St Alb *Pet* 78-81; TV Swinton St Pet *Man* 81-85; V Daisy Hill 85-92. *8 Westbury Close, Westhoughton, Bolton BL5 3UL* Tel (01942) 819057

STOKES, Terence Ronald. b 35. Linc Th Coll. **d** 69 **p** 70. C Bramley *Ripon* 69-72; C Osbournby w Scott Willoughby *Linc* 72-74; C Hykeham 74-77; V Birchwood 77-94; P-in-c Scopwick Gp from 94. *The Vicarage, Scopwick, Lincoln LN4 3NT* Tel (01526) 321047

STOKES, Preb Terence Walter (Terry). b 34. Bps' Coll Cheshunt 62. **d** 64 **p** 65. C Wanstead St Mary *Chelmsf* 64-67; C St Alb Abbey *St Alb* 67-70; Asst Dir RE *B & W* 70-75; Youth Chapl 70-75; P-in-c Yeovil 75-77; TV 77-82; TR Wellington and Distr from 82; RD Tone 89-96; Preb Wells Cathl from 90. *The Rectory, 72 High Street, Wellington, Somerset TA21 8RF* Tel (01823) 662248

STOKOE, Rodney James Robert. b 20. Dur Univ BSc46 BA48 DipTh49. Crozer Th Sem Penn ThM67 Atlantic Sch of Th Halifax (NS) Hon DD87. **d** 49 **p** 50. C W Hartlepool St Paul *Dur* 49-53; R Edin Ch Ch *Edin* 53-57; P-in-c Bishopwearmouth

St Gabr *Dur* 57-60; Canada from 60; Prof Div K Coll NS 60-71; Prof Past Th Atlantic Sch Th NS 71-85. *403 Prince Street, Ste 206, Truro, Nova Scotia, Canada, B2N 1E6* Tel Halifax (902) 895-0047

STOKOE, Wayne Jeffrey Jeff. b 56. Coll of Resurr Mirfield 94. **d** 96 **p** 97. C Sheff St Cath Richmond Road *Sheff* from 96. *35 Mason Crescent, Sheffield S13 8LH* Tel 0114-239 1168

STONE, Albert John. b 44. Loughb Univ BTech67 BSc. Sarum & Wells Th Coll 83. **d** 85 **p** 86. C Plymstock *Ex* 85-88; P-in-c Whitestone 88-92; P-in-c Oldridge 88-92; P-in-c Holcombe Burnell 88-92; P-in-c Tedburn St Mary 92; R Tedburn St Mary, Whitestone, Oldridge etc 93-94; P-in-c Yarcombe w Membury and Upottery 94; P-in-c Cotleigh 94; V Yarcombe, Membury, Upottery and Cotleigh from 95. *The Vicarage, Yarcombe, Honiton, Devon EX14 9BD* Tel (01404) 86561

STONE, Andrew Francis. b 43. AKC65. **d** 66 **p** 67. C Walthamstow St Mich *Chelmsf* 66-67; C Ealing St Barn *Lon* 67-70; C E Grinstead St Mary *Chich* 70-74; C-in-c The Hydneye CD 74-81; R Denton w S Heighton and Tarring Neville 81-93; V Eastbourne St Andr from 93. *St Andrew's Vicarage, 425 Seaside, Eastbourne, E Sussex BN22 7RT* Tel (01323) 723739

STONE, Christopher John. b 49. Lanc Univ MA89 Keele Univ MA92. Lambeth STh84 Linc Th Coll 78. **d** 81 **p** 82. C Bromley St Mark *Roch* 81-84; R Burgh-by-Sands and Kirkbampton w Kirkandrews etc *Carl* 84-89; Chapl N Staffs R Infirmary Stoke-on-Trent 89-93; Co-ord Staff Support Services N Staffs Hosp from 93. *4 Brackenberry, Newcastle, Staffs ST5 9PS* Tel (01782) 625134

STONE, Dr David Adrian. b 56. Or Coll Ox BA78 MA83 BM BCh83. Wycliffe Hall Ox 85. **d** 88 **p** 89. C Holborn St Geo w H Trin and St Bart *Lon* 88-91; C S Kensington St Jude 91-93; V from 93; AD Chelsea from 96. *St Jude's Vicarage, 20 Collingham Road, London SW5 0LX* Tel 0171-373 1693 or 370 1360 Fax 373 1693 E-mail 100031.2664@compuserve.com

STONE, Ernest Arthur. b 09. VRD60. AKC34 Open Univ BA81 MPhil91. **d** 34 **p** 35. C Saffron Walden *Chelmsf* 34-37; V Clavering w Langley 37-46; Chapl RNVR 44-64; V Clymping *Chich* 46-54; V Bexhill St Aug 54-74; Dioc RE Adv 54-80; rtd 74; Lic to Offic *Chich* 80-86; Perm to Offic from 89; RD Worthing 86-89. *56 Manor Road, Worthing, W Sussex BN11 4SQ* Tel (01903) 235120

STONE, Godfrey Owen. b 49. Ex Coll Ox BA71 MA75 W Midl Coll of Educn PGCE72. Wycliffe Hall Ox BA78. **d** 81 **p** 82. C Rushden w Newton Bromswold *Pet* 81-87; Dir Past Studies Wycliffe Hall Ox 87-92; TR Bucknall and Bagnall *Lich* from 92. *The Rectory, Werrington Road, Bucknall, Stoke-on-Trent ST2 9AQ* Tel (01782) 214455

STONE, Jeffrey Peter. b 34. Nottm Univ TCert72 BEd73. Lich Th Coll 58. **d** 61 **p** 62. C Newark St Mary *S'well* 61-65; C Sutton in Ashfield St Mich 65-69; Robert Smyth Sch Market Harborough 72-89; Perm to Offic *Leic* 88-90; R Waltham on the Wolds, Stonesby, Saxby etc 90-96; rtd 96. *18 Glebe Road, Queniborough, Leicester LE7 3FH* Tel 0116-260 6106

STONE, John Anthony. b 46. St Chad's Coll Dur BA68 DipTh69. **d** 69 **p** 70. C New Addington *Cant* 69-72; C Tewkesbury w Walton Cardiff *Glouc* 72-76; C-in-c Dedworth CD *Ox* 76-82; V Dedworth 82-86; TV Chipping Barnet w Arkley *St Alb* 86-95; R Baldock w Bygrave from 95. *The Rectory, 9 Pond Lane, Baldock, Herts SG7 5AS* Tel (01462) 894398

STONE, John Christopher. b 53. MSTSD74 MESB74 LGSM73 Newc Univ BA74 Birkb Coll Lon MA77. Oak Hill NSM Course 89. **d** 92 **p** 93. NSM Southfleet *Roch* from 92; Dioc Communications Officer from 96. *37 The Old Yews, New Barn Road, Longfield, Kent DA3 7JS* Tel (01474) 707511 Fax (01634) 402793

STONE, John Geoffrey Elliot. b 20. Ch Coll Cam BA41 MA45. Ridley Hall Cam 47. **d** 49 **p** 50. C Wellingborough St Barn *Pet* 49-51; C Bexhill St Pet *Chich* 51-56; C Ifield 56-59; V Southwater 59-70; V Thornham w Titchwell *Nor* 70-74; R Copdock w Washbrook and Belstead *St E* 74-77; P-in-c Therfield *St Alb* 77-82; P-in-c Kelshall 77-82; C Littlehampton St Jas *Chich* 82-85; C Littlehampton St Mary 82-85; C Wick 82-85; TV Littlehampton and Wick 86; rtd 86; C Compton, the Mardens, Stoughton and Racton *Chich* 86-92; Perm to Offic *Nor* 92-96; Perm to Offic *Chich* from 96. *1A Tuscan Avenue, Middleton-on-Sea, Bognor Regis, W Sussex PO22 7TD* Tel (01243) 582226

STONE, Michael Graham (Mike). b 33. FBCS. S Dios Minl Tr Scheme. **d** 83 **p** 84. NSM Chich St Paul and St Pet *Chich* 83-95; NSM Chichester from 95. *125 Cedar Drive, Chichester, W Sussex PO19 3EL* Tel (01243) 784484

STONE, Michael John. b 33. Trin Hall Cam MA56 LLB57. EAMTC 78. **d** 80 **p** 81. NSM Whitton and Thurleston w Akenham *St E* 80-84; NSM Westerfield and Tuddenham w Witnesham 84-95; Dioc Chr Stewardship Adv 93-95; P-in-c Coddenham w Gosbeck and Hemingstone w Henley from 95; Dioc Voc Adv from 95. *Chanters Mead, School Road, Coddenham, Ipswich IP6 9PS* Tel (01449) 7606312

STONE, Nigel John. b 57. Bedf Coll Lon BSc82 Lon Bible Coll MA95. St Jo Coll Nottm 82. **d** 85 **p** 86. C Battersea Park St Sav *S'wark* 85-87; C Battersea St Sav and St Geo w St Andr 87-89; P-in-c Brixton St Paul 89-92; V 92-97; Lay Tr Officer from 97. *11 Wilkinson Street, London SW8 1DD*

STONE, Noel Alfred William. b 33. St Jo Coll Morpeth 58. **d** 62 **p** 63. Australia 62-74; C The Quinton *Birm* 74-75; Hong Kong 75-78; New Zealand 78-85; P-in-c Witham Gp *Linc* 85; R 85-93; RD Beltisloe 90-93; rtd 93; Perm to Offic *Arg* from 93. *Allt and Bhruie, St Catherine's, Cairndow, Argyll PA25 8BA* Tel (01369) 86628

STONE, Peter James. b 54. Leic Univ BA75 Qu Coll Cam BA77 MA81. Westcott Ho Cam 76. **d** 78 **p** 79. C Bradford-on-Avon *Sarum* 78-81; R Corsley 81-83; Chapl Dauntsey's Sch Devizes 83-88; V Studley *Sarum* 89-94; Chapl Cheltenham Coll 94-95; Venezuela 95-96; V Upper Stratton *Bris* from 96. *The Vicarage, 67 Beechcroft Road, Swindon SN2 6RE* Tel (01793) 723095 Mobile 0402-342848

STONE, Philip William. b 58. Ridley Hall Cam 85. **d** 88 **p** 89. C Hackney Marsh *Lon* 88-97; V Kensal Rise St Mark and St Martin from 97. *Kensal Rise Vicarage, 93 College Road, London NW10 5EU* Tel 0181-969 4598

STONE, Richard Anthony. b 46. Hatf Coll Dur BA68 Nottm Univ DipTh71. Linc Th Coll 70. **d** 73 **p** 74. C Marske in Cleveland *York* 73-78; TV Haxby w Wigginton 78-87; V Osbaldwick w Murton 87-96; TV Willington Team *Newc* from 96. *The Vicarage, Berwick Drive, Wallsend, Tyne & Wear NE28 9ED* Tel 0191-262 7518

STONE, Rodney Cameron. b 32. Sarum Th Coll 67. **d** 69 **p** 70. C Milton *Portsm* 69-74; CF (TA) from 72; R Rowlands Castle *Portsm* 74-80; V Tividale *Lich* 80-81; C Weeke *Win* 81-88; V Win St Barn 89-97; rtd 97. *8 Lyndhurst Close, Harestock, Winchester, Hants SO22 6NA* Tel (01962) 883602

STONE, Rodney Milton Robertson. b 25. Ely Th Coll 51. **d** 53 **p** 54. C Stopsley *St Alb* 53-55; C S Ormsby w Ketsby, Calceby and Driby *Linc* 55-57; R Gunthorpe w Bale *Nor* 57-70; P-in-c Sharrington 62-70; R Tayport *St And* 70-90; R Newport-on-Tay 70-90; Can St Ninian's Cathl Perth 87-90; rtd 90; Lic to Offic *Newc* from 90. *12 Well Square, Tweedmouth, Berwick-upon-Tweed TD15 2AL* Tel (01289) 307791

STONEBANKS, David Arthur. b 34. Louvain Univ Belgium MA70. Coll of Resurr Mirfield 64. **d** 66 **p** 67. C Burgess Hill St Jo *Chich* 66-68; Chapl City Univ *Lon* 70-73; Chapl Strasbourg w Stuttgart and Heidelberg *Eur* 73-80; Chapl Geneva 80-86; Chapl Zurich w St Gallen and Winterthur 86-89; R Horsted Keynes *Chich* from 89. *The Rectory, Horsted Keynes, Haywards Heath, W Sussex RH17 7ED* Tel (01825) 790317

STONEHOUSE, Joseph Christopher. b 48. Chich Th Coll 68. **d** 71 **p** 72. C Beamish *Dur* 71-76; C Doncaster St Leon and St Jude *Sheff* 76-80; V Copmanthorpe *York* from 80. *The Vicarage, 17 Sutor Close, Copmanthorpe, York YO2 3TX* Tel (01904) 706280

STONES, John Graham. b 49. Southn Univ BSc72. SW Minl Tr Course 91. **d** 94 **p** 95. C Okehampton w Inwardleigh, Bratton Clovelly etc *Ex* 94-97; TV Sidmouth, Woolbrook, Salcombe Regis, Sidbury etc from 97. *All Saints Vicarage, All Saints Road, Sidmouth, Devon EX10 8ES* Tel (01395) 515963

STONESTREET, George Malcolm. b 38. AKC61. **d** 62 **p** 63. C Leeds St Pet *Ripon* 62-64; C Far Headingley St Chad 64-67; V Askrigg w Stallingbusk 67-82; V Bramley 82-85; TR 85-94; V Eskdale, Irton, Muncaster and Waberthwaite *Carl* from 94. *Eskdale Vicarage, Boot, Holmrook, Cumbria CA19 1TF* Tel (01946) 723242 Fax 723142

STONEY, The Ven Thomas Vesey. b 34. Or Coll Ox BA56 MA60. CITC 58. **d** 58 **p** 59. C Ballywillan *Conn* 58-61; C Carrickfergus 61-66; I Skerry w Rathcavan and Newtowncrommelin 66-92; Adn Dalriada 85-92; rtd 93. *Ardagh Lodge, Carrowbeg, Westport, Co Mayo, Irish Republic* Tel Westport (98) 41150

STOODLEY, Peter Bindon. b 47. Linc Th Coll 89. **d** 91 **p** 92. C Holbeck *Ripon* 91-94; P-in-c Osmondthorpe St Phil from 94. *St Philip's Vicarage, 68 Osmondthorpe Lane, Leeds LS9 9EF* Tel 0113-249 7371

STOPFORD, Eric. b 08. Tyndale Hall Bris 31. **d** 34 **p** 35. C Lower Broughton St Clem *Man* 34-37; C Horwich H Trin 37-39; R Newton Heath St Mark 39-46; V Bolton SS Simon and Jude 46-48; R Whitmore *Lich* 48-79; rtd 79. *Flat 7, Manor Court, Swan Road, Pewsey, Wilts SN9 5DW* Tel (01672) 64028

STOPPARD, Henry. b 16. Worc Ord Coll 60. **d** 61 **p** 62. C Ripley *Derby* 61-63; V Blackwell 63-83; rtd 83; Perm to Offic *Bris* from 83. *White Horse Cottage, 3 Church Hill, Olveston, Bristol BS12 3BX* Tel (01454) 615108

STOREY, Mrs Elizabeth Mary. b 37. Cam Univ DipRS80 Man Univ BA84. Local Minl Tr Course 81. **dss** 84 **d** 87 **p** 94. Liv All So Springwood *Liv* 84-87; Par Dn 87-91; C St Helens St Helen 91-94; C Garston 94-97; Asst Chapl Liv Univ from 94; C Mossley Hill St Matt and St Jas from 97. *27 Mentmore Road, Mossley Hill, Liverpool L18 4PU* Tel 0151-724 2075

STOREY, Gerard Charles Alfred. b 57. GRSC80 Thames Poly BSc80 Lon Univ PhD84. Wycliffe Hall Ox 84. **d** 87 **p** 88. C Broadwater St Mary *Chich* 87-92; TV 92-95; Chapl Northbrook Coll of Design and Tech 90-95; Oman from 95. *Oman Protestant Church, PO Box 1982, Ruwi 112, Sultanate of Oman*

STOREY, Michael. b 36. Chich Th Coll 73. **d** 75 **p** 76. C Illingworth *Wakef* 75-78; V Rastrick St Jo 78-87; V Crosland Moor from 87.

The Vicarage, Church Avenue, Crosland Moor, Huddersfield HD4 5DF Tel (01484) 422381

STOREY, Mrs Patricia Louise. b 60. TCD MA83. CITC BTh94. **d** 97. C Ballymena w Ballyclug *Conn* from 97. *38 Ballee Road East, Ballymena, Co Antrim BT42 3DH* Tel (01266) 47038

STOREY, Timothy (Tim). b 60. Trin Coll Bris DipHE94. **d** 94 **p** 95. C Bath Weston St Jo w Kelston *B & W* from 94. *3 Rosslyn Road, Bath BA1 3LQ* Tel (01225) 482757

STOREY, William Earl Cosbey. b 58. Kent Univ BA. CITC DipTh86. **d** 82 **p** 83. C Drumglass w Moygashel *Arm* 82-86; I Crinken *D & G* 86-96. *38 Ballee Road East, Ballymena, Co Antrim BT42 3DH* Tel (01266) 47038

STOREY, William Leslie Maurice. b 31. Oak Hill Th Coll 67. **d** 69 **p** 70. C Wembley St Jo *Lon* 69-71; C Ealing Dean St Jo 71-75; V W Derby St Luke *Liv* 75-80; V Hunts Cross 80-83; Hon C Brixton St Paul *S'wark* 83-86; P-in-c 87-88; P-in-c Brixton Hill St Sav 83-86; rtd 88; Perm to Offic *S'wark* from 88. *124 Surbiton Hill Park, Surbiton, Surrey KT5 8EP* Tel 0181-390 2821

STORR VENTER, Phillip. b 52. Called to the Bar (Gray's Inn) 74. S'wark Ord Course 90. **d** 93 **p** 94. NSM Bethnal Green St Barn *Lon* 93-97; Chapl Armenia and Georgia *Eur* from 97. *Bearsden, Tredegar Place, 109 Bow Road, London E3 2AN* Tel 0181-981 6195 Fax as telephone E-mail archisden@compuserve.com

STORY, Victor Leonard. b 45. BSc. Ripon Coll Cuddesdon. **d** 81 **p** 82. C Evesham *Worc* 81-85; P-in-c Ilmington w Stretton on Fosse and Ditchford *Cov* 85-90; P-in-c Ilmington w Stretton-on-Fosse etc 90-96; Chapl Vlissingen (Flushing) Miss to Seamen *Eur* from 96. *Amstelstraat 53, 4388 RK, Oost Souburg, The Netherlands* Tel Vlissingen (1184) 78788

STOTER, David John. b 43. AKC66. **d** 67 **p** 68. C Reading St Giles *Ox* 67-71; C Luton Lewsey St Hugh *St Alb* 71-73; Chapl Westmr Hosp Lon 73-79; Convenor of Chapls Notts Distr HA 79-94; Chapl Univ Hosp Nottm 79-94; Chapl Nottm Gen Hosp from 79; Chapl Qu Medical Cen Nottm Univ Hosp NHS Trust from 94. *University Hospital, Queen's Medical Centre, Nottingham NG7 2UH* Tel 0115-924 9924

STOTT, Antony. b 21. Bps' Coll Cheshunt 53. **d** 55 **p** 56. Australia 55-62; V Longbridge Deverill w Hill Deverill *Sarum* 62-66; V Bratton 66-74; R Marnhull 74-81; P-in-c Broad Chalke and Bower Chalke 81; P-in-c Ebbesbourne Wake w Fifield Bavant and Alvediston 81; P-in-c Berwick St John 81; V Chalke Valley W 81-87; rtd 87; Perm to Offic *Ex* from 87. *11 Luscombe Close, Ivybridge, Devon PL21 9TT* Tel (01752) 896142

STOTT, Christopher John (Chris). b 45. Lon Univ BD68. Tyndale Hall Bris. **d** 69 **p** 70. C Croydon Ch Ch Broad Green *Cant* 69-72; Ethiopia 73-76; Area Sec (SW) BCMS 76-78; Tanzania 78-85; R Harwell w Chilton *Ox* from 85; RD Wallingford 91-95. *The Rectory, Harwell, Didcot, Oxon OX11 0EW* Tel (01235) 835365

STOTT, Eric. b 36. ALCD62. **d** 62 **p** 63. C Penn Fields *Lich* 62-65; C Normanton *Derby* 65-71; R Lower Broughton St Clem w St Matthias *Man* 71-79; V Chadderton Em from 79. *Emmanuel Vicarage, 15 Chestnut Street, Chadderton, Oldham OL9 8HB* Tel 0161-681 1310

STOTT, Frederick. b 23. Bris Univ DipFE75 Univ of Wales (Cardiff) CQSW71. Sarum & Wells Th Coll 83. **d** 85 **p** 86. Hon C Sholing *Win* 85-90; Perm to Offic from 90; Perm to Offic *Portsm* from 89. *35 Broadwater Road, Southampton SO18 2DW* Tel (01703) 557193

STOTT, Dr John Robert Walmsley. b 21. Trin Coll Cam BA45 MA50. Lambeth DD83 Ridley Hall Cam 44. **d** 45 **p** 46. C St Marylebone All SS Pet and Jo *Lon* 45-50; R 50-75; Hon C 75-88; Hon C Langham Place All So from 88; Chapl to The Queen 59-91; Extra Chapl to The Queen from 91; Dir Lon Inst of Contemporary Christianity 82-86; Pres from 86; rtd 91. *12 Weymouth Street, London W1N 3FB* Tel 0171-580 1867

STOTT, Miss Teresa (Terrie). b 57. Linc Th Coll CMinlStuds94. **d** 94 **p** 95. C Lee-on-the-Solent *Portsm* 94-97; C Spalding St Jo w Deeping St Nicholas *Linc* from 97. *St John's House, 6 Wedgewood Drive, Wygate Park, Spalding, Lincs PE11 3FJ* Tel (01775) 714210

STOTT, Wilfrid. b 04. Lon Univ BA26 BD27 Linc Coll Ox BLitt62 DPhil66. Lon Coll of Div 26. **d** 27 **p** 28. C Kingsdown *Bris* 27-29; Tutor Tyndale Hall Bris 27-29; China 29-44; R Thorndon w Rishangles *St E* 44-45; Vice-Prin Tyndale Hall Bris 45-46; BCMS 46-51; R Dowdeswell *Glouc* 51-63; Lect St Mich Ho Ox 56-63; V Cambridge St Phil *Ely* 63-66; Kenya 66-71; rtd 71; P-in-c Croxton and Eltisley *Ely* 71-85. *12 Westfield, Harwell, Didcot, Oxon OX11 0LG* Tel (01235) 832791

STOW, John Mark. b 51. Selw Coll Cam BA73 MA77. Linc Th Coll 76. **d** 78 **p** 79. C Harpenden St Jo *St Alb* 78-82; TV Beaminster Area *Sarum* 82-87; P-in-c Hawkchurch 87-90; P-in-c Marshwood Vale 87-88; TR Marshwood Vale TM 88-91; Past Co-ord Millfield Jun Sch from 93. *Chestnut House, Edgarley Hall, Glastonbury, Somerset BA6 8LL* Tel (01458) 832245

STOW, Peter John. b 50. Oak Hill Th Coll. **d** 89 **p** 90. C Forest Gate St Mark *Chelmsf* 89-94; V from 94. *St Mark's Vicarage, Tylney Road, London E7 0LS* Tel 0181-555 2988

STOW, Archdeacon of. *See* WELLS, The Ven Roderick John

STOWE, Brian. b 32. Trin Coll Cam BA55 BA56 MA59. Ridley Hall Cam 55. **d** 57 **p** 58. C New Catton St Luke *Nor* 57-59; Chapl R Masonic Sch Bushey 59-70; Tutor Rickmansworth Sch Herts 70-71; Chapl Alleyn's Foundn Dulwich 71-75; Hon C Dulwich St Barn *S'wark* 71-75; Chapl Ellerslie Sch Malvern 75-92; Chapl Malvern Coll 92-93; TV Malvern Link w Cowleigh *Worc* 93-94; rtd 95; P-in-c Malvern St Andr *Worc* 95-96. *31 Park View, Grange Road, Malvern, Worcs WR14 3HG* Tel (01684) 568134

STOWE, Nigel James. b 36. Bris Univ BSc57. Clifton Th Coll 59. **d** 61 **p** 62. C Ware Ch Ch *St Alb* 61-64; C Reigate St Mary *S'wark* 64-67; V Islington St Jude Mildmay Park *Lon* 67-75; V Penn Street *Ox* from 75. *The Vicarage, Penn Street, Amersham, Bucks HP7 0PX* Tel (01494) 712194

STOWE, Canon Rachel Lilian. b 33. Qu Coll Birm 79. **dss** 83 **d** 87 **p** 94. Dean w Yelden, Melchbourne and Shelton *St Alb* 82-87; Pertenhall w Swineshead 82-87; Bp's Officer for NSM and Asst Dir of Ords 87-93; NSM The Stodden Churches 87-97; Hon Can St Alb 92-97; rtd 93. *Preston Cottage, East Cowton, Northallerton, N Yorkshire DL7 0BD* Tel (01325) 378173 Fax as telephone

STRACHAN, Donald Philip Michael. b 37. St D Coll Lamp 60. **d** 62 **p** 63. C Aberdeen St Mary *Ab* 62-64; P-in-c Aberdeen St Paul 64-66; Chapl St Andr Cathl 65-68; Itinerant Priest *Mor* 68-73; R Coatbridge *Glas* 73-85; Chapl HM Pris Glas (Barlinnie) 84-87; Dioc Supernumerary *Glas* 85-91; rtd 94; Perm to Offic *Arg* from 94. *Reul na Mara, Claddach Kirkibost, Lochmaddy, Isle of North Uist HS6 5EP*

✠**STRADLING, The Rt Revd Leslie Edward.** b 08. Qu Coll Ox BA30 MA31 Bp's Univ Lennoxville Hon DCL68. Wycliffe Hall Ox 32. **d** 33 **p** 34 **c** 45. C Stoke Newington St Andr *Lon* 33-38; V Camberwell St Luke *S'wark* 38-43; Chapl Camberwell Ho 38-43; V Wandsworth St Anne 43-45; S Africa from 45; Bp Masasi 45-52; Bp SW Tang 52-61; Bp Johannesburg 61-74; rtd 74. *Braehead House, Auburn Road, Kenilworth, 7700 South Africa* Tel Parow (21) 761-6251

STRAFFORD, Nigel Thomas Bevan. b 53. Univ of Wales (Lamp) BA80. Sarum & Wells Th Coll 80. **d** 82 **p** 94. C Kidderminster St Mary *Worc* 82; C Kidderminster St Mary and All SS, Trimpley etc 82-83; Hon C Stockton St Mark *Dur* 84-86; NSM Longwood *Wakef* 86-94; V Athersley 94-97; P-in-c Ferrybridge from 97. *St Andrew's Vicarage, 5 Pontefract Road, Knottingley, W Yorkshire WF11 8PN* Tel (01977) 672772

STRAIN, Christopher Malcolm (Chris). b 56. MLawSoc Southn Univ LLB77. Wycliffe Hall Ox 83. **d** 86 **p** 87. C Werrington *Pet* 86-89; C Broadwater St Mary *Chich* 89-94; TV Hampreston *Sarum* from 94. *The Vicarage, 19 Canford Bottom, Wimborne, Dorset BH21 2HA* Tel (01202) 884796

STRAIN, Dr Gregory John. b 62. Lon Hosp MB, BS86. Oak Hill Th Coll 94. **d** 96 **p** 97. C Wolverhampton St Luke *Lich* from 96. *36 Pencombe Drive, Wolverhampton WV4 5EW* Tel (01902) 337745

STRANACK, Canon David Arthur Claude. b 43. Chich Th Coll 65. **d** 68 **p** 69. C Forest Gate St Edm *Chelmsf* 68-69; C Colchester St Jas, All SS, St Nic and St Runwald 69-74; V Brentwood St Geo 74-82; V Nayland w Wiston *St E* from 82; Hon Can St E Cathl from 94. *The Vicarage, Bear Street, Nayland, Colchester CO6 4LA* Tel (01206) 262316

STRANACK, Dr Fay Rosemary. b 30. Lon Univ BSc55 PhD60. Westcott Ho Cam 88. **d** 89 **p** 94. NSM Denmead *Portsm* from 89. *35 Yew Tree Gardens, Denmead, Waterlooville, Hants PO7 6LH* Tel (01705) 256785

STRANACK, Richard Nevill. b 40. Leeds Univ BA63. Coll of Resurr Mirfield 63. **d** 65 **p** 66. C Bush Hill Park St Mark *Lon* 65-68; C Brighton St Martin *Chich* 68-72; P-in-c Toftrees w Shereford *Nor* 72-74; V 74-81; P-in-c Pensthorpe 72-74; R 74-81; V Hempton and Pudding Norton 72-81; RD Burnham and Walsingham 78-81; V Par *Truro* 81-94; P-in-c St Blazey 87-91; Hon Chapl Miss to Seamen from 81; V Stratton and Launcells *Truro* from 94. *The Vicarage, Diddies Road, Stratton, Bude, Cornwall EX23 9DW* Tel (01288) 352254

STRAND, Tyler Alan. b 51. Augustana Coll (USA) AB73. Gen Th Sem (NY) MDiv78 St Steph Ho Ox 74. **d** 77 **p** 78. USA 77-85 and from 93; W Germany 85-90; Chapl Helsinki w Moscow *Eur* 91-93. *1220 Cambia Drive 4108, Schaumburg, Illinois 60193, USA*

STRANGE, Alan Michael. b 57. Pemb Coll Ox BA79 MA89. Wycliffe Hall Ox BA84. **d** 84 **p** 85. C York St Paul *York* 84-87; Asst Chapl Brussels Cathl *Eur* 87-91; Assoc Chapl 91-95; P-in-c Heigham H Trin *Nor* from 95. *The Rectory, 17 Essex Street, Norwich NR2 2BL* Tel (01603) 622225

STRANGE, Bryan. b 26. Sarum & Wells Th Coll 73. **d** 75 **p** 76. C King's Worthy *Win* 75-78; C Wilton *B & W* 78-80; V Kewstoke w Wick St Lawrence 80-89; rtd 89; Hon C Tiverton St Andr *Ex* from 90. *29 Bluebell Avenue, Tiverton, Devon EX16 6SX*

STRANGE, Malcolm. b 58. Westmr Coll Ox MTh95. Sarum & Wells Th Coll 82. **d** 85 **p** 86. C Seaton Hirst *Newc* 85-88; C Ridgeway *Sarum* 88-89; TV 89-91; TV Newbury *Ox* from 91. *St George's Vicarage, 206 Andover Road, Newbury, Berks RG14 6NU* Tel (01635) 582911 Fax 524994

STRANGE, Mark Jeremy. b 61. Aber Univ LTh82. Linc Th Coll 87. **d** 89 **p** 90. C Worc St Barn w Ch Ch *Worc* 89-92; V Worc St Wulstan from 92. *St Wulstan's Vicarage, Cranham Drive, Worcester WR4 9PA* Tel (01905) 57806

STRANGE, Mrs Mary McKellar. b 53. FCA75 ATII77. St Jo Coll Nottm BTh93 Westcott Ho Cam 93. **d** 94 **p** 95. C Weston Favell *Pet* from 94. *5 Kestrel Close, Weston Favell, Northampton NN3 3JG* Tel (01604) 404986

STRANGE, Canon Peter Robert. b 48. Univ Coll Lon BA69 Ex Coll Ox BA71 MA76. Cuddesdon Coll 71. **d** 72 **p** 73. C Denton *Newc* 72-74; C Newc St Jo 74-79; Chapl for Arts and Recreation 79-90; R Wallsend St Pet 79-86; Can Res Newc Cathl from 86; Angl Adv Tyne Tees TV from 90. *55 Queen's Terrace, Jesmond, Newcastle upon Tyne NE2 2PL* Tel 0191-281 0181

STRANGE, Preb Robert Lewis. b 45. Sarum & Wells Th Coll 72. **d** 74 **p** 75. C Walthamstow St Barn and St Jas Gt *Chelmsf* 74-77; C Wickford 77-80; P-in-c Treverbyn *Truro* 80-83; V 83-86; Asst Stewardship Adv from 82; V Newlyn St Pet from 86; Miss to Seamen from 86; Preb St Endellion *Truro* from 95. *St Peter's Vicarage, Newlyn, Penzance, Cornwall TR18 5HT* Tel (01736) 62678

STRANGE, Dr William Anthony. b 53. Qu Coll Cam BA76 MA80 Win Coll CertEd77 Ox Univ DPhil89. Wycliffe Hall Ox. **d** 82 **p** 83. Tutor Wycliffe Hall Ox 82-87; Lic to Offic *Ox* 82-87; C Aberystwyth *St D* 87; TV 87-91; V Llandeilo and Taliaris 91-96; Hd of Relig Studies Trin Coll Carmarthen from 96. *Trinity College, Carmarthen SA31 3EP* Tel (01267) 237971

STRANGEWAYS, Canon David Inderwick. b 12. DSO43 OBE44. Trin Hall Cam BA33 MA36. Wells Th Coll 58. **d** 59 **p** 60. C Lee-on-the-Solent *Portsm* 59-61; R Symondsbury *Sarum* 61-65; V Bradford-on-Avon 65-73; Chapl Stockholm *Eur* 73-77; Chan Malta Cathl 77-81; rtd 81; Perm to Offic *St E* from 81; Perm to Offic *Nor* from 81. *10 Dowes Hill Close, Beccles, Suffolk NR34 9XL* Tel (01502) 716086

STRANRAER-MULL, The Very Revd Gerald Hugh. b 42. AKC69. St Aug Coll Cant 69. **d** 70 **p** 71. C Hexham *Newc* 70-72; C Corbridge w Halton 72; R Cruden Bay *Ab* from 72; R Ellon from 72; Can St Andr Cathl from 81; Dean Ab from 88. *The Rectory, Ellon, Aberdeenshire AB41 9NP* Tel (01358) 720366

STRAPPS, Canon Robert David. b 28. St Edm Hall Ox BA52 MA56. Wycliffe Hall Ox 52. **d** 54 **p** 55. C Low Leyton *Chelmsf* 54-57; C Ox St Aldate w H Trin *Ox* 57-60; V Sandal St Helen *Wakef* 60-94; RD Chevet 81-93; Hon Can Wakef Cathl 92-94; rtd 94; Perm to Offic *Wakef* from 94. *Brookside, Hill Road, Kemerton, Tewkesbury, Glos GL20 7JN* Tel (01386) 725515

STRASZAK, Edmund Norman. b 57. Coll of Resurr Mirfield 88. **d** 90 **p** 91. C Adlington *Blackb* 90-93; C Harrogate St Wilfrid and St Luke *Ripon* 93-95; V Chorley All SS *Blackb* from 95. *All Saints' Vicarage, Moor Road, Chorley, Lancs PR7 2LR* Tel (01257) 265665

STRATFORD, Mrs Anne Barbara. Southn Univ CertEd58. Qu Coll Birm. **d** 91 **p** 94. Officer Dioc Bd of Soc Resp (Family Care) *Lich* from 85; NSM Kinnerley w Melverley and Knockin w Maesbrook 91-95; Chapl Robert Jones and Agnes Hunt Orthopaedic Hosp from 95; NSM Maesbury *Lich* 95-96; P-in-c from 96; Chapl Moreton Hall Sch from 96. *Pentre Cleddar, Lower Hengoed, Oswestry, Shropshire SY10 7AB* Tel (01691) 655469

STRATFORD, The Ven Ralph Montgomery. b 30. TCD BA53 MA67. CITC 53. **d** 54 **p** 54. C Dioc C *C & O* 54-55; C Waterford Ch Ch 55-56; I Ballisodare w Collooney and Emlaghfad *T, K & A* from 56; RD Straid 61-66 and from 88; Adn Killala and Achonry from 69; Preb Kilmactalway St Patr Cathl Dublin from 85. *The Rectory, Ballysodare, Co Sligo, Irish Republic* Tel Sligo (71) 67260

STRATFORD, Terence Stephen (Terry). b 45. Chich Th Coll 67. **d** 69 **p** 70. C Old Shoreham *Chich* 69-73; C New Shoreham 69-73; C Uckfield 73-75; C Lt Horsted 73-75; C Isfield 73-75; P-in-c Waldron 76-80; R 80-82; V Blacklands Hastings Ch Ch and St Andr 82-89; P-in-c Ovingdean 89-95; Dioc Ecum Officer 89-95; P-in-c Staplefield Common from 95; Sussex Ecum Officer from 95. *14 Ledgers Meadow, Cuckfield, Haywards Heath, W Sussex RH17 5EW* Tel (01444) 456588

STRATFORD, Timothy Richard (Tim). b 61. York Univ BSc82. Wycliffe Hall Ox 83. **d** 86 **p** 87. C Mossley Hill St Matt and St Jas *Liv* 86-89; C St Helens St Helen 89-91; Bp's Dom Chapl 91-94; V W Derby Gd Shep from 94. *The Vicarage, 136 Carr Lane East, Liverpool L11 4SL* Tel 0151-546 7527

STRATFORD, William Anthony. b 23. Roch Th Coll 64. **d** 66 **p** 67. C Conisbrough *Sheff* 66-68; C Doncaster St Geo 68-71; V Arksey 71-75; R Armthorpe 75-80; R Harthill 80-82; R Harthill and Thorpe Salvin 82-85; rtd 85; Perm to Offic *Sheff* from 85. *Dulverton Hall, St Martin's Square, Scarborough, N Yorkshire YO11 2DB* Tel (01723) 366550

STRATHIE, Duncan John. b 58. Cranmer Hall Dur BA95. **d** 97. C Yateley *Win* from 97. *18 Hall Farm Crescent, Yateley, Hants GU46 6HT* Tel (01252) 876416 E-mail djstrathie@aol.com

STRATTA, Antony Charles (Tony). b 36. ACIS. S'wark Ord Course 82. **d** 85 **p** 86. C Southborough St Pet w Ch Ch and St Matt *Roch* 85-88; R Gt Mongeham w Ripple and Sutton by Dover *Cant* 88-96; rtd 96. *Well House, The Great Yard, Rougham Green, Bury St Edmunds, Suffolk IP30 9JP*

STRATTON, The Ven Basil. b 06. Hatf Coll Dur BA29 MA32. **d** 30 **p** 31. Tutor St Paul's Coll Burgh 30; C Grimsby St Steph *Linc* 30-32; India 32-47; CF 41-47; Hon CF 47; V Figheldean w Milston *Sarum* 48-53; V Drayton in Hales *Lich* 53-59; R Adderley 56-59; RD Hodnet 53-59; Adn Stafford 59-74; Can Res and Treas Lich Cathl 60-74; Chapl to The Queen 65-76; rtd 74. *The Ridge, Pettridge Lane, Mere, Warminster, Wilts BA12 6DG* Tel (01747) 860235

STRATTON, Geoffrey Frederick. b 25. ARICS52. Oak Hill Th Coll 78. **d** 81 **p** 82. NSM Chipping Barnet w Arkley *St Alb* 81-85; TV 85-90; rtd 90; Perm to Offic *Linc* from 90. *Witsend, 8 Thornton Crescent, Horncastle, Lincs LN9 6JP* Tel (01507) 525508

STRATTON, Henry William. b 39. Bris Univ CertEd74 BEd75. Glouc Sch of Min 80. **d** 83 **p** 84. NSM Cainscross w Selsley *Glouc* 83-87; C Odd Rode *Ches* 87-92; V Runcorn H Trin 92-96; V Lostock Gralam from 96. *The Vicarage, Station Road, Lostock Gralam, Northwich, Cheshire CW9 7PS* Tel (01606) 43806

STRATTON, Ian Herbert Shearing. b 27. St Jo Coll Dur BA52 DipTh53 MA78. **d** 53 **p** 54. C Shirley *Win* 53-58; Succ Bradf Cathl *Bradf* 58-60; Tutor St Aid Birkenhead 60-62; Vice-Prin 62-65; Perm to Offic *Sarum* 62-69; P-in-c Chettle 69-72; C Salisbury St Fran 72-80; C Harnham 81-87; rtd 88. *20 Bradley Road, Warminster, Wilts BA12 8BP* Tel (01985) 212785

STRATTON, John Jefferies. b 27. Bps' Coll Cheshunt 53. **d** 55 **p** 56. C Watford St Mich *St Alb* 55-60; C Stevenage 60-65; R Cottered w Broadfield and Throcking 65-82; RD Buntingford 75-82; V S Mimms St Mary and Potters Bar *Lon* 82-84; V Potters Bar *St Alb* 85-94; P-in-c Flamstead 94-96; rtd 94. *17 The Fairways, Sherford, Taunton, Somerset TA1 3PA*

STRATTON, Canon Leslie Verdun. b 16. Edin Th Coll 36. **d** 39 **p** 40. C Dundee St Mary Magd *Bre* 39-45; P-in-c Bo'ness *Edin* 45-50; P-in-c Linlithgow 45-50; P-in-c Dundee St Jo *Bre* 50-81; Can St Paul's Cathl Dundee 71-81; Hon Can from 81; Syn Clerk 71-81; rtd 81; Perm to Offic *Bre* from 81. *16 Argyle Street, Dundee DD4 7AL* Tel (01382) 462413

STRAUGHAN, Keith. b 60. Imp Coll Lon BSc81 Lon Univ PhD87 Imp Coll Lon ARCS81 CPhys87 MInstP87 Trin Coll Cam BA94. Westcott Ho Cam 94. **d** 97. C Abbots Langley *St Alb* from 97. *40 Kindersley Way, Abbots Langley, Herts WD5 0DQ* Tel (01923) 265729 Fax 261795 E-mail ks10019@cam.ac.uk

STREATER, David Arthur. b 33. Oak Hill Th Coll 67. **d** 68 **p** 69. C Lindfield *Chich* 68-71; S Africa 71-86; R Kingham w Churchill, Daylesford and Sarsden *Ox* 86-91; Dir Ch Soc and Sec Ch Soc Trust from 91; Lic to Offic *St Alb* from 91. *Dean Wace House, 16 Rosslyn Road, Watford WD1 7EY* Tel (01923) 213370

STREATFEILD, Francis Richard Champion. b 22. Qu Coll Cam BA48 MA59. Cuddesdon Coll 48. **d** 50 **p** 51. C Houghton le Spring *Dur* 50-53; India 53-70; V Sacriston *Dur* 70-79; Lic to Offic *Carl* 79-85; Area Sec (Dio Carl) USPG 79-85; C Carl St Aid and Ch Ch *Carl* 85-88; rtd 88; Perm to Offic *Carl* from 88. *Fenton Lane Head, How Mill, Carlisle CA4 9LD* Tel (01228) 70470

STREEK, Stanley James. b 11. Man Univ BD42. Wycliffe Hall Ox. **d** 42 **p** 43. C Horsforth *Ripon* 42-47; V Warmfield *Wakef* 47-51; V Holmebridge 51-76; rtd 76. *Bridgend, Laurieston, Castle Douglas, Kirkcudbrightshire DG7 2PW*

STREET, Anthony James (Tony). b 57. Trin Coll Bris DipHE81. **d** 85 **p** 87. SAMS 85-95; Chile 85-95; P-in-c Warley *Wakef* from 96. *The Vicarage, 466 Burnley Road, Warley, Halifax, W Yorkshire HX2 7LW* Tel (01422) 363623

STREET, David Grover. b 24. St Aid Birkenhead 49. **d** 54 **p** 55. C Everton St Tim *Liv* 54-56; Missr Shrewsbury Sch Miss Liv 56-62; Chapl The Cotswold Sch 62-64; Chapl Abingdon Sch 64-68; Warden Rugby Clubs Notting Hill 68-70; Chapl Milton Abbey Sch Dorset 70; Chapl St Lawr Coll Ramsgate 71; Community Cen Strabane Co Tyrone 73-74; Boys' Welfare Club Hartlepool 74-84; rtd 89; Perm to Offic *Dur* from 89. *80 Woodside, Barnard Castle, Co Durham DL12 8AP* Tel (01833) 37351

STREET, Peter Ernest. b 17. Oak Hill Th Coll 37. **d** 40 **p** 42. C Waltham Abbey *Chelmsf* 40-43; C Heigham H Trin *Nor* 43-44; Chapl RAFVR 44-48; C Cambridge St Andr Less *Ely* 48; Min Cam St Steph CD 48-52; V Lowestoft Ch Ch *Nor* 52-57; V Denton Holme *Carl* 57-68; V Cheadle Hulme St Andr *Ches* 68-73; CPAS Evang 74-78; rtd 78; Perm to Offic *Nor* from 78. *49 Eckling Grange, Dereham, Norfolk NR20 3BB* Tel (01362) 698896

STREET, Peter Jarman. b 29. K Coll Lon BD59 AKC59. **d** 59 **p** 60. C Highters Heath *Birm* 59-60; C Shirley 60-62; Lect Chesh Coll of Educn 62-66; St Pet Coll of Educn Birm 66-70; RE Adv Essex Co Coun 70-92; Hon C Gt Dunmow *Chelmsf* 71-85; Sen Insp RE and Humanities 74-92; R Gt w Lt Yeldham 85-92; RD Belchamp 90-92; rtd 92; Perm to Offic *Chelmsf* from 92. *18 Jubilee Court, Great Dunmow, Essex CM6 1DY* Tel (01371) 876871

STREET, Philip. b 47. Lon Univ BPharm68. NW Ord Course 75. **d** 78 **p** 79. C Heaton St Barn *Bradf* 78-81; C Evington *Leic* 82-84; P-in-c Wymondham w Edmondthorpe 84; P-in-c Buckminster w Sewstern, Sproxton and Coston 84; R Wymondham w Edmondthorpe, Buckminster etc 84-88; V Gosberton Clough and Quadring *Linc* 88-95; Asst Local Min Officer 88-95; V Buttershaw St Paul *Bradf* from 95. *The Vicarage, Wibsey Park Avenue, Bradford, W Yorkshire BD6 3QA* Tel (01274) 676735

STREETER, Christine Mary. *See* HADDON-REECE, Mrs Christine Mary

STREETER, David James. b 42. Pemb Coll Cam BA64 MA68. Qu Coll Birm 65. **d** 67 **p** 68. C Saffron Walden *Chelmsf* 67-71; C Shrub End 71-73; R Rayne 73-79; V Highams Park All SS 79-82; P-in-c Stradbroke w Horham and Athelington *St E* 82-87; R Stradbroke, Horham, Athelington and Redlingfield from 87; RD Hoxne from 91. *The Rectory, Doctors Lane, Stradbroke, Eye, Suffolk IP21 5HU* Tel (01379) 384363

STREETING, John William. b 52. ACertCM89 Cam Inst of Educn CertEd74 Birm Univ BEd77. St Steph Ho Ox 90. **d** 92 **p** 93. C Upminster *Chelmsf* 92-95; C Chingford SS Pet and Paul 95-97; C Chelsea St Luke and Ch Ch *Lon* from 97. *29 Burnsall Street, London SW3 3SR* Tel 0171-352 5608

STREETING, Laurence Storey. b 14. VRD65. St Jo Coll Dur BA39 DipTh40 MA42. **d** 40 **p** 41. C Bishopwearmouth St Gabr *Dur* 40-46; Chapl RNVR 42-46; S Africa 46-49; Chapl Garden City Woodford Bridge 49-51; Chapl Village Home Barkingside 49-51; Chapl RAF 51-56; Chapl RNR 56-90; Asst Chapl Eliz Coll Guernsey 56-60; Chapl Eshton Hall Sch Gargrave 60-64; Perm to Offic *Cant* 64-65; R Guernsey St Sampson *Win* 65-71; St Vincent 72-76; Chapl Madeira *Eur* 76-80; rtd 80; Perm to Offic *Win* from 79. *L'Amarrage, Marette Road, L'Islet, St Sampson, Guernsey GY2 4FR* Tel (01481) 47320

STRETCH, Richard Mark. b 53. LNSM course 91. **d** 93 **p** 94. NSM Stowmarket *St E* from 93. *91 Kipling Way, Stowmarket, Suffolk IP14 1TS* Tel (01449) 676219

STRETTON, George Peter. b 22. MBE. **d** 70 **p** 71. Malaysia 70-78; V Shireoaks *S'well* 79-85; Perm to Offic *B & W* from 86; rtd 87. *9 The Lerburne, Wedmore, Somerset BS28 4ED* Tel (01934) 713244

STRETTON, Reginald John. b 37. MRPharmS63 CBiol70 MIBiol70 Man Univ BSc62 Nottm Univ PhD65 SOSc. EMMTC 88. **d** 91 **p** 92. NSM Loughb Gd Shep *Leic* 91-94; P-in-c Burrough Hill Pars from 94. *The Rectory, 1 High Street, Somerby, Melton Mowbray, Leics LE14 2PZ* Tel (01664) 454318

STRETTON, Robert John. b 45. **d** 69 **p** 70. C Hendon St Ignatius *Dur* 69-73; C Middlesbrough St Thos *York* 73-77; OSB 77-78; V Brandon *Dur* 78-85; Lic to Offic 85-91; SSM from 85; Tr in Evang Ch in Wales 91-94; Perm to Offic *S'wark* from 91. *The Society of the Sacred Mission, 96 Vassall Road, London SW9 6IA* Tel 0171-582 2162

STREVENS, Brian Lloyd. b 49. St Jo Coll Dur BA70. Ripon Hall Ox 70. **d** 73 **p** 74. C Old Trafford St Jo *Man* 73-76; C Bolton St Pet 76-78; Org Sec Southn Coun of Community Service from 78; Perm to Offic *Win* 82-86; NSM Bitterne Park from 86. *186 Hill Lane, Southampton SO15 5DB* Tel (01703) 333301

STREVENS, Richard Ernest Noel. b 34. Nottm Univ BA60. Linc Th Coll 60. **d** 62 **p** 63. C St Botolph Aldgate w H Trin Minories *Lon* 62-66; C Ealing St Steph Castle Hill 66-68; Hon C St Botolph without Bishopgate 68-76; V Clent *Worc* 76-86; V Pirbright *Guildf* from 86. *The Vicarage, The Green, Pirbright, Woking, Surrey GU24 0JE* Tel (01483) 473332

STRIBLEY, William Charles Harold. b 29. SW Minl Tr Course. **d** 87 **p** 88. NSM Kenwyn St Geo *Truro* 87-92; NSM Truro St Paul and St Clem from 92. *54 Chirgwin Road, Truro, Cornwall TR1 1TT* Tel (01872) 72958

STRICKLAND, Derek. b 26. Bps' Coll Cheshunt 64. **d** 66 **p** 66. C Bray and Braywood *Ox* 66-67; C Hall Green Ascension *Birm* 67-70; V Hamstead St Bernard 70-76; Ind Chapl *St Alb* 76-93; rtd 93. *9 Dove House Crescent, Farnham Royal, Slough SL2 2PZ* Tel (01753) 521701

STRICKLAND (née CUTTS), Mrs Elizabeth Joan Gabrielle. b 61. St Jo Coll Dur BA83. Westcott Ho Cam 87. **d** 90 **p** 94. Par Dn Cayton w Eastfield *York* 90-92; NSM Biggin Hill *Roch* 93-96. *Address temp unknown*

STRICKLAND, Canon Ernest Armitage. b 24. Ch Coll Cam BA49 MA54. Wycliffe Hall Ox 49. **d** 51 **p** 52. C Bolton St Paul *Man* 51-53; C Hyson Green *S'well* 53-55; C-in-c Wollaton Park CD 55-57; V Wollaton Park 57-64; V Southport St Phil *Liv* 64-76; R Broughton *Linc* 76-90; RD Yarborough 81-86; Can and Preb Linc Cathl from 85; rtd 90; Perm to Offic *Linc* from 90. *143 Grimsby Road, Waltham, Grimsby, S Humberside DN37 0PU* Tel (01472) 821126

STRICKLAND, Canon Paul Lowndes. b 21. Linc Th Coll 46. **d** 49 **p** 50. C Oatlands *Guildf* 49-52; C Huddersfield St Jo *Wakef* 52-54; V Carlton 54-58; V Offton, Nettlestead and Willisham *St E* 58-61; CF (TA) 59-67; V Debenham *St E* 61-75; V Lakenheath 75-83; Hon Can St E Cathl 81-83; rtd 83. *4 Albany Gardens East, Clacton-on-Sea, Essex CO15 6HW* Tel (01255) 426303

STRIDE, Clifford Stephen. b 21. Ex & Truro NSM Scheme. **d** 81 **p** 82. NSM Chulmleigh *Ex* 81-83; NSM Hardham *Chich* 87-93; NSM Coldwaltham and Hardham from 93. *Ambleside, Sandy Lane, Watersfield, Pulborough, W Sussex RH20 1NF* Tel (01798) 831851

STRIDE, Desmond William Adair. b 15. Ch Coll Cam BA37 MA41. Ridley Hall Cam 38. **d** 39 **p** 40. C Alperton *Lon* 39-41; C St Marylebone All So w SS Pet and Jo 41-42; C Milton Regis St Mary *Cant* 42-45; Chapl Dover Coll 45-57; Warden St Mich Coll Tenbury 57-65; V Tenbury St Mich *Heref* 57-65; Asst Master Tre-Arddur Ho Sch 65-67; Chapl Heathfield Sch Ascot 67-80; rtd 80; Perm to Offic *Lon* 90; Perm to Offic *Chich* from 90. *5 Oakmede Way, Ringmer, Lewes, E Sussex BN8 5JL* Tel (01273) 813561

STRIDE, Edgar George. b 23. Tyndale Hall Bris 47. **d** 51 **p** 52. C Croydon Ch Ch Broad Green *Cant* 51-55; V W Thurrock *Chelmsf* 55-61; V Becontree St Mary 61-70; R Spitalfields Ch Ch w All SS *Lon* 70-89; rtd 89; Perm to Offic *Linc* from 89; Perm to Offic *Pet* from 89. *23 Pembroke Road, Stamford, Lincs PE9 1BS* Tel (01780) 56325

STRIDE, John David. b 46. Ex Univ BSc68. Oak Hill Th Coll DipHE88. **d** 88 **p** 89. C Ashtead *Guildf* 88-96; V Lodge Moor St Luke *Sheff* from 96. *St Luke's Vicarage, 18 Blackbrook Road, Sheffield S10 4LP* Tel 0114-230 5271

STRIDE, John Michael. b 48. Oak Hill Th Coll BA77. **d** 80 **p** 81. C Edmonton All SS *Lon* 80-82; C Edmonton All SS w St Mich 82-83; C Wembley St Jo 83-85; P-in-c Hockering *Nor* 85-89; R Hockering, Honingham, E and N Tuddenham 89-91; V Tuckswood 91-93; Chapl HM Pris Leeds 93-94; Chapl HM Pris Littlehey 94-96; V Heeley *Sheff* from 96. *The Vicarage, 151 Gleadless Road, Sheffield S2 3AE* Tel 0114-255 7718

STRIKE, Maurice Arthur. b 44. FRSA66 NDD66. Sarum & Wells Th Coll 85. **d** 87 **p** 88. C Chippenham St Andr w Tytherton Lucas *Bris* 87-91; R Corfe Castle, Church Knowle, Kimmeridge etc *Sarum* from 91. *The Rectory, Corfe Castle, Wareham, Dorset BH20 5EE* Tel (01929) 480257

STRINGER, Adrian Nigel. b 60. Univ of Wales (Cardiff) BD82 Lanc Univ PGCE83. Sarum & Wells Th Coll 86. **d** 88 **p** 89. C Barrow St Matt *Carl* 88-92; TV Westhoughton *Man* 92-94; I Inver w Mountcharles, Killaghtee and Killybegs *D & R* 94-96; V Tuckingmill *Truro* from 96. *All Saints' Vicarage, 35 Roskear, Camborne, Cornwall TR14 8DG* Tel (01209) 712114

STRINGER, Harold John. b 36. Peterho Cam BA58. Ripon Hall Ox 62. **d** 64 **p** 65. C Hackney St Jo *Lon* 64-68; C Roehampton H Trin *S'wark* 68-71; P-in-c Southampton St Mich w H Rood, St Lawr etc *Win* 71-73; TV Southampton (City Cen) 73-82; Ind Chapl 77-82; V Notting Hill St Jo *Lon* 82-87; V Notting Hill St Pet 82-87; V Notting Hill St Jo and St Pet from 87. *25 Ladbroke Road, London W11 3PD* Tel 0171-727 3439

STRINGER, Canon John Roden. b 33. AKC61. **d** 62 **p** 63. C Auckland St Helen *Dur* 62-63; C Hebburn St Cuth 63-67; V Cassop cum Quarrington 67-88; RD Sedgefield 84-88; V Lumley from 88; Hon Can Dur Cathl from 88. *The Vicarage, Great Lumley, Chester le Street, Co Durham DH3 4ER* Tel 0191-388 2228

STRINGER, Leonard Gordon. b 14. Westcott Ho Cam 64. **d** 66 **p** 67. C Bath Abbey w St Jas *B & W* 66-80; rtd 80; Perm to Offic *B & W* from 82. *8 Hockley Court, Weston Park West, Bath BA1 4AR* Tel (01225) 318286

STRINGER, Ralph Stuart. b 47. Chich Th Coll 82. **d** 84 **p** 85. C Hadleigh w Layham and Shelley *St E* 84-87; P-in-c Needham Market w Badley 87-89; V 89-95; RD Bosmere 94-95; R Rogate w Terwick and Trotton w Chithurst *Chich* from 95. *The Vicarage, Fyning Lane, Rogate, Petersfield, Hants GU31 5EE* Tel (01730) 821576

STRONG, Christopher Patteson. b 43. Ridley Hall Cam. **d** 83 **p** 84. C Dalton-in-Furness *Carl* 83-87; V Wootton *St Alb* from 87; RD Elstow from 94. *The Vicarage, Wootton, Bedford MK43 9HF* Tel (01234) 768391

STRONG, Donald Frederick. b 18. Oak Hill Th Coll 46. **d** 50 **p** 51. C Haydock St Mark *Liv* 50-52; C Toxteth Park St Philemon 52-53; Org Sec (Midl) CPAS 53-57; Public Preacher *Birm* 54-57; V Kirkdale St Lawr *Liv* 57-61; R Bedford St Jo *St Alb* 61-75; R Bedford St Jo and St Leon 75-81; rtd 81; Perm to Offic *St Alb* from 81. *1 Ramsay Hall, Byron Road, Worthing, W Sussex BN11 3HW*

STRONG, Jack. b 16. St Aid Birkenhead 52. **d** 54 **p** 55. C Radcliffe St Thos *Man* 54-58; V Chadderton St Mark 58-66; V Burgh-by-Sands w Kirkbampton *Carl* 66-83; R Burgh-by-Sands and Kirkbampton w Kirkandrews etc 83; rtd 83; Perm to Offic *Glouc* from 84. *Aballava, 18 Wincel Road, Winchcombe, Cheltenham, Glos GL54 5YE* Tel (01242) 603347

STRONG, Canon John David. b 34. Cuddesdon Coll 59. **d** 61 **p** 62. C Gosforth All SS *Newc* 61-65; Chapl Malvern Coll 65-71; R Welford w Weston on Avon *Glouc* 72-79; V Nailsworth from 79; RD Tetbury from 83; Hon Can Glouc Cathl from 91. *The Vicarage, Avening Road, Nailsworth, Stroud, Glos GL6 0PJ* Tel (01453) 832181

STRONG, Matthew John. b 60. Lon Univ BA81 Cam Univ BA84 MA89. Ridley Hall Cam 82. **d** 85 **p** 86. C Houghton *Carl* 85-89; C Hirwaun *Llan* 89-91; V Troedyrhiw w Merthyr Vale 91-95; Tutor Llan Ord Course 91-95. *92 Manor Abbey Road, Halesowen, W Midlands B62 0AA* Tel 0121-422 0970

STRONG, Neil. b 34. Bps' Coll Cheshunt 57. **d** 61 **p** 62. C Hunslet St Mary and Stourton *Ripon* 61-65; C Claxby w Normanby-le-Wold *Linc* 65-67; C Ludlow *Heref* 69-71; P-in-c Withern *Linc* 71-74; P-in-c N and S Reston 71-74; P-in-c Strubby 71-74; P-in-c Gayton le Marsh 71-74; P-in-c Authorpe 71-74; R Stanningley St Thos *Ripon* 74-76; P-in-c Bishop Wilton *York* 76-78; P-in-c Bishop Wilton w Full Sutton 76-80; V Holme-on-Spalding Moor 80-82; V Nunthorpe 82-85; rtd 85; Perm to Offic *York* from 85.

51 Reeth Road, Linthorpe, Middlesbrough, Cleveland TS5 5JU Tel (01642) 821433

STRONG, Rowan Gordon William. b 53. Victoria Univ Wellington BA76. St Jo Coll (NZ) LTh80 Melbourne Coll of Div ThM88. **d** 77 **p** 78. New Zealand 77-83; Australia 83-89; NSM Edin Old St Paul *Edin* from 89. *4 New Street, Edinburgh EH8 8BH* Tel 0131-557 3493

STRONG, Preb Stephen Charles. b 16. Em Coll Cam BA38 MA43. Lon Coll of Div 38. **d** 40 **p** 41. C Harborne Heath *Birm* 40-43; C Dublin St Kevin *D & G* 43-45; Hd Cam Univ Miss Bermondsey 45-52; V Upper Tulse Hill St Matthias *S'wark* 52-57; V Egham *Guildf* 57-66; V Heref St Pet w St Owen *Heref* 66-79; V Heref St Pet w St Owen and St Jas 79-82; Preb Heref Cathl 78-85; rtd 82; Perm to Offic *Heref* from 83. *162 Buckfield Road, Leominster, Herefordshire HR6 8UF* Tel (01568) 615534

STRONG, Capt William John Leonard. b 44. CA Tr Coll 64 Chich Th Coll 87. **d** 89 **p** 90. CA from 66; C Mayfield *Chich* 89-92; C Seaford w Sutton 92-94; V Crawley Down All SS from 94. *The Vicarage, Vicarage Road, Crawley Down, Crawley, W Sussex RH10 4JJ* Tel (01342) 713246

STROUD, The Ven Ernest Charles Frederick. b 31. St Chad's Coll Dur BA59 DipTh60. **d** 60 **p** 61. C S Kirkby *Wakef* 60-63; C Whitby *York* 63-66; C-in-c Chelmsf All SS CD *Chelmsf* 66-69; V Chelmsf All SS 69-75; V Leigh-on-Sea St Marg 75-83; Asst RD Southend 76-79; RD Hadleigh 79-83; Hon Can Chelmsf Cathl 82-83; Adn Colchester 83-97; rtd 97; Perm to Offic *Chelmsf* from 97. *S Therese, 67 London Road, Hadleigh, Benfleet, Essex SS7 2QL* Tel (01702) 554941 Fax 500789

STROUD, Canon Robert Owen. b 29. AKC56. **d** 57 **p** 58. C Aylesbury *Ox* 57-60; C Bexhill St Pet *Chich* 60-64; C Gosforth All SS *Newc* 64-66; V High Elswick St Phil 66-72; V Tynemouth Cullercoats St Paul 72-77; R Orlestone w Ruckinge w Warehorne *Cant* 77-81; RD N Lympne 79-81; V Folkestone H Trin w Ch Ch 81-83; TR Folkestone H Trin and St Geo w Ch Ch 83-90; R Folkestone H Trin w Ch Ch 90-93; RD Elham 90-93; Hon Can Cant Cathl 92-93; rtd 93; Perm to Offic *Ex* from 94. *The Old Barn, 8 Dares Orchard, Colyton, Devon EX13 6RN* Tel (01297) 553761

STROYAN, John Ronald Angus. b 55. MTh. Qu Coll Birm 81 Bossey Ecum Inst Geneva 82. **d** 83 **p** 84. C Cov E *Cov* 83-87; V Smethwick St Matt w St Chad *Birm* 87-94; V Bloxham w Milcombe and S Newington *Ox* from 94. *The Vicarage, Church Street, Bloxham, Banbury, Oxon OX15 4ET* Tel (01295) 720252

STRUDWICK, Canon Donald Frank. b 12. Leeds Univ BA33. Coll of Resurr Mirfield 33. **d** 35 **p** 37. C Wandsworth St Anne *S'wark* 35-39; C Plumstead Ascension 39-44; V Camberwell St Luke 44-49; V E Dulwich St Clem 49-85; RD Dulwich 57-67; Hon Can S'wark Cathl 73-85; rtd 85; Perm to Offic *Roch* from 85. *8 Mount Avenue, Yalding, Maidstone, Kent ME18 6JG* Tel (01622) 814514

STRUDWICK, Canon Vincent Noel Harold. b 32. Nottm Univ BA59 DipEd. Kelham Th Coll 52. **d** 59 **p** 60. Tutor Kelham Th Coll 59-63; Sub-Warden 63-70; C Crawley *Chich* 70-73; Adult Educn Adv 73-77; R Fittleworth 73-77; Planning Officer for Educn Milton Keynes 77-80; Dir of Educn *Ox* 80-89; Hon Can Ch Ch from 82; Continuing Minl Educn Adv 85-89; Dir Dioc Inst for Th Educn from 89; Prin Ox Min Course 89-94; Prin St Alb and Ox Min Course 94-96; Fell and Tutor Kellogg Coll Ox from 94; C Aylesbury w Bierton and Hulcott *Ox* from 97. *35 Windmill Street, Brill, Aylesbury, Bucks HP18 9TG* Tel (01844) 237748

STRUGNELL, Dr John Richard. b 30. Lon Univ BA52 Leeds Univ MA61 Queensland Univ PhD77. Wells Th Coll 54. **d** 56 **p** 57. C Leeds Halton St Wilfrid *Ripon* 56-59; C Moor Allerton 59-62; Australia from 65; rtd 95. *231 Grandview Road, Pullenvale, Queensland, Australia 4069* Tel Brisbane (7) 3374 1776

STRUTT, Mrs Susan. b 45. Glouc Sch of Min 87. **d** 90 **p** 94. NSM Eye, Croft w Yarpole and Lucton *Heref* 90-94; NSM Leominster 94; C 94-96; P-in-c Bosbury w Wellington Heath etc from 96. *The Vicarage, Bosbury, Ledbury, Herefordshire HR8 1QA* Tel (01531) 640225

STUART, Dr Angus Fraser. b 61. Bedf Coll Lon BA83 K Coll Lon PhD91. Cranmer Hall Dur BA92. **d** 93 **p** 94. C Twickenham St Mary *Lon* 93-96; Chapl Bris Univ *Bris* from 96; Hon C Bris St Mich and St Paul from 96. *67 Waverley Road, Redland, Bristol BS6 6ET* Tel 0117-924 4261 or 928 8823

STUART, Brother. *See* BURNS, Brother Stuart Maitland

STUART, Francis David. b 32. Barrister-at-Law Lon Univ BA54 AKC57. Ridley Hall Cam 62. **d** 64 **p** 65. C Addiscombe St Mildred *Cant* 64-67; Chapl RN 67-71; Lic to Offic *Liv* 76-80; TV Oldham *Man* 84-89; Chapl Oldham and Distr Gen Hosp 84-89; Chapl Oldham R Infirmary 86-89; Chapl R Oldham Hosp 89-94; Chapl Oldham NHS Trust from 94. *Royal Oldham Hospital, Rochdale Road, Oldham OL1 2JH, or Pine House, Barton Street, Oldham OL1 2NR* Tel 0161-624 0420 or 626 6804

STUART, Canon Herbert James. b 26. CB83. TCD BA48 MA55. **d** 49 **p** 50. C Sligo Cathl *K, E & A* 49-53; C Dublin Rathmines *D & G* 53-55; Chapl RAF 55-73; Asst Chapl-in-Chief RAF 73-80; Chapl-in-Chief and Archdeacon for the RAF 80-83; Can and Preb Linc Cathl *Linc* 81-83; R Cherbury *Ox* 83-87; Perm to Offic *Glouc* from 87; Perm to Offic *Ox* 87-96; rtd 91. *1 Abbot's Walk, Lechlade, Glos GL7 3DB* Tel (01367) 253299

STUART-BLACK, Veronica. *See* BRADSHAW, Mrs Veronica

STUART-FOX, The Ven Desmond. b 11. Selw Coll Cam BA33 MA37. Bps' Coll Cheshunt 33. **d** 34 **p** 35. C Leic St Pet *Leic* 34-37; C Lich St Mich *Lich* 37-40; Sacr Lich Cathl 37-40; CF (EC) 40-46; V W Bromwich St Andr *Lich* 46-49; Australia from 49. *5/24 Church Street, Goulburn, NSW, Australia 2580* Tel Goulburn (48) 211339

STUART-LEE, Nicholas (Nick). b 54. Wycliffe Hall Ox. **d** 83 **p** 84. C Costessey *Nor* 83-85; TV Dewsbury *Wakef* 85-90; R Rowlands Castle *Portsm* from 90. *The Rectory, 9 College Road, Rowland's Castle, Portsmouth PO9 6AJ* Tel (01705) 412605

STUART-SMITH, David. b 36. St Pet Coll Ox BA61 MA65. Tyndale Hall Bris. **d** 63 **p** 64. C Tooting Graveney St Nic *S'wark* 63-67; C Richmond H Trin 67-70; Lic to Offic 70-74; NSM Canonbury St Steph *Lon* 70-74; Travelling Sec IVF 70-74; Bangladesh 74-79; V Clapham Park St Steph *S'wark* 79-95; RD Streatham 83-87; P-in-c Wye w Brook *Cant* from 95; Chapl Wye Coll Kent from 95. *The Vicarage, Cherry Garden Crescent, Wye, Ashford, Kent TN25 5AS* Tel (01233) 812450

STUART-WHITE, William Robert. b 59. Ox Univ BA. Trin Coll Bris BA. **d** 86 **p** 87. C Upper Armley *Ripon* 86-91; P-in-c Austrey *Birm* 91-92; P-in-c Warton 91-92; V Austrey and Warton from 92. *The Vicarage, Austrey, Atherstone, Warks CV9 3EB* Tel (01827) 830572

STUBBINGS, Frank Edward. b 20. Fitzw Coll Cam BA48 MA53. Worc Ord Coll 60. **d** 61 **p** 62. C Rowbarton *B & W* 61-64; V Catcott 64-74; V Burtle 64-74; Chapl St Cath Sch Bramley 74-83; R Barkestone w Plungar, Redmile and Stathern *Leic* 83-87; rtd 87; Perm to Offic *B & W* 88-91; Hon C Lostwithiel, St Winnow w St Nectan's Chpl etc *Truro* from 91. *Gooseydown, Park Road, Lostwithiel, Cornwall PL22 0BU* Tel (01208) 872762

STUBBS, Anthony Richard Peter (Ælred). b 23. Ball Coll Ox BA49. Coll of Resurr Mirfield 51. **d** 54 **p** 54. Lic to Offic *Wakef* 54-57 and 82-94; CR from 54; Lic to Offic *Llan* 57-59; S Africa 60-77; Lesotho 77-81; rtd 94. *House of the Resurrection, Mirfield, W Yorkshire WF14 0BN* Tel (01924) 494318

STUBBS, Ian Kirtley. b 47. Man Univ DipAE90. Kelham Th Coll. **d** 70 **p** 71. C Chandler's Ford *Win* 70-75; C Farnham Royal *Ox* 75-80; Ind Chapl 75-80; Ind Chapl *Man* 81-86; TV Oldham 81-86; TR Langley and Parkfield 86-88; Community Work Officer Dioc Bd of Soc Resp 88-90; Dir Laity Development 90-96; Adv in Adult Educn Gen Syn Bd of Educn from 97. *Board of Education, Church House, Great Smith Street, London SW1P 3NZ, or 1 Barracks, Denshaw, Oldham OL3 5SR* Tel 0171-222 9011 or (01457) 870836 Fax 0171-233 1094 or (01457) 877341 E-mail ian_stubbs@compuserve.com

STUBBS, Stanley Peter Handley. b 23. Lon Univ BD52 Lille Univ LesL82. Ely Th Coll 55. **d** 55 **p** 56. C Fletton *Ely* 55-58; Hon Min Can Pet Cathl *Pet* 56-58; C Hounslow Heath St Paul *Lon* 58-63; CF (TA) 59-78; V Northampton St Alb *Pet* 63-76; R Brondesbury Ch Ch and St Laur *Lon* 76-93; rtd 93. *3 Westbury Lodge Close, Pinner, Middx HA5 3FG* Tel 0181-868 8296

STUBBS, Trevor Noel. b 48. AKC70. St Aug Coll Cant 73. **d** 74 **p** 75. C Heckmondwike *Wakef* 74-77; Australia 77-80; V Middleton St Cross *Ripon* 80-89; R Wool and E Stoke *Sarum* 89-95; TR Bridport from 95. *The Rectory, 84 South Street, Bridport, Dorset DT6 3NW* Tel (01308) 422138

STUBENBORD, Jess William. b 48. BA72. Trin Coll Bris 75. **d** 78 **p** 79. C Cromer *Nor* 78-82; C Gorleston St Mary 82-85; P-in-c Saxthorpe and Corpusty 85-89; P-in-c Blickling 86-89; R Saxthorpe w Corpusty, Blickling, Oulton etc 89-93; P-in-c Mulbarton w Kenningham from 93; PinC Flordon from 94; P-in-c Wreningham from 95. *The Rectory, The Common, Mulbarton, Norwich NR14 8JS* Tel (01508) 570296

STUBLEY, Dr Peter Derek. b 28. AKC57 Dur Univ MA79 PhD91. **d** 58 **p** 59. C Stockton St Chad *Dur* 58-61; V W Hartlepool St Oswald 61-66; Ind Chapl 66-76; Ind Chapl *York* 76-96; V Gt Totham *Chelmsf* 83; P-in-c Kingston upon Hull St Mary *York* 83-88; rtd 96; Perm to Offic *York* from 96. *8 Queens Way, Cottingham, N Humberside HU16 4EP* Tel (01482) 848718

STUCKES, Stephen. b 62. Trin Coll Bris. **d** 96 **p** 97. C Dunster, Carhampton and Withycombe w Rodhuish *B & W* from 96. *Carantoc House, Main Road, Carhampton, Minehead, Somerset TA24 6NB*

STUDD, Christopher Sidney. b 25. S'wark Ord Course. **d** 68 **p** 69. C Shenfield *Chelmsf* 68-73; R Stifford 73-83; P-in-c Bowers Gifford w N Benfleet 83-86; R 83-92; rtd 92; Perm to Offic *Chelmsf* from 92. *9 Stonehill Road, Roxwell, Chelmsford CM1 4PF* Tel (01245) 248824

STUDD, John Eric. b 34. Clare Coll Cam BA58 MA62. Coll of Resurr Mirfield 58. **d** 60 **p** 61. C Westmr St Steph w St Jo *Lon* 60-65; Australia 65-69; Hon C Kensington St Mary Abbots w St Geo *Lon* 70-71; P-in-c Monks Risborough *Ox* 72-77; P-in-c Gt and Lt Kimble 72-77; C Aylesbury 78; Chapl to the Deaf 78-82; Chapl Hants, Is of Wight and Channel Is Assn for Deaf 82-91; Perm to Offic *Guildf* from 82; Perm to Offic *Portsm* from 82; Chapl to the Deaf *Win* from 91. *Albion Lodge, Halterworth Lane, Romsey, Hants SO51 9AE* Tel (01794) 512575

STUDDERT, Michael John de Clare. b 39. Trin Coll Cam BA64 MA67. Cuddesdon Coll 64. **d** 66 **p** 67. C Langley All SS and Martyrs *Man* 66-69; C Fleet *Guildf* 69-73; Perm to Offic 73-77; Chapl Eagle Ho Sch Sandhurst 77-88. *Southlands, Churt Road, Hindhead, Surrey GU26 6PS* Tel (01428) 604620

STUDDERT, Canon Richard Charles Guy. b 03. Lon Coll of Div 26. **d** 28 **p** 30. C Clonmel *C & O* 28-32; C Kilnaboy w Kilkeedy *L & K* 32-34; I Tullow *C & O* 34-78; I Aghade w Ardoyne 62-75; Preb Ossory Cathl 47-70; Preb Leighlin Cathl 47-55; Treas 55-60; Chan 60-63; Prec 62-78; rtd 78. *Station House, Tullow, Co Carlow, Irish Republic* Tel Carlow (503) 51246

STUDDERT-KENNEDY, Andrew Geoffrey. b 59. Ch Ch Ox BA80 MA86. Ripon Coll Cuddesdon BA88. **d** 89 **p** 90. C Wimbledon *S'wark* 89-94; V Norbury St Oswald from 94. *220 Norbury Avenue, Thornton Heath, Surrey CR7 8AJ* Tel 0181-764 2853

STUDDERT-KENNEDY, Canon Christopher John. b 22. BNC Ox BA49 MA53. Wells Th Coll 49. **d** 51 **p** 52. C Bermondsey St Mary w St Olave and St Jo *S'wark* 51-54; C Clapham H Trin 54-56; V Putney St Marg 56-66; R Godstone 66-91; RD Godstone 76-88; Hon Can S'wark Cathl 80-91; rtd 91; Perm to Offic *Chich* from 91. *Orchard House, The Street, Washington, Pulborough, W Sussex RH20 4AS* Tel (01903) 892774

STUDHOLME, Muriel Isabel. **d** 96. NSM Bromfield w Waverton *Carl* from 96. *Yew Tree Cottage, Dundraw, Wigton, Cumbria CA7 0DP* Tel (01697) 320261

STURCH, Richard Lyman. b 36. Ch Ch Ox BA58 MA61 DPhil70. Ely Th Coll. **d** 62 **p** 63. C Hove All SS *Chich* 62-65; C Burgess Hill St Jo 65-66; C Ox St Mich w St Martin and All SS *Ox* 67-68; Tutor Ripon Hall Ox 67-71; Nigeria 71-74; Lect Lon Bible Coll 75-80; Lic to Offic *Lon* 75-80; TV Wolverton *Ox* 80-86; R Islip w Charlton on Otmoor, Oddington, Noke etc from 86. *The Rectory, 3 The Rise, Islip, Kidlington, Oxon OX5 2TG* Tel (01865) 372163

STURDY, William David Mark. b 28. Ch Coll Cam BA52 MA56. Qu Coll Birm. **d** 55 **p** 56. C Lutterworth w Cotesbach *Leic* 55-59; C Loughborough Em 59-61; V Thorpe Acre w Dishley 61-72; R Kegworth 72-82; V Cringleford *Nor* 82-85; R Colney 82-85; R Cringleford w Colney and Bawburgh 85-93; RD Humbleyard 87-93; rtd 94; Perm to Offic *Nor* from 94. *20 Valley Rise, Dersingham, Kings Lynn, Norfolk PE31 6PT* Tel (01485) 543762

STURMAN, Robert George. b 50. Nottm Univ BTh79. Linc Th Coll 75. **d** 79 **p** 80. C Cainscross w Selsley *Glouc* 79-83; TV Bottesford w Ashby *Linc* 83-88; V Prescot *Liv* 88-91; P-in-c Abenhall w Mitcheldean *Glouc* from 93. *St Michael's Rectory, Hawker Hill, Mitcheldean, Glos GL17 0BS* Tel (01594) 542434

STURT, Rock Andre Daniel. b 56. Liv Univ BSc79 Lon Univ CertEd80. Oak Hill Th Coll DipTh88 BA88. **d** 88 **p** 89. Chapl St Bede's Sch Cam 88-90; Par Dn Cambridge St Martin *Ely* 88-90; C 90-91; P-in-c Alwalton and Chesterton 91-96; TV The Ortons, Alwalton and Chesterton from 96. *Alwalton Rectory, Peterborough PE7 3UU* Tel (01733) 236205

STUTZ, Clifford Peter. b 25. **d** 83 **p** 84. NSM Cusop w Clifford, Hardwicke, Bredwardine etc *Heref* from 83. *Burnt House, Middlewood, Clifford, Hereford HR3 5SX* Tel (01497) 831472

STUTZ, Ms Sally Ann. b 64. Univ of Wales BSc88 Leeds Metrop Univ MSc93 Birm Univ BD95 SRD90. Qu Coll Birm 93. **d** 96 **p** 97. C Middleton St Mary *Ripon* from 96. *40 Manor Farm Gardens, Leeds LS10 3RA* Tel 0113-277 5276

STYLER, Geoffrey Marsh. b 15. CCC Ox BA37 MA40 Cam Univ MA44. Union Th Sem (NY) STM39 Cuddesdon Coll 40. **d** 41 **p** 42. C Heckmondwike *Wakef* 41-44; Vice-Prin Westcott Ho Cam 44-48; Fell CCC Cam from 48; Lect Th Cam Univ 53-82; Select Preacher Ox Univ 55-57; Select Preacher Cam Univ 58 and 63; rtd 82. *Middleton Cottage, Sidgwick Avenue, Cambridge CB3 9DA* Tel (01223) 358420

STYLER, Jamie Cuming. b 36. Sarum & Wells Th Coll 70. **d** 72 **p** 73. C Whipton *Ex* 72-75; C Paignton St Jo 76-78; V Topsham 78-88; V Plymouth St Simon from 88; Chapl Mt Gould Hosp Plymouth from 94. *St Simon's Vicarage, 86 Edith Avenue, Plymouth PL4 8TL* Tel (01752) 660654

STYLES, Clive William John. b 48. WMMTC 87. **d** 90 **p** 91. C Burslem *Lich* 90-94; TV Wednesfield from 94. *157 Stubby Lane, Wednesfield, Wolverhampton WV11 3NE* Tel (01902) 732763

STYLES, Canon Lawrence Edgar. b 19. AM88. Pemb Coll Cam BA48 MA52. Ridley Hall Cam. **d** 50 **p** 51. C Bishop's Stortford St Mich *St Alb* 50-53; V Tyldesley w Shakerley *Man* 53-60; Australia from 60; Can Melbourne from 82; rtd 86. *25 Carson Street, Kew, Victoria, Australia 3101* Tel Melbourne (3) 9853 9749

STYLES, Nigel Charles. b 57. Keele Univ BA79 Rob Coll Cam BA92. Ridley Hall Cam CTM93. **d** 95 **p** 96. C Bedford Ch Ch *St Alb* from 95. *9 Rothsay Road, Bedford MK40 3PP* Tel (01234) 720564

SUART, Geoffrey Hugh. b 49. Man Univ BSc70 Nottm Univ CertEd71. Oak Hill Th Coll DipHE83. **d** 83 **p** 84. C Ogley Hay *Lich* 83-86; TV Wenlock *Heref* 86-90; TR Kirby Muxloe *Leic* from 90. *The Rectory, 6 Station Road, Kirby Muxloe, Leicester LE9 2EJ* Tel 0116-238 6822

SUCH, Colin Royston. b 62. UEA LLB83. Ripon Coll Cuddesdon 94. **d** 97. C Streetly *Lich* from 97. *36 Foley Road East, Streetly, Sutton Coldfield, W Midlands B74 3JX* Tel 0121-352 0698

SUCH, Canon Howard Ingram James. b 52. Southn Univ BTh81. Sarum & Wells Th Coll 77. **d** 81 **p** 82. C Cheam *S'wark* 81-84; Prec Cant Cathl *Cant* 84-91; Hon Min Can Cant Cathl from 91; V Borden from 91. *The Vicarage, Borden, Sittingbourne, Kent ME9 8JS* Tel (01795) 472986

SUCH, Paul Nigel. b 52. FGA72 BTh84. Chich Th Coll 79. **d** 84 **p** 85. C Handsworth St Andr *Birm* 84-87; C Rugeley *Lich* 87-88; TV 88-91; R Longton from 91. *The Rectory, Rutland Road, Longton, Stoke-on-Trent ST3 1EH* Tel (01782) 595098

SUCH, Royston Jeffery. b 46. Solicitor Univ Coll Lon LLB67. Sarum & Wells Th Coll 83. **d** 83 **p** 84. NSM Ringwood *Win* 83-90; R Bishop's Sutton and Ropley and W Tisted from 90. *The Vicarage, Lyeway Lane, Ropley, Alresford, Hants SO24 0DW* Tel (01962) 772205

SUCKLING, Keith Edward. b 47. CChem FRSC Darw Coll Cam PhD71 Liv Univ BSc87 DSc89. Oak Hill NSM Course 91. **d** 94 **p** 95. NSM Digswell and Panshanger *St Alb* from 94. *291 Knightsfield, Welwyn Garden City, Herts AL8 7NH* Tel (01707) 330022

SUDBURY, Archdeacon of. *See* COX, The Ven John Stuart

SUDDABY, Mrs Susan Eveline. b 43. Cam Inst of Educn CertEd64 Bp Otter Coll Chich CertRE86. S'wark Ord Course 94. **d** 96 **p** 97. NSM Rusthall *Roch* from 96. *69 Hermitage Road, East Grinstead, W Sussex RH19 2BP* Tel (01342) 323467

SUDDARDS, John Martin. b 52. Barrister-at-Law 75 Trin Hall Cam BA74 MA77 Birm Univ DipTh89. Qu Coll Birm 86. **d** 89 **p** 90. C Halstead St Andr w H Trin and Greenstead Green *Chelmsf* 89-93; P-in-c Gt w Lt Yeldham from 93; P-in-c Toppesfield and Stambourne from 93. *The Rectory, Church Road, Great Yeldham, Halstead, Essex CO9 4PT* Tel (01787) 237358

SUDELL, Philip Henry. b 61. Thames Poly BScEng84 Lon Univ PGCE85. Wycliffe Hall Ox 89. **d** 92 **p** 93. C Worthing Ch the King *Chich* 92-96; C Muswell Hill St Jas w St Matt *Lon* from 96. *67 St James Lane, London N10 3QY* Tel 0181-883 7417

SUDWORTH, Frank. b 43. DipHE. Oak Hill Th Coll 76. **d** 78 **p** 79. C Deane *Man* 78-81; C Worksop St Jo *S'well* 82-85; V Wollaton Park 85-90; P-in-c Lenton Abbey 85-86; V 86-90; V Upper Armley *Ripon* 90-97; RD Armley 92-95; Chapl HM Pris Liv from 97. *14 Langdale Drive, Maghull, Merseyside L31 9BR* Tel 0151-520 0116

SUFFERN, Richard William Sefton. b 57. Reading Univ BSc79. Trin Coll Bris DipHE90. **d** 90 **p** 91. C Radipole and Melcombe Regis *Sarum* 90-94; TV Cheltenham St Mark *Glouc* from 94. *St Barnabas' Rectory, 152 Alstone Lane, Cheltenham, Glos GL51 8HL* Tel (01242) 694203

SUFFOLK, Archdeacon of. *See* ARRAND, The Ven Geoffrey William

SUFFRIN, Canon Arthur Charles Emmanuel. b 09. Selw Coll Cam BA30 MA34. Qu Coll Birm 34. **d** 35 **p** 36. C Winchmore Hill H Trin *Lon* 35-39; C Abbots Langley *St Alb* 39-42; CF (EC) 42-44; Public Preacher *St Alb* 44-47; C-in-c Luton St Chris Round Green CD 47-53; V Croxley Green All SS 53-63; V Hexton 63-68; V Pirton 68-74; Hon Can St Alb 65-75; RD Hitchin 71-74; rtd 74. *32 St Michael's Road, Melksham, Wilts SN12 6HN* Tel (01225) 708041

SUGDEN, Charles Edward. b 59. Magd Coll Cam MA81 PGCE82. Trin Coll Bris DipHE91. **d** 91 **p** 92. C Gidea Park *Chelmsf* 91-94; TV Melksham *Sarum* from 94. *St Andrew's Vicarage, 33 Church Lane, Melksham, Wilts SN12 7EF* Tel (01225) 702310

SUGDEN, Christopher Michael Neville. b 48. St Pet Coll Ox BA70 MA74 Nottm Univ MPhil74 PhD88. St Jo Coll Nottm 72. **d** 74 **p** 75. C Leeds St Geo *Ripon* 74-77; India 77-83; Lic to Offic *Ox* from 83. *Oxford Centre for Missionary Studies, PO Box 70, Oxford OX2 6HB* Tel (01865) 56071 Fax 510823

SUGDEN, Mrs Kerstin. b 58. Man Univ BSc81 W Midl Coll of Educn PGCE82. Trin Coll Bris BA91. **d** 91 **p** 96. NSM Gidea Park *Chelmsf* 91-94; NSM Melksham *Sarum* from 95. *St Andrew's Vicarage, 33 Church Lane, Melksham, Wilts SN12 7EF* Tel (01225) 702310

SULLIVAN, Adrian Michael. b 55. Sarum & Wells Th Coll 85. **d** 87 **p** 88. C Louth *Linc* 87-90; P-in-c E and W Keal 90; P-in-c Marden Hill Gp 90-92; R from 92; RD Bolingbroke from 97. *The Rectory, West Keal, Spilsby, Lincs PE23 4BJ* Tel (01790) 53534

SULLIVAN, Bernard George. b 24. St Jo Coll Dur BA50. **d** 51 **p** 52. C Dudley St Thos *Worc* 51-54; C Braunstone *Leic* 54-55; Chapl RAF 55-58; Chapl Ascham Ho Sch Gosforth 59-63; Chapl St Mary's Hosp Stannington 62-91; V Stannington *Newc* 63-91; rtd 91. *1 St Aidan's Crescent, Stobhill, Morpeth, Northd NE61 2UP*

SULLIVAN, Julian Charles. b 49. Lon Univ BSc74 CertEd75. Wycliffe Hall Ox 80. **d** 83 **p** 84. C Southall Green St Jo *Lon* 83-87; C Wells St Cuth w Wookey Hole *B & W* 87-90; V Sheff St Barn and St Mary *Sheff* 90-91; V Sheff St Mary w Highfield Trin 91-95; V Sheff St Mary Bramhall Lane from 95. *St Mary's Vicarage, 42 Charlotte Road, Sheffield S1 4TL* Tel 0114-272 4987

SULLIVAN, Miss Nicola Ann. b 58. SRN81 RM84. Wycliffe Hall Ox BTh95. **d** 95 **p** 96. C Earlham St Anne *Nor* from 95. *8 Corie Road, Norwich NR4 7JB* Tel (01603) 454509

SULLIVAN, Canon Trevor Arnold. b 40. CITC 69. **d** 70 **p** 71. C Lurgan Ch Ch *D & D* 71-72; C Tralee *L & K* 72-75; Irish Sch of Ecum 75-77; Ind Chapl *D & G* 77-80; I Ematris *Clogh* 80-84; I Aughrim w Ballinasloe etc *L & K* from 84; Can Limerick and Killaloe Caths from 89. *The Rectory, Aughrim, Ballinasloe, Co Galway, Irish Republic* Tel Ballinasloe (905) 73735 Mobile 087-412194 Fax as telephone

SULLY, Andrew Charles. b 67. Southn Univ BA88 Birm Univ DPS91 MPhil95. Qu Coll Birm 90. **d** 93 **p** 94. C Maindee *Mon* 93-96; V Llanfihangel w Llanafan and Llanwnnws etc *St D* from 96. *The Vicarage, Ysbyty Cynfyn, Ponterwyd, Aberystwyth SY23 3JR* Tel (01970) 890663

SULLY, Martin John. b 44. AIAS. St Jo Coll Nottm 80. **d** 82 **p** 83. C Lindfield *Chich* 82-86; V Walberton w Binsted from 86. *St Mary's Vicarage, The Street, Walberton, Arundel, W Sussex BN18 0PQ* Tel (01243) 551488

SUMMERS, John Ewart. b 35. MIMechE66 Ex Univ MA95. ALCD69. **d** 69 **p** 70. C Fulham St Matt *Lon* 69-72; Chapl RN 72-81; V Devonport St Barn *Ex* from 81. *St Barnabas' Vicarage, 10 De La Hay Avenue, Plymouth PL3 4HU* Tel (01752) 666544

SUMMERS, Paul Anthony. b 53. Coll of Resurr Mirfield 77. **d** 80 **p** 81. C Manston *Ripon* 80-83; Prec 83-88; Min Can Ripon Cathl 83-88; Chapl Univ Coll of Ripon and York St Jo 84-88; V Whitkirk *Ripon* 88-95; R Kirkby Overblow from 95. *The Rectory, Kirkby Overblow, Harrogate, N Yorkshire HG3 1HD* Tel (01423) 872314

SUMMERS, Raymond John (Ray). b 41. Univ of Wales TCert63 DPS88 Open Univ BA75. St Mich Coll Llan 77. **d** 77 **p** 78. NSM Mynyddislwyn *Mon* 77-81; NSM Abercarn 81-82; P-in-c 82-89; V 89-91; V Mynyddislwyn 91-95; TR Mynyddislwyn from 95; RD Bedwellty from 93. *The Vicarage, Tom-y-Moch Road, Pontllanfraith, Blackwood NP2 2DP* Tel (01495) 224240

SUMMERS, Thomas Gresley. b 25. Worc Coll Ox BA53 MA57. Cuddesdon Coll 53. **d** 55 **p** 56. C S Beddington St Mich *S'wark* 55-59; C New Charlton H Trin 59-63; OGS from 61; V Chesterton St Luke *Ely* 63-81; V Brownswood Park *Lon* 81-95; rtd 95. *306A Amhurst Road, London N16 7UE*

SUMMERS, Preb Ursula Jeanne. b 35. Birm Univ BA56 Liv Univ CertEd57. Glouc Sch of Min. **dss** 85 **d** 87 **p** 94. Fownhope *Heref* 85-87; Hon C 87; Brockhampton w Fawley 85-87; Hon C 87; C Marden w Amberley and Wisteston 88-94; P-in-c from 94; RD Heref Rural from 93; Preb Heref Cathl from 96. *99 Walkers Green, Marden, Hereford HR1 3EA* Tel (01432) 880497

SUMNER, Canon Gillian Mansell (Gill). b 39. St Anne's Coll Ox BA61 MA65 MLitt76. Wycliffe Hall Ox BA85. **dss** 86 **d** 87 **p** 94. Ox St Andr *Ox* 86-91; Hon C 87-91; Tutor Wycliffe Hall Ox 86-89; Prin Ox Area Chr Tr Scheme *Ox* 89-91; Vice-Prin Ox Min Course 89-91; Assoc Prin 91-94; Prin Ox Adnry Chr Tr Scheme 89-94; Hon C Kirtlington w Bletchingdon, Weston etc 91-94; Hon Can Ch Ch 94-95; Local Min Officer *Heref* from 95; P-in-c Wistanstow from 95; Preb Heref Cathl from 97. *The Rectory, Wistanstow, Craven Arms, Shropshire SY7 8DG* Tel (01588) 672067 Fax 672337

SUMNER, John Gordon. b 46. CCC Cam BA68 MA72. Ridley Hall Cam 69. **d** 72 **p** 73. C Liskeard w St Keyne *Truro* 72-75; C Caversham *Ox* 75-81; V Swallowfield 81-93; Asst Chapl Reading Univ 81-93; C Glastonbury w Meare, W Pennard and Godney *B & W* from 93; Ldr Quest Community from 93. *The White Cottage, 15 Bere Lane, Glastonbury, Somerset BA6 8BD* Tel (01458) 832377

SUMNERS, Ms Cristina Jordan. b 47. Vassar Coll (NY) BA73 BNC Ox MPhil85. Princeton Th Sem 73 Gen Th Sem (NY) MDiv76. **d** 78 **p** 82. USA 79-91; Asst Chapl K Edw Sch Witley from 93; Perm to Offic *Guildf* from 93. *South Haven, Woolmer Hill, Haslemere, Surrey GU27 1LT* Tel (01428) 641575

SUMPTER, Timothy Mark (Tim). b 62. St Jo Coll Nottm BTh95. **d** 95 **p** 96. C Ockbrook *Derby* from 95. *34 Rutland Avenue, Borrowash, Derby DE7 3JF* Tel (01332) 674252

SUNDERLAND, Christopher Allen. b 52. BA75 St Pet Coll Ox MA80 DPhil80 DipTh86. Trin Coll Bris 84. **d** 86 **p** 87. C Stratton St Margaret w S Marston etc *Bris* 86-90; V Barton Hill St Luke w Ch Ch from 90; RD Bris City from 94. *St Luke's Vicarage, 60 Barton Hill Road, Bristol BS5 0AW* Tel 0117-955 5947 E-mail 100704.601@compuserve.com

SUNDERLAND, Preb Geoffrey. b 21. St Edm Hall Ox BA43 MA47 DipTh47. St Steph Ho Ox 46. **d** 48 **p** 49. C Clifton All SS *Bris* 48-51; C Elland *Wakef* 52-54; C Devonport St Mark Ford *Ex* 55-56; C-in-c Plymouth St Jas Ham CD 56-59; V Plymouth St Jas Ham 59-63; Chapl K Coll Taunton 63-65; C Clifton All SS *Bris* 65-68; V Plymstock *Ex* 68-86; RD Plympton 76-81; Preb Ex Cathl 82-86; rtd 86; Perm to Offic *B & W* from 86; Perm to Offic *Ex* from 86. *22 Blackdown View, Sampford Peverell, Tiverton, Devon EX16 7BE* Tel (01884) 821688

SUNDERLAND, Archdeacon of. *See* WHITE, The Ven Francis

SURMAN, Malcolm Colin. b 48. Birm Univ CertEd72 Southn Univ BTh88. Sarum & Wells Th Coll 76. **d** 78 **p** 79. C Basingstoke *Win* 78-81; P-in-c Alton All SS 81-85; V from 85; Chapl Lord Mayor Treloar Hosp Alton from 84. *All Saints' Vicarage, Queen's Road, Alton, Hants GU34 1HU* Tel (01420) 83458

SURREY, Archdeacon of. *See* REISS, The Ven Robert Paul

SURRIDGE, Mrs Faith Thomas. b 45. Open Univ BA75 DipRD83 Lon Univ PGCE76 Ex Univ DipMathEd87. SW Minl Tr Course 83. **dss** 85 **d** 87 **p** 94. St Breoke and Egloshayle *Truro* 85-87; Hon C St Mawgan w St Ervan and St Eval from 91. *Lanvean Orchard, St Mawgan, Newquay, Cornwall TR8 4EY* Tel (01637) 860806

SURTEES, Geoffrey. b 06. St Chad's Coll Dur BA33 DipTh34 MA36. **d** 34 **p** 35. C Hebburn St Jo *Dur* 34-36; C Gosforth St Nic *Newc* 36-39; V Nether Hoyland St Andr *Sheff* 39-57; P-in-c Nether Hoyland St Pet 56-57; V Bridge Hill *Derby* 57-75; Chapl Community St Laur Belper 57-75; RD Duffield 57-70; rtd 75; Perm to Offic *Derby* from 75. *28 Penn Lane, Melbourne, Derby DE73 1EQ* Tel (01332) 862381

SURTEES, Timothy John de Leybourne. b 31. G&C Coll Cam BA54 MA58. Westcott Ho Cam 54. **d** 56 **p** 57. C Guisborough *York* 56-59; C Grantham St Wulfram *Linc* 59-61; V Cayton w Eastfield *York* 61-72; R Cheam *S'wark* 72-96; rtd 96. *Dove Cottage, Leysters, Leominster, Herefordshire HR6 0HW* Tel (01568) 750203

SUSTINS, Nigel. b 46. Lon Univ BEd70. S'wark Ord Course 86. **d** 88 **p** 90. Hon C Mitcham St Mark *S'wark* 89-93; Perm to Offic from 96. *Ivy Lodge, Morden Hall Road, Morden, Surrey SM4 5JD*

SUTCH, Christopher David. b 47. AKC69. St Aug Coll Cant 69. **d** 70 **p** 71. C Bris St Andr Hartcliffe *Bris* 70-75; C Swindon Dorcan 75-78; TV 78-79; P-in-c Alveston 79-83; V 83-89; RD Westbury and Severnside 86-89; TR Yate New Town from 89; RD Stapleton from 95. *The Rectory, Canterbury Close, Yate, Bristol BS17 5TU* Tel (01454) 311483

SUTCH, Canon Christopher Lang. b 21. Or Coll Ox BA47 MA47. Cuddesdon Coll 47. **d** 49 **p** 50. C Westbury-on-Trym H Trin *Bris* 49-53; V Bedminster Down 53-58; V Hanham 58-74; R Brinkworth w Dauntsey 74-86; RD Malmesbury 79-85; Hon Can Bris Cathl 82-86; rtd 86; Hon C E Bris from 86. *42 Henleaze Park Drive, Bristol BS9 4LL* Tel 0117-962 1952

SUTCLIFFE, Crispin Francis Henry. b 48. Keble Coll Ox BA69. Sarum & Wells Th Coll 73. **d** 74 **p** 75. C Truro St Paul *Truro* 74-77; S Africa 77-80; P-in-c Treslothan *Truro* 80-85; V 85-91; R Ilchester w Northover, Limington, Yeovilton etc *B & W* from 91. *The Rectory, Ilchester, Yeovil, Somerset BA22 8LJ* Tel (01935) 840296

SUTCLIFFE, Canon David. b 29. Lon Univ BD57. ALCD56. **d** 57 **p** 58. C Penn *Lich* 57-61; V Ashton St Pet *Man* 61-65; V Eccleshill *Bradf* 65-71; Lic to Offic 71-74; V Manningham St Luke 74-79; V Bolton St Jas w St Chrys 79-85; V Calverley 85-94; RD Calverley 88-93; Hon Can Bradf Cathl 89-94; rtd 94. *49 Galloway Lane, Pudsey, W Yorkshire LS28 7UG* Tel 0113-257 4053

SUTCLIFFE, Howard Guest. b 44. Fitzw Coll Cam BA66 MA70 Birm Univ MA75 Man Univ CertRS88. Westcott Ho Cam 73. **d** 74 **p** 75. C Chorlton-cum-Hardy St Clem *Man* 74-77; Chapl Chetham's Sch of Music 77-80; V Oldham St Paul *Man* 80-94; Lic to Offic from 94; Co-ord Werneth and Freehold Community Development Project from 94. *34 Lynn Street, Oldham OL9 7DW, or 155 Windsor Road, Oldham OL8 1RG* Tel 0161-628 2235

SUTCLIFFE, Ian. b 31. Surrey Univ BSc69. Qu Coll Birm 61. **d** 63 **p** 65. C W Wimbledon Ch Ch *S'wark* 63-65; C Battersea St Phil 65-66; C Kingston Hill St Paul 71-73; Lic to Offic *Carl* 75-96; rtd 96. *42 Hill Street, Arbroath, Angus DD11 1AB*

SUTCLIFFE, John Leslie. b 35. Liv Univ BA56. Sarum Th Coll 58. **d** 60 **p** 61. C Lytham St Cuth *Blackb* 60-62; C Altham w Clayton le Moors 62-65; C-in-c Penwortham St Leon CD 65-71; Ind Chapl *Liv* 71-74; V Orford St Andr 74-79; V Burnley St Cuth *Blackb* 79-88; Bp's Adv on UPA *Ripon* 88-94; Hon C Leeds Gipton Epiphany 88-94; I Carrickmacross w Magheracloone *Clogh* from 94. *The Rectory, Drumconrath Road, Carrickmacross, Co Monaghan, Irish Republic* Tel Carrickmacross (42) 61931

SUTCLIFFE, Peter John. b 58. BA. Linc Th Coll. **d** 82 **p** 83. C Skipton Ch Ch *Bradf* 82-85; C Tettenhall Regis *Lich* 85-86; TV 86-89; TV Warwick *Cov* 89-93; Relig Producer BBC Radio Cov & Warks 89-93; V Burley in Wharfedale *Bradf* from 93. *The Vicarage, Burley-in-Wharfedale, Ilkley, W Yorkshire LS29 7DR* Tel (01943) 863216

SUTCLIFFE, William Norman. b 09. Lich Th Coll 56. **d** 57 **p** 58. C Leek St Edw *Lich* 57-59; C Portishead *B & W* 59-60; V Northmoor Green 60-69; V Burrow Bridge 60-69; Perm to Offic *Sarum* 69-72; Lic to Offic 72-89; rtd 74. *The Bungalow, Hollis Hill, Broadwindsor, Beaminster, Dorset DT8 3QS* Tel (01308) 868476

SUTER, Richard Alan. b 48. Rhodes Univ BA72 St Jo Coll Dur BA74. Cranmer Hall Dur 72. **d** 75 **p** 76. C Darlington H Trin *Dur* 75-77; C Wrexham *St As* 77-82; R Llansantffraid Glan Conway and Eglwysfach 82-87; V Broughton 87-92; RD Wrexham 90-97; V Rossett from 92. *The Vicarage, Rossett, Wrexham LL12 0HE* Tel (01244) 570498

SUTHERLAND, Alan. b 55. Sarum & Wells Th Coll. **d** 80 **p** 81. C Hessle *York* 80-83; USA from 83. *501 South Phoenix, Russellville, Arkansas 72801, USA*

SUTHERLAND, Alistair Campbell. b 31. MIEE CEng Lon Univ BSc50 Ex Univ BA77. Wycliffe Hall Ox 77. **d** 78 **p** 79. C

Nottingham St Jude *S'well* 78-81; R Barton in Fabis 81-96; P-in-c Thrumpton 81; V 81-96; RD Bingham W 87-92; Dioc Adv on Ind Society 92-96; NSM Gotham 93-96; NSM Kingston and Ratcliffe-on-Soar 93-96; rtd 96. *Rosehayne, Musbury, Axminster, Devon EX13 6SR* Tel (01297) 552995

SUTHERLAND, Eric. b 54. AKC76. Sarum & Wells Th Coll 76. **d** 77 **p** 78. C Roehampton H Trin *S'wark* 77-80; C Tattenham Corner and Burgh Heath *Guildf* 80-84; V Guildf All SS 84-91; Dep Chapl HM Pris Wandsworth 91-92; Chapl HM Young Offender Inst Huntercombe and Finnamore from 92. *HM Young Offender Institution, Huntercombe Place, Nuffield, Henley-on-Thames, Oxon RG9 5SB* Tel (01491) 641711 or 641715 Fax 641902

SUTHERLAND, Mark Robert. b 55. Univ of NZ LLB77 Lon Univ DAC89. Ripon Coll Cuddesdon 82. **d** 85 **p** 86. C Pinner *Lon* 85-88; C Sudbury St Andr 88-91; Chapl Maudsley Hosp Lon 91-94; Chapl Bethlem R Hosp Beckenham 91-94; Chapl Bethlem and Maudsley NHS Trust Lon from 94; Perm to Offic *S'wark* 91-92. *The Maudsley Hospital, Denmark Hill, London SE5 8AZ* Tel 0171-919 2815

SUTTERS, Herbert John. b 15. St Jo Coll Ox BA37 MA40. St Steph Ho Ox 37. **d** 39 **p** 40. C Ox St Thos *Ox* 39-41; Lect St Steph Ho Ox 40-43; Lic to Offic *Ox* 41-43; C Fenny Stratford 43-49; Min Can Ripon Cathl *Ripon* 49-52; Chapl St Mary's Hosp Ripon 49-52; Asst Master Ripon Gr Sch 49-52; Chapl St Jo Hosp Ripon 50-52; PV Wells Cathl *B & W* 52-54; Chapl Wells Th Coll 52-54; Lic to Offic *B & W* 53-54; V Coleford 54-61; V Highbridge 61-73; Asst Master K Alfred Sch Highbridge 61-71; V St Margarets on Thames *Lon* 73-80; rtd 80; Perm to Offic *Ox* from 81. *22 Alexandra Road, Oxford OX2 0DB* Tel (01865) 723549

SUTTLE, Dr Neville Frank. b 38. Reading Univ BSc61 Aber Univ PhD64. **d** 76 **p** 77. NSM Penicuik *Edin* from 76. *44 St James's Gardens, Penicuik, Midlothian EH26 9DU* Tel (01968) 673819

SUTTON, Brian Ralph. b 33. Trin Coll Bris DPS81 Sarum & Wells Th Coll. **d** 83 **p** 84. NSM Timsbury *B & W* 83-84; NSM Timsbury and Priston 85-88; V Thorncombe w Winsham and Cricket St Thomas from 89. *The Vicarage, Chard Street, Thorncombe, Chard, Somerset TA20 4NE* Tel (01460) 30479

SUTTON, Charles Edwin. b 53. Bris Univ BEd77 Ox Univ. Ripon Coll Cuddesdon 77. **d** 80 **p** 81. C Stanwix *Carl* 80-84; Warden Marrick Priory *Ripon* 84-88. *7 Beech Close, Baldersby, Thirsk, N Yorkshire YO7 4QB* Tel (01765) 640616

SUTTON, Colin Phillip. b 51. Birm Univ BA73. Chich Th Coll 73. **d** 75 **p** 76. C Penarth All SS *Llan* 75-77; C Roath St Marg 77-80; C Caerau w Ely 80-84; V Rhydyfelin from 84. *St Luke's House, 6 Fairfield Lane, Hawthorn, Pontypridd CF37 5LN* Tel (01443) 852298

SUTTON, David Robert. b 49. Birm Univ BA69 Ox Univ CertEd72. St Steph Ho Ox 70. **d** 72 **p** 73. C Clitheroe St Mary *Blackb* 72-75; C Fleetwood 75-78; V Calderbrook *Man* 78-88; V Winton from 88; Chapl Salford Mental Health Services NHS Trust from 92. *The Vicarage, Albany Road, Eccles, Manchester M30 8DE* Tel 0161-788 8991

SUTTON, James William. b 41. Oak Hill Th Coll 81. **d** 84 **p** 85. NSM Chorleywood St Andr *St Alb* from 84. *Belmount, 7 Hillside Road, Chorleywood, Rickmansworth, Herts WD3 5AP* Tel (01923) 282806

SUTTON, Jeremy John Ernest. b 60. Ridley Hall Cam 83. **d** 86 **p** 87. C Seacombe *Ches* 86-88; C Northwich St Luke and H Trin 88-90; TV Birkenhead Priory 90-94; V Over St Chad from 94. *The Vicarage, 1 Over Hall Drive, Over, Winsford, Cheshire CW7 1EY* Tel (01606) 593222

SUTTON, John. b 47. St Jo Coll Dur BA70. Ridley Hall Cam 70. **d** 72 **p** 73. C Denton St Lawr *Man* 72-77; R 77-82; V High Lane *Ches* 82-88; V Sale St Anne 88-96; V Timperley from 96. *The Vicarage, 12 Thorley Lane, Timperley, Altrincham, Cheshire WA15 7AZ* Tel 0161-980 4330

SUTTON, John Stephen. b 33. Em Coll Cam BA57 MA61. Wycliffe Hall Ox 57. **d** 59 **p** 60. C Dagenham *Chelmsf* 59-62; C Bishopwearmouth St Gabr *Dur* 62-63; V Over Kellet *Blackb* 63-67; V Darwen St Barn 67-74; V Walthamstow St Jo *Chelmsf* 74-84; V Stebbing w Lindsell from 84; RD Dunmow from 94. *The Vicarage, High Street, Stebbing, Dunmow, Essex CM6 3SF* Tel (01371) 865468

SUTTON, Canon John Wesley. b 48. Rolle Coll CertEd71. All Nations Chr Coll DipMiss75. **d** 76 **p** 77. Chile 76-77; Peru 79-84; Area Sec SAMS 84-88; Youth Sec SAMS 88-91; Personnel Sec SAMS from 91; Asst Gen Sec SAMS from 91; Perm to Offic *Chelmsf* from 84; Perm to Offic *Ox* 85-96; Perm to Offic *St Alb* from 85; Hon Can Peru from 93. *88 Horn Lane, Woodford Green, Essex IG8 9AH* Tel 0181-505 7888 Fax (01892) 525797

✠**SUTTON, The Rt Revd Keith Norman.** b 34. Jes Coll Cam BA58 MA62. Ridley Hall Cam. **d** 59 **p** 60 **c** 78. C Plymouth St Andr *Ex* 59-61; Chapl St Jo Coll Cam 62-67; Uganda 68-72; Prin Ridley Hall Cam 73-78; Suff Bp Kingston *S'wark* 78-84; Bp Lich from 84. *Bishop's House, 22 The Close, Lichfield, Staffs WS13 7LG* Tel (01543) 262251 Fax 415801

SUTTON, Kingsley Edwin. b 70. TCD BTh94 CertAgric. **d** 97. C Belfast St Matt *Conn* from 97. *45 Lyndhurst Park, Belfast BT13 3PG* Tel (01232) 721581

SUTTON, Canon Malcolm David. b 26. Selw Coll Cam BA47 MA52. Ridley Hall Cam 48. **d** 50 **p** 51. C Owlerton *Sheff* 50-52; C Kew *S'wark* 52-54; C Hornchurch St Andr *Chelmsf* 54-56; V Roxeth Ch Ch *Lon* 56-63; R Beccles St Mich *St E* 63-82; TR 82-94; RD Beccles 65-73; Hon Can St E Cathl 70-94; rtd 94; Perm to Offic *Nor* from 95. *10 Merville, Carlton Colville, Lowestoft, Suffolk NR33 8UF*

SUTTON, Peter. b 20. Ely Th Coll 60. **d** 62 **p** 63. C Kippax *Ripon* 62-64; R Hamerton *Ely* 64-77; V Winwick 64-77; V Upton and Copmanford 70-77; V Bradworthy *Ex* 77-90; rtd 90. *Mowhay Villa, Chilsworthy, Holsworthy, Devon EX22 7BQ* Tel (01409) 254900

SUTTON, Peter Allerton. b 59. Ex Univ BA85. Linc Th Coll 85. **d** 87 **p** 88. C Fareham H Trin *Portsm* 87-90; C Alverstoke 90-93; Chapl HM Pris Haslar from 90; V Lee-on-the-Solent *Portsm* from 93; Warden of Readers from 96. *St Faith's Vicarage, Victoria Square, Lee-on-the-Solent, Hants PO13 9NF* Tel (01705) 550269

SUTTON, Philip Frank. b 55. Lon Univ HND76. St Alb and Ox Min Course CBTS95. **d** 95 **p** 96. NSM Akeman *Ox* 95-96; Chapl St Luke's Nursing Home Ox from 96; Chapl Ox Radcliffe Hosp NHS Trust from 96. *St Luke's Hospital, Latimer Road, Headington, Oxford OX3 7PF* Tel (01865) 750220 or 750904

SUTTON, Richard Alan. b 39. Reading Univ BSc61. Wycliffe Hall Ox 70. **d** 72 **p** 73. C Galleywood Common *Chelmsf* 72-76; Pakistan 76-79; C Walsall St Martin *Lich* 79-83; V Barton Hill St Luke w Ch Ch *Bris* 83-89; V Sidcup Ch Ch *Roch* 89-95; rtd 95; Perm to Offic *Roch* from 95. *117 Wren Road, Sidcup, Kent DA14 4NQ* Tel 0181-302 9233

SUTTON, Richard John. b 45. Lon Inst of Educn CertEd68. St Alb Minl Tr Scheme 77 Linc Th Coll 81. **d** 82 **p** 83. C Royston *St Alb* 82-87; C Hatfield 87-95; P-in-c Kempston from 95; P-in-c Biddenham from 95. *The Vicarage, Church End, Kempston, Bedford MK43 8RH* Tel (01234) 852241 E-mail backwater @argonet.co.uk

SUTTON, Ronald. b 27. FSCA. NW Ord Course 76. **d** 79 **p** 80. C Helsby and Dunham-on-the-Hill *Ches* 79-81; R Church Lawton 81-92; RD Congleton 91-92; rtd 92; Perm to Offic *Ches* from 92. *79 Thornton Avenue, Macclesfield, Cheshire SK11 7XL* Tel (01625) 430212

SWABEY, Brian Frank. b 44. BA. Oak Hill Th Coll 79. **d** 82 **p** 83. C Clapham St Jas *S'wark* 82-84; C Wallington H Trin 84-88; Chapl Mt Gould Hosp Plymouth 88-89; V Plymouth St Jude *Ex* 88-92; Chapl RN from 92. *Royal Naval Chaplaincy Service, Room 203, Victory Building, HM Naval Base, Portsmouth PO1 3LS* Tel (01705) 727903 Fax 727112

SWABY, Canon John Edwin. b 11. St Jo Coll Dur BA32 DipTh34 MA35 Leic Univ PhD83. **d** 34 **p** 35. C Louth w Welton-le-Wold *Linc* 34-40; V Scunthorpe St Jo 40-53; R Mablethorpe w Stain 53-60; P-in-c Theddlethorpe w Mablethorpe 53-54; R 54-60; RD E Louthesk 57-60; Acting RD Yarborough 64-70; V Barton upon Humber 60-71; Can and Preb Linc Cathl 69-77; V Barholm w Stowe 71-76; R Uffington 71-76; V Tallington 71-76; rtd 76; Perm to Offic *Pet* from 76; Perm to Offic *Linc* from 76. *6 Willoughby Drive, Empingham, Oakham, Leics LE15 8PZ* Tel (01780) 460719

SWABY, Keith Graham. b 48. Southn Univ BA75. St Steph Ho Ox 75. **d** 77 **p** 78. C Lt Stanmore St Lawr *Lon* 77-80; C Hove All SS *Chich* 80-83; C Haywards Heath St Wilfrid 83; TV 83-95; C Clayton w Keymer from 95. *11 The Spinney, Hassocks, W Sussex BN6 8EJ* Tel (01273) 846529

SWABY, Leward Anthony Woodrow. b 60. Trin Coll Bris 86 Ripon Coll Cuddesdon 89. **d** 92 **p** 93. C Wembley St Jo *Lon* 92-95; C Northampton St Matt *Pet* 95-97; TV Kingsthorpe w Northn St Dav from 97. *St Davids Vicarage, Eastern Avenue, Northampton NN2 7QB* Tel (01604) 714536

SWAIN, David Noel. b 36. Wellington Univ (NZ) BA63 MA66. Coll of Resurr Mirfield 65. **d** 67 **p** 68. C Clapham H Trin *S'wark* 67-70; New Zealand 70-75; P-in-c Hermitage *Ox* 75-76; P-in-c Hampstead Norris 75-76; V Hermitage w Hampstead Norreys 76-80; TR Hermitage and Hampstead Norreys, Cold Ash etc 80-82; R Bingham *S'well* 82-94; rtd 94. *20 Thorold Road, Barrowby, Grantham, Lincs NG32 1TD* Tel (01476) 560823

SWAIN, John Edgar. b 44. Lich Th Coll 67. **d** 69 **p** 70. C E Dereham w Hoe *Nor* 69-73; V Haugh *Linc* 73-74; R S Ormsby w Ketsby, Calceby and Driby 73-74; R Harrington w Brinkhill 73-74; R Oxcombe 73-74; R Ruckland w Farforth and Maidenwell 73-74; R Somersby w Bag Enderby 73-74; R Tetford and Salmonby 73-74; R Belchford 73-74; V W Ashby 73-74; C Attleborough *Nor* 74-78; Canada 78-90; P-in-c Kirton w Falkenham *St E* 90-95; Chapl Suffolk Constabulary from 90; P-in-c Gt and Lt Whelnetham w Bradfield St George from 95. *The Rectory, Little Whelnetham, Bury St Edmunds, Suffolk IP30 0DA* Tel (01284) 386332

SWAIN, Canon John Roger. b 29. Fitzw Ho Cam BA55 MA59. Bps' Coll Cheshunt 55. **d** 57 **p** 58. C Headingley *Ripon* 57-60; C Moor Allerton 60-65; V Wyther Ven Bede 65-75; V Horsforth 75-86; P-in-c Roundhay St Edm 86-88; V 88-95; RD Allerton 89-94; Hon Can Ripon Cathl 89-95; rtd 95. *36 Langtons Wharf, Leeds LS2 7EF* Tel 0113-246 1274

SWAIN, Canon Peter John. b 44. NCA63. Sarum & Wells Th Coll 86. **d** 88 **p** 89. C Beaminster Area *Sarum* 88-92; P-in-c Bromfield w Waverton *Carl* from 92; P-in-c W Newton from 92; Member Rural Life and Agric Team 93-96; Ldr Rural Life and Agric Team from 96; RD Solway from 95; Hon Can Carl Cathl from 96. *The Vicarage, Langrigg, Aspatria, Carlisle CA5 3NB* Tel (016973) 20261

SWAIN, Raymond Thomas. b 60. Oak Hill Th Coll BA89. **d** 89 **p** 90. C New Clee *Linc* 89-93; TV Cheltenham St Mark *Glouc* from 93. *St Aidan's Vicarage, 21 Brooklyn Road, Cheltenham, Glos GL51 8DT* Tel (01242) 574179

SWAIN, Ronald Charles Herbert. b 08. Dur Univ LTh32 BA42 MA50. St Aug Coll Cant 29. **d** 32 **p** 33. C S Wimbledon H Trin *S'wark* 32-34; China 34-40; Perm to Offic *Dur* 41-42; Perm to Offic *Newc* 41-42; P-in-c Padgate Ch Ch *Liv* 42-46; Perm to Offic *S'wark* 46-47; Chapl RAF 47-54; CF 54-62; V Walsham le Willows *St E* 62-70; V Shipley *Chich* 70-74; rtd 74; Perm to Offic *St E* from 74. *81 Westley Road, Bury St Edmunds, Suffolk IP33 3RU* Tel (01284) 761655

SWAIN, Mrs Sharon Juanita. b 46. Sussex Univ BA75 CertEd76. Glouc Sch of Min 84 Qu Coll Birm. **dss** 84 **d** 87 **p** 94. Upton St Leonards *Glouc* 84-87; C 87-88; Children's Officer *Worc* 88-95; Min Can Worc Cathl from 94; V Hanley Castle, Hanley Swan and Welland from 95. *The Vicarage, 5 Westmere, Hanley Swan, Worcester WR8 0DL* Tel (01684) 310321

SWAIN, William Allan. b 38. Kelham Th Coll 63. **d** 68 **p** 69. C Welwyn Garden City *St Alb* 68-72; C Romsey *Win* 72-74; C Weeke 74-78; V Bournemouth H Epiphany 78-91; P-in-c Moordown 91-94; V from 94. *St John's Vicarage, 2 Vicarage Road, Bournemouth BH9 2SA* Tel (01202) 546400

SWAINE, John Arthur. b 45. St Steph Ho Ox 68. **d** 71 **p** 72. C Kilburn St Aug *Lon* 71-74; C Lavender Hill Ascension *S'wark* 74-77; C Deptford St Paul 77-78; Hon C 78-80; Warden St Mark's Youth & Community Cen Deptford 78-80; V Leic St Chad *Leic* 80-86; V Leytonstone H Trin Harrow Green *Chelmsf* 86-94; rtd 94. *7 rue des Goelands, 17120 Mortagne-sur-Gironde, France* Tel France (33) 46 90 50 06

SWAINSON, Norman. b 38. Salford Univ MSc75. St Jo Coll Nottm 77. **d** 79 **p** 80. C Levenshulme St Pet *Man* 79-84; R Jarrow Grange *Dur* from 84. *Christ Church Rectory, Clayton Street, Jarrow, Tyne & Wear NE32 3JR* Tel 0191-489 4682

SWALES, David James. b 58. Warw Univ BA. Cranmer Hall Dur. **d** 84 **p** 85. C Eccleshill *Bradf* 84-88; C Prenton *Ches* 88-92; V Oakworth *Bradf* from 92. *The Vicarage, 18 Sunhurst Drive, Oakworth, Keighley, W Yorkshire BD22 7RG* Tel (01535) 647335

SWALES, Peter. b 52. ACIB78. Ridley Hall Cam 85. **d** 87 **p** 88. C Allestree *Derby* 87-91; P-in-c Horsley from 91. *The Vicarage, Horsley, Derby DE21 5BR* Tel (01332) 880284

SWALLOW, Mrs Alice Gillian. b 51. Birm Univ BA72 CertEd73. NE Ord Course 82. **dss** 84 **d** 87 **p** 94. Morpeth *Newc* 84-86; Uttoxeter w Bramshall *Lich* 86-88; Par Dn 87-88; Par Dn Rocester 88; Chapl to the Deaf *Man* 88-90; Par Dn Goodshaw and Crawshawbooth 88-93; C Barkisland w W Scammonden *Wakef* 93-95; V Ripponden 95-97; rtd 97. *11 Crossley Street, Brighouse, W Yorkshire HD6 3RE* Tel (01484) 719117

SWALLOW, John Brian. b 36. Trent Poly 78. **d** 84 **p** 85. C Cleveleys *Blackb* 84-87; V Blackpool St Mich 87-93; P-in-c Burnley St Steph from 93; RD Burnley from 97. *St Stephen's Vicarage, 154 Todmorden Road, Burnley, Lancs BB11 3ER* Tel (01282) 424733

SWALLOW, John Allen George. b 28. St Jo Coll Dur BA53 DipTh54. **d** 54 **p** 55. C Billericay St Mary *Chelmsf* 54-57; C Bishop's Stortford St Mich *St Alb* 57-59; V Roxwell *Chelmsf* 59-64; V S Weald 64-81; R W w E Mersea 81-93; rtd 93; Perm to Offic *Chelmsf* from 93. *72 Rembrandt Way, Bury St Edmunds, Suffolk IP33 2LT* Tel (01284) 725136

SWALLOW, Robert Andrew (Bob). b 52. Leeds Univ BA73 Sheff Univ PGCE74 Keele Univ MA76. Linc Th Coll 76. **d** 78 **p** 79. C Gt Wyrley *Lich* 78-81; C Blakenall Heath 81-83; TV 83-90; TV Fareham H Trin *Portsm* 90-92. *Address temp unknown*

SWAN, Duncan James. b 65. Imp Coll Lon BSc88 SS Coll Cam BA91. Ridley Hall Cam CTM92. **d** 92 **p** 93. C Stevenage St Andr and St Geo *St Alb* 92-95; C Harpenden St Nic from 95. *86 Tuffnells Way, Harpenden, Herts AL5 3HG* Tel (01582) 762485

SWAN, Owen. b 28. ACP71. Edin Th Coll 56. **d** 59 **p** 60. C Lewisham St Jo Southend *S'wark* 59-64; CF (TA) from 60; V Richmond St Luke *S'wark* 64-82; C-in-c Darlington St Hilda and St Columba CD *Dur* 82-84; R Feltwell *Ely* 84-87; R Holywell w Needingworth from 87. *The Rectory, Holywell, St Ives, Huntingdon, Cambs PE17 3TQ* Tel (01480) 494287

SWAN, Philip Douglas. b 56. Wye Coll Lon BSc78 Qu Coll Cam MA81 CertEd81 Nottm Univ DipTh87. St Jo Coll Nottm 86. **d** 88 **p** 89. C Birm St Martin w Bordesley St Andr *Birm* 88-92; C Selly Park St Steph and St Wulstan 92-96; P-in-c The Lickey from 96. *The Vicarage, 30 Lickey Square, Rednal, Birmingham B45 8HB* Tel 0121-445 1425

SWAN, Preb Ronald Frederick. b 35. St Cath Coll Cam BA59 MA. Coll of Resurr Mirfield. **d** 61 **p** 62. C Staveley *Derby* 61-66; Chapl Lon Univ *Lon* 66-72; C St Martin-in-the-Fields 72-77; V Ealing St Barn 77-88; V Ealing St Steph Castle Hill 81-88; AD Ealing E 84-87; V Harrow St Mary 88-97; AD Harrow 89-94; Preb St Paul's Cathl 91-97; Master R Foundation of St Kath in Ratcliffe from 97. *10 Great James Street, London WC1N 3DQ*

SWAN, Thomas Hugh Winfield. b 26. New Coll Ox BA50 MA62 Barrister 51. Ridley Hall Cam 63. **d** 65 **p** 66. C Yaxley *Ely* 65-68; P-in-c Sawtry 69; R 69-79; P-in-c Fordham St Mary 79-82; V 82-87; P-in-c Hilgay 79-82; R 82-87; P-in-c Southery 79-82; R 82-87; rtd 91. *24 Chiefs Street, Ely, Cambs CB6 1AT* Tel (01353) 668452

SWANBOROUGH, Alan William. b 38. Southn Univ BEd75. Sarum & Wells Th Coll 77. **d** 80 **p** 81. NSM Ventnor H Trin *Portsm* 80-85; NSM Ventnor St Cath 80-85; Chapl Upper Chine Sch Shanklin from 85; NSM Shanklin St Blasius *Portsm* 91-93; P-in-c from 93. *The Rectory, Rectory Road, Shanklin, Isle of Wight PO37 6NS* Tel (01983) 862407

SWANBOROUGH, Robert Charles. b 28. Sarum & Wells Th Coll 75. **d** 77 **p** 78. C Woodley St Jo the Ev *Ox* 77-78; C Bray and Braywood 79-80; V Gt Coxwell w Buscot, Coleshill & Eaton Hastings 80-96; rtd 96. *76 Foxcote, Finchampstead, Wokingham, Berks RG40 3PE* Tel (0118) 973 5465

SWANEPOEL, David John. b 41. Rhodes Univ BA62 UNISA BA64 DipHE80 BTh84. **d** 75 **p** 76. S Africa 75-94; Dean George 85-89; NSM Hellingly and Upper Dicker *Chich* from 94. *Providence House, Upper Dicker, Hailsham, E Sussex BN27 3QE* Tel (01323) 843887

SWANN, Antony Keith. b 34. Lon Univ DipTh60. St Aid Birkenhead 58. **d** 61 **p** 62. C Bilston St Leon *Lich* 61-66; Sierra Leone 66-70; V W Bromwich St Phil *Lich* 70-75; Nigeria 76-78; R Church Lench w Rous Lench and Abbots Morton *Worc* 78-88; Chapl HM Pris Coldingley 88-91; Chapl HM Pris Leyhill from 91. *HM Prison Leyhill, Wotton-under-Edge, Glos GL12 8BT* Tel (01454) 260681 Fax 261398

SWANN, The Ven Edgar John. b 42. TCD BA66 MA70 BD77. CITC 68. **d** 68 **p** 69. C Crumlin *Conn* 68-70; C Howth *D & G* 70-73; I Greystones from 73; Can Ch Ch Cathl Dublin from 90; Adn Glendalough from 93. *The Rectory, Greystones, Co Wicklow, Irish Republic* Tel Dublin (1) 287 4077 Mobile 087-557032 Fax 287 3766 E-mail edgarjswann@tinet.ie

SWANN, Canon Frederick David. b 38. **d** 69 **p** 70. C Lurgan Ch Ch *D & D* 69-77; I Ardmore w Craigavon 77-79; I Comber 79-85; I Drumglass w Moygashel *Arm* from 85; Preb Arm Cathl from 96. *The Rectory, 24 Circular Road, Dungannon, Co Tyrone BT71 6BE* Tel (01868) 722614

SWANN, Paul David James. b 59. Ch Ch Ox BA81 MA88. St Jo Coll Nottm DTS89 DPS90. **d** 90 **p** 91. C Old Hill H Trin *Worc* 90-94; V from 94. *The Vicarage, 58 Wrights Lane, Cradley Heath, Warley, W Midlands B64 6RD* Tel (01384) 412987

SWANNELL, George Alfred Roderick. b 20. St Edm Hall Ox BA47 MA51. Ridley Hall Cam 47. **d** 49 **p** 50. C Crowborough *Chich* 49-51; Chapl K Edw Sch Witley 51-55; C Sevenoaks St Nic *Roch* 55-57; Kenya 57-65; C St Marylebone All So w SS Pet and Jo *Lon* 65-68; V Hildenborough *Roch* 68-80; Lic to Offic from 80; Chapl Kent and Sussex Hosp Tunbridge Wells 80-86; rtd 85; Chapl Sevenoaks Hosp from 86; Chapl Sevenoaks Sch from 86; Chapl W Heath Sch Sevenoaks from 86. *68 Mount Ephraim, Tunbridge Wells, Kent TN4 8BG* Tel (01892) 529674

SWANSEA AND BRECON, Bishop of. *See* BRIDGES, The Rt Revd Dewi Morris

SWANTON, John Joseph. b 61. Bradf and Ilkley Coll BA84 MCIH89 MRSH95. S Dios Minl Tr Scheme 92. **d** 95 **p** 96. NSM Shalford *Guildf* from 95. *90 Busbridge Lane, Godalming, Surrey GU7 1QH* Tel (01483) 427160

SWARBRIGG, David Cecil. b 42. TCD BA64 MA67. **d** 65 **p** 66. C Lisburn Ch Ch *Conn* 65-67; C Thames Ditton *Guildf* 72-76; Chapl Hampton Sch Middx from 76. *The Chaplain's Office, Hampton School, Hampton, Middx TW12 3HD* Tel 0181-979 5526

SWART-RUSSELL, Dr Phoebe. b 58. Cape Town Univ BA79 MA82 DPhil88. Ox NSM Course 89. **d** 90 **p** 94. C Riverside *Ox* 90-95; Hon C Chenies and Lt Chalfont, Latimer and Flaunden from 96. *The Rectory, Latimer, Chesham, Bucks HP5 1UA* Tel (01494) 766109

SWEATMAN, John. b 44. Open Univ BA89. Oak Hill Th Coll 68. **d** 71 **p** 72. C Rayleigh *Chelmsf* 71-73; C Seaford w Sutton *Chich* 73-77; Chapl RN 77-82; CF 82-85; V Hellingly and Upper Dicker *Chich* 85-90; Hon C Mayfield 95-96; P-in-c Malborough w S Huish, W Alvington and Churchstow *Ex* from 96. *The Vicarage, Malborough, Kingsbridge, Devon TQ7 3RR* Tel (01548) 561234

SWEED, John William. b 35. Bernard Gilpin Soc Dur 58 Clifton Th Coll 59. **d** 62 **p** 63. C Shrewsbury St Julian *Lich* 62-64; C Sheff St Jo *Sheff* 64-70; V Doncaster St Jas 70-79; V Hatfield from 79; RD Snaith and Hatfield 84-93. *The Vicarage, Hatfield, Doncaster, S Yorkshire DN7 6RS* Tel (01302) 840280

SWEENEY, Andrew James. b 61. Wycliffe Hall Ox 96. **d** 96 **p** 97. C Bladon w Woodstock *Ox* from 96. *19 Park Close, Bladon, Oxford OX7 1RN* Tel (01993) 811075

SWEENEY, Robert Maxwell. b 38. Ch Ch Ox BA63 MA66 Birm Univ MA78. Cuddesdon Coll 63. **d** 65 **p** 66. C Prestbury *Glouc* 65-68; C Handsworth St Andr *Birm* 68-70; Asst Chapl Lancing Coll 70-73; Perm to Offic *Chich* 70-73; V Wotton St Mary *Glouc*

74-79; V Ox St Thos w St Frideswide and Binsey *Ox* from 79; Chapl Magd Coll Ox 82-88. *19 Botley Road, Oxford OX2 0BL* Tel (01865) 251403

SWEET, Canon John Philip McMurdo. b 27. New Coll Ox BA49 MA52 Lambeth DD94. Westcott Ho Cam 53 Yale Div Sch 54. **d** 55 **p** 56. C Mansfield St Mark *S'well* 55-58; Chapl Selw Coll Cam 58-83; Lic to Offic *Ely* from 58; Wiccamical Preb Chich Cathl *Chich* from 62; Asst Lect Div Cam Univ 60-63; Lect 64-94; Dean of Chapl Selw Coll Cam 83-94; rtd 94. *97 Barton Road, Cambridge CB3 9LL* Tel (01223) 353186

SWEET, Reginald Charles. b 36. Open Univ BA74. Ripon Hall Ox 61. **d** 62 **p** 63. C Styvechale *Cov* 62-65; Chapl RN 65-69 and 74-93; R Riddlesworth w Gasthorpe and Knettishall *Nor* 69-74; R Brettenham w Rushford 69-74; Perm to Offic 93-96. *Walnut Tree Cottage, Rushford, Thetford, Norfolk IP24 2SB* Tel (01842) 753346

SWEET, Vaughan Carroll. b 46. Aston Univ BSc69 MSc70. Linc Th Coll 89. **d** 91 **p** 92. C Uttoxeter w Bramshall *Lich* 91-95; P-in-c Hadley from 95. *The Vicarage, 19 Manor Road, Hadley, Telford, Shropshire TF1 4PN* Tel (01952) 254251

SWEET-ESCOTT, Richard Mark. b 28. Hertf Coll Ox BA51 MA53. Westcott Ho Cam 56. **d** 58 **p** 59. C Leeds St Pet *Ripon* 58-62; C Littlehampton St Mary *Chich* 62-65; C Seaford w Sutton 65-72; P-in-c Burpham 72-75; V Easebourne 75-79; V Crawley Down All SS 79-93; rtd 93; Perm to Offic *Chich* from 93. *8 Buttsfield Lane, East Hoathly, Lewes, E Sussex BN8 6EF* Tel (01825) 841052

SWEETMAN, Denis Harold. b 22. Roch Th Coll 61. **d** 63 **p** 64. C Riverhead *Roch* 63-70; C Dunton Green 67-70; Chapl Sevenoaks Hosp 70-72; R Eynsford w Lullingstone *Roch* 71-73; R Eynsford w Farningham and Lullingstone 73-89; rtd 89; Perm to Offic *Newc* from 89. *31 Gloster Park, Amble, Morpeth, Northd NE65 0JQ* Tel (01665) 711863

SWENARTON, Canon John Creighton. b 19. TCD BA41 MA45. **d** 42 **p** 43. C Lurgan Ch Ch *D & D* 42-45; C Belfast St Donard 45-46; C Donaghcloney w Waringstown 46-51; I Tullylish 51-60; I Donaghadee 60-84; Preb Down Cathl 81-84; rtd 84. *The Court, Culverhay, Wotton-under-Edge, Glos GL12 7LS* Tel (01453) 842038

SWENSSON, Sister Gerd Inger. b 51. Lon Univ MPhil Uppsala Univ 70. **dss** 74 **d** 87. In Ch of Sweden 74-75; Notting Hill *Lon* 75-77; CSA from 75; Abbey Ho Malmesbury 77-79; R Foundn of St Kath 79-81; Notting Hill All SS w St Columb *Lon* 81-84; Kensington St Mary Abbots w St Geo 85-89; C Bedford Park from 91. *2 Old Forge Mews, London W12 9JP* Tel 0181-740 0173

SWIDENBANK, Stephen. b 37. Lich Th Coll 58. **d** 61 **p** 62. C Penrith St Andr *Carl* 61-64; C Dalton-in-Furness 64-67; V Kells 67-76; V Staveley w Kentmere 76-85; rtd 85; Perm to Offic *Carl* from 86. *Flat 1, Engadine, New Road, Windermere, Cumbria LA23 2LA* Tel (015394) 46507

SWIFT, Ainsley. b 56. Liv Univ BEd80. Ripon Coll Cuddesdon DipMin94. **d** 94 **p** 95. C Prescot *Liv* from 94. *St Mary's House, West Street, Prescot, Merseyside L34 1LQ* Tel 0151-426 0716

SWIFT, Christopher James. b 65. Hull Univ BA86 Man Univ MA95. Westcott Ho Cam 89. **d** 91 **p** 92. C Longton *Blackb* 91-94; TV Chipping Barnet w Arkley *St Alb* 94-97; Chapl Wellhouse NHS Trust from 97. *4 High Street, Colney Heath, St Albans, Herts AL4 0NU* Tel (01727) 821647 or 0181-216 4355

SWIFT, Christopher John. b 54. Linc Coll Ox BA76 MA Selw Coll Cam BA80. Westcott Ho Cam 79. **d** 81 **p** 82. C Portsea N End St Mark *Portsm* 81-84; C Alverstoke 84-87; V Whitton SS Phil and Jas *Lon* 87-94; R Shepperton from 94. *The Rectory, Church Square, Shepperton, Middx TW17 9JY* Tel (01932) 220511

SWIFT, Francis Bernard. b 06. Dur Univ LTh32. Lich Th Coll 28. **d** 31 **p** 32. C Ravensthorpe *Wakef* 31-35; V Bromfield *Carl* 35-40; V Holme Cultram St Cuth 40-50; V Addingham 50-58; V Ireby w Uldale 58-72; rtd 72; Lic to Offic *Carl* 72-77; Perm to Offic 77-95. *5 Westhaven, Thursby, Carlisle CA5 6PH* Tel (01228) 710099

SWIFT, Ms Pamela Joan. b 47. Liv Univ BSc68. NE Ord Course 85. **d** 88 **p** 94. Par Dn Bermondsey St Jas w Ch Ch *S'wark* 88-91; Par Dn Middleton St Cross *Ripon* 91-92; Dioc Stewardship Adv 92-95; TR Bramley from 95. *6 St Peter's Gardens, Hough Lane, Leeds LS13 3EH* Tel 0113-256 7748

SWIFT, Richard Barrie. b 33. Selw Coll Cam BA58 MA64. Ripon Hall Ox. **d** 60 **p** 61. C Stepney St Dunstan and All SS *Lon* 60-64; C Sidmouth St Nic *Ex* 64-72; P-in-c W Hyde St Thos *St Alb* 72-77; V Mill End 72-77; V Mill End and Heronsgate w W Hyde 77-82; V Axminster *Ex* 82-83; P-in-c Chardstock 82-83; P-in-c Combe Pyne w Rousdon 82-83; TR Axminster, Chardstock, Combe Pyne and Rousdon 83-94; rtd 94; Perm to Offic *Ex* from 94. *Wheel Cottage, Exmouth Road, Colaton Raleigh, Sidmouth, Devon EX10 0LE*

SWIFT, Selwyn. b 41. Trin Coll Bris 73. **d** 76 **p** 77. C Melksham *Sarum* 76-79; TV 79-81; TV Whitton 81-84; V Derry Hill 84-89; R Bunwell, Carleton Rode, Tibenham, Gt Moulton etc *Nor* from 89; RD Depwade from 97. *The Rectory, Carleton Rode, Norwich NR16 1RN* Tel (01953) 789218

SWIFT, Stanley (Stan). b 47. ACIS71 Nottm Univ DipTh73 Open Univ BA86. Linc Th Coll 71. **d** 74 **p** 75. C Heaton St Barn *Bradf* 74-77; C Bexhill St Pet *Chich* 77-81; R Crowland *Linc* 81-86; RD Elloe W 82-86; R Upminster *Chelmsf* 86-95; P-in-c N Ockendon 94-95; V Rush Green from 95. *St Augustine's Vicarage, Birkbeck Road, Romford RM7 0QP* Tel (01708) 741460

SWINBURNE, Harold Noel. b 27. Univ Coll Lon BA49 St Chad's Coll Dur DipTh. **d** 53 **p** 54. C Cockerton *Dur* 53-57; C Wisbech St Aug *Ely* 57-59; V Chilton Moor *Dur* 59-71; Lect Relig Studies New Coll Dur 71-93; Lic to Offic *Dur* 71-85; V Bishopwearmouth St Nic 85-93; rtd 93. *39 Durham Moor Crescent, Durham DH1 5AS* Tel 0191-386 2603

SWINDELL, Anthony Charles. b 50. Selw Coll Cam BA73 MA77 Leeds Univ MPhil77. Ripon Hall Ox 73. **d** 75 **p** 76. C Hessle *York* 75-78; P-in-c Litlington w W Dean *Chich* 78-80; Adult Educn Adv E Sussex 78-80; TV Heslington *York* 80-81; Chapl York Univ 80-81; R Harlaxton *Linc* 81-91; RD Grantham 85-90; R Jersey St Sav *Win* from 91; Perm to Offic *Nor* from 93. *The Rectory, St Saviour, Jersey, Channel Islands JE2 7NP* Tel (01534) 36679

SWINDELL, Brian. b 35. St Jo Coll Nottm 86. **d** 88 **p** 89. C Wombwell *Sheff* 88-91; V Brinsworth w Catcliffe 91-93; TR Brinsworth w Catcliffe and Treeton from 93. *The Vicarage, 61 Whitehill Lane, Brinsworth, Rotherham, S Yorkshire S60 5JR* Tel (01709) 363850

SWINDELL, Richard Carl. b 45. FCollP87 Didsbury Coll Man CertEd67 Open Univ BA73 Leeds Univ MEd86. N Ord Course 79 Qu Coll Birm. **d** 82 **p** 83. Hd Teacher Moorside Jun Sch from 78; NSM Halifax St Aug *Wakef* 82-92; NSM Huddersfield H Trin from 92. *38 The Gardens, Heath Road, Halifax, W Yorkshire HX1 2PL* Tel (01422) 361972

SWINDELLS, Andrew Wallis (Andy). b 65. Peterho Cam BA88 MA92. Ridley Hall Cam 89. **d** 92 **p** 93. C Walworth *S'wark* 92-94; Asst Chapl Tonbridge Sch from 94. *Tonbridge School, High Street, Tonbridge, Kent TN9 1JP* Tel (01732) 365555

SWINDELLS, Philip John. b 34. St Edm Hall Ox BA56 MA60. Ely Th Coll 56. **d** 58 **p** 59. C Upton cum Chalvey *Ox* 58-62; C Bishops Hull St Jo *B & W* 62-66; C Stevenage St Geo *St Alb* 66-71; V Stevenage All SS Pin Green 71-78; R Clophill from 78; P-in-c Upper w Lower Gravenhurst from 83; P-in-c Shillington from 96. *The Rectory, Great Lane, Clophill, Bedford MK45 4BQ* Tel (01525) 860792

SWINDLEHURST, Canon Michael Robert Carol. b 29. Worc Coll Ox BA52 MA56. Cuddesdon Coll 61. **d** 63 **p** 64. C Havant *Portsm* 63-66; C Hellesdon *Nor* 66-69; V Brightlingsea *Chelmsf* 69-95; Miss to Seamen 69-95; RD St Osyth *Chelmsf* 84-94; Hon Can Chelmsf Cathl 89-95; rtd 95; Perm to Offic *Chelmsf* from 95. *9 Radwinter Road, Saffron Walden, Essex CB11 3HU* Tel (01799) 513788

SWINDLEY, Canon Geoffrey. b 25. St Mich Coll Llan 59. **d** 61 **p** 62. C Flint *St As* 61-68; V Buttington and Pool Quay 68-77; R Welshpool w Castle Caereinion 77-92; RD Pool 77-92; Hon Can St As Cathl 83-93; rtd 93. *2 Cobden Street, Welshpool SY21 7EH* Tel (01938) 555942

SWINDON, Archdeacon of. *See* MIDDLETON, The Ven Michael John

SWINDON, Suffragan Bishop of. *See* DOE, The Rt Revd Michael David

SWINGLER, Preb Jack Howell. b 19. St Jo Coll Cam BA41 MA47. Ridley Hall Cam 46. **d** 48 **p** 49. C Yeovil St Jo w Preston Plucknett *B & W* 48-53; V Henstridge 53-79; RD Merston 74-84; P-in-c Charlton Horethorne w Stowell 78-79; Preb Wells Cathl 79-85; R Henstridge and Charlton Horethorne w Stowell 79-85; rtd 85; Perm to Offic *B & W* from 85. *St Andrew's, March Lane, Galhampton, Yeovil, Somerset BA22 7AN* Tel (01963) 40842

SWINHOE, Terence Leslie (Terry). b 49. Man Univ BA71 PGCE72. N Ord Course. **d** 84 **p** 85. C Harborne St Pet *Birm* 84-87; V Warley *Wakef* 87-96; V Rastrick St Matt from 96. *St Matthew's Vicarage, 1 Vicarage Gardens, Ogden Lane, Brighouse, W Yorkshire HD6 3HD* Tel (01484) 713386

SWINN, Gerald Robert. b 40. Leeds Univ BSc60 Lon Univ BD70. Oak Hill Th Coll 63. **d** 66 **p** 67. C Weston-super-Mare Ch Ch *B & W* 66-69; C Harefield *Lon* 70-72; Lic to Offic *Sarum* from 72. *16 Heddington Drive, Blandford Forum, Dorset DT11 7TP* Tel (01258) 451637

SWINNERTON, Edward. b 26. St Aid Birkenhead 62. **d** 64 **p** 65. C Prescot *Liv* 64-67; C S Shore H Trin *Blackb* 67-69; V Hambleton 69-88; P-in-c Out Rawcliffe 84-88; V Hambleton w Out Rawcliffe 88-89; V Barnacre w Calder Vale 89-92; rtd 92; Perm to Offic *York* from 92. *136 Prince Rupert Drive, Tockwith, York YO5 8PU* Tel (01423) 358203

SWINNERTON, Ernest George Francis. b 33. Clare Coll Cam BA54 MA57. Linc Th Coll 56. **d** 58 **p** 59. C Kirkholt *Man* 58-61; C Swindon Ch Ch *Bris* 61-67; C-in-c Walcot St Andr CD 67-75; P-in-c Chilton Foliat *Sarum* 76; TV Whitton 76-85; V Bolton St Matt w St Barn *Man* 85-95; rtd 95. *9 Duddon Avenue, Breightmet, Bolton BL2 5EZ* Tel (01204) 381377

SWINTON, Garry Dunlop. b 59. SS Mark & Jo Coll Plymouth BA81 CertEd82. Ripon Coll Cuddesdon 85. **d** 88 **p** 89. C Surbiton St Andr and St Mark *S'wark* 88-92; Succ S'wark Cathl 92-97; P-in-c Wandsworth St Faith from 97. *2 Alma Road, London SW18 1AA* Tel 0181-874 8567

SWITHINBANK, Kim Stafford. b 53. SS Coll Cam BA77 MA80. Cranmer Hall Dur 78. **d** 80 **p** 81. C Heigham H Trin *Nor* 80-83;

Chapl Monkton Combe Sch Bath 83-85; C St Marylebone All So w SS Pet and Jo *Lon* 85-88; C Langham Place All So 88-89; R Stamford St Geo w St Paul *Linc* from 90. *St George's Rectory, Stamford, Lincs PE9 2BN* Tel (01780) 63351

SWITZERLAND, Archdeacon of. *See* HAWKER, The Ven Peter John

SWYER, David Martin. b 64. Univ of Wales (Abth) BA87 PGCE89. St Mich Coll Llan DipTh91. **d** 91 **p** 92. C Killay *S & B* 91-93; C Newton St Pet 93-95; R Albourne w Sayers Common and Twineham *Chich* from 95. *The Rectory, 5 The Twitten, Albourne, Hassocks, W Sussex BN6 9DF* Tel (01273) 832129

SWYER (née HARRIS), Mrs Rebecca Jane. b 67. **d** 91. C Sketty *S & B* 91-95. *The Rectory, 5 The Twitten, Albourne, Hassocks, W Sussex BN6 9DF* Tel (01273) 832129

SWYNNERTON, Brian Thomas. b 31. JP77. Ox Univ Inst of Educn 56 NY Univ BA74 PhD75 FRGS62 LCP62. Lich Th Coll 67. **d** 69 **p** 70. C Swynnerton *Lich* 69-71; CF (TAVR) 70-80; C Eccleshall *Lich* 71-74; C Croxton w Broughton 74-80; Chapl and Lect Stafford Coll 80-84; Chapl Naples w Sorrento, Capri and Bari *Eur* 84-85; Perm to Offic *Lich* from 85; Perm to Offic *Wakef* 85-88; Chapl Rishworth Sch Ripponden 85-88; Chapl Acton Reynald Sch Shrewsbury 88-96; Chapl Telford City Tech Coll from 96. *Hales Farm, Market Drayton, Shropshire TF9 2PP* Tel (01630) 657156

SYKES, Albert. b 08. Man Egerton Hall 33. **d** 35 **p** 36. C Levenshulme St Pet *Man* 35-41; V Bolton Sav 41-46; R St Dennis *Truro* 46-55; V Lostwithiel 55-67; V Pelynt 67-73; R Lanreath 67-73; rtd 73; Hon C St Austell *Truro* from 78. *32 Biscovey Road, Par, Cornwall PL24 2HW* Tel (01726) 814139

SYKES, Mrs Clare Mary. b 61. W of England Minl Tr Course 93. **d** 96 **p** 97. C Tupsley w Hampton Bishop *Heref* from 96. *The Vicarage, Breinton, Hereford HR4 7PG* Tel (01432) 273447

SYKES, Graham Timothy Gordon. b 59. ACIB89. St Jo Coll Nottm BTh92. **d** 92 **p** 93. C Kington w Huntington, Old Radnor, Kinnerton etc *Heref* 92-95; Dioc Co-ord for Evang from 95; C Breinton from 95. *The Vicarage, Breinton, Hereford HR4 7PG* Tel (01432) 273447

SYKES, Ian. b 44. Lon Univ DipTh Leic Univ DipEd. Bris Bapt Coll 64 Ripon Coll Cuddesdon 84. **d** 85 **p** 86. In Bapt Ch 64-84; C Headington *Ox* 85-88; TV Bourne Valley *Sarum* from 88. *The Rectory, High Street, Porton, Salisbury SP4 0LH* Tel (01980) 610305

SYKES, James Clement. b 42. Keble Coll Ox BA64 MA71. Westcott Ho Cam 65. **d** 67 **p** 68. C Bishop's Stortford St Mich *St Alb* 67-71; Chapl St Jo Sch Leatherhead 71-73; Bermuda 74-79; V Northaw *St Alb* 79-87; Chapl St Marg Sch Bushey from 87. *The Chaplain's House, St Margaret's School, Bushey, Herts WD2 1DT* Tel 0181-950 4616

SYKES, Miss Jean. b 45. Leeds Univ BA66 Bris Univ CertEd67. Ripon Coll Cuddesdon 86. **d** 88 **p** 94. C N Huddersfield *Wakef* 88-91; TD 91-93; TV Kippax w Allerton Bywater *Ripon* from 93. *The Vicarage, 134 Leeds Road, Allerton Bywater, Castleford, W Yorkshire WF10 2HB* Tel 0113-286 9415

SYKES, Jeremy Jonathan Nicholas. b 61. Girton Coll Cam BA83 MA86. Wycliffe Hall Ox. **d** 89 **p** 90. C Knowle *Birm* 89-92; Asst Chapl Oakham Sch from 92. *8 Ashwell Road, Oakham, Leics LE15 6QG* Tel (01572) 758624 Fax 758742

SYKES, Canon John. b 39. Man Univ BA62. Ripon Hall Ox 61. **d** 63 **p** 64. C Heywood St Luke *Man* 63-67; Chapl Bolton Colls of FE 67-71; C Bolton H Trin *Man* 67-71; R Reddish 71-78; V Saddleworth 78-87; TR Oldham from 87; Hon Can Man Cathl from 91; Chapl to The Queen from 95. *The Vicarage, 15 Grotton Hollow, Oldham OL4 4LN* Tel 0161-678 6767 or 624 4866

SYKES, John Trevor. b 35. Lich Th Coll 60. **d** 62 **p** 63. C Lillington *Cov* 62-65; C Cov St Marg 65-68; P-in-c Bubbenhall 68-77; V Ryton on Dunsmore 68-77; V Ryton on Dunsmore w Bubbenhall from 77. *The Vicarage, Ryton on Dunsmore, Coventry CV8 3ET* Tel (01203) 303570

✠**SYKES, The Rt Revd Stephen Whitefield.** b 39. St Jo Coll Cam BA61 MA65. Ripon Hall Ox 63. **d** 64 **p** 65 **c** 90. Fell and Dean St Jo Coll Cam 64-74; Asst Lect Div Cam Univ 64-68; Lect 68-74; Can Res Dur Cathl *Dur* 74-85; Van Mildert Prof Div Dur Univ 74-85; Regius Prof Div Cam Univ 85-90; Hon Can Ely Cathl *Ely* 85-90; Bp Ely from 90; Perm to Offic *Ban* from 90. *Bishop's House, Ely, Cambs CB7 4DW* Tel (01353) 662749 Fax 669477

SYKES, William George David (Bill). b 39. Ball Coll Ox BA63 MA68. Wycliffe Hall Ox 63. **d** 65 **p** 66. Chapl Bradf Cathl *Bradf* 65-69; Chapl Univ Coll *Lon* 69-78; Chapl Univ Coll Ox from 78. *The Senior Common Room, University College, Oxford OX1 4BH* Tel (01865) 276602

SYLVESTER, Jeremy Carl Edmund. b 56. Cape Town Univ BA78 HDipEd79. Coll of Resurr Mirfield 84. **d** 87 **p** 88. S Africa 87-96; P-in-c Stoke Newington St Olave *Lon* from 96. *St Olave's Vicarage, Woodberry Down, London N4 2TW* Tel 0181-800 1374

SYLVIA, Keith Lawrence Wilfred. b 63. Chich Th Coll 85. **d** 88 **p** 89. C Newbold w Dunston *Derby* 88-91; C Heston *Lon* 91-95; V Brighton St Matthias *Chich* from 95. *St Matthias's Vicarage, 45 Hollingbury Park Avenue, Brighton BN1 7JQ* Tel (01273) 508178

SYMES, Collin. b 20. Birm Univ BA47 MA48. Bps' Coll Cheshunt 56. **d** 58 **p** 59. C Enfield St Mich *Lon* 58-60; C Brondesbury St Anne w Kilburn H Trin 60-62; R Maidwell w Draughton *Pet* 62-66; R Yardley Hastings 66-68; V Denton 66-68; Hon C Rusthall *Roch* 68-85; Chapl W Kent Coll of FE 68-73; Chapl Chapl RN Sch Haslemere 81-84; rtd 84; Chapl St Elphin's Sch Matlock 85-86; Perm to Offic *Chich* from 86. *3 Eden Walk, Tunbridge Wells, Kent TN1 1TT* Tel (01892) 532283

SYMES, Percy Peter. b 24. Leeds Univ BA50. Coll of Resurr Mirfield 50. **d** 52 **p** 53. C Ox St Barn *Ox* 52-54; C Headington 54-56; C Abingdon w Shippon 56-61; V Reading St Luke 61-81; V Drayton St Pet (Berks) 81-89; rtd 89; Hon C Lower Windrush *Ox* from 94. *107 Abingdon Road, Standlake, Witney, Oxon OX8 7QN*

SYMES-THOMPSON, Hugh Kynard. b 54. Peterho Cam BA76 MA81 St Jo Coll Dur DipTh79. **d** 79 **p** 80. C Summerfield *Birm* 79-82; C Harlow New Town w Lt Parndon *Chelmsf* 82-83; Australia 84-89; TV Dagenham *Chelmsf* 89-95; R Cranfield and Hulcote w Salford *St Alb* from 95; Chapl Cranfield Univ from 95. *The Rectory, Court Road, Cranfield, Bedford MK43 0DR* Tel (01234) 750214

SYMINGTON, Patricia Ann. *See* TURNER, Mrs Patricia Ann

SYMMONS, Roderic Paul (Rod). b 56. Chu Coll Cam MA77. Oak Hill Th Coll BA83. **d** 83 **p** 84. C Ox St Aldate w St Matt *Ox* 83-88; USA 89-90; R Ardingly *Chich* from 90; RD Cuckfield from 95. *The Rectory, Church Lane, Ardingly, Haywards Heath, W Sussex RH17 6UR* Tel (01444) 892332

SYMON, Canon John Francis Walker. b 26. Edin Univ MA50. Edin Th Coll 50. **d** 52 **p** 53. C Edin St Cuth *Edin* 52-56; CF 56-59; R Forfar *St And* 59-68; R Dunblane 68-85; Can St Ninian's Cathl Perth 74-91; Chapl Trin Coll Glenalmond 85-91; rtd 91. *Westgarth, Tom-na-croich, Fortingall, Aberfeldy, Perthshire PH15 2LJ* Tel (01887) 830287

SYMON, Canon Roger Hugh Crispin. b 34. St Jo Coll Cam BA59. Coll of Resurr Mirfield 59. **d** 61 **p** 62. C Westmr St Steph w St Jo *Lon* 61-66; P-in-c Hascombe *Guildf* 66-68; Chapl Surrey Univ 66-74; V Paddington Ch Ch *Lon* 74-78; V Paddington St Jas 78-79; USPG 80-87; Abp Cant's Acting Sec for Angl Communion Affairs 87-94; Can Res Cant Cathl *Cant* from 94. *19 The Precincts, Canterbury CT1 2EP* Tel (01227) 459918 Fax as telephone

SYMONDS, Alan Jeffrey. b 56. Ridley Hall Cam CTM95. **d** 95 **p** 96. C Bath St Luke *B & W* from 95. *59 Longfellow Avenue, Bath BA2 4SH* Tel (01225) 480189

SYMONDS, Edward George. b 03. Launde Abbey 58. **d** 59 **p** 60. C Glen Parva and S Wigston *Leic* 59-64; V Leic All SS 64-74; rtd 74; Perm to Offic *Llan* from 74. *Skomer Residential Home, Marine Parade, Penarth CF64 3BG*

SYMONDS, James Henry (Jim). b 31. Ripon Hall Ox 67. **d** 69 **p** 70. C Southampton (City Cen) *Win* 69-71; CF 71-78; CF 79-90; P-in-c Arrington *Ely* 78-79; P-in-c Orwell 78-79; P-in-c Wimpole 78-79; P-in-c Croydon w Clopton 78-79; CF (R of O) 90-96; rtd 96. *Endex, 162 Curborough Road, Lichfield, Staffs WS13 7PW* Tel (01543) 254279

SYMONDS, Canon Robert Pinder. b 10. CCC Cam BA32 MA37. Linc Th Coll 32. **d** 34 **p** 35. C Hampton All SS *Lon* 34-36; C Willoughby *Linc* 36-38; C Hawarden *St As* 38-42; P-in-c Crowland *Linc* 42-46; OGS from 44; Tutor Linc Th Coll 46-51; Chapl 51-56; V Leic St Mary *Leic* 56-74; Hon Can Leic Cathl 73-74; Subwarden St Deiniol's Lib Hawarden 74-77; Chapl 77-78; rtd 75; Chapl Trin Hosp Retford 78-87; Perm to Offic *Chich* 87-92. *Flat 10, Stuart Court, High Street, Kibworth, Leicester LE8 0LE* Tel 0116-279 6380

SYMONS, Fernley Rundle. b 39. Peterho Cam BA61 MA71. St Steph Ho Ox 61. **d** 64 **p** 65. C Chesterton St Geo *Ely* 64-67; C Henleaze *Bris* 67-72; V Shirehampton from 72. *St Mary's Vicarage, 8 Priory Gardens, Bristol BS11 0BZ* Tel 0117-982 2737 E-mail 100333.2766@compuserve.com

SYMONS, James Edward. b 28. AKC57. **d** 58 **p** 59. C Benwell St Jas *Newc* 58-62; C Alnwick St Mich 62-65; C Prudhoe 65-67; V Mickley 67-95; rtd 95. *14 Moor Road, Prudhoe, Northd NE42 5LH* Tel (01661) 832978

SYMONS, Stewart Burlace. b 31. Keble Coll Ox BA55 MA59. Clifton Th Coll 55. **d** 57 **p** 58. C Hornsey Rise St Mary *Lon* 57-60; C Gateshead St Geo *Dur* 60-61; C Patcham *Chich* 61-64; R Stretford St Bride *Man* 64-71; V Waterloo St Jo *Liv* 71-83; R Ardrossan *Glas* 83-96; C-in-c Irvine St Andr LEP 83-96; Miss to Seamen 83-96; rtd 96; Perm to Offic *Carl* from 96. *8 Carlingdale, Burneside, Kendal, Cumbria LA9 6PW* Tel (01539) 728750

SYMS, Richard Arthur. b 43. Ch Coll Cam BA66 MA71. Wycliffe Hall Ox 66. **d** 68 **p** 69. C New Eltham All SS *S'wark* 68-72; Chapl to Arts and Recreation *Dur* 72-73; C Hitchin St Mary *St Alb* 73-76; TV Hitchin 77-78; Perm to Offic 78-97; P-in-c Datchworth w Tewin from 97. *94 Pondcroft Road, Knebworth, Herts SG3 6DE* Tel (01438) 811933

SYNNOTT, Alan Patrick Sutherland. b 59. **d** 85 **p** 86. C Lisburn Ch Ch *Conn* 85-88; CF 88-95; I Galloon w Drummully *Clogh* from 95. *The Rectory, Newtownbutler, Enniskillen, Co Fermanagh BT92 8JD* Tel (01365) 7245

SYNNOTT, Canon Patrick Joseph. b 18. **d** 52 **p** 54. C Ballymacarrett St Patr *D & D* 52-55; C Lurgan Ch Ch 55-60; I Scarva 60-63; I Magheralin 63-74; RD Shankill 70-74; I Belfast St Donard 74-89; Can Down Cathl 80-89; Chan Down Cathl 87-89; rtd 89; Lic to Offic *D & D* from 90. *7 Norwood Drive, Belfast BT4 2EA* Tel (01232) 652365

T

TABERN, James. b 23. St Aid Birkenhead 57. **d** 59 **p** 60. C Garston *Liv* 59-61; V Litherland St Paul Hatton Hill 61-72; V Gillingham St Mark *Roch* 72-79; V Lindow *Ches* 79-85; rtd 85; Perm to Offic *Liv* 86-91. *12 Dickinson Road, Formby, Merseyside L37 4BX* Tel (01704) 831131

TABERNACLE, Peter Aufrere. b 22. S'wark Ord Course 72. **d** 74 **p** 75. NSM Enfield St Geo *Lon* 74-80; C Corby Epiphany w St Jo *Pet* 80-83; V Wellingborough St Mark 83-88; P-in-c Wilby 83-88; rtd 88; Perm to Offic *Pet* from 88. *15 Archfield Court, Oxford Street, Wellingborough, Northants NN8 4HH* Tel (01933) 228570

TABOR, John Tranham. b 30. Ball Coll Ox BA56 MA58. Ridley Hall Cam 55. **d** 58 **p** 59. C Lindfield *Chich* 58-62; Tutor Ridley Hall Cam 62-63; Chapl 63-68; Warden Scargill Ho 68-75; R Berkhamsted St Mary *St Alb* 75-96; rtd 96. *2 Warwick Close, Aston Clinton, Aylesbury, Bucks HP22 5JF* Tel (01296) 631562

TABOR, Leonard Frank. b 15. St Steph Ho Ox 47. **d** 50 **p** 51. C Brentwood St Thos *Chelmsf* 50-55; V Bobbing w Iwade *Cant* 55-58; V S Norwood H Innocents 58-66; V Margate All SS 66-86; rtd 86; Perm to Offic *Cant* from 86. *Appleshaw, 18B Whitehall Gardens, Canterbury, Kent CT2 8BD* Tel (01227) 464342

TABRAHAM, Canon Albert John. b 14. Birm Univ DipTh71. Coll of Resurr Mirfield 55. **d** 56 **p** 57. C Oldbury *Birm* 56-59; V Stockland Green 59-70; RD Aston 68-70; V Acocks Green 70-80; RD Yardley 74-77; Hon Can Birm Cathl 78-80; rtd 80; Hon C Duns *Edin* from 80. *10 Gourlays Wynd, Duns, Berwickshire TD11 3AZ* Tel (01361) 82483

TADMAN, John Christopher. b 33. Lon Coll of Div 54. **d** 58 **p** 59. C Blackheath St Jo *S'wark* 58-61; C Surbiton Hill Ch Ch 61-64; R Cratfield w Heveningham and Ubbeston *St E* 65-70; R Kelsale w Carlton 70-74; R Ashurst *Roch* 74-76; V Fordcombe 74-77; P-in-c Penshurst 76-77; R Penshurst and Fordcombe 77-85; V Felsted *Chelmsf* 85-93; Resource Min Brentwood from 93; Chapl Warley Hosp Brentwood from 93. *The Rectory, 2 Church Road, Kelvedon Common, Brentwood, Essex CM14 5TJ*

TADMAN-ROBINS, Christopher Rodney (Chris). b 47. JP82. LRAM68 ARCM68 GNSM68 Lon Inst of Educn PGCE69 Westmr Coll Ox BA91 DipApTh93 Ox Univ MTh94. Ox NSM Course 86. **d** 89 **p** 90. NSM Burford w Fulbrook and Taynton *Ox* 89-94; NSM Burford w Fulbrook, Taynton, Asthall etc from 94. *Rest Harrow, Meadow Lane, Fulbrook, Burford, Oxon OX18 4BS* Tel (01993) 823551

TAGGART, Canon Justin Paul. b 11. Linc Th Coll 32. **d** 34 **p** 35. C Spittlegate *Linc* 34-40; C Linc St Nic w St Jo Newport 40-45; V Morton w Hacconby 45-52; V Woodhall Spa and Kirkstead 52-76; R Langton w Woodhall 52-76; Can and Preb Linc Cathl 68-76; rtd 76; Perm to Offic *S & M* from 76. *Reedsbeck, Droghadfayle Road, Port Erin, Isle of Man IM9 6EE* Tel (01624) 834204

TAGGART, William Joseph. b 54. DipFD. DipTh. **d** 85 **p** 86. C Belfast St Mich *Conn* 85-90; Chmn Dioc Youth Coun from 90; I Belfast St Kath from 90. *St Katharine's Rectory, 24 Lansdowne Road, Belfast BT15 4DB* Tel (01232) 777647

TAGUE, Russell. b 59. Aston Tr Scheme 90 Linc Th Coll 92. **d** 94 **p** 95. C Astley *Man* from 94. *42 Manor Road, Astley, Tyldesley, Manchester M29 7HT* Tel (01942) 878622

TAILBY, Mark Kevan. b 36. K Coll Lon 60. **d** 64 **p** 65. C Newbold on Avon *Cov* 64-67; C Stratford-on-Avon w Bishopton 67-70; CF 70-76; P-in-c S Shoebury *Chelmsf* 76-79; P-in-c Stambridge 79-89; Chapl Rochford Gen Hosp 79-89; TV Dovercourt and Parkeston *Chelmsf* 89-93; P-in-c Colchester St Botolph w H Trin and St Giles from 93; OCF from 93. *St Botolph's Vicarage, 50B Priory Street, Colchester CO1 2QB* Tel (01206) 868043

TAILBY, Peter Alan. b 49. Chich Th Coll 83. **d** 85 **p** 86. C Stocking Farm *Leic* 85-88; C Knighton St Mary Magd 88-90; P-in-c Thurnby Lodge from 90. *Christ Church Vicarage, 73 Nursery Road, Leicester LE5 2HQ* Tel 0116-241 3848

TAIT, James Laurence Jamieson. b 47. St Jo Coll Dur 78. **d** 80 **p** 81. C Heyside *Man* 80-81; C Westhoughton 81-84; R Aldingham and Dendron and Rampside *Carl* 84-88; V Flookburgh 88-92; New Zealand from 92. *St Peter's Vicarage, 229 Ruahine Street, Palmerston North, New Zealand* Tel Levin (6) 358 5403 or 358 9134 Fax 358 5403 E-mail stpeters@icon.nz

TAIT, Philip Leslie. b 52. Ex Univ BA73 Hull Univ PGCE74. NE Ord Course 87. **d** 90 **p** 91. NSM Osbaldwick w Murton *York* 90-92; Chapl Burnholme Sch York 90-92; Chapl and Hd Relig Studies Berkhamsted Sch Herts from 93. *The Chaplaincy, Mill Street, Berkhamsted, Herts HP4 2BA* Tel (01442) 878190

TAIT, Ruth Elizabeth. b 39. Moray Ord Course 88. **dss** 90 **d** 94 **p** 95. Elgin w Lossiemouth *Mor* 90-94; C 94-96; Min Dufftown *Ab* from 96. *30 Mayne Road, Elgin, Morayshire IV30 1PB* Tel (01343) 542919

TAIT, Thomas William. b 07. St Cath Soc Ox BA30 MA33. Clifton Th Coll 40 Edin Th Coll 42. **d** 43 **p** 44. C Elgin H Trin *Mor* 43-44; C Bordesley H Trin *Birm* 44-46; C Selly Oak St Mary 46-49; C Kingsbury 49-50; V Quarnford *Lich* 50-53; R Hevingham *Nor* 53-56; R Brampton 53-56; V Bordesley H Trin *Birm* 56-59; R Fitz *Lich* 59-64; R Church Lawton *Ches* 64-67; rtd 72. *43 Hanover Gardens, Cuckoofield Lane, Mulbarton, Norwich NR14 8DA* Tel (01508) 70598

TALBOT, Alan John. b 23. BNC Ox BA49 MA55. Coll of Resurr Mirfield 49. **d** 51 **p** 52. C Hackney Wick St Mary of Eton w St Aug *Lon* 51-54; C Portsea St Sav *Portsm* 54-63; Tanganyika 63-64; Tanzania 64-68; V Stepney St Aug w St Phil *Lon* 69-78; V Twickenham All Hallows 78-86; rtd 88; Perm to Offic *S'wark* from 88. *46 Brandon Street, London SE17 1NL* Tel 0171-703 0719

TALBOT, Derek Michael (Mike). b 55. St Jo Coll Dur BSc77 Nottm Univ DipTh85. St Jo Coll Nottm 84. **d** 87 **p** 88. C Rushden w Newton Bromswold *Pet* 87-90; C Barton Seagrave w Warkton 90-95; V Kettering Ch the King from 96. *The Vicarage, Deeble Road, Kettering, Northants NN15 7AA* Tel (01536) 512828 E-mail mtalbot@enterprise.net

TALBOT, George Brian. b 37. Qu Coll Birm 78. **d** 80 **p** 81. C Heref St Martin *Heref* 80-83; R Bishop's Frome w Castle Frome and Fromes Hill 83-90; P-in-c Acton Beauchamp and Evesbatch w Stanford Bishop 83-90; R Burstow *S'wark* from 90. *The Rectory, Church Road, Burstow, Horley, Surrey RH6 9RG* Tel (01342) 842224

TALBOT, John Frederick Gordon. b 12. Chich Th Coll 47. **d** 50 **p** 51. C Wolverhampton Ch Ch *Lich* 50-57; R Wednesbury St Jo 57-73; R W Felton 73-87; rtd 87. *8 Rose Hill Close, Whittington, Shropshire SY11 4DY* Tel (01691) 657962

TALBOT, John Herbert Boyle. b 30. TCD BA51 MA57. CITC 52. **d** 53 **p** 54. C Dublin St Pet *D & G* 53-57; Chan Vicar St Patrick's Cathl Dub 56-61; C Dublin Zion Ch 57-61; Chapl Asst St Thos Hosp Lon 61-64; Min Can and Sacr Cant Cathl *Cant* 64-67; R Brasted *Roch* 67-84; R Ightham 84-95; P-in-c Shipbourne 87-91; RD Shoreham 89-95; rtd 95. *12 Waterlakes, Edenbridge, Kent TN8 5BY* Tel (01732) 865729

TALBOT, Dr John Michael. b 23. FRSM FRCPath68 Lon Univ MD52. S'wark Ord Course 75. **d** 78 **p** 79. NSM S Croydon Em *Cant* 78-81; Perm to Offic *Nor* 82-85 and from 96; NSM Hethersett w Canteloff w Lt and Gt Melton 85-96. *3 White Gates Close, Hethersett, Norwich NR9 3JG* Tel (01603) 811709

TALBOT, Mrs June Phyllis. b 46. Ripon Coll of Educn CertEd67. NE Ord Course 88. **d** 91 **p** 94. NSM Cleadon *Dur* from 91. *66 Wheatall Drive, Whitburn, Sunderland SR6 7HQ* Tel 0191-529 2265

TALBOT (née KINGHAM), Mrs Mair Josephine. b 59. Univ Coll Lon BA84. Ridley Hall Cam 85. **d** 88 **p** 94. C Gt Yarmouth *Nor* 88-94; Sen Asst P The Raveningham Gp from 94; Chapl Norfolk Mental Health Care NHS Trust from 94. *The Rectory, Church Road, Thurlton, Norwich NR14 6RN* Tel (01508) 548648

TALBOT, Mrs Marian. b 25. Qu Coll Birm 76. **dss** 78 **d** 87 **p** 94. Droitwich *Worc* 78-87; Chapl Droitwich Hosps 83-88; Par Dn Droitwich Spa 87-88; Perm to Offic from 88; Asst Chapl Alexandra Hosp Redditch from 88. *Talbot House, Foredraught Lane, Tibberton, Droitwich, Worcs WR9 7NH* Tel (01905) 345404

TALBOT, The Very Revd Maurice John. b 12. TCD BA35 MA43. **d** 35 **p** 36. C Rathkeale w Nantenan *L & K* 35-43; I 43-52; I Killarney 52-54; Dean Limerick 54-71; Preb St Patr Cathl Dublin 59-73; C Kilmallock *L & K* 71-73; Lic to Offic 75-80; I Drumcliffe 80-84; Bp's C Banagher *M & K* 85-86; rtd 86. *Woodbrook, Lower Main Street, Abbeyleix, Co Laois, Irish Republic* Tel Abbeyleix (502) 31721

TALBOT, Stephen Richard. b 52. BSc. Trin Coll Bris DipHE. **d** 84 **p** 85. C Tonbridge SS Pet and Paul *Roch* 84-89; P-in-c Hemingford Grey *Ely* from 89; P-in-c Hemingford Abbots 89-96. *The Vicarage, Braggs Lane, Hemingford Grey, Huntingdon, Cambs PE18 9BW* Tel (01480) 467305

TALBOT, Ms Susan Gabriel. b 46. Leeds Univ BA69 Man Poly CertEd70 Lon Univ DipTh72. N Ord Course 91. **d** 94 **p** 95. C Wythenshawe St Martin *Man* from 94. *45 Amberwood Drive, Baguley, Manchester M23 9NZ* Tel 0161-998 3220

TALBOT-PONSONBY, Preb Andrew. b 44. Leeds Univ DipTh66. Coll of Resurr Mirfield 66. **d** 68 **p** 70. C Radlett *St Alb* 68-70; C Salisbury St Martin *Sarum* 70-73; P-in-c Acton Burnell w Pitchford *Heref* 73-80; P-in-c Frodesley 73-80; P-in-c Cound 73-80; Asst Youth Officer 73-80; P-in-c Bockleton w Leysters 80-81; V 81-92; P-in-c Kimbolton w Middleton-on-the-Hill 80-81; V Kimbolton w Hamnish and Middleton-on-the-Hill 81-92; P-in-c Wigmore Abbey 92-96; R Wigmore Abbey from 97;

Preb Heref Cathl from 87; RD Leominster from 97. *The Rectory, Watling Street, Leintwardine, Craven Arms, Shropshire SY7 0LL* Tel (01547) 540235

TALBOT-PONSONBY, Mrs Gillian (Jill). b 50. Sarum & Wells Th Coll 89. **d** 91 **p** 94. C Leominster *Heref* 91-92; NSM Wigmore Abbey from 92. *The Rectory, Watling Street, Leintwardine, Craven Arms, Shropshire SY7 0LL* Tel (01547) 540235

TALBOTT, Brian Hugh. b 34. RD78. St Pet Hall Ox BA57 MA64. Westcott Ho Cam. **d** 59 **p** 60. C Newc H Cross *Newc* 59-61; C Newc St Jo 61-64; Chapl RNR 63-77; Sen Chapl RNR 77-96; Chapl Barnard Castle Sch 64-71; Chapl Bishop's Stortford Coll 71-96; Hon C Bishop's Stortford St Mich *St Alb* 71-96; rtd 96; Perm to Offic *B & W* from 96. *2 The Croft, Wookey Hole, Wells, Somerset BA5 1BA* Tel (01749) 679678

TALBOTT, Simon John. b 57. Pontifical Univ Maynooth BD81. **d** 81 **p** 82. In RC Ch 81-87; C Headingley *Ripon* 88-91; V Gt and Lt Ouseburn w Marton-cum-Grafton 91-97; Chapl Qu Ethelburga's Coll York 91-97; V Markington w S Stainley and Bishop Thornton *Ripon* from 97; RD Ripon from 97. *The Vicarage, Westerns Lane, Markington, Harrogate, N Yorkshire HG3 3PB* Tel (01765) 677123 Fax 677623

TALENT, Canon Jack. b 23. AKC49. **d** 50 **p** 51. C Grantham St Wulfram *Linc* 50-59; R Corsley *Sarum* 59-62; S Africa from 62; Hon Can Kimberley and Kuruman from 81. *27 Armenia Crescent, Plattekloof Glen, Monta Vista, 7460 South Africa* Tel Cape Town (21) 559-1431

TALLANT, John. b 45. Edin Th Coll 86. **d** 88 **p** 89. C Cayton w Eastfield *York* 88-90; C N Hull St Mich 90-91; V Scarborough St Sav w All SS 91-93; V Fleetwood St Nic *Blackb* from 93. *St Nicholas's Vicarage, Highbury Avenue, Fleetwood, Lancs FY7 7DJ* Tel (01253) 874402

TAMBLING, Peter Francis. b 20. St Pet Hall Ox BA47. Westcott Ho Cam. **d** 49 **p** 50. C Stockport St Mary *Ches* 49-51; C Westbury *Sarum* 52-56; R Bishopstrow and Boreham 56-64; R Zeals and Stourton 64-73; P-in-c Bourton w Silton 71-73; R Upper Stour 73-74; R Glenfield *Leic* 74-85; RD Sparkenhoe III 76-81; rtd 85; Perm to Offic *B & W* 86-94. *20 Balsam Fields, Wincanton, Somerset BA9 9HF* Tel (01963) 34237

TAMPLIN, Peter Harry. b 44. Sarum & Wells Th Coll 71. **d** 73 **p** 74. C Digswell *St Alb* 73-76; C Chesterton St Luke *Ely* 76-82; V Chesterton St Geo 82-95; R Durrington *Sarum* from 95. *The Rectory, Church Street, Durrington, Salisbury SP4 8AL* Tel (01980) 652229

TAMS, Gordon Thomas Carl. b 37. LLCM76 Leeds Univ BMus60 Reading Univ CertEd61 Newc Univ MLitt84. Edin Dioc NSM Course 83. **d** 90 **p** 91. NSM Kelso *Edin* 90-92; P-in-c Coldstream from 92. *St Mary's Parsonage, 47 Lennel Mount, Coldstream, Berwickshire TD12 4NS* Tel (01890) 882479

TAMS, Paul William. b 56. Huddersfield Poly CertEd77. EAMTC 87. **d** 90 **p** 91. NSM Mildenhall *St E* from 90. *28 Raven Close, Mildenhall, Bury St Edmunds, Suffolk IP28 7LF* Tel (01638) 715475

TANBURN, John Walter. b 30. Jes Coll Cam BA53 MA57. Clifton Th Coll 54. **d** 56 **p** 57. C Orpington Ch Ch *Roch* 56-59; C-in-c St Paul's Cray St Barn CD 59-64; V St Paul's Cray St Barn 64-67; Chapl Stowe Sch Bucks 67-72; R Morley *Nor* 72-82; Chapl Wymondham Coll 72-82; rtd 95. *3 Town Road, Petham, Canterbury, Kent CT4 5QT*

TANKARD, Reginald Douglas Alan. b 37. Sarum Th Coll 60. **d** 62 **p** 63. C Howden *York* 62-65; C Heckmondwike *Wakef* 65-67; CF 67-70; C Thornbury *Bradf* 82-88; P-in-c Rockcliffe and Blackford *Carl* 88-90; V from 90. *The Vicarage, Rockcliffe, Carlisle CA6 4AA* Tel (01228) 74209

TANN, Canon David John. b 31. K Coll Lon BD57 AKC57. **d** 58 **p** 59. C Wandsworth St Anne *S'wark* 58-60; C Sholing *Win* 60-64; Asst Chapl Lon Univ *Lon* 64-65; C Fulham All SS 65-68; Hon C 72-82; Lic to Offic 68-72; Teacher Godolphin and Latymer Sch Hammersmith 68-73; Ealing Boys Gr Sch 69-73; Hd of RE Green Sch Isleworth 73-82; V Dudley St Jas *Worc* 82-95; Chapl Burton Rd Hosp Dudley 83-95; Hon Can Worc Cathl *Worc* 90-95; RD Dudley 93-95; rtd 95. *75 Parkview Court, Fulham High Street, London SW6 3LL* Tel 0171-736 6018

TANNER, Preb Alan John. b 25. OBE97. Linc Coll Ox BA52 MA65. Coll of Resurr Mirfield 52. **d** 54 **p** 55. C Hendon St Mary *Lon* 54-58; V S Harrow St Paul 58-60; Dir Coun for Chr Stewardship 60-65; Dir Lay Tr 65-71; Sec Coun for Miss and Unity 65-80; V St Nic Cole Abbey 66-78; Preacher of the Charterhouse from 73; Sec Gtr Lon Chs' Coun 76-83; P-in-c St Ethelburga Bishopgate *Lon* 78-85; R St Botolph without Bishopgate 78-97; P-in-c All Hallows Lon Wall 80-97; Bp's Ecum Officer from 81; AD The City 90-97; Preb St Paul's Cathl 91-97; rtd 97. *9 Sunningfields Road, London NW4 4QR* Tel 0171-588 3388 or 588 1053 Fax 638 1256

TANNER, Canon Frank Hubert. b 38. St Aid Birkenhead. **d** 66 **p** 67. C Ipswich St Marg *St E* 66-69; C Mansfield St Pet *S'well* 69-72; V Huthwaite 72-79; Chapl to the Deaf 79-92; Hon Can S'well Minster from 90; Chapl Northn and Rutland Miss to the Deaf from 92. *11 The Avenue, Spinney Hill, Northampton NN3 1BA* Tel (01604) 494366 or 250303

TANNER, Frederick James. b 24. **d** 64 **p** 65. Uganda 64-69; Hd Master Summerhill Jun Mixed Sch Bris from 69; Perm to Offic *Bris* 69-94; Hon C Chew Magna w Dundry *B & W* 81-86; Perm to Offic 86-94. *The Byre, Eastfields, Charlton, Horethorne, Sherborne, Dorset DT9 4PB* Tel (01963) 220641

TANNER, Canon Laurence Ernest. b 17. St Cath Coll Cam BA39 MA43. St Mich Coll Llan. **d** 40 **p** 41. C Pentyrch *Llan* 40-42; Chapl Cranleigh Sch Surrey 42-64; Lic to Offic *Guildf* 42-64; V Shamley Green 64-71; RD Cranleigh 68-71; Can Res Guildf Cathl 71-82; Sub-Dean 72-82; Dir of Ords 71-82; rtd 82; Perm to Offic *St E* from 82. *Homestead Cottage, South Green, Southwold, Suffolk IP18 6EU* Tel (01502) 722602

TANNER, Mark Stuart. b 59. Nottm Univ BA81. Sarum & Wells Th Coll. **d** 85 **p** 86. C Radcliffe-on-Trent *S'well* 85; C Radcliffe-on-Trent and Shelford etc 85-88; C Bestwood 88-89; TV 89-93; P-in-c S'well H Trin from 93; Bp's Research Officer 93-97. *Holy Trinity Vicarage, Westhorpe, Southwell, Notts NG25 0NB* Tel (01636) 813243

TANNER, Martin Philip. b 54. Univ Coll Lon BSc(Econ)75. Ridley Hall Cam 79. **d** 82 **p** 83. C Bitterne *Win* 82-85; C Weeke 85-88; V Long Buckby w Watford *Pet* 88-96; P-in-c Desborough from 96. *St Giles's Vicarage, Lower Street, Desborough, Kettering, Northants NN14 2NP* Tel (01536) 760324 Fax 760854

TANSILL, Canon Derek Ernest Edward. b 36. Univ of Wales (Lamp) BA61. Ripon Hall Ox 61. **d** 63 **p** 64. C Chelsea St Luke *Lon* 63-67; C-in-c Saltdean CD *Chich* 67-69; V Saltdean 69-73; V Billingshurst 73-82; RD Horsham 77-82 and 85-93; Can and Preb Chich Cathl from 81; R Bexhill St Pet 82-85; RD Battle and Bexhill 84-86; V Horsham 85-86; TR from 86. *The Vicarage, The Causeway, Horsham, W Sussex RH12 1HE* Tel (01403) 272919 or 253762

TAPLIN, John. b 35. St Alb Minl Tr Scheme 78. **d** 81 **p** 82. NSM Knebworth *St Alb* 81-88; C Braughing, Lt Hadham, Albury, Furneux Pelham etc 88; R Lt Hadham w Albury from 88. *The Vicarage, Parsonage Lane, Albury, Ware, Herts SG11 2HU* Tel (01279) 771361

TAPLIN, Kim. b 58. Lon Bible Coll BA79 Homerton Coll Cam PGCE84. S Dios Minl Tr Scheme 94. **d** 94 **p** 95. C Sholing *Win* from 94. *St Francis House, 75 Montague Avenue, Southampton SO19 0QB* Tel (01703) 443733

TAPPER, John A'Court. b 42. FCA64. Sarum & Wells Th Coll 89. **d** 91 **p** 92. C Ashford *Cant* 91-94; P-in-c Folkestone H Trin w Ch Ch 94-96; R from 96. *Holy Trinity Vicarage, 21 Manor Road, Folkestone, Kent CT20 2SA* Tel (01303) 253831

TARGETT, Kenneth. b 28. Qu Coll Birm 54. **d** 57 **p** 58. C Mansfield Woodhouse *S'well* 57-59; C Skipton Ch Ch *Bradf* 59-62; V Bradf St Jo 62-65; Perm to Offic 65-82; Australia 82-87; V Old Leake w Wrangle *Linc* 87-94; rtd 94. *The Sloop, Sea Lane, Old Leake, Boston, Lincs PE22 9JA*

TARLETON, Denis Reginald. b 12. TCD BA35 MA45. CITC 36. **d** 36 **p** 37. C Limerick St Mary *L & K* 36-38; C Egremont St Jo *Ches* 38-40; CF (EC) 40-46; CF (R of O) 50-61; I Kilcornan *L & K* 46-49; I Ardcanny 46-49; I Tullyaughnish w Milford *D & R* 49-51; I Dromore *D & D* 51-59; I Devenish w Boho *Clogh* 59-63; rtd 63; Perm to Offic *D & D* from 67. *33 Drumkeen Court, Belfast BT8 4TU* Tel (01232) 691003

TARLETON, Peter. b 46. TCD BA72 Div Test73 HDipEd77 MA80. **d** 73 **p** 74. C Cork St Luke w St Ann *C, C & R* 73-75; C Dublin Drumcondra *D & G* 75-78; I Limerick City *L & K* 78-82; I Drumgoon w Dernakesh, Ashfield etc *K, E & A* 82-85; Chapl HM Young Offender Inst Hindley 85-89; Chapl HM Pris Lindholme from 89. *HM Prison, Bawtry Road, Hatfield Woodhouse, Doncaster, S Yorkshire DN7 6EE* Tel (01302) 846600 Fax 843352

TARLING, Paul. b 53. Oak Hill Th Coll BA. **d** 85 **p** 86. C Old Hill H Trin *Worc* 85-89; V Walford w Bishopswood *Heref* 89-90; P-in-c Goodrich w Welsh Bicknor and Marstow 89-90; R Walford and St John w Bishopswood, Goodrich etc 90-96; RD Ross and Archenfield 95-96; P-in-c Kington w Huntington, Old Radnor, Kinnerton etc from 96. *The Vicarage, Kington, Herefordshire HR5 3AG* Tel (01544) 230525

TARPER, Ms Ann Jennifer. b 47. SRN71 Nottm Univ BCombStuds82. Linc Th Coll 79. **dss** 83 **d** 87 **p** 96. Stamford All SS w St Jo *Linc* 82-85; Witham *Chelmsf* 85-90; Par Dn 87-90; Min and Educn Adv to Newmarch Gp Min *Heref* 90-93; Perm to Offic 93-95; Dep Chapl HM Pris Dur 95-97; Chapl HM Pris Foston Hall from 97. *The Chaplaincy, HM Prison Foston Hall, Foston, Derby DE65 5DN* Tel (01283) 585802 Fax 585012

TARR, James Robert. b 39. Bps' Coll Cheshunt 64. **d** 67 **p** 68. C Wortley de Leeds *Ripon* 67-69; C Hunslet St Mary and Stourton St Andr 70-73; V Moorends *Sheff* 73-77; V Cross Stone *Wakef* 77-83; V Chilworth w N Baddesley *Win* 83-90; V Andover St Mich 90-93; V W Andover from 93. *St Michael's Vicarage, 13 The Avenue, Andover, Hants SP10 3EW* Tel (01264) 352553

TARRANT, Ian Denis. b 57. Cam Univ BA MA Nottm Univ DipTh. St Jo Coll Nottm 81. **d** 84 **p** 85. CMS from 79; C Ealing St Mary *Lon* 84-87; Republic of Congo from 88. *CAZ Arua, PO Box 21285, Nairobi, Kenya*

TARRANT, John Michael. b 38. St Jo Coll Cam BA59 MA63 Ball Coll Ox BA62 MA76. Ripon Hall Ox 60. **d** 62 **p** 63. C Chelsea All SS *Lon* 62-65; Chapl and Lect St Pet Coll Saltley 66-70; Br Honduras 70-73; Belize 73-74; V Forest Row *Chich* 75-87; Perm to Offic *Heref* from 93. *The Vicarage, Bridstow, Ross-on-Wye, Herefordshire HR9 6QE* Tel (01989) 65805

TARRANT, Paul John. b 57. Chich Th Coll. **d** 82 **p** 83. C Southgate Ch Ch *Lon* 82-85; C Hornsey St Mary w St Geo 85-90; USA 90-96; R Edin Old St Paul *Edin* 96-97. *Harbour View Cottage, Burnmouth, Eyemouth, Berwickshire TD14 5ST* Tel (01890) 781759

TARRIS, Canon Geoffrey John. b 27. Em Coll Cam BA50 MA55. Westcott Ho Cam 51. **d** 53 **p** 54. C Abbots Langley *St Alb* 53-55; Prec St E Cathl *St E* 55-59; V Bungay H Trin w St Mary 59-72; RD S Elmham 65-72; V Ipswich St Mary le Tower 72-78; Hon Can St E Cathl 74-82; V Ipswich St Mary le Tower w St Lawr and St Steph 78-82; Can Res St E Cathl 82-93; Dioc Dir of Lay Min and Warden of Readers 82-87; Dioc Dir of Ords 87-93; rtd 93; Perm to Offic *Nor* from 93. *53 The Close, Norwich NR1 4EG* Tel (01603) 622136

TARRY, Gordon Malcolm. b 54. Leeds Univ BSc75. Lon Bible Coll BA83 Ridley Hall Cam. **d** 85 **p** 86. C Gt Ilford St Andr *Chelmsf* 85-89; C Rainham 89-92; C Rainham w Wennington 92-93; V Gt Ilford St Jo from 93. *St John's Vicarage, 2 Regent Gardens, Ilford, Essex IG3 8UL* Tel 0181-590 5884

TASH, Stephen Ronald. b 56. Warw Univ BEd79. WMMTC 88. **d** 91 **p** 92. C Studley *Cov* 91-95; P-in-c Salford Priors from 95. *The Vicarage, Salford Priors, Evesham, Worcs WR11 5UX* Tel (01789) 772445

TASKER, Harry Beverley. b 41. BA76. Wycliffe Hall Ox 64. **d** 67 **p** 68. C Withington St Paul *Man* 67-71; C Bingley All SS *Bradf* 71-72; Chapl RAF 72-76; R Publow w Pensford, Compton Dando and Chelwood *B & W* 76-84; V Long Ashton from 84; RD Portishead 86-91. *The Vicarage, 7 Church Lane, Long Ashton, Bristol BS18 9LU* Tel 0117-939 3109

TASSELL, Douglas Rene. b 15. St Edm Hall Ox BA37 MA52. Wycliffe Hall Ox 37. **d** 39 **p** 40. C Kidderminster St Geo *Worc* 39-46; Chapl RAFVR 42-46; C Wilmslow *Ches* 46-49; PC Nether Peover 49-59; R Lexden *Chelmsf* 59-65; Asst RD Colchester 65; R Tattenhall *Ches* 65-69; R Delamere 69-74; RD Middlewich 69-74; P-in-c Welland *Worc* 75-79; Chapl St Jas Sch Malvern 77-81; rtd 80; Lic to Offic *Worc* 80-85. *12 Gardens Walk, Upton-upon-Severn, Worcester WR8 0LL* Tel (01684) 592205

TASSELL, Canon Dudley Arnold. b 16. K Coll Lon BD49 AKC49. **d** 49 **p** 50. C New Eltham All SS *S'wark* 49-55; V Catford St Andr 55-63; R Rotherhithe St Mary w All SS 63-77; RD Bermondsey 69-76; Hon Can S'wark Cathl 72-76; V Spring Park *Cant* 76-84; RD Croydon Addington 81-84; V Spring Park All SS *S'wark* 85-86; rtd 86; Perm to Offic *Guildf* from 86. *72 Sandy Lane, Woking, Surrey GU22 8BH* Tel (01483) 766154

TATE, Harold Richard. b 24. St Jo Coll Dur BA50. **d** 51 **p** 52. C Moss Side St Jas *Man* 51-54; C-in-c Langley St Aid CD 54-60; R Blackley St Pet 60-79; V Alsager Ch Ch *Ches* 79-89; rtd 89; Perm to Offic *Bradf* from 89. *57 Neville Road, Gargrave, Skipton, N Yorkshire BD23 3RE* Tel (01756) 748315

TATE, Henry Charles Osmond. b 13. K Coll Lon 64. **d** 65 **p** 66. C Boscombe St Andr *Win* 65-68; R Winfrith Newburgh w Chaldon Herring *Sarum* 68-78; V Chardstock *Ex* 78-82; rtd 82. *Manormead Residential Home, Tilford Road, Hindhead, Surrey GU26 6RA* Tel (01428) 604780

TATE, James (Jim). b 56. DipAD80. Oak Hill Th Coll DipHE95. **d** 95 **p** 96. C Hammersmith St Simon *Lon* from 95. *4 Mackenzie Trench House, 363 Lillie Road, London SW6 7PA* Tel 0171-381 9241

TATE, John Robert. b 38. Dur Univ BA61 MA71. Cranmer Hall Dur DipTh69. **d** 70 **p** 71. C Bare *Blackb* 70-73; V Over Darwen St Jas 73-81; V Caton w Littledale from 81. *The Vicarage, 153 Brookhouse Road, Brookhouse, Lancaster LA2 9NX* Tel (01524) 770300

TATE, Robert John Ward. b 24. St Jo Coll Morpeth ThL48. **d** 49 **p** 50. Australia from 49; Chapl RN 53-79; QHC 76-79; rtd 79. *58 Skye Point Road, Carey Bay, NSW, Australia 2283* Tel Maitland (49) 592921

TATHAM, Dr Andrew Francis. b 49. MSUC73 MSBC73 MICA86 Grey Coll Dur BA71 Southlands Coll Lon DAM80 K Coll Lon PhD84. S'wark Ord Course DipRS92. **d** 92 **p** 93. Hon C Headley w Box Hill *Guildf* from 92. *27 Newton Wood Road, Ashtead, Surrey KT21 1NN* Tel (01372) 274484

TATNALL, Alec James. b 09. Codrington Coll Barbados 51. **d** 52 **p** 53. Guyana 52-67; Belize 69-75; C Hale *Guildf* 75-79; rtd 79; Perm to Offic *Ex* 79-90; Chapl Livery Dole Almshouses 79-89. *15 Ashdown Close, Ashdown Road, Reigate, Surrey RH2 7QS* Tel (01737) 224964

TATTERSALL, Canon George Neville. b 10. Em Coll Cam BA32 MA36. Ridley Hall Cam 32. **d** 33 **p** 34. C Kersal Moor *Man* 33-37; C Flixton St Mich 37-39; R Cheetham St Mark 39-42; R Bucklesham w Brightwell and Foxhall *St E* 42-50; Dioc Youth Officer 42-50; V Batley All SS *Wakef* 50-85; Hon Can Wakef Cathl 68-85; rtd 85; Perm to Offic *Wakef* 85-86; Perm to Offic *Ely* from 86. *22 Beach Road, Grafham, Huntingdon, Cambs PE18 0BA* Tel (01480) 811013

TATTERSALL, James. b 31. Sheff Univ BSc53 DipEd54. Linc Th Coll 81. **d** 82 **p** 83. C Boston *Linc* 82-84; C Tyldesley w Shakerley *Man* 84-85; TV Sutton *Liv* 89-94; rtd 94; Perm to Offic *Blackb* from 94. *111 Croston Road, Garstang, Preston PR3 1HQ* Tel (01995) 600083

TATTON-BROWN, Simon Charles. b 48. Qu Coll Cam BA70 MA78 Man Univ CQSW72. Coll of Resurr Mirfield 78. **d** 79 **p** 80. C Ashton St Mich *Man* 79-82; P-in-c Prestwich St Gabr 82-87; V 87-88; Bp's Dom Chapl 82-88; TR Westhoughton 88-96; TR Westhoughton and Wingates from 97. *St Bartholomew's Rectory, Market Street, Westhoughton, Bolton BL5 3AZ* Tel (01942) 813280

TATTUM, Ian Stuart. b 58. N Lon Poly BA79 Lanc Univ DipRS86 Fitzw Coll Cam BA89. Westcott Ho Cam 87. **d** 90 **p** 91. C Beaconsfield *Ox* 90-94; C Bushey *St Alb* 94-96; P-in-c Pirton from 96. *The Vicarage, Crabtree Lane, Pirton, Hitchin, Herts SG5 3QE* Tel (01462) 712230

TAUNTON, Archdeacon of. *See* FRITH, The Ven Richard Michael Cokayne

TAUNTON, Suffragan Bishop of. *See* STEWART, The Rt Revd William Allen

TAVERNOR, James Edward. b 23. Lich Th Coll 41 St D Coll Lamp BA49. **d** 50 **p** 51. C Monmouth *Mon* 50-52; C Prestbury *Glouc* 52-53; C Newbold w Dunston *Derby* 53-55; C Buxton 67-69; Perm to Offic 70-75; Perm to Offic *Heref* 75-83; Perm to Offic *St D* 83-91; rtd 88. *12 Beech Close, Ludlow, Shropshire SY8 2PD* Tel (01584) 876502

TAVERNOR, William Noel. b 16. Lich Th Coll 37. **d** 40 **p** 41. C Ledbury *Heref* 40-43; C Kidderminster St Mary *Worc* 43-46; V Bettws-y-Crwyn w Newcastle *Heref* 46-50; V Upton Bishop 50-57; V Aymestrey and Leinthall Earles 57-65; P-in-c Shobdon 58-65; V Canon Pyon w Kings Pyon and Birley 65-88; rtd 88. *Vine Cottage, Kingsland, Leominster, Herefordshire HR6 9QS* Tel (01568) 708817

TAVINOR, Michael Edward. b 53. ARCO77 Univ Coll Dur BA75 Em Coll Cam CertEd76 K Coll Lon MMus77 AKC77 Ox Univ BA81 MA86. Ripon Coll Cuddesdon 79. **d** 82 **p** 83. C Ealing St Pet Mt Park *Lon* 82-85; Prec Ely Cathl *Ely* 85-90; Min Can and Sacr 85-90; P-in-c Stuntney 87-90; V Tewkesbury w Walton Cardiff *Glouc* from 90. *The Abbey House, Abbey Precinct, Tewkesbury, Glos GL20 5SR* Tel (01684) 293333

TAWN, Andrew. b 61. Trin Coll Cam BA83 Ox Univ BA88. Ripon Coll Cuddesdon 86. **d** 89 **p** 90. C Dovecot *Liv* 89-93; TV Dorchester *Ox* from 93; Student Supervisor Cuddesdon Coll from 93. *The Vicarage, Cherwell Road, Berinsfield, Oxford OX10 7PB* Tel (01865) 340460

TAYLOR, Alan Cecil. b 34. Keble Coll Ox BA57 MA63. Cuddesdon Coll 58. **d** 60 **p** 61. C Blackpool St Steph *Blackb* 60-63; C Chorley St Laur 63-65; V Burnley St Mark from 65. *St Mark's Vicarage, 9 Rossendale Road, Burnley, Lancs BB11 5DQ* Tel (01282) 428178

TAYLOR, Alan Clive. b 48. Southn Univ BTh79. Sarum Th Coll 69. **d** 74 **p** 75. C Watford St Pet *St Alb* 74-78; C Broxbourne w Wormley 78-83; Chapl to the Deaf 83-91; V Shefford 83-91; R Portishead *B & W* from 91. *The Rectory, Church Road South, Portishead, Bristol BS20 9PU* Tel (01275) 842284

TAYLOR, Alan Gerald. b 33. Roch Th Coll 61 St Aid Birkenhead 61. **d** 63 **p** 64. C W Bridgford *S'well* 63-66; C E w W Barkwith *Linc* 66-69; V E Stockwith 69-76; V Morton 69-76; Countryside Officer 69-88; R Ulceby w Fordington 76-88; R Willoughby w Sloothby w Claxby 76-88; R Woolpit w Drinkstone *St E* from 88; Rural Min Adv from 88. *The Rectory, Woolpit, Bury St Edmunds, Suffolk IP30 9QP* Tel (01359) 42244

TAYLOR, Alan Leonard. b 43. Chich Th Coll 67. **d** 69 **p** 70. C Walton St Mary *Liv* 69-73; C Toxteth St Marg 73-75; V Stanley 75-83; V Leeds St Aid *Ripon* from 84. *The Vicarage, Elford Place West, Leeds LS8 5QD* Tel 0113-248 6992

TAYLOR, Alfred Harry Bryant. b 17. St Deiniol's Hawarden 77. **d** 79 **p** 80. Hon C Woodchurch *Ches* 79-85; C 85-87; Hon C 87-92; Perm to Offic from 92. *111 New Hey Road, Birkenhead, Merseyside L49 7NE* Tel 0151-677 4933

TAYLOR, Andrew David. b 58. Ox Univ BA81 MA86 Toronto Univ MDiv92 K Coll Lon MTh95. Westcott Ho Cam 85. **d** 87 **p** 89. C Leckhampton SS Phil and Jas w Cheltenham St Jas *Glouc* 87-91; P-in-c Swindon w Uckington and Elmstone Hardwicke 92-93; C Highgate St Mich *Lon* 94-97; Chapl R Holloway and Bedf New Coll *Guildf* from 97. *10 Willow Walk, Egham, Surrey TW20 0DQ* Tel (01784) 432025 E-mail hatnat@aol.com

TAYLOR, Ms Anne Elizabeth. b 68. Ulster Univ BSc91. CITC BTh94. **d** 94 **p** 95. C Dublin Rathfarnham *D & G* from 94. *Rathfarnham Rectory, Rathfarnham Road, Terenure, Dublin 6W, Irish Republic* Tel Dublin (1) 490 5543 Fax as telephone

TAYLOR, Arthur Alfred. b 32. MA. Ox NSM Course. **d** 83 **p** 84. NSM Monks Risborough *Ox* from 83. *9 Place Farm Way, Monks Risborough, Princes Risborough, Bucks HP27 9JJ* Tel (01844) 347197

TAYLOR, Arthur John. b 17. Lon Univ BD39 BA52. ALCD39. **d** 40 **p** 41. C Walthamstow St Andr *Chelmsf* 40-42; C Hitchin H Sav *St Alb* 44-45; Asst Chapl Felsted Sch Essex 45-46; Asst Master K Sch Ely 56-80; Perm to Offic *Ely* 56-85; rtd 80; Perm to Offic *Mon* from 86. *44 Homeforge House, Goldwire Lane, Monmouth NP5 3HA* Tel (01600) 716269

TAYLOR, Arthur Robert. b 26. ACIS59. Oak Hill Th Coll 67. **d** 68 **p** 69. C Wilmington *Roch* 68-71; C Polegate *Chich* 71-73; R

Chesterton w Haddon *Ely* 73-80; P-in-c Alwalton 73-75; R 75-80; R Sawtry 80-91; rtd 91. *10 Faraday Ride, Tonbridge, Kent TN10 4RL* Tel (01732) 358694

TAYLOR, Bernard Richmond Hartley. b 30. Reading Univ MEd. S Dios Minl Tr Scheme 82. **d** 85 **p** 86. NSM Englefield Green *Guildf* 85-90; NSM Lyddington w Stoke Dry and Seaton *Pet* 90-95; rtd 95. *Middleton House, 40 Bond Street, Egham, Surrey TW20 0PY* Tel (01784) 435886

TAYLOR, Brian. b 38. MBIM Bris Univ BA60 Liv Univ BA70 Southn Univ MA90. Ridley Hall Cam 60. **d** 66 **p** 66. Nigeria 66-72; Perm to Offic *Derby* 74-78; Chapl Newbury Coll 76-94; P-in-c Shaw cum Donnington *Ox* 89-90; R from 90. *The Rectory, Well Meadow, Shaw, Newbury, Berks RG13 2DR* Tel (01635) 40450 or 41155

TAYLOR, Brian. b 42. St Deiniol's Hawarden 78. **d** 80 **p** 81. C Mold *St As* 80-84; V Bagillt from 84. *The Vicarage, Bagillt CH6 6BZ* Tel (01352) 732732

TAYLOR, Brian. b 61. St Mich Coll Llan DipTh91. **d** 94 **p** 95. C Aberdare St Jo *Llan* from 94. *9 College Street, Abernant, Aberdare CF44 0RN* Tel (01685) 882641

TAYLOR, Brian Valentine. b 34. St Deiniol's Hawarden 69. **d** 71 **p** 72. C Workington St Mich *Carl* 71-72; C Carl St Aid and Ch Ch 73-74; Chapl Rotterdam Miss to Seamen *Eur* 74-75; Asst Chapl Madrid 75-76; Chapl Marseille w St Raphael Aix-en-Provence etc 77-78; Chapl Alassio w Genoa and Rapallo 78-81; C Higher Broughton *Man* 82-83; P-in-c Cheetwood St Alb 83-84; Lic to Offic 84-85; rtd 85; Perm to Offic *Man* from 85. *Fosbrooke House, 8 Clifton Drive, Lytham St Annes, Lancs FY8 5RE*

TAYLOR, Charles Derek. b 36. Trin Hall Cam BA59 MA62. Ripon Hall Ox 59. **d** 61 **p** 62. C Nottingham All SS *S'well* 61-64; C Binley *Cov* 64-67; C Stoke 67-70; R Purley *Ox* 70-74; V Milton *B & W* 74-93; RD Locking 86-87 and 90-93; V Wells St Cuth w Wookey Hole from 93. *The Vicarage, 1 St Cuthbert Street, Wells, Somerset BA5 2AW* Tel (01749) 673136

TAYLOR, Canon Charles William. b 53. Selw Coll Cam BA74 MA78. Cuddesdon Coll 74. **d** 76 **p** 77. C Wolverhampton *Lich* 76-79; Chapl Westmr Abbey 79-84; V Stanmore *Win* 84-90; R N Stoneham 90-95; Can Res and Prec Lich Cathl *Lich* from 95. *23 The Close, Lichfield, Staffs WS13 7LD* Tel (01543) 263337

TAYLOR, Christopher Vincent Chris. b 47. Cen Sch Speech & Drama DipDA71. Cranmer Hall Dur 94. **d** 96 **p** 97. C Kendal St Geo *Carl* from 96. *78 Windermere Road, Kendal, Cumbria LA9 5EZ* Tel (01539) 726945

TAYLOR, Preb Clive Cavanagh. b 28. MBE91. Cranmer Hall Dur 61. **d** 63 **p** 64. C Wembley St Jo *Lon* 63-66; C Edmonton All SS 66-69; V Tottenham St Jo 69-76; RD E Haringey 73-76; Dir of Ords 76-85; Chapl Metrop Police Coll Hendon 76-93; Sen Chapl Metrop Police 78-93; V Temple Fortune St Barn 76-93; Preb St Paul's Cathl 78-93; AD W Barnet 79-85; rtd 93; Perm to Offic *Chich* from 93. *26 Wenthill Close, East Dean, Eastbourne, E Sussex BN20 0HT* Tel (01323) 422346

TAYLOR, Colin John. b 66. Witwatersrand Univ BCom87 HDipEd88 BTh94. Wycliffe Hall Ox MTh95. **d** 97. C Denton Holme *Carl* from 97. *118 Dalston Road, Carlisle CA2 5PJ* Tel (01228) 22938 Fax as telephone

TAYLOR, David. b 53. St Jo Coll Dur BA74 PGCE75. Sarum & Wells Th Coll DCM93. **d** 93 **p** 94. C Cheadle Hulme All SS *Ches* 93-97; V Macclesfield St Jo from 97. *St John's Vicarage, 25 Wilwick Lane, Macclesfield, Cheshire SK11 8RS* Tel (01625) 424185

TAYLOR, Dr David Christopher Morgan. b 56. Leeds Univ BSc77 Univ Coll Lon PhD80 Univ Coll Ches MEd96 SOSc. N Ord Course 91. **d** 94 **p** 95. NSM Waterloo Ch Ch and St Mary *Liv* from 94; Sen Tutor (Medicine) Liv Univ from 96. *20 Liverpool Road, Formby, Liverpool L37 4BW* Tel (01704) 873304 Fax 0151-794 5337 E-mail dcmt@liverpool.ac.uk

TAYLOR, Dennis James. b 31. ACIS62. Ripon Hall Ox 63. **d** 68 **p** 69. C Baswich *Lich* 68-77; P-in-c Hastings H Trin *Chich* 77-81; V 81-86; R Catsfield and Crowhurst from 86. *The Rectory, Church Lane, Catsfield, Battle, E Sussex TN33 9DR* Tel (01424) 892319

TAYLOR, The Very Revd Derek John. b 31. Univ of Wales (Lamp) BA52 Fitzw Ho Cam BA54 MA58 Ex Univ CertEd70 Birm Univ ACertEd92. St Mich Coll Llan 54. **d** 55 **p** 56. C Newport St Paul *Mon* 55-59; CF (TA) 57-59 and 62-64; CF 59-62; V Bettws *Mon* 62-64; V Exminster *Ex* 64-70; Hd of RE Heathcote Sch Tiverton 70-71; W Germany 71-75; Chapl R Russell Sch Croydon 75-79; Chapl St Andr Sch Croydon 79-84; P-in-c Croydon St Andr *Cant* 79-81; V 81-84; Chapl Bromsgrove Sch 84-89; Provost St Chris Cathl Bahrain from 90; Hon Chapl Miss to Seamen from 90; rtd 92. *19 Warwick Hall Gardens, Bromsgrove, Worcs B60 2AU* E-mail provost@batelco.com.bh

TAYLOR, Donald Alastair. b 26. Lon Univ BD Linc Coll Ox DPhil77. St Paul's Coll Mauritius. **d** 65 **p** 65. C Ware St Mary *St Alb* 65-66; Seychelles 66-78; SSJE from 68; Lect Relig Studies Middx Poly 78-92; rtd 91. *50 St Bartholomew's Road, Reading RG1 3QA* Tel 0118-966 1247

TAYLOR, Edward Frank. b 23. Lon Univ BSc44. Chich Th Coll 50. **d** 52 **p** 53. C Manston *Ripon* 52-55; Chapl Chich Th Coll 55-59; PV Chich Cathl *Chich* 57-59; C Ifield 59-63; V Hangleton 63-73; V Wivelsfield 73-88; rtd 88; Perm to Offic *Bradf* from 88. *4 Clarendon Street, Haworth, Keighley, W Yorkshire BD22 8PT* Tel (01535) 642493

TAYLOR, Eric Hargreaves. b 21. Oak Hill Th Coll 47. **d** 51 **p** 52. C Tranmere St Cath *Ches* 51-54; V Constable Lee *Man* 54-62; V Camerton H Trin W Seaton *Carl* 62-71; V Ramsgate Ch Ch *Cant* 71-85; Chapl Ramsgate Gen Hosp 71-85; rtd 85; Perm to Offic *Cant* 85-90; Perm to Offic *Blackb* 89-96. *130 Ellesmere Road, Walton, Warrington WA4 6EF* Tel (01925) 268100

TAYLOR, Frank. b 02. Kelham Th Coll 22. **d** 28 **p** 29. C W Hendon St Jo *Lon* 28-33; C Hanwell St Mellitus 33-37; Lon Dioc Home Missr E Hounslow St Mary 37-43; V Brondesbury St Anne 43-53; V Hammersmith St Jo 53-61; V Lambourn *Ox* 61-70; rtd 70; Perm to Offic *Ox* 74-91. *18 Bertie Road, Cumnor, Oxford OX2 9PS* Tel (01865) 863239

TAYLOR, Frank Hampton. b 49. St Jo Coll Nottm 80. **d** 82 **p** 83. C Hoole *Ches* 82-85; C Timperley 85-89; V Birkenhead Ch Ch 89-95. *9 Peckswood Road, Todmorden, Lancs OL14 7JR* Tel (01706) 817214

TAYLOR, George Davidson. b 27. St Aid Birkenhead 60. **d** 62 **p** 63. C Urmston *Man* 62-65; V Shuttleworth 65-71; V Litherland St Phil *Liv* 71-85; rtd 85. *34 Beckwith Crescent, Harrogate, N Yorkshire HG2 0BQ* Tel (01423) 560023

TAYLOR, George James Trueman. b 36. Ripon Hall Ox 66. **d** 69 **p** 70. C Wavertree H Trin *Liv* 69-73; V Newton-le-Willows 73-79; V Stoneycroft All SS 79-83; V Haigh from 83. *The Vicarage, Copperas Lane, Haigh, Wigan, Lancs WN2 1PA* Tel (01942) 831255

TAYLOR, Canon Godfrey Alan. b 36. Oak Hill Th Coll DipTh60. **d** 61 **p** 62. C Herne Bay Ch Ch *Cant* 61-64; C Tunbridge Wells St Jas *Roch* 64-68; V Guernsey H Trin *Win* 68-81; V Boscombe St Jo from 81; Hon Can Win Cathl from 96. *St John's Vicarage, 17 Browning Avenue, Bournemouth BH5 1NR* Tel (01202) 396667

TAYLOR, Canon Gordon. b 46. AKC68. St Aug Coll Cant 69. **d** 70 **p** 71. C Rotherham *Sheff* 70-74; P-in-c Brightside St Thos 74-79; P-in-c Brightside St Marg 77-79; V Brightside St Thos and St Marg 79-82; R Kirk Sandall and Edenthorpe 82-91; V Beighton 91-96; Hon Can Sheff Cathl from 93; V Goole from 96. *The Vicarage, 22 Clifton Gardens, Goole, N Humberside DN14 6AS* Tel (01405) 764259

TAYLOR, Gordon Clifford. b 15. VRD56 and Bars 66. FSA Ch Coll Cam BA37 MA41. Ripon Hall Ox 37. **d** 38 **p** 39. C Ealing St Steph Castle Hill *Lon* 38-40; Chapl RNVR 40-58; Asst Master Eton Coll 46-49; R St Giles-in-the-Fields *Lon* from 49; RD Finsbury and Holborn 54-67; Chapl RNR 58-70. *St Giles's Rectory, 15A Gower Street, London WC1E 6HG* Tel 0171-636 4646

TAYLOR, Graham Peter. b 58. NE Ord Course DipHE95. **d** 95 **p** 96. NSM Pickering *York* 95; NSM Pickering w Lockton and Levisham 95-96; C Whitby from 96. *19 Eskdale Road, Whitby, N Yorkshire YO22 4JH* Tel (01947) 603099

✠**TAYLOR, The Rt Revd Humphrey Vincent.** b 38. Pemb Coll Cam BA61 MA66 Lon Univ MA70. Coll of Resurr Mirfield 61. **d** 63 **p** 64 **c** 91. C N Hammersmith St Kath *Lon* 63-64; C Notting Hill St Mark 64-66; USPG 67-71; Malawi 67-71; Chapl Bp Grosseteste Coll Linc 72-74; Sec Chapls in HE Gen Syn Bd of Educn 75-80; Gen Sec USPG 80-91; Sec Miss Progr 80-84; Hon Can Bris Cathl *Bris* 86-91; Lic to Offic *S'wark* 89-91; Suff Bp Selby *York* from 91. *10 Precentor's Court, York YO1 2EJ* Tel (01904) 656592 Fax 655671

TAYLOR, Ian. b 53. Saltley Tr Coll Birm CertEd75. LNSM course 92. **d** 95 **p** 96. NSM Heywood St Luke w All So *Man* from 95. *818A Edenfield Road, Rochdale, Lancs OL12 7RB* Tel (01706) 355738

TAYLOR, James McMurray. b 16. TCD BA38 MA. **d** 39 **p** 40. C Belfast St Mary *Conn* 39-43; CF (EC) 43-47; P-in-c Upper Moville *D & R* 47-48; P-in-c Tamlaght O'Crilly 49-53; P-in-c Derrybrusk *Clogh* 53-55; I 55-57; I Castle Archdale and Killadeas 57-80; rtd 80. *Inan, Farnamullan Road, Lisbellaw, Co Fermanagh BT94 5ER* Tel (01365) 87259

TAYLOR, Jan William Karel. b 59. QUB BD82 MSocSc89 TCD DipTh84. **d** 84 **p** 85. C Belfast St Simon w St Phil *Conn* 84-87; I Belfast St Paul 87-92; Chapl RAF from 92. *Chaplaincy Services (RAF), HQ, Personnel and Training Command, RAF Innsworth, Gloucester GL3 1EZ* Tel (01452) 712612 ext 5164 Fax 510828

TAYLOR, Mrs Janette Elizabeth (Jan). b 44. Glouc Sch of Min 89. **d** 92 **p** 94. C Glouc St Geo w Whaddon *Glouc* 92-96; R Woolaston w Alvington and Aylburton from 96. *The Rectory, Main Road, Alvington, Lydney, Glos GL15 6AT* Tel (01594) 529387

TAYLOR (née PATTERSON), Sister Jennifer Mary. b 41. CA Tr Coll IDC65. **dss** 77 **d** 87. CA from 65; Chapl Asst HM Pris Holloway 75-79; Ho Mistress Ch Hosp Sch Hertf 78-79; Chapl Asst RAChD 80-90; Germany 90-96; rtd 96; Perm to Offic *Eur* from 96. *37 Paralela las Rosas, 38631 Las Galletas, Tenerife, Canary Islands* Tel Tenerife (22) 73 24 69

TAYLOR, John Alexander. b 54. S Dios Minl Tr Scheme 89. **d** 92 **p** 93. NSM Abbotts Ann and Upper and Goodworth Clatford *Win* from 92. *21 Sainsbury Close, Andover, Hants SP10 2LE* Tel (01264) 353339

TAYLOR, Canon John Ambrose. b 19. K Coll Lon 45. Coll of Resurr Mirfield 49. **d** 50 **p** 51. C Helmsley *York* 50-55; V Nether w Upper Poppleton 55-63; V Ches St Oswald w Lt St Jo *Ches* 63-72; P-in-c Ches Lt St Jo 63-67; TV Ches 72-74; Hon Can Gib Cathl *Eur* 74-91; V Withyham St Jo *Chich* 74-88; RD Rotherfield 77-87; P-in-c Withyham St Mich 87; rtd 88; Perm to Offic *Chich* from 88. *11 Park View, Buxted, Uckfield, E Sussex TN22 4LS* Tel (01825) 813475

TAYLOR, John Andrew. b 53. Linc Th Coll 86. **d** 88 **p** 89. C Stanley *Liv* 88-91; V Wigan St Jas w St Thos from 91. *St James' Vicarage, Poolstock Lane, Wigan, Lancs WN3 5HL* Tel (01942) 43896

TAYLOR, John Andrew Wemyss. b 27. RCS LDS51 PhD62. Sarum & Wells Th Coll 70. **d** 72 **p** 73. C Ashburton w Buckland-in-the-Moor *Ex* 72-76; P-in-c E Portlemouth 76-79; P-in-c S Pool w Chivelstone 76-79; R E Portlemouth, S Pool and Chivelstone 79-81; Miss to Seamen from 81; V Salcombe *Ex* 81-88; RD Woodleigh 83-88; Perm to Offic from 88; rtd 92. *Waverley, Grand View Road, Hope Cove, Kingsbridge, Devon TQ7 3HF* Tel (01548) 561332

✠**TAYLOR, The Rt Revd John Bernard.** b 29. Ch Coll Cam BA50 MA54 Jes Coll Cam 52 Hebrew Univ Jerusalem 54. Ridley Hall Cam 55. **d** 56 **p** 57 **c** 80. C Morden *S'wark* 56-59; V Henham *Chelmsf* 59-64; V Elsenham 59-64; Sen Tutor Oak Hill Th Coll 64-65; Vice-Prin 65-72; V Woodford Wells 72-75; Dioc Dir of Ords 72-80; Adn W Ham 75-80; Bp St Alb 80-95; High Almoner 88-95; rtd 95. *22 Conduit Head Road, Cambridge CB3 0EY* Tel (01223) 313783

TAYLOR, John Charles Browne. b 23. CEng58 MIEE58. Oak Hill Th Coll 81. **d** 82 **p** 83. NSM Havering-atte-Bower *Chelmsf* 82-85; NSM Collier Row St Jas and Havering-atte-Bower 86-89; rtd 89; Lic to Offic *Chelmsf* from 89. *Giffords, North Road, Havering-atte-Bower, Romford RM4 1PX* Tel (01708) 742072

TAYLOR, John Denys. b 20. Leeds Univ BA49. Coll of Resurr Mirfield. **d** 51 **p** 52. C Leeds St Marg *Ripon* 51-54; India 54-59; C Gt Grimsby St Jas *Linc* 59-66; New Zealand from 66. *4A Brunton Place, Glenfield, Auckland 1310, New Zealand* Tel Auckland (9) 443 1671 Fax as telephone

TAYLOR, Canon John Frederick. b 20. St Chad's Coll Dur 39. Ely Th Coll 59. **d** 61 **p** 62. C Grangetown *York* 61-64; V Middlesbrough St Cuth 64-71; V Skipsea w Ulrome 71-79; P-in-c Barmston w Fraisthorpe 77-79; Can and Preb York Minster 79-85; R Skipsea w Ulrome and Barmston w Fraisthorpe 79-82; V Hemingbrough 82-85; rtd 85. *19 Willow Garth, Eastrington, Goole, N Humberside DN14 7QP* Tel (01430) 410647

TAYLOR, Canon John Michael. b 30. St Aid Birkenhead 56. **d** 59 **p** 60. C Chorley St Jas *Blackb* 59-62; C Broughton 62-64; Chapl St Boniface Coll Warminster 64-68; V Altham w Clayton le Moors *Blackb* 68-76; RD Accrington 71-76; Can Res Blackb Cathl 76-96; rtd 96. *25 Gorse Road, Blackburn BB2 6LZ*

✠**TAYLOR, The Rt Revd John Mitchell.** b 32. Aber Univ MA54. Edin Th Coll 54. **d** 56 **p** 57 **c** 91. C Aberdeen St Marg *Ab* 56-58; R Glas H Cross *Glas* 58-64; R Glas St Ninian 64-73; R Dumfries 73-91; Chapl Dumfries and Galloway R Infirmary 73-91; Can St Mary's Cathl *Glas* 79-91; Bp Glas from 91. *Bishop's House, 25 Quadrant Road, Glasgow G43 2QP* Tel 0141-633 5877 or 637 5659 Fax 633 5877

TAYLOR, John Porter. b 48. Ex Univ BA71 MA76. Cranmer Hall Dur CTMin93. **d** 93 **p** 94. C Ossett cum Gawthorpe *Wakef* 93-96; R Crofton from 96. *The Rectory, 5 Hare Park Lane, Crofton, Wakefield, W Yorkshire WF4 1HW* Tel (01924) 862373

TAYLOR, John Ralph. b 48. St Jo Coll Nottm BTh74. **d** 74 **p** 75. C Clitheroe St Jas *Blackb* 74-77; C Kidsgrove *Lich* 77-79; C Hawkwell *Chelmsf* 79-82; V Linc St Geo Swallowbeck *Linc* 82-92; rtd 92. *The Gables, Beck Lane, South Hykeham, Lincoln LN6 9PQ* Tel (01522) 692043

TAYLOR, Canon John Rowland. b 29. OBE74. St Mich Coll Llan 57. **d** 58 **p** 59. C Caerau St Cynfelin *Llan* 58-59; C Aberdare St Jo 59-61; Miss to Seamen 61-88; Tanganyika 61-64; Tanzania 64-73; Adn Dar-es-Salaam 65-73; V-Gen 67-73; Thailand 73-84; Chapl Rotterdam w Schiedam *Eur* 84-88; V Warnham *Chich* from 88. *The Vicarage, Church Street, Warnham, Horsham, W Sussex RH12 3QW* Tel (01403) 265041

✠**TAYLOR, The Rt Revd John Vernon.** b 14. Trin Coll Cam BA36 St Cath Soc Ox BA38 MA41. Wycliffe Coll Toronto Hon DD64 Wycliffe Hall Ox 36. **d** 38 **p** 39 **c** 75. C St Marylebone All So w SS Pet and Jo *Lon* 38-40; C St Helens St Helen *Liv* 40-43; CMS 45-63; Gen Sec CMS 63-74; Bp Win 75-85; rtd 85; Perm to Offic *Ox* from 86. *Camleigh, 65 Aston Street, Oxford OX4 1EW* Tel (01865) 248502

TAYLOR, Joseph Robin Christopher. b 34. St Aid Birkenhead 58. **d** 61 **p** 62. C Aldershot St Mich *Guildf* 61-64; C Fleet 64-68; R Manaton *Ex* 69-74; R N Bovey 69-74; V Dawlish 74-87; P-in-c Christow, Ashton, Trusham and Bridford 87-88; R 88-95; Perm to Offic from 95. *Pound Cottage, Ramsley, South Zeal, Okehampton, Devon EX20 2LB* Tel (01837) 840589

TAYLOR, Justin Wray Lindsay. b 39. Moray Ord Course 77. **d** 84 **p** 87. Hon C Nairn *Mor* 84-87; Hon C Inverness St Andr from 87. *68 High Street, Ardersier, Inverness IV1 2QF* Tel (01667) 462509

TAYLOR, Kenneth Charles (Ken). b 24. St Deiniol's Hawarden 76. **d** 76 **p** 77. C Wilmslow *Ches* 76-79; V Willaston 79-93; Chapl Clatterbridge Hosp Wirral 86-93; rtd 93; Perm to Offic *Ches* from 93. *9 Windsor Drive, Whitby, South Wirral L65 6SH* Tel 0151-356 2477

TAYLOR, Kenneth Gordon. b 30. Selw Coll Cam BA54 MA58. Chich Th Coll 54. **d** 56 **p** 57. C S Lynn *Nor* 56-60; C Holbeck St Matt *Ripon* 60-62; C Moor Allerton 62-71; R Northwold *Ely* 71-81; P-in-c Harlton 81-87; R 87-89; P-in-c Haslingfield 81-87; V 87-89; P-in-c Thornage w Brinton w Hunworth and Stody *Nor* 89-92; P-in-c Briningham 89-92; P-in-c Melton Constable w Swanton Novers 89-92; R Brinton, Briningham, Hunworth, Stody etc 92-95; rtd 95; Perm to Offic *Nor* from 95. *Little Mount, Links Road, Mundesley, Norwich NR11 8AT* Tel (01263) 720402

TAYLOR, Kingsley Graham. b 55. Univ of Wales (Cardiff) BD93. St Mich Coll Llan 90. **d** 93 **p** 94. C Llanelli *St D* 93-97; V Whitland w Cyffig and Henllan Amgoed etc from 97. *The Vicarage, North Road, Whitland SA34 0BH* Tel (01994) 240494

TAYLOR, Lyndon John. b 49. St Mich Coll Llan 92 DipMin93. **d** 95 **p** 96. C Swansea St Nic *S & B* 95-96 and from 96. *27 Gelli Gwyn Road, Morriston, Swansea SA6 7PP* Tel (01792) 775898

TAYLOR, Canon Marcus Beresford. b 13. TCD BA35 MA43. CITC 36. **d** 36 **p** 37. C Glenageary *D & G* 36-39; C Dublin St Jas 39-47; I Stillorgan 47-78; Can Ch Ch Cathl Dublin 71-86; I Stillorgan w Blackrock 78-86; rtd 86. *78 Beech Trees, Galloping Green Lane, Stillorgan, Dublin, Irish Republic* Tel Dublin (1) 288 4196

TAYLOR, Marcus Iles. b 16. Ely Th Coll 48. **d** 49 **p** 50. C Bearsted *Cant* 49-53; V Cookham Dean *Ox* 56-71; rtd 81. *Kimbers, Budnick, Perranporth, Cornwall TR6 0AA* Tel (01872) 572143

TAYLOR, Mrs Marian Alexandra. b 62. Newc Univ BA85. Qu Coll Birm 89. **d** 91 **p** 96. C Earls Barton *Pet* 91-93; NSM Wellingborough St Barn 95-96; NSM Beaumont Leys *Leic* from 96. *11 Castlefields, Leicester LE4 1BN*

TAYLOR, Mark Edward. b 54. St Jo Coll Auckland LTh. **d** 78 **p** 79. New Zealand 78-86; Chapl RN 86-88; New Zealand from 88. *PO Box 547, Albany 1331, New Zealand* Tel Auckland (9) 413 8364 or 415 8244 Fax 415 4428

TAYLOR, Mark Frederick. b 62. N Ireland Poly BA84 TCD DipTh87. **d** 87 **p** 88. C Ballymacarrett St Patr *D & D* 87-90; C Dundela 90-93; Hon Chapl Miss to Seamen from 90; I Kilmore w Inch *D & D* from 93. *22 Church Road, Kilmore, Crossgar, Downpatrick, Co Down BT30 9HR* Tel (01396) 830371

TAYLOR, Martyn Andrew Nicholas. b 66. **d** 96 **p** 97. C Stamford St Geo w St Paul *Linc* from 96. *17 Turnpole Close, Stamford, Lincs PE9 1DT* Tel (01780) 57343

TAYLOR, Michael Alan. b 47. Bris Univ CertEd70 Lon Univ BD85. Trin Coll Bris 72. **d** 76 **p** 77. C Chilwell *S'well* 76-79; Chapl RAF 79-87; New Zealand from 87. *1 Merton Place, Bryndwr, Christchurch 8005, New Zealand* Tel Christchurch (3) 352 4788 or 355 6901 Fax 355 6908 E-mail strategic@chch.planet.org.nz

TAYLOR, Michael Allan. b 50. Nottm Univ BTh80. St Jo Coll Nottm 76. **d** 80 **p** 81. C Bowling St Jo *Bradf* 80-82; C Otley 82-85; P-in-c Low Moor St Mark 85-92; P-in-c Bris St Andr w St Bart *Bris* 92-96. *25 Cornfield Close, The Hawthornes, Bradley Stoke, Bristol BS12* Tel (01454) 618677

TAYLOR, Michael Barry. b 38. Bps' Coll Cheshunt 63. **d** 65 **p** 66. C Leeds St Cypr Harehills *Ripon* 65-68; C Stanningley St Thos 68-70; V Hunslet Moor St Pet and St Cuth 70-78; V Starbeck from 78. *The Vicarage, 78 High Street, Harrogate, N Yorkshire HG2 7LW* Tel (01423) 883036 or 889856

TAYLOR, Michael Frank Chatterton. b 30. St Aid Birkenhead 59. **d** 61 **p** 62. C Knighton St Jo *Leic* 61-65; V Briningham *Nor* 65-86; R Melton Constable w Swanton Novers 65-86; P-in-c Thornage w Brinton w Hunworth and Stody 85-86; R Lyng w Sparham 86-90; R Elsing w Bylaugh 86-90; R Lyng, Sparham, Elsing and Bylaugh 90-95; RD Sparham 92-95; rtd 95. *The Rhond, 33 Station Road, St Helens, Ryde, Isle of Wight PO33 1YF* Tel (01983) 873531

TAYLOR, Michael John. b 63. Lanc Univ BA85. Linc Th Coll 86. **d** 88 **p** 89. C Carl St Aid and Ch Ch *Carl* 88-91; C Loughton St Jo *Chelmsf* 91-93; V Eastwood St Dav from 93. *St David's Vicarage, 400 Rayleigh Road, Leigh-on-Sea, Essex SS9 5PT* Tel (01702) 523126

TAYLOR, Michael Joseph. b 49. Gregorian Univ Rome STB72 PhL74 Birm Univ MA81. English Coll Rome 67. **d** 72 **p** 73. In RC Ch 72-83; Hon C Newport Pagnell w Lathbury *Ox* 83-86; TV Langley Marish 86-90; Vice Prin E Midl Min Tr Course *S'well* 90-97; Prin from 97. *52 Parkside Gardens, Wollaton, Nottingham NG8 2PQ* Tel 0115-928 3111 or 951 4854 E-mail emmtc@nottingham.ac.uk

TAYLOR, Michael Laurence. b 43. ARCM68 Ch Coll Cam BA66 MA70 CertEd72 MPhil88. Cuddesdon Coll 66. **d** 68 **p** 69. C Westbury-on-Trym H Trin *Bris* 68-72; Asst Chapl Wellington Coll Berks 72-76; C St Helier *S'wark* 76-78; TV Bedminster *Bris* 78-82; P-in-c Chippenham St Andr w Tytherton Lucas 82-88; V 88-89; Dioc Ecum Officer *B & W* 89-90; P-in-c Rodney Stoke w Draycott 89-90. *21 Bath Road, Wells, Somerset BA5 2DJ* Tel (01749) 670348

TAYLOR, Michael Stewart. b 58. St Mich Coll Llan BTh. **d** 91 **p** 92. C Llangynnwr and Cwmffrwd *St D* 91-94; V Llansantffraed and Llanbadarn Trefeglwys etc from 94. *The Vicarage, 11 Maes Wyre, Llanrhystud SY23 5AH*

TAYLOR, Nancy. b 49. SRN70 SCM72. Ox Min Course 88. **d** 91 **p** 94. Chapl Asst Stoke Mandeville Hosp Aylesbury 91-94; Asst Chapl Aylesbury Vale Community Healthcare NHS Trust from 94; NSM Weston Turville *Ox* from 91. *Elmhurst, 23 School Lane, Weston Turville, Aylesbury, Bucks HP22 5SG* Tel (01296) 613384 or 316677

TAYLOR, Neil Hamish. b 48. Open Univ BA87. Linc Th Coll 72. **d** 75 **p** 76. C Rotherham *Sheff* 75-78; C Doncaster St Geo 78-82; P-in-c Knaresdale 82-87; V Alston cum Garrigill w Nenthead and Kirkhaugh *Newc* 82-87; TR Alston Team 87-88; V Maidstone St Paul *Cant* from 88; OCF 88-94. *St Paul's Vicarage, 130 Boxley Road, Maidstone, Kent ME14 2AH* Tel (01622) 691926

TAYLOR, Neville Patrick. b 40. Trin Coll Bris DipTh82. **d** 82 **p** 83. C Old Trafford St Jo *Man* 82-84; C Hurst 84-87; R Levenshulme St Mark from 87. *St Mark's Rectory, 331 Mount Road, Levenshulme, Manchester M19 3HW* Tel 0161-224 9551

TAYLOR, Nicholas James. b 46. St Chad's Coll Dur BA67 DipTh68. **d** 69 **p** 70. C Beamish *Dur* 69-74; C Styvechale *Cov* 74-77; P-in-c Wilmcote w Billesley 77-79; P-in-c Aston Cantlow 77-79; V Aston Cantlow and Wilmcote w Billesley 79-87; V Cov St Fran N Radford 87-97; RD Cov N 93-97; TR Wilton *B & W* from 97. *The Vicarage, Fons George, Wilton, Taunton, Somerset TA1 3JT* Tel (01823) 284253

TAYLOR, Nigel Thomas Wentworth. b 60. Bris Univ BA82 Ox Univ BA86. Wycliffe Hall Ox 84. **d** 87 **p** 88. C Ches Square St Mich w St Phil *Lon* 87-91; C Roxeth Ch Ch and Harrow St Pet 91-93; TV Roxeth 93-97; V S Mimms Ch Ch from 97. *Christ Church Vicarage, St Albans Road, Barnet, Herts EN5 4LA* Tel 0181-449 0832

TAYLOR, Norman. b 26. CCC Cam BA49 MA52. Cuddesdon Coll 49. **d** 51 **p** 52. C Clitheroe St Mary *Blackb* 51-54; C Pontesbury I and II *Heref* 54-55; R Lt Wilbraham *Ely* 55-71; Chapl St Faith's Sch Cam 71-86; Lic to Offic *Ely* 72-87; Hon C Chesterton St Andr 87-91; rtd 91; Hon C Lyme Regis *Sarum* 91-94. *Shire End West, Cobb Road, Lyme Regis, Dorset DT7 3JP* Tel (01297) 442922

TAYLOR, Norman Adrian. b 48. St D Coll Lamp DipTh73. **d** 73 **p** 74. C Fleur-de-Lis *Mon* 73-75; C W Drayton *Lon* 75-79; C-in-c Hayes St Edm CD 79-85; V Hayes St Edm 85-87; V Pilton w Ashford *Ex* 87-89; V Sidley *Chich* from 89. *All Saints Vicarage, All Saints Lane, Bexhill-on-Sea, E Sussex TN39 5HA* Tel (01424) 221071

TAYLOR, Norman Wyatt. b 23. Wells Th Coll 58. **d** 60 **p** 61. C Lawrence Weston *Bris* 60-63; V 63-69; V Bishop's Cannings *Sarum* 69-77; V Bishop's Cannings, All Cannings etc 77-80; V W Moors 80-87; rtd 88; Perm to Offic *Ex* from 89. *3 Kits Close, Chudleigh, Newton Abbot, Devon TQ13 0LG* Tel (01626) 852733

TAYLOR, Paul. b 63. RGN85. Sarum & Wells Th Coll 92 Linc Th Coll BTh95. **d** 95 **p** 96. C Boultham *Linc* from 95. *7 Earls Park, Boultham Park Road, Lincoln LN6* Tel (01522) 533644

TAYLOR, Paul Frank David. b 60. ARICS87 Leic Poly BSc84. Trin Coll Bris BA91. **d** 91 **p** 92. C Edin St Thos *Edin* 91-94; C Kempshott *Win* from 94. *12 Maplehurst Chase, Meadowcroft, Hatch Warren, Basingstoke, Hants RG22 4XQ* Tel (01256) 472632

TAYLOR, Paul Latham. b 11. **d** 49 **p** 50. C Monkseaton St Pet *Newc* 49-52; C Epsom St Barn *Guildf* 52-54; V Milford 54-72; Chapl K Geo V Hosp Godalming 54-70; Chapl Milford Chest Hosp 70-72; Warden Coll of St Barn Lingfield 72-77; rtd 77; Perm to Offic *Win* 83-95. *22 Halton Close, Bransgore, Christchurch, Dorset BH23 8HZ* Tel (01425) 72137

TAYLOR, Paul Stanley. b 53. Ox Univ BEd. Westcott Ho Cam. **d** 84 **p** 85. C Bush Hill Park St Steph *Lon* 84-88; Asst Dir Post Ord Tr Edmonton Episc Area 87-94; Dir Post Ord Tr from 94; V Southgate St Andr from 88. *St Andrew's Vicarage, 184 Chase Side, London N14 5HN* Tel 0181-886 7523

TAYLOR, Peter. b 35. Sussex Univ MA72. Wells Th Coll 58. **d** 60 **p** 61. C Godalming *Guildf* 60-62; C Epsom St Martin 62-65; R E Clandon 65-75; R W Clandon 65-75; rtd 96; P-in-c Burpham *Chich* from 96. *The Vicarage, Burpham, Arundel, W Sussex BN18 9RJ* Tel (01903) 882948 Fax as telephone

TAYLOR, Peter David. b 38. FCA. N Ord Course 77. **d** 80 **p** 81. C Penwortham St Mary *Blackb* 80-84; V Farington 84-92; V Euxton from 92. *The Vicarage, Wigan Road, Euxton, Chorley, Lancs PR7 6JH* Tel (01257) 262102

TAYLOR, Peter David. b 47. Liv Univ BEd74 Man Univ MEd78 Lanc Univ MA88. N Ord Course 78. **d** 81 **p** 82. C Formby H Trin *Liv* 81-84; V Stoneycroft All SS 84-91; Chapl St Kath Coll 91-96; Dioc RE Field Officer 91-96; Dioc Dir of Educn *Leic* from 96. *87 Main Street, Humberstone, Leicester LE5 1AE*

TAYLOR, The Ven Peter Flint. b 44. Qu Coll Cam BA65 MA69. Lon Coll of Div BD70. **d** 70 **p** 71. C Highbury New Park St Aug *Lon* 70-73; C Plymouth St Andr w St Paul and St Geo *Ex* 73-77; PC Ironville *Derby* 77-83; P-in-c Riddings 82-83; R Rayleigh *Chelmsf* 83-96; Chapl HM Young Offender Inst Bullwood Hall 85-90; RD Rochford *Chelmsf* 89-96; Adn Harlow from 96. *Glebe House, Church Lane, Sheering, Bishop's Stortford, Herts CM22 7NR* Tel (01279) 734524

TAYLOR, Peter Graham. b 45. Liv Univ 86 TCert69 CQSW69. Local Minl Tr Course 91. **d** 94 **p** 95. NSM Holywell *St As* from 94. *22 Nant Eos, Holway, Holywell CH8 7DA* Tel (01352) 712413

TAYLOR, Peter John. b 40. Oak Hill Th Coll 62. **d** 65 **p** 66. C St Paul's Cray St Barn *Roch* 65-69; C Woking St Jo *Guildf* 69-77; R Necton w Holme Hale *Nor* 77-94; P-in-c N Pickenham w S Pickenham etc 94; R Necton, Holme Hale w N and S Pickenham from 95; RD Breckland 86-94. *The Rectory, Necton, Swaffham, Norfolk PE37 8HT* Tel (01760) 722021

TAYLOR, Peter John. b 46. Trin Coll Bris 71. **d** 73 **p** 74. C Walshaw Ch Ch *Man* 73-75; C Rodbourne Cheney *Bris* 75-78; Asst Chapl HM Pris Pentonville 78-79; Chapl HM Borstal Roch 79-84; Chapl HM Pris Highpoint 84-90; Asst Chapl Gen of Pris from 90. *HM Prison Service Chaplaincy, PO Box 349, Stafford ST16 3DL* Tel (01785) 213456 Fax 227734

TAYLOR, Peter John. b 60. New Coll Edin LTh87. Edin Th Coll 83. **d** 87 **p** 88. C Edin SS Phil and Jas *Edin* 87-90; USA 90-92; R Glas St Oswald *Glas* from 92. *The Rectory, 1 King's Park Avenue, Glasgow G44 4UW* Tel 0141-632 1852

TAYLOR, Peter Joseph. b 41. Bps' Coll Cheshunt 66. **d** 68 **p** 69. C Wollaton *S'well* 68-71; C Cockington *Ex* 71-74; V Broadhembury 74-79; V Broadhembury w Payhembury 79-81; V Gt Staughton *Ely* 81-86; Chapl HM Young Offender Inst Gaynes Hall 81-91; R Offord D'Arcy w Offord Cluny *Ely* from 86; V Gt Paxton from 86. *The Rectory, Offord D'Arcy, Huntingdon, Cambs PE18 9RH* Tel (01480) 810588

TAYLOR (or URMSON-TAYLOR), Ralph Urmson. b 28. Tulsa Univ MA72 Man Coll of Educn DipEd74 TCert82. Kelham Th Coll DipTh56 BD56. **d** 56 **p** 57. C Redcar *York* 57-59; C Bridlington Quay H Trin 59-62; C Sewerby w Marton 60-62; USA from 62; rtd 93. *2136 East 22nd Place, Tulsa, Oklahoma 74114, USA* Tel Tulsa (918) 747-3876

TAYLOR, Raymond. b 34. Lon Coll of Div 62. **d** 65 **p** 66. C Pennington *Man* 65-70; P-in-c Wombridge *Lich* 70-80; R S Normanton *Derby* 80-88; RD Alfreton 86-88; V Youlgreave, Middleton, Stanton-in-Peak etc from 88. *The Vicarage, Youlgreave, Bakewell, Derbyshire DE45 1WL* Tel (01629) 636285

TAYLOR, Raymond Montgomery. b 43. Oak Hill Th Coll 77. **d** 80 **p** 81. Hon C Cricklewood St Pet *Lon* 80-85; Hon C Golders Green 85-87; V New Southgate St Paul from 87; AD Cen Barnet from 96. *St Paul's Vicarage, 11 Woodland Road, London N11 1PN* Tel 0181-361 1946

TAYLOR, Richard David. b 44. Worc Coll Ox BA67 MA70. Coll of Resurr Mirfield 67. **d** 69 **p** 70. C Barrow St Geo w St Luke *Carl* 69-73; C Gosforth All SS *Newc* 73-80; TR Newc Epiphany 80-83; V Tynemouth Priory 83-91; TR Benwell Team from 91. *Benwell Rectory, Benwell Lane, Newcastle upon Tyne NE15 6RS* Tel 0191-273 5021

TAYLOR, Preb Richard John. b 21. Kelham Th Coll 38. **d** 45 **p** 46. C Tunstall Ch Ch *Lich* 45-48; C Uttoxeter w Bramshall 48-52; V Croxden 52-57; V Willenhall H Trin 57-68; R Edgmond 68-77; V Streetly 77-87; Preb Lich Cathl 78-87; rtd 87; Perm to Offic *Lich* 87-96. *15 Covey Close, Lichfield, Staffs WS13 6BS* Tel (01543) 268558

TAYLOR, Richard John. b 46. Ripon Coll Cuddesdon 85. **d** 85 **p** 86. C Moseley St Mary *Birm* 85-87; V Kingsbury 87-91; TR Hodge Hill from 91. *The Rectory, Hodge Hill Common, Birmingham B36 8AG* Tel 0121-747 2094 or 747 9262

TAYLOR, Roger. b 21. Birkb Coll Lon BA50 Leeds Univ MA59 Essex Univ MPhil96. Oak Hill Th Coll 47. **d** 51 **p** 52. C Chadderton Ch Ch *Man* 51-55; V Bowling St Steph *Bradf* 55-63; SW Area Sec CPAS 63-68; V Felixstowe SS Pet and Paul *St E* 68-81; P-in-c Gt and Lt Thurlow w Lt Bradley 81-82; TV Haverhill w Withersfield, the Wrattings etc 82-84; R Hopton, Market Weston, Barningham etc 84-86; rtd 86; Perm to Offic *St E* from 87. *Chapel House, Lindsey, Ipswich IP7 6QA* Tel (01787) 211120

TAYLOR, Roger James Benedict. b 42. Glouc Sch of Min 89 WMMTC 95. **d** 96. Hon C Cromhall w Tortworth and Tytherington *Glouc* from 96. *14A Wortley Road, Wotton-under-Edge, Glos GL12 7JU* Tel (01453) 845366

TAYLOR, Canon Roland Haydn (Roly). b 29. St Chad's Coll Dur BA53 DipTh55. **d** 55 **p** 56. C N Gosforth *Newc* 55-58; C Barnsley St Mary *Wakef* 58-61; V Brotherton 61-68; V Purston cum S Featherstone 68-76; RD Pontefract 74-94; R Badsworth 76-97; Hon Can Wakef Cathl 81-97; rtd 97. *57 Fair View, Carleton, Pontefract, W Yorkshire WF8 3NU* Tel (01977) 796564

TAYLOR, Roy. b 63. Ex Coll Ox BA86 Ox Univ MA89 York Univ PGCE87 Univ of Wales (Cardiff) BD97. St Mich Coll Llan BD95. **d** 97. C Guisborough *York* from 97. *16 Lealholm Way, Guisborough, Cleveland TS14 8LN* Tel (01287) 635873

TAYLOR, Roy William. b 37. Ch Coll Cam BA61 MA64. Clifton Th Coll 61. **d** 63 **p** 64. C Blackb Sav *Blackb* 63-66; C Hensingham *Carl* 66-68; CMS 69-79; Taiwan 69-79; TV Bushbury *Lich* 79-85; OMF 85-93; Perm to Offic *Lich* 85-93; Hon C Wolverhampton St Jude 93-94; P-in-c Torquay St Jo and Ellacombe *Ex* from 94.

Christ Church Vicarage, 1A Lower Ellacombe Church Road, Torquay TQ1 1JH Tel (01803) 293441

TAYLOR, Mrs Stella Isabelle. b 31. S Dios Minl Tr Scheme 86. **d** 89 **p** 94. NSM Haworth *Bradf* 89-91; Par Dn Keighley St Andr 92-94; C 94-96; rtd 97. *Home Cottage, 4 Clarendon Street, Haworth, Keighley, W Yorkshire BD22 8PT* Tel (01535) 642493

TAYLOR, Stephen Gordon. b 35. Bris Univ BA60. Ridley Hall Cam 60. **d** 62 **p** 63. C Gt Baddow *Chelmsf* 62-65; C Portsdown *Portsm* 65-69; P-in-c Elvedon *St E* 69-70; R 70-75; P-in-c Eriswell 69-70; R 70-75; P-in-c Icklingham 69-70; R 70-75; Chapl St Felix Sch Southwold 75-77; R Lt Shelford *Ely* 77-96; rtd 96. *15 Church Close, Whittlesford, Cambridge CB2 4NY* Tel (01223) 830461

TAYLOR, Stephen James. b 48. Chich Th Coll 70. **d** 73 **p** 74. C Tottenham St Paul *Lon* 73-76; St Vincent 78-85; Grenada 85-88; C-in-c Hammersmith SS Mich and Geo White City Estate CD *Lon* 88-96; AD Hammersmith 92-96; P-in-c Hammersmith St Luke 94-96; Brazil from 96. *rua Amazonas 293 apt 102, Pituba 41830-380, Salvador BA, Brazil*

TAYLOR, Stephen Ronald. b 55. Cranmer Hall Dur 80. **d** 83 **p** 84. C Chester le Street *Dur* 83-87; V Newbottle 87-92; V Stranton from 92. *The Vicarage, Westbourne Road, Hartlepool, Cleveland TS25 5RE* Tel (01429) 263190 Fax 264829

TAYLOR, Stewart. b 51. St Jo Coll Dur 74. **d** 77 **p** 78. C Norwood St Luke *S'wark* 77-81; C Surbiton Hill Ch Ch 81-91; V Cambridge St Phil *Ely* from 91. *St Philip's Vicarage, 252 Mill Road, Cambridge CB1 3NF* Tel (01223) 247652

TAYLOR, Stuart Bryan. b 40. St Chad's Coll Dur BA64 DipTh66. **d** 66 **p** 67. C Portsea N End St Mark *Portsm* 66-70; C Epsom St Martin *Guildf* 70-76; Chapl Clifton Coll Bris 76-88; Dir Bloxham Project 88-93; Chapl Giggleswick Sch 93-95; Bp's Officer for Miss and Evang *Bris* from 96. *36 Benville Avenue, Coombe Dingle, Bristol BS9 2RX* Tel 0117-968 1426

TAYLOR, Mrs Susan Mary. b 48. Univ of Wales (Swansea) BA69 Univ of Wales (Lamp) LTh72. St D Coll Lamp 70. **dss** 72 **d** 87. Chepstow *Mon* 72-73; Mynyddislwyn 73-75; Perm to Offic *Lon* 75-79; Hayes St Edm 79-87; NSM Pilton w Ashford *Ex* 87-89; NSM Sidley *Chich* from 89. *All Saints' Vicarage, All Saints Lane, Sidley, Bexhill-on-Sea, Sussex TN39 5HA* Tel (01424) 221071

TAYLOR, Thomas (Tom). b 33. Sarum & Wells Th Coll 77. **d** 80 **p** 81. NSM Heatherlands St Jo *Sarum* 80-82; TV Kinson 82-88; TV Shaston from 88; Chapl Westmr Memorial Hosp Shaftesbury from 88. *The Vicarage, Motcombe, Shaftesbury, Dorset SP7 9NX* Tel (01747) 851442

TAYLOR, Thomas Fish. b 13. Glas Univ MA46. Kelham Th Coll 30. **d** 36 **p** 37. C Millfield St Mary *Dur* 36-38; C Middlesbrough All SS *York* 38-41; R Glas St Martin *Glas* 41-48; Chapl Priory of Our Lady Burford 48-50; Lic to Offic *Roch* 50-52; Chapl Mount Ephraim Distr Hosp Tunbridge Wells 50-52; V Chalford *Glouc* 52-58; R Over w Nether Compton and Trent *Sarum* 58-65; P-in-c Poughill w Stockleigh English *Ex* 67-69; P-in-c Rattery 69-79; rtd 79; Perm to Offic *Ex* 79-92. *Harleston House, St John's Hill, Wimborne, Dorset BH21 1DB* Tel (01202) 841596

TAYLOR, Thomas Ronald Bennett. b 23. TCD BA46 MA54. Div Test. **d** 47 **p** 48. C Larne and Inver *Conn* 47-49; Chapl RAF 49-65; I Narraghmore w Fontstown and Timolin *D & G* 65-68; I Tynan w Middletown *Arm* 68-85; rtd 85. *34 Kernan Park, Portadown, Co Armagh BT63 5QX* Tel (01762) 337230

TAYLOR, William Austin. b 36. Linc Th Coll 65. **d** 67 **p** 68. C Tyldesley w Shakerley *Man* 67-71; R Cheetham St Mark 71-79; TR Peel 79-90; AD Farnworth 83-90; V Pelton *Dur* 90-96; rtd 96. *36 Tynesbank, Worsley, Manchester M28 8SL* Tel 0161-790 5327

TAYLOR, William David. b 60. Southn Univ BTh90. Sarum & Wells Th Coll 87. **d** 90 **p** 91. C Washington *Dur* 90-94; P-in-c Heworth St Mary from 94. *The Vicarage, High Heworth Lane, Heworth, Gateshead, Tyne & Wear NE10 0PB* Tel 0191-469 2111

TAYLOR, William Henry. b 56. FRAS MA MTh PhD88. Westcott Ho Cam. **d** 83 **p** 84. C Maidstone All SS and St Phil w Tovil *Cant* 83-86; Abp's Adv on Orthodox Affairs 86-88; C St Marylebone All SS *Lon* 86-88; Chapl Guy's Hosp Lon 88; CMS 88-91; Jordan 88-91; V Ealing St Pet Mt Park *Lon* from 91; AD Ealing from 93. *St Peter's Vicarage, Mount Park Road, London W5 2RU* Tel 0181-997 1620

TAYLOR, William Richard de Carteret Martin (Bill). b 33. CCC Cam MA57. Westcott Ho Cam 58. **d** 59 **p** 60. C Eastney *Portsm* 59-63; Chapl RN 63-67 and 70-87; V Childe Okeford *Sarum* 67-70; V Manston w Hamoon 67-70; QHC from 83; TR Tisbury *Sarum* 87-89; Chapl Hatf Poly *St Alb* 89-92; Chapl Herts Univ from 92. *University of Hertfordshire, College Lane, Hatfield, Herts AL10 9AB* Tel (01707) 279000 or 279456 E-mail w.taylor@herts.ac.uk

TAYLOR, Capt William Thomas. b 61. Rob Coll Cam BA83 BA90. Ridley Hall Cam 88. **d** 91 **p** 92. C Bromley Ch Ch *Roch* 91-95; C St Helen Bishopsgate w St Andr Undershaft etc *Lon* from 95. *16 Ravensden Street, London SE11 4AR* Tel 0171-283 2231

TEAGUE, Dr Gaythorne Derrick. b 24. MRCGP53 Bris Univ MB, ChB49 DPH. **d** 74 **p** 75. NSM Bris St Andr Hartcliffe *Bris* 74-86; Perm to Offic *B & W* 79-86; NSM Blagdon w Compton Martin and Ubley from 86; Perm to Offic from 86. *Innisfree, Bell Square, Blagdon, Bristol BS18 6UB* Tel (01761) 462671

TEAGUE, Robert Hayden. b 15. Univ of Wales (Ban). Dorchester Miss Coll 36 St Deiniol's Hawarden. **d** 63 **p** 64. C Rhosddu *St As* 63-65; C Llanrhos 65-66; V Llangernyw, Gwytherin and Llanddewi 66-77; V Meliden and Gwaenysgor 77-83; rtd 83. *4 Ffordd Tanrallt, Melidan, Prestatyn LL19 8PR* Tel (01745) 857419

TEAL, Andrew Robert. b 64. Birm Univ BA85. Ripon Coll Cuddesdon 86. **d** 88 **p** 89. C Wednesbury St Paul Wood Green *Lich* 88-92; TV Sheff Manor *Sheff* 92-97; Tutor Ripon Coll Cuddesdon from 92; Asst Dioc Post Ord Tr Officer from 93; V Tickhill w Stainton *Sheff* from 97. *The Vicarage, 2 Sunderland Street, Tickhill, Doncaster, S Yorkshire DN11 9QJ* Tel (01302) 742224

TEALE, Adrian. b 53. Univ of Wales (Abth) BA74 CertEd77 MA80 Univ of Wales (Cardiff) MTh89. Wycliffe Hall Ox 78. **d** 80 **p** 81. C Betws w Ammanford *St D* 80-84; V Brynaman w Cwmllynfell from 84; RD Dyffryn Aman from 95. *The Vicarage, 23 Llandeilo Road, Brynaman SA18 1BA* Tel (01269) 822275

TEALE, Ernest Burdett. b 20. Keble Coll Ox BA42 MA46. Westcott Ho Cam 42. **d** 43 **p** 45. C Havant *Portsm* 43-48; C Melksham *Sarum* 48-54; R Bradford Peverell w Stratton 54-61; Asst Dir RE 61-64; R Morton *Derby* 64-69; P-in-c Radbourne 69-70; Adv for Primary and Middle Schs *Lon* 70-85; rtd 85; Lic to Offic *Lon* from 85. *103 Sandringham Gardens, London N12 0PA* Tel 0181-445 2037

TEARE, Canon Robert John Hugh. b 39. Bris Univ BSc62 Leeds Univ DipTh69. Coll of Resurr Mirfield 67. **d** 70 **p** 71. C Fareham SS Pet and Paul *Portsm* 70-73; Chapl K Alfred Coll *Win* 73-78; V Pokesdown St Jas 78-82; R Winnall from 82; RD Win from 89; Hon Can Win Cathl from 92. *The Rectory, 22 St John's Street, Winchester, Hants SO23 0HF* Tel (01962) 863891

TEARNAN, John Herman Janson. b 37. Bris Univ BSc59. Kelham Th Coll 62. **d** 66 **p** 67. C Kettering SS Pet and Paul *Pet* 66-71; Lic to Offic 71-85; Perm to Offic 85-94; Perm to Offic *St Alb* 82-85; Sub-Chapl HM Young Offender Inst Wellingborough 89-90; Chapl HM Young Offender Inst Glen Parva 90-94; Guyana from 94. *St Saviour's Vicarage, Smyth Street, Werk-en-Rust, Georgetown, Guyana* Tel Georgetown (02) 65527

TEASDALE, Keith. b 56. Cranmer Hall Dur 86. **d** 88 **p** 89. C Crook *Dur* 88-92; V Dunston from 92. *St Nicholas' Vicarage, Willow Avenue, Dunston, Gateshead, Tyne & Wear NE11 9UN* Tel 0191-460 0509

TEBBS, Richard Henry. b 52. Southn Univ BTh. Sarum & Wells Th Coll 75. **d** 78 **p** 79. C Cinderhill *S'well* 78-82; C Nor St Pet Mancroft *Nor* 82; C Nor St Pet Mancroft w St Jo Maddermarket 82-85; TV Bridport *Sarum* 85-94; TR Yelverton, Meavy, Sheepstor and Walkhampton *Ex* from 94. *The Rectory, Meavy Lane, Yelverton, Devon PL20 6AE* Tel (01822) 832362

TEBBUTT, Christopher Michael Chris. b 55. St Jo Coll Nottm BA94. **d** 96 **p** 97. C Catherington and Clanfield *Portsm* from 96. *23 Pipersmead, Clanfield, Waterlooville, Hants PO8 0FT* Tel (01705) 595018

TEBBUTT, Simon Albert. b 27. Qu Coll Birm 88. **d** 89 **p** 90. NSM Northampton St Matt *Pet* 89-92; TV Duston Team 92-94; rtd 94; NSM Gt and Lt Houghton w Brafield on the Green *Pet* 94-96; NSM Cogenhoe and Gt and Lt Houghton w Brafield from 96. *Tanners, Moulton Lane, Boughton, Northampton NN2 8RF* Tel (01604) 843240

TEDMAN, Alfred. b 33. AKC59. **d** 60 **p** 61. C Newington St Mary *S'wark* 60-64; C Milton *Portsm* 64-68; R Bonchurch from 68; RD E Wight 78-83; P-in-c Whitwell 79-82; P-in-c St Lawrence 82-84; V Wroxall from 84. *The Rectory, Bonchurch, Ventnor, Isle of Wight PO38 1NU* Tel (01983) 852357

TEE, John. b 59. **d** 82 **p** 83. C Walworth *S'wark* 82-85; Chapl RAF 85-89; CF from 89. *MOD Chaplains (Army), Trenchard Lines, Upavon, Pewsey, Wilts SN9 6BE* Tel (01980) 615804 Fax 615800

TEGGIN, John. b 26. **d** 83 **p** 84. NSM Dublin Sandford w Milltown *D & G* 84-93; Dir Leprosy Miss 86-96. *4 Temple Hill, Blackrock, Co Dublin, Irish Republic* Tel Dublin (1) 280 4008

TELFER, Andrew Julian. b 68. Essex Univ BA94. Wycliffe Hall Ox BTh97. **d** 97. C Skelmersdale St Paul *Liv* from 97. *6 Wilcove, Skelmersdale, Lancs WN8 8NF* Tel (01695) 726491

TELFER, Canon Frank Somerville. b 30. Trin Hall Cam BA53 MA58. Ely Th Coll 53. **d** 55 **p** 56. C Liv Our Lady and St Nic *Liv* 55-58; Chapl Down Coll Cam 58-62; Bp's Chapl *Nor* 62-65; Chapl Kent Univ *Cant* 65-73; Can Res Guildf Cathl *Guildf* 73-95; rtd 96; Perm to Offic *Nor* from 96. *Holbrook, Glandford, Holt, Norfolk NR25 7JP* Tel (01263) 740586

TELFORD, Alan. b 46. St Jo Coll Nottm. **d** 83 **p** 84. C Normanton *Derby* 83-86; TV N Wingfield, Pilsley and Tupton 86-90; TV N Wingfield, Clay Cross and Pilsley 90-92; P-in-c Oakwood 92-94; V Leic St Chris *Leic* from 94. *The Vicarage, 84A Marriott Road, Leicester LE2 6NU* Tel 0116-283 2679

TELFORD, Cyril Harry. b 22. S Dios Minl Tr Scheme. **d** 54 **p** 55. C Gt Crosby St Faith *Liv* 54-57; C Liv Our Lady and St Nic 57-60; V Lt Lever *Man* 60-94; rtd 94; Perm to Offic *Man* from 94. *1 Aintree Road, Little Lever, Bolton BL3 1EZ* Tel (01204) 72392

TELFORD, Canon Edward Cecil. b 17. Selw Coll Cam BA47 MA52. Linc Th Coll 47. **d** 49 **p** 50. C Laindon w Basildon *Chelmsf* 49-52; C-in-c Leytonstone St Aug CD 52-59; R Langdon Hills

59-70; R Shenfield 70-85; Hon Can Chelmsf Cathl 75-85; RD Brentwood 76-84; rtd 85; Perm to Offic *Ely* from 86. *13 Harlestones Road, Cottenham, Cambridge CB4 4TR* Tel (01954) 51184

TELFORD, John Edward. b 16. TCD BA40 MA46. CITC 40. **d** 41 **p** 42. C St Helens St Mark *Liv* 41-44; I Dublin Irishtown *D & G* 44-60; Chapl Miss to Adult Deaf and Dumb Dublin Area 44-60; rtd 60. *12 Woodbine Avenue, Blackrock, Co Dublin, Irish Republic* Tel Dublin (1) 269 1187

TELFORD, Richard Francis. b 46. K Coll Lon. **d** 69 **p** 70. C Barkingside H Trin *Chelmsf* 69-72; C Wickford 72-77; P-in-c Romford St Jo 77-80; V 80-82; Perm to Offic 93-96. *59 Hartswood Road, Brentwood, Essex CM14 5AG* Tel (01277) 214911

TELLINI, Canon Dr Gianfranco. b 36. Gregorian Univ Rome DTh65. Franciscan Sem Trent 57. **d** 61 **p** 61. In RC Ch 61-66; C Mill Hill Jo Keble Ch *Lon* 66; C Roxbourne St Andr 66-67; Lect Sarum Th Coll 67-69; Sen Tutor 69-74; Vice-Prin Edin Th Coll 74-82; Lect Th Edin Univ from 74; R Pittenweem *St And* 82-85; R Elie and Earlsferry 82-85; R Dunblane from 85; Can St Ninian's Cathl Perth from 90. *The Rectory, Smithy Loan, Dunblane, Perthshire FK15 0HQ* Tel (01786) 824225 E-mail gtellini@aol.com

TEMBEY, David. **d** 96. NSM Whitehaven *Carl* from 96. *2 High Street, Whitehaven, Cumbria CA28 7PZ* Tel (01946) 64738

TEMPERLEY, Robert Noble. b 29. JP. ACP52 St Jo Coll York CertEd50 Dur Univ DAES62. NE Ord Course 85. **d** 88 **p** 88. NSM Ryhope *Dur* from 88. *18 Withernsea Grove, Ryhope, Sunderland SR2 0BU* Tel 0191-521 1813

✠**TEMPLE, The Rt Revd Frederick Stephen.** b 16. Ball Coll Ox BA39 MA45 Trin Hall Cam BA47 MA52. Westcott Ho Cam 45. **d** 47 **p** 48 **c** 73. C Arnold *S'well* 47-49; C Newark w Coddington 49-51; R Birch St Agnes *Man* 51-53; Dean Hong Kong 53-59; Abp's Sen Chapl *Cant* 59-61; V Portsea St Mary *Portsm* 61-70; Hon Can Portsm Cathl 65-69; Adn Swindon *Bris* 70-73; Hon Can Bris Cathl 70-83; Suff Bp Malmesbury 73-83; rtd 83; Asst Bp Bris from 83; Asst Bp Sarum from 83. *7 The Barton, Wood Street, Wootton Bassett, Swindon SN4 7BG* Tel (01793) 851227

TEMPLE, The Ven George Frederick. b 33. Wells Th Coll 66. **d** 68 **p** 69. C Gt Bookham *Guildf* 68-70; C Penzance St Mary *Truro* 70-72; V St Just in Penwith 72-74; V Sancreed 72-74; V St Gluvias 74-81; Adn Bodmin 81-89; Hon Can Truro Cathl 81-89; V Saltash St Nich and St Faith 82-85; Dioc Dir of Ords 85-89; rtd 89; Perm to Offic *Truro* from 89. *50 Athelstan Park, Bodmin, Cornwall PL31 1DT* Tel (01208) 77568

TEMPLE, Mrs Sylvia Mary. b 48. Ex Univ BA70 Univ of Wales (Abth) PGCE71. St D Dioc Tr Course 93. **d** 94 **p** 97. NSM Tenby *St D* from 94. *Llwyn Onn, Trafalgar Road, Tenby SA70 7DW* Tel (01834) 842104

TEMPLEMAN, Peter Morton. b 49. Ch Ch Ox BA71 MA75 BTh75. Wycliffe Hall Ox 73. **d** 76 **p** 77. C Cheltenham St Mary, St Matt, St Paul and H Trin *Glouc* 76-79; Chapl St Jo Coll Cam 79-84; P-in-c Finchley St Paul Long Lane *Lon* 84-85; P-in-c Finchley St Luke 84-85; V Finchley St Paul and St Luke from 85. *St Paul's Vicarage, 50 Long Lane, London N3 2PU* Tel 0181-346 8729

TEMPLETON, Iain McAllister. b 57. **d** 85 **p** 86. In RC Ch 85-92; NSM Dornoch *Mor* 95; P-in-c Kirriemuir *St And* from 95. *The Rectory, 128 Glengate, Kirriemuir, Angus DD8 4JG* Tel (01575) 575515 Fax as telephone

TENNANT, Charles Roger. b 19. Open Univ PhD75. Linc Th Coll 49. **d** 51 **p** 52. C Belgrave St Pet *Leic* 51-54; Korea 54-62; V Bitteswell *Leic* 62-88; P-in-c Misterton w Walcote 80-88; rtd 88; Perm to Offic *Leic* from 88. *Middle House, Station Road, Ullesthorpe, Lutterworth, Leics LE17 5BS* Tel (01455) 209703

TENNANT, Cyril Edwin George. b 37. Keble Coll Ox BA59 MA63 Lon Univ BD61. Clifton Th Coll 59. **d** 62 **p** 63. C Stapleford *S'well* 62-65; C Felixstowe SS Pet and Paul *St E* 65-69; V Gipsy Hill Ch Ch *S'wark* 69-84; V Lee St Mildred 84-90; V Ilfracombe SS Phil and Jas w W Down *Ex* from 90; P-in-c Lundy Is 90-92. *St James's Vicarage, Kingsley Avenue, Ilfracombe, Devon EX34 8ET* Tel (01271) 863519

TENNANT, Osmond Roy. b 21. Worc Ord Coll 62. **d** 63 **p** 64. C S Molton w Nymet St George *Ex* 63-67; V Escot 67-89; R Talaton 67-89; P-in-c Clyst Hydon and Clyst St Lawrence 74-87; rtd 89; Perm to Offic *Ex* from 89. *Rockleigh, 29 West Clyst, Exeter EX1 3TL* Tel (01392) 65515

TER BLANCHE, Harold Daniel. b 35. St Paul's Grahamstown LTh85. **d** 63 **p** 64. S Africa 63-82; Miss to Seamen 82-84; Gen Preacher *Linc* from 84; Chapl Grimsby Distr Gen Hosp 84-94; Chapl Grimsby Health NHS Trust from 94. *Grimsby District General Hospital, Scartho Road, Grimsby, S Humberside DN33 2BA* Tel (01472) 875204

TERESA, Sister. *See* WHITE, Sister Teresa Joan

TERRANOVA, Jonathan Rossano. b 62. Sheff Poly BA85. Oak Hill Th Coll BA88. **d** 88 **p** 89. C Carl St Jo *Carl* 88-91; C Stoughton *Guildf* 91-94; R Ditton *Roch* from 94. *The Rectory, 2 The Stream, Ditton, Maidstone, Kent ME20 6AG* Tel (01732) 842027

TERRELL, Richard Charles Patridge. b 43. Wells Th Coll 69. **d** 71 **p** 72. C Shepton Mallet *B & W* 71-76; P-in-c Drayton 76-78; P-in-c Muchelney 76-78; TV Langport Area Chs 78-82; P-in-c Tatworth 82-89; V 89-96; R W Coker w Hardington Mandeville, E Chinnock etc from 96. *The Rectory, 7 Cedar Fields, West Coker, Yeovil, Somerset BA22 9DB* Tel (01935) 862328

TERRETT, Mervyn Douglas. b 43. AKC65. **d** 66 **p** 67. C Pet St Mary Boongate *Pet* 66-69; C Sawbridgeworth *St Alb* 69-74; V Stevenage H Trin 74-85; Perm to Offic from 86. *Red Roofs, 20 Woodfield Road, Stevenage, Herts SG1 4BP* Tel (01438) 720152

TERRY, Christopher Laurence. b 51. FCA80. St Alb Minl Tr Scheme. **d** 83 **p** 84. Hon C Dunstable *St Alb* 83-89; C Abbots Langley 89-92; TV Chambersbury (Hemel Hempstead) from 92; Chapl Abbot's Hill Sch Herts from 96. *St Mary's Vicarage, 31 Chipperfield Road, Apsley, Hemel Hempstead, Herts HP3 0AJ* Tel (01442) 61610

TERRY, Ian Andrew. b 53. St Jo Coll Dur BA74 St Jo Coll York PGCE75. Coll of Resurr Mirfield 78. **d** 80 **p** 81. C Beaconsfield *Ox* 80-83; C N Lynn w St Marg and St Nic *Nor* 83-84; Chapl & Head RE Eliz Coll Guernsey 84-89; Chapl St Jo Sch Leatherhead 89-92; R Bisley and W End *Guildf* from 92. *The Rectory, Clews Lane, Bisley, Woking, Surrey GU24 9DY* Tel (01483) 473377

TERRY, John Arthur. b 32. S'wark Ord Course. **d** 66 **p** 67. C Plumstead All SS *S'wark* 66-69; C Peckham St Mary Magd 69-72; V Streatham Vale H Redeemer 72-80; R Sternfield w Benhall and Snape *St E* 80-84; V Stevenage St Mary Shephall *St Alb* 84-86; V Stevenage St Mary Sheppall w Aston 86-90; V Cople w Willington from 90; Chapl Shuttleworth Agric Coll from 90. *The Vicarage, Cople, Bedford MK44 3TT* Tel (01234) 838431

TERRY, Justyn Charles. b 65. Keble Coll Ox BA86 St Jo Coll Dur BA95. Cranmer Hall Dur 92. **d** 95 **p** 96. C Paddington St Jo w St Mich *Lon* from 95. *12 Connaught Street, London W2 2AF* Tel 0171-706 4099 Fax 262 1732

TERRY, Stephen John. b 49. K Coll Lon BD72 AKC74. **d** 75 **p** 76. C Tokyngton St Mich *Lon* 75-78; C Hampstead St Steph w All Hallows 78-81; V Whetstone St Jo 81-89; TR Aldrington *Chich* from 89; OStJ from 89. *The Rectory, 77 New Church Road, Hove, E Sussex BN3 4BB* Tel (01273) 737915

TESTA, Luigi Richard Frederick. b 30. Nottm Univ CTPS85. **d** 85 **p** 86. NSM Castle Donington and Lockington cum Hemington *Leic* from 85. *40 Hillside, Castle Donington, Derby DE74 2NH* Tel (01332) 810823

TESTER, Clarence Albert. b 20. Qu Coll Birm 47. **d** 50 **p** 51. C Southmead *Bris* 50-53; C Knowle St Barn 53-55; Chapl Ham Green Hosp Bris 55-70; V Halberton *Ex* 70-85; rtd 85; Perm to Offic *B & W* from 86. *Brays Batch, Chewton Mendip, Bath BA3 4LH* Tel (01761) 241218

TESTER, Canon Francis Edward. b 24. Leeds Univ BA46. Coll of Resurr Mirfield 45. **d** 47 **p** 48. C Lon Docks St Pet w Wapping St Jo *Lon* 47-51; C Pimlico St Mary Graham Terrace 51-57; V Acton Green St Pet 58-64; V Hockerill *St Alb* 64-71; Chapl Highwood and St Faith's Hosps Brentwood 71-89; V Brentwood St Thos *Chelmsf* 71-89; RD Brentwood 84-89; Hon Can Chelmsf Cathl 87-89; rtd 89; Perm to Offic *Chelmsf* 89-92; Perm to Offic *Nor* 89-91 and from 94; P-in-c Toftrees w Shereford 91-94; P-in-c Hempton and Pudding Norton 91-94. *Wythe, Burnt Street, Wells-next-the-Sea, Norfolk NR23 1HW* Tel (01328) 711306

TETLEY, Brian. b 38. FCA BA. Cranmer Hall Dur 80. **d** 83 **p** 84. C Chipping Sodbury and Old Sodbury *Glouc* 83-86; Chapl and Succ Roch Cath *Roch* 86-89; R Gravesend H Family w Ifield 89-93; C Duxford *Ely* from 97; C Hinxton from 97; C Ickleton from 97. *201A Milton Road, Cambridge CB4 1XG* Tel (01223) 423633

TETLEY, Canon Joy Dawn. b 46. St Mary's Coll Dur BA68 Leeds Univ CertEd69 St Hugh's Coll Ox BA75 MA80 Dur Univ PhD88. NW Ord Course 77. **dss** 77 **d** 87 **p** 94. Bentley *Sheff* 77-79; Buttershaw St Aid *Bradf* 79-80; Dur Cathl *Dur* 80-83; Lect Trin Coll Bris 83-86; Chipping Sodbury and Old Sodbury *Glouc* 83-86; Dn Roch Cathl *Roch* 87-89; Hon Can Roch Cathl 90-93; Assoc Dir of Post Ord Tr 87-88; Dir Post Ord Tr 88-93; Hon Par Dn Gravesend H Family w Ifield 89-93; Prin E Anglian Minl Tr Course *Ely* from 93. *201A Milton Road, Cambridge CB4 1XG* Tel (01223) 423633 or 322633

TETLEY, Matthew David. b 61. Bucks Coll of Educn BSc83. Sarum & Wells Th Coll BTh89. **d** 87 **p** 88. C Kirkby *Liv* 87-90; C Hindley St Pet 90-93; TV Whorlton *Newc* 93-96; V Newbiggin Hall from 96. *St Wilfrid's House, Trevelyan Drive, Newcastle upon Tyne NE5 4DA* Tel 0191-286 0345

TETLOW, John. b 46. St Steph Ho Ox 73. **d** 76 **p** 77. C Stanwell *Lon* 76-77; C Hanworth All SS 77-80; C Somers Town St Mary 80-83; TV Wickford and Runwell *Chelmsf* 83-90; P-in-c Walthamstow St Mich 90-96. *6A Bushwood, London E11 3AY* Tel 0181-520 6328

TETLOW, Richard Jeremy. b 42. Trin Coll Cam MA66 Golds Coll Lon CQSW74. Qu Coll Birm 81. **d** 83 **p** 84. C Birm St Martin *Birm* 83-85; C Birm St Martin w Bordesley St Andr 85-88; V Birm St Jo Ladywood from 89. *St John's Vicarage, Darnley Road, Birmingham B16 8TF* Tel 0121-454 0973

TEWKESBURY, Alec. b 13. Dur Univ LTh38. ALCD36. **d** 36 **p** 37. C Leyton All SS *Chelmsf* 36-39; C Leic Martyrs *Leic* 39-42; C-in-c Leic St Chris CD 42-48; V Earl Shilton w Elmesthorpe 48-53;

Chapl Br Families Educn Service Germany 54-61; Chapl Thos Bennett Sch Crawley 61-70; C Crawley *Chich* 65-70; V Loxwood 70-78; rtd 78; Perm to Offic *Chich* from 78. *1 Stonefield Close, Crawley, W Sussex RH10 6AU* Tel (01293) 534420

TEWKESBURY, Noel. b 44. Hull Univ BA67. Wycliffe Hall Ox 70. **d** 72 **p** 73. C Bishops Waltham *Portsm* 72-76; C Havant 76-77; C Filey *York* 77-79; V Monk Fryston 79-84; V Hambleton 79-84; TV Bolventor *Truro* 84-86; TR 86-91; R N Elmham w Billingford and Worthing *Nor* from 91. *The Vicarage, Holt Road, North Elmham, Dereham, Norfolk NR20 5JQ* Tel (01362) 668244

TEWKESBURY, Suffragan Bishop of. *See* WENT, The Rt Revd John Stewart

THACKER, Ian David. b 59. DCR81 DRI84. Oak Hill Th Coll BA91. **d** 91 **p** 92. C Illogan *Truro* 91-94; C Eglwysilan *Llan* 94-96; TV Hornsey Rise Whitehall Park Team *Lon* 96-97; TV Upper Holloway from 97. *St Andrew's Vicarage, 43 Dresden Road, London N19 3BG* Tel 0171-281 8775

THACKER, James Robert. b 40. Cath Univ of America BA63 MDiv66 MSW76. Nashotah Ho. **d** 66 **p** 66. USA 66-90; Bermuda from 90. *PO Box FL 239, Smith's FL BX, Bermuda* Tel Bermuda (1-441) 236-8360 Fax 236-7148

THACKER, Jonathan William. b 53. Lon Univ BA74 Nottm Univ DipTh78. Linc Th Coll 76. **d** 79 **p** 80. C Bromyard *Heref* 79-82; C Penkridge w Stretton *Lich* 82-87; V Brothertoft Gp *Linc* 87-96; RD Holland W 92-95; P-in-c Crosby from 96. *St George's Vicarage, 87 Ferry Road, Scunthorpe, S Humberside DN15 8LY* Tel (01724) 843328

THACKER, Kenneth Ray. b 31. Open Univ BA73. Tyndale Hall Bris 56. **d** 59 **p** 60. C Penn Fields *Lich* 59-61; C Tipton St Martin 62-64; V Moxley 64-71; R Leigh 71-91; rtd 92; Perm to Offic *Lich* from 92. *24 Rugby Close, Newcastle-under-Lyme ST5 3JN* Tel (01782) 617812

THACKER, Roger Ailwyn Mackintosh. b 46. CCC Cam BA68 MA73. Westcott Ho Cam 68. **d** 70 **p** 71. C St Jo Wood *Lon* 70-74; P-in-c Hammersmith St Paul 74-79; V from 79. *21 Lower Mall, London W6 9DJ* Tel 0171-603 4303 or 748 3855

THACKRAY, John Adrian. b 55. ACIB84 Southn Univ BSc76. Coll of Resurr Mirfield 81. **d** 84 **p** 85. C Loughton St Jo *Chelmsf* 84-87; Chapl Bancroft's Sch Woodford Green 87-92; Sen Chapl K Sch Cant from 92; Hon Min Can Cant Cathl *Cant* from 93; Perm to Offic *Chelmsf* from 93. *14 Monastery Street, Canterbury, Kent CT1 1NJ* Tel (01227) 595613 or 595561

THACKRAY, Peter Michael. b 29. Coll of Resurr Mirfield BA52. **d** 54 **p** 55. C St Mary-at-Lambeth *S'wark* 54-57; C Primrose Hill St Mary w Avenue Road St Paul *Lon* 57-59; C-in-c S Kenton Annunciation CD 59-61; Chapl Pierrepont Sch Frensham 61-67; W Germany 67-73; CF 73-78; Lic to Offic *Eur* 78-84; Hon C Sellindge w Monks Horton and Stowting *Cant* 84-86; Hon C Lympne w W Hythe 84-86; Hon C Sellindge w Monks Horton and Stowting etc 86-91; Perm to Offic 91-95; rtd 94; Hon C Brabourne w Smeeth *Cant* 95. *The Rectory, Church Road, Smeeth, Ashford, Kent TN25 6SA* Tel (01303) 812126

THACKRAY, William Harry. b 44. Leeds Univ CertEd66. Chich Th Coll 70. **d** 73 **p** 74. C Sheff St Cuth *Sheff* 73-76; C Stocksbridge 76-78; P-in-c Newark St Leon *S'well* 79-80; TV Newark w Hawton, Cotham and Shelton 80-82; V Choral S'well Minster 82-85; V Bawtry w Austerfield 85; P-in-c Misson 85; V Bawtry w Austerfield and Misson 86-93; RD Bawtry 90-93; P-in-c Balderton from 93. *The Vicarage, Main Street, Balderton, Newark, Notts NG24 3NN* Tel (01636) 704811

THAKE, Preb Terence (Terry). b 41. ALCD65. **d** 66 **p** 67. C Gt Faringdon w Lt Coxwell *Ox* 66-70; C Aldridge *Lich* 70-73; V Werrington 73-82; Chapl HM Det Cen Werrington Ho 73-82; TR Chell *Lich* 82-94; Chapl Westcliffe Hosp 82-94; RD Stoke N 91-94; Preb Lich Cathl from 94; V Colwich w Gt Haywood from 94; P-in-c Colton from 95. *The Vicarage, Little Haywood, Stafford ST18 0TS* Tel (01889) 881262

THAME, Miss Margaret Eve. b 31. SRN54 SCM55. Glouc Sch of Min 85. **d** 88 **p** 94. NSM Cheltenham All SS *Glouc* 88-94; NSM Cheltenham St Mich from 94. *13 Brighton Road, Cheltenham, Glos GL52 6BA* Tel (01242) 241228

THATCHER, Barbara Mary. b 25. Lon Univ BCom. **d** 90 **p** 94. NSM Helensburgh *Glas* from 90. *228 West Princes Street, Helensburgh, Dunbartonshire G84 8HA* Tel (01436) 672003

THATCHER, Stephen Bert. b 58. ALCD87. St Jo Coll Nottm LTh87. **d** 87 **p** 88. C Bargoed and Deri w Brithdir *Llan* 87-89; C Llanishen and Lisvane 89-91; V Llanwnda, Goodwick, w Manorowen and Llanstinan *St D* 91-95; P-in-c Coberley w Cowley *Glouc* 95-96; P-in-c Colesborne 95-96; Dioc Rural Adv 95-96; V New Radnor and Llanfihangel Nantmelan etc *S & B* from 96. *The Vicarage, New Radnor, Presteigne LD8 2SS* Tel (01544) 21258

THAWLEY, The Very Revd David Laurie. b 24. St Edm Hall Ox BA47 MA49. Cuddesdon Coll 49. **d** 51 **p** 52. C Bitterne Park *Win* 51-56; C-in-c Andover St Mich CD 56-60; Australia from 60; Can Res Brisbane 64-72; Dean Wangaratta 72-89; rtd 89. *Lavender Cottage, 2 Bond Street, North Caulfield, Victoria, Australia 3161* Tel Melbourne (3) 9571 0513

THAYER, Michael David. b 52. Sarum & Wells Th Coll 77. **d** 80 **p** 81. C Minehead *B & W* 80-85; Chapl RN 85-89; TV Lowestoft and Kirkley *Nor* 89-92; Chapl St Helena's Hospice Colchester from 92. *St Helena's Hospice, Eastwood Drive, Highwoods, Colchester CO4 4JU* Tel (01206) 845566

THEAKSTON, Ms Sally Margaret. b 62. UEA BSc84 Ox Univ BA89 K Coll Lon MA94. Ripon Coll Cuddesdon 86. **d** 89 **p** 94. Par Dn Hackney *Lon* 89-93; Par Dn Putney St Mary *S'wark* 93-94; C 94-96; Chapl RN from 96. *Royal Naval Chaplaincy Service, Room 203, Victory Building, HM Naval Base, Portsmouth PO1 3LS* Tel (01705) 727903 Fax 727112

THELWELL, Canon John Berry. b 49. Univ of Wales (Ban) BD72. Qu Coll Birm 73. **d** 73 **p** 74. C Minera *St As* 73-80; Dioc Youth Chapl 78-86; V Gwernaffield and Llanferres 80-93; Chapl Clwyd Fire Service from 88; RD Mold 91-95; R Hawarden from 93; Can Cursal St As Cathl from 95. *The Rectory, 2 Birch Rise, Hawarden, Deeside CH5 3DD* Tel (01244) 531103 or 535816

THEOBALD, Graham Fitzroy. b 43. ALCD67. **d** 67 **p** 68. C Crookham *Guildf* 67-71; C York Town St Mich 71-74; V Wrecclesham 74-83; R Frimley 83-85; Perm to Offic *Ox* 90-92; C Easthampstead 92-97; Chapl E Berks Community Health NHS Trust from 97. *King Edward VII Hospital, Windsor, Berks SL4 3DP* Tel (01753) 860441

THEOBALD, Henry Charles. b 32. Lon Univ DBS63 DRBS63. S'wark Ord Course 60. **d** 63 **p** 64. C Battersea St Phil *S'wark* 63-65; C Caterham 65-68; C Reigate St Luke S Park 68-73; Chapl S Lon Hosp for Women & St Jas Hosp Balham 73-83; Chapl St Mary's Hosp Portsm 83-93; rtd 93. *141 Warren Avenue, Southsea, Hants PO4 8PP* Tel (01705) 817443

THEOBALD, John Walter. b 33. St Aid Birkenhead 62. **d** 65 **p** 66. C Hindley All SS *Liv* 65-68; C Beverley Minster *York* 68-71; R Loftus 71-86; P-in-c Carlin How w Skinningrove 73-86; Dep Chapl HM Pris Leeds 86-89; Chapl HM Pris Rudgate 89-93; Chapl HM Pris Thorp Arch 89-93; Chapl HM Pris Leeds 93-97; V Leeds St Cypr Harehills *Ripon* from 97. *St Cyprian's Vicarage, 43A Coldcotes Avenue, Leeds LS9 6ND* Tel 0113-249 3746

THEODOSIUS, Hugh John. b 32. Trin Coll Cam BA56 MA60. Cuddesdon Coll 56. **d** 58 **p** 59. C Milton *Win* 58-62; C Romsey 62-64; C Southampton Maybush St Pet 64-70; V Malden St Jo *S'wark* 70-81; V Billingborough *Linc* 81-94; V Horbling 81-94; V Sempringham w Pointon and Birthorpe 81-94; RD Aveland and Ness w Stamford 87-93. *Serupringham House, Wingland, East Bank, Sutton Bridge, Spalding, Lincs PE12 9YN* Tel (01775) 821735

THEODOSIUS, Richard Francis. b 35. Fitzw Coll Cam BA59. Lich Th Coll 69. **d** 71 **p** 72. C Bloxwich *Lich* 71-73; Chapl Blue Coat Comp Sch Walsall 71-73; Chapl Ranby Ho Sch Retford 73-96; Lic to Offic *S'well* 73-96; P-in-c Norton Cuckney from 96. *Downlea, 51 Town Street, Lound, Retford, Notts DN22 8RT* Tel (01777) 818744

THETFORD, Suffragan Bishop of. *See* de WAAL, The Rt Revd Hugo Ferdinand

THEWLIS, Andrew James. b 64. Man Univ BSc86. Cranmer Hall Dur 87. **d** 90 **p** 91. C Walshaw Ch Ch *Man* 90-95; P-in-c Jersey St Jo *Win* from 95. *The Rectory, La Rue des Landes, St John, Jersey, Channel Islands JE3 4AF* Tel (01534) 861677

THEWLIS, Brian Jacob. b 24. **d** 53 **p** 54. C Wednesbury St Jas *Lich* 53-57; C Sidley *Chich* 59-60; Australia from 61; rtd 94. *41 Sixth Street, Parkdale, Victoria, Australia 3195* Tel Melbourne (3) 9587 3095

THEWLIS, Dr John Charles. b 49. Van Mildert Coll Dur BA70 PhD75. N Ord Course 78. **d** 81 **p** 82. NSM Hull St Mary Sculcoates *York* 81-83; C Spring Park *Cant* 83-84; C Spring Park All SS *S'wark* 85-86; V Eltham Park St Luke from 86. *St Luke's Vicarage, 107 Westmount Road, London SE9 1XX* Tel 0181-850 3030 E-mail vicar@jctclerk.demon.co.uk

THICKE, James Balliston. b 43. Sarum & Wells Th Coll 74. **d** 77 **p** 78. C Wareham *Sarum* 77-80; TV 80-83; Dioc Youth Adv *Dur* 83-87; C Portishead *B & W* 87-90; V Westfield from 90. *Westfield Vicarage, Midsomer Norton, Bath BA3 4BJ* Tel (01761) 412105

✠**THIRD, The Rt Revd Richard Henry McPhail.** b 27. Em Coll Cam BA50 MA55 Kent Univ Hon DCL90. Linc Th Coll 50. **d** 52 **p** 53 **c** 76. C Mottingham St Andr *S'wark* 52-55; C Sanderstead All SS 55-59; V Sheerness H Trin w St Paul *Cant* 59-67; V Orpington All SS *Roch* 67-76; RD Orpington 73-76; Hon Can Roch Cathl 74-76; Suff Bp Maidstone *Cant* 76-80; Suff Bp Dover 80-92; rtd 92; Asst Bp B & W from 92. *25 Church Close, Martock, Somerset TA12 6DS* Tel (01935) 825519

THISELTON, Canon Prof Anthony Charles. b 37. Novi Testamenti Societas 75 Lon Univ BD59 K Coll Lon MTh64 Sheff Univ PhD77 Dur Univ DD93. Oak Hill Th Coll 58. **d** 60 **p** 61. C Sydenham H Trin *S'wark* 60-63; Tutor Tyndale Hall Bris 63-67; Sen Tutor 67-70; Lect Bibl Studies Sheff Univ 70-79; Sen Lect 79-85; Prof Calvin Coll Grand Rapids 82-83; Special Lect Th Nottm Univ 86-88; Prin St Jo Coll Nottm 86-88; Prin St Jo Coll w Cranmer Hall Dur 88-92; Prof Chr Th Nottm Univ from 93; Can Th Leic Cathl *Leic* from 94. *Department of Theology, Nottingham University, University Park, Nottingham NG7 2RD* Tel 0115-951 5852 Fax 951 5887

THISTLETHWAITE, Dr Nicholas John. b 51. Selw Coll Cam BA73 MA77 PhD80 Ox Univ BA78 MA83. Ripon Coll Cuddesdon BA78. **d** 79 **p** 80. C Newc St Gabr *Newc* 79-82; Lic to Offic *Ely* 82-90; Chapl G&C Coll Cam 82-90; V Trumpington

Ely from 90. *The Vicarage, Trumpington, Cambridge CB2 2LH* Tel (01223) 841262

THISTLEWOOD, Michael John. b 31. Ch Coll Cam BA53 MA57. Linc Th Coll 54. **d** 56 **p** 57. C N Hull St Mich *York* 56-59; C Scarborough St Mary 59-61; V Kingston upon Hull St Jude w St Steph 61-67; V Newland St Aug 67-72; Asst Master Bemrose Sch Derby 72-80; V Derby St Andr w St Osmund *Derby* 80-82; Lic to Offic *Ox* 84-95; rtd 88; Perm to Offic *Carl* from 88. *9 Lightburn Road, Ulverston, Cumbria LA12 0AU* Tel (01229) 584687

THODY, Charles Michael Jackson. b 62. Linc Th Coll BTh94. **d** 94 **p** 95. C Immingham *Linc* 94-97; P-in-c Leasingham from 97; P-in-c Cranwell from 97. *The Rectory, 3 Moor Lane, Leasingham, Sleaford, Lincs NG34 8JN* Tel (01529) 306756

THOM, Alastair George. b 60. ACA86 G&C Coll Cam BA81 MA84. Ridley Hall Cam 88. **d** 91 **p** 92. C Lindfield *Chich* 91-94; C Finchley St Paul and St Luke *Lon* from 94. *Church House, Howes Close, Mountfield Road, London N3 3BX* Tel 0181-346 0563

THOM, James. b 31. St Chad's Coll Dur BA53 DipTh57. **d** 57 **p** 58. C Middlesbrough St Thos *York* 57-60; C Hornsea and Goxhill 60-62; C S Bank 62-63; V Copmanthorpe 63-75; V Coxwold 75-77; RD Easingwold 77-82; V Coxwold and Husthwaite 77-87; Abp's Adv for Spiritual Direction 86-93; P-in-c Topcliffe 87-93; rtd 93. *34 Hellwath Grove, Ripon, N Yorkshire HG4 2JT* Tel (01765) 605083

THOM, Thomas Kennedy Dalziel. b 29. Pemb Coll Cam BA53 MA57. St Steph Ho Ox 60. **d** 61 **p** 62. C Colchester St Jas, All SS, St Nic and St Runwald *Chelmsf* 61-64; USPG 65-70; Ghana 65-70; SSJE 71-72; Chapl Essex Univ *Chelmsf* 73-80; Sec Chapls in HE Gen Syn Bd of Educn 81-87; Partnership Sec and Dep Gen Sec USPG 87-92; Chapl Burrswood Chr Cen *Roch* 93-94; rtd 95. *24 South Island Place, London SW9 0DX* Tel 0171-582 2798

THOMAS, Adrian Leighton. b 37. St D Coll Lamp BA62 DipTh. **d** 63 **p** 64. C Port Talbot St Theodore *Llan* 63-70; V Troedrhiwgarth 70-73; C Sandhurst *Ox* 73-77; V Streatley 77-84; P-in-c Moulsford 81-84; V Streatley w Moulsford 84-90; P-in-c Sutton Courtenay w Appleford from 90; RD Abingdon from 96. *The Vicarage, 3 Tullis Close, Sutton Courtenay, Abingdon, Oxon OX14 4BD* Tel (01235) 848297

THOMAS, Canon Alan. b 42. Univ of Wales (Cardiff) BA65. St Mich Coll Llan 65. **d** 67 **p** 68. C Fairwater *Llan* 67-69; C Llanishen and Lisvane 69-73; V Troedyrhiw w Merthyr Vale 73-77; V Pembroke Dock *St D* 77-93; P-in-c Cosheston w Nash and Upton 85-93; R 93; V Pembroke Dock from 93; Chapl S Pembrokeshire Hosp from 77; RD Castlemartin *St D* from 83; Can St D Cathl from 89. *The Vicarage, Church Street, Pembroke Dock SA72 6AR* Tel (01646) 682943

THOMAS, Alan William Charles. b 19. Liv Univ BA41. St Aid Birkenhead 42. **d** 43 **p** 44. C Everton Em *Liv* 43-45; C Fazakerley Em 45-50; V Everton St Benedict 50-56; V Tipton St Martin *Lich* 56-67; V Wolverhampton St Jude 67-87; rtd 87; Perm to Offic *Lich* 87-89; Perm to Offic *Ex* from 89. *Gable Cottage, Radway, Sidmouth, Devon EX10 8TW* Tel (01395) 513302

THOMAS, Albert Kenneth. b 18. St D Coll Lamp BA40 St Mich Coll Llan 40. **d** 42 **p** 43. C Griffithstown *Mon* 42-47; CF 47-67; R Charlton Musgrove *B & W* 67-80; P-in-c Cucklington w Stoke Trister and Bayford 79-80; R Charlton Musgrove, Cucklington and Stoke Trister 80-83; RD Bruton 71-77; rtd 83; Perm to Offic *B & W* 84-86. *Chelwood, 32 Shreen Way, Gillingham, Dorset SP8 4EL* Tel (01747) 822093

THOMAS, Aled Huw. b 59. Univ of Wales (Abth) BD81 DPS83. St Mich Coll Llan 84. **d** 85 **p** 86. C Llandeilo and Taliaris *St D* 85-86; P-in-c Llangrannog and Llandysiliogogo 86-88; Chapl RAF 88-92; R Ystradgynlais *S & B* 92-94; CF from 94. *MOD Chaplains (Army), Trenchard Lines, Upavon, Pewsey, Wilts SN9 6BE* Tel (01980) 615804 Fax 615800

THOMAS, Canon Alfred James Randolph. b 48. St D Coll Lamp DipTh71. **d** 71 **p** 72. C Cydweli and Llandyfaelog *St D* 71-74; C Carmarthen St Dav 74-76; TV Aberystwyth 76-81; V Betws w Ammanford 81-93; RD Dyffryn Aman 90-93; V Carmarthen St Pet from 93; Can St D Cathl from 96. *The Vicarage, Carmarthen SA31 1LJ* Tel (01267) 237117

THOMAS, Andrew Herbert Redding. b 41. Lon Coll of Div 66. **d** 69 **p** 70. C Cromer *Nor* 69-72; Holiday Chapl 72-76; R Grimston w Congham 76-83; R Roydon All SS 76-83; C-in-c Ewell St Paul Howell Hill CD *Guildf* 83-89; V Howell Hill 89-95; RD Epsom 93-95; TR Beccles St Mich *St E* from 95. *The Rectory, 53 Cromwell Avenue, Beccles, Suffolk NR34 9XF* Tel (01502) 716017

THOMAS, Arthur Norman. b 17. St Aid Birkenhead 54. **d** 56 **p** 57. C Chapel Allerton *Ripon* 56-59; V Wyther Ven Bede 59-65; R Seacroft 65-70; TR 70-76; R Thornton Watlass w Thornton Steward and E Witton 76-86; rtd 86. *10 St Andrew's Meadow, Kirkby Malzeard, Ripon, N Yorkshire HG4 3SW* Tel (01765) 658884

THOMAS, Canon Arthur Roy. b 25. St Steph Ho Ox 55. **d** 58 **p** 59. C Boston *Linc* 58-60; Lect 60-63; N Gp Org SPCK 63-64; Exec Officer Feed the Minds 64-67; C St Mary Aldermary *Lon* 66-72; Regional Officer SPCK 67-72; V Canning Town St Cedd *Chelmsf* 72-80; P-in-c Victoria Docks Ascension 78-79; P-in-c Runwell 80-81; P-in-c Wickford 80-81; TR Wickford and Runwell 81-85; V Gosfield 85-91; RD Halstead and Coggeshall 87-91; Hon Can Chelmsf Cathl 90-91; rtd 91; Perm to Offic *St E* from 91; Perm to Offic *Chelmsf* from 91. *1 Beech Cottage, Stoke by Nayland, Colchester CO6 4QH* Tel (01206) 262110

THOMAS, Austin George. b 23. Open Univ BA75. Wells Th Coll 65. **d** 67 **p** 68. C Brislington St Luke *Bris* 67-73; P-in-c Bris St Geo 73-74; P-in-c Bris St Leon Redfield 74-75; TV E Bris 75-80; R Lyddington w Wanborough 80-88; rtd 88; Perm to Offic *Bris* from 88. *11 College Road, Bristol BS16 2HN* Tel 0117-958 3511

THOMAS, Canon Barry Wilfred. b 41. Univ of Wales (Cardiff) BD75. St Mich Coll Llan 72. **d** 75 **p** 76. C Porthmadog *Ban* 75-78; V Llanegryn and Llanfihangel-y-Pennant etc 78-82; Sec Dioc Coun for Miss and Unity 81-94; R Llanbeblig w Caernarfon and Betws Garmon etc 82-94; Can Ban Cathl 89-94; Chapl Monte Carlo *Eur* from 95. *St Paul's Church, 22 Avenue de Grande-Bretagne, Monte-Carlo, MC 98000* Tel Monaco (377) 93 30 71 06 Fax 93 30 50 39

THOMAS, Bryan. b 36. Univ of Wales (Abth) BA59. St Deiniol's Hawarden 68. **d** 70 **p** 71. C Llangynwyd w Maesteg *Llan* 70-72; V Cwmllynfell *St D* 72-76; V Gors-las 76-82; R Yarnbury *Sarum* from 82; RD Wylye and Wilton from 94. *The Rectory, Steeple Langford, Salisbury SP3 4NH* Tel (01722) 790337

THOMAS, The Ven Charles Edward (Ted). b 27. Univ of Wales (Lamp) BA51. Coll of Resurr Mirfield 51. **d** 53 **p** 54. C Ilminster w Whitelackington *B & W* 53-56; Chapl St Mich Coll Tenbury 56-57; C St Alb St Steph *St Alb* 57-58; V Boreham Wood St Mich 58-66; R Monksilver w Brompton Ralph and Nettlecombe *B & W* 66-74; P-in-c Nettlecombe 68-69; R S Petherton w the Seavingtons 74-83; RD Crewkerne 77-83; Adn Wells, Can Res and Preb Wells Cathl 83-93; rtd 93; Perm to Offic *St D* from 93. *Geryfelin, Pentre, Tregaron SY25 6JG* Tel (01974) 298102

THOMAS, Charles Moray Stewart Reid. b 53. BNC Ox BA74 MA79. Wycliffe Hall Ox 75. **d** 78 **p** 79. C Bradf Cathl *Bradf* 78-81; C Barnsbury St Andr and H Trin w All SS *Lon* 81-90; TV Barnsbury from 90. *10 Thornhill Square, London N1 1BQ* Tel 0171-837 0720 or 609 5525

THOMAS, Cheeramattathu John. b 25. Travanscore Univ BA46 BT49 Serampore Coll BD55 United Th Coll Bangalore MA66. Andover Newton Th Coll. **d** 55 **p** 57. Singapore 55-60; Sarawak 60-65; C Eastham *Ches* 66-74; V Gt Sutton 75-83; USA from 83; rtd 91. *301 Eagle Lakes Drive, Friendswood, Texas 77546, USA* Tel (281) 996-7797

THOMAS, Clive Alexander. **d** 97. NSM Southwick *Chich* from 97. *26 Franklin Road, Shoreham-by-Sea, W Sussex BN43 6YD* Tel (01273) 706155

THOMAS, Colin Norman. b 41. Open Univ BA78. Trin Coll Bris 72. **d** 74 **p** 75. C Handforth *Ches* 74-77; C Bucknall and Bagnall *Lich* 77-80; TV 80-86; V Ogley Hay from 86. *St James's Vicarage, 37 New Road, Brownhills, Walsall WS8 6AT* Tel (01543) 372187

✠**THOMAS, The Rt Revd David.** b 42. Keble Coll Ox BA64 BA66 MA67. St Steph Ho Ox 64. **d** 67 **p** 68 **c** 96. C Hawarden *St As* 67-69; Lect St Mich Coll Llan 69-70; Chapl 70-75; Sec Ch in Wales Liturg Commn 70-75; Vice-Prin St Steph Ho Ox 75-79; Prin 82-87; V Chepstow *Mon* 79-82; Lic to Offic *Ox* 82-87; V Newton St Pet *S & B* 87-96; Can Brecon Cathl from 94; RD Clyne 96; Prov Asst Bp from 96. *3 Whites Close, Belmont Road, Abergavenny NP7 5HZ* Tel (01873) 858780 Fax 858269

THOMAS, David Brian. b 45. MIEEE. St D Dioc Tr Course 82. **d** 85 **p** 86. NSM Llandysul *St D* 85-87; NSM Lampeter Pont Steffan w Silian 88-92; NSM Lampeter and Ultra-Aeron 92-96; P-in-c Llanfihangel Genau'r-glyn and Llangorwen 96-97; V from 97. *The Vicarage, Maes y Garn, Bow Street SY24 5DS* Tel (01970) 828638

THOMAS, David Edward. b 60. Univ of Wales (Lamp) BA83 LTh85. St Mich Coll Llan DPS86. **d** 86 **p** 87. C Killay *S & B* 86-89; P-in-c Newbridge-on-Wye and Llanfihangel Brynpabuan 89-90; V 90-91; V Brecon St David w Llanspyddid and Llanilltyd from 91. *The Vicarage, 26 St David's Crescent, Ffrwdgrech Road, Brecon LD3 8DP*

THOMAS, Canon David Geoffrey. b 24. AKC48. **d** 49 **p** 50. C Milford Haven *St D* 49-52; Miss to Seamen 52-53 and 68-81; C Pembroke St Mary and St Mich 53-54; R Rhoscrowther and Pwllcrochan 54-68; V Milford Haven 68-89; Can St D Cathl 77-89; Treas 85-89; rtd 89. *49 Pill Lane, Milford Haven, Dyfed SA73 2LD* Tel (01646) 695792

THOMAS, David Geoffrey. b 37. Univ of Wales (Cardiff) BA58. Launde Abbey 70 Qu Coll Birm 71. **d** 71 **p** 72. Hon C Fenny Drayton *Leic* 71-75; Chapl Community of the H Family Baldslow Chich 75-77; Perm to Offic *Chich* 77-79; P-in-c Mill End and Heronsgate w W Hyde *St Alb* 79-81; Perm to Offic 82-91; Sen Lect Watford Coll 82-91; R Walgrave w Hannington and Wold and Scaldwell *Pet* from 91. *The Rectory, Lower Green, Walgrave, Northampton NN6 9QB* Tel (01604) 781974

THOMAS, Canon David Glynne. b 41. Dur Univ BSc63. Westcott Ho Cam 64. **d** 67 **p** 68. C St Jo Wood *Lon* 67-70; Min Can St Alb 70-72; Chapl Wadh Coll Ox 72-75; C Ox St Mary V w St Cross and St Pet *Ox* 72-75; Bp's Dom Chapl 75-78; P-in-c Burnham 78-82; TR Burnham w Dropmore, Hitcham and Taplow 82-83;

Australia 83-87; Can Res Worc Cathl *Worc* from 87. *The Chaplain's House, St Oswald's Close, The Tything, Worcester WR1 1HR* Tel (01905) 616619

THOMAS, David Godfrey. b 50. St Chad's Coll Dur BA71 Fitzw Coll Cam BA74 MA78. Westcott Ho Cam 72. **d** 75 **p** 76. C Kirkby *Liv* 75-78; TV Cov E *Cov* 78-88; TR Canvey Is *Chelmsf* 88-92; R Wivenhoe from 92. *The Rectory, 44 Belle Vue Road, Wivenhoe, Colchester CO7 9LD* Tel (01206) 825174

THOMAS, David John. b 34. Univ of Wales (Swansea) St D Coll Lamp. St D Dioc Tr Course 85. **d** 88 **p** 89. NSM Cwmaman *St D* 88-96; Public Preacher from 96. *9 New School Road, Garnant, Ammanford SA18 1LL* Tel (01269) 823936

THOMAS, Dr David Richard. b 48. BNC Ox BA71 MA74 Fitzw Coll Cam BA75 MA80 Lanc Univ PhD83. Ridley Hall Cam 73 Qu Coll Birm 79. **d** 80 **p** 81. C Anfield St Columba *Liv* 80-83; C Liv Our Lady and St Nic w St Anne 83-85; Chapl CCC Cam 85-90; V Witton *Blackb* 90-93; Bp's Adv on Inter-Faith Relns 90-93; Lect Cen for Study of Islam and Chr-Muslim Relns from 93; Perm to Offic *Birm* from 94. *15 Appletree Close, Birmingham B31 2YP* Tel 0121-472 4231

THOMAS, David Ronald Holt. b 28. Lich Th Coll 55. **d** 58 **p** 59. C Uttoxeter w Bramshall *Lich* 58-61; C Hednesford 61-66; R Armitage from 66; RD Rugeley 88-94. *The Rectory, Hood Lane, Armitage, Rugeley, Staffs WS15 4AG* Tel (01543) 490278

THOMAS, David Thomas. b 44. St Cath Coll Cam BA66 MA70 St Jo Coll Dur DipTh68. **d** 71 **p** 72. C Chorlton-cum-Hardy St Clem *Man* 71-74; Chapl Salford Tech Coll 74-79; P-in-c Pendleton St Thos *Man* 75-77; V 77-80; TR Gleadless *Sheff* 80-90; RD Attercliffe 86-90; V Benchill *Man* from 90. *St Luke's Vicarage, Brownley Road, Benchill, Manchester M22 4PT* Tel 0161-998 2071

THOMAS, Canon David William. b 17. Univ of Wales BA63 MA67. St D Coll Lamp BA38 St Mich Coll Llan 39. **d** 41 **p** 43. C Cynwyl Gaeo w Llansawel *St D* 41-46; C Llandysul 46-48; V Clydau and Penrhydd w Castellan 48-55; V Llanfihangel Geneu'r Glyn 55-67; V Llangynfelyn 58-62; V Pontyberem 67-76; V Llanilar w Rhostie and Llangwyryfon etc 76-83; Hon Can St D Cathl 78-83; rtd 83. *12 Stryd Margred, Ammanford SA18 2NN* Tel (01269) 594986

THOMAS, David William Wallace. b 51. St Chad's Coll Dur BA72. St Mich Coll Llan 72. **d** 75 **p** 76. C Bargoed and Deri w Brithdir *Llan* 75-79; Hon C 79-81; V Nantymoel w Wyndham 81-84; Chapl RN from 84. *Royal Naval Chaplaincy Service, Room 203, Victory Building, HM Naval Base, Portsmouth PO1 3LS* Tel (01705) 727903 Fax 727112

THOMAS, David Wynford. b 48. Univ of Wales (Abth) LLB70. Qu Coll Birm 76. **d** 79 **p** 80. C Swansea St Mary w H Trin and St Mark *S & B* 79-83; P-in-c Swansea St Mark 83-89; Lic to Offic 90. *74 Terrace Road, Swansea SA1 6HU*

THOMAS, Canon Dillwyn Morgan. b 26. Univ of Wales (Lamp) BA50. Qu Coll Birm 50. **d** 52 **p** 53. C Dowlais *Llan* 52-59; C Pontypridd St Cath 59-63; V Llanwynno 63-68; V Bargoed w Brithdir 68-74; V Bargoed and Deri w Brithdir 74-75; V Penarth All SS 75-88; Can Llan Cathl 86-88; rtd 88; Perm to Offic *Llan* from 88. *11 Baroness Place, Penarth CF64 3UL* Tel (01222) 704090

THOMAS, Canon Donald George. b 22. DFC44. Qu Coll Cam BA47 MA52. Ridley Hall Cam 47. **d** 49 **p** 50. C Drypool *York* 49-51; C Illogan *Truro* 51-52; C Cheltenham St Mary *Glouc* 52-55; V Cinderford St Steph w Littledean 55-61; V Runcorn All SS *Ches* 61-88; RD Frodsham 82-88; Hon Can Ches Cathl 84-88; rtd 88; Perm to Offic *Ches* from 88. *11 Parc Capel, Lixwm, Holywell CH8 8NA* Tel (01352) 780163

THOMAS, Edward Bernard Meredith. b 21. Leeds Univ BA44 Queensland Univ BEd68 BD72. Coll of Resurr Mirfield 47. **d** 49 **p** 50. C St Mary-at-Lambeth *S'wark* 49-54; C Portsea N End St Mark *Portsm* 54-56; V Portsea All SS 56-64; Australia from 64; rtd 92. *33 Highfield Street, Durack, Queensland, Australia 4077* Tel Brisbane (7) 3372 3517

THOMAS, Canon Edward Maldwyn. b 12. Univ of Wales BA34. St Mich Coll Llan 37. **d** 38 **p** 39. C Tylorstown w Ynyshir *Llan* 38-41; C Gabalfa 41-43; C Kingsbury *Birm* 43-49; Dioc Chapl 49-51; V Duddeston 51-83; Hon Can Birm Cathl 72-83; rtd 83; Perm to Offic *Birm* from 83. *3 Birchtree Grove, Solihull, W Midlands B91 1HD* Tel 0121-705 3706

THOMAS, Edward Walter Dennis. b 32. St Mich Coll Llan 61. **d** 63 **p** 64. C Lougher *S & B* 63-69; V Ystradfellte 69-74; V Dukinfield St Mark and St Luke *Ches* from 74; Chapl Gtr Man Police from 77; OCF from 88. *The Vicarage, 2 Church Square, Dukinfield, Cheshire SK16 4PX* Tel 0161-330 2783

THOMAS, Miss Eileen Anne Harwood. b 35. Univ of Wales (Swansea) BA59 Kent Univ MA80. Cant Sch of Min 80. **dss** 83 **d** 87 **p** 94. Mill Hill Jo Keble Ch *Lon* 83-86; The Lydiards *Bris* 86-92; Par Dn 87-92; C-in-c Woodgate Valley CD *Birm* 92-96; rtd 96. *2 Trelinnoe Gardens, South Petherwin, Launceston, Cornwall PL15 7TH* Tel (01566) 773380

THOMAS, Canon Eirwyn Wheldon. b 35. St Mich Coll Llan 58. **d** 61 **p** 62. C Glanadda *Ban* 61-67; R Llantrisant and Llandeusant 67-75; V Nefyn w Pistyll w Tudweiliog w Llandudwen etc from 75; Can Ban Cathl from 97. *The Vicarage, Nefyn, Pwllheli LL53 6BS* Tel (01758) 720494

THOMAS (née REEVES), Mrs Elizabeth Anne. b 45. Sheff Univ BA67 PGCE75. SW Minl Tr Course 87. **d** 90 **p** 94. Par Dn Stoke Damerel *Ex* 90-93; Dioc Children's Adv *Bradf* from 93; Par Dn Baildon 93-94; C 94-96; P-in-c Denholme Gate from 96. *The Vicarage, Halifax Road, Denholme, Bradford, W Yorkshire BD13 4EN* Tel (01274) 832813

THOMAS, Elwyn Bernard. b 45. Univ of Wales (Swansea) BSc68. St Mich Coll Llan BD71. **d** 71 **p** 72. C Aberdare St Fagan *Llan* 71-74; C Merthyr Dyfan 74-76; R Dowlais 76-86; V Llangynwyd w Maesteg from 86. *Yr Hen Ficerdy, Llangynwyd, Maesteg CF34 9SB* Tel (01656) 733194

THOMAS, Canon Ernest Keith. b 49. Univ of Wales (Cardiff) DipTh76. St Mich Coll Llan 73. **d** 76 **p** 77. C Swansea St Gabr *S & B* 76-79; C Killay 79-81; S Africa 81-92; V Aberdare St Jo *Llan* 93-96; S Africa from 96. *Address temp unknown*

✠**THOMAS, The Rt Revd Eryl Stephen.** b 10. St Jo Coll Ox BA32 MA38. Wells Th Coll 32. **d** 33 **p** 34 **c** 68. C Colwyn Bay *St As* 33-38; C Hawarden 38-43; V Risca *Mon* 43-48; Warden St Mich Coll Llan 48-54; Dean Llan 54-68; Bp Mon 68-71; Bp Llan 71-75; rtd 75; Asst Bp S & B from 88. *17 Orchard Close, Gilwern, Abergavenny NP7 0EN* Tel (01873) 831050

THOMAS, Euros Lloyd. b 53. Bris Poly LLB75. St Mich Coll Llan DipTh79. **d** 79 **p** 80. C Llanelli *St D* 79-84; R Cilgerran w Bridell and Llantwyd from 84; RD Cemais and Sub-Aeron from 93. *The Rectory, Cilgerran, Cardigan, Dyfed SA43 2RZ* Tel (01239) 614500

THOMAS, Frank Lowth. b 22. Lon Coll of Div 64. **d** 66 **p** 67. C Walthamstow St Mary *Chelmsf* 66-68; C Bickenhill w Elmdon *Birm* 68-71; R Carlton Colville *Nor* 71-81; R Smallburgh w Dilham w Honing and Crostwight 81-85; rtd 85; Perm to Offic *Nor* from 86. *7 Mill Close, Salhouse, Norwich NR13 6QB* Tel (01603) 720376

THOMAS, Geler Harries. b 28. St D Coll Lamp BA55. **d** 57 **p** 58. C Llanelli Ch Ch *St D* 57-62; V Llandyssilio and Egremont 62-69; V Llanedy 69-79; V Llangennech and Hendy 79-88; V Llanegwad w Llanfynydd 88-92; RD Llangadog and Llandeilo 89-90; rtd 92. *14 Llys-y-Ferin, Pont-ar-Gothi, Nantgaredig, Carmarthen SA32 7NF* Tel (01267) 290516

THOMAS, Geoffrey Brynmor. b 34. K Coll Lon BA56 AKC56. Ridley Hall Cam 58. **d** 60 **p** 61. C Harlow New Town w Lt Parndon *Chelmsf* 60-65; V Leyton All SS 65-74; V Halifax All So *Wakef* 74-82; R The Winterbournes and Compton Valence *Sarum* 82-89; TV Cheltenham St Mark *Glouc* 89-92; P-in-c Dowdeswell and Andoversford w the Shiptons etc 92-95; RD Northleach 92-95; rtd 95; Perm to Offic *B & W* from 96. *48 Riverside Walk, Midsomer Norton, Bath BA3 2PD* Tel (01761) 414146

THOMAS, Geoffrey Charles. b 30. St Jo Coll Nottm LTh ALCD64. **d** 64 **p** 65. C York St Paul *York* 64-67; C Cheltenham Ch Ch *Glouc* 67-70; V Whitgift w Adlingfleet *Sheff* 70-74; P-in-c Eastoft 72-74; V Mortomley St Sav 74-88; R Middleton Cheney w Chacombe *Pet* 88-93; rtd 94; Perm to Offic *York* from 94. *77 Penyghent Avenue, York YO3 0QH* Tel (01904) 414082

THOMAS, Canon Geoffrey Heale. b 29. St Mich Coll Llan 58. **d** 60 **p** 61. C Llansamlet *S & B* 60-63; Nigeria 63-67; V Swansea St Nic *S & B* 67-80; CF (TA) 72; V Oystermouth *S & B* from 80; Hon Can Brecon Cathl from 92. *The Vicarage, 9 Western Close, Mumbles, Swansea SA3 4HF* Tel (01792) 369971 or 361684

THOMAS, George. b 46. Leeds Univ BEd69. St Jo Coll Dur 75 Cranmer Hall Dur DipTh77. **d** 78 **p** 79. C Highfield *Liv* 78-83; V Chorley St Jas *Blackb* from 83. *St James's Vicarage, St James's Place, Chorley, Lancs PR6 0NA* Tel (01257) 263153

THOMAS, Glyn. b 36. Lon Univ BPharm61. St Deiniol's Hawarden 80. **d** 82 **p** 83. C Rhyl w St Ann *St As* 83-85; R Llanycil w Bala and Frongoch and Llangower etc from 85; RD Penllyn from 96. *The Rectory, Heol-y-Castell, Bala LL23 7YA* Tel (01678) 521047

THOMAS, Greville Stephen. b 64. Qu Coll Birm 94. **d** 96 **p** 97. C Hillingdon All SS *Lon* from 96. *19 Denecroft Crescent, Hillingdon, Uxbridge, Middx UB10 9HU* Tel (01895) 232708

THOMAS, Gwilym Ivor. b 20. St D Coll Lamp BA41 Univ of Wales MPhil95. **d** 43 **p** 44. C Llansadwrn w Llanwrda *St D* 43-47; C Llanedy 47-53; V Ambleston w St Dogwells 53-62; V Llansantffraed 62-70; V Llansantffraed and Llanbadarn Trefeglwys 70-80; V Llansantffraed and Llanbadarn Trefeglwys etc 80-85; RD Glyn Aeron 78-85; rtd 85. *Stanley House, 9 Hill Street, New Quay SA45 9QD* Tel (01545) 560167

THOMAS, Gwynfor. b 13. St D Coll Lamp BA40. **d** 46 **p** 47. C Ebbw Vale *Mon* 46-47; C Beaufort 47-48; C Blaenavon w Capel Newydd 48-51; C Trevethin 51-52; V Abercarn 52-61; R Ilchester w Northover *B & W* 61-69; P-in-c Limington 61-65; R 65-69; V Wookey 69-74; V Wookey w Henton 74-78; rtd 78; Lic to Offic *B & W* 79-95. *10 Fairfield, Somerton, Somerset TA11 7PE* Tel (01458) 72549

THOMAS, Harold Heath. b 08. Man Univ BA32 AKC47. Linc Th Coll 47. **d** 47 **p** 48. C Tranmere St Paul *Ches* 47-53; V Low Marple 53-75; rtd 75; Perm to Offic *Ches* from 75; Perm to Offic *Derby* from 75. *102 Hollins Lane, Marple Bridge, Stockport, Cheshire SK6 5DA* Tel 0161-449 8176

THOMAS, Herbert John. b 13. AKC42. **d** 42 **p** 43. C Hendford *B & W* 42-44; C Street 44-48; C-in-c Southdown St Barn CD 48-58; V Bath St Barn 58-62; V Bridgwater St Jo 62-73; R Compton Martin w Ubley 73-79; rtd 79; Perm to Offic *B & W* from 79. *25 Delmore Road, Frome, Somerset BA11 4EG* Tel (01373) 463762

THOMAS, Miss Hilary Faith. b 43. Ex Univ BA65 Southn Univ PGCE66. Trin Coll Bris DipHE92 DPS94. **d** 94 **p** 95. C Yeovil w Kingston Pitney *B & W* from 94. *67 Preston Grove, Yeovil, Somerset BA20 2BJ* Tel (01935) 25452

THOMAS, Howard Donald Lewis. b 19. Chich Th Coll 46. **d** 49 **p** 50. C Bramley *Ripon* 49-52; C Armley St Bart 52-54; V Kersey w Lindsey *St E* 61-67; R Hanborough *Ox* 67-84; rtd 84; Chapl Soc of All SS Sisters of the Poor 84-87; Perm to Offic *Ox* from 84. *7 Marlborough Crescent, Long Hanborough, Witney, Oxon OX8 8JP* Tel (01993) 881805

THOMAS, Hugh. b 14. St D Coll Lamp BA36. **d** 37 **p** 38. C Llanrhaiadr-yn-Mochnant *St As* 37-41; C Ruthin w Llanrhydd 41-50; R Clocaenog 50-55; R Clocaenog and Gyffylliog 55-79; RD Dyffryn Clwyd 70-79; rtd 79. *2 Hafan Deg, Clawdd Newydd, Ruthin LL15 2ND* Tel (01824) 5716

THOMAS, Hugh. b 25. St D Coll Lamp BA50. **d** 51 **p** 52. C Pen-bre *St D* 51-55; P-in-c Moelgrove and Monington 55-63; V Llanfynydd 63-74; V Pontyates 74-80; V Pontyates and Llangyndeyrn 80-90; rtd 91. *90 Priory Street, Kidwelly, Dyfed SA17 4TY* Tel (01554) 890114

THOMAS, Hugh Meredith. b 39. Univ of Wales (Lamp) BA61. St Mich Coll Llan 61. **d** 63 **p** 64. C Llandeilo Fawr and Llandefeisant *St D* 63-70; V Gwynfe and Llanddeusant 70-74; V Llanpumsaint 74-80; V Llanpumsaint w Llanllawddog 80-85; R Newport w Cilgwyn and Dinas w Llanllawer 85-91; V Llanarthne and Llanddarog from 91. *The Vicarage, Llanddarog, Carmarthen SA32 8PA* Tel (01267) 275268

THOMAS, Canon Huw Glyn. b 42. Univ of Wales (Lamp) BA62 Linacre Coll Ox BA65 MA69. Wycliffe Hall Ox 62. **d** 65 **p** 66. C Oystermouth *S & B* 65-68; Asst Chapl Solihull Sch 68-69; Chapl 69-73; Selection Sec ACCM 73-78; C Loughton St Jo *Chelmsf* 74-77; V Bury St Jo *Man* 78-83; Dir of Ords 82-87; V Bury St Jo w St Mark 83-86; Can Res and Treas Liv Cathl *Liv* 87-95; Ethiopia from 95. *St Matthews Church, PO Box 109, Addis Ababa, Ethiopia*

THOMAS, Ian Melville. b 50. Jes Coll Ox BA71 MA75. St Steph Ho Ox 71. **d** 73 **p** 74. PV St D Cathl *St D* 73-77; Chapl RAF 77-95; Asst Chapl-in-Chief RAF from 95. *Chaplaincy Services (RAF), HQ, Personnel and Training Command, RAF Innsworth, Gloucester GL3 1EZ* Tel (01452) 712612 ext 5164 Fax 510828

THOMAS, Ian William. b 53. Bedf Coll of Educn CertEd74. Ox Min Course 89. **d** 92 **p** 93. NSM Fenny Stratford *Ox* from 92. *5 Laburnum Grove, Bletchley, Milton Keynes MK2 2JW* Tel (01908) 644457

THOMAS, Idris. b 48. St D Coll Lamp DipTh71. **d** 71 **p** 72. C Llanbeblig w Caernarfon and Betws Garmon etc *Ban* 71-75; P-in-c Llanaelhaiarn 75-77; R Llanaelhaearn w Clynnog Fawr from 77; RD Arfon from 93. *The Rectory, Trefor, Caernarfon LL54 5HN* Tel (01286) 660547

THOMAS, The Ven Ilar Roy Luther. b 30. St D Coll Lamp BA51. St Mich Coll Llan 51. **d** 53 **p** 54. C Oystermouth *S & B* 53-56; C Gorseinon 56-59; R Llanbadarn Fawr and Llandegley 59-60; R Llanbadarn Fawr, Llandegley and Llanfihangel etc 60-66; CF (ACF) 62-90; Children's Adv *S & B* 63-77; RD Knighton 66-79; V Knighton and Norton 66-79; V Sketty 79-89; Can Brecon Cathl from 75; Treas 87-88; Chan 88-90; Adn Gower 90-95; rtd 95. *2 Druids Close, Mumbles, Swansea SA3 5TY*

THOMAS, Iris. b 18. Univ of Wales (Abth) BA39 DipEd40. **d** 80 **p** 97. Hon C Tylorstown *Llan* 80-84; Hon C Ferndale w Maerdy 84-85; rtd 85; Perm to Offic *Llan* from 86. *18 Richard Street, Maerdy, Ferndale CF43 4AU* Tel (01443) 755235

THOMAS, James Morris. b 02. **d** 37 **p** 38. Australia 37-47; C Mynyddislwyn *Mon* 47-51; R Henllys w Bettws 51-57; R Tintern Parva w Chapel Hill 57-73; rtd 73; Perm to Offic *Mon* 73-90; Perm to Offic *Heref* 74-90. *c/o 23 Dundee Court, Duncraig, Australia 6023*

THOMAS, Jennifer Monica (Jenny). b 58. Wilson Carlile Coll DipEvang82 Sarum & Wells Th Coll DipMin93. **d** 93 **p** 94. Par Dn Wandsworth St Paul *S'wark* 93-94; C 94-97; V Forest Hill from 97. *The Vicarage, 20 Gaynesford Road, London SE23 2UQ* Tel 0181-699 2576

THOMAS, John Arun. b 47. Bombay Univ BA69 MA72 Nottm Univ CertEd80. Oak Hill Th Coll 84. **d** 88 **p** 89. C Liv Ch Ch Norris Green *Liv* 88-89; C Wavertree St Mary 89-93; V St Mary Cray and St Paul's Cray *Roch* 93-96; India from 96. *11 Little Gibbs Road, Malabar Hill, Bombay 4000006, India*

THOMAS, John Bryn. b 37. Lich Th Coll 63. **d** 66 **p** 67. C Stoke upon Trent *Lich* 66-71; R Wotton *Guildf* 71-79; P-in-c Holmbury St Mary 78-79; R Wotton and Holmbury St Mary 79-86; C Easthampstead *Ox* 86-88; TV Chambersbury (Hemel Hempstead) *St Alb* from 88. *The Vicarage, Peascroft Road, Hemel Hempstead, Herts HP3 8EP* Tel (01442) 243934

THOMAS, Canon John Elwern. b 14. Univ of Wales BA35. Coll of Resurr Mirfield 35. **d** 37 **p** 38. C Conwy w Gyffin *Ban* 37-41; C Llandrillo-yn-Rhos *St As* 41-47; V Aberdare St Fagan *Llan* 47-55; R Dolgellau *Ban* 55-70; P-in-c Brithdir and Bryncoedifor 65-70; RD Ystumaner 58-70; Can Cursal Ban Cathl 68-70; Warden Ruthin w Llanrhydd *St As* 70-79; Can Cursal St As Cathl 77-79; rtd 79. *33 The Park, Ruthin LL15 1PN* Tel (01824) 703384

THOMAS, Canon John Herbert Samuel. b 34. Pemb Coll Cam BA57 MA64. St Mich Coll Llan 57. **d** 58 **p** 59. C Port Talbot St Theodore *Llan* 58-60; C Llantwit Major and St Donat's 60-67; P-in-c Barry All SS 67-74; V Dinas w Penygraig 74-85; V Pontypridd St Cath 85-90; V Pontypridd St Cath w St Matt from 90; RD Pontypridd from 90; Can Llan Cathl from 95. *St Catherine's Vicarage, Gelliwastad Grove, Pontypridd CF37 2BS* Tel (01443) 402021

THOMAS, Dr John Thurston. b 28. CChem FRSC65 Univ of Wales (Swansea) BSc48 DipEd49 Leeds Univ PhD58. Glouc Sch of Min 88. **d** 90 **p** 91. NSM S Cerney w Cerney Wick and Down Ampney *Glouc* from 90. *Samantha, Silver Street, South Cerney, Cirencester, Glos GL7 5TP* Tel (01285) 860382

THOMAS, Joseph Neville. b 33. Univ of Wales (Lamp) BA57. St Mich Coll Llan. **d** 59 **p** 60. C Porthmadog *Ban* 59-62; C Cardiff St Jo *Llan* 62-65; CF 65-88; R Sherfield-on-Loddon and Stratfield Saye etc *Win* from 88. *The Rectory, Breach Lane, Sherfield-on-Loddon, Basingstoke, Hants RG27 0EU* Tel (01256) 882209

THOMAS, June Marion. b 31. Univ of Wales BA53 DipEd54. NE Ord Course 83. **dss** 86 **d** 87 **p** 94. Stockton St Pet *Dur* 86-87; Hon Par Dn 87-89; NSM Stockton St Mark from 89. *50 Brisbane Grove, Stockton-on-Tees, Cleveland TS18 5BP* Tel (01642) 582408

THOMAS, Keith. b 55. Southlands Coll Lon TCert80. N Ord Course 92. **d** 95 **p** 96. NSM Knuzden *Blackb* from 95; Moorbrook Sch Preston from 95. *20 Duxbury Street, Darwen, Lancs BB3 2LA* Tel (01254) 776484

THOMAS, Leslie Richard. b 45. Lon Coll of Div 65. **d** 69 **p** 70. C Knotty Ash St Jo *Liv* 69-72; C Sutton 72-74; TV 74-77; V Banks 77-82; V Gt Crosby All SS 82-92; P-in-c Marthall *Ches* from 92; Chapl Dav Lewis Cen for Epilepsy from 92. *The Vicarage, Sandlebridge Lane, Marthall, Knutsford, Cheshire WA16 7SB* Tel (01625) 861462

THOMAS, Ms Margaret. b 41. Bris Univ BSc63 Leeds Univ CertEd64 Ex Univ ADC70. Cranmer Hall Dur 81. **dss** 83 **d** 87 **p** 94. Maghull *Liv* 83-86; Asst Chapl Liv Univ 86-89; St Luke in the City 86-87; Par Dn 87-89; Chapl Whiston Hosp 89-92; Chapl St Helen's and Knowsley HA 89-92; Chapl and Co-ord St Helen's and Knowsley Hosps Trust from 92. *Chapel House, Whiston Hospital, Warrington Road, Prescot, Merseyside L35 5DR* Tel 0151-430 1657 or 426 1600

THOMAS, Mark Wilson. b 51. Dur Univ BA72 Hull Univ MA89. Ripon Coll Cuddesdon 76. **d** 78 **p** 79. C Chapelthorpe *Wakef* 78-81; C Seaford w Sutton *Chich* 81-84; V Gomersal *Wakef* 84-92; TR Almondbury w Farnley Tyas from 92; RD Almondbury from 93. *The Vicarage, 2 Westgate, Almondbury, Huddersfield HD5 8XE* Tel (01484) 421753

THOMAS, Sister Mary Josephine. b 30. Ripon Dioc Tr Coll TCert50 Carl Dioc Tr Course 88. **d** 90 **p** 94. NSM Hawes Side *Blackb* 90-93; NSM St Annes St Marg from 93. *112 St Andrew's Road North, Lytham St Annes, Lancs FY8 2JQ* Tel (01253) 728016

THOMAS, Michael Longdon Sanby. b 34. Trin Hall Cam BA55 MA60. Wells Th Coll 56. **d** 58 **p** 59. C Sandal St Helen *Wakef* 58-60; Chapl Portsm Cathl *Portsm* 60-64; V Shedfield 64-69; V Portchester from 69. *The Vicarage, 164 Castle Street, Portchester, Fareham, Hants PO16 9QH* Tel (01705) 376289

THOMAS, Preb Owen. b 17. Selw Coll Cam BA40 MA58. St Mich Coll Llan 40. **d** 41 **p** 42. C Rhyl w St Ann *St As* 41-44; V Choral St As Cathl 44-48; C Welshpool 48-53; R Llanferres 53-65; R Welshpool w Castle Caereinion 65-77; RD Pool 76-77; Adn Montgomery 77-87; Preb St As Cathl 77-87; V Berriew and Manafon 80-87; rtd 87. *Oaklands, Fron, Montgomery SY15 6RZ* Tel (01686) 640675

THOMAS, Owen James. b 17. Univ of Wales BA38. Tyndale Hall Bris 38. **d** 40 **p** 41. C Wandsworth St Steph *S'wark* 40-43; C Dagenham *Chelmsf* 43-46; R Glas St Silas *Glas* 46-51; Tutor Lon Bible Coll 51-62; P-in-c Woburn Square Ch Ch *Lon* 51-52; Chapl and Lect Lon Bible Coll 62-76; Hon C Northwood Em 70-76; V Canonbury St Steph 76-85; rtd 85; Perm to Offic *Chich* from 85. *22 Woodland Way, Fairlight, Hastings, E Sussex TN35 4AU* Tel (01424) 813613

THOMAS, Ms Pamela Sybil (Pam). b 38. Ripon Coll Cuddesdon 88. **d** 90 **p** 94. Par Dn Preston w Sutton Poyntz and Osmington w Poxwell *Sarum* 90-94; C 94-96; P-in-c Weymouth St Edm from 96; Chapl Westhaven Hosp Weymouth from 96; P-in-c Abbotsbury, Portesham and Langton Herring *Sarum* from 97. *The Rectory, Portesham, Weymouth, Dorset DT3 4HB* Tel (01305) 871217

THOMAS, Mrs Patricia Margaret. b 44. Hockerill Coll Cam TCert65. Sarum & Wells Th Coll 79. **dss** 82 **d** 87 **p** 94. Verwood *Sarum* 82-87; Hon Par Dn 87-88; Chapl Asst Friern Hosp Lon 88-90; Par Dn Upton cum Chalvey *Ox* 90-94; C 94-95. *11 Cooper Way, Windsor Meadows, Slough SL1 9JA* Tel (01753) 538714

THOMAS, Dr Patrick Hungerford Bryan. b 52. St Cath Coll Cam BA73 MA77 Leeds Univ BA78 Univ of Wales PhD82. Coll of Resurr Mirfield 76. **d** 79 **p** 80. C Aberystwyth *St D* 79-81; C Carmarthen St Pet 81-82; R Llangeitho and Blaenpennal w Betws Leucu etc 82-84; Warden of Ords 83-86; R Brechfa w Abergorlech etc from 84. *The Rectory, Brechfa, Carmarthen SA32 7RA* Tel (01267) 202389

THOMAS, Paul Robert. b 42. N Ord Course. **d** 82 **p** 83. C Hull Newland St Jo *York* 82-84; P-in-c Rowley 84-87; Soc Resp Officer Hull 84-87; R Rowley w Skidby 87-88; TR Barking St Marg w St Patr *Chelmsf* 88-93; Gen Sec & Admin St Luke's Hosp for the Clergy from 93; Lic to Offic *Lon* from 93. *St Luke's Hospital for the Clergy, 14 Fitzroy Square, London W1P 6AH* Tel 0171-388 4954

THOMAS, Paul Wyndham. b 55. Or Coll Ox BA76 BTh78 MA80. Wycliffe Hall Ox 77. **d** 79 **p** 80. C Llangynwyd w Maesteg *Llan* 79-85; TV Langport Area Chs *B & W* 85-90; P-in-c Thorp Arch w Walton *York* 90-93; Clergy Tr Officer from 90; V Nether w Upper Poppleton from 93. *The Vicarage, 15 Nether Way, Upper Poppleton, York YO2 6JQ* Tel (01904) 794744

THOMAS, Peter George Hartley. b 38. AKC63. **d** 64 **p** 65. C Leigh Park St Fran CD *Portsm* 64-69; V Cosham 69-77; R Hayes *Roch* from 77. *The Rectory, Hayes Street, Bromley BR2 7LH* Tel 0181-462 1373

THOMAS, Peter James. b 53. Lon Univ BSc75. Trin Coll Bris 77. **d** 80 **p** 81. C Hucclecote *Glouc* 80-84; C Loughborough Em *Leic* 84-85; TV Parr *Liv* 85-92; V Eckington *Worc* from 92; V Defford w Besford from 92. *The Vicarage, Drakes Bridge Road, Eckington, Pershore, Worcs WR10 3BN* Tel (01386) 750203

THOMAS, Canon Peter Rhys. b 37. MInstPkg MIPM TCD BA59 MA72. **d** 72 **p** 73. C Cong *T, K & A* 73-75; I 75-77; C Bingley All SS *Bradf* 77-79; V Shelf 79-81; Producer Relig Broadcasting Viking Radio 81-84; P-in-c Croxton *Linc* 81-82; P-in-c Ulceby 81-82; P-in-c Wootton 81-82; P-in-c Ulceby Gp 82; V Ulceby Gp 82-84; R E and W Tilbury and Linford *Chelmsf* 84-89; I Celbridge w Straffan and Newcastle-Lyons *D & G* 89-93; I Youghal Union *C, C & R* from 93; Dio Info Officer (Cork) from 95; Preb Cork Cathl from 97; Preb Cloyne Cathl from 97. *The Rectory, Upper Strand, Youghal, Co Cork, Irish Republic* Tel Youghal (24) 92350 Fax as telephone

THOMAS, Peter Wilson. b 58. BD AKC. Ripon Coll Cuddesdon. **d** 82 **p** 83. C Stockton St Pet *Dur* 82-85; TV Solihull *Birm* 85-90; V Rednal from 90. *St Stephen's Vicarage, Edgewood Road, Rednal, Birmingham B45 8SG* Tel 0121-453 3347

THOMAS, Philip Harold Emlyn. b 41. Cant Univ (NZ) BA64 MA77 Dur Univ PhD82. Melbourne Coll of Div BD68. **d** 68 **p** 69. Australia 68-71; New Zealand 71-77; Fell and Chapl Univ Coll Dur 77-83; V Heighington *Dur* from 84; RD Darlington from 94. *The Vicarage, Heighington, Co Durham DL5 6PP* Tel (01325) 312134

THOMAS, Philip John. b 52. Liv Poly BSc74 Leeds Poly 77. Trin Coll Bris 94. **d** 96 **p** 97. C Skelton w Upleatham *York* from 96. *40 Eden Road, Skelton-in-Cleveland, Saltburn-by-the-Sea, Cleveland TS12 2NB* Tel (01287) 653959

THOMAS, Philip Sewell. b 09. Linc Coll Ox BA32 MA38. Ely Th Coll 32. **d** 33 **p** 34. C Odiham w S Warnborough *Win* 33-36; C Midsomer Norton *B & W* 36-42; PV Wells Cathl 42-46; C Easton 42-46; C Eastover 46-49; V Barton St David w Kingweston 49-91; rtd 91. *20 Brookside Close, Batheaston, Bath BA1 7HP* Tel (01225) 859588

THOMAS, Ralph Pilling. b 23. Univ of Wales (Lamp) BA49. Wycliffe Hall Ox 49. **d** 51 **p** 52. C S Shore H Trin *Blackb* 51-53; C Chorley St Geo 53-59; V Wellow *B & W* 59-63; V Hinton Charterhouse 59-63; R Coppull St Jo *Blackb* 63-68; Asst Chapl HM Pris Wandsworth 68-69; Chapl HM Pris Leeds 69-74; R Kirklington w Burneston and Wath *Ripon* 74-88; RD Wensley 85-88; rtd 88. *20 The Maltings, Staithe Road, Bungay, Suffolk NR35 1EJ* Tel (01986) 895118

THOMAS, Ramon Lorenzo. Oak Hill Th Coll. **d** 97. NSM Yateley *Win* from 97. *The Flat, Chaddisbrook House, 101 Reading Road, Yateley, Camberley, Surrey GU46 7LR* Tel (01252) 876255

THOMAS, Richard. b 45. St D Coll Lamp 68. **d** 71 **p** 72. C Llanelli St Paul *St D* 71-74; Chapl RN 74-90; V St Ishmael's w Llan-saint and Ferryside *St D* 90-93; V Maindee *Mon* 93-95; V St Clears w Llangynin and Llanddowror etc *St D* from 95. *The Vicarage, High Street, St Clears, Carmarthen SA33 4EE* Tel (01994) 230266

THOMAS, Richard Frederick. b 24. Qu Coll Cam BA45 MA49. Ridley Hall Cam 47. **d** 49 **p** 50. C S Croydon Em *Cant* 49-51; Chapl and Ho Master Haileybury Coll Herts 51-67; Jerusalem 67-73; Ho Master Bp Luffa Sch Chich 74-80; Lic to Offic *Chich* 75-77; Hon C Chich St Pancras and St Jo 78-80; R N Mundham w Hunston and Merston 80-89; rtd 89; C Compton, the Mardens, Stoughton and Racton *Chich* from 96; C Stansted from 96. *16 Brent Court, Emsworth, Hants PO10 7JA* Tel (01243) 430613

THOMAS, Richard Paul. b 50. MIPR. Wycliffe Hall Ox 74. **d** 76 **p** 77. C Abingdon w Shippon *Ox* 76-80; R Win All SS w Chilcomb and Chesil *Win* 80-88; Dioc Communications Officer 83-89; Dioc Communications Officer *Ox* from 89. *18 Eason Drive, Abingdon, Oxon OX14 3YD* Tel (01235) 553360 or (01865) 244566 Fax (01865) 790470

THOMAS, Robert Stanley. b 31. Lon Univ BD65 Man Univ MEd78. Sarum Th Coll 66. **d** 67 **p** 68. C Maltby *Sheff* 67-70; Lic to Offic *St Alb* 70-72; Lic to Offic *Man* 72-79; Lic to Offic *St As* 80-82; Dioc RE Adv 82-96; V Glyndyfrdwy and Llansantfraid Glyn Dyfrdwy 82-96; RD Edeyrnion 88-96; rtd 96. *East Lynne, New Road, New Broughton, Wrexham LL11 6SY*

THOMAS, Robin. b 27. Cen Sch of Art Lon NDD50. St Steph Ho Ox 89. **d** 89 **p** 90. NSM Clifton All SS w St Jo *Bris* 89-94; P-in-c Tintagel *Truro* from 94. *The Vicarage, Tintagel, Cornwall PL34 0DJ* Tel (01840) 770315

THOMAS, Roderick Charles Howell (Rod). b 54. LSE BSc75. Wycliffe Hall Ox 91. **d** 93 **p** 94. C Plymouth St Andr w St Paul and St Geo *Ex* 93-95; C Plymouth St Andr and St Paul Stonehouse from 95. *117 Lipson Road, Plymouth PL4 7NQ* Tel (01752) 661334

THOMAS, Roger James. b 37. Bris Univ BA59. Wells Th Coll 59. **d** 61 **p** 62. C Henbury *Bris* 61-64; C Stapleton 64-69; P-in-c Hardenhuish 69-71; R 71-75; P-in-c Kington 69-71; V 71-75; V Bris St Andr Hartcliffe 75-81; RD Bedminster 79-81; P-in-c Frenchay 81-86; P-in-c Winterbourne Down 81-86; R Frenchay and Winterbourne Down from 86. *The Rectory, Frenchay Common, Frenchay, Bristol BS16 1NB* Tel 0117-956 7616

THOMAS, Ronald Stuart. b 13. Univ of Wales BA35. St Mich Coll Llan 35. **d** 36 **p** 37. C Chirk *St As* 36-40; C Hanmer 40-42; R Manafon 42-54; V Eglwysfach *St D* 54-67; V Aberdaron and Bodferin *Ban* 67-72; R Aberdaron and Bodferin w Rhiw w Llanfaelrhys 72-78; rtd 78; Lic to Offic *Ban* from 78. *Cefn du Ganol, Llanfairynghornwy, Holyhead LL65 4LG* Tel (01407) 730943

THOMAS, Russen William. b 30. Univ of Wales (Lamp) BA55. St Mich Coll Llan 55. **d** 57 **p** 58. C Newport St Jo Bapt *Mon* 57-59; C Pembroke Dock *St D* 59-62; R St Florence and Redberth 62-69; V Newport St Julian *Mon* 69-79; V Stratton *Truro* 79-88; RD Stratton 83-88; V Lanteglos by Fowey 88-91; Miss to Seamen from 88; rtd 92; Chapl Puerto de la Cruz Tenerife *Eur* 93-95; Chapl Playa de Las Americas Tenerife 95-97. *Apartado de Correos 215, Los Cristianos 38650, Tenerife, Canary Islands* Tel Tenerife (22) 793143

THOMAS, Simon Jonathan Francklin. b 51. Sheff Univ BA72 Nottm Univ BA78. St Jo Coll Nottm 76. **d** 80 **p** 80. SAMS 80-82 and 83-95; Bolivia 80-82 and 83-95; C Camberwell All SS *S'wark* 82; C Ashtead *Guildf* from 96. *1 Oakfield Road, Ashtead, Surrey KT21 2RE* Tel (01372) 813334

THOMAS, Preb Stephen Blayney. b 35. St D Coll Lamp BA62. Bp Burgess Hall Lamp DipTh63. **d** 63 **p** 64. C Ledbury *Heref* 63-67; C Bridgnorth w Tasley 67-68; C Clun w Chapel Lawn, Bettws-y-Crwyn and Newcastle 68-73; C Clungunford w Clunbury and Clunton, Bedstone etc 68-73; V Worfield 73-84; RD Bridgnorth 81-83; R Kingsland 84-96; P-in-c Aymestrey and Leinthall Earles w Wigmore etc 84-96; P-in-c Eardisland 84-96; Preb Heref Cathl from 85; R Kingsland w Eardisland, Aymestrey etc from 97. *The Rectory, Kingsland, Leominster, Herefordshire HR6 9QW* Tel (01568) 708255

THOMAS, Stuart Grahame. b 54. Pemb Coll Cam BA77 MA81. Ridley Hall Cam 85. **d** 87 **p** 88. C Guildf H Trin w St Mary *Guildf* 87-91; V Churt 91-94; V Ewell St Fran from 94. *St Francis's Vicarage, 61 Ruxley Lane, Ewell, Surrey KT19 0JG* Tel 0181-393 5616

THOMAS, Canon Sydney Robert. b 44. Univ of Wales (Swansea) BA65 MA83. St D Coll Lamp LTh67. **d** 67 **p** 68. C Llanelli *St D* 67-77; V Pontyberem from 77; RD Cydweli from 94; Can St D Cathl from 94. *The Vicarage, 56 Llannon Road, Pontyberem, Llanelli SA15 5LY* Tel (01269) 870345

THOMAS, Telford Ifano. b 17. Univ of Wales BA38. St D Coll Lamp 38. **d** 40 **p** 41. C Llanegwad *St D* 40-45; C Llanddowror 45-46; C Llanelli Ch Ch 46-52; V Llansadwrn w Llanwrda 52-61; V Llangennech 61-79; V Llansteffan and Llan-y-bri etc 79-82; rtd 82. *33 Ty Rees, The Parade, Carmarthen SA31 1LY* Tel (01267) 221942

THOMAS, Theodore Eilir. b 36. Univ of Wales (Lamp) BA58. Sarum Th Coll 58. **d** 60 **p** 61. C Fenton *Lich* 60-63; C Stourport All SS and St Mich CD *Worc* 63-67; V Worc H Trin 67-74; P-in-c Dudley St Fran 74-79; V 79-83; R Plympton St Maurice *Ex* from 83. *St Maurice's Rectory, 31 Wain Park, Plympton, Plymouth PL7 3HX* Tel (01752) 346114

THOMAS, Thomas (Tom). b 68. Selw Coll Cam BA90. Wycliffe Hall Ox 91. **d** 93 **p** 94. C Much Woolton *Liv* 93-97; V Carr Mill from 97. *St David's Vicarage, 27 Erkdale Avenue, Carr Mill, St Helens, Merseyside WA11 7EN* Tel (01744) 32330

THOMAS, Thomas Alan. b 37. K Coll Lon BD60 AKC60. St Boniface Warminster 60. **d** 61 **p** 62. C Washington *Dur* 61-65; C Bishopwearmouth St Mary V w St Pet CD 65-70; V Ruishton w Thornfalcon *B & W* 70-82; R Hutton 82-94; V Frome Ch Ch 94-96; Chapl Victoria Hosp Frome 94-96; R Camerton w Dunkerton, Foxcote and Shoscombe *B & W* from 96. *The Rectory, Camerton, Bath BA3 1PU* Tel (01761) 470249

THOMAS, Thomas Hugh. b 25. Open Univ BA77 Westmr Coll Ox MTh94. St D Coll Lamp 59. **d** 60 **p** 61. C Cwmaman *St D* 60-63; V Martletwy and Lawrenny w Minwear 63-78; V Martletwy w Lawrenny and Minwear and Yerbeston 78-79; R Narberth w Mounton w Robeston Wathen and Crinow 79-95; RD Narberth

82-94; rtd 95. *27 Haven Road, Haverfordwest SA61 1DU* Tel (01437) 767182

THOMAS, Thomas John. b 15. St D Coll Lamp BA37 St Mich Coll Llan 37. **d** 38 **p** 39. C Abernant and Cynwyl Elfed *St D* 38-41; C Cardigan 41-45; P-in-c Talley and Taliaris 45-48; V 48-51; P-in-c Burry Port and Pwll 51-59; V 59-64; V St Benet Paul's Wharf *Lon* 64-82; C-in-c Paddington St Dav Welsh Ch 64-82; Perm to Offic *S'wark* 74-91; Chapl R Hosp and Home Putney 74-91; rtd 82. *5 Amberley Drive, Twyford, Reading RG10 9BX* Tel (0118) 934 5018

THOMAS, Thomas John Samuel. b 21. St D Coll Lamp BA48. **d** 49 **p** 50. C Dafen and Llwynhendy *St D* 49-50; Chapl RAF 52-77; QHC 73-85; V Horsham *Chich* 77-85; rtd 85; Perm to Offic *St D* from 85. *1 Glynhir Road, Llandybie, Ammanford SA18 2TA* Tel (01269) 850726

THOMAS, Canon Thomas Vernon. b 21. St D Coll Lamp BA42 Selw Coll Cam BA44 MA48. St Mich Coll Llan 44. **d** 45 **p** 46. C St Brides Minor *Llan* 45-47; Ripon Cathl *Ripon* 47-50; Min Can and Succ Ripon Cathl 47-50; C Leeds St Pet 50-55; V Beeston 55-77; Hon Can Ripon Cathl 75-89; R Spofforth w Kirk Deighton 77-89; rtd 89. *The Lodge, Main Street, East Keswick, Leeds LS17 9DB* Tel (01937) 573033

THOMAS, Tristan Emmanuel Douglas. b 38. Mysore Univ BA60. Bp's Coll Calcutta DipTh65. **d** 65 **p** 66. India 65-70; Miss to Seamen 70-72; Chapl Rotterdam w Schiedam etc *Eur* 70-71; C Gt Clacton *Chelmsf* 72-74; Chapl Hamburg w Kiel *Eur* 74-85; V Halliwell St Marg *Man* 85-93; V Brompton-by-Sawdon w Snainton, Ebberston etc *York* from 93. *The Vicarage, Pudding Lane, Snainton, Scarborough, N Yorkshire YO13 9AS* Tel (01723) 859805

THOMAS, Wallis Huw Wallis. b 06. Univ of Wales BA27. St Mich Coll Llan 30. **d** 31 **p** 32. C Bangor St Dav w Penrhosgarnedd *Ban* 31-35; Min Can Ban Cathl 35-46; Dom Chapl and Private Sec to Abp Wales 37-44; Chapl to Bp Ban 44-46; R Llanaber 46-56; R Llanaber w Caerdeon 56-66; Can and Preb Ban Cathl 55-59; Adn Meirionnydd 59-76; V Llanelltyd w Bontddu and Ganllwywd 66-76; rtd 76; Lic to Offic *Ban* from 76. *The Vicarage, Llanelltyd, Dolgellau LL40 2SU* Tel (01341) 422517

THOMAS, William Alwyn. b 11. St D Coll Lamp BA33 St Mich Coll Llan 33. **d** 34 **p** 35. C Cricklewood St Mich *Lon* 34-36; C Tottenham Ch Ch W Green 36-41; Chapl RAF 41-66; Prin RAF Chapl Sch and Asst Chapl-in-Chief 65-67; R Weyhill cum Penton Newsey *Win* 66-78; rtd 78; Perm to Offic *St D* from 78. *The Brow, Ferryside SA17 5RS* Tel (01267) 267369

THOMAS, William Brynmor. b 11. St D Coll Lamp BA33 BD41 Wycliffe Hall Ox 34. **d** 35 **p** 36. C Heworth H Trin *York* 35-42; V Forest Gate St Sav *Chelmsf* 42-45; V Herne Hill Road St Sav *S'wark* 45-53; P-in-c Denmark Hill St Matt 45-53; Hon CF from 49; Perm to Offic *York* from 76; V Belper *Derby* 53-76; rtd 76. *c/o Mrs G Ogle, 108 York Road, Haxby, York YO3 3EG* Tel (01904) 760309

THOMAS, William George. b 29. JP. FRSA Birm Univ BA50 CertEd51. EAMTC 82. **d** 85 **p** 86. NSM Brampton *Ely* 85-87; NSM Bluntisham w Earith 87-89; P-in-c Foxton from 89. *The Vicarage, 7 West Hill Road, Foxton, Cambridge CB2 6SZ* Tel (01223) 870375

THOMAS, William John. b 11. St D Coll Lamp BA48. **d** 49 **p** 50. C Mold *St As* 49-53; V Formby St Pet *Liv* 53-76; rtd 76. *Bro Gain, 49 Pen-y-Cefn Road, Caerwys, Mold CH7 5BH* Tel (01352) 720811

THOMAS, William John Charles. b 17. St D Coll Lamp BA50. **d** 51 **p** 52. C Fleur-de-Lis *Mon* 51-53; C Mynyddislwyn 53-55; C Pontypool 55-58; V Newport St Steph and H Trin 58-62; Chapl Springfield Hosp Lon 64-82; rtd 82; Perm to Offic *S'wark* 82-93. *101 Heybridge Avenue, London SW16 3DS*

THOMAS, The Ven William Jordison. b 27. K Coll Cam BA50 MA55. Cuddesdon Coll 51. **d** 53 **p** 54. C Byker St Ant *Newc* 53-56; C Berwick H Trin 56-59; V Alwinton w Holystone and Alnham 59-70; V Alston cum Garrigill w Nenthead and Kirkhaugh 70-80; P-in-c Lambley w Knaresdale 72-80; RD Bamburgh and Glendale 81-83; TR Glendale Gp 80-83; Adn Northd and Can Res Newc Cathl 83-92; rtd 92. *Wark Cottage, Whittingham, Alnwick, Northd NE66 4RB* Tel (0166574) 300

THOMAS, Canon William Kenneth. b 19. Mert Coll Ox BA40 MA44. Westcott Ho Cam 40. **d** 42 **p** 43. C Brislington St Luke *Bris* 42-47; C Westbury-on-Trym St Alb 47-52; CF 49-51; V Oldland *Bris* 52-71; V Longwell Green 52-71; V Minety w Oaksey 71-82; P-in-c 82-84; RD Malmesbury 73-79; Hon Can Bris Cathl 77-84; P-in-c Crudwell w Ashley 82-84; rtd 84; Perm to Offic *Bris* from 84. *27 Hamilton Road, Bristol BS3 4EN* Tel 0117-963 2198

THOMAS, William Phillip. b 43. Lich Th Coll 68. **d** 70 **p** 71. C Llanilid w Pencoed *Llan* 70-74; C Pontypridd St Cath 74-76; V Tonyrefail 76-84; Youth Chapl 78-80; RD Rhondda 81-84; R Neath w Llantwit from 84. *The Rectory, London Road, Neath SA11 1LE* Tel (01639) 644612

THOMAS, William Rhys Ithel Phillips. b 16. St Jo Coll Dur BA38 DipTh41 MA42. **d** 41 **p** 42. C Newport H Trin *Mon* 41-43; CF (EC) 43-48; C Usk *Mon* 48-49; V Llanishen w Trellech Grange 49-56; CF (TA) 49-56; CF 56-60; Area Sec (E Distr) Miss to Seamen 60-62; R Gt and Lt Saxham w Westley *St E* 62-68; Lic to Offic 68-78; Chapl Asst Addenbrooke's Hosp Cam 78-81; rtd 81; Perm to Offic *Ely* from 85. *19 Brooklyn Court, Cherry Hinton Road, Cambridge CB1 4HF* Tel (01223) 721246

THOMAS ANTHONY, Brother. *See* DE HOOP, Brother Thomas Anthony

THOMPSON, Anthony Edward. b 38. Bris Univ BA61. Ridley Hall Cam 61. **d** 63 **p** 64. C Peckham St Mary Magd *S'wark* 63-66; Paraguay 67-72; C Otley *Bradf* 72-75; TV Woughton *Ox* 75-82; P-in-c Lower Nutfield *S'wark* from 82; RD Reigate 91-93; Local Min Adv Croydon Episc Area from 93. *136 Mid Street, South Nutfield, Redhill RH1 5RP* Tel (01737) 822211

THOMPSON, Athol James Patrick. b 34. St Paul's Grahamstown 72. **d** 74 **p** 75. S Africa 74-83; P-in-c Dewsbury St Matt and St Jo *Wakef* 84; TV Dewsbury 84-93; Chapl Staincliffe and Dewsbury Gen Hosps Wakef 84-90; Chapl Dewsbury and Distr Hosp 90-93; V Shiregreen St Jas and St Chris *Sheff* from 93. *The Vicarage, 510 Bellhouse Road, Sheffield S5 0RG* Tel 0114-245 6526

THOMPSON, Barry (Brother Aidan). b 33. St Jo Coll Lusaka. **d** 69 **p** 70. SSF from 59; Zambia 69-76; Miss to Seamen from 76; Tanzania 76-81; Korea 81-82; Australia 83-85; Chapl Vlissingen (Flushing) Miss to Seamen *Eur* 85-95. *The Friary, Hilfield, Dorchester, Dorset DT2 7BE* Tel (01300) 341345

THOMPSON, Canon Barry Pearce. b 40. St Andr Univ BSc63 Ball Coll Ox PhD66 Hull Univ MA82. NW Ord Course 76. **d** 79 **p** 80. C Cottingham *York* 79-82; V Swine 82-83; Lect Th Hull Univ 83-88; Ind Chapl *York* 83-85; Abp's Adv on Ind Issues 85-88; Can Res Chelmsf Cathl *Chelmsf* from 88. *2 Harlings Grove, Waterloo Lane, Chelmsford CM1 1YQ* Tel (01245) 355041

THOMPSON, Brian. b 34. BSc. St Jo Coll Nottm. **d** 84 **p** 85. C Bletchley *Ox* 84-87; V Sneyd Green *Lich* from 87. *St Andrew's Vicarage, 42 Granville Avenue, Sneyd Green, Stoke-on-Trent ST1 6BH* Tel (01782) 215139

THOMPSON, David Arthur. b 37. Clifton Th Coll. **d** 69 **p** 70. C Finchley Ch Ch *Lon* 69-72; C Barking St Marg w St Patr *Chelmsf* 72-75; TV 75-81; V Toxteth Park St Clem *Liv* 81-91; TR Parr from 91. *The Rectory, Delta Road, St Helens, Merseyside WA9 2DZ* Tel (01744) 23726

THOMPSON, David Frank. b 44. Hull Univ BA65 MA69. St Steph Ho Ox 73. **d** 75 **p** 76. C Sidmouth, Woolbrook and Salcombe Regis *Ex* 75-78; C Lamorbey H Redeemer *Roch* 78-80; Chapl R Masonic Sch for Girls Rickmansworth from 81. *Royal Masonic School for Girls, Rickmansworth Park, Rickmansworth, Herts WD3 4HF* Tel (01923) 73168

THOMPSON, David John. b 17. Selw Coll Cam BA48 MA52. Ridley Hall Cam 48. **d** 50 **p** 51. C Denton Holme *Carl* 50-53; V Fulham St Mary N End *Lon* 53-62; V Wallington H Trin *S'wark* 62-74; R Hambledon *Guildf* 74-84; rtd 84; Perm to Offic *Chich* from 85. *1 Pond Willow, North Trade Road, Battle, E Sussex TN33 0HU* Tel (01424) 773000

THOMPSON, David John (Dave). b 64. Cranmer Hall Dur CTM95. **d** 95 **p** 96. C Poulton-le-Sands w Morecambe St Laur *Blackb* from 95. *31 Dallam Avenue, Morecambe, Lancs LA4 5BB* Tel (01524) 422974

THOMPSON, Miss Denise. b 50. Chich Th Coll 88. **d** 90. Par Dn Eighton Banks *Dur* 90-94. *1 Radlett Road, Sunderland SR5 5QZ* Tel 0191-549 0952

THOMPSON, Canon Donald Frazer. b 20. St Cath Coll Cam BA46 MA49. Coll of Resurr Mirfield 46. **d** 48 **p** 49. C Cheshunt *St Alb* 48-52; C Norton 52-56; V Wigan St Anne *Liv* 56-62; V Leeds St Aid *Ripon* 62-73; RD Allerton 70-73; R Adel 73-87; Hon Can Ripon Cathl 75-87; RD Headingley 85-87; rtd 87. *75 Cubbington Road, Leamington Spa, Warks CV32 7AQ* Tel (01926) 332935

THOMPSON, Edward Ronald Charles. b 25. AKC51. **d** 52 **p** 53. C Hinckley St Mary *Leic* 52-54; Jerusalem 54-55; Chapl St Boniface Coll Warminster 56-59; R Hawkchurch w Fishpond *Sarum* 59-63; V Camberwell St Mich w All So w Em *S'wark* 63-67; P-in-c St Mary le Strand w St Clem Danes *Lon* 67-74; R 74-93; rtd 93; Perm to Offic *S'wark* from 95. *3 Woodsyre, London SE26 6SS* Tel 0181-670 8289

THOMPSON, Eric John. b 41. Chich Th Coll 83. **d** 85 **p** 86. C Newbold w Dunston *Derby* 85-88; P-in-c Taddington and Chelmorton 88-90; P-in-c Earl Sterndale and Monyash 88-90; V Taddington, Chelmorton and Flagg, and Monyash 90-92; V Blackwell 92-95; P-in-c Walton on Trent w Croxall etc from 95. *The Rectory, 2 Station Lane, Walton-on-Trent, Swadlincote, Derbyshire DE12 8NA* Tel (01283) 712442

THOMPSON, Frederick Robert. b 15. Dur Univ LTh40. St Aug Coll Cant 37. **d** 40 **p** 41. C Northampton Ch Ch *Pet* 40-44; C Maidstone All SS *Cant* 44-46; India 46-57; Area Sec (Dios Birm and Lich) SPG 57-64; V Tutbury *Lich* 64-80; rtd 80. *1 Panorama Road, Poole, Dorset BH13 7RA* Tel (01202) 700735

THOMPSON, Garry. WMMTC. **d** 96 **p** 97. NSM Wilnecote *Lich* from 96. *37 Cornel, Amington, Tamworth, Staffs B77 4EF* Tel (01827) 65205

THOMPSON, Garry John. b 49. Qu Coll Birm. **d** 96 **p** 97. C Wilnecote *Lich* from 96. *87 Belgrave Road, Belgrave, Tamworth, Staffs B77 2LS* Tel (01827) 283174

✠THOMPSON, The Rt Revd Geoffrey Hewlett. b 29. Trin Hall Cam BA52 MA56. Cuddesdon Coll 52. **d** 54 **p** 55 **c** 74. C Northampton St Matt *Pet* 54-59; V Wisbech St Aug *Ely* 59-66; V

Folkestone St Sav *Cant* 66-74; Suff Bp Willesden *Lon* 74-79; Area Bp Willesden 79-85; Bp Ex from 85. *The Palace, Exeter EX1 1HY* Tel (01392) 272362 Fax 430923

THOMPSON, George Harry Packwood. b 22. Qu Coll Ox BA48 MA48 BTh49. Qu Coll Birm 50. **d** 51 **p** 52. Lect Qu Coll Birm 51-53; C Coleshill *Birm* 51-53; Lect 53-55; Chapl Sarum Th Coll 53-55; Vice-Prin 55-64; V Combe *Ox* 64-85; Perm to Offic from 85; rtd 87. *12 Briar Thicket, Woodstock, Oxon OX20 1NT* Tel (01993) 811915

THOMPSON, Preb Gordon Henry Moorhouse. b 41. Univ of Wales LLM95. K Coll Lon 63 St Boniface Warminster 66. **d** 67 **p** 68. C Leominster *Heref* 67-70; C Burford II w Greete and Hope Bagot 70-74; TV 74-89; C Burford III w Lt Heref 70-74; TV 74-89; C Tenbury 70-74; TV 74-89; TV Burford I 74-89; RD Ludlow 83-89; Preb Heref Cathl 85-97; rtd 89; Perm to Offic *Heref* from 89. *The Poplars, Bitterley, Ludlow, Shropshire SY8 3HQ* Tel (01584) 891093

THOMPSON, Harold Anthony. b 41. N Ord Course 84. **d** 87 **p** 88. C Leeds Belle Is St Jo and St Barn *Ripon* 87-90; V Leeds St Cypr Harehills 90-96; V Shadwell from 96. *The Vicarage, 2 Church Farm Garth, Leeds LS17 8HD* Tel 0113-273 7035

THOMPSON, Ian Charles. b 58. Wycliffe Hall Ox 80. **d** 83 **p** 84. C Knutsford St Jo and Toft *Ches* 83-86; C Birkenhead Ch Ch 86-88; V Balderstone *Man* from 88; AD Rochdale from 97. *The Sett, Badger Lane, Craiglands, Rochdale, Lancs OL16 4RD* Tel (01706) 49886

THOMPSON, Ian Malcolm. b 59. Wm Booth Memorial Coll CertEd79. Edin Th Coll 93. **d** 94 **p** 97. C Old Deer *Ab* 94-96; C Longside 94-96; C Strichen 94-96; Dioc Youth Chapl from 94; R Aberdeen St Mary from 96. *St Mary's Rectory, 28 Stanley Street, Aberdeen AB10 6UR* Tel (01224) 584123

THOMPSON, Father James. b 30. MNACH90 DipHyp84 Nottm Univ DipEd65 DipTh65. Paton Congr Coll Nottm 61 Wycliffe Hall Ox 66. **d** 66 **p** 67. C Woodlands *Sheff* 66-69; R Firbeck w Letwell 69-71; V Milnsbridge *Wakef* 71-80; Chapl St Luke's Hosp Huddersfield 71-80; NSM Dewsbury 80-84; Lect Huddersfield Coll FE 80-84; Dioc Chapl Aber Hosps 84-89; Dioc Supernumerary *Ab* 84-89; R Buckie 89-94; R Portsoy 89-94; rtd 95. *Peace Haven, Fron Park Road, Holywell, Flintwell CH8 7UY* Tel (01352) 713268

THOMPSON, James. b 37. Coll of Resurr Mirfield 64. **d** 67 **p** 68. C Shieldfield Ch Ch *Newc* 67-69; C Hendon *Dur* 69-74; V Gateshead St Chad Bensham 74-85; R Easington 85-90; Chapl Thorpe Hosp Easington 85-90; V Cassop cum Quarrington *Dur* from 90. *The Vicarage, Bowburn, Co Durham DH6 5DL* Tel 0191-377 0347

✠**THOMPSON, The Rt Revd James Lawton.** b 36. ACA59 FCA70 Em Coll Cam BA64 MA71 Hon DLitt89 Ex Univ Hon DD95. Cuddesdon Coll 64. **d** 66 **p** 67 **c** 78. C E Ham St Geo *Chelmsf* 66-68; Chapl Cuddesdon Coll 68-71; Lic to Offic *S'wark* 71-72; TR Thamesmead 72-78; Suff Bp Stepney *Lon* 78-79; Area Bp Stepney 79-91; Bp B & W from 91. *The Palace, Wells, Somerset BA5 2PD* Tel (01749) 672341 Fax 679355

THOMPSON, Jeremy James Thomas. b 58. Sunderland Univ BEd92. Cranmer Hall Dur 94. **d** 96 **p** 97. C Bedlington *Newc* from 96. *Berkswych, Front Street West, Bedlington, Northd NE22 5TT*

THOMPSON, John David. b 40. Lon Univ BD65 Ch Ch Ox DPhil69. St Steph Ho Ox 65. **d** 67 **p** 68. C Solihull *Birm* 67-71; C Biddestone w Slaughterford *Bris* 71-73; Lect Wells Th Coll 71-72; C Yatton Keynell *Bris* 71-73; C Castle Combe 71-73; V Braughing *St Alb* 74-77; R Digswell 77-82; TR Digswell and Panshanger from 82. *The Rectory, 354 Knightsfield, Welwyn Garden City, Herts AL8 7NG* Tel (01707) 326677

THOMPSON, John Michael. b 47. Nottm Univ BTh77 Hull Univ CLRHist90. Linc Th Coll 73. **d** 77 **p** 78. C Old Brumby *Linc* 77-80; C Grantham 80-81; TV 81-84; V Holton-le-Clay 84-94; V Holton-le-Clay and Tetney 94-97; R Humshaugh w Simonburn and Wark *Newc* from 97. *The Vicarage, Humshaugh, Hexham, Northd NE46 4AA* Tel (01434) 681304

THOMPSON, John Miller. b 26. St Deiniol's Hawarden. **d** 63 **p** 64. C Hawarden *St As* 63-66; C Connah's Quay 66-67; V Askern *Sheff* 67-72; P-in-c Moss 69-72; Ind Chapl 72-85; P-in-c Brightside St Marg 72-77; P-in-c Sheff Gillcar St Silas 77-88; Chapl Weston Park Hosp Sheff 85-93; C Ranmoor *Sheff* 88-93; Chapl to Homes for the Aged 88-93; rtd 93; Perm to Offic *Sheff* from 93. *2 Knab Close, Sheffield S7 2ER* Tel 0114-258 6790

THOMPSON, John Turrell. b 57. Sheff Univ BA(Econ)79 Southn Univ BTh88. Sarum & Wells Th Coll 83. **d** 86 **p** 87. C Tavistock and Gulworthy *Ex* 86-90; TV Pinhoe and Broadclyst 90-95; P-in-c Northam w Westward Ho! and Appledore 95-96; TV Bideford, Northam, Westward Ho!, Appledore etc from 96. *The Rectory, Fore Street, Northam, Bideford, Devon EX39 1AW* Tel (01237) 474379

THOMPSON, John Wilfred. b 44. CA Tr Coll 66 St Deiniol's Hawarden 84. **d** 85 **p** 86. C Rhyl w St Ann *St As* 85-87; R Fritwell w Souldern and Ardley w Fewcott *Ox* 87-97. *Address temp unknown*

THOMPSON (née LILLIE), Mrs Judith Virginia. b 44. LMH Ox BA66 Univ of E Africa DipEd67 Essex Univ MA73 Bris Univ DCouns92. Gilmore Course IDC82. **dss** 82 **d** 87 **p** 94. Lawrence Weston *Bris* 82-85; E Bris 85-95; Hon Par Dn 87-95; Chapl HM Rem Cen Pucklechurch 87-91; Chapl Asst Southmead Hosp Bris 91-94; Asst Chapl Bris NHS Trust 94-95; C Knowle St Barn and Holy Cross Inns Court *Bris* from 95; Adv in past care for clergy and their families from 97. *St Barnabas' Vicarage, Daventry Road, Bristol BS4 1DQ* Tel 0117-966 4139

THOMPSON, Kenneth. b 31. St Deiniol's Hawarden. **d** 87 **p** 88. Hon Par Dn Upton (Overchurch) *Ches* 87-90; NSM Tranmere St Cath 90-95; rtd 96; Perm to Offic *Ches* from 96. *33 Meadway, Upton, Wirral, Merseyside L49 6JQ* Tel 0151-677 6433

THOMPSON, Kenneth (Brother Nathanael). b 29. St Deiniol's Hawarden 76. **d** 78 **p** 79. SSF from 62; C Llanbeblig w Caernarfon *Ban* 78-80; C Swansea St Gabr *S & B* 84-87; C Swansea St Mary w H Trin 87; C Dolgellau w Llanfachreth and Brithdir etc *Ban* from 95. *Ty'r Ficer, Pencefn Road, Dolgellau LL40 2ER*

THOMPSON, Kevin. b 55. Sheff Univ BEd77. Oak Hill Th Coll DipHE89. **d** 89 **p** 90. C Brinsworth w Catcliffe *Sheff* 89-92; V Kimberworth Park 92-97; V Grenoside from 97. *St Mark's Vicarage, 19 Graven Close, Grenoside, Sheffield S30 3QT* Tel 0114-246 7513

THOMPSON, Mark William. b 52. St Jo Coll Nottm 77. **d** 81 **p** 82. C Barnsbury St Andr and H Trin w All SS *Lon* 81-84; C Addiscombe St Mary *Cant* 84; C Addiscombe St Mary *S'wark* 85-87; V Thorpe Edge *Bradf* 87-94; Chapl Essex Rivers Healthcare NHS Trust from 94. *Colchester General Hospital, Turner Road, Colchester CO4 5JL* Tel (01206) 853535

THOMPSON, Martin Eric. b 52. FCCA. Trin Coll Bris 95. **d** 97. C Heref St Pet w St Owen and St Jas *Heref* from 97. *Chycarne, Goodrich, Ross-on-Wye, Herefordshire HR9 6JE*

THOMPSON, Matthew. b 68. CCC Cam BA90 MA94 MPhil94. Ridley Hall Cam 91. **d** 94 **p** 95. C Hulme Ascension *Man* from 94. *The Arnott Centre, 2 Tarnbrook Walk, Manchester M15 6NL* Tel 0161-226 4694

THOMPSON, Mervyn Patrick. b 59. Wilson Carlile Coll 84 Coll of Resurr Mirfield 90. **d** 92 **p** 93. C Sheff St Cath Richmond Road *Sheff* 92-95; V Thurnscoe St Hilda from 95. *The Vicarage, Hanover Street, Thurnscoe, Rotherham, S Yorkshire S63 0HJ* Tel (01709) 893259

THOMPSON, Michael. b 49. NE Ord Course 83. **d** 86 **p** 87. C Ashington *Newc* 86-88; C Ponteland 88-91; TV Newc Epiphany from 91. *7 Fawdon Lane, Newcastle upon Tyne NE3 2RR* Tel 0191-285 5403

THOMPSON, Dr Michael Bruce. b 53. N Carolina Univ BA75 Ch Coll Cam PhD88. Dallas Th Sem ThM79 Virginia Th Sem 79. **d** 80 **p** 81. USA 80-83; Lect St Jo Coll Nottm 88-95; Dir of Studies Ridley Hall Cam from 95. *Dashwood House, Sidgwick Avenue, Cambridge CB3 9HG* Tel (01223) 65984 E-mail mbt2@cam.ac.uk

THOMPSON, Michael James. b 55. St Andr Univ MTh78. St Mich Coll Llan 78. **d** 79 **p** 80. C Aberavon *Llan* 79-81; C Kensington St Mary Abbots w St Geo *Lon* 81-85; Chapl Westmr Abbey 85-87; Sacrist 86-87; P-in-c Westmr St Marg 86-87; R Lowick w Sudborough and Slipton *Pet* 87-94; P-in-c Islip 87-94; V Sneinton St Steph w St Alb *S'well* from 96. *Sneinton Vicarage, Windmill Lane, Nottingham NG2 4QB* Tel 0115-958 0508

THOMPSON, Neil Hamilton. b 48. SS Hild & Bede Coll Dur BEd72 Leic Univ MA75. S'wark Ord Course 77. **d** 80 **p** 81. C Merton St Mary *S'wark* 80-82; C Dulwich St Barn 82-84; V Shooters Hill Ch Ch 84-87; V S Dulwich St Steph 87-96; R Limpsfield and Titsey from 96. *The Rectory, Limpsfield, Oxted, Surrey RH8 0DG* Tel (01883) 722812

THOMPSON, Patrick Arthur. b 36. Dur Univ BA59. Qu Coll Birm DipTh61. **d** 61 **p** 62. C W Wickham St Fran *Cant* 61-65; C Portchester *Portsm* 65-68; C Birchington w Acol *Cant* 68-71; V S Norwood St Mark 71-77; P-in-c Norbury St Oswald 77-81; V Norbury St Oswald *S'wark* 81-93; V Sutton New Town St Barn from 93. *St Barnabas' Vicarage, 37 St Barnabas' Road, Sutton, Surrey SM1 4NS* Tel 0181-661 9619

THOMPSON, Paul. b 58. Ox Univ BA. Ripon Coll Cuddesdon 80. **d** 83 **p** 84. Chapl Fazakerley Hosp 83-86; C Kirkby *Liv* 83-86; TV 86-89; Ind Chapl 86-89; Chapl Kirkby Coll of FE 86-89; CF from 89. *MOD Chaplains (Army), Trenchard Lines, Upavon, Pewsey, Wilts SN9 6BE* Tel (01980) 615804 Fax 615800

THOMPSON, Paul. b 65. TCD BA87. CITC 87. **d** 89 **p** 90. C Orangefield w Moneyreagh *D & D* 89-91; I Dromara w Garvaghy 91-97; I Ramoan w Ballycastle and Culfeightrin *Conn* from 97. *12 Novally Road, Ballycastle, Co Antrim BT54 6HB* Tel (01265) 762461

THOMPSON, Paul Noble. b 54. Univ of Wales (Cardiff) BMus77. Coll of Resurr Mirfield DipTh79. **d** 80 **p** 81. C Bargoed and Deri w Brithdir *Llan* 80-83; C Whitchurch 83-84; V Porth w Trealaw 84-89; V Llanharan w Peterston-super-Montem 89-97; C Barry All SS from 97; Youth Chapl from 97. *3A Park Road, Barry CF62 6NU* Tel (01446) 701814

THOMPSON, Mrs Pauline. b 44. EMMTC 81. **dss** 84 **d** 87 **p** 94. Derby St Aug *Derby* 84-87; Par Dn 87-88; Par Dn Boulton 88-90; Par Dn Allestree 91-94; C 94-97; Sub-Chapl HM Pris Sudbury from 92; P-in-c Hartington, Biggin and Earl Sterndale from 97. *The Vicarage, Hartington, Buxton, Derbyshire SK17 0AW* Tel (01298) 84280

THOMPSON, Peter Homer. b 17. Chich Th Coll 39. **d** 41 **p** 42. C Notting Hill St Mich and Ch Ch *Lon* 41-44; C Fulham St Pet 44-47; USA 47-50; C Kensington St Jo *Lon* 50-53; C-in-c Ruislip St Mary CD 53-59; V Ruislip St Mary 59-81; V Mullion *Truro* 81-87; rtd 87; Perm to Offic *Ex* from 94. *22 Parkside Drive, Exmouth, Devon EX8 4LB* Tel (01395) 266359

THOMPSON, Peter Kerr. b 32. Kelham Th Coll. **d** 56 **p** 57. Solomon Is 56-76; Adn Malaita and Outer E Solomon 62-68; Adn N Melanesia 68-70; Australia from 76. *28 Saunders Street, Point Vernon, Queensland, Australia 4655* Tel Brisbane (71) 243645

THOMPSON, Canon Dr Peter Ross. b 26. St Jo Coll Cam BA47 MB50 BChir50. Tyndale Hall Bris. **d** 60 **p** 61. C New Malden and Coombe *S'wark* 60-61; Burma 61-66; R Slaugham *Chich* 66-72; V Polegate 72-92; Can and Preb Chich Cathl 91-92; rtd 92; Perm to Offic *Guildf* from 92. *Tregenna, Barley Mow Lane, Knaphill, Woking, Surrey GU21 2HX* Tel (01483) 480595

THOMPSON, Randolph. b 25. Lich Th Coll 63. **d** 65 **p** 66. C Boultham *Linc* 65-68; V Paddock *Wakef* 68-69; P-in-c Cornholme 69-71; V 71-72; Chapl Barnsley Hall & Lea Hosps Bromsgrove 72-84; V Hanley Castle, Hanley Swan and Welland *Worc* 84-89; rtd 89; Perm to Offic *Lich* from 90. *37 Hampton Fields, Oswestry, Shropshire SY11 1TL* Tel (01691) 658484

THOMPSON, Raymond Craigmile. b 42. **d** 84 **p** 85. C Clooney *D & R* 84-86; I Urney w Sion Mills 86-92; I Derryvullen N w Castlearchdale *Clogh* from 92. *The Rectory, Enniskillen Road, Irvinestown, Co Fermanagh BT94 1GW* Tel (01365) 621225 Fax as telephone

THOMPSON, Richard Brian. b 60. Sheff Poly BSc83. Ripon Coll Cuddesdon 86. **d** 89 **p** 90. C Thorpe Bay *Chelmsf* 89-92; V Rushmere *St E* from 92. *The Vicarage, 253 Colchester Road, Rushmere, Ipswich IP4 4SH* Tel (01473) 270976

THOMPSON, Robert. b 36. AKC61. **d** 62 **p** 63. C Cockerton *Dur* 62-65; C Dur St Marg 65-70; V Wallsend St Jo *Newc* 70-78; V Norham and Duddo from 78. *The Vicarage, Norham, Berwick-upon-Tweed TD15 2LF* Tel (01289) 382325

THOMPSON, Robert Craig. b 72. Univ Coll Dur BA92. Westcott Ho Cam 94. **d** 96 **p** 97. C Wigan All SS *Liv* from 96. *The Glebe House, Wigan Hall, Wigan, Lancs WN1 1HH* Tel (01942) 243793

THOMPSON, Robert George. b 71. K Coll Cam BA93 MA97. Ripon Coll Cuddesdon MTh95. **d** 97. C Ruislip St Martin *Lon* from 97. *5 Whyteleaf Close, Ruislip, Middx HA4 7SP* Tel (01895) 633370

THOMPSON, Roger Quintin. b 63. St Jo Coll Nottm MA94 Aston Tr Scheme 92. **d** 96. C Easton H Trin w St Gabr and St Lawr and St Jude *Bris* from 96. *7 Villiers Road, Easton, Bristol BS5 0JH* Tel 0117-952 2894

THOMPSON, Ronald. b 08. DFC43. Linc Th Coll. **d** 60 **p** 61. C E Dereham w Hoe *Nor* 60-65; R Saham Toney 65-78; rtd 78; Perm to Offic *Nor* 79-96. *4 Oval Avenue, Norwich NR5 0DP* Tel (01603) 744139

THOMPSON, Dr Ross Keith Arnold. b 53. Sussex Univ BA75 Bris Univ PhD82. Coll of Resurr Mirfield 80. **d** 82 **p** 83. C Knowle *Bris* 82-85; TV E Bris 85-94; V Bristol St Aid w St Geo 94-95; V Knowle St Barn and Holy Cross Inns Court from 95. *St Barnabas' Vicarage, Daventry Road, Bristol BS4 1QD* Tel 0117-966 4139

THOMPSON, Miss Ruth Jean. b 47. St Alb Minl Tr Scheme 85. **d** 90 **p** 94. Par Dn Stonebridge St Mich *Lon* 90-94; C 94; C Ealing St Paul 94-96; TV W Slough *Ox* from 96. *St George's House, Long Furlong Drive, Slough SL2 2LX* Tel (01753) 525935

THOMPSON, Thomas. b 25. NE Ord Course. **d** 85 **p** 86. NSM Ford *Newc* 85-86; NSM Tweedmouth 86-93; rtd 93. *35 Magdalene Drive, Berwick-upon-Tweed TD15 1PX* Tel (01289) 305725

THOMPSON, Thomas Oliver. b 27. TCD 61. **d** 63 **p** 64. C Lisburn Ch Ch *Conn* 63-68; Chapl to Ch of Ireland Miss to Deaf and Dumb 68-76; I Glenavy w Tunny and Crumlin 77-92; rtd 92. *34 Strandview Avenue, Portstewart, Co Londonderry BT55 7LL* Tel (01265) 833267

THOMPSON, Canon Timothy. b 34. Fitzw Ho Cam BA59 MA64. Cuddesdon Coll 59. **d** 61 **p** 62. C Noel Park St Mark *Lon* 61-64; C Shrub End *Chelmsf* 64-67; New Zealand 67-70; R Tolleshunt Knights w Tiptree *Chelmsf* 70-81; R Colchester St Jas, All SS, St Nic and St Runwald 81-88; RD Colchester 84-88; Hon Can Chelmsf Cathl 85-88; Vice-Provost Chelmsf from 88; Can Res Chelmsf Cathl from 88. *115 Rainsford Road, Chelmsford CM1 2PH* Tel (01245) 267773

THOMPSON, Timothy Charles. b 51. Lon Univ BSc73 AKC. Westcott Ho Cam 75. **d** 78 **p** 79. C Ipswich St Mary at Stoke w St Pet & St Mary Quay *St E* 78-81; Ind Chapl *Nor* 81-88; C Lowestoft and Kirkley 81-83; TV 83-88; V Coney Hill *Glouc* 88-94; P-in-c Caister *Nor* from 94. *The Rectory, Caister-on-Sea, Great Yarmouth, Norfolk NR30 5EH* Tel (01493) 720287

THOMPSON, Timothy William. b 48. Bris Univ CertEd70 Open Univ BA78. EMMTC. **d** 88 **p** 89. C Scartho *Linc* 88-91; V Haxey 91-95; P-in-c Surfleet from 95; Asst Local Min Officer from 95. *The Vicarage, 11 Station Road, Surfleet, Spalding, Lincs PE11 4DA* Tel (01775) 680906

THOMPSON, Tom Malcolm. b 38. Dur Univ BA60. Bps' Coll Cheshunt 60. **d** 62 **p** 63. C Standish *Blackb* 62-65; C Lancaster St Mary 65-67; V Chorley All SS 67-72; V Barrowford 72-78; RD Pendle 75-78; R Northfield *Birm* 78-82; RD Kings Norton 79-82; V Longton *Blackb* 82-94; RD Leyland 89-94; V Nunthorpe *York* from 94. *The Vicarage, Nunthorpe, Middlesbrough, Cleveland TS7 0PD* Tel (01642) 346570

THOMPSON-McCAUSLAND, Marcus Perronet. b 31. Trin Coll Cam BA54 MA60. Coll of Resurr Mirfield 57. **d** 59 **p** 60. C Perry Barr *Birm* 59-65; V Rubery 65-72; R Cradley *Heref* 72-82; P-in-c Storridge 72-82; P-in-c Mathon 72-82; P-in-c Castle Frome 72-82; Hon C Camberwell St Giles *S'wark* 82-87; Hon C Lydbury N *Heref* 88-89; Hon C Lydbury N w Hopesay and Edgton 89-94; rtd 93. *18 Watling Street, Leintwardine, Craven Arms, Shropshire SY7 0LW* Tel (01547) 3228

THOMPSTONE, John Deaville. b 39. BNC Ox BA63 MA67. Ridley Hall Cam 63. **d** 65 **p** 66. C Hoole *Ches* 65-68; C Fulwood *Sheff* 68-71; V Skirbeck H Trin *Linc* 71-77; V Shipley St Pet *Bradf* 77-91; RD Airedale 82-88; V Poynton *Ches* from 91. *The Vicarage, 41 London Road North, Poynton, Cheshire SK12 1AF* Tel (01625) 872711

THOMSETT, Murray Richard. b 32. MBKSTS Kingston Tech Coll HND54. Oak Hill Th Coll 91. **d** 92 **p** 93. NSM Whitton SS Phil and Jas *Lon* 92-96; NSM Hampton All SS from 96. *27 Coombe Road, Hampton, Middx TW12 3PB* Tel 0181-979 7549

THOMSON, Alexander Keith. b 38. Cranmer Hall Dur BA63. **d** 64 **p** 65. C Middleton *Man* 64-68; Chapl Rannoch Sch Perthshire 68-72; P-in-c Kinloch Rannoch *St And* 68-72; Asst Chapl Oundle Sch from 72; Lic to Offic *Pet* from 73; Chapl Laxton Sch Oundle from 88. *34 Kings Road, Oundle, Peterborough PE8 4AY* Tel (01832) 273416

THOMSON, Andrew Maitland. b 43. CA(Z)67 Univ Coll of Rhodesia and Nyasaland DipApEc65. Westcott Ho Cam 78. **d** 80 **p** 81. Zimbabwe 80-92; P-in-c E w N and W Barsham *Nor* 92-95; P-in-c N and S Creake w Waterden 92-94; P-in-c Sculthorpe w Dunton and Doughton 92-94; R N and S Creake w Waterden, Syderstone etc from 95. *The Rectory, 18 Front Street, South Creake, Fakenham, Norfolk NR21 9PE* Tel (01328) 823433

THOMSON, Miss Celia Stephana Margaret. b 55. LMH Ox MA83 Birkb Coll Lon MA87 K Coll Lon MA94. Sarum & Wells Th Coll 89. **d** 91 **p** 94. Par Dn Southfields St Barn *S'wark* 91-94; C 94-95; V W Wimbledon Ch Ch from 95. *The Vicarage, 16 Copse Hill, London SW20 0HG* Tel 0181-946 4491

THOMSON, Preb Clarke Edward Leighton. b 19. TD65. Pemb Coll Ox BA41 MA45. Wycliffe Hall Ox 44. **d** 45 **p** 46. C Penge Lane H Trin *Roch* 45-47; Egypt 47-50; C Chelsea All SS *Lon* 50-51; V 51-92; CF (TA) 52-69; Preb St Paul's Cathl *Lon* 86-92; rtd 92. *15 Redburn Street, London SW3 4DA* Tel 0171-351 5371

THOMSON, Colin Hugh. b 21. **d** 91 **p** 92. C Galway w Kilcummin *T, K & A* 91-94; NSM Tuam from 94. *The Rectory, Luimnagh West, Corrandulla, Co Galway, Irish Republic* Tel Galway (91) 791482 Fax 791386

THOMSON, Dr David. b 52. Keble Coll Ox MA78 DPhil78 Selw Coll Cam BA80 MA84. Westcott Ho Cam 78. **d** 81 **p** 82. C Maltby *Sheff* 81-84; Sec Par and People 84-94; TV Banbury *Ox* 84-94; TR Cockermouth w Embleton and Wythop *Carl* from 94. *The Rectory, Lorton Road, Cockermouth, Cumbria CA13 9DU* Tel (01900) 823269

THOMSON, George Miller McMillan. b 33. Edin Th Coll 59. **d** 62 **p** 63. C Edin Old St Paul *Edin* 62-64; USA 64-68; C Brookfield St Mary *Lon* 68-72; V Noel Park St Mark 72-81; RD E Haringey 77-81; Chapl Newark Hosp 81-87; TR Newark w Hawton, Cotham and Shelton *S'well* 81-87; R Glas St Bride *Glas* from 87; rtd 94. *St Bride's Rectory, 25 Queensborough Gardens, Glasgow G12 9QP* Tel 0141-334 1401

THOMSON, John Bromilow. b 59. York Univ BA81. Wycliffe Hall Ox BA84 MA91. **d** 85 **p** 86. C Ecclesall *Sheff* 85-89; S Africa 89-92; V Doncaster St Mary *Sheff* from 93. *St Mary's Vicarage, 59 St Mary's Road, Doncaster, S Yorkshire DN1 2NR* Tel (01302) 342565

THOMSON, Julian Harley. b 43. AKC70. St Aug Coll Cant 70. **d** 71 **p** 72. C Wellingborough All Hallows *Pet* 71-74; Min Can, Prec and Sacr Ely Cathl *Ely* 74-80; P-in-c Stuntney 76-80; V Arrington 80-91; R Croydon w Clopton 80-91; R Orwell 80-91; R Wimpole 80-91; V Linton 91-96; R Bartlow 91-96; P-in-c Castle Camps 91-96; TR Linton from 96. *The Vicarage, Church Lane, Linton, Cambridge CB1 6JX* Tel (01223) 891291

THOMSON, Matthew James. b 63. Nottm Univ BA92 Univ of Wales (Ban). St Jo Coll Nottm 92. **d** 95 **p** 96. C Cosham *Portsm* from 95. *211 Hawthorn Crescent, Cosham, Portsmouth PO6 2TL* Tel (01705) 349609

THOMSON, Oliver Miles. b 38. Magd Coll Cam BA61 MA65. Wycliffe Hall Ox 61. **d** 63 **p** 64. C St Marylebone All So w SS Pet and Jo *Lon* 63-67; C Fulwood *Sheff* 67-70; R Wick w Doynton *Bris* 70-74; V Harold Wood *Chelmsf* 74-87; R Sevenoaks St Nic *Roch* from 87. *The Rectory, Rectory Lane, Sevenoaks, Kent TN13 1JA* Tel (01732) 740340 Fax 742810

THOMSON, Peter Ashley. b 36. Ridley Coll Melbourne ThL. **d** 59 **p** 60. Australia 59-62; C Fen Ditton *Ely* 62-63; V Upwood w Gt and Lt Raveley 63-64; Australia 64-96; C W Holloway St Luke

Lon from 96. *St Francis Church Centre, North Road, London N7 9EY* Tel 0171-700 5262

THOMSON, Peter Malcolm. b 44. Trin Coll Bris 75. **d** 78 **p** 79. C Tonbridge St Steph *Roch* 78-82; R Cobham w Luddesdowne and Dode 82-90; V Withall *Birm* 90-92; V Wythall from 92. *St Mary's Vicarage, 27 Lea Green Lane, Wythall, Birmingham B47 6HE* Tel (01564) 823381

THOMSON, Canon Richard Irving. b 32. Oak Hill Th Coll 57. **d** 60 **p** 61. C Kingston upon Hull H Trin *York* 60-63; C S Croydon Em *Cant* 63-66; V Shoreditch St Leon *Lon* 66-73; Chapl Vevey w Chateau d'Oex and Villars *Eur* 73-78; V Reigate St Mary *S'wark* from 78; Hon Can S'wark Cathl from 90. *St Mary's Vicarage, 76 Church Street, Reigate, Surrey RH2 0SP* Tel (01737) 242973

THOMSON, Richard William Byars. b 60. Birm Univ BA86. Ripon Coll Cuddesdon 86. **d** 88 **p** 89. C Moulsecoomb *Chich* 88-90; P-in-c Kirriemuir *St And* 90-94; P-in-c Piddletrenthide w Plush, Alton Pancras etc *Sarum* from 94; P-in-c Milborne St Andrew w Dewlish from 94. *The Vicarage, Piddletrenthide, Dorchester, Dorset DT2 7QX* Tel (01300) 348763 Fax as telephone

THOMSON, Robert Douglass. b 37. Dur Univ BEd75. Cranmer Hall Dur 76. **d** 79 **p** 80. NSM Shincliffe *Dur* from 79; Chapl St Aid Coll Dur from 95. *11 Hill Meadows, High Shincliffe, Durham DH1 2PE* Tel 0191-386 3358

THOMSON, Robin Alexander Stewart. b 43. Ch Coll Cam MA69 K Coll Lon MTh72. SEITE 94. **d** 96. NSM Wimbledon Em Ridgway Prop Chpl *S'wark* from 96. *2 Coppice Close, London SW20 9AS* Tel 0181-540 7748 Fax 770 9747

THOMSON, Canon Ronald. b 24. Leeds Univ BA49. Coll of Resurr Mirfield 49. **d** 51 **p** 52. C Sunderland *Dur* 51-54; C Attercliffe w Carbrook *Sheff* 54-57; V Shiregreen St Hilda 57-73; RD Ecclesfield 72-73; V Worsbrough 73-88; RD Tankersley 75-85; Hon Can Sheff Cathl 77-88; rtd 88; Perm to Offic *Sheff* from 88. *34 Kingwell Road, Worsbrough, Barnsley, S Yorkshire S70 4HF* Tel (01226) 203553

THOMSON, Ronald Arthur. b 29. G&C Coll Cam BA53 MA57. Ripon Hall Ox. **d** 57 **p** 58. C Sanderstead All SS *S'wark* 57-60; C Kidbrooke St Jas 60-62; Chapl RAF 62-68; C Amersham *Ox* 68; R Watton at Stone *St Alb* 68-94; rtd 94. *Ashby, 65 Edmonds Drive, Aston Brook, Stevenage, Herts SG2 9TJ*

THOMSON, Russell. b 39. AKC62. **d** 63 **p** 64. C Hackney *Lon* 63-66; C Plumstead Wm Temple Ch Abbey Wood CD *S'wark* 66-69; TV Strood *Roch* 69-75; V Gillingham St Mary 75-89; V Roch from 89; Chapl St Bart Hosp Roch from 89; Chapl Wisdom Hospice from 89. *The Vicarage, 138 Delce Road, Rochester, Kent ME1 2EH* Tel (01634) 845122 or 848900

THOMSON, Preb Sidney Seward Chartres. b 01. OBE44. St Geo Windsor. **d** 54 **p** 55. C Clun w Chapel Lawn *Heref* 54-56; V Worfield 56-72; RD Bridgnorth 65-71; Preb Heref Cathl 70-72; rtd 72; Perm to Offic *Heref* from 72. *Bradney House, Worfield, Bridgnorth, Shropshire WV15 5NT* Tel (01746) 765974

THOMSON, Mrs Winifred Mary. b 35. St Mary's Coll Dur BA57 MA58 Lon Univ 86. Qu Coll Birm 79. **dss** 82 **d** 87 **p** 94. Leic H Spirit *Leic* 82-86; Oadby 86-87; Par Dn 87-92; rtd 93; Perm to Offic *Leic* from 93. *140 Knighton Church Road, Leicester LE2 3JJ* Tel 0116-270 5863

THOMSON GIBSON, Thomas. *See* GIBSON, Thomas Thomson

THOMSON-GLOVER, Canon William Hugh. b 28. Trin Hall Cam BA52 MA56. Cuddesdon Coll 52. **d** 54 **p** 55. C Stepney St Dunstan and All SS *Lon* 54-58; C Tiverton St Andr *Ex* 58-60; P-in-c 60-63; Chapl Clifton Coll Bris 63-69; V Bris Lockleaze St Mary Magd w St Fran *Bris* 70-76; P-in-c Sherston Magna w Easton Grey 76-81; P-in-c Luckington w Alderton 76-81; V Sherston Magna, Easton Grey, Luckington etc 81-93; P-in-c Foxley w Bremilham 84-86; RD Malmesbury 88-93; Hon Can Bris Cathl 91-93; rtd 93; Perm to Offic *Ex* from 93. *Woodgate Farm House, Woodgate, Culmstock, Cullompton, Devon EX15 3HW* Tel (01884) 841465

THORBURN, Austin Noel. b 13. Trin Coll Cam BA36 MA40. Bps' Coll Cheshunt 36. **d** 38 **p** 39. C Hope St Jas *Man* 38-43; V Castleton All So 43-48; V Blackrod 48-52; SPG Pakistan 52-56; Lic to Offic Glouc, Lich and Worc 63-67; C Tettenhall Regis *Lich* 67-69; C Langley Marish *Ox* 71-76; TV 76-79; rtd 79; Perm to Offic *Carl* 79-88; Perm to Offic *Ox* from 88. *28 Blacklands Road, Benson, Wallingford, Oxon OX10 6NW* Tel (01491) 832365

THORBURN, Guy Douglas Anderson. b 50. Ridley Hall Cam. **d** 83 **p** 84. C Putney St Marg *S'wark* 83-87; R Moresby *Carl* from 87. *The Rectory, Low Moresby, Whitehaven, Cumbria CA28 6RR* Tel (01946) 693970

THORBURN, Peter Hugh. b 17. Worc Coll Ox BA41 MA43. Wells Th Coll 46. **d** 47 **p** 48. C Mill Hill Jo Keble Ch *Lon* 47-51; Lon Dioc Home Missr Colindale St Matthias 51; V 51-54; V Wigan St Mich *Liv* 54-65; USA 65-68; V Chipping Sodbury and Old Sodbury *Glouc* 68-72; Chapl Withington Hosp Man 72-82; rtd 82; Perm to Offic *B & W* from 83; Perm to Offic *Bris* from 85; Warden Servants of Ch the K from 89. *8 Stoberry Crescent, Wells, Somerset BA5 2TG* Tel (01749) 672919

THORBURN, Simon Godfrey. b 51. Newc Univ BSc73 Fitzw Coll Cam BA77 MA81. Westcott Ho Cam 75. **d** 78 **p** 79. C Stafford St Mary and St Chad *Lich* 78-79; C Stafford 79-82; C Tettenhall Regis 82-83; TV 83-90; Soc Resp Officer *S'wark* from 90. *104 Queens Road, London SW19 8LS* Tel 0181-543 8874

THORLEY, Barry. b 44. Westcott Ho Cam 70. **d** 73 **p** 74. C Camberwell St Giles *S'wark* 73-76; C Moseley St Mary *Birm* 76-78; V Birchfield 78-83; V Brixton St Matt *S'wark* 84-89; C Greenwich St Alfege w St Pet and St Paul from 96. *27 Haddo House, Haddo Street, London SE10 9SG* Tel 0181-858 8041

THORLEY-PAICE, Alan. b 26. AKC53. **d** 55 **p** 56. C Leek St Edw *Lich* 55-59; C Haslemere *Guildf* 59-63; C Eton w Boveney *Ox* 63-74; P-in-c Hawridge w Cholesbury 74-83; P-in-c Lee 74-83; V 83-86; P-in-c Aston Clinton St Leon 79-83; R Hawridge w Cholesbury and St Leonard 83-86; rtd 86. *Glaston, Kingstone, Hereford HR2 9ES* Tel (01981) 250195

THORN, Peter. b 50. Man Poly BEd79. Ridley Hall Cam 82. **d** 84 **p** 85. C Aughton Ch Ch *Liv* 84-87; C Skelmersdale St Paul 87-90; Dioc Children's Officer 87-92; P-in-c Croft w Southworth 90-92; C Streatley *St Alb* 92-95; R Blofield w Hemblington *Nor* 95-96; P-in-c from 96; Assoc Dioc Dir of Tr from 97. *The Rectory, 10 Oak Wood, Blofield, Norwich NR13 4JQ* Tel (01603) 713160

THORN, Robert Anthony D'Venning (Bob). b 54. AKC76. Chich Th Coll 75. **d** 77 **p** 78. C Bodmin *Truro* 77-80; TV N Hill w Altarnon, Bolventor and Lewannick 80-83; V Feock 83-90; Dioc Ecum Officer 83-90; Broadcasting Officer *Linc* 90-93; V Whitchurch *Bris* from 93. *The Vicarage, 780 Whitchurch Lane, Bristol BS14 0EU* Tel (01275) 832380

THORNBURGH, Richard Hugh Perceval. b 52. Sarum & Wells Th Coll. **d** 84 **p** 85. C Broadstone *Sarum* 84-87; TV Beaminster Area 87-95; TV Hanley H Ev *Lich* from 96. *St Luke's Vicarage, 18 Cromer Road, Stoke-on-Trent ST1 6QN*

THORNBURY, Peter Dawson. b 43. Open Univ BA84 TCD BTh93. CITC 90. **d** 93 **p** 94. C Annagh w Drumgoon, Ashfield etc *K, E & A* 93-96; I Clondehorkey w Cashel *D & R* from 96; I Mevagh w Glenalla from 96. *The Rectory, Ballymore, Letterkenny, Co Donegal, Irish Republic* Tel Letterkenny (74) 36185

THORNE, Mrs Anita Dawn. b 46. Trin Coll Bris 84. **dss** 86 **d** 87 **p** 94. Chapl Bris Poly *Bris* 86-88; Par Dn Olveston 88-94; P-in-c 94-96; P-in-c Portland All SS w St Pet *Sarum* from 96. *The Rectory, Straits, Easton, Portland, Dorset DT5 1HG* Tel (01305) 861285

THORNE, Clifford Graham. b 16. St Jo Coll Cam BA38 MA50. Westcott Ho Cam 78. **d** 78 **p** 79. Hon C Ponteland *Newc* from 78. *Dissington Old Hall, Dalton, Newcastle upon Tyne NE18 0BN* Tel (01661) 825258

THORNE, Mrs Marie Elizabeth. b 47. EMMTC 83. **dss** 86 **d** 87 **p** 94. Cleethorpes *Linc* 86-90; C 87-90; C Brigg 90-96; P-in-c New Waltham from 96. *The Vicarage, 41 Dunbar Avenue, New Waltham, Grimsby, S Humberside DN36 4PY* Tel (01472) 827765

THORNE, Canon Ralph Frederick. b 14. ALCD36 St Jo Coll Dur LTh36 BA37. **d** 37 **p** 38. C Harlesden All So *Lon* 37-41; C Heigham St Thos *Nor* 41-42; P-in-c N w S Wootton 42-44; V Middleton 45-49; V Newhey *Man* 49-62; R Heaton Reddish 62-80; Hon Can Man Cathl 74-80; rtd 80; Perm to Offic *Man* from 80. *9 Greenfield Road, Atherton, Manchester M46 9LW* Tel (01942) 873894

THORNETT, Frederick Charles. b 34. Harris Coll CQSW68. LNSM course. **d** 85 **p** 86. NSM Skegness and Winthorpe *Linc* 85-90; C New Sleaford 90-92; P-in-c Harlaxton 92-95; R Harlaxton Gp from 95. *The Rectory, Harlaxton, Grantham, Lincs NG32 1HD* Tel (01476) 575019

THORNEWILL, Canon Mark Lyon. b 25. ALCD56. **d** 56 **p** 58. C-in-c C Bradf Cathl *Bradf* 56-59; C-in-c Otley 59-62; R Lifton *Ex* 62-66; R Kelly w Bradstone 62-66; USA from 66; Hon Can Louisville Cathl from 70; rtd 90. *Yonder Cottage, 9701 Covered Bridge Prospect, Kentucky 40059, USA*

THORNEYCROFT, Mrs Pippa Hazel Jeanetta. b 44. Ex Univ BA65. Qu Coll Birm 85 WMMTC. **d** 88 **p** 94. NSM Albrighton *Lich* 88-90; NSM Beckbury, Badger, Kemberton, Ryton, Stockton etc 90-96; Dioc Adv for Women in Min from 93; P-in-c Shareshill from 96. *The Vicarage, 11 Brookhouse Lane, Featherstone, Wolverhampton WV10 7AW* Tel (01902) 727579 Fax as telephone

THORNILEY, Richard James Gordon. b 56. Portsm Poly BA78. St Jo Coll Nottm MTh95. **d** 97. C Bowbrook S *Worc* from 97. *The Parsonage, Church Lane, Tibberton, Droitwich, Worcs WR9 7NW* Tel (01905) 345868

THORNLEY, Arthur Richard. b 15. Selw Coll Cam BA38. Westcott Ho Cam 38. **d** 39 **p** 40. C St Mary-at-Lambeth *S'wark* 39-44; Chapl RNVR 44-47; Chapl RN 47-58; Chapl Malvern Coll 58-65; USA 65-66; Chapl RN 66-70; Chapl Lon Ho 70-75; PV Truro Cathl *Truro* 75-80; Chapl Truro Cathl Sch 75-80; rtd 80; Hon PV Truro Cathl *Truro* from 80; Perm to Offic *Chich* from 92. *54 Linkswood, Compton Place Road, Eastbourne, E Sussex BN21 1EF* Tel (01323) 647686

THORNLEY, David Howe. b 43. Wycliffe Hall Ox 77. **d** 79 **p** 80. C Burgess Hill St Andr *Chich* 79-83; P-in-c Amberley w N Stoke 83-84; P-in-c Parham and Wiggonholt w Greatham 83-84; V Amberley w N Stoke and Parham, Wiggonholt etc 84-92; P-in-c S w N Bersted from 92. *121 Victoria Drive, Bognor Regis, W Sussex PO21 2EH* Tel (01243) 862018

THORNLEY, Geoffrey Pearson. b 23. Pemb Coll Cam BA47 MA52. Cuddesdon Coll. **d** 50 **p** 51. C Stepney St Dunstan and All SS *Lon* 50-53; Chapl RN 53-73; Bp's Dom Chapl *Linc* 73-75; P-in-c Riseholme 73-78; P-in-c Scothern w Sudbrooke 77-78; V Dunholme 75-85; Hon PV Linc Cathl 75-85; rtd 85; Chapl Allnutt's Hosp Goring Heath 85-96. *18 Dolphin Court, Cliff Road, Meads, Eastbourne, E Sussex BN20 7XD* Tel (01323) 647115

THORNLEY, Nicholas Andrew. b 56. St Jo Coll Nottm BTh81. **d** 81 **p** 84. C Frodingham *Linc* 81-84; P-in-c Belton All SS 84-85; V 85-90; V Horncastle w Low Toynton from 90; RD Horncastle from 94. *The Vicarage, 9 Langton Drive, Horncastle, Lincs LN9 5AJ* Tel (01507) 525564 E-mail 100612.73@compuserve

THORNTON, Canon Cecil. b 26. Lon Univ BD PhD. Tyndale Hall Bris 47. **d** 50 **p** 51. C Kilmegan *D & D* 50-51; C Dromore Cathl 51-54; I Magherahamlet 54-60; I Inniskeel *D & R* 60-65; I Fahan Lower and Upper 65-88; RD Innishowen 67-88; Can Raphoe Cathl 79-88; rtd 88; Perm to Offic *Conn* from 91. *Cluain-Fois, 38 Ballywillan Road, Portrush, Co Antrim BT56 8JN* Tel (01265) 824270

THORNTON, David John Dennis. b 32. Kelham Th Coll 52. **d** 56 **p** 57. C New Eltham All SS *S'wark* 56-58; C Stockwell Green St Andr 58-62; V Tollesbury *Chelmsf* 62-74; P-in-c Salcot Virley 72-74; V Kelvedon from 74. *The Vicarage, Church Street, Kelvedon, Colchester CO5 9AL* Tel (01376) 570373

THORNTON, John. b 26. St Edm Hall Ox BA53 MA57. Westcott Ho Cam 53. **d** 55 **p** 56. C Woodhall Spa *Linc* 55-58; C Glouc St Steph *Glouc* 58-60; C Wotton St Mary 60-62; P-in-c Gt Witcombe 62-63; R 63-91; Chapl HM Pris Glouc 82-91; rtd 91; Perm to Offic *Glouc* from 91. *24 Spencer Close, Hucclecote, Gloucester GL3 3EA* Tel (01452) 619775

THORNTON, Canon Kenneth. b 27. Open Univ BA77. ALCD55. **d** 55 **p** 56. C Fazakerley Em *Liv* 55-61; V Widnes St Paul 61-69; V Childwall All SS 69-82; RD Childwall 79-82; V Ormskirk 82-92; Hon Can Liv Cathl 87-92; rtd 92; Perm to Offic *Carl* from 92. *14 Convent Close, Kenilworth, Warks CV8 2FQ* Tel (01926) 853147

THORNTON, Miss Magdalen Mary. b 69. Warw Univ BA90. Qu Coll Birm BD93. **d** 96 **p** 97. C Kirkby *Liv* from 96. *181 Gaywood Green, Kirkby, Liverpool L62 6RD*

THORNTON, Peter Stuart. b 36. St Pet Hall Ox BA59 MA67. Cuddesdon Coll 59. **d** 61 **p** 62. C Coatham *York* 61-64; C Scarborough St Martin 64-67; R Seaton Ross w Everingham and Bielby and Harswell 67-81; RD Weighton 75-85; P-in-c Thornton w Allerthorpe 80-81; R Seaton Ross Gp of Par 81-85; V York St Lawr w St Nic from 85. *St Lawrence's Vicarage, 11 Newland Park Close, York YO1 3HW* Tel (01904) 411916

THORNTON, Timothy Charles Gordon. b 35. Ch Ch Ox BA58 MA61. Linc Th Coll 60. **d** 62 **p** 63. C Kirkholt CD *Man* 62-64; Tutor Linc Th Coll 64-68; Chapl 66-68; Fiji 69-73; Chapl Brasted Place Coll Westerham 73-74; Can Missr *Guildf* 74-79; P-in-c Hascombe 74-79; V Chobham w Valley End 79-84; V Spelsbury and Chadlington *Ox* 84-87; V Chadlington and Spelsbury, Ascott under Wychwood from 87. *The Vicarage, Church Road, Chadlington, Chipping Norton, Oxon OX7 3LY* Tel (01608) 676572

THORNTON, Timothy Martin (Tim). b 57. Southn Univ BA78. St Steph Ho Ox 78. **d** 80 **p** 81. C Todmorden *Wakef* 80-82; P-in-c Walsden 82-85; Lect Univ of Wales (Cardiff) 85-87; Chapl 85-86; Sen Chapl 86-87; Bp's Chapl *Wakef* 87-91; Dir of Ords 88-91; Bp's Chapl *Lon* 91-94; Dep P in O from 91; Prin N Thames Minl Tr Course from 94; Lic to Offic *Lon* from 94. *4 Midhurst Avenue, London N10 3EN, or NTMTC, Chase Side, London N14 4PS* Tel 0181-444 3552 or 364 9442 Fax 0181-364 8889

THOROGOOD, John Martin. b 45. Birm Univ BA68 PGCE69. Ox NSM Course 82. **d** 85 **p** 86. NSM Sunningdale *Ox* 85-90; Chapl St Geo Sch Ascot 88-90; TV Camelot Par *B & W* from 90; RD Cary from 96; RD Bruton from 96. *The Rectory, Holton, Wincanton, Somerset BA9 8AN* Tel (01963) 32163

THOROLD, Henry Croyland. b 21. Ch Ch Ox 40 Lambeth MLitt94. Cuddesdon Coll 42. **d** 44 **p** 45. Chapl St Paul's Cathl Dundee *Bre* 44-46; Bp's Dom Chapl 44-46; Chapl RNVR 46-48; Chapl RN 48-49; Chapl Lancing Coll 49-68; Chapl Summer Fields Sch Ox 68-75; Lic to Offic *Ox* 69-81; rtd 81. *Marston Hall, Grantham, Lincs NG32 2HY* Tel (01400) 50225

THOROLD, John Robert Hayford. b 16. K Coll Cam BA43 MA45. Cuddesdon Coll 42. **d** 42 **p** 43. C Cheltenham St Mary *Glouc* 42-44; C Limehouse St Anne *Lon* 44-45; Tutor Ripon Hall Ox 47-52; V Mitcham SS Pet and Paul *S'wark* 52-86; OGS from 53; rtd 87; Perm to Offic *Blackb* 87-96. *St Deiniol's Library, Hawarden, Deeside CH5 3DF* Tel (01244) 531256

THOROLD, John Stephen. b 35. Bps' Coll Cheshunt 61. **d** 63 **p** 64. C Cleethorpes *Linc* 63-70; V Cherry Willingham w Greetwell 70-77; P-in-c Firsby w Gt Steeping 77-79; R 79-86; R Aswardby w Sausthorpe 77-86; R Halton Holgate 77-86; R Langton w Sutterby 77-86; V Spilsby w Hundleby 77-86; R Lt Steeping 79-86; R Raithby 79-86; V New Sleaford from 86; RD Lafford 87-96. *The Vicarage, Sleaford, Lincs NG34 7SH* Tel (01529) 302177

THOROLD, Trevor Neil. b 63. Hull Univ BA87. Ripon Coll Cuddesdon 87. **d** 89 **p** 90. C W Bromwich St Andr w Ch Ch *Lich* 89-93; C Oswestry H Trin 93-94; C Oswestry from 94. *Holy Trinity Vicarage, 29 Balmoral Crescent, Oswestry, Shropshire SY11 2XQ* Tel (01691) 652540

THORP, Adrian. b 55. Clare Coll Cam BA77 MA80 Lon Univ BD80. Trin Coll Bris 77. **d** 80 **p** 81. C Kendal St Thos *Carl* 80-83; C Handforth *Ches* 83-86; V Siddal *Wakef* 86-91; V Bishopwearmouth St Gabr *Dur* from 91. *The Vicarage, 1 St Gabriel's Avenue, Sunderland SR4 7TF* Tel 0191-567 5200

THORP, Catherine. b 57. St Luke's Coll Ex BEd79. Oak Hill Th Coll 93. **d** 96. NSM Watford Ch Ch *St Alb* from 96. *111 Barton Way, Croxley Green, Rickmansworth, Herts WD3 3PB* Tel (01923) 442713

THORP, Miss Eileen Margaret. b 31. **d** 95 **p** 96. NSM Daventry, Ashby St Ledgers, Braunston etc *Pet* from 95. *Waterside, Dark Lane, Braunston, Daventry, Northants NN11 7HJ* Tel (01788) 890321

THORP, Mrs Helen Mary. b 54. Bris Univ BA75 MA77 DipHE. Trin Coll Bris 78. **d** 87 **p** 94. NSM Siddal *Wakef* 87-91; NSM Bishopwearmouth St Gabr *Dur* from 91; Voc Adv from 93. *The Vicarage, 1 St Gabriel's Avenue, Sunderland SR4 7TF* Tel 0191-567 5200

THORP, Mrs Maureen Sandra. b 47. LNSM course 92. **d** 95 **p** 96. NSM Heywood St Marg *Man* from 95. *4 Lyn Grove, Heywood, Lancs OL10 4SS* Tel (01706) 366714

THORP, Norman Arthur. b 29. DMA63. Tyndale Hall Bris 63. **d** 65 **p** 66. C Southsea St Jude *Portsm* 65-68; C Braintree *Chelmsf* 68-73; P-in-c Tolleshunt D'Arcy w Tolleshunt Major 73-75; V 75-83; R N Buckingham *Ox* 83-95; RD Buckingham 90-95; rtd 95. *20 Swimbridge Lane, Furzton, Milton Keynes MK4 1JT*

THORP, Roderick Cheyne. b 44. Ch Ch Ox BA65 MA69. Ridley Hall Cam 66. **d** 69 **p** 70. C Reading Greyfriars *Ox* 69-73; C Kingston upon Hull St Martin *York* 73-76; C Heworth 76-79; C-in-c N Bletchley CD *Ox* 79-86; TV Washfield, Stoodleigh, Withleigh etc *Ex* 86-96; RD Tiverton 91-96; P-in-c Dolton from 96; P-in-c Iddesleigh w Dowland from 96; P-in-c Monkokehampton from 96. *The Rectory, Rectory Road, Dolton, Winkleigh, Devon EX19 8QL* Tel (01805) 804264

THORP, Stephen Linton. b 62. Lon Bible Coll CertRS88 Trin Coll Bris BA92. **d** 92 **p** 93. C Knutsford St Jo and Toft *Ches* 92-96; TV Newton Tracey, Horwood, Alverdiscott etc *Ex* from 96. *The Rectory, Beaford, Winkleigh, Devon EX19 8NN* Tel (01805) 603213

THORP, Thomas Malcolm (Tom). b 49. AKC. St Aug Coll Cant 71. **d** 72 **p** 73. C Derby St Bart *Derby* 72-76; C Newport Pagnell *Ox* 76-79; C Newport Pagnell w Lathbury 79; Dioc Youth and Community Officer 79-82; TV Schorne 82-92; TR from 92. *The Vicarage, White Horse Lane, Whitchurch, Aylesbury, Bucks HP22 4JZ* Tel (01296) 641768

THORP, Timothy. b 65. St Steph Ho Ox BTh93. **d** 96 **p** 97. C Jarrow *Dur* from 96. *St Andrew's House, Borough Road, Jarrow, Tyne & Wear NE32 5BL* Tel 0191-489 3279

THORPE, Christopher David Charles. b 60. Cov Poly BA83. Ripon Coll Cuddesdon 85. **d** 88 **p** 89. C Norton *St Alb* 88-92; TV Blakenall Heath *Lich* from 92. *St Aidan's Vicarage, 78A Chestnut Road, Leamore, Walsall WS3 1AP* Tel (01922) 407768

THORPE, Donald Henry. b 34. St Aid Birkenhead 57. **d** 60 **p** 61. C Mexborough *Sheff* 60-64; C Doncaster St Leon and St Jude 64-67; V Doncaster Intake 67-74; V Millhouses H Trin 74-85; Prec Leic Cathl *Leic* 85-89; TR Melton Gt Framland 89-93; rtd 93; Perm to Offic *Sheff* from 93. *18 All Hallows Drive, Tickhill, Doncaster, S Yorkshire DN11 9PP* Tel (01302) 743129

THORPE, Canon Harry Fletcher Cyprian. b 12. Kelham Th Coll 30. **d** 36 **p** 37. S Africa 36-73; R Ecton *Pet* 73-78; rtd 78; Perm to Offic *Portsm* 81-96. *11 Gracey Court, Woodland Road, Broadclyst, Exeter EX5 3LP* Tel (01392) 460988

THORPE, John Wellburn. b 31. Lich Th Coll 55. **d** 58 **p** 59. C Heref St Martin *Heref* 58-61; C Dudley St Fran *Worc* 61-65; R Gt w Lt Witley 65-70; C Tuffley *Glouc* 70-72; P-in-c Blaisdon w Flaxley 73-76; P-in-c Westbury-on-Severn w Flaxley and Blaisdon 76-77; V 77-84; P-in-c Walton on Trent w Croxall etc *Derby* 84-94; rtd 94. *3 Standing Butts Close, Walton-on-Trent, Swadlincote, Derbyshire DE12 8NJ*

THORPE, Kerry Michael. b 51. Lon Univ BD78. Oak Hill Th Coll DipTh76. **d** 78 **p** 79. C Upton (Overchurch) *Ches* 78-81; C Chester le Street *Dur* 81-84; V Fatfield 84-93; V Margate H Trin *Cant* from 93. *The Vicarage, 5 Offley Close, Northdown Park Road, Margate, Kent CT9 3UT* Tel (01843) 230318 or 230317

THORPE, Martin Xavier. b 66. Collingwood Coll Dur BSc87 GRSC87. Trin Coll Bris BA94. **d** 94 **p** 95. C Ravenhead *Liv* from 94. *8 Dawn Close, Thatto Heath, St Helens, Merseyside WA9 5JB* Tel (01744) 815128

THORPE, Michael William. b 42. Lich Th Coll 67. **d** 70 **p** 71. C Walthamstow St Mich *Chelmsf* 70-71; C Plaistow St Andr 71; P-in-c Plaistow St Mary 72-74; TV Gt Grimsby St Mary and St Jas *Linc* 74-78; Chapl Grimsby Distr Hosps 78-83; Chapl Roxbourne, Northwick Park and Harrow Hosps 83-87; Chapl St Geo Linc and Linc Co Hosps 87-92; Chapl Ipswich Hosp from 92. *339 Colchester Road, Ipswich IP4 4SE, or Ipswich Hospital, Heath Road, Ipswich IP4 5PD* Tel (01473) 713095 or 704100

THORPE, Richard Charles Ric. b 65. Birm Univ BSc87. Wycliffe Hall Ox 93. **d** 96 **p** 97. C Brompton H Trin w Onslow Square

St Paul *Lon* from 96. *Ground Floor Flat, St Paul's Church, Onslow Square, London SW7 3NX* Tel 0171-581 8255

THORPE, Trevor Cecil. b 21. Em Coll Cam BA47 MA52. Ridley Hall Cam 48. **d** 50 **p** 51. C Farnborough *Guildf* 50-53; C W Ham All SS *Chelmsf* 53-57; V N Weald Bassett from 57. *The Vicarage, Vicarage Lane, North Weald, Epping, Essex CM16 6AL* Tel (01992) 522246

THRALL, Canon Margaret Eleanor. b 28. Girton Coll Cam BA50 MA54 PhD60. **d** 82 **p** 97. Asst Chapl Univ of Wales (Ban) *Ban* 82-88; Lect Th Univ of Wales (Ban) from 83; Hon Can Ban Cathl *Ban* from 94. *25 Y Rhos, Bangor LL57 2LT* Tel (01248) 364957

THREADGILL, Alan Roy. b 31. St Alb Minl Tr Scheme 77. **d** 80 **p** 81. NSM Bedford St Andr *St Alb* 80-83; Chapl RAD 83-86; C Melton Gt Framland *Leic* 86-89; R Wymondham w Edmondthorpe, Buckminster etc 89-95; rtd 95; Perm to Offic *Leic* from 95. *The Corner House, 1 Stathern Lane, Harby, Melton Mowbray, Leics LE14 4DA*

THROSSELL, John Julian. b 30. Nottm Univ BSc53 Syracuse Univ PhD56. Oak Hill Th Coll 72. **d** 75 **p** 76. NSM Wheathampstead *St Alb* 75-82; V Codicote 82-88; rtd 91. *20 Dakings Drift, Halesworth, Suffolk IP19 8TQ* Tel (01986) 874602

THROWER, Clive Alan. b 41. CEng90 Sheff Univ BSc62. EMMTC 76. **d** 79 **p** 80. C Derby Cathl *Derby* 79-86; C Spondon 86-91; Soc Resp Officer 86-91; Faith in the City Link Officer 88-91; Dioc Rural Officer 91; P-in-c Ashford w Sheldon 91; V Ashford w Sheldon and Gt Longstone 92-93; V Ashford w Sheldon and Longstone from 93; Dioc Rural and Tourism Officer from 96. *The Vicarage, Ashford in the Water, Bakewell, Derbyshire DE45 1QN* Tel (01629) 812298 Fax 815402

THROWER, Philip Edward. b 41. Kelham Th Coll 61. **d** 66 **p** 67. C Hayes St Mary *Lon* 66-69; C Yeovil *B & W* 69-71; C Shirley St Jo *Cant* 71-77; P-in-c S Norwood St Mark 77-81; V 81-84; V S Norwood St Mark *S'wark* from 85. *St Mark's Vicarage, 101 Albert Road, London SE25 4JE* Tel 0181-656 9462

THUBRON, Thomas William. b 33. Edin Th Coll 62. **d** 65 **p** 66. C Gateshead St Mary *Dur* 65-66; C Shildon 66-67; E Pakistan 68-71; Bangladesh 71-80; V Wheatley Hill *Dur* 80-87; V Dur St Giles from 87. *St Giles's Vicarage, Durham DH1 1QH* Tel 0191-386 4241

THURBURN-HUELIN, David Richard. b 47. St Chad's Coll Dur BA69. Westcott Ho Cam 69. **d** 71 **p** 72. C Poplar *Lon* 71-76; Chapl Liddon Ho Lon 76-80; R Harrold and Carlton w Chellington *St Alb* 81-88; V Goldington 88-95; Dir LNSM *Truro* from 95. *The Vicarage, Mount Hawke, Truro, Cornwall TR4 8DE* Tel (01209) 890926

THURMER, Canon John Alfred. b 25. Or Coll Ox BA50 MA55 Ex Univ Hon DD91. Linc Th Coll 50. **d** 52 **p** 53. C Lt Ilford St Barn *Chelmsf* 52-55; Chapl and Lect Sarum Th Coll 55-64; Chapl Ex Univ *Ex* 64-73; Lect 64-85; Can Res and Chan Ex Cathl 73-91; rtd 91; Perm to Offic *Ex* from 91. *38 Velwell Road, Exeter EX4 4LD* Tel (01392) 272277

THURSFIELD, John Anthony. b 21. Magd Coll Ox BA47 MA51. Cuddesdon Coll 47. **d** 49 **p** 50. V Basing *Win* 60-72; Chapl Bonn w Cologne *Eur* 72-75; R E Clandon *Guildf* 75-79; R W Clandon 75-79; V Reydon *St E* 79-83; Perm to Offic *Heref* 84-93; rtd 86; Perm to Offic *Heref* from 96. *Little Homend, The Homend, Ledbury, Herefordshire HR8 1AR* Tel (01531) 632935

THURSTON, Colin Benedict. b 47. Chich Th Coll 88. **d** 90 **p** 91. C Up Hatherley *Glouc* 90-96; TV Redruth w Lanner and Treleigh *Truro* from 96. *37 Clinton Road, Redruth, Cornwall TR15 2LW* Tel (01209) 212627

THURSTON, Ian Charles. b 54. SS Hild & Bede Coll Dur CertEd78. S Dios Minl Tr Scheme 87. **d** 89 **p** 90. C St Chris Cathl Bahrain 89-91; C All Hallows by the Tower etc *Lon* 91-97; V Tottenham H Trin from 97. *Holy Trinity Vicarage, Philip Lane, London N15 4HZ* Tel 0181-801 3021 Fax 488 3333

TIBBO, George Kenneth. b 29. Reading Univ BA50 MA54. Coll of Resurr Mirfield 55. **d** 57 **p** 58. C W Hartlepool St Aid *Dur* 57-61; V Darlington St Mark 61-74; V Darlington St Mark w St Paul 74-75; R Crook 75-80; V Stanley 76-80; V Oldham St Chad Limeside *Man* 80-87; V Hipswell *Ripon* 87-95; OCF 90-95; rtd 95; P-in-c Nidd *Ripon* from 95. *The Vicarage, Nidd, Harrogate, N Yorkshire HG3 3BL* Tel (01423) 770060

TIBBOTT, Joseph Edwards. b 14. K Coll Lon. **d** 55 **p** 56. C Caterham Valley *S'wark* 55-59; V Stockwell St Mich 59-71; V Cwmddauddwr w St Harmon's and Llanwrthwl *S & B* 71-75; V Llangiwg 76-77; R Llangammarch w Garth, Llanlleonfel etc 77-80; rtd 80. *Pellingbridge Farm House, Scaynes Hill, Haywards Heath, W Sussex RH17 7NG* Tel (01444) 831381

TIBBS, Canon Howard Abraham Llewellyn Thomas. b 13. Univ of Wales BA39. Coll of Resurr Mirfield 39. **d** 41 **p** 42. C Middlesbrough St Oswald *York* 41-44; Chapl RAFVR 44-47; R Dunnington *York* 47-52; V Balsall Heath St Barn *Birm* 52-66; V Northampton H Sepulchre w St Andr *Pet* 66-76; RD Northn 70-79; Can Pet Cathl 75-85; V Northampton H Sepulchre w St Andr and St Lawr 76-85; rtd 85; Perm to Offic *Pet* from 85. *30 Fairway, Northampton NN2 7JZ* Tel (01604) 716863

TIBBS, Canon John Andrew. b 29. AKC53. **d** 54 **p** 55. C Eastbourne St Mary *Chich* 54-57; S Africa 57-62; C Bourne *Guildf* 62-64; Swaziland 64-68; V Sompting *Chich* 69-73; R Ifield 73-78; TR 78-83; V Elstow *St Alb* 83-89; rtd 90; Chapl Bedf Gen Hosp 90-95; Hon Can St Alb *St Alb* 91-95. *19 Adelaide Square, Bedford MK40 2RN* Tel (01234) 359579

TICE, Richard Ian (Rico). b 66. Bris Univ BA88. Wycliffe Hall Ox BTh94. **d** 94 **p** 95. C Langham Place All So *Lon* from 94. *20 Holcroft Court, Clipstone Street, London W1P 7DL* Tel 0171-580 1033

TICEHURST, David. b 29. K Coll Lon 50. **d** 55 **p** 56. C Gillingham St Mary *Roch* 55-57; Chapl Brunswick Sch 57-60; C Cove St Jo *Guildf* 60-63; C Chelsea Ch Ch *Lon* 63-64; Sen Master St Mich Sch Woking 65-67; Hd Master Hawley Place Camberley 67-76; P-in-c Bury and Houghton *Chich* 76-81; V 81-89; P-in-c Sutton w Bignor 78; P-in-c Barlavington 78; rtd 89; Perm to Offic *Chich* from 89. *43 Sheepdown Drive, Petworth, W Sussex GU28 0BX* Tel (01798) 344273

TICKLE, Robert Peter. b 51. St Chad's Coll Dur BA74. St Steph Ho Ox 74. **d** 76 **p** 77. *5 Bramley Court, Orchard Lane, Harrold, Bedford MK43 7BG* Tel (01234) 721417

TICKNER, Canon Colin de Fraine. b 37. Chich Th Coll. **d** 66 **p** 67. C Huddersfield St Pet and St Paul *Wakef* 66-68; C Dorking w Ranmore *Guildf* 68-74; V Shottermill 74-91; RD Godalming 89-91; R Ockley, Okewood and Forest Green from 91; Hon Can Guildf Cathl from 96. *The Rectory, Stane Street, Ockley, Dorking, Surrey RH5 5SY* Tel (01306) 711550

TICKNER, David Arthur. b 44. MBE89. AKC67. **d** 69 **p** 70. C Thornhill Lees *Wakef* 69-71; C Billingham St Aid *Dur* 71-74; TV 74-78; CF from 78. *MOD Chaplains (Army), Trenchard Lines, Upavon, Pewsey, Wilts SN9 6BE* Tel (01980) 615804 Fax 615800

TICKNER, Geoffrey John. b 55. BD. St Mich Coll Llan. **d** 82 **p** 83. C Bourne *Guildf* 82-85; C Grayswood 85-90; V New Haw from 90. *The Vicarage, 149 Woodham Lane, New Haw, Addlestone, Surrey KT15 3NJ* Tel (01932) 343187

TIDMARSH, Canon Peter Edwin. b 29. Keble Coll Ox BA52 MA56 DipEd. St Steph Ho Ox 52. **d** 54 **p** 55. C Stepney St Dunstan and All SS *Lon* 54-58; C Streatham St Pet *S'wark* 58-62; Chapl Shiplake Coll Henley 62-64; Hd Master All SS Choir Sch 64-68; C St Marylebone All SS *Lon* 64-68; V Cubert *Truro* from 68; Dir of Educn 69-85; Hon Can Truro Cathl from 73. *The Vicarage, St Cubert, Newquay, Cornwall TR8 5HA* Tel (01637) 830301

TIDMARSH, Philip Reginald Wilton. b 14. G&C Coll Cam BA36 MA40. Ridley Hall Cam 46. **d** 48 **p** 49. V Odiham w S Warnborough *Win* 66-76; P-in-c Abbotts Ann 76-79; Perm to Offic *Heref* from 79; rtd 86. *The Gravel Pit Bungalow, Broadheath, Presteigne LD8 2HG* Tel (01544) 267275

TIDY, The Very Revd John Hylton. b 48. AKC72 St Aug Coll Cant 72. **d** 73 **p** 74. C Newton Aycliffe *Dur* 73-78; V Auckland St Pet 78-84; V Burley in Wharfedale *Bradf* 84-92; Dean Jerusalem 92-97; V Surbiton St Andr and St Mark *S'wark* from 97. *St Mark's Vicarage, 1 Church Hill Road, Surbiton, Surrey KT6 4UG* Tel 0181-399 6053 Fax 390 4928

TIERNAN, Paul Wilson. b 54. Man Univ BA76. Coll of Resurr Mirfield 77. **d** 79 **p** 80. C Lewisham St Mary *S'wark* 79-83; V Sydenham St Phil from 83. *St Philip's Vicarage, 122 Wells Park Road, London SE26 6AS* Tel 0181-699 4930

TIGWELL, Brian Arthur. b 36. S'wark Ord Course 74. **d** 77 **p** 78. C Purley St Mark Woodcote *S'wark* 77-80; TV Upper Kennet *Sarum* 80-85; V Devizes St Pet from 85; Wilts Adnry Ecum Officer from 88; RD Devizes from 92. *The Vicarage, Bath Road, Devizes, Wilts SN10 2AP* Tel (01380) 722621

TILDESLEY, Edward William David. b 56. St Hild Coll Dur BEd79. St Alb and Ox Min Course 93. **d** 96 **p** 97. Chapl Shiplake Coll Henley from 96; NSM Emmer Green *Ox* from 96. *53 Tredegar Road, Caversham, Reading RG4 8PF* Tel (0118) 947 3101

TILL, Barry Dorn. b 23. Jes Coll Cam BA49 MA49. Westcott Ho Cam 48. **d** 50 **p** 51. C Bury St Mary *Man* 50-53; Fell Jes Coll Cam 53-60; Chapl 53-56; Dean 56-60; Lic to Offic *Ely* 53-60; Dean Hong Kong 60-64; Attached Ch Assembly 64-65; Prin Morley Coll Lon 66-87; Dir Baring Foundn 87-92; rtd 92. *44 Canonbury Square, London N1 2AW* Tel 0171-359 0708

TILL, The Very Revd Michael Stanley. b 35. Linc Coll Ox BA60 MA67. Westcott Ho Cam. **d** 64 **p** 65. C St Jo Wood *Lon* 64-67; Chapl K Coll Cam 67-70; Dean 70-80; AD Hammersmith *Lon* 81-86; V Fulham All SS 81-86; Adn Cant and Can Res Cant Cathl *Cant* 86-96; Dean Win from 96. *The Deanery, The Close, Winchester, Hants SO23 9LS* Tel (01962) 853738

TILLER, Charles Edgar Gregory. b 61. St Mich Coll Llan BD. **d** 89 **p** 90. C Ex St Thos and Em *Ex* 89-93; C Crediton and Shobrooke 93-95. *Address temp unknown*

TILLER, Edgar Henry. b 22. ACP71 Open Univ BA78. Wells Th Coll 57. **d** 59 **p** 60. C Weston-super-Mare St Jo *B & W* 59-62; V Stoke Lane 62-67; V Leigh upon Mendip 62-67; Perm to Offic *Ex* from 67; rtd 91. *3 Byron Close, Pilton, Barnstaple, Devon EX31 1QH* Tel (01271) 72483

TILLER, Canon John. b 38. Ch Ch Ox BA60 MA64 Bris Univ MLitt72. Tyndale Hall Bris 60. **d** 62 **p** 63. C Bedford St Cuth *St Alb* 62-65; C Widcombe *B & W* 65-67; Tutor Tyndale Hall Bris 67-71; Chapl 67-71; Lect Trin Coll Bris 71-73; P-in-c Bedford Ch Ch *St Alb* 73-78; Chief Sec ACCM 78-84; Hon Can St Alb

St Alb 79-84; Can Res and Chan Heref Cathl *Heref* from 84; Dioc Dir of Tr from 91. *The Canon's House, 3 St John Street, Hereford HR1 2NB* Tel (01432) 265659

TILLETT, Leslie Selwyn. b 54. Peterho Cam BA75 MA79 Leeds Univ BA80. Coll of Resurr Mirfield 78. **d** 81 **p** 82. C W Dulwich All SS and Em *S'wark* 81-85; R Purleigh, Cold Norton and Stow Maries *Chelmsf* 85-93; R Beddington *S'wark* from 93. *The Rectory, 18 Bloxworth Close, Wallington, Surrey SM6 7NL* Tel 0181-647 1973

TILLEY, David Robert. b 38. Kelham Th Coll 58. **d** 63 **p** 64. C Bournemouth St Fran *Win* 63-67; C Moulsecoomb *Chich* 67-70; C Ifield 70-75; TV Warwick *Cov* 76-85; P-in-c Alderminster 85-89; P-in-c Halford 85-89; Dioc Min Tr Adv from 85; Continuing Minl Educn Adv from 90; P-in-c Alderminster and Halford 90-96; C Willenhall from 96. *The Rectory, Church Road, Baginton, Coventry CV8 3AR* Tel (01203) 302508 Fax as telephone

TILLEY, Derise Ralph. b 21. Sarum Th Coll 55. **d** 57 **p** 58. C Moordown *Win* 57-61; C Penzance St Mary *Truro* 61-64; V Millbrook 64-80; P-in-c Antony w St Jo 76-80; R St John w Millbrook 80-90; rtd 90; Perm to Offic *Truro* from 90. *25 York Road, Torpoint, Cornwall PL11 2LG* Tel (01752) 815450

TILLEY, James Stephen (Steve). b 55. St Jo Coll Nottm BTh84. **d** 84 **p** 85. C Nottingham St Jude *S'well* 84-88; C Chester le Street *Dur* 88-92; Tr and Ed CYFA (CPAS) from 92; Perm to Offic *Cov* from 93. *CPAS, Athena Drive, Tachbrook Drive, Warwick CV34 6NG* Tel (01926) 334242 Fax 337613

TILLEY, Peter Robert. b 41. Bris Univ BA62. Sarum & Wells Th Coll 77. **d** 79 **p** 80. C Wandsworth St Paul *S'wark* 79-82; V Mitcham St Mark 82-91; RD Merton 89-91; R Walton St Mary *Liv* 91-92; TR Walton-on-the-Hill from 92. *The Rectory, Walton Village, Liverpool L4 6TJ* Tel 0151-525 3130

TILLIER, Mrs Jane Yvonne. b 59. New Hall Cam BA81 PhD85. Ripon Coll Cuddesdon BA90. **d** 91 **p** 94. Par Dn Sheff St Mark Broomhill *Sheff* 91-94; C 94-95; Chapl Glouc Cathl *Glouc* 95-97; Perm to Offic *Lich* 97; C Fradswell, Gayton, Milwich and Weston from 97. *52 St Leonard's Drive, Stafford ST17 4LT* Tel (01785) 245640

TILLMAN, Miss Mary Elizabeth. b 43. S Dios Minl Tr Scheme 86. **d** 89 **p** 95. NSM Bridgemary *Portsm* 89-93; NSM Portsea All SS from 93; Adv in Min to People w Disabilities from 93. *391 Fareham Road, Gosport, Hants PO13 0AD* Tel (01329) 232589

TILLOTSON, Simon Christopher. b 67. Lon Univ BA90 Trin Coll Cam BA93. Ridley Hall Cam 91. **d** 94 **p** 95. C Paddock Wood *Roch* from 94. *3 Ashcroft Road, Paddock Wood, Tonbridge, Kent TN12 6LG* Tel (01892) 833194

TILLYER, Desmond Benjamin. b 40. Ch Coll Cam BA63 MA67. Coll of Resurr Mirfield 64. **d** 66 **p** 67. C Hanworth All SS *Lon* 66-70; Chapl Liddon Ho Lon 70-74; V Pimlico St Pet w Westmr Ch Ch *Lon* from 74; AD Westmr St Marg 85-92. *1 St Peter's House, 119 Eaton Square, London SW1W 9AL* Tel 0171-235 4242

TILSON, Canon Alan Ernest. b 46. TCD. **d** 70 **p** 71. C Londonderry Ch Ch *D & R* 70-73; I Inver, Mountcharles and Killaghtee 73-79; I Leckpatrick w Dunnalong 79-89; Bermuda from 89; Hon Can Bermuda Cathl from 96. *Holy Trinity Rectory, PO Box CR 186, Hamilton Parish CR BX, Bermuda* Tel Bermuda (1-441) 293-1710 Fax 293-4363

TILSTON, Derek Reginald. b 27. NW Ord Course. **d** 73 **p** 74. NSM Bury St Mark *Man* 73-77; NSM Holcombe 77-82; NSM Bury St Jo 82-83; NSM Bury St Jo w St Mark 83-84; C Bramley *Ripon* 85-87; TV 87-90; R Tendring and Lt Bentley w Beaumont cum Moze *Chelmsf* 90-92; rtd 93. *Cobbler's Croft, 19 The Street, Wissett, Halesworth, Suffolk IP19 0JE* Tel (01986) 874693

TILTMAN, Alan Michael. b 48. Selw Coll Cam BA70 MA74. Cuddesdon Coll 71. **d** 73 **p** 74. C Chesterton Gd Shep *Ely* 73-77; C Preston St Jo *Blackb* 77-79; Chapl Lancs (Preston) Poly 77-79; TV Man Whitworth *Man* 79-86; Chapl Man Univ (UMIST) 79-86; V Urmston from 86. *St Clement's Vicarage, Manor Avenue, Urmston, Manchester M31 1HH* Tel 0161-748 3972 Fax as telephone

TIMBERLAKE, Neil Christopher. b 26. Kelham Th Coll 47. **d** 51 **p** 52. C Ardwick St Benedict *Man* 51-54; C Moss Side Ch Ch 54-55; C Stockport St Alb Hall Street *Ches* 55-57; C Cov St Jo *Cov* 57-60; V Heath *Derby* 60-68; Australia 68-70; C Leyland St Ambrose *Blackb* 70-72; C Bilborough w Strelley *S'well* 72-74; V Langold 74-86; rtd 86. *7 Thirlmere Avenue, Colne, Lancs BB8 7DD* Tel (01282) 863879

TIMBRELL, Keith Stewart. b 48. Edin Th Coll 72. **d** 74 **p** 75. C Chorley St Pet *Blackb* 74-77; C Altham w Clayton le Moors 77-79; Chapl Whittingham Hosp Preston 79-95; Chapl Dorset Healthcare NHS Trust from 95. *St Ann's Hospital, 69 Haven Road, Poole, Dorset BH13 7LN* Tel (01202) 708881

TIMBRELL, Maxwell Keith. b 28. St Jo Coll Morpeth ThL51. **d** 51 **p** 52. Australia 51-58 and 64-82; C Hanworth All SS *Lon* 59-63; V Ingleby Greenhow w Bilsdale Priory *York* 83-85; P-in-c Kildale 83-85; V Ingleby Greenhow w Bilsdale Priory, Kildale etc 85-96; rtd 96; Perm to Offic *York* from 96. *Jasmine House, Nunnington, York YO65 5US* Tel (01439) 748319

TIMINS, John Francis Holmer. b 03. Clare Coll Cam MA29. Ely Th Coll 33. **d** 34 **p** 35. C Thrumpton *S'well* 34-36; R Gt and Lt Glemham *St E* 36-48; CF (EC) 40-45; R Long Newnton *Bris* 48-52; R Martlesham *St E* 52-59; R Horringer cum Ickworth 59-65; Lic to Offic 67-75; rtd 68. *Four Seasons Residential Home, Back Lane, Mickleton, Chipping Campden, Glos GL55 6SJ*

TIMMINS, Susan Katherine. b 64. Leic Univ BScEng85 MICE91. St Jo Coll Nottm MTh94. **d** 96 **p** 97. C Iver *Ox* from 96. *St Leonard's House, St Leonard's Walk, Iver, Bucks SL0 9DD* Tel (01753) 653532

TIMMS, The Ven George Boorne. b 10. St Edm Hall Ox BA33 MA45. Coll of Resurr Mirfield 33. **d** 35 **p** 36. C Cov St Mary *Cov* 35-38; C Earley St Bart *Ox* 38-49; PV and Sacr S'wark Cathl *S'wark* 49-52; Succ S'wark Cathl 51-52; V Primrose Hill St Mary *Lon* 52-57; V Primrose Hill St Mary w Avenue Road St Paul 57-65; RD Hampstead 59-65; Preb St Paul's Cathl 64-71; Dir of Ords 64-81; V St Andr Holborn 65-81; Adn Hackney 71-81; Perm to Offic *Cant* from 78; rtd 81. *Cleve Lodge, Minster Road, Minster-in-Thanet, Ramsgate, Kent CT12 4BA* Tel (01843) 821777

TIMPERLEY, Patrick. b 65. St D Coll Lamp BA86. St Jo Coll Dur 86. **d** 88 **p** 89. C Pembroke St Mary and St Mich *St D* 88-91; C Higher Bebington *Ches* 91-93. *23 All Saints Road, Thurcaston, Leicester LE7 7JD* Tel 0116-236 3252

TINGAY, Kevin Gilbert Xavier. b 43. Sussex Univ BA79. Chich Th Coll 79. **d** 80 **p** 81. C W Tarring *Chich* 80-83; TV Worth 83-90; R Bradford w Oake, Hillfarrance and Heathfield *B & W* from 90; RD Tone from 96. *The Rectory, Bradford on Tone, Taunton, Somerset TA4 1HG* Tel (01823) 461423

TINGLE, Michael Barton. b 31. Bps' Coll Cheshunt 65. **d** 67 **p** 68. C Totteridge *St Alb* 67-70; C Hitchin St Mary 70-73; V Gt Gaddesden 73-78; V Belmont *Lon* 78-86; V Burford w Fulbrook and Taynton *Ox* 86-94; V Burford w Fulbrook, Taynton, Asthall etc from 94. *The Vicarage, Burford, Oxon OX18 4SE* Tel (01993) 822275

TINKER, Preb Eric Franklin. b 20. OBE89. Ex Coll Ox BA42 MA46 Lon Univ Hon DD89. Linc Th Coll 42. **d** 44 **p** 45. C Gt Berkhamsted *St Alb* 44-46; C Rugby St Andr *Cov* 46-48; CF 48-49; Lon Sec SCM 49-51; Chapl Lon Univ *Lon* 51-55; V Handsworth St Jas *Birm* 55-65; V Enfield St Andr *Lon* 65-69; Preb St Paul's Cathl 69-90; Sen Chapl Lon Univs and Polys 69-90; Dir of Educn (Dios Lon and S'wark) 72-80; Gen Sec Lon Dioc Bd of Educn 80-82; rtd 90; Hon C St Giles Cripplegate w St Bart Moor Lane etc *Lon* from 95. *35 Theberton Street, London N1 0QY* Tel 0171-359 4750

TINKER, Melvin. b 55. Hull Univ BSc Ox Univ MA. Wycliffe Hall Ox 80. **d** 83 **p** 84. C Wetherby *Ripon* 83-85; Chapl Keele Univ *Lich* 85-90; V Cheadle All Hallows *Ches* 90-94; V Hull Newland St Jo *York* from 94. *St John's Vicarage, Clough Road, Hull HU6 7PA* Tel (01482) 43658

TINKER, Michael Jonathan Russell. b 50. York Univ BA72. Qu Coll Birm DipTh74. **d** 75 **p** 76. C Castle Vale *Birm* 75-78; Bp's Dom Chapl 78-80; R Stretford All SS *Man* 80-88; V Stalybridge 88-97; AD Ashton-under-Lyne 94-97; P-in-c Saddleworth from 97. *The Vicarage, Station Road, Uppermill, Oldham OL3 6HQ* Tel (01457) 872412

TINKLER, Ian Henry. b 32. Selw Coll Cam BA57 MA61. Westcott Ho Cam. **d** 60 **p** 61. C Gosforth All SS *Newc* 60-65; Asst Chapl Brussels *Eur* 65-68; R S Ferriby *Linc* 68-85; V Horkstow 68-85; R Saxby All Saints 72-85; V Humberston from 85. *The Vicarage, 34 Tetney Road, Humberstone, Grimsby, S Humberside DN36 4JF* Tel (01472) 813158

TINSLEY, Bernard Murray. b 26. Nottm Univ BA51 Birm Univ DPS. Westcott Ho Cam 51. **d** 53 **p** 54. C Rotherham *Sheff* 53-56; C Goole 56-58; V Thorpe Hesley 58-61; R Alverdiscott w Huntshaw *Ex* 61-78; R Newton Tracey 61-78; R Beaford and Roborough 67-78; V St Giles in the Wood 67-78; V Yarnscombe 67-78; R Newton Tracey, Alverdiscott, Huntshaw etc 78-88; RD Torrington 81-86; rtd 88; Perm to Offic *Ex* from 88. *The Grange, Grange Road, Bideford, Devon EX39 4AS* Tel (01237) 471414

TINSLEY, Derek. b 31. ALCM65. NW Ord Course 73. **d** 76 **p** 77. C Gt Crosby St Faith *Liv* 76-80; V Wigan St Anne 80-85; V Colton w Satterthwaite and Rusland *Carl* 85-93; rtd 93; Perm to Offic *Liv* from 93. *Lyndale, 43 Renacres Lane, Ormskirk, Lancs L39 8SG*

TINSLEY, Preb Derek Michael. b 35. Lon Coll of Div ALCD66 LTh. **d** 66 **p** 67. C Rainhill *Liv* 66-68; C Chalfont St Peter *Ox* 68-74; R N Buckingham 74-82; RD Buckingham 78-82; P-in-c Alstonfield *Lich* 82-84; P-in-c Butterton 82-84; P-in-c Warslow and Elkstones 82-84; P-in-c Wetton 82-84; V Alstonfield, Butterton, Warslow w Elkstone etc 85-95; RD Alstonfield 82-95; Preb Lich Cathl from 91; V Cheddleton from 95. *The Vicarage, Hollow Lane, Cheddleton, Leek, Staffs ST13 7HP* Tel (01538) 360226

TINSLEY, Canon John. b 17. AKC49. **d** 49 **p** 50. C Putney St Mary *S'wark* 49-56; Youth Chapl 51-56; V Wandsworth St Paul 56-70; RD Wandsworth 69-70; V Redhill St Jo 70-80; RD Reigate 76-80; Hon Can S'wark Cathl 80-81; P-in-c Othery *B & W* 80; P-in-c Middlezoy 80; P-in-c Moorlinch w Stawell and Sutton Mallet 80; V Middlezoy and Othery and Moorlinch 81-85; rtd 85.

Cedar House, 1 Quantock Rise, Kingston St Mary, Taunton, Somerset TA2 8HJ Tel (01823) 451317

TIPLADY, Dr Peter. b 42. MRCGP72 FFPHM86 Dur Univ MB, BS65. Carl Dioc Tr Course 86. **d** 89 **p** 90. NSM Wetheral w Warw *Carl* from 89. *The Arches, The Green, Wetheral, Carlisle CA4 8ET* Tel (01228) 561611

TIPP, James Edward. b 45. Oak Hill Th Coll 73. **d** 75 **p** 76. C St Mary Cray and St Paul's Cray *Roch* 75-78; C Southborough St Pet w Ch Ch and St Matt 78-82; R Snodland All SS w Ch Ch from 82; RD Cobham from 96. *The Vicarage, 11 St Katherine's Lane, Snodland, Kent ME6 5EH* Tel (01634) 240232

TIPPER, Michael William. b 38. Hull Univ BSc59 MSc61. Em Coll Saskatoon 72. **d** 73 **p** 74. Canada 73-77, 79-80, 83-88 and from 91; R Amcotts *Linc* 77-79; V Aycliffe *Dur* 80-83; V Kneesall w Laxton and Wellow *S'well* 88-91. *Box 302, Cardston, Alberta, Canada, T0K 0K0* Tel Cardston (403) 653-1225

TIPPING, John Henry. b 27. St Mich Coll Llan 63. **d** 65 **p** 66. C Clydach *S & B* 65-68; C Oystermouth 68-70; R Llangynllo and Bleddfa 70-79; V Cwmddauddwr w St Harmon's and Llanwrthwl 79-80; R Ashton Gifford *Sarum* 80-97; rtd 97. *21 Norridge View, Warminster, Wilts BA12 8TA*

TIPPING, John Woodman. b 42. AKC65. **d** 66 **p** 67. C Croydon St Sav *Cant* 66-70; C Plaistow St Mary *Roch* 70-72; V Brockley Hill St Sav *S'wark* 72-83; P-in-c Sittingbourne St Mary *Cant* 83-86; V 86-94; P-in-c Mersham w Hinxhill from 94; P-in-c Sevington from 94; P-in-c Brabourne w Smeeth from 95; RD N Lympne from 95. *The Rectory, Bower Road, Mersham, Ashford, Kent TN25 6NN* Tel (01233) 502138

TITCOMBE, Peter Charles. *See* JONES, Peter Charles

TITFORD, Richard Kimber. b 45. UEA BA67. Ripon Coll Cuddesdon 78. **d** 80 **p** 80. C Middleton *Man* 80-83; P-in-c Edwardstone w Groton and Lt Waldingfield *St E* 83-90; R from 90. *The Rectory, Willow Corner, Edwardstone, Sudbury, Suffolk CO10 5PG* Tel (01787) 210026

TITLEY, David Joseph. b 47. Ex Univ BSc Surrey Univ PhD. Wycliffe Hall Ox. **d** 82 **p** 83. C Stowmarket *St E* 82-85; C Bloxwich *Lich* 85-90; TV 90-95; V Prees from 95; V Fauls from 95. *The Vicarage, Church Street, Prees, Whitchurch, Shropshire SY13 2EE* Tel (01948) 840243

TITLEY, Robert John. b 56. Ch Coll Cam BA78 MA82. Westcott Ho Cam DipTh83. **d** 85 **p** 86. C Lower Sydenham St Mich *S'wark* 85-88; C Sydenham All SS 85-88; Chapl Whitelands Coll of HE 88-94; V W Dulwich All SS from 94. *The Vicarage, 165 Rosendale Road, London SE21 8LN* Tel 0181-670 0826

TITTLEY, Donald Frank. b 22. ACP70 LCP74. NE Ord Course 78. **d** 80 **p** 81. NSM Tynemouth Cullercoats St Paul *Newc* from 80. *22 Selwyn Avenue, Whitley Bay, Tyne & Wear NE25 9DH* Tel 0191-252 6655

TIVEY, Nicholas. b 65. Liv Poly BSc89. Ridley Hall Cam CTM94. **d** 94 **p** 95. C Bromborough *Ches* from 94. *193 Allport Road, Wirral, Merseyside L62 6BA* Tel 0151-334 4181

TIZZARD, David John. b 40. LRAM. Sarum Th Coll 65. **d** 68 **p** 69. C Foley Park *Worc* 68-70; Hon C Gravesend St Geo *Roch* 70-73; Miss to Seamen 70-72; PV Truro Cathl *Truro* 73-75; TV Bemerton *Sarum* 75-79; Soc Resp Adv 79-85; Chapl to the Deaf 79-85; Can and Preb Sarum Cathl 84-85; R S Hill w Callington *Truro* 85-87; P-in-c Linkinhorne 86-87; Relig Affairs Producer BBC Radio Solent 87-94; V Portswood St Denys *Win* 87-94; P-in-c Distington *Carl* 94-96; Soc Resp Officer 94-96; Hon Can Carl Cathl 94-96; TV Beaminster Area *Sarum* from 96. *The Vicarage, Orchard Mead, Broadwindsor, Beaminster, Dorset DT8 3RA* Tel (01308) 868805

TIZZARD, Dudley Frank. b 19. Roch Th Coll 63. **d** 65 **p** 66. C Bearsted *Cant* 65-68; C Cant St Martin w St Paul 68-71; Chapl HM Pris Cant 68-71; V Petham w Waltham *Cant* 71-75; C Sevenoaks St Jo *Roch* 75-78; Perm to Offic *Cant* 78-84; rtd 84; Lic to Offic *Cant* from 84. *62 Knaves Acre, Headcorn, Ashford, Kent TN27 9TJ* Tel (01622) 891498

TIZZARD, Peter Francis. b 53. Oak Hill Th Coll DipHE88. **d** 90 **p** 91. C Letchworth St Paul w Willian *St Alb* 90-95; I Drumkeeran w Templecarne and Muckross *Clogh* from 95. *Drumkeeran Rectory, Tubrid, Kesh, Enniskillen, Co Fermanagh BT93 1BE* Tel (013656) 32315

TOAN, Robert Charles. b 50. Oak Hill Th Coll. **d** 84 **p** 85. C Upton (Overchurch) *Ches* 84-87; V Rock Ferry from 87; RD Birkenhead from 97. *The Vicarage, St Peter's Road, Birkenhead, Merseyside L42 1PY* Tel 0151-645 1622

TOBIAS, Edwin John Rupert. b 16. TCD BA40 MA59. **d** 40 **p** 41. C Donaghadee *D & D* 40-41; C Dublin Drumcondra *D & G* 41-44; C Cork St Fin Barre's Cathl *C, C & R* 44-47; I Durrus 47-49; I Lislee w Timoleague 49-55; C Dublin Rathmines *D & G* 55-59; Hon Clerical V Ch Ch Cathl Dublin 55-59; I Kilbixy *M & K* 59-77; I Killucan 77-82; rtd 82. *Sue Ryder House, Chalet 7, Ballyroan, Co Laois, Irish Republic* Tel Portlaoise (502) 31906

TOBIAS, William Trevor. b 10. St Steph Ho Ox 62. **d** 63 **p** 64. C Perivale *Lon* 63-69; P-in-c Hanwell St Mark 69-80; rtd 80; Perm to Offic *Lon* from 81. *58 Claremont Road, London W13 0DG* Tel 0181-997 6023

TOBIN, Richard Francis. b 44. CertEd. Chich Th Coll 76. **d** 78 **p** 79. C W Leigh CD *Portsm* 78-79; C Halstead St Andr *Chelmsf* 79; C Halstead St Andr w H Trin 79; C Halstead St Andr w H Trin and Greenstead Green 79-87; Youth Chapl 82-87; V S Shields St Simon *Dur* from 87. *St Simon's Vicarage, Wenlock Road, South Shields, Tyne & Wear NE34 9AL* Tel 0191-455 3164

TODD, Alastair. b 20. CMG71. CCC Ox BA45 Lon Univ DipTh65. Sarum & Wells Th Coll 71. **d** 73 **p** 74. C Willingdon *Chich* 73-77; P-in-c Brighton St Aug 77-78; V Brighton St Aug and St Sav 78-86; rtd 86; Perm to Offic *Chich* from 86. *59 Park Avenue, Eastbourne, E Sussex BN21 2XH* Tel (01323) 505843

TODD, Andrew John. b 61. Keble Coll Ox Univ Coll Dur BA84. Coll of Resurr Mirfield 85. **d** 87 **p** 88. C Thorpe *Nor* 87-91; Chapl K Alfred Coll *Win* 91-94; Sen Asst P E Dereham and Scarning *Nor* from 94; Dir Studies EAMTC 94-97; Vice-Prin from 97. *34 Laurel Close, Mepal, Ely, Cambs CB6 2BN* Tel (01353) 777293 or (01223) 741026 Fax (01223) 741027

TODD, Clive. b 57. Linc Th Coll 89. **d** 91 **p** 92. C Consett *Dur* 91-93; C Bensham 93-95; P-in-c S Hetton w Haswell from 95. *The Vicarage, South Hetton, Durham DH6 2SW* Tel 0191-526 1157

TODD, Edward Peter. b 44. Cranmer Hall Dur 86. **d** 88 **p** 89. C Hindley All SS *Liv* 88-91; P-in-c Wigan St Steph 91-96; V from 96. *St Stephen's Vicarage, 141 Whelley, Wigan, Lancs WN2 1BL* Tel (01942) 42579

TODD, George Robert. b 21. Sarum & Wells Th Coll 74. **d** 76 **p** 77. Hon C Wellington and Distr *B & W* 76-86; Perm to Offic from 86. *15 John Grinter Way, Wellington, Somerset TA21 9AR* Tel (01823) 662828

TODD, Jeremy Stephen Bevan (Jez). b 69. Kent Univ DipMan96. Trin Coll Bris BA92. **d** 97. NSM Tufnell Park St Geo and All SS *Lon* from 97. *St George's Centre, Crayford Road, London N7 0ND* Tel 0171-609 0121

TODD, Joy Gertrude. b 28. LNSM course. **d** 90 **p** 94. NSM Guildf H Trin w St Mary *Guildf* from 90. *165 Stoke Road, Guildford, Surrey GU1 1EY* Tel (01483) 67500

TODD, Nicholas Stewart (Nick). b 61. Huddersfield Poly HND84. Wycliffe Hall Ox 94. **d** 96 **p** 97. C Gt Wyrley *Lich* from 96. *6 Clover Ridge, Cheslyn Hay, Walsall WS6 7DP* Tel (01922) 419161

TODD, Canon Dr Norman Henry. b 19. PhC Lon Univ BPharm42 Fitzw Ho Cam BA50 MA55 Nottm Univ PhD78. Westcott Ho Cam 50. **d** 52 **p** 53. C Aspley *S'well* 52-54; Chapl Westcott Ho Cam 55-58; V Arnold *S'well* 58-65; V Rolleston w Morton 65-69; Can Res S'well Minster 65-69; R Elston w Elston Chapelry 71-76; R E Stoke w Syerston 72-76; V Sibthorpe 72-76; Bp's Adv on Tr 76-83; C Averham w Kelham 76-80; V Rolleston w Morton 80-83; P-in-c Upton 80-83; V Rolleston w Fiskerton, Morton and Upton 83-88; Hon Can S'well Minster 82-88; rtd 88; Abps' Adv for Bps' Min *Cant* 88-94. *39 Beacon Hill Road, Newark, Nottingham NG24 2JH* Tel (01636) 71857

TODD, William Colquhoun Duncan. b 26. AKC53 St Boniface Warminster 53. **d** 54 **p** 55. C Westmr St Steph w St Jo *Lon* 54-59; Win Coll Missr 60-72; C-in-c Leigh Park CD *Portsm* 59-69; V Leigh Park 69-72; R Hatfield *St Alb* from 72; Angl Adv Southern TV 62-72; Thames TV 72-92; Carlton TV from 93. *The Rectory, 1 Fore Street, Hatfield, Herts AL9 5AN* Tel (01707) 262072

TODD, Canon William Moorhouse. b 26. Lich Th Coll 54. **d** 57 **p** 58. C W Derby St Mary *Liv* 57-61; V Liv St Chris Norris Green 61-97; Hon Can Liv Cathl 92-97; rtd 97. *3 Haymans Grove, West Derby, Liverpool L12 7LD* Tel 0151-256 1712

TOFTS, Jack. b 31. Roch Th Coll 66. **d** 68 **p** 69. C Richmond *Ripon* 68-71; C Croydon *Cant* 71-74; P-in-c Welney *Ely* 74-78; P-in-c Upwell Ch Ch 74-79; V Gorefield 78-94; R Newton 78-94; R Tydd St Giles 78-94; rtd 96. *The Birches, Church Road, Walpole St Peter, Wisbech, Cambs PE14 7NU* Tel (01945) 780455

TOLL, Brian Arthur. b 35. Ely Th Coll 62 Linc Th Coll 64. **d** 65 **p** 66. C Cleethorpes *Linc* 65-68; C Hadleigh w Layham and Shelley *St E* 69-72; R Claydon and Barham 72-86; P-in-c Capel w Lt Wenham 86-94; P-in-c Holton St Mary w Gt Wenham 87-91; R Capel St Mary w Lt and Gt Wenham 94-96; Bp's Adv on Deliverance and Exorcism from 89; P-in-c Ipswich St Mary at the Elms from 96. *The Vicarage, 68 Black Horse Lane, Ipswich IP1 2EF* Tel (01473) 252822

TOLLER, Elizabeth Margery. b 53. Leeds Univ BA75. Ripon Coll Cuddesdon 84. **d** 87. Perm to Offic *Nor* from 87; Chapl Lt Plumstead Hosp 92-93; Asst Chapl HM Pris Nor 93-95; Chapl Co-ord Gt Yarmouth Coll of FE from 96. *The Rectory, 24 Rectory Road, Coltishall, Norwich NR12 7HL* Tel (01603) 737255

TOLLER, Heinz Dieter. b 52. Bonn Univ DipTh77. NE Ord Course 86. **d** 87 **p** 88. C Leeds Gipton Epiphany *Ripon* 87-90; R Coltishall w Gt Hautbois and Horstead *Nor* from 90. *The Rectory, 24 Rectory Road, Coltishall, Norwich NR12 7HL* Tel (01603) 737255

TOLLEY, Canon George. b 25. FRSC CBIM Lon Univ BSc45 MSc48 PhD52 Sheff Univ Hon DSc83. Linc Th Coll 65. **d** 67 **p** 68. C Sheff Sharrow *Sheff* 67-90; Hon Can Sheff Cathl from 76. *74 Furniss Avenue, Sheffield S17 3QP* Tel 0114-236 0538

TOLWORTHY, Colin. b 37. Chich Th Coll 64. **d** 67 **p** 68. C Hulme St Phil *Man* 67-70; C Lawton Moor 70-71; C Hangleton *Chich* 72-76; V Eastbourne St Phil 76-87; V Hastings H Trin from 87. *Holy Trinity Vicarage, 72 Priory Avenue, Hastings, E Sussex TN34 1UG* Tel (01424) 441766

TOMALIN, Stanley Joseph Edward. b 66. Oak Hill Th Coll BA93. **d** 96 **p** 97. C Bitterne *Win* from 96. *4 Aberdour Close, Bitterne, Southampton SO18 5PF* Tel (01703) 473436

TOMBLING, Canon Arthur John. b 32. St Jo Coll Cam BA54 MA58. Ridley Hall Cam 55. **d** 57 **p** 58. C Rushden *Pet* 57-59; Asst Chapl Repton Sch Derby 59-61; C Reigate St Mary *S'wark* 61-64; V Battersea Park St Sav 64-87; P-in-c Battersea St Geo w St Andr 74-87; RD Battersea 85-90; V Battersea St Sav and St Geo w St Andr 87-95; P-in-c Battersea Park All SS 89-95; Hon Can S'wark Cathl 89-95; rtd 95; Perm to Offic *Pet* from 95. *5 William Steele Way, Higham Ferrers, Rushden, Northants NN10 8LS* Tel (01933) 418072

TOMBS, Kenneth Roberts. b 42. Open Univ BA84. S Dios Minl Tr Scheme 92. **d** 95 **p** 96. Dep Hd Twyford C of E High Sch Acton from 86; NSM Ickenham *Lon* from 95. *91 Burns Avenue, Southall, Middx UB1 2LT* Tel 0181-574 3738

TOMKINS, Clive Anthony. b 47. Cant Sch of Min 85. **d** 88 **p** 89. C Eastry and Northbourne w Tilmanstone etc *Cant* 88-91; R 91-96; P-in-c 96-97; Chapl Eastry Hosp 91-93; Chapl Cant and Thanet Community Health Trust 93-97; P-in-c Woodchurch *Cant* from 97. *The Rectory, Woodchurch, Ashford, Kent TN26 3QJ* Tel (01233) 860257

TOMKINSON, Raymond David. b 47. RGN MSSCh. EAMTC 86. **d** 89 **p** 90. NSM Chesterton St Geo *Ely* 89-91; C Sawston 91-93; C Babraham 91-93; P-in-c Wimbotsham w Stow Bardolph and Stow Bridge etc 93-94; R from 94; RD Fincham from 94. *The Rectory, Wimbotsham, King's Lynn, Norfolk PE34 3QG* Tel (01366) 384279

TOMLIN, Graham Stuart. b 58. Linc Coll Ox MA80. Wycliffe Hall Ox BA85. **d** 86 **p** 87. C Ex St Leon w H Trin *Ex* 86-89; Tutor Wycliffe Hall Ox from 89; Chapl Jes Coll Ox 89-94. *Wycliffe Hall, Oxford OX2 6PW* Tel (01865) 274205

TOMLIN, Keith Michael. b 53. Imp Coll Lon BSc75. Ridley Hall Cam 77. **d** 80 **p** 81. C Heywood St Jas *Man* 80-83; C Rochdale 83-84; TV 84-85; Chapl Rochdale Tech Coll 83-85; R Benington w Leverton *Linc* from 85; Chapl HM Pris N Sea Camp from 97. *The Rectory, Main Road, Benington, Boston, Lincs PE22 0BT* Tel (01205) 760962

TOMLINE, Stephen Harrald. b 35. Dur Univ BA57. Cranmer Hall Dur DipTh61. **d** 61 **p** 62. C Blackley St Pet *Man* 61-66; V Audenshaw St Steph 66-90; V Newhey from 90. *St Thomas's Vicarage, Newhey, Rochdale, Lancs OL16 3QS* Tel (01706) 845159

TOMLINSON, Dr Anne Lovat. b 56. Edin Univ MA78 PhD85. St Jo Coll Nottm CertCS87. **d** 93. Tutor Edin Dioc Tr for Min Course from 93; Lic to Offic *Edin* from 93. *8 Buckstone Drive, Edinburgh EH10 6PD* Tel 0131-445 2942

TOMLINSON, Arthur John Faulkner. b 20. Clare Coll Cam BA41 MA45. Ridley Hall Cam 46. **d** 48 **p** 49. C Hampstead Em W End *Lon* 48-50; C Kensington St Helen w H Trin 50-54; V Furneux Pelham w Stocking Pelham *St Alb* 54-62; R Sarratt 62-85; rtd 85; Perm to Offic *Nor* from 85. *5 Mead Close, Buxton, Norwich NR10 5EL* Tel (01603) 279470

TOMLINSON, Barry William. b 47. Reading Univ DipTh. Clifton Th Coll 72. **d** 72 **p** 73. C Pennington *Man* 72-76; SAMS 76-80; Chile 77-80; C-in-c Gorleston St Mary CD *Nor* 80; Chapl Jas Paget Hosp Gorleston 81-87; V Gorleston St Mary *Nor* 80-88; P-in-c Gt w Lt Plumstead 88-89; R Gt w Lt Plumstead and Witton 89-93; R Gt and Lt Plumstead w Thorpe End and Witton from 93; Chapl Lt Plumstead Hosp 88-95; RD Blofield *Nor* from 96. *The Rectory, 9 Lawn Crescent, Thorpe End, Norwich NR13 5BP* Tel (01603) 434778

TOMLINSON, David Robert. b 60. Kent Univ BSc82 Chelsea Coll Lon PGCE83 Jes Coll Cam BA92 MA96. Ridley Hall Cam CTM93. **d** 93 **p** 94. C Godalming *Guildf* from 93. *St Mark's House, 29 Franklyn Road, Godalming, Surrey GU7 2LD* Tel (01483) 424710

TOMLINSON, Eric Joseph. b 45. Qu Coll Birm 70. **d** 73 **p** 74. C Cheadle *Lich* 73-76; C Sedgley All SS 77-79; V Ettingshall 79-94; P-in-c Longsdon 94; P-in-c Rushton 94; P-in-c Horton 94; V Horton, Lonsdon and Rushton Spencer from 94. *The Vicarage, Longsdon, Stoke-on-Trent ST9 9QF* Tel (01538) 385318

TOMLINSON, Frederick William (Fred). b 58. Glas Univ MA80 Edin Univ BD83. Edin Th Coll 80. **d** 83 **p** 84. C Cumbernauld *Glas* 83-86; C Glas St Mary 86-88; R Edin St Hilda *Edin* from 88; R Edin St Fillan from 88. *8 Buckstone Drive, Edinburgh EH10 6PD* Tel 0131-445 2942

TOMLINSON, Canon Geoffrey. b 15. Linc Coll Ox BA37 MA47. Westcott Ho Cam 37. **d** 39 **p** 40. C Whitworth w Spennymoor *Dur* 39-43; Chapl RNVR 43-47; P-in-c Dalton le Dale *Dur* 47; Bp's Dom Chapl *Linc* 47-50; V Market Rasen 50-56; P-in-c Linwood 52-53; R 53-56; V Westbury-on-Trym St Alb *Bris* 56-66; RD Clifton 61-66; V Lancaster St Mary *Blackb* 66-81; Hon Can Blackb Cathl 67-86; RD Lancaster 71-82; V Overton 81-86; rtd 86; Perm to Offic *Bradf* from 86; Perm to Offic *Blackb* from 87. *3 Kirk Beck Close, Brookhouse, Lancaster LA2 9JN* Tel (01524) 770051

TOMLINSON, Ian James. b 50. K Coll Lon AKC72 MA90. St Aug Coll Cant 72. **d** 73 **p** 74. C Thirsk w S Kilvington and Carlton Miniott etc *York* 73-76; C Harrogate St Wilfrid *Ripon* 76-79; R Appleshaw, Kimpton, Thruxton and Fyfield *Win* from 79. *The Rectory, Ragged Appleshaw, Andover, Hants SP11 9HX* Tel (01264) 772414

TOMLINSON, Mrs Jean Mary. b 32. K Coll Lon CertRK53 BEd75. S Dios Minl Tr Scheme 84. **d** 87 **p** 94. Hon Par Dn Spring Park All SS *S'wark* 87-92; Chapl HM Young Offender Inst Hatf from 92. *HM Young Offender Institution, Thorne Road, Hatfield, Doncaster DN7 6EL* Tel (01405) 812336 Fax 813325

TOMLINSON (née MILLS), Mrs Jennifer Clare. b 61. Trin Hall Cam BA82 MA86. Ridley Hall Cam 88. **d** 91 **p** 94. C Busbridge *Guildf* 91-95; C Godalming 95-97; Hon C from 97. *St Mark's House, 29 Franklyn Road, Godalming, Surrey GU7 2LD* Tel (01483) 424710

TOMLINSON, Canon John Coombes. b 34. Nottm Univ DipEd76. Lich Th Coll 60. **d** 62 **p** 63. C Cheadle *Lich* 62-66; Warden Lich Dioc Tr Cen 66-73; C Alstonfield 66-68; P-in-c Ilam w Blore Ray and Okeover 68-73; Dioc Youth Tr Officer 68-73; Bp's Youth Chapl *Derby* 73-84; Dep Dir of Educn 78-79; Dir 79-84; TR Buxton w Burbage and King Sterndale 84-96; Dioc Adv Past Care and Counselling from 85; RD Buxton 91-96; Hon Can Derby Cathl from 91; R Matlock from 96. *The Rectory, Church Street, Matlock, Derbyshire DE4 3BZ* Tel (01629) 582199

TOMLINSON, John Howard. b 54. MICE83 Newc Univ BSc76. Chich Th Coll 91. **d** 93 **p** 94. C Blewbury, Hagbourne and Upton *Ox* 93-96; C Cowley St Jas from 96. *85 Temple Road, Cowley, Oxford OX4 2EX* Tel (01865) 748915

TOMLINSON, John William Bruce. b 60. Univ of Wales (Abth) BA82 Man Univ MA90. Hartley Victoria Coll 87 Linc Th Coll 91. **d** 92 **p** 93. In Methodist Ch 90-91; C Sawley *Derby* 92-95; P-in-c Man Victoria Park *Man* from 95; Dioc CUF Officer from 95; Chapl St Anselm Hall Man Univ from 96. *The Rectory, 14 Moorgate Avenue, Withington, Manchester M20 1HE* Tel 0161-448 7219 or 832 5253 Fax 832 2869

TOMLINSON, Matthew Robert Edward. b 61. St Chad's Coll Dur BA83. St Mich Coll Llan BD94. **d** 94 **p** 95. C Abergavenny St Mary w Llanwenarth Citra *Mon* 94-96; Min Can Llan Cathl *Llan* from 96. *2 The White House, Cathedral Green, Llandaff, Cardiff CF5 2EB*

TOMLINSON, Peter Robert Willis. b 19. CertEd49. Linc Th Coll 53. **d** 55 **p** 56. C Matlock and Tansley *Derby* 55-57; R Risley 57-60; V Repton 60-70; V Foremark 60-70; V Barrow Gurney *B & W* 70-77; Asst Chapl and Lect Coll of St Matthias Bris 70-77; TV Langport Area Chs 78-80; R Flax Bourton 80-84; V Barrow Gurney 80-84; rtd 84. *Flat 2, Vernon Lodge, 87 Hampton Park, Bristol BS6 6LQ* Tel 0117-946 6011

TOMLINSON, Miss Thelma Marcelle. b 20. K Coll Lon 46. **dss** 67 **d** 87 **p** 94. Liv Cathl *Liv* 69-81; Liv Univ 69-75; Dioc Lay Min Adv 75-81; rtd 81; Hon C Worle *B & W* 81-87; Perm to Offic from 87. *Cranbrook, 16 Greenwood Road, Worle, Weston-super-Mare, Avon BS22 0EX* Tel (01934) 515112

TOMPKINS, David John. b 32. Oak Hill Th Coll 55. **d** 58 **p** 59. C Northampton St Giles *Pet* 58-61; C Heatherlands St Jo *Sarum* 61-63; V Selby St Jas *York* 63-73; V Wistow 63-73; V Retford *S'well* 73-87; P-in-c Clarborough w Hayton 84-87; V Kidsgrove *Lich* 87-90; V Tockwith and Bilton w Bickerton *York* 90-97; rtd 97. *49 Wentworth Drive, Oundle, Peterborough PE8 4QF* Tel (01832) 275176

TOMPKINS, Francis Alfred Howard. b 26. St Jo Coll Dur BA50 DipTh52. **d** 52 **p** 53. C Islington St Mary *Lon* 52-55; Argentina 55-61; Field Supt SAMS 61-65; V Donington *Linc* 65-79; RD Holland W 69-78; V Silloth *Carl* 79-91; rtd 91; Perm to Offic *Linc* from 91. *22 Silver Street, Branston, Lincoln LN4 1LR* Tel (01522) 791689

TOMPKINS, Michael John Gordon. b 35. JP76. Man Univ BSc58 MPS59. N Ord Course 82. **d** 85 **p** 86. C Abington *Pet* 85-87; TV Daventry 87-92; P-in-c Braunston 87-92; TV Daventry, Ashby St Ledgers, Braunston etc 92-93; R Paston from 93. *The Rectory, 236 Fulbridge Road, Peterborough PE4 6SN* Tel (01733) 571943

TOMPKINS, Peter Michael. b 58. Open Univ BA92 SS Hild & Bede Coll Dur CertEd79. St Jo Coll Nottm MA96. **d** 96 **p** 97. C Bromfield w Waverton *Carl* from 96. *West Garth House, Westnewton, Carlisle CA5 3PE* Tel (01697) 321812

TOMS, Sheila Patricia. b 33. Cam Univ TCert54 Univ of Wales (Cardiff) BEd77 Univ of Wales (Swansea) ADC74. Llan Ord Course 90. **dss** 91 **d** 94 **p** 97. Canton St Luke *Llan* 91-94; NSM Peterston-super-Ely w St Brides-super-Ely from 94. *East Wing, Dingestow Court, Dingestow, Monmouth NP5 4YD* Tel (01600) 740262

TONBRIDGE, Archdeacon of. *See* ROSE, The Ven Kathleen Judith

TONBRIDGE, Suffragan Bishop of. *See* SMITH, The Rt Revd Brian Arthur

TONES, Kevin Edward. b 64. Hertf Coll Ox BA85. Ridley Hall Cam 88. **d** 91 **p** 92. C Warmsworth *Sheff* 91-92; C Thorne 92-96; V Greasbrough from 96. *The Vicarage, 16 Church Street, Greasbrough, Rotherham, S Yorkshire S61 4DX* Tel (01709) 551288

TONG, Canon Peter Laurence. b 29. Lon Univ BA50. Oak Hill Th Coll 52. **d** 54 **p** 55. C Everton St Chrys *Liv* 54-56; P-in-c Liv St Sav 56-59; V Blackb Sav *Blackb* 59-65; Chapl Blackb R Infirmary 63-65; V Islington St Andr w St Thos and St Matthias *Lon* 65-75; V Welling *Roch* 75-82; TR Bedworth *Cov* 82-94; Hon

Can Cov Cathl 88-94; Hon Can Chile from 89; rtd 94; Perm to Offic *Roch* from 94. *46 Bladington Drive, Bexley, Kent DA5 3BP* Tel 0181-303 0085

TONGE, Brian. b 36. Dur Univ BA58. Ely Th Coll 59. **d** 61 **p** 62. C Fleetwood *Blackb* 61-65; Chapl Ranby Ho Sch Retford 65-69; Hon C Burnley St Andr w St Marg *Blackb* 69-97; rtd 97. *50 Fountains Avenue, Simonstone, Burnley, Lancs BB12 7PY* Tel (01282) 776518

TONGE, Lister. b 51. K Coll Lon AKC74 Man Univ DCouns92 Loyola Univ Chicago MPS95. St Aug Coll Cant 74. **d** 75 **p** 76. C Liv Our Lady and St Nic w St Anne *Liv* 75-78; S Africa 78-79; CR 79-91; Lic to Offic *Wakef* 83-91; Perm to Offic *Man* 89-94; USA 93-95; Perm to Offic *Liv* 95; Chapl Community of St Jo Bapt Windsor from 96. *The Cottage, Convent of St John the Baptist, Hatch Lane, Windsor, Berks SL4 3QS* Tel (01753) 860449

TONGUE, Canon Paul. b 41. St Chad's Coll Dur BA63 DipTh64. **d** 64 **p** 65. C Dudley St Edm *Worc* 64-69; C Sedgley All SS *Lich* 69-70; V Amblecote *Worc* from 70; Hon Can Worc Cathl from 93; RD Stourbridge from 96. *The Vicarage, 4 The Holloway, Amblecote, Stourbridge, W Midlands DY8 4DL* Tel (01384) 394057

TONKIN, The Ven David Graeme. b 31. Barrister-at-Law Univ of NZ LLB56 LLM57. Coll of Resurr Mirfield 57. **d** 59 **p** 60. C Hackney Wick St Mary of Eton w St Aug *Lon* 59-62; Chapl Worksop Coll Notts 62-68; Lic to Offic *S'well* 63-68; Jordan 68-74; New Zealand from 74; Can St Pet Cathl Waikato from 88; Adn Waitomo from 89; rtd 93. *Box 91, Owhango, New Zealand* Tel Owhango (7) 895 4738 Fax as telephone

TONKIN, Canon Richard John. b 28. Lon Coll of Div ALCD59 BD60. **d** 60 **p** 61. C Leic Martyrs *Leic* 60-63; C Keynsham *B & W* 63-66; V Hinckley H Trin *Leic* 66-74; RD Sparkenhoe II 71-74; R Oadby 74-84; Hon Can Leic Cathl 83-93; V Leic H Apostles 84-93; rtd 93; Perm to Offic *Leic* from 93. *39 Shackerdale Road, Wigston, Leicester LE8 1BQ* Tel 0116-281 2517

TONKINSON, Canon David Boyes. b 47. K Coll Lon BD71 AKC71. St Aug Coll Cant 71. **d** 72 **p** 73. C Surbiton St Andr *S'wark* 72-74; C Selsdon St Jo w St Fran *Cant* 75-81; V Croydon St Aug 81-84; V Croydon St Aug *S'wark* 85-89; C Easthampstead *Ox* 89-96; Ind Chapl 89-96; Chapl Bracknell Coll 93-96; Soc Resp Adv *Portsm* from 96; Hon Can Portsm Cathl from 96. *17 Squirrel Close, Sandhurst, Camberley, Surrey GU17 8DL* Tel (01252) 861722

TOOBY, Anthony Albert. b 58. Sarum & Wells Th Coll 89. **d** 91 **p** 92. C Warsop *S'well* 91-95; C Ollerton w Boughton from 95. *The Glebe House, Church Road, Broughton, Newark, Notts NG22 9RJ* Tel (01623) 836013

TOOGOOD, Ms Melanie Lorraine. b 57. K Coll Lon BD78 AKC78. Cuddesdon Coll DipMin94. **d** 96 **p** 97. C Shepperton *Lon* from 96. *Flat 2, The Rectory, Church Square, Shepperton, Middx TW17 9JY* Tel (01932) 241846

TOOGOOD, Noel Hare. b 32. Birm Univ BSc54. Wells Th Coll 59. **d** 61 **p** 62. C Rotherham *Sheff* 61-65; C Darlington St Jo *Dur* 65-70; V Burnopfield 70-81; P-in-c Roche *Truro* 81-84; P-in-c Withiel 81-84; R Roche and Withiel 84-91; RD St Austell 88-91; V Madron 91-96; rtd 96. *Acorn Cottage, Oakhill Road, Seaview, Isle of Wight PO34 5AP*

TOOGOOD, Robert Charles. b 45. AKC70. St Aug Coll Cant 70. **d** 71 **p** 72. C Shepperton *Lon* 71-74; C Kirk Ella *York* 74-76; P-in-c Levisham w Lockton 76-81; P-in-c Ebberston w Allerston 76-81; R Kempsey and Severn Stoke w Croome d'Abitot *Worc* 81-92; V Bramley *Win* from 92. *The Vicarage, Bramley, Basingstoke, Hants RG26 5DQ* Tel (01256) 881373

TOOGOOD, Robert Frederick (Bob). b 43. St Paul's Cheltenham CertEd65 DipPE65 Open Univ BA74. Trin Coll Bris DipHE95. **d** 95 **p** 96. C Southbroom *Sarum* from 95. *33 Brickley Lane, Devizes, Wilts SN10 3BH* Tel (01380) 729386

TOOKE, Mrs Sheila. b 44. EAMTC 89. **d** 91 **p** 94. NSM March St Wendreda *Ely* 91-95; P-in-c Upwell Ch Ch 95-97; P-in-c Welney 95-97; P-in-c Manea 95-97; R Christchurch and Manea and Welney from 97. *The Rectory, Church Road, Christchurch, Wisbech, Cambs PE14 9PQ* Tel (01354) 638379

TOOKEY, Preb Christopher Tom. b 41. AKC67. **d** 68 **p** 69. C Stockton St Pet *Dur* 68-71; C Burnham *B & W* 71-77; R Clutton w Cameley 77-81; V Wells St Thos w Horrington from 81; RD Shepton Mallet 86-95; Preb Wells Cathl from 90. *St Thomas's Vicarage, St Thomas's Street, Wells, Somerset BA5 2UZ* Tel (01749) 672193

TOOLEY, Geoffrey Arnold. b 27. Lon Coll of Div 55. **d** 58 **p** 59. C Chalk *Roch* 58-60; C Meopham 60-62; P-in-c Snodland and Paddlesworth 62-68; P-in-c Burham 68-76; C Riverhead w Dunton Green 76-79; C S w N Bersted *Chich* 79-83; C-in-c N Bersted CD 83-96; rtd 97. *Hawksworth, Charnwood Road, Bognor Regis, W Sussex PO22 9DN*

TOOLEY, Norman Oliver. b 27. Roch Th Coll. **d** 65 **p** 66. C Gravesend St Mary *Roch* 65-68; C Ormskirk *Liv* 68-73; Chapl Merseyside Cen for the Deaf 73-78; C Bootle Ch Ch 78-80; C W Ham *Chelmsf* 80-86; Chapl RAD 86-92; rtd 92; Perm to Offic *Roch* from 92. *6 Newton Terrace, Crown Lane, Bromley BR2 9PH* Tel 0181-303 0085

TOOMBS, Alan Trevor. b 33. Man Univ BA54. Ripon Hall Ox 54. **d** 56 **p** 57. C Hope St Jas *Man* 56-61; R Moston St Mary 61-74; V Weaste 74-81; R Newchurch from 81. *The Rectory, 539 Newchurch Road, Newchurch, Rossendale, Lancs BB4 9HH* Tel (01706) 215098

TOON, John Samuel. b 30. Bps' Coll Cheshunt 64. **d** 65 **p** 66. C Newark St Mary *S'well* 65-67; C Clewer St Andr *Ox* 67-69; Canada 70, 73-76 and from 78; R Osgathorpe *Leic* 70-72; C Maidstone All SS w St Phil and H Trin *Cant* 76-78; rtd 95. *804, 10th Street N W, Portage la Prairie, Manitoba, Canada, R1N 3K2* Tel Brandon (204) 857-4213

TOON, Dr Peter. b 39. K Coll Lon BD65 MTh67 Liv Univ MA72 Ch Ch Ox DPhil77 DD. Lambeth STh65 NW Ord Course 72. **d** 73 **p** 74. C Skelmersdale St Paul *Liv* 73-74; Lib Latimer Ho Ox 74-76; C Ox St Ebbe w St Pet *Ox* 74-76; Hon Lect St Giles-in-the-Fields *Lon* 76-82; Tutor Oak Hill Th Coll 76-82; Dir of Post-Ord Tr *St E* 82-87; P-in-c Boxford 82-88; V Staindrop *Dur* 88-91; USA from 91. *Nashotah Episcopal Seminary, 2777 Mission Road, Nashotah, Wisconsin 53058, USA*

TOOP, Alan Neil. b 49. St Alb Minl Tr Scheme 79 Linc Th Coll 82. **d** 83 **p** 84. C Kempston Transfiguration *St Alb* 83-87; C Ludlow *Heref* 87-92; P-in-c Stokesay from 92; P-in-c Sibdon Carwood w Halford from 92; P-in-c Acton Scott from 96; RD Condover from 96. *The Vicarage, Clun Road, Stokesay, Craven Arms, Shropshire SY7 9QW* Tel (01588) 672797

TOOP, William John. b 07. Lon Univ BSc27 K Coll Cam BA38 MA42. **d** 41 **p** 42. E Pakistan 41-44 and 46-47; Chapl Lahore Cathl 44; Ind Chapl *Man* 44-47; V Cofton *Ex* 48-52; R Torwood St Mark 52-79; P-in-c Torquay H Trin 74-79; R Torwood St Mark w H Trin 79; rtd 79; Lic to Offic *Ex* from 79. *Ardmore, Asheldon Road, Torquay TQ1 2QN* Tel (01803) 201387

TOOTH, Nigel David. b 47. Sarum & Wells Th Coll 71. **d** 74 **p** 75. C S Beddington St Mich *S'wark* 74-77; C Whitchurch *Bris* 77-83; TV Bedminster 83-87; Chapl Dorchester Hosps 87-94; Chapl Herrison Hosp Dorchester 87-94; Chapl W Dorset Gen Hosps NHS Trust from 94. *West Dorset Hospital, Damers Road, Dorchester, Dorset DT1 2JY* Tel (01305) 251150

TOOVEY, Preb Kenneth Frank. b 26. K Coll Lon BD51 AKC51. **d** 52 **p** 53. C Munster Square St Mary Magd *Lon* 52-60; V Upper Teddington SS Pet and Paul 60-70; V Ruislip St Martin 70-81; RD Hillingdon 75-81; V Greenhill St Jo 81-91; Preb St Paul's Cathl 83-91; rtd 91. *10 Fort Road, Northolt, Middx UB5 5HH* Tel 0181-842 2812

TOOZE, Margaret Elizabeth. b 27. St Mich Ho Ox 54. **dss** 83 **d** 89 **p** 94. Kenya 61-88; C Bath Walcot *B & W* 89-95; Perm to Offic from 95. *1 Victoria House, Weston Road, Bath BA1 2XY* Tel (01225) 465642

TOPALIAN, Berj. b 51. **d** 97. NSM Clifton Ch Ch w Em *Bris* from 97. *40 Fenshurst Gardens, Long Ashton, Bristol BS18 9AU* Tel (01275) 393899

TOPHAM, Paul Raby. b 31. MIL66 Columbia Pacific Univ LTh80 MA81. SSC. **d** 85 **p** 86. Chapl St Paul's Prep Sch Barnes 85-91; Chapl Toulouse w Biarritz, Cahors and Pau *Eur* 91-94; Perm to Offic *Lon* from 94; Perm to Offic *Eur* from 94; rtd 96; P-in-c St Margarets on Thames *Lon* from 97. *58 Gloucester Road, Hampton, Middx TW12 2UH* Tel 0181-979 4277

TOPPING, Kenneth Bryan Baldwin. b 27. Bps' Coll Cheshunt 58. **d** 59 **p** 60. C Fleetwood *Blackb* 59-63; V Ringley *Man* 63-70; V Cleator Moor w Cleator *Carl* 70-91; rtd 92; Perm to Offic *Blackb* from 92. *22 Sunningdale Avenue, Hest Bank, Lancaster LA2 6DF* Tel (01524) 822197

TOPPING, Norman. b 32. NW Ord Course 73. **d** 76 **p** 77. NSM Prenton *Ches* 76-79; C E Runcorn w Halton 79-80; C Halton 80; P-in-c Newton Flowery Field 80-81; V 81-86; V Bredbury St Mark 86-96; rtd 96; Perm to Offic *Ches* from 96. *18 Wellbank, Sandbach, Cheshire CW11 0EP* Tel (01270) 764771

TOPPING, Roy William. b 37. MBE92. S Dios Minl Tr Scheme 91. **d** 92 **p** 93. Bahrain 89-94; Chapl Miss to Seamen Milford Haven from 94. *7A Castle Pill Road, Steynton, Milford Haven SA73 1HE* Tel (01646) 697572

TORDOFF, Donald William. b 45. Nottm Univ BA69. Qu Coll Birm 69. **d** 71 **p** 72. C High Harrogate Ch Ch *Ripon* 71-75; C Moor Allerton 75-80; V Bilton 80-92; R Spennithorne w Finghall and Hauxwell from 92. *The Rectory, Spennithorne, Leyburn, N Yorkshire DL8 5PR* Tel (01969) 623010 E-mail 101355.546@compuserve.com

TORDOFF (née PARKER), Mrs Margaret Grace. b 40. SRN65 SCM67. Cranmer Hall Dur 81. **dss** 83 **d** 87 **p** 94. Bilton *Ripon* 83-87; C 87-92; Chapl Spennithorne Hall from 92; NSM Spennithorne w Finghall and Hauxwell from 92. *The Rectory, Spennithorne, Leyburn, N Yorkshire DL8 5PR* Tel (01969) 623010

TORODE, Brian Edward. b 41. FCollP93 St Paul's Cheltenham TCert63 Poitiers Univ DFStuds62. W of England Minl Tr Course 90. **d** 93 **p** 94. Hd Master Elmfield Sch Cheltenham from 82; NSM Up Hatherley *Glouc* 93-94; NSM Cheltenham St Steph 93-95; NSM Cheltenham Em 94-95; NSM Cheltenham Em w St Steph from 95. *23 Arden Road, Leckhampton, Cheltenham, Glos GL53 0HG* Tel (01242) 231212

TORRENS, Robert Harrington. b 33. Trin Coll Cam BA56 MA61. Ridley Hall Cam 56. **d** 58 **p** 59. C Bromley SS Pet and Paul *Roch*

58-60; C Aylesbury *Ox* 60-63; V Eaton Socon *St Alb* 63-73; Lic to Offic 73-75; V Cheltenham All SS *Glouc* 75-84; Chapl Frenchay Hosp Bris 84-94; Chapl Manor Park Hosp Bris 84-94; rtd 94; Chapl St Pet Hospice Bris from 94. *21 Church Road, Winterbourne Down, Bristol BS17 1BX* Tel (01454) 775445

TORRY, Alan Kendall. b 33. Ex & Truro NSM Scheme. **d** 77 **p** 79. NSM Truro St Paul *Truro* 77-80; TV Probus, Ladock and Grampound w Creed and St Erme 80-84; P-in-c Gulval 84-88; V from 88; P-in-c Marazion 85-88; V from 88. *The Vicarage, Gulval, Penzance, Cornwall TR18 3BG* Tel (01736) 62699

TORRY, Malcolm Norman Alfred. b 55. St Jo Coll Cam BA76 MA80 Lon Univ BD78 K Coll Lon MTh79 PhD90. Cranmer Hall Dur 79. **d** 80 **p** 81. C S'wark H Trin w St Matt *S'wark* 80-83; C S'wark Ch Ch 83-88; Ind Chapl 83-88; V Hatcham St Cath 88-96; V E Greenwich Ch Ch w St Andr and St Mich 96-97; TR E Greenwich from 97. *St George's Vicarage, 89 Westcombe Park Road, London SE3 7RZ* Tel 0181-858 3006

TOSTEVIN, Alan Edwin John. b 41. BA. Trin Coll Bris 83. **d** 86 **p** 87. C Hildenborough *Roch* 86-89; TV Ipsley *Worc* from 89. *29 Sheldon Road, Redditch, Worcs B98 7QS* Tel (01527) 501092

TOTNES, Archdeacon of. *See* GILPIN, The Ven Richard Thomas

TOTTEN, Andrew James. b 64. QUB BA87 TCD BTh90. CITC. **d** 90 **p** 91. C Newtownards *D & D* 90-94; CF from 94. *MOD Chaplains (Army), Trenchard Lines, Upavon, Pewsey, Wilts SN9 6BE* Tel (01980) 615804 Fax 615800

TOTTERDELL, Mrs Rebecca Helen. b 57. Lon Bible Coll BA80. Oak Hill Th Coll 88. **d** 91 **p** 94. Par Dn Broxbourne w Wormley *St Alb* 91-94; C 94-95; C Stevenage St Nic from 95. *68A Fairview Road, Stevenage, Herts SG1 2NR* Tel (01438) 313164

TOTTY, Canon Lawrence Harold. b 07. Tyndale Hall Bris 46. **d** 46 **p** 47. BCMS 46-64; R Kingswood *Glouc* 65-72; rtd 72; Perm to Offic *Glouc* from 72. *10 Kingscote Close, Cheltenham, Glos GL51 6JU* Tel (01242) 522809

TOUCHSTONE, Grady Russell. b 32. Univ of S California 51. Wells Th Coll 63. **d** 65 **p** 66. C Maidstone St Mich *Cant* 65-70; USA from 70; rtd 95. *1069 South Gramercy Place, Los Angeles, California 90019-3634, USA* Tel Los Angeles (213) 731-5822

TOURNAY, Ms Corinne Marie Eliane Ghislaine. b 57. Louvain Univ Belgium Lic82 STB90 MA90. Cuddesdon Coll DipMin94. **d** 94 **p** 95. C Redhill St Jo *S'wark* from 94. *15 Earlsbrook Road, Redhill RH1 6DR* Tel (01737) 778834

TOVAR, Miss Gillian Elaine. b 48. Sussex Univ CertEd69. Trin Coll Bris BA86. **dss** 86 **d** 87 **p** 94. Tonbridge SS Pet and Paul *Roch* 86-87; Par Dn 87-94; C from 94. *2 Larch Crescent, Tonbridge, Kent TN10 3NN* Tel (01732) 361204

TOVEY, John Hamilton. b 50. Cant Univ (NZ) BA72. St Jo Coll Nottm DipTh78 DPS80. **d** 80 **p** 81. C Hyson Green *S'well* 80-83; New Zealand from 83. *13 Halswater Drive, Churton Park, Wellington, New Zealand* Tel Wellington (4) 478 4099 Fax 478 4087

TOVEY, Phillip Noel. b 56. Societas Liturgica MSLS Lon Univ BA77 Nottm Univ MPhil88. Lon Bible Coll BA83 St Jo Coll Nottm 85 Lambeth STh95. **d** 87 **p** 88. C Beaconsfield *Ox* 87-90; C Banbury 90-91; TV 91-95; P-in-c Holton and Waterperry w Albury and Waterstock 95-97; TV Wheatley from 97. *The Rectory, Holton, Oxford OX33 1PR* Tel (01865) 872460

TOVEY, Canon Ronald. b 27. AKC51. **d** 52 **p** 53. C Glossop *Derby* 52-55; C Chorlton upon Medlock *Man* 55-57; C Hulme St Phil 55-57; C Hulme St Jo 55-57; C Hulme H Trin 55-57; Malawi 57-69; Lesotho 69-85; Adn S Lesotho 77-85; Hon Can Lesotho Cathl 85-92; R Reddish *Man* 85-92; rtd 92; Perm to Offic *Pet* from 92. *86 Kings Road, Oakham, Leics LE15 6PD* Tel (01572) 770628

TOWARD, Stanley. b 25. Cranmer Hall Dur 65. **d** 66 **p** 67. C S Westoe *Dur* 66-69; V Swalwell 69-74; R Ryton 74-86; R Ryton w Hedgefield 86-91; rtd 91. *3 Orchard Close, Rowlands Gill, Tyne & Wear NE39 1EQ* Tel (01207) 542092

TOWELL, Alan. b 37. Sarum & Wells Th Coll 86 WMMTC 87. **d** 89 **p** 90. C Boultham *Linc* 89-93; P-in-c Scunthorpe Resurr from 93. *The Vicarage, Mirfield Road, Scunthorpe, S Humberside DN15 8AN* Tel (01724) 842196

TOWELL, Geoffrey Leonard. b 37. K Coll Lon BA59. Linc Th Coll 59. **d** 61 **p** 62. C Ashbourne w Mapleton *Derby* 61-65; C Claxby w Normanby-le-Wold *Linc* 65-67; V Alkborough w Whitton 67-80; R W Halton 68-80; P-in-c Winteringham 75-80; V Alkborough 81-85; Dioc Ecum Officer 85-91; rtd 91. *40 Lady Frances Drive, Market Rasen, Lincoln LN8 3JJ* Tel (01673) 843983

TOWELL, Canon John William. b 16. St Jo Coll Dur BA38 MA41. **d** 39 **p** 40. C Stockton St Paul *Dur* 39-43; P-in-c Evenwood 43-44; Chapl RAFVR 44-47; P-in-c S Shields H Trin *Dur* 47-48; Tutor St Jo Coll Dur 48-50; PC Gateshead Ven Bede *Dur* 48-50; V Cambo *Newc* 50-59; P-in-c Kirkheaton 50-52; V Kirkharle 52-59; Chapl and Asst Master Harrogate Coll 59-67; Lic to Offic *Ripon* 59-67; R Leathley w Farnley *Bradf* 62-67; Can Res Bradf Cathl 67-77; rtd 77; Perm to Offic *Bradf* 77-94; Perm to Offic *S'wark* from 94. *22 Dobell Road, London SE9 1HE* Tel 0181-850 2408

TOWERS, Canon David Francis. b 32. G&C Coll Cam BA56 MA60. Clifton Th Coll 56. **d** 58 **p** 59. C Gresley *Derby* 58-63; V Brixton St Paul *S'wark* 63-75; V Chatteris *Ely* 75-87; RD March 82-87; Hon Can Ely Cathl 85-87; R Burnley St Pet *Blackb* from 87. *The Rectory, 42 Pasturegate, Burnley, Lancs BB11 4DE* Tel (01282) 413599

TOWERS, John Keble. b 19. Keble Coll Ox BA41 MA57. Edin Th Coll 41. **d** 43 **p** 44. Chapl Dundee St Paul *Bre* 43-47; India 47-62; R Edin Ch Ch-St Jas *Edin* 62-71; V Bradf St Oswald Chapel Green *Bradf* 71-78; P-in-c Holme Cultram St Mary *Carl* 78-80; V 80-85; rtd 85; Perm to Offic *Glas* 85-92; Hon C Moffat from 92. *Achnacarry, Harthope Place, Moffat, Dumfriesshire DG10 9HX* Tel (01683) 221232

TOWERS, Canon Patrick Leo. b 43. AKC68 Hull Univ CertEd69. **d** 74 **p** 75. Japan 74-81; TV Bourne Valley *Sarum* 81-83; Dioc Youth Officer 81-83; Chapl Oundle Sch 83-86; I Rathkeale w Askeaton and Kilcornan *L & K* 86-89; RD Limerick 88-89; I Nenagh from 89; Can Limerick, Killaloe and Clonfert Cathls from 97. *St Mary's Rectory, Church Road, Nenagh, Co Tipperary, Irish Republic* Tel Nenagh (67) 32598 Fax as telephone

TOWERS, Terence John. b 33. AKC60. **d** 61 **p** 62. C Bishopwearmouth Gd Shep *Dur* 61-65; V Runham *Nor* 65-67; R Stokesby w Herringby 65-67; V Ushaw Moor *Dur* 67-93; rtd 93. *8 Beech Court, Langley Park, Durham DH7 9XL* Tel 0191-373 0210

TOWLER, David George. b 42. Cranmer Hall Dur 73. **d** 76 **p** 77. C Newbarns w Hawcoat *Carl* 76-80; V Huyton St Geo *Liv* from 80. *St George's Vicarage, 1 St George's Road, Huyton, Liverpool L36 8BE* Tel 0151-489 1997

TOWLER, John Frederick. b 42. Bps' Coll Cheshunt 63. **d** 66 **p** 67. C Lowestoft St Marg *Nor* 66-71; R Horstead 71-77; Warden Dioc Conf Ho Horstead 71-77; Prec Worc Cathl *Worc* 77-81; Min Can Worc Cathl 78-81. *The Thatched Cottage, Ibsley Drove, Ibsley, Ringwood, Hants BH24 3NW* Tel (01425) 653299

TOWLSON, Arthur Stanley. b 20. St Jo Coll Dur LTh48 BA49 ALCD48. **d** 50 **p** 51. R Blithfield *Lich* 57-70; R Colton 57-70; R Longton St Jas 70-71; Lic to Offic 71-78; P-in-c Checkley 78-84; P-in-c Croxden 78-84; rtd 85; Perm to Offic *Lich* from 85. *4 The Close, Lichfield, Staffs WS13 7LD* Tel (01543) 258608

TOWLSON, George Eric. b 40. N Ord Course 80. **d** 83 **p** 84. NSM Wakef St Andr and St Mary *Wakef* 83-84; NSM Ox St Mich w St Martin and All SS *Ox* 84-86; Perm to Offic 86-87; NSM Hoar Cross w Newchurch *Lich* 87-93; C Wednesbury St Paul Wood Green from 93. *St Luke's House, 33 Oldbury Street, Wednesbury, W Midlands WS10 0QJ* Tel 0121-556 0443

TOWNDROW, The Ven Frank Noel. b 11. K Coll Cam BA34 MA38. Coll of Resurr Mirfield 35. **d** 37 **p** 38. C Chingford SS Pet and Paul *Chelmsf* 37-40; Chapl RAFVR 40-47; P-in-c Grangemouth *Edin* 47-48; R 48-51; V Kirton in Lindsey *Linc* 51-53; R Manton 51-53; R Greenford H Cross *Lon* 53-62; V E Haddon *Pet* 62-66; R Holdenby 62-66; V Ravensthorpe 63-66; Can Res Pet Cathl 66-77; Adn Oakham 67-77; Chapl to The Queen 75-81; rtd 77; Perm to Offic *Pet* 77-96. *17 Croake Hill, Swinstead, Grantham, Lincs NG33 4PE* Tel (01476) 550478

TOWNE, David William. b 34. St Jo Coll Dur BA58. Cranmer Hall Dur DipTh60. **d** 60 **p** 61. C Bromley St Jo *Roch* 60-63; Lect Watford St Mary *St Alb* 63-66; V Prestonville St Luke *Chich* 66-73; R Slaugham 73-79; V Wilmington *Roch* 79-85; V Otford 85-96; rtd 96; Perm to Offic *Chich* from 96; Perm to Offic *Roch* from 96. *Holly House, 7 The Coppice, Battle, E Sussex TN33 0UJ* Tel (01424) 775957

TOWNEND, John Philip. b 52. Southn Univ BTh95. Sarum & Wells Th Coll 89. **d** 91 **p** 92. C Sherborne w Castleton and Lillington *Sarum* 91-95; P-in-c Wool and E Stoke from 95. *The Vicarage, Wool, Wareham, Dorset BH20 6EB* Tel (01929) 462215

TOWNEND, Noel Alexander Fortescue. b 06. Selw Coll Cam BA28 MA32. Cuddesdon Coll 29. **d** 30 **p** 32. C Freemantle *Win* 30-34; Australia 34-40; Chapl RAFVR 40-47; R Week St Mary *Truro* 47-55; V Port Isaac 55-73; rtd 73; Hon C N Petherton w Northmoor Green *B & W* 73-95; Perm to Offic from 95. *4 Tappers Lane, North Petherton, Bridgwater, Somerset TA6 6SH* Tel (01278) 663279

TOWNER, Preb Paul. b 51. Bris Univ BSc72 BTh81. Oak Hill Th Coll 78. **d** 81 **p** 82. C Aspley *S'well* 81-84; R Gt Hanwood *Heref* from 84; RD Pontesbury from 93; Preb Heref Cathl from 96. *The Rectory, Hanwood, Shrewsbury SY5 8LJ* Tel (01743) 860074

TOWNLEY, Peter Kenneth. b 55. Sheff Univ BA78 Man Univ DSPT87. Ridley Hall Cam 78. **d** 80 **p** 81. C Ashton Ch Ch *Man* 80-83; C-in-c Holts CD 83-88; R Stretford All SS 88-96; V Ipswich St Mary-le-Tower *St E* from 96. *St Mary le Tower Vicarage, 8 Fonnereau Road, Ipswich IP1 3JP* Tel (01473) 252770

TOWNLEY, The Very Revd Robert Keith. b 44. St Jo Coll Auckland LTh67. **d** 67 **p** 68. New Zealand 67-70; C Lisburn Ch Ch *Conn* 71-74; C Portman Square St Paul *Lon* 75-80; Chan Cork Cathl *C, C & R* 82-94; Dean Ross 82-94; I Ross Union 82-94; Dean Kildare *M & K* from 95; Hon CF from 95; I Kildare, Edenderry, Naas and Newbridge *M & K* from 95. *Dean's House, Curragh Camp, Co Kildare, Irish Republic* Tel Kildare (45) 441654

TOWNLEY, Roger. b 46. Man Univ BSc York Univ MSc. St Deiniol's Hawarden 82. **d** 84 **p** 85. C Longton *Blackb* 84-88; V Penwortham St Leon 88-92; V Wrightington from 92; Chapl

Wrightington Hosp from 92. *The Vicarage, Church Lane, Wrightington, Wigan, Lancs WN6 9SL* Tel (01257) 451332

TOWNROE, Canon Edward John. b 20. St Jo Coll Ox BA42 MA48. Linc Th Coll 42. **d** 43 **p** 44. C Sunderland *Dur* 43-48; Chapl St Boniface Coll Warminster 48-56; Warden 56-69; Lic to Offic *Sarum* 48-93; Can and Preb Sarum Cathl 69-93; rtd 85. *St Boniface Lodge, Church Street, Warminster, Wilts BA12 8PG* Tel (01985) 212355

TOWNROE, Canon Michael Dakeyne. b 15. Linc Th Coll 35. **d** 38 **p** 39. C Grantham *Linc* 38-41; C W Grinstead *Chich* 41-44; C Pulborough 44-47; R Graffham w Woolavington 47-59; Chapl St Mich Sch Burton Park 47-59; RD Petworth *Chich* 56-59; R Bexhill St Pet 59-82; RD Battle and Bexhill 64-77; Can and Preb Chich Cathl 69-82; rtd 82; Perm to Offic *Chich* from 82. *Pax, Pett Road, Pett, Hastings, E Sussex TN35 4HE* Tel (01424) 813381

TOWNSEND, Allan Harvey. b 43. WMMTC 89. **d** 92 **p** 93. NSM Fenton *Lich* 92-96; C Tividale from 96. *14 Gladstone Drive, Tividale, Warley, W Midlands B69 3LF* Tel 0121-557 5402

TOWNSEND, Dr Anne Jennifer. b 38. MRCS60 LRCP60 Lon Univ MB, BS60. S'wark Ord Course 88. **d** 91 **p** 94. NSM Wandsworth St Paul *S'wark* from 91; Chapl Asst St Geo Hosp Tooting 91-92; Dean MSE from 93. *89E Victoria Drive, London SW19 6PT* Tel 0181-785 7675

TOWNSEND, Christopher Robin. b 47. St Jo Coll Nottm LTh74. **d** 74 **p** 75. C Gt Horton *Bradf* 74-77; C Heaton St Barn 77-78; C Wollaton *S'well* 78-80; V Slaithwaite w E Scammonden *Wakef* from 80. *The Vicarage, Station Road, Slaithwaite, Huddersfield HD7 5AW* Tel (01484) 842748

TOWNSEND, Dr Derek William (Bill). b 52. Fitzw Coll Cam BA74 Man Univ PhD89. St Jo Coll Nottm DTS91. **d** 91 **p** 92. C Hazlemere *Ox* 91-95; C Banbury 95; TV from 95. *St Paul's House, Prescott Avenue, Banbury, Oxon OX16 0LR* Tel (01295) 264003

TOWNSEND, Mrs Diane Rosalind (Di). b 45. Stockwell Coll of Educn CertEd66 K Alfred's Coll Win BEd88. Sarum Th Coll 93. **d** 96 **p** 97. NSM Botley *Portsm* from 96; NSM Curdridge from 96; NSM Durley from 96. *9 Daisy Lane, Locks Heath, Southampton SO31 6RA* Tel (01489) 574945

TOWNSEND, Canon John Clifford. b 24. St Edm Hall Ox BA48 MA49. Wells Th Coll. **d** 50 **p** 51. C Machen *Mon* 50-51; C Usk and Monkswood w Glascoed Chpl and Gwehelog 51-55; R Melbury Osmond w Melbury Sampford *Sarum* 55-60; Chapl RNVR 57-58; Chapl RNR 58-75; V Branksome St Aldhelm *Sarum* 60-70; R Melksham 70-73; TR 73-80; Can and Preb Sarum Cathl 72-90; RD Bradford 73-80; P-in-c Harnham 80-81; V 81-90; RD Salisbury 80-85; rtd 90. *19 Wyke Oliver Close, Preston, Weymouth, Dorset DT3 6DR* Tel (01305) 833641

TOWNSEND, John Elliott. b 39. ALCD63. **d** 64 **p** 65. C Harold Wood *Chelmsf* 64-68; C Walton *St E* 68-72; V Kensal Rise St Martin *Lon* 72-83; V Hornsey Ch Ch from 83. *Christ Church Vicarage, 32 Crescent Road, London N8 8AX* Tel 0181-340 1566

TOWNSEND, John Errington. b 20. St Aug Coll Cant 64. **d** 65 **p** 66. C Alverstoke *Portsm* 65-69; R Droxford 69-74; Soc Work Org Sec 74-78; Perm to Offic from 82; rtd 85. *Greytiles, Frogmore, East Meon, Petersfield, Hants GU32 1QQ* Tel (01730) 823374

TOWNSEND, Mark Timothy. b 67. Aston Tr Scheme 93 Cuddesdon Coll 93. **d** 96 **p** 97. C Ludlow, Ludford, Ashford Carbonell etc *Heref* from 96. *St Giles' Vicarage, Street Road, Ludlow, Shropshire SY8 1LR* Tel (01584) 876090

TOWNSEND, Peter. b 35. AKC63. **d** 64 **p** 65. C Norbury St Oswald *Cant* 64-67; C New Romney w Hope 67-69; C Westborough *Guildf* 69-74; P-in-c Wicken *Pet* 74-87; R Paulerspury 74-84; P-in-c Whittlebury w Silverstone 82-84; V Whittlebury w Paulerspury 84-87; V Greetham and Thistleton w Stretton and Clipsham from 87. *The Vicarage, Greetham, Oakham, Leics LE15 7NF* Tel (01572) 812015

TOWNSEND, Peter. b 37. Open Univ BA87. Wells Th Coll 67. **d** 69 **p** 70. C Desborough *Pet* 69-72; C Bramley *Ripon* 72-75; C-in-c Newton Hall LEP *Dur* 75-80; P-in-c Newton Hall 80-81; V Hartlepool St Luke from 81. *St Luke's Vicarage, 5 Tunstall Avenue, Hartlepool TS26 8NF* Tel (01429) 272893

TOWNSEND, Philip Roger. b 51. Sheff Univ BA78. Trin Coll Bris 78. **d** 80 **p** 81. C W Streatham St Jas *S'wark* 80-85; C Ardsley *Sheff* 85-88; V Crookes St Tim from 88. *St Timothy's Vicarage, 152 Slinn Street, Sheffield S10 1NZ* Tel 0114-266 1745

TOWNSEND, Robert William. b 68. Univ of Wales (Ban) BA90. St Mich Coll Llan BTh93. **d** 93 **p** 95. C Dolgellau w Llanfachreth and Brithdir etc *Ban* 93-94; Min Can Ban Cathl 94-96; P-in-c Amlwch from 96. *The Rectory, Bull Bay Road, Amlwch LL68 9EA* Tel (01407) 830740

TOWNSHEND, Charles Hume. b 41. St Pet Coll Ox BA64 MA69. Westcott Ho Cam 64. **d** 66 **p** 67. C Warlingham w Chelsham and Farleigh *S'wark* 66-75; R Old Cleeve, Leighland and Treborough *B & W* 75-85; R Bishops Lydeard w Bagborough and Cothelstone 85-95; V N Curry from 95. *The Vicarage, North Curry, Taunton, Somerset TA3 6JZ* Tel (01823) 490255

TOWNSHEND, David William. b 57. Lon Univ PGCE80 Ox Univ MA85. Cranmer Hall Dur 81. **d** 84 **p** 85. C Barking St Marg w St Patr *Chelmsf* 84-87; Canada from 87. *PO Box 116, 15 Carleton Street, Newboro, Ontario, Canada, K0G 1P0* Tel Kingston (613) 272-2664

TOWNSHEND, Edward George Hume. b 43. Pemb Coll Cam BA66 MA70. Westcott Ho Cam 68. **d** 70 **p** 71. C Hellesdon *Nor* 70-74; Ind Chapl 74-81; TV Lowestoft St Marg 74-79; TV Lowestoft and Kirkley 79-81; V Stafford St Jo *Lich* 81-85; P-in-c Tixall w Ingestre 81-85; V Stafford St Jo and Tixall w Ingestre 85-87; R Lich St Chad from 87; RD Lich from 94; P-in-c Hammerwich 94-96. *St Chad's Rectory, The Windings, Lichfield, Staffs WS13 7EX* Tel (01543) 262254

TOWNSON, Eric James. b 34. St Aid Birkenhead 60. **d** 62 **p** 63. C Heysham *Blackb* 62-65; C Preston St Jo 65-69; Rwanda 69-74; C Burley *Ripon* 74-85; V 85-87; P-in-c Kelbrook *Bradf* 87-94; Dioc Adv in Evang 87-94; rtd 94. *10 Nelson Street, Lytham, Lytham St Annes, Lancs FY8 4AB* Tel (01253) 731640

TOWSE, Anthony Norman Beresford. b 21. Linc Coll Ox BA48 MA72. Westcott Ho Cam 48. **d** 50 **p** 51. C Beeston *S'well* 50-55; C Norbury St Oswald *Cant* 57-60; C Tenterden St Mildred w Smallhythe 60-64; V Appledore 64-72; V Appledore w Stone in Oxney and Ebony 72-75; V Appledore w Stone in Oxney and Ebony etc 75-82; RD S Lympne 81-90; V Appledore w Brookland, Fairfield, Brenzett etc 82-90; rtd 90; Perm to Offic *Cant* from 90. *3 Oaks Road, Tenterden, Kent TN30 6RD* Tel (01580) 766402

TOY, Elizabeth Margaret. b 37. NDAD59 CQSW77. Oak Hill NSM Course 85. **d** 88 **p** 94. NSM Hildenborough *Roch* from 88. *2 Francis Cottages, London Road, Hildenborough, Tonbridge, Kent TN11 8NQ* Tel (01732) 833886

TOY, Canon John. b 30. Hatf Coll Dur BA53 MA62 Leeds Univ PhD82. Wells Th Coll 53. **d** 55 **p** 56. C Newington St Paul *S'wark* 55-58; S Sec SCM 58-60; Chapl Ely Th Coll 60-64; Chapl Gothenburg w Halmstad and Jonkoping *Eur* 65-69; Asst Chapl St Jo Coll York 69-72; Sen Lect 72-79; Prin Lect 79-83; Can Res and Chan York Minster *York* from 83. *4 Minster Yard, York YO1 2JF* Tel (01904) 620877

TOZE, Stephen James. b 51. Birm Univ BA79. Qu Coll Birm 76 Westcott Ho Cam 93. **d** 93 **p** 94. C Leominster *Heref* 93-94; R Gt Brickhill w Bow Brickhill and Lt Brickhill *Ox* from 94; Rural Officer Buckm Adnry from 95. *The Rectory, 6 Rushmere Close, Bow Brickhill, Milton Keynes MK17 9JB* Tel (01908) 642086

TOZER, Frank William. b 21. Open Univ BSc94. Wells Th Coll 61. **d** 63 **p** 64. C Kemp Town St Mark *Chich* 63-65; C Crawley 65-73; V Heathfield 73-87; rtd 87; Perm to Offic *Chich* from 87. *30 Orchid Close, Eastbourne, E Sussex BN23 8DE* Tel (01323) 768270

TOZER, Reginald Ernest. b 25. St Aid Birkenhead 57. **d** 59 **p** 60. C Plaistow St Andr *Chelmsf* 59-62; P-in-c Clayton *Lich* 62-69; V E Ham w Upton Park *Chelmsf* 69-75; V Hatfield Peverel w Ulting 75-91; rtd 91. *Basil's Place, 4 Church Road, Snape, Saxmundham, Suffolk IP17 1SZ* Tel (01728) 688895

TRACEY, Thomas Patrick. b 14. Sarum Th Coll 54. **d** 56 **p** 57. C Claines St Geo *Worc* 56-59; C Newbury St Jo *Ox* 59-61; V Edlesborough 61-71; R Rotherfield Peppard 71-75; P-in-c Stadhampton w Chislehampton 75-77; P-in-c Warborough 75-77; TV Dorchester 78-81; rtd 81; Perm to Offic *Ox* from 85. *Gracey Court, Woodland Road, Broadclyst, Exeter EX5 3LP* Tel (01392) 461714

TRAFFORD, Mrs Joyce. b 35. N Ord Course 84. **d** 87 **p** 94. Par Dn Chapelthorpe *Wakef* 87-94; C from 94. *1 Gillion Crescent, Durkar, Wakefield, W Yorkshire WF4 6PP* Tel (01924) 252033

TRAFFORD, Peter. b 39. Chich Th Coll. **d** 83 **p** 84. C Bath Bathwick *B & W* 83-86; Chapl RN 86-90; P-in-c Donnington *Chich* from 90. *The Vicarage, 65 Stockbridge Road, Donnington, Chichester, W Sussex PO20 2QE* Tel (01243) 776395

TRAFFORD-ROBERTS, Rosamond Jane (Ros). b 40. Qu Coll Birm 93. **d** 95 **p** 96. C Ledbury w Eastnor *Heref* from 95. *Old Colwall House, Malvern, Worcs WR13 6HF* Tel (01684) 540618 Fax as telephone

TRAILL, Geoffrey Conway. b 58. Ridley Coll Melbourne BA82 BTh87. **d** 85 **p** 85. Australia 85-87 and from 88; C Shrub End *Chelmsf* 87-88. *8 Rodborough Crescent, Corio, Victoria, Australia 3214* Tel Geelong (52) 754597

TRAPNELL, Canon Stephen Hallam. b 30. G&C Coll Cam BA53 MA57. Ridley Hall Cam 53 Virginia Th Sem BD56 MDiv70. **d** 56 **p** 57. C Upper Tulse Hill St Matthias *S'wark* 56-59; C Reigate St Mary 59-61; V Richmond Ch Ch 61-72; P-in-c Sydenham H Trin 72-80; R Worting *Win* 80-92; Field Officer Decade of Evang 92-96; Can Shyogwe (Rwanda) from 93; rtd 96. *Downs Cottage, Rivar Road, Shalbourne, Marlborough, Wilts SN8 3QE* Tel (01672) 870514 Fax as telephone

TRASK, Mrs Marion. b 54. Leic Univ BSc75 Brunel Univ PGCE76. Moorlands Bible Coll 82 Oak Hill Th Coll 93. **d** 96 **p** 97. C Bermondsey St Mary w St Olave, St Jo etc *S'wark* from 96. *22 Reverdy Road, London SE1 5QE* Tel 0171-237 9385

TRASLER, Graham Charles George. b 44. Ch Ch Ox BA65 MA69. Cuddesdon Coll 66. **d** 68 **p** 69. C Gateshead St Mary *Dur* 68-71; P-in-c Monkwearmouth St Pet 71-79; P-in-c Bentley *Guildf* 79; P-in-c Binsted *Win* 79; R Bentley and Binsted 80-84; R New Alresford w Ovington and Itchen Stoke from 84. *The Rectory, 37 Jacklyns Lane, Alresford, Hants SO24 9LF* Tel (01962) 732105

TRAVERS, Colin James. b 49. St Pet Coll Ox BA70 MA74. Ridley Hall Cam 70. **d** 72 **p** 73. C Hornchurch St Andr *Chelmsf* 72-75;

Youth Chapl 75-77; C Aldersbrook 75-77; V Barkingside St Laur 77-82; V Waltham Abbey 82-88; V S Weald 88-95; Co-ord N Thames Minl Tr Course from 95; Hon C Gt Warley and Ingrave St Nic from 95. *The Vicarage, Thorndon Gate, Ingrave, Brentwood, Essex CM13 3RG* Tel (01277) 812190

TRAVERS, John William. b 48. Open Univ BA84 Hull Univ MA86. Linc Th Coll 75. **d** 78 **p** 79. C Headingley *Ripon* 78-81; TV Louth *Linc* 81-89; P-in-c Shingay Gp of Par *Ely* 89; V 90-95; V Hamble le Rice *Win* from 95. *The Vicarage, Hamble, Southampton SO31 4JF* Tel (01703) 452148

TRAVERSE, Ernest. b 28. Oak Hill Th Coll 73. **d** 75 **p** 76. C Roby *Liv* 75-76; C Rainhill 76-78; V Wigan St Barn Marsh Green 78-80; TV Bemerton *Sarum* 80-83; C Hednesford *Lich* 83-86; rtd 86; Perm to Offic *Liv* from 86. *20 Ashgrove Crescent, Billinge, Wigan, Lancs WN5 7NH* Tel (01744) 894257

TRAVIS, Robert Leonard. b 15. Sarum Th Coll 55. **d** 56 **p** 57. C Rowner *Portsm* 56-57; P-in-c Bridgemary 57-58; V Everton Em *Liv* 59-61; Chapl Mill Road Hosp Everton 59-61; V Sevenoaks Weald *Roch* 61-66; rtd 66. *PO Box 680, Nelson, New Zealand*

TRAYNOR, Nigel Martin Arthur. b 58. St Jo Coll Nottm 94. **d** 96 **p** 97. C Wellington, All SS w Eyton *Lich* from 96. *1 Stile Rise, Shawbirch, Telford, Shropshire TF5 0LR* Tel (01952) 641229

TREADGOLD, The Very Revd John David. b 31. LVO90. Nottm Univ BA58. Wells Th Coll 58. **d** 59 **p** 60. V Choral S'well Minster *S'well* 59-64; CF (TA) 62-67 and 74-78; R Wollaton *S'well* 64-74; V Darlington St Cuth w St Hilda *Dur* 74-81; Chapl in the Gt Park 81-89; Can Windsor 81-89; Chapl to The Queen 81-89; Dean Chich from 89. *The Deanery, Chichester, W Sussex PO19 1PX* Tel (01243) 783286 or 787337

TREANOR, Canon Desmond Victor. b 28. St Jo Coll Dur BA53 DipTh54 MA59. **d** 54 **p** 55. C Oakwood St Thos *Lon* 54-57; C Sudbury St Andr 57-59; V Lansdown *B & W* 59-66; V Derby St Werburgh *Derby* 66-68; V Leic St Anne *Leic* 68-75; V Humberstone 75-86; Hon Can Leic Cathl 78-93; P-in-c Leic St Eliz Nether Hall 81-86; RD Christianity N 82-86; R Gt Bowden w Welham, Glooston and Cranoe 86-93; RD Gartree I 88-93; rtd 93; Perm to Offic *Leic* from 93; Perm to Offic *Pet* from 93. *5 Brookfield Way, Kibworth, Leicester LE8 0SA* Tel 0116-279 2750

TREANOR, Terence Gerald. b 29. St Jo Coll Ox BA52 MA56. Wycliffe Hall Ox 52. **d** 54 **p** 55. C Hornsey Ch Ch *Lon* 54-57; C Cambridge H Trin *Ely* 57-60; V Doncaster St Mary *Sheff* 60-66; Chapl Oakham Sch 66-94; Lic to Offic *Pet* 66-94; rtd 94; Perm to Offic *Leic* from 94; Perm to Offic *Linc* from 94; Perm to Offic *Pet* from 94. *35 Glebe Way, Oakham, Leics LE15 6LX* Tel (01572) 757495

TREASURE, Andrew Stephen. b 51. Or Coll Ox BA73 MA77. St Jo Coll Nottm BA76. **d** 77 **p** 78. C Beverley Minster *York* 77-81; C Cambridge H Trin *Ely* 81-84; C Cambridge H Trin w St Andr Gt 84-85; V Eccleshill *Bradf* from 85. *The Vicarage, Fagley Lane, Eccleshill, Bradford, W Yorkshire BD2 3NS* Tel (01274) 636403

TREASURE, Geoffrey. b 39. Hatf Coll Dur BA61 Univ of Wales (Cardiff) DipEd62. Oak Hill NSM Course 90. **d** 93 **p** 94. NSM Forty Hill Jes Ch *Lon* 93-94; Perm to Offic *B & W* from 94. *Gable Cottage, West Lyng, Taunton, Somerset TA3 5AP* Tel (01823) 490548

TREASURE, Mrs Joy Elvira. b 23. St Anne's Coll Ox MA50 CertEd. S Dios Minl Tr Scheme 80. **dss** 82 **d** 87 **p** 94. Tisbury *Sarum* 82-87; Hon Par Dn 87-91; rtd 92; Perm to Offic *Sarum* from 92. *Friars Lodge, The Friary, Salisbury SP1 2HU* Tel (01722) 333741

TREASURE, Ronald Charles. b 24. Or Coll Ox BA48 MA52. Cuddesdon Coll. **d** 50 **p** 51. C Whitby *York* 50-54; C-in-c N Hull St Mich 54-58; V 58-62; V New Malton 62-89; RD Malton 63-75; rtd 89; Perm to Offic *York* from 89. *Castle Walls, Castlegate, Kirkbymoorside, York YO6 6BW* Tel (01751) 32916

TREBLE, Harry. b 06. Lon Univ BD55 BA61. AKC32. **d** 32 **p** 33. C Stamford Hill St Bart *Lon* 32-34; C S Hackney St Jo w Ch Ch 34-42; V Epping Upland *Chelmsf* 42-49; CF 43-46; Hon CF 46; P-in-c Barkingside St Cedd *Chelmsf* 49-61; V 61-83; rtd 83. *8 Fairlight Avenue, Woodford Green, Essex IG8 9JP*

TREBY, David Alan. b 47. FIBMS72 Bris Poly MSc90. St Jo Coll Nottm DTS94 MA95. **d** 95 **p** 96. C Camborne *Truro* from 95. *6 St Meriadoc Road, Camborne, Cornwall TR14 7HL* Tel (01209) 613160

TREDENNICK, Angela Nicolette (Nicky). b 38. SRN62 SCM63 Lon Inst of Educn HVCert66. S'wark Ord Course 87. **d** 90 **p** 94. NSM Charlwood *S'wark* 90-92; Par Dn Roehampton H Trin 92-94; C from 94; RD Wandsworth from 95. *The Manse, Minstead Gardens, London SW15 4EB* Tel 0181-878 7682

TREE, Robin Leslie. b 46. S Dios Minl Tr Scheme 89. **d** 92 **p** 93. NSM St Leonards Ch Ch and St Mary *Chich* 92-95; NSM Hastings H Trin from 95. *30 The Links, St Leonards-on-Sea, E Sussex TN38 0UW* Tel (01424) 433289

TREEBY, Stephen Frank. b 46. Man Univ LLB67 Nottm Univ DipTh69. Cuddesdon Coll 69. **d** 71 **p** 72. C Ashbourne w Mapleton *Derby* 71-74; C Boulton 74-76; Chapl Trowbridge Coll *Sarum* 76-79; TV Melksham 79-87; V Dilton Marsh from 87; Chapl Westbury Hosp from 87. *The Vicarage, The Hollows, Dilton Marsh, Westbury, Wilts BA13 4BU* Tel (01373) 822560

TREEN, Anthony Robert. b 37. Chich Th Coll 72. **d** 74 **p** 75. C Haywards Heath St Rich *Chich* 74-77; Ind Chapl 77-80; V Burgess Hill St Jo 80-85; P-in-c Walpole St Andrew *Ely* 85-86; P-in-c Walpole St Peter 85-86; R Walpole St Peter w Walpole St Andrew from 86; P-in-c W Walton from 87; P-in-c Marshland St James 94-96; RD Lynn Marshland from 94. *The Rectory, Walpole St Peter, Wisbech, Cambs PE14 7NS* Tel (01945) 780252

TREEN, Preb Robert Hayes Mortlock. b 19. New Coll Ox BA46 MA46. Westcott Ho Cam 45. **d** 47 **p** 48. C Bath Abbey w St Jas *B & W* 47-52; PC Pill 52-61; R Bath St Sav 61-76; Preb Wells Cathl 74-84; V Bishops Hull 76-84; RD Taunton S 77-81; RD Taunton 81-84; rtd 84; Perm to Offic *B & W* from 84. *13 The Leat, Bishops Lydeard, Taunton, Somerset TA4 3NY* Tel (01823) 433437

TREETOPS, Ms Jacqueline. b 47. NE Ord Course 83. **dss** 86 **d** 87 **p** 94. Low Harrogate St Mary *Ripon* 86-87; C Roundhay St Edm 87-95; C Potternewton 95-97; rtd 97. *8 Granton Road, Leeds LS7 3LZ* Tel 0113-262 6225

TREFUSIS, Charles Rodolph. b 61. Hull Univ BA83. Wycliffe Hall Ox 85. **d** 90 **p** 91. C Blackheath St Jo *S'wark* 90-94; V Purley Ch Ch from 94. *The Vicarage, 38 Woodcote Valley Road, Purley, Surrey CR8 3AJ* Tel 0181-660 1790

TREHERNE, Canon Alan Thomas Evans. b 30. Univ of Wales (Lamp) BA53. Wycliffe Hall Ox. **d** 55 **p** 56. C Heref St Pet w St Owen *Heref* 55-57; India 57-72; C-in-c Netherley Ch Ch CD *Liv* 72-74; R Gateacre 74-75; TR 75-96; RD Farnworth 81-89; Hon Can Liv Cathl 94-96; rtd 96; Perm to Offic *Lich* from 96. *19 Smale Rise, Oswestry, Shropshire SY11 2YL*

TRELLIS, The Very Revd Oswald Fitz-Burnell (Ossie). b 35. Chich Th Coll 73. **d** 74 **p** 75. C Chelmsf All SS *Chelmsf* 74-78; C-in-c N Springfield CD 79-85; V Heybridge w Langford 85-94; Dean Georgetown from 94. *The Deanery, 79 Carmichael Street, Georgetown, Guyana*

TREMBATH, Martyn Anthony. b 65. Leeds Univ BA86. Ripon Coll Cuddesdon. **d** 90 **p** 91. C Bodmin w Lanhydrock and Lanivet *Truro* 90-91; C St Erth 92-96; C Phillack w Gwithian and Gwinear 94-96; C Hayle 94-96; Asst Chapl R Free Hampstead NHS Trust from 96. *The Chaplain's Office, Royal Free Hospital, Pond Street, London NW3 2QG* Tel 0171-794 0500

TREMELLING, Peter Ian. b 53. Ex & Truro NSM Scheme 94. **d** 96. NSM St Illogan *Truro* from 96. *88A Sunnyside Parc Illogan, Redruth, Cornwall TR15 3LX* Tel (01209) 213322

TREMLETT, Andrew. b 64. Pemb Coll Cam BA86 Qu Coll Ox BA88. Wycliffe Hall Ox 86. **d** 89 **p** 90. C Torquay St Matthias, St Mark and H Trin *Ex* 89-92; Miss to Seamen 92-94; Asst Chapl Rotterdam *Eur* 92-94; Chapl 94-95; TV Fareham H Trin *Portsm* from 95. *St Columba Vicarage, Hillson Drive, Fareham, Hants PO15 6PF* Tel (01329) 843705

TREMLETT, The Ven Anthony Frank (Tony). b 37. Ex & Truro NSM Scheme 78. **d** 81 **p** 82. C Southway *Ex* 81-82; P-in-c 82-84; V 84-88; RD Plymouth Moorside 86-88; Adn Totnes 88-94; Adn Ex and Preb Ex Cathl from 94. *St Matthew's House, Spicer Road, Exeter EX1 1TA* Tel (01392) 425432 Fax as telephone

TRENCHARD, Hubert John. b 26. S Dios Minl Tr Scheme. **d** 83 **p** 84. NSM Sturminster Marshall *Sarum* 83-87; NSM Blandford Forum and Langton Long 87-96. *20 Chapel Gardens, Blandford Forum, Dorset DT11 7UY* Tel (01258) 459576

TRENCHARD, Hugh. b 50. St Mich Coll Llan BD75. **d** 75 **p** 76. C Caerleon *Mon* 75-80; Dioc Chapl GFS 78-86; Asst Chapl Mon Sch 80-84; V Llanarth w Clytha, Llansantffraed and Bryngwyn *Mon* 80-84; TV Cyncoed 84-93; Prov Officer for Soc Resp 94-96; V Caerwent w Dinham and Llanfair Discoed etc from 96. *The Vicarage, Vicarage Gardens, Caerwent, Newport NP6 4BF* Tel (01291) 424984

TRENCHARD, Paul Charles Herbert Anstiss. b 53. Liv Univ LLB76. St Steph Ho Ox 77. **d** 80 **p** 81. C Torquay St Martin Barton *Ex* 80-84; R Ashprington, Cornworthy and Dittisham 84-92; R Barnwell w Tichmarsh, Thurning and Clapton *Pet* from 92. *The Rectory, Barnwell, Peterborough PE8 5PG* Tel (01832) 272374

TRENDALL, Peter John. b 43. Oak Hill Th Coll 66. **d** 69 **p** 70. C Beckenham Ch Ch *Roch* 69-73; C Bedworth *Cov* 73-76; V Hornsey Rise St Mary *Lon* 76-82; P-in-c Upper Holloway St Steph 80-82; V Hornsey Rise St Mary w St Steph 82-84; V Walthamstow St Mary w St Steph *Chelmsf* 84-85; TR 85-93; P-in-c Chigwell 93-94; TR Chigwell and Chigwell Row from 94. *The Rectory, 66 High Road, Chigwell, Essex IG7 6QB* Tel 0181-500 3510

TRENDER, Lawrence. b 37. Bps' Coll Cheshunt 64. **d** 66 **p** 67. C Petersham *S'wark* 66-71; C Malden St Jo 71-73; R Thornham Magna w Thornham Parva *St E* 73-81; P-in-c Mellis 73-81; P-in-c Gislingham 73-81; R Thornhams Magna and Parva, Gislingham and Mellis 81-87; RD Hartismere 85-87; R Skipsea w Ulrome and Barmston w Fraisthorpe *York* from 92. *The Rectory, Barmston, Driffield, N Humberside YO25 8PG* Tel (01262) 468188

TRENEER, Cyril George Howard. b 14. Leeds Univ BA36. Coll of Resurr Mirfield 36. **d** 38 **p** 39. C Plymouth St Pet *Ex* 38-45; C Cov St Jo *Cov* 45-46; C Paignton St Jo *Ex* 46-51; R S Molton w Nymet St George 51-60; R High Bray w Charles 55-60; V Plymouth St Gabr 60-79; rtd 79; Lic to Offic *Ex* from 79.

2 Headborough Road, Ashburton, Newton Abbot, Devon TQ13 7QP Tel (01364) 652159

TRESIDDER, Alistair Charles. b 65. Qu Coll Ox BA88. Cranmer Hall Dur DMinlStuds93. **d** 93 **p** 94. C Limehouse *Lon* from 93. *31 Kildare Walk, London E14 7DB* Tel 0171-515 9082

TRETHEWEY, Frederick Martyn. b 49. Lon Univ BA70 DipTh77. Lambeth STh79 Oak Hill Th Coll 75. **d** 78 **p** 79. C Tollington Park St Mark w St Anne *Lon* 78-82; C Whitehall Park St Andr Hornsey Lane 82-87; TV Hornsey Rise Whitehall Park Team 87-88; V Brockmoor *Lich* 88-93; V Brockmoor *Worc* from 93; Chapl Russells Hall Hosp Dudley from 88; RD Himley *Worc* from 96. *5 Leys Road, Brockmoor, Brierley Hill, W Midlands DY5 3UR* Tel (01384) 263327

TREVELYAN, Preb James William Irvine. b 37. Selw Coll Cam BA64 MA67. Cuddesdon Coll 62. **d** 65 **p** 66. C Heston *Lon* 65-68; C Folkestone St Sav *Cant* 68-72; R Lenham w Boughton Malherbe 72-78; P-in-c Honiton, Gittisham and Combe Raleigh *Ex* 78-79; R Honiton, Gittisham, Combe Raleigh and Monkton 79-83; TR Honiton, Gittisham, Combe Raleigh, Monkton etc from 83; P-in-c Farway w Northleigh and Southleigh 84-86; Preb Ex Cathl from 95. *The Rectory, Rookwood Close, Honiton, Devon EX14 8BH* Tel (01404) 42925

TREVOR, Canon Charles Frederic. b 27. Sarum Th Coll 54. **d** 56 **p** 57. C Sutton in Ashfield St Mich *S'well* 56-58; C Birstall *Leic* 58-61; V Prestwold w Hoton 61-66; V Thornton in Lonsdale w Burton in Lonsdale *Bradf* 66-74; V Kirkby Malham 74-85; P-in-c Coniston Cold 81-85; Hon Can Bradf Cathl 85-92; V Sutton 85-92; RD S Craven 86-91; C Embsay w Eastby 92; rtd 92. *5 Brooklyn, Threshfield, Skipton, W Yorkshire BD23 5ER* Tel (01756) 752640

TREVOR-MORGAN, Canon Basil Henry. b 27. Univ of Wales (Lamp) BA51. Wells Th Coll 51. **d** 53 **p** 54. C Chepstow *Mon* 53-56; C Halesowen *Worc* 56-59; CF (TA) 59-92; V Stourbridge St Thos *Worc* 59-76; Chapl Christchurch Hosp 76-92; V Christchurch *Win* 76-92; Hon Can Win Cathl 84-92; rtd 93. *31 West Walk, West Bay, Bridport, Dorset DT6 4HT* Tel (01308) 56461

TREW, Jeremy Charles. b 66. Univ of Wales (Abth) BSc89 Leeds Univ MSc92. St Jo Coll Nottm MA94. **d** 97. C Roundhay St Edm *Ripon* from 97. *1 Gledhow Grange View, Leeds LS8 1PH* Tel 0113-266 8212

TREW, Robin Nicholas. b 52. UWIST BSc74. St Jo Coll Nottm 87. **d** 89 **p** 90. C Cov H Trin *Cov* 89-93; V Snitterfield w Bearley from 93. *The Vicarage, Church Road, Snitterfield, Stratford-upon-Avon, Warks CV37 0LN* Tel (01789) 731263

TREWEEKS, Mrs Angela Elizabeth. b 35. Gilmore Ho IDC59. **dss** 59 **d** 87 **p** 94. Chapl Asst St Nic Hosp Newc 85-87; Chapl 87; Hon C Newc St Geo *Newc* 87-89; Chapl St Mary's Hosp Stannington 92-95; Hon C Rothbury *Newc* from 94; rtd 95. *The Nook, Pondicherry, Rothbury, Morpeth, Northd NE65 7YS* Tel (01669) 620393

TRIBE, Arthur Wilfrid Newton (Pip). b 03. Trin Coll Ox BA25 MA31. Ridley Hall Cam 25. **d** 27 **p** 28. C Spitalfields Ch Ch w All SS *Lon* 27-32; C Cambridge St Matt *Ely* 32-35; CMS 35-39; Rwanda 35-39; Chapl RAFVR 39-46; Chapl Seaford Coll E Sussex 46-49; Lic to Offic *Chich* 46-49; Lic to Offic *Ely* 49; C Morden *S'wark* 49-50; R Shustoke *Birm* 50-52; PC Merevale w Bentley 50-52; V Sevenoaks Weald *Roch* 52-61; R High Ongar w Norton Mandeville *Chelmsf* 61-76; rtd 76; Perm to Offic *Chelmsf* from 76. *19 Longfields, Ongar, Essex CM5 9BZ* Tel (01277) 364211

TRICKETT, Judith. b 50. St Jo Coll Nottm 89. **d** 91 **p** 94. Par Dn Kimberworth *Sheff* 91-93; D-in-c Worsbrough Common 93-94; V from 94. *The Vicarage, 9 Mount Close, Barnsley, S Yorkshire S70 4EE* Tel (01226) 282619

TRICKETT, Stanley Mervyn Wood. b 27. Lich Th Coll 64. **d** 66 **p** 67. C Kington w Huntington *Heref* 66-70; P-in-c Old Radnor 70-81; P-in-c Knill 70-81; V Shrewton *Sarum* 81-97; P-in-c Winterbourne Stoke 81-92; RD Wylye and Wilton 85-89. *Address temp unknown*

TRICKETT, Mrs Susan. b 42. JP89. S Dios Minl Tr Scheme 91. **d** 94 **p** 95. NSM Combe Down w Monkton Combe and S Stoke *B & W* from 94. *Granville House, Tyning Road, Combe Down, Bath BA2 5ER* Tel (01225) 833007

TRICKEY, The Very Revd Frederick Marc. b 35. Dur Univ BA62. Cranmer Hall Dur DipTh64. **d** 64 **p** 65. C Alton St Lawr *Win* 64-68; V Win St Jo cum Winnall 68-77; R Guernsey St Martin from 77; Angl Adv Channel TV from 77; Dean Guernsey *Win* from 95. *The Rectory, La Grande Rue, St Martin, Guernsey, Channel Islands GY4 6RR* Tel (01481) 38303

TRICKEY, Jolyon. b 57. Barrister-at-Law 80 Jes Coll Cam BA79 MA83. Trin Coll Bris BA90. **d** 90 **p** 91. C Chesham Bois *Ox* 90-94; R Busbridge *Guildf* from 94. *Busbridge Rectory, Brighton Road, Godalming, Surrey GU7 1XA* Tel (01483) 421267

TRICKLEBANK, Steven. b 56. Nottm Univ BTh88. Linc Th Coll 85. **d** 88 **p** 89. C Ditton St Mich *Liv* 88-91; C Wigan All SS 91-93; Chapl Aintree Hosps NHS Trust Liv 93-97; C-in-c St Edm Anchorage Lane CD *Sheff* from 97; Chapl Doncaster R Infirmary & Montague Hosp NHS Trust from 97. *St Edmunds House, Anchorage Lane, Doncaster, S Yorkshire DN5 8DT* Tel (01302) 781986

TRIGG, Jeremy Michael. b 51. Open Univ BA88. Ripon Coll Cuddesdon 80. **d** 81 **p** 82. C Roundhay St Edm *Ripon* 81-84; C Harrogate St Wilfrid and St Luke 84-87; TV Pocklington Team *York* 87-90; R Rowley w Skidby 90-97; Perm to Offic *Linc* from 91; TV Wolverton *Ox* from 97. *28 Harvester Close, Greenleys, Milton Keynes MK12 6LE* Tel (01908) 222802

TRIGG, John Alfred. b 29. Keble Coll Ox BA64 MA64. Ripon Hall Ox 64. **d** 65 **p** 66. C Dursley *Glouc* 65-67; C Glouc St Geo 67-68; C Swan *Ox* 68-72; P-in-c Stokenchurch and Cadmore End 72-76; V Stokenchurch and Ibstone 76-94; rtd 94. *Medbury, Tisbury Row, Tisbury, Salisbury SP3 6RZ* Tel (01747) 870707

TRIGG, Jonathan David. b 49. Ex Coll Ox BA71 MA75 Dur Univ PhD92. Cranmer Hall Dur BA82. **d** 83 **p** 84. C Enfield St Andr *Lon* 83-87; V Oakwood St Thos 87-96; AD Enfield 92-96; V Highgate St Mich from 96. *The Vicarage, 10 The Grove, London N6 6LB* Tel 0181-340 7279

TRILL, Barry. b 42. Chich Th Coll 65. **d** 68 **p** 69. C W Hackney St Barn *Lon* 68-73; TV Is of Dogs Ch Ch and St Jo w St Luke 73-78; P-in-c Hastings All So *Chich* 78-79; V from 79. *All Souls' Vicarage, 16 Berlin Road, Hastings, E Sussex TN35 5JD* Tel (01424) 421445

TRILL, Victor Alfred Mansfield. b 21. St Deiniol's Hawarden. **d** 81 **p** 82. Hon C Prestbury *Ches* 81-83; Hon C Church Hulme 83-85; V Marbury 85-90; rtd 90; Perm to Offic *Ches* from 90. *5 Maisterson Court, Nantwich, Cheshire CW5 5TZ* Tel (01270) 628948

TRIMBLE, Mrs Anne Inman. b 40. Kenton Lodge Tr Coll CertEd60 New Coll Dur DipRS84. NE Ord Course 89. **d** 92 **p** 94. NSM Longnewton w Elton *Dur* from 92. *3 Queen Anne Terrace, Stockton-on-Tees, Cleveland TS18 5HS* Tel (01642) 581141

TRIMBLE, Canon John Alexander. b 33. Lon Univ BD65. Edin Th Coll 55. **d** 58 **p** 59. C Glas St Mary *Glas* 58-60; C Edin St Jo *Edin* 60-65; R Baillieston *Glas* 65-69; R Falkirk *Edin* 69-86; R Troon *Glas* from 86; Can St Mary's Cathl from 91. *The Rectory, 70 Bentinck Drive, Troon, Ayrshire KA10 6HZ* Tel (01292) 313731

TRIMBLE, Canon Thomas Henry. b 36. TCD DipTh82 BTh90. CITC 79. **d** 82 **p** 83. C Seapatrick *D & D* 82-85; I Magheracross *Clogh* 85-90; Bp's Appeal Sec 89-90; I Donegal w Killymard, Lough Eske and Laghey *D & R* from 90; RD S Donegal from 91; Can Raphoe Cathl from 93. *The Rectory, Ballyshannon Road, Donegal, Co Donegal, Irish Republic* Tel Donegal (73) 21075

TRIMBY, George Henry. b 44. DipTh. Trin Coll Bris 84. **d** 86 **p** 87. C Newtown w Llanllwchaiarn w Aberhafesp *St As* 86-88; P-in-c Llanfair, Derwen, Llanelidan and Efenechtyd 88-90; V 90-95; V Llanasa from 95. *The Vicarage, Llanasa Road, Gronant, Prestatyn LL19 9TL* Tel (01745) 853512

TRINDER, John Derek. b 28. Glouc Th Course 74. **d** 77 **p** 78. C Forest of Dean Ch Ch w English Bicknor *Glouc* 77; Hon C 77-79; Hon C Chepstow *Mon* 79-81; C Newport St Paul 81-82; V Dingestow and Llangovan w Penyclawdd and Tregaer 82-87; V Kirton in Holland *Linc* 87-93; rtd 93; Perm to Offic *Linc* from 93. *96 Little London, Long Sutton, Spalding, Lincs PE12 9LF* Tel (01406) 363045

TRIPLOW, Keith John. b 44. Selw Coll Cam BA66 MA70. Chich Th Coll 70. **d** 72 **p** 73. C Ipswich All Hallows *St E* 72-76; C Dartford H Trin *Roch* 76-78; V Fyfield w Tubney and Kingston Bagpuize *Ox* from 78. *The Vicarage, Fyfield, Abingdon, Oxon OX13 5LR* Tel (01865) 390803

TRIST, Richard McLeod. b 55. Univ of NSW BSEd76. Ridley Coll Melbourne BTh83 DipMin83. **d** 87 **p** 87. Australia 87-96; C Langham Place All So *Lon* from 97. *2 St Paul's Court, 56 Manchester Street, London W1M 5PA* Tel 0171-486 0006

TRISTRAM, Canon Catherine Elizabeth (Kate). b 31. Somerville Coll Ox BA53 MA57. **dss** 83 **d** 87 **p** 94. Holy Is *Newc* 84-87; Hon C from 87; Hon Can Newc Cathl from 94. *Marygate House, Holy Island, Berwick-upon-Tweed TD15 2SD*

TRISTRAM, Geoffrey Robert. b 53. K Coll Lon BA76 Pemb Coll Cam BA78 MA80. Westcott Ho Cam 77. **d** 79 **p** 80. C Weymouth H Trin *Sarum* 79-82; C Gt Berkhamsted *St Alb* 83-85; OSB from 85; Lic to Offic *Pet* 86-91; Asst Chapl Oundle Sch 86-88; Sen Chapl 88-91; R Welwyn w Ayot St Peter *St Alb* from 91; Chapl Qu Victoria Hosp & Danesbury Home from 91. *The Rectory, 6 Hobbs Hill, Welwyn, Herts AL6 9DF* Tel (01438) 714150

TRISTRAM, Michael Anthony. b 50. Solicitor 76 Ch Coll Cam BA72 MA76. Ripon Coll Cuddesdon 79. **d** 82 **p** 83. C Stanmore *Win* 82-85; R Abbotts Ann and Upper and Goodworth Clatford 85-92; V Pershore w Pinvin, Wick and Birlingham *Worc* from 92. *The Vicarage, Church Street, Pershore, Worcs WR10 1DT* Tel (01386) 552071

TRIVASSE, Keith Malcolm. b 59. Man Univ BA81 CertEd82 MPhil90 Birm Univ DipTh86. Qu Coll Birm 84. **d** 86 **p** 87. C Prestwich St Marg *Man* 86-88; C Orford St Marg *Liv* 88-90; TV Sunderland *Dur* 90-91; P-in-c N Hylton St Marg Castletown 91-95; R Bothal and Pegswood w Longhirst *Newc* from 95. *Bothal Rectory, Longhirst Road, Pegswood, Morpeth, Northd NE61 6XF* Tel (01670) 510793

TRNKA, Oldrich Joseph. b 15. Inst of Th Olomouc 32. **d** 37 **p** 38. C Lambeth St Phil *S'wark* 52-55; P-in-c Lewisham St Mark 55-60; R Everdon w Farthingstone *Pet* 61-65; C Penton Street St Silas w

All SS *Lon* 66-68; rtd 68. *2 Carlton Court, Bosanquet Close, Cowley, Uxbridge, Middx UB8 3PF* Tel (01895) 254390

TRODDEN, Michael John. b 54. K Coll Lon BD77 AKC77 CertEd. Wycliffe Hall Ox 79. **d** 80 **p** 81. C Woodford St Mary w St Phil and St Jas *Chelmsf* 80-87; V Aldborough Hatch 87-96; R Ampthill w Millbrook and Steppingley *St Alb* from 96. *The Rectory, Rectory Lane, Ampthill, Bedford MK45 2EL* Tel (01525) 402320

TROLLOPE, David Harvey. b 41. BSc63. Lon Coll of Div 66. **d** 68 **p** 69. C Bermondsey St Jas w Ch Ch *S'wark* 68-71; Uganda 71-77; Kenya 77-82; V Gt Crosby St Luke *Liv* from 82. *St Luke's Vicarage, 71 Liverpool Road, Crosby, Liverpool L23 5SE* Tel 0151-924 1737

TROMANS, Kevin Stanley. b 57. St Martin's Coll Lanc BEd79. Aston Tr Scheme 90 Coll of Resurr Mirfield 92. **d** 94 **p** 95. C Rawdon *Bradf* 94-96; C Woodhall from 96. *34 The Lanes, Pudsey, W Yorkshire LS28 7AQ* Tel 0113-255 1080

TROOP, John Richard. b 37. Ely Th Coll 61. **d** 64 **p** 65. C Linc St Andr *Linc* 64-66; C Linc St Swithin 64-66; C Gt Grimsby St Andr and St Luke 66-70; V Wrangle 70-78; V S Moor *Dur* 78-85; Chapl Dur and Northd ATC from 82; V Darlington St Hilda and St Columba 85-95; P-in-c Southwick St Columba 95-97; V from 97. *St Columba's Vicarage, Cornhill Road, Southwick, Sunderland SR5 1RU* Tel 0191-516 0244

TROSS, Canon Julian Chamings. b 14. AKC35. Bps' Coll Cheshunt 37. **d** 37 **p** 38. C Limehouse St Anne *Lon* 37-43; C Finchley St Mary 43-46; V Mile End Old Town H Trin 46-55; R Datchworth *St Alb* 55-77; P-in-c Tewin 76-77; R Datchworth w Tewin 77-79; RD Stevenage 71-75; Hon Can St Alb 72-79; rtd 79; Perm to Offic *St Alb* 79-93. *63 Colestrete, Stevenage, Herts SG1 1RE* Tel (01438) 354150

TROTMAN, Anthony Edward Fiennes. b 11. Ex Coll Ox BA33 MA56. Wycliffe Hall Ox 46. **d** 48 **p** 49. C Ballymacarrett St Patr *D & D* 48-51; C Dundela 51-52; R Corsley *Sarum* 52-59; R Chilmark 59-76; P-in-c Teffont Evias and Teffont Magna 73-75; rtd 76. *17 Estcourt Road, Salisbury SP1 3AP* Tel (01722) 324857

TROTT, Stephen John. b 57. FRSA86 Hull Univ BA79 Fitzw Coll Cam BA83 MA87. Westcott Ho Cam 81. **d** 84 **p** 85. C Hessle *York* 84-87; C Kingston upon Hull St Alb 87-88; R Pitsford w Boughton *Pet* from 88; Sec Continuing Minl Educn 88-93; Chapl Northants Gr Sch from 91. *The Rectory, Humfrey Lane, Boughton, Northampton NN2 8RQ* Tel (01604) 821387 Fax 820637 E-mail stephentrott@mcmail.com

TROTTER, Harold Barrington (Barry). b 33. Sarum Th Coll 64. **d** 66 **p** 67. C Salisbury St Fran *Sarum* 66-69; Dioc Youth Officer 69-72; V Horton and Chalbury 69-73; R Frenchay *Bris* 73-81; V Henbury from 81. *St Mary's Vicarage, Station Road, Bristol BS10 7QQ* Tel 0117-950 0536

TROUNSON, Ronald Charles. b 26. Em Coll Cam BA48 MA52. Ripon Hall Ox 54. **d** 56 **p** 57. C Plymouth St Gabr *Ex* 56-58; Chapl Denstone Coll Uttoxeter 58-76; Bursar 76-78; Prin St Chad's Coll Dur 78-88; R Easton on the Hill, Collyweston w Duddington etc *Pet* 89-94; NSM from 94; RD Barnack 91-94; rtd 94. *The Rectory, 38 West Street, Easton On The Hill, Stamford, Lincs PE9 3LS* Tel (01780) 62616

TROUT, Keith. b 49. Trin Coll Bris DipHE92. **d** 92 **p** 93. C Pudsey St Lawr and St Paul *Bradf* 92-97; V Burley *Ripon* from 97. *St Matthias Vicarage, 271 Burley Road, Leeds LS4 3DZ* Tel 0113-278 5872 or 230 4408

TRUBY, David Charles. b 57. BA79 Nottm Univ DipTh80. Linc Th Coll 79. **d** 82 **p** 83. C Stanley *Liv* 82-85; C Hindley St Pet 85-90; R Brimington *Derby* from 90. *The Rectory, Brimington, Chesterfield, Derbyshire S43 1JG* Tel (01246) 273103

TRUDGILL, Harry Keith. b 25. LCP54 Leeds Univ DipEd49 Lon Univ BD61. St Deiniol's Hawarden 76. **d** 76 **p** 76. C Glas St Marg *Glas* 76-78; R Lenzie 78-86; rtd 86; Perm to Offic *Bradf* from 86. *4 High Bank, Grassington, Skipton, N Yorkshire BD23 5BU* Tel (01756) 752371

TRUEMAN, Reginald. b 24. K Coll Cam BA47 MA49 Man Univ BD53. St Jo Coll Winnipeg Hon DD58 Ely Th Coll 48 Union Th Sem (NY) STM50. **d** 50 **p** 51. C Bolton St Pet *Man* 50-53; Hong Kong 53-61; Prin Union Th Coll 57-61; Lect K Coll Lon 61-74; Sen Lect N Co Coll of Educn 75-78; Teacher Manor Park Sch Newc 78-82; Lesotho 84-86; rtd 92. *22 The Square, Petersfield, Hants GU32 3HS* Tel (01730) 261341

TRUMPER, Roger David. b 52. Ex Univ BSc74 K Coll Lon MSc75 Ox Univ BA80 MA85. Wycliffe Hall Ox 78. **d** 81 **p** 82. C Tunbridge Wells St Jo *Roch* 81-84; C Slough *Ox* 84-87; TV Shenley and Loughton 87-88; TV Watling Valley 88-93; R Byfleet *Guildf* from 93. *The Rectory, 81 Rectory Lane, West Byfleet, Surrey KT14 7LX* Tel (01932) 342374

TRUNDLE, Herbert Edward. b 11. Lich Th Coll 33. **d** 36 **p** 37. C Gt Ilford St Jo *Chelmsf* 36-40; C Cheam *S'wark* 40-44; V Battersea St Steph 44-52; V Cheam Common St Phil 52-76; rtd 76. *Westlands, Mappowder, Sturminster Newton, Dorset DT10 2EH* Tel (01258) 817694

TRURO, Bishop of. *See* IND, The Rt Revd William

TRURO, Dean of. *See* SHEARLOCK, The Very Revd David John

TRUSS, Charles Richard. b 42. Reading Univ BA63 K Coll Lon MPhil79 Linacre Coll Ox BA66 MA69. Wycliffe Hall Ox 64. **d** 66 **p** 67. C Leic H Apostles *Leic* 66-69; C Hampstead St Jo *Lon* 69-72; V Belsize Park 72-79; V Wood Green St Mich 79-82; TR Wood Green St Mich w Bounds Green St Gabr etc 82-85; R Shepperton 85-94; V Waterloo St Jo w St Andr *S'wark* from 94; RD Lambeth from 95. *St John's Vicarage, 1 Secker Street, London SE1 8UF* Tel 0171-928 2003

TRUSTRAM, Canon David Geoffrey. b 49. Pemb Coll Ox BA71 MA76 Qu Coll Cam BA73 MA77. Westcott Ho Cam 74. **d** 75 **p** 76. C Surbiton St Mark *S'wark* 75-77; C Surbiton St Andr and St Mark 77-78; C Richmond St Mary 78-79; C Richmond St Mary w St Matthias and St Jo 79-82; P-in-c Eastry *Cant* 82-88; R Eastry and Northbourne w Tilmanstone etc 88-90; Chapl Eastry Hosp 82-90; V Tenterden St Mildred w Smallhythe *Cant* from 90; Hon Can Cant Cathl from 96. *The Vicarage, Church Road, Tenterden, Kent TN30 6AT* Tel (01580) 763118

TSIPOURAS, John George. b 38. Trin Coll Bris 76. **d** 78 **p** 79. C Cheadle Hulme St Andr *Ches* 78-82; V Hurdsfield from 82. *197A Hurdsfield Road, Macclesfield, Cheshire SK10 2PY* Tel (01625) 424587

TUAM, Archdeacon of. *See* PREVITE, The Ven Anthony Michael Allen

TUAM, Dean of. *See* CORBETT, The Very Revd Ian Deighton

TUAM, KILLALA AND ACHONRY, Bishop of. *Vacant*

TUAM, Provost of. *See* MacCARTHY, The Very Revd Robert Brian

TUBBS, Preb Brian Ralph. b 44. AKC66. **d** 67 **p** 68. C Ex St Thos *Ex* 67-72; TV Sidmouth, Woolbrook and Salcombe Regis 72-77; R Ex St Jas 77-96; RD Christianity 89-95; Preb Ex Cathl from 95; V Paignton St Jo from 96. *The Vicarage, Palace Place, Paignton, Devon TQ3 3AQ* Tel (01803) 559059

TUBBS, Canon Christopher Norman. b 25. G&C Coll Cam BA51 MA54. Wycliffe Hall Ox. **d** 52 **p** 53. C Neston *Ches* 52-55; C Nor St Pet Mancroft *Nor* 55-59; V Scalby *York* 59-68; V Scalby w Ravenscar and Staintondale 68-95; RD Scarborough 76-82; Can and Preb York Minster 85-96; rtd 95. *9 Mill Lane, West Ayton, Scarborough, N Yorkshire YO13 9JT* Tel (01723) 863211

TUBBS, Peter Alfred. b 22. G&C Coll Cam BA48 MA53. Linc Th Coll 55. **d** 57 **p** 58. C Tettenhall Regis *Lich* 57-60; C Wellington Ch Ch 60-64; Asst Chapl Keele Univ 65-69; V Cardington *St Alb* 69-85; RD Elstow 77-82; C Sandy 85-89; rtd 89; Perm to Offic *St Alb* from 89. *1 Foster Grove, Sandy, Beds SG19 1HP* Tel (01767) 682803

TUCK, Andrew Kenneth. b 42. Kelham Th Coll 63. **d** 68 **p** 69. C Poplar *Lon* 68-74; TV 74-76; V Walsgrave on Sowe *Cov* 76-90; R Farnham *Guildf* from 90; Chapl Farnham Hosp Guildf from 90. *The Rectory, Upper Church Lane, Farnham, Surrey GU9 7PW* Tel (01252) 715412

TUCK, David John. b 36. St Cath Coll Cam BA61 MA65. Cuddesdon Coll 61. **d** 63 **p** 64. C Kelling w Salthouse *Nor* 63-69; C Holt 63-69; Zambia 69-73; V Sprowston *Nor* 73-84; R Beeston St Andr 73-84; RD Nor N 81-84; V Pinner *Lon* from 84. *The Vicarage, 2 Church Lane, Pinner, Middx HA5 3AA* Tel 0181-866 3869 or 866 2676

TUCK, Gillian (Gill). b 40. SRN64 SCM66. Llan Dioc Tr Scheme 93. **d** 97. NSM Pontypridd St Cath w St Matt *Llan* from 97. *4 Maes Glas, Coed y Cwm, Pontypridd CF37 3EJ* Tel (01443) 791049

TUCK, Nigel Graham. b 57. Chich Th Coll 82. **d** 85 **p** 86. C Port Talbot St Theodore *Llan* 85-87; C Llantrisant 87-90; TV Duston Team *Pet* 90-95; C Aldwick *Chich* from 95. *59 Westminster Drive, Aldwick, Bognor Regis, W Sussex PO21 3RE* Tel (01243) 830124

TUCK, Ralph Thomas. b 42. Worc Coll Ox BA64 Bris Univ CertEd66 Leeds Univ DipFE81. N Ord Course 87. **d** 90 **p** 91. NSM S Crosland *Wakef* from 90; NSM Helme from 90. *5 Nields Road, Slaithwaite, W Yorkshire HD7 5HT* Tel (01484) 843583

TUCK, Ronald James. b 47. S'wark Ord Course 75. **d** 78 **p** 79. C Upper Holloway St Pet *Lon* 78-79; C Upper Holloway St Pet w St Jo 79-81; P-in-c Scottow *Nor* 81-88; P-in-c Swanton Abbott w Skeyton 81-88; R Bradwell from 88. *The Rectory, Church Walk, Bradwell, Great Yarmouth, Norfolk NR31 8QQ* Tel (01493) 663219

TUCKER, Andrew Michael. b 64. K Coll Lon BD87. Wycliffe Hall Ox DipMin95. **d** 95 **p** 96. C Moreton *Ches* 95-96; C Poynton from 96. *11 Deva Close, Poynton, Stockport, Cheshire SK12 1HH* Tel (01625) 871958

TUCKER, Anthony Ian. b 50. CYCW78. CA Tr Coll 73 S'wark Ord Course 81. **d** 85 **p** 86. NSM E Ham w Upton Park St Alb *Chelmsf* 85-86; NSM S'well Minster *S'well* 86-90; C Rolleston w Fiskerton, Morton and Upton 90-93; P-in-c Teversal 93-96; Chapl Sutton Cen 93-96; P-in-c Norwell w Ossington, Cromwell and Caunton from 96; Dioc Tourism Officer from 96. *The Vicarage, Main Street, Norwell, Newark, Notts NG23 6JT* Tel (01636) 636329

TUCKER, Desmond Robert. b 29. Bris Sch of Min 83. **d** 86 **p** 87. C Bris St Mich *Bris* 86-88; P-in-c 88-94; rtd 94; Perm to Offic *Bris* from 94. *94 Fremantle House, Dove Street, Bristol BS2 8LH* Tel 0117-924 6803

TUCKER, Douglas Greening. b 17. Lon Univ DipTh53. St Aid Birkenhead 49. **d** 52 **p** 53. C Jesmond Clayton Memorial *Newc* 52-56; C Fenham St Jas and St Basil 56-58; V Cowgate 58-62; V Elsham *Linc* 62-85; V Worlaby 62-85; V Bonby 73-85; rtd 85.

Balintore, Main Street, Bowsden, Northd TD15 2TW Tel (01289) 88630

TUCKER, Harold George. b 21. St Aug Coll Cant 48 Sarum Th Coll 50. **d** 51 **p** 52. C S Molton w Nymet St George *Ex* 51-56; V Mariansleigh and Romansleigh w Meshaw 56-64; R Bratton Fleming 64-73; P-in-c Goodleigh 67-73; P-in-c Stoke Rivers 67-73; P-in-c Parracombe 69-73; P-in-c Martinhoe 69-73; R Whimple 73-86; rtd 86; Perm to Offic *Ex* from 86. *Lansdowne, The Crescent, Widemouth Bay, Bude, Cornwall EX23 0AE* Tel (01288) 361396

TUCKER, Ian Malcolm. b 46. Bris Coll HND69 ONC66. S Dios Minl Tr Scheme 86. **d** 89 **p** 90. NSM Pill w Easton in Gordano and Portbury *B & W* 89-95; C Frome St Jo and St Mary from 95. *St Mary's House, Innox Hill, Frome, Somerset BA11 2LN* Tel (01373) 463525

TUCKER, John Yorke Raffles. b 24. Magd Coll Cam BA49 MA56. Westcott Ho Cam 49. **d** 51 **p** 52. C Shadwell St Paul w Ratcliffe St Jas *Lon* 51-54; C Preston Ascension 54-58; V S Hackney St Mich 58-67; V Belmont 67-78; V Sunbury 78-89; rtd 89; Perm to Offic *Ex* 89-93; Perm to Offic *B & W* from 93. *Tudor Cottage, Fivehead, Taunton, Somerset TA3 6PJ* Tel (01460) 281330

TUCKER, Michael. b 33. MA. **d** 84 **p** 85. NSM Sawston *Ely* 84-87; C Ely 87-90; P-in-c Barton Bendish w Beachamwell and Shingham from 90; P-in-c Wereham from 90. *The Rectory, Barton Bendish, King's Lynn, Norfolk PE33 9DP* Tel (013664) 363

TUCKER, Dr Michael Owen. b 42. Lon Univ BSc66 Surrey Univ PhD69. Glouc Sch of Min 81. **d** 84 **p** 85. Hon C Uley w Owlpen and Nympsfield *Glouc* 84-92; P-in-c Amberley from 92; Dioc NSM Officer from 94. *The Rectory, Amberley, Stroud, Glos GL5 5JG* Tel (01453) 878515

TUCKER, Nicholas Harold (Nick). b 41. Reading Univ BSc66. N Ord Course 90. **d** 93 **p** 94. NSM Ilkley All SS *Bradf* from 93. *Waddington House, 2 Margerison Road, Ilkley, W Yorkshire LS29 8QU* Tel (01943) 609472 Fax 609829

TUCKER, Richard Parish. b 51. Cam Univ BA72 MA76 Lon Univ BD83. Wycliffe Hall Ox 80. **d** 83 **p** 84. C Wellington w Eyton *Lich* 83-84; C Walsall 84-88; TV Dronfield *Derby* 88-90; TV Dronfield w Holmesfield from 90. *11 Rothay Close, Dronfield Woodhouse, Sheffield S18 5PR* Tel (01246) 416893

TUCKER, Stephen Reid. b 51. New Coll Ox MA76. Ripon Coll Cuddesdon DipTh76. **d** 77 **p** 78. C Hove All SS *Chich* 77-80; Lect Chich Th Coll 80-86; V Portsea St Alb *Portsm* 86-90; Chapl and Dean of Div New Coll Ox 90-95; P-in-c Ovingdean *Chich* from 96; Bp's Adv Continuing Minl Educn from 96. *St Wulfran's Rectory, 43 Ainsworth Avenue, Brighton BN2 7BG* Tel (01273) 303633

TUCKER, Mrs Susan (Sue). b 53. Stockwell Coll of Educn CertEd74. **d** 97. C Taunton St Andr *B & W* from 97. *1 Peter Street, Taunton, Somerset TA2 7BZ* Tel (01823) 337662

TUCKER, Vivian Clive Temple. b 39. **d** 96 **p** 97. NSM Gresford *St As* from 96. *8 Snowdon Drive, Ty Gwyn, Wrexham LL11 2UY*

TUCKETT, Prof Christopher Mark. b 48. Qu Coll Cam MA71 Lanc Univ PhD79. Westcott Ho Cam 71. **d** 75 **p** 76. C Lancaster St Mary *Blackb* 75-77; Chapl and Fell Qu Coll Cam 77-79; Lect NT Man Univ 79-89; Sen Lect 89-91; Prof Bibl Studies from 91; Perm to Offic *Ches* from 93. *Kidd Road Farm, Moorfield, Glossop, Derbyshire SK13 9PN* Tel (01457) 860150

TUCKEY, John William Townsend. b 19. TCD BA41 MA. **d** 43 **p** 44. C Dublin Rathfarnham *D & G* 43-45; C Ballymacarrett St Martin *D & D* 45-50; P-in-c Shandon St Ann *C, C & R* 50-52; Chapl Kirwan Ho Dublin 52-59; Hon Clerical V Ch Ch Cathl Dublin *D & G* 55-59; C Monkstown 59-60; C Weston-super-Mare St Paul *B & W* 60-63; C Kewstoke 63-65; V Milton 65-74; P-in-c E Brent 74-75; R E Brent w Lympsham 75-81; Deanery C Glastonbury 81-84; rtd 84; Perm to Offic *B & W* from 85. *7 Parkfields, Butleigh, Glastonbury, Somerset BA6 8SZ* Tel (01458) 851107

TUDBALL, Arthur James. b 28. AKC54. **d** 54 **p** 55. C Munster Square St Mary Magd *Lon* 54-56; Malaysia 63-73 and 75-79; Brunei 73-75; Singapore from 79; rtd 89. *Orchard Point, PO Box 160, Singapore 9123* Tel Singapore (65) 259-4298

TUDGE, Paul Quartus. b 55. Leeds Univ BEd78. Cranmer Hall Dur 84. **d** 87 **p** 88. C Roundhay St Edm *Ripon* 87-90; C Leeds St Pet 90; C Leeds City 91; V Woodside from 91; Warden of Readers from 96. *St James's Vicarage, 1 Scotland Close, Horsforth, Leeds LS18 5SG* Tel 0113-258 2433

TUDGEY, Stephen John. b 51. St Jo Coll Nottm BTh81 LTh. **d** 81 **p** 82. C Grays Thurrock *Chelmsf* 81-83; C Grays SS Pet and Paul, S Stifford and W Thurrock 83-84; C Grays Thurrock 84; C Madeley *Heref* 84-87; R Chilcompton w Downside and Stratton on the Fosse *B & W* from 87. *The Rectory, The Street, Chilcompton, Bath BA3 4HN* Tel (01761) 232219

TUDOR, David Charles Frederick. b 42. Sarum Th Coll 70. **d** 73 **p** 74. C Plymouth St Pet *Ex* 73-75; C Reddish *Man* 75-78; P-in-c Hamer 78-80; V Goldenhill *Lich* 80-87; V Meir 87-91; Chapl Asst Nottm City Hosp 91-94; Chapl Cen Sheff Univ Hosps NHS Trust 94-96; V Nottingham St Geo w St Jo *S'well* from 96. *St George's Vicarage, Strome Close, Nottingham NG2 1HD* Tel 0115-986 4881

TUDOR, David St Clair. b 55. K Coll Lon BD77 AKC77 K Coll Lon MTh89. Ripon Coll Cuddesdon 77. **d** 78 **p** 79. C Plumstead St Nic *S'wark* 78-80; C Redhill St Matt 80-83; C-in-c Reigate St Phil CD 83-87; Asst Sec Gen Syn Bd for Miss and Unity 87-88; Perm to Offic *S'wark* from 94. *11 St Martin's Close, Erith, Kent DA18 4DZ*

TUDOR, Malcolm George Henry Booth. b 36. Nottm Univ BA71. Linc Th Coll 72. **d** 60 **p** 61. In RC Ch 60-71; C Cinderhill *S'well* 72-74; P-in-c Broxtowe 74-78; P-in-c E Drayton w Stokeham 78-86; R E Markham and Askham 78-86; P-in-c Headon w Upton 78-86; V Llandinam w Trefeglwys w Penstrowed *Ban* from 86. *The Vicarage, Llandinam SY17 5BS* Tel (01686) 688341

TUFFEL, Kennedy Joseph. b 20. Worc Ord Coll 64. **d** 66 **p** 67. C Belmont *Lon* 66-68; C Goring-by-Sea *Chich* 68-72 and 81-89; NSM 89-96; V Barnham 72-78; Hon C W Worthing St Jo 78-81; rtd 89; Perm to Offic *Chich* from 96. *15 Mill House Gardens, Mill Road, Worthing, W Sussex BN11 4NE* Tel (01903) 700671

TUFFIELD, Canon Basil Thomas. b 23. Fitzw Ho Cam BA49 MA54. Wells Th Coll 50. **d** 52 **p** 53. C Charlton St Luke w St Paul *S'wark* 52-58; C Carshalton 58-65; V Carshalton Beeches 65-79; P-in-c Crosscanonby *Carl* 79-82; V 82-90; P-in-c Allonby w W Newton 81-82; V Allonby 82-90; RD Solway 84-90; Hon Can Carl Cathl 87-90; rtd 90; Perm to Offic *Carl* from 90. *Hafod y Cwm, Nannerch, Mold CH7 5RP* Tel (01352) 741234

TUFFIN, Mrs Gillian Patricia. b 43. S Dios Minl Tr Scheme 91. **d** 94 **p** 95. C Gidea Park *Chelmsf* from 94. *109 Carlton Road, Romford RM2 5AU* Tel (01708) 769669

TUFFNELL, Nigel Owen. b 65. Teesside Poly BSc90. St Jo Coll Nottm 91. **d** 94 **p** 95. C Guisborough *York* 94-97; P-in-c Northwold *Ely* from 97; P-in-c Stoke Ferry w Wretton from 97; P-in-c Whittington from 97. *The Vicarage, Low Road, Wretton, Kings Lynn, Norfolk PE33 9QN* Tel (01366) 501075

TUFNELL, Edward Nicholas Pember. b 45. Chu Coll Cam MA68. St Jo Coll Nottm BA73. **d** 73 **p** 74. C Ealing St Mary *Lon* 73-76; BCMS 76-88; Tanzania 76-88; P-in-c Lt Thurrock St Jo *Chelmsf* 89-91; V Grays North from 91; Chapl Thurrock Hosp from 89. *St John's Vicarage, Victoria Avenue, Grays, Essex RM16 2RP* Tel (01375) 372101

TUFT, Preb Patrick Anthony. b 31. Selw Coll Cam BA56 MA60. Edin Th Coll 56. **d** 58 **p** 59. C Keighley *Bradf* 58-63; PV Chich Cathl *Chich* 63-68; Min Can St Paul's Cathl *Lon* 68-74; Hon Min Can St Paul's Cathl from 74; V Chiswick St Nic w St Mary from 74; PV Westmr Abbey 74-79; AD Hounslow *Lon* 87-93; P-in-c Chiswick St Paul Grove Park 88-90; Preb St Paul's Cathl from 95. *Chiswick Vicarage, The Mall, London W4 2PJ* Tel 0181-995 4717

TUGWELL, Elizabeth Ann. b 36. **d** 94 **p** 95. NSM Carbis Bay w Lelant *Truro* from 94. *Buslasson, Enys Close, Carbis Bay, St Ives, Cornwall TR26 2SD* Tel (01736) 798551

TULL, Preb Christopher Stuart. b 36. Hertf Coll Ox BA60 MA64. Oak Hill Th Coll 60. **d** 62 **p** 63. C Stoodleigh *Ex* 62-71; C Washfield 62-71; TV Washfield, Stoodleigh, Withleigh etc 71-74; RD Tiverton 74-75; R Bishops Nympton w Rose Ash 75-77; V Mariansleigh 75-77; TR Bishopsnympton, Rose Ash, Mariansleigh etc from 77; RD S Molton 80-87 and from 95; Preb Ex Cathl from 84. *The Rectory, Bishops Nympton, South Molton, Devon EX36 4NY* Tel (01769) 550427

TULLETT, Peter Watts. b 46. Qu Coll Birm 92. **d** 94 **p** 95. C Worle *B & W* 94-96; Chapl HM Young Offender Inst Portland from 96. *HM Young Offender Institution, Easton Portland, Dorset DT5 1DL* Tel (01305) 823718 Fax 823718

TULLOCH, Richard James Anthony. b 52. Wadh Coll Ox BA74 Selw Coll Cam BA79. Ridley Hall Cam 76. **d** 79 **p** 80. C Morden *S'wark* 79-83; C Jesmond Clayton Memorial *Newc* 83-94; V New Borough and Leigh *Sarum* from 94. *The Vicarage, 15 St John's Hill, Wimborne, Dorset BH21 1BX* Tel (01202) 883490

TULLOCH, Walter Harold. b 16. AIMLS53 MRSH62. St Deiniol's Hawarden 79. **d** 79 **p** 80. NSM Maghull *Liv* 79-86; Hon C from 88; rtd 86; Perm to Offic *Liv* 86-88. *8 Tailor's Lane, Maghull, Liverpool L31 3HD* Tel 0151-526 1936

TULLY, David John. b 56. St Jo Coll Dur BA77 Nottm Univ PGCE78. Ridley Hall Cam 81. **d** 84 **p** 85. C Gosforth St Nic *Newc* 84-86; C Newburn 86-90; TV Whorlton 90-96; V from 96. *St John's Vicarage, Whorlton, Newcastle upon Tyne NE5 1NN* Tel 0191-286 9648

TULLY, Ross. b 22. Clare Coll Cam BA44 MA48. Ridley Hall Cam 47. **d** 49 **p** 50. C Beckenham Ch Ch *Roch* 49-52; Pakistan 53-73; Chapl St Bernard's Hosp Southall 74-80; C Eastbourne H Trin *Chich* 80-86; rtd 87. *Venn House, 17 Boyne Park, Tunbridge Wells, Kent TN4 8EL* Tel (01892) 534729

TUNBRIDGE, Dr Genny Louise. b 64. Clare Coll Cam BA85 St Cross Coll Ox DPhil93 Birm Univ BD95. Qu Coll Birm 93. **d** 96 **p** 97. C Boston *Linc* from 96. *2 Tower Street, Boston, Lincs PE21 8RX* Tel (01205) 362524

TUNBRIDGE, John Stephen. b 31. Keble Coll Ox BA54 MA59. Ely Th Coll 54. **d** 56 **p** 57. C Upper Norwood All SS w St Marg *Cant* 56-57; C Ramsgate St Geo 57-60; P-in-c 76-84; C Folkestone St Mary and St Eanswythe 60-62; R Gt Chart 62-67; V Womenswold 67-76; C-in-c Aylesham CD 67-76; R Harbledown 84-94; Perm to Offic *St D* from 94; rtd 96. *Ashdown,*

11 Castle Road, St Ishmaels, Haverfordwest SA62 3SF Tel (01646) 636584

TUNLEY, Timothy Mark (Tim). b 61. Oak Hill Th Coll DipHE84 Ridley Hall Cam CTM92. **d** 92 **p** 93. C Aldborough w Boroughbridge and Roecliffe *Ripon* 92-95; C Knaresborough from 95. *39 Birkdale Avenue, Knaresborough, N Yorkshire HG5 0LS* Tel (01423) 864484

TUNNICLIFFE, Mrs Jean Sarah. b 36. RGN69. Glouc Sch of Min 89. **d** 92 **p** 94. NSM Dixton *Heref* from 92. *Bryn Awelon, 21 Ridgeway, Wyesham, Monmouth NP5 3JX* Tel (01600) 714115

TUNNICLIFFE, Canon Martin Wyndham. b 31. Keele Univ BA56. Qu Coll Birm 59. **d** 60 **p** 61. C Castle Bromwich SS Mary and Marg *Birm* 60-65; V Shard End 65-73; R Over Whitacre w Shustoke 73-78; V Tanworth from 78; RD Solihull 89-94; Hon Can Birm Cathl from 91. *The Vicarage, Tanworth-in-Arden, Solihull, W Midlands B94 5EB* Tel (01564) 742565

TUNSTALL, Barry Anthony. b 29. Sarum Th Coll 53. **d** 55 **p** 56. C Croxley Green All SS *St Alb* 55-58; C Apsley End 58-63; V N Mymms 63-81; P-in-c Kirkby Overblow *Ripon* 81; R Kirkby Overblow 81-94; rtd 94; Perm to Offic *Glouc* from 94. *22 Roman Row, Whichford, Shipston-on-Stour, Warks CV36 5PJ* Tel (01608) 684362

TUPPER, Michael Heathfield. b 20. St Edm Hall Ox BA41 MA46. Ridley Hall Cam 41. **d** 43 **p** 44. C Win Ch Ch *Win* 43-45; Chapl Monkton Combe Sch Bath 45-48; Asst Chapl Shrewsbury Sch 48-59 and 60-79; Kenya 59-60; Hon C Bayston Hill *Lich* from 80. *9 Eric Lock Road, Bayston Hill, Shrewsbury SY3 0HQ* Tel (01743) 722674

TURAY, Prince Eddie Solomon. b 60. Sierra Leone Th Hall 82. **d** 85 **p** 87. Sierra Leone 85-91; Hon C Gt Cambridge Road St Jo and St Jas *Lon* 94-97; C Edmonton St Aldhelm from 97. *73 Haselbury Road, London N18 1PZ* Tel 0181-807 5336

✠**TURNBULL, The Rt Revd Anthony Michael Arnold.** b 35. Keble Coll Ox BA58 MA62. Cranmer Hall Dur DipTh60. **d** 60 **p** 61 **c** 88. C Middleton *Man* 60-61; C Luton w E Hyde *St Alb* 61-65; Dir of Ords *York* 65-69; Abp's Dom Chapl 65-69; Chapl York Univ 69-76; V Heslington 69-76; Chief Sec CA 76-84; Can Res Roch Cathl *Roch* 84-88; Adn Roch 84-88; Bp Roch 88-94; Bp Dur from 94. *Auckland Castle, Bishop Auckland, Co Durham DL14 7NR* Tel (01388) 602576 Fax 605264

TURNBULL, Brian Robert. b 43. Chich Th Coll 71. **d** 74 **p** 75. C Norbury St Phil *Cant* 74-76; C Folkestone St Sav 76-77; Hon C Tong *Lich* 83-88; C Jarrow *Dur* 88-89; TV 89-94; P-in-c Hartlepool St Oswald 94-96; V from 96. *St Oswald's Clergy House, Brougham Terrace, Hartlepool, Cleveland TS24 8EU* Tel (01429) 273201

TURNBULL, Charles Philip. b 13. Ely Th Coll 37. **d** 38 **p** 39. C Pembury *Roch* 38-42; C Notting Hill St Mich and Ch Ch *Lon* 42-47; C Ely 47-50; V Gorefield 50-52; P-in-c Camden Square St Paul *Lon* 52-54; R Coveney *Ely* 54-64; V Hornsey St Pet *Lon* 64-76; Chapl Laleham Abbey 76-79; rtd 79; Perm to Offic *Chich* from 79. *White Lodge, South Strand, East Preston, Littlehampton, W Sussex BN16 1PN* Tel (01903) 784415

TURNBULL, The Ven David Charles. b 44. Leeds Univ BA65. Chich Th Coll 67. **d** 69 **p** 70. C Jarrow St Paul *Dur* 69-74; V Carlinghow *Wakef* 74-83; V Penistone 83-86; TR Penistone and Thurlstone 86-93; RD Barnsley 88-93; Hon Can Wakef Cathl 92-93; Adn Carl and Can Res Carl Cathl *Carl* from 93. *2 The Abbey, Carlisle CA3 8TZ* Tel (01228) 23026 Fax 594899

TURNBULL, James. b 19. St Aug Coll Cant 57. **d** 58 **p** 59. C Brighton St Pet *Chich* 58-61; V Sayers Common 61-75; R Twineham 61-75; P-in-c Kingston Buci 75-80; Perm to Offic *B & W* from 80; rtd 84. *34 Hood Close, Glastonbury, Somerset BA6 8ES* Tel (01458) 833796

TURNBULL, James Awty. b 28. Solicitor Bradf Univ HonDLaws97. Cranmer Hall Dur 89. **d** 89 **p** 90. NSM Bolton Abbey *Bradf* from 89. *Deerstones Cottage, Deerstones, Skipton, N Yorkshire BD23 6JB*

TURNBULL, Canon John Smith Gardiner. b 13. Kelham Th Coll 30. **d** 36 **p** 37. C Whitwood Mere *Wakef* 36-38; C Sunderland *Dur* 38-43; V W Hartlepool St Aid 43-51; Australia 51-53; V Auckland St Helen *Dur* 53-78; Hon Can Dur Cathl 58-78; rtd 79. *32 The Ridgeway, Mount Park Drive, Lanchester, Durham DH7 0PT* Tel (01207) 520541

TURNBULL, Peter Frederick. b 64. SS Mark & Jo Coll Plymouth BA85. Sarum & Wells Th Coll 89. **d** 91 **p** 92. C Upper Norwood All SS *S'wark* 91-95; Chapl HM Pris Dorchester from 95; C Dorchester *Sarum* from 95. *The Vicarage, Maiden Newton, Dorchester, Dorset DT2 0AT* Tel (01305) 320284

TURNBULL, Richard Duncan. b 60. Reading Univ BA82 MICAS85 Dur Univ PhD97. Cranmer Hall Dur BA92. **d** 94 **p** 95. C Portswood Ch Ch *Win* from 94. *6 Royston Close, Southampton SO17 1TB* Tel (01703) 595015

TURNBULL, Stephen. b 40. Nottm Univ BTh74. Linc Th Coll 70. **d** 74 **p** 75. C Kirkstall *Ripon* 74-76; C Fairfield *Derby* 76-79; TV Seacroft *Ripon* 79-84; Lic to Offic *Derby* from 84; Chapl Derby City Hosp 84-94; Chapl Derby City Gen Hosp NHS Trust from 94; Chapl Derbyshire Children's Hosp from 84. *Derby City General Hospital, Uttoxeter Road, Derby DE22 3NE* Tel (01332) 340131

TURNBULL, William George. b 25. Lich Th Coll 63. **d** 65 **p** 66. C Nunhead St Silas *S'wark* 65-69; C Portishead *B & W* 69-73; C Holsworthy w Cookbury *Ex* 73-76; P-in-c Bridgerule 76-79; P-in-c Pyworthy w Pancraswyke 77-79; P-in-c Pyworthy, Pancrasweek and Bridgerule 79-80; R 80-81; V Otterton and Colaton Raleigh 81-90; rtd 90; Chapl Convent Companions Jes Gd Shep W Ogwell 90-94; Lic to Offic *Ex* 90-94; Perm to Offic *Chich* from 94. *College of St Barnabas, Blackberry Lane, Lingfield, Surrey RH7 6NJ* Tel (01342) 870260

TURNER, Alan James. b 40. Oak Hill Th Coll BA81. **d** 81 **p** 82. C Bradley *Wakef* 81-84; C Sandal St Helen 84-86; P-in-c Sileby *Leic* 86-87; TR Sileby, Cossington and Seagrave 87-94; R Hollington St Leon *Chich* from 94. *The Rectory, Tile Barn Road, St Leonards-on-Sea, E Sussex TN38 9PA* Tel (01424) 852257

TURNER, Albert Edward. b 41. Glouc Sch of Min 83. **d** 89 **p** 90. C Woodford St Mary w St Phil and St Jas *Chelmsf* 89-91; R Greatworth and Marston St Lawrence etc *Pet* from 91. *The Rectory, Marston St Lawrence, Banbury, Oxon OX17 2DA* Tel (01295) 712279

TURNER, Andrew John. b 52. St Jo Coll Nottm LTh. **d** 83 **p** 84. C Framlingham w Saxtead *St E* 83-86; P-in-c Badingham w Bruisyard and Cransford 86-88; P-in-c Dennington 86-88; R Badingham w Bruisyard, Cransford and Dennington 88-91; Chapl RAF from 91. *Chaplaincy Services (RAF), HQ, Personnel and Training Command, RAF Innsworth, Gloucester GL3 1EZ* Tel (01452) 712612 ext 5164 Fax 510828

TURNER, Mrs Ann Elizabeth Hamer. b 38. Ex Univ BA59 PGCE60. Trin Coll Bris 84. **dss** 86 **d** 87 **p** 94. Bath St Luke *B & W* 86-87; Hon C 87-91; Chapl Dorothy Ho Foundn 89-91; C Bath Twerton-on-Avon 91-94; TV 94-96. *24 Edgeworth Road, Bath BA2 2LY* Tel (01225) 424234

TURNER, Anthony John. b 49. St Mich Coll Llan 89. **d** 91 **p** 92. C Coity w Nolton *Llan* 91-95; R Castlemartin w Warren and Angle etc *St D* from 95. *The Rectory, Angle, Pembroke SA71 5AN* Tel (01646) 641368

TURNER, The Ven Antony Hubert Michael (Tony). b 30. FCA63 Lon Univ DipTh56. Tyndale Hall Bris 54. **d** 56 **p** 57. C Nottingham St Ann *S'well* 56-58; C Cheadle *Ches* 58-62; PC Macclesfield Ch Ch 62-68; Lic to Offic *S'wark* 68-74; Home Sec BCMS 68-74; V Southsea St Jude *Portsm* 74-86; P-in-c Portsea St Luke 75-80; RD Portsm 79-84; Hon Can Portsm Cathl 85-86; Adn Is of Wight 86-96; rtd 96. *15 Avenue Road, Hayling Island, Hants PO11 0LX* Tel (01705) 465881

TURNER, Benjamin John. b 45. Bolton Inst of Tech CEng MICE. N Ord Course 82. **d** 85 **p** 86. C Worsley *Man* 85-88; V Elton St Steph 88-95; C Greystoke, Matterdale, Mungrisdale etc *Carl* from 95. *The Rectory, Patterdale, Penrith, Cumbria CA11 0NL* Tel (017684) 82209

TURNER, Mrs Beryl Rose. b 31. Nottm Univ CertEd75 BEd76. **dss** 84 **d** 87 **p** 94. Mortomley St Sav *Sheff* 84-86; Whitgift w Adlingfleet and Eastoft 86; The Marshland 86-87; Par Dn Goole 87-94; C 94; rtd 95; Perm to Offic *Sheff* from 95. *49 Colonel's Walk, Goole, N Humberside DN14 6HJ* Tel (01405) 769193

TURNER, Carl Francis. b 60. St Chad's Coll Dur BA81. St Steph Ho Ox 83. **d** 85 **p** 86. C Leigh-on-Sea St Marg *Chelmsf* 85-88; C Brentwood St Thos 88-90; TV Plaistow 90-95; P-in-c 95-96; TR Plaistow and N Canning Town from 96. *St Martin's Rectory, 34 St Martin's Avenue, London E6 3DX* Tel 0181-471 9381

TURNER, Charles Maurice Joseph. b 13. **d** 79 **p** 80. Hon C Brislington St Luke *Bris* 79-83; Hon C Bris Ch Ch w St Ewen and All SS 83-84; Hon C Bris St Steph w St Nic and St Leon 83-84; Hon C City of Bris 84-89; Perm to Offic from 89. *31 Eagle Road, Bristol BS4 3LQ* Tel 0117-977 6329

TURNER, Mrs Christine. EMMTC. **d** 94 **p** 95. Asst Chapl Qu Medical Cen Nottm Univ Hosp NHS Trust from 94. *Bridge Farm, Hickling, Melton Mowbray, Leics LE14 3AH* Tel (01949) 81304

TURNER, Christopher Gilbert. b 29. New Coll Ox BA52 MA55. Ox Min Course 91. **d** 92 **p** 93. Hon C Hook Norton w Gt Rollright, Swerford etc *Ox* from 92. *Rosemullion, High Street, Great Rollright, Chipping Norton, Oxon OX7 5RQ* Tel (01608) 737359

TURNER, Christopher James Shepherd. b 48. Ch Ch Ox BA70 MA74. Wycliffe Hall Ox 71. **d** 74 **p** 75. C Rusholme H Trin *Man* 74-78; C Chadderton Ch Ch 78-80; V 80-89; V Selly Park St Steph and St Wulstan *Birm* from 89. *St Stephen's Vicarage, 20 Elmdon Road, Birmingham B29 7LF* Tel 0121-472 0050

TURNER, Colin Peter John. b 42. Clifton Th Coll 63. **d** 66 **p** 67. C Kinson *Sarum* 66-68; C York St Paul *York* 68-72; Org Sec (SE Area) CPAS 73-78; TV Weymouth St Jo *Sarum* 78-87; TV Radipole and Melcombe Regis 78-87; R Radstock w Writhlington *B & W* from 90; R Kilmersdon w Babington from 90. *The Rectory, 1 Bristol Road, Radstock, Bath BA3 3EF* Tel (01761) 433182

TURNER, David. b 40. St Andr Univ BSc63. Ridley Hall Cam 63. **d** 65 **p** 66. C Bootle St Matt *Liv* 65-68; C Wigan St Barn Marsh Green 68-73; V Huyton St Geo 73-79; V Meltham Mills *Wakef* 79-89; V Wilshaw 79-89; P-in-c Helme 81-85; P-in-c Meltham 85-89; V Gawber 89-95; Asst Chapl Wirral Hosp NHS Trust from 96; Perm to Offic *Ches* from 96. *Arrowe Park Hospital,*

Arrowe Park Road, Upton, Wirral, Merseyside L49 5PE Tel 0151-678 5111

TURNER, Canon David Stanley. b 35. MISM69 MISE69 Lon Univ CertRK69 Westmr Coll Ox BA84. WMMTC 86. **d** 87 **p** 88. In Free Ch of England 75-77; NSM Worc St Mich *Worc* 87-90; Min Shelfield St Mark CD *Lich* 90-95; C Walsall Wood 90-95; Chapl St Woolos Cathl *Mon* 95-97; V Tredegar St Jas from 97; Hon Can St Bart's Cathl Barrackpore from 97. *St James's Vicarage, Poplar Road, Tredegar NP2 4LH* Tel (01495) 252510

TURNER, Derek John. b 54. Univ of Wales (Ban) BSc81 PhD86. St Jo Coll Nottm. **d** 87 **p** 88. C Pelsall *Lich* 87-91; C Stratford-on-Avon w Bishopton *Cov* from 91. *6 Verney Drive, Stratford-upon-Avon, Warks CV37 0DX* Tel (01789) 269874

TURNER, Donald. b 29. S'wark Ord Course. **d** 71 **p** 72. C Hounslow St Steph *Lon* 71-76; Hon C Isleworth St Jo 76-78; C Brighton St Pet w Chpl Royal *Chich* 78-80; C Brighton St Pet w Chpl Royal and St Jo 80-85; P-in-c St Leonards SS Pet and Paul 85-87; V 87-91; rtd 91. *The Vicarage, West Alvington, Kingsbridge, Devon TQ7 3PZ* Tel (01548) 857658

TURNER, Douglas John. b 15. Ely Th Coll 45. **d** 47 **p** 48. C Ipswich St Matt *St E* 47-50; V Shotesham *Nor* 50-53; R Blakeney w Lt Langham 53-58; RD Walsingham 55-58; Australia 58-59; R Hethersett w Canteloff *Nor* 59-66; V Ketteringham 59-66; V Ventnor H Trin *Portsm* 66-72; V Ventnor St Cath 66-72; V Ryde All SS 72-81; rtd 81; Perm to Offic *Chich* 81-94; Perm to Offic *Nor* from 94. *29 Primrose Avenue, Mulbarton, Norwich NR14 8BJ* Tel (01508) 570185

TURNER, Canon Edward Robert. b 37. Em Coll Cam BA62 BTh66 MA67. Westcott Ho Cam 64. **d** 66 **p** 67. C Salford St Phil w St Steph *Man* 66-69; Chapl Tonbridge Sch 69-81; Adv for In-Service Tr *Roch* 81-89; Dir of Educn 81-96; Can Res Roch Cathl 81-97; Vice-Dean Roch Cathl from 88; Dioc Adv on Community Affairs from 96. *1 King's Orchard, The Precinct, Rochester, Kent ME1 1TG* Tel (01634) 842756 or 830333

TURNER, Mrs Eileen Margaret. b 45. Golds Coll Lon TCert66. N Ord Course 90. **d** 93 **p** 94. Par Dn Sandal St Cath *Wakef* 93-94; C 94-96; P-in-c Hammerwich *Lich* from 96; Dir Local NSM Course from 96. *3 Blackroot Close, Hammerwich, Walsall WS7 0LA* Tel (01543) 677708

TURNER, Miss Elizabeth Jane. b 67. Leeds Univ BEng88. Trin Coll Bris 93. **d** 96 **p** 97. C Eccles *Man* 96; C Eccles from 96. *34 Waterslea, Eccles, Manchester M30 0SR* Tel 0161-789 8148

TURNER, Canon Francis Edwin. b 29. Sarum Th Coll 54. **d** 57 **p** 58. C Cheriton Street *Cant* 57-61; C Willesborough w Hinxhill 61-64; P-in-c Betteshanger w Ham 64-65; R Northbourne w Betteshanger and Ham 64-70; R Northbourne, Tilmanstone w Betteshanger and Ham 70-74; V Sittingbourne St Mich 74-94; RD Sittingbourne 78-84; Hon Can Cant Cathl 84-94; rtd 94. *6 Cherry Grove, Hungerford, Berks RG17 0HP* Tel (01488) 682683

TURNER, Frederick Charles Jesse. b 07. St Boniface Warminster 31. **d** 36 **p** 37. C Ponders End St Matt *Lon* 36-38; C Hayes St Mary 38-46; V Tottenham H Trin 46-59; V Lynch w Iping Marsh *Chich* 59-65; R Ninfield 65-74; V Hooe 65-74; rtd 74. *1 Birchwood Road, Malvern, Worcs WR14 1LD* Tel (01886) 832453

TURNER, Canon Frederick Glynne. b 30. Univ of Wales (Lamp) BA52. St Mich Coll Llan 52. **d** 54 **p** 55. C Aberaman *Llan* 54-60; C Oystermouth *S & B* 60-64; V Abercynon *Llan* 64-71; V Ton Pentre 71-73; V Ystradyfodwg 73-77; R Caerphilly 77-82; V Whitchurch 82-96; Can Llan Cathl from 84; Prec from 95. *83 Newborough Avenue, Llanishen, Cardiff CF4 5DA*

TURNER, Miss Gaynor. b 44. LNSM course 93. **d** 96 **p** 97. NSM Salford Sacred Trin *Man* from 96; Asst Chapl to the Deaf from 96. *28 Monaco Drive, Northenden, Manchester M22 4FG* Tel 0161-872 2323 Textphone 0161-945 1487

TURNER, Geoffrey. b 46. St Deiniol's Hawarden 86. **d** 87 **p** 88. C Lougher *S & B* 87-89; C Swansea St Pet 89-90; V New Radnor and Llanfihangel Nantmelan etc 90-96; V Ystalyfera from 96. *The Vicarage, Ystalyfera, Swansea SA9 3EP* Tel (01639) 842257

TURNER, Geoffrey. b 51. Selw Coll Cam BA75 PGCE75 MA78. N Ord Course 90. **d** 93 **p** 94. C E Crompton *Man* 93-96; C Heywood St Luke w All So from 96. *St Luke's Vicarage, 26 Heywood Hall Road, Heywood, Lancs OL10 4UU* Tel (01706) 360182

TURNER, Dr Geoffrey Edwin. b 45. Aston Univ BSc68 Newc Univ MSc69 PhD72. Cranmer Hall Dur BA74 DipTh75. **d** 75 **p** 76. C Wood End *Cov* 75-79; V Huyton Quarry *Liv* 79-86; Press and Communications Officer *Ely* 86-94; P-in-c Gt w Lt Abington 86-94; P-in-c Hildersham 86-94; V Letchworth St Paul w Willian *St Alb* from 94. *St Paul's Vicarage, 177 Pixmore Way, Letchworth, Herts SG6 1QT* Tel (01462) 683083 Fax 894172

✠**TURNER, The Rt Revd Geoffrey Martin.** b 34. Oak Hill Th Coll 60. **d** 63 **p** 64 **c** 94. C Tonbridge St Steph *Roch* 63-66; C Heatherlands St Jo *Sarum* 66-69; V Derby St Pet *Derby* 69-73; V Chadderton Ch Ch *Man* 73-79; R Bebington *Ches* 79-93; Hon Can Ches Cathl 89-93; RD Wirral N 89-93; Adn Ches 93-94; Suff Bp Stockport from 94. *Bishop's Lodge, Back Lane, Dunham Town, Altrincham, Cheshire WA14 4SG* Tel 0161-928 5611 Fax 929 0692

TURNER, Canon Gerald Garth. b 38. Univ of Wales (Lamp) BA61 St Edm Hall Ox BA63 MA67. St Steph Ho Ox 63. **d** 65 **p** 66. C Drayton in Hales *Lich* 65-68; Chapl Prebendal Sch Chich 68-70; PV Chich Cathl *Chich* 68-70; C Forest Row 70-72; V Hope *Derby* 72-78; Prec Man Cathl *Man* 78-86; Can Res 78-86; R Tattenhall and Handley *Ches* from 86. *The Rectory, Tattenhall, Chester CH3 9QE* Tel (01829) 70328

TURNER, Graham Colin. b 55. Bradf Univ BTech. Oak Hill Th Coll BA81. **d** 81 **p** 82. C Upper Armley *Ripon* 81-86; V Bordesley Green *Birm* from 86. *The Vicarage, 405 Belcher's Lane, Bordesley Green, Birmingham B9 5SY* Tel 0121-772 0418 Fax 766 5401

TURNER, Mrs Heather Winifred. b 43. SRN65. Cant Sch of Min 89. **d** 90 **p** 94. Par Dn Orpington All SS *Roch* 90-93; Chapl to the Deaf from 93; P-in-c Wrotham from 95. *The Rectory, Borough Green Road, Wrotham, Sevenoaks, Kent TN15 7RA* Tel (01732) 882211 (Voice) (01732) 887188 (Minicom) Fax 882211

TURNER, Henry John Mansfield. b 24. Magd Coll Cam BA45 MA48 Man Univ PhD85. Westcott Ho Cam 48. **d** 50 **p** 51. C Crosby *Linc* 50-52; C Chorlton upon Medlock *Man* 52-55; Inter-Colleg Sec SCM (Man) 52-55; C Leigh St Mary *Man* 55-57; V Rochdale Gd Shep 57-62; India 63-67; V Becontree St Geo *Chelmsf* 67-71; R Weeley 71-79; Chapl St Deiniol's Lib Hawarden 79-80; Sub-Warden 80-86; Perm to Offic *St As* 86-87; Perm to Offic *Chelmsf* from 86; Hon C St Botolph without Bishopgate *Lon* from 87. *Merrywood, 25 Fourth Avenue, Frinton-on-Sea, Essex CO13 9DU* Tel (01255) 677554

TURNER, James Alfred (Jim). b 34. Ox Coll FE MCIPS76. Ox Min Course 91. **d** 94 **p** 95. NSM Kidlington w Hampton Poyle *Ox* from 94. *11 St Mary's Close, Kidlington, Oxford OX5 2AY* Tel (01865) 375562

TURNER, Miss Jessica Mary. b 60. SS Coll Cam BA81 PGCE82. Trin Coll Bris 88. **d** 91 **p** 94. Par Dn Preston Em *Blackb* 91-94; Par Dn Bamber Bridge St Aid 94; C 94-95; Chapl Preston Acute Hosps NHS Trust from 95. *Royal Preston Hospital, Sharoe Green Lane North, Fulwood, Preston PR2 4HT* Tel (01772) 710435 or 716565 Fax 710162

TURNER, Miss Jessie Irene. b 06. Qu Mary Coll Lon BSc29 DipEd30. **dss** 60 **d** 87. Coleford w Staunton *Glouc* 60-69; Chingford St Edm *Chelmsf* 69-87; Hon Par Dn 87-93; Perm to Offic from 93. *57 Normanshire Drive, London E4 9HE* Tel 0181-524 4108

TURNER, John David Maurice. b 22. Keble Coll Ox BA45 MA48. Ripon Hall Ox 69. **d** 70 **p** 71. C Crowthorne *Ox* 70-73; V Cropredy w Gt Bourton 73-79; V Cropredy w Gt Bourton and Wardington 80-83; Perm to Offic from 83; Perm to Offic *Pet* from 83; rtd 87. *Appletree Cottage, The Close, Greatworth, Banbury, Oxon OX17 2EB* Tel (01295) 711326

TURNER, John Edward. b 19. S Dios Minl Tr Scheme. **d** 82 **p** 83. NSM Radipole and Melcombe Regis *Sarum* 82-91; Perm to Offic from 91. *95 Weymouth Bay Avenue, Weymouth, Dorset DT3 5AD* Tel (01305) 771024

TURNER, John Gilbert. b 06. Cranmer Hall Dur. **d** 66 **p** 67. C Holme Pierrepont w Adbolton *S'well* 66-69; C Radcliffe-on-Trent 69-71; C Tithby w Cropwell Butler 71-77; C Colston Bassett 71-77; C Cropwell Bishop 71-77; C Langar 71-77; C Granby w Elton 71-77; rtd 77; Perm to Offic *S'well* from 79. *Landyke, Tythby Road, Cropwell Butler, Nottingham NG14 7AR* Tel 0115-933 3166

TURNER, John William. b 43. Sheff Univ BSc73. Wycliffe Hall Ox 86. **d** 88 **p** 89. C Clayton *Bradf* 88-91; C Horton 91-92; V Bankfoot from 92. *The Vicarage, Carbottom Road, Bankfoot, Bradford, W Yorkshire BD5 9AA* Tel (01274) 726529

TURNER, Keith Howard. b 50. Southn Univ BA71. Wycliffe Hall Ox 72. **d** 75 **p** 76. C Enfield Ch Ch Trent Park *Lon* 75-79; C Chilwell *S'well* 79-83; P-in-c Linby w Papplewick 83-90; R from 90. *The Rectory, Main Street, Linby, Nottingham NG15 8AE* Tel 0115-963 2346

TURNER, Lawrence John. b 43. Kelham Th Coll 65. **d** 70 **p** 71. C Lower Gornal *Lich* 70-73; C Wednesbury St Paul Wood Green 73-74; C Porthill 75-77; C Wilton *York* 77-80; P-in-c 80-82; R Jersey St Martin *Win* from 82; Chmn Jersey Miss to Seamen from 82. *St Martin's Rectory, Jersey, Channel Islands JE3 6HW* Tel (01534) 854294

TURNER, Leslie. b 29. NE Lon Poly BSc87. St Jo Coll Dur 50 St Aid Birkenhead 51. **d** 54 **p** 55. C Darwen St Cuth *Blackb* 54-56; C Haslingden w Grane and Stonefold 56-59; V Oswaldtwistle St Paul 59-65; Chapl Belmont and Henderson Hosps Sutton 65-71; St Ebba's Hosp Epsom 65-71; Qu Mary's Carshalton 67-71; Lic to Offic *Pet* 71-94; Chapl Princess Marina & St Crispin's Hosps 71-87; Chapl Northn Gen Hosp 87-94; Chapl Manfield Hosp Northn 87-94; Chapl St Edm Hosp Northn 87-94; rtd 94; Perm to Offic *Pet* from 94. *20 Banbury Close, Northampton NN4 9UA* Tel (01604) 769233

TURNER, Mark. b 60. Aston Tr Scheme 87 Sarum & Wells Th Coll BTh92. **d** 92 **p** 93. C New Sleaford *Linc* 92-94; C Bottesford and Muston *Leic* from 94; C Harby, Long Clawson and Hose from 94; C Barkestone w Plungar, Redmile and Stathern from 94. *The Rectory, 1 Boyers Orchard, Harby, Melton Mowbray, Leics LE14 4BA*

TURNER, Mark Richard Haythornthwaite. b 41. TCD MA67 Linc Coll Ox BA68. Wycliffe Hall Ox 65. **d** 68 **p** 69. C Birtley *Newc* 68-71; C Cambridge Gt St Mary w St Mich *Ely* 71-74; Chapl Loughb Univ *Leic* 74-79; P-in-c Keele *Lich* 80-85; Chapl Keele Univ 80-85; P-in-c Ashley 85-95; P-in-c Mucklestone 86-95; R Farnborough *Roch* from 95. *The Rectory, Farnborough Hill, Orpington, Kent BR6 7EQ* Tel (01689) 853471

TURNER, Martin John. b 34. Trin Hall Cam BA55 MA59. Cuddesdon Coll 58. **d** 60 **p** 61. C Rugby St Andr *Cov* 60-65; C Cov Cathl 65-68; USA 68-70; V Rushmere *St E* 70-82; V Monkwearmouth St Pet *Dur* 82-90; V Bathford *B & W* from 90. *Bathford Vicarage, Ostlings Lane, Bath BA1 7RW* Tel (01225) 859575

TURNER, Mrs Maureen. b 55. Leeds Univ BA78. St Jo Coll Nottm 84. **d** 87 **p** 94. Par Dn Darlaston St Lawr *Lich* 87-91; C Stratford-on-Avon w Bishopton *Cov* from 91. *6 Verney Drive, Stratford-upon-Avon, Warks CV37 0DX* Tel (01789) 269874

TURNER, Maurice William. b 27. Sarum Th Coll 53. **d** 56 **p** 57. C Thornhill *Wakef* 56-60; V Gawber 60-71; V Alverthorpe 71-74; V Oxon and Shelton *Lich* 74-81; P-in-c Battlefield w Albrighton 81-82; V Leaton 81-82; V Leaton and Albrighton w Battlefield 82-92; rtd 92; Perm to Offic *Lich* 93-96; Perm to Offic *Heref* from 96. *10 Melbourne Rise, Bicton Heath, Shrewsbury SY3 5DA* Tel (01743) 352667

TURNER, Michael Andrew. b 34. K Coll Cam BA59 MA62. Cuddesdon Coll 59. **d** 61 **p** 62. C Luton St Andr *St Alb* 61-64; V 70-77; C-in-c Northolt St Mary *Lon* 64-70; Perm to Offic *St Alb* 77-93; Dep Hd and Chapl Greycoat Hosp Sch 86-93; Perm to Offic *Lon* 86-93; P-in-c Shilling Okeford *Sarum* from 93; Chapl Croft Ho Sch Shillingstone from 93. *The Rectory, Shillingstone, Blandford Forum, Dorset DT11 0SL* Tel (01258) 860261

TURNER, Michael John Royce. b 43. St Jo Coll Dur BA65. Chich Th Coll 65. **d** 67 **p** 68. C Hodge Hill *Birm* 67-71; C Eling, Testwood and Marchwood *Win* 71-72; TV 72-77; R Kirkwall *Ab* 77-85; R Laurencekirk *Bre* from 85; R Drumtochty from 85; R Fasque from 85; R Drumlithie from 85. *Beattie Lodge, Laurencekirk, Kincardineshire AB30 1HJ* Tel (01561) 377380

TURNER, Canon Nicholas Anthony. b 51. Clare Coll Cam BA73 MA77 Keble Coll Ox BA77 MA81. Ripon Coll Cuddesdon 76. **d** 78 **p** 79. C Stretford St Matt *Man* 78-80; Tutor St Steph Ho Ox 80-84; V Leeds Richmond Hill *Ripon* 84-91; Ascension Is 91-96; Offg Chapl RAF 91-96; Can Th St Helena Cathl from 94; V Raynes Park St Sav *S'wark* from 96. *St Saviour's Vicarage, Church Walk, London SW20 9DG* Tel 0181-542 2787 Fax 543 8330

TURNER (née SYMINGTON), Mrs Patricia Ann. b 46. SRN68 RMN71 SCM72 Cam Univ DipRS82. St Steph Ho Ox 82. **dss** 84 **d** 87. Buttershaw St Aid *Bradf* 84-87; TD Manningham 87-91; Ascension Is 91-96; Par Dn Raynes Park St Sav *S'wark* from 96. *St Saviour's Vicarage, Church Walk, London SW20 9DG* Tel 0181-542 2787 Fax 543 8330

TURNER, Peter Carpenter. b 39. Oak Hill Th Coll 63. **d** 66 **p** 67. C Chadwell *Chelmsf* 66-69; C Braintree 69-73; R Fyfield 73-87; P-in-c Moreton 77-87; C-in-c Bobbingworth 82-87; P-in-c Willingale w Shellow and Berners Roding 84-87; P-in-c E Ham St Geo from 87. *The Vicarage, Buxton Road, London E6 3NB* Tel 0181-472 2111

TURNER, The Ven Peter Robin. b 42. Open Univ BA79. AKC65. **d** 66 **p** 67. C Crediton *Ex* 66-69; Chapl RAF 70-88; Asst Chapl-in-Chief RAF 88-95; QHC from 92; Chapl-in-Chief RAF from 95. *Chaplaincy Services (RAF), HQ, Personnel and Training Command, RAF Innsworth, Gloucester GL3 1EZ* Tel (01452) 712612 ext 5164 Fax 510828

TURNER, Philip William. b 25. CM65. Worc Coll Ox BA50 MA62. Chich Th Coll 49. **d** 51 **p** 52. C Armley St Bart *Ripon* 51-56; P-in-c Crawley *Chich* 56-62; V Northampton St Matt *Pet* 62-66; Relig Broadcasting Org BBC Midl Region 66-71; Asst Master Brian Mill Sch Droitwich 71-73; Chapl Eton Coll 73-75; Chapl Malvern Coll 75-84; Chapl St Jas & Abbey Schs Malvern 84-86; rtd 90. *181 West Malvern Road, Malvern, Worcs WR14 4AY* Tel (01684) 563852

TURNER, Canon Robert Edgar. b 20. TCD BA42 MA51. Linc Th Coll 44. **d** 45 **p** 46. C Kings Heath *Birm* 45-51; Min Can Belf Cathl 51-63; Dean of Res QUB 51-58; Bp's Dom Chapl *D & D* 56-67; I Belfast St Geo *Conn* 58-90; Can Belf Cathl 71-76; Preb Clonmethan St Patr Cathl Dublin 76-90; Dioc Registrar *Conn* from 82; rtd 90. *19 Cricklewood Park, Belfast BT9 5GU* Tel (01232) 663214

TURNER, Robin Edward. b 35. Selw Coll Cam BA57 MA63. Qu Coll Birm DipTh63. **d** 63 **p** 64. C Aveley *Chelmsf* 63-67; C Upminster 67-71; R Goldhanger w Lt Totham 71-80; R Lt Baddow from 80; Hon Chapl New Hall Sch Essex from 80. *The Rectory, Colam Lane, Little Baddow, Chelmsford CM3 4SY* Tel (01245) 223488

TURNER, Roger Dyke. b 39. Trin Coll Bris 79. **d** 81 **p** 82. C Clevedon St Andr *B & W* 81-82; C Clevedon St Andr and Ch Ch 83-85; R Freshford, Limpley Stoke and Hinton Charterhouse 85-88; V Kenilworth St Jo *Cov* from 88; RD Kenilworth from 90. *St John's Vicarage, Clarke's Avenue, Kenilworth, Warks CV8 1HX* Tel (01926) 53203

TURNER, St John Alwin. b 31. Dur Univ BA57 MA61. Cranmer Hall Dur DipTh58. **d** 59 **p** 60. C W Hartlepool St Paul *Dur* 59-62; C S Shore H Trin *Blackb* 62-65; V Huncoat 65-67; Org Sec (Dios Ripon and York) CMS 67-72; V Harrogate St Mark *Ripon* 72-94; rtd 96. *2 The Tilney, Whaplode, Spalding, Lincs PE12 6UW* Tel (01406) 371390

TURNER, Susan. b 58. Man Univ BA89. N Ord Course 89. **d** 92 **p** 93. NSM Balderstone *Man* 92-93; NSM E Crompton 93-94; Hon C 94-96; Chapl Man Coll of Arts and Tech 92-96; Asst Chapl S Man Univ Hosps NHS Trust 96-97; Chapl Burnley Healthcare NHS Trust from 97. *St Luke's Vicarage, 26 Heywood Hall Road, Heywood, Lancs OL10 4UU* Tel (01706) 360182 or (01282) 425071

TURNER (formerly BENBOW), Mrs Susan Catherine (Sue). b 47. Birm Univ BEd70. St Alb Minl Tr Scheme 82. **dss** 85 **d** 87 **p** 94. Gt Wyrley *Lich* 85-87; Par Dn 87-88; Par Dn Whitstable *Cant* 88-92; Par Dn Eastry and Northbourne w Tilmanstone etc 92-94; C 94-96; P-in-c Gt Mongeham w Ripple and Sutton by Dover from 96. *The Rectory, Northbourne Road, Great Mongeham, Deal, Kent CT14 0HB* Tel (01304) 360170

TURNER, Sylvia Jean. b 46. Lon Univ 72 Open Univ BA77. Westcott Ho Cam CTM95. **d** 95 **p** 96. C Whitstable *Cant* from 95. *64 Cromwell Road, Whitstable, Kent CT5 1NN* Tel (01227) 262590

TURNER, Walter. b 21. Lich Th Coll 51. **d** 53 **p** 54. C Barrow St Jas *Carl* 53-56; C Penrith 56-58; V Haverthwaite 58-65; V Frizington 65-70; V Underbarrow w Helsington and Crook 70-77; V Allithwaite 77-79; TV Kirkby Lonsdale 79-82; TV Penrith w Newton Reigny and Plumpton Wall 82-86; rtd 86; Perm to Offic *Carl* from 86. *69 Lansdowne Crescent, Carlisle CA3 9ES* Tel (01228) 401177

TURNER, Canon Walter John. b 29. Bris Univ BA53. Clifton Th Coll 49. **d** 54 **p** 55. C W Bromwich All SS *Lich* 54-58; C-in-c Oxley 58-60; V 60-65; V Wednesfield St Thos 65-74; RD Shifnal 75-83; V Boningale 75-83; V Shifnal 75-83; Preb Lich Cathl 80-83; Can Res and Prec Lich Cathl 83-94; rtd 94; Perm to Offic *Lich* from 94. *9 Kestrel Close, Newport, Shropshire TF10 8QE* Tel (01952) 820758

TURNER, William Edward (Bill). b 41. Keble Coll Ox BA63 MA73. Linc Th Coll 76. **d** 78 **p** 79. C Lich St Chad *Lich* 78-80; Chapl Trent (Nottm) Poly *S'well* 80-89; Chapl Lancs (Preston) Poly *Blackb* 89-92; Chapl Cen Lancs Univ from 92. *10 Queens Road, Fulwood, Preston PR2 3EA* Tel (01772) 717791 or 892615 Fax 202073

TURNOCK, Geoffrey. MSOSc Leeds Univ BSc61 PhD64. EMMTC 84. **d** 87 **p** 88. NSM Oadby *Leic* from 87. *51 Brambling Way, Oadby, Leicester LE2 5PB* Tel 0116-271 4115

TURP, Paul Robert. b 48. Oak Hill Th Coll BA79. **d** 79 **p** 80. C Southall Green St Jo *Lon* 79-83; V Shoreditch St Leon w St Mich 83-88; TR Shoreditch St Leon and Hoxton St Jo from 88. *The Vicarage, 36 Hoxton Square, London N1 6NN* Tel 0171-739 2063

TURPIN, John Richard. b 41. St D Coll Lamp BA63 Magd Coll Cam BA65 MA70. Cuddesdon Coll 65. **d** 66 **p** 67. C Tadley St Pet *Win* 66-71; V Southampton Thornhill St Chris 71-85; V Ringwood from 85. *The Vicarage, 65 Southampton Road, Ringwood, Hants BH24 1HE* Tel (01425) 473219

TURRALL, Albert Thomas George. b 19. Linc Th Coll 64. **d** 66 **p** 67. C Rowley Regis *Birm* 66-69; R Astley *Worc* 69-74; V Montford w Shrawardine *Lich* 74-77; R Montford w Shrawardine and Fitz 77-84; rtd 84; Perm to Offic *Heref* from 86; Perm to Offic *Lich* from 86. *15 Highbury Close, Shrewsbury SY2 6SN* Tel (01743) 249831

TURTON, Arthur Bickerstaffe. b 19. Oak Hill Th Coll 46. **d** 48 **p** 49. C Rawtenstall St Mary *Man* 48-51; C Islington St Mary *Lon* 51-52; V Lozells St Silas *Birm* 52-56; V Streatham Park St Alb *S'wark* 56-60; Org Sec CPAS Metrop Area 60-64; V Southborough St Pet *Roch* 64-68; P-in-c Southborough St Matt 67-68; V Southborough St Pet w Ch Ch and St Matt 68-76; V Histon *Ely* 76-82; rtd 84; Perm to Offic *Chich* 82-88; Perm to Offic *Ely* from 88. *20 St Peter's Drive, Chatteris, Cambs PE16 6BY* Tel (01354) 695551

TURTON, Douglas Walter. b 38. Kent Univ BA77 Surrey Univ MSc90. Oak Hill Th Coll 77. **d** 78 **p** 79. C Cant St Mary Bredin *Cant* 78-80; P-in-c Thornton Heath St Paul 80-81; V 81-84; V Thornton Heath St Paul *S'wark* 85-91; R Eastling w Ospringe and Stalisfield w Otterden *Cant* from 91. *The Rectory, Newnham Lane, Eastling, Faversham, Kent ME13 0AS* Tel (01795) 890487

TURTON, Neil Christopher. b 45. Wycliffe Hall Ox 77. **d** 79 **p** 80. C Guildf Ch Ch *Guildf* 79-83; C Godalming 83-86; V Wyke 86-92; R Frimley from 92; RD Surrey Heath from 97. *The Rectory, Parsonage Way, Frimley, Camberley, Surrey GU16 5AG* Tel (01276) 23309

TURTON, Paul Edward. b 26. St Pet Hall Ox BA50 MA55. Qu Coll Birm 50. **d** 52 **p** 53. C Selly Oak St Mary *Birm* 52-55; C Ward End 55-57; I Netherton CD *Liv* 57-64; V Brockley Hill St Sav *S'wark* 64-68; Perm to Offic 68-70; Dir of Educn *Nor* 70-75; Dep Dir Nat Soc Cen Camberwell 75-77; Dir Nat Soc RE Cen Kensington 78-84; C Eastbourne St Mary *Chich* 84-86; rtd 86;

Perm to Offic *Chich* from 87. *32 Churchill Close, Eastbourne, E Sussex BN20 8AJ* Tel (01323) 638089

✠**TUSTIN, The Rt Revd David.** b 35. Magd Coll Cam BA57 MA61. Cuddesdon Coll 58. **d** 60 **p** 61 **c** 79. C Stafford St Mary *Lich* 60-63; C St Dunstan in the West *Lon* 63-67; Asst Gen Sec C of E Coun on Foreign Relns 63-67; V Wednesbury St Paul Wood Green *Lich* 67-71; V Tettenhall Regis 71-79; RD Trysull 76-79; Suff Bp Grimsby *Linc* from 79; Can and Preb Linc Cathl from 79. *Bishop's House, Church Lane, Irby-upon-Humber, Grimsby, S Humberside DN37 7JR* Tel (01472) 371715 Fax 371716

TUTTON, Canon John Knight. b 30. Man Univ BSc51. Ripon Hall Ox 53. **d** 55 **p** 56. C Tonge w Alkrington *Man* 55-57; C Bushbury *Lich* 57-59; R Blackley St Andr *Man* 59-67; R Denton Ch Ch 67-95; Hon Can Man Cathl 90-95; rtd 95. *The Rectory, Cheriton Bishop, Exeter EX6 6HY* Tel (01647) 24651

✠**TUTU, The Rt Revd Desmond Mpilo.** b 31. UNISA BA K Coll Lon BD MTh FKC78. St Pet Rosettenville LTh. **d** 60 **p** 61 **c** 76. S Africa 60-62; C Golders Green St Alb *Lon* 62-65; C Bletchingley *S'wark* 65-66; S Africa 67-70; Lesotho 70-72; Assoc Dir Th Educn Fund WCC 72-75; C Lee St Aug *S'wark* 72-75; Dean Johannesburg 75-76; Bp Lesotho 76-78; Asst Bp Johannesburg 78-85; Bp Johannesburg 85-86; Abp Cape Town 86-96; rtd 96. *PO Box 3162, Cape Town, 8000 South Africa*

TWADDELL, Canon William Reginald. b 33. TCD 61. **d** 62 **p** 63. C Belfast Whiterock *Conn* 62-65; I Loughgilly w Clare *Arm* 65-71; I Milltown 71-84; I Portadown St Mark from 84; RD Kilmore from 86; Preb Arm Cathl 88-96; Treas Arm Cathl from 96. *The Rectory, Brownstown Road, Portadown, Co Armagh BT62 3QA* Tel (01762) 332368

TWEDDLE, David William Joseph. b 28. ATCL56 Dur Univ BSc50. Wycliffe Hall Ox 54. **d** 56 **p** 57. C Darlington H Trin *Dur* 56-60; P-in-c Prestonpans *Edin* 60-63; PV Linc Cathl *Linc* 63-65; C Pet St Jo *Pet* 65-71; Hon Min Can Pet Cathl 68-93; V Southwick w Glapthorn 71-83; P-in-c Benefield 80-83; R Benefield and Southwick w Glapthorn 83-93; RD Oundle 84-89; rtd 94; Perm to Offic *Ely* from 94; Perm to Offic *Pet* from 94. *6 Barton Square, Ely, Cambs CB7 4DF* Tel (01353) 668020

TWEED, Andrew. b 48. Univ of Wales (Cardiff) BA69 Trin Coll Carmarthen MA97. St Deiniol's Hawarden. **d** 81 **p** 84. NSM Llandrindod w Cefnllys *S & B* 81-87; NSM Llandrindod w Cefnllys and Disserth from 87. *Gwenallt, Wellington Road, Llandrindod Wells LD1 5NB* Tel (01597) 823671

TWEEDIE-SMITH, Ian David. b 60. Newc Univ BA83. Wycliffe Hall Ox 83. **d** 85 **p** 86. C Hatcham St Jas *S'wark* 85-89; C Bury St Edmunds St Mary *St E* from 89. *St Mary's House, 18 Vinery Road, Bury St Edmunds, Suffolk IP33 2JR* Tel (01284) 705035

TWIDELL, William James. b 30. St Mich Coll Llan 58. **d** 60 **p** 61. C Tonge w Alkrington *Man* 60-63; C High Wycombe All SS *Ox* 63-65; P-in-c Elkesley w Bothamsall *S'well* 65-66; V Bury St Thos *Man* 66-72; V Daisy Hill 72-84; R Flixton St Mich from 84; AD Stretford from 88; Hon Can Man Cathl from 97. *The Rectory, 348 Church Road, Flixton, Urmston, Manchester M31 3HR* Tel 0161-748 2884

TWISLETON, Dr John Fiennes. b 48. St Jo Coll Ox MA73 DPhil73. Coll of Resurr Mirfield DipTh75. **d** 76 **p** 77. C New Bentley *Sheff* 76-79; P-in-c Moorends 79-80; V 80-86; USPG 86-90; Coll of the Ascension Selly Oak 86-87; Guyana 87-90; V Holbrooks *Cov* 90-96; Edmonton Area Missr *Lon* from 96. *St Saviour's Vicarage, 268 Alexandra Park Road, London N22 4BG* Tel 0181-888 5683

TWISLETON, Peter. b 50. Linc Th Coll. **d** 84 **p** 85. C Bodmin w Lanhydrock and Lanivet *Truro* 84-87; C Par 87-90; R St Breoke and Egloshayle 90-93; R Bude Haven and Marhamchurch 93-97. *Elmore Abbey, Church Lane, Speen, Newbury, Berks RG13 1SA* Tel (01635) 33080

TWISLETON-WYKEHAM-FIENNES, Oliver William. *See* FIENNES, The Very Revd the Hon Oliver William

TWISS, Dorothy Elizabeth. Gilmore Ho 68 Linc Th Coll 70. **d** 87 **p** 94. Chapl Asst RAF 78-91; TV Pewsey TM *Sarum* 91-95; Chapl HM Pris Drake Hall from 95. *The Chaplain's Office, HM Prison Drake Hall, Eccleshall, Stafford ST21 6LQ* Tel (01785) 850621 Ext 238 Fax 851931

TWITTY, Miss Rosamond Jane. b 54. Univ of Wales (Ban) BSc75 CertEd76. Trin Coll Bris BA89. **d** 90 **p** 94. Par Dn Lt Thurrock St Jo *Chelmsf* 90-94; C 94-95; C Upper Armley *Ripon* from 95. *115A Heights Drive, Leeds LS12 3TG* Tel 0113-263 7240

TWOHIG, Brian Robert. b 48. La Trobe Univ Victoria BA77 PhD86. St Mich Th Coll Crafers 70. **d** 72 **p** 73. Australia 72-78 and 80-82; C Leatherhead *Guildf* 78-80; TV New Windsor *Ox* 82-92; V Sheff St Cuth *Sheff* 92-97; rtd 97. *26A Bloomsbury Street, Brighton BN2 1HQ*

TWOMEY, Jeremiah Francis (Derry). b 50. Man Poly BA83 Univ of Wales (Ban) PGCE85 Real Colegio de Escoceses Valladolid Spain. NE Ord Course 92. **d** 94 **p** 95. C Beverley St Nic *York* 94-96; V Anlaby Common St Mark from 96. *St Mark's Vicarage, 1055 Anlaby Road, Hull HU4 7PP* Tel (01482) 351977

TWOMEY, Jeremiah Thomas Paul. b 46. CITC 87. **d** 87 **p** 88. C Derryloran *Arm* 87-90; I Brackaville w Donaghendry and Ballyclog 90-97; I Mohill w Farnaught, Aughavas, Oughteragh etc *K, E & A* from 97. *St Mary's Rectory, Mohill, Carrick-on-Shannon, Co Leitrim, Irish Republic* Tel Leitrim (078) 31012

TWYCROSS, Stephen Jervis. b 33. Nottm Univ BEd73 Leic Univ MA85. Lambeth STh88 Kalk Bay Bible Inst S Africa 56 Wycliffe Hall Ox 58. **d** 60 **p** 61. C Hinckley H Trin *Leic* 60-64; V Barlestone 64-71; NSM Dio Leic 71-87; P-in-c Stokesay *Heref* 87-91; P-in-c Sibdon Carwood w Halford 87-91; Chapl Utrecht w Amersfoort, Harderwijk & Zwolle *Eur* 91-94; V Llanwddyn and Llanfihangel and Llwydiarth *St As* 94-96; rtd 96; Perm to Offic *Ban* from 96. *1 Britannia Place, Porthmadog LL49 9LY* Tel (01766) 514682

TWYFORD, Canon Arthur Russell. b 36. ALCD60. **d** 60 **p** 61. C Speke All SS *Liv* 60-64; Asst Dioc Youth Officer *Ox* 64-70; R Maids Moreton w Foxcote 64-72; P-in-c Lillingstone Dayrell w Lillingstone Lovell 70-72; V Desborough *Pet* 72-88; P-in-c Braybrook 73-77; P-in-c Brampton Ash w Dingley 73-77; R Brampton Ash w Dingley and Braybrooke 77-88; RD Kettering 79-87; Can Pet Cathl 81-95; R Stanwick w Hargrave 88-95; rtd 95; Perm to Offic *Pet* from 95. *1 Laws Lane, Finedon, Wellingborough, Northants NN9 5LU* Tel (01933) 682116

TYDEMAN, Canon Richard. b 16. St Jo Coll Ox BA39 MA43. Ripon Hall Ox 38. **d** 39 **p** 40. C Langley St Mich *Birm* 39-41; C Ipswich All SS *St E* 41-45; P-in-c Ipswich St Helen 45-46; V Woodbridge St Jo 46-53; V Newmarket All SS 53-63; RD Newmarket 54-63; Hon Can St E Cathl 59-63; R St Sepulchre w Ch Ch Greyfriars etc *Lon* 63-81; Dep Min Can St Paul's Cathl 63-81; Preacher Lincoln's Inn 72-81; rtd 81; Perm to Offic *St E* from 82. *10 Colneis Road, Felixstowe, Suffolk IP11 9HF* Tel (01394) 283214

TYE, Eric John. b 37. St Alb Minl Tr Scheme. **d** 81 **p** 82. NSM Rushden w Newton Bromswold *Pet* from 81. *31 Morris Avenue, Rushden, Northants NN10 9PB* Tel (01933) 53274

TYE, John Raymond. b 31. Lambeth STh64 Linc Th Coll 66. **d** 68 **p** 69. C Crewe St Mich *Ches* 68-71; C Wednesfield St Thos *Lich* 71-76; P-in-c Petton w Cockshutt 76-79; P-in-c Hordley 79; P-in-c Weston Lullingfield 79; R Petton w Cockshutt and Weston Lullingfield etc 79-81; V Hadley 81-84; R Ightfield w Calverhall 84-89; V Ash 84-89; R Calton, Cauldon, Grindon and Waterfall 89-96; RD Alstonfield 95-96; rtd 96. *Oak Lodge, Weston Lullingfields, Shrewsbury SY4 2AA*

TYE, Leslie Bernard. b 14. AKC40. **d** 40 **p** 41. C Edmonton St Alphege *Lon* 40-42; C Hornsey St Mary 42-43; C Whetstone St Jo 43-47; C Hawarden *St As* 47-52; C Addlestone *Guildf* 52-59; V Ault Hucknall *Derby* 59-69; V Ambergate 69-79; rtd 79; Perm to Offic *Derby* from 79. *31 Cromwell Drive, Swanwick, Derby DE55 1DB* Tel (01773) 602895

TYERS, Canon Gerald Seymour. b 22. St Pet Hall Ox BA46 MA49. Linc Th Coll 47. **d** 49 **p** 50. C Perry Street *Roch* 49-52; C Gillingham St Aug 52-53; V 60-67; V Orpington St Andr 53-60; V Erith Ch Ch 67-82; Chapl Erith and Distr Hosp 67-82; RD Erith 79-82; R Foots Cray *Roch* 82-91; Hon Can Roch Cathl 82-91; rtd 91; Perm to Offic *Roch* from 91. *Yew Tree Cottage, Castle Hill, Hartley, Dartford DA3 7BH* Tel (01474) 707923

TYERS, Canon John Haydn. b 31. Lon Univ BSc51. Ridley Hall Cam 53. **d** 55 **p** 56. C Nuneaton St Nic *Cov* 55-58; C Rugby St Andr 58-62; V Cov St Anne 62-71; V Keresley and Coundon 71-78; V Atherstone 78-85; P-in-c Pleshey *Chelmsf* 85-91; Warden Pleshey Retreat Ho 85-91; Hon Can Chelmsf Cathl *Chelmsf* 86-91; P-in-c Ash *Lich* 91-96; P-in-c Ightfield w Calverhall 91-96; rtd 96. *7 Brook Road, Pontesbury, Shrewsbury SY5 0QZ* Tel (01743) 790354

TYERS, Philip Nicolas. b 56. Nottm Univ BTh84. St Jo Coll Nottm 80. **d** 84 **p** 85. C Rugby St Matt *Cov* 84-88; TV Cov E 88-95; P-in-c Preston St Matt *Blackb* 95-96; TR Preston Risen Lord from 96. *St Matthew's Vicarage, 20 Fishwick Road, Preston PR1 4YA* Tel (01772) 794222

TYLDESLEY, Douglas Wilfred. b 31. CCC Cam BA54 MA58. Oak Hill Th Coll 54. **d** 56 **p** 57. C Skellingthorpe *Linc* 56-58; C Doddington 57-58; C Beckenham St Jo *Roch* 58-61; V Walthamstow St Luke *Chelmsf* 61-66; V Prestwold w Hoton *Leic* 66-72; R Sapcote 72-83; R Sapcote and Sharnford w Wigston Parva 83-96; rtd 96; Perm to Offic *Ex* from 96. *8 West Grove Road, Exeter EX2 4LU* Tel (01392) 274881

TYLER, Alan William. b 60. Univ of Wales (Ban) DipTh84. Ridley Hall Cam 84. **d** 86 **p** 87. C Bedwellty *Mon* 86-89; C St Mellons and Michaelston-y-Fedw 89-92; V Abersychan and Garndiffaith from 92. *The Vicarage, Abersychan, Pontypool NP4 8PL* Tel (01495) 772213

TYLER, Alison Ruth. b 51. Keele Univ BA74 Birm Univ DipSocWork78 CQSW78. S'wark Ord Course 93. **d** 95 **p** 96. NSM Hatcham St Cath *S'wark* from 95. *75 Erlanger Road, London SE14 5TQ* Tel 0171-207 0756

TYLER, Andrew. b 57. Univ of Wales (Lamp) BA79 Warw Univ MA80 Man Univ BD86. Coll of Resurr Mirfield 83. **d** 87 **p** 88. C Glen Parva and S Wigston *Leic* 87-90; C Didcot All SS *Ox* 90-92; Asst Chapl Chu Hosp Ox 92-93; NSM Caversham St Andr *Ox*

93-97; Co-ord Tr Portfolio (Berks) 96-97; P-in-c Nor St Giles *Nor* from 97. *44 Heigham Road, Norwich NR2 3AU* Tel (01603) 623724

TYLER, Brian Sidney. b 32. MIPI79. Chich Th Coll 62. **d** 64 **p** 65. C Brighton St Mich *Chich* 64-69; C-in-c Southwick St Pet 69-75; Perm to Offic 80; NSM Brighton Resurr 93-94; Chapl St Dunstan's Hosp Brighton 93-95; C Brighton St Matthias *Chich* from 95. *318 Ditchling Road, Brighton BN1 6JG* Tel (01273) 559292

TYLER (née FOSTER), Mrs Frances Elizabeth. b 55. Linc Th Coll 81. **dss** 84 **d** 87 **p** 94. Hampton All SS *Lon* 84-87; Par Dn Brentford 87-91; NSM Walsgrave on Sowe *Cov* from 91. *The Vicarage, 4 Farber Road, Coventry CV2 2BG* Tel (01203) 615152 or 618845

TYLER, Mrs Gaynor. b 46. Univ of Wales (Abth) BA68. S'wark Ord Course 87. **d** 90 **p** 94. NSM Reigate St Luke S Park *S'wark* 90-97; Maelienydd *S & B* from 97. *Dyffryn Farm, Llanwrthwl, LLandrindod Wells LD1 6NU* Tel (01597) 811017

TYLER, Graham Reginald. b 25. CEng65 Aber Univ CertCS95. Moray Ord Course 90. **d** 95. Hon C Thurso *Mor* from 95; Hon C Wick from 95. *11 Houston Terrace, Thurso, Caithness KW14 8PX* Tel (01847) 893876

TYLER, John Arthur Preston. b 19. Em Coll Cam BA42 MA46. Wycliffe Hall Ox 42. **d** 44 **p** 45. C Rodbourne Cheney *Bris* 44-47; C Worthing Ch Ch *Chich* 48-50; C Streatham Park St Alb *S'wark* 50-59; R Wickhambreaux and Stodmarsh *Cant* 59-65; R Ickham w Wickhambreaux and Stodmarsh 65-85; rtd 85; Perm to Offic *Ox* 86-89; Perm to Offic *Cant* from 89. *Church Orchard, Church Lane, Kingston, Canterbury, Kent CT4 6HY* Tel (01227) 830193

TYLER, John Thorne. b 46. Selw Coll Cam BA68 MA71 Ex Univ DipEd70. Sarum & Wells Th Coll 70. **d** 72 **p** 73. C Frome St Jo *B & W* 72-74; Chapl Huish Coll Taunton 74-93; Hon C Stoke St Gregory w Burrowbridge and Lyng *B & W* 77-93; P-in-c Shepton Beauchamp w Barrington, Stocklinch etc 93-94; TV Ilminster and District from 94. *The Rectory, Church Street, Shepton Beauchamp, Ilminster, Somerset TA19 0LQ* Tel (01460) 240338

TYLER, The Ven Leonard George. b 20. Liv Univ BA41 Ch Coll Cam BA46 MA50. Westcott Ho Cam. **d** 43 **p** 44. C Toxteth Park Ch Ch *Liv* 43-44; Ceylon 46-50; R Bradford cum Beswick *Man* 50-55; V Leigh St Mary 55-66; RD Leigh 57-62; Adn Rochdale 62-66; Prin Wm Temple Coll 66-73; R Easthampstead *Ox* 73-85; rtd 85; Perm to Offic *Ox* from 85. *11 Ashton Place, Kintbury, Newbury, Berks RG15 0XS* Tel (01488) 58510

TYLER, Malcolm. b 56. Kent Univ BSc77 Cam Univ BA84. Ridley Hall Cam 82. **d** 85 **p** 86. C Twickenham St Mary *Lon* 85-88; C Acton St Mary 88-91; V Walsgrave on Sowe *Cov* from 91. *The Vicarage, 4 Farber Road, Coventry CV2 2BG* Tel (01203) 615152 or 618845

TYLER, Paul Graham Edward. b 58. Cranmer Hall Dur. **d** 83 **p** 84. C Stranton *Dur* 83-86; C Collierley w Annfield Plain 86-89; V Esh 89-92; V Hamsteels 89-92. *Address temp unknown*

TYLER, Samuel John. b 32. Lon Univ BD57. Oak Hill Th Coll 57. **d** 58 **p** 59. C W Ham All SS *Chelmsf* 58-61; V Berechurch 61-64; R Aythorpe w High and Leaden Roding 64-72; Perm to Offic 73-74; P-in-c Gt Ilford St Jo 74-76; V 76-92; rtd 92. *21 Ash Green, Canewdon, Rochford, Essex SS4 3QN* Tel (01702) 258526

TYLER (née WAITE), Mrs Sheila Margaret. b 25. SRN47 Lon Univ DipTh73. Trin Coll Bris. **dss** 79 **d** 87 **p** 94. Easton H Trin w St Gabr and St Lawr *Bris* 79-80; Westbury-on-Trym St Alb 81-85; rtd 85; Hon Par Dn Henleaze *Bris* 87-94; Hon C 94-95; Chapl Stoke Park and Purdown Hosps Stapleton 88-90; Perm to Offic *Bris* from 95; Perm to Offic *B & W* from 95. *7 Ramenham Drive, Bristol BS9 4HY* Tel 0117-962 8394

TYLER, William Stanley. b 12. Ripon Hall Ox 54. **d** 55 **p** 56. C Upton *Ex* 55-58; V E Stonehouse 58-68; R Woodleigh and Loddiswell 68-76; rtd 76. *258 Hillbury Road, Warlingham, Surrey CR6 9TP*

TYMMS, Canon Wilfrid Widdas. b 18. Ch Coll Cam BA40 MA44. Linc Th Coll 40. **d** 41 **p** 42. C Gateshead St Jas *Dur* 41-45; Cam Staff Sec SCM 45-47; Hon C Cambridge St Benedict *Ely* 45-47; S Africa 47-53; R Stella *Dur* 53-59; V Stockton St Pet 59-70; Chapl Stockton and Thornaby Hosp 59-70; R Middleton St Geo 70-78; Hon Can Dur Cathl 72-78; Can Res Dur Cathl 78-83; rtd 83. *4 Piggy Lane, Gainford, Darlington, Co Durham DL2 3DW* Tel (01325) 730086

TYNDALE-BISCOE, John Annesley. b 08. Cam Univ BA33 MA61. Westcott Ho Cam 34. **d** 34 **p** 35. C Bredon *Worc* 34-38; Burma 38-46; Perm to Offic *Lon* 53-60; R Gilston w Eastwick *St Alb* 60-76; rtd 76; Perm to Offic *Chelmsf* from 76. *33 Hadleigh Road, Frinton-on-Sea, Essex CO13 9HQ* Tel (01255) 671520

TYNDALE-BISCOE, William Francis. b 04. Trin Coll Ox BA25 MA29. Westcott Ho Cam 27. **d** 28 **p** 29. SSF from 37; Lic to Offic *Sarum* 45-62; Cen Africa 62-74; Australia 74-77 and from 86; Melanesia 77-86; rtd 86. *Hermitage of St Bernadine, Stroud, NSW, Australia 2425* Tel Cessnock (49) 945372 Fax 945404

TYNDALL, Daniel Frank. b 61. Aston Tr Scheme 90 Sarum & Wells Th Coll BTh93. **d** 93 **p** 94. C Wolverhampton *Lich* 93-96; C Bris St Mary Redcliffe w Temple etc *Bris* from 96. *2 Colston Parade, Bristol BS1 6RA* Tel 0117-926 2770

TYNDALL, Mrs Elizabeth Mary. b 30. St Andr Univ MA51 Hughes Hall Cam CertEd52 Birm Univ DPS81. Qu Coll Birm 81. **dss** 83 **d** 87 **p** 94. Rugby St Andr *Cov* 83-87; Par Dn Feltham *Lon* 87-91; rtd 92; NSM Vale of White Horse Deanery *Ox* from 93. *The Cobbler's Cottage, 18 Stanford Road, Faringdon, Oxon SN7 7AQ* Tel (01367) 240977

TYNDALL, Jeremy Hamilton. b 55. St Jo Coll Nottm BTh81 LTh81. **d** 81 **p** 82. C Oakwood St Thos *Lon* 81-84; C Upper Holloway St Pet w St Jo 84-87; TV Halewood *Liv* 87-96; P-in-c Yardley St Edburgha *Birm* from 96. *The Vicarage, 541 Church Road, Yardley, Birmingham B33 8PH* Tel 0121-628 9548

TYNDALL, Simon James. b 54. Lon Univ BSc(Econ)77 PGCE82. St Jo Coll Nottm 88. **d** 90 **p** 91. C Yeovil w Kingston Pitney *B & W* 90-94; V Rastrick St Jo *Wakef* from 94. *St John's Vicarage, 2 St John Street, Brighouse, W Yorkshire HD6 1HN* Tel (01484) 715889

TYNDALL, Canon Timothy Gardner. b 25. Jes Coll Cam BA50. Wells Th Coll 50. **d** 51 **p** 52. C Warsop *S'well* 51-55; R Newark St Leon 55-60; V Sherwood 60-75; P-in-c Bishopwearmouth St Mich w St Hilda *Dur* 75-85; RD Wearmouth 75-85; Hon Can Dur Cathl 83-90; Chief Sec ACCM 85-90; rtd 90; Perm to Offic *Lon* from 90; Perm to Offic *S'wark* from 90. *29 Kingswood Road, London W4 5EU* Tel 0181-994 4516

TYNEY, Canon James Derrick. b 33. TCD. **d** 62 **p** 63. C Ballynafeigh St Jude *D & D* 62-64; C Bangor St Comgall 64-69; I Clonallon w Warrenpoint 69-75; I Groomsport from 75; RD Bangor from 91; Can Belf Cathl from 93; Dioc Registrar *D & D* from 95. *32 Bangor Road, Groomsport, Bangor, Co Down BT19 6JF* Tel (01247) 464476

TYRER, Ms Jayne Linda. b 59. Golds Coll Lon BA81 CertEd82. Sarum & Wells Th Coll 85. **d** 87 **p** 95. C Rochdale *Man* 87-88; Par Dn Heywood St Luke w All So 88-91; Hon Par Dn Burneside *Carl* from 91; Chapl Kendal Hosps from 91. *St Oswald's Vicarage, Burneside, Kendal, Cumbria LA9 6QX* Tel (01539) 722015

TYRREL, John Cockett. b 16. Qu Coll Cam BA38 MA42. Ridley Hall Cam 38. **d** 40 **p** 41. C Southall H Trin *Lon* 40-43; Chapl RNVR 43-46; S Africa 46-50; Australia from 50; rtd 81. *20/58 Shackleton Cct, Mawson, NSW, Australia 2607* Tel Canberra (6) 286 1317

TYRRELL, The Very Revd Charles Robert. b 51. SRN73 Open Univ BA80. Oak Hill Th Coll 74. **d** 77 **p** 78. C Halewood *Liv* 77-80; C St Helens St Helen 80-83; V Banks 83-88; New Zealand from 88; Can Wellington 88-94; Dean Nelson from 94. *The Deanery, 365 Trafalgar Street, Nelson, New Zealand* Tel Nelson (3) 548 8574 or 548 1008 Fax 548 3264

TYRRELL, Frank Englefield. b 20. DSC44 VRD. Qu Coll Birm 70. **d** 72 **p** 73. C S Gillingham *Roch* 72-76; Chapl N Staffs R Infirmary Stoke-on-Trent 76-78; Chapl Stoke-on-Trent City Gen Hosp 76-78; rtd 86. *Flat 34, The Moorings, Stone, Staffs ST15 8FZ* Tel (01785) 811457

TYRRELL, John Patrick Hammond. b 42. Cranmer Hall Dur 62. **d** 65 **p** 66. C Edin St Jo *Edin* 65-68; Chapl RN 68-72; Hong Kong 72-74 and 79-82; R Westborough *Guildf* 74-78; C Yateley *Win* 82-83; C-in-c Darby Green CD 83-88; V Darby Green 88-96; V Chineham 96-97. *18 Sepen Meade, Church Crookham, Fleet, Hants GU13 0YS* Tel (01252) 628440

TYRRELL, Stephen Jonathan. b 39. Sheff Univ BA62. Clifton Th Coll. **d** 65 **p** 66. C Rodbourne Cheney *Bris* 65-68; C Lillington *Cov* 68-72; P-in-c Bishop's Itchington 73-78; V 78-86; V Kingston upon Hull St Nic *York* 86-92; TV Cheltenham St Mary, St Matt, St Paul and H Trin *Glouc* from 92. *85 Brunswick Street, St Paul's, Cheltenham, Glos GL50 4HA* Tel (01242) 524572

TYSOE, James Raymond. b 19. Qu Coll Birm 70. **d** 75 **p** 76. NSM Cov E *Cov* 75-85; NSM Cov Cathl 85-87; Perm to Offic *Glouc* from 87. *Wisma Mulia, Bridge Road, Frampton on Severn, Gloucester GL2 7HE* Tel (01452) 740890

TYSON, Mrs Nigella Jane. d 97. NSM Aylesham w Adisham *Cant* from 97. *Oak Tree Cottage, 5 Boyes Lane, Goodnestone, Kent CT3 1PD* Tel (01304) 841870

TYSON, Canon William Edward Porter. b 25. St Cath Coll Cam BA49 MA52. Ridley Hall Cam 49. **d** 51 **p** 52. C Wilmslow *Ches* 51-54; C Astbury 54-57; V Macclesfield St Pet 57-62; V Over Tabley 62-70; V High Legh 62-70; CF (TA) 64-91; V Church Hulme *Ches* 70-91; Chapl Cranage Hall Hosp 70-91; Hon Can Ches Cathl *Ches* 82-91; RD Congleton 85-90; rtd 91; Perm to Offic *Ches* from 91; Perm to Offic *Carl* from 91. *59 Kirkhead Road, Allithwaite, Grange-over-Sands, Cumbria LA11 7DD* Tel (015395) 35291

TYTE, The Ven Keith Arthur Edwin. b 31. St D Coll Lamp BA55. **d** 57 **p** 58. C Mynyddislwyn *Mon* 57-61; C Llanfrechfa All SS 61-64; V Bettws 64-71; V Griffithstown 71-77; RD Pontypool 74-77; Can St Woolos Cathl 77-86; V Malpas 77-87; Adn Mon 86-93; R Llanmartin 87-93; Adn Newport from 93. *The Archdeaconry, 93 Stow Hill, Newport NP9 4EA* Tel (01633) 215012

TYZACK, Canon Leonard George. b 37. BA DipTh. Chich Th Coll. **d** 63 **p** 64. C Folkestone St Mary and St Eanswythe *Cant* 63-67; Abp's Dom Chapl 67-69; C-in-c Buckland Valley CD 69-72; R Buckland in Dover w Buckland Valley from 72; RD Dover 81-86; Hon Can Cant Cathl from 83; Dir of Ords *Eur* 86-94. *St Andrew's Rectory, London Road, Dover, Kent CT17 0TF* Tel (01304) 201324

U

UCHIDA, Job Minoru. b 28. St Paul's Univ Tokyo BA51. **d** 54 **p** 55. Japan 54-56 and 59-89; SSM 56-58; Chapl to Japanese in UK from 89; Hon C W Acton St Martin *Lon* from 95. *St Martin's Cottage, Hale Gardens, London W3 9SQ* Tel 0181-993 4227

UDAL, Miss Joanna Elizabeth Margaret. b 64. SS Hild & Bede Coll Dur BSc86. Ripon Coll Cuddesdon BTh94. **d** 97. C Whitton St Aug *Lon* from 97. *60 Powder Mill Lane, Whitton, Twickenham, Middx TW2 6ED* Tel 0181-255 8299

UDY, John Francis. b 24. EMMTC 78. **d** 81 **p** 82. NSM Kirton in Holland *Linc* 81-89; NSM Sutterton w Fosdyke and Algarkirk 89-94. *26 Grosvenor Road, Frampton, Boston, Lincs PE20 1DB* Tel (01205) 722043

UFFINDELL, David Wilfred George. b 37. Qu Coll Birm 72. **d** 75 **p** 76. NSM Harlescott *Lich* from 75. *13 Kenley Avenue, Heath Farm, Shrewsbury SY1 3HA* Tel (01743) 352029

UFFINDELL, Harold David. b 61. Down Coll Cam MA87. Wycliffe Hall Ox BA86 MA91 Oak Hill Th Coll 86. **d** 87 **p** 88. C Kingston Hill St Paul *S'wark* 87-91; C Surbiton St Matt from 91. *127 Hamilton Avenue, Surbiton, Surrey KT6 7QA* Tel 0181-397 4294

ULLMANN, Clair. *See* FILBERT-ULLMANN, Mrs Clair

UNDERDOWN, Steven. Hull Univ BSc75 CertEd76. **d** 88. CSWG from 82; Lic to Offic *Chich* from 88. *The Monastery, Crawley Down, Crawley, W Sussex RH10 4LH* Tel (01342) 712074

UNDERHILL, Edward Mark Thomas. b 24. Univ Coll Dur BA50. St Aid Birkenhead 50. **d** 52 **p** 53. C Meopham *Roch* 52-54; Kenya 55-57; PC Gateshead St Geo *Dur* 57-68; V Gateshead St Geo from 68. *St George's Vicarage, 327 Durham Road, Gateshead, Tyne & Wear NE9 5AJ* Tel 0191-487 5587

UNDERHILL, Stanley Robert. b 27. Cant Sch of Min. **d** 82 **p** 83. C New Addington *Cant* 82-84; C Cannock *Lich* 84-86; TV 86-88; R Dymchurch w Burmarsh and Newchurch *Cant* 88-92; rtd 92; Chapl Menorca *Eur* 92-94. *Casa Pequena Es Barranc, Officina de Correos, 07710 San Luis, Menorca, Spain* Tel Mahon (71) 150889

UNDERWOOD, Brian. b 35. Dur Univ BA57 Keble Coll Ox PGCE76 Dur Univ MA72. Clifton Th Coll 57. **d** 59 **p** 60. C Blackpool Ch Ch *Blackb* 59-61; C New Malden and Coombe *S'wark* 61-64; Travel Sec Pathfinders 64-68; Chapl Chantilly *Eur* 68-69; Home Sec CCCS 69-71; P-in-c Gatten St Paul *Portsm* 71-72; Chapl Lyon w Grenoble and Aix-les-Bains *Eur* 72-75; Asst Chapl Trent Coll Nottm 76-80; Lic to Offic *Derby* 76-80; Chapl Qu Eliz Gr Sch Blackb 80-85; Lic to Offic *Blackb* 80-85; R Bentham St Jo *Bradf* 85-92; V St Alb Ch Ch *St Alb* from 92. *Christ Church Vicarage, 5 High Oaks, St Albans, Herts AL3 6DJ* Tel (01727) 857592

UNDERWOOD, Charles Brian. b 23. Leeds Univ BA48 CertEd. Coll of Resurr Mirfield 48. **d** 50 **p** 51. C Tilehurst St Mich *Ox* 50-53; C Leic St Paul *Leic* 53-54; Youth Chapl 54-61; V Leic St Geo 57-59; R Harby 59-61; New Zealand 61-62; Dioc Youth Chapl *Bradf* 63-72; R Carleton-in-Craven 63-76; V Twyning *Glouc* 76-88; RD Tewkesbury 81-88; rtd 88. *9 Ellendene Drive, Pamington, Tewkesbury, Glos GL20 8LU* Tel (01684) 72504

UNDERWOOD, David Richard. b 47. AKC69 St Osyth Coll of Educn PGCE72. St Aug Coll Cant 69. **d** 70 **p** 92. C Witham *Chelmsf* 70-71; Teacher 71-82; Hd Teacher Gt Heath Sch Mildenhall 82-91; NSM Chevington w Hargrave and Whepstead w Brockley *St E* 82-91; Par Dn Haverhill w Withersfield, the Wrattings etc 91-92; TV 92-94; P-in-c Bury St Edmunds St Jo from 94; RD Thingoe from 95. *The Vicarage, 37 Well Street, Bury St Edmunds, Suffolk IP33 1EQ* Tel (01284) 754335

UNDERWOOD, Jack Maurice. b 13. Leeds Univ BA36 Lon Univ BD41. Coll of Resurr Mirfield 36. **d** 38 **p** 39. C Kidderminster St Mary and All SS, Trimpley etc *Worc* 38-40; C Hornsey St Mary *Lon* 40-42; Chapl RAFVR 42-46; V Middleton *Birm* 50-53; Prin Stroud Court Ox 60-71; Perm to Offic *Eur* 73-78; rtd 78. *Willow Lea, Hatford, Faringdon, Oxon SN7 8JF* Tel (01367) 710364

UNDERWOOD, Luke William. b 21. SW Minl Tr Course. **d** 85 **p** 86. NSM Duloe w Herodsfoot *Truro* 85-87; P-in-c 87-89; rtd 89; Perm to Offic *Truro* from 89. *Harewold, Tredinnick, Duloe, Liskeard, Cornwall PL14 4PJ* Tel (01503) 263541

UNGOED-THOMAS, Peter. b 27. Pemb Coll Ox BA51 MA67. St Mich Coll Llan. **d** 60 **p** 61. C Llangeinor *Llan* 60-64; I Dublin Donnybrook *D & G* 64-67; RAChD 67-70; Chapl Leigh C of E Schs 70-74; C Leigh St Mary *Man* 70-74; Lect Warley Coll 74-86; Perm to Offic *Birm* from 75; Perm to Offic *St D* from 75; Lect Sandwell Coll of F&HE from 86; rtd 94. *93 Heol Felin-Foel, Llanelli SA15 3JQ*

UNSWORTH, Philip James. b 41. UEA BEd81 Nottm Coll of Educn CertEd72 DipEd72. EAMTC 94. **d** 97. NSM Hethersett w Canteloff w Lt and Gt Melton *Nor* from 97. *32 Harman Close, Hethersett, Norwich NR9 3PR* Tel (01603) 812354

UNSWORTH, Thomas Foster. b 28. Lon Univ BA56. Lich Th Coll 60. **d** 62 **p** 63. C Northfield *Birm* 62-64; C The Lickey 64-66; V Forcett *Ripon* 66-68; V Leyburn 68-73; V Bellerby 68-73; Chapl Whittingham Hosp Preston 73-79; V Freckleton *Blackb* 79-83; V S Yardley St Mich *Birm* 83-86; V Sutton w Carlton and Normanton upon Trent etc *S'well* 86-90; rtd 90; Chapl St Raphael *Eur* 90-97. *9 Chelsea Court, South Road, Hythe, Kent CT21 6AH, or 16 rue Emile Zola, Lou Roucas, 83520 Roquebrune-sur-Argens, France* Tel (01303) 230183 or France (33) 94 44 05 67

UNWIN, Christopher Michael Fairclough. b 31. Dur Univ BA57. Linc Th Coll 65. **d** 67 **p** 68. C S Shields St Hilda w St Thos *Dur* 67-73; R Tatsfield *S'wark* 73-81; RE Adv to Ch Secondary Schs 73-81; V Newc St Gabr *Newc* 81-96; RD Newc E 96; rtd 96. *2 The Cottage, West Row, Greatham, Hartlepool TS25 2HW*

UNWIN, Christopher Philip. b 17. TD63. Magd Coll Cam BA39 MA63. Qu Coll Birm 39. **d** 40 **p** 41. C Benwell St Jas *Newc* 40-44; V 55-63; C Sugley 44-47; V Horton 47-55; Adn Northd and Can Res Newc Cathl 63-82; rtd 82. *60 Sandringham Avenue, Benton, Newcastle upon Tyne NE12 8JX* Tel 0191-270 0418

UNWIN, The Ven Kenneth. b 26. St Edm Hall Ox BA48 MA52. Ely Th Coll 49. **d** 51 **p** 52. C Leeds All SS *Ripon* 51-55; C Dur St Marg *Dur* 55-59; V Dodworth *Wakef* 59-69; V Royston 69-73; V Wakef St Jo 73-82; Hon Can Wakef Cathl 80-82; RD Wakef 80-81; Adn Pontefract 82-92; rtd 92; Perm to Offic *Bradf* from 92; Perm to Offic *Wakef* from 92. *2 Rockwood Close, Skipton, N Yorkshire BD23 1UG* Tel (01756) 791323

UPCOTT, Derek Jarvis. b 26. CEng FIMechE FBIM. S'wark Ord Course 81. **d** 84 **p** 85. NSM Gt Chesham *Ox* from 84; Perm to Offic *St Alb* from 90. *Bluff Cottage, Blackthorne Lane, Ballinger, Great Missenden, Bucks HP16 9LN* Tel (01494) 837505

UPHILL, Ms Ann Carol. b 54. Westcott Ho Cam 95. **d** 97. C Strood St Nic w St Mary *Roch* from 97. *12 Cadnam Close, Strood, Rochester, Kent ME2 3TS* Tel (01634) 724248

UPHILL, Keith Ivan. b 35. Keble Coll Ox BA70 MA74. Wycliffe Hall Ox 67. **d** 70 **p** 71. C Maghull *Liv* 70-73; V Wroxall *Portsm* 73-77; TV Fareham H Trin 77-82; C Havant 82-84; P-in-c Merton St Jo *S'wark* 84-85; V 85-95; rtd 95. *20 Wilby Lane, Anchorage Park, Portsmouth PO3 5UF* Tel (01705) 666998

UPRICHARD, Jervis. b 17. **d** 42 **p** 43. C Kilmegan w Maghera *D & D* 42-45; C Ballymacarrett St Patr 45-46; C Kilmegan 46-47; C Belfast St Aid *Conn* 48-50; I Naas w Killashee *M & K* 50-53; I Outeragh w Fenagh *K, E & A* 53-60; V Edgeside *Man* 60-66; rtd 82; Perm to Offic *Man* from 82. *c/o Miss A Uprichard, 161 Main Street, Salsburgh, Shotts, Lanarkshire ML7 4LS*

UPTON, Anthony Arthur. b 30. Leic Univ MA97. Wells Th Coll 61. **d** 63 **p** 64. C Milton *Portsm* 63-67; Chapl RN 67-83; V Foleshill St Laur *Cov* 83-91; rtd 91. *Redlands Bungalow, Banbury Road, Lighthorne, Warwick CV35 0AH*

UPTON, Ms Caroline Tracey (Carrie). b 67. Lon Univ BMus90 Edin Univ BD94. Edin Th Coll 91. **d** 94 **p** 95. C Edin St Martin *Edin* 94-96; Hon C Edin St Pet from 97. *6 Cadzow Place, Edinburgh EH7 5SN* Tel 0131-661 9346

UPTON, Christopher Martin. b 53. Bp Grosseteste Coll CertEd74. EAMTC 94. **d** 97. NSM Gorleston St Andr *Nor* from 97. *27 Curlew Way, Bradwell, Great Yarmouth, Norfolk NR31 8QX* Tel (01493) 668184

UPTON, Clement Maurice. b 49. Linc Th Coll 88. **d** 90 **p** 91. C Northampton St Alb *Pet* 90-93; V Laxey *S & M* 93-96; V Lonan 93-96; V Hipswell *Ripon* from 96. *The Vicarage, 7 Forest Drive, Catterick Garrison, N Yorkshire DL9 4PN* Tel (01748) 833320

UPTON, Donald George Stanley. b 16. Peterho Cam BA38 MA44. Westcott Ho Cam 39. **d** 40 **p** 41. C Ashbourne w Mapleton *Derby* 40-43; V Mackworth All SS 43-51; Chapl Bps' Coll Cheshunt 51-54; Chapl Haileybury Coll Herts 54-58; Qu Eliz Gr Sch Barnet 59-60; Alleyne's Gr Sch Stevenage 60-69; Lic to Offic *St Alb* from 69; Chapl St Alb High Sch for Girls 69-73; Ch Hosp Sch Hertf 73-80; rtd 80. *2 The Square, Braughing, Ware, Herts SG11 2QS*

UPTON, Miss Julie. b 61. Ripon Coll Cuddesdon 87. **d** 88 **p** 94. C Kirkstall *Ripon* 88-91; Par Dn E Greenwich Ch Ch w St Andr and St Mich *S'wark* 91-94; C 94. *3 Prestwood House, Drummond Road, London SE16 4BX* Tel 0171-237 9608

UPTON, Kenneth Roy. b 19. K Coll Cam BA40 MA48. Oak Hill Th Coll 46. **d** 48 **p** 49. C Litherland St Jo and St Jas *Liv* 48-51; C Darfield *Sheff* 51-54; V Gresley *Derby* 54-65; V Derby St Chad 65-86; rtd 86; Perm to Offic *Derby* from 86. *31 Stone Hill Road, Derby DE23 6TJ* Tel (01332) 343765

UPTON, Michael Gawthorne. b 29. AKC53. **d** 54 **p** 55. C Middleton *Man* 54-57; C Plymouth St Andr *Ex* 57-59; Dep Dir of Educn *Cant* 59-63; Hon C Riverhead *Roch* 63-70; Youth Chapl 63-70; Lic to Offic *Ex* from 70; Chr Aid Area Sec (Devon and Cornwall) 70-94; Chr Aid SW Region Co-ord 73-89; rtd 94. *Otter Dell, Harpford, Sidmouth, Devon EX10 0NH* Tel (01395) 568448

UPTON-JONES, Peter John. b 38. Selw Coll Cam BA63 MA67 Liv Univ CertEd64. N Ord Course 90. **d** 92 **p** 93. NSM Formby H Trin *Liv* from 92. *25 Greenloons Drive, Formby, Liverpool L37 2LX* Tel (01704) 874510

URMSON-TAYLOR, Ralph. *See* TAYLOR, Ralph Urmson

URQUHART, David Andrew. b 52. BA77. Wycliffe Hall Ox 82. **d** 84 **p** 85. C Kingston upon Hull St Nic *York* 84-87; TV Drypool 87-92; V Cov H Trin *Cov* from 92. *The Vicarage, 6 Davenport Road, Coventry CV5 6PY* Tel (01203) 674996 or 220418

URQUHART, Edmund Ross. b 39. Univ Coll Ox BA62 DipTh63 MA68. St Steph Ho Ox 62. **d** 64 **p** 65. C Milton *Win* 64-69; C Norton *Derby* 69-73; V Bakewell from 73; RD Bakewell and Eyam from 95. *The Vicarage, Bakewell, Derbyshire DE45 1FD* Tel (01629) 812256

URSELL, David John. b 45. R Agric Coll Cirencester NDA70 MRAC70. SW Minl Tr Course 92. **d** 95 **p** 96. NSM Dolton *Ex* from 95. *Aller Farm, Dolton, Winkleigh, Devon EX19 8PP* Tel (01805) 4414

URSELL, Philip Elliott. b 42. Univ of Wales BA66 Ox Univ MA82. St Steph Ho Ox 66. **d** 68 **p** 69. C Newton Nottage *Llan* 68-71; Asst Chapl Univ of Wales (Cardiff) 71-77; Chapl Wales Poly 74-77; Lic to Offic *Llan* from 77; Chapl Em Coll Cam 77-82; Prin Pusey Ho Ox from 82; Lic to Offic *Ox* from 82. *Pusey House, Oxford OX1 3LZ* Tel (01865) 278415 Fax 270708

URWIN, John Hope. b 09. Lich Th Coll 29. **d** 32 **p** 33. C Wednesbury St Paul Wood Green *Lich* 32-33; C Willenhall St Steph 33-35; C Walsall St Matt 35-37; Miss to Seamen 37-44; Lic to Offic *Lich* 37-44; V Ogley Hay 44-50; V Hints 50-60; R Weeford 50-60; V Trysull 60-74; rtd 74; Perm to Offic *Lich* from 74. *77 Fountain Fold, Gnosall, Stafford ST20 0DR* Tel (01785) 822601

✠**URWIN, The Rt Revd Lindsay Goodall.** b 55. Ripon Coll Cuddesdon 77. **d** 80 **p** 81 **c** 93. C Walworth *S'wark* 80-83; V N Dulwich St Faith 83-88; Dioc Missr *Chich* 88-93; OGS from 91; Area Bp Horsham *Chich* from 94. *Bishop's House, 21 Guildford Road, Horsham, W Sussex RH12 1LU* Tel (01403) 211139 Fax 217349

URWIN, Preb Roger Talbot. b 22. Ex Coll Ox BA43 MA47. Sarum Th Coll 48. **d** 50 **p** 50. C Weymouth H Trin *Sarum* 50-53; V Netheravon w Fittleton 53-57; CF (R of O) 56-77; V Townstall w Dartmouth *Ex* 57-66; V Dartmouth St Petrox 58-66; RD Ipplepen 61-66; V Littleham w Exmouth 66-72; TR 72-87; RD Aylesbeare 69-73; P-in-c Withycombe Raleigh 72-74; Preb Ex Cathl 82-87; rtd 87; Perm to Offic *Truro* from 87. *Bishop's Lodge, Kelly Park, St Mabyn, Bodmin, Cornwall PL30 3RL* Tel (0120884) 606

USHER, George. b 30. Univ of Wales (Swansea) BSc51. St Deiniol's Hawarden 73. **d** 75 **p** 76. NSM Clun w Chapel Lawn *Heref* 75-78; NSM Clun w Chapel Lawn, Bettws-y-Crwyn and Newcastle 79-80; C Shrewsbury St Giles *Lich* 80-83; C Shrewsbury St Giles w Sutton and Atcham 83-84; R Credenhill w Brinsop, Mansel Lacey, Yazor etc *Heref* 84-95; P-in-c Bishopstone 86-95; P-in-c Kenchester and Bridge Sollers 86-95; R Credenhill w Brinsop and Wormsley etc from 95. *St Mary's Rectory, Credenhill, Hereford HR4 7DL* Tel (01432) 760687

USHER, Graham Barham. b 70. Edin Univ BSc93 CCC Cam BA95. Westcott Ho Cam CTM93. **d** 96 **p** 97. C Nunthorpe *York* from 96. *15 Ripon Road, Nunthorpe, Middlesbrough, Cleveland TS7 0HX* Tel (01642) 310834 Fax as telephone

USHER, Robin Reginald. b 50. AKC74. St Aug Coll Cant 75. **d** 76 **p** 77. C Hulme Ascension *Man* 76-80; P-in-c Newall Green 80-85; C Atherton 85-87; TV 87-90; V Leigh St Jo from 90; Chapl Leigh Infirmary Lancs from 93. *The Vicarage, 156 Gordon Street, Leigh, Lancs WN7 1RT* Tel (01942) 672868

USHER-WILSON, Neville. **d** 96 **p** 96. NSM Shill Valley and Broadshire *Ox* from 96. *The Tallet, Westwell, Burford, Oxon OX18 4JJ*

UTLEY, Canon Edward Jacob. b 24. AKC52. **d** 53 **p** 54. C Pontefract St Giles *Wakef* 53-56; C Bexhill St Pet *Chich* 56-60; Chapl Asst Bexhill Hosp 56-60; Chapl Dudley Road Hosp Birm 60-89; RD Birm City *Birm* 75-82; Hon Can Birm Cathl 80-89; rtd 89; Perm to Offic *Birm* from 89. *St Raphael, 50 Wheatsheaf Road, Birmingham B16 0RY* Tel 0121-454 2666

UTTLEY, Mrs Valerie Gail. b 43. Man Univ BA64. N Ord Course 80. **dss** 83 **d** 87 **p** 94. Otley *Bradf* 83-87; Hon Par Dn 87-89; Par Dn Calverley 89-92; Ind Chapl *Ripon* 92-97; C Kirkstall 95-97; V Lofthouse from 97. *The Vicarage, 8 Church Farm Close, Lofthouse, Wakefield, W Yorkshire WF3 3SA* Tel (01924) 823286

V

VAIL, David William. b 30. Dur Univ BA56 Sheff Univ DipEd71. Oak Hill Th Coll 56. **d** 58 **p** 59. C Toxteth Park St Bede *Liv* 58-61; Kenya 61-77; Chapl Versailles *Eur* 77-82; Gen Sec Rwanda Miss 82-88; V Virginia Water *Guildf* 88-96; rtd 96. *36 Silverthorne Drive, Caversham, Reading RG4 7NS* Tel (01189) 546667

VAIZEY, Martin John. b 37. AKC64. **d** 65 **p** 66. C Bishopwearmouth Gd Shep *Dur* 65-69; C Darlington H Trin 69-72; V Easington Colliery 72-80; C-in-c Bishopwearmouth St Mary V w St Pet CD 80-85; V Sunderland Springwell w Thorney Close 85-88; R Witton Gilbert 88-96; P-in-c Wingate Grange from 96. *The Vicarage, Wingate, Co Durham TS28 5BW* Tel (01429) 838338

VALE, Thomas Stanley George. b 52. Chich Th Coll 85. **d** 87 **p** 88. C Leic St Phil *Leic* 87-90; C Knighton St Mary Magd 90-93; P-in-c Leic St Chad from 93. *St Chad's Clergy House, 145 Coleman Road, Leicester LE5 4LH* Tel 0116-276 6062

VALENTINE, Derek William. b 24. S'wark Ord Course 65. **d** 68 **p** 69. NSM Battersea St Luke *S'wark* 68-77; NSM Fenstanton *Ely* 77-88; Perm to Offic *Bradf* from 88. *4 Woodland Drive, Skipton, N Yorkshire BD23 1QU* Tel (01756) 799399

VALENTINE, Hugh William James. b 56. Bradf Univ BA83 CQSW. S'wark Ord Course 86. **d** 89 **p** 90. NSM Stoke Newington Common St Mich *Lon* 89-92; NSM Westmr St Jas from 92. *4 Leigh House, 1 Halcrow Street, London E1 2HF* Tel 0171-377 7500 E-mail 73064.471@compuserve.com

VALENTINE, Jeremy Wilfred. b 38. NW Ord Course 76. **d** 79 **p** 80. C Cundall *Ripon* 79-82; TV Huntington *York* 82-87; V Sand Hutton from 87. *The Vicarage, Sand Hutton, York YO4 1LB* Tel (01904) 468443 Fax 468670

VALENTINE, John Harvey. b 63. Ch Ch Ox BA85 MA85. Ridley Hall Cam BA92. **d** 93 **p** 94. C Heigham H Trin *Nor* 93-97; C Ches Square St Mich w St Phil *Lon* from 97. *72A Warwick Way, London SW1V 1RZ* Tel 0171-821 9781

VALLINS, Christopher. b 43. Lich Th Coll 63. **d** 66 **p** 67. C Cuddington *Guildf* 66-70; C Aldershot St Mich 70-73; V W Ewell 73-81; R Worplesdon 81-89; Chapl Merrist Wood Coll of Agric 81-89; RD Guildf 86-89; Chapl Epsom Healthcare NHS Trust from 89; Chapl Horton Hosp Epsom from 95; Perm to Offic *S'wark* from 96; Bp's Adv on Healing *Guildf* from 97. *The Chaplain's Office, Epsom General Hospital, Dorking Road, Epsom, Surrey KT18 7EG* Tel (01372) 735322 or 726100 Fax 735187

VAMPLEW, Peter Gordon. b 33. Jes Coll Cam BA57 MA61. Ridley Hall Cam 57. **d** 59 **p** 60. C Tooting Graveney St Nic *S'wark* 59-65; C Poole *Sarum* 70-76; rtd 95. *187 High Street, Amersham, Bucks HP7 0EB*

VAN CARRAPIETT, Timothy Michael James. b 39. Chich Th Coll 60. **d** 63 **p** 64. C Sugley *Newc* 63-65; C Newc St Fran 65-69; P-in-c Wrangbrook w N Elmsall CD *Wakef* 69-74; P-in-c Flushing *Truro* 74-75; P-in-c Mylor w Flushing 75-76; P-in-c St Day 76-82; R Aldrington *Chich* 82-87; V Bexhill St Barn from 87. *The Vicarage, Cantelupe Road, Bexhill-on-Sea, E Sussex TN40 1JG* Tel (01424) 212036

VAN CULIN, Canon Samuel. b 30. Princeton Univ AB52. Virginia Th Sem DB55 Hon DD. **d** 55 **p** 56. USA 55-83; Hon Can Cant Cathl *Cant* from 83; Sec Gen ACC from 83; Hon C All Hallows by the Tower etc *Lon* from 89. *ACC, Partnership House, 157 Waterloo Road, London SE1 8UT* Tel 0171-620 1110 Fax 620 1070

VAN DE KASTEELE, Peter John. b 39. Magd Coll Cam BA61 MA65. Clifton Th Coll 61. **d** 63 **p** 64. C Eastbourne H Trin *Chich* 63-66; C N Pickenham w S Pickenham etc *Nor* 66-70; R Mursley w Swanbourne and Lt Horwood *Ox* 70-80; Perm to Offic *Glouc* 83-88; Admin Sec Clinical Th Assn from 83; Gen Dir from 88; Hon C Westcote w Icomb and Bledington 88-92; Perm to Offic from 92. *St Mary's House, Church Westcote, Chipping Norton, Oxon OX7 6SF* Tel (01993) 830209

van de WEYER, Robert William Bates. b 50. Lanc Univ BA76. S'wark Ord Course 78. **d** 81 **p** 82. Warden Lt Gidding Community from 77; Hon C Gt w Lt Gidding and Steeple Gidding *Ely* 81-83; P-in-c Winwick 83-93; P-in-c Hamerton 83-93; P-in-c Upton and Copmanford 83-93; Perm to Offic from 93. *Woodend, Upton, Huntingdon, Cambs PE17 5YF* Tel (01480) 890333

VAN DEN BERG, Jan Jacob. b 56. Sarum & Wells Th Coll 86. **d** 88 **p** 89. C Glouc St Aldate *Glouc* 88-91; C Ollerton w Boughton *S'well* 91-95; P-in-c Scrooby from 95; P-in-c Blyth from 97. *The Vicarage, 7 Arundel Drive, Ranskill, Retford, Notts DN22 8PG* Tel (01777) 818470

van der LINDE, Herbert John. b 43. Rhodes Univ BA66. Coll of Resurr Mirfield. **d** 68 **p** 69. C Kingston St Luke *S'wark* 68-75; C Chipping Campden w Ebrington *Glouc* 75-78; V Cheltenham St Pet 78-84; V Bussage from 84. *St Michael's Vicarage, Bussage, Stroud, Glos GL6 8BB* Tel (01453) 883556

VAN DER PUMP, Charles Lyndon. b 25. FRCM. S'wark Ord Course 86. **d** 88 **p** 89. NSM Primrose Hill St Mary w Avenue

Road St Paul *Lon* from 88. *48 Canfield Gardens, London NW6 3EB* Tel 0171-624 4517

van der VALK, Jesse. b 59. Nottm Univ BTh84 Avery Hill Coll PGCE85 Birm Univ MPhil88. St Jo Coll Nottm 81. **d** 88 **p** 89. C Droitwich Spa *Worc* 88-92; V Hartshead and Hightown *Wakef* 92-96; R Woolwich St Mary w St Mich *S'wark* from 96; USPG Co-worker (Lewisham Adnry) from 97. *The Rectory, 43 Rectory Place, London SE18 5DA* Tel 0181-854 2302 or 316 4338

VAN DONGEN, Wilhelmina Gerardina. b 26. Qu Wilhelmina Coll Rotterdam Gen Teacher 45. St Chris Coll Blackheath 51. **dss** 76 **d** 96. Harold Hill St Geo *Chelmsf* 74-84; Hon Asst Rotterdam *Eur* 84-95; NSM Elmstead *Chelmsf* from 96. *14 Churchfield Road, Coggeshall, Colchester CO6 1QE* Tel (01376) 562919

VAN GORDER, Lloyd Franklin. b 11. **d** 73 **p** 74. V Hartley Wintney and Elvetham *Win* 74-76; Perm to Offic *Chich* 76-78; Perm to Offic *Portsm* 79-94. *Address temp unknown*

VAN LEEUWEN, Canon Dirk Willem. b 45. Utrecht Univ LLD71. Th Faculty Brussels 71 S'wark Ord Course 80. **d** 82 **p** 83. Asst Chapl Brussels Cathl *Eur* 82-84; Chapl Haarlem 84-93; Chapl Antwerp St Boniface from 94; Charleroi from 94; Can Brussels Cathl from 96; P-in-c Ypres from 97. *Grétrystraat 39, 2018 Antwerp, Belgium* Tel Antwerp (3) 239-3339 Fax 281-3946 E-mail dirk.vanleeuwen@ping.be

VAN STRAATEN, Christopher Jan (Chris). b 55. Bris Univ BA77 Natal Univ HDipEd78. Oak Hill Th Coll DipHE92. **d** 92 **p** 93. C Woodley *Ox* 92-96; V Gillingham St Aug *Roch* from 96. *St Augustine's Vicarage, Rock Avenue, Gillingham, Kent ME7 5PW* Tel (01634) 850288

VANDERSTOCK, Alan. b 31. St Jo Coll Dur BA57. Cranmer Hall Dur DipTh59. **d** 59 **p** 60. C Kersal Moor *Man* 59-62; C-in-c Lower Kersal CD 63-67; Lic Preacher *Cant* from 67; Sen Tutor Heath Clark High Sch Croydon 73-83; Dep Hd Teacher Norbury Manor High Sch Croydon 83-86; Sen Master Shirley High Sch Croydon 86-92; rtd 92. *11 State Farm Avenue, Orpington, Kent BR6 7TN* Tel (01689) 862643

VANDYCK, Mrs Salli Diane Seymour. b 39. Grenoble Univ DFStuds57 Inst of Travel & Tourism DipTT77 AIL75 CertFE93. S'wark Ord Course 93 SEITE 93. **d** 96 **p** 97. NSM Chertsey *Guildf* from 96. *6 Alderside Walk, Egham, Surrey TW20 0LY* Tel (01784) 434548

VANE, Walter Brian. b 21. Liv Univ BSc46 MA50. Coll of Resurr Mirfield 51. **d** 53 **p** 54. C Leigh St Mary *Man* 53-56; C Wolverhampton St Pet *Lich* 56-58; R Abbey Hey *Man* 58-62; V Prestwich St Hilda 62-65; Hon C Heaton Norris Ch Ch 66-70; Lic to Offic 71-84; Lic to Offic *Ches* 71-84; Chapl Costa del Sol W *Eur* 84-88; rtd 88; Perm to Offic *Glouc* from 88. *6 The Mead, Cirencester, Glos GL7 2BB* Tel (01285) 653235

VANN, Ms Cherry Elizabeth. b 58. ARCM78 GRSM80. Westcott Ho Cam 86. **d** 89 **p** 94. Par Dn Flixton St Mich *Man* 89-92; Chapl Bolton Inst of F&HE from 92; Par Dn Bolton St Pet 92-94; C from 94. *1 Bramcote Avenue, Bolton BL2 1LF* Tel (01204) 535279

VANN, Paul. b 41. St D Coll Lamp DipTh65. **d** 65 **p** 66. C Griffithstown *Mon* 65-67; C Llanfrechfa All SS 67-71; Dioc Youth Chapl 69-74; Chapl St Woolos Cathl 71-72; P-in-c Llanrumney 72-76; V 76-97; Asst Chapl HM Pris Cardiff 75-78; RD Bassaleg *Mon* from 90; R Machen from 97. *The Rectory, Rectory Gardens, Newport NP1 8SU* Tel (01633) 440321

VANNOZZI, Peter. b 62. Lon Univ BA83 Ox Univ BA86. Ripon Coll Cuddesdon 84. **d** 87 **p** 88. C Kenton *Lon* 87-90; C Fleet *Guildf* 90-93; V Northwood Hills St Edm *Lon* 93-97; AD Harrow 95-97; V S Dulwich St Steph *S'wark* from 97. *St Stephen's Vicarage, College Road, London SE21 7HN* Tel 0181-693 3797

VANSTON, The Ven William Francis Harley. b 24. TCD BA48 MA52. **d** 48 **p** 49. C Belfast St Mary *Conn* 48-51; C Dublin Rathfarnham *D & G* 51-58; I Narraghmore w Fontstown and Timolin 58-65; I Arklow 65-67; I Arklow w Inch 67-73; I Arklow w Inch and Kilbride 73-89; RD Rathdrum 77-89; Adn Glendalough 83-89; rtd 89. *11 Seabank Court, Sandycove, Dun Laoghaire, Co Dublin, Irish Republic* Tel Dublin (1) 280 4575

VANSTONE, Walford David Frederick. b 38. Open Univ BA81. AKC69. **d** 70 **p** 71. C Feltham *Lon* 70-75; TV E Runcorn w Halton *Ches* 75-80; V Grange St Andr 80-82; V Hampton All SS *Lon* from 82; AD Hampton from 95. *All Saints' Vicarage, 40 The Avenue, Hampton, Middx TW12 3RS* Tel 0181-979 2102

VANSTONE, Canon William Hubert. b 23. Ball Coll Ox BA48 MA St Jo Coll Cam BA50 MA. Lambeth DD88 Westcott Ho Cam 48 Union Th Sem (NY) STM50. **d** 50 **p** 51. C Halliwell St Thos *Man* 50-55; C-in-c Kirkholt CD 55-64; V Kirkholt 64-76; Hon Can Man Cathl 68-76; V Hattersley *Ches* 77-78; Can Res Ches Cathl 78-90; Six Preacher Cant Cathl *Cant* from 83; rtd 91; Perm to Offic *Glouc* from 91. *6 Hodges Close, Tetbury, Glos GL8 8HL* Tel (01666) 502689

VARAH, Preb Edward Chad. b 11. OBE69 CBE95. Keble Coll Ox BA33 MA46 Leic Univ Hon LLD79 St Andr Univ Hon LLD93 City Univ Hon DSc93. Linc Th Coll 34. **d** 35 **p** 36. C Linc St Giles *Linc* 35-38; C Putney St Mary *S'wark* 38-40; C Barrow St Jo *Carl* 40-42; V Blackb H Trin *Blackb* 42-49; V Battersea St Paul *S'wark* 49-53; P-in-c St Steph Walbrook and St Swithun etc *Lon* 53-54; R from 54; Founder The Samaritans 53; Dir 53-74; Preb St Paul's Cathl *Lon* from 75. *St Stephen's Vestry, 39 Walbrook, London EC4N 8BP* Tel 0171-283 4444 or 626 8242

VARAH, Paul Hugh. b 46. St Deiniol's Hawarden 83. **d** 85 **p** 86. C Prestatyn *St As* 85-87; P-in-c Hawarden 87-88; TV 88-89; V Esclusham 89-96; V Connah's Quay from 96. *The Vicarage, Church Hill, Connah's Quay, Deeside CH5 1AZ*

VARGAS, Eric Arthur Dudley. b 27. BD. S Dios Minl Tr Scheme 81. **d** 83 **p** 84. C Farncombe *Guildf* 83-86; R Ockley, Okewood and Forest Green 86-90; V Kirdford *Chich* 90-93; rtd 93; Perm to Offic *Portsm* from 93; Perm to Offic *Chich* from 93. *5 Bath Road, Emsworth, Hants PO10 7EP* Tel (01243) 376284

VARGESON, Peter Andrew. b 53. Wycliffe Hall Ox 85. **d** 87 **p** 88. C Yateley *Win* 87-92; V Bursledon from 92. *The Vicarage, School Road, Bursledon, Southampton SO31 8BW* Tel (01703) 402821

VARLEY (née TRIM), Elizabeth Ann. b 52. Homerton Coll Cam BEd75 Van Mildert Coll Dur PhD85 St Jo Coll Dur BA96. NE Ord Course 94. **d** 96. C Sedgefield *Dur* from 96. *9 Belsay Court, Sedgefield, Stockton-on-Tees, Cleveland TS21 2JA* Tel (01740) 620829

VARLEY, Robert. b 36. St Jo Coll Cam BA57 MA64. NW Ord Course 71. **d** 74 **p** 75. C Wallasey St Hilary *Ches* 74-77; V Rock Ferry 77-81; Perm to Offic *Man* 82-83; Hon C E Farnworth and Kearsley 83-86; Hon C Walkden Moor 86-87; C 87-89; V Lt Hulton 89-90. *66 Normanby Road, Worsley, Manchester M28 7TS* Tel 0161-790 8420

VARNEY, Donald James (Don). b 35. Chich Th Coll 84. **d** 86. Hon C Liss *Portsm* from 86. *12 Birch Close, Liss, Petersfield, Hants GU33 7HS* Tel (01730) 893945

VARNEY, Peter David. b 38. Dur Univ BA61 MA64 Birm Univ DipTh63. Qu Coll Birm 61. **d** 64 **p** 65. C Newington St Paul *S'wark* 64-66; C Camberwell St Mich w All So w Em 66-67; Malaysia 67-68; Hon C Croxley Green All SS *St Alb* 69; Perm to Offic *Roch* 69-72 and 74-84; Asst Chapl Chapl Community St Jo Bapt Clewer 72-73; Asst Sec Chrs Abroad 74-79; Dir Bloxham Project 84-86; Perm to Offic *Cant* 84-85; Perm to Offic *S'wark* 85-86; P-in-c Thornage w Brinton w Hunworth and Stody *Nor* 87; P-in-c Briningham 87; P-in-c Melton Constable w Swanton Novers 87; Perm to Offic from 89; Chapl Yare and Norvic Clinics and St Andr Hosp Nor from 90. *8 High Green, Norwich NR1 4AP* Tel (01603) 34855

VARNEY, Stephen Clive. b 59. Qu Mary Coll Lon BSc80 Sussex Univ MSc82 Southn Univ BTh88. Sarum & Wells Th Coll 83. **d** 86 **p** 87. C Riverhead w Dunton Green *Roch* 86-91; V Bostall Heath from 91. *St Andrew's Parsonage, 276 Brampton Road, Bexleyheath, Kent DA7 5SF* Tel 0181-303 9332

VARNEY, Wilfred Davies. b 10. Sarum & Wells Th Coll 71. **d** 71 **p** 72. C Glouc St Paul *Glouc* 71-74; V Lydbrook 74-77; rtd 77; Hon C Felpham w Middleton *Chich* 77-80; Hon C Overbury w Alstone, Teddington and Lt Washbourne *Worc* 80-82; P-in-c Nor St Andr *Nor* 87-91; Perm to Offic 82-87 and 91-93; Perm to Offic *Guildf* from 93. *11 Manormead, Tilford Road, Hindhead, Surrey GU26 6RA* Tel (01428) 606652

VARNEY, William James Granville. b 22. St D Coll Lamp 62. **d** 65 **p** 66. C Burry Port and Pwll *St D* 65-68; V Strata Florida 68-71; V Llandyfriog, Llanfair Trelygen, Troedyraur etc 71-78; OCF 78; R Aberporth w Tremain and Blaenporth *St D* 78-87. P-in-c Penbryn and Betws Ifan w Bryngwyn 88-92; rtd 92. *Alma, Tan y Groes, Cardigan SA43 2JT* Tel (01239) 810217

VARNHAM, Gerald Stanley. b 29. Sarum & Wells Th Coll 74. **d** 77 **p** 78. Hon C Portchester *Portsm* 77-86; Perm to Offic from 88. *15 Southampton Road, Fareham, Hants PO16 7DZ* Tel (01329) 234182

VARNON, Nicholas Charles Harbord. b 45. St Luke's Coll Ex CertEd71 Open Univ BA83 BPhil91 MA94. St Mich Coll Llan DipTh91. **d** 93 **p** 94. C Pontypridd St Cath w St Matt *Llan* 93-97; P-in-c Sutton St Nicholas w Sutton St Michael *Heref* from 97; P-in-c Withington w Westhide from 97. *The Rectory, Sutton St Nicholas, Hereford HR1 3BA* Tel (01432) 880253

VARTY, John Eric. b 44. Tyndale Hall Bris 68. **d** 71 **p** 72. C Barrow St Mark *Carl* 71-74; C Cheadle *Ches* 74-82; V Cheadle All Hallows 82-89; V Alsager Ch Ch from 89. *Christ Church Vicarage, 43 Church Road, Alsager, Stoke-on-Trent ST7 2HS* Tel (01270) 873727

VARTY, Robert. b 46. LRAM. Sarum & Wells Th Coll 84. **d** 86 **p** 87. C Plympton St Mary *Ex* 86-89; TV Northam w Westward Ho! and Appledore 89-95; P-in-c Wigginton *St Alb* from 95; TV Tring from 95. *The Vicarage, Wigginton, Tring, Herts HP23 6DZ* Tel (01442) 823273

VASEY, Michael Richard. b 46. Ball Coll Ox BA68 MA71. Wycliffe Hall Ox 68. **d** 71 **p** 72. C Tonbridge SS Pet and Paul *Roch* 71-75; Tutor St Jo Coll Dur from 75; Lic to Offic *Dur* from 75. *St John's College, 3 South Bailey, Durham DH1 3RJ* Tel 0191-374 3584 or 384 0593 Fax 374 3573

VASS, Robert James Templeton. b 28. Lon Coll of Div 62. **d** 64 **p** 68. C Horsell *Guildf* 64-65; Kenya from 72. *PO Box 11860, Nairobi, Kenya*

VAUGHAN, Andrew Christopher James. b 61. Univ of Wales (Lamp) BA82. Linc Th Coll CMM84. **d** 84 **p** 85. C Caerleon *Mon* 84-86; C Magor w Redwick and Undy 86-88; Ind Chapl 84-94;

Linc Ind Miss *Linc* from 94. *4 Grange Close, Canwick, Lincoln LN4 2RH* Tel (01522) 528266

✠**VAUGHAN, The Rt Revd Benjamin Noel Young.** b 17. Univ of Wales (Lamp) BA40 St Edm Hall Ox BA42 MA46. Westcott Ho Cam 42. **d** 43 **p** 44 **c** 61. C Llan-non *St D* 43-45; C Carmarthen St Dav 45-48; Barbados 48-52; Lect St D Coll Lamp 52-55; Trinidad and Tobago 55-61; Dean Port of Spain 55-61; Jamaica 61-67; Suff Bp Mandeville 61-67; Adn S Middx 61-64; Bp Br Honduras 67-71; Dean Ban 71-76; Asst Bp Ban 71-76; Bp S & B 76-87; Pres Coun of Ch for Wales 79-82; rtd 87. *4 Caswell Drive, Newton, Swansea SA3 4RJ* Tel (01792) 360646

VAUGHAN, Brian John. b 38. Lich Th Coll 65. **d** 68 **p** 69. C Fisherton Anger *Sarum* 68-70; C Wareham w Arne 70-73; Australia from 73. *St Martin's Rectory, PO Box 114, Manjimup, W Australia 6258* Tel Perth (9) 771 1015

VAUGHAN, Charles Jeremy Marshall. b 52. Man Univ BSc75 LTh. St Jo Coll Nottm 83. **d** 85 **p** 86. C Epsom Common Ch Ch *Guildf* 85-88; C Woking Ch Ch 88-93; R Worting *Win* from 93. *The Rectory, Glebe Lane, Basingstoke, Hants RG23 8QA* Tel (01256) 331531

VAUGHAN, Idris Samuel. b 46. Sarum Th Coll 70. **d** 72 **p** 73. C Workington St Jo *Carl* 72-76; C Foley Park *Worc* 76-79; P-in-c Hayton St Mary *Carl* 79; V 79-85; Chapl Asst Univ Hosp Nottm 85-90; Chapl Asst Nottm Gen Hosp 85-90; Chapl Stafford Distr Gen Hosp 90-94; Chapl Chase Hosp Cannock 90-94; Chapl Mid Staffs Gen Hosps NHS Trust from 94. *The Chaplain's Office, Stafford District General Hospital, Weston Road, Stafford ST16 3RS* Tel (01785) 257731

VAUGHAN, Jeffrey Charles. b 45. S'wark Ord Course 85. **d** 88 **p** 89. NSM Tottenham St Paul *Lon* 88-91; C Hendon St Alphage 91-95; V Enfield SS Pet and Paul from 95. *The Vicarage, 177 Ordnance Road, Enfield, Middx EN3 6AB* Tel (01992) 719770 Fax 0181-292 8456

VAUGHAN, John. b 30. Sarum Th Coll 53. **d** 56 **p** 57. C Wigan St Andr *Liv* 56-59; Australia 59-64; P-in-c Riddings *Derby* 64-71; R Hasland 71-80; V Temple Normanton 71-80; TV Dronfield 80-86; V Bradwell 86-95; rtd 95; Perm to Offic *Derby* from 95. *11 Millstone Close, Dronfield Woodhouse, Sheffield S18 5ZL* Tel (01246) 415647

VAUGHAN, Canon Dr Patrick Handley. b 38. TCD BA60 BD65 Selw Coll Cam BA62 MA66 Nottm Univ PhD88. Ridley Hall Cam 61. **d** 63 **p** 64. Min Can Bradf Cathl *Bradf* 63-66; Uganda 67-73; P-in-c Slingsby *York* 74-77; Tutor NW Ord Course 74-77; P-in-c Hovingham *York* 74-77; Prin E Midl Min Tr Course *S'well* 77-90; Hon Can Leic Cathl *Leic* 87-90. *50 Crescent Road, Sheffield S7 1HN* Tel 0114-258 2110

✠**VAUGHAN, The Rt Revd Peter St George.** b 30. Selw Coll Cam BA55 MA59 BNC Ox MA63. Ridley Hall Cam. **d** 57 **p** 58 **c** 89. C Birm St Martin *Birm* 57-63; Chapl Ox Pastorate 63-67; Asst Chapl BNC Ox 63-67; Ceylon 67-72; New Zealand 72-75; Prin Crowther Hall CMS Tr Coll Selly Oak 75-83; Lic to Offic *Birm* 75-83; Adn Westmorland and Furness *Carl* 83-89; Hon Can Carl Cathl 83-89; Area Bp Ramsbury *Sarum* from 89; Can and Preb Sarum Cathl from 89. *Bishop's House, High Street, Urchfont, Devizes, Wilts SN10 4QH* Tel (01380) 840373 Fax 848247

VAUGHAN, Roger Maxwell. b 39. AKC62. **d** 63 **p** 64. C W Bromwich All SS *Lich* 63-65; C Wolverhampton 65-70; V Tunstall Ch Ch 70-79; V Tunstall 79; V Abbots Bromley 79-86; P-in-c Blithfield 85-86; V Abbots Bromley w Blithfield 86-93; V Stafford St Jo and Tixall w Ingestre from 93. *St John's Vicarage, Westhead Avenue, Stafford ST16 3RP* Tel (01785) 53493

VAUGHAN, Ronald Alfred (Ron). b 38. S'wark Ord Course 78. **d** 81 **p** 82. NSM Stepney St Pet w St Benet *Lon* 81-86; Asst P St Jo on Bethnal Green from 87; Dep Dioc Sec 90-95; Projects Officer (Stepney Area) from 97. *St Bartholomew's Vicarage, Buckhurst Street, London E1 5QT* Tel 0171-247 8013 Fax as telephone

VAUGHAN, Trevor. b 41. TD91. Cen Lancs Univ BA91. Linc Th Coll 66. **d** 69 **p** 70. C Wyken *Cov* 69-72; C Stratford-on-Avon w Bishopton 72-73; P-in-c Monks Kirby w Withybrook and Copston Magna 73-75; P-in-c Wolvey, Burton Hastings and Stretton Baskerville 73-77; P-in-c Withybrook w Copston Magna 73-77; V Heyhouses *Blackb* 77-80; CF (TA) from 79; V Chorley St Geo *Blackb* 80-83; R Bolton by Bowland w Grindleton *Bradf* 83-89; V Settle 89-91; R Broughton, Marton and Thornton from 91. *The Rectory, Broughton, Skipton, N Yorkshire BD23 3AN* Tel (01282) 842332

VAUGHAN-JONES, Canon Geraint James. b 29. JP77. St D Coll Lamp 50 St Deiniol's Hawarden 68. **d** 70 **p** 71. C Llanaber w Caerdeon *Ban* 70-73; TV Dolgellau w Llanfachreth and Brithdir etc 73-76; R Mallwyd w Cemais and Llanymawddwy 76-96; RD Cyfeiliog and Mawddwy 85-96; Can Ban Cathl from 86; Prec Ban Cathl from 89; rtd 96. *4 Brynymor Terrace, Aberystwyth SY23 2HU* Tel (01970) 627535

VAUGHAN-JONES, Canon John Paschal. b 18. Keble Coll Ox BA39 MA43. St Steph Ho Ox 39. **d** 41 **p** 42. C Laindon w Basildon *Chelmsf* 41-43 and 47-49; CF 43-47; R Chipping Ongar *Chelmsf* 49-83; R Shelley 49-83; RD Ongar 72-82; Hon Can Chelmsf Cathl 78-83; rtd 83. *Ryecroft, Old Harwich Road, Little Bentley, Colchester CO7 8SX* Tel (01206) 250238

VAUGHAN-WILSON, Jane Elizabeth. b 61. Magd Coll Ox MA87. Cranmer Hall Dur. **d** 89 **p** 94. Par Dn Ormesby *York* 89-93; D-in-c Middlesbrough St Agnes 93-94; P-in-c 94-95; TV Basingstoke *Win* from 95. *St Gabriel's Vicarage, Tewkesbury Close, Basingstoke, Hants RG24 9DU* Tel (01256) 24734

VAYRO, Mark Shaun. b 66. Aston Tr Scheme 88 Linc Th Coll BTh93. **d** 93 **p** 94. C Northampton St Mich w St Edm *Pet* 93-96; TV Duston Team from 96. *St Francis House, Eastfield Road, Duston, Northampton NN5 6TQ* Tel (01604) 753679

VEAZEY, Harry Christopher Hurford. b 11. Westcott Ho Cam 33. **d** 35 **p** 36. C Sutton New Town St Barn *S'wark* 35-38; C Newington St Mary 38-41; V Nunhead St Silas 41-57; V Doddington w Wychling *Cant* 57-80; V Newnham 57-80; RD Ospringe 78-80; rtd 80; Perm to Offic *Cant* from 80. *Five Oaks, Pluckley Road, Charing, Ashford, Kent TN27 0AJ* Tel (01233) 713009

VEITCH, Thomas. b 12. Glas Univ MA37. **d** 40 **p** 41. C Glas St Mary *Glas* 40-41; C Ayr 41-43; P-in-c Prestwick 43-46; R Girvan 46-49; R Peterhead *Ab* 49-56; Chapl HM Pris Peterhead 49-53; R Edin St Paul and St Geo *Edin* 56-84; I Edin St Vin 60-71; rtd 85. *10 Lasswade Road, Liberton, Edinburgh EH16 6RZ* Tel 0131-664 4034

VELLACOTT, John Patrick Millner. b 29. Ox NSM Course 86. **d** 89 **p** 90. NSM Cholsey *Ox* 89-93; Chapl Nerja *Eur* 93-97; rtd 97. *13 Calle de Jilguera, Almijara 2, 29780 Nerja, Spain* Tel Malaga (52) 525406

VELLACOTT, Peter Graham. b 37. Seale-Hayne Agric Coll NDA59. EMMTC 90. **d** 93 **p** 94. NSM Framlingham w Saxtead *St E* 93-95; NSM Brandeston w Kettleburgh from 95. *Soham House, Brandeston, Woodbridge, Suffolk IP13 7AX* Tel (01728) 685423

VENABLES, Arthur Peter. b 20. Vancouver Sch of Th LTh47. **d** 49 **p** 50. Canada 49-54; C Beckenham St Geo *Roch* 54-56; C Brighton St Martin *Chich* 56-58; C Paddington St Mary Magd *Lon* 58-59; C Penton Street St Silas w All SS 59-61; C Willesden St Andr 61-63; C Chesterfield St Aug *Derby* 63-66; V Kensington St Phil Earl's Court *Lon* 69-74; P-in-c Uxbridge Moor 74-82; rtd 82; Perm to Offic *Lon* from 82. *4 Wharf Court, Iver Lane, Cowley, Middx UB8 2JD*

VENABLES, Dudley James. b 17. Cant Sch of Min 77. **d** 80 **p** 81. NSM Ramsgate H Trin *Cant* 80-82; Chapl Asst St Aug Hosp Cant 83-88; NSM Wye w Brook 83-88; Perm to Offic from 88; Chapl Cant and Thanet Mental Health Unit from 93. *48 Abbots Walk, Wye, Ashford, Kent TN25 5ES* Tel (01233) 813000

✠**VENABLES, The Rt Revd Gregory James (Greg).** b 49. Lon Univ CertEd74. **d** 84 **p** 84 **c** 93. SAMS from 77; Paraguay 78-90; C Rainham *Chelmsf* 90-92; C Rainham w Wennington 92-93; Aux Bp Peru and Bolivia 93-95; Bp Bolivia from 95; Asst Primate of S Cone from 95. *Iglesia Anglicana de Bolivia, Casilla 9574, La Paz, Bolivia* Tel La Paz (2) 371414 Fax as telephone

VENABLES, Mrs Margaret Joy. b 37. ADB. Bp Otter Coll CertEd57 S Dios Minl Tr Scheme 86. **d** 89 **p** 94. NSM Wilton *B & W* 89-91; NSM Taunton St Andr 91-92; C from 92. *11 Henley Road, Taunton, Somerset TA1 5BN* Tel (01823) 335023

VENABLES, Philip Richard Meredith. b 58. Magd Coll Ox BA79 CertEd80. Wycliffe Hall Ox 85. **d** 88 **p** 89. C Gillingham St Mark *Roch* 88-93; V Penge St Jo from 93. *The Vicarage, St John's Road, London SE20 7EQ* Tel 0181-778 6176

VENESS, Allan Barry. **d** 97. NSM Felpham w Middleton *Chich* from 97. *95 Limmer Lane, Felpham, Bognor Regis, W Sussex PO22 7LP* Tel (01243) 583230

VENESS, David Roger. b 48. Brunel Univ BTech70. St Jo Coll Nottm 73. **d** 75 **p** 76. C Selly Hill St Steph *Birm* 75-80; V Colney Heath St Mark *St Alb* from 80; RD Hatfield 88-93. *St Mark's Vicarage, Colney Heath, St Albans, Herts AL4 0NQ* Tel (01727) 822040

✠**VENNER, The Rt Revd Stephen Squires.** b 44. Birm Univ BA65 Linacre Coll Ox BA67 MA71 Lon Univ PGCE72. St Steph Ho Ox 65. **d** 68 **p** 69 **c** 94. C Streatham St Pet *S'wark* 68-71; C Streatham Hill St Marg 71-72; C Balham Hill Ascension 72-74; Bp's Chapl to Overseas Students 74-76; V Clapham St Pet 74-76; P-in-c Studley *Sarum* 76; V 76-82; V Weymouth H Trin 82-94; RD Weymouth 88-93; Can and Preb Sarum Cathl 89-94; Suff Bp Middleton *Man* from 94. *The Hollies, Manchester Road, Rochdale, Lancs OL11 3QY* Tel (01706) 358550 Fax 354851 E-mail +stephen@middtn.demon.co.uk

VENNING, Nigel Christopher. b 50. K Coll Lon BD75 AKC75. St Aug Coll Cant 75. **d** 76 **p** 77. C Minehead *B & W* 76-80; C Fawley *Win* 80-83; P-in-c Combe St Nicholas w Wambrook *B & W* 83-89; P-in-c Whitestaunton 83-89; R Staplegrove from 89; RD Taunton from 96. *The Rectory, Rectory Drive, Staplegrove, Taunton, Somerset TA2 6AP* Tel (01823) 272787

VENUS, John Charles. b 29. AKC53. **d** 54 **p** 55. C Havant *Portsm* 54-59; S Africa 60-65; Chapl RN 66-70 and 78-83; Chapl Trin Coll Glenalmond 70-78; R Abinger cum Coldharbour *Guildf* 83-93; rtd 93; Perm to Offic *Guildf* from 93. *Dora Cottage, Beech Hill, Hambledon, Godalming, Surrey GU8 4HL* Tel (01428) 682087

VERE HODGE, Preb Francis. b 19. MC43. Worc Coll Ox BA46 MA46. Cuddesdon Coll 46. **d** 48 **p** 49. C Battle *Chich* 48-54; R

Iping 54-58; R Linch 54-58; V Kingswood *S'wark* 58-65; V Moorlinch w Stawell and Sutton Mallet *B & W* 65-79; R Greinton 68-79; RD Glastonbury 75-79; Preb Wells Cathl from 79; P-in-c Lydeard St Lawrence w Combe Florey and Tolland 79-84; rtd 84; Perm to Offic *B & W* from 84. *Rose Cottage, Ham Street, Baltonsborough, Glastonbury, Somerset BA6 8PN* Tel (01458) 850032

✠**VERNEY, The Rt Revd Stephen Edmund.** b 19. MBE45. Ball Coll Ox BA48 MA48. **d** 50 **p** 51 **c** 77. C Gedling *S'well* 50-52; C-in-c Clifton CD 52-57; V Clifton St Fran 57-58; Dioc Missr *Cov* 58-64; V Leamington Hastings 58-64; Can Res Cov Cathl 64-70; Can Windsor 70-77; Suff Bp Repton *Derby* 77-85; Hon Can Derby Cathl 77-85; Dioc Dir of Post-Ord Tr 83-85; rtd 86; Perm to Offic *Ox* 86-91; Asst Bp Ox from 91. *Charity School House, Church Road, Blewbury, Didcot, Oxon OX11 9PY* Tel (01235) 850004

VERNON, Bryan Graham. b 50. Qu Coll Cam BA72 MA76. Qu Coll Birm DipTh74. **d** 75 **p** 76. C Newc St Gabr *Newc* 75-79; Chapl Newc Univ 79-91; Chmn Newc Mental Health Trust from 91. *34 Queens Road, Newcastle upon Tyne NE2 2PQ* Tel 0191-281 3861

VERNON, John Christie. b 40. Lon Univ BSc62. Linc Th Coll 63. **d** 65 **p** 66. C Barnard Castle *Dur* 65-69; CF 69-92; Chapl Ellesmere Coll Shropshire from 92. *Ellesmere College, Ellesmere, Shropshire SY12 9AB* Tel (01691) 622321

VERNON, Mark Nicolas. b 66. St Jo Coll Dur BSc89 Ox Univ BTh93. St Steph Ho Ox 90. **d** 93 **p** 94. C Billingham St Cuth *Dur* 93-95. *St Barnabas' Vicarage, 38 Calton Avenue, London SE21 7DG*

VERNON, Matthew James. b 71. Collingwood Coll Dur BSc93. Westcott Ho Cam BA96 CTM97. **d** 97. C Guildf H Trin w St Mary *Guildf* from 97. *27 Pewley Way, Guildford, Surrey GU1 3PX* Tel (01483) 568477

VERNON, Robert Leslie. b 47. Sarum & Wells Th Coll 73. **d** 76 **p** 77. C Hartlepool St Luke *Dur* 76-79; C Birm St Geo *Birm* 79-82; V Bordesley Green 82-86; Dioc Youth Officer *Carl* 86-89; P-in-c Holme 86-89; Dioc Youth Adv *Newc* 89-95; V Widdrington from 95; V Ulgham from 95. *The Vicarage, Grangemoor Road, Widdrington, Morpeth, Northd NE61 5PU* Tel (01670) 790389

VESEY, Nicholas Ivo. b 54. Bris Univ BSc73. Cranmer Hall Dur 95. **d** 97. C Tunbridge Wells St Mark *Roch* from 97. *2 Tudor Court, Tunbridge Wells, Kent TN2 5QH* Tel (01892) 517969 E-mail nicholasvesey@msn.com

VESSEY, Andrew John. b 45. Bp Otter Coll CertEd67 Sarum & Wells Th Coll 84. **d** 86 **p** 87. C Framlingham w Saxtead *St E* 86-89; V Catshill and Dodford *Worc* 89-94; P-in-c Areley Kings from 94. *The Rectory, Areley Kings, Stourport-on-Severn, Worcs DY13 0TH* Tel (01299) 822868

VESSEY, Peter Allan Beaumont. b 36. R Agric Coll Cirencester DipEM56. Lon Coll of Div ALCD65 LTh74. **d** 64 **p** 65. C Rayleigh *Chelmsf* 64-67; C Cambridge H Trin *Ely* 67-71; V Kingston upon Hull St Aid Southcoates *York* 71-80; V Swanwick and Pentrich *Derby* 80-94; Perm to Offic from 94; rtd 96. *Hillview Cottage, 30 Chapel Hill, Cromford, Matlock, Derbyshire DE4 3QG* Tel (01629) 825572 Fax 823988

VETTERS, Miss Shirley Jacqueline Margaret. b 34. S'wark Ord Course 85. **d** 88 **p** 94. NSM E Ham w Upton Park St Alb *Chelmsf* 88-91; C Birm St Martin w Bordesley St Andr *Birm* from 91; Chapl to the Markets from 91. *341 George Road, Erdington, Birmingham B23 7RY* Tel 0121-382 4109

VEVAR, Canon John Harvard. b 14. Univ of Wales BA36. St Mich Coll Llan 37. **d** 38 **p** 40. C Llanfechell w Bodewryd, Rhosbeirio etc *Ban* 38-42; C Newtown w Llanllwchaiarn *St As* 42-46; P-in-c Llanfairynghornwy w Llanrhwydrys *Ban* 46-51; R Mellteyrn w Botwnnog 51-55; R Mellteyrn w Botwnnog and Llandygwnnin etc 55-84; P-in-c Llandudwen 67-73; Can Ban Cathl 78-84; rtd 84; Perm to Offic *Ban* from 84. *Gwynant, Tudweiliog, Pwllheli LL53 8AJ* Tel (01758) 87270

VEVERS, Eric. b 22. Oak Hill Th Coll 54. **d** 56 **p** 57. C Dagenham *Chelmsf* 56-58; C E Ham St Paul 58-60; V Fulham Ch Ch *Lon* 60-68; V Ealing St Mary 68-78; V Sidmouth All SS *Ex* 78-88; rtd 88; Perm to Offic *Guildf* from 88. *16 Clayton Drive, Guildford, Surrey GU2 6TZ* Tel (01483) 506269

VEVERS, Geoffrey Martin. b 51. Oak Hill Th Coll. **d** 82 **p** 83. C Wealdstone H Trin *Lon* 82-84; C Harrow Trin St Mich 84-88; V Wandsworth St Steph *S'wark* 88-96; V Battersea Fields from 96. *St Saviour's Vicarage, 351A Battersea Park Road, London SW11 4LH* Tel 0171-498 1642

VEYSEY, John Norris. b 14. **d** 47 **p** 48. C Cov St Jo *Cov* 48-50; Chapl to the Deaf *B & W* 50-79; rtd 79; Perm to Offic *B & W* 80-95. *8 Richmond Place, Lansdown, Bath BA1 5PZ* Tel (01225) 313965

VIBERT, Simon David Newman. b 63. Oak Hill Th Coll BA89. **d** 89 **p** 90. C Houghton *Carl* 89-92; C-in-c Buxton Trin Prop Chpl *Derby* from 92. *37 Temple Road, Buxton, Derbyshire SK17 9BA* Tel (01298) 23461

VICARS, David. b 22. Leeds Univ BA48. Coll of Resurr Mirfield 48. **d** 50 **p** 51. C Newington St Paul *S'wark* 50-54; C Kingston St Luke 54-56; C Cirencester *Glouc* 56-59; Malaysia 59-66; Area Sec (Llan, Mon, St D and S & B) USPG 67-77; R Coychurch w Llangan and St Mary Hill *Llan* 77-90; rtd 90; Perm to Offic *Llan* from 90. *43 Bryn Rhedyn, Pencoed, Bridgend CF35 6TL* Tel (01656) 860920

VICARY, Canon Douglas Reginald. b 16. Trin Coll Ox BA38 BSc39 DipTh40 MA42. Wycliffe Hall Ox 39. **d** 40 **p** 41. Asst Chapl St Lawr Coll Ramsgate 40-45; C Collingtree w Courteenhall *Pet* 40-45; Tutor Wycliffe Hall Ox 45-47; Chapl Hertf Coll Ox 45-48; Chapl Wycliffe Hall Ox 47-48; Dir of Educn *Roch* 48-57; Min Can Roch Cathl 49-52; Can Res Roch Cathl 52-57; Dir Post Ord Tr 52-57; Hd Master K Sch Roch 57-75; Hon Can Roch Cathl *Roch* 57-75; Can Res and Prec Wells Cathl *B & W* 75-88; Chapl to The Queen 77-87; rtd 88; Perm to Offic *B & W* from 88. *8 Tor Street, Wells, Somerset BA5 2US* Tel (01749) 679137

VICK, Samuel Kenneth Lloyd. b 31. Univ of Wales (Lamp) BA53. Linc Th Coll. **d** 55 **p** 56. C Shotton *St As* 55-56; C Wrexham 56-61; C Knowle H Nativity *Bris* 61-67; V Mirfield Eastthorpe St Paul *Wakef* 67-78; V Altofts from 78. *The Vicarage, Altofts, Normanton, W Yorkshire WF6 2QG* Tel (01924) 892299

VICKERMAN, John. b 42. Chich Th Coll 69. **d** 72 **p** 73. C Horbury *Wakef* 72-76; C Elland 76-78; V Glasshoughton 78-89; V Bruntcliffe 89-96; V King Cross from 96. *The Vicarage, West Royd Avenue, Halifax, W Yorkshire HX1 3NU* Tel (01422) 352933

VICKERS, Dennis William George. b 30. RIBA72 York Univ MA91. Glouc Th Course 83. **d** 86 **p** 87. NSM Stokesay *Heref* 86-88; NSM Bucknell w Chapel Lawn, Llanfair Waterdine etc 88-92; NSM Wigmore Abbey from 93. *Reeves Holding, Reeves Lane, Stanage, Knighton LD7 1NA* Tel (015474) 530577

VICKERS, Mrs Janice Audrey Maureen. b 56. Guildf Dioc Min Course 93. **d** 96 **p** 97. NSM Woking Ch Ch *Guildf* from 96. *7 Langdale Close, Woking, Surrey GU21 4RS* Tel (01483) 720873

VICKERS, Mrs Mary Janet. b 57. Westmr Coll Ox MTh97. St Jo Coll Nottm BTh85. **dss** 85 **d** 87. Worc City St Paul and Old St Martin etc *Worc* 85-89; Par Dn 87-89; World Miss Officer *Worc* 89-92; USPG from 92; Lic to Offic *Eur* from 95. *41 Wakefords Park, Church Crookham, Fleet, Hants GU13 0EY* Tel (01252) 620457 Fax as telephone E-mail revsvickers@msn.com

✠**VICKERS, The Rt Revd Michael Edwin.** b 29. Worc Coll Ox BA56 MA56 Dur Univ DipTh59. **d** 59 **p** 60 **c** 88. C Bexleyheath Ch Ch *Roch* 59-62; Chapl Lee Abbey 62-67; V Hull Newland St Jo *York* 67-81; AD W Hull 72-81; Can and Preb York Minster 81-88; Adn E Riding 81-88; Area Bp Colchester *Chelmsf* 88-94; rtd 94; Asst Bp Blackb from 94. *2 Collingham Park, Lancaster LA1 4PD* Tel (01524) 848492

VICKERS, Peter. b 56. St Jo Coll Nottm LTh85. **d** 85 **p** 86. C Worc St Barn w Ch Ch *Worc* 85-88; TV Kidderminster St Mary and All SS w Trimpley etc 88-92; Ind Chapl 88-92; CF from 92. *MOD Chaplains (Army), Trenchard Lines, Upavon, Pewsey, Wilts SN9 6BE* Tel (01980) 615804 Fax 615800 E-mail revsvickers@msn.com

VICKERS, Peter George. b 41. Local Minl Tr Course 90. **d** 93 **p** 94. Hon C Cobham *Guildf* from 93. *24 Station Road, Stoke D'Abernon, Cobham, Surrey KT11 3BN* Tel (01932) 862497

VICKERS, Randolph. b 36. FCIM FInstD Newc Univ MA93. St Alb Minl Tr Scheme 77. **d** 80 **p** 82. NSM Hitchin *St Alb* 80-87; NSM Luton Lewsey St Hugh 87-89; NSM Shotley *Newc* from 89; Prin Northumbrian Cen of Prayer for Chr Healing from 89. *Beggar's Roost, 26 Painshawfield Road, Stocksfield, Northd NE43 7PF* Tel (01661) 842364 Fax as telephone E-mail 101317.2746@compuserve.com

VICKERSTAFF, John Joseph. b 60. Westcott Ho Cam. **d** 97. C Halesworth w Linstead, Chediston, Holton etc *St E* from 97. *St Ursula House, 64 Old Station Road, Halesworth, Suffolk IP19 8JQ* Tel (01986) 874480

VICKERY, Jonathan Laurie. b 58. Bretton Hall Coll CertEd79 Leeds Univ BEd80. Wycliffe Hall Ox 81. **d** 84 **p** 85. C Gorseinon *S & B* 84-86; P-in-c Whitton and Pilleth and Cascob etc 86-87; V 87-91; V Crickhowell w Cwmdu and Tretower from 91. *The Rectory, Crickhowell NP8 1DW* Tel (01873) 811224

VICKERY, Robin Francis. b 48. K Coll Lon BD73 AKC73. **d** 74 **p** 75. C Clapham St Jo *S'wark* 74-77; C Clapham Ch Ch and St Jo 75-77; C Reigate St Luke S Park 77-79; Hon C Clapham H Spirit 80-87; Hon C Clapham TM from 87. *Norfolk House, 13 Chelsham Road, London SW4 6NR* Tel 0171-622 4792

VICKERY, Trevor Hopkin. b 17. Univ of Wales BA39. St Mich Coll Llan 39. **d** 40 **p** 41. C Ban St Jas *Ban* 40-43; Lic to Offic 43-47; Lic to Offic *Cant* 48-51; Chapl RN 43-47; C Heacham *Nor* 47-48; Chapl Cranbrook Sch Kent 48-51; R Staplehurst *Cant* 51-91; Chapl HM Det Cen Blantyre Ho 54-80; rtd 91; Perm to Offic *Cant* from 91; Perm to Offic *Chich* from 91. *Park View, Cranbrook Road, Staplehurst, Kent TN12 0EJ* Tel (01580) 891091

VIDAL-HALL, Roderic Mark. b 37. Sheff Univ BSc60 Birm Univ DPS70. Lich Th Coll 62. **d** 64 **p** 65. C Ilkeston St Mary *Derby* 64-67; C Nether and Over Seale 67-70; V Chellaston 70-84; C Marchington w Marchington Woodlands *Lich* 84-97; C Kingstone w Gratwich 85-97; TV Uttoxeter Area from 97. *13 Moisty Lane, Marchington, Uttoxeter, Staffs ST14 8JY* Tel (01283) 820030

VIGAR, Gilbert Leonard. b 12. Lon Univ BD46 BA50 MA52 Nottm Univ MPhil72. Kelham Th Coll 32. **d** 38 **p** 39. C Sheff St Cuth *Sheff* 38-42; P-in-c Herringthorpe 42-47; V Bradwell *Derby* 47-52; V Ault Hucknall 52-55; P-in-c Heath 52-55; V Winshill 55-57; V Madingley *Ely* 57-61; Asst Dir Educn 57-61; Prin Lect Bp Grosseteste Coll Linc 61-77; rtd 77; Hon C Win H Trin *Win* 79-85; Hon C Eastbourne St Sav and St Pet *Chich* 85-88; Perm to Offic from 88. *5 Chatsworth Gardens, Eastbourne, E Sussex BN20 7JP* Tel (01323) 644121

VIGARS, Anthony Roy (Tony). b 54. St Jo Coll Dur BA75. Trin Coll Bris 77. **d** 78 **p** 79. C Barking St Marg w St Patr *Chelmsf* 78-81; C Littleover *Derby* 81-84; C-in-c Stapenhill Immanuel CD 84-90; V Meltham *Wakef* 90-97; V Reading St Jo *Ox* from 97. *St John's Vicarage, 50 London Road, Reading RG1 5AS* Tel 0118-987 2366

VIGEON, Canon Owen George. b 28. Peterho Cam BA52 MA57. Ely Th Coll 52. **d** 54 **p** 55. C Barrow St Luke *Carl* 54-58; Chapl St Jo Coll York 58-61; V Burnley St Steph *Blackb* 61-69; V Bilsborrow 69-73; Asst Dir RE 69-73; V St Annes 74-85; RD Fylde 80-85; R Halton w Aughton 85-93; Hon Can Blackb Cathl 92-93; rtd 93. *19 Lynden Close, Bromsgrove, Worcs B61 8PD* Tel (01527) 574520

VIGERS, Neil Simon. b 62. K Coll Lon BD84 MTh87. Linc Th Coll 88. **d** 90 **p** 91. C Chelsea St Luke and Ch Ch *Lon* 90-93; C Staines St Mary and St Pet 93-96; P-in-c Hook *Win* from 96. *The Rectory, London Road, Hook, Basingstoke, Hants RG27 9EG* Tel (01256) 762268

VIGOR, Ms Margaret Ann. b 45. Ripon Coll Cuddesdon 85. **d** 87 **p** 96. Chapl Asst All SS Convent Ox 87-89; Par Dn Basildon St Martin w Nevendon *Chelmsf* 89-91; Bp's Ho Iona 91. *15 Mitchell Street, Hartlepool, Cleveland TS26 9EZ* Tel (01429) 867458

VILE, John Frederick. b 48. Univ of Wales (Cardiff) DipTh74. St Mich Coll Llan 71. **d** 74 **p** 75. C Roath St German *Llan* 74-78; C Newton Nottage 78-80; V Landore *S & B* 80-84; SSF 85-94; Hon C Clifton All SS w St Jo *Bris* 88-91; C Tile Hill *Cov* 91-94. *7 Hanbury Road, Clifton, Bristol BS8 2EW* Tel 0117-973 8700

VILLAGE, Dr Andrew. b 54. Collingwood Coll Dur BSc75 Edin Univ PhD80. Trin Coll Bris BA92. **d** 92 **p** 93. C Northampton St Giles *Pet* 92-95; R Middleton Cheney w Chacombe from 95. *The Rectory, 3 High Street, Middleton Cheney, Banbury, Oxon OX17 2PB* Tel (01295) 710254

VILLER, Allan George Frederick. b 38. EAMTC 78. **d** 81 **p** 82. NSM Ely 81-85; V Emneth 85-92; V Littleport from 92. *St George's Vicarage, 30 Church Lane, Littleport, Ely, Cambs CB6 1PS* Tel (01353) 860207 E-mail allan@agfv.demon.co.uk

VILLIERS, Preb Tony. b 35. Lich Th Coll 59. **d** 62 **p** 63. C Shifnal *Lich* 62-65; C Wednesbury St Paul Wood Green 65-67; R Llanymynech from 67; V Morton from 72; RD Oswestry 82-87; Preb Lich Cathl from 89. *Llanymynech Rectory, Pant, Oswestry, Shropshire SY10 9RA* Tel (01691) 830446

VINCE, Mrs Barbara Mary Tudor. b 29. St Alb Minl Tr Scheme 79. **dss** 82 **d** 87 **p** 94. Northwood H Trin *Lon* 82-86; Belmont 86-87; Par Dn 87-89; rtd 90; Perm to Offic *Lon* from 90. *22 St Mary's Avenue, Northwood, Middx HA6 3AZ* Tel (01923) 825730

VINCE, David Eric. b 59. Birm Univ BA81 Nottm Univ BCombStuds85 Golds Coll Lon PGCE90. Linc Th Coll 82. **d** 85 **p** 86. C Gt Malvern St Mary *Worc* 85-88; C All Hallows by the Tower etc *Lon* 88-90; Min St Giles Cripplegate w St Bart Moor Lane etc 90-92; R Salwarpe and Hindlip w Martin Hussingtree *Worc* 92-97; R Willersey, Saintbury, Weston-sub-Edge etc *Glouc* from 97. *The Rectory, Weston-sub-Edge, Chipping Campden, Glos GL55 6QH* Tel (01386) 840292

VINCE, Raymond Michael. b 45. Lon Univ BD69 Bris Univ MA72 K Coll Lon MTh80 LSE MSc83. Tyndale Hall Bris 66. **d** 71 **p** 72. C Southsea St Jude *Portsm* 71-75; Hon C Islington St Mary *Lon* 75-83; Chapl N Lon Poly 75-83; USA from 83. *906 South Orleans Drive, Tampa, Florida 33606, USA*

VINCENT, Preb Alfred James. b 30. Bris Univ BA54 Lon Univ BD56. Tyndale Hall Bris 50. **d** 54 **p** 55. C Shrewsbury St Julian *Lich* 54-56; C Camborne *Truro* 56-59; V Kenwyn 59-68; Lic to Offic *St Alb* 68; Lect Qu Coll Birm 68-70; Lic to Offic *Birm* 68-70; V Bordesley St Oswald 70-76; V S Shields St Hilda w St Thos *Dur* 76-84; Miss to Seamen 84-92; V Bude Haven *Truro* 84-89; R Bude Haven and Marhamchurch 89-92; RD Stratton 88-92; Preb St Endellion 90-95; rtd 92; P-in-c Chacewater *Truro* 92-95; Perm to Offic from 95. *5 Raymond Road, Redruth, Cornwall TR15 2HD* Tel (01209) 209263

VINCENT, Bruce Matthews. b 24. Univ of Wales (Swansea) DipYW50 Open Univ BA76 Surrey Univ MPhil83. **d** 88 **p** 88. Hon C Sidcup St Jo *Roch* from 88. *497 Footscray Road, London SE9 3UH* Tel 0181-850 5450

VINCENT, Christopher Robin. b 30. Sarum Th Coll 57. **d** 60 **p** 61. C Frome St Jo *B & W* 60-64; V Puxton w Hewish St Ann and Wick St Lawrence 64-70; V Buckland Dinham w Elm 70-71; V Buckland Dinham w Elm, Orchardleigh etc 71-77; P-in-c Frome H Trin 77-90; Chapl St Adhelm's Hosp Frome 77-88; RD Frome *B & W* 85-89; V Kewstoke w Wick St Lawrence 90-94; rtd 94; Perm to Offic *B & W* from 94. *Willows Edge, 2 Westwood Close, Weston-super-Mare, Avon BS22 0JU* Tel (01934) 517425

VINCENT, David Cyril. b 37. Selw Coll Cam BA60 MA64. Coll of Resurr Mirfield 60. **d** 62 **p** 63. C Cheetwood St Alb *Man* 62-65; C Lawton Moor 65-67; V Wandsworth Common St Mary *S'wark* 67-84; RD Tooting 75-80; R Stoke D'Abernon *Guildf* from 84. *The Rectory, Blundell Lane, Stoke D'Abernon, Cobham, Surrey KT11 2SE* Tel (01932) 862502

VINCENT, George William Walter. b 13. ALCD40. **d** 40 **p** 41. C Hammersmith St Simon *Lon* 40-44; C Stowmarket *St E* 44-47; R Earl Stonham 47-55; R Alderton w Ramsholt and Bawdsey 55-86; rtd 86; Perm to Offic *St E* from 86. *c/o B Vincent Esq, Rectory House, Alderton, Woodbridge, Suffolk IP12 3BL* Tel (01394) 411306

VINCENT, Henry William Gordon. b 16. Leeds Univ BA42. Coll of Resurr Mirfield 42. **d** 44 **p** 45. C Bridgwater St Jo *B & W* 44-46; C Greenford H Cross *Lon* 46-52; C Teddington St Alb 52-55; V N Hammersmith St Kath 55-64; V Whitton St Aug 64-81; rtd 81. *20 West Mills Road, Dorchester, Dorset DT1 1SR* Tel (01305) 263933

VINCENT, John Leonard. b 61. Univ of Wales (Lamp) BA83 Southn Univ BTh87. Chich Th Coll 84. **d** 87 **p** 88. C Hampton All SS *Lon* 87-90; C Shepperton 90-95; V Whitton SS Phil and Jas from 95. *The Vicarage, 205 Kneller Road, Twickenham TW2 7DY* Tel 0181-894 1932

VINCENT, Michael Francis. b 48. CertEd70 Open Univ BA83. Sarum & Wells Th Coll 85. **d** 87 **p** 88. C Nuneaton St Mary *Cov* 87-90; C Stockingford 90-91; P-in-c from 91. *The Vicarage, Church Road, Stockingford, Nuneaton, Warks CV10 8LG* Tel (01203) 383024

VINCENT, Canon Noel Thomas. b 36. Fitzw Ho Cam BA63 MA67. Ridley Hall Cam 60. **d** 63 **p** 64. C Fenham St Jas and St Basil *Newc* 63-67; C Prudhoe 67-70; V Holbrooke *Derby* 70-74; P-in-c Lt Eaton 72-74; P-in-c Osmaston w Edlaston 74-78; Hon C 78-85; Dioc Info Officer 74-78; Sen Producer Relig Progr BBC Man 82-91; Hon C Brailsford w Shirley and Osmaston w Edlaston *Derby* 85-86; Hon Can Derby Cathl 85-86; Perm to Offic *Ches* 86-92; Chief Producer BBC Relig Progr Lon 91-93; Hon C Twickenham St Mary *Lon* 92-95; Chief Asst to Hd BBC Relig Broadcasting 93-95; Can Res and Treas Liv Cathl *Liv* from 95. *2 Cathedral Close, Liverpool L1 7BR* Tel 0151-708 0932

VINCENT, Roy David. b 37. Univ of Wales (Swansea) DipYW. Chich Th Coll 81. **d** 83 **p** 84. C Atherton *Man* 83-86; V E Crompton 86-95; P-in-c Burwash *Chich* from 95. *The Rectory, Burwash, Etchingham, E Sussex TN19 7BH* Tel (01435) 882301

VINCENT, Canon William Alfred Leslie. b 11. Bris Univ BA33 St Edm Hall Ox BLitt44 DPhil68. **d** 39 **p** 40. Chapl R Wanstead Sch 39-41; C S Woodford H Trin CD *Chelmsf* 39-41; Lic to Offic *Mon* from 42; Chapl Ch Ch Ox 45-51; Chapl Dioc Tr Coll Ches 51-64; Lic to Offic *Ches* from 52; Can Res Bris Cathl *Bris* 74-77; Lic to Offic 77-94. *Address temp unknown*

VINCER, Michael (Mike). b 41. Sarum & Wells Th Coll 77. **d** 80 **p** 81. Hon C Littleham w Exmouth *Ex* 80-92; Miss to Seamen 80-92; Area Sec (Dios Ex and Truro) USPG 86-92; Ind Chapl Gtr Man Ind Miss *Man* from 92; Chapl Man Airport from 92; Lic Preacher from 92; Perm to Offic *Ches* from 92. *10 Highfield Crescent, Wilmslow, Cheshire SK9 2JL* Tel (01625) 525982 or 0161-489 2838 Fax 0161-489 3813

VINE, John. b 24. Keble Coll Ox BA45 MA50. St Steph Ho Ox 45. **d** 48 **p** 49. C Hackney Wick St Mary of Eton w St Aug *Lon* 48-50; C Holborn St Alb w Saffron Hill St Pet 50-53; Chapl Ely Th Coll 53-56; Vice-Prin Ely Th Coll 56-60; Hon C St Leonards Ch Ch *Chich* 60-62; Chapl Lich Th Coll 62-67; R Wrington *B & W* 67-69; V Earl's Court St Cuth w St Matthias *Lon* from 69. *St Cuthbert's Clergy House, 50 Philbeach Gardens, London SW5 9EB* Tel 0171-370 3263

VINE, Michael Charles. b 51. Worc Coll Ox BA73 MA80. Cuddesdon Coll 73. **d** 76 **p** 77. C Wallsend St Luke *Newc* 76-79; C Denton 79-81; V Sugley 81-91; V Shiremoor from 91. *St Mark's Vicarage, Brenkley Avenue, Shiremoor, Newcastle upon Tyne NE27 0PP* Tel 0191-253 3291

VINE, Michael Derek. b 35. Ch Ch Ox BA58 MA63. Ely Th Coll 58. **d** 60 **p** 61. C Syston *Leic* 60-63; C S Ascot *Ox* 63-66; Chapl RN 66-70; Perm to Offic *Portsm* 71-74; Perm to Offic *Lon* 74-91; C Chepstow *Mon* 91-94; V Llantillio Pertholey w Bettws Chpl etc from 94. *St Teilo's Vicarage, Llantillio Pertholey, Abergavenny NP7 6NY* Tel (01873) 854323

VINE, Neville Peter. b 54. K Coll Lon BD80 AKC80. Linc Th Coll 80. **d** 81 **p** 82. C Peterlee *Dur* 81-86; Chapl Peterlee Coll 84-86; V Auckland St Pet *Dur* 86-89; Perm to Offic 89-91; R Easington from 91. *The Rectory, 5 Tudor Grange, Easington, Peterlee, Co Durham SR8 3DF* Tel 0191-527 0287

VINER, Canon Leonard Edwin. b 20. Univ Coll Dur LTh41 BA43. St Aug Coll Cant 38. **d** 43 **p** 44. C W Molesey *Guildf* 43-45; Nyasaland 46-56 and 58-64; Malawi 64-71; C Roxbourne St Andr *Lon* 56-58; R Honing w Crostwight *Nor* 71-75; P-in-c E Ruston 71-73; V 73-75; P-in-c Witton w Ridlington 71-73; V 73-75; C Corby Epiphany w St Jo *Pet* 75-79; V Brigstock w Stanion 79-86; rtd 86; Asst Chapl Lisbon *Eur* 86-87; Chapl Tangier 87-89; Perm to Offic *Pet* from 90. *8 Clive Close, Kettering, Northants NN15 5BQ* Tel (01536) 519734

VINEY, Arthur William. b 32. BEd. S Dios Minl Tr Scheme. **d** 82 **p** 83. NSM Clayton w Keymer *Chich* 82-86; NSM Streat w Westmeston 86-94; rtd 94; Perm to Offic *Chich* from 94. *3 The Almshouses of the Holy Name, Brighton Road, Hurstpierpoint, Hassocks, W Sussex BN6 9EF* Tel (01273) 832570

VINEY, Peter. b 43. Ox NSM Course. **d** 76 **p** 77. NSM High Wycombe *Ox* from 76. *5 Avery Avenue, Downley, High Wycombe, Bucks HP13 5UE* Tel (01494) 436065

VIPOND, Canon John. b 17. Lon Univ BD48. ALCD48. **d** 48 **p** 49. C Roxeth Ch Ch *Lon* 48-51; V 51-56; V Pudsey St Lawr *Bradf* 56-73; Hon Can Bradf Cathl 67-73; V St Austell *Truro* 73-83; rtd 83; Perm to Offic *Truro* from 83. *Wisteria, 15 Coffeelake Meadow, Lostwithiel, Cornwall PL22 0LT* Tel (01208) 873141

VIRGO, Canon Leslie Gordon. b 25. Linc Th Coll 56. **d** 58 **p** 59. C Hatcham Park All SS *S'wark* 58-61; C Selsdon *Cant* 61-65; Chapl Warlingham Park Hosp Croydon 65-73; Dioc Adv on Past Care and Counselling from 74; R Chelsfield *Roch* from 74; Hon Can Roch Cathl from 83. *The Rectory, Skibbs Lane, Orpington, Kent BR6 7RH* Tel (01689) 825749

VIRTUE, Thomas James. b 32. QUB BA56 TCD 58 Liv Univ DipRS80. **d** 58 **p** 59. C Belfast St Mich *Conn* 58-61; C Belfast St Bart 61-63; I Tempo *Clogh* 63-66; P-in-c Glynn w Raloo and Templecorran *Conn* 66-70; TV Ellesmere Port *Ches* 70-74; TV Ches Team 74-83; V Gt Sutton from 83. *St John's Vicarage, 1 Church Lane, Great Sutton, South Wirral L66 4RE* Tel 0151-339 9916

VITTLE, Cyril Wilfred. b 13. **d** 55 **p** 56. C Bishopsworth *Bris* 55-57; C Henbury 57-59; V Fishponds All SS 59-69; V Brislington St Cuth 69-76; C Thornbury *Glouc* 76-79; rtd 79; Perm to Offic *Glouc* 80-90. *39 Hyde Avenue, Thornbury, Avon BS12 1HZ* Tel (01454) 415614

VIVASH, Peter Henry. b 57. Hockerill Coll of Educn CertEd78 Chelmer Inst of HE CQSW85. Cranmer Hall Dur 90. **d** 92 **p** 93. C Malpas *Mon* 92-95; V Bettws from 95. *St David's Rectory, Bettws Hill, Bettws, Newport NP9 6BP* Tel (01633) 855193

VIVIAN, Adrian John. b 42. K Coll Lon BD65 AKC66. **d** 66 **p** 67. C Bromley St Andr *Roch* 66-69; C Egg Buckland *Ex* 69-73; Perm to Offic 73-84; P-in-c Newton Ferrers w Revelstoke 84-87. *The Parsonage Farm, Parsonage Road, Newton Ferrers, Plymouth PL8 1AT*

VIVIAN, Thomas Keith. b 27. St Jo Coll Cam BA48 MA52. St Deiniol's Hawarden 76. **d** 80 **p** 81. Hd Master Lucton Sch Leominster 62-85; Lic to Offic *Heref* 80-85; P-in-c Chew Stoke w Nempnett Thrubwell *B & W* 85-88; R 88-97; P-in-c Norton Malreward 85-88; R 88-97; RD Chew Magna 92-97; rtd 97. *Timberley, Sidmouth Road, Lyme Regis, Dorset DT7 3ES* Tel (01297) 443547

VIVIAN, Victor Ivan. b 38. Nottm Poly LLB87. EMMTC DTPS94. **d** 94 **p** 95. NSM Bestwood *S'well* from 94. *12 Deepdale Road, Nottingham NG8 2FU* Tel 0115-928 3954

VOAKE, Andrew James Frederick. b 28. Dur Univ BA55. Oak Hill Th Coll 51. **d** 55 **p** 56. C Uxbridge St Marg *Lon* 55; C Fulham St Matt 55-58; C Hove Bp Hannington Memorial Ch *Chich* 58-61; V Kirkdale St Lawr *Liv* 61-63; Chapl Millfield Sch Somerset 63-71; R Bp Latimer Memorial Ch *Birm* 71-73; R Birm Bishop Latimer w All SS 73-80; V Crondall and Ewshot *Guildf* 80-90; rtd 90; Perm to Offic *B & W* from 90. *1 St Aubyns Avenue, Weston-super-Mare, Avon BS23 4UJ* Tel (01934) 620587

VOCKINS, Michael David. b 44. OBE96. Univ of Wales (Abth) BSc69. Glouc Sch of Min 85. **d** 88 **p** 89. NSM Cradley w Mathon and Storridge *Heref* from 88; Perm to Offic *Worc* from 88. *Birchwood Lodge, Birchwood, Storridge, Malvern, Worcs WR13 5EZ* Tel (01886) 884366

✠**VOCKLER, The Rt Revd John Charles.** b 24. Queensland Univ BA53. ACT ThL48 ThD61 Gen Th Sem (NY) STB54 STM56 Hon STD61 St Jo Coll Morpeth 48. **d** 48 **p** 48 **c** 59. Australia 48-53 and 56-62 and 75-81; USA 54-56 and from 81; Bp Coadjutor Adelaide 59-62; Adn Eyre Peninsula 59-62; Bp Polynesia 62-68; SSF 69-90; Perm to Offic *Sarum* 69-72; Asst Bp Worc 71-72; Perm to Offic *Lon* 72-75; Asst Bp Chelmsf 72-73; Asst Bp S'wark 73-75; Hon Can S'wark Cathl 75; rtd 90; Asst Bp Quincy from 90; Superior Franciscan Order Divine Compassion from 90. *Holyrood Seminary, PO Box 111, Liberty, New York 12754-0111, USA*

VODEN, Capt Raymond William Lang. b 35. CQSW74. SW Minl Tr Course 85. **d** 88 **p** 89. CA from 60; NSM Bideford *Ex* 88-94; C Northlew w Ashbury 94; C Bratton Clovelly w Germansweek 94; TV Okehampton w Inwardleigh, Bratton Clovelly etc from 94. *The Vicarage, Northlew, Okehampton, Devon EX20 3NJ* Tel (01409) 221714

VOGEL, Charles Edward. b 06. Trin Coll Ox BA28 MA31. Cuddesdon Coll 64. **d** 65 **p** 65. C Lt Missenden *Ox* 65-69; P-in-c Childrey 69-75; P-in-c Sparsholt w Kingston Lisle 73-75; rtd 75. *Flat 12, Ellesborough Manor, Butlers Cross, Aylesbury, Bucks HP17 0XF* Tel (01296) 696125

VOGT, Charles William Derek. b 36. Portsm Poly DipSocWork76 Sheff Sch of Counselling & Psychology CertAnPsych85. EMMTC 83. **d** 86 **p** 87. NSM Ilkeston H Trin *Derby* 86-87; C Derby St Anne and St Jo 87-90; TV Staveley and Barrow Hill 90-95; P-in-c Hasland 95-96; R from 97; P-in-c Temple Normanton 95-96; V from 97. *The Rectory, 49 Churchside, Hasland, Chesterfield, Derbyshire S41 0JX* Tel (01246) 232486

VOGT, Robert Anthony. b 25. Jes Coll Cam BA50 MA54. S'wark Ord Course 60. **d** 63 **p** 64. C Sutton New Town St Barn *S'wark* 63-67; C Kidbrooke St Jas 67-72; V Wood End *Cov* 72-80; RD Cov E 77-80; R Kidbrooke St Jas *S'wark* 80-85; TR Kidbrooke 85-90; rtd 90; Perm to Offic *S'wark* from 90. *16 Tristan Square, London SE3 9UB* Tel 0181-297 2361

VOKES, Prof Frederick Ercolo. b 10. FTCD74 St Jo Coll Cam BA33 MA46 BD53 TCD MA67. Westcott Ho Cam 33. **d** 34 **p** 35. C Whippingham w E Cowes *Portsm* 34-37; Cranbrook Sch Kent 37-42; Stamford Sch 42-43; K Edw VI Sch Retford 43-44; R Wittering w Thornhaugh and Wansford *Pet* 44-47; R Forncett St Mary w St Pet *Nor* 47-55; Prof of Th and Hebrew St D Coll Lamp 55-57; Prof of Div TCD 57-80; Fell 74-80; Dean of Faculty of Arts 76-80; rtd 80; Perm to Offic *Blackb* from 80. *Flat 24, The Hastings, Greaves Road, Lancaster LA1 4TF* Tel (01524) 69428

VON BENZON, Charles Nicholas. b 54. Solicitor 79 Kent Univ BA78. S'wark Ord Course 82. **d** 85 **p** 86. NSM Bromley SS Pet and Paul *Roch* 85-87; Perm to Offic *Chich* 87-93; Ed Newsletter among Ministers at Work 89-93; Asst to RD Dallington 93-95; C The Deverills *Sarum* 95; TV Cley Hill Warminster from 95. *The Rectory, 6 Homefield Close, Longbridge Deverill, Warminster, Wilts BA12 7DQ* Tel (01985) 840278

VON MALAISE, Nicolas Christoph Axel. b 62. Univ Coll Ox BA84. Ripon Coll Cuddesdon BA86. **d** 87 **p** 88. C Oxhey St Matt *St Alb* 87-90; C Northfield *Birm* 90-92; Asst Chapl Win Coll from 92. *Winchester College, Winchester, Hants SO23 9LX* Tel (01962) 884056

VONBERG, Canon Michael. b 27. Lon Univ BA51. Wells Th Coll 58. **d** 59 **p** 60. C Bournemouth St Andr *Win* 59-61; C Milton 61-64; V Camberwell St Geo *S'wark* 64-74; V Kenley 75-94; RD Croydon S 85-93; Hon Can S'wark Cathl 89-94; rtd 94; Perm to Offic *Guildf* from 94. *81 Christchurch Mount, Epsom, Surrey KT19 8LP*

VOOGHT, Canon Michael George Peter. b 38. St Pet Hall Ox BA61 MA65. Chich Th Coll 61. **d** 63 **p** 64. C E Dulwich St Jo *S'wark* 63-66; C Prestbury *Glouc* 66-72; R Minchinhampton 72-85; RD Stonehouse 79-85; V Thornbury from 85; Hon Can Glouc Cathl from 86. *The Vicarage, Castle Street, Thornbury, Bristol BS12 1HQ* Tel (01454) 413209

VORLEY, Kenneth Arthur. b 27. Sarum Th Coll 65. **d** 67 **p** 68. C Ashbourne w Mapleton and Clifton *Derby* 67-71; R W Hallam and Mapperley 71-77; V Hemingford Grey *Ely* 78-88; rtd 88; Perm to Offic *Carl* from 88. *The Old Manor, Little Braithwaite, Keswick, Cumbria CA12 5SR* Tel (01768) 782535

VOSS, Mrs Philomena Ann. b 35. Edge Hill Coll of HE CertEd55. St Alb Minl Tr Scheme 87 EAMTC 95. **d** 96 **p** 97. NSM Tye Green w Netteswell *Chelmsf* from 96. *21 Queen's Road, Hertford SG13 8AZ* Tel (01992) 554676

VOUSDEN, Alan Thomas. b 48. K Coll Lon BSc69. Qu Coll Birm DipTh71. **d** 72 **p** 73. C Orpington All SS *Roch* 72-76; C Belvedere All SS 76-80; R Cuxton and Halling 80-86; V Bromley St Mark from 86; Chapl Bromley Hosp 86-94; Chapl Bromley Hosps NHS Trust from 94. *St Mark's Vicarage, 51 Hayes Road, Bromley BR2 9AE* Tel 0181-460 6220

VOUT, Victor Alan. b 25. Lon Univ BA53 Hull Univ BA56. Ripon Hall Ox 63. **d** 65 **p** 66. C Norton Woodseats St Paul *Sheff* 65-70; V Clifton St Jas 70-92; rtd 92; Perm to Offic *Sheff* from 92. *87 Spinneyfield, Moorgate, Rotherham, S Yorkshire S60 3LZ* Tel (01709) 839258

VOWLES, Miss Patricia. b 50. S'wark Ord Course 84. **d** 87 **p** 94. USPG 70-91; NSM Nunhead St Antony w St Silas *S'wark* 87-91; Par Dn Newington St Mary 91; D-in-c Camberwell St Mich w All So w Em 91; Par Dn 91-94; V from 94. *St Michael's Vicarage, 128 Bethwin Road, London SE5 0YY* Tel 0171-703 8686

VOWLES, Canon Peter John Henry. b 25. Magd Coll Ox BA50 MA55. Westcott Ho Cam 50. **d** 52 **p** 53. C Kings Heath *Birm* 52-56; C Huddersfield St Pet *Wakef* 56-57; PC Perry Beeches *Birm* 57-64; V 64-72; R Cottingham *York* 72-83; R Man St Ann *Man* 83-91; Hon Can Man Cathl 83-91; rtd 91; Perm to Offic *Man* from 91. *10 Redshaw Close, Fallowfield, Manchester M14 6JB* Tel 0161-257 2065

VYSE, Canon Jack Walter Miller. b 15. CCC Cam BA37 MA41. Westcott Ho Cam 38. **d** 39 **p** 40. C Southampton St Mary w H Trin *Win* 39-43; C Clee *Linc* 43-47; R Gt Braxted *Chelmsf* 47-61; R Lt Braxted 48-61; RD Witham 55-61; V St Mary Abchurch *Lon* 61-70; Vice-Prin S'wark Ord Course 66-70; P-in-c Alby w Thwaite *Nor* 70-81; V Aylsham 70-88; Chapl St Mich Hosp Aylsham 70-88; RD Ingworth *Nor* 74-88; Hon Can Nor Cathl 81-88; rtd 88; Perm to Offic *Linc* from 88; RD Louthesk 89-94. *The Old Post Office, Magna Mile, Ludford, Market Rasen, Lincs LN8 6AD* Tel (01507) 313740

VYVYAN, John Philip. b 28. New Coll Ox BA51 MA59. Cuddesdon Coll 57. **d** 59 **p** 60. C Notting Hill St Mark *Lon* 59-61; USPG (Sarawak & Borneo) 61-64; V Adderbury w Milton *Ox* 64-93; rtd 93; Perm to Offic *Truro* from 93. *Treliever Farm, Carnon Valley, Truro, Cornwall TR3 6LG* Tel (01872) 865740

W

WADDINGTON, Gary Richard. b 69. St Chad's Coll Dur BSc91. St Steph Ho Ox BTh93. **d** 96 **p** 97. C Southsea H Spirit *Portsm* from 96. *Church House, 219 Fawcett Road, Southsea, Hants PO4 0DH* Tel (01705) 812128

WADDINGTON, The Very Revd Robert Murray. b 27. Selw Coll Cam BA51 MA55. Ely Th Coll 51. **d** 53 **p** 54. C Bethnal Green St Jo w St Simon *Lon* 53-56; Australia 56-59 and 61-71; C Chesterton St Luke *Ely* 59-61; OGS from 60; Can Res Carl Cathl *Carl* 72-77; Bp's Adv for Educn 72-77; Hon Can Carl Cathl 77-84; Gen Sec Gen Syn Bd of Educn 77-84; Gen Sec Nat Soc 77-84; Dean Man 84-93; rtd 93. *6 Waverley Street, York YO3 7QZ* Tel (01904) 670200

WADDINGTON-FEATHER, John Joseph. b 33. FRSA87 Leeds Univ BA54 Keele Univ PGCE74. St Deiniol's Hawarden 75. **d** 77 **p** 78. NSM Longden and Annscroft w Pulverbatch *Heref* 77-84 and from 85; Chapl Asst HM Pris Shrewsbury 77-84 and from 85; Sudan 84-85; Chapl Prestfelde Sch Shrewsbury 86-96; rtd 96. *Fair View, Old Coppice, Lyth Bank, Bayston Hill, Shrewsbury SY3 0BW* Tel (01743) 872177 Fax as telephone E-mail john@feather.enta.net.

WADDLE, William. b 31. Linc Th Coll 64. **d** 66 **p** 67. C Tynemouth Priory *Newc* 66-69; C Longbenton St Bart 69-75; V Denton 75-81; V Beadnell 81; V Beadnell w Ellingham 81-93; RD Bamburgh and Glendale 83-92; rtd 93. *Kilmartin, 58J Church Street, Berwick-upon-Tweed TD15 1DU* Tel (01289) 305908

WADDLETON, Edwin Henry. b 12. Clifton Th Coll 37. **d** 39 **p** 40. C Bris St Phil and St Jacob w Em *Bris* 39-42; CF (EC) 42-46; Hon CF 46; V Birm Bp Ryder *Birm* 47-49; V Tytherington *Glouc* 49-54; Chapl HM Pris Falfield 51-54; Chapl HM Pris Leyhill 50-54; V Bishopsworth *Bris* 54-65; R Chippenham St Paul w Langley Burrell 65-77; rtd 77; Perm to Offic *Bris* from 77. *66 Sadler's Mead, Chippenham, Wilts SN15 3PL* Tel (01249) 653721

WADDY, Richard Patteson Stacy. b 04. Ball Coll Ox BA26 MA30. Cuddesdon Coll 26. **d** 27 **p** 28. C Leic St Pet *Leic* 27-30; India 30-47; R Ampthill *St Alb* 47-52; RD Ampthill 51-52; Warden Coll of the Ascension Selly Oak 52-59; Hon Can Birm Cathl *Birm* 54-59; R Morley *Derby* 59-67; Hon Can Derby Cathl 63-67; Chapl Qu Anne's Sch Caversham 67-72; rtd 72; Chapl Community of All Hallows Ditchingham 72-79. *Manormead, Tilford Road, Hindhead, Surrey GU26 6RA* Tel (01428) 604780

WADE, Andrew John. b 50. Trin Coll Bris. **d** 86 **p** 87. C St Keverne *Truro* 86-89; TV Probus, Ladock and Grampound w Creed and St Erme 89-92; V Constantine from 92. *The Vicarage, Charlbury Heights, Constantine, Falmouth, Cornwall TR11 5AN* Tel (01326) 40259

WADE, Anthony Austen. b 14. Leeds Univ BA36 MA38. Coll of Resurr Mirfield 36. **d** 38 **p** 39. C Ruislip Manor St Paul *Lon* 38-45; V Whitton SS Phil and Jas 46-58; V W Hendon St Jo 58-68; V Sudbury St Andr 68-79; rtd 79; Perm to Offic *Bris* 88-92. *15 Stuart Court, High Street, Kibworth, Leicester LE8 0LE* Tel 0116-279 6369

WADE, Christopher John. b 54. ARICS82 ACIArb88 Basford Coll Nottm ONC76 Trent Poly BSc81. Aston Tr Scheme 88 Trin Coll Bris DipHE92. **d** 92 **p** 93. C Barnsley St Geo *Wakef* 92-95; C Whittle-le-Woods *Blackb* from 95. *60 Schoolfield, Bamber Bridge, Preston PR5 8BH* Tel (01772) 322692

WADE, David Peter (Dave). b 65. St Jo Coll Nottm LTh92 DCM92. **d** 92 **p** 93. C Victoria Docks Ascension *Chelmsf* 92-95; P-in-c Victoria Docks St Luke 95-97; V from 97. *St Luke's Vicarage, 105 Tarling Road, London E16 1HN* Tel 0171-476 2076

WADE, Canon John Martin. b 22. Wells Th Coll. **d** 54 **p** 55. C Felixstowe St Jo *St E* 54-57; P-in-c Bury St Edmunds All SS CD 57-60; V Nayland w Wiston 60-74; Chapl Jane Walker Hosp Nayland 62-74; V Shrivenham w Watchfield and Bourton *Ox* 74-88; RD Vale of White Horse 83-87; Hon Can Ch Ch 86-88; rtd 88; Perm to Offic *Ox* from 88; Perm to Offic *Glouc* from 90. *Cranham, 13 Besbury Park, Minchinhampton, Stroud, Glos GL6 9EN* Tel (01453) 885449

WADE, Walter. b 29. Oak Hill Th Coll 64. **d** 66 **p** 67. C Denton Holme *Carl* 66-69; V Jesmond H Trin *Newc* 69-78; R Moresby *Carl* 78-87; P-in-c Langdale 87-94; Member Rural Life and Agric Team 93-94; rtd 94; Perm to Offic *Carl* from 94. *Manor Cottage, Fellside, Caldbeck, Wigton, Cumbria CA7 8HA* Tel (016974) 78214

WADE-STUBBS, Edward Pomery Flood. b 17. St Jo Coll Dur LTh39 BA40. Tyndale Hall Bris 36. **d** 40 **p** 41. C Burslem St Jo *Lich* 40-42; C Handsworth St Jas *Birm* 42-44; C Hawkhurst *Cant* 44-46; C Cheltenham St Mark *Glouc* 51-53; R Gt Witcombe 53-62; Canada 62-63; R Sutton Veny *Sarum* 63-66; V Norton Bavant 63-66; R Sutton Veny 63-66; rtd 69; Perm to Offic *Sarum* 90-95. *44 All Saints Road, Hawkhurst, Cranbrook, Kent TN18 4HT*

WADGE, Alan. b 46. Grey Coll Dur BA68 MA72 St Chad's Coll Dur DipTh69. **d** 70 **p** 71. C Cockerton *Dur* 70-74; C Whitworth w Spennymoor 74-75; P-in-c Shipton Moyne w Westonbirt and Lasborough *Glouc* 75-80; Chapl Westonbirt Sch 75-80; V Dean Forest H Trin *Glouc* 80-83; Chapl Gresham's Sch Holt 83-91; R Ridgeway *Ox* from 91; RD Wantage from 95. *The Rectory, Letcombe Regis, Wantage, Oxon OX12 9LD* Tel (01235) 763805

WADHAM, Philip Andrew. b 41. Vancouver Sch of Th BTh80. **d** 79 **p** 80. Canada 80-82 and 85-88; Ecuador 82-85; Area Sec (Dios Wakef and Bradf) USPG 88-92; Perm to Offic *Bradf* from 88. *6 Glenhurst Road, Shipley, W Yorkshire BD18 4DZ* Tel (01274) 588935

WADLAND, Douglas Bryan. b 33. CQSW62 K Coll Dur BA61 Liv Univ DSA62. Oak Hill Th Coll 90. **d** 91 **p** 92. NSM Cowley *Lon* 91-93; Asst Chapl Hillingdon Hosp Uxbridge from 91; P-in-c Wembley St Jo from 93. *The Vicarage, 3 Crawford Avenue, Wembley, Middx HA0 2HX* Tel 0181-902 0273

WADSWORTH (née REID), Mrs Alison Margaret. b 36. Bris Univ CertEd57. LNSM course 95. **d** 97. NSM Cley Hill Warminster *Sarum* from 97. *2 Saxon's Acre, Warminster, Wilts BA12 8HT* Tel (01985) 212510

WADSWORTH, Andrew James. b 56. St Jo Coll Dur BA79 Cam Univ CertEd80. Sarum & Wells Th Coll 84 Chich Th Coll 86 Lambeth STh95. **d** 87 **p** 88. NSM Forest Row *Chich* 87-89; NSM E Grinstead St Swithun 87-89; C Shrewsbury St Chad w St Mary *Lich* 89-91; TV Honiton, Gittisham, Combe Raleigh, Monkton etc *Ex* 91-97; V Bulkington w Shilton and Ansty *Cov* from 97. *The Vicarage, School Lane, Bulkington, Nuneaton, Warks CV12 9JB* Tel (01203) 312396

WADSWORTH, Jean. b 44. Cranmer Hall Dur BA71 St Jo Coll Dur. **d** 87 **p** 94. Par Dn Thamesmead *S'wark* 87-92; Par Dn Rotherhithe H Trin 92-94; C from 94. *7 Howland Way, London SE16 1HN* Tel 0171-252 2995

WADSWORTH, Michael Philip. b 43. Qu Coll Ox BA65 MA68 DPhil75 Cam Univ PhD78. Ripon Hall Ox 67. **d** 70 **p** 71. C Sutton St Mich *York* 70-73; Lect Sussex Univ 73-78; Fell 78-81; Hon C Hove St Jo *Chich* 75-78; Chapl SS Coll Cam 78-81; Dir Th Studies 79-81; CF (TA) from 80; C Ditton St Mich *Liv* 81; TV 82-84; Dioc Lay Tr Officer 83-89; V Orford St Marg 84-89; V Haddenham *Ely* from 89; V Wilburton from 89; RD Ely from 94. *The Vicarage, Haddenham, Ely, Cambs CB6 3TB* Tel (01353) 740309

WADSWORTH, Norman Charles. b 26. Bps' Coll Cheshunt 62. **d** 64 **p** 65. C Leighton Buzzard *St Alb* 64-69; P-in-c Wing *Ox* 69-73; P-in-c Grove St Mic 69-73; P-in-c Wingrave 69-74; V Wing w Grove 73-79; R Didcot All SS 79-91; rtd 91. *25 Snipewood, Eccleston, Chorley, Lancs PR7 5RQ* Tel (01257) 450162

WADSWORTH, Peter Richard. b 52. Qu Coll Ox BA73 MA77. Cuddesdon Coll 74 English Coll Rome 76. **d** 77 **p** 78. C High Wycombe *Ox* 77-81; C Farnham Royal w Hedgerley 81-84; Dioc Ecum Officer *Portsm* 84-90; V E Meon 84-96; V Langrish 84-96; V Elson from 96; RD Gosport from 96. *St Thomas's Vicarage, 21 Elson Road, Gosport, Hants PO12 4BL* Tel (01705) 582824

WADSWORTH, Roy. b 37. NE Ord Course 89. **d** 89 **p** 90. NSM Alne *York* from 89; Ind Chapl from 94. *The Rosery, Tollerton, York YO6 2DX* Tel (01347) 838212

WAGGETT, Geoffrey James. b 49. Sarum & Wells Th Coll 83. **d** 85 **p** 86. C Newton Nottage *Llan* 85-88; TV Glyncorrwg w Afan Vale and Cymmer Afan 88-89; R from 89. *The Vicarage, Church Street, Glyncorrwg, Port Talbot SA13 3BW* Tel (01639) 851301

WAGHORN, Geoffrey Brian. b 28. St Aid Birkenhead 62. **d** 64 **p** 65. C Gillingham H Trin *Roch* 64-66; C St Mary Cray and St Paul's Cray 66-68; C Lenton w Ingoldsby *Linc* 68-70; V Messingham 70-77; R Fishtoft 77-85; R Durley *Portsm* 85-93; V Curdridge 85-93; rtd 93. *17 Waters Edge, Hedge End, Southampton SO30 4AE* Tel (01489) 782795

WAGHORNE, Frederick Charles. b 07. St Jo Coll Dur BA32 MA35 DipTh35. **d** 33 **p** 34. C S'wark St Geo *S'wark* 33-37; C Tooting All SS 38-41; V W Wickham St Mary *Cant* 41-63; V Bearsted 63-73; rtd 73; Perm to Offic *Cant* 73-93. *Townfield, Burleigh Road, Charing, Ashford, Kent TN27 0JB* Tel (01233) 713130

WAGNER, Canon Peter Frederick. b 33. Lon Univ BSc56. Westcott Ho Cam. **d** 60 **p** 61. C Longbridge *Birm* 60-64; V Nechells 64-70; Rhodesia 70-80; Zimbabwe from 80; Dean Gweru 84-87. *PO Box 75, Kwekwe, Zimbabwe* Tel Kwekwe (55) 2535

WAGSTAFF, Alan Robert Joseph. b 21. Lon Univ DipTh69. S'wark Ord Course 67. **d** 70 **p** 71. C St Paul's Cray St Barn *Roch* 70-76; V Southborough St Pet w Ch Ch and St Matt 76-86; RD Tunbridge Wells 83-86; rtd 86; Perm to Offic *Chich* from 86; Perm to Offic *Roch* from 86. *27A The Green, St Leonards-on-Sea, E Sussex TN38 0SX* Tel (01424) 425895

WAGSTAFF, Andrew Robert. b 56. K Coll Lon BD79 AKC79. Coll of Resurr Mirfield 81. **d** 83 **p** 84. C Newark w Hawton, Cotham and Shelton *S'well* 83-86; C Dublin St Bart w Leeson Park *D & G* 86-89; V Nottingham St Geo w St Jo *S'well* 89-95; V Worksop Priory from 95. *The Vicarage, Cheapside, Worksop, Notts S80 2HX* Tel (01909) 472180

WAGSTAFF, The Ven Christopher John Harold. b 36. St D Coll Lamp BA62 DipTh63. **d** 63 **p** 64. C Queensbury All SS *Lon* 63-68; V Tokyngton St Mich 68-73; V Coleford w Staunton *Glouc*

73-83; RD Forest S 76-82; Adn Glouc from 83; Hon Can St Andr Cathl Njombe (Tanzania) from 93. *Glebe House, Church Road, Maisemore, Gloucester GL2 8EY* Tel (01452) 528500

WAGSTAFF, Miss Joan. b 33. Gilmore Ho. **dss** 75 **d** 87 **p** 94. Ellesmere Port *Ches* 86-87; Par Dn 87-93; rtd 93; Perm to Offic *Ches* from 93. *41 Heywood Road, Great Sutton, South Wirral L66 3PS* Tel 0151-348 0884

WAGSTAFF, Michael. b 59. R Holloway Coll Lon BA81. Coll of Resurr Mirfield 86. **d** 89 **p** 90. C Worksop Priory *S'well* 89-92; C Ab Kettleby Gp *Leic* 92-94; TV Leic Resurr from 94. *St Alban's House, Weymouth Street, Leicester LE4 6FN* Tel 0116-266 1002

WAGSTAFF, Robert William. b 36. Edin Th Coll 61. **d** 63 **p** 64. C Harringay St Paul *Lon* 63-64; C Mill Hill Jo Keble Ch 64-69; Perm to Offic *S'wark* 76-81; Lic to Offic *Worc* from 81; NSM Ombersley w Doverdale from 94. *The Red House, Quarry Bank, Hartlebury, Kidderminster, Worcs DY11 7TE* Tel (01299) 250883

WAGSTAFFE, Eric Herbert. b 25. St Aid Birkenhead 55. **d** 57 **p** 58. C Harpurhey Ch Ch *Man* 57-60; R 60-69; V Pendlebury St Jo 69-84; V Hoghton *Blackb* 84-91; rtd 91; Perm to Offic *Blackb* from 91. *3 Chelwood Close, Bolton BL1 7LN* Tel (01204) 596048

WAIN, Frank. b 13. Leeds Univ BA35. Coll of Resurr Mirfield 35. **d** 37 **p** 38. C Shrewsbury H Cross *Lich* 37-39; C Walsall St Andr 39-42; St Vincent 42-48; Grenada 48-49; C Rushall *Lich* 49-51; C Edgmond 51-53; P-in-c Cov St Fran N Radford CD *Cov* 53-55; R Kinwarton w Gt Alne and Haselor 55-83; rtd 83; Perm to Offic *Cov* from 83. *21 Queensway, Bidford-on-Avon, Alcester, Warks B50 4BA* Tel (01789) 778586

WAIN, Phillip. b 54. Aston Tr Scheme 89 Linc Th Coll CMinlStuds93. **d** 93 **p** 94. C Witton *Ches* from 93. *The Curate's House, 162 Middlewich Road, Rudheath, Northwich, Cheshire CW9 7DX* Tel (01606) 41965

WAINAINA, Francis Samson Kamoko. b 51. BA84 Dur Univ MA89. Oak Hill Th Coll 81. **d** 84 **p** 85. Kenya 84-88; C Upton (Overchurch) *Ches* 89-92; V Ellesmere St Pet *Sheff* 92-95; C York St Mich-le-Belfrey *York* from 95. *13 Hempland Drive, York YO3 0AY* Tel (01904) 422418

✠**WAINE, The Rt Revd John.** b 30. KCVO96. Man Univ BA51. Ridley Hall Cam 53. **d** 55 **p** 56 **c** 75. C W Derby St Mary *Liv* 55-58; C Sutton 58-60; V Ditton St Mich 60-64; V Southport H Trin 64-69; V Kirkby 69-71; TR 71-75; Suff Bp Stafford *Lich* 75-78; Preb Lich Cathl 75-78; Bp St E 78-86; Bp Chelmsf 86-96; Clerk of the Closet 89-96; rtd 96. *Broadmere, Ipswich Road, Grundisburgh, Woodbridge, Suffolk IP13 6TJ* Tel (01473) 738296

WAINE, Stephen John. b 59. Westcott Ho Cam 81. **d** 84 **p** 85. C Wolverhampton *Lich* 84-88; Min Can and Succ St Paul's Cathl *Lon* 88-93; V Romford St Edw *Chelmsf* from 93. *St Edward's Vicarage, 15 Oaklands Avenue, Romford RM1 4DB* Tel (01708) 740385

WAINWRIGHT, David Bernard Pictor. b 25. St Jo Coll Dur BA50 MA53. Chich Th Coll 50. **d** 51 **p** 52. C Redditch St Geo *Worc* 51-53; C Aveley *Chelmsf* 53-55; P-in-c Belhus Park 55-56; V Harlow St Mary Magd 56-61; Soc Resp Adv *Ripon* 62-69; C Leeds St Jo Ev 65-69; Sen Soc Worker Bd for Soc Resp Man 69-73; V Scouthead *Man* 69-72; Asst Sec Gen Syn Bd for Soc Resp 74-78; Dep Sec 78-79; P-in-c Charlton on Otmoor and Oddington *Ox* 79-85; Soc Resp Officer 79-88; RD Bicester and Islip 82-85; Sec Ox Dioc Bd for Soc Resp 85-88; rtd 88. *8 St Robert's Gardens, Knaresborough, N Yorkshire HG5 8EH* Tel (01423) 865236

WAINWRIGHT, Frank Alan. b 18. Leeds Univ BA39. Coll of Resurr Mirfield 39. **d** 41 **p** 42. C Glouc St Paul *Glouc* 41-46; C Perry Hill St Geo *S'wark* 46-47; V 47-57; V N Dulwich St Faith 57-64; Chapl Maudsley Hosp Lon 60-62; Chapl St Gabr Coll Camberwell 62-64; V Woodham *Guildf* 64-72; rtd 83; Perm to Offic *Truro* from 83. *Menhay, Pendoggett, St Kew, Bodmin, Cornwall PL30 3HH* Tel (01208) 880528

WAINWRIGHT, John Pounsberry. b 42. St Steph Ho Ox 64. **d** 66 **p** 67. C Palmers Green St Jo *Lon* 66-70; C Primrose Hill St Mary w Avenue Road St Paul 70-71; P-in-c St Jo Wood All SS 71-73; V Hendon All SS Childs Hill from 73. *All Saints' Vicarage, Church Walk, London NW2 2JT* Tel 0171-435 3182

WAINWRIGHT, Joseph Allan. b 21. K Coll Lon BD50 AKC50 Columbia Pacific Univ PhD82 Sussex Univ DPhil85. **d** 50 **p** 51. C Boston *Linc* 50-53; Chapl St Paul's Coll Cheltenham 53-62; Educn Sec BCC 62-66; Lect Moray Ho Coll of Educn Edin 66-78; Perm to Offic *Chich* 79-88; rtd 86. *Beggar's Roost, Lewes, E Sussex BN7 1LX* Tel (01273) 477453

WAINWRIGHT, Kevin Frank. b 46. Linc Th Coll 73. **d** 75 **p** 76. C Stand *Man* 75-78; C Radcliffe St Thos and St Jo 78-80; V Kearsley Moor from 80. *St Stephen's Vicarage, Blair Street, Kearsley, Bolton BL4 8QP* Tel (01204) 72535

WAINWRIGHT, Maurice Sidney. b 30. Lon Univ BSc54. Bps' Coll Cheshunt 54. **d** 56 **p** 57. C Twickenham St Mary *Lon* 56-59; C Caversham *Ox* 59-61; Public Preacher *Chelmsf* 61-95; rtd 95. *60 Eastwood Road, London E18 1BU* Tel 0181-989 1529

WAINWRIGHT, Miss Pauline Barbara. b 40. St Deiniol's Hawarden 83. **dss** 84 **d** 87 **p** 94. New Ferry *Ches* 84-87; Par Dn 87-90; Par Dn Hallwood 90-94; C from 94. *39 Badger Close, Palace Fields, Runcorn, Cheshire WA7 2QW* Tel (01928) 715688

WAINWRIGHT, Raymond Laycock. b 25. Lon Univ BD60. Ho of Resurr Mirfield 55. **d** 56 **p** 57. C Bingley All SS *Bradf* 56-58; C Almondbury *Wakef* 58-60; V Gawthorpe and Chickenley Heath 60-74; V New Mill 74-89; V Thurstonland 74-89; TV Upper Holme Valley 89-91; rtd 91; Perm to Offic *Wakef* from 91. *7 Greenlaws Close, Holmfirth, Huddersfield HD7 2GB* Tel (01484) 683779

WAIT, Alan Clifford. b 33. St Cath Soc Ox BA58 MA70. Coll of Resurr Mirfield. **d** 60 **p** 61. C Charlton St Luke w St Paul *S'wark* 60-67; C Caterham 67-72; V N Dulwich St Faith 72-83; RD Dulwich 78-83; V Purley St Barn from 83; RD Croydon S from 93. *St Barnabas's Vicarage, 84 Higher Drive, Purley, Surrey CR8 2HJ* Tel 0181-660 3251

WAITE, John Langton (Tony). b 10. Solicitor 34 ACP37 Man Univ 30. Wycliffe Hall Ox 37. **d** 39 **p** 40. C Hove Bp Hannington Memorial Ch *Chich* 39-41; C Walcot *B & W* 41-42; V Blackheath St Jo *S'wark* 42-48; V Leeds St Geo *Ripon* 48-58; V Woking St Jo *Guildf* 58-76; rtd 76; Perm to Offic *Portsm* from 82. *11 The Crescent, Alverstoke, Gosport, Hants PO12 2DH* Tel (01705) 521458

WAITE, Julian Henry. b 47. Brasted Th Coll 68 Ridley Hall Cam 70. **d** 72 **p** 73. C Wollaton *S'well* 72-76; C Herne Bay Ch Ch *Cant* 76-79; P-in-c Mersham 79-87; P-in-c Sevington 79-87; R Mersham w Hinxhill 87; V Marden 87-93; Chapl HM Pris Blantyre Ho 90-93. *Address temp unknown*

WAITE, Sheila Margaret. *See* TYLER, Mrs Sheila Margaret

WAIYAKI, Mrs Jennie. b 34. MBE88. ALA64. NE Ord Course 89. **d** 92 **p** 94. NSM Ulgham *Newc* 92-97; NSM Widdrington 92-97; NSM Longhorsley and Hebron from 97. *6 Woodburn Street, Stobswood, Morpeth, Northd NE61 5QD* Tel (01670) 791066

WAKE, Colin Walter. b 50. Or Coll Ox BA72 MA. Cuddesdon Coll 74. **d** 75 **p** 76. C Sandhurst *Ox* 75-78; C Faversham *Cant* 79-80; TV High Wycombe *Ox* 80-89; R Weston Favell *Pet* from 89; Chapl St Jo Hosp Weston Favell from 89. *The Rectory, Churchway, Weston Favell, Northampton NN3 3BX* Tel (01604) 784679 or 787117

WAKEFIELD, Allan. b 31. Qu Coll Birm 72. **d** 74 **p** 75. C Kingsthorpe w Northn St Dav *Pet* 74-77; TV Clifton *S'well* 77-81; V Bilborough St Jo 81-85; R Bere Ferrers *Ex* 85-91; R Mevagissey and St Ewe *Truro* 91-96; rtd 96; Perm to Offic *Truro* from 96. *15 Marshallen Road, Mount Hawke, Truro, Cornwall TR4 8EF* Tel (01209) 890757

WAKEFIELD, Andrew Desmond. b 55. K Coll Lon BD77 AKC77. Coll of Resurr Mirfield 77. **d** 78 **p** 79. C Mitcham Ascension *S'wark* 78-81; C Putney St Mary 81-86; TV Wimbledon 86-91; Ind Chapl from 90; Dioc Urban Missr from 91; P-in-c S Wimbledon St Andr from 91. *St Andrew's Vicarage, 47 Wilton Grove, London SW19 3QU* Tel 0181-542 1794

WAKEFIELD, Anne Frances. b 58. St Aid Coll Dur BSc79 Sheff Univ PGCE80. NTMTC 97. **d** 97. NSM Danbury *Chelmsf* from 97. *10 Chestwood Close, Billericay, Essex CM12 0PB* Tel (01277) 652659

WAKEFIELD, David Geoffrey. b 43. AMIC90. S'wark Ord Course 84. **d** 87 **p** 88. C Addiscombe St Mildred *S'wark* 87-89; C Reigate St Luke S Park 89-93; Chapl HM Pris Bullingdon 93-96; Chapl HM Pris Ranby from 96. *HM Prison Ranby, Retford, Notts DN22 8EU* Tel (01773) 706721

WAKEFIELD, Gavin Tracy. b 57. Van Mildert Coll Dur BSc Sheff Univ CertEd Nottm Univ DipTh. St Jo Coll Nottm 83. **d** 86 **p** 87. C Anston *Sheff* 86-89; C Aston cum Aughton and Ulley 89-91; TV Billericay and Lt Burstead *Chelmsf* from 91. *10 Chestwood Close, Billericay, Essex CM12 0PB* Tel (01277) 652659

WAKEFIELD, Kenneth (Ken). b 54. St Jo Coll Dur BA95. **d** 95 **p** 96. C E and W Leake, Stanford-on-Soar, Rempstone etc *S'well* from 95. *The Rectory, Stanford on Soar, Loughborough, Leics LE12 5PY* Tel (01509) 266794

WAKEFIELD, Canon Kenneth Eyles. b 25. St Jo Coll Dur BA50 DipTh51 MA56. **d** 51 **p** 52. C Redhill H Trin *S'wark* 51-54; C Attenborough w Bramcote and Chilwell *S'well* 54-56; V Leyton St Edw *Chelmsf* 56-59; Chapl Bartlet Hosp Felixstowe 59-89; V Walton *St E* 59-88; Hon Chapl Miss to Seamen 64-88; RD Colneys *St E* 73-86; Hon Can St E Cathl 75-88; rtd 89. *14 Fleetwood Road, Felixstowe, Suffolk IP11 7EQ* Tel (01394) 672113

WAKEFIELD, Peter. b 48. Nottm Univ BTh72 DipAdEd85. St Jo Coll Nottm 68 ALCD72. **d** 72 **p** 73. C Hinckley H Trin *Leic* 72-75; C Kirby Muxloe 75-78; V Barlestone 78-85; TV Padgate *Liv* 85-88; V Quinton w Marston Sicca *Glouc* 91-97; rtd 97. *18 Pampas Close, Stratford-upon-Avon, Warks CV37 0TM* Tel (01789) 267390

WAKEFIELD, Bishop of. *See* McCULLOCH, The Rt Revd Nigel Simeon

WAKEFIELD, Provost of. *See* NAIRN-BRIGGS, The Very Revd George Peter

WAKEHAM, Geoffrey. **d** 96. Asst Chapl Torrevieja *Eur* from 96. *Calle Nerbion 20, Torrejon Alto, 03180 Torrevieja, Alicante, Spain* Tel (66) 700135

WAKELIN, Alan Frank. b 32. Univ of Wales (Lamp) BA58. Coll of Resurr Mirfield 58. **d** 60 **p** 61. C Northampton St Matt *Pet* 60-63;

C Pet All SS 63-65; C Spalding *Linc* 65-68; R Skirbeck St Nic 68-97; rtd 97. *Woodview Cottage, Tattershall Road, Woodhall Spa, Lincoln LN10 6TP* Tel (01526) 354957

WAKELIN, Paul Edward. b 60. St Steph Ho Ox 90. **d** 92 **p** 93. C Sevenoaks St Jo *Roch* 92-96; V Perry Street from 96. *All Saints' Vicarage, Perry Street, Gravesend, Kent DA11 8RD* Tel (01474) 534398

WAKELING, Bruce. b 50. Lon Univ BA74. Westcott Ho Cam 74. **d** 77 **p** 78. C Weymouth H Trin *Sarum* 77-82; TV Oakdale 82-89; R Clopton w Otley, Swilland and Ashbocking *St E* from 89. *The Rectory, Clopton, Woodbridge, Suffolk IP13 6SE* Tel (01473) 735765

WAKELING, Hugh Michael. b 42. CEng82 FIChemE94 Cape Town Univ BSc63. Wycliffe Hall Ox 71. **d** 74 **p** 75. C Kennington St Mark *S'wark* 74-78; C Surbiton Hill Ch Ch 78-80; Hon C Richmond H Trin and Ch Ch 80-84; Hon C California *Ox* 85-89; Hon C Arborfield w Barkham from 89. *Pine Lodge, 52 Pine Drive, Wokingham, Berks RG40 3LE* Tel (0118) 973 4078

WAKELING, Joan. b 44. Hockerill Coll Cam CertEd65 Lon Univ DipTh79. S'wark Ord Course 76. **dss** 79 **d** 90 **p** 94. Surbiton Hill Ch Ch *S'wark* 79-80; Richmond H Trin and Ch Ch 80-84; California *Ox* 84-89; Arborfield w Barkham 89-90; NSM from 90; Chapl Luckley-Oakfield Sch Wokingham from 90. *Pine Lodge, 52 Pine Drive, Wokingham, Berks RG40 3LE* Tel (0118) 973 4078

✠**WAKELING, The Rt Revd John Denis.** b 18. MC45. St Cath Coll Cam BA40 MA44 Nottm Univ Hon DD84. Ridley Hall Cam 46. **d** 47 **p** 48 **c** 70. C Barwell w Potters Marston and Stapleton *Leic* 47-50; Chapl Clare Coll Cam 50-52; Lic to Offic *Ely* 50-52; V Plymouth Em *Ex* 52-59; Preb Ex Cathl 57-59; V Barking St Marg *Chelmsf* 59-65; P-in-c Barking St Patr 60-65; Adn W Ham 65-70; Bp S'well 70-85; rtd 85. *50 St Anne Place, Salisbury SP1 2SU* Tel (01722) 322016

WAKELY, Marcus. b 40. Solicitor 62 FRSA88. EMMTC 84. **d** 87 **p** 88. NSM Carrington *S'well* 87-91; C Worksop Priory 91-95; V Sheff St Matt *Sheff* from 95. *29 Winchester Road, Sheffield S10 4EE* Tel 0114-230 5641

WAKELY, Roger. b 42. St Paul's Cheltenham CertEd. S'wark Ord Course 67. **d** 70 **p** 71. C Ealing St Mary *Lon* 70-76; Chapl Bp Wand's Sch Sunbury-on-Thames 76-82; R Gaulby *Leic* 82-87; V Galleywood Common *Chelmsf* 87-95; Warden of Ords 89-95; rtd 95; Perm to Offic *Chelmsf* from 95. *72 Vicarage Lane, Great Baddow, Chelmsford CM2 8HY*

WAKELY, Simon Nicolas. b 66. K Alfred's Coll Win BA88. St Jo Coll Nottm DTS91 DipMM92. **d** 92 **p** 93. C Wymondham *Nor* 92-95; P-in-c Babbacombe *Ex* from 95. *Babbacombe Vicarage, Cary Park, Torquay TQ1 3NH* Tel (01803) 323002

WAKEMAN, Canon Hilary Margaret. b 38. EAMTC. **dss** 85 **d** 87 **p** 94. Heigham St Thos *Nor* 85-87; C 87-90; C Nor St Mary Magd w St Jas 90-91; D-in-c Norwich-over-the-Water Colegate St Geo 90-91; TD Norwich Over-the-Water 91-94; TV 94-96; Hon Can Nor Cathl 94-96; I Kilmoe Union *C, C & R* from 96. *Altar Rectory, Toormore, Goleen, Co Cork, Irish Republic* Tel Skibbereen (28) 28249

WAKERELL, Richard Hinton. b 55. Qu Coll Birm. **d** 84 **p** 85. C Gillingham St Mary *Roch* 84-87; C Kingswinford St Mary *Lich* 87-93; V Rickerscote 93. *18 Ellis Drive, New Romney, Kent TN28 8XH*

WALDEN, John Edward Frank. b 38. FInstSMM. Oak Hill Th Coll 67. **d** 69 **p** 70. C Rainham *Chelmsf* 69-73; P-in-c Bris H Cross Inns Court *Bris* 73-78; Conf and Publicity Sec SAMS 78-81; Hon C Southborough St Pet w Ch Ch and St Matt *Roch* 78-81; Exec Sec Spanish and Portuguese Ch Aid Soc 80-81; Hon C Tonbridge St Steph 81-84; R Earsham w Alburgh and Denton *Nor* 84-89. *c/o Michael Hall & Co, Garsett House, Norwich NR3 1AU* Tel (01603) 617772

WALDEN, Samuel (Sam). b 15. Richmond Th Coll 45. **d** 57 **p** 58. USA 57-71; R Blackley H Trin *Man* 71-74; Chapl Prestwich Hosp Man 74-80; rtd 80; Perm to Offic *Bradf* from 90. *5 Castlegate, New Brook Street, Ilkley, W Yorkshire LS29 8DF* Tel (01943) 601860

WALDRON, Geoffrey Robert. b 15. Selw Coll Cam BA37 MA41. Ely Th Coll 37. **d** 38 **p** 39. C Gainsborough St Jo *Linc* 38-41; PV and Sacr S'wark Cathl *S'wark* 41-44; Asst Chapl Guy's Hosp Lon 41-44; P-in-c S'wark St Mich *S'wark* 42-44; C Leamington Priors All SS *Cov* 44-48; C Portsea St Alb *Portsm* 48-50; C Stoke-in-Teignhead and Combe-in-Teignhead *Ex* 50-52; C-in-c Milber St Luke CD 52-55; Chapl Beaulieu-sur-Mer *Eur* 55-57; R Gt w Lt Gransden *Ely* 57-63; R Barwick *B & W* 63-76; R Closworth 63-76; P-in-c Charlton Adam w Charlton Mackrell 76-78; R Charlton Adam w Charlton Mackrell and Kingsdon 78-80; rtd 80; Perm to Offic *B & W* from 81. *Roseland, Castle Street, Keinton Mandeville, Somerton, Somerset TA11 6DX* Tel (01458) 223224

WALDRON, Laurence Charles. b 22. Bps' Coll Cheshunt 58. **d** 59 **p** 60. C Gravelly Hill *Birm* 59-63; C-in-c Lea Hall CD 63-66; V Lea Hall 66-77; V Wiggenhall St Mary Magd *Ely* 77-87; V Wiggenhall St Germans and Islington 77-87; rtd 87; Perm to Offic *Lich* from 90. *16 Heath Gardens, Stone, Staffs ST15 0AW* Tel (01785) 818237

WALES, David Neville. b 55. Rhodes Univ BA78. Coll of Resurr Mirfield 80. **d** 82 **p** 83. Zimbabwe 82-88; C Linslade *Ox* 89-91; P-in-c Weston Turville from 91. *The Rectory, Church Walk, Weston Turville, Aylesbury, Bucks HP22 5SH* Tel (01296) 613212

WALES, Archbishop of. *See* JONES, The Most Revd Alwyn Rice

WALFORD, Mrs Angela. b 44. Whitelands Coll Lon CertEd76. S Dios Minl Tr Scheme 85. **d** 92 **p** 94. NSM Boyatt Wood *Win* from 92. *St Peter's Church House, 53 Sovereign Way, Eastleigh, Hants SO50 4SA* Tel (01703) 642188

WALFORD, David. b 45. S'wark Ord Course 75. **d** 78 **p** 79. NSM Hackbridge and N Beddington *S'wark* 78-83; C Fawley *Win* 83-87; C-in-c Boyatt Wood CD 87-90; V Boyatt Wood from 90. *St Peter's Church House, 53 Sovereign Way, Eastleigh, Hants SO50 4SA* Tel (01703) 642188

WALFORD, David John. b 47. St Luke's Coll Ex CertEd68 AKC71. St Aug Coll Cant. **d** 72 **p** 73. C Oxton *Ches* 72-77; C Neston 77-80; Youth Chapl 80-81; V Backford 80-81; C Woodchurch 81; Chapl Fulbourn Hosp and Ida Darw Hosp Cam 82-83; Chapl N Man Gen Hosp 83-86; Distr Chapl in Mental Health Ex HA from 86; Chapl R Devon and Ex Hosp (Wonford) 86-94; Chapl R Devon and Ex Health Care NHS Trust from 94; Chapl Ex and Distr Community Health Service NHS Trust from 94; Lic to Offic *Ex* from 86. *Royal Devon and Exeter Hospital, Exeter EX2 5DW, or Dean Clarke House, Southernhay East, Exeter EX1 1PQ* Tel (01392) 402024 or 411222

WALFORD, David Sanderson. b 23. BEM49. Chich Th Coll 78. **d** 79 **p** 80. Hon C Chich St Pet *Chich* 79-81; C Chich St Paul and St Pet 81-83; P-in-c Wisbech St Aug *Ely* 83-86; rtd 88. *Sibford, Church Hill, Marnhull, Sturminster Newton, Dorset DT10 1PU* Tel (01258) 820201

WALFORD, Dr Frank Roy. b 35. Birm Univ MB, ChB58. Qu Coll Birm 78. **d** 80 **p** 81. Hon C Walsall Pleck and Bescot *Lich* 80-85; Chr Healing Cen Bordon 85-88; Dep Medical Dir St Wilfrid's Hospice Chich from 88; Perm to Offic *Chich* from 88. *15 Grove Road, Chichester, W Sussex PO19 2AR* Tel (01243) 533947

WALFORD, Robin Peter. b 46. Qu Coll Birm 75. **d** 78 **p** 79. C Radcliffe-on-Trent *S'well* 78-81; TV Newark w Hawton, Cotham and Shelton 81-84; P-in-c Forest Town 84-92; Co-ord Chapl Leeds Community and Mental Health Services 92-97. *2A Weetwood Lane, Leeds LS16 5LS* Tel 0113-278 9953

WALKER, Alan David. b 44. Bretton Hall Coll CertEd65. EAMTC 92. **d** 95 **p** 96. NSM Ashill w Saham Toney *Nor* from 95. *4 Orchard Close, Ashill, Thetford, Norfolk IP25 7AP* Tel (01760) 441554

WALKER, Alan Robert Glaister. b 52. K Coll Cam BA76 MA79 New Coll Ox MA84 Poly Cen Lon LLB91 Heythrop Coll Lon MTh93 Univ of Wales LLM96. St Steph Ho Ox 82. **d** 84 **p** 85. C St Jo Wood *Lon* 84-86; Chapl Poly Cen Lon 87-92; Chapl Univ Westmr 92-94; Chapl Univ Ch Ch the K 87-94; V Hampstead Garden Suburb from 94. *The Vicarage, 1 Central Square, London NW11 7AH* Tel 0181-455 7206 Fax as telephone E-mail fatheralan@compuserve.com

WALKER, Albert William John. b 14. Linc Th Coll 43. **d** 45 **p** 46. C Ches St Mary *Ches* 45-48; C Hoylake 48-51; V Lower Tranmere 51-56; V Plumstead St Nic *S'wark* 56-66; V Merton St Jas 66-67; V Kingston St Luke 67-74; V Mickleton *Glouc* 74-79; rtd 79; Chapl Convent of St Mary at the Cross Edgware 79-87; Lic to Offic *Lon* 79-87; Perm to Offic *Carl* 87-95; Perm to Offic *Truro* from 95. *Shepherd's Fold, 4 Treza Road, Porthleven, Helston, Cornwall TR13 9HB* Tel (01326) 562104

WALKER, Allen Ross. b 46. Chich Th Coll 86. **d** 88. C Cosham *Portsm* 88-91; Chapl Portsm Mental Health Community 91-97; Dn Portsm Deanery 91-97; Community Chapl Burnham Deanery *Ox* from 97. *21 Palmeston Avenue, Langley, Slough SL3 7PU* Tel (01753) 522807

WALKER, Andrew Stephen. b 58. St Chad's Coll Dur BA80. St Steph Ho Ox 83. **d** 85 **p** 86. C Fareham SS Pet and Paul *Portsm* 85-87; C St Jo Wood *Lon* 87-93; V Streatham St Pet *S'wark* from 93. *St Peter's Vicarage, 113 Leigham Court Road, London SW16 2NX* Tel 0181-769 2922

WALKER, Anthony Charles St John (Tony). b 55. Trin Coll Ox MA80. Wycliffe Hall Ox 78. **d** 81 **p** 82. C Bradf Cathl *Bradf* 81-84; C Nottingham St Ann w Em *S'well* 84-88; V Retford from 88. *St Saviour's Vicarage, 31 Richmond Road, Retford, Notts DN22 6SJ* Tel (01777) 703800

WALKER, Canon Arthur Keith. b 33. Dur Univ BSc57 Fitzw Ho Cam BA60 MA64 Leeds Univ PhD68 FRSA94. Lich Th Coll 62. **d** 63 **p** 64. C Slaithwaite w E Scammonden *Wakef* 63-66; Lect Wells Th Coll 66-71; V N Wootton *B & W* 66-71; Can Res and Prec Chich Cathl *Chich* 71-80; TV Basingstoke *Win* 81-87; Can Res Win Cathl from 87. *5 The Close, Winchester, Hants SO23 9LS* Tel (01962) 864923

WALKER, Barry Donovan. b 28. Linc Coll Ox BA52 MA56. Linc Th Coll 52. **d** 54 **p** 55. C Enfield St Mich *Lon* 54-58; C Hornsey St Mary 58-61; V Kensal Rise St Martin 61-71; V Palmers Green St Jo 71-83; R Takeley w Lt Canfield *Chelmsf* 83-88; rtd 88; Perm to Offic *Chelmsf* from 88. *122 Waterfall Road, London N14 7JN* Tel 0181-886 1695

WALKER, Miss Bethany Helen. b 58. RGN80 DON80 Lon Univ DN83. Cranmer Hall Dur 86. **d** 89 **p** 94. C Newark *S'well* 89-93; rtd 93. *Julian House, 76 Peveril Road, Beeston, Nottingham NG9 2HU* Tel 0115-922 8806

WALKER, Brian Cecil. b 28. FCA62. Cranmer Hall Dur 68. **d** 70 **p** 71. C Heworth w Peasholme St Cuth *York* 70-73; C Attenborough w Chilwell *S'well* 73-75; C Chilwell 75-78; R Trowell 78-89; rtd 89. *1 Kendal Close, Bromsgrove, Worcs B60 2HW* Tel (01527) 579382

WALKER, Charles Edward Cornwall. b 18. Selw Coll Cam BA39 MA43. Cuddesdon Coll 40. **d** 41 **p** 42. C Gillingham *Sarum* 41-46; C Evesham *Worc* 46-48; V Gt Amwell *St Alb* 48-81; P-in-c Stanstead St Marg 74-81; V Gt Amwell w St Marg 81-94; rtd 94. *Jubilee Cottage, Great Amwell, Ware, Herts SG12 9SF* Tel (01902) 870139

WALKER, Christopher James Anthony. b 43. Sarum & Wells Th Coll 85. **d** 87 **p** 88. Hon C Durrington *Sarum* 87-89; CF from 87. *MOD Chaplains (Army), Trenchard Lines, Upavon, Pewsey, Wilts SN9 6BE* Tel (01980) 615804 Fax 615800

WALKER, Christopher John. b 52. ALA74. Chich Th Coll 75. **d** 78 **p** 79. C Reading All SS *Ox* 78-82; C Stony Stratford 82-84; C Wokingham All SS 84-90; V Headington St Mary from 90. *St Mary's Vicarage, Bayswater Road, Oxford OX3 9EY* Tel (01865) 61886

WALKER, Christopher John Deville. b 42. St Jo Coll Dur BA69. Westcott Ho Cam 69. **d** 71 **p** 72. C Portsea St Mary *Portsm* 71-75; C Saffron Walden w Wendens Ambo and Littlebury *Chelmsf* 75-77; C St Martin-in-the-Fields *Lon* 77-80; V Riverhead w Dunton Green *Roch* 80-89; V Chatham St Steph from 89. *St Stephen's Vicarage, 55 Pattens Lane, Chatham, Kent ME4 6JR* Tel (01634) 849791

WALKER, David. b 48. Linc Th Coll 71. **d** 74 **p** 75. C Arnold *S'well* 74-77; C Crosby *Linc* 77-79; V Scrooby *S'well* 79-86; V Sutton in Ashfield St Mary 86-94; P-in-c Sutton in Ashfield St Mich 89-94; TR Birkenhead Priory *Ches* from 94. *St Anne's Vicarage, 29 Park Road West, Birkenhead, Merseyside L43 1UR* Tel 0151-652 1309

WALKER, David Andrew. b 52. St Andr Univ MTh75 MA. Linc Th Coll 79. **d** 81 **p** 82. C Hessle *York* 81-84; C N Hull St Mich 84-86; V from 86. *St Michael's Vicarage, 214 Orchard Park Road, Hull HU6 9BX* Tel (01482) 803375

WALKER, Canon David Grant. b 23. FSA60 FRHistS62 Bris Univ BA49 Ball Coll Ox DPhil54. **d** 62 **p** 62. Hon C Swansea St Mary w H Trin *S & B* 62-86; Chapl and Lect Univ of Wales (Swansea) 62; Sen Lect 63-82; Dir of Post-Ord Tr 65-93; Can Brecon Cathl from 72; Prec 79-90; Chan 90-93; Chapl Univ of Wales (Swansea) 75-76; Dir of In-Service Tr from 77; P-in-c Caereithin 86-87. *52 Eaton Crescent, Swansea SA1 4QN* Tel (01792) 472624

WALKER, David Ian. b 41. DipCMus. Bernard Gilpin Soc Dur 64 Bps' Coll Cheshunt 65. **d** 68 **p** 69. C Todmorden *Wakef* 68-72; V Rastrick St Jo 72-77; V Crosland Moor 77-86; V Kirton in Lindsey *Linc* from 86; R Grayingham from 86; R Manton from 86; OCF from 88. *The Vicarage, 28 Southcliffe Road, Kirton-in-Lindsey, Gainsborough, Lincs DN21 4NR* Tel (01652) 648009

WALKER, David John. b 47. St Jo Coll Nottm 88. **d** 90 **p** 91. C Strood St Fran *Roch* 90-94; V Larkfield from 94. *The Vicarage, 206 New Hythe Lane, Larkfield, Maidstone, Kent ME20 6PT* Tel (01732) 843349

WALKER, David Stuart. b 57. Cam Univ MA. Qu Coll Birm DipTh. **d** 83 **p** 84. C Handsworth *Sheff* 83-86; TV Maltby 86-91; Ind Chapl 86-91; V Bramley and Ravenfield 91-95; R Bramley and Ravenfield w Hooton Roberts etc from 95. *The Vicarage, 88 Main Street, Bramley, Rotherham, S Yorkshire S66 0SQ* Tel (01709) 542028

WALKER, Dennis Richard. b 25. Bp Gray Coll Cape Town LTh57. **d** 57 **p** 58. S Africa 57-73; V Catterick *Ripon* 73-78; V Manston 78-86; rtd 86; Perm to Offic *York* from 90. *Micklegarth, Cliff Road, Sewerby, Bridlington, N Humberside YO15 1EW* Tel (01262) 678417

WALKER, Derek Fred. b 46. Trin Coll Bris 71. **d** 74 **p** 75. C St Paul's Cray St Barn *Roch* 74-78; C Rushden w Newton Bromswold *Pet* 78-80; R Kirkby Thore w Temple Sowerby and Newbiggin *Carl* 80-83; V Coppull *Blackb* 83-87; V New Ferry *Ches* 87-96; R Akeman *Ox* from 96. *The Rectory, Chesterton, Bicester, Oxon OX6 8UW* Tel (01869) 252387

WALKER, Douglas. b 36. Lich Th Coll 61. **d** 63 **p** 64. C Bris St Ambrose Whitehall *Bris* 63-68; P-in-c Easton All Hallows 68-71; V Penhill 71-79; P-in-c Crundale w Godmersham *Cant* 79-83; P-in-c Elmsted w Hastingleigh 79-83; V Sheerness H Trin w St Paul from 83. *The Vicarage, 241 High Street, Sheerness, Kent ME12 1UR* Tel (01795) 662589

WALKER, Duncan Andrew. b 59. **d** 90 **p** 91. C Gorseinon *S & B* 90-91; C Morriston 92-94; V Llanelli Ch Ch *St D* from 94. *Christ Church Vicarage, New Dock Road, Llanelli SA15 2HE* Tel (01554) 774264

WALKER, Mrs Edna Bilbie. b 20. Nottm Univ BEd76. **d** 88 **p** 94. NSM Oakham, Hambleton, Egleton, Braunston and Brooke *Pet* from 88. *Chestnut Cottage, Braunston, Oakham, Leics LE15 8QZ* Tel (01572) 722365

✠**WALKER, The Rt Revd Edward William Murray (Dominic).** b 48. AKC73. **d** 72 **p** 72. CGA 67-83; C Wandsworth St Faith *S'wark* 72-73; Bp's Dom Chapl 73-76; R Newington St Mary 76-85; RD S'wark and Newington 80-85; OGS from 83; Superior from 90; V Brighton St Pet w Chpl Royal and St Jo *Chich* 85-86; P-in-c Brighton St Nic 85-86; TR Brighton St Pet and St Nic w Chpl Royal 86-97; RD Brighton 85-97; Can and Preb Chich Cathl 85-97; Area Bp Reading *Ox* from 97. *Bishop's House, Tidmarsh Lane, Tidmarsh, Reading RG8 8HA* Tel 0118-984 1216 Fax 984 1218

WALKER, Mrs Elizabeth. b 42. Sunderland Poly CQSW85. NE Ord Course 91. **d** 94. NSM Stockton St Chad *Dur* from 94. *29 Bramble Road, Stockton-on-Tees, Cleveland TS19 0NQ* Tel (01642) 615332

WALKER, Mrs Elizabeth Margaret Rea. b 49. Ch Ch Coll Cant CertEd70. S'wark Ord Course 89. **d** 92 **p** 94. NSM Ash *Roch* 92-97; NSM Ridley 92-97; Asst Chapl St Geo Sch Gravesend 92-97; P-in-c Burham and Wouldham *Roch* from 97. *The Rectory, 266 Rochester Road, Burham, Rochester, Kent ME1 3RJ* Tel (01634) 666862 Mobile 0421-940283 Fax 868749

WALKER, Ernest Alwyn. b 18. Clifton Th Coll 54. **d** 56 **p** 57. C Brixton Road Ch Ch *S'wark* 56-59; V Kingston upon Hull St Barn *York* 59-70; V Shiptonthorpe w Hayton 70-77; V Daubhill *Man* 77-84; rtd 84; Perm to Offic *Bradf* from 84. *1 Hillside View, Pudsey, W Yorkshire LS28 9DH* Tel 0113-257 8468

WALKER, Gavin Russell. b 43. FCA78. Coll of Resurr Mirfield 76. **d** 78 **p** 79. C Wakef St Jo *Wakef* 78-81; C Northallerton w Kirby Sigston *York* 81-83; V Whorlton w Carlton and Faceby 83-85; Chapl Pontefract Gen Infirmary 85-89; P-in-c Brotherton *Wakef* 85-89; V Earl's Heaton 89-97; TV Dewsbury from 97. *45 Chatsworth Terrace, Dewsbury, W Yorkshire WF12 8BH* Tel (01924) 461490

WALKER, Canon George Percival John. b 13. Dur Univ LTh38. St Boniface Warminster 35. **d** 38 **p** 39. C Brislington St Anne *Bris* 38-42; Antigua 42-50 and 51-52; Perm to Offic *Win* 51; St Kitts-Nevis 52-78; Hon Can Antigua 55-78; Adn St Kitts 64-78; rtd 78. *St Peter's Cottage, Monkey Hill, St Kitts* Tel St Kitts (1809) 461-4091

WALKER, Gerald Roger. b 41. K Coll Lon BD67 AKC67. **d** 68 **p** 69. C High Elswick St Phil *Newc* 68-70; C Goring-by-Sea *Chich* 70-75; R Selsey 75-81; V Hove St Andr Old Ch 81-91; V Copthorne 91-95; rtd 95; NSM Streat w Westmeston *Chich* from 95. *Rectory Bungalow, Streat, Hassocks, W Sussex BN6 8RX* Tel (01273) 890607

WALKER, Canon Graham. b 35. Ex Coll Ox BA58 BTh60 MA62 Leeds Univ MPhil80. Sarum Th Coll 60. **d** 61 **p** 62. C Guiseley *Bradf* 61-64; C Ingrow cum Hainworth 64-68; Lic to Offic 68-80; V Hellifield from 80; RD Bowland 86-95; Hon Can Bradf Cathl from 89; P-in-c Gisburn from 94. *The Vicarage, Hellifield, Skipton, N Yorkshire BD23 4HY* Tel (01729) 850243

WALKER, Canon Harvey William. b 26. Edin Univ MA52. St Steph Ho Ox 58. **d** 60 **p** 61. C Newc St Matt w St Mary *Newc* 60-64; V 64-94; Hon Can Newc Cathl 80-94; rtd 95. *21 Grosvenor Drive, Whitley Bay, Tyne & Wear NE26 2JP* Tel 0191-252 1858

WALKER, Helen Margaret. *See* WALKER, Miss Bethany Helen

WALKER, Ian Richard Stevenson. b 51. Univ of Wales (Lamp) BA73. Qu Coll Birm DipTh75. **d** 76 **p** 77. C Stainton-in-Cleveland *York* 76-79; C Fulford 79-81; C Kidderminster St Mary *Worc* 81-82; TV Kidderminster St Mary and All SS, Trimpley etc 82-86; R Keyingham w Ottringham, Halsham and Sunk Is *York* from 86; RD S Holderness from 94. *The Rectory, Keyingham, Hull HU12 9RX* Tel (01964) 622171

WALKER, Jack. b 21. Kelham Th Coll 37. **d** 45 **p** 46. C Tynemouth Ch Ch *Newc* 45-49; C Wallsend St Luke 49-51; C Linthorpe *York* 51-55; V Newbald 55-96; V Sancton 55-96; rtd 96. *10 Molescroft Avenue, Beverley, N Humberside HU17 7HH*

WALKER, Jill Dorothy Ann. b 36. RGN58 Westmr Coll Ox 93. St Alb Minl Tr Scheme 89. **d** 96. NSM E Barnet *St Alb* from 96. *2 Dean's Gardens, St Albans, Herts AL4 9LS* Tel (01727) 834436

WALKER, John. b 49. Sheff Univ BSc74. Qu Coll Birm DipTh77. **d** 78 **p** 79. C Loughborough Em *Leic* 78-81; C Nottingham All SS *S'well* 81-84; V Radford St Pet 84-95; V Carrington from 95. *Carrington Vicarage, 6 Watcombe Circus, Nottingham NG5 2DT* Tel 0115-962 1291

WALKER, John. b 51. Aber Univ MA74. Edin Th Coll BD78. **d** 78 **p** 79. C Broughty Ferry *Bre* 78-81; P-in-c Dundee St Jo 81-85; Ind Chapl 83-88; R Dundee St Luke 85-95; R Inverurie *Ab* from 95; R Kemnay from 95; R Alford from 95; R Auchindoir from 95. *The Rectory, St Mary's Place, Inverurie, Aberdeenshire AB51 3NW* Tel (01467) 620470

WALKER, John Anthony Patrick. b 58. Trin Coll Bris BA86. **d** 86 **p** 87. C Canford Magna *Sarum* 86-90; TV Glyncorrwg w Afan Vale and Cymmer Afan *Llan* 90-96. *78 Bloom Street, Edgeley, Stockport, Cheshire SK3 9LQ*

WALKER, Canon John Cameron. b 31. St Andr Univ MA52. Edin Th Coll 63. **d** 65 **p** 66. C Edin H Cross *Edin* 65-67; C Perth St Jo *St And* 67-70; Chapl Angl Students Glas 70-74; Youth Chapl Warks Educn Cttee 75-77; Officer Gen Syn Bd of Educn 78-82; C W Hendon St Jo *Lon* 79-82; PV Westmr Abbey 82-84; Chapl Ghent w Ypres *Eur* 84-92; Chapl Ghent from 92; Miss to Seamen from 84; Can Brussels Cathl *Eur* from 93. *Blankenbergestraat 39, B-9000 Ghent, Belgium* Tel Ghent (9) 222-3659 Fax 220-8004

WALKER, John David. b 44. St Jo Coll Dur BA76 DipTh77. **d** 77 **p** 78. C Heworth *York* 77-81; P-in-c Barmby on the Moor w Fangfoss 81-83; P-in-c Allerthorpe 81-83; TV Pocklington Team 84-89; P-in-c Hovingham 89; TV Street TM 89-92; R Dunnington from 92. *The Rectory, Church Street, Dunnington, York YO1 5PW* Tel (01904) 489349

WALKER, John Frank. b 53. Leeds Univ BEd76 Ripon Coll of Educn CertEd75. NW Ord Course 78. **d** 81 **p** 82. NSM Whitkirk *Ripon* 81-82; C 82-85; V Sutton Courtenay w Appleford *Ox* 85-90; Dioc Children's Adv *S'wark* 90-94; V Walworth St Jo from 94; Youth and Children's Officer Woolwich Episc Area from 95. *St John's Vicarage, 18 Larcom Street, London SE17 1NQ* Tel 0171-703 4375

WALKER, John Frederick. b 21. St Jo Coll Dur BA47 DipTh49 MA51. **d** 49 **p** 50. C Normanton *Wakef* 49-51; C Northowram 51-53; V Gawthorpe and Chickenley Heath 53-59; V Halifax All So 59-74; V Hampsthwaite *Ripon* 74-86; P-in-c Killinghall 76-86; rtd 86; Perm to Offic *Bradf* from 86. *36 Rockwood Drive, Skipton, N Yorkshire BD23 1UW* Tel (01756) 799835

WALKER, John Howard. b 47. Brasted Th Coll 67 Clifton Th Coll 69. **d** 72 **p** 73. C Upton (Overchurch) *Ches* 72-76; Asst Chapl Liv Univ *Liv* 76-79; V Everton St Chrys 79-82; C Parr Mt 83-86; SAMS 86-94; Area Sec (NE and E Midl) SAMS 86-89; Paraguay 89-94; V Calverley *Bradf* from 95. *The Vicarage, Town Gate, Calverley, Pudsey, W Yorkshire LS28 5NF* Tel 0113-257 7968

WALKER, John Hugh. b 34. K Coll Lon BD57 AKC57 K Coll Lon MTh75 MA85 Lon Inst of Educn PGCE68. St Boniface Warminster 57. **d** 58 **p** 59. C Southend St Alb *Chelmsf* 58-61; V Gt Ilford St Alb 61-67; Perm to Offic 67-68; Hon C Forest Gate St Edm 68-74; Perm to Offic *Cant* 75-82 and from 87; R Dymchurch w Burmarsh and Newchurch 82-87; rtd 94. *Aberfeldy, Covet Lane, Kingston, Canterbury, Kent CT4 6HU* Tel (01227) 830818

WALKER, John Michael. b 32. Qu Coll Birm. **d** 57 **p** 58. C Ruddington *S'well* 57-60; C Horsham *Chich* 60-64; C Sullington 64-70; C Storrington 64-70; V Peasmarsh 70-73; V Washington 73-77; R Ashington, Washington and Wiston with Buncton from 77. *The Rectory, Ashington, Pulborough, W Sussex RH20 3BH* Tel (01903) 892304

WALKER, John Percival. b 45. CITC 68. **d** 71 **p** 72. C Belfast St Clem *D & D* 71-74; C Magheraculmoney *Clogh* 74-78; C Lisburn St Paul *Conn* 78-81; I Belfast St Ninian 81-88; I Belfast St Mary 88-89; I Belfast St Mary w H Redeemer from 89. *558 Crumlin Road, Belfast BT14 7GL* Tel (01232) 391120 or 748423

WALKER, John Robert. b 50. NE Lon Poly BSc74 K Coll Lon PhD77. Trin Coll Bris BA93 MA95. **d** 96 **p** 97. C Bushbury *Lich* from 96. *27 Morrison Avenue, Bushbury, Wolverhampton WV10 9TZ* Tel (01902) 864548

WALKER, Keith. b 48. Linc Th Coll 82. **d** 84 **p** 85. C Whickham *Dur* 84-87; C Trimdon Station 87; P-in-c 87-89; V 89-90; R Penshaw from 90; P-in-c Shiney Row 92-95; P-in-c Herrington 93-95. *All Saints' Rectory, Penshaw, Houghton le Spring, Tyne & Wear DH4 7ER* Tel 0191-584 2631

WALKER, The Ven Kingsley. b 17. St Chad's Coll Dur MA46. St Paul's Grahamstown LTh47. **d** 47 **p** 48. S Africa 47-53; V Finham *Cov* 53-60; Adn Seychelles 60-63; Feed the Minds (N Sec) 63-68; V Preston-on-Stour w Whitchurch *Cov* 68-73; S Africa 73-91; rtd 91; Perm to Offic *Chich* from 92. *17 Uplands Park, Broad Oak, Heathfield, E Sussex TN21 8SJ* Tel (01435) 882270

WALKER, Mrs Lesley Ann. b 53. S Dios Minl Tr Scheme 85. **d** 88 **p** 94. Par Dn Oakdale *Sarum* 88-92; TD Bridgnorth, Tasley, Astley Abbotts, Oldbury etc *Heref* 92-94; TV from 94. *32 Goodwood Avenue, Bridgnorth, Shropshire WV15 5BD* Tel (01746) 765874

WALKER, Mrs Margaret Joy (Margi). b 44. Avery Hill Coll DipHE80 Newc Univ MA93. CA Tr Coll 80. **dss** 86 **d** 87 **p** 94. Scargill Ho 86-87; Hon Par Dn Monkwearmouth St Andr *Dur* 87; Hon Par Dn Chester le Street 87-93; NSM Wells Cathl *B & W* from 94. *6 The Liberty, Wells, Somerset BA5 2SU* Tel (01749) 672224

WALKER, Mark Robert Joseph George. b 66. Nottm Univ BA88. CITC 90. **d** 92 **p** 93. C Larne and Inver *Conn* 92-95. *Address temp unknown*

WALKER, Martin Frank. b 39. St Jo Coll Nottm 71. **d** 73 **p** 74. C Penn *Lich* 73-78; V Bentley 78-82; V Kinver 82-88; R Kinver and Enville 88-91; V Harlescott from 91. *Harlescott Vicarage, Meadow Farm Drive, Shrewsbury SY1 4NG* Tel (01743) 362883

WALKER, Martin John. b 52. Linc Coll Ox BA73 PGCE74 Chateau de Bossey Geneva DipEcum78. Cranmer Hall Dur BA78. **d** 79 **p** 80. C Harlow New Town w Lt Parndon *Chelmsf* 79-81; C Dorchester *Ox* 81-83; Chapl City of Bath Coll of FE 83-89; TV Southampton (City Cen) *Win* 89-91; Adv in RE and Resources *Sarum* 91-92; Chapl Bancroft's Sch Woodford Green from 92; Hon C Northolt St Mary *Lon* from 92. *St Mary's Rectory, Ealing Road, Northolt, Middx UB5 6AA* Tel 0181-841 5691

WALKER, Michael John. b 39. Univ of Wales (Lamp) BA61. St Aid Birkenhead 61. **d** 63 **p** 64. C Clifton *York* 63-66; C Marfleet 66-69; V Salterhebble St Jude *Wakef* 69-83; V Llangollen w Trevor and Llantysilio *St As* 83-93; RD Llangollen 87-93; V Kerry and Llanmerewig and Dolfor from 93. *The Vicarage, Kerry, Newtown SY16 4NY* Tel (01806) 670466

WALKER, Canon Michael John Maynard. b 32. BNC Ox BA55 MA59. Clifton Th Coll 55. **d** 57 **p** 58. C Patcham *Chich* 57-61; V Stapleford *S'well* 61-66; R Saxmundham *St E* 66-71; V New Beckenham St Paul *Roch* 71-78; V Bury St Edmunds St Mary *St E* 78-92; Hon Can St E Cathl 86-94; V Debenham w Aspall and Kenton 92-94; rtd 94. *Martletts, 3 Rembrandt Gardens, Bury St Edmunds, Suffolk IP33 2LX* Tel (01284) 724236

WALKER, Michael Sykes. b 10. TD. Trin Hall Cam BA33 MA40. Wycliffe Hall Ox. **d** 49 **p** 50. C Northowram *Wakef* 49-51; C Castleford All SS 51-53; R Birdsall w Langton *York* 53-61; R Escrick 61-75; RD Escrick 66-73; rtd 75; Hon C Ryther *York* 75-80; Perm to Offic from 80. *2 Rawcliffe Grove, Clifton Lane, York YO3 6NR* Tel (01904) 636453

WALKER, Canon Nigel Maynard. b 39. ALCD66. **d** 67 **p** 68. C Southsea St Jude *Portsm* 67-70; S Africa 70-76; C Abingdon w Shippon *Ox* 76-80; V Upton (Overchurch) *Ches* 80-94; Chan Brussels Cathl *Eur* from 94; Chapl Brussels from 94. *Avenue Parmentier 240/4, B-1150 Brussels, Belgium* Tel Brussels (2) 770-7715 or 511-7183 Fax 511-1028

WALKER, Mrs Pamela Sarah. b 52. Somerville Coll Ox BA73 MA77 St Jo Coll Dur BA78. Cranmer Hall Dur 76. **dss** 79 **d** 87 **p** 94. Harlow New Town w Lt Parndon *Chelmsf* 79-81; Dorchester *Sarum* 82-83; Bath St Bart *B & W* 85-88; Hon Par Dn 87-88; Par Dn Warmley *Bris* 88-89; Par Dn Bitton 88-89; Par Dn Southampton (City Cen) *Win* 89-92; Par Dn Northolt St Mary *Lon* 92-94; R from 94. *St Mary's Rectory, Ealing Road, Northolt, Middx UB5 6AA* Tel 0181-841 5691

WALKER, Paul Gary. b 59. Lon Univ BD. St Jo Coll Nottm 82. **d** 84 **p** 85. C Bowling St Steph *Bradf* 84-87; C Tong 87-90; P-in-c Oakenshaw cum Woodlands from 90. *589 Bradford Road, Oakenshaw, Bradford, W Yorkshire BD12 7ES* Tel (01274) 676410 E-mail sqwalker@netcom.ca

WALKER, Paul Laurence. b 63. St Chad's Coll Dur BA84. Chich Th Coll BTh90. **d** 88 **p** 89. C Shildon w Eldon *Dur* 88-91; C Barnard Castle w Whorlton 91-93; C Silksworth 93-96; C-in-c Moorside St Wilfrid CD from 96. *24 Midhurst Close, Sunderland SR3 2QD* Tel 0191-528 8845

WALKER, Pauline Ann. b 51. Open Univ BA87. St As Minl Tr Course 88. **d** 93 **p** 97. NSM Bistre *St As* from 93. *Mountain Farm, Foxes Lane, Alltami, Mold CH7 6RT* Tel (01244) 550638

WALKER, Pauline Jean. b 49. St Hild Coll Dur BSc72 Homerton Coll Cam PGCE73 Nottm Univ MA96. All Nations Chr Coll 89 St Jo Coll Nottm 94. **d** 96. C Bitterne *Win* from 96. *39 Whites Road, Southampton SO19 7NR* Tel (01703) 447929

WALKER, Peter Anthony. b 57. Pemb Coll Cam BA79 MA83 St Jo Coll Dur BA86. Cranmer Hall Dur 84. **d** 87 **p** 88. C Chesham Bois *Ox* 87-90; Chapl Bradf Cathl *Bradf* 90-93; TV W Swindon and the Lydiards *Bris* from 93. *6 Springhill Close, Westlea, Swindon SN5 7BG* Tel (01793) 872932

WALKER, Peter Anthony Ashley. b 46. Chich Th Coll 67. **d** 70 **p** 71. C Stamford Hill St Thos *Lon* 70-74; C Bethnal Green St Matt 74-77; V Hackney Wick St Mary of Eton w St Aug 77-84; Warden Rydal Hall *Carl* 84-95; P-in-c Rydal 84-95; P-in-c Porthleven w Sithney *Truro* from 95; RD Kerrier from 96. *The Vicarage, Pendeen Road, Porthleven, Helston, Cornwall TR13 9AL* Tel (01326) 562419

WALKER, Peter Jeffrey. b 46. Kelham Th Coll 65. **d** 70 **p** 71. C Middlesbrough All SS *York* 70-75 and 77-78; SSF 75-77; C-in-c Wrangbrook w N Elmsall CD *Wakef* 78-82; V Athersley 82-86; Perm to Offic *Blackb* 86-87; Perm to Offic *Dur* 87-89; V Hartlepool H Trin 89-95; OGS from 95; Dep Chapl HM Pris Birm 95-96; Chapl HM Pris Moorland from 96. *HM Prison Moorland, Bowtry Road, Hatfield Woodhouse, Doncaster, S Yorkshire DN7 6EE* Tel (01302) 351500

✠**WALKER, The Rt Revd Peter Knight.** b 19. Qu Coll Ox BA47 MA47 Cam Univ Hon DD78. Westcott Ho Cam 53. **d** 54 **p** 55 **c** 72. Asst Master Merchant Taylors' Sch Lon 50-56; C Hemel Hempstead St Mary *St Alb* 56-58; Fell Dean and Lect Th CCC Cam 58-62; Asst Tutor 59-62; Prin Westcott Ho Cam 62-72; Hon Can Ely Cathl *Ely* 66-72; Suff Bp Dorchester *Ox* 72-77; Can Res Ch Ch 72-77; Bp Ely 77-89; rtd 89; Asst Bp Ox from 89. *19 St Mark's Court, Barton Road, Cambridge CB3 9LE* Tel (01223) 363041

WALKER, Peter Sidney Caleb. b 50. DipMin80. St Mich Th Coll Crafers 76. **d** 80 **p** 81. Australia 80-88; R Swallow *Linc* 88-94; R Selworthy and Timberscombe and Wootton Courtenay *B & W* 94-95; R Luccombe 94-95; R Selworthy, Timberscombe, Wootton Courtenay etc from 95. *The Rectory, Selworthy, Minehead, Somerset TA24 8TL* Tel (01643) 862445

WALKER, Peter Stanley. b 56. SRN RMN Nottm Univ BCombStuds. Linc Th Coll 80. **d** 83 **p** 84. C Woodford St Barn *Chelmsf* 83-86; C Brentwood St Thos 86-88; V Colchester St Barn 88-94; P-in-c Colchester St Jas, All SS, St Nic and St Runwald 94-96; R Colchester St Jas and St Paul w All SS etc from 96. *The Rectory, 76 East Hill, Colchester CO1 2QW* Tel (01206) 866802

WALKER, Peter William Leyland. b 61. CCC Cam BA82 MA86 PhD87. Wycliffe Hall Ox 87. **d** 89 **p** 90. C Tonbridge SS Pet and Paul *Roch* 89-93; Fell Tyndale Ho Cam 93-96; Tutor Wycliffe Hall Ox from 96. *Wycliffe Hall, 54 Banbury Road, Oxford OX2 6PW* Tel (01865) 274214

WALKER, Canon Philip Geoffrey. b 47. St Jo Coll Dur BA70 Or Coll Ox BA72 MA76 Newc Univ MA93. Ripon Hall Ox 70. **d** 74 **p** 75. C Sheff St Geo *Sheff* 74-77; C Cambridge Gt St Mary w St Mich *Ely* 77-81; V Monkwearmouth St Andr *Dur* 81-87; R Chester le Street 87-93; RD Chester-le-Street 89-93; Dioc Missr *B & W* from 93; Can Res Wells Cathl from 94. *6 The Liberty, Wells, Somerset BA5 2SU* Tel (01749) 672224

WALKER, Philip Kingsley. b 47. Ox Univ BA70 Univ of Wales DPS90. St Mich Coll Llan. **d** 90 **p** 91. C Maindee *Mon* 90-92; C Llanmartin 92-94; R Bishton from 94. *The Vicarage, Station Road, Llanwern, Newport NP6 2DW* Tel (01633) 413457

WALKER, Raymond. b 28. Carl Dioc Tr Inst 83. **d** 86 **p** 87. NSM Gt Salkeld w Lazonby *Carl* 86-91; C Greystoke, Matterdale, Mungrisdale etc 91-92; TV 92-95; rtd 95. *Brackenrigg, Town Head, Lazonby, Penrith, Cumbria CA10 1AT* Tel (01768) 898314

WALKER, Richard David. Hull Univ BSc. S Dios Minl Tr Scheme. **d** 95 **p** 96. Hon C Horfield St Greg *Bris* from 95. *10 Saxon Way, Bradley Stoke, Bristol BS12 9AS* Tel (01454) 202139

WALKER, Richard Mainprize. b 43. Keele Univ BA DipEd. Wycliffe Hall Ox 84. **d** 86 **p** 87. C Guildf Ch Ch *Guildf* 86-90; V Bradley St Martin *Lich* from 90. *St Martin's Vicarage, King Street, Bradley, Bilston, W Midlands WV14 8PQ* Tel (01902) 493109

WALKER, Robert Edward Lea. b 23. Qu Coll Ox MA49. Wycliffe Hall Ox 49. **d** 51 **p** 52. C Witney *Ox* 51-61; V Wroxton w Balscott 61-80; P-in-c Shenington and Alkerton w Shutford 79-80; R Wroxton w Balscote and Shenington w Alkerton 80-88; rtd 88. *11 Tanners Court, Charlbury, Chipping Norton, Oxon OX7 3RP* Tel (01608) 810461

WALKER, Mrs Ruth Elizabeth. b 58. St Jo Coll Dur BA79 Cam Univ CertEd81. St Jo Coll Nottm 86. **d** 88 **p** 94. Par Dn Princes Risborough w Ilmer *Ox* 88-90; Chapl Bradf Cathl *Bradf* 90-93; C The Lydiards *Bris* 93-94; Hon C W Swindon and the Lydiards 94-96; C Swindon St Jo and St Andr from 96. *6 Springhill Close, Westlea, Swindon SN5 7BG* Tel (01793) 872932

WALKER, Simon Patrick. b 71. Ch Ch Ox BA93. Wycliffe Hall Ox BTh94. **d** 97. C Abingdon *Ox* from 97. *33 Mattock Way, Abingdon, Oxon OX14 2PQ* Tel (01235) 510993 Fax as telephone E-mail simon_walker@cin.org.uk

WALKER, Stanley Frederick. b 48. St Jo Coll Nottm. **d** 84 **p** 85. C Ellesmere Port *Ches* 84-89; V Seacombe 89-97; C Lache cum Saltney from 97. *89 Sandy Lane, Saltney, Chester CH4 8UA* Tel (01244) 680308

WALKER, Canon Stephen. b 09. St Jo Coll Dur BA30 DipTh31 MA33. **d** 32 **p** 33. C Horsforth *Ripon* 32-35; C Upper Armley 35-36; V Birmingham St Barn *Birm* 36-40; V Monkwearmouth All SS *Dur* 40-43; V Bruntcliffe *Wakef* 43-50; V N Ferriby *York* 50-58; V Beverley St Mary 58-77; Chapl Westwood Hosp 59-77; RD Beverley 63-73; Can and Preb York Minster 64-77; rtd 77; Perm to Offic *York* from 77; Perm to Offic *Dur* from 77. *Dulverton Hall, St Martin's Square, Scarborough, N Yorkshire YO11 2DB* Tel (01723) 373082

WALKER, Stephen Michael Maynard. b 62. St Jo Coll Dur BA84. Trin Coll Bris 86. **d** 88 **p** 89. C Eastwood *S'well* 88-92; CF from 92; Perm to Offic *Chich* from 92. *MOD Chaplains (Army), Trenchard Lines, Upavon, Pewsey, Wilts SN9 6BE* Tel (01980) 615804 Fax 615800

WALKER, Stephen Patrick. b 62. York Univ BSc83 PGCE84. St Jo Coll Nottm DipTh89 DPS90. **d** 90 **p** 91. C Hull Newland St Jo *York* 90-94; Min Grove Green LEP *Cant* from 94; Children's Min Adv from 96. *7 Samphire Close, Weavering, Maidstone, Kent ME14 5UD* Tel (01622) 739294

WALKER, Mrs Susan Joy. b 52. Univ of Wales (Lamp) BA73 Hull Univ MA91. Qu Coll Birm 75. **dss** 83 **d** 87 **p** 94. Kidderminster St Mary and All SS, Trimpley etc *Worc* 83-86; Keyingham w Ottringham, Halsham and Sunk Is *York* 86-87; Hon Par Dn 87-94; Hon C from 94; Chapl Hull Coll of FE from 89. *The Rectory, Keyingham, Hull HU12 9RX* Tel (01964) 622171

WALKER, The Ven Thomas Overington (Tom). b 33. Keble Coll Ox BA58 MA61. Oak Hill Th Coll 58. **d** 60 **p** 61. C Woking St Paul *Guildf* 60-62; C St Leonards St Leon *Chich* 62-64; Travelling Sec IVF 64-67; Succ Birm Cathl *Birm* 67-70; Hon Can Birm Cathl 80-91; V Harborne Heath 70-91; P-in-c Edgbaston St Germain 83-91; RD Edgbaston 89-91; Adn Nottingham *S'well* 91-96; rtd 96. *6 Cornbrook, Clee Hill, Ludlow, Shropshire SY8 3QQ* Tel (01584) 890176

WALKER, Trevor John. b 51. Southn Univ BTh80. Sarum & Wells Th Coll 75. **d** 78 **p** 79. C Standish *Blackb* 78-81; P-in-c N Somercotes *Linc* 81-82; P-in-c S Somercotes 81-82; V Somercotes 82-85; R Binbrook Gp from 85. *The Rectory, Binbrook, Lincoln LN3 6BJ* Tel (01472) 398227 Fax as telephone E-mail priest1@compuserve.com

WALKER, Canon Walter Stanley. b 21. AKC42. Cuddesdon Coll 42. **d** 44 **p** 45. C Southport All SS *Liv* 44-47; Miss to Seamen 47-48; C-in-c Kelsall CD *Ches* 48-53; V Birkenhead St Mary w St Paul 53-61; Chapl Barony Hosp Nantwich 61-66; R Wistaston 61-66; R Bromborough 66-77; R Wallasey St Hilary 77-86; RD Wallasey 77-86; Hon Can Ches Cathl 80-86; rtd 86; Perm to Offic *Ches* from 86. *39 Lyndhurst Road, Wallasey, Merseyside L45 6XB* Tel 0151-630 4237

WALKER, William. b 10. FCIM48. **d** 51 **p** 52. C Gotham *S'well* 51-58; Chapl, Lect and Tutor Stanford Hall Loughb 52-70; C-in-c Normanton on Soar 58-65; V Daybrook 70-80; rtd 80; Perm to Offic *S'well* from 80. *278 Rutland Road, Nottingham NG2 5EB* Tel 0115-986 9353

WALKER, Canon William George Leslie. b 10. TCD BA39 MA42. **d** 39 **p** 40. C Dublin St Kevin *D & G* 39-42; C Bangor St Comgall *D & D* 42-43; CF (EC) 43-46; I Saul w Inch *D & D* 46-52; I Magheradroll 52-66; I Knockbreda 59-78; RD Hillsborough 66-70; Can Down Cathl 70-78; rtd 78. *Larch House, 160 Ballylesson Road, Belfast BT8 8JU* Tel (01232) 826578

WALKEY, Malcolm Gregory Taylor. b 44. Lon Univ DipTh68. Kelham Th Coll 63. **d** 68 **p** 69. C Oadby *Leic* 68-72; TV Corby SS Pet and Andr w Gt and Lt Oakley *Pet* 72-79; R Ashton w Hartwell 79-86; TR Halesworth w Linstead, Chediston, Holton etc *St E* 86-91; 91-93; P-in-c Laxfield from 93. *The Vicarage, 15 Noyes Avenue, Laxfield, Woodbridge, Suffolk IP13 8EB* Tel (01986) 798218

WALKLATE, Keith. b 46. FCIB MIEx FRSA. Ox Min Course 92. **d** 95 **p** 96. NSM Wykeham *Ox* from 95. *Holly Tree House, 17 Old Glebe, Upper Tadmarton, Banbury, Oxon OX15 5TH* Tel (01295) 780273

WALL, Canon David Oliver. b 39. TD JP. OStJ. Bps' Coll Cheshunt 62. **d** 65 **p** 66. C Lt Ilford St Mich *Chelmsf* 65-68; CF 68-73; R Sudbourne w Orford *St E* 73-76; R Orford w Sudbourne and Chillesford w Butley 76-79; P-in-c Iken 76-79; P-in-c Ipswich St Bart 77-79; R Drinkstone 79-82; R Rattlesden 79-82; R Chedburgh w Depden, Rede and Hawkedon from 82; Chapl to Suffolk Fire Service from 91; Hon Can St E Cathl from 96. *The Rectory, Rede, Bury St Edmunds, Suffolk IP29 4BE* Tel (01284) 89342

✠**WALL, The Rt Revd Eric St Quintin.** b 15. BNC Ox BA37 MA46. Wells Th Coll 37. **d** 38 **p** 39 **c** 72. C Boston *Linc* 38-41; Chapl RAFVR 41-45; V Sherston Magna w Easton Grey *Bris* 44-53; RD Malmesbury 51-53; V Cricklade w Latton 53-60; Bp's Chapl 60-66; Dioc Adv in Chr Stewardship 60-66; Hon Can Bris Cathl 60-72; V Westbury-on-Trym St Alb 66-72; RD Clifton 67-72; Suff Bp Huntingdon *Ely* 72-80; Can Res Ely Cathl 72-80; rtd 80; Perm to Offic *Nor* from 80; Perm to Offic *St E* from 81; Perm to Offic *Ely* from 86. *7 Peregrine Close, Diss, Norfolk IP22 3PG* Tel (01379) 644331

WALL, James Leach. b 19. Leeds Univ BA40. **d** 64 **p** 65. Hong Kong 64-66; C Prenton *Ches* 66-71; C Auckland St Andr and St Anne *Dur* 71-74; V Hart w Elwick Hall 74-80; rtd 81. *191 Park Road, Hartlepool, Cleveland TS26 9LP* Tel (01429) 275105

WALL, John Caswallen. b 60. York Univ BA83 MA85 Ox Univ BA89. St Steph Ho Ox 86. **d** 89 **p** 90. C Ifield *Chich* 89-94; C Brighton St Pet and St Nic w Chpl Royal from 94. *40 Kemp Street, Brighton, E Sussex BN1 4EF* Tel (01273) 675684

WALL, Martyn Philip Lucas. b 17. Hertf Coll Ox BA38 MA43. Wells Th Coll 69. **d** 71 **p** 72. C Highworth w Sevenhampton and Inglesham etc *Bris* 71-74; R Wick w Doynton 74-85; rtd 85; Perm to Offic *B & W* from 85. *9 Woburn Close, Trowbridge, Wilts BA14 9TJ* Tel (01225) 754323

WALL, Nicholas John. b 46. Brasted Th Coll 69 Trin Coll Bris 71. **d** 73 **p** 74. C Morden *S'wark* 73-78; R Dunkeswell and Dunkeswell Abbey *Ex* 78-83; V Sheldon 78-83; P-in-c Luppitt 81-83; V Dunkeswell, Sheldon and Luppitt from 83. *The Rectory, Dunkeswell, Honiton, Devon EX14 0RE* Tel (01404) 891243

WALL, Mrs Pauline Ann. b 39. Bris Sch of Min 87. **dss** 85 **d** 87 **p** 94. Bris Ch the Servant Stockwood *Bris* 85-87; Hon Par Dn 87-94; Hon C from 94; Chapl St Brendan's Sixth Form Coll from 90. *41 Ladman Road, Bristol BS14 8QD* Tel (01275) 833083

WALL, Philip John. b 12. St Chad's Coll Dur BA34 DipTh35 MA37. **d** 35 **p** 36. C Fleur-de-Lis *Mon* 35-38; C Roath St Sav *Llan* 38-39; C Newport *Ex* 39-41; C Usk and Gwernesney w Llangeview 41-43; V Newport St Julian *Mon* 43-63; Chapl HM Pris Holloway 63-68; P-in-c Norwood St Mary *Lon* 68-69; R 69-81; RD Ealing W 74-80; rtd 81; Perm to Offic *Lon* 82-91; Perm to Offic *Ox* from 89. *9 Hervines Court, Amersham, Bucks HP6 5HH* Tel (01494) 728124

WALL, Robert William. b 52. Ex Coll Ox MA Ex Univ BPhil77. Trin Coll Bris 80. **d** 83 **p** 84. C Blackb Sav *Blackb* 83-86; C Edgware *Lon* 86-89; C Barnsbury 89-90; TV from 90. *43 Matilda Street, London N1 0LA* Tel 0171-278 5208 or 607 4552

WALLACE, Preb Alastair Robert. b 50. St Cath Coll Cam BA71 MA75 Lon Univ BD75. Trin Coll Bris 72. **d** 75 **p** 76. C Ex St Leon w H Trin *Ex* 75-79; Chapl Ridley Hall Cam 79-80; R Bath St Mich w St Paul *B & W* 83-96; RD Bath 90-96; Hon Asst Dioc Missr from 96; Sub-Dean Wells from 96; Preb Wells Cathl from 96. *The Lower Mill, Long Street, Croscombe, Wells, Somerset BA5 3QQ* Tel (01749) 344198

WALLACE, Mrs Ann. b 29. CITC 92. **d** 95 **p** 96. Aux Min Abbeyleix w Old Church, Ballyroan etc *C & O* from 95. *Knapton, Abbeyleix, Portlaoise, Co Laois, Irish Republic* Tel Portlaoise (502) 31010

WALLACE, Mrs Brenda Claire. b 52. Linc Th Coll 73 S'wark Ord Course 78. **dss** 80 **d** 87 **p** 94. Sutton at Hone *Roch* 80-83; Borstal 83-87; Hon Par Dn 87-89; HM Pris Cookham Wood 83-89; Asst Chapl 87-89; NSM Stansted Mountfitchet *Chelmsf* 89-96; NSM Stansted Mountfitchet w Birchanger and Farnham 97; C Hutton from 97. *The Rectory, 175 Rayleigh Road, Hutton, Brentwood, Essex CM13 1LX* Tel (01277) 215115 Fax 263407

WALLACE, David Alexander Rippon. b 39. Ox Min Course 94. **d** 96. NSM Haddenham w Cuddington, Kingsey etc *Ox* from 96. *11 Station Road, Haddenham, Aylesbury, Bucks HP17 8AN* Tel (01844) 290670 E-mail wallace@nildram.co.uk

WALLACE, Derek George. b 33. Glas Univ MA55. Edin Th Coll 55. **d** 57 **p** 58. C Falkirk *Edin* 57-60; C Ayr *Glas* 60-62; Chapl Netherton Tr Sch Morpeth 62-67; V Oldham St Jo *Man* 67-70; R Burravoe *Ab* 70-78; R Lerwick 70-78; R Port Glas 78-94; Miss to Seamen 78-94; rtd 94. *39 Coronation Crescent, Margate, Kent CT9 5PN* Tel (01843) 223869

WALLACE, Hugo. b 31. Trin Coll Cam BA54 MA59. Ridley Hall Cam 54. **d** 56 **p** 57. C Hornchurch St Andr *Chelmsf* 56-58; Uganda 58-60; C Bermondsey St Mary w St Olave and St Jo *S'wark* 61; S Africa from 61. *Shalom, 7 Ixia Avenue, Kommetjie Cape, 7976 South Africa* Tel Cape Town (21) 831466

WALLACE, Julie Michele. b 58. Cam Univ DipRS82 Lon Univ DCouns88 DipApTh92 CCouns92 Ox Univ MTh93. CA Tr Coll 77. **d** 88 **p** 94. Chapl Middx Poly *Lon* 86-90; Voc Adv CA 90-92; Member CA Counselling Service 92-96; NSM Bellingham St Dunstan *S'wark* 91-96; TV Kidbrooke from 96. *66A Whetstone Road, London SE3 8PZ* Tel 0181-856 6317

WALLACE, The Ven Martin William. b 48. K Coll Lon BD70 AKC70. St Aug Coll Cant 70. **d** 71 **p** 72. C Attercliffe *Sheff* 71-74; C New Malden and Coombe *S'wark* 74-77; V Forest Gate St Mark *Chelmsf* 77-93; RD Newham 82-91; P-in-c Forest Gate Em w Upton Cross 85-89; Hon Can Chelmsf Cathl from 89; P-in-c Forest Gate All SS 91-93; Dioc ACUPA Link Officer 91-97; P-in-c Bradwell on Sea 93-97; Ind Chapl Maldon and Dengie Deanery 93-97; Adn Colchester from 97. *63 Powers Hall End, Witham, Essex CM8 1NH* Tel (01376) 513130

WALLACE, Nicholas Robert. b 56. Trin Coll Bris DipHE95. **d** 95 **p** 96. C Fishponds St Jo *Bris* from 95. *5 Lodgeside Gardens, Bristol BS15 1NY* Tel 0117-961 5707

WALLACE, Raymond Sherwood. b 28. Selw Coll Dunedin (NZ). **d** 52 **p** 54. New Zealand 52-58; C St Pancras H Cross w St Jude and St Pet *Lon* 58-64; C N Harrow St Alb 64-67; V Stroud Green H Trin 67-79; V Penwerris *Truro* 79-84; R Wymington w Podington *St Alb* 84-87; rtd 87; Perm to Offic *St Alb* from 87. *141 Dunsmore Road, Luton LU1 5JX* Tel (01582) 455882

WALLACE, Richard Colin. b 39. Mert Coll Ox BA61 MA64. St Chad's Coll Dur 69. **d** 71 **p** 72. Tutor St Chad's Coll Dur 71-72; P-in-c Kimblesworth *Dur* 72-74; Chapl Bradf Univ *Bradf* 74-79; C Bingley All SS 79-80; TV 80-89; V Earby from 89. *The Vicarage, Earby, Colne, Lancs BB8 6JL* Tel (01282) 842291

WALLACE, Richard John. b 56. Coll of Resurr Mirfield. **d** 82 **p** 83. C Catford St Laur *S'wark* 82-85; C Bellingham St Dunstan 85-87; V 87-95; TR Stanley *Dur* from 95. *St Andrew's Rectory, Churchbank, Stanley, Co Durham DH9 0DU* Tel (01207) 233936

WALLACE, Richard Samuel. b 17. TCD BA39 MA53. **d** 41 **p** 42. C Belfast St Steph *Conn* 41-43; C Hammersmith St Pet *Lon* 43-44; India 44-51; Perivale *Lon* 51-54; V Notting Hill St Mark 54-60; V Teddington St Mark 60-83; rtd 83; Perm to Offic *Ex* from 83. *St Christopher, 17 Hartley Road, Exmouth, Devon EX8 2SG* Tel (01395) 279595

WALLACE, Robert (Bob). b 52. Sussex Univ BSc73 Nottm Univ DipTh75. Linc Th Coll 73. **d** 76 **p** 77. C Plaistow St Mary *Roch* 76-79; C Dartford H Trin 79-83; Chapl The Foord Almshouses 83-89; V Borstal *Roch* 83-89; Chapl HM Pris Cookham Wood 83-89; V Stansted Mountfitchet *Chelmsf* 89-96; P-in-c Farnham 89-96; R Stansted Mountfitchet w Birchanger and Farnham 97; R Hutton from 97. *The Rectory, 175 Rayleigh Road, Hutton, Brentwood, Essex CM3 1LX* Tel (01277) 215115 Fax 263407

WALLACE-HADRILL, David Sutherland. b 20. CCC Ox BA41 MA45 Man Univ BD44 DD60. **d** 43 **p** 44. C Flixton St Mich *Man* 43-45; C Walthamstow St Mary *Chelmsf* 45-47; V Hornchurch H Cross 47-50; Chapl Aldenham Sch Herts 50-55; Ho Master 62-72; Asst Master 72-85; V Eston *York* 55-62; Lic to Offic *St Alb* from 62; rtd 85. *1 The Almshouse, High Street, Elstree, Borehamwood, Herts WD6 3EY* Tel 0181-207 2919

WALLER, David Arthur. b 61. Leeds Univ BA83. Chich Th Coll 89. **d** 91 **p** 92. C Aldwick *Chich* 91-95; TV Crawley from 95. *7 The Parade, Crawley, W Sussex RH10 2DT* Tel (01293) 520620

WALLER, David James. b 58. Whitelands Coll Lon BA85 K Coll Lon MA95. Ripon Coll Cuddesdon 85. **d** 88 **p** 89. C Tettenhall Regis *Lich* 88-91; Chapl Greenwich Univ *S'wark* 92-97; P-in-c Yiewsley *Lon* from 97. *The Vicarage, 93 High Street, Yiewsley, Middx UB7 7QH* Tel (01895) 442093

WALLER, Derek James Keith. b 54. Em Coll Cam BA75 PGCE76. Trin Coll Bris 88. **d** 91 **p** 92. C Church Stretton *Heref* 91-95; R The Appleby Gp *Leic* from 95. *The Rectory, Rectory Lane, Appleby Magna, Swadlincote, Derbyshire DE12 7BQ* Tel (01530) 270482

WALLER, Miss Elizabeth Jean (Liz). b 58. Keswick Hall Coll BEd BTh. Linc Th Coll 84. **d** 87 **p** 94. Par Dn Mile End Old Town H Trin *Lon* 87-90; Manna Chr Cen 90-91; Chapl LSE *Lon* 91-96; CARA from 96; NSM Notting Dale St Clem w St Mark and St Jas *Lon* from 96. *Flat 3, 80A Southampton Row, London WC1B 4BA* Tel 0171-831 9288

WALLER, John. b 60. Man Univ BA84. St Jo Coll Nottm 85. **d** 87 **p** 88. C Chorlton-cum-Hardy St Clem *Man* 87-90; R Openshaw 90-95; Chapl Ancoats Hosp Man 93-95; TV Watling Valley *Ox* 95-96; TR from 96. *114 Blackmoor Gate, Furzton, Milton Keynes MK4 1DN* Tel (01908) 502871

WALLER, John Pretyman. b 41. Sarum Th Coll 68. **d** 71 **p** 72. C Ipswich St Jo *St E* 71-74; R Waldringfield w Hemley 74-78; P-in-c Newbourn 74-78; R Waldringfield w Hemley and Newbourn from 78. *The Rectory, Mill Road, Waldringfield, Woodbridge, Suffolk IP12 4PY* Tel (01473) 36247

✠**WALLER, The Rt Revd John Stevens.** b 24. Peterho Cam BA48 MA53. Wells Th Coll 48. **d** 50 **p** 51 **c** 79. C Hillingdon St Jo *Lon* 50-52; C Twerton *B & W* 52-55; C-in-c Weston-super-Mare St Andr Bournville CD 55-59; V Weston-super-Mare St Andr Bournville 59-60; R Yarlington 60-63; Youth Chapl 60-63; Tr Officer C of E Youth Coun 63-67; V Frindsbury w Upnor *Roch* 67-72; P-in-c Strood St Fran 67-72; P-in-c Strood St Mary 67-72; P-in-c Strood St Nic 67-72; TR Strood 72-73; RD Strood 67-73; R Harpenden St Nic *St Alb* 73-79; Suff Bp Stafford *Lich* 79-87; Asst Bp B & W from 87; P-in-c Long Sutton w Long Load 87-88; TV Langport Area Chs 88-89; rtd 89. *102 Harnham Road, Salisbury SP2 8JW* Tel (01722) 329739

WALLER, Canon John Watson. b 35. Qu Mary Coll Lon BSc57 St Cath Soc Ox DipTh60. Wycliffe Hall Ox 59. **d** 61 **p** 62. C Pudsey St Lawr *Bradf* 61-65; V 74-82; V Mortomley St Sav *Sheff* 65-74; V Pudsey St Lawr and St Paul *Bradf* 82-88; Hon Can Bradf Cathl 84-88; RD Calverley 84-88; V Kingston upon Hull H Trin *York* from 88; AD Cen and N Hull from 94; Can and Preb York Minster from 95; RD Hull from 96. *Holy Trinity Vicarage, 66 Pearson Park, Hull HU5 2TQ* Tel (01482) 42292

WALLER, Orlando Alfred. b 12. St Aid Birkenhead 39. **d** 41 **p** 42. C Birkenhead St Pet *Ches* 41-42; C Crewe St Barn 42-45; C Gatley 45-49; Min Heald Green St Cath CD 49-51; V Haslington w Crewe Green 51-54; Australia 54-59; V Runcorn St Jo Weston *Ches* 59-63; V Merrington *Dur* 63-70; P-in-c Bearpark 70-71; V 71-76; rtd 77. *22 Thornley Close, Broom Park, Durham DH7 7NN*

WALLER, Philip Thomas. b 56. Ex Coll Ox BA78 MA88. St Jo Coll Dur BA87. **d** 88 **p** 89. C Enfield St Andr *Lon* 88-91; C Belper *Derby* 91-95; P-in-c Oakwood from 95. *The Vicarage, 239 Morley Road, Oakwood, Derby DE21 4TB* Tel (01332) 667803

WALLES, Bruce Andrew. b 54. Coll of Resurr Mirfield 90. **d** 92 **p** 93. C Maidstone St Martin *Cant* 92-96; TV Banbury *Ox* from 96. *St Leonard's Vicarage, Middleton Road, Banbury, Oxon OX16 8RG* Tel (01295) 262120

WALLING, Mrs Caroline. b 47. **d** 86 **p** 87. Saudi Arabia 89 and 94-96; Par Dn Mottingham St Andr *S'wark* 90; Par Dn Battersea St Mary 91-94; C Lee Gd Shep w St Pet 96. *50 Queen of Denmark Court, Finland Street, London SE16 1TB* Tel 0171-231 3873

WALLINGTON, Paul. b 62. Birm Univ BCom83 ACA86. Trin Coll Bris BA94. **d** 94 **p** 95. C Chorley St Laur *Blackb* 94-97; C Darwen St Pet w Hoddlesden from 97. *St Paul's Vicarage, Johnson New Road, Hoddlesden, Darwen, Lancs BB3 3NN* Tel (01254) 702598

WALLIS, Benjamin John. b 55. Wimbledon Sch of Art BA79. Chich Th Coll 92. **d** 94 **p** 95. C Battersea Ch Ch and St Steph *S'wark* from 94. *Christ Church Flat, Cabul Road, London SW11 2PN* Tel 0171-350 0851

WALLIS, Dr Ian George. b 57. Sheff Univ BA79 PhD92 St Edm Ho Cam MLitt87. Ridley Hall Cam 88. **d** 90 **p** 91. C Armthorpe *Sheff* 90-92; Chapl SS Coll Cam 92-95; Lic to Offic *Ely* 93-95; Hon C Chesterton Gd Shep 95; R Houghton le Spring *Dur* from 95. *The Rectory, Dairy Lane, Houghton le Spring, Tyne & Wear DH4 5BH* Tel 0191-584 2198 Fax 512 1685

WALLIS, Canon John. b 13. Pemb Coll Ox BA36 MA40. Wells Th Coll 36. **d** 37 **p** 38. C Airedale w Fryston *Wakef* 37-39; C Birstall 39-47; V Heckmondwike 47-69; RD Birstall 59-79; Hon Can Wakef Cathl 65-79; V Hartshead 69-79; rtd 79; Perm to Offic *Wakef* 79-94. *Bank Chambers, Albion Road, Ramshill, Scarborough, N Yorkshire YO11 2BX* Tel (01723) 500922

WALLIS, John Anthony. b 36. St Pet Coll Ox BA60 MA65. Clifton Th Coll 60. **d** 62 **p** 63. C Blackpool St Mark *Blackb* 62-65; C Leeds St Geo *Ripon* 65-69; Korea 69-74; Nat Sec (Scotland) OMF 75-78; Home Dir OMF 78-89; Hon C Sevenoaks St Nic *Roch* 78-89; Chapl The Hague *Eur* 89-95; V Northwood Em *Lon* from 95. *Emmanuel Vicarage, 3 Gatehill Road, Northwood, Middx HA6 3QB* Tel (01923) 821598

WALLIS, Paul Justin. b 65. St Jo Coll Nottm BTh90. **d** 90 **p** 91. C Somers Town St Mary *Lon* 90-93; P-in-c Southsea St Pet *Portsm* 93-94. *25 Britannia Road North, Southsea, Hants PO5 1SL*

WALLIS, Raymond Christopher. b 38. Moor Park Coll Farnham 61. Sarum Th Coll 63. **d** 66 **p** 67. C Allerton *Bradf* 66-68; C

Langley Marish *Ox* 68-69; C Caister *Nor* 69-73; P-in-c E w W Bradenham 73-80; R Outwell *Ely* 80-84; R Upwell St Pet 80-84; V Bishopstone *Chich* 84-97; rtd 97; Perm to Offic *Chich* from 97. *The Moorings, Rattle Road, Westham, Eastbourne, E Sussex BN24 5DS*

WALLIS, Roderick Vaughan. b 37. Leic Univ BA79 Warw Univ MA80 Leeds Univ CertEd82 E Lon Poly DCouns90. Lich Th Coll 64. **d** 66 **p** 67. C Cookham *Ox* 66-70; C Daventry *Pet* 70-72; TV Northampton Em 72-76; Hon C 81-89; Hon C Northampton St Matt 76-81; Perm to Offic from 89. *28 Lingswood Park, Northampton NN3 4TA* Tel (01604) 401578

WALLIS, Roland Seabon. b 17. MBE44. Lon Univ BSc38 Ex Univ BSc57. St Aug Coll Cant 75. **d** 77 **p** 78. Hon C Whitstable All SS w St Pet *Cant* 77-84; Hon C Whitstable 84-87; Perm to Offic from 87. *22 Mickleburgh Avenue, Herne Bay, Kent CT6 6HA* Tel (01227) 372263

WALLMAN, Jane Elizabeth. b 61. Homerton Coll Cam BEd83 Bell Educational Trust CertTESOL85 Open Univ ADEd88 Drama Studio Lon DipThe88. St Steph Ho Ox 89 Sarum & Wells Th Coll BTh92. **d** 93 **p** 94. C Woodbridge St Mary *St E* 93-96; V Ipswich St Thos from 96. *St Thomas's Vicarage, 102 Cromer Road, Ipswich IP1 5EP* Tel (01473) 741215

WALLS, Canon Michael Peter. b 38. Cape Town Univ BA57 Lon Univ DipTh61. Wells Th Coll 59. **d** 61 **p** 62. C Morecambe St Barn *Blackb* 61-64; C Birm St Paul *Birm* 64-66; Ind Chapl 64-74; V Temple Balsall 66-74; Chapl Wroxall Abbey Sch 72-74; V Kings Heath *Birm* 74-76; Hon C Small Heath St Greg 76-78; Chapl Oakham Sch 78-83; P-in-c Leic St Sav *Leic* 83-85; P-in-c Knossington and Cold Overton 85-87; P-in-c Owston and Withcote 85-87; V Tilton w Lowesby 85-87; P-in-c 87; V Whatborough Gp of Par 87-90; Bp's Adv Relns w People of Other Faiths 89-93; Hon Can Leic Cathl 89-93; V Leic St Mary 90-93. *358 Aylestone Road, Leicester LE2 8BL*

WALLS, Canon Raymond William. b 10. AKC35. **d** 35 **p** 36. C Bromley St Andr *Roch* 35-38; C Selsdon *Cant* 38-42; P-in-c Bromley St Andr *Roch* 42-45; C Aylesford 45-46; R Eriswell *St E* 46-52; R Glemsford 52-59; P-in-c Somerton 54-59; R Ufford 59-77; Chapl St Audry's Hosp Melton 59-77; Hon Can St E Cathl *St E* 65-77; rtd 77. *4 St Florence Cottages, St Florence, Tenby SA70 8NQ* Tel (01834) 871064

WALLS, Simon Conor. b 67. Dur Univ BA89 TCD MPhil90. **d** 91 **p** 92. C Castleknock and Mulhuddart, w Clonsilla *D & G* 91-93; Chapl Asst Maidstone Hosp 93-95; Chapl R Sussex Co Hosp Brighton from 95. *Royal Sussex County Hospital, Eastern Road, Brighton BN2 5BE* Tel (01273) 696955

WALMISLEY, Andrew John. b 55. Ex Univ BA75. Ridley Hall Cam 76. **d** 78 **p** 79. C W Brompton St Mary w St Pet *Lon* 78-81; USA from 81. *2601 Derby Street, Berkeley, California 94705, USA*

WALMSLEY, Derek. b 57. Oak Hill Th Coll DipHE91. **d** 91 **p** 92. C Bletchley *Ox* 91-95; C Utley *Bradf* from 95. *194 Skipton Road, Keighley, W Yorkshire BD21 2SY* Tel (01535) 681448

WALMSLEY, George Bernard. b 07. Leeds Univ BA29. Coll of Resurr Mirfield 25. **d** 31 **p** 32. C Llandysilio (or Menai Bridge) *Ban* 31-33; C Llandudno 33-39; V Beddgelert 39-46; R Pentraeth and Llanddyfnan 46-51; P-in-c S Yardley St Mich *Birm* 51-55; V Witton 55-59; V Meerbrook *Lich* 59-72; P-in-c Quarnford 65-72; rtd 72; Perm to Offic *Lich* from 72. *46 Parker Street, Leek, Staffs ST13 6LB* Tel (01538) 373927

WALMSLEY, John William. b 37. Hull Univ BA71 MA73 PhD81. Wycliffe Hall Ox 71. **d** 72 **p** 73. C Clifton *York* 72-74; C Acomb St Steph 74-76; P-in-c Newton upon Ouse 76-81; P-in-c Shipton w Overton 76-81; V York St Thos w St Maurice 81-89; V Barkingside St Laur *Chelmsf* 89-92; Dir Romanian Children's Aid from 92. *Unit 2/1 Thirsk Industrial Park, York Road, Thirsk, N Yorkshire YO7 3BX* Tel (01845) 526272

WALMSLEY-McLEOD, Paul Albert. b 56. St Cuth Soc Dur BA82 Cam Univ CertEd83. Westcott Ho Cam 85. **d** 87 **p** 88. C Gt Bookham *Guildf* 87-90; Asst Chapl St Chris Hospice Sydenham 90-93; Soc Care Team Member Phoenix Ho Fountain Project 93-95; Perm to Offic *S'wark* 93-95; C Catford (Southend) and Downham 95-96; TV from 96. *St Barnabas Vicarage, 1 Churchdown, Bromley, Kent BR1 5PS* Tel 0181-698 4851

WALNE, John Clifford. b 29. Wycliffe Hall Ox. **d** 87 **p** 88. NSM Hedsor and Bourne End *Ox* 87-88; Hon C Lezayre St Olave Ramsey *S & M* 88-92; Hon C Bride 88-92; P-in-c Berrington and Betton Strange *Heref* 92-97; rtd 97. *2 Bell Close, Beaconsfield, Bucks HP9 1AT* Tel (01494) 670120

WALROND-SKINNER, Susan Mary. b 42. Bris Univ BA63 CertEd68 Univ of Wales DASS70. Bris Minl Tr Scheme 82 Ripon Coll Cuddesdon. **dss** 84 **d** 87 **p** 94. Assoc Dir of Ords *Bris* 84-86; Continuing Minl Educn Officer 87-91; Dir Past Care and Counselling *S'wark* from 91. *St Michael's Vicarage, 78 Stockwell Park Road, London SW9 0DA* Tel 0171-733 867

WALSALL, Archdeacon of. *Vacant*

WALSER, Emil Jonathan. b 16. St Jo Coll Dur LTh38 BA39 MA43. Oak Hill Th Coll 35. **d** 39 **p** 40. C Holloway St Mary Magd *Lon* 39-42; C Pudsey St Lawr *Bradf* 42-46; R Whalley Range St Edm *Man* 46-52; V Mackworth All SS *Derby* 52-65; P-in-c Kirk Langley 57-59; R 59-65; V Baslow 65-82; RD Bakewell and Eyam 78-81; rtd 82. *2 Almond Grove, Filey, N Yorkshire YO14 9EH* Tel (01723) 515582

WALSER (née SHIELS), Mrs Rosalinde Cameron. b 47. Edin Univ MA68 Moray Ho Coll of Educn PGCE69. N Ord Course 92. **d** 95 **p** 96. NSM Scarborough St Mary w Ch Ch and H Apostles *York* from 95. *29 Sea Cliff Road, Scarborough, N Yorkshire YO11 2XU* Tel (01723) 372382

WALSH, Bertram William Nicholas. b 21. TCD BA44. CITC 46. **d** 46 **p** 47. C Dublin St Pet w St Matthias *D & G* 46-47; Min Can St Patr Cathl Dublin 47-49; C Dublin St Jas *D & G* 47-49; Res Preacher Cork Cathl *C, C & R* 49-52; C Dublin St Bart *D & G* 52-54; Clerical V Ch Ch Cathl Dublin 54-58; Chapl St Columba's Coll Dub 60-87; rtd 87. *130 Grange Road, Rathfarnham, Dublin 14, Irish Republic* Tel Dublin (1) 493 1229

✠**WALSH, The Rt Revd Geoffrey David Jeremy.** b 29. Pemb Coll Cam BA53 MA58. Linc Th Coll 53. **d** 55 **p** 56 **c** 86. C Southgate Ch Ch *Lon* 55-58; SCM Sec Cam 58-61; C Cambridge Gt St Mary w St Mich *Ely* 58-61; V Moorfields *Bris* 61-66; R Marlborough *Sarum* 66-76; Can and Preb Sarum Cathl 73-76; Adn Ipswich *St E* 76-86; R Elmsett w Aldham 76-80; Suff Bp Tewkesbury *Glouc* 86-95; rtd 95. *6 Warren Lane, Martlesham Heath, Ipswich IP5 7SH* Tel (01473) 620797

WALSH, Geoffrey Malcolm. b 46. Sarum & Wells Th Coll 82. **d** 84 **p** 85. C Wellington and Distr *B & W* 84-87; TV Axminster, Chardstock, Combe Pyne and Rousdon *Ex* 87-90; Chapl RN 90-94; R Huntspill *B & W* from 94. *The Rectory, Church Road, West Huntspill, Highbridge, Somerset TA9 3RN* Tel (01278) 793950

WALSH, John Alan. b 37. Chich Th Coll 63. **d** 66 **p** 67. C Wigan St Anne *Liv* 66-69; C Newport w Longford *Lich* 69-73; V Dunstall 73-83; V Rangemore 73-83; P-in-c Tatenhill 77-83; R Dunstall w Rangemore and Tatenhill 83; V Hartshill from 83. *Holy Trinity Vicarage, Hartshill, Stoke-on-Trent ST4 7NJ* Tel (01782) 616965

WALSH, Julia Christine (Sister Julian). b 20. K Coll Lon DipTh49. Gilmore Ho 46. **dss** 56 **d** 87 **p** 94. CSA 53-90; rtd 96. *St Andrew's House, 2 Tavistock Road, London W11 1BA* Tel 0171-229 2662

WALSH, Peter. b 64. Liv Univ BA86 Nottm Univ BTh90. Linc Th Coll 87. **d** 90 **p** 91. C Cantley *Sheff* 90-93; C Poulton-le-Fylde *Blackb* 93-95; V Blackpool St Steph from 95. *The Vicarage, St Stephen's Avenue, Blackpool FY2 9RB* Tel (01253) 351484

WALSHE, Canon Brian. b 28. AKC49. St Boniface Warminster. **d** 54 **p** 55. C Southsea St Pet *Portsm* 54-57; C Portsea St Jo Rudmore 57-58; Warden Wellington Coll Miss Walworth 58-62; V Chesterfield St Aug *Derby* 62-68; R Langley Marish *Ox* 68-76; Chapl Manfield Hosp Northn 76-88; V Northampton St Alb *Pet* 76-88; Dir Mountbatten Community Trust from 76; Chief Exec Lon Youth Trust from 87; rtd 88; Perm to Offic *Pet* 88-93; Perm to Offic *Chich* from 93. *9/10 Warrior Court, 16 Warrior Way, St Leonards-on-Sea, E Sussex TN37 6BS*

WALT, Trevor. RMN74 RNT79. Ox NSM Course 83. **d** 86 **p** 87. NSM Crowthorne *Ox* from 86; Chapl Asst Broadmoor Hosp Crowthorne 86-89; Chapl from 89. *Broadmoor Hospital, Crowthorne, Berks RG45 7EG* Tel (01344) 773111 or 773999

WALTER, Christopher Stuart Radclyffe (Chris). b 47. Sarum & Wells Th Coll DipTh93. **d** 93 **p** 94. C Fakenham w Alethorpe *Nor* 93-96; P-in-c Buxton w Oxnead, Lammas and Brampton from 96. *The Vicarage, Back Lane, Buxton, Norwich NR10 5HD* Tel (01603) 279394

WALTER, Donald Alex. b 34. Ripon Hall Ox 57. **d** 60 **p** 61. C Ealing St Steph Castle Hill *Lon* 60-63; Jamaica 63-80; V Twickenham Common H Trin *Lon* from 81. *Holy Trinity Vicarage, 1 Vicarage Road, Twickenham TW2 5TS* Tel 0181-898 1168

WALTER, Giles Robert. b 54. Cam Univ MA76. Cranmer Hall Dur 78. **d** 82 **p** 83. C Finchley Ch Ch *Lon* 82-86; C Cambridge H Sepulchre w All SS *Ely* 86-92; C Cambridge H Sepulchre 92-93; P-in-c Tunbridge Wells St Jo *Roch* 93-95; V from 95. *St John's Vicarage, 1 Amherst Road, Tunbridge Wells, Kent TN4 9LG* Tel (01892) 521183

WALTER, Ian Edward. b 47. Edin Univ MA69 Keble Coll Ox BA71 MA78. Cuddesdon Coll 71. **d** 73 **p** 74. C Greenock *Glas* 73-76; C Glas St Mary 76-79; Chapl Angl Students Glas 76-79; R Paisley St Barn 79-84; P-in-c Bolton St Phil *Man* 84-86; V 86-91; Bp's Ecum Adv from 89; V Elton All SS from 91. *All Saints' Vicarage, 90 Tottington Road, Bury, Lancs BL8 1LR* Tel 0161-764 1431

WALTER, Michael. b 36. AKC62. **d** 63 **p** 64. C Middlesbrough St Jo the Ev *York* 63-65; C Sherborne *Win* 65-68; C Bournemouth St Fran 68-69; Prec Newc Cathl *Newc* 69-71; C Dur St Marg *Dur* 72-74; P-in-c Deaf Hill cum Langdale 74-77; V Newington w Dairycoates *York* 77-88; Perm to Offic 88-92; C Feltham *Lon* 92-96; Perm to Offic from 96. *52 Royal Road, Teddington, Middx TW11 0SB* Tel 0181-943 4212

WALTER, Noel. b 41. St D Coll Lamp DipTh66. **d** 66 **p** 67. C Mitcham Ascension *S'wark* 66-71; C Caterham 71-74; V Welling 74-82; C Warlingham w Chelsham and Farleigh 82-88; Chapl Warlingham Park Hosp Croydon 82-88; Chapl R Earlswood Hosp Redhill 88-90; Chapl Redhill Gen Hosp 88-91; Chapl E Surrey Hosp Redhill 88-96; Sen Chapl Gt Ormond Street Hosp for Children NHS Trust from 96. *Great Ormond Street Hospital, Great Ormond Street, London WC1N 3JH, or 3 Carleton Villas, Leighton Grove, London NW5 2QU* Tel 0171-405 9200, 813 8232 or 4822133

WALTER, Peter John. b 44. CEng MIGasE. Chich Th Coll 80. **d** 82 **p** 83. C Leominster *Heref* 82-85; P-in-c Brimfield 85-90; P-in-c Orleton 85-90; R Orleton w Brimfield 91-95. *12 Rainbow Street, Leominster, Herefordshire HR6 8DQ*

WALTER, Robin. b 37. Univ Coll Dur BA63 MA90 Linacre Coll Ox BA65 MA69. St Steph Ho Ox 63. **d** 66 **p** 68. C Peckham St Jo *S'wark* 66-69; Chapl Lon Univ *Lon* 69-70; C Dur St Marg *Dur* 70-74; R Burnmoor 74-79; Asst Master Barnard Castle Sch 79-97; Lic to Offic 79-82; Hon C Whorlton 82-88; NSM Barnard Castle Deanery 88-97; P-in-c Redmarshall from 97; P-in-c Bishopton w Gt Stainton from 97. *The Rectory, Redmarshall, Stockton-on-Tees, Cleveland TS21 1EP* Tel (01740) 30810

WALTERS, Andrew Farrar. b 42. ACP67 St Luke's Coll Ex CertEd71. **d** 81 **p** 82. Hd Master and Warden St Mich Coll Tenbury 77-85; Chapl Ex Cathl Sch 85-87; Hd Master Homefield Sch Sutton 87-92; Hd Master Lich Cathl Sch from 92; Hon C Sutton St Nic *S'wark* 87-92. *Lichfield Cathedral School, The Palace, Lichfield, Staffs WS13 7LH* Tel (01543) 263326

WALTERS, Christopher John Linley. b 24. St Pet Hall Ox BA47 MA49. Linc Th Coll 48. **d** 50 **p** 51. C Dartford Ch Ch *Roch* 50-53; C Oswestry St Oswald *Lich* 53-56; V Weston Rhyn 56-61; V Newcastle St Paul 61-70; V Pattingham 70-85; P-in-c Patshull 77-85; V Pattingham w Patshull 85-89; rtd 89; Perm to Offic *Heref* from 93. *Old School House, 19 Cardington, Church Stretton, Shropshire SY6 7JZ* Tel (01694) 771528

WALTERS, David Michael Trenham. b 46. Open Univ BA86. St D Coll Lamp DipTh69. **d** 69 **p** 70. C Killay *S & B* 69-72; CF 72-89 and from 91; Chapl Eagle Ho Prep Sch Crowthorne 89-91. *MOD Chaplains (Army), Trenchard Lines, Upavon, Pewsey, Wilts SN9 6BE* Tel (01980) 615804 Fax 615800

WALTERS, David Trevor. b 37. Ex Coll Ox BA58 MA62. St Steph Ho Ox 62. **d** 64 **p** 65. C Cardiff St Mary *Llan* 64-69; C Brecon w Battle *S & B* 69-73; Min Can Brecon Cathl 69-73; V Llanddew and Talachddu 73-78; V Cefncoed and Capel Nantddu 78-80; V Cefn Coed and Capel Nantddu w Vaynor etc 80-87; V Talgarth and Llanelieu from 87. *The Vicarage, 10 Bronant, Talgarth, Brecon LD3 0HF* Tel (01874) 711249

WALTERS, Canon Douglas Lewis. b 20. Univ of Wales BA41. St Mich Coll Llan 41. **d** 43 **p** 44. C Milford Haven *St D* 43-48; C Llanelli 48-52; R Llangwm 52-58; V Kidwelly 58-80; RD Cydweli 77-85; Can St D Cathl 78-86; V Cydweli and Llandyfaelog 80-86; rtd 86. *83 Ashburnham Road, Burry Port SA16 0TW* Tel (01554) 834139

WALTERS, Canon Francis Raymond. b 24. Ball Coll Ox BA49 MA54. Wycliffe Hall Ox 51. **d** 53 **p** 54. C Boulton *Derby* 53-56; Lect Qu Coll Birm 56-64; Succ Birm Cathl *Birm* 56-58; C Harborne St Pet 58-64; V Leic St Nic *Leic* 64-74; Chapl Leic Univ 64-74; R Appleby 74-77; Dioc Dir of Educn 77-89; Hon Can Leic Cathl 77-91; P-in-c Swithland 77-91; rtd 91; Perm to Offic *Nor* from 91. *2 Beeston Common, Sheringham, Norfolk NR26 8ES* Tel (01263) 824414

WALTERS, Ian Robert. b 51. ACA75 FCA81. LNSM course 80. **d** 85 **p** 86. NSM Ingoldsby *Linc* from 85. *Dairy Farmhouse, Westby, Grantham, Lincs NG33 4EA* Tel (0147685) 542

WALTERS, John Morgan. b 09. **d** 34 **p** 35. New Zealand 34-37; C Folke w Long Burton, N Wootton and Haydon *Sarum* 39; C Lt Bardfield *Chelmsf* 39-40; C Radlett *St Alb* 40-42; P-in-c Watford St Jas 42-43; V Dean w Shelton 43-48; V Hexton 48-52; R Higham Gobion 48-52; V High Wych 52-74; RD Bishop's Stortford 63-67; rtd 74; Perm to Offic *St E* from 75. *5 Cannonfields, Bury St Edmunds, Suffolk IP33 1JX* Tel (01284) 761010

WALTERS, John Philip Hewitt. b 50. Coll of Resurr Mirfield 72. **d** 73 **p** 74. C Llangiwg *S & B* 73-76; Min Can Brecon Cathl 76-79; C Brecon w Battle 76-79; V Merthyr Cynog and Dyffryn Honddu etc 79-83; V Llandeilo Tal-y-bont from 83. *The Vicarage, 28 Bolgoed Road, Pontardulais, Swansea SA4 1JE* Tel (01792) 882468

WALTERS, Leslie Ernest Ward. b 27. Wadh Coll Ox BA51 MA55. Ridley Hall Cam 55. **d** 57 **p** 58. C Heref St Pet w St Owen *Heref* 57-59; C Morden *S'wark* 59-61; V Felbridge 61-68; V Streatham Immanuel w St Anselm 68-81; V Cotmanhay *Derby* 81-92; Chapl Ilkeston Gen Hosp 81-88; Chapl Ilkeston Community Hosp 88-92; rtd 92; Perm to Offic *Nor* from 93. *Rokeby, Taverham Road, Felthorpe, Norwich NR10 4DR* Tel (0160548) 5134

WALTERS, Canon Michael William. b 39. Dur Univ BSc61. Clifton Th Coll 61. **d** 63 **p** 64. C Aldershot H Trin *Guildf* 63-66; C Upper Armley *Ripon* 66-69; NE Area Sec CPAS 69-75; V Hyde St Geo *Ches* 75-82; V Knutsford St Jo and Toft from 82; Hon Can Ches Cathl from 94. *The Vicarage, 11 Gough's Lane, Knutsford, Cheshire WA16 8QL* Tel (01565) 632834

WALTERS, Nicholas Humphrey. b 45. K Coll Lon BD67 AKC67. **d** 68 **p** 69. C Weston *Guildf* 68-71; Chapl and Lect NE Surrey Coll of Tech Ewell 71-77; Hon C Ewell 71-77; Warden Moor Park Coll Farnham 77-80; Tutor Surrey Univ *Guildf* from 80; Dir of Studies Guildf Inst from 82; Lic to Offic from 84. *9 Valley View, Godalming, Surrey GU7 1RD* Tel (01483) 415106

WALTERS, Peter. b 27. Leeds Univ BSc48 Univ of Wales (Abth) MSc52. Ripon Coll Cuddesdon 78. **d** 79 **p** 80. C Kingswood *Bris* 79-82; R Stanton St Quintin, Hullavington, Grittleton etc 82-88; rtd 88; Perm to Offic *Glouc* from 88. *Newcombes End, Elkstone, Cheltenham, Glos GL53 9PD* Tel (01242) 870258

WALTERS, Peter Shane. b 54. SS Paul & Mary Coll Cheltenham DipRS83 Univ of Wales (Cardiff) BD87. St Mich Coll Llan 84. **d** 87 **p** 88. C Newport St Julian *Mon* 87-90; Asst Admin of Shrine of Our Lady of Walsingham 91-93; Lic to Offic *Nor* 91-93; Colombia from 93. *Address temp unknown*

WALTERS, The Very Revd Rhys Derrick Chamberlain. b 32. OBE94. LSE BSc55. Ripon Hall Ox. **d** 57 **p** 58. C Manselton *S & B* 57-58; C Swansea St Mary and H Trin 58-62; Chapl Univ of Wales (Swansea) 58-62; V Totley *Sheff* 62-67; V Boulton *Derby* 67-74; Dioc Missr *Sarum* 74-83; P-in-c Burcombe 74-79; Can and Preb Sarum Cathl 77-79; Can Res and Treas Sarum Cathl 79-83; Dean Liv from 83. *The Deanery, 1 Cathedral Close, Liverpool L1 7BR* Tel 0151-708 0924

WALTERS, Mrs Rosemary Anne. b 38. JP72 DL85. Oak Hill Th Coll 93. **d** 96 **p** 97. NSM Lambourne w Abridge and Stapleford Abbotts *Chelmsf* from 96. *31 Connaught Avenue, Loughton, Essex IG10 4DS* Tel 0181-508 2543 Fax 282 0660

WALTERS, Mrs Sheila Ann Beatrice. b 37. Bris Univ DipEd58. EMMTC 85. **d** 89 **p** 94. NSM Ashby-de-la-Zouch St Helen w Coleorton *Leic* from 89. *115 Loughborough Road, Coleorton, Coalville, Leics LE67 8HH* Tel (01530) 832267

WALTERS, Thomas. b 24. St Deiniol's Hawarden. **d** 79 **p** 80. NSM Bardsley *Man* 79-94; rtd 90; Perm to Offic *Man* from 90. *49 Fir Tree Avenue, Oldham, Lancs OL8 2QS* Tel 0161-652 4108

WALTHEW, Mrs Nancy Jennifer. b 39. Leeds Inst of Educn CertEd59 Ripon Coll of Educn RTC59. N Ord Course 92. **d** 95 **p** 96. NSM Wilmslow *Ches* from 95. *Ashburn, 13 Priory Road, Wilmslow, Cheshire SK9 5PS* Tel (01625) 525462

WALTON, Mrs Alison Claire (Ali). b 59. Homerton Coll Cam BEd82. Lon Bible Coll DPS87 Oak Hill Th Coll DipHE89 BA90 MPhil92. **d** 92. C Bedford Ch Ch *St Alb* 92-94; Perm to Offic 94-95; Perm to Offic *S'well* from 95. *1 Peache Way, Chilwell Lane, Bramcote, Nottingham NG9 3DX* Tel 0115-922 9499

WALTON, Brian. b 53. Sarum & Wells Th Coll 83. **d** 85 **p** 86. C Silksworth *Dur* 85-86; C Bishopwearmouth St Mich w St Hilda 86-88; Chapl RN 88-92; V Sugley *Newc* 92-95; Chapl Lemington Hosp 92-95; CF from 95. *MOD Chaplains (Army), Trenchard Lines, Upavon, Pewsey, Wilts SN9 6BE* Tel (01980) 615804 Fax 615800

WALTON, The Ven Geoffrey Elmer. b 34. Dur Univ BA59. Qu Coll Birm DipTh61. **d** 61 **p** 62. C Warsop *S'well* 61-65; Dioc Youth Chapl 65-69; V Norwell 65-69; Recruitment Sec ACCM 69-75; V Weymouth H Trin *Sarum* 75-82; RD Weymouth 79-82; Can and Preb Sarum Cathl from 81; Adn Dorset from 82; P-in-c Witchampton and Hinton Parva, Long Crichel etc from 82; V Witchampton, Stanbridge and Long Crichel etc from 96. *The Vicarage, Witchampton, Wimborne, Dorset BH21 5AP* Tel (01258) 840422

WALTON, John Victor. b 45. Lon Univ BSc67. Linc Th Coll 79. **d** 81 **p** 82. C Stevenage St Mary Shephall *St Alb* 81-85; TV Bourne Valley *Sarum* 85-95; P-in-c Puddletown and Tolpuddle from 95. *The Vicarage, The Square, Puddletown, Dorchester, Dorset DT2 8SL* Tel (01305) 848216

WALTON, Kevin Anthony. b 64. St Chad's Coll Dur BA87. Trin Coll Bris BA91. **d** 92 **p** 93. C Stranton *Dur* 92-95; C Hartlepool H Trin 95-96; V Sunderland St Mary and St Pet from 96. *St Mary's Clergy House, Springwell Road, Sunderland SR2 4DY* Tel 0191-528 3754

WALTON, Maurice James. b 31. RIBA54 MRTPI55 Liv Univ BArch53 MCD54. Wycliffe Hall Ox 93. **d** 94 **p** 95. NSM Billing *Pet* 94-97; NSM Church Brampton, Chapel Brampton, Harleston etc from 97. *Caldecote, Garrick Road, Northampton NN1 5ND* Tel (01604) 20760

WALTON, Philip William. b 28. Dur Univ BScAgr52. Tyndale Hall Bris 54. **d** 56 **p** 58. C Clerkenwell St Jas and St Jo w St Pet *Lon* 56-57; C St Alb St Paul *St Alb* 57-59; C Haydock St Mark *Liv* 58-60; V Wiggenhall St Mary Magd *Ely* 60-66; Sec CCCS 66-69; Chapl Maisons-Laffitte w Versailles and Caen *Eur* 69-74; V Worthing Ch Ch *Chich* 74-85; R Wigmore Abbey *Heref* 85-92; rtd 92; Perm to Offic *Heref* from 92. *Larkey Lodge, The Cwm, Knighton LD7 1HF*

WALTON, Reginald Arthur. b 40. St Jo Coll Nottm 80. **d** 81 **p** 82. C Woodthorpe *S'well* 81-84; P-in-c Nottingham St Andr 84-85; V 85-91; R Moreton *Ches* from 91. *The Rectory, Dawpool Drive, Moreton, South Wirral L46 0PH* Tel 0151-677 3540

WALTON, Stephen John (Steve). b 55. Birm Univ BSc76 Fitzw Coll Cam BA79 MA82 Sheff Univ PhD97. Ridley Hall Cam 77. **d** 83 **p** 84. C Bebington *Ches* 83-86; Voc and Min Adv CPAS 86-92; Lic to Offic *St Alb* 86-94; Bp's Dom Chapl 94-95; Lect St Jo Coll Nottm from 95; Public Preacher *S'well* from 95. *St John's College, Chilwell Lane, Bramcote, Nottingham NG9 3DS* Tel 0115-925 1114 or 922 9499 Fax 943 6438

WALTON, Wilfred James. b 14. St Jo Coll Dur BA39 MA51. **d** 39 **p** 40. C Tipton St Matt *Lich* 39-42; C Bloxwich 42-45; P-in-c Walsall St Mark 45-47; Kenya 47-52; V Bloxwich *Lich* 52-60; R Newport w Longford 60-61; Asst Master Aston Comp Sch 61-79;

Lic to Offic *Sheff* from 68; rtd 79; Perm to Offic *Derby* from 79. *25 Main Avenue, Totley, Sheffield S17 4FH* Tel 0114-236 7183

WAMBUNYA, Timothy Livingstone (Amboko). b 66. Simon of Cyrene Th Inst 93 Oak Hill Th Coll DipHE94 BA94. **d** 97. C Southall Green St Jo *Lon* from 97. *9 Derley Road, Southall, Middx UB2 5EJ* Tel 0181-574 5016 Mobile 0370-887232

WANDSWORTH, Archdeacon of. *See* GERRARD, The Ven David Keith Robin

WANJIE, Lukas Macharia. b 50. Fitzw Coll Cam BA79 MA83. St Paul's Coll Limuru 72 Ridley Hall Cam 76. **d** 75 **p** 76. Kenya 75-76 and 80-91; Prin Trin Bib Coll Nairobi 85-91; C Mill End and Heronsgate w W Hyde *St Alb* 79; C St Alb St Steph 91-94; Perm to Offic 94-95. *59 Manor Road, London Colney, St Albans, Herts AL2 1PP* Tel (01727) 824340

WANN, Canon Denis Francis. b 27. TCD BA55 MA77. Div Test. **d** 56 **p** 57. C Belfast St Donard *D & D* 56-58; Tanzania 58-65; The Philippines 65-72; Hon Can Moro from 72; C Lurgan Ch the Redeemer *D & D* 72-73; Australia 73-91 and from 95; Adn Wollongong and Camden 82-84; I Bailieborough w Knockbride, Shercock and Mullagh *K, E & A* 91-95. *35 Lackersteen Street, Callala Bay, NSW, Australia 2540* Tel Callala Bay (44) 466179

WANSTALL, Noelle Margaret. *See* HALL, Canon Noelle Margaret

WARBRICK, Quentin David. b 66. Jes Coll Ox BA88. Cranmer Hall Dur 89. **d** 92 **p** 93. C Birm St Martin w Bordesley St Andr *Birm* 92-96; C Handsworth St Jas from 96. *51 Westbourne Road, Handsworth, Birmingham B21 8AU* Tel 0121-253 3439

WARBURTON, Andrew James. b 44. Oak Hill Th Coll 64. **d** 69 **p** 70. C New Milverton *Cov* 69-72; C Fulham St Matt *Lon* 72-76; C Chesham St Mary *Ox* 76-80; TV Gt Chesham 80-94; Chapl Paris St Mich *Eur* 94-97. *Address temp unknown*

WARBURTON, John Bryce. b 33. St Aid Birkenhead 64. **d** 66 **p** 67. C Padiham *Blackb* 66-69; C Burnley St Pet 69-70; V Tideswell *Derby* 70-81; V Bollington St Jo *Ches* 81-91; V Capesthorne w Siddington and Marton from 91. *The Vicarage, School Lane, Marton, Macclesfield, Cheshire SK11 9HD* Tel (01260) 224447

WARBURTON, Piers Eliot de Dutton. b 30. Cranmer Hall Dur BA65. **d** 65 **p** 66. C Grassendale *Liv* 65-68; Bermuda 68-71; R Sherborne *Win* 71-76; V Yateley 76-82; R Guernsey St Andr 82-89; V Hartley Wintney, Elvetham, Winchfield etc from 89. *The Vicarage, Church Lane, Hartley Wintney, Basingstoke, Hants RG27 8DZ* Tel (01252) 842670

WARBURTON, Canon Robert Tinsley. b 23. MBE66 TD69. Jes Coll Cam BA47 MA52. Oak Hill Th Coll 47. **d** 47 **p** 48. C Ipswich St Marg *St E* 47-50; R Dallinghoo and Pettistree 50-54; P-in-c Playford w Culpho and Tuddenham St Martin 52-54; V Attenborough w Bramcote *S'well* 54-67; RD Beeston 60-67; CF (TA) from 55; RD Mansfield *S'well* 67-92; P-in-c Teversal 68-72; Hon Can S'well Minster from 72; V Mansfield St Pet from 97. *The Vicarage, Lindhurst Lane, Mansfield, Notts NG18 4JE* Tel (01623) 21600

WARBURTON, Walter George. b 16. Bede Coll Dur BA40 DipTh42 MA43. **d** 41 **p** 42. C Witton *Blackb* 41-45; C Accrington Ch Ch 45-46; V Bolton St Barn *Man* 46-52; V Stonefold *Blackb* 52-60; V Gt Marsden 60-81; rtd 81; Lic to Offic *Blackb* from 81. *145 Halifax Road, Nelson, Lancs BB9 0EL* Tel (01282) 697589

WARCHUS, Michael Edward George. b 37. Lon Univ DipTh67. Roch Th Coll 65. **d** 68 **p** 69. C Buckhurst Hill *Chelmsf* 68-71; C Stainton-in-Cleveland *York* 71-76; V Carlton and Drax 76-86; V Acomb St Steph from 86. *The Vicarage, 32 Carr Lane, Acomb, York YO2 5HX* Tel (01904) 798106

WARD, Alan William. b 56. Trin Coll Bris 80. **d** 81 **p** 82. C New Ferry *Ches* 81-86; Dioc Youth Officer 86-91; C Charlesworth and Dinting Vale *Derby* 91-96; V Mickleover All SS from 96. *All Saints' Vicarage, Etwall Road, Mickleover, Derby DE3 5DL* Tel (01332) 513793

WARD, Albert George. b 27. K Coll Lon BD54 AKC54. **d** 55 **p** 56. C Birstall *Wakef* 55-57; C Gt Berkhamsted *St Alb* 57-60; V Corby St Columba *Pet* 60-66; R Walgrave w Hannington and Wold 66-69; TR Usworth *Dur* 69-78; V S Shields St Simon 78-86; C Darlington St Cuth 86-88; rtd 88. *25 West Crescent, Darlington, Co Durham DL3 7PS* Tel (01325) 351572

WARD, Alfred John. b 37. Coll of Resurr Mirfield. **d** 93 **p** 94. C Hendon St Mary *Lon* from 93. *St Mary's Cottage, 48 Church End, London NW4 4JX* Tel 0181-203 4673

WARD, Mrs Alisoun Mary. b 52. Univ of Wales BA74. Ridley Hall Cam 94. **d** 96 **p** 97. C S Woodham Ferrers *Chelmsf* from 96. *25 Benbow Drive, South Woodham Ferrers, Chelmsford CM3 5FP* Tel (01245) 325593

WARD, Anthony Colin (Tony). b 55. Wycliffe Hall Ox 78. **d** 80 **p** 81. Zimbabwe 80-85; S Africa 85-90; Asst P Leic H Trin w St Jo *Leic* 90-96; R Rainham w Wennington *Chelmsf* from 96. *The Vicarage, Broadway, Rainham, Essex RM13 9YW* Tel (01708) 552752

WARD, Anthony Peter. b 46. Bris Univ BSc67 Ox Univ DipEd68. St Jo Coll Nottm. **d** 82 **p** 83. C Hellesdon *Nor* 82-85; P-in-c Nor St Aug w St Mary 85-91; P-in-c Norwich-over-the-Water Colegate St Geo 85-90; Norfolk Churches' Radio Officer 85-95; TV Norwich Over-the-Water 91-95; V Gorleston St Andr from 95. *The Vicarage, Duke Road, Gorleston, Great Yarmouth, Norfolk NR31 6LL* Tel (01493) 663477

WARD, The Ven Arthur Frederick. b 12. Armstrong Coll Dur BA33. Ridley Hall Cam 33. **d** 35 **p** 36. C Byker St Mich *Newc* 35-40; R Harpurhey Ch Ch *Man* 40-44; V Nelson in Lt Marsden *Blackb* 44-55; V Paignton Ch Ch *Ex* 55-62; Adn Barnstaple 62-70; R Shirwell w Loxhore 62-70; Preb Ex Cathl 70-89; Adn Ex and Can Res Ex Cathl 70-81; Prec 72-81; rtd 81; Perm to Offic *Ex* from 89. *Melrose, Christow, Exeter EX6 7LY* Tel (01647) 252498

WARD, Arthur John. b 32. Lon Univ BD57. St Aid Birkenhead 57. **d** 57 **p** 58. C Ecclesfield *Sheff* 57-60; C Fulwood 60-63; Tutor St Aid Birkenhead 63-66; R Denton St Lawr *Man* 66-74; CMS 74-82; TV Wolverhampton *Lich* 82-90; V Edgbaston SS Mary and Ambrose *Birm* 90-96; rtd 96. *Bramble Cottage, 6 Lower Forge, Eardington, Bridgnorth, Shropshire WV16 5LQ* Tel (01746) 764758

WARD, Canon Calvin. b 34. Univ of Wales BA57 DipEd60 Fitzw Ho Cam BA63 MA67. Westcott Ho Cam 61. **d** 64 **p** 65. C Handsworth St Mich *Birm* 64-66; C Shaw Hill 66-69; V Windhill *Bradf* 69-76; V Esholt 76-81; V Oakworth 81-91; V Allerton from 91; Hon Can Bradf Cathl from 94. *The Vicarage, Leytop Lane, Allerton, Bradford, W Yorkshire BD15 7LT* Tel (01274) 541948

WARD, Christopher John William. b 36. Bps' Coll Cheshunt 66 Qu Coll Birm 68. **d** 69 **p** 70. C Wednesbury St Bart *Lich* 69-73; CF 73-93; rtd 93; Perm to Offic *Sarum* from 93. *6 Meadow View, Blandford Forum, Dorset DT11 7JB* Tel (01258) 455140

WARD, David. b 40. St Jo Coll Nottm 83. **d** 85 **p** 86. C Aspley *S'well* 85-89; V from 89. *St Margaret's Vicarage, 319 Aspley Lane, Nottingham NG8 5GA* Tel 0115-929 2920

WARD, David Conisbee. b 33. St Jo Coll Cam BA54 MA59. S'wark Ord Course 77. **d** 80 **p** 81. NSM Surbiton St Matt *S'wark* 80-83; C Streatham Immanuel w St Anselm 83-84; P-in-c 84-87; V Hook 87-93; rtd 93; Perm to Offic *S'wark* from 94; Perm to Offic *Chich* from 94. *50 Elgar Avenue, Surbiton, Surrey KT9 9JN* Tel 0181-399 9679

WARD, David Robert. b 51. Oak Hill Th Coll 74. **d** 77 **p** 78. C Kirkheaton *Wakef* 77-81; V Earl's Heaton 81-88; V Bradley from 88. *The Vicarage, 87 Bradley Road, Huddersfield HD2 1RA* Tel (01484) 427838

WARD, David Towle Greenfield. b 22. Ch Coll Cam BA47 MA49. Linc Th Coll 47. **d** 49 **p** 50. C Heigham St Barn *Nor* 49-53; C Diss 53-55; V Gayton 55-64; V Potter Heigham 64-77; V Repps 64-77; R Ditchingham w Pirnough 77-87; R Broome 77-87; R Hedenham 77-87; rtd 87; Perm to Offic *Nor* from 87. *Manor Cottage, 58 Mount Street, Diss, Norfolk IP22 3QQ* Tel (01379) 651328

WARD, The Ven Edwin James Greenfield. b 19. LVO63. Ch Coll Cam BA46 MA48. Ridley Hall Cam 46. **d** 48 **p** 49. C E Dereham w Hoe *Nor* 48-50; V N Elmham w Billingford 50-55; Chapl to The Queen 55-90; Extra Chapl to The Queen from 90; R W Stafford w Frome Billet *Sarum* 67-84; Can and Preb Sarum Cathl 67-84; Adn Sherborne 67-84; rtd 85. *14 Arle Close, Alresford, Hants SO24 9BG* Tel (01962) 735501

WARD, Ms Frances Elizabeth Fearn. b 59. St Andr Univ MTh83 Jes Coll Cam DipTh89. Westcott Ho Cam 87. **d** 89 **p** 94. Par Dn Westhoughton *Man* 89-93; Tutor Practical Th N Coll Man from 93; Hon C Bury St Pet from 94. *142 Manchester Road, Bury, Lancs BL9 0TL* Tel 0161-761 4541

WARD, Frank Neal. b 16. EAMTC 78. **d** 80 **p** 81. NSM Weybourne w Upper Sheringham *Nor* 80-84; NSM Kelling w Salthouse 80-84; NSM Briningham 84-92; NSM Brinton, Briningham, Hunworth, Stody etc from 92. *The Street, Sharrington, Melton Constable, Norfolk NR24 2AB* Tel (01263) 860337

WARD, Frank Wyatt. b 30. Oak Hill NSM Course 84. **d** 92 **p** 94. NSM Paddington St Pet *Lon* from 92. *82 Hill Rise, Greenford, Middx UB6 8PE* Tel 0181-575 5515

WARD, Geoffrey. b 35. Cranmer Hall Dur 77. **d** 79 **p** 80. C Garforth *Ripon* 79-81; V Holmfield *Wakef* 81-85; TV Thornaby on Tees *York* 85-91; V Linc St Jo *Linc* from 91. *St John's Vicarage, Sudbrooke Drive, Lincoln LN2 2EF* Tel (01522) 525621

WARD, Geoffrey Edward. b 30. Linc Th Coll 62. **d** 64 **p** 65. C Oundle *Pet* 64-68; C Weston Favell 68-70; TV 70-72; R Cottingham w E Carlton 72-95; rtd 95; Perm to Offic *Pet* from 95. *4 Sovereigns Court, Saxonfields, Kettering, Northants NN16 9SS* Tel (01536) 520498

WARD, Graham John. b 55. Fitzw Coll Cam BA80 Selw Coll Cam MA83. Westcott Ho Cam 87. **d** 90 **p** 91. C Bris St Mary Redcliffe w Temple etc *Bris* 90-92; Chapl Ex Coll Ox 92-94; Dean Peterho Cam from 95. *Peterhouse, Cambridge CB2 1RD* Tel (01223) 338200 Fax 337578 E-mail gjw21@cam.ac.uk

WARD, Ian Stanley. b 62. K Coll Lon BD83. Cranmer Hall Dur 84. **d** 86 **p** 87. C Moreton *Ches* 86-89; Chapl RAF from 89. *Chaplaincy Services (RAF), HQ, Personnel and Training Command, RAF Innsworth, Gloucester GL3 1EZ* Tel (01452) 712612 ext 5164 Fax 510828

WARD, Jack. b 08. Tyndale Hall Bris. **d** 57 **p** 58. C Bucknall and Bagnall *Lich* 57-60; C Tettenhall Wood 60-61; V Mow Cop 61-79; rtd 79; Perm to Offic *Lich* from 79. *9 Wentworth Drive, Rookery, Stoke-on-Trent ST7 4SU* Tel (01782) 773316

WARD, John Frederick. b 55. St Mich Coll Llan 81. **d** 84 **p** 85. C Pembroke Dock *St D* 84-86; PV Llan Cathl *Llan* 86-89; R St Brides Minor w Bettws 89-97; V Shard End *Birm* from 97. *The Vicarage, 47 Shustoke Road, Birmingham B34 7BA* Tel 0121-747 3299

WARD, John Raymond. b 31. St Jo Coll Dur BA54 DipTh56. **d** 56 **p** 57. C Leeds St Pet *Ripon* 56-60; C Seacroft 60-63; V Kirkstall 63-75; V Bramhope 75-95; rtd 96. *94 Leeds Road, Bramhope, Leeds LS16 9AN* Tel 0113-230 0356

WARD, Prof John Stephen Keith. b 38. Univ of Wales (Cardiff) BA62 Linacre Coll Ox BLitt68 Trin Hall Cam MA72. Westcott Ho Cam 72. **d** 72 **p** 73. Hon C Hampstead St Jo *Lon* 72-75; Dean Trin Hall Cam 75-82; Prof Moral and Soc Th K Coll Lon 82-85; Prof Hist and Philosophy of Religion 85-91; Regius Prof Div Ox Univ from 91; Can Ch Ch *Ox* from 91. *Christ Church, Oxford OX1 1DP* Tel (01865) 276246 or 722208

WARD, John Stewart. b 43. St Jo Coll Dur BA66. Ripon Coll Cuddesdon 77. **d** 79 **p** 80. C High Harrogate Ch Ch *Ripon* 79-82; V Ireland Wood 82-86; Chapl Wells Cathl Sch 86-88; V Menston w Woodhead *Bradf* 88-95; R Bolton Abbey from 95. *The Beeches, Bolton Abbey, Skipton, N Yorkshire BD26 6EX* Tel (01756) 710326

WARD, Keith Raymond. b 37. Dur Univ BSc60. Chich Th Coll 63. **d** 65 **p** 66. C Wallsend St Luke *Newc* 65-68; C Wooler 68-74; V Dinnington 74-81; V Bedlington 81-93; V Stannington from 93. *The Vicarage, Stannington, Morpeth, Northd NE61 6HL* Tel (01670) 789222

WARD, Kenneth Arthur. b 22. St D Coll Lamp BA50 Chich Th Coll 50. **d** 52 **p** 53. C Wellingborough St Barn *Pet* 52-55; C Stevenage *St Alb* 55-58; R Daventry *Pet* 58-72; RD Daventry 68-76; R Daventry w Norton 73-79; R Daventry 79-82; V Pattishall w Cold Higham 82-88; rtd 88; Perm to Offic *Pet* from 89. *43 Inlands Rise, Daventry, Northants NN11 4DQ*

WARD, Dr Kevin. b 47. Edin Univ MA69 Trin Coll Cam PhD76. **d** 78 **p** 79. CMS 75-92; Uganda 76-90; Qu Coll Birm 91; Perm to Offic *Birm* 91; C Halifax *Wakef* 91-92; P-in-c Charlestown 92-95; Lect Leeds Univ from 95. *8 North Grange Mews, Leeds LS26 2EW* Tel 0113-278 7801

WARD, Canon Leslie Alan James. b 38. AKC61. **d** 62 **p** 63. C Earlham St Anne *Nor* 62-65; C Gt Yarmouth 65-70; R Belton 70-83; R Burgh Castle 71-83; Chapl Norfolk and Nor Hosp 83-94; Chapl W Norwich and Colman Hosp 83-94; Chapl Norfolk and Nor Healthcare NHS Trust from 94; Hon Can Nor Cathl *Nor* from 86. *Norfolk & Norwich Hospital, Brunswick Road, Norwich NR1 3SR, or 24 Carnoustie, Norwich NR4 6AY* Tel (01603) 286286 or 58245

WARD, Lionel Owen. b 37. Univ of Wales (Cardiff) BA58 Univ of Wales (Swansea) DipEd59 MA65 Lon Univ PhD70. St Mich Coll Llan 83. **d** 85 **p** 86. NSM Swansea St Mary w H Trin *S & B* 85-89; P-in-c Swansea St Matt w Greenhill from 89; Asst Dir of Educn from 92. *96 Glanbrydan Avenue, Uplands, Swansea SA2 0JH* Tel (01792) 208081

WARD, Louis Arthur. b 13. Ripon Hall Ox 72. **d** 73 **p** 74. C Corsham *Bris* 73-77; Bp's Chapl for the Arts 76-80; V Bitton 78-80; rtd 80; Perm to Offic *Bris* from 80; Perm to Offic *Glouc* 86-96. *10 Orchard Close, Westbury-on-Trym, Bristol BS9 1AS* Tel 0117-962 8332

WARD, Mrs Marjorie. b 38. Univ of Wales (Abth) BA59 DipEd60. N Ord Course 83. **dss** 86 **d** 87 **p** 94. Keighley St Andr *Bradf* 86-87; Hon Par Dn 87-88; Hon Par Dn Oakworth 88-90; C Allerton from 91. *The Vicarage, Leytop Lane, Allerton, Bradford, W Yorkshire BD15 7LT* Tel (01274) 541948

WARD, Mark. b 62. ACGI84 Imp Coll Lon BScEng84. Wycliffe Hall Ox BTh93. **d** 93 **p** 94. C Parkham, Alwington, Buckland Brewer etc *Ex* 93-96; C S Molton w Nymet St George, High Bray etc from 96. *The Vicarage, East Street, South Molton, Devon EX36 3HX* Tel (01598) 740325

WARD, Matthew Alan James. b 69. Nottm Poly BSc91. Ridley Hall Cam 94. **d** 97. C Birchwood *Linc* from 97. *Plot 24, Sycamore Crescent, Doddington Park, Lincoln LN6 0RR* Tel (01522) 688274

WARD, Canon Michael Anthony. b 42. Sarum Th Coll 67. **d** 70 **p** 71. C Bridport *Sarum* 70-74; TV Swanborough 74-77; P-in-c Chute w Chute Forest 77-79; P-in-c Shalbourne w Ham 77-79; TR Wexcombe 79-86; V Southbroom from 86; Can and Preb Sarum Cathl from 95. *Southbroom Vicarage, London Road, Devizes, Wilts SN10 1LT* Tel (01380) 723891

WARD, Michael Reginald. b 31. BNC Ox BA54 MA58. Tyndale Hall Bris 54. **d** 56 **p** 57. C Ealing St Mary *Lon* 56-59; C Morden *S'wark* 59-61; Area Sec (Midl and E Anglia) CCCS 61-66; V Chelsea St Jo *Lon* 66-73; P-in-c Chelsea St Andr 72-73; V Chelsea St Jo w St Andr 73-76; P-in-c Hawkesbury *Glouc* 76-80; P-in-c Alderley w Hillesley 79-80; P-in-c Bibury w Winson and Barnsley 80-85; V Barkby and Queniborough *Leic* 85-90; R Gunthorpe w Bale w Field Dalling, Saxlingham etc *Nor* from 90. *The Rectory, Bale, Fakenham, Norfolk NR21 0QJ* Tel (01328) 878292

WARD, Nigel Andrew. b 50. Peterho Cam BA72 MA76. Oak Hill NSM Course 89. **d** 92 **p** 93. NSM Frogmore *St Alb* from 92. *15 Park Street, St Albans, Herts AL2 2PE* Tel (01727) 872667

WARD, Patricia. b 43. **d** 91 **p** 97. NSM Swansea St Mary w H Trin *S & B* from 91. *96 Glanbrydan Avenue, Uplands, Swansea SA2 0JH* Tel (01792) 208081

WARD, Peter Garnet. b 28. GRSM51 LRAM. Ridley Hall Cam 59. **d** 61 **p** 62. C Maghull *Liv* 61-64; Kenya 64-73; Master St Leon Mayfield Sch Sussex 73-83; Perm to Offic *Chich* 74-75; P-in-c Coleman's Hatch 75-77; Lic to Offic 77-83; P-in-c Herstmonceux 83-84; P-in-c Wartling 83-84; R Herstmonceux and Wartling 84-94; rtd 94; Perm to Offic *Chich* from 94. *Old Jesolo, Cross Lane, Ticehurst, Wadhurst, E Sussex TN5 7HQ* Tel (01580) 201340

WARD, Canon Philip Paul Ben. b 35. Toronto Univ BA61. ALCD66. **d** 66 **p** 67. C Chenies and Lt Chalfont *Ox* 66-68; C Ardsley *Sheff* 68-70; C Finham *Cov* 70-73; V Terrington St Clement *Ely* 73-81; Canada from 81. *369 Main Street, St John, New Brunswick, Canada, E2K 1J1*

WARD, Philip Percival Ford. b 33. City Univ BSc61. Wells Th Coll 67. **d** 69 **p** 70. C Clifton All SS *Bris* 69-72; P-in-c Bedminster Down 72-76; V 76-77; P-in-c Fishponds All SS 77-80; V Fishponds St Jo 77-83; V Walney Is *Carl* 83-90; V Hambleton w Out Rawcliffe *Blackb* from 90. *The Vicarage, Church Lane, Hambleton, Poulton-le-Fylde, Lancs FY6 9BZ* Tel (01253) 700231

WARD, Richard. b 09. St Aug Coll Cant 63. **d** 64 **p** 65. C Lt Stanmore St Lawr *Lon* 64-69; V Hoar Cross *Lich* 69-78; P-in-c Newborough w Ch Ch on Needwood 76-78; rtd 78. *Hoar Cross Nursing Home, Hoar Cross, Burton-on-Trent, Staffs DE13 8QS* Tel (01283) 75210

WARD, Robert. b 60. Em Coll Cam BA81 MA85. Chich Th Coll. **d** 86 **p** 87. C Horfield H Trin *Bris* 86-90; C Stantonbury and Willen *Ox* 90; TV 90-96; V Knowle St Martin *Bris* from 96. *St Martin's Vicarage, St Martin's Road, Knowle, Bristol BS4 2NH* Tel 0117-977 6275

WARD, Robert Arthur Philip. b 53. Lon Univ BD82 Open Univ BA88. Qu Coll Birm 77. **d** 79 **p** 80. C Balsall Heath St Paul *Birm* 79-82; Chapl RAF from 82. *Chaplaincy Services (RAF), HQ, Personnel and Training Command, RAF Innsworth, Gloucester GL3 1EZ* Tel (01452) 712612 ext 5164 Fax 510828

WARD, Robert Charles Irwin. b 48. Leic Univ LLB70. St Jo Coll Dur 78. **d** 80 **p** 81. C Byker St Mich w St Lawr *Newc* 80-85; Perm to Offic from 86; Perm to Offic *Dur* from 91. *1 Hawthorn Villas, The Green, Wallsend, Tyne & Wear NE28 7NT* Tel 0191-234 3969

WARD, Robin. b 66. Magd Coll Ox BA87 MA91. St Steph Ho Ox 88. **d** 91 **p** 92. C Romford St Andr *Chelmsf* 91-94; C Willesden Green St Andr and St Fran of Assisi *Lon* 94-96; V Sevenoaks St Jo *Roch* from 96. *St John's Vicarage, 62 Quakers Hall Lane, Sevenoaks, Kent TN13 3TX* Tel (01732) 451710

WARD, Stanley. b 34. NE Ord Course. **d** 84 **p** 85. NSM Jarrow *Dur* 84-90; P-in-c Thornley from 90. *The Vicarage, 10 Church Walk, Thornley, Durham DH6 3EN* Tel (01429) 820363 or 821766

WARD, Stanley Gordon. b 21. Qu Coll Cam BA43 MA47. EMMTC 76. **d** 79 **p** 80. NSM Wollaton *S'well* 79-83; NSM Plympton St Mary *Ex* 84-88; Perm to Offic from 88. *60 Wain Park, Plympton, Plymouth PL7 3HX* Tel (01752) 344042

WARD, Mrs Susan Elizabeth. b 50. N Ord Course 92. **d** 95 **p** 96. NSM Heyside *Man* from 95. *45 Fold Green, Chadderton, Oldham OL9 9DX* Tel 0161-620 2839

WARD, Timothy John Conisbee (Tim). b 62. New Coll Ox BA85 PGCE86. Wycliffe Hall Ox BA91. **d** 92 **p** 93. C Dorking St Paul *Guildf* 92-96; C Herne Hill *S'wark* from 96. *1 Finsen Road, London SE5 9AX* Tel 0171-274 3663 Fax 586 0105

WARD, Timothy William. b 49. Open Univ BA74. St Deiniol's Hawarden 78. **d** 79 **p** 80. Hon C Handsworth St Mary *Birm* 79-95; Perm to Offic from 95; Hon C Gt Barr *Lich* from 95. *3 Dale Close, Birmingham B43 6AS* Tel 0121-358 1880

WARD, William. b 13. Wycliffe Hall Ox 63. **d** 64 **p** 65. C Helmsley *York* 64-66; V Stillington w Marton and Farlington 68-73; V Langtoft w Foxholes, Butterwick and Cottam 73-78; rtd 78; Perm to Offic *York* from 78. *14 Park Close, Easingwold, York YO6 3BR* Tel (01347) 823009

WARD, William Edward. b 48. FSAScot71. AKC71. **d** 72 **p** 73. C Heref St Martin *Heref* 72-77; C Blakenall Heath *Lich* 77-78; TV 78-82; V Astley, Clive, Grinshill and Hadnall 82-91; R Edgmond w Kynnersley and Preston Wealdmoors from 91; Chapl Harper Adams Agric Coll from 96. *The Rectory, Edgmond, Newport, Shropshire TF10 8JR* Tel (01952) 820217

WARD, William Francis. b 35. Ely Th Coll 61 Coll of Resurr Mirfield 64. **d** 64 **p** 65. C Byker St Ant *Newc* 64-67; C Glas St Marg *Glas* 67-69; R Glas Ascension 69-74; Chapl RNR 72-74; Chapl RN 74-78; R Arbroath *Bre* from 78; Hon Chapl Miss to Seamen from 78; P-in-c Auchmithie *Bre* 79-90. *The Rectory, 2 Springfield Terrace, Arbroath DD11 1EL* Tel (01241) 873392 Fax 434849 E-mail revdwfward@aol.com

WARD-BODDINGTON, Canon Douglas. b 20. MBE97. S'wark Ord Course 69. **d** 72 **p** 73. C S'wark Ch Ch *S'wark* 72-77; Admin S Lon Ind Miss 72-77; Chapl Algarve *Eur* 77-80 and 83-89; V Gen to Bp Eur 80-83; Can Gib Cathl 80-97; rtd 89; Chapl Oporto *Eur* 89-97. *The College of St Barnabas, Blackberry Lane, Lingfield, Surrey RH7 6NJ* Tel (01342) 870973 Mobile 0140-405481

WARDALE, Dr Harold William (Harry). b 40. BSc PhD. Wycliffe Hall Ox 83. **d** 85 **p** 86. C Bedminster St Mich *Bris* 85-89; C Bishopston 89; TV 89-96; V Lawrence Weston from 96. *The Vicarage, 335 Long Cross, Bristol BS11 0NN* Tel 0117-982 5863

WARDALE, Robert Christopher. b 46. Newc Univ BA69. Coll of Resurr Mirfield 77. **d** 79 **p** 80. C Cockerton *Dur* 79-84; P-in-c Hedworth 84-87; V 87-92; V Darlington H Trin from 92. *Holy Trinity Vicarage, 45 Milbank Road, Darlington, Co Durham DL3 9NL* Tel (01325) 480444

WARDEN, John Michael. b 41. Univ Coll Lon BA63 Trin Coll Ox BA65 MA. NE Ord Course 80. **d** 82 **p** 83. NSM Osmotherley w E Harlsey and Ingleby Arncliffe *York* 82-86; V Kirkdale from 86. *Kirkdale Vicarage, Nawton, York YO6 5ST* Tel (01439) 71206

WARDEN, Richard James. b 57. BA MTh. Wycliffe Hall Ox 81. **d** 83 **p** 84. C Fulham St Mary N End *Lon* 83-85; CF 85-89; Chapl Wycombe Abbey Sch High Wycombe from 89. *Wycombe Abbey School, High Wycombe, Bucks HP11 1PE* Tel (01494) 520381 Fax 473836

WARDLE, Edward Christian. b 13. **d** 62 **p** 63. C Farnley *Ripon* 62-64; C Wortley de Leeds 64-66; R Llanwyddelan w Manafon *St As* 66-79; P-in-c Stottesdon *Heref* 79-82; Perm to Offic *Ripon* 82-92. *The Gables Nursing Home, Swinnow Road, Pudsey, Leeds LS28 9AP* Tel 0113-257 0123

WARDLE, Canon John Alexander (Jack). b 30. TD73. Lon Univ BA59 Man Univ MA81. Oak Hill Th Coll 53. **d** 57 **p** 58. C Blackpool St Mark *Blackb* 57-60; C Tunbridge Wells St Jo *Roch* 60-62; V Maidstone St Luke *Cant* 62-69; CF (TA) 62-73; V Hartford *Ches* 69-79; R Barton Seagrave w Warkton *Pet* 79-96; Can Pet Cathl 94-96; rtd 96; Perm to Offic *Eur* from 96. *Iglesia San Jorge, Calle San Juan de la Salle 41, Horacio 38, 08022 Barcelona, Spain* Tel Barcelona (3) 409 855 336

WARDLE, John Argyle. b 47. ARCM67 St Jo Coll Dur BA71 CertEd73. Cranmer Hall Dur DipTh72. **d** 73 **p** 74. C Mansfield St Pet *S'well* 73-77; Chapl St Felix Sch Southwold 77-87; TV Haverhill w Withersfield, the Wrattings etc *St E* 87-90; V Choral S'well Minster *S'well* from 90; Bp's Adv on Healing from 94. *3 Vicars' Court, Southwell, Notts NG25 0HP* Tel (01636) 813767

WARDLE-HARPUR, Canon James. b 31. St Jo Coll Dur BA55. Wells Th Coll 55. **d** 56 **p** 57. C Sheff Parson Cross St Cecilia *Sheff* 56-59; C Maltby 59-61; V Doncaster St Jude 61-64; Pakistan 64-68; R Man Victoria Park *Man* 68-75; V Foxton w Gumley and Laughton *Leic* 75-79; V Foxton w Gumley and Laughton and Lubenham 79-82; TR Leic Resurr 82-88; V Burrough Hill Pars 88-94; Hon Can Leic Cathl 88-94; rtd 96. *Laburnum Cottage, 1 Coates Lane, Starbotton, Skipton, N Yorkshire BD23 5HZ* Tel (01756) 760401

WARDMAN, Carol Joy. b 56. Lon Univ BA79. Nor Ord Course 91. **d** 94 **p** 95. NSM Hebden Bridge *Wakef* from 94. *3 The Pond, Triangle, Sowerby Bridge, W Yorkshire HX6 3NM* Tel (01422) 835464

WARDROBE, Bevan. b 26. Hatf Coll Dur BA53. Cuddesdon Coll 53. **d** 54 **p** 55. C Southgate Ch Ch *Lon* 54-59; PV Lich Cathl *Lich* 59-67; Asst Master Cathl Sch 59-67; Hd Master York Minster Song Sch 67-85; V Choral York Minster *York* 67-85; Chapl Rome *Eur* 85-91; rtd 91; Chapl San Remo *Eur* 91-96. *3 Regency Gardens, Sandford Road, Cheltenham, Glos GL53 7AJ* Tel (01242) 242355

WARDROP, David John. b 34. RN Coll Dartmouth RN Eng Coll Plymouth GIMechE56 ALCD59. **d** 59 **p** 60. C Harrow Weald All SS *Lon* 59-62; Chapl RNR 61-95; V Ernesettle *Ex* 62-64; V Broadclyst 64-67; Dioc Miss and Ecum Officer 64-67; Asst Gen Sec Ind Chr Fellowship 67-76; P-in-c Pertenhall w Swineshead *St Alb* 76-80; R Wymington w Podington 80-83; R Cavendish *St E* 83-89; P-in-c Clare w Poslingford 86-89; P-in-c Stoke by Clare w Wixoe 86-89; R Clare w Poslingford, Cavendish etc 89-91; RD Clare 87-91; Chapl Aquitaine *Eur* 91-95; rtd 95. *Cotswold, 6 Shreen Way, Gillingham, Dorset SP8 4EL* Tel (01747) 822189 Fax as telephone

WARE, Austin Neville. b 14. St D Coll Lamp BA37 St Mich Coll Llan 37. **d** 39 **p** 41. C Seven Sisters *Llan* 39-42; C Drypool St Andr and St Pet *York* 42-44; C Leeds St Geo *Ripon* 44-45; C Loughborough Em *Leic* 45-47; R Elton *Derby* 47-55; V Winster 49-55; V Kingston upon Hull St Barn *York* 55-58; V Knapton 58-75; R W and E Heslerton w Knapton 75-79; P-in-c Yedingham 75-79; rtd 79; Perm to Offic *Ban* from 79. *Craigsmoor, Lon Crecrist, Trearddur Bay, Holyhead LL65 2BQ* Tel (01407) 860106

WARE, Canon John Lawrence. b 37. Nottm Univ BA59. Ridley Hall Cam 62. **d** 62 **p** 63. C Attercliffe *Sheff* 62-66; C Ranmoor 66-68; R Liddington *Bris* 68-74; Soc and Ind Adv 74-79; P-in-c City of Bris 74-79; Hon Can Bris Cathl from 76; V Kingswood 79-88; RD Bitton 85-87; P-in-c Broad Blunsdon 88-94; RD Cricklade 88-94; R Broad Blunsdon 94; P-in-c Blunsdon 94; R The Blunsdons from 94. *The Rectory, Church Way, Blunsdon, Bristol SN2 4DU* Tel (01793) 729592

WARE, Stephen John. b 55. Univ of Wales (Lamp) BA76. Ripon Coll Cuddesdon 77. **d** 79 **p** 80. C Lighthorne *Cov* 79-82; Chapl RAF from 82. *Chaplaincy Services (RAF), HQ, Personnel and Training Command, RAF Innsworth, Gloucester GL3 1EZ* Tel (01452) 712612 ext 5164 Fax 510828

WAREHAM, Mrs Caroline. b 32. Lightfoot Ho Dur 55. **dss** 80 **d** 87 **p** 94. Stanwell *Lon* 80-87; Par Dn 87-88; C Epsom St Barn *Guildf* 88-95; C Aldershot St Mich from 95. *Ascension Church House, Ayling Hill, Aldershot, Hants GU11 3LL* Tel (01252) 330224

WAREHAM, Mrs Sheila. b 36. CertEd56. N Ord Course 85. **d** 88 **p** 94. NSM Lostock Hall *Blackb* 88-90; NSM Allithwaite *Carl* 90-91; NSM Windermere RD 91-94; NSM Colton w Satterthwaite and Rusland 94-95; NSM Colton 95-96. *Lyng Nook, Church Road, Allithwaite, Grange-over-Sands, Cumbria LA11 7RD* Tel (015395) 35237

WARING, Graham George Albert. b 37. ACII62. Portsm Dioc Tr Course 86. **d** 87. Chapl Asst Qu Alexandra Hosp Portsm 87-92; NSM Portsea All SS *Portsm* 92-94; NSM Widley w Wymering 94-95; NSM Wisbech St Aug *Ely* from 95. *1 Ivesdyke Close, Leverington, Wisbech, Cambs PE13 5EQ*

WARING, Jeffery Edwin. b 53. Trin Coll Bris 80. **d** 83 **p** 84. C Harpurhey Ch Ch *Man* 83-86; TV Eccles 86-92; P-in-c Hamworthy *Sarum* from 92. *The Rectory, 323 Blandford Road, Hamworthy, Poole, Dorset BH15 4HP* Tel (01202) 674878

WARING, John Valentine. b 29. St Deiniol's Hawarden 65. **d** 67 **p** 68. C Bistre *St As* 67-71; C Blackpool St Thos *Blackb* 71-72; R Levenshulme St Pet *Man* 72-87; R Caerwys and Bodfari *St As* 87-94; rtd 94. *13 St Mellors Road, Southdown Park, Buckley CH7 2ND* Tel (01244) 547290

WARING, Roger. b 32. ACP66 CertEd56 Open Univ BA74. SW Minl Tr Course 83. **d** 86 **p** 87. NSM Ex St Sidwell and St Matt *Ex* 86-90; NSM Tavistock and Gulworthy 90-96; NSM Axminster, Chardstock, Combe Pyne and Rousdon from 96. *The Vicarage, Chardstock, Axminster, Devon EX13 7BY* Tel (01460) 220005

WARING, Mrs Ruth. b 44. Keele Univ CertEd65. SW Minl Tr Course 86. **d** 90 **p** 94. Par Dn Tavistock and Gulworthy *Ex* 90-94; C 94-96; TV Axminster, Chardstock, Combe Pyne and Rousdon from 96. *The Vicarage, Chardstock, Axminster, Devon EX13 7BY* Tel (01460) 220005

WARING, Mrs Sheila May. b 29. SS Paul & Mary Coll Cheltenham CertEd49. Oak Hill Th Coll 85. **dss** 86 **d** 87 **p** 94. Eastwood *Chelmsf* 86-92; NSM 87-92; Chapl Rochford Hosp from 87; NSM Prittlewell St Pet *Chelmsf* 92-96; NSM Prittlewell w Westcliff from 96. *42 Manchester Drive, Leigh-on-Sea, Essex SS9 3HR* Tel (01702) 711046

WARKE, Alistair Samuel John. b 66. Ulster Univ BA89. CITC BTh92. **d** 92 **p** 93. C Arm St Mark w Aghavilly *Arm* 92-95; I Killyman from 95; Hon V Choral Arm Cathl from 95. *St Andrew's Rectory, 85 Dungorman Road, Killyman, Dungannon, Co Tyrone BT71 6SE* Tel (01868) 722500

✠**WARKE, The Rt Revd Robert Alexander.** b 30. TCD BA52 BD60. Union Th Sem (NY) DipEcum60. **d** 53 **p** 54 **c** 88. C Newtownards *D & D* 53-56; C Dublin St Cath w St Victor *D & G* 56-58; C Dublin Rathfarnham 58-64; Min Can St Patr Cathl Dublin 59-64; I Dunlavin w Ballymore Eustace and Hollywood *D & G* 64-67; I Dublin Drumcondra w N Strand 67-71; I Dublin St Barn 67-71; I Dublin Zion Ch 71-88; RD Taney 77-80; Adn Dublin 80-88; Bp C, C & R from 88. *The Palace, Bishop Street, Cork, Irish Republic* Tel Cork (21) 316114 Fax 273437

WARLAND, Preb Cyril John. b 21. St Cath Soc Ox BA43 MA56. Cuddesdon Coll. **d** 44 **p** 45. C Bradf St Wilfrid Lidget Green *Bradf* 44-46; C Goldthorpe *Sheff* 47-56; R Mary Tavy *Ex* 56-88; RD Tavistock 77-88; P-in-c Walkhampton 80-83; Preb Ex Cathl 82-88; R Peter Tavy 82-88; rtd 88; Lic to Offic *Ex* from 88. *2 Rowantree Road, Newton Abbot, Devon TQ1 4LL* Tel (01626) 55369

WARLAND, Peter William. b 35. K Coll Lon 56. **d** 60 **p** 61. C Pemberton St Jo *Liv* 60-64; C Warrington St Elphin 64-66; V Farnworth All SS *Man* 66-71; Chapl RN 71-92; Hon Chapl to The Queen 88-92; Chapl Greenbank and Freedom Fields Hosps Ex from 92; Chapl St Luke's Hospice Plymouth from 94; Perm to Offic *Ex* from 94. *122 Wingfield Road, Plymouth PL3 4ER* Tel (01752) 561381

WARMAN, Canon Cyril Aidan Oswald. b 08. Pemb Coll Ox BA30 MA35. Ridley Hall Cam 30. **d** 31 **p** 32. C Battersea St Mary *S'wark* 31-33; C Rugby St Andr *Cov* 33-37; V Shepshed *Leic* 37-46; V Manningham St Luke *Bradf* 46-52; V Normanton *Wakef* 52-66; RD Wakef 59-66; Hon Can Wakef Cathl 62-74; V Kellington w Whitley 66-74; rtd 74; Perm to Offic *York* from 74. *Dulverton Hall, St Martin's Square, Scarborough, N Yorkshire YO11 2DB* Tel (01723) 371040

WARMAN, Canon John Richard. b 37. Pemb Coll Ox BA61 MA. Ridley Hall Cam 61. **d** 63 **p** 64. C Huyton St Mich *Liv* 63-67; Asst Chapl Liv Univ 67-68; Chapl 68-74; P-in-c Holbrooke *Derby* 74-80; P-in-c Lt Eaton 74-80; R Sawley 80-96; RD Ilkeston 82-92; Hon Can Derby Cathl from 91; V Allestree from 96. *St Edmund's Vicarage, Kings Croft, Allestree, Derby DE22 2FN* Tel (01332) 557396

WARMAN, Miss Marion Alice. b 20. Newnham Coll Cam BA43 MA50. S'wark Ord Course 76. **dss** 79 **d** 87 **p** 94. Spring Grove St Mary *Lon* 79-87; Hon Par Dn 87-93; Chapl Asst W Middx Hosp Isleworth from 80; Perm to Offic from 93. *43 Thornbury Road, Isleworth, Middx TW7 4LE* Tel 0181-560 5905

WARNER, Alan Winston. b 51. Lon Univ BSc73 Leeds Univ DipTh75. Coll of Resurr Mirfield 73. **d** 76 **p** 77. C Willenhall

St Anne *Lich* 76-78; C Baswich 78-81; V Wednesfield St Greg 81-87; Chapl Frimley Park Hosp 87-94; Chapl Frimley Park Hosp NHS Trust from 94. *14 The Cloisters, Frimley, Camberley, Surrey GU16 5JR* Tel (01276) 64685 or 692777

WARNER, Andrew Compton. b 35. Fitzw Ho Cam BA58 MA62. Westcott Ho Cam 59. **d** 60 **p** 61. C Addlestone *Guildf* 60-64; C-in-c Ash Vale CD 64-71; V Hinchley Wood 71-80; R Gt Bookham from 80; RD Leatherhead 88-93. *The Rectory, 2A Fife Way, Leatherhead, Surrey KT23 3PH* Tel (01372) 452405

WARNER, Clifford Chorley. b 38. Hull Univ MA88. EMMTC 76. **d** 79 **p** 80. NSM Swanwick and Pentrich *Derby* 79-88; NSM Allestree from 88. *17 Amber Heights, Ripley, Derbyshire DE5 3SP* Tel (01773) 745089

WARNER, David. b 40. AKC63. **d** 64 **p** 65. C Castleford All SS *Wakef* 64-68; Warden Hollowford Tr and Conf Cen Sheff 68-72; R Wombwell *Sheff* 72-83; V Wortley 83-84; V Wortley w Thurgoland 84-95; RD Tankersley 88-93; V Worsbrough from 95. *St Mary's Vicarage, Church Lane, Worsbrough, Barnsley, S Yorkshire S70 5LU* Tel (01226) 203113

WARNER, David Leonard John. b 24. Kelham Th Coll 47. **d** 51 **p** 52. C Mill Hill St Mich *Lon* 51-54; C Pimlico St Sav 54-56; S Africa 56-68; V Bournemouth H Epiphany *Win* 68-78; V Whitchurch w Tufton and Litchfield 78-89; RD Whitchurch 79-89; rtd 89. *9 Sparkford Close, Winchester, Hants SO22 4NH* Tel (01962) 867343

WARNER, Dennis Vernon. b 46. Lon Univ BA68 K Coll Lon BD71. **d** 72 **p** 73. C W Bromwich All SS *Lich* 72-75; C Uttoxeter w Bramshall 75-79; Lic to Offic from 79. *17 Shrewsbury Road, Stretton, Swadlincote, Derbyshire DE13 0JF* Tel (01283) 48058

WARNER, Canon George Francis. b 36. Trin Coll Ox BA60 MA64 Qu Coll Cam BA63. Westcott Ho Cam 61. **d** 63 **p** 64. C Birm St Geo *Birm* 63-66; C Maidstone All SS w St Phil and H Trin *Cant* 66-69; Chapl Wellington Coll Berks 69-78; TR Coventry Caludon *Cov* 78-95; Hon Can Cov Cathl from 85; RD Cov E 89-95; P-in-c Leamington Priors All SS from 95; P-in-c Leamington Spa and Old Milverton from 95. *Holy Trinity Vicarage, Clive House, Kenilworth Road, Leamington Spa, Warks CV32 5TL* Tel (01926) 424016

WARNER, James Morley (Jim). b 32. S'wark Ord Course 66. **d** 69 **p** 70. C S Mymms K Chas *Lon* 69-72; C Bush Hill Park St Steph 72-75; V W Hendon St Jo from 75. *St John's Vicarage, Vicarage Road, London NW4 3PX* Tel 0181-202 8606

WARNER, John Philip. b 59. Keble Coll Ox BA80 MA85. St Steph Ho Ox. **d** 83 **p** 84. C Brighton Resurr *Chich* 83-87; C Paddington St Mary *Lon* 87-90; V Teddington St Mark and Hampton Wick St Jo from 90. *The Vicarage, 23 St Mark's Road, Teddington, Middx TW11 9DE* Tel 0181-977 4067

WARNER, Martin Clive. b 58. St Chad's Coll Dur BA80 MA85. St Steph Ho Ox. **d** 84 **p** 85. C Plymouth St Pet *Ex* 84-88; TV Leic Resurr *Leic* 88-93; Admin of Shrine of Our Lady of Walsingham from 93; Lic to Offic *Nor* from 92. *The College, Walsingham, Norfolk NR22 6EF* Tel (01328) 820266

WARNER, Dr Mary. b 52. Univ of Wales (Swansea) BSc73 Aber Univ PhD77. NE Ord Course 90. **d** 93 **p** 94. C Bensham *Dur* 93-96; Asst Chapl R Victoria Infirmary and Assoc Hosps NHS Trust from 96. *Royal Victoria Infirmary, Queen Victoria Road, Newcastle upon Tyne NE1 4LP* Tel 0191-232 5131

WARNER, Michael John William. b 41. Sarum Th Coll 68. **d** 71 **p** 72. C Plympton St Mary *Ex* 71-75; V St Goran w St Mich Caerhays *Truro* 75-78; V Bishops Tawton *Ex* 78-79; V Newport 78-79; Perm to Offic *Truro* 79-83; V St Stythians w Perranarworthal and Gwennap 83-93; P-in-c Budock from 93; Sec Dioc Adv Cttee from 93. *The Vicarage, School Lane, Budock Water, Falmouth, Cornwall TR11 5DJ* Tel (01326) 372227 Fax 376955

WARNER, Nigel Bruce. b 51. ALCM67 St Jo Coll Cam BA72 DipTh73 MA76. Wycliffe Hall Ox 75. **d** 77 **p** 78. C Luton St Mary *St Alb* 77-80; Prec Dur Cathl *Dur* 80-84; R St John Lee *Newc* 84-91; V Lamesley *Dur* from 91. *The Vicarage, Lamesley, Gateshead, Tyne & Wear NE11 0EU* Tel 0191-487 6490

WARNER, Canon Robert William. b 32. TCD BA54 MA65 BD65. TCD Div Sch Div Test56. **d** 56 **p** 57. C Wythenshawe St Martin CD *Man* 56-60; R Hulme St Steph w St Mark 60-66; R Droylsden St Mary 66-76; R Stand 76-97; AD Radcliffe and Prestwich 85-96; Hon Can Man Cathl 87-97; rtd 97. *28 Cow Lees, Westhoughton, Bolton BL5 3EG* Tel (01942) 818823

WARNER, Canon Samuel John. b 10. TCD BA34 MA50. **d** 34 **p** 35. C Portadown St Mark *Arm* 34-39; I Dunmanway St Edm *C, C & R* 39-43; I Heynestown *Arm* 43-47; I Ballymore 47-64; Hon V Choral Armagh Cathl 57-64; I Laghey *D & R* 64-79; Can Raphoe Cathl 72-79; rtd 79. *Coolkelure, Laghey, Donegal, Irish Republic* Tel Laghey (73) 21808

WARNER, Terence. b 36. LNSM course. **d** 92 **p** 93. NSM Leek and Meerbrook *Lich* from 92. *5 School Close, Leek, Staffs ST13 8HS* Tel (01538) 387336

WARNES, Brian Leslie Stephen. b 40. Natal Univ BSocSc76. Kelham Th Coll 59. **d** 67 **p** 68. C Tonge Moor *Man* 67-71; S Africa 71-87; V Blean *Cant* 87-94; New Zealand from 94. *St John's Vicarage, 47 George Street, Te Awamutu, New Zealand* Tel Te Awamutu (7) 871 4627 or 871 5568 Fax 871 4620

WARNES, Miss Marjorie. b 32. Leeds Inst of Educn CertEd53. St Jo Coll Nottm 85. **d** 87 **p** 94. C Leamington Priors St Mary *Cov* from 87. *78 Lewis Road, Radford Semele, Leamington Spa, Warks CV31 1UQ* Tel (01926) 420811

WARNES, Warren Hugh. b 23. St Barn Coll Adelaide ThL49. **d** 50 **p** 50. Australia 50-58 and 60-62; C Northolt St Mary *Lon* 58-60 and 62-64; V Kings Heath *Pet* 64-71; V Rockingham w Caldecote 71-73; V Gretton w Rockingham and Caldecote 73-83; V Marston St Lawrence w Warkworth and Thenford 83-89; rtd 89; Perm to Offic *Pet* from 89. *17 Thorpe Road, Earls Barton, Northampton NN6 0PJ* Tel (01604) 812935

WARR, Timothy Gerald (Tim). b 59. Trin Coll Bris BA86. **d** 88 **p** 89. C Yateley *Win* 88-91; C Chapel Allerton *Ripon* 91-93; V Wortley de Leeds from 93. *The Vicarage, Dixon Lane Road, Leeds LS12 4RU* Tel 0113-263 8867

WARREN, The Very Revd Alan Christopher. b 32. CCC Cam BA56 MA60. Ridley Hall Cam 56. **d** 57 **p** 58. C Cliftonville *Cant* 57-59; C Plymouth St Andr *Ex* 59-62; Chapl Kelly Coll Tavistock 62-64; V Leic H Apostles *Leic* 64-72; Hon Can Cov Cathl *Cov* 72-78; Dioc Missr 72-78; Provost Leic 78-92; rtd 92; Perm to Offic *Nor* from 92. *9 Queen's Drive, Hunstanton, Norfolk PE36 6EY* Tel (01485) 534533

WARREN, Canon Christopher Bruce. TCD BA58 MA61 HDipEd60. **d** 62 **p** 63. C Waterford H Trin *C & O* 62-64; I Askeaton w Shanagolden and Loghill *L & K* 64-66; I Kilcolman 66-73; I Dublin St Werburgh *D & G* 73-74; I Kilrossanty *C & O* 74-80; I Fenagh w Myshall, Aghade and Ardoyne 80-86; Preb Ossory and Leighlin Cathls 85-88; I Castlecomer w Colliery Ch, Mothel and Bilbo 86-88; Finland 88-94 and from 96; I Omey w Ballynakill, Errislannan and Roundstone *T, K & A* 94-96; rtd 96. *Virkamiehenkatu 15, 35800 Mänttä, Finland* Tel Mänttä (3) 474 8607 Fax 488 8551

WARREN, Clifford Frederick. b 32. Univ of Wales (Lamp) BA53. St Mich Coll Llan 54. **d** 56 **p** 57. C Whitchurch *Llan* 56-68; Lic to Offic 68-70; C Llanedeyrn *Mon* 70-76; R Machen 76-97; rtd 97. *1 Drury Close, Thornhill, Cardiff CF4 9BJ*

WARREN, David. b 39. S'wark Ord Course. **d** 87 **p** 88. NSM Mottingham St Andr *S'wark* from 87. *26 Longcroft, London SE9 3BQ* Tel 0181-851 4824

WARREN, Desmond Benjamin Moore. b 22. TCD BA44 MA49. Bps' Coll Cheshunt 46. **d** 48 **p** 49. C Moulsham St Jo *Chelmsf* 48-52; C Colchester St Mary V 52-55; V Elmstead 55-63; R Sandy *St Alb* 63-78; P-in-c Gt Munden 78-79; P-in-c Westmill 78-79; R Westmill w Gt Munden 79-84; rtd 84; Lic to Offic (Lismore) *C & O* 84-90; Perm to Offic *C, C & R* from 91. *Dysert, Ardmore, Youghal, Co Cork, Irish Republic* Tel Youghal (24) 94110

WARREN, Eric Anthony. b 28. MBE. Ex & Truro NSM Scheme. **d** 83 **p** 84. NSM Chudleigh *Ex* 83-88; Perm to Offic from 88. *Lower Radway House, Bishopsteignton, Teignmouth, Devon TQ14 9SS* Tel (01626) 772135 or 779277

WARREN, Ernest Bruce. b 24. K Coll Lon BD54 AKC54. **d** 54 **p** 55. C St Austell *Truro* 54-58; C Hitchin St Mary *St Alb* 58-62; P-in-c Talland *Truro* 62-67; P-in-c Lansallos 62-64; R 64-67; V Lostwithiel 67-77; V Perranzabuloe 77-89; rtd 89; Perm to Offic *Truro* from 89. *22 Coombe Road, Saltash, Cornwall PL12 4ER* Tel (01752) 844058

WARREN, Canon Frederick Noel. b 30. TCD BA52 MA58 BD66 QUB PhD72. **d** 53 **p** 54. C Belfast St Matt *Conn* 53-56; C Belfast St Geo 56-59; I Castlewellan *D & D* 59-65; I Clonallon w Warrenpoint 65-69; I Newcastle 69-87; Can Belf Cathl 73-76; Preb Wicklow St Patr Cathl Dublin 76-88; I Dunfanaghy, Raymunterdoney and Tullaghbegley *D & R* 87-97; Preb Swords St Patr Cathl Dublin 89-97; rtd 97. *Runclevin, Dunfanaghy, Letterkenny, Co Donegal* Tel Letterkenny (74) 36635

WARREN, Geoffrey Richard. b 44. Middx Poly MA91. Bps' Coll Cheshunt 66 Qu Coll Birm 68. **d** 69 **p** 70. C Waltham Cross *St Alb* 69-73; C Radlett 73-78; C Tring 78-80; TV Tring 80-95; V Watford St Andr from 95. *St Andrew's Vicarage, 18 Park Road, Watford WD1 3QN* Tel (01923) 224858

WARREN, Mrs Gillian (Jill). b 53. Sheff Univ BA74 PGCE75. WMMTC 89. **d** 92 **p** 94. Par Dn Tettenhall Regis *Lich* 92-94; C 94-95; TV Bilston from 95. *43 Willenhall Road, Bilston, W Midlands WV14 6NW* Tel (01902) 490255

WARREN, Gordon Lenham (Bunny). b 45. Wycliffe Hall Ox DipMin93. **d** 93 **p** 94. C Sunbury *Lon* 93-96; C Laleham from 96. *22 Sunmead Road, Sunbury-on-Thames, Middx TW16 6PE* Tel (01932) 772882

WARREN, Preb Henry Fiennes. b 21. Keble Coll Ox BA42 MA47. Cuddesdon Coll 42. **d** 48 **p** 49. C Weston-super-Mare St Jo *B & W* 48-53; R Exford 53-75; RD Wiveliscombe 65-73; Preb Wells Cathl from 73; R W Monkton 75-86; rtd 86; Perm to Offic *B & W* from 86. *6 Brookside, Broadway, Ilminster, Somerset TA19 9RT* Tel (01460) 57922

WARREN, James Randolph. b 54. St Paul's Cheltenham CertEd75 Bris Univ BEd76 Birm Univ MEd84. Ridley Hall Cam CTM92. **d** 92 **p** 93. C Boldmere *Birm* 92-95; V Torpoint *Truro* from 95. *The Vicarage, 3 Grove Park, Torpoint, Cornwall PL11 2PP* Tel (01752) 812418

WARREN, Malcolm Clive. b 46. St D Coll Lamp DipTh74. **d** 74 **p** 75. C Newport St Andr *Mon* 74-78; C Risca 78-79; V St Hilary

Greenway 79-84; TV Grantham *Linc* 84-90; Ind Chapl 87-90; Ind Chapl *Worc* 90-96; P-in-c Dudley St Aug Holly Hall 95-96. *9 Tansley Hill Road, Dudley, W Midlands DY2 7ER* Tel (01384) 261026

WARREN, Martin John. b 59. Ch Coll Cam BA81 MA85 LTh DPS. St Jo Coll Nottm 83. **d** 86 **p** 87. C Littleover *Derby* 86-90; C Hermitage and Hampstead Norreys, Cold Ash etc *Ox* 90-91; TV from 91. *The Rectory, Yattendon, Newbury, Berks RG16 0UR* Tel (01635) 201213

WARREN, Michael John. b 40. Kelham Th Coll 59. **d** 64 **p** 65. C Withington St Chris *Man* 64-67; C Worsley 67-69; C Witney *Ox* 69-72; V S Hinksey 72-80; Canada from 80. *Box 1117, Fort McLeod, Alberta, Canada, T0L 0Z0*

WARREN, Michael Philip. b 62. Nottm Univ DipPhys87. Oak Hill Th Coll BA91. **d** 94 **p** 95. C Tunbridge Wells St Jo *Roch* from 94. *112 Stephens Road, Tunbridge Wells, Kent TN4 9QA* Tel (01892) 521767

WARREN, The Ven Norman Leonard. b 34. CCC Cam BA58 MA62. Ridley Hall Cam 58. **d** 60 **p** 61. C Bedworth *Cov* 60-63; V Leamington Priors St Paul 63-77; R Morden *S'wark* 77-88; TR 88-89; RD Merton 86-89; Adn Roch from 89; Can Res Roch Cathl from 89. *The Archdeaconry, Rochester, Kent ME1 1SX* Tel (01634) 842527

WARREN, Canon Paul Kenneth. b 41. Selw Coll Cam BA63 MA67. Cuddesdon Coll 64. **d** 67 **p** 68. C Lancaster St Mary *Blackb* 67-70; Chapl Lanc Univ 70-78; V Langho Billington 78-83; Bp's Dom Chapl 83-88; Chapl Whalley Abbey 83-88; R Standish from 88; Hon Can Blackb Cathl from 91; RD Chorley from 92. *The Rectory, 13 Rectory Lane, Standish, Wigan, Lancs WN6 0XA* Tel (01257) 421396

WARREN, Peter. b 40. FCA64. Oak Hill Th Coll 77. **d** 79 **p** 80. C Newcastle w Butterton *Lich* 79-82; TV Sutton St Jas and Wawne *York* 82-87; V Ledsham w Fairburn 87-95; R Ainderby Steeple w Yafforth and Kirby Wiske etc *Ripon* from 95. *The Rectory, Ainderby Steeple, Northallerton, N Yorkshire DL7 9PY* Tel (01609) 773346

WARREN, Peter John. b 55. CertEd76 BA86. Trin Coll Bris 83. **d** 86 **p** 87. C W Streatham St Jas *S'wark* 86-91; P-in-c Edin Clermiston Em *Edin* from 91. *127 Clermiston Road, Edinburgh EH12 6UR* Tel 0131-316 4706

WARREN, Canon Robert. b 54. TCD BA78 MA81. CITC 76. **d** 78 **p** 79. C Limerick City *L & K* 78-81; Dioc Youth Adv (Limerick) 79-86; I Adare w Kilpeacon and Croom 81-88; Bp's Dom Chapl 81-95; Dioc Registrar (Limerick etc) from 81; Dioc Registrar (Killaloe etc) from 86; I Tralee w Ballymacelligott, Kilnaughtin etc from 88; RD Tralee from 89; Can Limerick, Killaloe and Clonfert Cathls 95-96; Chan from 97. *St John's Rectory, Ashe Street, Tralee, Co Kerry, Irish Republic* Tel Tralee (66) 22245 Mobile 088-521133 Fax 29004

WARREN, Robert Geoffrey. b 51. DipHE. Trin Coll Bris 79. **d** 82 **p** 83. C Felixstowe SS Pet and Paul *St E* 82-86; V Gazeley w Dalham, Moulton and Kentford 86-90; P-in-c Ipswich St Clem w St Luke and H Trin from 90. *42 Clapgate Lane, Ipswich IP3 0RD* Tel (01473) 723467

WARREN, Robert Irving. b 38. Univ of BC BA58 Ox Univ MA73. Angl Th Coll (BC) LTh61. **d** 61 **p** 63. Canada 61-89; R Northfield *Birm* from 89. *The Rectory, Rectory Road, Birmingham B31 2NA* Tel 0121-477 3111 or 475 1518

WARREN, Canon Robert Peter Resker. b 39. Jes Coll Cam BA63 MA. ALCD65. **d** 65 **p** 66. C Rusholme H Trin *Man* 65-68; C Bushbury *Lich* 68-71; V Crookes St Thos *Sheff* 71-90; TR 90-93; RD Hallam 78-83; Hon Can Sheff Cathl 82-93; Can Th Sheff Cathl from 93; Nat Officer for Evang from 93. *16 Connaught Road, Market Harborough, Leics LE16 7NG* Tel (01858) 431947

WARREN, William Frederick. b 55. Sarum & Wells Th Coll 83. **d** 86 **p** 87. C E Greenwich Ch Ch w St Andr and St Mich *S'wark* 86-91; C Richmond St Mary w St Matthias and St Jo 91-95; TV from 96. *22A Cambrian Road, Richmond, Surrey TW10 6JQ* Tel 0181-948 7217

WARRICK, Mark. b 54. Aston Univ BSc76 Nottm Univ BCombStuds83. Linc Th Coll 80. **d** 83 **p** 84. C Grantham *Linc* 83-87; C Cirencester *Glouc* 87-91; V Over *Ely* from 91. *The Vicarage, Over, Cambridge CB4 5NX* Tel (01954) 230329

WARRILLOW, Brian Ellis. b 39. Linc Th Coll 81. **d** 83 **p** 84. C Tunstall Ch Ch *Lich* 83; C Tunstall 83-85; C Shrewsbury H Cross 86-87; P-in-c Tilstock 88; P-in-c Whixall 88; V Tilstock and Whixall 89-92; TV Hanley H Ev 92-94; rtd 94. *46 Meakin Avenue, Newcastle-under-Lyme, Staffs ST1 6SL* Tel (01782) 634476

WARRILOW, Mrs Christine. b 42. Lanc Univ BA86. N Ord Course 86. **d** 89 **p** 94. C Netherton *Liv* 89-92; C Cantril Farm 92-94; V 94-96; V Hindley Green from 96. *The Vicarage, 848 Atherton Road, Hindley, Wigan, Lancs WN2 4SA* Tel (01942) 255833

WARRINER, Leonard. b 15. Ox NSM Course. **d** 79 **p** 80. NSM Chalfont St Peter *Ox* from 79. *Briar Rose, Winkers Lane, Chalfont St Peter, Gerrards Cross, Bucks SL9 0AJ* Tel (01753) 884443

WARRINGTON, Gwynfa Lewis Jones. b 44. St D Coll Lamp 64. **d** 67 **p** 68. C Gorseinon *S & B* 67-70; C Pembroke Dock *St D* 70-74; V Rosemarket and Freystrop 74-78; R Llangwm and Freystrop 78-79; V Ystradfellte *S & B* 79-84; V Abercynon *Llan* 84-87; V Beguildy and Heyope *S & B* from 87. *The Vicarage, Beguildy, Knighton LD7 1YE* Tel (01547) 7252

WARRINGTON, Katherine Irene. **d** 95. NSM Knighton and Norton *S & B* from 95. *The Vicarage, Knighton LD7 1AG*

WARRINGTON, Archdeacon of. *See* WOODHOUSE, The Ven Charles David Stewart

WARRINGTON, Suffragan Bishop of. *See* PACKER, The Rt Revd John Richard

WARWICK, Gordon Melvin. b 31. N Ord Course 79. **d** 80 **p** 81. NSM Darrington w Wentbridge *Wakef* 80-87; TV Almondbury w Farnley Tyas 87-95; rtd 95. *Andante, Christon Bank, Alnwick, Northd NE66 3EZ* Tel (01665) 576742

WARWICK, Canon John Michael. b 37. Fitzw Ho Cam BA58 MA62. Ely Th Coll 58. **d** 60 **p** 61. C Towcester w Easton Neston *Pet* 60-63; C Leighton Buzzard *St Alb* 63-64; C Boston *Linc* 64-66; P-in-c Sutterton 66-72; V 72-74; V Sutton St Mary 74-84; V Bourne from 84; Chapl Bourne Hosps Lincs from 84; Can and Preb Linc Cathl *Linc* from 89; RD Aveland and Ness w Stamford from 93. *The Vicarage, Bourne, Lincs PE10 9LX* Tel (01778) 422412

WARWICK, Archdeacon of. *See* PAGET-WILKES, The Ven Michael Jocelyn James

WARWICK, Suffragan Bishop of. *See* PRIDDIS, The Rt Revd Anthony Martin

WASH, John. **d** 81 **p** 83. Hon C Newington St Mary *S'wark* from 81. *15 Canterbury Place, London SE17 3AD* Tel 0171-582 9280

WASHINGTON, Patrick Leonard. b 44. Nottm Univ BSc66. St Steph Ho Ox 65. **d** 68 **p** 69. C Fleet *Guildf* 68-71; C Farnham 71-74; TV Staveley and Barrow Hill *Derby* 74-83; V Norbury St Phil *Cant* 83-84; V Norbury St Phil *S'wark* from 85; RD Croydon N from 90. *St Philip's Vicarage, 66 Pollards Hill North, London SW16 4NY* Tel 0181-764 1812

WASSALL, Keith Leonard. b 45. Bede Coll Dur TCert67. Chich Th Coll 68. **d** 71 **p** 72. C Upper Gornal *Lich* 71-74; C Codsall 74-75; C Shelton 75-76; TV Hanley All SS 76-79; Bermuda 79-81; V Rickerscote *Lich* 81-92; P-in-c Coven from 92; Asst Chapl HM Pris Featherstone from 92. *St Paul's New Vicarage, Church Lane, Coven, Wolverhampton WV9 5DD* Tel (01902) 790230 or 790991

WASSELL, Miss Leonora Jane. b 55. La Sainte Union Coll CertEd76. N Ord Course 91. **d** 94 **p** 95. NSM High Harrogate St Pet *Ripon* from 94. *7 Rydal Road, Harrogate, N Yorkshire HG1 4SQ* Tel (01423) 886570

WASTELL, Canon Eric Morse. b 33. St Mich Coll Llan DipTh62. **d** 62 **p** 63. C Oystermouth *S & B* 62-65; Antigua 65-74; Hon Can Antigua 71-74; V Swansea St Gabr *S & B* from 74; RD Clyne 88-96; Can Brecon Cathl from 90. *St Gabriel's Vicarage, Bryn Road, Brynmill, Swansea SA2 0AP* Tel (01792) 464011

WASTIE, Canon David Vernon. b 37. BA84. Chich Th Coll 79. **d** 81 **p** 82. C Bitterne Park *Win* 81-83; TV Chambersbury (Hemel Hempstead) *St Alb* 83-87; V Jersey St Luke *Win* 87-95; P-in-c Jersey St Jas 87-93; V 93-95; Hon Can Bukavu from 94; V Southbourne St Kath *Win* from 95. *St Katharine's Vicarage, 7 Wollaston Road, Bournemouth BH6 4AR* Tel (01202) 423986

WATCHORN, Canon Brian. b 39. Em Coll Cam BA61 MA65 Ex Coll Ox BA62. Ripon Hall Ox 61. **d** 63 **p** 64. C Bolton St Pet *Man* 63-66; Chapl G&C Coll Cam 66-74; V Chesterton St Geo *Ely* 75-82; Fell Dean and Chapl Pemb Coll Cam from 82; Lic to Offic *Ely* from 82; Hon Can Ely Cathl from 94. *Pembroke College, Cambridge CB2 1RF* Tel (01223) 338100

WATERER, Anthony Tatham. b 14. ARCA38. Cuddesdon Coll 45. **d** 47 **p** 48. C Arundel w Tortington and S Stoke *Chich* 47-48; C Henfield 48-50; V Farnham *Ripon* 50-73; Asst Chapl Scotton Banks Sanatorium 50-51; R Staveley w Copgrove 53-73; Perm to Offic *Win* from 72; R Rawreth w Rettendon *Chelmsf* 73-82; Chapl Rawreth Rehabilitation Cen 74-79; rtd 82; Perm to Offic *Chich* from 83; Hon Asst P Clayton w Keymer from 83. *9 Stafford Way, Hassocks, W Sussex BN6 8QG* Tel (01273) 844341

WATERFORD, Dean of. *See* NEILL, The Very Revd William Benjamin Alan

WATERHOUSE, Eric Thomas Benjamin. b 24. Lon Univ DipTh60. Qu Coll Birm 50. **d** 51 **p** 52. C Wolverhampton St Pet *Lich* 51-56; C Lower Gornal 56-57; V Walsall St Mark 57-60; R Kington w Dormston *Worc* 60-64; R Worc St Clem 64-77; P-in-c Abberton, Naunton Beauchamp and Bishampton etc 77-80; R 80-92; rtd 92. *7 Hazel Avenue, Evesham, Worcs WR11 6XT* Tel (01386) 421312

WATERHOUSE, Peter. b 46. Leeds Univ DipTh68. Linc Th Coll 68. **d** 70 **p** 71. C Consett *Dur* 70-73; C Heworth St Mary 73-76; V Stockton St Chad 76-83; V Lanchester from 83; RD Lanchester from 90. *The Vicarage, 1 Lee Hill Court, Lanchester, Durham DH7 0QE* Tel (01207) 521170

WATERMAN, Canon Albert Thomas. b 33. Roch Th Coll 61. **d** 64 **p** 65. C Dartford St Alb *Roch* 64-67; V from 79; V Ilkeston St Jo *Derby* 67-75; V Mackworth St Fran 75-79; RD Dartford *Roch* from 84; Hon Can Roch Cathl from 96. *St Alban's Vicarage, 51 Watling Street, Dartford DA1 1RW* Tel (01322) 224052

WATERMAN, Mrs Jacqueline Mahalah. b 45. ALCM71. Cant Sch of Min 82. **dss** 85 **d** 87 **p** 94. Wavertree H Trin *Liv* 85-87; Par Dn 87-90; Par Dn Anfield St Columba 90-94; C 94; TV Speke St Aid

94-97; P-in-c Walton St Jo from 97. *St John's Vicarage, 472 Rice Lane, Walton, Liverpool L9 2BW* Tel 0151-525 3458

WATERS, Arthur Brian. b 34. St Deiniol's Hawarden 71. **d** 73 **p** 74. C Bedwellty *Mon* 73-76; P-in-c Newport All SS 76-81; V Mynyddislwyn 81-91; C-in-c Maesglas Newport CD 91-95; I Maesglas and Duffryn from 95. *The Vicarage, Old Cardiff Road, Newport NP9 3AT*

WATERS, Charles Eric. b 14. Hatf Coll Dur LTh37 BA38. St Aug Coll Cant 34. **d** 38 **p** 39. C Gateshead St Cuth *Dur* 38-41; C Whitburn 41-46; V Witton le Wear 46-55; V E Grafton *Sarum* 55-62; V Tidcombe w Fosbury 55-62; R Bromham 62-79; P-in-c Chittoe 72-73; V 73-79; rtd 79. *3 St Mary's Court, Silver Street, Bridgwater, Somerset TA6 3EG* Tel (01278) 453675

WATERS, Charles Theodore Newton. b 27. **d** 51 **p** 52. C Becontree St Mary *Chelmsf* 51-53; C Lewisham St Jo Southend *S'wark* 62-63; C Clapham H Trin 63-66; C Morden 66-68; rtd 96; Perm to Offic *S'wark* from 96. *75 Bardsley Close, Croydon CR0 5PT* Tel 0181-680 2914

WATERS, David Keith. b 46. S Wales Bapt Coll DipTh73 DPS73 St Mich Coll Llan 93. **d** 93 **p** 94. In Bapt Ch 73-90; C Caerphilly *Llan* from 93. *St Andrew's House, Troed-y-Bryn, Penyrheol, Caerphilly CF83 2PX* Tel (01222) 884103

WATERS, Miss Jill Christine. b 43. CertEd64. Cranmer Hall Dur 82. **dss** 82 **d** 87 **p** 94. New Milverton *Cov* 82-86; Draycott-le-Moors w Forsbrook *Lich* 86-96; Par Dn 87-94; C 94-96; P-in-c Mow Cop from 96. *The Vicarage, 5 Congleton Road, Mow Cop, Stoke-on-Trent ST7 3PJ* Tel (01782) 515077

WATERS, John Michael. b 30. Qu Coll Cam BA53 MA58. Ridley Hall Cam 53. **d** 55 **p** 56. C Southport Ch Ch *Liv* 55-57; C Farnworth 57-62; V Blackb H Trin *Blackb* 63-70; Sec Birm Coun Chr Chs 70-77; Chapl Birm Cathl *Birm* 70-74; Dioc Ecum Officer 74-77; V Hednesford *Lich* 77-93; RD Rugeley 78-88; rtd 93; NSM Etton w Dalton Holme *York* from 93. *The Rectory, Etton, Beverley, N Humberside HU17 7PQ* Tel (01430) 810735

WATERS, Mark. b 51. Sarum & Wells Th Coll. **d** 82 **p** 83. C Clifton All SS w St Jo *Bris* 82-85; P-in-c Brislington St Anne 85-91; Dioc Soc Resp Officer *Sheff* 91-94; Community Org Citizen Organisation Foundn from 94; NSM Rotherham from 94. *9 The Copse, Bramley, Rotherham, S Yorkshire S66 0TB* Tel (01709) 548867

WATERS, Nicholas Marshall Stephenson. b 35. Selw Coll Cam BA59 MA63. Wells Th Coll 59. **d** 61 **p** 62. C Eastbourne St Mary *Chich* 61-64; Asst Chapl Ardingly Coll Haywards Heath 64-93; P-in-c Slindon, Eartham and Madehurst *Chich* from 93. *The Rectory, Dyers Lane, Slindon, Arundel, W Sussex BN18 0RE* Tel (01243) 814275

WATERS, Stephen. b 49. Chich Th Coll 83. **d** 85 **p** 86. C Baildon *Bradf* 85-87; C Altrincham St Geo *Ches* 87-89; TV Ellesmere Port 89-91; P-in-c Crewe St Jo 91-93; V Mossley from 93. *The Vicarage, 79 Leek Road, Congleton, Cheshire CW12 3HX* Tel (01260) 273182 E-mail stephen@frwaters.demon.co.uk

WATERS, William Paul. b 52. Aston Tr Scheme 84 Chich Th Coll 86. **d** 88 **p** 89. C Tottenham St Paul *Lon* 88-91; C Stroud Green H Trin 91-95; TV Wickford and Runwell *Chelmsf* from 95; Chapl Runwell Hosp Essex from 95. *St Mary's Vicarage, Church End Lane, Runwell, Wickford, Essex SS11 7JQ* Tel (01268) 732068

WATERSON, Raymond Arthur. b 25. Wells Th Coll 69. **d** 70 **p** 71. C Wotton St Mary *Glouc* 70-74; C Cirencester 74-79; P-in-c Falfield w Rockhampton 79-90; P-in-c Oldbury-on-Severn 85-90; rtd 90; Perm to Offic *B & W* from 90. *91 Brampton Way, Portishead, Bristol BS20 9YT* Tel 0117-984 5134

WATERSTONE, Canon Albert Thomas. b 23. TCD BA45 BD67. CITC 46. **d** 46 **p** 47. C Kilkenny St Canice Cathl *C & O* 46-50; P-in-c Borris-in-Ossory w Aghavoe 50-51; I 52-54; I Fiddown w Kilmacow 54-64; RD Durrow *M & K* 59-64; I Tullamore w Lynally and Rahan 64-73; I Tullamore w Durrow, Newtownfertullagh, Rahan etc 73-90; Can Meath 81-90; rtd 90. *Lynally House, Mocklagh, Blue Ball, Tullamore, Co Offaly, Irish Republic* Tel Tullamore (506) 21367

WATERSTREET, Canon John Donald. b 34. Trin Hall Cam BA58 MA62. Lich Th Coll 58. **d** 60 **p** 61. C Blackheath *Birm* 60-64; C Aston SS Pet and Paul 64-67; R Sheldon 67-77; RD Coleshill 75-77; V Selly Oak St Mary 77-89; RD Edgbaston 84-89; Hon Can Birm Cathl from 86; R The Whitacres and Shustoke from 89. *The Rectory, Dog Lane, Coleshill, Birmingham B46 2DU* Tel (01675) 481252

WATHEN, Mark William Gerard. b 12. TD45. ACIB. K Coll Lon 31. **d** 82 **p** 82. Hon C Broadford *Arg* 82-91; Hon C Fort William 82-91; Hon C Portree 82-96; rtd 96. *Talisker House, Carbost, Isle of Skye IV47 8SF* Tel (01478) 640245

WATHEN, Sydney Gordon. Open Univ BA FRSA94. EMMTC. **d** 86 **p** 87. NSM W Hallam and Mapperley *Derby* from 86. *40 Station Road, West Hallam, Ilkeston, Derbyshire DE7 6GW* Tel 0115-932 9255

WATHERSTON, Peter David. b 42. FCA76 Lon Univ BSc69. Ridley Hall Cam 75. **d** 77 **p** 78. C Barnsbury St Andr *Lon* 77-78; C Barnsbury St Andr w H Trin 79-80; C Barnsbury St Andr and H Trin w All SS 81; Chapl Mayflower Family Cen Canning Town *Chelmsf* 81-96; Perm to Offic from 96. *264 Plashet Grove, London E6 1DH* Tel 0181-470 6868

WATKIN, David William. b 42. FCA70. Qu Coll Birm 84. **d** 86 **p** 87. C Tunstall *Lich* 86-89; Camberwell Deanery Missr *S'wark* 89-95; V Trent Vale *Lich* from 95. *The Vicarage, Crosby Road, Stoke-on-Trent ST4 6JY* Tel (01782) 747669

WATKIN, Thomas Glyn. b 52. Barrister-at-Law (Middle Temple) 76 Pemb Coll Ox BA74 BCL75 MA77. Llan Dioc Tr Scheme 89. **d** 92 **p** 94. NSM Roath St Martin *Llan* from 92. *49 Cyncoed Road, Penylan, Cardiff CF2 6AB* Tel (01222) 495662

WATKINS, Alfred Felix Maceroni. b 20. Glouc Th Course 70. **d** 72 **p** 73. C Yate *Glouc* 72-75; V Dean Forest St Paul 75-90; rtd 90; Perm to Offic *Heref* from 93. *Leylines, 26 Southbank Road, Hereford HR1 2TJ* Tel (01432) 341014

WATKINS, Anthony John. b 42. St D Coll Lamp BA64 St Steph Ho Ox 64. **d** 66 **p** 67. C E Dulwich St Jo *S'wark* 66-71; C Tewkesbury w Walton Cardiff *Glouc* 71-75; Prec 75-81; Chapl Choral Ches Cathl *Ches* 75-81; V Brixworth w Holcot *Pet* from 81. *The Vicarage, Station Road, Brixworth, Northampton NN6 9DF* Tel (01604) 880286

WATKINS, Ms Betty Anne. b 45. Leeds Univ BA66 Nottm Univ PGCE67. EAMTC 94. **d** 97. C Ipswich St Aug *St E* from 97. *18 Fitzmaurice Road, Ipswich IP3 9AX* Tel (01473) 719562

WATKINS, Christopher. b 43. Sarum & Wells Th Coll 88. **d** 90 **p** 91. C Abergavenny St Mary w Llanwenarth Citra *Mon* 90-94; TV Cwmbran 94-96. *40 Pen-y-Fon Street, Morfa, Llanelli SA15 2HR* Tel (01554) 751261

WATKINS, David James Hier. b 39. Trin Coll Carmarthen CertEd60 Univ of Wales DipEd67 BEd76. **d** 90 **p** 91. NSM Oystermouth *S & B* from 90. *10 Lambswell Close, Langland, Swansea SA3 4HJ* Tel (01792) 369742

WATKINS, Gordon Derek. b 29. **d** 53 **p** 54. Australia 53-61; C Harrogate St Wilfrid *Ripon* 61-63; V Upton Park *Chelmsf* 63-67; V Gt and Lt Bentley 67-73; R Gt Canfield 73-78; Dioc Past Sec *Lon* 78-84; Sec Dioc Adv Cttee 84-94; PV Westmr Abbey 84-89; P-in-c St Martin Ludgate *Lon* 84-89; P in O 84-94; rtd 94. *21 Cramond Place, Dalgety Bay, Dunfermline, Fife KY11 5LS* Tel (01383) 822634

WATKINS, Mrs Gwyneth. b 35. Univ of Wales (Swansea) BA MEd. St Mich Coll Llan. **d** 91 **p** 97. NSM Llanbadarn Fawr w Capel Bangor and Goginan *St D* 91-94; P-in-c Maenordeifi and Capel Colman w Llanfihangel etc 94-97; R from 97. *The Rectory, Manordeifi, Cardigan SA43 2PN* Tel (01239) 682830

WATKINS, Herbert Ernest. b 22. Clifton Th Coll 39 Oak Hill Th Coll 43. **d** 46 **p** 47. C Buttershaw St Paul *Bradf* 46-48; C Rodbourne Cheney *Bris* 48-49; C Lenton *S'well* 49-52; V Upper Armley *Ripon* 52-58; V Rodbourne Cheney *Bris* 58-73; V Bilton St Helen *York* 73-77; V Tockwith 73-77; V Hurdsfield *Ches* 77-82; V Pott Shrigley 82-87; rtd 87; Perm to Offic *Cov* 87-88; Chapl to the Deaf *Bradf* from 88; Perm to Offic *Ches* from 88. *41 Hawkclife View, Silsden, Keighley, W Yorkshire BD20 0BS* Tel (01535) 656284

WATKINS, Jonathan. b 58. Padgate Coll of Educn BEd79. Trin Coll Bris DipHE92. **d** 92 **p** 93. C Wallington H Trin *S'wark* 92-97; C Hartley Wintney, Elvetham, Winchfield etc *Win* from 97. *40 Pool Road, Hartley Wintney, Hook, Hants RG27 8RD* Tel (01252) 843602

WATKINS, Miss Lorna Ann Francis Charles. b 59. Trin Coll Carmarthen BEd82. St Steph Ho Ox 82. **d** 84 **p** 97. C Tenby and Gumfreston *St D* 84-89; C Pembroke Dock 89-91; D-in-c Cosheston w Nash and Upton 91-92; C Bassaleg *Mon* 92-94; C Mynyddislwyn 94-95; TV Mynyddislwyn from 95. *Church House, 12 Orchard Court, Pontllanfraith, Blackwood NP2 2NG* Tel (01495) 221409

WATKINS, Dr Michael Morris. b 32. MRCS60 LRCP60. St Jo Coll Nottm DPS78. **d** 81 **p** 81. C Hornchurch St Andr *Chelmsf* 81-84; P-in-c Snitterfield w Bearley *Cov* 84-90; V 90-92; rtd 93; Perm to Offic *Cov* from 93. *Glaslyn, Riverside, Tiddington Road, Stratford-upon-Avon, Warks CV37 7BD* Tel (01789) 298085

WATKINS, Peter. b 51. Oak Hill Th Coll BA. **d** 82 **p** 83. C Whitnash *Cov* 82-86; V Wolston and Church Lawford from 86; RD Rugby from 94. *The Vicarage, Brook Street, Wolston, Coventry CV8 3HD* Tel (01203) 542722

WATKINS, Peter Gordon. b 34. St Pet Coll Ox BA57 MA61. Wycliffe Hall Ox 58. **d** 59 **p** 60. C Wolverhampton St Geo *Lich* 59-60; C Burton St Chad 60-61; C Westmr St Jas *Lon* 61-63; USA 63-65; V Ealing Common St Matt *Lon* from 67. *St Matthew's Vicarage, 7 North Common Road, London W5 2QA* Tel 0181-567 3820

WATKINS, Robert Henry. b 30. New Coll Ox BA54 MA60. Westcott Ho Cam 59. **d** 60 **p** 61. C Newc H Cross *Newc* 60-63; C Morpeth 63-67; V Delaval 67-80; V Lanercost w Kirkcambeck and Walton *Carl* 80-90; rtd 90; Perm to Offic *Carl* from 90. *Lowpark, Loweswater, Cockermouth, Cumbria CA13 0RU* Tel (01900) 85242

WATKINS, Walter. b 27. St Deiniol's Hawarden 80. **d** 81 **p** 82. C Lache cum Saltney *Ches* 81-84; P-in-c Over Tabley and High Legh 84-93; rtd 93; Perm to Offic *Ches* from 93; Perm to Offic *Lich* from 93. *30 St Matthew's Drive, Derrington, Stafford ST18 9LU* Tel (01785) 46349

WATKINS, Canon William Hywel. b 36. St D Coll Lamp BA58. Wycliffe Hall Ox 58. **d** 61 **p** 62. C Llanelli *St D* 61-68; V

Llwynhendy 68-78; V Slebech and Uzmaston w Boulston from 78; Asst Chapl OStJ 82-87; Sub-Chapl from 87; RD Daugleddau *St D* from 87; Hon Can St D Cathl 91-93; Can St D Cathl from 93. *The Vicarage, Uzmaston, Haverfordwest SA62 4AE* Tel (01437) 762325

WATKINS-JONES, Arthur Basil. b 24. Sarum Th Coll 67. **d** 69 **p** 70. C Broadstone *Sarum* 69-73; P-in-c Winterbourne Stickland and Turnworth etc 73-76; R 76-78; P-in-c Lilliput 78-82; V 82-89; rtd 89. *Oak Cottage, 31 Danecourt Road, Poole, Dorset BH14 0PG* Tel (01202) 746074

WATKINS-WRIGHT, Richard Kenneth David. b 39. Westcott Ho Cam 66. **d** 70 **p** 71. C Bilton *Cov* 70-74; Asst Chapl St Geo Hosp Lon 74-75; Chapl Oakwood Hosp Maidstone 76-78; R Gt w Lt Gransden *Ely* 78-97. *Halsou, De Lisle Close, Papworth Everard, Cambs CB3 8UT* Tel (01480) 830746

WATLING, His Honour Brian. b 35. QC79. K Coll Lon LLB56 Barrister 57. **d** 87 **p** 88. Hon C Lavenham *St E* 87-90; Hon C Nayland w Wiston from 90. *The Manse, Nayland, Suffolk CO6 4HX*

WATLING, Sister Rosemary Dawn. b 32. Newnham Coll Cam BA70 MA73. Gilmore Course 70. **dss** 85 **d** 87 **p** 94. CSA 79-90; Paddington St Mary *Lon* 85-86; E Bris 86-87; Hon Par Dn 87; Par Dn Clifton H Trin, St Andr and St Pet 87-94; C 94-95; rtd 95; NSM Wraxall *B & W* from 96. *Wraxall Rectory, Wraxall Hill, Wraxhall, Bristol BS19 1NA* Tel 0117-985 7086

WATSON, Canon Alan. b 34. Lon Univ LLB58. Linc Th Coll 58. **d** 60 **p** 61. C Spring Park *Cant* 60-63; C Sheerness H Trin w St Paul 63-68; R Allington 68-73; P-in-c Maidstone St Pet 73; R Allington and Maidstone St Pet from 73; Hon Can Cant Cathl from 85; RD Sutton 86-92. *The Rectory, 35 Poplar Grove, Allington, Maidstone, Kent ME16 0DE* Tel (01622) 758704

WATSON, Albert Victor. b 44. Ridley Hall Cam 85. **d** 87 **p** 88. C Hornchurch St Andr *Chelmsf* 87-94; P-in-c Tye Green w Netteswell 94-95; R from 95. *The Rectory, Tawneys Road, Harlow, Essex CM18 6QR* Tel (01279) 425138

WATSON, Alfred Keith. b 39. Birm Univ BSc61. Ox Min Course 93. **d** 96 **p** 97. NSM Aylesbury w Bierton and Hulcott *Ox* from 96. *3 Cottesloe Close, Wing, Leighton Buzzard, Beds LU7 0TB* Tel (01296) 688578

WATSON, Andrew John. b 61. CCC Cam BA82 MA90. Ridley Hall Cam 84. **d** 87 **p** 88. C Ipsley *Worc* 87-91; C Notting Hill St Jo and St Pet *Lon* 91-96; V E Twickenham St Steph from 96. *St Stephen's Vicarage, 21 Cambridge Park, Twickenham TW1 2JE* Tel 0181-892 5258

WATSON, Basil Alderson. b 16. OBE65. Selw Coll Cam BA38 MA44. Westcott Ho Cam 39. **d** 40 **p** 41. C Cambridge H Trin *Ely* 40-41; C Sugley *Newc* 41-44; Chapl RNVR 44-46; Chapl RN 46-70; V St Lawr Jewry *Lon* 70-86; RD The City 76-79; rtd 86. *19 Straightsmouth, London SE10 9LB* Tel 0181-853 0643

WATSON, The Very Revd Derek Richard. b 38. Selw Coll Cam BA61 MA65. Cuddesdon Coll 62. **d** 64 **p** 65. C New Eltham All SS *S'wark* 64-66; Chapl Ch Coll Cam 66-70; Bp's Dom Chapl *S'wark* 70-73; V Surbiton St Mark 73-77; V Surbiton St Andr and St Mark 77-78; Can Res and Treas S'wark Cathl 78-82; Dioc Dir of Ords 78-82; P-in-c Chelsea St Luke *Lon* 82-85; R 85-87; P-in-c Chelsea Ch Ch 86-87; R Chelsea St Luke and Ch Ch 87-96; AD Chelsea 94-96; Dean Sarum from 96. *The Deanery, 7 The Close, Salisbury SP1 2EF* Tel (01722) 322457

WATSON, Derek Stanley. b 54. NE Ord Course DipHE95. **d** 95 **p** 96. C W Acklam *York* from 95. *41 Ambleside Grove, Middlesborough, Cleveland TS5 7DQ* Tel (01642) 816997

WATSON, Mrs Diane Elsie. b 44. N Ord Course 92. **d** 95 **p** 96. C Grange St Andr *Ches* from 95; C Runcorn H Trin from 96. *Holy Trinity Vicarage, Grange Park Avenue, Runcorn, Cheshire WA7 5UT* Tel (01928) 572299

WATSON, Preb Donald Wace. b 17. Qu Coll Cam BA39 MA43. Lich Th Coll 39. **d** 41 **p** 42. C W Bromwich St Andr *Lich* 41-43; C Fenton 43-47; C-in-c Birches Head CD 47-48; V Smethwick St Steph *Birm* 48-51; R Kingstone w Gratwich *Lich* 51-55; V Kinver 55-82; Preb Lich Cathl 78-82; rtd 82; Perm to Offic *Heref* from 89. *The Stables, King Street, Much Wenlock, Shropshire TF13 6BL* Tel (01952) 728364

WATSON, Douglas John Muirhead. b 29. Keble Coll Ox BA52 MA56 DipEd. Ely Th Coll 58. **d** 60 **p** 61. C Charlton-by-Dover SS Pet and Paul *Cant* 60-62; C St Peter-in-Thanet 62-66; V W Wickham St Fran 66-72; V Headcorn 72-94; rtd 94; Perm to Offic *Cant* from 95. *4 Hastings Place, Sandwich, Kent CT2 0RE* Tel (01304) 614841

WATSON, Edward John. b 48. Chu Coll Cam BA70 MA74. Chich Th Coll 79. **d** 81 **p** 82. C Liv Our Lady and St Nic w St Anne *Liv* 81-84; C Clayton w Keymer *Chich* 84-87; V Frizington and Arlecdon *Carl* 87-94. *Tiraghoil Cottage, Bunessan, Isle of Mull PA67 6DU* Tel (01681) 700581

WATSON, Mrs Elsada Beatrice (Elsie). b 30. Westhill Coll Birm CPS86. WMMTC. **d** 89 **p** 94. NSM Birm St Pet *Birm* 89-90; NSM Lozells St Paul and St Silas 90-93; Par Dn 93-94; C 94-96; Perm to Offic from 96; rtd 96. *4 Maidstone Road, Birmingham B20 3EH* Tel 0121-356 0626

WATSON, Geoffrey. b 48. Liv Univ BEd71. Linc Th Coll 81. **d** 83 **p** 84. C Hartlepool St Luke *Dur* 83-87; P-in-c Shadforth 87-94; Soc Resp Officer 87-94; Dioc Rural Development Adv 90-94; V Staveley, Ings and Kentmere *Carl* from 94. *The Vicarage, Kentmere Road, Staveley, Kendal, Cumbria LA8 9PA* Tel (01539) 821267

WATSON, Gordon Mark Stewart. b 67. Wolv Poly BA90 DipEd. CITC BTh95. **d** 95 **p** 96. C Ballymoney w Finvoy and Rasharkin *Conn* from 95. *14 Queen's Avenue, Ballymoney, Co Antrim BT53 6DF* Tel (01265) 664329

WATSON, Graeme Campbell Hubert. b 35. Ch Ch Ox BA58 MA61. Coll of Resurr Mirfield 59. **d** 61 **p** 62. C Edin St Mary *Edin* 61-63; C Carrington *S'well* 63-67; Tanzania 67-77; P-in-c Kingston St Mary w Broomfield *B & W* 77-80; V 80-81; R Kingston St Mary w Broomfield etc 81-95; P-in-c Feock *Truro* from 95; Tutor SW Minl Tr Course from 95. *The Vicarage, Feock, Truro, Cornwall TR3 6SD* Tel (01872) 862044

WATSON, Hartley Roger. b 40. K Coll Lon. **d** 64 **p** 65. C Noel Park St Mark *Lon* 64-67; C Munster Square St Mary Magd 67-68; C Stamford Hill St Jo 68-70; Chapl RAF 70-76; R St Breoke *Truro* 76-84; P-in-c Egloshayle 82-84; R Wittering w Thornhaugh and Wansford *Pet* from 84. *The Rectory, Wittering, Peterborough PE8 6AQ* Tel (01780) 782428

WATSON, Henry Stanley. b 36. **d** 72 **p** 74. Hon C Bethnal Green St Jas Less *Lon* 72-83; Hon C Old Ford St Paul w St Steph and St Mark 83-88; Hon C Bethnal Green St Jas Less 89-93; Hon C Scarborough St Mary w Ch Ch and H Apostles *York* from 93. *36 Ashville Avenue, Scarborough, N Yorkshire YO12 7NF* Tel (01723) 375852

WATSON, Ian Leslie Stewart. b 50. Wycliffe Hall Ox 79. **d** 81 **p** 82. C Plymouth St Andr w St Paul and St Geo *Ex* 81-85; TV Ipsley *Worc* 85-90; V Woodley St Jo the Ev *Ox* 90-92; TR Woodley 92-95; Chapl Amsterdam w Den Helder and Heiloo *Eur* from 95. *Bouwmeester 2, 1188 DT, Amstelveen, The Netherlands* Tel Amsterdam (20) 441-0355 or 624-8877 Fax as telephone E-mail info@christchurch.nl

WATSON, James Valentine John Giles. b 65. Newc Univ BA87. Ripon Coll Cuddesdon BA91. **d** 92 **p** 93. C Newc St Geo *Newc* 92-95; TV Daventry, Ashby St Ledgers, Braunston etc *Pet* from 95. *The Rectory, High Street, Braunston, Daventry, Northants NN11 4HT* Tel (01788) 890235

WATSON, The Ven Jeffrey John Seagrief (Jeff). b 39. Em Coll Cam BA61 MA65. Clifton Th Coll 62. **d** 65 **p** 66. C Beckenham Ch Ch *Roch* 65-69; C Southsea St Jude *Portsm* 69-71; V Win Ch Ch *Win* 71-81; V Bitterne 81-93; RD Southn 83-93; Hon Can Win Cathl 91-93; Adn Ely from 93; Hon Can Ely Cathl from 93. *St Botolph's Rectory, 1A Summerfield, Cambridge CB3 9HE* Tel (01223) 350684

WATSON, John. b 16. Oak Hill Th Coll 76. **d** 78 **p** 79. Hon C Lexden *Chelmsf* 78-81; Perm to Offic *Ches* 81-85; Hon C Alsager St Mary from 85. *9 Woolaston Drive, Alsager, Stoke-on-Trent ST7 2PL* Tel (01270) 874565

WATSON, John. b 34. **d** 60 **p** 61. C Stockton St Pet *Dur* 60-64; C Darlington H Trin 64-66; V Swalwell 66-68; Perm to Offic 68-69; Perm to Offic *Leic* 69-74; Perm to Offic *Man* 74-76; rtd 96. *27 Fairlyn Drive, Bolton BL5 1HJ*

WATSON, John Davidson. b 25. Kelham Th Coll. **d** 58 **p** 59. C St Marychurch *Ex* 58-61; C Brixham 61-70; V Treverbyn *Truro* 70-73; V S Shields St Jude *Dur* 73-78; V Rekendyke 78-84; V Coleford w Holcombe *B & W* 84-91; rtd 91. *La Ribouilliere, 53510 Chatillon sur Colmont, France*

WATSON, Canon John Derrick. b 35. K Coll Lon 56. Edin Th Coll 60. **d** 61 **p** 62. C Fulham St Etheldreda *Lon* 61-64; P-in-c Stevenage H Trin *St Alb* 64-71; V 71-74; V Leagrave 74-84; RD Luton 80-82; V Eaton Socon from 84; Hon Can St Alb from 93; RD Biggleswade 94-96. *St Mary's Vicarage, 34 Drake Road, Eaton Socon, St Neots, Huntingdon, Cambs PE19 3HS* Tel (01480) 212219

WATSON, Preb John Francis Wentworth. b 28. St Jo Coll Nottm LTh59. **d** 59 **p** 60. C Egham *Guildf* 59-62; C-in-c Ewell St Paul Howell Hill CD 62-66; R Ashtead 66-72; V Plymouth St Andr w St Paul and St Geo *Ex* 72-94; Angl Adv TV SW 83-93; Westcountry TV 93-94; Preb Ex Cathl 84-94; rtd 94. *Woodland House, Western Road, Ivybridge, Devon PL21 9AL* Tel (01752) 893735

WATSON, John Lionel. b 39. G&C Coll Cam BA61 MA65. Ridley Hall Cam 62. **d** 64 **p** 65. C Toxteth Park St Philemon w St Silas *Liv* 64-69; C Morden *S'wark* 69-73; C Cambridge St Phil *Ely* 73-74; Chapl Elstree Sch Woolhampton 74-77; R Woolhampton w Midgham *Ox* 77-81; R Woolhampton w Midgham and Beenham Valance 81-95. *Westfield House, Littleton Road, Crawley, Winchester, Hants SO21 2QD* Tel (01962) 776892

WATSON, Canon John Robertson Thomas. b 27. CITC 68. **d** 70 **p** 71. C Belfast St Steph *Conn* 71-73; Bp's C Swanlinbar w Templeport *K, E & A* 73-82; I Arvagh w Carrigallen, Gowna and Columbkille from 82; Preb Kilmore Cathl from 88. *The Rectory, Arva, Cavan, Irish Republic* Tel Cavan (49) 35233

WATSON, Jonathan Ramsay George. b 38. Or Coll Ox BA61 MA65 DipEd62. Ridley Hall Cam 88. **d** 90 **p** 91. C Locks Heath *Portsm* 90-94; V Erith St Paul *Roch* from 94. *The Vicarage, 44A Colyers Lane, Erith, Kent DA8 3NP* Tel (01322) 332809

WATSON, Kenneth Roy. b 27. CEng68 MIMechE68. EMMTC 83. **d** 86 **p** 87. NSM Ashby-de-la-Zouch St Helen w Coleorton *Leic* 86-90; R Breedon cum Isley Walton and Worthington 90-93; rtd

93; Perm to Offic *Leic* from 93; Perm to Offic *Derby* from 93. *2 Meadow Gardens, Atherstone Road, Measham, Swadlincote, Derbyshire DE12 7EG* Tel (01530) 273263

WATSON, Laurence Leslie. b 31. Keble Coll Ox BA55 MA59. Ely Th Coll. **d** 57 **p** 58. C Solihull *Birm* 57-60; C Digswell *St Alb* 60-62; V Smethwick St Steph *Birm* 62-67; V Billesley Common 67-95; rtd 95. *10 Redwing Close, Bishopton, Stratford-upon-Avon, Warks CV37 9EX* Tel (01789) 294569

WATSON, Leonard Alexander David. b 37. Man Univ BSc59. Coll of Resurr Mirfield 62. **d** 64 **p** 65. C Rawmarsh w Parkgate *Sheff* 64-68; S Africa 69-74; TV E Runcorn w Halton *Ches* 74-79; TV Sanderstead All SS *S'wark* 79-86; TR Selsdon St Jo w St Fran from 86; RD Croydon Addington 90-95. *The Rectory, Upper Selsdon Road, South Croydon, Surrey CR2 8DD* Tel 0181-657 2343

WATSON, Michael Henry. b 44. Victoria Univ Wellington BA65 MA66. Wycliffe Hall Ox 75. **d** 77 **p** 78. C Farnborough *Roch* 77-81; New Zealand from 81. *PO Box 7023, Wellington South, New Zealand* Tel Wellington (4) 389 2760 or 389 9603 Fax 389 2109

WATSON, Michael Paul (Mike). b 58. Trin Coll Bris DipHE93. **d** 93 **p** 94. C Derby St Alkmund and St Werburgh *Derby* from 93. *54 Park Grove, Derby DE22 1HF* Tel (01332) 372408

WATSON, Nicholas Edgar (Nick). b 67. St Cath Coll Cam BA88 MA92. Wycliffe Hall Ox BA91. **d** 92 **p** 93. C Benfieldside *Dur* 92-95; C-in-c Stockton Green Vale H Trin CD 95-96; P-in-c Stockton H Trin from 96; Chapl Ian Ramsey Sch Stockton from 95. *4 Greymouth Close, Stockton-on-Tees, Cleveland TS18 5LF* Tel (01642) 585749

WATSON, Paul Frederick. b 44. MRCVS69 RVC(Lon) BSc66 BVetMed69 Sydney Univ PhD73. Oak Hill NSM Course 86. **d** 88 **p** 89. Hon C Muswell Hill St Jas w St Matt *Lon* from 88. *43 Grasmere Road, London N10 2DH* Tel 0181-444 7158

WATSON, Paul William. b 55. Huddersfield Poly BA. St Jo Coll Nottm. **d** 86 **p** 87. C Meltham Mills *Wakef* 86-89; C Meltham 89-90; TV Borehamwood *St Alb* 90-96; V Oswaldtwistle Immanuel and All SS *Blackb* from 96. *Immanuel Vicarage, New Lane, Oswaldtwistle, Accrington, Lancs BB5 3QN* Tel (01254) 233962

WATSON, Philip. b 60. RGN83. Qu Coll Birm 86. **d** 89 **p** 90. C Ordsall *S'well* 89-93; TV Benwell Team *Newc* from 93. *14 Bentinck Road, Newcastle upon Tyne NE4 6UU* Tel 0191-273 2055

✠**WATSON, The Rt Revd Richard Charles Challinor (Dick).** b 23. New Coll Ox BA48 MA48. Westcott Ho Cam 50. **d** 51 **p** 52 **c** 70. C Stratford St Jo *Chelmsf* 51-53; Tutor and Chapl Wycliffe Hall Ox 54-57; Chapl to Ox Pastorate 57-61; Chapl Wadh Coll Ox 57-62; V Hornchurch St Andr *Chelmsf* 62-70; R Burnley St Pet *Blackb* 70-77; Suff Bp Burnley 70-87; Hon Can Blackb Cathl 70-88; Asst Bp Ox from 87; rtd 88. *6 Church Road, Thame, Oxon OX9 3AJ* Tel (01844) 213853

WATSON, Richard Frederick. b 66. Avery Hill Coll BA87. Trin Coll Bris ADMT93. **d** 93 **p** 94. C Kempston Transfiguration *St Alb* 93-97; TV Dunstable from 97. *The Vicarage, 83 Halfmoon Lane, Dunstable, Beds LU5 4AE* Tel (01582) 668019

WATSON, Richard Rydill. b 47. Sarum & Wells Th Coll 74. **d** 77 **p** 78. C Cayton w Eastfield *York* 77-80; C Howden TM 80-82; P-in-c Burton Pidsea and Humbleton w Elsternwick 82-83; V Dormanstown 83-87; V Cotehill and Cumwhinton *Carl* 87-89; Chapl Harrogate Distr and Gen Hosp 89-94; Chapl Harrogate Health Care NHS Trust from 94. *Harrogate General Hospital, Knaresborough Road, Harrogate, N Yorkshire HG2 7ND* Tel (01423) 885959 or 864816

WATSON, Robert Bewley. b 34. Bris Univ BA59. Clifton Th Coll 56. **d** 61 **p** 62. C Bebington *Ches* 61-65; C Woking St Jo *Guildf* 65-68; V Knaphill from 68. *Trinity House, Trinity Road, Knaphill, Woking, Surrey GU21 2SY* Tel (01483) 473489

WATSON, Mrs Sheila Anne. b 53. St Andr Univ MA75 MPhil80. Edin Th Coll 79. **dss** 79 **d** 87 **p** 94. Bridge of Allan *St And* 79-80; Alloa 79-80; Monkseaton St Mary *Newc* 80-84; Adult Educn Officer *Lon* 84-87; Hon C Chelsea St Luke and Ch Ch from 87; Selection Sec ABM 92-93; Sen Selection Sec ABM from 93. *29 Burnstall Street, London SW3 3SR, or Church House, Great Smith Street, London SW1P 3NZ* Tel 0171-352 6331 or 222 9011 Fax 799 2714

WATSON, Miss Stephanie Abigail. b 61. Heriot-Watt Univ BA84 Dur Univ CCSk90. Cranmer Hall Dur 86. **d** 90 **p** 94. C Bishop's Castle w Mainstone *Heref* 90-93; Dep Chapl HM Pris Dur 93-95; Chapl HM Rem Cen Low Newton from 95. *The Chaplaincy, HM Remand Centre, Low Newton, Brasside, Durham DH1 5SD* Tel 0191-386 1141 Fax 386 2620

WATSON, Terence David. b 38. Jes Coll Ox BA61 MA67. Chich Th Coll 73. **d** 74 **p** 75. C Sidley *Chich* 74-78; C Woodham *Guildf* 78-86; C Willesborough w Hinxhill *Cant* 86-87; C Willesborough 87-93; C Maidstone St Mich 93-94; C Clacton St Jas *Chelmsf* from 94. *8 Trafalgar Road, Clacton-on-Sea, Essex CO15 1LR* Tel (01255) 434763

WATSON, Thomas Anthony. b 23. Chich Th Coll 50. **d** 52 **p** 53. C Ashburton w Buckland-in-the-Moor *Ex* 52-54; C Bideford 54-57; V Bishops Nympton 57-59; R Rose Ash 57-59; N Rhodesia 59-64; Zambia 64-65; V Honicknowle *Ex* 65-72; R Butterleigh 72-90; R Silverton 72-90; rtd 90; Chapl Palermo w Taormina *Eur* 90-93; Perm to Offic *Ex* from 93. *13A Lower North Street, Exeter EX4 3ET* Tel (01392) 424423

WATSON, Timothy Patrick. b 38. ALCD66. **d** 66 **p** 67. C Northwood Em *Lon* 66-70; TV High Wycombe *Ox* 70-76; Gen Sec Intercon Ch Soc 76-82; R Bath Weston All SS w N Stoke *B & W* 82-93; R Bath Weston All SS w N Stoke and Langridge 93-94; TR Cheltenham St Mary, St Matt, St Paul and H Trin *Glouc* from 94. *The Rectory, 18 Park Place, Cheltenham, Glos GL50 2QT* Tel (01242) 512208

WATSON, Miss Violet Hazel. b 29. SRN52 SCM54 RSCN59. Linc Th Coll 83. **dss** 85 **d** 87. Hammersmith SS Mich and Geo White City Estate CD *Lon* 85-86; Sunbury 86; Fulham St Dionis Parson's Green 86-87; Par Dn 87; Perm to Offic *St Alb* 88-90. *4 Hayes Terrace, Crown Lane, Shorne, Gravesend, Kent DA12 3DZ*

WATSON, William. b 36. Ripon Hall Ox 64. **d** 66 **p** 67. C Leamington Priors H Trin *Cov* 66-69; V Salford Priors 69-74; V Malin Bridge *Sheff* 74-79; Chapl Shrewsbury R Hosps 79-89; Chapl R Hallamshire Hosp Sheff 89-92; Chapl Cen Sheff Univ Hosps NHS Trust 92-93; P-in-c Alveley and Quatt *Heref* 93-96; rtd 96; Chapl N Gen Hosp NHS Trust Sheff from 96; Chapl Weston Park Hosp Sheff from 96. *396 Stannington Road, Stannington, Sheffield S6 5QQ* Tel 0114-232 4005

WATSON, William Lysander Rowan. b 26. TCD BA47 MA50 Clare Coll Cam MA52 St Pet Hall Ox MA57. **d** 49 **p** 50. C Chapelizod and Kilmainham *D & G* 49-51; Tutor Ridley Hall Cam 51-55; Chapl 55-57; Chapl St Pet Coll Ox 57-93; Fell and Tutor 59-93; Sen Tutor 77-81; Vice Master 83-85; Lect Th Ox Univ 60-93; rtd 93. *19 Cobden Crescent, Oxford OX1 4LJ* Tel (01865) 721895

WATSON-PEGMAN, John Basil. b 24. **d** 58 **p** 59. C Far Headingley St Chad *Ripon* 58-61; R Slingsby *York* 61-64; V Hovingham 61-64; R Guisborough 64-68; Miss to Seamen 68-87; E Regional Dir 74-87; Lic to Offic *Chelmsf* 69-74; Lic to Offic *Linc* 74-87; V Skelsmergh w Selside and Longsleddale *Carl* 87-90; rtd 90. *c/o Dale Cottage, Slingsby Walk, Harrogate, N Yorkshire HG2 8LS*

WATSON WILLIAMS, Richard Hamilton Patrick. b 31. SS Coll Cam BA57 MA62. St Aug Coll Cant. **d** 59 **p** 60. C Dorking St Paul *Guildf* 59-63; C Portsea St Mary *Portsm* 63-66; V Culgaith *Carl* 66-71; V Kirkland 66-71; V Wigton 72-79; Warden Dioc Conf Ho Crawshawbooth *Man* 79-82; P-in-c Crawshawbooth 79-82; Master Lady Kath Leveson Hosp from 82; P-in-c Temple Balsall *Birm* 82-84; V from 84. *The Master's House, Knowle, Solihull, W Midlands B93 0AL* Tel (01564) 772415

WATT, The Very Revd Alfred Ian. b 34. FRSA95. Edin Th Coll 57. **d** 60 **p** 61. Chapl St Paul's Cathl Dundee *Bre* 60-63; Prec 63-66; P-in-c Dundee H Cross 64-66; R Arbroath 66-69; R Perth St Ninian *St And* 69-82; Provost St Ninian's Cathl Perth 69-82; Can St Ninian's Cathl Perth from 82; R Kinross 82-95; Dean St Andr from 89. *33 Stirling Road, Milnathort, Kinross KY13 7XS* Tel (01577) 865711

WATT, Prof William Montgomery. b 09. Edin Univ MA30 PhD44 Ball Coll Ox BA32 BLitt36 MA36 Aber Univ Hon DD66. Cuddesdon Coll 38. **d** 39 **p** 40. C W Brompton St Mary *Lon* 39-41; C Edin Old St Paul *Edin* 41-43; Hon C 46-60; Jerusalem 43-46; Lect Edin Univ 46-53; Reader 53-64; Prof Arabic and Islamic Studies 64-91; Hon C Edin St Columba *Edin* 60-67; Hon C Dalkeith 80-93; Hon C Lasswade 80-93; rtd 93. *The Neuk, 2 Bridgend, Dalkeith, Midlothian EH22 1JT* Tel 0131-663 3197

WATT-WYNESS, Gordon. b 25. Cranmer Hall Dur 70 St Jo Coll Dur 70. **d** 72 **p** 73. C Scarborough St Mary w Ch Ch, St Paul and St Thos *York* 72-76; R Rossington *Sheff* 76-90; rtd 90. *29 Church Street, Filey, N Yorkshire YO14 9ED* Tel (01723) 516608

WATTERSON, Mrs Susan Mary. b 50. S & M Dioc Inst 84. **d** 87 **p** 94. NSM Rushen *S & M* 87-89; Hon Par Dn Castletown 89-94; C 94-96; Dioc Youth Officer 87-91; Bp's Adv for Healing Min 91-94; Chapl (Asst) Bris Univ *Bris* from 96; Hon C Bris St Mich and St Paul from 96. *12 St Paul's Road, Clifton, Bristol BS8 1LR* Tel 0117-973 3963 or 928 8823

WATTERSON, William Howard. b 16. Dur Univ LTh39 BA47 MA58. St Aid Birkenhead 36. **d** 39 **p** 40. C Wakef St Andr *Wakef* 39-41; C Seacombe *Ches* 41-43; Chapl RAFVR 43-46; Perm to Offic *Dur* 46-47; Ho Master and Hd of Div Qu Eliz Gr Sch Ashbourne 48-53; Hd of RE Waterloo Gr Sch 53-72; Lic to Offic *Liv* 70-81; Hd of RE Aylesbury High Sch Bucks 72-77; Perm to Offic *Ox* 72-77; rtd 81; Perm to Offic *Liv* from 81. *10 Dinorwic Road, Southport, Merseyside PR8 4DL* Tel (01704) 65682

WATTHEY, Arthur Edward. b 20. St Cath Coll Cam BA45 MA48. St Aug Coll Cant 73. **d** 73 **p** 74. NSM Glen Magna w Stretton Magna *Leic* 73-76; NSM Carlton Curlieu, Illston on the Hill etc 76-81; Perm to Offic from 81; Perm to Offic *Pet* 85-96; Bp's Insp of Par Registers and Records *Leic* from 90. *2 The Chase, Great Glen, Leicester LE8 9EQ* Tel 0116-259 2603

WATTLEY, Jeffery Richard. b 57. Univ of Wales (Abth) BSc(Econ)79. Trin Coll Bris BA92. **d** 92 **p** 93. C Reading Greyfriars *Ox* 92-96; V Wonersh *Guildf* from 96. *The Vicarage,*

The Street, Wonersh, Guildford, Surrey GU5 0PF Tel (01483) 893131

WATTON, Robert Newman Kingsley. b 45. Qu Coll Birm 72. **d** 74 **p** 75. C Madron w Morvah *Truro* 74-78; Dioc Adv in RE 78-81; P-in-c Lostwithiel 78-83; P-in-c Lanhydrock 81-83; P-in-c Lanivet 81-82; V Launceston 83-91; RD Trigg Major 89-91; R Kingston, Langton Matravers and Worth Matravers *Sarum* from 91. *The Rectory, St George's Close, Langton Matravers, Swanage, Dorset BH19 3HZ* Tel (01929) 422559

WATTS, Anthony George (Tony). b 46. K Coll Lon BD69 AKC69 Lon Univ CertEd70. Sarum & Wells Th Coll 82. **d** 84 **p** 85. C Wimborne Minster and Holt *Sarum* 84-87; P-in-c Shilling Okeford 87-92; Chapl Croft Ho Sch Shillingstone 87-92; R W Parley *Sarum* from 92. *The Rectory, 250 New Road, West Parley, Ferndown, Dorset BH22 8EW* Tel (01202) 873561

WATTS, Anthony John. b 30. AKC59. **d** 60 **p** 61. C Whitburn *Dur* 60-63; C Croxdale 63-65; V Warrington St Pet *Liv* 65-70; V Peel *Man* 70-78; P-in-c Bury St Mark 78-81; V Davyhulme Ch Ch from 81. *Christ Church Vicarage, 14 Welbeck Avenue, Urmston, Manchester M41 0GJ* Tel 0161-748 2018

WATTS, Canon Arthur James. b 08. Hatf Coll Dur BA30 MA47. **d** 32 **p** 33. Chapl All Hallows Sch Honiton 32-34; C Ex St Jas *Ex* 34-36; C Sidmouth St Nic 36-40; V Townstall w Dartmouth 40-45; V Watlington *Ox* 45-51; R Harpsden w Bolney 51-77; Chapl Henley War Memorial Hosp 53-77; Dir of Educn 56-65; Hon Can Ch Ch 59-77; RD Henley 64-73; rtd 77. *c/o C J F Watts Esq, 18 Meadow Road, Salisbury SP2 7BN* Tel (01722) 330965

WATTS, David Henry. b 27. Ex Coll Ox BA50 MA55. Wells Th Coll 51. **d** 53 **p** 54. C Haslemere *Guildf* 53-55; C Chelmsf Cathl *Chelmsf* 55-58; Succ Chelmsf Cathl 55-58; V Chessington *Guildf* 58-62; Educn Officer Essex Educn Cttee 62-70; HMI of Schs 70-87; Hon C Wetherby *Ripon* 79-87; P-in-c Healaugh w Wighill, Bilbrough and Askham Richard *York* 87-89; Chapl HM Pris Askham Grange 87-96; rtd 89. *3 Westwood Way, Boston Spa, Wetherby, W Yorkshire LS23 6DX* Tel (01937) 845005

WATTS, Canon Frank Walter. b 30. St Boniface Warminster 53 AKC54. **d** 54 **p** 55. C Llandough w Leckwith *Llan* 54-56; C Llanishen and Lisvane 56-59; C Gt Marlow *Ox* 59-60; R Black Bourton 60-63; V Carterton 60-63; C-in-c Brize Norton 61-63; V Brize Norton and Carterton 63-69; Australia from 69; Hon Can Perth from 78; rtd 95. *1 Allambi Way, South Yunderup, W Australia 6208* Tel Perth (9) 537 8178 Fax as telephone

WATTS, Dr Fraser Norman. b 46. FBPsS80 CPsychol89 Magd Coll Ox BA68 MA74 Lon Univ MSc70 PhD75 Magd Coll Cam DipTh90. Westcott Ho Cam 88. **d** 90 **p** 91. NSM Harston w Hauxton *Ely* 90-95; P-in-c 91-95; Lect Cam Univ from 94; Fell Qu Coll Cam from 94; Chapl Cam St Edw Prop Chpl *Ely* from 95. *81 Church Road, Hauxton, Cambridge CB2 5HS* Tel (01223) 871810

WATTS, Gordon Sidney Stewart. b 40. CITC 63. **d** 66 **p** 67. C Belfast St Steph *Conn* 66-69; CF 69-94; V Boldre w S Baddesley *Win* 94-96; P-in-c Warmfield *Wakef* from 96. *The Vicarage, Kirkthorpe, Wakefield, W Yorkshire WF1 5SZ* Tel (01924) 896327

WATTS, Canon Horace Gordon. b 20. TCD BA42 MA52. **d** 43 **p** 44. C Tralee *L & K* 43-46; I Dunmanway St Edm *C, C & R* 46-51; I Drimoleague w Caheragh 51-56; I Fanlobbus Union 56-76; Can Cloyne Cathl 67-68; Preb Cork Cathl 67-88; Treas Cloyne Cathl 68-88; I Douglas w Frankfield 76-86; I Douglas Union w Frankfield 86-88; rtd 88. *St Anton, 29 Carrigcourt, Carrigaline, Co Cork, Irish Republic* Tel Cork (21) 373406

WATTS, Ian Charles. b 63. Hull Univ BA85. Linc Th Coll 86. **d** 88 **p** 89. C W Kirby St Bridget *Ches* 88-93; V High Lane from 93. *The Vicarage, 85 Buxton Road, High Lane, Stockport, Cheshire SK6 8DX* Tel (01663) 762627

WATTS, Ian Harold. b 15. St Pet Coll Ox BA39 MA47. Wycliffe Hall Ox. **d** 65 **p** 66. Nigeria 65-68; Chapl Uppingham Sch Leics 68-73; Hon C Mirfield *Wakef* 73-79; Chapl Cannes *Eur* 80-87; rtd 87. *3 Golf Court, High Street, Aberlady, Longniddry, East Lothian EH32 0SQ* Tel (01875) 870681

WATTS, John Robert. b 39. Leeds Univ BSc60 MSc63 DipEd63. Oak Hill Th Coll 88. **d** 90 **p** 91. C Partington and Carrington *Ches* 90-93; P-in-c Tintwistle from 93. *The Vicarage, Tintwistle, Hadfield, Hyde, Cheshire SK14 7JR* Tel (01457) 852575

WATTS, John Harry. b 24. St Aid Birkenhead 57. **d** 59 **p** 60. C Fairfield *Derby* 59-61; C King Sterndale 59-61; C Wirksworth w Carsington 61-65; V S Wingfield 65-86; C-in-c Wessington CD 77-86; V S Wingfield and Wessington 86-89; rtd 89; Perm to Offic *Derby* from 89. *57 Abbotts Road, Alfreton, Derbyshire DE55 7HD* Tel (01773) 521063

WATTS, John Stanley. b 28. LCP62 Birm Univ DipEd65 MEd72 Nottm Univ MPhil83. Qu Coll Birm 83. **d** 86 **p** 87. Hon C Dudley St Fran *Worc* 86-91; Hon C Sedgley St Mary *Lich* 91-93; Hon C Sedgley St Mary *Worc* from 93. *5 Warren Drive, Sedgley, Dudley, W Midlands DY3 3RQ* Tel (01902) 661265

WATTS, Kenneth Francis. b 17. St Fran Coll Brisbane ThL39. **d** 40 **p** 41. Australia 40-55; C Maidstone All SS *Cant* 55-58; R Elmstone w Preston 58-63; R Stourmouth 59-63; V Cheriton Street 63-78; V Cheriton All So w Newington 78-80; New Zealand from 80; rtd 82. *4/41 Admiral Crescent, Hamilton, New Zealand*

WATTS, Mrs Mary Kathleen. b 31. Lon Univ DipRS73 BA86. Gilmore Ho 73. **dss** 77 **d** 87 **p** 94. Lower Streatham St Andr *S'wark* 77-88; C 87-88; C Streatham Immanuel w St Anselm 87-88; C Streatham Immanuel and St Andr 90-91; rtd 91; Perm to Offic *S'wark* 91-94; Hon C Norbury St Oswald from 94. *25 Hilldown Road, London SW16 3DZ* Tel 0181-764 6165

WATTS, Paul George. b 43. Nottm Univ BA67. Wells Th Coll 67. **d** 69 **p** 70. C Sherwood *S'well* 69-74; Chapl Trent (Nottm) Poly 74-80; V Nottingham All SS 80-84; Public Preacher from 84. *16 Grosvenor Avenue, Nottingham NG5 3DX* Tel 0115-960 9964

WATTS, Canon Peter Alan Witney. b 37. Dur Univ BA59 Birm Univ MSocSc83. Qu Coll Birm DipTh61. **d** 61 **p** 62. C Hamstead St Paul *Birm* 61-65; C Ward End 65-66; V Burney Lane 66-73; V Sutton Coldfield St Chad from 73; Hon Can Birm Cathl from 89. *The Vicarage, 41 Hollyfield Road, Sutton Coldfield, W Midlands B75 7SN* Tel 0121-329 2995

WATTS, Raymond Ivor. b 31. DIM. LNSM course. **d** 85 **p** 86. NSM Scotter w E Ferry *Linc* from 85. *5 St Peter's Road, Scotter, Gainsborough, Lincs DN21 3SG* Tel (01724) 762691

WATTS, Rebecca Harriet. b 61. St Cath Coll Cam BA83 MA Welsh Coll of Music & Drama 84. Wycliffe Hall Ox 87. **d** 90 **p** 94. C Goldsworth Park *Guildf* 90-94; Chapl Wadh Coll Ox from 94; C Ox St Mary V w St Cross and St Pet *Ox* 94-97. *156 Kingston Road, Oxford OX2 6RP* Tel (01865) 513803 or 277905

WATTS, Roger Edward. b 39. S'wark Ord Course 85. **d** 88 **p** 89. C Belmont *S'wark* 88-92; R Godstone from 92. *The Rectory, 17 Ivy Mill Lane, Godstone, Surrey RH9 8NK* Tel (01883) 742354

WATTS, Roger Mansfield. b 41. CEng76 MIEE76 Univ of Wales (Cardiff) BSc63 Southn Univ. Chich Th Coll 89. **d** 91 **p** 92. C Chippenham St Andr w Tytherton Lucas *Bris* 91-93; C Henfield w Shermanbury and Woodmancote *Chich* 93-96; R Jedburgh *Edin* from 96. *The Rectory, 46 Castlegate, Jedburgh, Roxburghshire TD8 6BB* Tel (01835) 863892

WATTS, Ronald Horace (Ron). b 57. CITC DTh92. **d** 92 **p** 93. C Sligo *K, E & A* 92-93; C Limerick City *L & K* 94-95; I Holmpatrick w Balbriggan and Kenure *D & G* from 95. *Holmpatrick Rectory, Miller's Lane, Skerries, Co Dublin, Irish Republic* Tel Dublin (1) 849 2247

WATTS, Mrs Valerie Anne. b 44. UEA BEd79. EAMTC 90. **d** 93 **p** 94. NSM N Walsham w Antingham *Nor* from 93. *15 Millfield Road, North Walsham, Norfolk NR28 0EB* Tel (01692) 405119

WATTS, Wilfred Richard James. b 11. St Mich Coll Llan 64. **d** 66 **p** 66. C Coleford w Staunton *Glouc* 66-69; V Viney Hill 69-82; rtd 82; Perm to Offic *Glouc* from 82. *5 Lambert Drive, Shurdington, Cheltenham, Glos GL51 5SP* Tel (01242) 862377

WATTS, William Henry Norbury. b 51. CertEd. St Jo Coll Nottm 87. **d** 89 **p** 90. C S Molton w Nymet St George, High Bray etc *Ex* 89-93; TV Swanage and Studland *Sarum* from 93. *The Vicarage, School Lane, Studland, Swanage, Dorset BH19 3AJ* Tel (01929) 450441

WAUD, John David. b 31. N Ord Course 82. **d** 85 **p** 86. C Cayton w Eastfield *York* 85-88; R Brandesburton 88-93; R Beeford w Frodingham and Foston from 93. *The Rectory, Rectory Lane, Beeford, Driffield, N Humberside YO25 8BA* Tel (01262) 488042

WAUDBY, Miss Christine. b 45. TCert66. Trin Coll Bris DipHE. **d** 90 **p** 94. C Weston-super-Mare Ch Ch *B & W* 90-94; C Blackheath *Birm* from 94. *25 Garland Crescent, Halesowen, W Midlands B62 9NJ* Tel 0121-421 4821

WAUGH, Mrs Jane Leitch. b 38. DMusEd60 CertEd61 Toronto Univ MDiv83. Trin Coll Toronto 80. **d** 84 **p** 94. Canada 84-87; Par Dn Dunnington *York* 88-90; Perm to Offic 90-93; NSM York St Olave w St Giles 93-96. *Moonrakers, Rectory Corner, Brandsby, York YO6 4RJ* Tel (01347) 888637

WAUGH, Canon Nigel John William. b 56. TCD BA78 MA81. CITC 76. **d** 79 **p** 80. C Ballymena *Conn* 79-82; C Ballyholme *D & D* 82-84; I Bunclody w Kildavin *C & O* 84-86; I Bunclody w Kildavin and Clonegal 86-91; I Bunclody w Kildavin, Clonegal and Kilrush from 91; RD New Ross from 86; Preb Ferns Cathl 88-91; Treas 91-96; Radio Officer (Cashel) 90-91; (Ferns) from 92; Dioc Info Officer (Ferns) from 91; Prec Ferns Cathl from 96. *St Mary's Rectory, Bunclody, Enniscorthy, Co Wexford, Irish Republic* Tel Enniscorthy (54) 77652 Mobile 088-627915 Fax 76151 E-mail nwaugh@iol.ie

WAXHAM, Derek Frank. b 33. Oak Hill Th Coll 76. **d** 79 **p** 80. Hon C Old Ford St Paul w St Steph *Lon* 79-82; Hon C Old Ford St Paul w St Steph and St Mark 82-89; NSM Bow w Bromley St Leon from 89. *39 Hewlett Road, London E3 5NA* Tel 0181-980 1748

WAY, Albert James. b 27. St D Coll Lamp BA61 DipTh63. **d** 63 **p** 64. C Neath w Llantwit *Llan* 63-68; C Watford St Jo *St Alb* 68; R Clayhidon *Ex* 68-76; V Llanbadog and Llanllowell *Mon* 76-83; V Llanhilleth from 83. *The Rectory, Aberbeeg, Abertillery NP3 2DA* Tel (01495) 214236

WAY, Andrew Lindsay. b 43. Linc Th Coll 76. **d** 78 **p** 79. C Shenfield *Chelmsf* 78-82; C Waltham *Linc* 82-84; V New Waltham 84-89; R Duxford *Ely* 89-94; V Hinxton 89-94; V Ickleton 89-94; P-in-c Doddington w Benwick 94-97; P-in-c Wimblington 94-97; R Doddington w Benwick and Wimblington from 97. *The Rectory,*

Ingle's Lane, Doddington, March, Cambs PE15 0TE Tel (01354) 740692

WAY, Anthony Hilton (Tony). b 21. ARIBA. Chich Th Coll 57. **d** 59 **p** 60. C Chich St Paul and St Bart *Chich* 59-61; C Hangleton 61-63; V Horam 63-70; V Ditchling 70-77; Asst Dioc Sec 77-83; Chapl Dioc Ch Ho 79-83; V Linchmere 83-91; rtd 91; Perm to Offic *Chich* from 91. *59 Finches Garden, Lindfield, Haywards Heath, W Sussex RH16 2PB* Tel (01444) 484584

WAY, Mrs Barbara Elizabeth. b 47. Open Univ BA82 Hull Univ PGCE86. Linc Th Coll IDC78. **dss** 78 **d** 87 **p** 94. Shenfield *Chelmsf* 78-82; Adult Educn Adv *Linc* 82-85; Dioc Lay Min Adv 85; New Waltham 82-89; Min 87-89; Tetney 86-89; Min 87-89; NSM Duxford *Ely* 89-94; NSM Ickleton 89-94; NSM Hinxton 89-94; Dir of Past Studies E Anglian Min Tr Course 91-94; Min Pampisford 92-94; P-in-c Coates 94-95; TV Whittlesey, Pondersbridge and Coates from 95. *The Rectory, North Green, Coates, Whittlesey, Peterborough PE7 2BQ* Tel (01733) 840254

WAY, Colin George. b 31. St Cath Coll Cam BA55 MA59 Lon Inst of Educn PGCE58. EAMTC. **d** 84 **p** 85. NSM Hempnall *Nor* 84-87; C Gaywood, Bawsey and Mintlyn 87-90; R Acle w Fishley and N Burlingham 90-96; RD Blofield 95-96; rtd 96; Perm to Offic *Nor* from 96. *The Swan House, Topcroft, Bungay, Suffolk NR35 2BL* Tel (01508) 482222

WAY, David Charles. b 61. St Mich Coll Llan BTh94. **d** 97. C Cardiff St Mary and St Steph w St Dyfrig etc *Llan* from 97. *43 Pentre Street, Grangetown, Cardiff CF1 7QX* Tel (01222) 230054

WAY, David Victor. b 54. Pemb Coll Ox MA DPhil. Cranmer Hall Dur BA Cuddesdon Coll 83. **d** 85 **p** 86. C Chenies and Lt Chalfont *Ox* 85-87; C Chenies and Lt Chalfont, Latimer and Flaunden 87-88; Tutor and Dir of Studies Sarum & Wells Th Coll 88-93; Selection Sec ABM from 94; Sec Minl Educn Cttee from 94. *Church House, Great Smith Street, London SW1P 3NZ* Tel 0171-222 9011 Fax 799 2714

WAY, Lawrence William. b 32. St Mich Coll Llan 77. **d** 79 **p** 80. C Merthyr Dyfan *Llan* 79-82; V Abercynon 82-84; TV Cwmbran *Mon* 84-86; V Caerwent w Dinham and Llanfair Discoed etc 86-90; V Pontnewydd 90-93; rtd 93. *8 Ceredig Court, Llanyrafon, Cwmbran NP44 8SA* Tel (01633) 865309

WAY, Michael David. b 57. K Coll Lon BD78 AKC78. St Steph Ho Ox 79. **d** 80 **p** 83. C Bideford *Ex* 80-81; Hon C Wembley Park St Aug *Lon* 81-84; C Kilburn St Aug w St Jo 84-89; V Earlsfield St Jo *S'wark* 89-92; Project Co-ord CARA from 92. *13 Sparkford House, Sunbury Lane, London SW11 3NQ* Tel 0171-792 8299

WAYNE, Kenneth Hammond. b 31. Bps' Coll Cheshunt 58. **d** 61 **p** 62. C Eyres Monsell CD *Leic* 61-62; C Loughborough Em 62-65; C-in-c Staunton Harold 65-73; R Breedon w Isley Walton 65-73; V Leic St Phil 73-85; V Ault Hucknall *Derby* 85-95; rtd 95. *The Haven, 3 Burton Walk, East Leake, Loughborough, Leics LE12 6LB* Tel (01509) 852848

WAYTE, Alleyn Robert. b 33. Trin Coll Ox BA56 MA60. Westcott Ho Cam 60. **d** 61 **p** 62. C Cannock *Lich* 61-66; P-in-c Dawley 66-75; V Stretton w Claymills 75-92; rtd 92; Perm to Offic *Derby* from 92. *2 Church Close, Willington, Derby DE65 6EN* Tel (01283) 701815

WAYTE, Christopher John. b 28. Lon Univ BSc54. Wells Th Coll 54. **d** 56 **p** 57. C Maidstone St Martin *Cant* 56-60; C W Wickham St Jo 60-61; C Birchington w Acol 61-64; C-in-c Buckland Valley CD 64-68; R Biddenden 68-80; P-in-c Boughton Monchelsea 80-85; V St Margarets-at-Cliffe w Westcliffe etc 85-91; rtd 92; Perm to Offic *Cant* from 92. *9 St John's Road, Hythe, Kent CT21 4BE* Tel (01303) 263060

WEALE, Colin Alexander. b 26. Univ of Wales (Lamp) BA49 Lon Univ DipRS77 Open Univ MPhil87 Middx Univ PhD96. Lambeth STh81 Sarum Th Coll 49. **d** 51 **p** 52. C Swansea St Mary and H Trin *S & B* 51-55; Min Can Brecon Cathl 55-59; C Brecon w Battle 55-59; V Llanbister and Llanbadarn Fynydd w Llananno 59-61; R Bengeo H Trin *St Alb* 61-69; R Bengeo 69-93; rtd 93; Perm to Offic *Nor* from 93. *1 Diana Way, Caister-on-Sea, Great Yarmouth, Norfolk NR30 5TP* Tel (01493) 377946

WEARE, Sydney Vincent. b 17. Solicitor 39 Linc Coll Ox BA48 MA52 Univ of W Aus MA57. Westcott Ho Cam 48. **d** 50 **p** 51. C St Jo Wood *Lon* 50-55; CF (TA) 54-55; Australia from 55; P-in-c Lolworth *Ely* 80-81; P-in-c Fen Drayton w Conington 80-81; rtd 81; Perm to Offic *Ely* from 81. *42 Rosalie Street, Shenton Park, W Australia 6008, or 63 Cedars Road, Beckenham, Kent BR3 4JG* Tel Perth (9) 381-2696 or 0181-650 8856

WEARMOUTH, Alan Wilfred. b 54. St Paul's Cheltenham CertEd75 Bris Univ BEd76. Glouc Sch of Min 85. **d** 88 **p** 89. Hon C Coleford w Staunton *Glouc* from 88. *22 Forest Patch, Christchurch, Coleford, Glos GL16 8RB* Tel (01594) 832660

WEARMOUTH, Paul Frederick. b 37. Bede Coll Dur 57 RCM Man 59. Wells Th Coll 60. **d** 62 **p** 63. C Bradford Ch Ch *Man* 62; C Bedford Leigh 63-66; C Prestbury *Ches* 66-67; Ho Master Castleview Sch Sunderland 68-84; rtd 84; Perm to Offic *Dur* from 84. *9 Withernsea Grove, Ryhope, Sunderland SR2 0BU* Tel 0191-521 0127

WEARN, William Frederick. b 51. S Dios Minl Tr Scheme. **d** 85 **p** 86. NSM Hythe *Win* 85-94; Asst Chapl HM Pris Liv 94-95; Chapl HM Pris Wakef 95-96; Chapl HM Pris Garth 96-97; rtd 97. *66 Sussex Road, Southport, Merseyside PR9 0SP*

WEATHERHEAD, The Very Revd Thomas Leslie. b 13. Hatf Coll Dur BA37 LTh37. St Aug Coll Cant 32. **d** 37 **p** 38. C Beeston Hill H Spirit *Ripon* 37-40; C Wensley 40-42; Chapl RAFVR 42-47; C Leeds Halton St Wilfrid *Ripon* 47-48; V New Mills *Derby* 48-59; R Staveley 59-65; Dean and V-Gen Nassau 65-72; R Felmingham *Nor* 72-79; P-in-c Suffield 72-74; R 74-79; P-in-c Colby w Banningham and Tuttington 72-74; R 74-79; RD Tunstead 76-79; rtd 79. *St Nicholas' Lodge, 25 Bishopton Lane, Ripon, N Yorkshire HG4 2QN* Tel (01765) 600413

WEATHERLEY, Miss Mary Kathleen. b 36. SRN57 SCM59 MTD72. SW Minl Tr Course 78. **dss** 82 **d** 87 **p** 94. Littleham w Exmouth *Ex* 82-84; Heavitree w Ex St Paul 85-87; Hon Par Dn 87-88; Chapl Asst R Devon and Ex Hosp 85-93; Lic to Offic *Ex* 88-94; NSM Littleham w Exmouth from 94. *Flat 5, 36 Douglas Avenue, Exmouth, Devon EX8 2HB* Tel (01395) 265528

WEATHRALL, Ian Charles. b 22. OBE75. AKC47. **d** 47 **p** 48. C Southampton St Mary w H Trin *Win* 47-51; India from 51; Brotherhood of Ascension from 51; Hd 70-88; rtd 92. *7 Court Lane, Delhi 110 054, India* Tel Delhi (11) 251-8515

WEAVER, Alan William. b 63. Brighton Poly HNC88. Linc Th Coll CMinlStuds95. **d** 95 **p** 96. C Seaford w Sutton *Chich* from 95. *29 Stafford Road, Seaford, E Sussex BN25 1UE* Tel (01323) 891831

WEAVER (née ROBBINS), Ms Angela Mary. b 48. WMMTC 92. **d** 95 **p** 96. C Hill *Birm* from 95. *3 Dower Road, Sutton Coldfield, W Midlands B75 1SH* Tel 0121-308 0759

WEAVER, Prof Arthur Kenneth (Ken). b 17. MRAeS Trin Coll Cam MA. Wycliffe Hall Ox 81 Ox NSM Course 81. **d** 81 **p** 82. NSM Ashbury, Compton Beauchamp and Longcot w Fernham *Ox* from 81. *White Lodge, King's Lane, Longcot, Faringdon, Oxon SN7 7SS* Tel (01793) 782364

WEAVER, Brian John. b 34. Oak Hill Th Coll 82. **d** 84 **p** 85. C Nailsea H Trin *B & W* 84-88; R Nettlebed w Bix and Highmore *Ox* from 88. *The Rectory, Nettlebed, Henley-on-Thames, Oxon RG9 5DD* Tel (01491) 641575

WEAVER, David Anthony. b 43. Hatf Coll Dur BSc65. Lich Th Coll 68. **d** 71 **p** 72. C Walsall Wood *Lich* 71-75; C Much Wenlock w Bourton *Heref* 75-76; Canada 76-79 and 82; V Mow Cop *Lich* 79-82; P-in-c Burntwood from 82; Chapl St Matt Hosp Burntwood 83-95. *The Vicarage, Church Road, Burntwood, Walsall WS7 9EA* Tel (01543) 675014

WEAVER, Duncan Charles. b 60. St Jo Coll Nottm DipTh94. **d** 94 **p** 95. C Watford *St Alb* from 94. *8A Lammas Road, Watford WD1 8BA* Tel (01923) 232979

WEAVER, The Ven John. b 28. Ex Coll Ox BA51 MA55. St Steph Ho Ox 52. **d** 55 **p** 56. C Ex St Dav *Ex* 55-58; S Africa from 58; Adn Midl from 84. *PO Box 21, Himeville, 4585 South Africa* Tel Himeville (33722) 13

WEAVER, Canon Michael Howard. b 39. Leeds Univ DipArch63 DipTh66 DipL&A69 Southn Univ MPhil95. Chich Th Coll 63. **d** 66 **p** 67. C Kidderminster St Jo *Worc* 66-69; Br Honduras 69-71; TV Droitwich *Worc* 71-76; V Arundel w Tortington and S Stoke *Chich* 76-96; Sub-Chapl HM Pris Ford 77-96; P-in-c Clymping 84-87; RD Arundel and Bognor 88-93; Hon Can Enugu from 94; V Lymington *Win* from 96. *The Vicarage, Grove Road, Lymington, Hants SO41 9RF* Tel (01590) 673847

WEAVER, Raymond Alexander (Ray). b 30. Bris Univ BA51 CertEd52. **d** 86 **p** 87. NSM Weymouth H Trin *Sarum* 86-96; Perm to Offic from 96. *10 Windsor Court, Westerhall Road, Weymouth, Dorset DT4 7SZ* Tel (01305) 783681

WEAVER, Canon William. b 40. Man Univ BA63 BD65. **d** 74 **p** 75. Lect Th Leeds Univ 67-91; Hon C Clifford *York* 82-86; Chapl K Edw Sch Birm 91-94; Provost Woodard Schs (Midl Division) from 94; Hon Can Derby Cathl *Derby* from 96. *2 Nidd View, Cattal, York YO5 8DZ* Tel (01423) 358512

WEBB, Canon Albert (Bertie). b 22. AKC49. **d** 50 **p** 51. C Warsop *S'well* 50-52; V Cleeve Prior *Worc* 52-59; V Foley Park 59-66; V Evesham 66-87; RD Evesham 73-79; Hon Can Worc Cathl 75-87; rtd 87. *2 Dolphin Close, Worcester WR2 6BG* Tel (01905) 422230

WEBB, Anthony John. b 24. Sarum & Wells Th Coll 79. **d** 81 **p** 82. C Yeovil *B & W* 81-84; P-in-c Cossington 84-87; P-in-c Woolavington 84-87; P-in-c Bawdrip 87; V Woolavington w Cossington and Bawdrip 87-91; rtd 91; Perm to Offic *B & W* from 91. *4 Brue Crescent, Burnham-on-Sea, Somerset TA8 1LR* Tel (01278) 787483

WEBB, Arthur Robert. b 33. FRSA LCP67 Lanc Univ MA82. Wells Th Coll 69. **d** 70 **p** 70. C W Drayton *Lon* 70-72; Hd Master St Jas Cathl Sch Bury St Edmunds 72-86; Min Can St E Cathl *St E* 72-87; Succ St E Cathl 81-87; P-in-c Seend and Bulkington *Sarum* 87-88; V 88-91; R Heytesbury and Sutton Veny 91-96; rtd 96. *27 Marlborough Buildings, Bath BA1 2LY* Tel (01225) 484042

WEBB, Christopher Scott. b 70. Univ of Wales (Abth) BSc. Trin Coll Bris. **d** 96 **p** 97. C Dafen *St D* from 96. *25 Brynelli, Dafen, Llanelli SA14 8PW*

WEBB, Cyril George. b 19. Roch Th Coll 64. **d** 66 **p** 67. C Bournemouth St Andr *Win* 66-71; V Micheldever 71-72; V Micheldever and E Stratton, Woodmancote etc 72-79; V

Bubwith w Ellerton and Aughton *York* 79-83; I Tomregan w Drumlane *K, E & A* 83-86; rtd 86; Perm to Offic *Cant* from 90. *62 Columbia Avenue, Whitstable, Kent CT5 4EH* Tel (01227) 264687

WEBB, David Basil. b 30. Ch Coll Cam BA54 MA58. Ripon Hall Ox 54. **d** 55 **p** 56. C Wimbledon *S'wark* 55-57; Chapl Em Coll Cam 57-60; V Langley Mill *Derby* 60-64; R Farnborough *Roch* 64-73; R Dunstable *St Alb* 73-78; TR 78-84; RD Dunstable 81-84; TR Bemerton *Sarum* 84-90; V Haslingden w Grane and Stonefold *Blackb* 90-96; RD Accrington 92-95; rtd 96; Perm to Offic *Bradf* from 96. *22 Thwaites Avenue, Ilkley, W Yorkshire LS29 8EH* Tel (01943) 609762

WEBB, David William. b 30. MRINA Kent Univ DipTh84. Cant Sch of Min 86. **d** 89 **p** 90. NSM Sittingbourne St Mary *Cant* 89-95; Hon C Iwade from 95. *16 School Lane, Iwade, Sittingbourne, Kent ME9 8SE* Tel (01795) 424502

WEBB, Mrs Diane. b 45. LNSM course 91. **d** 93 **p** 94. NSM Stowmarket *St E* from 93. *36 Wordsworth Road, Stowmarket, Suffolk IP14 1TT* Tel (01449) 677880

WEBB, Dominic Mark. b 68. Or Coll Ox BA91. Wycliffe Hall Ox BA93. **d** 96 **p** 97. C Cradley *Worc* from 96. *2 Doverdale Close, Halesowen, W Midlands B63 2AT* Tel (01384) 567601

WEBB, Frances Mary. *See* BATTIN, Mrs Frances Mary

WEBB, Mrs Gillian Anne. b 49. Whitelands Coll Lon CertEd71. St Alb Minl Tr Scheme 83. **dss** 86 **d** 87 **p** 94. Kempston Transfiguration *St Alb* 86-87; NSM from 87. *2 Hillson Close, Marston Moreteyne, Bedford MK43 0QN* Tel (01234) 767256

WEBB, Gregory John. b 55. Man Univ LLB77. Oak Hill Th Coll 89. **d** 91 **p** 92. C Bury St Edmunds St Geo *St E* 91-94; P-in-c Bury St Edmunds All SS from 94. *All Saints Vicarage, 59 Bennett Avenue, Bury St Edmunds, Suffolk IP33 3JJ* Tel (01284) 701063

WEBB, Harold William. b 37. St Chad's Coll Dur BA59. St Steph Ho Ox 59. **d** 61 **p** 62. C Plumstead St Nic *S'wark* 61-65; S Africa 65-70; Sacr Wakef Cathl *Wakef* 71-72; P-in-c Lane End *Ox* 72-76; V Lane End w Cadmore End 76-84; Chapl to the Deaf *Guildf* 84-96; V Roade and Ashton w Hartwell *Pet* from 96. *The Vicarage, 18 Hartwell Road, Roade, Northampton NN7 2NT* Tel (01604) 862284

WEBB (née EDWARDS), Mrs Helen Glynne. b 57. SRN79 RMN81. Wycliffe Hall Ox 88. **d** 90 **p** 94. Par Dn Clapham St Jas *S'wark* 90-94; Chapl Asst Southmead Health Services NHS Trust Bris 94-97. *157 Ratcliffe Drive, Stoke Gifford, Bristol BS12 6TZ* Tel 0117-931 1847

WEBB, Jason Stephen. b 72. Southlands Coll Lon BA93. St Steph Ho Ox DipMin95. **d** 95 **p** 96. C Leeds St Aid *Ripon* from 95. *St Aidan's House, 84 Copgrove Road, Leeds LS8 2ST* Tel 0113-248 0050

WEBB, Jennifer Rose. b 48. Leeds Univ BA70 Bedf Coll Lon CQSW72. LNSM course 93. **d** 96. Hon C Ham St Rich *S'wark* from 96. *3 Locksmeade Road, Ham, Richmond, Surrey TW10 7YT* Tel 0181-948 0031

WEBB, John Christopher Richard. b 38. ACA63 FCA74. Wycliffe Hall Ox 64. **d** 67 **p** 68. C Hendon St Paul Mill Hill *Lon* 67-71; CF 71-93; R Bentworth and Shalden and Lasham *Win* from 93. *The Rectory, Bentworth, Alton, Hants GU34 5RB* Tel (01420) 563218

WEBB, Dr Kenneth Gordon Webb (Ken). b 47. DRCOG73 Lon Univ MB, BS71. Trin Coll Bris BA92 ADPS93. **d** 93 **p** 94. C Cheltenham St Mark *Glouc* 93-97; Thailand from 97. *PO Box 19, Ban Chang Post Office, Rayong, Thailand*

WEBB, Marjorie Valentine (Sister Elizabeth). b 31. Bedf Coll Lon. **d** 88 **p** 94. CSF from 55; Rev Mother 71-86; Lic to Bp Heref 86-90; Perm to Offic *Lon* 88-90; Lic to Offic *Lich* 90-91; Lic to Offic *B & W* 91-95; Perm to Offic *Cant* from 95; Perm to Offic *B & W* from 95; rtd 96. *St Francis House, 113 Gillott Road, Birmingham B16 0ET* Tel 0121-454 8302

WEBB, Martin George. b 46. SS Mark & Jo Coll Chelsea CertEd MEd. N Ord Course 82. **d** 85 **p** 86. NSM Brotherton *Wakef* 85-87; Perm to Offic *York* from 95. *Melrose, 3 Argyle Road, Whitby, N Yorkshire YO21 3HS* Tel (01947) 603541

WEBB, Michael David. b 59. K Coll Lon BD82 PGCE83. Ripon Coll Cuddesdon 88. **d** 90 **p** 91. C Broughton Astley *Leic* 90-93; C Hugglescote w Donington, Ellistown and Snibston 93-94; TV from 94. *St James's Vicarage, Highfield Street, Coalville, Leics LE67 3BN* Tel (01530) 832679

WEBB, Michael John. b 49. Linc Coll Ox BA70 MA74. Linc Th Coll 70. **d** 72 **p** 73. C Tring *St Alb* 72-75; C Chipping Barnet 75-78; C Chipping Barnet w Arkley 78-82; TV Cullercoats St Geo *Newc* 82-89; V Newc H Cross 89-97; V Newc St Gabr from 97; RD Newc E from 97. *St Gabriel's Vicarage, 9 Holderness Road, Heaton, Newcastle upon Tyne NE6 5RH* Tel 0191-276 3957

WEBB, Mrs Pauline Nikola. b 49. WMMTC. **d** 87 **p** 94. C Walsgrave on Sowe *Cov* 87-91; TD Grantham *Linc* 91-94; Ind Chapl 91-96; TV Grantham 94-96. *18 Dudley Road, Grantham, Lincs NG31 9AA*

WEBB, Peter Henry. b 55. Nottm Univ BA77. St Steph Ho Ox 77. **d** 79 **p** 80. C Lancing w Coombes *Chich* 79-82; C The Hydneye CD 82-84; C-in-c 84-86; Chapl Sunderland Distr Gen Hosp 86-94; Chapl City Hosps Sunderland NHS Trust from 94. *The Chaplain's Office, Sunderland District General Hospital, Kayll Road, Sunderland SR4 7TP* Tel 0191-565 6256 or 569 9180

WEBB, Richard. b 38. Oak Hill NSM Course 91. **d** 94 **p** 95. NSM Hanwell St Mary w St Chris *Lon* from 94. *46 Graham Avenue, London W13 9TQ* Tel 0181-579 9798

WEBB, Richard Frederick. b 42. Cant Sch of Min. **d** 84 **p** 85. C Ipswich St Clem w H Trin *St E* 84-87; R Rougham and Beyton w Hessett 87-91; R Rougham, Beyton w Hessett and Rushbrooke 91-92; P-in-c Woodbridge St Jo from 92. *St John's Vicarage, St John's Hill, Woodbridge, Suffolk IP12 1HS* Tel (01394) 382083

WEBB, Richard Lacey. b 09. ALCD30. **d** 32 **p** 33. C Keynsham *B & W* 32-35; R Wacton Magna w Parva *Nor* 36-41; V Castle Acre w Newton 41-49; R Garboldisham 49-66; R Blo' Norton 49-66; RD Rockland 63-66; V Lakenham St Alb 66-77; rtd 77; Hon C Nor St Andr *Nor* 83-86; Perm to Offic from 86. *32 Ipswich Road, Norwich NR4 6QR* Tel (01603) 51348

WEBB, Rowland James. b 33. Roch Th Coll 64. **d** 67 **p** 68. C Tavistock and Gulworthy *Ex* 67-70; Chapl RN 70-86; R Mundford w Lynford *Nor* 86-90; V Burnham *Chelmsf* from 90. *The Vicarage, 2A Church Road, Burnham-on-Crouch, Essex CM0 8DA* Tel (01621) 782071

WEBB, William John. b 43. Cuddesdon Coll 68. **d** 71 **p** 72. C Weston Favell *Pet* 71-73; C Newport w Longford *Lich* 74-77; C Baswich 77-79; P-in-c Stonnall 79-83; P-in-c Wall 79-83; V Fauls 83-95; V Prees 83-95; V St Martin's from 95. *The Vicarage, St Martins, Oswestry, Shropshire SY11 3AP* Tel (01691) 772295

WEBBER, David Price. b 39. Chich Th Coll 90. **d** 91 **p** 92. NSM Shoreham Beach *Chich* 91-93; NSM Hove St Patr from 93. *69 Grinstead Lane, Lancing, W Sussex BN15 9DT* Tel (01903) 753950

WEBBER, The Very Revd Eric Michael. b 16. Lon Univ BD54 ATh(SA)55 Univ of Tasmania MEd77 MHums85. AKC43. **d** 43 **p** 44. C Clapham H Spirit *S'wark* 43-47; C Wimbledon 47-50; S Africa 50-58; Australia from 58; Dean Hobart 59-71; Sen Lect Relig Studies Tasmanian Coll Adv Educn 71-81. *1 Hean Street, Hobart, Tasmania, Australia 7004* Tel Hobart (2) 236413

WEBBER, John Arthur. b 45. Keble Coll Ox BA67 MA71. Gen Th Sem (NY) STM85 Cuddesdon Coll 70. **d** 71 **p** 72. C Penarth All SS *Llan* 71-74; USPG 75-91; Bangladesh 75-91; Asst P Stepney St Dunstan and All SS *Lon* 91-97; Bp's Adv on Inter-Faith Relns from 91; P-in-c Bethnal Green St Barn from 97. *16 Rhonda Grove, London E3 5AP* Tel 0181-980 8628

WEBBER, Canon Lionel Frank. b 35. Kelham Th Coll St Mich Coll Llan. **d** 60 **p** 61. C Bolton Sav *Man* 60-63; C Aberavon *Llan* 63-65; R Salford Stowell Memorial *Man* 65-69; V Aberavon H Trin *Llan* 69-74; TV Stantonbury *Ox* 74-76; TR Basildon St Martin w H Cross and Laindon *Chelmsf* 76-79; P-in-c Nevendon 77-79; RD Basildon 79-89; R Basildon St Martin w Nevendon 79-95; R Basildon St Martin from 95; Hon Can Chelmsf Cathl from 84; Chapl to The Queen from 94. *The Rectory, Pagel Mead, Basildon, Essex SS14 1DX* Tel (01268) 280039

WEBBER, Michael Champneys Wilfred. b 48. Man Univ BA71 MA(Theol)78. Cuddesdon Coll 73. **d** 75 **p** 76. C Caterham *S'wark* 75-79; P-in-c Kidbrooke St Jas 79-84; TV 84-85; V Earls Barton *Pet* from 87. *The Vicarage, 7 High Street, Earls Barton, Northampton NN6 0JG* Tel (01604) 810447

WEBBER, Peter Cecil. b 21. Lon Coll of Div ALCD55 LTh. **d** 55 **p** 56. C Wimbledon St Luke *S'wark* 55-58; V Beckenham St Jo *Roch* 58-67; V Foord St Jo *Cant* 67-86; RD Elham 80-83; rtd 86; Perm to Offic *Chich* from 86. *15 Goodwin Close, Hailsham, E Sussex BN27 3DE* Tel (01323) 848668

WEBBER, Raymond John. b 40. Lon Univ DipTh65. Linc Th Coll 84. **d** 85 **p** 86. C Helston *Truro* 85; C Helston and Wendron 85-90; TV 90-93; R Kenton, Mamhead, Powderham, Cofton and Starcross *Ex* from 93. *The Vicarage, 1 Staplake Rise, Starcross, Exeter EX6 8SJ* Tel (01626) 890331

WEBER, Douglas John Craig. b 20. Ex Coll Ox BA46 MA46. Sarum Th Coll. **d** 49 **p** 50. C Portsea N End St Mark *Portsm* 49-52; C Alverstoke 52-55; V Hook w Warsash 55-88; rtd 88; Perm to Offic *Portsm* from 88. *1 Trevose Way, Titchfield, Fareham, Hants PO14 4NG* Tel (01489) 583065

WEBLEY, Robin Bowen. b 32. Univ of Wales (Cardiff) DPS. St Mich Coll Llan 87. **d** 89 **p** 90. C St D Cathl *St D* 89-91; Min Can St D Cathl 89-91; R Castlemartin w Warren and Angle etc 91-94; Succ St D Cathl from 94. *The Archdeaconry, St Davids, Haverfordwest SA62 6PE* Tel (01437) 720456

WEBSTER, The Very Revd Alan Brunskill. b 18. KCVO88. Qu Coll Ox BA39 MA43 BD54 City Univ Hon DD. Westcott Ho Cam 41. **d** 42 **p** 43. C Attercliffe w Carbrook *Sheff* 42-44; C Sheff Arbourthorne 44-46; Chapl and Lib Westcott Ho Cam 46-48; Vice-Prin 48-53; V Barnard Castle *Dur* 53-59; RD Barnard Castle 54-59; Warden Linc Th Coll 59-70; Can and Preb Linc Cathl *Linc* 64-70; Dean Nor 70-78; Dean St Paul's *Lon* 78-87; rtd 88. *20 Beechbank, Norwich NR2 2AL* Tel (01603) 55833

WEBSTER, David Edward. b 39. K Coll Lon 60 Edin Th Coll 62. **d** 64 **p** 65. C Maghull *Liv* 64-69; R Wavertree St Mary 69-76; TV Greystoke, Matterdale and Mungrisdale *Carl* 76-81; R Lowton St Luke *Liv* 81-88; Chapl Nat Agric Cen from 88; R Stoneleigh w

Ashow and Baginton *Cov* from 88. *The Rectory, Church Lane, Stoneleigh, Coventry CV8 3DN* Tel (01203) 415506

WEBSTER, David Robert. b 32. Selw Coll Cam BA56 MA60. Linc Th Coll 56. **d** 58 **p** 59. C Billingham St Cuth *Dur* 58-61; C Doncaster St Geo *Sheff* 61-64; Chapl Doncaster R Infirmary 61-64; V Lumley *Dur* 64-76; V Belmont 76-93; rtd 93. *25 Eldon Grove, Hartlepool, Cleveland TS26 9LY* Tel (01429) 275698

WEBSTER, Dennis Eric. b 39. Fitzw Ho Cam BA60 MA64 Linacre Coll Ox MA70 Lon Univ CertEd61. Wycliffe Hall Ox 62. **d** 65 **p** 66. C Herne Bay Ch Ch *Cant* 65-68; C Tulse Hill H Trin *S'wark* 68-69; Kenya 70-75; Chapl Pierrepont Sch Frensham 75-91; R Chiddingfold *Guildf* from 91. *The Rectory, Coxcombe Lane, Chiddingfold, Godalming, Surrey GU8 4QA* Tel (01428) 682008

WEBSTER, Derek Herbert. b 34. FRSA82 Hull Univ BA55 Lon Univ BD55 Leic Univ MEd68 PhD73. Lambeth STh67 Linc Th Coll 76. **d** 76 **p** 77. Lect Hull Univ from 72; Hon C Cleethorpes *Linc* from 76. *60 Queen's Parade, Cleethorpes, S Humberside DN35 0DG* Tel (01472) 693786

WEBSTER, Mrs Diane Margaret. b 43. Oak Hill NSM Course 91. **d** 94 **p** 95. NSM Welwyn Garden City *St Alb* from 94. *26 Dellcott Close, Welwyn Garden City, Herts AL8 7BD* Tel (01707) 323103

WEBSTER, Geoffrey William. b 36. St Alb Minl Tr Scheme 77. **d** 80 **p** 81. NSM Harlington *St Alb* 80-82; C Belmont *Dur* 82-86; R Gateshead Fell 86-94; P-in-c Hamsterley 94-95; V Hamsterley and Witton-le-Wear from 95. *The Vicarage, Hamsterley, Bishop Auckland, Co Durham DL13 3PP* Tel (01388) 488418

WEBSTER, Canon Glyn Hamilton. b 51. SRN73. Cranmer Hall Dur 74 St Jo Coll Dur 74. **d** 77 **p** 78. C Huntington *York* 77-81; V York St Luke 81-92; Chapl York Distr Hosp 81-92; Sen Chapl York Health Services NHS Trust from 92; Can and Preb York Minster *York* from 94; RD City of York from 97. *York District Hospital, Wiggington Road, York YO3 7HE, or 22 Markham Crescent, York YO3 7NS* Tel (01904) 631313 or 632380

WEBSTER, Prof John Bainbridge. b 55. Clare Coll Cam MA81 PhD82. **d** 83 **p** 84. Chapl and Dep Sen Tutor St Jo Coll Dur 83-86; Hon C Bearpark *Dur* 83-86; Assoc Prof Systematic Th Wycliffe Coll Toronto 86-93; Prof Systematic Th 93-95; Ramsay Armitage Prof Systematic Th 95-96; Lady Marg Prof Div Ox Univ from 96. *Christ Church, Oxford OX1 1DP* Tel (01865) 276247

WEBSTER, John Maurice. b 34. Sarum & Wells Th Coll 73. **d** 76 **p** 77. Hon C Hythe *Win* from 76. *Avery Lodge, Long Lane, Marchwood, Southampton SO40 4WR* Tel (01703) 862388

WEBSTER, Martin Duncan. b 52. Nottm Univ BSc74 DipTh76. Linc Th Coll 75. **d** 78 **p** 79. C Thundersley *Chelmsf* 78-81; C Canvey Is 81-82; TV 82-86; V Nazeing from 86; RD Harlow from 88. *The Vicarage, Betts Lane, Nazeing, Waltham Abbey, Essex EN9 2DB* Tel (01992) 893167

WEBSTER, Mrs Monica. b 39. DipCOT60. WMMTC 94. **d** 97. NSM Wolverton w Norton Lindsey and Langley *Cov* from 97; Asst Chapl to the Deaf from 97. *The Parsonage, Church Lane, Stoneleigh, Coventry CV8 3DN* Tel (01203) 415506 Fax as telephone

WEBSTER, Mrs Patricia Eileen. b 34. St Gabr Coll Lon TCert54. Gilmore Ho 56. **d** 87 **p** 94. Par Dn Belmont *Dur* 87-93; rtd 93. *25 Eldon Grove, Hartlepool, Cleveland TS26 9LY* Tel (01429) 275698

WEBSTER, Peter. b 26. FASI. Cranmer Hall Dur 68. **d** 70 **p** 71. C Tickhill w Stainton *Sheff* 70-72; C Conisbrough 72-73; V Walkley 73-77; V Rawcliffe 77-84; V Barrow-on-Humber *Linc* 84; P-in-c Goxhill 84; V Barrow and Goxhill 84-91; rtd 91; Perm to Offic *York* from 91; Perm to Offic *Sheff* from 91. *17 Kirkham Court, Goole, N Humberside DN14 6JU* Tel (01405) 766513

WEBSTER, Sarah Vernoy (Sally). b 38. Univ of Georgia BSc61. S'wark Ord Course 87. **d** 90 **p** 94. NSM Primrose Hill St Mary w Avenue Road St Paul *Lon* from 90. *15 Elsworthy Rise, London NW3 3QY* Tel 0171-722 5756

WEBSTER, Mrs Sheila Mary. b 22. Bedf Coll Lon CSocStuds43. Gilmore Ho 69. **dss** 81 **d** 87. Patcham *Chich* 77-83; Hove All SS 84-90; Hon Par Dn 87-90; rtd 90; Perm to Offic *Chich* from 90. *108 Surrenden Road, Brighton BN1 6WB* Tel (01273) 561222

WEBSTER-SMITH, Preb Alfred William. b 10. St Chad's Coll Dur BA32 DipTh33 MA35. **d** 33 **p** 34. C Riddlesdown *S'wark* 33-36; Tanganyika 36-51; Gen Sec UMCA 51-59; Lic to Offic *S'wark* 51-59; Hon Can Masasi from 57; Zambia 59-66; Can N Rhodesia 60-62; R Pontesbury I and II *Heref* 66-76; RD Pontesbury 66-76; Preb Heref Cathl 73-81; rtd 76; Perm to Offic *S'wark* from 80. *6 Frederick Gardens, Cheam, Surrey SM1 2HX* Tel 0181-641 0226

WEDDERSPOON, The Very Revd Alexander Gillan. b 31. Jes Coll Ox BA54 MA61 Lon Univ BD62. Cuddesdon Coll. **d** 61 **p** 62. C Kingston All SS *S'wark* 61-63; Lect RE Lon Univ 63-66; Educn Adv C of E Sch Coun 66-70; Can Res Win Cathl *Win* 70-87; Vice-Dean 80-87; Treas 80-85; Dean Guildf from 87. *1 Cathedral Close, Guildford, Surrey GU2 5TL* Tel (01483) 60328 or 65287 Fax 303350

WEDGBURY, John William. b 53. RMCS BSc78. St Jo Coll Nottm 84. **d** 87 **p** 88. C Foord St Jo *Cant* 87-91; V Mangotsfield *Bris* 91-92. *138 Wessex Oval, Wareham, Dorset BH20 4ET* Tel (01929) 552880

WEDGEWORTH, Michael John. b 40. Nottm Univ BSc62. Wesley Ho Cam MA66. **d** 93 **p** 94. In Meth Ch 66-93; NSM Feniscowles *Blackb* from 93; Sec DBF from 95. *46 Preston New Road, Blackburn BB2 6AH* Tel (01254) 260078 Fax 392597 E-mail dio.sec@blackburn.anglican.org.uk.

WEDGWOOD, Preb Charles Mervyn. b 16. Selw Coll Cam BA38 MA46. Wycliffe Hall Ox 38. **d** 40 **p** 41. C Melton Mowbray w Burton Lazars, Freeby etc *Leic* 40-46; Chapl RAFVR 42-46; V Copt Oak *Leic* 46-50; Chapl Towle Recovery Homes Woodhouse Eaves 46-50; R Kirby Muxloe 50-54; RD Sparkenhoe III 53-54; V Claughton cum Grange *Ches* 54-56; V Keynsham w Queen Charlton *B & W* 56-67; R Burnett 56-67; Chapl Keynsham Hosp 56-67; Preb Wells Cathl 63-81; V Wellington w W Buckland and Nynehead 67-72; Chapl Wellington Hosps 67-72; V Combe Down w Monkton Combe 73-81; V Combe Down w Monkton Combe and S Stoke 81; RD Bath 76-81; rtd 81; Perm to Offic *B & W* from 81; Perm to Offic *Ex* 86-93. *126 Kingsgate, Pennsylvania Road, Exeter EX4 6DH*

WEDGWOOD, George Peter. b 26. St Jo Coll Dur BA51 DipTh52 MA56. **d** 52 **p** 53. C Barrow St Mark *Carl* 52-54; Chapl Sedbergh Sch 54-57; P-in-c Dur St Cuth *Dur* 57-63; Chapl Dur Sch 58-63; Hd of Div and Sen Lect 63-69; Chapl St Kath Coll *Liv* 63-69; Prin Lect St Kath Coll 69-83; Lic to Offic *Bradf* 83-86; Hd of Div Liv Coll of HE 84-86; P-in-c Kirkoswald, Renwick and Ainstable *Carl* 86-88; rtd 88; Perm to Offic *Carl* 88-92; Perm to Offic *Liv* from 92. *Chameutre, 71250 Bergesserin, Saone-et-Loire, France*

WEDGWOOD, Keith. b 20. Hertf Coll Ox BA42 MA46. Wycliffe Hall Ox 42. **d** 43 **p** 44. C Hartlebury *Worc* 43-46; C Worc St Martin 46-49; Succ Derby Cathl *Derby* 49-52; V Choral Sarum Cathl *Sarum* 52-68; Succ 55-68; Canada 68-72; P-in-c Osmington w Poxwell *Sarum* 72-77; TV The Iwernes and Sutton Waldron 77-78; P-in-c 78-81; V The Iwernes, Sutton Waldron and Fontmell Magna 81-85; rtd 85. *18 Walton Road, Bournemouth BH10 4BJ* Tel (01202) 532116

WEDGWOOD GREENHOW, Stephen John Francis. b 57. Man Univ BA82. Edin Th Coll MTh84. **d** 84 **p** 85. C Wythenshawe Wm Temple Ch *Man* 84-87; USA from 87. *2548 Walnut Avenue 9, Carmichael, CA, 95608 USA*

WEEDEN, Simon Andrew. b 55. York Univ BA79. Wycliffe Hall Ox 88. **d** 90 **p** 91. C Gt Chesham *Ox* 90-94; P-in-c Haversham w Lt Linford, Tyringham w Filgrave 94-97; R Lamp from 97. *The Rectory, High Street, Haversham, Milton Keynes MK19 7DT* Tel (01908) 312136

WEEDING, Paul Stephen. b 62. Leic Poly BSc. Ripon Coll Cuddesdon. **d** 90 **p** 91. C Llanishen and Lisvane *Llan* 90-93; C Merthyr Tydfil Ch Ch 93-97; V Abercynon from 97. *The Vicarage, 67 Groversfield, Abercynon, Mountain Ash CF45 4PP* Tel (01443) 740207

✠**WEEKES, The Rt Revd Ambrose Walter Marcus.** b 19. CB70. AKC41 Linc Th Coll 41. **d** 42 **p** 43 **c** 77. C New Brompton St Luke *Roch* 42-44; Chapl RNVR 44-46; Chapl RN 46-69; Chapl of the Fleet and Adn for the RN 69-72; QHC from 69; Can Gib Cathl *Eur* 71-73; Chapl Tangier 72-73; Dean Gib 73-77; Aux Bp Eur 77-80; Asst Bp Eur from 89; Suff Bp Eur 80-86; Dean Brussels 81-86; rtd 86; Asst Bp Roch 86-88; Chapl Montreux w Gstaad *Eur* 89-92. *c/o All Saints' Vicarage, 7 Margaret Street, London W1N 8JQ* Tel 0171-580 6467

WEEKES, The Very Revd Cecil William. b 31. CITC. **d** 78 **p** 79. NSM Glenageary *D & G* 78-80; Bp's V Kilkenny Cathl *C & O* 80-83; I Carlow w Urglin and Staplestown 83-90; Preb Leighlin Cathl 88-96; Preb Ossory Cathl 88-96; I Lismore w Cappoquin, Kilwatermoy, Dungarvan etc 90-96; Dean Lismore 90-96; Chan Cashel Cathl 90-96; Prec Waterford Cathl 90-96; rtd 96. *The Cottage, Danesford Road, Bennettsbridge, Co Kilkenny, Irish Republic*

WEEKES, David John. b 34. Magd Coll Cam BA59 MA68 Lon Univ PGCE68 Aber Univ MTh79. Clifton Th Coll 62. **d** 64 **p** 65. C Cheadle *Ches* 64-68; Uganda 69-73; Perm to Offic *St And* 73-74; Chapl and Hd of RE Fettes Coll Edin 74-94; Lic to Offic *Edin* 74-94; Warden Lee Abbey International Students' Club Kensington from 94; Perm to Offic *Lon* from 94. *Lee Abbey International Students' Club, 57-67 Lexham Gardens, London W8 6JJ* Tel 0171-373 7242 or 244 8758 Fax 244 8702

WEETMAN, John Charles. b 66. Qu Coll Ox BA87. Trin Coll Bris BA91. **d** 91 **p** 92. C Hull Newland St Jo *York* 91-95; V Boosbeck w Moorsholm from 95. *The Vicarage, Boosbeck, Saltburn-by-the-Sea, Cleveland TS12 1AR* Tel (01287) 651728

WEIR, David Alexander. b 69. City Univ BSc91 Fitzw Coll Cam BA94. Westcott Ho Cam CTM. **d** 95 **p** 97. C Locks Heath *Portsm* 95-96; C W Leigh from 96. *4 White Oak Walk, Havant, Hants PO9 5PL* Tel (01705) 484711

WEIR, Graham Francis. b 52. GSM LASI. N Ord Course 88. **d** 91 **p** 92. NSM High Crompton *Man* 91-92; NSM Heyside from 92; Asst Chapl Bolton Hosps NHS Trust from 94. *Bolton General Hospital, Minerva Road, Farnworth, Bolton BL4 0JR* Tel (01204) 390770 or 390390

WEIR, John Michael Vavasour. b 48. K Coll Lon BD72 AKC72. **d** 73 **p** 74. C Hatfield Hyde *St Alb* 73-76; C Watford St Mich 76-79; Asst Chapl Oslo St Edm *Eur* 80-81; V Bethnal Green St Pet w St Thos *Lon* from 81; Chapl Qu Eliz Hosp for Children

Lon from 81. *St Peter's Vicarage, St Peter's Close, London E2 7AE* Tel 0171-739 2717

WEIR, John William Moon. b 36. St Luke's Coll Ex CertEd69 Ex Univ BEd76. SW Minl Tr Course 82. **d** 85 **p** 86. NSM Meavy, Sheepstor and Walkhampton *Ex* 85-87; NSM Yelverton, Meavy, Sheepstor and Walkhampton from 87; Hd Master Princetown Primary Sch from 87; Sub-Chapl HM Pris Dartmoor from 87. *Goblin's Green, Dousland, Yelverton, Devon PL20 6ND* Tel (01822) 852671

WEIR, William Daniel Niall. b 57. BA. Ripon Coll Cuddesdon. **d** 83 **p** 84. C Chelsea St Luke *Lon* 83-87; PV Westmr Abbey 85-89; C Poplar *Lon* 87-88; TV 88-93; P-in-c Forest Gate Em w Upton Cross *Chelmsf* 93-97; V from 97. *Emmanuel Vicarage, 2B Margery Park Road, London E7 9JY* Tel 0181-536 0244

WELANDER, Canon David Charles St Vincent. b 25. FSA. Lon Coll of Div BD47 ALCD47. **d** 48 **p** 49. C Heigham H Trin *Nor* 48-51; Tutor Oak Hill Th Coll 51-52; Tutor 52-56; Chapl Lon Coll of Div 52-56; V Iver *Ox* 56-63; V Cheltenham Ch Ch *Glouc* 63-75; RD Cheltenham 73-75; Can Res Glouc Cathl 75-91; rtd 91; Perm to Offic *Glouc* from 91; Perm to Offic *Bris* from 91. *Willow Cottage, 1 Sandpits Lane, Sherston Magna, Malmesbury, Wilts SN16 0NN* Tel (01666) 840180

WELBOURN, David Anthony. b 41. K Coll Lon BD63 AKC63 DMS. **d** 64 **p** 65. C Stockton St Chad *Dur* 64-67; C S Westoe 69-74; Ind Chapl 69-80; Ind Chapl *Nor* 80-90; Ind and Commerce Officer *Guildf* from 90. *81 Collingwood Crescent, Guildford, Surrey GU1 2NU* Tel (01483) 570600

WELBY, Justin Portal. b 56. MACT84 Trin Coll Cam BA78 MA90. Cranmer Hall Dur BA91 DMinlStuds92. **d** 92 **p** 93. C Chilvers Coton w Astley *Cov* 92-95; R Southam from 95; RD Southam from 97. *The Rectory, Park Lane, Southam, Leamington Spa, Warks CV33 0JA* Tel (01926) 812413

WELBY, Peter Edlin Brown. b 34. Open Univ BA75. St Jo Coll Dur 75. **d** 77 **p** 78. C Auckland St Andr and St Anne *Dur* 77-79; C S Westoe 79-81; V Tudhoe 81-93; R Croxdale and Tudhoe from 93. *21 York Villas, Tudhoe Village, Spennymoor, Co Durham DL16 6LP* Tel (01388) 818418

WELBY, Richard Alexander Lyon (Alex). b 58. St Jo Coll Nottm BTh81 LTh Leeds Univ MA93. Ridley Hall Cam 83. **d** 84 **p** 85. C Stoke Bishop *Bris* 84-88; V Bowling St Steph *Bradf* 88-95; P-in-c Hatherleigh, Meeth, Exbourne and Jacobstowe *Ex* from 95. *The Rectory, Hatherleigh, Okehampton, Devon EX20 3JY* Tel (01837) 810314

WELCH, Derek. b 27. Keble Coll Ox BA51 MA57. Coll of Resurr Mirfield 51. **d** 53 **p** 54. C Middlesbrough St Jo the Ev *York* 53-58; C Oswaldtwistle Immanuel *Blackb* 58-59; V Accrington St Andr 59-65; V Salesbury 66-72; V Heyhouses on Sea 73-92; rtd 92; Perm to Offic *Blackb* from 92. *76 St Thomas's Road, Lytham St Annes, Lancs FY8 1JR* Tel (01253) 781469

WELCH, Francis Hughan. b 16. Lon Univ BD67. S'wark Ord Course 67. **d** 70 **p** 71. Lic to Offic *St Alb* 70-71; C St Alb St Steph 71-75; P-in-c 75-80; Chapl St Alb City Hosp 80-90; Perm to Offic *Lon* 80-90; rtd 81; Perm to Offic *St Alb* 80-81 and 90-93; Hon C St Alb St Pet 81-89; Hon C St Alb St Mich 89-90; Perm to Offic *St D* from 93. *Bryntelor, Sarnau, Llandysul SA44 6QN* Tel (01239) 654573

WELCH, Frederick George. b 23. St Cath Coll Cam BA44 MA48 Lon Univ BD59. St Aug Coll Cant 63. **d** 74 **p** 75. Kenya 74-87; rtd 87; Asst Chapl Tenerife *Eur* 87-88; Hon C Tamworth *Lich* 88-89; Hon C Hordle *Win* 89-92; Perm to Offic from 92. *8 Cruse Close, Sway, Lymington, Hants SO41 6AY* Tel (01590) 682134

WELCH, Gordon Joseph. b 47. Man Univ BSc68 PhD72. N Ord Course 84. **d** 87 **p** 88. NSM Upton Ascension *Ches* from 87. *6 St James Avenue, Chester CH2 1NA* Tel (01244) 382196

WELCH, Canon Grant Keith. b 40. AKC63. **d** 64 **p** 65. C Nottingham St Mary *S'well* 64-68; V Cinderhill 68-73; Master St Jo Hosp Weston Favell 73-88; R Weston Favell *Pet* 73-88; Can Pet Cathl 83-88; P-in-c Gt Houghton 84-85; V Wymondham *Nor* 88; C Loughton St Jo *Chelmsf* 89-92; TR from 92. *The Rectory, Church Lane, Loughton, Essex IG10 1PD* Tel 0181-508 1224

WELCH, Harold Gerald. b 16. St Cath Soc Ox BA48 MA53. Wycliffe Hall Ox 48. **d** 50 **p** 51. C Ipswich St Jo *St E* 50-53; V Offton, Nettlestead and Willisham 53-58; V Lozells St Paul *Birm* 58-66; V Austrey 66-83; V Warton 66-83; rtd 83; Perm to Offic *Birm* from 88; Perm to Offic *Lich* 88-94. *2 Clifford Close, Tamworth, Staffs B77 2DD* Tel (01827) 53678

WELCH, John Harry. b 52. Oak Hill Th Coll 85. **d** 87 **p** 88. C Parr *Liv* 87-90; V W Derby St Luke from 90. *St Luke's Vicarage, Princess Drive, West Derby, Liverpool L14 8XG* Tel 0151-228 6025

WELCH, Canon Michael Robin. b 33. MBE81. St Chad's Coll Dur BSc55. Wells Th Coll 57. **d** 59 **p** 60. C S Shields St Hilda *Dur* 59-63; CF (R of O) 61-88; Warden and Tr Officer Dioc Youth Cen *Newc* 63-68; Soc and Ind Adv *Portsm* 68-96; V Portsea All SS 72-85; V Swanmore St Barn 85-96; RD Bishops Waltham 88-93; Hon Can Portsm Cathl 92-96; rtd 96. *Southwell, Church Street, Mere, Warminster, Wilts BA12 6LS*

WELCH, Paul Baxter. b 47. Lanc Univ BEd74 MA75. St Alb Minl Tr Scheme 80. **d** 83 **p** 84. NSM Heath and Reach *St Alb* 83-84; Bp's Sch Adv *Win* 84-89; P-in-c Clungunford w Clunbury and Clunton, Bedstone etc *Heref* 89-93; V Wellingborough All SS *Pet* from 93. *The Vicarage, 154 Midland Road, Wellingborough, Northants NN8 1NF* Tel (01933) 227101

WELCH, Stephan John. b 50. Hull Univ BA74. Qu Coll Birm DipTh76. **d** 77 **p** 78. C Waltham Cross *St Alb* 77-80; P-in-c Reculver *Cant* 80-86; P-in-c Herne Bay St Bart 82-86; V Reculver and Herne Bay St Bart 86-92; V Hurley and Stubbings *Ox* from 92. *St Mary's Vicarage, High Street, Hurley, Maidenhead, Berks SL6 6AB* Tel (01628) 829032

✠**WELCH, The Rt Revd William Neville.** b 06. Keble Coll Ox BA27 MA32. Wycliffe Hall Ox 27. **d** 29 **p** 30 **c** 68. C Kidderminster *Worc* 29-32; C St Alb St Mich *St Alb* 32-34; Miss to Seamen 34-39; V Grays Thurrock *Chelmsf* 39-43; V Gt Ilford St Clem 43-53; RD Barking 46-53; Hon Can Chelmsf Cathl 51-53; V Gt Burstead 53-56; Adn Southend 53-72; Suff Bp Bradwell 68-73; rtd 73; Perm to Offic *Nor* 73-97; Perm to Offic *Chelmsf* from 73. *59 Moorfield Court, Newland Street, Witham, Essex CM8 1AE* Tel (01376) 503681

WELCHMAN, Richard Neville de Beaufort. b 11. St Pet Hall Ox BA33 DipTh34 MA37. Wycliffe Hall Ox 33. **d** 34 **p** 35. C Plymouth St Andr *Ex* 34-40; CF 40-45; P-in-c Yelverton *Ex* 45-54; R Lifton 54-62; R Kelly w Bradstone 59-62; V Pinhoe 62-76; rtd 77; Lic to Offic *Ex* from 77. *8 Culvert Road, Stoke Canon, Exeter EX5 4BD* Tel (01392) 841503

WELDON, William Ernest. b 41. TCD BA62 MA66. **d** 64 **p** 65. C Belfast Trin Coll Miss *Conn* 64-67; C Carnmoney 67-71; Chapl RN 71-96; QHC 93-96; Hon C Holbeton *Ex* from 96. *Church Hill House, Holbeton, Plymouth PL8 1LN* Tel (01752) 830528

WELFORD, Alan Traviss. b 14. St Jo Coll Cam BA35 MA39 ScD64. **d** 37 **p** 38. C Crayford *Roch* 37-38; Chapl St Jo Coll Cam 38-45; Fell 56-68; Australia 68-79; rtd 79; Perm to Offic *Win* 87-90. *187A High Street, Aldeburgh, Suffolk IP15 5AL* Tel (01394) 278536

WELHAM, Clive Richard. b 54. **d** 80 **p** 81. C Bellingham St Dunstan *S'wark* 80-84; Chapl Golds Coll Lon 84-95; V Plumstead Ascension from 95. *The Ascension Vicarage, Thornhill Avenue, London SE18 2HS* Tel 0181-854 3395

WELLER, David Christopher. b 60. UWIST BSc83. St Jo Coll Nottm MA94. **d** 96 **p** 97. C Wednesfield Heath *Lich* from 96. *220 Bushbury Road, Heath Town, Wolverhampton WV10 0NT* Tel (01902) 735689

WELLER, John Beresford. b 15. Lon Univ BD52. Tyndale Hall Bris 39. **d** 42 **p** 43. C Worthing H Trin *Chich* 42-44; V Hemingford Grey *Ely* 44-49; I Wimbledon Em Ridgway Prop Chpl *S'wark* 49-54; R Heigham H Trin *Nor* 54-60; V Harlow St Mary and St Hugh w St Jo the Bapt *Chelmsf* 60-77; Chapl Hillingdon Hosp Uxbridge 60-75; Chapl Harlow Tertiary Coll 61-65; RD Harlow *Chelmsf* 73-80; V Hatfield Broad Oak 77-80; rtd 80; Hon C Duffield *Derby* 81-94; Perm to Offic from 95. *8 Chadfield Road, Duffield, Belper, Derbyshire DE56 4DU* Tel (01332) 842271

WELLER, Canon John Christopher. b 25. St Pet Hall Ox BA49 MA52 Nottm Univ BD57. Qu Coll Birm 50. **d** 51 **p** 52. C Nottingham All SS *S'well* 51-54; C-in-c Porchester St Jas CD 54-58; S Rhodesia 58-64; Zambia 64-71; V W Heath *Birm* 71-81; Warden and Chapl Resthaven Home Stroud 81-84; P-in-c Duddeston 84-85; Zimbabwe 85-90; Can Harare 87-90; rtd 90; P-in-c Ward End *Birm* from 96. *42 Mallard Close, Acocks Green, Birmingham B27 6BN* Tel 0121-706 7535

WELLER, Richard Morton. b 33. Selw Coll Cam BA57 MA61. Wells Th Coll 61. **d** 63 **p** 64. C Stockingford *Cov* 63-66; C Pontefract St Giles *Wakef* 66-68; C-in-c Stockton St Jas CD *Dur* 68-74; V E Ardsley *Wakef* 74-83; V Heckmondwike 83-91; V Birstall 91-96; RD Birstall 92-96; V Gawber from 96. *The Vicarage, Church Street, Gawber, Barnsley, S Yorkshire S75 2RL* Tel (01226) 207140

WELLER, Ronald Howden. b 18. Wycliffe Hall Ox. **d** 60 **p** 61. C Edgbaston St Bart *Birm* 60-63; V Broxbourne *St Alb* 63-70; Singapore 70-74; New Zealand from 74; rtd 83. *4 Rydal Street, Hoon Hay, Christchurch 2, New Zealand*

WELLER, William John France. b 12. MBE58. Ridley Hall Cam 60. **d** 61 **p** 62. C Plymouth St Aug *Ex* 61-63; C Ringwood *Win* 63-65; R Stratfield Saye 65-73; R Stratfield Saye w Hartley Wespall 73-74; C-in-c Hartley Wespall w Stratfield Turgis 65-74; RD Odiham 69-74; P-in-c Southwick w Boarhunt *Portsm* 75-77; rtd 77; Perm to Offic *Ex* 78-94. *8 Moor View, North Tawton, Devon EX20 2HW* Tel (01837) 82873

WELLING, Anthony Wyndham. b 29. Ely Th Coll 55. **d** 58 **p** 83. C Coppenhall St Paul *Ches* 58-60; Lic to Offic *Ox* 82; Hon C Cookham from 83. *Broadway Barn, High Street, Ripley, Woking, Surrey GU23 6AQ* Tel (01483) 225384

WELLINGTON, Canon James Frederick. b 51. Leic Univ LLB72 Fitzw Coll Cam BA76. Ridley Hall Cam 74. **d** 77 **p** 78. C Mill Hill Jo Keble Ch *Lon* 77-80; C Wood Green St Mich 80-82; C Wood Green St Mich w Bounds Green St Gabr etc 82-83; V Stocking Farm *Leic* 83-90; V Gt Glen, Stretton Magna and Wistow etc from 90; Warden of Readers 91-97; Hon Can Leic Cathl from 94; RD Gartree II from 96. *St Cuthbert's Vicarage, Church Road, Great Glen, Leicester LE8 9FE* Tel 0116-259 2238

WELLS, Andrew Stuart. b 48. St Jo Coll Dur BA71. Cranmer Hall Dur DipTh73. **d** 74 **p** 75. C Walmsley *Man* 74-77; C Failsworth H Family 77-79; R Openshaw 79-90; V Hindsford from 90.

St Anne's Vicarage, Powys Street, Atherton, Manchester M46 9AR Tel (01942) 883902

WELLS, Anthony Martin Giffard. b 42. St Jo Coll Nottm 72. **d** 74 **p** 75. C Orpington Ch Ch *Roch* 74-78; P-in-c Odell *St Alb* 78-82; R 82-86; P-in-c Pavenham 78-82; V 82-86; RD Sharnbrook 81-86; R Angmering *Chich* from 86; RD Arundel and Bognor from 93. *The Rectory, Rectory Lane, Angmering, Littlehampton, W Sussex BN16 4JU* Tel (01903) 784979

WELLS, Antony Ernest (Tony). b 36. Oak Hill Th Coll 58. **d** 61 **p** 62. C Bethnal Green St Jas Less *Lon* 61-64; SAMS 64-69; Paraguay 64-69; V Kirkdale St Athanasius *Liv* 69-73; SAMS 73-75; Argentina 73-75; V Warfield *Ox* 75-81; V Fairfield *Liv* 81-83; C Rainhill 83-85; TV Cheltenham St Mark *Glouc* 85-89; P-in-c Forest of Dean Ch Ch w English Bicknor 89-95; rtd 97. *56 Averill Close, Broadway, Worcs WR12 7RA*

WELLS, Bryan Arthur. b 47. Golds Coll Lon BMus72 DipEd83 MA85. Coll of Resurr Mirfield 77. **d** 79 **p** 82. C Leigh-on-Sea St Marg *Chelmsf* 79-80; Hon C Limpsfield and Titsey *S'wark* 81-85; C Weymouth St Paul *Sarum* 86-89; TV Selsdon St Jo w St Fran *S'wark* from 89. *St Francis's Vicarage, Tedder Road, South Croydon, Surrey CR2 8AH* Tel 0181-657 7864

WELLS, Miss Cecilia Isabel. b 24. Bedf Coll Lon BA45. St Mich Ho Ox 56. **dss** 62 **d** 87. Chester le Street *Dur* 74-84; rtd 84; Perm to Offic *Ches* from 84. *12 Rectory Close, Nantwich, Cheshire CW5 5SW* Tel (01270) 627258

WELLS, Charles Francis (Charlie). b 39. Oak Hill Th Coll DipHE. **d** 85 **p** 86. C Southend St Sav Westcliff *Chelmsf* 85-89; P-in-c E and W Horndon w Lt Warley 89-96; V E and W Horndon w Lt Warley and Childerditch from 96. *The Rectory, Thorndon Avenue, Brentwood, Essex CM13 3TR* Tel (01277) 811223

WELLS, David Henry Nugent. b 20. St Chad's Coll Dur BA42 MA46 DipTh47. **d** 47 **p** 48. C Wednesbury St Paul Wood Green *Lich* 47-48; C Rugeley 48-50; C Hanley All SS 50-53; R Leigh 53-57; R Ashley 57-64; V Hales 57-64; V Alrewas 64-73; V Wychnor 64-73; R Upton Magna 73-81; V Withington 73-81; P-in-c Uffington 81; R Uffington, Upton Magna and Withington 81-85; rtd 85; Perm to Offic *Lich* from 85. *13 Belvidere Avenue, Shrewsbury SY2 5PF* Tel (01743) 365822

WELLS, Canon Edward Arthur. b 23. MBE97. SRN. Oak Hill Th Coll. **d** 57 **p** 58. C Wednesfield Heath *Lich* 57-60; R Mettingham w Ilketshall St John *St E* 60-62; R Sproughton w Burstall 62-74; V Ipswich St Nic 74-80; Hon Can St E Cathl 80-88; Chapl Ipswich Hosp 80-90; rtd 88. *74 Christchurch Street, Ipswich IP4 2DH* Tel (01473) 254046

WELLS, George Reginald. b 11. K Coll Cam BA33. Cuddesdon Coll 33. **d** 34 **p** 35. C Penistone w Midhope *Wakef* 34-37; India 38-61; V Hagbourne *Ox* 61-74; P-in-c Gt Coxwell 74-80; P-in-c Buscot 74-80; P-in-c Coleshill 74-80; P-in-c Eaton Hastings 74-80; rtd 80; Perm to Offic *Glas* from 80. *8 Greystone Avenue, Dumfries DG1 1PE* Tel (01387) 68294

WELLS, Jeremy Stephen. b 47. Nottm Univ BA69 Univ of Wales (Cardiff) DPS87 UWE MSc97. Chich Th Coll 72. **d** 73 **p** 74. C S Yardley St Mich *Birm* 73-76; C St Marychurch *Ex* 76-78; P-in-c Bridgwater H Trin *B & W* 78-82; P-in-c Brent Knoll 82-84; P-in-c E Brent w Lympsham 82-84; R Brent Knoll, E Brent and Lympsham from 84. *The Rectory, Church Road, East Brent, Highbridge, Somerset TA9 4HZ* Tel (01278) 760271

WELLS, Jo Bailey. b 65. CCC Cam BA87 Minnesota Univ MA90 St Jo Coll Dur BA92. Cranmer Hall Dur DMinlStuds93. **d** 95 **p** 96. Chapl Clare Coll Cam from 95; Acting Dean from 97. *Clare College, Cambridge CB2 1TL* Tel (01223) 333200 Fax 333219 E-mail jbw21@cam.ac.uk

WELLS, John Michael. b 35. Mert Coll Ox BA58 MA61. Westcott Ho Cam 60. **d** 62 **p** 63. C Hornchurch St Andr *Chelmsf* 62-64; C Barking St Marg 64-66; C Wanstead H Trin Hermon Hill 66-69; V Elm Park St Nic Hornchurch 69-76; Offg Chapl RAF 69-76; R Wakes Colne w Chappel *Chelmsf* 76-79; Project Officer Cathl Cen for Research and Tr 79-81; Hon Chapl Chelmsf Cathl 79-81; Area Sec (Dios Chelmsf and Ely) CMS 81-88; E Cen Co-ord 85-91; Area Sec (Dios Chelmsf and St E) 88-91; Public Preacher *Chelmsf* 82-91; V Hanging Heaton *Wakef* 92-96. *2 Clarkesmead, Tiptree, Colchester CO5 0BX* Tel (01621) 819899

WELLS, The Ven John Rowse David. b 27. Kelham Th Coll 53. **d** 57 **p** 58. SSM from 57; Lic to Offic *S'well* 57-59; Australia 59-65; Basutoland 65-66; Lesotho from 66; Can SS Mary and Jas Cathl Maseru from 77; Adn Cen Lesotho from 85. *PO Box 1579, Maseru, Lesotho 100* Tel Lesotho (266) 315979

WELLS, Mark Wynne-Eyton. b 20. Peterho Cam BA48 MA54. Westcott Ho Cam 48. **d** 50 **p** 51. C Heene *Chich* 50-53; C Sullington 53-57; R Slinfold 57-59; S Rhodesia 59-62; V Stoke by Nayland w Leavenheath *St E* 62-88; RD Hadleigh 71-76 and 85-86; rtd 88; Perm to Offic *Nor* from 88. *Red House, The Street, Great Snoring, Fakenham, Norfolk NR21 0AH* Tel (01328) 820641

WELLS, Michael John. b 46. Solicitor 74 Univ Coll Ox BA68 MA73. S Dios Minl Tr Scheme 92. **d** 95 **p** 96. NSM Brighton St Pet and St Nic w Chpl Royal *Chich* from 95. *35 Park Crescent, Brighton BN2 3HB* Tel (01273) 600735

WELLS, Nicholas Anthony. b 60. Cranmer Hall Dur 88. **d** 91 **p** 92. C Accrington St Jo w Huncoat *Blackb* 91-94; C Douglas St Geo and St Barn *S & M* 94-97; V Onchan from 97. *The Vicarage, Church Road, Onchan, Douglas, Isle of Man IM3 1BF* Tel (01624) 675797

WELLS, Norman Charles. b 18. Keble Coll Ox BA40 MA44. St Steph Ho Ox 40. **d** 42 **p** 43. C Teddington St Alb *Lon* 42-46; C S Kensington St Aug 46-52; V Fulham St Pet 52-62; V St Margarets on Thames 62-73; V Highbridge *B & W* 73-84; RD Burnham 76-82; rtd 84; Perm to Offic *B & W* 85-95. *40 Mount Road, Nether Stowey, Bridgwater, Somerset TA5 1LU* Tel (01278) 732609

WELLS, Oswald Bertie (Bert). b 18. Linc Th Coll. **d** 48 **p** 49. C Leigh St Mary *Man* 48-51; P-in-c Plaistow St Andr *Chelmsf* 57-59; Father Guardian SSF 59-66; C Loughton St Jo 81-84; Hon C from 84; rtd 84. *2 Baldwins Hill, Loughton, Essex IG10 1SD* Tel 0181-508 4602

WELLS, Peter Robert. b 59. Wilson Carlile Coll 78 Sarum & Wells Th Coll 87. **d** 89 **p** 90. CA from 81; C Mortlake w E Sheen *S'wark* 89-93; Dir St Marylebone Healing and Counselling Cen from 93. *17 Marylebone Road, London NW1 5LT* Tel 0171-935 6374

WELLS, Philip Anthony. b 57. BA MPhil. Coll of Resurr Mirfield. **d** 84 **p** 85. C Wylde Green *Birm* 84-87; Chapl and Succ Birm Cathl 87-91; Bp's Dom Chapl 91-97; V Polesworth from 97. *Polesworth Vicarage, Tamworth, Staffs B78 1DU* Tel (01827) 892340

WELLS, Richard John. b 46. St Mich Coll Llan DipTh70 Cuddesdon Coll 70. **d** 71 **p** 72. C Kingston upon Hull St Alb *York* 71-75; C Addlestone *Guildf* 75-80; V Weston 80-88; V Milford 88-96; Chapl Milford Hosp Surrey 88-96; R Westbourne *Chich* from 96. *The New Rectory, Westbourne Road, Emsworth, Hants PO10 8UL* Tel (01243) 372867

WELLS, Robert Crosby. b 28. St Jo Coll Dur BA52. **d** 54 **p** 55. C S Shore H Trin *Blackb* 54-59; C-in-c Lea CD 59-69; V Ribby w Wrea 69-93; rtd 93; Perm to Offic *Blackb* from 93. *4 Myra Road, Fairhaven, Lytham St Annes, Lancs FY8 1EB* Tel (01253) 739851

WELLS, The Ven Roderick John. b 36. Dur Univ BA63 Hull Univ MA85. Cuddesdon Coll 63. **d** 65 **p** 66. C Lambeth St Mary the Less *S'wark* 65-68; P-in-c 68-71; R Skegness *Linc* 71-77; P-in-c Winthorpe 77; R Skegness and Winthorpe 77-78; TR Gt and Lt Coates w Bradley 78-89; RD Grimsby and Cleethorpes 83-89; Can and Preb Linc Cathl from 86; Adn Stow from 89; V Hackthorn w Cold Hanworth 89-93; P-in-c N w S Carlton 89-93. *The Vicarage, Hackthorn, Lincoln LN2 3PF* Tel (01673) 860382

WELLS, Ronald Charles (Ron). b 20. AKC50. **d** 51 **p** 52. C Prittlewell St Mary *Chelmsf* 51-56; C-in-c Leigh-on-Sea St Aid CD 56; V Leigh-on-Sea St Aid 56-65; R Springfield All SS 65-80; Chapl Southend Gen Hosp 80-91; V Prittlewell St Pet *Chelmsf* 80-90; P-in-c 91; rtd 91; Perm to Offic *Chelmsf* from 91. *61 Byrne Drive, Southend-on-Sea SS2 6SA* Tel (01702) 338006

WELLS, Mrs Sally Ursula. b 40. St Mark's Coll Canberra BTh93 Ripon Coll Cuddesdon 96. **d** 97. Asst Chapl Vienna *Eur* from 97. *Plenergasse 4/13, A-1180 Vienna, Austria* Tel Vienna (1) 40 66354

WELLS, Samuel Martin Bailey. b 65. Mert Coll Ox BA87. Edin Th Coll 88. **d** 91 **p** 92. C Wallsend St Luke *Newc* 91-95; C Cherry Hinton St Andr *Ely* 95-97; P-in-c Earlham St Eliz *Nor* from 97. *St Elizabeth's Vicarage, 75 Cadge Road, North Earlham, Norwich NR5 8DQ* Tel (01603) 250764

WELLS, Stephen Glossop. b 22. CCC Ox BA48 MA48. Westcott Ho Cam 48. **d** 50 **p** 51. C Poplar All SS w St Frideswide *Lon* 50-56; R Saltford *B & W* 56-80; P-in-c Corston w Newton St Loe 76-80; RD Chew Magna 80-85; R Saltford w Corston and Newton St Loe 80-87; Preb Wells Cathl 84-90; TV Wellington and Distr 87-90; rtd 90. *57 Meadow Road, Berkhamsted, Herts HP4 1JL* Tel (01442) 870981

WELLS, Terry Roy John. b 45. EAMTC 89. **d** 92 **p** 93. C Martlesham w Brightwell *St E* 92-95; R Higham, Holton St Mary, Raydon and Stratford from 95. *The Rectory, School Lane, Stratford St Mary, Colchester CO7 6LZ* Tel (01206) 322128

WELLS, Canon William David Sandford. b 41. JP. Or Coll Ox BA64 MA66. Ridley Hall Cam 63. **d** 65 **p** 66. C Gt Malvern St Mary *Worc* 65-70; V Crowle 70-84; P-in-c Himbleton w Huddington 78-84; V E Bowbrook 84-89; Hon Can Worc Cathl from 84; RD Droitwich 84-96; R Bowbrook S from 89. *The Vicarage, Church Road, Crowle, Worcester WR7 4AT* Tel (01905) 381617

WELLS, Archdeacon of. *See* ACWORTH, The Ven Richard Foote

WELLS, Dean of. *See* LEWIS, The Very Revd Richard

WELSBY, Canon Paul Antony. b 20. Univ Coll Dur BA42 MA45 Sheff Univ PhD58. Linc Th Coll 42. **d** 44 **p** 45. C Boxley *Cant* 44-47; C Ipswich St Mary le Tower *St E* 47-52; R Copdock w Washbrook and Belstead 52-66; RD Samford 64-66; Can Res Roch Cathl *Roch* 66-88; Dir Post Ord Tr 66-88; Chapl to The Queen 80-90; rtd 88; Bp's Dom Chapl *Roch* 88-90; Perm to Offic from 90. *20 Knights Ridge, Pembury, Tunbridge Wells, Kent TN2 4HP* Tel (01892) 823053

WELSH, Angus Alexander. b 30. Trin Coll Cam BA54 MA59 St Jo Coll Dur DipTh56. **d** 56 **p** 57. C Jesmond Clayton Memorial *Newc* 56-60; C Fenham St Jas and St Basil 60-62; V Bacup St Jo *Man* 62-68; Tristan da Cunha 68-71; St Vincent 72-78; R Heysham *Blackb* 78-88; V Blackb St Steph 88-96; rtd 96. *23 Low Stobhill, Morpeth, Northd NE61 2SF*

WELSH, Jennifer Ann. b 48. Univ Coll Lon BA. **d** 81. NSM Newport St Matt *Mon* 81-85; NSM Risca from 85. *470 Caerleon Road, Newport NP9 7LW* Tel (01633) 258287

WELSH, Jennifer Lee (Jenny). b 59. Calgary Univ BSc81. Cam Episc Div Sch (USA) MDiv87. **d** 87 **p** 88. Canada 87-89; Asst Chapl HM Pris Linc 89-94. *The Rectory, Church Street, Basingstoke, Hants RG21 1QT* Tel (01256) 26654

WELSH, Miss Mary Elizabeth. b 22. St Hilda's Coll Ox BA44 MA48 Lon Univ DipEd45 BD50. Lambeth STh64. **dss** 68 **d** 87 **p** 94. Ex St Mark *Ex* 70-82; Lic to Offic 82-85; Yatton Moor *B & W* 85-87; Perm to Offic from 87. *26 Rectory Way, Yatton, Bristol BS19 4JF* Tel (01934) 833329

WELSH, Maxwell Wilfred. b 29. Bp's Coll Calcutta 55. **d** 58 **p** 59. India 58-72; C Cannock *Lich* 73-76; C Wednesfield 76-79; V Milton 79-86; V Croxton w Broughton and Adbaston from 86. *The Vicarage, Croxton, Stafford ST21 6PF* Tel (01630) 620231

WELSH, Philip Peter. b 48. Keble Coll Ox BA69 MA73 Selw Coll Cam BA72 MA76. Westcott Ho Cam 71. **d** 73 **p** 74. C W Dulwich All SS and Em *S'wark* 73-76; C Surbiton St Andr 76-77; C Surbiton St Andr and St Mark 77-79; India 79-81; V Malden St Jo *S'wark* 81-87; Min Officer *Linc* 87-94; TR Basingstoke *Win* from 94. *The Rectory, Church Street, Basingstoke, Hants RG21 1QT* Tel (01256) 26654

WELSH, Robert Leslie. b 32. Sheff Univ BA54 St Jo Coll Dur DipTh58. **d** 58 **p** 59. C S Westoe *Dur* 58-62; C Darlington St Cuth 62-66; CF (TA) 64-67; V E Rainton *Dur* 66-85; R W Rainton 66-85; R Wolsingham and Thornley from 85. *The Rectory, 14 Rectory Lane, Wolsingham, Bishop Auckland, Co Durham DL13 3AJ* Tel (01388) 527340

WELTON, Peter Abercrombie. b 62. Ball Coll Ox BA84. Qu Coll Birm 84. **d** 86 **p** 87. C Walthamstow St Pet *Chelmsf* 86-89; Community Priest 89-93. *c/o Citizens, PO Box 459, Wolverhampton WV10 0YY*

WEMYSS, Gary. b 52. St Jo Coll Dur 79. **d** 80 **p** 81. C Blackb St Jas *Blackb* 80-83; C Padiham 83-86; V Stalmine 86-90; P-in-c Egton-cum-Newland and Lowick *Carl* from 90. *The Vicarage, Penny Bridge, Ulverston, Cumbria LA12 7RQ* Tel (01229) 861285

WENHAM, David. b 45. MA PhD. Ridley Hall Cam. **d** 84 **p** 85. Lic to Offic *Ox* 84-96; Tutor Wycliffe Hall Ox from 84; NSM Shelswell *Ox* from 96. *Wycliffe Hall, 54 Banbury Road, Oxford OX2 6PW* Tel (01865) 274200/5/8 Fax 274215

WENHAM, Michael Timothy. b 49. Pemb Coll Cam MA75. Wycliffe Hall Ox DipTh85. **d** 86 **p** 87. C Norbury *Ches* 86-89; V Stanford in the Vale w Goosey and Hatford *Ox* from 89. *The Vicarage, Stanford in the Vale, Faringdon, Oxon SN7 8HU* Tel (01367) 710267

WENSLEY, Mrs Beryl Kathleen. b 29. CertRK55. Selly Oak Coll 53. **dss** 76 **d** 87 **p** 94. Raynes Park St Sav *S'wark* 76-83; Chapl Asst St Geo Hosp Lon 83-89; rtd 89; Chapl R Hants Co Hosp Win 89-94; Chapl Win HA 89-94. *22 Orchard Walk, Winchester, Hants SO22 6DL* Tel (01962) 883405

✠**WENT, The Rt Revd John Stewart.** b 44. CCC Cam BA66 MA70. Oak Hill Th Coll 67. **d** 69 **p** 70 **c** 96. C Northwood Em *Lon* 69-75; V Margate H Trin *Cant* 75-83; Vice-Prin Wycliffe Hall Ox 83-89; Adn Surrey *Guildf* 89-96; Chmn Dioc Coun for Unity and Miss 90-96; Suff Bp Tewkesbury *Glouc* from 96. *Green Acre, 166 Hempstead Lane, Gloucester GL2 6LG* Tel (01452) 521824 Fax 505554

WENZEL, Peggy Sylvia. STh. Gilmore Ho. **d** 88 **p** 94. Perm to Offic *Sarum* from 88; rtd 92. *Church Cottage, Church Street, Pewsey, Wilts SN9 5DL* Tel (01672) 63834

WERNER, David Robert Edmund. b 33. Clifton Th Coll 61. **d** 63 **p** 64. C Holywell *St As* 63-68; C Llanrhos 68-70; R Tedburn St Mary *Ex* 71-91; RD Kenn 80-83; Perm to Offic from 92. *The Old Rectory, Tedburn St Mary, Exeter EX6 6EN* Tel (01647) 61253

WERNER, Donald Kilgour. b 39. Univ of Wales BA61 Linacre Coll Ox BA64 MA67. Wycliffe Hall Ox 61. **d** 64 **p** 65. C Wrexham *St As* 64-69; Chapl Brasted Place Coll Westerham 69-73; Chapl Bris Univ *Bris* 73-76; Hon C Clifton St Paul 73-76; Chapl Keele Univ *Lich* 77-79; P-in-c Keele 77-79; C York St Mich-le-Belfrey *York* 79-83; Dir of Evang 79-83; R Holborn St Geo w H Trin and St Bart *Lon* from 83. *13 Doughty Street, London WC1N 2PL* Tel 0171-831 0588

WERRELL, Ralph Sidney. b 29. Tyndale Hall Bris 54. **d** 56 **p** 57. C Penn Fields *Lich* 56-60; C Champion Hill St Sav *S'wark* 60-61; R Danby Wiske w Yafforth *Ripon* 61-65; P-in-c Hutton Bonville *York* 61-65; R Combs *St E* 65-75; V Bootle Ch Ch *Liv* 75-80; R Scole w Billingford and Thorpe Parva *Nor* 80; P-in-c Brockdish w Thorpe Abbots 80; R Scole, Brockdish, Billingford, Thorpe Abbots etc 80-83; R Southam w Stockton *Cov* 83-89; R Southam 89-94; rtd 95; Perm to Offic *Birm* from 95; Perm to Offic *Cov* from 95. *2A Queens Road, Kenilworth, Warks CV8 1JQ* Tel (01926) 58677

WERWATH, Wolfgang Albert Richard Kurt. b 22. Ripon Hall Ox 54. **d** 56 **p** 57. C Hamer *Man* 56-58; C N Reddish 58-59; V Chadderton St Luke 59-67; V Whitfield *Derby* 67-75; V Bretby w Newton Solney 75-88; rtd 88; Perm to Offic *Derby* from 88. *28 D'Ayncourt Walk, Farnsfield, Newark, Notts NG22 8DP* Tel (01623) 882635

WESSON, Basil. b 24. **d** 83 **p** 84. NSM Belper Ch Ch and Milford *Derby* 83-96; Perm to Offic from 96. *Wescot, Belper Lane End, Belper, Derbyshire DE56 2DL* Tel (01773) 827566

WESSON, John Graham. b 38. St Pet Coll Ox BA62 DipTh63 MA68. Clifton Th Coll 63. **d** 65 **p** 66. C Southport Ch Ch w St Andr *Liv* 65-68; C Ox St Ebbe w St Pet *Ox* 68-71; Chapl Poly Cen Lon 71-76; C-in-c Edin St Thos *Edin* 76-82; Dir Past Studies Trin Coll Bris 82-86; R Birm St Martin w Bordesley St Andr *Birm* 86-96; RD Birm City 88-95; Hon Can Birm Cathl 91-96; Dir Post-Ord Tr *Lich* from 96; Dir Continuing Minl Educn from 96; C Lich St Mary w St Mich 96; C Lich St Mich w St Mary and Wall from 96. *200E St John Street, Lichfield, Staffs WS14 9EF* Tel (01543) 414551 Fax 250935

WEST, Alan David. b 61. Southn Univ BTh92. Aston Tr Scheme 87 Sarum & Wells Th Coll 89. **d** 92 **p** 93. C S'wark St Geo the Martyr w St Jude *S'wark* 92-94; C S'wark St Geo the Martyr w St Alphege & St Jude 95-96; V Boscoppa *Truro* from 96. *St Luke's House, 5 David Penhaligon Way, St Austell, Cornwall PL25 3AR* Tel (01726) 69857

WEST, Andrew Victor. b 59. Wycliffe Hall Ox 87. **d** 90 **p** 91. C Leyland St Andr *Blackb* 90-94; C Blackpool St Jo 94-96; TV Bedworth *Cov* from 96. *St Andrew's House, Smorrall Lane, Bedworth, Nuneaton, Warks CV12 0JN* Tel (01203) 363322

WEST, Arthur. b 20. Linc Th Coll 59. **d** 60 **p** 61. C Cottingham *York* 60-64; V Ruswarp w Sneaton 64-68; V Nether w Upper Poppleton 68-85; RD Ainsty 77-85; rtd 85; Perm to Offic *York* from 85. *8 River View, Linton on Ouse, York YO6 2BJ* Tel (01347) 848463

WEST, Bernard Kenneth. b 31. Linc Th Coll. **d** 67 **p** 68. C E Ham St Geo *Chelmsf* 67-71; Australia from 71; rtd 89. *Lot 33, Mitchell Street, Wooroloo, W Australia 6558*

WEST, Bryan Edward. b 39. Avery Hill Coll CertEd69 BEd80 Kent Univ MA86. Cant Sch of Min 85. **d** 88 **p** 89. NSM Gravesend H Family w Ifield *Roch* 88-92; C Gravesend St Geo 92-95; NSM Hatcham Park All SS *S'wark* from 95; Perm to Offic *Chelmsf* from 95. *Flat 6, 76 Wickham Road, London SE4 1LS* Tel 0181-692 8897

WEST, Miss Caroline Elisabeth. b 61. RGN84. Wycliffe Hall Ox DipMin95. **d** 95. C Eastrop *Win* from 95. *19 Beaulieu Court, Riverdene, Basingstoke, Hants RG21 2DQ*

WEST, Mrs Christine Cecily. TCD BA60 MA63 HDipEd61. CITC 91. **d** 94 **p** 95. NSM Bray *D & G* 94-96; NSM Kilternan from 96. *55 Beech Park Road, Foxrock, Dublin 18, Irish Republic* Tel Dublin (1) 289 6374

WEST, Canon Clive. QUB BD75. CITC. **d** 64 **p** 65. C Lisburn Ch Ch Cathl *Conn* 64-68; Asst Master Lisnagarvey Sec Sch Lisburn 68-70; C Belfast All SS 70-75; I from 84; Can Belf Cathl from 95; I Mullabrack w Kilcluney *Arm* 76-84. *All Saints Rectory, 25 Rugby Road, Belfast BT7 1PT* Tel (01232) 323327

WEST, David Marshall. b 48. St Jo Coll Dur BA70. Qu Coll Birm DipTh72. **d** 73 **p** 74. C Wylde Green *Birm* 73-76; C Wokingham St Paul *Ox* 76-79; V Hurst 79-88; V Maidenhead St Luke 88-95; C Whitley Ch Ch from 95. *32 Bourne Avenue, Reading RG2 0DU* Tel 0118-987 2935

WEST, Derek Elvin. b 47. Hull Univ BA69. Westcott Ho Cam 71. **d** 73 **p** 74. C Walthamstow St Pet *Chelmsf* 73-77; C Chingford SS Pet and Paul 77-80; TV W Slough *Ox* 80-88; Slough Community Chapl 88-95; TV Upton cum Chalvey from 95. *St Peter's Vicarage, Montem Lane, Slough SL1 2QJ* Tel (01753) 520725

WEST, Eric Edward. b 32. Leeds Univ BA60. Bps' Coll Cheshunt 63. **d** 64 **p** 65. C Biscot *St Alb* 64-71; V from 71. *The Vicarage, 161 Bishopscote Road, Luton LU3 1PD* Tel (01582) 573421

WEST, Eric Robert Glenn. b 55. QUB BA79 Man Univ DipEd80. CITC BTh92. **d** 92 **p** 93. C Enniskillen *Clogh* 92-95; I Lisbellaw from 95. *The Rectory, Lisbellaw, Enniskillen, Co Fermanagh BT94 5BS* Tel (01365) 387219

✠**WEST, The Rt Revd Francis Horner.** b 09. Magd Coll Cam BA31 MA35. Ridley Hall Cam 31. **d** 33 **p** 34 **c** 62. C Burmantofts St Steph and St Agnes *Ripon* 33-36; C Cambridge H Trin *Ely* 36; Chapl and Tutor Ridley Hall Cam 36-38; V Starbeck *Ripon* 38-42; CF (R of O) 39-46; V Upton *S'well* 46-51; Adn Newark 47-62; V E Retford 51-54; RD Retford 51-53; R Dinder *B & W* 62-71; Preb Wells Cathl 62-77; Suff Bp Taunton 62-77; rtd 77. *11 Castle Street, Aldbourne, Marlborough, Wilts SN8 2DA* Tel (01672) 40630

WEST, Gerald Eric. b 18. ACII48. St Deiniol's Hawarden. **d** 80 **p** 81. Hon C Bramhall *Ches* 80-82; C 82-87; rtd 87; Perm to Offic *Ches* from 87. *255 Bramhall Moor Lane, Hazel Grove, Stockport, Cheshire SK7 5JL* Tel 0161-439 3029

WEST, Harold Reginald. b 15. Dur Univ BA43 MA46. Coll of Resurr Mirfield 43. **d** 45 **p** 46. C Tynemouth H Trin W Town *Newc* 45-48; C Sugley 48-55; V Cresswell 55-61; V Newc St Luke 61-82; rtd 82. *42 Linden Road, Gosforth, Newcastle upon Tyne NE3 4HB* Tel 0191-284 4291

WEST, Henry Cyrano. b 28. K Coll Lon. **d** 51 **p** 52. C Braunstone *Leic* 51-53; C Wandsworth St Anne *S'wark* 53-55; C Raynes Park St Sav 55-58; CF 58-63; V Sculcoates *York* 63-71; P-in-c Kingston upon Hull St Jude w St Steph 67-71; Lic to Offic *Cov* 71-75; Lic to Offic *Man* 75-87; Hon C Hulme Ascension from 87; rtd 91; Perm to Offic *Man* from 91. *6 King's Drive, Middleton, Manchester M24 4PB* Tel 0161-643 4410

WEST, Keith. b 63. Sunderland Poly BSc86. Chich Th Coll 92 Coll of Resurr Mirfield BTh95. **d** 95 **p** 96. C Rawmarsh w Parkgate *Sheff* 95-96; C Armley w New Wortley *Ripon* from 96. *20 Wesley Road, Leeds LS12 1UN* Tel 0113-279 7377

WEST (formerly WINDIATE), Mrs Mary Elizabeth. b 49. Linc Th Coll CMinlStuds94. **d** 94 **p** 95. C Loughton St Jo *Chelmsf* from 94. *2 Doubleday Road, Loughton, Essex IG10 2LG* Tel 0181-508 0690

WEST, Canon Michael Brian. b 39. Bris Univ BSc60. Linc Th Coll 64. **d** 66 **p** 67. C Hatfield *St Alb* 66-69; Ind Chapl 69-81; Hon Can St Alb 78-81; Sen Ind Chapl *Sheff* from 81; Hon Can Sheff Cathl from 81. *21 Endcliffe Rise Road, Sheffield S11 8RU* Tel 0114-266 1921

WEST, Canon Michael Frederick. b 50. Trin Coll Ox BA72 MA76 UEA DPhil96. Westcott Ho Cam 72. **d** 74 **p** 75. C Wolverhampton *Lich* 74-78; C Wolverhampton 78; C Hanley H Ev 78-79; TV 79-82; Dioc Youth Officer *St E* 83-88; V Ipswich St Thos 88-95; Prin LNSM Scheme from 96; Hon Can St E Cathl from 96. *The Rectory, School Road, Coddenham, Ipswich IP6 9PS* Tel (01449) 760419

WEST, Michael John. b 33. ARSM54 CEng60 FIMM68 FEng89 Imp Coll Lon BScEng54. S'wark Ord Course 85. **d** 88 **p** 89. Hon C Caterham *S'wark* from 88. *1 Church Road, Kenley, Surrey CR8 5DW* Tel 0181-668 1548

WEST, Michael Oakley. b 31. Bris Bapt Coll 53 Wells Th Coll 62. **d** 63 **p** 64. C Swindon Ch Ch *Bris* 63-66; Libya 66-68; R Lydiard Millicent w Lydiard Tregoz *Bris* 68-75; V Breage w Germoe *Truro* 75-82; CMS 82-91; Chapl Tel Aviv 82-89; Chapl Shiplake Coll Henley 91-94; Asst Chapl Bryanston Sch Dorset 94-95; Belgium 95-96; rtd 96; Perm to Offic *Eur* from 96. *10 Rossetti House, Erasmus Street, London SW1P 4HT* Tel 0171-834 4266

WEST, Miss Penelope Anne Margaret (Penny). b 44. City of Birm Coll CertEd68. Glouc Sch of Min 74 Ridley Hall Cam 85. **dss** 86 **d** 87 **p** 94. Portishead *B & W* 86-87; C 87-92; C Bath Abbey w St Jas 92-95; Chapl Bath Gp Hosps 92-95; V Kewstoke w Wick St Lawrence *B & W* from 95. *The Vicarage, 35 Kewstoke Road, Kewstoke, Weston-super-Mare, Avon BS22 9YE* Tel (01934) 416162

WEST, Peter Harcourt. b 29. **d** 59 **p** 60. C Histon *Ely* 59-60; C Hampreston *Sarum* 60-61; C Braintree *Chelmsf* 61-63; Perm to Offic from 72; rtd 94. *Westgates, 139 Witham Road, Black Notley, Braintree, Essex CM7 8LR* Tel (01376) 323048

WEST, Philip William. b 48. Magd Coll Ox BA70 MA78. St Jo Coll Nottm BA74 DPS75. **d** 75 **p** 76. C Rushden w Newton Bromswold *Pet* 75-79; C Pitsmoor w Ellesmere *Sheff* 79-83; V Attercliffe 83-89; Ind Chapl 85-90; P-in-c Darnall H Trin 86-89; V Stannington from 89; RD Hallam from 96. *The Vicarage, 214 Oldfield Road, Stannington, Sheffield S6 6DY* Tel 0114-234 5586 or 232 4490

WEST, Reginald Roy. b 28. St Deiniol's Hawarden 74. **d** 74 **p** 75. C Abergavenny St Mary w Llanwenarth Citra *Mon* 74-77; V Tredegar St Jas 77-96; rtd 96. *2 Croesonen Park, Abergavenny NP7 6PD*

WEST, Reginald George. b 14. ACA39 FCA57. Worc Ord Coll 66. **d** 68 **p** 69. C Oundle *Pet* 68-73; V Weedon Lois w Plumpton and Moreton Pinkney 73-79; rtd 79; Perm to Offic *Lich* from 91. *57 Greenacres Way, Newport, Shropshire TF10 7PH* Tel (01952) 812645

WEST, Richard Wilfrid Anthony. b 20. Magd Coll Cam BA41 MA45. Wells Th Coll 41. **d** 43 **p** 44. C Dorking *Guildf* 43-47; C Leatherhead 47-49; V Brockham Green *S'wark* 50-86; P-in-c Betchworth 81-86; rtd 86. *2 Abbotts Walk, Cerne Abbas, Dorchester, Dorset DT2 7JN* Tel (01300) 341567

WEST, Canon Ronald Cameron. b 06. AKC33. **d** 33 **p** 34. C Blackheath *Birm* 33-36; C Yardley Wood 36-38; C Banbury *Ox* 38-39; V Wroxton w Balscott 39-50; V Enstone 50-55; V Freeland 55-80; RD Woodstock 76-80; Hon Can Ch Ch 79-80; rtd 80; Perm to Offic *Truro* from 80. *Flat 22, Chynance, Alexandra Road, Penzance, Cornwall TR18 4LY* Tel (01736) 366612

WEST, Stephen Peter. b 52. Liv Univ CertEd74. Oak Hill Th Coll 87. **d** 89 **p** 90. C Gateacre *Liv* 89-92; V Liv All So Springwood from 92. *Springwood Vicarage, Mather Avenue, Liverpool L19 4TF* Tel 0151-427 5699

WEST, Thomas Roderic. b 55. DipTh BTh90. TCD Div Sch. **d** 86 **p** 87. C Dromore Cathl *D & D* 86-89; I Carrowdore w Millisle 89-95; I Moira from 95. *1 Main Street, Moira, Craigavon, Co Armagh BT67 0LE* Tel (01846) 611268

WEST, Timothy Ralph (Tim). b 53. Bath Univ BSc75. Ridley Hall Cam 82. **d** 85 **p** 86. C Mildenhall *St E* 85-88; TV Melbury *Sarum* 88-92; TR from 92. *The Rectory, Summer Lane, Evershot, Dorchester, Dorset DT2 0JP* Tel (01935) 83238

WEST CUMBERLAND, Archdeacon of. *See* DAVIS, The Ven Alan Norman

WEST HAM, Archdeacon of. *See* FOX, The Ven Michael John

WEST-LINDELL, Stein Eric. b 54. BA. Linc Th Coll 82. **d** 84 **p** 85. C Allington and Maidstone St Pet *Cant* 84-87; R Orlestone w Snave and Ruckinge w Warehorne 87-93; R Byfield w Boddington and Aston le Walls *Pet* from 93. *The Rectory, Church Street, Byfield, Daventry, Northants NN11 6XN* Tel (01327) 60204

WESTALL, Canon Michael Robert. b 39. Qu Coll Cam BA62 MA66. Cuddesdon Coll 63 Harvard Div Sch 65. **d** 66 **p** 67. C Heref St Martin *Heref* 66-70; India 70-83; Vice Prin Bp's Coll Calcutta 76-79; Prin 79-83; Tanzania 84-92; Prin St Mark's Th Coll Dar-es-Salaam 84-92; R Alfrick, Lulsley, Suckley, Leigh and Bransford *Worc* from 93. *The Rectory, Leigh, Worcester WR6 5LE* Tel (01886) 832355

WESTBROOK, Canon Colin David. b 36. Or Coll Ox BA59. St Steph Ho Ox DipTh60 MA63. **d** 61 **p** 62. C Roath St Martin *Llan* 61-66; C Roath St Marg 66-74; V Llantarnam *Mon* 74-79; V Newport St Jo Bapt from 79; Hon Can St Woolos Cathl 88-91; Can St Woolos Cathl from 91; Warden of Ords from 91. *St John's Vicarage, Oakfield Road, Newport NP9 4LP* Tel (01633) 265581

WESTBROOK (née REED), Mrs Ethel Patricia Ivy. b 42. Bris Univ CertEd63. Cant Sch of Min 82. **dss** 84 **d** 87 **p** 94. Fawkham and Hartley *Roch* 84-85; Asst Dir of Educn 84-86; Cliffe at Hoo w Cooling 85-86; Corby SS Pet and Andr w Gt and Lt Oakley *Pet* 86-87; Par Dn 87-90; Par Dn Roch 90-94; C 94; C Rainham from 94. *60 Childscroft Road, Rainham, Gillingham, Kent ME8 7SN* Tel (01634) 363631

WESTBROOK, Richard Henry. b 09. **d** 67 **p** 68. C Gt Bowden w Welham *Leic* 67-70; R Carlton Curlieu, Illston on the Hill etc 70-81; rtd 81; Perm to Offic *Roch* from 90. *Providence House, 60 Childscroft Road, Gillingham, Kent ME8 7SN* Tel (01634) 363631

WESTCOTT, Cuthbert Philip Brooke. b 09. Magd Coll Ox BA32 MA36. Westcott Ho Cam 36. **d** 36 **p** 37. C Kingsthorpe *Pet* 36-39; C Pershore w Wick *Worc* 39-41; Chapl RAFVR 41-47; Chapl Harborne Colleg Sch 47-48; Asst Chapl St Jo Sch Leatherhead 48-50; India 50-56; Chapl Milan *Eur* 62-65; Chapl San Remo w Bordighera 71-74; Chapl Palermo 75-77; rtd 77; Chapl St Jean-de-Luz w Pau and Biarritz *Eur* 77-80; Perm to Offic *Birm* 81-86; Perm to Offic *Linc* from 87; Perm to Offic *Pet* from 87. *c/o Henry and Marigold Lamin, Belmont, 10 Oakham Road, Greetham, Oakham, Leics LE15 7NN* Tel (01572) 812276

WESTCOTT, Donald Ralph. b 27. Bris Univ BA51. Ridley Hall Cam 51. **d** 53 **p** 54. C Marfleet *York* 53-56; C New Windsor St Jo *Ox* 56-57; R Ardwick St Thos *Man* 57-63; CF (TA) 58-60; V Benchill *Man* 63-70; R Islip *Ox* 70-86; R Noke 70-86; P-in-c Woodeaton 70-86; R Roydon St Remigius *Nor* 86-90; rtd 90; Perm to Offic *Heref* from 90. *54 Arosa Drive, Malvern, Worcs WR14 3QF* Tel (01684) 568653

WESTCOTT, James John. b 55. St Jo RC Sem Surrey 76. **d** 81 **p** 82. In RC Ch 81-93; C Westmr St Steph w St Jo *Lon* 93-96; P-in-c Haggerston St Chad from 96. *St Chad's Vicarage, Dunloe Street, London E2 8JR* Tel 0171-739 3878

WESTERN, Robert Geoffrey. b 37. Man Univ BSc60. Qu Coll Birm DipTh62. **d** 62 **p** 63. C Sedbergh *Bradf* 62-65; PV Linc Cathl *Linc* 65-73; Hd Master Linc Cathl Sch 74-97; Can and Preb Linc Cathl *Linc* 74-97. *Address temp unknown*

WESTLAKE, Michael Paul. b 34. Ex Coll Ox BA56 MA64. Wells Th Coll 59. **d** 61 **p** 62. C Southmead *Bris* 61-67; V Eastville St Thos 67-74; V Eastville St Thos w St Anne 74-83; P-in-c Easton St Mark 79-83; V Marshfield w Cold Ashton and Tormarton etc from 83. *The Vicarage, Church Lane, Marshfield, Chippenham, Wilts SN14 8NT* Tel (01225) 891850

WESTLAKE, Peter Alan Grant. b 19. CMG72 MC43. FRAS CCC Ox MA48 Univ of Wales (Ban) BD81 MSc81. **d** 81 **p** 82. Hon C Llandegfan w Llandysilio *Ban* from 81. *53 Church Street, Beaumaris LL58 8AB* Tel (01248) 810114

WESTLAND, Richard Theodore. b 27. LNSM course. **d** 87 **p** 88. NSM Freiston w Butterwick *Linc* from 87. *76 Brand End Road, Butterwick, Boston, Lincs PE22 0JD* Tel (01205) 760572

WESTLEY, Stuart. b 24. Em Coll Cam BA48 MA52 Man Univ DASE84. Wells Th Coll 49. **d** 50 **p** 51. C Prestwich St Marg *Man* 50-53; C Tonge w Alkrington 53-55; C-in-c Oldham St Ambrose 55-58; Lic to Offic *Blackb* 58-70; Chapl Arnold Sch Blackpool 58-66; Asst Chapl Denstone Coll Uttoxeter 70-73; Chapl Ermysted's Gr Sch Skipton 73-85; Hon C Blackpool St Mich *Blackb* 75-77; Perm to Offic *Bradf* 77-78; Lic to Offic 78-85; C Padiham *Blackb* 85-89; rtd 89; Perm to Offic *Blackb* from 89. *20 Crichton Place, Blackpool FY4 1NS* Tel (01253) 347962

WESTMACOTT, Preb Ian Field. b 19. Wells Th Coll 60. **d** 60 **p** 61. C Weston-super-Mare Cen Par *B & W* 60-63; V Long Ashton 63-84; RD Portishead 72-82; Preb Wells Cathl 77-84; rtd 84; Perm to Offic *Bris* from 84; Perm to Offic *B & W* from 85. *8A York Place, Bristol B58 1AH* Tel 0117-973 6057

WESTMINSTER, Archdeacon of. *See* HARVEY, The Ven Anthony Ernest

WESTMINSTER, Dean of. *Vacant*

WESTMORLAND AND FURNESS, Archdeacon of. *See* JENKINS, The Ven David Thomas Ivor

WESTNEY, Michael Edward William. b 29. Lich Th Coll 64. **d** 65 **p** 66. C Hughenden *Ox* 65-68; C Banbury 68-71; TV Trunch *Nor* 71-78; V Reading St Matt *Ox* 78-83; TV W Slough 83-88; TR 88-94; rtd 94. *59 Portland Close, Burnham, Slough SL2 2LT* Tel (01628) 660052

WESTON, Christopher James. b 20. G&C Coll Cam BA46 MA49. Ridley Hall Cam 47. **d** 49 **p** 50. C Neasden cum Kingsbury St Cath *Lon* 49-53; Singapore 53-55; Chapl Cheltenham Coll

56-63; V Clifton St Jas *Sheff* 63-70; P-in-c Stevenage St Nic *St Alb* 70-71; V 71-87; rtd 87; Perm to Offic *Ely* from 87. *15 Coltsfoot Close, Cherry Hinton, Cambridge CB1 4YH* Tel (01223) 242604

WESTON, Canon David Wilfrid Valentine. b 37. Lanc Univ PhD93. **d** 67 **p** 68. OSB 60-84; Lic to Offic *Ox* 67-84; Prior Nashdom Abbey 71-74; Abbot 74-84; C Chorley St Pet *Blackb* 84-85; V Pilling 85-89; Bp's Dom Chapl *Carl* 89-94; Can Res Carl Cathl from 94. *3 The Abbey, Carlisle CA3 8TZ* Tel (01228) 21834

WESTON, The Ven Frank Valentine. b 35. Qu Coll Ox BA60 MA64. Lich Th Coll 60. **d** 61 **p** 62. C Atherton *Man* 61-65; Chapl USPG Coll of the Ascension Selly Oak 65-69; Prin 69-76; Prin Edin Th Coll 76-82; Can St Mary's Cathl *Edin* 76-82; Adn Ox and Can Res Ch Ch *Ox* from 82. *Archdeacon's Lodging, Christ Church, Oxford OX1 1DP* Tel (01865) 276185 Fax 276276

WESTON, Frederick Victor Henry. b 41. Qu Coll Cam BA63 MA67. St D Coll Lamp LTh65. **d** 65 **p** 66. C Grangetown *Llan* 65-67; C Cwmmer w Abercregan CD 67-69; C Haverhill *St E* 69-74; R Gt and Lt Whelnetham 74-79; Perm to Offic from 84. *154 Southgate Street, Bury St Edmunds, Suffolk IP33 2AF*

WESTON, Harold John. b 24. Worc Ord Coll 65. **d** 67 **p** 68. C Northampton St Mich *Pet* 67-71; C Pet St Jo 71-74; R Peakirk w Glinton 75-89; rtd 89. *8 Delph Court, Delph Street, Whittlesey, Peterborough PE7 1QQ* Tel (01733) 205516

WESTON, Ivan John. b 45. MBE88. Chich Th Coll 71. **d** 74 **p** 75. C Harlow St Mary Magd *Chelmsf* 74-77; Chapl RAF from 77; Perm to Offic *Nor* from 93. *Chaplaincy Services (RAF), HQ, Personnel and Training Command, RAF Innsworth, Gloucester GL3 1EZ* Tel (01452) 712612 ext 5164 Fax 510828

WESTON, John Oglivy. b 30. St Pet Coll Ox BA66 MA70. Linc Th Coll 71. **d** 71 **p** 72. Lect Trent (Nottm) Poly 66-82; Hon C Long Clawson and Hose *Leic* 71-82; Hon C Bingham *S'well* 82-85; Lic to Offic 85-91; rtd 91; Perm to Offic *Heref* from 91. *The Cliffords Farm House, Nash, Ludlow, Shropshire SY8 3DE* Tel (01584) 811491

WESTON, Mrs Judith. b 36. MSR56 Open Univ BA75. St Jo Coll Nottm 84. **dss** 85 **d** 87 **p** 94. Huddersfield H Trin *Wakef* 85-87; Par Dn 87-91; Par Dn Wakef St Andr and St Mary 91-94; C 94-95; Chapl Huddersfield NHS Trust from 95; rtd 96. *Overcroft, 8A Newland Road, Huddersfield HD5 0QT* Tel (01484) 453591

WESTON, Canon Keith Aitken Astley. b 26. Trin Hall Cam BA51 MA55. Ridley Hall Cam 51. **d** 53 **p** 54. C Weston-super-Mare Ch Ch *B & W* 53-56; C Cheltenham St Mark *Glouc* 56-59; PC Clevedon Ch Ch *B & W* 59-64; R Ox St Ebbe w H Trin and St Pet *Ox* 64-85; RD Ox 71-76; Hon Can Ch Ch 81-85; Dir of Post-Ord Tr *Nor* 85-90; Dioc Dir of Ords 85-91; P-in-c Nor St Steph 85-91; Hon Brigade Chapl to Norfolk Co Fire Service from 90; rtd 91. *18 Moor End Lane, Thame, Oxon OX9 3BQ* Tel (01844) 215441

WESTON, Neil. b 51. Jes Coll Ox BA73 MA78. Ridley Hall Cam 74. **d** 76 **p** 77. C Ealing St Mary *Lon* 76-80; P-in-c Pertenhall w Swineshead *St Alb* 80-89; P-in-c Dean w Yelden, Melchbourne and Shelton 80-89; R The Stodden Churches 89-91; R Newhaven *Chich* from 91; Miss to Seamen from 91. *The Rectory, 36 Second Avenue, Newhaven, E Sussex BN9 9HN* Tel (01273) 515251

WESTON, Paul David Astley. b 57. Trin Hall Cam BA80 MA83 Westmr Coll Ox MPhil92. Wycliffe Hall Ox 83. **d** 85 **p** 86. C New Malden and Coombe *S'wark* 85-89; Lect Oak Hill Th Coll 89-97; Vice-Prin from 97. *Oak Hill College, Chase Side, London N14 4PS* Tel 0181-449 0467 Fax 441 5996

WESTON, Ralph Edward Norman. b 30. Worc Ord Coll 67. **d** 69 **p** 70. C Harborne St Pet *Birm* 69-71; CF 71-75; Chapl Oswestry Sch 75-85; Chapl Rotherham Distr Gen Hosp 85-95; CF (ACF) 87-95; TV Thorverton, Cadbury, Upton Pyne etc *Ex* from 95; rtd 95. *The Vicarage, Newton St Cyres, Exeter EX5 5BN*

WESTON, Stephen. b 48. St Steph Ho Ox 74. **d** 77 **p** 78. C Wigston Magna *Leic* 77-82; C Corringham *Chelmsf* 82-84; V Southtown *Nor* 84-89; R Catfield 90-92; R Sutton w Ingham and Catfield from 92. *The Rectory, Fenside, Catfield, Great Yarmouth, Norfolk NR29 5DB* Tel (01692) 582290

WESTON, Stephen John Astley. b 55. Aston Univ BSc77. Ridley Hall Cam 78. **d** 81 **p** 82. C Gt Chesham *Ox* 81-85; C Southport Ch Ch *Liv* 85-87; P-in-c Gayhurst w Ravenstone, Stoke Goldington etc *Ox* 87-91; R 91-96; RD Newport 92-95; V Chipping Norton from 96. *The Vicarage, Church Street, Chipping Norton, Oxon OX7 5NT* Tel (01608) 642688

WESTON, Mrs Virginia Anne. b 58. UEA BSc79. Wycliffe Hall Ox 84. **d** 87. Par Dn New Malden and Coombe *S'wark* 87-89; Lic to Offic *Lon* from 89. *Oak Hill College, Chase Side, London N14 4PS* Tel 0181-449 0467 Fax 441 5996

WESTRUP, Wilfrid Allan. b 08. Ch Coll Cam BA30 MA34. Westcott Ho Cam 30. **d** 32 **p** 33. C E Wickham *S'wark* 32-34; C Crofton Park St Hilda 34-39; V Hazelwell *Birm* 39-52; Chapl Cranbrook Sch Kent 52-64; rtd 73. *Sharon, Hartley Hill, Cranbrook, Kent TN17 3QD* Tel (01580) 712595

WESTWELL, The Ven George Leslie Cedric. b 31. Lich Th Coll 59. **d** 61 **p** 63. C Rothwell *Ripon* 61-63; C Armley St Bart 63-66; C Maidstone St Martin *Cant* 65-68; V 72-77; R Otham 68-72; V Bethersden w High Halden 77-79; R Lichborough w Maidford and Farthingstone *Pet* 79-80; Perm to Offic *Chich* 80-81; Perm to Offic *Cant* 80-81; Perm to Offic *Llan* 81-83; Chapl Florence w Siena *Eur* 83-92; Adn Italy 85-92; rtd 92. *Flat 5, 7 Chatsworth Gardens, Eastbourne, E Sussex BN20 7JP* Tel (01323) 736306

WESTWOOD, Canon John Richard. b 55. Clare Coll Cam BA77 MA81. Lambeth DipTh93 Ripon Coll Cuddesdon 77. **d** 79 **p** 80. C Oakham w Hambleton and Egleton *Pet* 79-81; C Oakham, Hambleton, Egleton, Braunston and Brooke 81-83; V Gt w Lt Harrowden and Orlingbury 83-90; V Wellingborough St Andr from 90; RD Wellingborough from 92; Can Pet Cathl from 97. *The Vicarage, Berrymoor Road, Wellingborough, Northants NN8 2HU* Tel (01933) 222692

WESTWOOD, Peter. b 38. Open Univ BA76. AKC64. **d** 65 **p** 66. C Acomb St Steph *York* 65-68; Chapl HM Youth Cust Cen Onley 69-73; Chapl HM Pris Leic 73-77; Chapl HM Pris Maidstone 77-81; Chapl HM Pris Dur 81-87; Chapl HM Pris Brixton 87-93; Chapl HM Pris Wormwood Scrubs from 93. *HM Prison Wormwood Scrubs, PO Box 757, Du Cane Road, London W12 0AE* Tel 0181-743 0311 Fax 749 5655

✠**WESTWOOD, The Rt Revd William John.** b 25. Em Coll Cam BA50 MA55 Leic Univ Hon LLD91. Westcott Ho Cam 50. **d** 52 **p** 53 **c** 75. C Kingston upon Hull H Trin *York* 52-57; R Lowestoft St Marg *Nor* 57-65; RD Lothingland 59-65; V Nor St Pet Mancroft 65-75; RD Nor 66-71; Hon Can Nor Cathl 68-75; Suff Bp Edmonton *Lon* 75-79; Area Bp Edmonton 79-84; Bp Pet 84-95; rtd 95. *102 Thwaite Street, Cottingham, N Humberside HU16 4RQ* Tel (01482) 876263

WETHERALL, Canon Cecil Edward (Ted). b 29. St Jo Coll Dur 49. **d** 56 **p** 57. C Ipswich St Aug *St E* 56-59; R Hitcham 59-79; P-in-c Brettenham 61-63; P-in-c Kettlebaston 71-91; R Hitcham w Lt Finborough 79-91; Hon Can St E Cathl 83-93; P-in-c Preston 85-91; rtd 92; Asst Chapl Athens w Kifissia, Patras, Thessaloniki & Voula *Eur* 92-96. *Villa Lily, D Solomou 4, Tolo Nafplio, 21056 Argolis, Greece*

WETHERALL, Nicholas Guy. b 52. Lon Univ BMus73 Ox Univ CertEd75. Chich Th Coll 82. **d** 84 **p** 85. C Cleobury Mortimer w Hopton Wafers *Heref* 84-87; TV Leominster 87-92; V Cuckfield *Chich* from 92. *The Vicarage, Broad Street, Cuckfield, Haywards Heath, W Sussex RH17 5LL* Tel (01444) 454007

WETHERELL, Ms Eileen Joyce. b 44. Westf Coll Lon BSc66. S Dios Minl Tr Scheme 89. **d** 92 **p** 94. Par Dn Southampton Maybush St Pet *Win* 92-94; C 94-96; TV Totton from 96. *The Vicarage, Cooks Lane, Calmore, Southampton SO40 2RU* Tel (01703) 812702

WETHERELL, Philip Anthony. b 45. Leic Univ MPhil87. AKC72. **d** 73 **p** 74. C Walthamstow St Sav *Chelmsf* 73-75; Chapl Bp Namibia and Tutor Namibia Internat Peace Cen 75-76; C Knighton St Mary Magd *Leic* 76-80; TV Southampton (City Cen) *Win* 80-84; Miss Personnel Sec USPG from 84; Perm to Offic *S'wark* from 84. *19 Bassett Green Road, Southampton SO16 3DJ* Tel (01703) 552783 Fax 0171-928 2371

WETZ, Peter Joseph Patrick. b 37. **d** 62 **p** 62. C Hatfield Hyde *St Alb* 85; C Stevenage St Pet Broadwater 85-87; V Irlam *Man* from 87. *The Vicarage, Vicarage Road, Irlam, Manchester M44 6WA* Tel 0161-775 2461

WEYMAN, John Derek Henry. b 31. Wells Th Coll 69. **d** 70 **p** 71. C Headley All SS *Guildf* 70-76; V Westcott from 76; RD Dorking 84-89. *The Vicarage, Guildford Road, Westcott, Dorking, Surrey RH4 3QB* Tel (01306) 885309

WEYMAN, Richard Darrell George. b 46. Lon Univ BA Bris Univ PhD. Sarum & Wells Th Coll. **d** 84 **p** 85. C Sherborne w Castleton and Lillington *Sarum* 84-88; V Malden St Jo *S'wark* 88-92; P-in-c Marnhull *Sarum* from 92; Dir Post Ord Tr from 92. *The Rectory, Conyers Place, Marnhull, Sturminster Newton, Dorset DT10 1PZ* Tel (01258) 821130

WEYMONT, Miss Gillian. b 41. SRN67. Trin Coll Bris 88. **d** 90 **p** 94. C Wincanton *B & W* 90-94; P-in-c Middlezoy and Othery and Moorlinch from 94; RD Glastonbury from 97. *The Vicarage, North Lane, Othery, Bridgwater, Somerset TA7 0QG* Tel (01823) 698073

WEYMONT, Martin Eric. b 48. St Jo Coll Dur BA69 MA74 CertEd73 Lon Univ PhD88. Westcott Ho Cam 71. **d** 73 **p** 74. C Blackheath *Birm* 73-76; Hon C Willesden St Matt *Lon* 76-77; Hon C Belmont 76-79; P-in-c W Twyford 79-85; P-in-c Cricklewood St Mich 85-88; Chapl St Pet Colleg Sch Wolv 88-91; Hon C Wolverhampton *Lich* 88-91; NSM Bickershaw *Liv* from 91. *Bickershaw Vicarage, 582 Bickershaw Lane, Bickershaw, Wigan, Lancs WN2 4AE* Tel (01942) 866139

WHALE, Desmond Victor. b 35. Bris Sch of Min 81. **d** 84 **p** 85. Lic to Offic *Bris* 84-88; C Parr *Liv* 88-91; R Winfarthing w Shelfanger w Burston w Gissing etc *Nor* from 91; RD Redenhall from 97. *The Rectory, Winfarthing, Diss, Norfolk IP22 2EA* Tel (01379) 642543

WHALE, Canon Jeffery Walter George. b 33. Lon Univ BSc60. Cuddesdon Coll 60. **d** 62 **p** 63. C Rugby St Andr *Cov* 62-68; C-in-c Britwell St Geo CD *Ox* 68-77; P-in-c Datchet 77-78; TR Riverside 78-88; RD Burnham 83-87; Hon Can Ch Ch from 85; TR New Windsor from 88. *The Rectory, Park Street, Windsor, Berks SL4 1LU* Tel (01753) 864572

WHALE, Dr Peter Richard. b 49. Down Coll Cam BA74 MA78 Auckland Univ BSc71 MA72 Otago Univ BD78 Ex Univ PhD89. St Jo Coll Auckland 75. **d** 77 **p** 78. New Zealand 77-85; TV Saltash *Truro* 85-90; Jt Dir SW Min Tr Course Truro 86-90; Preb

St Endellion 89-90; Prin WMMTC 90-92. *83 Chaddesley Court, Coventry CV5 7JP*

WHALER, Herbert Riggall. b 13. St Andr Pampisford 47. **d** 49 **p** 50. C Horncastle w Low Toynton *Linc* 49-51; R Bucknall w Tupholme 52-82; R Horsington w Stixwould 52-82; R Kirkby-on-Bain 61-82; V Martin w Thornton 61-82; R Roughton w Haltham 61-82; R Scrivelsby w Dalderby 66-82; P-in-c Thimbleby 80-82; rtd 82. *Stocks Hill Lodge, Stixwould, Lincoln LN3 5HP* Tel (01526) 352064

WHALES, Jeremy Michael. b 31. Bris Univ MA82. Lambeth STh72 Wycliffe Hall Ox 59. **d** 61 **p** 62. C W Wimbledon Ch Ch *S'wark* 61-64; Lect St Paul's Coll Cheltenham 64-67; Asst Chapl and Sen Lect 67-74; Chapl 74-78; Assoc Chapl & Sen Lect Coll of St Mary & St Paul 78-84; V Cheltenham St Luke and St Jo *Glouc* 85-92; rtd 92; Perm to Offic *Glouc* from 92; Clergy Widows' Officer from 96. *5 Robert Burns Avenue, Benhall, Cheltenham, Glos GL52 6NU*

WHALEY, Stephen John. b 57. York Univ BA79. Cranmer Hall Dur BA85. **d** 86 **p** 87. C Selby Abbey *York* 86-90; V Derringham Bank from 90. *110 Calvert Road, Hull HU5 5DH* Tel (01482) 52175

WHALLEY, Anthony Allen (Tony). b 41. Linc Th Coll 77. **d** 79 **p** 80. C Upton cum Chalvey *Ox* 79-83; R Newton Longville w Stoke Hammond and Whaddon 83-96; R Winslow w Gt Horwood and Addington from 96. *The Vicarage, Vicarage Road, Winslow, Buckingham MK18 3BJ* Tel (01296) 712564

WHALLEY, George Peter. b 40. LNSM course 82. **d** 86 **p** 86. NSM Ellon *Ab* from 86; NSM Cruden Bay from 86. *128 Braehead Drive, Cruden Bay, Aberdeenshire AB42 7NW* Tel (01779) 812511

WHALLEY, Jonathan Peter Lambert. b 60. St Jo Coll Nottm BA95. **d** 97. C Hattersley *Ches* from 97. *58 Callington Drive, Hyde, Cheshire SK14 3EL* Tel 0161-366 7036

WHALLEY, Michael Thomas. b 30. AKC55. **d** 56 **p** 57. C Nottingham All SS *S'well* 56-58; C Clifton St Fran 58-60; C Mansfield St Pet 60; V N Wilford St Faith 60-66; Asst Chapl HM Pris Man 66-67; Chapl HM Youth Cust Cen Dover 67-69; Lic to Offic *Linc* 70-75; Chapl HM Pris Aylesbury 75-79; C Aylesbury *Ox* 79-83; P-in-c Bierton w Hulcott 83-89; TV Aylesbury w Bierton and Hulcott 89-95; rtd 95. *17 Willowfield Avenue, Nettleham, Lincoln LN2 2TH* Tel (01522) 595372

WHARTON, Christopher Joseph. b 33. Keble Coll Ox BA57 MA61. **d** 79 **p** 80. NSM Harpenden St Nic *St Alb* 79-93; R Kimpton w Ayot St Lawrence from 93. *The Vicarage, 11 High Street, Kimpton, Hitchin, Herts SG4 8RA* Tel (01438) 833419

WHARTON, Miss Gillian Vera. b 66. TCD BTh93. CITC 90. **d** 93 **p** 94. C Glenageary *D & G* 93-96; PV Ch Ch Cathl Dublin from 96; Dioc Youth Officer (Dublin) from 96; C Lucan w Leixlip from 96. *280 River Forest, Leixlip, Co Kildare, Irish Republic* Tel Dublin (1) 624 5412. Mobile 087-2300767

✠**WHARTON, The Rt Revd John Martin.** b 44. Van Mildert Coll Dur BA69 Linacre Coll Ox BTh71 MA76. Ripon Hall Ox 69. **d** 72 **p** 73 **c** 92. C Birm St Pet *Birm* 72-75; C Croydon *Cant* 76-77; Dir Past Studies Ripon Coll Cuddesdon 77-83; C Cuddesdon *Ox* 79-83; Sec to Bd of Min and Tr *Bradf* 83-92; Dir Post-Ord Tr 84-92; Hon Can Bradf Cathl 84-92; Can Res Bradf Cathl 92; Bp's Officer for Min and Tr 92; Area Bp Kingston *S'wark* 92-97; Bp Newc from 97. *Bishop's House, 29 Moor Road South, Newcastle-upon-Tyne NE3 1PA* Tel 0191-285 2220 Fax 0191-213 0728

WHARTON, Thomas Anthony. b 21. Bps' Coll Cheshunt 49. **d** 52 **p** 53. C Beeston *S'well* 52-55; C Ambleside w Rydal *Carl* 55-58; V Northowram *Wakef* 58-65; V Chipping Norton *Ox* 65-86; Chapl Berne *Eur* 86-89; rtd 89; Perm to Offic *Glouc* from 89. *4 Bowling Green Crescent, Cirencester, Glos GL7 2HA* Tel (01285) 659043

WHATELEY, Thomas Roderick Rod. b 52. St Jo Coll Nottm 94. **d** 96 **p** 97. C Willesborough *Cant* from 96. *11 Earlsworth Road, South Willesborough, Ashford, Kent CT24 0DF* Tel (01233) 646702

WHATLEY, Preb Henry Lawson. b 16. Worc Coll Ox BA38. Wells Th Coll 38. **d** 39 **p** 40. C Bromsgrove St Jo *Worc* 39-43; CF (EC) 44-47; R Aston Ingham *Heref* 45-47; R Aston Ingham w The Lea 47-63; R Colwall 63-82; Preb Heref Cathl 76-82; rtd 82; Perm to Offic *Heref* 84-90. *Manormead Nursing Home, Tilford Road, Hindhead, Surrey GU26 6RA* Tel (01428) 604780

WHATLEY, Roger James. b 49. Chich Th Coll 94. **d** 96. NSM Newport St Jo *Portsm* from 96. *Beechcroft, 46 Trafalgar Road, Newport, Isle of Wight PO30 1QG* Tel (01983) 825938

WHATMORE, Michael John. b 30. Bris Univ BA51 St Cath Soc Ox BA53 MA54. Wycliffe Hall Ox 56. **d** 56 **p** 58. C Bexley St Mary *Roch* 56-57; C Keston 57-59; C Bromley St Mark 59-61; Distr Sec (GB) Bible Soc 61-64; R Stanningley St Thos *Ripon* 64-67; V Speke All SS *Liv* 67-70; Teacher & Sen Tutor Barton Peveril Coll 70-92; rtd 92. *26 Grebe Close, Milford on Sea, Lymington, Hants SO41 0XA* Tel (01590) 644892

WHATMOUGH, Michael Anthony (Tony). b 50. ARCO71 Ex Univ BA72. Edin Th Coll BD81. **d** 81 **p** 82. C Edin St Hilda *Edin* 81-84; C Edin St Fillan 81-84; C Salisbury St Thos and St Edm *Sarum* 84-86; R 86-93; RD Salisbury 90-93; V Bris St Mary Redcliffe w Temple etc *Bris* from 93. *The Vicarage, 10 Redcliffe Parade West, Bristol BS1 6SP* Tel 0117-929 1487 E-mail 100652.2602@compuserve.com

WHATSON, Mark Edwin Chadwick. b 57. CEng83 MIMechE83 Southn Univ BSc79. N Ord Course 86. **d** 88 **p** 91. NSM Church Hulme *Ches* 88-95; NSM Hardwicke, Quedgeley and Elmore w Longney *Glouc* from 95. *2 Carters Orchard, Quedgeley, Gloucester GL2 6WB*

WHAWELL, Arthur Michael. b 38. SRN59. Sarum & Wells Th Coll 74. **d** 76 **p** 77. C Cottingham *York* 76-79; P-in-c Bessingby 79-84; P-in-c Carnaby 79-84; V Birchencliffe *Wakef* 84-87; Chapl Huddersfield R Infirmary 84-87; V St Bart Less *Lon* 87-95; Chapl St Bart Hosp Lon 87-95; P-in-c Wormingford, Mt Bures and Lt Horkesley *Chelmsf* from 95. *The Vicarage, Church Road, Wormingford, Colchester CO6 3AZ* Tel (01787) 227398

WHEALE, Alan Leon. b 43. HNC65 AKC69 Hull Univ MA92. St Aug Coll Cant 69 DipMin89. **d** 70 **p** 71. C Tamworth *Lich* 70-73; C Cheddleton 73-75; V Garretts Green *Birm* 75-78; V Perry Beeches 78-83; V Winshill *Derby* 83-84; Deputation Appeals Org (E Midl) CECS 84-86; C Arnold *S'well* 86-88; V Daybrook 88-96; R Clifton Campville w Edingale and Harlaston *Lich* from 96; P-in-c Thorpe Constantine from 96; P-in-c Nomans Heath from 96. *The Rectory, Main Street, Clifton Campville, Tamworth, Staffs B79 0AP* Tel (01827) 373257

WHEALE, Canon Gerald Arnold. b 32. MBE93. St Jo Coll Dur BA56 Man Univ MEd74 PhD79. Ridley Hall Cam 56. **d** 58 **p** 59. C Tonge w Alkrington *Man* 58-60; Nigeria 60-62; R Moss Side St Jas *Man* 62-73; R Moss Side St Jas w St Clem from 73; AD Hulme 82-95; Hon Can Man Cathl from 84. *The Rectory, 68 Dudley Road, Whalley Range, Manchester M16 8DE* Tel 0161-226 1684 or 226 4211

WHEALE, Sarah Ruth. *See* BULLOCK, Mrs Sarah Ruth

WHEAT, Charles Donald Edmund. b 37. Nottm Univ BA70 Sheff Univ MA76. Kelham Th Coll 57. **d** 62 **p** 63. C Sheff Arbourthorne *Sheff* 62-67; Lic to Offic *S'well* 67-70; SSM 69-97; Chapl St Martin's Coll Lanc 70-73; Prior SSM Priory Sheff 73-75; Lic to Offic *Sheff* 73-97; C Ranmoor 75-77; Asst Chapl Sheff Univ 75-77; Chapl 77-80; Prov SSM in England 81-91; Dir 82-89; Lic to Offic *Blackb* 81-88; V Middlesbrough All SS *York* 88-95; Roehampton Inst *S'wark* 96-97; Chapl Order of the Holy Paraclete from 97. *30 Castle Road, Whitby, N Yorkshire YO22 3QN*

WHEATLEY, Canon Arthur. b 31. Edin Th Coll 68. **d** 70 **p** 70. C Dundee St Salvador *Bre* 70-71; C Dundee St Martin 70-71; P-in-c Dundee St Ninian 71-76; R Elgin H Trin *Mor* 76-80; R Lossiemouth 76-80; Can St Andr Cathl Inverness 78-80 and from 83; Provost 80-83; R Inverness St Andr 80-83; Chapl HM Pris Inverness from 80; P-in-c Grantown-on-Spey *Mor* from 83; P-in-c Rothiemurchus from 83. *West Curr Cottage, Dulnain Bridge, Grantown-on-Spey, Morayshire PH26 3LX* Tel (01479) 851273

WHEATLEY, Gordon Howard. b 29. Trin Coll Cam MA52. Lon Bible Coll DipTh58. **d** 90 **p** 91. C Cockley Cley w Gooderstone *Nor* 90-94; C Didlington 90-94; C Gt and Lt Cressingham w Threxton 90-94; C Hilborough w Bodney 90-94; C Oxborough w Foulden and Caldecote 90-94; P-in-c Mundford w Lynford from 94; P-in-c Ickburgh w Langford from 94; P-in-c Cranwich from 94. *The Rectory, St Leonard's Street, Mundford, Thetford, Norfolk IP26 5HG* Tel (01842) 878220

WHEATLEY, Ian James. b 62. Chich Th Coll BTh94. **d** 94 **p** 95. C Braunton *Ex* 94-97; Chapl RN from 97. *Royal Naval Chaplaincy Service, Room 203, Victory Building, HM Naval Base, Portsmouth PO1 3LS* Tel (01705) 727903 Fax 727112

WHEATLEY, James. b 40. Open Univ BA95. Brasted Th Coll 64 Linc Th Coll 66. **d** 68 **p** 69. C Morpeth *Newc* 68-72; C Cowgate 72-74; C Tynemouth Cullercoats St Paul 74-76; V Newsham 76-84; R Bothal 84-89; C Newc St Geo 89-91; C Mexborough *Sheff* 91-92; Perm to Offic *Newc* 93-95; C Sheff Parson Cross St Cecilia *Sheff* 95-96; rtd 96. *132 Hangingwater Road, Sheffield S11 7ES* Tel 0114-230 2720

WHEATLEY, John. b 14. **d** 77 **p** 78. NSM Cambois *Newc* 77-87; rtd 87; Perm to Offic *Newc* from 87. *20 Cypress Gardens, Blyth, Northd NE24 2LP* Tel (01670) 353353

WHEATLEY, Canon Maurice Samuel. b 13. AKC36. Chich Th Coll 36. **d** 37 **p** 38. C Coggeshall w Markshall *Chelmsf* 37-39; Madagascar 39-49; CF 40-46; Prin St Paul's Th Coll Ambat 46-49; SPG Area Sec (Dios Derby, Leic and S'well) 50-54; Youth and Educn Sec 54-60; Cand Sec 60-64; Appt and Tr Sec 64-72; Bermuda 72-80; Hon Can N Queensland from 62; rtd 80. *Abbeyfield, Friars Moor, Sturminster Newton, Dorset DT10 1BH* Tel (01258) 473066

WHEATLEY, The Ven Paul Charles. b 38. Dur Univ BA61. Linc Th Coll 61. **d** 63 **p** 64. C Bishopston *Bris* 63-68; Youth Chapl 68-73; V Swindon St Paul 73-77; TR Swindon Dorcan 77-79; R Ross *Heref* 79-81; P-in-c Brampton Abbotts 79-81; RD Ross and Archenfield 79-91; TR Ross w Brampton Abbotts, Bridstow and Peterstow 81-91; Preb Heref Cathl 87-91; Adn Sherborne *Sarum* from 91; P-in-c W Stafford w Frome Billet from 91. *The Rectory, West Stafford, Dorchester, Dorset DT2 8AB* Tel (01305) 264637

WHEATLEY, The Ven Peter William. b 47. Qu Coll Ox BA69 MA73 Pemb Coll Cam BA71 MA75. Ripon Hall Ox 72. **d** 73 **p** 74. C Fulham All SS *Lon* 73-78; V St Pancras H Cross w St Jude and St Pet 78-82; P-in-c Hampstead All So 82-90; P-in-c Kilburn St Mary 82-90; P-in-c Kilburn St Mary w All So 90-95;

V W Hampstead St Jas 82-95; Dir Post-Ord Tr from 85; AD N Camden (Hampstead) 88-93; Adn Hampstead from 95. *27 Thurlow Road, London NW3 5PP* Tel 0171-435 5890

WHEATLEY, Sarah Jane. d 96 p 97. NSM Meppershall w Campton and Stondon *St Alb* from 96. *16 Queen Street, Stotfold, Hitchin, Herts SG5 4NX* Tel (01462) 731170

WHEATLEY PRICE, Canon John. b 31. Em Coll Cam BA54 MA58. Ridley Hall Cam 54. **d** 56 **p** 57. C Drypool St Andr and St Pet *York* 56-59; CMS 59-74; Uganda 60-74; Adn Soroti 72-74; Hon Can Soroti 78-97; Can Emer Soroti from 97; Kenya 74-76; Adn N Maseno 74-76; V Clevedon St Andr *B & W* 76-82; V Clevedon St Andr and Ch Ch 82-87; Chapl Amsterdam *Eur* 87-92; P-in-c Cromford *Derby* 92-95; P-in-c Matlock Bath 92-95; V Matlock Bath and Cromford 95-96; rtd 96. *2 Murray Walk, Melksham, Wilts SN12 7AZ* Tel (01225) 704294

WHEATON, Christopher. b 49. St Jo Coll Nottm BTh80 LTh80. **d** 80 **p** 81. C Hatcham St Jas *S'wark* 80-83; C Warlingham w Chelsham and Farleigh 83-87; V Carshalton Beeches from 87. *The Vicarage, 38 Beeches Avenue, Carshalton, Surrey SM5 3LW* Tel 0181-647 6056

WHEATON, Canon David Harry. b 30. St Jo Coll Ox BA53 MA56 Lon Univ BD55. Oak Hill Th Coll 58. **d** 59 **p** 60. Tutor Oak Hill Th Coll 59-62; Prin 71-86; C Enfield Ch Ch Trent Park *Lon* 59-62; R Ludgershall *Ox* 62-66; V Onslow Square St Paul *Lon* 66-71; Chapl Brompton Hosp 69-71; Hon Can St Alb *St Alb* from 76; V Ware Ch Ch 86-96; RD Hertford 88-91; Chapl to The Queen from 90; rtd 96. *43 Rose Drive, Chesham, Bucks HP5 1RR* Tel (01494) 783862

WHEATON, Canon Ralph Ernest. b 32. St Jo Coll Dur BA54. Cranmer Hall Dur DipTh58. **d** 58 **p** 59. C Evington *Leic* 58-63; V Bardon Hill 63-71; V Whitwick St Jo the Bapt 71-81; RD Akeley S 79-81; V Blyth *S'well* 81-96; P-in-c Scofton w Osberton 83-86; V 86-96; RD Worksop 83-93; Hon Can S'well Minster 86-96; P-in-c Langold 86-91; rtd 96. *Petriburg, Main Street, Hayton, Retford, Notts DN22 9LL* Tel (01777) 705910

WHEBLE, Eric Clement. b 23. S'wark Ord Course 68. **d** 71 **p** 72. C Croydon H Trin *Cant* 71-78; Hon C Croydon St Sav 78-80; Hon C Norbury St Oswald 80-81; TV Selsdon St Jo w St Fran 81-84; TV Selsdon St Jo w St Fran *S'wark* 85-88; rtd 88. *20 Michael's Way, Fair Oak, Eastleigh, Hants S05 7NT* Tel (01703) 693239

WHEELDON, John Graham. b 32. Sarum & Wells Th Coll 86. **d** 87 **p** 88. C Winchcombe, Gretton, Sudeley Manor etc *Glouc* 87-90; R Huntley and Longhope 90-91; rtd 91. *17 Mitton Way, Mitton, Tewkesbury, Glos GL20 8AW*

WHEELDON, William Dennis. b 25. Leeds Univ BA51. Coll of Resurr Mirfield 52. **d** 54 **p** 56. CR 55-76; Barbados 59-66; Prin Coll of Resurr Mirfield 66-75; P-in-c New Whittington *Derby* 83-87; P-in-c Belper Ch Ch and Milford 87-90; rtd 90; Perm to Offic *Bradf* from 90. *10 Brooklyn, Threshfield, Skipton, N Yorkshire BD23 5ER* Tel (01756) 753187

WHEELER, Alban Massy. b 19. Dur Univ 40. Bps' Coll Cheshunt 40. **d** 43 **p** 44. C Buckie *Ab* 43-45; C Aldrington *Chich* 45-47; C Chailey 47-49; C Hove St Thos 49-52; C Farnham *Guildf* 53-56; C Overton w Laverstoke and Freefolk *Win* 56-57; C Highcliffe w Hinton Admiral 57-59; C Epsom *Guildf* 59-62; C Leckhampton SS Phil and Jas *Glouc* 62-64 and 66-67; Perm to Offic 68-81; Perm to Offic *Ex* 81-84; rtd 84. *Bell Memorial Home, South Street, Lancing, W Sussex BN15 8AZ*

WHEELER, Alexander Quintin Henry (Alastair). b 51. Lon Univ BA73 Nottm Univ DipTh75. St Jo Coll Nottm 74. **d** 77 **p** 78. C Kenilworth St Jo *Cov* 77-80; C Madeley *Heref* 80-83; P-in-c Draycott-le-Moors *Lich* 83-84; P-in-c Forsbrook 83-84; R Draycott-le-Moors w Forsbrook 84-91; V Nailsea Ch Ch *B & W* 91-96; R Nailsea Ch Ch w Tickenham from 96; RD Portishead from 95. *The Rectory, Christ Church Close, Nailsea, Bristol BS19 2DL* Tel (01275) 853187 Fax 855888

WHEELER, Andrew Charles. b 48. CCC Cam MA69 Makerere Univ Kampala MA72 Leeds Univ CertEd72. Trin Coll Bris BA88. **d** 88 **p** 88. CMS from 76; C Whitton *Sarum* 88-89; Egypt 89-90; Sudan from 90. *PO Box 52802, Nairobi, Kenya*

WHEELER, Anthony William (Tony). b 28. **d** 76 **p** 77. NSM Shirehampton *Bris* from 76; Chmn Avonmouth Miss to Seamen from 76. *Flat 3, The Priory, Priory Gardens, Bristol BS11 0BZ* Tel 0117-982 2261

WHEELER (née MILLAR), Mrs Christine. b 55. City of Lon Poly BSc76 DipCOT81. S Dios Minl Tr Scheme 84. **d** 87 **p** 94. NSM Kingston Buci *Chich* 87-89; Par Dn Merstham and Gatton *S'wark* 89-94; C 94-96; R Rockland St Mary w Hellington, Bramerton etc *Nor* from 96. *The Rectory, 2 Rectory Lane, Rockland St Mary, Norwich NR14 7EY* Tel (01508) 538619

WHEELER, Dr David Ian. b 49. Southn Univ BSc70 PhD78. N Ord Course 87. **d** 90 **p** 91. C Blackpool St Jo *Blackb* 90-94; R Old Trafford St Jo *Man* from 94. *St John's Rectory, Lindum Avenue, Old Trafford, Manchester M16 9NQ* Tel 0161-872 0500

WHEELER, David James. b 49. S Dios Minl Tr Scheme 87. **d** 90 **p** 91. C Hythe *Cant* 90-92; C Knaresborough *Ripon* from 92. *9 Castle Yard, Knaresborough, N Yorkshire HG5 8AS* Tel (01423) 864678

WHEELER, David Robert. b 62. Birm Univ BSc84. Oak Hill Th Coll BA95. **d** 95 **p** 96. C Lancaster St Thos *Blackb* 95-96. *30 Connaught Road, Lancaster LA1 4BQ* Tel (01524) 381837

WHEELER, Desmond Reginald Sessel. b 18. Rhodes Univ BA49. St Paul's Grahamstown LTh51. **d** 50 **p** 51. S Africa 50-53; C Whitley Ch Ch *Ox* 54-56; C S Kensington St Aug *Lon* 56-58; R Zeal Monachorum *Ex* 60-63; R Bondleigh w Brushford 60-63; V Sutton on Plym 63-70; V Bishopsteignton 71-85; rtd 85; Perm to Offic *Ex* from 85. *30 Odlehill Grove, Abbotskerswell, Newton Abbot, Devon TQ12 5NJ* Tel (01626) 51162

WHEELER, Sister Eileen Violet. b 28. TCert48 Newnham Coll Cam MA52. Chich Th Coll 85. **dss** 86 **d** 87 **p** 95. Bexhill St Pet *Chich* 86-87; Hon Par Dn 87-90; Par Dn 90-94; NSM 94-95; rtd 94; Hon C Bexhill St Mark *Chich* from 95. *1 The Briary, St Peter's Crescent, Bexhill-on-Sea, E Sussex TN40 2EG* Tel (01424) 215115

WHEELER, Graham John. b 39. St Mich Coll Llan DipTh66 BD78. **d** 66 **p** 67. C Roath St Martin *Llan* 66-71; C Cadoxton-juxta-Barry 71-75; Perm to Offic 75-79; C Highcliffe w Hinton Admiral *Win* 79-83; C Milton 83-90; P-in-c Bournemouth St Ambrose from 90. *St Ambrose Vicarage, 72 West Cliff Road, Bournemouth BH4 8BE* Tel (01202) 764957

WHEELER, James Albert. b 49. Sarum & Wells Th Coll 74. **d** 76 **p** 77. C Orpington All SS *Roch* 76-79; C Roch 79-81; C Bexley St Jo 81-84; V Penge Lane H Trin 84-93; P-in-c Tunbridge Wells St Luke from 93. *St Luke's Vicarage, 158 Upper Grosvenor Road, Tunbridge Wells, Kent TN1 2EQ* Tel (01892) 521374

WHEELER, John David. b 31. Selw Coll Cam BA54 MA58. Ely Th Coll 54. **d** 56 **p** 57. C Charlton St Luke w St Paul *S'wark* 56-60; C Northolt St Mary *Lon* 61-63; V Bush Hill Park St Mark 64-71; V Ealing St Pet Mt Park 71-74; V Truro St Paul *Truro* 74-79; V Truro St Paul and St Clem 79-80; P-in-c Hammersmith St Sav *Lon* 80-83; V Cobbold Road St Sav w St Mary 83-96; rtd 96; Perm to Offic *Heref* from 96. *37 St Martin's Street, Hereford HR2 7RD*

WHEELER, Julian Aldous. b 48. Nottm Univ BTh74. Kelham Th Coll 70. **d** 75 **p** 76. C Bideford *Ex* 75-79; Lic to Offic 79-86; Hon C Parkham, Alwington, Buckland Brewer etc from 86. *Forge Cottage, Pump Lane, Abbotsham, Bideford, Devon EX39 5AY* Tel (01237) 473948

WHEELER, Preb Madeleine. b 42. Gilmore Course 76. **dss** 78 **d** 87 **p** 94. Ruislip Manor St Paul *Lon* 78-87; Par Dn 87-91; TD 91-92; Chapl for Women's Min (Willesden Episc Area) 86-95; P-in-c N Greenford All Hallows from 94; Preb St Paul's Cathl from 95. *All Hallows' Vicarage, 72 Horsenden Lane North, Greenford, Middx UB6 0PD* Tel 0181-422 3183

WHEELER, Michael. b 26. Qu Coll Cam MA54 Lon Univ PGCE53. Sarum & Wells Th Coll 93. **d** 94 **p** 95. NSM Redhorn *Sarum* from 94. *Dominie's, Wilsford, Pewsey, Wilts SN9 6HB* Tel (01672) 851373

WHEELER, Nicholas Gordon Timothy. b 59. BCombStuds84. Linc Th Coll. **d** 84 **p** 85. C Hendon St Alphage *Lon* 84-87; C Wood Green St Mich w Bounds Green St Gabr etc 87-89; TV 89-93; R Cranford from 93. *The Rectory, 34 High Street, Cranford, Hounslow TW5 9RG* Tel 0181-897 8836

WHEELER, Nicholas Paul. b 60. Ox Univ BA86 MA91. Wycliffe Hall Ox 83. **d** 87 **p** 88. C Wood Green St Mich w Bounds Green St Gabr etc *Lon* 87-91; Chapl to Bp Edmonton 91-96; P-in-c Somers Town St Mary from 96; P-in-c Old St Pancras w Bedford New Town St Matt from 96; P-in-c Camden Town St Mich w All SS and St Thos from 96; P-in-c Camden Square St Paul from 96. *The Vicarage, 191 St Pancras Way, London NW1 9NH* Tel 0171-485 6837

WHEELER, Richard Anthony. b 23. St Chad's Coll Dur BA46 MA48 DipTh48. **d** 48 **p** 49. C Kingswinford St Mary *Lich* 48-52; C Toxteth Park St Agnes *Liv* 52-54; V Upholland 54-64; R Dorchester H Trin w Frome Whitfield *Sarum* 64-73; TV Dorchester 73-87; rtd 87. *25 Victoria Road, Dorchester, Dorset DT1 1SB* Tel (01305) 262803

WHEELER, Canon Richard Roy. b 44. K Coll Lon BD72. St Aug Coll Cant. **d** 74 **p** 74. C Brixton St Matt *S'wark* 74-78; Dir St Matt Meeting Place Brixton 78-79; Sec BCC Community Work Resource Unit 79-82; TV Southampton (City Cen) *Win* 83-88; TR from 88; Hon Can Win Cathl from 94. *St Michael's Vicarage, 55 Bugle Street, Southampton SO14 2AG* Tel (01703) 224242

WHEELER, Mrs Sally Ann. b 59. Westmr Coll Ox BEd81. St Alb and Ox Min Course 94. **d** 97. NSM Chippenham St Paul w Hardenhuish etc *Bris* from 97. *15 Tavinor Drive, Chippenham, Wilts SN15 3FT* Tel (01249) 446899

WHEELER, Sally Ann Violet. b 59. **d** 97. NSM Chippenham St Paul w Hardenhuish etc *Bris* from 97. *15 Tavinor Drive, Chippenham, Wilts SN15 3FT* Tel (01249) 446899

WHEELHOUSE, Brian Clifford Dunstan. b 69. St Steph Ho Ox BTh93. **d** 96 **p** 97. C Brighton Resurr *Chich* from 96. *107 Hartington Road, Brighton BN2 3PA* Tel (01273) 673811

WHEELOCK, Canon John Richard. b 18. TCD BA41 MA51. CITC 42. **d** 42 **p** 43. C Drumgoon and Ashfield *K, E & A* 42-44; I Clongish 44-51; I Swanlinbar w Templeport 51-56; I Annagh Union 56-83; RD Kilmore S 64-77; Kilmore E 71-77; Preb Kilmore Cathl 72-83; P-in-c Cloverhill 74-83; rtd 83. *c/o Mrs J*

Elliott, Tomkin Road, Belturbet, Co Cavan, Irish Republic Tel Cavan (49) 22865

WHEELWRIGHT, Michael Harvey. b 39. Bps' Coll Cheshunt 64. **d** 67 **p** 68. C Glen Parva and S Wigston *Leic* 67-70; C Evington 70-74; V Leic St Eliz Nether Hall 74-79; Chapl Prudhoe Hosp Northd from 79; Perm to Offic *Dur* from 95. *Prudhoe Hospital, Prudhoe, Northd NE42 5NT, or 61 Dene Road, Wylam, Northd NE41 8HB* Tel (01661) 32501 or 852508

WHELAN, Canon John Bernard. b 17. Dur Univ LTh41. Oak Hill Th Coll 38. **d** 47 **p** 48. C Ambleside w Rydal *Carl* 47-49; C Barrow St Geo 49-54; Korea 54-66; Japan 66-67; C Bury St Mary *Man* 68-71; Asst Chapl Crumpsall Hosp Man 71-73; Chapl N Man Gen Hosp 73-82; rtd 82; Chapl Las Palmas *Eur* 82-84; Asst Chapl Valletta w Sliema 84-93; Can Malta Cathl 87-93. *146 Rudolphe Street, Sliema SLM02, Malta* Tel Malta (356) 330214

WHELAN, Miss Patricia Jean (Pat). b 33. ACA55 FCA82. Dalton Ho Bris 58. **dss** 64 **d** 87 **p** 94. Stapleford *S'well* 62-69; Aylesbury *Ox* 69-75; Bushbury *Lich* 75-77; Patchway *Bris* 77-81; Trin Coll Bris 81-82; W Swindon LEP 82-86; High Wycombe *Ox* 86-87; Par Dn 87-91; Par Dn Ox St Ebbe w H Trin and St Pet 91-93; rtd 93. *81 Cogges Hill Road, Witney, Oxon OX8 6XU* Tel (01993) 779099

WHELAN, Peter Warwick Armstrong. b 34. Southn Univ BTh80 Open Univ BA80. Sarum Th Coll 69. **d** 71 **p** 72. C Salisbury St Mark *Sarum* 71-73; C Solihull *Birm* 73-77; TR Shirley 77-86; Chapl Whittington Hosp NHS Trust from 86; Chapl Camden & Islington Community & Health NHS Trust from 86. *51 Tytherton Road, London N19 4PZ* Tel 0171-272 5309 or 288 5337

WHELAN, Raymond Keith (Ray). b 40. Cant Sch of Min 85. **d** 88 **p** 91. C Eastbourne St Andr *Chich* 88-93; C-in-c Parklands St Wilfrid CD 93-95; TV Chichester from 95. *St Wilfrid's House, 7 Durnford Close, Chichester, W Sussex PO19 3AG* Tel (01243) 783853

WHERRY, Anthony Michael (Tony). b 44. Nottm Univ BA65 Univ Coll Lon DAA66. WMMTC 88. **d** 91 **p** 92. NSM Worc City St Paul and Old St Martin etc *Worc* 91-95; NSM Worc E Deanery from 95. *2 Redfern Avenue, Worcester WR5 1PZ* Tel (01905) 358532

WHETTEM, Canon John Curtiss. b 27. Peterho Cam BA50 MA55. Wycliffe Hall Ox 50. **d** 52 **p** 53. C Clifton Ch Ch *Bris* 52-55; C Wandsworth All SS *S'wark* 55-58; V Soundwell *Bris* 58-63; Youth Chapl 63-68; Chapl Bris Cathl 64-68; R N Mundham w Hunston *Chich* 68-80; P-in-c Oving w Merston 75-80; TR Swanborough *Sarum* 80-92; RD Pewsey 84-89; rtd 92. *32 Hogshill Street, Beaminster, Dorset DT8 3AA* Tel (01308) 863050

WHETTER, Michael Arnold. b 30. Bris Univ BA51. Wells Th Coll 53. **d** 55 **p** 56. C Dursley *Glouc* 55-58; C Coppenhall *Ches* 58-61; R Ches H Trin 61-71; V Stockport St Alb Hall Street 72-90; V Offerton 90-91; Chapl Cherry Tree Hosp Stockport 72-91; Chapl Offerton Hosp Stockport 72-91; V Bollington St Jo *Ches* from 91. *The Vicarage, Shrigley Road, Bollington, Macclesfield, Cheshire SK10 5RD* Tel (01625) 573162

WHETTINGSTEEL, Raymond Edward. b 44. S Dios Minl Tr Scheme 79. **d** 82 **p** 83. NSM Sholing *Win* 82-84; C Southampton Maybush St Pet 84-89; V Hatherden w Tangley, Weyhill and Penton Mewsey from 89. *The Rectory, Penton Mewsey, Andover, Hants SP11 0RD* Tel (01264) 773554

WHETTON, Nicholas John. b 56. St Jo Coll Nottm 83. **d** 86 **p** 87. C Hatfield *Sheff* 86-90; V Cornholme *Wakef* 90-96; P-in-c Livesey *Blackb* from 96; P-in-c Ewood from 96. *St Andrew's Vicarage, 112 Full View, Blackburn BB2 4QB* Tel (01254) 259422

WHIFFEN, Canon William Timothy (Bill). b 25. SS Coll Cam BA50 MA54 FRSA94. Linc Th Coll. **d** 52 **p** 53. C Wigan St Mich *Liv* 52-56; India 57-69; V Clay Cross *Derby* 69-74; Sec (Overseas Division) USPG 74-79; TR Woughton *Ox* 79-85; P-in-c Seer Green and Jordans 85-91; Hon Can Ch Ch 91-92; rtd 91. *90 Booker Avenue, Bradwell Common, Milton Keynes MK13 8EF* Tel (01908) 677466

✠**WHINNEY, The Rt Revd Michael Humphrey Dickens.** b 30. Pemb Coll Cam BA55 MA59. Gen Th Sem (NY) STM90 Ridley Hall Cam 55. **d** 57 **p** 58 **c** 82. C Rainham *Chelmsf* 57-60; Hd Cam Univ Miss Bermondsey 60-67; Chapl 67-73; V Bermondsey St Jas w Ch Ch *S'wark* 67-73; Adn S'wark 73-82; Suff Bp Aston *Birm* 82-85; Bp S'well 85-88; Asst Bp Birm 88-95; Can Res Birm Cathl 92-95; rtd 96; Asst Bp Birm from 96. *3 Moor Green Lane, Moseley, Birmingham B13 8NE* Tel 0121-449 2856

WHINTON, William Francis Ivan. b 35. N Ord Course 77. **d** 80 **p** 81. NSM Stockport St Mary *Ches* 80-82; NSM Disley 82-87; V Birtles from 87; Dioc Officer for Disabled from 89. *The Vicarage, Birtles, Macclesfield, Cheshire SK10 4RX* Tel (01625) 861238

WHIPP, Anthony Douglas (Tony). b 46. Leeds Univ BSc68. Ripon Coll Cuddesdon 84. **d** 86 **p** 87. C Dalston *Carl* 86-89; V Holme Cultram St Mary 89-96; V Holme Cultram St Cuth 89-96; V Kells from 96. *St Peter's Vicarage, Cliff Road, Whitehaven, Cumbria CA28 9ET* Tel (01946) 692496 E-mail tony @chezwhip.demon.co.uk

WHIPP, Dr Margaret Jane. b 55. MRCP82 FRCR86 LMH Ox BA76 Sheff Univ MB, ChB79. N Ord Course 87. **d** 90 **p** 94. NSM Wickersley *Sheff* from 90. *7 Scholey Road, Wickersley, Rotherham, S Yorkshire S66 0HU* Tel (01709) 548661

WHITAKER, David Arthur Edward. b 27. New Coll Ox BA50 MA55. Wells Th Coll 51. **d** 53 **p** 54. C W Bridgford *S'well* 53-56; CF 56-58; V Clifton St Fran *S'well* 58-63; Basutoland 63-66; Lesotho 66-69; R Buckerell *Ex* 69-76; R Feniton 69-76; P-in-c Tiverton St Pet 76-79; R 79-92; rtd 92; Perm to Offic *Heref* from 92. *The Cottage, Hereford Road, Weobley, Hereford HR4 8SW* Tel (01544) 318669

WHITAKER, Michael Benjamin (Ben). b 60. Nottm Univ BA83. Sarum & Wells Th Coll 85. **d** 87 **p** 88. C Gt Grimsby St Mary and St Jas *Linc* 87-91; C Abingdon *Ox* 91-95; Chapl to the Deaf *Sarum* from 95. *2 Orchard Mews, Gillingham, Dorset SP8 4TQ* Tel (01747) 825375

WHITBY, Suffragan Bishop of. *See* BATES, The Rt Revd Gordon

WHITCOMBE, Michael George Stanley. b 34. Keble Coll Ox BA58 MA62. Wycliffe Hall Ox DipTh59. **d** 60 **p** 61. C Nuneaton St Nic *Cov* 60-63; Malaysia 63-67; V Warwick St Paul *Cov* 67-68; Hong Kong 68-72; V Lightcliffe *Wakef* 72-79; R Largs *Glas* 79-81; P-in-c Ipswich St Fran *St E* 81-82; TR 82-93; TV Mildenhall from 93. *The Vicarage, Worlington, Bury St Edmunds, Suffolk IP28 8RU* Tel (01638) 713510

WHITCOMBE, Stanley Edward Cuthbert. b 07. K Coll Lon 42. **d** 42 **p** 42. C Glouc St Jas *Glouc* 42-45; V Pauntley w Upleadon 45-47; V Gorsley w Cliffords Mesne 47-54; R Shipton Oliffe w Shipton Sollars 54-56; C Stratford-on-Avon *Cov* 56-59; R Brinklow 59-65; R Harborough Magna 60-61; R Bourton w Frankton 65-72; rtd 72; Perm to Offic *Wakef* 73-79 and from 81; Perm to Offic *Glas* 79-81. *c/o Mrs A G V Bradley, 26 Holly Bank, Ackworth, Pontefract, W Yorkshire WF7 7PE* Tel (01977) 613643

WHITCROFT, Graham Frederick. b 42. Oak Hill Th Coll 64. **d** 66 **p** 67. C Cromer *Nor* 66-69; C Attercliffe *Sheff* 69-72; V Kimberworth Park 72-85; V Lepton *Wakef* from 85. *The Vicarage, 138 Wakefield Road, Lepton, Huddersfield HD8 0EJ* Tel (01484) 602172

WHITE, Alan. b 18. Man Univ BSc39 MSc40 St Cath Soc Ox BA42 MA46 Leeds Univ MEd52. Ripon Hall Ox 40. **d** 42 **p** 43. C Leic St Marg *Leic* 42-45; Chapl and Asst Master Leeds Gr Sch 45-56; Lic to Offic *Worc* 56-89; Asst Master Bromsgrove Sch 56-72; Chapl 72-83; rtd 83; P-in-c Tardebigge *Worc* from 89. *25 Leadbetter Drive, Bromsgrove, Worcs B61 7JG* Tel (01527) 877955

WHITE, Alan. b 43. Ex Univ BA65. Chich Th Coll 65. **d** 68 **p** 69. C Upper Clapton St Matt *Lon* 68-72; C Southgate Ch Ch 72-76; P-in-c Friern Barnet St Pet le Poer 76-79; V 79-85; TR Ex St Thos and Em *Ex* from 85. *St Thomas's Vicarage, 57 Cowick Street, Exeter EX4 1HR* Tel (01392) 55219

WHITE, Mrs Alison Mary. b 56. St Aid Coll Dur BA78. Cranmer Hall Dur 83. **d** 86 **p** 94. NSM Chester le Street *Dur* 86-89; Hon Par Dn Birtley 89-93; Adv in Local Miss 89-93; Dir Past Studies Cranmer Hall Dur from 93. *St John's Vicarage, 6 Ruskin Road, Birtley, Chester le Street, Co Durham DH3 1AD* Tel 0191-410 2115 or 374 3500 Fax 374 3573

WHITE, Andrew Paul Bartholomew. b 64. MIOT85 ABIST85 St Thos Hosp Lon DipSurg84 DA84 CertMBiol84. Ridley Hall Cam 86. **d** 90 **p** 91. C Battersea Rise St Mark *S'wark* 90-93; P-in-c Balham Hill Ascension from 93. *Ascension Vicarage, 22 Malwood Road, London SW12 8EN* Tel 0181-673 7666

WHITE, Andrew Peter. b 65. Lon Univ BA87. Sarum & Wells Th Coll BTh94. **d** 94 **p** 95. C Croydon St Matt *S'wark* 94-96; C S Wimbledon H Trin and St Pet from 96. *50 Evelyn Road, London SW19 8BT* Tel 0181-688 8675

WHITE, Charles William Langston. b 13. Lon Coll of Div 52. **d** 54 **p** 55. C Streatham Immanuel w St Anselm *S'wark* 54-57; V Guildf St Sav *Guildf* 57-68; R St Leonards St Leon *Chich* 68-76; Jerusalem 76-78; rtd 78. *The Gatehouse, Terrys Cross House, Woodmancote, Henfield, W Sussex BN5 9SX* Tel (01273) 495401

WHITE, Canon Christopher Norman Hessler. b 32. TD76. St Cath Coll Cam BA56 MA60. Cuddesdon Coll 57. **d** 59 **p** 60. C Solihull *Birm* 59-62; C Leeds St Aid *Ripon* 62-65; CF (TA) 64-85; V Aysgarth *Ripon* 65-74; R Richmond 74-76; P-in-c Hudswell w Downholme and Marske 75-76; R Richmond w Hudswell from 76; RD Richmond 75-80 and from 93; Hon Can Ripon Cathl from 89; Chapl St Fran Xavier Sch Richmond from 89. *The Rectory, Church Wynd, Richmond, N Yorkshire DL10 7AQ* Tel (01748) 823398

WHITE, Clement. b 25. AKC50. **d** 51 **p** 52. C Gosforth All SS *Newc* 51-54; C Newc St Andr 54-56; C Seaton Hirst 56-59; V Tynemouth St Jo 59-69; V Monkseaton St Pet 69-89; rtd 89. *18 Beach Road, Tynemouth, Tyne & Wear NE30 2NS* Tel 0191-258 7505

WHITE, Colin Davidson. b 44. St And Dioc Tr Course 86 Coates Hall Edin 90. **d** 88 **p** 89. NSM Glenrothes *St And* 88-89; P-in-c 89-90; P-in-c Leven 90-92; R 92-95; V Grimethorpe *Wakef* from 95. *The Vicarage, High Street, Grimethorpe, Barnsley, S Yorkshire S72 7JA* Tel (01226) 711331

WHITE, Crispin Michael. b 42. FRSA94. Bps' Coll Cheshunt 62. **d** 65 **p** 66. C S Harrow St Paul *Lon* 65-67; C Mill Hill St Mich 67-68; Canada 68-71; Toc H Padre (W Region) 71-75; (E Midl

Region) 75-82; Ind Chapl *Portsm* from 82. *11 Burnham Wood, Fareham, Hants PO16 7UD* Tel (01329) 239390 Fax 238711

WHITE, David Christopher. b 51. Lon Univ LLB73. St Jo Coll Nottm 86. **d** 88 **p** 89. C Bulwell St Mary *S'well* 88-92; V Nottingham All SS from 92. *The Vicarage, 16 All Saints' Street, Nottingham NG7 4DP* Tel 0115-970 4197 or 978 6362

WHITE, David John. b 26. Leeds Univ BA53. Coll of Resurr Mirfield 53. **d** 55 **p** 56. C Brighton St Pet *Chich* 55-58; C Wednesbury St Jas *Lich* 58-60; C Bishops Hull St Jo *B & W* 60-61; R Morton *Derby* 61-62; In RC Ch 62-73; Perm to Offic *Nor* 73-75; Lect Whitelands Coll Lon 72-75; R Tregony w St Cuby and Cornelly *Truro* 75-79; R Castle Bromwich SS Mary and Marg *Birm* 79-83; V Plymouth St Simon *Ex* 83-88; R Lapford, Nymet Rowland and Coldridge 88-93; RD Chulmleigh 93; rtd 93; Perm to Offic *Ex* from 94. *The Belvedere, Peak Hill Road, Sidmouth, Devon EX10 8RZ* Tel (01395) 513365

WHITE, David Martin. b 50. St Jo Coll Dur BA72. Cranmer Hall Dur DipTh73. **d** 74 **p** 75. C Ripley *Derby* 74-78; C Normanton 78-80; C-in-c Sinfin 78-80; P-in-c 80; V 80-88; P-in-c Belper 88-91; V from 91; RD Duffield 96-97. *St Peter's Vicarage, Chesterfield Road, Belper, Derbyshire DE56 1FD* Tel (01773) 822148

WHITE, David Paul. b 58. Oak Hill Th Coll. **d** 84 **p** 85. C Toxteth Park St Clem *Liv* 84-87; C Woodford Wells *Chelmsf* 87-89; C Woodside Park St Barn *Lon* 89-90; TV Canford Magna *Sarum* 90-93; V York St Mich-le-Belfrey *York* from 93. *St Helen's Vicarage, 12 Muncastergate, York YO3 9LA* Tel (01904) 430428

WHITE, Derek. b 35. MBE97. **d** 84 **p** 85. Hon C St Marylebone St Cypr *Lon* 84-87; C 87-96; Bp's Chapl for the Homeless from 87; P-in-c St Mary le Strand w St Clem Danes from 96. *80 Coleraine Road, London SE3 7BE, or 17 Homer Row, London W1H 1HU* Tel 0181-858 3622 or 0171-723 3501

WHITE, Derek James. KCT93. Birm Univ BA56. Chich Th Coll 56. **d** 58 **p** 59. C Stanmer w Falmer and Moulsecoomb *Chich* 58-61; Asst Chapl Ardingly Coll Haywards Heath 61-63; Chapl 63-72; C Glynde, W Firle and Beddingham *Chich* 72-73; R Bramber w Botolphs 73-87; V Upper Beeding 73-87; R Beeding and Bramber w Botolphs from 87. *The Rectory, Church Lane, Beeding, Steyning, W Sussex BN44 3HP* Tel (01903) 815474

WHITE, Douglas Richard Leon (Rick). b 49. Linc Th Coll. **d** 83 **p** 84. C Warsop *S'well* 83-88; V Kirkby in Ashfield St Thos 88-93; Asst Chapl Qu Medical Cen Nottm Univ Hosp NHS Trust from 93; Chapl Highbury Hosp Nottm from 93. *University Hospital, Queen's Medical Centre, Nottingham NG7 2UH* Tel 0115-942 9924

WHITE, Dudley William. b 33. Univ of Wales (Ban) BSc53. St Mich Coll Llan BD69. **d** 59 **p** 60. C Sketty *S & B* 59-66; R New Radnor and Llanfihangel Nantmelan 66-70; V Penyfai w Tondu *Llan* 70-77; V Swansea St Jude *S & B* from 77. *St Jude's Vicarage, Hillside Crescent, Swansea SA2 0RD* Tel (01792) 473154

WHITE, The Ven Francis (Frank). b 49. Univ of Wales (Cardiff) BSc(Econ)70 DSocStuds71. St Jo Coll Nottm DipTh78. **d** 80 **p** 81. C Dur St Nic *Dur* 80-84; C Chester le Street 84-87; Chapl Dur and Ches le Street Hosps 87-89; V Birtley *Dur* 89-97; RD Chester-le-Street from 93; Hon Can Dur Cathl from 97; Adn Sunderland from 97. *St John's Vicarage, 6 Ruskin Road, Birtley, Chester le Street, Co Durham DH3 1AD* Tel 0191-410 2115 or 374 3500 Fax 374 3573

WHITE, Frederick William Hartland. b 22. MBE62. Kelham Th Coll 39. **d** 45 **p** 46. C Newc St Jo *Newc* 45-50; CF 50-70; Asst Chapl Gen 70-74; QHC from 73; V Harrow St Mary *Lon* 74-87; rtd 87. *Whitesfield House, 5 Seend Cleeve, Melksham, Wilts SN12 6PS*

WHITE, Canon Gavin Donald. b 27. Toronto Univ BA49 Lon Univ PhD70. Trin Coll Toronto BD61 Gen Th Sem (NY) STM68 St Steph Ho Ox 51. **d** 53 **p** 54. Canada 53-58; Zanzibar 59-62; Kenya 62-66; C Hampstead St Steph *Lon* 68-70; Lect Glas Univ 71-92; Lic to Offic *Glas* 71-90; rtd 92; Hon Can St Mary's Cathl *Glas* from 92; Hon C St Andrews St Andr *St And* from 94. *85D Market Street, St Andrews, Fife KY16 9NX* Tel (01334) 477338

WHITE, Geoffrey Brian. b 54. Jes Coll Ox BA76 MA80. St Steph Ho Ox 76. **d** 79 **p** 80. C Huddersfield St Pet *Wakef* 79-82; C Flixton St Mich *Man* 82-84; TV Westhoughton 84-91; V Stevenage St Mary Sheppall w Aston *St Alb* from 91. *St Mary's Vicarage, 148 Hydean Way, Sheppall, Stevenage, Herts SG2 9YA* Tel (01438) 351963

WHITE, Canon Geoffrey Gordon. b 28. Selw Coll Cam BA50 MA54. Cuddesdon Coll 51. **d** 53 **p** 54. C Bradford-on-Avon *Sarum* 53-56; C Kennington St Jo *S'wark* 56-61; V Leeds St Wilfrid *Ripon* 61-63; Chapl K Coll Hosp Lon 63-66; V Aldwick *Chich* 66-76; V Brighton Gd Shep Preston 76-93; Can and Preb Chich Cathl 90-93; rtd 93; Hon C Stepney St Dunstan and All SS *Lon* from 94. *Flat 65, Telfords Yard, 6/8 The Highway, London E1 9BQ* Tel 0171-480 6585

WHITE, Gordon Benjamin James. b 13. Worc Ord Coll 60. **d** 62 **p** 63. C Stroud *Glouc* 62-65; V Leonard Stanley 65-83; RD Stonehouse 67-79; rtd 83. *The Old Vicarage, Honeyhill, Wootton Bassett, Swindon SN4 7DY* Tel (01793) 851363

WHITE, Howard Christopher Graham. b 43. Leeds Univ BA65. Coll of Resurr Mirfield 67. **d** 67 **p** 68. C Friern Barnet St Jas *Lon* 67-71; P-in-c Uxbridge Moor 71-73; Asst Chapl RADD 73-77; Hon C Corringham *Chelmsf* 73-77; Team Ldr St Sav Cen for the Deaf Acton 77-84; Perm to Offic *Guildf* 86-94; Perm to Offic *Chich* from 94. *Drake Cottage, Hook Hill Lane, Woking, Surrey GU22 0PS*

WHITE, Hugh Richard Bevis. b 55. New Coll Ox BA78 Ox Univ DPhil85. S'wark Ord Course 93. **d** 96. NSM Westcote Barton w Steeple Barton, Duns Tew etc *Ox* from 96. *28 Duns Tew, Bicester, Oxon OX6 4JR* Tel (01869) 347889

WHITE, Ian Terence. b 56. CertEd. Ripon Coll Cuddesdon 83. **d** 86 **p** 87. C Maidstone St Martin *Cant* 86-89; C Earley St Pet *Ox* 89-91; TV Schorne 91-96; V St Osyth *Chelmsf* from 96. *The Vicarage, The Bury, St Osyth, Clacton-on-Sea, Essex CO16 8NX* Tel (01255) 820348

WHITE, Dr Jack Chapman. b 27. St Louis Univ BSc49 Univ of Cincinnati PhD82. **d** 54 **p** 55. USA 54-62 and 65-94; Can Res American Cathl Paris 62-65; Chapl Izmir (Smyrna) w Bornova *Eur* 95-96; rtd 96. *PO Box 18997, Washington DC, 20036-8997, USA*

WHITE, Miss Janice. b 49. Trin Coll Bris IDC76. **d** 91 **p** 94. C Claygate *Guildf* from 91. *The Church Hall Flat, Church Road, Claygate, Esher, Surrey KT10 0JP* Tel (01372) 464894

WHITE, Jeremy Spencer. b 54. St Luke's Coll Ex BEd78. Wycliffe Hall Ox 81. **d** 84 **p** 85. C S Molton w Nymet St George, High Bray etc *Ex* 84-87; TV 87-95; V Sway *Win* from 95. *The Vicarage, Station Road, Sway, Lymington, Hants SO41 6BA* Tel (01590) 682358

WHITE, Canon John Austin. b 42. Hull Univ BA64. Coll of Resurr Mirfield 64. **d** 66 **p** 67. C Leeds St Aid *Ripon* 66-69; Asst Chapl Leeds Univ 69-73; Chapl N Ord Course 73-82; Can and Prec Windsor from 82. *8 The Cloisters, Windsor Castle, Windsor, Berks SL4 1NJ* Tel (01753) 860409

WHITE, John Christopher. b 62. Keble Coll Ox BA84. Wycliffe Hall Ox 86. **d** 89 **p** 90. C Southway *Ex* 89-93; TV Plymouth Em, St Paul Efford and St Aug from 93. *St Paul's Vicarage, 1 Yeo Close, Blandford Road, Plymouth PL3 6ER* Tel (01752) 785576

WHITE, John Cooper. b 58. LTCL79 K Alfred's Coll Win BEd82 Lon Univ MA92 FRSA94. St Steph Ho Ox 86. **d** 89 **p** 90. C Christchurch *Win* 89-93; P-in-c Bournemouth St Alb 93-94; V from 94. *St Alban's Vicarage, 17 Linwood Road, Bournemouth BH9 1DW* Tel (01202) 534193

WHITE, John Francis. b 47. Qu Coll Cam BA69 MA73. Cuddesdon Coll 72. **d** 72 **p** 73. Sacr Wakef Cathl *Wakef* 72-73; Prec 73-76; V Thurlstone 76-82; P-in-c Hoyland Swaine 81-82; V Chapelthorpe from 82; RD Chevet from 96. *The Vicarage, Church Lane, Chapelthorpe, Wakefield, W Yorkshire WF4 3JB* Tel (01924) 255360

WHITE, John Malcolm. b 54. Aston Univ BSc77. Trin Coll Bris BA87. **d** 87 **p** 88. C Harborne Heath *Birm* 87-91; C S Harrow St Paul *Lon* 91-93; TV Roxeth 93-96; V Derby St Alkmund and St Werburgh *Derby* from 96. *The Vicarage, 200 Duffield Road, Derby DE22 1BL* Tel (01332) 348339

WHITE, John McKelvey. b 57. QUB BA TCD DipTh82. **d** 82 **p** 83. C Clooney *D & R* 82-84; C Belfast H Trin *Conn* 84-86; I Kilcronaghan w Draperstown and Sixtowns *D & R* 86-94; I Ballybeen *D & D* from 94. *1 Grahamsbridge Road, Dundonald, Belfast BT16 0DB* Tel (01232) 489297

WHITE, Canon John Neville. b 41. Edin Univ MA63. Cranmer Hall Dur DipTh65. **d** 65 **p** 66. C Sedgefield *Dur* 65-68; C Stoke *Cov* 68-72; V Wrose *Bradf* 72-90; V Farsley from 90; RD Calverley from 93; Hon Can Bradf Cathl from 96. *The Vicarage, 9 St John's Avenue, Farsley, Pudsey, W Yorkshire LS28 5DJ* Tel 0113-257 4009

WHITE, Jonathan Roger. b 36. Lon Univ BSc61. Cuddesdon Coll 63. **d** 65 **p** 66. C Swinton St Pet *Man* 65-67; C Prestwich St Mary 67-70; R Salford Stowell Memorial 70-74; TV Swan *Ox* 74-78; P-in-c Monks Risborough 78-84; P-in-c Gt and Lt Kimble 78-84; P-in-c Prestwood 84-87; P-in-c Gt w Lt Hampden 85-87; P-in-c Prestwood and Gt Hampden 87-93; R from 93; RD Wendover 89-94. *The Rectory, 140 Wycombe Road, Prestwood, Great Missenden, Bucks HP16 0HJ* Tel (01494) 862130

WHITE, Canon Joseph George. b 19. Liv Univ DPA50 Leeds Univ CertEd57. St Deiniol's Hawarden 61. **d** 61 **p** 62. C Frodsham *Ches* 61-65; V Rainow w Saltersford 65-72; P-in-c Macclesfield Forest w Wildboarclough 66-72; TV Ches 72-75; Dir of Educn 74-88; Hon Can Ches Cathl 79-88; P-in-c Capenhurst 79-87; rtd 88; Perm to Offic *Ches* from 88. *17 Endsleigh Close, Chester CH2 1LX* Tel (01244) 382376

WHITE, Julian Edward Llewellyn. b 53. St D Coll Lamp BA79 Chich Th Coll 79. **d** 79 **p** 80. C Newport St Mark *Mon* 79-83; TV Llanmartin 83-86; R Llandogo and Tintern from 86. *The Rectory, Llandogo, Monmouth NP5 4TW* Tel (01594) 530887

WHITE, Keith. b 54. Liv Poly BA78 Lon Univ BD82. Wycliffe Hall Ox 78. **d** 81 **p** 82. C Edin St Thos *Edin* 81-84; C Fulwood *Sheff* 84-87; R Heigham H Trin *Nor* 87-95; Zimbabwe 95-97; V Ipswich St Jo *St E* from 97. *St John's Vicarage, Cauldwell Hall Road, Ipswich IP4 4QE* Tel (01473) 728034

WHITE, Keith Robert. b 48. St Jo Coll Nottm. **d** 84 **p** 85. C Erith St Paul *Roch* 84-88; Chapl Salisbury Coll of Tech *Sarum* 88. *22 Chapel Hill, Dartford DA1 4BY* Tel (01322) 523779

WHITE, Kenneth Charles. b 15. TD. FCIS FHSM. St Deiniol's Hawarden 76. **d** 77 **p** 78. Hon C Upton Ascension *Ches* 77-79; R Warburton 79-82; rtd 82; Perm to Offic *Ches* from 82; Chapl Asst Countess of Ches Hosp from 84. *13 Queen's Park House, Queen's Park View, Handbridge, Chester CH4 7DB* Tel (01244) 680348

WHITE, Kenneth Charles. b 26. Tyndale Hall Bris 48. **d** 54 **p** 56. Uganda 54-55; Kenya 55-57; C Morden *S'wark* 57-60; V Ramsey St Mary's w Ponds Bridge *Ely* 60-66; V Leyton Ch Ch *Chelmsf* 66-81; V Totland Bay *Portsm* 81-91; rtd 91; Perm to Offic *Llan* from 91. *30 Pendwyallt Road, Whitchurch, Cardiff CF4 7EG* Tel (01222) 611529

WHITE, Malcolm Robert. b 46. Man Univ BSc68. St Jo Coll Dur 74. **d** 77 **p** 78. C Linthorpe *York* 77-81; C Sutton St Jas and Wawne 81-83; V Upper Holloway St Pet w St Jo *Lon* 83-95; TV Burnham w Dropmore, Hitcham and Taplow *Ox* from 95. *12 Hatchgate Gardens, Burnham, Slough SL1 8DD* Tel (01628) 662739

WHITE, Marilyn. d 88 **p** 94. NSM Westbury-on-Severn w Flaxley and Blaisdon *Glouc* from 88. *Beacon View, Northwood Green, Westbury-on-Severn, Glos GL14 1NA* Tel (01452) 760419

WHITE, Mrs Maureen Barbara. b 42. Bris Univ BA63 Ox Univ DipEd64. Oak Hill Th Coll 87. **d** 89. NSM Wallington H Trin *S'wark* 89-91. *20 Woodcote Avenue, Wallington, Surrey SM6 0QY* Tel 0181-647 1639

WHITE, Nicolas John. b 54. BEd. Wycliffe Hall Ox. **d** 83 **p** 84. C Islington St Mary *Lon* 83-87; Chapl Univ Coll 87-89. *3 Carleton Villas, Leighton Grove, London NW5 2TU* Tel 0171-482 2133

WHITE, Noel Louis. b 11. TCD BA45 MA58. CITC 46. **d** 46 **p** 47. C Ballymacarrett St Patr *D & D* 46-50; Sudan 50-59; C Lisburn St Paul *Conn* 60-62; I Belfast St Silas 62-74; Asst Gen Sec CMS Ireland 74-81; Lic to Offic *D & D* 75-82; rtd 82; Hon C Newtownards *D & D* from 82. *Achlon, 90 Hamilton Road, Bangor, Co Down BT20 4LG* Tel (01247) 450121

WHITE, Patrick George Hilliard. Toronto Univ BA67 DMin93. Wycliffe Coll Toronto MDiv77. **d** 77 **p** 78. Canada 77-97; Bermuda from 97. *St John's Rectory, 15 Langton Hill, Pembroke HM 13, Bermuda*

WHITE, Paul Raymond. b 49. Canberra Coll BTh86 DipMin87 Heythrop Coll Lon MTh89. **d** 85 **p** 86. Australia 85-87 and 89-92; P-in-c Reigate St Phil *S'wark* 87-89; V Redhill St Matt 92-97; Australia from 97; V E Ivanhoe St Geo Dio Melbourne from 97. *46 Warncliffe Road, East Ivanhoe, Victoria 3079, Australia* Tel Launceston (03) 9497 1290 or 9499 5904 Fax 9497 4242

WHITE, Peter Francis. b 27. St Edm Hall Ox BA51 MA55. Ridley Hall Cam 51. **d** 53 **p** 54. C Drypool St Columba *York* 53-56; V Dartford St Edm *Roch* 56-62; CF 62-78; R Barming *Roch* 78-89; rtd 89; Perm to Offic *Wakef* from 89. *Middleton House Cottage, Middleton on the Hill, Ludlow, Shropshire SY8 4BE* Tel (01568) 750454

WHITE, Canon Peter John. b 23. Hertf Coll Ox BA45 MA49. Wycliffe Hall Ox 45. **d** 47 **p** 48. C Bowling St Steph *Bradf* 47-49; C Upton *Ex* 49-52; V Devonport St Boniface 52-59; V Mancetter *Cov* 59-62; Area Sec (Dios Glouc, Heref and Worc) CMS 62-69; V Chipping Campden *Glouc* 69-75; P-in-c Ebrington 69-75; RD Campden 73-88; V Chipping Campden w Ebrington 75-88; Hon Can Glouc Cathl 86-88; rtd 88. *70 Northmoor Way, Wareham, Dorset BH20 4EG* Tel (01929) 553502

WHITE, Peter John. b 26. St Aid Birkenhead 57. **d** 60 **p** 61. C Toxteth Park St Gabr *Liv* 60-62; C Huyton St Mich 62-63; V Thornham w Gravel Hole *Man* 63-68; C Keighley *Bradf* 68-71; C Newington w Dairycoates *York* 71-75; C Frodingham *Linc* 75-80; R Mareham-le-Fen and Revesby 80-86; V Wrawby 86-91; V Melton Ross w New Barnetby 86-91; rtd 91; Perm to Offic *Linc* 91-95. *3 Park Avenue, Wakefield, W Yorkshire WF2 8DS* Tel (01924) 201438

WHITE, Philip William. b 53. Bede Coll Dur CertEd75. St Jo Coll Nottm DCM91. **d** 91 **p** 92. C Clifton *York* 91-95; TV Heworth from 95. *St Wulstans Vicarage, 8 Abbotsway, York YO3 9LD* Tel (01904) 425188

WHITE, Canon Phillip George. b 33. Univ of Wales (Lamp) BA54. St Mich Coll Llan 54. **d** 56 **p** 57. C Tongwynlais *Llan* 56-58; C Mountain Ash 58-60; C Aberavon 60-62; Area Sec (Middx) CMS 62-64; V Treherbert *Llan* 64-76; P-in-c Treorchy 75-76; V Treherbert w Treorchy 76-77; V Pyle w Kenfig from 77; RD Margam from 86; Can Llan Cathl from 91. *The Vicarage, Pyle, Bridgend CF33 6PG* Tel (01656) 740500

WHITE, Mrs Priscilla Audrey. b 62. St Hugh's Coll Ox BA84. Wycliffe Hall Ox 87. **d** 89 **p** 94. Par Dn Southway *Ex* 89-93; NSM Plymouth Em, St Paul Efford and St Aug from 93. *St Paul's Vicarage, 1 Yeo Close, Blandford Road, Plymouth PL3 6ER* Tel (01752) 785576

WHITE, Richard Alfred. b 49. DipSocWork CQSW. St Jo Coll Nottm. **d** 90 **p** 91. C Leic St Phil *Leic* 90-95; C Old Dalby and Nether Broughton from 95. *The Vicarage, Old Dalby, Melton Mowbray, Leics LE14 3LB* Tel 0116-482 2878

WHITE, Richard Allen. b 25. Open Univ BA78 Southn Univ MPhil88 MTh95. Sarum & Wells Th Coll 78. **d** 81 **p** 82. NSM Bursledon *Win* 81-85; C W End 85-90; C Fareham SS Pet and Paul *Portsm* 90-95; Chapl St Chris Hosp Fareham from 92; rtd 96. *11 Quayhaven, Lower Swanwick, Southampton SO3 7DE* Tel (01489) 576529

WHITE, Canon Robert Bruce (Bob). b 42. Sarum & Wells Th Coll 71. **d** 73 **p** 74. C Woodford St Barn *Chelmsf* 73-75; Youth Chapl 75-79; C-in-c Sutton 75-78; P-in-c 78-79; C-in-c Shopland 75-78; P-in-c 78-79; TR Southend St Jo w St Mark, All SS w St Fran etc 79-82; P-in-c Southend St Alb 80-82; TR Southend 82-89; P-in-c Brentwood St Thos from 89; RD Brentwood from 93; Hon Can Chelmsf Cathl from 97. *The Vicarage, 91 Queen's Road, Brentwood, Essex CM14 4EY* Tel (01277) 225700

WHITE, Canon Robert Charles (Bob). b 61. Mansf Coll Ox BA83. St Steph Ho Ox 83. **d** 85 **p** 86. C Forton *Portsm* 85-88; C Portsea N End St Mark 88-92; V Warren Park St Clare from 92; P-in-c Leigh Park 94-96; V from 96; Hon Can Portsm Cathl from 97. *St Clare's House, Strouden Court, Havant, Hants PO9 4JX* Tel (01705) 451762

WHITE, The Ven Robin Edward Bantry. b 47. TCD BA70 BD79. CITC 72. **d** 72 **p** 73. C Dublin Zion Ch *D & G* 72-76; Min Can St Patr Cathl Dublin 76-79; C Taney Ch Ch *D & G* 76-79; I Abbeystrewry Union *C, C & R* 79-89; RD Mid W Cork 87-89; I Douglas Union w Frankfield from 89; Preb Ross Cathl 89-93; Preb Cork Cathl 89-93; RD Cork City from 89; Adn Cork, Cloyne and Ross from 93. *The Rectory, Carrigaline Road, Douglas, Cork, Irish Republic* Tel Cork (21) 891539 Fax as telephone

WHITE, Roderick Harry. b 55. Trin Coll Bris BA86. **d** 86 **p** 87. C Northampton St Giles *Pet* 86-89; C Godley cum Newton Green *Ches* 89-93; P-in-c from 93; RD Woodleigh *Ex* from 95. *The Vicarage, 43 Sheffield Road, Hyde, Cheshire SK14 2PR* Tel 0161-368 2159

WHITE, Roger Charles. b 37. St Alb Minl Tr Scheme 77. **d** 80 **p** 81. NSM Wilshamstead and Houghton Conquest *St Alb* from 80. *30 Wood End Road, Wood End, Kempston, Bedford MK43 9BB* Tel (01234) 852472

WHITE, Roger David. b 37. St Mich Coll Llan DipTh66. **d** 66 **p** 67. C Mountain Ash *Llan* 66-71; C Port Talbot St Theodore 71-74; V Caerhun w Llangelynin *Ban* 74-85; R Llanbedrog w Llannor w Llanfihangel etc 85-88; V Llangeinor *Llan* 88-90; V Spittal w Trefgarn and Ambleston w St Dogwells *St D* from 90. *The Vicarage, West Gate, Spittal, Haverfordwest SA26 5QP* Tel (01437) 741505

WHITE, Roger Ian Scott. b 41. Leeds Univ BA62 Culham Coll Ox PGCE70. Coll of Resurr Mirfield 62. **d** 64 **p** 65. C Wotton-under-Edge *Glouc* 64-69; NSM Rugby St Andr *Cov* 71-80; W Germany 80-82; P-in-c Brinklow *Cov* 82-86; R 86-90; P-in-c Harborough Magna 82-86; R 86-90; P-in-c Monks Kirby w Pailton and Stretton-under-Fosse 82-86; V 86-90; Germany 90-92; V St Anne Lydgate w Ch Ch Friezland *Man* from 92. *The Vicarage, Stockport Road, Lydgate, Oldham OL4 4JJ* Tel (01457) 872117

✠**WHITE, The Rt Revd Roger John.** b 41. Kelham Th Coll. **d** 66 **p** 67 **c** 84. C Manston *Ripon* 66-69; USA from 69; Bp Milwaukee from 85. *804 East Juneau Avenue, Milwaukee, Wisconsin 53202, USA*

WHITE, Ronald Henry. b 36. Bris Univ BSc58 Ox Univ DipEd59 Lon Univ DipTh64. SW Minl Tr Course 82. **d** 85 **p** 86. C Ivybridge *Ex* 85-87; C Ivybridge w Harford 87-88; V Blackawton and Stoke Fleming 88-95; V Stoke Fleming, Blackawton and Strete from 95. *The Vicarage, Stoke Fleming, Dartmouth, Devon TQ6 0QB* Tel (01803) 770361

WHITE, Canon Roy Sidney. b 34. Sarum Th Coll 62. **d** 65 **p** 66. C Selsdon *Cant* 65-68; C Ranmoor *Sheff* 68-72; V Croydon St Andr *Cant* 72-78; Dir Abp Coggan Tr Cen 78-85; Dir of Chr Stewardship *S'wark* 85-91; Hon Can S'wark Cathl 85-91; Can Res S'wark Cathl from 91; Vice Provost S'wark from 91. *73 St George's Road, London SE1 6EQ* Tel 0171-735 8322 or 407 3708 Fax 357 7389

WHITE, Simon Inigo Dexter. b 58. York Univ BA80 Nottm Univ PGCE81. St Jo Coll Nottm 87. **d** 90 **p** 91. C Chadkirk *Ches* 90-94; C Stockport St Geo 94; Chapl Stockport Gr Sch from 94; TV Stockport SW *Ches* from 94. *19 Frewland Avenue, Stockport, Cheshire SK3 8TZ* Tel 0161-456 9356

WHITE, The Very Revd Stephen Ross. b 58. Hull Univ BA Ox Univ BA QUB DPhil93. Ripon Coll Cuddesdon 82. **d** 85 **p** 86. C Redcar *York* 85-88; P-in-c Gweedore, Carrickfin and Templecrone *D & R* 88-92; Bp's Dom Chapl 91-92; Dean Raphoe from 92; I Raphoe w Raymochy and Clonleigh from 93. *The Deanery, Raphoe, Lifford, Co Donegal, Irish Republic* Tel Raphoe (74) 45226

WHITE, Sister Teresa Joan. b 36. Wellesley Coll (USA) BA58 Harvard Univ STB61 Lon Univ CertEd74 Hon DD86. **dss** 75 **d** 87 **p** 94. CSA from 72; Teacher Burlington-Danes Sch 74-76; Lect Inst of Chr Studies *Lon* 76-78; Gen Sec World Congress of Faiths 77-81; Lect Dioc Readers' Course *S'wark* 81-89; Asst Abp's Sec for Ecum Affairs 81-82; Ed Distinctive Diaconate from 81; Ed DIAKONIA News from 87. *St Andrew's House, 2 Tavistock Road, London W11 1BA* Tel 0171-229 2662

WHITE, Trevor John. b 37. St Pet Coll Ox BA61 MA65. Wycliffe Hall Ox. **d** 63 **p** 64. C Walsall *Lich* 63-67; V Greasbrough *Sheff* 67-73; Chapl Nat Nautical Sch Portishead 73-82; Chapl Bris Cathl Sch from 82; Perm to Offic *B & W* from 82. *4 Gardner Road, Portishead, Bristol BS20 9ER* Tel (01275) 847855

WHITE, Canon Vernon Philip. b 53. Clare Coll Cam BA75 MA79 Or Coll Ox MLitt80. Wycliffe Hall Ox DipTh76. **d** 77 **p** 78. Tutor

Wycliffe Hall Ox 77-83; Chapl and Lect Ex Univ 83-87; R Wotton and Holmbury St Mary *Guildf* 87-93; Dir of Ords 87-93; Can Res and Chan Linc Cathl *Linc* from 93. *The Chancery, 11 Minster Yard, Lincoln LN2 1PJ* Tel (01522) 525610

WHITE, William John. b 54. BSc. Wycliffe Hall Ox. **d** 84 **p** 85. C Bowdon *Ches* 84-87; C Chadkirk 87-90; R Wistaston from 90. *The Rectory, 44 Church Lane, Wistaston, Crewe CW2 8HA* Tel (01270) 67119

WHITE SPUNNER, Mrs Jessie Janet. b 37. SRN59 SCM61. CITC 91. **d** 94 **p** 95. NSM Shinrone w Aghancon etc *L & K* from 94. *Milltown Park, Shinrone, Birr, Co Offaly, Irish Republic* Tel Birr (505) 47143

WHITEFIELD, Dr Keith Russell. b 60. Aber Univ MA83 PhD91 Edin Univ BD91. Edin Th Coll 88. **d** 91 **p** 93. C Haddington *Edin* 91-94; C Dunbar 91-94; Miss Priest Wester Hailes St Luke from 94. *24/3 Wester Hailes Park, Edinburgh EH14 3AF* Tel 0131-453 4265

WHITEHEAD, Barry. b 30. Or Coll Ox BA53 MA62. St Steph Ho Ox 53. **d** 55 **p** 56. C Edge Hill St Dunstan *Liv* 55-58; C Upholland 58-61; Ind Chapl 61-90; CF (TA) 64-78; V Aspull *Liv* 77-96; rtd 96; Perm to Offic *Blackb* from 96; Perm to Offic *Liv* from 96. *5 Sedgely, Standish, Wigan, Lancs WN6 0BZ* Tel (01257) 427160

WHITEHEAD, Brian. b 36. DipTh SRN. S'wark Ord Course 74. **d** 75 **p** 77. C Croydon St Aug *Cant* 75-78; C St Marychurch *Ex* 78-80; V Devonport St Mark Ford 80-87; V Castle Donington and Lockington cum Hemington *Leic* from 87. *The Vicarage, 6 Delven Lane, Castle Donington, Derby DE74 2LJ* Tel (01332) 810364

WHITEHEAD, Christopher Martin Field. b 36. ALCD62. **d** 62 **p** 63. C Higher Openshaw *Man* 62-63; C Halliwell St Pet 64-66; V Owlerton *Sheff* 66-75; V Hunmanby w Muston *York* 75-95; RD Scarborough 91-94; R Lockington and Lund and Scorborough w Leconfield from 95. *The Rectory, Lockington, Driffield, N Humberside YO25 9SU* Tel (01430) 810604

WHITEHEAD, Canon Denys Gordon. b 22. Pemb Coll Ox BA50 MA55. Linc Th Coll 49. **d** 52 **p** 53. C Sheff St Swithun *Sheff* 52-54; C Rawmarsh 54-57; Man Sec SCM 57-60; C Chorlton upon Medlock *Man* 57-60; Zambia from 60; Adn S Zambia 80-89; rtd 89; Hon Can Zambia from 93. *PO Box 60648, Livingstone, Zambia* Tel Livingstone (3) 323565

WHITEHEAD, Canon Dr Derek. b 27. St Jo Coll Cam BA50 MA55 Lon Univ BD60 Lanc Univ PhD73. Wells Th Coll 55. **d** 56 **p** 57. C Lower Broughton Ascension *Man* 56-59; Chapl Highgate Sch Lon 63-65; Lect Div Preston Poly 65-79; Dir of Educn *Chich* 79-94; Can and Preb Chich Cathl 82-94; NSM Fletching 93-94; rtd 94. *The Rectory, Fletching, Uckfield, E Sussex TN22 3SR* Tel (01825) 722498

WHITEHEAD, Frederick Keith. b 35. K Coll Lon BD58 AKC58. St Boniface Warminster 58. **d** 59 **p** 60. C S Shore H Trin *Blackb* 59-63; C Whitfield *Derby* 63-66; Lic to Offic 66-93; V Glossop from 93; Chapl Shire Hill Hosp Glossop from 93. *The Vicarage, Church Street South, Glossop, Derbyshire SK13 9RU* Tel (01457) 852146

WHITEHEAD, Gordon James. b 42. Clifton Th Coll 66. **d** 73 **p** 74. Chile 73-87; C Coleraine *Conn* 87-94; I Errigle Keerogue w Ballygawley and Killeshil *Arm* from 94. *Richmond Rectory, 24 Old Omagh Road, Ballygawley, Co Tyrone BT70 2AA* Tel (01662) 568670

WHITEHEAD, Mrs Hazel. b 54. K Coll Lon AKC76 BD76 Lon Univ CertTESOL89 Lambeth MA97. Oak Hill Th Coll 93. **d** 94 **p** 95. NSM Oatlands *Guildf* 94; C 95-96; Tutor Guildf Dioc Min Course 94-96; C Oatlands from 96; Prin Dioc Min Course from 96. *The Vicarage, 5 Burwood Road, Walton-on-Thames, Surrey KT12 4AA* Tel (01932) 269343

WHITEHEAD, Ian Richard. b 63. St Jo Coll Nottm BA95. **d** 95 **p** 96. C Hillmorton *Cov* 95-97; C Whitnash from 97. *13 Palmer Road, Whitnash, Leamington Spa, Warks CV31 2HP* Tel (01926) 425366

WHITEHEAD, John Stanley. b 38. Jes Coll Cam BA63 MA67 MPhil. Westcott Ho Cam 63. **d** 64 **p** 65. C Batley All SS *Wakef* 64-67; C Mitcham St Mark *S'wark* 67-70; C Frindsbury w Upnor *Roch* 70-72; TV Strood 72-75; R Halstead 75-82; V Betley *Lich* 82-85; Asst Chapl Keele Univ from 82; V Betley and Keele from 85. *The Vicarage, Church Lane, Betley, Crewe CW3 9AX* Tel (01270) 820245

WHITEHEAD, Canon Matthew Alexander (Alex). b 44. Leeds Univ BA65 St Chad's Coll Dur DipEd66 Birm Univ MA75. Qu Coll Birm DipTh68. **d** 69 **p** 70. C Bingley All SS *Bradf* 69-72; C Keele *Lich* 72-74; Asst Chapl Keele Univ 72-74; Bp's Dom Chapl *Dur* 74-80; V Escomb 74-80; V Witton Park 74-80; V Birtley 80-89; RD Chester-le-Street 84-89; V Stockton St Pet from 89; Hon Can Dur Cathl from 96. *The Vicarage, 77 Yarm Road, Stockton-on-Tees, Cleveland TS18 3PJ* Tel (01642) 676625

WHITEHEAD, Canon Michael Hutton. b 33. St Chad's Coll Dur 54. **d** 58 **p** 59. C Southwick St Columba *Dur* 58-64; V Hendon St Ignatius 64-70; P-in-c Sunderland 67-80; V Hendon 70-80; V Hendon and Sunderland 80-87; Hon Can Dur Cathl from 84; V Hartlepool St Aid from 87; RD Hartlepool 91-95. *The Vicarage, St Aidan's Street, Hartlepool, Cleveland TS25 1SN* Tel (01429) 273539

WHITEHEAD, Nicholas James. b 53. AIB. Ridley Hall Cam 86. **d** 88 **p** 89. C Bourne *Guildf* 88-92; V Hersham from 92. *The Vicarage, 5 Burwood Road, Hersham, Walton-on-Thames, Surrey KT12 4AA* Tel (01932) 227445

WHITEHEAD, Paul Conrad. b 60. St Jo Coll Nottm LTh92. **d** 92 **p** 93. C Mansfield Woodhouse *S'well* 92-96; C Carlton-in-the-Willows from 96; C Netherfield w Colwick 96; C Colwick from 96. *84 Hillside Road, Beeston, Nottingham NG9 3AT* Tel 0115-925 2762

WHITEHEAD, Philip. b 34. Kelham Th Coll 55. **d** 59 **p** 60. C Sugley *Newc* 59-62; C Alnwick St Paul 62-63; C Newc St Gabr 63-66; C Gosforth All SS 66-67; V Kenton Ascension 67-75; V Spittal 75-88; P-in-c Scremerston 81-88; V Cresswell and Lynemouth 88-96; rtd 96. *13 Abbey Gate, Morpeth, Northd NE61 2XL* Tel (01670) 514953

WHITEHEAD, Robin Lawson. b 53. Bris Univ BA76. St Steph Ho Ox 77. **d** 80 **p** 81. C Cheshunt *St Alb* 80-83; C E Grinstead St Swithun *Chich* 83-85; V Friern Barnet St Pet le Poer *Lon* 85-92; R Friern Barnet St Jas 92-95; C Wood Green St Mich w Bounds Green St Gabr etc from 96. *20 Cornwall Avenue, London N22 4DA* Tel 0181-881 0484

WHITEHEAD, Roger Milton. b 25. Pemb Coll Ox BA50 MA54. Ely Th Coll 50. **d** 52 **p** 53. C Gateshead Ch Ch *Dur* 52-55; C N Lynn w St Marg and St Nic *Nor* 55-56; C-in-c Clifton H Trin CD *S'well* 56-59; TR Clifton 59-61; R Elston w Elston Chapelry 61-64; R E Stoke w Syerston 61-64; V Oakfield St Jo *Portsm* 64-72; V Albrighton *Lich* 72-80; R Euston w Barnham and Fakenham *St E* 80-85; R Euston w Barnham, Elvedon and Fakenham Magna 85-89; rtd 89; Perm to Offic *Nor* from 89. *Groveways, Spur Road, Barnham Broom, Norwich NR9 4BY* Tel (0160545) 779

WHITEHORN, Arthur Basil. b 24. WMMTC. **d** 84 **p** 85. Asst Chapl Bromsgrove & Redditch Health Auth 84-89; NSM Bromsgrove St Jo *Worc* 84-94; Perm to Offic from 94. *15 Perry Lane, Bromsgrove, Worcs B61 7JL* Tel (01527) 74857

WHITEHORN, Jean Margaret. b 28. Lon Univ DipSocSc49 Cam Univ TCert70 Lon Univ DipRS85. S'wark Ord Course 87. **d** 89 **p** 94. NSM Orsett *Chelmsf* 89-90; NSM Orsett and Bulphan 90-93; NSM Orsett and Bulphan and Horndon on the Hill from 93. *46 Monks Haven, Stanford-le-Hope, Essex SS17 7EF* Tel (01375) 676074

WHITEHOUSE, Alan Edward. b 35. CEng66. Glouc Sch of Min 89. **d** 92 **p** 93. NSM Evesham *Worc* 92-96; NSM Evesham w Norton and Lenchwick from 96. *99 Greenhill, Evesham, Worcs WR11 4NB* Tel (01386) 442427

WHITEHOUSE, Nigel Andrew. b 57. St Mary's RC Sem Birm 75. **d** 80 **p** 81. In RC Ch 81-87; C Whittlesey and Pondersbridge *Ely* 92-94; P-in-c Newton from 94; P-in-c Gorefield from 94; P-in-c Tydd St Giles from 94. *The Rectory, Newton, Wisbech, Cambs PE13 5EX* Tel (01945) 870205

WHITEHOUSE, Robert Edward. b 64. Oak Hill Th Coll BA. **d** 91 **p** 92. C Sheff Norwood St Leon *Sheff* 91-94; P-in-c Birchencliffe *Wakef* from 94; Dioc Youth Officer from 94; Bp's Chapl for Youth from 94. *The Vicarage, 191 Birkby Road, Huddersfield HD2 2BX*

WHITEHOUSE, Miss Susan Clara. b 48. R Holloway Coll Lon BA70. Westcott Ho Cam 87. **d** 89 **p** 94. Par Dn Farnley *Ripon* 89-93; Dioc Development Rep from 92; C Bedale 93-96; C Thornton Watlass w Thornton Steward 93-96; V Aysgarth and Bolton cum Redmire from 96. *The Vicarage, Carperby, Leyburn, N Yorkshire DL8 4DQ* Tel (01969) 663235

WHITELEY, Alan. b 42. ACII. Lich Th Coll 68. **d** 71 **p** 72. C Wales *Sheff* 71-75; TV Frecheville and Hackenthorpe 75-79; V Malin Bridge 79-95; V Ellesmere St Pet from 95. *85 Malton Street, Sheffield S4 7EA* Tel 0114-276 2555

WHITELEY, Donal Royston. b 27. Qu Coll Birm 54. **d** 57 **p** 58. C Handsworth St Mary *Birm* 57-60; C Kingswinford St Mary *Lich* 60-63; R Norton Canes 63-71; V Wetley Rocks 71-96; rtd 96. *7 Balmoral Road, Burton-on-Trent, Staffs DE15 0JN* Tel (01283) 548312

WHITELEY, Robert. b 36. Dur Univ BA67. Cranmer Hall Dur 62. **d** 67 **p** 68. C Maidstone All SS w St Phil and H Trin *Cant* 67-70; Asst Chapl K Sch Roch 70-71; Chapl 71-82. *c/o Mrs L E Walton, 10 Greenway, Wilmslow, Cheshire SK9 1LU* Tel (01625) 524019

WHITELEY, Canon Robert Louis. b 28. Leeds Univ BA48. Coll of Resurr Mirfield 50. **d** 52 **p** 53. C Hollinwood *Man* 52-55; Br Honduras 56-61; V Illingworth *Wakef* 61-68; V Westgate Common 68-75; Can Res Wakef Cathl 75-80; Hon Can Wakef Cathl 80-93; V Almondbury 80-82; TR Almondbury w Farnley Tyas 82-92; RD Almondbury 81-93; rtd 93; Perm to Offic *Wakef* from 93. *12 Woodland Avenue, Lepton, Huddersfield HD8 0HZ* Tel (01484) 608050

WHITEMAN, Canon Cedric Henry. b 28. Lich Th Coll 59. **d** 61 **p** 62. C Abington *Pet* 61-64; V Kettering St Andr 64-79; RD Kettering 73-79; Can Pet Cathl 77-79; V Rotherham *Sheff* 79-87; RD Rotherham 79-86; Hon Can Sheff Cathl from 85; Bp's Dom Chapl from 86; V Wentworth 87-91; rtd 91. *11 Thornbrook Close, Chapeltown, Sheffield S30 4BB* Tel 0114-245 7479

WHITEMAN, Christopher Henry Raymond. b 51. Portsm Poly BA73 Worc Coll of Educn PGCE74. St Jo Coll Nottm DipTh90. **d** 90 **p** 91. C Rockland St Mary w Hellington, Bramerton etc *Nor*

90-93; P-in-c Gillingham w Geldeston, Stockton, Ellingham etc 93-94; R from 94. *The Rectory, The Street, Geldeston, Beccles, Suffolk NR34 0LN* Tel (01502) 712255

WHITEMAN, The Ven Rodney David Carter. b 40. Ely Th Coll 61. **d** 64 **p** 65. C Kings Heath *Birm* 64-70; V Rednal 70-79; V Erdington St Barn 79-89; RD Aston 81-86 and 88-89; Hon Can Birm Cathl 85-89; Adn Bodmin *Truro* from 89; P-in-c Cardynham from 89; P-in-c Helland from 89; Hon Can Truro Cathl from 89. *The Rectory, Cardinham, Bodmin, Cornwall PL30 4BL* Tel (01208) 821614 Fax 821602

WHITESIDE, Canon Peter George. b 30. St Cath Coll Cam BA55 MA61. Cuddesdon Coll 55. **d** 57 **p** 58. C Westmr St Steph w St Jo *Lon* 57-61; Chapl Clifton Coll Bris 61-70; Hd Master Linc Cathl Sch 71-73; Australia 74-92; TV Brentford *Lon* 92-97; rtd 97. *Flat 2, 17 Mount Park Road, London W5 2RP*

WHITFIELD, Charles. b 25. St Pet Hall Ox BA49 MA53. Ridley Hall Cam 49. **d** 51 **p** 52. C Ecclesfield *Sheff* 51-54; C Grassendale *Liv* 54-56; C Neasden cum Kingsbury St Cath *Lon* 56-58; C St Martin-in-the-Fields 58-59; V Bromley H Trin *Roch* 59-68; V Egg Buckland *Ex* 68-90; rtd 90. *23 Chapel Meadow, Buckland Monachorum, Yelverton, Devon PL20 7LR*

WHITFIELD, George Joshua Newbold. b 09. Lon Univ AKC30 MA35. Bps' Coll Cheshunt. **d** 62 **p** 63. Hon C Hampton St Mary *Lon* 62-74; Gen Sec Gen Syn Bd of Educn 69-74; rtd 74; Lic to Offic *Ex* from 78. *Bede Lodge, 31A Rolle Road, Exmouth, Devon EX8 2AW* Tel (01395) 274162

WHITFIELD, Joy Verity. *See* CHAPMAN, Mrs Joy Verity

WHITFIELD, Trevor. b 48. Bedf Coll Lon BSc71 Bris Univ PGCE73 Fitzw Coll Cam BA78 MA88. Ridley Hall Cam 76. **d** 79 **p** 80. C Battersea St Pet and St Paul *S'wark* 79-82; Chapl Stockholm w Uppsala *Eur* 82-83; C-in-c Roundshaw CD *S'wark* 83-89; Asst Chapl R Victoria Infirmary Newc 89-92; Asst Chapl Berne w Neuchatel *Eur* 92-95; Chapl Utrecht w Amersfoort, Harderwijk & Zwolle from 95. *V Hogendorpstraat 26, 3581 KE Utrecht, The Netherlands* Tel Utrecht (30) 513424

WHITFORD, William Laurence. b 56. Open Univ BA92 Liv Univ DipApTh96. N Ord Course 92. **d** 95 **p** 96. C Hindley All SS *Liv* from 95. *45 Woodland Avenue, Wigan, Lancs WN2 4PP* Tel (01942) 254824

WHITING, Antony Gerald Stroud. b 26. CITC 81. **d** 86 **p** 87. NSM Clonmel Union *C, C & R* 86-87; Cork St Fin Barre's Union 87-88; Lic to Offic 88-92; Bp's C Mallow Union 92-97; I from 97. *The Rectory, Lower Bearforest, Mallow, Co Cork, Irish Republic* Tel Mallow (22) 21473 Fax 50044

WHITING, Graham James. b 58. Bris Univ BSc81. Chich Th Coll 83. **d** 86 **p** 88. C Portslade St Nic and St Andr *Chich* 86-87; C W Tarring 87-91; C Seaford w Sutton 91-94; P-in-c Bournemouth St Clem *Win* from 94. *The Vicarage, St Clement's Road, Bournemouth BH1 4DZ* Tel (01202) 392851

WHITING, Joseph Alfred. b 41. Oak Hill Th Coll 82. **d** 85 **p** 86. Hon C Sidcup St Andr *Roch* 85-88; C Southborough St Pet w Ch Ch and St Matt 88-92; C Aldridge *Lich* 92-97; TV Rye *Chich* from 97. *Camber Vicarage, Lydd Road, Camber, Rye, E Sussex TN31 7RN* Tel (01797) 225386

WHITLEY, Eric Keir. b 47. Salford Univ BSc68. Trin Coll Bris 77. **d** 79 **p** 80. C Nottingham St Ann w Em *S'well* 79-83; V Donisthorpe and Moira w Stretton-en-le-Field *Leic* 83-91; V Thorpe Acre w Dishley from 91. *The Vicarage, Knightthorpe Road, Loughborough, Leics LE11 0LF* Tel (01509) 214553

WHITLEY, John Duncan Rooke. b 29. Trin Coll Cam BA51 MA55 Jordan Hill Coll Glas CertEd82. Coll of Resurr Mirfield 52. **d** 54 **p** 55. C Ashington *Newc* 54-59; C Chiswick St Nic w St Mary *Lon* 59-61; V Ware St Mary *St Alb* 61-71; Can Missr St Mary's Cathl Edin 71-74; Chapl Edin R Infirmary 71-74; Dioc Educn Officer *Edin* 71-74; Lic to Offic from 74; Asst Chapl Edin Healthcare NHS Trust from 95. *114 Viewforth, Edinburgh EH10 4LN* Tel 0131-229 0130 Mobile 0802-446264 Fax 229 6528 E-mail 100430.66@compuserve.com

WHITLEY, John William. b 46. TCD BA68. Cranmer Hall Dur BA71. **d** 71 **p** 72. C Belfast St Mary Magd *Conn* 71-73; C Toxteth St Philemon w St Gabr *Liv* 73-78; P-in-c Toxteth Park St Cleopas 78-88; TV Toxteth St Philemon w St Gabr and St Cleopas 89-95; P-in-c Litherland St Paul Hatton Hill from 95. *St Paul's Vicarage, Watling Avenue, Liverpool L21 9NU* Tel 0151-928 2705

WHITLEY (née ALLISON), Rosemary Jean. b 45. LTCL67. Trin Coll Bris 75 St Jo Coll Nottm 94. **d** 95 **p** 96. NSM Loughb Gd Shep *Leic* from 95. *Thorpe Acre Vicarage, Knightthorpe Road, Loughborough, Leics LE11 0JS* Tel (01509) 214553

WHITLOCK, James Frederick. b 44. Ch Coll Cam BA75 MA78. Westcott Ho Cam 73. **d** 76 **p** 77. C Newquay *Truro* 76-79; P-in-c St Mawgan w St Ervan and St Eval 79-81; R 81; Bp's Dom Chapl 82-85; Dioc Dir of Ords 82-85; V Leagrave *St Alb* 85-89; TR Probus, Ladock and Grampound w Creed and St Erme *Truro* 89-95; V Penzance St Mary w St Paul from 95. *St Mary's Vicarage, Chapel Street, Penzance, Cornwall TR18 4AP* Tel (01736) 63079

WHITLOW, The Very Revd Brian William. b 14. St Edm Hall Ox BA36 DipTh37 Bp's Univ Lennoxville MEd52 BD59 DD67. Westcott Ho Cam 37. **d** 38 **p** 39. C Leeds St Aid *Ripon* 38-41; Chapl RAFVR 41-46; Canada from 46; Dean Ch Ch Cathl Victoria 55-80. *1347 Craigdarroch Road, Victoria, British Columbia, Canada, V8S 2A6* Tel Victoria (604) 592-6109

WHITMORE, Benjamin Nicholas. b 66. Imp Coll Lon BEng88. Cranmer Hall Dur 89. **d** 92 **p** 93. C Gt Wyrley *Lich* 92-95; C Hednesford from 95. *554 Littleworth Road, Rawnsley, Cannoch, Staffs WS12 5JD* Tel (01543) 879686

WHITMORE, Mrs Dorothy Mary. b 28. Sheff Univ BA49 DipEd50. Gilmore Course 79. **dss** 81 **d** 87 **p** 94. Marston Green *Birm* 81-87; NSM 87-96; Perm to Offic from 96. *106 Needlers End Lane, Balsall Common, Coventry CV7 7AB* Tel (01676) 534305

WHITMORE, Edward James. b 36. Lon Univ BD66. Tyndale Hall Bris. **d** 68 **p** 69. Tanzania 68-76; Lic to Offic *Blackb* from 77. *74 Greencroft, Penwortham, Preston PR1 9LB* Tel (01772) 746522

WHITMORE, Miss Jane Frances. b 30. **dss** 79 **d** 87 **p** 94. Elloughton and Brough w Brantingham *York* 79-83; Foley Park *Worc* 83-87; C Frimley *Guildf* 87-96; rtd 96. *The Grange, 26 Middleton Road, Marlpool, Kidderminster, Worcs DY11 5EY*

WHITMORE, Stephen Andrew. b 53. Sheff Univ BSc74. St Jo Coll Nottm DTS89. **d** 91 **p** 92. C Newbury *Ox* 91-95; TV High Wycombe from 95. *70 Marlow Road, High Wycombe, Bucks HP11 1TH* Tel (01494) 528207

WHITNALL, Robert Edward (Dominic). b 14. Magd Coll Ox BA37. Cuddesdon Coll 37. **d** 38 **p** 39. C Staveley *Derby* 38-44; S Africa 47-66; CR from 47; Hon C Battyeford *Wakef* from 68; rtd 84. *House of the Resurrection, Mirfield, W Yorkshire WF14 0BN* Tel (01924) 494318

WHITROW, Capt Henry Thomas. b 32. RMA 50. Oak Hill Th Coll 61. **d** 63 **p** 64. C Burley *Ripon* 63-65; CF 65-66; C Reading St Jo *Ox* 68-69; rtd 94. *Grenfell, Ellesborough Manor, Aylesbury, Bucks HP17 0XF*

WHITTA, Rex Alfred Rought. b 28. Leeds Inst of Educn CertEd52 Open Univ BA88 Lon Univ CertTESOL89. Qu Coll Birm DipTh63. **d** 63 **p** 64. C Newland St Aug *York* 63-66; V Elloughton 66-68; P-in-c Brantingham 66-68; V Elloughton and Brough w Brantingham 68-74; TR Redcar w Kirkleatham 74-78; V Redcar 78-84; V Bassenthwaite, Isel and Setmurthy *Carl* 84-86; P-in-c Cloughton *York* 86-88; P-in-c Hackness w Harwood Dale 86-88; rtd 89. *14 Candler Street, Scarborough, N Yorkshire YO12 7DF* Tel (01723) 375740

WHITTAKER, Arthur. b 30. Oak Hill Th Coll. **d** 60 **p** 61. C Bispham *Blackb* 60-64; V Edge Hill St Cypr *Liv* 64-73; Area Sec (Dios Ban, St As, Ches and S & M) CMS 73-74; C Maghull *Liv* 74; V Bilsborrow *Blackb* 74-96; rtd 96; Perm to Offic *Blackb* from 96. *33 Hamers Wood Drive, Catterall, Preston PR3 1YN*

WHITTAKER, Arthur George. b 14. MRIPHH38 LTCL57 Man Univ 48. **d** 60 **p** 61. C Ibstock *Leic* 60-62; C Leic St Phil 62-63; V Hadfield *Derby* 63-72; V Coldham *Ely* 72-81; V Friday Bridge 72-81; rtd 81; Perm to Offic *Glouc* from 81. *27 Mosley Crescent, Cashes Green, Stroud, Glos GL5 4LT* Tel (01453) 763622

WHITTAKER, Brian Lawrence. b 39. Clifton Th Coll 63. **d** 66 **p** 67. C Whitton and Thurleston w Akenham *St E* 66-69; C Normanton *Wakef* 69-74; P-in-c Castle Hall *Ches* 74-77; P-in-c Dukinfield Ch Ch 74-77; P-in-c Stalybridge H Trin and Ch Ch 74-77; V 77-83; TR Bucknall and Bagnall *Lich* 83-91; R Draycott-le-Moors w Forsbrook from 91. *The Rectory, 7 Cheadle Road, Blythe Bridge, Stoke-on-Trent ST11 9PW* Tel (01782) 392259

WHITTAKER, Bryan. b 58. Southn Univ BTh82. Chich Th Coll 82. **d** 84 **p** 85. C Whitleigh *Ex* 84-88; C Corringham *Chelmsf* 88-92; V Rush Green 92-94. *361 Dagenham Road, Romford RM7 0XX*

WHITTAKER, Derek. b 30. OBE85. Liv Univ BEng51 PhD58 CEng65. **d** 93 **p** 95. Zambia 93-96; NSM Broom Leys *Leic* from 97. *84 Blackwood, Broom Leys, Coalville, Leics LE67 4RF* Tel (01530) 838403

WHITTAKER, Garry. b 59. St Jo Coll Nottm DCM91. **d** 91 **p** 92. C Denton Ch Ch *Man* 91-95; P-in-c Waterhead from 95. *Holy Trinity Vicarage, Church Street East, Waterhead, Oldham OL4 2JQ* Tel 0161-624 4011

WHITTAKER, James Rawstron. b 14. Worc Coll Ox BA38 MA46. Wells Th Coll 38. **d** 40 **p** 41. C York St Mary Bishophill Senior *York* 40-43; Hornsea w Bewholme 43-47; R Neen Sollars w Milson *Heref* 47-55; V Annscroft 55-70; R Pontesbury III 55-70; V Longden 55-70; V Almeley 70-80; P-in-c Kinnersley w Norton Canon 74-80; rtd 81; Perm to Offic *Heref* from 82. *Eign Gate House, 142 Eign Street, Hereford HR4 0AP* Tel (01432) 268961

WHITTAKER, Jeremy Paul. b 59. Ox Univ MA. Ripon Coll Cuddesdon 82. **d** 84 **p** 85. C Crowthorne *Ox* 84-87; C Westborough *Guildf* 87-88; TV 88-91; Chapl Pierrepont Sch Frensham 91-95; Perm to Offic *Guildf* from 95. *6 Springhaven Close, Guildford, Surrey GU1 2JP*

WHITTAKER, Canon John. b 20. Ch Coll Cam BA47 MA49. Ridley Hall Cam 46. **d** 48 **p** 49. C Astley Bridge *Man* 48-51; C Kersal Moor 51-53; R Birch St Agnes 53-66; V New Bury 66-75; Hon Can Man Cathl 71-87; R Middleton 75-87; rtd 87; Perm to Offic *Man* from 87. *5 Farnborough Road, Bolton BL1 7HJ* Tel (01204) 595499

WHITTAKER, John. b 27. Oak Hill Th Coll 53. **d** 55 **p** 56. C Blackpool St Thos *Blackb* 55-57; C St Helens St Helen *Liv* 58-60; V Hensingham *Carl* 60-67; V Skelmersdale St Paul *Liv*

67-77; V Gt Faringdon w Lt Coxwell *Ox* 77-83; RD Vale of White Horse 80-83; rtd 83; Perm to Offic *Ox* 83-88; C Broughton Poggs w Filkins, Broadwell etc 88-95; C Shill Valley and Broadshire 95-96. *26 The Pines, Faringdon, Oxon SN7 8AU* Tel (01367) 241009

WHITTAKER, Karl Paul. b 55. CITC BTh95. **d** 95 **p** 96. C Killowen *D & R* from 95. *27 Ballycranny Drive, Coleraine, Co Londonderry BT51 3JX* Tel (01265) 52006

WHITTAKER, Canon Peter Harold. b 39. AKC62. **d** 63 **p** 64. C Walton St Mary *Liv* 63-67; C Ross *Heref* 67-70; R Bridgnorth St Mary 70-78; P-in-c Oldbury 70-78; TR Bridgnorth, Tasley, Astley Abbotts and Oldbury 78-81; RD Bridgnorth 78-81; Preb Heref Cathl 80-81; V Leighton Buzzard w Eggington, Hockliffe etc *St Alb* 81-92; RD Dunstable 84-85; R Barton-le-Cley w Higham Gobion and Hexton from 92; Hon Can St Alb from 92. *The Rectory, Church Road, Barton-le-Clay, Bedford MK45 4LA* Tel (01582) 881226

WHITTAKER, Robert Andrew. b 49. DipEd Open Univ BA75 Nottm Univ MA83. Linc Th Coll 85. **d** 87 **p** 88. C Mansfield Woodhouse *S'well* 87-90; V Norwell w Ossington, Cromwell and Caunton 90-95; Chapl Ranby Ho Sch Retford from 95. *East Lodge, Ranby House School, Ranby, Retford, Notts DN22 8HX* Tel (01777) 701455

WHITTAKER, William Paul. *See* STAFFORD-WHITTAKER, William Paul

WHITTAM, Canon Kenneth Michael. b 26. Ball Coll Ox BA50 MA54. Cuddesdon Coll 50. **d** 52 **p** 53. C Adlington *Blackb* 52-55; C St Annes 55-58; R Halton w Aughton 58-62; R Colne St Bart 62-66; Chapl Highgate Sch Lon 66-75; V Shotwick *Ches* 75-89; Can Res Ches Cathl and Dioc Missr 75-85; Hon Can Ches Cathl 85-90; Clergy Study Officer 85-91; rtd 91; Perm to Offic *Ches* from 91. *22 Warwick Close, Little Neston, South Wirral L64 0SR*

WHITTINGHAM, Peter. b 58. Sheff Univ BA79. St Jo Coll Nottm 88. **d** 90 **p** 91. C Northowram *Wakef* 90-93; C Airedale w Fryston 93-96; V Wrenthorpe from 96. *The Vicarage, 121 Wrenthorpe Road, Wrenthorpe, Wakefield, W Yorkshire WF2 0JS* Tel (01924) 373758

WHITTINGHAM, Ronald Norman. b 43. Linc Coll Ox BA65 MA68. Coll of Resurr Mirfield 65. **d** 67 **p** 68. C Horninglow *Lich* 67-69; C Drayton in Hales 69-70; C Uttoxeter w Bramshall 71-75; P-in-c Burton St Paul 75-80; V Shareshill 80-83; V Silverdale and Knutton Heath 83-89; P-in-c Alsagers Bank 83-89; V Silverdale and Alsagers Bank 89-92; V Honley *Wakef* from 92. *The Vicarage, St Mary's Road, Honley, Huddersfield HD7 2AZ* Tel (01484) 661178

WHITTINGTON, Canon David John. b 45. Qu Coll Ox BA67 MA71. Coll of Resurr Mirfield 69. **d** 71 **p** 72. Chapl St Woolos Cathl *Mon* 71-72; C Ox St Mary V w St Cross and St Pet *Ox* 72-76; Chapl Qu Coll Ox 72-76; V Stockton *Dur* from 77; Hon Can Dur Cathl from 93. *61 Bishopton Road, Stockton-on-Tees, Cleveland TS18 4PD* Tel (01642) 617420

WHITTINGTON, Peter Graham. b 68. Ox Poly BA90. Trin Coll Bris BA95. **d** 95 **p** 96. C Gateacre *Liv* from 95. *14 Egremont Lawn, Liverpool L27 5RB* Tel 0151-487 3391

WHITTINGTON, Richard Hugh (Dick). b 47. MBE74. Sarum & Wells Th Coll DipTh93. **d** 93 **p** 94. C Enfield St Jas *Lon* 93-96; P-in-c Ightham *Roch* 96-97; R from 97. *The Rectory, Tonbridge Road, Ightham, Sevenoaks, Kent TN15 9BG* Tel (01732) 884176

WHITTLE, Alan. b 29. K Coll Lon BD52 AKC52. **d** 53 **p** 54. C Combe Down *B & W* 53-55; C Bath Twerton-on-Avon 55-57; Australia 57-66; R Aston Rowant w Crowell *Ox* 66-68; Lic to Offic *S'wark* 69-72; V Mitcham Ch Ch 72-92; rtd 92; Perm to Offic *S'wark* from 92. *117 May Cross Avenue, Morden, Surrey SM4 4DF*

WHITTLE, Fred. b 17. Keble Coll Ox BA40 MA44. Cuddesdon Coll 40. **d** 41 **p** 42. C Northampton St Matt *Pet* 41-47; C W Molesey *Guildf* 47-49; C Isham *Pet* 49-51; V Warmington 51-58; R Orlingbury w Pytchley 58-71; R Gt w Lt Addington 71-82; rtd 82; Lic to Offic *Pet* 82-85; Perm to Offic from 85. *6 Coleman Street, Raunds, Wellingborough, Northants NN9 6NJ* Tel (01933) 624989

WHITTLE, Ian Christopher. b 60. Univ Coll Dur BA81 Fitzw Coll Cam BA87. Ridley Hall Cam. **d** 88 **p** 89. C S Petherton w the Seavingtons *B & W* 88-91; Asst Chapl The Hague *Eur* from 91. *Kijkdionsestraat 858, 2554 AB The Hague, The Netherlands* Tel The Hague (70) 356-1653

WHITTLE, John William. b 46. Qu Mary Coll Lon BA68. Sarum & Wells Th Coll 84. **d** 86 **p** 87. C Blandford Forum and Langton Long etc *Sarum* 86-88. *Leslie House, The Tabernacle, Blandford Forum, Dorset DT11 7DW* Tel (01258) 451943

WHITTLE, Robin Jeffrey. b 51. Bris Univ BA72 Leic Univ CQSW75. Sarum & Wells Th Coll 85. **d** 87 **p** 88. C Henbury *Bris* 87-91; V Capel *Guildf* 91-96; Chapl to the Deaf from 96. *24 Cleardene, Dorking, Surrey RH4 2BY* Tel (01306) 888004

WHITTOCK, Michael Graham. b 47. Hull Univ BA69 Fitzw Ho Cam BA71 MA76. Westcott Ho Cam 69 Union Th Sem Richmond 71. **d** 72 **p** 73. C Kirkby *Liv* 72-76; C Prescot 76-79; R Methley w Mickletown *Ripon* 79-92; RD Whitkirk 88-92; V Morley St Pet w Churwell *Wakef* from 92. *St Peter's Vicarage, Rooms Lane, Morley, Leeds LS27 9PA* Tel 0113-253 2052

WHITTOME, Donald Marshall. b 26. Cam Univ BA50 MA53. S Dios Minl Tr Scheme. **d** 84 **p** 85. NSM Henfield w Shermanbury and Woodmancote *Chich* 84-93; P-in-c Poynings w Edburton, Newtimber and Pyecombe 93-97; rtd 97; Perm to Offic *Chich* from 97. *Quaker's Rest, 7 Dean Court Road, Rottingdean, Brighton BN2 7DE* Tel (01273) 705508

WHITTON, Eric. b 33. N Lon Poly 78. Lon Coll of Div ALCD59 Western Th Sem Michigan 60. **d** 60 **p** 61. C Mortlake w E Sheen *S'wark* 60-64; C Surbiton St Matt 64-66; Youth Officer *Lon* 66-72; Tr Officer Gen Syn Bd of Educn 73-78; Visiting Lect Roehampton Inst of HE from 80; rtd 94. *31 Ovington Street, London SW3 2JA* Tel 0171-584 8819

WHITTON, Robert Archibald. b 17. Edin Univ MA37. Moray Ho Edin TCert60 Edin Th Coll 38. **d** 40 **p** 41. C Ayr *Glas* 40-43; R Stromness *Ab* 43-51; R Kirkwall 45-51; Adn Orkney 47-51; R Helensburgh *Glas* 51-59; Chapl Fettes Coll Edin 59-60; Perm to Offic *Edin* from 60. *36 Bryce Road, Currie, Midlothian EH14 5LW* Tel 0131-449 4303

WHITTY, Gordon William. b 35. WMMTC. **d** 82 **p** 83. NSM Willenhall St Giles *Lich* 82-84; NSM Coseley Ch Ch 84-85; C 85-87; TV Hanley H Ev 87-91; P-in-c Meir from 91. *The Vicarage, 715 Uttoxeter Road, Meir, Stoke-on-Trent ST3 5PY* Tel (01782) 313347

WHITTY, Harold George. b 41. TCD BA64 MA67. CITC Div Test65. **d** 65 **p** 66. C Willowfield *D & D* 65-68; C Lisburn Ch Ch *Conn* 68-71; Bp's Dom Chapl 70-71; Asst Dir Exhibitions CMJ 71-72; C Enfield Ch Ch Trent Park *Lon* 72-75; TV Washfield, Stoodleigh, Withleigh etc *Ex* 75-83; R Washfield, Stoodleigh, Withleigh etc 83-84; TR 84-93; RD Tiverton 82-84; P-in-c Allithwaite *Carl* from 93. *The Vicarage, Boarbank Lane, Allithwaite, Grange-over-Sands, Cumbria LA11 7QR* Tel (015395) 32437

WHITWAM, Miss Diana Morgan. b 28. MCSP54 Brighton Poly DCouns82. Local Minl Tr Course 88. **d** 93 **p** 94. NSM Stoke-next-Guildf from 93. *27 Acacia Road, Guildford, Surrey GU1 1HL* Tel (01483) 36443

WHITWELL, Canon John Peter. b 36. Qu Coll Birm 62. **d** 65 **p** 66. C Stepney St Dunstan and All SS *Lon* 65-68; C Chingford SS Pet and Paul *Chelmsf* 68-71; V Walthamstow St Sav 71-78; P-in-c Lt Ilford St Mich 78-88; R from 88; RD Newham 91-97; Hon Can Chelmsf Cathl from 96. *The Rectory, Church Road, London E12 6HA* Tel 0181-478 2182

WHITWELL, Martin Corbett. b 32. Pemb Coll Ox BA55 MA59. Clifton Th Coll 55. **d** 57 **p** 58. C Wolverhampton St Jude *Lich* 57-60; C Aldridge 60-66; Chapl Sandbach Co Secondary Sch 68-74; C Chipping Campden *Glouc* 70-71; Perm to Offic *Chich* 74-75; Perm to Offic *Bris* 75-76; C Tranmere St Cath *Ches* 76-80; V Lt Leigh and Lower Whitley 80-90; rtd 90; Perm to Offic *Ches* from 90; Perm to Offic *Heref* from 93; Perm to Offic *Lich* from 93. *11 Hollies Drive, Bayston Hill, Shrewsbury SY3 0HN* Tel (01743) 874241

WHITWORTH, Benjamin Charles Battams (Ben). b 49. CCC Ox BA71 MA85. Linc Th Coll 83. **d** 85 **p** 86. C Swanborough *Sarum* 85-88; C Sherborne w Castleton and Lillington 88-91; V Milborne Port w Goathill *B & W* from 91. *The Vicarage, Bathwell Lane, Milborne Port, Sherborne, Dorset DT9 5AN* Tel (01963) 250248

WHITWORTH, Canon Duncan. b 47. K Coll Lon BD69 AKC69. **d** 70 **p** 71. C Tonge Moor *Man* 70-73; C Upper Norwood St Jo *Cant* 73-78; Asst Chapl Madrid *Eur* 78-82; Chapl Br Emb Ankara 82-83; V Douglas St Matt *S & M* from 84; RD Douglas from 91; Can St German's Cathl from 96. *St Matthew's Vicarage, Alexander Drive, Douglas, Isle of Man IM2 3QN* Tel (01624) 676310

WHITWORTH, Canon Patrick John. b 51. Ch Ch Ox BA72 MA76 St Jo Coll Dur DipTh75 MA78. **d** 76 **p** 77. C York St Mich-le-Belfrey *York* 76-79; C Brompton H Trin w Onslow Square St Paul *Lon* 79-84; V Gipsy Hill Ch Ch *S'wark* 84-95; Hon Can Bauchi from 95; R Bath Weston All SS w N Stoke and Langridge *B & W* from 95. *The Vicarage, Weston, Bath BA1 4BU* Tel (01225) 421159

WHITWORTH-HARRISON, Bernard. b 05. St Cath Coll Ox BA36 MA38. St Chad's Coll Dur 28 K Coll Lon 28. **d** 34 **p** 36. C Chilton All SS *Ox* 34-49; C Kingsbury *Birm* 49-52; V Crondall *Guildf* 52-58; V Cornish Hall End *Chelmsf* 58-62; R Langham 62-75; rtd 75; Perm to Offic *Ely* from 75. *19 Trinity Close, Balsham, Cambridge CB1 6DW* Tel (01223) 893921

WHYBORN, Robert. b 42. Loughb Coll of Educn CSD69. N Ord Course 87. **d** 90 **p** 91. NSM Milnrow *Man* from 90. *5 Delamere Avenue, Shaw, Oldham OL2 8HN* Tel (01706) 843644

WHYBRAY, Prof Roger Norman. b 23. Keble Coll Ox BA44 MA48 DPhil62 BD81 DD81. Linc Th Coll 44. **d** 46 **p** 47. C Basingstoke *Win* 46-48; USA 48-50; Lect Qu Coll Birm 51-52; C Harborne St Pet *Birm* 51-52; Japan 52-65; Lect Th Hull Univ 65-71; Reader 71-78; Prof Hebrew and OT 78-82. *45 Hills Lane, Ely, Cambs CB6 1AY* Tel (01353) 663897

WHYBROW, Paul Andrew. b 59. St Paul's Cheltenham BEd80. Oak Hill Th Coll DipMin89 BA90 Wycliffe Hall Ox MTh95. **d** 97. C Magor w Redwick and Undy *Mon* from 97. *3 The Meadows, Magor, Newport NP6 3LA* Tel (01633) 881714

WHYMAN, Oliver. b 27. ALCM52 LCP57. S'wark Ord Course 60. **d** 63 **p** 64. C Streatham Ch Ch *S'wark* 63-68; Lic to Offic 68-87; NSM Sutton New Town St Barn 87-92; rtd 92. *37 Jubilee Court, London Road, Thornton Heath, Surrey CR7 6JL* Tel 0181-684 5320

WHYTE, Alastair John. b 61. Coll of Ripon & York St Jo BA83. Sarum & Wells Th Coll 83. **d** 85 **p** 86. C Chorley St Geo *Blackb* 85-88; C Poulton-le-Fylde 88-91; V Wesham from 91; Chapl Wesham Park Hosp Blackb from 91. *The Vicarage, Mowbreck Lane, Wesham, Preston PR4 3HA* Tel (01772) 682206

WHYTE, Duncan Macmillan. b 25. St Jo Coll Dur BA49 St Cath Soc Ox BA51 MA57. Wycliffe Hall Ox 49. **d** 51 **p** 53. C Garston *Liv* 51-56; C St Leonards St Leon *Chich* 56-59; V Southsea St Simon *Portsm* 59-66; Gen Sec Lon City Miss 66-92; Hon C Blackheath St Jo *S'wark* 66-92; rtd 92. *1 The Meadows, Salisbury SP1 2SS* Tel (01722) 330528

WHYTE, Henry Lewis. b 38. Lon Coll of Div ALCD70 LTh74. **d** 70 **p** 71. C Crawley *Chich* 70-74; V Bermondsey St Jas w Ch Ch *S'wark* 74-82; V Kingston Hill St Paul 82-94; V Blackheath Park St Mich from 94. *St Michael's Vicarage, 2 Pond Road, London SE3 9JL* Tel 0181-852 5287

WHYTE, Canon Herbert Blayney. b 21. TCD BA43 MA53. **d** 44 **p** 45. C Dublin Crumlin *D & G* 44-47; Succ St Patr Cathl Dublin 47-50; Dioc Registrar (Ossory, Ferns and Leighlin) *C & O* 50-58; Bp's V and Lib Kilkenny Cathl 50-58; Bp Ossory Dom Chapl 50-58; RD Offerlane 55-58; RD Fiddown 55-58; Preb Ossory Cathl 56-58; I Maryborough 58-68; Clerical V Ch Ch Cathl Dublin *D & G* 68-91; I Dublin Crumlin 68-91; Can Ch Ch Cathl Dublin 80-86; Chan 86-91; rtd 91. *238 Redford Park, Greystones, Co Wicklow, Irish Republic* Tel Dublin (1) 287 7264

WHYTE, Canon Malcolm Dorrance. b 29. Man Univ BA50 BD53. Wycliffe Hall Ox 57. **d** 57 **p** 58. C Roch St Pet w St Marg *Roch* 57-60; V Ravenhead *Liv* 60-67; V Southport Em 67-95; RD N Meols 78-89; AD 89-95; Hon Can Liv Cathl 91-96; rtd 96; Perm to Offic *Blackb* from 96; Perm to Offic *Liv* from 96. *13 Ruskin Close, Tarleton, Preston PR4 6XY* Tel (01772) 813017

WHYTE, Robert Euan. b 44. St Pet Coll Ox BA67. Cuddesdon Coll 67. **d** 69 **p** 70. C Blackheath Ascension *S'wark* 69-73; NSM Lewisham St Swithun 73-76; NSM Heston *Lon* 76-77; NSM Rusthall *Roch* 77-87; C 87-88; V from 88; RD Tunbridge Wells 91-96. *The Vicarage, Bretland Road, Rusthall, Tunbridge Wells, Kent TN4 8PB* Tel (01892) 521357

WHYTE, Thomas Arthur. b 15. Man Univ BA48. Wycliffe Hall Ox 56. **d** 56 **p** 57. C Ormskirk *Liv* 56-59; V Hunts Cross 59-71; V Roby 71-83; rtd 83; Perm to Offic *Liv* from 83; Perm to Offic *Ches* 83-90; NSM Aston by Sutton from 90. *11 Acres Crescent, Westbrook Park, Kingsley, Warrington WA6 3DZ* Tel (01928) 788194

WIBBERLEY, Anthony Norman. b 36. K Coll Lon BSc58 AKC58. Sarum & Wells Th Coll 76. **d** 79 **p** 80. Hon C Tavistock and Gulworthy *Ex* 79-86; R Hoby cum Rotherby w Brooksby, Ragdale & Thru'ton *Leic* 86-90; V Ingol *Blackb* 90-96. *13 Missleton Court, Cherry Hinton Road, Cambridge CB1 4BL*

WIBREW, Mrs Janet Anne (Jan). b 48. Win Sch of Arts NDAD89. S Dios Minl Tr Scheme 89. **d** 92 **p** 94. NSM Basingstoke *Win* from 92. *High Meadows, Green Lane, Ellisfield, Basingstoke, Hants RG25 2QW* Tel (01256) 381387

WIBROE, Andrew Peter. b 56. K Coll Lon BD83 AKC83 Thames Poly PGCE91. Ripon Coll Cuddesdon 83. **d** 86 **p** 87. C Purley St Mark Woodcote *S'wark* 86-88; C Boyne Hill *Ox* 89-90; Hon C Milton next Gravesend Ch Ch *Roch* from 90. *15 Pinnocks Avenue, Gravesend, Kent DA11 7QD* Tel (01474) 354321

WICK, Patricia Anne. b 54. Lon Bible Coll BA80 Oak Hill Th Coll DipHE86. **dss** 86 **d** 87 **p** 94. Halliwell St Luke *Man* 86-87; Par Dn 87-91; Par Dn Drypool *York* 91-94; C 94-95; TV from 95. *3 Caledonia Park, Hull HU9 1TE* Tel (01482) 589786

WICKENS, Andrew St Lawrence John. b 63. Mert Coll Ox BA85. Qu Coll Birm 89. **d** 92 **p** 93. C Birchfield *Birm* 92-96; Perm to Offic 96-97; Zambia from 97. *UCZ Theological College, PO Box 20429, Kitwe, Zambia*

WICKENS, John Philip. b 33. Open Univ BA76. K Coll Lon 57. **d** 61 **p** 62. C Hatcham Park All SS *S'wark* 61-64; USA 64-66; Tutor Richmond Fellowship Coll 66-95; Hon C Sutton Ch Ch *S'wark* 68-83; Hon C Benhilton 83-95; rtd 95. *West Villa, 196 West Malvern Road, West Malvern, Worcs WR14 4AZ* Tel (01684) 574043

WICKENS, Mrs Moira. b 56. S Dios Minl Tr Scheme 91. **d** 94. NSM Ifield *Chich* 94-96; C Saltdean from 96. *129 Rodmell Avenue, Saltdean, Brighton BN2 8PH* Tel (01273) 309546

WICKHAM, Lionel Ralph. b 32. LRAM St Cath Coll Cam BA57 MA61 PhD. Westcott Ho Cam 57. **d** 59 **p** 60. C Boston *Linc* 59-61; Tutor Cuddesdon Coll 61-63; V Cross Stone *Wakef* 63-67; Lect Th Southn Univ 67-78; Sen Lect 78-81; V Honley 81-87; Lect Cam Univ from 87; NSM W Wratting *Ely* from 89; NSM Weston Colville from 89. *The Vicarage, The Causeway, West Wratting, Cambridge CB1 5NA* Tel (01223) 290001

WICKHAM, Nicholas John. b 27. Trin Coll Cam BA51 MA56. Coll of Resurr Mirfield 54 Ox NSM Course 85. **d** 87 **p** 88. NSM Banbury *Ox* 87-92; rtd 92. *19 Britannia Wharf, Britannia Road, Banbury, Oxon OX16 8DS* Tel (01295) 256537

WICKHAM, Canon Norman George. b 25. Kelham Th Coll 42. **d** 51 **p** 52. C Syston *Leic* 51-54; V Leic St Gabr 54-57; R Wingerworth *Derby* 57-69; TP Edin St Jo *Edin* 69-79; Can and Vice-Provost St Mary's Cathl Edin 74-79; R Edin Ch Ch 79-88; Can St Mary's Cathl 86-91; rtd 88; Hon Can St Mary's Cathl *Edin* from 91. *Linton Mill, Mill Wynd, East Linton, East Lothian EH40 3AE* Tel (01620) 860142

WICKINGS, Luke Iden. b 59. Sheff Poly BA81. Oak Hill Th Coll BA90. **d** 90 **p** 91. C Fulham St Mary N End *Lon* 90-94; C Bletchley *Ox* from 94. *1 Ashburnam Place, Bletchley, Milton Keynes MK3 7TR* Tel (01908) 371373

WICKS, Christopher Blair. b 59. BA. Oak Hill Th Coll 85. **d** 88 **p** 89. C Edmonton All SS w St Mich *Lon* 88-92; C Southborough St Pet w Ch Ch and St Matt *Roch* 92-96; TV from 96. *72 Powder Mill Lane, Southborough, Tunbridge Wells, Kent TN4 9EJ* Tel (01892) 529098

WICKSTEAD, Gavin John. b 46. St Chad's Coll Dur BA67. Linc Th Coll 82. **d** 84 **p** 85. C Louth *Linc* 84-87; P-in-c E Markham and Askham *S'well* 87-89; P-in-c Headon w Upton 87-89; P-in-c Grove 87-89; R E Markham w Askham, Headon w Upton and Grove 90-92; P-in-c Skegness and Winthorpe *Linc* 92-97; R from 97. *The Rectory, 31 Lumley Avenue, Skegness, Lincs PE25 2AT* Tel (01754) 760566

WIDDAS, Preb John Anderson. b 38. Kelham Th Coll 58. **d** 63 **p** 64. C Willenhall H Trin *Lich* 63-66; C Tamworth 66-69; V 86-96; V Chesterton 69-74; R Lich St Chad 74-86; RD Lich 77-86; Preb Lich Cathl from 80; P-in-c Gentleshaw 80-82; P-in-c Farewell 80-82; RD Tamworth 91-95; V Walsall Wood from 96. *The Vicarage, St John's Close, Walsall Wood, Walsall WS9 9LP* Tel (01543) 372284

WIDDECOMBE, Canon Malcolm Murray. b 37. Tyndale Hall Bris 57. **d** 62 **p** 63. C Bris H Trin *Bris* 62-65; C Barton Hill St Luke w Ch Ch 65-67; P-in-c Bris St Phil and St Jacob w Em 67-74; V from 74; RD Bris City 79-85; Hon Can Bris Cathl from 86. *The Vicarage, 7 King's Drive, Bristol BS7 8JW* Tel 0117-924 3169

WIDDESS, Mrs Margaret Jennifer. b 48. Bedf Coll Lon BA70 Clare Coll Cam PGCE75. EAMTC 94. **d** 97. NSM Cambridge St Botolph *Ely* from 97. *69 Gwydir Street, Cambridge CB1 2LG* Tel (01223) 313908

WIDDICOMBE, Alexander Charles Ernest. b 11. Jes Coll Cam BA32 MA36. Wells Th Coll 33. **d** 34 **p** 35. C Rock Ferry *Ches* 34-35; C Audlem 35-36; Min Can Ely Cathl *Ely* 36-39; S Africa 39-59; R Flempton w Hengrave and Lackford *St E* 59-62; C-in-c Bury St Edmunds St Geo CD 62-66; R Chedburgh w Depden and Rede 66-71; S Africa from 72; rtd 79. *PO Box 20, Saldanha, 7395 South Africa* Tel Vredenburg (2281) 42662

WIDDOWS, David Charles Roland. b 52. Hertf Coll Ox BA75 MA79. St Jo Coll Nottm BA77. **d** 79 **p** 80. C Blackley St Andr *Man* 79-83; P-in-c Rochdale Deeplish St Luke 83-84; V 84-92; TR Stoke Gifford *Bris* from 92. *The Vicarage, 24 North Road, Stoke Gifford, Bristol BS12 6PB* Tel 0117-923 6395 or 969 2486

WIDDOWS, Edward John. b 45. Lon Coll of Div 66. **d** 70 **p** 71. C Formby St Pet *Liv* 70-72; C Uckfield *Chich* 72-73; C Isfield 72-73; C Lt Horsted 72-73; C Babbacombe *Ex* 73-76; V Sithney *Truro* 76-78; RD Kerrier 77-78; V Bude Haven 78-84; P-in-c Laneast w St Clether and Tresmere 84-85; P-in-c N Hill w Altarnon, Bolventor and Lewannick 84-85; P-in-c Boyton w N Tamerton 84-85; P-in-c N Petherwin 84-85; R Collingham w S Scarle and Besthorpe and Girton *S'well* 85-92; R Guernsey St Michel du Valle *Win* from 92. *The Rectory, L'Abbaye, Vale, Guernsey, Channel Islands GY3 5SF* Tel (01481) 44088

WIDDOWS, Heather Susan. b 45. Moray Ord Course. **d** 96 **p** 97. NSM Poolewe *Mor* from 96. *2 Fasaich, Gairloch, Ross-shire IV21 2BD* Tel (01445) 712176

WIDDOWS, John Christopher (Kit). b 46. Trin Coll Cam BA69 MA72. Cuddesdon Coll 69. **d** 71 **p** 72. C Herrington *Dur* 71-76; Chapl Nat Exhibition Cen 76-80; TV Chelmsley Wood *Birm* 76-80; V Halifax St Hilda *Wakef* 80-95; RD Halifax 92-95; Newc Cen Deanery *Newc* from 95; RD Newc Cen from 95; C-in-c Master Newc St Thos Prop Chpl from 95. *9 Chester Crescent, Newcastle upon Tyne NE2 1DH* Tel 0191-232 9789

WIDDOWSON, Charles Leonard. b 28. ALCD62. **d** 62 **p** 63. C Radcliffe-on-Trent *S'well* 62-66; R Newark Ch Ch 66-69; Australia from 69; rtd 93. *241 Tooronga Road, Malvern, Victoria, Australia 3144* Tel Melbourne (3) 824-7086

WIDDOWSON, Robert William. b 47. Linc Th Coll 83. **d** 85 **p** 86. C Syston *Leic* 85-88; R Husbands Bosworth w Mowsley and Knaptoft etc 88-93; R Asfordby from 93; P-in-c Ab Kettleby Gp from 93; P-in-c Old Dalby and Nether Broughton from 95. *The Rectory, Church Lane, Asfordby, Melton Mowbray, Leics LE14 3RU* Tel (01664) 812327

WIFFEN, Richard Austin. b 58. St Pet Coll Ox BA80. Trin Coll Bris BA90. **d** 90 **p** 91. C Bowdon *Ches* 90-93; C Ellesmere Port 93-94; TV from 94. *4 Deeside Close, Ellesmere Port, South Wirral L65 6TH* Tel 0151-355 5661

WIFFEN, Susan Elizabeth. b 51. Edin Th Coll 93. **d** 96 **p** 97. NSM Jedburgh *Edin* from 96. *26 South Myrescroft, Ancrum, Jedburgh, Roxburghshire TD8 6XE* Tel (01835) 53298

WIGFIELD, Thomas Henry Paul. b 26. Edin Th Coll 46. **d** 49 **p** 50. C Seaham w Seaham Harbour *Dur* 49-52; C Dur St Marg 52-54; V Fatfield 54-63; Asst Dir Chr TV Cen 63-79; Perm to Offic *Lon*

63-91; Perm to Offic *St Alb* 66-91; Hd of Services Foundn for Chr Communication 79-84; Chs' Liaison Officer 84-91; rtd 91. *16 Fishers Field, Buckingham MK18 1SF* Tel (01280) 817893

WIGGEN, Richard Martin. b 42. Open Univ BA78 Hull Univ MA86. Qu Coll Birm 64. **d** 67 **p** 68. C Penistone w Midhope *Wakef* 67-70; C Leeds St Pet *Ripon* 70-73; Asst Youth Chapl *Glouc* 73-76; Youth Officer *Liv* 76-80; V Kirkstall *Ripon* 80-90; V Meanwood from 90. *Meanwood Vicarage, 9 Parkside Green, Leeds LS6 4NY* Tel 0113-275 7885

WIGGINS, Karl Patrick. b 38. FRICS64 Lon Univ BD72. Trin Coll Bris 71. **d** 72 **p** 73. C Hildenborough *Roch* 72-76; Hon C Reading St Barn *Ox* 76-78; Lic to Offic 78-83; NSM Beech Hill, Grazeley and Spencers Wood from 83. *93 Crescent Road, Reading RG1 5SC* Tel 0118-966 3832

WIGGINTON, Canon Peter Walpole. b 20. Dur Univ LTh44. Edin Th Coll 40. **d** 43 **p** 44. C Derby St Jas *Derby* 43-46; C Brimington 46; C Gedling *S'well* 46-49; PV S'well Minster 49-52; V Rolleston w Morton 52-56; R W Keal *Linc* 56-83; R E Keal 57-83; RD Bolingbroke 66-88; Can and Preb Linc Cathl 77-88; R E and W Keal 83-88; R Bolingbroke 83-88; R Toynton All Saints w Toynton St Peter 83-88; rtd 88; Chapl Trin Hosp Retford from 88. *The Rectory Farm, Rectory Road, Retford, Notts DN22 7AY* Tel (01777) 860352

WIGGLESWORTH, Mark. b 60. Clare Coll Cam BA82. St Jo Coll Nottm DTS91 DipMM92. **d** 92 **p** 93. C Brinsworth w Catcliffe *Sheff* 92-93; C Brinsworth w Catcliffe and Treeton 93-95; C Goole 95-96; V Askern from 96. *The Vicarage, Askern, Doncaster, S Yorkshire DN6 0PH* Tel (01302) 700404

WIGGS, Robert James. b 50. Pemb Coll Cam BA72 MA CertEd. Qu Coll Birm 78. **d** 80 **p** 81. C Stratford St Jo and Ch Ch w Forest Gate St Jas *Chelmsf* 80-83; C E Ham w Upton Park St Alb 83-86; TV 86-91; TR Grays Thurrock from 91. *The Rectory, 10 High View Avenue, Grays, Essex RM17 6RU* Tel (01375) 373215

WIGHT, Dennis Marley. b 53. Southn Univ BTh87. Sarum & Wells Th Coll 82. **d** 85 **p** 86. C Gillingham *Sarum* 85-87; Appeals Org CECS from 87; Perm to Offic *Birm* 89-90; V Coseley Ch Ch *Lich* 90-93; V Coseley *Worc* 93-94; R Stoke Prior, Wychbold and Upton Warren from 94; RD Droitwich from 96. *The Rectory, Fish House Lane, Stoke Prior, Bromsgrove, Worcs B60 4JT* Tel (01527) 832501

WIGHT (née JONES), Mrs Sian Hilary. b 54. CertEd75 Birm Univ BEd76 Southn Univ BTh87. Sarum & Wells Th Coll 82. **dss** 85 **d** 87 **p** 94. Ex St Sidwell and St Matt *Ex* 85-87; Par Dn 87-88; Perm to Offic *Lich* 89-90 and 93-96; Hon Par Dn Coseley Ch Ch 90-93; Hon Par Dn Coseley *Worc* 93-94; NSM Stoke Prior, Wychbold and Upton Warren from 94. *The Rectory, Fish House Lane, Stoke Prior, Bromsgrove, Worcs B60 4JT* Tel (01527) 832501

WIGHTMAN, The Very Revd William David. b 39. Birm Univ BA61. Wells Th Coll 61. **d** 63 **p** 64. C Rotherham *Sheff* 63-67; C Castle Church *Lich* 67-70; V Buttershaw St Aid *Bradf* 70-76; V Cullingworth 76-83; R Peterhead *Ab* 83-91; R Strichen 90-91; R Old Deer 90-91; R Longside 90-91; Provost St Andr Cathl from 91; R Aberdeen St Andr from 91; P-in-c Aberdeen St Ninian from 91; Hon Can Ch Ch Cathl Connecticut from 91. *15 Morningfield Road, Aberdeen AB15 4AP* Tel (01224) 314765 or 640119

WIGLEY, Brian Arthur. b 31. Qu Coll Birm. **d** 82 **p** 83. C Houghton le Spring *Dur* 82-85; C Louth *Linc* 85-86; TV 86-89; Chapl City Hosp NHS Trust Birm 89-95; rtd 95; Perm to Offic *Ex* from 95. *3 Willows Close, Frogmore, Kingsbridge, Devon TQ7 2NY* Tel (01548) 531374

WIGLEY, Canon Harry Maxwell (Max). b 38. Oak Hill Th Coll 61. **d** 64 **p** 65. C Upton (Overchurch) *Ches* 64-67; C Gateacre *Liv* 67-69; C Chadderton Ch Ch *Man* 67; V Gt Horton *Bradf* 69-88; Hon Can Bradf Cathl from 85; V Pudsey St Lawr and St Paul 88-96; V Yeadon St Jo from 96. *St John's Vicarage, Barcroft Grove, Yeadon, Leeds LS19 7SE* Tel 0113-250 2272

WIGLEY, Ms Jennifer. b 53. Bris Univ BA74 Birm Univ MA75 Ox Univ CertEd76. Qu Coll Birm 86. **d** 87 **p** 97. C Llangollen w Trevor and Llantysilio *St As* 87-89; C Swansea St Jas *S & B* 89-94; NSM Aberystwyth *St D* from 95. *39 Maesceinion, Waunfawr, Aberystwyth SY23 3QQ* Tel (01970) 617296

WIGRAM, Andrew Oswald. b 39. Lon Univ BD64. Bps' Coll Cheshunt 61. **d** 64 **p** 65. C Marton-in-Cleveland *York* 64-69; Kenya 69-82; V Westcliff St Mich *Chelmsf* 82-95; RD Southend-on-Sea 89-94; R Cropwell Bishop w Colston Bassett, Granby etc *S'well* from 95. *The Vicarage, 2 Dobbin Close, Cropwell Bishop, Nottingham NG12 3GR* Tel 0115-989 3172

WIGRAM, Canon Sir Clifford Woolmore, Bt. b 11. Trin Coll Cam BA32 MA36. Ely Th Coll 33. **d** 34 **p** 35. C Brondesbury St Anne *Lon* 34-37; Chapl Ely Th Coll 37-40; Perm to Offic *Ox* 40; C Long Ashton *B & W* 40-42; C Kensington St Jo *Lon* 42-45; V Marston w Warkworth *Pet* 45-75; V Marston St Lawrence w Warkworth and Thenford 75-83; Can Pet Cathl 73-83; rtd 83; Perm to Offic *B & W* 84-94; Perm to Offic *Pet* from 94. *Flat 8, Emden House, Barton Lane, Headington, Oxford OX3 9JU* Tel (01865) 750887

WIGRAM, Miss Ruth Margaret. b 41. CertEd63. Cranmer Hall Dur 83. **dss** 84 **d** 87 **p** 94. Shipley St Paul and Frizinghall *Bradf* 84-87; Par Dn 87-90; Asst Dioc Dir of Ords 90-96; C Skipton H Trin 90-96; V Easby w Brompton on Swale and Bolton on Swale *Ripon* from 96. *The Vicarage, St Paul's Drive, Brompton on Swale, Richmond, N Yorkshire DL10 7HQ* Tel (01748) 811840

WIGSTON, Kenneth Edmund. b 28. Lich Th Coll 55. **d** 58 **p** 59. C Sheff Sharrow *Sheff* 58-61; C Kidlington *Ox* 61-68; R Airdrie *Glas* 68-78; R Gartcosh 68-78; R Glas St Oswald 78-85; R Onich *Arg* 85-94; R Glencoe 85-94; R Ballachulish 85-94; rtd 94; Perm to Offic *Arg* from 94. *Old Croft Cottage, 18 Tighphuirt, Glencoe, Argyll PA39 4HN* Tel (01855) 811503

WIKELEY, Canon John Roger Ian. b 41. AKC64. **d** 65 **p** 66. C Southport H Trin *Liv* 65-69; C Padgate Ch Ch 69-71; TV Padgate 71-73; R 73-74; TR 74-85; TR W Derby St Mary from 85; AD W Derby from 89; Hon Can Liv Cathl from 94. *The Rectory, West Derby, Liverpool L12 5EA* Tel 0151-256 6600

WIKNER, Richard Hugh. b 46. MSI. St Alb Minl Tr Scheme 79. **d** 94 **p** 95. NSM Lt Heath *St Alb* from 94. *Koinonia, 5 The Avenue, Potters Bar, Herts EN6 1EG* Tel (01707) 650437

WILBOURNE, David Jeffrey. b 55. Jes Coll Cam BA78 MA82. Westcott Ho Cam 79. **d** 81 **p** 82. C Stainton-in-Cleveland *York* 81-85; Chapl Asst Hemlington Hosp 81-85; R Monk Fryston and S Milford *York* 85-91; Abp's Dom Chapl from 91; Dir of Ords from 91. *Brew House Cottage, Bishopthorpe, York YO2 1QE, or Bishopthorpe Palace, Bishopthorpe, York YO2 1QE* Tel York (01904) 706822 or 707021 Fax 709204

WILBOURNE, Geoffrey Owen. b 29. Lich Th Coll 60. **d** 62 **p** 63. C Marfleet *York* 62-65; V Ellerton Priory w Aughton and E Cottingwith 65-70; TV Scalby w Ravenscar and Staintondale 70-73; V Kingston upon Hull St Nic 73-76; V Keyingham 76-85; V Hemingbrough 85-91; rtd 91; Perm to Offic *Derby* from 91. *4 Eastleigh Court, Hasland, Chesterfield, Derbyshire S41 0BH* Tel (01246) 239939

WILBRAHAM, David. b 59. Oak Hill Th Coll BA88. **d** 88 **p** 89. C Ince Ch Ch *Liv* 88-91; C St Helens St Helen 91-93; Perm to Offic *Guildf* from 93. *28 Tyndalls Estate, Hindhead, Surrey GU26 6AP*

WILBY, Mrs Jean (Sister Davina). b 38. Open Univ BA82. Wycliffe Hall Ox 83. **dss** 85 **d** 87 **p** 94. Maidenhead St Andr and St Mary *Ox* 85-87; C 87; TD Hermitage and Hampstead Norreys, Cold Ash etc 87-91; Lic to Offic 92-95; All SS Convent Ox 91-95; NSM Iffley *Ox* 94-95; C Denham from 95. *St Francis House, Oxford Road, Uxbridge, Middx UB9 4DW* Tel (01895) 258867

WILBY, Timothy David. b 59. Univ Coll Dur BA80 MA87. Ripon Coll Cuddesdon 81. **d** 83 **p** 84. C Standish *Blackb* 83-86; CF 86-89; V Chorley All SS *Blackb* 89-95; V Penwortham St Leon from 95. *St Leonard's Vicarage, Marshall's Brow, Penwortham, Preston PR1 9HY* Tel (01772) 742367

WILBY, Mrs Wendy Ann. b 49. ARCM69 LRAM72 St Hugh's Coll Ox BA71. NE Ord Course. **d** 90 **p** 94. Par Dn Barwick in Elmet *Ripon* 90-93; C High Harrogate St Pet 93-94; V Birstwith 94; P-in-c from 94; Chapl St Aid Sch Harrogate from 94. *The Vicarage, Wreaks Road, Birstwith, Harrogate, N Yorkshire HG3 3AN* Tel (01423) 772315

WILCOCK, Michael Jarvis. b 32. Dur Univ BA54. Tyndale Hall Bris 60. **d** 62 **p** 63. C Southport Ch Ch *Liv* 62-65; C St Marylebone All So w SS Pet and Jo *Lon* 65-69; V Maidstone St Faith *Cant* 69-77; Dir Past Studies Trin Coll Bris 77-82; V Dur St Nic *Dur* from 82. *St Nicholas' Vicarage, Kepier Rise, Durham DH1 1JP* Tel 0191-384 6066

WILCOCK, Paul Trevor. b 59. Bris Univ BA. Trin Coll Bris 83. **d** 87 **p** 88. C Kirkheaton *Wakef* 87-90; Chapl Huddersfield Poly 90-92; Chapl Huddersfield Univ 92-93; Dir Student Services from 93; NSM Huddersfield H Trin from 92. *Huddersfield University, Queensgate, Huddersfield HD1 3DH* Tel (01484) 422288

WILCOCKSON, Stephen Anthony. b 51. Nottm Univ BA73 Ox Univ BA75 MA81. Wycliffe Hall Ox 73. **d** 76 **p** 77. C Pudsey St Lawr *Bradf* 76-78; C Wandsworth All SS *S'wark* 78-81; V Rock Ferry *Ches* 81-86; V Lache cum Saltney 86-95; V Howell Hill *Guildf* from 95. *St Paul's Vicarage, 17 Northey Avenue, Cheam, Surrey SM2 7HS* Tel 0181-224 9927

WILCOX, Anthony Gordon (Tony). b 41. Lon Coll of Div LTh67 ALCD67. **d** 67 **p** 68. C Cheltenham Ch Ch *Glouc* 67-72; C Beccles St Mich *St E* 72-74; TV 74-81; V Ipswich All SS from 81. *All Saints' Vicarage, 264 Norwich Road, Ipswich IP1 4BT* Tel (01473) 252975

WILCOX, Brian Howard. b 46. Westcott Ho Cam 71. **d** 73 **p** 74. C Kettering SS Pet and Paul *Pet* 73-78; V Eye 78-82; R Clipston w Naseby and Haselbech w Kelmarsh 82-90; V Hornsea w Atwick *York* from 90; RD N Holderness from 95. *The Vicarage, 9 Newbeggin, Hornsea, N Humberside HU18 1AB* Tel (01964) 532531

WILCOX, Colin John. b 43. St Mich Coll Llan 84. **d** 86 **p** 87. C Newport St Andr *Mon* 86-88; C Llanmartin 88-90; TV 90-92; V Griffithstown from 92. *St Hilda's Vicarage, 2 Sunnybank Road, Griffithstown, Pontypool NP4 5LT* Tel (01495) 763641

✠**WILCOX, The Rt Revd David Peter.** b 30. St Jo Coll Ox BA52 MA56. Linc Th Coll 52. **d** 54 **p** 55 **c** 86. C St Helier *S'wark* 54-56; C Ox St Mary V *Ox* 56-59; Tutor Linc Th Coll 59-60; Chapl 60-61; Sub-Warden 61-63; India 64-70; R Gt w Lt Gransden *Ely* 70-72; Can Res Derby Cathl *Derby* 72-77; Warden EMMTC 73-77; Prin Ripon Coll Cuddesdon 77-85; V Cuddesdon *Ox* 77-85; Suff Bp Dorking *Guildf* 86-95; rtd 95; Asst Bp Chich from

95. *4 The Court, Hoo Gardens, Willingdon, Eastbourne, E Sussex BN20 9AX*

WILCOX, David Thomas Richard. b 42. Down Coll Cam BA63 Regent's Park Coll Ox BA66 Tubingen Univ. **d** 95 **p** 96. C Bris St Mary Redcliffe w Temple etc *Bris* 95-97; TV Yate New Town from 97. *The Vicarage, Shorthill Road, Westerleigh, Bristol BS17 4QN* Tel (01454) 312152

WILCOX, Graham James. b 43. Qu Coll Ox BA64 MA75. Ridley Hall Cam 64. **d** 66 **p** 67. C Edgbaston St Aug *Birm* 66-69; C Sheldon 69-72; Asst Chapl Wrekin Coll Shropshire 72-74; C Asterby w Goulceby *Linc* 74-77; P-in-c 77; R 77-81; R Benniworth w Market Stainton and Ranby 77-81; R Donington on Bain 77-81; R Stenigot 77-81; R Gayton le Wold w Biscathorpe 77-81; V Scamblesby w Cawkwell 77-81; R Asterby Gp 81-88; V Sutton le Marsh 88-90; R Sutton, Huttoft and Anderby from 90. *The Vicarage, Huttoft Road, Mablethorpe, Lincs LN12 2RU* Tel (01507) 441169

WILCOX, Haydon Howard. b 56. Sarum & Wells Th Coll. **d** 82 **p** 83. C Fishponds St Jo *Bris* 82-85; TV Hucknall Torkard *S'well* 85-91; R Bilsthorpe from 91; R Eakring from 91; P-in-c Maplebeck from 91; P-in-c Winkburn from 91. *The Rectory, Church Hill, Bilsthorpe, Newark, Notts NG22 8RU* Tel (01623) 870256

WILCOX, Canon Hugh Edwin. b 37. St Edm Hall Ox BA62 MA66. St Steph Ho Ox 62. **d** 64 **p** 65. C Colchester St Jas, All SS, St Nic and St Runwald *Chelmsf* 64-66; Hon C Clifton St Paul *Bris* 66-68; SCM 66-68; Sec Internat Dept BCC 68-76; Asst Gen Sec 74-76; V Ware St Mary *St Alb* from 76; Hon Can St Alb from 96. *The Vicarage, 31 Thunder Court, Milton Road, Ware, Herts SG12 0PT* Tel (01920) 464817

WILCOX, Jeffry Reed. b 40. K Coll Lon AKC65 BA78. **d** 66 **p** 67. C Ryhope *Dur* 66-69; C Cockerton 69-71; P-in-c Pallion 71-82; R Streatham St Leon *S'wark* from 82; RD Streatham from 92. *The Rectory, 1 Becmead Avenue, London SW16 1UH* Tel 0181-769 4366 or 769 1216

WILCOX, Joe. b 21. ACT LTh62 Lich Th Coll. **d** 62 **p** 63. C Tamworth *Lich* 62-66; C Tettenhall Wood 66-67; V Leek St Luke 67-75; P-in-c Ellington *Ely* 75-80; P-in-c Spaldwick w Barham and Woolley 75-80; P-in-c Easton 75-80; P-in-c Grafham 75-80; R Holywell w Needingworth 80-86; rtd 86; Perm to Offic *Ely* from 87. *16 Silver Birch Avenue, St Ives, Huntingdon, Cambs PE17 4TS* Tel (01480) 496846

WILCOX, John Bower. b 28. AKC55. **d** 58 **p** 59. C Orford St Marg *Liv* 58-60; C W Derby St Mary 60-63; Ind Chapl *Linc* 63-74; R Aisthorpe w W Thorpe and Scampton 63-74; R Brattleby 64-74; Ind Chapl *York* 74-89; P-in-c Middlesbrough St Cuth 89-93; Urban Development Officer 89-93; rtd 93; Perm to Offic *York* from 93. *5 Duncan Avenue, Redcar, Cleveland TS10 5BX* Tel (01642) 489683

WILCOX, Peter Jonathan. b 61. St Jo Coll Dur BA84 MA91 St Jo Coll Ox DPhil93. Ridley Hall Cam BA86. **d** 87 **p** 88. C Preston on Tees *Dur* 87-90; NSM Ox St Giles and SS Phil and Jas w St Marg *Ox* 90-93; TV Gateshead *Dur* from 93; Dir Urban Miss Cen Cranmer Hall from 93. *St Columba House, Peterborough Close, Gateshead, Tyne & Wear NE8 1RB* Tel 0191-478 5116

WILCOX, Raymond Trevor. b 22. St D Coll Lamp BA47. **d** 48 **p** 49. C Llanfrechfa All SS *Mon* 48-50; C Griffithstown 50-52; C Walsall St Paul *Lich* 52-54; CF 54-57; P-in-c Bentley *Lich* 57-58; V 58-78; P-in-c Blithfield 78-84; P-in-c Colton 78-84; V Llanddewi Rhydderch w Llangattock-juxta-Usk etc *Mon* 84-87; rtd 87; Perm to Offic *Lich* from 91. *8 Orchard Close, Uttoxeter, Staffs ST14 7QZ* Tel (01889) 566308

WILD, Hilda Jean. b 48. Linc Th Coll CMinlStuds95. **d** 95 **p** 96. C Newark *S'well* from 95. *28 Harewood Avenue, Newark, Notts NG24 4AN* Tel (01636) 700396

WILD, Roger Bedingham Barratt. b 40. Hull Univ MA94. ALCD64. **d** 65 **p** 66. C Shipley St Pet *Bradf* 65-68; C Pudsey St Lawr 68-71; P-in-c Rawthorpe *Wakef* 71-73; V 73-78; V Ripon H Trin *Ripon* 78-93; RD Ripon 86-93; R Barwick in Elmet from 93. *The Rectory, Main Street, Barwick in Elmet, Leeds LS15 4JR* Tel 0113-281 2218

WILDE, David Wilson. b 37. Lon Coll of Div ALCD61 BD62. **d** 62 **p** 63. C Kirkheaton *Wakef* 62-66; C Attenborough w Chilwell *S'well* 66-72; P-in-c Bestwood Park 72-83; R Kimberley from 83. *The Rectory, Kimberley, Nottingham NG16 2LL* Tel 0115-938 3565

WILDEY, Ian Edward. b 51. St Chad's Coll Dur BA72. Coll of Resurr Mirfield 72. **d** 74 **p** 75. C Westgate Common *Wakef* 74-77; C Barnsley St Mary 77-81; V Ravensthorpe 81-95; R Barnsley St Mary from 95; Dir of Educn from 96. *The Rectory, 30 Victoria Road, Barnsley, S Yorkshire S70 2BU* Tel (01226) 282270

WILDING, Miss Anita Pamela. b 38. Blackpool and Fylde Coll of Further Tech TCert61. CMS Tr Coll Chislehurst 65. **dss** 89 **d** 92 **p** 93. CMS from 87; Kenya from 87. *St Andrew's College, PO Box 6, Kerugoya, Kenya* Tel Kerugoya (163) 21025

WILDING, David. b 43. K Coll Lon BD67 AKC67. **d** 68 **p** 69. C Thornhill *Wakef* 68-70; C Halifax St Jo Bapt 70-72; V Scholes 72-79; V Lightcliffe from 79. *The Vicarage, Wakefield Road, Lightcliffe, Halifax, W Yorkshire HX3 8TH* Tel (01422) 202424

WILDING, Joseph. b 14. Edin Th Coll 50. **d** 52 **p** 53. C Dumbarton *Glas* 52-56; R Alexandria 56-80; P-in-c 80-84; rtd 84; Perm to Offic *Blackb* from 84. *Ash House Farm, Ulnes Walton, Preston PR5 3LU*

WILDING, Michael Paul. b 57. Chich Th Coll 82. **d** 85 **p** 86. C Treboeth *S & B* 85-87; C Llangiwg 87-88; V Defynnog w Rhydybriw and Llandilo'r-fan from 88. *The Vicarage, Sennybank, Sennybridge, Brecon LD3 8PP* Tel (01874) 638927

WILDS, Canon Anthony Ronald (Tony). b 43. Dur Univ BA64. Bps' Coll Cheshunt 64. **d** 66 **p** 67. C Newport Pagnell *Ox* 66-72; Zambia 72-75; V Chandler's Ford *Win* 75-85; V Andover w Foxcott 85-97; RD Andover 89-94; Hon Can Win Cathl 91-97; TR Solihull *Birm* from 97. *The Rectory, Church Hill Road, Solihull, W Midlands B91 3RQ* Tel 0121-705 0069 or 705 5350

WILES, David James. b 50. Univ Coll Lon BSc72 K Coll Lon CertEd73. St Jo Coll Nottm 85. **d** 88 **p** 89. C Clapham Park St Steph *S'wark* 88-92; V Wimbledon St Luke from 92. *St Luke's Vicarage, 28 Farquhar Road, London SW19 8DA* Tel 0181-946 3396

WILES, Canon Prof Maurice Frank. b 23. FBA Ch Coll Cam BA47 MA52 DD. Ridley Hall Cam 48. **d** 50 **p** 51. C Stockport St Geo *Ches* 50-52; Chapl Ridley Hall Cam 52-55; Nigeria 55-59; Dean Clare Coll Cam 59-67; Lect Div Cam Univ 59-67; Prof Chr Doctrine K Coll Lon 67-70; Can Res Ch Ch *Ox* 70-91; Regius Prof Div Ox Univ 70-91; rtd 91. *11 Baytree Close, Oxford OX4 4DT* Tel (01865) 777091

WILKES, Jonathan Peter. b 66. Leic Poly BA88. Cuddesdon Coll BTh93 Bossey Ecum Inst Geneva 94. **d** 96 **p** 97. C Hackney *Lon* from 96. *21B Blurton Road, London E5 0NL* Tel 0181-533 2454

WILKES, Canon Keith Reid. b 30. FBIM75 Pemb Coll Cam BA53 MA60 Bris Univ MA71 Bris Poly DipEdMan74. Linc Th Coll 53. **d** 55 **p** 56. C Welwyn Garden City *St Alb* 55-59; Chapl St Fran Hall Birm Univ 59-64; SCM Sec Birm Univ 59-64; Chapl Birm Coll Adv Tech 62-64; Chapl St Matthias's Coll Bris 64-69; Dir of Educn *Bris* 70-80; Chapl Bris Cathl 70-74; Hon Can Bris Cathl 74-80; R Bris Ch Ch w St Ewen 70-74; R Bris Ch Ch w St Ewen and All SS 74-80; Hon Chapl Bp Bris 73-76; Provost Woodard Schs (Midl Division) 80-94; Perm to Offic *S'well* 80-94; Perm to Offic *Derby* 80-94; Lic to Offic *Lich* 80-94; rtd 94. *The Mount, St John's Hill, Ellesmere, Shropshire SY12 0EY* Tel (01691) 622466

WILKES, Robert Anthony (Bob). b 48. Trin Coll Ox BA70 MA73. Wycliffe Hall Ox 71. **d** 74 **p** 75. C Netherton *Liv* 74-77; V 77-81; Bp's Dom Chapl 81-85; CMS from 85; Pakistan 85-86; Regional Sec Middle E and Pakistan from 87; Perm to Offic *S'wark* 87-90; Perm to Offic *Ox* from 90. *28 Lonsdale Road, Oxford OX2 7EW* Tel (01865) 59362/0171-928 8681 Fax 0171-401 3215

WILKIE, Alan James. b 17. Chich Th Coll 39. **d** 42 **p** 43. C Wednesbury St Paul Wood Green *Lich* 42-44; C Porthill 44-52; C Stoke-upon-Trent 52-54; Chapl Stoke-on-Trent City Gen Hosp 52-54; Lic to Offic *Guildf* 54-65; Lic to Offic *Nor* 66-68; Hd Badingham Coll Leatherhead 54-65; Wymondham 65-68; V Lindale *Carl* 69-71; P-in-c Field Broughton 71; V Lindale w Field Broughton 71-85; rtd 85; Perm to Offic *Carl* from 85. *Fernlea, Beckermet, Cumbria CA21 2YF* Tel (01946) 841284

WILKIN, Kenneth. b 54. S'wark Ord Course 86 Wilson Carlile Coll. **d** 88 **p** 89. C Wolverhampton *Lich* 88-92; V W Bromwich St Andr w Ch Ch from 92. *St Andrew's Vicarage, Oakwood Street, West Bromwich, W Midlands B70 9SN* Tel 0121-553 1871

WILKIN, Paul John. b 56. Linc Th Coll 88. **d** 90 **p** 91. C Leavesden All SS *St Alb* 90-93; C Jersey St Brelade *Win* from 93. *The Parsonage, High Street, St Aubin, Jersey, Channel Islands JE3 8BR* Tel (01534) 44009 E-mail branwall@itl.net

WILKIN, Rose Josephine. *See* HUDSON-WILKIN, Mrs Rose Josephine

WILKINS, Mrs Janice Joy. b 49. St D Coll Lamp 90. **d** 93 **p** 97. NSM Tredegar St Jas *Mon* 93-96; NSM Newbridge from 96. *Ty-Heddwch, Fflorens Road, Newbridge, Newport NP1 4DU* Tel (01495) 245199

WILKINS, Ralph Herbert. b 29. Lon Univ BD61. St Aug Coll Cant 72. **d** 73 **p** 74. C Epsom Common Ch Ch *Guildf* 73-76; C Haslemere 77-79; P-in-c Market Lavington and Easterton *Sarum* 79-82; V 82-90; P-in-c Puddletown and Tolpuddle 90-94; P-in-c Milborne St Andrew w Dewlish 92-94; P-in-c Piddletrenthide w Plush, Alton Pancras etc 92-94; rtd 94; Perm to Offic *Ab* from 94. *Spiggie Lodge, Scousburgh, Dunrossness, Shetland ZE2 9JE* Tel (01950) 60563

WILKINS, Miss Susan Stafford (Sue). b 47. Dur Univ BA. Sarum Th Coll. **dss** 82 **d** 87 **p** 94. Redlynch and Morgan's Vale *Sarum* 82-87; Hon Par Dn 87-88; Hon Par Dn Bemerton 88-90; Par Dn Hilperton w Whaddon and Staverton etc 90-94; C 94; TV Worle *B & W* from 94. *The Vicarage, 6 Gannet Road, Worle, Weston-super-Mare, Avon BS22 8UR* Tel (01934) 521765

WILKINS, Vernon Gregory. b 53. Trin Coll Cam MA74 Ox Univ BA88. Wycliffe Hall Ox 86. **d** 89 **p** 90. C Boscombe St Jo *Win* 89-91; C Bursledon 91-94; V Ramsgate St Luke *Cant* from 94. *St Luke's Vicarage, St Luke's Avenue, Ramsgate, Kent CT11 7JX* Tel (01843) 592562

WILKINSON, Adrian Mark. b 68. TCD BA90 NUI HDipEd91. CITC BTh94. **d** 94 **p** 95. C Douglas Union w Frankfield *C, C & R* 94-97; I Dunboyne w Kilcock, Maynooth, Moyglare etc *M & K* from 97; Chapl St Patr Coll Maynooth from 97; Min Can St Patr

Cathl Dublin from 97. *The Rectory, Lismahon, Batterstown, Co Meath, Irish Republic* Tel Dublin (1) 825 0020 Fax as telephone

WILKINSON, Canon Alan Bassindale. b 31. St Cath Coll Cam BA54 MA58 PhD59 DD97. Coll of Resurr Mirfield 57. **d** 59 **p** 60. C Kilburn St Aug *Lon* 59-61; Chapl St Cath Coll Cam 61-67; V Barrow Gurney *B & W* 67-70; Asst Chapl and Lect St Matthias's Coll Bris 67-70; Prin Chich Th Coll 70-74; Can and Preb Chich Cathl *Chich* 70-74; Warden Verulam Ho 74-75; Dir of Aux Min Tr *St Alb* 74-75; Sen Lect Crewe and Alsager Coll of HE 75-78; Hon C Alsager St Mary *Ches* 76-78; Dioc Dir of Tr *Ripon* 78-84; P-in-c Thornthwaite w Thruscross and Darley 84-88; Hon Can Ripon Cathl 84-88; Perm to Offic *Portsm* from 88; Hon P Portsm Cathl from 88; Hon Dioc Th from 93; Hon Chapl Portsm Cathl from 94; rtd 96. *Hope Cottage, 27 Great Southsea Street, Portsmouth PO5 3BY* Tel (01705) 825788

WILKINSON, Alice Margaret Marion. *See* BISHOP, Mrs Alice Margaret Marion

WILKINSON, Andrew Wilfrid. b 66. Nottm Univ BTh96. Linc Th Coll 93. **d** 96 **p** 97. C Longridge *Blackb* from 96. *94 Higher Road, Longridge, Preston PR3 3SY* Tel (01772) 784832

WILKINSON (née PHILPOTT), Mrs Barbara May. b 48. Leeds Univ BA69 CertEd70 MA90. N Ord Course 90. **d** 93 **p** 94. NSM Carleton and Lothersdale *Bradf* 93-96; C Steeton from 96; Asst Chapl Airedale Gen Hosp from 96. *37 Aire Valley Drive, Bradley, Keighley, W Yorkshire BD20 9HY* Tel (01535) 636339 or 657157

WILKINSON, David Andrew. b 62. Edge Hill Coll of HE BA83. Oak Hill Th Coll BA85. **d** 88 **p** 89. C Upton (Overchurch) *Ches* 88-91; C Fulham St Matt *Lon* 91-94; V Duffield *Derby* from 94. *St Alkmund's Vicarage, Vicarage Lane, Duffield, Belper, Derbyshire DE56 4EB* Tel (01332) 841168

WILKINSON, David Edward Paul. b 36. Univ of Wales (Swansea) BSc57. St Mich Coll Llan 57. **d** 59 **p** 60. C Brecon w Battle *S & B* 59-60; Min Can Brecon Cathl 60-66; R Llanelwedd w Llanfaredd, Cwmbach Llechryd etc 66-72; V Tycoch 72-74; Asst Master Churchmead Sch Datchet 75-82; Perm to Offic *Ox* 80-82; TV Seacroft *Ripon* from 82. *St Paul's Vicarage, 58 Whinmoor Crescent, Leeds LS14 1EW* Tel 0113-265 5649

WILKINSON, David James. b 45. St D Coll Lamp 65 Wycliffe Hall Ox 68. **d** 69 **p** 70. C Swansea St Thos and Kilvey *S & B* 69-73; C Clydach 73-76; R Llanbadarn Fawr, Llandegley and Llanfihangel etc 76-81; V Swansea St Nic 81-88; V Killay 88-94; V Ilston w Pennard from 94. *The Vicarage, 88 Pennard Road, Pennard, Swansea SA3 2AD* Tel (01792) 232928

WILKINSON, Edward. b 55. Cranmer Hall Dur 86. **d** 88 **p** 89. C Bishopwearmouth St Nic *Dur* 88-92; P-in-c Newbottle from 92. *The Vicarage, Newbottle, Houghton le Spring, Tyne & Wear DH4 4EP* Tel 0191-584 3244

WILKINSON, Edwin. b 29. Oak Hill Th Coll 53. **d** 56 **p** 57. C Blackb Ch Ch *Blackb* 56-58; C Cheltenham St Mark *Glouc* 58-61; V Tiverton St Geo *Ex* 61-66; V Rye Harbour *Chich* 66-73; V Camber and E Guldeford 73-79; V Westf 79-87; V Bexhill St Steph 87-93; rtd 93; Perm to Offic *Chich* from 93. *51 Anderida Road, Eastbourne, E Sussex BN22 0PZ* Tel (01323) 503083

WILKINSON, Guy Alexander. b 48. Magd Coll Cam BA69. Ripon Coll Cuddesdon 85. **d** 87 **p** 88. C Coventry Caludon *Cov* 87-90; P-in-c Ockham w Hatchford *Guildf* 90-91; R 91-94; Bp's Dom Chapl 90-94; V Small Heath *Birm* from 94. *St Aidan's Clergy House, 172 Herbert Road, Birmingham B10 0PR* Tel 0121-772 0318

WILKINSON, Canon James Noel Batthews. b 30. LRAM66 TCD BA53 MA65 BD65. CITC 55. **d** 55 **p** 56. C Dundonald *D & D* 55-57; C Lurgan Ch Ch 57-62; R Harrington *Carl* 62-66; C Antrim All SS *Conn* 66-70; I Belfast Ardoyne 70-79; Min Can Belf Cathl 72-88; RD M Belfast *Conn* 78-79; I Derryvolgie 79-93; Can Belf Cathl 88-93; rtd 93. *68 Orangefield Road, Belfast BT5 6DD* Tel (01232) 654075

WILKINSON, John Andrew. b 59. Pemb Coll Ox BA83 MA87 St Jo Coll Dur BA86. Cranmer Hall Dur 84. **d** 87 **p** 88. C Broadheath *Ches* 87-91; TV Worthing Ch the King *Chich* 91-97; Chapl Chantilly *Eur* from 97. *7A avenue du Bouteiller, 60500 Chantilly, France* Tel France (33) 3 44 58 53 22

WILKINSON, John David. b 36. AKC59. **d** 60 **p** 61. C Wythenshawe Wm Temple Ch CD *Man* 60-63; C Morley St Pet w Churwell *Wakef* 63-65; V Roberttown 65-75; V Battyeford 75-88; V Airedale w Fryston from 88. *The Vicarage, The Mount, Airedale, Castleford, W Yorkshire WF10 3JL* Tel (01977) 553157

WILKINSON, Canon John Donald. b 29. Mert Coll Ox BA54 MA56 Louvain Univ Belgium LTh59 Lon Univ PhD82 FSA80. Gen Th Sem (NY) Hon STD63 Cuddesdon Coll 54. **d** 56 **p** 57. C Stepney St Dunstan and All SS *Lon* 56-59; Jerusalem 61-63; Gen Ed USPG 63-69; Dean St Geo Coll Jerusalem 69-75; Can Jerusalem 73-75; P-in-c S Kensington H Trin w All SS *Lon* 75-78; Bp's Dir of Clergy Tr 75-79; Dir Br Sch of Archaeology Jerusalem 79-83; USA 83-91; NSM Kensington St Mary Abbots w St Geo *Lon* 91-94; rtd 94; Hon C St Marylebone St Cypr *Lon* from 94. *7 Tenniel Close, London W2 3LE* Tel 0171-229 9205 Fax as telephone

WILKINSON, John Lawrence. b 43. Ch Coll Cam BA65 MA69 Birm Univ MLitt91. Qu Coll Birm DipTh68 Gen Th Sem (NY) STB69. **d** 69 **p** 70. C Braunstone *Leic* 69-71; C Hodge Hill *Birm* 71-74; P-in-c Aston St Jas 75-84; Tutor Qu Coll Birm 85-95; Hon C Birm St Geo *Birm* 86-95; V Kings Heath from 95. *All Saints' Vicarage, 2 Vicarage Road, Birmingham B14 7RA* Tel 0121-444 1207

WILKINSON, John Stoddart. b 47. Univ of Wales (Cardiff) CQSW83. St D Coll Lamp DipTh70. **d** 70 **p** 71. C Kells *Carl* 70-72; C Barrow St Geo w St Luke 72-74; Perm to Offic *Mon* 74-89; Sub-Chapl HM Young Offender Inst Hewell Grange 89-90; Sub-Chapl HM Rem Cen Brockhill 89-90. *Address temp unknown*

WILKINSON, Jonathan Charles. b 61. Leeds Univ BA83. Wycliffe Hall Ox 85. **d** 87 **p** 88. C Plymouth St Andr w St Paul and St Geo *Ex* 87-90; C Oulton Broad *Nor* 90-93; V Hallwood *Ches* from 93. *The Vicarage, 6 Kirkstone Crescent, Runcorn, Cheshire WA7 3JQ* Tel (01928) 713101

WILKINSON, Miss Julia Mary. b 52. Cam Inst of Educn CertEd73 Open Univ BA85 Univ of Wales (Ban) BD89. Linc Th Coll CMM92. **d** 92 **p** 94. Par Dn High Wycombe *Ox* 92-94; C 94-96; TV from 96. *The Vicarage, Micklefield Road, High Wycombe, Bucks HP13 7HU* Tel (01494) 531141

WILKINSON, Canon Keith Howard. b 48. Hull Univ BA70 Em Coll Cam MA74 FRSA94. Westcott Ho Cam 74. **d** 76 **p** 77. C Pet St Jude *Pet* 76-79; Chapl Eton Coll 79-84; Perm to Offic *Pet* 82-94; Chapl Malvern Coll 84-89; Hd Master Berkhamsted Colleg Sch Herts 89-96; Lic to Offic *St Alb* 89-96; Hd Master K Sch Cant from 96; Hon Can Cant Cathl *Cant* from 96. *The King's School, Canterbury, Kent CT1 2ES* Tel (01227) 595501

WILKINSON, The Ven Kenneth Samuel. b 31. TCD BA60 MA69. CITC 60. **d** 60 **p** 61. C Dublin St Michan w St Paul *D & G* 60-63; Min Can St Patr Cathl Dublin 62-67; C Dublin Ch Ch Leeson Park *D & G* 63-67; I Killegney *C & O* 67-70; I Enniscorthy w Clone, Clonmore, Monart etc from 70; Preb Ferns Cathl 83-88; Adn Ferns from 88; Dio Dir Ords from 94. *The Rectory, Enniscorthy, Co Wexford, Irish Republic* Tel Enniscorthy (54) 33249 Fax as telephone

WILKINSON, Miss Marlene Sandra. b 45. SRN71 Huddersfield Poly NDN86 Leeds Univ DipTh91 Sheff Univ DBS93. Trin Coll Bris IDC78. **dss** 78 **d** 93 **p** 94. Wrose *Bradf* 78-82; Chapl St Luke's Hosp Bradf 78-82; Past Tutor Aston Tr Sch 79-81; W Yorkshire CECS 82-84; Westgate Common *Wakef* 84-86; E Ardsley 86-92; Wakef St Jo 92-94; NSM 93-94; C Barrow St Geo w St Luke *Carl* 94; TV from 94. *The Vicarage, 98A Roose Road, Barrow-in-Furness, Cumbria LA13 9RL* Tel (01229) 821258

WILKINSON, Michael Alan. b 27. Selw Coll Cam BA51. Westcott Ho Cam 52. **d** 53 **p** 54. C Swindon Ch Ch *Bris* 53-57; C Knowle St Barn 57-59; C Eltham St Jo *S'wark* 59-65; C Sydenham St Bart 65-77; Perm to Offic *Ex* 77-84; P-in-c Yealmpton 84-91; P-in-c Brixton 87-91; V Yealmpton and Brixton 91-97; RD Ivybridge 91-93; rtd 97. *The Old Forge, Kingston, Kingsbridge, Devon TQ7 4PT*

WILKINSON, Paul. b 51. Sarum & Wells Th Coll 75. **d** 78 **p** 79. C Allerton *Bradf* 78-80; C Baildon 80-83; V Hengoed w Gobowen *Lich* 83-90; V Potterne w Worton and Marston *Sarum* from 90; Chapl Roundway Hosp Devizes from 92. *The Vicarage, 4 Rookes Lane, Potterne, Devizes, Wilts SN10 5NF* Tel (01380) 723189

WILKINSON, Paul Martin. b 56. Brunel Univ BSc. Wycliffe Hall Ox 83. **d** 86 **p** 87. C Hinckley H Trin *Leic* 86-90; V Newbold on Avon *Cov* from 90. *The Vicarage, Main Street, Newbold, Rugby, Warks CV21 1HH* Tel (01788) 543055

WILKINSON, Peter David Lloyd. b 67. Trin Coll Ox BA89 MA93. Ridley Hall Cam BA94 CTM95. **d** 95 **p** 96. C Brampton St Thos *Derby* from 95. *1 Rhodesia Road, Chesterfield, Derbyshire S40 3AL* Tel (01246) 231089

WILKINSON, Peter Francis. b 20. Cuddesdon Coll 63. **d** 65 **p** 66. C Chobham w Valley End *Guildf* 65-78; V Yalding *Roch* 68-72; V Yalding w Collier Street 72-87; rtd 87; Perm to Offic *Chich* from 87; Perm to Offic *Roch* from 87. *Chartfield, Flimwell, Wadhurst, E Sussex TN5 7PA* Tel (01580) 870372

WILKINSON, Peter Howarth. b 32. St Pet Hall Ox BA54 MA58. Ridley Hall Cam 56. **d** 58 **p** 59. C Cheadle *Ches* 58-62; V Nettlebed *Ox* 62-68; rtd 68; Hon C Cheadle *Ches* 69-82. *10 Norbreck Avenue, Cheadle, Cheshire SK8 2ET* Tel 0161-428 7699

WILKINSON, Robert Ian (Bob). b 43. MIMunE73 MICE84 CEng73. Oak Hill NSM Course. **d** 88 **p** 89. NSM Hawkwell *Chelmsf* 88-89; NSM Thundersley 89-91; C New Thundersley 91-94; V Berechurch St Marg w St Mich from 94. *The Vicarage, 348 Mersea Road, Colchester CO2 8RA* Tel (01206) 576859

WILKINSON, Canon Robert Matthew. b 21. TCD BA46. CITC 47. **d** 47 **p** 48. C Limerick St Lawr w H Trin and St Jo *L & K* 47-49; C Arm St Mark *Arm* 49-51; I Mullavilly 51-55; I Derryloran 55-73; Can Arm Cathl 67-73; I Ballymore 73-87; Treas Arm Cathl 73-75; Chan 75-83; Prec 83-87; rtd 87. *60 Coleraine Road, Portrush, Co Antrim BT56 8HN* Tel (01265) 822758

WILKINSON, Robert Samuel (Rob). b 52. Wycliffe Hall Ox DipMin94. **d** 94 **p** 95. C Boughton Monchelsea *Cant* 94-96; C Parkwood CD 95-96; C Plymouth St Andr and St Paul

Stonehouse *Ex* from 96. *18 Glenhurst Road, Plymouth PL3 5LT* Tel (01752) 267025

WILKINSON, Roger. b 46. K Coll Lon BA68 AKC68 AKC72. St Aug Coll Cant 72. **d** 73 **p** 74. C Lt Stanmore St Lawr *Lon* 73-76; Asst Chapl St Geo Hosp Lon 76-78; Chapl Hounslow and Spelthorne HA 78-88; TV Langley and Parkfield *Man* 88-89; C Shelf and C Buttershaw St Aid *Bradf* 89-90; Chapl Asst Ipswich Hosp 90-94; Perm to Offic *St E* 90-94; C Fingringhoe w E Donyland and Abberton etc *Chelmsf* from 94. *St Lawrence House, Rectory Road, Rowhedge, Colchester CO5 7HR* Tel (01206) 728071

WILKINSON, Roy Geoffrey. b 42. Sarum Th Coll 67. **d** 70 **p** 71. C Belsize Park *Lon* 70-73; C Heston 73-75; C Hythe *Cant* 75-79; P-in-c Croydon Woodside 79-81; V 81-84; V Croydon Woodside *S'wark* 85-86. *Sundown, Church Lane, Skegness, Lincs PE25 1EG* Tel (01754) 766727

WILKINSON, Simon Evelyn. b 49. Nottm Univ BA74. Cuddesdon Coll 74. **d** 76 **p** 77. C Cheam *S'wark* 76-78; P-in-c Warlingham w Chelsham and Farleigh 78-83; Radley Coll Oxon 83-89; R Bishops Waltham *Portsm* from 89; R Upham from 89. *The Rectory, Bishops Waltham, Southampton SO32 1EE* Tel (01489) 892618

WILKINSON, Walter Edward Robert. b 38. St Andr Univ MA60. Lon Coll of Div BD63 ALCD63. **d** 63 **p** 64. C High Wycombe *Ox* 63-70; PV, Succ and Sacr Roch Cathl *Roch* 70-73; P-in-c Asby w Ormside *Carl* 73-80; R Cherry Burton *York* 80-95; RD Beverley 88-94; P-in-c Grasmere *Carl* from 95. *The Rectory, Grasmere, Ambleside, Cumbria LA22 9SW* Tel (015394) 35326

WILKINSON, Canon Wilfred Badger. b 21. K Coll Lon BD50 AKC50. **d** 50 **p** 51. C Luton St Mary *St Alb* 50-53; C Gt Berkhamsted 53-57; C-in-c Wythenshawe Wm Temple Ch CD *Man* 57-65; R Clifton w Glapton *S'well* 65-71; TR Clifton 71-86; Hon Can S'well Minster 83-86; rtd 86; Perm to Offic *S'well* from 86. *13 Farthingate Close, Southwell, Notts NG25 0HU* Tel (01636) 814047

WILKS, Eric Percival. b 32. Wells Th Coll 67. **d** 68 **p** 69. C Fladbury w Throckmorton, Wyre Piddle and Moor *Worc* 68-70; Perm to Offic from 70. *4 Catherine Cottages, Droitwich Road, Hartlebury, Kidderminster, Worcs DY10 4EL* Tel (01299) 251580

WILKS, Ernest Howard. b 26. Oak Hill Th Coll 64. **d** 66 **p** 67. C Slough *Ox* 66-69; R Gressenhall w Longham and Bittering Parva *Nor* 69-77; Area Sec (Dios St E & I and Nor) CMS 77-83; P-in-c Deopham w Hackford *Nor* 83-84; P-in-c Morley 83-84; P-in-c Wicklewood and Crownthorpe 83-84; R Morley w Deopham, Hackford, Wicklewood etc 84-88; CMS 89-91; Nigeria 89-91; rtd 91; Perm to Offic *Nor* from 91. *Corner Cottage, Carbrooke Road, Griston, Thetford, Norfolk IP25 6QE* Tel (01953) 881413

WILL, Nicholas James. b 53. Birm Univ LLB75. Qu Coll Birm 93. **d** 95 **p** 96. C Bridgnorth, Tasley, Astley Abbotts, Oldbury etc *Heref* from 95. *9 Fir Trees, Bridgnorth, Shropshire WR15 5EA* Tel (01746) 761069

WILLANS, Jonathan Michael Arthur. b 60. QUB BD. CITC 83. **d** 85 **p** 86. C Larne and Inver *Conn* 85-88; R Hawick *Edin* 88-91; P-in-c Brockham Green *S'wark* from 91; P-in-c Leigh from 91. *The Vicarage, Clayhill Road, Leigh, Reigate, Surrey RH2 8PD* Tel (01306) 611224

WILLARD, John Fordham. b 38. K Coll Lon BD62 AKC62. **d** 63 **p** 64. C Balham Hill Ascension *S'wark* 63-67; C Leigh Park *Portsm* 67-73; C-in-c Leigh Park St Clare CD 73-75; R Bishops Waltham 75-87; P-in-c Upham 78-79; R 79-87; V Dalston H Trin w St Phil *Lon* 87-97; P-in-c Haggerston All SS 90-97; P-in-c Fairford *Glouc* from 97. *The Vicarage, The Croft, Fairford, Glos GL7 4BB* Tel (01285) 712467

WILLCOCK, Albert. b 13. St D Coll Lamp BA41. **d** 41 **p** 42. C Royton St Anne *Man* 41-44; C Tonge w Alkrington 44-47; C Melton Mowbray w Burton Lazars, Freeby etc *Leic* 47-49; V Waterfoot *Man* 49-53; V Long Clawson *Leic* 53-61; V Long Clawson and Hose 61-74; R Stonton Wyville w Glooston, Slawston and Cranoe 74-78; rtd 78; Perm to Offic *Linc* from 78; Perm to Offic *Leic* 78-80. *19 Teesdale Road, Grantham, Lincs NG31 8ES* Tel (01476) 573774

WILLCOCK, Richard William. b 39. Hertf Coll Ox BA62 MA66. Ripon Hall Ox 62. **d** 64 **p** 65. C Ashton St Mich *Man* 64-68; Bp's Dom Chapl 68-72; V Charlestown 72-73; V Charlestown 73-75; Chapl Casterton Sch Lancs 75-80; V Bamford *Man* 80-92; R Framlingham w Saxtead *St E* from 92; RD Loes 95-97. *The Rectory, Framlingham, Woodbridge, Suffolk IP13 9BJ* Tel (01728) 621082

WILLCOX, Canon Frederick John (Fred). b 29. Kelham Th Coll 49. **d** 54 **p** 55. C Tranmere St Paul *Ches* 54-56; Lic to Offic *S'well* 57-61; S Africa 62-70; P-in-c Derby St Andr w St Osmund *Derby* 70-74; V 74-80; V Netherton St Andr *Worc* 80-94; Hon Can Worc Cathl 91-94; rtd 94. *48 Meadow Croft, West Hagley, Stourbridge, W Midlands DY9 0LJ* Tel (01562) 887255

WILLCOX, Ralph Arthur. b 32. Westhill Coll Birm CertYS59 Cranfield Inst of Tech MSc80. St Alb Minl Tr Scheme 86. **d** 89 **p** 90. NSM Aspley Guise w Husborne Crawley and Ridgmont *St Alb* 89-92; Chapl HM Pris Bedf from 92. *HM Prison, St Loyes, Bedford MK40 1HG* Tel (01234) 358671 Fax 273568

WILLCOX, Dr Richard John Michael. b 39. Birm Univ BSc62 PhD67. Qu Coll Birm 78. **d** 80 **p** 81. C Boldmere *Birm* 80-83; V Edgbaston SS Mary and Ambrose 83-89; V Evercreech w Chesterblade and Milton Clevedon *B & W* 89-97; Dioc Development Rep from 90; V Bridgwater H Trin from 97. *Holy Trinity Vicarage, Hamp Street, Bridgwater, Somerset TA6 6AR* Tel (01278) 422610

WILLCOX, Canon Sydney Harold. b 36. Univ of Wales (Lamp) BA58. St Mich Coll Llan. **d** 60 **p** 61. C Pwllheli *Ban* 60-62; C Llandegfan w Beaumaris and Llanfaes 62-65; R Llanenddwyn 65-70; R Dolgellau, Llanfachreth, Brithdir etc 70-76; TR Ridgeway *Sarum* 76-86; RD Marlborough 81-86; TR Cockermouth w Embleton and Wythop *Carl* 86-94; RD Derwent 89-94; Hon Can Carl Cathl 91-94; V Chalke Valley W *Sarum* from 94. *The Vicarage, Broad Chalke, Salisbury SP5 5DS* Tel (01722) 780262

WILLESDEN, Area Bishop of. *See* DOW, The Rt Revd Geoffrey Graham

WILLETT, Canon Allen Gardiner. b 20. Bris Univ BA51 Lon Univ BD54. Clifton Th Coll 47. **d** 54 **p** 55. C Rawtenstall St Mary *Man* 54-57; Nigeria 57-58; Tutor Clifton Th Coll 58-60; C Wallington H Trin *S'wark* 60-62; Tutor All Nations Miss Coll Taplow 62-63; V Bedminster St Luke w St Silas *Bris* 63-68; V Galleywood Common *Chelmsf* 68-87; RD Chelmsf 81-86; Hon Can Chelmsf Cathl 85-87; rtd 87; Perm to Offic *Pet* from 87; Perm to Offic *Ely* from 90; Perm to Offic *Linc* from 90. *4 Abbotts Grove, Werrington, Peterborough PE4 5BT* Tel (01733) 77532

WILLETT, Frank Edwin. b 45. Lon Univ DipTh68. Kelham Th Coll 64. **d** 68 **p** 69. C Oswestry H Trin *Lich* 68-71; C Bilston St Leon 71-74; USPG Coll of the Ascension Selly Oak 74-75; USPG 74-80; Zambia 75-80; V Curbar and Stoney Middleton *Derby* 80-88; Area Sec (Dios Derby and Leic) USPG 88-91; V Chesterfield St Aug *Derby* from 91; Chapl Walton Hosp from 91. *St Augustine's Vicarage, 1 Whitecotes Lane, Chesterfield, Derbyshire S40 3HJ* Tel (01246) 273942

WILLETT, Canon Geoffrey Thomas. b 38. Dur Univ BA59 MA82. Cranmer Hall Dur DipTh61. **d** 62 **p** 63. C Widnes St Paul *Liv* 62-65; C Harborne Heath *Birm* 65-68; V Wakef St Andr and St Mary *Wakef* 68-75; V Hinckley H Trin *Leic* 75-89; TR 89; RD Sparkenhoe II 84-87; RD Sparkenhoe W 87-89; Hon Can Leic Cathl from 87; P-in-c Markfield 89-90; R from 90; RD Sparkenhoe E from 91; P-in-c Thornton, Bagworth and Stanton from 96. *The Rectory, The Nook, Markfield, Leics LE67 9WE* Tel (01530) 242844

WILLETT, John Ivon. b 40. Ch Ch Ox BA63 MA65. Chich Th Coll 61. **d** 63 **p** 64. C Leic St Andr *Leic* 63-66; C Bordesley St Alb *Birm* 66-72; Min Can, Prec and Sacr Pet Cathl *Pet* 72-82; R Uppingham w Ayston and Wardley w Belton from 82. *The Rectory, Uppingham, Oakham, Leics LE15 9TJ* Tel (01572) 823381

WILLETT, Michael John Farquhar. b 32. St Mich Coll Llan DMinlStuds92. **d** 92 **p** 93. NSM Llangorse, Cathedine, Llanfihangel Talyllyn etc *S & B* from 92. *Beaufort House, Llangynidr, Crickhowell NP8 1NT* Tel (01874) 730449

WILLETT, Stephen John. b 54. Ridley Hall Cam 88. **d** 90 **p** 91. C Chapeltown *Sheff* 90-94; V Hackenthorpe from 94. *The Vicarage, 63 Sheffield Road, Sheffield S12 4LR* Tel 0114-248 4486

WILLETTS, Alfred. b 15. **d** 62 **p** 63. C Canton St Jo *Llan* 62-65; V Afan Vale 65-67; R Man St Phil w St Mark *Man* 67-75; R Man Apostles 75-84; rtd 85; Perm to Offic *Ches* from 85; Perm to Offic *Man* from 85. *22 Larne Drive, Broughton, Chester CH4 0QF* Tel (01244) 533485

WILLEY, David Geoffrey. b 53. Imp Coll Lon BSc74 BA86. Oak Hill Th Coll 83. **d** 86 **p** 87. C Cromer *Nor* 86-90; R High Halstow w All Hallows and Hoo St Mary *Roch* 90-94; R Gravesend St Geo from 94. *St George's Rectory, Gravesend, Kent DA11 0DJ* Tel (01474) 534965

WILLEY, Graham John. b 38. Moray Ord Course 91. **d** 93 **p** 94. Hon C W Coast Jt Congregations Moray *Mor* from 93. *Harbour View, Badachro, Gairloch, Ross-shire IV21 2AA* Tel (01445) 741316

WILLIAMS, Alan Ronald Norman. b 60. RMN85. Linc Th Coll CMinlStuds95. **d** 95 **p** 96. C Malvern Link w Cowleigh *Worc* from 95. *17 Bosbury Road, Malvern, Worcs WR14 1TR* Tel (01684) 569890

WILLIAMS, Aled Jones. b 56. Univ of Wales (Ban) BA77 Univ of Wales (Cardiff) DipTh79. St Mich Coll Llan 77. **d** 79 **p** 80. C Conwy w Gyffin *Ban* 79-82; R Llanrug 82-86; R Machynlleth and Llanwrin 86-87; Member L'Arche Community 88-95; V Ynyscynhaearn w Penmorfa and Porthmadog from 95. *The Vicarage, Ffordd Penamser, Porthmadog LL49 9PA* Tel (01766) 514951

WILLIAMS, Aled Wyn. b 47. Univ of Wales (Abth) BA69. St Mich Coll Llan 69. **d** 71 **p** 72. C Llanelli *St D* 71-73; P-in-c Capel Colman w Llanfihangel Penbedw etc 73-74; V 74-81; V Llanddewi Brefi w Llanbadarn Odwyn 81-84; V Llanddewi Brefi w Llanbadarn Odwyn, Cellan etc from 84; RD Lampeter and Ultra-Aeron from 96. *The Vicarage, Llanddewi Brefi, Tregaron SY25 6PE* Tel (01974) 298937

WILLIAMS, Alexander Ernest. b 14. Fitzw Ho Cam BA35 MA46 Regent's Park Coll Ox 35. Coll of Resurr Mirfield 79. **d** 79 **p** 80. Hon C Carshalton Beeches *S'wark* 79-87; rtd 87; Perm to Offic *S'wark* from 87. *88 Grosvenor Avenue, Carshalton, Surrey SM5 3EP* Tel 0181-647 8446

WILLIAMS, Alfred Donald. b 26. St Aid Birkenhead 57. **d** 59 **p** 60. C Ordsall *S'well* 59-62; V Ladybrook 62-70; P-in-c Newark Ch Ch 70-71; R Gotham 72-88; P-in-c W Leake w Kingston-on-Soar and Ratcliffe-on-Soar 72-81; rtd 88; Perm to Offic *Bradf* from 88. *20 Grassington Road, Skipton, N Yorkshire BD23 1LL* Tel (01756) 794496

WILLIAMS, Alfred George. b 21. St D Coll Lamp BA42. **d** 46 **p** 47. C Ruabon *St As* 46-49; C Lache cum Saltney *Ches* 49-52; V Millbrook 52-54; V Aston by Sutton 54-64; V Rock Ferry 64-77; V Lache cum Saltney 77-86; rtd 86; Perm to Offic *Ches* from 86. *7 Lache Park Avenue, Chester CH4 8HR* Tel (01244) 678768

WILLIAMS, Allen Philpin. b 10. St D Coll Lamp BA32 St Mich Coll Llan. **d** 34 **p** 35. C Llandysul *St D* 34-37; C Llanelli Ch Ch 37-40; P-in-c Talley 40-48; V Llanfair-ar-y-Bryn 48-58; V Manordeilo 58-70; V Manordeilo and Taliaris 70-78; rtd 78. *7 Diana Road, Llandeilo SA19 6RR* Tel (01558) 822376

WILLIAMS, Amanda Clare. *See* WILLIAMS-POTTER, Mrs Amanda Clare

WILLIAMS, Andrew David. b 67. Univ of Wales (Lamp) BA91. Linc Th Coll CMM93. **d** 93 **p** 94. C Perry Street *Roch* 93-96; C Ealing St Pet Mt Park *Lon* from 96. *56B Mount Park Road, London W5 2RU* Tel 0181-998 7493

WILLIAMS, Andrew Gibson. b 31. Edin Univ MA57. Edin Th Coll 56. **d** 59 **p** 60. C Todmorden *Wakef* 59-61; C Clitheroe St Mary *Blackb* 61-63; V Burnley St Jas 63-65; CF (TA) 64-65; CF 65-71; R Winterslow *Sarum* 71-84; P-in-c Condover *Heref* 84-88; P-in-c Acton Burnell w Pitchford 84-88; P-in-c Frodesley 84-88; R Condover w Frodesley, Acton Burnell etc 88-90; R Whimple, Talaton and Clyst St Lawr *Ex* 90-94; rtd 94; Perm to Offic *Ex* from 94. *6 Culvery Close, Woodbury, Exeter EX5 1LZ* Tel (01395) 233079

WILLIAMS, Andrew Joseph. b 55. St Jo Coll Nottm BTh81. **d** 81 **p** 82. C Hollington St Leon *Chich* 81-84; C Sutton Coldfield H Trin *Birm* 84-87; Perm to Offic from 87; Chapl Blue Coat Comp Sch Walsall from 91. *139 Rectory Road, Sutton Coldfield, W Midlands B75 7RV* Tel 0121-378 2962

WILLIAMS, Mrs Anthea Elizabeth. b 50. Trevelyan Coll Dur BA71. Linc Th Coll 72. **dss** 79 **d** 87 **p** 94. St Marylebone Ch Ch *Lon* 79-84; Maidstone St Martin *Cant* 84-87; Par Dn 87-91; Par Dn Rolvenden 91; D-in-c 91-94; P-in-c from 94. *The Vicarage, Rolvenden, Cranbrook, Kent TN17 4ND* Tel (01580) 241235

WILLIAMS, Dr Anthony David. b 38. MRCGP68 LRCP62 MRCS62 DRCOG65 FPACert65. S Dios Minl Tr Scheme 87. **d** 90 **p** 91. Hon C Jersey St Pet *Win* 90-92; NSM Jersey St Helier from 92. *Beau Vallon, Mont de la Rosiere, St Saviour, Jersey, Channel Islands JE2 7HF* Tel (01534) 863859

WILLIAMS, Anthony Francis. b 21. Trin Coll Ox BA49 MA53. Coll of Resurr Mirfield 49. **d** 51 **p** 52. C Paignton St Jo *Ex* 51-54; C Cov H Trin *Cov* 54-60; V Cov All SS 60-67; V Lindridge *Worc* 67-77; P-in-c Bluntisham w Earith *Ely* 77-79; R 79-88; rtd 88; Perm to Offic *Ely* from 88. *21 Kings Hedges, St Ives, Huntingdon, Cambs PE17 6XU* Tel (01480) 467686

WILLIAMS, Anthony Riley. b 36. Univ of Wales BA60. Chich Th Coll 57. **d** 59 **p** 60. C Llandinorwic *Ban* 59-61; C Llandegfan w Beaumaris and Llanfaes 61-64; R Ludchurch and Templeton *St D* 64-72; V Lamphey w Hodgeston 72-83; RD Castlemartin 75-83; V Llanelli from 83; Can St D Cathl from 86; Chapl Bryntirion Hosp Llanelli from 90; Chan St D Cathl *St D* from 93. *The Vicarage, 11 Old Road, Llanelli SA14 3HW* Tel (01554) 772072

WILLIAMS, Arfon. b 58. Univ of Wales (Abth) BD83 Univ of Wales (Ban) MA84. Wycliffe Hall Ox 83. **d** 84 **p** 85. C Carmarthen St Dav *St D* 84-86; TV Aberystwyth 86-88; V Glanogwen *Ban* 88-94; Dir Oast Ho Retreat Cen *Chich* from 95; Asst to RD Rye from 95; C Ewhurst from 95; Co-ord for Adult Educn (E Sussex Area) from 97. *6 Weald View, Staplecross, Robertsbridge, E Sussex TN32 5QW* Tel (01580) 830653

WILLIAMS, Preb Arthur Edwin. b 33. Leeds Univ BA57. Coll of Resurr Mirfield 57. **d** 59 **p** 60. C Wednesfield St Thos *Lich* 59-62; C Codsall 62-65; V from 83; V Coseley St Chad 65-73; R Kingswinford H Trin 73-81; TR Wordsley 81-83; RD Himley 77-83; Preb Lich Cathl from 82; RD Penkridge 89-94. *The Vicarage, Church Road, Codsall, Wolverhampton WV8 1EH* Tel (01902) 842168

WILLIAMS, Canon Arthur James Daniel. b 24. Univ of Wales (Lamp) BA49. St Mich Coll Llan 49. **d** 51 **p** 52. C Pontlottyn *Llan* 51-54; C Caerphilly 54-60; Dioc Youth Sec 55-62; V Gilfach Goch w Garden Village 60-66; Youth Chapl 62-67; V Llantwit Fadre 66-89; RD Pontypridd 84-88; Can Llan Cathl 86-89; rtd 89; Perm to Offic *Llan* from 89. *Ty Pica, Efail Isaf, Church Village, Pontypridd CF38 1BA* Tel (01443) 480423

WILLIAMS, Barrie. b 33. Em Coll Cam BA54 MA58 Bris Univ MLitt71. Lambeth STh75 Ripon Hall Ox 62. **d** 63 **p** 64. C Penwortham St Mary *Blackb* 63-65; Hon C Salisbury St Martin *Sarum* 65-77; Chapl St Edw K and Martyr Cam *Ely* 77-84; Asst Chapl Trin Hall Cam 77-84; R Ashley w Weston by Welland and Sutton Bassett *Pet* 84-85; Asst Chapl St Hilda's Sch Whitby from 85. *Flat 5, Crinkle Court, 9 Chubb Hill, Whitby, N Yorkshire YO21 1JU* Tel (01947) 600766

WILLIAMS, Benjamin Clive. b 24. Lon Univ BD59. Westcott Ho Cam 59. **d** 61 **p** 62. C Bury St Mark *Man* 61-63; C Christchurch *Win* 63-66; R Denton w S Heighton and Tarring Neville *Chich* 66-74; Dioc Stewardship Adv 74-81; P-in-c Clapham w Patching 76-81; V Ticehurst and Flimwell 81-89; rtd 89; Perm to Offic *Chich* from 89. *14 Lindfield Avenue, Seaford, E Sussex BN25 4DY* Tel (01323) 491019

WILLIAMS, Brian. b 48. WMMTC. **d** 83 **p** 84. NSM Lich St Chad *Lich* from 83. *82 Walsall Road, Lichfield, Staffs WS13 8AF* Tel (01543) 253120

WILLIAMS, Brian Luke. b 54. AKC75. St Steph Ho Ox 76. **d** 77 **p** 78. C Kettering St Mary *Pet* 77-80; C Walsall St Gabr Fulbrook *Lich* 80-83; P-in-c Sneyd 83-85; V from 85; RD Stoke N from 94. *Sneyd Vicarage, Hamil Road, Stoke-on-Trent ST6 1AP* Tel (01782) 825841

WILLIAMS, Brian Thomas. b 48. GSM69. Linc Th Coll 89. **d** 91 **p** 92. C Liss *Portsm* 91-95; C Portsea N End St Mark from 95. *St Nicholas' House, 90A Compton Road, Portsmouth PO2 0SR* Tel (01705) 660657

WILLIAMS, Ms Carol Jean. b 45. FIPM89. Ox NSM Course 86. **d** 89 **p** 94. NSM High Wycombe *Ox* 89-97; P-in-c Penn from 97. *3 Pimms Close, High Wycombe, Bucks HP13 7EG* Tel (01494) 814571

WILLIAMS, Cecil Augustus Baldwin. b 09. TCD BA31 MA39. CITC 32. **d** 32 **p** 33. C Belfast St Mary Magd *Conn* 32-36; BCMS Kapoeta Sudan 36-39; I Schull *C, C & R* 40-49; Sec Ch of Ireland Jews' Soc 49-54; I Dublin St Luke *D & G* 54-71; BCMS Sec 56-63; I Crinken 71-81; rtd 81. *3 St John's Close, Portstewart, Co Londonderry BT55 7HJ* Tel (01265) 834249

WILLIAMS, Dr Cecil Peter. b 41. TCD BA63 MA67 Lon Univ BD67 PhD86 Bris Univ MLitt77. Clifton Th Coll 64. **d** 67 **p** 68. C Maghull *Liv* 67-70; Lic to Offic *Bris* 70-91; Tutor Clifton Th Coll 70-72; Tutor Trin Coll Bris 72-91; Lib 73-81; Course Ldr 81-85; Vice-Prin 85-91; V Ecclesall *Sheff* from 91. *Ecclesall Vicarage, Ringinglow Road, Sheffield S11 7PQ* Tel 0114-236 0084 Fax as telephone

WILLIAMS, Clifford Smith. b 48. Univ of Wales (Ban) BD79. St Deiniol's Hawarden 79. **d** 80 **p** 81. C Llanbeblig w Caernarfon and Betws Garmon etc *Ban* 80-82; R Llanfair Mathafarn Eithaf w Llanbedrgoch 82-97. *The Rectory, Bay View Road, Tyn-y-Gongl LL74 8TT* Tel (01248) 852348

WILLIAMS, Clive Gregory. b 45. Trin Coll Bris 83. **d** 85 **p** 86. C Bedhampton *Portsm* 85-88; V Highley *Heref* from 88; RD Bridgnorth from 96. *The Vicarage, Church Street, Highley, Bridgnorth, Shropshire WV16 6NA* Tel (01746) 861612

WILLIAMS, Colin Henry. b 52. Pemb Coll Ox BA73 MA78. St Steph Ho Ox BA80. **d** 81 **p** 82. C Liv St Paul Stoneycroft *Liv* 81-84; TV Walton St Mary 84-89; Chapl Walton Hosp Liv 86-89; Bp's Dom Chapl *Blackb* 89-94; Chapl Whalley Abbey 89-94; V Poulton-le-Fylde from 94. *The Vicarage, 7 Vicarage Road, Poulton-le-Fylde, Blackpool FY6 7BE* Tel (01253) 883086

WILLIAMS, Creswell. b 13. Univ of Wales BA36. St D Coll Lamp 37. **d** 38 **p** 39. C Ystradyfodwg *Llan* 38-42; CF (EC) 42-46; C Abercynon *Llan* 46-49; CF 49-67; V Eglwysfach and Llangynfelin *St D* 67-78; rtd 78; Lic to Offic *Ban* from 78. *4 Londonderry Terrace, Machynlleth SY20 8BG* Tel (01654) 702349

WILLIAMS, Cyril. b 06. Univ of Wales BA34. St Mich Coll Llan 34. **d** 35 **p** 36. C Mostyn *St As* 35-38; C Llangollen 38-46; V Llandrillo 46-51; V Tremeirchion 51-61; R Denbigh 61-77; rtd 77. *Bryniog, 13 Nant y Patrick, St Asaph LL17 0BN* Tel (01745) 730264

WILLIAMS, David. b 19. **d** 66 **p** 67. Hon C Dean Forest St Paul *Glouc* 66-78; Hon C Coleford w Staunton 78-83; Perm to Offic from 83. *The Nook, Parkend Road, Bream, Lydney, Glos GL15 6JZ* Tel (01594) 562240

WILLIAMS, David. b 33. Ch Coll Cam BA56 MA60 Cranfield Inst of Tech MSc72. Sarum & Wells Th Coll 71. **d** 73 **p** 74. C Ex St Jas *Ex* 73-75; Lic to Offic 75-84; Teacher St Wilfrid Sch Ex 75-76; Teacher Hele's Sch Ex 76-84; TV Thorverton, Cadbury, Upton Pyne etc 84-92; TR 92-93; rtd 93. *1 Wrefords Close, Exeter EX4 5AY* Tel (01392) 435759

WILLIAMS, David. b 43. ACA65 K Coll Lon AKC69 BD70. St Aug Coll Cant 69. **d** 70 **p** 71. C Walkden Moor *Man* 70-72; C Deane 72-75; V Horwich St Cath 75-81; Hon C Chorley All SS *Blackb* 84-86; P-in-c Weeton 86-87; V Singleton w Weeton from 87. *St Michael's Vicarage, Church Road, Weeton, Preston PR4 3WD* Tel (01253) 836249

WILLIAMS, Canon David. b 49. BTh DTechM. **d** 88 **p** 89. C Lurgan etc w Ballymachugh, Kildrumferton etc *K, E & A* 88-91; I Kinsale Union *C, C & R* from 91; Miss to Seamen from 91; Can Cork and Cloyne Cathls *C, C & R* 95-97; Treas Cork Cathl from 97. *St Multose Rectory, Abbey Court, Kinsale, Co Cork, Irish Republic* Tel Cork (21) 772220

WILLIAMS, David Albert. b 15. St D Coll Lamp BA35 St Mich Coll Llan 36. **d** 38 **p** 39. C Penrhosgarnedd *Ban* 38-40; C Glanadda 38-40; C Llanbadarn Fawr *St D* 40-49; Chapl RAF 49-58; Perm to Offic *Birm* 58-59; Malaya 59-61; Perm to Offic

Heref 61-69; Lic to Offic 69-80; rtd 80; Perm to Offic *St D* 81-94; P-in-c Cil-y-Cwm and Ystrad-ffin w Rhandir-mwyn etc 94-95; P-in-c Llanegwad w Llanfynydd 94-95; Perm to Offic from 95. *London House, Llanwrda SA19 8AA* Tel (01550) 777671

WILLIAMS, Dr David Alun. b 65. St Thos Hosp Lon MB, BS88. Wycliffe Hall Ox BTh94. **d** 94 **p** 95. C Ware Ch Ch *St Alb* from 94. *10 Cromwell Road, Ware, Herts SG12 7JZ* Tel (01920) 467918

WILLIAMS, David Frank. b 48. S Dios Minl Tr Scheme 91. **d** 94 **p** 95. NSM Romsey *Win* from 94. *24 Feltham Close, Romsey, Hants SO51 8PB* Tel (01794) 524050

WILLIAMS, David Gareth. b 58. Lon Univ BD81. Ripon Coll Cuddesdon 82. **d** 84 **p** 85. C Chandler's Ford *Win* 84-88; C Alton St Lawr 88-90; R Crawley and Littleton and Sparsholt w Lainston from 90. *The Rectory, Church Lane, Littleton, Winchester, Hants SO22 6QY* Tel (01962) 881898

WILLIAMS, Canon David Gerald Powell. b 35. St Mich Coll Llan DipTh62. **d** 62 **p** 63. C Canton St Jo *Llan* 62-64; Field Tr Officer Ch in Wales Prov Youth Coun 63-70; Prov Youth Chapl 65-70; V Treharris *Llan* 70-75; R Flemingston w Gileston and St Hilary 75-78; Warden of Ords 77-80; Dir Past Studies and Chapl St Mich Coll Llan 78-80; Sub-Warden 79-80; Dir Ch in Wales Publications and Communications 80-85; Prov Dir of Educn Ch in Wales 80-85; Dir of Miss Ch in Wales 85-87; Hon Can Llan Cathl *Llan* 84-93; V Pendoylan and Welsh St Donats 87-93; R Llandudno *Ban* 93-95; Press Officer to Abp of Wales from 93. *39 Cathedral Road, Cardiff CF1 9XF*

WILLIAMS, Canon David Gordon. b 43. Selw Coll Cam BA65 MA69. Oak Hill Th Coll 66. **d** 68 **p** 69. C Maidstone St Luke *Cant* 68-71; C Rugby St Matt *Cov* 71-73; P-in-c Budbrooke 73-74; V 74-81; V Lenton *S'well* 81-87; TR Cheltenham St Mark *Glouc* from 87; Hon Can Glouc Cathl from 96. *St Mark's Rectory, Fairmount Road, Cheltenham, Glos GL51 7AQ* Tel (01242) 255110

WILLIAMS, David Grant. b 61. Bris Univ BSocSc83. Wycliffe Hall Ox 86. **d** 89 **p** 90. C Ecclesall *Sheff* 89-92; V Dore from 92; RD Ecclesall from 97. *The Vicarage, 51 Vicarage Lane, Dore, Sheffield S17 3GY* Tel 0114-236 3335

WILLIAMS, David Henry. b 33. Trin Coll Cam BA56 MA60 PhD77. St D Coll Lamp 67. **d** 69 **p** 70. C Monmouth *Mon* 69-70; Chapl St Woolos Cathl 70-71; P-in-c Six Bells 71-76; Libya 76-79; P-in-c Crumlin *Mon* 79-80; R Llanddewi Skirrid w Llanvetherine etc 80-83; Perm to Offic 83-87; Guest Master Caldey Abbey 83-87; V Buttington and Pool Quay *St As* 87-95; Chapl Warsaw *Eur* from 95. *VL Zakopiansha, 12A, 03-958 Warsaw, Poland* Tel Warsaw (2) 625-4150 or 617-8367

WILLIAMS, Canon David Humphrey. b 23. Em Coll Cam BA49 MA54. St Steph Ho Ox 49. **d** 51 **p** 52. C Daybrook *S'well* 51-55; C-in-c Bilborough St Jo Bapt CD 55-62; V Bilborough St Jo 62-63; RD Bulwell 70-88; P-in-c Bestwood Park 71-78; R Hucknall Torkard 63-71; TR 71-88; Hon Can S'well Minster 75-88; rtd 88. *12 Wollaton Paddocks, Trowell Road, Nottingham NG8 2ED* Tel 0115-928 0639

WILLIAMS, David James. b 42. Chich Th Coll 67. **d** 70 **p** 71. C Charlton-by-Dover St Bart *Cant* 70-74; C Dorking w Ranmore *Guildf* 74-77; C Guildf H Trin w St Mary 77-78; P-in-c E Molesey St Paul 78-88; V Burpham 88-94; rtd 95. *1 Taleworth Close, Ashtead, Surrey KT21 2PU* Tel (01372) 278056

WILLIAMS, David John. b 30. Open Univ BA79. St D Coll Lamp 64. **d** 66 **p** 67. C Mold *St As* 66-69; C Llanrhos 69-71; R Llangynhafal and Llanbedr Dyffryn Clwyd 71-86; P-in-c Llanynys w Llanychan 77-95; RD Dyffryn Clwyd 86-95; R Ruthin w Llanrhydd 86-95; rtd 95. *16 The Park, Ruthin LL15 1PW* Tel (01824) 705746

WILLIAMS, David John. b 38. AKC62. **d** 63 **p** 64. C Benchill *Man* 63-66; C Heywood St Jas 66-69; V Leesfield 69-73; Chapl TS Arethusa 73-74; TV Southend St Jo w St Mark, All SS w St Fran etc *Chelmsf* 74-80; V Horndon on the Hill 80-93; RD Thurrock 83-92; P-in-c Rochford from 93; RD Rochford from 96. *The Rectory, 36 Millview Meadows, Rochford, Essex SS4 1EF* Tel (01702) 530621

WILLIAMS, David John. b 43. Wadh Coll Ox BA64. St Jo Coll Nottm 73. **d** 75 **p** 76. C Newcastle w Butterton *Lich* 75-79; P-in-c Oulton 79-89; P-in-c Stone Ch Ch 84-89; V Stone Ch Ch and Oulton 89-96; P-in-c Ashley from 96; P-in-c Mucklestone from 96. *The Rectory, Ashley, Market Drayton, Shropshire TF9 4LQ* Tel (01630) 872210

WILLIAMS, David John. b 52. N Ord Course 92. **d** 95 **p** 96. C Gt Crosby St Luke *Liv* from 95. *20 Ascot Park, Crosby, Liverpool L23 2HX* Tel 0151-931 4907

WILLIAMS, David Leslie. b 35. ALCD63. **d** 63 **p** 64. C Bexleyheath Ch Ch *Roch* 63-64; C Gt Faringdon w Lt Coxwell *Ox* 64-66; CMS 67-76; Uganda 67-73; C Shortlands *Roch* 73-74; Fiji 74-76; V Bromley H Trin *Roch* 77-86; R Meopham w Nurstead 86-96; RD Cobham 86-96; Chapl N Kent Health Care NHS Trust from 96. *107 Ploughmans Way, Rainham, Kent ME8 8LT* Tel (01634) 372545

WILLIAMS, David Michael Rochfort. b 40. Hull Univ DipTh81. St Mich Coll Llan DipTh65. **d** 65 **p** 66. C Pembroke Dock *St D* 65-68; Miss to Seamen 68-71; Ind Chapl *St D* 68-71; P-in-c Walwyn's Castle w Robeston W 68-70; R 70-71; Ind Chapl *Mon* 71-74; Hon Chapl St Woolos Cathl 71-74; V Blaenavon w Capel Newydd 74-77; Ind Chapl *St As* 77-88; V Whitford 81-87; V Ruabon 87-92; TR Cen Telford *Lich* from 92. *The Rectory, Church Road, Dawley, Telford, Shropshire TF4 2AS* Tel (01952) 501655

WILLIAMS, David Norman. b 54. Lanc Univ BSc Leeds Univ BA. Coll of Resurr Mirfield. **d** 84 **p** 85. C Ireland Wood *Ripon* 84-87; C Beeston 87-91; V Cross Roads cum Lees *Bradf* from 91. *The Vicarage, Cross Roads, Keighley, W Yorkshire BD22 9DL* Tel (01535) 642210

WILLIAMS, David Paul. *See* HOWELL, David Paul

WILLIAMS, David Roger. b 49. St D Coll Lamp DipTh73. **d** 73 **p** 74. C Llansamlet *S & B* 73-76; C Oystermouth 76-79; V Aberedw w Llandeilo Graban and Llanbadarn etc 79-81; V Brynmawr 81-89; V Newport St Julian *Mon* from 89. *St Julian's Vicarage, 41 St Julian's Avenue, Newport NP9 7JT* Tel (01633) 258046

WILLIAMS, Derek. b 27. Man Univ BSc49. St Deiniol's Hawarden 76. **d** 78 **p** 79. NSM Abergele *St As* 78-97; rtd 97. *48 Eldon Drive, Abergele LL22 7DA* Tel (01745) 833479

WILLIAMS, Derek Howard. b 24. Leeds Univ BSc49. Coll of Resurr Mirfield 49. **d** 51 **p** 52. C Dundee St Salvador *Bre* 51-54; CR 54-57 and 60-61; S Africa 57-60; S Rhodesia 62-65; Rhodesia 65-80; Zimbabwe from 80; Dean Mutare 84-86; rtd 95. *Box 530, Mutare, Zimbabwe* Tel Mutare (20) 62682

WILLIAMS, Derek Lawrence. b 45. Lon Univ DipTh68. Tyndale Hall Bris 65. **d** 69 **p** 70. C Cant St Mary Bredin *Cant* 69-71; Gen Sec Inter-Coll Chr Fellowship 71-75; Lic to Offic *St Alb* 78-84; Lic to Offic *Bris* 85-92; Perm to Offic *Pet* from 92. *58 Clarence Avenue, Northampton NN2 6NZ* Tel (01604) 710404

WILLIAMS, Derwyn Gavin. b 69. Trin Coll Cam BA89 MA93. Ripon Coll Cuddesdon DipMin94. **d** 94 **p** 95. C Harpenden St Nic *St Alb* from 94. *37 St James Road, Harpenden, Herts AL5 4PB* Tel (01582) 761657

WILLIAMS, Diana Mary (Di). b 36. Bris Univ CertEd56 Leeds Univ BSc57. Oak Hill Th Coll 86. **d** 87 **p** 94. NSM S Mymms K Chas *St Alb* 87-93; Par Dn 93-94; C 94-95; V from 95. *The Vicarage, 40 Dugdale Hill Lane, Potters Bar, Herts EN6 2DW* Tel (01707) 654219

WILLIAMS, Ms Diane Patricia. b 53. Dur Univ CertEd74 Liv Univ DipRE83 Lanc Univ MA84. Cranmer Hall Dur 84. **dss** 86 **d** 87 **p** 94. Clubmoor *Liv* 86-87; Par Dn 87-90; Par Dn Everton St Geo 90-94; Dioc Lay Tr Officer 90-96; C Everton St Geo 94-96; Chapl Lanc Univ *Blackb* from 96. *6 Beechwood Gardens, Lancaster LA1 4PH* Tel (01524) 66295

WILLIAMS, Diane Ruth. b 52. Hull Univ BA80. Linc Th Coll. **d** 94 **p** 95. Par Dn Stokesley *York* 94; C from 94. *25 Riversdene, Stokesley, Middlesbrough, Cleveland TS9 5DD* Tel (01642) 710911

WILLIAMS, Doiran George. b 26. Barrister-at-Law (Gray's Inn) 52. W of England Minl Tr Course 91. **d** 93 **p** 94. NSM Edvin Loach w Tedstone Delamere etc *Heref* from 93. *Howberry, Whitbourne, Worcester WR6 5RZ* Tel (01886) 821189

WILLIAMS, The Ven Edward Bryan. b 36. Univ of Wales (Lamp) BA58. St Mich Coll Llan 58. **d** 60 **p** 61. C Rhyl w St Ann *St As* 60-68; Dioc Youth Chapl 66-78; V Dyserth and Trelawnyd and Cwm 68-77; R Denbigh 77-82; Can St As Cathl 81-87; R Denbigh and Nantglyn 82-87; Adn Wrexham from 87; V Bwlchgwyn from 87. *The Vicarage, 8 Whiteoaks, Bwlchgwyn, Wrexham LL11 5UB* Tel (01978) 752627

WILLIAMS, Edward Ffoulkes (Peter). b 34. ALA65. Chich Th Coll 71. **d** 73 **p** 74. C Kidderminster St Geo *Worc* 73-78; TV Worc St Barn w Ch Ch 78-82; V Exhall w Wixford *Cov* from 82; V Temple Grafton w Binton from 82. *The Vicarage, Temple Grafton, Alcester, Warks B49 6PA* Tel (01789) 772314

WILLIAMS, Edward Heaton. b 18. St Aid Birkenhead 56. **d** 58 **p** 59. C Timperley *Ches* 58-62; V Macclesfield St Pet 62-66; Sec Dioc Miss Bd 63-67; R Wistaston 66-81; Dioc Bd for Miss and Unity 67-69; V Burton 81-85; rtd 85; Perm to Offic *Ox* 85-94; Perm to Offic *Pet* from 85. *4 Bowmens Lea, Aynho, Banbury, Oxon OX17 3AG* Tel (01869) 810533

WILLIAMS, Prof Edward Sydney. b 23. FRCP FRCR K Coll Lon BSc PhD MB, BS MD AKC. Sarum & Wells Th Coll 84. **d** 87 **p** 88. NSM Bramley and Grafham *Guildf* 87-89; Hon C Shamley Green 89-94; Perm to Offic from 94. *Bisney Cottage, Shamley Green, Guildford, Surrey GU5 0TB* Tel (01483) 892591

WILLIAMS, Elfed Owain. b 24. Newc Univ DipAdEd74. St Deiniol's Hawarden 79. **d** 81 **p** 82. Hon C Whorlton *Newc* 81-82; Hon C Elham w Denton and Wootton *Cant* 82-86; R Barham w Bishopsbourne and Kingston 86-91; rtd 91. *Chusan, 31 Ryecroft Way, Wooler, Northd NE71 6DY* Tel (01668) 81253

WILLIAMS, Eric Rees. b 30. Roch Th Coll 60 St Deiniol's Hawarden 71. **d** 72 **p** 73. C Llanelli *St D* 72-75; P-in-c Tregaron 75-76; V 76-82; RD Lampeter and Ultra-Aeron 82-87; V Tregaron w Ystrad Meurig and Strata Florida 82-87; V St Dogmael's w Moylgrove and Monington from 87. *The Vicarage, St Dogmael's, Cardigan SA43 3DX* Tel (01239) 612030

WILLIAMS, Evelyn Joyce. b 37. Cant Sch of Min 86. **d** 89 **p** 94. NSM Sittingbourne H Trin w Bobbing *Cant* from 89. *32 Rock Road, Sittingbourne, Kent ME10 1JF* Tel (01795) 470372

WILLIAMS, Frederick Errol. b 41. MBIM80. Sarum & Wells Th Coll 86. **d** 88 **p** 89. C Milton *Win* 88-91; P-in-c Chilbolton cum Wherwell 91-94; R from 94. *The Rectory, Chilbolton, Stockbridge, Hants SO20 6BA* Tel (01264) 860258

WILLIAMS, Fredric Barry. b 41. Man Univ BSc62 CertEd63 Man Poly DMEd87. N Ord Course 79. **d** 82 **p** 83. NSM Darwen St Cuth *Blackb* 82-85; NSM Darwen St Cuth w Tockholes St Steph 85-88; V Rillington w Scampston, Wintringham etc *York* from 88; RD Buckrose from 90. *The Vicarage, 2 High Street, Rillington, Malton, N Yorkshire YO17 8LA* Tel (01944) 758891

WILLIAMS, Gareth Wynn. b 67. St D Coll Lamp BA88 Hull Univ MA89. Westcott Ho Cam 89. **d** 91 **p** 92. C Mold *St As* 91-93; TV Hawarden 93-95; Ecum Chapl Glam Univ *Llan* from 95. *Neuadd Maes y Eglwys, Upper Church Village, Pontypridd CF38 1EB* Tel (01443) 480480 or 208784 E-mail gwwillia@glam.ac.uk

WILLIAMS, Gavin John. b 61. Barrister-at-Law 85 Down Coll Cam BA84. Wycliffe Hall Ox BA88. **d** 89 **p** 90. C Muswell Hill St Jas w St Matt *Lon* 89-92; Asst Chapl Shrewsbury Sch from 92. *Flat B, Lindisfarne, 6 Kennedy Road, Shrewsbury SY3 7AD* Tel (01743) 364393

WILLIAMS, Canon Geoffrey Ainsworth. b 16. Univ Coll Dur BA38 MA41. **d** 39 **p** 40. C Bury St Mary *Man* 39-49; V Habergham All SS *Blackb* 49-65; RD Burnley 61-65; Can Res and Chan Blackb Cathl 65-90; Warden of Readers 65-89; Warden Whalley Abbey 77-90; rtd 90; Perm to Offic *Blackb* from 90. *22 Buncer Lane, Blackburn BB2 6SE* Tel (01254) 256706

WILLIAMS, Geoffrey Thomas. b 35. Ox NSM Course 77. **d** 80 **p** 81. NSM Earley St Bart *Ox* 80-82; NSM Reading St Luke 82-85; C Wembley Park St Aug *Lon* 85-86; C-in-c S Kenton Annunciation CD 86-90; V Streatham Hill St Marg *S'wark* from 90. *St Margaret's Vicarage, 165 Barcombe Avenue, London SW2 3BH* Tel 0181-674 7348

WILLIAMS, George Harold. b 20. Lon Univ BSc49. **d** 67 **p** 68. C Bishopsworth *Bris* 67-70; V Weston-super-Mare Ch Ch *B & W* 70-85; rtd 85; Perm to Offic *B & W* from 86. *15 Elmhurst Road, Hutton, Weston-super-Mare, Avon BS24 9RJ* Tel (01934) 813342

WILLIAMS, Preb George Maxwell Frazer. b 42. TCD BA65 MA69. Cuddesdon Coll 65. **d** 67 **p** 68. C Bolton St Jas w St Chrys *Bradf* 67-70; C Lich St Chad *Lich* 70-73; V Shawbury 73-79; P-in-c Moreton Corbet 73-79; V Willenhall H Trin 79-86; TR 86-88; V Penn from 88; Preb Lich Cathl from 96. *St Bartholemew's Vicarage, 68 Church Hill, Penn, Wolverhampton WV4 5JD* Tel (01902) 341399

WILLIAMS, George Melvin (Kim). b 24. Worc Ord Coll 64. **d** 66 **p** 67. C Holdenhurst *Win* 66-70; V Yateley 70-75; V St Leonards and St Ives 75-90; rtd 90. *20 Hillside Drive, Christchurch, Dorset BH23 4RU* Tel (01202) 484930

WILLIAMS, Dr George Ola. b 55. Bradf Univ PhD90 Waterloo Luth Univ MA83. St Jo Coll Nottm CTMin94 MTh95. **d** 96 **p** 97. C Enfield St Jas *Lon* from 96. *Glebe House, 146 Hertford Road, Enfield, Middx EN3 5AY* Tel 0181-804 3100

WILLIAMS, Canon Giles Peter. b 54. Lon Univ BA77 MA78. Trin Coll Bris 80. **d** 82 **p** 83. C Reading Greyfriars *Ox* 82-85; Rwanda Miss 85-90; Mid-Africa Min (CMS) 90-94; Can Kigali Cathl Rwanda from 90; V Woking St Jo *Guildf* from 95. *The Vicarage, St John's Hill Road, Woking, Surrey GU21 1RQ* Tel (01483) 761253

WILLIAMS, Glyn. b 54. K Coll Lon BD77 AKC77. Ripon Coll Cuddesdon 77. **d** 78 **p** 79. C Coppenhall *Ches* 78-81; C Northampton St Alb *Pet* 81-82; TV Birkenhead Priory *Ches* 82-85; Chapl RAF 85-90 and from 96; Dep Chapl HM Pris Wandsworth 90-91; Chapl HM Pris Elmley 91-95. *Chaplaincy Services (RAF), HQ, Personnel and Training Command, RAF Innsworth, Gloucester GL3 1EZ* Tel (01452) 712612 ext 5164 Fax 510828

WILLIAMS, Glyn Alun. b 17. St D Coll Lamp BA40. **d** 41 **p** 42. C Gors-las *St D* 41-46; C Llangyfelach and Morriston *S & B* 46-48; C Llansadwrn w Llanwrda *St D* 48-50; V Llandyssilio 50-57; V Llangyndeyrn 57-71; V Pencarreg and Llanycrwys 71-73; rtd 73. *11 Tirwaun, Pwll, Llanelli SA15 4AY* Tel (01554) 759850

WILLIAMS, Graham Ivor. b 23. Jes Coll Ox BA48 MA48. Cuddesdon Coll 48. **d** 49 **p** 50. C Swansea St Mary and H Trin *S & B* 49-53; C Edgbaston St Bart *Birm* 53-55; R Nutfield *S'wark* from 55. *The Rectory, Blechingley Road, Nutfield, Redhill RH1 4HN* Tel (01737) 822286

WILLIAMS, Graham Parry. b 46. Bp Burgess Hall Lamp 67 St D Coll Lamp DipTh70. **d** 70 **p** 71. C Ebbw Vale *Mon* 70-73; C Trevethin 73-74; V Nantyglo 74-76; Chapl RN 76-85; R Northlew w Ashbury *Ex* 85-87; R Bratton Clovelly w Germansweek 85-87; TV Pontypool *Mon* 88-90; C Skegness and Winthorpe *Linc* 90-91; V Sutton Bridge 91-94; P-in-c Witham Gp 94-97; P-in-c Ruskington from 97. *The Rectory, Ruskington, Sleaford, Lincs NG34 9AE* Tel (01526) 832463

WILLIAMS, Gwenllian. *See* GILES, Mrs Gwenllian

WILLIAMS, Gwilym Elfed. b 33. Univ of Wales (Lamp) BA53. St Mich Coll Llan 53. **d** 56 **p** 57. C Llandudno *Ban* 56-59; C Aberdare St Jo *Llan* 59-63; C Penarth All SS 63-65; R Eglwysilan 65-70; V Mountain Ash 70-81; V Llanblethian w Cowbridge and Llandough etc 81-93; P-in-c St Hilary 87-91; V Lisvane from 93. *The Vicarage, 2 Llwynpia Road, Lisvane, Cardiff CF4 5SY* Tel (01222) 753338

WILLIAMS, Canon Gwilym Kenneth. b 12. Univ of Wales BA34. St Mich Coll Llan 34. **d** 35 **p** 36. C Llansadwrn w Llanwrda *St D* 35-38; C Llandingat 38-42; P-in-c Henllan Amgoed and Llangan 42-44; R Brechfa 44-52; R Brechfa and Abergorlech 52-59; R Brechfa w Abergorlech etc 59-60; R Borth 60-80; RD Llanbadarn Fawr 71-80; Can St D Cathl 75-80; rtd 80. *2 Clos-y-Drindod, Buarth Road, Aberystwyth SY23 1NB* Tel (01970) 615756

WILLIAMS, The Ven Harold Edgar. b 17. Univ of Wales (Lamp) BA39. AKC42. **d** 42 **p** 43. C Leytonstone St Jo *Chelmsf* 42-45; C Barnes St Mary *S'wark* 45-46; Chapl RNVR 46-51 and 55-58; Chapl RN 51-55; C Swansea St Jude *S & B* 48-51; Bp's Messenger 55-56; R Llanhamlach and Llansantffraed-juxta-Usk 55-61; Dir of Ords 55-79; Dir of Post-Ord Tr 56; V Hay 61-67; V Brynmawr 67-76; Can Brecon Cathl 72-83; Sec Prov Selection Bd for Ords 73-76; V Newton St Pet 76-87; Chan Brecon Cathl 79-83; Adn Gower 83-87; rtd 87. *10 Budehaven Terrace, Mumbles, Swansea SA3 5PY* Tel (01792) 404728

WILLIAMS, Harry Abbott. b 19. Trin Coll Cam BA41 MA45. Cuddesdon Coll 41. **d** 43 **p** 44. C Pimlico St Barn *Lon* 43-45; C St Marylebone All SS 45-48; Chapl and Tutor Westcott Ho Cam 48-51; Fell and Lect Trin Coll Cam 51-69; Dean of Chpl and Tutor 58-69; CR from 72; Lic to Offic *Wakef* from 80; rtd 89. *House of the Resurrection, Mirfield, W Yorkshire WF14 0BN* Tel (01924) 493272

WILLIAMS, Haydn Clifford. b 32. Univ of Wales (Abth) BA54 DipEd55. EMMTC 89. **d** 95 **p** 96. Hon C Anstey *Leic* from 95. *42 Ashfield Drive, Anstey, Leicester LE7 7TA* Tel 0116-236 3894

WILLIAMS, Mrs Heather Marilyn. b 42. Oak Hill Th Coll 82. **dss** 85 **d** 87 **p** 94. Taunton Lyngford *B & W* 85-87; Hon C 87-89; C Worle 89-94; V Weston-super-Mare St Andr Bournville from 94. *St Andrew's Vicarage, Coniston Crescent, Weston-super-Mare, Avon BS23 3RX* Tel (01934) 627818

WILLIAMS, Helena Maria Alija. b 43. **d** 88 **p** 95. NSM Roath St Marg *Llan* 88-91; Westcott Ho Cam 91-92; Asst Chapl Univ Hosp of Wales Cardiff 92-95; Chapl United Bris Healthcare NHS Trust from 95. *Bristol Royal Hospital for Children, St Michael's Hill, Bristol BS2 8BJ* Tel 0117-921 5411 or 928 5323

WILLIAMS, Henry Gordon. b 33. JP83. St Aid Birkenhead 57. **d** 60 **p** 61. C Radcliffe St Mary *Man* 60-63; Australia from 63; OStJ from 78. *PO Box 259, Northampton, W Australia 6535* Tel Northampton (99) 341259 Fax 341507

WILLIAMS, The Ven Henry Leslie. b 19. Univ of Wales (Lamp) BA41. St Mich Coll Llan 41. **d** 43 **p** 44. C Aberdovey *Ban* 43-45; C Ban Cathl Par 45-48; Chapl RN 48-49; C Ches St Mary *Ches* 49-53; V Barnston 53-84; CF (TA) 54-62; RD Wirral N *Ches* 67-75; Hon Can Ches Cathl 72-75; Adn Ches 75-88; rtd 88; Perm to Offic *Ches* from 88. *1 Bartholomew Way, Westminster Park, Chester CH4 7RJ* Tel (01244) 675296

WILLIAMS, Herbert Brian. b 18. BNC Ox BA39 MA48. Linc Th Coll 80. **d** 81 **p** 82. NSM Asterby Gp *Linc* 81-94; rtd 88; Lic to Offic *Linc* from 94. *55 Upgate, Louth, Lincs LN11 9HD* Tel (01507) 608093

WILLIAMS, Canon Howard. b 08. Univ of Wales BA29 MA32 St Jo Coll Cam MLitt45. St Steph Ho Ox 30. **d** 31 **p** 32. C Aberystwyth St Mich *St D* 31-36; Perm to Offic *Ely* 36-38; V Llan-non *St D* 38-49; Lect Univ of Wales 49-50; V Betws w Ammanford 49-57; V Llanelli 57-75; Chapl Llanelli Hosps 57-75; Can St D Cathl 60-75; Treas 73-75; rtd 75. *Cwm Eithin, 53 Maes Hendre, Waunfawr, Aberystwyth SY23 3PS* Tel (01970) 615311

WILLIAMS, Howell Mark. b 56. Univ of Wales (Cardiff) BD87. St Mich Coll Llan 84. **d** 87 **p** 88. C Swansea St Thos and Kilvey *S & B* 87-89; TV Aberystwyth *St D* 89-93; V Hirwaun *Llan* from 93. *The Vicarage, High Street, Hirwaun, Aberdare CF44 9SL* Tel (01685) 811316

WILLIAMS, Canon Hugh. b 27. MRIPHH ACP48. AKC53. **d** 54 **p** 55. C Kirkby *Liv* 54-57; C Blackpool St Jo *Blackb* 57-58; V Foulridge 58-65; V Over Darwen H Trin 65-74; P-in-c Hoddlesden 65-74; P-in-c Over Darwen St Jo 68-74; P-in-c Darwen St Geo 69-74; TR Darwen St Pet w Hoddlesden 74-77; RD Darwen 75-77; R Burnley St Pet 77-85; RD Burnley 78-85; Hon Can Blackb Cathl 78-92; V Bolton le Sands 85-92; rtd 92; Bp's Officer for Rtd Clergy (Blackb Adnry) *Blackb* from 92. *37 Albert Street, Brierfield, Nelson, Lancs BB9 5JF*

WILLIAMS, Hugh Martin. b 45. AKC73. St Aug Coll Cant 73. **d** 74 **p** 75. C Heston *Lon* 74-78; Chapl City Univ 78-84; PV Westmr Abbey 82-84; V Newquay *Truro* 84-93; V Christchurch *Win* from 93. *The Priory Vicarage, Quay Road, Christchurch, Dorset BH23 1BU* Tel (01202) 483102

WILLIAMS, Hugh Wynford. b 16. Selw Coll Cam BA40 MA44. St D Coll Lamp BA38 St Mich Coll Llan 40. **d** 41 **p** 42. C Kirkburton *Wakef* 41-43; C Skipton H Trin *Bradf* 43-44; Perm to Offic 44-51; Perm to Offic *Pet* 51-74; Chapl Oundle Sch 54-74; R Tichmarsh *Pet* 74-88; P-in-c Clapton 77-88; rtd 88; Perm to Offic *Pet* from 88. *28 Church Street, Tichmarsh, Kettering, Northants NN14 3DB* Tel (01832) 734529

WILLIAMS, Ian Geoffrey. b 50. Lon Univ BD71 AKC71 PGCE73 DPS74 Derby Univ MA94 PhD97. St Jo Coll Nottm 72. **d** 74 **p** 75. C Harborne Heath *Birm* 74-77; C Hazlemere *Ox* 77-84; V Littleover *Derby* 84-90; Hd of RE Woodlands Sch Derby 90-95; Hd of Relig Studies Qu Eliz Mercian High Sch Tamworth 95-97; Visiting Lect Derby Univ Derby from 96; Lect Relig Studies Univ Coll Ches from 97. *30 Redshaw Street, Derby DE1 3SG* Tel (01332) 343987 or (01244) 375444 E-mail i.g.williams1@student.derby.ac.uk

WILLIAMS, Ian Kenneth. b 44. MMS83 MBIM87. EMMTC 84. **d** 87 **p** 88. NSM Corby Glen *Linc* from 87. *6 Market Place, Corby Glen, Grantham, Lincs NG33 4NH* Tel (01476) 550595

WILLIAMS, Ian Withers. b 43. Linc Th Coll 68. **d** 69 **p** 70. C Burney Lane *Birm* 69-72; C Cleobury Mortimer w Hopton Wafers *Heref* 72-75; P-in-c Coreley w Doddington 75-79; V Knowbury 75-79; V Lich Ch Ch *Lich* from 79. *Christ Church Vicarage, Lichfield, Staffs WS13 8AL* Tel (01543) 264431 Mobile 0860-105541 Fax 411862 E-mail williams@homemail.com

WILLIAMS, Ieuan Merchant. b 13. St D Coll Lamp BA36. **d** 39 **p** 40. C Ardsley *Sheff* 39-42; C Wombwell 42-48; R N and S Wheatley w W Burton *S'well* 48-55; R W Leake w Kingston-on-Soar and Ratcliffe-on-Soar 55-59; V Burton Joyce w Bulcote 59-71; R Brightwell Baldwin *Ox* 71-80; R Cuxham w Easington 72-80; P-in-c Britwell Salome 76-80; P-in-c Ewelme 76-80; rtd 80; Perm to Offic *Ox* from 80. *5 The Cloisters, Ewelme, Oxford OX10 6HS* Tel (01491) 838897

WILLIAMS, Ifan. b 24. St D Coll Lamp 54. **d** 56 **p** 57. C Llangefni w Tregaean *Ban* 56-60; R Llanfachreth 60-67; Dioc Youth Officer 62-65; Area Sec (Merioneth) USPG 63-89; P-in-c Brithdir and Bryncoedifor *Ban* 65-67; V Ffestiniog w Blaenau Ffestiniog 67-89; RD Ardudwy 80-89; rtd 89; Lic to Offic *Ban* from 89. *Cil y Coed, 6 Penrallt, Llanystumdwy, Criccieth LL52 0SR* Tel (01766) 522978

WILLIAMS, Jack. b 26. Univ of Wales (Ban) BSc50. St Mich Coll Llan 50. **d** 52 **p** 53. C Buckley *St As* 52-55; C Llanrhos 55-59; V Bronnington and Bettisfield 59-61; C Ripponden *Wakef* 61-65; Chapl Rishworth Sch Ripponden 65-68; Hd Master Rishworth Sch Ripponden 68-86; V Halifax St Jo *Wakef* 86-89; rtd 89; Perm to Offic *Ban* from 89. *36 Tros-yr-Afon, Llangoed, Beaumaris LL58 8AT* Tel (01248) 490839

WILLIAMS, James Einon. b 18. St Mary's Univ (NS) BEd63. St D Coll Lamp BA39. **d** 46 **p** 47. C Kidwelly *St D* 46-48; Canada 48-70; Chapl RCN 52-70; V Mydroilyn and Llanarth w Llanina *St D* 73-80; rtd 80. *105-7633 Central Saannich Road, Saanichton, British Columbia, Canada, V8M 2B6*

WILLIAMS, James Llanfair Warren. b 48. St Mich Coll Llan DMinlStuds92. **d** 92 **p** 93. C Pembroke Dock *St D* 92-93; C Pembroke Dock w Cosheston w Nash and Upton 93-95; V Cwmaman from 95. *Cwmaman Vicarage, Vicarage Road, Twyn, Ammanford SA18 1JQ* Tel (01269) 822107

WILLIAMS, James Nicholas Owen (Nick). b 39. MBE. CEng DipTh. S'wark Ord Course. **d** 82 **p** 83. C Petersfield w Sheet *Portsm* 82-86; TV Droitwich *Worc* 86-87; TV Droitwich Spa 87-88; R Church Lench w Rous Lench and Abbots Morton 88-94; V Milton *B & W* from 94. *St Peter's Vicarage, Baytree Road, Weston-super-Mare, Avon BS22 8QW* Tel (01934) 624247

WILLIAMS, Preb John. b 31. AKC56. **d** 57 **p** 58. C Cockerton *Dur* 57-60; C Camberwell St Geo *S'wark* 60-62; C Stockton St Chad *Dur* 62-65; V 65-68; R Longnewton 68-75; Soc Resp Officer 68-83; Hon Can Dur Cathl 80-83; Bp's Officer for Min *Lich* 83-96; Preb Lich Cathl 83-96; C Lich St Mary w St Mich 95-96; rtd 96. *2 Fox Spring Rise, Edinburgh EH10 6NE* Tel 0131-445 2983

WILLIAMS, Dr John Anthony. b 53. G&C Coll Cam BA75 MA79 St Jo Coll Dur BA83 PhD86. Cranmer Hall Dur 81. **d** 86 **p** 87. C Beverley Minster *York* 86-89; C Cloughton 89-90; P-in-c 90-93; Clergy Tr Officer E Riding 89-93; P-in-c Emley *Wakef* from 93; Dioc Minl Tr Officer from 93; Wakef Min Scheme Officer from 97. *The Rectory, 14 Grange Drive, Emley, Huddersfield HD8 9SF* Tel (01924) 848301

WILLIAMS, John Barrie. b 38. Lon Univ DSocStuds68 Univ of Wales (Cardiff) MSc77 DipEd80. St Mich Coll Llan 89. **d** 87 **p** 88. NSM Newcastle *Llan* 87-89; C Port Talbot St Theodore 89; Perm to Offic from 89. *Shorncliffe, 11 Priory Oak, Bridgend, M Glam CF31 2HY* Tel (01656) 660369

WILLIAMS, John Beattie. b 42. Univ of Wales BA66. Cuddesdon Coll 67. **d** 69 **p** 69. C St Helier *S'wark* 69-70; C Yeovil H Trin *B & W* 70-76; P-in-c Ebbesbourne Wake w Fifield Bavant and Alvediston *Sarum* 76-78; Chapl to the Deaf 76-78; Chapl to the Deaf *B & W* 78-83; TV Fareham H Trin *Portsm* 83-94; R W Wittering and Birdham w Itchenor *Chich* from 94. *The Rectory, Cakeham Road, West Wittering, Chichester, W Sussex PO20 8AD* Tel (01243) 514057

WILLIAMS, The Ven John Charles. b 12. Univ Coll Ox 34 St D Coll Lamp BA34. Qu Coll Birm 36. **d** 37 **p** 38. C Birm Ch Ch Summerfield *Birm* 37-39; C Halesowen *Worc* 39-43; V Reddal Hill St Luke 43-48; V Redditch St Steph 48-59; R Halesowen 59-70; Hon Can Worc Cathl 65-75; Adn Dudley 68-75; V Dodderhill 70-75; RD Bromsgrove 58-59; Adn Worc and Can Res Worc Cathl 75-80; Dir of Ords 75-79; rtd 80; Lic to Offic *Worc* from 80; Perm to Offic *Cov* from 80; Asst Chapl HM Pris Long Lartin 82-87. *The Old Vicarage, Church Lane, Norton, Evesham, Worcs WR11 4TL* Tel (01386) 870213

WILLIAMS, John David Anthony. b 55. St Steph Ho Ox 85. **d** 87 **p** 88. C Paignton St Jo *Ex* 87-90; C Heavitree w Ex St Paul 90-91; TV from 91. *St Lawrence Vicarage, Lower Hill Barton Road, Exeter EX1 3EH* Tel (01392) 466302

WILLIAMS, John Edward. b 31. Univ of Wales (Abth) DipTh55. St Deiniol's Hawarden 76. **d** 76 **p** 77. C Llansamlet *S & B* 76-78; V Aberffraw and Llangwyfan w Llangadwaladr *Ban* 78-83; rtd 83. *17 Pontwillim Estate, Brecon LD3 9BT*

WILLIAMS, John Elwyn Askew. b 09. St Jo Coll Cam BA32 MA36. Ridley Hall Cam 32. **d** 34 **p** 35. C Roch St Marg *Roch* 34-37; C Lenton *S'well* 37-40; CF (EC) 40-46; P-in-c Eakring *S'well* 46-47; R 47-55; V Winkburn 47-55; V Sutton on the Forest *York* 55-61; V Whitchurch w Creslow *Ox* 61-81; rtd 81; Perm to Offic *Ox* from 81. *15 Manor Park, Maids Moreton, Buckingham MK18 1QY* Tel (01280) 814101

WILLIAMS, John Francis Meyler. b 34. St Jo Coll Cam BA56 MA60. Sarum & Wells Th Coll 79. **d** 81 **p** 82. C Hadleigh w Layham and Shelley *St E* 81-84; P-in-c Parham w Hacheston 84-87; P-in-c Campsey Ashe and Marlesford 84-87; R Campsea Ashe w Marlesford, Parham and Hacheston 87-95; P-in-c Kedington from 95. *The Rectory, Kedington, Haverhill, Suffolk CB9 7NN* Tel (01440) 712052

WILLIAMS, Canon John Francis Oliver. b 15. TCD BA40 MA43. **d** 40 **p** 41. C Shankill *C & O* 40-42; C Oldcastle *M & K* 42-44; P-in-c Clonfadfornan w Castletown 44-46; I Athboy w Girley and Kildalkey 46-54; Sec Ch of Ireland Jews' Soc 54-56; I Dublin Irishtown *D & G* 56-73; I Dalkey St Patr 73-82; RD Dublin St Mark 69-82; Can Ch Ch Cathl Dublin 81-82; rtd 82. *Wayside, Church Road, Greystones, Co Wicklow, Irish Republic* Tel Dublin (1) 287 4953

WILLIAMS, Dr John Frederick Arthur. b 26. Lon Univ BSc50 Southn Univ PhD53. Ridley Hall Cam 63. **d** 65 **p** 66. C Cambridge H Sepulchre w All SS *Ely* 65-66; P-in-c Cambridge St Mark 66-67; V Portswood Ch Ch *Win* 67-90; Assoc V 90-93; C Win Ch Ch 93-96; rtd 96. *120 Bellemoor Road, Southampton SO1 2QY* Tel (01703) 771482

WILLIAMS, John Gilbert. b 36. St Aid Birkenhead 64. **d** 67 **p** 68. C Bollington St Jo *Ches* 67-69; C Oxton 69-72; P-in-c Acton Beauchamp and Evesbatch 72-76; P-in-c Castle Frome *Heref* 72-76; P-in-c Bishop's Frome 72-76; R Kingsland 76-83; P-in-c Eardisland 77-83; P-in-c Aymestry and Leinthall Earles 82-83; R Cradley w Mathon and Storridge 83-94; R Norton St Philip w Hemington, Hardington etc *B & W* from 94. *The Rectory, Vicarage Lane, Norton St Philip, Bath BA3 6LY* Tel (01373) 834447

WILLIAMS, John Glyn. b 18. Lon Univ BA47. St Mich Coll Llan 46. **d** 49 **p** 50. C Aberdare w Cwmbach *Llan* 49-59; Clerical Org Sec (S Wales) CECS 59-83; Lic to Offic *Llan, St D, Mon* and *S & B* from 59; P-in-c Llanharry *Llan* from 83. *St Caron's, 40 Parkfields Road, Bridgend CF31 4BJ* Tel (01656) 654110

WILLIAMS, John Gordon. b 06. Lon Univ BA27. Ridley Hall Cam 30. **d** 32 **p** 33. C Bermondsey St Luke *S'wark* 32-34; C Rotherhithe H Trin 34-40; Asst to Relig Dir BBC 40-50; Field Sec Nat Soc 50-53; V Anfield St Columba *Liv* 53-57; Chapl and Educn Officer SPCK 57-72; Hon Min Can Ripon Cathl *Ripon* 72; rtd 72. *2 Sunnybank Place, Borrage Lane, Ripon, N Yorkshire HG4 2PZ* Tel (01765) 603352

WILLIAMS, Canon John Heard. b 35. Bris Univ BA58. Clifton Th Coll 59. **d** 59 **p** 60. C Tunbridge Wells Ch Ch *Roch* 59-65; V Forest Gate St Sav *Chelmsf* 65-75; P-in-c W Ham St Matt 72-75; TR Forest Gate St Sav w W Ham St Matt from 75; Hon Can Chelmsf Cathl from 82. *St Saviour's Rectory, Sidney Road, London E7 0EF* Tel 0181-534 6109

WILLIAMS, John Herbert. b 19. LVO89. St D Coll Lamp BA41 Sarum & Wells Th Coll 41. **d** 43 **p** 44. Chapl HM Pris Birm 57-64; Chapl HM Pris Wormwood Scrubs 64-71; SE Regional Chapl 71-74; Chapl HM Remand Cen Latchmere Ho 71-74; Dep Chapl Gen of Pris 74-83; P in O 79-83; Chapl RVO 83-89; Chapl to RVO and Qu Chpl of the Savoy 83-89; Chapl to The Queen 87-89; rtd 89. *75 Monks Drive, London W3 0ED* Tel 0181-992 5206

WILLIAMS, John James. b 08. Qu Coll Cam BA31 MA35. Ely Th Coll 31. **d** 32 **p** 33. C Harrow St Pet *Lon* 32-35; C Hampstead Garden Suburb 35-36; C W Hampstead St Jas 36-38; C Abingdon w Shippon *Ox* 38-44; V Speen 44-50; R Lathbury 50-62; R Newport Pagnell 50-62; R Wokingham St Paul 62-73; P-in-c N w S Moreton 73-77; rtd 77; Perm to Offic *Ox* from 77. *Iona, Coopers Lane, Wantage, Oxon OX12 8HQ* Tel (01235) 767904

WILLIAMS, Canon John James. b 20. TD61. Linc Coll Ox BA42 MA46. St Mich Coll Llan 42. **d** 44 **p** 45. C Rhosymedre *St As* 44-47; C Flint 47-50; CF 49-62; C Llanrhos *St As* 50-53; V Whixall *Lich* 53-57; V Prees 57-64; Sen CF (TA) 62-67; CF (TA) 67-68; V Powyke *Worc* 64-85; Hon Can Worc Cathl 77-85; rtd 85; Perm to Offic *Worc* from 85. *9 St Nicholas's Road, Peopleton, Pershore, Worcs WR10 2EN* Tel (01905) 840032

WILLIAMS, John Keith. b 63. MISM89. Ridley Hall Cam 95. **d** 97. C Potters Bar *St Alb* from 97. *11 Otways Close, Potters Bar, Herts EN6 1TE* Tel (01707) 646505 Fax as telephone

WILLIAMS, John Mark Gruffydd. MA MSc DPhil. **d** 89 **p** 90. NSM Girton *Ely* 89-91; Perm to Offic *Ban* from 91. *Department of Psychology, University of Wales, Bangor LL57 2DG* Tel (01248) 351151

WILLIAMS, John Michael. b 44. MBASW Univ of Wales (Cardiff) CQSW74. St Deiniol's Hawarden 80. **d** 83 **p** 84. NSM Llanrhos *St As* 83-94; P-in-c Brynymaen w Trofarth 94-95; V from 95. *The Vicarage, Brynymaen, Colwyn Bay LL28 5EW* Tel (01492) 532567

WILLIAMS, John Peter Philip. b 49. Univ of Wales (Ban) DipTh70 Open Univ BA84. Chich Th Coll 71. **d** 72 **p** 73. C Abergele *St As* 72-77; R Henllan and Llannefydd 77-82; R Henllan and Llannefydd and Bylchau from 82. *The Rectory, Henllan, Denbigh LL16 5BB* Tel (01745) 812628

WILLIAMS, John Richard. b 48. Rhodes Univ BA68 K Coll Lon BD72 AKC72. **d** 73 **p** 74. S Africa 73-76; C Addington *Cant* 77-80; C Minster in Sheppey 80-86; R Temple Ewell w Lydden 86-90; V Hound *Win* 90-94; V Highcliffe w Hinton Admiral from 94. *The Vicarage, 33 Nea Road, Christchurch, Dorset BH23 4NB* Tel (01425) 272761

WILLIAMS, John Roger. b 31. Bris Univ BA55 Lon Univ BD57. Tyndale Hall Bris 57. **d** 57 **p** 58. C Islington H Trin Cloudesley Square *Lon* 57-60; Travelling Sec IVF 60-64; V Selly Hill St Steph *Birm* 64-74; P-in-c Chilwell *S'well* 74-75; V 75-90; Dioc Tourism Officer 90-95; P-in-c Perlethorpe 90-95; P-in-c Norton Cuckney 90-95; rtd 95. *Derwent Lights, 4 Wyntor Avenue, Winster, Matlock, Derbyshire DE4 2DU* Tel (01629) 650142

WILLIAMS, Canon John Roger. b 37. Westmr Coll Ox MTh97. Lich Th Coll 60. **d** 63 **p** 64. C Wem *Lich* 63-66; C Wolverhampton St Pet 66-69; R Pudleston w Hatf *Heref* 69-74; P-in-c Stoke Prior and Ford w Humber 69-74; P-in-c Docklow 69-74; V Fenton *Lich* 74-81; P-in-c Honington w Idlicote *Cov* 81; P-in-c Shipston-on-Stour w Tidmington 81; R Shipston-on-Stour w Honington and Idlicote 81-92; RD Shipston 83-90; Hon Can Cov Cathl from 90; R Lighthorne from 92; V Chesterton from 92; V Newbold Pacey w Moreton Morrell from 92. *The Rectory, Church Lane, Lighthorne, Warwick CV35 0AR* Tel (01926) 651279

WILLIAMS, John Strettle. b 44. DipEd73 BA84. N Ord Course 77. **d** 80 **p** 81. NSM Liv St Paul Stoneycroft *Liv* 80-83; Chapl Cen Liv Coll of FE from 80; Hon C Liv Our Lady and St Nic w St Anne from 83; Chapl RNR 84-90; Chapl City Coll of FE Liv from 85. *28 Brook Street, Whiston, Prescot, Merseyside L35 5AP* Tel 0151-426 9598

WILLIAMS, John Trefor. b 23. Worc Ord Coll 65. **d** 67 **p** 68. C Paignton St Jo *Ex* 67-72; V Winkleigh 72-80; P-in-c Ashreigney 73-79; R 79-80; P-in-c Brushford 75-79; V 79-80; R Broadwoodkelly 79-80; P-in-c Berrynarbor 80-81; P-in-c Combe Martin 80-81; R Combe Martin and Berrynarbor 81-92; rtd 92; Perm to Offic *Ex* from 92. *97 Littleham Road, Exmouth, Devon EX8 2RA* Tel (01395) 264460

WILLIAMS, Jonathan Simon. b 60. Univ of Wales (Cardiff) BSc81. Coll of Resurr Mirfield 83. **d** 86 **p** 87. C Gelligaer *Llan* 86-89; C Cwmbran *Mon* 89-90; TV 90-97; V Marshfield and Peterstone Wentloog etc from 97. *The Vicarage, Church Lane, Marshfield, Cardiff CF3 8UF* Tel (01633) 680257

WILLIAMS, Miss Joy Margaret. b 30. Lon Univ BD69. Linc Th Coll 82. **dss** 83 **d** 87 **p** 94. Pershore w Pinvin, Wick and Birlingham *Worc* 83-87; Par Dn 87-88; Par Dn Dudley St Jo 88-90; rtd 90. *Pixie Cottage, 40 Ridge Street, Pershore, Worcs WR10 1AT* Tel (01386) 556867

WILLIAMS, Julian Thomas. b 65. Clare Coll Cam BA87. Wycliffe Hall Ox BA90. **d** 91 **p** 92. Min Can St D Cathl *St D* 91-94; C St D Cathl 91-94; V Cil-y-Cwm and Ystrad-ffin w Rhandir-mwyn etc from 94. *The Vicarage, Cil-y-Cwm, Llandovery SA20 0SP* Tel (01550) 721109

WILLIAMS, Keith. b 37. St Jo Coll Nottm 83. **d** 85 **p** 86. C Holbeck *Ripon* 85-88; R Swillington 88-95; V Batley All SS *Wakef* from 95; P-in-c Purlwell from 95. *The Vicarage, Churchfield Street, Batley, W Yorkshire WF17 5DL* Tel (01924) 473049

WILLIAMS, Keith Douglas. b 41. EMMTC 86. **d** 89 **p** 90. NSM Netherfield w Colwick *S'well* from 89; Chapl Nottm Healthcare NHS Trust from 93; NSM Gedling *S'well* from 95. *15 Mile End Road, Nottingham NG4 2DW* Tel 0115-961 4850

WILLIAMS, Keith Graham. b 38. ARICS62 Reading Univ MSc70 St Jo Coll Dur DipTh77. **d** 77 **p** 78. C Almondbury *Wakef* 77-81; C Chapelthorpe 81-82; V Ryhill 82-88; V E Ardsley from 88. *The Vicarage, Church Lane, East Ardsley, Wakefield, W Yorkshire WF3 2LJ* Tel (01924) 822184

WILLIAMS, Kelvin George John. b 36. ALCD62. **d** 62 **p** 63. C Bath Abbey w St Jas *B & W* 62-65; CF (TA) 64-65 and 70-79; Chapl R Nat Hosp for Rheumatic Diseases Bath 64-65; CF 65-68; C Clevedon St Andr *B & W* 68-70; V Ston Easton w Farrington Gurney 70-74; P-in-c Bradford 74-75; R Bradford w Oake, Hillfarrance and Heathfield 75-76; NSM Puriton and Pawlett 89-91; V from 92; NSM Bridgwater Deanery 91-92. *The Vicarage, 1 The Rye, Puriton, Bridgwater, Somerset TA7 8BZ* Tel (01278) 683500

WILLIAMS, Lloyd. b 43. Oak Hill Th Coll 71. **d** 74 **p** 75. C Laisterdyke *Bradf* 74-77; C Hoole *Ches* 77-80; V Rawthorpe *Wakef* 80-84; HM Pris Leeds 84-85; Chapl HM Pris Cardiff 85-88; R Aldington w Bonnington and Bilsington *Cant* 88-95; Chapl HM Pris Aldington 88-95; RD N Lympne *Cant* 94-95; Hong Kong from 95. *c/o St Andrew's Church, Nathan Road, Kowloon, Hong Kong* E-mail 100043.3001@compuserve.com

WILLIAMS, Mrs Louise Margaret. b 66. Lanc Univ BA87. St Jo Coll Nottm DPS91. **d** 91 **p** 94. Par Dn W Ham *Chelmsf* 91-94; C Harold Hill St Geo 94-95; NSM Southend St Sav Westcliff from 95; Chapl Asst Southend Health Care NHS Trust from 97. *St Saviour's Vicarage, 33 King's Road, Southend-on-Sea SS0 8LL* Tel (01702) 342920

WILLIAMS, Malcolm Kendra. b 34. Oak Hill NSM Course. **d** 85 **p** 86. NSM Margate H Trin *Cant* 85-87; P-in-c Austrey *Birm* 87-90; V Wonersh *Guildf* 90-95; Zimbabwe from 95. *Address temp unknown*

WILLIAMS, Mark. b 64. St Mich Coll Llan BTh94. **d** 97. C Mountain Ash *Llan* from 97. *The Church House, Toncoch Terrace, Cefn Pennar, Mountain Ash CF45 4DY* Tel (01443) 473108

WILLIAMS, Mark Naylor. b 28. CCC Cam BA52 MA56 CertEd. Ripon Hall Ox 58. **d** 59 **p** 60. C Dorchester *Ox* 59-65; R Gt and Lt Braxted *Chelmsf* 65-70; R E Kilbride *Glas* 70-74; R Norton *Sheff* 74-89; R Lt w Gt Ellingham w Rockland *Nor* 89-95; rtd 95; Perm to Offic *Chelmsf* from 95. *15 Olivia Drive, Leigh-on-Sea, Essex SS9 3EF* Tel (01702) 78734

WILLIAMS, The Ven Martin Inffeld. b 37. SS Coll Cam BA62. Chich Th Coll 62. **d** 64 **p** 65. C Greenford H Cross *Lon* 64-70; Tutor Chich Th Coll 70-75; Vice-Prin 75-77; V Roath St German *Llan* 77-92; Adn Margam from 92; Treas Llan Cathl from 92; V Penydarren from 92. *The Vicarage, Church Street, Penydarren, Merthyr Tydfil CF47 9HS* Tel (01685) 386258

WILLIAMS, Maxwell Holman Bentley. b 24. Reading Univ BA50. Cuddesdon Coll 56. **d** 58 **p** 59. C Melksham *Sarum* 58-62; Chapl HM Youth Cust Cen Erlestoke 62-67; V Erlestoke *Sarum* 62-66; P-in-c Gt Cheverell 66-67; R 67; P-in-c Erlestoke 66-67; V 67; R Bemerton 67-75; rtd 89. *1 Three Yards Close, Portland, Dorset DT5 1JN* Tel (01305) 821055

WILLIAMS, Mervyn Rees. b 28. Univ of Wales (Swansea) BA49 Lon Univ PGCE54. St Deiniol's Hawarden 68. **d** 72 **p** 73. NSM Llangollen w Trevor and Llantysilio *St As* 72-94; rtd 94. *12 Wern Road, Llangollen LL20 8DU* Tel (01978) 860369

WILLIAMS, Meurig Llwyd. b 61. Univ of Wales (Abth) BA83 PGCE84 Univ of Wales (Cardiff) BD90. Westcott Ho Cam 90. **d** 92 **p** 93. C Holyhead w Rhoscolyn w Llanfair-yn-Neubwll *Ban* 92-95; P-in-c Denio w Abererch 95-96; V from 96. *The Vicarage, Yr Ala, Pwllheli LL53 5BL* Tel (01758) 612305

WILLIAMS, Michael Dermot Andrew. b 57. Ex Univ BA86. Ripon Coll Cuddesdon 90. **d** 92 **p** 93. C Leominster *Heref* 92; NSM Christow, Ashton, Trusham and Bridford *Ex* 92-97; Chief Exec Radcliffe Infirmary NHS Trust from 97. *21 Staunton Road, Oxford OX3 7TL* Tel (01865) 761957 or 224193 Mobile 0385-748561

WILLIAMS, Michael John. b 31. St Edm Hall Ox BA53 MA57. Wells Th Coll 53. **d** 55 **p** 56. C Wood Green St Mich *Lon* 55-59; C Bedminster St Aldhelm *Bris* 59-62; C Witney *Ox* 62-65; C Thatcham 66-70; Perm to Offic *Ex* 70-81; C Rainhill *Liv* 81-86; Chapl Whiston Hosp 83-86; rtd 86; Perm to Offic *Ex* from 86. *1 Bramble Lane, Crediton, Devon EX17 1DA* Tel (01363) 774005

WILLIAMS, Canon Michael Joseph. b 42. Cranmer Hall Dur BA68. **d** 70 **p** 71. C Toxteth Park St Philemon *Liv* 70-75; TV Toxteth St Philemon w St Gabr 75-78; Dir Past Studies St Jo Coll Dur 78-89; Prin N Ord Course from 89; Hon Can Liv Cathl *Liv* from 92; Perm to Offic *Ches* from 89. *75 Framingham Road, Brooklands, Sale, Cheshire M33 3RH* Tel 0161-962 7513 or 225 6668 Fax 248 9201 E-mail mike@noc2.u-net.com

WILLIAMS, Michael Robert John. b 41. Cranmer Hall Dur 67. **d** 70 **p** 71. C Middleton *Man* 70-73; C-in-c Blackley White Moss St Mark CD 73-79; R Blackley White Moss St Mark 79-86; R Gorton Em 86-96; R Gorton Em w St Jas from 96. *Emmanuel Rectory, 35 Blackwin Street, Manchester M12 5LD* Tel 0161-223 3510

WILLIAMS, Nicholas Jolyon. b 68. Univ of Wales (Swansea) BA89. Wycliffe Hall Ox BTh96. **d** 96 **p** 97. C Ditton *Roch* from 96. *Old School Cottage, 79 New Road, Ditton, Aylesford, Kent ME20 6AE* Tel (01732) 847669

WILLIAMS, Nigel Howard. b 63. Llys Fasi Agric Coll NCA81. St Mich Coll Llan DipTh95. **d** 95 **p** 96. C Denbigh and Nantglyn *St As* from 95. *34 Trewen, Denbigh LL16 3HF* Tel (01745) 812262

WILLIAMS, Norman Ernest. b 23. IEng FIEEE AMIEE Cardiff Coll of Tech HNC. Llan Dioc Tr Scheme 78. **d** 82 **p** 83. NSM Llanblethian w Cowbridge and Llandough etc *Llan* 82-93; rtd 93; Perm to Offic *Llan* from 93. *The Poplars, Cowbridge CF7 7BD* Tel (01446) 772107

WILLIAMS, Norman Henry. b 17. Bris Univ BA43. Qu Coll Birm 77. **d** 77 **p** 78. NSM Cov Cathl *Cov* from 77. *63 Daventry Road, Coventry CV3 5DH* Tel (01203) 502448

WILLIAMS, Norman Leigh. b 26. Open Univ BA86 Trin Coll Carmarthen 83. **d** 85 **p** 86. NSM Lougher *S & B* 85-96; NSM Adnry Gower 87-96; rtd 96. *Gorwydd Villa, 13 The Woodlands, Gowerton, Swansea SA4 3DP* Tel (01792) 874853

WILLIAMS, Ogwen Lloyd. b 20. Univ of Wales (Ban) BA42. St Mich Coll Llan 42. **d** 44 **p** 45. C Mostyn *St As* 44-47; C Colwyn 47-50; C Connah's Quay 50-56; V Llanfair D C 56-65; V Bistre 65-80; V Llansantffraid and Llanarmon and Pontfadog 80-85; rtd 85; Perm to Offic *St D* from 85. *Gwendraeth, 3 Heol y Gof, Newcastle Emlyn SA38 9HW* Tel (01239) 710295

WILLIAMS, Owen David. b 38. S'wark Ord Course 72. **d** 75 **p** 76. NSM Tatsfield *S'wark* 75-80; C Maidstone All SS w St Phil and H Trin *Cant* 80-81; C Maidstone All SS and St Phil w Tovil 81-82; V St Nicholas at Wade w Sarre and Chislet w Hoath 82-92; TV Bruton and Distr *B & W* from 92. *The Parsonage, Gold Hill, Batcombe, Shepton Mallet, Somerset BA4 6HF* Tel (01749) 850671

WILLIAMS, Paul Andrew. b 62. Oak Hill Th Coll BA91. **d** 91 **p** 92. C Ware Ch Ch *St Alb* 91-94; C Harold Wood *Chelmsf* from 94. *48 Harold Court Road, Harold Wood, Romford RM3 0YX*

WILLIAMS, Paul Gavin. b 68. Grey Coll Dur BA89. Wycliffe Hall Ox MPhil93. **d** 92 **p** 93. C Muswell Hill St Jas w St Matt *Lon* 92-96; C Clifton Ch Ch w Em *Bris* from 96. *62 Clifton Park Road, Clifton, Bristol BS8 3HN* Tel 0117-973 9640

WILLIAMS, Paul Rhys. b 58. St Andr Univ MTh82. Westcott Ho Cam 83. **d** 86 **p** 87. Asst Chapl Selw Coll Cam 86-87; C Chatham St Steph *Roch* 87-90; V Gillingham St Aug 90-95; Bp's Dom Chapl from 95. *22 St Margaret's Street, Rochester, Kent ME1 1TS* Tel (01634) 828344

WILLIAMS, Peris Llewelyn. b 39. Univ of Wales (Lamp) BA59. Qu Coll Birm 59. **d** 62 **p** 63. C Upton (Overchurch) *Ches* 62-65; C Davenham 65-68; C Grange St Andr 68-73; TV E Runcorn w Halton 73-74; V Backford 74-80; Youth Chapl 74-80; V Witton 80-86; V Hoylake 86-93; R Ches H Trin from 93. *Holy Trinity Rectory, Norris Road, Chester CH1 5DZ* Tel (01244) 372721

WILLIAMS, Peter David. b 32. K Coll Lon BSc56 AKC56 PhD62 St Jo Coll Cam PGCE69 Lon Univ BD70. Clifton Th Coll 62. **d** 64 **p** 65. C Southport St Phil *Liv* 64-70; Chapl St Ninian's Sch Dumfriesshire 70-74; Chapl Crawfordton Sch Dumfriesshire 74-75; CMS 75-93; Kenya 76-88; Tanzania 88-92; rtd 93; NSM Kirriemuir *St And* from 93. *3/4 Lilybank, Brechin Road, Kirriemuir, Angus DD8 4BW* Tel (01575) 574025

WILLIAMS, Peter Hurrell. b 34. Keble Coll Ox BA58 MA61. Tyndale Hall Bris 62. **d** 64 **p** 65. C Sparkbrook Ch Ch *Birm* 64-67; C Rushden St Pet 67-70; P-in-c Clapham Park All SS *S'wark* 70-78; R Stanford-le-Hope w Mucking *Chelmsf* 78-92; P-in-c Gt Oakley w Wix 92-96; R Gt Oakley w Wix and Wrabness from 96. *The Rectory, Wix Road, Great Oakley, Harwich, Essex CO12 5BJ* Tel (01255) 880230

WILLIAMS, Peter John. b 55. Southn Univ BTh80 Univ of Wales (Swansea) DSocStuds90. Chich Th Coll 76. **d** 80 **p** 81. C Chepstow *Mon* 80-84; C Morriston *S & B* 84-85; V Glantawe 85-88; R Reynoldston w Penrice and Llangennith from 88; Dioc Soc Resp Officer from 88. *The Vicarage, Llangennith SA3 1HU* Tel (01792) 386391

WILLIAMS, Peter Rodney. b 22. Chich Th Coll 60. **d** 62 **p** 63. C Seaford w Sutton *Chich* 62-65; P-in-c Wivelsfield 65-72; V Eastbourne St Jo 72-87; rtd 87; Perm to Offic *Chich* from 87. *Sussex Cottage, 14 Michel Dene Road, East Dean, Eastbourne, E Sussex BN20 0JN* Tel (01323) 422417

WILLIAMS, Philip Allan. b 48. Bris Univ BSc69 CertEd74. Trin Coll Bris 86. **d** 88 **p** 89. C Heref St Pet w St Owen and St Jas *Heref* 88-93; R Peterchurch w Vowchurch, Turnastone and Dorstone 93-96; P-in-c Holmer w Huntington from 96. *The Vicarage, Holmer, Hereford HR4 9RG* Tel (01432) 273200

WILLIAMS, Philip Andrew. b 64. Sheff Univ BA86. St Jo Coll Dur 88. **d** 90 **p** 91. C Hillsborough and Wadsley Bridge *Sheff* 90-94; C Lenton Abbey *S'well* 94-96; C Wollaton Park 94-96; P-in-c Lenton Abbey from 96. *St Barnabas' Vicarage, Derby Road, Lenton Abbey, Beeston, Nottingham NG9 2SN* Tel 0115-925 4995

WILLIAMS, Philip James. b 52. St Chad's Coll Dur BA73. Coll of Resurr Mirfield 74. **d** 76 **p** 77. C Stoke upon Trent *Lich* 76-80; TV 80; Chapl N Staffs Poly 80-84; TV Stoke-upon-Trent 80-84; R Shrewsbury St Giles w Sutton and Atcham from 84. *St Giles's Rectory, 127 Abbey Foregate, Shrewsbury SY2 6LY* Tel (01743) 356426

WILLIAMS, Ray. b 23. Birm City Tech Coll DipMechEng41 Lon Univ DipEd46. St Aid Birkenhead 56. **d** 58 **p** 59. C Sparkhill St Jo *Birm* 58-60; Area Sec (Dios St Alb and Chelmsf) CMS 60-65; V Shenstone *Lich* 65-73; New Zealand from 73. *Monkton Combe, Wakamarina Road, Canvastown, RD1 Havelock 7154, New Zealand* Tel Christchurch (3) 574 2714

WILLIAMS, Raymond Howel (Ray). b 27. St Jo Coll Cam BA49 MA51 Ball Coll Ox BLitt63. St Jo Coll Nottm 72 NW Ord Course 73. **d** 73 **p** 74. C Derby St Pet *Derby* 73-76; C Enfield Ch Ch Trent Park *Lon* 75-81; V S Mymms K Chas *St Alb* 81-94; NSM 94-95; rtd 94. *The Vicarage, 40 Dugdale Hill Lane, Potters Bar, Herts EN6 2DW* Tel (01707) 654219

WILLIAMS, Richard Dennis. b 57. LTCL79. Coll of Resurr Mirfield 79. **d** 82 **p** 83. C Roath St Marg *Llan* 82-85; C Penarth w Lavernock 85-88; V Abertillery *Mon* 88-95; V Tredunnoc and Llantrisant w Llanhennock etc from 95. *The Rectory, Tredunnock, Usk NP3 1LY* Tel (01633) 49231

WILLIAMS, Richard Elwyn. b 57. Hull Univ BA79. Coll of Resurr Mirfield 79. **d** 81 **p** 82. C Altrincham St Geo *Ches* 81-84; C Stockport St Thos 84-85; C Stockport St Thos w St Pet 86; R Withington St Crispin *Man* 86-95; V Alveston *Cov* from 95. *The Vicarage, Alveston, Stratford-upon-Avon, Warks CV37 7QB* Tel (01789) 292777

WILLIAMS, Canon Richard Glyndwr. b 18. St D Coll Lamp BA39 BD50. **d** 41 **p** 42. C Kidwelly *St D* 41-46; C Llandudno *Ban* 46-52; R Trefriw 52-55; V Llandinorwic 55-62; Sec Dioc Coun for Educn 58-62; Warden Ch Hostel Ban 62-70; Chapl Univ of Wales (Ban) *Ban* 62-70; Dir of Ords 62-70 and 84-86; Prec Ban Cathl 68-88; Can from 68; R Llanbeblig w Caernarfon 70-71; R Llanbeblig w Caernarfon and Betws Garmon etc 71-81; V Llandysilio and Llandegfan 81-88; RD Tindaethwy 82-88; rtd 88; Lic to Offic *Ban* from 88. *Borth, 9 Cae Cil Melyn, Penrhos, Bangor LL57 2HD* Tel (01248) 362883

WILLIAMS, Canon Richard Henry Lowe. b 31. Liv Univ BA52. K Coll (NS) BD64 Ridley Hall Cam 54. **d** 56 **p** 57. C Drypool St Andr and St Pet *York* 56-59; Canada 59-64; V Kirkdale St Athanasius *Liv* 64-68; R Much Woolton 68-79; R Croft w Southworth 79-89; Dioc Communications Officer 79-97; Hon Can Liv Cathl 88-97; R Wavertree St Mary 89-97; rtd 97. *16 Childwall Crescent, Liverpool L16 7PQ* Tel 0151-722 7962

WILLIAMS, Richard Huw (Rick). b 63. Bradf and Ilkley Coll BA85. St Jo Coll Nottm LTh88 DPS89. **d** 89 **p** 90. C Forest Gate St Edm *Chelmsf* 89-90; C Plaistow 90-92; C Canning Town St Matthias 92-96; V Southend St Sav Westcliff from 96. *St Saviour's Vicarage, 33 King's Road, Southend-on-Sea SS0 8LL* Tel (01702) 342920

WILLIAMS, Richard Lawrence. b 62. Warw Univ BSc83 ACA87. Wycliffe Hall Ox 95. **d** 97. C Wallington H Trin *S'wark* from 97. *14 Harcourt Road, Wallington, Surrey SM6 8BA* Tel 0181-647 0132 Fax as telephone

WILLIAMS, Robert. d 97. C W Derby St Mary *Liv* from 97. *2 The Village, West Derby, Liverpool L12 5HW*

WILLIAMS, Canon Robert. b 20. OBE90. Univ of Wales (Ban) BA43. St Mich Coll Llan 43. **d** 45 **p** 46. C Holyhead w Rhoscolyn *Ban* 45-55; R Llangwnnadl w Penllech and Bryncroes 55-90; RD Llyn 76-90; Hon Can Ban Cathl 84-90; R Aberdaron and Bodferin w Rhiw w Llanfaelrhys 89-90; rtd 90; Lic to Offic *Ban* from 90. *Hendre Bach, Aberdaron, Pwllheli LL53 8BL* Tel (01758) 86624

WILLIAMS, Robert David. b 05. St D Coll Lamp BA32. **d** 33 **p** 34. C Llandinorwic *Ban* 33-38; C Meyllteyrn 38-42; R Llanddona w Llaniestyn 42-48; V Llanerchymedd w Rhodogeidio and Gwredog 48-57; V Dolwyddelan 57-62; V Llandysilio (or Menai Bridge) 62-75; rtd 75; Lic to Offic *Ban* from 75. *31 Parc Henblas, Llanfairfechan LL33 0RW* Tel (01248) 680102

WILLIAMS, Canon Robert Edward. b 17. St Mich Coll Llan 45. **d** 47 **p** 48. C Llangeinwen *Ban* 47-52; C Machynlleth and Llanwrin 52-55; V Llanwnda w Llanfaglan 55-87; Hon Can Ban Cathl 86-87; rtd 87; Lic to Offic *Ban* from 87. *Bodfryn, 49 Llwyn Beuno, Bontnewydd, Caernarfon LL49 2UH* Tel (01286) 673877

WILLIAMS, Robert Edward. b 42. Ex Univ BA63. Lich Th Coll. **d** 65 **p** 66. C Wednesbury St Paul Wood Green *Lich* 65-67; C Whitchurch 67-69; P-in-c Whixall 69-72; P-in-c Edstaston 69-72; CF 72-91; R Cheriton w Tichborne and Beauworth *Win* from 91. *The Rectory, Cheriton, Alresford, Hants SO24 0QH* Tel (01962) 771226

WILLIAMS, Robert Edward. b 50. Univ of Wales (Ban) DipTh71. St Mich Coll Llan BD74 CertEd79. **d** 74 **p** 75. C Flint *St As* 74-77; Asst Chapl Sandbach Sch 79-80; Chapl and Hd RE 80-88; Perm to Offic *Ches* 86-88; Perm to Offic *St As* 87-88; CF from 88. *MOD Chaplains (Army), Trenchard Lines, Upavon, Pewsey, Wilts SN9 6BE* Tel (01980) 615804 Fax 615800

WILLIAMS, Robert Ellis Greenleaf. b 12. St D Coll Lamp BA34 Lich Th Coll 34. **d** 36 **p** 37. C S Banbury *Ox* 36-39; Australia 39-54; R Croydon w Clopton *Ely* 54-58; V Tadlow w E Hatley 54-58; R Hatley 54-58; V Oldham St Ambrose *Man* 58-66; V Rochdale St Aid 66-75; TV Weston-super-Mare Cen Par *B & W* 75-78; P-in-c Castleton All So *Man* 78-80; rtd 80; Perm to Offic *Man* from 81. *18 Barrowdale Drive, Rochdale, Lancs OL11 3JZ* Tel (01706) 356582

WILLIAMS, Robert George Dibdin. b 20. St Mich Coll Llan 56. **d** 58 **p** 59. C Welshpool *St As* 58-63; R Nannerch 63-68; V Cilcain and Nannerch 68-75; V Gwersyllt 75-85; rtd 85. *30 Ffordd y Gaer, Bradley, Wrexham LL11 4BW* Tel (01978) 754007

WILLIAMS, Robert Gwynne. b 15. St D Coll Lamp BA38. **d** 41 **p** 42. C Tenby *St D* 41-51; R Goodrich w Welsh Bicknor and Marstow *Heref* 51-81; rtd 81; Perm to Offic *Heref* from 92. *The Arch Bungalow, Goodrich, Ross-on-Wye, Herefordshire HR9 6HY* Tel (01600) 890285

WILLIAMS, Robert Jeffrey Hopkin. b 62. ALAM Univ of Wales (Abth) BA84. Chich Th Coll BTh90. **d** 90 **p** 91. C Eastbourne St Mary *Chich* 90-94; R Upper St Leonards St Jo from 94. *53 Brittany Road, St Leonards-on-Sea, E Sussex TN38 0RD* Tel (01424) 423367

WILLIAMS, Canon Robert John. b 51. Cartrefle Coll of Educn CertEd73 Univ of Wales (Ban) BEd. St Mich Coll Llan BD76. **d** 76 **p** 77. C Swansea St Mary and H Trin *S & B* 76-78; Chapl

Univ of Wales (Swansea) 78-84; Children's Adv 81-88; Asst Dir of Educn 81-88; Bp's Chapl for Th Educn 83-88; R Reynoldston w Penrice and Llangennith 84-88; R Denbigh and Nantglyn *St As* 88-94; V Sketty *S & B* from 94; Dir of Ords from 94; Can Brecon Cathl from 95. *The Vicarage, De la Beche Road, Sketty, Swansea SA2 9AR* Tel (01792) 202767

WILLIAMS, Roger Anthony. b 54. Univ of Wales (Lamp) BA76. Bp Burgess Hall Lamp 72 Qu Coll Birm 76. **d** 78 **p** 79. C Llanelli *St D* 78-82; V Monkton 82-86; Chapl to the Deaf *B & W* 86-90; Chapl to the Deaf *Ox* from 90. *Denchworth House, Denchworth, Wantage, Oxon OX12 0DX* Tel (01235) 868248

WILLIAMS, Roger Stewart. b 54. Qu Coll Cam BA75 MA79. Wycliffe Hall Ox BA78 MA82. **d** 79 **p** 80. C Hamstead St Paul *Birm* 79-82; C Barking St Marg w St Patr *Chelmsf* 82-85; V Mildmay Grove St Jude and St Paul *Lon* 85-95; P-in-c Charles w Plymouth St Matthias *Ex* from 95; Chapl Plymouth Univ from 95. *The Vicarage, 6 St Lawrence Road, Plymouth PL4 6HN* Tel (01752) 665640

WILLIAMS, Ronald Hywel. b 35. St D Coll Lamp BA62. **d** 63 **p** 64. C Machynlleth and Llanwrin *Ban* 63-66; C Llanaber 66-69; C Hawarden *St As* 69-73; R Llansantffraid Glan Conway and Eglwysfach 73-77; V Rhosllannerchrugog 77-88; R Cilcain and Nannerch and Rhyd-y-mwyn 88-92; V Llanbadarn Fawr w Capel Bangor and Goginan *St D* 92-95; V Llanbadarn Fawr from 95; RD Llanbadarn Fawr from 94. *The New Vicarage, Llanbadarn Fawr, Aberystwyth SY23 3QU* Tel (01970) 623368

✠**WILLIAMS, The Rt Revd Rowan Douglas.** b 50. FBA90 Ch Coll Cam BA71 MA75 Wadh Coll Ox DPhil75 DD89. Coll of Resurr Mirfield 75. **d** 77 **p** 78 **c** 92. Tutor Westcott Ho Cam 77-80; Hon C Chesterton St Geo *Ely* 80-83; Lect Div Cam Univ 80-86; Dean Clare Coll Cam 84-86; Can Th Leic Cathl *Leic* 81-92; Can Res Ch Ch *Ox* 86-92; Lady Marg Prof Div Ox Univ 86-92; Bp Mon from 92. *Bishopstow, Newport NP9 4EA* Tel (01633) 263510

WILLIAMS, Canon Roy. b 28. Lon Univ DipTh60. Ely Th Coll 58. **d** 60 **p** 61. C Daybrook *S'well* 60-63; V Bilborough St Jo 63-73; V Arnold 73-92; Hon Can S'well Minster 85-92; rtd 92. *10 Maris Drive, Burton Joyce, Nottingham NG14 5AJ* Tel 0115-931 2030

WILLIAMS, Royce. b 35. Leeds Univ BA56 Lanc Univ MA82. St Steph Ho Ox 58. **d** 60 **p** 61. C Ardwick St Benedict *Man* 60-62; C Bedford Leigh 62-64; V Blackb St Pet *Blackb* 64-68; Perm to Offic 70-78; Chapl W R Tuson Coll Preston 75-78; V Burnley St Cath 78-81; P-in-c Burnley St Alb w St Paul 78-81; V Burnley St Cath w St Alb and St Paul 81-95. *2 Westmoreland Avenue, Thornton-Cleveleys, Blackpool FY5 2LX* Tel (01253) 823107

WILLIAMS, Shamus Frank Charles. b 57. St Cath Coll Cam BA79 MA83. Ripon Coll Cuddesdon 81. **d** 84 **p** 85. C Swanage and Studland *Sarum* 84-87; C St Alb St Pet *St Alb* 87-90; TV Saffron Walden w Wendens Ambo and Littlebury *Chelmsf* 90-95; V Shingay Gp of Par *Ely* from 95. *The Vicarage, Church Street, Guilden Morden, Royston, Herts SG8 0JP* Tel (01763) 852747

WILLIAMS, Preb Sidney Austen. b 12. CVO79. St Cath Coll Cam BA36 MA56. Westcott Ho Cam 36. **d** 37 **p** 38. C Harringay St Paul *Lon* 37-40; Chapl Toc H 40-48; C All Hallows Barking *Lon* 45-46; Hon C St Martin-in-the-Fields 46-48; C 49-50; V Westbury-on-Trym St Alb *Bris* 51-56; V St Martin-in-the-Fields *Lon* 56-84; Chapl to The Queen 61-82; Extra Chapl to The Queen from 82; Preb St Paul's Cathl *Lon* 73-84; rtd 84; Perm to Offic *S'wark* from 84. *37 Tulsemere Road, London SE27 9EH* Tel 0181-670 7945

WILLIAMS, Stephen Clark (Steve). b 47. Univ of Wales (Cardiff) BSc(Econ)69 Warw Univ MSc70. Wycliffe Hall Ox DipMin93. **d** 93 **p** 94. C High Wycombe *Ox* 93-96; C Walton H Trin from 96. *The Parsonage, 60 Grenville Road, Aylesbury, Bucks HP21 8EY* Tel (01296) 24175

WILLIAMS, Stephen Geoffrey. b 54. St Jo Coll Nottm BTh79 LTh79. **d** 79 **p** 80. C Skelmersdale St Paul *Liv* 79-81; C Burley *Ripon* 81-86. *24 Coronation Drive, Penketh, Warrington WA5 2DD* Tel (01925) 723599

WILLIAMS, Stephen Grant. b 51. K Coll Lon BD73 AKC73. **d** 75 **p** 76. C Paddington Ch Ch *Lon* 75-78; C Paddington St Jas 78-80; Chapl LSE 80-91; Chapl (Sen) Lon Univs from 91. *15 Wilmington Square, London WC1X 0ER* Tel 0171-837 1782 or 387 0670

WILLIAMS, The Ven Stephen Heath. b 51. LTh DipRE DipMin. **d** 74 **p** 75. Australia 74-76 and from 78; Adn Wagga Wagga from 89; C Leigh Park *Portsm* 76-78. *The Rectory, Church Street, Wagga Wagga, NSW, Australia 2650* Tel Wagga Wagga (69) 212323 Fax 216259

WILLIAMS, Stephen James. b 52. Lon Univ BSc73. Ridley Hall Cam 73. **d** 78 **p** 79. C Waltham Abbey *Chelmsf* 78-82; C Bedford St Paul *St Alb* 82-86; P-in-c Chalgrave 86-88; V Harlington from 86. *The Vicarage, Church Road, Harlington, Dunstable, Beds LU5 6LE* Tel (01525) 872413

WILLIAMS, Stephen John. b 49. Univ of NSW BA73 Cam Univ MA81. Ridley Hall Cam 75. **d** 78 **p** 79. Uganda 78; C Brompton H Trin w Onslow Square St Paul *Lon* 79-82; Australia from 82. *11 Moore Avenue, West Lindfield, NSW, Australia 2070* Tel Sydney (2) 416 5729 Fax 416 6926

WILLIAMS, Stephen Lionel. b 48. St Kath Coll Liv CertEd73 Open Univ BA77. N Ord Course 93. **d** 96 **p** 97. NSM Ditton St Mich *Liv* from 96. *355 Upton Lane, Widnes, Cheshire WA8 9AQ* Tel 0151-420 3352

WILLIAMS, Stephen Stuart. b 60. Magd Coll Ox BA82 Dur Univ BA88. Cranmer Hall Dur 86. **d** 89 **p** 90. C W Derby Gd Shep *Liv* 89-93; TV Liv Our Lady and St Nic w St Anne from 93. *43 Bisphan House, Lace Street, Liverpool L3 2BP* Tel 0151-236 3420

WILLIAMS, Susan (Sue). b 50. Swansea Coll of Educn CertEd72. Ban Ord Course 94. **d** 97. NSM Criccieth w Treflys *Ban* from 97. *Tal Eifion, High Street, Criccieth LL52 0RN* Tel (01766) 523183

WILLIAMS, Terence. b 36. Univ of Wales (Abth) BSc57 Univ of Wales (Cardiff) MA67 Aston Univ PhD71. Glouc Sch of Min 78. **d** 81 **p** 81. NSM Deerhurst, Apperley w Forthampton and Chaceley *Glouc* 81-87; NSM Tarrington w Stoke Edith, Aylton, Pixley etc *Heref* 87-88; P-in-c Upper and Lower Slaughter w Eyford and Naunton *Glouc* 88-91; P-in-c Redmarley D'Abitot, Bromesberrow w Pauntley etc 91-95; R from 95; RD Forest N from 95. *The Rectory, Redmarley, Gloucester GL19 3HS* Tel (01531) 650630

WILLIAMS, Terence John. b 36. Univ of Wales BSc62. St Deiniol's Hawarden 85. **d** 86 **p** 87. C Llangyfelach *S & B* 86-88; C Morriston 88-89; V Llanwrtyd w Llanddulas in Tir Abad etc 89-91; V Llanedi w Tycroes and Saron *St D* from 91. *The Vicarage, 37 Hendre Road, Tycroes, Ammanford SA18 3LF* Tel (01269) 592384

WILLIAMS, Thomas Bruce. b 41. Oak Hill Th Coll 74. **d** 76 **p** 77. C Liskeard w St Keyne and St Pinnock *Truro* 76-79; Australia from 79. *213 Thompson Street, (PO Box 165), Tennant Creek, NT, Australia 0861* Tel Tennant Creek (89) 621101

WILLIAMS, Canon Thomas Gerald. b 14. Ex Coll Ox BA35 MA39. Chich Th Coll 35. **d** 37 **p** 38. C Teynham *Cant* 37-44; C Whitstable All SS 44-49; V Sturry 49-56; P-in-c Fordwich 49-52; P-in-c Sevington 56-79; R Willesborough 56-62; P-in-c Hinxhill w Brook 59-62; R Willesborough w Hinxhill 62-80; Chapl Willesborough Hosp 56-80; Hon Can Cant Cathl 73-81; rtd 80; Perm to Offic *Cant* from 81. *2 Heathfield Court, Heathfield Road, Ashford, Kent TN24 8QD* Tel (01233) 639328

WILLIAMS, Timothy John. b 54. BEd83. Trin Coll Carmarthen. **d** 89 **p** 90. NSM Llansamlet *S & B* 89-97; P-in-c Bryngwyn and Newchurch and Llanbedr etc from 97. *The Rectory, Rhosgoch, Builth Wells LD2 3JU* Tel (01497) 851260

WILLIAMS, Timothy John. b 64. Kent Univ BA86. St Mich Coll Llan BD89. **d** 89 **p** 90. C Killay *S & B* 89-91; C Llwynderw 91-94; V Knighton and Norton from 94. *The Vicarage, Knighton LD7 1AG* Tel (01547) 528566

WILLIAMS, Tom David. b 19. St D Coll Lamp BA41 St Mich Coll Llan 41. **d** 43 **p** 45. C Llanbeblig *Ban* 43-47; C Aberdovey 47-49; C Llanengan and Llangian 49; C Llandegai 49-53; R Llangybi w Llanarmon 53-60; V Llanidloes 60-75; P-in-c Llangurig 66-72; V 72-75; RD Arwystli 73-75; R Criccieth w Treflys 75-82; V Llanfihangel Ysgeifiog and Llanffinan etc 82-84; rtd 84; Perm to Offic *Ban* from 84. *Trefri Fach, Llangaffo, Gaerwen LL60 6LT* Tel (01248) 79687

WILLIAMS, Trevor Russell. b 48. TCD BA71. St Jo Coll Nottm BA73. **d** 74 **p** 75. C Maidenhead St Andr and St Mary *Ox* 74-77; Asst Chapl QUB 78-80; Relig Broadcasting Producer BBC 81-88; Lic to Offic *Conn* 81-88; I Newcastle *D & D* 88-93; Leader Corrymeela Community from 93. *54 North Parade, Ormeau Road, Belfast BT7 2GG* Tel (01232) 208054 Fax (01265) 762626 E-mail belfast@corrymeela.org.uk

WILLIAMS, Canon Trevor Stanley Morlais. b 38. Jes Coll Ox BA63 Univ of E Africa MA67. Westcott Ho Cam BA67. **d** 67 **p** 68. C Clifton St Paul *Bris* 67-70; Asst Chapl Bris Univ 67-70; Chapl and Fell Trin Coll Ox from 70; Hon Can Ch Ch *Ox* from 95. *Trinity College, Oxford OX1 3BH* Tel (01865) 279886 E-mail trevor.williams@trinity.ox.ac.uk

WILLIAMS, Vincent Handley. b 24. LRAM LLCM ARCM CertEd. St Deiniol's Hawarden 76. **d** 78 **p** 79. Hon C Barrow *Ches* 78-81; C Dodleston 81-83; V Lostock Gralam 83-90; rtd 90; Perm to Offic *Ches* from 90. *2 Springfield Close, Higher Kinnerton, Chester CH4 9BU* Tel (01244) 660983

WILLIAMS, Walter Haydn. b 31. Univ of Wales (Lamp) BA53 Selw Coll Cam BA55 MA60. St Mich Coll Llan 55. **d** 56 **p** 57. C Denbigh *St As* 56-58; V Choral St As Cathl 58-61; C St As 58-61; R Llanfyllin and Bwlchycibau 61-68; V Northop 68-73; V Mold 73-86; RD Mold 79-86; Can St As Cathl 77-82; Prec 81-82; Preb and Chan 82-86; R Overton and Erbistock and Penley 86-94; Chmn Ch of Wales Liturg Cttee 86-94; rtd 94. *2 Park Lane, Craig y Don, Llandudno LL30 1PQ* Tel (01492) 877294

WILLIAMS, William Arwyn. b 15. Univ of Wales (Abth) BA37. Clifton Th Coll 38. **d** 40 **p** 41. C Romford Gd Shep Collier Row *Chelmsf* 40-42; CF (EC) 42-48; CF 48-72; Dep Asst Chapl Gen 60-65; Asst Chapl Gen 65-72; Hon Chapl to The Queen 69-72; Chapl Salisbury Hosps 72-84; rtd 84; Perm to Offic *B & W* 84-94; Perm to Offic *Bris* 85-94. *The Coach House, Entry Hill Drive, Bath BA2 5NJ* Tel (01225) 312658

WILLIAMS, William David Brynmor. b 48. Univ of Wales (Swansea) DipTh71 Open Univ BA89. St D Coll Lamp 71. **d** 72 **p** 73. C Killay *S & B* 72-74; C Wokingham All SS *Ox* 74-75; CF 75-77; C Spilsby w Hundleby *Linc* 83-87; R Meppershall w Campton and Stondon *St Alb* 87-90; V Hemsby *Nor* 90-96; P-in-c

Winterton w E and W Somerton and Horsey 94-96; rtd 96. *The Gables, The Green, Stokesby, Great Yarmouth, Norfolk NR29 3EX*

WILLIAMS, William John. b 23. Fitzw Ho Cam BA50 MA55. Wycliffe Hall Ox. **d** 54 **p** 55. V Cholsey *Ox* 69-73; rtd 88. *38 Hordley Road, Wellington, Telford, Shropshire TF1 3NR* Tel (01952) 242210

WILLIAMS-HUNTER, Ian Roy. b 44. Trin Coll Bris 71. **d** 73 **p** 74. C Redhill H Trin *S'wark* 73-75; C Deane *Man* 76-80; R Hartshorne *Derby* from 80. *The Rectory, 74 Woodville Road, Hartshorne, Swadlincote, Derbyshire DE11 7ET* Tel (01283) 217866

WILLIAMS-POTTER, Mrs Amanda Clare (Mandy). b 69. Univ of Wales (Ban) BD90. Westcott Ho Cam CTM92. **d** 92 **p** 97. C Carmarthen St Dav *St D* 92-94; Chapl Trin Coll Carmarthen from 94. *Llwynon, College Road, Carmarthen SA31 3EQ* Tel (01267) 238175

WILLIAMSON, Alfred Michael. b 28. Kelham Th Coll 53. **d** 58 **p** 59. C Nottingham St Geo w St Jo *S'well* 58-64; SSM 60-64; V Kenwyn St Geo *Truro* 64-73; V St Agnes 73-87; Australia from 87; rtd 93. *PO Box 76, Pacific Palms, NSW, Australia 2428* Tel Pacific Palms (65) 542239

WILLIAMSON, Andrew John. b 39. MRPharmS. St Alb Minl Tr Scheme 82. **d** 85 **p** 86. NSM Oxhey All SS *St Alb* 85-88; NSM Bricket Wood from 88. *148 Penrose Avenue, Watford WD1 5AH* Tel 0181-421 0623

WILLIAMSON, Canon Anthony William (Tony). b 33. OBE77. Trin Coll Ox BA56 MA60. Cuddesdon Coll 56. **d** 60 **p** 61. Hon C Cowley St Jas *Ox* 60-79; TV 79-89; Dir of Educn (Schs) from 89; Hon Can Ch Ch from 94. *9 The Goggs, Watlington, Oxon OX9 5JX* Tel (01491) 612143

WILLIAMSON, David Barry. b 56. St Jo Coll Nottm 80. **d** 83 **p** 84. C N Mymms *St Alb* 83-86; C Burley *Ripon* 86-92; Project Worker CECS 92-96; Youth and Children's Adv *B & W* from 96. *35 Orchard Road, Street, Somerset BA16 0BT* Tel (01458) 446435

WILLIAMSON, Edward McDonald. b 42. CITC 67. **d** 69 **p** 70. C Limerick St Mary *L & K* 69-70; CF 70-73; C Penzance St Mary w St Paul *Truro* 73-76; V Mullion 76-81; rtd 81; Perm to Offic *Truro* from 81. *Hazelmere, The Commons, Mullion, Helston, Cornwall TR12 7HZ* Tel (01326) 240865

WILLIAMSON, Gavin Leslie. b 59. FRSA Hull Univ BA82 TCD DipTh85. **d** 85 **p** 86. C Stillorgan w Blackrock *D & G* 85-87; Min Can St Patr Cathl Dublin 86-96; Warden Guild of Lay Readers 86-96; I Dunboyne w Kilcock, Maynooth, Moyglare etc *M & K* 87-96; Treas St Patr Cathl Dublin 90-96; Dioc Tutor for Tr of Aux Min (Meath) *M & K* 93-96; Prec Cant Cathl *Cant* from 96; Hon Min Can Cant Cathl from 96. *10 The Precincts, Canterbury, Kent CT1 2EE* Tel (01227) 762862

WILLIAMSON, Henry Lyttle. b 47. Lon Bible Coll DipTh91. **d** 95 **p** 96. NSM Edin St Marg *Edin* from 96. *12 Jubilee Crescent, Gorebridge, Midlothian EH23 4XD* Tel (01875) 820170

WILLIAMSON, Ivan Alister. b 63. TCD BTh90 Ulster Univ HNC87. CITC 87. **d** 90 **p** 91. C Lisburn St Paul *Conn* 90-95; C Roxbourne St Andr *Lon* from 95; Lect QUB from 95. *108 Malvern Avenue, South Harrow, Middx HA2 9EY* Tel 0181-423 0761

WILLIAMSON, Mrs Jennifer Irene. b 44. Glas Univ MA66 Sunderland Poly DipT79. NE Ord Course 89. **d** 92 **p** 94. NSM Easby w Brompton on Swale and Bolton on Swale *Ripon* 92-95; P-in-c Gilling and Kirkby Ravensworth from 95. *The Vicarage, Gilling West, Richmond, N Yorkshire DL10 5JG* Tel (01748) 824466

WILLIAMSON, John. b 33. Bede Coll Dur. NE Ord Course 81. **d** 84 **p** 85. NSM Beamish *Dur* 84-85; C Sedgefield 85-88; P-in-c Trimdon 88-89; V 89-94; rtd 94. *9 Beamish View, Stanley, Co Durham DH9 0XB* Tel (01207) 237380

WILLIAMSON, Dr John Brian Peter. b 30. CEng FIMechE FIEE FInstP FWeldI Selw Coll Cam PhD55. WMMTC. **d** 84 **p** 87. NSM Malvern H Trin and St Jas *Worc* 84-94; Perm to Offic from 94. *Monkfield House, Newland, Malvern, Worcs WR13 5BB* Tel (01905) 830522

WILLIAMSON, John Mark. b 43. FCP87 Birm Univ BA65 Univ of Wales (Cardiff) MEd75 MA82. St D Coll Lamp LTh67. **d** 67 **p** 68. C Shepton Mallet *B & W* 67-70; Hon C Dinder 70-71; Chapl Clifton Coll Bris 71-75; Lect All SS Bris 75-78; Chapl Bris Cathl *Bris* 77-78; Perm to Offic *Pet* 78-84; Perm to Offic *B & W* from 84. *6 Upper Lansdown Mews, Bath BA1 5HG* Tel (01225) 429938

WILLIAMSON, Michael John. b 39. ALCD63. **d** 64 **p** 65. C Pennington *Man* 64-67; C Higher Openshaw 67-69; P-in-c Man St Jerome w Ardwick St Silas 69-72; C-in-c Holts CD 72-77; R Droylsden St Mary from 77; Hon Can Man Cathl from 97. *The Rectory, Dunkirk Street, Droylsden, Manchester M35 7FB* Tel 0161-370 1569

WILLIAMSON, Nigel. b 65. Qu Coll Ox BA87. Cranmer Hall Dur CTMin93. **d** 93 **p** 94. C Stannington *Sheff* 93-96; P-in-c Nether Hoyland St Andr from 96. *The Vicarage, Market Street, Hoyland, Barnsley, S Yorkshire S74 0ET* Tel (01226) 742126

WILLIAMSON, Paul Nicholas. b 55. Univ of Otago BTh79. St Jo Coll Auckland 80. **d** 80 **p** 81. New Zealand 80-86 and from 88; C Selston *S'well* 86-88. *94 Hamilton Road, Hataitai, Wellington 3, New Zealand* Tel Wellington (4) 386 2140 or 386 3042 E-mail dalepaul@ihug.co.nz

WILLIAMSON, Paul Stewart. b 48. K Coll Lon BD71 AKC71. **d** 72 **p** 73. C Deptford St Paul *S'wark* 72-75; Hon C Kennington St Jo 76-77; C Hoxton H Trin w St Mary *Lon* 78-83; C St Marylebone All SS 83-84; C Willesden St Mary 84-85; Perm to Offic 86-89; C Hanworth St Geo 89-92; P-in-c from 92. *The Rectory, 7 Blakewood Close, Feltham, Middx TW13 7NL* Tel 0181-844 0457

WILLIAMSON, Peter Barry Martin. b 21. Wycliffe Hall Ox 61. **d** 62 **p** 63. C Billericay St Mary *Chelmsf* 62-68; V Bentley Common 68-77; V Lt Thurrock St Jo 77-86; rtd 86; Perm to Offic *St E* from 86. *Corner Cottage, The Street, Kelsale, Saxmundham, Suffolk IP17 2PB* Tel (01728) 602963

WILLIAMSON, Ralph James. b 62. LSE BSc(Econ)84. Ripon Coll Cuddesdon BA89 MA97. **d** 90 **p** 91. C Southgate St Andr *Lon* 90-93; TV Ross w Brampton Abbotts, Bridstow, Peterstow etc *Heref* 93-97; Chapl Ch Ch Ox from 97. *Christ Church, Oxford OX1 1DP* Tel (01865) 276236

WILLIAMSON, Robert John. b 55. K Coll Lon BA77. Coll of Resurr Mirfield 78. **d** 79 **p** 80. C Kirkby *Liv* 79-82; C Warrington St Elphin 82-84; P-in-c Burneside *Carl* 84-90; V Walney Is from 90. *The Vicarage, Promenade, Walney, Barrow-in-Furness, Cumbria LA14 3QU* Tel (01229) 471268

✠**WILLIAMSON, The Rt Revd Robert Kerr (Roy).** b 32. Oak Hill Th Coll 61. **d** 63 **p** 64 **c** 84. C Crowborough *Chich* 63-66; V Hyson Green *S'well* 66-72; V Nottingham St Ann w Em 72-76; V Bramcote 76-79; Adn Nottingham 78-84; Bp Bradf 84-91; Bp S'wark from 91. *Bishop's House, 38 Tooting Bec Gardens, London SW16 1QZ* Tel 0181-769 3256 Fax 769 4126 E-mail bishops.house@dswark.org.uk

WILLIAMSON, Canon Thomas George. b 33. AKC57. **d** 58 **p** 59. C Winshill *Derby* 58-61; C Hykeham *Linc* 61-64; V Brauncewell w Dunsby 64-78; R S w N Leasingham 64-78; RD Lafford 78-87; V Cranwell 78-80; R Leasingham 78-80; V Billinghay 80-87; V Gosberton 87-97; Can and Preb Linc Cathl from 94; V Gosberton, Gosberton Clough and Quadrin from 97. *The Vicarage, Wargate Way, Gosberton, Spalding, Lincs PE11 4NH* Tel (01775) 840694

WILLIE, Andrew Robert. b 43. Bris Univ BA65 Fitzw Coll Cam BA73 MA77. Ridley Hall Cam 71. **d** 74 **p** 75. Chapl St Woolos Cathl *Mon* 74-79; Chapl St Woolos Hosp Newport 75-79; V Newbridge *Mon* 79-85; V Mathern and Mounton w St Pierre from 85; Post-Ord Tr Officer from 85; Warden of Readers from 91. *St Tewdric's Vicarage, Mathern, Chepstow NP6 6JA* Tel (01291) 622317

WILLIMENT, Paul. b 47. Leeds Univ BSc68. St Steph Ho Ox 70. **d** 73 **p** 74. C Guiseley *Bradf* 73-76; C Northampton St Mary *Pet* 76-79; Malaysia from 80. *Box 347, Kuching, Sarawak, Malaysia*

WILLINK, Simon Wakefield. b 29. Magd Coll Cam BA52 MA55. Cuddesdon Coll 52. **d** 54 **p** 55. C Thornbury *Glouc* 54-57; C Tetbury w Beverston 57-60; R Siddington w Preston 60-64; New Zealand 65-71; Perm to Offic *Ex* 90-92; NSM Sidmouth, Woolbrook, Salcombe Regis, Sidbury etc from 92; rtd 95. *Willows, 6 Ridgeway Close, Sidbury, Sidmouth, Devon EX10 0SN* Tel (01395) 597545

WILLIS, Andrew Lyn. b 48. Univ of Wales (Lamp) BA73. **d** 74 **p** 75. C Swansea St Mary w H Trin and St Mark *S & B* 74-81; V Glasbury and Llowes 81-83; Chapl RAF from 83; Perm to Offic *Ban* from 83. *Chaplaincy Services (RAF), HQ, Personnel and Training Command, RAF Innsworth, Gloucester GL3 1EZ* Tel (01452) 712612 ext 5164 Fax 510828

WILLIS, Anthony David (Tony). b 40. Sarum & Wells Th Coll 87. **d** 89 **p** 90. C Ivybridge w Harford *Ex* 89-92; C Catherington and Clanfield *Portsm* 92-94; R Ellesborough, The Kimbles and Stoke Mandeville *Ox* from 94. *The Rectory, Ellesborough, Butlers Cross, Aylesbury, Bucks HP17 0XA* Tel (01296) 622110

WILLIS, Anthony John. b 38. Univ of Wales (Lamp) BA62. Qu Coll Birm DipTh74. **d** 64 **p** 65. C Kidderminster St Jo *Worc* 64-68; C Dunstable *St Alb* 68-72; V Rubery *Birm* 72-80; R Salwarpe and Hindlip w Martin Hussingtree *Worc* 80-92; Chapl of Agric and Rural Life from 85. *Glebe House, Grafton Flyford, Worcester WR7 4PG* Tel (01905) 381460

WILLIS, Christopher Charles Billopp (Chris). b 32. MITD. Bps' Coll Cheshunt 57. **d** 59 **p** 60. C Golders Green St Alb *Lon* 59-61; C N Harrow St Alb 61-64; V Shaw and Whitley *Sarum* 64-69; Ind Chapl *Ex* 69-77; C Swimbridge 70-77; Lic to Offic 77-92; Chapl W Buckland Sch Barnstaple 77-92; rtd 97; Perm to Offic *Ex* from 97. *Lower Upcott, Chittlehampton, Umberleigh, Devon EX37 9RX* Tel (01769) 540289

WILLIS, David George. b 45. Oak Hill Th Coll BA79. **d** 79 **p** 80. C Wallington H Trin *S'wark* 79-84; V Ramsgate St Mark *Cant* 84-89; Hon C Woodnesborough w Worth and Staple from 94. *75 Poulders Gardens, Sandwich, Kent CT13 0AJ* Tel (01304) 611959

WILLIS, Geoffrey Stephen Murrell. b 58. Sussex Univ BA80. Wycliffe Hall Ox 83. **d** 86 **p** 87. C Ashtead *Guildf* 86-89; Chapl Lee Abbey 89-94; Lic to Offic *Ex* 89-94; R Dunsfold *Guildf* from 94. *The Rectory, Church Green, Dunsfold, Godalming, Surrey GU8 4LT* Tel (01483) 200207

WILLIS, Preb George Arnold. b 16. Liv Univ BVSc46. Ely Th Coll 52. **d** 53 **p** 53. C Ipswich St Matt *St E* 53-55; R Brantham 55-60; V Cheltenham St Steph *Glouc* 60-64; R Ex St Martin, St Steph, St Laur etc *Ex* 64-74; Dep PV Ex Cathl 64-73; Preb Ex Cathl 73-81; TV Cen Ex 74-78; TR 78-81; rtd 81; Perm to Offic *Ox* 90-94; Hon C Binfield from 94. *11 Knox Green, Binfield, Bracknell, Berks RG42 4NZ* Tel (01344) 428522

WILLIS, Joyce Muriel. b 42. CQSW73 Open Univ BA86. EAMTC 86. **d** 89 **p** 94. NSM Hadleigh *St E* from 89. *26 Ramsey Road, Hadleigh, Ipswich IP7 6AN* Tel (01473) 823165

WILLIS, Peter Ambrose Duncan. b 34. Kelham Th Coll 55 Lich Th Coll 58. **d** 59 **p** 60. C Sevenoaks St Jo *Roch* 59-63; Trinidad and Tobago 63-68; P-in-c Diptford *Ex* 68-69; R 69-85; P-in-c N Huish 68-69; R 69-85; R Diptford, N Huish, Harberton and Harbertonford 85-96. *Sun Cottage, Church Street, Modbury, Ivybridge, Devon PL21 0QR* Tel (01548) 830541

WILLIS, The Very Revd Robert Andrew. b 47. Warw Univ BA68 Worc Coll Ox DipTh71. Cuddesdon Coll 70. **d** 72 **p** 73. C Shrewsbury St Chad *Lich* 72-75; V Choral Sarum Cathl *Sarum* 75-78; TR Tisbury 78-87; Chapl Cranborne Chase Sch Wilts 78-92; RD Chalke *Sarum* 82-87; V Sherborne w Castleton and Lillington 87-92; Can and Preb Sarum Cathl 88-92; RD Sherborne 91-92; Dean Heref from 92; P-in-c Heref St Jo from 92. *The Deanery, The Cloisters, Hereford HR1 2NG* Tel (01432) 272525

WILLIS, Mrs Rosemary Ann. b 39. LNSM course 89. **d** 93 **p** 96. NSM Fressingfield, Mendham, Metfield, Weybread etc *St E* from 93. *Priory House, Fressingfield, Eye, Suffolk IP21 5PH* Tel (01379) 586254

WILLIS, Thomas Charles (Tom). b 30. Bps' Coll Cheshunt 55. **d** 58 **p** 59. C Anlaby Common St Mark *York* 58-61; C Middlesbrough St Martin 61-63; V Kingston upon Hull St Paul w Sculcoates Ch Ch 63-69; P-in-c Sculcoates St Silas 67-69; V Sculcoates St Paul w Ch Ch and St Silas 69-80; V Bridlington H Trin and Sewerby w Marton 80-96; rtd 96. *23 Hillcrest Drive, Beverley, N Humberside HU17 7JL* Tel (01482) 888511

WILLMINGTON, John Martin Vanderlure. b 45. St D Coll Lamp BA69. St Steph Ho Ox 69. **d** 71 **p** 72. C Upper Teddington SS Pet and Paul *Lon* 71-75; C Kensington St Mary Abbots w St Geo 75-83; R Perivale 83-91; V Acton Green from 91. *206 St Alban's Avenue, London W4 5JU* Tel 0181-994 5735

WILLMONT, Anthony Vernon. b 35. Lich Th Coll 62. **d** 63 **p** 64. C Yardley St Edburgha *Birm* 63-65; C Smethwick H Trin w St Alb 65-68; V Ropley w W Tisted *Win* 68-77; V Ipswich St Aug *St E* 77-84; R King's Worthy *Win* 84-90; R Headbourne Worthy 84-90; R Lapworth *Birm* from 90; R Baddesley Clinton from 90. *The Rectory, Church Lane, Lapworth, Solihull, W Midlands B94 5NX* Tel (01564) 782098

WILLMOT, Philip Boulton. b 15. St Pet Hall Ox BA36 MA41. Westcott Ho Cam 38. **d** 38 **p** 39. C Totton *Win* 38-42; Chapl Magd Coll Ox and Sch 42-50; Chapl Win Coll 50-77; Lic to Offic *Win* 60-84; Chapl St Jo and St Mary Hosps Win 79-80; rtd 80; Perm to Offic *Win* from 84. *34 Hatherley Road, Winchester, Hants SO22 6RT* Tel (01962) 852360

WILLMOTT, Robert Owen Noel (Bob). b 41. Lich Th Coll 65. **d** 68 **p** 69. C Perry Hill St Geo *S'wark* 68-71; C Denham *Ox* 71-76; P-in-c Tingewick w Water Stratford 76-77; P-in-c Radclive 76-77; R Tingewick w Water Stratford, Radclive etc 77-89; R Wingrave w Rowsham, Aston Abbotts and Cublington from 89. *The Rectory, Leighton Road, Wingrave, Aylesbury, Bucks HP22 4PA* Tel (01296) 681623

WILLMOTT, The Ven Trevor. b 50. St Pet Coll Ox BA71 MA74. Westcott Ho Cam DipTh73. **d** 74 **p** 75. C Norton *St Alb* 74-77; Asst Chapl Chapl Oslo w Bergen, Trondheim and Stavanger *Eur* 78-79; Chapl Naples w Sorrento, Capri and Bari 79-83; Warden Ecton Ho 83-89; R Ecton *Pet* 83-89; Dir of Post-Ord Tr 86-97; Dir of Ords 86-97; Can Res, Prec and Sacr Pet Cathl from 86-97; Adn Dur and Can Res from 97. *15 The College, Durham DH1 3EQ* Tel 0191-384 7534

WILLOUGHBY, The Ven David Albert. b 31. St Jo Coll Dur BA53. DipTh57. **d** 57 **p** 58. C Shipley St Pet *Bradf* 57-61; C Barnoldswick w Bracewell 61-62; R Moston St Chad *Man* 62-72; V Marown *S & M* 72-80; Dioc Stewardship Adv 76-96; V Douglas St Geo and St Barn 80-96; RD Douglas 80-82; Adn Man 82-96; rtd 96; Perm to Offic *S & M* from 96. *19 Glen Vine Park, Glen Vine, Douglas, Isle of Man IM4 4EZ* Tel (01624) 852493

WILLOUGHBY, Francis Edward John. b 38. St Jo Coll Nottm. **d** 83 **p** 84. C Tonbridge SS Pet and Paul *Roch* 83-87; V Sutton at Hone from 87. *The Vicarage, Main Road, Sutton at Hone, Dartford DA4 9HQ* Tel (01322) 862253

WILLOUGHBY, The Ven George Charles. b 20. TCD BA43 MA46. CITC 44. **d** 44 **p** 45. C Conwall *D & R* 44-47; C Derry Cathl 47-51; RD Raphoe 57-59; RD Londonderry 62-69; I Clooney 59-85; Dioc Dir of Ords 62-72; Adn Derry 79-85; rtd 85. *21 Tyler Avenue, Limavady, Co Londonderry BT49 0DT* Tel (01504) 765382

✠WILLOUGHBY, The Rt Revd Noel Vincent. b 26. TCD BA48 MA52. TCD Div Sch Div Test48. **d** 50 **p** 51 **c** 80. C Drumglass *Arm* 50-53; C Dublin St Cath *D & G* 53-55; C Bray Ch Ch 55-59; I Delgany 59-69; I Glenageary 69-80; Treas St Patr Cathl Dublin 77-80; Adn Dub 78-80; Bp C & O 80-97; rtd 97. *Newcastle, Ferrycarrig, Crossabeg, Co Wexford, Irish Republic* Tel Wexford (53) 20008

WILLOUGHBY, Paul Moore. b 60. DipTh BA. **d** 86 **p** 87. C Dublin St Patr Cathl Gp *D & G* 86-90; C Glenageary 90-92; I Dublin Booterstown 92-94; I Kilmocomogue Union *C, C & R* from 94. *The Rectory, Durrus, Bantry, Co Cork, Irish Republic* Tel Bantry (27) 61011 Fax as telephone E-mail revpmw @indigo.ie

WILLOUGHBY, Mrs Serena Louise. b 72. Oak Hill Th Coll BA93. **d** 96 **p** 97. C St Paul's Cray St Barn *Roch* from 96. *Church House, Rushet Road, St Paul's Cray, Orpington, Kent BR5 2PT* Tel (01689) 833706

WILLOWS, David Keith. b 70. St Jo Coll Dur BA90 K Coll Lon MA94. Wycliffe Hall Ox DipMin94. **d** 95 **p** 96. C Ox St Mary V w St Cross and St Pet *Ox* 95-97; Asst Chapl Littlemore Hosp Ox from 97; Asst Chapl Warneford Park Hosp Ox from 97. *74 Godstow Road, Wolvercote, Oxford OX2 8NY* Tel (01865) 556847

WILLOWS, Michael John. b 35. Sarum & Wells Th Coll 70. **d** 72 **p** 73. C Pershore w Wick *Worc* 72-75; P-in-c Astley 75-81; Ind Chapl from 75; P-in-c Hallow 81-85; V 85-88; V Wollaston from 88. *The Vicarage, 46 Vicarage Road, Wollaston, Stourbridge, W Midlands DY8 4NP* Tel (01384) 395674

WILLOX, Peter. b 63. Sunderland Poly BSc85. St Jo Coll Dur 86. **d** 89 **p** 90. C Bradley *Wakef* 89-92; C Utley *Bradf* 92-95; TV Bingley All SS from 95. *The Vicarage, Winston Grange, Eldwick, Bingley, W Yorkshire BD16 3EQ* Tel (01274) 568266

WILLS, David (Dave). b 58. Oak Hill Th Coll DipHE94. **d** 94 **p** 95. C Chadwell *Chelmsf* from 94. *7 Cedar Road, Grays, Essex RM16 4ST* Tel (01375) 850877

WILLS, David Ernest. b 37. St Jo Coll Cam BA58 MA62. Ridley Hall Cam 58. **d** 60 **p** 61. C Kenilworth St Jo *Cov* 60-63; C Northwood Em *Lon* 63-66; V Huyton St Geo *Liv* 66-73; V Littleover *Derby* 73-84; V Mossley Hill St Matt and St Jas *Liv* 84-97; TR Walbrook Epiphany *Derby* from 97. *St Augustine's Rectory, 155 Almond Street, Derby DE23 6LY* Tel (01332) 766603

WILLS, Preb David Stuart Ralph. b 36. Chich Th Coll 64. **d** 66 **p** 67. C Bodmin *Truro* 66-70; V Bude Haven 70-78; TV Banbury *Ox* 78-83; Accredited Counsellor from 81; V Launceston St Steph w St Thos *Truro* 83-88; P-in-c Kenwyn St Geo 88-93; V Truro St Geo and St Jo 93-96; Preb St Endellion from 95; rtd 96. *Garden Cottage, Penwinnick Road, St Agnes, Cornwall TR5 0PA* Tel (01872) 553020

WILLS, Herbert Ashton Peter. b 24. St Edm Hall Ox BA46 MA50. Qu Coll Birm 60. **d** 60 **p** 61. C Stocksbridge *Sheff* 60-63; Chapl Repton Sch Derby 64-69; Chapl St Matthias's Coll Bris 69-78; Asst Chapl Sheff Univ *Sheff* 78-80; Chapl 80-84; R Flax Bourton *B & W* 84-92; V Barrow Gurney 84-92; rtd 92; Perm to Offic *Glouc* from 92. *2 The Pavilions, Sansford Road, Cheltenham, Glos GL53 7AV* Tel (01242) 263748

WILLS, Ian Leslie. b 49. Wycliffe Hall Ox 77. **d** 80 **p** 81. C Henbury *Bris* 80; C Gtr Corsham 80-83; C Whitchurch 83-86; Chapl HM Rem Cen Pucklechurch 86-96; P-in-c Pucklechurch and Abson w Dyrham *Bris* 86-87; V Pucklechurch and Abson from 87. *The Vicarage, Westerleigh Road, Pucklechurch, Bristol BS17 3RD* Tel 0117-937 2260 Fax 937 2729

WILLS, Morley. b 35. Ex & Truro NSM Scheme. **d** 80 **p** 81. NSM St Enoder *Truro* 80-82; NSM Kenwyn St Geo 82-85; NSM Truro St Paul and St Clem 85-88; NSM Crantock from 89. *The Vicarage, Beach Road, Crantock, Newquay, Cornwall TR8 5RE* Tel (01637) 830174

WILLSON, Andrew William. b 64. Or Coll Ox BA85 Nottm Univ BTh90. Linc Th Coll 87. **d** 90 **p** 91. C Northampton St Mary *Pet* 90-93; C Cov E *Cov* 93-96; NSM from 96. *St Catherine's House, 7 St Catherine's Close, Coventry CV3 1EH* Tel (01203) 635737

WILLSON, Stephen Geoffrey. b 63. Nottm Univ BTh90. St Jo Coll Nottm. **d** 90 **p** 91. C Newport St Andr *Mon* 90-92; C Risca 92-94; TV Cyncoed 94-96; Dioc Youth Chapl from 96. *13 Clos Alyn, Cardiff CF2 7LB* Tel (01222) 540071

WILLSON, Stuart Leslie. b 61. Nottm Univ BA83. Sarum & Wells Th Coll 83. **d** 84 **p** 85. C Llandrindod w Cefnllys *S & B* 84-85; Asst Chapl Angl Students Univ of Wales (Swansea) 85-88; C Llwynderw 85-88; Chapl Gatwick Airport *Chich* 88-95; Nene Coll of HE Northn from 95. *24 The Leys, Long Buckby, Northampton NN6 7YR* Tel (01327) 844132

WILMAN, Arthur Garth. b 37. EAMTC 84. **d** 87 **p** 88. NSM Swavesey *Ely* 87-90; NSM Fen Drayton w Conington 87-90; NSM Hardwick from 90; NSM Toft w Caldecote and Childerley from 90. *37 Prentice Close, Longstanton, Cambridge CB4 5DY* Tel (01954) 781400

WILMAN, Mrs Dorothy Ann Jane. b 38. Reading Univ BSc60 Lon Univ DipTh67. Westcott Ho Cam 89. **d** 90 **p** 94. NSM Toft w Caldecote and Childerley *Ely* from 90; Chapl Trin Hall Cam from 93. *37 Prentice Close, Longstanton, Cambridge CB4 5DY* Tel (01954) 781400

WILMAN, Leslie Alan. b 37. Selw Coll Cam BA61 MA65. Ridley Hall Cam 61. **d** 63 **p** 64. C Skipton H Trin *Bradf* 63-67; C Guiseley 67-69; V Morton St Luke 69-79; R Swanton Morley w Worthing *Nor* 79-82; P-in-c E Bilney w Beetley 79-82; P-in-c Hoe 80-82; R

Swanton Morley w Worthing, E Bilney, Beetley etc 82-89; R Swanton Morley w Beetley w E Bilney and Hoe from 89; RD Brisley and Elmham 87-93. *The Rectory, Beetley, Dereham, Norfolk NR20 4AB* Tel (01362) 860328

WILMER, John Watts. b 26. Lich Th Coll 56. **d** 58 **p** 59. C Wolverhampton Ch Ch *Lich* 58-60; C Fenton 60-63; V Dresden 63-76; TV Sutton St Jas and Wawne *York* 76-80; R Bishop Wilton w Full Sutton 80; P-in-c Kirby Underdale w Bugthorpe 80; R Bishop Wilton w Full Sutton, Kirby Underdale etc 80-87; V York St Hilda 87-91; rtd 92; Perm to Offic *York* from 92. *27 Hunters Way, Dringhouses, York YO2 2JL* Tel (01904) 709591

WILMOT, David Mark Baty. b 60. Liv Univ BA82. Sarum & Wells Th Coll 84. **d** 87 **p** 88. C Penrith w Newton Reigny and Plumpton Wall *Carl* 87-91; C St Alb St Pet *St Alb* 91-93; Chapl City Coll St Alb 92-93; V Milton *Lich* from 93; RD Leek from 96. *The Vicarage, Baddeley Green Lane, Stoke-on-Trent ST2 7EY* Tel (01782) 534062

WILMOT, Jonathan Anthony de Burgh. b 48. St Jo Coll Nottm LTh73 BTh74. **d** 74 **p** 75. C Cambridge St Martin *Ely* 74-77; Chapl Chantilly *Eur* 77-82; Asst Chapl Chapl Paris St Mich 80-82; Chapl Versailles 82-87; V Blackheath St Jo *S'wark* 88-95; V Reading Greyfriars *Ox* from 95. *Greyfriars Vicarage, 64 Friar Street, Reading RG1 1EH* Tel 0118-957 3822

WILMOT, Stuart Leslie. b 42. Oak Hill Th Coll 64. **d** 68 **p** 69. C Spitalfields Ch Ch w All SS *Lon* 68-71; C Islington St Mary 71-74; P-in-c Brixton St Paul *S'wark* 75-81; R Mursley w Swanbourne and Lt Horwood *Ox* 81-91; P-in-c Bermondsey St Jas w Ch Ch *S'wark* 91-96; V from 96; P-in-c Bermondsey St Anne 91-93; P-in-c Bermondsey St Anne and St Aug 93-96; V from 96; RD Bermondsey from 96. *The Vicarage, 10 Thorburn Square, London SE1 5QH* Tel 0171-237 3950

WILSON, Dr Alan Thomas Lawrence. b 55. St Jo Coll Cam BA77 MA81 Ball Coll Ox DPhil89. Wycliffe Hall Ox 77. **d** 79 **p** 80. Hon C Eynsham *Ox* 79-81; C 81-82; C Caversham and Mapledurham 82-89; V Caversham St Jo 89-92; R Sandhurst from 92. *The Rectory, 155 High Street, Sandhurst, Camberley, Surrey GU17 8HR* Tel (01252) 872168 E-mail atwilson @macline.co.uk

WILSON, Canon Cecil Alfred Michael Sykes. b 32. Jes Coll Cam BA56 MA61. Ridley Hall Cam 56. **d** 58 **p** 59. C Fulwood *Sheff* 58-63; V Gt Horton *Bradf* 63-69; R Rushden w Newton Bromswold *Pet* 69-76; RD Higham 75-83; P-in-c Rushden St Pet 75-77; R Rushden w Newton Bromswold 77-83; Can Pet Cathl from 77; R Preston and Ridlington w Wing and Pilton from 83; RD Rutland 85-95. *The Rectory, Preston, Oakham, Leics LE15 9NN* Tel (01572) 737287

WILSON, Andrew Alan. b 47. Nottm Univ BA68. St Steph Ho Ox 68. **d** 71 **p** 72. C Streatham St Paul *S'wark* 71-75; TV Catford (Southend) and Downham 75-80; V Malden St Jas 80-89; Chapl Croydon Community Mental Health Unit from 89; Chapl Warlingham Park Hosp Croydon from 89. *Warlingham Park Hospital, Croydon CR6 9YR, or 7 Leas Road, Warlingham, Surrey CR6 9LN* Tel (01883) 622101

WILSON, Andrew Kenneth. b 62. CertJourn. Oak Hill Th Coll BA91. **d** 91 **p** 92. C Springfield H Trin *Chelmsf* 91-96; V Sidcup Ch Ch *Roch* from 96. *The Vicarage, 16 Christchurch Road, Sidcup, Kent DA15 7HE* Tel 0181-308 0835

WILSON, Andrew Marcus William. b 69. Ex Coll Ox BA91 CCC Cam BA93. Westcott Ho Cam CTM94. **d** 94 **p** 95. C Forest Gate Em w Upton Cross *Chelmsf* from 94. *52 Bolton Road, London E15 4JY* Tel 0181-522 0425

WILSON, Arthur Guy Ross. b 28. St Aid Birkenhead 58. **d** 59 **p** 60. C Bexley St Mary *Roch* 59-63; C Gravesend St Geo 63-66; C Belvedere All SS 66-70; V Brighton St Matthias *Chich* 70-77; V Bradf St Clem *Bradf* 77-84; Lic to Offic 84-87; C Baildon 87-88; V Skirwith, Ousby and Melmerby w Kirkland *Carl* 88-93; C Menston w Woodhead *Bradf* 93-96; Chapl High Royds Hosp Menston 93-96; rtd 96; Perm to Offic *Derby* from 96. *The Old School House, Ashbourne Road, Mayfield, Ashbourne, Derbyshire DE6 2LG*

WILSON, Arthur Neville. b 43. ACGI Lon Univ BScEng65 Linacre Coll Ox BA70 MA74. St Steph Ho Ox 68. **d** 71 **p** 72. C Whitton St Aug *Lon* 71-73; C Chiswick St Nic w St Mary 73-76; C Littlehampton St Jas *Chich* 76-81; C Littlehampton St Mary 76-81; C Wick 76-81; V Whitworth *Man* 81-88; V Shaw from 88. *The Vicarage, 13 Church Road, Shaw, Oldham OL2 7AT* Tel (01706) 847369

WILSON, Barry Frank. b 58. Man Metrop Univ BA89 MPhil91 Keele Univ PGCE90. N Ord Course 94. **d** 97. NSM Stone St Mich w Aston St Sav *Lich* from 97. *13 Powderham Close, Packmoor, Stoke-on-Trent ST6 6XN* Tel (01782) 819768

WILSON, Barry Richard. b 46. WMMTC 88. **d** 91 **p** 92. NSM Leek and Meerbrook *Lich* 91-93; C Styvechale *Cov* from 93. *55 Watercall Avenue, Coventry CV3 5AX* Tel (01203) 417920

WILSON, Bernard Martin. b 40. St Jo Coll Cam BA63 MA68 Lon Univ CertEd67. Ripon Hall Ox 72. **d** 73 **p** 74. C Bilton *Cov* 73-77; Dioc Development Officer *Birm* 78-83; Soc Resp Officer *Derby* 83-90; V Darley Abbey 83-90; Chapl Derbyshire R Infirmary 88-90; Educn Unit Dir Traidcraft Exchange 91; V Mickleover St Jo *Derby* from 92. *St John's Vicarage, 7 Onslow Road, Mickleover, Derby DE3 5JJ* Tel (01332) 516545

WILSON, Brian Arthur. b 37. Portsm Dioc Tr Course 84 Chich Th Coll. **d** 85. NSM S w N Hayling *Portsm* 85-88; Chapl Asst RN from 88. *Royal Naval Chaplaincy Service, Room 203, Victory Building, HM Naval Base, Portsmouth PO1 3LS* Tel (01705) 727903 Fax 727112

WILSON, Cecil Henry. b 40. CITC 67. **d** 69 **p** 70. C Lurgan St Jo *D & D* 69-72; Min Can Dromore Cathl 72-75; Youth Sec CMS Ireland 75-80; N Regional Sec 80-87; Gen Sec from 87. *20 Knockbreda Road, Belfast BT6 0JA* Tel (01232) 644011 or 324581 Fax 321756

WILSON, Canon Cecil Moffat. b 26. TCD BA51. **d** 52 **p** 53. C Urney *K, E & A* 52-54; I Templeharry *L & K* 56-59; I Cloughjordan 59-64; I Mountmellick *M & K* 64-76; Can Kildare Cathl 72-75; Adn Kildare 75-76; I Raheny w Coolock *D & G* 76-91; Preb Dunlavin St Patr Cathl Dublin 88-91; rtd 91. *3A Galway Mews, Comber Road, Dundonald, Belfast BT16 0AU* Tel (01232) 484967

WILSON, Charles Michael. b 39. Magd Coll Ox BA63 MA66. NE Ord Course 76. **d** 79 **p** 80. NSM Darlington St Jas *Dur* from 79. *29 Prescott Street, Darlington, Co Durham DL1 2ND* Tel (01325) 460442

WILSON, Charles Roy. b 30. Brasted Place Coll 56. St Aid Birkenhead 57. **d** 59 **p** 60. C Kirkdale St Paul N Shore *Liv* 59-62; C St Helens St Mark 62-66; V Wolverhampton St Matt *Lich* 66-74; V Ripley *Derby* 74-88; V Willington 88-95; V Findern 88-95; rtd 95; Perm to Offic *Derby* from 95. *12 Oak Tree Close, Swanwick, Alfreton, Derbyshire DE55 1FG* Tel (01773) 541822

WILSON, Mrs Christine Louise. **d** 97. NSM Henfield w Shermanbury and Woodmancote *Chich* from 97. *Willow House, 118 Parsonage Road, Henfield, W Sussex BN5 9HZ* Tel (01273) 493954

WILSON, Christopher Harry. b 59. Man Univ MusB80. Wycliffe Hall Ox 88. **d** 91 **p** 92. C S Lafford *Linc* 91-95; P-in-c Billingborough 95-96; P-in-c Sempringham w Pointon and Birthorpe 95-96; P-in-c Horbling 95-96; V Billingborough Gp from 96. *The Vicarage, 13 High Street, Billingborough, Sleaford, Lincs NG34 0QG* Tel (01529) 240750

WILSON, Mrs Claire Frances. b 43. Hull Univ BA65. SW Minl Tr Course 85. **d** 87 **p** 94. Par Dn Belsize Park *Lon* 87-94; C 94-97; C Chingford SS Pet and Paul *Chelmsf* from 97. *Old Church House, Priory Avenue, London E4 8AA* Tel 0181-529 0110

WILSON, Colin Edward. b 63. Ripon Coll Cuddesdon BTh94. **d** 94 **p** 95. C High Wycombe *Ox* from 94. *7 Totteridge Road, High Wycombe, Bucks HP13 6DR* Tel (01494) 452953

WILSON, David Brian. b 47. QUB BA68. CITC 71. **d** 71 **p** 72. C Ballyholme *D & D* 71-74; C Guildf Ch Ch *Guildf* 74-78; I Arvagh w Carrigallen, Gowna and Columbkille *K, E & A* 78-81; I Clogherney w Seskinore and Drumnakilly *Arm* 81-95; I Caledon w Brantry from 95. *The Rectory, 36 Church Hill Road, Caledon, Co Tyrone BT68 4UY* Tel (01861) 568205

WILSON, David Gordon. b 40. Man Univ BSc61 Clare Coll Cam BA63 MA68. Ridley Hall Cam 63. **d** 65 **p** 66. C Clapham Common St Barn *S'wark* 65-69; C Onslow Square St Paul *Lon* 69-73; V Leic H Apostles *Leic* 73-84; V Spring Grove St Mary *Lon* from 84; Chapl Brunel Univ from 90; AD Hounslow from 97. *St Mary's Vicarage, Osterley Road, Isleworth, Middx TW7 4PW* Tel 0181-560 3555

WILSON, David Mark. b 53. Lon Univ BSc75. Wycliffe Hall Ox BA77 MA82. **d** 78 **p** 79. C Romford Gd Shep Collier Row *Chelmsf* 78-81; C Cheadle Hulme St Andr *Ches* 81-85; V Huntington 85-95; Chapl Bp's Blue Coat C of E High Sch 85-95; V Birkenhead Ch Ch *Ches* from 95. *Christ Church Vicarage, 7 Palm Grove, Birkenhead, Merseyside L43 1TE* Tel 0151-652 5647 or 652 3990

WILSON, David Merritt. b 26. S'wark Ord Course 61. **d** 64 **p** 65. C Brixton St Paul *S'wark* 64-69; Perm to Offic from 69. *18 Calais Street, London SE5 9LP* Tel 0171-274 5707

WILSON, Derrick. b 33. Oak Hill Th Coll 69. **d** 71 **p** 72. C Lurgan Ch the Redeemer *D & D* 71-74; C Willowfield 74-75; I 83-88; I Knocknamuckley 75-83; I Tullylish from 88. *Tullylish Rectory, 100 Banbridge Road, Gilford, Craigavon, Co Armagh BT63 6DL* Tel (01762) 831298

WILSON, Mrs Dorothy Jean. b 35. St Mary's Coll Dur BA57 DipEd58 Newc Poly LLB78. NE Ord Course 86. **d** 88 **p** 96. NSM Dur St Giles *Dur* from 88; Perm to Offic *Newc* from 88; Chapl Univ of Northumbria at Newc from 94. *86 Gilesgate, Durham DH1 1HY* Tel 0191-386 5016

WILSON, Edith Yvonne. b 43. **d** 97. NSM Skerton St Chad *Blackb* from 97. *7 Edenvale Road, Lancaster LA1 2NN* Tel (01524) 60534

WILSON, Edward Thomas. b 48. Southn Univ BTh82. Chich Th Coll 78. **d** 82 **p** 83. C Cardiff St Jo *Llan* 82-86; V Aberavon H Trin 86-92; R St Nicholas w Bonvilston and St George-super-Ely from 92. *The Rectory, 8 Ger-y-Llan, St Nicholas, Cardiff CF5 6SY* Tel (01446) 760728

WILSON, Erik. b 51. Lanc Univ BA72. Trin Coll Bris 83. **d** 85 **p** 86. C Linthorpe *York* 85-89; V Hull St Martin w Transfiguration from 89; AD W Hull from 96. *St Martin's Vicarage, 942 Anlaby Road, Hull HU4 6AH* Tel (01482) 352995

WILSON, Francis. b 34. ACP67. Cuddesdon Coll 71. **d** 73 **p** 74. C Newc St Fran *Newc* 73-79; V Wallsend St Jo from 79. *St John's Vicarage, Station Road, Wallsend, Tyne & Wear NE28 8DT* Tel 0191-262 3944

WILSON, Frederick John. b 25. Lon Univ BScEng45. Oak Hill Th Coll 68. **d** 70 **p** 71. C Wandsworth All SS *S'wark* 70-75; P-in-c Garsdon w Lea and Cleverton *Bris* 75-84; P-in-c Charlton w Brokenborough and Hankerton 80-84; Chapl Barn Fellowship Whatcombe Ho 84-87; C Corby Epiphany w St Jo *Pet* 87-92; rtd 92; Perm to Offic *Linc* from 93; Perm to Offic *Pet* from 93. *2 Thorseby Close, Netherton, Peterborough PE3 9QS* Tel (01733) 263386

WILSON, Geoffrey Samuel Alan. b 46. TCD BA69 QUB DipEd70 TCD MA72. CITC BTh93. **d** 96. C Glendermott *D & R* from 96. *42 Ferndale Park, Portstewart, Co Londonderry BT55 7JB* Tel (01265) 833542 or (01504) 348557

✠**WILSON, The Rt Revd Godfrey Edward Armstrong.** b 26. Linc Th Coll. **d** 54 **p** 55 **c** 80. C Sheff St Geo and St Steph *Sheff* 54-58; New Zealand from 57; Asst Bp Auckland 80-91. *30 Maryland Street, Point Chevalier, Auckland 1002, New Zealand* Tel Auckland (9) 846 4669

WILSON, Graham Whitelaw. b 46. Glas Sch of Art DA70 Leeds Univ CertEd77. EMMTC DTPS95. **d** 95 **p** 96. NSM Burbage w Aston Flamville *Leic* 95-97; C from 97. *2 Beales Close, Stapleton, Leicester LE9 8JG* Tel (01455) 843677

WILSON, Canon Harold (Harry). b 29. St Jo Coll Ox BA53 MA57. Ridley Hall Cam 57. **d** 59 **p** 60. C Leamington Priors St Mary *Cov* 59-61; C Walsgrave on Sowe 61-64; V Potters Green 64-67; Chapl Barcelona *Eur* 67-73; V Bursledon *Win* 73-83; RD Eastleigh 75-83; V Yateley 83-94; RD Odiham 85-88; Hon Can Win Cathl 87-94; rtd 94. *11 Hill Meadow, Overton, Basingstoke, Hants RG25 3JD* Tel (01256) 771825

WILSON, Harold Marcus. b 32. St Jo Coll Dur BA55 DipTh57. **d** 57 **p** 58. C Adlington *Blackb* 57-60; Miss to Seamen 60-81; Iraq 60-63; Japan 63-67; P-in-c Crowfield w Stonham Aspal and Mickfield *St E* 81-97; rtd 97. *16 Victoria Road, Oundle, Peterborough PE8 4AY* Tel (01832) 272431

WILSON, Ian Andrew. b 57. Nottm Univ BTh89. Linc Th Coll 86. **d** 89 **p** 90. C Whitton and Thurleston w Akenham *St E* 89-93; P-in-c Elmsett w Aldham from 93. *The Rectory, Hadleigh Road, Elmsett, Ipswich IP7 6ND* Tel (01473) 658219

WILSON, James Andrew Christopher. b 48. Ex & Truro NSM Scheme. **d** 82 **p** 83. NSM Plymouth Crownhill Ascension *Ex* 82-83; NSM Yelverton 83-85; C Plymstock 85-87; R Lifton 87-92; R Kelly w Bradstone 87-92; V Broadwoodwidger 87-92; R Calstock *Truro* from 92. *The Rectory, Sand Lane, Calstock, Cornwall PL18 9QX* Tel (01822) 832518

WILSON, James Charles. TCD BA82 MA84 DipTh85 BD87. **d** 85 **p** 86. C Bangor Abbey *D & D* 85-88; C Dublin Rathfarnham *D & G* 88-91; I Desertcreat *Arm* 91-95; Bp's C Rathmolyon w Castlerickard, Rathcore and Agher *M & K* from 95. *Address excluded by request*

WILSON, James Kenneth. b 47. **d** 88 **p** 89. C Holyhead w Rhoscolyn w Llanfair-yn-Neubwll *Ban* 88-91; Chapl RAF from 91. *Chaplaincy Services (RAF), HQ, Personnel and Training Command, RAF Innsworth, Gloucester GL3 1EZ* Tel (01452) 712612 ext 5164 Fax 510828

WILSON, James Lewis. b 39. TCD BA62 HDipEd63 MA65 BD71. TCD Div Sch Div Test74. **d** 74 **p** 75. C Enniskillen *Clogh* 74-76; C Belfast St Matt *Conn* 76-79; I Killeshandra w Killegar *K, E & A* 79-81; I Derrylane 79-81; I Loughgilly w Clare *Arm* from 81. *The Rectory, 124 Gosford Road, Loughgilly, Armagh BT60 2DE* Tel (01861) 507265

WILSON, James Phillip Maclean. b 31. RMA 52 MBIM75. Glouc Sch of Min 89. **d** 91 **p** 92. NSM Quinton w Marston Sicca *Glouc* from 91. *The Old Bakery, Upper Quinton, Stratford-upon-Avon, Warks CV37 8SX* Tel (01789) 720224

WILSON, James Robert. b 36. CITC. **d** 66 **p** 67. C Ballywillan *Conn* 67-73; I Drummaul 73-79; I Drummaul w Duneane and Ballyscullion from 79; RD Antrim from 93; Preb Conn Cathl 96; Treas Lisburn Ch Ch Cathl from 96. *The Vicarage, 1A Glenkeen, Randalstown, Antrim BT41 3JX* Tel (01849) 472561

WILSON, Miss Jane Jennifer. b 43. Ch Ch Coll Cant TCert65 Open Univ BA84. Wycliffe Hall Ox 89. **d** 91 **p** 94. Par Dn Northwood Em *Lon* 91-94; C from 94. *27 Foxfield Close, Northwood, Middx HA6 3NU* Tel (01923) 825390

WILSON, John Anthony. b 34. Linc Th Coll. **d** 83 **p** 84. C Nunthorpe *York* 83-85; V Whorlton w Carlton and Faceby 85-94; V Coatham from 94. *The Vicarage, 9 Blenheim Terrace, Redcar, Cleveland TS10 1QP* Tel (01642) 482870

WILSON, Canon John Christopher Heathcote. b 13. Qu Coll Ox BA39 MA41. Cuddesdon Coll 40. **d** 41 **p** 42. C Bradf St Wilfrid Lidget Green *Bradf* 41-44; C Skipton H Trin 44-47; CF 47-50; V Kingston upon Hull St Nic *York* 50-59; V Kirk Ella 59-88; AD W Hull 72-79; Can and Preb York Minster 79-95; rtd 88; Perm to Offic *York* from 95. *14 Tremayne Avenue, Brough, N Humberside HU15 1BL* Tel (01482) 668481

WILSON, John Clifford. b 32. AKC56. **d** 57 **p** 58. C Bordesley St Andr *Birm* 57-59; C Kings Norton 59-61; Somalia and Aden 61-63; V Lydbrook *Glouc* 64-67; TV Bow w Bromley St Leon *Lon* 69-73; P-in-c Stepney St Pet w St Benet 73-80; P-in-c Long Marton w Dufton and w Milburn *Carl* 80-81; R 81-87; V Annesley Our Lady and All SS *S'well* 87-95; V Annesley w Newstead 95-97; rtd 97. *Cwmwell Cottage, Upper Cwm, Little Dewchurch, Hereford HR2 6PS* Tel (01432) 840559

WILSON, John Frederick. b 33. Qu Coll Birm 58. **d** 61 **p** 62. C Jarrow St Paul *Dur* 61-65; C Monkwearmouth All SS 65-68; Br Honduras 68-71; V Scunthorpe Resurr *Linc* 71-90; Chapl Divine Healing Miss Crowhurst 90-91; V Terrington St Clement *Ely* from 91; Bp's Officer for Rtd Clergy and Widows *Nor* from 95. *The Vicarage, 27 Sutton Road, Terrington St Clement, King's Lynn, Norfolk PE34 4RQ* Tel (01553) 828430

WILSON, Canon John Hamilton. b 29. St Chad's Coll Dur BA53. Sarum Th Coll 53. **d** 55 **p** 56. C W End *Win* 55-59; C Fishponds St Mary *Bris* 59-64; V Bedminster St Fran 64-73; RD Bedminster 68-73; R Horfield H Trin 73-96; Hon Can Bris Cathl 77-96; rtd 96; Perm to Offic *Bris* from 96. *2 West Croft, Bristol BS9 4PQ* Tel 0117-962 9204

WILSON, Canon John Hewitt. b 24. CB77. TCD BA46 Div Test47 MA61. **d** 47 **p** 48. C Dublin St Geo *D & G* 47-50; Chapl RAF 50-73; Chapl-in-Chief RAF 73-80; QHC 73-80; Can and Preb Linc Cathl *Linc* 74-80; R The Heyfords w Rousham and Somerton *Ox* 81-93; rtd 93. *Glencree, Philcote Street, Deddington, Oxford OX15 0TB* Tel (01869) 38903

WILSON, John Lake. b 34. Linc Th Coll 74. **d** 76 **p** 77. C N Lynn w St Marg and St Nic *Nor* 76-80; V Narborough w Narford 80-85; V Pentney St Mary Magd w W Bilney 80-85; V Lakenham St Mark 85-93; P-in-c Trowse 92-93; V Lakenham St Mark w Trowse from 93; Chapl Whitlingham Hosp from 93. *The Vicarage, 2 Conesford Drive, Bracondale, Norwich NR1 2BB* Tel (01603) 622579

WILSON, Dr John Michael. b 16. MRCP48 Lon Univ MB, BS42 MD48. **d** 53 **p** 56. C Leigh St Mary *Man* 53-57; C St Martin-in-the-Fields *Lon* 58-63; Lect 63-67; Birm Univ Research Fell 67-71; Lect 71-78; Sen 78-81; rtd 81. *4 Eastern Road, Birmingham B29 7JP* Tel 0121-472 1051

WILSON, John Stafford. b 21. Bible Churchmen's Coll 49. **d** 51 **p** 52. C Mile Cross *Nor* 51-53; Casablanca *Eur* 53-54 and 66-68; Demnat 54-66; V Packington w Normanton-le-Heath *Leic* 68-72; V Worthing St Geo *Chich* 72-84; P-in-c Ashby w Fenby and Brigsley *Linc* 84; P-in-c Beelsby 84; P-in-c E and W Ravendale w Hatcliffe 84; R Ravendale Gp 84-87; rtd 88; Perm to Offic *Chich* from 88. *88 Bruce Avenue, Worthing, W Sussex BN11 5LA* Tel (01903) 245844

WILSON, Canon John Walter. b 25. St Jo Coll Dur BA67 Hatf Coll Dur MSc74. Cranmer Hall Dur. **d** 67 **p** 68. C Auckland St Helen *Dur* 67-69; V S Hetton 69-75; Lect Sunderland Poly 75-82; V Ormesby w Scratby *Nor* 82-92; RD Flegg (Gt Yarmouth) 89-92; Hon Can Nor Cathl 91-92; rtd 92; Perm to Offic *Nor* from 92; Bp's Officer for Rtd Clergy and Widows from 95. *4 Rectory Lane, Chedgrave, Norwich NR14 6NE* Tel (01508) 20259

WILSON, Joseph William Sidney. b 23. St Aid Birkenhead 62. **d** 64 **p** 65. C Gt Sankey *Liv* 64-66; Chapl Rotterdam w Schiedam etc *Eur* 67-68; C Birkdale St Jo *Liv* 68-71; V Eppleton *Dur* 71-78; V Riccall *York* 78-84; V Freckleton *Blackb* 84-87; rtd 87; Perm to Offic *Ches* from 87. *27 Sandy Lane, Wallasey, Merseyside L45 3JY* Tel 0151-639 9083

WILSON, Miss Judith Anne. b 48. Keele Univ BA71 Leic Univ PGCE72. S Dios Minl Tr Scheme 92. **d** 95 **p** 96. NSM Slaugham *Chich* 95-96; Sub Chapl HM Pris Wandsworth 95-96; Chapl HM Young Offender Inst Hollesley Bay Colony from 96. *Chaplain's Office, Hollesley Bay Colony, Hollesley, Woodbridge, Suffolk IP12 3JW* Tel (01394) 411741 ext 325 Fax 411071

WILSON, Keith. b 38. UEA BA87 MA90. Chich Th Coll 60. **d** 63 **p** 64. C W Bromwich St Fran *Lich* 63-66; C Kirkley *Nor* 66-70; R Swainsthorpe w Newton Flotman 70-75; R Acle 75-89; R Fishley 77-89; RD Blofield 79-87; P-in-c Burlingham St Andr w St Pet 85-89; R Acle w Fishley and N Burlingham 89; TV Thetford from 89; Ind Chapl from 89; Dioc Rep for Abp's Commn on UPA from 91. *44 Monksgate, Thetford, Norfolk IP24 1BY* Tel (01842) 766074

WILSON, Kenneth. b 59. ARICS84 Selw Coll Cam MA82 DipRS88. S'wark Ord Course 86. **d** 89 **p** 90. C Walthamstow St Pet *Chelmsf* 89-92; TV Wolverhampton *Lich* 92-97. *6 Westland Road, Wolverhampton WV3 9NY* Tel (01902) 561485

WILSON, Malcolm Richard Milburn. b 30. Edin Th Coll 57. **d** 59 **p** 60. C Dumbarton *Glas* 59-61; India 62-63; C Dunfermline *St And* 63-65; R Newport-on-Tay 65-70; R Tayport 65-70; R Baillieston *Glas* 70-74; R Milngavie 74-84; R Bearsden 74-84; R Dalbeattie 84-88; R Gourock 88-94; rtd 94. *20 Dougalston Gardens North, Milngavie, Glasgow G62 6HN* Tel 0141-956 4138

WILSON, Marjorie Jayne. *See* SHIPTON, Mrs Marjorie Jayne

WILSON, Mark Anthony John. b 56. TCD BA80. CITC 75. **d** 80 **p** 81. C Dublin Rathfarnham *D & G* 80-83; Bp's C Dublin Finglas 83-85; I Celbridge w Straffan and Newcastle-Lyons 85-88; CF 88-93; I Dundalk w Heynestown *Arm* from 93. *The Rectory, Old Golf Links Road, Blackrock, Co Louth, Irish Republic* Tel Dundalk (42) 21402

WILSON, The Ven Mark John Crichton. b 46. Clare Coll Cam BA67 MA70. Ridley Hall Cam 67. **d** 69 **p** 70. C Luton w E Hyde *St Alb* 69-72; C Ashtead *Guildf* 72-77; Chapl Epsom Coll 77-81; V Epsom Common Ch Ch *Guildf* 81-96; RD Epsom 87-91; Adn Dorking from 96. *Littlecroft, Heathside Road, Woking, Surrey GU22 7EZ* Tel (01483) 772713

WILSON, Canon Mavis Kirby. b 42. Cam Univ CertEd71 Ex Univ BA64. S Dios Minl Tr Scheme 82. **dss** 84 **d** 87 **p** 94. Chessington *Guildf* 84-85; Epsom St Martin 85-86; Epsom Common Ch Ch 86-87; C 87-96; Dioc Adv in Miss and Evang from 90; Hon Can Guildf Cathl from 94. *Littlecroft, Heathside Road, Woking, Surrey GU22 7EZ* Tel (01483) 772713

WILSON, Mervyn Raynold Alwyn. b 33. Qu Coll Cam BA57 MA61. Ripon Hall Ox 57. **d** 59 **p** 60. C Rubery *Birm* 59-62; C Kings Norton 62-63; V Hamstead St Bernard 63-69; R Bermondsey St Mary w St Olave, St Jo etc *S'wark* 69-78; R Bulwick, Blatherwycke w Harringworth and Laxton *Pet* from 78. *The Rectory, Church Lane, Bulwick, Corby, Northants NN17 3DY* Tel (01780) 285249

WILSON, The Very Revd Mervyn Robert. b 22. Bris Univ BA51 Lon Univ BD58. Tyndale Hall Bris 52. **d** 52 **p** 53. C Ballymacarrett St Patr *D & D* 52-56; C Donaghcloney 56-59; C Newtownards 59-61; I Ballyphilip w Ardquin 61-70; I Newry St Patr 70-92; RD Newry and Mourne 77-83; RD Kilbroney 77-83; Preb Dromore Cathl 83-85; Can Belf Cathl 85-89; Dean Dromore *D & D* 90-92; rtd 92. *31 Manor Drive, Lisburn, Co Antrim BT28 1JH* Tel (01846) 666361

WILSON, Michael. b 13. Trin Coll Cam BA35 MA39. Westcott Ho Cam 37. **d** 38 **p** 39. C Eastleigh *Win* 38-41; CF (EC) 41-46; V St Mary Bourne w Litchfield *Win* 45-52; N Rhodesia 52-61; R Kingsland *Heref* 61-65; Zambia 66-68; C Bournemouth St Clem w St Mary *Win* 68-73; V Appleshaw 73-78; rtd 78. *The Friary, 19 St Cross Road, Winchester, Hants SO23 9JA* Tel (01962) 860172

WILSON, Canon Michael. b 44. Liv Univ BA66 Fitzw Coll Cam BA68 MA73. Westcott Ho Cam. **d** 69 **p** 70. C Worksop Priory *S'well* 69-71; C Gt Malvern St Mary *Worc* 71-75; V Leic St Anne *Leic* 75-85; TR Leic Ascension 85-88; Hon Can Leic Cathl 85-88; Can Res and Treas from 88. *7 St Martins East, Leicester LE1 5FX* Tel 0116-253 0580

WILSON, Neil. b 61. Newc Univ BA83. Ripon Coll Cuddesdon 85. **d** 88 **p** 89. C Wallsend St Luke *Newc* 88-91; C Monkseaton St Pet 91-93; V Earsdon and Backworth from 93. *Earsdon Vicarage, 5 Front Street, Whitley Bay, Tyne & Wear NE25 9JU* Tel 0191-252 9393

WILSON, Paul Edward. b 43. Ridley Hall Cam 81. **d** 83 **p** 84. C Brighstone and Brooke w Mottistone *Portsm* 83-86; C Shorwell w Kingston 83-86; TV Tring *St Alb* 86-90; P-in-c Renhold 90-91; Chapl HM Pris Bedf 90-91; V Buckfastleigh w Dean Prior *Ex* 91-96; P-in-c Stockland, Dalwood, Kilmington and Shute from 96. *The Vicarage, Kilmington, Axminster, Devon EX13 7RF* Tel (01297) 33156

WILSON, Paul Hugh. b 26. Glouc Sch of Min 80. **d** 83 **p** 84. NSM Much Birch w Lt Birch, Much Dewchurch etc *Heref* 83-86; C 86-92; rtd 92; Perm to Offic *Heref* from 92. *Cherry Lyn, Staunton-on-Wye, Hereford HR4 7LR* Tel (01981) 500231

WILSON, Paul Thomas Wardley. b 43. AKC67. St Aug Coll Cant. **d** 70 **p** 71. C Tokyngton St Mich *Lon* 70-74; Soc Community Worker *Roch* 74-81; Perm to Offic 81-90; Lic to Offic *Cant* 83-88; Sen Adv Coun for Soc Resp from 83; Chief Exec Carr Gomm Soc from 88. *Carr Gomm Society, Telegraph Hill Centre, Kitto Road, London SE14 5TY* Tel 0171-277 5050

WILSON, Peter John. b 43. CertEd76 BEd84. Linc Th Coll. **d** 71 **p** 72. C Stretford St Matt *Man* 71-73; C Rugby St Andr *Cov* 73-76; TV 86-92; Hon C Bilton 76-79; Asst Dir of Educn *Blackb* 79-81; P-in-c Accrington St Paul 79-81; Dioc Officer for Stewardship *Carl* from 92; P-in-c Dacre from 95. *Dacre Vicarage, Stainton, Penrith, Cumbria CA11 0ES* Tel (01768) 63179 or (01228) 22573 Fax (01228) 48769

WILSON, Peter Sheppard. b 39. TCD BA61. CITC 62. **d** 62 **p** 63. C Killowen *D & R* 62-68; C Portadown St Columba *Arm* 68-70; I Convoy w Monellan and Donaghmore *D & R* 70-78; P-in-c Castletown *S & M* 78; V 78-83; R Kilmacolm *Glas* 83-84; R Bridge of Weir 83-84; I Camus-juxta-Bann *D & R* 85-92; Bp's Dom Chapl 90-92; I Maguiresbridge w Derrybrusk *Clogh* from 92; RD Enniskillen from 95. *9 Drumgoon Road, Maguiresbridge, Co Fermanagh BT94 4PJ* Tel (01365) 721250

WILSON, Quentin Harcourt. b 45. FTCL75 K Coll Lon AKC68 BD76. St Aug Coll Cant 69. **d** 70 **p** 71. C Is of Dogs Ch Ch and St Jo w St Luke *Lon* 70-72; C Muswell Hill St Jas 72-77; Succ and Sacr Ex Cathl *Ex* 77-81; Min Can Windsor 81-84; V Langho Billington *Blackb* from 84; Chapl Brockhall Hosp Blackb from 85; RD Whalley *Blackb* 89-95. *St Leonard's Vicarage, Whalley Road, Billington, Clitheroe, Lancs BB7 9NA* Tel (01254) 822246

WILSON, Robert Brian. b 29. AKC55. **d** 56 **p** 57. C Wortley de Leeds *Ripon* 56-60; C Chapel Allerton 60-63; V Hunslet Moor St Pet and St Cuth 63-70; V Bilton 70-80; V Gt and Lt Ouseburn w Marton-cum-Grafton 80-90; rtd 90. *56 Church Avenue, Harrogate, N Yorkshire HG1 4HG* Tel (01423) 504398

WILSON, Canon Robert Malcolm (Robin). b 35. St Andr Univ MA59. ALCD62. **d** 62 **p** 63. C Wallington H Trin *S'wark* 62-66; C Dur St Nic *Dur* 66-70; V Colchester St Pet *Chelmsf* from 70; RD Colchester from 93; Hon Can Chelmsf Cathl from 94. *The Vicarage, Balkerne Close, Colchester CO1 1NZ* Tel (01206) 572641

WILSON, Robert Michael. b 33. Linc Th Coll 73. **d** 75 **p** 76. C Knottingley *Wakef* 75-78; Ind Chapl 78-94; P-in-c Cleckheaton St Luke 78-84; V Cleckheaton St Luke and Whitechapel 84-86; V Batley All SS 86-94; RD Dewsbury 90-93; rtd 94. *1 White Lee Side, Heckmondwike, W Yorkshire WF16 9PD* Tel (01924) 411778

WILSON, Robert Stoker. b 39. Dur Univ BSc62. Oak Hill Th Coll 62. **d** 64 **p** 65. C High Elswick St Paul *Newc* 64-68; C Kirkheaton 68-70; Youth Chapl *Liv* 70-73; P-in-c S Shields St Steph *Dur* 73-78; R 78-83; Youth Chapl 73-77; P-in-c S Shields St Aid 81-83; V Greenside 83-94; P-in-c Fatfield from 94. *49 Larchwood, Harraton, Washington, Tyne & Wear NE38 9BT* Tel 0191-416 3134

✠**WILSON, The Rt Revd Roger Plumpton.** b 05. KCVO74. Keble Coll Ox BA28 MA34. Lambeth DD49 Westcott Ho Cam 35. **d** 35 **p** 36 **c** 49. C Prince's Park St Paul *Liv* 35-38; C Westmr St Jo 38-39; V S Shore H Trin *Blackb* 39-44; V Radcliffe-on-Trent *S'well* 44-49; Adn Nottingham 44-49; V Shelford 46-49; Bp Wakef 49-58; Bp Chich 58-74; Clerk of the Closet 63-74; rtd 74; Asst Bp B & W from 74. *40 Rosemont Road, Richmond, Surrey TW10 6QL* Tel 0181-940 2616

WILSON, Canon Ronald. b 11. St Aid Birkenhead. **d** 51 **p** 52. C Lenton *S'well* 51-53; C Worksop St Anne 53-55; V Lenton Abbey 55-63; V Pinchbeck *Linc* 63-78; Can and Preb Linc Cathl 72-78; rtd 78. *14 Windermere Gardens, Linslade, Leighton Buzzard, Beds LU7 7QP* Tel (01525) 379676

WILSON, Stephen Charles. b 51. Newc Univ BA73 Cam Univ MA82. Westcott Ho Cam BA78. **d** 79 **p** 80. C Fulham All SS *Lon* 79-82; C W Hampstead St Jas 82-85; P-in-c Alexandra Park St Sav 85-93; V Preston next Faversham, Goodnestone and Graveney *Cant* from 93. *The Vicarage, Preston Lane, Faversham, Kent ME13 8LG* Tel (01795) 536801

WILSON, Stephen John. b 45. Bradf Univ BTech69. Trin Coll Bris DipHE92. **d** 92 **p** 93. C Marple All SS *Ches* 92-96; P-in-c Moulton from 96; Chapl Leighton Hosp Crewe from 96. *The Vicarage, Moulton, Northwich, Cheshire CW9 8NR* Tel (01606) 593355

WILSON, Thomas Irven. b 30. TCD BA51 MA58. **d** 53 **p** 54. C Ballymena *Conn* 53-56; Chapl RAF 56-85; QHC from 80; rtd 85. *Rathclaren House, Kilbrittain, Co Cork, Irish Republic* Tel Clonakilty (23) 49689

WILSON, Canon Thomas Roderick. b 26. St Pet Hall Ox BA50 MA55. Sarum Th Coll 50. **d** 52 **p** 53. C Poulton-le-Sands *Blackb* 52-56; C Altham w Clayton le Moors 56-58; V Habergham Eaves H Trin 58-78; RD Burnley 70-78; Hon Can Blackb Cathl 75-89; V Bare 78-81; P-in-c Accrington St Jas 81-82; P-in-c Accrington St Paul 81-82; V Accrington St Jas w St Paul 82-89; rtd 89; Perm to Offic *Blackb* from 89. *33 Nook Terrace, Cherry Tree, Blackburn BB2 4SW* Tel (01254) 209390

WILSON, Timothy Charles. b 62. Oak Hill Th Coll BA90. **d** 90 **p** 91. C Highley *Heref* 90-94; C Margate H Trin *Cant* from 94. *4 Sandhurst Road, Margate, Kent CT9 3HR* Tel (01843) 221178

WILSON, Timothy John (Tim). b 58. St Pet Coll Ox MA80. Trin Coll Bris 81. **d** 83 **p** 84. C Gt Horton *Bradf* 83-86; C Handforth *Ches* 86-90; V Salterhebble All SS *Wakef* from 90. *All Saints' Vicarage, Greenroyd Avenue, Halifax, W Yorkshire HX3 0LP* Tel (01422) 365805

WILSON, Victor Isaac. b 23. St Deiniol's Hawarden 69. **d** 71 **p** 72. C Davenham *Ches* 71-75; V Latchford Ch Ch 75-80; V Stalybridge St Paul 80-88; rtd 88. *215 Huddersfield Road, Stalybridge, Cheshire SK15 3DY* Tel 0161-38 2386

WILSON, Walter. b 33. **d** 60 **p** 61. C Sheff St Swithun *Sheff* 60-64; Ind Chapl 64-66; C Attercliffe 66-69; R Swallow w Cabourn *Linc* 69-72; Dioc Youth Officer *Heref* 72-77; Chapl Ipswich Sch 77-94; rtd 94; Perm to Offic *St E* from 94. *Riverside Cottage, Mendlesham Green, Stowmarket, Suffolk IP14 5RF* Tel (01449) 766198

WILSON, William Adam (Bill). b 53. Sheff Univ BA74 St Jo Coll Dur BA84. Cranmer Hall Dur 82. **d** 85 **p** 86. C S Croydon Em *S'wark* 85-89; C Wandsworth All SS 89-93; Chapl Fontainebleau *Eur* from 93. *21 Quai Franklin Roosevelt, 77920 Samois sur Seine, France* Tel France (33) 64 24 81 57 Fax as telephone

WILSON, William Bell. b 04. AKC28. **d** 27 **p** 28. C Newc St Mary *Newc* 27-29; C Burgh Heath w Nork and Banstead *Guildf* 30-32; C Earlsdon *Cov* 32-34; Min Cov St Geo 34-39; V 39-71; Chapl RAFVR 41-45; rtd 71; Perm to Offic *Cov* from 71. *c/o E H Whitehead Esq, 7 Warwick Road, Stratford-upon-Avon, Warks CV37 6YW* Tel (01789) 294867

WILSON, William Gerard (Bill). b 42. St Chad's Coll Dur BA65 DipTh67. **d** 67 **p** 68. C Hollinwood *Man* 67-71; V Oldham St Jas 71-79; R Birch w Fallowfield 79-93; V Paddington St Jas *Lon* from 93; AD Westmr Paddington from 97. *The Vicarage, 6 Gloucester Terrace, London W2 3DD* Tel 0171-723 8119

✠**WILSON, The Rt Revd William Gilbert.** b 18. TCD BA39 MA44 BD44 PhD49. TCD Div Sch Div Test40. **d** 41 **p** 42 **c** 81. C Belfast St Mary Magd *Conn* 41-44; C Bangor St Comgall *D & D* 44-47; I Armoy w Loughguile *Conn* 47-76; Preb Conn Cathl 64-76; I Lisburn Ch Ch 76-81; Dean Conn 76-81; Bp K, E & A 81-93; rtd

93. *24 Pennington Park, Cairnshill Road, Belfast BT8 4GJ* Tel (01232) 701742

WILSON, William John (Bill). b 25. CEng MIEE MRTS. S Dios Minl Tr Scheme 79. **d** 82 **p** 83. NSM Weeke *Win* 82-88; NSM Win St Barn from 89. *23 Buriton Road, Winchester, Hants SO22 6JE* Tel (01962) 881904

WILSON-BROWN, Nigel. **d** 97. C Wimbledon Em Ridgway Prop Chpl *S'wark* from 97. *25 Richmond Road, London SW20 0PG* Tel 0181-946 9940

WILTON, Albert Edward. b 10. St Paul's Grahamstown 69. **d** 67 **p** 68. Rhodesia 67-68; S Africa 69-77; rtd 77; Perm to Offic *St E* 77-86; Perm to Offic *Chich* from 92. *College of St Barnabas, Blackberry Lane, Lingfield, Surrey RH7 6NJ* Tel (01342) 870609

WILTON, Gary Ian. b 60. Bath Univ BSc83. Trin Coll Bris MA93 Wycliffe Hall Ox 85. **d** 88 **p** 89. C Clevedon St Andr and Ch Ch *B & W* 88-92; Lect Univ of the W of England, Bris 92-93; TV Bath Twerton-on-Avon *B & W* from 93. *The Ascension Vicarage, 35A Claude Avenue, Bath BA2 1AF* Tel (01225) 421971

WILTON (née ADAMS), Mrs Gillian Linda. b 57. SRN79 SCM81. Trin Coll Bris DipHE84 DPS85. **dss** 85 **d** 87 **p** 94. Easton H Trin w St Gabr and St Lawr and St Jude *Bris* 85-87; Par Dn 87-91; Regional Adv (Dios B & W and Bris) CMJ from 91; Perm to Offic *B & W* 92-93; NSM Bath Twerton-on-Avon from 93. *The Ascension Vicarage, 35A Claude Avenue, Bath BA2 1AF* Tel (01225) 421971

WILTON, Glenn Warner Paul. b 33. Miami Univ Ohio BSc55 Univ of Washington Seattle MSW76 Cath Univ of America 69. Ch Div Sch of the Pacific (USA) 77 Pontifical Beda Coll Rome 66. **d** 65 **p** 66. In RC Ch 65-72; USA 77-81; Chapl Pastures Hosp Derby 82-88; Chapl St Martin's Hosp Cant 89-93; Chapl St Aug Hosp Cant 89-93; Chapl Cant and Thanet Community Health Trust from 93. *St Martin's Hospital, Littlebourne Road, Canterbury, Kent CT1 1TD* Tel (01227) 459584 or 454230

WILTON, Harry Owens (Hal). b 22. St Aid Birkenhead 43. **d** 46 **p** 47. C Edge Hill St Cypr *Liv* 46-49; C Kingston upon Hull H Trin *York* 49-51; Area Sec (NW England) CCCS 51-53; V Southport All So *Liv* 53-56. *Crantock, Mansfield's Land, Kinsale, Co Cork, Irish Republic* Tel Cork (21) 773417 Fax 773418

WILTSE, Joseph August Jean Paul. b 41. Leeds Univ BA64. Coll of Resurr Mirfield 64. **d** 66 **p** 67. C Airedale w Fryston *Wakef* 66-70; Canada from 70. *6983 Richmond Street, Powell River, British Columbia, Canada, V8A 1H7*

WILTSHIRE, Albert. b 19. Qu Coll Birm 49. **d** 51 **p** 52. C Stockton St Jo *Dur* 51-55; C Brandon 55-57; PC Monkwearmouth Ven Bede 57-59; V Carlinghow *Wakef* 59-63; V Woodhorn w Newbiggin *Newc* 63-71; V Chatton w Chillingham 71-75; Chapl OHP 75-77; P-in-c Felton *Newc* 77-80; V Cornhill w Carham 80-85; V Branxton 80-85; rtd 85. *The Levers, Yeavering, Wooler, Northd NE71 6HG* Tel (01668) 216427

WILTSHIRE, John Herbert Arthur. b 27. S'wark Ord Course 63. **d** 66 **p** 67. C Lee Gd Shep w St Pet *S'wark* 66-69; Min W Dulwich Em CD 69-79; R Coulsdon St Jo 79-93; rtd 93; Perm to Offic *Ches* from 93. *66 Meadow Lane, Willaston, South Wirral L64 2TZ* Tel 0151-327 6668

WILTSHIRE, Robert Michael (Bob). b 50. WMMTC. **d** 89 **p** 90. NSM Droitwich Spa *Worc* 89-94; Chapl HM Pris Standford Hill from 94. *HM Prison Standford Hill, Church Road, Eastchurch, Sheerness, Kent ME12 4AA* Tel (01795) 880441 Fax 880267

WILTSHIRE, Archdeacon of. *See* SMITH, The Ven Brian John

WIMBUSH, Canon Timothy. b 44. JP. St Steph Ho Ox. **d** 68 **p** 69. C Hobs Moat *Birm* 68-71; C W Wycombe *Ox* 71-76; R Wykeham from 76; RD Deddington from 86; Hon Can Ch Ch from 95. *The Rectory, Sibford Gower, Banbury, Oxon OX15 5RW* Tel (01295) 780555

WIMMER, Michael John. b 41. Natal Univ BA64. Coll of Resurr Mirfield 65. **d** 67 **p** 68. S Africa 67-86; Canada from 86; Miss to Seamen from 86. *c/o Missions to Seamen, 50 North Dunlevy Avenue, Vancouver, BC, Canada, V6A 3R1*

WIMSETT, Paul. b 58. Univ of Wales (Abth) BSc(Econ)79 Hull Univ MA86. St Jo Coll Nottm DipTh83. **d** 85 **p** 86. C Nuneaton St Nic *Cov* 85-89; C Loughborough Em *Leic* 89-92; TV Totnes, Bridgetown and Berry Pomeroy etc *Ex* from 92. *The Vicarage, Week, Dartington, Totnes, Devon TQ9 6JL* Tel (01803) 868304

WIMSHURST, Michael Alexander. b 33. St Jo Coll Ox BA58. Westcott Ho Cam 59. **d** 60 **p** 61. C Lewisham St Mary *S'wark* 60-65; India 66-70; V Battersea St Pet *S'wark* 71-73; V Battersea St Pet and St Paul from 73. *St Peter's Vicarage, Plough Road, London SW11 2DE* Tel 0171-228 8027

WINBOLT LEWIS, Martin John. b 46. Fitzw Coll Cam BA69 MA72. St Jo Coll Nottm LTh75. **d** 75 **p** 76. C Highbury Ch Ch *Lon* 75-78; C Nottingham St Nic *S'well* 79-82; R Carlton Colville *Nor* 82-83; R Carlton Colville w Mutford and Rushmere 83-88; V Burley *Ripon* 88-96; Asst Chapl Pinderfields Hosps NHS Trust from 96. *Pinderfields General Hospital, Aberford Road, Wakefield, W Yorkshire WF1 4DG* Tel (01924) 201688 Fax 814864

WINCH, Victor Edward. b 17. AIB41 Selw Coll Cam BA47 MA52. Ridley Hall Cam. **d** 48 **p** 49. C Gt Baddow *Chelmsf* 48-50; SW Area Sec CPAS 50-54; V Hastings Em *Chich* 54-69; V Hastings St Mary in the Castle 54-69; Chapl Buchanan Hosp 59-69; V Kirdford 69-82; rtd 82; Perm to Offic *Heref* from 83. *Flat 26, Gracey Court, Woodland Road, Broadclyst, Exeter EX5 3LP* Tel (01392) 469650

WINCHESTER, Gordon Law. b 50. LTCL LRAM ARCM. Trin Coll Bris. **d** 82 **p** 83. C Cheadle *Ches* 82-84; Asst Chapl Amsterdam *Eur* 84-88; C Hove Bp Hannington Memorial Ch *Chich* 88-96; V Wandsworth All SS *S'wark* from 96. *Wandsworth Vicarage, 11 Rusholme Road, London SW15 3JX* Tel 0181-788 7400

WINCHESTER, Paul. b 44. St Pet Coll Ox BA66 MA70. Ridley Hall Cam 67. **d** 69 **p** 70. C Wednesfield Heath *Lich* 69-72; Perm to Offic *Sarum* 73-84; R Tushingham and Whitewell *Ches* from 84. *The Vicarage, Tushingham, Whitchurch, Shropshire SY13 4QS* Tel (01948) 85328

WINCHESTER, Paul Marc. b 53. Univ of Wales (Lamp) BA80 DipTh. St Mich Coll Llan 82. **d** 84 **p** 85. C Bedwellty *Mon* 84-86; C Chepstow 86-89; V Cwmcarn 89-93; V Fleur-de-Lis from 93. *The Vicarage, Commercial Street, Fleur-de-Lis, Blackwood NP2 1TX* Tel (01443) 830467

WINCHESTER, Archdeacon of. *See* CLARKSON, The Ven Alan Geoffrey

WINCHESTER, Bishop of. *See* SCOTT-JOYNT, The Rt Revd Michael Charles

WINCHESTER, Dean of. *See* TILL, The Very Revd Michael Stanley

WINDEBANK, Clive Leonard. b 41. New Coll Ox BA62 MA85. Ox NSM Course 75. **d** 78 **p** 79. Kuwait 78-83; NSM Brompton H Trin w Onslow Square St Paul *Lon* 83-84; NSM Basildon w Aldworth and Ashampstead *Ox* 85-88; NSM Streatley w Moulsford from 88. *The Coombe House, The Coombe, Streatley, Reading RG8 9QL* Tel (01491) 872174

WINDER, John William. b 15. SS Coll Cam BA37 MA41. Ridley Hall Cam 37. **d** 39 **p** 40. C Huddersfield H Trin *Wakef* 39-43; C Sowerby Bridge w Norland 43-48; V Stainland 48-53; V Manningham St Paul *Bradf* 53-66; R Bolton by Bowland 66-81; rtd 81; Perm to Offic *Bradf* from 81. *2 Croft Rise, Menston, Ilkley, W Yorkshire LS29 6LU* Tel (01943) 872084

WINDIATE, Mary Elizabeth. *See* WEST, Mrs Mary Elizabeth

WINDLE, Christopher Rodney. b 45. Univ of Wales (Lamp) BA66. Qu Coll Birm DipTh68. **d** 70 **p** 71. C Lache cum Saltney *Ches* 70-73; C Stockton Heath 73-76; P-in-c Bredbury St Barn 76-83; V from 83. *St Barnabas' Vicarage, Osborne Street, Stockport, Cheshire SK6 2DA* Tel 0161-494 1191

WINDLEY, Caroline Judith. b 62. Trent Poly BA84 CQSW84 Nottm Univ MA97. St Jo Coll Nottm MA96. **d** 97. C Kidderminster St Geo *Worc* from 97. *c/o The Rectory, 30 Leswell Street, Kidderminster, Worcs DY10 1RP*

WINDMILL, Roy Stanley. b 17. Sarum Th Coll. **d** 54 **p** 55. C Wells St Cuth w Coxley and Wookey Hole *B & W* 54-58; R Honiley *Cov* 58-64; PC Wroxall 58-64; V Meriden 64-66; C Cov H Trin 66-70; P-in-c Kineton 70-75; P-in-c Combroke w Compton Verney 70-75; C Wraxall *B & W* 76-78; P-in-c Holton 78-82; rtd 82; Perm to Offic *B & W* from 82. *21 Rectory Drive, Burnham-on-Sea, Somerset TA8 2DT* Tel (01278) 782715

WINDRIDGE, Michael Harry. b 47. Sarum & Wells Th Coll DCM93. **d** 93 **p** 94. C Hempnall *Nor* 93-96; NSM Twickenham St Mary *Lon* from 96. *27 Strafford Road, Twickenham TW1 3AD* Tel 0181-891 1709

WINDRIDGE, Peter William Roland. b 23. ACGI MIMechE BScEng. Sarum & Wells Th Coll 82. **d** 84 **p** 85. NSM Shirley St Jo *Cant* 84; NSM Shirley St Jo *S'wark* 85-86; NSM New Addington 86-95; rtd 95. *83 Orchard Avenue, Croydon CR0 7NF* Tel 0181-655 0872

WINDROSS, Andrew (Andy). b 49. Univ of Wales (Ban) BA71. Cuddesdon Coll 71. **d** 74 **p** 75. C Wakef St Jo *Wakef* 74-78; C Bromley All Hallows *Lon* 78-83; V De Beauvoir Town St Pet from 83; AD Hackney 89-94. *St Peter's Vicarage, 86 De Beauvoir Road, London N1 5AT* Tel 0171-254 5670

WINDROSS, Anthony Michael (Tony). b 50. CCC Cam BA72 MA75 Birm Univ PGCE73. S Dios Minl Tr Scheme 90. **d** 93 **p** 94. NSM Eastbourne St Mary *Chich* 93-97; C E Grinstead St Swithun from 97. *St Luke's House, Holtye Avenue, East Grinstead, W Sussex RH19 3EG* Tel (01342) 323800

WINDSLOW, Miss Kathryn Alison. b 62. Southn Univ BTh83. Linc Th Coll 84. **dss** 86 **d** 87 **p** 94. Littlehampton and Wick *Chich* 86-87; Par Dn 87-89; D-in-c Scotton w Northorpe *Linc* 89-94; Asst Local Min Officer from 89; P-in-c Scotton w Northorpe from 94. *The Rectory, Scotton, Gainsborough, Lincs DN21 3QP* Tel (01724) 764020

WINDSOR, Dean of. *See* MITCHELL, The Very Revd Patrick Reynolds

WINFIELD, Ms Flora Jane Louise. b 64. Univ of Wales (Lamp) BA85. Ripon Coll Cuddesdon 87. **d** 89 **p** 94. Par Dn Stantonbury and Willen *Ox* 89-92; Co Ecum Officer for Glouc 92-94; Chapl Mansf Coll Ox from 94. *Mansfield College, Oxford OX1 3TF* Tel (01865) 282889

WINFIELD, Miss June Mary. b 29. Gilmore Ho 57. **dss** 66 **d** 87 **p** 94. Is of Dogs Ch Ch and St Jo w St Luke *Lon* 66-68; Bracknell *Ox* 68-74; Dean of Women's Min 74-80; St Marylebone w H Trin *Lon* 80-82; Ind Chapl 82-89; rtd 89; NSM Ealing St Steph Castle Hill *Lon* from 89; Asst Dioc Dir Ords Willesden Area from 94. *Kaire, 3 Clementine Close, London W13 9UB* Tel 0181-840 5696

WING, Miss Myra Susan (Sue). b 45. Cranmer Hall Dur 92. **d** 94 **p** 95. C Appledore w Brookland, Fairfield, Brenzett etc *Cant* from 94; Hon C Wittersham w Stone-in-Oxney and Ebony from 95. *Puddleglum, Rheewall, Brenzett, Romney Marsh, Kent TN29 9VB* Tel (01797) 344125

WINGATE, Canon Andrew David Carlile. b 44. Worc Coll Ox BA66 MPhil68 MA71. Linc Th Coll 70. **d** 72 **p** 73. C Halesowen *Worc* 72-75; India 76-82; Prin WMMTC 82-90; Prin Coll of Ascension Selly Oak from 90; Hon Can Birm Cathl *Birm* from 97. *The College of the Ascension, Weoley Park Road, Birmingham B29 6RD* Tel 0121-472 1667 Fax 472 4320

WINGATE, Canon David Hugh. b 22. Qu Coll Cam BA48 MA53. Qu Coll Birm 47. **d** 49 **p** 50. C Cov St Mary *Cov* 49-52; V Wolston 52-56; V Cov All SS 56-60; R Patterdale *Carl* 60-66; Chapl United Leeds Hosp 66-71; Chapl Garlands Cumberland and Westmoreland Hosps 71-86; V Cotehill and Cumwhinton *Carl* 72-86; Hon Can Carl Cathl 85-86; rtd 87; Perm to Offic *Carl* from 87. *26 Beechwood Avenue, Carlisle CA3 9BW* Tel (01228) 38061

WINGFIELD, Christoper Laurence (Chris). b 57. Ripon Coll Cuddesdon DipMin95. **d** 95 **p** 96. C Hadleigh w Layham and Shelley *St E* from 95. *74 Ann Beaumont Way, Hadleigh, Ipswich IP7 6SB* Tel (01473) 823235

WINGFIELD, Eric John. b 16. Queensland Univ BA51. ACT ThL43 St Fran Coll Brisbane. **d** 44 **p** 44. Australia 44-57; C Westmr St Matt *Lon* 57-58; R Wadingham w Snitterby *Linc* 59-77; V Cowbit 77-78; P-in-c Moulton St Jas 77-78; P-in-c Weston 78; V Cowbit (united benefice) 78-81; rtd 81. *1A Fallowfield, Luton LU3 1UL* Tel (01582) 592208

WINGFIELD-DIGBY, Andrew Richard. b 50. Keble Coll Ox BA72. Wycliffe Hall Ox 74. **d** 77 **p** 78. C Cockfosters Ch Ch CD *Lon* 77-80; C Enfield Ch Ch Trent Park 80-84; Dir Chrs in Sport from 84; Hon C Ox St Aldate w St Matt *Ox* 84-94; Hon C Ox St Aldate from 95; Six Preacher Cant Cathl *Cant* from 97. *Christians in Sport, PO Box 93, Oxford OX2 7YP* Tel (01865) 311211

WINGFIELD DIGBY, The Very Revd Richard Shuttleworth. b 11. Ch Coll Cam BA35 MA39. Westcott Ho Cam 35. **d** 36 **p** 37. C Rugby St Andr *Cov* 36-46; CF (EC) 40-45; V Newmarket All SS *St E* 46-53; R Bury St Mary *Man* 53-66; RD Bury 62-66; Hon Can Man Cathl 65-66; Dean Pet 66-80; rtd 80; Perm to Offic *B & W* from 81. *Byways, Higher Holton, Wincanton, Somerset BA9 8AP* Tel (01963) 32137

WINKETT, Miss Lucy Clare. b 68. ARCM92 Selw Coll Cam BA90 MA94. Qu Coll Birm BD94. **d** 95 **p** 96. C Lt Ilford St Mich *Chelmsf* from 95. *3 Toronto Avenue, London E12 5JF* Tel 0181-553 4627

WINKS, Paul David. b 45. Ex Univ BA67. Cuddesdon Coll 68. **d** 70 **p** 71. C Rickerscote *Lich* 70-73; Chapl RAF 73-75; C Yate *Bris* 76-77; TV Yate New Town 77-83; P-in-c Leigh upon Mendip w Stoke St Michael *B & W* 83-84; V from 84. *The Vicarage, Leigh Street, Leigh upon Mendip, Bath BA3 5QP* Tel (01373) 812559

WINLO, Ronald. b 14. Open Univ BA74. AKC41. **d** 41 **p** 42. C Egham Hythe *Guildf* 41-44; CF (EC) 44-48; Hon CF 48; S Rhodesia 48-52; C Ditcheat *B & W* 53-54; V Paulton 54-61; Australia 61-65; V Kirkby Malzeard w Dallow Gill *Ripon* 66-81; rtd 81. *12 Roslyn Road, Harrogate, N Yorkshire HG2 7SB* Tel (01423) 884442

WINN, Mrs Jean Elizabeth. b 58. Man Univ BSc80. Wycliffe Hall Ox 85. **d** 88. C W Derby St Luke *Liv* 88-89. *St Thomas's Vicarage, Elm Road, Liverpool L21 1BH* Tel 0151-928 1889

WINN, Paul William James. b 44. Liv Univ BSc66. EMMTC 86. **d** 89 **p** 90. NSM Spalding St Paul *Linc* from 89. *10 Holland Road, Spalding, Lincs PE11 1UL* Tel (01775) 722802

WINN, Peter Anthony. b 60. Worc Coll Ox BA82 MA86. Wycliffe Hall Ox 83. **d** 86 **p** 87. C W Derby Gd Shep *Liv* 86-89; V Seaforth from 89. *St Thomas's Vicarage, Elm Road, Liverpool L21 1BH* Tel 0151-928 1889

WINNARD, Jack. b 30. Oak Hill Th Coll 79. **d** 81 **p** 82. C Skelmersdale St Paul *Liv* 81-84; C Goose Green 84-85; V Wigan St Barn Marsh Green from 85. *St Barnabas' Vicarage, Lancaster Road, Wigan, Lancs WN5 0PT* Tel (01942) 222092

WINNINGTON-INGRAM, David Robert. b 59. Hertf Coll Ox BA82 MA85 K Coll Cam BA89. Westcott Ho Cam 87. **d** 90 **p** 91. C Bishop's Cleeve *Glouc* 90-94; TV Colyton, Southleigh, Offwell, Widworthy etc *Ex* from 94. *The Rectory, Offwell, Honiton, Devon EX14 9SB* Tel (01404) 831480

WINSLADE, Richard Clive. b 69. Aston Tr Scheme 91 Linc Th Coll BTh93. **d** 96 **p** 97. C Waltham Cross *St Alb* from 96. *103 Northfield Road, Waltham Cross, Herts EN8 8RD* Tel (01992) 627246

WINSOR, Anthony Geoffrey. b 56. Nottm Univ BTh87 Middx Univ MA92. Linc Th Coll 84. **d** 87 **p** 88. C Cobbold Road St Sav w St Mary *Lon* 87-88; Barnardo's CANDL Project 88-89. *2 The Bench, Ham Street, Richmond, Surrey TW10 7HX* Tel 0181-940 9978

WINSPER, Arthur William (Brother Benedict). b 46. Glas NSM Course 89. **d** 91 **p** 92. SSF from 70; NSM Barrowfield *Glas* from 91. *16 Dalserf Street, Barrowfield, Glasgow G31 4AS* Tel 0141-550 1202

✠**WINSTANLEY, The Rt Revd Alan Leslie.** b 49. Nottm Univ BTh72. St Jo Coll Nottm 68 ALCD72. **d** 72 **p** 73 **c** 88. C Livesey *Blackb* 72-75; C Gt Sankey *Liv* 75-77; P-in-c Penketh 75-77; V 78-81; SAMS 81-93; Peru 88-93; Bp Bolivia and Peru 88-93; V Eastham *Ches* from 94; Asst Bp Ches from 94. *The Vicarage, Ferry Road, Eastham, Wirral, Merseyside L62 0AJ* Tel 0151-327 2182

WINSTANLEY, Canon Cyril Henry. b 04. Liv Univ BA26 MA30. Ridley Hall Cam 30. **d** 32 **p** 33. C Everton St Sav *Liv* 32-34; C Edge Hill St Cypr 34-36; V Bootle St Matt 36-41; V Liv Ch Ch Norris Green 41-72; RD W Derby 61-71; Hon Can Liv Cathl 66-72; rtd 72; Perm to Offic *Liv* from 83. *49 Menlove Gardens West, Liverpool L18 2ET* Tel 0151-722 9177

WINSTANLEY, John Graham. b 47. K Coll Lon 67. **d** 71 **p** 72. C Wandsworth St Paul *S'wark* 71-74; Chapl Salford Univ *Man* 75-79; R Kersal Moor 79-87. *14 Lyndhurst Avenue, Prestwich, Manchester M25 8DF* Tel 0161-740 2715

WINSTON, Jeremy Hugh. b 54. Univ of Wales BEd76. St Steph Ho Ox BA78. **d** 79 **p** 80. C Bassaleg *Mon* 79-83; Dioc Children's Adv from 79; V Itton and St Arvans w Penterry and Kilgwrrwg etc 83-93; V Abergavenny St Mary w Llanwenarth Citra from 93. *St Mary's Vicarage, Monk Street, Abergavenny NP7 5ND* Tel (01873) 853168

WINSTONE, Canon Peter John. b 30. Jes Coll Ox BA52 MA56. Ridley Hall Cam 53. **d** 55 **p** 56. C Bitterne *Win* 55-58; C Keighley *Bradf* 58-60; PC Fairweather Green 60-67; V Clapham 67-84; R Leathley w Farnley, Fewston and Blubberhouses 84-95; Hon Can Bradf Cathl 89-95; rtd 95. *7 Kingfisher Close, Worcester WR5 3RY* Tel (01905) 763114

WINTER, Anthony Cathcart. b 28. FCA. Ridley Hall Cam 54. **d** 56 **p** 57. C Childwall St Dav *Liv* 56-58; C Hackney St Jo *Lon* 58-63; V Newmarket All SS *St E* 63-73; Lic to Offic 74-81; Perm to Offic *Lon* 78-81; Hon C St Andr-by-the-Wardrobe w St Ann, Blackfriars 81-86; Hon C Smithfield St Bart Gt from 86. *246 Crescent House, London EC1Y 0SL* Tel 0171-250 0741

WINTER, Dagmar. b 63. Heidelberg Univ DTh96. Herborn Th Sem 93. **d** 96 **p** 97. C Bromley St Mark *Roch* from 96. *25 Matfield Close, Bromley, Kent BR2 9DY* Tel 0181-466 5827 Fax as telephone

WINTER, Canon David Brian. b 29. K Coll Lon BA53 CertEd54. Oak Hill NSM Course. **d** 87 **p** 88. Hon C Finchley St Paul and St Luke *Lon* 87-89; Hd of Relig Broadcasting BBC 87-89; Bp's Officer for Evang *Ox* 89-95; P-in-c Ducklington 89-95; Hon Can Ch Ch 95; rtd 95; NSM Hermitage and Hampstead Norreys, Cold Ash etc *Ox* from 95. *The Vicarage, Cold Ash Hill, Cold Ash, Newbury, Berks RG16 9PT* Tel (01635) 864395

WINTER, Canon Dennis Graham St Leger. b 33. K Coll Lon BSc54 AKC54. Tyndale Hall Bris BD62. **d** 61 **p** 62. C Pennycross *Ex* 61-64; C Maidstone St Faith *Cant* 64-66; V Paddock Wood *Roch* from 66; RD Tonbridge 89-95; Hon Can Roch Cathl from 90; RD Paddock Wood from 95. *The Vicarage, 169 Maidstone Road, Paddock Wood, Tonbridge, Kent TN12 6DZ* Tel (01892) 833917

WINTER, Ernest Philip. b 18. Bris Univ BA49 St Cath Coll Ox BLitt54 MA56. Worc Ord Coll 57. **d** 58 **p** 59. C Worc St Barn w Ch Ch *Worc* 58-61; V Reddal Hill St Luke 61-79; P-in-c Upper Arley 79-86; P-in-c Wribbenhall 81-83; rtd 86; Perm to Offic *Worc* from 86; Perm to Offic *Heref* from 87. *4 Summit Road, Clows Top, Kidderminster, Worcs DY14 9HN* Tel (01299) 832342

WINTER, Henry David. b 24. Sarum Th Coll 51. **d** 53 **p** 54. C Hope St Jas *Man* 53-55; C Heywood St Luke 55-58; R Hulme St Mich 58-63; Chapl Essex Co Hosp Colchester 63-85; V Colchester St Paul *Chelmsf* 63-95; rtd 95; Perm to Offic *Chelmsf* from 95. *24 Valley Crescent, West Bergholt, Colchester CO6 3ED* Tel (01206) 242455

WINTER, Jonathan Gay. b 37. AKC64. **d** 65 **p** 66. C W Dulwich All SS and Em *S'wark* 65-69; Asst Master Kidbrooke Sch 69-77; Norwood Sch from 77; Hon C Dulwich St Barn from 90. *160 Turney Road, London SE21 7JJ* Tel 0171-274 3060

WINTER, Norman Gladwyn. b 50. Ch Ch Ox BA72 MA76. Wycliffe Hall Ox 72. **d** 76 **p** 77. C Huyton St Mich *Liv* 76-80; C-in-c Skelmersdale Ecum Cen 80-82; V Skelmersdale Ch at Cen 82-87; Producer BBC Relig Broadcasting Unit Man from 87. *43 Falstone Close, Birchwood, Warrington WA3 6SU* Tel 0161-244 3212 Fax 244 3207

WINTER, Raymond McMahon. b 23. FSA73 Selw Coll Cam BA52 MA60. Wycliffe Hall Ox 59. **d** 61 **p** 62. C Gaywood, Bawsey and Mintlyn *Nor* 61-64; P-in-c Horstead w Frettenham w Stanninghall 64-71; Youth Chapl 64-71; Warden Dioc Conf Ho 64-71; Chapl Loretto Sch Musselburgh 71-74; P-in-c Latchingdon w Mundon and N Fambridge *Chelmsf* 74-75; P-in-c Brettenham w Rushford *Nor* 75-83; P-in-c Riddlesworth w Gasthorpe and Knettishall 76-83; P-in-c Garboldisham w Blo' Norton 77-83; Chapl Bedgebury Sch Kent 83-91; Hon C Kilndown *Cant* 83-87; Hon C Goudhurst w Kilndown 87-91; Warden Coll of St Barn Lingfield 88-94; rtd 91; Perm to Offic *Nor* from 94. *27 Breydon Road, Norwich NR7 8EF* Tel (01602) 484889

WINTER, Stephen Christopher. b 55. Southn Univ BA76. Trin Coll Bris 85. **d** 88 **p** 89. C Birm St Luke *Birm* 88-92; TV Kings Norton from 92. *93 Westhill Road, Birmingham B38 8SX* Tel 0121-459 3098

WINTER, Thomas Andrew. b 24. Wadh Coll Ox BA51 MA63. Ely Th Coll 51. **d** 53 **p** 54. C Horninglow *Lich* 53-56; S Africa 56-83; R Woodston *Ely* 83-90; rtd 90; Perm to Offic *Ely* from 90; Perm to Offic *Chich* from 90. *6 The Close, Shoreham-by-Sea, W Sussex BN43 5AH* Tel (01273) 452606

WINTERBOTHAM, Canon Anthony James Marshall (Tony). b 27. Magd Coll Cam BA51 MA55. Wells Th Coll 55. **d** 57 **p** 58. C Portsea St Mary *Portsm* 57-63; Asst Chapl Wellington Coll Berks 63-67; Hon Chapl Portsm Cathl *Portsm* from 67; Hon Can 90-91; Chapl and Hd of RE Portsm Gr Sch 67-91; rtd 92. *4 Poynings Place, St Nicholas Street, Portsmouth PO1 2PB* Tel (01705) 825068

WINTERBOTTOM, Canon Ian Edmund. b 42. St Andr Univ MA66 Nottm Univ DipTh68. Linc Th Coll 66. **d** 68 **p** 69. C Blackb St Steph *Blackb* 68-71; C Wingerworth *Derby* 71-73; P-in-c Brimington 73-77; R 77-89; RD Bolsover and Staveley 86-93; R Pleasley 89-94; P-in-c Shirebrook 92-94; TR E Scarsdale from 94; Hon Can Derby Cathl from 95. *The Vicarage, Main Street, Shirebrook, Notts NG20 8DN* Tel (01623) 742395

WINTERBOURNE, George. b 20. S'wark Ord Course 64. **d** 67 **p** 68. C Cove St Jo *Guildf* 67-71; Perm to Offic 72; Hon C Aldershot St Mich 73-78; Perm to Offic *B & W* 79-80; Lic to Offic 80-87; rtd 87; Perm to Offic *Glouc* from 87. *4 Lawn Crescent, Shurdington, Cheltenham, Glos GL51 5UR* Tel (01242) 862671

WINTERBURN, Derek Neil. b 60. Bris Univ BSc82 Ox Univ BA85. Wycliffe Hall Ox 83. **d** 86 **p** 87. C Mildmay Grove St Jude and St Paul *Lon* 86-89; C Hackney Marsh 89-91; TV 91-96; V Hampton St Mary from 96. *St Mary's Vicarage, Church Street, Hampton, Middx TW12 2EB* Tel 0181-979 3071

WINTERBURN, Ieuan Thomas. b 16. Univ of Wales BA37 Univ of S Africa BA48 Witwatersrand Univ MA52. K Coll Lon 37. **d** 39 **p** 40. C Llanelli *St D* 39-44; S Africa 44-59 and 70-72; C Cheam *S'wark* 59-60; V Champion Hill St Sav 60-64; Seychelles 64-68; Adn Seychelles 64-68; Dean Mahe 66-68; Deputations Sec (Dio Win) USPG 68-69; Rhodesia 72-80; Zimbabwe 80-81; V Borth and Eglwys-fach w Llangynfelyn *St D* 81-85; rtd 85. *209 Wilsborough Mansions, Seaview Street, Durban 4000, South Africa*

WINTERBURN, Maurice. b 14. Oak Hill Th Coll 61. **d** 62 **p** 63. C Bethnal Green St Jas Less *Lon* 62-65; C Ealing St Mary 65-68; V Stambermill *Worc* 68-79; P-in-c The Lye 74-79; rtd 79; Perm to Offic *Worc* from 79. *36 Whittingham Road, Halesowen, W Midlands B63 3TF* Tel 0121-550 0434

WINTERSGILL, Allan Vernon. b 19. St Jo Coll Dur BA49. Ely Th Coll 49. **d** 50 **p** 51. C Old Street St Luke w St Mary Charterhouse etc *Lon* 50-52; C S Harrow St Paul 52-55; C Ilkeston St Mary *Derby* 55-57; V Pet St Barn *Pet* 57-70; V Northampton St Jas 70-81; V Staverton w Helidon and Catesby 81-89; rtd 89; Perm to Offic *Pet* from 89. *20 Church Lane, Nether Heyford, Northampton NN7 3LQ* Tel (01327) 40796

WINTLE, Anthony Robert. b 44. K Coll Lon 64. St Mich Coll Llan DipTh68. **d** 68 **p** 69. C Llandaff N *Llan* 68-70; C Baglan 70-75; V Treharris 75-86; V Treharris w Bedlinog 86-90; R St Fagans w Michaelston-super-Ely from 90. *The Rectory, Greenwood Lane, St Fagans, Cardiff CF5 6EL* Tel (01222) 565869

WINTLE, David Robert. b 56. Open Univ BA84. Qu Coll Birm 93. **d** 95 **p** 96. C Cov St Mary *Cov* from 95. *193 Allesley Old Road, Coventry CV5 8FL* Tel (01203) 691392

WINTLE, Graham. b 52. Bris Univ BSc73. Oak Hill Th Coll BA86. **d** 86 **p** 87. C Southgate *Chich* 86-89; C New Malden and Coombe *S'wark* 89-92; V Surbiton Hill Ch Ch from 92. *Christ Church Vicarage, 7 Christ Church Road, Surbiton, Surrey KT5 8JJ* Tel 0181-399 3444

WINTLE, Canon Ruth Elizabeth. b 31. Westf Coll Lon BA53 St Hugh's Coll Ox BA67 MA74. St Mich Ho Ox 63. **dss** 72 **d** 87 **p** 94. Tutor St Jo Coll Dur 72-74; Selection Sec ACCM 74-83; St Jo in Bedwardine *Worc* 83-87; Par Dn 87-94; Dir of Ords 84-92; Hon Can Worc Cathl 87-94; rtd 95; Bp's Adv on Women's Min *Worc* from 95. *72 Henwick Road, Worcester WR2 5NT* Tel (01905) 422841 Fax 612302

WINTON, Alan Peter. b 58. Sheff Univ BA83 PhD87. Linc Th Coll CMM91. **d** 91 **p** 92. C Southgate Ch Ch *Lon* 91-95; P-in-c St Paul's Walden *St Alb* from 95; Dir Continuing Minl Educn from 95. *The Vicarage, Bendish Lane, Whitwell, Hitchin, Herts SG4 8HX* Tel (01438) 871658

WINTON, Ms Philippa Mary (Pippa). b 56. Nottm Univ BA78. Trin Coll Bris DipHE82. **dss** 83 **d** 87 **p** 94. Sheff St Jo *Sheff* 83-86; Sheff Gillcar St Silas 86-87; Hon Par Dn 87-90; Chapl Asst R Hallamshire Hosp Sheff 87; Hon Par Dn Linc St Faith and St Martin w St Pet *Linc* 90-92; Chapl Asst W Middx Univ Hosp Isleworth 92-93; Perm to Offic *Lon* from 93. *62 Oakfield Road, London N14 6LX* Tel 0181-886 3346

WINTON, Stanley Wootton. b 30. Sarum & Wells Th Coll 70. **d** 72 **p** 73. C Birkenhead St Jas w St Bede *Ches* 72-75; V 75-79; TR Ellesmere Port 79-88; Chapl Ellesmere Port and Manor Hosps 79-95; R Delamere *Ches* 88-95; rtd 95; Perm to Offic *Ches* from 95. *26 Wimborne Avenue, Thingwall, Wirral, Merseyside L61 7UL* Tel 0151-648 0176

WINWARD, Stuart James. b 36. Open Univ BA85. Lich Th Coll 65. **d** 68 **p** 69. C Lytham St Cuth *Blackb* 68-71; C Padiham 71-73; V Musbury 73-84; R Old Trafford St Hilda *Man* 84-89; V Davyhulme St Mary from 89. *St Mary's Vicarage, Vicarage Road, Davyhulme, Manchester M41 5TP* Tel 0161-748 2210

WIPPELL, David Stanley. b 46. Queensland Univ BSc67 Selw Coll Cam BA77 MA. Westcott Ho Cam. **d** 78 **p** 79. C Wolvercote w Summertown *Ox* 78-80; Asst Chapl St Edw Sch Ox from 78; Housemaster 85-97; Chapl St Hugh's Coll Ox 80-85. *St Edward's School, Woodstock Road, Oxford OX2 7NN* Tel (01865) 319204

WISBECH, Archdeacon of. *See* RONE, The Ven James

WISE, David Reginald. b 46. Glas Univ BSc68 QUB PhD74 LRAM67. Edin Th Coll 72. **d** 74 **p** 75. Chapl St Andr Cathl *Ab* 74-75; C Ayr *Glas* 75-78; R Airdrie 78-81; P-in-c Gartcosh 78-81; P-in-c Leic St Nic *Leic* 81-82; Chapl Leic Univ 81-89; TV Leic H Spirit 82-89; Chapl St Hilda's Priory and Sch Whitby 89-96; TV Louth *Linc* from 96. *St Michael's Vicarage, Little Lane, Louth, Lincs LN11 9DU* Tel (01507) 601340

WISE, Ms Pamela Margaret. b 51. CertEd73 BA79. Ripon Coll Cuddesdon 89. **d** 91 **p** 94. Par Dn Tokyngton St Mich *Lon* 91-94; C N Greenford All Hallows 94; C Bedford All SS *St Alb* from 94. *9 Wingfield Close, Bedford MK40 4PD* Tel (01234) 354631

WISE, The Very Revd Randolph George. b 25. VRD64. MBIM Qu Coll Ox BA49 MA55. Linc Th Coll 49. **d** 51 **p** 52. C Walworth Lady Marg w St Mary *S'wark* 51-53; V 55-60; C Stocksbridge *Sheff* 53-55; V 60-66; Ind Chapl *Lon* 66-76; V St Botolph without Aldersgate 72-76; TR Notting Hill 76-81; Dean Pet 81-92; rtd 92; Perm to Offic *Pet* from 92. *2 Derwent Drive, Oakham, Leics LE15 6SA* Tel (01572) 756263

WISEMAN, David John. b 51. Lon Univ BD80 Birm Univ DipIslam87. Cranmer Hall Dur 77. **d** 80 **p** 81. C Bilston *Lich* 80-84; P-in-c W Bromwich St Phil 84-86; V 86-89; P-in-c Cheetham St Mark *Man* 89-94; Dioc Community Relns Officer from 89; P-in-c Ashton H Trin from 94. *Holy Trinity Vicarage, Dean Street, Ashton-under-Lyne, Lancs OL6 7HD* Tel 0161-344 0075

WISEMAN, John. b 56. Sarum & Wells Th Coll 80. **d** 83 **p** 84. C Swinton St Pet *Man* 83-87; C Swinton and Pendlebury 87-88; TV Atherton 88-93; V Bedford Leigh from 93. *St Thomas's Vicarage, 121 Green Lane, Leigh, Lancs WN7 2TW* Tel (01942) 673519

WISHART, Michael Leslie. b 45. St Mich Coll Llan DipTh73. **d** 73 **p** 74. C Llangyfelach *S & B* 73-76; Chapl RN 77-80 and from 85; Chapl RNR 80-85; V Beguildy and Heyope *S & B* 80-84; V Gowerton 84-85; R Dowlais *Llan* from 97. *The Rectory, Gwernllwyn Uchaf, Dowlais, Merthyr Tydfil CF48 3NA* Tel (01685) 722118

WISKEN, Canon Brian Leonard. b 34. Dur Univ BA58. Linc Th Coll 58. **d** 60 **p** 61. C Lobley Hill *Dur* 60-63; C Ipswich All Hallows *St E* 63-65; P-in-c Scunthorpe All SS *Linc* 65-69; V 69-71; Dioc Stewardship Adv 70-75; R Panton w Wragby 71-75; V Langton by Wragby 71-75; R Cleethorpes 75-77; TR Cleethorpes 77-89; Can and Preb Linc Cathl from 88; V Linc St Nic w St Jo Newport from 89. *St Nicholas Vicarage, 103 Newport, Lincoln LN1 3EE* Tel (01522) 525653

WISKEN, Robert Daniel. b 30. ACT. **d** 60 **p** 60. Australia 60-63; V Winton *Man* 63-65; R Luddington w Hemington and Thurning *Pet* 65-69; P-in-c Clopton *St E* 66-69; V Ipswich All SS 69-73; V Sompting *Chich* 74-78; Org Sec (SW England) CECS 78-80; R Edmundbyers w Muggleswick *Dur* 80-83; R Wexham *Ox* 83-86; Australia from 86; rtd 95. *St Swithin's House, 5 Pearl Avenue, Kallangur, Queensland, Australia 4503*

WISKER, George Richard. b 35. S'wark Ord Course 69. **d** 72 **p** 73. C Croydon Ch Ch Broad Green *Cant* 72-76; C Barking St Erkenwald *Chelmsf* 76-77; P-in-c 77-82; V from 82. *St Erkenwald's Vicarage, Levett Road, Barking, Essex IG11 9JZ* Tel 0181-594 2271

WITCHELL, David William. b 47. St Jo Coll Nottm BTh75 LTh75. **d** 75 **p** 76. C Northampton St Mary *Pet* 75-78; C Oakham w Hambleton and Egleton 78-81; C Oakham, Hambleton, Egleton, Braunston and Brooke 81-82; V Weedon Bec w Everdon 82-90; V Wellingborough St Barn from 90. *St Barnabas' Vicarage, St Barnabas Street, Wellingborough, Northants NN8 3HB* Tel (01933) 226337

WITCHER, Ian. b 49. CertEd93. **d** 97. NSM Shaston *Sarum* from 97. *7 Old Boundary Road, Shaftesbury, Dorset SP7 8ND* Tel (01747) 854878

WITCOMBE, John Julian. b 59. Cam Univ MA84. St Jo Coll Nottm BA83 DPS84. **d** 84 **p** 85. C Birtley *Dur* 84-87; C Chilwell *S'well* 87-91; V Lodge Moor St Luke *Sheff* 91-95; Chapl Lodge Moor Hosp 91-95; TR Uxbridge *Lon* from 95. *The Rectory, Nursery Way, Uxbridge, Middx UB8 2BJ* Tel (01895) 239055

WITCOMBE, Mrs Maureen Dorothy (Mo). b 56. CertEd77 Nottm Univ BTh83. St Jo Coll Nottm 80. **dss** 84 **d** 87 **p** 94. Birtley *Dur* 84-85; Hon Par Dn Chilwell *S'well* 87-91; Par Dn Lodge Moor St Luke *Sheff* 91-94; C 94-95; Asst Chapl R Hallamshire Hosp Sheff 91-92; Asst Chapl Cen Sheff Univ Hosps NHS Trust 92-94; Chapl Brunel Univ *Lon* from 96. *The Rectory, Nursery Way, Uxbridge, Middx UB8 2BJ* Tel (01895) 239055

WITCOMBE, Michael David. b 53. Univ of Wales (Lamp) BA76. Qu Coll Birm 76. **d** 78 **p** 79. C Neath w Llantwit *Llan* 78-80; C Whitchurch 80-83; V Newcastle from 83; P-in-c Ewenny 84-86.

The Vicarage, 1 Walters Road, Bridgend CF31 4HE Tel (01656) 655999

WITCOMBE, Simon Christopher. b 61. Dundee Univ MA83 PGCE84 Dur Univ BA90. St Jo Coll Dur 88. **d** 91 **p** 92. C Earlham St Anne *Nor* 91-95; Assoc P Skegness and Winthorpe *Linc* from 95; Gen Preacher from 95. *St Clement's Parsonage, 134 Lincoln Road, Skegness, Lincs PE25 2DN* Tel (01750) 761966 Fax 763875

WITHERIDGE, John Stephen. b 53. Kent Univ BA76 Ch Coll Cam BA78 MA82. Ridley Hall Cam 78. **d** 79 **p** 80. C Luton St Mary *St Alb* 79-82; Asst Chapl Marlborough Coll 82-84; Abp's Chapl *Cant* 84-87; Conduct Eton Coll 87-96; Hd Charterhouse Godalming from 96. *Charterhouse, Godalming, Surrey GU7 2DN* Tel (01483) 291501

WITHERS, Mrs Christine Mary. b 37. ALA60. Gilmore Ho DipRS81. **dss** 81 **d** 87 **p** 94. Chorleywood Ch Ch *St Alb* 81-86; Darley *Derby* 86-92; C 87-92; Chapl HM Pris Drake Hall 92-95; P-in-c Standon and Cotes Heath *Lich* from 96. *Hill Farm, Badenhall, Eccleshall, Stafford ST21 6LG* Tel (01785) 850925

WITHERS, Geoffrey Edward. b 68. QUB BSc90 TCD BTh93. CITC 90. **d** 93 **p** 94. C Ballymena w Ballyclug *Conn* 93-97; I Monkstown from 97. *22 Rosemount Crescent, Newtownabbey, Co Antrim BT37 0NH* Tel (01232) 865160

WITHERS, Gillian. b 58. BEd80. **d** 97. Aux Min Mossley *Conn* from 97. *Culmore Hall, Stranmillis College, Belfast BT9 5DY* Tel (01232) 662421 or (01960) 362869

WITHERS, John Geoffrey. b 39. St Jo Coll Dur BA61 Birm Univ CertEd63 Reading Univ DipEdG70 CQSW72. SW Minl Tr Course 84. **d** 87 **p** 88. NSM Drewsteignton *Ex* from 87. *Broomhill, Chagford, Newton Abbot, Devon TQ13 8DD* Tel (01647) 432340

WITHERS, Michael. b 41. TCD BA66 Edin Univ BD70 QUB MTh83. Union Th Sem (NY) STM71. **d** 71 **p** 73. C Seagoe *D & D* 71-77; C Seapatrick 77-80; I Belfast St Chris 80-89; I Movilla 89-96; rtd 96. *11 Earlswood Road, Belfast BT4 3DL* Tel (01232) 471037

WITHERS, Michael Selby. b 36. Sheff Univ BA61 PGCE62 Univ of Wales (Swansea) 75. St Alb and Ox Min Course 93. **d** 96 **p** 97. NSM Bletchley *Ox* from 96. *17 Baccara Grove, Bletchley, Milton Keynes MK2 3AS* Tel (01908) 270669

WITHERS GREEN, Timothy. b 30. K Coll Lon 51. **d** 55 **p** 56. C Greenhill St Jo *Lon* 55-58; C St Helier *S'wark* 58-61; V Belmont 61-79; CF (TA) 71-79; R Hexham *Newc* 79-84; R Weldon w Deene *Pet* 84-95; rtd 95; Perm to Offic *Pet* from 95. *2 Benefield Road, Oundle, Peterborough PE8 4ET* Tel (01832) 273957

WITHEY, Michael John. b 45. Open Univ BA80 Westmr Coll Ox DipApTh95. Oak Hill Th Coll 71. **d** 74 **p** 75. C St Alb St Paul *St Alb* 74-76; C Luton St Mary 77; C Luton St Fran 77-80; V Woodside w E Hyde 80-87; CF (TA) 83-87; Dioc Stewardship Adv *Ox* 87-89; Chapl HM Young Offender Inst Onley 89-91; V Hengoed w Gobowen *Lich* 91-95; Chapl Robert Jones and Agnes Hunt Orthopaedic Hosp 91-95; P-in-c Chasetown *Lich* from 95. *The Vicarage, 158A High Street, Chase Town, Walsall WS7 8XG* Tel (01543) 686276

WITHINGTON, Brian James. b 54. Sheff Poly DipSocWork76 CQSW76. EAMTC CertRS94. **d** 97. NSM Pet St Jo *Pet* from 97. *8 Livermore Green, Werrington, Peterborough PE4 5DG* Tel (01733) 322918

WITHINGTON, George Kenneth. b 37. Birm Univ BA59. Wells Th Coll 59. **d** 61 **p** 62. C Hartcliffe St Andr CD *Bris* 61-65; V Swindon St Jo 65-73; V Cricklade w Latton 73-97; RD Cricklade 94-97; rtd 97. *7 Pear Tree Close, Malvern, Worcs WR14 4AW* Tel (01684) 563711

WITHINGTON, Canon Keith. b 32. Univ of Wales (Lamp) BA55. Qu Coll Birm 55. **d** 57 **p** 58. C Bournville *Birm* 57-61; V from 61; RD Moseley 81-91; Hon Can Birm Cathl from 83. *The Vicarage, 61 Linden Road, Birmingham B30 1JT* Tel 0121-472 1209 or 472 7215

WITHNELL, Roderick David. b 55. Leic Univ CTPS89. EMMTC 86 Ridley Hall Cam 89. **d** 90 **p** 91. C Shenfield *Chelmsf* 90-94; C Woodleigh and Loddiswell *Ex* 94-95; TV Modbury, Bigbury, Ringmore w Kingston etc from 95. *The Vicarage, 3 Little Gate, Loddiswell, Kingsbridge, Devon TQ7 4RB* Tel (01548) 550841

WITHY, John Daniel Forster. b 38. Bible Tr Inst Glas CertRK61 ALCD64. **d** 64 **p** 65. C Belfast St Aid *Conn* 64-68; Dir Chr Conf Cen Sion Mills from 68. *Zion House, 120 Melmont Road, Strabane, Co Tyrone BT82 9ET* Tel (016626) 58672

WITT, Bryan Douglas. b 52. St Mich Coll Llan BD84. **d** 84 **p** 85. C Betws w Ammanford *St D* 84-87; V Llanllwni 87-91; V Llangennech and Hendy from 91. *The Vicarage, Mwrwg Road, Llangennech, Llanelli SA14 8UA* Tel (01554) 820324

✠**WITT, The Rt Revd Howell Arthur John.** b 20. Leeds Univ BA42. Coll of Resurr Mirfield 42. **d** 44 **p** 45 **c** 65. C Usk and Monkswood w Glascoed Chpl and Gwehelog *Mon* 44-48; C Camberwell St Geo *S'wark* 48-49; Australia from 49; Bp NW Aus 65-81; Bp Bathurst 81-89; rtd 89. *U20 DGV, 99 McCabe Street, Mosman Park, W Australia 6012* Tel Perth (9) 383 3301

WITTER, Mrs Tania Judy Ingram. b 37. Girton Coll Cam BA58 MA63. St Jo Coll Nottm DipPC95 Oak Hill Th Coll 94. **d** 95 **p** 96. NSM Highbury Ch Ch w St Jo and St Sav Lon from 95. *27 Arvon Road, London N5 1PL* Tel 0171-607 3156 Fax as telephone

WITTS, Donald Roger. b 47. Cranmer Hall Dur 86. **d** 88 **p** 89. C Leyland St Ambrose *Blackb* 88-90; C Staines St Mary and St Pet *Lon* 90-93; Ind Missr *Man* 93-95; P-in-c Blean *Cant* from 95; Dioc Communications Officer from 95. *The Vicarage, 24 Tyler Hill Road, Blean, Canterbury, Kent CT2 9HT* Tel (01227) 763373 Fax as telephone E-mail don.witts@ukonline.co.uk

WITTS, Graham Robert. b 53. Newc Univ BEd. Linc Th Coll 79. **d** 82 **p** 83. C Horncastle w Low Toynton *Linc* 82-85; TV Gt Grimsby St Mary and St Jas 85-89; TR Yelverton, Meavy, Sheepstor and Walkhampton *Ex* 89-93; C Glastonbury w Meare, W Pennard and Godney *B & W* from 93. *The Parsonage, St Mary's Road, Meare, Glastonbury, Somerset BA5 9SR* Tel (01458) 860276

WITTS, Paul Michael. b 58. Man Univ MA(Theol)95 Sheff Poly BN86 Sheff Univ MSc88 RMN79 RGN86 DipEd83. St Steph Ho Ox 94. **d** 96 **p** 97. C Bamber Bridge St Aid *Blackb* from 96. *17 Station Road, Bamber Bridge, Preston PR5 6QR* Tel (01772) 312663 Fax as telephone

WIXON, Jack. b 44. Lich Th Coll 68. **d** 71 **p** 72. C Adlington *Blackb* 71-74; C St Annes 74-76; V Chorley St Jas 76-82; V Preston Em 82-94; V Ribby w Wrea from 94. *The Vicarage, 1 Vicarage Close, Wrea Green, Preston PR4 2PQ* Tel (01772) 687644

WOADDEN, Christopher Martyn. b 56. St Jo Coll Nottm LTh. **d** 87 **p** 88. C Mickleover All SS *Derby* 87-90; C Wirksworth w Alderwasley, Carsington etc 90-92; C Wirksworth 92; TV Gt and Lt Coates w Bradley *Linc* from 92. *The Vicarage, Wingate Road, Grimsby DN37 9EL* Tel (01472) 885709

WOAN, Miss Susan Ann. b 52. Univ of Wales (Abth) BSc71 Ch Ch Coll Cant MA91 Rob Coll Cam BA95. Ridley Hall Cam BA93 CTM93. **d** 96. C Histon *Ely* 96-97; C Radipole and Melcombe Regis *Sarum* from 97. *1 Campion Close, Weymouth, Dorset DT4 7UE* Tel (01305) 781307

WODEHOUSE, Armine Boyle. b 24. Oak Hill Th Coll 83. **d** 86 **p** 86. NSM Gt Parndon *Chelmsf* 86-92; Perm to Offic *Eur* 89-92; Chapl Menton from 92. *103 Orient Place, 1 rue de la Republique, 06500 Menton, France* Tel France (33) 93 35 77 41 Fax as telephone

WODEHOUSE, Lady Carol Lylie. b 51. St Hugh's Coll Ox BA73 CertEd74 MA77. Ripon Coll Cuddesdon 87. **d** 89 **p** 94. NSM Hambleden Valley *Ox* from 89. *Kingswood, Henley Road, Medmenham, Marlow, Bucks SL7 2EU* Tel (01628) 476291

WODEMAN, Cyril Peter Guy. b 28. ARCO54 LRAM58 ARCM58 Qu Coll Cam BA50 MA55. Cranmer Hall Dur 72. **d** 73 **p** 74. C Penwortham St Mary *Blackb* 73-77; V Burnley St Steph 77-85; V Hornby w Claughton 85-93; rtd 93; Perm to Offic *Blackb* from 93; Perm to Offic *Carl* from 93. *5 Harling Bank, Kirkby Lonsdale, Carnforth, Lancs LA6 2DJ* Tel (01524) 272474

WOLFE, Dr Kenneth Wesley. b 19. QUB MB42. Linc Th Coll 52. **d** 57 **p** 61. C Dunleckney *C & O* 57-58; C Portishead *B & W* 60-63; C Branksome St Aldhelm *Sarum* 68-76; C Rugby St Matt *Cov* 76-80; Hon C Northampton St Alb *Pet* 80-84; rtd 84; Perm to Offic *Pet* from 84. *40 Greenfield Avenue, Northampton NN3 2AF* Tel (01604) 406369

WOLFE, Canon Michael Matheson. b 29. Pemb Coll Ox BA49 MA53. Cuddesdon Coll 51. **d** 53 **p** 54. C Moorfields *Bris* 53-57; P-in-c Fochabers *Mor* 57-58; Sub-Warden Aberlour Orphanage 58-59; V Southport St Paul *Liv* 59-65; V Upholland 65-73; TR 73-82; RD Ormskirk 78-82; Hon Can Liv Cathl 78-82; Can Res Liv Cathl 82-96; Merseyside Ecum Officer 82-96; AD Toxteth and Wavertree 89-96; rtd 96; Perm to Offic *Liv* from 97; Hon Chapl Liv Cathl from 97. *23 Hunters Lane, Liverpool L15 8HL* Tel 0151-733 1541

WOLFENDEN, Peter Graham. b 40. St Pet Coll Ox BA63 MA66. Linc Th Coll 62. **d** 64 **p** 65. C Adlington *Blackb* 64-66; Asst Master Barton Peveril Gr Sch 66-69; Chapl Bp Wordsworth Sch Salisbury 69-72; Hon C Ponteland *Newc* from 72; Hd Master Coates Middle Sch Ponteland from 78. *16 Fern Avenue, Jesmond, Newcastle upon Tyne NE2 2QT* Tel 0191-281 9346

WOLLASTON, Canon Barbara Kathleen. b 30. LSE BSc(Soc)64. Gilmore Ho 51. **d** 87 **p** 94. Dir Past Studies Qu Coll Birm 80-89; Dioc Dir of Ords *S'wark* 89-94; rtd 94. *6 Chapel Street, Wem, Shropshire SY4 5ER* Tel (01939) 232229

WOLLEY, John. BSc. **d** 85 **p** 86. Hon C Croydon St Aug *S'wark* 85-89; Perm to Offic *Linc* from 89. *7 Royal Oak Court, Upgate, Louth, Lincs LN11 9JA* Tel (01507) 601614

WOLLEY, Richard. b 33. Ox Univ MA. S Dios Minl Tr Scheme 82. **d** 85 **p** 86. NSM Brighton Resurr *Chich* 85-88; C 88-89; C Brighton St Geo w St Anne and St Mark 89-91; R Buxted and Hadlow Down from 91. *St Mary's Vicarage, Buxted, Uckfield, E Sussex TN22 4LP* Tel (01825) 733103

WOLSTENCROFT, Canon Alan. b 37. Cuddesdon Coll. **d** 69 **p** 70. C Halliwell St Thos *Man* 69-71; C Stand 71-73; V Wythenshawe St Martin 73-80; AD Withington 78-91; Chapl Wythenshawe Hosp Man 80-89; V Baguley *Man* 80-91; Hon Can Man Cathl from 86; V Bolton St Pet from 91. *St Peter's Vicarage, Churchgate, Bolton BL1 1PS* Tel (01204) 533847

WOLSTENHULME, Arthur James. b 20. Leeds Univ BA42. Coll of Resurr Mirfield 42. **d** 44 **p** 46. C Tonge Moor *Man* 44-45; C Hollinwood 45-48; C Walsall St Mary and All SS Palfrey *Lich* 48-52; V Cov St Pet *Cov* 52-56; V New Bilton 56-66; R Kingsthorpe *Pet* 66-73; TR Kingsthorpe w Northn St Dav 73-86; rtd 86; Perm to Offic *Pet* from 86. *2 Springbanks Way, Northampton NN4 0QA* Tel (01604) 766405 Fax as telephone

WOLVERHAMPTON, Area Bishop of. *See* BOURKE, The Rt Revd Michael Gay

WOLVERSON, Marc Ali Morad. b 68. BA91. Cuddesdon Coll DipMin93. **d** 96 **p** 97. C Nantwich *Ches* from 96. *22 Beatty Road, Nantwich, Cheshire CW5 5JP* Tel (01270) 623620

WOMERSLEY, Walter John. b 28. AKC52. **d** 53 **p** 54. C Linc St Pet-at-Gowts *Linc* 53-59; S Rhodesia 59-65; Rhodesia 65-69; S Africa 70-86; C E and W Keal *Linc* 87-90; Chapl St Jas Choir Sch Grimsby 90-92; rtd 92; Perm to Offic *Linc* from 95. *6 Abbey Park Road, Grimsby, S Humberside DN32 0HR* Tel (01472) 354289

WONNACOTT, Charles Edward. b 14. Wycliffe Hall Ox 62. **d** 63 **p** 64. C Blackpool St Paul *Blackb* 63-66; C Ringwood *Win* 66-68; C Sidley *Chich* 70-73; P-in-c Peasmarsh 73-76; R Beckley and Peasmarsh 76-81; rtd 81; Perm to Offic *Win* from 81. *The Grove, 3 Cedar Avenue, St Leonards, Ringwood, Hants BH24 2QF* Tel (01202) 895457

WOOD, Mrs Ann Rene. b 49. St Deiniol's Hawarden 87. **d** 90 **p** 94. Par Dn Bamber Bridge St Aid *Blackb* 90-93; C W Burnley 93-95; V Marton Moss from 95. *The Vicarage, 187 Common Edge Road, Blackpool FY4 5DL* Tel (01253) 762658

WOOD, Anthony James. b 38. Kelham Th Coll 58. **d** 63 **p** 64. C Shrewsbury St Alkmund *Lich* 63; C Harlescott 63-66; C Porthill 66-70; P-in-c Priorslee 70-76; Chapl Telford Town Cen 73-74; V Barton-under-Needwood 76-97; V Barton under Needwood w Dunstall from 97. *The Vicarage, Church Lane, Barton under Needwood, Burton-on-Trent, Staffs DE13 8HU* Tel (01283) 712359

WOOD, The Ven Arnold. b 18. Clifton Th Coll 66. **d** 65 **p** 66. C Kirkheaton *Wakef* 65-67; V Mount Pellon 67-73; R Lanreath *Truro* 73-81; V Pelynt 73-81; RD W Wivelshire 76-81; Lib Truro Cathl 81-88; Can Res Truro Cathl 81-88; Adn Cornwall 81-88; Warden Community of the Epiphany Truro from 85; rtd 88. *Cobblers, Quethiock, Liskeard, Cornwall PL14 3SQ* Tel (01579) 344788

WOOD, Barry. b 56. CQSW81 CYCW81 Open Univ BA87. St Steph Ho Ox 87. **d** 89 **p** 90. C Tranmere St Paul w St Luke *Ches* 89-92; TV Ches Team 92-94; P-in-c S Tawton and Belstone *Ex* from 94. *The Vicarage, South Tawton, Okehampton, Devon EX20 2LQ* Tel (01837) 840337

WOOD, Beresford Donald Richard. b 32. Leeds Univ BA58. Cant Sch of Min 91. **d** 94 **p** 95. C Folkestone St Mary and St Eanswythe *Cant* from 94. *St Katherine's Cottage, Pound Lane, Elham, Canterbury, Kent CT4 6TS* Tel (01303) 840817

WOOD, Miss Beryl Jean. b 54. Linc Th Coll 85. **d** 87 **p** 94. C Gaywood, Bawsey and Mintlyn *Nor* 87-92; C Gaywood St Faith 92-93; Asst Chapl Univ Hosp Nottm 93-95; R Shipdham w E and W Bradenham *Nor* from 95. *The Rectory, Church Close, Shipdham, Thetford, Norfolk IP25 7LX* Tel (01362) 820234

WOOD, Canon Brian Frederick. b 31. Leeds Univ BA52. Coll of Resurr Mirfield 55. **d** 57 **p** 58. C Wigan St Anne *Liv* 57-60; C Elland *Wakef* 60-63; V Carlinghow 63-73; V Drighlington 73-94; RD Birstall 83-92; Hon Can Wakef Cathl 89-94; rtd 94; Perm to Offic *Bradf* from 94; Perm to Offic *Wakef* from 94. *10 Grove Road, Menston, Ilkley, Yorks LS29 6JD* Tel (01943) 872820

WOOD, Charles Laver. b 14. Wells Th Coll 66. **d** 68 **p** 69. C Stoke *Cov* 68-71; V Ramsey w Lt Oakley *Chelmsf* 71-85; P-in-c Wrabness w Wix 82-85; V Ramsey w Lt Oakley and Wrabness 85-88; RD Harwich 81-87; rtd 88. *9 Richards Way, Salisbury SP2 8NT*

WOOD, Christopher William. b 44. Rhodes Univ BA66 Univ of S Africa BTh82. St Bede's Coll Umtata 79. **d** 80 **p** 82. S Africa 80-87; C Houghton Regis *St Alb* from 87. *The New Clergy House, Lowry Drive, Houghton Regis, Dunstable, Beds LU5 5SJ* Tel (01582) 863292

WOOD, Colin Arthur. b 41. CEng MICE68 MIStructE68. S'wark Ord Course 86. **d** 89 **p** 90. C Tadworth *S'wark* 89-93; TV Morden from 93. *49 Cambourne Road, Morden, Surrey SM4 4JL* Tel 0181-542 2966

WOOD, Canon David Abell. b 25. Qu Coll Cam BA50 MA54. Wells Th Coll 50. **d** 50 **p** 51. C Bodmin *Truro* 50-52; Ind Chapl *Lich* 52-55; P-in-c Wolverhampton St Geo 55-56; Warden St Geo Ho Wolv 56-67; V Wolverhampton St Geo 56-67; Perm to Offic *Heref* 67-70; Warden Communicare Ho *Newc* 70-88; V Mitford 88-93; Chapl Northgate Mental Handicap Unit Morpeth 88-93; Hon Can Newc Cathl *Newc* 88-93; rtd 93. *3 Fontburn Cottages, Ewesley, Morpeth, Northd NE61 4PL*

WOOD, David Arthur. b 30. Man Univ BA51 DSA55. Lich Th Coll 59. **d** 61 **p** 62. C Ashton Ch Ch *Man* 61-64; C Elton All SS 64-68; Dioc Youth Adv *Newc* 68-72; R Cramlington 72-73; TR 73-83; V Wylam 83-86; TV Egremont and Haile *Carl* 86-94; rtd 94; Perm to Offic *Carl* from 94. *6 John Street, Maryport, Cumbria CA15 6JT* Tel (01900) 816706

WOOD, David Christopher. b 52. Oak Hill Th Coll DipHE91. **d** 91 **p** 92. C Kendal St Thos *Carl* 91-95; P-in-c Crosby Ravensworth from 95; P-in-c Asby from 95; P-in-c Bolton from 95. *The Vicarage, Crosby Ravensworth, Penrith, Cumbria CA10 3JA* Tel (01931) 715226

WOOD, David Michael. b 39. Chich Th Coll. **d** 82 **p** 83. C Epping St Jo *Chelmsf* 82-85; C Totton *Win* 85-88; V Southway *Ex* from 88. *The Vicarage, 70 Inchkeith Road, Plymouth PL6 6EJ* Tel (01752) 771938

WOOD, Dennis William. b 28. Qu Mary Coll Lon BSc53 Glas Univ PhD57. NE Ord Course 82. **d** 85 **p** 85. NSM Stanhope *Dur* 85-86; NSM Stanhope w Frosterley 86-94; NSM Eastgate w Rookhope 86-94; NSM Melrose *Edin* from 94. *Gordonlee, Ormiston Terrace, Melrose, Roxburghshire TD6 9SP* Tel (01896) 823835

WOOD, Donald. b 40. **d** 95 **p** 96. NSM Caldicot *Mon* from 95. *6 St Mary's Crescent, Rogiet, Newport NP6 3TB* Tel (01291) 421749

WOOD, Edward Berryman. b 33. Ely Th Coll 54. **d** 57 **p** 58. C Aldershot St Mich *Guildf* 57-60; C Worplesdon 60-62; V Littleport St Matt *Ely* 62-64; V Balham St Jo Bedf Hill *S'wark* 64-71; V New Eltham All SS 71-84; RD Eltham (Sub-Deanery) 79-82; P-in-c Woldingham from 84. *The Rectory, The Crescent, Station Road, Woldingham, Caterham, Surrey CR3 7DB* Tel (01883) 652192

WOOD, Edward Francis. b 28. Chich Th Coll 56. **d** 58 **p** 59. C Newc St Fran *Newc* 58-62; C High Elswick St Phil 62-64; C Delaval 64-67; C-in-c Shiremoor CD 67-68; Dioc Broadcasting Adv 68-78; V Shiremoor 68-78; C Newc St Geo 78-82; C Newc Epiphany 82-93; rtd 93. *52 Albemarle Avenue, Jesmond, Newcastle upon Tyne NE2 3NQ* Tel 0191-284 5338

WOOD, Elizabeth Lucy. b 35. WMMTC 89. **d** 92 **p** 94. NSM Wellingborough St Mark *Pet* 92-95; P-in-c Stanwick w Hargrave from 95. *46 Finedon Road, Wellingborough, Northants NN8 4AA* Tel (01933) 223143

WOOD, Eric Basil. b 25. St Edm Hall Ox BA50 MA50. Cuddesdon Coll 50. **d** 51 **p** 52. C Cheshunt *St Alb* 51-54; C St Pancras w St Jas and Ch Ch *Lon* 54-57; C Leatherhead *Guildf* 57-62; V Mapledurham *Ox* 62-68; P-in-c Drayton St Pet (Berks) 68-72; V 72-81; P-in-c Buckland 81-84; V 84-88; P-in-c Littleworth 81-84; V 84-88; P-in-c Pusey 81-84; R 84-88; Master Hugh Sexey's Hosp Bruton 88-95; rtd 89. *2 Bedwardine House, Henwick Road, Worcester WR2 5NT* Tel (01905) 748207

WOOD, Eric Stanley. b 16. AKC40. **d** 40 **p** 41. C Wavertree St Bridget *Liv* 40-42; C Aintree St Pet 42-43; C Sutton 43-48; C Prescot 48-50; V Banks 50-55; R Newton in Makerfield Em 55-64; R Lowton St Luke 64-81; rtd 81. *5 Lavender Lane, Carluke, Lanarkshire ML8 5TA* Tel (01555) 752461

WOOD, Ernest Charles Anthony. b 06. RMA 25. Wycliffe Hall Ox 52. **d** 53 **p** 54. C Roch St Pet w St Marg *Roch* 53-55; R Nurstead w Ifield 55-78; rtd 78. *14 Maryland Drive, Barming, Maidstone, Kent ME16 9EW* Tel (01622) 727120

WOOD, Frederick Leonard. b 19. BEM59. Worc Ord Coll. **d** 64 **p** 65. C Paignton St Paul Preston *Ex* 64-68; V Charles w Plymouth St Matthias 68-81; rtd 82; Perm to Offic *B & W* 85-92. *Oaklands, 1 Windrush Heights, Sandhurst, Camberley, Surrey GU17 8ET* Tel (01344) 762368

WOOD, Geoffrey. b 33. Tyndale Hall Bris 56. **d** 61 **p** 62. C Tranmere St Cath *Ches* 61-64; C Newburn *Newc* 64-68; R Gt Smeaton w Appleton upon Wiske *Ripon* 69-79; P-in-c Cowton w Birkby 73-79; P-in-c Danby Wiske w Yafforth and Hutton Bonville 76-79; R Gt Smeaton w Appleton Wiske and Birkby etc 79-89; P-in-c Bishop Monkton and Burton Leonard 89; R Fressingfield, Mendham, Metfield, Weybread etc *St E* from 92. *The Vicarage, Metfield, Harleston, Norfolk IP20 0JY* Tel (01379) 853442

WOOD, Geoffrey James. b 47. N Ord Course 88. **d** 91 **p** 92. C Stainton-in-Cleveland *York* 91-94; V Middlesbrough St Oswald from 94. *St Oswald's Vicarage, Lambton Road, Middlesbrough, Cleveland TS4 2RG* Tel (01642) 816156

WOOD, George Albert. b 22. St Paul's Grahamstown. **d** 54 **p** 55. S Africa 54-60 and 63-77; C Cheam *S'wark* 60-63; Area Sec (Dio Chich) USPG from 78; TV Littlehampton and Wick *Chich* 86-88; rtd 88; Perm to Offic *Chich* from 88. *3 Orchard Gardens, Rustington, Littlehampton, W Sussex BN16 3HS* Tel (01903) 787746

WOOD, George Robert. b 26. Em Coll Cam BA52. Oak Hill Th Coll 52. **d** 53 **p** 54. C Denton Holme *Carl* 53-56; V Cambridge St Matt *Ely* 56-60; NW Area Sec CPAS 60-61; R Watermillock *Carl* 61-74; V Holme Eden 74-76; Chapl Lindley Lodge 76-78; C Kingston upon Hull H Trin *York* 78-80; V Chipping *Blackb* 80-81; P-in-c Whitewell 80-81; V Chipping and Whitewell 82-83; R Bunwell w Carleton Rode and Tibenham *Nor* 83-88; P-in-c Wray w Tatham Fells *Blackb* 88-89; rtd 89; Perm to Offic *Carl* from 89. *5 Rimington Way, Penrith, Cumbria CA11 8TG* Tel (01768) 890177

WOOD, Gordon Cooper. b 20. St Pet Hall Ox BA43 MA46. Wycliffe Hall Ox. **d** 44 **p** 45. C Armley St Bart *Ripon* 44-46; CF 46-49; V Sheepscar *Ripon* 49-65; V Roundhay St Jo 65-90; rtd 90. *Flat 55, Moorland Drive, Leeds LS17 6JP* Tel 0113-266 6994

WOOD, Lt Col Gordon Edward. b 12. Ely Th Coll 63. **d** 64 **p** 65. C Ely 64-66; R Houghton 66-74; R Wyton 66-74; V Billingborough *Linc* 74-80; V Horbling 75-80; V Sempringham w Pointon and

Birthorpe 75-80; rtd 80; C Broughton *Ely* 81-91; Perm to Offic from 91. *4 Kings Hedges, St Ives, Huntingdon, Cambs PE17 4XR* Tel (01480) 461806

WOOD, Miss Helen Ruth. b 54. Bedf Coll Lon BA75 Ex Univ PGCE77. Glouc Sch of Min 87. **d** 91 **p** 94. NSM Up Hatherley *Glouc* from 91; Chapl Cheltenham Ladies' Coll from 91. *17 Naunton Terrace, Cheltenham, Glos GL53 7NU* Tel (01242) 242793

WOOD, Mrs Jennifer Sarah. b 40. Sarum Dioc Tr Coll CertEd60. Oak Hill Th Coll DipHE94. **d** 94 **p** 95. C St Illogan *Truro* from 94. *46 Bosmeor Park, Illogan, Redruth, Cornwall TR15 3JN* Tel (01209) 219268

WOOD, John. b 37. LNSM course 75. **d** 77 **p** 79. NSM Dunbar *Edin* from 77; NSM Haddington from 77. *7 Herdmanflatt, Haddington, East Lothian EH41 3LN* Tel (01620) 822838

WOOD, John Anthony Scriven. b 48. Leeds Univ BSc70. St Jo Coll Nottm 76. **d** 79 **p** 80. C Colwich *Lich* 79-82; C W Bridgford *S'well* 82-90; V Gamston and Bridgford 90-95; Chapl Kings Mill Cen NHS Trust from 95. *64 Henry Road, Nottingham NG2 7ND* Tel 0115-982 0969

WOOD, John Arthur. b 23. Roch Th Coll 68. **d** 70 **p** 71. C Wetherby *Ripon* 70-71; P-in-c Sheff Arbourthorne *Sheff* 71-75; TV Sheff Manor 75-81; R Rodney Stoke w Draycott *B & W* 81-88; rtd 88; Perm to Offic *Sheff* from 88. *Flat 36, The Glen, Endcliffe Vale Road, Sheffield S10 3FN* Tel 0114-266 5173

WOOD, John Maurice. b 58. Qu Coll Cam BA80 MA83. Wycliffe Hall Ox BA87. **d** 87 **p** 88. C Northwood Em *Lon* 87-91; C Muswell Hill St Jas w St Matt 91-94; P-in-c S Tottenham St Ann from 94. *St Ann's Vicarage, South Grove, London N15 5QG* Tel 0181-800 3506

WOOD, John Samuel. b 47. Lanchester Poly BSc69 Sheff Univ DipEd. Westcott Ho Cam 72. **d** 81 **p** 82. NSM Haverhill *St E* 81-83; C Haverhill w Withersfield, the Wrattings etc 83; C Whitton and Thurleston w Akenham 83-86; P-in-c Walsham le Willows 86-88; P-in-c Finningham w Westhorpe 86-88; R Walsham le Willows and Finningham w Westhorpe 88-94; Min Can St E Cathl 89-94; TR Whitstable *Cant* from 94. *The Vicarage, Church Street, Whitstable, Kent CT5 1PG* Tel (01227) 272308

WOOD, Keith. b 49. St Steph Ho Ox 76. **d** 78 **p** 79. C Bognor *Chich* 78-81; C Hangleton 81-83; R W Blatchington 83-87; V W Worthing St Jo 87-96; R Winchelsea and Icklesham from 96. *The Rectory, St Thomas Street, Winchelsea, E Sussex TN36 4EB* Tel (01797) 226254

WOOD, Keith Ernest. b 33. Qu Coll Ox BA55 BCL56 DipTh57 MA70. Wycliffe Hall Ox 56. **d** 58 **p** 59. C Barking St Marg *Chelmsf* 58-61; Min Basildon St Andr ED 61-70; V Brampton Bierlow *Sheff* 70-82; R Grasmere *Carl* 82-94; RD Windermere 89-94; Hon Can Carl Cathl 91-94; Bp's Dom Chapl from 94. *Plumpton Vicarage, Plumpton, Penrith, Cumbria CA11 9PA* Tel (01768) 894273

WOOD, Laurence Henry. b 27. Kelham Th Coll 47. **d** 52 **p** 53. C Ravensthorpe *Wakef* 52-55; C Almondbury 55-58; V Linthwaite 58-64; R Bonsall *Derby* 64-70; V Cromford 64-70; V Longwood *Wakef* 70-76; V Liversedge 76-92; rtd 92; Perm to Offic *Wakef* from 92. *203 The Rock, Gillroyd Lane, Linthwaite, Huddersfield HD7 5SR* Tel (01484) 843499

WOOD, Mrs Lorna. b 43. EAMTC 85. **d** 88 **p** 94. Hon C Sprowston *Nor* 88-90; Hon C Sprowston w Beeston 90-95; P-in-c Nor St Helen from 95; Chapl Gt Hosp Nor from 95. *39 Inman Road, Norwich NR7 8JT* Tel (01603) 408710

✠**WOOD, The Rt Revd Maurice Arthur Ponsonby.** b 16. DSC44. Qu Coll Cam BA38 MA42. Ridley Hall Cam 40. **d** 40 **p** 41 **c** 71. C Portman Square St Paul *Lon* 40-43; Chapl RNVR 43-46; R Ox St Ebbe *Ox* 47-52; V Islington St Mary *Lon* 52-61; RD Islington 52-61; Prin Oak Hill Th Coll 61-71; Preb St Paul's Cathl *Lon* 69-71; Bp Nor 71-85; Chapl RNR from 71; rtd 85; Asst Bp Lon from 85; Res P Theale and Englefield 87-94; Asst Bp Ox from 89. *41 Fir Tree Walk, Enfield, Middx EN1 3TZ* Tel 0181-363 4491

WOOD, Michael. Dur Univ BA PGCE. Coll of Resurr Mirfield. **d** 96 **p** 97. NSM Battyeford *Wakef* from 96. *9 Dorchester Road, Fixby, Huddersfield HD2 2JZ* Tel (01484) 536496

WOOD, Michael Frank. b 55. Nottm Univ BCombStuds. Linc Th Coll. **d** 84 **p** 85. C Marton *Blackb* 84-88; TV Ribbleton 88-93; V Blackpool St Mary from 93; RD Blackpool from 96. *St Mary's Vicarage, 59 Stony Hill Avenue, Blackpool FY4 1PR* Tel (01253) 342713

WOOD, Nicholas Martin. b 51. AKC74. **d** 75 **p** 76. C E Ham w Upton Park St Alb *Chelmsf* 75-78; C Leyton St Luke 78-81; V Rush Green 81-91; Chapl Barking Tech Coll 81-91; TR Elland *Wakef* from 91; RD Brighouse and Elland from 96. *Elland Rectory, 50 Victoria Road, Elland, W Yorkshire HX5 0QA* Tel (01422) 372133

WOOD, Paul Dominic. b 52. R Agric Coll Cirencester DipAgr74 Tasmania Coll of Advanced Educn DipEd80. Ridley Coll Melbourne BTh87. **d** 87 **p** 88. Australia 87-92 and from 95; TV Ifield *Chich* 92-95. *8 Rodborough Crescent, Corio 324, Melbourne, Victoria, Australia*

WOOD, Peter Palmer. b 36. Nottm Univ BA58. Bps' Coll Cheshunt 58. **d** 60 **p** 61. C Aldrington *Chich* 60-64; C Brighton St Matthias 64-67; C Lewes St Anne 67-70; C The Quinton *Birm* 70-72; V Kirkby Wharfe *York* 72-85; V Riccall 85-94; rtd 94; Perm to Offic *York* from 94. *28 Hallcroft Lane, Copmanthorpe, York YO2 3UQ* Tel (01904) 703457

WOOD, Preb Peter Thomas. b 31. Clifton Th Coll 57. **d** 60 **p** 61. C Woodford Wells *Chelmsf* 60-63; SAMS 63-72; Chile 63-72; V Clevedon Ch Ch *B & W* 72-82; Chapl St Brandon's Sch Clevedon 72-82; Chapl Heref Gen Hosp 82-93; Chapl Heref Hosps NHS Trust from 93; V Heref St Pet w St Owen and St Jas *Heref* from 82; Police Chapl from 86; RD Heref City 90-96; Preb Heref Cathl from 91. *St James's Vicarage, 102 Green Street, Hereford HR1 2QW* Tel (01432) 273676

WOOD, Philip Hervey. b 42. Sarum & Wells Th Coll 73. **d** 74 **p** 75. C Cov H Trin *Cov* 74-75; C Finham 75-77; C Wandsworth Common St Mary *S'wark* 78-81; R Bodiam *Chich* 81-87; R Ewhurst 81-87; Dep Chapl HM Pris Wandsworth 88-90; Chapl HM Rem Cen Latchmere Ho 88-90; Lic to Offic *Chich* from 90; Chapl R Berks and Battle Hosps NHS Trust from 90. *24 Knebworth Road, Bexhill-on-Sea, E Sussex TN39 4JJ* Tel (01424) 730031

WOOD, Canon Philip James. b 48. Bris Univ BSc69. Oak Hill Th Coll 71. **d** 74 **p** 75. C Islington St Mary *Lon* 74-77; C Stapenhill w Cauldwell *Derby* 77-80; V Walthamstow St Luke *Chelmsf* 80-94; RD Waltham Forest 89-94; Can Chelmsf Cathl 93-94. *c/o 86 Aldersbrook Road, London E12 5DH*

WOOD, Raymond John Lee. b 28. ACII55 ACIArb. Linc Th Coll 66. **d** 68 **p** 69. C Beaconsfield *Ox* 68-72; CF 70-72; V Wath-upon-Dearne w Adwick-upon-Dearne *Sheff* 72-77; R St Tudy w Michaelstow *Truro* 77-86; P-in-c St Mabyn 82-86; R St Tudy w St Mabyn and Michaelstow 86-95; Chapl Bodmin Fire Brigade from 91; rtd 95; Perm to Offic *Truro* from 96. *Lamellen Lodge, St Tudy, Bodmin, Cornwall PL30 3NR* Tel (01208) 850107

WOOD, Reginald John. b 16. Worc Ord Coll 61. **d** 63 **p** 64. C Weston-super-Mare St Jo *B & W* 63-65; C Radstock 65-68; V The Seavingtons w Lopen 68-80; rtd 81; Perm to Offic *Ex* from 82. *Downside, 11 Station Road, Budleigh Salterton, Devon EX9 6RW* Tel (01395) 442389

✠**WOOD, The Rt Revd Richard James.** b 20. Wells Th Coll 51. **d** 52 **p** 53 **c** 73. C Calne *Sarum* 52-55; S Africa 55-73; Namibia 73-77; Suff Bp Damaraland 73-77; V Kingston upon Hull St Mary *York* 77-79; Chapl Hull Coll of HE 77-79; Tanzania 79-85; rtd 85; Asst Bp York 79 and from 85. *90 Park Lane, Cottingham, N Humberside HU16 5RX* Tel (01482) 843928

WOOD, Richard Olivier Ronald. b 19. TCD BA42 MA51. **d** 43 **p** 44. C Belfast St Bart *Conn* 43-45; CF (EC) 45-47; CF 47-74; V Kemble w Poole Keynes *Glouc* 74-77; V Kemble, Poole Keynes, Somerford Keynes etc 77-81; rtd 81. *73 Newbarn Lane, Prestbury, Cheltenham, Glos GL52 3LB* Tel (01242) 57752

WOOD, Roger Graham. b 49. K Coll Lon BD. Chich Th Coll 74. **d** 76 **p** 77. C Skipton H Trin *Bradf* 76-79; Dioc Youth Chapl 79-87; V Queensbury 87-96; P-in-c Langcliffe w Stainforth and Horton from 96. *The Vicarage, Stainforth, Settle, N Yorkshire BD24 9PG* Tel (01729) 823010

WOOD, Roger William. b 43. Leeds Univ BA65 MA67 Fitzw Coll Cam BA69 MA75. Westcott Ho Cam 67. **d** 70 **p** 71. C Bishop's Stortford St Mich *St Alb* 70-74; C Sundon w Streatley 75-79; V Streatley from 80. *17 Sundon Road, Streatley, Luton LU3 3PL* Tel (01582) 882780

WOOD, Ronald Ernest (Ron). b 49. Sarum & Wells Th Coll 79. **d** 81 **p** 82. C Weston-super-Mare Cen Par *B & W* 81-84; C Forest of Dean Ch Ch w English Bicknor *Glouc* 84-88; R Handley w Gussage St Andrew and Pentridge *Sarum* from 88. *The Vicarage, 60 High Street, Sixpenny Handley, Salisbury SP5 5ND* Tel (01725) 552608

WOOD, Shane Grant Lindsay. b 60. Southn Univ BTh91. St Steph Ho Ox 95. **d** 97. C Parkstone St Pet w Branksea and St Osmund *Sarum* from 97. *79 Church Road, Lower Parkstone, Poole, Dorset BH14 0HS* Tel (01202) 743016

WOOD, Stanley Charles. b 26. Glouc Th Course. **d** 83 **p** 84. NSM Lower Cam w Coaley *Glouc* 83-87; P-in-c Shipton Moyne w Westonbirt and Lasborough 87-91; rtd 92; Perm to Offic *Glouc* from 92. *8 The Vennings, Cam, Dursley, Glos GL11 5NQ* Tel (01453) 544873

✠**WOOD, The Rt Revd Stanley Mark.** b 19. Univ of Wales BA40. Coll of Resurr Mirfield 40. **d** 42 **p** 43 **c** 71. C Cardiff St Mary *Llan* 42-45; S Africa 45-55; S Rhodesia 55-65; Rhodesia 65-77; Can Mashonaland 61-65; Dean Salisbury 65-71; Bp Matabeleland 71-77; Asst Bp Heref 77-81; Preb Heref Cathl 77-87; Suff Bp Ludlow 81-87; Adn Ludlow 82-83; rtd 87; Perm to Offic *Llan* from 87. *13 Bruton Place, Llandaff, Cardiff CF5 2ER* Tel (01222) 560632

WOOD, Stella Margaret. **d** 97. NSM Mere w W Knoyle and Maiden Bradley *Sarum* from 97. *19 Church Street, Maiden Bradley, Warminster, Wilts BA12 7HW* Tel (01985) 844456

WOOD, Stuart Hughes. b 32. ACIB64. Guildf Dioc Min Course 93. **d** 95 **p** 96. NSM Camberley St Martin Old Dean *Guildf* from 95. *30 Diamond Ridge, Camberley, Surrey GU15 4LD* Tel (01276) 22115 E-mail stuart.wood@mintsoft.dircon.co.uk

WOOD, Mrs Sylvia Marian. b 40. Gilmore Ho 77. **dss** 80 **d** 87 **p** 94. Tolleshunt Knights w Tiptree *Chelmsf* 80-83; Leigh-on-Sea St Jas 83-86; Canvey Is 86-87; Par Dn 87-92; Miss to Seamen 87-92; Warden of Ords *Chelmsf* 89-92; Par Dn Hutton 92-94;

Continuing Minl Educn Officer 92-94; C Hutton 94-97; Ind Chapl from 97. *15 Shelley Road, Chelmsford CM2 6ER* Tel (01245) 351813

WOOD, Thomas Henry. Glassboro Coll (USA) BEcon84. St D Coll Lamp 57. **d** 60 **p** 61. C Pontnewynydd *Mon* 60-62; C Middlesbrough All SS *York* 64-69; C Fleetwood *Blackb* 69-73; V Ferndale *Llan* 73-77; C Sheff Parson Cross St Cecilia *Sheff* 88-93; V St Hilary Greenway *Mon* from 93. *St Hilary's Vicarage, 38 Rhyl Road, Cardiff CF3 8PA* Tel (01222) 793460

WOOD, Canon Thomas Patrick Scarborough. b 19. TCD BA41 BD54. **d** 42 **p** 43. C Portarlington w Ballykean and Cloneyhurke *M & K* 42-44; C Dublin St Geo *D & G* 44-46; I Rathaspick w Russagh and Streete *K, E & A* 46-56; P-in-c Ballysumaghan 46-49; I Calry 56-94; RD S Elphin 67-75; Preb Elphin Cathl 67-83; Preb Mulhuddart St Patr Cathl Dublin 83-94; rtd 94. *7 Glenmullen Court, Church Street, Sligo, Irish Republic* Tel Sligo (71) 42656

✠**WOOD, The Rt Revd Wilfred Denniston.** b 36. Lambeth DipTh62 Gen Th Sem NY Hon DD86 FRSA93. Codrington Coll Barbados 57. **d** 61 **p** 62 **c** 85. C Hammersmith St Steph *Lon* 62-63; C Shepherd's Bush St Steph w St Thos 63-74; Bp's Chapl for Community Relns 67-74; V Catford St Laur *S'wark* 74-82; Hon Can S'wark Cathl 77-82; RD E Lewisham 77-82; Boro Dean S'wark 82-85; Adn S'wark 82-85; Suff Bp Croydon 85-91; Area Bp Croydon from 91. *53 Stanhope Road, Croydon CR0 5NS* Tel 0181-686 1822 or 681 5496 Fax 686 2074

WOOD, William. b 03. St Jo Coll Morpeth 28 ACT ThL31. **d** 31 **p** 32. Brotherhood of the Gd Shep (NSW) from 28; Australia 31-37; Hon C Fulham All SS *Lon* 37-38; C Brighton St Steph *Chich* 38-39; Perm to Offic *Sarum* 39-41 and 45-69; P-in-c Devizes St Jo w St Mary 41-45; Missr and Chairman Lon Healing Miss 49-68; Chapl and Trustee 68-71; rtd 71; Perm to Offic *Ox* 83-96; Perm to Offic *S'wark* 83-91. *32 The Maltings, Kennet Road, Newbury, Berks RG14 5HZ* Tel (01635) 523447

WOOD, William George. b 31. Oak Hill Th Coll 61. **d** 63 **p** 64. C Woking St Jo *Guildf* 63-69; V Camberwell All SS *S'wark* 69-88; R Horne 88-97; P-in-c Outwood 88-97; rtd 97. *43 Kingston Way, Seaford, E Sussex BN25 4NG* Tel (01323) 490572

WOODALL, Hugh Gregory. b 11. Keble Coll Ox BA33 MA37. Cuddesdon Coll 33. **d** 34 **p** 35. C Horsham *Chich* 34-37; C Guildf Cathl *Guildf* 37-40; C Hurstpierpoint *Chich* 40-41; CF (EC) 41-46; C-in-c Hampden Park CD *Chich* 46-52; V Beddingham w W Firle 52-55; V Boston Spa *York* 55-80; Chapl HM Pris Askham Grange 58-65; RD Tadcaster *York* 72-78; rtd 80; Perm to Offic *York* from 80. *Kirklea, Gracious Street, Huby, York YO6 1HR* Tel (01347) 810705

WOODALL, Reginald Homer. b 38. Univ of Wales DipTh59. St Mich Coll Llan 59. **d** 61 **p** 62. C Newtown w Llanllwchaiarn w Aberhafesp *St As* 61-65; C Rhosddu 65-66; C Hawarden 66-70; CF 70-74; C Thornton Heath St Jude *Cant* 74-77; TV Cannock *Lich* 77-79; TV Basildon St Martin w H Cross and Laindon etc *Chelmsf* 79-84; P-in-c Canning Town St Cedd 84-93; rtd 93. *64 Stephens Road, London E15 3JL*

WOODBRIDGE, Trevor Geoffrey. b 31. Lon Univ BSc52. ALCD57. **d** 58 **p** 59. C Bitterne *Win* 58-61; C Ilkeston St Mary *Derby* 61-65; Area Sec (Dios Ex and Truro) CMS 65-81; SW Regional Sec 70-81; TV Clyst St George, Aylesbeare, Clyst Honiton etc *Ex* 82-84; V Aylesbeare, Rockbeare, Farringdon etc 85-95; rtd 95; Perm to Offic *Ex* from 95. *19 Marlborough Road, Exeter EX2 4TJ*

WOODCOCK, John Charles Gerard. b 31. Kelham Th Coll 52. **d** 56 **p** 57. SSM 56-88; S Africa 56-62 and 76-83; Lesotho 62-76; Chapl Bede Ho Staplehurst 83-87; C Auckland St Andr and St Anne *Dur* 87-88. *3 Helena Terrace, Cockton Hill, Bishop Auckland, Co Durham DL14 6BP* Tel (01388) 604956

WOODCOCK, Michael David. b 67. Avery Hill Coll BEd91. Wycliffe Hall Ox BTh96. **d** 96 **p** 97. C Orpington Ch Ch *Roch* from 96. *43 Haileybury Road, Orpington, Kent BR6 9EZ* Tel (01689) 823774

WOODCOCK, Nicholas Ethelbert (Nick). b 46. FRSA90. Cant Sch of Min 80. **d** 90 **p** 91. Chief Exec and Co Sec Keston Coll Kent 89-92; NSM Clerkenwell H Redeemer w St Phil *Lon* 90-92; NSM Clerkenwell H Redeemer and St Mark 92-93; Chapl RN from 93. *Royal Naval Chaplaincy Service, Room 203, Victory Building, HM Naval Base, Portsmouth PO1 3LS* Tel (01705) 727903 Fax 727112

WOODERSON, Mrs Marguerite Ann. b 44. RGN SCM. Qu Coll Birm 86. **d** 89 **p** 94. Par Dn Stoneydelph St Martin CD *Lich* 89-90; Par Dn Glascote and Stonydelph 90-91; Par Dn Chasetown 91-94; C 94. *15 Spring Gardens, Sallins Road, Naas, Co Kildare, Irish Republic* Tel Naas (45) 897206

WOODERSON, Preb Michael George. b 39. Southn Univ BA61. Lon Coll of Div BD69. **d** 69 **p** 70. C Morden *S'wark* 69-73; C Aldridge *Lich* 73-81; V Chasetown 81-94; RD Lich 86-94; Preb Lich Cathl 89-94; P-in-c Hammerwich 91-94; I Naas w Kill and Rathmore *M & K* from 94. *15 Spring Gardens, Sallins Road, Naas, Co Kildare, Irish Republic* Tel Naas (45) 897206 Fax as telephone

WOODFIELD, Robert Ronald. b 13. Ch Coll Cam BA35 MA49. Ridley Hall Cam 35. **d** 37 **p** 38. C Poulton-le-Sands w Morecambe St Laur *Blackb* 37-39; C Habergham All SS 39-42; C High Wycombe All SS *Ox* 42-43; Chapl Watts Naval Tr Sch N Elmham 43-48; C Gt Faringdon w Lt Coxwell 48-49; C Newbury St Nic 50-53; R Shaw cum Donnington 53-71; R Leadenham *Linc* 71-78; R Welbourn 73-78; rtd 78; Perm to Offic *Roch* from 78. *Upper Treasurer's House, 42 Bromley College, London Road, Bromley BR1 1PE* Tel 0181-290 1544

WOODGATE, Douglas Digby. b 09. Bris Univ BA32. Wells Th Coll 33. **d** 34 **p** 35. C Lewisham St Mary *S'wark* 34-36; C Notting Hill *Lon* 36-42; C Bilborough w Strelley *S'well* 42-45; V Elkesley w Bothamsall 45-80; rtd 80; Perm to Offic *S'well* from 80. *4 Elm Tree Court, Potter Street, Worksop, Notts S80 2HL* Tel (01909) 484740

WOODGER, John McRae. b 36. Tyndale Hall Bris 60. **d** 63 **p** 64. C Heref St Pet w St Owen *Heref* 63-66; C Macclesfield St Mich *Ches* 66-69; V Llangarron w Llangrove *Heref* 69-74; P-in-c Garway 70-74; R Church Stretton 74-84; Preb Heref Cathl 82-84; V Watford *St Alb* from 84. *St Mary's Vicarage, 14 Cassiobury Drive, Watford WD1 3AB* Tel (01923) 254005 or 225189

WOODGER, John Page. b 30. Master Mariner 56 Lon Univ DipTh58. St Aid Birkenhead 56. **d** 59 **p** 60. C Kimberworth *Sheff* 59-62; Chapl HM Borstal Pollington 62-70; C Goole *Sheff* 62-63; V Balne 63-70; C Halesowen *Worc* 70-74; V Cookley 74-81; TV Droitwich 81-85; TV Bedminster *Bris* 85-93; rtd 93; Perm to Offic *Bris* from 93. *1 Barbel Crescent, Worcester WR5 3QU*

WOODGER, Richard William. b 50. Sarum & Wells Th Coll 76. **d** 79 **p** 80. C Chessington *Guildf* 79-82; C Frimley 82-85; C Frimley Green 82-85; V N Holmwood 85-90; TR Headley All SS from 90. *All Saints Rectory, High Street, Headley, Bordon, Hants GU35 8PP* Tel (01428) 717321

WOODHALL, Peter. b 32. Edin Th Coll 57. **d** 60 **p** 61. C Carl St Barn *Carl* 60-63; Hon Chapl Estoril St Paul *Eur* 63-65; Chapl RN 66-82; TR Is of Scilly *Truro* 82-90; V Mithian w Mt Hawke 90-95; rtd 97. *Tregarth, 4 Peverell Road, Porthleven, Helston, Cornwall TR13 9DH*

WOODHAM, Richard Medley Swift. b 43. Master Mariner 70 DipTh. S'wark Ord Course 71. **d** 73 **p** 74. C Gravesend St Aid *Roch* 73-75; C Chessington *Guildf* 75-78; Warden Dioc Conf Ho Horstead *Nor* 78-87; R Horstead 78-87; Youth Chapl from 78; V Nor St Mary Magd w St Jas 87-91; TR Norwich Over-the-Water from 91. *The Vicarage, Crome Road, Norwich NR3 4RQ* Tel (01603) 625699 or 661381

WOODHAMS, Roy Owen. b 57. GRSM78 ARCM86 Lon Inst of Educn TCert79. Ripon Coll Cuddesdon DipMin93. **d** 93 **p** 94. C Deal St Leon and St Rich and Sholden *Cant* 93-97; P-in-c Cherbury *Ox* from 97. *The Rectory, Longworth, Abingdon, Oxon OX13 5DX* Tel (01865) 820213

WOODHAMS, Mrs Sophie Harriet. b 27. Cranmer Hall Dur 66. **dss** 80 **d** 87. Raveningham *Nor* 80-81; Henleaze *Bris* 81-87; rtd 87. *31 Hanover Close, Shaftgate Avenue, Shepton Mallet, Somerset BA4 5YQ* Tel (01749) 344124

WOODHEAD, Christopher Godfrey. b 26. Pemb Coll Cam BA50 MA55. Ely Th Coll 50. **d** 52 **p** 53. C Barnsley St Edw *Wakef* 52-54; C Mill Hill St Mich *Lon* 54-58; C Sandridge *St Alb* 58-66; R Earl Stonham *St E* 66-72; V Hoo St Werburgh *Roch* 72-88; C Cheam *S'wark* 88-91; rtd 91; Perm to Offic *Cant* from 91. *4 Eastgate Close, Herne Bay, Kent CT6 7ER* Tel (01227) 374137

WOODHEAD, Miss Helen Mary. b 35. Bedf Coll Lon BA57. Westcott Ho Cam 86. **d** 87 **p** 94. Par Dn Daventry *Pet* 87-90; C Godalming *Guildf* 90-95; Asst Dioc Dir of Ords from 90; C Worplesdon from 95. *St Albans House, 96 Oak Hill, Wood Street Village, Guildford, Surrey GU3 3ES* Tel (01483) 235136

WOODHEAD, Canon Henry Hamilton (Harry). b 22. TCD BA45. **d** 47 **p** 48. C Seagoe *D & D* 47-50; I Donagh w Cloncha and Clonmany *D & R* 50-57; I Badoney Lower w Greenan and Badoney Upper 57-65; I Killowen 65-91; Can Derry Cathl 81-91; rtd 91; Miss to Seamen from 91. *7 Woodland Park, Coleraine, Co Londonderry BT52 1JG* Tel (01265) 51382

WOODHEAD, Michael. b 51. St Jo Coll Nottm 88. **d** 90 **p** 91. C Stannington *Sheff* 90-93; V Deepcar from 93. *St John's Vicarage, 27 Carr Road, Deepcar, Sheffield S30 5PQ* Tel 0114-288 5138

WOODHEAD, Mrs Sandra Buchanan. b 42. Man Poly BA82 Man Univ BD85. St Deiniol's Hawarden. **dss** 86 **d** 87 **p** 94. High Lane *Ches* 86-87; Hon Par Dn 87-90; C Brinnington w Portwood 91-94; V from 94. *St Luke's Vicarage, Brinnington Road, Stockport, Cheshire SK5 8BS* Tel 0161-430 4164

WOODHEAD-KEITH-DIXON, James Addison. b 25. St Aid Birkenhead 44. **d** 48 **p** 49. C Upperby St Jo *Carl* 48-50; C Dalton-in-Furness 50-52; V Blawith w Lowick 52-59; V Lorton 59-80; Chapl Puerto de la Cruz Tenerife *Eur* 80-82; TV Bellingham/Otterburn Gp *Newc* 82-83; TR 83-91; TR N Tyne and Redesdale Team 91-92; rtd 92. *Cree Grange, Cree Bridge, Newton Stewart, Wigtownshire DG8 6NR*

WOODHOUSE, Miss Alison Ruth. b 43. Bedf Coll of Educn CertEd64 Lon Univ DipTh70. Dalton Ho Bris 68. **dss** 79 **d** 87 **p** 94. Bayston Hill *Lich* 79-81; W Derby St Luke *Liv* 81-86; Burscough Bridge 86-95; Par Dn 87-94; C 94-95; V Formby St Luke from 95. *St Luke's Vicarage, St Luke's Church Road, Formby, Liverpool L37 2DE* Tel (01704) 877655

WOODHOUSE, The Ven Andrew Henry. b 23. DSC45. Qu Coll Ox BA48 MA49. Linc Th Coll 48. **d** 50 **p** 51. C Poplar All SS w St Frideswide *Lon* 50-56; V W Drayton 56-70; RD Hillingdon

67-70; Adn Ludlow *Heref* 70-82; R Wistanstow 70-82; P-in-c Acton Scott 70-73; Can Res Heref Cathl 82-91; Treas 82-85; Adn Heref 82-91; rtd 91; Perm to Offic *Guildf* from 91. *Orchard Cottage, Bracken Close, Woking, Surrey GU22 7HD* Tel (01483) 760671

WOODHOUSE, Andrew Laurence. b 40. NW Ord Course. **d** 82 **p** 83. NSM Bedale *Ripon* from 82. *86 South End, Bedale, N Yorkshire DL8 2DS* Tel (01677) 423573

WOODHOUSE, The Ven Charles David Stewart. b 34. Kelham Th Coll 55. **d** 59 **p** 60. C Leeds Halton St Wilfrid *Ripon* 59-63; Youth Chapl *Liv* 63-66; Bermuda 66-69; Asst Gen Sec CEMS 69-70; Gen Sec 70-76; Bp's Dom Chapl *Ex* 76-81; R Ideford, Luton and Ashcombe 76-81; V Hindley St Pet *Liv* 81-92; Adn Warrington from 81; Hon Can Liv Cathl from 83. *22 Rob Lane, Newton-le-Willows, Merseyside WA12 0DR* Tel (01925) 229247

WOODHOUSE, Canon David. b 36. FRSA FCollP Selw Coll Cam BA60 MA64. St Steph Ho Ox 60. **d** 62 **p** 63. C Boston *Linc* 62-64; C Pimlico St Gabr *Lon* 64-66; Chapl Woodbridge Sch 66-73; V Heap Bridge *Man* 73-75; Can Res Wakef Cathl *Wakef* 76-85; Dir of Educn 76-85; Hon Can Liv Cathl *Liv* from 85; Dir of Educn from 85. *5 Cathedral Close, Liverpool L1 7BR* Tel 0151-708 0942

WOODHOUSE, David Edwin. b 45. Lon Univ BSc68. Cuddesdon Coll 68. **d** 71 **p** 72. C E Dulwich St Jo *S'wark* 71-74; Lic to Offic 74-77; Perm to Offic *Bris* 77-79; Lic to Offic 79-93. *St Augustine's Vicarage, Morris Street, Swindon SN2 2HT* Tel (01793) 522741

WOODHOUSE, David Maurice. b 40. Lon Univ BA62. Clifton Th Coll 63. **d** 65 **p** 66. C Wellington w Eyton *Lich* 65-69; C Meole Brace 69-71; V Colwich 71-82; P-in-c Gt Haywood 78-82; R Clitheroe St Jas *Blackb* 82-88; Ellel Grange Chr Healing Cen 88-91; V The Lye and Stambermill *Worc* from 91. *The Vicarage, High Street, Lye, Stourbridge, W Midlands DY9 8LF* Tel (01384) 423142 E-mail david@oakland.ftech.co.uk

WOODHOUSE, Hugh Frederic. b 12. TCD BA34 BD37 DD52. **d** 37 **p** 38. C Belfast St Donard *D & D* 37-39; C Bangor 40-44; I Aghalee 44-46; I Newtownards 46-51; Canada 51-63; Regius Prof Div TCD 63-82; rtd 82. *4591 West 16th Avenue, Vancouver, British Columbia, Canada, V6R 3E8* Tel Vancouver (604) 224-4812

WOODHOUSE, James. b 29. Lon Univ BA52. Lich Th Coll. **d** 61 **p** 62. C Whitby *York* 61-64; C Pocklington w Yapham-cum-Meltonby, Owsthorpe etc 64-66; P-in-c Roos w Tunstall 66-69; R 69-72; C Garton w Grimston and Hilston 66-69; V 69-72; V Nunthorpe 72-82; V Pocklington w Yapham-cum-Meltonby, Owsthorpe etc 82-83; P-in-c Millington w Gt Givendale 82-83; TR Pocklington Team 84-89; RD Pocklington 84-86; RD S Wold 86-90; V Coatham 89-94; rtd 94; Perm to Offic *York* from 94. *5 Cleveland Avenue, Stokesley, Middlesbrough, Cleveland TS9 5EZ* Tel (01642) 712310

WOODHOUSE, Canon Keith Ian. b 33. K Coll Lon 54. **d** 58 **p** 59. C Stockton St Chad CD *Dur* 58-61; C Man St Aid *Man* 61-64; V Peterlee *Dur* from 64; RD Easington from 72; Hon Can Dur Cathl from 79. *The Vicarage, Manor Way, Peterlee, Co Durham SR8 5QW* Tel 0191-586 2630

WOODHOUSE, Patrick Henry Forbes. b 47. Ch Ch Ox BA69 MA81. St Jo Coll Nottm 69 Lon Coll of Div ALCD71 LTh71. **d** 72 **p** 73. C Birm St Martin *Birm* 72-74; C Whitchurch *Bris* 75-76; C Harpenden St Nic *St Alb* 76-80; Tanzania 80-81; Soc Resp Officer *Carl* 81-85; P-in-c Dean 81-85; Dir Soc Resp *Win* 85-90; V Chippenham St Andr w Tytherton Lucas *Bris* from 90. *The Vicarage, 54A St Mary Street, Chippenham, Wilts SN15 3JW* Tel (01249) 656834

WOODHOUSE, Thomas Mark Bews. b 66. Aston Tr Scheme 90 Westcott Ho Cam CTM95. **d** 95 **p** 96. C Cainscross w Selsley *Glouc* from 95. *Church House, 13 Frome Gardens, Stroud, Glos GL5 4LE* Tel (01453) 756290

WOODHOUSE, William Henry. b 12. SS Coll Cam BA36 MA40. Chich Th Coll 36. **d** 38 **p** 39. C St Margarets on Thames *Lon* 38-47; Chapl RNVR 40-47; R Southery *Ely* 47-51; V Wisbech St Mary 51-61; RD Wisbech 57-61; R Yate *Bris* 61-74; P-in-c Wapley w Codrington and Dodington 67-71; R N Cerney w Bagendon *Glouc* 74-82; RD Cirencester 77-82; rtd 82; Perm to Offic *Glouc* from 82. *2 Burford Road, Cirencester, Glos GL7 1AF* Tel (01285) 658938

WOODING JONES, Andrew David. b 61. Oak Hill Th Coll BA91. **d** 91 **p** 92. C Welling *Roch* 91-95; TV Crookes St Thos *Sheff* from 95. *79 Glebe Road, Sheffield S10 1FB* Tel 0114-268 3463

WOODLAND, Robert Alan. b 29. Bps' Coll Cheshunt 59. **d** 61 **p** 62. C Cheshunt *St Alb* 61-66; V Oxhey All SS 66-76; V Hainault *Chelmsf* 76-81; R Bicknoller w Crowcombe and Sampford Brett *B & W* 81-89; rtd 90; Perm to Offic *B & W* from 90. *13 Paganel Close, Minehead, Somerset TA24 5HD* Tel (01643) 704598

WOODLEY, David James. b 38. K Coll Lon BD61 AKC61. **d** 62 **p** 63. C Lancing St Jas *Chich* 62-64; C St Alb St Pet *St Alb* 64-67; Malaysia 67-70; Lic to Offic *Linc* 71-72; V Westoning w Tingrith *St Alb* 72-77; Asst Chapl HM Pris Wormwood Scrubs 77-78; Chapl HM Pris Cardiff 78-84; Chapl HM Rem Cen Risley 84-92; Chapl HM Pris Styal from 92. *HM Prison, Styal, Wilmslow, Cheshire SK9 4HR* Tel (01625) 532141 Fax 548060

WOODLEY, Canon John Francis Chapman. b 33. Univ of Wales (Lamp) BA58. Edin Th Coll 58. **d** 60 **p** 61. C Edin All SS *Edin* 60-65; Chapl St Andr Cathl *Ab* 65-67; Prec 67-71; R Glas St Oswald *Glas* 71-77; P-in-c Cumbernauld 77-93; Can St Mary's Cathl from 82; CSG from 82; R Dalbeattie *Glas* from 93. *The Rectory, 319 High Street, Dalbeattie, Kirkcudbrightshire DG5 4DT* Tel (01556) 610671

WOODLEY, The Ven Ronald John. b 25. Bps' Coll Cheshunt 50. **d** 53 **p** 54. C Middlesbrough St Martin *York* 53-58; C Whitby 58-61; C-in-c Middlesbrough Berwick Hills CD 61-66; V Middlesbrough Ascension 66-71; R Stokesley 71-85; RD Stokesley 77-85; Can and Preb York Minster from 82; Adn Cleveland 85-91; rtd 91. *52 South Parade, Northallerton, N Yorkshire DL7 8SL* Tel (01609) 778818

WOODMAN, Dr Brian Baldwin. b 35. Leeds Univ BA57 PhD73. N Ord Course 84. **d** 87 **p** 88. C Guiseley w Esholt *Bradf* 87-90; TV Bingley All SS 90-94; NSM St Merryn *Truro* from 94. *The Vicarage, St Merryn, Padstow, Cornwall PL28 8ND* Tel (01841) 520379

WOODMAN, Christopher James. b 65. Chich Th Coll BTh93. **d** 93 **p** 94. C Leigh-on-Sea St Marg *Chelmsf* 93-97; TV Canvey Is from 97. *St Anne's House, 51 St Anne's Road, Canvey Island, Essex SS8 7LS* Tel (01268) 514412

WOODMAN, Oliver Nigel. b 47. FIPM MIPM73 HNC73. Sarum Th Coll 67. **d** 70 **p** 82. C Stepney St Dunstan and All SS *Lon* 70-71; NSM Ovingdean w Rottingdean and Woodingdean *Chich* 81-87; NSM Eastbourne St Sav and St Pet 88-93; Asst to RD Eastbourne from 93. *56 Upper Kings Drive, Eastbourne, E Sussex BN20 9AS* Tel (01323) 507208

WOODMAN, The Ven Peter Wilfred. b 36. Univ of Wales (Lamp) BA58. Wycliffe Hall Ox 58. **d** 60 **p** 61. C New Tredegar *Mon* 60-61; C Newport St Paul 61-64; C Llanfrechfa All SS 64-66; Abp of Wales's Messenger 66-67; V Llantillio Pertholey w Bettws Chpl etc *Mon* 67-74; V Bassaleg 74-90; Can St Woolos Cathl from 84; V Caerwent w Dinham and Llanfair Discoed etc 90-96; Adn Mon from 93; V Mamhilad and Llanfihangel Pontymoile from 96. *The Rectory, 1 Millbrook Court, Little Mill, Pontypool NP4 0HT* Tel (01495) 785528

WOODMANSEY, Michael Balfour. b 55. Leic Univ BSc. Ridley Hall Cam. **d** 83 **p** 84. C St Paul's Cray St Barn *Roch* 83-89; C S Shoebury *Chelmsf* 89-93; R Stifford from 93. *The Rectory, High Road, North Stifford, Grays, Essex RM16 1UE* Tel (01375) 372733

WOODROFFE, Ian Gordon. b 46. Edin Th Coll 69. **d** 72 **p** 73. C Soham *Ely* 72-75; P-in-c Swaffham Bulbeck 75-80; Youth Chapl 75-80; V Cambridge St Jas 80-87; Chapl Mayday Univ Hosp Thornton Heath 87-94; Chapl Mayday Healthcare NHS Trust Thornton Heath from 94. *Mayday Hospital, Mayday Road, Thornton Heath, Surrey CR7 7YE* Tel 0181-401 3105 or 401 3000

WOODROW, Canon Norman Wilson. b 21. TCD BA44 MA50. CITC 46. **d** 46 **p** 47. C Newcastle *D & D* 46-50; C Leytonstone St Jo *Chelmsf* 50-54; R Pitsea 54-63; C Newtownards *D & D* 63-64; I Saintfield 64-93; RD Killinchy 79-93; Can Belf Cathl 85-93; rtd 93. *Kingswood, 12 The Grange, Saintfield, Co Down BT24 7NF* Tel (01238) 510447

WOODS, Canon Alan Geoffrey. b 42. TD93. ACCA65 FCCA80. Sarum Th Coll 67. **d** 70 **p** 71. C Bedminster St Fran *Bris* 70-73; Youth Chapl 73-76; Warden Legge Ho Res Youth Cen 73-76; P-in-c Neston 76-79; TV Gtr Corsham 79-81; CF (TA) 80-94; P-in-c Charminster *Sarum* 81-83; V Charminster and Stinsford 83-90; RD Dorchester 85-90; Chapl Dorchester Hosps 86-87; V Calne and Blackland *Sarum* 90-96; RD Calne 90-96; Chapl St Mary's Sch Calne 90-96; Can and Preb Sarum Cathl *Sarum* 92-96; Sen Chapl Malta and Gozo *Eur* from 96; Chan Malta Cathl from 96. *Chancellor's Lodge, St Paul's Anglican Pro-Cathedral, Independence Square, Valletta VLT12, Malta GC* Tel Malta (356) 225714 Fax as telephone

WOODS, Albert. b 12. St Paul's Coll Burgh St Chad's Coll Regina LTh47. **d** 41 **p** 42. Canada 41-50; C Huyton Quarry *Liv* 50-51; V Litherland St Andr 51-56; Chapl Whiston Co Hosp Prescot 50-51; CF (TA) 50-78; V Rainbow Hill St Barn *Worc* 56-61; P-in-c Tolladine 58-61; V Elmley Castle w Netherton and Bricklehampton 61-63; Dioc Adv on Chr Stewardship 58-63; Dir Chr Stewardship 63-66; V Gt and Lt Hampton 66-71; V Upper w Nether Swell *Glouc* 71-78; rtd 78; Perm to Offic *Liv* 85-91. *3 Lygon Lodge, Beauchamp Community, Newland, Malvern, Worcs WR13 5AX* Tel (01684) 562100

WOODS, Allan Campbell. b 32. MIEH59. Ox NSM Course 85. **d** 89 **p** 90. NSM W Wycombe w Bledlow Ridge, Bradenham and Radnage *Ox* from 89. *4 Pitcher's Cottages, Bennett End, Radnage, High Wycombe, Bucks HP14 4EF* Tel (01494) 482083

WOODS, Charles William. b 31. Lich Th Coll 55. **d** 58 **p** 59. C Hednesford *Lich* 58-62; V Wilnecote 62-67; V Basford 67-76; V Chasetown 76-81; P-in-c Donington 81-83; V 83-96; V Boningale 83-96; RD Shifnal 84-89; rtd 96; Perm to Offic *Lich* from 96. *17 Campion Drive, Telford, Shropshire TF2 7RH* Tel (01952) 677134

WOODS, Christopher Guy Alistair. b 35. Dur Univ BA60. Clifton Th Coll 60. **d** 62 **p** 63. C Rainham *Chelmsf* 62-65; C Edin St Thos *Edin* 65-69; Sec Spanish and Portuguese Ch Aid Soc 69-79; C Willesborough w Hinxhill *Cant* 75-80; P-in-c Murston w Bapchild and Tonge 80-87; R 87-90; R Gt Horkesley *Chelmsf* from 90; RD Dedham and Tey from 91. *The Rectory, Ivy Lodge Road, Great Horkesley, Colchester CO6 4EN* Tel (01206) 271242

WOODS, Christopher Samuel. b 43. Cant Univ (NZ) BA. Qu Coll Birm 75. **d** 76 **p** 77. C Childwall All SS *Liv* 76-79; V Parr Mt from 79. *The Vicarage, Traverse Street, St Helens, Merseyside WA9 1BW* Tel (01744) 22778

WOODS, David Arthur. b 28. Bris Univ BA52. Tyndale Hall Bris 48. **d** 53 **p** 54. C Camborne *Truro* 53-56; C Bromley Ch Ch *Roch* 56-58; V Tewkesbury H Trin *Glouc* 58-66; V Stapleford *S'well* 66-70; Miss to Seamen 70-93; Hon Chapl Miss to Seamen 70-93; V Fowey *Truro* 70-93; RD St Austell 80-88; rtd 93; Hon C Pelynt *Truro* from 93. *Linden, 7 Richmond Road, Pelynt, Looe, Cornwall PL13 2NH* Tel (01503) 220374

WOODS, David Benjamin. b 42. Linc Th Coll 88. **d** 90 **p** 91. C Louth *Linc* 90-93; P-in-c Ingoldmells w Addlethorpe 93-97; R from 97. *The Rectory, 73 Elmwood Drive, Ingoldmells, Skegness, Lincs PE25 1QG* Tel (01754) 773906

WOODS, David Edward. b 36. City Univ FBCO61 FSMC61. SW Minl Tr Course 83 S Dios Minl Tr Scheme 94. **d** 95 **p** 96. NSM Bemerton *Sarum* from 95. *13B Bower Gardens, Salisbury SP1 2RL* Tel (01722) 334482

WOODS, Edward Christopher John. b 44. NUI BA67. CITC 66. **d** 67 **p** 68. C Drumglass *Arm* 67-70; C Belfast St Mark *Conn* 70-73; I Kilcolman *L & K* 73-78; RD Killarney 75-78; I Portarlington w Cloneyhurke and Lea *M & K* 78-84; Chan Kildare Cathl 81-84; I Killiney Ballybrack *D & G* 85-92; RD Killiney 90-93; I Dublin Rathfarnham from 93. *Rathfarnham Rectory, Rathfarnham, Terenure, Dublin 6W, Irish Republic* Tel Dublin (1) 490 5543 Fax as telephone

WOODS, Eric John. b 51. Magd Coll Ox BA72 MA77 Trin Coll Cam BA77 MA83 FRSA94. Westcott Ho Cam 75. **d** 78 **p** 79. C Bris St Mary Redcliffe w Temple etc *Bris* 78-81; Hon C Clifton St Paul 81-83; Asst Chapl Bris Univ 81-83; R Wroughton 83-93; RD Wroughton 88-93; V Sherborne w Castleton and Lillington *Sarum* from 93; Chapl Sherborne Sch for Girls from 93; Chapl Yeatman Hosp from 93; RD Sherborne *Sarum* from 96. *The Vicarage, Abbey Close, Sherborne, Dorset DT9 3LQ* Tel (01935) 812452

WOODS, Frederick James (Fred). b 45. Southn Univ BA66 MPhil74 Fitzw Coll Cam BA76 MA79. Ridley Hall Cam 74. **d** 77 **p** 78. C Stratford-on-Avon w Bishopton *Cov* 77-81; V Warminster Ch Ch *Sarum* 81-96; RD Heytesbury 95-96; TR Woodley *Ox* from 96. *The Rectory, 36 Church Road, Woodley, Reading RG5 4QJ* Tel 0118-969 2316

WOODS, Geoffrey Edward. b 49. Lon Univ BD70 K Coll Lon MA94. Tyndale Hall Bris 67. **d** 73 **p** 74. C Gipsy Hill Ch Ch *S'wark* 73-76; C Uphill *B & W* 76-79; R Swainswick w Langridge and Woolley 79-84; Perm to Offic *Bris* 84-96; NSM Colerne w N Wraxall from 96. *22 Watergates, Colerne, Chippenham, Wilts SN14 8DR* Tel (01225) 743675

WOODS, Canon John Mawhinney. b 19. Edin Th Coll 55. **d** 58 **p** 59. C Kirkcaldy *St And* 58-60; R Walpole St Peter *Ely* 60-75; R Inverness St Andr *Mor* 75-80; Provost St Andr Cathl Inverness 75-80; Hon Can St Andr Cathl Inverness from 80; V The Suttons w Tydd *Linc* 80-85; rtd 85; Perm to Offic *Nor* 85-93. *4 Trenowarth Place, King Street, King's Lynn, Norfolk PE30 1HL* Tel (01553) 762569

WOODS, John William Ashburnham. b 22. Reading Univ BSc50. NW Ord Course 73 St Jo Coll Lusaka 69. **d** 71 **p** 74. Zambia 71-72; C Goole *Sheff* 73-75; P-in-c Firbeck w Letwell 75-76; R 76-82; P-in-c Woodsetts 75-76; V 76-82; Bp's Rural Adv 80-92; R Barnburgh w Melton on the Hill 82-92; RD Wath 86-92; rtd 92; NSM Birdsall w Langton *York* 93-96; NSM Settrington w N Grimston, Birdsall w Langton from 96. *The Vicarage, 2 Cromarty Cottages, Birdsall, Malton, N Yorkshire YO17 9NN* Tel (01944) 768374

WOODS, Joseph Richard Vernon. b 31. Solicitor 57. Cuddesdon Coll 58. **d** 60 **p** 61. C Newc St Gabr *Newc* 60-63; Trinidad and Tobago 63-67; Chapl Long Grove Hosp Epsom 67-76; P-in-c Ewell St Fran *Guildf* 76-79; V 79-87; V Englefield Green 87-96; rtd 96. *8 Wren Close, Christchurch, Dorset BH23 4BD* Tel (01425) 270799

WOODS, Canon Michael Spencer. b 44. K Coll Lon BD66 AKC66 Hull Univ DipMin88. **d** 67 **p** 68. C Sprowston *Nor* 67-70; Malaysia 70-74; TV Hempnall *Nor* 74-79; TV Halesworth w Linstead and Chediston *St E* 79-80; TV Halesworth w Linstead, Chediston, Holton etc 80-85; TR Braunstone *Leic* 85-92; RD Sparkenhoe E 89-91; TR Gt Yarmouth *Nor* from 92; Hon Can Nor Cathl from 96. *The Rectory, 1 Osborne Avenue, Great Yarmouth, Norfolk NR30 4EE* Tel (01493) 850666

WOODS, Canon Norman Harman. b 35. K Coll Lon BD62 AKC62. **d** 63 **p** 64. C Poplar All SS w St Frideswide *Lon* 63-68; C-in-c W Leigh CD *Portsm* 68-76; V Hythe *Cant* from 76; RD Elham 83-89; Hon Can Cant Cathl from 90. *St Leonard's Vicarage, Oak Walk, Hythe, Kent CT21 5DN* Tel (01303) 266217

WOODS, Richard Thomas Evelyn Brownrigg. b 51. St Steph Ho Ox 83. **d** 85 **p** 86. C Southgate Ch Ch *Lon* 85-88; C Northampton All SS w St Kath *Pet* 88-89; V Maybridge *Chich* from 89. *56 The Boulevard, Worthing, W Sussex BN13 1LA* Tel (01903) 249463

✠**WOODS, The Rt Revd Robert Wylmer.** b 14. KCMG89 KCVO71. Trin Coll Cam BA37 MA40. Westcott Ho Cam 37. **d** 38 **p** 39 **c** 71. C St Edm the King w St Nic Acons etc *Lon* 38-39; C Hoddesdon *St Alb* 39-42; CF (EC) 42-46; V Glen Parva and S Wigston *Leic* 46-51; Adn Singapore 51-58; R Tankersley *Sheff* 58-62; Adn Sheff 58-62; Dean of Windsor and Dom Chapl to The Queen 62-71; Bp Worc 71-81; rtd 81; Asst Bp Glouc from 81. *Torsend House, Tirley, Gloucester GL19 4EU* Tel (01452) 780327

WOODS, The Ven Samuel Edward. b 10. Trin Coll Cam BA34 MA37. Westcott Ho Cam 35. **d** 36 **p** 37. New Zealand 36-46 and from 55; V Southport H Trin *Liv* 46-50; R Hatfield *St Alb* 50-55; Adn Rangiora and Westland 55-59 and 63-68; Adn Sumner 59-63; Adn Timaru 68-71; Adn Akaroa and Asburton 74-77. *18 Wren Street, Parkwood, Waikanae, New Zealand* Tel Wellington (4) 293 1035

WOODS, Theodore Frank Spreull. b 37. Wells Th Coll 60. **d** 62 **p** 63. C Stocking Farm CD *Leic* 62-67; Papua New Guinea 67-77; V Knighton St Jo *Leic* 77-80; Australia from 80. *257 Bennetts Road, Norman Park, Queensland, Australia 4170* Tel Brisbane (7) 395-5723 or 354-3422

WOODS, Timothy James. b 52. AIB75 PACTA88 Poly Cen Lon BA78 MSc79. Qu Coll Birm 81. **d** 83 **p** 84. C Brierley Hill *Lich* 83-86; C Stoneydelph St Martin CD 86-88; World Development Officer 86-88; Chr Aid Area Sec (SE Lon) 88-91; Perm to Offic *S'wark* 88-91; Perm to Offic *Roch* 88-91; Perm to Offic *Chelmsf* 88-91; V Estover *Ex* from 91. *The Vicarage, 1 Hallerton Court, Hallerton Close, Plymouth PL6 8NP* Tel (01752) 703713

WOODS, Mrs Valerie Irene. b 44. Trin Coll Bris DipHE84. **dss** 84 **d** 87 **p** 94. Coleford w Staunton *Glouc* 84-88; C 87-88; TD Bedminster *Bris* 88-94; TV 94-95; Chapl HM Rem Cen Pucklechurch 95-96; Chapl HM Pris Eastwood Park from 96. *HM Prison, Eastwood Park, Falfield, Wotton-under-Edge, Glos GL12 8DB* Tel (01454) 260771 Fax 261027

WOODSFORD, Canon Andrew Norman. b 43. Nottm Univ BA65. Ridley Hall Cam 65. **d** 67 **p** 68. C Radcliffe-on-Trent *S'well* 67-70; P-in-c Ladybrook 70-73; P-in-c Barton in Fabis 73-81; P-in-c Thrumpton 73-81; R Gamston w Eaton and W Drayton 81-88; Chapl Bramcote Sch Notts 81-93; Warden of Readers *S'well* from 88; Hon Can S'well Minster from 93; RD Retford from 93. *The Rectory, Gamston, Retford, Notts DN22 0QB* Tel (01777) 838706

WOODSIDE, David. b 60. St Jo Coll Dur BA81. Cranmer Hall Dur 87. **d** 90 **p** 91. C Stoke Newington St Mary *Lon* 90-92. *2A South Park Street, Chatteris, Cambs PE16 6AR* Tel (01354) 695948

WOODWARD, Anthony John. b 50. Salford Univ BSc78. St Jo Coll Nottm DipTh79. **d** 81 **p** 82. C Deane *Man* 81-84; CF 84-87; R Norris Bank *Man* 87-90; V Lostock St Thos and St Jo 92-96; rtd 96. *5 Kintyre Drive, Ladybridge, Bolton BL3 4PE* Tel (01204) 650381

WOODWARD, Arthur Robert Harry (Bob). b 28. **d** 76 **p** 77. Rhodesia 76-80; Zimbabwe 80-87; Adn E Harare 82-87; R Wymington w Podington *St Alb* from 87; RD Sharnbrook from 89. *The Rectory, Manor Lane, Wymington, Rushden, Northants NN10 9LL* Tel (01933) 57800

WOODWARD, Geoffrey Wallace. b 23. St Jo Coll Cam BA47 MA50. Westcott Ho Cam 47. **d** 49 **p** 50. C Middlesbrough St Jo the Ev *York* 49-52; C Rugeley *Lich* 52-54; C Edgmond 54-55; V Whorlton *York* 55-59; V Middlesbrough St Thos 59-65; V Nunthorpe 65-72; V Scarborough St Martin 72-79; V Goathland 79-88; rtd 88; Perm to Offic *York* from 88; Chapl E Netherlands *Eur* 89-93. *Yemscroft, 2 Grange Drive, Cottingham, N Humberside HU16 5RE* Tel (01482) 841423

WOODWARD, Ian. **d** 97. NSM Queen Thorne *Sarum* from 97. *The Willows, Sandford Orcas, Sherborne, Dorset DT9 4RU* Tel (01963) 220468

WOODWARD, James Welford. b 61. K Coll Lon BD82 AKC82 Birm Univ MPhil91. Westcott Ho Cam 83 Lambeth STh85. **d** 85 **p** 86. C Consett *Dur* 85-87; Bp's Dom Chapl *Ox* 87-90; Chapl Qu Eliz Psychiatric Hosp Birm 90-96; Distr Chapl Co-ord S Birm HA 90-96; Chapl Manager Univ Hosp Birm NHS Trust 92-96; P-in-c Middleton *Birm* from 96; P-in-c Wishaw from 96; Bp's Adv for Health and Soc Care from 96. *The Rectory, Coppice Lane, Middleton, Birmingham B78 2AR* Tel 0121-323 3022

WOODWARD, Canon John Clive. b 35. Univ of Wales (Lamp) BA56. St Jo Coll Dur 56. **d** 58 **p** 59. C Risca *Mon* 58-63; C Chepstow 63-66; V Ynysddu 66-74; V Newport Ch Ch 74-84; Can St Woolos Cathl from 82; R Cyncoed from 84. *The Rectory, 256 Cycoed Road, Cardiff CF2 6RU* Tel (01222) 752138

WOODWARD, Maurice George. b 29. Selw Coll Cam BA56 MA58. Wells Th Coll 56. **d** 58 **p** 59. C Gedling *S'well* 58-61; Succ Leic Cathl *Leic* 61-64; Chapl Leic R Infirmary 62-64; CF (R of O) 63-94; V Barrow upon Soar *Leic* 64-77; Hon Chapl Leic Cathl 64-77; V Clare w Poslingford *St E* 77-85; P-in-c Stoke by Clare w Wixoe 84-85; R How Caple w Sollarshope, Sellack etc *Heref* 85-94; rtd 94; Perm to Offic *Glouc* from 95. *Wynfield, 16 Sherwood Road, Tetbury, Glos GL8 8BU* Tel (01666) 505717

WOODWARD, Canon Peter Cavell. b 36. St Cath Coll Cam BA58 MA62. Bps' Coll Cheshunt 58. **d** 60 **p** 61. C Chingford St Anne *Chelmsf* 60-63; Madagascar 63-75; V Weedon Bec *Pet* 75-76;

P-in-c Everdon 75-76; V Weedon Bec w Everdon 76-81; RD Daventry 79-81; Can Pet Cathl from 81; V Brackley St Pet w St Jas from 81; Chapl Brackley Cottage Hosp from 81; RD Brackley 82-88. *The Vicarage, Old Town, Brackley, Northants NN13 5BZ* Tel (01280) 702767

WOODWARD, Reginald Charles Huphnill. b 19. FRGS Lon Univ BA41 DipEd. Wells Th Coll 41. **d** 43 **p** 44. C Linc St Giles *Linc* 43-46; Succ St Mary's Cathl *Edin* 46-51; Hd Master St Mary's Cathl Choir Sch Edin 47-53; Lic to Offic *Linc* 53-95; Teacher K Sch Grantham 53-74; Hd Master K Lower Sch Grantham 74-79; rtd 79. *104 Harrowby Road, Grantham, Lincs NG31 9DS* Tel (01476) 571912

WOODWARD, Richard Tharby. b 39. Man Univ BA60. Chich Th Coll 60. **d** 62 **p** 63. C Mansfield St Mark *S'well* 62-65; Chapl Liddon Ho Lon 65-69; C-in-c Beaconsfield St Mich CD *Ox* 69-76; TV Beaconsfield 76-94; rtd 94. *10 Baring Crescent, Beaconsfield, Bucks HP9 2NG* Tel (01494) 670690

WOODWARD, Roger David. b 38. WMMTC 87. **d** 90 **p** 91. C Castle Bromwich SS Mary and Marg *Birm* 90-93; C Kingstanding St Luke from 93; C Kingstanding St Mark from 93. *77 Bannersgate Road, Sutton Coldfield, W Midlands B73 6TY* Tel 0121-355 8497

WOODWARD-COURT, John Blunden. b 13. Ripon Hall Ox 52. **d** 53 **p** 54. C Nuneaton St Mary *Cov* 53-55; P-in-c Snitterfield w Bearley 55-74; P-in-c Barton-on-the-Heath 74-83; R Barcheston 76-83; R Cherington w Stourton 76-83; V Wolford w Burmington 76-83; rtd 83; Perm to Offic *Cov* from 83; Perm to Offic *Glouc* from 83; Perm to Offic *Ox* from 84. *2 Orchard Close, Lower Brailes, Banbury, Oxon OX15 5AH* Tel (01608) 685411

WOODWARDS, Canon David George. b 36. K Coll Lon BD62 MTh73. Oak Hill Th Coll 62. **d** 64 **p** 65. C Heworth H Trin *York* 64-66; Nigeria 67-71; V Edwardstone w Groton *St E* 72-82; RD Sudbury 81-88; R Glemsford 82-88; P-in-c Stanstead w Shimplingthorne and Alpheton 85-86; P-in-c Hartest w Boxted 85-86; P-in-c Lawshall 85-86; P-in-c Hartest w Boxted, Somerton and Stanstead 86-88; Hon Can St E Cathl from 87; R Thorndon w Rishangles, Stoke Ash, Thwaite etc 88-94; RD Hartismere 88-93. *4 Cricketers Close, Sudbury, Suffolk CO10 6AL* Tel (01787) 374160

WOOKEY, Stephen Mark. b 54. Em Coll Cam BA76 MA80. Wycliffe Hall Ox 77. **d** 80 **p** 81. C Enfield Ch Ch Trent Park *Lon* 80-84; Asst Chapl Paris St Mich *Eur* 84-87; C Langham Place All So *Lon* 87-96; R Moreton-in-Marsh w Batsford, Todenham etc *Glouc* from 96. *The Rectory, Bourton Road, Moreton-in-Marsh, Glos GL56 0BG* Tel (01608) 652680

WOOLCOCK, Mrs Annette Elisabeth. b 56. Qu Coll Birm BTh94. **d** 94 **p** 95. C Hethersett w Canteloff w Lt and Gt Melton *Nor* 94-96; C Stourport and Wilden *Worc* from 96. *26 Bewdley Road, Stourport-on-Severn, Worcs DY13 8XQ* Tel (01299) 822705

WOOLCOCK, Christine Ann. *See* FROUDE, Mrs Christine Ann

WOOLCOCK, John. b 47. DipRK70 Open Univ BA82 BA86. Wm Temple Coll Rugby 69 Sarum & Wells Th Coll 70. **d** 72 **p** 73. C Kells *Carl* 72-76; C Barrow St Matt 76-78; R Distington 78-86; V Staveley w Kentmere 86-93; V Staveley, Ings and Kentmere 93; Soc Resp Officer 89-93; Hon Can Carl Cathl 91-93; TR Egremont and Haile from 93. *The Rectory, Grove Road, Egremont, Cumbria CA22 2LU* Tel (01946) 820268

WOOLDRIDGE, Derek Robert. b 33. Nottm Univ BA57. Oak Hill Th Coll. **d** 59 **p** 60. C Chesterfield H Trin *Derby* 59-63; C Heworth w Peasholme St Cuth *York* 63-70; R York St Paul from 70. *St Paul's Rectory, 100 Acomb Road, York YO2 4ER* Tel (01904) 792304

WOOLDRIDGE, John Bellamy. b 27. Tyndale Hall Bris 54. **d** 56 **p** 57. C Norbury *Ches* 56-58; C Bramcote *S'well* 58-60; R Eccleston *Ches* 60-66; NW Area Sec CPAS 66-68; P-in-c Knutsford St Jo *Ches* 68-71; V Knutsford St Jo and Toft 71-79; V Gt Clacton *Chelmsf* 79-82; V Disley *Ches* 82-88; Min Buxton Trin Prop Chpl *Derby* 88-92; rtd 92; Lic to Offic *S'well* from 92; Perm to Offic *Derby* from 92. *227 Bramcote Lane, Nottingham NG8 2QL* Tel 0115-928 8332

WOOLFENDEN, Dennis George. b 12. Leeds Univ BSc35. Cranmer Hall Dur 66. **d** 68 **p** 69. C Barking St Marg *Chelmsf* 68-72; R Wakes Colne w Chappel 72-76; V Elm Park St Nic Hornchurch 76-80; rtd 80; Perm to Offic *Chich* from 80; Perm to Offic *Portsm* 90-96. *2 Tollhouse Close, Chichester, W Sussex PO19 1SE* Tel (01243) 528593

WOOLHOUSE, Kenneth (Ken). b 38. BNC Ox BA61 MA65. Cuddesdon Coll 61. **d** 64 **p** 65. C Old Brumby *Linc* 64-67; W Germany 67-68; Chapl Cov Cathl *Cov* 68-75; C-in-c Hammersmith SS Mich and Geo White City Estate CD *Lon* 75-81; Dir Past Studies Chich Th Coll 81-86; P-in-c Birdham w W Itchenor *Chich* 81-86; Chapl W Sussex Inst of HE 86-95; TV N Lambeth *S'wark* from 95. *22 Wincott Street, London SE11 4NT* Tel 0171-582 4915

WOOLHOUSE, Miss Linda June. b 49. ACP76 CertEd70. WMMTC 85. **d** 88 **p** 94. Hon Par Dn Old Swinford Stourbridge *Worc* 88-92; Par Dn 93-94; Community Chapl 92-93; C Old Swinford Stourbridge 94-96; Black Country Urban Ind Miss *Lich* from 96; Res Min W Bromwich All SS from 96. *7 Hopkins Drive, West Bromwich, W Midlands B71 3RR* Tel 0121-588 3744

WOOLLARD, Miss Bridget Marianne. b 56. K Coll Cam BA77 MA80 Sheff Univ PGCE78 St Jo Coll Dur BA81 Birm Univ MPhil87. Cranmer Hall Dur 79. **dss** 82 **d** 87 **p** 94. Battersea St Pet and St Paul *S'wark* 82-84; Chapl Southn Univ *Win* 84-89; Tutor Past Th and Dir Past Studies Qu Coll Birm 89-92; Telford Chr Coun Officer for Ind and Commerce *Lich* from 92; Perm to Offic *Heref* from 92. *Meeting Point House, Southwater Square, Town Centre, Telford, Shropshire TF3 4HS* Tel Telford (01952) 291904 or 243205 Fax 290617

WOOLLARD, David John. b 39. Leic Univ BSc62. Trin Coll Bris DipHE88. **d** 88 **p** 89. C Clifton *York* 88-91; C York St Luke 91-94; V Selby St Jas from 94; V Wistow 94-96. *St James's Vicarage, 14 Leeds Road, Selby, N Yorkshire YO8 0HX* Tel (01757) 702861

WOOLLASTON, Brian. b 53. CertEd76 DipTh83. St Paul's Grahamstown 81. **d** 83 **p** 84. C Kington w Huntington, Old Radnor, Kinnerton etc *Heref* 88-89; C Tupsley 89-91; V Newbridge-on-Wye and Llanfihangel Brynpabuan etc *S & B* from 91. *The Vicarage, Newbridge-on-Wye, Llandrindod Wells LD1 6LY* Tel (01597) 89272

WOOLLCOMBE, Mrs Juliet. b 38. St Mary's Coll Dur BA60 DipEd61. Gilmore Course 74. **dss** 77 **d** 87 **p** 94. St Marylebone Ch Ch *Lon* 77-80; Dean of Women's Min (Lon Area) 87-89; D-in-c Upton Snodsbury and Broughton Hackett etc *Worc* 89-94; NSM Pershore w Pinvin, Wick and Birlingham from 94. *19 Ashdale Avenue, Pershore, Worcs WR10 1PL* Tel Pershore (02386) 556550

✠**WOOLLCOMBE, The Rt Revd Kenneth John.** b 24. St Jo Coll Ox BA49 MA53 S Sewanee Univ STD63 Trin Coll Hartford (USA) Hon DD75. Westcott Ho Cam 49. **d** 51 **p** 52 **c** 71. C Gt Grimsby St Jas *Linc* 51-53; Fell Chapl and Lect St Jo Coll Ox 53-60; Tutor St Jo Coll Ox 56-60; USA 60-63; Prof Dogmatic Th Gen Th Sem NY 60-63; Prin Edin Th Coll 63-71; Can St Mary's Cathl *Edin* 63-71; Bp Ox 71-78; Asst Bp Lon 78-81; Can Res and Prec St Paul's Cathl 81-89; rtd 89; Asst Bp Worc from 89. *19 Ashdale Avenue, Pershore, Worcs WR10 1PL* Tel (01386) 556550

WOOLLEY, Canon Christopher Andrew Lempriere. b 15. Ch Ch Ox BA37 MA70. Ely Th Coll 37. **d** 39 **p** 40. C Kilburn St Aug *Lon* 39-46; Tanganyika 46-64; Tanzania 64-70; Adn Njombe 64-70; Can Liuli 65-70; Hon Can from 70; P-in-c Hanwell *Ox* 70-84; V Horley w Hornton 70-84; rtd 84; Perm to Offic *B & W* 86-91. *Springfield, Street Road, Glastonbury, Somerset BA6 9EG* Tel (01458) 835175

WOOLLEY, Francis Bertram Hopkinson. b 43. Sarum & Wells Th Coll 75. **d** 78 **p** 79. C Halesowen *Worc* 78-81; TV Droitwich 81-86; TV Cambridge Ascension *Ely* 86-92; R Leverington from 92; P-in-c Wisbech St Mary from 92. *The Rectory, Gorefield Road, Leverington, Wisbech, Cambs PE13 5AS* Tel (01945) 581486

WOOLLEY, John Alexander. b 28. St Deiniol's Hawarden 61. **d** 63 **p** 64. C Garston *Liv* 63-65; C-in-c Gt Crosby St Luke 65-71; R Croft w Southworth 71-75; Chapl Cherry Knowle & Ryhope Hosps Sunderland 75-83; Chapl Cell Barnes Hosp St Alb 83-93; Chapl Hill End Hosp St Alb 83-93; rtd 93; NSM Niton *Portsm* from 95; NSM Whitwell from 95; NSM St Lawrence from 95. *The Vicarage, Ashknowle Lane, Whitwell, Ventnor, Isle of Wight PO38 2PP* Tel (01983) 730745

WOOLMER, John Shirley Thursby. b 42. Wadh Coll Ox BA63 MA69. St Jo Coll Nottm 70. **d** 71 **p** 72. Asst Chapl Win Coll 72-75; C Ox St Aldate w H Trin *Ox* 75-82; C Ox St Aldate w St Matt 82; R Shepton Mallet w Doulting *B & W* from 82. *The Rectory, Peter Street, Shepton Mallet, Somerset BA4 5BL* Tel (01749) 342163

WOOLSTENHOLMES, Cyril Esmond. b 16. Bede Coll Dur BA37 DipTh38 MA41. **d** 39 **p** 40. C Leadgate *Dur* 39-44; C Darlington St Cuth 44-46; C W Hartlepool St Paul 46-50; V Tudhoe Grange 50-67; R Shadforth 67-82; rtd 82. *12 Wearside Drive, The Sands, Durham DH1 1LE* Tel 0191-384 3763

WOOLVEN, Ronald (Ron). b 36. Oak Hill Th Coll 60. **d** 63 **p** 64. C Romford Gd Shep Collier Row *Chelmsf* 63-68; C Widford 68-73; P-in-c Barling w Lt Wakering 73-84; V from 84. *154 Little Wakering Road, Great Wakering, Southend-on-Sea SS3 0JN* Tel (01702) 219200

WOOLVERIDGE, Gordon Hubert. b 27. Barrister-at-Law 52 CCC Cam BA51 MA55. S Dios Minl Tr Scheme 81. **d** 84 **p** 85. NSM St Edm the King w St Nic Acons etc *Lon* 84-85; NSM Chich St Paul and St Pet *Chich* 85-88; P-in-c Greatham w Empshott *Portsm* 88-90; P-in-c Hawkley w Prior's Dean 88-90; P-in-c Greatham w Empshott and Hawkley w Prior's Dean 90-92; rtd 92. *Brook House, Winfrith Newburgh, Dorchester, Dorset DT2 8JH* Tel (01305) 853633

WOOLWICH, Area Bishop of. *See* BUCHANAN, The Rt Revd Colin Ogilvie

WOON, Edward Charles. b 43. LNSM course 94. **d** 96 **p** 97. NSM Tuckingmill *Truro* from 96. *25 Pendarves Street, Beacon, Camborne, Cornwall TR14 7SQ* Tel (01209) 715910

WOOSTER, Patrick Charles Francis. b 38. Qu Coll Birm 63. **d** 65 **p** 66. C Chippenham St Andr w Tytherton Lucas *Bris* 65-70; C Cockington *Ex* 70-72; V Stone w Woodford *Glouc* 72-73; P-in-c

Hill 72-73; V Stone w Woodford and Hill from 73. *The Vicarage, Stone, Berkeley, Glos GL13 9LB* Tel (01454) 260277

WORCESTER, Archdeacon of. *See* BENTLEY, The Ven Frank William Henry

WORCESTER, Bishop of. *See* SELBY, The Rt Revd Peter Stephen Maurice

WORCESTER, Dean of. *See* MARSHALL, The Very Revd Peter Jerome

WORDSWORTH, Jeremy Nathaniel. b 30. Clare Coll Cam BA54 MA58. Ridley Hall Cam 54. **d** 56 **p** 57. C Gt Baddow *Chelmsf* 56-59; Chapl Felsted Sch Essex 59-63; Chapl Sherborne Sch 63-71; PV and Succ S'wark Cathl *S'wark* 71-73; P-in-c Stone *Worc* 73-77; V Malvern St Andr 77-82; V Combe Down w Monkton Combe and S Stoke *B & W* 82-95; rtd 95. *4 The Glebe, Hinton Charterhouse, Bath BA3 6AB* Tel (01225) 722520

WORDSWORTH, Paul. b 42. Birm Univ BA64 Hull Univ DipMin89. Wells Th Coll 64. **d** 66 **p** 67. C Anlaby St Pet *York* 66-71; C Marfleet 71-72; TV 72-77; V Sowerby 77-90; P-in-c Sessay 77-90; V York St Thos w St Maurice from 90; Dioc Community Miss Project Ldr from 90; Abp's Miss Adv from 96. *St Thomas's Vicarage, 157 Haxby Road, York YO3 7JL* Tel (01904) 652228

WORGAN, Maurice William. b 40. Ely Th Coll 62 Sarum Th Coll 64. **d** 65 **p** 66. C Cranbrook *Cant* 65-69; C Maidstone St Martin 69-72; P-in-c Stanford w Postling and Radegund 72-73; R Lyminge w Paddlesworth 72-73; R Lyminge w Paddlesworth, Stanford w Postling etc 73-88; V Cant St Dunstan w H Cross from 88. *St Dunstan's Vicarage, 5 Harkness Drive, Canterbury, Kent CT2 7RW* Tel (01227) 463654

WORKMAN, David Andrew. b 22. MICS49 AMBIM78 FBIM80. Arm Aux Min Course 87. **d** 90 **p** 91. C Dundalk w Heynestown *Arm* 90-97; rtd 97. *Dunbeag, Togher, Drogheda, Co Louth, Irish Republic* Tel Drogheda (41) 52171

WORKMAN, John Lewis. b 26. St Deiniol's Hawarden 82. **d** 83 **p** 84. C Brecon St Mary and Battle w Llanddew *S & B* 83-86; Min Can Brecon Cathl 83-86; P-in-c Swansea St Luke 86-87; V 87-95; rtd 95. *69 Belgrave Court, Walter Road, Uplands, Swansea SA1 4PZ* Tel (01792) 473649

WORLEY, William. b 37. TD89. Cranmer Hall Dur 69. **d** 72 **p** 73. C Consett *Dur* 72-76; V Seaton Carew from 76; CF (TA) from 77. *The Vicarage, 11 Ruswarp Grove, Seaton Carew, Hartlepool, Cleveland TS25 2BA* Tel (01429) 262463

WORMALD, Roy Henry. b 42. Chich Th Coll 64. **d** 67 **p** 68. C Walthamstow St Mich *Chelmsf* 67-69; C Cov St Thos *Cov* 69-72; C Cov St Jo 69-72; C Wood Green St Mich *Lon* 72-77; P-in-c Hanwell St Mellitus 77-80; P-in-c Hanwell St Mellitus w St Mark 80-81; V 81-95; C Hillingdon St Jo from 95. *Glebe House, Royal Lane, Uxbridge, Middx UB8 3QR* Tel (01895) 256427

WORN, Nigel John. b 56. Sarum & Wells Th Coll. **d** 84 **p** 85. C Walworth St Jo *S'wark* 84-88; Succ S'wark Cathl 88-92; V Mitcham Ascension from 92. *The Parsonage, Sherwood Park Road, Mitcham, Surrey CR4 1NE* Tel 0181-764 1258

WORRALL, Frederick Rowland. b 27. **d** 86 **p** 87. NSM Chellaston *Derby* from 86; NSM Barrow-on-Trent w Twyford and Swarkestone from 94. *37 St Peter's Road, Chellaston, Derby DE7 1UU* Tel (01332) 701890

WORRALL, Peter Henry. b 62. CA Tr Coll DipEvang88 WMMTC 93. **d** 95 **p** 96. C Bromsgrove St Jo *Worc* from 95. *6 Rock Hill, Bromsgrove, Worcs B61 7LJ* Tel (01527) 832087

WORRALL, Suzanne. *See* SHERIFF, Mrs Suzanne

WORSDALL, John Robin. b 33. Dur Univ BA57. Linc Th Coll 62. **d** 63 **p** 64. C Manthorpe w Londonthorpe *Linc* 63-66; C Folkingham w Laughton 66-68; V New Bolingbroke w Carrington 68-74; P-in-c S Somercotes 74-80; V N Somercotes 74-80; P-in-c Stickney 80-82; P-in-c E Ville and Mid Ville 80-82; P-in-c Stickford 80-82; V Stickney Gp from 82. *The Rectory, Horbling Lane, Stickney, Boston, Lincs PE22 8DQ* Tel (01205) 480049

WORSDELL, William Charles (<u>Bill</u>). b 35. AKC59. **d** 60 **p** 61. C Glouc St Aldate *Glouc* 60-66; V Devonport St Barn *Ex* 66-72; R Uplyme 72-77; R Withington and Compton Abdale w Haselton *Glouc* 77-87; V Badgeworth w Shurdington 87-95; R Badgeworth, Shurdington and Witcombe w Bentham 95; rtd 95. *6 Tidcombe Close, Tiverton, Devon EX16 4RA* Tel (01884) 252153

WORSFOLD, Ms Caroline Jayne. b 61. St Steph Ho Ox. **d** 88 **p** 94. Chapl Asst Leic R Infirmary 88-90; C Sunderland Pennywell St Thos *Dur* 90-91; Sunderland HA Chapl 90-94; Chapl Priority Healthcare Wearside NHS Trust from 94. *Cherry Knowle Hospital, Ryhope, Sunderland SR2 0NB* Tel 0191-565 6256

WORSFOLD, John. b 24. Keble Coll Ox BA50 MA50. Cuddesdon Coll 50. **d** 51 **p** 52. C Clapham H Spirit *S'wark* 51-62; C Richmond St Mary w St Matthias and St Jo 62-63; C Shirley St Geo *Cant* 63-80; C Croydon H Sav 80-84; C Croydon H Sav *S'wark* 85-89; rtd 90; Perm to Offic *S'wark* from 90. *26 Links Road, West Wickham, Kent BR4 0QW* Tel 0181-777 7463

WORSFOLD, Richard Vernon. b 64. Ex Univ LLB86. Cranmer Hall Dur BA94 DMS95. **d** 95 **p** 96. C Countesthorpe w Foston *Leic* from 95. *12 The Hawthorns, Countesthorpe, Leicester LE8 5RY* Tel 0116-277 6066

WORSLEY, Mrs Christine Anne. b 52. Hull Univ BA73 Bris Univ CertEd74 Birm Univ MPhil94. WMMTC 82. **dss** 84 **d** 87 **p** 94. Smethwick St Mary *Birm* 84-87; Par Dn 87; Par Dn Smethwick H Trin w St Alb 87-89; Par Dn Coventry Caludon *Cov* 89-91; Chapl Myton Hamlet Hospice 92-95; Tutor WMMTC from 95; Perm to Offic *Birm* from 95. *Wyken Vicarage, 56 Wyken Croft, Coventry CV2 3AD* Tel (01203) 602332 or 0121-452 2604

WORSLEY, Howard John. b 61. Man Univ BA83 Leeds Univ PGCE85. St Jo Coll Nottm DTS92 MA93. **d** 93 **p** 94. C Huthwaite *S'well* 93-96; V Radford St Pet from 96. *St Peter's Vicarage, 183 Hartley Road, Nottingham NG7 3DW* Tel 0115-978 4450

WORSLEY, James Duncan. b 14. Dur Univ LTh40. Tyndale Hall Bris 37. **d** 40 **p** 41. C Lower Broughton St Clem *Man* 40-41; C Halliwell St Pet 41-43; C Bucknall and Bagnall *Lich* 43-47; V Biddulph 47-54; Chapl Biddulph Grange Orthopaedic Hosp 50-54; V Launceston St Thos *Truro* 54-61; V Ullenhall cum Aspley *Cov* 61-72; V Wappenbury w Weston under Wetherley 72-79; V Hunningham 72-79; Chapl Weston-under-Wetherley Hosp 72-79; rtd 79. *24 Banneson Road, Nether Stowey, Bridgwater, Somerset TA5 1NW* Tel (01278) 732169

WORSLEY, Malcolm. b 37. Carl Dioc Tr Inst 94. **d** 96 **p** 97. NSM Hawes Side *Blackb* from 96. *14 Winslow Avenue, Carleton, Poulton-le-Fylde, Lancs FY6 7PQ* Tel (01253) 882208 or 21859 Fax 751156 E-mail philippi@dial.pipex.com

WORSLEY, Richard John. b 52. Qu Coll Cam BA74 MA78. Qu Coll Birm DipTh79. **d** 80 **p** 81. C Styvechale *Cov* 80-84; V Smethwick H Trin w St Alb *Birm* 84-89; TV Coventry Caludon *Cov* 89-96. *Wyken Vicarage, 56 Wyken Croft, Coventry CV2 3AD* Tel (01203) 602332

WORSLEY, Mrs Ruth Elizabeth. b 62. **d** 96. C Basford w Hyson Green *S'well* from 96. *St Peter's Vicarage, 183 Hartley Road, Nottingham NG7 3DW* Tel 0115-978 4450

WORSNIP, Harry. b 29. Oldham Tech Coll HNC50. St Alb Minl Tr Scheme 89. **d** 92 **p** 93. NSM Arlesey w Astwick *St Alb* 92-96; NSM Goldington from 96. *28 Milburn Road, Bedford MK41 0NZ* Tel (01234) 266422

WORSSAM, Richard Mark. b 61. St Jo Coll Dur BA83 Selw Coll Cam BA92. Ridley Hall Cam CTM93. **d** 93 **p** 94. C Green Street Green and Pratts Bottom *Roch* from 93. *9 Ringwood Avenue, Orpington, Kent BR6 7SY* Tel (01689) 861742

WORSTEAD, Eric Henry. b 14. Lon Univ BD44 BA46 MTh54. **d** 64 **p** 64. Niger 64-66; Hon C Southborough St Thos *Roch* 67-72; Dep Prin Whitelands Coll Lon 67-72; P-in-c High Hurstwood *Chich* 72-78; rtd 78. *Flat 2, Waterside, Crowborough Hill, Crowborough, E Sussex TN6 2RS* Tel (01892) 664330

WORTH, Preb Frederick <u>Stuart</u>. b 30. Oak Hill Th Coll 60. **d** 62 **p** 63. C Okehampton w Inwardleigh *Ex* 62-68; R Dunkeswell and Dunkeswell Abbey 68-78; P-in-c Luppitt 69-72; P-in-c Upottery 72-76; V Sheldon 73-78; RD Honiton 77-84 and 86-90; R Uplyme 78-86; R Uplyme w Axmouth from 86; Preb Ex Cathl from 96. *The Rectory, Rhode Lane, Uplyme, Lyme Regis, Dorset DT7 3TX* Tel (01297) 443256

WORTH, Thomas (<u>Tom</u>). b 23. Glouc Sch of Min 90. **d** 91 **p** 92. NSM Bourton-on-the-Water w Clapton *Glouc* 91-94; Perm to Offic from 94. *7 Station Meadow, Bourton-on-the-Water, Cheltenham, Glos GL54 2HG* Tel (01451) 822342

WORTHEN, Dr Jeremy Frederick. b 65. Rob Coll Cam BA86 MPhil88 Toronto Univ PhD92. Ripon Coll Cuddesdon DipTh93 DipMin94. **d** 94 **p** 95. C Bromley SS Pet and Paul *Roch* from 94. *13 Rochester Avenue, Bromley BR1 3DB* Tel 0181-464 9532

WORTHEN, Peter Frederick. b 38. Oak Hill Th Coll 71. **d** 71 **p** 72. C Tonbridge SS Pet and Paul *Roch* 71-75; P-in-c High Halstow w Hoo St Mary 75-76; R High Halstow w All Hallows and Hoo St Mary 76-83; V Welling 83-93; TV Stantonbury and Willen *Ox* from 93. *Bradwell Church House, 1A Atterbrook, Bradwell, Milton Keynes MK13 9EY* Tel (01908) 320850

WORTHINGTON, George. b 35. AKC60. **d** 61 **p** 62. C Stockton St Pet *Dur* 61-65; C Poulton-le-Fylde *Blackb* 65-67; V Trawden 67-76; P-in-c Gressingham 76-78; P-in-c Arkholme 76-78; P-in-c Whittington 77-78; V Whittington w Arkholme and Gressingham 78-91; V Warton St Paul from 91. *The Vicarage, Church Road, Warton, Preston PR4 1BD* Tel (01772) 632227

WORTHINGTON, John Clare. b 17. St Jo Coll Cam BA39 MA46. Westcott Ho Cam 39 46. **d** 48 **p** 49. C Rotherham *Sheff* 48-51; CF 51-65; V Ellingham and Harbridge and Ibsley *Win* 65-85; RD Christchurch 79-82; rtd 85; Perm to Offic *Win* 85-95. *Moorland Cottage, Godshill, Fordingbridge, Hants SP6 2LG* Tel (01425) 654448

WORTHINGTON, Mark. b 55. Solicitor 80 Leeds Poly BA77. Cranmer Hall Dur CTMin93. **d** 93 **p** 94. C Monkwearmouth St Andr *Dur* 93-96; C Chester le Street from 96. *2 Glencoe Avenue, Chester le Street, Co Durham DH2 2JJ* Tel 0191-388 0931

WORTLEY, Prof John Trevor. b 34. FRHistS Dur Univ BA57 MA60 DD86 Lon Univ PhD69. Edin Th Coll 57. **d** 59 **p** 60. C Huddersfield St Jo *Wakef* 59-64; Canada from 64; Prof Hist Manitoba Univ from 69. *298 Yale Avenue, Winnipeg, Canada, R3M 0M1, or Manitoba University, Winnipeg, Canada, R3T 2N2* Tel Winnipeg (204) 284-7554 or 474-9830

WORTON, David Reginald (Brother Paschal). b 56. St Steph Ho Ox 88. **d** 90 **p** 90. SSF from 77. *The Friary, Alnmouth, Alnwick, Northd NE66 3NJ* Tel (01665) 830213

WORTON, Norman. b 10. ALCD38. **d** 38 **p** 39. C Croydon Ch Ch Broad Green *Cant* 38-41; CMS 41-47; Egypt 41-47; C Durrington *Chich* 47-49; C Horsham 49-53; R Westbourne 53-59; V Stansted 57-59; V Hove St Phil 59-65; Australia from 65; rtd 75. *1/12 Rawson Street, Mosman, NSW, Australia 2088* Tel Sydney (2) 9969 5587

WORWOOD, Canon Frank Edward. b 11. ALCD34. **d** 34 **p** 35. C Lyncombe *B & W* 34-39; V Battersea St Geo w St Andr *S'wark* 39-48; V Portsdown *Portsm* 48-61; R W Bridgford *S'well* 61-81; RD Bingham W 61-81; Hon Can S'well Minster 72-81; rtd 81; Perm to Offic *S'well* from 81. *1 Eastwood Road, Radcliffe-on-Trent, Nottingham NG12 2FZ* Tel 0115-933 5647

WOSTENHOLM, Dr David Kenneth. b 56. Edin Univ BSc77 MB, ChB80 Southn Univ BTh88. Chich Th Coll 82. **d** 85 **p** 86. C Leytonstone St Marg w St Columba *Chelmsf* 85-90; V Brighton Annunciation *Chich* from 90. *Annunciation Vicarage, 89 Washington Street, Brighton BN2 2SR* Tel (01273) 681341

WOTHERSPOON, David Colin. b 36. Portsm Coll of Tech CEng65 MIMechE65. St Jo Coll Dur 76. **d** 78 **p** 79. C Blackb St Gabr *Blackb* 78-81; V Witton 81-90; Chapl Berne w Neuchatel *Eur* from 90. *St Ursula, Jubiläumsplatz 2, 3005 Berne, Switzerland* Tel Berne (31) 351-0343 or 352-8567 Fax 352-8567

WOTTON, David Ashley. b 44. Chich Th Coll 71. **d** 74 **p** 75. C Allington and Maidstone St Pet *Cant* 74-77; C Ham St Andr *S'wark* 78-79; Chapl HM Rem Cen Latchmere Ho 78-79; C Tattenham Corner and Burgh Heath *Guildf* 85-88; P-in-c E Molesey St Mary 88-93; R Headley w Box Hill from 93; Offg Chapl RAF from 93. *The Rectory, Headley, Epsom, Surrey KT18 6LE* Tel (01372) 377327

WOULDHAM, Ralph Douglas Astley. b 19. Leeds Univ BA48. Coll of Resurr Mirfield 48. **d** 50 **p** 51. C Leeds Halton St Wilfrid *Ripon* 50-53; Perm to Offic *Newc* 53-56; V Bolam 56-62; TR Usworth *Dur* 62-69; V Cleadon 69-79; V Lowick and Kyloe w Ancroft *Newc* 79-84; rtd 84. *55 Northumberland Road, Tweedmouth, Berwick-upon-Tweed TD15 2AS* Tel (01289) 308240

WRAGG, John Gordon. b 17. Sheff Univ BA39. ALCD41. **d** 41 **p** 42. C Scotswood *Newc* 41-43; C Menston w Woodhead *Bradf* 43-46; S Africa 46-49 and 56-62; C Ashbourne w Mapleton *Derby* 49-53; V Rosherville *Roch* 53-56; V Spittal *Newc* 62-75; R Wark 75-82; P-in-c Birtley 75-77; V 77-82; rtd 82. *21 The Croft, Filey, N Yorkshire YO14 9LT* Tel (01723) 514824

WRAGG, Peter Robert. b 46. Lon Univ BSc68. Sarum & Wells Th Coll 71. **d** 74 **p** 75. C Feltham *Lon* 74-79; TV Hackney 79-85; P-in-c Isleworth St Mary 85-94; V Feltham from 94. *The Vicarage, Cardinal Road, Feltham, Middx TW13 5AL* Tel 0181-890 6681 or 890 2011

WRAIGHT, John Radford. b 38. St Chad's Coll Dur BA62 DipTh64. **d** 64 **p** 65. C Shildon *Dur* 64-67; C Newton Aycliffe 67-70; C Darlington St Jo 70-75; P-in-c Livingston LEP *Edin* 75-80; TV Carl H Trin and St Barn *Carl* 80-85; P-in-c Lindale w Field Broughton 85-95; R Middleton Tyas w Croft and Eryholme *Ripon* from 95. *The Rectory, 13 Kneeton Park, Middleton Tyas, Richmond, N Yorkshire DL10 6SB* Tel (01325) 377562

WRAKE, John. b 28. RMA. Clifton Th Coll 56. **d** 59 **p** 60. C Gt Baddow *Chelmsf* 59-62; CF 62-66; V Tilton w Lowesby *Leic* 66-73; R Maresfield *Chich* 73-79; rtd 93. *Parkfield, Batts Ridge Road, Maresfield, Uckfield, E Sussex TN22 2HJ* Tel (01825) 762727

WRAPSON, Donald. b 36. St Aid Birkenhead 61. **d** 65 **p** 66. C Bacup St Sav *Man* 65-69; C Wolverhampton St Matt *Lich* 69-72; C Normanton *Derby* 72-78; V Dordon *Birm* 78-82; Chapl Birm Accident Hosp 82-93; Chapl Selly Oak Hosp Birm 82-93; Chapl S Birm Acute Unit Birm Gen Hosp from 93. *37 Walkers Heath Road, Kings Norton, Birmingham B38 0AB* Tel 0121-458 2995 or 442 4321

WRATTEN, Martyn Stephen. b 34. AKC58 St Boniface Warminster 58. **d** 59 **p** 60. C Wandsworth Common St Mary *S'wark* 59-62; C Putney St Mary 62-65; C Pembury *Roch* 65-70; R Stone 70-76; Chapl Joyce Green Hosp Dartford 70-73; Stone Ho Hosp Kent 73-76; Hillcrest Hosp and Netherne Hosp Coulsdon 76-87; Hon C Netherne St Luke CD *S'wark* 76-87; V Gt Doddington *Pet* 87-88; V Gt Doddington and Wilby 88-95; Hon C N Petherton w Northmoor Green *B & W* 95-96; rtd 95; Perm to Offic *B & W* from 96. *Rose Cottage, Clare Street, North Petherton, Bridgwater, Somerset TA6 6RG* Tel (01278) 662135

WRAW, John Michael. b 59. Linc Coll Ox BA81 Fitzw Ho Cam BA84. Ridley Hall Cam 82. **d** 85 **p** 86. C Bromyard *Heref* 85-88; TV Sheff Manor *Sheff* 88-92; V Clifton St Jas from 92. *Clifton Vicarage, 10 Clifton Crescent North, Rotherham, S Yorkshire S65 2AS* Tel (01709) 363082 or 836308

WRAY, Christopher. b 48. Hull Univ BA70 New Coll Ox DipTh73. Cuddesdon Coll 70. **d** 73 **p** 74. C Brighouse *Wakef* 73-76; C Almondbury 76-78; C Tong *Bradf* 78-80; V Ingleton w Chapel le Dale 80-86; R Brompton Regis w Upton and Skilgate *B & W* 86-91; V Yoxford and Peasenhall w Sibton *St E* 91-94; Perm to Offic *Carl* from 94. *2 Greystoke, Penrith, Cumbria CA11 0TP* Tel (01768) 483188

WRAY, Christopher Brownlow. b 46. Open Univ BA91. Oak Hill Th Coll 86. **d** 88 **p** 89. C Quidenham *Nor* 88-91; TV Chippenham St Paul w Hardenhuish etc *Bris* from 91. *Hardenhuish Vicarage, 141 Malmesbury Road, Chippenham, Wilts SN15 1QA* Tel (01249) 650787

WRAY, Karl. b 51. St And Coll Greystoke 72 Ian Ramsey Coll 74 Coll of Resurr Mirfield 75. **d** 78 **p** 79. C Salford St Phil w St Steph *Man* 78-83; CF 83-86 and 89-92; V Sculcoates St Paul w Ch Ch and St Silas *York* 86-89; V Carl St Luke Morton *Carl* from 92. *St Luke's Vicarage, Brownrigg Drive, Carlisle CA2 6PA* Tel (01228) 515693

WRAY, Kenneth Martin. b 43. Linc Th Coll 72. **d** 75 **p** 76. C Shipley St Paul *Bradf* 75-79; V Edlington *Sheff* 79-85; V Nether Hoyland St Pet 85-97; V Up Hatherley *Glouc* from 97. *St James House, The Reddings, Cheltenham, Glos GL51 6PA* Tel (01452) 856980 Fax as telephone

WRAY, Martin John. b 51. St Steph Ho Ox 86. **d** 88 **p** 89. C E Boldon *Dur* 88-90; C Seaham w Seaham Harbour 90-92; P-in-c Chopwell 92-95; V 95-97. *18 Bannockburn Way, Billingham, Cleveland TS23 3QP*

WRAY, Michael. b 49. Univ of Wales (Cardiff) BSc(Econ)77 Keele Univ PGCE78 RGN87. Ripon Coll Cuddesdon 80. **d** 82 **p** 83. C Blackpool St Steph *Blackb* 82-83; C Torrisholme 83-84; NSM Headington Quarry *Ox* 93-95; C Kennington *Cant* from 95; CF (TA) from 95. *158 Canterbury Road, Kennington, Ashford, Kent TN24 9QE* Tel (01233) 638058

WRAYFORD, Geoffrey John. b 38. Ex Coll Ox BA61 MA65. Linc Th Coll 61. **d** 63 **p** 64. C Cirencester *Glouc* 63-69; Chapl Chelmsf Cathl *Chelmsf* 69-74; V 70-74; V Canvey Is 74-76; TR 76-80; P-in-c Woodlands *B & W* 80-88; V 89-92; P-in-c Frome St Jo 80-88; P-in-c Frome Ch Ch 80-85; P-in-c Frome St Mary 85-88; V Frome St Jo and St Mary 89-92; V Minehead from 92. *The Vicarage, 7 Paganel Road, Minehead, Somerset TA24 5ET* Tel (01643) 703530

WREN, Christopher John. b 54. Dur Univ BEd76 MA85. St Steph Ho Ox 77. **d** 79 **p** 80. C Stockton St Pet *Dur* 79-82; C Newton Aycliffe 82-85; V Gateshead St Chad Bensham 85-91; TR Bensham from 91. *St Chad's Vicarage, Dunsmuir Grove, Gateshead, Tyne & Wear NE8 4QL* Tel 0191-477 1964

WREN, Douglas Peter. b 59. Lanc Univ BA82. Trin Coll Bris BA88. **d** 88 **p** 89. C Nantwich *Ches* 88-91; C Chatham St Phil and St Jas *Roch* 91-94; R Kingsdown from 94. *The Rectory, School Lane, West Kingsdown, Sevenoaks, Kent TN15 6JB* Tel (01474) 852265

WREN, John Aubrey. b 46. St Chad's Coll Dur BA69. Cuddesdon Coll 72. **d** 74 **p** 75. C Fenny Stratford and Water Eaton *Ox* 74-77; TV Brighton Resurr *Chich* 77-84; V Eastbourne St Andr 84-92; V Hove St Barn and St Agnes 92-96. *24 Marlborough Road, Lowestoft, Suffolk NR32 3BU* Tel (01502) 539274

WREN, Canon Kathleen Ann. b 50. St Steph Ho Ox 83. **dss** 85 **d** 87. Gateshead St Cuth w St Paul *Dur* 85-86; Gateshead St Chad Bensham 86-91; Par Dn 87-91; Adv for Women's Min from 90; Par Dn Bensham 91-94; C from 94; Hon Can Dur Cathl from 93. *St Chad's Vicarage, Dunsmuir Grove, Gateshead, Tyne & Wear NE8 4QL* Tel 0191-477 1964

WREN, Richard. b 35. S Dios Minl Tr Scheme. **d** 90 **p** 91. NSM Tisbury *Sarum* from 90. *Gaston House, Tisbury, Salisbury SP3 6LG* Tel (01747) 870674

WRENBURY, The Revd and Rt Hon Lord (John Burton Buckley). b 27. Solicitor 52 K Coll Cam BA48 MA48. S'wark Ord Course 87. **d** 90 **p** 91. NSM Brightling, Dallington, Mountfield etc *Chich* from 90. *Oldcastle, Dallington, Heathfield, E Sussex TN21 9JP* Tel (01435) 830400

WRENN, Peter Henry. b 34. Lon Univ BA56. Qu Coll Birm 58. **d** 60 **p** 61. C Dronfield *Derby* 60-64; C Hessle *York* 64-65; V Loscoe *Derby* 65-70; Asst Chapl Solihull Sch 71-77; Chapl 77-97; rtd 97; Perm to Offic *Birm* from 97. *63 Shakespeare Drive, Shirley, Solihull, W Midlands B90 2AN* Tel 0121-744 3941

WREXHAM, Archdeacon of. *See* WILLIAMS, The Ven Edward Bryan

WRIGHT, Alan James. b 38. Chich Th Coll 63. **d** 66 **p** 67. C Edge Hill St Dunstan *Liv* 66-69; Swaziland 69-71; P-in-c Seaforth *Liv* 71-76; V Taunton All SS *B & W* 76-95. *Bethel, Langford Lane, Norton Fitzwarren, Taunton, Somerset TA2 6NZ* Tel (01823) 326558

WRIGHT, Alan Richard. b 31. LNSM course 95. **d** 96. NSM Quidenham Gp *Nor* from 96. *Upgate Farm, Carleton Rode, Norwich NR16 1NJ* Tel (01953) 860300

WRIGHT, Alan William. b 44. AMusTCL71 Hull Univ BA66 Bris Univ PGCE67. Local Minl Tr Course 87. **d** 95 **p** 96. NSM Barton upon Humber *Linc* from 95. *1 Birchdale, Barton-upon-Humber, S Humberside DN18 5ED* Tel (01652) 632364

WRIGHT, Alfred John. b 22. Wycliffe Hall Ox 66. **d** 66 **p** 67. C Newbury St Jo *Ox* 66-71; V E Challow 71-91; Chapl Community of St Mary V Wantage 75-89; rtd 91. *3 Latton Close, Southmoor, Abingdon, Oxon OX13 5AE* Tel (01865) 820625

WRIGHT, Andrew David Gibson. b 58. St Andr Univ MTheol81. Ridley Hall Cam. **d** 83 **p** 84. C W Derby Gd Shep *Liv* 83-86; C Carl H Trin and St Barn *Carl* 86-88; V Wigan St Jas w St Thos

Liv 88-91; Chapl St Edw Sch Ox from 91. *34 Oakthorpe Road, Oxford OX2 7BE, or St Edward's School, Oxford OX2 7NN* Tel Oxford (01865) 319266 or 319204

WRIGHT, Miss Anne. b 39. Dalton Ho Bris 67. **dss** 76 **d** 87 **p** 94. BCMS 71-88; Uganda 71-77; N Area Sec BCMS 78-88; Pudsey St Lawr and St Paul *Bradf* 82-87; Hon Par Dn 87-88; Par Dn Kingston upon Hull H Trin *York* 88-93; Hd of Min amongst Women CPAS from 93; Perm to Offic *Cov* from 93; CPAS Consultant (W Midl) from 96; Perm to Offic *Birm* from 96. *CPAS, Athena Drive, Tachbrook Park, Warwick CV34 6NG* Tel (01926) 334242 Fax 337613 E-mail awright@cpas.org.uk

WRIGHT, Antony John. b 31. St Pet Coll Saltley CertEd53. Chan Sch Truro 76. **d** 79 **p** 80. NSM St Breoke *Truro* 79-84; TV Probus, Ladock and Grampound w Creed and St Erme 84-89; V Perranzabuloe 89-95; rtd 96; Perm to Offic *Truro* from 96. *Gazebo, Tinners Way, New Polzeath, Wadebridge, Cornwall PL27 6UE* Tel (01208) 863565

WRIGHT, Anthony John. b 47. ACA70 FCA77. Ripon Coll Cuddesdon 86. **d** 88 **p** 89. C Kidderminster St Mary and All SS w Trimpley etc *Worc* 88-91; P-in-c Offenham and Bretforton 91-96; R Backwell w Chelvey and Brockley *B & W* from 96. *The Rectory, 72 Church Lane, Backwell, Bristol BS19 3JJ* Tel (01275) 462391

WRIGHT, Canon Anthony Robert. b 49. Lanchester Poly BA70. St Steph Ho Ox 70. **d** 73 **p** 74. C Amersham on the Hill *Ox* 73-76; C Reading St Giles 76-78; P-in-c Prestwood 78-84; P-in-c Wantage 84-87; V 87-92; RD Wantage 84-92; P-in-c W w E Hanney 88-91; V Portsea St Mary *Portsm* from 92; Hon Can Portsm Cathl from 96. *St Mary's Vicarage, Fratton Road, Portsmouth PO1 5PA* Tel (01705) 822687

WRIGHT, Canon Aubrey Kenneth William. b 21. K Coll Lon BD43 AKC43 BA44. Linc Th Coll 43. **d** 44 **p** 45. C Croydon H Trin *Cant* 44-47; C Addington 47-49; C-in-c Spring Park 49-57; V 57-58; V Cheriton Street 58-63; R W Wickham St Jo 63-72; RD Croydon Cen 66-72; RD E Charing 72-81; Hon Can Cant Cathl 72-86; V Ashford 72-81; R Barham w Bishopsbourne and Kingston 81-86; rtd 86; Perm to Offic *Cant* from 86. *28 The Gateway, Dover, Kent CT16 1LG* Tel (01304) 202097

WRIGHT, Canon Barry Owen. b 38. S'wark Ord Course 66. **d** 69 **p** 70. C Plumstead Ascension *S'wark* 69-74; Hon C Welling 74-89; Hon Can S'wark Cathl 79-89; Sen Chapl W Midl Police *Birm* 89-93; Sen Chapl Metrop Police *Lon* from 93; Lic to Offic from 93. *St Barnabas Vicarage, 7 Oakfields Road, London NW11 0JA* Tel 0181-458 7828 or 200 2077 Fax 458 7828

WRIGHT, Miss Caroline Peggy. b 34. RMN75. Gilmore Ho 57. **dss** 59 **d** 88 **p** 94. Badsey *Worc* 62-66; Wickhamford 62-66; Wolverley 66-67; Warden St Mary's Abbey Leiston 67-74; Perm to Offic *St E* 74-88; Par Dn Bungay H Trin w St Mary 88-94; C from 94. *4 Kerrison Road, Bungay, Suffolk NR35 1RZ* Tel (01986) 892023

WRIGHT, Catherine Jane. b 62. **d** 97. C Highworth w Sevenhampton and Inglesham etc *Bris* from 97. *24 Lismore Road, Highworth, Swindon SN6 7HU* Tel (01793) 764729

WRIGHT, Charles Frederick Peter. b 16. Qu Coll Ox BA39 MA42. Westcott Ho Cam 40. **d** 41 **p** 42. C Stocksbridge *Sheff* 41-43; C Goole 43-47; C Ecclesall 47-50; R Brown and Chilton Candover w Northington etc *Win* 50-54; V Sutton St Mary *Linc* 54-61; V Welton 61-69; Lect Linc Th Coll 61-63; Lic to Offic *Linc* from 69; rtd 81. *The Hermitage, Snelland, Lincoln LN3 5AA* Tel (01673) 885325

WRIGHT, Charles Kenneth (Ken). b 38. CEng73 MIMechE73 MBIM91. Sarum & Wells Th Coll DCM93. **d** 93 **p** 94. C Bridgwater St Mary, Chilton Trinity and Durleigh *B & W* 93-96; Chapl Workington *Carl* from 96; C Camerton, Seaton and W Seaton from 96. *40 Moorlands Drive, Stainburn, Workington, Cumbria CA14 4UJ* Tel (01900) 606286

WRIGHT, Dr Christopher Joseph Herbert (Chris). b 47. St Cath Coll Cam BA69 MA73 PhD77. Ridley Hall Cam 75. **d** 77 **p** 78. C Tonbridge SS Pet and Paul *Roch* 77-81; Perm to Offic *St Alb* from 82; India 83-88; Tutor and Dir Studies All Nations Chr Coll Ware 88-93; Prin from 93. *All Nations Christian College, Easneye, Ware, Herts SG12 8LX* Tel (01920) 461243 Fax 462997

WRIGHT, Christopher Nigel. b 39. Kelham Th Coll 60. **d** 65 **p** 66. C Ellesmere Port *Ches* 65-69; C Latchford Ch Ch 69-72; C Gt Budworth 72-75; C Wigan St Andr *Liv* 75-76; V New Springs 77-82; C Dovecot 82-85; C Rainford 85-89; rtd 89; Perm to Offic *Liv* from 89. *105 Ilfracombe Road, Sutton Leach, St Helens, Merseyside WA9 4NN* Tel (01744) 821199

WRIGHT, Canon Clifford Nelson. b 35. K Coll Lon BD59 AKC59. **d** 60 **p** 61. C Stevenage *St Alb* 60-67; V Camberwell St Luke *S'wark* 67-81; RD Camberwell 75-80; Hon Can S'wark Cathl 79-80; TR Basingstoke *Win* 81-93; RD Basingstoke 84-93; Hon Can Win Cathl from 89; R Win St Matt from 93. *The Rectory, 44 Cheriton Road, Winchester, Hants SO22 5AY* Tel (01962) 854849

WRIGHT, David Evan Cross. b 35. K Coll Lon BD64 AKC64. **d** 65 **p** 66. C Morpeth *Newc* 65-69; C Benwell St Jas 69-70; C Bushey *St Alb* 70-74; V High Wych 74-77; R High Wych and Gilston w Eastwick 77-80; V St Alb St Mary Marshalswick 80-89; P-in-c Sandridge 87-89; R Lenham w Boughton Malherbe *Cant* from 89. *The Vicarage, Old Ashford Road, Lenham, Maidstone, Kent ME17 2PX* Tel (01622) 858245

WRIGHT, David Henry. b 23. Keble Coll Ox BA48. St Steph Ho Ox 52. **d** 54 **p** 55. C Penton Street St Silas w All SS *Lon* 54-57; V Barnsbury St Clem 57-66; V Wandsworth St Anne *S'wark* 66-73; P-in-c Stanley *St And* 73-75; R Dunkeld 73-92; R Strathtay 75-92; rtd 92. *Ground Flat, 83 Henderson Street, Bridge of Allan, Stirling FK9 4HG* Tel (01786) 833954

WRIGHT, David William. b 63. Barrister 86 Liv Univ LLB85 Fitzw Coll Cam BA92 Cam Univ MA96. Westcott Ho Cam 90. **d** 93 **p** 94. C Chorlton-cum-Hardy St Clem *Man* 93-97; P-in-c Donnington Wood *Lich* from 97. *The Vicarage, St George's Road, Donnington Wood, Telford, Shropshire TF2 7NJ* Tel (01952) 604239

WRIGHT, Derek Anthony. b 35. ACP66 Lon Univ CertEd57. Cranmer Hall Dur 80. **d** 81 **p** 82. C Auckland St Andr and St Anne *Dur* 81-83; V Cornforth 83-87; P-in-c Thornley 87-88; R Gt and Lt Glemham, Blaxhall etc *St E* 88-90; V Evenwood *Dur* 90-93; P-in-c Satley and Tow Law 93-95; V from 95. *The Vicarage, 3 Church Lane, Tow Law, Bishop Auckland, Co Durham DL13 4HE* Tel (01388) 730335

WRIGHT, Edward Maurice. b 54. **d** 88 **p** 91. C Maidstone St Luke *Cant* 88-93; R Cliffe at Hoo w Cooling *Roch* from 93. *St Helen's Rectory, Church Street, Cliffe, Rochester, Kent ME3 7PY* Tel (01634) 220220

WRIGHT, Edward Michael. b 37. St Cath Soc Ox BA61 MA65. Cuddesdon Coll DipTh63. **d** 64 **p** 65. C Willesden St Andr *Lon* 64-68; Bahamas 68-71; V Lewisham St Steph and St Mark *S'wark* 72-80; V Ox St Barn and St Paul *Ox* from 80. *St Barnabas' Vicarage, St Barnabas Street, Oxford OX2 6BG* Tel (01865) 57530

WRIGHT, Frank Albert. b 51. Sarum & Wells Th Coll 80. **d** 83 **p** 84. C Buckingham *Ox* 83-86; C Newport Pagnell w Lathbury and Moulsoe 86-89; TV W Slough 89-95; TR from 95. *298 Stoke Poges Lane, Slough SL1 3LL* Tel (01753) 539062

WRIGHT, Canon Frank Sidney. b 22. St Pet Hall Ox BA45 MA47. Westcott Ho Cam 47. **d** 49 **p** 50. C Bishopwearmouth St Mich *Dur* 49-53; C Barnard Castle 53-55; R Stretford St Matt *Man* 55-66; Can Res Man Cathl 66-74; Sub-Dean 72-74; Min Can 74-83; Tutor Man Univ 74-83; Angl Adv Granada TV from 82; rtd 83; Perm to Offic *Carl* from 83; Perm to Offic *Ches* from 87. *Windyridge, Aaronstown Lonning, Brampton, Cumbria CA8 1QR*

WRIGHT, Frederic Ian. b 64. City Univ BSc85. Wycliffe Hall Ox BTh94. **d** 94 **p** 95. C Carl St Jo *Carl* from 94. *68 Greystone Road, Carlisle CA1 2DG* Tel (01228) 20893 or 595792

WRIGHT, Frederick John. b 15. AKC42. **d** 42 **p** 43. C Brierley Hill *Lich* 42-45; C Walsall Pleck and Bescot 45-49; V W Bromwich Gd Shep 49-54; R Headless Cross *Worc* 54-67; R Romsley 67-80; rtd 80. *Rosevear, 3 Dury Lane, Colne, Huntingdon, Cambs PE17 3NB* Tel (01487) 840518

WRIGHT, George Frederick. b 12. Kelham Th Coll 30. **d** 36 **p** 37. C Bethnal Green St Matt *Lon* 36-38; C Chiswick St Nic w St Mary 38-43; C Holborn St Alb w Saffron Hill St Pet 43-45; Perm to Offic 45-48; C Bethnal Green St Jas the Gt w St Jude 48-52; V Finsbury St Clem w St Barn and St Matt 52-62; R E Markham and Askham *S'well* 62-77; P-in-c Headon w Upton 76-77; rtd 77; Perm to Offic *S'well* from 77. *Rutland House, Low Street, Collingham, Newark, Notts NG23 7NL* Tel (01636) 892876

WRIGHT, Gerald Grattan. b 32. Delaware State Coll BSc72. Ripon Hall Ox 73. **d** 76 **p** 77. Hon C Wolvercote w Summertown *Ox* 76-87; NSM from 88; C Ox St Mich w St Martin and All SS 87-88. *28 Davenant Road, Oxford OX2 8BX* Tel (01865) 52617

WRIGHT, Graham. b 50. Oak Hill Th Coll 73. **d** 76 **p** 77. C Northampton St Giles *Pet* 76-79; C Man Resurr *Man* 79-82; V Barkingside St Laur *Chelmsf* 82-88; Chapl K Geo V Hosp Ilford 82-88; P-in-c Yoxford *St E* 88-90; Chapl Suffolk Constabulary 88-90. *8-10 Dixons Fold, North Walsham Road, Norwich NR6 7QD* Tel (01603) 459960

WRIGHT, Graham Ewen. b 44. Lon Univ DipRS. S'wark Ord Course 86. **d** 89 **p** 90. NSM Aveley and Purfleet *Chelmsf* from 89. *2 Palmers, Corringham, Stanford-le-Hope, Essex SS17 7JA* Tel (01375) 671747

WRIGHT, Mrs Heather Margaret. b 47. EAMTC 93. **d** 96 **p** 97. NSM Heigham St Thos *Nor* from 96. *302 Gertrude Road, Norwich NR3 4RY* Tel (01603) 404194

WRIGHT, Howard John Douglas. b 64. BA85. Trin Coll Bris BA94. **d** 96 **p** 97. C Ipswich St Matt *St E* from 96. *70 Orford Street, Ipswich IP1 3PE* Tel (01473) 210539

WRIGHT, Hugh Edward. b 57. BNC Ox BA79 MA87 Ex Univ CertEd81. Sarum & Wells Th Coll 85. **d** 87 **p** 88. C Hobs Moat *Birm* 87-90; C W Drayton *Lon* 90-92; V Oakfield St Jo *Portsm* from 92. *St John's Vicarage, Victoria Crescent, Ryde, Isle of Wight PO33 1DQ* Tel (01983) 562863

WRIGHT, Mrs Jean. b 41. Man Univ BA63 CertEd64. Carl Dioc Tr Inst 88. **d** 91 **p** 94. NSM Kirkby Stephen w Mallerstang etc *Carl* from 91. *Mains View, Crosby Garrett, Kirkby Stephen, Cumbria CA17 4PR* Tel (017683) 71457

WRIGHT, John Alastair. b 30. FRSA72. Cranmer Hall Dur 62. **d** 64 **p** 65. C Thornton-le-Fylde *Blackb* 64-67; Miss to Seamen 67-72; V Darlington St Luke *Dur* 72-78; Community Chapl

Darlington 78-89; rtd 89. *4 Grasmere, Agar Nook, Coalville, Leics LE67 4SH* Tel (01530) 837390

WRIGHT, John Douglas. b 42. Birm Univ BSc64 CertEd66. St Steph Ho Ox 69. **d** 69 **p** 70. C Swanley St Mary *Roch* 69-74; C Stockwell Green St Andr *S'wark* 74-79; V Leigh St Jo *Man* 79-82; P-in-c Whitehawk *Chich* from 82. *St Cuthman's Vicarage, 1 St Cuthman's Close, Whitehawk, Brighton BN2 5LJ* Tel (01273) 699424

WRIGHT, John Gordon. b 27. Birm Univ MA51. St D Coll Lamp BA50. **d** 52 **p** 53. C Walsall St Mary and All SS Palfrey *Lich* 52-54; C Cambridge St Giles w St Pet *Ely* 55-57; Perm to Offic *Chelmsf* 57-60; Hon C Limpsfield and Titsey *S'wark* 60-62; Chapl St Mary's Hosp Gt Ilford 62-68; Chapl St Olave's and St Sav Schs Orpington 68-86; Hon C Crayford *Roch* 68-76; Lic to Offic 76-86; R Whimple *Ex* 87-88; R Whimple, Talaton and Clyst St Lawr 89-90; rtd 90; Perm to Offic *Lich* 90-96; Perm to Offic *Heref* 90-93. *Danesford, High Street, Albrighton, Wolverhampton WV7 3LA* Tel (01902) 373709

WRIGHT, John Harold. b 36. ATCL Dur Univ BA58 ACertCM. Ely Th Coll 58. **d** 61 **p** 62. C Boston *Linc* 61-64; C Willesborough w Hinxhill *Cant* 64-68; V Westwell 68-75; R Eastwell w Boughton Aluph 68-75; V Rolvenden 75-84; R Cheriton from 84. *St Martin's Rectory, Horn Street, Folkestone, Kent CT20 3JJ* Tel (01303) 238509

WRIGHT, Canon John Richard Martin. b 12. St Jo Coll Dur BA34 MA37 DipTh35. **d** 35 **p** 36. C Hook *S'wark* 35-38; C Purley Ch Ch 38-41; C St E Cathl *St E* 41-45; R Bradfield St Geo w Rushbrooke 45-53; R Barrow 53-76; V Denham St Mary 53-76; R Edmundbyers w Muggleswick *Dur* 76-80; rtd 80; Perm to Offic *St E* from 80. *The Grange, 140 St Cross Road, Winchester, Hants SO23 9RJ*

WRIGHT, Canon Joseph James. b 16. Lon Univ BD39 AKC39. Ely Th Coll 39. **d** 39 **p** 40. C Bethnal Green St Andr *Lon* 39-46; C Prittlewell St Mary *Chelmsf* 46-49; Min Prittlewell St Steph CD 49-50; V Forest Gate Em 50-62; P-in-c Upton Cross 60-62; V Forest Gate Em w Upton Cross 62-84; Hon Can Chelmsf Cathl 82-84; rtd 84; Perm to Offic *Chelmsf* from 84. *87 Burnham Road, Southminster, Essex CM0 7ES* Tel (01621) 773640

WRIGHT, Canon Kenneth William. b 13. Coll of Resurr Mirfield 37. **d** 39 **p** 40. C Clerkenwell H Redeemer w St Phil *Lon* 39-42; C Acton Green St Pet 42-45; C Boyne Hill *Ox* 45-50; V Stony Stratford St Mary 50-57; R Fenny Stratford 54-74; TR Fenny Stratford and Water Eaton 74-79; P-in-c Lt Brickhill 57-58; RD Bletchley 63-70; P-in-c Simpson w Woughton on the Green 69-72; RD Milton Keynes 70-72; Hon Can Ch Ch 70-79; rtd 80; Perm to Offic *S'well* 80-92. *St Martin's, Station Road, Collingham, Newark, Notts NG23 7RA* Tel (01636) 892800

WRIGHT, Canon Kenyon Edward. b 32. Glas Univ MA53 Fitzw Coll Cam BA55 Serampore Coll MTh61. Wesley Ho Cam 53. **d** 71 **p** 71. In Meth Ch 57-71; India 57-71; Dir Urban Min Cov Cathl *Cov* 71-81; Dir of Internat Min and Can Res 72-81; Public Preacher 72-74; Gen Sec Scottish Chs Coun 81-90; Dir Scottish Chs Ho Dunblane 81-90; Dir Kairos Trust 90-92; Hon C Knightswood H Cross Miss *Glas* from 91; rtd 92; P-in-c Glencarse *Bre* from 94. *The Rectory, Glencarse, Perth PH2 7LX* Tel (01738) 860386 Fax as telephone

WRIGHT, Leslie Frank. b 08. Coll of Resurr Mirfield 71. **d** 71 **p** 72. Hon C Northampton St Alb *Pet* 71-78; Lic to Offic *Lich* 78-81; Perm to Offic *Ex* from 96. *24 Audley Rise, Milber, Newton Abbot, Devon TQ12 4JW*

WRIGHT, Leslie Vandernoll. b 24. Trin Hall Cam MA50. Ridley Hall Cam 49. **d** 51 **p** 52. C Aldershot H Trin *Guildf* 51-53; C Cambridge H Trin *Ely* 53-57; V Marston *Ox* 57-59; Asst Master Castle Ct Sch Parkstone 59-61; Asst Chapl Stowe Sch Bucks 61-64; Hd Master St Mich Prep Sch Five Oaks Jersey 64-66; Chapl Windlesham Ho Sch Sussex 66-68; Chapl Vevey *Eur* 68-73; Hd St Geo Sch Clarens 73-89; rtd 89; Chapl Lugano *Eur* 89-92. *18 avenue Schubert, Domine de Tournon, 83440 Montauroux, France*

WRIGHT, Mrs Louisa Mary (Lisa). b 33. S'wark Ord Course. **d** 87 **p** 94. NSM Streatham Hill St Marg *S'wark* 87-95; Hon C Streatham St Leon from 95. *19 Hillside Road, London SW2 3HL* Tel 0181-671 8037

WRIGHT, Preb Martin Neave. b 37. AKC61 Leic Univ DSRS67. St Boniface Warminster. **d** 62 **p** 63. C Corby St Columba *Pet* 62-65; Ind Chapl 65-71; Nigeria 71-75; P-in-c Honiley *Cov* 75-84; P-in-c Wroxall 75-84; Ind Chapl 75-84; Soc Resp Officer 84-96; Hon Can Cov Cathl 95-96; Bp's Dom Chapl *B & W* from 96; Preb Wells Cathl from 96. *The Palace, Wells, Somerset BA5 2PD* Tel (01749) 672341 Fax 679355

WRIGHT, Canon Michael. b 30. St Chad's Coll Dur BA55 DipTh56. **d** 56 **p** 57. C New Cleethorpes *Linc* 56-59; C Skegness 59-62; V Louth St Mich 62-73; R Stewton 62-73; R Warmsworth *Sheff* 73-86; Warden Dioc Readers' Assn 81-86; Hon Can Sheff Cathl 82-95; V Wath-upon-Dearne w Adwick-upon-Dearne 86-94; V Wath-upon-Dearne 94-95; RD Wath 92-95; rtd 95. *17 Ashfield Road, Sleaford, Lincs NG34 7DZ* Tel (01529) 415698

WRIGHT, Michael Christopher. b 44. Leeds Univ BA65 CertEd67 MSc75 FRSA95. Wells Th Coll 65. **d** 67 **p** 68. C Dormanstown *York* 67-69; Perm to Offic *Linc* 69-88; Perm to Offic *Sheff* from 71; Hd Master Eastmoor High Sch Wakef 84-87; Hd Master Carleton High Sch Pontefract 87-95; C-in-c St Edm Anchorage Lane CD 95-96; Chapl Doncaster R Infirmary & Montague Hosp NHS Trust from 95. *Orchard End, Finkle Street, Hensall, Goole, N Humberside DN14 0QY* Tel (01977) 661900 or (01302) 661900 Fax as telephone

WRIGHT, Michael John. b 38. DipTM. Chich Th Coll 59. **d** 62 **p** 63. C Yate *Glouc* 62-65; C Kirby Moorside w Gillamoor *York* 65-68; V 68-72; V Bransdale cum Farndale 68-72; V Kirkbymoorside w Gillamoor, Farndale etc 72-73; Dioc Communications Officer 72-74; V Ormesby 74-80; P-in-c Middlesbrough St Cuth 81-88; Perm to Offic 88-90; NSM W Acklam from 91. *25 Thornfield Road, Middlesbrough, Cleveland TS5 5DD* Tel (01642) 816247

WRIGHT, Nicholas John. b 65. Liv Univ BA87. Wycliffe Hall Ox 89. **d** 92 **p** 93. C Burley *Ripon* 92-95; C Brightside w Wincobank *Sheff* 95-97; TV Sheff Manor from 97. *The Vicarage, 2 Manor Lane, Sheffield S2 1UF* Tel 0114-272 4676

WRIGHT, Nicholas Mark (Nick). b 59. Loughb Univ BSc80. Qu Coll Birm 82. **d** 85 **p** 86. C Coney Hill *Glouc* 85-89; C Rotherham *Sheff* 89-91; TV Worc SE *Worc* from 91. *The Vicarage, 4 Silverdale Avenue, Worcester WR5 1PY* Tel (01905) 353432

WRIGHT, The Very Revd Nicholas Thomas (Tom). b 48. Ex Coll Ox BA71 MA75 DPhil81. Wycliffe Hall Ox BA73. **d** 75 **p** 76. Fell Mert Coll Ox 75-78; Chapl 76-78; Chapl and Fell Down Coll Cam 78-81; Asst Prof NT Studies McGill Univ Montreal 81-86; Chapl and Fell Worc Coll Ox and Univ Lect Th 86-93; Tutor 86-93; Can Th Cov Cathl *Cov* from 92; Dean Lich from 93. *The Deanery, The Close, Lichfield, Staffs WS13 7LD* Tel (01543) 256120 Fax 250935

WRIGHT, Patricia. b 46. SRN68 DN68 DipHV69. S'wark Ord Course 80. **dss** 85 **d** 89. Chapl R Lon Hosp (Mile End) 83-89; Bethnal Green St Matt w St Jas the Gt *Lon* 85-87; St Botolph Aldgate w H Trin Minories 88-89; C from 89. *8 Royal Mint Street, London E1 8LG* Tel 0171-265 1814

WRIGHT, Paul. b 54. K Coll Lon BD78 AKC78 Heythrop Coll Lon MTh90. Ripon Coll Cuddesdon 78. **d** 79 **p** 80. C Beckenham St Geo *Roch* 79-83; Chapl Ch Sch Richmond 83-85; C Richmond St Mary w St Matthias and St Jo *S'wark* 83-85; V Gillingham St Aug *Roch* 85-90; R Crayford from 90; RD Erith from 93. *The Rectory, 1 Claremont Crescent, Crayford, Dartford DA1 4RJ* Tel (01322) 522078

WRIGHT, Paul Stephen. b 66. Cen Lancs Univ BA88 Liv Univ MA96. Westcott Ho Cam 90. **d** 93 **p** 94. C Upholland *Liv* 93-96; CF from 96. *MOD Chaplains (Army), Trenchard Lines, Upavon, Pewsey, Wilts SN9 6BE* Tel (01980) 615804 Fax 615800

WRIGHT, Canon Peter. b 35. Hull Univ MA. AKC61 St Boniface Warminster. **d** 62 **p** 63. C Goole *Sheff* 62-67; V Norton Woodseats St Chad 67-80; R Aston cum Aughton 80-84; P-in-c Ulley 80-84; R Aston cum Aughton and Ulley 84-93; TR Aston cum Aughton w Swallownest, Todwick etc from 93; RD Laughton 85-93; Hon Can Sheff Cathl from 92. *The Rectory, 91 Worksop Road, Aston, Sheffield S31 0EB* Tel 0114-287 2272

WRIGHT, Peter Gordon. b 27. St Aid Birkenhead 55. **d** 57 **p** 58. C Mansfield Woodhouse *S'well* 57-61; V Coddington w Barnby in the Willows from 61. *All Saints' Vicarage, Coddington, Newark, Notts NG24 2QF* Tel (01636) 703084

WRIGHT, Peter Reginald. b 34. St Chad's Coll Dur BA60. Linc Th Coll 60. **d** 62 **p** 63. C Lt Ilford St Mich *Chelmsf* 62-65; C Billingham St Aid *Dur* 65-68; TV 68-71; TR 71-76; Chapl Portsm Poly *Portsm* 76-87; Sec Chapls in HE Gen Syn Bd of Educn 88-95; rtd 95. *6 Garden Lane, Southsea, Hants PO5 3DP* Tel (01705) 736651

WRIGHT, Peter Westrope. b 24. Kelham Th Coll 43. **d** 48 **p** 49. C Pimlico St Barn *Lon* 48-50; C Sidley *Chich* 50-59; R E Blatchington 59-73; P-in-c Lewes St Mich 73-75; TV Lewes All SS, St Anne, St Mich and St Thos 75-84; TR 84-87; rtd 89; Perm to Offic *Chich* from 89. *9 Powis Villas, Brighton BN1 3HD* Tel (01273) 321768

WRIGHT, Philip. b 32. G&C Coll Cam BA53 MA57. Wells Th Coll 56. **d** 57 **p** 58. C Barnard Castle *Dur* 57-60; C Heworth St Mary 60-64; V Tow Law 64-70; V Tanfield 70-78; V Gateshead Ch Ch from 78. *Christ Church Vicarage, Bewick Road, Gateshead, Tyne & Wear NE8 4DR* Tel 0191-477 1840

WRIGHT, Robert Charles. b 31. Roch Th Coll 65. **d** 67 **p** 68. C Manston *Ripon* 67-70; C Moor Allerton 70-74; P-in-c Terrington St John *Ely* 74-79; P-in-c Walpole St Andrew 74-75; P-in-c Tilney All Saints w Tilney St Lawrence 79; V Terrington St John 80-91; V Tilney St Lawrence 80-91; V Tilney All Saints 80-91; R Stiffkey and Cockthorpe w Morston, Langham etc *Nor* 91-96; rtd 96; Perm to Offic *Nor* from 96. *Glenfinnan, 83 Childs Way, Sheringham, Norfolk NR26 8TX* Tel (01263) 822535

WRIGHT, Canon Robert Doogan. b 24. TCD BA46. **d** 47 **p** 48. C Carnmoney *Conn* 47-49; C Belfast St Jas 49-51; C Belfast St Matt 51-53; P-in-c Belfast Whiterock 53-57; I Magheragall 57-64; I Belfast St Mark 64-70; I Carrickfergus 70-82; Can Conn Cathl 79-86; I Killead w Gartree 82-86; Chan Conn Cathl 83-86; rtd 86. *123 Station Road, Greenisland, Carrickfergus, Co Antrim BT38 8UN* Tel (01232) 862779

✠**WRIGHT, The Rt Revd Royston Clifford.** b 22. Univ of Wales BA42. St Steph Ho Ox 43. **d** 45 **p** 46 **c** 86. C Bedwas *Mon* 45-47; C

Newport St Jo Bapt 47-49; C Walton St Jo *Liv* 49-51; Chapl RNVR 50-51; Chapl RN 51-68; V Blaenavon w Capel Newydd *Mon* 68-74; RD Pontypool 73-74; Can St Woolos Cathl 74-77; R Ebbw Vale 74-77; Adn Newport 77-86; Adn Mon 77-86; Bp Mon 86-91; rtd 91. *23 Rupert Brook Drive, Newport NP9 3HP* Tel (01633) 250770

WRIGHT, Canon Simon Christopher. b 44. AKC67. **d** 68 **p** 69. C Bitterne Park *Win* 68-72; C Kirkby 72-74; V Wigan St Anne *Liv* 74-79; Abp's Dom Chapl *York* 79-84; Dir of Ords 79-84; V W Acklam from 84; RD Middlesbrough from 87; Can and Preb York Minster from 94. *The Vicarage, 50 Church Lane, Middlesbrough, Cleveland TS5 7EB* Tel (01642) 817150

WRIGHT, Stephen Irwin. b 58. Ex Coll Ox BA80 MA84 Selw Coll Cam BA85 MA90. Ridley Hall Cam 83. **d** 86 **p** 87. C Newbarns w Hawcoat *Carl* 86-90; C Burton and Holme 90-94; NSM Esh *Dur* from 94; NSM Hamsteels from 94. *The Vicarage, Church Street, Langley Park, Durham DH7 9TZ* Tel 0191-373 6019

WRIGHT, Stephen Mark. b 60. Keele Univ BA83. Trin Coll Bris 86. **d** 89 **p** 90. C Thorne *Sheff* 89-92; CMS from 92; Nigeria from 93. *Bishopscourt, Cable Point, PO Box 216, Asaba, Delta State, Nigeria*

WRIGHT, Thomas Stephen (Tom). b 31. Fitzw Ho Cam BA54 MA58. Bps' Coll Cheshunt 56. **d** 57 **p** 58. C Bishop's Stortford St Mich *St Alb* 57-61; C St E Cathl *St E* 61-64; R Hartest w Boxted 64-82; Chapl RAF 64-71; RD Sudbury *St E* 70-81; P-in-c Somerton 71-82; P-in-c Stansfield 82-91; V Denston w Stradishall and Stansfield from 91; Min Can St E Cathl from 82. *The Rectory, Cornerstone Grove, Stradishall, Newmarket, Suffolk CB8 8YN* Tel (01440) 820580

WRIGHT, Tim Stanley. b 63. Derby Coll of Educn BEd86. St Jo Coll Dur 89. **d** 92 **p** 93. C Eccleshill *Bradf* 92-96; TV Southend *Chelmsf* from 96. *All Saints Vicarage, 1 Sutton Road, Southend-on-Sea SS2 5PA* Tel (01702) 613440

WRIGHT, Timothy. b 63. NUU BSc85. Cranmer Hall Dur 86. **d** 89 **p** 90. C Bramcote *S'well* 89-93; I Glenavy w Tunny and Crumlin *Conn* from 93. *Glenavy Vicarage, 30 Crumlin Road, Glenavy, Crumlin, Co Antrim BT29 4LG* Tel (01849) 422361

WRIGHT, Timothy John. b 41. K Coll Lon BD63 AKC63. **d** 64 **p** 65. C Highfield *Ox* 64-68; Asst Chapl Worksop Coll Notts 68-71; Chapl Malvern Coll 71-77; Ho Master and Asst Chapl 77-87; Hd Master Jo Lyon Sch Harrow from 86. *Capers Mead, Whitmore Road, Harrow, Middx HA1 4AA* Tel 0181-864 9964

WRIGHT, Timothy John. b 54. Nottm Univ BA76. Ripon Coll Cuddesdon 90. **d** 92 **p** 93. C Dawlish *Ex* 92-95; TV Teignmouth, Ideford w Luton, Ashcombe etc from 95. *The Vicarage, 3 Moors Park, Bishopsteignton, Teignmouth, Devon TQ14 9RH* Tel (01626) 775247

WRIGHT, Mrs Vyvienne Mary. b 35. S Dios Minl Tr Scheme 80. **dss** 83 **d** 87 **p** 94. Martock w Ash *B & W* 83-87; Hon C from 87. *29 North Street, Martock, Somerset TA12 6DH* Tel (01935) 823292

WRIGHT, William Charles Stuart. b 53. Ulster Poly BSc81. CITC BTh95. **d** 95 **p** 96. C Ballyholme *D & D* from 95. *5 Shandon Park West, Bangor, Co Down BT20 5JD* Tel (01247) 271922

WRIGHT, William Easton. b 20. Linc Th Coll 52. **d** 53 **p** 54. C Petrockstowe w Peters Marland *Ex* 53-56; R Farway w Northleigh and Southleigh 56-69; RD Honiton 65-68; R Offwell w Widworthy 69-72; P-in-c Cotleigh 69-72; R Offwell, Widworthy, Cotleigh, Farway etc 72-85; rtd 85; Perm to Offic *Ex* from 85. *17 North Street, Ottery St Mary, Devon EX11 1DR* Tel (01404) 813744

WRIGHT, Canon William Hutchinson. b 27. St Jo Coll Dur BA50 DipTh52. **d** 55 **p** 56. C Kimberworth *Sheff* 55-59; Ind Chapl *Dur* 59-92; Hon Can Dur Cathl 72-92; rtd 92. *109 Bishopton Road, Stockton-on-Tees, Cleveland TS18 4PL* Tel (01642) 678817

WRIGHT, William Samuel. b 59. TCD DipTh87 BTh89. **d** 87 **p** 88. C Belfast St Aid *Conn* 87-91; Sec Dioc Bd of Miss 90-91; I Cleenish w Mullaghdun *Clogh* from 91. *Cleenish Rectory, Bellanaleck, Enniskillen, Co Fermanagh BT92 2BP* Tel (01365) 348259

WRIGHTSON, Bernard. b 25. Linc Th Coll. **d** 83 **p** 84. Hon C Alford w Rigsby *Linc* 83-86; Perm to Offic 86-89; NSM Mablethorpe w Trusthorpe 89-94; Perm to Offic from 94. *Pipits Acre, 64 Church Lane, Mablethorpe, Lincs LN12 2NU* Tel (01507) 472394

WRIGLEY, William Vickers. b 10. K Coll Cam BA32 MA36. Wells Th Coll 32. **d** 33 **p** 35. C Hinckley St Mary *Leic* 33-35; C Newport w Longford *Lich* 35-37; S Africa 38-52; CF 40-45; C Northallerton w Deighton and Romanby *York* 52-53; R Hawnby w Old Byland 53-57; V Hutton Buscel 57-70; V Wykeham 57-70; V Old Malton 70-75; rtd 76; Hon C Rillington w Scampston, Wintringham etc *York* 76-83; RD Buckrose 77-80; Perm to Offic from 83. *Beech House, Low Moorgate, Rillington, Malton, N Yorkshire YO17 8JW* Tel (01944) 758513

WRISDALE, Jean May. b 40. LNSM course. **d** 90 **p** 94. NSM Fotherby *Linc* from 90. *The Meadows, Livesey Road, Ludborough, S Humberside DN36 5SG* Tel (01472) 840474

WRIST-KNUDSEN, Svend Michael. b 61. Copenhagen Univ DipTh87. St Jo Coll Dur BA91. **d** 91 **p** 92. C Newton Aycliffe *Dur* 91-95; P-in-c Penzance St Jo *Truro* from 95. *11 Pendarves Road, Penzance, Cornwall TR18 2AJ* Tel (01736) 65836

WROE, Mark. b 69. Surrey Univ BA92. Ridley Hall Cam 94. **d** 96 **p** 97. C Chilvers Coton w Astley *Cov* from 96. *126 Coventry Road, Nuneaton, Warks CV10 7AD* Tel (01203) 383086

WYATT, Colin. b 27. Ex Coll Ox BA54 MA55 Lon Univ BD62. Tyndale Hall Bris 60. **d** 63 **p** 64. C Radipole *Sarum* 63-66; C Southborough St Pet *Roch* 66-67; V Tetsworth *Ox* 67-72; Lect Bible Tr Inst Glas 72-74; R Hurworth *Dur* 74-79; P-in-c Dinsdale w Sockburn 74-76; R 76-79; R Sadberge 79-84; R Bacton w Wyverstone and Cotton *St E* 84-92; rtd 92. *20 Harrogate Road, Ripon, N Yorkshire HG4 1SR* Tel (01765) 606810

WYATT, Canon David Stanley Chadwick. b 36. Fitzw Ho Cam BA59 MA71. Ely Th Coll 59. **d** 61 **p** 62. C Rochdale *Man* 61-63; Bp's Dom Chapl 63-68; R Salford St Paul w Ch Ch from 68; Hon Can Man Cathl from 82; P-in-c Salford Ordsall St Clem from 91; AD Salford from 97. *St Paul's Church House, Broadwalk, Salford M6 5AN* Tel 0161-736 8868

WYATT, Peter John. b 38. Kelham Th Coll 58. **d** 64 **p** 65. C N Stoneham *Win* 64-68; C Brixham *Ex* 68-69; Dominica 69-75; Zambia 76-78; P-in-c Ettington *Cov* 78-79; V Butlers Marston and the Pillertons w Ettington 79-86; V Codnor and Loscoe *Derby* 86-91; Chapl to the Deaf from 91. *10 Kirkstead Close, Oakwood, Derby DE21 2HN* Tel (01332) 280922

WYATT, Richard Norman. b 21. LVCM. **d** 84 **p** 85. C Puttenham and Wanborough *Guildf* 84-90; rtd 91; Perm to Offic *Chich* 91-93; P-in-c Stedham w Iping 93-97. *Trenethick, June Lane, Midhurst, W Sussex GU29 9EL* Tel (01730) 813447

WYATT, Royston Dennis. b 36. FRICS67. Sarum & Wells Th Coll 74. **d** 77 **p** 78. NSM Canford Magna *Sarum* 77-82; V Abbotsbury, Portesham and Langton Herring 82-88; Dioc Missr *Linc* 88-95; R Welford w Weston and Clifford Chambers *Glouc* from 95; RD Campden from 96. *The Rectory, Church Lane, Welford on Avon, Stratford-upon-Avon, Warks CV37 8EL* Tel (01789) 750808

WYBREW, Canon Hugh Malcolm. b 34. Qu Coll Ox BA58 MA. Linc Th Coll 59. **d** 60 **p** 61. C E Dulwich St Jo *S'wark* 60-64; Tutor St Steph Ho Ox 65-71; Chapl Bucharest *Eur* 71-73; V Pinner *Lon* 73-83; Sec Fellowship of SS Alb and Sergius 84-86; Dean Jerusalem 86-89; V Ox St Mary Magd *Ox* from 89; Hon Can Gib Cathl *Eur* from 89. *15 Beaumont Street, Oxford OX1 2NA* Tel (01865) 247836

WYER, Keith George. b 45. St Paul's Cheltenham CertEd66 K Coll Lon BD71 AKC71. St Aug Coll Cant 71. **d** 72 **p** 73. C Moseley St Mary *Birm* 72-76; Chapl RNR 73-92; C Walsall *Lich* 76-77; Min Walsall St Martin 77-79; Chapl Colston's Sch Bris 79-86; Chapl Kelly Coll Tavistock 86-92; Lic to Offic *Ex* 86-92; R Combe Martin and Berrynarbor 92-95; TR Combe Martin, Berrynarbor, Lynton, Brendon etc from 96; RD Shirwell from 95. *The Rectory, Rectory Road, Combe Martin, Devon EX34 0NS* Tel (01271) 883203

WYLAM, John. b 43. AKC66. **d** 67 **p** 68. C Derby St Bart *Derby* 67-70; SSF 70-73; C Seaton Hirst *Newc* 74-77; V Byker St Silas 77-83; V Alwinton w Holystone and Alnham from 83. *The Vicarage, Alwinton, Morpeth, Northd NE65 7BE* Tel (01669) 50203

WYLD, Kevin Andrew. b 58. St Cath Coll Ox BA79 MA85 Univ Coll Dur MSc83 Edin Univ BD85. Edin Th Coll 82. **d** 85 **p** 86. C Winlaton *Dur* 85-87; C Houghton le Spring 87-90; V Medomsley 90-95; V High Spen and Rowlands Gill from 95. *St Patrick's Vicarage, High Spen, Rowlands Gill, Tyne & Wear NE39 2AA* Tel (01207) 542815

WYLD, Peter Houldsworth. b 20. Magd Coll Ox BA53 MA53. Cuddesdon Coll 53. **d** 55 **p** 56. C Stafford St Chad *Lich* 55-60; C Stafford St Mary 55-60; N Rhodesia 60-64; Zambia 64-65; USPG 66-74; Gen Ed 71-74; Dir C of E Enquiry Cen 74-78; C Hatfield *St Alb* 78-79; R Appleton *Ox* 79-89; P-in-c Besselsleigh w Dry Sandford 85-89; rtd 89. *2 Jubilee Terrace, Oxford OX1 4LN* Tel (01865) 792506

WYLIE, Alan. b 47. Is of Man Tr Inst 88. **d** 92 **p** 93. NSM Douglas St Geo and St Barn *S & M* 92-96; Perm to Offic *Glas* from 97. *2 Boreland Anworth, Gatehouse of Fleet, Castle Douglas DG7 2EJ* Tel (01557) 330913

WYLIE, Clive George. b 64. QUB BSc TCD BTh MITD MA. CITC. **d** 90 **p** 91. C Drumglass w Moygashel *Arm* 90-93; Bp's C Arm St Mark w Aghavilly from 93; I from 95; Hon V Choral Arm Cathl from 93. *The Rectory, 16 Derryhaw Road, Tynan, Armagh BT60 4SS* Tel (01861) 568619

WYLIE, David Victor. b 61. ACA86 LSE BSc(Econ)82 Leeds Univ BA91. Coll of Resurr Mirfield 89. **d** 92 **p** 93. C Kilburn St Aug w St Jo *Lon* 92-95; C Heston from 95. *24 Hogarth Gardens, Hounslow TW5 0QS*

WYLIE, Nigel Bruce. b 62. Trin Coll Bris 88. **d** 91 **p** 92. C Selly Park St Steph and St Wulstan *Birm* 91-94. *10 Regent Court, Winn Road, Southampton SO17 1GG* Tel (01703) 556456

WYLIE-SMITH, Ms Megan Judith. b 52. BD74. S'wark Ord Course 88. **d** 91 **p** 94. C Greenstead juxta Colchester *Chelmsf* 91-94; C W Ham from 94. *St Thomas' House, 29A Mortham Street, London E15 3LS* Tel 0181-519 2118

WYNBURNE, John Paterson Barry. b 48. St Jo Coll Dur BA70. Wycliffe Coll Toronto MDiv72 Ridley Hall Cam 72. **d** 73 **p** 74. C Gt Stanmore *Lon* 73-76; Chapl Bucharest w Sofia *Eur* 76-77; C Dorking w Ranmore *Guildf* 77-80; V Send 80-88; V York Town St Mich 88-93; V Camberley St Mich Yorktown 93-95; TR

Beaconsfield *Ox* from 95. *The Rectory, Wycombe End, Beaconsfield, Bucks HP9 1NB* Tel (01494) 673949

WYNES, Michael John. b 33. AKC57. **d** 58 **p** 59. C Gt Berkhamsted *St Alb* 58-62; C Silverhill St Matt *Chich* 62-65; C Wilton *B & W* 65-68; R Berkley w Rodden 68-77; V Priddy 77-86; V Westbury sub Mendip w Easton 77-86; C Milton 86-93; rtd 93; Perm to Offic *B & W* from 95. *23A Fairways, Wells, Somerset BA5 2DF* Tel (01749) 673778

WYNGARD, Canon Ernest Clive. b 30. Leeds Univ BA52. Coll of Resurr Mirfield 52. **d** 54 **p** 55. C Bishopwearmouth St Mich *Dur* 54-59; C Winlaton 59-61; V Castleside 61-67; V Beamish 67-80; RD Lanchester 74-80; V Dur St Giles 80-87; Hon Can Dur Cathl from 83; V Greatham 87-94; Master Greatham Hosp 87-94; rtd 94. *16 Langholm Road, East Boldon, Tyne & Wear NE36 0ED* Tel 0191-536 5275

WYNN-EVANS, James Naylor. b 34. Magd Coll Ox BA55 MA59. Linc Th Coll 57. **d** 59 **p** 60. C Goole *Sheff* 59-62; C Hatfield 62-63; Chapl HM Borstal Hatf 62-67; C-in-c Dunscroft CD *Sheff* 63-67; Bp's Dom Chapl *Edin* 67-75; C Edin St Columba 67-69; R Edin St Marg 69-85; P-in-c Edin SS Phil and Jas 76-85; P-in-c Edin St Dav from 85; Can St Mary's Cathl 86-95. *1 Gayfield Place, Edinburgh EH7 4AB* Tel 0131-556 1566 or 225 6357 Fax 346 7247 E-mail scot_epis_church@ecunet.org

WYNNE, Alan John. b 46. St Luke's Coll Ex CertEd71. St Steph Ho Ox BA71 MA75. **d** 71 **p** 72. C Watford St Pet *St Alb* 71-74; Chapl Liddon Ho Lon 74-75; Chapl Abp Tenison's Gr Sch Kennington 75-86; Hon C St Marylebone Annunciation Bryanston Street *Lon* 81-86; V Hoxton St Anne w St Columba 86-94; TR Poplar from 94. *Poplar Rectory, Newby Place, London E14 0EY* Tel 0171-987 3133 or 538 9198 Fax 987 1605

WYNNE, Frederick John Gordon. b 44. Chu Coll Cam BA66 MA70. CITC DipTh84. **d** 84 **p** 85. C Dublin St Patr Cathl Gp *D & G* 84-86; C Romsey *Win* 86-89; R Broughton, Bossington, Houghton and Mottisfont 89-97; I Dunleckney w Nurney, Lorum and Kiltennel *C & O* from 97. *The Rectory, Dunleckney, Muine Bheag, Co Carlow, Irish Republic* Tel Carlow (503) 21570

WYNNE, Preb Geoffrey. b 41. K Coll Lon BD64 AKC64 Lon Univ BSc(Soc)75 Heythrop Coll Lon MTh86. **d** 66 **p** 67. C Wolverhampton St Pet *Lich* 66-70; Chapl Wolv Poly 70-79; Sen Chapl 79-92; Sen Chapl Wolv Univ from 92; Dir of Ords 76-83; Preb Lich Cathl from 83. *The Principal's House, 1 Compton Park, Wolverhampton WV3 9DU* Tel Wolverhampton (0902) 712051/25747

WYNNE, James Arthur Hill. b 13. BSP45. **d** 47 **p** 48. C Kilmore w Drumsnatt *Clogh* 47-50; C Tydavnet 47-50; C Darlington St Hilda *Dur* 50-52; V S Shields St Oswin 52-67; V Coundon 67-82; rtd 82; Perm to Offic *Dur* from 82; Perm to Offic *Newc* from 82. *44 Hermiston, Monkseaton, Whitley Bay, Tyne & Wear NE25 9AN* Tel 0191-253 0302

WYNNE, Canon Richard William Maurice. b 19. TCD BA44 MA68 LLD. TCD Div Sch Div Test44. **d** 44 **p** 45. C Dublin Clontarf *D & G* 44-49; C Dublin Rathmines 49-52; I Delgany 52-58; I Monkstown St Mary 58-78; Founder Member Irish Samaritans 59; Preb Dunlavin St Patr Cathl Dublin 76-87; I Dublin St Ann w St Mark and St Steph *D & G* 78-87; Chmn, Nat Sec and Deputation Sec Miss to Seamen from 83; rtd 87. *17 Brookville Park, Stradbrook, Blackrock, Co Dublin, Irish Republic* Tel Dublin (1) 289 2315

WYNNE, Canon Ronald Charles. b 16. Selw Coll Cam BA38 MA42 Cape Town Univ MA79. Bp's Coll Calcutta 41. **d** 42 **p** 43. Ceylon 42-45; C Basingstoke *Win* 46-50; C Fleet *Guildf* 50-56; V Lockerley w E Dean *Win* 56-61; St Vincent 61-67; Botswana 68-82; rtd 82; Perm to Offic *Glouc* from 83. *19 Ricardo Road, Minchinhampton, Stroud, Glos GL6 9BY* Tel (01453) 883372

WYNNE, Trefor. b 35. St Mich Coll Llan 72. **d** 74 **p** 75. C Llangynwyd w Maesteg *Llan* 74-77; V Trealaw 77-83; R Llanbeulan w Llanfaelog and Tal-y-Llyn *Ban* 83-96; RD Llifon and Talybolion 93-96; rtd 96. *3 St John's Drive, Ton Pentre, Pentre CF41 7EU*

WYNNE-GREEN, Roy Rowland. b 36. Chich Th Coll 67. **d** 70 **p** 71. C Fleetwood *Blackb* 70-73; C Cen Torquay *Ex* 73-75; Chapl SW Hosp & Chapl Asst St Thos Hosp Lon 75-85; Chapl R Surrey Co Hosp Guildf 85-94; Chapl R Surrey County and St Luke's Hosps NHS Trust from 94; Chapl Heathlands Mental Health Trust Surrey from 94. *Surrey Hospital, Egerton Road, Guildford GU2 5XX, or 14 Broadacres, Guildford, Surrey GU3 3AZ* Tel (01483) 571122

WYNNE-JONES, Dyfed. b 56. St Mich Coll Llan DipTh79. **d** 79 **p** 80. C Porthmadog *Ban* 79-82; R Llangelynnin w Rhoslefain 82-86; Dioc Youth Officer 82-88; V Llanllechid 86-88; Chapl RAF from 88. *Chaplaincy Services (RAF), HQ, Personnel and Training Command, RAF Innsworth, Gloucester GL3 1EZ* Tel (01452) 712612 ext 5164 Fax 510828

WYNNE-JONES, Nicholas Winder. b 45. Jes Coll Ox BA67 MA72. Oak Hill Th Coll 69. **d** 72 **p** 73. C St Marylebone All So w SS Pet and Jo *Lon* 72-75; Chapl Stowe Sch Bucks 75-83; V Gt Clacton *Chelmsf* 83-95; V Beckenham Ch Ch *Roch* from 95. *Christ Church Vicarage, 18 Court Downs Road, Beckenham, Kent BR3 2LR* Tel 0181-650 3847

WYNTER, Michael Pallant. b 48. Ripon Coll Cuddesdon DipMin95. **d** 95 **p** 96. C Hughenden *Ox* from 95. *Pipers Cottage, Pipers Lane, Great Kingshill, High Wycombe, Bucks HP15 6LW* Tel (01494) 714758

WYSS, Mrs Joan. b 30. St Chris Coll Blackheath. **d** 88. NSM Woodhorn w Newbiggin *Newc* 88-92; rtd 90. *11 Sandridge, Newbiggin-by-the-Sea, Northd NE64 6DX* Tel (01670) 813356

Y

YABBACOME, David Wallace. b 55. Bp Otter Coll BEd Linc Th Coll DipTh. **d** 83 **p** 84. C Egham Hythe *Guildf* 83-86; C Cen Telford *Lich* 86-87; TV 87-92; R Cheadle w Freehay from 92. *The Rectory, Church Street, Cheadle, Stoke-on-Trent ST10 1HU* Tel (01538) 753337

YABSLEY, Mrs Janet. b 42. St Alb Minl Tr Scheme 81. **dss** 84 **d** 87 **p** 94. Luton St Andr *St Alb* 84-87; Hon C Luton St Aug Limbury from 87. *11 Dale Road, Dunstable, Beds LU5 4PY* Tel (01582) 661480

YACOMENI, Peter Frederick. b 34. Worc Coll Ox BA58 MA61. Wycliffe Hall Ox 58. **d** 60 **p** 61. C New Malden and Coombe *S'wark* 60-64; C Bethnal Green St Jas Less *Lon* 64-68; V Barton Hill St Luke w Ch Ch *Bris* 68-75; V Bishopsworth 75-86; RD Bedminster 84-86; P-in-c Wick w Doynton 86-87; V Wick w Doynton and Dyrham from 87; RD Bitton from 95. *The Vicarage, 78A High Street, Wick, Bristol BS15 5QH* Tel 0117-973 3281

YAHAYA, Haruna. b 62. St Fran Coll Nigeria DipTh88 Trin Coll Bris 93. **d** 81 **p** 92. Nigeria 81-93; C Hirwaun *Llan* 93 and from 94. *St Winifred's Church Flat, 5 Shopping Centre, Pen y Waun, Aberdare CF44 9HD* Tel (01685) 814249

YALLOP, John. b 47. BA79. Oak Hill Th Coll 79. **d** 79 **p** 80. C Brinsworth w Catcliffe *Sheff* 79-81; C Heeley 81-83; C Pitsmoor Ch Ch 83-86; V Ellesmere St Pet 86-88; C Worksop St Jo *S'well* 90-94; P-in-c Cliftonville *Cant* from 94. *St Paul's Vicarage, Northdown Road, Margate, Kent CT9 2RD* Tel (01843) 220857

YATES, Andrew Martin. b 55. St Chad's Coll Dur BA77. Linc Th Coll 78. **d** 80 **p** 81. C Brightside St Thos and St Marg *Sheff* 80-83; TV Haverhill w Withersfield, the Wrattings etc *St E* 84-90; Ind Chapl 84-90; R Aylesham w Adisham *Cant* 90-96; P-in-c Dudley St Aug Holly Hall *Worc* from 96; Chapl Merry Hill Shopping Cen from 96. *St James's Vicarage, The Parade, Dudley, W Midlands DY1 3JA* Tel (01384) 253570

YATES, Anthony Hugh. b 39. Univ of Wales BA62. Wycliffe Hall Ox 62. **d** 65 **p** 66. C Withington St Crispin *Man* 65-68; C Sheff Parson Cross St Cecilia *Sheff* 68-73; V Middlesbrough St Thos *York* 73-82; V Fenton *Lich* 82-95; V Kilburn St Aug w St Jo *Lon* from 95. *St Augustine's House, Kilburn Park Road, London NW6 5XB* Tel 0171-624 1637

YATES, Dr Arthur Stanley. b 11. Lon Univ BD43 BA45 Leeds Univ PhD49. Ripon Hall Ox. **d** 61 **p** 62. C Gidea Park *Chelmsf* 61-63; Sen Lect Coll of SS Jo and Mark Plymouth 63-77; Lic to Offic *Ex* from 74; rtd 77; Ex Univ *Ex* from 77. *The Homestead, Thornhill Road, Plymouth PL3 5NA* Tel (01752) 663774

YATES, David. b 56. Oak Hill Th Coll DipHE90. **d** 90 **p** 91. C Parkham, Alwington, Buckland Brewer etc *Ex* 90-93; C Watling Valley *Ox* 93-95; TV from 95. *3 Daubeney Gate, Shenley Church End, Milton Keynes MK5 6EH* Tel (01908) 505812

YATES, David Herbert. b 10. **d** 70 **p** 73. Rhodesia 70-80; rtd 80; C Verwood *Sarum* 80-85; Perm to Offic from 85. *Denewood House, 14 Denewood Road, West Moors, Wimborne, Dorset BH22 0LX* Tel (01202) 871483

YATES, Francis Edmund (Frank). b 49. Ox Univ BEd72 Sheff Univ MEd88. Linc Th Coll CMinlStuds95. **d** 95 **p** 96. C Chesterfield St Mary and All SS *Derby* from 95. *5 Queen Street, Chesterfield, Derbyshire S40 4SF* Tel (01246) 279063

YATES, James Ainsworth. b 21. Bps' Coll Cheshunt 56. **d** 58 **p** 59. C Dunstable *St Alb* 58-60; V Shillington 60-79; V Upper Gravenhurst 62-72; R Lower Gravenhurst 62-72; RD Shefford 69-79; V Upper w Lower Gravenhurst 72-79; V Sandon and Wallington w Rushden 79; R Sandon, Wallington and Rushden w Clothall 79-87; rtd 87. *97 Grove Road, Hitchin, Herts SG5 1SQ* Tel (01462) 434959

YATES, Miss Joanna Mary. b 49. St Anne's Coll Ox BA71 MA74 K Coll Lon PGCE72. S'wark Ord Course 89. **d** 91 **p** 94. Promotions and Publications Officer Nat Soc 85-95; Chapl Ch Ho Westmr 91-95; C Regent's Park St Mark *Lon* 91-95; C Finchley St Mary from 95. *28 Hendon Lane, London N3 1TR* Tel 0181-371 0361

✠**YATES, The Rt Revd John.** b 25. Jes Coll Cam BA49 MA52 Cheltenham & Glouc Coll of HE Hon DLitt92. Linc Th Coll 49. **d** 51 **p** 52 **c** 72. C Southgate Ch Ch *Lon* 51-54; Lic to Offic *Linc* 54-59; Tutor Linc Th Coll 54-59; Chapl 56-59; V Bottesford *Linc* 59-65; Prin Lich Th Coll 66-72; Preb Lich Cathl *Lich* 72; Lic to Offic 66-72; Suff Bp Whitby *York* 72-75; Bp Glouc 75-91; Bp at Lambeth (Hd of Staff) *Cant* 91-94; rtd 94. *14 Belle Vue Road, Andover, Hants SP10 2DF* Tel (01264) 354996

YATES, Canon John Dennis. b 28. Wells Th Coll. **d** 57 **p** 58. C Elton All SS *Man* 57-60; C Cannock *Lich* 60-62; R Moston St Jo *Man* 62-73; V Bury St Pet 73-76; R Ipswich St Mary at Stoke w St Pet & St Mary Quay *St E* 76-80; TR Ipswich St Mary at Stoke w St Pet & St Mary Quay 80-85; TR Ipswich St Mary at Stoke w St Pet 85-94; P-in-c Wherstead 77-94; Hon Can St E Cathl 87-94; rtd 94. *41 Princethorpe Road, Ipswich IP3 8NX* Tel (01473) 721394

YATES, Keith Leonard. b 36. K Coll Lon BD AKC61 Nottm Univ MPhil79. Wells Th Coll. **d** 69 **p** 70. C Luton Ch Ch *St Alb* 69-73; Hon C Luton St Andr 73-76; R Grimoldby w Manby *Linc* 76-80; P-in-c Yarburgh 76-78; R 78-80; P-in-c Alvingham w N and S Cockerington 76-78; V 78-80; P-in-c Gt w Lt Carlton 77-78; R 78-80; Lect Sarum & Wells Th Coll 80-87; R Upper Chelsea H Trin w St Jude *Lon* 87-96; rtd 96. *17 Redlands Drive, Broadwindsor, Beaminster, Dorset DT8 3ST* Tel (01308) 868892

YATES, Kenneth. b 44. Leeds Univ CQSW80. Kelham Th Coll 65. **d** 70 **p** 71. C Leeds City *Ripon* 70-74; C Worksop Priory *S'well* 74-75; Hon C Bawtry w Austerfield 75-78; Hon C Cantley *Sheff* 80-83; Hon C Doncaster St Jude 83-86; Hon C Ashford St Matt *Lon* 86-88; TV Brighton Resurr *Chich* 88-95; R E Blatchington from 95. *The Rectory, 86 Belgrave Road, Seaford, E Sussex BN25 2HE* Tel (01323) 892964

YATES, Michael Anthony. b 48. Oak Hill Th Coll. **d** 82 **p** 83. C Hebburn St Jo *Dur* 82-85; C Sheldon *Birm* 85-87; V Lea Hall 87-92; TV Old Brampton and Loundsley Green *Derby* from 92. *Church House, 6 Arden Close, Loundsley Green, Chesterfield, Derbyshire S40 4NE* Tel (01246) 276805

YATES, Michael John Whitworth. b 39. Selw Coll Cam BA62. Oak Hill Th Coll 62. **d** 64 **p** 65. C New Catton St Luke *Nor* 64-68; C Lowestoft St Jo 68-74; Perm to Offic *Bradf* from 75. *5 Belle Hill, Giggleswick, Settle, N Yorkshire BD24 0BA* Tel (01729) 822690

YATES, Michael Peter. b 47. Leeds Univ BA69 MA70 MPhil85. Coll of Resurr Mirfield 69. **d** 71 **p** 72. C Crewe St Andr *Ches* 71-76; V Wheelock 76-79; Chapl Rainhill Hosp Liv 79-89; Chapl Barnsley Distr Gen Hosp 89-94; Chapl Barnsley Distr Gen Hosp NHS Trust from 94. *The Chaplain's Office, Barnsley Hospital, Gawber Road, Barnsley, S Yorkshire S75 2EP* Tel (01226) 730000

YATES, Dr Paul David. b 47. Sussex Univ BA73 DPhil80. Sarum & Wells Th Coll 88. **d** 91 **p** 92. NSM Lewes All SS, St Anne, St Mich and St Thos *Chich* from 91. *17 St Swithun's Terrace, Lewes, E Sussex BN7 1UJ* Tel (01273) 473463

YATES, Peter Francis. b 47. Sheff Univ BA69 Nottm Univ DipTh71. Kelham Th Coll 69. **d** 74 **p** 75. C Mexborough *Sheff* 74-78; C Sevenoaks St Jo *Roch* 78-81; CSWG from 81; Lic to Offic *Chich* from 86. *The Monastery, Crawley Down, Crawley, W Sussex RH10 4LH* Tel (01342) 712074

YATES, Raymond Paul (Ray). b 55. Oak Hill Th Coll BA88. **d** 88 **p** 89. C Bootle St Mary w St Paul *Liv* 88-91; C Drypool *York* 91-92; TV from 92. *383 Southcoates Lane, Hull HU9 3UN* Tel (01482) 781090

YATES, Dr Roger Alan. b 47. MRCP77 Trin Coll Cam BA68 MB71 BChir71 MA72 Bris Univ PhD75. N Ord Course 84. **d** 87 **p** 88. NSM Wilmslow *Ches* from 87. *3 Racecourse Park, Wilmslow, Cheshire SK9 5LU* Tel (01625) 520246

YATES, Mrs Rosamund. b 63. Rob Coll Cam BA84 MA88. Oak Hill Th Coll BA93. **d** 93. C Holloway St Mary Magd *Lon* 93-95; NSM Tervuren w Liege *Eur* from 95. *71 Seward Road, London W7 2JP* Tel 0181-567 2518

YATES, Mrs Sian. b 57. Univ of Wales (Ban). Linc Th Coll 78. **d** 80 **p** 94. C Risca *Mon* 80-83; Chapl Ch Hosp Horsham 83-85; TD Haverhill w Withersfield, the Wrattings etc *St E* 85-90; Dioc Youth Chapl *Cant* 90-93; C Cant St Martin and St Paul 93-96; P-in-c Dudley St Jas *Worc* from 96; Educn Chapl from 96. *St James's Vicarage, The Parade, Dudley, W Midlands DY1 3JA* Tel (01384) 253570

YATES, Canon Timothy Edward. b 35. Magd Coll Cam BA59 MA62 Uppsala Univ DTh78. Ridley Hall Cam 58. **d** 60 **p** 61. C Tonbridge SS Pet and Paul *Roch* 60-63; Tutor St Jo Coll Dur 63-71; Warden Cranmer Hall Dur 71-79; P-in-c Darley w S Darley *Derby* 79-82; R Darley 82-90; Dioc Dir of Ords 85-95; Hon Can Derby Cathl from 89; C Ashford w Sheldon and Longstone from 90. *Great Longstone Vicarage, Bakewell, Derbyshire DE45 1TB* Tel (01629) 640257

YATES, Warwick John (Ricky). b 52. Univ of Wales (Lamp) BA78. Wycliffe Hall Ox 87. **d** 89 **p** 90. C Hoddesdon *St Alb* 89-93; R Finmere w Mixbury, Cottisford, Hardwick etc *Ox* 93-95; R Shelswell from 96. *The Rectory, Finmere, Buckingham MK18 4AT* Tel (01280) 847184

YATES, William Herbert. b 35. Man Univ BA59. Chich Th Coll 60. **d** 61 **p** 62. C Blackpool St Steph *Blackb* 61-65; C Wednesbury St Jo *Lich* 65-69; V Porthill 69-78; R Norton in the Moors 78-84; R Church Aston from 84. *St Andrew's Rectory, Church Aston, Newport, Shropshire TF10 9JG* Tel (01952) 810942

YATES-ROUND, Joseph Laurence John. b 25. S'wark Ord Course 75. **d** 76 **p** 77. NSM Tonbridge SS Pet and Paul *Roch* 76-83; Chapl Palma and Balearic Is w Ibiza etc *Eur* 83-90; rtd 90; Perm to Offic *Ches* from 90. *5 Willowtree Grove, Road Heath, Alsager, Stoke-on-Trent ST7 3TE* Tel (01270) 883425

YEATS, Charles. b 56. Natal Univ BCom77 Witwatersrand Univ MBA79 Ball Coll Ox MA85 K Coll Lon MTh90. Wycliffe Hall Ox 85. **d** 87 **p** 88. C Islington St Mary *Lon* 87-90; Research Fell Whitefield Inst Ox 90-92; Chapl and Fell Univ Coll Dur from 92. *University College, The Castle, Durham DH1 3RW* Tel 0191-374 3800 Fax 374 4740

YEATS, Peter Derek. b 62. Leeds Univ BA84. Cranmer Hall Dur 85. **d** 87 **p** 88. C Tynemouth Cullercoats St Paul *Newc* 87-90; USPG from 90. *USPG, Partnership House, 157 Waterloo Road, London SE1 8XA* Tel 0171-928 8681 Fax 928 2371

YEEND, Walter Archibald John. b 12. AKC40. **d** 40 **p** 41. C W Molesey *Guildf* 40-42; V from 45; C Westmr St Matt *Lon* 43-45. *The Vicarage, 518 Walton Road, West Molesey, Surrey KT8 0QF* Tel 0181-979 2805

YELDHAM, Anthony Paul Richard. *See* KYRIAKIDES-YELDHAM, Anthony Paul Richard

YENDALL, John Edward Thomas. b 52. St Jo Coll Dur BA88. Cranmer Hall Dur. **d** 88 **p** 89. C Ban 88-90; C Mellteyrn w Botwnnog and Llandygwnnin etc 90-91; R Trefdraeth w Aberffraw and Llangwyfan etc from 91. *The Rectory, 1 Maes Glas, Bethel, Bodorgan, Anglesey LL62 5ER* Tel (01407) 840190

YEO (née HARRISSON), Mrs Jennifer Marjorie. b 40. SRN62. Cant Sch of Min 87. **d** 90 **p** 97. NSM Kemsing w Woodlands *Roch* 90-91; Chapl Stone Ho Hosp Kent 90-91; NSM Totnes, Bridgetown and Berry Pomeroy etc *Ex* from 95. *Clematis Cottage, 2 Brooking Barn, Ashprington, Totnes, Devon TQ9 7UL* Tel (01803) 732770

YEO, Lester John. b 55. Ex Coll Ox BA77 MA81. Coll of Resurr Mirfield 78. **d** 80 **p** 81. C Plymstock *Ex* 80-83; C Northam w Westward Ho! and Appledore 83-85; TV 85-89; P-in-c Devonport St Mark Ford 89-93; TV Thorverton, Cadbury, Upton Pyne etc 93-95; TR from 95. *The Vicarage, Thorveton, Exeter EX5 5NP* Tel (01392) 8605332

YEO, Richard Ellery. b 25. Ex Coll Ox MA49 DipEd49. Cant Sch of Min 86. **d** 89 **p** 90. NSM Broadstairs *Cant* 89-92; NSM Totnes, Bridgetown and Berry Pomeroy etc *Ex* from 95. *Clematis Cottage, 2 Brooking Barn, Ashprington, Totnes, Devon TQ9 7UL* Tel (01803) 732770

YEOMAN, David. b 44. Univ of Wales DipTh69. St Mich Coll Llan 66. **d** 70 **p** 71. C Cardiff St Jo *Llan* 70-72; C Caerphilly 72-76; V Ystrad Rhondda w Ynyscynon 76-81; V Mountain Ash 81-96; R Coity w Nolton from 96. *Nolton Rectory, 5 Merthyr Mawr Road North, Bridgend CF31 3NH* Tel (01656) 652247

YEOMAN, Douglas. b 35. ACII63. **d** 77 **p** 78. NSM Edin St Martin *Edin* 77-90; NSM Edin St Luke 79-90; Chapl Gogarburn Hosp from 95; C Edin St Cuth *Edin* from 96. *6 Craiglockhart Crescent, Edinburgh EH14 1EY* Tel 0131-443 5449

YEOMAN, Miss Ruth Jane. b 60. Sheff Univ BSc82 MSc85 Dur Univ PGCE83. Ripon Coll Cuddesdon BA90. **d** 91 **p** 94. C Coleshill *Birm* 91-95; C Hodge Hill from 95; Bp's Adv for Children's Work from 95. *1 Ayala Croft, Bromford Bridge, Birmingham B36 8SN* Tel 0121-747 9320

YEOMANS, Robert John. b 44. AKC66. **d** 67 **p** 68. C Pontesbury I and II *Heref* 67-70; Asst Youth Officer *St Alb* 70-72; Project Officer (Dio St Alb) Gen Syn Bd of Educn 73-77; V Is of Dogs Ch Ch and St Jo w St Luke *Lon* 77-87; V Waterloo St Jo w St Andr *S'wark* 87-93; Chapl United Bris Healthcare NHS Trust from 93. *The Chaplaincy Office, Bristol Royal Infirmary, Marlborough Street, Bristol BS2 8HW* Tel 0117-923 0000 or 924 5275

YERBURGH, Canon David Savile. b 34. Magd Coll Cam BA57 MA61. Wells Th Coll 57. **d** 59 **p** 60. C Cirencester *Glouc* 59-63; C Bitterne Park *Win* 63-67; V Churchdown St Jo *Glouc* 67-74; RD Glouc N 73-74; V Charlton Kings St Mary 74-85; R Minchinhampton 85-95; Hon Can Glouc Cathl 86-95; rtd 95. *2 Mill Race Close, Mill Road, Salisbury SP2 7RX* Tel (01722) 320064

YERBURGH, Peter Charles. b 31. Magd Coll Cam BA53 MA57. Wells Th Coll 53. **d** 55 **p** 56. C Southbroom *Sarum* 55-58; Chapl Wells Cathl Sch 58-71; Chapl Durlston Court Sch Barton on Sea 71-91; rtd 91. *2 Mill Race Close, Mill Road, Salisbury SP2 7RX* Tel (01722) 327796

YERBURY, Gregory Howard Greg. b 67. Trin Coll Bris BA93. St Jo Coll Nottm 94. **d** 96 **p** 97. C Crofton *Portsm* from 96. *Carefree, 46 Carisbrooke Avenue, Stubbington, Fareham, Hants PO14 3PR* Tel (01329) 668577

YEWDALL, Mrs Mary Doreen. b 23. Nottm Univ DipEd71 BTh85. EMMTC 76. **dss** 79 **d** 87 **p** 94. Kirkby in Ashfield St Thos *S'well* 79-81; Daybrook 81-87; Par Dn 87-89; rtd 89; Hon Par Dn Bilsthorpe *S'well* 89-91; Hon Par Dn Eakring 89-91; Hon Par Dn Winkburn 89-91; Hon Par Dn Maplebeck 89-91; NSM Norton juxta Malton *York* from 92. *The Rectory, Crambe, York YO6 7JR* Tel (01653) 618647

YIEND, Paul Martin. b 57. UEA BA80. St Jo Coll Nottm DTS92. **d** 92 **p** 94. C Bushbury *Lich* 92-95; France *Eur* from 95. *Boulevard de Metz 76/34, 59000 Lille, France* Tel France (33) 20 57 23 19 Fax 20 42 94 22

YIN, Canon Roy Henry Bowyer. b 10. K Coll Cam BA32 MA36. Cuddesdon Coll 32. **d** 33 **p** 34. C Cambridge St Giles w St Pet *Ely* 33-37; Chapl K Coll Cam 33-37; Chapl Hurstpierpoint Coll Hassocks 37-46; Ceylon 46-62; Singapore from 64; rtd 75; Hon

Can Singapore from 80. *114-A Newton Road, Singapore 307980* Tel Singapore (65) 253-4080

YODER, John Henry. b 36. **d** 76 **p** 77. USA 76-79 and from 80; C Wolverhampton *Lich* 79-80. *108 East 39th, Paterson, New Jersey 07514, USA*

YONGE, James Mohun (Brother Amos). b 47. Keele Univ BA71. WMMTC 91. **d** 94. SSF from 76. *The Society of St Francis, Glasshampton, Shrawley, Worcester WR6 6TQ* Tel (01299) 896345

YORK, Canon Humphrey Bowmar. b 28. St Chad's Coll Dur BA54. **d** 55 **p** 56. C Beamish *Dur* 55-57; C Tettenhall Regis *Lich* 57-62; P-in-c Lansallos w Pelynt *Truro* 62-63; R Lanreath 62-67; V Pelynt 63-67; P-in-c Lanlivery 67-74; P-in-c Luxulyan 67-74; P-in-c Lanlivery w Luxulyan 74-83; RD Bodmin 76-82; R Antony w Sheviock 83-93; Hon Can Truro Cathl 90-93; rtd 93; Perm to Offic *Truro* from 93. *8 Huntingdon Street, Bradford-on-Avon, Wilts BA15 1RF*

YORK, Archbishop of. *See* HOPE, The Most Revd and Rt Hon David Michael

YORK, Archdeacon of. *See* AUSTIN, The Ven George Bernard

YORK, Dean of. *See* FURNELL, The Very Revd Raymond

YORKE, John Andrew. b 47. Cranmer Hall Dur 70. **d** 73 **p** 74. C Spitalfields Ch Ch w All SS *Lon* 73-78; Canada 78-92; V Totland Bay *Portsm* from 92; P-in-c Thorley from 95; V from 96. *The Vicarage, Alum Bay New Road, Totland Bay, Isle of Wight PO39 0ES* Tel (01983) 752031

YORKE, The Very Revd Michael Leslie. b 39. Magd Coll Cam BA62 MA66. Cuddesdon Coll 62. **d** 64 **p** 65. C Croydon *Cant* 64-68; Succ Chelmsf Cathl *Chelmsf* 68-69; Prec and Chapl 69-73; Dep Dir Cathl Cen for Research and Tr 72-74; P-in-c Ashdon w Hadstock 74-76; R 76-78; Can Res Chelmsf Cathl 78-88; Vice-Provost 84-88; P-in-c N Lynn w St Marg and St Nic *Nor* 88-92; P-in-c King's Lynn St Marg w St Nic 92-94; Chmn Dioc Adv Bd for Min 90-94; Hon Can Nor Cathl 93-94; Provost Portsm from 94. *Provost's House, 13 Pembroke Road, Portsmouth P01 2NS* Tel (01705) 824400 or 823300 Fax 295480

YORKSTONE, Peter. b 48. Loughb Univ BTech72. Oak Hill Th Coll 79. **d** 81 **p** 82. C Blackpool St Thos *Blackb* 81-85; V Copp from 85. *St Anne's Vicarage, Copp Lane, Great Eccleston, Preston PR3 0ZN* Tel (01995) 670231

YOUATT, Jennifer Alison. *See* MONTGOMERY, Mrs Jennifer Alison

YOUDE, Paul Crosland. b 47. Birm Univ LLB68. W of England Minl Tr Course 93. **d** 96. NSM Cheltenham St Luke and St Jo *Glouc* from 96. *107 Painswick Road, Cheltenham, Glos GL50 2EX* Tel (01242) 527233

YOUENS, Edward. *See* MONTAGUE-YOUENS, Canon Hubert Edward

YOUINGS, Dr Adrian. b 65. Ex Univ BSc86 Bath Univ PhD90. Wycliffe Hall Ox 93. **d** 96 **p** 97. C Dorking St Paul *Guildf* from 96. *6 Falkland Road, Dorking, Surrey RH4 3AB* Tel (01306) 889513

YOULD, Dr Guy Martin. b 38. FSAScot75 Keble Coll Ox BA61 DipTh62 MA65 Magd Coll Ox BD68 Hull Univ PhD80. Lambeth STh75 St Steph Ho Ox 61. **d** 63 **p** 64. C Middlesbrough St Jo the Ev *York* 63-65; Chapl Magd Coll Ox 65-68; C Cowley St Jo *Ox* 65-68; Lic to Offic 68-71 and 87-93; Asst Chapl Radley Coll Oxon 68-71; C W Kirby St Bridget *Ches* 71-74; Chapl Loretto Sch Musselburgh 74; V Liscard St Mary w St Columba *Ches* 74-78; Australia 78-80; C Doncaster St Leon and St Jude *Sheff* 80-81; V Brodsworth w Hooton Pagnell, Frickley etc 81-87; Chapl St Mary's Sch Wantage 87-93; Lic to Offic *Ox* 87-93; R Chapel Chorlton, Maer and Whitmore *Lich* from 93. *Whitmore Rectory, Snape Hall Road, Whitmore Heath, Newcastle, Staffs ST5 5HS* Tel (01782) 680258

YOUNG, Andrew John. b 50. St Jo Coll Dur BA73. Westcott Ho Cam 73. **d** 75 **p** 89. C Nailsworth *Glouc* 75-76; NSM Yeovil w Kingston Pitney *B & W* 89-93; NSM Tintinhull w Chilthorne Domer, Yeovil Marsh etc from 93. *17 Stone Lane, Yeovil, Somerset BA21 4NN* Tel (01935) 76394

YOUNG, Aubrey William. b 38. **d** 91 **p** 92. NSM Tallaght *D & G* 91-96; NSM Kill from 96. *27 Flower Grove, Dun Laoghaire, Irish Republic* Tel Dublin (1) 285 5069

YOUNG, Brian Thomas. b 42. Linc Th Coll 67. **d** 70 **p** 71. C Monkseaton St Mary *Newc* 70-73; C Berwick H Trin 73-77; P-in-c Gt Broughton *Carl* 77-80; P-in-c Gt Broughton and Broughton Moor 80; V 80-83; V Chorley *Ches* 83-90; V Alderley Edge from 90; RD Knutsford from 96. *The Vicarage, Church Lane, Alderley Edge, Cheshire SK9 7UZ* Tel (01625) 583249

YOUNG, Canon Charles John. b 24. Qu Coll Birm 52. **d** 55 **p** 56. C Dudley St Thos *Worc* 55-58; C Beeston *S'well* 58-61; V Lady Bay 61-66; R Kirkby in Ashfield 66-75; V Balderton 75-92; RD Newark 82-90; Hon Can S'well Minster 84-92; rtd 92; Bp's Chapl for Rtd Clergy *S'well* from 92. *9 The Paddocks, London Road, Newark, Notts NG24 1SS* Tel (01636) 613445

YOUNG, The Ven Clive. b 48. St Jo Coll Dur BA70. Ridley Hall Cam 70. **d** 72 **p** 73. C Neasden cum Kingsbury St Cath *Lon* 72-75; C Hammersmith St Paul 75-79; P-in-c Old Ford St Paul w St Steph 79-82; V Old Ford St Paul w St Steph and St Mark 82-92; AD Tower Hamlets 88-92; Adn Hackney from 92; V St Andr Holborn from 92. *St Andrew's Vicarage, 5 St Andrew Street, London EC4A 3AB* Tel 0171-353 3544 Fax 583 2750

YOUNG, Daniel George Harding. b 52. New Coll Ox BA73 MA83. Cranmer Hall Dur 77. **d** 80 **p** 81. C Bushbury *Lich* 80-83; Chapl Dean Close Sch Cheltenham from 83. *The White House, 2 Church Road, St Marks, Cheltenham, Glos GL51 7AH* Tel (01242) 528922

YOUNG, Dr David. b 37. Open Univ PhD89. Lambeth STh79 Ely Th Coll 61 Linc Th Coll 64. **d** 67 **p** 68. C Crofton *Wakef* 67-68; C Heckmondwike 68-71; V Stainland 71-76; R Patrington w Winestead *York* 76-80; Gen Preacher *Linc* from 80; Chapl St Jo Hosp Linc 80-90; Chapl N Lincs Mental Health Unit from 90; Chapl Witham Court ESMI Unit 90-93; Chapl Linc Distr Healthcare NHS Trust from 93. *Westview, Ainsthorpe, Lincoln LN1 2SG, or Witham Court, Fen Lane, North Hykeham, Lincoln LN6 8UZ* Tel (01522) 730912 or 500690

YOUNG, David Charles. b 44. Or Coll Ox BA66 MA70. S'wark Ord Course 74. **d** 77 **p** 78. C Harborne St Pet *Birm* 77-81; P-in-c Edgbaston St Germain 81-83; P-in-c Birm St Paul 83-85; Perm to Offic *St Alb* from 85. *18 Tamar Walk, Leighton Buzzard, Beds LU7 8DD* Tel (01525) 382881

YOUNG, David John. b 43. Nottm Univ BA64 MPhil89. Lambeth STh87 Coll of Resurr Mirfield 64. **d** 66 **p** 67. C Warsop *S'well* 66-68; C Harworth 68-71; P-in-c Hackenthorpe Ch Ch *Derby* 71-73; TV Frecheville and Hackenthorpe 73-75; V Chaddesden St Phil 75-83; R Narborough and Huncote *Leic* 83-89; RD Guthlaxton I 87-90; Chapl Leic Univ 90-95; V Eyres Monsell from 95. *St Hugh's Vicarage, Pasley Road, Leicester LE2 9BU* Tel 0116-278 2954

✠**YOUNG, The Rt Revd David Nigel de Lorentz.** b 31. Ball Coll Ox BA54 MA58. Wycliffe Hall Ox 57. **d** 59 **p** 60 **c** 77. C Allerton *Liv* 59-62; C St Marylebone St Mark Hamilton Terrace *Lon* 62-63; CMS 63-67; Perm to Offic *Ches* 67-70; Perm to Offic *Man* 67-70; Lect Man Univ 67-70; V Burwell *Ely* 70-75; Hon Can Ely Cathl 75-77; Adn Huntingdon 75-77; V Gt w Lt Gidding and Steeple Gidding 75-77; R Hemingford Abbots 77; Bp Ripon from 77. *Bishop Mount, Ripon, N Yorkshire HG4 5DP* Tel (01765) 602045 Fax 700758

YOUNG, Derek John. b 42. St D Coll Lamp DipTh73. **d** 73 **p** 74. C Griffithstown *Mon* 73-76; C Ebbw Vale 76-77; V Penmaen 77-81; V Penmaen and Crumlin 81-87; Chapl Oakdale Hosp Gwent from 83; V New Tredegar *Mon* from 87. *The Vicarage, Gorse Terrace, New Tredegar NP2 6NR* Tel (01443) 821087

YOUNG, Desmond Terence. b 17. TCD BA40. **d** 41 **p** 42. C Hadfield *Derby* 41-44; C Derby St Werburgh 44-47; CF 47-55; I Fertagh *C & O* 55-62; I Inistioge w the Rower 62-74; P-in-c Thomastown 62-74; RD Kells 65-74; C Roundhay St Edm *Ripon* 74-77; V Leeds Gipton Epiphany 77-83; rtd 83; Perm to Offic *Guildf* 83-94. *102 Wallace Avenue, Worthing, W Sussex BN11 5QA* Tel (01903) 246973

YOUNG, Frederick Charles (Eric). b 32. TCD BA56 MA59 MLitt63 DTh68. **d** 58 **p** 59. C Dublin Donnybrook *D & G* 58-63; C Taney Ch Ch 63-66; I Bray 66-70; I Dalkey St Patr 70-73; C Upper Norwood All SS w St Marg *Cant* 81-84; Warden Coll of Preachers 84-93; Dir 94-97; P-in-c Morton w Hacconby *Linc* 84-90; V 90-93; rtd 97. *Wilsthorpe Manor, Wilsthorpe, Stamford, Lincs PE9 4PE*

YOUNG, Canon Geoffrey Maxwell. b 12. Ch Coll Cam BA34 MA38. Westcott Ho Cam 34. **d** 35 **p** 36. C Bradf St Wilfrid Lidget Green *Bradf* 35-38; C Guiseley 38-45; CF (EC) 40-45; V Thornbury *Bradf* 45-49; V Farningham *Roch* 49-57; Chapl Parkwood Hosp Swanley 50-57; V Kemsing 57-66; P-in-c Woodlands 66; V W Malling w Offham 67-81; P-in-c Leybourne 72-76; Hon Can Roch Cathl 73-81; rtd 81; Perm to Offic *Roch* 82-84; Hon PV Roch Cathl from 84. *4 Albany Road, Rochester, Kent ME1 3ET* Tel (01634) 844608

YOUNG, George William. b 31. Lon Coll of Div ALCD55 LTh74. **d** 56 **p** 57. C Everton Em *Liv* 56-58; C Halliwell St Pet *Man* 58-61; V Newburn *Newc* 61-67; P-in-c Tylers Green *Ox* 67-69; V 69-80; Lic to Offic 80-84; Area Sec (W England) SAMS 80-84; Hon C Purley Ch Ch *S'wark* 84-87; V Beckenham St Jo *Roch* 87-92; rtd 92; Perm to Offic *S'wark* from 92. *9 Shortacres, High Street, Nutfield, Redhill RH1 4HJ* Tel (01737) 822363

YOUNG, Henry Lawrence. b 19. TCD MA46. **d** 47 **p** 48. C Ballywillan *Conn* 47-49; C Urney w Denn and Derryheen *K, E & A* 49-50; I 50-51; CF 51-60; I Donegal w Killymard, Lough Eske and Laghey *D & R* 60-64; R Gt and Lt Casterton w Pickworth and Tickencote *Pet* 64-70; rtd 70; Hon C Perth St Jo *St And* from 70. *6 Pullar Terrace, Hillyland, Perth PH1 2QF* Tel (01738) 636797

YOUNG, Iain Clavering. b 56. Newc Poly BA79. Coll of Resurr Mirfield 80. **d** 83 **p** 84. C Wallsend St Luke *Newc* 83-86; C Horton 86-87; V 87-92; V Friern Barnet St Pet le Poer *Lon* 92-95; C Holborn St Alb w Saffron Hill St Pet 96-97; P-in-c Hoxton H Trin w St Mary from 97. *Holy Trinity Vicarage, 3 Bletchley Street, London N1 7QG* Tel 0171-253 4796

YOUNG, Jeremy Michael. b 54. Ch Coll Cam BA76 MA80 Lon Univ MTh94. Coll of Resurr Mirfield 78. **d** 80 **p** 81. C Whitworth w Spennymoor *Dur* 80-83; C Boxmoor St Jo *St Alb* 83-86; V Croxley Green St Oswald 86-94; Dir Theol CITC from 94. *27 Rostrevor Road, Rathgar, Dublin 6, Irish Republic* Tel Dublin (1) 497 0331

YOUNG, Canon John David. b 37. DLC60 Lon Univ BD65 Sussex Univ MA77. Clifton Th Coll 62. **d** 65 **p** 66. C Plymouth St Jude *Ex* 65-68; Hd of RE Northgate Sch Ipswich 68-71; Lic to Offic *St E* 68-71; Chapl and Sen Lect Bp Otter Coll Chich 71-81; Chapl and Sen Lect W Sussex Inst of HE 77-81; Chapl and Sen Lect Coll of Ripon and York St Jo 81-87; C York St Paul *York* 87-88; Dioc Ev from 88; Can and Preb York Minster from 92. *73 Middlethorpe Grove, York YO2 2JX* Tel (01904) 704195

YOUNG, John Kenneth. Edin Th Coll 62. **d** 64 **p** 65. C Gosforth All SS *Newc* 64-67; C Newc St Gabr 67-69; R Bowers Gifford *Chelmsf* 69-72; R Bowers Gifford w N Benfleet 72-75; P-in-c Kirkwhelpington *Newc* 75-79; P-in-c Kirkheaton 75-79; P-in-c Cambo 77-79; P-in-c Kirkharle 77-79; V Kirkwhelpington, Kirkharle, Kirkheaton and Cambo 79-82; V Gosforth St Nic 82-92; V Healey and Slaley 92-97; rtd 97. *20 Mitford Way, Dinnington, Newcastle upon Tyne NE13 7LW*

YOUNG, Canon Jonathan Frederick. b 25. Univ of Wales (Lamp) BA51 Birm Univ MA81. St Mich Coll Llan 51. **d** 53 **p** 54. C Roath St Martin *Llan* 53-59; Lic to Offic *Ox* 59-74; SSJE 62-71; Bp's Chapl for Community Relns *Birm* 71-74; Chapl Coun for Soc Resp 74-85; Hon Can Birm Cathl 84-85; USA from 85; rtd 90. *52 Harvard Road, Belmont, MA 02178, USA*

YOUNG, Jonathan Priestland. b 44. AKC68. **d** 69 **p** 70. C Clapham H Trin *S'wark* 69-73; C Mitcham St Mark 73-74; V Godmanchester *Ely* 74-82; P-in-c Cambridge St Giles w St Pet 82; P-in-c Chesterton St Luke 82; TR Cambridge Ascension from 82; Chapl St Jo Coll Sch Cam 88-93. *Ascension Rectory, Cambridge CB4 3PS* Tel (01223) 361919 Fax 322710

YOUNG, Kathleen Margaret. b 40. QUB BD BTh. **d** 88 **p** 90. C Carrickfergus *Conn* 88-92; I Belfast St Paul w St Barn from 92. *The Parsonage, 50 Sunningdale Park, Belfast BT14 6RW* Tel (01232) 715413

YOUNG, Mark Gilbert Campbell. b 60. Mert Coll Ox BA88. Wycliffe Hall Ox 86. **d** 91 **p** 92. C Holborn St Geo w H Trin and St Bart *Lon* 91-95; C St Pancras w St Jas and Ch Ch from 95. *Flat 3, 58 Lambs Conduit Street, London WC1N 3LW* Tel 0171-831 7234

YOUNG, Martin Edward. b 20. Or Coll Ox BA41 MA45. Cuddesdon Coll 41. **d** 43 **p** 44. C Newbury *Ox* 43-45; C Wymondham *Nor* 45-49; C Gt Berkhamsted *St Alb* 49-51; V Littlemore *Ox* 51-64; R Wootton w Quinton *Pet* 64-72; R Wootton w Quinton and Preston Deanery 72-78; V Welford w Sibbertoft 78-82; V Welford w Sibbertoft and Marston Trussell 82-88; rtd 88; Perm to Offic *Pet* from 88. *2 Knutsford Lane, Long Buckby, Northampton NN6 7RL* Tel (01327) 843929

YOUNG, Canon Noel. b 26. St Aid Birkenhead 53. **d** 56 **p** 57. C Garston *Liv* 56-59; C Oldham St Paul *Man* 59-61; R Goldhanger w Lt Totham *Chelmsf* 61-65; C-in-c Leigh-on-Sea St Aid CD 65-69; V Leigh-on-Sea St Aid 69-72; I Kilnasoolagh *L & K* 73-78; I Tullow w Shillelagh, Aghold and Mullinacuff *C & O* 79-88; Preb Leighlin Cathl 83-88; Preb Ossory Cathl 83-88; Treas Ossory and Leighlin Cathls 85-88; I Templemore w Thurles and Kilfithmone 88-94; rtd 94. *31 Cherryfield, Coolgreany Road, Arklow, Co Wicklow, Irish Republic* Tel Arklow (402) 33242

YOUNG, Norman Keith. b 35. EAMTC 85. **d** 87 **p** 88. C Burwell *Ely* 87-91; V Swaffham Bulbeck and Swaffham Prior w Reach 91-92; V Barnby Dun *Sheff* from 92; Ind Chapl from 92. *The Vicarage, Stainforth Road, Barnby Dun, Doncaster, S Yorkshire DN3 1AA* Tel (01302) 882835

YOUNG, Peter John. b 26. Pemb Coll Cam BA49 MA54. Ridley Hall Cam 49. **d** 51 **p** 52. C Cheadle *Ches* 51-54; Malaya 54-63; Malaysia from 63; rtd 92. *Peti Syrat 498, Jalan Sultan, 46760 Petaling Jaya, Selangor, Malaysia* Tel Kuala Lumpur (3) 274-6172

YOUNG, Canon Raymond Grant. b 11. MBE81. **d** 43 **p** 44. C Ince Ch Ch *Liv* 43-45; C Pemberton St Jo 46; Chapl to Deaf (Dios Win and Portsm) 46-49; Perm to Offic *Portsm* 48-59; V Marchwood *Win* 59-70; Chapl to Deaf (Dios Win and Portsm) 70-81; Hon Can Win Cathl *Win* 77-81; rtd 81; Perm to Offic *Win* 81-95. *66 Chalvington Road, Eastleigh, Hants SO53 3DT* Tel (01703) 261519

YOUNG, Richard Michael. **d** 96 **p** 97. NSM Brunswick *Man* from 96. *2 Birch Grove, Rusholme, Manchester M14 5JY* Tel 0161-225 0884

YOUNG, Roger Edward. b 40. Dur Univ BSc62. Cuddesdon Coll 64. **d** 66 **p** 67. C Eglwysilan *Llan* 66-68; C Llanishen and Lisvane 68-74; C-in-c Rhydyfelin CD 74-78; TV Ystradyfodwg 78-81; V 81-88; Chapl Tyntyla, Llwynypia and Porth and Distr Hosps from 81; Dir of Tr for the NSM from 86; R Peterston-super-Ely w St Brides-super-Ely *Llan* from 88. *The Rectory, Peterston-super-Ely, Cardiff CF5 6LH* Tel (01446) 760297

YOUNG, Canon Stanley. b 14. St Jo Coll Dur BA36. Ely Th Coll 36. **d** 37 **p** 38. C Camberwell St Luke *S'wark* 37-40; Min Can Carl Cathl *Carl* 40-45; Warden St Anne's Ch Ho Soho 45-48; C Pimlico St Mary Graham Terrace *Lon* 48-50; Warden Pemb Coll Miss Walworth *S'wark* 50-53; V Aldermaston w Wasing *Ox* 53-69; RD Bradfield 63-68; V Long Crendon 70-80; P-in-c Chearsley w Nether Winchendon 77-80; V Long Crendon w Chearsley and Nether Winchendon 80-94; Hon Can Ch Ch 81-94; rtd 94. *The Pightle, Church Lane, Chearsley, Aylesbury, Bucks HP18 0DH* Tel (01844) 208402

YOUNG, Stephen. b 33. St Edm Hall Ox MA61. St Jo Coll Nottm 75 ALCD77. **d** 77 **p** 78. C Crofton *Portsm* 77-81; C Rainham *Chelmsf* 81-87; V Ramsgate Ch Ch *Cant* from 87. *The Vicarage, 23 Pegwell Road, Ramsgate, Kent CT11 0JB* Tel (01843) 589848

YOUNG, Stephen Edward. b 52. K Coll Lon BD73 AKC73 Ch Ch Coll Cant CertEd74. **d** 75 **p** 76. C Walton St Mary *Liv* 75-79; C St Marylebone All SS *Lon* 83; C Pimlico St Gabr 83-85; Chapl Whitelands Coll of HE *S'wark* 85-88; Asst Chapl St Paul's Sch Barnes 88-91; Chapl from 91; P in O from 91; NSM Pimlico St Mary Graham Terrace *Lon* from 94. *St Mary's Presbytery, 30 Bourne Street, London SW1W 8JJ* Tel 0171-730 4886

YOUNG, Stuart Kincaid. b 59. **d** 95 **p** 96. C Letchworth St Paul w Willian *St Alb* from 95. *89 Howard Drive, Letchworth, Herts SG6 2BX* Tel (01462) 673888

YOUNG, Walter Howlett. b 08. Clifton Th Coll 32. **d** 34 **p** 35. C Bath St Sav *B & W* 34-37; C Bath Abbey w St Jas 37-38; R Hinton Blewett 38-43; Chapl RNVR 43-46; Chapl HM Pris Leyhill 46-50; C Wraxall *B & W* 50-67; V Compton Dando 67-73; R Chelwood 67-73; rtd 73; Perm to Offic *B & W* 73-94. *69 Yew Tree Gardens, Nailsea, Bristol BS19 2XR* Tel (01275) 855797

YOUNG, William Maurice. b 32. St Jo Coll Nottm 80. **d** 81 **p** 82. C Harlescott *Lich* 81-84; V Hadley 84-94; rtd 94; Perm to Offic *Heref* from 94. *Old Chapel School, Newport Street, Clun, Craven Arms, Shropshire SY7 8JZ* Tel (01588) 640846

YOUNGER, Jeremy Andrew. b 46. Nottm Univ BA68 Bris Univ MA71. Wells Th Coll 68. **d** 70 **p** 71. C Basingstoke *Win* 70-74; C Harpenden St Nic *St Alb* 74-76; Dir Communications & Chapl Sarum & Wells Th Coll 77-81; V Clifton All SS w St Jo *Bris* 81-84; Relig Affairs Producer BBC Radio Nottm *S'well* 84-86; C Bow w Bromley St Leon *Lon* 86-88; Projects and Min Manager St Jas Piccadilly from 89; Hon C St Marylebone All SS from 89. *90 Harvist Road, London NW6 6HA* Tel 0181-964 2930

YOUNGMAN, Donald Arthur. b 10. AKC37. **d** 37 **p** 38. C Tilbury Docks *Chelmsf* 37-39; P-in-c Barking St Patr 39-43; Chapl RAFVR 43-47; C Almondbury *Wakef* 47-48; C-in-c Prittlewell St Luke CD *Chelmsf* 48-51; Chapl RAF 51-57; R Long Stanton w St Mich *Ely* 57-69; P-in-c Rampton 69-74; rtd 74. *4 Church Close, Hunstanton, Norfolk PE36 6BE* Tel (01485) 533322

YOUNGSON, David Thoms. b 38. Cuddesdon Coll 71. **d** 73 **p** 74. C Norton St Mary *Dur* 73-76; C Hartlepool St Paul 76-79; P-in-c Stockton St Jo CD 79-84; V Stockton St Jo 84-86; V Owton Manor 86-90; rtd 90; Perm to Offic *Dur* from 90. *36 Stokesley Road, Seaton Carew, Hartlepool, Cleveland TS24 1EE*

YULE, John David. b 49. G&C Coll Cam BA70 MA74 PhD76. Westcott Ho Cam 79. **d** 81 **p** 82. C Cherry Hinton St Andr *Ely* 81-84; C Almondbury w Farnley Tyas *Wakef* 84-87; V Swavesey *Ely* 87-95; V Fen Drayton w Conington 87-95; R Fen Drayton w Conington and Lolworth etc from 95. *The Vicarage, Honey Hill, Fen Drayton, Cambridge CB4 5SF* Tel (01954) 231903

YULE, Robert White. b 49. FCMA81. St Jo Coll Nottm LTh88. **d** 88 **p** 89. C Wilford *S'well* 88-91; TV Bestwood 91-96; P-in-c Selston from 96. *The Vicarage, Church Lane, Selston, Nottingham NG16 6EW* Tel (01773) 810247

Z

ZACHAU, Eric. b 31. AKC57. **d** 58 **p** 59. C Bishopwearmouth St Mich *Dur* 58-62; C Ryhope 62-63; V Beadnell *Newc* 63-69; V Earsdon 69-81; V Bamburgh and Lucker 81-95; V Bamburgh and Beadnell from 95; RD Bamburgh and Glendale 92-97. *The Vicarage, 7 The Wynding, Bamburgh, Northd NE69 7DB* Tel (01668) 214295

ZAIR, Richard George. b 52. Newc Univ BSc74. Trin Coll Bris 75 St Jo Coll Dur 79. **d** 80 **p** 81. C Bishopsworth *Bris* 80-83; C New Malden and Coombe *S'wark* 83-91; Dir of Evang CPAS from 91; Perm to Offic *Cov* from 91. *64 Kingsway, Leamington Spa, Warks CV31 3LE* Tel (01926) 424634 Fax (01926) 337613

ZAMMIT, Mark Timothy Paul. b 60. Aston Tr Scheme 90 Sarum & Wells Th Coll DCTM94. **d** 94 **p** 95. C Bitterne Park *Win* from 94. *25 Lacon Close, Southampton SO18 1JA* Tel (01703) 583540

ZAREK, Jennifer Hilary. b 51. Newnham Coll Cam MA76 Southn Univ MSc73 PhD78 Garnett Coll Lon CertEd83 DipEd87 Birkb Coll Lon DipRS91. St Steph Ho Ox 95. **d** 97. C Caterham *S'wark* from 97. *70 Spencer Road, Caterham, Surrey CR3 5LB* Tel (01883) 340882

ZASS-OGILVIE, Ian David. b 38. ARICS72 FRICS80. AKC65. **d** 66 **p** 67. C Washington *Dur* 66-70; Bp's Soc and Ind Adv for N Dur 70-73; Lic to Offic *Newc* 73-75; V Tynemouth St Jo 75-78; Hon C St Marylebone St Mary *Lon* 78-81; V Bromley St Jo *Roch* 81-84; R Keith *Mor* 84-88; R Huntly 84-88; R Aberchirder 84-88; R Edin St Pet *Edin* from 88. *3 Bright's Crescent, Edinburgh EH9 2DB* Tel 0131-667 6224 Fax as telephone

ZEAL, Stanley Allan. b 33. Leeds Univ BA55. Coll of Resurr Mirfield. **d** 57 **p** 58. C Perry Hill St Geo *S'wark* 57-61; C Cobham *Guildf* 61-64; V Ash Vale 64-69; R Ash 64-69; Chapl Northfield Hosp Aldershot from 69; V Aldershot St Mich *Guildf* from 69. *St Michael's Vicarage, 120 Church Lane East, Aldershot, Hants GU11 3SS* Tel (01252) 20108

ZIETSMAN, Sheila. **d** 90 **p** 91. C Geashill w Killeigh and Ballycommon *M & K* 90-91; C Mullingar, Portnashangan, Moyliscar, Kilbixy etc 91-96; Chapl Wilson's Hosp Sch Multyfarnham 91-96; Chapl E Glendalough Sch from 96. *East Glendalough School, Station Road, Wicklow, Irish Republic* Tel Wicklow (404) 69608 Fax 68180

ZORAB, Mark Elston. b 53. FRICS77 MRAC75. Mon Dioc Tr Scheme 92. **d** 94. NSM Itton and St Arvans w Penterry and Kilgwrrwg etc *Mon* from 94. *Oak Cottage, Itton Road, Chepstow NP6 6BQ* Tel (01291) 620919 Fax as telephone

ZOTOV, Mrs Carolyn Ann. b 47. Lady Mabel Coll CertEd68 Open Univ BA78 Nottm Univ DSpEd86. EMMTC CTPS91. **d** 92 **p** 94. NSM Hykeham *Linc* 92-94; NSM Aisthorpe w Scampton w Thorpe le Fallows etc 94; C Ingham w Cammeringham w Fillingham from 94. *2 The Green, Ingham, Lincoln LN1 2XT* Tel (01522) 730765

ZUCCA, Peter Rennie. b 73. **d** 96 **p** 97. NSM Spotland *Man* from 96. *19 Judith Street, Rochdale, Lancs OL12 7HS* Tel (01706) 359327

ZWALF, Willem Anthony Louis. b 46. AKC68. **d** 71 **p** 72. C Fulham St Etheldreda w St Clem *Lon* 71-74; Chapl City Univ 74-78; V Coalbrookdale *Heref* 78; P-in-c Ironbridge 78; P-in-c Lt Wenlock 78; R Coalbrookdale, Iron-Bridge and Lt Wenlock 78-90; V Wisbech SS Pet and Paul *Ely* from 90. *The Vicarage, Love Lane, Wisbech, Cambs PE13 1HP* Tel (01945) 583559

DEACONESSES

The biographies of women clergy are to be found in the preceding section.

ANDERSON, Mary. b 15. St Mary's Ho Dur 38. **dss** 43. Warden Dioc Ho *S'wark* 66-70; Clapham H Trin 70-75; rtd 75. *1 Barrett Crescent, Wokingham, Berks RG40 1UR* Tel (0118) 978 3676

BENNETT, Miss Doreen. b 29. St Mich Ho Ox 60. **dss** 79. Moreton *Ches* 79-80; Dewsbury Moor *Wakef* 80-86; W Germany 86-90; Germany 90-91; rtd 89; Perm to Offic *Blackb* from 95. *6B Fairlawn Road, Lytham, Lytham St Annes, Lancs FY8 5PT* Tel (01253) 795217

BLACKBURN, Mary Paterson. b 16. St Chris Coll Blackheath 45 Wm Temple Coll Rugby 59. **dss** 76. Sawston *Ely* 74-78; rtd 78. *30 Maple Avenue, Sawston, Cambridge CB2 4TB* Tel (01223) 833843

BRIERLY, Margaret Ann. b 32. Dalton Ho Bris 54. **dss** 85. Wreningham *Nor* 85-86; Tetsworth, Adwell w S Weston, Lewknor etc *Ox* 86-95; rtd 95. *85 Coombe Hill Crescent, Thame, Oxon OX9 2EQ* Tel (01844) 261871

BUTLER, Miss Ann. b 41. St Mich Ho Ox 67 Dalton Ho Bris IDC69. **dss** 82. Bucknall and Bagnall *Lich* 82-87; Leyton St Mary w St Edw *Chelmsf* 89-97; Leyton St Mary w St Edw and St Luke from 97. *14 Vicarage Road, London E10 5EA* Tel 0181-558 4200

BYATT, Margaret Nelly. b 18. Bedf Coll Lon BA40. Lon Bible Coll DipTh50 Gilmore Ho 59. **dss** 62. Lee Gd Shep w St Pet *S'wark* 66-78; rtd 78. *41 Woodlands, Overton, Basingstoke, Hants RG25 3HW* Tel (01256) 770347

COLEBROOK, Vera Gwendoline. b 06. Greyladies Coll Gilmore Ho 45. **dss** 49. Charlton St Luke w St Paul *S'wark* 49-59; Welling 56-62; Lewisham St Steph 61-67; rtd 67. *Flat 57, Charles Clore Court, 139 Appleford Road, Reading RG3 3NT* Tel 0118-958 3960

COOK, Gwendoline. b 14. Greyladies Coll 50 St Andr Ho Ox 51. **dss** 56. Eltham St Sav *S'wark* 56-58; Malden St Jo 58-64; Asst Warden Dss Home Staines 64-69; Dss Ho Hindhead 69-74; rtd 74; Perm to Offic *S'wark* from 74. *2 Lancaster Avenue, London SW19 5DE* Tel 0181-947 1096

COOPER, Janet Pamela. b 46. Glos Coll of Educn TCert67 Ox Poly CertEdD79. Trin Coll Bris DipHE83. **dss** 83. Patchway *Bris* 83-88; Perm to Offic *Glouc* from 90. *Bethel, Kington Mead Farm, Kington Road, Thornbury, Bristol BS12 1PQ* Tel (01454) 414230

CUZNER, Amabel Elizabeth Callow. b 17. Gilmore Ho 63. **dss** 72. Catshill *Worc* 72-82; rtd 82; Perm to Offic *Worc* from 82. *12 Blake Road, Catshill, Bromsgrove, Worcs B61 0LZ* Tel (01527) 835063

DAVIDSON, Helen Beatrice. b 98. Greyladies Coll 40. **dss** 45. Norbury St Steph *Cant* 48-50; rtd 50; Perm to Offic *Chich* 50-70. *Ridgemead House Nursing Home, Ridgemead Road, Egham, Surrey TW20 0YH* Tel (01784) 433463

DEE, Mary. b 21. **dss** 55. Cumnor *Ox* 76-81; rtd 81. *Flat 4, 45 Oxford Avenue, Bournemouth BH6 5HT* Tel (01202) 424240

DENCE, Barbara Irene (Sister Verity). b 20. **dss** 52. CSA from 48. *St Andrew's House, 2 Tavistock Road, London W11 1BA* Tel 0171-229 2662

DOROTHY, Sister. *See* WARR, Sister Dorothy Lilian Patricia

DUCKERING, Alice Muriel. b 07. Gilmore Ho 43. **dss** 46. USPG 45-70; Kegworth *Leic* 71-77; rtd 77. *23 Stuart Court, Kibworth, Leicester LE8 0LN*

ENTWISTLE, Phyllis. b 18. Gilmore Ho 49. **dss** 54. Northallerton w Kirby Sigston *York* 70-78; rtd 78. *15 Kent Road, Harrogate, N Yorkshire HG1 2LH* Tel (01423) 560564

ESSAM, Susan Catherine. b 46. Southn Univ BA67 CertEd68. Linc Th Coll DipTh74. **dss** 80. CMS from 83; Nigeria from 83. *c/o Bishopscourt, PO Box 6283, Jos, Plateau State, Nigeria* Tel Jos (73) 52221

EVANS, Mrs Diana. b 59. Somerville Coll Ox BA81 MA85. St Steph Ho Ox 81. **dss** 84. Sherborne w Castleton and Lillington *Sarum* 84-88; Northampton St Paul *Pet* from 93. *St Paul's Vicarage, 104 Semilong Road, Northampton NN2 6EX* Tel (01604) 712688

EVENDEN, Joyce Nellie. b 15. Ranyard Tr Ho 46. **dss** 63. Battersea Ch Ch *S'wark* 62-67; Wembley St Jo *Lon* 67-72; Warden Dss Ho Staines 72-76; rtd 76. *Manormead Nursing Home, Tilford Road, Hindhead, Surrey GU26 6RA*

FINDER, Miss Patricia Constance. b 30. Dalton Ho Bris 63. **dss** 79. Clapham St Jas *S'wark* 79-90; rtd 90. *8 Brighton Road, Ilkley, W Yorkshire LS29 8PS* Tel (01943) 607023

FISH, Margaret. b 18. St Mich Ho Ox 49. **dss** 77. rtd 78; Perm to Offic *Nor* 78-89. *35 Ashwell Court, Norwich NR5 9BS* Tel (01603) 746123

FROST, Constance Mary. b 09. Gilmore Ho 34. **dss** 37. Walworth St Jo *S'wark* 36-40; Fenton *Lich* 41-47; Gt Wyrley 47-49; Bilston 49-73; rtd 73; Perm to Offic *Chich* from 73. *17 Church Way, Worthing, W Sussex BN13 1HD* Tel (01903) 201596

GOUGH, Mrs Janet Ainley. b 46. SRN RSCN SCM Lon Univ CertRK73. Trin Coll Bris 70. **dss** 76. Leic H Apostles *Leic* 73-80; USA 80-81; Perm to Offic *Leic* 81-96. *410 Hinckley Road, Leicester LE3 0WA* Tel 0116-285 4284 Fax as telephone

GREAVES, Dorothea Mary. b 16. St Denys Warminster 39. **dss** 62. Willesden St Andr *Lon* 63-76; rtd 76; Perm to Offic *Chich* from 76. *5 Norfolk House, Ellenslea Road, St Leonards-on-Sea, E Sussex TN37 6HZ* Tel (01424) 432965

GRIERSON, Miss Janet. b 13. Westf Coll Lon BA34. Lambeth STh37 MA82 Greyladies Coll 34 K Coll Lon 34. **dss** 48. Prin Lect RE Summerfield Coll Kidderminster 63-75; rtd 75. *Flat 8, Parkview, Abbey Road, Malvern, Worcs WR14 3HG* Tel (01684) 569341

HAMBLY, Miss Winifred Kathleen. b 18. Lambeth DipTh55 Gilmore Ho 54. **dss** 55. Cricklewood St Pet *Lon* 55-78; Eastbourne St Mich *Chich* from 78. *4 Tutts Barn Court, Tutts Barn Lane, Eastbourne, E Sussex BN22 8XP* Tel (01323) 640735

HAMILTON, Miss Pamela Moorhead. b 43. SRN64 SCM66. Trin Coll Bris DipTh75. **dss** 77. Derby St Pet and Ch Ch w H Trin *Derby* 77-84; Bedworth *Cov* from 85. *10 William Street, Bedworth, Nuneaton, Warks CV12 9DS* Tel (01203) 491608

HARRIS, Audrey Margaret. *See* STOKES, Audrey Margaret

HARRISON, Mrs Ann. b 55. Ex Univ BSc77. Linc Th Coll DipHE81. **dss** 82. Acomb H Redeemer *York* 82-83; Lic to Offic *Wakef* 83-91. *The Rectory, 8 Viking Road, Stamford Bridge, York YO4 1BR* Tel (01759) 371353

HEDLEY, Elsie. b 16. Lon Univ DipTh51. St Chris Coll Blackheath 46. **dss** 58. Whitton St Aug *Lon* 58-65; St D Cathl *St D* 65-74; Bradford-on-Avon *Sarum* 74-75; rtd 75. *13A Connaught Road, Sidmouth, Devon EX10 8TT* Tel (01395) 516963

HEWITT, Miss Joyce Evelyn. b 30. SRN51 SCM55. St Mich Ho Ox IDC61. **dss** 67. Spitalfields Ch Ch w All SS *Lon* 67-70; CMJ 71-73; Canonbury St Steph *Lon* 73-75; Chorleywood RNIB Coll for Blind Girls 75-80; rtd 90. *38 Ashridge Court, Station Road, Newbury, Berks RG14 7LL* Tel (01635) 47829

HIDER, Margaret Joyce Barbara. b 25. St Mich Ho Ox 52. **dss** 77. Bris H Cross Inns Court *Bris* 77-84; Uphill *B & W* 84-89; rtd 89; Perm to Offic *B & W* 89-95. *Bethany, 8 Uphill Way, Weston-super-Mare, Avon BS23 4TH* Tel (01934) 414191

HILDEGARD, Sister. *See* MOORE, Sister Hildegard

HINDE, Miss Mavis Mary. b 29. Lightfoot Ho Dur. **dss** 65. Hitchin St Mary *St Alb* 65-68; Ensbury *Sarum* 69-70; Portsea St Alb *Portsm* 70-76; Houghton Regis *St Alb* 77-85; Eaton Socon 85-94; rtd 94. *8 Burnt Close, Eynesbury, St Neots, Huntingdon, Cambs PE19 2LZ* Tel (01480) 218219

HOWARD, Jean Elizabeth. b 37. Man Univ BA59 Univ of Wales (Cardiff) TDip61 Lon Univ DipTh BD86. St Mich Ho Ox 61. **dss** 82. Hanger Lane St Ann *Lon* 82-84; Dagenham *Chelmsf* 88-90; Perm to Offic from 90. *c/o Miss E Neeve, 4 Lavenham House, Brettenham Road, London E17 5AS* Tel 0181-527 3013

JAMES, Grace. b 18. **dss** 72. Chatham St Wm *Roch* 70-78; rtd 79. *46 Oastview, Gillingham, Kent ME8 8JQ* Tel (01634) 360276

KELLY, Miss Philippa. b 14. St Chris Coll Blackheath 37. **dss** 61. Jamaica 69-71; Kidderminster St Mary *Worc* 72-75; rtd 75. *Dulverton Hall, St Martin's Square, Scarborough, N Yorkshire YO11 2DB* Tel (01723) 501806

LEACH, Edith. b 22. St Mich Ho Ox 51. **dss** 81. Halliwell St Luke *Man* 77-83; rtd 82. *13 London Road, Blackpool FY3 8DL* Tel (01253) 34616

McCLATCHEY, Mrs Diana. b 20. LMH Ox MA44 DPhil49 Lon Univ DBRS69. **dss** 71. Adv for Women's Min *Dur* 70-74; Adv Lay Min *Worc* 74-80; Wilden 80-85; rtd 85. *10 Bellars Lane, Malvern, Worcs WR14 2DN* Tel (01684) 560336

MacCORMACK, Mrs June Elizabeth. b 45. LNSM course 82 St Jo Coll Nottm 85. **dss** 86. Bieldside *Ab* from 86. *5 Overton Park, Dyce, Aberdeen AB2 0FT* Tel (01224) 722691

MOORE (née STOWE), Mrs Ann Jessica Margaret. b 41. St Mich Ho Ox. **dss** 87. Watford *St Alb* 87-88; Spitalfields Ch Ch w All SS *Lon* 88-89; rtd 89. *168 Thorpe Road, Kirby Cross, Frinton-on-Sea, Essex CO13 0NQ* Tel (01255) 851933

MOORE, Sister Hildegard. b 03. St Andr Ho Ox CWWCh38. **dss** 41. CSA from 41; Perm to Offic *Lon* from 41. *St Andrew's House, 2 Tavistock Road, London W11 1BA* Tel 0171-229 2662

MOORHOUSE, Olga Marian. b 28. Dalton Ho Bris. **dss** 63. Wolverhampton St Matt *Lich* 62-68; Fazakerley Em *Liv* 68-70; Huyton St Geo 70-76; Blurton *Lich* 76-88; rtd 88. *37 Rosalind Grove, Wednesfield, Wolverhampton WV11 3RZ* Tel (01902) 630128

MORGAN, Beryl. b 19. Dalton Ho Bris 47. **dss** 77. Princess Marg Hosp Swindon 69-79; rtd 79. *Ty Clyd, Llanfihangel, Nant-Bran, Brecon LD3 9NA* Tel (01874) 82500

MULLER, Louise Irmgard. b 12. **dss** 64. Prestonville St Luke *Chich* 65-72; rtd 73; Perm to Offic *Chich* from 73. *24 Clifton Road, Worthing, W Sussex BN11 4DP* Tel (01903) 206541

NELSON, Olive Margaret. b 21. **dss** 52. Auckland St Andr and St Anne *Dur* 76; Heanor *Derby* 76-78; Littleover 78-82; rtd 82; Blagreaves St Andr CD *Derby* 82. *Address temp unknown*

OBEE, Sister Monica May. b 37. **dss** 82. Radford *Cov* 82-97; rtd 97. *14 The Hill, Great Walsingham, Norfolk NR22 6DF* Tel (01328) 821033

OLD, Constance Nellie. b 11. St Cath Coll Lon 37 St Mich Ho Ox 38. **dss** 40. Bris H Trin *Bris* 40-44; Surbiton St Matt *S'wark* 44-47; Pakistan 47-71; Gt Ilford St Andr *Chelmsf* 72-86; rtd 86. *230 Wanstead Park Road, Ilford, Essex IG1 3TT* Tel 0181-554 2781

OLIVER, Miss Kathleen Joyce. b 44. Man Univ BA65. N Ord Course 80. **dss** 83. Littleborough *Man* from 83; Perm to Offic from 83. *Littleborough Christian Care Centre, Lee House, Todmorden Road, Littleborough, Lancs OL15 9EA* Tel (01706) 376477 Fax 374074

OLPHIN, Miss Maureen Rose. b 30. Lon Univ BSc Sheff Univ DipEd Man Univ DipTh. **dss** 84. Sheff St Barn and St Mary *Sheff* 84-90; rtd 90. *41A Queen Street, Mosborough, Sheffield S19 5BP* Tel 0114-247 3009

PALMER, Kathleen. b 09. Gilmore Ho 43. **dss** 65. Chapl Asst S Ockendon Hosp 65-70; S Ockendon *Chelmsf* 65-70; rtd 70; Lee St Marg *S'wark* 70-80; Lewisham St Mary 70-80. *25 Stuart Court, Kibworth, Leicester LE8 0LN* Tel 0116-279 6326

PATRICK, Ruby Olivia. b 16. Gilmore Ho 69. **dss** 72. E Ham w Upton Park *Chelmsf* 72-74; Becontree St Elisabeth 74-75; Trinidad and Tobago 75-82; rtd 82. *41A New River Crescent, London N13 5RD* Tel 0181-882 5146

PIERSON, Mrs Valerie Susan (Sue). b 44. CertEd65. Trin Coll Bris 76. **dss** 79. Fulham St Matt *Lon* from 79. *48 Peterborough Road, London SW6 3EB* Tel 0171-736 4421

PLATT, Marjorie. b 18. Qu Coll Birm 76. **dss** 78. Hinckley St Mary *Leic* 78-91; Burbage w Aston Flamville from 91. *216 Brookside, Burbage, Hinckley, Leics LE10 2TW* Tel (01455) 233928

POLLARD, Shirley Ann. b 27. Wm Temple Coll Rugby 67 Cranmer Hall Dur 69. **dss** 84. Cramlington *Newc* 78-85; rtd 85. *3 Buttermere Drive, Worcester WR4 9HX* Tel (01905) 610724

RAIKES, Miss Gwynneth Marian Napier. b 51. Somerville Coll Ox MA72 Lon Univ BD81. Trin Coll Bris 79. **dss** 81. Asst Chapl Bris Poly *Bris* 81-86; Beckenham Ch Ch *Roch* from 86. *25 Rectory Road, Beckenham, Kent BR3 1HL* Tel 0181-650 8025

RAINEY, Miss Irene May. b 14. SRN36 SCM38. Gilmore Ho 69. **dss** 72. Filton *Bris* 70-74; Crowthorne *Ox* 74-79; rtd 79. *12 Stevens Close, Cottenham, Cambridge CB4 4TT* Tel (01954) 51634

RANSLEY, Frances Mary. b 12. St Andr Ho Portsm 52. **dss** 61. Portsea St Mary *Portsm* 61-63; Widley w Wymering 63-65; Jamaica 65-69; Linc St Jo *Linc* 69-72; rtd 72; Lic to Offic *Portsm* 72-80. *The Home of Comfort, 17 Victoria Grove, Southsea, Hants PO5 1NF* Tel (01705) 820920

ROBINSON, Philippa. b 09. R Holloway Coll Lon BA31 Nottm Univ CTPS76. **dss** 75. Branksome St Aldhelm *Sarum* 76-83; Lic to Offic from 83; Tutor Bp's Cert 84-86. *132 Parkstone Avenue, Poole, Dorset BH14 9LS* Tel (01202) 748415

SAMPSON, Miss Hazel. b 35. Lightfoot Ho Dur 58. **dss** 64. Fenton *Lich* 64-67; Gt Wyrley 67-69; Chapl Asst Manor Hosp Walsall 69-76; Lich St Mary w St Mich 76-95; rtd 95; Perm to Offic *Lich* from 95. *107 Walsall Road, Lichfield, Staffs WS13 8DD* Tel (01543) 419664

SCHMIEGELOW, Mrs Patricia Kate Lunn (Patti). b 37. St Mich Ho Ox IDC65. **dss** 86. The Hague *Eur* 86-89; Perm to Offic *Glouc* from 90; Gen Sec Intercon Ch Soc 92-97; rtd 97. *Waterside, Coln St Aldwyns, Cirencester, Glos GL7 5AJ* Tel (01285) 750218 Fax as telephone

SELWOOD, Miss Eveline Mary. b 34. **dss** 71. Huddersfield St Jo *Wakef* 76-79; King Cross 79-85; rtd 94. *27 Alverthorpe Road, Wakefield, W Yorkshire WF2 9NW* Tel (01924) 378364

SILL, Grace Mary. b 11. St Chris Coll Blackheath 53. **dss** 62. Lawrence Weston *Bris* 55-63; Southmead Hosp Bris 63-77; rtd 77. *10 Tyndale Court, Chertsey Road, Bristol BS6 6NF* Tel 0117-973 2903

SNOW, Marjorie Eveline. b 07. St Chris Coll Blackheath 30. **dss** 45. Eastbourne Ch Ch *Chich* 40-57; Jamaica 57-72; rtd 72. *Linden Lodge, 2 Tennyson Road, Worthing, W Sussex BN11 4BY* Tel (01903) 233446

SPROSON, Doreen. b 31. St Mich Ho Ox IDC58. **dss** 70. Wandsworth St Mich *S'wark* 68-71; Women's Sec CMS 71-74; Goole *Sheff* 74-76; Kirby Muxloe *Leic* 76-77; Perm to Offic *S'wark* from 85; rtd 91. *Flat 1, 27 St Leonards Road, London SW14 7LY* Tel 0181-876 4281

STOKES, Audrey Margaret. b 39. Dalton Ho Bris 68. **dss** 82. Collier Row St Jas *Chelmsf* 82-85; Woking St Mary *Guildf* 85-95; rtd 95. *1 Greet Park Close, Southwell, Notts NG25 0EE*

STOWE, Ann Jessica Margaret. *See* MOORE, Mrs Ann Jessica Margaret

SYMES, Miss Annabel. b 41. AIMLS68. S Dios Minl Tr Scheme 79. **dss** 85. Barford St Martin, Dinton, Baverstock etc *Sarum* from 89; Chapl Asst Salisbury Hosps from 85. *7 Shaftesbury Road, Barford St Martin, Salisbury SP3 4BL* Tel (01722) 744110

TAYLOR, Miss Jean. b 37. St Andr Coll Pampisford 62. **dss** 68. CSA 62-79; E Crompton *Man* 79-97; Chadderton St Luke from 97. *1A Crossley Street, Shaw, Oldham OL2 8EN* Tel (01706) 844061

TAYLOR, Muriel. b 28. CA Tr Coll 48. **dss** 76. Gateshead Fell *Dur* 76-86; Gateshead Harlow Green 86-88; rtd 88. *18 Beechwood Avenue, Gateshead, Tyne & Wear NE9 6PP* Tel 0191-487 6902

THUMWOOD, Janet Elizabeth. b 30. STh60 DipRE61. Trin Coll Toronto 58. **dss** 62. Canada 62-63; Mile End Old Town H Trin *Lon* 63-65; CSF 66-77; rtd 90. *66 Headley Grove, Tadworth, Surrey KT20 5JF* Tel (01737) 371076

TURNER, Miss Rosie (Poppy). b 22. St Mich Ho Ox 56. **dss** 61. Hornsey Rise St Mary *Lon* 61-62; Wealdstone H Trin 62-70; CMJ 71-72; CMS 73-74; Dss Ho Hindhead 74-76; Sutton Ch Ch *S'wark* 77-80; rtd 80. *Bungalow 16, Huggens' College, College Road, Northfleet, Gravesend, Kent DA11 9DL* Tel (01474) 357722

VERITY, Sister. *See* DENCE, Barbara Irene

WARR, Sister Dorothy Lilian Patricia. b 14. Selly Oak Coll 38. **dss** 53. St Etheldreda's Children's Home Bedf 51-59; CSA from 53; Goldington *St Alb* 54-59; S'wark St Sav w All Hallows *S'wark* 59-65; St Mich Convalescent Home Westgate-on-Sea 65-74; rtd 75. *St Andrew's House, 2 Tavistock Road, London W11 1BA* Tel 0171-229 2662

WEBB, Sybil Janet. b 20. SRN42 SCM43. Gilmore Course 69. **dss** 77. Worthing St Geo *Chich* 77-80; rtd 80; Perm to Offic *Chich* from 80. *42 Ham Road, Worthing, W Sussex BN11 2QX* Tel (01903) 202997

WRIGHT, Edith Mary. b 22. St Hugh's Coll Ox MA46 DipEd46. Gilmore Ho STh58. **dss** 61. St Marylebone St Mary *Lon* 58-71; Lect Linc Th Coll 71-73; Oatlands *Guildf* 73-76; Roehampton H Trin *S'wark* 76-82; rtd 82. *39A Radnor Road, Harrow, Middx HA1 1SA* Tel 0181-863 7320

WRIGHT, Gloria Mary. b 40. **dss** 83. Smethwick St Matt w St Chad *Birm* 83-84; Tottenham H Trin *Lon* 84-86. *3 Barelees Cottages, Cornhill-on-Tweed, Northd TD12 4SF* Tel (01890) 820327

BISHOPS IN ENGLAND, WALES, SCOTLAND AND IRELAND

CHURCH OF ENGLAND

BATH AND WELLS
Bishop of Bath and Wells — J L THOMPSON
Honorary Assistant Bishops — P E COLEMAN, A K HAMILTON, C C W JAMES, J R G NEALE, W M D PERSSON, J RICHARDS, R H M THIRD, J S WALLER, R P WILSON
Suffragan Bishop of Taunton — W A STEWART

BIRMINGHAM
Bishop of Birmingham — M SANTER
Honorary Assistant Bishops — A C DUMPER, A P HALL, M H D WHINNEY
Suffragan Bishop of Aston — J M AUSTIN

BLACKBURN
Bishop of Blackburn — A D CHESTERS
Assistant Bishop — D P NESTOR
Honorary Assistant Bishops — G K GIGGALL, M E VICKERS
Suffragan Bishop of Burnley — M W JARRETT
Suffragan Bishop of Lancaster — *Vacant*

BRADFORD
Bishop of Bradford — D J SMITH

BRISTOL
Bishop of Bristol — B ROGERSON
Honorary Assistant Bishops — P J FIRTH, J GIBBS, J R G NEALE, F S TEMPLE
Suffragan Bishop of Swindon (formerly Malmesbury) — M D DOE

CANTERBURY
Archbishop of Canterbury, Primate of All England and Metropolitan — G L CAREY
Bishop at Lambeth — F P SARGEANT
Honorary Assistant Bishop — R D SAY
Suffragan Bishop of Dover — J R A LLEWELLIN
Suffragan Bishop of Maidstone — G H REID
Suffragan Bishop of Ebbsfleet (Provincial Episcopal Visitor) — J RICHARDS
Suffragan Bishop of Richborough (Provincial Episcopal Visitor) — E R BARNES

CARLISLE
Bishop of Carlisle — I HARLAND
Honorary Assistant Bishops — I M GRIGGS, G L HACKER, J R SATTERTHWAITE
Suffragan Bishop of Penrith — R GARRARD

CHELMSFORD
Bishop of Chelmsford — J F PERRY
Honorary Assistant Bishops — J N JOHNSON
Area Bishop of Barking — R F SAINSBURY
Area Bishop of Bradwell — L A GREEN
Area Bishop of Colchester — E HOLLAND

CHESTER
Bishop of Chester — P R FORSTER
Honorary Assistant Bishop — A L WINSTANLEY
Suffragan Bishop of Birkenhead — M L LANGRISH
Suffragan Bishop of Stockport — G M TURNER

CHICHESTER
Bishop of Chichester — E W KEMP
Honorary Assistant Bishops — M E ADIE, D R J EVANS, M GREEN, J W HIND, E G KNAPP-FISHER, C C LUXMOORE, M H St J MADDOCKS, M R J MANKTELOW, M E MARSHALL, S W PHIPPS, D P WILCOX
Area Bishop of Horsham — L G URWIN
Area Bishop of Lewes — W P BENN

COVENTRY
Bishop of Coventry — *Vacant*
Suffragan Bishop of Warwick — A M PRIDDIS

DERBY
Bishop of Derby — J S BAILEY
Honorary Assistant Bishops — R M C BEAK, K J F SKELTON
Suffragan Bishop of Repton — F H A RICHMOND

DURHAM
Bishop of Durham — A M A TURNBULL
Suffragan Bishop of Jarrow — A SMITHSON

ELY
Bishop of Ely — S W SYKES
Honorary Assistant Bishops — P S DAWES, R L FISHER, J B TAYLOR
Suffragan Bishop of Huntingdon — J R FLACK

EXETER
Bishop of Exeter — G H THOMPSON
Honorary Assistant Bishops — R F CARTWRIGHT, I C DOCKER, P J PASTERFIELD, R C O GOODCHILD
Suffragan Bishop of Crediton — R S HAWKINS
Suffragan Bishop of Plymouth — J H GARTON

GLOUCESTER
Bishop of Gloucester — D E BENTLEY
Honorary Assistant Bishops — C D BOND, C W J BOWLES, J GIBBS, W S LLEWELLYN, M A MANN, J R G NEALE, R W WOODS
Suffragan Bishop of Tewkesbury — J S WENT

GUILDFORD
Bishop of Guildford — J W GLADWIN
Suffragan Bishop of Dorking — I J BRACKLEY

HEREFORD
Bishop of Hereford — J K OLIVER
Suffragan Bishop of Ludlow — J C SAXBEE

LEICESTER
Bishop of Leicester — T F BUTLER
Assistant Bishop — W J D DOWN
Honorary Assistant Bishop — J E L MORT

LICHFIELD
Bishop of Lichfield — K N SUTTON
Honorary Assistant Bishops — R O BOWLBY, K C ORAM
Area Bishop of Shrewsbury — D M HALLATT
Area Bishop of Stafford — C J HILL
Area Bishop of Wolverhampton — M G BOURKE

LINCOLN
Bishop of Lincoln — R M HARDY
Honorary Assistant Bishops — J E BROWN, D G SNELGROVE
Suffragan Bishop of Grantham — *Vacant*
Suffragan Bishop of Grimsby — D TUSTIN

LIVERPOOL
Bishop of Liverpool — *Vacant*
Honorary Assistant Bishops — R BROWN, J W ROXBURGH
Suffragan Bishop of Warrington — J R PACKER

LONDON
Bishop of London — R J C CHARTRES
Honorary Assistant Bishops — D S ARDEN, M BAUGHEN, R N COOTE, M E MARSHALL, M A P WOOD
Area Bishop of Edmonton — B J MASTERS
Suffragan Bishop of Fulham — J C BROADHURST
Area Bishop of Kensington — M J COLCLOUGH
Area Bishop of Stepney — J M SENTAMU
Area Bishop of Willesden — G G DOW

MANCHESTER
Bishop of Manchester — C J MAYFIELD
Suffragan Bishop of Hulme — C J F SCOTT
Suffragan Bishop of Middleton — S S VENNER
Suffragan Bishop of Bolton — D BONSER

NEWCASTLE
Bishop of Newcastle — J M WHARTON
Assistant Bishop — K E GILL

NORWICH
Bishop of Norwich — P J NOTT
Honorary Assistant Bishop — D G HAWKER
Suffragan Bishop of Lynn — D J CONNER
Suffragan Bishop of Thetford — H F de WAAL

OXFORD
Bishop of Oxford — R D HARRIES
Honorary Assistant Bishops — K A ARNOLD, L J ASHTON, J BONE, J P BURROUGH, A K CRAGG, A R M GORDON, J RICHARDS, S E VERNEY, R C C WATSON
Area Bishop of Buckingham — C J BENNETTS
Area Bishop of Dorchester — A J RUSSELL
Area Bishop of Reading — E W M WALKER

PETERBOROUGH
Bishop of Peterborough — I P M CUNDY
Suffragan Bishop of Brixworth — P E BARBER

PORTSMOUTH
Bishop of Portsmouth — K W STEVENSON
Honorary Assistant Bishops — M E ADIE, H D HALSEY, E E CURTIS, E J K ROBERTS

RIPON
Bishop of Ripon — D N de L YOUNG
Honorary Assistant Bishops — R EMMERSON, J S GAISFORD, D E JENKINS, J W A HOWE
Suffragan Bishop of Knaresborough — *Vacant*

ROCHESTER
Bishop of Rochester — M J NAZIR-ALI
Honorary Assistant Bishop — D R J EVANS
Suffragan Bishop of Tonbridge — B A SMITH

ST ALBANS
Bishop of St Albans — C W HERBERT
Honorary Assistant Bishops — E R BARNES, D J FARMBROUGH, R A K RUNCIE
Suffragan Bishop of Bedford — J H RICHARDSON
Suffragan Bishop of Hertford — R J N SMITH

ST EDMUNDSBURY AND IPSWICH
Bishop of St Edmundsbury & Ipswich — J H R LEWIS
Suffragan Bishop of Dunwich — T J STEVENS

SALISBURY
Bishop of Salisbury — D S STANCLIFFE
Honorary Assistant Bishop — J K CAVELL
Area Bishop of Ramsbury — P St G VAUGHAN
Area Bishop of Sherborne — J D G KIRKHAM

SHEFFIELD
Bishop of Sheffield — J NICHOLLS
Honorary Assistant Bishops — K H PILLAR, K J F SKELTON
Suffragan Bishop of Doncaster — M F GEAR

SODOR AND MAN
Bishop of Sodor and Man — N D JONES

SOUTHWARK
Bishop of Southwark — R K WILLIAMSON
Honorary Assistant Bishops — J T HUGHES, H W MONTEFIORE, S W PHIPPS, E M H CAPPER
Area Bishop of Kingston-upon-Thames — *Vacant*
Area Bishop of Woolwich — C O BUCHANAN
Area Bishop of Croydon — W D WOOD

SOUTHWELL
Bishop of Southwell — P B HARRIS
Honorary Assistant Bishops — R J MILNER, J W H FLAGG
Suffragan Bishop of Sherwood — A W MORGAN

TRURO
Bishop of Truro — W IND
Honorary Assistant Bishop — R F CARTWRIGHT
Suffragan Bishop of St Germans — G R JAMES

WAKEFIELD
Bishop of Wakefield — N S McCULLOCH
Honorary Assistant Bishop — R A M GENDERS
Suffragan Bishop of Pontefract — J T FINNEY

WINCHESTER
Bishop of Winchester — M C SCOTT-JOYNT
Honorary Assistant Bishops — J A BAKER, S BURROWS, H B DEHQANI-TAFTI, L L REES, J YATES
Suffragan Bishop of Basingstoke — D G ROWELL
Suffragan Bishop of Southampton — J M GLEDHILL

WORCESTER
Bishop of Worcester — P S M SELBY
Honorary Assistant Bishops — C D BOND, G C BRIGGS, K J WOOLLCOMBE, J A A MAUND
Area Bishop of Dudley — R W N HOARE

YORK
Archbishop of York, Primate of England and Metropolitan — D M HOPE
Honorary Assistant Bishops — C C BARKER, R G G FOLEY, D G GALLIFORD, R J WOOD
Suffragan Bishop of Hull — J S JONES
Suffragan Bishop of Selby — H V TAYLOR
Suffragan Bishop of Whitby — G BATES
Suffragan Bishop of Beverley (Provincial Episcopal Visitor) — J S GAISFORD

GIBRALTAR IN EUROPE
Bishop of Gibraltar in Europe — J W HIND
Suffragan Bishop in Europe — H W SCRIVEN
Assistant Bishops — E M H CAPPER, D P dos S de PINA CABRAL, M R J MANKTELOW, J W ROWTHORN, A W M WEEKES

CHURCH IN WALES

ST ASAPH
Bishop of St Asaph — A R JONES

BANGOR
Bishop of Bangor — B C MORGAN

ST DAVIDS
Bishop of St Davids — D H JONES

LLANDAFF
Bishop of Llandaff — R T DAVIES

MONMOUTH
Bishop of Monmouth — R D WILLIAMS

SWANSEA AND BRECON
Bishop of Swansea and Brecon — D M BRIDGES

SCOTTISH EPISCOPAL CHURCH

ABERDEEN AND ORKNEY
Bishop of Aberdeen and Orkney — A B CAMERON

ARGYLL AND THE ISLES
Bishop of Argyll and the Isles — D M CAMERON

BRECHIN
Bishop of Brechin — N CHAMBERLAIN

EDINBURGH
Bishop of Edinburgh — R F HOLLOWAY
Assistant Bishop — P C RODGER

GLASGOW AND GALLOWAY
Bishop of Glasgow and Galloway — J M TAYLOR

MORAY, ROSS AND CAITHNESS
Bishop of Moray, Ross and Caithness — G MACGREGOR

ST ANDREWS, DUNKELD AND DUNBLANE
Bishop of St Andrews, Dunkeld and Dunblane — M H G HENLEY

CHURCH OF IRELAND

ARMAGH
Archbishop of Armagh and Primate of All Ireland and Metropolitan — R H A EAMES

CASHEL AND OSSORY
Bishop of Cashel and Ossory — J R W NEILL

CLOGHER
Bishop of Clogher — B D A HANNON

CONNOR
Bishop of Connor — J E MOORE

CORK, CLOYNE AND ROSS
Bishop of Cork, Cloyne and Ross — R A WARKE

DERRY AND RAPHOE
Bishop of Derry and Raphoe — J MEHAFFEY

DOWN AND DROMORE
Bishop of Down and Dromore — H C MILLER

DUBLIN AND GLENDALOUGH
Archbishop of Dublin, Bishop of Glendalough, Primate of Ireland and Metropolitan — W N F EMPEY

KILMORE, ELPHIN AND ARDAGH
Bishop of Kilmore, Elphin and Ardagh — M H G MAYES

LIMERICK AND KILLALOE
Bishop of Limerick and Killaloe — E F DARLING

MEATH AND KILDARE
Bishop of Meath and Kildare — R L CLARKE

TUAM, KILLALA AND ACHONRY
Bishop of Tuam, Killala and Achonry — *Vacant*

BISHOPS IN THE HOUSE OF LORDS

The Archbishops of Canterbury and York, and the Bishops of London, Durham and Winchester always have seats in the House of Lords. Twenty-one of the remaining Diocesan Bishops also sit in the Upper House, and they do so according to their dates of seniority. When a vacancy arises, it is filled by the senior Diocesan Bishop without a seat, and the vacated See is placed at the foot of the list of those awaiting seats. Translation of a Bishop from one See to another does not affect his right to sit in the House of Lords.

The Bishop of Sodor and Man and the Bishop of Gibraltar in Europe are not eligible to sit in the House of Lords, but the former has a seat in the Upper House of the Tynwald, Isle of Man.

ARCHBISHOPS

	Enthroned	Entered House of Lords
CANTERBURY	1991	1991
YORK	1995	1990

BISHOPS SITTING IN THE HOUSE OF LORDS

(as at 1 December 1997)

	Became Diocesan Bishop	Entered House of Lords
LONDON	1995	1996
DURHAM	1988	1994
WINCHESTER	1995	1996
CHICHESTER	1974	1979
RIPON	1977	1984
SOUTHWARK	1984	1988
LICHFIELD	1984	1989
EXETER	1985	1990
BRISTOL	1985	1990
NORWICH	1985	1991
LINCOLN	1987	1993
OXFORD	1987	1993
BIRMINGHAM	1987	1994
SOUTHWELL	1988	1996
BLACKBURN	1989	1995
CARLISLE	1989	1996
ELY	1990	1996
HEREFORD	1990	1997
LEICESTER	1991	1997
BATH AND WELLS	1991	1997
WAKEFIELD	1992	1997
BRADFORD	1992	awaiting introduction
MANCHESTER	1993	awaiting introduction
SALISBURY	1993	awaiting introduction

BISHOPS AWAITING SEATS IN THE HOUSE OF LORDS

(in order of seniority)

	Became Diocesan Bishop
GLOUCESTER	1993
ROCHESTER	1994
GUILDFORD	1994
PORTSMOUTH	1995
DERBY	1995
ST ALBANS	1995
CHELMSFORD	1996
PETERBOROUGH	1996
CHESTER	1996
ST EDMUNDSBURY AND IPSWICH	1997
TRURO	1997
WORCESTER	1997
NEWCASTLE	1997
SHEFFIELD	1997
COVENTRY	*Vacant*
LIVERPOOL	*Vacant*

HISTORICAL SUCCESSION OF ARCHBISHOPS AND BISHOPS

In a number of dioceses, especially for the medieval period, the dating of some episcopal appointments is not known for certain. For ease of reference, the date of consecration is given where known; or, in the case of more modern appointments, the date of confirmation of election. More information on the dates of individual bishops can be found in the Royal Historical Society's *Handbook of British Chronology*.

ENGLAND

PROVINCE OF CANTERBURY

Canterbury

597 Augustine
604 Laurentius
619 Mellitus
624 Justus
627 Honorius
655 Deusdedit
668 Theodorus
693 Berhtwald
731 Tatwine
735 Nothelm
740 Cuthbert
761 Bregowine
765 Jaenberht
793 Æthelheard
805 Wulfred
832 Feologild
833 Ceolnoth
870 Æthelred
890 Plegmund
914 Æthelhelm
923 Wulfhelm
942 Oda
959 Ælfsige
959 Byrhthelm
960 Dunstan
*c.*988 Athelgar
990 Sigeric Serio
995 Ælfric
1005 Ælfheah
1013 Lyfing [Ælfstan]
1020 Æthelnoth
1038 Eadsige
1051 Robert of Jumièges
1052 Stigand
1070 Lanfranc
1093 Anselm
1114 Ralph d'Escures
1123 William de Corbeil
1139 Theobald of Bec
1162 Thomas Becket
1174 Richard [of Dover]
1184 Baldwin
1193 Hubert Walter
1207 Stephen Langton
1229 Richard le Grant
1234 Edmund Rich
1245 Boniface of Savoy
1273 Robert Kilwardby
1279 John Pecham
1294 Robert Winchelsey
1313 Walter Reynolds
1328 Simon Mepham
1333 John Stratford
1349 Thomas Bradwardine
1349 Simon Islip
1366 Simon Langham
1368 William Whittlesey
1375 Simon Sudbury
1381 William Courtenay
1396 Thomas Arundel[1]
1398 Roger Walden
1414 Henry Chichele
1443 John Stafford
1452 John Kempe
1454 Thomas Bourgchier
1486 John Morton
1501 Henry Deane
1503 William Warham
1533 Thomas Cranmer
1556 Reginald Pole
1559 Matthew Parker
1576 Edmund Grindal
1583 John Whitgift
1604 Richard Bancroft
1611 George Abbot
1633 William Laud
1660 William Juxon
1663 Gilbert Sheldon
1678 William Sancroft
1691 John Tillotson
1695 Thomas Tenison
1716 William Wake
1737 John Potter
1747 Thomas Herring
1757 Matthew Hutton
1758 Thomas Secker
1768 Frederick Cornwallis
1783 John Moore
1805 Charles Manners Sutton
1828 William Howley
1848 John Bird Sumner
1862 Charles Thomas Longley
1868 Archibald Campbell Tait
1883 Edward White Benson
1896 Frederick Temple
1903 Randall Thomas Davidson
1928 Cosmo Gordon Lang
1942 William Temple
1945 Geoffrey Francis Fisher
1961 Arthur Michael Ramsey
1974 Frederick Donald Coggan
1980 Robert Alexander Kennedy Runcie
1991 George Leonard Carey

London

Theanus
Eluanus
Cadar
Obinus
Conanus
Palladius
Stephanus
Iltutus
Theodwinus
Theodredus
Hilarius
314 Restitutus
Guitelinus
Fastidius
Vodinus
Theonus
*c.*604 Mellitus
664 Cedd[2]
666 Wini
675 Eorcenwald
693 Waldhere
716 Ingwald
745 Ecgwulf
772 Wigheah
782 Eadbeorht
789 Eadgar
793 Coenwalh
796 Eadbald
798 Heathoberht
803 Osmund
*c.*811 Æthelnoth
824 Ceolberht
862 Deorwulf
898 Swithwulf
898 Heahstan
900 Wulfsige
*c.*926 Æthelweard
926 Leofstan
926 Theodred
— Wulfstan I
953 Brihthelm
959 Dunstan
964 Ælfstan
996 Wulfstan II
1004 Ælfhun
1014 Ælfwig
1035 Ælfweard
1044 Robert of Jumièges
1051 William
1075 Hugh of Orival
1086 Maurice
1108 Richard de Belmeis
1128 Gilbert [the Universal]
1141 Robert de Sigillo
1152 Richard de Belmeis II
1163 Gilbert Foliot
1189 Richard Fitz Neal
1199 William of Ste-Mere-Eglise
1221 Eustace de Fauconberg
1229 Roger Niger
1244 Fulk Basset
1260 Henry Wingham
1263 Henry of Sandwich
1274 John Chishull
1280 Richard Gravesend
1306 Ralph Baldock
1313 Gilbert Segrave
1317 Richard Newport
1319 Stephen Gravesend
1338 Richard Bintworth
1355 Michael Northburgh
1362 Simon Sudbury
1375 William Courtenay
1382 Robert Braybrooke
1404 Roger Walden
1406 Nicholas Bubwith
1407 Richard Clifford
1421 John Kempe
1426 William Gray
1431 Robert Fitz-Hugh

[1] On 19 October 1399 Boniface IX annulled Arundel's translation to St Andrews and confirmed him in the See of Canterbury.
[2] See vacant for a term of years.

1436 Robert Gilbert
1450 Thomas Kempe
1489 Richard Hill
1496 Thomas Savage
1502 William Warham
1504 William Barons [Barnes]
1506 Richard Fitz-James
1522 Cuthbert Tunstall [Tonstall]
1530 John Stokesley
1540 Edmund Bonner
1550 Nicholas Ridley
1553 Edmund Bonner (restored)
1559 Edmund Grindal
1570 Edwin Sandys
1577 John Aylmer
1595 Richard Fletcher
1597 Richard Bancroft
1604 Richard Vaughan
1607 Thomas Ravis
1610 George Abbot
1611 John King
1621 George Monteigne [Mountain]
1628 William Laud
1633 William Juxon
1660 Gilbert Sheldon
1663 Humfrey Henchman
1676 Henry Compton
1714 John Robinson
1723 Edmund Gibson
1748 Thomas Sherlock
1761 Thomas Hayter
1762 Richard Osbaldeston
1764 Richard Terrick
1778 Robert Lowth
1787 Beilby Porteus
1809 John Randolph
1813 William Howley
1828 Charles James Blomfield
1856 Archibald Campbell Tait
1869 John Jackson
1885 Frederick Temple
1897 Mandell Creighton
1901 Arthur Foley Winnington-Ingram
1939 Geoffrey Francis Fisher
1945 John William Charles Wand
1956 Henry Colville Montgomery Campbell
1961 Robert Wright Stopford
1973 Gerald Alexander Ellison
1981 Graham Douglas Leonard
1991 David Michael Hope
1995 Richard John Carew Chartres

†Westminster

1540 Thomas Thirlby

Winchester

BISHOPS OF THE WEST SAXONS

634 Birinus
650 Ægilberht

BISHOPS OF WINCHESTER

660 Wine
670 Leutherius
676 Haedde
705 Daniel
744 Hunfrith
756 Cyneheard
778 Æthelheard
778 Ecbald
785 Dudd
*c.*785 Cyneberht
803 Eahlmund
814 Wigthegn
825 Herefrith[1]
838 Eadmund
*c.*838 Eadhun
839 Helmstan
852 Swithhun
867 Ealhferth
877 Tunberht
879 Denewulf
909 Frithestan
931 Byrnstan
934 Ælfheah I
951 Ælfsige I
960 Brihthelm
963 Æthelwold I
984 Ælfheah II
1006 Cenwulf
1006 Æthelwold II
*c.*1014 Ælfsige II
1032 Ælfwine
1043 Stigand
Ælfsige III?
1070 Walkelin
1107 William Giffard
1129 Henry of Blois
1174 Richard of Ilchester (Toclyve)
1189 Godfrey de Lucy
1205 Peter des Roches
1244 Will. de Raleigh
1260 Aymer de Valance [of Lusignan]
1262 John Gervaise
1268 Nicholas of Ely
1282 John of Pontoise
1305 Henry Merewell [or Woodlock]
1316 John Sandale
1320 Rigaud of Assier
1323 John Stratford
1333 Adam Orleton
1346 William Edendon [Edington]
1367 William of Wykeham
1404 Henry Beaufort
1447 William of Waynflete
1487 Peter Courtenay
1493 Thomas Langton
1501 Richard Fox
1529 Thomas Wolsey
1531 Stephen Gardiner (deposed)
1551 John Ponet [Poynet]
1553 Stephen Gardiner (restored)
1556 John White (deposed)
1561 Robert Horne
1580 John Watson
1584 Thomas Cowper [Cooper]
1595 William Wickham [Wykeham]
1596 William Day
1597 Thomas Bilson
1616 James Montague
1619 Lancelot Andrewes
1628 Richard Neile
1632 Walter Curll
1660 Brian Duppa
1662 George Morley
1684 Peter Mews
1707 Jonathan Trelawney
1721 Charles Trimnell
1723 Richard Willis
1734 Benjamin Hoadly
1761 John Thomas
1781 Brownlow North
1820 George Pretyman Tomline
1827 Charles Richard Sumner
1869 Samuel Wilberforce
1873 Edward Harold Browne
1891 Anthony Wilson Thorold
1895 Randall Thomas Davidson
1903 Herbert Edward Ryle
1911 Edward Stuart Talbot
1923 Frank Theodore Woods
1932 Cyril Forster Garbett
1942 Mervyn George Haigh
1952 Alwyn Terrell Petre Williams
1961 Sherard Falkner Allison
1975 John Vernon Taylor
1985 Colin Clement Walter James
1995 Michael Charles Scott-Joynt

Bath and Wells

BISHOPS OF WELLS

909 Athelm
925 Wulfhelm I
928 Ælfheah
938 Wulfhelm II
956 Byrhthelm
974 Cyneweard
979 Sigegar
997 Ælfwine
999 Lyfing
1013 Æthelwine (ejected)
1013 Beorhtwine (deposed)
Æthelwine (restored)
Beorhtwine (restored)
1024 Brihtwig [also Merehwit]
1033 Duduc
1061 Gisa
1088 John of Tours [de Villula]

BISHOPS OF BATH

1090 John of Tours [de Villula]
1123 Godfrey
1136 Robert
1174 Reg. Fitz Jocelin
1192 Savaric FitzGeldewin

BATH AND GLASTONBURY

1206 Jocelin of Wells

BATH AND WELLS

1244 Roger of Salisbury
1248 William Bitton I
1265 Walter Giffard
1267 William Bitton II
1275 Robert Burnell
1293 William of March
1302 Walter Hasleshaw
1309 John Droxford
1329 Ralph of Shrewsbury
1364 John Barnet
1367 John Harewell
1386 Walter Skirlaw
1388 Ralph Erghum
1401 Henry Bowet
1407 Nicholas Bubwith
1425 John Stafford
1443 Thomas Beckington
1466 Robert Stillington
1492 Richard Fox
1495 Oliver King
1504 Adriano de Castello [di Corneto]
1518 Thomas Wolsey
1523 John Clerk
1541 William Knight
1548 William Barlow
1554 Gilbert Bourne
1560 Gilbert Berkeley
1584 Thomas Godwin
1593 John Still
1608 James Montague
1616 Arthur Lake
1626 William Laud
1628 Leonard Mawe
1629 Walter Curll
1632 William Piers

† Indicates a diocese no longer extant, or united with another diocese.
[1] Never signed without Wigthegn.

1670 Robert Creighton
1673 Peter Mews
1685 Thomas Ken (deposed)
1691 Richard Kidder
1704 George Hooper
1727 John Wynne
1743 Edward Willes
1774 Charles Moss
1802 Richard Beadon
1824 George Henry Law
1845 Richard Bagot
1854 Robert John Eden, Lord Auckland
1869 Arthur Charles Hervey
1894 George Wyndham Kennion
1921 St John Basil Wynne Wilson
1937 Francis Underhill
1943 John William Charles Wand
1946 Harold William Bradfield
1960 Edward Barry Henderson
1975 John Monier Bickersteth
1987 George Leonard Carey
1991 James Lawton Thompson

Birmingham

1905 Charles Gore
1911 Henry Russell Wakefield
1924 Ernest William Barnes
1953 John Leonard Wilson
1969 Laurence Ambrose Brown
1978 Hugh William Montefiore
1987 Mark Santer

Bristol

1542 Paul Bush
1554 John Holyman
1562 Richard Cheyney
1581 John Bullingham (held Gloucester and Bristol 1586-9)
1589 Richard Fletcher
[See vacant for ten years]
1603 John Thornborough
1617 Nicholas Felton
1619 Rowland Searchfield
1623 Robert Wright
1633 George Coke
1637 Robert Skinner
1642 Thomas Westfield
1644 Thomas Howell
1661 Gilbert Ironside
1672 Guy Carleton
1679 William Gulston
1684 John Lake
1685 Jonathan Trelawney
1689 Gilbert Ironside
1691 John Hall
1710 John Robinson
1714 George Smalridge
1719 Hugh Boulter
1724 William Bradshaw
1733 Charles Cecil
1735 Thomas Secker
1737 Thomas Gooch
1738 Joseph Butler
1750 John Conybeare
1756 John Hume
1758 Philip Yonge
1761 Thomas Newton
1782 Lewis Bagot
1783 Christopher Wilson
1792 Spencer Madan
1794 Henry Reginald Courtenay
1797 Ffolliott Herbert Walker Cornewall
1803 George Pelham
1807 John Luxmoore
1808 William Lort Mansel
1820 John Kaye
1827 Robert Gray
1834 Joseph Allen
[1836 to 1897 united with **Gloucester**]
1897 George Forrest Browne
1914 George Nickson
1933 Clifford Salisbury Woodward
1946 Frederick Arthur Cockin
1959 Oliver Stratford Tomkins
1976 Ernest John Tinsley
1985 Barry Rogerson

Chelmsford

1914 John Edwin Watts-Ditchfield
1923 Frederic Sumpter Guy Warman
1929 Henry Albert Wilson
1951 Sherard Falkner Allison
1962 John Gerhard Tiarks
1971 Albert John Trillo
1986 John Waine
1996 John Freeman Perry

Chichester

BISHOPS OF SELSEY

681 Wilfrid
716 Eadberht
731 Eolla
733 Sigga [Sigeferth]
765 Aaluberht
*c.*765 Oswald [Osa]
780 Gislhere
786 Tota
*c.*789 Wihthun
*c.*811 Æthelwulf
824 Cynered
845 Guthheard
900 Wighelm
909 Beornheah
931 Wulfhun
943 Ælfred
955 Daniel
956 Brihthelm
963 Eadhelm
980 Æthelgar
990 Ordbriht
1009 Ælfmaer
1032 Æthelric I
1039 Grimketel
1047 Heca
1058 Æthelric II
1070 Stigand

BISHOPS OF CHICHESTER

1075 Stigand
1088 Godfrey
1091 Ralph Luffa
1125 Seffrid I [d'Escures Pelochin]
1147 Hilary
1174 John Greenford
1180 Seffrid II
1204 Simon FitzRobert
1215 Richard Poore
1218 Ranulf of Wareham
1224 Ralph Nevill
1245 Richard Wich
1254 John Climping
1262 Stephen Bersted [or Pagham]
1288 Gilbert de St Leofard
1305 John Langton
1337 Robert Stratford
1362 William Lenn
1369 William Reade
1386 Thomas Rushock
1390 Richard Mitford
1396 Robert Waldby
1397 Robert Reade
1417 Stephen Patrington
1418 Henry de la Ware
1421 John Kempe
1421 Thomas Polton
1426 John Rickingale
1431 Simon Sydenham
1438 Richard Praty
1446 Adam de Moleyns
1450 Reginald Pecock
1459 John Arundel
1478 Edward Story
1504 Richard Fitz-James
1508 Robert Sherburne
1536 Richard Sampson
1543 George Day (deposed)
1552 John Scory
1553 George Day (restored)
1557 John Christopherson
1559 William Barlow
1570 Richard Curtis
1586 Thomas Bickley
1596 Anthony Watson
1605 Lancelot Andrewes
1609 Samuel Harsnett
1619 George Carleton
1628 Richard Montague
1638 Brian Duppa
1642 Henry King
1670 Peter Gunning
1675 Ralph Brideoake
1679 Guy Carleton
1685 John Lake
1689 Simon Patrick
1691 Robert Grove
1696 John Williams
1709 Thomas Manningham
1722 Thomas Bowers
1724 Edward Waddington
1731 Francis Hare
1740 Matthias Mawson
1754 William Ashburnham
1798 John Buckner
1824 Robert James Carr
1831 Edward Maltby
1836 William Otter
1840 Philip Nicholas Shuttleworth
1842 Ashurst Turner Gilbert
1870 Richard Durnford
1896 Ernest Roland Wilberforce
1908 Charles John Ridgeway
1919 Winfrid Oldfield Burrows
1929 George Kennedy Allen Bell
1958 Roger Plumpton Wilson
1974 Eric Waldram Kemp

Coventry

1918 Huyshe Wolcott Yeatman-Biggs
1922 Charles Lisle Carr
1931 Mervyn George Haigh
1943 Neville Vincent Gorton
1956 Cuthbert Killick Norman Bardsley
1976 John Gibbs
1985 Simon Barrington-Ward

Derby

1927 Edmund Courtenay Pearce
1936 Alfred Edward John Rawlinson
1959 Geoffrey Francis Allen
1969 Cyril William Johnston Bowles
1988 Peter Spencer Dawes
1995 Jonathan Sansbury Bailey

Dorchester[1]

634 Birinus
650 Agilbert
*c.*660 Ætla
*c.*888 Ahlheard

Ely

1109 Hervey
1133 Nigel
1174 Geoffrey Ridel
1189 William Longchamp
1198 Eustace
1220 John of Fountains
1225 Geoffrey de Burgo
1229 Hugh of Northwold
1255 William of Kilkenny
1258 Hugh of Balsham
1286 John of Kirkby
1290 William of Louth
1299 Ralph Walpole
1303 Robert Orford
1310 John Ketton
1316 John Hotham
1337 Simon Montacute
1345 Thomas de Lisle
1362 Simon Langham
1367 John Barnet
1374 Thomas Arundel
1388 John Fordham
1426 Philip Morgan
1438 Lewis of Luxembourg
1444 Thomas Bourgchier
1454 William Grey
1479 John Morton
1486 John Alcock
1501 Richard Redman
1506 James Stanley
1515 Nicholas West
1534 Thomas Goodrich
1555 Thomas Thirlby
1559 Richard Cox
1600 Martin Heton
1609 Lancelot Andrewes
1619 Nicolas Felton
1628 John Buckeridge
1631 Francis White
1638 Matthew Wren
1667 Benjamin Laney
1675 Peter Gunning
1684 Francis Turner
1691 Simon Patrick
1707 John Moore
1714 William Fleetwood
1723 Thomas Greene
1738 Robert Butts
1748 Thomas Gooch
1754 Matthias Mawson
1771 Edmund Keene
1781 James Yorke
1808 Thomas Dampier
1812 Bowyer Edward Sparke
1836 Joseph Allen
1845 Thomas Turton
1864 Edward Harold Browne
1873 James Russell Woodford
1886 Alwyne Frederick Compton
1905 Frederick Henry Chase
1924 Leonard Jauncey White-Thomson
1934 Bernard Oliver Francis Heywood
1941 Harold Edward Wynn
1957 Noel Baring Hudson
1964 Edward James Keymer Roberts
1977 Peter Knight Walker
1990 Stephen Whitefield Sykes

Exeter

BISHOPS OF CORNWALL

870 Kenstec
893 Asser
931 Conan
950 Æthelge[ard]
*c.*955 Daniel
963 Wulfsige Comoere
990 Ealdred
1009 Æthelsige
1018 Buruhwold
1027 Lyfing, Bishop of Crediton Cornwall and Worcester
1046 Leofric Bishop of Crediton and Cornwall
[See transferred to Exeter 1050]

BISHOPS OF CREDITON

909 Eadwulf
934 Æthelgar
953 Ælfwold I
973 Sideman
979 Ælfric
987 Ælfwold II
1008 Ælfwold III
1015 Eadnoth
1027 Lyfing
1046 Leofric[2]

BISHOPS OF EXETER

1050 Leofric
1072 Osbern Fitz-Osbern
1107 Will. Warelwast
1138 Robert Warelwast
1155 Robert II of Chichester
1161 Bartholomew
1186 John the Chanter
1194 Henry Marshall
1214 Simon of Apulia
1224 William Brewer
1245 Richard Blund
1258 Walter Bronescombe
1280 Peter Quinel [Wyvill]
1292 Thomas Bitton
1308 Walter Stapeldon
1327 James Berkeley
1328 John Grandisson
1370 Thomas Brantingham
1395 Edmund Stafford
1419 John Catterick
1420 Edmund Lacy
1458 George Nevill
1465 John Booth
1478 Peter Courtenay
1487 Richard Fox
1493 Oliver King
1496 Richard Redman
1502 John Arundel
1505 Hugh Oldham
1519 John Veysey (resigned)
1551 Miles Coverdale
1553 John Veysey (restored)
1555 James Turberville
1560 William Alley [or Allei]
1571 William Bradbridge
1579 John Woolton
1595 Gervase Babington
1598 William Cotton
1621 Valentine Carey
1627 Joseph Hall
1642 Ralph Brownrigg
1660 John Gauden
1662 Seth Ward
1667 Anthony Sparrow
1676 Thomas Lamplugh
1689 Jonathan Trelawney
1708 Offspring Blackall
1717 Lancelot Blackburn
1724 Stephen Weston
1742 Nicholas Claget
1747 George Lavington
1762 Frederick Keppel
1778 John Ross
1792 William Buller
1797 Henry Reginald Courtenay
1803 John Fisher
1807 George Pelham
1820 William Carey
1830 Christopher Bethell
1831 Henry Phillpotts
1869 Frederick Temple
1885 Edward Henry Bickersteth
1901 Herbert Edward Ryle
1903 Archibald Robertson
1916 Rupert Ernest William Gascoyne Cecil
1936 Charles Edward Curzon
1949 Robert Cecil Mortimer
1973 Eric Arthur John Mercer
1985 Geoffrey Hewlett Thompson

Gloucester

1541 John Wakeman *alias* Wiche
1551 John Hooper
1554 James Brooks
1562 Richard Cheyney[3]
1581 John Bullingham[4]
1598 Godfrey Goldsborough
1605 Thomas Ravis
1607 Henry Parry
1611 Giles Thompson
1612 Miles Smith
1625 Godfrey Goodman
1661 William Nicolson
1672 John Pritchett
1681 Robert Frampton
1691 Edward Fowler
1715 Richard Willis
1721 Joseph Wilcocks
1731 Elias Sydall
1735 Martin Benson
1752 James Johnson
1760 William Warburton
1779 James Yorke
1781 Samuel Hallifax
1789 Richard Beadon
1802 George Isaac Huntingford
1815 Henry Ryder
1824 Christopher Bethell
1830 James Henry Monk
[1836 to 1897, united with Bristol]

BISHOPS OF GLOUCESTER AND BRISTOL

1836 James Henry Monk
1856 Charles Baring
1861 William Thomson
1863 Charles John Ellicott[5]

BISHOPS OF GLOUCESTER

1897 Charles John Ellicott
1905 Edgar Charles Sumner Gibson
1923 Arthur Cayley Headlam
1946 Clifford Salisbury Woodward
1954 Wilfred Marcus Askwith
1962 Basil Tudor Guy
1975 John Yates
1992 Peter John Ball
1993 David Edward Bentley

Guildford

1927 John Harold Greig
1934 John Victor Macmillan

[1] Originally a West Saxon, after Ahlheard's time a Mercian, bishopric. See transferred to Lincoln 1077.
[2] Removed See from Crediton. [3] Also Bishop of Bristol. [4] Held Gloucester and Bristol 1581-9. [5] Gloucester only from 1897.

1949 Henry Colville Montgomery Campbell
1956 Ivor Stanley Watkins
1961 George Edmund Reindorp
1973 David Alan Brown
1983 Michael Edgar Adie
1994 John Warren Gladwin

Hereford

676 Putta
688 Tyrhtel
710 Torhthere
c.731 Wahistod
736 Cuthberht
741 Podda
c.758 Acca
c.770 Headda
777 Aldberht
786 Esne
c.788 Ceolmund
c.798 Utel
801 Wulfheard
824 Beonna
c.832 Eadwulf
c.839 Cuthwulf
866 Mucel
c.866 Deorlaf
888 Cynemund
890 EadBar
c.931 Tidhelm
940 Wulfhelm
c.940 Ælfric
971 Æthelwulf
1016 Æthelstan
1056 Leofgar
1056 Ealdred, Bishop of Hereford and Worcester
1060 Walter
1079 Robert Losinga
1096 Gerard
1107 Reinhelm
1115 Geoffrey de Clive
1121 Richard de Capella
1131 Robert de Bethune
1148 Gilbert Foliot
1163 Robert of Melun
1174 Robert Foliot
1186 William de Vere
1200 Giles de Braose
1216 Hugh of Mapenore
1219 Hugh Foliot
1234 Ralph Maidstone
1240 Peter d'Aigueblanche
1269 John Breton
1275 Thomas Cantilupe
1283 Richard Swinfeld
1317 Adam Orleton
1327 Thomas Chariton
1344 John Trilleck
1361 Lewis Charleton
1370 William Courtenay
1375 John Gilbert
1389 John Trefnant
1404 Robert Mascall
1417 Edmund Lacy
1420 Thomas Polton
1422 Thomas Spofford
1449 Richard Beauchamp
1451 Reginald Boulers
1453 John Stanbury
1474 Thomas Milling
1492 Edmund Audley
1502 Adriano de Castello [di Corneto]
1504 Richard Mayeu
1516 Charles Booth
1535 Edward Fox
1539 John Skip
1553 John Harley
1554 Robert Parfew or Wharton
1559 John Scory
1586 Herbert Westfaling
1603 Robert Bennett
1617 Francis Godwin
1634 Augustine Lindsell
1635 Matthew Wren
1635 Theophilus Field
1636 George Coke
1661 Nicolas Monk
1662 Herbert Croft
1691 Gilbert Ironside
1701 Humphrey Humphries
1713 Philip Bisse
1721 Benjamin Hoadly
1724 Henry Egerton
1746 James Beauclerk
1787 John Harley
1788 John Butler
1803 Ffolliott Herbert Walker Cornewall
1808 John Luxmoore
1815 George Isaac Huntingford
1832 Edward Grey
1837 Thomas Musgrave
1848 Renn Dickson Hampden
1868 James Atlay
1895 John Percival
1918 Herbert Hensley Henson
1920 Martin Linton Smith
1931 Charles Lisle Carr
1941 Richard Godfrey Parsons
1949 Tom Longworth
1961 Mark Allin Hodson
1974 John Richard Gordon Eastaugh
1990 John Keith Oliver

Leicester

see also under Lincoln

NEW FOUNDATION

1927 Cyril Charles Bowman Bardsley
1940 Guy Vernon Smith
1953 Ronald Ralph Williams
1979 Cecil Richard Rutt
1991 Thomas Frederick Butler

Lichfield

BISHOPS OF MERCIA

656 Diuma[1]
658 Ceollach
659 Trumhere
662 Jaruman

BISHOPS OF LICHFIELD

669 Chad[2]
672 Winfrith
676 Seaxwulf
691 Headda[3]
731 Aldwine
737 Hwita
757 Hemele
765 Cuthfrith
769 Berhthun
779 Hygeberht[4]
801 Aldwulf
816 Herewine
818 Æthelwald
830 Hunberht
836 Cyneferth
845 Tunberht
869 Eadberht
883 Wulfred
900 Wigmund or Wilferth
915 Ælfwine
941 Wulfgar
949 Cynesige
964 Wynsige
975 Ælfheah
1004 Godwine
1020 Leofgar
1026 Brihtmaer
1039 Wulfsige
1053 Leofwine
1072 Peter

BISHOPS OF LICHFIELD, CHESTER, AND COVENTRY[5]

1075 Peter
1086 Robert de Limesey[5]
1121 Robert Peche
1129 Roger de Clinton
1149 Walter Durdent
1161 Richard Peche
1183 Gerard La Pucelle
1188 Hugh Nonant
1198 Geoffrey Muschamp
1215 William Cornhill
1224 Alex. Stavensby
1240 Hugh Pattishall
1246 Roger Weseham
1258 Roger Longespee
1296 Walter Langton
1322 Roger Northburgh
1360 Robert Stretton
1386 Walter Skirlaw
1386 Richard le Scrope
1398 John Burghill
1415 John Catterick
1420 William Heyworth
1447 William Booth
1452 Nicholas Close
1453 Reginald Boulers
1459 John Hales
1493 William Smith
1496 John Arundel
1503 Geoffrey Blyth
1534 Rowland Lee
1541 [**Chester** formed as a bishopric]
1543 Richard Sampson
1554 Ralph Baynes
1560 Thomas Bentham
1580 William Overton
1609 George Abbot
1610 Richard Neile
1614 John Overall
1619 Thomas Morton
1632 Robert Wright
1644 Accepted Frewen
1661 John Hackett
1671 Thomas Wood
1692 William Lloyd
1699 John Hough
1717 Edward Chandler
1731 Richard Smalbroke

[1] Archbishop of the Mercians, the Lindisfari, and the Middle Angles.
[2] Bishop of the Mercians and Lindisfari.
[3] Bishop of Lichfield and Leicester.
[4] Archbishop of Lichfield after 787.
[5] 1102 Robert de Limesey, Bishop of Lichfield, moved the See to Coventry. Succeeding Bishops are usually termed *of Coventry* until 1228. Then *Coventry and Lichfield* was the habitual title until the Reformation. *Chester* was used by some 12th-century Bishops, and popularly afterwards. After the Reformation *Lichfield and Coventry* was used until 1846.

1750 Fred. Cornwallis
1768 John Egerton
1771 Brownlow North
1775 Richard Hurd
1781 James Cornwallis [4th Earl Cornwallis]
1824 Henry Ryder
1836 [Coventry transferred to Worcester diocese]
1836 Samuel Butler
1840 James Bowstead
1843 John Lonsdale
1868 George Augustus Selwyn
1878 William Dalrymple Maclagan
1891 Augustus Legge
1913 John Augustine Kempthorne
1937 Edward Sydney Woods
1953 Arthur Stretton Reeve
1975 Kenneth John Fraser Skelton
1984 Keith Norman Sutton

Lincoln

BISHOPS OF LINDSEY

634 Birinus
650 Agilbert
660 Aetlai
678 Eadhaed
680 Æthelwine
693 (?)Edgar
731 (?)Cyneberht
733 Alwig
750 Aldwulf
767 Ceolwulf
796 Eadwulf
839 Beorhtred
869 Burgheard
933 Ælfred
953 Leofwine
996 Sigefrith

BISHOPS OF LEICESTER

664 Wilfrid, translated from York
679 Cuthwine
691 Headda[1] (founder of Lichfield Cathedral 705-37)
727 Aldwine
737 Torhthelm
764 Eadberht
785 Unwona
803 Wernberht
816 Raethhun
840 Ealdred
844 Ceolred
874 [See of Leicester removed to Dorchester]

BISHOPS OF DORCHESTER

(after it became a Mercian See)

*c.*888 Ahlheard
900 Wigmund or Wilferth
909 Cenwulf
925 Wynsige
*c.*951 Osketel
953 Leofwine
975 Ælfnoth
979 Æscwig
1002 Ælfheln
1006 Eadnoth I
1016 Æthelric
1034 Eadnoth II
1049 Ulf
1053 Wulfwig
1067 Remigius

BISHOPS OF LINCOLN

1072 Remigius
1094 Robert Bloett
1123 Alexander
1148 Robert de Chesney
1183 Walter de Coutances
1186 Hugh of Avalon
1203 William of Blois
1209 Hugh of Wells
1235 Robert Grosseteste
1254 Henry Lexington [Sutton]
1258 Richard Gravesend
1280 Oliver Sutton [Lexington]
1300 John Dalderby
1320 Henry Burghersh
1342 Thomas Bek
1347 John Gynewell
1363 John Bokyngham [Buckingham]
1398 Henry Beaufort
1405 Philip Repingdon
1420 Richard Fleming
1431 William Gray
1436 William Alnwick
1450 Marmaduke Lumley
1452 John Chedworth
1472 Thomas Rotherham [Scott]
1480 John Russell
1495 William Smith
1514 Thomas Wolsey
1514 William Atwater
1521 John Longland
1547 Henry Holbeach [Rands]
1552 John Taylor
1554 John White
1557 Thomas Watson
1560 Nicholas Bullingham
1571 Thomas Cooper
1584 William Wickham
1595 William Chaderton
1608 William Barlow
1614 Richard Neile
1617 George Monteigne [Mountain]
1621 John Williams
1642 Thomas Winniffe
1660 Robt. Sanderson
1663 Benjamin Laney
1667 William Fuller
1675 Thomas Barlow
1692 Thomas Tenison
1695 James Gardiner
1705 William Wake
1716 Edmund Gibson
1723 Richard Reynolds
1744 John Thomas
1761 John Green
1779 Thomas Thurlow
1787 George Pretyman [Pretyman Tomline after June 1803]
1820 George Pelham
1827 John Kaye
1853 John Jackson
1869 Christopher Wordsworth
1885 Edward King
1910 Edward Lee Hicks
1920 William Shuckburgh Swayne
1933 Frederick Cyril Nugent Hicks
1942 Henry Aylmer Skelton
1946 Leslie Owen
1947 Maurice Henry Harland
1956 Kenneth Riches
1975 Simon Wilton Phipps
1987 Robert Maynard Hardy

Norwich

BISHOPS OF DUNWICH

631 Felix
648 Thomas
*c.*653 Berhtgils [Boniface]
*c.*670 Bisi
*c.*673 Æcce
693 Alric (?)
716 Eardred
731 Aldbeorht I
747 Æscwulf
747 Eardwulf
775 Cuthwine
775 Aldbeorht II
781 Ecglaf
781 Heardred
793 Ælfhun
798 Tidferth
824 Waermund[2]
825 Wilred
836 Husa
870 Æthelwold

BISHOPS OF ELMHAM

673 Beaduwine
706 Nothberht
*c.*731 Heathulac
736 Æthelfrith
758 Eanfrith
*c.*781 Æthelwulf
*c.*785 Alhheard
814 Sibba
824 Hunferth
824 Hunbeorht
836 Cunda[3]
*c.*933 Ælfred[4]
*c.*945 Æthelweald
956 Eadwulf
970 Ælfric I
974 Theodred I
982 Theodred II
997 Æthelstan
1001 Ælfgar
1021 Ælfwine
1038 Ælfric II
1039 Ælfric III
1043 Stigand[5]
1043 Grimketel[6]
1044 Stigand (restored)
1047 Æthelmaer

BISHOPS OF THETFORD

1070 Herfast
1086 William de Beaufai
1091 Herbert Losinga

BISHOPS OF NORWICH

1091 Herbert Losinga
1121 Everard of Montgomery
1146 William de Turbe
1175 John of Oxford
1200 John de Gray
1222 Pandulf Masca
1226 Thomas Blundeville
1239 William Raleigh
1245 Walter Suffield or Calthorp
1258 Simon Walton
1266 Roger Skerning
1278 William Middleton
1289 Ralph Walpole
1299 John Salmon
1325 [Robert de Baldock]
1325 William Ayermine

[1] Bishop of Leicester and Lichfield.
[2] Bishop of Dunwich or Elmham.
[3] Bishop of Elmham or Dunwich.
[4] Bishop of Elmham or Lindsey.
[5] Deposed before consecration.
[6] Bishop of Selsey and Elmham.

1337 Anthony Bek
1344 William of Norwich [Bateman]
1356 Thomas Percy
1370 Henry Spencer [Dispenser]
1407 Alexander Tottington
1413 Richard Courtenay
1416 John Wakeryng
1426 William Ainwick
1436 Thomas Brown
1446 Walter Lyhert [le Hart]
1472 James Goldwell
1499 Thomas Jane
1501 Richard Nykke
1536 William Reppes [Rugge]
1550 Thomas Thirlby
1554 John Hopton
1560 John Parkhurst
1575 Edmund Freke
1585 Edmund Scambler
1595 William Redman
1603 John Jegon
1618 John Overall
1619 Samuel Harsnett
1629 Francis White
1632 Richard Corbet
1635 Matthew Wren
1638 Richard Montagu
1641 Joseph Hall
1661 Edward Reynolds
1676 Antony Sparrow
1685 William Lloyd
1691 John Moore
1708 Charles Trimnell
1721 Thomas Green
1723 John Leng
1727 William Baker
1733 Robert Butts
1738 Thomas Gooch
1748 Samuel Lisle
1749 Thomas Hayter
1761 Philip Yonge
1783 Lewis Bagot
1790 George Horne
1792 Charles Manners Sutton
1805 Henry Bathurst
1837 Edward Stanley
1849 Samuel Hinds
1857 John Thomas Pelham
1893 John Sheepshanks
1910 Bertram Pollock
1942 Percy Mark Herbert
1959 William Launcelot Scott Fleming
1971 Maurice Arthur Ponsonby Wood
1985 Peter John Nott

Oxford

1542 Robert King[1]
1558 [Thomas Goldwell]
1567 Hugh Curen [Curwen]
1589 John Underhill
1604 John Bridges
1619 John Howson
1628 Richard Corbet
1632 John Bancroft
1641 Robert Skinner
1663 William Paul
1665 Walter Blandford
1671 Nathaniel Crewe [Lord Crewe]
1674 Henry Compton
1676 John Fell
1686 Samuel Parker
1688 Timothy Hall
1690 John Hough
1699 William Talbot
1715 John Potter
1737 Thomas Secker
1758 John Hume
1766 Robert Lowth
1777 John Butler
1788 Edward Smallwell
1799 John Randolph
1807 Charles Moss
1812 William Jackson
1816 Edward Legge
1827 Charles Lloyd
1829 Richard Bagot
1845 Samuel Wilberforce
1870 John Fielder Mackarness
1889 William Stubbs
1901 Francis Paget
1911 Charles Gore
1919 Hubert Murray Burge
1925 Thomas Banks Strong
1937 Kenneth Escott Kirk
1955 Harry James Carpenter
1971 Kenneth John Woollcombe
1978 Patrick Campbell Rodger
1987 Richard Douglas Harries

Peterborough

1541 John Chamber
1557 David Pole
1561 Edmund Scambler
1585 Richard Howland
1601 Thomas Dove
1630 William Piers
1633 Augustine Lindsell
1634 Francis Dee
1639 John Towers
1660 Benjamin Laney
1663 Joseph Henshaw
1679 William Lloyd
1685 Thomas White
1691 Richard Cumberland
1718 White Kennett
1729 Robert Clavering
1747 John Thomas
1757 Richard Terrick
1764 Robert Lambe
1769 John Hinchliffe
1794 Spencer Madan
1813 John Parsons
1819 Herbert Marsh
1839 George Davys
1864 Francis Jeune
1868 William Connor Magee
1891 Mandell Creighton
1897 Edward Carr Glyn
1916 Frank Theodore Woods
1924 Cyril Charles Bowman Bardsley
1927 Claude Martin Blagden
1949 Spencer Stottisbury Gwatkin Leeson
1956 Robert Wright Stopford
1961 Cyril Eastaugh
1972 Douglas Russell Feaver
1984 William John Westwood
1996 Ian Patrick Martyn Cundy

Portsmouth

1927 Ernest Neville Lovett
1936 Frank Partridge
1942 William Louis Anderson
1949 William Launcelot Scott Fleming
1960 John Henry Lawrence Phillips
1975 Archibald Ronald McDonald Gordon
1985 Timothy John Bavin
1995 Kenneth William Stevenson

Rochester

604 Justus
624 Romanus
633 Paulinus
644 Ithamar
664 Damianus
669 Putta
676 Cwichelm
678 Gebmund
716 Tobias
727 Aldwulf
741 Dunn
747 Eardwulf
772 Diora
785 Waermund I
805 Beornmod
844 Tatnoth
868 Badenoth
868 Waermund II
868 Cuthwulf
880 Swithwulf
900 Ceolmund
*c.*926 Cyneferth
*c.*934 Burhric
949 Beorhtsige
955 [Daniel?] Rochester or Selsey
964 Ælfstan
995 Godwine I
1046 Godwine II
1058 Siward
1076 Arnost
1077 Gundulf
1108 Ralph d'Escures
1115 Ernulf
1125 John
1137 John II
1142 Ascelin
1148 Walter
1182 Waleran
1185 Gilbert Glanvill
1215 Benedict of Sausetun [Sawston]
1227 Henry Sandford
1238 Richard Wendene
1251 Lawrence of St Martin
1274 Walter Merton
1278 John Bradfield
1283 Thomas Ingoldsthorpe
1292 Thomas of Wouldham
1319 Hamo Hethe
1353 John Sheppey
1362 William of Whittlesey
1364 Thomas Trilleck
1373 Thomas Brinton
1389 William Bottlesham [Bottisham]
1400 John Bottlesham
1404 Richard Young
1419 John Kempe
1422 John Langdon
1435 Thomas Brouns
1437 William Wells
1444 John Low
1468 Thomas Rotherham [otherwise Scott]
1472 John Alcock
1476 John Russell
1480 Edmund Audley
1493 Thomas Savage
1497 Richard Fitz-James
1504 John Fisher
1535 John Hilsey [Hildesleigh]
1540 Nicolas Heath
1544 Henry Holbeach
1547 Nicholas Ridley
1550 John Ponet [Poynet]
1551 John Scory
1554 Maurice Griffith
1560 Edmund Gheast [Guest]

[1] Bishop Rheon. *in partibus*. Of Oseney 1542-5. See transferred to Oxford 1545.

1572 Edmund Freke
1576 John Piers
1578 John Young
1605 William Barlow
1608 Richard Neile
1611 John Buckeridge
1628 Walter Curil
1630 John Bowle
1638 John Warner
1666 John Dolben
1683 Francis Turner
1684 Thomas Sprat
1713 Francis Atterbury
1723 Samuel Bradford
1731 Joseph Wilcocks
1756 Zachary Pearce
1774 John Thomas
1793 Samuel Horsley
1802 Thomas Dampier
1809 Walker King
1827 Hugh Percy
1827 George Murray
1860 Joseph Cotton Wigram
1867 Thomas Legh Claughton
1877 Anthony Wilson Thorold
1891 Randall Thomas Davidson
1895 Edward Stuart Talbot
1905 John Reginald Harmer
1930 Martin Linton Smith
1940 Christopher Maude Chavasse
1961 Richard David Say
1988 Anthony Michael Arnold Turnbull
1994 Michael James Nazir-Ali

St Albans

1877 Thomas Legh Claughton
1890 John Wogan Festing
1903 Edgar Jacob
1920 Michael Bolton Furse
1944 Philip Henry Loyd
1950 Edward Michael Gresford Jones
1970 Robert Alexander Kennedy Runcie
1980 John Bernard Taylor
1995 Christopher William Herbert

St Edmundsbury and Ipswich

1914 Henry Bernard Hodgson
1921 Albert Augustus David
1923 Walter Godfrey Whittingham
1940 Richard Brook
1954 Arthur Harold Morris
1966 Leslie Wilfrid Brown
1978 John Waine
1986 John Dennis
1997 John Hubert Richard Lewis

Salisbury

BISHOPS OF SHERBORNE

705 Ealdhelm
709 Forthhere
736 Hereweald
774 Æthelmod
793 Denefrith
801 Wigberht
825 Ealhstan
868 Heahmund
877 Æthelheah
889 Wulfsige I
900 Asser
*c.*909 Æthelweard
*c.*909 Waerstan
925 Æthelbald
925 Sigehelm
934 Ælfred
943 Wulfsige II
958 Ælfwold I
979 Æthelsige I
992 Wulfsige III
1002 Æthelric
1012 Æthelsige II
1017 Brihtwine I
1017 Ælfmaer
1023 Brihtwine II
1045 Ælfwold II
1058 Hereman, Bp of Ramsbury

BISHOPS OF RAMSBURY

909 Æthelstan
927 Oda
949 Ælfric I
951 Osulf
970 Ælfstan
981 Wulfgar
986 Sigeric
993 Ælfric II
1005 Brihtwold
1045 Hereman[1]

BISHOPS OF SALISBURY

1078 Osmund
Osmer
1107 Roger
1142 Jocelin de Bohun
1189 Hubert Walter
1194 Herbert Poore
1217 Richard Poore
1229 Robert Bingham
1247 William of York
1257 Giles of Bridport
1263 Walter de la Wyle
1274 Robert Wickhampton
1284 Walter Scammel
1287 Henry Brandeston
1289 William de la Corner
1292 Nicholas Longespee
1297 Simon of Ghent
1315 Roger de Mortival
1330 Robert Wyville
1375 Ralph Erghum
1388 John Waltham
1395 Richard Mitford
1407 Nicholas Bubwith
1407 Robert Hallum
1417 John Chaundler
1427 Robert Nevill
1438 William Aiscough
1450 Richard Beauchamp
1482 Lionel Woodville
1485 Thomas Langton
1494 John Blythe
1500 Henry Deane
1502 Edmund Audley
1525 Lorenzo Campeggio
1535 Nicholas Shaxton
1539 John Salcot [Capon]
1560 John Jewell
1571 Edmund Gheast [Guest]
1577 John Piers
1591 John Coldwell
1598 Henry Cotton
1615 Robert Abbot
1618 Martin Fotherby
1620 Robert Townson [Toulson]
1621 John Davenant
1641 Brian Duppa
1660 Humfrey Henchman
1663 John Earle
1665 Alexander Hyde
1667 Seth Ward
1689 Gilbert Burnet
1715 William Talbot
1721 Richard Wilis
1723 Benjamin Hoadly
1734 Thomas Sherlock
1748 John Gilbert
1757 John Thomas
1761 Robert Hay Drummond
1761 John Thomas
1766 John Hume
1782 Shute Barrington
1791 John Douglas
1807 John Fisher
1825 Thomas Burgess
1837 Edward Denison
1854 Walter Kerr Hamilton
1869 George Moberly
1885 John Wordsworth
1911 Frederic Edward Ridgeway
1921 St Clair George Alfred Donaldson
1936 Ernest Neville Lovett
1946 Geoffrey Charles Lester Lunt
1949 William Louis Anderson
1963 Joseph Edward Fison
1973 George Edmund Reindorp
1982 John Austin Baker
1993 David Staffurth Stancliffe

Southwark

1905 Edward Stuart Talbot
1911 Hubert Murray Burge
1919 Cyril Forster Garbett
1932 Richard Godfrey Parsons
1942 Bertram Fitzgerald Simpson
1959 Arthur Mervyn Stockwood
1980 Ronald Oliver Bowlby
1991 Robert Kerr Williamson

Truro

1877 Edward White Benson
1883 George Howard Wilkinson
1891 John Gott
1906 Charles William Stubbs
1912 Winfrid Oldfield Burrows
1919 Frederic Sumpter Guy Warman
1923 Walter Howard Frere
1935 Joseph Wellington Hunkin
1951 Edmund Robert Morgan
1960 John Maurice Key
1973 Graham Douglas Leonard
1981 Peter Mumford
1990 Michael Thomas Ball
1997 William Ind

Worcester

680 Bosel
691 Oftfor
693 Ecgwine
718 Wilfrid I
745 Milred
775 Waermund
777 Tilhere
781 Heathured
798 Deneberht
822 Heahberht
845 Alhhun
873 Waerferth
915 Æthelhun
922 Wilferth II
929 Cenwald
957 Dunstan
961 Oswald
992 Ealdwulf
1002 Wulfstan I
1016 Leofsige
1027 Lyfing
1033 Brihtheah
1040 Æltric Puttoc, Bp of York and Worcester

[1] Ramsbury was added to Sherborne in 1058 when Hereman became Bishop of Sherborne. The See was moved to Salisbury in 1078.

1041 Lyfing (restored)
1046 Ealdred Bp of Hereford and Worcester 1056-60
1062 Wulfstan II
1096 Samson
1115 Theulf
1125 Simon
1151 John of Pagham
1158 Aldred
1164 Roger of Gloucester
1180 Baldwin
1186 William of Northolt
1191 Robert Fitz Ralph
1193 Henry de Sully
1196 John of Coutances
1200 Mauger
1214 Walter de Gray
1216 Silvester of Evesham
1218 William of Blois
1237 Walter Cantilupe
1266 Nicolas of Ely
1268 Godfrey Giffard
1302 Walter Gainsborough
1308 Walter Reynolds
1313 Walter Maidstone
1317 Thomas Cobham
1327 Adam Orleton
1334 Simon Montacute
1337 Thomas Hempnall
1339 Wulstan Bransford
1350 John Thoresby
1353 Reginald Brian
1362 John Barnet
1364 William of Whittlesey
1369 William Lenn
1375 Henry Wakefield
1396 Robert Tideman of Winchcomb
1401 Richard Clifford
1407 Thomas Peverel
1419 Philip Morgan
1426 Thomas Polton
1435 Thomas Bourgchier
1444 John Carpenter
1476 John Alcock
1487 Robert Morton
1497 Giovanni de' Gigli
1499 Silvestro de' Gigli
1521 Julius de Medici Guilio de Medici (administrator)
1523 Geronimo Ghinucci
1535 Hugh Latimer
1539 John Bell
1544 Nicholas Heath (deposed)
1552 John Hooper
1554 Nicholas Heath (restored)
1555 Richard Pates
1559 Edwin Sandys
1571 Nicholas Bullingham
1577 John Whitgift
1584 Edmund Freke
1593 Richard Fletcher
1596 Thomas Bilson
1597 Gervase Babington
1610 Henry Parry
1617 John Thornborough
1641 John Prideaux
1660 George Morley
1662 John Gauden
1662 John Earle
1663 Robert Skinner
1671 Walter Blandford
1675 James Fleetwood
1683 William Thomas
1689 Edward Stillingfleet
1699 William Lloyd
1717 John Hough
1743 Isaac Maddox
1759 James Johnson
1774 Brownlow North
1781 Richard Hurd
1808 Ffoliott Herbert Walker Cornewall
1831 Robert James Carr
1841 Henry Pepys
1861 Henry Philpott
1891 John James Stewart Perowne
1902 Charles Gore
1905 Huyshe Wolcott Yeatman-Biggs
1919 Ernest Harold Pearce
1931 Arthur William Thomson Perowne
1941 William Wilson Cash
1956 Lewis Mervyn Charles-Edwards
1971 Robert Wylmer Woods
1982 Philip Harold Ernest Goodrich
1997 Peter Stephen Maurice Selby

PROVINCE OF YORK

York

BISHOPS

314 Eborius
625 Paulinus
[Vacancy 633-64]
664 Cedda
664 Wilfrid I
678 Bosa (retired)
686 Bosa (restored)
691 Wilfrith (restored)
706 John of Beverley
718 Wilfrid II

ARCHBISHOPS

734 Egberht
767 Æthelberht
780 Eanbald I
796 Eanbald II
808 Wulfsige
837 Wigmund
854 Wulfhere
900 Æthelbald
*c.*928 Hrothweard
931 Wulfstan I
956 Osketel
971 Oswald
971 Edwald
992 Ealdwulf[1]
1003 Wulfstan II
1023 Ælfric Puttoc
1041 Æthelric
1051 Cynesige
1061 Ealdred
1070 Thomas I of Bayeux
1100 Gerard
1109 Thomas II
1119 Thurstan
1143 William Fitzherbert
1147 Henry Murdac
1153 William Fitzherbert (restored)
1154 Roger of Pont l'Eveque
1191 Geoffrey Plantagenet
1215 Walter de Gray
1256 Sewal de Bovill
1258 Godfrey Ludham [Kineton]
1266 Walter Giffard
1279 William Wickwane
1286 John Romanus [le Romeyn]
1298 Henry Newark
1300 Thomas Corbridge
1306 William Greenfield
1317 William Melton
1342 William de la Zouche
1352 John Thoresby
1374 Alexander Neville
1388 Thomas Arundel
1396 Robert Waldby
1398 Richard le Scrope
1407 Henry Bowet
1426 John Kempe
1452 William Booth
1464 George Nevill
1476 Lawrence Booth
1480 Thomas Rotherham [Scott]
1501 Thomas Savage
1508 Christopher Bainbridge
1514 Thomas Wolsey
1531 Edward Lee
1545 Robert Holgate
1555 Nicholas Heath
1561 Thomas Young
1570 Edmund Grindal
1577 Edwin Sandys
1589 John Piers
1595 Matthew Hutton
1606 Tobias Matthew
1628 George Montaigne [Mountain]
1629 Samuel Harsnett
1632 Richard Neile
1641 John Williams
1660 Accepted Frewen
1664 Richard Sterne
1683 John Dolben
1688 Thomas Lamplugh
1691 John Sharp
1714 William Dawes
1724 Lancelot Blackburn
1743 Thomas Herring
1747 Matthew Hutton
1757 John Gilben
1761 Roben Hay Drummond
1777 William Markham
1808 Edward Venables Vernon Harcourt
1847 Thomas Musgrave
1860 Charles Thomas Longley
1863 William Thomson
1891 William Connor Magee
1891 William Dalrymple Maclagan
1909 Cosmo Gordon Lang
1929 William Temple
1942 Cyril Forster Garbett
1956 Arthur Michael Ramsey
1961 Frederick Donald Coggan
1975 Stuart Yarworth Blanch
1983 John Stapylton Habgood
1995 David Michael Hope

Durham

BISHOPS OF LINDISFARNE[2]

635 Aidan
651 Finan
661 Colman
664 Tuda
[Complications involving Wilfrid and Chad]
681 Eata

[1] Ealdwulf and Wulfstan II held the Sees of York and Worcester together. Ælfric Puttoc held both 1040-41 and Ealdred 1060-61.
[2] See transferred to Chester-le-Street 883.

685 Cuthberht
[Vacancy during which Wilfrid administered the see]
688 Eadberht
698 Eadfenh
731 Æthelweald
740 Cynewulf
781 Higbald
803 Ecgberht
821 Heathwred
830 Ecgred
845 Eanberht
854 Eardwulf

BISHOPS OF HEXHAM

664 Wilfrith
678 Eata
681 Tunberht
684 Cuthbert
685 Eata (restored)
687 John of Beverley
709 Acca
734 Frithoberht
767 Ahimund
781 Tilberht
789 Æthelberht
797 Heardred
800 Eanberht
813 Tidferth

BISHOPS OF CHESTER-LE-STREET[1]

899 Eardwulf
899 Cutheard
915 Tilred
925 Wigred
944 Uhtred
944 Seaxhelm
944 Ealdred
968 Ælfsige
990 Aldhun

BISHOPS OF DURHAM

990 Aldhun d. 1018
[See vacant 1018-1020]
1020 Edmund
c.1040 Eadred
1041 Æthelric
1056 Æthelwine
1071 Walcher
1081 William of Saint Calais
1099 Ralph [Ranulf] Flambard
1133 Geoffrey Rufus
1143 William of Sainte-Barbe
1153 Hugh of le Puiset
1197 Philip of Poitiers
1217 Richard Marsh
1228 Richard Poore
1241 Nicholas Farnham
1249 Walter Kirkham
1261 Robert Stichill
1274 Robert of Holy Island
1284 Anthony Bek
1311 Richard Kellaw
1318 Lewis de Beaumont
1333 Richard of Bury
1345 Thomas Hatfield
1382 John Fordham
1388 Walter Skirlaw
1406 Thomas Langley
1438 Robert Nevill
1457 Lawrence Booth
1476 William Dudley
1485 John Shirwood
1494 Richard Fox
1502 William Senhouse [Sever]
1507 Christopher Bainbridge
1509 Thomas Ruthall
1523 Thomas Wolsey
1530 Cuthbert Tunstall
1561 James Pilkington
1577 Richard Barnes
1589 Matthew Hutton
1595 Tobias Matthew
1606 William James
1617 Richard Neile
1628 George Monteigne [Mountain]
1628 John Howson
1632 Thomas Morton
1660 John Cosin
1674 Nathaniel Crew [Lord Crew]
1721 William Talbot
1730 Edward Chandler
1750 Joseph Butler
1752 Richard Trevor
1771 John Egerton
1787 Thomas Thurlow
1791 Shute Barrington
1826 William Van Mildert
1836 Edward Maltby
1856 Chaarles Thomas Longley
1860 Henry Montagu Villiers
1861 Charles Baring
1879 Joseph Barber Lightfoot
1890 Brooke Foss Westcott
1901 Handley Carr Glyn Moule
1920 Herbert Hensley Henson
1939 Alwyn Terrell Petre Williams
1952 Arthur Michael Ramsey
1956 Maurice Henry Harland
1966 Ian Thomas Ramsey
1973 John Stapylton Habgood
1984 David Edward Jenkins
1994 Anthony Michael Arnold Turnbull

Blackburn

1926 Percy Mark Herbert
1942 Wilfred Marcus Askwith
1954 Walter Hubert Baddeley
1960 Charles Robert Claxton
1972 Robert Arnold Schürhoff Martineau
1982 David Stewart Cross
1989 Alan David Chesters

Bradford

1920 Arthur William Thomson Perowne
1931 Alfred Walter Frank Blunt
1956 Frederick Donald Coggan
1961 Clement George St Michael Parker
1972 Ross Sydney Hook
1981 Geoffrey John Paul
1984 Robert Kerr Williamson
1992 David James Smith

Carlisle

1133 Æthelwulf
1203 Bernard
1219 Hugh of Beaulieu
1224 Walter Mauclerc
1247 Silvester Everdon
1255 Thomas Vipont
1258 Robert de Chause
1280 Ralph Ireton
1292 John of Halton
1325 John Ross
1332 John Kirkby
1353 Gilbert Welton
1363 Thomas Appleby
1396 Robert Reade
1397 Thomas Merks
1400 William Strickland
1420 Roger Whelpdale
1424 William Barrow
1430 Marmaduke Lumley
1450 Nicholas Close
1452 William Percy
1462 John Kingscote
1464 Richard le Scrope
1468 Edward Story
1478 Richard Bell
1496 William Senhouse [Sever]
1504 Roger Layburne
1508 John Penny
1521 John Kite
1537 Robert Aldrich
1556 Owen Oglethorpe
1561 John Best
1570 Richard Barnes
1577 John May
1598 Henry Robinson
1616 Robert Snowden
1621 Richard Milbourne
1624 Richard Senhouse
1626 Francis White
1629 Barnabas Potter
1642 James Ussher
1660 Richard Sterne
1664 Edward Rainbowe
1684 Thomas Smith
1702 William Nicolson
1718 Samuel Bradford
1723 John Waugh
1735 George Fleming
1747 Richard Osbaldeston
1762 Charles Lyttleton
1769 Edmund Law
1787 John Douglas
1791 Edward Venables Vernon [Harcourt]
1808 Samuel Goodenough
1827 Hugh Percy
1856 Henry Montagu Villiers
1860 Samuel Waldegrave
1869 Harvey Goodwin
1892 John Wareing Bardsley
1905 John William Diggle
1920 Henry Herbert Williams
1946 Thomas Bloomer
1966 Sydney Cyril Bulley
1972 Henry David Halsey
1989 Ian Harland

Chester

1541 John Bird
1554 George Cotes
1556 Cuthbert Scott
1561 William Downham
1579 William Chaderton
1595 Hugh Bellott
1597 Richard Vaughan
1604 George Lloyd
1616 Thomas Morton
1619 John Bridgeman
1660 Brian Walton
1662 Henry Ferne
1662 George Hall
1668 John Wilkins
1673 John Pearson
1686 Thomas Cartwright
1689 Nicolas Stratford
1708 William Dawes
1714 Francis Gastrell
1726 Samuel Peploe
1752 Edmund Keene
1771 William Markham
1777 Beilby Porteus
1788 William Cleaver
1800 Henry William Majendie
1810 Bowyer Edward Sparke
1812 George Henry Law

[1] See transferred to Durham 995.

1824 Charles James Blomfield
1828 John Bird Sumner
1848 John Graham
1865 William Jacobson
1884 William Stubbs
1889 Francis John Jayne
1919 Henry Luke Paget
1932 Geoffrey Francis Fisher
1939 Douglas Henry Crick
1955 Gerald Alexander Ellison
1974 Hubert Victor Whitsey
1982 Michael Alfred Baughen
1996 Peter Robert Forster

Liverpool

1880 John Charles Ryle
1900 Francis James Chavasse
1923 Albert Augustus David
1944 Clifford Arthur Martin
1966 Stuart Yarworth Blanch
1975 David Stuart Sheppard

Manchester

1848 James Prince Lee
1870 James Fraser
1886 James Moorhouse
1903 Edmund Arbuthnott Knox
1921 William Temple
1929 Frederic Sumpter Guy Warman
1947 William Derrick Lindsay Greer
1970 Patrick Campbell Rodger
1979 Stanley Eric Francis Booth-Clibborn
1993 Christopher John Mayfield

Newcastle

1882 Ernest Roland Wilberforce
1896 Edgar Jacob
1903 Arthur Thomas Lloyd
1907 Norman Dumenil John Straton
1915 Herbert Louis Wild
1927 Harold Ernest Bilbrough
1941 Noel Baring Hudson
1957 Hugh Edward Ashdown
1973 Ronald Oliver Bowlby
1981 Andrew Alexander Kenny Graham
1997 John Martin Wharton

Ripon

*c.*678 Eadheath

NEW FOUNDATION

1836 Charles Thomas Longley
1857 Robert Bickersteth
1884 William Boyd Carpenter
1912 Thomas Wortley Drury
1920 Thomas Banks Strong
1926 Edward Arthur Burroughs
1935 Geoffrey Charles Lester Lunt
1946 George Armitage Chase
1959 John Richard Humpidge Moorman
1975 Stuart Hetley Price
1977 David Nigel de Lorentz Young

Sheffield

1914 Leonard Hedley Burrows
1939 Leslie Stannard Hunter
1962 Francis John Taylor
1971 William Gordon Fallows
1980 David Ramsay Lunn
1997 John Nicholls

Sodor and Man[1]

447 Germanus
Conindrius
Romulus
Machutus
Conanus
Contentus
Baldus
Malchus
Torkinus
Brendanus
[Before 1080 Roolwer]
William
Hamond
1113 Wimund
1151 John
1160 Gamaliel
Ragnald
Christian of Argyle
Michael
1203 Nicholas de Meaux
Nicholas II
1217 Reginald
1226 John
1229 Simon of Argyle
1252 Richard
1275 Mark of Galloway
1305 Alan
1321 Gilbert Maclelan
1329 Bernard de Linton
1334 Thomas
1348 William Russell
1387 John Donegan
1387 Michael
1392 John Sproten
1402 Conrad
1402 Theodore Bloc
1429 Richard Messing Andrew
1435 John Seyre
1455 Thomas Burton
1458 Thomas Kirklam
1472 Angus
1478 Richard Oldham
1487 Hugh Blackleach
1513 Hugh Hesketh
1523 John Howden
1546 Henry Man
1556 Thomas Stanley
1570 John Salisbury
1576 John Meyrick
1600 George Lloyd
1605 John Philips
1634 William Forster
1635 Richard Parr
1661 Samuel Rutter
1663 Isaac Barrow
1671 Henry Bridgman
1683 John Lake
1685 Baptist Levinz
1698 Thomas Wilson
1755 Mark Hildesley
1773 Richard Richmond
1780 George Mason
1784 Claudius Crigan
1814 George Murray
1828 William Ward
1838 James Bowstead
1840 Henry Pepys
1841 Thomas Vowler Short
1847 Walter Augustus Shirley
1847 Robert John Eden
1854 Horatio Powys
1877 Rowley Hill
1887 John Wareing Bardsley
1892 Norman Dumenil John Straton
1907 Thomas Wortley Drury
1912 James Denton Thompson
1925 Charles Leonard Thornton-Duesbery
1928 William Stanton Jones
1943 John Ralph Strickland Taylor
1954 Benjamin Pollard
1966 George Eric Gordon
1974 Vernon Sampson Nicholls
1983 Arthur Henry Attwell
1989 Noel Debroy Jones

Southwell

1884 George Ridding
1904 Edwyn Hoskyns
1926 Bernard Oliver Francis Heywood
1928 Henry Mosley
1941 Frank Russell Barry
1964 Gordon David Savage
1970 John Denis Wakeling
1985 Michael Humphrey Dickens Whinney
1988 Patrick Burnet Harris

Wakefield

1888 William Walsham How
1897 George Rodney Eden
1928 James Buchanan Seaton
1938 Campbell Richard Hone
1946 Henry McGowan
1949 Roger Plumpton Wilson
1958 John Alexander Ramsbotham
1968 Eric Treacy
1977 Colin Clement Walter James
1985 David Michael Hope
1992 Nigel Simeon McCulloch

[1] Included in the province of York by Act of Parliament 1542. Prior to Richard Oldham there is some uncertainty as to several names and dates. From 1425 to 1553 there was an English and Scottish succession. It is not easy to say which claimant was Bishop either *de jure* or *de facto*.

BISHOPS SUFFRAGAN IN ENGLAND

Aston (Birmingham)

1954 Clement George St Michael Parker
1962 David Brownfield Porter
1972 Mark Green
1982 Michael Humphrey Dickens Whinney
1985 Colin Ogilvie Buchanan
1989-92 *no appointment*
1992 John Michael Austin

Barking (Chelmsford)

[in St Albans diocese to 1914]

1901 Thomas Stevens
1919 James Theodore Inskip
1948 Hugh Rowlands Gough
1959 William Frank Percival Chadwick
1975 Albert James Adams
1983 James William Roxburgh
1991 Roger Frederick Sainsbury

Barrow-in-Furness (Carlisle)

1889 Henry Ware
1909 Campbell West-Watson
1926 Henry Sidney Pelham
1944 *in abeyance*

Basingstoke (Winchester)

1973 Colin Clement Walter James
1977 Michael Richard John Manktelow
1994 Douglas Geoffrey Rowell

Bedford (St Albans)

1537 John Hodgkins[1]
1560-1879 *in abeyance*
1879 William Walsham How[2]
1888 Robert Claudius Billing[3]
1898-1935 *in abeyance*
1935 James Lumsden Barkway
1939 Aylmer Skelton
1948 Claude Thomas Thellusson Wood
1953 Angus Campbell MacInnes
1957 Basil Tudor Guy
1963 Albert John Trillo
1968 John Tyrrell Holmes Hare
1977 Andrew Alexander Kenny Graham
1981 David John Farmbrough
1994 John Henry Richardson

Berwick (Durham)

1536 Thomas Sparke
1572 *in abeyance*

Beverley (York)

1889 Robert Jarratt Crosthwaite
1923-94 *in abeyance*
1994 John Scott Gaisford

Birkenhead (Chester)

1965 Eric Arthur John Mercer
1974 Ronald Brown
1993 Michael Laurence Langrish

Bolton (Manchester)

1984 David George Galliford
1991 David Bonser

Bradwell (Chelmsford)

1968 William Neville Welch
1973 John Gibbs
1976 Charles Derek Bond
1993 Laurence Alexander Green

Bristol (Worcester)

1538 Henry Holbeach [Rands]
1542 *became diocesan see*

Brixworth (Peterborough)

1989 Paul Everard Barber

Buckingham (Oxford)

1914 Edward Domett Shaw
1921 Philip Herbert Eliot
1944 Robert Milton Hay
1960 Gordon David Savage
1964 George Christopher Cutts Pepys
1974 Simon Hedley Burrows
1994 Colin James Bennetts

Burnley (Blackburn)

[in Manchester diocese to 1926]

1901 Edwyn Hoskyns
1905 Alfred Pearson
1909 Henry Henn
1931 Edgar Priestley Swain
1950 Charles Keith Kipling Prosser
1955 George Edward Holderness
1970 Richard Charles Challinor Watson
1988 Ronald James Milner
1994 Martyn William Jarrett

Colchester (Chelmsford)

[in London diocese to 1845
in Rochester diocese to 1877
in St Albans diocese 1877-1914]

1536 William More
1541-91 *in abeyance*
1592 John Sterne
1608-1882 *in abeyance*
1882 Alfred Blomfield
1894 Henry Frank Johnson
1909 Robert Henry Whitcombe
1922 Thomas Alfred Chapman
1933 Charles Henry Ridsdale
1946 Frederick Dudley Vaughan Narborough
1966 Roderic Norman Coote
1988 Michael Edwin Vickers
1995 Edward Holland

Coventry (Worcester)

see also under Lichfield

1891 Henry Bond Bowlby
1894 Edmund Arbuthnott Knox
1903-18 *no appointment*
1918 *became diocesan see*

Crediton (Exeter)

1897 Robert Edward Trefusis
1930 William Frederick Surtees
1954 Wilfred Arthur Edmund Westall
1974 Philip John Pasterfield
1984 Peter Everard Coleman
1996 Richard Stephen Hawkins

Croydon (Southwark)

(in Canterbury diocese to 1985)

1904 Henry Horace Pereira
1924-30 *no appointment*
1930 Edward Sydney Woods
1937 William Louis Anderson
1942 Maurice Henry Harland
1947 Cuthbert Killick Norman Bardsley
1957 John Taylor Hughes
1977 Geoffrey Stuart Snell
1985 Wilfred Denniston Wood

Derby (Southwell)

1889 Edward Ash Were
1909 Charles Thomas Abraham
1927 *became diocesan see*

Doncaster (Sheffield)

1972 Stuart Hetley Price
1976 David Stewart Cross
1982 William Michael Dermot Persson
1993 Michael Frederick Gear

Dorchester (Oxford)

see also under Dorchester (*diocesan see*) *and* Lincoln

1939 Gerald Burton Allen
1952 Kenneth Riches
1957 David Goodwin Loveday
1972 Peter Knight Walker
1979 Conrad John Eustace Meyer
1988 Anthony John Russell

Dorking (Guildford)

[in Winchester diocese to 1927]

1905 Cecil Henry Boutflower
1909-68 *in abeyance*
1968 Kenneth Dawson Evans
1986 David Peter Wilcox
1996 Ian James Brackley

Dover (Canterbury)

1537 Richard Yngworth
1545 Richard Thornden
1557-69 *no appointment*
1569 Richard Rogers
1597-1870 *in abeyance*
1870 Edward Parry
1890 George Rodney Eden
1898 William Walsh
1916 Harold Ernest Bilbrough
1927 John Victor Macmillan
1935 Alfred Careywollaston Rose
1957 Lewis Evan Meredith
1964 Anthony Paul Tremlett
1980 Richard Henry McPhail Third
1992 John Richard Allan Llewellin

Dudley (Worcester)

1974 Michael Ashley Mann
1977 Anthony Charles Dumper
1993 Rupert William Noel Hoare

Dunwich (St Edmundsbury and Ipswich)

see also under Norwich

1934 Maxwell Homfray Maxwell-Gumbleton
1945 Clement Mallory Ricketts
1955 Thomas Herbert Cashmore
1967 David Rokeby Maddock
1977 William Johnston
1980 Eric Nash Devenport
1992 Jonathan Sansbury Bailey
1995 Timothy John Stevens

Ebbsfleet (Canterbury)

1994 John Richards

Edmonton (London)

1970 Alan Francis Bright Rogers
1975 William John Westwood
1985 Brian John Masters

[1] Appointed for the diocese of London.
[2] Appointed for the diocese of London.
[3] Appointed for the diocese of London, and retained title after resigning his suffragan duties in 1895.

Fulham (London)[1]

1926 Basil Staunton Batty
1947 William Marshall Selwyn
1949 George Ernest Ingle
1955 Robert Wright Stopford
1957 Roderic Norman Coote
1966 Alan Francis Bright Rogers
1970 John Richard Satterthwaite[2]
1980-1982 *no appointment*
1982 Brian John Masters
1985 Charles John Klyberg
1996 John Charles Broadhurst

Grantham (Lincoln)

1905 Welbore MacCarthy
1920 John Edward Hine
1930 Ernest Morell Blackie
1935 Arthur Ivan Greaves
1937 Algernon Augustus Markham
1949 Anthony Otter
1965 Ross Sydney Hook
1972 Dennis Gascoyne Hawker
1987 William Ind

Grimsby (Lincoln)

1935 Ernest Morell Blackie
1937 Anhur Ivan Greaves
1958 Kenneth Healey
1966 Gerald Fitzmaurice Colin
1979 David Tustin

Guildford (Winchester)

1874 John Sutton Utterton
1888 George Henry Sumner
1909 John Hugh Granville Randolph
1927 *became diocesan see*

Hertford (St Albans)

1968 Albert John Trillo
1971 Hubert Victor Whitsey
1974 Peter Mumford
1982 Kenneth Harold Pillar
1990 Robin Jonathan Norman Smith

Horsham (Chichester)

1968 Simon Wilton Phipps
1975 Ivor Colin Docker
1991 John William Hind
1993 Lindsay Goodall Urwin

Hull (York)

1538 Robert Sylvester (Pursglove)
1579-1891 *in abeyance*
1891 Richard Frederick Lefevre Blunt
1910 John Augustus Kempthome
1913 Francis Gurdon
1929-31 *no appointment*
1931 Bemard Oliver Francis Heywood
1934 Henry Townsend Vodden
1957 George Fredenck Townley
1965 Hubert Laurence Higgs
1977 Geoffrey John Paul
1981 Donald George Snelgrove
1994 James Stuart Jones

Hulme (Manchester)

1924 John Charles Hill
1930 Thomas Sherwood Jones
1945 Hugh Leycester Homby
1953 Kenneth Venner Ramsey
1975 David George Galliford
1984 Colin John Fraser Scott

Huntingdon (Ely)

1966 Robert Amold Schürhoff Martineau
1972 Eric St Quintin Wall
1980 William Gordon Roe
1997 John Robert Flack

Ipswich (Norwich)

1536 Thomas Manning[3]
?-1899 *in abeyance*[4]
1899 George Carnac Fisher
1906 Henry Luke Paget
1909 *no appointment*
1914 *became diocesan see with St Edmundsbury*

Islington (London)

1898 Charles Henry Turner
1923 *in abeyance*

Jarrow (Durham)

1906 George Nickson
1914 John Nathaniel Quirk
1924 Samuel Kirshbaum Knight
1932 James Geoffrey Gordon
1939 Leslie Owen
1944 David Colin Dunlop
1950 John Alexander Ramsbotham
1958 Mervyn Armstrong
1965 Alexander Kenneth Hamilton
1980 Michael Thomas Ball
1990 Alan Smithson

Kensington (London)

1901 Frederic Edward Ridgeway
1911 John Primatt Maud
1932 Bertram Fitzgerald Simpson
1942 Henry Colville Montgomery Campbell
1949 Cyril Eastaugh
1962 Edward James Keymer Roberts
1964 Ronald Cedric Osbourne Goodchild
1981 Mark Santer
1987 John George Hughes
1994-96 *no appointment*
1996 Michael John Colclough

Kingston upon Thames (Southwark)

1905 Cecil Hook
1915 Samuel Mumford Taylor
1922 Percy Mark Herbert
1927 Frederick Ochterlony Taylor Hawkes
1952 William Percy Gilpin
1970 Hugh William Montefiore
1978 Keith Norman Sutton
1984 Peter Stephen Maurice Selby
1992 John Martin Wharton

Knaresborough (Ripon)

1905 Lucius Fredenck Moses Bottomley Smith
1934 Paul Fulcrand Dalacour de Labilliere
1938 John Norman Bateman-Champain
1948 Henry Handley Vully de Candole
1965 John Howard Cruse
1972 Ralph Emmerson
1979 John Dennis
1986 Malcolm James Menin

Lancaster (Blackburn)

1936 Benjamim Pollard
1955 Anthony Leigh Egerton Hoskyns-Abrahall
1975 Dennis Fountain Page
1985 Ian Harland
1990 John Nicholls

Leicester (Peterborough)

see also under Lichfield *and* Lincoln

1888 Francis Henry Thicknesse
1903 Lewis Clayton
1913 Norman MacLeod Lang
1927 *became diocesan see*

Lewes (Chichester)

1909 Leonard Hedley Burrows
1914 Herbert Edward Jones
1920 Henry Kemble Southwell
1926 Thomas William Cook
1929 William Champion Streatfield
1929 Hugh Maudsley Hordern
1946 Geoffrey Hodgson Warde
1959 James Herbert Lloyd Morrell
1977 Peter John Ball
1992 Ian Patrick Martyn Cundy
1997 Wallace Parke Benn

Ludlow (Hereford)

1981 Stanley Mark Wood
1987 Ian Macdonald Griggs
1994 John Charles Saxbee

Lynn (Norwich)

1963 William Somers Llewellyn
1972 William Aubrey Aitken
1986 David Edward Bentley
1994 David John Conner

Maidstone (Canterbury)

1944 Leslie Owen
1946-56 *no appointment*
1956 Stanley Woodley Betts
1966-69 *no appointment*
1969 Geoffrey Lewis Tiarks
1976 Richard Henry McPhail Third
1980 Robert Maynard Hardy
1987 David James Smith
1992 Gavin Hunter Reid

Malmesbury (Bristol)

1927 Ronald Erskine Ramsay
1946 Ivor Stanley Watkins
1956 Edward James Keymer Roberts
1962 Clifford Leofric Purdy Bishop
1973 Frederick Stephen Temple

[1] From 1926 to 1980 exercised the Bishop of London's extra-diocesan jurisdiction over chaplaincies in Northern and Central Europe.
[2] Bishop of Fulham and Gibraltar.
[3] Manning does not appear to have acted as a suffragan bishop in the diocese of Norwich.
[4] The date of Manning's death is not known.

1983 Peter James Firth
1994 *renamed* Swindon

Marlborough

1537 Thomas Morley (Bickley)[1]
*c*1561-1888 *in abeyance*
1888 Alfred Earle[2]
1919 *in abeyance*

Middleton (Manchester)

1927 Richard Godfrey Parsons
1932 Cecil Wilfred Wilson
1938 Arthur Fawssett Alston
1943 Edward Worsfold Mowll
1952 Frank Woods
1958 Robert Nelson
1959 Edward Ralph Wickham
1982 Donald Alexander Tytler
1994 Stephen Squires Venner

Nottingham (Lincoln)

[in York diocese to 1837]

1567 Richard Barnes
1570-1870 *in abeyance*
1870 Henry Mackenzie
1877 Edward Trollope
1893 *in abeyance*

Penrith (Carlisle)

see also under Richmond

1537 John Bird[3]
1539-1888 *in abeyance*
1888 John James Pulleine[4]
1939 Grandage Edwards Powell
1944 Herbert Victor Turner
1959 Sydney Cyril Bulley
1967 Reginald Foskett
1970 William Edward Augustus Pugh
1979 George Lanyon Hacker
1994 Richard Garrard

Plymouth (Exeter)

1923 John Howard Bertram Masterman
1934 Francis Whitfield Daukes
1950 Norman Harry Clarke
1962 Wilfred Guy Sanderson
1972 Richard Fox Cartwright
1982 Kenneth Albert Newing
1988 Richard Stephen Hawkins
1996 John Henry Garton

Pontefract (Wakefield)

1931 Campbell Richard Hone
1939 Tom Longworth
1949 Arthur Harold Morris
1954 George William Clarkson
1961 Eric Treacy
1968 William Gordon Fallows
1971 Thomas Richard Hare
1993 John Thornley Finney

Ramsbury (Salisbury)

see also under Salisbury

1974 John Robert Geoffrey Neale
1989 Peter St George Vaughan

Reading (Oxford)

1889 James Leslie Randall
1909-42 *in abeyance*
1942 Arthur Groom Parham
1954 Eric Henry Knell
1972 Eric Wild
1982 Ronald Graham Gregory Foley
1989 John Frank Ewan Bone
1997 Edward William Murray Walker

Repton (Derby)

1965 William Warren Hunt
1977 Stephen Edmund Verney
1986 Francis Henry Arthur Richmond

Richborough (Canterbury)

1995 Edwin Ronald Barnes

Richmond (Ripon)

1889 John James Pulleine[5]
1913 Francis Charles Kilner
1921 *in abeyance*

St Germans (Truro)

1905 John Rundle Cornish
1918-74 *in abeyance*
1974 Cecil Richard Rutt
1979 Reginald Lindsay Fisher
1985 John Richard Allan Llewellin
1993 Graham Richard James

Selby (York)

1939 Henry St John Stirling Woollcombe
1941 Carey Frederick Knyvett
1962 Douglas Noel Sargent
1972 Morris Henry St John Maddocks
1983 Clifford Conder Barker
1991 Humphrey Vincent Taylor

Shaftesbury (Salisbury)

[in Bristol diocese 1542-1836]

1539 John Bradley
? *in abeyance*[6]

Sheffield (York)

1901 John Nathaniel Quirk
1914 *became diocesan see*

Sherborne (Salisbury)

1925 Robert Crowther Abbott
1928 Gerald Burton Allen
1936 Harold Nickinson Rodgers
1947 John Maurice Key
1960 Victor Joseph Pike
1976 John Dudley Galtrey Kirkham

Sherwood (Southwell)

1965 Kenneth George Thompson
1975 Harold Richard Darby
1989 Alan Wyndham Morgan

Shrewsbury (Lichfield)

1537 Lewis Thomas[7]
1561-1888 *in abeyance*
1888 Sir Lovelace Tomlinson Stamer
1905-40 *in abeyance*
1940 Eric Knightley Chetwode Hamilton
1944 Robert Leighton Hodson
1959 William Alonzo Parker
1970 Francis William Cocks
1980 Leslie Lloyd Rees
1987 John Dudley Davies
1994 David Marrison Hallatt

Southampton (Winchester)

1895 William Awdry
1896 George Carnac Fisher
1898 The Hon Arthur Temple Lyttelton
1903 James Macarthur
1921 Cecil Henry Boutflower
1933 Arthur Baillie Lumsdaine Karney
1943 Edmund Robert Morgan
1951 Kenneth Edward Norman Lamplugh
1972 John Kingsmill Cavell
1984 Edward David Cartwright
1989 John Freeman Perry
1996 Jonathan Michael Gledhill

Southwark (Rochester)

1891 Huyshe Wolcott Yeatman-Biggs
1905 *became diocesan see*

Stafford (Lichfield)

1909 Edward Ash Were
1915 Lionel Payne Crawfurd
1934 Douglas Henry Crick
1938 Lemprière Durell Hammond
1958 Richard George Clitherow
1975 John Waine
1979 John Stevens Waller
1987 Michael Charles Scott-Joynt
1996 Christopher John Hill

Stepney (London)

1895 George Forrest Browne
1897 Arthur Foley Winnington-Ingram
1901 Cosmo Gordon Lang
1909 Henry Luke Paget
1919 Henry Mosley
1928 Charles Edward Curzon
1936 Robert Hamilton Moberly
1952 Joost de Blank
1957 Francis Evered Lunt
1968 Ernest Urban Trevor Huddleston
1978 James Lawton Thompson
1992 Richard John Carew Chartres
1996 John Mugabi Sentamu

Stockport (Chester)

1949 Frank Jackson Okell
1951 David Henry Saunders Saunders-Davies
1965 Rupert Gordon Strutt

1 Appointed for the diocese of London.
2 Appointed for the diocese of London, but retained the title while Dean of Exeter 1900-18.
3 Appointed for the diocese of Lichfield.
4 Appointed for the diocese of Ripon.
5 His suffragan title was changed from Penrith to Richmond by Royal Warrant.
6 The date of Bradley's death is not known.
7 Not appointed for Lichfield, but probably for Llandaff.

1984 Frank Pilkington Sargeant
1994 Geoffrey Martin Turner

Swindon (Bristol)

1994 Michael David Doe

Taunton (Bath and Wells)

1538 William Finch
1559-1911 *in abeyance*
1911 Charles Fane de Salis
1931 George Arthur Hollis
1945 Harry Thomas
1955 Mark Allin Hodson
1962 Francis Horner West
1977 Peter John Nott
1986 Nigel Simeon McCulloch
1992 John Hubert Richard Lewis
1997 William Allen Stewart

Tewkesbury (Gloucester)

1938 Augustine John Hodson
1955 Edward Barry Henderson
1960 Forbes Trevor Horan
1973 Thomas Carlyle Joseph Robert Hamish Deakin
1986 Geoffrey David Jeremy Walsh
1996 John Stewart Went

Thetford (Norwich)

see also under Norwich

1536 John Salisbury
1570-1894 *in abeyance*
1894 Arthur Thomas Lloyd
1903 John Philips Alcott Bowers
1926-45 *no appointment*
1945 John Walker Woodhouse
1953 Manin Patrick Grainge Leonard
1963 Eric William Bradley Cordingly
1977 Hugh Charles Blackburne
1981 Timothy Dudley-Smith
1992 Hugo Ferdinand de Waal

Tonbridge (Rochester)

1959 Russell Berridge White
1968 Henry David Halsey
1973 Philip Harold Ernest Goodrich
1982 David Henry Bartleet
1993 Brian Arthur Smith

Warrington (Liverpool)

1918 Martin Linton Smith
1920 Edwin Hone Kempson
1927 Herbert Gresford Jones
1946 Charles Robert Claxton
1960 Laurence Ambrose Brown
1970 John Monier Bickersteth
1976 Michael Henshall
1996 John Richard Packer

Warwick (Coventry)

1980 Keith Appleby Arnold
1990 Clive Handford
1996 Anthony Martin Priddis

Whalley (Blackburn)

[in Manchester diocese to 1926]

1909 Atherton Gwillym Rawstorne
1936 *in abeyance*

Whitby (York)

1923 Harry St John Stirling Woollcombe
1939 Harold Evelyn Hubbard
1947 Walter Hubert Baddeley
1954 Philip William Wheeldon
1961 George D'Oyly Snow
1972 John Yates
1976 Clifford Conder Barker
1983 Gordon Bates

Willesden (London)

1911 William Willcox Perrin
1929 Guy Vernon Smith
1940 Henry Colville Montgomery Campbell
1942 Edward Michael Gresford Jones
1950 Gerald Alexander Ellison
1955 George Ernest Ingle
1964 Graham Douglas Leonard
1974 Geoffrey Hewlett Thompson
1985 Thomas Frederick Butler
1992 Geoffrey Graham Dow

Wolverhampton (Lichfield)

1979 Barry Rogerson
1985 Christopher John Mayfield
1994 Michael Gay Bourke

Woolwich (Southwark)

1905 John Cox Leeke
1918 William Woodcock Hough
1932 Arthur Llewellyn Preston
1936 Leslie Hamilton Lang
1947 Robert William Stannard
1959 John Arthur Thomas Robinson
1969 David Stuart Sheppard
1975 Michael Eric Marshall
1984 Albert Peter Hall
1996 Colin Ogilvie Buchanan

WALES

Archbishops of Wales

1920 Alfred George Edwards (St Asaph, 1889–1934)
1934 Charles Alfred Howell Green (Bangor, 1928–44)
1944 David Lewis Prosser (St Davids, 1927–50)
1949 John Morgan (Llandaff, 1939–57)
1957 Alfred Edwin Morris (Monmouth, 1945–67)
1968 William Glyn Hughes Simon (Llandaff, 1957–71)
1971 Gwilym Owen Williams (Bangor, 1957–82)
1983 Derrick Greenslade Childs (Monmouth, 1972–87)
1987 George Noakes (St Davids, 1982–91)
1991 Alwyn Rice Jones (St Asaph 1982–)

Bangor[1]

c.550 Deiniol [Daniel]
c.775 Elfod [Elbodugen]
1092 Herve
[*Vacancy* 1109–20]
1120 David the Scot
1140 Maurice (Meurig)
[*Vacancy* 1161–77]
1177 Guy Rufus [Gwion Goch]
[*Vacancy* c1190–95]
1195 Alan [Alban]
1197 Robert of Shrewsbury
[*Vacancy* 1212–15]
1215 Cadwgan
1237 Richard
1267 Anian [or Einion]
1307 Gruflydd ab Iowerth
1309 Anian [Einion] Sais
1328 Matthew de Englefield
1357 Thomas de Ringstead
1366 Gervase de Castro
1371 Hywel ap Gronwy
1372 John Gilbert
1376 John Swaffham
1400 Richard Young
[*Vacancy* c1404–8]
1408 Benedict Nicolls
1418 William Barrow
1425 John Cliderow
1436 Thomas Cheriton
1448 John Stanbury
1453 James Blakedon
1465 Richard Edenham
1495 Henry Dean
1500 Thomas Pigot
1505 Thomas Penny
1509 Thomas Skevington
1534 John Salcot [or Capon]
1539 John Bird
1542 Arthur Bulkeley
1555 William Glynn
1559 Rowland Meyrick
1566 Nicholas Robinson
1586 Hugh Bellot
1596 Richard Vaughan
1598 Henry Rowlands
1616 Lewis Bayly
1632 David Dolben
1634 Edmund Griffith
1637 William Roberts
1666 Robert Morgan
1673 Humphrey Lloyd
1689 Humphrey Humphreys
1702 John Evans
1716 Benjamin Hoadley
1721 Richard Reynolds
1723 William Baker
1728 Thomas Sherlock
1734 Charles Cecil
1738 Thomas Herring
1743 Matthew Hutton
1748 Zachary Pearce
1756 John Egerton
1769 John Ewer
1775 John Moore
1783 John Warren
1800 William Cleaver

[1] Very few of the names of the Celtic bishops have been preserved.

1807 John Randolph
1809 Henry William Majendie
1830 Christopher Bethell
1859 James Colquhoun Campbell
1890 Daniel Lewis Lloyd
1899 Watkin Herbert Williams
1925 Daniel Davies
1928 Charles Alfred Howell Green (Archbishop of Wales 1934)
1944 David Edwardes Davies
1949 John Charles Jones
1957 Gwilym Owen Williams (Archbishop of Wales 1971)
1982 John Cledan Mears
1993 Barry Cennydd Morgan

Llandaff[1]

c.550 Teiliau
c.872 Cyfeiliag
c.880 Libiau
c.940 Marchlwys
982 Gwyzan
c.995 Bledri
1027 Joseph
1056 Herewald
1107 Urban
[*Vacancy of six years*]
1140 Uchtryd
1148 Nicolas ap Gwrgant
[*Vacancy of two years*]
1186 William Saltmarsh
1193 Henry of Abergavenny
1219 William of Goldcliff
1230 Elias of Radnor
1245 William de Burgh
1254 John de Ware
1257 William of Radnor
1266 Willam de Breuse [or Brus]
1297 John of Monmouth
1323 John of Eaglescliffe
1344 John Paschal
1361 Roger Cradock
1383 Thomas Rushook
1386 William Bottesham
1389 Edmund Bromfield
1393 Tideman de Winchcomb
1395 Andrew Barret
1396 John Burghill
1398 Thomas Peverel
1408 John de la Zouch [Fulford]
1425 John Wells
1441 Nicholas Ashby
1458 John Hunden
1476 John Smith
1478 John Marshall
1496 John Ingleby
1500 Miles Salley
1517 George de Athequa
1537 Robert Holdgate [or Holgate]
1545 Anthony Kitchin
1567 Hugh Jones
1575 William Blethin
1591 Gervase Babington
1595 William Morgan
1601 Francis Godwin
1618 George Carleton
1619 Theophilus Field
1627 William Murray
1640 Morgan Owen
1660 Hugh Lloyd
1667 Francis Davies
1675 William Lloyd
1679 William Beaw
1706 John Tyler
1725 Robert Clavering
1729 John Harris
1739 Matthias Mawson
1740 John Gilbert
1749 Edward Cressett
1755 Richard Newcome
1761 John Ewer
1769 Jonathan Shipley
1769 Shute Barrington
1782 Richard Watson
1816 Herbert Marsh
1819 William Van Mildert
1826 Charles Richard Sumner
1828 Edward Copleston
1849 Alfred Ollivant
1883 Richard Lewis
1905 Joshua Pritchard Hughes
1931 Timothy Rees
1939 John Morgan (Archbishop of Wales 1949)
1957 William Glyn Hughes Simon (Archbishop of Wales 1968)
1971 Eryl Stephen Thomas
1975 John Richard Worthington Poole-Hughes
1985 Roy Thomas Davies

Monmouth

1921 Charles Alfred Howell Green
1928 Gilbert Cunningham Joyce
1940 Alfred Edwin Monahan
1945 Alfred Edwin Morris (Archbishop of Wales 1957)
1968 Eryl Stephen Thomas
1972 Derrick Greenslade Childs (Archbishop of Wales 1983)
1986 Royston Clifford Wright
1992 Rowan Douglas Williams

St Asaph[2]

c.560 Kentigern
c.573 Asaph
1143 Gilbert
1152 Geoffrey of Monmouth
1154 Richard
1160 Godfrey
1175 Adam
1183 John I
1186 Reiner
1225 Abraham
1235 Hugh
1242 Hywel Ab Ednyfed
1249 Anian I [or Einion]
1267 John II
1268 Anian II
1293 Llywelyn de Bromfield
1315 Dafydd ap Bleddyn
1346 John Trevor I
1357 Llywelyn ap Madoc ab Ellis
1377 William de Spridlington
1382 Lawrence Child
1390 Alexander Bache
1395 John Trevor II
1411 Robert de Lancaster
1433 John Lowe
1444 Reginald Pecock
1451 Thomas Bird *alias* Knight
1471 Richard Redman
1496 Michael Deacon
1500 Dafydd ab lorwerth
1504 Dafydd ab Owain
1513 Edmund Birkhead
1518 Henry Standish
1536 Robert Warton [or Parfew]
1555 Thomas Goldwell
1560 Richard Davies
1561 Thomas Davies
1573 William Hughes
1601 William Morgan
1604 Richard Parry
1624 John Hanmer
1629 John Owen
1660 George Griffith
1667 Henry Glemham
1670 Isaac Barrow
1680 William Lloyd
1692 Edward Jones
1703 George Hooper
1704 William Beveridge
1708 Will. Fleetwood
1715 John Wynne
1727 Francis Hare
1732 Thomas Tanner
1736 Isaac Maddox
1744 Samuel Lisle
1748 Robert Hay Drummond
1761 Richard Newcome
1769 Jonathan Shipley
1789 Samuel Hallifax
1790 Lewis Bagot
1802 Samuel Horsley
1806 William Cleaver
1815 John Luxmore
1830 William Carey
1846 Thomas Vowler Short
1870 Joshua Hughes
1889 Alfred George Edwards (Archbishop of Wales 1920)
1934 William Thomas Havard
1950 David Daniel Bartlett
1971 Harold John Charles
1982 Alwyn Rice Jones (Archbishop of Wales 1991)

St Davids[3]

c.601 David
c.606 Cynog
831 Sadyrnfyw
Meurig
c.840 Novis
?Idwal
c.906 Asser
Llunwerth
944 Eneuris
c.961 Rhydderch
c.999 Morgeneu
1023 Morgeneu
1023 Erwyn
1039 Tramerin
1061 Joseph
1061 Bleddud
1072 Sulien
1078 Abraham
1080 Sulien
1085 Wilfrid
1115 Bernard
1148 David Fitz-Gerald
1176 Peter de Leia
1203 Geoffrey de Henlaw
1215 Gervase [Iorwerth]
1231 Anselm le Gras
1248 Thomas le Waleys
1256 Richard de Carew
1280 Thomas Bek
1296 David Martin
1328 Henry Gower
1347 John Thoresby
1350 Reginald Brian
1352 Thomas Fastolf
1362 Adam Houghton
1389 John Gilbert
1397 Guy de Mohne
1408 Henry Chichele

[1] The traditional list of bishops of the Celtic Church has little historical foundation. But the names of the following, prior to Urban, may be regarded as fairly trustworthy, though the dates are very uncertain.
[2] Prior to the Norman period there is considerable uncertainty as to names and dates.
[3] The following names occur in early records though the dates given cannot always be reconciled.

1414 John Catterick
1415 Stephen Patrington
1418 Benedict Nichols
1434 Thomas Rodburn [Rudborne]
1442 William Lindwood
1447 John Langton
1447 John de la Bere
1460 Robert Tully
1482 Richard Martin
1483 Thomas Langton
1485 Hugh Pavy
1496 John Morgan [Young]
1505 Robert Sherborn
1509 Edward Vaughan
1523 Richard Rawlins
1536 William Barlow
1548 Robert Ferrar
1554 Henry Morgan
1560 Thomas Young
1561 Richard Davies
1582 Marmaduke Middleton
1594 Anthony Rudd
1615 Richard Milbourne
1621 William Laud
1627 Theophilus Field
1636 Roger Mainwaring
1660 William Lucy
1678 William Thomas
1683 Laurence Womock
1686 John Lloyd
1687 Thomas Watson
[*Vacancy* 1699–1705]
1705 George Bull
1710 Philip Bisse
1713 Adam Ottley
1724 Richard Smallbrooke
1731 Elias Sydall
1732 Nicholas Claggett
1743 Edward Willes
1744 Richard Trevor
1753 Anthony Ellis
1761 Samuel Squire
1766 Robert Lowth
1766 Charles Moss
1774 James Yorke
1779 John Warren
1783 Edward Smallwell
1788 Samuel Horsley
1794 William Stewart
1801 George Murray
1803 Thomas Burgess
1825 John Banks Jenkinson
1840 Connop Thirlwall
1874 William Basil Tickell Jones
1897 John Owen
1927 David Lewis Prosser (Archbishop of Wales 1944)
1950 William Thomas Havard
1956 John Richards Richards
1971 Eric Matthias Roberts
1982 George Noakes (Archbishop of Wales 1987)
1991 John Ivor Rees
1996 David Huw Jones

Swansea and Brecon

1923 Edward Latham Bevan
1934 John Morgan
1939 Edward William Williamson
1953 William Glyn Hughes Simon
1958 John James Absalom Thomas
1976 Benjamin Noel Young Vaughan
1988 Dewi Morris Bridges

SCOTLAND

Sources: Bp Dowden's *The Bishops of Scotland* (Glasgow 1912), for all the sees up to the Reformation, and for Aberdeen and Moray to the present time.

For bishops after the Reformation (and for a few of the earliest ones before Queen Margaret)—Grub, *Ecclesiastical History of Scotland* (Edinburgh 1861, 4 Vols.) and Bp Keith and Bp Russel, *Scottish Bishops* (2nd ed. Edinburgh 1824).

Scottish episcopal elections became subject immediately to Roman confirmation in 1192. The subordination of the Scottish Church to York became less direct in 1165, and its independence was recognized in a bill of Celestine III in 1192. St Andrews was raised to metropolitan rank on 17 August 1472 and the Archbishop became primate of all Scotland with the same legative rights as the Archbishop of Canterbury on 27 March 1487.

The dates in the margin are those of the consecration or translation to the particular see of the bishops named; or in the case of bishops elect, who are not known to have been consecrated, they are those of the election; or in the case of titular bishops, of the date of their appointment.

The date of the death has been given where there was a long interregnum, or where there is dislocation (as at the Reformation and at the Revolution), or for some special reason to make the history intelligible.

The extra information in the list of College Bishops is given for the reason just stated.

St Andrews

St Andrews, Dunkeld and Dunblane

906 Cellach I
915(?) Fothad I
955 Malisius I
963 Maelbridge
970 Cellach II
996(?) Malasius II
(?) Malmore
1025 Alwyn
1028 Maelduin
1055 Tuthald or Tuadal
1059 Fothad II
1077 to 1107 Gregory (elect)
Catharas (elect)
Edmarus (elect)
Godricus (elect)
1109 Turgot
1120 Eadmer (elect)
1127 Robert
1159 Waldeve (elect)
1160 Ernald
1165 Richard
1178 Hugh
1180 John the Scot
1198 Roger de Beaumon
1202 William Malveisin
1238 Geoffrey (elect)
1240 David de Bernham
1253 Robert de Stuteville (elect)
1254 Abel de Golin
1255 Gamelin
1273 William Wischard
1280 William Fraser
1298 William de Lamberton
1328 James Bennet
1342 William de Laundels
1385 Stephen de Pay (elect)
1386(?) Walter Trayl
1388 Alexander de Neville
1398 Thomas de Arundel
1401 Thomas Stewart (elect)
1402 Walter de Danielston (elect)
1403(?) Gilbert Greenlaw
1403 Henry Wardlaw
1408 John Trevor
1440 James Kennedy

ARCHBISHOPS

1465 Patrick Graham
1478 William Scheves
1497 James Stewart (elect)
1504 Alexander Stewart (elect)
1513 John Hepburn (elect)
1513 Innocenzo Cibo (elect)
1514 Andrew Forman
1522 James Betoun
1538 David Betoun [coadjutor]
1547 John Hamilton
1551 Gavin Hamilton [coadjutor] died 1571
1572 John Douglas (titular)
1576 Patrick Adamson (titular) died 1592
1611 George Gladstanes
1615 John Spottiswoode, died 1639
1661 James Sharp
1679 Alexander Burnet
1684 Arthur Rose, died 1704

BISHOPS OF FIFE

[1704–26 See vacant]
1726 James Rose
1733 Robert Keith
1743 Robert White
1761 Henry Edgar

BISHOPS OF ST ANDREWS

1842 Patrick Torry
1853 Charles Wordsworth
1893 George Howard Wilkinson
1908 Charles Edward Plumb
1931 Edward Thomas Scott Reid
1938 James Lumsden Barkway
1949 Arnold Brian Burrowes
1955 John William Alexander Howe
1969 Michael Geoffrey Hare Duke
1995 Michael Harry George Henley

†Dunkeld

849(?) Tuathal
865(?) Flaithbertach
1114 Cormac
1147 Gregory
1170 Richard I
1178 Walter de Bidun (elect)
1183(?) John I, the Scot
1203 Richard II, de Prebenda

† Indicates a diocese no longer extant, or united with another diocese.

1212(?) John II, de Leycester
1214(?) Hugh de Sigillo
1229 Matthew Scot (elect)
1229 Gilbert
1236(?) Geoffrey de Liberatione
1252 Richard III, of Inverkeithing
1273(?) Robert de Stuteville
1283(?) Hugh de Strivelin [Stirling] (elect)
1283 William
1288 Matthew de Crambeth
1309 John de Leek (elect)
1312 William Sinclair
1337 Malcolm de Innerpeffray (elect)
1344 Richard de Pilmor
1347 Robert de Den (elect)
1347(?) Duncan de Strathearn
1355 John Luce
1370 John de Carrick (elect)
1371(?) Michael de Monymusk
1377(?) Andrew Umfray (elect)
1379 John de Peblys [? of Peebles]
1379 Robert de Derling
1390(?) Nicholas Duffield
1391 Robert Sinclair
1398(?) Robert de Cardeny
1430 William Gunwardby
1437 Donald MacNaughton (elect)
1438 James Kennedy
1440(?) Thomas Livingston
1440 Alexander de Lawedre [Lauder] (elect)
1442 James de Brois [Brewhous]
1447 William Turnbull (elect)
1448 John Ralston
1452(?) Thomas Lauder
1476 James Livingston
1483 Alexander Inglis (elect)
1484 George Brown
1515 Andrew Stewart (elect)
1516 Gavin Dougias
1524 Robert Cockburn
1526(?) George Crichton
1546 John Hamilton
1552 Robert Crichton
1572 James Paton (titular)
1585 Peter Rollock (titular)
1607 James Nicolson (titular)
1611(?) Alexander Lindsay (deposed 1638)
1662 George Haliburton
1665 Henry Guthrie
1677 William Lindsay
1679 Andrew Bruce
1686 John Hamilton
1717 Thomas Rattray
1743 John Alexander
1776(?) Charles Rose
1792 Jonathan Watson
1808 Patrick Torry
1842 Held with **St Andrews**

†Dunblane

1162 Laurence
*c.*1180 Symon
1196 W[illelmus]
1198 Jonathan
1215 Abraham
1225 Ralph (elect)
1227 Osbert
1233 Clement
1259 Robert de Prebenda
1284 William I
1296 Alpin
1301 Nicholas
1307 Nicholas de Balmyle
1318(?) Roger de Balnebrich (elect)
1322 Maurice
*c.*1347 William II
*c.*1361 Walter de Coventre
*c.*1372 Andrew
*c.*1380 Dougal
1403(?) Finlay or Dermoch
1419 William Stephen
1430 Michael Ochiltree
1447(?) Robert Lauder
1468 John Hepburn
1487 James Chisolm
1527 William Chisolm I
1561 William Chisom II [coadjutor]
1575 Andrew Graham (titular)
1611 George Graham
1616 Adam Bellenden
1636 James Wedderburn
1661 Robert Leighton
1673 James Ramsay
1684 Robert Douglas
[1716–31 See vacant]
1731 John Gillan
1735 Robert White
1744 Thomas Ogilvie (elect)
1774 Charles Rose, died 1791
1776 Held with **Dunkeld**

Edinburgh

1634 William Forbes
1634 David Lindsay
1662 George Wishart
1672 Alexander Young
1679 John Paterson
1687 Alexander Rose
1720 John Fullarton
1727 Arthur Millar
1727 Andrew Lumsden
1733 David Freebairn
[1739–76 See vacant]
1776 William Falconer
1787 William Abernethy Drummond
1806 Daniel Sandford
1830 James Walker
1841 Charles Hughes Terrot
1872 Henry Cotterill
1886 John Dowden
1910 George Henry Somerset Walpole
1929 Harry Seymour Reid
1939 Ernest Denny Logie Danson
1947 Kenneth Charles Harman Warner
1961 Kenneth Moir Carey
1975 Alastair Iain Macdonald Haggart
1986 Richard Frederick Holloway

Aberdeen

Aberdeen and Orkney

BISHOPS AT MURTHLAC

(?) Beyn [Beanus]
(?) Donort
(?) Cormac

BISHOPS AT ABERDEEN

1132 Nechtan
*c.*1150 Edward
*c.*1172 Matthew
*c.*1201 John
*c.*1208 Adam de Kalder
1228 Matthew Scot (elect)
1230 Gilbert de Strivelyn
1240 Radulf de Lamley
1247 Peter de Ramsey
1258 Richard de Pottun
1272 Hugh de Bennum
1282 Henry le Chene
1329 Walter Herok (elect)
1329 Alexander I, de Kyninmund
1344 William de Deyn
1351 John de Rate
1356 Alexander II, de Kyninmund
1380 Adam de Tynyngham
1391 Gilbert de Grenlaw
1422 Henry de Lychton [Leighton]
*c.*1441 Ingram de Lindsay
1458 Thomas Spens
1480 Robert Blackadder (elect)
1488 William Elphinstone
1515 Robert Forman (elect)
1516 Alexander Gordon
1519 Gavin Dunbar
1529 George Learmonth [coadjutor]
1533 William Stewart
1547 William Gordon
1577 David Cunningham (elect)
1611 Peter Blackburn
1616 Alexander Forbes
1618 Patrick Forbes of Corse
1635 Adam Bellenden [Bannatyne]
1662 David Mitchell
1663 Alexander Burnet
1664 Patrick Scougal
1682 George Halyburton
[1715–21 See vacant]
1721 Archibald Campbell
1724 James Gadderar
1733 William Dunbar
1746 Andrew Gerard
1768 Robert Kilgour
1786 John Skinner
1816 William Skinner
1857 Thomas George Spink Suther
1883 Arthur Gascoigne Douglas
1906 Rowland Ellis
1912 Anthony Mitchell
1917 Frederic Llewellyn Deane
1943 Herbert William Hall
1956 Edward Frederick Easson
1973 Ian Forbes Begg
1978 Frederick Charles Darwent
1992 Andrew Bruce Cameron

†Orkney

1035 Henry
1050 Turolf
1072 John I
1072 Adalbert
1073 Radulf
1102 William I, 'the Old'
1108 Roger
1114 Radulf Novell
1168(?) William II
1188(?) Bjarni
1224 Jofreyrr
1248 Henry I
1270 Peter
1286 Dolgfinn
1310 William III
*c.*1369 William IV
*c.*1384 Robert Sinclair
1384(?) John
1394 Henry II
1396(?) John Pak
1407 Alexander Vaus (elect)
1415 William Stephenson
1420 Thomas Tulloch
1461 William Tulloch
1477 Andrew Painter
1500 Edward Stewart
1524 John Benston [coadjutor]
1526(?) Robert Maxwell
1541 Robert Reid
1559 Adam Bothwell
1611 James Law
1615 George Graham
1639 Robert Barron (elect)
1661 Thomas Sydserf
1664 Andrew Honeyman

1677 Murdo Mackenzie
1688 Andrew Bruce, See afterwards administered with **Caithness**
1857 Held with **Aberdeen**

Brechin

1153(?) Samson
1178 Turpin
1202 Radulf
1215 Hugh
1218 Gregory
1246 Albin
1269(?) William de Crachin (elect)
1275 William Comyn
1296 Nicholas
1298 John de Kyninmund
1328 Adam de Moravia
1350 Philip Wilde
1351 Patrick de Locrys [Leuchars]
1383 Stephen de Cellario
1411 Walter Forrester
1426 John de Crannach
1455 George Schoriswood
1464 Patrick Graham
1465 John Balfour
1489 William Meldrum
1523 John Hepburn
1557 Donald Campbell (elect)
1565(?) John Sinclair (elect)
1566 Alexander Campbell (titular)
1610 Andrew Lamb
1619 David Lindsay
1634 Thomas Sydserf
1635 Walter Whitford
1662 David Strachan
1672 Robert Laurie
1678 George Haliburton
1682 Robert Douglas
1684 Alexander Cairncross
1684 James Drummond
1695–1709 Held with **Edinburgh**
1709 John Falconar
1724 Robert Norrie
1726 John Ochterlonie
1742 James Rait
1778 George Innes
1787 William Abernethy Drummond
1788 John Strachan
1810 George Gleig
1840 David Moir
1847 Alexander Penrose Forbes
1876 Hugh Willoughby Jermyn
1904 Walter John Forbes Robberds
1935 Kenneth Donald Mackenzie
1944 Eric Graham
1959 John Chappell Sprott
1975 Lawrence Edward Luscombe
1990 Robert Taylor Halliday
1997 Neville Chamberlain

Moray

Moray, Ross and Caithness

1114 Gregory
1153(?) William
1164 Felix
1172 Simon de Tonei
1187 Richard de Lincoln
1203 Brice de Douglas
1224(?) Andrew de Moravia
1244(?) Simon
1251 Radulf de Leycester (elect)
1253 Archibald
1299 David de Moravia
1326 John de Pilmor
1363 Alexander Bur
1397 William de Spyny
1407 John de Innes
1415 Henry Leighton
1422 Columba de Dunbar
1437 John de Winchester
1460(?) James Stewart
1463 David Stewart
1477 William de Tulloch
1487 Andrew Stewart
1501(?) Andrew Forman
1516(?) James Hepburn
1525 Robert Shaw
1532(?) Alexander Stewart
1538(?) Patrick Hepburn
1574 George Douglas
1611 Alexander Douglas
1623 John Guthrie
1662 Murdo Mackenzie
1677 James Aitken
1680 Colin Falconer
1687 Alexander Rose
1688 William Hay
1707 Held with **Edinburgh**
1725 Held with **Aberdeen**
1727 William Dunbar
1737 George Hay (elect)
1742 William Falconar
1777 Arthur Petrie
1787 Andrew Macfarlane
1798 Alexander Jolly
1838 Held with **Ross**
1851 Robert Eden
1886 James Butler Knill Kelly
1904 Arthur John Maclean
1943 Piers Holt Wilson
1953 Duncan Macinnes
1970 George Minshull Sessford
1994 Gregor Macgregor

†Ross

1131(?) Macbeth
1150(?) Simon
1161 Gregory
1195 Reginald
1213 Andrew de Moravia (elect)
1215(?) Robert I
1250 Robert II
1272 Matthew
1275(?) Robert II de Fyvin
1295(?) Adam de Derlingtun (elect)
1297(?) Thomas de Dundee
1325 Roger
1351 Alexander Stewart
1372 Alexander de Kylwos
1398(?) Alexander de Waghorn
1418 Thomas Lyell (elect)
Griffin Yonge (elect)
1420 John Bulloch
1441(?) Andrew de Munro (elect)
1441(?) Thomas Tulloch
1464(?) Henry Cockburn
1478 John Wodman
1481 William Elphinstone (elect)
1483 Thomas Hay
1492 John Guthrie
1498 John Frisel [Fraser]
*c.*1507 Robert Cockburn
1525 James Hay
*c.*1539 Robert Cairncross
1552 David Painter
1561(?) Henry Sinclair
1566 John Lesley
1575 Alexander Hepburn
1611 David Lindsay
1613 Patrick Lindsay
1633 John Maxwell
1662 John Paterson
1679 Alexander Young
1684 James Ramsay
1696 See vacant or held with **Caithness** until 1727
1727 Held with **Moray**
1742 Held with **Caithness**
1762 Robert Forbes
1777 Held with **Moray**
1819 David Low
1851 Held with **Moray**

†Caithness

*c.*1146 Andrew
*c.*1187 John
1214 Adam
1223(?) Gilbert de Moravia
1250(?) William
1263 Walter de Baltrodin
1273(?) Nicholas (elect)
1275 Archibald Herok
1278 Richard (elect)
1279(?) Hervey de Dundee (elect)
1282 Alan de St Edmund
1295 John or James (elect)
1296 Adam de Derlingtun
1297 Andrew
1306 Fercard Belegaumbe
1328(?) David
1341 Alan de Moravia
1343 Thomas de Fingask
1370 Malcolm de Dumbrek
1381 Alexander Man
1414 Alexander Vaus
1425 John de Crannach
1428 Robert Strabrok
1446 John Innes
1448 William Mudy
1478(?) Prospero Camogli de Medici
1484(?) John Sinclair (elect)
1502 Andrew Stewart I
1517(?) Andrew Stewart II
1542 Robert Stewart (elect)
1600 George Gledstanes (elect)
1611 Alexander Forbes
1616 John Abernethy
1662 Patrick Forbes
1680 Andrew Wood
[1695 See vacant]
1731 Robert Keith
1741 Wm. Falconas
1762 Held with **Ross**
[1742 See Vacant]
1777 Held with **Moray**

Glasgow

Glasgow and Galloway

550(?) Kentigern or Mungo (no record of his successors)
1114(?) (Michael)
1118(?) John
1147 Herbert
1164 Ingram
1175 Jocelin
1199 Hugh de Roxburgh (elect)
1200 William Malveisin
1202 Florence (elect)
1208 Walter de St Albans
1233 William de Bondington
1259 Nicholas de Moffat (elect)
1259 John de Cheam
1268 Nicholas de Moffat (elect)
1271 William Wischard (elect)
1273 Robert Wischard
1317 Stephen de Donydouer (elect)
1318 John de Eglescliffe
1323 John de Lindsay
1337 John Wischard
1339 William Rae
1367 Walter Wardlaw
1388 Matthew de Glendonwyn
1391 John Framisden (titular)
1408 William Lauder
1427 John Cameron
1447 James de Brois [Brewhouse]
1448 William Turnbull

1456 Andrew de Durrisdeer
1475 John Laing
1483 George Carmichael (elect)

ARCHBISHOPS

1483 Robert Blackadder (Archbishop 9 Jan 1492)
1509 James Betoun I
1525 Gavin Dunbar
1551 Alexander Gordon
1552 James Betoun II (restored 1587)
1571 John Porterfield (titular)
1573 James Boyd (titular)
1581 Robert Montgomery (titular)
1585 William Erskine (titular)
1610 John Spottiswoode
1615 James Law
1633 Patrick Lindsay
1661 Andrew Fairfoul
1664 Alexander Burnet (restored 1674)
1671 Robert Leighton, died 1684 (resigned 1674)
1679 Arthur Rose
1684 Alexander Cairncross, died 1701
1687 John Paterson,[1] died 1708
[1708 Vacant]

BISHOPS

1731 Alexander Duncan, died 1733
[1733 Vacant]
1787 Held with **Edinburgh**
1805 William Abernethy Drummond
1809–37 Held with **Edinburgh**
1837 Michael Russell
1848 Walter John Trower
1859 William Scott Wilson
1888 William Thomas Harrison
1904 Archibald Ean Campbell
1921 Edward Thomas Scott Reid
1931 John Russell Darbyshire
1938 John Charles Halland How
1952 Francis Hamilton Moncreiff
1974 Frederick Goldie
1981 Derek Alec Rawcliffe
1991 John Mitchell Taylor

†Galloway or Candida Casa or Whithorn[2]

Ninian, died 432(?)
(?) Octa
681 Trumwine
731 Penthelm, died 735(?)
735 Frithowald, died 764
763 Pehtwine, died 776
777 Ethelbert
791 Beadwulf
1140 Gilla-Aldan
1154 Christian
1189 John
1214 Walter
1235 Odo Ydonc (elect)
1235 Gilbert
1255 Henry
1294 Thomas de Kircudbright [de Daltoun]
1327 Simon de Wedale
1355 Michael Malconhalgh
1359(?) Thomas Macdowell (elect)
1359 Thomas
1364 Adam de Lanark
(?) David Douglas, died 1373
(?) James Carron (resigned 1373)
1378 Ingram de Kethnis (elect)
1379 Oswald
1380 Thomas de Rossy
(?) Francis Ramsay, died 1402
1406 Elisaeus Adougan
1414(?) Gilbert Cavan (elect)
1415 Thomas de Butil
1422 Alexander Vaus
1451 Thomas Spens
1457(?) Thomas Vaus (elect)
1459 Ninian Spot
1482(?) George Vaus
1508(?) James Betoun (elect)
1509(?) David Arnot
1526 Henry Wemyss
1541(?) Andrew Dury
1559(?) Alexander Gordon
1610 Gavin Hamilton
1612(?) William Couper
1619 Andrew Lamb
1635 Thomas Sydserf
1661 James Hamilton
1675 John Paterson
1679 Arthur Rose
1680 James Aitken
1688 John Gordon, died 1726
1697 Held with **Edinburgh**
1837 Held with **Glasgow**

Argyll or Lismore

Argyll and The Isles

1193 Harald
1240 William
1253 Alan
1268 Laurence de Erganis
1300 Andrew
1342 Angusde Ergadia (elect)
1344 Martinde Ergaill
1387 John Dugaldi
1397(?) Bean Johannis
1420(?) Finlay de Albany
1428 George Lauder
1476 Robert Colquhoun
1504 David Hamilton
1532 Robert Montgomery
1539(?) William Cunningham (elect)
1553(?) James Hamilton (elect)
1580 Neil Campbell (titular)
1611 John Campbell (titular)
1613 Andrew Boyd
1637 James Fairlie
1662 David Fletcher
1665 John Young (elect)
1666 William Scroggie
1675 Arthur Rose
1679 Colin Falconer
1680 Hector Maclean
1688 Alexander Monro (elect)
Held with **Ross**
1847 Alexander Ewing
1874 George Mackarness
1883 James Robert Alexander Chinnery-Haldane
1907 Kenneth Mackenzie
1942 Thomas Hannay
1963 Richard Knyvet Wimbush
1977 George Kennedy Buchanan Henderson
1993 Douglas MacLean Cameron

†The Isles

900 Patrick
1080 Roolwer
1080 William
1095 Hamundr
1138 Wimund
1152 John I
1152(?) Ragnald
1154 Gamaliel
1170 Christian
1194 Michael
1210 Nicholas I
1219 Nicholas II of Meaux
1226(?) Reginald
1226 Simon
1249 Laurence (elect)
1253 Richard
1275 Gilbert (elect)
1275 Mark
1305 Alan
1324 Gilbert Maclelan
1328 Bernard de Linton
1331 Thomas de Rossy
1349 William Russell
1374 John Donkan
1387 Michael
1392 John Sproten (**Man**) (titular)
1402(?) Conrad (**Man**) (titular)
1402(?) Theodore Bloc (**Man**) (titular)
1410 Richard Messing (**Man**)
1422 Michael Anchire
1425(?) John Burgherlinus (**Man**)
1428 Angus I
1441(?) John Hectoris [McCachane] Macgilleon
1472 Angus II
1487 John Campbell
1511 George Hepburn
1514 John Campbell (elect)
1530(?) Ferchar MacEachan (elect)
1550(?) Roderick Maclean
1553(?) Alexander Gordon
1567 John Carswell (titular)
1573 John Campbell
1605 Andrew Knox
1619 Thomas Knox
1628 John Leslie
1634 Neil Campbell
1662 Robert Wallace
1677 Andrew Wood
1680 Archibald Graham [or McIlvernock]
Held with **Orkney** and **Caithness**
1819 Held with **Argyll**

College Bishops, Consecrated without Sees

1705 John Sage, died 1711
1705 John Fullarton (**Edinburgh** 1720), died 1727
1709 Henry Christie, died 1718
1709 John Falconar (**Fife** 1720), died 1723
1711 Archibald Campbell (**Aberdeen** 1721), died 1744
1712 James Gadderar (**Aberdeen** 1725, **Moray** 1725), died 1733
1718 Arthur Millar (**Edinburgh** 1727), died 1727
1718 William Irvine, died 1725
1722 Andrew Cant, died 1730
1722 David Freebairn (**Edinburgh** 1733)
1726 John Ochterlonie (**Brechin** 1731), died 1742
1726 James Ross (**Fife** 1731), died 1733

[1] After the deposition of John Paterson at the Revolution the See ceased to be Archiepiscopal.
[2] The traditional founder of the See is St Ninian, but nothing authentic is known of the bishops prior to the accession of Gilla-Aldan between 1133 and 1140.

1727 John Gillan
(**Dunblane** 1731), died 1735
1727 David Ranken, died 1728

Bishops who have held the Office of Primus

1704 Alexander Rose (**Edinburgh** 1704–20)
1720 John Fullarton (**Edinburgh** 1720–27)
1727 Arthur Millar (**Edinburgh** 1727)
1727 Andrew Lumsden (**Edinburgh** 1727–33)
1731 David Freebairn (**Edinburgh** 1733–39)
1738 Thomas Rattray (**Dunkeld** 1727–43)
1743 Robert Keith (**Caithness** 1731–41)
1757 Robert White (**Dunblane** 1735–43, **St Andrews** 1743–61)
1762 William Falconar (**Orkney** and **Caithness** 1741–62)
1782 Robert Kilgour (**Aberdeen** 1768–86)
1788 John Skinner (**Aberdeen** 1786–1816)
1816 George Gleig (**Brechin** 1810–40)
1837 James Walker (**Edinburgh** 1880–41)
1841 William Skinner (**Aberdeen** 1816–57)
1857 Charles Hughes Terrot (**Edinburgh** 1841–72)
1862 Robert Eden (**Moray, Ross, and Caithness** 1851–86)
1886 Hugh Willoughby Jermyn (**Brechin** 1875–1903)
1901 James Butler Knill Kelly (**Moray, Ross, and Caithness** 1886–1904)
1904 George Howard Wilkinson (**St Andrews, Dunkeld, and Dunblane** 1893–1907)
1908 Walter John Forbes Robberds (**Brechin** 1904–34)
1935 Arthur John Maclean (**Moray, Ross, and Caithness** 1904–43)
1943 Ernest Denny Logie Danson (**Edinburgh** 1939–46)
1946 John Charles Halland How (**Glasgow and Galloway** 1938–52)
1952 Thomas Hannay (**Argyll and The Isles** 1942–62)
1962 Francis Hamilton Moncreiff (**Glasgow and Galloway** 1952–74)
1974 Richard Knyvet Wimbush (**Argyll and The Isles** 1963–77)
1977 Alastair Iain Macdonald Haggart (**Edinburgh** 1975–85)
1985 Lawrence Edward Luscombe (**Brechin** 1975–)
1990 George Kennedy Buchanan Henderson (**Argyll and The Isles** 1977–1992)
1992 Richard Frederick Holloway (**Edinburgh** 1986–)

IRELAND

PROVINCE OF ARMAGH

†Achonry

BISHOPS

c.558 Cathfuidh
1152 Mael Ruanaid ua Ruadain
1159 Gille na Naehm O Ruadain [Gelasius]
1208 Clemens O Sniadaig
1220 Connmach O Torpaig [Carus]
1226 Gilla Isu O Cleirig [Gelasius]
1237 Tomas O Ruadhan
1238 Oengus O Clumain [Elias]
1251 Tomas O Maicin
1266 Tomas O Miadachain [Dionysus]
1286 Benedict O Bracain
1312 David of Kilheny
1348 David II
1348 Nicol Alias Muircheartach O hEadhra
1374 William Andrew
1385 Simon
c.1390 Tomas mac Muirgheasa MacDonn-chadha
1401 Brian mac Seaain O hEadhra
1410 Maghnus O h Eadhra
1424 Donatus
1424 Richard Belmer
1436 Tadhg O Dalaigh
1442 James Blakedon
1449 Cornelius O Mochain
1463 Brian O hEasdhra [Benedictus]
1470 Nicholas Forden
1475 Robert Wellys
1484 Thomas fitzRichard
1484 Tomas O Conghalain
1489 John Bustamente
1492 Thomas Ford
1508 Eugenius O Flannagain
1522 Cormac O Snighe
1547 Thomas O Fihilly
1562 Eugene O'Harte
1613 Miler Magrath (with **Cashel**)
United to **Killala** 1622

†Annadown

BISHOPS

1189 Conn ua Mellaig [Concors]
1202 Murchad ua Flaithbertaig
1242 Tomas O Mellaig
1251 Conchobar [Concors]
1283 John de Ufford
1308 Gilbert O Tigernaig
1323 Jacobus O Cethernaig
1326 Robert Petit
1328 Albertus
1329 Tomas O Mellaig
1359 Dionysius
1393 Johannes
1394 Henry Trillow
1402 John Bryt
1408 John Wynn
1421 John Boner [Camere]
1425 Seean Mac Braddaigh
1428 Seamus O Lonnghargain
1431 Donatus O Madagain
1446 Thomas Salscot
1450 Redmund Bermingham
1458 Thomas Barrett
1496 Francis Brunand
1540 John Moore
United to **Tuam** c.1555

†Ardagh

454 Mel
c.670 Erard
874 Faelghus
Cele 1048
1152 Mac Raith ua Morain
1172 Gilla Crist O hEothaig [Christianus]
O'Tirlenain 1187
ua hEislinnen
Annud O Muiredaig 1216
1217 Robert
1224 M.
1228 Loseph mac Teichthechain
1229 Mac Raith Mac Serraig
1232 Gilla Isu mac in Scelaige O Tormaid [Gelasius]
1232 Iocelinus
1238 Brendan Mac Teichthechain
1256 Milo of Dunstable
1290 Matha O'h-Eothaig [Mattheus]
1323 Robert Wirsop (did not get possession)
1324 Mac Eoaighseoan
1347 Eoghan O Ferghail [Audovenus]
1368 William Mac Carmaic
1373 Cairbre O'Ferghail [Charles]
1373 John Aubrey
1392 Henry Nony (did not get possession)
1396 Comedinus Mac Bradaigh [Gilbert]
1400 Adam Leyns
1419 Conchobar O'Ferghail [Cornelius]
1425 Risdeard O'Ferghail
[1444 O'Murtry, not consecrated resigned]
1445 Cormac Mac Shamhradhain
1462 Seaan O'Ferghail
1467 Donatus O'Ferghail
1482 William O'Ferghail
1517 Ruaidri O'Maoileoin
1517 Rory O'Mallone [Roger O Melleine]
1541 Richard O'Ferrall
1553 Patrick MacMahon

† Indicates a diocese no longer extant or united with another diocese.

[1572 John Garvey, not consecrated]
1583 Lysach O'Ferrall
1604 Robert Draper
1613 Thomas Moigne
1679 William Bedell
1633 John Richardson
1661 Robert Maxwell
1673 Francis Marsh
1682 William Sheridan
1692 Ulysses Burgh
1604–33, 1661–92 and 1692–1751 Held by the Bishops of **Kilmore**
1751–1839 Held by the Archbishops of **Tuam**
United to **Kilmore** 1839

Armagh

BISHOPS

444 Patrick
Benignus 467
Jarlath 481
Cormac 497
Dubthach 513
Ailill I 526
Ailill II 536
David O'Faranan 551
Carlaen 588
MacLaisre 623
–640 Thomian MacRonan
Segeni 688
Suibhne 730
–732 Congusa
Affinth 794
–811 Nundha
–818 Artri
835 Forannan
Mael Patraic I 862
Fethgna 875
Cathasach MacRobartach 883
Mochta 893
900 Maelaithghin
Cellach
Mael Ciarain 915
Joseph 936
Mael Patraic II 936
Cathasach MacDolgen 966
Maelmiure 994
Airindach 1000
Maeltuile 1032
1032 Hugh O'Ferris
Mael Patraic III 1096
1099 Caincomrac O'Boyle

ARCHBISHOPS

1105 Cellach mac Aeda meic Mael Isu [Celsus]
1132 Mael maedoc Ua Morgair [Malachais]
1137 Gilla Meic Liac mac Diarmata meic Ruaidri [Gelasius]
1174 Conchobar O Conchaille [Concors]
1175 Gille in Coimhedh O Caran [Gilbertus]
1180 Tomaltach O Conchobair [Thomas]
1184 Mael Isu Ua Cerbaill [Malachias]
1202 Echdonn mac Gilla Uidir [Eugenius]
1217 Lucas Neterville
1227 Donatus O Fidabra
1240 Albert Suebeer of Cologne
1247 Reginald
1258 Abraham O'Conallain
1261 Mael Patraic O Scannail
1270 Nicol Mac Mael Isu
1303 Michael MacLochlainn (not confirmed)
1304 Dionysius (not confirmed)
1306 John Taaffe
1307 Walter Jorz
1311 Roland Jorz
1324 Stephen Segrave
1334 David Mag Oireachtaigh
1347 Richard FitzRalph
1362 Milo Sweetman
1383 John Colton
1404 Nicholas Fleming
1418 John Swayne
1439 John Prene
1444 John Mey
1457 John Bole [Bull]
1471 John Foxhalls or Foxholes
1475 Edmund Connesburgh
1480 Ottaviano Spinelli [de Palatio]
1513 John Kite
1521 George Cromer
1543 George Dowdall
1552 Hugh Goodacre
1553 George Dowdall (again)
[1560 Donat MacTeague, not recognized by the Crown, 1562]
1563 Adam Loftus
1568 Thomas Lancaster
1584 John Long
1589 John Garvey
1595 Henry Ussher
1613 Christopher Hampton
1625 James Ussher
[Interregnum 1656–61]
1661 John Bramhall
1663 James Margetson
1679 Michael Boyle
1703 Narcissus Marsh
1714 Thomas Lindsay
1724 Hugh Boulter
1742 John Hoadly
1747 George Stone
1765 Richard Robinson [afterwards Baron Rokeby]
1795 William Newcome
1800 William Stuart
1822 John George Beresford
United to **Clogher** 1850–86
1862 Marcus Gervais Beresford
1886 Robert Bentknox
1893 Robert Samuel Gregg
1896 William Alexander
1911 John Baptist Crozier
1920 Charles Frederick D'Arcy
1938 John Godfrey FitzMaurice Day
1939 John Allen Fitzgerald Gregg
1959 James McCann
1969 George Otto Simms
1980 John Ward Armstrong
1986 Robert Henry Alexander Eames

Clogher

*c.*493 MacCarthinn or Ferdachrioch
Ailill 869
1135 Cinaeth O Baigill
1135 Gilla Crist O Morgair [Christianus] (moved his see to Louth)

BISHOPS OF LOUTH

1135 Gilla Crist O Morgair [Christianus]
1138 Aed O Ceallaide [Edanus]
1178 Mael Isu O Cerbaill [Malachias]
1187 Gilla Crist O Mucaran [Christinus]
1194 Mael Isu Ua Mael Chiarain
1197 Gilla Tigernaig Mac Gilla Ronain [Thomas]

BISHOPS OF CLOGHER

1218 Donatus O Fidabra
1228 Nehemias
1245 David O Bracain
1268 Michael Mac an tSair
1287 Matthew Mac Cathasaigh I
–1310 Henricus
1316 Gelasius O Banain
1320 Nicholas Mac Cathasaigh
1356 Brian Mac Cathmaoil [Bernard]
1362 Matthew Mac Cathasaigh II
— Aodh O hEothaigh [*alias* O Neill]
1373 John O Corcrain [Wurzburg]
1390 Art Mac Cathmhail
1433 Piaras Mag Uidhir [Petrus]
1450 Rossa mac Tomais Oig Mag Uidhir [Rogerius]
1475 Florence Woolley
[1484 Niall mac Seamuis Mac Mathghamna]
1484 John Edmund de Courci
1494 Seamus Mac Pilip Mac Mathghamna
1500 Andreas
1502 Nehemias O Cluainin
1504 Giolla Padraig O Conalaigh [Patrick]
1505 Eoghan Mac Cathmhail [Eugenius]
1517 Padraig O Cuilin
1535 Aodh O Cearbhalain [Odo]
1517 Patrick O'Cullen
1535 Hugh O'Carolan
1570 Miler Magrath
1605 George Montgomery
1621 James Spottiswood
1645 Henry Jones
1661 John Leslie
1671 Robert Leslie
1672 Roger Boyle
1691 Richard Tennison
1697 St George Ashe
1717 John Stearne
1745 Robert Clayton
1758 John Garnett
1782 John Hotham
1796 William Foster
1797 John Porter
1819 John George Beresford
1820 Percy Jocelyn
1822 Robert Ponsonby Tottenham Luftus
United to **Armagh** 1850–86
1886 Charles Maurice Stack
1903 Charles Frederick D'Arcy
1908 Maurice Day
1923 James MacManaway
1944 Richard Tyner
1958 Alan Alexander Buchanan
1970 Richard Patrick Crosland Hanson
1973 Robert William Heavener
1980 Gordon McMullan
1986 Brian Desmond Anthony Hannon

Connor

506 Oengus MacNessa 514
Lughadh 543
640 Dimma Dubh [the Black]
Duchonna the Pious 725
Cunnen or Cuinden 1038
Flann O'Sculu 1117
1124 Mael Maedoc Ua Morgair [Malachias]

–1152 MaelPatraic O'Banain
1172 Nehemias
1178 Reginaldus
1226 Eustacius
1242 Adam
1245 Isaac de Newcastle-on-Tyne
1258 William de Portroyal
1261 William de Hay [or la Haye]
1263 Robert de Flanders
1275 Peter de Dunach
1293 Johannes
1320 Richard
1321 James de Couplith
1323 John de Eglecliff
1323 Robert Wirsop
1324 Jacabus O Cethernaig
1353 William Mercier
1374 Paulus
1389 Johannes
[1420 Seaan O Luachrain, not consecrated]
1423 Eoghan O'Domhnaill
1429 Domhnall O'Meraich
1431 John Fossade [Festade]
1459 Patricius
1459 Simon Elvington
United to **Down** 1441
1945 Charles King Irwin
1956 Robert Cyril Hamilton Glover Elliott
1969 Arthur Hamilton Butler
1981 William John McCappin
1987 Samuel Greenfield Poyntz
1995 James Edward Moore

Derry

Derry and Raphoe

Caencomhrac 927
–937 Finachta MacKellach
–949 Mael Finnen

BISHOPS OF MAGHERA

(Where the See was in the twelfth and the thirteenth centuries)
1107 Mael Coluim O Brolchain
— Mael Brigte O Brolchain
1152 O Gormgaile Muiredach O Cobthaig [Mauricius]
1173 Amhlaim O Muirethaig
1185 Fogartach O Cerballain [Florentius]
c.1230 Gilla in Coimhded O Cerballain [Germanus]
c.1280 Fogartach O Cerballain II [Florentius]

BISHOPS OF DERRY

(Where the See was resettled)
1295 Enri Mac Airechtaig [O'Reghly] [of Ardagh]
1297 Gofraid MacLochlainn [Godfrey]
1316 Aed O Neill [Odo]
1319 Michael Mac Lochlainn [Maurice]
1349 Simon
1391 Johannes
1391 John Dongan
1394 Seoan O Mochain
1398 Aodh [Hugo]
1401 Seoan O Flannabhra
1415 Domhnall Mac Cathmhail
1419 Domhnall O Mearaich
1429 Eoghan O Domhnaill [Eugenius]
1433 John Oguguin
[1456 John Bole, appointment not completed, translated to Armagh]
1458 Bartholomew O Flannagain
c.1464 Johannes
1467 Nicholas Weston
1485 Domhnall O Fallamhain
1501 Seamus mac Pilip Mac Mathghamna [MacMahon]
1520 Ruaidhri O Domhnaill
1520 Rory O'Donnell
1554 Eugene O'Doherty
1568 F. [doubtful authority]
1569 Redmond O'Gallagher
[1603 Denis Campbell, not consecrated]
1605 George Montgomery
1610 Brutus Babington
[1611 Christopher Hampton, consecrated]
1613 John Tanner
1617 George Downham
1634 John Bramhall
1661 George Wild
1666 Robert Mossom
1680 Michael Ward
1681 Ezekiel Hopkins
1691 William King
1703 Charles Hickman
1714 John Hartstonge
1717 St George Ashe
1718 William Nicolson
1727 Henry Downes
1735 Thomas Rundle
1743 Carew Reynell
1745 George Stone
1747 William Barnard
1768 Frederick Augustus Hervey [afterwards Earl of Bristol]
1803 William Knox
1831 Richard Ponsonby
Raphoe united to Derry from 1834
1853 William Higgin
1867 William Alexander
1896 George Alexander Chadwick (resigned)
1916 Joseph Irvine Peacocke
1945 Robert M'Neil Boyd
1958 Charles John Tyndall
1970 Cuthbert Irvine Peacocke
1975 Robert Henry Alexander Eames
1980 James Mehaffey

Down

Down and Dromore

Fergus 584
Suibhne 825
Graithene 956
Finghin 964
Flaithbertach 1043
MaelKevin 1086
— Mael Muire 1117
Oengus Ua Gormain 1123
— [Anonymous]
c.1124 Mael Maedoc O Morgair [Malachias]
1152 Mael Isu mac in Chleirig Chuirr [Malachias]
1175 Gilla Domangairt Mac Cormaic
c.1176 Echmilid [Malachias]
c.1202 Radulfus
1224 Thomas
1251 Randulphus
1258 Reginaldus
1265 Thomas Lydel
1277 Nicholas le Blund
1305 Thomas Ketel
1314 Thomas Bright
1328 John of Baliconingham
1329 Ralph of Kilmessan
1353 Richard Calf I
1365 Robert of Aketon
1367 William White
1369 Richard Calf [II]
1386 John Ross
1394 John Dongan
1413 John Cely [or Sely]
1445 Ralph Alderle

BISHOPS OF DOWN AND CONNOR

1441 John Fossard
1447 Thomas Pollard
1451 Richard Wolsey
1456 Thomas Knight
1469 Tadhg O Muirgheasa [Thaddaeus]
1489 Tiberio Ugolino
1520 Robert Blyth
1542 Eugene Magennis
1565 James MacCawell
1569 John Merriman
1572 Hugh Allen
1593 Edward Edgeworth
1596 John Charden
1602 Roben Humpston
1607 John Todd (resigned)
1612 James Dundas
1613 Robert Echlin
1635 Henry Leslie
1661 Jeremy Taylor
1667 Roger Boyle
1672 Thomas Hacket
1694 Samuel Foley
1695 Edward Walkington
1699 Edward Smyth
1721 Francis Hutchinson
1739 Carew Reynell
1743 John Ryder
1752 John Whitcombe
1752 Robert Downes
1753 Arthur Smyth
1765 James Traill
1784 William Dickson
1804 Nathaniel Alexander
1823 Richard Mant

BISHOPS OF DOWN, CONNOR AND DROMORE

1849 Robert Bent Knox
1886 William Reeves
1892 Thomas James Welland
1907 John Baptist Crozier
1911 Charles Frederick D'Arcy
1919 Charles Thornton Primrose Grierson
1934 John Frederick McNeice
1942 Charles King Irwin

BISHOPS OF DOWN AND DROMORE

1945 William Shaw Kerr
1955 Frederick Julian Mitchell
1970 George Alderson Quin
1980 Robert Henry Alexander Eames
1986 Gordon McMullan
1997 Harold Creeth Miller

†Dromore

Mael Brighde 974
Riagan 1101
1197 Ua Ruanada
1227 Geraldus
1245 Andreas
1284 Tigernach I
1290 Gervasius
— Tigernach II
1309 Florentius Mac Donnocain
1351 Anonymous

1366 Milo
1369 Christophorus Cornelius 1382
1382 John O'Lannoy
1398 Thomas Orwell
1400 John Waltham
1402 Roger Appleby
1408 Richard Payl
1410 Marcus
1411 John Chourles
1414 Seaan O Ruanadha
1419 Nicholas Wartre
1429 Thomas Rackelf
1431 William
1431 David Chirbury
1450 Thomas Scrope [Bradley]
1450 Thomas Radcliff
1456 Donatus O h-Anluain [Ohendua]
1457 Richard Messing
1463 William Egremond
— Aonghus [Aeneas] 1476
1476 Robert Kirke
1480 Yvo Guillen
1483 George Braua
1511 Tadhg O Raghallaigh [Thaddeus]
1536 Quintin O Quigley [Cogley]
1539 Roger McHugh
1540 Arthur Magennis
1607 John Todd
[1613 John Tanner, not consecrated]
1613 Theophilus Buckworth
1661 Robert Leslie
1661 Jeremy Taylor (administered the diocese)
1667 George Rust
1671 Essex Digby
1683 Capel Wiseman
1695 Tobias Pullein
1713 John Stearne
1717 Ralph Lambert
1727 Charles Cobbe
1732 Henry Maule
1744 Thomas Fletcher
1745 Jemmett Browne
1745 George Marlay
1763 John Oswald
1763 Edward Young
1765 Henry Maxwell
1766 William Newcome
1775 James Hawkins
1780 William de la Poer Beresford
1782 Thomas Percy
1811 George Hall
1812 John Leslie
1819 James Saurin
United to **Down** since 1842

†Elphin

Domnall mac Flannacain Ua Dubhthaig 1136
Muiredach O Dubhthaig 1150
1152 Mael Isu O Connachtain
Flannacan O Dubhthaig 1168
c.1177 Tomaltach mac Aeda Ua Conchobhair [Thomas]
c.1180 Florint Ua Riacain Ui Maelrvanaid
1206 Ardgar O Conchobhair
1226 Dionysius O Mordha
c.1230 Alanus
1231 Donnchad mac Fingein O Conchobhair [Dionysius Donatus]
1245 Eoin O Mugroin
1247 Tomaltach macToirrdelbaig O Conchobhair [Thomas]
1260 Mael Sechlainn O Conchobhair [Milo]
1262 Tomas mac Fergail mac Diarmata
1266 Muiris O Conchobhair
[1285 Amiaim O Tommaltaig, not consecrated]
1285 Gilla Isu mac in Liathana O Conchobhair
1297 Maelsechlainn mac Briain [Malachias]
1303 Donnchad O Flannacain, [Donatus]
1307 Cathal O Conchobhair
1310 Mael Sechlainn Mac Aedha
1313 Lurint O Lachtnain [Laurence]
1326 Sean O Finnachta
1355 Carolus
1357 Gregory O Mochain
1372 Thomas Barrett
1383 Seoan O Mochain
1407 Seaan O Grada
1405 Gerald Caneton
1412 Thomas Colby
1418 Robert Fosten
1421 Edmund Barrett
1427 Johannes
1429 Laurence O Beolain
1429 William O hEidighean
1448 Conchobhar O Maolalaidh
1458 Nicholas O Flanagan
1487 Hugo Arward
1492 Rlocard mac Briain O gCuanach
1499 George Brana
1501 Cornelius O Flannagain
1508 Christopher Fisher
1525 John Maxey
1539 William Maginn 1541(?)
1539 Gabriel de Sancto Serio
1541 Conach or Con O'Negall or O'Shyagall
1552 Roland Burke [de Burgo]
1582 Thomas Chester
1583 John Lynch
1611 Edward King
1639 Henry Tilson
1661 John Parker
1667 John Hodson
1691 Simon Digby
1720 Henry Downes
1724 Theophilus Bolton
1730 Robert Howard
1740 Edward Synge
1762 William Gore
1772 Jemmett Browne
1775 Charles Dodgson
1795 John Law
1810 Power le Poer Trench
1819 John Leslie 1854
United to **Kilmore** and **Ardagh** on the death of Bishop Beresford in 1841, when Bishop Leslie became Bishop of the united dioceses.

†Killala

Muiredach
Kellach
O Maolfogmair I 1137
O Maolfogmair II 1151
Imar O Ruaidhin 1176
1179 O Maolfogmair III
1199 Domnall Ua Becdha
1207 Cormac O'Tarpy
O'Kelly 1214
1226 Aengus O Maolfogmair [Elias]
Gille Cellaig O Ruaidhin
1253 Seoan O Laidlg
1281 Donnchad O Flaithbertaig [Donatus]
1307 John Tankard
Sean O Flaithim 1343
1344 James Bermingham
1347 William O Dubhda
1351 Robert Elyot
1381 Thomas Lodowys
1383 Conchobar O Coineoil [Cornelius]
1390 Thomas Horwell [Orwell]
1400 Thomas Barrett
1403 Muircheartach Cleirach mac Donnchadha O Dubhda
Connor O'Connell 1423
1427 Fergal Mac Martain
1431 Thaddaeus Mac Creagh
1432 Brian O Coneoil
1447 Robert Barrett
1452 Ruaidhri Bairead [Barrett]
1453 Thomas
1459 Richard Viel
Miler O'Connell
1461 Donatus O Conchobhair
1470 Tomas Bairead [Barrett]
1487 John de Tuderto [Seaan O Caissin]
1500 Thomas Clerke
1508 Malachias O Clumhain
1513 Risdeard Bairead
1545 Redmond O'Gallagher
1570 Donat O'Gallagher
1580 John O'Casey
1592 Owen O'Conor
1613 Miler Magrath
Achonry united to Killala 1622
1623 Archibald Hamilton
1630 Archibald Adair (deposed, but subsequently restored)
164? John Maxwell
1661 Henry Hall
1664 Thomas Bayly
1671 Thomas Otway
1680 John Smith
1681 William Smyth
1682 Richard Tennison
1691 William Lloyd
1717 Henry Downes
1720 Charles Cobbe
1727 Robert Howard
1730 Robert Clayton
173? Mordecai Cary
175? Richard Robinson [afterwards Baron Rokeby]
1759 Samuel Hutchinson
1781 William Cecil Pery
1784 William Preston
1787 John Law
1795 John Porter
1798 Joseph Stock
1810 James Verschoyle
United to **Tuam** since 1834

Kilmore

Kilmore, Elphin and Ardagh

— Aed Ua Finn 1136
— Muirchenach Ua Maelmoeherge 1149
1152 Tuathal Ua Connachtaig [Thadeus]
1202 Mi Ua Dobailen
— Flann O Connachtaig [Florentius] 1231
1237 Congalach Mac Idneoil
1251 Simon O Ruairc
1286 Mauricius
— Matha Mac Duibne 1314
1320 Padraig O Cridecain
— Conchobhar Mac Conshnamha [Ford] 1355
1356 Richard O Raghilligh
1373 Johannes
1388 Thomas Rushook
1392 Sean O Raghilligh I [John]

1398 Nicol Mac Bradaigh
1401 Sean O'Raghilligh II
1407 John Stokes
1409 David O'Fairchellaigh
1422 Domhnall O Gabhann
1445 Aindrias Mac Bradaigh
1455 Fear Sithe Mag Dhuibhne
1465 Sean O Raghilligh II
1476 Cormac Mag Shamhradhain
1480 Tomas MacBradaigh
1512 Diarmaid O Raghilligh
1530 Edmund Nugent
1540 Sean Mac Bradaigh
1585 John Garvey
1604 Robert Draper
1613 Thomas Moigne
1629 William Bedell
1643 Robert Maxwell
1673 Francis Marsh
1682 William Sheridan
1693 William Smyth
1699 Edward Wetenhall
1715 Timothy Godwin
1727 Josiah Hott
1742 Joseph Story
1757 John Cradock
1772 Denison Cumberland
1775 George Lewis Jones
1790 William Foster
1796 Charles Broderick
1802 George de la Poer Beresford
Ardagh united to Kilmore 1839
Elphin united to Kilmore 1841
1841 John Leslie
1854 Marcus Gervais Beresford
1862 Hamilton Verschoyle
1870 Charles Leslie
1870 Thomas Carson
1874 John Richard Darley
1884 Samuel Shone
1897 Alfred George Elliott
1915 William Richard Moore
1930 Arthur William Barton
1939 Albert Edward Hughes
1950 Frederick Julian Mitchell
1956 Charles John Tyndall
1959 Edward Francis Butler Moore
1981 William Gilbert Wilson
1993 Michael Hugh Gunton Mayes

†Mayo

Gerald 732
Muiredach [or Murray]
Mcinracht 732
Aidan 773
1172 Gilla Isu Ua Mailin
Cele O Dubhthaig 1210
1210 ?Patricius
1428 William Prendergast
1430 Nicholas 'Wogmay'
1439 Odo O h-Uiginn
1432 Martin Campania
1457 Simon de Duren
1493 John Bel
1541 Eugenius Macan Brehon
United to **Tuam** 1559

†Raphoe

Sean O Gairedain
Donell O Garvan
Felemy O Syda
Oengus O'Lappin 959
1150 Muiredhach O'Cofley
1156 Gille in Coimhded Ua Carain [Gilbertus]
— Anonymous
1204 Mael Isu Ua Doirig
— Anonymous
1253 Mael Padraig O Scannail [Patricius]
1263 John de Alneto
1265 Cairpre O Scuapa
1275 Fergal O Firghil [Florentius]
1306 Enri Mac-in-Chrossain [Henricus]
1319 Tomas Mac Carmaic Ui Domhnaill
1363 Padraig Mac Maonghail
1367 Conchobar Mac Carmaic Ui Domhnaill [Cornelius]
1397 Seoan MacMenmain
1400 Eoin MacCarmaic [Johannes]
–1413 Anthony
–1414 Robert Rubire
1416 John McCormic
1420 Lochlainn O Gallchobhair I [Laurentius]
1440 Cornelius Mac Giolla Brighde
1443 Lochlainn O Gallchobhair II [Laurentius]
1479 John de Rogeriis
1482 Meanma Mac Carmail [Menclaus Mac Carmacain]
1514 Conn O Cathain [Cornelius]
1534 Eamonn O Gallchobhair
1547 Arthur o'Gallagher
1563 Donnell Magonigle [or McCongail]
[1603 Denis Campbell, not consecrated]
1605 George Montgomery
1611 Andrew Knox
1633 John Leslie
1661 Robert Leslie
1671 Ezekiel Hopkins
1682 William Smyth
1693 Alexander Cairncross
1701 Robert Huntington
1702 John Pooley
1713 Thomas Lindsay
1714 Edward Synge
1716 Nicholas Forster
1744 William Barnard
1747 Philip Twysden
1753 Robert Downes
1763 John Oswald
1780 James Hawkins
1807 John George Beresford
1819 William Magee
1822 William Bissett
United to **Derry** since 1834

Tuam

Tuam, Killala and Achonry

BISHOPS

Murrough O'Nioc 1032
Hugh O'Hessian 1085
Cathusach Ua Conaill 1117
O Clerig 1137
Muiredach Ua Dubhthaig 1150

ARCHBISHOPS

1152 Aed Ua h-Oisin [Edanus]
1167 Cadhla Ua Dubhthaig [Catholicus]
1202 Felix Ua Ruanada
1236 Mael Muire O Lachtain [Marianus]
1250 Flann Mac Flainn [Florentius]
[1256 James O'Laghtnan, not confirmed or consecrated]
1257 Walter de Salerno
1258 Tomaltach O Conchobair [Thomas]
1286 Stephen de Fulbourn
1289 William de Bermingham
1312 Mael Sechlainn Mac Aeda
1348 Tomas MacCerbhaill [MacCarwill]
1364 Eoin O Grada
1372 Gregory O Mochain I
1384 Gregory O Mochain II
1387 William O Cormacain
1393 Muirchertach mac Pilb O Cellaigh
1410 John Babingle
1411 Cornelius
1430 John Bermingham [Winfield]
1438 Tomas mac Muirchearthaigh O Cellaigh
1441 John de Burgo
1452 Donatus O Muiredaigh
1485 William Seoighe [Joyce]
1503 Philip Pinson
1506 Muiris O Fithcheallaigh
1514 Tomas O Maolalaidh
1537 Christopher Bodkin
1573 William O'Mullally [or Lealy]
Annadown united to Tuam *c.*1555
Mayo united to Tuam 1559
1595 Nehemiah Donnellan
1609 William O'Donnell [or Daniel]
1629 Randolph or Ralph Barlow
1638 Richard Boyle
1645 John Maxwell
1661 Samuel Pullen
1667 John Parker
1679 John Vesey
1716 Edward Synge
1742 Josiah Hort
1752 John Ryder
1775 Jemmett Browne
1782 Joseph Dean Bourke [afterwards Earl of Mayo]
1794 William Beresford [afterwards Baron Decies]
1819 Power le Poer Trench
Killala united to Tuam from 1834

BISHOPS

1839 Thomas Plunket [afterwards Baron Plunket]
1867 Charles Brodrick Bernard
1890 James O'Sullivan
1913 Benjamin John Plunket
1920 Arthur Edwin Ross
1923 John Ort
1928 John Mason Harden
1932 William Hardy Holmes
1939 John Winthrop Crozier
1958 Arthur Hamilton Butler
1970 John Coote Duggan
1986 John Robert Winder Neill

PROVINCE OF DUBLIN

†Ardfert

BISHOPS

Anmchad O h-Anmchada 1117
1152 Mael Brenain Ua Ronain
Gilla Mac Aiblen O'Anmehadha 1166
Domnall O Connairche 1193
1200 David Ua Duibdithrib
Anonymous 1217
1218 John
1218 Gilbertus

1237 Brendan
1253 Christianus
1257 Philippus
1265 Johannes
1286 Nicolaus
1288 Nicol O Samradain
1336 Ailin O hEichthighirn
1331 Edmund of Caermaerthen
1348 John de Valle
1372 Cornelius O Tigernach
1380 William Bull
1411 Nicholas FitzMaurice
1404 Nicholas Ball
1405 Tomas O Ceallaigh
1409 John Attilburgh [Artilburch]
1450 Maurice Stack
1452 Maurice O Conchobhair
1461 John Stack
1461 John Pigge
1473 Philip Stack
1495 John FitzGerald
[See vacant in 1534]
1536 James FitzMaurice
1588 Nicholas Kenan
1600 John Crosbie
1622 John Steere
1628 William Steere
1641 Thomas Fulwar
United to **Limerick** 1661

†Ardmore

1153 Eugenius
Incorporated with **Lismore** 1192

Cashel

Cashel, Waterford, Lismore, Ossory, Ferns and Leighlin

BISHOPS

Cormac MacCuillenan 908
Donnell O'Heney 1096 *or* 1098

ARCHBISHOPS

*c.*1111 Mael los Ua h-Ainmire
Mael losa Ua Fogludha [Mauricius] 1131
Domnall Ua Conaing 1137
Gilla Naomh O'Marty 1149
–1152 Donat O'Lonergan I
– *c.*1160 M.
1172 Domnall O h-Ualla-chain [Donatus]
1186 Muirghes O h-Enna [Matheus]
*c.*1208 Donnchad Ua Longargain I [Donatus]
1216 Donnchad Ua Longargain II [Donatus]
1224 Mairin O Briain [Marianus]
1238 David mac Ceallaig [O'Kelly]
1254 David Mac Cearbaill [Mac Carwill]
1290 Stiamna O Bracain
1303 Maurice Mac Cearbaill
1317 William FitzJohn
1327 Seoan Mac Cerbaill
1329 Walter le Rede
1332 Eoin O Grada
1346 Radulphus O Cellaigh [Kelly]
1362 George Roche [de Rupe]
1365 Tomas Mac Cearbhaill
1374 Philip of Torrington
1382 Michael
1384 Peter Hackett
1406 Richard O Hedian
1442 John Cantwell I
1452 John Cantwell II
1484 David Creagh
1504 Maurice FitzGerald
1525 Edmund Butler
1553 Roland Baron or FitzGerald
1567 James MacCawell
Emly united to Cashel 1569
1571 Miler Magrath (Bishop of Cashel and Waterford from 1582)
1623 Malcolm Hamilton
1630 Archibald Hamilton
1661 Thomas Fulwar
1667 Thomas Price
[See vacant 1685–91]
1691 Narcissus Marsh
1694 William Palliser
[1727 William Nicolson, not enthroned]
1727 Timothy Goodwin
1730 Theophilus Bolton
1744 Arthur Price
1752 John Whitcombe
1754 Michael Cox
1779 Charles Agar
1801 Charles Brodrick
1822 Richard Laurente
Waterford and **Lismore** united to Cashel from 1833; on the death of Abp Laurence in 1838 the province was united to Dublin and the see ceased to be an Archbishopric

BISHOPS

1839 Stephen Creagh Sandes
1843 Robert Daly
1872 Maurice FitzGerald Day
1900 Henry Stewart O'Hara
1919 Robert Miller
1931 John Frederick McNeice
1935 Thomas Arnold Harvey
1958 William Cecil De Pauley
1968 John Ward Armstrong
Ossory united to Cashel 1977
1980 Noel Vincent Willoughby
1997 John Robert Winder Neill

†Clonfert

Moena, or Moynean, or Moeinend 572
Cummin the Tall 662
Ceannfaeladh 807
Laithbheartach 822
Ruthnel or Ruthme 826
Cormac MacEdain 922
Ciaran O'Gabbla 953
Cathal 963
Eochu 1031
O'Corcoran 1095
Muiredach Ua h-Enlainge 1117
Gille Patraic Ua Ailcinned 1149
*c.*1152 Petrus Ua Mordha
1172 Mail Isu mac in Baird
1179 Celechair Ua h-Armedaig
Muirchertach Ua'Maeluidir 1187
Domnall Ua Finn 1195
Muirchertach Ua Carmacain 1204
1205 Mael Brigte Ua hErurain
1224 Cormac O Luimlin [Carus]
1248 Thomas
1259 Tomas mac Domnaill Moire O Cellaig
1266 Johannes de Alatre
1296 Robert
*c.*1302 John
1308 Gregorius O Brocaig
1320 Robert Le Petit
1322 Seoan O Leaain
1347 Tomas mac Gilbert O Cellaigh I
1378 Muircheartach mac Pilib O Cellaigh [Maurice]
1393 William O Cormacain
1398 David Corre
1398 Enri O Conmaigh
1405 Tomasi O Cellaigh II
1410 Cobhthach O Madagain
1438 Seaan O hEidin
1441 John White
1447 Conchobhar O Maolalaidh
1448 Cornelius O Cuinnlis
1463 Matthaeus Mag Raith
1508 David de Burgo
1509 Dionysius O'Mordha
1534 Roland de Burgo
1536 Richard Nangle
1580 Hugh
1582 Stephen Kirwan
1602 Roland Lynch
1627 Robert Dawson
1644 William Baily
1665 Edward Wolley
1691 William FitzGerald
1722 Theophilus Bolton
1724 Arthur Price
1730 Edward Synye
1732 Mordecai Cary
1716 John Whitcombe
1752 Arthur Smyth
1753 William Carmichael
1758 William Gote
1762 John Oswald
1763 Denison Cumberland
1772 Walter Cope
1782 John Law
1787 Richard Marlay
1795 Charles Broderick
1796 Hugh Hamilton
1798 Matthew Young
1801 George de la l'oer Beresford
1802 Nathaniel Alexander
1804 Christopher Butson
United to **Killaloe** since 1834

†Clonmacnoise

–663 Baitan O'Cormac
–839 Joseph [of Rossmore]
Maclodhar 890
Cairbre Crom 904
Loingsech 919
–940 Donough I
–953 Donough II
–966 Cormae O Cillin
Maenach 971
Conaing O'Cosgraigh 998
Male Poil 1001
Flaithbertach 1038
Celechar 1067
O'Mallaen 1093
Christian Aherne 1104
?1111 Domnall mac Flannacain Ua Dubthaig
1152 Muirchertach Ua Maeluidir
Cathal Ua Maeileoin 1207
*c.*1207 Muirchertach Ua Muiricen
1214 Aed O Maeileoin I
1227 Aed O Maeileoin II [Elias]
1236 Thomas Fitzpatrick
1252 Tomas O Cuinn
1280 Anonymous
1282 Gilbert (not consecrated)
1290 William O Dubhthaig
1298 William O Finnein
1303 Domnall O Braein
1324 Lughaid O Dalaigh
1337 Henricus
1349 Simon
1369 Richard [Braybroke]

1371 Hugo
1388 Philippus O Maoil
1389 Milo Corr
1397 O'Gallagher
1397 Philip Nangle
1423 David Prendergast
1426 Cormac Mac Cochlain [Cornelius]
1444 Sean O Dalaigh
1449 Thomas
1458 Robertus
1458 William
1459 John
1487 Walter Blake
1509 Tomas O Maolalaidh
1516 Quintin O h-Uiginn
1539 Richard O'Hogan
1539 Florence Kirwan
1556 Peter Wall [Wale]
United to **Meath** 1569

†Cloyne

Reachtaidh 887
1148 Gilla na Naem O Muirchertaig [Nehemias]
Ua Dubcroin 1159
Ua Flannacain 1167
1177 Matthaeus Ua Mongaig
1201 Laurence Ua Suilleabain
1205 C.
1281 Luke
*c.*1224 Florence
1226 Daniel
1237 David mac Cellaig [O'Kelly]
1240 Ailinn O Suilleabain
1247 Daniel
1265 Reginaldus
1275 Alan O Longain
1284 Nicholas of Effingham
1323 Maurice O Solchain
1333 John Brid
1351 John Whitekot
1363 John Swaffham
1376 Richard Wye
1394 Gerard Caneton
1413 Adam Payn
United to **Cork** 1418–1638
1638 George Synge
1661–78 Held by the Bishops of Cork
1679 Patrick Sheridan
1683 Edward Jones
1693 William Palliser
1694 Tobias Pullein
1695 St George Ashe
1697 John Pooley
1702 Charles Crow
1726 Henry Maule
1732 Edward Synge
1734 George Berkeley
1753 James Stopford
1759 Robert Johnson
1767 Frederick Augustus Hervery
1768 Charles Agar
1780 George Chinnery
1781 Richard Woodward
1794 William Bennett
1820 Charles Mongan Warhurton
1826 John Brinkley
United to **Cork** on the death of Bp Brinkley in 1835

Cork

Cork, Cloyne and Ross

Donnell 876
Soer Bhreatach 892
Dubhdhurn O'Stefam 959
Cathmogh 969
Mugron O'Mutan 1057
1138 Gregory
? Ua Menngorain 1147
1148 Gilla Aedha Ua Maigin
1174 [Gregorius] O h-Aedha [O Hea]
*c.*1182 Reginaldus I
1187 Aicher
1192 Murchad Ua h-Aedha
Anonymous 1214
1215 Mairin Ua Briain [Marianus]
1225 Gilbertus
1248 Laurentius
1265 William of Jerpoint
1267 Reginaldus
1277 Robert Mac Donnchada
1302 Seoan Mac Cearbaill [Mac Carwill]
1321 Philip of Slane
1327 Walter le Rede
1330 John of Ballyconingham
1347 John Roche
1359 Gerald de Barri
1396 Roger Ellesmere
1406 Richard Kynmoure
1409 Patrick Fox
1409 Milo fitzJohn
1425 John Paston
1418 Adam Payn
1429 Jordan Purcell
1472 William Roche (Coadjutor)
1463 Gerald FitzGerald
1490 Tadhg Mac Carthaigh
1499 John FitzEdmund FitzGerald
1499 Patrick Cant
1523 John Benet
1536 Dominic Tyrre [Tirrey]
1562 Roger Skiddy
1570 Richard Dyxon
1572 Matthew Sheyn
Ross united to Cork 1583
1583 William Lyon
1618 John Boyle
1620 Richard Boyle
1638 William Chappell
1661 Michael Boyle
1663 Edward Synge
1679 Edward Wetenhall
1699 Dive Downes
1710 Peter Browne
1735 Robert Clayton
1745 Jemmett Browne
1772 Isaac Mann
1789 Euseby Cleaver
1789 William Foster
1790 William Bennet
1794 Thomas Stopford
1805 John George Beresford
1807 Thomas St Laurence
1831 Samuel Kyle
Cloyne united to Cork from 1835
1848 James Wilson
1857 William FitzGerald
1862 John Gregg
1878 Robert Samuel Gregg
1894 William Edward Meade
1912 Charles Benjamin Dowse
1933 William Edward Flewett
1938 Robert Thomas Hearn
1952 George Otto Sims
1957 Richard Gordon Perdue
1978 Samuel Greenfield Poyntz
1988 Robert Alexander Warke

Dublin

Dublin and Glendalough

BISHOPS

Sinhail 790
*c.*1028 Dunan [Donatus]
1074 Gilla Patraic
1085 Donngus
1096 Samuel Ua'h-Aingliu

ARCHBISHOPS

1121 Grene [Gregorius]
1162 Lorcan Ua'Tuathail [Laurentius]
1182 John Cumin
1213 Henry de Loundres
Glendalough united to Dublin
1230 Luke
125? Fulk de Sandford
1279 John de Derlington
1286 John de Sandford
1295 Thomas de Chadworth
1296 William de Hotham
1299 Richard de Ferings
[1307 Richard de Havering, not consecrated]
1311 John de Leche
1317 Alexander de Bicknor
1349 John de St Paul
1363 Thomas Minot
1376 Robert de Wikeford
1391 Robert Waldeby
1396 Richard Northalis
1397 Thomas Cranley
1418 Richard Talbot
1451 Michael Tregury
1472 John Walton
1484 Walter Fitzsimons
1512 William Rokeby
1521 Hugh Inge
1529 John Alan
1535 George Browne
1555 Hugh Curwin
1567 Adam Loftus
1605 Thomas Jones
1619 Lancelot Bulkeley
1661 James Margetson
1663 Michael Boyle
1679 John Parker
1682 Francis Marsh
1694 Narcissus Marsh
1703 William King
1730 John Hoadly
1743 Charles Cobbe
1765 William Carmichael
1766 Arthur Smyth
1772 John Cradock
1779 Robert Fowler
1801 Charles Agar [Earl of Normanton]
1809 Euseby Cleaver
1820 John George Beresford
1822 William Magee
1831 Richard Whately
Kildare united to Dublin 1846
1864 Richard Chenevix Trench (resigned)
1885 William Conyngham [Lord Plunket]
1897 Joseph Ferguson Peacocke
1915 John Henry Bernard
1919 Charles Frederick D'Arcy
1920 John Allen Fitzgerald Gregg
1939 Arthur William Barton
1956 George Otto Simms
1969 Alan Alexander Buchanan
1977 Henry Robert McAdoo
1985 Donald Arthur Richard Caird
1996 Walton Newcome Francis Empey

†Emly

Raidghil 881
Ua Ruaich 953
Faelan 980
MaelFinan 1030
Diarmait Ua Flainnchua 1114

1152 Gilla in Choimhded Ua h-Ardmhail Mael Isu Ua Laigenain 1163
1172 Ua Meic Stia
1177 Charles O'Buacalla
1177 Isaac O'Hamery
1192 Ragnall Ua Flainnchua
1205 M.
1209 William
1212 Henry
1227 John Collingham
1238 Daniel
1238 Christianus
1251 Gilbert O'Doverty
1266 Florence or Laurence O'hAirt
1272 Matthew MacGormain
1275 David O Cossaig
1286 William de Clifford
1306 Thomas Cantock [Quantock]
1309 William Roughead
1335 Richard le Walleys
1353 John Esmond
1363 David Penlyn [Foynlyn]
1363 William
1405 Nicholas Ball
1421 John Rishberry
1422 Robert Windell
1428 Thomas de Burgo
1428 Robert Portland
1445 Cornelius O Cuinnlis
1444 Robert
1448 Cornelius O Maolalaidh
1449 William O Hetigan
1476 Pilib O Cathail
1494 Donatus Mac Briain
1498 Cinneidigh Mac Briain
1507 Tomas O hUrthaille
1543 Angus O'Hernan
1551 Raymond de Burgo
United to **Cashel** 1569
Transferred to **Limerick** 1976

†Ferns

–598 Edar [or Maedoc or Hugh]
Maeldogair 676
Coman 678
Diratus 693
Cillenius 715
Cairbre O'Kearney 1095
Ceallach Ua Colmain 1117
Mael Eoin Ua Dunacain 1125
Ua Cattain 1135
1178 Loseph Ua h-Aeda
1186 Ailbe Ua Maelmuaid [Albinus]
1224 John of St John
1254 Geoffrey of St John
1258 Hugh of Lamport
1283 Richard of Northampton
1304 Simon of Evesham
1305 Robert Walrand
1312 Adam of Northampton
1347 Hugh de Saltu [of Leixlip]
1347 Geoffrey Grandfeld
1349 John Esmond
1350 William Charnells
1363 Thomas Dene
1400 Patrick Barret
1418 Robert Whittey
1453 Tadhg O Beirn
1457 John Purcell I
1479 Laurence Nevill
1505 Edmund Comerford
1510 Nicholas Comyn
1519 John Purcell II
1539 Alexander Devereux
1566 John Devereux
1582 Hugh Allen
Leighlin united to Ferns 1597
1600 Robert Grave
1601 Nicholas Statford
1605 Thomas Ram
1635 George Andrews
1661 Robert Price
1667 Richard Boyle
1683 Narcissus Marsh
1691 Bartholomew Vigors
1722 Josiah Hort
1727 John Hoadly
1730 Arthur Price
1734 Edward Synge
1740 George Stone
1743 William Cottrell
1744 Robert Downes
1752 John Garnet
1758 William Carmichael
1758 Thomas Salmon
1759 Richard Robinson
1761 Charles Jackson
1765 Edward Young
1772 Joseph Deane Bourke
1782 Walter Cope
1787 William Preston
1789 Euseby Cleaver
1809 Percy Jocelyn
1820 Robert Ponsonby Tottenham Loftus
1822 Thomas Elrington
United to **Ossory** 1835

†Glendalough

Dairchell 678
Eterscel 814
Dungal 904
Cormac 927
Nuadha 920 [or Neva]
Gilda Na Naomh *c.*1080
Cormac O'Mail 1101
Aed Ua Modain 1126
1140 Anonymous
1152 Gilla na Naem
1157 Cinaed O Ronain [Celestinus]
1176 Maelcallann Ua Cleirchen [Malchus]
1186 Macrobius
1192 William Piro
1214 Robert de Bedford
United to **Dublin**
After the union with Dublin some rival bishops appear
*c.*1216 Bricheus
1468 John
1475 Michael
1481 Denis White
John 1494
1494 Ivo Ruffi
1495 John
1500 Francis Fitzjohn of Corduba

†Iniscattery (Scattery Island)

861 Aidan
959 Cinaeda O'Chommind
973 Scandlam O'Lenz
O'Bruil 1069
O'Bruil II 1081
Dermot O Lennain 1119
Aed Ua Bechain I 1188
Cearbhal Ua'h-Enna [Carolus] 1193
1360 Tomas Mac Mathghamhna
1392 John Donkan
1414 Richard Belmer
Dionysius 1447
1447 John Grene
Incorporated with **Limerick**

†Kells

Mael Finnen 968
*c.*1152 Tuathal Ua Connachtarg
1185 Anonymous
1202 M. Ua Dobailen
Incorporated with **Meath**

†Kildare

Conlaedh 520
Hugh [or Hed] the Black 639
Maeldoborcon 709
Eutigern 762
Lomthiull 787
Snedbran 787
Tuatchar 834
Orthanach 840
Aedgene Britt 864
Macnghal 870
Lachtnan 875
Suibhne 881
Scannal 885
Lergus 888
Mael Findan 950
Annchadh 981
Murrough McFlan 986
1030 MaelMartain
MaelBrighde 1042
Finn 1085
MaelBrighde O Brolchan 1097
Hugh [Heremon] 1100
Ferdomnach 1101
Cormac O Cathassaig 1146
Ua Duibhin 1148
1152 Finn mac Mael Muire Mac Cianain
Fin mac Gussain Ua Gormain
1161 Malachias Ua Brain
1177 Nehemias
1206 Cornelius Mac Fealain
1223 Ralph of Bristol
1233 John of Taunton
1258 Simon of Kilkenny
1280 Nicholas Cusack
1300 Walter Calf [de Veel]
1333 Richard Houlot
1352 Thomas Giffard
1366 Robert of Aketon [Acton]
1404 John Madock
1431 William fitzEdward
1449 Geoffrey Hereford
1456 John Bole [Bull]
1464 Richard Lang
1474 David Cone
1475 James Wall
William Barret
1480 Edward Lane
1526 Thomas Dillon
1529 Walter Wellesley
1540 William Miagh
1550 Thomas Lancaster
1555 Thomas Leverous
1560 Alexander Craik
1564 Robert Daly
1583 Daniel Neylan
1604 William Pilsworth
1636 Robert Ussher
1644 William Golborne
1661 Thomas Price
1667 Ambrose Jones
1679 Anthony Dopping
1682 William Moreton
1705 Welbore Ellis
1731 Charles Cobbe
1743 George Stone
1745 Thomas Fletcher
1761 Richard Robinson
1765 Charles Jackson
1790 George Lewis Jones
1804 Charles Lindsay
United to **Dublin** after the death of Bp Lindsay in 1846
1976 Separated from Dublin and united to **Meath**

†Kilfenora

1172 Anonymous
1205 F.
1224 Johannes
1254 Christianus
Anonymous 1264
1266 Mauricius
1273 Florentius O Tigernaig
1281 Congalach [O Lochlainn]
1291 G.
1299 Simon O Cuirrin
1303 Maurice O Briain
1323 Risdeard O Lochlainn
c.1355 Dionysius
1372 Henricus
Cornelius
1390 Patricius
1421 Feidhlimidh mac Mathghamhna O Lochlainn [Florentius]
1433 Fearghal
1434 Dionysius O Connmhaigh
1447 John Greni
1476 [? Denis] O Tombaigh
1491 Muircheartach mac Murchadha O Briain [Mauricius]
1514 Maurice O'Kelly
1541 John O'Neylan
–1585 Daniel, bishop-elect
1606 Bernard Adams [with Limerick q.v.]
1617 John Steere
1622 William Murray
[1628 Richard Betts, not consecrated]
1630 James Heygate
1638 Robert Sibthorp
1661–1741 Held by the Archbishops of Tuam
1742–52 Held by the Bishop of Clonfert
United to **Killaloe** 1752

†Killaloe

BISHOPS

O'Gerruidher 1054
Domnall Ua hEnna 1098
Mael Muire O Dunain 1117
Domnall Ua Conaing 1131
Domnall Ua Longargain 1137
Tadg Ua Longargain 1161
Donnchad mac Diarmata Ua Briain 1164
1179 Constantin mac Toirrdelbaig Ua Briain
1194 Diarmait Ua Conaing
1201 Conchobhar Ua h-Enna [Cornelius]
1217 Robert Travers
1221 Domnall Ua h-Enna [Donatus]
1231 Domnall O Cenneitig [Donatus]
1253 Isoc O Cormacain [Isaac]
1268 Mathgamain O h-Ocain [O Hogan]
1281 Maurice O h-Ocain
1299 David Mac Mathghamna [Mac Mahon]
1317 Tomas O Cormacain I
1323 Brian O Cosgraig
1326 David Mac Briain [David of Emly]
?1326 Natus O Heime
1343 Tomas O h-Ogain
1355 Tomas O Cormacain II
1389 Mathghamain Mag Raith
1400 Donatus Mag Raith
1409 Robert Mulfield
1418 Eugenius O Faolain
1423 Thadeus Mag Raith I
1429 Seamus O Lonnghargain
1443 Donnchadh mac Toirdhealbhaigh O Briain
1460 Thadeus Mag Raith II
1463 Matthaeus O Griobhtha
1483 Toirdhealbhach mac Mathghamhna O Briain [Theodoricus]
1523 Thadeus
1526 Seamus O Cuirrin
1546 Cornelius O Dea
1554 Turlough [or Terence] O'Brien II
1570 Maurice [or Murtagh] O'Brien-Arra
1613 John Rider
1633 Lewis Jones
1647 Edward Parry
1661 Edward Worth
1669 Daniel Wytter
1675 John Roan
1693 Henry Ryder
1696 Thomas Lindsay
1713 Thomas Vesey
1714 Nicholas Forster
1716 Charles Carr
1740 Joseph Story
1742 John Ryder
1743 Jemmet Browne
1745 Richard Chenevix
1746 Nicholas Synge
Kilfenora united to Killaloe 1752
1771 Robert Fowler
1779 George Chinnery
1780 Thomas Barnard
1794 William Knox
1803 Charles Dalrymple Lindsay
1804 Nathaniel Alexander
1804 Robert Ponsonby Tottenham Loftus
1820 Richard Mant
1823 Alexander Arbuthnot
1828 Richard Ponsonby
1831 Edmund Knox [with Clonfert]
Clonfert united to Killaloe 1834
Kilmacduagh united to Killaloe 1834
1834 Christopher Butson
1836 Stephen Crengh Sandes
1839 Ludlow Tonson [afterwards Baron Riversdale]
1862 William FitzGerald
1884 William Bennet Chester
1893 Frederick Richards Wynne
1897 Mervyn Archdall
1912 Charles Benjamin Dowse
1913 Thomas Sterling Berry (resigned)
1924 Henry Edmund Patton
1943 Robert M'Neil Boyd
1945 Hedley Webster
1953 Richard Gordon Perdue
1957 Henry Arthur Stanistreet
1972 Edwin Owen
1976 United to **Limerick**

†Kilmacduagh

? Ua Cleirig 1137
Imar Ua Ruaidin 1176
Rugnad O'Rowan 1178
1179 Mac Gilla Cellaig Ua Ruaidin
1206 Ua Cellaig
Mael Muire O Connmaig 1224
1227 Aed [Odo]
Conchobhar O Muiredaig 1247
1248 Gilla Cellaig O Ruaidin [Gilbertus]
1249 David yFredrakern
1254 Mauricius O Leaain
1284 David O Setachain
1290 Luirint O Lachtnain [Laurentius]
1307 Lucas
1326 Johannes
1360 Nicol O Leaain
1394 Gregory O Leaain
1405 Enri O Connmhaigh
1409 Dionysius
1409 Eugene O Faolain
1418 Diarmaid O Donnchadha
1419 Nicol O Duibhghiolla
1419 Seaan O Connmhaigh
1441 Dionysius O Donnchadha
1479 Cornelius O Mullony
1503 Matthaeus O Briain
1533 Christopher Bodkin
1573 Stephen O'Kirwan
[1584 Thomas Burke, not consecrated]
1587 Roland Lynch
1627–1836 Held in commendam by the Bishops of Clonfert
United to **Killaloe** since 1834

†Leighlin

–633 Laserian or Molaise
–865 Mainchin
–940 Conella McDonegan
Daniel 969
Cleitic O'Muinic 1050
c.1096 Ferdomnac
Mael Eoin Ua Dunacain 1125
Sluaigedach Ua Cathain 1145
1152 Dungal O Caellaide
1192 Johannes
1197 Johannes
1202 Herlewin
1217 Richard [Fleming]
1228 William le Chauniver
1252 Thomas
1275 Nicholas Chever
1309 Maurice de Blanchville
1321 Meiler le Poer
1344 Radulphus O Ceallaigh
1349 Thomas of Brakenberg
1360 Johannes
1362 William (not consecrated)
1363 John Young
1371 Philip FitzPeter
1385 John Griffin
1398 Thomas Peverell
1400 Richard Bocomb
1419 John Mulgan
1432 Thomas Fleming
— Diarmaid 1464
1464 Milo Roche
1490 Nicholas Magwyr
1513 Thomas Halsey
1524 Mauricius O Deoradhain
1527 Matthew Sanders
1550 Robert Travers
1555 Thomas O'Fihelly
1567 Donnell or Daniel Cavanagh
1589 Richard Meredith
United to **Ferns** since 1597 on the death of Bp Meredith

Limerick

Limerick, Ardfert, Aghadoe, Killaloe, Kilfenora, Clonfert, Kilmacduagh and Emly

–1106 Gilli alias Gilla Espaic
1140 Patricius
1150 Erolb [? = Harold]

1152 Torgesius
1179 Brictius
1203 Donnchad Ua'Briain [Donatus]
1207 Geoffrey
–1215 Edmund
1223 Hubert de Burgo
1252 Robert de Emly or Neil
1273 Gerald [or Miles] de Mareshall
1302 Robert de Dundonald
1312 Eustace de Aqua or de l'Eau
1336 Maurice de Rochfort
1354 Stephen Lawless
1360 Stephen Wall [de Valle]
1369 Peter Curragh
1399 Bernardus O Conchobhair
1400 Conchobhar O Deadhaidh
1426 John Mothel (resigned)
Iniscattery incorporated with Limerick
1456 Thomas Leger
1458 William Russel, *alias* Creagh
1463 Thomas Arthur
[1486 Richard Stakpoll, not consecrated]
1486 John Dunowe
1489 John O'Phelan [Folan]
1524 Sean O Cuinn
1551 William Casey
1557 Hugh de Lacey or Lees (deposed)
1571 William Casey
1594 John Thornburgh
1604 Bernard Adams
1626 Francis Gough
1634 George Webb
1643 Robert Sibthorp
Ardfert united to Limerick 1661
1661 Edward Synge
1664 William Fuller
1667 Francis Marsh
1673 John Vesey
1679 Simon Digby
1692 Nathaniel Wilson
1695 Thomas Smyth
1725 William Burscough
1755 James Leslie
1771 James Averill
1772 William Gore
1784 William Cecil Pery
1794 Thomas Barnard
1806 Charles Morgan Warburton
1820 Thomas Elrington
1823 John Jebb
1834 Edmund Knox
1849 William Higgin
1854 Henry Griffin
1866 Charles Graves
1899 Thomas Bunbury
1907 Raymond D'Audemra Orpen
1921 Harry Vere White
1934 Charles King Irwin
1942 Evelyn Charles Hodges
1961 Robert Wyse Jackson
1970 Donald Arthur Richard Caird
Killaloe united to Limerick 1976
Emly transferred to Limerick 1976
1976 Edwin Owen
1981 Walton Newcome Francis Empey
1985 Edward Flewett Darling

†Lismore

Ronan 764
Cormac MacCuillenan 918
–999 Cinneda O'Chonmind
Niall mac Meic Aedacain 1113
Ua Daightig 1119
1121 Mael Isu Ua h-Ainmere
Mael Muire Ua Loingsig 1150
1151 Gilla Crist Ua Connairche [Christianus]
1179 Felix
Ardmore incorporated with Lismore 1192
1203 Malachias, O'Heda or O'Danus
1216 Thomas
1219 Robert of Bedford
1228 Griffin Christopher
1248 Ailinn O Suilleabain
1253 Thomas
1270 John Roche
1280 Richard Corre
1309 William Fleming
1310 R.
1322 John Leynagh
1356 Roger Cradock, provision annulled
1358 Thomas le Reve
United to **Waterford** 1363

Meath

Meath and Kildare

BISHOPS OF THE SEE OF CLONARD

Senach 588
–640 Colman 654
Dubhduin O'Phelan 718
Tole 738
–778 Fulartach 779
Clothcu 796
Clemens 826
Cormac MacSuibhne
Cumsuth 858
Suarlech 870
Ruman MacCathasaid 922
Colman MacAilild 926
Tuathal O'Dubhamaigh 1028

BISHOPS OF MEATH

1096 Mael Muire Ua Dunain
1128 Eochaid O Cellaig
1151 Etru Ua Miadacain [Eleuzerius]
1177 Echtigern mac Mael Chiarain [Eugenius]
1192 Simon Rochfort
(The See was transferred from Clonard to Newtown near Trim, 1202)
Kells incorporated with Meath
1224 Donan De [Deodatus] (not consecrated)
1227 Ralph Petit
1231 Richard de la Corner
1253 Geoffrey Cusack
1255 Hugo de Taghmon
1283 Walter de Fulburn
1287 Thomas St Leger
1322 Seoan Mac Cerbaill [John MacCarwill]
1327 William de Paul
1350 William St Leger
1353 Nicholas [Allen]
1369 Stephen de Valle [Wall]
1380 William Andrew
1385 Alexander Petit [or de Balscot]
1401 Robert Montayne
1412 Edward Dantesey
[1430 Thomas Scurlog, apparently not consecrated]
1430 William Hadsor
1435 William Silk
1450 Edmund Ouldhall
1460 William Shirwood
1483 John Payne
1507 William Rokeby
1512 Hugh Inge
1523 Richard Wilson
1529 Edward Staples
1554 William Walsh
1563 Hugh Brady
Clonmacnoise united to Meath 1569
1584 Thomas Jones
1605 Roger Dod
1612 George Montgomery
1621 James Usher
1625 Anthony Martin
[Interregnum 1650–61]
1661 Henry Leslie
1661 Henry Jones
1682 Anthony Dopping
1697 Richard Tennison
1705 William Moreton
1716 John Evans
1724 Henry Downes
1727 Ralph Lambert
1732 Welbore Ellis
1734 Arthur Price
1744 Henry Maule
1758 William Carmichael
1765 Richard Pococke
1765 Arthur Smyth
1766 Henry Maxwell
1798 Thomas Lewis O'Beirne
1823 Nathaniel Alexander
1840 Charles Dickinson
1842 Edward Stopford
1850 Thomas Stewart Townsend
1852 James Henderson Singer
1866 Samuel Butcher
1876 William Conyngham, Lord Plunket
1885 Charles Parsons Reichel
1894 Joseph Ferguson Peacocke
1897 James Bennett Keene
1919 Benjamin John Plunket
1926 Thomas Gibson George Collins
1927 John Orr
1938 William Hardy Holmes
1945 James McCann
1959 Robert Bonsall Pike
Kildare united to Meath 1976
1976 Donald Arthur Richard Caird
1985 Walton Newcome Francis Empey
1996 Richard Lionel Clarke

†Ossory

Dermot 973
1152 Domnall Ua Fogartaig
1180 Felix Ua Duib Slaine
1202 Hugo de Rous [Hugo Rufus]
1220 Peter Mauveisin
1231 William of Kilkenny
1233 Walter de Brackley
1245 Geoffrey de Turville
1251 Hugh de Mapilton
1260 Geoffrey St Leger
1287 Roger of Wexford
1289 Michael d'Exeter
1303 William FitzJohn
1317 Richard Ledred
1361 John de Tatenhale
1366 William
— John of Oxford
1371 Alexander Petit [de Balscot]
1387 Richard Northalis
1396 Thomas Peverell
1399 John Waltham
1400 John Griffin
1400 John
1401 Roger Appleby
1402 John Waltham

1407 Thomas Snell
1417 Patrick Foxe
1421 Dionysius O Deadhaidh
1427 Thomas Barry
1460 David Hacket
1479 Seaan O hEidigheain
1487 Oliver Cantwell
1528 Milo Baron [or FitzGerald]
1553 John Bale
1554 John Tonory
1567 Christopher Gaffney
1577 Nicholas Walsh
1586 John Horsfall
1610 Richard Deane
1613 Jonas Wheeler
1641 Griffith Williams
1672 John Parry
1678 Benjamin Parry
1678 Michael Ward
1680 Thomas Otway
1693 John Hartstonge
1714 Thomas Vesey
1731 Edward Tennison
1736 Charles Este
1741 Anthony Dopping
1743 Michael Cox
1754 Edward Maurice
1755 Richard Pococke
1765 Charles Dodgson
1775 William Newcome
1779 John Hotham
1782 William Heresford
1795 Thomas Lewis O'Beirne
1799 Hugh Hamilton
1806 John Kearney
1813 Robert Fowler
Ferns united to Ossory 1835
1842 James Thomas O'Brien
1874 Robert Samuel Gregg
1878 William Fakenham Walsh
1897 John Baptist Crozier
1907 Charles Frederick D'Arcy
1911 John Henry Bernard
1915 John Allen Fitzgerald Gregg
1920 John Godfrey FitzMaurice Day
1938 Ford Tichbourne
1940 John Percy Phair
1962 Henry Robert McAdoo
United to **Cashel** 1977

†Ross

Nechtan MacNechtain 1160
Isaac O'Cowen 1161
O'Carroll 1168
1177 Benedictus
1192 Mauricius
1198 Daniel
1224 Fineen O Clothna [Florentius]
*c.*1250 Malachy
1254 Mauricius
1269 Walter O Mithigein
1275 Peter O h-Uallachain [? Patrick]
1291 Laurentius
1310 Matthaeus O Finn
1331 Laurentius O h-Uallachain
1336 Dionysius
1379 Bernard O Conchobhair
1399 Peter Curragh
1400 Thadeus O Ceallaigh
1401 Mac Raith O hEidirsgeoil [Macrobius]
1402 Stephen Brown
1403 Matthew
1418 Walter Formay
1424 John Bloxworth
1426 Conchobhar Mac Fhaolchadha [Cornelius]
Maurice Brown 1431
1431 Walter of Leicester
1434 Richard Clerk
1448 Domhnall O Donnobhain
John 1460
1460 Robert Colynson
–1464 Thomas
1464 John Hornse *alias* Skipton
1473 Aodh O hEidirsgeoil [Odo]
1482 Tadhg Mac Carthaigh
1494 John Edmund Courci
1517 Seaan O Muirthile
1519 Tadgh O Raghallaigh [Thaddeus]
1523 Bonaventura
1526 Diarmaid Mac Carthaigh
1544 Dermot McDonnell
1551 John
1554 Maurice O'Fihelly
1559 Maurice O'Hea
1561 Thomas O'Herlihy
1582 William Lyon [with Cork and Cloyne after 1581]
United to **Cork** 1583

†Waterford

1096 Mael lus Ua h-Ainmere
1152 Toistius
1175 Augustinus Ua Selbaig
Anonymous 1199
1200 Robert I
1204 David the Welshman
1210 Robert II [Breathnach]
1223 William Wace
1227 Walter
1232 Stephen
1250 Henry
1252 Philip
1255 Walter de Southwell
1274 Stephen de Fulbourn
1286 Walter de Fulbourn
1308 Matthew
1323 Nicholas Welifed
1338 Richard Francis
1349 Robert Elyot
1350 Roger Cradock
Lismore united to Waterford 1363
1363 Thomas le Reve
1394 Robert Read
1396 Thomas Sparklord
1397 John Deping
1400 Thomas Snell
1407 Roger of Appleby (*see under* **Ossory**)
1409 John Geese
1414 Thomas Colby
1421 John Geese
1426 Richard Cantwell
1446 Robert Poer
1473 Richard Martin
1475 John Bulcomb
1480 Nicol O hAonghusa
1483 Thomas Purcell
1519 Nicholas Comyn
1551 Patrick Walsh
1579 Marmaduke Middleton
1582 Miler Magrath (Bishop of Cashel and Waterford)
1589 Thomas Wetherhead [or Walley]
1592 Miler Magrath
1608 John Lancaster
1619 Michael Boyle
1636 John Atherton
1641 Archibald Adair
1661 George Baker
1666 Hugh Gore
1691 Nathaniel Foy
1708 Thomas Mills
1740 Charles Este
1746 Richard Chenevix
1779 William Newcome
1795 Richard Marlay
1802 Power le Poer Trench
1810 Joseph Stock
1813 Richard Bourke
United to **Cashel** under Church Temporalities Act 1833

CATHEDRALS

CHURCH OF ENGLAND

(BATH AND) WELLS (St Andrew) **Dean** R LEWIS, **Cans Res** THE VEN R F ACWORTH, P G WALKER, P DE N LUCAS

BIRMINGHAM (St Philip) **Provost** P A BERRY, **Cans Res** THE VEN C J G BARTON, G O'NEILL, D J LEE, **Chapl** V A CORY

BLACKBURN (St Mary) **Provost** D FRAYNE, **Cans Res** J R HALL, A D HINDLEY, G D S GALILEE

BRADFORD (St Peter) **Provost** J S RICHARDSON, **Cans Res** C G LEWIS, G SMITH

BRISTOL (Holy Trinity) **Dean** R W GRIMLEY, **Cans Res** P F JOHNSON, A L J REDFERN, J L SIMPSON

CANTERBURY (Christ) **Dean** J A SIMPSON, **Cans Res** P G C BRETT, M J CHANDLER, R H C SYMON, THE VEN J L PRITCHARD, **Prec** G L WILLIAMSON

CARLISLE (Holy Trinity) **Dean** H E C STAPLETON, **Cans Res** R A CHAPMAN, D W V WESTON, THE VEN D C TURNBULL, C HILL

CHELMSFORD (St Mary, St Peter and St Cedd) **Provost** P S M JUDD, **Cans Res** D C KNIGHT, B P THOMPSON, T THOMPSON, **Chapl** J D JONES

CHESTER (Christ and Blessed Virgin Mary) **Dean** S S SMALLEY, **Cans Res** T J DENNIS, J W S NEWCOME, O A CONWAY, R M REES

CHICHESTER (Holy Trinity) **Dean** J D TREADGOLD, **Cans Res** R T GREENACRE, F J HAWKINS, THE VEN J M BROTHERTON, P G ATKINSON, **PV** D NASON

COVENTRY (St Michael) **Provost** J F PETTY, **Cans Res** P OESTREICHER, V F FAULL, J C BURCH

DERBY (All Saints) **Provost** B H LEWERS, **Cans Res** G A CHESTERMAN, G O MARSHALL, R M PARSONS, I GATFORD

DURHAM (Christ and Blessed Virgin Mary) **Dean** J R ARNOLD, **Cans Res** D W BROWN, R L COPPIN, G S PEDLEY, M C PERRY, THE VEN T WILLMOTT, **Prec** D J MEAKIN, **Min Cans** M PARKER, M H J HAMPEL

ELY (Holy Trinity) **Dean** M J HIGGINS, **Cans Res** D J GREEN, J C INGE, **Prec and Sacr** P J MOGER, **Chapl** J E MCFARLANE

EXETER (St Peter) **Dean** K B JONES, **Cans Res** A C MAWSON, K C PARRY, D J ISON

GLOUCESTER (St Peter and Holy Trinity) **Dean** N A S BURY, **Cans Res** N CHATFIELD, N C HEAVISIDES, R D M GREY, C H MORGAN, **Chapl** J F HUBBARD-JONES

GUILDFORD (Holy Spirit) **Dean** A G WEDDERSPOON, **Cans Res** J M SCHOFIELD, M F PALMER, C P COLLINGWOOD

HEREFORD (Blessed Virgin Mary and St Ethelbert) **Dean** R A WILLIS, **Cans Res** P R ILES, J TILLER, THE VEN L G MOSS, J F BUTTERWORTH, **Can** A R OSBORNE, **Succ** A C HUTCHINSON

LEICESTER (St Martin) **Provost** D N HOLE, **Cans Res** M T H BANKS, M WILSON, **Prec** J N CRAIG

LICHFIELD (Blessed Virgin Mary and St Chad) **Dean** N T WRIGHT, **Cans Res** A N BARNARD, THE VEN R B NINIS, C W TAYLOR

LINCOLN (Blessed Virgin Mary) **Dean** *Vacant*, **Cans Res** B R DAVIS, A J STOKES, V P WHITE

LIVERPOOL (Christ) **Dean** R D C WALTERS, **Cans Res** D J HUTTON, M C BOYLING, N T VINCENT

LONDON (St Paul) **Dean** J H MOSES, **Cans Res** THE VEN G H CASSIDY, R J HALLIBURTON, M J SAWARD, S J OLIVER, **Min Cans** J R LEES, J M PAUL

MANCHESTER (St Mary, St Denys and St George) **Dean** K J RILEY, **Cans Res** J R ATHERTON, THE VEN R B HARRIS, A E RADCLIFFE, P DENBY

NEWCASTLE (St Nicholas) **Provost** N G COULTON, **Cans Res** R LANGLEY, P R STRANGE, I F BENNETT, THE VEN P ELLIOTT

NORWICH (Holy Trinity) **Dean** S G PLATTEN, **Cans Res** C J OFFER, R J HANMER, M F PERHAM

OXFORD (Christ Church) **Dean** J H DRURY, **Cans Res** O M T O'DONOVAN, J M PEIRCE, J S K WARD, THE VEN F V WESTON, THE VERY REVD R M C JEFFERY, J B WEBSTER, **Prec** A C BALLARD

PETERBOROUGH (St Peter, St Paul and St Andrew) **Dean** M BUNKER, **Cans Res** T R CHRISTIE, J HIGHAM, T WILLMOTT

PORTSMOUTH (St Thomas of Canterbury) **Provost** M L YORKE, **Cans Res** C J BRADLEY, J B HEDGES, D T ISAAC, **Prec** S W LEWIS

RIPON (St Peter and St Wilfrid) **Dean** J A R METHUEN, **Cans Res** M R GLANVILLE-SMITH, K PUNSHON, J H BELL, **Min Cans** E D MURFET, D G PATON-WILLIAMS, P M DRIVER

ROCHESTER (Christ and Blessed Virgin Mary) **Dean** E F SHOTTER, **Cans Res** J M ARMSON, R J R LEA, E R TURNER, THE VEN N L WARREN

ST ALBANS (St Alban) **Dean** C A LEWIS, **Cans Res** C GARNER, G R S RITSON, M C SANSOM, C R J FOSTER, A K BERGQUIST, **Prec** D L MUNCHIN

ST EDMUNDSBURY (St James) **Provost** J E ATWELL, **Cans Res** M E MINGINS, A M SHAW, **Chapl** R H DAVEY

SALISBURY (Blessed Virgin Mary) **Dean** D R WATSON, **Cans Res** D J C DAVIES, D M K DURSTON, J OSBORNE

SHEFFIELD (St Peter and St Paul) **Provost** M SADGROVE, **Cans Res** T M PAGE, THE VEN S R LOWE, J E M SINCLAIR, C M SMITH

SODOR AND MAN (St German) **Dean** THE BISHOP, **Can Prec** B H KELLY

SOUTHWARK (St Saviour and St Mary Overie) **Provost** C B SLEE, **Cans Res** M KITCHEN, D S PAINTER, R S WHITE, H M CUNLIFFE, **Succ** G D SWINTON

SOUTHWELL (Blessed Virgin Mary) **Provost** D LEANING, **Cans Res** I G COLLINS, D P KEENE, **V Choral** J A WARDLE

TRURO (St Mary) **Dean** D J SHEARLOCK, **Cans Res** P R GAY, K P MELLOR

WAKEFIELD (All Saints) **Provost** G P NAIRN-BRIGGS, **Cans Res** R CAPPER, R E GAGE

WINCHESTER (Holy Trinity, St Peter, St Paul and St Swithun) **Dean** M S TILL, **Cans Res** A F KNIGHT, C STEWART, P B MORGAN, A K WALKER

WORCESTER (Christ and Blessed Virgin Mary) **Dean** P J MARSHALL, **Cans Res** THE VEN F W H BENTLEY, I M MACKENZIE, D G THOMAS, **Prec** C R OWEN

YORK (St Peter) **Dean** R FURNELL, **Cans Res** R METCALFE, E R NORMAN, J TOY, P J FERGUSON

Collegiate Churches

WESTMINSTER ABBEY
ST GEORGE'S CHAPEL, WINDSOR
See Royal Peculiars, p. 831.

Diocese in Europe

GIBRALTAR (Holy Trinity) **Dean** B W HORLOCK

MALTA Valletta (St Paul) Pro-Cathedral **Chan** A G WOODS

BRUSSELS (Holy Trinity) Pro-Cathedral **Chan** N M WALKER

CHURCH IN WALES

The name of the Dean is given, together with other clergy holding full-time appointments.

BANGOR (St Deiniol) **Dean** T E P EDWARDS, **Min Can** H J DAVIES
LLANDAFF (St Peter and St Paul) **Dean** J ROGERS, **Min Can** M R E TOMLINSON, **PV** R C PARRISH
MONMOUTH Newport (St Woolos) **Dean** R D FENWICK, **Chapl** D C MATTHEWS, S H LODWICK
ST ASAPH (St Asaph) **Dean** T R K GOULSTONE, **Min Can** C A MITCHELL
ST DAVIDS (St David and St Andrew) **Dean** J W EVANS, **Succ** R B WEBLEY, **Min Can** R P DAVIES
(SWANSEA AND) BRECON (St John the Evangelist) **Dean** J HARRIS, **Can Res** E C JOHN, **Min Can** N HOOK

SCOTTISH EPISCOPAL CHURCH

For the members of the chapter the *Scottish Episcopal Church Directory* should be consulted.

Aberdeen and Orkney
ABERDEEN (St Andrew) **Provost** W D WIGHTMAN

Argyll and The Isles
OBAN (St John) **Provost** A M MACLEAN
CUMBRAE (Holy Spirit) Cathedral of The Isles **Provost** D M CAMERON *Bishop of Argyll and The Isles*

Brechin
DUNDEE (St Paul) **Provost** *Vacant*

Edinburgh
EDINBURGH (St Mary) **Provost** G J T FORBES, **Chapl** J CUTHBERT

Glasgow and Galloway
GLASGOW (St Mary) **Provost** *Vacant*

Moray, Ross and Caithness
INVERNESS (St Andrew) **Provost** M E GRANT

St Andrews, Dunkeld and Dunblane
PERTH (St Ninian) **Provost** K G FRANZ

CHURCH OF IRELAND

Most cathedrals are parish churches, and the dean is usually, but not always, the incumbent. For the members of the chapter the *Church of Ireland Directory* should be consulted. The name of the dean is given, together with other clergy holding full-time appointments.

NATIONAL CATHEDRAL OF ST PATRICK, Dublin **Dean** M E STEWART, **Dean's Vicar** P R CAMPION
CATHEDRAL OF ST ANNE, Belfast J SHEARER
(St Anne's is a cathedral of the dioceses of Down and Dromore and of Connor)

Tuam, Killala and Achonry
TUAM (St Mary) I D CORBETT
KILLALA (St Patrick) E G ARDIS
ACHONRY (St Crumnathy) *Vacant*

Province of Armagh

Armagh
ARMAGH (St Patrick) H CASSIDY

Clogher
CLOGHER (St Macartan) T R MOORE
ENNISKILLEN (St Macartin) T R MOORE *Dean of Clogher*

Derry and Raphoe
DERRY (St Columb) *Vacant*
RAPHOE (St Eunan) S R WHITE

Down and Dromore
DOWN (Holy and Undivided Trinity) J F DINNEN, **Can Res** J A B MAYNE
DROMORE (Christ the Redeemer) D R CHILLINGWORTH, THE VEN W B NEILL

Connor
LISBURN (Christ) F J RUSK *Dean of Connor*, **Can** J T McCAMMON

Kilmore, Elphin and Ardagh
KILMORE (St Fethlimidh) D S G GODFREY
SLIGO (St Mary and St John the Baptist) S I McGEE *Dean of Elphin and Ardagh*

Province of Dublin

Dublin and Glendalough
DUBLIN (Holy Trinity) Christ Church J T F PATERSON

Meath and Kildare
TRIM (St Patrick) A W U FURLONG *Dean of Clonmacnoise*
KILDARE (St Brigid) R K TOWNLEY

Cashel and Ossory
CASHEL (St John the Baptist) P J KNOWLES
WATERFORD (Blessed Trinity) Christ Church W B A NEILL
LISMORE (St Carthage) J C HEALEY
KILKENNY (St Canice) N N LYNAS *Dean of Ossory*
LEIGHLIN (St Laserian) C A FAULL
FERNS (St Edan) L D A FORREST

Cork, Cloyne and Ross
CORK (St Fin Barr) M G St A JACKSON
CLOYNE (St Colman) G P St J HILLIARD
ROSS (St Fachtna) R C A HENDERSON

Limerick and Killaloe
LIMERICK (St Mary) J M G SIRR
KILLALOE (St Flannan) N M CUMMINS

ROYAL PECULIARS, CLERGY OF THE QUEEN'S HOUSEHOLD, etc

Royal Peculiars

Collegiate Church of St Peter Westminster (Westminster Abbey) Dean A W CARR **Cans** D C GRAY, THE VEN A E HARVEY, D H HUTT **Prec** B D FENTON **Chapl and Sacr** J M GOODALL

Queen's Free Chapel of St George Windsor Castle (St George's Chapel) Dean P R MITCHELL **Cans** M A MOXON, D M STANESBY, J A WHITE, L F P GUNNER **Min Cans** T J HARVEY, A G GYLE

The Queen's Household

Royal Almonry

High Almoner THE RT REVD J B TAYLOR

Sub-Almoner W J BOOTH

The College of Chaplains

Clerk of the Closet THE RT REVD J BAILEY (Bishop of Derby)

Deputy Clerk of the Closet W J BOOTH

Chaplains to The Queen

J D A ADAMS	R G GILBERT	M A MOXON
P L ASHFORD	D C GRAY	B C OSBORNE
D L BARTLES-SMITH	D N GRIFFITHS	D G PALMER
F W H BENTLEY	G R HALL	G S PEDLEY
R A BOWDEN	I A HARDAKER	K S POUND
E BUCHANAN	J G HASLAM	J C PRIESTLEY
D J BURGESS	C A C HILL	J P ROBSON
R A CHAPMAN	C J HILL	I G SMITH-CAMERON
R S CLARKE	K HUXLEY	J A STANLEY
J O COLLING	G JONES	J SYKES
A CRAIG	I KNOX	L F WEBBER
D FLEMING	M E MINGINS	D H WHEATON

Extra Chaplains to The Queen

A D CAESAR	J G M W MURPHY	E J G WARD
E A JAMES	J R W STOTT	S A WILLIAMS

Chapels Royal

Dean of the Chapels Royal THE BISHOP OF LONDON

Sub-Dean of the Chapels Royal W J BOOTH

Priests in Ordinary R D E BOLTON, P M HUNT, S E YOUNG

Deputy Priests M D OAKLEY, T M THORNTON, M M H MOORE, A H MEAD, P R C ABRAM

Domestic Chaplain, Buckingham Palace W J BOOTH

Domestic Chaplain, Windsor Castle THE DEAN OF WINDSOR

Domestic Chaplain, Sandringham G R HALL

Chaplain, Royal Chapel, Windsor Great Park M A MOXON

Chaplain, Hampton Court Palace M M H MOORE

Chaplain, HM Tower of London P R C ABRAM

The Queen's Chapel of the Savoy

Chaplain J P ROBSON

Royal Memorial Chapel, Sandhurst

Chaplain A J HEAGERTY

Royal Foundation of St Katharine in Ratcliffe

Master R F SWAN

DIOCESAN OFFICES

CHURCH OF ENGLAND

BATH AND WELLS	Diocesan Office, The Old Deanery, Wells, Somerset BA5 2UG Tel (01749) 670777 Fax 674240 E-mail wellsdbf@globalnet.co.uk
BIRMINGHAM	Diocesan Office, 175 Harborne Park Road, Harborne, Birmingham B17 0BH Tel 0121-427 5141 Fax 428 1114
BLACKBURN	Church House, Cathedral Close, Blackburn BB1 5AA Tel (01254) 54421 Fax 667309 E-mail blackburn@churchnet1.ucsm.ac.uk
BRADFORD	Diocesan Office, Cathedral Hall, Stott Hill, Bradford, W Yorkshire BD1 4ET Tel (01274) 725958 Fax 726343
BRISTOL	Diocesan Church House, 23 Great George Street, Bristol BS1 5QZ Tel 0117-921 4411 Fax 925 0460
CANTERBURY	Diocesan House, Lady Wootton's Green, Canterbury, Kent CT1 1NQ Tel (01227) 459401 Fax 450964
CARLISLE	Church House, West Walls, Carlisle CA3 8UE Tel (01228) 22573 Fax 48769
CHELMSFORD	Guy Harlings, 53 New Street, Chelmsford CM1 1AT Tel (01245) 266731 Fax 492786
CHESTER	Diocesan House, Raymond Street, Chester CH1 4PN Tel (01244) 379222 Fax 383835
CHICHESTER	Diocesan Church House, 211 New Church Road, Hove, E Sussex BN3 4ED Tel (01273) 421021 Fax 421041
COVENTRY	Church House, Palmerston Road, Coventry CV5 6FJ Tel (01203) 674328 Fax 691760
DERBY	Derby Church House, Full Street, Derby DE1 3DR Tel (01332) 382233 Fax 292969
DURHAM	Diocesan Office, Auckland Castle, Market Place, Bishop Auckland, Co Durham DL14 7QJ Tel (01388) 604515 Fax 603695
ELY	Diocesan Office, Bishop Woodford House, Barton Road, Ely, Cambs CB7 4DX Tel (01353) 663579 Fax 666148 E-mail tom.ambrose@ely.anglican.org
EUROPE	Diocesan Office, 14 Tufton Street, Westminster, London SW1P 3QZ Tel 0171-976 8001 Fax 976 8002 E-mail 100642.731@compuserve.com
EXETER	Diocesan House, Palace Gate, Exeter EX1 1HX Tel (01392) 272686 Fax 499594
GLOUCESTER	Church House, College Green, Gloucester GL1 2LY Tel (01452) 410022 Fax 308324 E-mail glosdioc@star.co.uk
GUILDFORD	Diocesan House, Quarry Street, Guildford, Surrey GU1 3XG Tel (01483) 571826 Fax 567896
HEREFORD	Diocesan Office, The Palace, Hereford HR4 9BL Tel (01432) 353863 Fax 352952
LEICESTER	Church House, 3/5 St Martin's East, Leicester LE1 5FX Tel 0116-262 7445 Fax 253 2889 E-mail chouse@leicester.anglican.org
LICHFIELD	St Mary's House, The Close, Lichfield, Staffs WS13 7LD Tel (01543) 414551 Fax 250935
LINCOLN	Diocesan Office, The Old Palace, Lincoln LN2 1PU Tel (01522) 529241 Fax 512717
LIVERPOOL	Church House, 1 Hanover Street, Liverpool L1 3DW Tel 0151-709 9722 Fax 709 2885
LONDON	Diocesan House, 36 Causton Street, London SW1P 4AU Tel 0171-932 1100 Fax 932 1112
MANCHESTER	Diocesan Church House, 90 Deansgate, Manchester M3 2GH Tel 0161-833 9521 Fax 833 2751
NEWCASTLE	Church House, Grainger Park Road, Newcastle upon Tyne NE4 8SX Tel 0191-273 0120 Fax 256 5900 E-mail church_house@newcastle.anglican.org
NORWICH	Diocesan House, 109 Dereham Road, Easton, Norwich NR9 5ES Tel (01603) 880853 Fax 881083
OXFORD	Diocesan Church House, North Hinksey, Oxford OX2 0NB Tel (01865) 244566 Fax 790470 E-mail thomasrp@thomasrp.demon.co.uk

PETERBOROUGH	The Palace, Peterborough PE1 1YB Tel (01733) 64448 Fax 555271
PORTSMOUTH	Cathedral House, St Thomas's Street, Portsmouth PO1 2HA Tel (01705) 825731 Fax 752967
RIPON	Ripon Diocesan Office, St Mary's Street, Leeds LS9 7DP Tel 0113-248 7487 Fax 249 1129 E-mail 101355.546@compuserve.com
ROCHESTER	St Nicholas Church, Boley Hill, Rochester, Kent ME1 1SL Tel (01634) 830333 Fax 829463 E-mail thomson@mbox.gaiacom.co.uk
ST ALBANS	Holywell Lodge, 41 Holywell Hill, St Albans, Herts AL1 1HE Tel (01727) 854532 Fax 844469 E-mail stalbans@cix.compulink.co.uk
ST EDMUNDSBURY AND IPSWICH	Diocesan House, 13/15 Tower Street, Ipswich IP1 3BG Tel (01473) 211028 Fax 232407
SALISBURY	Church House, Crane Street, Salisbury SP1 2QB Tel (01722) 411922 Fax 411990
SHEFFIELD	Diocesan Church House, 95/99 Effingham Street, Rotherham, S Yorkshire S65 1BL Tel (01709) 511116 Fax 512550
SODOR AND MAN	1 Kelly Close, Ramsey, Isle of Man IM8 2AR Tel (01624) 816545 Fax as telephone
SOUTHWARK	Trinity House, 4 Chapel Court, Borough High Street, London SE1 1HW Tel 0171-403 8686 Fax 403 4770 E-mail trinity@dswark.org.uk
SOUTHWELL	Dunham House, Westgate, Southwell, Notts NG25 OJL Tel (01636) 814331 Fax 815084 E-mail sdbf@john316.com
TRURO	Diocesan House, Kenwyn, Truro, Cornwall TR1 3DU Tel (01872) 274351 Fax 222510
WAKEFIELD	Church House, 1 South Parade, Wakefield, W Yorkshire WF1 1LP Tel (01924) 371802 Fax 364834
WINCHESTER	Church House, 9 The Close, Winchester, Hants SO23 9LS Tel (01962) 844644 Fax 841815 E-mail 100517.721@compuserve.com
WORCESTER	The Old Palace, Deansway, Worcester WR1 2JE Tel (01905) 20537 or 28764 Fax 612302
YORK	Church House, Ogleforth, York YO1 2JE Tel (01904) 611696 Fax 620375 E-mail 100517.72@compuserve.com

CHURCH IN WALES

BANGOR	Diocesan Centre, Cathedral Close, Bangor LL57 1RL Tel (01248) 354999 Fax 353882
LLANDAFF	Llandaff Diocesan Board of Finance, Heol Fair, Llandaff, Cardiff CF5 2EE Tel (01222) 578899 Fax 576198
MONMOUTH	Diocesan Office, 64 Caerau Road, Newport NP9 4HJ Tel (01633) 267490 Fax 265586
ST ASAPH	St Asaph Diocesan Board of Finance, High Street, St Asaph LL17 0RD Tel (01745) 582245 Fax 583556
ST DAVIDS	Diocesan Office, Abergwili, Carmarthen SA31 2JG Tel (01267) 236145 Fax 223046
SWANSEA AND BRECON	Swansea and Brecon Diocesan Board of Finance, House of the Good Shepherd, Eastmoor, Clyne Common, Swansea SA3 3JA Tel (01792) 402616 Fax as telephone

SCOTTISH EPISCOPAL CHURCH

ABERDEEN AND ORKNEY	Diocesan Centre, 39 King's Crescent, Aberdeen AB24 3HP Tel (01224) 636653 Fax 636186
ARGYLL AND THE ISLES	The Pines, Ardconnel Road, Oban, Argyll PA34 5DR Tel (01631) 66912 Fax as telephone
BRECHIN	The Bishop's Room, St Paul's Cathedral, 1 High Street, Dundee DD1 1TD Tel (01382) 229230 (mornings only) Fax 203446
EDINBURGH	Diocesan Centre, 21A Grosvenor Crescent, Edinburgh EH12 5EL Tel 0131-538 7033 Fax 538 7088

GLASGOW AND GALLOWAY	Diocesan Office, 5 St Vincent Place, Glasgow G1 2DH Tel 0141-221 5720 or 221 2694 Fax 221 7014
MORAY AND CAITHNESS	Diocesan Office, 11 Kenneth Street, Inverness IV3 5NR Tel (01463) 226255 (mornings only) Fax as telephone
ST ANDREWS, DUNKELD AND DUNBLANE	Perth Diocesan Centre, 28A Balhousie Street, Perth PH1 5HJ Tel (01738) 443173 Fax 443174

CHURCH OF IRELAND

PROVINCE OF ARMAGH

ARMAGH	Church House, 46 Abbey Street, Armagh BT61 7DZ Tel (01861) 522858 Fax 527823
CLOGHER	The Deanery, 10 Augher Road, Clogher, Co Tyrone BT76 0AD Tel (01662) 548235 Fax as telephone
CONNOR	Diocesan Office, 61/67 Donegall Street, Belfast BT1 2QH Tel (01232) 322268 or 323188 Fax 323554
DERRY AND RAPHOE	Diocesan Office, London Street, Londonderry BT48 6RQ Tel (01504) 262440
DOWN AND DROMORE	Diocesan Office, 61/67 Donegall Street, Belfast BT1 2QH Tel (01232) 322268 or 323188 Fax 323554
KILMORE	Killinagh Rectory, Blacklion, Sligo, Irish Republic Tel Bundoran (72) 53010 Fax as telephone
ELPHIN AND ARDAGH	Carrowkeel Lodge, Castlebaldwin, Co Sligo, Irish Republic Tel Castlebaldwin (79) 66015 Fax as telephone
TUAM, KILLALA AND ACHONRY	Stonehall House, Ballisodare, Co Sligo, Irish Republic Tel Sligo (71) 67280 Fax 30264

PROVINCE OF DUBLIN

CASHEL, WATERFORD, LISMORE, OSSORY AND LEIGHLIN	Diocesan Office, St Canice's Library, Kilkenny, Irish Republic Tel Kilkenny (56) 61910 or 27248 Fax 64399
CORK, CLOYNE AND ROSS	St Nicholas House, 14 Cove Street, Cork, Irish Republic Tel Cork (21) 272262 Fax 968467
DUBLIN AND GLENDALOUGH	Diocesan Office, Church of Ireland House, Church Avenue, Rathmines, Dublin 6, Irish Republic Tel Dublin (1) 496 6981 Fax 497 2865
FERNS	Garranvabby, The Rower, Thomastown, Co Kilkenny, Irish Republic Tel Waterford (51) 423637
KILLALOE, CLONFERT, LIMERICK AND ARDFERT	St Cronan's Rectory, Roscrea, Co Tipperary, Irish Republic Tel Roscrea (505) 21725 Fax 21993
MEATH AND KILDARE	Mrs K Seaman, 28 Celbridge Abbey, Celbridge, Co Kildare, Irish Republic Tel Dublin (1) 627 0631 Fax as telephone

ARCHDEACONRIES, DEANERIES AND RURAL DEANS OF THE CHURCH OF ENGLAND AND THE CHURCH IN WALES

The numbers given to the deaneries below correspond to those given in the benefice entries in the combined benefice and church index for England (page 843) and for Wales (page 1016). Where an archdeaconry comes within the jurisdiction of suffragan or area bishop under an established scheme, the respective bishop is indicated.

The dioceses of Liverpool, London and Manchester and the three Nottingham deaneries in the diocese of Southwell, use the title Area Dean.

CHURCH OF ENGLAND

BATH AND WELLS

ARCHDEACONRY OF WELLS

1. AXBRIDGE V L DALEY
2. BRUTON J M THOROGOOD
3. CARY J M THOROGOOD
4. FROME J G PESCOD
5. GLASTONBURY G WEYMONT
6. IVELCHESTER T J FARMILOE
7. MERSTON M D ELLIS
8. SHEPTON MALLET R R B PLOWMAN

ARCHDEACONRY OF BATH

9. BATH D F PERRYMAN
10. CHEW MAGNA G R W HALL
11. LOCKING G W HOBDEN
12. MIDSOMER NORTON P M HAND
13. PORTISHEAD A Q H WHEELER

ARCHDEACONRY OF TAUNTON

14. BRIDGWATER R E J PACKER
15. CREWKERNE AND ILMINSTER M S KIVETT
16. EXMOOR B E PRIORY
17. QUANTOCK J D A STEVENS
18. TAUNTON N C VENNING
19. TONE K G X TINGAY

BIRMINGHAM

ARCHDEACONRY OF BIRMINGHAM

1. BIRMINGHAM CITY J G PENDORF
2. EDGBASTON I M MICHAEL
3. HANDSWORTH R J MORRIS
4. KINGS NORTON C J W JACKSON
5. MOSELEY H J OSBORNE
6. SHIRLEY M G B C CADDY
7. WARLEY M C W GORICK

ARCHDEACONRY OF ASTON

8. ASTON D E NEWSOME
9. BORDESLEY S A HOLLOWAY
10. COLESHILL C J BOYLE
11. POLESWORTH D R CARRIVICK
12. SOLIHULL A J M DOW
13. SUTTON COLDFIELD R D HINDLEY
14. YARDLEY R H POSTILL

BLACKBURN

ARCHDEACONRY OF BLACKBURN

1. ACCRINGTON P H DEARDEN
2. BLACKBURN S D BESSANT
3. BURNLEY J B SWALLOW
4. CHORLEY P K WARREN
5. DARWEN R P CARTMELL
6. LEYLAND A F RANSON
7. PENDLE G S INGRAM
8. WHALLEY P A SMITH

ARCHDEACONRY OF LANCASTER

9. BLACKPOOL M F WOOD
10. GARSTANG R G GREENALL
11. KIRKHAM J H CATLEY
12. LANCASTER P J BALLARD
13. POULTON D E REEVES
14. PRESTON J R POWELL
15. TUNSTALL W G BOWNESS

BRADFORD

ARCHDEACONRY OF BRADFORD

1. AIREDALE S R CROWE
2. BOWLING AND HORTON W HOLLIDAY
3. CALVERLEY J N WHITE
4. OTLEY P J C MARSHALL

ARCHDEACONRY OF CRAVEN

5. BOWLAND G D RHODES
6. EWECROSS J M BEARPARK
7. SKIPTON C J HAYWARD
8. SOUTH CRAVEN P J ENDALL

BRISTOL

ARCHDEACONRY OF BRISTOL

1. BEDMINSTER B E PEARCE
2. BITTON P F YACOMENI
3. BRISLINGTON K NEWTON
4. BRISTOL CITY C A SUNDERLAND
5. CLIFTON F SMITH
6. HORFIELD D D HOLLOWAY
7. STAPLETON C D SUTCH
8. WESTBURY AND SEVERNSIDE D B HARREX

ARCHDEACONRY OF SWINDON

9. CHIPPENHAM A D FENSOME
10. CRICKLADE R W ADAMS
11. HIGHWORTH B J DUCKETT
12. MALMESBURY R K EAST
13. WROUGHTON M A JOHNSON

CANTERBURY

ARCHDEACONRY OF CANTERBURY

1. EAST BRIDGE R GILBERT
2. WEST BRIDGE C C BARLOW
3. CANTERBURY P T MACKENZIE
4. DOVER P W A BOWERS
5. ELHAM R G HUMPHRISS
6. OSPRINGE J W R MOWLL
7. RECULVER R W COTTON
8. SANDWICH B A HAWKINS
9. THANET M W HAYTON

ARCHDEACONRY OF MAIDSTONE

10. CHARING, EAST C G PREECE
11. CHARING, WEST B BARNES
12. LYMPNE NORTH J W TIPPING
13. LYMPNE SOUTH L J HAMMOND
14. SITTINGBOURNE G H SPENCER
15. SUTTON G H SIDAWAY

CARLISLE

ARCHDEACONRY OF CARLISLE

1. APPLEBY C R LEVEY
2. BRAMPTON A S PYE
3. CARLISLE G P RAVALDE
4. PENRITH R P H FRANK

ARCHDEACONRY OF WEST CUMBERLAND

5. CALDER J H BAKER
6. DERWENT M R BRAITHWAITE
7. SOLWAY P J SWAIN

ARCHDEACONRY OF WESTMORLAND AND FURNESS

8. FURNESS D SANDERSON
9. KENDAL G A HOWE
10. WINDERMERE C L V ATKINSON

CHELMSFORD

ARCHDEACONRY OF WEST HAM (BISHOP OF BARKING)

1. BARKING AND DAGENHAM J A A FLETCHER
2. HAVERING B J LEWIS
3. NEWHAM A R EASTER
4. REDBRIDGE T H SHANNON
5. WALTHAM FOREST D S AINGE

ARCHDEACONRY OF SOUTHEND (BISHOP OF BRADWELL)

6. BASILDON P D ASHTON
7. BRENTWOOD R B WHITE
8. CHELMSFORD NORTH C E HOPKINSON
9. CHELMSFORD SOUTH D J ATKINS
10. HADLEIGH P J SANDBERG
11. MALDON AND DENGIE P J MASON
12. ROCHFORD D J WILLIAMS
13. SOUTHEND-ON-SEA M A BALLARD
14. THURROCK E R LITTLER

ARCHDEACONRY (AND BISHOP) OF COLCHESTER

15. BRAINTREE J F H SHEAD
16. COLCHESTER R M WILSON
17. DEDHAM AND TEY C G A WOODS
18. DUNMOW J S SUTTON
19. HINCKFORD B E ROSE
20. HARWICH S HARDIE
21. NEWPORT AND STANSTED C BISHOP
22. SAFFRON WALDEN J D SAVILLE
23. ST OSYTH N G E ISSBERNER
24. WITHAM C J SLY

ARCHDEACONRY OF HARLOW (BISHOP OF BARKING)

25. EPPING FOREST D DRISCOLL
26. HARLOW M D WEBSTER
27. ONGAR E J SIBSON

CHESTER

ARCHDEACONRY OF CHESTER

1. BIRKENHEAD R C TOAN
2. CHESTER C W J SAMUELS
3. FRODSHAM A R RIDLEY
4. GREAT BUDWORTH J T OWEN
5. MALPAS J M G DAVIES
6. MIDDLEWICH P D GARDNER
7. WALLASEY R ORTON
8. WIRRAL NORTH R J SHIMWELL
9. WIRRAL SOUTH H J ALDRIDGE

ARCHDEACONRY OF MACCLESFIELD

10. BOWDON B R McCONNELL
11. CONGLETON R N W ELBOURNE
12. KNUTSFORD B T YOUNG
13. MACCLESFIELD D W MOIR
14. MOTTRAM J H DARCH
15. NANTWICH D ROSTRON
16. CHADKIRK M A LOWE
17. CHEADLE S P ISHERWOOD
18. STOCKPORT J M ROFF

CHICHESTER

ARCHDEACONRY OF CHICHESTER

1. ARUNDEL AND BOGNOR A M G WELLS
2. BRIGHTON B L BRANDIE
3. CHICHESTER V R CASSAM
4. HOVE J M P CALDICOTT
5. WORTHING R G RUSSELL

ARCHDEACONRY OF HORSHAM

6. CUCKFIELD R P SYMMONS
7. EAST GRINSTEAD A F HAWKER
8. HORSHAM J D MORRIS
9. HURST R L CLARKE
10. MIDHURST M C JUDGE
11. PETWORTH D S POLLARD
12. STORRINGTON G A EVANS
13. WESTBOURNE T J INMAN

ARCHDEACONRY OF LEWES AND HASTINGS

14. BATTLE AND BEXHILL J W COTTON
15. DALLINGTON R G H PORTHOUSE
16. EASTBOURNE G T RIDEOUT
17. HASTINGS C L J RICHARDSON
18. LEWES AND SEAFORD H M MOSELEY
19. ROTHERFIELD A C J CORNES
20. RYE M SHEPPARD
21. UCKFIELD G T DAINTREE

COVENTRY

ARCHDEACONRY OF COVENTRY

1. COVENTRY EAST D J HOWARD
2. COVENTRY NORTH B KEETON
3. COVENTRY SOUTH C H KNOWLES
4. KENILWORTH R D TURNER
5. NUNEATON J D PHILPOTT
6. RUGBY P WATKINS

ARCHDEACONRY OF WARWICK

7. ALCESTER J F GANJAVI
8. FOSSE S A BEAKE
9. SHIPSTON N J MORGAN
10. SOUTHAM J P WELBY
11. WARWICK AND LEAMINGTON B MERRINGTON

DERBY

ARCHDEACONRY OF CHESTERFIELD

1. ALFRETON D W ASHTON
2. BAKEWELL AND EYAM E R URQUHART
3. BOLSOVER AND STAVELEY J EASTON
4. BUXTON M F H HULBERT
5. CHESTERFIELD T B JOHNSON
6. GLOSSOP D M ROWLEY
7. WIRKSWORTH M SMITH

ARCHDEACONRY OF DERBY

8. ASHBOURNE D H SANSUM
9. DERBY NORTH T G REILLY
10. DERBY SOUTH D C MACDONALD
11. DUFFIELD D PERKINS
12. HEANOR C L BLAKEY
13. ILKESTON G R PERCY
14. LONGFORD S L RAYNER
15. MELBOURNE R J HARRIS
16. REPTON J H LISTER

DURHAM

ARCHDEACONRY OF DURHAM

1. DURHAM D J BELL
2. EASINGTON K I WOODHOUSE
3. HARTLEPOOL D C COULING
4. LANCHESTER P WATERHOUSE
5. SEDGEFIELD P A BALDWIN

ARCHDEACONRY OF AUCKLAND

6. AUCKLAND J S BAIN
7. BARNARD CASTLE T J D OLLIER
8. DARLINGTON P H E THOMAS
9. STANHOPE A FEATHERSTONE
10. STOCKTON R I SMITH

ARCHDEACONRY OF SUNDERLAND

11. CHESTER-LE-STREET F WHITE
12. GATESHEAD H DITCHBURN
13. GATESHEAD WEST T L JAMIESON
14. HOUGHTON-LE-SPRING M L BECK
15. JARROW E G STEPHENSON
16. WEARMOUTH R I DAVISON

ELY

ARCHDEACONRY OF ELY

1. BOURN R STEPHENSON
2. CAMBRIDGE M L DIAMOND
3. FORDHAM M N HAWORTH
4. LINTON W N C GIRARD
5. NORTH STOWE H K McCURDY
6. QUY F J KILNER
7. SHELFORD K F M FISHER
8. SHINGAY *Vacant*

ARCHDEACONRY OF HUNTINGDON

9. HUNTINGDON W R KING
10. LEIGHTONSTONE J HINDLEY
11. ST IVES S O LEEKE
12. ST NEOTS B CURRY
13. YAXLEY M SOULSBY

ARCHDEACONRY OF WISBECH

14. ELY M P WADSWORTH
15. FELTWELL D J KIGHTLEY
16. FINCHAM R D TOMKINSON
17. LYNN MARSHLAND A R TREEN
18. MARCH P BAXANDALL
19. WISBECH R D BULL

EXETER

ARCHDEACONRY OF EXETER

1. AYLESBEARE J CLAPHAM
2. CADBURY A E GEERING
3. CHRISTIANITY L M BATE
4. CULLOMPTON B PETTY
5. HONITON N H FREATHY
6. KENN C R EVANS
7. OTTERY T W BRIGHTON
8. TIVERTON M J PARTRIDGE

ARCHDEACONRY OF TOTNES

9. HOLSWORTHY L BROOKHOUSE
10. IPPLEPEN P W DARBY
11. MORETON P J GREGSON
12. OKEHAMPTON R C CHAMBERLAIN
13. TOTNES J CRUSE
14. WOODLEIGH R H WHITE

ARCHDEACONRY OF BARNSTAPLE

15. BARNSTAPLE N JACKSON-STEVENS
16. HARTLAND G J HANSFORD
17. SHIRWELL K G WYER
18. SOUTH MOLTON C S TULL
19. TORRINGTON R J P ACWORTH

ARCHDEACONRY OF PLYMOUTH

20. IVYBRIDGE R J CARLTON
21. PLYMOUTH DEVONPORT S PHILPOTT
22. PLYMOUTH MOORSIDE J F RICHARDS
23. PLYMOUTH SUTTON S R DINSMORE
24. TAVISTOCK G M COTTER

GLOUCESTER

ARCHDEACONRY OF GLOUCESTER

1. BISLEY B C E COKER
2. DURSLEY S G RICHARDS
3. FOREST NORTH T WILLIAMS
4. FOREST SOUTH A N JAMES
5. GLOUCESTER CITY M W BUTLER
6. GLOUCESTER NORTH J O'BRIEN
7. HAWKESBURY D B SMALL
8. STONEHOUSE G G C MINORS
9. TEWKESBURY P L SIBLEY

ARCHDEACONRY OF CHELTENHAM

10. CHELTENHAM E A CROFTON
11. CAMPDEN R D WYATT
12. CIRENCESTER H J MORRIS
13. FAIRFORD A M ROSS
14. NORTHLEACH D W HUTCHIN
15. STOW R F ROTHERY
16. TETBURY J D STRONG
17. WINCHCOMBE M J PAGE

GUILDFORD

ARCHDEACONRY OF SURREY

1. ALDERSHOT M S KING
2. CRANLEIGH N P NICHOLSON
3. FARNHAM J R H HUBBARD
4. GODALMING F J ASHE
5. GUILDFORD J J R COLLINGWOOD
6. SURREY HEATH N C TURTON

ARCHDEACONRY OF DORKING

7. DORKING A S W CULLIS
8. EMLY J T HENDERSON
9. EPSOM D A SMETHURST
10. LEATHERHEAD D J EATON
11. RUNNYMEDE A J MAGOWAN
12. WOKING M F HERBERT

HEREFORD

ARCHDEACONRY OF HEREFORD

1. ABBEYDORE P W M BYLLAM-BARNES
2. BROMYARD D W GOULD
3. HEREFORD CITY J D REESE
4. HEREFORD RURAL U J SUMMERS
5. KINGTON AND WEOBLEY S HOLLINGHURST
6. LEDBURY C L BEEVERS
7. LEOMINSTER A TALBOT-PONSONBY
8. ROSS AND ARCHENFIELD S R ASHTON

ARCHDEACONRY OF LUDLOW

9. BRIDGNORTH C G WILLIAMS
10. CLUN FOREST R T SHAW
11. CONDOVER A N TOOP
12. LUDLOW D S DORMOR
13. PONTESBURY P TOWNER
14. TELFORD SEVERN GORGE D P SMITH

LEICESTER

ARCHDEACONRY OF LEICESTER

1. CHRISTIANITY (LEICESTER) NORTH J J LEONARD
2. CHRISTIANITY (LEICESTER) SOUTH R J FREEMAN
3. FRAMLAND (Melton) G SPENCER
4. GARTREE FIRST DEANERY (Harborough) S R LONG
5. GARTREE SECOND DEANERY (Wigston) J F WELLINGTON
6. GOSCOTE N BAINES

ARCHDEACONRY OF LOUGHBOROUGH

7. AKELEY EAST (Loughborough) S A CHERRY
8. AKELEY SOUTH (Coalville) K C EMMETT
9. AKELEY WEST (Ashby) C P DOBBIN
10. GUTHLAXTON FIRST DEANERY (Blaby) P BURROWS
11. GUTHLAXTON SECOND DEANERY (Lutterworth) P J C CLEMENTS
12. SPARKENHOE EAST G T WILLETT
13. SPARKENHOE WEST (Hinckley and Bosworth) B DAVIS

LICHFIELD

ARCHDEACONRY OF LICHFIELD

1. LICHFIELD E G H TOWNSHEND
2. PENKRIDGE T H GREEN
3. RUGELEY A F CREBER
4. TAMWORTH B R F ROCHE

ARCHDEACONRY OF STOKE-ON-TRENT

5. ALSTONFIELD A C F NICOLL
6. CHEADLE N JEFFERYES
7. ECCLESHALL M J POPE
8. LEEK D M B WILMOT
9. NEWCASTLE W G H GARDINER
10. STAFFORD G K SMITH
11. STOKE NORTH B L WILLIAMS
12. STOKE J W PAWSON
13. TRENTHAM G L SIMPSON
14. TUTBURY P J JEFFERIES
15. UTTOXETER J B HALL

ARCHDEACONRY OF SALOP

16. EDGMOND D J BUTTERFIELD
17. ELLESMERE M W H GRAY
18. HODNET J H GRAHAM
19. OSWESTRY D B CROWHURST
20. SHIFNAL R B BALKWILL
21. SHREWSBURY R W D BIDDLE
22. TELFORD D P SMITH
23. WEM AND WHITCHURCH N MacGREGOR
24. WROCKWARDINE C S COOKE

ARCHDEACONRY OF WALSALL

25. TRYSULL M J HUNTER
26. WALSALL P A R HAMMERSLEY
27. WEDNESBURY I B COOK
28. WEST BROMWICH M C RUTTER
29. WOLVERHAMPTON P J CHAPMAN

LINCOLN

ARCHDEACONRY OF STOW

1. AXHOLME, ISLE OF J D BROWN
2. CORRINGHAM G S RICHARDSON
3. LAWRES I R HOWITT
4. MANLAKE A G D HAYDAY
5. WEST WOLD M J CARTWRIGHT
6. YARBOROUGH S PHILLIPS

ARCHDEACONRY OF LINDSEY

7. BOLINGBROKE A M SULLIVAN
8. CALCEWAITHE AND CANDLESHOE P F COATES
9. GRIMSBY AND CLEETHORPES J W ELLIS
10. HAVERSTOE H W P HALL
11. HORNCASTLE N A THORNLEY
12. LOUTHESK S D HOLDAWAY

ARCHDEACONRY OF LINCOLN

13. AVELAND AND NESS w STAMFORD J M WARWICK
14. BELTISLOE A T HAWES
15. CHRISTIANITY A J KERSWILL
16. ELLOE EAST P HILL
17. ELLOE WEST P G F NORWOOD
18. GRAFFOE R G BILLINGHURST
19. GRANTHAM R S EYRE
20. HOLLAND EAST W G PAGE
21. HOLLAND WEST M A BARSLEY
22. LAFFORD S H SPEERS
23. LOVEDEN G R SHRIMPTON

LIVERPOOL

ARCHDEACONRY OF LIVERPOOL

1. BOOTLE C H JONES
2. HUYTON J A STANLEY
3. LIVERPOOL NORTH G J BUTLAND
4. LIVERPOOL SOUTH J V ROBERTS
5. SEFTON F A BRISCOE
6. TOXTETH AND WAVERTREE D C KIRKWOOD
7. WALTON A B HAWLEY
8. WEST DERBY J R I WIKELEY

ARCHDEACONRY OF WARRINGTON

9. NORTH MEOLS J M BURGESS
10. ST HELENS C H B BYWORTH
11. ORMSKIRK M J SMOUT
12. WARRINGTON J O COLLING
13. WIDNES B ROBINSON
14. WIGAN EAST K M FORREST
15. WIGAN WEST D LYON
16. WINWICK R BRITTON

LONDON

ARCHDEACONRY OF LONDON

1. THE CITY J OATES

ARCHDEACONRY OF CHARING CROSS
(BISHOP OF FULHAM)

2. WESTMINSTER PADDINGTON W G WILSON
3. WESTMINSTER ST MARGARET A C C COURTAULD
4. WESTMINSTER ST MARYLEBONE J SLATER

ARCHDEACONRY OF HACKNEY
(BISHOP OF STEPNEY)

5. HACKNEY W M MACNAUGHTON
6. ISLINGTON S J W COX
7. TOWER HAMLETS C T J CHESSUN

ARCHDEACONRY OF MIDDLESEX
(BISHOP OF KENSINGTON)

8. CHELSEA D A STONE
9. HAMMERSMITH J J CLARK
10. HAMPTON W D F VANSTONE
11. HOUNSLOW D G WILSON
12. KENSINGTON I L ROBSON
13. SPELTHORNE D C PEMBERTON

ARCHDEACONRY OF HAMPSTEAD
(BISHOP OF EDMONTON)

14. BARNET, CENTRAL R M TAYLOR
15. BARNET, WEST P G BAKER
16. CAMDEN, NORTH (Hampstead) P J W BUCKLER
17. CAMDEN, SOUTH (Holborn and St Pancras) C G POPE
18. ENFIELD R C KNOWLING
19. HARINGEY, EAST R B PEARSON
20. HARINGEY, WEST G B SEABROOK

ARCHDEACONRY OF NORTHOLT
(BISHOP OF WILLESDEN)

21. BRENT J B ROOT
22. EALING W H TAYLOR
23. HARROW P M REECE
24. HILLINGDON P J BALL

MANCHESTER

ARCHDEACONRY OF MANCHESTER

1. ARDWICK W NELSON
2. ECCLES N JONES
3. HEATON A PUGMIRE
4. HULME R J GILPIN
5. MANCHESTER, NORTH C S FORD
6. SALFORD D S C WYATT
7. STRETFORD W J TWIDELL
8. WITHINGTON N W DAWSON

ARCHDEACONRY OF BOLTON

9. BOLTON R F OLDFIELD
10. BURY I M ROGERSON
11. DEANE D W GATENBY
12. FARNWORTH A E BALLARD
13. LEIGH P W LEAKEY
14. RADCLIFFE AND PRESTWICH C H ELLIS
15. ROSSENDALE J A ARMES
16. WALMSLEY D J BRIERLEY

ARCHDEACONRY OF ROCHDALE

17. ASHTON-UNDER-LYNE R CASSIDY
18. HEYWOOD AND MIDDLETON I McVEETY
19. OLDHAM C H RAZZALL
20. ROCHDALE I C THOMPSON
21. SADDLEWORTH C W M BARLOW
22. TANDLE D SHARPLES

NEWCASTLE

ARCHDEACONRY OF NORTHUMBERLAND

1. BEDLINGTON J R PRINGLE
2. BELLINGHAM T R HARPER
3. CORBRIDGE M F FENWICK
4. HEXHAM V G ASHWIN
5. NEWCASTLE CENTRAL J C WIDDOWS
6. NEWCASTLE EAST M J WEBB
7. NEWCASTLE WEST B C HURST
8. TYNEMOUTH W N STOCK

ARCHDEACONRY OF LINDISFARNE

9. ALNWICK B COWEN
10. BAMBURGH AND GLENDALE A J HUGHES
11. MORPETH R A FERGUSON
12. NORHAM J W SHEWAN

NORWICH

ARCHDEACONRY OF NORWICH

1. NORWICH EAST H R G COOKE
2. NORWICH NORTH M H STAGG
3. NORWICH SOUTH P R OLIVER

ARCHDEACONRY OF NORFOLK

4. BLOFIELD B W TOMLINSON
5. DEPWADE S SWIFT
6. GREAT YARMOUTH C W COUSINS
7. HUMBLEYARD P J STEPHENS
8. LODDON C R CHAPMAN
9. LOTHINGLAND M C GRAY
10. REDENHALL D V WHALE
11. THETFORD AND ROCKLAND J HANDLEY
12. ST BENET AT WAXHAM AND TUNSTEAD M W SMITH

ARCHDEACONRY OF LYNN

13. BRECKLAND J H RICHARDSON
14. BRISLEY AND ELMHAM B R A COLE
15. BURNHAM AND WALSINGHAM A J BELL
16. HEACHAM AND RISING G R HALL
17. HINGHAM AND MITFORD D W A RIDER
18. HOLT P J G BARNES-CLAY
19. INGWORTH P B FOREMAN
20. LYNN S R NAIRN
21. REPPS D F HAYDEN
22. SPARHAM J P P ILLINGWORTH

OXFORD

ARCHDEACONRY OF OXFORD (BISHOP OF DORCHESTER)

1. ASTON AND CUDDESDON J Y CROWE
2. BICESTER AND ISLIP G G CHAPMAN
3. CHIPPING NORTON G G B CANNING
4. COWLEY A R PRICE
5. DEDDINGTON T WIMBUSH
6. HENLEY P E NIXON
7. OXFORD A M GANN
8. WITNEY C J BUTLAND
9. WOODSTOCK G J H B van der WEEGEN

ARCHDEACONRY OF BERKSHIRE (BISHOP OF READING)

10. ABINGDON A L THOMAS
11. BRACKNELL D S JONES
12. BRADFIELD R B HOWELL
13. MAIDENHEAD D D J ROSSDALE
14. NEWBURY C T SCOTT-DEMPSTER
15. READING B SHENTON
16. SONNING J W RATINGS
17. VALE OF WHITE HORSE C R RUDD
18. WALLINGFORD J MORLEY
19. WANTAGE A WADGE

ARCHDEACONRY (AND BISHOP) OF BUCKINGHAM

20. AMERSHAM N A RUSSELL
21. AYLESBURY T J HIGGINS
22. BUCKINGHAM D G MEARA
23. BURNHAM AND SLOUGH S N D BROWN
24. CLAYDON J M REES
25. MILTON KEYNES I J PUSEY
26. MURSLEY N J COTTON
27. NEWPORT M C STANTON-SARINGER
28. WENDOVER A W BENNETT
29. WYCOMBE C D BULL

PETERBOROUGH

ARCHDEACONRY OF NORTHAMPTON

1. BRACKLEY J H ROBERTS
2. BRIXWORTH B LEE
3. DAVENTRY D EVANS
4. NORTHAMPTON K E ANDERSON
5. TOWCESTER M H CHAMPNEYS
6. WELLINGBOROUGH J R WESTWOOD
7. WOOTTON R J ORMSTON

ARCHDEACONRY OF OAKHAM

8. BARNACK B HARRIS
9. CORBY R D HOWE
10. HIGHAM D R BIRD
11. KETTERING J SIMMONS
12. OUNDLE M A McADAM
13. PETERBOROUGH H C SMART
14. RUTLAND M H W ROGERS

PORTSMOUTH

ARCHDEACONRY OF PORTSMOUTH

1. BISHOPS WALTHAM D E HENLEY
2. FAREHAM I JAGGER
3. GOSPORT P R WADSWORTH
4. HAVANT P HANCOCK
5. PETERSFIELD C LOWSON
6. PORTSMOUTH J R PINDER

ARCHDEACONRY OF ISLE OF WIGHT

7. WIGHT, EAST A P MENNISS
8. WIGHT, WEST J W RUSSELL

RIPON

ARCHDEACONRY OF RICHMOND

1. HARROGATE A C BETTS
2. RICHMOND C N H WHITE
3. RIPON S J TALBOTT
4. WENSLEY C W MALPASS

ARCHDEACONRY OF LEEDS

5. ALLERTON C R CORNWELL
6. ARMLEY J N O HORTON
7. HEADINGLEY M A CROSS
8. WHITKIRK K A PAYNE

ROCHESTER

ARCHDEACONRY OF ROCHESTER

1. COBHAM J E TIPP
2. DARTFORD A T WATERMAN
3. GILLINGHAM P T KERR
4. GRAVESEND C D GOBLE
5. ROCHESTER C D COLLINS
6. STROOD D A LOW

ARCHDEACONRY OF TONBRIDGE

7. MALLING R B STEVENSON
8. PADDOCK WOOD D G St L WINTER
9. SEVENOAKS B E S GODFREY
10. SHOREHAM C C HORN
11. TONBRIDGE R J BAWTREE
12. TUNBRIDGE WELLS F R CUMBERLEGE

ARCHDEACONRY OF BROMLEY

13. BECKENHAM D S R REDMAN
14. BROMLEY P H D'A LOCK
15. ERITH P WRIGHT
16. ORPINGTON P MILLER
17. SIDCUP D L KNIGHT

ST ALBANS

ARCHDEACONRY OF ST ALBANS

1. ALDENHAM S PURVIS
2. BERKHAMSTED J A S PAYNE COOK
3. HEMEL HEMPSTEAD P V HUGHES
4. HITCHIN F J C MERCURIO
5. RICKMANSWORTH B L DRIVER
6. ST ALBANS A R HURLE
7. WATFORD J B BROWN
8. WHEATHAMPSTEAD T PURCHAS

ARCHDEACONRY OF BEDFORD

9. AMPTHILL N JEFFERY
10. BEDFORD J R BROWN
11. BIGGLESWADE R F SIBSON
12. DUNSTABLE G H NEWTON
13. ELSTOW C P STRONG
14. LUTON R I CHEETHAM

15. SHARNBROOK A R H WOODWARD
16. SHEFFORD J K DIXON

ARCHDEACONRY OF HERTFORD

17. BARNET G R HUDDLESTON
18. BISHOP'S STORTFORD C P SLAUGHTER
19. BUNTINGFORD L D HARMAN
20. CHESHUNT J H SPRINGBETT
21. HATFIELD P J SMITH
22. HERTFORD AND WARE J RISBY
23. STEVENAGE M BARNSLEY

ST EDMUNDSBURY AND IPSWICH

ARCHDEACONRY OF IPSWICH

1. BOSMERE R J DEDMAN
2. COLNEYS G L GRANT
3. HADLEIGH S C MORRIS
4. IPSWICH D CUTTS
5. SAMFORD R F PALLANT
6. STOWMARKET N J HARTLEY
7. WOODBRIDGE R W CLIFTON

ARCHDEACONRY OF SUDBURY

8. CLARE E J BETTS
9. IXWORTH D M B MATHERS
10. LAVENHAM D M STIFF
11. MILDENHALL G C SMITH
12. SUDBURY L R PIZZEY
13. THINGOE D R UNDERWOOD

ARCHDEACONRY OF SUFFOLK

14. BECCLES AND SOUTH ELMHAM J M S FALKNER
15. HALESWORTH L W DOOLAN
16. HARTISMERE M P BEEK
17. HOXNE D J STREETER
18. LOES R J DIXON
19. SAXMUNDHAM R S SMITH

SALISBURY

ARCHDEACONRY OF SHERBORNE

1. BEAMINSTER E G A W PAGE-TURNER
2. DORCHESTER K J SCOTT
3. LYME BAY E G A W PAGE-TURNER
4. SHERBORNE E J WOODS
5. WEYMOUTH K A HUGO

ARCHDEACONRY OF DORSET

6. BLACKMORE VALE W T RIDDING
7. MILTON AND BLANDFORD G S M SQUAREY
8. POOLE V R BARRON
9. PURBECK P G HARDMAN
10. WIMBORNE D R PRICE

ARCHDEACONRY OF SARUM

11. ALDERBURY M C GALLAGHER
12. AVON M J BRIDGER
13. CHALKE M E RIDLEY
14. HEYTESBURY M J FLIGHT
15. SALISBURY D P SCRACE
16. WYLYE AND WILTON B THOMAS

ARCHDEACONRY OF WILTS

17. BRADFORD C F BROWN
18. CALNE B J SMITH
19. DEVIZES B A TIGWELL
20. MARLBOROUGH H G PEARSON
21. PEWSEY D M RYDER

SHEFFIELD

ARCHDEACONRY OF SHEFFIELD

1. ATTERCLIFFE R F BLACKBURN
2. ECCLESALL D G WILLIAMS
3. ECCLESFIELD T W ELLIS
4. HALLAM P W WEST
5. LAUGHTON H J PATRICK
6. ROTHERHAM B H COOPER
7. TANKERSLEY L M ATKINSON

ARCHDEACONRY OF DONCASTER

8. ADWICK-LE-STREET R A FITZHARRIS
9. DONCASTER J C BARNES
10. DONCASTER, WEST G J MARCER
11. SNAITH AND HATFIELD J M OSGERBY
12. WATH C W M BALDOCK

SODOR AND MAN

1. CASTLETOWN AND PEEL B H KELLY
2. DOUGLAS D WHITWORTH
3. RAMSEY J H SHEEN

SOUTHWARK

ARCHDEACONRY OF LEWISHAM
(BISHOP OF WOOLWICH)

1. DEPTFORD W G CORNECK
2. GREENWICH SOUTH J E NEAL
3. GREENWICH THAMESIDE G S HARCOURT
4. LEWISHAM, EAST D GARLICK
5. LEWISHAM, WEST J O ARDLEY

ARCHDEACONRY OF SOUTHWARK
(BISHOP OF WOOLWICH)

6. BERMONDSEY S L WILMOT
7. CAMBERWELL R W G BOMFORD
8. DULWICH W C HEATLEY
9. SOUTHWARK AND NEWINGTON G D SHAW

ARCHDEACONRY OF LAMBETH
(BISHOP OF KINGSTON)

10. BRIXTON L DENNEN
11. CLAPHAM D J HOUGHTON
12. LAMBETH C R TRUSS
13. MERTON J M SHEPHERD
14. STREATHAM J R WILCOX

ARCHDEACONRY OF WANDSWORTH
(BISHOP OF KINGSTON)

15. BATTERSEA P CLARK
16. KINGSTON P A HOLMES
17. RICHMOND AND BARNES R AMES-LEWIS
18. TOOTING B M C BROGGIO
19. WANDSWORTH A N TREDENNICK

ARCHDEACONRY (AND BISHOP) OF CROYDON

20. CROYDON ADDINGTON A H R QUINN
21. CROYDON CENTRAL G S DERRIMAN
22. CROYDON SOUTH A C WAIT
23. CROYDON NORTH P L WASHINGTON
24. SUTTON D V LEWIS

ARCHDEACONRY OF REIGATE
(BISHOP OF CROYDON)

25. CATERHAM J E SMITH
26. GODSTONE D A RICHARDSON
27. REIGATE R H McLEAN

SOUTHWELL

ARCHDEACONRY OF NEWARK

1. BAWTRY J A BRITTON
2. MANSFIELD J M BURGESS
3. NEWARK A A CONN
4. NEWSTEAD F G GREEN
5. RETFORD A N WOODSFORD
6. WORKSOP G E JONES

ARCHDEACONRY OF NOTTINGHAM

7. BEESTON *Vacant*
8. BINGHAM G B BARRODALE
9. BINGHAM SOUTH T SISSON
10. BINGHAM WEST S J SMITH
11. GEDLING W G CALTHROP-OWEN
12. NOTTINGHAM CENTRAL S E DYAS
13. NOTTINGHAM NORTH C GALE
14. NOTTINGHAM WEST A S G HART
15. SOUTHWELL P HILL

TRURO

ARCHDEACONRY OF CORNWALL

1. ST AUSTELL F M BOWERS
2. CARNMARTH NORTH R C BUSH
3. CARNMARTH SOUTH R G GILBERT
4. KERRIER P A A WALKER
5. PENWITH M H FISHER
6. POWDER T M GOULDSTONE
7. PYDAR J G SLEE

ARCHDEACONRY OF BODMIN

8. STRATTON B G DORRINGTON
9. TRIGG MAJOR A J M BROWNRIDGE
10. TRIGG MINOR AND BODMIN I H MORRIS
11. WIVELSHIRE, EAST R OAKES
12. WIVELSHIRE, WEST D J LOEWENDAHL

WAKEFIELD

ARCHDEACONRY OF HALIFAX

1. ALMONDBURY M W THOMAS
2. BRIGHOUSE AND ELLAND N M WOOD
3. CALDER VALLEY P N CALVERT
4. HALIFAX A A ROSS
5. HUDDERSFIELD E O ROBERTS
6. KIRKBURTON D BARRACLOUGH

ARCHDEACONRY OF PONTEFRACT

7. BARNSLEY J L HUDSON
8. BIRSTALL I M GASKELL
9. CHEVET J F WHITE
10. DEWSBURY L C DEW
11. PONTEFRACT W T HICKS
12. WAKEFIELD B S ELLIS

WINCHESTER

ARCHDEACONRY OF BASINGSTOKE

1. ALRESFORD C R SMITH
2. ALTON J RICHARDS
3. ANDOVER M HARLEY
4. BASINGSTOKE A D PICTON
5. ODIHAM N D BEAMER
6. WHITCHURCH N P CUMMING

ARCHDEACONRY OF WINCHESTER

7. BOURNEMOUTH A F J CHAMBERS
8. CHRISTCHURCH A SESSFORD
9. EASTLEIGH A G HARBIDGE
10. LYNDHURST M G ANDERSON
11. ROMSEY D B KINGTON
12. SOUTHAMPTON B J HARTNELL
13. WINCHESTER R J H TEARE

CHANNEL ISLANDS

14. GUERNSEY F M TRICKEY
15. JERSEY J N SEAFORD

WORCESTER

ARCHDEACONRY OF WORCESTER

1. EVESHAM G S CROSS
2. MALVERN P C G BILLINGHAM
3. MARTLEY AND WORCESTER WEST G T M NOTT
4. PERSHORE K A BOYCE
5. UPTON C G HARDWICK
6. WORCESTER EAST M A O LEWIS

ARCHDEACONRY OF DUDLEY

7. BROMSGROVE D C SALT
8. DROITWICH D M WIGHT
9. DUDLEY J C EVEREST
10. HIMLEY F M TRETHEWEY
11. KIDDERMINSTER G SHILVOCK
12. STOURBRIDGE P TONGUE
13. STOURPORT B GILBERT

YORK

ARCHDEACONRY OF YORK (BISHOP OF SELBY)

1. AINSTY, NEW J A RENDALL
2. BUCKROSE F B WILLIAMS
3. BULMER AND MALTON E T CHAPMAN
4. DERWENT F G HUNTER
5. EASINGWOLD G C GALLEY
6. SELBY D G RICHARDSON
7. SOUTH WOLD D S COOK
8. YORK, CITY OF G H WEBSTER

ARCHDEACONRY OF EAST RIDING (BISHOP OF HULL)

9. BEVERLEY M L KAVANAGH
10. BRIDLINGTON J C MEEK
11. HARTHILL H L ARTLEY
12. HOLDERNESS, NORTH B H WILCOX
13. HOLDERNESS, SOUTH I R S WALKER
14. HOWDEN D C BAILEY
15. HULL J W WALLER
16. SCARBOROUGH M D B LONG

ARCHDEACONRY OF CLEVELAND (BISHOP OF WHITBY)

17. GUISBOROUGH T N EVANS
18. HELMSLEY D E NEWTON
19. MIDDLESBROUGH S C WRIGHT
20. MOWBRAY D G BILES
21. PICKERING F J A HEWITT
22. STOKESLEY D F LICKESS
23. WHITBY N N JONES

CHURCH IN WALES

ST ASAPH

ARCHDEACONRY OF ST ASAPH

1. ST ASAPH R W ROWLAND
2. DENBIGH C W EVANS
3. DYFFRYN CLWYD J B DAVIES
4. HOLYWELL J W K SOMERVILLE
5. LLANRWST T E MART
6. RHOS D J ROBERTS

ARCHDEACONRY OF MONTGOMERY

7. CEDEWAIN J R GUY
8. CAEREINION G MORGAN
9. LLANFYLLIN C F CARTER
10. POOL R A BIRD

ARCHDEACONRY OF WREXHAM

11. BAN ISYCOED P R OWENS
12. EDEYRNION *Vacant*
13. LLANGOLLEN G C JONES
14. MOLD J B JONES
15. PENLLYN G THOMAS
16. WREXHAM D GRIFFITHS

BANGOR

ARCHDEACONRY OF BANGOR

1. ARFON I THOMAS
2. ARLLECHWEDD P R JONES
3. LIFTON AND TALYBOLION C M EVANS
4. MENAI AND MALLTRAETH J F W JONES
5. TINDAETHWY G M HUGHES
6. TWRCELYN G W EDWARDS

ARCHDEACONRY OF MEIRIONNYDD

7. ARDUDWY R A BEACON
8. ARWYSTLI D J PARRY
9. CYFEILIOG AND MAWDDWY E W ROWLANDS
10. EIFIONYDD W JONES
11. LLYN W L JONES
12. YSTUMANER J M RILEY

ST DAVIDS

ARCHDEACONRY OF ST DAVIDS

1. CASTLEMARTIN A THOMAS
2. DAUGLEDDAU W H WATKINS
3. DEWISLAND AND FISHGUARD R J E W REES
4. NARBERTH M BUTLER
5. ROOSE A CRAVEN

ARCHDEACONRY OF CARDIGAN

6. CEMAIS AND SUB-AERON E L THOMAS
7. EMLYN J H ROWLANDS
8. GLYN AERON M L REES
9. LAMPETER AND ULTRA-AERON A W WILLIAMS
10. LLANBADARN FAWR R H WILLIAMS

ARCHDEACONRY OF CARMARTHEN

11. CARMARTHEN J K DAVIES
12. CYDWELI S R THOMAS
13. DYFFRYN AMAN A TEALE
14. LLANGADOG AND LLANDEILO B T RICE
15. ST CLEARS M G R MORRIS

LLANDAFF

ARCHDEACONRY OF LLANDAFF

1. BRIDGEND E J EVANS
2. CAERPHILLY M J SHORT
3. CARDIFF H G CLARKE
4. LLANTWIT MAJOR AND COWBRIDGE D V GINN
5. LLANDAFF W G BARLOW
6. PENARTH AND BARRY N H COLLINS

ARCHDEACONRY OF MARGAM

7. ABERDARE S J RYAN
8. MARGAM P G WHITE
9. MERTHYR TYDFIL S S MORGAN
10. NEATH P RAIKES
11. PONTYPRIDD J H S THOMAS
12. RHONDDA P N COLEMAN

MONMOUTH

ARCHDEACONRY OF MONMOUTH

1. ABERGAVENNY D K POPE
2. CHEPSTOW J P HARRIS
3. MONMOUTH J K C DENERLEY
4. NETHERWENT T H J PALMER
5. RAGLAN-USK C R F CALE

ARCHDEACONRY OF NEWPORT

6. BASSALEG P VANN
7. BEDWELLTY R J SUMMERS
8. BLAENAU GWENT D J JONES
9. NEWPORT K W SHARPE
10. PONTYPOOL D G BRUNNING

SWANSEA AND BRECON

ARCHDEACONRY OF BRECON

1. BRECON B M JONES
2. BUILTH P A C PEARCEY
3. CRICKHOWELL J R ELLIS
4. HAY P DIXON
5. MAELIENYDD G M H HUGHES

ARCHDEACONRY OF GOWER

6. CLYNE R BRITTON
7. CWMTAWE D H E MOSFORD
8. GOWER J W GRIFFIN
9. LLWCHWR C J COLEBROOK
10. PENDERI A G LEE
11. SWANSEA A G HOWELLS

ENGLISH BENEFICES AND CHURCHES

An index of benefices, conventional districts, local ecumenical projects, and proprietary chapels (all shown in bold type), together with entries for churches and other licensed places of worship listed on the Parish Index of the Central Board of Finance. Where the church name is the same as that of the benefice (or as that of the place whose name forms the beginning of the benefice name), the church entry is omitted. Church dedications are indicated in brackets.

The benefice entry gives the full legal name, followed by the diocese, its deanery number (page 835), the patron(s), and the name(s) and appointment(s) of clergy serving there (if there are none, the telephone number of the parsonage house is given). The following are the main abbreviations used; for others see the full list of abbreviations.

C	Curate	**P**	Patron(s)
C-in-c	Curate-in-charge	**P-in-c**	Priest-in-charge
Dn-in-c	Deacon-in-charge	**Par Dn**	Parish Deacon
Dss	Deaconess	**R**	Rector
Hon C	Honorary Curate	**TM**	Team Minister
Hon Par Dn	Honorary Parish Deacon	**TR**	Team Rector
Min	Minister	**TV**	Team Vicar
NSM	Non-stipendiary Minister	**V**	Vicar

Listed below are the elements in place names which are not normally treated as substantive in the index:

CENTRAL	**HIGHER**	**MUCH**	**OVER**
EAST	**LITTLE**	**NETHER**	**SOUTH**
GREAT	**LOW**	**NEW**	**THE**
GREATER	**LOWER**	**NORTH**	**UPPER**
HIGH	**MIDDLE**	**OLD**	**WEST**

Thus, WEST WIMBLEDON (Christ Church) appears as **WIMBLEDON, WEST (Christ Church)** and CENTRAL TELFORD as **TELFORD, CENTRAL**. The only exception occurs where the second element of the place name is a common noun; thus NEW LANE remains as **NEW LANE**, and WEST TOWN as **WEST TOWN.**

AB KETTLEBY Group, The (St James) *Leic 3* **P** *V Rothley, K J M Madocks-Wright Esq, and MMCET (jt)* **P-in-c** R W WIDDOWSON

ABBAS and Templecombe w Horsington *B & W 2* **P** *Bp and Ch Trust Fund (jt)* **R** A J ROSE

ABBERLEY (St Mary) *see* Shrawley, Witley, Astley and Abberley *Worc*

ABBERLEY (St Michael) *as above*

ABBERTON (St Andrew) *see* Fingringhoe w E Donyland and Abberton etc *Chelmsf*

ABBERTON (St Edburga), The Flyfords, Naunton Beauchamp and Bishampton w Throckmorton *Worc 4* **P** *Bp and Croome Estate Trustees (1 turn), and Ld Chan (1 turn)* **R** D E HASSELL

ABBESS RODING (St Edmund) *see* Leaden Roding and Abbess Roding etc *Chelmsf*

ABBEY CHAPEL (St Mary) *see* Annesley w Newstead *S'well*

ABBEY HEY (St George) *Man 1* **P** *Bp* **P-in-c** I C J GORTON

ABBEY HULTON (St John) *see* Bucknall and Bagnall *Lich*

ABBEY WOOD (St Michael and All Angels) *S'wark 3* **P** *Bp* **V** M W NEALE, **NSM** D C ROBINSON

ABBEY WOOD (William Temple) *see* Thamesmead *S'wark*

ABBEYDALE (St John the Evangelist) *Sheff 2* **P** *Lady Judith Roberts, Mrs C Longworth, P Hayward Esq and J Roebuck Esq (jt)* **V** G G MacINTOSH

ABBEYDALE (St Peter) *see* Sheff Abbeydale St Pet *Sheff*

ABBEYDORE (St Mary) *see* Ewyas Harold w Dulas, Kenderchurch etc *Heref*

ABBOTS BICKINGTON (St James) and Bulkworthy *Ex 9* **P** *Bp* **V** *Vacant*

ABBOTS BROMLEY (St Nicholas) w Blithfield *Lich 3* **P** *Bp and D&C (jt)* **P-in-c** S C DAVIS

ABBOTS LANGLEY (St Lawrence) *St Alb 7* **P** *Bp* **V** B K ANDREWS, **C** K STRAUGHAN

ABBOTS LEIGH (Holy Trinity) w Leigh Woods *Bris 5* **P** *Bp* **P-in-c** T J DAPLYN

ABBOTS MORTON (St Peter) *see* Church Lench w Rous Lench and Abbots Morton *Worc*

ABBOTS RIPTON (St Andrew) w Wood Walton *Ely 9* **P** *Lord de Ramsey (2 turns), D&C (1 turn)* **P-in-c** B J HYDER-SMITH

ABBOTSBURY (St Mary) *see* Highweek and Teigngrace *Ex*

ABBOTSBURY (St Nicholas), Portesham and Langton Herring *Sarum 5* **P** *Hon Charlotte Morrison and P R FitzGerald Esq (jt), and Bp (alt)* **P-in-c** P S THOMAS

ABBOTSHAM (St Helen) *see* Parkham, Alwington, Buckland Brewer etc *Ex*

ABBOTSKERSWELL (Blessed Virgin Mary) *Ex 11* **P** *Ld Chan* **P-in-c** J G A IVE, **C** P F IVE

ABBOTSLEY (St Margaret) *Ely 12* **P** *Ball Coll Ox* **P-in-c** B CURRY

ABBOTSWOOD (St Nicholas Family Centre) *see* Yate New Town *Bris*

ABBOTTS ANN (St Mary) and Upper Clatford and Goodworth Clatford *Win 3* **P** *Exors T P de Paravicini Esq and Bp (jt)* **R** P M GILKS, **NSM** N J JUDD, J A TAYLOR

ABDON (St Margaret) *Heref 12* **P** *Bp* **R** I E GIBBS

ABENHALL (St Michael) w Mitcheldean *Glouc 3* **P** *DBP* **P-in-c** R G STURMAN

ABERFORD (St Ricarius) *see* Aberford w Micklefield *York*

ABERFORD (St Ricarius) w Micklefield *York 6* **P** *Abp and Or Coll Ox (jt)* **V** D G MOORE, **P-in-c** D G MOORE

ABINGDON (Christ Church) (St Helen) (St Michael and All Angels) (St Nicholas) *Ox 10* **P** *Patr Bd* **TR** M A J GOODE, **TV** G N MAUGHAN, P E BRADLEY, M LOVERING, **C** J M LOVERING, S P WALKER, R S MARTIN, **NSM** M C SAMS

ABINGER (St James) cum Coldharbour *Guildf 7* **P** *Ch Patr Trust and J P M H Evelyn Esq (alt)* **R** A N BERRY

ABINGTON (St Peter and St Paul) *Pet 4* **P** *Bp* **R** *Vacant* (01604) 31041

ABINGTON, GREAT (St Mary the Virgin) w LITTLE (St Mary) *Ely 4* **P** *MMCET* **P-in-c** G C MILLS

ABINGTON PIGOTTS (St Michael and All Angels) *see* Shingay Gp of Par *Ely*

ABNEY (Mission Room) *see* Bradwell *Derby*

ABRAM (St John) *Liv 14* **P** *R Wigan* **V** S A MATHER

ABRIDGE (Holy Trinity) *see* Lambourne w Abridge and Stapleford Abbotts *Chelmsf*

ABSON (St James the Great) *see* Pucklechurch and Abson *Bris*

ABTHORPE (St John the Baptist) *see* Silverstone and Abthorpe w Slapton *Pet*

ACASTER MALBIS (Holy Trinity) *York 1* **P** *R A G Raimes Esq* **V** P RATHBONE

ACASTER SELBY (St John) *see* Appleton Roebuck w Acaster Selby *York*

ACCRINGTON (Christ Church) *Blackb 1* **P** *Bp and V S Shore H Trin (jt)* **V** K LOGAN

ACCRINGTON (St James) (St Paul) (St Andrew) (St Peter) *Blackb 1* **P** *DBP* **TV** A D LYON

ACCRINGTON (St John) w Huncoat (St Augustine) *Blackb 1* **P** *Bp and V Accrington St Jas w St Paul (jt)* **C** G BILLINGTON

ACCRINGTON (St Mary Magdalen) Milnshaw *Blackb 1* **P** *V Accrington St Jas* **P-in-c** P FORD

ACKLAM (St John the Baptist) *see* Burythorpe, Acklam and Leavening w Westow *York*

ACKLAM, WEST (St Mary) *York 19* **P** *Trustees* **V** S C WRIGHT, **C** D S WATSON, **NSM** M J WRIGHT

ACKLETON (Mission Room) *see* Worfield *Heref*

ACKLINGTON (St John the Divine) *see* Warkworth and Acklington *Newc*

ACKWORTH (All Saints) (St Cuthbert) *Wakef 11* **P** *Duchy of Lanc* **R** P HARTLEY

ACLE (St Edmund) w Fishley and North Burlingham *Nor 4* **P** *Bp and Ch Soc Trust (jt)* **R** *Vacant* (01493) 750393

ACOCKS GREEN (St Mary) *Birm 14* **P** *Trustees* **V** R H POSTILL

ACOL (St Mildred) *see* Birchington w Acol and Minnis Bay *Cant*

ACOMB (Holy Redeemer) *York 8* **P** *The Crown* **V** J BEECH

ACOMB (St Stephen) *York 8* **P** *Trustees* **V** M E G WARCHUS, **C** V POLLARD

ACOMB MOOR (James the Deacon) *York 8* **P** *Abp* **V** R W A GUIVER

ACRISE (St Martin) *see* Hawkinge w Acrise and Swingfield *Cant*
ACTON (All Saints) w Great Waldingfield *St E 12* **P** *Bp* **V** P J LILEY, **NSM** D L C RUTHERFORD
ACTON (St Mary) *Lon 22* **P** *Bp* **R** J F FOX, **C** S M MAINA, **NSM** P M SMEDLEY
ACTON (St Mary) and Worleston, Church Minshull and Wettenhall *Ches 15* **P** *Bp, V Over St Chad, and R C Roundell Esq (jt)* **V** M J RYLANDS, **C** A C RYLANDS
ACTON, EAST (St Dunstan w St Thomas) *Lon 22* **P** *Bp* **V** N J BLANDFORD-BAKER
ACTON, NORTH (St Gabriel) *Lon 22* **P** *Bp* **V** E J ALCOCK, **NSM** J H ROBINSON
ACTON, WEST (St Martin) *Lon 22* **P** *Bp* **V** N P HENDERSON, **Hon C** J M UCHIDA
ACTON BEAUCHAMP (St Giles) and Evesbatch w Stanford Bishop *Heref 2* **P** *Bp and MMCET (alt)* **P-in-c** F M RIGBY
ACTON BURNELL (St Mary) *see* Condover w Frodesley, Acton Burnell etc *Heref*
ACTON GREEN (St Alban) (St Peter) (All Saints) *Lon 22* **P** *Bp* **V** J M V WILLMINGTON, **C** R M REEVE
ACTON ROUND (St Mary) *Heref 9* **P** *DBP* **Hon C** H J PATTERSON
ACTON SCOTT (St Margaret) *Heref 11* **P** *DBP* **P-in-c** A N TOOP
ACTON TRUSSELL (St James) *see* Penkridge Team *Lich*
ACTON TURVILLE (St Mary) *see* Badminton w Lt Badminton, Acton Turville etc *Glouc*
ADBASTON (St Michael and All Angels) *see* Croxton w Broughton and Adbaston *Lich*
ADDERBURY (St Mary) w Milton *Ox 5* **P** *New Coll Ox* **V** J E HOLBROOK
ADDERLEY (St Peter), Ash, Calverhall, Ightfield and Moreton Say *Lich 18* **P** *C C Russell Esq, A E H Heber-Percy Esq, T C Heywood-Lonsdale Esq, and R Whitchurch (jt)* **C** P J KNIGHT
ADDINGHAM (St Michael), Edenhall, Langwathby and Culgaith *Carl 4* **P** *D&C* **V** R A MOATT, **NSM** A R BEAUMONT
ADDINGHAM (St Peter) *Bradf 4* **P** *J R Thompson-Ashby Esq* **R** M J CASTERTON, **Hon C** J E LLOYD
ADDINGTON (St Margaret) *see* Birling, Addington, Ryarsh and Trottiscliffe *Roch*
ADDINGTON (St Mary) *see* Winslow w Gt Horwood and Addington *Ox*
ADDINGTON (St Mary) *S'wark 21* **P** *Abp* **V** P ADAMS, **C** J C BANISTER, **NSM** B J HESELTINE
ADDINGTON, GREAT (All Saints) w LITTLE (St Mary the Virgin) and Woodford *Pet 10* **P** *Bp and DBP (alt)* **R** G M JESSOP, **NSM** P R NEEDLE
ADDINGTON, NEW (St Edward) *S'wark 21* **P** *Bp* **V** J A F GALBRAITH, **C** A O NICOLL, P M BALLAMAN
ADDISCOMBE (St Mary Magdalene) *S'wark 22* **P** *Trustees* **V** M R McKINNEY, **C** R W J MYERS, H H NESBITT
ADDISCOMBE (St Mildred) *S'wark 22* **P** *Bp* **V** V M HAMER
ADDLESTONE (St Augustine) (St Paul) *Guildf 11* **P** *Bp* **V** W M POWELL, **NSM** A G BARDELL, D GODDARD
ADDLETHORPE (St Nicholas) *see* Ingoldmells w Addlethorpe *Linc*
ADEL (St John the Baptist) *Ripon 7* **P** *Brig R G Lewthwaite, D R Lewthwaite Esq, and J V Lewthwaite Esq (jt)* **R** G C DARVILL
ADEYFIELD (St Barnabas) *see* Hemel Hempstead *St Alb*
ADFORTON (St Andrew) *see* Wigmore Abbey *Heref*
ADISHAM (Holy Innocents) *see* Aylesham w Adisham *Cant*
ADLESTROP (St Mary Magdalene) *see* Broadwell, Evenlode, Oddington and Adlestrop *Glouc*
ADLINGFLEET (All Saints) *see* The Marshland *Sheff*
ADLINGTON (St John's Mission Church) *see* Prestbury *Ches*
ADLINGTON (St Paul) *Blackb 4* **P** *Bp* **V** D F C MORGAN
ADSTOCK (St Cecilia) *see* Lenborough *Ox*
ADSTONE (All Saints) *see* Blakesley w Adstone and Maidford etc *Pet*
ADSWOOD (St Gabriel's Mission Church) *see* Stockport SW *Ches*
ADVENT (St Adwena) *see* Lanteglos by Camelford w Advent *Truro*
ADWELL (St Mary) *see* Tetsworth, Adwell w S Weston, Lewknor etc *Ox*
ADWICK-LE-STREET (StLaurence) w Skelbrooke *Sheff 8* **P** *J C M Fullerton Esq and Bp (alt)* **R** P A INGRAM
ADWICK-UPON-DEARNE (St John the Baptist) *see* Barnburgh w Melton on the Hill etc *Sheff*
AFFPUDDLE (St Lawrence) *see* Bere Regis and Affpuddle w Turnerspuddle *Sarum*
AIGBURTH (St Anne) *Liv 4* **P** *Trustees* **V** J C ANDERS
AIKTON (St Andrew) *Carl 3* **P** *Earl of Lonsdale* **C** G M HART
AINDERBY STEEPLE (St Helen) w Yafforth and Kirby Wiske w Maunby *Ripon 4* **P** *Bp and Duke of Northd (jt)* **R** P WARREN
AINSDALE (St John) *Liv 9* **P** *R Walton, Bp, and Adn (jt)* **V** A RENSHAW
AINSTABLE (St Michael and All Angels) *see* Kirkoswald, Renwick and Ainstable *Carl*
AINSWORTH (Christ Church) *Man 14* **P** *Bp* **V** A T FLAHERTY
AINTREE (St Giles) *Liv 7* **P** *Bp* **V** *Vacant* 0151-526 7908
AINTREE (St Peter) *Liv 7* **P** *R Sefton* **P-in-c** R A BYWORTH
AIREDALE (Holy Cross) w Fryston *Wakef 11* **P** *Bp* **V** J D WILKINSON, **C** S A MOOR
AIRMYN (St David), Hook and Rawcliffe *Sheff 11* **P** *Bp and Ch Soc Trust (jt)* **V** G HOLLINGSWORTH
AISHOLT (All Saints) *see* Spaxton w Charlynch, Goathurst, Enmore etc *B & W*
AISLABY (St Margaret) and Ruswarp *York 23* **P** *Abp* **V** *Vacant* (01947) 810350
AISTHORPE (St Peter) w Scampton w Thorpe le Fallows w Brattleby *Linc 3* **P** *DBP and J M Wright Esq (jt)* **R** *Vacant*
AKELEY (St James) *see* N Buckingham *Ox*
AKEMAN *Ox 2* **P** *New Coll and Ch Ch (1 turn), Qu Coll, St Jo Coll, and Period and Country Houses Ltd (1 turn)* **R** D F WALKER, **C** J N ASHWORTH
ALBERBURY (St Michael and All Angels) w Cardeston *Heref 13* **P** *Bp and Sir Michael Leighton Bt (alt)* **V** *Vacant*
ALBOURNE (St Bartholomew) w Sayers Common and Twineham *Chich 9* **P** *Bp (2 turns), Ex Coll Ox (1 turn)* **R** D M SWYER
ALBRIGHTON (St John the Baptist) *see* Leaton and Albrighton w Battlefield *Lich*
ALBRIGHTON (St Mary Magdalene) *Lich 20* **P** *Haberdashers' Co and Ch Hosp Horsham (alt)* **V** R B BALKWILL
ALBURGH (All Saints) *see* Earsham w Alburgh and Denton *Nor*
ALBURY (St Helen) Tiddington *see* Wheatley *Ox*
ALBURY (St Mary) *see* Lt Hadham w Albury *St Alb*
ALBURY (St Peter and St Paul) (St Martha) *Guildf 2* **P** *Duke of Northumberland, W F P Hugonin Esq, and the Hon M Q Ridley (jt)* **R** *Vacant* (0148641) 2533
ALBY (St Ethelbert) *see* Erpingham w Calthorpe, Ingworth, Aldborough etc *Nor*
ALCESTER (St Nicholas) and Arrow w Oversley and Weethley *Cov 7* **P** *Marquess of Hertf* **R** D C CAPRON
ALCISTON (not known) *see* Berwick w Selmeston and Alciston *Chich*
ALCOMBE (St Michael the Archangel) *B & W 16* **P** *Bp* **V** A F MILLS
ALCONBURY (St Peter and St Paul) w Alconbury Weston *Ely 9* **P** *D&C Westmr* **V** *Vacant* (01480) 890284
ALDBOROUGH (St Andrew) w Boroughbridge and Roecliffe *Ripon 3* **P** *D&C York and Bp (alt)* **V** R T COOPER, **C** P J SMITH
ALDBOROUGH (St Mary) *see* Erpingham w Calthorpe, Ingworth, Aldborough etc *Nor*
ALDBOROUGH HATCH (St Peter) *Chelmsf 4* **P** *The Crown* **V** T COLEMAN
ALDBOURNE (St Michael) *see* Whitton *Sarum*
ALDBROUGH (St Bartholomew) and Mappleton w Goxhill and Withernwick *York 12* **P** *Ld Chan, Abp, and Adn E Riding (by turn)* **NSM** S FOSTER
ALDBROUGH (St Paul) *see* Forcett and Aldbrough and Melsonby *Ripon*
ALDBURY (St John the Baptist) *see* Tring *St Alb*
ALDEBURGH (St Peter and St Paul) w Hazlewood *St E 19* **P** *Mrs A C V Wentworth* **V** A H MOORE, **NSM** J A BIRCH
ALDEBY (St Mary) *see* The Raveningham Gp *Nor*
ALDENHAM (St John the Baptist) *St Alb 1* **P** *Lord Aldenham* **P-in-c** G H BOLT, **NSM** M V BOLT
ALDERBROOK (St Richard) *see* Crowborough *Chich*
ALDERBURY (St Mary the Virgin) *see* Alderbury Team *Sarum*
ALDERBURY Team, The (St Mary the Virgin) *Sarum 11* **P** *Patr Bd* **TR** G ROWSTON, **TV** M I CLUTTERBUCK, **Hon C** L M CATER
ALDERCAR (St John) *see* Langley Mill *Derby*
ALDERFORD (St John the Baptist) w Attlebridge and Swannington *Nor 22* **P** *Bp and D&C (alt)* **P-in-c** J P P ILLINGWORTH
ALDERHOLT (St James) *Sarum 10* **P** *DBP* **V** P J MARTIN
ALDERLEY (St Kenelm) *see* Kingswood w Alderley and Hillesley *Glouc*
ALDERLEY (St Mary) *Ches 12* **P** *Trustees* **P-in-c** B C REEVE
ALDERLEY EDGE (St Philip) *Ches 12* **P** *Trustees* **V** B T YOUNG
ALDERMASTON (St Mary the Virgin) w Wasing and Brimpton *Ox 12* **P** *Bp, DBP, Sir William Mount Bt, and Worc Coll Ox (jt)* **P-in-c** P G STEELE

ALDERMINSTER (St Mary and Holy Cross) and Halford *Cov 9* **P** *Bp and SMF (jt)* **P-in-c** E B SAVIGEAR

ALDERNEY (St Anne) *Win 14* **P** *The Crown* **V** S C INGHAM

ALDERSBROOK (St Gabriel) *Chelmsf 4* **P** *DBP* **V** D J DALAIS, **NSM** G A CLARKE

ALDERSHOT (Holy Trinity) *Guildf 1* **P** *CPAS* **V** R F PARKER

ALDERSHOT (St Augustine) *Guildf 1* **P** *Bp* **V** K M HODGES

ALDERSHOT (St Michael) (Ascension) *Guildf 1* **P** *Bp* **V** S A ZEAL, **C** C WAREHAM

ALDERSLEY (Christ the King) *see* Tettenhall Regis *Lich*

ALDERTON (St Andrew) w Ramsholt and Bawdsey *St E 7* **P** *Sir Anthony Quilter Bt (1 turn), F G A Beckett Esq (2 turns), and Bp (1 turn)* **P-in-c** M H INMAN

ALDERTON (St Giles) *see* Sherston Magna, Easton Grey, Luckington etc *Bris*

ALDERTON (St Margaret) *see* Stoke Bruerne w Grafton Regis and Alderton *Pet*

ALDERTON (St Margaret of Antioch), Great Washbourne, Dumbleton and Wormington *Glouc 17* **P** *M A E Casey Esq (1 Turn), Bp (2 turns), and Hon S K L Evetts (1 turn)* **R** P W SMITH

ALDERWASLEY (All Saints) *see* Wirksworth *Derby*

ALDFIELD (St Lawrence) *see* Fountains Gp *Ripon*

ALDFORD (St John the Baptist) and Bruera *Ches 5* **P** *Duke of Westmr and D&C (alt)* **P-in-c** C J REES

ALDHAM (St Margaret and St Catherine) *see* Marks Tey w Aldham and Lt Tey *Chelmsf*

ALDHAM (St Mary) *see* Elmsett w Aldham *St E*

ALDINGBOURNE (St Mary the Virgin), Barnham and Eastergate *Chich 1* **P** *Bp and D&C (jt)* **R** S P HOLLAND, **NSM** C R S HARDING

ALDINGHAM (St Cuthbert) and Dendron and Rampside and Urswick *Carl 8* **P** *Prime Min (1 turn), V Dalton-in-Furness and Resident Landowners of Urswick (1 turn)* **P-in-c** C E POTTER

ALDINGTON (St Martin) w Bonnington and Bilsington *Cant 12* **P** *Abp* **P-in-c** P FOSTER

ALDRIDGE (St Mary the Virgin) (St Thomas) *Lich 26* **P** *MMCET* **R** N J H REEVES, **C** G R DAVIES

ALDRINGHAM (St Andrew) w Thorpe, Knodishall w Buxlow and Friston *St E 19* **P** *Mrs A C V Wentworth, Ch Patr Trust, and Ch Soc Trust (by turn)* **P-in-c** C E BROOKS

ALDRINGTON (St Leonard) *Chich 4* **P** *Bp* **TR** S J TERRY, **TV** T P J BODKIN

ALDSWORTH (St Bartholomew) *see* Sherborne, Windrush, the Barringtons etc *Glouc*

ALDWARK (St Stephen) *see* Alne *York*

ALDWICK (St Richard) *Chich 1* **P** *Bp* **V** L C J NAGEL, **C** N G TUCK

ALDWINCLE (St Peter) w Thorpe Achurch and Pilton w Wadenhoe and Stoke Doyle *Pet 12* **P** *Soc Merchant Venturers Bris (2 turns), G C Capron Esq (1 turn), and Wadenhoe Trust (1 turn)* **P-in-c** J A ROSE

ALDWORTH (St Mary the Virgin) *see* Basildon w Aldworth and Ashampstead *Ox*

ALEXANDRA PARK (St Andrew) *Lon 20* **P** *Bp* **V** A F PYBUS

ALFINGTON (St James and St Anne) *see* Ottery St Mary, Alfington, W Hill, Tipton etc *Ex*

ALFOLD (St Nicholas) and Loxwood *Guildf 2* **P** *Bp and CPAS (jt)* **R** K A SHORT

ALFORD (All Saints) *see* Six Pilgrims *B & W*

ALFORD (St Wilfrid) w Rigsby *Linc 8* **P** *Bp* **V** A READER-MOORE, **C** R J BENSON

ALFRETON (St Martin) *Derby 1* **P** *Bp* **P-in-c** H J DOBBIN

ALFRICK (St Mary Magdalene) and Lulsley and Suckley and Leigh and Bransford *Worc 3* **P** *Prime Min and Bp (alt)* **R** M R WESTALL

ALFRISTON (St Andrew) w Lullington, Litlington and West Dean *Chich 18* **P** *Ld Chan (3 turns), R A Brown Esq (1 turn), and Duke of Devonshire (1 turn)* **R** F J FOX-WILSON

ALGARKIRK (St Peter and St Paul) *see* Sutterton w Fosdyke and Algarkirk *Linc*

ALHAMPTON (Mission Church) *see* Ditcheat w E Pennard and Pylle *B & W*

ALKBOROUGH (St John the Baptist) *Linc 4* **P** *Em Coll Cam and Bp (alt)* **V** G P GUNNING

ALKERTON (St Michael and All Angels) *see* Ironstone *Ox*

ALKHAM (St Anthony) w Capel le Ferne and Hougham *Cant 4* **P** *Abp* **P-in-c** G M CALVER

ALKMONTON (St John), Cubley, Marston, Montgomery and Yeaveley *Derby 14* **P** *Bp (3 turns), V Shirley (1 turn)* **P-in-c** M G HUGGETT

ALL CANNINGS (All Saints) *see* Bishop's Cannings, All Cannings etc *Sarum*

ALL SAINTS *see* Highertown and Baldhu *Truro*

ALL STRETTON (St Michael and All Angels) *see* Church Stretton *Heref*

ALLENDALE (St Cuthbert) w Whitfield *Newc 4* **P** *Viscount Allendale and J C Blackett-Ord Esq (alt)* **R** J E HAMPSON

ALLENS CROSS (St Bartholomew) *Birm 4* **P** *Bp* **P-in-c** D W JAMES

ALLENS GREEN (Mission Church) *see* High Wych and Gilston w Eastwick *St Alb*

ALLEN'S ROUGH (Worship Centre) *see* Willenhall H Trin *Lich*

ALLENSMORE (St Andrew) *see* Kingstone w Clehonger, Eaton Bishop etc *Heref*

ALLENTON (St Edmund) and Shelton Lock *Derby 15* **P** *Bp* **V** A LUKE

ALLER (St Andrew) *see* Langport Area Chs *B & W*

ALLERSTON (St John) *see* Brompton-by-Sawdon w Snainton, Ebberston etc *York*

ALLERTHORPE (St Botolph) *see* Barmby Moor w Allerthorpe, Fangfoss and Yapham *York*

ALLERTON (All Hallows) *Liv 4* **P** *J Bibby Esq* **V** G J BUTLAND, **NSM** A M SMITH

ALLERTON (not known) *see* Mark w Allerton *B & W*

ALLERTON (St Peter) (St Francis of Assisi) *Bradf 1* **P** *Bp* **V** C WARD, **C** M WARD

ALLERTON BYWATER (St Mary) *see* Kippax w Allerton Bywater *Ripon*

ALLESLEY (All Saints) *Cov 2* **P** *J R W Thomson-Bree Esq* **R** J T H BRITTON, **C** T J PULLEN

ALLESLEY PARK (St Christopher) and Whoberley *Cov 3* **P** *Bp* **V** F J CURTIS

ALLESTREE (St Edmund) *Derby 11* **P** *Bp* **V** J R WARMAN, **NSM** C C WARNER, A J CLARK

ALLESTREE (St Nicholas) *Derby 11* **P** *Bp* **V** W F BATES

ALLEXTON (St Peter) *see* Hallaton w Horninghold, Allexton, Tugby etc *Leic*

ALLHALLOWS (All Saints) *Carl 7* **P** *Bp* **P-in-c** C S SIMS

ALLINGTON (St John the Baptist) *see* Bourne Valley *Sarum*

ALLINGTON (St Nicholas) and Maidstone St Peter *Cant 15* **P** *Abp* **R** A WATSON, **C** D A IRVINE

ALLINGTON (St Swithin) *see* Bridport *Sarum*

ALLINGTON, EAST (St Andrew) *see* Modbury, Bigbury, Ringmore w Kingston etc *Ex*

ALLINGTON, WEST (Holy Trinity) *see* Saxonwell *Linc*

ALLITHWAITE (St Mary) *Carl 10* **P** *Bp* **P-in-c** H G WHITTY

ALLONBY (Christ Church) *Carl 7* **P** *D&C and V Bromfield w Waverton (jt)* **V** J LEONARDI

ALMELEY (St Mary) *see* Lyonshall w Titley, Almeley and Kinnersley *Heref*

ALMER (St Mary) *see* Red Post *Sarum*

ALMONDBURY (St Michael and St Helen) (St Mary) (All Hallows) w Farnley Tyas *Wakef 1* **P** *DBP* **TR** M W THOMAS, **TV** S V BROOKS, **C** P A HOLMES

ALMONDSBURY (St Mary the Virgin) *Bris 8* **P** *Bp* **V** P W ROWE, **Hon C** S M J CROSSMAN

ALNE (St Mary) *York 5* **P** *CPAS and MMCET (alt)* **NSM** R WADSWORTH

ALNE, GREAT (St Mary Magdalene) *see* Kinwarton w Gt Alne and Haselor *Cov*

ALNHAM (St Michael and All Angels) *see* Alwinton w Holystone and Alnham *Newc*

ALNMOUTH (St John the Baptist) *see* Lesbury w Alnmouth *Newc*

ALNWICK (St Michael and St Paul) *Newc 9* **P** *Trustees of the late Duke of Northd* **P-in-c** M N F HAIG

ALPERTON (St James) *Lon 21* **P** *CPAS* **V** J B ROOT, **C** C T MAIN, **NSM** A S JACOB

ALPHAMSTONE (not known) w Lamarsh and Pebmarsh *Chelmsf 19* **P** *Earl of Verulam and Ld Chan (alt)* **R** *Vacant* (01787) 269646

ALPHETON (St Peter and St Paul) *see* Lawshall w Shimplingthorne and Alpheton *St E*

ALPHINGTON (St Michael and All Angels) *Ex 3* **P** *DBP* **R** L M BATE

ALRESFORD (St Andrew) *Chelmsf 23* **P** *Bp* **R** G R COBB, **NSM** J R PANTRY

ALRESFORD, NEW (St John the Baptist) w Ovington and Itchen Stoke *Win 1* **P** *Bp* **R** G C G TRASLER, **NSM** J A BROWNING

ALRESFORD, OLD (St Mary) and Bighton *Win 1* **P** *Bp* **P-in-c** T M W PINNER

ALREWAS (All Saints) *Lich 1* **P** *Bp* **V** S J MORRIS

ALSAGER (Christ Church) *Ches 11* **P** *Bp* **V** J E VARTY

ALSAGER (St Mary Magdalene) (St Patrick's Mission Church) *Ches 11* **P** *Bp* **Hon C** J WATSON

ALSAGERS BANK (St John) *see* Silverdale and Alsagers Bank *Lich*

ALSOP EN LE DALE (St Michael and All Angels) *see* Parwich w Alsop en le Dale *Derby*

ALSTON Team, The (St Augustine) *Newc 4* **P** *Bp* **P-in-c** J R KELLY

ALSTONE (St Margaret) *see* Overbury w Teddington, Alstone etc *Worc*
ALSTONFIELD (St Peter), Butterton, Warslow w Elkstone and Wetton *Lich 5* **P** *Miss A I M Harpur-Crewe, Bp, and V Mayfield (jt)* **P-in-c** D MARSH
ALSWEAR (not known) *see* Bishopsnympton, Rose Ash, Mariansleigh etc *Ex*
ALTARNON (St Nonna) w Bolventor, Laneast and St Clether *Truro 9* **P** *Bp, D&C, and SMF (jt)* **V** *Vacant* (01566) 86108
ALTCAR (St Michael and All Angels) *Liv 5* **P** *Bp* **P-in-c** R J LEE
ALTHAM (St James) w Clayton le Moors *Blackb 1* **P** *DBP and Trustees (alt)* **V** P H DEARDEN, **C** S P C COOPER
ALTHORNE (St Andrew) *see* Creeksea w Althorne, Latchingdon and N Fambridge *Chelmsf*
ALTHORPE (St Oswald) *see* N Axholme Gp *Linc*
ALTOFTS (St Mary Magdalene) *Wakef 9* **P** *Meynall Ingram Trustees* **V** S K L VICK
ALTON (All Saints) *Win 2* **P** *Bp* **V** M C SURMAN
ALTON (St Lawrence) *Win 2* **P** *D&C* **V** R W S L GUSSMAN, **C** E M V RUSSELL
ALTON (St Peter) w Bradley-le-Moors and Oakamoor w Cotton *Lich 6* **P** *Earl of Shrewsbury and Talbot, DBP, and R Cheadle (jt)* **V** D J R FLEET
ALTON BARNES (St Mary the Virgin) *see* Swanborough *Sarum*
ALTON COMMON (Mission Room) *see* Alton w Bradley-le-Moors and Oakamoor w Cotton *Lich*
ALTON PANCRAS (St Pancras) *see* Piddletrenthide w Plush, Alton Pancras etc *Sarum*
ALTRINCHAM (St George) *Ches 10* **P** *V Bowdon* **V** B R McCONNELL, **C** S J ARTUS
ALTRINCHAM (St John the Evangelist) *Ches 10* **P** *Bp* **P-in-c** R E CORK, **NSM** P M PULLAN
ALVANLEY (St John the Evangelist) *Ches 3* **P** *Bp* **P-in-c** A R RIDLEY, **C** J A KENDALL
ALVASTON (St Michael and All Angels) *Derby 15* **P** *PCC* **P-in-c** C F MEEHAN, **C** N K PRITCHARD
ALVECHURCH (St Lawrence) *Worc 7* **P** *Bp* **R** D H MARTIN
ALVEDISTON (St Mary) *see* Chalke Valley W *Sarum*
ALVELEY (St Mary the Virgin) and Quatt *Heref 9* **P** *J W H Thompson Esq and Lady Labouchere (jt)* **P-in-c** N P ARMSTRONG
ALVERDISCOTT (All Saints) *see* Newton Tracey, Horwood, Alverdiscott etc *Ex*
ALVERSTOKE (St Faith) (St Francis) (St Mary) *Portsm 3* **P** *Bp* **R** E A GOODYER, **C** C B RANKINE, **NSM** R A FORSE
ALVERSTONE (Church Hall) *see* Brading w Yaverland *Portsm*
ALVERTHORPE (St Paul) *Wakef 12* **P** *Bp* **V** A MAUCHAN
ALVESCOT (St Peter) *see* Shill Valley and Broadshire *Ox*
ALVESTON (St Helen) *Bris 8* **P** *D&C* **V** D J POLE
ALVESTON (St James) *Cov 8* **P** *R Hampton Lucy w Charlecote and Loxley* **V** R E WILLIAMS
ALVINGHAM (St Adelwold) *see* Mid Marsh Gp *Linc*
ALVINGTON (St Andrew) *see* Woolaston w Alvington and Aylburton *Glouc*
ALVINGTON, WEST (All Saints) *see* Malborough w S Huish, W Alvington and Churchstow *Ex*
ALWALTON (St Andrew) *see* The Ortons, Alwalton and Chesterton *Ely*
ALWINGTON (St Andrew) *see* Parkham, Alwington, Buckland Brewer etc *Ex*
ALWINTON (St Michael and All Angels) w Holystone and Alnham *Newc 9* **P** *Ld Chan and Trustees of the late Duke of Northd (alt)* **V** J WYLAM
ALWOODLEY (St Barnabas) *see* Moor Allerton *Ripon*
AMBERGATE (St Anne) and Heage *Derby 11* **P** *V Duffield and Exors M A T Johnson Esq* **P-in-c** R J I PAGET
AMBERLEY (Holy Trinity) *Glouc 8* **P** *DBP* **P-in-c** M O TUCKER
AMBERLEY (no dedication) *see* Marden w Amberley and Wisteston *Heref*
AMBERLEY (St Michael) w North Stoke and Parham, Wiggonholt and Greatham *Chich 12* **P** *Bp and Parham Estate Trustees (jt)* **V** *Vacant* (01798) 831500
AMBLE (St Cuthbert) *Newc 9* **P** *Bp* **V** *Vacant* (01665) 710273
AMBLECOTE (Holy Trinity) *Worc 12* **P** *Bp* **V** P TONGUE, **C** J A CORKER
AMBLESIDE (St Mary) w Brathay *Carl 10* **P** *DBP* **V** W R F COKE, **C** J W DANIELS
AMBROSDEN (St Mary the Virgin) w Merton and Piddington *Ox 2* **P** *Trustees F A W Page-Turner Esq, Ex Coll Ox, and DBF (jt)* **V** G G CHAPMAN, **NSM** L K ROSE
AMCOTTS (St Mark) *see* N Axholme Gp *Linc*
AMERSHAM (St Mary the Virgin) *Ox 20* **P** *Capt F Tyrwhitt Drake* **R** T J L HARPER
AMERSHAM ON THE HILL (St Michael and All Angels) *Ox 20* **P** *Bp* **V** P D RODERICK, **C** J E CHRICH-SMITH
AMESBURY (St Mary and St Melor) *Sarum 12* **P** *D&C Windsor* **V** P R LEWIS
AMINGTON (St Editha) *Birm 11* **P** *Bp* **V** M A HARRIS
AMOTHERBY (St Helen) *see* Street TM *York*
AMPFIELD (St Mark) *see* Hursley and Ampfield *Win*
AMPLEFORTH (St Hilda) and Oswaldkirk and Gilling East *York 18* **P** *Abp and Trin Coll Cam (jt)* **R** D E NEWTON
AMPNEYS (St Mary) (St Peter) (Holy Rood) w Driffield and Poulton, The *Glouc 13* **P** *Bp and Col Sir Piers Bengough (jt)* **R** P H NAYLOR
AMPORT (St Mary), Grateley, Monxton and Quarley *Win 3* **P** *D&C Chich, Exors T P de Paravicini Esq, Mrs C E Land, Bp, and R Foundn of St Kath (jt)* **P-in-c** C F PETTET
AMPTHILL (St Andrew) w Millbrook and Steppingley *St Alb 9* **P** *Ld Chan* **R** M J TRODDEN, **C** J H HEARN
AMPTON (St Peter) *see* Blackbourne *St E*
AMWELL, GREAT (St John the Baptist) w St Margaret's and Stanstead Abbots *St Alb 22* **P** *Bp, Peache Trustees, and Haileybury Coll (jt)* **V** B F J GOODWIN, **NSM** J E KNIGHT
AMWELL, LITTLE (Holy Trinity) *St Alb 22* **P** *Ch Patr Trust* **V** R W BOWEN, **NSM** M HARDING
ANCASTER (St Martin) *see* Ancaster Wilsford Gp *Linc*
ANCASTER WILSFORD Group, The *Linc 23* **P** *Bp (2 turns), DBP (1 turn), and Mrs G V Hoare (1 turn)* **P-in-c** J R HAWKINS, **C** G P POND, **NSM** J E COULTHURST
ANCHORSHOLME (All Saints) *Blackb 9* **P** *Bp, V Bispham, and Ch Soc Trust (jt)* **V** P R NUNN
ANCOATS (All Souls) *see* Manchester Gd Shep and St Barn *Man*
ANCROFT (St Anne) *see* Lowick and Kyloe w Ancroft *Newc*
ANDERBY (St Andrew) *see* Sutton, Huttoft and Anderby *Linc*
ANDOVER (St Mary the Virgin) (St Thomas) w Foxcott *Win 3* **P** *St Mary's Coll Win* **C** M A AIKMAN, D DUNN
ANDOVER, WEST (St Michael and All Angels) *Win 3* **P** *Bp* **V** J R TARR
ANDREAS (St Andrew) *S & M 4* **P** *The Crown* **R** R C GEDDES
ANDREAS (St Jude Chapelry) *S & M 4* **P** *R Andreas* **V** R C GEDDES
ANERLEY Christ Church *Roch 13* **P** *CPAS* **V** M E PORTER
ANFIELD (St Columba) *Liv 7* **P** *Bp* **V** P B CAVANAGH, **NSM** K L MILLER, N F FRANCES
ANFIELD (St Margaret) *Liv 3* **P** *Bp* **P-in-c** M E J ABREY
ANGELL TOWN (St John the Evangelist) *S'wark 10* **P** *Bp* **V** M S ARMITAGE, **NSM** D J DERRICK
ANGERSLEIGH (St Michael) *see* Trull w Angersleigh *B & W*
ANGMERING (St Margaret) *Chich 1* **P** *J F P Somerset Esq and Ch Patr Trust (jt)* **R** A M G WELLS, **C** M J T PAYNE
ANLABY (St Peter) *York 15* **P** *Trustees* **V** F A GORDON-KERR, **NSM** D J W BATH
ANLABY COMMON (St Mark) Hull *York 15* **P** *Abp* **V** J F TWOMEY
ANMER (St Mary) *see* Dersingham w Anmer and Shernborne *Nor*
ANNESLEY (Our Lady and All Saints) w Newstead *S'well 4* **P** *Exors Major R P Chaworth-Musters* **V** J C WILSON
ANNFIELD PLAIN (St Aidan) *see* Collierley w Annfield Plain *Dur*
ANNSCROFT (Christ Church) *see* Longden and Annscroft w Pulverbatch *Heref*
ANSFORD (St Andrew) *see* Castle Cary w Ansford *B & W*
ANSLEY (St Lawrence) *Cov 5* **P** *Ch Patr Trust* **V** *Vacant* (01203) 396403
ANSLOW (Holy Trinity) *Lich 14* **P** *MMCET* **V** M D BIRT
ANSTEY (St George) *see* Hormead, Wyddial, Anstey, Brent Pelham etc *St Alb*
ANSTEY (St Mary) *Leic 12* **P** *R Thurcaston* **R** J E HALL, **Hon C** H C WILLIAMS
ANSTEY, EAST (St Michael) *see* Bishopsnympton, Rose Ash, Mariansleigh etc *Ex*
ANSTEY, WEST (St Petrock) *as above*
ANSTON (St James) *Sheff 5* **P** *Bp* **V** P J COGHLAN, **C** S G MILLWOOD
ANSTY (St James) *see* Bulkington w Shilton and Ansty *Cov*
ANSTY (St James) *see* Tisbury *Sarum*
ANSTY (St John) *see* Cuckfield *Chich*
ANTINGHAM (St Mary) *see* Trunch *Nor*
ANTONY (St James the Great) w Sheviock *Truro 11* **P** *Bp and Col Sir John Carew-Pole Bt (alt)* **NSM** K J PIPER
ANTROBUS (St Mark) *Ches 4* **P** *V Gt Budworth* **P-in-c** M E REAVIL
ANWICK (St Edith) *see* Kirkby Laythorpe *Linc*
APETHORPE (St Leonard) *Pet 12* **P** *Lord Brassey* **V** *Vacant*
APLEY (St Andrew) *see* Bardney *Linc*
APPERLEY (Holy Trinity) *see* Deerhurst, Apperley w Forthampton and Chaceley *Glouc*

APPLEBY (St Bartholomew) *see* Winterton Gp *Linc*
APPLEBY (St Lawrence) *Carl 1* **P** *D&C and Bp (jt)* **V** P E P NORTON, **C** E M SMITH, **NSM** R A COLLINSON
APPLEBY GROUP, The *Leic 9* **P** *DBP, MMCET, Bp, and Ld Chan (by turn)* **R** D J K WALLER, **NSM** S C POLASHEK
APPLEBY MAGNA (St Michael and All Angels) *see* The Appleby Gp *Leic*
APPLEDORE (St Mary) *see* Bideford, Northam, Westward Ho!, Appledore etc *Ex*
APPLEDORE (St Peter and St Paul) w Brookland and Fairfield and Brenzett w Snargate and Kenardington *Cant 13* **P** *Abp* **V** L J HAMMOND, **C** M S WING, **NSM** K FAZZANI
APPLEDRAM (St Mary the Virgin) *Chich 3* **P** *D&C* **P-in-c** M A COLLIS
APPLEFORD (St Peter and St Paul) *see* Sutton Courtenay w Appleford *Ox*
APPLESHAW (St Peter) and Kimpton and Thruxton and Fyfield *Win 3* **P** *Bp, D&C, and M H Routh Esq (jt)* **R** I J TOMLINSON
APPLETHWAITE (St Mary) *see* Windermere St Mary and Troutbeck *Carl*
APPLETON (All Saints) *see* Street TM *York*
APPLETON (St Lawrence) *Ox 10* **P** *Magd Coll Ox* **P-in-c** R G PENMAN
APPLETON (St Mary Magdalene) *see* Stockton Heath *Ches*
APPLETON-LE-MOORS (Christ Church) *see* Lastingham w Appleton-le-Moors, Rosedale etc *York*
APPLETON ROEBUCK (All Saints) w Acaster Selby *York 1* **P** *Abp* **P-in-c** J M RODEN
APPLETON THORN (St Cross) *see* Stretton and Appleton Thorn *Ches*
APPLETON WISKE (St Mary) *see* Gt Smeaton w Appleton Wiske and Birkby etc *Ripon*
APPLETREEWICK (St John the Baptist) *see* Burnsall w Rylstone *Bradf*
APPLEY BRIDGE (All Saints) *Blackb 4* **P** *Bp* **V** I J J DEWAR
APULDRAM (St Mary the Virgin) *see* Appledram *Chich*
ARBORFIELD (St Bartholomew) w Barkham *Ox 16* **P** *DBP* **P-in-c** D B ROWE, **Hon C** H M WAKELING, **NSM** J WAKELING
ARBORY (St Columba) *S & M 1* **P** *The Crown* **V** G B CLAYTON, **C** C L BARRY
ARBOURTHORNE (St Paul) *see* Sheff Manor *Sheff*
ARDELEY (St Lawrence) *St Alb 19* **P** *D&C St Paul's* **V** *Vacant* (0143886) 286
ARDINGLY (St Peter) *Chich 6* **P** *MMCET* **R** R P SYMMONS, **NSM** K I GOSS
ARDINGTON (Holy Trinity) *see* Wantage Downs *Ox*
ARDLEIGH (St Mary the Virgin) and Bromleys, The *Chelmsf 20* **P** *Ld Chan (2 turns), CR (1 turn), Wadh Coll Ox (1 turn)* **R** *Vacant* (01206) 230344
ARDLEIGH GREEN (All Saints) *see* Squirrels Heath *Chelmsf*
ARDLEY (St Mary) *see* Fritwell w Souldern and Ardley w Fewcott *Ox*
ARDSLEY (Christ Church) *Sheff 12* **P** *R Darfield* **V** R G R EVANS
ARDSLEY, EAST (St Gabriel) (St Michael) *Wakef 12* **P** *E C S J G Brudenell Esq* **V** K G WILLIAMS
ARDSLEY, WEST *Wakef 10* **P** *E C S J G Brudenell Esq* **V** T R KING
ARDWICK (St Benedict) *Man 1* **P** *Keble Coll Ox* **P-in-c** J HAY
ARDWICK (St Jerome and St Silas) *see* Manchester Gd Shep and St Barn *Man*
ARELEY KINGS (St Bartholomew) *Worc 13* **P** *R Martley* **P-in-c** A J VESSEY
ARKENDALE (St Bartholomew) *see* Farnham w Scotton, Staveley, Copgrove etc *Ripon*
ARKENGARTHDALE (St Mary) *see* Swaledale *Ripon*
ARKESDEN (St Mary the Virgin) *see* Clavering w Langley and Arkesden *Chelmsf*
ARKHOLME (St John the Baptist) *see* Whittington w Arkholme and Gressingham *Blackb*
ARKLEY (St Peter) *see* Chipping Barnet w Arkley *St Alb*
ARKSEY (All Saints) *Sheff 8* **P** *DBP* **V** C J A HICKLING
ARLECDON (St Michael) *see* Frizington and Arlecdon *Carl*
ARLESEY (St Andrew) (St Peter) w Astwick *St Alb 16* **P** *DBP* **V** S D EDWARDS, **NSM** C M EAGGER
ARLEY (St Michael) (St Wilfred) *Cov 5* **P** *A C D Ransom Esq and N W H Sylvester Esq (jt)* **R** G F KIMBER, **C** G M KIMBER
ARLEY, UPPER (St Peter) *see* Kidderminster St Mary and All SS w Trimpley etc *Worc*
ARLINGHAM (St Mary the Virgin) *see* Frampton on Severn, Arlingham, Saul etc *Glouc*
ARLINGTON (St James) *see* Shirwell, Loxhore, Kentisbury, Arlington, etc *Ex*
ARLINGTON (St Pancras), Folkington and Wilmington *Chich 18* **P** *Bp Lon, Mrs M P Gwynne-Longland, and Duke of Devonshire (by turn)* **P-in-c** J D E SMITH
ARMATHWAITE (Christ and St Mary) *see* Hesket-in-the-Forest and Armathwaite *Carl*
ARMINGHALL (St Mary) *see* Stoke H Cross w Dunston, Arminghall etc *Nor*
ARMITAGE (Holy Trinity) (St John the Baptist) *Lich 3* **P** *Bp* **R** D R H THOMAS
ARMITAGE BRIDGE (St Paul) *see* Newsome and Armitage Bridge *Wakef*
ARMLEY (St Bartholomew) w New Wortley *Ripon 6* **P** *Bp, DBP, and Hyndman Trustees (jt)* **V** T W LIPSCOMB, **C** K WEST
ARMLEY, UPPER (Christ Church) *Ripon 6* **P** *Ch Patr Trust* **C** R J TWITTY
ARMLEY HEIGHTS (Church of the Ascension) *see* Upper Armley *Ripon*
ARMTHORPE (St Leonard and St Mary) *Sheff 9* **P** *Bp* **R** J C BARNES
ARNCLIFFE (St Oswald) *see* Kettlewell w Conistone, Hubberholme etc *Bradf*
ARNE (St Nicholas) *see* Wareham *Sarum*
ARNESBY (St Peter) w Shearsby and Bruntingthorpe *Leic 10* **P** *Bp* **P-in-c** A W JOHNSON, **Hon C** J C DUDLEY
ARNOLD (St Mary) *S'well 11* **P** *Bp* **V** A CLARKE
ARNSIDE (St James) *Carl 9* **P** *Bp* **V** *Vacant* (01524) 761319
ARRETON (St George) *Portsm 7* **P** *Bp* **V** D H HEATLEY
ARRINGTON (St Nicholas) *Ely 8* **P** *Bp and DBP (alt)* **V** N A BRICE
ARROW (Holy Trinity) *see* Alcester and Arrow w Oversley and Weethley *Cov*
ARTHINGTON (St Peter) *see* Pool w Arthington *Ripon*
ARTHINGWORTH (St Andrew) and Harrington w Oxendon and East Farndon *Pet 2* **P** *St Jo Coll Cam (2 turns), E G Nugee Esq (2 turns), and Bp (1 turn)* **R** T H ROPER
ARTHURET (St Michael and All Angels) *Carl 2* **P** *Sir Charles Graham Bt* **P-in-c** W KELLY
ARUNDEL (St Nicholas) w Tortington and South Stoke *Chich 1* **P** *Bp (2 turns), Duke of Norfolk (1 turn)* **V** K D RICHARDS
ASBY (St Peter) *Carl 1* **P** *Bp* **P-in-c** D C WOOD
ASCOT, NORTH (St Mary and St John) *see* Ascot Heath *Ox*
ASCOT, SOUTH (All Souls) *Ox 11* **P** *Bp* **V** D S JONES, **C** S J JONES
ASCOT HEATH (All Saints) *Ox 11* **P** *Bp* **R** P le S V NASH-WILLIAMS
ASCOTT UNDER WYCHWOOD (Holy Trinity) *see* Chadlington and Spelsbury, Ascott under Wychwood *Ox*
ASFORDBY (All Saints) *Leic 3* **P** *DBP* **R** R W WIDDOWSON
ASGARBY (St Andrew) *see* Kirkby Laythorpe *Linc*
ASH (Christ Church) *see* Adderley, Ash, Calverhall, Ightfield etc *Lich*
ASH (Holy Trinity) *see* Martock w Ash *B & W*
ASH (St Nicholas) w Westmarsh *Cant 1* **P** *Abp* **V** D J BARNES
ASH (St Peter) *Guildf 1* **P** *Win Coll* **R** J H FROST
ASH (St Peter and St Paul) *Roch 1* **P** *J R A B Scott Esq* **R** L W G KEVIS
ASH (Thomas Chapel) *see* Sampford Peverell, Uplowman, Holcombe Rogus etc *Ex*
ASH PRIORS (Holy Trinity) *see* Lydeard St Lawrence w Brompton Ralph etc *B & W*
ASH VALE (St Mary) *Guildf 1* **P** *Bp* **V** P C BAKER
ASHAMPSTEAD (St Clement) *see* Basildon w Aldworth and Ashampstead *Ox*
ASHBOCKING (All Saints) *see* Clopton w Otley, Swilland and Ashbocking *St E*
ASHBOURNE (St John the Baptist) *Derby 8* **P** *Wright Trustees* **V** D H SANSUM
ASHBOURNE (St Oswald) w Mapleton *Derby 8* **P** *Bp* **V** D H SANSUM
ASHBRITTLE (St John the Baptist) *see* Wellington and Distr *B & W*
ASHBURNHAM (St Peter) w Penhurst *Chich 14* **P** *Ashburnham Chr Trust* **P-in-c** K L BARHAM
ASHBURTON (St Andrew) w Buckland in the Moor and Bickington *Ex 11* **P** *D&C* **V** P J GREGSON
ASHBURY (St Mary the Virgin), Compton Beauchamp and Longcot w Fernham *Ox 17* **P** *Ld Chan* **P-in-c** K M SINGLETON, **NSM** A K WEAVER
ASHBY (St Catherine) *see* Bottesford w Ashby *Linc*
ASHBY (St Mary) *see* Somerleyton, Ashby, Fritton, Herringfleet etc *Nor*
ASHBY (St Mary) *see* Thurton *Nor*
ASHBY (St Paul) *see* Bottesford w Ashby *Linc*
ASHBY, WEST (All Saints) *see* Hemingby *Linc*
ASHBY-BY-PARTNEY (St Helen) *see* Partney *Linc*
ASHBY-CUM-FENBY (St Peter) *see* Ravendale Gp *Linc*
ASHBY DE LA LAUNDE (St Hibald) *see* Digby *Linc*

ASHBY-DE-LA-ZOUCH (Holy Trinity) *Leic 9* **P** *Bp* **V** L A DUTTON, **NSM** D FLOWER
ASHBY-DE-LA-ZOUCH (St Helen) w Coleorton *Leic 9* **P** *D A G Shields Esq* **V** C P DOBBIN, **C** P D S MASSEY, **NSM** S A B WALTERS
ASHBY FOLVILLE (St Mary) *see* S Croxton Gp *Leic*
ASHBY MAGNA (St Mary) *see* Willoughby Waterleys, Peatling Magna etc *Leic*
ASHBY PARVA (St Peter) *see* Leire w Ashby Parva and Dunton Bassett *Leic*
ASHBY PUERORUM (St Andrew) *see* Fulletby w Greetham and Ashby Puerorum *Linc*
ASHBY ST LEDGERS (St Mary) *see* Daventry, Ashby St Ledgers, Braunston etc *Pet*
ASHCHURCH (St Nicholas) *Glouc 9* **P** *K Storey Esq* **R** R E ROBERTS
ASHCOMBE (St Nectan) *see* Teignmouth, Ideford w Luton, Ashcombe etc *Ex*
ASHCOTT (All Saints) *see* Shapwick w Ashcott and Burtle *B & W*
ASHDON (All Saints) w Hadstock *Chelmsf 22* **P** *E H Vestey Esq and Ld Chan (alt)* **R** J D SAVILLE
ASHE (Holy Trinity and St Andrew) *see* N Waltham and Steventon, Ashe and Deane *Win*
ASHEN (St Augustine) *see* Ridgewell w Ashen, Birdbrook and Sturmer *Chelmsf*
ASHENDON (St Mary) *see* Ludgershall w Wotton Underwood and Ashendon *Ox*
ASHFIELD, GREAT (All Saints) *see* Badwell Ash w Gt Ashfield, Stowlangtoft etc *St E*
ASHFIELD CUM THORPE (St Mary) *see* Earl Soham w Cretingham and Ashfield cum Thorpe *St E*
ASHFORD (St Hilda) *Lon 13* **P** *Bp* **V** S J BLOOD
ASHFORD (St Mary the Virgin) *Cant 10* **P** *Abp* **V** J W EVERETT
ASHFORD (St Matthew) *Lon 13* **P** *Ld Chan* **V** R E HORTON
ASHFORD (St Peter) *see* Pilton w Ashford *Ex*
ASHFORD, South (St Francis of Assisi) *Cant 10* **P** *Abp* **P-in-c** I L GARRETT, **C** C J GARRETT
ASHFORD, SOUTH (Christ Church) *Cant 10* **P** *Abp* **C** M J ASQUITH
ASHFORD BOWDLER (St Andrew) *see* Ludlow, Ludford, Ashford Carbonell etc *Heref*
ASHFORD CARBONELL (St Mary) *as above*
ASHFORD COMMON (St Benedict) *see* Upper Sunbury St Sav *Lon*
ASHFORD HILL (St Paul) w Headley *Win 6* **P** *V Kingsclere* **V** B G G MARSHALL
ASHFORD IN THE WATER (Holy Trinity) w Sheldon and Great Longstone *Derby 2* **P** *V Bakewell* **V** C A THROWER, **C** T E YATES
ASHILL (Blessed Virgin Mary) *see* Ilminster and District *B & W*
ASHILL (St Nicholas) w Saham Toney *Nor 13* **P** *Bp and New Coll Ox (alt)* **R** M J DOWN, **NSM** A D WALKER, S D H MAWDITT
ASHILL (St Stephen) *see* Uffculme *Ex*
ASHINGDON (St Andrew) w South Fambridge *Chelmsf 12* **P** *CCC Cam* **R** *Vacant* (01702) 544327
ASHINGTON (Holy Sepulchre) *Newc 11* **P** *Bp* **V** C H KNIGHTS, **C** L BEADLE
ASHINGTON (St Matthew) *see* Canford Magna *Sarum*
ASHINGTON (St Peter and St Paul), Washington and Wiston w Buncton *Chich 12* **P** *Bp and R H Goring Esq (alt)* **R** J M WALKER
ASHINGTON (St Vincent) *see* Chilton Cantelo, Ashington, Mudford, Rimpton etc *B & W*
ASHLEWORTH (St Bartholomew) *see* Hasfield w Tirley and Ashleworth *Glouc*
ASHLEY (St Elizabeth) *see* Hale and Ashley *Ches*
ASHLEY (St James), Crudwell, Hankerton, Long Newnton and Oaksey *Bris 12* **P** *Trustees* **R** B RAVEN
ASHLEY (St John the Baptist) *Lich 7* **P** *Meynell Ch Trustees* **P-in-c** D J WILLIAMS
ASHLEY (St Mary the Virgin) *see* Stoke Albany w Wilbarston and Ashley etc *Pet*
ASHLEY (St Mary) w Silverley *Ely 4* **P** *Bp and DBP (alt)* **R** C A SINDALL
ASHLEY (St Peter and St Paul) *see* Somborne w Ashley *Win*
ASHLEY GREEN (St John the Evangelist) *see* Gt Chesham *Ox*
ASHMANHAUGH (St Swithin) *see* Horning w Beeston St Laurence and Ashmanhaugh *Nor*
ASHMANSWORTH (St James) *see* Highclere and Ashmansworth w Crux Easton *Win*
ASHMORE (St Nicholas) *see* Tollard Royal w Farnham, Gussage St Michael etc *Sarum*
ASHMORE PARK (St Alban) *see* Wednesfield *Lich*
ASHOVER (All Saints) and Brackenfield *Derby 5* **P** *Revd J J C Nodder and DBF (jt)* **R** T B JOHNSON, **NSM** R SMITH
ASHOW (Assumption of Our Lady) *see* Stoneleigh w Ashow and Baginton *Cov*
ASHPERTON (St Bartholomew) *see* Bosbury w Wellington Heath etc *Heref*
ASHPRINGTON (St David), Cornworthy and Dittisham *Ex 13* **P** *Bp* **P-in-c** R A KING
ASHREIGNEY (St James) *Ex 19* **P** *DBP* **R** P J NORMAN
ASHTEAD (St George) (St Giles) *Guildf 10* **P** *Bp* **R** C C HUGHES, **C** S J F THOMAS, T H PATTERSON, J G PERKIN
ASHTON (Annunciation) *see* Breage w Germoe *Truro*
ASHTON (Chapel) *see* Oundle *Pet*
ASHTON (St John the Baptist) *see* Christow, Ashton, Trusham and Bridford *Ex*
ASHTON (St Michael and All Angels) *see* Roade and Ashton w Hartwell *Pet*
ASHTON, WEST (St John) *see* Trowbridge St Thos and W Ashton *Sarum*
ASHTON GATE (St Francis) *see* Bedminster *Bris*
ASHTON GIFFORD *Sarum 16* **P** *DBP, Ld Chan, and Pemb Coll Ox (by turn)* **NSM** G I DUFF
ASHTON HAYES (St John the Evangelist) *Ches 2* **P** *Keble Coll Ox* **P-in-c** K HARRIS
ASHTON-IN-MAKERFIELD (Holy Trinity) *Liv 15* **P** *Bp* **R** D R ABBOTT
ASHTON-IN-MAKERFIELD (St Thomas) *Liv 15* **P** *R Ashton-in-Makerfield H Trin* **V** D G MELLORS, **C** W FORSTER, **NSM** D HART
ASHTON KEYNES (Holy Cross), Leigh and Minety *Bris 12* **P** *Bp* **V** P S HUGHES
ASHTON ON MERSEY (St Mary Magdalene) *Ches 10* **P** *Trustees* **V** G J SKINNER, **C** G R PATCHELL, S B RANKIN
ASHTON-ON-RIBBLE (St Andrew) *Blackb 14* **P** *Trustees* **V** J R POWELL
ASHTON-ON-RIBBLE (St Michael and All Angels) w Preston St Mark *Blackb 14* **P** *Bp* **V** W G GRIMES
ASHTON UNDER HILL (St Barbara) *see* Overbury w Teddington, Alstone etc *Worc*
ASHTON-UNDER-LYNE (Christ Church) *Man 17* **P** *Bp* **V** C LAYCOCK, **C** M E DICKER
ASHTON-UNDER-LYNE (Holy Trinity) *Man 17* **P** *Trustees* **P-in-c** D J WISEMAN, **C** R L PRAVISANI
ASHTON-UNDER-LYNE (St James) (Queen Victoria Memorial Church) *Man 17* **P** *Bp and Lord Deramore (jt)* **P-in-c** L ADAM
ASHTON-UNDER-LYNE (St Michael and All Angels) (St Gabriel) *Man 17* **P** *Lord Deramore* **R** *Vacant* 0161-330 1172
ASHTON-UNDER-LYNE (St Peter) *Man 17* **P** *R Ashton-under-Lyne St Mich* **V** *Vacant* 0161-330 4285
ASHTON UPON MERSEY (St Martin) *Ches 10* **P** *SMF* **R** R J E CLACK
ASHURST (St James) *Chich 12* **P** *MMCET* **R** P M RAMPTON
ASHURST (St Martin of Tours) *see* Speldhurst w Groombridge and Ashurst *Roch*
ASHURST WOOD (St Dunstan) *see* Forest Row *Chich*
ASHWATER (St Peter ad Vincula), Halwill, Beaworthy, Clawton and Tetcott w Luffincott *Ex 9* **P** *Ld Chan (1 turn), Major L J Melhuish, Lt-Col Sir John Molesworth-St Aubyn Bt, and Bp (jt) (2 turns)* **R** L BROOKHOUSE
ASHWELL (St Mary) *see* Cottesmore and Barrow w Ashwell and Burley *Pet*
ASHWELL (St Mary the Virgin) w Hinxworth and Newnham *St Alb 19* **P** *Bp, R Smyth Esq, and N J A Farr Esq (jt) (1 turn), Bp (3 turns)* **R** P J M BRIGHT, **NSM** C H BROWNLIE
ASHWELLTHORPE (All Saints) *see* Wreningham *Nor*
ASHWICK (St James) w Oakhill and Binegar *B & W 8* **P** *Bp* **P-in-c** J C ANDREWS
ASHWICKEN (All Saints) *see* Gayton Gp of Par *Nor*
ASHWORTH (St James) *see* Norden w Ashworth *Man*
ASKAM (St Peter) *see* Ireleth w Askam *Carl*
ASKERN (St Peter) *Sheff 8* **P** *Bp* **V** M WIGGLESWORTH
ASKERSWELL (St Michael), Loders and Powerstock *Sarum 3* **P** *Ld Chan, Lady Laskey, Bp, and D&C (by turn)* **R** E G A W PAGE-TURNER
ASKHAM (Church Centre) *see* Ireleth w Askam *Carl*
ASKHAM (St Nicholas) *see* E Markham w Askham, Headon w Upton and Grove *S'well*
ASKHAM (St Peter) *see* Lowther and Askham and Clifton and Brougham *Carl*
ASKHAM BRYAN (St Nicholas) *York 1* **P** *Trustees of Revd G Nussey* **NSM** G G HOLMAN
ASKHAM RICHARD (St Mary) *see* Healaugh w Wighill, Bilbrough and Askham Richard *York*

ASKRIGG (St Oswald) w Stallingbusk *Ripon 4* **P** *V Aysgarth* **V** C W MALPASS
ASLACKBY (St James) *see* Billingborough Gp *Linc*
ASLACTON (St Michael) *see* Bunwell, Carleton Rode, Tibenham, Gt Moulton etc *Nor*
ASLOCKTON (St Thomas) *see* Whatton w Aslockton, Hawksworth, Scarrington etc *S'well*
ASPALL (St Mary of Grace) *see* Debenham w Aspall and Kenton *St E*
ASPATRIA (St Kentigern) w Hayton *Carl 7* **P** *Bp* **P-in-c** B ROWE, **NSM** J M BEAZLEY
ASPENDEN (St Mary), Buntingford and Westmill *St Alb 19* **P** *CPAS, MCET, and K Coll Lon (jt)* **R** N J RICHARDS, **NSM** M CAPEL-EDWARDS, P J ALEXANDER
ASPLEY (St Margaret) *S'well 14* **P** *Trustees* **V** D WARD
ASPLEY GUISE (St Botolph) w Husborne Crawley and Ridgmont *St Alb 9* **P** *Ld Chan (1 turn), Trustees Bedf Estates (1 turn), and Bp (2 turns)* **R** J E INGHAM
ASPULL (St Elizabeth) *Liv 14* **P** *R Wigan* **V** *Vacant* (01942) 831236
ASSINGTON (St Edmund) w Newton Green and Little Cornard *St E 12* **P** *DBP (1 turn), Peterho Cam (1 turn), and Bp (2 turns)* **R** A R GEORGE
ASTBURY (St Mary) and Smallwood *Ches 11* **P** *Sir Richard Baker Wilbraham Bt* **R** E J A BRAZIER
ASTERBY Group, The *Linc 11* **P** *Bp, DBP, J N Heneage Esq, F Smith Esq, and Mrs J Fox (jt)* **P-in-c** I D McGRATH
ASTHALL (St Nicholas) *see* Burford w Fulbrook, Taynton, Asthall etc *Ox*
ASTLEY (St Mary the Virgin) *see* Chilvers Coton w Astley *Cov*
ASTLEY (St Mary), Clive, Grinshill and Hadnall *Lich 23* **P** *D R B Thompson Esq* **V** S W DEANE
ASTLEY (St Peter) *see* Shrawley, Witley, Astley and Abberley *Worc*
ASTLEY (St Stephen) *Man 13* **P** *V Leigh St Mary* **V** C A BRACEGIRDLE, **C** R TAGUE
ASTLEY ABBOTTS (St Calixtus) *see* Bridgnorth, Tasley, Astley Abbotts, Oldbury etc *Heref*
ASTLEY BRIDGE (St Paul) *Man 16* **P** *The Crown* **V** T P CHALLIS, **C** K R GOVAN, **NSM** B E HAWORTH
ASTON (St Giles) *see* Wigmore Abbey *Heref*
ASTON (St Mary) *see* Woore and Norton in Hales *Lich*
ASTON (St Mary) *see* Stevenage St Mary Sheppall w Aston *St Alb*
ASTON (St Saviour) *see* Stone St Mich w Aston St Sav *Lich*
ASTON, LITTLE (St Peter) *Lich 1* **P** *Patr Bd* **V** S HUYTON
ASTON, NORTH (St Mary the Virgin) *see* Steeple Aston w N Aston and Tackley *Ox*
ASTON ABBOTS (St James the Great) *see* Wingrave w Rowsham, Aston Abbotts and Cublington *Ox*
ASTON BOTTERELL (St Michael and All Angels) *see* Ditton Priors w Neenton, Burwarton etc *Heref*
ASTON BY SUTTON (St Peter) *Ches 3* **P** *B H Talbot Esq* **P-in-c** M E REAVIL, **NSM** T A WHYTE
ASTON CANTLOW (St John the Baptist) and Wilmcote w Billesley *Cov 7* **P** *SMF* **V** *Vacant*
ASTON CLINTON (St Michael and All Angels) w Buckland and Drayton Beauchamp *Ox 22* **P** *Exors Major S W Jenney, Jes Coll Ox, and Bp (by turn)* **R** A W BENNETT, **NSM** I CORNISH
ASTON CUM AUGHTON (All Saints) w Swallownest, Todwick and Ulley *Sheff 5* **P** *Bp* **TR** P WRIGHT, **TV** D C BLISS, A P FEREDAY, H LIDDLE
ASTON EYRE (not known) *see* Morville w Aston Eyre *Heref*
ASTON FLAMVILLE (St Peter) *see* Burbage w Aston Flamville *Leic*
ASTON INGHAM (St John the Baptist) *see* Linton w Upton Bishop and Aston Ingham *Heref*
ASTON JUXTA BIRMINGHAM (St James) *Birm 8* **P** *V Aston* **P-in-c** E J FURNESS
ASTON JUXTA BIRMINGHAM (St Peter and St Paul) *Birm 8* **P** *Aston Trustees* **V** G K SINCLAIR
ASTON LE WALLS (St Leonard) *see* Byfield w Boddington and Aston le Walls *Pet*
ASTON-ON-TRENT (All Saints) and Weston-on-Trent *Derby 15* **P** *Winterbottom Trustees and Bp (alt)* **R** B H MUNRO
ASTON ROWANT (St Peter and St Paul) *see* Chinnor w Emmington and Sydenham etc *Ox*
ASTON SANDFORD (St Michael and All Angels) *see* Haddenham w Cuddington, Kingsey etc *Ox*
ASTON SOMERVILLE (St Mary) *see* Childswyckham w Aston Somerville, Buckland etc *Glouc*
ASTON-SUB-EDGE (St Andrew) *see* Willersey, Saintbury, Weston-sub-Edge etc *Glouc*
ASTON TIRROLD (St Michael) *see* S w N Moreton, Aston Tirrold and Aston Upthorpe *Ox*
ASTON UPTHORPE (All Saints) *as above*
ASTWICK (St Guthlac) *see* Arlesey w Astwick *St Alb*
ASTWOOD (St Peter) *see* Sherington w Chicheley, N Crawley, Astwood etc *Ox*
ASTWOOD BANK (St Matthias and St George) *Worc 7* **P** *DBP* **P-in-c** P G HARRISON, **NSM** I J MERRY
ASWARBY (St Denys) *see* S Lafford *Linc*
ASWARDBY (St Helen) w Sausthorpe *Linc 7* **P** *DBP* **R** G ROBSON
ATCHAM (St Eata) *see* Shrewsbury St Giles w Sutton and Atcham *Lich*
ATHELINGTON (St Peter) *see* Stradbroke, Horham, Athelington and Redlingfield *St E*
ATHERINGTON (St Mary) *see* Newton Tracey, Horwood, Alverdiscott etc *Ex*
ATHERSLEY (St Helen) *Wakef 7* **P** *Bp* **V** *Vacant* (01226) 245361
ATHERSTONE (St Mary) *Cov 5* **P** *V Mancetter* **V** P I HARRIS
ATHERTON (St John the Baptist) (St George) (St Philip) *Man 13* **P** *Bp* **TR** W BALDWIN
ATLOW (St Philip and St James) *see* Hulland, Atlow, Bradley and Hognaston *Derby*
ATTENBOROUGH (St Mary the Virgin) *S'well 7* **P** *CPAS* **V** B DAWSON
ATTERCLIFFE (St Alban) (Hill Top Chapel), Darnall and Tinsley *Sheff 1* **P** *Patr Bd* **TR** M L FUDGER, **TV** C T GIBSON
ATTLEBOROUGH (Assumption of the Blessed Virgin Mary) w Besthorpe *Nor 11* **P** *CR and Mrs S P J Scully (jt)* **R** J A AVES
ATTLEBOROUGH (Holy Trinity) *Cov 5* **P** *V Nuneaton* **V** C JONES
ATTLEBRIDGE (St Andrew) *see* Alderford w Attlebridge and Swannington *Nor*
ATWICK (St Lawrence) *see* Hornsea w Atwick *York*
ATWORTH (St Michael and All Angels) w Shaw and Whitley *Sarum 17* **P** *D&C Bris and R Melksham (alt)* **P-in-c** G R J FORCE-JONES
AUBOURN (St Peter) w Haddington *Linc 18* **P** *Capt H N Nevile* **V** M J N HOWES, **NSM** J R D SCARBOROUGH
AUCKLAND (St Andrew) (St Anne) *Dur 6* **P** *Bp* **V** J MARSHALL
AUCKLAND (St Helen) *Dur 6* **P** *Bp* **V** R I McTEER
AUCKLAND (St Peter) *Dur 6* **P** *The Crown* **V** P K LEE
AUCKLEY (St Saviour) *see* Finningley w Auckley *S'well*
AUDENSHAW (St Hilda) *Man 17* **P** *Bp* **V** J H KERSHAW
AUDENSHAW (St Stephen) *Man 17* **P** *Bp* **V** P R DIXON
AUDLEM (St James the Great) *Ches 15* **P** *Bp* **V** D ROSTRON
AUDLEY (St James the Great) *Lich 9* **P** *Ch Soc Trust* **V** P T W DAVIES, **NSM** K M BURGESS
AUGHTON (All Saints) *see* Bubwith w Skipwith *York*
AUGHTON (Christ Church) *Liv 11* **P** *R Aughton St Mich* **V** R MOUGHTIN, **C** J L ROBERTS
AUGHTON (St Michael) *Liv 11* **P** *Bp* **R** M J SMOUT, **C** J L McKELVEY
AUGHTON (St Saviour) *see* Halton w Aughton *Blackb*
AUKBOROUGH (St John the Baptist) *see* Alkborough *Linc*
AUKBOROUGH (St John the Baptist) *as above*
AULT HUCKNALL (St John the Baptist) *Derby 3* **P** *Duke of Devonshire* **P-in-c** A L BELL
AUNSBY (St Thomas of Canterbury) *see* S Lafford *Linc*
AUST (not known) *see* Olveston *Bris*
AUSTERFIELD (St Helen) *see* Bawtry w Austerfield and Misson *S'well*
AUSTREY (St Nicholas) and Warton (Holy Trinity) *Birm 11* **P** *Ld Chan and V Polesworth St Editha (alt)* **V** W R STUART-WHITE
AUSTWICK (Epiphany) *see* Clapham-with-Keasden and Austwick *Bradf*
AVEBURY (St James) *see* Upper Kennet *Sarum*
AVELEY (St Michael) and Purfleet *Chelmsf 14* **P** *Bp* **V** C J NORRIS, **NSM** G E WRIGHT
AVENING (Holy Cross) w Cherington *Glouc 16* **P** *E A Tarlton Esq (1 turn), D&C (2 turns)* **NSM** C CARTER
AVERHAM (St Michael and All Angels) w Kelham *S'well 3* **P** *DBP* **P-in-c** A C ARMSTRONG, **NSM** M B ARMSTRONG
AVETON GIFFORD (St Andrew) *see* Modbury, Bigbury, Ringmore w Kingston etc *Ex*
AVINGTON (St Mary) *see* Itchen Valley *Win*
AVON DASSETT (St Peter and St Clare) w Farnborough and Fenny Compton *Cov 8* **P** *G V L Holbech Esq and Mrs A D Seyfried (jt), CCC Ox, and Bp(alt)* **R** D P PYM
AVON VALLEY *Sarum 12* **P** *Bp (3 turns), MOD (2 turns), and Ch Hosp (1 turn)* **V** R MANN, **NSM** M EDWARDS
AVONMOUTH (St Andrew) *Bris 8* **P** *Bp* **V** *Vacant* 0117-982 2302

AWBRIDGE (All Saints) w Sherfield English *Win 11* **P** *Bp and CPAS (jt)* **R** D E APPLIN
AWLISCOMBE (St Michael and All Angels) *see* Honiton, Gittisham, Combe Raleigh, Monkton etc *Ex*
AWRE (St Andrew) *see* Newnham w Awre and Blakeney *Glouc*
AWSWORTH (St Peter) w Cossall *S'well 7* **P** *Bp* **P-in-c** D McMANN
AXBRIDGE (St John the Baptist) w Shipham and Rowberrow *B & W 1* **P** *Bp and D&C (alt)* **R** D J RICHARDS, **NSM** P R ROGERS
AXFORD (St Michael) *see* Whitton *Sarum*
AXHOLME Group, The NORTH *Linc 1* **P** *The Crown* **V** *Vacant* (01724) 783612
AXMINSTER (St Mary), Chardstock, Combe Pyne and Rousdon *Ex 5* **P** *Bp* **TR** J H GOOD, **TV** R WARING, **NSM** R WARING
AXMOUTH (St Michael) *see* Uplyme w Axmouth *Ex*
AYCLIFFE (Church Centre) *see* Dover St Mary *Cant*
AYCLIFFE, GREAT (St Andrew) (St Clare) *Dur 5* **P** *Patr Bd* **TV** N A CHAMBERLAIN, C JAY, **NSM** M FERGUSON
AYLBURTON (St Mary) *see* Woolaston w Alvington and Aylburton *Glouc*
AYLBURTON COMMON (Mission Church) *see* Lydney *Glouc*
AYLESBEARE (Blessed Virgin Mary), Rockbeare, Farringdon, Clyst Honiton and Sowton *Ex 1* **P** *Bp and D&C (jt)* **Hon C** J C COPUS, **NSM** P PULLIN
AYLESBURY (St Mary the Virgin) w Bierton and Hulcott *Ox 21* **P** *Bp and Patr Bd (jt)* **TR** T J HIGGINS, **TV** P C FAULKNER, V J HICKS, P D ATKINSON, **C** V N H STRUDWICK, **NSM** A K WATSON
AYLESBY (St Lawrence) *see* Keelby w Riby and Aylesby *Linc*
AYLESFORD (St Peter and St Paul) *Roch 7* **P** *D&C* **V** P E FRANCIS, **NSM** C M HAYDON
AYLESHAM (St Peter) w Adisham *Cant 1* **P** *Abp* **NSM** N J TYSON
AYLESTONE (St Andrew) w St James *Leic 2* **P** *Bp* **R** A RACE, **C** H BRADLEY, J M BROWN
AYLESTONE PARK (Church of the Nativity) *see* Aylestone St Andr w St Jas *Leic*
AYLMERTON (St John the Baptist) w Runton *Nor 21* **P** *Bp* **R** P H ATKINS
AYLSHAM (St Michael) *Nor 19* **P** *D&C Cant* **V** R D BRANSON
AYLTON (not known) *see* Tarrington w Stoke Edith, Aylton, Pixley etc *Heref*
AYMESTREY (St John the Baptist and St Alkmund) *see* Kingsland w Eardisland, Aymestrey etc *Heref*
AYNHO (St Michael) and Croughton w Evenley and Farthinghoe and Hinton-in-the-Hedges w Steane *Pet 1* **P** *Bp (2 turns), Mrs E A J Cartwright-Hignett (1 turn), Magd Coll Ox (1 turn), and Ld Chan (1 turn)* **R** P A M GOMPERTZ
AYOT ST LAWRENCE (St Lawrence) *see* Kimpton w Ayot St Lawrence *St Alb*
AYOT ST PETER (St Peter) *see* Welwyn w Ayot St Peter *St Alb*
AYSGARTH (St Andrew) and Bolton cum Redmire *Ripon 4* **P** *Trin Coll Cam and R Wensley (alt)* **V** S C WHITEHOUSE, **Hon C** J H RICHARDSON
AYSTON (St Mary the Virgin) *see* Uppingham w Ayston and Wardley w Belton *Pet*
AYTHORPE RODING (St Mary) *see* Gt Canfield w High Roding and Aythorpe Roding *Chelmsf*
AYTON, EAST (St John the Baptist) *see* Seamer w E Ayton *York*
AYTON, GREAT (All Saints) (Christ Church) w Easby and Newton in Cleveland *York 22* **P** *Abp* **V** P H PEVERELL, **NSM** G S JAQUES
BABBACOMBE (All Saints) *Ex 10* **P** *V St Marychurch* **P-in-c** S N WAKELY
BABCARY (Holy Cross) *see* Six Pilgrims *B & W*
BABRAHAM (St Peter) *Ely 7* **P** *H R T Adeane Esq* **P-in-c** R L POWELL
BABWORTH (All Saints) w Sutton-cum-Lound *S'well 5* **P** *Bp and Sir James Whitaker Bt (jt)* **R** *Vacant* (01777) 703253
BACKFORD (St Oswald) and Capenhurst *Ches 9* **P** *Bp* **P-in-c** G F PARSONS
BACKWELL (St Andrew) w Chelvey and Brockley *B & W 13* **P** *DBP* **R** A J WRIGHT
BACKWORTH (St John) *see* Earsdon and Backworth *Newc*
BACONSTHORPE (St Mary) *see* Barningham w Matlaske w Baconsthorpe etc *Nor*
BACTON (St Andrew) w Edingthorpe w Witton and Ridlington *Nor 12* **P** *Duchy of Lanc (1 turn), Bp and Earl of Kimberley (1 turn)* **P-in-c** J M S PICKERING
BACTON (St Faith) *see* Ewyas Harold w Dulas, Kenderchurch etc *Heref*
BACTON (St Mary the Virgin) w Wyverstone and Cotton *St E 6* **P** *MMCET, Ld Chan, and J C S Priston Esq (by turn)* **P-in-c** R W JACK, **NSM** B B BILSTON
BACUP (Christ Church) *Man 15* **P** *Trustees* **P-in-c** M L GOODER
BACUP (St John the Evangelist) *Man 15* **P** *Wm Hulme Trustees* **V** M HOLT
BACUP (St Saviour) *Man 15* **P** *Ch Soc Trust* **P-in-c** S E BROOK
BADBY (St Mary) w Newham and Charwelton w Fawsley and Preston Capes *Pet 3* **P** *Bp* **R** S P ADAMS
BADDESLEY, NORTH (All Saints' Mission Church) *see* Chilworth w N Baddesley *Win*
BADDESLEY, NORTH (St John the Baptist) *see* Valley Park *Win*
BADDESLEY, SOUTH (St Mary the Virgin) *see* Boldre w S Baddesley *Win*
BADDESLEY CLINTON (St Michael) *Birm 6* **P** *T W Ferrers-Walker Esq* **R** A V WILLMONT
BADDESLEY ENSOR (St Nicholas) w Grendon *Birm 11* **P** *Bp, V Polesworth, and PCC (jt)* **V** K HODSON
BADDILEY (St Michael) and Wrenbury w Burleydam *Ches 15* **P** *V Acton and Bp (alt)* **V** M ROWLANDS
BADDOW, GREAT (Meadgate Church Centre) (St Mary the Virgin) (St Paul) *Chelmsf 9* **P** *Patr Bd* **TR** A D McGREGOR, **TV** M D MOORE
BADDOW, LITTLE (St Mary the Virgin) *Chelmsf 9* **P** *Bp* **R** R E TURNER
BADGER (St Giles) *see* Beckbury, Badger, Kemberton, Ryton, Stockton etc *Lich*
BADGEWORTH (Holy Trinity), Shurdington and Witcombe w Bentham *Glouc 6* **P** *Bp and M W Hicks Beach Esq (jt)* **R** D E S PRIMROSE, **NSM** P F SMITH
BADGWORTH (St Congar) *see* Crook Peak *B & W*
BADINGHAM (St John the Baptist) w Bruisyard, Cransford and Dennington *St E 18* **P** *R C Rous Esq (1 turn), DBP (2 turns)* **P-in-c** M PICKERING
BADLESMERE (St Leonard) *see* Selling w Throwley, Sheldwich w Badlesmere etc *Cant*
BADMINTON (St Michael and All Angels) w Little Badminton, Acton Turville and Hawkesbury *Glouc 7* **P** *Duke of Beaufort* **P-in-c** P R BERROW
BADMINTON, LITTLE (St Michael and All Angels) *see* Badminton w Lt Badminton, Acton Turville etc *Glouc*
BADSEY (St James) w Aldington and Offenham and Bretforton *Worc 1* **P** *Bp and Ch Ch Ox (jt)* **V** A M HOUGH
BADSHOT LEA (St George) *see* Hale *Guildf*
BADSWORTH (St Mary the Virgin) *Wakef 11* **P** *DBP* **R** *Vacant* (01977) 643642
BADWELL ASH (St Mary) w Great Ashfield, Stowlangtoft, Langham and Hunston *St E 9* **P** *Bp (2 turns), DBP (1 turn)* **P-in-c** M G CLARKE
BAG ENDERBY (St Margaret) *see* S Ormsby Gp *Linc*
BAGBOROUGH (St Pancras) *see* Bishops Lydeard w Bagborough and Cothelstone *B & W*
BAGBY (St Mary) *see* Thirkleby w Kilburn and Bagby *York*
BAGENDON (St Margaret) *see* Stratton, N Cerney, Baunton and Bagendon *Glouc*
BAGINTON (St John the Baptist) *see* Stoneleigh w Ashow and Baginton *Cov*
BAGNALL (St Chad) *see* Bucknall and Bagnall *Lich*
BAGSHOT (Good Shepherd) *see* Wexcombe *Sarum*
BAGSHOT (St Anne) *Guildf 6* **P** *Ld Chan* **V** *Vacant* (01276) 473348
BAGULEY Brooklands (St John the Divine) *Man 8* **P** *Bp and A W Hargreaves Esq (jt)* **V** J C FINDON, **C** T SHEPHERD, **NSM** A W HARGREAVES
BAGWORTH (The Holy Rood) *see* Thornton, Bagworth and Stanton *Leic*
BAILDON (St John the Evangelist) (St Hugh Mission Church) (St James) *Bradf 1* **P** *S H K Butcher Esq* **V** J D NOWELL, **C** N W STOCKBRIDGE, **NSM** K N MEDHURST
BAINTON (St Andrew) w North Dalton, Middleton-on-the-Wolds and Kilnwick *York 11* **P** *Abp, St Jo Coll Ox, and Exors M P Winter (jt)* **R** H L ARTLEY, **NSM** C CONNER
BAINTON (St Mary) *see* Barnack w Ufford and Bainton *Pet*
BAKEWELL (All Saints) *Derby 2* **P** *D&C Lich* **V** E R URQUHART, **NSM** L E ELLSWORTH
BALBY (St John the Evangelist) *Sheff 10* **P** *Bp* **V** G J MARCER
BALCOMBE (St Mary) *Chich 6* **P** *P A D Secretan Esq* **R** N G PRINT
BALDERSBY (St James) *see* Topcliffe w Baldersby, Dalton, Dishforth etc *York*
BALDERSTONE (St Leonard) *Blackb 2* **P** *V Blackb* **V** D E ASHFORTH
BALDERSTONE (St Mary) *Man 20* **P** *Trustees* **V** I C THOMPSON, **C** G J CROSSLEY, **NSM** D OATES

BALDERTON (St Giles) *S'well 3* **P** *Ld Chan* **P-in-c** W H THACKRAY
BALDHU (St Michael) *see* Highertown and Baldhu *Truro*
BALDOCK (St Mary the Virgin) w Bygrave *St Alb 23* **P** *Marquess of Salisbury and Bp (alt)* **R** J A STONE
BALDWIN (St Luke) *see* Marown *S & M*
BALE (All Saints) *see* Gunthorpe w Bale w Field Dalling, Saxlingham etc *Nor*
BALHAM (St Mary and St John the Divine) *S'wark 18* **P** *Bp and Keble Coll Ox (jt)* **V** D A NICHOLSON, **NSM** J B SMITH
BALHAM HILL (Ascension) *S'wark 18* **P** *Bp* **P-in-c** A P B WHITE, **C** M S NICHOLS
BALKWELL (St Peter) *Newc 8* **P** *Bp* **V** P S McCONNELL
BALLAM (St Matthew) *see* Ribby w Wrea *Blackb*
BALLAUGH (St Mary) (St Mary Old Church) *S & M 3* **P** *The Crown* **R** *Vacant* (0162489) 7873
BALLIDON (All Saints) *see* Wirksworth *Derby*
BALLINGER (St Mary Mission Hall) *see* Gt Missenden w Ballinger and Lt Hampden *Ox*
BALLINGHAM (St Dubricius) *see* Heref S Wye *Heref*
BALSALL COMMON (St Peter) *Birm 12* **P** *Bp* **V** A S MONTGOMERIE
BALSALL HEATH (St Barnabas) *see* Sparkbrook St Agatha w Balsall Heath St Barn *Birm*
BALSALL HEATH (St Paul) *Birm 5* **P** *Bp* **V** J D HANNAH, **C** P M HOLLINGSWORTH
BALSCOTE (St Mary Magdalene) *see* Ironstone *Ox*
BALSHAM (Holy Trinity) *Ely 4* **P** *Charterhouse* **R** W N C GIRARD
BALTERLEY (All Saints' Memorial Church) *see* Barthomley *Ches*
BALTONSBOROUGH (St Dunstan) w Butleigh and West Bradley *B & W 5* **P** *Bp* **V** *Vacant* (01458) 50409
BAMBER BRIDGE (St Aidan) *Blackb 6* **P** *Bp* **V** M L HARTLEY, **C** P M WITTS
BAMBER BRIDGE (St Saviour) *Blackb 6* **P** *V Blackb* **V** W T BARNES
BAMBURGH (St Aidan) and Beadnell *Newc 10* **P** *Lady Armstrong and Newc Dioc Soc (alt)* **V** E ZACHAU
BAMFORD (St John the Baptist) *Derby 2* **P** *A C H Barnes Esq* **R** N P GOWER
BAMFORD (St Michael) *Man 20* **P** *Bp* **V** S B GREY
BAMFURLONG (Good Shepherd) *see* Abram *Liv*
BAMPTON (Holy Trinity) (St James) (St Mary) w Clanfield *Ox 8* **P** *Bp, DBP, St Jo Coll Ox, D&C Ex, and B Babington-Smith Esq (jt)* **V** D J LLOYD
BAMPTON (St Michael and All Angels), Morebath, Clayhanger and Petton *Ex 8* **P** *DBP and D&C (jt)* **V** P P OCKFORD
BAMPTON (St Patrick) *see* Shap w Swindale and Bampton w Mardale *Carl*
BAMPTON ASTON (St James) *see* Bampton w Clanfield *Ox*
BAMPTON LEW (Holy Trinity) *as above*
BAMPTON PROPER (St Mary) *as above*
BANBURY (St Mary) *Ox 5* **P** *Bp* **TR** D A INESON, **TV** D W TOWNSEND, L R COLLINSON, B A WALLES, **C** C KNIGHT, D JACKSON, **NSM** S R FAIRBAIRN, V W BALL, W M JOHNSTON
BANHAM (St Mary) *see* Quidenham Gp *Nor*
BANKFOOT (St Matthew) *Bradf 2* **P** *Bp* **V** J W TURNER
BANKS (St Stephen in the Banks) *Liv 9* **P** *R N Meols* **V** *Vacant* (01704) 28985
BANNINGHAM (St Botolph) *see* Felmingham, Skeyton, Colby, Banningham etc *Nor*
BANSTEAD (All Saints) *Guildf 9* **P** *Bp* **V** D N CHANCE, **C** W D GULLIFORD
BANWELL (St Andrew) *B & W 11* **P** *D&C Bris* **V** D R G LOCKYER
BAPCHILD (St Lawrence) *see* Murston w Bapchild and Tonge *Cant*
BAR HILL (not known) *Ely 5* **P** *Bp* **P-in-c** G J RENISON
BARBON (St Bartholomew) *see* Kirkby Lonsdale *Carl*
BARBOURNE (St Stephen) *Worc 6* **P** *Bp* **V** S W CURRIE, **C** M BADGER
BARBROOK (St Bartholomew) *see* Combe Martin, Berrynarbor, Lynton, Brendon etc *Ex*
BARBY (St Mary) w Kilsby *Pet 3* **P** *Bp* **R** *Vacant* (01788) 890252
BARCHESTON (St Martin) *Cov 9* **P** *Bp* **P-in-c** R K SMITH, **C** R D HOLDER
BARCOMBE (St Francis) (St Mary the Virgin) *Chich 18* **P** *Ld Chan* **R** D PEARSON-MILES, **NSM** R A MOORE
BARDFIELD (St Peter and St Paul) *see* Gt and Lt Bardfield w Gt and Lt Saling *Chelmsf*
BARDFIELD, GREAT (St Mary the Virgin) and Little (St Katherine) w Great and Little (Bardfield) Saling *Chelmsf 18* **P** *Ch Union Trust, and Bp (jt)* **V** M J ATKINSON
BARDNEY (St Laurence) *Linc 11* **P** *DBP (1 turn), Bp (2 turns), and St Jo Coll Cam (1 turn)* **R** *Vacant* (01526) 398595
BARDON HILL (St Peter) *see* Coalville and Bardon Hill *Leic*
BARDSEA (Holy Trinity) *see* Pennington and Lindal w Marton and Bardsea *Carl*
BARDSEY (All Hallows) *Ripon 1* **P** *G L Fox Esq* **V** R J PEARSON
BARDSLEY (Holy Trinity) *Man 17* **P** *Wm Hulme Trustees* **V** L S IRELAND, **Hon C** L A IRELAND
BARDWELL (St Peter and St Paul) *see* Blackbourne *St E*
BARE (St Christopher) *Blackb 12* **P** *Bp* **V** D L HEAP
BARFORD (St Botolph) *see* Barnham Broom *Nor*
BARFORD (St John) *see* Deddington w Barford, Clifton and Hempton *Ox*
BARFORD (St Michael) *as above*
BARFORD (St Peter) w Wasperton and Sherbourne *Cov 8* **P** *Major J M Mills, R Hampton Lucy, and Lady Jeryl Smith-Ryland (jt)* **P-in-c** D C JESSETT
BARFORD, GREAT (All Saints) *see* Roxton w Gt Barford *St Alb*
BARFORD ST MARTIN (St Martin), Dinton, Baverstock and Burcombe *Sarum 13* **P** *All So Coll Ox, A K I Mackenzie-Charrington Esq, Bp, and St Jo Hosp Wilton (jt)* **R** J LEEMING, **Dss** A SYMES
BARFREYSTONE (St Nicholas) *see* Eythorne and Elvington w Waldershare etc *Cant*
BARHAM (St Giles) *see* Spaldwick w Barham and Woolley *Ely*
BARHAM (St John the Baptist) w Bishopsbourne and Kingston *Cant 1* **P** *Abp* **R** A A DUKE
BARHAM (St Mary) *see* Claydon and Barham *St E*
BARHOLME (St Martin) *see* Uffington Gp *Linc*
BARKBY (St Mary) *see* Syston TM *Leic*
BARKESTONE (St Peter and St Paul) w Plungar, Redmile and Stathern *Leic 3* **P** *The Crown and Peterho Cam (alt)* **P-in-c** G SPENCER, **C** M TURNER, D F MILLS
BARKHAM (St James) *see* Arborfield w Barkham *Ox*
BARKING (St Erkenwald) *Chelmsf 1* **P** *Bp* **V** G R WISKER
BARKING (St Margaret) (St Patrick) *Chelmsf 1* **P** *Patr Bd* **P-in-c** J B PARSONS, **C** A R B JOWITT, M BARKER
BARKING (St Mary) *see* Ringshall w Battisford, Barking w Darmsden etc *St E*
BARKINGSIDE (Holy Trinity) *Chelmsf 4* **P** *V Gt Ilford* **V** *Vacant* 0181-550 2669
BARKINGSIDE (St Cedd) *Chelmsf 4* **P** *Bp* **P-in-c** P A REILY
BARKINGSIDE (St Francis of Assisi) *Chelmsf 4* **P** *Bp* **V** M JENNINGS
BARKINGSIDE (St George) *Chelmsf 4* **P** *Bp* **V** J V FISHER
BARKINGSIDE (St Laurence) *Chelmsf 4* **P** *Bp* **V** G R LOCK
BARKISLAND (Christ Church) w West Scammonden *Wakef 4* **P** *V Halifax* **V** *Vacant*
BARKSTON (St Nicholas) and Hough Group, The *Linc 23* **P** *Capt Sir Anthony Thorold Bt, Revd J R H and Revd H C Thorold, Lord Brownlow, and Sir Lyonel Tollemache Bt* **R** G R SHRIMPTON
BARKSTON ASH (Holy Trinity) *see* Sherburn in Elmet w Saxton *York*
BARKWAY (St Mary Magdalene), Reed and Buckland w Barley *St Alb 19* **P** *The Crown and DBP (alt)* **R** B KNIGHT
BARKWITH Group, The *Linc 5* **P** *D&C, J N Heneage Esq, K Coll Lon, and DBP (by turn)* **R** I S PARTRIDGE
BARKWITH, EAST (St Mary) *see* Barkwith Gp *Linc*
BARLASTON (St John the Baptist) *Lich 13* **P** *Countess of Sutherland* **V** G L SIMPSON
BARLAVINGTON (St Mary), Burton w Coates and Sutton w Bignor *Chich 11* **P** *Lord Egremont and Miss J B Courtauld (jt)* **P-in-c** R D PAYNE
BARLBOROUGH (St James) *Derby 3* **P** *S R Sitwell Esq* **P-in-c** A J SIDEBOTTOM
BARLBY (All Saints) w Riccall *York 4* **P** *Abp and V Hemingbrough (jt)* **V** C J SIMMONS, **NSM** F LOFTUS
BARLESTONE (St Giles) *Leic 13* **P** *Bp* **P-in-c** L R CARPENTER
BARLEY (St Margaret of Antioch) *see* Barkway, Reed and Buckland w Barley *St Alb*
BARLING (All Saints) w Little Wakering *Chelmsf 12* **P** *D&C St Paul's and Bp (alt)* **V** R WOOLVEN
BARLING MAGNA (All Saints) *see* Barling w Lt Wakering *Chelmsf*
BARLINGS (St Edward) *Linc 3* **P** *DBP (2 turns), Earl of Scarborough (1 turn)* **V** R G SPAIGHT
BARLOW (not known) *see* Brayton *York*
BARLOW, GREAT (St Lawrence) *see* Newbold w Dunston and Gt Barlow *Derby*
BARLOW MOOR (Emmanuel) *see* Didsbury St Jas and Em *Man*
BARMBY MARSH (St Helen) *see* Howden TM *York*

BARMBY MOOR (St Catherine) w Allerthorpe, Fangfoss and Yapham *York 7* **P** *Abp* **R** V P HEWETSON
BARMING (St Margaret of Antioch) w West Barming *Roch 7* **P** *Ld Chan* **R** A DAUNTON-FEAR
BARMING HEATH (St Andrew) *Cant 15* **P** *Abp* **V** B REED
BARMSTON (All Saints) *see* Skipsea w Ulrome and Barmston w Fraisthorpe *York*
BARNACK (St John the Baptist) w Ufford and Bainton *Pet 8* **P** *Bp and St Jo Coll Cam (alt)* **R** G B AUSTEN
BARNACRE (All Saints) w Calder Vale *Blackb 10* **P** *Bp and Mrs V O Shepherd-Cross (alt)* **P-in-c** P J PIKE
BARNARD CASTLE (St Mary) w Whorlton *Dur 7* **P** *Trin Coll Cam* **V** P W LIND-JACKSON, **NSM** G KIRTLEY
BARNARDISTON (All Saints) *see* Hundon w Barnardiston *St E*
BARNBURGH (St Peter) w Melton on the Hill and Aldwick-upon-Dearne *Sheff 12* **P** *Ld Chan (2 turns), Bp (1 turn)* **R** J R SMITH
BARNBY (St John the Baptist) *see* Worlingham w Barnby and N Cove *St E*
BARNBY, EAST (Mission Chapel) *see* Lythe w Ugthorpe *York*
BARNBY DUN (St Peter and St Paul) *Sheff 9* **P** *Bp* **V** N K YOUNG
BARNBY IN THE WILLOWS (All Saints) *see* Coddington w Barnby in the Willows *S'well*
BARNEHURST (St Martin) *Roch 15* **P** *Bp* **V** D F SPRINGTHORPE
BARNES (Holy Trinity) *S'wark 17* **P** *R Barnes St Mary* **P-in-c** G HOLDSTOCK
BARNES (St Mary) *S'wark 17* **P** *D&C St Paul's* **P-in-c** R AMES-LEWIS, **C** E J RANCE
BARNES (St Michael and All Angels) *S'wark 17* **P** *D&C St Paul's* **V** J P HAWES, **NSM** A J ROBERTS
BARNET (Christ Church) *see* S Mimms Ch Ch *Lon*
BARNET (St Stephen) *see* Chipping Barnet w Arkley *St Alb*
BARNET, EAST (St Mary the Virgin) *St Alb 17* **P** *The Crown* **R** A J PROUD, **C** A K MATTHEWS, **NSM** J D A WALKER
BARNET, NEW (St James) *St Alb 17* **P** *Ch Patr Trust* **V** B R PENFOLD
BARNET VALE (St Mark) *St Alb 17* **P** *Bp* **V** C J GAY
BARNETBY LE WOLD (St Barnabas) *see* N Wolds Gp *Linc*
BARNEY (St Mary), Fulmodeston w Croxton, Hindringham, Thursford, Great and Little Snoring w Kettlestone and Pensthorpe *Nor 15* **P** *Lord Hastings, St Jo Coll Cam, D&C, DBP, and CCC Cam (by turn)* **R** J P S DENNY
BARNHAM (St Gregory) *see* Blackbourne *St E*
BARNHAM (St Mary) *see* Aldingbourne, Barnham and Eastergate *Chich*
BARNHAM BROOM (St Peter and St Paul) *Nor 17* **P** *Patr Bd* **TR** C H MILFORD, **Hon C** A H REYNOLDS
BARNINGHAM (St Andrew) *see* Hopton, Market Weston, Barningham etc *St E*
BARNINGHAM (St Mary the Virgin) w Matlaske w Baconsthorpe w Plumstead w Hempstead *Nor 18* **P** *Duchy of Lanc (1 turn), Sir Charles Mott-Radclyffe, CPAS, and D&C (jt) (1 turn)* **P-in-c** P J BELL
BARNINGHAM (St Michael and All Angels) w Hutton Magna and Wycliffe *Ripon 2* **P** *Bp and V Gilling and Kirkby Ravensworth (jt)* **R** W A CLAYTON
BARNINGHAM, LITTLE (St Andrew), Blickling, Edgefield, Itteringham w Mannington, Oulton w Irmingland, Saxthorpe w Corpusty and Wickmere w Wolterton *Nor 19* **P** *Bp, Lord Walpole, SMF, MMCET (2 turns), and Pemb Coll Cam (1 turn)* **R** K A HAWKES
BARNINGHAM WINTER (St Mary the Virgin) *see* Barningham w Matlaske w Baconsthorpe etc *Nor*
BARNOLDBY LE BECK (St Helen) *Linc 10* **P** *Ld Chan* **P-in-c** I R SHELTON
BARNOLDSWICK (Holy Trinity) (St Mary le Gill) w Bracewell *Bradf 7* **P** *Bp* **V** J R LANCASTER
BARNSBURY (St Andrew) *Lon 6* **P** *Patr Bd* **TR** A E HARVEY, **TV** C M S R THOMAS, R W WALL
BARNSLEY Old Town (St Paul) *see* Barnsley St Mary *Wakef*
BARNSLEY (St Edward the Confessor) *Wakef 7* **P** *Bp* **V** G H HALL
BARNSLEY (St George's Parish Church Centre) *Wakef 7* **P** *Bp* **V** P J MUNBY
BARNSLEY (St Mary) *see* Bibury w Winson and Barnsley *Glouc*
BARNSLEY (St Mary) *Wakef 7* **P** *Bp* **R** I E WILDEY, **C** J R JENKINS
BARNSLEY (St Peter and St John the Baptist) *Wakef 7* **P** *Bp* **V** A BRISCOE
BARNSTAPLE (St Peter and St Mary Magdalene) (Holy Trinity) w Goodleigh, Landkey and Sticklepath *Ex 15* **P** *DBP* **P-in-c** C PUCKRIN, **TV** M J PEARSON, G CHAVE-COX, **Hon C** P D PILDITCH, **NSM** G F SQUIRE
BARNSTON (Christ Church) *Ches 8* **P** *Bp* **V** G P BENSON, **C** N A J BELCHER
BARNSTON (not known) *see* Gt Dunmow and Barnston *Chelmsf*
BARNSTONE (St Mary Mission Room) *see* Cropwell Bishop w Colston Bassett, Granby etc *S'well*
BARNT GREEN (St Andrew) *see* Cofton Hackett w Barnt Green *Birm*
BARNTON (Christ Church) *Ches 4* **P** *Bp* **P-in-c** A P MANNING, **NSM** G H BUCHAN
BARNWELL (All Saints) (St Andrew) w Tichmarsh, Thurning and Clapton *Pet 12* **P** *Soc of Merchant Venturers, MMCET, Em Coll Cam, and DBP (by turn)* **R** P C H A TRENCHARD
BARNWOOD (St Lawrence) *Glouc 5* **P** *D&C* **V** M S RILEY, **Hon C** K I MORGAN
BARR, GREAT (St Margaret) *Lich 26* **P** *E G A Farnham Esq* **V** J S REANEY, **Hon C** T W WARD
BARRINGTON (All Saints) *Ely 8* **P** *Trin Coll Cam* **V** M W BAKER
BARRINGTON (Blessed Virgin Mary) *see* Ilminster and District *B & W*
BARRINGTON, GREAT (St Mary) *see* Sherborne, Windrush, the Barringtons etc *Glouc*
BARRINGTON, LITTLE (St Peter) *as above*
BARROW (All Saints) w Denham St Mary and Higham Green *St E 13* **P** *Bp, St Jo Coll Cam, and D W Barclay Esq (by turn)* **R** J B DAVIS
BARROW and Goxhill *Linc 6* **P** *Ld Chan* **V** C MACDONALD
BARROW (St Bartholomew) *Ches 2* **P** *D Okell Esq* **P-in-c** P T CHANTRY, **NSM** H F CHANTRY
BARROW (St Giles) *see* Broseley w Benthall, Jackfield, Linley etc *Heref*
BARROW, NORTH (St Nicholas) *see* Six Pilgrims *B & W*
BARROW, SOUTH (St Peter) *as above*
BARROW GURNEY (Blessed Virgin Mary and St Edward King and Martyr) *B & W 13* **P** *Major M A Gibbs* **P-in-c** J B BISHOP
BARROW HILL (St Andrew) *see* Staveley and Barrow Hill *Derby*
BARROW-IN-FURNESS (St Aidan) *Carl 8* **P** *Bp* **P-in-c** I GRAINGER
BARROW-IN-FURNESS (St George) (St Luke) *Carl 8* **P** *Bp* **P-in-c** P E MANN, **TV** M S WILKINSON
BARROW-IN-FURNESS (St James) *Carl 8* **P** *DBP* **P-in-c** C J LAXON
BARROW-IN-FURNESS (St John the Evangelist) *Carl 8* **P** *DBP* **P-in-c** I DAVIES, **C** M A EDWARDS
BARROW-IN-FURNESS (St Mark) *Carl 10* **P** *Bp* **V** P G DAY
BARROW-IN-FURNESS (St Mary the Virgin) *see* Walney Is *Carl*
BARROW-IN-FURNESS (St Matthew) *Carl 8* **P** *Bp* **P-in-c** D G KENNEDY
BARROW-ON-HUMBER (Holy Trinity) *see* Barrow and Goxhill *Linc*
BARROW-ON-TRENT (St Wilfrid) w Twyford and Swarkestone *Derby 15* **P** *Repton Sch and Miss A I M Harpur-Crewe (jt)* **P-in-c** R HILL, **NSM** F R WORRALL
BARROW UPON SOAR (Holy Trinity) w Walton le Wolds *Leic 7* **P** *St Jo Coll Cam and DBP (jt)* **R** S J MITCHELL
BARROWBY (All Saints) and Gonerby, Great *Linc 19* **P** *R Grantham, and Duke of Devonshire (by turn)* **R** P HOPKINS
BARROWDEN (St Peter) and Wakerley w South Luffenham *Pet 8* **P** *Burghley Ho Preservation Trust and Ball Coll Ox (alt)* **R** B SCOTT
BARROWFORD (St Thomas) *Blackb 7* **P** *DBF* **V** B MORGAN
BARSHAM (Holy Trinity) *see* Wainford *St E*
BARSHAM, EAST (All Saints) *see* Walsingham, Houghton and Barsham *Nor*
BARSHAM, NORTH (All Saints) *as above*
BARSHAM, WEST (The Assumption of the Blessed Virgin Mary) *as above*
BARSTON (St Swithin) *Birm 12* **P** *MMCET* **P-in-c** E W RUSSELL
BARTHOMLEY (St Bertoline) *Ches 11* **P** *Lord O'Neill* **R** *Vacant* (01270) 872479
BARTLEY (Mission Church) *see* Copythorne and Minstead *Win*
BARTLEY GREEN (St Michael and All Angels) *Birm 2* **P** *Bp* **V** C E MANSLEY
BARTLOW (St Mary) *see* Linton *Ely*
BARTON (St Cuthbert w St Mary) and Manfield and Cleasby w Stapleton *Ripon 2* **P** *Bp, D&C, and V Forcett and Stanwick w Aldbrough (jt)* **V** R W GROSSE
BARTON (St Lawrence) *Blackb 10* **P** *DBP* **V** J H RANDELL

BARTON (St Mark's Chapel) w Peel Green (St Michael and All Angels) (St Catherine) *Man 2* **P** *Bp and TR Eccles* **P-in-c** R J SMITH
BARTON (St Martin) *see* Torquay St Martin Barton *Ex*
BARTON (St Michael), Pooley Bridge and Martindale *Carl 4* **P** *Bp and Earl of Lonsdale (jt)* **P-in-c** J M STAGG
BARTON (St Paul) *Portsm 8* **P** *R Whippingham* **P-in-c** P E PIMENTEL
BARTON (St Peter) *Ely 1* **P** *Ld Chan* **V** H D SEARLE
BARTON, GREAT (Holy Innocents) *St E 13* **P** *Sir Michael Bunbury Bt* **P-in-c** D W HERRICK
BARTON BENDISH (St Andrew) w Beachamwell and Shingham *Ely 16* **P** *Bp and DBP (alt)* **P-in-c** M TUCKER
BARTON HARTSHORN (St James) *see* Swan *Ox*
BARTON HILL (St Luke w Christ Church) *Bris 4* **P** *V Bris St Phil (2 turns) and CPAS (1 turn)* **V** C A SUNDERLAND
BARTON IN FABIS (St George) *S'well 10* **P** *Ld Chan* **P-in-c** R A SPRAY, **NSM** J M GORICK
BARTON-LE-CLEY (St Nicholas) w Higham Gobion and Hexton *St Alb 9* **P** *The Crown (3 turns), Mrs F A A Cooper (1 turn)* **R** P H WHITTAKER
BARTON-LE-STREET (St Michael) *see* Street TM *York*
BARTON MILLS (St Mary) *see* Mildenhall *St E*
BARTON-ON-THE-HEATH (St Lawrence) *see* Long Compton, Whichford and Barton-on-the-Heath *Cov*
BARTON SEAGRAVE (St Botolph) w Warkton *Pet 11* **P** *Ch Soc Trust (2 turns), Duke of Buccleuch (1 turn)* **R** J M PERRIS, **C** S J DAVIES, **Hon C** G MORGAN, **NSM** H EASTWOOD
BARTON ST DAVID (St David) *see* Keinton Mandeville w Lydford-on-Fosse etc *B & W*
BARTON STACEY (All Saints) and Bullington and Hurstbourne Priors and Longparish *Win 6* **P** *Bp, D&C, and J Woodcock Esq (jt)* **V** W ROBSON
BARTON TURF (St Michael) *see* Neatishead, Barton Turf and Irstead *Nor*
BARTON UNDER NEEDWOOD (St James) w Dunstall *Lich 14* **P** *Bp and Sir Rupert Hardy Bt (jt)* **V** A J WOOD
BARTON UPON HUMBER (St Mary) *Linc 6* **P** *Bp* **V** E J P HEPWORTH, **C** N G BATCOCK, **NSM** A W WRIGHT
BARTON UPON IRWELL (St Catherine) *see* Barton w Peel Green *Man*
BARWELL (St Mary) w Potters Marston and Stapleton *Leic 13* **P** *R J W Titley Esq* **R** A C DEEGAN
BARWICK (St Mary Magdalene) *see* Yeovil H Trin w Barwick *B & W*
BARWICK IN ELMET (All Saints) *Ripon 8* **P** *Duchy of Lanc* **R** R B B WILD
BASCHURCH (All Saints) and Weston Lullingfield w Hordley *Lich 17* **P** *Ch Patr Trust and Bp (jt)* **R** J H ROBINSON
BASCOTE HEATH (Chapel) *see* Radford Semele and Ufton *Cov*
BASEGREEN (St Peter) *see* Gleadless *Sheff*
BASFORD (St Aidan) *S'well 13* **P** *Bp* **P-in-c** P HEMSTOCK
BASFORD (St Leodegarius) w Hyson Green *S'well 13* **P** *Bp and CPAS (jt)* **P-in-c** G J BURTON, **C** E A CARRINGTON, R E WORSLEY
BASFORD (St Mark) *Lich 9* **P** *Bp* **V** I NICKLIN
BASFORD, NEW (St Augustine) *see* Basford w Hyson Green *S'well*
BASHLEY (St John) *see* Milton *Win*
BASILDON (St Andrew) (Holy Cross) *Chelmsf 6* **P** *Bp* **V** J R CARR
BASILDON (St Martin of Tours) *Chelmsf 6* **P** *Bp* **R** L F WEBBER, **C** P M A PEELING
BASILDON (St Stephen) w Aldworth and Ashampstead *Ox 12* **P** *St Jo Coll Cam, Simeon's Trustees, and DBF (by turn)* **P-in-c** M O M MILLS-POWELL
BASING (St Mary) *Win 4* **P** *Magd Coll Ox* **V** A D PICTON, **NSM** C E EDMONDS
BASINGSTOKE (All Saints) (St Michael) *Win 4* **P** *Patr Bd* **TR** P P WELSH, **TV** T H ROBERTS, M D BAILEY, A M BURDEN, J E VAUGHAN-WILSON, **C** S T HORNE, **NSM** E A GEORGE, J A WIBREW
BASINGSTOKE Brighton Hill (Christ the King) *see* Basingstoke *Win*
BASINGSTOKE Popley (Bethlehem Chapel) *as above*
BASINGSTOKE South Ham (St Peter) *as above*
BASLOW (St Anne) w Curbar and Stoney Middleton *Derby 2* **P** *Duke of Devonshire and V Hathersage (jt)* **V** G R ORCHARD
BASSENTHWAITE (St Bega) (St John), Isel and Setmurthy *Carl 6* **P** *Bp, D&C, and Miss M E Burkett (by turn)* **P-in-c** C S SIMS
BASSINGBOURN (St Peter and St Paul) *Ely 8* **P** *D&C Westmr* **P-in-c** J E ARMSTRONG
BASSINGHAM (St Michael and All Angels) *Linc 18* **P** *CCC Ox* **R** M J N HOWES, **NSM** J R D SCARBOROUGH
BASSINGTHORPE (St Thomas a Becket) *see* Ingoldsby *Linc*
BASTON (St John the Baptist) *see* Ness Gp *Linc*
BASWICH or Berkswich (Holy Trinity) *Lich 10* **P** *Bp* **V** M V ROBERTS, **C** P H MYERS
BATCOMBE (Blessed Virgin Mary) *see* Bruton and Distr *B & W*
BATCOMBE (St Mary) *see* Yetminster w Ryme Intrinseca and High Stoy *Sarum*
BATH Abbey (St Peter and St Paul) w St James *B & W 9* **P** *Simeon's Trustees* **R** R G ASKEW, **C** C R M ROBERTS, N M COULTHARD
BATH Bathwick (St John the Baptist) (Blessed Virgin Mary) *B & W 9* **P** *Bp* **R** D J PROTHERO, **C** L A PINFIELD
BATH (Christ Church) Proprietary Chapel *B & W 11* **P** *R Walcot* **NSM** C R BURROWS
BATH (Holy Trinity) *B & W 9* **P** *SMF* **R** G OAKES
BATH Odd Down (St Philip and St James) w Combe Hay *B & W 9* **P** *Simeon's Trustees* **V** A BAIN, **NSM** T D H CATCHPOOL, M JOYCE
BATH (St Barnabas) w Englishcombe *B & W 9* **P** *Bp* **V** R ATTLEY
BATH (St Bartholomew) *B & W 9* **P** *Simeon's Trustees* **V** I R LEWIS
BATH (St Luke) *B & W 9* **P** *Simeon's Trustees* **V** D F PERRYMAN, **C** A J SYMONDS
BATH St Mary Magdalene Holloway (Extra-parochial Chapelry) *B & W 11* **P** *Bath Municipal Charities for Ld Chan,* W G BURMAN
BATH (St Michael) w St Paul *B & W 9* **P** *CPAS* **R** M C LLOYD WILLIAMS
BATH (St Saviour) w Swainswick and Woolley *B & W 9* **P** *Ch Patr Trust and Or Coll Ox (jt)* **R** P J SOURBUT, **C** T M STAPLES, **Hon C** D L JOHN, **NSM** N J L PEARCE
BATH (St Stephen) *see* Charlcombe w Bath St Steph *B & W*
BATH Twerton-on-Avon (Ascension) (St Michael) *B & W 9* **P** *Patr Bd* **TR** K L SHILL, **TV** G I WILTON, **C** R T MORGAN, **NSM** G L WILTON
BATH Walcot (St Andrew) (St Swithin) *B & W 9* **P** *Simeon's Trustees* **R** H KOPSCH
BATH Weston (All Saints) w North Stoke and Langridge *B & W 9* **P** *Ld Chan* **R** P J WHITWORTH, **C** J A J SOPER
BATH Weston (St John the Evangelist) (Emmanuel) w Kelston *B & W 9* **P** *Ld Chan* **R** C D G PATTERSON, **C** T STOREY
BATH Widcombe (St Matthew) (St Thomas a Becket) *B & W 9* **P** *Simeon's Trustees* **V** R A RUSSELL, **NSM** P J BETTS
BATHAMPTON (St Nicholas) w Claverton *B & W 9* **P** *D&C Bris and Personal Reps R L D Skrine Esq (jt)* **R** P BURDEN
BATHEALTON (St Bartholomew) *see* Wellington and Distr *B & W*
BATHEASTON (St John the Baptist) (St Catherine) *B & W 9* **P** *Ch Ch Ox* **V** J W B PERRY
BATHFORD (St Swithun) *B & W 9* **P** *D&C Bris* **V** M J TURNER
BATLEY (All Saints) *Wakef 10* **P** *E C S J G Brudenell Esq and Trustees D Stubley Esq (jt)* **V** K WILLIAMS
BATLEY (St Thomas) *Wakef 10* **P** *V Batley* **V** *Vacant* (01924) 473901
BATLEY CARR (Holy Trinity) *see* Dewsbury *Wakef*
BATSFORD (St Mary) *see* Moreton-in-Marsh w Batsford, Todenham etc *Glouc*
BATTERSEA (Christ Church and St Stephen) *S'wark 15* **P** *Bp and V Battersea St Mary (alt)* **V** P CLARK, **C** B J WALLIS
BATTERSEA (St Luke) *S'wark 15* **P** *Bp* **Hon C** J A BAKER, **NSM** J DEVERILL
BATTERSEA (St Mary) *S'wark 15* **P** *Earl Spencer* **C** T J GADEN
BATTERSEA (St Michael) Wandsworth Common *S'wark 15* **P** *V Battersea St Mary* **V** A C HORTON
BATTERSEA (St Peter) (St Paul) *S'wark 15* **P** *V Battersea St Mary* **V** M A WIMSHURST
BATTERSEA (St Philip w St Bartholomew) *S'wark 15* **P** *Bp* **V** I R FORSTER
BATTERSEA FIELDS (St Saviour) (All Saints) *S'wark 15* **P** *Bp, CPAS, and Ch Patr Trust (jt)* **V** G M VEVERS, **C** A BAKER, A J GADD, **Hon C** I G SMITH-CAMERON
BATTERSEA PARK (All Saints) *see* Battersea Fields *S'wark*
BATTERSEA PARK (St Saviour) *as above*
BATTERSEA RISE (St Mark) *S'wark 15* **P** *V Battersea St Mary* **V** P J S PERKIN, **C** A J BAUGHEN
BATTISFORD (St Mary) *see* Ringshall w Battisford, Barking w Darmsden etc *St E*
BATTLE (Church of the Ascension) (St Mary the Virgin) *Chich 14* **P** *The Crown* **V** W A V CUMMINGS
BATTLE HILL (Good Shepherd) *see* Willington Team *Newc*
BATTLESDEN (St Peter and All Saints) *see* Woburn w Eversholt, Milton Bryan, Battlesden etc *St Alb*

BATTYEFORD (Christ the King) *Wakef 10* **P** *V Mirfield* **V** D B FOSS, **Hon C** R E WHITNALL, **NSM** M WOOD
BAUGHURST (St Stephen) and Ramsdell and Wolverton w Ewhurst and Hannington *Win 4* **P** *Ld Chan, Duke of Wellington, and Bp (by turn)* **R** A E BARTON
BAULKING (St Nicholas) *see* Uffington, Shellingford, Woolstone and Baulking *Ox*
BAUMBER (St Swithin) *see* Hemingby *Linc*
BAUNTON (St Mary Magdalene) *see* Stratton, N Cerney, Baunton and Bagendon *Glouc*
BAVERSTOCK (St Editha) *see* Barford St Martin, Dinton, Baverstock etc *Sarum*
BAWBURGH (St Mary and St Walstan) *see* Cringleford w Colney and Bawburgh *Nor*
BAWDESWELL (All Saints) *see* Lyng, Sparham, Elsing, Bylaugh, Bawdeswell etc *Nor*
BAWDRIP (St Michael and All Angels) *see* Woolavington w Cossington and Bawdrip *B & W*
BAWDSEY (St Mary) *see* Alderton w Ramsholt and Bawdsey *St E*
BAWTRY (St Nicholas) w Austerfield and Misson *S'well 1* **P** *Bp* **V** J N GREEN, **Hon C** P E SARGAN
BAXENDEN (St John) *Blackb 1* **P** *Bp* **V** M C IRELAND
BAXTERGATE (St Ninian) *see* Whitby *York*
BAXTERLEY (not known) w Hurley and Wood End and Merevale w Bentley *Birm 11* **P** *Ld Chan (1 turn), Bp and Sir William Dugdale Bt (1 turn)* **R** D R CARRIVICK, **NSM** J M FATHERS
BAYDON (St Nicholas) *see* Whitton *Sarum*
BAYFORD (Mission Room) *see* Charlton Musgrove, Cucklington and Stoke Trister *B & W*
BAYFORD (St Mary) *see* Lt Berkhamsted and Bayford, Essendon etc *St Alb*
BAYLHAM (St Peter) *see* Gt and Lt Blakenham w Baylham and Nettlestead *St E*
BAYSTON HILL (Christ Church) *Lich 21* **P** *V Shrewsbury H Trin w St Julian* **V** G C GRIFFITHS, **Hon C** M H TUPPER
BAYSWATER (St Matthew) *Lon 2* **P** *Exors Dame Jewell Magnus-Allcroft* **V** G M EVANS
BAYTON (St Bartholomew) *see* Mamble w Bayton, Rock w Heightington etc *Worc*
BEACHAMPTON (Assumption of the Blessed Virgin Mary) *see* Buckingham *Ox*
BEACHAMWELL (St Mary) *see* Barton Bendish w Beachamwell and Shingham *Ely*
BEACHLEY (St John the Evangelist) *see* Tidenham w Beachley and Lancaut *Glouc*
BEACONSFIELD (St Mary and All Saints) (St Michael and All Angels) *Ox 20* **P** *Patr Bd* **TR** J P B WYNBURNE, **TV** H EDEN, R A CADDELL, **NSM** W T EVANS, R A JOHNSON, G R ANDERSON, A M CAW
BEADLAM (St Hilda) *see* Kirkdale *York*
BEADNELL (St Ebba) *see* Bamburgh and Beadnell *Newc*
BEAFORD (All Saints) *see* Newton Tracey, Horwood, Alverdiscott etc *Ex*
BEALINGS, GREAT (St Mary) and LITTLE (All Saints) w Playford and Culpho *St E 7* **P** *Lord Cranworth (1 turn), Bp (3 turns)* **Dn-in-c** C M EVERETT
BEAMINSTER AREA (St Mary of the Annunciation) *Sarum 3* **P** *Patr Bd* **TR** T M F BILES, **TV** R LEGG, D J TIZZARD
BEAMISH (St Andrew) *see* Stanley *Dur*
BEARD (St James the Less) *see* New Mills *Derby*
BEARLEY (St Mary the Virgin) *see* Snitterfield w Bearley *Cov*
BEARPARK (St Edmund) and Ushaw Moor *Dur 1* **P** *D&C and Bp (alt)* **TR** L G BARRON
BEARSTED (Holy Cross) w Thurnham *Cant 15* **P** *Abp* **V** G H SIDAWAY, **C** P J HESKETH
BEARWOOD (St Catherine) *Ox 16* **P** *Bp* **R** H D ETCHES
BEARWOOD (St Mary the Virgin) *Birm 7* **P** *V Smethwick* **V** A H PERRY
BEAUCHAMP RODING (St Botolph) *see* Leaden Roding and Abbess Roding etc *Chelmsf*
BEAUDESERT (St Nicholas) and Henley-in-Arden w Ullenhall *Cov 7* **P** *MMCET, Bp, and High Bailiff of Henley-in-Arden (jt)* **R** J F GANJAVI
BEAULIEU (Blessed Virgin and Holy Child) and Exbury and East Boldre *Win 10* **P** *Bp and Lord Montagu of Beaulieu (jt)* **V** D T P ABERNETHY, **Hon C** E M SINGLETON
BEAUMONT CUM MOZE (St Leonard and St Mary) *see* Tendring and Lt Bentley w Beaumont cum Moze *Chelmsf*
BEAUMONT LEYS (Christ the King) *Leic 2* **P** *Bp* **V** C R OXLEY, **C** P J OXLEY, **NSM** M A TAYLOR
BEAUWORTH (St James) *see* Cheriton w Tichborne and Beauworth *Win*
BEAUXFIELD (St Peter) *see* Whitfield w Guston *Cant*
BEAWORTHY (St Alban) *see* Ashwater, Halwill, Beaworthy, Clawton etc *Ex*
BEBINGTON (St Andrew) *Ches 8* **P** *Ch Soc Trust* **R** S L JAMES, **C** G J COUSINS, P M FROGGATT
BEBINGTON, HIGHER (Christ Church) *Ches 8* **P** *C J C Saunders-Griffiths Esq* **V** N P CHRISTENSEN, **C** G D MASSEY, **Hon C** R RAWLINSON
BECCLES (St Michael the Archangel) (St Luke's Church Centre) *St E 14* **P** *Patr Bd* **TR** A H R THOMAS
BECK ROW (St John) *see* Mildenhall *St E*
BECKBURY (St Milburga), Badger, Kemberton, Ryton, Stockton and Sutton Maddock *Lich 20* **P** *Lord Hamilton of Dalzell, Or Coll Ox, and MMCET (2 turns), Ld Chan (1 turn)* **R** D F CHANTREY, **NSM** A W BRYANT
BECKENHAM (Christ Church) *Roch 13* **P** *Ch Trust Fund Trust* **V** N W WYNNE-JONES, **C** S M C DOWDY, **Hon C** J T ANSCOMBE, **Dss** G M N RAIKES
BECKENHAM (Holy Trinity) *see* Penge Lane H Trin *Roch*
BECKENHAM (St Barnabas) *Roch 13* **P** *Keble Coll Ox* **V** P MARR
BECKENHAM (St George) *Roch 13* **P** *Bp* **R** D G E CARPENTER, **C** R M DAY, S E McCARTHY
BECKENHAM (St James) Elmers End *Roch 13* **P** *Bp* **V** L C STAPLETON
BECKENHAM (St John the Baptist) Eden Park *Roch 13* **P** *Ch Trust Fund Trust, Bp and Adn Bromley (jt)* **V** M L JEFFERIES, **C** P J AVANN
BECKENHAM (St Michael and All Angels) w St Augustine *Roch 13* **P** *SMF and Bp (jt)* **V** R S FAYERS
BECKENHAM, NEW (St Paul) *Roch 13* **P** *Bp* **V** J FROST
BECKERMET (St Bridget) (St Bridget Old Church) (St John) w Ponsonby *Carl 5* **P** *Bp, Adn W Cumberland, P Stanley Esq, and PCCs of Beckermet St Jo and St Bridget (jt)* **V** P EVANS
BECKFORD (St John the Baptist) *see* Overbury w Teddington, Alstone etc *Worc*
BECKHAM, WEST (St Helen and All Saints) *see* Weybourne Gp *Nor*
BECKINGHAM (All Saints) *see* Brant Broughton and Beckingham *Linc*
BECKINGHAM (All Saints) w Walkeringham *S'well 1* **P** *Bp and Ld Chan (alt)* **V** D HOLLIS
BECKINGTON (St George) w Standerwick, Berkley, Rodden, Lullington and Orchardleigh *B & W 4* **P** *Bp (3 turns), Ch Soc Trust (1 turn), and Exors A Duckworth Esq* **R** A F HOGARTH
BECKLEY (All Saints) and Peasmarsh *Chich 20* **P** *Univ Coll Ox and SS Coll Cam (alt)* **R** C F HOPKINS
BECKLEY (Assumption of the Blessed Virgin Mary) *see* Wheatley *Ox*
BECKTON (St Mark) *Chelmsf 3* **P** *Bp* **V** R J SHIRRAS
BECKWITHSHAW (St Michael and All Angels) *see* Pannal w Beckwithshaw *Ripon*
BECONTREE (St Elisabeth) *Chelmsf 1* **P** *Bp* **P-in-c** N JOHN
BECONTREE (St George) *see* Dagenham *Chelmsf*
BECONTREE (St Mary) *Chelmsf 1* **P** *CPAS* **V** R HERBERT, **C** H R F MARTIN, A NEWTON
BECONTREE SOUTH (St Alban) (St John the Divine) (St Martin) *Chelmsf 1* **P** *Patr Bd* **TR** P HAWORTH, **NSM** V D DRURY, R G GIBBS
BECONTREE WEST (St Cedd) (St Thomas) *Chelmsf 1* **P** *DBP* **TV** D P RITCHIE
BEDALE (St Gregory) *Ripon 4* **P** *Sir Henry Beresford-Peirce Bt* **R** M D EMMEL, **C** D P RYAN, **NSM** A L WOODHOUSE
BEDDINGHAM (St Andrew) *see* Glynde, W Firle and Beddingham *Chich*
BEDDINGTON (St Francis' Church Hall) *see* S Beddington St Mich *S'wark*
BEDDINGTON (St Mary) *S'wark 24* **P** *K Bond Esq* **R** L S TILLETT
BEDDINGTON, SOUTH (St Michael and All Angels) *S'wark 24* **P** *Bp* **V** *Vacant* 0181-647 1201
BEDFIELD (St Nicholas) *see* Worlingworth, Southolt, Tannington, Bedfield etc *St E*
BEDFONT, EAST (St Mary the Virgin) *Lon 11* **P** *Ld Chan* **V** P G HUTTON
BEDFORD (All Saints) *St Alb 10* **P** *Bp* **V** N J ELDER, **C** P M WISE
BEDFORD (Christ Church) *St Alb 10* **P** *Bp* **V** D R HARRIS, **C** N C STYLES
BEDFORD (St Andrew) *St Alb 10* **P** *Ld Chan* **V** C M DENT
BEDFORD (St John the Baptist) (St Leonard) *St Alb 10* **P** *MMCET* **R** M J PARKER, **C** M C NEWBON, **NSM** E M HOUGHTON
BEDFORD (St Mark) *St Alb 10* **P** *Bp* **V** C ROYDEN
BEDFORD (St Martin) *St Alb 10* **P** *Bp* **V** M P R LINSKILL
BEDFORD (St Michael and All Angels) *St Alb 10* **P** *Bp* **P-in-c** S J MANLEY-COOPER
BEDFORD (St Paul) *St Alb 10* **P** *Bp* **V** C P COLLINGWOOD, **C** P SHAYLER-WEBB, **NSM** M H BULL

BEDFORD (St Peter de Merton) w St Cuthbert *St Alb 10* **P** *Ld Chan* **R** G E W BUCKLER
BEDFORD LEIGH (St Thomas) (All Saints' Mission) *Man 13* **P** *V Leigh St Mary* **V** J WISEMAN, **C** A C BEDELL
BEDFORD PARK (St Michael and All Angels) *Lon 11* **P** *Bp* **V** K J MORRIS, **C** G I SWENSSON
BEDGROVE (Holy Spirit) *Ox 21* **P** *DBP* **V** W F MASON
BEDHAMPTON (St Nicholas's Mission Church) (St Thomas) *Portsm 4* **P** *Bp* **R** D P LITTLE
BEDINGFIELD (St Mary) *St E 16* **P** *MMCET* **R** *Vacant*
BEDINGHAM (St Andrew) *see* Hempnall *Nor*
BEDLINGTON (St Cuthbert) *Newc 1* **P** *D&C Dur* **V** M D J SAVAGE, **C** J J T THOMPSON
BEDMINSTER (St Aldhelm) (St Paul) *Bris 1* **P** *Bp* **TR** R V HEADING, **TV** G H SAUNDERS, D P LLOYD
BEDMINSTER (St Michael and All Angels) *Bris 1* **P** *Bp* **V** D S MOSS
BEDMINSTER DOWN (St Oswald) *see* Bishopsworth and Bedminster Down *Bris*
BEDMONT (Ascension) *see* Abbots Langley *St Alb*
BEDNALL (All Saints) *see* Penkridge Team *Lich*
BEDSTONE (St Mary) *see* Clungunford w Clunbury and Clunton, Bedstone etc *Heref*
BEDWORTH (All Saints) *Cov 5* **P** *Patr Bd* **TR** K I HOBBS, **TV** A V WEST, **Dss** P M HAMILTON
BEDWYN, GREAT (St Mary), Little Bedwyn and Savernake Forest *Sarum 21* **P** *Bp* **V** T SALISBURY
BEDWYN, LITTLE (St Michael) *see* Gt and Lt Bedwyn and Savernake Forest *Sarum*
BEECH (St Peter) *see* Alton St Lawr *Win*
BEECH, HIGH (Holy Innocents) *see* Waltham H Cross *Chelmsf*
BEECH HILL (St Mary the Virgin), Grazeley and Spencers Wood *Ox 15* **P** *Bp* **P-in-c** G O SHAW, **NSM** K P WIGGINS, A S HOLMES
BEECHDALE ESTATE (St Chad) *see* Blakenall Heath *Lich*
BEECHINGSTOKE (St Stephen) *see* Swanborough *Sarum*
BEEDING (St Peter) and Bramber w Botolphs *Chich 12* **P** *Bp* **R** D J WHITE
BEEDING, LOWER (Holy Trinity) (St John the Evangelist) *Chich 8* **P** *Bp* **P-in-c** S GALLAGHER
BEEDON (St Nicholas) and Peasemore w West Ilsley and Farnborough *Ox 14* **P** *Bp* **P-in-c** A L CRETNEY, **NSM** B D SIMS
BEEFORD (St Leonard) w Frodingham and Foston *York 12* **P** *Abp and Ch Soc Trust (jt)* **R** J D WAUD
BEELEY (St Anne) and Edensor *Derby 2* **P** *Duke of Devonshire* **P-in-c** M C GOWDEY
BEELSBY (St Andrew) *see* Ravendale Gp *Linc*
BEENHAM VALENCE (St Mary) *see* Woolhampton w Midgham and Beenham Valance *Ox*
BEER (St Michael) and Branscombe *Ex 5* **P** *Lord Clinton and D&C (jt)* **V** N H FREATHY
BEER HACKETT (St Michael) *see* Bradford Abbas and Thornford w Beer Hackett *Sarum*
BEERCROCOMBE (St James) *see* Hatch Beauchamp w Beercrocombe, Curry Mallet etc *B & W*
BEESANDS (St Andrew) *see* Stokenham w Sherford and Beesands, and Slapton *Ex*
BEESBY (St Andrew) *see* Saleby w Beesby and Maltby *Linc*
BEESTON (St Andrew) *see* Sprowston w Beeston *Nor*
BEESTON (St John the Baptist) *S'well 7* **P** *Duke of Devonshire* **V** S A LOWE
BEESTON (St Laurence) *see* Horning w Beeston St Laurence and Ashmanhaugh *Nor*
BEESTON (St Mary the Virgin) *Ripon 6* **P** *V Leeds St Pet* **V** P J BRINDLE, **C** R E HAYES
BEESTON HILL (Holy Spirit) *Ripon 6* **P** *V Leeds St Pet* **P-in-c** J P GUTTERIDGE
BEESTON NEXT MILEHAM (St Mary the Virgin) *see* Litcham w Kempston, E and W Lexham, Mileham etc *Nor*
BEESTON REGIS (All Saints) *Nor 21* **P** *Duchy of Lanc* **R** S H GILBERT
BEESTON RYLANDS (St Mary) *see* Beeston *S'well*
BEETHAM (St Michael and All Angels) *Carl 9* **P** *Bp* **P-in-c** P K BARBER
BEETLEY (St Mary) *see* Swanton Morley w Beetley w E Bilney and Hoe *Nor*
BEGBROKE (St Michael) *see* Yarnton w Begbroke and Shipton on Cherwell *Ox*
BEIGHTON (All Saints) *see* Freethorpe w Wickhampton, Halvergate etc *Nor*
BEIGHTON (St Mary the Virgin) *Sheff 1* **P** *Bp* **V** M J CAMERON
BEKESBOURNE (St Peter) *see* Patrixbourne w Bridge and Bekesbourne *Cant*
BELAUGH (St Peter) *see* Wroxham w Hoveton and Belaugh *Nor*
BELBROUGHTON (Holy Trinity) w Fairfield and Clent *Worc 12* **P** *Ld Chan and St Jo Coll Ox (alt)* **R** D SHARPLES
BELCHALWELL (St Aldheim) *see* Hazelbury Bryan and the Hillside Par *Sarum*
BELCHAMP (St Paul and St Andrew) *see* Belchamp Otten w Belchamp Walter and Bulmer etc *Chelmsf*
BELCHAMP OTTEN (St Ethelbert and All Saints) w Belchamp Walter and Bulmer w Belchamp St Paul and Ovington *Chelmsf 19* **P** *DBP, D&C Windsor, M M J Raymond Esq, and Trustees of the late Miss W M N Brett (jt)* **R** *Vacant* (01787) 277210
BELCHAMP WALTER (St Mary the Virgin) *see* Belchamp Otten w Belchamp Walter and Bulmer etc *Chelmsf*
BELCHFORD (St Peter and St Paul) *Linc 11* **P** *Ld Chan* **R** *Vacant*
BELFIELD (St Ann) *Man 20* **P** *Bp* **V** D K BARNES
BELFORD (St Mary) and Lucker *Newc 10* **P** *V Bamburgh and Beadnell and Bp (alt)* **V** A J HUGHES
BELGRAVE (St Gabriel) *see* Leic Resurr *Leic*
BELGRAVE (St Michael and All Angels) *as above*
BELGRAVE (St Paul) *see* Wilnecote *Lich*
BELGRAVE (St Peter) *see* Leic Resurr *Leic*
BELHUS PARK (All Saints) *Chelmsf 14* **P** *Bp* **P-in-c** R W SPRINGETT, **C** D J PALMER
BELLE GREEN (Mission) *see* Ince Ch Ch *Liv*
BELLE ISLE (St John and St Barnabas) *see* Leeds Belle Is St Jo and St Barn *Ripon*
BELLEAU (St John the Baptist) *see* Wold-Marsh Gp *Linc*
BELLERBY (St John) *see* Leyburn w Bellerby *Ripon*
BELLFIELD (St Mark) *see* Sutton St Jas and Wawne *York*
BELLINGDON (St John the Evangelist) *see* Gt Chesham *Ox*
BELLINGHAM (St Cuthbert) *see* N Tyne and Redesdale Team *Newc*
BELLINGHAM (St Dunstan) *S'wark 4* **P** *Bp* **V** P D BUTLER, **Hon C** J R W ACKLAND
BELMONT (St Anselm) *Lon 23* **P** *Bp* **V** W M DAVIES, **C** G CLARKE
BELMONT (St John) *S'wark 24* **P** *R Cheam* **V** E C PROBERT, **C** S H L CAWDELL
BELMONT (St Mary Magdalene) *Dur 1* **P** *The Crown* **V** J W ELLIOTT
BELMONT (St Peter) *Man 16* **P** *V Bolton-le-Moors St Pet* **P-in-c** D J BRIERLEY, **NSM** D R JONES
BELPER (Christ Church) (St Faith's Mission Church) and Milford *Derby 11* **P** *Bp* **P-in-c** D PERKINS
BELPER (St Peter) *Derby 11* **P** *V Duffield* **V** D M WHITE, **C** L M PLAYER, M G W HAYES, **NSM** S M BAILEY
BELSIZE PARK (St Peter) *Lon 16* **P** *D&C Westmr* **V** J P F HARRIS
BELSTEAD (St Mary the Virgin) *see* Copdock w Washbrook and Belstead *St E*
BELSTONE (St Mary) *see* S Tawton and Belstone *Ex*
BELTINGHAM (St Cuthbert) *see* Haydon Bridge and Beltingham w Henshaw *Newc*
BELTON (All Saints) and Burgh Castle *Nor 6* **P** *Bp and Ld Chan (alt)* **R** J J QUINN
BELTON in the Isle of Axholme (All Saints) *Linc 1* **P** *Bp* **V** *Vacant* (01427) 872207
BELTON (St John the Baptist) *see* Hathern, Long Whatton and Diseworth w Belton etc *Leic*
BELTON (St Peter) *see* Uppingham w Ayston and Wardley w Belton *Pet*
BELTON (St Peter and St Paul) *see* Barkston and Hough Gp *Linc*
BELVEDERE (All Saints) *Roch 15* **P** *DBP* **V** I SHAW
BELVEDERE (St Augustine) *Roch 15* **P** *Bp* **V** P ROYSTON-BALL
BEMBRIDGE (Holy Trinity) (St Luke's Mission Church) *Portsm 7* **P** *V Brading* **V** A P MENNISS
BEMERTON (St Andrew) (St John the Evangelist) (St Michael and All Angels) *Sarum 15* **P** *Prime Min (2 turns) and Bp (1 turn)* **P-in-c** A R ARCHER, **C** P D NEWTON, **NSM** P CURZEN, D E WOODS
BEMPTON (St Michael) w Flamborough, Reighton w Speeton *York 10* **P** *Patr Bd* **V** J JORDAN
BEN RHYDDING (St John the Evangelist) *Bradf 4* **P** *V Ilkey* **V** B GREGORY
BENCHILL (St Luke) *Man 8* **P** *Bp* **V** D T THOMAS, **C** C MacLAREN
BENEFIELD (St Mary the Virgin) and Southwick w Glapthorn *Pet 12* **P** *Mrs G S Watts-Russell and G C Capron Esq (alt)* **R** *Vacant* (01832) 274026
BENENDEN (St George and St Margaret) *Cant 11* **P** *Abp* **V** C F SMITH, **NSM** J T M DESROSIERS
BENFIELDSIDE (St Cuthbert) *Dur 4* **P** *Bp* **V** M JACKSON, **C** A J HUTCHINSON
BENFLEET, SOUTH (St Mary the Virgin) *Chelmsf 10* **P** *D&C Westmr* **V** M E GALLOWAY

BENGEO (Holy Trinity) (St Leonard) and Christ Church *St Alb 22* **P** *R M A Smith Esq* **R** I PEARSON
BENGEWORTH (St Peter) *Worc 1* **P** *Bp* **V** *Vacant* (01386) 446164
BENHALL (St Mary) *see* Sternfield w Benhall and Snape *St E*
BENHILTON (All Saints) *S'wark 24* **P** *Bp* **V** M A J OADES
BENINGTON (All Saints) w Leverton *Linc 20* **P** *Ld Chan* **R** K M TOMLIN
BENINGTON (St Peter) w Walkern *St Alb 23* **P** *Trustees Ripon Coll Ox and K Coll Cam (alt), and Bp* **P-in-c** J N PRICE
BENNIWORTH (St Julian) *see* Asterby Gp *Linc*
BENSHAM (St Chad) *Dur 12* **P** *Bp* **TR** C J WREN, **TV** R A COLLINS, **C** K A WREN
BENSINGTON (St Helen) *see* Benson *Ox*
BENSON (St Helen) *Ox 1* **P** *Ch Ch Ox* **V** A R HAWKEN
BENTHALL (St Bartholomew) *see* Broseley w Benthall, Jackfield, Linley etc *Heref*
BENTHAM (St John the Baptist) *Bradf 6* **P** *Bp* **P-in-c** M J BAMFORTH
BENTHAM (St Margaret) *Bradf 6* **P** *Bp* **V** J M BEARPARK
BENTILEE (St Stephen) *see* Bucknall and Bagnall *Lich*
BENTLEY (Emmanuel) *Lich 29* **P** *Bp, Mrs H G Jenkins, and A D Owen Esq (jt)* **V** N J CARTER
BENTLEY (St Mary) and Binsted *Win 2* **P** *Adn Surrey and D&C (jt)* **R** J M CAMPBELL
BENTLEY (St Mary) w Tattingstone *St E 5* **P** *Bp and DBP (alt)* **P-in-c** A S JONES, J P DRUCE
BENTLEY (St Peter) *Sheff 8* **P** *Bp* **V** R A FITZHARRIS
BENTLEY (St Peter) *see* Rowley w Skidby *York*
BENTLEY, GREAT (St Mary the Virgin) and Frating w Thorrington *Chelmsf 23* **P** *St Jo Coll Cam and Bp (alt)* **R** W B METCALFE
BENTLEY, LITTLE (St Mary) *see* Tendring and Lt Bentley w Beaumont cum Moze *Chelmsf*
BENTLEY, LOWER (St Mary) *see* Tardebigge *Worc*
BENTLEY, NEW (St Philip and St James) *Sheff 8* **P** *Bp* **V** S P DICKINSON
BENTLEY COMMON (St Paul) *Chelmsf 7* **P** *Bp* **P-in-c** R A L ROSE
BENTLEY HEATH (St James) *see* Dorridge *Birm*
BENTWORTH (St Mary) and Shalden and Lasham *Win 2* **P** *J L Jervoise Esq* **R** J C R WEBB
BENWELL Team, The (St James) (St John) (Venerable Bede) *Newc 7* **P** *Bp* **TR** R D TAYLOR, **TV** A P RUGG, P WATSON
BEOLEY (St Leonard) (St Andrew's Church Centre) *Worc 7* **P** *Patr Bd* **V** D ROGERS, **C** G DEW
BEPTON (St Mary) *see* Cocking, Bepton and W Lavington *Chich*
BERDEN (St Nicholas) *see* Manuden w Berden *Chelmsf*
BERE ALSTON (Holy Trinity) *see* Bere Ferrers *Ex*
BERE FERRERS (St Andrew) *Ex 24* **P** *DBP* **R** N C LAW
BERE REGIS (St John the Baptist) and Affpuddle w Turnerspuddle *Sarum 7* **P** *Ball Coll Ox (2 turns), Bp (1 turn)* **R** G H ROBLIN
BERECHURCH (St Margaret w St Michael) *Chelmsf 16* **P** *Bp* **V** R I WILKINSON
BERGH APTON (St Peter and St Paul) *see* Thurton *Nor*
BERGHOLT, EAST (St Mary the Virgin) *St E 5* **P** *Em Coll Cam* **R** J P DRUCE
BERGHOLT, WEST (St Mary the Virgin) *Chelmsf 17* **P** *Bp* **R** W C FREWIN
BERINSFIELD (St Mary and St Berin) *see* Dorchester *Ox*
BERKELEY (St Mary the Virgin) w Wick, Breadstone and Newport *Glouc 2* **P** *R J G Berkeley Esq and Sir Hugo Huntington-Whiteley (jt)* **V** S G RICHARDS, **NSM** R P CHIDLAW
BERKHAMSTED (St Mary) *St Alb 2* **P** *Duchy of Cornwall* **R** P W HART
BERKHAMSTED, GREAT (All Saints) (St Peter) *St Alb 2* **P** *Bp* **R** M P J BONNEY, **C** R A R FIGG, **NSM** J MACPHERSON
BERKHAMSTED, LITTLE (St Andrew) and Bayford, Essendon and Ponsbourne *St Alb 22* **P** *Marquess of Salisbury (2 turns), CPAS (1 turn), and Bp (1 turn)* **P-in-c** P M HIGHAM
BERKHAMSYTCH (St Mary and St John) *see* Ipstones w Berkhamsytch and Onecote w Bradnop *Lich*
BERKLEY (Blessed Virgin Mary) *see* Beckington w Standerwick, Berkley, Rodden etc *B & W*
BERKSWELL (St John the Baptist) *Cov 4* **P** *Trustees Col C J H Wheatley* **R** G BAISLEY, **Hon C** B P BAISLEY
BERKSWICH (Holy Trinity) *see* Baswich *Lich*
BERMONDSEY (St Anne) *S'wark 6* **P** *Bp and F W Smith Esq (alt)* **V** S L WILMOT
BERMONDSEY (St Crispin w Christ Church) *S'wark 6* **P** *Hyndman Trustees* **V** P GRAY
BERMONDSEY (St Hugh) Charterhouse Mission Conventional District *S'wark 5 Vacant*
BERMONDSEY (St James w Christ Church) *S'wark 6* **P** *The Crown, Bp, and R Bermondsey St Mary (by turn)* **V** S L WILMOT, **C** I J DAVOLL, R D BAINBRIDGE
BERMONDSEY (St Katharine) w St Bartholomew *S'wark 6* **P** *Bp and R Rotherhithe St Mary w All SS (jt)* **V** T HOPPERTON
BERMONDSEY (St Mary Magdalen w St Olave, St John and St Luke) *S'wark 6* **P** *Ch Patr Soc (2 turns), Ld Chan (1 turn), and Bp (1 turn)* **R** J A BRADSHAW, **C** M TRASK
BERNEY, GREAT (St John) *see* Langdon Hills *Chelmsf*
BERRICK SALOME (St Helen) *see* Chalgrove w Berrick Salome *Ox*
BERRINGTON (All Saints) and Betton Strange *Heref 11* **P** *DBP* **R** *Vacant* (0174375) 214
BERROW (Blessed Virgin Mary) and Breane *B & W 1* **P** *Adn Wells* **R** S LOW
BERROW (St Faith) w Pendock, Eldersfield, Hollybush and Birtsmorton *Worc 5* **P** *Bp, D&C, and Sir Berwick Lechmere Bt (jt)* **R** J R PARKINSON
BERRY POMEROY (St Mary) *see* Totnes, Bridgetown and Berry Pomeroy etc *Ex*
BERRYNARBOR (St Peter) *see* Combe Martin, Berrynarbor, Lynton, Brendon etc *Ex*
BERSTED, NORTH (Holy Cross) Conventional District *Chich 1 Vacant*
BERSTED, SOUTH (St Mary Magdalene) w NORTH (St Peter) *Chich 1* **P** *Abp* **P-in-c** D H THORNLEY
BERWICK (Holy Trinity) (St Mary) *Newc 12* **P** *Bp (2 turns), D&C Dur (1 turn)* **V** A HUGHES
BERWICK (St John) *see* Chalke Valley W *Sarum*
BERWICK (St Michael and All Angels) w Selmeston and Alciston *Chich 18* **P** *Miss I M Newson and Miss R Fitzherbert (1 turn), D&C (1 turn)* **R** P SMITH
BERWICK PARK (Good Shepherd) *see* Wood Green St Mich w Bounds Green St Gabr etc *Lon*
BERWICK ST JAMES (St James) *see* Lower Wylye and Till Valley *Sarum*
BESFORD (St Peter's Chapelry) *see* Defford w Besford *Worc*
BESSACARR, WEST (St Francis of Assisi) *Sheff 9* **P** *Bp* **V** A C GRIFFITHS
BESSELSLEIGH (St Lawrence) w Dry Sandford *Ox 10* **P** *Ox Ch Trust* **P-in-c** R G PENMAN
BESSINGBY (St Magnus) (St Mark) *York 10* **P** *Reps George Wright Esq* **V** T J DAVIDSON
BESSINGHAM (St Mary) *see* Roughton and Felbrigg, Metton, Sustead etc *Nor*
BESTHORPE (All Saints) *see* Attleborough w Besthorpe *Nor*
BESTHORPE (Holy Trinity) *see* Collingham w S Scarle and Besthorpe and Girton *S'well*
BESTWOOD (no dedication) (St Mark) (St Matthew on the Hill) (St Philip) (Emmanuel) *S'well 13* **P** *Patr Bd* **TR** S J GRIFFITHS, **TV** B A STARK, S LEES, N G SHAW, **C** K J HITCHMAN, **NSM** V I VIVIAN
BESTWOOD/RISE PARK Local Ecumenical Project *S'well 10 Vacant*
BESWICK (St Margaret) *see* Hutton Cranswick w Skerne, Watton and Beswick *York*
BETCHWORTH (St Michael and All Angels) *S'wark 26* **P** *D&C Windsor* **P-in-c** S J BAILEY
BETHERSDEN (St Margaret) w High Halden *Cant 11* **P** *Abp* **V** D W FLEWKER
BETHESDA (Shared Church) *see* Hallwood *Ches*
BETHNAL GREEN (St Barnabas) *Lon 7* **P** *D&C Cant* **P-in-c** J A WEBBER, **NSM** F M ROLLINSON
BETHNAL GREEN (St James the Less) *Lon 7* **P** *CPAS* **P-in-c** B S CASTLE, **Hon C** W C HARRAP
BETHNAL GREEN (St John) *see* St Jo on Bethnal Green *Lon*
BETHNAL GREEN (St Matthew w St James the Great) *Lon 7* **P** *Bp* **C** J SCOTT
BETHNAL GREEN (St Peter) (St Thomas) *Lon 7* **P** *City Corp* **V** J M V WEIR
BETLEY (St Margaret) and Keele *Lich 9* **P** *T G H Howard-Sneyd Esq and DBP (jt)* **V** J S WHITEHEAD, **NSM** T E BIDDINGTON
BETTESHANGER (St Mary the Virgin) *see* Eastry and Northbourne w Tilmanstone etc *Cant*
BETTISCOMBE (St Stephen) *see* Marshwood Vale TM *Sarum*
BETTON STRANGE (St Margaret) *see* Berrington and Betton Strange *Heref*
BETTWS-Y-CRWYN (St Mary) *see* Clun w Bettws-y-Crwyn and Newcastle *Heref*
BEVENDEAN (Holy Nativity) *see* Moulsecoomb *Chich*
BEVERLEY (St Mary) *York 9* **P** *Abp* **V** D W HOSKIN, **Hon C** H A HALL
BEVERLEY (St Nicholas) *York 9* **P** *Abp* **V** M L KAVANAGH, **C** L C MUNT
BEVERLEY MINSTER (St John and St Martin) *York 9* **P** *Simeon's Trustees* **C** G D C LANE, C B GARDNER

BEVERSTON (St Mary the Virgin) *see* Tetbury w Beverston *Glouc*
BEWBUSH (Community Centre) *see* Ifield *Chich*
BEWCASTLE (St Cuthbert), Stapleton and Kirklinton w Hethersgill *Carl 2* **P** *Bp, D&C, and DBP (jt)* **R** J R REPATH
BEWDLEY (St Anne) *see* Ribbesford w Bewdley and Dowles *Worc*
BEWERLEY GRANGE (Chapel) *see* Upper Nidderdale *Ripon*
BEWHOLME (St John the Baptist) *see* Sigglesthorne and Rise w Nunkeeling and Bewholme *York*
BEWICK, OLD (Holy Trinity) *see* Glendale Gp *Newc*
BEXHILL (All Saints) *see* Sidley *Chich*
BEXHILL (St Augustine) *Chich 14* **P** *Bp* **V** E F P BRYANT, **C** S R EARL
BEXHILL (St Barnabas) *Chich 14* **P** *Bp* **V** T M J VAN CARRAPIETT
BEXHILL (St Mark) *Chich 14* **P** *Bp* **R** J J W EDMONDSON, **Hon C** E V WHEELER
BEXHILL (St Peter) (St Michael) (Good Shepherd) (St Andrew) *Chich 14* **P** *Bp* **TR** J W COTTON, **C** N P CHATFIELD
BEXHILL (St Stephen) *Chich 14* **P** *Bp* **V** D R FROST
BEXLEY (St John the Evangelist) *Roch 17* **P** *The Crown* **V** J A PEAL, **NSM** J PEAL
BEXLEY (St Mary) *Roch 17* **P** *Bp* **V** D L KNIGHT, **Hon C** G ATFIELD
BEXLEYHEATH (Christ Church) *Roch 15* **P** *Bp* **V** M G GRIBBLE, **C** T M MASON
BEXLEYHEATH (St Peter) *Roch 15* **P** *Bp* **V** M H C LUMGAIR
BEXWELL (St Mary) *see* Downham Market w Bexwell *Ely*
BEYTON (All Saints) *see* Rougham, Beyton w Hessett and Rushbrooke *St E*
BIBURY (St Mary) w Winson and Barnsley *Glouc 13* **P** *Bp and W H Wykeham-Musgrave Esq (alt)* **P-in-c** G R MARTIN
BICESTER (St Edburg) w Bucknell, Caversfield and Launton *Ox 2* **P** *Patr Bd* **TV** J D NIXON, S P HALL
BICKENHILL (St Peter) *Birm 12* **P** *Birm Dioc Trustees* **P-in-c** A J EYLES
BICKER (St Swithin) and Wigtoft *Linc 21* **P** *Bp and D&C (alt)* **V** *Vacant* (01775) 820574
BICKERSHAW (St James and St Elizabeth) *Liv 14* **P** *Bp* **V** S A MATHER, **NSM** M E WEYMONT
BICKERSTAFFE Four Lane Ends (not known) *see* Bickerstaffe and Melling *Liv*
BICKERSTAFFE (Holy Trinity) and Melling *Liv 11* **P** *Lord Derby and R Halsall (jt)* **V** N K LEIPER
BICKERTON (Holy Trinity) w Bickley *Ches 5* **P** *DBP, Marchioness of Cholmondeley, Adn, and Bp (jt)* **P-in-c** D R BUCKLEY
BICKINGTON (St Andrew) *see* Fremington *Ex*
BICKINGTON (St Mary the Virgin) *see* Ashburton w Buckland in the Moor and Bickington *Ex*
BICKINGTON, HIGH (St Mary) *see* Newton Tracey, Horwood, Alverdiscott etc *Ex*
BICKLEIGH Roborough (St Mary the Virgin) and Shaugh Prior *Ex 20* **P** *Patr Bd* **TR** R J CARLTON, **C** R OLLIFF
BICKLEIGH (St Mary) *see* Silverton, Butterleigh, Bickleigh and Cadeleigh *Ex*
BICKLEIGH DOWN (School) *see* Bickleigh (Roborough) and Shaugh Prior *Ex*
BICKLEY (St George) *Roch 14* **P** *SMF* **V** D A S HERBERT
BICKLEY (St Wenefrede) *see* Bickerton w Bickley *Ches*
BICKNACRE (St Andrew) *see* Woodham Ferrers and Bicknacre *Chelmsf*
BICKNOLLER (St George) w Crowcombe and Sampford Brett *B & W 17* **P** *Bp and V Stogumber (jt)* **R** M D BOLE
BICKNOR (St James) *see* Bredgar w Bicknor and Frinsted w Wormshill etc *Cant*
BICTON (Holy Trinity), Montford w Shrawardine and Fitz *Lich 21* **P** *Earl of Powis, N E E Stephens Esq, and C J Wingfield Esq (jt)* **P-in-c** R W D BIDDLE, **C** R N REEVE
BICTON (St Mary) *see* E Budleigh w Bicton and Otterton *Ex*
BIDBOROUGH (St Lawrence) *Roch 11* **P** *Mabledon Trust* **R** M R HODGE
BIDDENDEN (All Saints) and Smarden *Cant 11* **P** *Abp* **R** *Vacant* (01580) 291454
BIDDENHAM (St James) *St Alb 10* **P** *Bp* **P-in-c** R J SUTTON, **NSM** D G MASON
BIDDESTONE (St Nicholas) w Slaughterford *Bris 9* **P** *Win Coll* **P-in-c** R V C LEWIS
BIDDISHAM (St John the Baptist) *see* Crook Peak *B & W*
BIDDLESDEN (St Margaret) *see* Westbury w Turweston, Shalstone and Biddlesden *Ox*
BIDDULPH (St Lawrence) *Lich 8* **P** *MMCET* **V** A J PIGGOTT, **C** N D GREW
BIDDULPH MOOR (Christ Church) *Lich 8* **P** *MMCET* **R** J McGUIRE
BIDEFORD (St Mary) (St Peter East the Water), Northam, Westward Ho!, Appledore, Weare Giffard, Littleham and Landcross *Ex 16* **P** *Patr Bd* **TV** G J HANSFORD, J T THOMPSON, T E JESSIMAN, J EWINGTON, **C** I W MACKENZIE
BIDFORD-ON-AVON (St Laurence) *Cov 7* **P** *Bp* **V** D A HALL
BIDSTON (St Oswald) *Ches 1* **P** *Bp* **V** S M MANSFIELD, **C** S CHESTERS
BIELBY (St Giles) *see* Seaton Ross Gp of Par *York*
BIERLEY (St John the Evangelist) *Bradf 2* **P** *DBP* **V** I R LANE, **C** T H C MEYRICK
BIERLEY, EAST (St Luke) *see* Birkenshaw w Hunsworth *Wakef*
BIERTON (St James the Great) *see* Aylesbury w Bierton and Hulcott *Ox*
BIGBURY (St Lawrence) *see* Modbury, Bigbury, Ringmore w Kingston etc *Ex*
BIGBY (All Saints) *see* N Wolds Gp *Linc*
BIGGIN (St Thomas) *see* Hartington, Biggin and Earl Sterndale *Derby*
BIGGIN HILL (St Mark) *Roch 14* **P** *Bp* **V** C W KITCHENER, **C** S D BURTON-JONES
BIGGLESWADE (St Andrew) *St Alb 11* **P** *Bp* **V** R F SIBSON, **C** N D BARNES
BIGHTON (All Saints) *see* Old Alresford and Bighton *Win*
BIGNOR (Holy Cross) *see* Barlavington, Burton w Coates, Sutton and Bignor *Chich*
BIGRIGG (St John) *see* Egremont and Haile *Carl*
BILBOROUGH (St John the Baptist) *S'well 14* **P** *Bp* **V** A S G HART, **C** E P BAILEY
BILBOROUGH (St Martin) w Strelley *S'well 14* **P** *SMF* **P-in-c** D J HOWARD
BILBROOK (Holy Cross) *see* Codsall *Lich*
BILBROUGH (St James) *see* Healaugh w Wighill, Bilbrough and Askham Richard *York*
BILDESTON (St Mary Magdalene) w Wattisham *St E 3* **P** *Abp, Bp, and CPAS (by turn)* **P-in-c** J NEWHAM
BILHAM *Sheff 12* **P** *Bp, Major W Warde-Aldam, W G A Warde-Norbury Esq, and Mrs S Grant-Dalton (jt)* **V** G K BOSTOCK
BILLERICAY (Christ Church) (Emmanuel) (St John the Divine) (St Mary Magdalen) and Little Burstead *Chelmsf 6* **P** *Bp* **TR** P D ASHTON, **TV** J E EATON, G T WAKEFIELD, **C** M J A HOWARD, **NSM** M L ASHTON
BILLESDON (St John the Baptist) and Skeffington *Leic 4* **P** *Bp* **V** D V OSBORNE
BILLESLEY COMMON (Holy Cross) *Birm 5* **P** *Bp* **P-in-c** G L HODKINSON
BILLING, GREAT (St Andrew) w LITTLE (All Saints) *Pet 4* **P** *BNC Ox and Bp (alt)* **R** K P ASHBY, **C** R P STOCKITT
BILLINGBOROUGH Group, The (St Andrew) *Linc 13* **P** *Prime Min (2 turns), Bp and St Jo Coll Dur (1 turn)* **V** C H WILSON
BILLINGE (St Aidan) *Liv 15* **P** *R Wigan* **V** D LYON
BILLINGFORD (St Leonard) *see* Scole, Brockdish, Billingford, Thorpe Abbots etc *Nor*
BILLINGFORD (St Peter) *see* N Elmham w Billingford and Worthing *Nor*
BILLINGHAM (St Aidan) (St Luke) *Dur 10* **P** *Patr Bd* **TV** T P PARKER, **C** N M EDWARDS
BILLINGHAM (St Cuthbert) *Dur 10* **P** *D&C* **V** R I SMITH
BILLINGHAM (St Mary Magdalene) *see* Wolviston *Dur*
BILLINGHAY (St Michael) *Linc 22* **P** *Sir Stephen Hastings* **P-in-c** P J GREEN
BILLINGSHURST (St Mary the Virgin) *Chich 8* **P** *Bp* **V** D C PAIN
BILLINGSLEY (St Mary) w Sidbury, Middleton Scriven, Chetton, Glazeley, Deuxhill and Chelmarsh *Heref 9* **P** *Bp and Woodard Schools (jt)* **R** *Vacant* (01746) 718625
BILLINGTON (St Michael and All Angels) *see* Leighton Buzzard w Eggington, Hockliffe etc *St Alb*
BILLOCKBY (All Saints) *see* Rollesby w Burgh w Billockby w Ashby w Oby etc *Nor*
BILLY MILL (St Aidan) *see* Cullercoats St Geo *Newc*
BILNEY, EAST (St Mary) *see* Swanton Morley w Beetley w E Bilney and Hoe *Nor*
BILSBORROW (St Hilda) *Blackb 10* **P** *V St Michael's-on-Wyre* **P-in-c** G A CROSSLEY
BILSBY (Holy Trinity) w Farlesthorpe *Linc 8* **P** *Bp* **V** A READER-MOORE
BILSDALE MIDCABLE (St John) *see* Upper Ryedale *York*
BILSDALE PRIORY (St Hilda) *see* Ingleby Greenhow w Bilsdale Priory, Kildale etc *York*
BILSINGTON (St Peter and St Paul) *see* Aldington w Bonnington and Bilsington *Cant*
BILSON (Mission Church) *see* Cinderford St Steph w Littledean *Glouc*

BILSTHORPE (St Margaret) *S'well 15* **P** *DBP* **R** H H WILCOX
BILSTON (St Leonard) (St Chad) (St Mary the Virgin) *Lich 29* **P** *Patr Bd* **TR** P J CHAPMAN, **TV** G E MORRIS, G WARREN, **C** I D HOUGHTON
BILTON (St John the Evangelist) and St Luke *Ripon 1* **P** *Bp* **V** A L GLASBY, **C** M GUBBINS, N D BEER, **NSM** K A FITZSIMONS
BILTON (St Mark) *Cov 6* **P** *N M Assheton Esq* **R** C S HARPER, **C** S P MOULT, **NSM** J E K MOULT
BILTON, NEW (St Oswald) *Cov 6* **P** *Dioc Trustees* **P-in-c** G J HARDWICK, **Hon C** S F HARDWICK
BILTON-IN-AINSTY (St Helen) *see* Tockwith and Bilton w Bickerton *York*
BILTON IN HOLDERNESS (St Peter) *York 13* **P** *Abp* **V** R J E MAJOR
BINBROOK Group, The (St Mary) *Linc 10* **P** *Ld Chan, DBP and M M Sleight Esq (alt)* **R** T J WALKER
BINCOMBE (Holy Trinity) w Broadwey, Upwey and Buckland Ripers *Sarum 5* **P** *G&C Coll Cam (2 turns), Miss M B F Frampton (1 turn), and Bp (1 turn)* **R** R A C SIMMONS, **NSM** P A JONES
BINEGAR (Holy Trinity) *see* Ashwick w Oakhill and Binegar *B & W*
BINFIELD (All Saints) (St Mark) *Ox 11* **P** *Ld Chan* **Hon C** G A WILLIS
BINGFIELD (St Mary) *see* St Oswald in Lee w Bingfield *Newc*
BINGHAM (St Mary and All Saints) *S'well 8* **P** *The Crown* **R** D L HARPER, **Hon C** J B DAVIS, **NSM** Y E GLASS
BINGLEY (All Saints) *Bradf 1* **P** *Bp* **TR** S P KELLY, **TV** P WILLOX
BINGLEY (Holy Trinity) *Bradf 1* **P** *Bp* **P-in-c** A J CLARKE
BINHAM (St Mary) *see* Stiffkey and Cockthorpe w Morston, Langham etc *Nor*
BINLEY (St Bartholomew) *Cov 1* **P** *Bp* **V** D J HOWARD, **C** T D BUCKLEY, G L PRINGLE
BINLEY WOODS Local Ecumenical Project *Cov 1* **Min** T D BUCKLEY
BINSEY (St Margaret) *see* Ox St Thos w St Frideswide and Binsey *Ox*
BINSTEAD (Holy Cross) *Portsm 7* **P** *Bp* **R** S M CHALONER
BINSTED (Holy Cross) *see* Bentley and Binsted *Win*
BINSTED (St Mary) *see* Walberton w Binsted *Chich*
BINTON (St Peter) *see* Temple Grafton w Binton *Cov*
BINTREE (St Swithin) *see* Twyford, Guist, Bintree, Themelthorpe etc *Nor*
BIRCH (St Agnes) w Longsight St John w St Cyprian *Man 3* **P** *Prime Min and Bp (alt)* **R** C D NEWELL, **C** M K J SMITH
BIRCH (St James) w Fallowfield *Man 4* **P** *Bp* **R** W G RAINES
BIRCH (St Mary) *see* Rhodes *Man*
BIRCH w Layer Breton and Layer Marney *Chelmsf 24* **P** *Col J G Round, N S Charrington Esq, and Bp (jt)* **R** *Vacant* (01206) 330241
BIRCHAM, GREAT (St Mary the Virgin) *see* Docking, The Birchams, Stanhoe and Sedgeford *Nor*
BIRCHAM NEWTON (All Saints) *as above*
BIRCHANGER (St Mary the Virgin) *see* Stansted Mountfitchet w Birchanger and Farnham *Chelmsf*
BIRCHENCLIFFE (St Philip the Apostle) *Wakef 5* **P** *V Lindley* **P-in-c** R E WHITEHOUSE
BIRCHES HEAD (St Matthew) *see* Hanley H Ev *Lich*
BIRCHFIELD (Holy Trinity) *Birm 3* **P** *Bp* **V** R W HUNT, **C** G R MENSINGH
BIRCHILLS, THE (St Andrew) *see* Walsall St Andr *Lich*
BIRCHIN COPPICE (St Peter) *see* Kidderminster St Jo and H Innocents *Worc*
BIRCHINGTON (All Saints) w Acol and Minnis Bay *Cant 9* **P** *Abp* **V** F R SMALE, **C** S D MANSFIELD
BIRCHMOOR (St John) *see* Polesworth *Birm*
BIRCHOVER (St Michael) *see* Youlgreave, Middleton, Stanton-in-Peak etc *Derby*
BIRCHWOOD (Mission Church) *see* Churchstanton, Buckland St Mary and Otterford *B & W*
BIRCHWOOD (St Luke) *Linc 15* **P** *Bp* **P-in-c** J B PAVEY, **C** A M PAVEY, M A J WARD
BIRCHWOOD (Transfiguration) *Liv 12* **P** *Bp, Adn, and R Warrington (jt)* **V** R C HARDCASTLE
BIRCLE (St John the Baptist) *Man 10* **P** *R Middleton St Leon* **V** A R BROCKBANK
BIRDBROOK (St Augustine) *see* Ridgewell w Ashen, Birdbrook and Sturmer *Chelmsf*
BIRDHAM (St James) *see* W Wittering and Birdham w Itchenor *Chich*
BIRDINGBURY (St Leonards) *see* Leamington Hastings and Birdingbury *Cov*
BIRDLIP (St Mary in Hamlet) *see* Brimpsfield w Birdlip, Syde, Daglingworth, etc *Glouc*
BIRDSALL (St Mary) *see* Settrington w N Grimston, Birdsall w Langton *York*
BIRKBY (St Peter) *see* Gt Smeaton w Appleton Wiske and Birkby etc *Ripon*
BIRKDALE Carr Lane (St Mary) *see* Birkdale St Jo *Liv*
BIRKDALE (St James) *Liv 9* **P** *Trustees* **V** J S BELLAMY, **NSM** I D DAWSON
BIRKDALE (St John) *Liv 9* **P** *Trustees* **V** *Vacant* (01704) 68318
BIRKDALE (St Peter) *Liv 9* **P** *Trustees* **V** M I STOCKLEY
BIRKENHEAD (Christ Church) *Ches 1* **P** *Bp* **V** D M WILSON
BIRKENHEAD (St James) w St Bede *Ches 1* **P** *Trustees* **V** S T PENDLEBURY, **C** D R NUGENT
BIRKENHEAD (St Winifred) Welsh Church *Ches 1 Vacant*
BIRKENHEAD PRIORY (Christ the King) *Ches 1* **P** *Bp, Simeon's Trustees, and Ch Patr Trust (jt)* **TR** D WALKER, **TV** T JORDAN, **NSM** S HUGHES
BIRKENSHAW (St Paul) w Hunsworth *Wakef 8* **P** *V Birstall* **V** I M GASKELL
BIRKIN (St Mary) *see* Haddlesey w Hambleton and Birkin *York*
BIRLEY (St Peter) *see* Canon Pyon w Kings Pyon and Birley *Heref*
BIRLING (All Saints), Addington, Ryarsh and Trottiscliffe *Roch 7* **P** *Bp* **R** G C M MILES, **NSM** B E HURD
BIRLING, LOWER (Christ Church) *see* Snodland All SS w Ch Ch *Roch*
BIRLINGHAM (St James the Great) *see* Pershore w Pinvin, Wick and Birlingham *Worc*
BIRMINGHAM *see* Univ of Cen England in Birm *Birm*
BIRMINGHAM (Bishop Latimer w All Saints) *Birm 1* **P** *St Martin's Trustees* **R** R F BASHFORD
BIRMINGHAM (St George) *Birm 1* **P** *St Martin's Trustees* **R** *Vacant* 0121-359 2000
BIRMINGHAM (St John the Evangelist) Ladywood *Birm 1* **P** *R Birm St Martin w Bordesley* **V** R J TETLOW, **C** J M MASON
BIRMINGHAM (St Luke) *Birm 1* **P** *Trustees* **V** A G LENOX-CONYNGHAM, **C** E A JOHNSEN
BIRMINGHAM (St Martin) w Bordesley St Andrew *Birm 1* **P** *St Martin's Trustees* **R** A NEWMAN, **C** S J M VETTERS, E C CLINES, J M S CLINES
BIRMINGHAM (St Paul) *Birm 1* **P** *St Martin's Trustees* **V** D L CLARINGBULL
BIRMINGHAM (St Peter) *Birm 1* **P** *Bp* **V** C F MORTON
BIRSTALL (St James the Greater) and Wanlip *Leic 6* **P** *Bp and C A Palmer-Tomkinson Esq (jt)* **V** C A BRADSHAW, **C** H C BAKER
BIRSTALL (St Peter) *Wakef 8* **P** *Bp* **V** *Vacant* (01924) 473715
BIRSTWITH (St James) *Ripon 1* **P** *Miss S J Greenwood* **P-in-c** W A WILBY
BIRTLES (St Catherine) *Ches 13* **P** *Bp* **V** W F I WHINTON
BIRTLEY (St Giles) *see* Chollerton w Birtley and Thockrington *Newc*
BIRTLEY (St John the Evangelist) *Dur 11* **P** *R Chester-le-Street* **C** D M JOHNSON
BIRTSMORTON (St Peter and St Paul) *see* Berrow w Pendock, Eldersfield, Hollybush etc *Worc*
BIRWOOD (Mission church) *see* Churcham w Bulley and Minsterworth *Glouc*
BISBROOKE (St John the Baptist) *see* Morcott w Glaston and Bisbrooke *Pet*
BISCATHORPE (St Helen) *see* Asterby Gp *Linc*
BISCOT (Holy Trinity) *St Alb 14* **P** *Bp* **V** E E WEST
BISHAM (All Saints) *see* Gt Marlow w Marlow Bottom, Lt Marlow and Bisham *Ox*
BISHAMPTON (St James) *see* Abberton, The Flyfords, Naunton Beauchamp etc *Worc*
BISHOP AUCKLAND (St Andrew) (St Anne) *see* Auckland St Andr and St Anne *Dur*
BISHOP AUCKLAND (St Peter) *see* Auckland St Pet *Dur*
BISHOP AUCKLAND Woodhouse Close Area of Ecumenical Experiment (Conventional District) *Dur 10* **C-in-c** P SINCLAIR
BISHOP BURTON (All Saints) w Walkington *York 9* **P** *Abp and DBP (alt)* **R** D G KIRBY
BISHOP CAUNDLE (not known) *see* The Caundles w Folke and Holwell *Sarum*
BISHOP MIDDLEHAM (St Michael) *Dur 5* **P** *Ld Chan* **P-in-c** V SHEDDEN
BISHOP MONKTON (St John the Baptist) and Burton Leonard *Ripon 3* **P** *D&C* **V** *Vacant* (01765) 677372
BISHOP NORTON (St Peter), Waddingham and Snitterby *Linc 6* **P** *Bp and The Crown (alt)* **P-in-c** D J ATKINSON
BISHOP SUTTON (Holy Trinity) and Stanton Drew and Stowey *B & W 10* **P** *Bp and Adn Bath (alt)* **V** J HIGGINS
BISHOP THORNTON (St John the Evangelist) *see* Markington w S Stainley and Bishop Thornton *Ripon*

BISHOP WILTON (St Edith) w Full Sutton, Kirby Underdale and Bugthorpe *York 7* **P** *Abp, D&C, and Earl of Halifax (jt) (3 turns), Ld Chan (1 turn)* **R** J C FINNEMORE
BISHOPDALE (Mission Room) *see* Aysgarth and Bolton cum Redmire *Ripon*
BISHOPHILL JUNIOR (St Mary) *see* Micklegate H Trin and Bishophill Junior St Mary *York*
BISHOP'S CANNINGS (St Mary the Virgin), All Cannings and Etchilhampton *Sarum 19* **P** *DBP* **P-in-c** A P JEANS
BISHOP'S CASTLE (St John the Baptist) w Mainstone *Heref 10* **P** *Earl of Powis and Ld Chan (alt)* **V** K M CROUCH, **C** K B COLLINS
BISHOP'S CLEEVE (St Michael and All Angels) *Glouc 9* **P** *DBP* **R** J H MEAD, **C** M JOHNSON
BISHOP'S FROME (St Mary the Virgin) w Castle Frome and Fromes Hill *Heref 2* **P** *Bp* **P-in-c** F M RIGBY
BISHOPS GREEN (Community Church) *see* Burghclere w Newtown and Ecchinswell w Sydmonton *Win*
BISHOP'S HATFIELD (St Etheldreda) *see* Hatfield *St Alb*
BISHOP'S HULL (St John the Evangelist) *see* Taunton St Jo *B & W*
BISHOPS HULL (St Peter and St Paul) *B & W 18* **P** *Adn Taunton* **V** C M S RANDALL
BISHOP'S ITCHINGTON (St Michael) *Cov 10* **P** *Bp* **P-in-c** M C GREEN
BISHOP'S LAVINGTON (All Saints) *see* W Lavington and the Cheverells *Sarum*
BISHOPS LYDEARD (Blessed Virgin Mary) w Bagborough and Cothelstone *B & W 18* **P** *D&C (3 turns), Ms P M G Mitford (1 turn)* **R** D A BURTON
BISHOPS NORTON (St John the Evangelist) *see* Twigworth, Down Hatherley, Norton, The Leigh etc *Glouc*
BISHOP'S STORTFORD (Holy Trinity) *St Alb 18* **P** *Bp* **R** J R HAYNES
BISHOP'S STORTFORD (St Michael) *St Alb 18* **P** *Bp* **V** R A V MARCHAND, **C** L KLIMAS, **NSM** D C HINGE
BISHOP'S SUTTON (St Nicholas) and Ropley and West Tisted *Win 1* **P** *Peache Trustees* **R** R J SUCH
BISHOP'S TACHBROOK (St Chad) *Cov 10* **P** *Bp* **V** W R LARGE
BISHOPS TAWTON (St John the Baptist) *see* Newport, Bishops Tawton and Tawstock *Ex*
BISHOPS WALTHAM (St Peter) *Portsm 1* **P** *Bp* **R** S E WILKINSON, **C** G E D HITCHINS
BISHOP'S WOOD (St Mary) *see* Hartlebury *Worc*
BISHOPSBOURNE (St Mary) *see* Barham w Bishopsbourne and Kingston *Cant*
BISHOPSNYMPTON (St Mary the Virgin), Rose Ash, Mariansleigh, Molland, Knowstone, East Anstey and West Anstey *Ex 18* **P** *DBP* **TR** C S TULL, **TV** R E SHORTER
BISHOPSTEIGNTON (St John the Evangelist) *see* Teignmouth, Ideford w Luton, Ashcombe etc *Ex*
BISHOPSTOKE (St Mary) (St Paul) *Win 9* **P** *Bp* **R** D J COTTRILL, **C** M MULLINS
BISHOPSTON (Church of the Good Shepherd) *Bris 6* **P** *Patr Bd* **P-in-c** P R BAILEY
BISHOPSTONE (St Andrew) *Chich 18* **P** *Bp Lon* **V** *Vacant* (01323) 892972
BISHOPSTONE (St John the Baptist) *see* Chalke Valley W *Sarum*
BISHOPSTONE (St Lawrence) *see* Credenhill w Brinsop and Wormsley etc *Heref*
BISHOPSTROW (St Aldhelm) and Boreham *Sarum 14* **P** *DBP* **P-in-c** D R A BRETT
BISHOPSWOOD (All Saints) *see* Walford and St John w Bishopswood, Goodrich etc *Heref*
BISHOPSWOOD (St John the Evangelist) *Lich 2* **P** *V Brewood* **V** T H GREEN
BISHOPSWORTH (St Peter) and Bedminster Down *Bris 1* **P** *Bp* **V** P G HUZZEY, **TV** J M LEWIS, **NSM** P J BEVAN
BISHOPTHORPE (St Andrew) *York 1* **P** *Abp* **V** P RATHBONE
BISHOPTON (St Peter) w Great Stainton *Dur 10* **P** *Ld Chan* **P-in-c** R WALTER
BISHOPWEARMOUTH (Christ Church) *Dur 16* **P** *Bp* **V** R I DAVISON, **NSM** B J ABBOTT
BISHOPWEARMOUTH (Good Shepherd) *Dur 16* **P** *Bp* **V** *Vacant* 0191-565 6870
BISHOPWEARMOUTH (St Gabriel) *Dur 16* **P** *V Sunderland* **V** A THORP, **C** R G E BRADSHAW, **NSM** H M THORP
BISHOPWEARMOUTH (St Luke Pallion) *see* Millfield St Mark and Pallion *Dur*
BISHOPWEARMOUTH (St Mary) *see* Millfield St Mary *Dur*
BISHOPWEARMOUTH (St Nicholas) *Dur 16* **P** *Bp* **V** *Vacant* 0191-522 6444
BISLEY (All Saints), Oakridge, Miserden and Edgeworth *Glouc 1* **P** *Major M T N H Wills, Ld Chan, and Bp (by turn)* **V** I E D FARROW
BISLEY (St John the Baptist) and West End (Holy Trinity) *Guildf 6* **P** *Bp* **R** I A TERRY, **NSM** D H ROBINSON
BISPHAM (All Hallows) *Blackb 9* **P** *Ch Soc Trust* **R** S J COX, **C** J W MORLEY, **Hon C** L FRASER
BISTERNE (St Paul) *see* Ringwood *Win*
BITCHFIELD (St Mary Magdalene) *see* Ingoldsby *Linc*
BITTADON (St Peter) *see* Ilfracombe, Lee, Woolacombe, Bittadon etc *Ex*
BITTERING PARVA (St Peter and St Paul) *see* Gressenhall w Longham w Wendling etc *Nor*
BITTERLEY (St Mary) w Middleton, Stoke St Milborough w The Heath and Hopton Cangeford, Clee St Margaret and Cold Weston *Heref 12* **P** *Bp, DBP, Walcott Trustees, and Miss M F Rouse-Boughton (jt)* **R** A G SEABROOK
BITTERNE (Holy Saviour) *Win 12* **P** *Bp* **V** P HARRIS, **C** S J E TOMALIN, P J WALKER
BITTERNE PARK (All Hallows) (Ascension) *Win 12* **P** *Bp* **V** J R EVANS, **C** M T P ZAMMIT, P A RICKMAN, **NSM** B L STREVENS
BITTESWELL (St Mary) *Leic 11* **P** *Haberdashers' Co* **P-in-c** M H W COUSSENS
BITTON (St Mary) *see* Warmley, Syston and Bitton *Bris*
BIX (St James) *see* Nettlebed w Bix and Highmore *Ox*
BLABY (All Saints) *Leic 10* **P** *Bp* **P-in-c** J G GIBBINS
BLACK BOURTON (St Mary the Virgin) *see* Shill Valley and Broadshire *Ox*
BLACK NOTLEY (St Peter and St Paul) *Chelmsf 15* **P** *St Jo Coll Cam* **R** A G MORRISON
BLACK TORRINGTON (St Mary), Bradford w Cookbury, Thornbury and Highampton *Ex 9* **P** *DBP* **P-in-c** H J MAYELL
BLACKAWTON (St Michael) *see* Stoke Fleming, Blackawton and Strete *Ex*
BLACKBIRD LEYS (Holy Family) *Ox 4* **P** *Bp* **V** J A RAMSAY
BLACKBOURNE *St E 9* **P** *Patr Bd* **TR** P M OLIVER, **TV** R H NORBURN, E S FOGDEN, **NSM** A DAY
BLACKBURN (Christ Church w St Matthew) *Blackb 2* **P** *Bp* **V** J G RILEY, **Hon Par Dn** L A RILEY
BLACKBURN (Church of the Redeemer) *Blackb 2* **P** *Bp* **V** S D BESSANT
BLACKBURN (Saviour) *Blackb 2* **P** *CPAS* **V** P R CARTER, **NSM** C L CARTER
BLACKBURN (St Aidan) *Blackb 5* **P** *Bp* **V** A FISHWICK
BLACKBURN (St Andrew) *see* Livesey *Blackb*
BLACKBURN (St Barnabas) *Blackb 2* **P** *Bp* **V** H H DANIEL
BLACKBURN (St Bartholomew) *see* Ewood *Blackb*
BLACKBURN (St Gabriel) *Blackb 2* **P** *Bp* **V** J CORBYN, **C** B R McCONKEY
BLACKBURN (St James) *Blackb 2* **P** *Bp* **V** T B ENSOR
BLACKBURN (St Luke) w St Philip *Blackb 2* **P** *Bp* **V** P S GRIERSON
BLACKBURN (St Michael and All Angels) (Holy Trinity Worship Centre) w St John the Evangelist *Blackb 2* **P** *V Blackb* **V** S J LOCKE, **NSM** E G HUNT
BLACKBURN (St Silas) *Blackb 2* **P** *Trustees* **V** B STEVENSON
BLACKBURN (St Stephen) *Blackb 2* **P** *Trustees* **V** *Vacant* (01254) 255546
BLACKBURN St Thomas (St Jude) *Blackb 2* **P** *Bp and Trustees (alt)* **V** P R HAPGOOD-STRICKLAND
BLACKDOWN (Holy Trinity) *see* Beaminster Area *Sarum*
BLACKFEN (Good Shepherd) *see* Lamorbey H Redeemer *Roch*
BLACKFORD (Holy Trinity) *see* Wedmore w Theale and Blackford *B & W*
BLACKFORD (St John the Baptist) *see* Rockcliffe and Blackford *Carl*
BLACKFORD (St Michael) *see* Camelot Par *B & W*
BLACKFORDBY (St Margaret) and Woodville *Leic 9* **P** *Bp* **V** M J PENNY
BLACKHALL (St Andrew) *Dur 2* **P** *Bp* **V** W E L BROAD
BLACKHAM (All Saints) *see* Withyham St Mich *Chich*
BLACKHEATH (All Saints) *S'wark 4* **P** *V Lewisham St Mary* **V** H K BURGIN
BLACKHEATH (Ascension) *S'wark 4* **P** *V Lewisham St Mary* **P-in-c** D J FUDGER, **Hon C** E R NEWNHAM, **NSM** J M PRESTON
BLACKHEATH (St John the Evangelist) *S'wark 2* **P** *CPAS* **V** M D MARSHALL, **Hon C** J McALLEN, **NSM** A M BESWETHERICK
BLACKHEATH (St Martin) and Chilworth *Guildf 2* **P** *Bp* **V** E GIBBONS
BLACKHEATH (St Paul) *Birm 7* **P** *Bp* **V** D H GARNER, **C** C WAUDBY

BLACKHEATH PARK (St Michael and All Angels) *S'wark 2* **P** *Bp* **V** H L WHYTE, **NSM** A SCOTT, M J CALLAGHAN
BLACKLAND (St Peter) *see* Calne and Blackland *Sarum*
BLACKLANDS Hastings (Christchurch and St Andrew) *Chich 17* **P** *Ch Patr Trust* **V** P J LE SUEUR
BLACKLEY (Holy Trinity) *Man 5* **P** *Bp* **R** P A STAMP
BLACKLEY (St Andrew) *Man 5* **P** *Bp* **R** D J ERRIDGE
BLACKLEY (St Paul) *Man 5* **P** *Bp* **R** *Vacant* 0161-740 1518
BLACKLEY (St Peter) *Man 5* **P** *D&C* **R** L St J R AITKEN
BLACKLEY White Moss (St Mark) *Man 5* **P** *D&C* **R** R LEATHERBARROW
BLACKMOOR (St Matthew) *Portsm 5* **P** *Earl of Selborne* **P-in-c** A D RICHARDS
BLACKMORE (St Laurence) and Stondon Massey *Chelmsf 27* **P** *Bp* **V** I E CRAWFORD
BLACKPOOL (Christ Church w All Saints) (St Andrew) *Blackb 9* **P** *Bp and Trustees (jt)* **V** P GASCOIGNE
BLACKPOOL (Holy Cross) South Shore *Blackb 9* **P** *Bp* **V** S EDWARDS
BLACKPOOL (Holy Trinity) *see* S Shore H Trin *Blackb*
BLACKPOOL (St John) *Blackb 9* **P** *Trustees* **V** M A MANLEY, **C** F E GREEN
BLACKPOOL (St Mark) *Blackb 9* **P** *CPAS* **V** E W GRAY
BLACKPOOL (St Mary) South Shore *Blackb 9* **P** *Bp* **V** M F WOOD, **Hon C** N SMITH
BLACKPOOL (St Michael and All Angels) *Blackb 9* **P** *Bp* **V** D H JENKINS, **C** L H SIMPSON
BLACKPOOL St Paul *Blackb 9* **P** *Trustees* **C** D M HANKEY
BLACKPOOL (St Peter) *see* S Shore St Pet *Blackb*
BLACKPOOL (St Stephen on the Cliffs) *Blackb 9* **P** *Bp, R Bispham All Hallows, and Ch Wardens (jt)* **V** P WALSH
BLACKPOOL (St Thomas) *Blackb 9* **P** *CPAS* **V** G A FISHER, **C** G P H NEWTON, R G SHRINE
BLACKPOOL (St Wilfrid) Mereside *Blackb 9* **P** *Bp* **V** P H HUDSON
BLACKROD (St Catherine) (Scot Lane School) *Man 11* **P** *V Bolton-le-Moors St Pet* **V** R C COOPER
BLACKTOFT (Holy Trinity) *see* Howden TM *York*
BLACKWATER (St Barnabas) *see* Arreton *Portsm*
BLACKWELL (All Saints) and Salutation Conventional District *Dur 12* **C-in-c** J R DOBSON
BLACKWELL (St Catherine) *see* The Lickey *Birm*
BLACKWELL (St Werburgh) *Derby 1* **P** *Bp* **P-in-c** M N W EDWARDS
BLACON (Holy Trinity) *see* Ches H Trin *Ches*
BLADON (St Martin) w Woodstock *Ox 9* **P** *Duke of Marlborough* **R** R J HUMPHREYS, **C** A J SWEENEY, **NSM** C A W SANDERS
BLAGDON (St Andrew) w Compton Martin and Ubley *B & W 10* **P** *Bp and Sir John Wills Bt (jt)* **R** H A MATTHEWS, **C** M J SLADE, **NSM** G D TEAGUE
BLAGREAVES (St Andrew) *Derby 10* **P** *Bp, Churchwardens, and CPAS (jt)* **V** K W HORLESTON
BLAISDON (St Michael and All Angels) *see* Westbury-on-Severn w Flaxley and Blaisdon *Glouc*
BLAKEDOWN (St James the Great) *see* Churchill-in-Halfshire w Blakedown and Broome *Worc*
BLAKEMERE (St Leonard) *see* Madley w Tyberton, Preston-on-Wye and Blakemere *Heref*
BLAKENALL HEATH (Christ Church) *Lich 26* **P** *Patr Bd* **TV** C D C THORPE, **C** C M MASON
BLAKENEY (All Saints) *see* Newnham w Awre and Blakeney *Glouc*
BLAKENEY (St Nicholas w St Mary and St Thomas) w Cley, Wiveton, Glandford and Letheringsett *Nor 18* **P** *Bp and Keble Coll Ox (jt)* **R** N R MARTIN, **NSM** R H ROE
BLAKENHALL (St Luke) *see* Wolverhampton St Luke *Lich*
BLAKENHAM, GREAT (St Mary) and LITTLE (St Mary) w Baylham and Nettlestead *St E 1* **P** *Bp and MMCET (jt)* **Dn-in-c** H N BROWN
BLAKESLEY (St Mary) w Adstone and Maidford and Farthingstone *Pet 5* **P** *Sons of Clergy Corp, Bp, Hertf Coll Ox, and Capt R Grant-Renwick (by turn)* **R** A F RIDLEY
BLANCHLAND (St Mary's Abbey) w Hunstanworth and Edmundbyers and Muggleswick *Newc 3* **P** *D E Scott-Harden Esq, Lord Crewe's Trustees and D&C (alt)* **R** M A CUMING
BLANDFORD FORUM (St Peter and St Paul) and Langton Long *Sarum 7* **P** *Bp* **R** B W J LOMAX, **C** M W FEARN, **Hon C** M C MILES
BLANDFORD ST MARY (St Mary) *see* Spetisbury w Charlton Marshall etc *Sarum*
BLANKNEY (St Oswald) *see* Metheringham w Blankney and Dunston *Linc*
BLASTON (St Giles) *see* Six Saints circa Holt *Leic*
BLATCHINGTON, EAST (St John the Evangelist) (St Peter) *Chich 19* **P** *Bp* **R** K YATES
BLATCHINGTON, WEST (St Peter) *Chich 4* **P** *Bp* **R** M S PORTEOUS, **NSM** J FOX

BLAXHALL (St Peter) *see* Gt and Lt Glemham, Blaxhall etc *St E*
BLEADON (St Peter and St Paul) *B & W 11* **P** *Guild of All So* **R** D T PARKINSON
BLEAN (St Cosmus and St Damian) *Cant 3* **P** *Master of Eastbridge Hosp* **P-in-c** D R WITTS
BLEASBY (St Mary) *see* Thurgarton w Hoveringham and Bleasby etc *S'well*
BLEASDALE (St Eadmor) *see* Whitechapel w Admarsh-in-Bleasdale *Blackb*
BLEATARN (Chapel of Ease) *see* Brough w Stainmore, Musgrave and Warcop *Carl*
BLEDINGTON (St Leonard) *see* Westcote w Icomb and Bledington *Glouc*
BLEDLOW (Holy Trinity) w Saunderton and Horsenden *Ox 21* **P** *Lord Carrington* **R** *Vacant* (01844) 344762
BLEDLOW RIDGE (St Paul) *see* W Wycombe w Bledlow Ridge, Bradenham and Radnage *Ox*
BLENDON (St James) *see* Bexley St Jo *Roch*
BLENDON (St James the Great) *Roch 17* **P** *The Crown* **V** A KEELER
BLENDWORTH (Holy Trinity) w Chalton w Idsworth *Portsm 4* **P** *Bp* **P-in-c** R W REED, **NSM** F J HEAL
BLETCHINGDON (St Giles) *see* Akeman *Ox*
BLETCHINGLEY (St Andrew) (St Mary) *S'wark 25* **P** *Em Coll Cam* **R** D C EDWARDS, **NSM** P H BRADSHAW
BLETCHLEY (St Mary) *Ox 25* **P** *DBP* **R** I J PUSEY, **C** A MACKENZIE, L I WICKINGS, S J L CANSDALE, **NSM** M S WITHERS
BLETCHLEY, NORTH (Whaddon Way Church) Conventional District *Ox 25* **NSM** J M LAWRENCE
BLETSOE (St Mary) *see* Riseley w Bletsoe *St Alb*
BLEWBURY (St Michael and All Angels), Hagbourne and Upton *Ox 18* **P** *Bp* **R** E G CLEMENTS, **NSM** W D PLATT
BLICKLING (St Andrew) *see* Lt Barningham, Blickling, Edgefield etc *Nor*
BLIDWORTH (St Mary) *S'well 2* **P** *Ld Chan* **V** R BEARDALL
BLIDWORTH, NEW (St Andrew) *see* Blidworth *S'well*
BLINDLEY HEATH (St John the Evangelist) *S'wark 25* **P** *R Godstone* **V** *Vacant* (01342) 832337
BLISLAND (St Protus and St Hyacinth) w St Breward *Truro 10* **P** *SMF and D&C (alt)* **P-in-c** R D REED
BLISWORTH (St John the Baptist) *Pet 5* **P** *MMCET* **R** *Vacant* (01604) 858412
BLITHFIELD (St Leonard) *see* Abbots Bromley w Blithfield *Lich*
BLO' NORTON (St Andrew) *see* Guiltcross *Nor*
BLOCKLEY (St Peter and St Paul) w Aston Magna and Bourton on the Hill *Glouc 10* **P** *Lord Dulverton and DBP (jt)* **V** G A NEALE
BLOFIELD (St Andrew) w Hemblington *Nor 4* **P** *G&C Coll Cam* **P-in-c** P THORN
BLOOMSBURY (St George) w Woburn Square (Christ Church) *Lon 17* **P** *Ld Chan* **P-in-c** P A BUTLER
BLORE RAY (St Bartholomew) *see* Ilam w Blore Ray and Okeover *Lich*
BLOXHAM (Our Lady of Bloxham) w Milcombe and South Newington *Ox 5* **P** *Ex Coll Ox and Eton Coll (jt)* **V** J R A STROYAN
BLOXHOLME (St Mary) *see* Digby *Linc*
BLOXWICH (All Saints) (Holy Ascension) *Lich 26* **P** *Patr Bd* **TR** S C RAWLING, **TV** M H HAWKSWORTH, M D ALLABY
BLOXWORTH (St Andrew) *see* Red Post *Sarum*
BLUBBERHOUSES (St Andrew) *see* Leathley w Farnley, Fewston and Blubberhouses *Bradf*
BLUCHER (St Cuthbert) *see* Newburn *Newc*
BLUE BELL HILL (St Alban) *see* Chatham St Wm *Roch*
BLUNDELLSANDS (St Michael) *Liv 5* **P** *Trustees* **V** P C N CONDER
BLUNDELLSANDS (St Nicholas) *Liv 5* **P** *Trustees* **V** R D BAKER
BLUNDESTON (St Mary) *see* Somerleyton, Ashby, Fritton, Herringfleet etc *Nor*
BLUNHAM (St Edmund King and Martyr and St James) w Tempsford and Little Barford *St Alb 11* **P** *Ball Coll Ox and The Crown (alt)* **P-in-c** R D SEYMOUR-WHITELEY
BLUNSDONS, The (St Leonard) (St Andrew) *Bris 10* **P** *Bp* **R** J L WARE
BLUNTISHAM (St Mary) cum Earith w Colne and Woodhurst *Ely 11* **P** *Ch Ch Ox* **R** C BACKHOUSE
BLURTON (St Bartholomew) (St Alban) *Lich 13* **P** *Bp* **V** P J MOCKFORD, **C** M R M CALLADINE
BLYBOROUGH (St Alkmund) *see* Glentworth Gp *Linc*
BLYFORD (All Saints) *see* Halesworth w Linstead, Chediston, Holton etc *St E*
BLYMHILL (St Mary) w Weston-under-Lizard *Lich 2* **P** *Earl of Bradf* **P-in-c** J R McMANUS, **Hon C** R C W DAMPIER

BLYTH (St Cuthbert) *Newc 1* **P** *Bp* **V** *Vacant* (01670) 352410
BLYTH (St Mary) *Newc 1* **P** *Bp* **V** B BENISON
BLYTH (St Mary and St Martin) *S'well 6* **P** *Trin Coll Cam* **P-in-c** J J VAN DEN BERG
BLYTHBURGH (Holy Trinity) w Reydon *St E 15* **P** *Exors Earl of Stradbroke (2 turns), Sir Charles Blois Bt (1 turn)* **P-in-c** J B NAYLOR, **Hon C** A K E SORENSEN
BLYTON (St Martin) *see* Corringham and Blyton Gp *Linc*
BOARHUNT (St Nicholas) *see* Southwick w Boarhunt *Portsm*
BOARSTALL (St James) *see* Brill, Boarstall, Chilton and Dorton *Ox*
BOBBING (St Bartholomew) *see* Sittingbourne H Trin w Bobbing *Cant*
BOBBINGTON (Holy Cross) *see* Wombourne w Trysull and Bobbington *Lich*
BOBBINGWORTH (St Germain) *see* Fyfield, Moreton w Bobbingworth etc *Chelmsf*
BOCKING (St Mary) *Chelmsf 15* **P** *Abp Cant* **R** P A NEED
BOCKING (St Peter) *Chelmsf 15* **P** *Abp Cant* **V** T C DIAPER
BOCKLETON (St Michael) w Leysters *Heref 7* **P** *Bp* **P-in-c** W R PRIDIE
BOCONNOC (not known) *see* Lostwithiel, St Winnow w St Nectan's Chpl etc *Truro*
BODDINGTON (St John the Baptist) *see* Byfield w Boddington and Aston le Walls *Pet*
BODDINGTON (St Mary Magdalene) *see* Staverton w Boddington and Tredington etc *Glouc*
BODENHAM (St Michael and All Angels) w Hope-under-Dinmore, Felton and Preston Wynne *Heref 4* **P** *Bp* **P-in-c** C M HILL
BODHAM (All Saints) *see* Weybourne Gp *Nor*
BODIAM (St Giles) *Chich 20* **P** *All So Coll Ox* **P-in-c** R K BAKER
BODICOTE (St John the Baptist) *Ox 5* **P** *New Coll Ox* **V** B L M PHILLIPS
BODINNICK (St John) *see* Lanteglos by Fowey *Truro*
BODLE STREET GREEN (St John the Evangelist) *see* Warbleton and Bodle Street Green *Chich*
BODMIN (St Leonard) (St Petroc) w Lanhydrock and Lanivet *Truro 10* **P** *DBP* **TR** K ROGERS, **TV** S R F DRAKELEY, R S MITCHELL, **NSM** F B J COOMBES
BODNEY (St Mary) *see* Hilborough w Bodney *Nor*
BOGNOR (St Wilfrid) *Chich 1* **P** *Abp* **P-in-c** R P CALDER, **C** J R PHILLIPS
BOLAM (St Andrew) *see* Heighington *Dur*
BOLAM (St Andrew) w Whalton and Hartburn w Meldon *Newc 11* **P** *Ld Chan (2 turns), J I K Walker Esq (1 turn), and D&C Dur (1 turn)* **R** G F REVETT
BOLAS MAGNA (St John the Baptist) *see* Tibberton w Bolas Magna and Waters Upton *Lich*
BOLDMERE (St Michael) *Birm 13* **P** *Birm Dioc Trustees* **C** G R HOCKEN
BOLDON (St Nicholas) *Dur 15* **P** *Bp* **R** T A MIDDLETON
BOLDON, EAST (St George) *Dur 15* **P** *Bp* **V** E G STEPHENSON
BOLDRE (St John the Baptist) w South Baddesley *Win 10* **P** *Bp and Lord Teynham (jt)* **V** *Vacant* (01590) 673484
BOLDRE, EAST (St Paul) *see* Beaulieu and Exbury and E Boldre *Win*
BOLDRON (Mission Room) *see* Startforth and Bowes and Rokeby w Brignall *Ripon*
BOLE (St Martin) *see* N Wheatley, W Burton, Bole, Saundby, Sturton etc *S'well*
BOLINGBROKE (St Peter and St Paul) *see* Marden Hill Gp *Linc*
BOLINGBROKE, NEW (St Peter) *see* Sibsey w Frithville *Linc*
BOLLINGHAM (St Silas) *see* Eardisley w Bollingham, Willersley, Brilley etc *Heref*
BOLLINGTON (Holy Trinity) *see* Rostherne w Bollington *Ches*
BOLLINGTON (St John the Baptist) *Ches 13* **P** *V Prestbury* **V** M A WHETTER
BOLLINGTON CROSS (St Oswald) *see* Bollington St Jo *Ches*
BOLNEY (St Mary Magdalene) *Chich 6* **P** *K Coll Lon* **V** A R HARCUS
BOLNHURST (St Dunstan) *see* Keysoe w Bolnhurst and Lt Staughton *St Alb*
BOLSOVER (St Mary and St Laurence) *Derby 3* **P** *Bp* **V** J EASTON
BOLSTERSTONE (St Mary) *Sheff 7* **P** *R B Rimington Wilson Esq* **V** K J F BARNARD, **C** C E BARNARD, **Hon C** P B MIALL
BOLTBY (Holy Trinity) *see* Felixkirk w Boltby *York*
BOLTON (All Saints) *Carl 1* **P** *V Morland w Thrimby etc* **P-in-c** D C WOOD
BOLTON (All Saints) w Ireby and Uldale *Carl 6* **P** *Earl of Lonsdale, D&C, and Qu Coll Ox (by turn)* **P-in-c** C S SIMS, **C** J M FEARNLEY
BOLTON Breightmet (St James) *Man 16* **P** *The Crown* **V** *Vacant* (01204) 525640
BOLTON Chapel (unknown) *see* Whittingham and Edlingham w Bolton Chapel *Newc*
BOLTON (St Chad) *see* Tonge Fold *Man*
BOLTON (St James w St Chrysostom) *Bradf 3* **P** *Bp* **V** B LOFTHOUSE
BOLTON (St John the Evangelist) Top o' th' Moss *Man 16* **P** *The Crown* **V** H CALLAGHAN
BOLTON (St Thomas) *Man 9* **P** *Trustees* **V** D R OTTLEY, **NSM** A PIERCE
BOLTON ABBEY (St Mary and St Cuthbert) *Bradf 7* **P** *Duke of Devonshire* **R** J S WARD, **NSM** J A TURNBULL
BOLTON BY BOWLAND (St Peter and St Paul) w Grindleton *Bradf 5* **P** *Bp and V Hurst Green and Mitton (jt)* **R** D W MEWIS
BOLTON LE MOORS (St Bede) *Man 11* **P** *Bp* **P-in-c** A BORSBEY
BOLTON LE MOORS (St Matthew w St Barnabas) *Man 9* **P** *Bp* **P-in-c** S C NEAL
BOLTON LE MOORS (St Paul) (Emmanuel) *Man 9* **P** *Patr Bd* **TR** *Vacant* (01204) 842303
BOLTON LE MOORS (St Peter) *Man 9* **P** *Bp* **V** A WOLSTENCROFT, **C** C E VANN
BOLTON LE MOORS (St Philip) *Man 9* **P** *Bp and Hulme Trustees (alt)* **V** M W J HILLS, **NSM** G BUSH
BOLTON LE MOORS (St Simon and St Jude) *Man 9* **P** *Trustees* **V** F G DOWNING
BOLTON LE SANDS (Holy Trinity) *Blackb 15* **P** *Bp* **V** R D HACKING, **NSM** R FOSTER
BOLTON ON SWALE (St Mary) *see* Easby w Brompton on Swale and Bolton on Swale *Ripon*
BOLTON PERCY (All Saints) *York 1* **P** *Abp* **P-in-c** F A R MINAY
BOLTON-UPON-DEARNE (St Andrew the Apostle) *Sheff 12* **P** *Meynall Ch Trust* **V** D G STAFFORD
BOLVENTOR (Holy Trinity) *see* Altarnon w Bolventor, Laneast and St Clether *Truro*
BOMERE HEATH (Mission Room) *see* Leaton and Albrighton w Battlefield *Lich*
BONBY (St Andrew) *Linc 6* **P** *DBP* **P-in-c** G A PLUMB
BONCHURCH (St Boniface) (St Boniface Old Church) *Portsm 7* **P** *Ch Patr Trust* **R** A TEDMAN
BONDLEIGH (St James the Apostle) *see* N Tawton, Bondleigh, Sampford Courtenay etc *Ex*
BONINGALE (St Chad) *Lich 20* **P** *MMCET* **V** *Vacant*
BONNINGTON (St Rumwold) *see* Aldington w Bonnington and Bilsington *Cant*
BONSALL (St James the Apostle) *see* Wirksworth *Derby*
BOOKER (St Birinus' Mission Church) *see* High Wycombe *Ox*
BOOKHAM, GREAT (St Nicholas) *Guildf 10* **P** *Bp* **R** A C WARNER, **C** M E BIDE
BOOKHAM, LITTLE (not known) *see* Effingham w Lt Bookham *Guildf*
BOONGATE (St Mary) *see* Pet St Mary Boongate *Pet*
BOOSBECK (St Aidan) w Moorsholm *York 17* **P** *Abp* **V** J C WEETMAN
BOOTHBY GRAFFOE (St Andrew) *see* Graffoe Gp *Linc*
BOOTHBY PAGNELL (St Andrew) *see* Ingoldsby *Linc*
BOOTHSTOWN (St Andrew's Church Institute) *see* Worsley *Man*
BOOTLE (Christ Church) *Liv 1* **P** *Bp* **V** T RICH
BOOTLE (St Leonard) *Liv 1* **P** *Simeon's Trustees* **V** *Vacant* 0151-922 1434
BOOTLE (St Mary w St Paul) *Liv 1* **P** *Bp and Trustees (jt)* **V** P H JORDAN, **C** C I KIDD
BOOTLE (St Matthew) *Liv 1* **P** *Bp* **V** C H JONES, **C** D A HEWITSON
BOOTLE (St Michael and All Angels), Corney, Whicham and Whitbeck *Carl 5* **P** *Earl of Lonsdale* **R** M C RIDYARD
BORASTON (not known) *see* Burford I *Heref*
BORDEN (St Peter and St Paul) *Cant 14* **P** *SMF* **V** H I J SUCH
BORDESLEY (St Alban and St Patrick) *see* Highgate *Birm*
BORDESLEY (St Benedict) *Birm 9* **P** *Keble Coll Ox* **P-in-c** M O C JOY
BORDESLEY (St Oswald of Worcester) *see* Small Heath *Birm*
BORDESLEY GREEN (St Paul) *Birm 14* **P** *The Crown* **V** G C TURNER
BORDON (St Mark) *see* Headley All SS *Guildf*
BOREHAM (St Andrew) *Chelmsf 9* **P** *Bp* **P-in-c** D W A KING
BOREHAM (St John the Evangelist) *see* Bishopstrow and Boreham *Sarum*
BOREHAMWOOD (All Saints) (Holy Cross) (St Michael and All Angels) *St Alb 1* **P** *Patr Bd* **TR** S PURVIS, **TV** R C A LESLIE, M E PARTRIDGE
BORLEY (not known) *see* Pentlow, Foxearth, Liston and Borley *Chelmsf*

BOROUGH GREEN (Good Shepherd) *Roch 10* **P** *Bp* **V** A J POWELL
BOROUGHBRIDGE (St James) *see* Aldborough w Boroughbridge and Roecliffe *Ripon*
BORROWASH (St Stephen's Chapel) *see* Ockbrook *Derby*
BORROWDALE (St Andrew) *Carl 6* **P** *V Crosthwaite* **P-in-c** J T ROOKE
BORSTAL (St Matthew) *Roch 5* **P** *V Rochester St Marg* **V** J KING
BORWICK (St Mary) *see* Warton St Oswald w Yealand Conyers *Blackb*
BOSBURY (Holy Trinity) w Wellington Heath, Stretton Grandison, Ashperton and Canon Frome *Heref 6* **P** *Bp and D&C (jt)* **P-in-c** S STRUTT
BOSCASTLE w Davidstow *Truro 10* **P** *Duchy of Cornwall (1 turn), DBP (2 turns)* **TR** J M AYLING, **Hon C** S W DORAN
BOSCOMBE (St Andrew) *see* Bourne Valley *Sarum*
BOSCOMBE (St Andrew) *Win 7* **P** *Bp* **V** N A CARTER
BOSCOMBE (St John) *Win 7* **P** *Peache Trustees* **V** G A TAYLOR, **C** T D HANSON, **NSM** P H DRAPER
BOSCOPPA *Truro 1* **P** *Prime Min* **V** A D WEST
BOSHAM (Holy Trinity) *Chich 13* **P** *Bp* **V** T J INMAN, **NSM** J V EMERSON
BOSLEY (St Mary the Virgin) and North Rode (St Michael) w Wincle (St Michael) and Wildboarclough (St Saviour) *Ches 13* **P** *Bp, V Prestbury, and Earl of Derby (jt)* **P-in-c** D W MOIR
BOSSALL (St Botolph) *see* Sand Hutton *York*
BOSSINGTON (St James) *see* Broughton, Bossington, Houghton and Mottisfont *Win*
BOSTALL HEATH (St Andrew) *Roch 15* **P** *DBP* **V** S C VARNEY
BOSTON (Holy Trinity) *see* Skirbeck H Trin *Linc*
BOSTON (St Botolph) (St Christopher) *Linc 20* **P** *Bp* **V** C C DALLISTON, **C** G L TUNBRIDGE, J S KNEE
BOSTON (St Nicholas) *see* Skirbeck St Nic *Linc*
BOSTON (St Thomas) *see* Skirbeck Quarter *Linc*
BOSTON SPA (St Mary) *York 1* **P** *Ch Ch Ox* **V** R M C SEED
BOTCHERBY (St Andrew) *see* Carl St Aid and Ch Ch *Carl*
BOTESDALE (St Botolph) *see* Redgrave cum Botesdale w Rickinghall *St E*
BOTHAL (St Andrew) and Pegswood w Longhirst *Newc 11* **P** *Bp* **R** K M TRIVASSE
BOTHAMSALL (Our Lady and St Peter) *see* Elkesley w Bothamsall *S'well*
BOTHENHAMPTON (Holy Trinity) *see* Bridport *Sarum*
BOTLEY (All Saints) *Portsm 1* **P** *Bp* **R** I G COOMBER, **C** C J POWELL, **NSM** D R TOWNSEND
BOTLEY (St Peter and St Paul) *see* N Hinksey and Wytham *Ox*
BOTLEYS and Lyne (Holy Trinity) *Guildf 11* **P** *Bp* **V** A B OLSEN
BOTOLPHS (St Botolph) *see* Beeding and Bramber w Botolphs *Chich*
BOTTESFORD (St Mary the Virgin) and Muston *Leic 3* **P** *Duke of Rutland* **P-in-c** G SPENCER, **C** M TURNER, **NSM** J C HILL
BOTTESFORD (St Peter) w Ashby *Linc 4* **P** *Patr Bd* **TR** M J BOUGHTON, **TV** D C PEACOCK, A I JOHNSTON, **C** N H BALLARD, **NSM** M L MILLSON
BOTTISHAM (Holy Trinity) and Lode with Longmeadow *Ely 6* **P** *Trin Coll Cam and Bp (jt)* **P-in-c** V B A BRECHIN
BOTUS FLEMING (St Mary) *see* Landrake w St Erney and Botus Fleming *Truro*
BOUGHTON (All Saints) *Ely 16* **P** *Bp* **R** *Vacant*
BOUGHTON (St John the Baptist) *see* Pitsford w Boughton *Pet*
BOUGHTON (St Matthew) *see* Ollerton w Boughton *S'well*
BOUGHTON ALUPH (All Saints) *see* Westwell, Hothfield, Eastwell and Boughton Aluph *Cant*
BOUGHTON ALUPH (St Christopher) *as above*
BOUGHTON MALHERBE (St Nicholas) *see* Lenham w Boughton Malherbe *Cant*
BOUGHTON MONCHELSEA (St Augustine) (St Peter) *Cant 15* **P** *Abp* **V** R G DAVIS
BOUGHTON UNDER BLEAN (St Barnabas) (St Peter and St Paul) w Dunkirk and Hernhill *Cant 6* **P** *Abp* **V** J W R MOWLL, **Hon C** P J JACOBS
BOULGE (St Michael) w Burgh and Grundisburgh *St E 7* **P** *Bp and DBP (jt)* **R** N DAVIS
BOULMER (St Andrew) *see* Longhoughton w Howick *Newc*
BOULTHAM (Holy Cross) (St Helen) (St Mary Magdalene) (St Matthew) *Linc 15* **P** *DBP* **P-in-c** D J OSBOURNE, **C** P TAYLOR
BOULTON (St Mary the Virgin) *Derby 15* **P** *Bp* **P-in-c** R J HARRIS, **C** S J RADLEY
BOUNDSTONE (Mission Church) *see* Wrecclesham *Guildf*
BOURN (St Helena and St Mary) and Kingston w Caxton and Longstowe *Ely 1* **P** *Bp, Ch Coll Cam, D&C Windsor, and Selw Coll Cam (jt)* **R** J C B PEMBERTON, **NSM** C M PEMBERTON
BOURNE (St Peter and St Paul) *Linc 13* **P** *DBP* **V** J M WARWICK, **C** J C GIRTCHEN
BOURNE (St Thomas on the Bourne) *Guildf 3* **P** *Adn Surrey* **V** J R H HUBBARD, **C** A P C DOYE, H S HOUSTON, **NSM** A J GAUNT
BOURNE, LOWER (St Martin) *see* Bourne *Guildf*
BOURNE END (St John) *see* Sunnyside w Bourne End *St Alb*
BOURNE END (St Mark) *see* Hedsor and Bourne End *Ox*
BOURNE STREET (St Mary) *see* Pimlico St Mary Graham Terrace *Lon*
BOURNE VALLEY *Sarum 11* **P** *Patr Bd* **TR** S P BURTWELL, **TV** I SYKES
BOURNEMOUTH (All Saints) *see* Pokesdown All SS *Win*
BOURNEMOUTH (Christ Church) *see* Westbourne Ch Ch CD *Win*
BOURNEMOUTH (Holy Epiphany) *Win 7* **P** *Bp* **V** R S COSSINS, **Hon C** D G KINGSLAND
BOURNEMOUTH Queen's Park (St Barnabas) *see* Holdenhurst *Win*
BOURNEMOUTH (St Alban) *Win 7* **P** *Bp* **V** J C WHITE
BOURNEMOUTH (St Ambrose) *Win 7* **P** *Bp* **P-in-c** G J WHEELER
BOURNEMOUTH (St Andrew) Bennett Road *Win 7* **P** *Trustees* **V** A R ROAKE, **Hon C** D K BOAK
BOURNEMOUTH (St Augustine) *Win 7* **P** *Bp* **P-in-c** P MANHOOD
BOURNEMOUTH (St Clement) *Win 7* **P** *DBP* **P-in-c** G J WHITING
BOURNEMOUTH (St Francis) *Win 7* **P** *CR* **V** P G BERRETT, **NSM** A J JORDAN
BOURNEMOUTH (St James) *see* Pokesdown St Jas *Win*
BOURNEMOUTH (St John) (St Michael and All Angels) *Win 7* **P** *Bp and S R Willcox Esq (jt)* **V** K J RANDALL, **C** K E W MATHERS, **Hon C** K D MATHERS
BOURNEMOUTH (St Luke) *Win 7* **P** *Bp* **V** S HOLMES
BOURNEMOUTH (St Peter) (St Stephen) w St Swithun and Holy Trinity *Win 7* **P** *Patr Bd* **TR** J J RICHARDSON, **TV** J H S STEVEN, R C N HARGER, **Hon C** H G JAMES
BOURNVILLE (St Andrew) *see* Weston-super-Mare St Andr Bournville *B & W*
BOURNVILLE (St Francis) *Birm 5* **P** *Bp* **V** K WITHINGTON
BOURTON (Holy Trinity) *see* Wenlock *Heref*
BOURTON (St George) *see* Upper Stour *Sarum*
BOURTON (St James) *see* Shrivenham w Watchfield and Bourton *Ox*
BOURTON (St Peter) w Frankton and Stretton on Dunsmore w Princethorpe *Cov 6* **P** *Bp (2 turns), Simeon's Trustees (1 turn), and Mrs J H Shaw-Fox (1 turn)* **R** R C ROGERS
BOURTON, GREAT (All Saints) *see* Shires' Edge *Ox*
BOURTON ON THE HILL (St Lawrence) *see* Blockley w Aston Magna and Bourton on the Hill *Glouc*
BOURTON-ON-THE-WATER (St Lawrence) w Clapton *Glouc 15* **P** *Wadh Coll Ox* **R** *Vacant* (01242) 820386
BOVEY, NORTH (St John the Baptist) *see* Moretonhampstead, Manaton, N Bovey and Lustleigh *Ex*
BOVEY TRACEY (St John the Evangelist) w Chudleigh Knighton and Heathfield *Ex 11* **P** *DBP and Guild of All So (jt)* **P-in-c** D J STANTON
BOVEY TRACEY (St Peter and St Paul and St Thomas of Canterbury) w Hennock *Ex 11* **P** *Prime Min (2 turns), MMCET (1 turn)* **V** C H SARALIS, **NSM** C V L CURD
BOVINGDON (St Lawrence) *St Alb 5* **P** *Ch Soc Trust* **V** T J MARSHALL, **Hon C** R H METCALFE
BOW (Holy Trinity) (All Hallows) *Lon 7* **P** *Patr Bd* **TR** J M PEET
BOW (St Bartholomew) w Broad Nymet *Ex 2* **P** *DBP* **R** J C HALL
BOW (St Mary) w Bromley (St Leonard) *Lon 7* **P** *Bp* **R** G W GARNER, **NSM** D F WAXHAM
BOW BRICKHILL (All Saints) *see* Gt Brickhill w Bow Brickhill and Lt Brickhill *Ox*
BOW COMMON (St Paul) *Lon 7* **P** *Bp* **P-in-c** D G ROSS
BOWBROOK NORTH: Feckenham and Hanbury and Stock and Bradley *Worc 8* **P** *Bp and D&C (jt)* **R** E J ROTHWELL
BOWBROOK SOUTH: Crowle w Bredicot and Hadzor w Oddingley and Tibberton and Himbleton and Huddington *Worc 8* **P** *Bp, D&C, R J G Berkeley Esq, and J F Bennett Esq (jt)* **R** W D S WELLS, **C** R J G THORNILEY
BOWBURN (Christ the King) *see* Cassop cum Quarrington *Dur*
BOWDEN, GREAT (St Peter and St Paul) w Welham, Glooston and Cranoe *Leic 4* **P** *Bp and E Brudenell Esq* **P-in-c** I W Y GEMMELL
BOWDEN, LITTLE (St Hugh) *see* Market Harborough Transfiguration *Leic*
BOWDEN, LITTLE (St Nicholas) *as above*
BOWDEN HILL (St Anne) *see* Lacock w Bowden Hill *Bris*

BOWDON (St Luke) (St Mary the Virgin) *Ches 10* **P** *Bp* **V** K E HINE, **C** I SPARKS
BOWERCHALKE (Holy Trinity) *see* Chalke Valley W *Sarum*
BOWERS GIFFORD (St John) (St Margaret) w North Benfleet *Chelmsf 6* **P** *Em Coll Cam and Brig R H C Bryhers CBE (alt)* **R** *Vacant* (01268) 552219
BOWES (St Giles) *see* Startforth and Bowes and Rokeby w Brignall *Ripon*
BOWES PARK (St Michael-at-Bowes) *see* Wood Green St Mich w Bounds Green St Gabr etc *Lon*
BOWLEE (St Thomas) *see* Rhodes *Man*
BOWLING (St John) *Bradf 2* **P** *V Bradford* **V** H K ASTIN
BOWLING (St Stephen) *Bradf 2* **P** *CPAS* **V** C W W BARBER
BOWNESS (St Michael) *Carl 3* **P** *Earl of Lonsdale* **P-in-c** J T SPENCE
BOWTHORPE (St Michael) *Nor 3* **P** *Bp and CPAS (jt)* **V** *Vacant*
BOX (St Barnabas) *see* Minchinhampton *Glouc*
BOX (St Thomas a Becket) w Hazlebury and Ditteridge *Bris 9* **P** *Bp* **R** J R FLORY, **NSM** J AYERS, J D POTTER
BOX HILL (St Andrew) *see* Headley w Box Hill *Guildf*
BOXFORD (St Andrew) *see* Welford w Wickham and Gt Shefford, Boxford etc *Ox*
BOXFORD (St Mary) *St E 12* **P** *The Crown* **R** E C HAMLYN
BOXGROVE (St Mary and St Blaise) *Chich 3* **P** *Duke of Richmond and Gordon* **V** J M HASELOCK, **NSM** J K GAVIGAN
BOXLEY (St Mary the Virgin and All Saints) w Detling *Cant 15* **P** *Abp* **V** M M BRADSHAW
BOXMOOR (St John the Evangelist) *St Alb 3* **P** *Bp* **P-in-c** P V HUGHES, **C** J M HALLOWS, **NSM** E J HUGHES
BOXTED (Holy Trinity) *see* Glem Valley United Benefice *St E*
BOXTED (St Peter) w Langham *Chelmsf 17* **P** *Bp and Duchy of Lanc (alt)* **R** J A CARDELL-OLIVER
BOXWELL (St Mary the Virgin), Leighterton, Didmarton, Oldbury-on-the-Hill and Sopworth *Glouc 16* **P** *Duke of Beaufort and J F B Hutley Esq (alt)* **R** N C J MULHOLLAND
BOXWORTH (St Peter) *Ely 1* **P** *G E P Thornhill Esq* **R** *Vacant* (019547) 226
BOYATT WOOD (St Peter) *Win 9* **P** *Bp* **V** D WALFORD, **NSM** A WALFORD
BOYLESTONE (St John the Baptist) *see* Ch Broughton w Barton Blount, Boylestone etc *Derby*
BOYNE HILL (All Saints) *Ox 13* **P** *Bp* **V** N J BROWN, **C** A K SILLIS
BOYNTON (St Andrew) *see* Rudston w Boynton and Kilham *York*
BOYTHORPE (St Francis) *see* Chesterfield St Aug *Derby*
BOYTON (Holy Name), North Tamerton, Werrington w St Giles-in-the-Heath and Virginstow *Truro 9* **P** *Duke of Cornwall, MMCET, Ld Chan, and R Williams Esq (by turn)* **R** A J M BROWNRIDGE
BOYTON (St Andrew) w Capel St Andrew and Hollesley *St E 7* **P** *Mary Warner Charity and DBP (alt)* **R** J M GATES
BOYTON (St Mary the Virgin) *see* Ashton Gifford *Sarum*
BOZEAT (St Mary) w Easton Maudit *Pet 6* **P** *Bp and Marquess of Northn (alt)* **V** P H BLIGH
BRABOURNE (St Mary the Blessed Virgin) w Smeeth *Cant 12* **P** *Abp* **P-in-c** J W TIPPING, **Hon C** R L LE ROSSIGNOL
BRACEBOROUGH (St Margaret) *see* Uffington Gp *Linc*
BRACEBRIDGE (All Saints) *Linc 15* **P** *Mrs B M Ellison-Lendrum* **V** A J KERSWILL
BRACEBRIDGE HEATH (St John the Evangelist) *Linc 15* **P** *Bp* **P-in-c** H C MIDDLETON, **NSM** J M CLARK
BRACEBY (St Margaret) *see* Sapperton w Braceby *Linc*
BRACEWELL (St Michael) *see* Barnoldswick w Bracewell *Bradf*
BRACKENFIELD (Holy Trinity) *see* Ashover and Brackenfield *Derby*
BRACKLEY (St Peter w St James) *Pet 1* **P** *Bp* **V** P C WOODWARD, **C** L M S McCLEAN
BRACKNELL (Holy Trinity) *Ox 11* **P** *Bp* **TV** A J DUFF, C ALLSOPP, **C** T D COCKELL, H F COCKELL
BRACON ASH (St Nicholas) *see* Wreningham *Nor*
BRADBOURNE (All Saints) *see* Wirksworth *Derby*
BRADDAN (St Brendan) *S & M 2* **P** *Bp* **V** P S FREAR
BRADDEN (St Michael) *see* Greens Norton w Bradden and Lichborough *Pet*
BRADELEY (St Mary and All Saints), Church Eaton and Moreton *Lich 10* **P** *Bp and V Gnosall (jt)* **R** T W B FOX
BRADENHAM (St Botolph) *see* W Wycombe w Bledlow Ridge, Bradenham and Radnage *Ox*
BRADENHAM, WEST (St Andrew) *see* Shipdham w E and W Bradenham *Nor*
BRADENSTOKE (St Mary) *see* Lyneham w Bradenstoke *Sarum*
BRADFIELD (St Andrew) and Stanford Dingley *Ox 12* **P** *Ch Soc Trust* **P-in-c** H W ELLIS
BRADFIELD (St Clare) *see* Cockfield w Bradfield St Clare, Felsham etc *St E*
BRADFIELD (St Giles) *see* Trunch *Nor*
BRADFIELD (St Laurence) *see* Mistley w Manningtree and Bradfield *Chelmsf*
BRADFIELD (St Nicholas) *Sheff 7* **P** *V Ecclesfield* **R** G V LETTS
BRADFIELD COMBUST (All Saints) *see* Hawstead and Nowton w Stanningfield etc *St E*
BRADFIELD ST GEORGE (St George) *see* Gt and Lt Whelnetham w Bradfield St George *St E*
BRADFORD (All Saints) *see* Black Torrington, Bradf w Cookbury etc *Ex*
BRADFORD (St Augustine) Undercliffe *Bradf 3* **P** *V Bradf* **V** A P BOWSHER, **C** S P DOWSON
BRADFORD (St Clement) *Bradf 3* **P** *Bp (2 turns) and Trustees (1 turn)* **P-in-c** D P BANBURY
BRADFORD (St Columba w St Andrew) *Bradf 2* **P** *Bp* **V** C I JUDD
BRADFORD (St Giles) w Oake, Hillfarrance and Heathfield *B & W 19* **P** *Bp and M V Spurway Esq (jt)* **R** K G X TINGAY
BRADFORD (St Oswald) Chapel Green *Bradf 2* **P** *Bp* **P-in-c** W HOLLIDAY
BRADFORD (St Wilfrid) Lidget Green *Bradf 2* **P** *Bp* **V** P M BILTON, **NSM** G A BRIGHOUSE
BRADFORD, WEST (St Catherine) *see* Waddington *Bradf*
BRADFORD ABBAS (St Mary the Virgin) and Thornford w Beer Hackett *Sarum 4* **P** *Major K S D Wingfield Digby and Win Coll (alt)* **R** D A K GREENE
BRADFORD-ON-AVON (Christ Church) *Sarum 17* **P** *V Bradf H Trin* **V** D R R SEYMOUR, **NSM** B F CHAPMAN
BRADFORD-ON-AVON (Holy Trinity) *Sarum 17* **P** *D&C* **V** W A MATTHEWS
BRADFORD ON TONE (St Giles) *see* Bradford w Oake, Hillfarrance and Heathfield *B & W*
BRADFORD PEVERELL (Church of the Assumption), Stratton, Frampton and Sydling St Nicholas *Sarum 2* **P** *Win Coll and Bp (alt)* **R** K J SCOTT, **NSM** S C CHALK, M J RIDGEWELL, P A STEAR
BRADING (St Mary the Virgin) w Yaverland *Portsm 7* **P** *Hon Mrs I S T Monck and Trin Coll Cam (jt)* **R** D M LOW
BRADLEY (All Saints) *see* Hulland, Atlow, Bradley and Hognaston *Derby*
BRADLEY (All Saints) *see* The Candover Valley *Win*
BRADLEY (St George) *see* Gt and Lt Coates w Bradley *Linc*
BRADLEY (St John the Baptist) *see* Bowbrook N *Worc*
BRADLEY (St Martin) *Lich 29* **P** *Baldwin Pugh Trustees* **V** R M WALKER
BRADLEY (St Mary) *see* Cononley w Bradley *Bradf*
BRADLEY (St Thomas) *Wakef 5* **P** *Bp* **V** D R WARD
BRADLEY, GREAT (St Mary the Virgin) *see* Haverhill w Withersfield, the Wrattings etc *St E*
BRADLEY, LITTLE (All Saints) *as above*
BRADLEY, NORTH (St Nicholas) Southwick and Heywood *Sarum 17* **P** *Win Coll* **V** J R PARKER
BRADLEY, WEST (not known) *see* Baltonsborough w Butleigh and W Bradley *B & W*
BRADLEY-LE-MOORS (St Leonard) *see* Alton w Bradley-le-Moors and Oakamoor w Cotton *Lich*
BRADLEY STOKE (Christ the King) *see* Stoke Gifford *Bris*
BRADMORE (Mission Room) *see* Bunny w Bradmore *S'well*
BRADNINCH (St Denis) and Clyst Hydon *Ex 4* **P** *D&C and D&C Windsor (jt)* **R** D L D ROBOTTOM
BRADNOP (Mission Church) *see* Ipstones w Berkhamsytch and Onecote w Bradnop *Lich*
BRADOC (Blessed Virgin Mary) *see* Liskeard, St Keyne, St Pinnock, Morval etc *Truro*
BRADPOLE (Holy Trinity) *see* Bridport *Sarum*
BRADSHAW (St John the Evangelist) *Wakef 4* **P** *Bp* **V** C HAYNES
BRADSHAW (St Maxentius) *Man 16* **P** *V Bolton-le-Moors St Pet* **V** D M DUNN, **C** S C EDWARDS, S HAWORTH
BRADWELL (St Barnabas) *Derby 2* **P** *D&C Lich* **P-in-c** N P GOWER
BRADWELL (St Barnabas) *see* Wolstanton *Lich*
BRADWELL (St Laurence and Methodist United) *see* Stantonbury and Willen *Ox*
BRADWELL (St Nicholas) *Nor 6* **P** *Bp* **R** R J TUCK
BRADWELL, NEW (St James) *see* Stantonbury and Willen *Ox*
BRADWELL AND PATTISWICK (Holy Trinity) *see* Stisted w Bradwell and Pattiswick *Chelmsf*
BRADWELL ON SEA (St Thomas) *Chelmsf 11* **P** *Bp* **R** *Vacant* (01621) 776203
BRADWORTHY (St John the Baptist) *Ex 9* **P** *The Crown* **P-in-c** N P G LAST

BRAFFERTON (St Peter) w Pilmoor, Myton on Swale and Thormanby *York 5* **P** *Abp and Sir Anthony Milnes Coates (jt)* **V** *Vacant* (01423) 360244
BRAFIELD ON THE GREEN (St Laurence) *see* Cogenhoe and Gt and Lt Houghton w Brafield *Pet*
BRAILES (St George) *Cov 9* **P** *Provost and Chapter* **V** N J MORGAN, **NSM** J W ROLFE
BRAILSFORD (All Saints) w Shirley and Osmaston w Edlaston *Derby 8* **P** *Bp, Earl Ferrers, and Sir Peter Walker-Okeover, Bt (by turn)* **R** I ALDERSLEY, **NSM** C L JOHNSON
BRAINTREE (St Michael) *Chelmsf 15* **P** *Ch Trust Fund Trust* **V** B DAVIES, **C** A McHAFFIE
BRAINTREE (St Paul) *Chelmsf 15* **P** *Ch Trust Fund Trust* **V** S R LLOYD
BRAISHFIELD (All Saints) *see* Michelmersh, Timsbury, Farley Chamberlayne etc *Win*
BRAITHWAITE (St Herbert) *see* Thornthwaite cum Braithwaite and Newlands *Carl*
BRAITHWELL (St James) *see* Bramley and Ravenfield w Hooton Roberts etc *Sheff*
BRAMBER (St Nicholas) *see* Beeding and Bramber w Botolphs *Chich*
BRAMBLETON (not known) *see* Bourne *Guildf*
BRAMCOTE (St Michael and All Angels) *S'well 7* **P** *CPAS* **NSM** D EDINBOROUGH, J HENDERSON, J P SMITHURST
BRAMDEAN (St Simon and St Jude) *see* Hinton Ampner w Bramdean and Kilmeston *Win*
BRAMDEAN COMMON (Church in the Wood) *as above*
BRAMERTON (St Peter) *see* Rockland St Mary w Hellington, Bramerton etc *Nor*
BRAMFIELD (St Andrew) *see* Thorington w Wenhaston, Bramfield etc *St E*
BRAMFIELD (St Andrew) w Stapleford and Waterford *St Alb 22* **P** *R M A Smith Esq and Grocers' Co (alt)* **P-in-c** B H GWINN
BRAMFORD (St Mary the Virgin) *St E 1* **P** *D&C Cant* **P-in-c** R J DEDMAN, **NSM** A M BAIRD
BRAMHALL (St Michael and All Angels) (Hall Chapel) *Ches 17* **P** *Trustees* **C** R J ISHERWOOD, T S McCABE, **NSM** L M DADSON
BRAMHAM (All Saints) *York 1* **P** *G Lane Fox Esq* **V** J R D SHAW
BRAMHOPE (St Giles) *Ripon 7* **P** *Trustees* **V** D M ROBINSON
BRAMLEY (Holy Trinity) and Grafham *Guildf 2* **P** *Ld Chan* **V** M F H GODWIN
BRAMLEY (St Francis) and Ravenfield w Hooton Roberts and Braithwell *Sheff 6* **P** *Patr Bd* **R** D S WALKER, **TV** P J HOPPER
BRAMLEY (St James) *Win 4* **P** *Qu Coll Ox* **V** R C TOOGOOD
BRAMLEY (St Peter) *Ripon 6* **P** *DBP* **TR** P J SWIFT, **TV** J M LEAK, H FIELDEN
BRAMPFORD SPEKE (St Peter) *see* Thorverton, Cadbury, Upton Pyne etc *Ex*
BRAMPTON (St Mark) *Derby 5* **P** *Bp* **P-in-c** M J LEWIS
BRAMPTON (St Martin) and Farlam and Castle Carrock w Cumrew *Carl 2* **P** *Bp, D&C, Mrs J M Matthews, and Mrs S C Dean (jt)* **R** N N STEADMAN, **C** J L HIGGINS
BRAMPTON (St Mary Magdalene) *Ely 9* **P** *Bp* **R** M R GREENFIELD
BRAMPTON (St Peter) *see* Buxton w Oxnead, Lammas and Brampton *Nor*
BRAMPTON (St Peter) *see* Hundred River *St E*
BRAMPTON (St Thomas the Martyr) *Derby 5* **P** *Bp* **R** C J C FRITH, **C** A C BROOM, P D L WILKINSON, **NSM** J A HENDERSON
BRAMPTON, OLD (St Peter and St Paul) (Cutthorpe Institute) and Loundsley Green *Derby 5* **P** *Bp* **TR** P J BOWLES, **TV** M A YATES
BRAMPTON ABBOTTS (St Michael) *see* Ross w Brampton Abbotts, Bridstow, Peterstow etc *Heref*
BRAMPTON ASH (St Mary) w Dingley and Braybrooke *Pet 11* **P** *Earl Spencer (2 turns), DBP (1 turn)* **NSM** N M CLARKE
BRAMPTON BIERLOW (Christ Church) *Sheff 12* **P** *V Wath-upon-Dearne* **V** C W M BALDOCK, **C** L D BOULNOIS
BRAMPTON BRYAN (St Barnabas) *see* Wigmore Abbey *Heref*
BRAMSHALL (St Laurence) *see* Uttoxeter Area *Lich*
BRAMSHAW (St Peter) and Landford w Plaitford *Sarum 11* **P** *Bp and D&C (alt)* **R** D P CLACEY
BRAMSHILL (Mission Church) *see* Eversley *Win*
BRAMSHOTT (St Mary the Virgin) and Liphook *Portsm 5* **P** *Qu Coll Ox* **R** R A EWBANK
BRANCASTER (St Mary the Virgin) *see* Hunstanton St Mary w Ringstead Parva etc *Nor*
BRANCEPETH (St Brandon) *Dur 1* **P** *Bp* **P-in-c** A J DORBER
BRANCEPETH, NEW (St Catherine) *see* Brandon *Dur*
BRANDESBURTON (St Mary) and Leven w Catwick *York 12* **P** *St Jo Coll Cam, Exors Sir Henry Strickland-Constable Bt, and Simeon's Trustees (jt)* **R** M P DUNNING
BRANDESTON (All Saints) w Kettleburgh *St E 18* **P** *Capt J L Round-Turner (2 turns), C Austin Esq (1 turn)* **P-in-c** R J DIXON, **NSM** P G VELLACOTT
BRANDLESHOLME (St Francis House Chapel) *see* Elton All SS *Man*
BRANDON (Chapel) *see* Barkston and Hough Gp *Linc*
BRANDON (St John the Evangelist) *Dur 1* **P** *R Brancepeth* **V** D B GODSELL, **C** P BROWN
BRANDON (St Peter) and Santon Downham w Elveden *St E 11* **P** *Exors Earl of Iveagh* **R** S J ABBOTT
BRANDON PARVA (All Saints) *see* Barnham Broom *Nor*
BRANDSBY (All Saints) *see* Crayke w Brandsby and Yearsley *York*
BRANDWOOD (St Bede) *Birm 4* **P** *Bp* **V** N H BENSON, **NSM** H C BENSON
BRANKSEA ISLAND (St Mary) *see* Parkstone St Pet w Branksea and St Osmund *Sarum*
BRANKSOME (St Aldhelm) (St Francis) *Sarum 8* **P** *Bp* **V** S D LAKE, **C** H H D PRYSE
BRANKSOME (St Clement) (St Barnabas) *Sarum 8* **P** *MMCET* **V** J G V FOSTER
BRANKSOME PARK (All Saints) *Sarum 8* **P** *MMCET* **P-in-c** C M DAY
BRANSCOMBE (St Winifred) *see* Beer and Branscombe *Ex*
BRANSDALE (St Nicholas) *see* Kirkbymoorside w Gillamoor, Farndale etc *York*
BRANSFORD (St John the Baptist) *see* Alfrick, Lulsley, Suckley, Leigh and Bransford *Worc*
BRANSGORE (St Mary the Virgin) *Win 8* **P** *P W J Jesson Esq* **V** P C ELKINS
BRANSHOLME (St John) *see* Sutton St Jas and Wawne *York*
BRANSTON (All Saints) w Nocton and Potterhanworth *Linc 18* **P** *Stowe Sch (2 turns), Ld Chan (1 turn), and Nocton Ltd (1 turn)* **R** D F REAGON
BRANSTON (St Saviour) w Tatenhill *Lich 14* **P** *Bp and Simeon's Trustees (jt)* **V** D B SIMMONDS
BRANSTON BY BELVOIR (St Guthlac) *see* High Framland Parishes *Leic*
BRANT BROUGHTON (St Helen) and Beckingham *Linc 23* **P** *Bp, Exors Sir Richard Sutton Bt, and Revd J R H and Revd H C Thorold (by turn)* **P-in-c** A C E KNIGHT, **C** S N SHRIMPTON
BRANT ROAD (Church Centre) *see* Bracebridge *Linc*
BRANTHAM (St Michael and All Angels) w Stutton *St E 5* **P** *Bp and Em Coll Cam (alt)* **R** A S JONES, **NSM** I D FRYER
BRANTINGHAM (All Saints) *see* Elloughton and Brough w Brantingham *York*
BRANXTON (St Paul) *Newc 12* **P** *Abp* **V** R W HOWE
BRASSINGTON (St James) *see* Wirksworth *Derby*
BRASTED (St Martin) *Roch 9* **P** *Abp* **P-in-c** S M BANNISTER
BRATHAY (Holy Trinity) *see* Ambleside w Brathay *Carl*
BRATOFT (St Peter and St Paul) w Irby-in-the-Marsh *Linc 8* **P** *Bp* **R** T STEELE
BRATTLEBY (St Cuthbert) *see* Aisthorpe w Scampton w Thorpe le Fallows etc *Linc*
BRATTON (St James the Great) (Oratory), Edington and Imber, Erlestoke and Coulston *Sarum 19* **P** *Bp and V Westbury (jt)* **R** D J BELCHER, **Hon C** A LLOYD-DAVIES
BRATTON CLOVELLY (St Mary the Virgin) *see* Okehampton w Inwardleigh, Bratton Clovelly etc *Ex*
BRATTON FLEMING (St Peter) *see* Shirwell, Loxhore, Kentisbury, Arlington, etc *Ex*
BRATTON ST MAUR (St Nicholas) *see* Bruton and Distr *B & W*
BRAUGHING (St Mary the Virgin) w Furneux Pelham and Stocking Pelham *St Alb 18* **P** *Bp and Lord Hamilton (alt)* **R** R H NOKES
BRAUNSTON (All Saints) *see* Daventry, Ashby St Ledgers, Braunston etc *Pet*
BRAUNSTON (All Saints) *see* Oakham, Hambleton, Egleton, Braunston and Brooke *Pet*
BRAUNSTONE (St Peter) (St Crispin) *Leic 12* **P** *Bp* **TR** R K DANIEL, **TV** D A T MACGREGOR
BRAUNTON (St Brannock) *Ex 15* **P** *Bp* **V** R P REEVE, **Hon C** L A BUTTLE
BRAXTED, GREAT (All Saints) *see* Tolleshunt Knights w Tiptree and Gt Braxted *Chelmsf*
BRAXTED, LITTLE (St Nicholas) *see* Wickham Bishops w Lt Braxted *Chelmsf*
BRAY (St Michael) and Braywood *Ox 13* **P** *Bp* **V** G D REPATH, **C** J F RAMSBOTTOM
BRAY, HIGH (All Saints) *see* S Molton w Nymet St George, High Bray etc *Ex*
BRAYBROOKE (All Saints) *see* Brampton Ash w Dingley and Braybrooke *Pet*

BRAYDESTON (St Michael) *see* Brundall w Braydeston and Postwick *Nor*
BRAYTON (St Wilfrid) *York 6* **P** *Abp* **TR** D H REYNOLDS, **TV** P E GRIGSBY, **NSM** K MANNERS
BREADSALL (All Saints) *Derby 13* **P** *Miss A I M Harpur-Crewe* **P-in-c** R T SHORTHOUSE
BREADSTONE (St Michael and All Angels) *see* Berkeley w Wick, Breadstone and Newport *Glouc*
BREAGE (St Breaca) w Germoe *Truro 4* **P** *The Crown* **P-in-c** P J NICKOLS-RAWLE
BREAM (St James) *Glouc 4* **P** *Bp* **V** A G KENDALL, **NSM** M M HALE
BREAMORE (St Mary) *Win 8* **P** *Sir Westrow Hulse Bt* **P-in-c** G F W NEWELL of Staffa
BREAN (St Bridget) *see* Berrow and Breane *B & W*
BREARTON (St John the Baptist) *see* Knaresborough *Ripon*
BREASTON (St Michael) *see* Wilne and Draycott w Breaston *Derby*
BRECKLES (St Margaret) *see* Caston, Griston, Merton, Thompson etc *Nor*
BREDBURY (St Barnabas) *Ches 16* **P** *V Bredbury St Mark* **V** C R WINDLE
BREDBURY (St Mark) *Ches 16* **P** *Bp* **P-in-c** A R GARNER, **NSM** S J OSGOOD
BREDE (St George) w Udimore *Chich 20* **P** *Bp and Mrs M E Crook (alt)* **R** R W COTTON
BREDENBURY (St Andrew) w Grendon Bishop and Wacton, Edwyn Ralph, Collington, Thornbury, Pencombe and Marston Stannett and Little Cowarne *Heref 2* **P** *DBP, V Bromyard, and Lt-Col H H Barneby (jt)* **R** C I FLETCHER
BREDFIELD (St Andrew) *see* Ufford w Bredfield and Hasketon *St E*
BREDGAR (St John the Baptist) w Bicknor and Frinsted w Wormshill and Milsted *Cant 14* **P** *Abp, Lord Kingsdown, M Nightingale Esq, and S McCandlish Esq (jt)* **R** P N S HAYNES
BREDHURST (St Peter) *see* S Gillingham *Roch*
BREDICOT (St James the Less) *see* Bowbrook S *Worc*
BREDON (St Giles) w Bredon's Norton *Worc 4* **P** *Bp* **R** C J RIDOUT
BREDON'S NORTON (not known) *see* Bredon w Bredon's Norton *Worc*
BREDWARDINE (St Andrew) *see* Cusop w Clifford, Hardwicke, Bredwardine etc *Heref*
BREDY, LITTLE (St Michael and All Angels) *see* Bride Valley *Sarum*
BREEDON-ON-THE-HILL (St Mary and St Hardulph) cum Isley Walton and Worthington *Leic 9* **P** *D A G Shields Esq and Ch Coll Cam (alt)* **R** S J D FOSTER, **NSM** J W A DAWSON
BREIGHTMET (St James) *see* Bolton Breightmet St Jas *Man*
BREIGHTMET Top o' th' Moss (St John the Evangelist) *see* Bolton St Jo *Man*
BREINTON (St Michael) (Mission Hall) *Heref 4* **P** *Bp* **C** G T G SYKES
BREMHILL (St Martin) *see* Derry Hill w Bremhill and Foxham *Sarum*
BRENCHLEY (All Saints) *Roch 8* **P** *D&C Cant* **V** J F BOYCE
BRENDON (St Brendon) *see* Combe Martin, Berrynarbor, Lynton, Brendon etc *Ex*
BRENT, EAST (The Blessed Virgin Mary) *see* Brent Knoll, E Brent and Lympsham *B & W*
BRENT, SOUTH (St Petroc) and Rattery *Ex 13* **P** *Bp and Sir R V Carew, Bt (jt)* **V** J H HARPER, **Hon C** D G H HAMBLIN
BRENT ELEIGH (St Mary) *see* Monks Eleigh w Chelsworth and Brent Eleigh etc *St E*
BRENT KNOLL (St Michael) and East Brent and Lympsham *B & W 1* **P** *Adn Wells (1 turn), Bp (2 turns)* **R** J S WELLS
BRENT PELHAM (St Mary the Virgin) *see* Hormead, Wyddial, Anstey, Brent Pelham etc *St Alb*
BRENT TOR (Christ Church) *see* Peter Tavy, Mary Tavy, Lydford and Brent Tor *Ex*
BRENT TOR (St Michael) *as above*
BRENTFORD (St Paul w St Lawrence and St George) (St Faith) *Lon 11* **P** *Bp* **TR** D J SIMPSON, **Hon C** J S BOWDEN
BRENTRY (St Mark) *see* Henbury *Bris*
BRENTS (St John the Evangelist) and Davington w Oare and Luddenham, The *Cant 6* **P** *Abp and Ld Chan (alt)* **P-in-c** I C BLACK
BRENTWOOD (St George the Martyr) *Chelmsf 7* **P** *DBP* **V** G F JENKINS
BRENTWOOD (St Thomas) *Chelmsf 7* **P** *DBP* **P-in-c** R B WHITE, **C** P C BANKS
BRENZETT (St Eanswith) *see* Appledore w Brookland, Fairfield, Brenzett etc *Cant*
BRERETON (St Michael) *Lich 3* **P** *R Rugeley* **P-in-c** D J P ISIORHO
BRERETON (St Oswald) w Swettenham *Ches 11* **P** *DBP and MMCET (jt)* **R** J M INNES

BRESSINGHAM (St John the Baptist) w North and South Lopham and Fersfield *Nor 10* **P** *R D A Woode Esq, MMCET, and St Jo Coll Cam (by turn)* **P-in-c** R J MELLOWSHIP
BRETBY (St Wystan) w Newton Solney *Derby 16* **P** *Bp and DBP (alt)* **Hon C** A T REDMAN
BRETFORTON (St Leonard) *see* Badsey w Aldington and Offenham and Bretforton *Worc*
BRETHERTON (St John the Baptist) *Blackb 4* **P** *R Croston* **P-in-c** D P NESTOR
BRETTENHAM (St Andrew) *see* E w W Harling, Bridgham w Roudham, Larling etc *Nor*
BRETTENHAM (St Mary) *see* Rattlesden w Thorpe Morieux and Brettenham *St E*
BRETTON PARK (St Bartholomew) *see* Woolley *Wakef*
BREWHAM, SOUTH (St John the Baptist) *see* Bruton and Distr *B & W*
BREWOOD (St Mary and St Chad) *Lich 2* **P** *Bp* **V** T H GREEN
BRICETT, GREAT (St Mary and St Lawrence) *see* Ringshall w Battisford, Barking w Darmsden etc *St E*
BRICKENDON (Holy Cross and St Alban) *see* Lt Berkhamsted and Bayford, Essendon etc *St Alb*
BRICKET WOOD (St Luke) *St Alb 1* **P** *CPAS* **V** N M LADD, **NSM** A J WILLIAMSON, A de C LADD
BRICKHILL, GREAT (St Mary) w Bow Brickhill and Little Brickhill *Ox 26* **P** *Sir Philip Duncombe, Bt, Bp, and St Edw Sch Ox (by turn)* **R** S J TOZE
BRICKHILL, LITTLE (St Mary Magdalene) *see* Gt Brickhill w Bow Brickhill and Lt Brickhill *Ox*
BRICKHILL, NORTH (St Mark) *see* Bedf St Mark *St Alb*
BRICKLEHAMPTON (St Michael) *see* Elmley Castle w Bricklehampton and Combertons *Worc*
BRIDE VALLEY *Sarum 3* **P** *Patr Bd* **TR** J D ATKINSON, **TV** A J ASHWELL
BRIDEKIRK (St Bridget) *Carl 6* **P** *Trustees* **V** *Vacant* (01900) 826557
BRIDESTOWE (St Bridget) *see* Okehampton w Inwardleigh, Bratton Clovelly etc *Ex*
BRIDFORD (St Thomas a Becket) *see* Christow, Ashton, Trusham and Bridford *Ex*
BRIDGE (St Peter) *see* Patrixbourne w Bridge and Bekesbourne *Cant*
BRIDGE SOLLARS (St Andrew) *see* Kenchester and Bridge Sollers *Heref*
BRIDGEMARY (St Matthew) *Portsm 3* **P** *Bp* **V** J D JONES
BRIDGERULE (St Bridget) *see* Pyworthy, Pancrasweek and Bridgerule *Ex*
BRIDGETOWN (St John the Evangelist) *see* Totnes, Bridgetown and Berry Pomeroy etc *Ex*
BRIDGFORD, EAST (St Peter) and Kneeton *S'well 8* **P** *Magd Coll Ox (2 turns), C G Neale Esq (1 turn)* **R** A HAYDOCK
BRIDGFORD, WEST (St Giles) (St Luke) *S'well 10* **P** *Waddington Trustees* **R** P N HUMPHREYS, **NSM** D M FISHER
BRIDGHAM (St Mary) *see* E w W Harling, Bridgham w Roudham, Larling etc *Nor*
BRIDGNORTH (St Mary Magdalene) (St Leonard) (St James), Tasley, Astley Abbotts, Oldbury and Quatford *Heref 9* **P** *DBP (3 turns) and Ld Chan (1 turn)* **TR** A A ROBERTS, **TV** M J KNEEN, L A WALKER, **C** N J WILL, **Hon C** W A D BAKER
BRIDGWATER (Holy Trinity) *B & W 14* **P** *Bp* **V** R J M WILLCOX, **NSM** J K L POWELL
BRIDGWATER (St Francis of Assisi) *B & W 14* **P** *Bp* **V** D ARNOTT
BRIDGWATER (St John the Baptist) *B & W 14* **P** *Bp* **V** I G PIDOUX
BRIDGWATER (St Mary) and Chilton Trinity and Durleigh *B & W 14* **P** *Ld Chan* **V** R E J PACKER, **C** H T ANGOVE
BRIDLINGTON (Emmanuel) *York 10* **P** *Trustees* **V** M EXLEY
BRIDLINGTON (Holy Trinity) and Sewerby w Marton *York 10* **P** *Abp* **V** *Vacant* (01262) 675725
BRIDLINGTON (St Mary's Priory Church) *York 10* **P** *Simeon's Trustees* **R** J C MEEK
BRIDLINGTON QUAY (Christ Church) *York 10* **P** *R Bridlington Priory* **V** J G COUPER
BRIDPORT (St Mary) *Sarum 3* **P** *Patr Bd (2 turns) and Ld Chan (1 turn)* **TR** T N STUBBS, **TV** M A ALLCHIN, R W SHAMBROOK, **Hon C** J A FRY
BRIDSTOW (St Bridget) *see* Ross w Brampton Abbotts, Bridstow, Peterstow etc *Heref*
BRIERCLIFFE (St James) *Blackb 3* **P** *Hulme Trustees* **V** P H HALLAM
BRIERFIELD (St Luke) *Blackb 7* **P** *Bp* **V** E A SAVILLE
BRIERLEY (St Paul) *see* Felkirk w Brierley *Wakef*
BRIERLEY HILL (St Michael) (St Paul) *Worc 10* **P** *TR Wordsley* **R** C S MINCHIN

BRIGG (St John the Evangelist), Wrawby and Cadney cum Howsham *Linc 6* **P** *Bp* **V** M J SILLEY, **C** M S POSKITT
BRIGHAM (St Bridget) *Carl 6* **P** *Earl of Lonsdale* **V** C GODDARD
BRIGHOUSE (St Martin) (St Chad) and Clifton *Wakef 2* **P** *Bp* **TR** W G HARRIS-EVANS, **TV** D C BROOKES, G MANN
BRIGHSTONE (St Mary the Virgin) and Brooke w Mottistone *Portsm 8* **P** *Bp (2 turns), D&C St Paul's (1 turn)* **R** T W EADY
BRIGHTLING (St Thomas of Canterbury) Dallington, Mountfield and Netherfield *Chich 15* **P** *Bp, Adn Lewes and Hastings, Mrs R Hope Grissell, P S Wilmot-Sitwell Esq, and N S Cobbold Esq (jt)* **R** S BAKER, **NSM** J SHERWIN, J B B WRENBURY
BRIGHTLINGSEA (All Saints) (St James) *Chelmsf 23* **P** *Ld Chan* **V** R M SALENIUS
BRIGHTON (Annunciation) *Chich 2* **P** *Wagner Trustees* **V** D K WOSTENHOLM
BRIGHTON (Good Shepherd) Preston *Chich 2* **P** *Bp* **V** J D F GREENER
BRIGHTON (Resurrection) (St Alban) (St Luke) (St Martin w St Wilfrid) *Chich 2* **P** *Patr Bd* **TR** B L BRANDIE, **TV** K G PERKINTON, G J BUTTERWORTH, **C** W P STAFFORD-WHITTAKER, B C D WHEELHOUSE
BRIGHTON (St Augustine and St Saviour) *Chich 2* **P** *Bp* **V** T G BUXTON
BRIGHTON (St Bartholomew) *Chich 2* **P** *Wagner Trustees* **V** V W HOUSE, **NSM** H N ANNIS
BRIGHTON (St George w St Anne and St Mark) *Chich 2* **P** *Bp and V Brighton (jt)* **V** A H MANSON-BRAILSFORD, **C** C J MIDLANE
BRIGHTON (St John) *see* Preston *Chich*
BRIGHTON (St Mary the Virgin) *see* Kemp Town St Mary *Chich*
BRIGHTON (St Matthias) *Chich 2* **P** *V Preston* **V** K L W SYLVIA, **C** B S TYLER
BRIGHTON (St Michael and All Angels) *Chich 2* **P** *V Brighton* **V** S M MASTERS, **NSM** D G HEWETSON, J F KEYS
BRIGHTON (St Paul) *Chich 2* **P** *Wagner Trustees* **V** G R O'LOUGHLIN, **Hon C** J N BALDRY
BRIGHTON (St Peter) (St Nicholas) (Chapel Royal) *Chich 2* **P** *Bp* **TV** W R D CAPSTICK, D F MOODY, **C** J C WALL, **NSM** M J WELLS
BRIGHTON, NEW (All Saints) *Ches 7* **P** *DBP* **V** *Vacant* 0151-639 2748
BRIGHTON, NEW (St James) (Emmanuel) *Ches 7* **P** *Bp* **V** C A BOYCE, **C** B D HARRY
BRIGHTSIDE (St Thomas and St Margaret) w Wincobank *Sheff 3* **P** *The Crown and Sheff Ch Burgesses (alt)* **V** M V GILBERT, **NSM** M CAUNT
BRIGHTWALTON (All Saints) w Catmore, Leckhampstead, Chaddleworth and Fawley *Ox 14* **P** *Bp, P L Wroughton Esq, and D&C Westmr (jt)* **R** A A D SMITH
BRIGHTWELL (St Agatha) w Sotwell *Ox 18* **P** *Bp* **R** *Vacant* (01491) 837110
BRIGHTWELL (St John the Baptist) *see* Martlesham w Brightwell *St E*
BRIGHTWELL BALDWIN (St Bartholomew) *see* Ewelme, Brightwell Baldwin, Cuxham w Easington *Ox*
BRIGNALL (St Mary) *see* Startforth and Bowes and Rokeby w Brignall *Ripon*
BRIGSLEY (St Helen) *see* Ravendale Gp *Linc*
BRIGSTOCK (St Andrew) w Stanion and Lowick and Sudborough *Pet 9* **P** *Bp (2 turns), L G Stopford Sackville Esq (1 turn)* **R** R D HOWE
BRILL (All Saints), Boarstall, Chilton and Dorton *Ox 21* **P** *Sir John Aubrey-Fletcher, Bt and Earl Temple of Stowe (jt)* **V** P R BUGG
BRILLEY (St Mary) *see* Eardisley w Bollingham, Willersley, Brilley etc *Heref*
BRIMFIELD (St Michael) *see* Orleton w Brimfield *Heref*
BRIMINGTON (St Michael) *Derby 3* **P** *V Chesterfield* **R** D C TRUBY, **NSM** J V LEWIS
BRIMPSFIELD (St Michael) w Birdlip, Syde, Daglingworth, The Duntisbournes and Winstone *Glouc 12* **P** *Ld Chan, Bp, DBP, and CCC Ox (by turn)* **R** P NEWING, **NSM** J M FRANCIS
BRIMPTON (St Peter) *see* Aldermaston w Wasing and Brimpton *Ox*
BRIMSCOMBE (Holy Trinity) *see* Woodchester and Brimscombe *Glouc*
BRINDLE (St James) *Blackb 4* **P** *Trustees* **P-in-c** A SOWERBUTTS
BRINGHURST (St Nicholas) *see* Six Saints circa Holt *Leic*
BRINGTON (All Saints) w Molesworth and Old Weston *Ely 10* **P** *Bp* **P-in-c** C M FURLONG
BRINGTON (St Mary w St John) w Whilton and Norton *Pet 3* **P** *Earl Spencer and DBP (alt)* **P-in-c** D A J MacPHERSON
BRININGHAM (St Maurice) *see* Brinton, Briningham, Hunworth, Stody etc *Nor*
BRINKBURN (not known) *see* Longframlington w Brinkburn *Newc*
BRINKHILL (St Philip) *see* S Ormsby Gp *Linc*
BRINKLEY (St Mary), Burrough Green and Carlton *Ely 4* **P** *St Jo Coll Cam, Mrs B O Killander, and E H Vestey Esq (by turn)* **P-in-c** J S ASKEY
BRINKLOW (St John the Baptist) *Cov 6* **P** *Ld Chan* **R** P S RUSSELL
BRINKWORTH (St Michael and All Angels) w Dauntsey *Bris 12* **P** *Bp* **R** D ORMSTON
BRINNINGTON (St Luke) w Portwood St Paul *Ches 18* **P** *Bp* **V** S B WOODHEAD, **NSM** W S ATKINSON
BRINSCALL (St Luke) *see* Heapey St Barnabas and Withnell St Paul *Blackb*
BRINSLEY (St James the Great) w Underwood *S'well 4* **P** *Bp* **P-in-c** E F CULLY
BRINSOP (St George) *see* Credenhill w Brinsop, Mansel Lacey, Yazor etc *Heref*
BRINSWORTH (St Andrew) w Catcliffe and Treeton *Sheff 6* **P** *Patr Bd* **TR** B SWINDELL, **TV** L E G BONIFACE, **C** M J SNOW
BRINTON (St Andrew), Briningham, Hunworth, Stody, Swanton Novers and Thornage *Nor 18* **P** *J S Howlett Esq, Lord Hastings, and DBP (by turn)* **NSM** F N WARD
BRISLEY (St Bartholomew) *see* Colkirk w Oxwick w Pattesley, Whissonsett etc *Nor*
BRISLINGTON (St Anne) *Bris 3* **P** *Bp* **V** *Vacant* 0117-977 6667
BRISLINGTON (St Christopher) *Bris 3* **P** *Simeon's Trustees* **P-in-c** C R EDWARDS
BRISLINGTON (St Cuthbert) *Bris 3* **P** *Bp* **P-in-c** G R M FISON
BRISLINGTON (St Luke) *Bris 3* **P** *Bp* **P-in-c** S W JONES
BRISTOL *see* Univ of the W of England *Bris*
BRISTOL (Christ the Servant) Stockwood *Bris 3* **P** *Bp* **Hon C** P A WALL
BRISTOL Lockleaze (St Mary Magdalene w St Francis) *Bris 6* **P** *Bp* **P-in-c** K A MacKINNON
BRISTOL Redfield (St Leonard) *see* E Bris *Bris*
BRISTOL St Aidan w St George *Bris 2* **P** *Bp and SMF* **V** B D JOY
BRISTOL (St Andrew) Hartcliffe *Bris 1* **P** *Bp* **V** J J HASLER, **C** R C NIXSON
BRISTOL (St Andrew w St Bartholomew) *Bris 6* **P** *Bp* **P-in-c** P R BAILEY
BRISTOL (St Mary the Virgin) Redcliffe w Temple and Bedminster St John the Baptist *Bris 1* **P** *Bp* **V** M A WHATMOUGH, **C** D F TYNDALL, **NSM** G G STIMPSON, W C BEAVER
BRISTOL (St Matthew and St Nathanael) (St Katharine) *Bris 6* **P** *Bp and CPAS (jt)* **V** R V BRAZIER
BRISTOL (St Michael the Archangel on the Mount Without) (St Paul) *Bris 5* **P** *Bp and Bris Ch Trustees (jt)* **Hon C** A F STUART, S M WATTERSON
BRISTOL St Paul's (St Agnes) *Bris 4* **P** *Ld Chan and Patr Bd (alt)* **TR** D C SELF, **TV** J M FRANCIS, **NSM** P BARTLE-JENKINS
BRISTOL (St Philip and St Jacob w Emmanuel) *Bris 4* **P** *Trustees* **V** M M WIDDECOMBE
BRISTOL, The City of (Christ Church w St George) (St James w St Peter) (St Stephen w St James and St John the Baptist) *Bris 4* **P** *Ld Chan (1 turn), Trustees (2 turns)* **R** *Vacant* 0117-973 6576
BRISTOL, EAST (St Aidan) *see* Bristol St Aid w St Geo *Bris*
BRISTOL, EAST (St Ambrose) (St Matthew) (St Leonard) *Bris 2* **P** *Patr Bd* **TR** R D JAMES, **C** D A IZZARD, **Hon C** C L SUTCH, N G BAILEY, C R PIPE-WOLFERSTAN
BRISTOL, EAST (St George) *see* Bristol St Aid w St Geo *Bris*
BRISTON (All Saints) w Burgh Parva and Melton Constable *Nor 18* **P** *Bp and Lord Hastings (jt)* **R** H J BLACKER
BRITFORD (St Peter) *see* Chalke Valley W *Sarum*
BRITWELL (St George) *see* W Slough *Ox*
BRITWELL SALOME (St Nicholas) *see* Icknield *Ox*
BRIXHAM (St Mary) (All Saints) w Churston Ferrers and Kingswear *Ex 10* **P** *The Crown* **TV** A S ALLEN, D R MILTON
BRIXTON (St Mary) *see* Yealmpton and Brixton *Ex*
BRIXTON (St Matthew) *S'wark 10* **P** *Abp* **V** C B OXENFORTH
BRIXTON (St Paul) *S'wark 10* **P** *Ch Soc Trust* **V** *Vacant* 0171-274 6907
BRIXTON, EAST (St Jude) *S'wark 10* **P** *Ch Soc Trust* **V** W P NASH
BRIXTON, NORTH (Christ Church) *see* Brixton Road Ch Ch *S'wark*
BRIXTON DEVERILL (St Michael) *see* Cley Hill Warminster *Sarum*

BRIXTON HILL (St Saviour) *S'wark 10* **P** *Ch Soc Trust* **P-in-c** S F COUGHTREY
BRIXTON ROAD (Christ Church) *S'wark 10* **P** *CPAS* **V** N P GODFREY
BRIXWORTH (All Saints) w Holcot *Pet 2* **P** *Bp* **V** A J WATKINS
BRIZE NORTON (St Britius) *see* Minster Lovell and Brize Norton *Ox*
BROAD Town (Christ Church), Clyffe Pypard, Hilmarton and Tockenham *Sarum 18* **P** *Ld Chan, DBP, and Prime Min (by turns)* **R** A G CAPES
BROAD BLUNSDON (St Leonard) *see* The Blunsdons *Bris*
BROAD CAMPDEN (St Michael and All Angels) *see* Chipping Campden w Ebrington *Glouc*
BROAD HINTON (St Peter ad Vincula) *see* Upper Kennet *Sarum*
BROAD LANE (Licensed Room) *see* Wybunbury w Doddington *Ches*
BROAD OAK (St George) *see* Heathfield *Chich*
BROADBOTTOM (St Mary Magdalene) *see* Mottram in Longdendale *Ches*
BROADBRIDGE HEATH (St John) *see* Horsham *Chich*
BROADCHALKE (All Saints) *see* Chalke Valley W *Sarum*
BROADCLYST (St John the Baptist) *see* Pinhoe and Broadclyst *Ex*
BROADFIELD (Christ the Lord) *see* Southgate *Chich*
BROADHEATH (Christ Church), Crown East and Rushwick *Worc 3* **P** *Bp and D&C (jt)* **V** G T M NOTT
BROADHEATH (St Alban) *Ches 10* **P** *Bp* **V** J BEANEY, **C** A R ROWE
BROADHEMBURY (St Andrew the Apostle and Martyr), Payhembury and Plymtree *Ex 7* **P** *W Drewe Esq, Ex Coll Ox, and Or Coll Ox (by turn)* **R** A M ROBERTS
BROADHEMPSTON (St Peter and St Paul), Woodland, Staverton w Landscove and Littlehempston *Ex 13* **P** *Prime Min (1 turn), D&C and Bp (1 turn)* **R** J CRUSE
BROADMAYNE (St Martin), West Knighton, Owermoigne and Warmwell *Sarum 2* **P** *Major G A M Cree (1 turn), MMCET (2 turns), and Sir Robert Williams, Bt (1 turn)* **R** R B GREGORY
BROADOAK (St Paul) *see* Symondsbury and Chideock *Sarum*
BROADSTAIRS (Holy Trinity) *Cant 9* **P** *V St Peter-in-Thanet* **R** M W HAYTON
BROADSTONE (not known) *see* Diddlebury w Munslow, Holdgate and Tugford *Heref*
BROADSTONE (St John the Baptist) *Sarum 8* **P** *Bp* **V** M FREDRIKSEN, **C** V T LEONARD, **NSM** D J MADDOX
BROADWAS (St Mary Magdalene) *see* Martley and Wichenford, Knightwick etc *Worc*
BROADWATER (St Mary) (St Stephen) *Chich 5* **P** *Patr Bd* **TR** P J DOMINY, **TV** S C COUPLAND, J M NEVILL, **C** T J GREENSLADE
BROADWATER DOWN *see* Tunbridge Wells St Mark *Roch*
BROADWATERS (St Oswald) *see* Kidderminster St Mary and All SS w Trimpley etc *Worc*
BROADWAY (St Aldhem and St Eadburga) *see* Ilminster and District *B & W*
BROADWAY (St Eadburgha) (St Michael and All Angels) w Wickhamford *Worc 1* **P** *Peache Trustees and Ch Ch Ox (jt)* **V** P J BURCH
BROADWELL (Good Shepherd) *see* Coleford w Staunton *Glouc*
BROADWELL (St Paul), Evenlode, Oddington and Adlestrop *Glouc 15* **P** *Bp, Ch Soc Trust, Lord Leigh, and DBP (jt)* **R** *Vacant* (01451) 831866
BROADWELL (St Peter and St Paul) *see* Shill Valley and Broadshire *Ox*
BROADWEY (St Nicholas) *see* Bincombe w Broadwey, Upwey and Buckland Ripers *Sarum*
BROADWINDSOR (St John the Baptist) *see* Beaminster Area *Sarum*
BROADWOODKELLY (All Saints) *Ex 19* **P** *DBP* **R** P J NORMAN
BROADWOODWIDGER (St Nicholas) *Ex 24* **P** *Bp* **P-in-c** J H HEATH
BROCKDISH (St Peter and St Paul) *see* Scole, Brockdish, Billingford, Thorpe Abbots etc *Nor*
BROCKENHURST (St Nicholas) (St Saviour) *Win 10* **P** *E J F Morant Esq* **V** G C BOWYER, **Hon C** R DROWN
BROCKHALL (St Peter and St Paul) *see* Heyford w Stowe Nine Churches and Flore etc *Pet*
BROCKHAM GREEN (Christ Church) *S'wark 26* **P** *Hon J L Hamilton* **P-in-c** J M A WILLANS
BROCKHAMPTON (Chapel) *see* Bromyard *Heref*
BROCKHAMPTON (All Saints) *see* Fownhope w Mordiford, Brockhampton etc *Heref*
BROCKHOLES (St George) *see* Honley *Wakef*
BROCKLESBY PARK (All Saints) *Linc 6* **P** *Earl of Yarborough* **V** S PHILLIPS, **C** H A JONES, **Hon C** S W ANDREW
BROCKLEY (St Andrew) *see* Chevington w Hargrave and Whepstead w Brockley *St E*
BROCKLEY HILL (St Saviour) *S'wark 5* **P** *V Forest Hill Ch Ch* **V** C G SMITH, **NSM** R O SMITH, R G TURPIN
BROCKMOOR (St John) *Worc 10* **P** *Prime Min* **V** F M TRETHEWEY
BROCKWORTH (St George) *Glouc 6* **P** *DBP* **V** M M ENNIS, **C** W F P PERRY
BROCTON (All Saints) *see* Baswich *Lich*
BRODSWORTH (St Michael and All Angels) *see* Bilham *Sheff*
BROKENBOROUGH (St John the Baptist) *see* Malmesbury w Westport and Brokenborough *Bris*
BROKERS WOOD (All Saints) *see* Dilton Marsh *Sarum*
BROMBOROUGH (St Barnabas) *Ches 9* **P** *D&C* **R** W J HOGG, **C** N TIVEY
BROME (St Mary) *see* N Hartismere *St E*
BROMESWELL (St Edmund) *see* Eyke w Bromeswell, Rendlesham, Tunstall etc *St E*
BROMFIELD (St Mary the Virgin) *see* Culmington w Onibury, Bromfield etc *Heref*
BROMFIELD (St Mungo) w Waverton *Carl 7* **P** *Bp* **P-in-c** P J SWAIN, **C** P M TOMPKINS, **NSM** M I STUDHOLME
BROMFORD FIRS (not Known) *see* Hodge Hill *Birm*
BROMHAM (St Nicholas), Chittoe and Sandy Lane *Sarum 18* **P** *DBP and S Spicer Esq (jt)* **R** R G BROWN
BROMHAM (St Owen) w Oakley and Stagsden *St Alb 13* **P** *Bp* **V** D V DRAPER, **C** P M QUINT
BROMLEY (All Hallows) *see* Bow H Trin and All Hallows *Lon*
BROMLEY (Christ Church) *Roch 14* **P** *CPAS* **V** M C LAWSON, **C** R B C STANDRING, R Q EDWARDS, **Hon C** N E BAINES, **NSM** C D HARLEY
BROMLEY (Holy Trinity Mission Church) *see* Pensnett *Worc*
BROMLEY (St Andrew) *Roch 14* **P** *Bp* **V** H A ATHERTON
BROMLEY (St John the Evangelist) *Roch 14* **P** *Bp* **V** C D ELLIOTT
BROMLEY (St Mark) *Roch 14* **P** *V Bromley SS Pet & Paul* **V** A T VOUSDEN, **C** D WINTER
BROMLEY (St Peter and St Paul) *Roch 14* **P** *Bp* **V** P H D'A LOCK, **C** J F WORTHEN
BROMLEY, GREAT (St George) *see* Ardleigh and The Bromleys *Chelmsf*
BROMLEY COMMON (Holy Trinity) *Roch 14* **P** *The Crown* **V** H P C BROADBENT, **NSM** K C BARNES
BROMLEY COMMON (St Augustine) *Roch 14* **P** *Bp* **V** B J ASH
BROMLEY COMMON (St Luke) *Roch 14* **P** *Bp* **V** G D GRAHAM, **C** H HESELWOOD
BROMLEY CROSS (St Andrew's Mission Church) *see* Walmsley *Man*
BROMPTON (Holy Trinity) w Onslow Square St Paul *Lon 8* **P** *Bp and MMCET (jt)* **V** J A K MILLAR, **C** N G P GUMBEL, S G DOWNHAM, J P T PETERS, N K LEE, R C THORPE
BROMPTON (St Thomas) w Deighton *York 20* **P** *D&C Dur* **V** M S SNOWBALL
BROMPTON, NEW (St Luke) *Roch 3* **P** *Bp* **V** J L C ABLEWHITE
BROMPTON, WEST (St Mary) (St Peter) *Lon 8* **P** *Bp* **V** G C BEAUCHAMP
BROMPTON-BY-SAWDON (All Saints) w Snainton, Ebberston and Allerston *York 21* **P** *Abp* **V** T E D THOMAS
BROMPTON ON SWALE (St Paul) *see* Easby w Brompton on Swale and Bolton on Swale *Ripon*
BROMPTON RALPH (The Blessed Virgin Mary) *see* Lydeard St Lawrence w Brompton Ralph etc *B & W*
BROMPTON REGIS (Blessed Virgin Mary) w Upton and Skilgate *B & W 16* **P** *Bp, Em Coll Cam, and Keble Coll Ox (jt)* **P-in-c** J CLOWES
BROMSBERROW (St Mary the Virgin) *see* Redmarley D'Abitot, Bromesberrow w Pauntley etc *Glouc*
BROMSGROVE (All Saints) *Worc 7* **P** *V Bromsgrove St Jo* **V** J E COOK
BROMSGROVE (St John the Baptist) *Worc 7* **P** *D&C* **V** J H DAVIES, **C** P H WORRALL, **NSM** G GILES
BROMWICH, WEST (All Saints) (St Mary Magdalene) *Lich 28* **P** *Bp* **V** M MORETON, **C** R K BELL, L J WOOLHOUSE
BROMWICH, WEST (Good Shepherd w St John) *Lich 28* **P** *Bp* **P-in-c** N G MARNS, **C** R J HUDSON-WILKIN
BROMWICH, WEST (Holy Trinity) *Lich 28* **P** *Peache Trustees* **V** *Vacant* 0121-525 3595
BROMWICH, WEST (St Andrew) (Christ Church) *Lich 28* **P** *Bp and V W Bromwich All SS (jt)* **V** K WILKIN, **C** D GRASBY

BROMWICH, WEST (St Francis of Assisi) *Lich 28* **P** *Bp* **V** R G DAVIES, **C** K H JOHNSON
BROMWICH, WEST St James Hill Top *Lich 28* **P** *Bp* **V** M C RUTTER, **C** J MITSON
BROMWICH, WEST (St Paul) Golds Hill *Lich 28* **P** *V Tipton St Martin* **P-in-c** M C RUTTER
BROMWICH, WEST (St Peter) *Lich 28* **P** *Bp* **P-in-c** G D STARKEY
BROMWICH, WEST (St Philip) *Lich 28* **P** *Bp* **V** R C DESON
BROMYARD (St Peter) *Heref 2* **P** *Bp* **V** D W GOULD, **C** P CUBITT
BROMYARD DOWNS (Mission Church) *see* Bromyard *Heref*
BRONDESBURY (Christ Church) (St Laurence) *Lon 21* **P** *Ld Chan* **P-in-c** E V LAKE
BRONDESBURY St Anne w Kilburn (Holy Trinity) *Lon 21* **P** *Bp and Ch Patr Soc (alt)* **P-in-c** F B CAPIE, **NSM** D NEW
BROOK (St Mary) *see* Wye w Brook *Cant*
BROOKE (St Mary the Virgin) *see* Brighstone and Brooke w Mottistone *Portsm*
BROOKE (St Peter) *see* Oakham, Hambleton, Egleton, Braunston and Brooke *Pet*
BROOKE (St Peter), Kirstead, Mundham w Seething and Thwaite *Nor 5* **P** *G&C Coll Cam, Gt Hosp and Countess Ferrers and Ld Chan (by turn)* **R** P E HALLS
BROOKE STREET (St Alban the Martyr) *see* Holborn St Alb w Saffron Hill St Pet *Lon*
BROOKEND (Mission Room) *see* Sharpness w Purton and Brookend *Glouc*
BROOKFIELD (St Anne), Highgate Rise *Lon 17* **P** *Bp* **P-in-c** C G POPE, **C** J W BESWICK
BROOKFIELD (St Margaret) *York 22* **P** *Abp* **V** R W SMITH
BROOKFIELD (St Mary) *Lon 17* **P** *Bp* **V** C G POPE, **C** J W BESWICK
BROOKHURST (St Peter's Chapel) *see* Eastham *Ches*
BROOKING (St Barnabas) *see* Totnes, Bridgetown and Berry Pomeroy etc *Ex*
BROOKLAND (St Augustine) *see* Appledore w Brookland, Fairfield, Brenzett etc *Cant*
BROOKLANDS *see* Baguley *Man*
BROOKMANS PARK (St Michael) *see* N Mymms *St Alb*
BROOKSBY (St Michael and All Angels) *see* Upper Wreake *Leic*
BROOKSIDE (Pastoral Centre) *see* Cen Telford *Lich*
BROOKWOOD (St Saviour) *see* Woking St Jo *Guildf*
BROOM (St Matthew) *see* Bidford-on-Avon *Cov*
BROOM LEYS (St David) *Leic 8* **P** *Bp* **V** J W STEVENSON, **NSM** D WHITTAKER
BROOM VALLEY (St Barnabas) *see* Rotherham *Sheff*
BROOME (St Michael) *see* Ditchingham, Hedenham and Broome *Nor*
BROOME (St Peter) *see* Churchill-in-Halfshire w Blakedown and Broome *Worc*
BROOMFIELD (St Margaret) *see* Hollingbourne and Hucking w Leeds and Broomfield *Cant*
BROOMFIELD (St Mary and All Saints) *see* Kingston St Mary w Broomfield etc *B & W*
BROOMFIELD (St Mary w St Leonard) *Chelmsf 8* **P** *Bp* **P-in-c** A W D RITSON
BROOMFLEET (St Mary) *see* S Cave and Ellerker w Broomfleet *York*
BROOMHILL (St Mark) *see* Sheff St Mark Broomhill *Sheff*
BROSELEY (All Saints) w Benthall, Jackfield, Linley, Willey and Barrow *Heref 14* **P** *Patr Bd* **R** M A KINNA, **C** T J STEAD, **NSM** A A BRACE
BROTHERTOFT Group, The (Christ Church) (St Gilbert of Sempringham) *Linc 21* **P** *Bp (2 turns), V Algarkirk (1 turn)* **NSM** D J CLARKE
BROTHERTON (St Edward the Confessor) *Wakef 11* **P** *D&C York* **P-in-c** D ROBINSON
BROTTON PARVA (St Margaret) *York 17* **P** *Abp* **R** E SMITS
BROUGH (All Saints) *see* Elloughton and Brough w Brantingham *York*
BROUGH (St Michael) w Stainmore, Musgrave and Warcop *Carl 1* **P** *Bp (2 turns) and Lord Hothfield (1 turn)* **C** D B de M LEATHES
BROUGHAM (St Wilfrid Chapel) *see* Lowther and Askham and Clifton and Brougham *Carl*
BROUGHTON (All Saints) *see* Warboys w Broughton and Bury w Wistow *Ely*
BROUGHTON (All Saints), Marton and Thornton *Bradf 7* **P** *Ch Ch Ox and Exors Dame Harriet Nelson (jt)* **R** T VAUGHAN
BROUGHTON (St Andrew) w Loddington and Cransley and Thorpe Malsor *Pet 11* **P** *Ld Chan (1 turn), Bp (2 turns), and Keble Coll Ox (1 turn)* **R** R M GILES
BROUGHTON (St James) (St Clement and St Matthias) (St John the Baptist) *Man 6* **P** *Patr Bd* **TR** J APPLEGATE, **TV** C W READ
BROUGHTON (St John the Baptist) *Blackb 14* **P** *Trustees* **V** S J FINCH, **C** J E C PERCIVAL, **NSM** A RHODES
BROUGHTON (St Mary) *Lich 23* **P** *D R B Thompson Esq* **P-in-c** E A HADLEY
BROUGHTON (St Mary) *Linc 6* **P** *MMCET* **R** J W COTTON
BROUGHTON (St Mary Magdalene) (Holy Innocents) and Duddon *Carl 8* **P** *V Millom, Lt-Col D A S Pennefather, and Ch Patr Trust (by turn)* **V** P F BARNES
BROUGHTON (St Mary the Virgin) *see* Wykeham *Ox*
BROUGHTON (St Mary) w Bossington and Houghton and Mottisfont *Win 11* **P** *Ld Chan (1 turn), Mr and Mrs R G L Pugh, A Humbert Esq and Miss R A Humbert (jt) (2 turns)* **R** *Vacant* Carlow (503) 21570
BROUGHTON (St Peter) *see* Croxton w Broughton and Adbaston *Lich*
BROUGHTON, GREAT (Christ Church) and Broughton Moor *Carl 7* **P** *Bp* **P-in-c** J V HINE
BROUGHTON, LOWER (Ascension) *Man 6* **P** *Trustees* **P-in-c** P R S BOLTON
BROUGHTON, NETHER (St Mary the Virgin) *see* Old Dalby and Nether Broughton *Leic*
BROUGHTON, UPPER (St Luke) *see* Hickling w Kinoulton and Broughton Sulney *S'well*
BROUGHTON ASTLEY (St Mary) and Croft w Stoney Stanton *Leic 10* **P** *Patr Bd* **TR** P BURROWS, **C** N M HUNT
BROUGHTON GIFFORD (St Mary the Virgin), Great Chalfield and Holt St Katharine *Sarum 17* **P** *D&C Bris (3 turns), Ld Chan (2 turns), and R C Floyd Esq (1 turn)* **R** R G HART
BROUGHTON HACKETT (St Leonard) *see* Peopleton and White Ladies Aston w Churchill etc *Worc*
BROUGHTON IN FURNESS (St Mary Magdalene) *see* Broughton and Duddon *Carl*
BROUGHTON MILLS (Holy Innocents) *as above*
BROUGHTON MOOR (St Columba) *see* Gt Broughton and Broughton Moor *Carl*
BROUGHTON POGGS (St Peter) *see* Shill Valley and Broadshire *Ox*
BROWN CANDOVER (St Peter) *see* The Candover Valley *Win*
BROWN EDGE (St Anne) *Lich 8* **P** *Bp* **V** D J FAIRWEATHER
BROWNHILL (St Saviour) *Wakef 10* **P** *V Batley* **V** R ADAIR
BROWNSWOOD PARK (St John the Evangelist) *Lon 5* **P** *City Corp* **P-in-c** M S STARKEY
BROXBOURNE (St Augustine) w Wormley *St Alb 20* **P** *Bp and Peache Trustees (jt)* **R** R A POTTER, **C** B E C PATE
BROXHOLME (All Saints) *see* Saxilby Gp *Linc*
BROXTED (St Mary the Virgin) w Chickney and Tilty and Great and Little Easton *Chelmsf 18* **P** *Mrs F Spurrier (2 turns), DBP (1 turn), and MMCET (1 turn)* **R** J M FILBY
BROXTOWE (St Martha) *S'well 14* **P** *Bp* **V** J S M HARDING
BRUERA (St Mary) *see* Aldford and Bruera *Ches*
BRUISYARD (St Peter) *see* Badingham w Bruisyard, Cransford and Dennington *St E*
BRUMBY (St Hugh) (All Saints) *Linc 4* **P** *Bp* **TR** A G D HAYDAY, **TV** H P JONES, **C** M N HOLDEN
BRUNDALL (St Lawrence) w Braydeston and Postwick *Nor 4* **P** *Bp and MMCET (jt)* **R** R M BAKER, **C** R J ESPIN-BRADLEY
BRUNDISH (St Lawrence) *see* Wilby w Brundish *St E*
BRUNSTEAD (St Peter) *see* Stalham and E Ruston w Brunstead *Nor*
BRUNSWICK (Christ Church) *Man 4* **P** *Ch Soc Trust* **R** S J T GATENBY, **NSM** R M YOUNG
BRUNSWICK (St Cuthbert) *see* Ch the King in the Dio of Newc *Newc*
BRUNTCLIFFE (St Andrew) *Wakef 8* **P** *V Batley and V St Peter Morley (alt)* **P-in-c** D E CRAIG-WILD
BRUNTINGTHORPE (St Mary) *see* Arnesby w Shearsby and Bruntingthorpe *Leic*
BRUNTON PARK (St Aidan) *see* Ch the King in the Dio of Newc *Newc*
BRUSHFORD (St Mary the Virgin) *Ex 19* **P** *D&C* **V** P J NORMAN
BRUSHFORD (St Nicholas) *see* Dulverton and Brushford *B & W*
BRUTON (Blessed Virgin Mary) and District *B & W 2* **P** *Patr Bd* **TV** O D WILLIAMS, **C** J F M MILES
BRYANSTON SQUARE (St Mary) w St Marylebone (St Mark) *Lon 4* **P** *The Crown* **R** D EVANS
BRYANSTON STREET (Annunciation) *see* St Marylebone Annunciation Bryanston Street *Lon*
BRYHER (All Saints) *see* Is of Scilly *Truro*
BRYMPTON (St Andrew) *see* Odcombe, Brympton, Lufton and Montacute *B & W*

BRYN (St Chad) *see* Clun w Bettws-y-Crwyn and Newcastle *Heref*
BRYN (St Peter) *Liv 15* **P** *Bp* **V** D J HOOTON
BUBBENHALL (St Giles) *see* Ryton on Dunsmore w Bubbenhall *Cov*
BUBWITH (All Saints) w Skipwith *York 4* **P** *Abp and D&C, and Ld Chan (alt)* **V** B EVES
BUCKDEN (St Mary) *Ely 12* **P** *Bp* **V** R C BENDING, **Hon C** M FALLA
BUCKENHAM, NEW (St Martin) *see* Quidenham Gp *Nor*
BUCKENHAM, OLD (All Saints) *as above*
BUCKERELL (St Mary and St Giles) *see* Feniton, Buckerell and Escot *Ex*
BUCKFAST SANCTUARY (not known) *see* Buckfastleigh w Dean Prior *Ex*
BUCKFASTLEIGH (Holy Trinity) (St Luke's Mission) w Dean Prior *Ex 13* **P** *D&C (2 turns), DBP (1 turn)* **V** D J ROWLAND, **NSM** J N C IRWIN
BUCKHORN WESTON (St John the Baptist) *see* Gillingham *Sarum*
BUCKHURST HILL (St Elisabeth) (St John the Baptist) (St Stephen) *Chelmsf 25* **P** *Patr Bd* **P-in-c** K P HALLETT, **C** T V ROBERTS, A COMFORT, **NSM** P ROBERTS
BUCKINGHAM (St Peter and St Paul) *Ox 22* **P** *Bp, New Coll, G&C Coll Cam, Mrs S A J Doulton, and Adn (jt)* **R** D G MEARA, **C** P HARDY, M MOWFORTH, **NSM** R M BUNDOCK
BUCKINGHAM, NORTH *Ox 22* **P** *Ch Soc Trust, Mrs J M Williams, and D J Robarts Esq (by turn)* **R** R H KENT
BUCKLAND (All Saints) *see* Aston Clinton w Buckland and Drayton Beauchamp *Ox*
BUCKLAND (St Mary the Virgin) *Ox 17* **P** *DBP, Bp and Or Coll Ox (by turn)* **V** C R RUDD, **C** S W HALL
BUCKLAND (St Mary the Virgin) *S'wark 26* **P** *All So Coll Ox* **P-in-c** S J BAILEY
BUCKLAND (St Michael) *see* Childswyckham w Aston Somerville, Buckland etc *Glouc*
BUCKLAND, EAST (St Michael) *see* S Molton w Nymet St George, High Bray etc *Ex*
BUCKLAND, WEST (Blessed Virgin Mary) *see* Wellington and Distr *B & W*
BUCKLAND, WEST (St Peter) *see* Swimbridge and W Buckland *Ex*
BUCKLAND BREWER (St Mary and St Benedict) *see* Parkham, Alwington, Buckland Brewer etc *Ex*
BUCKLAND DINHAM (St Michael and All Angels) *see* Mells w Buckland Dinham, Elm, Whatley etc *B & W*
BUCKLAND FILLEIGH (St Mary and Holy Trinity) *see* Shebbear, Buckland Filleigh, Sheepwash etc *Ex*
BUCKLAND IN DOVER (St Andrew) w Buckland Valley (St Nicholas) *Cant 4* **P** *Abp* **R** L G TYZACK, **C** G G GILL
BUCKLAND IN THE MOOR (St Peter) *see* Ashburton w Buckland in the Moor and Bickington *Ex*
BUCKLAND MONACHORUM (St Andrew) *Ex 24* **P** *Bp* **V** G M COTTER
BUCKLAND NEWTON (Holy Rood) *see* Dungeon Hill *Sarum*
BUCKLAND RIPERS (St Nicholas) *see* Bincombe w Broadwey, Upwey and Buckland Ripers *Sarum*
BUCKLAND ST MARY (Blessed Virgin Mary) *see* Churchstanton, Buckland St Mary and Otterford *B & W*
BUCKLAND TOUT SAINTS (St Peter) *see* Charleton w Buckland Tout Saints etc *Ex*
BUCKLAND VALLEY (St Nicholas) *see* Buckland in Dover w Buckland Valley *Cant*
BUCKLEBURY (St Mary) w Marlston *Ox 14* **P** *C J Pratt Esq* **V** A D R HOLMES
BUCKLEBURY, UPPER (All Saints) *see* Bucklebury w Marlston *Ox*
BUCKLERS HARD (St Mary) *see* Beaulieu and Exbury and E Boldre *Win*
BUCKLESHAM (St Mary) *see* Nacton and Levington w Bucklesham and Foxhall *St E*
BUCKMINSTER (St John the Baptist) *see* Wymondham w Edmondthorpe, Buckminster etc *Leic*
BUCKNALL (St Margaret) *see* Woodhall Spa Gp *Linc*
BUCKNALL (St Mary the Virgin) and Bagnall *Lich 12* **P** *Patr Bd* **TR** G O STONE, **TV** M R EAST, G F SMALL, M K ELLOR
BUCKNELL (St Mary) w Chapel Lawn, Llanfair Waterdine and Stowe *Heref 10* **P** *Earl of Powis, Grocers' Co, and J Coltman Rogers Esq (jt)* **P-in-c** E LLOYD
BUCKNELL (St Peter) *see* Bicester w Bucknell, Caversfield and Launton *Ox*
BUCKS MILLS (St Anne) *see* Parkham, Alwington, Buckland Brewer etc *Ex*
BUCKWORTH (All Saints) *Ely 9* **P** *Bp* **R** *Vacant*
BUDBROOKE (St Michael) *Cov 4* **P** *MMCET* **V** *Vacant* (01926) 494002
BUDE HAVEN (St Michael and All Angels) and Marhamchurch *Truro 8* **P** *Bp and PCC (jt)* **R** *Vacant* (01288) 352318
BUDLEIGH, EAST (All Saints) w Bicton and Otterton *Ex 1* **P** *Lord Clinton* **V** M A J HARDING
BUDLEIGH SALTERTON (St Peter) *Ex 1* **P** *Lord Clinton* **V** R S J CHARLES
BUDOCK (St Budock) *Truro 3* **P** *Bp* **P-in-c** M J W WARNER
BUDWORTH, GREAT (St Mary and All Saints) *Ches 4* **P** *Ch Ch Ox* **V** G D MILLS
BUDWORTH, LITTLE (St Peter) *see* Whitegate w Lt Budworth *Ches*
BUGBROOKE (St Michael and All Angels) w Rothersthorpe *Pet 3* **P** *Exors E W Harrison (2 turns), DBP (1 turn)* **R** T R PARTRIDGE
BUGLAWTON (St John the Evangelist) *Ches 11* **P** *R Astbury* **V** M L EAMAN
BUGTHORPE (St Andrew) *see* Bishop Wilton w Full Sutton, Kirby Underdale etc *York*
BUILDWAS (Holy Trinity) *see* Wrockwardine Deanery *Lich*
BULCOTE (Holy Trinity) *see* Burton Joyce w Bulcote and Stoke Bardolph *S'well*
BULFORD (St Leonard) *see* Avon Valley *Sarum*
BULKELEY (All Saints) *see* Bickerton w Bickley *Ches*
BULKINGTON (Christ Church) *see* Seend and Bulkington *Sarum*
BULKINGTON (St James) w Shilton and Ansty *Cov 5* **P** *Ld Chan* **V** A J WADSWORTH
BULKWORTHY (St Michael) *see* Abbots Bickington and Bulkworthy *Ex*
BULLEY (St Michael and All Angels) *see* Churcham w Bulley and Minsterworth *Glouc*
BULLINGHOPE, UPPER (St Peter) *see* Heref S Wye *Heref*
BULLINGTON (St Michael and All Angels) *see* Barton Stacey and Bullington etc *Win*
BULMER (St Andrew) *see* Belchamp Otten w Belchamp Walter and Bulmer etc *Chelmsf*
BULMER (St Martin) w Dalby, Terrington and Welburn *York 3* **P** *Abp and Hon S B G Howard (jt)* **R** E T CHAPMAN
BULPHAN (St Mary the Virgin) *see* Orsett and Bulphan and Horndon on the Hill *Chelmsf*
BULWELL (St John the Divine) *S'well 13* **P** *Bp* **V** J P FEWKES
BULWELL (St Mary the Virgin and All Souls) *S'well 13* **P** *Bp* **R** W S BEASLEY
BULWICK (St Nicholas) and Blatherwycke w Harringworth and Laxton *Pet 8* **P** *G T G Conant Esq (3 turns), F & A George Ltd (1 turn)* **R** M R A WILSON
BUNBURY (St Boniface) and Tilstone Fearnall *Ches 5* **P** *Haberdashers' Co* **V** J E W BOWERS
BUNCTON (All Saints) *see* Ashington, Washington and Wiston with Buncton *Chich*
BUNGAY (Holy Trinity) w St Mary *St E 14* **P** *DBP* **V** I S MORGAN, **C** C P WRIGHT
BUNNY (St Mary the Virgin) w Bradmore *S'well 9* **P** *Ld Chan* **P-in-c** J H MOORE
BUNWELL (St Michael and All Angels), Carleton Rode, Tibenham, Great Moulton and Aslacton *Nor 5* **P** *Bp and DBP (alt)* **R** S SWIFT
BURBAGE (All Saints) *see* Wexcombe *Sarum*
BURBAGE (Christ Church) *see* Buxton w Burbage and King Sterndale *Derby*
BURBAGE (St Catherine) w Aston Flamville *Leic 13* **P** *Ball Coll Ox* **R** F D JENNINGS, **C** A S REED, G W WILSON, **Dss** M PLATT
BURCOMBE (St John the Baptist) *see* Barford St Martin, Dinton, Baverstock etc *Sarum*
BURES (St Mary the Virgin) *St E 12* **P** *DBP* **V** R L C KING, **NSM** K M KING
BURFORD First Portion *Heref 12* **P** *DBP, Bp Birm, Bp, and J J C Caldwell Esq (jt)* **R** D S DORMOR
BURFORD Second Portion (St Mary) w Greete and Hope Bagot *Heref 12* **P** *DBP* **R** D S DORMOR
BURFORD (St John the Baptist) w Fulbrook, Taynton, Asthall, Swinbrook and Widford *Ox 8* **P** *Bp and Capt D Mackinnon (jt)* **V** M B TINGLE, **NSM** C R TADMAN-ROBINS
BURFORD Third Portion (St Mary) w Little Hereford *Heref 12* **P** *DBP and Bp Birm (jt)* **R** D S DORMOR
BURGATE (St Mary) *see* N Hartismere *St E*
BURGESS HILL (St Andrew) *Chich 9* **P** *Bp* **V** I G PRIOR, **C** S CHRISTOU, **NSM** S C M McLARNON
BURGESS HILL (St John the Evangelist) (St Edward) *Chich 9* **P** *Patr Bd* **TR** M C KNOWLES, **TV** T L PESKETT
BURGH (St Botolph) *see* Boulge w Burgh and Grundisburgh *St E*

BURGH (St Margaret and St Mary) *see* Rollesby w Burgh w Billockby w Ashby w Oby etc *Nor*
BURGH (St Peter) *see* The Raveningham Gp *Nor*
BURGH-BY-SANDS (St Michael) and Kirkbampton w Kirkandrews on Eden, Beaumont and Grinsdale *Carl 3* **P** *DBP and Earl of Lonsdale (jt)* **R** D R KING, **C** G M HART
BURGH CASTLE (St Peter and St Paul) *see* Belton and Burgh Castle *Nor*
BURGH HEATH (St Mary the Virgin) *see* Tattenham Corner and Burgh Heath *Guildf*
BURGH LE MARSH (St Peter and St Paul) *Linc 8* **P** *Bp* **V** T STEELE
BURGH-NEXT-AYLSHAM (St Mary) *see* Marsham w Burgh-next-Aylsham *Nor*
BURGH-ON-BAIN (St Helen) *see* Asterby Gp *Linc*
BURGH PARVA (St Mary) *see* Briston w Burgh Parva and Melton Constable *Nor*
BURGHCLERE (Ascension) (All Saints) w Newtown and Ecchinswell w Sydmonton *Win 6* **P** *Earl of Carnarvon* **R** C A LE PREVOST
BURGHFIELD (St Mary the Virgin) *Ox 12* **P** *Earl of Shrewsbury* **R** A B GRUNDY, **NSM** J N COOPER
BURGHILL (St Mary the Virgin) *Heref 4* **P** *DBP* **P-in-c** J W R MORRISON
BURGHWALLIS (St Helen) *Sheff 8* **P** *Mrs E H I Ellison-Anne* **P-in-c** A D LENNON
BURHAM (Methodist Church) and Wouldham *Roch 5* **P** *Bp and Ld Chan (alt)* **P-in-c** E M R WALKER
BURITON (St Mary the Virgin) *Portsm 5* **P** *Bp* **R** C LOWSON, **C** O E ANDERSON
BURLESCOMBE (St Mary) *see* Sampford Peverell, Uplowman, Holcombe Rogus etc *Ex*
BURLEY (St Matthias) *Ripon 7* **P** *G M Bedford Esq, J C Yeadon Esq, E Beety Esq, Mrs M E Dunham, and Mrs L M Rawse (jt)* **V** K TROUT, **C** A B CHAPMAN
BURLEY IN WHARFEDALE (St Mary the Virgin) *Bradf 4* **P** *Bp* **V** P J SUTCLIFFE
BURLEY VILLE (St John the Baptist) *Win 8* **P** *V Ringwood* **V** A G CLARKSON
BURLEYDAM (St Mary and St Michael) *see* Baddiley and Wrenbury w Burleydam *Ches*
BURLINGHAM (St Andrew) *see* Acle w Fishley and N Burlingham *Nor*
BURLINGHAM (St Edmund King and Martyr) w Lingwood, Strumpshaw w Hassingham and Buckenham *Nor 4* **P** *Ch Soc Trust, MMCET, and Bp (jt)* **P-in-c** V M ELPHICK
BURLTON (St Anne) *see* Loppington w Newtown *Lich*
BURMANTOFTS (St Stephen and St Agnes) *Ripon 5* **P** *Ch Trust Fund Trust* **V** J CHEVERTON, **C** R H JAMIESON
BURMARSH (All Saints) *see* Dymchurch w Burmarsh and Newchurch *Cant*
BURMINGTON (St Nicholas and St Barnabas) *see* Wolford w Burmington *Cov*
BURNAGE (St Margaret) *Man 3* **P** *Bp* **R** A PUGMIRE, **C** A R BRADLEY
BURNAGE (St Nicholas) *Man 8* **P** *Trustees* **R** L CONNOLLY
BURNBY (St Giles) *York 7* **P** *Trustees* **P-in-c** J C MELLING
BURNESIDE (St Oswald) *Carl 9* **P** *J A Cropper Esq, Mrs E Bingham, and Mrs B Baines (jt)* **V** N L DAVIES, **Hon Par Dn** J L TYRER
BURNESTON (St Lambert) *see* Kirklington w Burneston and Wath and Pickhill *Ripon*
BURNETT (St Michael) *see* Keynsham *B & W*
BURNEY LANE (Christ Church) *Birm 14* **P** *Bp* **V** M CHESTER, **C** P PETERSON
BURNHAM (St Andrew) *B & W 1* **P** *D&C* **V** R E PITT
BURNHAM (St Mary the Virgin) *Chelmsf 11* **P** *N D Beckett Esq and Walsingham Coll Trust (jt)* **V** R J WEBB
BURNHAM (St Peter) w Dropmore, Hitcham and Taplow *Ox 23* **P** *Patr Bd* **TR** S N D BROWN, **TV** A C DIBDEN, T R HEWSON, M R WHITE, **NSM** G M EDEN, S SMITH
BURNHAM DEEPDALE (St Mary) *see* Hunstanton St Mary w Ringstead Parva etc *Nor*
BURNHAM NORTON (St Margaret) *see* Burnham Gp of Par *Nor*
BURNHAM-ON-CROUCH (St Mary the Virgin) *see* Burnham *Chelmsf*
BURNHAM-ON-SEA (St Andrew) *as above*
BURNHAM OVERY (St Clement) *see* Burnham Gp of Par *Nor*
BURNHAM THORPE (All Saints) *as above*
BURNHAM ULPH (All Saints) *as above*
BURNHAM WESTGATE (St Mary), Burnham Norton, Burnham Overy, Burnham Thorpe, and Burnham Sutton w Ulph (The Burnham Group of Parishes) *Nor 15* **P** *Ch Coll Cam (1 turn), Ld Chan (2 turns), and DBP (1 turn)* **P-in-c** J CHARLES
BURNLEY Habergham Eaves (St Matthew the Apostle) (Holy Trinity) *Blackb 3* **P** *R Burnley* **V** *Vacant* (01282) 424849
BURNLEY (St Andrew) w St Margaret *Blackb 3* **P** *R Burnley* **V** *Vacant* (01282) 423185
BURNLEY (St Catherine) (St Alban) and St Paul *Blackb 3* **P** *R Burnley* **P-in-c** A I DALTON
BURNLEY (St Cuthbert) *Blackb 3* **P** *R Burnley* **V** H LEE
BURNLEY (St James) *Blackb 3* **P** *The Crown* **V** *Vacant* (01282) 24758
BURNLEY (St Mark) *Blackb 3* **P** *Bp* **V** A C TAYLOR
BURNLEY (St Peter) *Blackb 3* **P** *Bp* **R** D F TOWERS
BURNLEY (St Stephen) *Blackb 3* **P** *R Burnley* **P-in-c** J B SWALLOW
BURNLEY, WEST (All Saints) *Blackb 3* **P** *Bp and V Burnley St Pet (jt)* **V** C A ROGERS, **C** B A EATON
BURNMOOR (St Barnabas) *Dur 14* **P** *Lord Lambton* **R** *Vacant* 0191-385 2695
BURNOPFIELD (St James) *Dur 4* **P** *Bp* **V** R G BIRCHALL
BURNSALL (St Wilfrid) w Rylstone *Bradf 7* **P** *Exors Earl of Craven and CPAS (jt)* **R** *Vacant* (01756) 720331
BURNT OAK (St Alphage) *see* Hendon St Alphage *Lon*
BURNT YATES (St Andrew) *see* Ripley *Ripon*
BURNTWOOD (Christ Church) *Lich 1* **P** *D&C* **P-in-c** D A WEAVER, **C** P S DAVIES
BURPHAM (St Luke) Guildford *Guildf 5* **P** *Bp* **V** C J MATTHEWS, **C** D A MINNS
BURPHAM (St Mary the Virgin) *Chich 1* **P** *D&C* **P-in-c** P TAYLOR
BURRADON (Good Shepherd) *see* Weetslade *Newc*
BURRILL (Mission Church) *see* Bedale *Ripon*
BURRINGTON (Holy Trinity) *see* Chulmleigh, Chawleigh w Cheldon, Wembworthy etc *Ex*
BURRINGTON (Holy Trinity) and Churchill *B & W 11* **P** *D&C Bris and Burrington PCC (jt)* **V** J C ABDY, **C** C J HORDER
BURRINGTON (St George) *see* Wigmore Abbey *Heref*
BURROUGH GREEN (St Augustine of Canterbury) *see* Brinkley, Burrough Green and Carlton *Ely*
BURROUGH HILL Parishes, The: Burrough on the Hill, Great Dalby, Little Dalby, Pickwell and Somerby *Leic 3* **P** *Bp, DBP, and Mrs M Burdett Fisher (jt)* **P-in-c** R J STRETTON
BURROUGH ON THE HILL (St Mary the Virgin) *see* Burrough Hill Pars *Leic*
BURROWBRIDGE (St Michael) *see* Stoke St Gregory w Burrowbridge and Lyng *B & W*
BURRSVILLE (St Mark) *see* Gt Clacton *Chelmsf*
BURSCOUGH BRIDGE (St John) (St Andrew) (St Cyprian) *Liv 11* **P** *V Ormskirk* **V** N R SHORT
BURSDON MOOR (St Martin) *see* Parkham, Alwington, Buckland Brewer etc *Ex*
BURSEA (Chapel) *see* Holme-on-Spalding Moor *York*
BURSLEDON Pilands Wood (St Paul) *see* Bursledon *Win*
BURSLEDON (St Leonard) *Win 9* **P** *Bp* **V** P A VARGESON
BURSLEM (St John the Baptist) (St Paul) *Lich 11* **P** *Bp and MMCET (jt)* **R** C R JOHNSON, **C** D P COOPER
BURSLEM (St Werburgh) *Lich 11* **P** *Bp* **V** K L ROUND
BURSTALL (St Mary the Virgin) *see* Sproughton w Burstall *St E*
BURSTEAD, GREAT (St Mary Magdalene) *Chelmsf 6* **P** *Bp* **V** B J RODWELL
BURSTEAD, LITTLE (St Mary) *see* Billericay and Lt Burstead *Chelmsf*
BURSTOCK (St Andrew) *see* Beaminster Area *Sarum*
BURSTON (St Mary) *see* Winfarthing w Shelfanger w Burston w Gissing etc *Nor*
BURSTON (St Rufin) *see* Salt and Sandon w Burston *Lich*
BURSTOW (St Bartholomew) *S'wark 26* **P** *Ld Chan* **R** G B TALBOT, **Hon C** K W RAMSAY
BURSTWICK (All Saints) w Thorngumbald *York 13* **P** *Abp* **V** F W R LA TOUCHE
BURTLE (St Philip and St James) *see* Shapwick w Ashcott and Burtle *B & W*
BURTON (All Saints) w Christ Church *Lich 14* **P** *CPAS and Ch Soc Trust (jt)* **V** R P OAKLEY, **C** N D J LINES
BURTON (St James) and Holme *Carl 9* **P** *Simeon's Trustees* **V** J J C NODDER
BURTON (St Luke) and Sopley *Win 8* **P** *Bp and D&C Cant (alt)* **V** A SESSFORD
BURTON (St Nicholas) and Shotwick *Ches 9* **P** *D&C (1 turn) and St Jo Hosp Lich (2 turns)* **V** H J ALDRIDGE
BURTON w COATES (St Agatha) *see* Barlavington, Burton w Coates, Sutton and Bignor *Chich*
BURTON AGNES (St Martin) w Harpham and Lowthorpe w Ruston Parva *York 11* **P** *Ld Chan (2 turns), C T Legard Esq (1 turn)* **R** D S HAWKINS
BURTON BRADSTOCK (St Mary) *see* Bride Valley *Sarum*
BURTON BY LINCOLN (St Vincent) *Linc 2* **P** *Lord Monson* **R** *Vacant*
BURTON COGGLES (St Thomas a Becket) *see* Ingoldsby *Linc*
BURTON DASSETT (All Saints) *Cov 8* **P** *Bp* **V** P T FRANCIS

BURTON FLEMING (St Cuthbert) w Fordon, Grindale and Wold Newton *York 10* **P** *Abp and MMCET (jt)* **V** J R BROADHURST, **C** C J HAYES
BURTON GREEN (Chapel of Ease) *see* Kenilworth St Nic *Cov*
BURTON HASTINGS (St Botolph) *see* Wolvey w Burton Hastings, Copston Magna etc *Cov*
BURTON IN LONSDALE (All Saints) *see* Thornton in Lonsdale w Burton in Lonsdale *Bradf*
BURTON JOYCE (St Helen) w Bulcote and Stoke Bardolph *S'well 11* **P** *MMCET* **V** A GRAHAM
BURTON LATIMER (St Mary the Virgin) *Pet 11* **P** *Bp* **R** J SIMMONS
BURTON LAZARS (St James) *see* Melton Mowbray *Leic*
BURTON LEONARD (St Leonard) *see* Bishop Monkton and Burton Leonard *Ripon*
BURTON-ON-TRENT (All Saints) *see* Burton All SS w Ch Ch *Lich*
BURTON-ON-TRENT (St Aidan) *see* Shobnall *Lich*
BURTON-ON-TRENT (St Chad) *Lich 14* **P** *Bp* **V** M P SKILLINGS
BURTON-ON-TRENT (St Modwen) (St Paul) *Lich 14* **P** *Bp and Lord Burton (jt)* **V** D M MORRIS, **C** A R BAILEY, **Hon Par Dn** V R MORRIS
BURTON OVERY (St Andrew) *see* Gaulby *Leic*
BURTON PEDWARDINE (St Andrew and the Blessed Virgin Mary and St Nicholas) *see* Heckington *Linc*
BURTON PIDSEA (St Peter) and Humbleton w Elsternwick *York 13* **P** *Ld Chan and D&C (alt)* **V** J L CAMPBELL
BURTON UPON STATHER (St Andrew) *see* Flixborogh w Burton upon Stather *Linc*
BURTONWOOD (St Michael) *Liv 16* **P** *R Warrington* **V** R S NAYLOR, **Hon C** F H BOARDMAN
BURWARDSLEY (St John) *see* Harthill and Burwardsley *Ches*
BURWASH (St Bartholomew) *Chich 14* **P** *BNC Ox* **P-in-c** R D VINCENT
BURWASH WEALD (St Philip) *Chich 15* **P** *Bp* **V** *Vacant* (01435) 883287
BURWELL (St Andrew) (St Mary) *Ely 3* **P** *DBP* **V** S G F EARL
BURY (All Saints) *see* Elton All SS *Man*
BURY (Christ the King) *Man 10* **P** *Patr Bd* **V** P R FRENCH
BURY (Holy Cross) *see* Warboys w Broughton and Bury w Wistow *Ely*
BURY (Holy Trinity) *Man 10* **P** *Patr Bd* **P-in-c** D A HAILES
BURY (St John the Evangelist) and Houghton *Chich 11* **P** *Pemb Coll Ox* **P-in-c** R F ROBINSON
BURY (St John w St Mark) *Man 10* **P** *R Bury St Mary* **V** R W LAWRANCE
BURY (St Mary the Virgin) *Man 10* **P** *Earl of Derby* **R** J R SMITH
BURY St Paul *Man 10* **P** *Trustees* **P-in-c** C R DUXBURY
BURY (St Peter) *Man 10* **P** *R Bury St Mary* **V** G G ROXBY, **C** M A MORRIS, **Hon C** F E F WARD, **NSM** J M SMITH
BURY (St Stephen) *see* Elton St Steph *Man*
BURY, NEW (St James) *Man 12* **P** *Bp* **C** A COMBER, **NSM** D N BIRD
BURY ST EDMUNDS (All Saints) *St E 13* **P** *Bp* **P-in-c** G J WEBB
BURY ST EDMUNDS (Cathedral of St James) District *St E 13* **C** V A HERRICK
BURY ST EDMUNDS (Christ Church) Moreton Hall *St E 13* **P** *Bp, V Bury St Edm St Jas, and V Bury St Edm St Mary (jt)* **V** J L ALDERTON-FORD, **NSM** N T CORWIN
BURY ST EDMUNDS (St George) *St E 13* **P** *Bp* **V** *Vacant* (01284) 750321
BURY ST EDMUNDS (St John the Evangelist) *St E 13* **P** *Bp* **P-in-c** D R UNDERWOOD, **NSM** D MAUDLIN
BURY ST EDMUNDS (St Mary) (St Peter's District Church) *St E 13* **P** *Hyndman Trustees* **P-in-c** J D HAYDEN, **C** I D TWEEDIE-SMITH
BURYTHORPE (All Saints), Acklam and Leavening w Westow *York 2* **P** *Abp* **R** *Vacant* (0165385) 220
BUSBRIDGE (St John the Baptist) *Guildf 4* **P** *DBP* **R** J TRICKEY
BUSCOT (St Mary) *see* Gt Coxwell w Buscot, Coleshill & Eaton Hastings *Ox*
BUSH END (St John the Evangelist) *see* Hatfield Broad Oak and Bush End *Chelmsf*
BUSH HILL PARK (St Mark) *Lon 18* **P** *Bp* **V** P C ATHERTON
BUSH HILL PARK (St Stephen) *Lon 18* **P** *V Edmonton All SS* **V** R J ANNIS
BUSHBURY (St Mary) *Lich 29* **P** *Patr Bd* **TR** R A HINTON, **TV** N R HOGG, P I DENNISON, **C** J R WALKER, S J OSBOURNE
BUSHEY (Holy Trinity) (St James) (St Paul) *St Alb 1* **P** *Bp* **R** I C COOPER, **C** T S MOORE, **Hon C** W A PENNEY
BUSHEY HEATH (St Peter) *St Alb 1* **P** *Bp* **V** W R LOW
BUSHLEY (St Peter) *see* Longdon, Castlemorton, Bushley, Queenhill etc *Worc*
BUSHMEAD Conventional District *St Alb 20* **C-in-c** M A SLATER
BUSSAGE (St Michael and All Angels) *Glouc 1* **P** *Bp* **V** H J van der LINDE
BUTCOMBE (St Michael and All Angels) *see* Wrington w Butcombe *B & W*
BUTLEIGH (St Leonard) *see* Baltonsborough w Butleigh and W Bradley *B & W*
BUTLERS MARSTON (St Peter and St Paul) and the Pillertons w Ettington *Cov 9* **P** *Ch Ch Ox (1 turn), Bp, Major and Mrs J E Shirley, and Miss M L P Shirley (jt) (1 turn), and Mr and Mrs G Howell (1 turn)* **P-in-c** E B SAVIGEAR
BUTLEY (St John the Baptist) *see* Orford w Sudbourne, Chillesford, Butley and Iken *St E*
BUTTERCRAMBE (St John the Evangelist) *see* Sand Hutton *York*
BUTTERLEIGH (St Matthew) *see* Silverton, Butterleigh, Bickleigh and Cadeleigh *Ex*
BUTTERMERE (St James) *see* Lorton and Loweswater w Buttermere *Carl*
BUTTERMERE (St James the Great) *see* Wexcombe *Sarum*
BUTTERSHAW (St Aidan) *see* Shelf St Mich w Buttershaw St Aid *Bradf*
BUTTERSHAW (St Paul) *Bradf 2* **P** *Bp* **V** P STREET, **NSM** M HARGREAVES
BUTTERTON (St Bartholomew) *see* Alstonfield, Butterton, Warslow w Elkstone etc *Lich*
BUTTERTON (St Thomas) *see* Newcastle w Butterton *Lich*
BUTTERWICK (Mission Chapel) *see* Street TM *York*
BUTTERWICK (St Andrew) *see* Freiston w Butterwick *Linc*
BUTTERWICK (St Nicholas) *see* Langtoft w Foxholes, Butterwick, Cottam etc *York*
BUTTERWICK, EAST (St Andrew) *see* Messingham *Linc*
BUTTERWICK, WEST (St Mary) *Linc 1* **P** *V Owston* **V** *Vacant*
BUTTSBURY (St Mary) *see* Ingatestone w Buttsbury *Chelmsf*
BUXHALL (St Mary) w Shelland *St E 6* **P** *Bp* **R** *Vacant* (014493) 236
BUXTED (St Margaret the Queen) (St Mary) and Hadlow Down *Chich 21* **P** *Abp, Bp, and Wagner Trustees (jt)* **R** R WOLLEY
BUXTON (St Andrew) w Oxnead, Lammas and Brampton *Nor 19* **P** *Bp* **P-in-c** C S R WALTER
BUXTON (St Anne) (St John the Baptist) (St Mary the Virgin) w Burbage and King Sterndale *Derby 4* **P** *Patr Bd* **TR** J H K NORTON, **TV** C M SCARGILL
BUXTON (Trinity Chapel) Proprietary Chapel *Derby 4* **C-in-c** S D N VIBERT
BUXWORTH (St James) *see* Chinley w Buxworth *Derby*
BYERS GREEN (St Peter) *Dur 6* **P** *Bp* **R** *Vacant* (01388) 606659
BYFIELD (Holy Cross) w Boddington and Aston le Walls *Pet 1* **P** *Bp, CCC Ox, and Em Coll Cam (by turn)* **R** S E WEST-LINDELL
BYFLEET (St Mary) *Guildf 12* **P** *Ld Chan* **R** R D TRUMPER, **C** M A McCAGHREY, **NSM** A G BARDELL
BYFLEET, WEST (St John) *Guildf 12* **P** *Bp* **V** L S SMITH
BYFORD (St John the Baptist) *see* Letton w Staunton, Byford, Mansel Gamage etc *Heref*
BYGRAVE (St Margaret of Antioch) *see* Baldock w Bygrave *St Alb*
BYKER (St Anthony) *Newc 6* **P** *Bp* **V** D C MUMFORD, **C** J DRAY
BYKER St Mark and Walkergate (St Oswald) *Newc 6* **P** *Bp and Ch Trust Fund Trust (jt)* **V** K MOULDER, **C** H A CHARTERIS
BYKER (St Martin) Newcastle upon Tyne *Newc 6* **P** *Bp* **P-in-c** R BEST, **C** D M IND
BYKER (St Michael w St Lawrence) *Newc 6* **P** *Bp* **P-in-c** S J LIDDLE
BYKER (St Silas) *Newc 6* **P** *Bp* **P-in-c** J H ADAMS
BYLAND, OLD (All Saints) *see* Upper Ryedale *York*
BYLAUGH (St Mary) *see* Lyng, Sparham, Elsing, Bylaugh, Bawdeswell etc *Nor*
BYLEY CUM LEES (St John the Evangelist) *see* Middlewich w Byley *Ches*
BYRNESS (St Francis) *see* N Tyne and Redesdale Team *Newc*
BYTHAM, LITTLE (St Medardus) *see* Castle Bytham w Creeton *Linc*
BYTHORN (St Lawrence) *see* Keyston and Bythorn *Ely*
BYTON (St Mary) *see* Pembridge w Moorcourt, Shobdon, Staunton etc *Heref*
BYWELL (St Peter) *Newc 3* **P** *Adn Northd* **V** T EMMETT
BYWORTH (St Francis) *see* Farnham *Guildf*
CABLE STREET (St Mary) *see* St Geo-in-the-East St Mary *Lon*
CABOURN (St Nicholas) *see* Swallow *Linc*

CADBROKE GROVE (St Michael and All Angels) *see* Notting Hill St Mich and Ch Ch *Lon*
CADBURY (St Michael and All Angels) *see* Thorverton, Cadbury, Upton Pyne etc *Ex*
CADBURY, NORTH (St Michael the Archangel) *see* Camelot Par *B & W*
CADBURY, SOUTH (St Thomas a Becket) *as above*
CADDINGTON (All Saints) *St Alb 14* **P** *D&C St Paul's* **V** A J D SMITH, **Hon C** A K GARVIE
CADEBY (All Saints) *see* Market Bosworth, Cadeby w Sutton Cheney etc *Leic*
CADELEIGH (St Bartholomew) *see* Silverton, Butterleigh, Bickleigh and Cadeleigh *Ex*
CADGWITH (St Mary) *see* St Ruan w St Grade and Landewednack *Truro*
CADISHEAD (St Mary the Virgin) *Man 2* **P** *Bp* **V** D RIDLEY, **C** L RIDLEY
CADMORE END (St Mary le Moor) *see* Lane End w Cadmore End *Ox*
CADNEY (All Saints) *see* Brigg, Wrawby and Cadney cum Howsham *Linc*
CADOGAN SQUARE (St Simon Zelotes) *see* Upper Chelsea St Simon *Lon*
CAERHAYS (St Michael) *see* St Goran w St Mich Caerhays *Truro*
CAGE GREEN (Church Hall) *see* Tonbridge SS Pet and Paul *Roch*
CAINSCROSS (St Matthew) w Selsley *Glouc 8* **P** *Bp and Sir Charles Marling, Bt (alt)* **V** G G C MINORS, **C** T M B WOODHOUSE
CAISTER NEXT YARMOUTH (Holy Trinity) (St Edmund) *Nor 6* **P** *SMF* **P-in-c** T C THOMPSON
CAISTOR (St Peter and St Paul) w Clixby *Linc 5* **P** *Bp* **P-in-c** I ROBINSON
CAISTOR ST EDMUNDS (St Edmund) *see* Stoke H Cross w Dunston, Arminghall etc *Nor*
CALBOURNE (All Saints) w Newtown *Portsm 8* **P** *Bp* **V** *Vacant*
CALCOT (St Birinus) *Ox 15* **P** *Magd Coll Ox* **V** A D BARNES
CALDBECK (St Mungo) (Fellside), Castle Sowerby and Sebergham *Carl 3* **P** *Bp and D&C (alt)* **R** R C JOHNS
CALDECOTE (All Saints) *St Alb 11* **P** *Grocers' Co* **P-in-c** R J DOULTON
CALDECOTE (St Michael and All Angels) *see* Toft w Caldecote and Childerley *Ely*
CALDECOTE (St Theobald and St Chad) *see* Weddington and Caldecote *Cov*
CALDECOTT (St John the Evangelist) *see* Lyddington w Stoke Dry and Seaton w Caldecott *Pet*
CALDER GROVE (St John the Divine) *see* Chapelthorpe *Wakef*
CALDER VALE (Mission) *see* Barnacre w Calder Vale *Blackb*
CALDER VALE (St John the Evangelist) *as above*
CALDERBROOK (St James the Great) *Man 20* **P** *Bp* **P-in-c** M C HODSON
CALDMORE (St Michael and All Angels) *Lich 26* **P** *Bp* **P-in-c** F R MILLER
CALDWELL (Chapel) *see* Forcett and Aldbrough and Melsonby *Ripon*
CALDWELL (St Giles) *see* Stapenhill w Cauldwell *Derby*
CALDY (Church of the Resurrection and All Saints) *see* W Kirby St Bridget *Ches*
CALEDONIAN ROAD (All Saints Hall) *see* Barnsbury *Lon*
CALIFORNIA (St Mary and St John) *Ox 16* **P** *DBP* **P-in-c** A J BURDON, **Dn-in-c** P M BURDON
CALLINGTON (St Mary) *see* S Hill w Callington *Truro*
CALLOW END (St James) *see* Powyke *Worc*
CALMORE (St Anne) *see* Totton *Win*
CALNE (Holy Trinity) (St Mary the Virgin) and Blackland *Sarum 18* **P** *Bp* **V** R A KENWAY, **C** M T B EVANS, S P V CADE
CALOW (St Peter) and Sutton cum Duckmanton *Derby 3* **P** *Bp and V Chesterfield (jt)* **R** N V JOHNSON
CALSHOT (St George) *see* Fawley *Win*
CALSTOCK (St Andrew) *Truro 11* **P** *Duchy of Cornwall* **R** J A C WILSON, **C** A G BASHFORTH
CALSTONE WELLINGTON (St Mary the Virgin) *see* Oldbury *Sarum*
CALTHORPE (Our Lady w St Margaret) *see* Erpingham w Calthorpe, Ingworth, Aldborough etc *Nor*
CALTHWAITE (All Saints) *see* Hesket-in-the-Forest and Armathwaite *Carl*
CALTON (St Mary the Virgin), Cauldon, Grindon and Waterfall *Lich 5* **P** *Bp* **P-in-c** P W DAVEY
CALUDON *see* Coventry Caludon *Cov*
CALVELEY CHURCH (not known) *see* Bunbury and Tilstone Fearnall *Ches*
CALVERHALL or CORRA (Holy Trinity) *see* Adderley, Ash, Calverhall, Ightfield etc *Lich*
CALVERLEIGH (St Mary the Virgin) *see* Washfield, Stoodleigh, Withleigh etc *Ex*
CALVERLEY (St Wilfrid) *Bradf 3* **P** *Bp* **V** J H WALKER
CALVERTON (All Saints) *Ox 25* **P** *DBP* **R** C H J CAVELL-NORTHAM
CALVERTON (St Wilfrid) *S'well 15* **P** *Bp* **P-in-c** P HILL, **C** T J RENSHAW
CAM (St George) w Stinchcombe *Glouc 2* **P** *Bp* **V** C M MALKINSON
CAM, LOWER (St Bartholomew) w Coaley *Glouc 2* **P** *Bp* **V** I A ROBB
CAMBER (St Thomas) *see* Rye *Chich*
CAMBERLEY (St Martin) Old Dean *Guildf 6* **P** *Bp* **V** P A DOBSON, **NSM** S H WOOD
CAMBERLEY (St Michael) Yorktown *Guildf 6* **P** *Bp* **V** J P B WYNBURNE, B NICOLE
CAMBERLEY (St Paul) (St Mary) *Guildf 6* **P** *Bp* **TR** R S CROSSLEY, **TV** P D BRYER, J H G CARTER, **C** M C BREADMORE, **Hon C** A C LONG, **NSM** C SIMONS
CAMBERLEY HEATHERSIDE (Community Centre) *see* Camberley St Paul *Guildf*
CAMBERWELL (All Saints) Blenheim Grove *S'wark 7* **P** *Ch Trust Fund Trust* **P-in-c** R HURLEY
CAMBERWELL (Christ Church) *S'wark 7* **P** *Trustees* **V** H R BALFOUR
CAMBERWELL (St George) *S'wark 7* **P** *Bp and Trin Coll Cam (jt)* **V** S J ROBERTS, **C** B A HOPKINS, **Hon C** J E PAWSEY
CAMBERWELL (St Giles) (St Matthew) *S'wark 7* **P** *Bp* **V** R W G BOMFORD, **C** S M SICHEL, **Hon C** S D HAINES, **NSM** H D POTTER
CAMBERWELL (St Luke) *S'wark 7* **P** *Bp* **V** J D JELLEY
CAMBERWELL (St Matthew) *see* Herne Hill *S'wark*
CAMBERWELL (St Michael and All Angels w All Souls w Emmanuel) *S'wark 9* **P** *DBP* **V** P VOWLES
CAMBERWELL (St Philip) and St Mark *S'wark 6* **P** *The Crown* **V** N A W DAVIS
CAMBO (Holy Trinity) *see* Kirkwhelpington, Kirkharle, Kirkheaton and Cambo *Newc*
CAMBOIS (St Peter) (St Andrew's Mission Church) *Newc 1* **P** *D&C* **V** *Vacant* (01670) 813526
CAMBORNE (St Martin and St Meriadoc) *Truro 2* **P** *Ch Soc Trust* **R** N J POCOCK, **C** D A TREBY, **Hon C** G E BOTTOMLEY, **NSM** D E HARVEY
CAMBRIDGE Ascension (St Giles) (St Luke the Evangelist) (St Augustine of Canterbury) (All Souls Chapel) *Ely 2* **P** *Bp* **TR** J P YOUNG, **C** P A KING, **NSM** O R SPENCER-THOMAS
CAMBRIDGE (Holy Cross) *Ely 2* **P** *Bp* **V** A L HARGRAVE
CAMBRIDGE (Holy Sepulchre) (St Andrew the Great) *Ely 2* **P** *PCC* **V** M H ASHTON, **C** G R WALTER, C J DAVIS, C E SANDOM
CAMBRIDGE (Holy Trinity) *Ely 2* **P** *D&C and Peache Trustees (jt)* **V** C D HANCOCK, **C** N G JONES
CAMBRIDGE (St Andrew the Less) (Christ Church) *Ely 2* **P** *Ch Trust Fund Trust* **V** M L DIAMOND
CAMBRIDGE (St Barnabas) *Ely 2* **P** *V Cam St Paul* **V** L J BROWNE, **C** G A COLLINS, **NSM** J E KEILLER
CAMBRIDGE (St Benedict) *Ely 2* **P** *CCC Cam* **V** R A L SMYTH
CAMBRIDGE (St Botolph) *Ely 2* **P** *Qu Coll Cam* **NSM** W HORBURY, M J WIDDESS
CAMBRIDGE (St Clement) *Ely 2* **P** *Jes Coll Cam* **V** *Vacant*
CAMBRIDGE (St Edward King and Martyr) Proprietary Chapel *Ely 2*, F N WATTS
CAMBRIDGE (St James) *Ely 2* **P** *Bp* **V** H W DAWES, **C** S SHAKESPEARE
CAMBRIDGE (St John the Evangelist) *see* Cherry Hinton St Jo *Ely*
CAMBRIDGE (St Mark) *Ely 2* **P** *DBP* **V** C M FARRINGTON, **NSM** L J E GOODHEW
CAMBRIDGE (St Martin) (St Thomas) *Ely 2* **P** *V Cam St Paul* **V** S D ARMSTRONG
CAMBRIDGE (St Mary the Great) w St Michael *Ely 2* **P** *Trin Coll Cam* **V** J R BINNS, **C** R E AVERY, J N CLARK-KING, D L GOSLING
CAMBRIDGE (St Mary the Less) *Ely 2* **P** *Peterho Cam* **V** R A H GREANY, **NSM** N J HANCOCK
CAMBRIDGE (St Matthew) *Ely 2* **P** *V Cam St Andr the Less* **V** E P J FOSTER
CAMBRIDGE (St Paul) *Ely 2* **P** *Ch Trust Fund Trust* **V** M S BECKETT
CAMBRIDGE (St Philip) (St Stephen) *Ely 2* **P** *Ch Trust Fund Trust* **V** S TAYLOR, **C** N CUTLER, **NSM** T R MONTGOMERY
CAMDEN SQUARE (St Paul) *Lon 17* **P** *D&C St Paul's* **P-in-c** N P WHEELER, **C** E G GREER

CAMDEN TOWN (St Michael) (All Saints and St Thomas) *Lon 17* **P** *D&C St Paul's* **V** A R B PAGE, **P-in-c** N P WHEELER
CAMEL, WEST (All Saints) *see* Queen Camel w W Camel, Corton Denham etc *B & W*
CAMELFORD (St Julitta) *see* Lanteglos by Camelford w Advent *Truro*
CAMELFORD (St Thomas of Canterbury) *as above*
CAMELOT Parishes, The *B & W 3* **P** *Patr Bd* **TV** J M THOROGOOD, **C** A CUNNINGHAM, **NSM** K L BRUTON
CAMELSDALE (St Paul) *see* Lynchmere and Camelsdale *Chich*
CAMERTON (St Peter) w Dunkerton, Foxcote and Shoscombe *B & W 12* **P** *Bp* **R** T A THOMAS
CAMERTON (St Peter), Seaton and West Seaton *Carl 7* **P** *D&C and Ch Trust Fund Trust (jt)* **V** J D KELLY, **C** C K WRIGHT
CAMMERINGHAM (St Michael) *see* Ingham w Cammeringham w Fillingham *Linc*
CAMP HILL (St Mary and St John) w Galley Common *Cov 5* **P** *Bp* **V** S D SNEATH
CAMPBELL ROOMS (not known) *see* Parr Mt *Liv*
CAMPSALL (St Mary Magdalene) *Sheff 8* **P** *Bp* **V** P J BOULTON-LEA
CAMPSEA ASHE (St John the Baptist) w Marlesford, Parham and Hacheston *St E 18* **P** *Prime Min, Ch Soc Trust, and J S Schreiber Esq (by turn)* **P-in-c** H V EDWARDS
CAMPTON (All Saints) *see* Meppershall w Campton and Stondon *St Alb*
CANDLESBY (St Benedict) *see* Partney *Linc*
CANDOVER VALLEY, THE *Win 1* **P** *D&C and Lord Ashburton (jt)* **R** C R SMITH
CANEWDON (St Nicholas) w Paglesham *Chelmsf 12* **P** *D&C Westmr and Hyndman Trustees (jt)* **V** N J KELLY
CANFIELD, GREAT (St Mary) w High Roding and Aythorpe Roding *Chelmsf 18* **P** *A Sainthill Esq, Ch Soc Trust, and Bp (by turn)* **R** T G LYNDS
CANFIELD, LITTLE (All Saints) *see* Takeley w Lt Canfield *Chelmsf*
CANFORD CLIFFS (Transfiguration) and Sandbanks *Sarum 8* **P** *Bp* **P-in-c** J C OAKES
CANFORD HEATH (St Paul) *see* Oakdale *Sarum*
CANFORD MAGNA (Bearwood) (Lantern) *Sarum 10* **P** *Patr Bd* **TR** P H LAWRENCE, **TV** A D EDWARDS, R J GROVES, **NSM** A SIMPSON, D A PHILLIPS, I CHALLIS
CANLEY (St Stephen) *Cov 3* **P** *Bp* **V** P H SMITH
CANNING TOWN (St Cedd) *see* Plaistow and N Canning Town *Chelmsf*
CANNING TOWN (St Matthias) *as above*
CANNINGTON (Blessed Virgin Mary), Otterhampton, Combwich and Stockland *B & W 14* **P** *Bp* **R** P MARTIN, **NSM** R H BARBER
CANNOCK (St Luke) *Lich 3* **P** *Patr Bd* **TV** C A GILBERT, P A GRAYSMITH, N PURVEY-TYRER, **C** M A HOLDSWORTH, A J BETTS, H M LEWIS
CANON FROME (St James) *see* Bosbury w Wellington Heath etc *Heref*
CANON PYON (St Lawrence) w Kings Pyon and Birley *Heref 7* **P** *Bp and D&C (alt)* **V** C M BURKE
CANONBURY (St Stephen) *Lon 6* **P** *V Islington St Mary* **V** D J P MOORE, **NSM** M E EVANS
CANTERBURY (All Saints) *Cant 3* **P** *Abp* **V** B J COOPER
CANTERBURY (St Dunstan w Holy Cross) *Cant 3* **P** *Abp* **V** M W WORGAN
CANTERBURY (St Martin) (St Paul) *Cant 3* **P** *Abp* **R** P T MACKENZIE
CANTERBURY (St Mary Bredin) *Cant 3* **P** *Simeon's Trustees* **C** M J BURRELL
CANTERBURY (St Peter w St Alphege) (St Mildred) and St Margaret w St Mary de Castro *Cant 3* **P** *The Crown* **R** D M H HAYES
CANTERBURY (St Stephen) *see* Hackington *Cant*
CANTLEY (St Margaret) *see* Reedham w Cantley w Limpenhoe and Southwood *Nor*
CANTLEY (St Wilfrid) *Sheff 9* **P** *Guild of All So* **V** R J OAKLEY, **C** T A PARKINSON
CANTLEY, NEW (St Hugh of Lincoln) *Sheff 9* **P** *Guild of All So* **V** K SMITH
CANTRIL FARM (St Jude) *Liv 2* **P** *Bp and R W Derby (jt)* **V** A T JUDD
CANVEY ISLAND (St Anne) (St Katherine's Worship Centre) (St Nicholas) *Chelmsf 10* **P** *Bp and Patr Bd (jt)* **TR** D J ELLA, **TV** C J WOODMAN
CANWELL (St Mary, St Giles and All Saints) *Lich 4* **P** *Bp* **V** H J BAKER
CANWICK (All Saints) *see* Washingborough w Heighington and Canwick *Linc*
CAPEL (St John the Baptist) *Guildf 7* **P** *Ld Chan* **P-in-c** J M MASKELL
CAPEL St Mary w Little Wenham and Great Wenham *St E 5* **P** *Bp and SMF (jt)* **R** *Vacant* (01473) 310236
CAPEL LE FERNE (St Radigund) *see* Alkham w Capel le Ferne and Hougham *Cant*
CAPENHURST (Holy Trinity) *see* Backford and Capenhurst *Ches*
CAPESTHORNE (Holy Trinity) w Siddington and Marton *Ches 13* **P** *W A B Davenport Esq* **V** J B WARBURTON
CAR COLSTON (St Mary) w Screveton *S'well 8* **P** *H S Blagg Esq* **R** J PULMAN
CARBIS BAY (St Anta and All Saints) w Lelant (St Uny) *Truro 5* **P** *Bp* **V** R M ELKS, **NSM** E A TUGWELL
CARBROOKE (St Peter and St Paul) *see* Watton w Carbrooke and Ovington *Nor*
CARBURTON (St Giles) *see* Worksop Priory *S'well*
CARDESTON (St Michael) *see* Alberbury w Cardeston *Heref*
CARDINGTON (St James) *Heref 11* **P** *Rt Hon Sir Frederick Corfield* **V** M BROMFIELD
CARDINGTON (St Mary) *St Alb 13* **P** *S C Whitbread Esq* **V** N P MORRELL, **Hon C** L R MOORE
CARDYNHAM (St Mewbud) *Truro 10* **P** *DBP and Personal Reps R M Coode Esq (jt)* **P-in-c** R D C WHITEMAN
CAREBY (St Stephen) *see* Castle Bytham w Creeton *Linc*
CARHAM (St Cuthbert) *see* Cornhill w Carham *Newc*
CARHAMPTON (St John the Baptist) *see* Dunster, Carhampton and Withycombe w Rodhuish *B & W*
CARHARRACK (St Piran's Mission Church) *see* Chacewater w St Day and Carharrack *Truro*
CARISBROOKE (St John the Baptist) *see* Newport St Jo *Portsm*
CARISBROOKE (St Mary the Virgin) *Portsm 8* **P** *Qu Coll Ox* **P-in-c** M A J EXELL
CARISBROOKE St Nicholas in the Castle *Portsm 8* **P** *Qu Coll Ox* **V** *Vacant*
CARLBY (St Stephen) *see* Ryhall w Essendine and Carlby *Pet*
CARLECOATES (St Anne) *see* Penistone and Thurlstone *Wakef*
CARLETON (St Mary the Virgin) and Lothersdale *Bradf 7* **P** *Ch Ch Ox* **R** S G HOARE
CARLETON (St Michael) *Wakef 11* **P** *V Pontefract* **P-in-c** S A STACEY
CARLETON (St Peter) *see* Rockland St Mary w Hellington, Bramerton etc *Nor*
CARLETON, EAST (St Mary) *see* Swardeston w E Carleton, Intwood, Keswick etc *Nor*
CARLETON IN CRAVEN *see* Carleton and Lothersdale *Bradf*
CARLETON RODE (All Saints) *see* Bunwell, Carleton Rode, Tibenham, Gt Moulton etc *Nor*
CARLIN HOW (St Helen) *see* Loftus and Carlin How w Skinningrove *York*
CARLINGHOW (St John the Evangelist) *Wakef 10* **P** *V Brownhill and V Batley (alt)* **P-in-c** R S STOKES
CARLISLE Belah (St Mark) *see* Stanwix *Carl*
CARLISLE Harraby (St Elizabeth) *see* Harraby *Carl*
CARLISLE (Holy Trinity) (St Barnabas) *Carl 3* **P** *Patr Bd* **TV** G M DYER, **NSM** T N DYER
CARLISLE (St Aidan) and Christ Church *Carl 3* **P** *Bp* **V** N M E CLAPP
CARLISLE (St Cuthbert) *Carl 3* **P** *D&C* **P-in-c** R D PRATT
CARLISLE (St Herbert) w St Stephen *Carl 3* **P** *Bp* **V** G F GILCHRIST
CARLISLE (St James) *see* Denton Holme *Carl*
CARLISLE (St John the Evangelist) *Carl 3* **P** *CPAS* **V** P J BYE, **C** F I WRIGHT, **NSM** C G Y HYSLOP
CARLISLE (St Luke) Morton *Carl 3* **P** *Bp* **V** K WRAY
CARLISLE Stanwix (St Michael) *see* Stanwix *Carl*
CARLISLE Upperby (St John the Baptist) *see* Upperby St Jo *Carl*
CARLTON (St Aidan) *see* Helmsley *York*
CARLTON (St Andrew) *see* Nailstone and Carlton w Shackerstone *Leic*
CARLTON (St Bartholomew) *see* Guiseley w Esholt *Bradf*
CARLTON (St Botolph) *see* Whorlton w Carlton and Faceby *York*
CARLTON (St John the Baptist) *S'well 11* **P** *Bp* **V** A M LUCKCUCK
CARLTON (St John the Evangelist) *Wakef 7* **P** *DBP* **P-in-c** J L HUDSON
CARLTON (St Mary) *see* Harrold and Carlton w Chellington *St Alb*
CARLTON (St Peter) *see* Brinkley, Burrough Green and Carlton *Ely*
CARLTON (St Peter) *see* Kelsale-cum-Carlton, Middleton-cum-Fordley etc *St E*
CARLTON, EAST (St Peter) *see* Cottingham w E Carlton *Pet*
CARLTON, GREAT (St John the Baptist) *see* Mid Marsh Gp *Linc*

CARLTON, NORTH (St Luke) w SOUTH (St John the Baptist) *Linc 3* **P** *Lord Monson* **V** *Vacant*
CARLTON BY SNAITH (St Mary) and Drax *York 6* **P** *Abp and Ch Trust Fund Trust (jt)* **P-in-c** J H MDUMULLA
CARLTON COLVILLE (St Peter) w Mutford and Rushmere *Nor 9* **P** *Bp, G&C Coll Cam, and Simeon's Trustees (jt)* **R** *Vacant* (01502) 565217
CARLTON CURLIEU (St Mary the Virgin) *see* Gaulby *Leic*
CARLTON FOREHOE (St Mary) *see* Barnham Broom *Nor*
CARLTON HUSTHWAITE (St Mary) *see* Coxwold and Husthwaite *York*
CARLTON-IN-LINDRICK (St John the Evangelist) *S'well 6* **P** *Ld Chan* **R** J OGLEY, **Hon C** J H SIMPSON
CARLTON-IN-THE-WILLOWS (St Paul) *S'well 11* **P** *MMCET* **R** J F McGINLEY, **C** P C WHITEHEAD
CARLTON-LE-MOORLAND (St Mary) w Stapleford *Linc 18* **P** *Lord Middleton* **V** M J N HOWES, **NSM** J R D SCARBOROUGH
CARLTON MINIOTT (St Lawrence) *see* Thirsk *York*
CARLTON-ON-TRENT (St Mary) *see* Sutton w Carlton and Normanton upon Trent etc *S'well*
CARLTON SCROOP (St Nicholas) *see* Caythorpe *Linc*
CARNABY (St John the Baptist) *York 10* **P** *Abp* **V** T J DAVIDSON
CARNFORTH (Christ Church) *Blackb 15* **P** *Bp* **V** S L JONES
CARR CLOUGH (St Andrew) *see* Kersal Moor *Man*
CARR MILL (St David) *Liv 10* **P** *V St Helens St Mark and Bp (jt)* **V** T THOMAS
CARRINGTON (St John the Evangelist) *S'well 13* **P** *Bp* **V** J WALKER
CARRINGTON (St Paul) *see* Sibsey w Frithville *Linc*
CARSHALTON (All Saints) *S'wark 24* **P** *Bp* **R** L C EDWARDS
CARSHALTON BEECHES (Good Shepherd) *S'wark 24* **P** *Bp* **V** C WHEATON
CARSINGTON (St Margaret) *see* Wirksworth *Derby*
CARTERTON (St John the Evangelist) *Ox 8* **P** *Ch Ch Ox* **V** R K BILLINGS, **C** R J ROGERS
CARTMEL (St Mary and St Michael) *Carl 10* **P** *R H Cavendish Esq* **V** C L V ATKINSON, **NSM** A BAKER
CARTMEL FELL (St Anthony) *Carl 9* **P** *Bp* **P-in-c** W F GREETHAM
CASSINGTON (St Peter) *see* Eynsham and Cassington *Ox*
CASSOP CUM QUARRINTON *Dur 5* **P** *Bp* **V** J THOMPSON
CASTERTON (Holy Trinity) *see* Kirkby Lonsdale *Carl*
CASTERTON, GREAT (St Peter and St Paul) and LITTLE (All Saints) w Pickworth and Tickencote *Pet 8* **P** *Burghley Ho Preservation Trust (2 turns), Lord Chesham (1 turn), and Bp (1 turn)* **R** B HARRIS
CASTLE ACRE (St James) w Newton, Rougham and Southacre *Nor 14* **P** *Viscount Coke, T F North Esq, Bp and H Birkbeck Esq (jt) (by turn)* **P-in-c** S R NAIRN
CASTLE ASHBY (St Mary Magdalene) *see* Yardley Hastings, Denton and Grendon etc *Pet*
CASTLE BOLTON (St Oswald) *see* Aysgarth and Bolton cum Redmire *Ripon*
CASTLE BROMWICH (St Clement) *Birm 10* **P** *Bp* **V** W J SILLITOE, **Hon C** M W MORECROFT, **NSM** P A SILLITOE
CASTLE BROMWICH (St Mary and St Margaret) *Birm 10* **P** *Earl of Bradf* **R** C J BOYLE
CASTLE BYTHAM (St James) w Creeton *Linc 14* **P** *D&C, Bp, Ld Chan, and DBP (by turn)* **R** B J BENNETT
CASTLE CAMPS (All Saints) *see* Linton *Ely*
CASTLE CARROCK (St Peter) *see* Brampton and Farlam and Castle Carrock w Cumrew *Carl*
CASTLE CARY (All Saints) w Ansford *B & W 3* **P** *Bp* **V** P W M REVELL
CASTLE CHURCH (St Mary) *Lich 10* **P** *Bp* **V** J T H PYE, **NSM** G E PYE
CASTLE COMBE (St Andrew) *Bris 9* **P** *Bp* **P-in-c** R V C LEWIS
CASTLE DONINGTON (St Edward the King and Martyr) and Lockington cum Hemington *Leic 7* **P** *Lady Gretton and C H C Coaker Esq (jt)* **V** B WHITEHEAD, **NSM** L R F TESTA
CASTLE EATON (St Mary the Virgin) *see* Meysey Hampton w Marston Meysey and Castle Eaton *Glouc*
CASTLE EDEN (St James) w Monkhesleden *Dur 2* **P** *Bp* **R** *Vacant* (01429) 836846
CASTLE FROME (St Michael) *see* Bishop's Frome w Castle Frome and Fromes Hill *Heref*
CASTLE HEDINGHAM (St Nicholas) *see* Sible Hedingham w Castle Hedingham *Chelmsf*
CASTLE HILL (St Philip) *see* Hindley All SS *Liv*
CASTLE RISING (St Lawrence) *Nor 16* **P** *G Howard Esq* **P-in-c** G R HALL
CASTLE SOWERBY (St Kentigern) *see* Caldbeck, Castle Sowerby and Sebergham *Carl*
CASTLE TOWN (St Thomas and St Andrew) *Lich 10* **P** *Hyndman Trustees* **V** A L HUGHES
CASTLE VALE (St Cuthbert of Lindisfarne) *Birm 13* **P** *Bp* **V** S W POWELL
CASTLE VIEW ESTATE (St Francis) *see* Langley Marish *Ox*
CASTLECROFT (The Good Shepherd) *see* Tettenhall Wood *Lich*
CASTLEFORD (All Saints) *Wakef 11* **P** *Duchy of Lanc* **R** *Vacant* (01977) 552401
CASTLEFORD (St Michael and All Angels) *see* Smawthorpe St Mich *Wakef*
CASTLEMORTON (St Gregory) *see* Longdon, Castlemorton, Bushley, Queenhill etc *Worc*
CASTLESIDE (St John the Evangelist) *Dur 4* **P** *Bp* **V** *Vacant* (01207) 508242
CASTLETHORPE (St Simon and St Jude) *see* Hanslope w Castlethorpe *Ox*
CASTLETON (St Edmund) *see* Hope and Castleton *Derby*
CASTLETON (St Mary Magdalene) *see* Sherborne w Castleton and Lillington *Sarum*
CASTLETON (St Michael and St George) *see* Danby *York*
CASTLETON MOOR (St Martin) *Man 18* **P** *Bp* **V** I McVEETY, **NSM** E SHORT
CASTLETOWN (St Margaret) *see* N Hylton St Marg Castletown *Dur*
CASTLETOWN (St Mary) *S & M 1* **P** *Bp* **V** S T M R DEAN, **NSM** J R GULLAND
CASTON (St Cross), Griston, Merton, Thompson, Stow Bedon, Breckles and Great Hockham *Nor 13* **P** *Bp and DBP (jt)* **R** J H RICHARDSON
CASTOR (St Kyneburgha) w Sutton and Upton w Marholm *Pet 13* **P** *Sir Stephen Hastings (2 turns), Mrs V S V Gunnery (1 turn)* **R** W S D BURKE
CATCLIFFE (St Mary) *see* Brinsworth w Catcliffe and Treeton *Sheff*
CATCOTT (St Peter) *see* W Poldens *B & W*
CATERHAM (St Mary the Virgin) (St Laurence) (St Paul) *S'wark 25* **P** *Bp* **P-in-c** M A HART, **C** G P REEVES, J H ZAREK, **Hon C** E M HILL, M J WEST, P D JONES, **NSM** J M MALES
CATERHAM VALLEY (St John the Evangelist) *S'wark 25* **P** *Bp* **P-in-c** C M S SNOW
CATESBY (St Mary) *see* Daventry, Ashby St Ledgers, Braunston etc *Pet*
CATFIELD (All Saints) *see* Sutton w Ingham and Catfield *Nor*
CATFORD (St Andrew) *S'wark 4* **P** *Bp* **V** R B JORDAN
CATFORD (St John) and Downham *S'wark 4* **P** *Bp* **TR** J BOARDMAN, **TV** P A WALMSLEY-McLEOD, P H ALLEN, **NSM** F M NEAL, D E RHYS
CATFORD (St Laurence) *S'wark 4* **P** *Bp* **V** C F PICKSTONE, **C** C A M BRADDICK-SOUTHGATE
CATHERINGTON (All Saints) and Clanfield *Portsm 4* **P** *Bp* **V** C BEARDSLEY, **C** C M TEBBUTT, B D GOLDSMITH
CATHERSTON LEWESTON (St Mary) *see* Charmouth and Catherston Leweston *Sarum*
CATON (St Paul) w Littledale *Blackb 12* **P** *V Lanc* **V** J R TATE
CATSFIELD (St Laurence) and Crowhurst *Chich 14* **P** *Bp and J P Papillon (alt)* **R** D J TAYLOR
CATSHILL (Christ Church) and Dodford *Worc 7* **P** *Bp and V Bromsgrove St Jo (alt)* **P-in-c** R M HARDING, **C** W J RIOCH
CATTERICK (St Anne) *Ripon 2* **P** *Bp* **V** W R HOGG
CATTHORPE (St Thomas) *see* Swinford w Catthorpe, Shawell and Stanford *Leic*
CATTISTOCK (St Peter and St Paul) *see* Melbury *Sarum*
CATTON (All Saints) *see* Stamford Bridge Gp of Par *York*
CATTON (St Nicholas and the Blessed Virgin Mary) *see* Walton on Trent w Croxall etc *Derby*
CATTON, NEW (Christ Church) *Nor 2* **P** *R Colegate St Geo* **P-in-c** K G CROCKER, **NSM** E M CANNON
CATTON, NEW (St Luke) *Nor 2* **P** *CPAS* **V** D A G G DOLMAN
CATTON, OLD (St Margaret) *Nor 2* **P** *D&C* **V** S J BETTS, **NSM** T I PATIENT
CATWICK (St Michael) *see* Brandesburton and Leven w Catwick *York*
CATWORTH, GREAT *see* Catworth Magna *Ely*
CATWORTH MAGNA (St Leonard) *Ely 10* **P** *BNC Ox* **P-in-c** J HINDLEY, **NSM** B A BEARCROFT, J RAWLINSON
CAULDON (St Mary and St Laurence) *see* Calton, Cauldon, Grindon and Waterfall *Lich*
CAUNDLE MARSH (St Peter and St Paul) *see* The Caundles w Folke and Holwell *Sarum*
CAUNDLES w Folke and Holwell, The *Sarum 4* **P** *Major K S D Wingfield Digby, Bp, and D&C (jt)* **R** D J HILLIER

CAUNTON (St Andrew) *see* Norwell w Ossington, Cromwell and Caunton *S'well*
CAUSEWAY HEAD (St Paul) *see* Silloth *Carl*
CAUTLEY (St Mark) *see* Sedbergh, Cautley and Garsdale *Bradf*
CAVENDISH (St Mary) *see* Clare w Poslingford, Cavendish etc *St E*
CAVENHAM (St Andrew) *see* Mildenhall *St E*
CAVERSFIELD (St Laurence) *see* Bicester w Bucknell, Caversfield and Launton *Ox*
CAVERSHAM (St Andrew) *Ox 15* **P** *Bp* **R** W B CARPENTER
CAVERSHAM (St John the Baptist) *Ox 15* **P** *Bp* **V** S M B ROWE, **NSM** C E ROWE
CAVERSHAM (St Peter) (Park Church) and Mapledurham *Ox 15* **P** *Eton Coll (1 turn) and Ch Ch Ox (3 turns)* **R** R J KINGSBURY, **C** P J ABREY, S J NUNN, **NSM** C PYNN
CAVERSHAM HEIGHTS (St Andrew) *see* Caversham St Andr *Ox*
CAVERSHAM PARK Local Ecumenical Project *Ox 15* **Min** P J ABREY
CAVERSWALL (St Peter) and Weston Coyney w Dilhorne *Lich 6* **P** *D&C* **V** N JEFFERYES, **C** S K SPENCE, **NSM** J A JEFFERYES
CAWOOD (All Saints) *York 6* **P** *Abp* **P-in-c** A STOKER
CAWSAND (St Andrew's Mission Church) *see* Maker w Rame *Truro*
CAWSTON (St Agnes) w Booton and Brandiston, Haveringland andHeydon *Nor 19* **P** *Pemb Coll Cam (3 turns), DBP (1 turn)* **R** M C KING
CAWTHORNE (All Saints) *Wakef 7* **P** *S W Fraser Esq* **V** *Vacant* (01226) 790235
CAXTON (St Andrew) *see* Bourn and Kingston w Caxton and Longstowe *Ely*
CAYNHAM (St Mary) *see* Ludlow, Ludford, Ashford Carbonell etc *Heref*
CAYTHORPE (St Aidan) *see* Lowdham w Caythorpe, and Gunthorpe *S'well*
CAYTHORPE (St Vincent) *Linc 23* **P** *Bp, J F Fane Esq, and S J Packe-Drury-Lowe Esq (by turn)* **P-in-c** B H LUCAS, **NSM** B HANCOCK
CAYTON (St John the Baptist) w Eastfield *York 16* **P** *Abp* **V** M D B LONG, **C** E C R BURGE
CENTRAL *see under substantive place name*
CERNE ABBAS (St Mary) w Godmanstone and Minterne Magna *Sarum 2* **P** *Adn Sherborne (1 turn), D H C Batten Esq (1 turn), Lord Digby (2 turns), and G E H Gallia Esq (1 turn)* **P-in-c** E G LONGMAN
CERNEY, NORTH (All Saints) *see* Stratton, N Cerney, Baunton and Bagendon *Glouc*
CERNEY, SOUTH (All Hallows) w Cerney Wick and Down Ampney *Glouc 13* **P** *Bp and Ch Ch Ox (alt)* **V** J R CALVERT, **NSM** J T THOMAS
CERNEY WICK (Holy Trinity) *see* S Cerney w Cerney Wick and Down Ampney *Glouc*
CHACELEY (St John the Baptist) *see* Deerhurst, Apperley w Forthampton and Chaceley *Glouc*
CHACEWATER (St Paul) w St Day and Carharrack *Truro 2* **P** *D&C and R Kenwyn w St Allen (jt)* **V** A S GOUGH
CHACOMBE (St Peter and St Paul) *see* Middleton Cheney w Chacombe *Pet*
CHADDERTON (Christ Church) (St Saviour) *Man 22* **P** *Trustees* **V** D P BANTING, **C** D K PHILLIPS
CHADDERTON (Emmanuel) (St George) *Man 22* **P** *Trustees* **V** E STOTT
CHADDERTON (St Luke) *Man 22* **P** *Bp* **V** G G MARSHALL, **Dss** J TAYLOR
CHADDERTON (St Mark) *Man 22* **P** *The Crown* **V** A COOKE
CHADDERTON (St Matthew) *Man 22* **P** *The Crown* **V** R W BAILEY
CHADDESDEN (St Mary) *Derby 9* **P** *MMCET* **V** D W BAILEY, **C** T M BINLEY
CHADDESDEN (St Philip) *Derby 9* **P** *Bp* **V** T G REILLY
CHADDESLEY CORBETT (St Cassian) and Stone *Worc 11* **P** *Ld Chan* **V** J A COX
CHADDLEWORTH (St Andrew) *see* Brightwalton w Catmore, Leckhampstead etc *Ox*
CHADKIRK (St Chad) *Ches 16* **P** *R Stockport St Mary* **V** T D BARLOW, **C** T R PARKER
CHADLINGTON (St Nicholas) and Spelsbury, Ascott under Wychwood *Ox 3* **P** *Bp and Ch Ch Ox (alt)* **V** T C G THORNTON
CHADSMOOR (St Aidan) *see* Cannock *Lich*
CHADSMOOR (St Chad) *as above*
CHADWELL (Emmanuel) (St Mary) *Chelmsf 14* **P** *Ch Soc Trust* **R** N T B DEANE, **C** D WILLS
CHADWELL HEATH (St Chad) *Chelmsf 1* **P** *Vs Dagenham and Ilford (alt)* **V** J A A FLETCHER, **C** D A BAKER
CHAFFCOMBE (St Michael and All Angels) *see* Chard Furnham w Chaffcombe, Knowle St Giles etc *B & W*
CHAGFORD (St Michael) w Gidleigh and Throwleigh *Ex 12* **P** *Lady Anne Hayter-Hames, Guild of All So, and Bp (jt)* **R** P L BAYCOCK
CHAILEY (St Peter) *Chich 21* **P** *J P B Tillard Esq* **R** C R ABBOTT
CHALBURY (All Saints) *see* Horton, Chalbury, Hinton Martel and Holt St Jas *Sarum*
CHALDON (St Peter and St Paul) *S'wark 25* **P** *Bp* **P-in-c** M A HART
CHALDON HERRING (St Nicholas) *see* The Lulworths, Winfrith Newburgh and Chaldon *Sarum*
CHALE (St Andrew) *Portsm 8* **P** *Keble Coll Ox* **R** J W RUSSELL, **NSM** S C HENDERSON
CHALFIELD, GREAT (All Saints) *see* Broughton Gifford, Gt Chalfield and Holt *Sarum*
CHALFONT, LITTLE (St George) *see* Chenies and Lt Chalfont, Latimer and Flaunden *Ox*
CHALFONT ST GILES (St Giles) *Ox 20* **P** *Bp* **R** P W POOLE
CHALFONT ST PETER (St Peter) *Ox 20* **P** *St Jo Coll Ox* **R** J K GREASLEY, **C** S J DAVIES, **NSM** L WARRINER
CHALFORD (Christ Church) and France Lynch *Glouc 1* **P** *Adn Glouc and DBP (jt)* **V** P R KESLAKE
CHALGRAVE (All Saints) *St Alb 12* **P** *DBP* **P-in-c** K A STEELE
CHALGROVE (St Mary) w Berrick Salome *Ox 1* **P** *Ch Ch Ox* **V** I G H COHEN
CHALK (St Mary) *Roch 4* **P** *R Milton* **V** J R FRY, **NSM** D HITCHCOCK
CHALKE VALLEY West *Sarum 13* **P** *Bp, DBP, and K Coll Cam (by turn)* **V** S H WILLCOX, **TV** R C REDDING, G SOUTHGATE, **NSM** K S CURNOCK
CHALLACOMBE (Holy Trinity) *see* Shirwell, Loxhore, Kentisbury, Arlington, etc *Ex*
CHALLOCK (St Cosmas and St Damian) *see* Chilham w Challock and Molash *Cant*
CHALLOW, EAST (St Nicolas) *see* Hanney, Denchworth and E Challow *Ox*
CHALLOW, WEST (St Laurence) *see* Ridgeway *Ox*
CHALTON (St Michael and All Angels) *see* Blendworth w Chalton w Idsworth *Portsm*
CHALVEY (St Peter) *see* Upton cum Chalvey *Ox*
CHALVINGTON (St Bartholomew) *see* Laughton w Ripe and Chalvington *Chich*
CHAMBERSBURY Hemel Hempstead (Holy Trinity) (St Mary) (St Benedict) *St Alb 3* **P** *DBP* **TR** D T N PARRY, **TV** C L TERRY, J B THOMAS, **Hon C** D A BUTLER
CHANDLER'S FORD (St Boniface) (St Martin in the Wood) *Win 9* **P** *Bp* **V** A G HARBIDGE, **C** J H T de GARIS, **NSM** V L MOFFITT
CHANTRY (Holy Trinity) *see* Mells w Buckland Dinham, Elm, Whatley etc *B & W*
CHAPEL ALLERTON (St Matthew) *Ripon 5* **P** *V Leeds St Pet* **V** S JARRATT, **C** R A M T QUICK
CHAPEL CHORLTON (St Laurence), Maer and Whitmore *Lich 7* **P** *Bp and R G D Cavenagh-Mainwaring Esq (jt)* **R** G M YOULD
CHAPEL-EN-LE-FRITH (St Thomas a Becket) *Derby 4* **P** *PCC* **V** N R BRALESFORD
CHAPEL HOUSE (Holy Nativity) *Newc 7* **P** *Bp* **V** S H CONNOLLY
CHAPEL LAWN (St Mary) *see* Bucknell w Chapel Lawn, Llanfair Waterdine etc *Heref*
CHAPEL LE DALE (St Leonard) *see* Ingleton w Chapel le Dale *Bradf*
CHAPEL PLAISTER (not known) *see* Box w Hazlebury and Ditteridge *Bris*
CHAPEL ST LEONARDS (St Leonard) w Hogsthorpe *Linc 8* **P** *V Willoughby St Helen* **V** J D DUCKETT
CHAPELTHORPE (St James) *Wakef 9* **P** *V Sandal* **V** J F WHITE, **C** J TRAFFORD
CHAPELTOWN (St John the Baptist) *Sheff 7* **P** *Bp* **V** S HOPE, **NSM** I G BIRKINSHAW, H A FRANKLIN
CHAPMANSLADE (St Philip and St James) *see* Cley Hill Warminster *Sarum*
CHAPPEL (St Barnabas) *see* Gt Tey and Wakes Colne w Chappel *Chelmsf*
CHARBOROUGH (St Mary) *see* Red Post *Sarum*
CHARD (Blessed Virgin Mary) *B & W 15* **P** *Bp* **V** M S KIVETT
CHARD Furnham (Good Shepherd) w Chaffcombe, Knowle St Giles and Cricket Malherbie *B & W 15* **P** *R Shepton Beauchamp etc and R Bishops Lydeard etc (jt)* **P-in-c** F R HAZELL

CHARDSTOCK (All Saints) *see* Axminster, Chardstock, Combe Pyne and Rousdon *Ex*
CHARDSTOCK (St Andrew) *as above*
CHARFIELD (St John) *Glouc 7* **P** *R W Neeld Esq* **P-in-c** R C PESTELL
CHARFORD (St Andrew) *see* Bromsgrove St Jo *Worc*
CHARING (St Peter and St Paul) w Charing Heath (Holy Trinity) and Little Chart *Cant 10* **P** *Abp and D&C (jt)* **V** B CHALMERS
CHARLBURY (St Mary the Virgin) w Shorthampton *Ox 3* **P** *St Jo Coll Ox* **V** J K FRENCH, **NSM** N J READ
CHARLCOMBE (Blessed Virgin Mary) w Bath (St Stephen) *B & W 9* **P** *DBP and Simeon's Trustees (jt)* **R** R OSBORNE
CHARLECOTE (St Leonard) *see* Hampton Lucy w Charlecote and Loxley *Cov*
CHARLES (St John the Baptist) *see* S Molton w Nymet St George, High Bray etc *Ex*
CHARLES w Plymouth St Matthias *Ex 23* **P** *Ch Patr Trust* **P-in-c** R S WILLIAMS, **C** G M LOOMES
CHARLESTOWN (St George) *see* Pendleton *Man*
CHARLESTOWN (St Paul) *Truro 1* **P** *The Crown* **Hon C** A D J JAGO, **NSM** D C B PECKETT
CHARLESTOWN (St Thomas the Apostle) *Wakef 4* **P** *V Halifax* **V** *Vacant* (01422) 348188
CHARLESWORTH (St John the Evangelist) and Dinting Vale *Derby 6* **P** *The Crown (2 turns), Bp (1 turn)* **V** M A ROYLE, **C** M K MADELEY, **NSM** S M McLEOD
CHARLETON (St Mary) w Buckland Tout Saints, East Portlemouth, South Pool and Chivelstone *Ex 14* **P** *Ld Chan (2 turns), E Roberts Esq, S Tyler Esq and N Tyler Esq (1 turn), Bp (1 turn), and DBP (1 turn)* **P-in-c** B J DANSIE
CHARLTON (Holy Trinity) *see* Wantage *Ox*
CHARLTON (St John) *see* Cropthorne w Charlton *Worc*
CHARLTON (St John the Baptist) *see* Garsdon, Lea and Cleverton and Charlton *Bris*
CHARLTON (St John the Baptist) *see* The Donheads *Sarum*
CHARLTON (St Luke w Holy Trinity) (St Richard) *S'wark 3* **P** *Viscount Gough* **R** J G HESKINS, **C** K RAMSAY, **NSM** J R GRIFFITHS
CHARLTON (St Peter) *see* Uphavon w Rushall and Charlton *Sarum*
CHARLTON (St Thomas the Apostle) *see* Andover w Foxcott *Win*
CHARLTON (All Saints) *see* Chalke Valley W *Sarum*
CHARLTON, OLD (St Thomas) *see* Woolwich St Thos *S'wark*
CHARLTON, SOUTH (St James) *see* Glendale Gp *Newc*
CHARLTON ABBOTS (St Martin) *see* Sevenhampton w Charlton Abbotts and Hawling etc *Glouc*
CHARLTON ADAM (St Peter and St Paul) *see* Somerton w Compton Dundon, the Charltons etc *B & W*
CHARLTON HORETHORNE (St Peter and St Paul) *see* Henstridge and Charlton Horethorne w Stowell *B & W*
CHARLTON-IN-DOVER (St Peter and St Paul) *Cant 4* **P** *Keble Coll Ox* **R** N D L DE KEYSER
CHARLTON KINGS (Holy Apostles) *Glouc 14* **P** *R Cheltenham* **P-in-c** R COPPING
CHARLTON KINGS (St Mary) *Glouc 11* **P** *Bp* **V** G T BRYANT
CHARLTON MACKRELL (Blessed Virgin Mary) *see* Somerton w Compton Dundon, the Charltons etc *B & W*
CHARLTON MARSHALL (St Mary the Virgin) *see* Spetisbury w Charlton Marshall etc *Sarum*
CHARLTON MUSGROVE (St John) (St Stephen), Cucklington and Stoke Trister *B & W 2* **P** *Bp* **R** *Vacant* (01963) 33233
CHARLTON ON OTMOOR (St Mary) *see* Islip w Charlton on Otmoor, Oddington, Noke etc *Ox*
CHARLWOOD (St Nicholas) *S'wark 26* **P** *DBP* **R** W G CAMPEN, **Hon C** R C GAUNT
CHARMINSTER (St Mary the Virgin) and Stinsford *Sarum 2* **P** *Hon Charlotte Morrison and P R FitzGerald (jt), and Bp (alt)* **P-in-c** B R CONAWAY
CHARMOUTH (St Andrew) and Catherston Leweston *Sarum 3* **P** *MMCET* **P-in-c** R H BLANKLEY
CHARNEY BASSETT (St Peter) *see* Cherbury *Ox*
CHARNOCK RICHARD (Christ Church) *Blackb 4* **P** *DBF* **P-in-c** R A PETTITT
CHARSFIELD w Debach (St Peter), Monewden, Hoo, Dallinghoo and Letheringham *St E 18* **P** *MMCET and CPAS, Ld Chan, and Ch Patr Trust (by turn)* **V** G R ADDINGTON HALL
CHART, GREAT (St Mary) *Cant 10* **P** *Abp* **R** A J DAVIS, **C** M A McLAUGHLIN
CHART, LITTLE (St Mary) *see* Charing w Charing Heath and Lt Chart *Cant*
CHART SUTTON (St Michael) *see* Sutton Valence w E Sutton and Chart Sutton *Cant*
CHARTERHOUSE-ON-MENDIP (St Hugh) *see* Blagdon w Compton Martin and Ubley *B & W*
CHARTHAM (St Mary) *Cant 2* **P** *Abp* **R** C C BARLOW
CHARWELTON (Holy Trinity) *see* Badby w Newham and Charwelton w Fawsley etc *Pet*
CHASETOWN (St Anne) (St John) *Lich 1* **P** *V Burntwood* **P-in-c** M J WITHEY, **C** D B LEAKE
CHASTLETON (St Mary the Virgin) *see* Lt Compton w Chastleton, Cornwell etc *Ox*
CHATBURN (Christ Church) *Blackb 8* **P** *DBF* **V** W DRAIN
CHATHAM (Christ the King) *see* Prince's Park CD *Roch*
CHATHAM (St Mary and St John) *Roch 5* **P** *D&C* **R** R C PAGET
CHATHAM (St Paul w All Saints) *Roch 5* **P** *Bp* **V** B T KNAPP, **C** R A KNAPP
CHATHAM (St Philip and St James) *Roch 5* **P** *Ch Soc Trust* **V** G J ACKERLEY, **C** V C SHORT
CHATHAM (St Stephen) *Roch 5* **P** *Bp* **V** C J D WALKER, **Hon C** O MATON
CHATHAM (St William) (St Alban) (St David) *Roch 5* **P** *Bp* **V** S F MORRIS
CHATTERIS (St Peter and St Paul) *Ely 18* **P** *G&C Coll Cam* **V** C J MYHILL
CHATTISHAM (All Saints and St Margaret) *see* Hadleigh *St E*
CHATTON (Holy Cross) *see* Glendale Gp *Newc*
CHAULDEN (St Stephen) *see* Hemel Hempstead *St Alb*
CHAVEY DOWN (St Martin) *see* Winkfield and Cranbourne *Ox*
CHAWLEIGH (St James) *see* Chulmleigh, Chawleigh w Cheldon, Wembworthy etc *Ex*
CHAWTON (St Nicholas) and Farringdon *Win 2* **P** *Bp* **R** *Vacant* (0142058) 398
CHEADLE (All Hallows) (St Philip's Mission Church) *Ches 17* **P** *R Cheadle* **V** R I McLAREN, **C** J N FIELDER
CHEADLE (St Cuthbert) (St Mary) *Ches 17* **P** *Ch Soc Trust* **R** D S ALLISTER, **C** J E M NEWMAN, M I A SMITH, **NSM** S POOLE, N C HALL
CHEADLE (St Giles) w Freehay *Lich 6* **P** *DBP* **R** D W YABBACOME, **C** S A ANSELL
CHEADLE HEATH (St Augustine) *Ches 18* **P** *Bp* **P-in-c** C E LARSEN
CHEADLE HULME (All Saints) *Ches 17* **P** *Bp* **V** H B EALES
CHEADLE HULME (Emmanuel) Conventional District *Ches 17* **Min** P G BURROWS
CHEADLE HULME (St Andrew) *Ches 17* **P** *R Cheadle* **V** C P COOK, **C** D W GUEST
CHEAM (St Dunstan) (St Alban the Martyr) (St Oswald) *S'wark 24* **P** *St Jo Coll Ox* **R** C A FRENCH, **C** H R NAUNTON
CHEAM COMMON (St Philip) *S'wark 24* **P** *R Cheam* **C** S H CAWDELL
CHEARSLEY (St Nicholas) *see* Long Crendon w Chearsley and Nether Winchendon *Ox*
CHEBSEY (All Saints), Ellenhall and Seighford-with-Creswell *Lich 7* **P** *D&C, Trustees Earl of Lich, Personal Reps Major C Eld, and Qu Eliz Grant Trustees (jt)* **V** G G HODSON
CHECKENDON (St Peter and St Paul) *see* Langtree *Ox*
CHECKLEY (Mission Room) *see* Fownhope w Mordiford, Brockhampton etc *Heref*
CHECKLEY (St Mary and All Saints) *see* Uttoxeter Area *Lich*
CHEDBURGH (All Saints) w Depden, Rede and Hawkedon *St E 8* **P** *Bp (1 turn), Ld Chan (4 turns)* **R** D O WALL
CHEDDAR (St Andrew) *B & W 1* **P** *D&C* **V** V L DALEY, **C** R M HOVEY, **NSM** R D H BURSELL
CHEDDINGTON (St Giles) w Mentmore and Marsworth *Ox 26* **P** *Bp and Earl of Rosebery (jt)* **R** R A HALE
CHEDDLETON (St Edward the Confessor) *Lich 8* **P** *Bp* **V** D M TINSLEY
CHEDDON FITZPAINE (The Blessed Virgin Mary) *see* Kingston St Mary w Broomfield etc *B & W*
CHEDGRAVE (All Saints) w Hardley and Langley *Nor 8* **P** *Gt Hosp (1 turn), Sir Christopher Beauchamp, Bt (2 turns)* **P-in-c** C R CHAPMAN
CHEDISTON (St Mary) *see* Halesworth w Linstead, Chediston, Holton etc *St E*
CHEDWORTH (St Andrew), Yanworth and Stowell, Coln Rogers and Coln St Denys *Glouc 14* **P** *Ld Chan (2 turns), Qu Coll Ox (1 turn)* **NSM** D W HUTCHIN
CHEDZOY (The Blessed Virgin Mary) *see* Weston Zoyland w Chedzoy *B & W*
CHEETHAM (St John the Evangelist) *Man 5* **P** *Bp* **P-in-c** D M SEBER
CHEETHAM (St Mark) (Hamilton Memorial Hall) and Lower Crumpsall *Man 5* **P** *Patr Bd* **R** H W MAYOR
CHEETWOOD *Man 6* **P** *D&C* **R** *Vacant*
CHELBOROUGH, EAST (St James) *see* Melbury *Sarum*
CHELBOROUGH, WEST (St Andrew) *as above*
CHELDON (St Mary) *see* Chulmleigh, Chawleigh w Cheldon, Wembworthy etc *Ex*
CHELFORD (St John the Evangelist) w Lower Withington *Ches 12* **P** *J M Dixon Esq* **V** J F ELLIS

CHELL (St Michael) *Lich 11* **P** *Patr Bd* **TR** C S BUTLER, **TV** E M BARNES, **C** R H PARSONAGE
CHELL HEATH (Saviour) *see* Chell *Lich*
CHELLASTON (St Peter) *Derby 15* **P** *Bp* **V** N GUTHRIE, **C** A A ERDAL, **NSM** F R WORRALL
CHELLS (St Hugh) *see* Stevenage St Hugh and St Jo *St Alb*
CHELLS (St John) *as above*
CHELMARSH (St Peter) *see* Billingsley w Sidbury, Middleton Scriven etc *Heref*
CHELMONDISTON (St Andrew) and Erwarton w Harkstead *St E 5* **P** *Ld Chan (1 turn), Bp (2 turns)* **R** R D NEWTON, **NSM** R FREEMAN
CHELMORTON AND FLAGG (St John the Baptist) *see* Taddington, Chelmorton and Flagg, and Monyash *Derby*
CHELMSFORD (All Saints) (St Michael's Church Centre) *Chelmsf 8* **P** *Bp* **P-in-c** A P SHACKERLEY, **C** D W LOWMAN
CHELMSFORD (Ascension) *Chelmsf 8* **P** *Bp* **V** I L MORRIS, **C** D W LOWMAN
CHELMSFORD (St Andrew) *Chelmsf 8* **P** *Bp* **P-in-c** A L COZENS
CHELMSLEY WOOD (St Andrew) *Birm 10* **P** *Bp* **TR** D T SHAW, **C** J D R COX
CHELSEA (All Saints) (Old Church) *Lon 8* **P** *R Chelsea St Luke and Earl Cadogan (jt)* **V** P D ELVY
CHELSEA (St John w St Andrew) (St John) *Lon 8* **P** *CPAS and Lon Coll of Div (jt)* **V** J O S SMITH
CHELSEA (St Luke) (Christ Church) *Lon 8* **P** *Earl Cadogan* **R** C C KEVILL-DAVIES, **C** J W STREETING, **Hon C** S A WATSON
CHELSEA (St Saviour) *see* Upper Chelsea St Sav *Lon*
CHELSEA, UPPER (Holy Trinity) (St Jude) *Lon 8* **P** *Earl Cadogan* **P-in-c** M E MARSHALL
CHELSEA, UPPER (St Saviour) *Lon 8* **P** *R Upper Chelsea Holy Trin w St Jude* **P-in-c** M H McGOWAN
CHELSEA, UPPER (St Simon Zelotes) *Lon 8* **P** *Hyndman Trustees* **P-in-c** M H McGOWAN
CHELSFIELD (St Martin of Tours) *Roch 16* **P** *All So Coll Ox* **R** L G VIRGO, **Hon C** R S BODY
CHELSHAM (St Christopher) *see* Warlingham w Chelsham and Farleigh *S'wark*
CHELSHAM (St Leonard) *as above*
CHELSTON (St Peter) *see* Cockington *Ex*
CHELSWORTH (All Saints) *see* Monks Eleigh w Chelsworth and Brent Eleigh etc *St E*
CHELTENHAM (All Saints) *Glouc 11* **P** *Bp* **V** W J JENNINGS
CHELTENHAM (Christ Church) *Glouc 11* **P** *Simeon's Trustees* **V** E A CROFTON, **C** R J CORNFIELD, **NSM** F M BAYNE
CHELTENHAM (Emmanuel) (St Stephen) *Glouc 10* **P** *Bp* **V** I E BURBERY, **C** R NORTHING, **NSM** B E TORODE
CHELTENHAM (St Luke and St John) *Glouc 11* **P** *R Cheltenham and Simeon's Trustees (alt)* **P-in-c** M J LODGE, **NSM** P C YOUDE
CHELTENHAM (St Mark) (St Silas) (St Barnabas) (St Aidan) (Emmanuel) *Glouc 11* **P** *Patr Bd* **TR** D G WILLIAMS, **TV** R J AVERY, R T SWAIN, R W S SUFFERN, **C** R J FACER, **NSM** H J DAVIES, B E HORNE
CHELTENHAM (St Mary) (St Matthew) (St Paul) (Holy Trinity) *Glouc 11* **P** *Patr Bd* **TR** T P WATSON, **TV** M R BAILEY, S J TYRRELL, **C** M J SCHORAH, **NSM** A B MARTIN-DOYLE
CHELTENHAM (St Michael) *Glouc 11* **P** *Bp* **V** D I LAWRENCE, **NSM** M E THAME
CHELTENHAM (St Peter) *Glouc 11* **P** *DBP* **V** W F J EVERITT, **NSM** M J FRENCH
CHELVESTON (St John the Baptist) *see* Higham Ferrers w Chelveston *Pet*
CHELVEY (St Bridget) *see* Backwell w Chelvey and Brockley *B & W*
CHELWOOD (St Leonard) *see* Publow w Pensford, Compton Dando and Chelwood *B & W*
CHELWOOD GATE (not known) *see* Danehill *Chich*
CHENIES (St Michael) and Little Chalfont, Latimer and Flaunden *Ox 23* **P** *Bedf Estates Trustees and Lord Chesham (jt)* **R** D F LAMBERT, **C** A W BAINES, **Hon C** P SWART-RUSSELL
CHEQUERBENT (St Thomas) *see* Westhoughton and Wingates *Man*
CHEQUERFIELD (St Mary) *see* Pontefract St Giles *Wakef*
CHERBURY *Ox 17* **P** *Bp, Jes Coll Ox, and Worc Coll Ox (jt)* **P-in-c** R O WOODHAMS
CHERHILL (St James the Great) *see* Oldbury *Sarum*
CHERINGTON (St John the Baptist) w Stourton *Cov 9* **P** *Bp* **P-in-c** R K SMITH, **C** R D HOLDER
CHERINGTON (St Nicholas) *see* Avening w Cherington *Glouc*
CHERITON (All Souls) w Newington *Cant 5* **P** *Abp* **V** G H GREEN
CHERITON (St Martin) *Cant 5* **P** *Abp* **R** J H WRIGHT
CHERITON (St Michael and All Angels) w Tichborne and Beauworth *Win 1* **P** *The Crown* **R** R E WILLIAMS
CHERITON, NORTH (St John the Baptist) *see* Camelot Par *B & W*
CHERITON BISHOP (St Mary) *see* Tedburn St Mary, Whitestone, Oldridge etc *Ex*
CHERITON FITZPAINE (St Matthew) *see* N Creedy *Ex*
CHERRY BURTON (St Michael) *York 9* **P** *R H Burton Esq* **P-in-c** E A CULLING
CHERRY HINTON (St Andrew) *Ely 2* **P** *Peterho Cam* **V** C D BOULTON, **Hon C** W G PRENTICE
CHERRY HINTON (St John the Evangelist) *Ely 2* **P** *Bp* **C** R A DARMODY
CHERRY WILLINGHAM (St Peter and St Paul) w Greetwell *Linc 3* **P** *D&C* **P-in-c** K N JAMES
CHERTSEY (St Peter w All Saints) *Guildf 11* **P** *Haberdashers' Co* **V** D L H HEAD, **C** T J HILLIER, B STEADMAN-ALLEN, **NSM** S D S VANDYCK
CHESELBORNE (St Martin) *see* Milton Abbas, Hilton w Cheselbourne etc *Sarum*
CHESHAM, GREAT (Christ Church) (Emmanuel) (St Mary the Virgin) *Ox 20* **P** *Patr Bd* **TR** R J SALISBURY, **TV** J A HAWKINS, W M C STILEMAN, **C** S N AUSTEN, M M HALL, **NSM** A DAVIS, A W MEEK, D J UPCOTT, J O EDIS
CHESHAM BOIS (St Leonard) *Ox 20* **P** *Peache Trustees* **R** G C ROWLANDSON, **C** S P DUST, **NSM** D J BUTLER, C CLARE
CHESHUNT (St Mary the Virgin) *St Alb 20* **P** *Marquess of Salisbury* **V** B M BLACKSHAW, **C** J V ANDERSON, **NSM** D R PEPPER
CHESSINGTON (St Mary the Virgin) *Guildf 9* **P** *Mert Coll Ox* **V** P M FLYNN
CHESTER (Holy Trinity without the Walls) *Ches 2* **P** *Bp* **R** P L WILLIAMS, **C** D W GOODWIN
CHESTER (St Mary on the Hill) *Ches 2* **P** *Duke of Westmr* **R** C W J SAMUELS, **Hon C** J R CARHART
CHESTER (St Paul) *Ches 2* **P** *R Ches* **V** N W PYATT
CHESTER Team, The (Christ Church) (St Barnabas) (St John the Baptist) (St Peter) (St Thomas of Canterbury) *Ches 2* **P** *DBP* **TR** A J POULTER, **TV** C M POTTER, J L GOODE, **NSM** W J T HAMILTON
CHESTER LE STREET (St Mary and St Cuthbert) *Dur 11* **P** *St Jo Coll Dur* **R** S K PRIOR, **C** M WORTHINGTON, S A K ALLABY, J A ATKINSON
CHESTER SQUARE (St Michael) (St Philip) *Lon 3* **P** *Duke of Westmr* **V** C C MARNHAM, **C** C P GUINNESS, J H VALENTINE
CHESTERBLADE (The Blessed Virgin Mary) *see* Evercreech w Chesterblade and Milton Clevedon *B & W*
CHESTERFIELD (Holy Trinity) (Christ Church) *Derby 5* **P** *CPAS* **R** N D GREENWOOD, **C** S M POTTER
CHESTERFIELD (St Augustine) *Derby 5* **P** *Bp* **V** F E WILLETT, **C** J H A KIRBY
CHESTERFIELD (St Mary and All Saints) *Derby 5* **P** *Bp* **V** M R KNIGHT, **C** F E YATES, **NSM** D KING, J E HUNT
CHESTERFORD, GREAT (All Saints) w LITTLE (St Mary the Virgin) *Chelmsf 22* **P** *Bp* **V** A KEMP
CHESTERTON (Good Shepherd) *Ely 2* **P** *Bp* **V** A R McKEARNEY, **C** G J GILES
CHESTERTON (Holy Trinity) (St Chad) *Lich 9* **P** *Prime Min* **V** *Vacant* (01782) 562479
CHESTERTON (St Andrew) *Ely 2* **P** *Trin Coll Cam* **C** L DAZELEY
CHESTERTON (St George) *Ely 2* **P** *Bp* **V** P K REED
CHESTERTON (St Giles) *Cov 8* **P** *Lady Willoughby de Broke* **V** J R WILLIAMS
CHESTERTON (St Lawrence) *see* Cirencester *Glouc*
CHESTERTON (St Michael) *see* The Ortons, Alwalton and Chesterton *Ely*
CHESTERTON, GREAT (St Mary) *see* Akeman *Ox*
CHESWARDINE (St Swithun), Childs Ercall, Hales, Hinstock, Sambrook and Stoke on Tern *Lich 18* **P** *Bp, Adn Salop, R Edgmond w Kynnersley and Preston Wealdmoors, C C Corbet Esq, and R N C Hall Esq (jt)* **R** B PEACE, **C** N C PEDLEY
CHETNOLE (St Peter) *see* Yetminster w Ryme Intrinseca and High Stoy *Sarum*
CHETTISHAM (St Michael and All Angels) *see* Ely *Ely*
CHETTLE (St Mary) *see* Tollard Royal w Farnham, Gussage St Michael etc *Sarum*
CHETTON (St Giles) *see* Billingsley w Sidbury, Middleton Scriven etc *Heref*
CHETWODE (St Mary and St Nicholas) *see* Swan *Ox*
CHETWYND (St Michael and All Angels) *see* Newport w Longford, Chetwynd and Forton *Lich*

CHEVELEY (St Mary) *Ely 4* **P** *DBP and Mrs D A Bowlby (alt)* **R** C A SINDALL
CHEVENING (St Botolph) *Roch 9* **P** *Abp* **R** C F JOHNSON
CHEVERELL, GREAT (St Peter) *see* W Lavington and the Cheverells *Sarum*
CHEVERELL, LITTLE (St Peter) *as above*
CHEVINGTON (All Saints) w Hargrave and Whepstead w Brockley *St E 13* **P** *DBP (1 turn), Guild of All So (2 turns), and Bp (2 turns)* **R** J W MOTT
CHEVINGTON (St John the Divine) *Newc 9* **P** *Bp* **V** J P H CLARK
CHEVITHORNE (St Thomas) *see* Tiverton St Pet and Chevithorne w Cove *Ex*
CHEW MAGNA (St Andrew) w Dundry *B & W 10* **P** *Mrs D H F Luxmoore-Ball* **V** M W MATTHEWS
CHEW STOKE (St Andrew) w Nempnett Thrubwell *B & W 10* **P** *Bp and SMF (jt)* **R** *Vacant* (01275) 332554
CHEWTON (Mission Church) *see* Keynsham *B & W*
CHEWTON MENDIP (St Mary Magdalene) w Ston Easton, Litton and Emborough *B & W 8* **P** *Earl Waldegrave (2 turns), Bp (1 turn)* **P-in-c** V S ROBERTS
CHEYLESMORE (Christ Church) *Cov 3* **P** *Ch Trust Fund Trust* **V** A F MUNDEN
CHICHELEY (St Laurence) *see* Sherington w Chicheley, N Crawley, Astwood etc *Ox*
CHICHESTER (St Pancras and St John) *Chich 3* **P** *Simeon's Trustees (2 turns), St Jo Chpl Trustees (1 turn)* **R** R B M GRIFFITHS
CHICHESTER (St Paul) (St Wilfrid) *Chich 3* **P** *Patr Bd* **TR** K W CATCHPOLE, **TV** J P COOPER, R K WHELAN, **C** C M B HUXTABLE, **NSM** M G STONE
CHICKERELL (St Mary) w Fleet *Sarum 5* **P** *Bp* **P-in-c** N T POLLOCK
CHICKLADE (All Saints) *see* Tisbury *Sarum*
CHIDDINGFOLD (St Mary) *Guildf 4* **P** *Ld Chan* **R** D E WEBSTER
CHIDDINGLY (not known) w East Hoathly *Chich 21* **P** *Bp* **P-in-c** P CLARK
CHIDDINGSTONE (St Mary) w Chiddingstone Causeway *Roch 11* **P** *Abp and Bp (jt)* **R** J R LEE, **NSM** E J LORIMER
CHIDDINGSTONE CAUSEWAY (St Luke) *see* Chiddingstone w Chiddingstone Causeway *Roch*
CHIDEOCK (St Giles) *see* Symondsbury and Chideock *Sarum*
CHIDHAM (St Mary) *Chich 13* **P** *Bp* **P-in-c** B R COOK
CHIEVELEY (St Mary the Virgin) w Winterbourne and Oare *Ox 14* **P** *Adn Berks* **V** C T SCOTT-DEMPSTER
CHIGNAL SMEALEY (St Nicholas) *see* The Chignals w Mashbury *Chelmsf*
CHIGNALS w Mashbury, The *Chelmsf 8* **P** *CPAS (2 turns), Bp (1 turn)* **P-in-c** A L COZENS
CHIGWELL (St Mary) (St Winifred) see 8/76bx *Chelmsf 25* **P** *Bp* **TR** *Vacant* 0181-500 3510
CHIGWELL (St Mary) (St Winifred) and Chigwell Row *Chelmsf 25* **P** *The Crown, and Patr Bd (by turn)* **TR** P J TRENDALL, **TV** S MARSHALL, **C** E R STEINBERG, **NSM** V N ARNOLD
CHIGWELL ROW (All Saints) *see* Chigwell and Chigwell Row *Chelmsf*
CHILBOLTON (St Mary) cum Wherwell *Win 3* **P** *Bp and Marquess of Camden (alt)* **R** F E WILLIAMS
CHILCOMB (St Andrew) *see* Win All SS w Chilcomb and Chesil *Win*
CHILCOMBE (not known) *see* Bride Valley *Sarum*
CHILCOMPTON (St John the Baptist) w Downside and Stratton on the Fosse *B & W 12* **P** *Bp, MMCET, and V Midsomer Norton (jt)* **R** S J TUDGEY
CHILCOTE (St Matthew's Chapel) *see* Clifton Campville w Edingale and Harlaston *Lich*
CHILDE OKEFORD (St Nicholas), Okeford Fitzpaine, Manston, Hammoon and Handford *Sarum 6* **P** *G A L Pitt-Rivers Esq and DBP (alt)* **P-in-c** P J RAHILLY
CHILDERDITCH (All Saints and St Faith) *see* E and W Horndon w Lt Warley and Childerditch *Chelmsf*
CHILDREY (St Mary the Virgin) *see* Ridgeway *Ox*
CHILDS ERCALL (St Michael and All Angels) *see* Cheswardine, Childs Ercall, Hales, Hinstock etc *Lich*
CHILDS HILL (All Saints) *see* Hendon All SS Childs Hill *Lon*
CHILDSWYCKHAM (St Mary the Virgin) w Aston Somerville, Buckland and Snowshill *Glouc 17* **P** *Bp* **P-in-c** P PHILLIPS
CHILDWALL (All Saints) *Liv 4* **P** *Bp* **V** E BRAMHALL, **C** M S J CANNAM
CHILDWALL (St David) *Liv 4* **P** *Bp* **V** S W C GOUGH, **C** U R SHONE
CHILDWALL VALLEY (St Mark) *see* Gateacre *Liv*
CHILDWICK (St Mary) *see* St Alb St Mich *St Alb*
CHILFROME (Holy Trinity) *see* Melbury *Sarum*
CHILHAM (St Mary) w Challock and Molash *Cant 2* **P** *Abp and Viscount Massereene and Ferrard (jt)* **V** C R DUNCAN
CHILLENDEN (All Saints) *see* Nonington w Wymynswold and Goodnestone etc *Cant*
CHILLESFORD (St Peter) *see* Orford w Sudbourne, Chillesford, Butley and Iken *St E*
CHILLINGHAM (St Peter) *see* Glendale Gp *Newc*
CHILLINGTON (St James) *see* Ilminster and District *B & W*
CHILMARK (St Margaret of Antioch) *see* Tisbury *Sarum*
CHILTHORNE DOMER (Blessed Virgin Mary) *see* Tintinhull w Chilthorne Domer, Yeovil Marsh etc *B & W*
CHILTINGTON, EAST (not known) *see* Plumpton w E Chiltington cum Novington *Chich*
CHILTINGTON, WEST (St Mary) *Chich 12* **P** *Bp* **R** G A EVANS
CHILTON (All Saints) *see* Harwell w Chilton *Ox*
CHILTON (St Aidan) *Dur 5* **P** *Bp* **V** *Vacant* (01388) 720243
CHILTON (St Mary) *see* Brill, Boarstall, Chilton and Dorton *Ox*
CHILTON CANTELO (St James) w Ashington, Mudford, Rimpton and Marston Magna *B & W 7* **P** *DBP and D&C, D&C Bris, and Bp Lon (by turn)* **R** *Vacant* (01935) 850381
CHILTON FOLIAT (St Mary) *see* Whitton *Sarum*
CHILTON MOOR (St Andrew) *Dur 14* **P** *Bp* **V** P D DAVEY
CHILTON POLDEN (St Edward) *see* W Poldens *B & W*
CHILTON TRINITY (Holy Trinity) *see* Bridgwater St Mary, Chilton Trinity and Durleigh *B & W*
CHILVERS COTON (All Saints) w Astley *Cov 5* **P** *Viscount Daventry* **V** J D PHILPOTT, **C** M WROE
CHILWELL (Christ Church) *S'well 7* **P** *CPAS* **V** I S CHISHOLM, **C** G B McGUINNESS, I D MOUNTFORD
CHILWORTH (St Denys) w North Baddesley *Win 11* **P** *Mrs P M A T Chamberlayne-Macdonald* **V** P B C SALISBURY
CHILWORTH (St Thomas) *see* Blackheath and Chilworth *Guildf*
CHINEHAM (Christ Church) *Win 4* **P** *Bp* **V** *Vacant* (01256) 474280
CHINESE CONGREGATION *see* St Martin-in-the-Fields *Lon*
CHINGFORD (All Saints) (St Peter and St Paul) *Chelmsf 5* **P** *Bp* **R** N J EDWARDS, **C** W G CAMPBELL-TAYLOR, C F WILSON, R E HAMPSON, J BASKERVILLE
CHINGFORD (St Anne) *Chelmsf 5* **P** *Bp* **V** J A L HARRISSON
CHINGFORD (St Edmund) *Chelmsf 5* **P** *Bp* **V** E C FORD
CHINLEY (St Mary) w Buxworth *Derby 6* **P** *Bp* **P-in-c** E D PACKHAM
CHINNOCK, EAST (Blessed Virgin Mary) *see* W Coker w Hardington Mandeville, E Chinnock etc *B & W*
CHINNOCK, MIDDLE (St Margaret) *see* Norton sub Hamdon, W Chinnock, Chiselborough etc *B & W*
CHINNOCK, WEST (Blessed Virgin Mary) *as above*
CHINNOR (St Andrew) w Emmington and Sydenham and Aston Rowant w Crowell *Ox 1* **P** *Bp, DBP, and Peache Trustees (jt)* **R** R A CARTMILL, **C** J M MALDOOM
CHIPPENHAM (St Andrew) w Tytherton Lucas *Bris 9* **P** *Ch Ch Ox* **V** P H F WOODHOUSE
CHIPPENHAM (St Margaret) *Ely 3* **P** *Mrs A Crawley* **V** *Vacant* (01638) 720550
CHIPPENHAM (St Paul) w Hardenhuish and Langley Burrell *Bris 9* **P** *Patr Bd* **TR** J A SMITH, **TV** C B WRAY, **Hon C** G H EDWARDS, **NSM** S A WHEELER, S A V WHEELER
CHIPPENHAM (St Peter) *Bris 9* **P** *Bp* **V** A D FENSOME, **C** M CREGAN
CHIPPERFIELD (St Paul) *St Alb 5* **P** *Trustees* **P-in-c** A M BUTLER
CHIPPING (St Bartholomew) and Whitewell (St Michael) *Blackb 8* **P** *Bp and Hulme Trustees (jt)* **V** A SIDDALL
CHIPPING BARNET (St John the Baptist) w Arkley *St Alb 17* **P** *The Crown* **TR** A G K ESDAILE, **TV** K M EMERY, J N DAY, **C** J E STEEN
CHIPPING CAMPDEN (St James) w Ebrington *Glouc 10* **P** *Peache Trustees (1 turn), Earl of Harrowby (2 turns)* **V** S J OBERST, **C** H M FLINT
CHIPPING NORTON (St Mary the Virgin) *Ox 3* **P** *D&C Glouc* **V** S J A WESTON, **C** C E CERRATTI
CHIPPING ONGAR (St Martin) w Shelley *Chelmsf 27* **P** *Guild of All So and Keble Coll Ox* **R** E J SIBSON
CHIPPING SODBURY (St John the Baptist) and Old Sodbury *Glouc 7* **P** *D&C Worc* **NSM** E P A GREEN
CHIPPING WARDEN (St Peter and St Paul) *see* Culworth w Sulgrave and Thorpe Mandeville etc *Pet*
CHIPSTABLE (All Saints) *see* Wiveliscombe w Chipstable, Huish Champflower etc *B & W*
CHIPSTEAD (Good Shepherd) *see* Chevening *Roch*
CHIPSTEAD (St Margaret of Antioch) *S'wark 26* **P** *Abp* **R** J M P GOODDEN
CHIRBURY (St Michael) *Heref 13* **P** *Sir David Wakeman, Bt and Bp (alt)* **V** P D HARRATT

CHIRTON (St John the Baptist) *see* Redhorn *Sarum*
CHISELBOROUGH (St Peter and St Paul) *see* Norton sub Hamdon, W Chinnock, Chiselborough etc *B & W*
CHISHILL, GREAT (St Swithun) *see* Heydon, Gt and Lt Chishill, Chrishall etc *Chelmsf*
CHISHILL, LITTLE (St Nicholas) *as above*
CHISLEDON (Holy Cross) *see* Ridgeway *Sarum*
CHISLEHURST (Annunciation) *Roch 14* **P** *Keble Coll* **V** W B BEER
CHISLEHURST (Christ Church) *Roch 14* **P** *CPAS* **V** J M ADAMS, **C** D J LITTLE, **NSM** R M LITTLE
CHISLEHURST (St Nicholas) *Roch 14* **P** *Bp* **NSM** J B HURN
CHISLET (St Mary the Virgin) *see* St Nicholas at Wade w Sarre and Chislet w Hoath *Cant*
CHISWICK (St Michael) *Lon 11* **P** *V St Martin-in-the-Fields* **P-in-c** N C FINCHAM
CHISWICK (St Michael and All Angels) *see* Bedford Park *Lon*
CHISWICK (St Nicholas w St Mary Magdalene) *Lon 11* **P** *D&C St Paul's* **V** P A TUFT
CHISWICK (St Paul) Grove Park *Lon 11* **P** *V Chiswick* **V** M C RILEY
CHITHURST (St Mary) *see* Rogate w Terwick and Trotton w Chithurst *Chich*
CHITTERNE (All Saints and St Mary) *see* Tilshead, Orcheston and Chitterne *Sarum*
CHITTERNE (St Mary) *as above*
CHITTLEHAMHOLT (St John) *see* S Molton w Nymet St George, High Bray etc *Ex*
CHITTLEHAMPTON (St Hieritha) *as above*
CHITTS HILL (St Cuthbert) *Lon 19* **P** *CPAS* **V** D M DALEY
CHIVELSTONE (St Sylvester) *see* Charleton w Buckland Tout Saints etc *Ex*
CHOBHAM (St Lawrence) w Valley End *Guildf 6* **P** *Bp and Brig R W Acworth (alt)* **V** A BODY
CHOLDERTON (St Nicholas) *see* Bourne Valley *Sarum*
CHOLESBURY (St Lawrence) *see* Hawridge w Cholesbury and St Leonard *Ox*
CHOLLERTON w Birtley and Thockrington *Newc 2* **P** *Mrs P I Enderby (2 turns), Newc Dioc Soc (1 turn)* **R** *Vacant* (01434) 681721
CHOLSEY (St Mary) *Ox 18* **P** *Ld Chan* **V** A M PETIT
CHOPPARDS (Mission Room) *see* Upper Holme Valley *Wakef*
CHOPPINGTON (St Paul the Apostle) *Newc 1* **P** *D&C* **NSM** J M GRIEVE
CHOPWELL (St John the Evangelist) *Dur 13* **P** *Bp* **V** *Vacant* (01207) 561248
CHORLEY (All Saints) *Blackb 4* **P** *Bp* **V** E N STRASZAK
CHORLEY (St George) *Blackb 4* **P** *R Chorley* **V** K BARRETT
CHORLEY (St James) *Blackb 4* **P** *R Chorley* **V** G THOMAS
CHORLEY (St Laurence) *Blackb 4* **P** *Bp* **R** J R K FENWICK
CHORLEY (St Peter) *Blackb 4* **P** *R Chorley* **V** L T ATHERTON
CHORLEY (St Philip) *see* Alderley Edge *Ches*
CHORLEYWOOD (Christ Church) *St Alb 5* **P** *CPAS* **V** J S KINGSLEY-SMITH, **C** T A STACEY, **Hon C** J L C COWLEY
CHORLEYWOOD (St Andrew) *St Alb 5* **P** *Bp* **V** M W G STIBBE, **C** B J KISSELL, M O KNIGHT, **NSM** J W SUTTON, M S McCRUM
CHORLTON-CUM-HARDY (St Clement) (St Barnabas) *Man 4* **P** *D&C* **R** R J GILPIN
CHORLTON-CUM-HARDY (St Werburgh) *Man 4* **P** *Bp* **P-in-c** A P JOHNSON
CHRISHALL (Holy Trinity) *see* Heydon, Gt and Lt Chishill, Chrishall etc *Chelmsf*
CHRIST THE KING in the Diocese of Newcastle *Newc 5* **P** *Patr Bd* **TR** R K KENNEDY, **TV** C J CLINCH, G G KEYES, **NSM** J SKINNER
CHRISTCHURCH (Christ Church) and Manea and Welney *Ely 18* **P** *Bp and R T Townley Esq (jt)* **R** S TOOKE
CHRISTCHURCH (Holy Trinity) *Win 8* **P** *Bp* **V** H M WILLIAMS, **C** P A BARLOW, M S LOWE, P A MacCARTY
CHRISTCHURCH Stourvale (St George) *see* Christchurch *Win*
CHRISTIAN MALFORD (All Saints) *see* Draycot *Bris*
CHRISTLETON (St James) *Ches 2* **P** *Bp* **R** K P LEE
CHRISTON (Blessed Virgin Mary) *see* Crook Peak *B & W*
CHRISTOW (St James), Ashton, Trusham and Bridford *Ex 6* **P** *SMF, MMCET, Viscount Exmouth, Bp, and E A Beard Esq (jt)* **P-in-c** G K MAYER
CHUDLEIGH (St Mary and St Martin) *Ex 11* **P** *MMCET* **V** C T PIDSLEY
CHUDLEIGH KNIGHTON (St Paul) *see* Bovey Tracey St John, Chudleigh Knighton etc *Ex*
CHULMLEIGH (St Mary Magdalene), Chawleigh w Cheldon, Wembworthy w Eggesford, and Burrington *Ex 18* **P** *Bp, DBP, MMCET, and G A L Cruwys Esq* **R** R A GRINSTED, **C** K A ELLIOTT
CHURCH ASTON (St Andrew) *Lich 16* **P** *R Edgmond* **R** W H YATES
CHURCH BRAMPTON (St Botolph) w Chapel Brampton and Harleston, East Haddon and Holdenby *Pet 2* **P** *Earl Spencer, Bp, Prim Min, and CCC Ox (by turn)* **NSM** M J WALTON
CHURCH BROUGHTON (St Michael and All Angels) w Barton Blount, Boylestone, Sutton on the Hill and Trusley *Derby 14* **P** *C G Buckston Esq, Worc Coll Ox, D Coke-Steel Esq (2 turns each), Miss C M Auden and J W Pratt Esq (1 turn each)* **P-in-c** P M BISHOP
CHURCH CONISTON (St Andrew) *Carl 8* **P** *Peache Trustees* **P-in-c** M H CANNON
CHURCH EATON (St Editha) *see* Bradeley, Church Eaton and Moreton *Lich*
CHURCH HONEYBOURNE (St Ecgwyn) *see* Pebworth w Dorsington and Honeybourne *Glouc*
CHURCH HULME (St Luke) *Ches 11* **P** *V Sandbach* **V** J EARDLEY
CHURCH KIRK (St James) *Blackb 1* **P** *Hulme Trustees* **R** N A ASHTON
CHURCH KNOWLE (St Peter) *see* Corfe Castle, Church Knowle, Kimmeridge etc *Sarum*
CHURCH LANGTON (St Peter) w Tur Langton, Thorpe Langton and Stonton Wyville *Leic 4* **P** *Bp and E Brudenell Esq (jt)* **P-in-c** I W Y GEMMELL, K F SHEPHERD
CHURCH LAWFORD (St Peter) *see* Wolston and Church Lawford *Cov*
CHURCH LAWTON (All Saints) *Ches 11* **P** *J A Lawton Esq* **R** G L JOYCE
CHURCH LENCH (All Saints) w Rous Lench and Abbots Morton *Worc 1* **P** *Bp* **P-in-c** F R HIGGINS
CHURCH MINSHULL (St Bartholomew) *see* Acton and Worleston, Church Minshull etc *Ches*
CHURCH OAKLEY (St Leonard) and Wootton St Lawrence *Win 4* **P** *Qu Coll Ox and D&C (alt)* **R** B W NICHOLSON, **C** T M HUMPHREY
CHURCH PREEN (St John the Baptist) *see* Wenlock *Heref*
CHURCH STRETTON (St Laurence) *Heref 11* **P** *Ch Patr Trust* **R** M S STEDMAN, **C** T A CANNON, **NSM** D E JANES
CHURCHAM (St Andrew) w Bulley and Minsterworth *Glouc 3* **P** *Bp and D&C (alt)* **V** G P JENKINS
CHURCHDOWN (St Andrew) (St Bartholomew) *Glouc 6* **P** *D&C* **V** T E MASON
CHURCHDOWN (St John the Evangelist) *Glouc 6* **P** *Bp* **V** E F GILES
CHURCHILL (All Saints) *see* Kingham w Churchill, Daylesford and Sarsden *Ox*
CHURCHILL (St John the Baptist) *see* Burrington and Churchill *B & W*
CHURCHILL (St Michael) *see* Peopleton and White Ladies Aston w Churchill etc *Worc*
CHURCHILL-IN-HALFSHIRE (St James) w Blakedown and Broome *Worc 12* **P** *Viscount Cobham and N A Bourne Esq (alt)* **R** N J DAVIS
CHURCHOVER (Holy Trinity) w Willey *Cov 6* **P** *Bp* **R** *Vacant* (01788) 832420
CHURCHSTANTON (St Peter and St Paul), Buckland St Mary and Otterford *B & W 18* **P** *DBP and Mrs M E Mcdonald (jt)* **R** *Vacant* (01823) 601570
CHURCHSTOKE (St Nicholas) w Hyssington and Sarn *Heref 10* **P** *The Crown (1 turn), Earl of Powis (2 turns)* **V** W T BRYAN, **NSM** I R BALL, G LLOYD
CHURCHSTOW (St Mary) *see* Malborough w S Huish, W Alvington and Churchstow *Ex*
CHURSTON FERRERS (St Mary the Vigin) *see* Brixham w Churston Ferrers and Kingswear *Ex*
CHURT (St John the Evangelist) *Guildf 3* **P** *Adn Surrey* **V** C H PONTIN
CHURWELL (All Saints) *see* Morley St Pet w Churwell *Wakef*
CHUTE (St Nicholas) *see* Wexcombe *Sarum*
CHYNGTON (St Luke) *see* Seaford w Sutton *Chich*
CINDERFORD (St John the Evangelist) *Glouc 4* **P** *The Crown* **V** J W HOLDER
CINDERFORD (St Stephen) w Littledean *Glouc 4* **P** *Ch Patr Trust* **V** S N CRONK, **NSM** B J DAVIES
CINDERHILL (Christ Church) *S'well 14* **P** *Bp* **P-in-c** M J O'CONNELL
CINNAMON BROW (Resurrection) *Liv 12* **P** *Bp, Adn, and R Warrington (jt)* **V** S W ELSTOB
CIPPENHAM (St Andrew) *see* W Slough *Ox*
CIRENCESTER (St John the Baptist) *Glouc 12* **P** *Bp* **V** H S RINGROSE, **C** G D OSBORNE, R S HARRIS, J G LEWIS-ANTHONY
CLACTON, GREAT (St John the Baptist) *Chelmsf 23* **P** *Ch Patr Trust* **V** *Vacant* (01255) 423435

CLACTON, LITTLE (St James) *see* Weeley and Lt Clacton *Chelmsf*
CLACTON-ON-SEA (St Christopher) (St James) *Chelmsf 23* **P** *Bp* **V** A P D SPOONER, **C** T D WATSON, **NSM** I A O LEE
CLACTON-ON-SEA (St Paul) *Chelmsf 23* **P** *Ch Patr Trust* **V** N G E ISSBERNER, **Hon C** D W HART
CLAINES (St George w St Mary Magdalene) *see* Worc St Geo w St Mary Magd *Worc*
CLAINES (St John the Baptist) *Worc 6* **P** *Bp* **V** A W BROOKSBANK
CLANDON, EAST (St Thomas of Canterbury) and WEST (St Peter and St Paul) *Guildf 5* **P** *Earl of Onslow and Bp (alt)* **R** J B SMITH
CLANFIELD (St James) *see* Catherington and Clanfield *Portsm*
CLANFIELD (St Stephen) *see* Bampton w Clanfield *Ox*
CLANNABOROUGH (St Petrock) *see* N Creedy *Ex*
CLAPHAM (St James) *S'wark 11* **P** *CPAS* **Hon C** J MARSHALL
CLAPHAM (St Mary the Virgin) *see* Findon w Clapham and Patching *Chich*
CLAPHAM (St Thomas of Canterbury) *St Alb 13* **P** *MMCET* **V** R T BASHFORD
CLAPHAM Team Ministry, The (Christ Church and St John) (Holy Spirit) (Holy Trinity) (St John the Evangelist) (St Paul) (St Peter) *S'wark 11* **P** *Patr Bd* **TR** D O ISHERWOOD, **TV** J P H ALLAIN CHAPMAN, P J ROSE-CASEMORE, D J HOUGHTON, **C** J GARTON, A BIENFAIT, **Hon C** R F VICKERY, **NSM** S MOSS
CLAPHAM COMMON (St Barnabas) *S'wark 15* **P** *Ch Trust Fund Trust* **V** D PAGE
CLAPHAM PARK (All Saints) *S'wark 11* **P** *CPAS and TR Clapham (jt)* **V** N COOPER
CLAPHAM PARK (St Stephen) *S'wark 12* **P** *Trustees* **V** S P GATES
CLAPHAM-WITH-KEASDEN (St James) and Austwick *Bradf 6* **P** *Bp* **V** J DALBY
CLAPTON (St James) *see* Bourton-on-the-Water w Clapton *Glouc*
CLAPTON (St Peter) *see* Barnwell w Tichmarsh, Thurning and Clapton *Pet*
CLAPTON, UPPER (St Matthew) *Lon 5* **P** *D&C Cant* **V** L W S PHILLIPS
CLARBOROUGH (St John the Baptist) w Hayton *S'well 5* **P** *Bp* **P-in-c** R GOODHAND
CLARE (St Peter and St Paul) w Poslingford, Cavendish, Stoke by Clare w Wixoe *St E 8* **P** *Lady Loch* **R** W J A RANKIN, **C** J R ELLIS
CLARENDON PARK (St John the Baptist) w Knighton (St Michael and All Angels) *Leic 2* **P** *Bp* **TR** M W STEPHENSON, **TV** S I SKIDMORE, **Hon C** A J BALLARD, **NSM** N A McINTOSH
CLATFORD, UPPER (All Saints) *see* Abbotts Ann and Upper and Goodworth Clatford *Win*
CLATWORTHY (St Mary Magdalene) *see* Wiveliscombe w Chipstable, Huish Champflower etc *B & W*
CLAUGHTON (St Chad) *see* Hornby w Claughton *Blackb*
CLAUGHTON VILLAGE (St Bede) *see* Birkenhead St Jas w St Bede *Ches*
CLAVERDON (St Michael and All Angels) w Preston Bagot *Cov 7* **P** *Bp* **P-in-c** C P C HUNT
CLAVERHAM (St Barnabas) *see* Yatton Moor *B & W*
CLAVERING (St Mary and St Clement) w Langley and Arkesden *Chelmsf 21* **P** *Ch Hosp and Keble Coll Ox (alt)* **V** D S McGUFFIE
CLAVERLEY (All Saints) (Heathton Mission) w Tuckhill *Heref 9* **P** *Bp and E M A Thompson Esq (jt)* **V** *Vacant* (01746) 710268
CLAVERTON (Blessed Virgin Mary) *see* Bathampton w Claverton *B & W*
CLAVERTON DOWN (St Hugh) *as above*
CLAWTON (St Leonard) *see* Ashwater, Halwill, Beaworthy, Clawton etc *Ex*
CLAXBY (St Mary) *see* Walesby *Linc*
CLAXTON (St Andrew) *see* Rockland St Mary w Hellington, Bramerton etc *Nor*
CLAY CROSS (St Bartholomew *see* N Wingfield, Clay Cross and Pilsley *Derby*
CLAY HILL (St John the Baptist) (St Luke) *Lon 18* **P** *V Enfield St Andr and Bp (jt)* **V** J H NODDINGS
CLAYBROOKE (St Peter) cum Wibtoft and Frolesworth *Leic 11* **P** *The Crown and Adn Loughb (by turn)* **R** J M BRADSHAW
CLAYDON and Barham *St E 1* **P** *G R Drury Esq* **R** T W BROADBENT, **C** S M EVANS
CLAYDON (St James the Great) *see* Shires' Edge *Ox*
CLAYDONS, The (St Mary) (All Saints) *Ox 24* **P** *Sir Ralph Verney, Bt* **R** C DRAPER
CLAYGATE (Holy Trinity) *Guildf 8* **P** *Ch Patr Trust* **V** J T HENDERSON, **C** J WHITE
CLAYHANGER (St Peter) *see* Bampton, Morebath, Clayhanger and Petton *Ex*
CLAYHIDON (St Andrew) *see* Hemyock w Culm Davy, Clayhidon and Culmstock *Ex*
CLAYPOLE (St Peter) *Linc 23* **P** *DBP* **R** G MUNN
CLAYTON (St Cross w St Paul) *see* Man Clayton St Cross w St Paul *Man*
CLAYTON (St James the Great) *Lich 9* **P** *Bp* **V** R K LEGG, **C** P H SMITH
CLAYTON (St John the Baptist) *Bradf 2* **P** *V Bradf* **V** J A N B HOWELL
CLAYTON (St John the Baptist) w Keymer *Chich 9* **P** *BNC Ox* **R** R L CLARKE, **C** K G SWABY, **Hon C** A T WATERER
CLAYTON BROOK (Community Church) *see* Whittle-le-Woods *Blackb*
CLAYTON LE MOORS (All Saints) *see* Altham w Clayton le Moors *Blackb*
CLAYTON LE MOORS (St James) *as above*
CLAYTON WEST w HIGH HOYLAND (All Saints) *see* High Hoyland, Scissett and Clayton W *Wakef*
CLAYWORTH (St Peter) *see* Everton and Mattersey w Clayworth *S'well*
CLEADON (All Saints) *Dur 15* **P** *R Whitburn* **V** N SHAW, **NSM** J P TALBOT
CLEADON PARK (St Mark and St Cuthbert) *Dur 15* **P** *Bp* **V** P R C HAMILTON MANON
CLEARWELL (St Peter) *see* Newland and Redbrook w Clearwell *Glouc*
CLEASBY (St Peter) *see* Barton and Manfield and Cleasby w Stapleton *Ripon*
CLEATOR MOOR (St John the Evangelist) w Cleator (St Leonard) *Carl 5* **P** *Earl of Lonsdale and Bp (alt)* **P-in-c** R BOWLZER, **C** A M ARMSTRONG
CLECKHEATON (St John the Evangelist) *Wakef 8* **P** *V Birstall* **V** M G INMAN
CLECKHEATON (St Luke) (Whitechapel) *Wakef 8* **P** *Bp and Sir Martin Wilson (jt)* **V** D ACKROYD
CLEDFORD (Mission Room) *see* Middlewich w Byley *Ches*
CLEE, NEW (St John the Evangelist) (St Stephen) *Linc 9* **P** *Bp* **V** J W ELLIS
CLEE, OLD (Holy Trinity and St Mary the Virgin) *Linc 9* **P** *Bp* **V** *Vacant* (01472) 691800
CLEE HILL (St Peter's Mission Room) *see* Wigmore Abbey *Heref*
CLEE ST MARGARET (St Margaret) *see* Bitterley w Middleton, Stoke St Milborough etc *Heref*
CLEETHORPE (Christ Church) *see* Clee *Linc*
CLEETHORPES St Aidan *Linc 9* **P** *Bp* **V** H P JANSMA
CLEETHORPES (St Francis) (St Peter) *Linc 9* **P** *Bp* **TR** T H ROBINSON, **TV** T H ATKINSON, **Hon C** D H WEBSTER
CLEETON (St Mary) *see* Stottesdon w Farlow, Cleeton and Silvington *Heref*
CLEEVE (Holy Trinity) *see* Yatton Moor *B & W*
CLEEVE, OLD (St Andrew), Leighland and Treborough *B & W 16* **P** *Selw Coll Cam (2 turns), Personal Reps G R Wolseley Esq (1 turn)* **R** *Vacant* (01984) 640576
CLEEVE HILL (St Peter) *see* Bishop's Cleeve *Glouc*
CLEEVE PRIOR (St Andrew) and The Littletons *Worc 1* **P** *D&C and Ch Ch Ox (alt)* **V** D R EVANS
CLEHONGER (All Saints) *see* Kingstone w Clehonger, Eaton Bishop etc *Heref*
CLENCHWARTON (St Margaret) and West Lynn *Ely 17* **P** *DBP* **R** A J DAVEY
CLENT (St Leonard) *see* Belbroughton w Fairfield and Clent *Worc*
CLEOBURY MORTIMER (St Mary the Virgin) w Hopton Wafers, Neen Sollars and Milson, Neen Savage w Kinlet *Heref 12* **P** *Patr Bd (2 turns), Ld Chan (1 turn)* **R** R A HORSFIELD, **C** P E HUNT, **NSM** B H GADD
CLEOBURY NORTH (St Peter and St Paul) *see* Ditton Priors w Neenton, Burwarton etc *Heref*
CLERKENWELL (Holy Redeemer) (St Mark) *Lon 6* **P** *Trustees and City Corp (jt)* **P-in-c** P A BAGOTT
CLERKENWELL (St James and St John) (St Peter) *Lon 6* **P** *Ch Patr Trust and PCC (jt)* **V** *Vacant* 0171-253 1568
CLEVEDON (St Andrew) (Christ Church) (St Peter) *B & W 13* **P** *Simeon's Trustees (1 turn), Ld Chan (2 turns)* **V** T J BAILLIE
CLEVEDON (St John the Evangelist) *B & W 13* **P** *SMF* **V** D S M SMITH, **C** C D EPPS
CLEVEDON, EAST (All Saints) and Walton w Weston w Clapton in Gordano *B & W 13* **P** *Bp and SMF (jt)* **R** J F SMART
CLEVELEYS (St Andrew) *Blackb 13* **P** *Trustees* **V** D E REEVES, **C** J E SHAW

CLEWER (St Andrew) *Ox 13* **P** *Eton Coll* **P-in-c** I N RANDALL
CLEWER (St Stephen) *see* New Windsor *Ox*
CLEY (St Margaret) *see* Blakeney w Cley, Wiveton, Glandford etc *Nor*
CLEY HILL Warminster (Team Ministry) *Sarum 14* **P** *Patr Bd* **TR** R SHARPE, **TV** C N VON BENZON, **C** G COGGINS, **NSM** A M WADSWORTH
CLIBURN (St Cuthbert) *see* Morland, Thrimby, Gt Strickland and Cliburn *Carl*
CLIDDESDEN (St Lawrence) and Ellisfield w Farleigh Wallop and Dummer *Win 4* **P** *Earl of Portsm and DBP (jt)* **P-in-c** J H P HAMILTON
CLIFFE (St Andrew) *see* Hemingbrough *York*
CLIFFE, SOUTH (St John) *see* N Cave w Cliffe *York*
CLIFFE AT HOO (St Helen) w Cooling *Roch 6* **P** *D&C* **R** E M WRIGHT
CLIFFE VALE (St Stephen) *see* Hartshill *Lich*
CLIFFORD (St Luke) *York 1* **P** *G Lane-Fox Esq* **P-in-c** R M C SEED
CLIFFORD (St Mary the Virgin) *see* Cusop w Clifford, Hardwicke, Bredwardine etc *Heref*
CLIFFORD CHAMBERS (St Helen) *see* Welford w Weston and Clifford Chambers *Glouc*
CLIFFORDS MESNE (St Peter) *see* Newent and Gorsley w Cliffords Mesne *Glouc*
CLIFFSEND (St Mary the Virgin) *see* St Laur in Thanet *Cant*
CLIFTON (All Saints) and Southill *St Alb 16* **P** *Bp and S C Whitbread Esq (jt)* **R** J K DIXON, **NSM** W A HEANEY
CLIFTON (All Saints w St John) *Bris 5* **P** *Bp* **V** P G COBB, **NSM** R DURBIN
CLIFTON (Christ Church w Emmanuel) *Bris 5* **P** *Simeon's Trustees* **C** P G WILLIAMS, R D JAMES, **NSM** B TOPALIAN
CLIFTON (Holy Trinity) *Derby 8* **P** *Mrs M F Stanton, T W Clowes Esq, and V Ashbourne (by turn)* **P-in-c** A H HART
CLIFTON (Holy Trinity, St Andrew the Less and St Peter) *Bris 5* **P** *Simeon's Trustees* **V** G G HOWARD
CLIFTON (Mission Church) *see* Conisbrough *Sheff*
CLIFTON (St Anne) *Man 2* **P** *Bp* **P-in-c** P J BARNETT
CLIFTON (St Cuthbert) *see* Lowther and Askham and Clifton and Brougham *Carl*
CLIFTON (St Francis) (St Mary the Virgin) *S'well 10* **P** *DBP* **TR** E P FORSHAW, **TV** L A de POMERAI, **NSM** G CLEAVER, D I M de POMERAI, L FOX
CLIFTON (St James) *Sheff 6* **P** *Bp* **V** J M WRAW, **C** G R HOLMES
CLIFTON (St John the Evangelist) *see* Brighouse and Clifton *Wakef*
CLIFTON (St Luke) *Carl 4* **P** *R Workington* **V** P M BADEN
CLIFTON (St Michael) *see* Bris St Mich and St Paul *Bris*
CLIFTON (St Philip and St James) *York 8* **P** *Trustees* **V** R G FLETCHER, **C** A W ALLINGTON, N E ECKERSLEY
CLIFTON (St Paul) *see* Bris St Mich and St Paul *Bris*
CLIFTON, NEW (Holy Trinity) *see* Clifton *S'well*
CLIFTON, NORTH (St George) *see* Harby w Thorney and N and S Clifton *S'well*
CLIFTON CAMPVILLE (St Andrew) w Edingale and Harlaston *Lich 4* **P** *Bp and Major F C Pipe-Wolferstan* **R** A L WHEALE, **Hon C** C M J IBALL
CLIFTON GREEN (St Thomas) *Man 2* **P** *Bp* **V** *Vacant* 0161-794 1986
CLIFTON HAMPDEN (St Michael and All Angels) *see* Dorchester *Ox*
CLIFTON-ON-TEME (St Kenelm), Lower Sapey and the Shelsleys *Worc 3* **P** *Bp and A F Evans Esq (jt)* **P-in-c** P C OWEN
CLIFTON REYNES (St Mary the Virgin) *see* Lavendon w Cold Brayfield, Clifton Reynes etc *Ox*
CLIFTON UPON DUNSMORE (St Mary) and Newton *Cov 6* **P** *H A F W Boughton Leigh Esq* **V** *Vacant*
CLIFTONVILLE (St Paul) *Cant 9* **P** *Ch Patr Trust* **P-in-c** J YALLOP
CLIPPESBY (St Peter) *see* Rollesby w Burgh w Billockby w Ashby w Oby etc *Nor*
CLIPSHAM (St Mary) *see* Greetham and Thistleton w Stretton and Clipsham *Pet*
CLIPSTON (All Saints) w Naseby and Haselbech w Kelmarsh *Pet 2* **P** *Ch Coll Cam, DBP, Mrs M F Harris, Exors Miss C V Lancaster (by turn)* **R** D W FAULKS
CLIPSTONE (All Saints) *S'well 2* **P** *Bp* **V** C F GREEN
CLITHEROE (St James) *Blackb 8* **P** *Trustees* **R** R PHILPOTT
CLITHEROE (St Mary Magdalene) *Blackb 8* **P** *J R Peel Esq* **NSM** P W SHEPHERD
CLITHEROE (St Paul) Low Moor *Blackb 8* **P** *Bp* **V** R NICHOLSON
CLIVE (All Saints) *see* Astley, Clive, Grinshill and Hadnall *Lich*
CLIVE VALE (All Souls) *see* Hastings All So *Chich*
CLODOCK (St Clydog) and Longtown w Craswall, Llanveynoe, St Margaret's, Michaelchurch Escley and Newton *Heref 1* **P** *DBP (2 turns), MMCET (1 turn)* **V** F E RODGERS, **NSM** G G DAVIES
CLOFORD (St Mary) *see* Nunney and Witham Friary, Marston Bigot etc *B & W*
CLOPHILL (St Mary the Virgin) *St Alb 16* **P** *Ball Coll Ox* **R** P J SWINDELLS
CLOPTON (St Mary) w Otley, Swilland and Ashbocking *St E 7* **P** *Ld Chan and Bp (alt)* **R** B WAKELING
CLOSWORTH (All Saints) *see* E Coker w Sutton Bingham and Closworth *B & W*
CLOTHALL (St Mary Virgin) *see* Sandon, Wallington and Rushden w Clothall *St Alb*
CLOUGHTON (St Mary) and Burniston w Ravenscar and Staintondale *York 16* **P** *Abp* **V** S RICHARDSON
CLOVELLY (All Saints) *see* Parkham, Alwington, Buckland Brewer etc *Ex*
CLOVELLY (St Peter) *as above*
CLOWNE (St John the Baptist) *Derby 3* **P** *Ld Chan* **R** L R R HARRIS
CLOWS TOP (Mission Room) *see* Mamble w Bayton, Rock w Heightington etc *Worc*
CLUBMOOR (St Andrew) *Liv 8* **P** *Bp* **V** S McGANITY
CLUMBER PARK (St Mary the Virgin) *see* Worksop Priory *S'well*
CLUN (St George) w Bettws-y-Crwyn and Newcastle *Heref 10* **P** *Earl of Powis* **V** R T SHAW, **Hon C** J E M ROBERTS
CLUNBURY (St Swithin) *see* Clungunford w Clunbury and Clunton, Bedstone etc *Heref*
CLUNGUNFORD (St Cuthbert) w Clunbury and Clunton, Bedstone and Hopton Castle *Heref 10* **P** *Earl of Powis, Mrs S B Rocke, M S C Brown Esq, and Sir HughRipley Bt (jt)* **P-in-c** S B BELL
CLUNTON (St Mary) *see* Clungunford w Clunbury and Clunton, Bedstone etc *Heref*
CLUTTON (St Augustine of Hippo) w Cameley *B & W 10* **P** *Earl of Warw (2 turns), Exors J P Hippisley Esq (1 turn)* **R** A V SAUNDERS, **NSM** J P KNOTT
CLYFFE PYPARD (St Peter) *see* Broad Town, Clyffe Pypard, Hilmarton etc *Sarum*
CLYMPING (St Mary the Virgin) and Yapton w Ford *Chich 1* **P** *Bp (2 turns), Ld Chan (1 turn)* **V** *Vacant* (01243) 552962
CLYST HONITON (St Michael and All Angels) *see* Aylesbeare, Rockbeare, Farringdon etc *Ex*
CLYST HYDON (St Andrew) *see* Bradninch and Clyst Hydon *Ex*
CLYST ST GEORGE (St George) *see* Clyst St Mary, Clyst St George etc *Ex*
CLYST ST LAWRENCE (St Lawrence) *see* Whimple, Talaton and Clyst St Lawr *Ex*
CLYST ST MARY (St Mary), Clyst St George and Woodbury Salterton *Ex 1* **P** *Lord Wraxall, D&C, and S Radcliffe Esq (jt)* **R** G L ROWE
COALBROOKDALE (Holy Trinity), Iron-Bridge and Little Wenlock *Heref 14* **P** *Bp, Lord Forester, and Vs Madeley and Much Wenlock (jt)* **R** *Vacant* (01952) 433309
COALEY (St Bartholomew) *see* Lower Cam w Coaley *Glouc*
COALPIT HEATH (St Saviour) *Bris 7* **P** *Bp* **P-in-c** A N GRAHAM
COALVILLE (Christ Church) and Bardon Hill *Leic 8* **P** *Simeon's Trust and R Hugglescote (jt)* **P-in-c** T L RINGLAND
COATES (Holy Trinity) *see* Whittlesey, Pondersbridge and Coates *Ely*
COATES (St Edith) *see* Stow Gp *Linc*
COATES (St Matthew), Rodmarton and Sapperton w Frampton Mansell *Glouc 12* **P** *Bp, Lord Bathurst, and Guild of All So (jt)* **R** R A BOWDEN, **NSM** J M FRANCIS, S G EMSON
COATES, GREAT (St Nicholas) and LITTLE (Bishop Edward King Church) (St Michael) w Bradley *Linc 9* **P** *Patr Bd* **TR** A V DOUGLAS, **TV** C M WOADDEN, J C NEALE, **NSM** L A KOLOGARAS
COATES, NORTH (St Nicholas) *see* The North-Chapel Parishes *Linc*
COATHAM (Christ Church) *York 17* **P** *Trustees* **V** J A WILSON
COATHAM, EAST (Christ Church) *see* Coatham *York*
COBBOLD ROAD (St Saviour) (St Mary) *Lon 9* **P** *Bp* **V** M J BULMAN
COBERLEY (St Giles), Cowley, Colesbourne and Elkstone *Glouc 12* **P** *H W G Elwes Esq (2 turns), Ld Chan (1 turn), and W/Cdr H T Price (1 turn)* **P-in-c** D N GREEN
COBHAM Sole Street (St Mary's Church Room) *see* Cobham w Luddesdowne and Dode *Roch*

COBHAM (St Andrew) (St John the Divine) *Guildf 10* **P** *D C H Combe Esq* **V** B L PREECE, **C** J V PERCIVAL, **Hon C** P G VICKERS
COBHAM (St Mary Magdalene) w Luddesdowne and Dode *Roch 1* **P** *Earl of Darnley and CPAS (alt)* **R** S P DAVIE, **NSM** A E BEETY
COBRIDGE (Christ Church) *see* Hanley H Ev *Lich*
COCKAYNE HATLEY (St John the Baptist) *see* Potton w Sutton and Cockayne Hatley *St Alb*
COCKERHAM (St Michael) w Winmarleigh St Luke and Glasson Christ Church *Blackb 12* **P** *Bp (2 turns), Trustees (1 turn)* **V** R N HAMBLIN
COCKERINGTON, SOUTH (St Leonard) *see* Mid Marsh Gp *Linc*
COCKERMOUTH (All Saints) (Christ Church) w Embleton and Wythop *Carl 6* **P** *Patr Bd* **TR** D THOMSON, **TV** I M RUMSEY, **C** D J HYNDMAN, **NSM** J M CHAMBERLIN
COCKERNHOE (St Hugh) *see* Luton St Fran *St Alb*
COCKERTON (St Mary) *Dur 8* **P** *Bp* **V** S D CONWAY, **C** M L DENT
COCKFIELD (St Mary) *Dur 7* **P** *Bp* **R** M J SHEARING
COCKFIELD (St Peter) w Bradfield St Clare, Felsham and Gedding *St E 10* **P** *St Jo Coll Cam (3 turns), Bp (2 turns), and Lt-Col J G Aldous (1 turn)* **P-in-c** P BARHAM, **NSM** H M FORD
COCKFOSTERS (Christ Church) Trent Park *see* Enfield Ch Ch Trent Park *Lon*
COCKING (not known), Bepton and West Lavington *Chich 10* **P** *Ld Chan, Bp and Cowdray Trust (alt)* **P-in-c** F J R OTTO
COCKINGTON (St George and St Mary) (St Matthew) *Ex 10* **P** *Bp* **V** A K F MACEY
COCKLEY CLEY (All Saints) w Gooderstone *Nor 13* **P** *Bp* **P-in-c** G R DRAKE
COCKSHUTT (St Simon and St Jude) *see* Petton w Cockshutt, Welshampton and Lyneal etc *Lich*
COCKYARD (Church Hall) *see* Chapel-en-le-Frith *Derby*
CODDENHAM (St Mary) w Gosbeck and Hemingstone w Henley *St E 1* **P** *Pemb Coll Cam (2 turns), Lord de Saumarez (1 turn)* **P-in-c** M J STONE
CODDINGTON (All Saints) *see* Colwall w Upper Colwall and Coddington *Heref*
CODDINGTON (All Saints) w Barnby in the Willows *S'well 3* **P** *Bp* **V** P G WRIGHT
CODDINGTON (St Mary) *see* Farndon and Coddington *Ches*
CODFORD (St Mary) *see* Ashton Gifford *Sarum*
CODFORD (St Peter) *as above*
CODICOTE (St Giles) *St Alb 21* **P** *Abp* **V** P J SMITH
CODNOR (St James) *Derby 12* **P** *The Crown* **V** M M MOOKERJI
CODSALL (St Nicholas) *Lich 2* **P** *Bp and Lady Wrottesley (jt)* **V** A E WILLIAMS, **C** G E T BENNETT
CODSALL WOOD (St Peter) *see* Codsall *Lich*
COFFEEHALL (Community Church) *see* Woughton *Ox*
COFFINSWELL (St Bartholomew) *see* Kingskerswell w Coffinswell *Ex*
COFTON (St Mary) *see* Kenton, Mamhead, Powderham, Cofton and Starcross *Ex*
COFTON HACKETT (St Michael) w Barnt Green *Birm 4* **P** *Bp* **P-in-c** R S FIELDSON
COGENHOE (St Peter) and Great Houghton and Little Houghton w Brafield on the Green *Pet 7* **P** *C G V Davidge Esq, Mrs A C Usher, Magd Coll Ox, and DBP (jt)* **NSM** S A TEBBUTT
COGGES (St Mary) and Leigh, South *Ox 8* **P** *Bp and Payne Trustees (jt)* **V** S L BESSENT, **C** A J GODDARD, E A GODDARD
COGGESHALL (St Peter ad Vincula) w Markshall *Chelmsf 17* **P** *Bp (2 turns), SMF (1 turn)* **V** D A M BEETON
COGGESHALL, LITTLE (St Nicholas) *see* Coggeshall w Markshall *Chelmsf*
COKER, EAST (St Michael and All Angels) w Sutton Bingham and Closworth *B & W 7* **P** *D&C Ex* **V** D J HUNT
COKER, WEST (St Martin of Tours) w Hardington Mandeville, East Chinnock and Pendomer *B & W 7* **P** *MMCET and Ox Chs Trust, and DBP (alt)* **R** R C P TERRELL
COLATON RALEIGH (St John the Baptist) *see* Newton Poppleford, Harpford and Colaton Raleigh *Ex*
COLBURN (St Cuthbert) *see* Hipswell *Ripon*
COLBURY (Christ Church) *Win 10* **P** *Mrs A V Barker-Mill* **P-in-c** B L PICKETT
COLBY (Belle Abbey Church) *see* Arbory *S & M*
COLBY (St Giles) *see* Felmingham, Skeyton, Colby, Banningham etc *Nor*
COLCHESTER (Christ Church w St Mary at the Walls) *Chelmsf 16* **P** *Bp* **R** A J ROSE
COLCHESTER (St Anne) *Chelmsf 16* **P** *Bp* **V** *Vacant* (01206) 860931
COLCHESTER (St Barnabas) Old Heath *Chelmsf 16* **P** *Bp* **V** R W F BEAKEN
COLCHESTER (St Botolph w Holy Trinity and St Giles) *Chelmsf 16* **P** *Bp* **P-in-c** M K TAILBY, **Hon C** P B J GREGORY
COLCHESTER (St James) *see* Colchester St Jas and St Paul w All SS etc *Chelmsf*
COLCHESTER (St James) (St Paul) w All Saints, St Nicholas and St Runwald *Chelmsf 16* **P** *Bp* **R** P S WALKER
COLCHESTER (St John the Evangelist) *Chelmsf 16* **P** *Adn Colchester* **NSM** P H ADAMS
COLCHESTER (St Michael) Myland *Chelmsf 16* **P** *Ball Coll Ox* **R** J F BLORE
COLCHESTER (St Paul) *see* Colchester St Jas and St Paul w All SS etc *Chelmsf*
COLCHESTER (St Peter) *Chelmsf 16* **P** *Simeon's Trustees* **V** R M WILSON
COLCHESTER (St Stephen) *see* Colchester, New Town and The Hythe *Chelmsf*
COLCHESTER, New Town and The Hythe (St Stephen, St Mary Magdalen and St Leonard) *Chelmsf 16* **P** *Ball Coll Ox (2 turns), Ld Chan (1 turn)* **P-in-c** I A HILTON
COLD ASH (St Mark) *see* Hermitage and Hampstead Norreys, Cold Ash etc *Ox*
COLD ASHBY (St Denys) *see* Guilsborough w Hollowell and Cold Ashby *Pet*
COLD ASHTON (Holy Trinity) *see* Marshfield w Cold Ashton and Tormarton etc *Bris*
COLD ASTON (St Andrew) w Notgrove and Turkdean *Glouc 14* **P** *Ld Chan (2 turns), Bp (1 turn)* **P-in-c** D C NYE, **NSM** P G W PRIDGEON
COLD BRAYFIELD (St Mary) *see* Lavendon w Cold Brayfield, Clifton Reynes etc *Ox*
COLD HIGHAM (St Luke) *see* Pattishall w Cold Higham and Gayton w Tiffield *Pet*
COLD KIRBY (St Michael) *see* Upper Ryedale *York*
COLD NORTON (St Stephen) *see* Purleigh, Cold Norton and Stow Maries *Chelmsf*
COLD OVERTON (St John the Baptist) *see* Whatborough Gp of Par *Leic*
COLD SALPERTON (All Saints) *see* Dowdeswell and Andoversford w the Shiptons etc *Glouc*
COLDEAN (St Mary Magdalene) *see* Moulsecoomb *Chich*
COLDEN (Holy Trinity) *Win 9* **P** *V Twyford* **V** A C MILLAR
COLDHAM (St Etheldreda) *Ely 19* **P** *Bp* **V** *Vacant*
COLDHARBOUR (Christ Church) *see* Abinger cum Coldharbour *Guildf*
COLDHURST (Holy Trinity) *see* Oldham *Man*
COLDRED (St Pancras) *see* Eythorne and Elvington w Waldershare etc *Cant*
COLDRIDGE (St Matthew) *see* Lapford, Nymet Rowland and Coldridge *Ex*
COLDWALTHAM (St Giles) and Hardham *Chich 12* **P** *D&C and Col Sir Brian Barttelot Bt (jt)* **P-in-c** R F ROBINSON, **NSM** C S STRIDE
COLEBROOKE (St Andrew) *Ex 2* **P** *D&C* **V** J C HALL
COLEBY (All Saints) *see* Graffoe Gp *Linc*
COLEFORD (Holy Trinity) w Holcombe *B & W 12* **P** *Bp and V Kilmersdon (jt)* **V** P M DOWN
COLEFORD (St John the Evangelist) w Staunton *Glouc 4* **P** *Bp* **V** P W SEMPLE, **Hon C** A W WEARMOUTH
COLEGATE (St George) *see* Norwich Over-the-Water *Nor*
COLEHILL (St Michael and All Angels) *Sarum 10* **P** *Wimborne Minster Sch* **V** J W GOODALL, **C** D J J R LINAKER
COLEMAN'S HATCH (Holy Trinity) *see* Hartfield w Coleman's Hatch *Chich*
COLEORTON (St Mary the Virgin) *see* Ashby-de-la-Zouch St Helen w Coleorton *Leic*
COLERNE (St John the Baptist) w North Wraxall *Bris 9* **P** *New Coll Ox and Or Coll Ox (alt)* **P-in-c** A V I BERNERS-WILSON, **NSM** G E WOODS
COLESBOURNE (St James) *see* Coberley, Cowley, Colesbourne and Elkstone *Glouc*
COLESHILL (All Saints) *see* Amersham *Ox*
COLESHILL (All Saints) *see* Gt Coxwell w Buscot, Coleshill and Eaton Hastings *Ox*
COLESHILL (St Peter and St Paul) *Birm 10* **P** *K S D Wingfield Digby Esq* **V** R G BOLLARD
COLEY Norwood Green (St George) *see* Coley *Wakef*
COLEY (St John the Baptist) *Wakef 2* **P** *V Halifax* **V** A M EARNSHAW, **Hon C** R C DOWSON
COLGATE (St Saviour) *see* Rusper w Colgate *Chich*
COLINDALE (St Matthias) *Lon 15* **P** *Bp* **V** M R POOLE
COLKIRK (St Mary) w Oxwick w Pattesley, Whissonsett, Horningtoft and Brisley *Nor 14* **P** *DBP, Ch Coll Cam, and C S P D Lane Esq (jt)* **NSM** K D BLOGG
COLLATON (St Mary the Virgin) *see* Stoke Gabriel and Collaton *Ex*

COLLIER ROW (St James) and Havering-atte-Bower *Chelmsf 2* **P** *CPAS and Bp (jt)* **V** C G T HERBERT, **C** R J GARNETT
COLLIER STREET (St Margaret) *see* Yalding w Collier Street *Roch*
COLLIERLEY (St Thomas) w Annfield Plain *Dur 4* **P** *Bp and The Crown (alt)* **V** G H LAWES
COLLIERS END (St Mary) *see* High Cross *St Alb*
COLLIERS WOOD (Christ Church) *see* Mitcham Ch Ch *S'wark*
COLLINGBOURNE DUCIS (St Andrew) *see* Wexcombe *Sarum*
COLLINGBOURNE KINGSTON (St Mary) *as above*
COLLINGHAM (All Saints) (St John the Baptist) w South Scarle and Besthorpe and Girton *S'well 3* **P** *Ld Chan and D&C Pet (alt)* **R** A A CONN, **NSM** S A DAVENPORT
COLLINGHAM (St Oswald) w Harewood *Ripon 1* **P** *Earl of Harewood and G H H Wheler Esq (jt)* **V** P F ROBERTS
COLLINGTON (St Mary) *see* Bredenbury w Grendon Bishop and Wacton etc *Heref*
COLLINGTREE (St Columba) w Courteenhall and Milton Malsor *Pet 7* **P** *Major Sir Hereward Wake, G Phipps-Walker, and Hyndman Trustees (by turn)* **R** R J ORMSTON
COLLYHURST (The Saviour) *Man 5* **P** *Bp and Trustees (jt)* **R** M A DONALDSON, **NSM** M B ROGERS
COLLYWESTON (St Andrew) *see* Easton on the Hill, Collyweston w Duddington etc *Pet*
COLMWORTH (St Denys) *see* Wilden w Colmworth and Ravensden *St Alb*
COLN ROGERS (St Andrew) *see* Chedworth, Yanworth and Stowell, Coln Rogers etc *Glouc*
COLN ST ALDWYNS (St John the Baptist), Hatherop, Quenington, Eastleach and Southrop *Glouc 13* **P** *Earl St Aldwyn, D&C, Wadh Coll Ox, and DBP (jt)* **V** A M ROSS
COLN ST DENYS (St James the Great) *see* Chedworth, Yanworth and Stowell, Coln Rogers etc *Glouc*
COLNBROOK (St Thomas) *see* Riverside *Ox*
COLNE (Christ Church) *Blackb 7* **P** *DBF* **V** J C PRIESTLEY
COLNE (Holy Trinity) *Blackb 7* **P** *Bp* **V** G S INGRAM, **NSM** K ALLEN
COLNE (St Bartholomew) *Blackb 7* **P** *DBF* **R** P J MOTT
COLNE (St Helen) *see* Bluntisham cum Earith w Colne and Woodhurst *Ely*
COLNE, THE UPPER, Parishes of Great Yeldham, Little Yeldham, Stambourne, Tilbury-juxta-Clare and Toppesfield *Chelmsf 19* **P** *Prime Min, Ld Chan, Bp, Duchy of Lancaster, and Trustees of the late Miss W M N Brett (by turn)* **R** *Vacant* (01787) 237358
COLNE ENGAINE (St Andrew) *see* Earls Colne w White Colne and Colne Engaine *Chelmsf*
COLNEY (St Andrew) *see* Cringleford w Colney and Bawburgh *Nor*
COLNEY (St Peter) *St Alb 1* **P** *Bp* **V** M T BEER, **Hon C** J M BEER, **NSM** R W HEINZE
COLNEY HEATH (St Mark) *St Alb 21* **P** *Trustees* **V** D R VENESS, **Hon C** A D T GORTON, **NSM** B R McMAHON
COLSTERWORTH Group, The (St John the Baptist) *Linc 14* **P** *Bp (2 turns), Mrs R S McCorquodale and Revd J R H and Revd H C Thorold (1 turn)* **R** J COOK, **NSM** P C HOLLINGSHEAD
COLSTON BASSETT (St John the Divine) *see* Cropwell Bishop w Colston Bassett, Granby etc *S'well*
COLTISHALL (St John the Baptist) w Great Hautbois and Horstead *Nor 19* **P** *D&C and K Coll Cam (jt)* **R** H D TOLLER, **NSM** N H KHAMBATTA
COLTON (Holy Trinity) *Carl 10* **P** *Landowners* **NSM** D HARRISON
COLTON (St Andrew) *see* Easton w Colton and Marlingford *Nor*
COLTON (St Mary the Virgin) *Lich 3* **P** *Bp* **P-in-c** T THAKE
COLTON (St Paul) *see* Bolton Percy *York*
COLWALL (St Crispin's Chapel) (St James the Great) w Upper Colwall (Good Shepherd) and Coddington *Heref 6* **P** *Bp* **R** C N H ATTWOOD
COLWALL, UPPER (Good Shepherd) *see* Colwall w Upper Colwall and Coddington *Heref*
COLWICH (St Michael and All Angels) w Great Haywood *Lich 3* **P** *Bp and Trustees (jt)* **V** T THAKE
COLWICK (St John the Baptist) *S'well 11* **P** *DBP* **R** J F McGINLEY, **C** P C WHITEHEAD
COLYFORD (St Michael) *see* Colyton, Southleigh, Offwell, Widworthy etc *Ex*
COLYTON (St Andrew), Southleigh, Offwell, Widworthy, Farway, Northleigh and Musbury *Ex 5* **P** *Patr Bd* **TR** D A GUNN-JOHNSON, **TV** D R WINNINGTON-INGRAM, **NSM** A RICHMOND, G A SMITH
COMBE (St Lawrence) *see* Stonesfield w Combe *Ox*
COMBE (St Swithin) *see* W Woodhay w Enborne, Hampstead Marshall etc *Ox*
COMBE DOWN (Holy Trinity) (St Andrew) w Monkton Combe and South Stoke *B & W 9* **P** *R Bath, Ox Chs Trust, and Comdr H R Salmer (jt)* **V** P J LANGHAM, **C** E M C BOWES-SMITH, **NSM** S TRICKETT
COMBE FLOREY (St Peter and St Paul) *see* Lydeard St Lawrence w Brompton Ralph etc *B & W*
COMBE HAY (not known) *see* Bath Odd Down w Combe Hay *B & W*
COMBE-IN-TEIGNHEAD (All Saints) *see* Stoke-in-Teignhead w Combe-in-Teignhead etc *Ex*
COMBE MARTIN (St Peter), Berrynarbor, Lynton, Brendon, Countisbury, Parracombe, Martinhoe and Trentishoe *Ex 17* **P** *Patr Bd* **TR** K G WYER, **TV** P J RINGER
COMBE PYNE (St Mary the Virgin) *see* Axminster, Chardstock, Combe Pyne and Rousdon *Ex*
COMBE RALEIGH (St Nicholas) *see* Honiton, Gittisham, Combe Raleigh, Monkton etc *Ex*
COMBE ST NICHOLAS (St Nicholas) w Wambrook *B & W 15* **P** *Bp and T V D Eames Esq (jt)* **P-in-c** P REGAN
COMBERFORD (St Mary and St George) *see* Wigginton *Lich*
COMBERTON (St Mary) *Ely 1* **P** *Jes Coll Cam* **V** R STEPHENSON, **NSM** M J REISS
COMBERTON, GREAT (St Michael) *see* Elmley Castle w Bricklehampton and Combertons *Worc*
COMBERTON, LITTLE (St Peter) *as above*
COMBROKE (St Mary and St Margaret) w Compton Verney *Cov 8* **P** *Bp* **V** C A HOST
COMBS (St Mary) *St E 6* **P** *Bp* **P-in-c** A L FOWLER
COMBWICH (St Peter) *see* Cannington, Otterhampton, Combwich and Stockland *B & W*
COMER GARDENS (St David) *see* Worc St Clem *Worc*
COMMONDALE (St Peter) *see* Danby *York*
COMPSTALL (St Paul) *see* Werneth *Ches*
COMPTON (All Saints) and Otterbourne *Win 13* **P** *Bp and Mrs P M A T Chamberlayne-Macdonald (jt)* **R** P L S BARRETT
COMPTON (St Mary) *see* Farnham *Guildf*
COMPTON (St Mary and St Nicholas) w East Ilsley *Ox 14* **P** *Bp* **V** *Vacant* (01635) 578256
COMPTON (St Mary), the Mardens, Stoughton and Racton *Chich 13* **P** *Bp Lon (1 turn), Bp (2 turns)* **P-in-c** A N STAMP, **C** R F THOMAS
COMPTON (St Nicholas) w Shackleford and Peper Harow *Guildf 4* **P** *Bp and Major J R More-Molyneux (jt)* **R** J M FELLOWS
COMPTON, LITTLE (St Denys) w Chastleton, Cornwell, Little Rollright and Salford *Ox 3* **P** *Ch Ch Ox, DBP, and Bp (by turn)* **P-in-c** G P EVANS, **NSM** H M WILLIAMS
COMPTON, NETHER (St Nicholas) *see* Queen Thorne *Sarum*
COMPTON, OVER (St Michael) *as above*
COMPTON ABBAS (St Mary the Virgin) *see* Shaston *Sarum*
COMPTON ABDALE (St Oswald) *see* Withington and Compton Abdale w Haselton *Glouc*
COMPTON BASSETT (St Swithin) *see* Oldbury *Sarum*
COMPTON BEAUCHAMP (St Swithun) *see* Ashbury, Compton Beauchamp and Longcot w Fernham *Ox*
COMPTON BISHOP (St Andrew) *see* Crook Peak *B & W*
COMPTON CHAMBERLAYNE (St Michael) *see* Fovant, Sutton Mandeville and Teffont Evias etc *Sarum*
COMPTON DANDO (Blessed Virgin Mary) *see* Publow w Pensford, Compton Dando and Chelwood *B & W*
COMPTON DUNDON (St Andrew) *see* Somerton w Compton Dundon, the Charltons etc *B & W*
COMPTON GREENFIELD (All Saints) *see* Pilning w Compton Greenfield *Bris*
COMPTON MARTIN (St Michael) *see* Blagdon w Compton Martin and Ubley *B & W*
COMPTON PAUNCEFOOT (Blessed Virgin Mary) *see* Camelot Par *B & W*
COMPTON VALENCE (St Thomas a Beckett) *see* The Winterbournes and Compton Valence *Sarum*
CONCHAN (St Peter) *see* Onchan *S & M*
CONDICOTE (St Nicholas) *see* Longborough, Sezincote, Condicote and the Swells *Glouc*
CONDOVER (St Andrew and St Mary) w Frodesley, Acton Burnell and Pitchford *Heref 11* **P** *Bp, Revd E W Serjeantson, and Mrs C R Colthurst (jt)* **R** F T RUMBALL
CONEY HILL (St Oswald) *Glouc 5* **P** *The Crown* **V** I F CALDER, **C** M SHARLAND
CONEY WESTON (St Mary) *see* Hopton, Market Weston, Barningham etc *St E*
CONEYSTHORPE (Chapel) *see* Street TM *York*
CONGERSTONE (St Mary the Virgin) *see* Market Bosworth, Cadeby w Sutton Cheney etc *Leic*
CONGHAM (St Andrew) *see* Grimston, Congham and Roydon *Nor*

CONGLETON (St James) *Ches 11* **P** *Bp* **P-in-c** A J BURTON
CONGLETON (St Peter) *Ches 1* **P** *Simeon's Trustees* **V** *Vacant* (01260) 273212
CONGLETON (St Stephen) *Ches 11* **P** *Bp* **V** *Vacant* (01260) 272994
CONGRESBURY (St Andrew) w Puxton and Hewish St Ann *B & W 11* **P** *MMCET* **V** R H SALMON
CONINGSBY (St Michael and All Angels) w Tattershall *Linc 11* **P** *DBP and Baroness Willoughby de Eresby (alt)* **P-in-c** J R MOORE, **NSM** M DONE
CONINGTON (St Mary) *see* Fen Drayton w Conington and Lolworth etc *Ely*
CONISBROUGH (St Peter) *Sheff 10* **P** *Bp* **V** P A JEPPS, **C** E A MORRIS
CONISCLIFFE (St Edwin) *Dur 8* **P** *Bp* **P-in-c** P CRICK
CONISHOLME (St Peter) *see* Somercotes and Grainthorpe w Conisholme *Linc*
CONISTON (St Andrew) *see* Church Coniston *Carl*
CONISTON COLD (St Peter) *see* Kirkby-in-Malhamdale w Coniston Cold *Bradf*
CONISTONE (St Mary) *see* Kettlewell w Conistone, Hubberholme etc *Bradf*
CONONLEY (St John the Evangelist) w Bradley *Bradf 8* **P** *Bp* **V** J C PEET
CONSETT (Christ Church) *Dur 4* **P** *Bp* **V** *Vacant* (01207) 502235
CONSTABLE LEE (St Paul) *Man 15* **P** *CPAS* **V** P HEYWOOD
CONSTANTINE (St Constantine) *Truro 4* **P** *D&C* **V** A J WADE
COOKBURY (St John the Baptist and the Seven Maccabes) *see* Black Torrington, Bradf w Cookbury etc *Ex*
COOKHAM (Holy Trinity) *Ox 13* **P** *Mrs K E Rogers* **V** D D J ROSSDALE, **Hon C** A W WELLING
COOKHAM DEAN (St John the Baptist) *Ox 13* **P** *V Cookham* **V** J F W V COPPING
COOKHILL (St Paul) *see* Inkberrow w Cookhill and Kington w Dormston *Worc*
COOKLEY (St Michael and All Angels) *see* Cratfield w Heveningham and Ubbeston etc *St E*
COOKLEY (St Peter) *see* Wolverley and Cookley *Worc*
COOKRIDGE (Holy Trinity) *Ripon 7* **P** *R Adel* **V** J F HAMILTON
COOMBE (Christ Church) *see* New Malden and Coombe *S'wark*
COOMBE BISSET (St Michael and All Angels) *see* Chalke Valley W *Sarum*
COOMBES (not known) *see* Lancing w Coombes *Chich*
COOMBS WOOD (St Ambrose) *see* Blackheath *Birm*
COOPERSALE (St Alban) *see* Epping Distr *Chelmsf*
COPDOCK (St Peter) w Washbrook and Belstead *St E 5* **P** *DBP* **R** *Vacant*
COPFORD (St Michael and All Angels) w Easthorpe and Messing w Inworth *Chelmsf 24* **P** *Ld Chan, Duchy of Lanc, and DBP (by turn)* **R** C J GARLAND
COPGROVE (St Michael) *see* Farnham w Scotton, Staveley, Copgrove etc *Ripon*
COPLE (All Saints) w Willington *St Alb 11* **P** *Bp and D&C Ox (alt)* **V** J A TERRY
COPLEY *Wakef 4* **P** *V Halifax* **V** *Vacant* (01422) 652964
COPMANTHORPE (St Giles) *York 1* **P** *R Micklegate H Trin* **V** J C STONEHOUSE
COPNOR (St Alban) *see* Portsea St Alb *Portsm*
COPNOR (St Cuthbert) *see* Portsea St Cuth *Portsm*
COPP (St Anne) *Blackb 10* **P** *V St Michael's-on-Wyre* **V** P YORKSTONE
COPPENHALL (All Saints and St Paul) *see* Crewe All SS and St Paul *Ches*
COPPENHALL (St Laurence) *see* Penkridge Team *Lich*
COPPENHALL (St Michael) *Ches 15* **P** *Bp* **R** J MACKEY, **C** J D ADEY
COPPULL (not known) *Blackb 4* **P** *R Standish* **V** J HUDSON
COPPULL (St John) *Blackb 4* **P** *R Standish* **R** J STEWART
COPSTON MAGNA (St John) *see* Wolvey w Burton Hastings, Copston Magna etc *Cov*
COPT OAK (St Peter) *see* Oaks in Charnwood and Copt Oak *Leic*
COPTHORNE (St John the Evangelist) *Chich 7* **P** *Bp* **V** A M CUTTING
COPYTHORNE (St Mary) and Minstead *Win 10* **P** *Bp Liv and J P Green Esq (jt)* **P-in-c** J W PRAGNELL, P F MURPHY
CORBRIDGE w Halton (St Andrew) and Newton Hall *Newc 3* **P** *D&C Carl* **V** M J MORPHY, **NSM** H H HUNTER, J KINNAIRD
CORBY (Epiphany) (St John the Baptist) *Pet 9* **P** *E Brudenell Esq* **R** *Vacant* (01536) 203314
CORBY (St Columba and the Northern Saints) *Pet 9* **P** *Bp* **V** M W EDEN
CORBY (St Peter and St Andrew) (Kingswood Church) w Great and Little Oakley *Pet 9* **P** *Bp, Boughton Estates, and H W G de Capell Brooke Esq (jt)* **TR** M A CRAGGS
CORBY GLEN (St John the Evangelist) *Linc 14* **P** *Ld Chan (2 turns), Sir Simon Benton Jones, Bt (1 turn)* **NSM** I K WILLIAMS
CORELEY (St Peter) w Doddington *Heref 12* **P** *DBP and Mrs R C Woodward (jt)* **P-in-c** D M BURGESS
CORFE (St Nicholas) *see* Pitminster w Corfe *B & W*
CORFE CASTLE (St Edward the Martyr), Church Knowle, Kimmeridge Steeple w Tyneham *Sarum 9* **P** *Major M J A Bond and Major J C Mansel (jt)* **R** M A STRIKE
CORFE MULLEN (St Hubert) *Sarum 10* **P** *Bp* **R** A B ELKINS, **NSM** J K ELKINS
CORHAMPTON (not known) *see* Meonstoke w Corhampton cum Exton *Portsm*
CORLEY (not known) *see* Fillongley and Corley *Cov*
CORNARD, GREAT (St Andrew) *St E 12* **P** *Bp* **P-in-c** P F HOCKING
CORNARD, LITTLE (All Saints) *see* Assington w Newton Green and Lt Cornard *St E*
CORNELLY (St Cornelius) *see* Tregony w St Cuby and Cornelly *Truro*
CORNEY (St John the Baptist) *see* Bootle, Corney, Whicham and Whitbeck *Carl*
CORNFORTH (Holy Trinity) *Dur 5* **P** *Bp* **V** *Vacant* (01740) 654591
CORNHILL (St Helen) w Carham *Newc 12* **P** *Abp (2 turns), E M Straker-Smith Esq (1 turn)* **V** R W HOWE
CORNHOLME (St Michael and All Angels) *Wakef 3* **P** *DBP* **V** *Vacant* (01706) 813604
CORNISH HALL END (St John the Evangelist) *see* Finchingfield and Cornish Hall End etc *Chelmsf*
CORNWELL (St Peter) *see* Lt Compton w Chastleton, Cornwell etc *Ox*
CORNWOOD (St Michael and All Angels) *Ex 20* **P** *Bp* **NSM** D HALL
CORNWORTHY (St Peter) *see* Ashprington, Cornworthy and Dittisham *Ex*
CORONATION SQUARE (St Aidan) *see* Cheltenham St Mark *Glouc*
CORRA (Holy Trinity) *see* Adderley, Ash, Calverhall, Ightfield etc *Lich*
CORRINGHAM (St John the Evangelist) (St Mary the Virgin) *Chelmsf 14* **P** *SMF* **P-in-c** M HUME, **C** K R HAVEY
CORRINGHAM (St Lawrence) and Blyton Group, The *Linc 2* **P** *Ld Chan (2 turns), Bp (1 turn), Meynell Ch Trustees (1 turn)* **V** M W PAGE-CHESTNEY, **NSM** S V PAGE-CHESTNEY
CORSCOMBE (St Mary the Virgin) *see* Melbury *Sarum*
CORSE (St Margaret) *see* Hartpury w Corse and Staunton *Glouc*
CORSENSIDE (All Saints) *see* N Tyne and Redesdale Team *Newc*
CORSENSIDE (St Cuthbert) *as above*
CORSHAM, GREATER (St Bartholomew) *Bris 9* **P** *Patr Bd* **TR** R G CLIFTON, **C** V J HOWLETT
CORSLEY (St Mary the Virgin) *see* Cley Hill Warminster *Sarum*
CORSLEY (St Mary the Virgin) *as above*
CORSTON (All Saints) *see* Saltford w Corston and Newton St Loe *B & W*
CORSTON (All Saints) *see* Gt Somerford, Lt Somerford, Seagry, Corston etc *Bris*
CORTON (St Bartholomew) *see* Hopton w Corton *Nor*
CORTON (St Bartholomew) *see* Abbotsbury, Portesham and Langton Herring *Sarum*
CORTON DENHAM (St Andrew) *see* Queen Camel w W Camel, Corton Denham etc *B & W*
CORYTON (St Andrew) *see* Marystowe, Coryton, Stowford, Lewtrenchard etc *Ex*
COSBY (St Michael and All Angels) *Leic 10* **P** *Bp* **V** S B HEYGATE
COSELEY (Christ Church) (St Cuthbert) *Worc 10* **P** *Bp* **V** M T C BAYNES, **C** R J ROSOMAN
COSELEY (St Chad) *Worc 10* **P** *Bp* **V** A HOWES
COSGROVE (St Peter and St Paul) *see* Potterspury, Furtho, Yardley Gobion and Cosgrove *Pet*
COSHAM (St Philip) *Portsm 6* **P** *Bp* **P-in-c** P R ELLMORE, **C** M J THOMSON
COSSALL (St Catherine) *see* Awsworth w Cossall *S'well*
COSSINGTON (All Saints) *see* Sileby, Cossington and Seagrave *Leic*
COSSINGTON (Blessed Virgin Mary) *see* Woolavington w Cossington and Bawdrip *B & W*
COSTESSEY (St Edmund) *Nor 2* **P** *Gt Hosp Nor* **V** N J S PARRY, **C** C J PRICE
COSTESSEY, NEW (St Helen) *see* Costessey *Nor*

COSTOCK (St Giles) *see* E and W Leake, Stanford-on-Soar, Rempstone etc *S'well*
COSTON (St Andrew) *see* Wymondham w Edmondthorpe, Buckminster etc *Leic*
COTEBROOKE (St John and Holy Cross) *see* Tarporley *Ches*
COTEHELE HOUSE (Chapel) *see* Calstock *Truro*
COTEHILL (St John the Evangelist) and Cumwhinton *Carl 2* **P** *The Crown* **Hon C** P N DOWNHAM
COTES HEATH (St James) *see* Standon and Cotes Heath *Lich*
COTESBACH (St Mary) *see* Lutterworth w Cotesbach *Leic*
COTGRAVE (All Saints) *S'well 8* **P** *DBP* **R** G B BARRODALE, **C** S SPENCER
COTHAM (St Saviour w St Mary) *Bris 5* **P** *Bp* **V** G N BOUNDY, **Hon C** T E McCLURE
COTHELSTONE (St Thomas of Canterbury) *see* Bishops Lydeard w Bagborough and Cothelstone *B & W*
COTHERIDGE (St Leonard) *see* Martley and Wichenford, Knightwick etc *Worc*
COTHERSTONE (St Cuthbert) *see* Romaldkirk w Laithkirk *Ripon*
COTLEIGH (St Michael and All Angels) *see* Yarcombe, Membury, Upottery and Cotleigh *Ex*
COTMANHAY (Christ Church) *Derby 13* **P** *Bp* **V** J D HOLT
COTON (St Peter) *Ely 1* **P** *St Cath Coll Cam* **R** H D SEARLE
COTON IN THE ELMS (St Mary) *see* Walton on Trent w Croxall etc *Derby*
COTTAM (Holy Trinity) *see* Rampton w Laneham, Treswell, Cottam and Stokeham *S'well*
COTTENHAM (All Saints) *Ely 5* **P** *Bp* **R** I M G FRIARS
COTTERED (St John the Baptist) w Broadfield and Throcking *St Alb 19* **P** *Bp* **Dn-in-c** C POLHILL
COTTERIDGE (St Agnes) *Birm 4* **P** *R Kings Norton* **V** M W BLOOD, **NSM** R R COLLINS, J M ADAMS
COTTERSTOCK (St Andrew) *see* Warmington, Tansor, Cotterstock and Fotheringhay *Pet*
COTTESBROOKE (All Saints) w Great Creaton and Thornby *Pet 2* **P** *Bp (2 turns), MacDonald-Buchanan Trustees (1 turn)* **P-in-c** W G GIBBS, B LEE
COTTESMORE (St Nicholas) and Barrow w Ashwell and Burley *Pet 14* **P** *E R Hanbury Esq, Viscount Downe, and DBP (by turn)* **R** M H W ROGERS
COTTIMORE (St John) *see* Walton-on-Thames *Guildf*
COTTINGHAM (St Mary) *York 15* **P** *Abp* **R** T G GRIGG, **C** G R DREWERY
COTTINGHAM (St Mary Magdalene) w East Carlton *Pet 9* **P** *BNC Ox and Sir Geoffrey Palmer Bt (alt)* **P-in-c** J L SMITH
COTTINGLEY (St Michael and All Angels) *Bradf 1* **P** *Bp* **V** J M FRANCIS
COTTINGWITH, EAST (St Mary) *see* Elvington w Sutton on Derwent and E Cottingwith *York*
COTTISFORD (St Mary the Virgin) *see* Shelswell *Ox*
COTTON (St Andrew) *see* Bacton w Wyverstone and Cotton *St E*
COTTON (St John the Baptist) *see* Alton w Bradley-le-Moors and Oakamoor w Cotton *Lich*
COTTON MILL (St Julian) *see* St Alb St Steph *St Alb*
COUGHTON (St Peter) *Cov 7* **P** *Bp* **P-in-c** F J BALLINGER
COULSDON (St Andrew) *S'wark 23* **P** *Bp* **V** M R GOODLAD, **Hon C** K V McKIE
COULSDON (St John) *S'wark 23* **P** *Abp* **R** S H MASLEN, **C** R W HARE
COULSTON, EAST (St Thomas of Canterbury) *see* Bratton, Edington and Imber, Erlestoke etc *Sarum*
COUND (St Peter) *Heref 11* **P** *Bp* **R** *Vacant*
COUNDON (St James) *Dur 6* **P** *Bp* **V** H HUTCHINSON
COUNTESS WEAR (St Luke) *Ex 3* **P** *V Topsham* **V** P J S CROCKETT
COUNTESTHORPE (St Andrew) w Foston *Leic 10* **P** *DBP and Bp (alt)* **V** A W JOHNSON, **C** R V WORSFOLD, **NSM** M D GILLESPIE
COUNTISBURY (St John the Evangelist) *see* Combe Martin, Berrynarbor, Lynton, Brendon etc *Ex*
COURTEENHALL (St Peter and St Paul) *see* Collingtree w Courteenhall and Milton Malsor *Pet*
COVE (St John the Baptist) (St Christopher) *Guildf 1* **P** *Bp* **TR** M S KING, **TV** J P STEWART, B APPLETON, **C** H O'SULLIVAN
COVEHITHE (St Andrew) *see* Wrentham w Benacre, Covehithe, Frostenden etc *St E*
COVEN (St Paul) *Lich 2* **P** *V Brewood* **P-in-c** K L WASSALL
COVEN HEATH (Mission Church) *see* Bushbury *Lich*
COVENEY (St Peter ad Vincula) *Ely 14* **P** *Bp* **R** *Vacant*
COVENHAM (Annunciation of the Blessed Virgin Mary) *see* Fotherby *Linc*
COVENT GARDEN (St Paul) *Lon 3* **P** *Bp* **R** D ELLIOTT
COVENTRY Caludon *Cov 1* **P** *Bp and Ld Chan (alt)* **TR** M W BRYANT, **TV** M M CLARKE, **C** C R PETERS
COVENTRY Holbrooks (St Luke) *see* Holbrooks *Cov*
COVENTRY (Holy Trinity) *Cov 2* **P** *Ld Chan* **V** D A URQUHART, **C** A D BRADLEY, P J HARWOOD
COVENTRY (St Francis of Assisi) North Radford *Cov 2* **P** *Bp* **NSM** M J ROWBERRY
COVENTRY (St George) *Cov 2* **P** *Bp* **V** L N JANICKER
COVENTRY (St John the Baptist) *Cov 2* **P** *Trustees* **R** B KEETON
COVENTRY (St Mary Magdalen) *Cov 3* **P** *Bp* **V** C H KNOWLES, **C** D R WINTLE
COVENTRY (St Nicholas) *see* Radford *Cov*
COVENTRY EAST (St Anne and All Saints) (St Barnabas) (St Margaret) (St Peter) *Cov 1* **P** *Patr Bd* **TV** N A J BLACKWELL, P G EDWARDS, S MUKHERJEE, L A HUMPHREYS, **C** S EDWARDS, **NSM** P N ASPINALL, A W WILLSON
COVERACK (St Peter) *see* St Keverne *Truro*
COVERDALE (St Botolph) *see* Middleham w Coverdale and E Witton *Ripon*
COVINGHAM (St Paul) *see* Swindon Dorcan *Bris*
COVINGTON (All Saints) *Ely 10* **P** *Sir Stephen Hastings* **P-in-c** J HINDLEY, **NSM** B A BEARCROFT, J RAWLINSON
COWARNE, LITTLE (not known) *see* Bredenbury w Grendon Bishop and Wacton etc *Heref*
COWARNE, MUCH (St Mary the Virgin) *see* Stoke Lacy, Moreton Jeffries w Much Cowarne etc *Heref*
COWBIT (St Mary) *Linc 17* **P** *Ld Chan and DBP (alt)* **V** D J SPICER
COWCLIFFE (St Hilda) *see* N Huddersfield *Wakef*
COWDEN (St Mary Magdalene) w Hammerwood *Chich 7* **P** *Ch Soc Trust* **P-in-c** P D F HORNER
COWES (Holy Trinity) and Cowes (St Mary the Virgin) *Portsm 8* **P** *Trustees and V Carisbrooke St Mary the Virgin (jt)* **V** R J EMBLIN, **NSM** D L DENNIS
COWES (St Faith) *Portsm 8* **P** *Bp* **NSM** R S NETHERWAY
COWES, EAST (St James) *see* Whippingham w E Cowes *Portsm*
COWESBY (St Michael) *York 20* **P** *Abp* **P-in-c** P R A R HOARE
COWFOLD (St Peter) *Chich 9* **P** *Bp Lon* **V** G L DRIVER
COWGATE (St Peter) *Newc 7* **P** *Bp* **V** *Vacant* 0191-286 9913
COWGILL (St John the Evangelist) *see* Dent w Cowgill *Bradf*
COWICK (Holy Trinity) *see* Gt Snaith *Sheff*
COWLAM (St Mary) *see* Sledmere and Cowlam w Fridaythorpe, Fimer etc *York*
COWLEIGH (St Peter) *see* Malvern Link w Cowleigh *Worc*
COWLEY (St James) (St Francis) *Ox 4* **P** *Patr Bd* **TR** S W M HARTLEY, **C** J H TOMLINSON, P D STANWAY, **NSM** W CHAND
COWLEY (St John) (St Alban) (St Bartholomew) (St Mary and St John) *Ox 4* **P** *St Steph Ho Ox* **V** C P IRVINE, **C** P M DOLL, **NSM** A L FORBES
COWLEY (St Laurence) *Lon 24* **P** *Bp* **P-in-c** R N LEACH
COWLEY (St Mary) *see* Coberley, Cowley, Colesbourne and Elkstone *Glouc*
COWLEY CHAPEL (St Antony) *see* Thorverton, Cadbury, Upton Pyne etc *Ex*
COWLING (Holy Trinity) *Bradf 8* **P** *Bp* **V** R D CARTER
COWLINGE (St Margaret) *see* Wickhambrook w Lydgate, Ousden and Cowlinge *St E*
COWPEN (St Benedict) *see* Horton *Newc*
COWPLAIN (St Wilfrid) *Portsm 4* **P** *Bp* **V** P HANCOCK, **C** A P MARSDEN, **NSM** A MATHESON
COWTONS, The (All Saints) (St Luke's Pastoral Centre) *Ripon 2* **P** *V Gilling (1 turn), DBP (2 turns)* **P-in-c** S T GRIFFITHS
COX GREEN (Good Shepherd) *Ox 13* **P** *Bp* **P-in-c** V J BROOKS
COXHEATH (Holy Trinity) w East Farleigh, Hunton and Linton *Roch 7* **P** *Abp, Ld Chan and Lord Cornwallis (by turn)* **R** R J CASTLE, **NSM** G R ELLMORE
COXHOE (St Mary) *see* Kelloe and Coxhoe *Dur*
COXLEY (Christ Church), Henton and Wookey *B & W 8* **P** *Bp* **V** R R B PLOWMAN
COXWELL, GREAT (St Giles) w Buscot, Coleshill and Eaton Hastings *Ox 17* **P** *Bp and Lord Faringdon (jt)* **P-in-c** I S BECKWITH
COXWELL, LITTLE (St Mary) *see* Gt Faringdon w Lt Coxwell *Ox*
COXWOLD (St Michael) and Husthwaite *York 5* **P** *Abp* **V** D F JOHNSON
CRABBS CROSS (St Peter) *see* Redditch, The Ridge *Worc*
CRADLEY (St James) w Mathon and Storridge *Heref 6* **P** *Bp and D&C Westmr (jt)* **P-in-c** G P HOWELL, **NSM** M D VOCKINS
CRADLEY (St Peter) (St Katherine's Mission Church) *Worc 9* **P** *R Halesowen* **V** D J BLACKBURN, **C** D M WEBB
CRADLEY HEATH (St Luke) *see* Reddal Hill St Luke *Worc*

CRAGG VALE (St John the Baptist in the Wilderness) *see* Halifax St Jo *Wakef*
CRAKEHALL (St Gregory) *Ripon 4* **P** *Sir Henry Beresford-Peirse, Bt* **V** *Vacant*
CRAMBE (St Michael) *see* Whitwell w Crambe, Flaxton, Foston etc *York*
CRAMLINGTON (St Nicholas) *Newc 1* **P** *Bp* **TR** J A MACNAUGHTON, **TV** A PATTISON, E J NOBLE
CRAMPMOOR (St Swithun) *see* Romsey *Win*
CRANBORNE (St Mary and St Bartholomew) w Boveridge, Edmondsham, Wimborne St Giles and Woodlands *Sarum 10* **P** *Marquess of Salisbury, Earl of Shaftesbury, and Mrs C M Medlycott (jt)* **R** B R DIXON
CRANBOURNE (St Peter) *see* Winkfield and Cranbourne *Ox*
CRANBROOK (St Dunstan) *Cant 11* **P** *Abp* **V** G S BRIDGEWATER, **NSM** J P MOY
CRANFIELD (St Peter and St Paul) and Hulcote w Salford *St Alb 13* **P** *MMCET* **R** H K SYMES-THOMPSON
CRANFORD (Holy Angels) (St Dunstan) *Lon 11* **P** *R J G Berkeley Esq and Sir Hugo Huntingdon-Whiteley (jt)* **R** N G T WHEELER
CRANFORD (St John the Baptist) w Grafton Underwood and Twywell *Pet 11* **P** *Boughton Estates, DBP, and Sir John Robinson (by turn)* **R** D H P FOOT
CRANHAM (All Saints) *Chelmsf 2* **P** *St Jo Coll Ox* **P-in-c** T W PAGE, **C** A J D E ABSALOM, **NSM** G K ARBER
CRANHAM (St James the Great) *see* Painswick w Sheepscombe and Cranham *Glouc*
CRANHAM PARK Moor Lane (not known) *see* Cranham Park *Chelmsf*
CRANHAM PARK (St Luke) *Chelmsf 2* **P** *Bp* **V** J F DUNNETT
CRANLEIGH (St Nicolas) *Guildf 2* **P** *Bp* **R** N P NICHOLSON, **C** S N PAUL
CRANMORE, WEST (St Bartholomew) *see* Shepton Mallet w Doulting *B & W*
CRANOE (St Michael) *see* Gt Bowden w Welham, Glooston and Cranoe *Leic*
CRANSFORD (St Peter) *see* Badingham w Bruisyard, Cransford and Dennington *St E*
CRANSLEY (St Andrew) *see* Broughton w Loddington and Cransley etc *Pet*
CRANTOCK (St Carantoc) *Truro 7* **P** *SMF* **NSM** M WILLS
CRANWELL (St Andrew) *Linc 22* **P** *DBP* **P-in-c** C M J THODY
CRANWICH (St Mary) *Nor 13* **P** *CPAS* **P-in-c** G H WHEATLEY
CRANWORTH (St Mary the Virgin) *see* Reymerston w Cranworth, Letton, Southburgh etc *Nor*
CRASSWALL (St Mary) *see* Clodock and Longtown w Craswall, Llanveynoe etc *Heref*
CRASTER (Mission Church) *see* Embleton w Rennington and Rock *Newc*
CRATFIELD (St Mary) w Heveningham and Ubbeston w Huntingfield and Cookley *St E 15* **P** *Hon Mrs S Peel and Simeon's Trustees (alt)* **P-in-c** L M HIPKINS
CRATHORNE (All Saints) *York 22* **P** *Lord Crathorne, Hon David Dugdale, and J Southern Esq (jt)* **P-in-c** P KITCHING
CRAWCROOK (Church of the Holy Spirit) *see* Greenside *Dur*
CRAWFORD (District Church) *see* Upholland *Liv*
CRAWLEY (St John the Baptist) *Chich 7* **P** *Bp* **TV** R C MARSH, B L HACKSHALL, J BROWN, D A WALLER, **C** P G J HUGHES, **Hon C** I W NATHANIEL
CRAWLEY (St Mary) and Littleton and Sparsholt w Lainston *Win 13* **P** *Ld Chan and DBP (alt)* **R** D G WILLIAMS
CRAWLEY, NORTH (St Firmin) *see* Sherington w Chicheley, N Crawley, Astwood etc *Ox*
CRAWLEY DOWN (All Saints) *Chich 7* **P** *R Worth* **V** W J L STRONG
CRAWSHAWBOOTH (St John) *see* Goodshaw and Crawshawbooth *Man*
CRAY (St Barnabas) *see* St Paul's Cray St Barn *Roch*
CRAY (St Mary and St Paulinus) *see* St Mary Cray and St Paul's Cray *Roch*
CRAY, NORTH (St James) w Ruxley *Roch 17* **P** *Bp* **R** P H ROLTON
CRAYFORD (St Paulinus) *Roch 15* **P** *Bp* **R** P WRIGHT, **C** J M HULME, S SHOOTER, J PEAL
CRAYKE (St Cuthbert) w Brandsby and Yearsley *York 5* **P** *The Crown and Abp (alt)* **NSM** R W DAVILL
CRAZIES HILL (Mission Room) *see* Wargrave *Ox*
CREACOMBE (St Michael and All Angels) *see* Witheridge, Thelbridge, Creacombe, Meshaw etc *Ex*
CREAKE, NORTH (St Mary) and SOUTH (St Mary) w Waterden, Syderstone w Barmer and Sculthorpe *Nor 15* **P** *Bp, Earl Spencer, Earl of Leicester, Guild of All So, J Labouchere Esq, Mrs M E Russell, and DBP (jt)* **R** A M THOMSON
CREATON, GREAT (St Michael and All Angels) *see* Cottesbrooke w Gt Creaton and Thornby *Pet*
CREDENHILL (St Mary) w Brinsop and Wormsley, Mansel Lacey and Yazor, Kenchester, Bridge Sollers and Bishopstone *Heref 4* **P** *R M Ecroyd Esq, Major D J C Davenport and Bp (3 turns), Ld Chan (1 turn)* **R** G USHER
CREDITON (Holy Cross) (St Lawrence) and Shobrooke *Ex 2* **P** *12 Govs of Crediton Ch* **R** A E GEERING
CREECH ST MICHAEL (St Michael) *B & W 18* **P** *MMCET* **V** D G MANNING
CREED (St Crida) *see* Probus, Ladock and Grampound w Creed and St Erme *Truro*
CREEDY, NORTH: Cheriton Fitzpaine, Woolfardisworthy East, Kennerleigh, Washford Pyne, Puddington, Poughill, Stockleigh English, Morchard Bishop, Stockleigh Pomeroy, Down St Mary and Clannaborough *Ex 2* **P** *Ld Chan (1 turn), DBP (3 turns)* **TR** B SHILLINGFORD, **TV** S G C SMITH, A R GARDINER
CREEKMOOR (Christ Church) *see* Oakdale *Sarum*
CREEKSEA (All Saints) w Althorne and Latchingdon w North Fambridge *Chelmsf 11* **P** *Bp, Abp and Ld Chan (by turn)* **V** S A ROBERTSON, **NSM** D I GORDON
CREETING (St Peter) *see* Creeting St Mary, Creeting St Peter etc *St E*
CREETING ST MARY (St Mary), Creeting (St Peter) and Earl Stonham w Stonham Parva *St E 1* **P** *DBP (2 turns), Pemb Coll Cam (1 turn)* **R** A PYKE
CREETON (St Peter) *see* Castle Bytham w Creeton *Linc*
CREGNEISH (St Peter) *see* Rushen *S & M*
CRESSAGE (Christ Church) *see* Wenlock *Heref*
CRESSBROOK (St John the Evangelist) *see* Tideswell *Derby*
CRESSING (All Saints) *Chelmsf 15* **P** *Bp* **R** J R CORBYN
CRESSINGHAM, GREAT (St Michael) and LITTLE (St Andrew), w Threxton *Nor 13* **P** *Bp and Sec of State for Defence* **P-in-c** G R DRAKE
CRESSWELL (St Bartholomew) and Lynemouth *Newc 11* **P** *Bp* **P-in-c** T D DAWSON
CRESWELL (St Mary Magdalene) *see* Elmton *Derby*
CRETINGHAM (St Peter) *see* Earl Soham w Cretingham and Ashfield cum Thorpe *St E*
CREWE (All Saints and St Paul) *Ches 15* **P** *Bp* **V** P D BRADBROOK
CREWE (Christ Church) (St Peter) *Ches 15* **P** *Bp* **V** W C W FOSS
CREWE (St Andrew w St John the Baptist) *Ches 15* **P** *Bp* **V** W J BAKER
CREWE (St Barnabas) *Ches 15* **P** *Bp* **V** R D POWELL
CREWE GREEN (St Michael and All Angels) *see* Haslington w Crewe Green *Ches*
CREWKERNE (St Bartholomew) w Wayford *B & W 15* **P** *Ld Chan* **R** P B CURTIS
CREWTON (St Peter) *see* Boulton *Derby*
CRICH (St Mary) *Derby 1* **P** *Ch Trust Fund Trust* **P-in-c** P D BROOKS
CRICK (St Margaret) and Yelvertoft w Clay Coton and Lilbourne *Pet 2* **P** *MMCET and St Jo Coll Cam (jt)* **R** R M BARLOW
CRICKET MALHERBIE (St Mary Magdalene) *see* Chard Furnham w Chaffcombe, Knowle St Giles etc *B & W*
CRICKET ST THOMAS (St Thomas) *see* Thorncombe w Winsham and Cricket St Thomas *B & W*
CRICKLADE (St Sampson) w Latton *Bris 10* **P** *D&C, Bp, and Hon P N Eliot (by turn)* **V** S J ORAM, **NSM** A EVANS
CRICKLEWOOD (St Gabriel and St Michael) *Lon 21* **P** *Bp* **P-in-c** M R ALDRIDGE, **C** C RAMSAY, **NSM** S P MNGOMEZULU
CRICKLEWOOD (St Peter) *Lon 21* **P** *Bp* **V** P D RABIN
CRIFTINS (St Matthew) w Dudleston and Welsh Frankton *Lich 17* **P** *Bp and V Ellesmere (jt)* **C** A C NETHERWOOD
CRIMPLESHAM (St Mary) w Stradsett *Ely 16* **P** *Bp* **V** P F KEELING
CRINGLEFORD (St Peter) w Colney and Bawburgh *Nor 7* **P** *Gt Hosp Nor, Exors E H Barclay Esq and D&C (alt)* **R** C J BLACKMAN
CROCKENHILL (All Souls) *Roch 2* **P** *Bp* **V** *Vacant* (01322) 662157
CROCKERNWELL (Holy Trinity) *see* Tedburn St Mary, Whitestone, Oldridge etc *Ex*
CROCKHAM HILL (Holy Trinity) *Roch 11* **P** *J St A Warde Esq* **P-in-c** S A J MITCHELL, **C** R JONES
CROFT (All Saints) *see* The Wainfleet Gp *Linc*
CROFT (Christ Church) w Southworth *Liv 16* **P** *Bp* **R** W R D ALEXANDER
CROFT (St Michael and All Angels) *see* Eye, Croft w Yarpole and Lucton *Heref*
CROFT (St Michael and All Angels) *see* Broughton Astley and Croft w Stoney Stanton *Leic*

CROFT (St Peter) *see* Middleton Tyas w Croft and Eryholme *Ripon*
CROFTON (All Saints) *Wakef 9* **P** *Duchy of Lanc* **R** J P TAYLOR
CROFTON (Holy Rood) (St Edmund) *Portsm 2* **P** *Bp* **V** M T CHRISTIAN-EDWARDS, **C** G H YERBURY, **Hon C** O B STARES
CROFTON (St Paul) *Roch 16* **P** *V Orpington* **V** C J REED
CROFTON PARK (St Hilda w St Cyprian) *S'wark 5* **P** *V Lewisham St Mary* **V** S G BATES, **NSM** R O SMITH
CROGLIN (St John the Baptist) *Carl 2* **P** *D&C* **P-in-c** J S CASSON
CROMER (St Peter and St Paul) *Nor 21* **P** *CPAS* **V** D F HAYDEN, **C** T MITCHELL, **Hon C** E C BAILEY
CROMFORD (St Mary) *see* Matlock Bath and Cromford *Derby*
CROMHALL (St Andrew) w Tortworth and Tytherington *Glouc 7* **P** *Earl of Ducie, Or Coll Ox, and MMCET (jt)* **P-in-c** P M LYES-WILSDON, **Hon C** R J B TAYLOR
CROMPTON, EAST (St James) *Man 22* **P** *Bp* **V** D PEEL, **C** R F I CRAM, **NSM** G W LINDLEY
CROMPTON, HIGH (St Mary) *Man 22* **P** *Bp* **V** H S EDWARDS
CROMPTON FOLD (St Saviour) *see* E Crompton *Man*
CROMWELL (St Giles) *see* Norwell w Ossington, Cromwell and Caunton *S'well*
CRONDALL (All Saints) and Ewshot *Guildf 3* **P** *Bp* **V** P M RICH
CROOK (St Catherine) *Carl 9* **P** *CPAS* **V** R A MACHIN
CROOK (St Catherine) *Dur 9* **P** *R Brancepeth* **R** A FEATHERSTONE, **C** J V HALLETT
CROOK PEAK *B & W 1* **P** *Ld Chan, Bp, Bp Lon, and R M Dod Esq (by turn)* **R** G GOULD
CROOKES (St Thomas) *Sheff 4* **P** *Patr Bd* **TR** M J BREEN, **TV** A D WOODING JONES
CROOKES (St Timothy) *Sheff 4* **P** *Sheff Ch Burgesses* **V** P R TOWNSEND
CROOKHAM (Christ Church) *Guildf 1* **P** *V Crondall and Ewshot* **V** F J M EVANS
CROOKHORN (Good Shepherd) *Portsm 4* **P** *Simeon's Trustees* **V** *Vacant* (01705) 267647
CROPREDY (St Mary the Virgin) *see* Shires' Edge *Ox*
CROPTHORNE (St Michael) w Charlton *Worc 4* **P** *D&C (2 turns), Bp (1 turn)* **P-in-c** K A BOYCE, **C** I SCOTT
CROPTON (St Gregory) *see* Lastingham w Appleton-le-Moors, Rosedale etc *York*
CROPWELL BISHOP (St Giles) w Colston Bassett, Granby w Elton, Langar cum Barnstone and Tythby w Cropwell Butler *S'well 8* **P** *CPAS and Bp, Ld Chan (alt)* **R** A O WIGRAM, **NSM** J A CONLEY, B E F CLANCEY
CROSBY (St George) (St Michael) *Linc 4* **P** *Sir Reginald Sheffield, Bt* **P-in-c** J W THACKER
CROSBY, GREAT (All Saints) *Liv 5* **P** *R Sefton, Bp, V St Luke, and CPAS (jt)* **V** N J PATTERSON
CROSBY, GREAT (St Faith) *Liv 1* **P** *St Chad's Coll Dur* **C** C KETLEY, **Hon C** D A SMITH, **NSM** G GILFORD
CROSBY, GREAT (St Luke) *Liv 5* **P** *R Sefton* **V** D H TROLLOPE, **C** D J WILLIAMS, **NSM** W J PIERCE
CROSBY GARRETT (St Andrew) *see* Kirkby Stephen w Mallerstang etc *Carl*
CROSBY-ON-EDEN (St John the Evangelist) *see* Irthington, Crosby-on-Eden and Scaleby *Carl*
CROSBY RAVENSWORTH (St Lawrence) *Carl 1* **P** *DBP* **P-in-c** D C WOOD
CROSCOMBE (Blessed Virgin Mary) *see* Pilton w Croscombe, N Wootton and Dinder *B & W*
CROSLAND, SOUTH (Holy Trinity) *Wakef 1* **P** *R Almondbury* **V** M C RUSSELL, **NSM** R T TUCK
CROSLAND MOOR (St Barnabas) *Wakef 5* **P** *Bp* **V** M STOREY, **NSM** D A KIRBY
CROSS GREEN (St Hilda) *see* Leeds Richmond Hill *Ripon*
CROSS GREEN (St Saviour) *as above*
CROSS HEATH (St Michael and All Angels) *Lich 9* **P** *Bp* **P-in-c** N B JAMIESON-HARVEY
CROSS IN HAND (St Bartholomew) *see* Waldron *Chich*
CROSS ROADS cum Lees (St James) *Bradf 8* **P** *Bp* **V** D N WILLIAMS
CROSS STONE (St Paul) *see* Todmorden *Wakef*
CROSSCANONBY (St John the Evangelist) *Carl 7* **P** *D&C* **V** J LEONARDI
CROSSCRAKE (St Thomas) and Preston Patrick *Carl 9* **P** *Bp and V Heversham and Milnthorpe (jt)* **P-in-c** H BROWN
CROSSENS (St John) *Liv 9* **P** *Trustees* **V** *Vacant* (01704) 27662
CROSSFLATTS (St Aidan) *see* Bingley All SS *Bradf*
CROSSPOOL (St Columba) *Sheff 4* **P** *Bp* **V** M R BURKE
CROSTHWAITE (St Kentigern) Keswick *Carl 6* **P** *Bp* **V** R T HUGHES
CROSTHWAITE (St Mary) Kendal *Carl 9* **P** *DBP* **P-in-c** W F GREETHAM
CROSTON (St Michael and All Angels) *Blackb 4* **P** *M G Rawstorne Esq* **R** R J BRUNSWICK
CROSTWICK (St Peter) *see* Spixworth w Crostwick and Frettenham *Nor*
CROSTWIGHT (All Saints) *see* Smallburgh w Dilham w Honing and Crostwight *Nor*
CROUCH END HILL (Christ Church) *see* Hornsey Ch Ch *Lon*
CROUGHTON (All Saints) *see* Aynho and Croughton w Evenley etc *Pet*
CROWAN (St Crewenna) w Godolphin *Truro 4* **P** *Bp and D L C Roberts Esq (alt)* **V** P DOUGLASS
CROWBOROUGH (All Saints) *Chich 19* **P** *Ld Chan* **V** A C J CORNES, **C** A RAYNES, **NSM** J A HOBBS
CROWCOMBE (Holy Ghost) *see* Bicknoller w Crowcombe and Sampford Brett *B & W*
CROWELL (Nativity of the Blessed Virgin Mary) *see* Chinnor w Emmington and Sydenham etc *Ox*
CROWFIELD (All Saints) w Stonham Aspal and Mickfield *St E 1* **P** *DBP, Bp, and Lord de Saumarez (alt)* **R** *Vacant* (01449) 711409
CROWHURST (St George) *see* Catsfield and Crowhurst *Chich*
CROWHURST (St George) *see* Lingfield and Crowhurst *S'wark*
CROWLAND (St Mary and St Bartholomew and St Guthlac) *Linc 17* **P** *Earl of Normanton* **R** *Vacant* (01733) 210499
CROWLE (St John the Baptist) *see* Bowbrook S *Worc*
CROWLE (St Oswald) *Linc 1* **P** *Bp* **V** D SCHOFIELD, **Hon C** D E CORNELIUS
CROWMARSH GIFFORD (St Mary Magdalene) *see* Wallingford w Crowmarsh Gifford etc *Ox*
CROWN EAST AND RUSHWICK (St Thomas) *see* Broadheath, Crown East and Rushwick *Worc*
CROWNHILL (Ascension) *see* Plymouth Crownhill Ascension *Ex*
CROWTHORNE (St John the Baptist) *Ox 16* **P** *Bp* **V** B R SPENCE, **NSM** T WALT
CROWTON (Christ Church) *see* Norley and Crowton *Ches*
CROXALL-CUM-OAKLEY (St John the Baptist) *see* Walton on Trent w Croxall etc *Derby*
CROXBY (All Saints) *see* Swallow *Linc*
CROXDALE (St Bartholomew) and Tudhoe *Dur 6* **P** *D&C* **R** P E B WELBY
CROXDEN (St Giles) *see* Rocester and Croxden w Hollington *Lich*
CROXLEY GREEN (All Saints) *St Alb 5* **P** *V Rickmansworth* **V** L G-H LEE
CROXLEY GREEN (St Oswald) *St Alb 5* **P** *Bp* **V** A M LOVEGROVE
CROXTETH (St Paul) *Liv 8* **P** *R W Derby and Bp (jt)* **V** I G BROOKS
CROXTON (All Saints) *see* Thetford *Nor*
CROXTON Group, The SOUTH (St John the Baptist) *Leic 3* **P** *DBP, Ch Soc Trust, and MMCET (jt)* **R** M E LAMBERT
CROXTON (St James) and Eltisley *Ely 1* **P** *Bp* **R** *Vacant* (0148087) 252
CROXTON (St John the Evangelist) *Linc 6* **P** *Ld Chan* **Hon C** S W ANDREW
CROXTON (St Paul) w Broughton and Adbaston *Lich 7* **P** *Bp and J Hall Esq* **V** M W WELSH
CROXTON KERRIAL (St Botolph and St John the Baptist) *see* High Framland Parishes *Leic*
CROYDE (St Mary Magdalene) *see* Georgeham *Ex*
CROYDON (All Saints) w Clopton *Ely 8* **P** *Bp and DBP (alt)* **R** N A BRICE
CROYDON (Christ Church) Broad Green *S'wark 22* **P** *Simeon's Trustees* **V** C J ROSEWEIR, **C** S M HODGES, **Hon C** J K EYNON
CROYDON (Holy Saviour) *S'wark 24* **P** *Bp* **V** X SOOSAINAYAGAM, **NSM** P L GIBBS
CROYDON (St Andrew) *S'wark 22* **P** *Trustees* **V** P D HENDRY
CROYDON (St Augustine) *S'wark 22* **P** *Bp* **V** G S DERRIMAN, **NSM** A SMITH
CROYDON (St John the Baptist) *S'wark 22* **P** *Abp* **V** C J L BOSWELL, **C** P J BROWN, T J JEFFREYS, P W HOLLAND, **Hon C** S J F GEDGE, K V G SMITH, **NSM** P D F SMITH
CROYDON (St Matthew) *S'wark 22* **P** *V Croydon* **V** P C GULVIN
CROYDON (St Michael and All Angels w St James) *S'wark 22* **P** *Trustees* **V** D P MINCHEW
CROYDON (St Peter) *S'wark 22* **P** *V Croydon* **V** S J KNOWERS, **NSM** R C IVES
CROYDON Woodside (St Luke) *S'wark 24* **P** *Bp* **V** P EVANS, **C** P I D GRANT

CROYDON, SOUTH (Emmanuel) *S'wark 23* **P** *Ch Trust Fund Trust* **V** R A HIGGINS, **C** J E G DASH, **NSM** D J RICHARDSON
CROYDON, SOUTH (St Augustine) *see* Croydon St Aug *S'wark*
CROYLAND (St Mary and St Bartholomew and St Guthlac) *see* Crowland *Linc*
CRUDGINGTON (St Mary Mission Church) *see* Wrockwardine Deanery *Lich*
CRUDWELL (All Saints) *see* Ashley, Crudwell, Hankerton, Long Newnton etc *Bris*
CRUMPSALL (St Matthew w St Mary) *Man 5* **P** *Bp* **P-in-c** A-M C BIRD
CRUMPSALL, LOWER (St Thomas) *see* Cheetham and Lower Crumpsall *Man*
CRUNDALE (St Mary the Blessed Virgin) w Godmersham *Cant 2* **P** *Abp* **P-in-c** R I MARTIN
CRUWYS MORCHARD (Holy Cross) *see* Washfield, Stoodleigh, Withleigh etc *Ex*
CRUX EASTON (St Michael and All Angels) *see* Highclere and Ashmansworth w Crux Easton *Win*
CUBBINGTON (St Mary) *Cov 11* **P** *Bp* **V** K LINDOP
CUBERT (St Cubert) *Truro 7* **P** *DBP* **V** P E TIDMARSH
CUBLEY (St Andrew) *see* Alkmonton, Cubley, Marston, Montgomery etc *Derby*
CUBLINGTON (St Nicholas) *see* Wingrave w Rowsham, Aston Abbotts and Cublington *Ox*
CUCKFIELD (Holy Trinity) *Chich 6* **P** *Bp* **V** N G WETHERALL
CUCKLINGTON (St Lawrence) *see* Charlton Musgrove, Cucklington and Stoke Trister *B & W*
CUDDESDON (All Saints) *see* Wheatley *Ox*
CUDDINGTON (St Mary) *Guildf 9* **P** *Bp* **V** B P OWEN
CUDDINGTON (St Nicholas) *see* Haddenham w Cuddington, Kingsey etc *Ox*
CUDHAM (St Peter and St Paul) and Downe *Roch 16* **P** *Ch Soc Trust and Bp (jt)* **V** T R HATWELL, **NSM** N K HINTON
CUDWORTH (St John) *Wakef 7* **P** *Bp* **V** *Vacant* (01226) 710279
CUDWORTH (St Michael) *see* Ilminster and District *B & W*
CUFFLEY (St Andrew) *see* Northaw *St Alb*
CULBONE (St Beuno) *see* Oare w Culbone *B & W*
CULFORD (St Mary), West Stow and Wordwell w Flempton, Hengrave and Lackford *St E 13* **P** *Bp (2 turns), R W Gough Esq (1 turn)* **P-in-c** D P BURRELL, **NSM** E M ELLIOTT
CULGAITH (All Saints) *see* Addingham, Edenhall, Langwathby and Culgaith *Carl*
CULHAM (St Paul) *see* Dorchester *Ox*
CULLERCOATS (St George) *Newc 8* **P** *Patr Bd* **TV** J T SHONE, M SLACK, **Hon C** R A MACEY, **NSM** D HOOD
CULLERCOATS (St Paul) *see* Tynemouth Cullercoats St Paul *Newc*
CULLINGWORTH (St John the Evangelist) *Bradf 8* **P** *Bp* **P-in-c** M COWGILL
CULLOMPTON (St Andrew) (Langford Chapel) *Ex 4* **P** *CPAS* **C** A DELANEY
CULM DAVY (St Mary's Chapel) *see* Hemyock w Culm Davy, Clayhidon and Culmstock *Ex*
CULMINGTON (All Saints) w Onibury, Bromfield and Stanton Lacy *Heref 12* **P** *O T M Rogers-Coltman (1 turn), Earl of Plymouth (2 turns)* **R** K J M EWEN, **NSM** E H M PERKS
CULMSTOCK (All Saints) *see* Hemyock w Culm Davy, Clayhidon and Culmstock *Ex*
CULPHO (St Botolph) *see* Gt and Lt Bealings w Playford and Culpho *St E*
CULWORTH (St Mary the Virgin) w Sulgrave and Thorpe Mandeville and Chipping Warden w Edgcote *Pet 1* **P** *Ch Patr Trust (1 turn), T M Sergison-Brooke Esq (1 turn), DBP (2 turns), and D L P Humfrey Esq (1 turn)* **R** B M EAVES
CUMBERWORTH (St Helen) *see* Sutton, Huttoft and Anderby *Linc*
CUMBERWORTH (St Nicholas), Denby and Denby Dale *Wakef 6* **P** *Bp and V Penistone (jt)* **R** D J CLARKSON
CUMDIVOCK (St John) *see* Dalston *Carl*
CUMMERSDALE (St James) *see* Denton Holme *Carl*
CUMNOR (St Michael) *Ox 10* **P** *St Pet Coll Ox* **V** N D DURAND, **C** L E FLETCHER, **NSM** C H HOLMES
CUMREW (St Mary the Virgin) *see* Brampton and Farlam and Castle Carrock w Cumrew *Carl*
CUMWHINTON (St John's Hall) *see* Cotehill and Cumwhinton *Carl*
CUMWHITTON (St Mary the Virgin) *see* Hayton w Cumwhitton *Carl*
CUNDALL (St Mary and All Saints) *see* Kirby-on-the-Moor, Cundall w Norton-le-Clay etc *Ripon*
CURBAR (All Saints) *see* Baslow w Curbar and Stoney Middleton *Derby*
CURBRIDGE (St Barnabas) *see* Sarisbury *Portsm*
CURBRIDGE (St John the Baptist) *see* Witney *Ox*
CURDRIDGE (St Peter) *Portsm 1* **P** *D&C Win* **NSM** D R TOWNSEND
CURDWORTH (St Nicholas and St Peter ad Vincula) (St George) *Birm 13* **P** *Bp and Lord Norton (jt)* **R** M GARLAND, **NSM** C HOARE
CURRY, NORTH (St Peter and St Paul) *B & W 18* **P** *D&C* **V** C H TOWNSHEND
CURRY MALLET (All Saints) *see* Hatch Beauchamp w Beercrocombe, Curry Mallet etc *B & W*
CURRY RIVEL (St Andrew) w Fivehead and Swell *B & W 15* **P** *D&C Bris (1 turn), P G H Speke Esq (2 turns)* **R** P C LAMBERT, **C** A M GRIGOR
CURY (St Corentine) and Gunwalloe w St Mawgan-in-Meneage *Truro 4* **P** *Bp* **R** P R LONG
CUSOP (St Mary) w Clifford, Hardwicke, Bredwardine, Brobury and Moccas *Heref 1* **P** *CPAS, MMCET, P M I S Trumper Esq, S Penoyre Esq, and Mrs P Chester-Master (jt)* **R** P W M BYLLAM-BARNES, **Hon C** S F BARNES, **NSM** C P STUTZ
CUTCOMBE (St John the Evangelist) *see* Exton and Winsford and Cutcombe w Luxborough *B & W*
CUTSDEAN (St James) *see* The Guitings, Cutsdean and Farmcote *Glouc*
CUXHAM (Holy Rood) *see* Ewelme, Brightwell Baldwin, Cuxham w Easington *Ox*
CUXTON (St Michael and All Angels) and Halling *Roch 6* **P** *Bp and D&C (jt)* **R** R I KNIGHT
CUXWOLD (St Nicholas) *see* Swallow *Linc*
CWM HEAD (St Michael) *see* Wistanstow *Heref*
DACRE (Holy Trinity) w Hartwith and Darley w Thornthwaite *Ripon 3* **P** *Bp, D&C, V Masham and Healey, and Mrs K A Dunbar (jt)* **V** F A CHAPPELL
DACRE (St Andrew) *Carl 4* **P** *Trustees* **P-in-c** P J WILSON
DADLINGTON (St James) *see* Stoke Golding w Dadlington *Leic*
DAGENHAM (St Luke) (St Peter and St Paul) *Chelmsf 1* **P** *Patr Bd* **TR** R M REITH, **TV** S L SMALLWOOD, **C** E N COOMBS
DAGENHAM (St Martin) *see* Becontree S *Chelmsf*
DAGLINGWORTH (Holy Rood) *see* Brimpsfield w Birdlip, Syde, Daglingworth, etc *Glouc*
DAGNALL (All Saints) *see* Kensworth, Studham and Whipsnade *St Alb*
DAISY HILL (St James) *Man 11* **P** *Bp* **V** R COWARD
DALBURY (All Saints) *see* Longford, Long Lane, Dalbury and Radbourne *Derby*
DALBY (St James) *see* Patrick *S & M*
DALBY (St Lawrence and Blessed Edward King) *see* Partney *Linc*
DALBY (St Peter) *see* Bulmer w Dalby, Terrington and Welburn *York*
DALBY, GREAT (St Swithun) *see* Burrough Hill Pars *Leic*
DALBY, LITTLE (St James) *as above*
DALBY, OLD (St John the Baptist) and Nether Broughton *Leic 3* **P** *Bp* **P-in-c** R W WIDDOWSON, **C** R A WHITE
DALE ABBEY (All Saints) *see* Stanton-by-Dale w Dale Abbey *Derby*
DALE HEAD (St James) *see* Long Preston w Tosside *Bradf*
DALHAM (St Mary) *see* Gazeley w Dalham, Moulton and Kentford *St E*
DALLAM (St Mark) *Liv 12* **P** *R Warrington and Bp (jt)* **V** P J MARSHALL
DALLINGHOO (St Mary) *see* Charsfield w Debach, Monewden, Hoo etc *St E*
DALLINGTON (St Giles) *see* Brightling, Dallington, Mountfield etc *Chich*
DALLINGTON (St Mary) *Pet 7* **P** *Earl Spencer* **V** A E PANTON
DALLOWGILL (St Peter) *see* Fountains Gp *Ripon*
DALSTON (Holy Trinity) (St Philip) *Lon 5* **P** *Bp* **V** *Vacant* 0171-254 5062
DALSTON (St Mark w St Bartholomew) *Lon 5* **P** *Ch Patr Trust* **V** D H PATEMAN
DALSTON (St Michael) *Carl 3* **P** *Bp* **P-in-c** P KYBIRD, **C** H J CARTER
DALTON (Holy Trinity) *see* Newburn *Newc*
DALTON (Holy Trinity) *Sheff 6* **P** *Bp* **V** M O BLACKMAN
DALTON (St James) *see* Gilling and Kirkby Ravensworth *Ripon*
DALTON (St John the Evangelist) *see* Topcliffe w Baldersby, Dalton, Dishforth etc *York*
DALTON (St Michael and All Angels) *Liv 11* **P** *Bp* **V** T C BARTON

DALTON, NORTH (All Saints) *see* Bainton w N Dalton, Middleton-on-the-Wolds etc *York*
DALTON, SOUTH *see* Dalton le Dale *Dur*
DALTON HOLME (St Mary) *see* Etton w Dalton Holme *York*
DALTON-IN-FURNESS (St Mary) *Carl 8* **P** *Bp* **V** S J SKINNER, **C** I K HOOK, **NSM** J M SKINNER
DALTON LE DALE (Holy Trinity) (St Andrew) *Dur 2* **P** *D&C* **P-in-c** A MILNE
DALWOOD (St Peter) *see* Stockland, Dalwood, Kilmington and Shute *Ex*
DAMERHAM (St George) *see* W Downland *Sarum*
DANBURY (St John the Baptist) *Chelmsf 9* **P** *Lord Fitzwalter* **P-in-c** M G BLYTH, **NSM** A F WAKEFIELD
DANBY (St Hilda) *York 23* **P** *Viscount Downe* **P-in-c** R LEWIS
DANBY WISKE (not known) *see* Gt Smeaton w Appleton Wiske and Birkby etc *Ripon*
DANEHILL (All Saints) *Chich 21* **P** *Ch Soc Trust* **P-in-c** J M REX
DANESMOOR (St Barnabas) *see* N Wingfield, Clay Cross and Pilsley *Derby*
DARBY END (St Peter) *Worc 9* **P** *Bp* **V** N LAMBERT
DARBY GREEN (St Barnabas) *Win 5* **P** *Bp* **V** *Vacant* (01252) 877817
DARENTH (St Margaret) *Roch 2* **P** *D&C* **V** R J FORD
DARESBURY (All Saints) *Ches 4* **P** *D G Greenhall Esq* **V** D W SMITH
DARFIELD (All Saints) *Sheff 12* **P** *MMCET* **R** J G BLAKELEY
DARLASTON (All Saints) *Lich 27* **P** *Simeon's Trustees* **P-in-c** D A STEVENSON
DARLASTON (St Lawrence) *Lich 27* **P** *Bp and Simeon's Trustees (jt)* **R** G W LLOYD
DARLEY (Christ Church) *see* Dacre w Hartwith and Darley w Thornthwaite *Ripon*
DARLEY (St Helen) *Derby 7* **P** *Bp* **R** R E QUARTON
DARLEY, SOUTH (St Mary the Virgin), Elton and Winster *Derby 7* **P** *Bp and DBF (jt)* **P-in-c** A H CARR
DARLEY ABBEY (St Matthew) *Derby 9* **P** *DBP* **V** D MOWBRAY
DARLINGSCOTT (St George) *see* Tredington and Darlingscott w Newbold on Stour *Cov*
DARLINGTON (Holy Trinity) *Dur 8* **P** *Adn Dur* **V** R C WARDALE, **C** C M BLAKESLEY
DARLINGTON (St Cuthbert) *Dur 8* **P** *Lord Barnard* **V** G V MILLER
DARLINGTON St Hilda and (St Columba) *Dur 8* **P** *Bp* **P-in-c** S C FOSTER
DARLINGTON (St James) *Dur 8* **P** *The Crown* **V** I L GRIEVES, **NSM** C M WILSON
DARLINGTON (St Mark) w St Paul *Dur 8* **P** *Bp and St Jo Coll Dur* **V** *Vacant* (01325) 382400
DARLINGTON (St Matthew) and St Luke *Dur 8* **P** *Bp* **V** J R RICE-OXLEY, **NSM** B HOLMES
DARLINGTON, EAST (St John) (St Herbert) *Dur 8* **P** *The Crown* **TR** J CLASPER, **TV** J E HOWES
DARLTON (St Giles) *see* Dunham-on-Trent w Darlton, Ragnall etc *S'well*
DARNALL (Church of Christ) *see* Attercliffe, Darnall and Tinsley *Sheff*
DARRINGTON (St Luke and All Saints) w Wentbridge *Wakef 11* **P** *Bp* **V** C DAWSON
DARSHAM (All Saints) *St E 19* **P** *Exors Earl of Stradbroke* **V** R J GINN
DARTFORD (Christ Church) *Roch 2* **P** *V Dartford H Trin* **V** D B KITLEY, **NSM** C CROOK
DARTFORD (Holy Trinity) *Roch 2* **P** *Bp* **V** M J HENWOOD
DARTFORD (St Alban) *Roch 2* **P** *V Dartford H Trin* **V** A T WATERMAN
DARTFORD (St Edmund the King and Martyr) *Roch 2* **P** *Bp* **V** R P CALLAGHAN
DARTINGTON (Old St Mary's Church Tower) *see* Totnes, Bridgetown and Berry Pomeroy etc *Ex*
DARTINGTON (St Mary) *as above*
DARTMOUTH (St Petrox) (St Saviour) *Ex 13* **P** *DBP and Sir John Seale, Bt (jt)* **V** R E FLOWER, **Hon C** P A RILEY
DARTON (All Saints) *Wakef 7* **P** *Bp* **V** W R PLIMMER
DARWEN (St Barnabas) *Blackb 5* **P** *Bp* **V** P H SMITH
DARWEN (St Cuthbert) w Tockholes St Stephen *Blackb 5* **P** *Bp* **V** *Vacant* (01254) 775039
DARWEN (St Peter) w Hoddlesden St Paul *Blackb 5* **P** *V Blackburn and DBP (jt)* **TR** K P ARKELL, **C** P WALLINGTON, C PETER
DARWEN, LOWER (St James) *Blackb 5* **P** *V Blackb* **V** R P CARTMELL
DARWEN, OVER (St James) *Blackb 5* **P** *V Blackb* **V** J FARADAY
DASSETT MAGNA (All Saints) *see* Burton Dassett *Cov*
DATCHET (St Mary the Virgin) *see* Riverside *Ox*
DATCHWORTH (All Saints) w Tewin *St Alb 5* **P** *Bp and Jes Coll Cam (alt)* **P-in-c** R A SYMS
DAUBHILL (St George the Martyr) *Man 9* **P** *Trustees* **V** S J ABRAM
DAUNTSEY (St James Great) *see* Brinkworth w Dauntsey *Bris*
DAVENHAM (St Wilfrid) *Ches 6* **P** *Bp* **R** *Vacant* (01606) 42450
DAVENTRY (Holy Cross), Ashby St Ledgers, Braunston, Catesby, Hellidon, Staverton and Welton *Pet 3* **P** *Patr Bd* **TR** K SMALLDON, **TV** J V J G WATSON, J W HARGREAVES, I W JONES, **C** P MOSELING, **NSM** E M THORP
DAVIDSTOW (St David) *see* Boscastle w Davidstow *Truro*
DAVINGTON (St Mary Magdalene) *see* The Brents and Davington w Oare and Luddenham *Cant*
DAVYHULME (Christ Church) *Man 7* **P** *Bp* **V** A J WATTS
DAVYHULME (St Mary) *Man 7* **P** *Bp* **V** S J WINWARD
DAWDON (St Hild and St Helen) *Dur 2* **P** *Bp* **V** J C G POLLOCK
DAWLEY (Holy Trinity) *see* Cen Telford *Lich*
DAWLEY (St Jerome) *Lon 24* **P** *Hyndman Trustees* **P-in-c** D HONOUR
DAWLISH (St Gregory) *Ex 6* **P** *D&C* **V** .W D S LARK, **Hon C** C R EVANS
DAWLISH WARREN (Church Hall) *see* Kenton, Mamhead, Powderham, Cofton and Starcross *Ex*
DAYBROOK (St Paul) *S'well 13* **P** *Bp* **P-in-c** W D MILNER
DAYLESFORD (St Peter) *see* Kingham w Churchill, Daylesford and Sarsden *Ox*
DE BEAUVOIR TOWN (St Peter) *Lon 5* **P** *Bp* **V** A WINDROSS, **NSM** I C CZERNIAWSKA EDGECUMBE
DEAL (St Andrew) *Cant 8* **P** *Abp* **R** J D KING
DEAL (St George the Martyr) *Cant 8* **P** *Abp* **C** A R DODDS
DEAL (St Leonard) (St Richard) and Sholden *Cant 8* **P** *Abp* **R** G D KENDREW, **C** G F MACK
DEAN (All Hallows) *see* The Stodden Churches *St Alb*
DEAN (St Oswald) *Carl 6* **P** *A R Sherwen Esq and R Workington (jt)* **R** P M BADEN
DEAN, EAST (St Simon and St Jude) w Friston and Jevington *Chich 16* **P** *Duke of Devonshire (1 turn), D&C (2 turns)* **P-in-c** S J MORGAN
DEAN, EAST (St Winifred) *see* Lockerley and E Dean w E and W Tytherley *Win*
DEAN, WEST (All Saints) *see* Alfriston w Lullington, Litlington and W Dean *Chich*
DEAN, WEST (St Mary) *see* Alderbury Team *Sarum*
DEAN COURT (St Andrew) *see* Cumnor *Ox*
DEAN FOREST (Christ Church) *see* Forest of Dean Ch Ch w English Bicknor *Glouc*
DEAN FOREST (Holy Trinity) *Glouc 4* **P** *The Crown* **V** A N JAMES
DEAN FOREST (St Paul) *Glouc 4* **P** *Bp* **V** I L DAVIES
DEAN PRIOR (St George the Martyr) *see* Buckfastleigh w Dean Prior *Ex*
DEANE (All Saints) *see* N Waltham and Steventon, Ashe and Deane *Win*
DEANE (St Mary the Virgin) *Man 11* **P** *Patr Bd* **TR** R B JACKSON, **TV** P ELLIS, **C** C D MOORE
DEANSHANGER (Holy Trinity) *see* Passenham *Pet*
DEARHAM (St Mungo) *Carl 7* **P** *Bp* **P-in-c** K KITCHIN
DEARNLEY (St Andrew) *Man 20* **P** *Bp* **P-in-c** P F DAVEY
DEBDEN (St Mary the Virgin) and Wimbish w Thunderley *Chelmsf 22* **P** *Bp* **R** A K GAIR
DEBENHAM (St Mary Magdalene) w Aspall and Kenton *St E 18* **P** *Lord Henniker (2 turns), Bp (1 turn)* **P-in-c** G E NOBLE
DEDDINGTON (St Peter and St Paul) Barford, Clifton and Hempton *Ox 5* **P** *D&C Windsor and Bp (jt)* **V** K G REEVES, **C** E J NEWELL
DEDHAM (St Mary the Virgin) *Chelmsf 17* **P** *Duchy of Lanc and Lectureship Trustees (alt)* **V** G G MOATE
DEDWORTH (All Saints) *Ox 13* **P** *Bp* **P-in-c** L M BROWN
DEEPCAR (St John the Evangelist) *Sheff 7* **P** *Bp* **V** M WOODHEAD
DEEPING, WEST (St Andrew) *see* Uffington Gp *Linc*
DEEPING ST JAMES (St James) *Linc 13* **P** *Burghley Ho Preservation Trust* **V** *Vacant* (01778) 347995
DEEPING ST NICHOLAS (St Nicholas) *see* Spalding St Jo w Deeping St Nicholas *Linc*
DEEPLISH (St Luke) *see* Rochdale Deeplish St Luke *Man*
DEERHURST (St Mary) and Apperley w Forthampton and Chaceley *Glouc 9* **P** *Bp, Exors G J Yorke Esq, and V Longdon (jt)* **V** J E FORRYAN
DEFFORD (St James) w Besford *Worc 4* **P** *D&C Westmr* **V** P J THOMAS
DEIGHTON (All Saints) *see* Brompton w Deighton *York*
DELABOLE (St John the Evangelist) *see* St Teath *Truro*

DELAMERE (St Peter) *Ches 6* **P** *The Crown* **P-in-c** P F REYNOLDS
DELAVAL (Our Lady) *Newc 1* **P** *Lord Hastings* **V** M S JONES, **Hon C** F R HOWE
DEMBLEBY (St Lucia) *see* S Lafford *Linc*
DENABY, OLD (Mission Church) *see* Mexborough *Sheff*
DENABY MAIN (All Saints) *Sheff 8* **P** *Bp* **V** R C DAVIES
DENBURY (St Mary the Virgin) *see* Ogwell and Denbury *Ex*
DENBY (St John the Evangelist) *see* Cumberworth, Denby and Denby Dale *Wakef*
DENBY (St Mary the Virgin) *Derby 12* **P** *Mrs L B Palmer* **P-in-c** D J PHYPERS
DENBY DALE (Holy Trinity) *see* Cumberworth, Denby and Denby Dale *Wakef*
DENCHWORTH (St James) *see* Hanney, Denchworth and E Challow *Ox*
DENDRON (St Matthew) *see* Aldingham, Dendron, Rampside and Urswick *Carl*
DENESIDE (All Saints) *see* Seaham w Seaham Harbour *Dur*
DENFORD (Holy Trinity) w Ringstead *Pet 10* **P** *L Stopford-Sackville Esq* **V** F COLEMAN
DENGIE (St James) w Asheldham *Chelmsf 11* **P** *Bp* **P-in-c** I M FINN
DENHAM (St John the Baptist) *see* Hoxne w Denham, Syleham and Wingfield *St E*
DENHAM (St Mark) (St Mary the Virgin) *Ox 20* **P** *L J Way Esq* **R** J A HIRST, **C** J WILBY
DENHAM (St Mary) *see* Barrow w Denham St Mary and Higham Green *St E*
DENHAM, NEW (St Francis) *see* Denham *Ox*
DENHOLME GATE (St Paul) *Bradf 8* **P** *Bp* **P-in-c** E A THOMAS
DENMARK PARK (St Saviour) *see* Peckham St Sav *S'wark*
DENMEAD (All Saints) *Portsm 4* **P** *Ld Chan* **NSM** F R STRANACK
DENNINGTON (St Mary) *see* Badingham w Bruisyard, Cransford and Dennington *St E*
DENSHAW (Christ Church) *Man 21* **P** *Bp* **V** S C L CLAYTON
DENSTON (St Nicholas) w Stradishall and Stansfield *St E 8* **P** *Mrs G S M MacRae and Ld Chan (alt)* **V** T S WRIGHT, **NSM** P W de VOIL
DENSTONE (All Saints) w Ellastone and Stanton *Lich 15* **P** *Bp and Col Sir Walter Bromley-Davenport (jt)* **V** J R CLATWORTHY
DENT (St Andrew) w Cowgill *Bradf 6* **P** *Bp and Sidesmen of Dent (alt)* **V** C A MITCHELL
DENTON (Christ Church) *Man 17* **P** *Bp* **P-in-c** D J COX
DENTON Dane Bank (St George) *see* Denton Ch Ch *Man*
DENTON (Holy Spirit) *Newc 7* **P** *Bp* **V** B C HURST, **C** G R KELSEY
DENTON (St Andrew) *see* Harlaxton Gp *Linc*
DENTON (St Helen) *see* Weston w Denton *Bradf*
DENTON (St Lawrence) *Man 17* **P** *Earl of Wilton* **R** R CASSIDY
DENTON (St Leonard) w South Heighton and Tarring Neville *Chich 18* **P** *MMCET and Bp (alt)* **R** N A MANNING
DENTON (St Margaret) *see* Yardley Hastings, Denton and Grendon etc *Pet*
DENTON (St Mary) *see* Earsham w Alburgh and Denton *Nor*
DENTON (St Mary Magdalene) *see* Elham w Denton and Wootton *Cant*
DENTON, NETHER (St Cuthbert) *see* Gilsland w Nether Denton *Carl*
DENTON HOLME (St James) *Carl 3* **P** *Trustees* **V** J R LIBBY, **C** C J TAYLOR
DENVER (St Mary) *Ely 16* **P** *G&C Coll Cam* **P-in-c** J K ISAACS
DENVILLE (Christchurch Centre) *see* Havant *Portsm*
DEOPHAM (St Andrew) *see* High Oak *Nor*
DEPDEN (St Mary the Virgin) *see* Chedburgh w Depden, Rede and Hawkedon *St E*
DEPTFORD Brockley (St Peter) *S'wark 3* **P** *Bp* **C** B A ABAYOMI-COLE
DEPTFORD Edward Street (St Mark) *see* Deptford St Paul *S'wark*
DEPTFORD (St John) (Holy Trinity) *S'wark 3* **P** *Peache Trustees and Ch Trust Fund Trust (jt)* **V** A I KEECH, **C** C I RUSSELL
DEPTFORD (St Nicholas) (St Luke) *S'wark 3* **P** *MMCET, Peache Trustees, and CPAS (jt)* **V** W G CORNECK
DEPTFORD (St Paul) (St Mark) *S'wark 3* **P** *Bp* **R** P W FELLOWS
DERBY (St Alkmund and St Werburgh) *Derby 9* **P** *Simeon's Trustees* **V** J M WHITE, **C** M P WATSON
DERBY (St Andrew w St Osmund) *Derby 10* **P** *Bp* **V** D C MACDONALD
DERBY (St Anne) (St John the Evangelist) *Derby 9* **P** *Bp* **V** C M G BRINKWORTH
DERBY (St Augustine) *see* Walbrook Epiphany *Derby*
DERBY (St Barnabas) *Derby 9* **P** *Bp* **P-in-c** R J ELGAR
DERBY (St Bartholomew) *Derby 10* **P** *Bp* **V** A G MESSOM
DERBY (St Luke) *Derby 9* **P** *Bp* **V** M J P CAIN, **C** J H FLINT
DERBY (St Mark) *Derby 9* **P** *Bp* **V** L N CHILDS
DERBY (St Paul) *Derby 9* **P** *Bp* **V** J F LEE
DERBY (St Peter and Christ Church w Holy Trinity) *Derby 10* **P** *CPAS* **V** *Vacant* (01332) 347821
DERBY (St Thomas) *see* Walbrook Epiphany *Derby*
DERBY, WEST (Good Shepherd) *Liv 8* **P** *Bp and R W Derby (jt)* **V** T R STRATFORD, **C** A R BECK
DERBY, WEST (St James) *Liv 8* **P** *Trustees* **V** P W PLUNKETT
DERBY, WEST St John *Liv 8* **P** *Trustees* **V** T P E NENER
DERBY, WEST (St Luke) *Liv 2* **P** *Bp* **V** J H WELCH, **C** M K ROGERS
DERBY, WEST (St Mary) *Liv 8* **P** *Bp* **TR** J R I WIKELEY, **TV** T M LATHAM, **C** R WILLIAMS, J E BOWEN
DERBYHAVEN (Chapel) *see* Malew *S & M*
DEREHAM, EAST (St Nicholas) and Scarning *Nor 17* **P** *Ld Chan* **R** D W A RIDER, **C** C I GREEN
DEREHAM, WEST (St Andrew) *Ely 16* **P** *Bp* **P-in-c** J K ISAACS
DERRINGHAM BANK (Ascension) *York 15* **P** *Abp* **V** S J WHALEY, **C** P N A SENIOR, **Hon C** J BRAY
DERRINGTON (St Matthew), Haughton and Ranton *Lich 10* **P** *Bp, Mrs M N Nutt, and Trustees Earl of Lich (jt)* **R** G K SMITH
DERRY Hill (Christ Church) w Bremhill and Foxham *Sarum 18* **P** *Prime Min and V Calne and Blackland* **V** J R CARDWELL, **NSM** J W SCOTT
DERSINGHAM (St Nicholas) w Anmer and Shernborne *Nor 16* **P** *Ld Chan* **R** T P JARDINE
DESBOROUGH (St Giles) *Pet 11* **P** *Bp* **P-in-c** M P TANNER, **C** J P LEADER, **NSM** N M CLARKE
DESFORD (St Martin) and Peckleton w Tooley *Leic 12* **P** *Ld Chan* **R** *Vacant* (01455) 822276
DETHICK (St John the Baptist) *see* Tansley, Dethick, Lea and Holloway *Derby*
DETLING (St Martin) *see* Boxley w Detling *Cant*
DEVIZES (St John) (St Mary) *Sarum 19* **P** *Ld Chan* **R** *Vacant* (01380) 723705
DEVIZES (St Peter) *Sarum 19* **P** *Bp* **V** B A TIGWELL
DEVONPORT (St Aubyn) *Ex 21* **P** *The Crown and R Stoke Damerel (alt)* **P-in-c** G D CRYER, **C** P A W JONES, **Hon C** J GODFREY
DEVONPORT (St Barnabas) *Ex 21* **P** *R Stoke Damerel* **V** J E SUMMERS
DEVONPORT (St Bartholomew) *Ex 21* **P** *Bp* **P-in-c** J M ROBINSON
DEVONPORT (St Boniface) (St Philip) *Ex 21* **P** *Bp* **TR** P J LOW, **TV** N R C PEARKES
DEVONPORT (St Budeaux) *Ex 21* **P** *V Plymouth St Andr w St Paul and St Geo* **V** M D D JONES
DEVONPORT (St Mark) Ford *Ex 21* **P** *Trustees* **P-in-c** J M ROBINSON
DEVONPORT (St Michael) Stoke *Ex 21* **P** *R Stoke Damerel* **P-in-c** R J HILL
DEVORAN (St John the Evangelist and St Petroc) *Truro 6* **P** *Bp* **V** M C PALMER
DEWCHURCH, LITTLE (St David) *see* Heref S Wye *Heref*
DEWCHURCH, MUCH (St David) *see* Much Birch w Lt Birch, Much Dewchurch etc *Heref*
DEWLISH (All Saints) *see* Milborne St Andrew w Dewlish *Sarum*
DEWSALL (St Michael) *see* Heref S Wye *Heref*
DEWSBURY (All Saints) (St Mark) (St Matthew and St John the Baptist) *Wakef 11* **P** *Bp, Adn Pontefract, RD Dewsbury, and Lay Chmn Dewsbury Deanery Syn (jt)* **TR** *Vacant* (01924) 465491 or 457057
DEWSBURY (St Matthew and St John the Baptist) *see* Dewsbury *Wakef*
DEWSBURY (All Saints) *as above*
DEWSBURY (St Mark) *as above*
DEWSBURY MOOR (St John the Evangelist) *as above*
DHOON (Christ Church) *see* Maughold *S & M*
DIBDEN (All Saints) *Win 10* **P** *MMCET* **R** J D ALDERMAN, **C** M R POWIS
DIBDEN PURLIEU (St Andrew) *see* Dibden *Win*
DICKER, UPPER (Holy Trinity) *see* Hellingly and Upper Dicker *Chich*
DICKLEBURGH (All Saints) w Langmere and Shimpling, Thelveton w Frenze, Rushall *Nor 10* **P** *Ld Chan, Bp, Trin Coll Cam, MMCET, and Lady Mann (by turn)* **R** *Vacant* (01379) 741313
DIDBROOK (St George) *see* Toddington, Stanton, Didbrook w Hailes etc *Glouc*

DIDCOT (All Saints) *Ox 18* **P** *BNC Ox* **P-in-c** P A DALLAWAY, **C** J M IMPEY
DIDCOT (St Peter) *Ox 18* **P** *Bp* **P-in-c** N J GANDY, **C** R M A HANCOCK
DIDDINGTON (St Laurence) *Ely 12* **P** *G E P Thornhill Esq* **V** *Vacant*
DIDDLEBURY (St Peter) w Munslow, Holdgate and Tugford *Heref 12* **P** *Bp (3 turns), D&C(1 turn)* **R** I E GIBBS
DIDLINGTON (St Michael) *Nor 13* **P** *CPAS* **P-in-c** G R DRAKE
DIDMARTON (St Lawrence) *see* Boxwell, Leighterton, Didmarton, Oldbury etc *Glouc*
DIDSBURY (Christ Church) Barlow Moor Road *Man 8* **P** *Trustees* **R** C J S JONES
DIDSBURY (St James) (Emmanuel) *Man 8* **P** *Patr Bd* **TR** D M HUGHES, **TV** J K MILLS
DIGBY (St Thomas of Canterbury) *Linc 22* **P** *DBP and Mrs H E Gillatt (alt)* **P-in-c** R J MORRISON
DIGMOOR (Christ the Servant) *see* Upholland *Liv*
DIGSWELL (St John the Evangelist) (Christ the King) and Panshanger *St Alb 21* **P** *Patr Bd* **TR** J D THOMPSON, **TV** R A FLETCHER, **NSM** G G BROWN, K E SUCKLING, J M ANNIS
DILHAM (St Nicholas) *see* Smallburgh w Dilham w Honing and Crostwight *Nor*
DILHORNE (All Saints) *see* Caverswall and Weston Coyney w Dilhorne *Lich*
DILSTON (St Mary Magdalene) *see* Corbridge w Halton and Newton Hall *Newc*
DILTON or LEIGH (Holy Saviour) *see* Westbury *Sarum*
DILTON MARSH (Holy Trinity) *Sarum 14* **P** *Bp* **V** S F TREEBY
DILWYN AND STRETFORD (St Mary the Virgin) *see* Leominster *Heref*
DINDER (St Michael and All Angels) *see* Pilton w Croscombe, N Wootton and Dinder *B & W*
DINEDOR (St Andrew) *see* Heref S Wye *Heref*
DINGLEY (All Saints) *see* Brampton Ash w Dingley and Braybrooke *Pet*
DINNINGTON (St Leonard) *Sheff 5* **P** *J C Athorpe Esq* **R** S K PROCTOR, **C** A NASCIMENTO de JESUS
DINNINGTON (St Matthew) *see* Ch the King in the Dio of Newc *Newc*
DINNINGTON (St Nicholas) *see* Merriott w Hinton, Dinnington and Lopen *B & W*
DINSDALE (St John the Baptist) w Sockburn *Dur 8* **P** *D&C and Sherburn Hosp (alt)* **R** R R A GRAHAM
DINTING VALE (Holy Trinity) *see* Charlesworth and Dinting Vale *Derby*
DINTON (St Mary) *see* Barford St Martin, Dinton, Baverstock etc *Sarum*
DINTON (St Peter and St Paul) *see* Stone w Dinton and Hartwell *Ox*
DIPTFORD (St Mary the Virgin), North Huish, Harberton and Harbertonford *Ex 13* **P** *Mrs E P Buchanan-Allen, D&C, and Bp (jt)* **Hon C** J T GEORGE, D A LAWES
DIPTON (St John the Evangelist) and Leadgate *Dur 4* **P** *Bp* **V** D G HERON
DISCOED (St Michael) *see* Presteigne w Discoed, Kinsham and Lingen *Heref*
DISEWORTH (St Michael and All Angels) *see* Hathern, Long Whatton and Diseworth w Belton etc *Leic*
DISHFORTH (Christ Church) *see* Topcliffe w Baldersby, Dalton, Dishforth etc *York*
DISHLEY (All Saints) *see* Thorpe Acre w Dishley *Leic*
DISLEY (St Mary the Virgin) *Ches 16* **P** *Lord Newton* **V** P S DANIEL
DISS Heywood (St James the Great) *see* Diss *Nor*
DISS (St Mary) *Nor 10* **P** *Bp* **R** G C JAMES, **NSM** B J SASADA
DISTINGTON (Holy Spirit) *Carl 7* **P** *Earl of Lonsdale* **R** *Vacant* (01946) 830384
DITCHEAT (St Mary Magdalene) w East Pennard and Pylle *B & W 8* **P** *Bp and Canon D S Salter (jt)* **P-in-c** S M MUNNS
DITCHINGHAM (St Mary), Hedenham and Broome *Nor 5* **P** *Countess Ferrers and Bp (jt)* **P-in-c** J S READ
DITCHLING (St Margaret) *Chich 9* **P** *Bp* **V** K C JEFFERY
DITTERIDGE (St Christopher) *see* Box w Hazlebury and Ditteridge *Bris*
DITTISHAM (St George) *see* Ashprington, Cornworthy and Dittisham *Ex*
DITTON (St Michael) *Liv 13* **P** *Patr Bd* **TR** D R LESLIE, **TV** R S BRIDSON, **C** D J ROSCOE, **NSM** S L WILLIAMS
DITTON (St Peter ad Vincula) *Roch 7* **P** *Ch Trust Fund Trust* **R** J R TERRANOVA, **C** N J WILLIAMS
DITTON PRIORS (St John the Baptist) w Neenton, Burwarton, Cleobury North, Aston Botterell, Wheathill and Loughton *Heref 9* **P** *Bp, Viscount Boyne, and Princess Josephine zu Loewenstein (jt)* **P-in-c** D H GOOD
DIXTON (St Peter) *Heref 8* **P** *DBP* **V** B E D W PHILLIPS, **NSM** J S TUNNICLIFFE
DOBCROSS (Holy Trinity) w Scouthead (St Paul) *Man 21* **P** *Bp* **V** C W M BARLOW
DOBWALLS (St Peter) *see* Liskeard, St Keyne, St Pinnock, Morval etc *Truro*
DOCCOMBE (Chapel) *see* Moretonhampstead, Manaton, N Bovey and Lustleigh *Ex*
DOCK (Mission Church) *see* Immingham *Linc*
DOCKENFIELD (Church of the Good Shepherd) *see* Frensham *Guildf*
DOCKING (St Mary), the Birchams, Stanhoe and Sedgeford *Nor 16* **P** *Bp, D&C, and Mrs A J Ralli (3 turns), The Crown (1 turn)* **V** M P ADAMS
DOCKLOW (St Bartholomew) *see* Leominster *Heref*
DODBROOKE (St Thomas a Beckett) *see* Kingsbridge and Dodbrooke *Ex*
DODDERHILL (St Augustine) *see* Droitwich Spa *Worc*
DODDINGHURST (All Saints) and Mountnessing *Chelmsf 7* **P** *Bp* **P-in-c** A J ABBEY, **NSM** S M GRIDLEY
DODDINGTON (All Saints) *see* Quantoxhead *B & W*
DODDINGTON (St John) *see* Wybunbury w Doddington *Ches*
DODDINGTON (St John the Baptist) *see* Coreley w Doddington *Heref*
DODDINGTON (St John the Baptist), Newnham and Wychling *Cant 6* **P** *Abp, Adn, and Exors Sir John Croft, Bt (jt)* **V** *Vacant* (01795) 886265
DODDINGTON (St Mary and St Michael) *see* Glendale Gp *Newc*
DODDINGTON (St Mary) w Benwick and Wimblington *Ely 18* **P** *Bp, St Jo Coll Dur, and R Raynar Esq (jt)* **R** A L WAY
DODDINGTON (St Peter) *see* Skellingthorpe w Doddington *Linc*
DODDINGTON, GREAT (St Nicholas) and Wilby *Pet 6* **P** *Exors Lt-Col H C M Stockdale and Ld Chan (alt)* **V** D H JOHNSTON
DODDISCOMBSLEIGH (St Michael) *see* Tedburn St Mary, Whitestone, Oldridge etc *Ex*
DODFORD (Holy Trinity and St Mary) *see* Catshill and Dodford *Worc*
DODFORD (St Mary the Virgin) *see* Weedon Bec w Everdon and Dodford *Pet*
DODLESTON (St Mary) *Ches 2* **P** *D&C* **R** K G HORSWELL
DODWORTH (St John the Baptist) *Wakef 7* **P** *V Silkstone* **V** P HUMPLEBY
DOGMERSFIELD (All Saints) *see* Hartley Wintney, Elvetham, Winchfield etc *Win*
DOLPHINHOLME (St Mark) w Quernmore St Peter *Blackb 12* **P** *Bp and V Lanc (alt)* **V** L J HAKES
DOLTON (St Edmund King and Martyr) *Ex 19* **P** *Ch Soc Trust* **P-in-c** R C THORP, **NSM** D J URSELL
DONCASTER Holy Trinity *Sheff 9* **P** *SMF* **V** J P F HARRIS
DONCASTER Intake (All Saints) *Sheff 9* **P** *Bp* **V** *Vacant* (01302) 323167
DONCASTER (St George) (St Edmund's Church Centre) *Sheff 9* **P** *Bp* **V** H J J BIRD
DONCASTER (St James) *Sheff 10* **P** *Hyndman Trustees* **V** D POLLARD
DONCASTER (St Jude) *Sheff 10* **P** *Bp* **V** A J GILBERT
DONCASTER (St Leonard and St Jude) *Sheff 8* **P** *The Crown* **V** N J PAY
DONCASTER (St Mary) *Sheff 9* **P** *Hyndman Trustees* **V** J B THOMSON
DONHEAD ST ANDREW (St Andrew) *see* The Donheads *Sarum*
DONHEAD ST MARY (St Mary the Virgin) *as above*
DONHEADS, The *Sarum 13* **P** *DBP and New Coll Ox (alt)* **P-in-c** T C CURRY
DONINGTON (St Cuthbert) *Lich 20* **P** *MMCET* **P-in-c** G FROST, **C** R C HENSON
DONINGTON (St Mary and the Holy Rood) *Linc 21* **P** *Simeon's Trustees* **V** *Vacant* (01775) 820418
DONINGTON-ON-BAIN (St Andrew) *see* Asterby Gp *Linc*
DONISTHORPE (St John) and Moira w Stretton-en-le-Field *Leic 9* **P** *Ch Soc Trust (1 turn), and Bp (3 turns)* **V** A J BURGESS, **Hon C** W POPEJOY
DONNINGTON (St George) *Chich 3* **P** *Bp* **P-in-c** P TRAFFORD
DONNINGTON WOOD (St Matthew) *Lich 22* **P** *Bp* **P-in-c** D W WRIGHT
DONNISON (School) *see* Sunderland *Dur*
DONYATT (The Blessed Virgin Mary) *see* Ilminster and District *B & W*
DONYLAND, EAST (St Lawrence) *see* Fingringhoe w E Donyland and Abberton etc *Chelmsf*

DORCHESTER (St George) (St Mary the Virgin) (St Peter, Holy Trinity and All Saints) *Sarum 2* **P** *Patr Bd (3 turns), Ld Chan (1 turn)* **TR** R E H JOHNSON, **TV** D J LETCHER, A HAWTHORNE, **C** T J COOK, P F TURNBULL, **NSM** G J MUGRIDGE
DORCHESTER (St Peter and St Paul) *Ox 1* **P** *Patr Bd* **TR** J Y CROWE, **TV** A TAWN, W J M COOMBS, M P PULESTON, **NSM** R M GODFREY, M C R BRAYBROOKE, M D CHAPMAN
DORDON (St Leonard) *Birm 11* **P** *V Polesworth* **V** J D POTTER
DORE (Christ Church) *Sheff 2* **P** *Sir Stephen Hastings* **V** D G WILLIAMS, **C** M J PORTER
DORKING (St Martin) w Ranmore *Guildf 7* **P** *Bp* **V** M J FARRANT, **C** A J FORAN
DORKING (St Paul) *Guildf 7* **P** *Ch Patr Trust* **V** A S W CULLIS, **C** A YOUINGS
DORMANSLAND (St John) *S'wark 25* **P** *Bp* **V** D A RICHARDSON
DORMANSTOWN (All Saints) *York 17* **P** *Abp* **V** W BARNES
DORMINGTON (St Peter) *see* Fownhope w Mordiford, Brockhampton etc *Heref*
DORMSTON (St Nicholas) *see* Inkberrow w Cookhill and Kington w Dormston *Worc*
DORNEY (St James the Less) *see* Riverside *Ox*
DORRIDGE (St Philip) *Birm 6* **P** *Bp* **V** J A STEVENS, **C** P D HALL
DORRINGTON (St Edward) w Leebotwood, Longnor, Stapleton, Smethcote and Woolstaston *Heref 11* **P** *DBP and J J C Coldwell Esq (jt)* **R** R S PAYNE, **NSM** M G GILLIONS
DORRINGTON (St James) *see* Digby *Linc*
DORSINGTON (St Peter) *see* Pebworth w Dorsington and Honeybourne *Glouc*
DORSTONE (St Faith) *see* Peterchurch w Vowchurch, Turnastone and Dorstone *Heref*
DORTON (St John the Baptist) *see* Brill, Boarstall, Chilton and Dorton *Ox*
DOSTHILL (St Paul) *Birm 11* **P** *Bp* **V** R G SHARPE
DOTTERY (St Saviour) *see* Askerswell, Loders and Powerstock *Sarum*
DOUGLAS (Christ Church) *Blackb 4* **P** *Bp* **V** B E HARDING
DOUGLAS (St George) and St Barnabas w (All Saints) *S & M 2* **P** *Bp* **V** B H PARTINGTON, **Hon C** J P HEBDEN, **NSM** R HARPER
DOUGLAS (St Matthew the Apostle) *S & M 2* **P** *Bp* **V** D WHITWORTH, **Hon C** J W R C SARKIES, **NSM** N PILLING
DOUGLAS (St Ninian) *S & M 2* **P** *CPAS* **V** G C GRINHAM, **NSM** G B QUINN
DOUGLAS (St Thomas the Apostle) *S & M 2* **P** *Bp* **V** A J FITCH, **C** D A GUEST
DOUGLAS-IN-PARBOLD (Christ Church) *see* Douglas *Blackb*
DOULTING (St Aldhelm) *see* Shepton Mallet w Doulting *B & W*
DOVE HOLES (St Paul) *see* Wormhill, Peak Forest w Peak Dale and Dove Holes *Derby*
DOVECOT (Holy Spirit) *Liv 2* **P** *Bp* **V** D G R BEARDSLEY, **C** N J ANDREWES
DOVER Buckland Valley (St Nicholas) *see* Buckland in Dover w Buckland Valley *Cant*
DOVER (St Martin) *Cant 4* **P** *CPAS* **V** K G GARRETT
DOVER (St Mary the Virgin) *Cant 4* **P** *Abp, Ld Warden of Cinque Ports, and Ld Lt of Kent (jt)* **V** G J BATTEN
DOVER (St Peter and St Paul) *see* Charlton-in-Dover *Cant*
DOVERCOURT (All Saints) and Parkeston w Harwich *Chelmsf 20* **P** *Bp and DBP (alt)* **R** S HARDIE, **C** K L JUSTICE, **NSM** G C GREENSLADE
DOVERDALE (St Mary) *see* Ombersley w Doverdale *Worc*
DOVERIDGE (St Cuthbert) *Derby 14* **P** *Duke of Devonshire* **P-in-c** D MILNER, **NSM** P R JONES
DOVERSGREEN (St Peter) *see* Reigate St Luke S Park *S'wark*
DOWDESWELL (St Michael) and Andoversford w the Shiptons and Cold Salperton *Glouc 14* **P** *Mrs L E Evans, MMCET, and Bp (jt)* **P-in-c** R A B MORRIS
DOWLAND (not known) *see* Iddesleigh w Dowland *Ex*
DOWLES Button Oak (St Andrew) *see* Ribbesford w Bewdley and Dowles *Worc*
DOWLISHWAKE (St Andrew) *see* Ilminster and District *B & W*
DOWN, East (St John the Baptist) *see* Shirwell, Loxhore, Kentisbury, Arlington, etc *Ex*
DOWN AMPNEY (All Saints) *see* S Cerney w Cerney Wick and Down Ampney *Glouc*
DOWN HATHERLEY (St Mary and Corpus Christi) *see* Twigworth, Down Hatherley, Norton, The Leigh etc *Glouc*
DOWN ST MARY (St Mary the Virgin) *see* N Creedy *Ex*
DOWNDERRY (St Nicholas) *see* St Germans *Truro*
DOWNE (St Mary Magdalene) *see* Cudham and Downe *Roch*
DOWNEND (Christ Church) (Church Centre) *Bris 7* **P** *Peache Trustees* **V** A O JOYCE, **C** H A C MORSE, R H HAYES, **Hon C** G C HART
DOWNHAM (St Barnabas) *see* Catford (Southend) and Downham *S'wark*
DOWNHAM (St Leonard) *Blackb 8* **P** *Lord Clitheroe* **V** *Vacant* (01200) 41379
DOWNHAM (St Leonard) *Ely 14* **P** *Bp* **R** *Vacant* (01353) 699337
DOWNHAM (St Luke) *see* Catford (Southend) and Downham *S'wark*
DOWNHAM (St Margaret) w South Hanningfield *Chelmsf 9* **P** *Bp* **R** D J ATKINS, **NSM** J M ALLWRIGHT
DOWNHAM, NORTH (St Mark) *see* Catford (Southend) and Downham *S'wark*
DOWNHAM MARKET (St Edmund) w Bexwell *Ely 16* **P** *Bp* **R** P F KEELING
DOWNHEAD (All Saints) *see* Leigh upon Mendip w Stoke St Michael *B & W*
DOWNHOLME (St Michael and All Angels) and Marske *Ripon 2* **P** *Bp* **C** H C STOKER
DOWNLEY (St James the Great) *see* High Wycombe *Ox*
DOWNS BARN and NEAT HILL (Community Church) *see* Stantonbury and Willen *Ox*
DOWNSBY (St Andrew) *see* Billingborough Gp *Linc*
DOWNSIDE (St Michael's Chapel) *see* Ockham w Hatchford *Guildf*
DOWNSWAY (All Souls Worship Centre) *see* Southwick *Chich*
DOWNTON (St Giles) *see* Wigmore Abbey *Heref*
DOWNTON (St Lawrence) *Sarum 11* **P** *Win Coll* **V** M C GALLAGHER
DOXEY (St Thomas and St Andrew) *see* Castle Town *Lich*
DOYNTON (Holy Trinity) *see* Wick w Doynton and Dyrham *Bris*
DRAKES BROUGHTON (St Barnabas) *see* Stoulton w Drake's Broughton and Pirton etc *Worc*
DRAUGHTON (St Augustine) *see* Skipton H Trin *Bradf*
DRAUGHTON (St Catherine) *see* Maidwell w Draughton, Lamport w Faxton *Pet*
DRAX (St Peter and St Paul) *see* Carlton and Drax *York*
DRAYCOT *Bris 9* **P** *Bp, D&C Sarum, and R W Neeld Esq (jt)* **R** T W HARRIS
DRAYCOTT (St Mary) *see* Wilne and Draycott w Breaston *Derby*
DRAYCOTT (St Peter) *see* Rodney Stoke w Draycott *B & W*
DRAYCOTT IN THE CLAY (St Augustine) *see* Hanbury w Newborough and Rangemore *Lich*
DRAYCOTT-LE-MOORS (St Margaret) w Forsbrook *Lich 6* **P** *Bp* **R** B L WHITTAKER
DRAYTON (Iron Mission Room) *see* Chaddesley Corbett and Stone *Worc*
DRAYTON (St Catherine) *see* Langport Area Chs *B & W*
DRAYTON (St Leonard and St Catherine) *see* Dorchester *Ox*
DRAYTON (St Margaret) w Felthorpe *Nor 2* **P** *Bp* **R** P H HARRISON, **C** M M KINGSTON
DRAYTON (St Peter) *see* Ironstone *Ox*
DRAYTON (St Peter) Berks *Ox 10* **P** *Bp* **NSM** T A SCOTT
DRAYTON, EAST (St Peter) *see* Dunham-on-Trent w Darlton, Ragnall etc *S'well*
DRAYTON, LITTLE (Christ Church) *Lich 18* **P** *V Drayton in Hales* **V** J O DAVIES
DRAYTON, WEST (St Martin) *Lon 24* **P** *Bp* **V** T SAMUEL
DRAYTON, WEST (St Paul) *see* Gamston w Eaton and W Drayton *S'well*
DRAYTON BASSETT (St Peter) *Lich 4* **P** *Bp* **R** H J BAKER, **C** P E R HALL
DRAYTON-BEAUCHAMP (St Mary the Virgin) *see* Aston Clinton w Buckland and Drayton Beauchamp *Ox*
DRAYTON IN HALES (St Mary) *Lich 18* **P** *C C Corbet Esq* **P-in-c** G D PRICE, **NSM** J T SMITH
DRAYTON PARSLOW (Holy Trinity) *see* Stewkley w Soulbury and Drayton Parslow *Ox*
DRESDEN (Resurrection) *Lich 12* **P** *V Blurton* **V** H F HARPER
DREWSTEIGNTON (Holy Trinity) *Ex 12* **P** *Exors B Drewe* **R** C J L NAPIER, **NSM** J G WITHERS
DRIFFIELD (St Mary) *see* The Ampneys w Driffield and Poulton *Glouc*
DRIFFIELD, GREAT (All Saints) and LITTLE (St Peter) *York 11* **P** *Abp* **V** R E CARLILL, **C** S E CEELY, **Hon C** A J E KIDD
DRIGG (St Peter) *see* Seascale and Drigg *Carl*
DRIGHLINGTON (St Paul) *Wakef 8* **P** *Bp* **V** P A CRABB
DRIMPTON (St Mary) *see* Beaminster Area *Sarum*
DRINGHOUSES (St Edward the Confessor) *York 8* **P** *Abp* **V** A M GIRLING

DRINKSTONE (All Saints) *see* Woolpit w Drinkstone *St E*
DROITWICH SPA (St Andrew w St Mary de Witton) (St Nicholas) (St Peter) (St Richard) *Worc 8* **P** *Bp* **TR** P BRISTOW, **TV** S K BANYARD, **Hon C** S W GODFREY
DRONFIELD (St John the Baptist) w Holmesfield *Derby 5* **P** *Ld Chan* **TR** B GREEN, **TV** R P TUCKER, P R SANDFORD, M D LILES
DROPMORE (St Anne) *see* Burnham w Dropmore, Hitcham and Taplow *Ox*
DROXFORD (St Mary and All Saints) *Portsm 1* **P** *Bp* **R** D E HENLEY, **NSM** P FLETCHER
DROYLSDEN (St Andrew) *Man 17* **P** *Bp* **R** I BLAY
DROYLSDEN (St Martin) *Man 17* **P** *Bp* **V** B LIPSCOMBE
DROYLSDEN (St Mary) (St John) *Man 17* **P** *Bp* **R** M J WILLIAMSON
DRY DODDINGTON (St James) *see* Claypole *Linc*
DRY DRAYTON (St Peter and St Paul) *Ely 5* **P** *MMCET* **R** *Vacant*
DRY SANDFORD (St Helen) *see* Besselsleigh w Dry Sandford *Ox*
DRYBROOK (Holy Trinity) *see* Dean Forest H Trin *Glouc*
DRYPOOL (St Columba) (St John) *York 15* **P** *Patr Bd* **TR** P R W HARRISON, **TV** R P YATES, P A WICK, **C** J A EVANS
DUCKLINGTON (St Bartholomew) *Ox 8* **P** *DBP* **P-in-c** C HORSEMAN, **NSM** R J EDY
DUCKMANTON (St Peter and St Paul) *see* Calow and Sutton cum Duckmanton *Derby*
DUDDENHOE END (The Hamlet Church) *see* Heydon, Gt and Lt Chishill, Chrishall etc *Chelmsf*
DUDDESTON St Matthew w Nechells *Birm 8* **P** *Bp and V Aston-juxta-Birm (jt)* **P-in-c** S R PALMER, **C** M O HEFFERNAN
DUDDINGTON (St Mary) *see* Easton on the Hill, Collyweston w Duddington etc *Pet*
DUDDO (All Saints) *see* Norham and Duddo *Newc*
DUDDON (St Peter) *see* Tarvin *Ches*
DUDLESTON (St Mary) *see* Criftins w Dudleston and Welsh Frankton *Lich*
DUDLEY (St Andrew) *see* Netherton St Andr *Worc*
DUDLEY (St Augustine) Holly Hall *Worc 9* **P** *V Dudley* **P-in-c** A M YATES
DUDLEY (St Barnabas) *Worc 9* **P** *Bp* **V** P G GREEN
DUDLEY (St Edmund King and Martyr) *Worc 9* **P** *V Dudley* **V** M C BRAIN
DUDLEY (St Francis) *Worc 9* **P** *Bp* **V** J G PRYSOR-JONES, **NSM** G S JOHNSTON
DUDLEY (St James the Great) Eve Hill *Worc 9* **P** *V Dudley* **Dn-in-c** S YATES
DUDLEY (St John) Kate's Hill *Worc 9* **P** *V Dudley* **V** J W KNIGHTS
DUDLEY (St Paul) *see* Weetslade *Newc*
DUDLEY (St Thomas and St Luke) *Worc 9* **P** *Bp* **V** M J GOSS
DUDLEY WOOD (St John) *Worc 9* **P** *V Netherton* **V** S G F OWENS
DUFFIELD (St Alkmund) *Derby 11* **P** *Ch Soc Trust* **V** D A WILKINSON
DUFTON (St Cuthbert) *see* Long Marton w Dufton and w Milburn *Carl*
DUKINFIELD (St John) (St Alban Mission Church) *Ches 14* **P** *R Stockport St Mary* **P-in-c** T J HAYES
DUKINFIELD (St Mark) (St Luke) *Ches 14* **P** *Bp* **V** E W D THOMAS
DULAS (St Michael) *see* Ewyas Harold w Dulas, Kenderchurch etc *Heref*
DULCOTE (All Saints) *see* Wells St Cuth w Wookey Hole *B & W*
DULLINGHAM (St Mary) *Ely 4* **P** *P B Taylor Esq* **P-in-c** J S ASKEY
DULOE (St Cuby) w Herodsfoot *Truro 12* **P** *Ball Coll Ox* **P-in-c** D J BURLEIGH
DULVERTON (All Saints) and Brushford *B & W 16* **P** *D&C and Bp (jt)* **R** A R N APPLEBY
DULWICH (St Barnabas) *S'wark 8* **P** *Bp* **V** R M CATTLEY, **C** D L HARTLEY, **Hon C** J G WINTER, M E JACKSON, **NSM** J BROTHWOOD
DULWICH (St Clement) St Peter *S'wark 8* **P** *Bp* **V** P J E MACAN, **C** J M McLAREN
DULWICH, EAST (St John) *S'wark 8* **P** *Ripon Coll Cuddesdon* **C** P E COLLIER, **Hon C** C HAYWARD
DULWICH, NORTH (St Faith) *S'wark 8* **P** *Bp* **V** S M BURDETT, **C** G W GODDARD
DULWICH, SOUTH (St Stephen) *S'wark 8* **P** *Dulwich Coll* **V** P VANNOZZI
DULWICH, WEST (All Saints) *S'wark 14* **P** *Bp* **V** R J TITLEY, **C** S J ROBBINS-COLE
DULWICH, WEST (Emmanuel) *S'wark 14* **P** *Bp* **V** K G A ANSAH, **Hon C** H O KIMBER
DUMBLETON (St Peter) *see* Alderton, Gt Washbourne, Dumbleton etc *Glouc*
DUMMER (All Saints) *see* Cliddesden and Ellisfield w Farleigh Wallop etc *Win*
DUNCHIDEOCK (St Michael and All Angels) and Shillingford St George w Ide *Ex 6* **P** *D&C and Mrs J M Michelmore (alt)* **R** *Vacant* (01392) 832589
DUNCHURCH (St Peter) *Cov 6* **P** *Bp* **V** R P C ELVERSON, **NSM** J W T ROGERS
DUNCTON (Holy Trinity) *Chich 11* **P** *Lord Egremont* **P-in-c** C D BIDDELL
DUNDRY (St Michael) *see* Chew Magna w Dundry *B & W*
DUNGEON HILL *Sarum 4* **P** *DBP, Col J L Yeatman, Mrs C B Ireland-Smith, and N G Halsey Esq (jt)* **R** D HOPLEY
DUNHAM, GREAT (St Andrew) and LITTLE (St Margaret), w Great and Little Fransham and Sporle *Nor 14* **P** *Hertf Coll Ox, Ch Soc Trust, Magd Coll Cam, and DBP (by turn)* **R** B R A COLE
DUNHAM MASSEY (St Margaret) (St Mark) (All Saints) *Ches 10* **P** *J G Turnbull Esq* **P-in-c** B HIGGINS
DUNHAM-ON-THE-HILL (St Luke) *see* Helsby and Dunham-on-the-Hill *Ches*
DUNHAM-ON-TRENT (St Oswald) w Darlton, Ragnall, Fledborough and East Drayton *S'well 5* **P** *Bp (2 turns), D&C York (1 turn)* **P-in-c** J CALVERT
DUNHOLME (St Chad) *see* Welton and Dunholme w Scothern *Linc*
DUNKERTON (All Saints) *see* Camerton w Dunkerton, Foxcote and Shoscombe *B & W*
DUNKESWELL (Holy Trinity) (St Nicholas), Sheldon and Luppitt *Ex 5* **P** *MMCET and Bp (jt)* **V** N J WALL
DUNMOW, GREAT (St Mary the Virgin) and Barnston *Chelmsf 18* **P** *Ld Chan (2 turns), CPAS (1 turn)* **R** K G HOLLOWAY, **NSM** R DREW
DUNMOW, LITTLE (not known) *see* Felsted and Lt Dunmow *Chelmsf*
DUNNINGTON (not known) *see* Salford Priors *Cov*
DUNNINGTON (St Nicholas) *see* Beeford w Frodingham and Foston *York*
DUNNINGTON (St Nicholas) *York 4* **P** *Abp* **R** J D WALKER
DUNS TEW (St Mary Magdalene) *see* Westcote Barton w Steeple Barton, Duns Tew etc *Ox*
DUNSBY (All Saints) *see* Ringstone in Aveland Gp *Linc*
DUNSCROFT (St Edwin) *Sheff 11* **P** *Bp* **V** S J RAINE, **P-in-c** A WATSON
DUNSDEN (All Saints) *see* Shiplake w Dunsden *Ox*
DUNSFOLD (St Mary and All Saints) *Guildf 2* **P** *Ld Chan* **R** G S M WILLIS
DUNSFORD (St Mary) *see* Tedburn St Mary, Whitestone, Oldridge etc *Ex*
DUNSFORTH (St Mary) *see* Aldborough w Boroughbridge and Roecliffe *Ripon*
DUNSLAND (Mission Church) *see* Ashwater, Halwill, Beaworthy, Clawton etc *Ex*
DUNSLEY (Mission Room) *see* Aislaby and Ruswarp *York*
DUNSMORE (Chapel of the Ressurection) *see* Ellesborough, The Kimbles and Stoke Mandeville *Ox*
DUNSOP BRIDGE (St George) *see* Slaidburn *Bradf*
DUNSTABLE (St Augustine of Canterbury) (St Fremund the Martyr) (St Peter) *St Alb 12* **P** *Bp* **TR** G H NEWTON, **TV** A J M SINCLAIR, J H HARRIS, R F WATSON
DUNSTALL (St Mary) *see* Barton under Needwood w Dunstall *Lich*
DUNSTAN (St Leonard) *see* Penkridge Team *Lich*
DUNSTAN (St Peter) *see* Metheringham w Blankney and Dunston *Linc*
DUNSTER (St George), Carhampton and Withycombe w Rodhuish *B & W 16* **P** *Bp* **R** M P GRANTHAM, **C** S STUCKES
DUNSTON (Church House) *see* Newbold w Dunston and Gt Barlow *Derby*
DUNSTON (St Nicholas) w (Christ Church) *Dur 13* **P** *Bp* **V** K TEASDALE
DUNSTON (St Remigius) *see* Stoke H Cross w Dunston, Arminghall etc *Nor*
DUNSWELL (St Faith's Mission Church) *see* Hull Newland St Jo *York*
DUNTERTON (All Saints) *see* Milton Abbot, Dunterton, Lamerton etc *Ex*
DUNTISBOURNE ABBOTS (St Peter) *see* Brimpsfield w Birdlip, Syde, Daglingworth, etc *Glouc*
DUNTISBOURNE ROUS (St Michael and All Angels) *as above*
DUNTON (St Martin) *see* Schorne *Ox*
DUNTON (St Mary Magdalene) w Wrestlingworth and Eyeworth *St Alb 11* **P** *Ld Chan and DBP (alt)* **P-in-c** D K DAWES
DUNTON BASSETT (All Saints) *see* Leire w Ashby Parva and Dunton Bassett *Leic*
DUNWICH (St James) *see* Westleton w Dunwich *St E*

DURHAM (St Cuthbert) *Dur 1* **P** *D&C* **V** D J BELL, **C** R N INNES, **NSM** B MIDDLEBROOK
DURHAM (St Giles) *Dur 1* **P** *D&C* **V** T W THUBRON, **NSM** D J WILSON
DURHAM (St Margaret of Antioch) *Dur 1* **P** *D&C* **P-in-c** D C GLOVER
DURHAM (St Nicholas) *Dur 1* **P** *CPAS* **V** M J WILCOCK, **C** D R HANSON
DURHAM (St Oswald King and Martyr) *Dur 1* **P** *D&C* **V** B J H de la MARE, **C** J HIRST
DURLEIGH (not known) *see* Bridgwater St Mary, Chilton Trinity and Durleigh *B & W*
DURLEY (Holy Cross) *Portsm 1* **P** *Ld Chan* **NSM** D R TOWNSEND
DURNFORD (St Andrew) *see* Woodford Valley *Sarum*
DURRINGTON (All Saints) *Sarum 12* **P** *D&C Win* **R** P H TAMPLIN
DURRINGTON (St Symphorian) *Chich 5* **P** *Bp* **V** R N AITON, **C** K SMITH
DURSLEY (St James the Great) *Glouc 2* **P** *Bp* **R** J B HUNNISETT
DURSTON (St John the Baptist) *see* N Newton w St Michaelchurch, Thurloxton etc *B & W*
DURWESTON (St Nicholas) *see* Pimperne, Stourpaine, Durweston and Bryanston *Sarum*
DUSTON Team, The (St Francis) (St Luke) *Pet 7* **P** *Bp* **TR** N C DENT, **TV** M S VAYRO, A Q MICKLETHWAITE, **NSM** Y H CHAPMAN
DUSTON, NEW (Mission Church) *see* Duston Team *Pet*
DUTTON (Licensed Room) *see* Lt Leigh and Lower Whitley *Ches*
DUXFORD (St Peter) w St John *Ely 7* **P** *Bp* **R** J E E CHARMAN, **C** B TETLEY, **NSM** P F NEWLAND
DYMCHURCH (St Peter and St Paul) w Burmarsh and Newchurch *Cant 13* **P** *Abp* **R** P N ASHMAN
DYMOCK (St Mary the Virgin) w Donnington and Kempley *Glouc 3* **P** *Pemb Coll Ox, Bp, and R D Marcon Esq (by turn)* **P-in-c** R HART
DYRHAM (St Peter) *see* Wick w Doynton and Dyrham *Bris*
EAGLE (All Saints) *see* Swinderby *Linc*
EAKRING (St Andrew) *S'well 15* **P** *DBP* **R** H H WILCOX
EALING (All Saints) *Lon 22* **P** *Bp* **V** N P HENDERSON, **C** R W BUCKLEY
EALING (Ascension) *see* Hanger Hill Ascension and W Twyford St Mary *Lon*
EALING (Christ the Saviour) *Lon 22* **P** *Bp* **V** A F DAVIS, **C** J B PENMAN, **NSM** D E BIRT
EALING (St Barnabas) *Lon 22* **P** *Bp* **V** G A REDDINGTON, **NSM** M H GREEN
EALING (St Mary) *Lon 22* **P** *Bp* **V** D R HOLT, **C** J E PETERSEN
EALING (St Paul) *Lon 22* **P** *Bp* **V** M P MELLUISH, **C** A W KILPATRICK
EALING (St Peter) Mount Park *Lon 22* **P** *Bp* **V** W H TAYLOR, **C** A D WILLIAMS
EALING (St Stephen) Castle Hill *Lon 22* **P** *D&C St Paul's* **V** J E CLARK, **NSM** J M WINFIELD
EALING, WEST (St John) w St James *Lon 22* **P** *Bp* **V** I N FISHWICK, **TV** D E SMITH, **C** M Q BRATTON, **NSM** G M DALLOW
EALING COMMON (St Matthew) *Lon 22* **P** *Bp* **V** P G WATKINS
EARBY (All Saints) *Bradf 7* **P** *Bp* **V** R C WALLACE
EARDISLAND (St Mary the Virgin) *see* Kingsland w Eardisland, Aymestrey etc *Heref*
EARDISLEY (St Mary Magdalene) w Bollingham, Willersley, Brilley, Michaelchurch, Whitney and Winforton *Heref 5* **P** *Bp, Mrs C E Hope, and Exors Mrs A M Dew (jt)* **P-in-c** J S POLLOCK
EARL SHILTON (St Simon and St Jude) w Elmesthorpe *Leic 13* **P** *Bp* **V** G GITTINGS
EARL SOHAM (St Mary) w Cretingham and Ashfield cum Thorpe *St E 18* **P** *Lord Henniker, Ld Chan, and Wadh Coll Ox (by turn)* **R** *Vacant* (01728) 685778
EARL STERNDALE (St Michael and All Angels) *see* Hartington, Biggin and Earl Sterndale *Derby*
EARL STONHAM (St Mary) *see* Creeting St Mary, Creeting St Peter etc *St E*
EARLESFIELD (The Epiphany) *see* Grantham *Linc*
EARLESTOWN (St John the Baptist) *Liv 16* **P** *R Wargrave* **V** M BUCKLEY
EARLEY (St Nicolas) *Ox 15* **P** *DBP* **P-in-c** T C PLATTS, **Hon C** W P COOPER
EARLEY (St Peter) *Ox 15* **P** *DBP* **V** R R D SPEARS, **C** J R HICKS
EARLEY Trinity *Ox 15* **P** *DBP* **P-in-c** S C HOWARD
EARLEY, LOWER Trinity Church Local Ecumenical Project *Ox 15 Vacant*
EARLHAM (St Anne) *Nor 3* **P** *Bp* **V** P R OLIVER, **C** N A SULLIVAN
EARLHAM (St Elizabeth) *Nor 3* **P** *Bp* **P-in-c** S M B WELLS
EARLHAM (St Mary) *Nor 3* **P** *Trustees* **P-in-c** P G RUTHERFORD
EARLS BARTON (All Saints) *Pet 6* **P** *DBP* **V** M C W WEBBER
EARLS COLNE (St Andrew) w White Colne and Colne Engaine *Chelmsf 19* **P** *DBP, Ch Hosp, and Keble Coll Ox (by turn)* **R** J E F JASPER
EARL'S COURT (St Cuthbert) (St Matthias) *Lon 12* **P** *Trustees* **V** J VINE, **NSM** W J A KIRKPATRICK
EARLS CROOME (St Nicholas) *see* Ripple, Earls Croome w Hill Croome and Strensham *Worc*
EARL'S HEATON *see* Dewsbury *Wakef*
EARL'S HEATON (St Peter) *as above*
EARLSDON (St Barbara) *Cov 3* **P** *Bp* **V** T C BROOKE
EARLSFIELD (St Andrew) *S'wark 19* **P** *Bp* **V** C W PRITCHARD
EARLSFIELD (St John the Divine) *S'wark 19* **P** *Bp* **V** C E ROBERTS
EARLY (St Bartholomew) *see* Reading St Luke w St Bart *Ox*
EARNLEY (not known) and East Wittering *Chich 3* **P** *Bp (2 turns), Bp Lon (1 turn)* **R** J H LYON
EARNSHAW BRIDGE (St John) *see* Leyland St Jo *Blackb*
EARSDON (St Alban) and Backworth *Newc 8* **P** *Bp* **V** N WILSON
EARSHAM (All Saints) w Alburgh and Denton *Nor 10* **P** *Abp, J M Meade Esq, and St Jo Coll Cam (by turn)* **R** J S READ
EARSWICK, NEW (St Andrew) *see* Huntington *York*
EARTHAM (St Margaret) *see* Slindon, Eartham and Madehurst *Chich*
EASBY (Chapel) *see* Gt Ayton w Easby and Newton in Cleveland *York*
EASBY (St Agatha) w Brompton on Swale and Bolton on Swale *Ripon 2* **P** *Bp* **V** R M WIGRAM
EASEBOURNE (St Mary) *Chich 10* **P** *Cowdray Trust* **V** M C JUDGE
EASINGTON (All Saints) w Liverton *York 17* **P** *Ld Chan* **R** P F LANGFORD
EASINGTON (All Saints) w Skeffling, Kilnsea and Holmpton *York 13* **P** *Ld Chan* **R** W J G HEALE
EASINGTON (St Hugh) *see* Banbury *Ox*
EASINGTON (St Mary) *Dur 2* **P** *Bp* **R** N P VINE
EASINGTON (St Peter) *see* Ewelme, Brightwell Baldwin, Cuxham w Easington *Ox*
EASINGTON COLLIERY (Ascension) *Dur 2* **P** *Bp* **V** *Vacant* 0191-527 0272
EASINGWOLD (St John the Baptist and All Saints) w Raskelfe *York 5* **P** *Abp* **V** T HART
EAST *see also under substantive place name*
EAST DEAN (All Saints) *Chich 13* **P** *Bp* **V** P M JENKINS
EAST FERRY (St Mary the Virgin) *see* Scotter w E Ferry *Linc*
EAST HAM (St Bartholomew) (St Mary Magdalene) w Upton Park *Chelmsf 3* **P** *Patr Bd* **TV** Q B D PEPPIATT, J BROWN, **C** S I LAMB
EAST HAM (St George w St Ethelbert) *Chelmsf 3* **P** *Bp* **P-in-c** P C TURNER
EAST HAM (St Paul) *Chelmsf 3* **P** *Ch Patr Trust* **V** J R ALLCOCK
EAST LANE (St Mary) *see* W Horsley *Guildf*
EAST ORCHARD (St Thomas) *see* Shaston *Sarum*
EASTBOURNE (All Saints) *Chich 16* **P** *Trustees* **V** G T RIDEOUT, **C** P J COEKIN, **Hon C** P S PLUNKETT
EASTBOURNE (All Souls) *Chich 16* **P** *Ch Soc Trust and J H Cordle Esq (jt)* **V** R H G MASON
EASTBOURNE (Christ Church) *Chich 16* **P** *V Eastbourne* **V** P A S FORDHAM
EASTBOURNE (Holy Trinity) *Chich 16* **P** *V Eastbourne* **V** K H BLYTH, **C** P DUNTHORNE, **NSM** K C LEFROY
EASTBOURNE (St Andrew) *Chich 16* **P** *Bp* **V** A F STONE, **C** R J S CATCHPOLE
EASTBOURNE (St Elisabeth) *Chich 16* **P** *Bp* **P-in-c** D W PROUT
EASTBOURNE (St John) Meads *Chich 16* **P** *Trustees* **V** A McCABE, **NSM** B H JEFFORD
EASTBOURNE (St Mary) *Chich 16* **P** *Bp* **V** N S READE, **C** K R C AGNEW
EASTBOURNE (St Michael and All Angels) Ocklynge *Chich 16* **P** *V Eastbourne* **V** J C T HARRINGTON, **Dss** W K HAMBLY
EASTBOURNE (St Philip) *Chich 16* **P** *Bp* **V** R C COLES
EASTBOURNE (St Richard of Chichester) *see* Langney *Chich*
EASTBOURNE (St Saviour and St Peter) *Chich 16* **P** *Keble Coll Ox* **V** D MOTTERSHEAD, **Hon Par Dn** B R RUNDLE
EASTBURY (St James the Great) and East Garston *Ox 14* **P** *Bp and Ch Ch Ox (alt)* **P-in-c** W J STEWART
EASTCHURCH (All Saints) w Leysdown and Harty *Cant 14* **P** *Abp and Keble Coll Ox (jt)* **R** L C MEPSTED

EASTCOMBE (St Augustine) *see* Bussage *Glouc*
EASTCOTE (St Lawrence) *Lon 24* **P** *Bp* **V** D COLEMAN, **C** A V COLEMAN, M F BOLLEY
EASTER, HIGH (St Mary the Virgin) and Good Easter w Margaret Roding *Chelmsf 18* **P** *Bp Lon, Trustees R K Shepherd Esq, and D&C St Paul's (by turn)* **R** *Vacant* (01245) 231429
EASTERGATE (St George) *see* Aldingbourne, Barnham and Eastergate *Chich*
EASTERN GREEN (St Andrew) *Cov 3* **P** *R Allesley* **V** J A DAVIES
EASTERTON (St Barnabas) *see* Market Lavington and Easterton *Sarum*
EASTFIELD (Holy Nativity) *see* Cayton w Eastfield *York*
EASTGATE (All Saints) w Rookhope *Dur 9* **P** *Bp and Ld Chan (alt)* **C** J D F INKPIN, **Hon C** P H JONES
EASTHAM (St Mary the Blessed Virgin) (St Peter's Chapel) (Chapel of the Holy Spirit) *Ches 9* **P** *D&C* **V** A L WINSTANLEY, **C** D W JACKSON
EASTHAM (St Peter and St Paul) *see* Teme Valley S *Worc*
EASTHAMPSTEAD (St Michael and St Mary Magdalene) *Ox 11* **P** *Ch Ch Ox* **R** O SIMON, **C** R G BURGESS
EASTHOPE (St Peter) *see* Wenlock *Heref*
EASTHORPE (St Mary the Virgin) *see* Copford w Easthorpe and Messing w Inworth *Chelmsf*
EASTINGTON (St Michael and All Angels) and Frocester *Glouc 8* **P** *Lady Cooper and DBP (alt)* **P-in-c** N E L BAKER
EASTLEACH (St Andrew) *see* Coln St Aldwyns, Hatherop, Quenington etc *Glouc*
EASTLEIGH (All Saints) *Win 9* **P** *Bp* **V** R P DAVIES, **C** P R LECKEY
EASTLEIGH Nightingale Avenue (St Francis) *see* Eastleigh *Win*
EASTLING (St Mary) w Ospringe and Stalisfield w Otterden *Cant 6* **P** *The Crown* **R** D W TURTON, **NSM** P A FENTON, P J POLLARD
EASTMOORS (St Mary Magdalene) *see* Helmsley *York*
EASTNEY (St Margaret) *Portsm 6* **P** *Bp* **V** *Vacant* (01705) 731316
EASTNOR (St John the Baptist) *see* Ledbury w Eastnor *Heref*
EASTOFT (St Bartholomew) *see* The Marshland *Sheff*
EASTOKE (St Andrew) *see* Hayling Is St Andr *Portsm*
EASTON (All Hallows) *Bris 4* **P** *R Bris St Steph* **P-in-c** K NEWTON
EASTON (All Saints) *see* Wickham Market w Pettistree and Easton *St E*
EASTON (Holy Trinity w St Gabriel and St Lawrence and St Jude) *Bris 4* **P** *Trustees* **V** W R DONALDSON, **C** R Q THOMPSON
EASTON (St Mary) *see* Itchen Valley *Win*
EASTON (St Paul) *see* Westbury sub Mendip w Easton *B & W*
EASTON (St Peter) *Ely 10* **P** *Bp* **P-in-c** J ALFORD
EASTON (St Peter) w Colton and Marlingford *Nor 17* **P** *Ld Chan, E C Evans-Lombe Esq, and Adn Norfolk (by turn)* **P-in-c** J B LUMBY
EASTON, GREAT (St Andrew) *see* Six Saints circa Holt *Leic*
EASTON, GREAT (St John and St Giles) *see* Broxted w Chickney and Tilty etc *Chelmsf*
EASTON, LITTLE (not known) *as above*
EASTON GREY (not known) *see* Sherston Magna, Easton Grey, Luckington etc *Bris*
EASTON IN GORDANO (St George) *see* Pill w Easton in Gordano and Portbury *B & W*
EASTON MAUDIT (St Peter and St Paul) *see* Bozeat w Easton Maudit *Pet*
EASTON NESTON (St Mary) *see* Towcester w Easton Neston *Pet*
EASTON ON THE HILL (All Saints) and Collyweston w Duddingtonand Tixover *Pet 8* **P** *Ld Chan, Bp, and Burghley Ho Preservation Trust (by turn)* **NSM** R C TROUNSON
EASTON ROYAL (Holy Trinity) *see* Pewsey TM *Sarum*
EASTRINGTON (St Michael) *see* Howden TM *York*
EASTROP (St Mary) *Win 4* **P** *CPAS* **R** C L HAWKINS, **C** C E WEST
EASTRY (St Mary Blessed Virgin) and Northbourne w Tilmanstone and Betteshanger w Ham *Cant 8* **P** *Abp and Lord Northbourne (jt)* **Hon C** J A GOSLING, **NSM** R C NELSON
EASTTHORPE (St Paul) and Upper Hopton *Wakef 10* **P** *V Mirfield* **V** S G D PARKINSON
EASTVILLE (St Anne w St Mark and St Thomas) *Bris 4* **P** *Bp* **V** P J HAYWARD
EASTVILLE (St Paul) *see* Stickney Gp *Linc*
EASTWELL (St Michael) *see* Scalford w Goadby Marwood and Wycombe etc *Leic*
EASTWICK (St Botolph) *see* High Wych and Gilston w Eastwick *St Alb*
EASTWOOD (St David) *Chelmsf 10* **P** *Bp* **V** M J TAYLOR
EASTWOOD (St Laurence and All Saints) *Chelmsf 10* **P** *Ld Chan* **V** N L RANSOM
EASTWOOD (St Mary) *S'well 4* **P** *J N Plumptre Esq* **R** E A C CARDWELL, **C** J CURRIN
EATON (All Saints) *see* Gamston w Eaton and W Drayton *S'well*
EATON (Christ Church) and Hulme Walfield *Ches 11* **P** *Bp and R Astbury (alt)* **V** R B ROBERTS
EATON (Christ Church) (St Andrew) *Nor 3* **P** *D&C* **V** A BEARDSMORE, **C** J B SCOTT, J M HOFFMANN
EATON (St Denys) *see* Scalford w Goadby Marwood and Wycombe etc *Leic*
EATON (St Thomas) *see* Tarporley *Ches*
EATON, LITTLE (St Paul) *see* Holbrook and Lt Eaton *Derby*
EATON BISHOP (St Michael and All Angels) *see* Kingstone w Clehonger, Eaton Bishop etc *Heref*
EATON BRAY (St Mary the Virgin) w Edlesborough *St Alb 12* **P** *DBP* **V** M R ABBOTT
EATON HASTINGS (St Michael and All Angels) *see* Gt Coxwell w Buscot, Coleshill & Eaton Hastings *Ox*
EATON SOCON (St Mary) *St Alb 11* **P** *E W Harper Esq* **V** J D WATSON, **C** V E RAYMER
EATON SQUARE (St Peter) *see* Pimlico St Pet w Westmr Ch Ch *Lon*
EATON-UNDER-HEYWOOD (St Edith) *see* Hope Bowdler w Eaton-under-Heywood *Heref*
EBBERSTON (St Mary) *see* Brompton-by-Sawdon w Snainton, Ebberston etc *York*
EBBESBOURNE WAKE (St John the Baptist) *see* Chalke Valley W *Sarum*
EBCHESTER (St Ebba) *Dur 4* **P** *Bp* **R** A E HARRISON
EBERNOE (Holy Trinity) *see* N Chapel w Ebernoe *Chich*
EBONY (St Mary the Virgin) *see* Wittersham w Stone-in-Oxney and Ebony *Cant*
EBREY WOOD (Mission Chapel) *see* Wrockwardine Deanery *Lich*
EBRINGTON (St Eadburgha) *see* Chipping Campden w Ebrington *Glouc*
ECCHINSWELL (St Lawrence) *see* Burghclere w Newtown and Ecchinswell w Sydmonton *Win*
ECCLES (St Mary the Virgin) *see* Quidenham Gp *Nor*
ECCLES (St Mary the Virgin) (St Andrew) *Man 2* **P** *Patr Bd* **TR** N JONES, **TV** M W SAUNDERS, J R BAXENDALE, **C** E J TURNER
ECCLESALL (St Gabriel) *see* Greystones *Sheff*
ECCLESALL BIERLOW (All Saints) *Sheff 2* **P** *Provost Sheff* **V** C P WILLIAMS, **C** E HOPE, A M SAVAGE
ECCLESFIELD (St Mary the Virgin) *Sheff 3* **P** *DBF* **V** J O FORRESTER
ECCLESFIELD (St Paul) *see* Sheff St Paul Wordsworth Avenue *Sheff*
ECCLESHALL (Holy Trinity) *Lich 7* **P** *Bp* **V** J S COOKE
ECCLESHILL (St Luke) *Bradf 3* **P** *V Bradf* **V** A S TREASURE, **C** C FISHER-BAILEY
ECCLESTON (Christ Church) *Liv 10* **P** *F Webster Esq, Lord Blanch, Canon J A Lawton, Revd D G Mellors, and Bp (jt)* **V** C D HENDRICKSE
ECCLESTON (St Luke) *Liv 10* **P** *Trustees* **V** A W HARDY
ECCLESTON (St Mary the Virgin) *Blackb 4* **P** *DBP* **R** A H McMICHAEL
ECCLESTON (St Mary the Virgin) and Pulford *Ches 2* **P** *Duke of Westmr* **R** F H LINN
ECCLESTON (St Thomas) *Liv 10* **P** *Bp* **V** S P ATTWATER
ECCLESTON, GREAT *see* Copp *Blackb*
ECCLESTON PARK (St James) *Liv 10* **P** *Bp* **V** A OVEREND
ECKINGTON (Holy Trinity) *Worc 4* **P** *D&C Westmr* **V** P J THOMAS
ECKINGTON (St Peter and St Paul) w Handley and Ridgeway *Derby 3* **P** *The Crown and Patr Bd (alt)* **TR** N R HARVEY, **TV** H E PATTEN
ECKINGTON, UPPER (St Luke) *see* Eckington w Handley and Ridgeway *Derby*
ECTON (St Mary Magdalene) *Pet 6* **P** *The Crown* **R** *Vacant* (01604) 406442
EDALE (Holy and Undivided Trinity) *Derby 2* **P** *Rep Landowners* **P-in-c** A J G MURRAY-LESLIE
EDBURTON (St Andrew) *see* Poynings w Edburton, Newtimber and Pyecombe *Chich*
EDENBRIDGE (St Peter and St Paul) *Roch 11* **P** *Bp* **V** S A J MITCHELL, **C** R JONES
EDENFIELD (not known) and Stubbins *Man 10* **P** *Bp* **V** G N HIGHAM
EDENHALL (St Cuthbert) *see* Addingham, Edenhall, Langwathby and Culgaith *Carl*
EDENHAM (St Michael) w Witham-on-the-Hill *Linc 13* **P** *Bp and Baroness Willoughby de Eresby (alt)* **V** A T HAWES
EDENSOR (St Paul) *Lich 12* **P** *Prime Min* **V** C CRUMPTON
EDENSOR (St Peter) *see* Beeley and Edensor *Derby*
EDGBASTON (St Augustine) *Birm 2* **P** *Bp* **V** R F PRICE

EDGBASTON (St Bartholomew) *Birm 2* **P** *Sir Euan Anstruther-Gough-Calthorpe, Bt* **V** E D COOMBES
EDGBASTON (St George w St Michael) (St Michael's Hall) *Birm 2* **P** *Sir Euan Anstruther-Gough-Calthorpe, Bt* **V** *Vacant* 0121-454 2303
EDGBASTON (St Germain) *Birm 2* **P** *Trustees* **V** A P NORRIS, **C** D J SMITH
EDGBASTON (St Mary and St Ambrose) *Birm 2* **P** *Bp and Sir Euan Anstruther-Gough-Calthorpe, Bt (jt)* **P-in-c** H L SAVAGE
EDGCOTE (St James) *see* Culworth w Sulgrave and Thorpe Mandeville etc *Pet*
EDGCOTT (St Michael) *see* Swan *Ox*
EDGE, THE (St John the Baptist), Pitchcombe, Harescombe and Brookthorpe *Glouc 1* **P** *Bp and D&C (jt)* **P-in-c** E A POWELL
EDGE HILL (St Cyprian w Christ Church) *see* Toxteth St Cypr w Ch Ch *Liv*
EDGE HILL (St Dunstan) Earle Road *Liv 6* **P** *Trustees* **V** R F JONES
EDGE HILL (St Mary) *Liv 3* **P** *Bp* **V** A GODSON
EDGEFIELD (School Room) *see* Worsley *Man*
EDGEFIELD (St Peter and St Paul) *see* Lt Barningham, Blickling, Edgefield etc *Nor*
EDGESIDE (St Anne) *Man 15* **P** *Trustees* **P-in-c** R J CARMYLLIE
EDGEWORTH (St Mary) *see* Bisley, Oakridge, Miserden and Edgeworth *Glouc*
EDGMOND (St Peter) w Kynnersley and Preston Wealdmoors *Lich 16* **P** *Bp, Adn Salop, Chan Lich, MMCET, and Preston Trust Homes Trustees (jt)* **R** W E WARD
EDGTON (St Michael the Archangel) *see* Lydbury N w Hopesay and Edgton *Heref*
EDGWARE (St Alphege) *see* Hendon St Alphage *Lon*
EDGWARE (St Andrew) (St Margaret) (St Peter) *Lon 15* **P** *MMCET* **R** C M BEDFORD, **C** R A LEE, R J POWELL
EDINGALE (Holy Trinity) *see* Clifton Campville w Edingale and Harlaston *Lich*
EDINGLEY (St Giles) w Halam *S'well 15* **P** *Bp* **P-in-c** I G COLLINS
EDINGTHORPE (All Saints) *see* Bacton w Edingthorpe w Witton and Ridlington *Nor*
EDINGTON (St George) *see* W Poldens *B & W*
EDINGTON (St Mary, St Katharine and All Saints) *see* Bratton, Edington and Imber, Erlestoke etc *Sarum*
EDITH WESTON (St Mary) w North Luffenham and Lyndon w Manton *Pet 14* **P** *Baroness Willoughby de Eresby, Sir John Conant, and Em CollCam (by turn)* **R** B A NICHOLLS
EDITHMEAD (Mission) *see* Burnham *B & W*
EDLASTON (St James) *see* Brailsford w Shirley and Osmaston w Edlaston *Derby*
EDLINGHAM (St John the Baptist w Bolton Chapel) *see* Whittingham and Edlingham w Bolton Chapel *Newc*
EDLINGTON (St Helen) *see* Hemingby *Linc*
EDLINGTON (St John the Baptist) *Sheff 10* **P** *Bp* **V** J T ARCHER
EDMONDSHAM (St Nicholas) *see* Cranborne w Boveridge, Edmondsham etc *Sarum*
EDMONDTHORPE (St Michael and All Angels) *see* Wymondham w Edmondthorpe, Buckminster etc *Leic*
EDMONTON (All Saints) (St Michael) *Lon 18* **P** *D&C St Paul's* **V** B W OAKLEY, **C** D O AGBELUSI
EDMONTON (St Aldhelm) *Lon 18* **P** *V Edmonton All SS* **V** J E HALL, **C** P E S TURAY
EDMONTON (St Alphege) *Lon 18* **P** *Bp* **V** T G CLEMENT
EDMONTON (St Mary w St John) (St Mary's Centre) *Lon 18* **P** *D&C St Paul's* **V** D W GOUGH, **Hon C** J S ALDIS
EDMONTON (St Peter w St Martin) *Lon 18* **P** *Bp* **V** B M SMITH
EDMUNDBYERS (St Edmund) *see* Blanchland w Hunstanworth and Edmundbyers etc *Newc*
EDSTASTON (St Mary the Virgin) *see* Tilstock, Edstaston and Whixall *Lich*
EDSTON (St Michael) *see* Kirby Misperton w Normanby, Edston and Salton *York*
EDVIN LOACH (St Mary) w Tedstone Delamere, Tedstone Wafer, Upper Sapey, Wolferlow and Whitbourne *Heref 2* **P** *Bp, BNC Ox, Sir Francis Winnington Bt, and D P Barneby Esq (jt)* **NSM** D G WILLIAMS
EDWALTON (Holy Rood) *S'well 9* **P** *Exors Major R P Chaworth-Musters* **V** D C BIGNELL, **NSM** P A EDWARDS
EDWARDSTONE (St Mary the Virgin) w Groton and Little Waldingfield *St E 12* **P** *DBP (2 turns) and Hon Thomas Lindsay (1 turn)* **R** R K TITFORD
EDWINSTOWE (St Mary) w Carburton *S'well 6* **P** *Earl Manvers' Trustees* **P-in-c** A J COOPER, **NSM** D M PORTER
EDWYN RALPH (St Michael) *see* Bredenbury w Grendon Bishop and Wacton etc *Heref*
EFFINGHAM (St Lawrence) w Little Bookham *Guildf 10* **P** *Keble Coll Ox* **V** C A E LAWRENCE
EFFORD (St Paul) *see* Plymouth Em, St Paul Efford and St Aug *Ex*
EGDEAN (St Bartholomew) *Chich 11* **P** *Bp* **R** *Vacant*
EGERTON (St James) w Pluckley *Cant 10* **P** *Abp* **R** M J HIGGS
EGG BUCKLAND (St Edward) *Ex 22* **P** *Ld Chan* **V** T R J DICKENS
EGGESFORD (All Saints) *see* Chulmleigh, Chawleigh w Cheldon, Wembworthy etc *Ex*
EGGINTON (St Michael) *see* Leighton Buzzard w Eggington, Hockliffe etc *St Alb*
EGGINTON (St Wilfrid) *see* Etwall w Egginton *Derby*
EGGLESCLIFFE (St John the Baptist) *Dur 10* **P** *Bp* **R** R V CHADWICK
EGGLESTON (Holy Trinity) *Dur 7* **P** *The Crown* **V** J E G CLARK
EGHAM (St John the Baptist) *Guildf 11* **P** *Ch Soc Trust* **V** A J MAGOWAN, **C** M J BROADLEY, **Hon C** J H GOODING
EGHAM HYTHE (St Paul) *Guildf 11* **P** *Bp* **V** A J BUTCHER
EGLETON (St Edmund) *see* Oakham, Hambleton, Egleton, Braunston and Brooke *Pet*
EGLINGHAM (St Maurice) *see* Glendale Gp *Newc*
EGLOSHAYLE (St Petroc) *see* St Breoke and Egloshayle *Truro*
EGLOSKERRY (St Petrock and St Keri), North Petherwin, Tremaine and Tresmere *Truro 9* **P** *Duchy of Cornwall and Bp (alt)* **V** G PENGELLY
EGMANTON (Our Lady of Egmanton) *S'well 3* **P** *SMF* **V** C C LEVY
EGREMONT (St John) *Ches 7* **P** *Bp* **V** B E LEE
EGREMONT (St Mary and St Michael) and Haile *Carl 5* **P** *Patr Bd* **TR** J WOOLCOCK, **TV** N J P HAYTON, **C** M E IVEY, **NSM** B J JEAPES
EGTON (St Hilda) w Grosmont *York 23* **P** *Abp* **V** D C KING
EGTON-CUM-NEWLAND (St Mary the Virgin) and Lowick *Carl 8* **P** *Trustees* **P-in-c** G WEMYSS
EIGHT ASH GREEN (All Saints) *see* Fordham *Chelmsf*
EIGHTON BANKS (St Thomas) *Dur 12* **P** *Bp* **V** A W HODGSON, **NSM** E CARR
ELBERTON (St John) *see* Littleton on Severn w Elberton *Bris*
ELBURTON (St Matthew) *Ex 23* **P** *CPAS* **V** K H S COOMBE
ELDENE (not known) *see* Swindon Dorcan *Bris*
ELDERSFIELD (St John the Baptist) *see* Berrow w Pendock, Eldersfield, Hollybush etc *Worc*
ELDON (St Mark) *see* Shildon w Eldon *Dur*
ELDWICK (St Lawrence) *see* Bingley All SS *Bradf*
ELFORD (St Peter) *Lich 4* **P** *Bp* **R** *Vacant* (01827) 383212
ELHAM (St Mary the Virgin) w Denton and Wootton *Cant 5* **P** *Abp and Mert Coll Ox (jt)* **P-in-c** J V H RUSSELL
ELING (St Mary) *see* Totton *Win*
ELKESLEY (St Giles) w Bothamsall *S'well 5* **P** *SMF* **V** *Vacant* (01777) 838293
ELKINGTON, SOUTH (All Saints) *see* Louth *Linc*
ELKSTONE (St John the Baptist) *see* Alstonfield, Butterton, Warslow w Elkstone etc *Lich*
ELKSTONE (St John the Evangelist) *see* Coberley, Cowley, Colesbourne and Elkstone *Glouc*
ELLACOMBE (Christ Church) *see* Torquay St Jo and Ellacombe *Ex*
ELLAND (All Saints) (St Mary the Virgin) *Wakef 2* **P** *Bp, Adn Halifax, and V Halifax (jt)* **TR** N M WOOD, **TV** M R FREEMAN, **C** J R GARRARD
ELLASTONE (St Peter) *see* Denstone w Ellastone and Stanton *Lich*
ELLEL (St John the Evangelist) *Blackb 12* **P** *V Cockerham* **P-in-c** A J GWILLIM
ELLENBROOK (St Mary's Chapel) *see* Worsley *Man*
ELLENHALL (St Mary) *see* Chebsey, Ellenhall and Seighford-with-Creswell *Lich*
ELLERBURNE (St Hilda) *see* Thornton Dale w Ellerburne and Wilton *York*
ELLERBY (St James) *see* Swine *York*
ELLERKER (not known) *see* S Cave and Ellerker w Broomfleet *York*
ELLESBOROUGH (St Peter and St Paul), The Kimbles and Stoke Mandeville *Ox 28* **P** *Chequers Trustees, Hon I Hope-Morley, and D&C Linc (by turn)* **R** A D WILLIS, **NSM** D J FREEMAN, H W HESLOP, N M DICK
ELLESMERE (St Mary) *Lich 17* **P** *Bp* **V** P J EDGE, **Hon C** M W H GRAY
ELLESMERE (St Peter) *Sheff 3* **P** *Bp* **V** A WHITELEY, **NSM** J L BROWN
ELLESMERE PORT *Ches 9* **P** *Bp* **TV** R A WIFFEN, **C** M LEWIS

ELLINGHAM (St Mary) *see* Gillingham w Geldeston, Stockton, Ellingham etc *Nor*
ELLINGHAM (St Mary and All Saints) and Harbridge and Hyde w Ibsley *Win 8* **P** *Earl of Normanton and Keble Coll Ox (jt)* **V** B R CASSIDY
ELLINGHAM (St Maurice) *Newc 10* **P** *D&C Dur* **V** A J HUGHES
ELLINGHAM, GREAT (St James), LITTLE (St Peter), Rockland All Saints, Rockland St Peter and Shropham w Snetterton *Nor 11* **P** *Bp, Major E H C Garnier, and CCC Cam (jt)* **R** A KNIGHT
ELLINGTON (All Saints) *Ely 10* **P** *Peterho Cam* **P-in-c** J ALFORD
ELLISFIELD (St Martin) *see* Cliddesden and Ellisfield w Farleigh Wallop etc *Win*
ELLISTOWN (St Christopher) *see* Hugglescote w Donington, Ellistown and Snibston *Leic*
ELLOUGHTON (St Mary) and Brough w Brantingham *York 14* **P** *Abp and D&C Dur (jt)* **V** W E J MASH
ELM (All Saints) *Ely 19* **P** *Bp* **V** *Vacant* (01945) 860382
ELM (St Mary Magdalene) *see* Mells w Buckland Dinham, Elm, Whatley etc *B & W*
ELM PARK (St Nicholas) Hornchurch *Chelmsf 2* **P** *Bp* **V** R B LLOYD, **NSM** M S McCREADY, R MORTON
ELMBRIDGE (St Mary) *see* Elmley Lovett w Hampton Lovett and Elmbridge etc *Worc*
ELMDON (St Nicholas) *see* Heydon, Gt and Lt Chishill, Chrishall etc *Chelmsf*
ELMDON (St Nicholas) (St Stephen's Church Centre) (St Nicholas' Hall) *Birm 12* **P** *Ch Trust Fund Trust* **R** A S GRAESSER
ELMDON HEATH (St Francis of Assisi) *see* Solihull *Birm*
ELMESTHORPE (St Mary) *see* Earl Shilton w Elmesthorpe *Leic*
ELMHAM, NORTH (St Mary) w Billingford and Worthing *Nor 14* **P** *Bp (1 turn), Viscount Coke (2 turns), and G & C Coll Cam (1 turn)* **R** N TEWKESBURY
ELMHAM, SOUTH (St Cross) (St James) (St Margaret) (St Peter) (St Michael and All Angels) and Ilketshall *St E 14* **P** *Bp (3 turns), Ld Chan (1 turn), and Duke of Norfolk (1 turn)* **R** J M S FALKNER, **NSM** R A FINCH, C S LEE, S M ELLIS
ELMHURST (Mission Room) *see* Lich St Chad *Lich*
ELMLEY CASTLE (St Mary) w Bricklehampton and the Combertons *Worc 4* **P** *Bp* **R** *Vacant* (01386) 710394
ELMLEY LOVETT (St Michael) w Hampton Lovett and Elmbridge w Rushdock *Worc 8* **P** *Bp and Ch Coll Cam (alt)* **P-in-c** J READER
ELMORE (St John the Baptist) *see* Hardwicke, Quedgeley and Elmore w Longney *Glouc*
ELMSALL, NORTH (St Margaret) *see* Badsworth *Wakef*
ELMSALL, SOUTH (St Mary the Virgin) *Wakef 11* **P** *Bp* **V** M E ROGERS
ELMSETT (St Peter) w Aldham *St E 3* **P** *Bp and MMCET (alt)* **P-in-c** I A WILSON
ELMSTEAD (St Anne and St Laurence) *Chelmsf 20* **P** *Jes Coll Cam* **NSM** W G VAN DONGEN
ELMSTED (St James the Great) w Hastingleigh *Cant 2* **P** *Abp* **P-in-c** P G COX
ELMSTONE (not known) *see* Wingham w Elmstone and Preston w Stourmouth *Cant*
ELMSTONE HARDWICKE (St Mary Magdalene) *see* Swindon w Uckington and Elmstone Hardwicke *Glouc*
ELMSWELL (St John) *St E 10* **P** *MMCET* **R** J A C PERROTT
ELMTON (St Peter) *Derby 3* **P** *Bp* **V** B M CROWTHER-ALWYN
ELSDON (St Cuthbert) *see* N Tyne and Redesdale Team *Newc*
ELSECAR (Holy Trinity) *Sheff 7* **P** *Sir Stephen Hastings* **V** J G FAIRHURST
ELSENHAM (St Mary the Virgin) *see* Henham and Elsenham w Ugley *Chelmsf*
ELSFIELD (St Thomas of Canterbury) *see* Marston w Elsfield *Ox*
ELSHAM (All Saints) *see* N Wolds Gp *Linc*
ELSING (St Mary) *see* Lyng, Sparham, Elsing, Bylaugh, Bawdeswell etc *Nor*
ELSON (St Thomas) *Portsm 3* **V** P R WADSWORTH, **C** J A GORDON
ELSTEAD (St James) *Guildf 4* **P** *Adn Surrey* **R** W D LANG
ELSTED (St Paul) *see* Harting w Elsted and Treyford cum Didling *Chich*
ELSTERNWICK (St Laurence) *see* Burton Pidsea and Humbleton w Elsternwick *York*
ELSTON (All Saints) w Elston Chapelry *S'well 3* **P** *J C S Darwin Esq* **R** G A FIRTH
ELSTOW (St Mary and St Helena) *St Alb 13* **P** *S C Whitbread Esq* **V** R W HUBAND
ELSTREE (St Nicholas) *St Alb 1* **P** *Ld Chan* **R** W J ELLIOTT
ELSWICK, HIGH (St Paul) *Newc 7* **P** *Trustees* **P-in-c** G R CURRY
ELSWICK, HIGH (St Philip) *see* Newc St Phil and St Aug *Newc*
ELSWICK, LOW (St Stephen) *Newc 7* **P** *Ch Soc Trust* **V** G R CURRY
ELSWORTH (Holy Trinity) w Knapwell *Ely 1* **P** *Bp (4 turns), The Crown (1 turn)* **R** *Vacant*
ELTHAM (Holy Trinity) *S'wark 2* **P** *Bp* **V** J P H JOHN, **C** G W OWEN, **Hon C** A GURNEY
ELTHAM (St Barnabas) *S'wark 2* **P** *Bp* **V** J E NEAL
ELTHAM (St John the Baptist) *S'wark 2* **P** *DBP* **V** P V L JOHNSTONE
ELTHAM (St Saviour) *S'wark 2* **P** *Bp* **V** S M CAPLE
ELTHAM, NEW (All Saints) *S'wark 2* **P** *Bp* **V** B M BRANCHE, **NSM** G S LYONS
ELTHAM PARK (St Luke) *S'wark 2* **P** *Bp* **V** J C THEWLIS, **NSM** M J MABBS, I NASH
ELTISLEY (St Pandionia and St John the Baptist) *see* Croxton and Eltisley *Ely*
ELTON (All Saints) *see* S Darley, Elton and Winster *Derby*
ELTON (All Saints) *Ely 13* **P** *Sir Peter Proby* **R** P O POOLEY
ELTON (All Saints) *Man 10* **P** *R Bury St Mary* **V** I E WALTER, **Hon C** P J BEDDINGTON
ELTON (no dedication) *see* Longnewton w Elton *Dur*
ELTON (St Mary the Virgin) *see* Wigmore Abbey *Heref*
ELTON (St Stephen) *Man 10* **P** *V Elton All SS* **P-in-c** A BRADBROOK
ELTON-ON-THE-HILL (St Michael) *see* Cropwell Bishop w Colston Bassett, Granby etc *S'well*
ELVASTON (St Bartholomew) and Shardlow *Derby 15* **P** *Earl of Harrington and DBP (alt)* **V** *Vacant* (01332) 571790
ELVEDEN (St Andrew and St Patrick) *see* Brandon and Santon Downham w Elveden *St E*
ELVINGTON (Holy Trinity) w Sutton on Derwent and East Cottingwith *York 4* **P** *Lt Col J Darlington* **R** S E MUTCH
ELWICK HALL (St Peter) *see* Hart w Elwick Hall *Dur*
ELWORTH (St Peter) and Warmingham *Ches 11* **P** *V Sandbach, Q H Crewe Esq and J C Crewe Esq (alt)* **R** C D JEFFERSON
ELY (Holy Trinity w St Mary) (St Peter) *Ely 14* **P** *Patr Bd* **TR** F J KILNER, **TV** M E RABY, **C** J M SAVAGE
EMBERTON (All Saints) *see* Lamp *Ox*
EMBLETON (Holy Trinity) w Rennington and Rock *Newc 9* **P** *Mert Coll Ox* **V** J M MOUNTNEY
EMBLETON (St Cuthbert) *see* Cockermouth w Embleton and Wythop *Carl*
EMBROOK (Community of St Nicholas) *see* Wokingham St Paul *Ox*
EMBSAY (St Mary the Virgin) w Eastby *Bradf 7* **P** *R Skipton H Trin* **P-in-c** A KITCHEN
EMERY DOWN (Christ Church) *see* Lyndhurst and Emery Down *Win*
EMLEY (St Michael the Archangel) *Wakef 6* **P** *Lord Savile* **P-in-c** J A WILLIAMS
EMMER GREEN (St Barnabas) *Ox 15* **P** *Bp* **R** N J HARDCASTLE, **NSM** E W D TILDESLEY, J D S DUDLEY
EMMINGTON (St Nicholas) *see* Chinnor w Emmington and Sydenham etc *Ox*
EMNETH (St Edmund) and Marshland St James *Ely 19* **P** *Bp* **V** J A COOMBS
EMPINGHAM (St Peter) and Exton w Horn w Whitwell *Pet 14* **P** *Bp and Earl of Gainsborough (alt)* **P-in-c** B FERNYHOUGH
EMPSHOTT (Holy Rood) *see* Greatham w Empshott and Hawkley w Prior's Dean *Portsm*
EMSCOTE (All Saints) *Cov 11* **P** *Earl of Warw* **V** A P LURY, **C** A G R BRISTOW
EMSWORTH (St James) *see* Warblington and Emsworth *Portsm*
ENBORNE (St Michael and All Angels) *see* W Woodhay w Enborne, Hampstead Marshall etc *Ox*
ENDCLIFFE (St Augustine) *Sheff 2* **P** *Ch Burgesses* **V** M R GOATER, **Hon C** C A COLLINS
ENDERBY (St John the Baptist) w Lubbesthorpe and Thurlaston *Leic 10* **P** *Bp and F B Drummond Esq* **V** R A SHELLEY, **Hon C** T J R KING
ENDON (St Luke) w Stanley *Lich 8* **P** *R Leek and Meerbrook* **V** E OSMAN, **NSM** J FORRESTER
ENFIELD (Christ Church) Trent Park *Lon 18* **P** *Ch Trust Fund Trust* **V** P A E REES, **C** J E ROBSON, A G PURSER, N M GENDERS
ENFIELD (St Andrew) *Lon 18* **P** *Trin Coll Cam* **V** M M EDGE, **C** O A FAGBEMI, **Hon C** O R COPE
ENFIELD (St George) *Lon 18* **P** *Bp* **V** J S CLARKE
ENFIELD (St James) (St Barnabas) *Lon 18* **P** *V Enfield* **V** J M BOWERS, **C** G O WILLIAMS, L HOLLAND

ENFIELD (St John the Baptist) *see* Clay Hill St Jo and St Luke *Lon*
ENFIELD (St Luke) *as above*
ENFIELD (St Mark) *see* Bush Hill Park St Mark *Lon*
ENFIELD (St Matthew) *see* Ponders End St Matt *Lon*
ENFIELD (St Michael and All Angels) *Lon 18* **P** *V Enfield* **V** G H G PLASTOW
ENFIELD (St Peter and St Paul) *Lon 18* **P** *Bp* **V** J C VAUGHAN
ENFIELD (St Stephen) *see* Bush Hill Park St Steph *Lon*
ENFIELD CHASE (St Mary Magdalene) *Lon 18* **P** *Bp* **V** J A SAMPFORD, **NSM** R H DUNN
ENFORD (All Saints) *see* Avon Valley *Sarum*
ENGLEFIELD (St Mark) *see* Theale and Englefield *Ox*
ENGLEFIELD GREEN (St Jude) *Guildf 11* **P** *Bp* **V** L C SMITH
ENGLISH BICKNOR (St Mary) *see* Forest of Dean Ch Ch w English Bicknor *Glouc*
ENGLISHCOMBE (St Peter) *see* Bath St Barn w Englishcombe *B & W*
ENHAM ALAMEIN (St George) *see* Smannell w Enham Alamein *Win*
ENMORE (St Michael) *see* Spaxton w Charlynch, Goathurst, Enmore etc *B & W*
ENMORE GREEN (St John the Evangelist) *see* Shaston *Sarum*
ENNERDALE (St Mary) *see* Lamplugh w Ennerdale *Carl*
ENSBURY PARK (St Thomas) *Sarum 8* **P** *Bp* **V** E FARROW
ENSTONE (St Kenelm) and Heythrop *Ox 3* **P** *Bp* **V** A R MOORE
ENVILLE (St Mary the Virgin) *see* Kinver and Enville *Lich*
EPPERSTONE (Holy Cross) *S'well 11* **P** *Bp, Ld Chan, and Comdr M B P Francklin (by turn)* **R** M J BROCK, **C** T J RENSHAW
EPPING District (All Saints) (St John the Baptist) *Chelmsf 25* **P** *Patr Bd* **TR** P W NOKES, **TV** C F J BARD, J M GLASSPOOL, **C** A J HODGSON, **NSM** P A EVANS
EPPLETON (All Saints) and Hetton le Hole *Dur 14* **P** *Prime Min and Bp (alt)* **R** M L BECK, **NSM** G M BECK
EPSOM (St Barnabas) *Guildf 9* **P** *Bp* **V** M C PRESTON
EPSOM (St Martin) (St Stephen on the Downs) *Guildf 9* **P** *Bp* **V** D A SMETHURST, **C** R C HOAD, **Hon C** M D RANKEN
EPSOM COMMON (Christ Church) *Guildf 9* **P** *Bp* **V** J D ANDERSON
EPWELL (St Anne) *see* Wykeham *Ox*
EPWORTH (St Andrew) and Wroot *Linc 1* **P** *Prime Min (2 turns), Ld Chan (1 turn)* **P-in-c** J D BROWN
ERCALL, HIGH (St Michael and All Angels) *see* Wrockwardine Deanery *Lich*
ERDINGTON (St Barnabas) *Birm 8* **P** *Aston Trustees* **V** P R SPENCER, **C** J S CURRY
ERDINGTON (St Chad) *Birm 8* **P** *Bp* **V** A R BROOKS
ERIDGE GREEN (Holy Trinity) *see* Frant w Eridge *Chich*
ERISWELL (St Laurence and St Peter) *see* Mildenhall *St E*
ERITH (Christ Church) *Roch 15* **P** *Bp* **V** J DRAYCOTT
ERITH (St John the Baptist) *Roch 15* **P** *Bp* **V** J DAY
ERITH (St Paul) Northumberland Heath *Roch 15* **P** *CPAS* **V** J R G WATSON, **C** I F DURNDELL
ERLESTOKE (Holy Saviour) *see* Bratton, Edington and Imber, Erlestoke etc *Sarum*
ERMINGTON (St Peter and St Paul) and Ugborough *Ex 20* **P** *Prime Min (1 turn), Bp and Grocers' Co (jt) (3 turns)* **V** E J PERRY
ERNESETTLE (St Aidan) *Ex 21* **P** *Bp* **V** G J SMITH
ERPINGHAM (St Mary) w Calthorpe, Ingworth, Aldborough, Thurgarton and Alby w Thwaite *Nor 19* **P** *Bp, Lord Walpole, Gt Hosp Nor, Mrs S M Lilly, and DBP (by turn)* **R** B T FAULKNER
ERWARTON (St Mary the Virgin) *see* Chelmondiston and Erwarton w Harkstead *St E*
ERYHOLME (St Mary) *see* Middleton Tyas w Croft and Eryholme *Ripon*
ESCOMB (no dedication) *Dur 6* **P** *Bp* **V** N M J-W BEDDOW
ESCOT (St Philip and St James) *see* Feniton, Buckerell and Escot *Ex*
ESCRICK (St Helen) and Stillingfleet w Naburn *York 4* **P** *Abp, D&C, and N C Forbes Adam Esq (jt)* **R** R M KIRKMAN
ESH (St Michael and All Angels) *Dur 4* **P** *The Crown* **Dn-in-c** G M POCOCK, **NSM** S I WRIGHT
ESHER (Christ Church) (St George) *Guildf 8* **P** *Wadh Coll Ox* **R** C M SCOTT
ESHOLT (St Paul) *see* Guiseley w Esholt *Bradf*
ESKDALE (St Catherine) (St Bega's Mission), Irton, Muncaster and Waberthwaite *Carl 5* **P** *Bp, Adn W Cumberland, Mrs P Gordon-Duff-Pennington, and P Stanley Esq (jt)* **V** G M STONESTREET, **NSM** I M HALL
ESKDALESIDE (St John) w Ugglebarnby and Sneaton *York 23* **P** *Abp* **V** N N JONES
ESSENDINE (St Mary the Virgin) *see* Ryhall w Essendine and Carlby *Pet*
ESSENDON (St Mary the Virgin) *see* Lt Berkhamsted and Bayford, Essendon etc *St Alb*
ESSINGTON (St John the Evangelist) *Lich 2* **P** *Bp, R Bushbury, R Wednesfield, and Simeon's Trustees (jt)* **V** B PRENTICE
ESTON (Christ Church) w Normanby *York 19* **P** *Abp* **TR** A G C LEIGHTON, **TV** L N CAVAN
ESTOVER (Christ Church) *Ex 22* **P** *Bp* **V** T J WOODS
ETAL (St Mary the Virgin) *see* Ford and Etal *Newc*
ETCHILHAMPTON (St Andrew) *see* Bishop's Cannings, All Cannings etc *Sarum*
ETCHING HILL (The Holy Spirit) *see* Rugeley *Lich*
ETCHINGHAM (Assumption and St Nicholas) *Chich 15* **P** *Bp* **R** B C GURD
ETHERLEY (St Cuthbert) *Dur 6* **P** *Bp* **R** *Vacant* (01388) 832350
ETON (St John the Evangelist) *see* Riverside *Ox*
ETON WICK (St John the Baptist) *as above*
ETTINGSHALL (Holy Trinity) *Lich 29* **P** *Bp* **V** A J JONES
ETTINGTON (Holy Trinity and St Thomas of Canterbury) *see* Butlers Marston and the Pillertons w Ettington *Cov*
ETTON (St Mary) w Dalton Holme *York 9* **P** *Lord Hotham* **NSM** J M WATERS
ETTON (St Stephen) w Helpston and Maxey *Pet 13* **P** *Sir Stephen Hastings (2 turns), D&C (1 turn)* **R** D G BARTHOLOMEW
ETWALL (St Helen) w Egginton *Derby 14* **P** *Bp, Sir Henry Every Bt, Major J W Chandos-Pole, and DBP (by turn)* **P-in-c** S L RAYNER
EUSTON (St Genevieve) *see* Blackbourne *St E*
EUXTON (not known) *Blackb 4* **P** *Bp* **V** P D TAYLOR
EVE HILL (St James the Great) *see* Dudley St Jas *Worc*
EVEDON (St Mary) *see* Kirkby Laythorpe *Linc*
EVENLEY (St George) *see* Aynho and Croughton w Evenley etc *Pet*
EVENLODE (St Edward King and Martyr) *see* Broadwell, Evenlode, Oddington and Adlestrop *Glouc*
EVENWOOD (St Paul) *Dur 7* **P** *Bp* **V** G LIDDLE
EVERCREECH (St Peter) w Chesterblade and Milton Clevedon *B & W 2* **P** *DBP* **V** *Vacant* (01749) 830322
EVERDON (St Mary) *see* Weedon Bec w Everdon and Dodford *Pet*
EVERINGHAM (St Everilda) *see* Seaton Ross Gp of Par *York*
EVERSDEN, GREAT (St Mary) *see* Haslingfield w Harlton and Gt and Lt Eversden *Ely*
EVERSDEN, LITTLE (St Helen) *as above*
EVERSHOLT (St John the Baptist) *see* Woburn w Eversholt, Milton Bryan, Battlesden etc *St Alb*
EVERSHOT (St Osmund) *see* Melbury *Sarum*
EVERSLEY (St Mary) *Win 5* **P** *DBP* **R** *Vacant* (0118) 973 3237
EVERTON (Holy Trinity) and Mattersey w Clayworth *S'well 1* **P** *Ld Chan (2 turns), Bp (2 turns)* **R** *Vacant* (01777) 817364
EVERTON (St George) *Liv 3* **P** *Bp* **V** P H SPIERS, **NSM** I CASSIDY
EVERTON (St John Chrysostom) (Emmanuel) *Liv 3* **P** *Adn, CPAS, and PCC (jt)* **V** S ELLIS
EVERTON (St Mary) *see* Milford *Win*
EVERTON (St Mary) w Tetworth *Ely 12* **P** *Clare Coll Cam* **P-in-c** B CURRY
EVERTON (St Peter) *Liv 3* **P** *Patr Bd* **TR** H CORBETT
EVESBATCH (St Andrew) *see* Acton Beauchamp and Evesbatch w Stanford Bishop *Heref*
EVESHAM (All Saints w St Lawrence) w Norton and Lenchwick *Worc 1* **P** *Bp and D&C (jt)* **V** R N ARMITAGE, **NSM** A E WHITEHOUSE
EVINGTON (St Denys) *Leic 1* **P** *Bp* **V** C FINCH, **C** R D STAPLEFORD, **Hon C** S A PATERSON
EVINGTON (St Stephen) *see* Twigworth, Down Hatherley, Norton, The Leigh etc *Glouc*
EVINGTON, NORTH (St Stephen) *Leic 1* **P** *Bp* **P-in-c** I St C RICHARDS, **NSM** W C BURLEIGH, L M HUGHES
EWELL (St Francis of Assisi) Ruxley Lane *Guildf 9* **P** *Bp* **V** S G THOMAS
EWELL (St Mary the Virgin) *Guildf 9* **P** *Bp* **V** W R HANFORD, **Hon Par Dn** A J LYNN
EWELL, WEST (All Saints) *Guildf 9* **P** *Bp* **V** A J HURD
EWELME (St Mary the Virgin), Brightwell Baldwin, Cuxham w Easington *Ox 1* **P** *F D Wright Esq and Mert Coll Ox, Prime Min (alt)* **R** M W GARNER
EWERBY (St Andrew) *see* Kirkby Laythorpe *Linc*
EWHURST (St James the Great) *Chich 20* **P** *K Coll Cam* **P-in-c** R K BAKER, **C** A WILLIAMS
EWHURST (St Peter and St Paul) *Guildf 2* **P** *Ld Chan* **R** D H LEWIS

EWOOD (St Bartholomew) *Blackb 5* **P** *Bp* **P-in-c** N J WHETTON, **C** K HOWLES
EWSHOT (St Mary the Virgin) *see* Crondall and Ewshot *Guildf*
EWYAS HAROLD (St Michael and All Angels) w Dulas, Kenderchurch, Abbeydore, Bacton, Kentchurch, Llangua, Rowlestone, Llancillo, Walterstone, Kilpeck, St Devereux and Wormbridge *Heref 1* **P** *Patr Bd* **P-in-c** A L MOORE, **NSM** H E BAKER
EXBOURNE (St Mary the Virgin) *see* Hatherleigh, Meeth, Exbourne and Jacobstowe *Ex*
EXBURY (St Katherine) *see* Beaulieu and Exbury and E Boldre *Win*
EXE, WEST (St Paul) *Ex 8* **P** *Peache Trustees* **P-in-c** M J PARTRIDGE
EXE VALLEY *see* Washfield, Stoodleigh, Withleigh etc *Ex*
EXETER (St David) (St Michael and All Angels) *Ex 3* **P** *D&C* **V** J M HENTON, **C** T C HUNT, **NSM** P A LEE
EXETER (St James) *Ex 3* **P** *D&C* **P-in-c** P G SMITH, **C** C E DEACON
EXETER (St Leonard w Holy Trinity) *Ex 3* **P** *CPAS* **R** J C SKINNER, **C** A D M PAINE, **NSM** J F SEARLE
EXETER (St Mark) (St Matthew) (St Sidwell) *Ex 3* **P** *Bp and D&C (jt)* **R** S CROFT, **C** P K CRANCH, **NSM** R J A BARRETT
EXETER (St Mary Steps) *Ex 3* **P** *SMF* **R** *Vacant* (01392) 277685
EXETER (St Paul) *see* Heavitree w Ex St Paul *Ex*
EXETER (St Thomas the Apostle) (Emmanuel) (St Andrew) (St Philip) *Ex 3* **P** *Bp* **TR** A WHITE, **TV** D B M GILL, **C** N T MACNEILL
EXETER, CENTRAL (St Martin) (St Mary Arches) (St Olave) (St Pancras) (St Petrock) (St Stephen) *Ex 3* **P** *Patr Bd* **TR** M R SELMAN, **Hon C** M J HATT, **NSM** A A HALL
EXFORD (St Mary Magdalene), Exmoor, Hawkridge and Withypool *B & W 16* **P** *Bp (1 turn), Peterho Cam (2 turns)* **R** R J RAY
EXHALL (St Giles) *Cov 5* **P** *Bp* **V** W M SMITH, **C** S L BUSHELL
EXHALL (St Giles) w Wixford *Cov 7* **V** E F WILLIAMS
EXMINSTER (St Martin) and Kenn *Ex 6* **P** *Mrs M P L Bate and 12 Govs of Crediton Ch (jt)* **P-in-c** I C MORTER
EXMOOR (St Luke) *see* Exford, Exmoor, Hawkridge and Withypool *B & W*
EXMOUTH (All Saints) *see* Withycombe Raleigh *Ex*
EXMOUTH (Holy Trinity) *see* Littleham w Exmouth *Ex*
EXMOUTH (St Andrew) *as above*
EXMOUTH (St Saviour) *as above*
EXNING (St Agnes) *see* Newmarket St Mary w Exning St Agnes *St E*
EXNING (St Martin) (St Philip) w Landwade *St E 11* **P** *D&C Cant* **V** C T CATTON, **C** C R NORBURN, **NSM** C T McCARTY
EXTON (St Andrew) *see* Woodbury *Ex*
EXTON (St Peter and St Paul) *see* Empingham and Exton w Horn w Whitwell *Pet*
EXTON (St Peter and St Paul) *see* Meonstoke w Corhampton cum Exton *Portsm*
EXTON (St Peter) and Winsford and Cutcombe w Luxborough *B & W 16* **P** *Ld Chan (2 turns), Em Coll Cam (1 turn), and G A Warren Esqand D M Warren Esq (1 turn)* **R** C J BUDDEN
EXWICK (St Andrew) *Ex 3* **P** *Lord Wraxall* **V** J FAIRWEATHER
EYAM (St Lawrence) *Derby 2* **P** *Earl Temple* **R** D G SHAW
EYDON (St Nicholas) *see* Woodford Halse w Eydon *Pet*
EYE (St Matthew) *Pet 13* **P** *Bp* **V** *Vacant* (01733) 222334
EYE (St Peter and St Paul) w Braiseworth and Yaxley *St E 16* **P** *SMF* **V** *Vacant* (01379) 870277
EYE (St Peter and St Paul), Croft w Yarpole and Lucton *Heref 7* **P** *Exors Mrs E Parr (2 turns), Ld Chan (2 turns), Lucton Sch (1 turn)* **P-in-c** M W HOOPER
EYEWORTH (All Saints) *see* Dunton w Wrestlingworth and Eyeworth *St Alb*
EYKE (All Saints) w Bromeswell, Rendlesham, Tunstall and Wantisden *St E 7* **P** *Bp, Mrs R M L Darling, J H Kemball Esq, and MMCET (jt)* **P-in-c** N D G DEAR
EYNESBURY (St Mary) *Ely 12* **P** *Bp* **R** T J McCABE
EYNSFORD (St Martin) w Farningham and Lullingstone *Roch 10* **P** *D&C* **R** R A FREEMAN, **NSM** C H SALMON
EYNSHAM (St Leonard) and Cassington *Ox 9* **P** *Wycliffe Hall Ox and Ch Ch Ox (alt)* **V** I R BENTLEY, **C** T R DAVIES
EYPE (St Peter) *see* Symondsbury and Chideock *Sarum*
EYRES MONSELL (St Hugh) *Leic 2* **P** *Bp* **V** D J YOUNG
EYTHORNE (St Peter and St Paul) and Elvington w Waldershare and Barfreystone w Sherdswell and Coldred *Cant 4* **P** *Abp, St Jo Coll Ox, and Earl of Guilford (jt)* **NSM** P M O OLIVER, M M MOWER
EYTON (All Saints) *see* Leominster *Heref*
EYTON (St Catherine) *see* Wellington, All SS w Eyton *Lich*
FACCOMBE (St Barnabas) *see* Hurstbourne Tarrant, Faccombe, Vernham Dean etc *Win*
FACEBY (St Mary Magdalene) *see* Whorlton w Carlton and Faceby *York*
FACIT (St John the Evangelist) (St Michael the Archangel) *Man 20* **P** *Bp* **P-in-c** J A READ
FAILAND (St Bartholomew) *see* Wraxall *B & W*
FAILSWORTH (Holy Family) *Man 19* **P** *Bp* **R** P R LOMAS
FAILSWORTH (Holy Trinity) *Man 19* **P** *The Crown* **R** R W STEPHENS
FAILSWORTH (St John) (St John the Evangelist) *Man 19* **P** *Bp* **P-in-c** J S HOLLAND
FAIR OAK (St Thomas) *Win 9* **P** *Bp* **V** D S SNUGGS
FAIRBURN (St James) *see* Ledsham w Fairburn *York*
FAIRFIELD (St John the Divine) *Liv 3* **P** *MMCET* **P-in-c** J R SKINNER
FAIRFIELD (St Mark) *see* Belbroughton w Fairfield and Clent *Worc*
FAIRFIELD (St Matthew) *Linc 9* **P** *Bp* **V** D P ROWETT
FAIRFIELD (St Peter) *Derby 4* **P** *Ch Govs* **P-in-c** C P CRAVEN, **NSM** P D BRIDGWATER
FAIRFIELD (St Thomas a Becket) *see* Appledore w Brookland, Fairfield, Brenzett etc *Cant*
FAIRFORD (St Mary the Virgin) *Glouc 13* **P** *D&C* **P-in-c** J F WILLARD
FAIRHAVEN (St Paul) *Blackb 11* **P** *J C Hilton Esq* **P-in-c** G ROUSE
FAIRLIGHT, Guestling and Pett *Chich 20* **P** *Patr Bd* **R** J R BALCH
FAIRSEAT (Holy Innocents) *see* Stansted w Fairseat and Vigo *Roch*
FAIRSTEAD (St Mary) w Terling and White Notley w Faulkbourne *Chelmsf 24* **P** *Bp, Exors Lord Rayleigh, and C W O Parker Esq (by turn)* **R** J M HALL
FAIRWARP (Christ Church) *Chich 21* **P** *Bp* **P-in-c** I GIBSON
FAIRWEATHER GREEN (St Saviour) *Bradf 1* **P** *Bp* **V** S BETSON
FAKENHAM (St Peter and St Paul) w Alethorpe *Nor 15* **P** *Trin Coll Cam* **R** A J BELL
FAKENHAM MAGNA (St Peter) *see* Blackbourne *St E*
FALCONWOOD (Bishop Ridley Church) *Roch 15* **P** *Bp* **V** R J IRETON
FALDINGWORTH (All Saints) *see* Wickenby Gp *Linc*
FALFIELD (St George) w Rockhampton *Glouc 7* **P** *Adn Glouc, V Thornbury, J Leigh Esq, and Bp (by turn)* **P-in-c** R W MARTIN
FALINGE (St Edmund) *see* Rochdale *Man*
FALKENHAM (St Ethelbert) *see* Kirton w Falkenham *St E*
FALMER (St Laurence) *see* Stanmer w Falmer *Chich*
FALMOUTH (All Saints) *Truro 3* **P** *Bp* **V** J S SCANTLEBURY
FALMOUTH (King Charles the Martyr) *Truro 3* **P** *Bp* **R** R G GILBERT, **C** J SAVAGE, **NSM** J B BENNETTS
FALSTONE (St Peter) *see* N Tyne and Redesdale Team *Newc*
FAMBRIDGE, NORTH (Holy Trinity) *see* Creeksea w Althorne, Latchingdon and N Fambridge *Chelmsf*
FAMBRIDGE, SOUTH (All Saints) *see* Ashingdon w S Fambridge *Chelmsf*
FANGFOSS (St Martin) *see* Barmby Moor w Allerthorpe, Fangfoss and Yapham *York*
FAR FOREST (Holy Trinity) *see* Mamble w Bayton, Rock w Heightington etc *Worc*
FAR HEADINGLEY St Chad (St Oswald) *Ripon 7* **P** *Lord Grimthorpe* **V** B M OVEREND, **C** A W SEWELL
FARCET (St Mary) *see* Stanground and Farcet *Ely*
FAREHAM (Holy Trinity) (St Columba) *Portsm 2* **P** *Bp* **TR** I JAGGER, **TV** A TREMLETT, **C** S E LITJENS, **Hon C** A P BURR, **NSM** D M JACKSON, R V JAGGER
FAREHAM (St John the Evangelist) *Portsm 2* **P** *CPAS* **V** H CHANT
FAREHAM (St Peter and St Paul) *Portsm 2* **P** *Bp* **V** R C H FRANKLIN, **Hon C** R CHAPMAN
FAREWELL (St Bartholomew) *Lich 1* **P** *MMCET* **P-in-c** M J BUTT
FARFORTH (St Peter) *see* S Ormsby Gp *Linc*
FARINGDON, GREAT (All Saints) w Little Coxwell *Ox 17* **P** *Simeon's Trustees* **V** A J BAILEY, **NSM** M R STARR
FARINGDON, LITTLE (not known) *see* Shill Valley and Broadshire *Ox*
FARINGTON (St Paul) *Blackb 6* **P** *V Penwortham* **V** P E M HOLLANDS
FARLAM (St Thomas a Becket) *see* Brampton and Farlam and Castle Carrock w Cumrew *Carl*
FARLEIGH (St Mary) *see* Warlingham w Chelsham and Farleigh *S'wark*
FARLEIGH, EAST (not known) *see* Coxheath w E Farleigh, Hunton and Linton *Roch*

FARLEIGH, WEST (All Saints) *see* Wateringbury w Teston and W Farleigh *Roch*
FARLEIGH HUNGERFORD (St Leonard) *see* Rode Major *B & W*
FARLEIGH WALLOP (St Andrew) *see* Cliddesden and Ellisfield w Farleigh Wallop etc *Win*
FARLESTHORPE (St Andrew) *see* Bilsby w Farlesthorpe *Linc*
FARLEY (All Saints) *see* Alderbury Team *Sarum*
FARLEY CHAMBERLAYNE (St John) *see* Michelmersh, Timsbury, Farley Chamberlayne etc *Win*
FARLEY GREEN (St Michael) *see* Albury w St Martha *Guildf*
FARLEY HILL (St John the Baptist) *St Alb 14* **P** *Bp* **V** R E MERRY
FARLEY HILL (St John the Evangelist) *see* Swallowfield *Ox*
FARLINGTON (St Andrew) (Church of the Resurrection) *Portsm 6* **P** *Dr R A L Leatherdale and E G Nugee Esq (jt)* **R** J R PINDER, **C** A C LEONARD, **NSM** J L FELLOWS
FARLINGTON (St Leonard) *see* Sheriff Hutton, Farlington, Stillington etc *York*
FARLOW (St Giles) *see* Stottesdon w Farlow, Cleeton and Silvington *Heref*
FARMBOROUGH (All Saints) and Marksbury and Stanton Prior *B & W 9* **P** *MMCET (3 turns), Duchy of Cornwall (1 turn), and DBF (1 turn)* **R** A KENNEDY
FARMCOTE (St Faith) *see* The Guitings, Cutsdean and Farmcote *Glouc*
FARMINGTON (St Peter) *see* Northleach w Hampnett and Farmington *Glouc*
FARMOOR (St Mary) *see* Cumnor *Ox*
FARNBOROUGH (All Saints) *see* Beedon and Peasemore w W Ilsley and Farnborough *Ox*
FARNBOROUGH (St Botolph) *see* Avon Dassett w Farnborough and Fenny Compton *Cov*
FARNBOROUGH (St Giles) (St Nicholas) *Roch 16* **P** *Em Coll Cam* **R** M R H TURNER, **C** M D PALMER
FARNBOROUGH, NORTH (St Peter) (Good Shepherd) *Guildf 1* **P** *Patr Bd* **TR** A C P BODDINGTON, **TV** S D PAYNTER, **C** E B PHILLIPS, **NSM** M JAMES, S J CRABTREE
FARNBOROUGH, SOUTH (St Mark) *Guildf 1* **P** *Bp* **V** I C HEDGES
FARNCOMBE (St John the Evangelist) *Guildf 4* **P** *Bp* **R** T W KING, **C** D HENLEY
FARNDALE (St Mary) *see* Kirkbymoorside w Gillamoor, Farndale etc *York*
FARNDON (St Chad) and Coddington *Ches 5* **P** *Duke of Westmr and D&C (jt)* **V** D A BOYD
FARNDON (St Peter) w Thorpe, Hawton and Cotham *S'well 3* **P** *Ld Chan* **R** J B QUARRELL
FARNDON, EAST (St John the Baptist) *see* Arthingworth, Harrington w Oxendon and E Farndon *Pet*
FARNHAM (St Andrew) *Guildf 3* **P** *Bp* **R** A K TUCK, **C** M S NICHOLLS, M BLAKE
FARNHAM (St Laurence) *see* Tollard Royal w Farnham, Gussage St Michael etc *Sarum*
FARNHAM (St Mary) *see* Gt and Lt Glemham, Blaxhall etc *St E*
FARNHAM (St Mary the Virgin) *see* Stansted Mountfitchet w Birchanger and Farnham *Chelmsf*
FARNHAM (St Oswald) w Scotton and Staveley and Copgrove and Arkendale *Ripon 1* **P** *Bp, DBP, R Knaresborough, MMCET, and Major Sir Arthur Collins (jt)* **R** P GARNER
FARNHAM COMMON (St John the Evangelist) *see* Farnham Royal w Hedgerley *Ox*
FARNHAM ROYAL (St Mary the Virgin) w Hedgerley *Ox 23* **P** *Bp and Eton Coll (jt)* **R** M D SMITH, **C** P A ROBERTS, **NSM** S F BEDWELL
FARNHAM ROYAL SOUTH (St Michael) *see* W Slough *Ox*
FARNINGHAM (St Peter and St Paul) *see* Eynsford w Farningham and Lullingstone *Roch*
FARNLEY (All Saints) *see* Leathley w Farnley, Fewston and Blubberhouses *Bradf*
FARNLEY (St Michael) *Ripon 6* **P** *Bp* **R** C C GARRUD
FARNLEY, NEW (St James) *see* Farnley *Ripon*
FARNLEY TYAS (St Lucias) *see* Almondbury w Farnley Tyas *Wakef*
FARNSFIELD (St Michael) *S'well 15* **P** *Bp* **V** D J BARTLETT, **NSM** F CLARKE
FARNWORTH (St George) *see* New Bury *Man*
FARNWORTH (St Luke) (Bold Mission) (Cronton Mission) *Liv 13* **P** *V Prescot St Mary* **V** M C FREEMAN, **C** P MAKIN
FARNWORTH, EAST (All Saints) (St John) (St Peter) (St Thomas) and Kearsley *Man 12* **P** *Bp (2 turns), Ld Chan (1 turn)* **TV** B HARTLEY, F M SHAW, **NSM** P S CASTLE
FARRINGDON (All Saints) *see* Chawton and Farringdon *Win*
FARRINGDON (St Petrock and St Barnabas) *see* Aylesbeare, Rockbeare, Farringdon etc *Ex*
FARRINGTON GURNEY (St John the Baptist) *B & W 12* **P** *Bp* **V** R E INGLESBY
FARSLEY (St John the Evangelist) *Bradf 3* **P** *V Calverley* **V** J N WHITE
FARTHINGHOE (St Michael and All Angels) *see* Aynho and Croughton w Evenley etc *Pet*
FARTHINGSTONE (St Mary the Virgin) *see* Blakesley w Adstone and Maidford etc *Pet*
FARWAY (St Michael and All Angels) *see* Colyton, Southleigh, Offwell, Widworthy etc *Ex*
FATFIELD (St George) *Dur 11* **P** *Lord Lambton* **P-in-c** R S WILSON, **C** A J FARISH
FAULKBOURNE (St Germanus) *see* Fairstead w Terling and White Notley etc *Chelmsf*
FAULS (Holy Emmanuel) *Lich 23* **P** *V Prees* **V** D J TITLEY
FAVERSHAM (St Mary of Charity) *Cant 6* **P** *D&C* **V** G R D MANLEY, **C** A J EVANS
FAWDON (St Mary the Virgin) *see* Newc Epiphany *Newc*
FAWKENHURST *Cant 12* **P** *DBP* **R** *Vacant*
FAWKHAM (St Mary) and Hartley *Roch 1* **P** *Bp and D&C (jt)* **R** G B McCORMACK
FAWLEY (All Saints) *Win 10* **P** *Bp* **R** G J PHILBRICK, **C** S ARMITAGE
FAWLEY (St Mary) *see* Brightwalton w Catmore, Leckhampstead etc *Ox*
FAWLEY (St Mary the Virgin) *see* Hambleden Valley *Ox*
FAWSLEY (St Mary the Virgin) *see* Badby w Newham and Charwelton w Fawsley etc *Pet*
FAZAKERLEY (Emmanuel) (St Paul) *Liv 7* **P** *Patr Bd* **TR** D H HARRISON, **TV** R J DRIVER, J E DUFFIELD
FAZAKERLEY Sparrow Hall (St George) *see* Fazakerley Em *Liv*
FAZAKERLEY (St Nathanael) *see* Walton-on-the-Hill *Liv*
FAZELEY (St Paul) (St Barnabas) *Lich 4* **P** *Bp* **V** H J BAKER
FEATHERSTONE (All Saints) *Wakef 11* **P** *Ch Ch Ox* **V** N CLEWS
FEATHERSTONE (School Chapel) *see* Haltwhistle and Greenhead *Newc*
FECKENHAM (St John the Baptist) *see* Bowbrook N *Worc*
FEERING (All Saints) *Chelmsf 24* **P** *Bp* **V** A R MOODY
FELBRIDGE (St John) *S'wark 25* **P** *DBP* **V** S G BOWEN
FELBRIGG (St Margaret) *see* Roughton and Felbrigg, Metton, Sustead etc *Nor*
FELIXKIRK (St Felix) w Boltby *York 20* **P** *Abp* **P-in-c** P R A R HOARE
FELIXSTOWE (St John the Baptist) (St Edmund) *St E 2* **P** *Bp* **V** K FRANCIS, **NSM** I H CAMPBELL
FELIXSTOWE (St Peter and St Paul) (St Andrew) (St Nicholas) *St E 2* **P** *Ch Trust Fund Trust* **P-in-c** P S LAWRIE
FELKIRK (St Peter) w Brierley *Wakef 7* **P** *Bp* **V** A N DAWKINS
FELLING (Christ Church) *Dur 12* **P** *CPAS* **V** *Vacant* 0191-469 2440
FELLISCLIFFE (Mission Church) *see* Hampsthwaite and Killinghall *Ripon*
FELMERSHAM (St Mary) *St Alb 15* **P** *Bp* **P-in-c** D E CLAYPOLE WHITE
FELMINGHAM (St Andrew), Skeyton, Colby, Banningham, Tuttington and Suffield *Nor 12* **P** *Bp, D&C, P H C Barber Esq, and J T D Shaw Esq (jt)* **R** P I IMPEY
FELPHAM (St Mary the Virgin) w Middleton *Chich 1* **P** *D&C* **R** R D HARRIS, **NSM** A B VENESS
FELSHAM (St Peter) *see* Cockfield w Bradfield St Clare, Felsham etc *St E*
FELSTED (Holy Cross) and Little Dunmow *Chelmsf 18* **P** *CPAS* **NSM** A C BUSHELL
FELTHAM (Christ Church) (St Dunstan) *Lon 11* **P** *Bp* **V** P R WRAGG
FELTHORPE (St Margaret) *see* Drayton w Felthorpe *Nor*
FELTON (St Katharine and the Noble Army of Martyrs) *see* Winford w Felton Common Hill *B & W*
FELTON (St Michael and All Angels) *Newc 9* **P** *Bp* **P-in-c** P A G ETTERLEY
FELTON (St Michael the Archangel) *see* Bodenham w Hope-under-Dinmore, Felton etc *Heref*
FELTON, WEST (St Michael) *Lich 19* **P** *Bp* **P-in-c** D R NORTH, **NSM** J F EDGE
FELTWELL (St Mary) w St Nicholas *Ely 15* **P** *Bp* **P-in-c** D J KIGHTLEY
FEN DITTON (Holy Cross) (St Mary Magdalene) (St Mary the Virgin) *Ely 6* **P** *Bp* **R** L A MARSH
FEN DRAYTON (St Mary the Virgin) w Conington and Lolworth and Swavesey *Ely 5* **P** *The Crown, Jes Coll Cam, SMF, and Ch Coll Cam (by turn)* **R** J D YULE, **NSM** A F JESSON
FENCE-IN-PENDLE (St Anne) and Newchurch-in-Pendle *Blackb 7* **P** *Ld Chan* **V** T N HOWARD
FENCOTE (St Andrew) *see* Kirkby Fleetham w Langton on Swale and Scruton *Ripon*

FENHAM (St James and St Basil) *Newc 7* **P** *Bp* **V** *Vacant* 0191-274 5078
FENISCLIFFE (St Francis) *Blackb 5* **P** *Bp* **V** J G O'CONNOR
FENISCOWLES (Immanuel) *Blackb 5* **P** *V Blackb* **V** J R CREE, **NSM** M J WEDGEWORTH
FENITON (St Andrew), Buckerell and Escot *Ex 7* **P** *DBP, D&C and J M Kennaway Esq (jt)* **P-in-c** R J GORDON
FENNY BENTLEY (St Edmund King and Martyr), Kniveton, Thorpe and Tissington *Derby 8* **P** *Bp and Sir John FitzHerbert, Bt (jt)* **P-in-c** C D HARRISON
FENNY DRAYTON (St Michael and All Angels) *see* Higham-on-the-Hill w Fenny Drayton and Witherley *Leic*
FENNY STRATFORD (St Martin) *Ox 25* **P** *Bp* **V** S L HUCKLE, **NSM** I W THOMAS
FENSTANTON (St Peter and St Paul) *Ely 9* **P** *Bp* **V** P S G CAMERON
FENTON (All Saints) *see* Brant Broughton and Beckingham *Linc*
FENTON (Christ Church) *Lich 12* **P** *R Stoke-on-Trent* **V** D A CAMERON
FENWICK and MOSS (St John) *see* Fishlake w Sykehouse, Kirk Bramwith, Fenwick etc *Sheff*
FEOCK (St Feock) *Truro 6* **P** *Bp* **P-in-c** G C H WATSON, **Hon C** I F FRITH
FERHAM PARK (St Paul) *see* Masbrough *Sheff*
FERNDOWN (St Mary) *see* Hampreston *Sarum*
FERNHAM (St John the Evangelist) *see* Ashbury, Compton Beauchamp and Longcot w Fernham *Ox*
FERNHURST (St Margaret) *Chich 10* **P** *Cowdray Trust* **V** W S CROFT
FERNILEE (Holy Trinity) *see* Whaley Bridge *Ches*
FERRIBY, NORTH (All Saints) *York 15* **P** *Patr Bd* **TR** C J ASTILL, **TV** R H O HILL
FERRIBY, SOUTH (St Nicholas) *Linc 6* **P** *Bp* **P-in-c** G A PLUMB
FERRING (St Andrew) *Chich 5* **P** *D&C* **V** A K McNICOL
FERRYBRIDGE (St Andrew) *Wakef 11* **P** *D&C York* **P-in-c** N T B STRAFFORD
FERRYHILL (St Luke) (St Martha and St Mary) *Dur 5* **P** *D&C* **V** K LUMSDON
FERSFIELD (St Andrew) *see* Bressingham w N and S Lopham and Fersfield *Nor*
FETCHAM (St Mary) *Guildf 10* **P** *Bp* **R** P H BOUGHTON
FEWSTON (St Michael and St Lawrence) *see* Leathley w Farnley, Fewston and Blubberhouses *Bradf*
FIDDINGTON (St Martin) *see* Stogursey w Fiddington *B & W*
FIELD BROUGHTON (St Peter) *see* Lindale w Field Broughton *Carl*
FIELD DALLING (St Andrew) *see* Gunthorpe w Bale w Field Dalling, Saxlingham etc *Nor*
FIFEHEAD MAGDALEN (St Mary Magdalene) *see* Gillingham *Sarum*
FIFEHEAD NEVILLE (All Saints) *see* Hazelbury Bryan and the Hillside Par *Sarum*
FIFIELD (St John the Baptist) *see* Shipton-under-Wychwood w Milton-under-Wychwood *Ox*
FIFIELD BAVANT (St Martin) *see* Chalke Valley W *Sarum*
FIGHELDEAN (St Michael and All Angels) *see* Avon Valley *Sarum*
FILBY (All Saints), Thrigby, Mautby, Stokesby, Runham and Burgh w Billockby *Nor 6* **P** *Bp, Adn Nor, DBP, Mrs Z K Cognetti, R T Daniel Esq, and I F M Lucas Esq (jt)* **R** J E ANDERSON
FILEY (St John) (St Oswald) *York 16* **P** *PCC* **V** C W HUMPHRIES
FILKINS (St Peter) *see* Shill Valley and Broadshire *Ox*
FILLEIGH (St Paul) *see* S Molton w Nymet St George, High Bray etc *Ex*
FILLINGHAM (St Andrew) *see* Ingham w Cammeringham w Fillingham *Linc*
FILLONGLEY (St Mary and All Saints) and Corley *Cov 5* **P** *Bp and Ch Soc Trust (jt)* **V** J F LAW
FILTON (St Peter) *Bris 6* **P** *Bp* **R** B R ARMAN, **NSM** E M DESMOND
FIMBER (St Mary) *see* Sledmere and Cowlam w Fridaythorpe, Fimer etc *York*
FINBOROUGH, GREAT (St Andrew) w Onehouse and Harleston *St E 6* **P** *Bp* **P-in-c** N J HARTLEY
FINBOROUGH, LITTLE (St Mary) *see* Hitcham w Lt Finborough *St E*
FINCHAM (St Martin) *Ely 16* **P** *Bp* **P-in-c** G PARROTT
FINCHAMPSTEAD (St James) *Ox 16* **P** *DBP* **R** *Vacant* (0118) 973 2102
FINCHFIELD (St Thomas) *see* Tettenhall Wood *Lich*
FINCHINGFIELD (St John the Baptist) and Cornish Hall End and Wethersfield w Shalford *Chelmsf 15* **P** *Mrs E M Bishop and Bp (alt)* **V** J F H SHEAD
FINCHLEY (Christ Church) *Lon 14* **P** *Ch Patr Trust* **V** T D ATKINS
FINCHLEY (Holy Trinity) *Lon 16* **P** *Bp* **V** L B HILL
FINCHLEY (St Barnabas) *see* Woodside Park St Barn *Lon*
FINCHLEY (St Mary) *Lon 14* **P** *Bp* **R** D J BARNETT, **C** J M YATES
FINCHLEY (St Paul) (St Luke) *Lon 14* **P** *Simeon Trustees and Ch Patr Trust (jt)* **V** P M TEMPLEMAN, **C** A G THOM
FINCHLEY, EAST (All Saints) *Lon 14* **P** *Bp* **V** C R HARDY
FINDERN (All Saints) *Derby 16* **P** *Bp* **P-in-c** D J T RYMER
FINDON (St John the Baptist) w Clapham and Patching *Chich 5* **P** *Abp, Bp, and J E P Somerset Esq (jt)* **V** Z E ALLEN
FINDON VALLEY (All Saints) *Chich 5* **P** *Bp* **V** *Vacant* (01903) 872900
FINEDON (St Mary the Virgin) *Pet 10* **P** *Bp* **V** *Vacant* (01933) 680285
FINGEST (St Bartholomew) *see* Hambleden Valley *Ox*
FINGHALL (St Andrew) *see* Spennithorne w Finghall and Hauxwell *Ripon*
FINGRINGHOE (St Andrew) w East Donyland and Abberton w Langenhoe *Chelmsf 16* **P** *Bp (3 turns), Ld Chan (1 turn)* **R** R J HANDSCOMBE, **C** R WILKINSON
FINHAM (St Martin in the Fields) *Cov 3* **P** *Bp* **V** D T PETTIFOR, **C** D E KERR
FINMERE (St Michael) *see* Shelswell *Ox*
FINNINGHAM (St Bartholomew) *see* Walsham le Willows and Finningham w Westhorpe *St E*
FINNINGLEY (Holy Trinity and St Oswald) w Auckley *S'well 1* **P** *DBP* **P-in-c** D OTTEWELL
FINSBURY (St Clement) (St Barnabas) (St Matthew) *Lon 5* **P** *D&C St Paul's* **P-in-c** L S A MARSH
FINSBURY PARK (St Thomas) *Lon 5* **P** *Abp* **V** S R COLES
FINSTALL (St Godwald) *Worc 7* **P** *V Stoke Prior* **P-in-c** P A HARVEY
FINSTHWAITE (St Peter) *see* Leven Valley *Carl*
FIR TREE (St Mary the Virgin) *see* Howden-le-Wear and Hunwick *Dur*
FIR VALE (St Cuthbert) *see* Sheff St Cuth *Sheff*
FIRBANK (St John the Evangelist), Howgill and Killington *Bradf 6* **P** *Ld Chan and V Sedbergh (alt)* **V** L FOSTER, **Hon C** A W FELL
FIRBECK (St Martin) w Letwell *Sheff 5* **P** *Bp* **R** P IRESON
FIRLE, WEST (St Peter) *see* Glynde, W Firle and Beddingham *Chich*
FIRSBY (St Andrew) w Great Steeping *Linc 7* **P** *Mrs J M Fox-Robinson* **R** G ROBSON
FISH HALL (Mission Church) *see* Tonbridge SS Pet and Paul *Roch*
FISHBOURNE, NEW (St Peter and St Mary) *Chich 3* **P** *Ld Chan* **R** M A COLLIS
FISHBURN (St Catherine) *see* Sedgefield *Dur*
FISHERMEAD (Trinity Church) *see* Woughton *Ox*
FISHERTON ANGER (St Paul) *Sarum 15* **P** *Ch Patr Trust* **P-in-c** R A CHARKHAM, **C** T C DAVIS, **NSM** M G HUXTABLE
FISHLAKE (St Cuthbert) w Sykehouse, Kirk Bramwith, Fenwick and Moss *Sheff 11* **P** *Duchy of Lanc (1 turn), D&C Dur (2 turns), and Bp (1 turn)* **R** J M OSGERBY, **NSM** E S ATHERFOLD
FISHLEY (St Mary) *see* Acle w Fishley and N Burlingham *Nor*
FISHPOND (St John the Baptist) *see* Marshwood Vale TM *Sarum*
FISHPONDS (All Saints) *Bris 7* **P** *Bp* **V** R J BURBRIDGE, **Hon C** J A KINGS
FISHPONDS (St John) *Bris 7* **P** *Bp* **V** J G BRAY, **C** N R WALLACE
FISHPONDS (St Mary) *Bris 7* **P** *Bp* **V** R G MINSON
FISHTOFT (St Guthlac) *Linc 20* **P** *DBP* **R** M A COOPER
FISKERTON (St Clement) w Reepham *Linc 3* **P** *D&C and Mercers' Co (jt)* **R** M K ROBERTS
FITTLETON (All Saints) *see* Avon Valley *Sarum*
FITTLEWORTH (St Mary the Virgin) *see* Stopham and Fittleworth *Chich*
FITTON HILL (St Cuthbert) *see* Bardsley *Man*
FITZ (St Peter and St Paul) *see* Bicton, Montford w Shrawardine and Fitz *Lich*
FITZHEAD (St James) *see* Milverton w Halse and Fitzhead *B & W*
FITZWILLIAM (St Maurice) *see* Kinsley w Wragby *Wakef*
FIVE ASHES (Church of the Good Shepherd) *see* Mayfield *Chich*
FIVE OAK GREEN (St Luke) *see* Tudeley w Capel *Roch*
FIVEHEAD (St Martin) *see* Curry Rivel w Fivehead and Swell *B & W*
FIXBY (St Francis) *see* N Huddersfield *Wakef*
FLACKWELL HEATH (Christ Church) *Ox 29* **P** *DBP* **P-in-c** C D BULL

FLADBURY (St John the Baptist), Wyre Piddle and Moor *Worc 4* **P** *Bp* **R** K A BOYCE, **NSM** S J GIBBONS
FLAGG (School Mission Room) *see* Taddington, Chelmorton and Flagg, and Monyash *Derby*
FLAMBOROUGH (St Oswald) *see* Bempton w Flamborough, Reighton w Speeton *York*
FLAMSTEAD (St Leonard) *St Alb 8* **P** *Univ Coll Ox* **C** D J KERR, **Hon C** G H KING
FLAUNDEN (St Mary Magdalene) *see* Chenies and Lt Chalfont, Latimer and Flaunden *Ox*
FLAWBOROUGH (St Peter) *see* Staunton w Flawborough *S'well*
FLAX BOURTON (St Michael and All Angels) *B & W 13* **P** *Lord Wraxall* **P-in-c** J B BISHOP
FLAXLEY (St Mary the Virgin) *see* Westbury-on-Severn w Flaxley and Blaisdon *Glouc*
FLAXTON (St Lawrence) *see* Whitwell w Crambe, Flaxton, Foston etc *York*
FLECKNEY (St Nicholas) and Kilby *Leic 5* **P** *Bp and Hon Ann Brooks (jt)* **V** B R GLOVER, **Hon C** C E SOUTHALL
FLECKNOE (St Mark) *see* Grandborough w Willoughby and Flecknoe *Cov*
FLEET (All Saints) (St Philip and St James) *Guildf 1* **P** *Bp* **V** D HOLT, **C** P P MOYSE, **NSM** R W DYER
FLEET (Holy Trinity) *see* Chickerell w Fleet *Sarum*
FLEET (St Mary Magdalene) w Gedney *Linc 16* **P** *The Crown and DBP (alt)* **R** D F BRATLEY
FLEETWOOD (St David) *Blackb 13* **P** *Bp and Meynell Trustees (jt)* **V** E K SILLIS
FLEETWOOD (St Nicholas) *Blackb 13* **P** *Bp and Meynell Trustees (jt)* **V** J TALLANT
FLEETWOOD (St Peter) *Blackb 13* **P** *Meynell Trustees* **V** *Vacant* (01253) 771642
FLEMPTON (St Catherine of Alexandria) *see* Culford, W Stow and Wordwell w Flempton etc *St E*
FLETCHAMSTEAD (St James) *Cov 3* **P** *Bp* **V** R J COOKE, **C** E A SMITH
FLETCHING (St Mary and St Andrew) *Chich 21* **P** *Abp* **NSM** J D GRAY
FLETTON (St Margaret) *Ely 13* **P** *Sir Stephen Hastings* **P-in-c** D G STEVENS
FLIMBY (St Nicholas) *Carl 7* **P** *Bp* **P-in-c** A BUTLER
FLIMWELL (St Augustine of Canterbury) *see* Ticehurst and Flimwell *Chich*
FLINTHAM (St Augustine of Canterbury) *S'well 8* **P** *M T Hildyard Esq* **V** J PULMAN
FLITCHAM (St Mary the Virgin) *see* Sandringham w W Newton and Appleton etc *Nor*
FLITTON (St John the Baptist) *see* Silsoe, Pulloxhill and Flitton *St Alb*
FLITWICK (St Andrew) (St Peter and St Paul) *St Alb 9* **P** *DBP* **V** M F J BRADLEY, **C** S MORTON
FLIXBOROUGH (All Saints) w Burton upon Stather *Linc 4* **P** *Sir Reginald Sheffield, Bt* **Hon C** D E CORNELIUS
FLIXTON (St John) *Man 7* **P** *Bp* **V** K J MASSEY, **NSM** R W GREEN, B R CORKE
FLIXTON (St Mary) *see* S Elmham and Ilketshall *St E*
FLIXTON (St Michael) *Man 7* **P** *Bp* **R** W J TWIDELL, **C** A J HARDY, **NSM** A H CLEPHANE
FLOCKTON (St James the Great) cum Denby Grange *Wakef 6* **P** *R Carter's Trustees* **V** *Vacant* (01924) 848349
FLOOKBURGH (St John the Baptist) *Carl 10* **P** *R H Cavendish Esq* **P-in-c** N J ASH
FLORDON (St Michael) *see* Tasburgh w Tharston, Forncett and Flordon *Nor*
FLORE (All Saints) *see* Heyford w Stowe Nine Churches and Flore etc *Pet*
FLOWTON (St Mary) *see* Somersham w Flowton and Offton w Willisham *St E*
FLUSHING (St Peter) *see* Mylor w Flushing *Truro*
FLYFORD FLAVELL (St Peter) *see* Abberton, The Flyfords, Naunton Beauchamp etc *Worc*
FOBBING (St Michael) *Chelmsf 14* **P** *The Crown* **R** *Vacant* (01375) 672002
FOLESHILL (St Laurence) *Cov 2* **P** *Ld Chan* **V** M R CLEVELAND
FOLESHILL (St Paul) *Cov 2* **P** *Ld Chan* **V** A J CANNING
FOLEY PARK (Holy Innocents) *see* Kidderminster St Jo and H Innocents *Worc*
FOLKE (St Lawrence) *see* The Caundles w Folke and Holwell *Sarum*
FOLKESTONE Foord (St John the Baptist) *see* Foord St Jo *Cant*
FOLKESTONE (Holy Trinity w Christ Church) *Cant 5* **P** *Abp* **R** J C TAPPER
FOLKESTONE (St Augustine) (St Mary and St Eanswythe) *Cant 5* **P** *Abp* **V** J W DILNOT, **Min** D G RIDLEY, **C** B D R WOOD
FOLKESTONE (St George) *see* Sandgate St Paul w Folkestone St Geo *Cant*
FOLKESTONE (St Peter) *Cant 5* **P** *Trustees* **V** M A HOUGHTON
FOLKESTONE (St Saviour) *Cant 5* **P** *Abp* **V** G J BUTLER
FOLKESWORTH (St Helen) *see* Stilton w Denton and Caldecote etc *Ely*
FOLKINGHAM (St Andrew) *see* S Lafford *Linc*
FOLKINGTON (St Peter ad Vincula) *see* Arlington, Folkington and Wilmington *Chich*
FOLKTON (St John) *see* Willerby w Ganton and Folkton *York*
FOLLIFOOT (St Joseph and St James) *see* Spofforth w Kirk Deighton *Ripon*
FONTHILL BISHOP (All Saints) *see* Tisbury *Sarum*
FONTHILL GIFFORD (Holy Trinity) *as above*
FONTMELL MAGNA (St Andrew) *see* The Iwernes, Sutton Waldron and Fontmell Magna *Sarum*
FOOLOW (St Hugh) *see* Eyam *Derby*
FOORD (St John the Baptist) *Cant 5* **P** *CPAS* **V** H W J HARLAND, **C** D P MOUNCER
FOOTS CRAY (All Saints) *Roch 17* **P** *Ld Chan* **R** G S COLVILLE
FORCETT (St Cuthbert) and Aldbrough and Melsonby *Ripon 2* **P** *DBP and Univ Coll Ox (alt)* **R** M D GRAY
FORD (St Andrew) *see* Clymping and Yapton w Ford *Chich*
FORD (St John of Jerusalem) *see* Leominster *Heref*
FORD (St John the Evangelist) *see* Colerne w N Wraxall *Bris*
FORD (St Mark) *see* Devonport St Mark Ford *Ex*
FORD (St Michael) *Heref 13* **P** *Bp* **V** *Vacant* (01743) 850254
FORD (St Michael and All Angels) and Etal *Newc 12* **P** *Lord Joicey* **R** V T DICKINSON
FORD END (St John the Evangelist) *see* Gt Waltham w Ford End *Chelmsf*
FORDCOMBE (St Peter) *see* Penshurst and Fordcombe *Roch*
FORDHAM (All Saints) *Chelmsf 17* **P** *Reform Ch Trust, Ball Coll Ox (alt)* **R** M R J NEVILLE
FORDHAM (St Peter and St Mary Magdalene) *Ely 3* **P** *Jes Coll Cam* **V** A HASELHURST
FORDHOUSES (St James) *see* Bushbury *Lich*
FORDINGBRIDGE (St Mary) *Win 8* **P** *K Coll Cam* **P-in-c** T E DAYKIN, **C** S W MILLER, **NSM** C E ROLFE
FORDON (St James) *see* Burton Fleming w Fordon, Grindale etc *York*
FOREBRIDGE (St Paul) *see* Stafford St Paul Forebridge *Lich*
FOREMARK (St Saviour) *Derby 16* **P** *Mrs M Burdett Fisher (1 turn), Miss I A M Harpur-Crewe (2 turns)* **V** J R P BARKER
FOREST (St Stephen) *see* Rainow w Saltersford and Forest *Ches*
FOREST GATE (All Saints) (St Edmund) *Chelmsf 3* **P** *Bp* **P-in-c** B K SHIPSIDES
FOREST GATE (Emmanuel w St Peter) Upton Cross *Chelmsf 3* **P** *Bp* **V** W D N WEIR, **C** A M W WILSON, **NSM** A R EASTER
FOREST GATE (St James) *see* Stratford St Jo and Ch Ch w Forest Gate St Jas *Chelmsf*
FOREST GATE (St Mark) *Chelmsf 3* **P** *Ch Patr Trust* **V** P J STOW, **NSM** S A LAW
FOREST GATE (St Saviour) w West Ham St Matthew *Chelmsf 3* **P** *Patr Bd* **TR** J H WILLIAMS
FOREST GREEN (Holy Trinity) *see* Ockley, Okewood and Forest Green *Guildf*
FOREST HILL (Christ Church) (St Paul) *S'wark 5* **P** *Bp and Earl of Dartmouth (jt)* **V** J M THOMAS, **NSM** T G BURMAN
FOREST HILL (St Augustine) Honor Oak Park *S'wark 5* **P** *Bp* **V** M J R COUNSELL, **Hon C** S COOK, **NSM** R O SMITH, K G SIMS
FOREST HILL (St Nicholas) *see* Wheatley *Ox*
FOREST-IN-TEESDALE (St Mary the Virgin) *see* Middleton-in-Teesdale w Forest and Frith *Dur*
FOREST OF DEAN (Christ Church) w English Bicknor *Glouc 4* **P** *The Crown (3 turns), SMF (1 turn)* **P-in-c** C P COPELAND
FOREST OF DEAN (Holy Trinity) *see* Dean Forest H Trin *Glouc*
FOREST ROW (Holy Trinity) *Chich 7* **P** *V E Grinstead* **V** R N HARLEY, **NSM** A W B LEACH
FOREST TOWN (St Alban) *S'well 2* **P** *Bp* **P-in-c** H R SMITH
FORESTSIDE (Christ Church) *see* Stansted *Chich*
FORMBY (Holy Trinity) *Liv 5* **P** *Trustees* **V** C A QUINE, **C** D A LAMB, **NSM** P J UPTON-JONES
FORMBY (St Luke) *Liv 5* **P** *Bp* **V** A R WOODHOUSE
FORMBY (St Peter) *Liv 5* **P** *R Walton* **V** P W ORMROD
FORNCETT (St Peter) *see* Tasburgh w Tharston, Forncett and Flordon *Nor*
FORNCETT END (St Edmund) *as above*
FORNHAM ALL SAINTS (All Saints) and Fornham St Martin w Timworth *St E 13* **P** *Bp* **NSM** E M ELLIOTT

FORNHAM ST MARTIN (St Martin) *see* Fornham All SS and Fornham St Martin w Timworth *St E*
FORRABURY (St Symphorian) *see* Boscastle w Davidstow *Truro*
FORSBROOK (St Peter) *see* Draycott-le-Moors w Forsbrook *Lich*
FORTHAMPTON (St Mary) *see* Deerhurst, Apperley w Forthampton and Chaceley *Glouc*
FORTON (All Saints) *see* Newport w Longford, Chetwynd and Forton *Lich*
FORTON (St John the Evangelist) *Portsm 3* **P** *DBP* **NSM** D KING
FORTY HILL (Jesus Church) *Lon 18* **P** *V Enfield* **V** P N L PYTCHES
FOSDYKE (All Saints) *see* Sutterton w Fosdyke and Algarkirk *Linc*
FOSTON (All Saints) *see* Whitwell w Crambe, Flaxton, Foston etc *York*
FOSTON (St Bartholomew) *see* Countesthorpe w Foston *Leic*
FOSTON (St Peter) *see* Saxonwell *Linc*
FOSTON-ON-THE-WOLDS (St Andrew) *see* Beeford w Frodingham and Foston *York*
FOTHERBY (St Mary) *Linc 12* **P** *Ld Chan (1 turn), DBP, MMCET and M M Sleight Esq (1 turn), and Bp (1 turn)* **P-in-c** M E BURSON-THOMAS, **NSM** A HUNDLEBY, J M WRISDALE
FOTHERINGHAY (St Mary and All Saints) *see* Warmington, Tansor, Cotterstock and Fotheringhay *Pet*
FOULDEN (All Saints) *see* Oxborough w Foulden and Caldecote *Nor*
FOULNESS (St Mary the Virgin) *see* Gt Wakering w Foulness *Chelmsf*
FOULRIDGE (St Michael and All Angels) *Blackb 7* **P** *Bp* **V** G SENIOR
FOULSHAM (Holy Innocents) Hindolveston and Guestwick *Nor 22* **P** *Lord Hastings, Mrs M E E Bulwer-Long and D&C (alt)* **P-in-c** C J ENGELSEN
FOUNTAINS Group, The *Ripon 3* **P** *D&C* **R** T KEDDIE, **C** M J STEWART
FOUR ELMS (St Paul) *see* Hever, Four Elms and Mark Beech *Roch*
FOUR MARKS (Good Shepherd) *Win 2* **P** *Bp* **V** C M NOYCE
FOUR OAKS (All Saints) *Birm 13* **P** *Bp* **V** D E McCORMACK
FOURSTONES (St Aidan) *see* Warden w Newbrough *Newc*
FOVANT (St George), Sutton Mandeville and Teffont Evias w Teffont Magna and Compton Chamberlayne *Sarum 13* **P** *Reformation Ch Trust, Bp, and Ch Soc Trust (jt)* **R** J C EADE
FOWEY (St Fimbarrus) *Truro 1* **P** *Ch Soc Trust* **V** D J N MADDOCK
FOWLMERE (St Mary) *Ely 8* **P** *Bp* **P-in-c** J B MYNORS
FOWNHOPE (St Mary) w Mordiford, Brockhampton and Fawley and Woolhope *Heref 4* **P** *D&C (4 turns), and Major R J Hereford (1 turn)* **R** A E DICKSON, **NSM** M M DEES
FOXCOTE (St James the Less) *see* Camerton w Dunkerton, Foxcote and Shoscombe *B & W*
FOXDALE (St Paul) *S & M 3* **P** *The Crown and Bp (alt)* **V** P J BENNETT
FOXEARTH (St Peter and St Paul) *see* Pentlow, Foxearth, Liston and Borley *Chelmsf*
FOXHAM (St John the Baptist) *see* Derry Hill w Bremhill and Foxham *Sarum*
FOXHILL (Chapel) *see* Frodsham *Ches*
FOXHOLE (St Boniface) *see* Paignton St Jo *Ex*
FOXHOLES (St Mary) *see* Langtoft w Foxholes, Butterwick, Cottam etc *York*
FOXLEY (not known) *see* Sherston Magna, Easton Grey, Luckington etc *Bris*
FOXLEY (St Thomas) *see* Lyng, Sparham, Elsing, Bylaugh, Bawdeswell etc *Nor*
FOXT (St Mark the Evangelist) w Whiston *Lich 6* **P** *Mrs G I A Dalrymple-Hamilton and Mrs C I Townley (alt)* **P-in-c** J B HARROP
FOXTON (St Andrew) w Gumley and Laughton and Lubenham *Leic 4* **P** *Bp, A M Finn Esq, and D&C Linc (by turn)* **P-in-c** S M LEE, **C** I L JOHNSON
FOXTON (St Laurence) *Ely 8* **P** *Bp* **P-in-c** W G THOMAS, R M NANCARROW
FOY (St Mary) *see* How Caple w Sollarshope, Sellack etc *Heref*
FRADLEY (St Stephen) *see* Alrewas *Lich*
FRADSWELL (St James the Less), Gayton, Milwich and Weston on Trent *Lich 10* **P** *Bp, Personal Reps of Earl of Harrowby, Hertf Coll Ox and T J A Dive Esq (jt)* **P-in-c** J H STERLING, **C** J M OAKES, J Y TILLIER
FRAISTHORPE (St Edmund) *see* Skipsea w Ulrome and Barmston w Fraisthorpe *York*
FRAMFIELD (St Thomas a Becket) *Chich 21* **P** *Mrs E R Wix* **V** G T DAINTREE
FRAMILODE (St Peter) *see* Frampton on Severn, Arlingham, Saul etc *Glouc*
FRAMINGHAM EARL (St Andrew) *see* Poringland *Nor*
FRAMINGHAM PIGOT (St Andrew) *see* Thurton *Nor*
FRAMLAND Parishes, The HIGH *Leic 3* **P** *Duke of Rutland and Sir Lyonel Tollemache Bt (jt)* **P-in-c** S SAMUEL, **C** P L BOTTING
FRAMLINGHAM (St Michael) w Saxtead *St E 18* **P** *Pemb Coll Cam* **R** R W WILLCOCK, **NSM** R L COURT
FRAMPTON (St Mary) *see* Bradford Peverell, Stratton, Frampton etc *Sarum*
FRAMPTON (St Mary) (St Michael) w Kirton in Holland *Linc 21* **P** *Mercers Co (2 turns), Trustees (1 turn)* **P-in-c** E HORNER
FRAMPTON COTTERELL (St Peter) *Bris 7* **P** *SMF* **P-in-c** S E RUSHTON
FRAMPTON MANSELL (St Luke) *see* Coates, Rodmarton and Sapperton etc *Glouc*
FRAMPTON ON SEVERN (St Mary), Arlingham, Saul, Fretherne and Framilode *Glouc 8* **P** *DBP, V Standish w Haresfield etc, Brig Sir Jeffrey Darell, Bt, and Bp (jt)* **V** P CHEESMAN
FRAMSDEN (St Mary) *see* Helmingham w Framsden and Pettaugh w Winston *St E*
FRAMWELLGATE MOOR (St Aidan) *see* Dur St Cuth *Dur*
FRANCE LYNCH (St John the Baptist) *see* Chalford and France Lynch *Glouc*
FRANCHE (St Barnabas) *see* Kidderminster St Mary and All SS w Trimpley etc *Worc*
FRANKBY (St John the Divine) w Greasby St Nicholas *Ches 8* **P** *D&C* **V** G M BREFFITT, **C** M R SHORT, E C HALL
FRANKLEY (St Leonard) *Birm 4* **P** *Bp* **R** M T DENNY
FRANKTON (St Nicholas) *see* Bourton w Frankton and Stretton on Dunsmore etc *Cov*
FRANSHAM, GREAT (All Saints) *see* Gt and Lt Dunham w Gt and Lt Fransham and Sporle *Nor*
FRANSHAM, LITTLE (St Mary) *as above*
FRANT (St Alban) w Eridge *Chich 19* **P** *Bp and Marquess of Abergavenny (jt)* **R** E G DORE
FREASLEY (St Mary) *see* Dordon *Birm*
FRECHEVILLE (St Cyprian) *Sheff 2* **P** *Bp* **R** M J GILLINGHAM
FRECKENHAM (St Andrew) *see* Mildenhall *St E*
FRECKLETON (Holy Trinity) *Blackb 11* **P** *Bp* **V** S F BRIAN
FREEBY (St Mary) *see* Melton Mowbray *Leic*
FREEHAY (St Chad) *see* Cheadle w Freehay *Lich*
FREELAND (St Mary the Virgin) *see* Hanborough and Freeland *Ox*
FREEMANTLE (Christ Church) *Win 12* **P** *Bp* **P-in-c** N J COATES, **NSM** T LANE
FREETHORPE (All Saints) w Wickhampton, Halvergate, Tunstall, Beighton and Moulton *Nor 4* **P** *Bp, Ch Soc Trust, and K M Mills Esq (jt)* **R** R F GIBSON, **Hon C** T J N HULL
FREISTON (St James) w Butterwick *Linc 20* **P** *Bp* **V** B R GRELLIER, **NSM** L HALL, R T WESTLAND
FREMINGTON (St Peter) *Ex 15* **P** *MMCET* **V** P H HOCKEY
FRENCHAY (St John the Baptist) and Winterbourne Down *Bris 7* **P** *St Jo Coll Ox and SMF (jt)* **R** R J THOMAS
FRENSHAM (St Mary the Virgin) *Guildf 3* **P** *Ld Chan* **V** A L PETTERSEN, **NSM** J C NEWELL PRICE
FRESHFORD (St Peter) w Limpley Stoke and Hinton Charterhouse *B & W 9* **P** *Simeon's Trustees and V Norton St Phil (jt)* **R** D J CLARK, **C** N A SCHEMANOFF
FRESHWATER (All Saints) (St Agnes) *Portsm 8* **P** *St Jo Coll Cam* **R** B W E BANKS, **NSM** D K BELLAMY
FRESSINGFIELD (St Peter and St Paul), Menham, Metfield, Weybread and Withersdale *St E 17* **P** *Bp, Em Coll Cam, Ch Soc Trust, and SMF (jt)* **R** G WOOD, **NSM** P A SCHWIER, C D BURKE, R A WILLIS
FRESTON (St Peter) *see* Holbrook w Freston and Woolverstone *St E*
FRETHERNE (St Mary the Virgin) *see* Frampton on Severn, Arlingham, Saul etc *Glouc*
FRETTENHAM (St Swithin) *see* Spixworth w Crostwick and Frettenham *Nor*
FRIAR PARK (St Francis of Assisi) *see* W Bromwich St Fran *Lich*
FRIARMERE (St Thomas) *Man 21* **P** *Bp* **P-in-c** J R BROCKLEHURST
FRICKLEY (All Saints) *see* Bilham *Sheff*
FRIDAY BRIDGE (St Mark) *Ely 19* **P** *Bp* **V** *Vacant* (01945) 860382
FRIDAYTHORPE (St Mary) *see* Sledmere and Cowlam w Fridaythorpe, Fimer etc *York*

FRIERN BARNET (All Saints) *Lon 14* **P** *Bp* **V** A V BENJAMIN
FRIERN BARNET (St James the Great) (St John the Evangelist) *Lon 14* **P** *D&C St Paul's* **R** S J POTHEN, **C** C M CHIVERS
FRIERN BARNET (St Peter le Poer) *Lon 14* **P** *D&C St Paul's* **V** G J GILES
FRIESTHORPE (St Peter) *see* Wickenby Gp *Linc*
FRIETH (St John the Baptist) *see* Hambleden Valley *Ox*
FRIEZLAND (Christ Church) *see* St Anne Lydgate w Ch Ch Friezland *Man*
FRILSHAM (St Frideswide) *see* Hermitage and Hampstead Norreys, Cold Ash etc *Ox*
FRIMLEY (St Francis) (St Peter) *Guildf 6* **P** *R Ash* **R** N C TURTON, **C** B M JONES, **Hon C** H E B SKEET
FRIMLEY GREEN (St Andrew) *Guildf 6* **P** *Bp* **V** B K BESSANT
FRINDSBURY (All Saints) w Upnor (St Phillip and St James) *Roch 6* **P** *Bp* **V** W J N DURANT
FRING (All Saints) *see* Snettisham w Ingoldisthorpe and Fring *Nor*
FRINGFORD (St Michael) *see* Shelswell *Ox*
FRINSTED (St Dunstan) *see* Bredgar w Bicknor and Frinsted w Wormshill etc *Cant*
FRINTON (St Mary Magdalene) (St Mary the Virgin Old Church) *Chelmsf 23* **P** *CPAS* **R** A D ROSE, **C** S P CLARKE
FRISBY-ON-THE-WREAKE (St Thomas of Canterbury) *see* Upper Wreake *Leic*
FRISKNEY (All Saints) *Linc 8* **P** *Bp* **P-in-c** J DUMAT
FRISTON (St Mary Magdalene) *see* Aldringham w Thorpe, Knodishall w Buxlow etc *St E*
FRISTON (St Mary the Virgin) *see* E Dean w Friston and Jevington *Chich*
FRITCHLEY (Mission Room) *see* Crich *Derby*
FRITHELSTOCK (St Mary and St Gregory) *see* Gt and Lt Torrington and Frithelstock *Ex*
FRITHVILLE (St Peter) *see* Sibsey w Frithville *Linc*
FRITTENDEN (St Mary) *see* Sissinghurst w Frittenden *Cant*
FRITTON (St Catherine) *see* Hempnall *Nor*
FRITTON (St Edmund) *see* Somerleyton, Ashby, Fritton, Herringfleet etc *Nor*
FRITWELL (St Olave) w Souldern and Ardley w Fewcott *Ox 2* **P** *DBP, St Jo Coll Cam, and Wadh Coll Ox (by turn)* **R** *Vacant* (01869) 346739
FRIZINGHALL (St Margaret) *see* Shipley St Paul and Frizinghall *Bradf*
FRIZINGTON (St Paul) and Arlecdon *Carl 5* **P** *Bp* **P-in-c** R BOWLZER, **C** A M ARMSTRONG
FROCESTER (St Andrew) *see* Eastington and Frocester *Glouc*
FRODESLEY (St Mark) *see* Condover w Frodesley, Acton Burnell etc *Heref*
FRODINGHAM (St Lawrence) *Linc 4* **P** *Lord St Oswald* **V** M P COONEY, **C** S V MERCER-LESLIE, **NSM** M DUNFORD
FRODINGHAM, NORTH (St Elgin) *see* Beeford w Frodingham and Foston *York*
FRODSHAM (St Lawrence) *Ches 3* **P** *Ch Ch Ox* **V** M H MILLS
FROGMORE (Holy Trinity) *St Alb 1* **P** *CPAS* **V** G R BARTER, **NSM** N A WARD
FROLESWORTH (St Nicholas) *see* Claybrooke cum Wibtoft and Frolesworth *Leic*
FROME (Christ Church) *B & W 4* **P** *Bp* **V** P N RAPSEY
FROME (Holy Trinity) *B & W 4* **P** *Bp* **V** R D M MARTIN
FROME (St John the Baptist) (Blessed Virgin Mary) *B & W 4* **P** *Bp and DBP (jt)* **V** J G PESCOD, **C** I M TUCKER, **NSM** P E LAWLESS
FROME ST QUINTON (St Mary) *see* Melbury *Sarum*
FROME VAUCHURCH (St Mary) *as above*
FROMES HILL (St Matthew) *see* Bishop's Frome w Castle Frome and Fromes Hill *Heref*
FROSTENDEN (All Saints) *see* Wrentham w Benacre, Covehithe, Frostenden etc *St E*
FROSTERLEY (St Michael and All Angels) *see* Stanhope w Frosterley *Dur*
FROXFIELD (All Saints) *see* Whitton *Sarum*
FROXFIELD (St Peter) *see* Steep and Froxfield w Privett *Portsm*
FROXFIELD (St Peter on the Green) *as above*
FROYLE (Assumption of the Blessed Virgin Mary) and Holybourne *Win 2* **P** *Guild of All So and D&C (jt)* **V** J S CROFT
FRYERNING (St Mary the Virgin) w Margaretting *Chelmsf 7* **P** *Wadh Coll Ox* **P-in-c** J D BROWN, **NSM** F DRAKE
FRYSTON (St Peter) *see* Airedale w Fryston *Wakef*
FUGGLESTONE (St Peter) *see* Wilton w Netherhampton and Fugglestone *Sarum*
FULBECK (St Nicholas) *see* Caythorpe *Linc*
FULBOURN (St Vigor w All Saints) *Ely 6* **P** *St Jo Coll Cam* **R** B E KERLEY
FULBROOK (St Gabriel) *see* Walsall St Gabr Fulbrook *Lich*
FULBROOK (St James the Great) *see* Burford w Fulbrook, Taynton, Asthall etc *Ox*
FULFORD (St Oswald) *York 8* **P** *Abp* **V** R A HALL, **NSM** M COOPER
FULFORD-IN-STONE (St Nicholas) w Hilderstone *Lich 13* **P** *D&C* **V** M N GRIFFIN
FULHAM (All Saints) *Lon 9* **P** *Bp* **V** K N BOWLER
FULHAM (Christ Church) *Lon 9* **P** *CPAS* **P-in-c** S C R LEES
FULHAM (St Alban) (St Augustine) *Lon 9* **P** *Bp and City Corp (jt)* **V** G PALMER, **Hon C** G R J SHEA
FULHAM (St Andrew) Fulham Fields *Lon 9* **P** *Bp* **V** D R PAGET
FULHAM (St Dionis) Parson's Green *Lon 9* **P** *Bp* **P-in-c** A S ATKINS, **C** K D MENTZEL
FULHAM (St Etheldreda) (St Clement) *Lon 9* **P** *Bp* **P-in-c** J F H HENLEY
FULHAM (St Mary) North End *Lon 9* **P** *Ch Soc Trust* **V** R W CURL
FULHAM (St Matthew) *Lon 9* **P** *Ch Patr Trust* **V** G Q D PIPER, **C** N D BEYNON, **Dss** V S PIERSON
FULHAM (St Peter) *Lon 9* **P** *Bp* **V** *Vacant* 0171-385 2045
FULKING (Good Shepherd) *see* Poynings w Edburton, Newtimber and Pyecombe *Chich*
FULL SUTTON (St Mary) *see* Bishop Wilton w Full Sutton, Kirby Underdale etc *York*
FULLETBY (St Andrew) w Greetham and Ashby Puerorum *Linc 11* **P** *D&C (2 turns), Keble Coll Ox (1 turn)* **R** *Vacant* (01507) 588671
FULMER (St James) *see* Gerrards Cross and Fulmer *Ox*
FULMODESTON (Christ Church) *see* Barney, Fulmodeston w Croxton, Hindringham etc *Nor*
FULSHAW (St Anne) *see* Wilmslow *Ches*
FULSTOW (St Laurence) *see* Fotherby *Linc*
FULWELL (St Michael and St George) *see* Teddington SS Pet and Paul and Fulwell *Lon*
FULWOOD (Christ Church) *Blackb 14* **P** *V Lanc* **V** E J BURNS
FULWOOD (Christ Church) *Sheff 4* **P** *CPAS* **V** P H HACKING, **C** H PALMER, M J H MEYNELL
FULWOOD Lodge Moor (St Luke) *see* Lodge Moor St Luke *Sheff*
FULWOOD (St Cuthbert) *see* Preston St Cuth *Blackb*
FUNDENHALL (St Nicholas) *see* Wreningham *Nor*
FUNTINGTON (St Mary) and Sennicotts *Chich 13* **P** *Bp* **V** D A JOHNSON
FUNTLEY (St Francis) *see* Fareham SS Pet and Paul *Portsm*
FURNACE GREEN (St Andrew) *see* Southgate *Chich*
FURNESS VALE (St John) *see* Disley *Ches*
FURNEUX PELHAM (St Mary the Virgin) *see* Braughing w Furneux Pelham and Stocking Pelham *St Alb*
FURNHAM (Good Shepherd) *see* Chard Furnham w Chaffcombe, Knowle St Giles etc *B & W*
FURTHO (St Bartholomew) *see* Potterspury, Furtho, Yardley Gobion and Cosgrove *Pet*
FURZE PLATT (St Peter) *Ox 13* **P** *Bp* **NSM** M W SKINNER
FURZEBANK (Worship Centre) *see* Willenhall H Trin *Lich*
FURZTON (not known) *see* Watling Valley *Ox*
FYFIELD (St Nicholas) *see* Upper Kennet *Sarum*
FYFIELD (St Nicholas) *see* Appleshaw, Kimpton, Thruxton and Fyfield *Win*
FYFIELD (St Nicholas) w Tubney and Kingston Bagpuize *Ox 10* **P** *St Jo Coll Ox* **V** K J TRIPLOW
FYFIELD (St Nicholas), Moreton w Bobbingworth and Willingale w Shellow and Berners Roding *Chelmsf 27* **P** *Ld Chan, St Jo Coll Cam, MMCET, and Major G N Capel-Cure (by turn)* **R** R MORGAN
FYLINGDALES (St Stephen) and Hawsker cum Stainsacre *York 23* **P** *Abp* **V** L C CARBERRY
GADDESBY (St Luke) *see* S Croxton Gp *Leic*
GADDESDEN, GREAT (St John the Baptist) and LITTLE (St Peter and St Paul) *St Alb 2* **P** *N G Halsey Esq and Bp (jt)* **P-in-c** R P HOLLINGSHURST
GADEBRIDGE (St Peter) *see* Hemel Hempstead *St Alb*
GAINFORD (St Mary) *Dur 7* **P** *Trin Coll Cam* **V** T J D OLLIER
GAINSBOROUGH (All Saints) *Linc 2* **P** *Bp* **V** P W DADD
GAINSBOROUGH (St George) *Linc 2* **P** *Bp* **V** *Vacant* (01427) 612717
GAINSBOROUGH (St John the Divine) *Linc 2* **P** *Bp* **V** *Vacant* (01427) 612847
GALLEY COMMON (St Peter) *see* Camp Hill w Galley Common *Cov*
GALLEYWOOD (Junior School Worship Centre) *see* Galleywood Common *Chelmsf*
GALLEYWOOD COMMON (St Michael and All Angels) *Chelmsf 9* **P** *CPAS* **V** S BAILEY, **C** M I McNAMARA
GALMINGTON (St Michael) *see* Wilton *B & W*

GALMPTON (Chapel of The Good Shepherd) *see* Brixham w Churston Ferrers and Kingswear *Ex*
GAMBLESBY (St John) *see* Addingham, Edenhall, Langwathby and Culgaith *Carl*
GAMESLEY (Bishop Geoffrey Allen Church and County Centre) *see* Charlesworth and Dinting Vale *Derby*
GAMLINGAY (St Mary the Virgin) w Hatley (St George) and East Hatley *Ely 12* **P** *Bp and Down Coll Cam (jt)* **P-in-c** A J COLE
GAMLINGAY HEATH (St Sylvester) *see* Gamlingay w Hatley St Geo and E Hatley *Ely*
GAMSTON and Bridgford *S'well 5* **P** *DBP* **V** S D SILVESTER
GAMSTON (St Peter) w Eaton and West Drayton *S'well 5* **P** *D&C York and Bp (alt)* **R** C F ANDREWS
GANAREW (St Swithin) *see* Llangarron w Llangrove, Whitchurch and Ganarew *Heref*
GANTON (St Nicholas) *see* Willerby w Ganton and Folkton *York*
GARBOLDISHAM (St John the Baptist) *see* Guiltcross *Nor*
GARFORD (St Luke) *see* Marcham w Garford *Ox*
GARFORTH (St Mary the Virgin) *Ripon 8* **P** *DBP* **R** R G N PLANT
GARGRAVE (St Andrew) *Bradf 5* **P** *Bp* **P-in-c** M W BULL
GARRETTS GREEN (St Thomas) *Birm 10* **P** *Bp* **V** A E ASH
GARRIGILL (St John) *see* Alston Team *Newc*
GARSDALE (St John the Baptist) *see* Sedbergh, Cautley and Garsdale *Bradf*
GARSDON (All Saints), Lea and Cleverton and Charlton *Bris 12* **P** *Ch Soc Trust and Bp (jt)* **R** R K EAST
GARSINGTON (St Mary) *see* Wheatley *Ox*
GARSTANG (St Helen) Churchtown *Blackb 10* **P** *A R Pedder Esq* **V** R BRAITHWAITE
GARSTANG (St Thomas) *Blackb 10* **P** *V Churchtown St Helen* **V** R G GREENALL
GARSTON (St Michael) *Liv 4* **P** *Trustees* **V** W N LETHEREN
GARSTON, EAST (All Saints) *see* Eastbury and E Garston *Ox*
GARSWOOD (St Andrew) *see* Ashton-in-Makerfield H Trin *Liv*
GARTHORPE (St Mary) *see* Wymondham w Edmondthorpe, Buckminster etc *Leic*
GARTHORPE (St Mary) *see* N Axholme Gp *Linc*
GARTON IN HOLDERNESS (St Michael) *see* Roos and Garton in Holderness w Tunstall etc *York*
GARTON-ON-THE-WOLDS (St Michael and All Angels) *see* Wetwang and Garton-on-the-Wolds w Kirkburn *York*
GARVESTON (St Margaret) *see* Barnham Broom *Nor*
GARWAY (St Michael) *see* St Weonards w Orcop, Garway, Tretire etc *Heref*
GASTARD (St John the Baptist) *see* Gtr Corsham *Bris*
GATCOMBE (St Olave) *Portsm 8* **P** *Qu Coll Ox* **R** J W RUSSELL, **NSM** S C HENDERSON
GATE BURTON (St Helen) *see* Lea Gp *Linc*
GATE HELMSLEY (St Mary) *see* Sand Hutton *York*
GATEACRE (St Stephen) *Liv 4* **P** *Bp* **TR** P H JANVIER, **TV** V E HUGHES, A W ROBINSON, **C** P G WHITTINGTON
GATEFORTH (St Mary's Mission Room) *see* Haddlesey w Hambleton and Birkin *York*
GATELEY (St Helen) *see* Gt and Lt Ryburgh w Gateley and Testerton *Nor*
GATESHEAD (Christ Church) *Dur 12* **P** *Bp* **V** P WRIGHT
GATESHEAD Harlow Green (St Ninian) *Dur 12* **P** *Bp* **V** *Vacant* 0191-487 6685
GATESHEAD Lobley Hill (All Saints) *see* Lobley Hill *Dur*
GATESHEAD (St Chad) *see* Bensham *Dur*
GATESHEAD (St Edmund's Chapel w Holy Trinity) (Venerable Bede) *Dur 12* **P** *Bp and The Crown (alt)* **TR** K HUXLEY, **TV** P J WILCOX, H DITCHBURN
GATESHEAD (St George) *Dur 12* **P** *Trustees* **V** E M T UNDERHILL
GATESHEAD (St Helen) *Dur 12* **P** *Bp* **V** B M HARRISON
GATESHEAD FELL (St John) *Dur 12* **P** *Bp* **R** M HOUGH
GATLEY (St James) *Ches 17* **P** *R Stockport St Thos* **V** P O MOULTON
GATTEN (St Paul) *Portsm 7* **P** *Ch Patr Trust* **V** P G ALLEN
GATTON (St Andrew) *see* Merstham and Gatton *S'wark*
GAULBY (St Peter) *Leic 5* **P** *MMCET, Ch Soc Trust, and Sir Geoffrey Palmer, Bt (jt)* **R** A F B CHEESMAN
GAUTBY (All Saints) *see* Bardney *Linc*
GAWBER (St Thomas) *Wakef 7* **P** *V Darton* **V** R M WELLER, **NSM** B BENFORD
GAWCOTT (Holy Trinity) *see* Lenborough *Ox*
GAWSWORTH (St James) *Ches 13* **P** *T R R Richards Esq* **R** K V POVEY
GAWTHORPE (St Mary) and Chickenley Heath *Wakef 10* **P** *Bp* **V** S MITCHELL
GAYDON (St Giles) w Chadshunt *Cov 8* **P** *Bp* **V** P T FRANCIS
GAYHURST (St Peter) w Ravenstone, Stoke Goldington and Weston Underwood *Ox 27* **P** *Bp and Lord Hesketh (jt)* **R** A E D MURDOCH
GAYTON Group of Parishes, The: Gayton (St Nicholas), Gayton Thorpe w East Walton, Westacre, Ashwicken w Leziate and Bawsey (Eastern) *Nor 20* **P** *Bp and Capt H Birkbeck (alt)* **R** *Vacant* (01553) 636227
GAYTON (St Mary) *see* Pattishall w Cold Higham and Gayton w Tiffield *Pet*
GAYTON (St Peter) *see* Fradswell, Gayton, Milwich and Weston *Lich*
GAYTON LE WOLD (St Peter) *see* Asterby Gp *Linc*
GAYTON THORPE (St Mary) *see* Gayton Gp of Par *Nor*
GAYWOOD (St Faith) King's Lynn *Nor 20* **P** *Patr Bd* **TR** P I ALLTON, **TV** P M FARROW, **C** L A HUMPHREYS, **NSM** K M LEES
GAZELEY (All Saints) w Dalham, Moulton and Kentford *St E 11* **P** *Bp (2 turns), Personal Reps Major the Hon J P Philipps (1 turn), and Ch Coll Cam (1 turn)* **V** B R W HAYES
GEDDING (St Mary the Virgin) *see* Cockfield w Bradfield St Clare, Felsham etc *St E*
GEDDINGTON (St Mary Magdalene) w Weekley *Pet 11* **P** *Boughton Estates* **V** R B DORRINGTON
GEDLING (All Hallows) *S'well 11* **P** *DBP* **R** M H F BEACH, **C** K GRIFFIN, **NSM** K D WILLIAMS, G M MYERS
GEDNEY (St Mary Magdalene) *see* Fleet w Gedney *Linc*
GEDNEY DROVE END (Christ Church) *see* Lutton w Gedney Drove End, Dawsmere *Linc*
GEDNEY HILL (Holy Trinity) (St Polycarp) *Linc 16* **P** *Bp* **P-in-c** J MONTAGUE
GEE CROSS (Holy Trinity) (St Philip's Mission Room) *Ches 14* **P** *V Werneth* **V** G D OSGOOD, **C** R H CHAMBERLAIN
GELDESTON (St Michael) *see* Gillingham w Geldeston, Stockton, Ellingham etc *Nor*
GENTLESHAW (Christ Church) *Lich 1* **P** *MMCET* **P-in-c** M J BUTT
GEORGEHAM (St George) *Ex 15* **P** *MMCET* **R** D W T RUDMAN, **NSM** G C PHILLIPS
GERMAN (St German) *S & M 3* **P** *Bp* **V** B H KELLY
GERMAN (St John the Baptist) *S & M 3* **P** *Bp* **V** P J BENNETT
GERMANSWEEK (St German) *see* Okehampton w Inwardleigh, Bratton Clovelly etc *Ex*
GERMOE (St Germoe) *see* Breage w Germoe *Truro*
GERRANS (St Gerran) w St Anthony in Roseland *Truro 6* **P** *Bp* **Dn-in-c** D POWELL
GERRARDS CROSS (St James) and Fulmer *Ox 20* **P** *Bp and Simeon's Trustees (jt)* **R** N A RUSSELL, **C** B E STANNARD, A J CHRICH-SMITH
GESTINGTHORPE (St Mary) *see* Gt and Lt Maplestead w Gestingthorpe *Chelmsf*
GIDDING, GREAT (St Michael) w LITTLE (St John) and Steeple Gidding *Ely 10* **P** *Sir Stephen Hastings and Bp (alt)* **P-in-c** C M FURLONG, **NSM** I D M GIBSON
GIDEA PARK (St Michael) *Chelmsf 2* **P** *Bp* **V** E R PILKINGTON, **C** G P TUFFIN
GIDLEIGH (Holy Trinity) *see* Chagford w Gidleigh and Throwleigh *Ex*
GIGGETTY LANE (The Venerable Bede) *see* Wombourne w Trysull and Bobbington *Lich*
GIGGLESWICK (St Alkelda) and Rathmell w Wigglesworth *Bradf 5* **P** *Bp and Ch Trust Fund Trust (jt)* **V** G D RHODES
GILCRUX (St Mary) *see* Plumbland and Gilcrux *Carl*
GILDERSOME (St Peter) *Wakef 8* **P** *V Batley* **V** D R D MARTINEAU
GILLAMOOR (St Aidan) *see* Kirkbymoorside w Gillamoor, Farndale etc *York*
GILLCAR (St Silas) *see* Sheff St Silas Broomhall *Sheff*
GILLING (St Agatha) and Kirkby Ravensworth *Ripon 2* **P** *Bp and A C P Wharton Esq (jt)* **Dn-in-c** J I WILLIAMSON
GILLING EAST (Holy Cross) *see* Ampleforth and Oswaldkirk and Gilling E *York*
GILLINGHAM (Holy Trinity) *Roch 3* **P** *Bp* **V** D W GREEN, **NSM** H J CONNELL
GILLINGHAM (St Augustine) *Roch 3* **P** *Bp* **V** C J VAN STRAATEN, **NSM** P MATTHIAS
GILLINGHAM (St Barnabas) *Roch 3* **P** *Bp* **V** D F PRESTON
GILLINGHAM (St Luke) *see* New Brompton St Luke *Roch*
GILLINGHAM (St Mark) *Roch 3* **P** *Hyndman Trustees* **C** P T KERR, J KERR
GILLINGHAM (St Mary Magdalene) *Roch 3* **P** *DBP* **V** O P HARVEY
GILLINGHAM (St Mary the Virgin) *Sarum 6* **P** *Bp* **TR** J McNEISH, **TV** P BIRT, W T RIDDING, **NSM** J R HEDGES
GILLINGHAM (St Mary) w Geldeston w Stockton w Ellingham St Mary and Kirby Cane *Nor 8* **P** *Ld Chan (1 turn), Bp,*

MMCET and Ch Trust Fund Trust (1 turn) **R** C H R WHITEMAN, **NSM** R D HARVEY
GILLINGHAM, SOUTH (St Matthew) *Roch 3* **P** *Patr Bd* **TV** G E HOVENDEN, A C OEHRING
GILLOW HEATH (Mission Room) *see* Biddulph *Lich*
GILMORTON (All Saints) w Peatling Parva and Kimcote cum Walton *Leic 11* **P** *Bp and Guild All So (jt)* **P-in-c** A M HUGHES
GILSLAND (St Mary Magdalene) w Nether Denton *Carl 2* **P** *Bp* **R** *Vacant* (016977) 47657
GILSTEAD (St Wilfrid) *see* Bingley H Trin *Bradf*
GILSTON (St Mary) *see* High Wych and Gilston w Eastwick *St Alb*
GIMINGHAM (All Saints) *see* Trunch *Nor*
GIPPING (Chapel of St Nicholas) *see* Old Newton w Stowupland *St E*
GIPSY HILL (Christ Church) *S'wark 14* **P** *CPAS* **V** M C R CRIPPS
GIPTON (Church of the Epiphany) *see* Leeds Gipton Epiphany *Ripon*
GIRLINGTON (St Philip) *Bradf 1* **P** *Simeon's Trustees* **V** *Vacant* (01274) 544987
GIRTON (St Andrew) *Ely 5* **P** *Ld Chan* **R** R G J MACKINTOSH
GIRTON (St Cecilia) *see* Collingham w S Scarle and Besthorpe and Girton *S'well*
GISBURN (St Mary the Virgin) *Bradf 5* **P** *Bp* **P-in-c** G WALKER, **NSM** G L HALL
GISLEHAM (Holy Trinity) *see* Kessingland w Gisleham *Nor*
GISLINGHAM (St Mary) *see* Thornhams Magna and Parva, Gislingham and Mellis *St E*
GISSING (St Mary the Virgin) *see* Winfarthing w Shelfanger w Burston w Gissing etc *Nor*
GITTISHAM (St Michael) *see* Honiton, Gittisham, Combe Raleigh, Monkton etc *Ex*
GIVENDALE, GREAT (St Ethelberga) *see* Pocklington and Owsthorpe and Kilnwick Percy etc *York*
GLAISDALE (St Thomas) *York 23* **P** *Abp* **V** B HARRISON
GLANDFORD (St Martin) *see* Blakeney w Cley, Wiveton, Glandford etc *Nor*
GLANTON (St Peter) *see* Whittingham and Edlingham w Bolton Chapel *Newc*
GLAPTHORN (St Leonard) *see* Benefield and Southwick w Glapthorn *Pet*
GLAPWELL (St Andrew) *see* Ault Hucknall *Derby*
GLASCOTE (St George) and Stonydelph *Lich 4* **P** *Patr Bd* **TR** B R F ROCHE, **TV** C E BERESFORD, D S McDONOUGH
GLASSHOUGHTON (St Paul) *Wakef 11* **P** *Bp* **V** *Vacant* (01977) 551031
GLASSON (Christ Church) *see* Cockerham w Winmarleigh and Glasson *Blackb*
GLASTON (St Andrew) *see* Morcott w Glaston and Bisbrooke *Pet*
GLASTONBURY (St John the Baptist) (St Benedict) w Meare, West Pennard and Godney *B & W 5* **P** *Bp* **V** P J RILEY, **C** G R WITTS, J G SUMNER
GLATTON (St Nicholas) *see* Sawtry and Glatton *Ely*
GLAZEBURY (All Saints) w Hollinfare *Liv 16* **P** *Bp and R Warrington (jt)* **R** B C CLARK
GLAZELEY (St Bartholomew) *see* Billingsley w Sidbury, Middleton Scriven etc *Heref*
GLEADLESS (Christ Church) *Sheff 1* **P** *DBP* **TR** C J W HEDLEY, **NSM** S D HOLDAWAY
GLEADLESS VALLEY (Holy Cross) *Sheff 1* **P** *DBP* **P-in-c** G CREASEY
GLEMHAM, GREAT (All Saints) and LITTLE (St Andrew), Blaxhall, Stratford St Andrew and Farnham *St E 19* **P** *Earl of Guilford, C J V Hope Johnstone Esq, and P M Cobbold Esq (1 turn), and DBP (1 turn)* **R** M I BLACKALL
GLEMSFORD (St Mary the Virgin), Hartest w Boxted, Somerton and Stanstead (Glem Valley United Benefice) *St E 12* **P** *Bp, Prime Min, and Ch Soc Trust (by turn)* **P-in-c** P J PRIGG
GLEN AULDYN (Mission Church) *see* Lezayre *S & M*
GLEN MAGNA (St Cuthbert) *see* Gt Glen, Stretton Magna and Wistow etc *Leic*
GLEN PARVA and South Wigston *Leic 5* **P** *Bp* **V** P DAY, **C** S A HOY, **NSM** P G HOLMES
GLENDALE Group, The *Newc 10* **P** *Patr Bd (4 turns), Ld Chan (1 turn)* **TR** R B S BURSTON, **TV** B E SEAMAN, M D CATLING, **C** J R GLOVER, **NSM** T R ROCHESTER
GLENFIELD (St Peter) *Leic 12* **P** *Bp* **R** J E SHARPE
GLENHOLT (St Anne) *see* Bickleigh (Roborough) and Shaugh Prior *Ex*
GLENTHAM (St Peter) *see* Owmby Gp *Linc*
GLENTWORTH Group, The (St Michael) *Linc 2* **P** *Bp, Earl of Scarbrough, MMCET, and Ch Soc Trust (jt)* **P-in-c** M DAWSON
GLINTON (St Benedict) *see* Peakirk w Glinton and Northborough *Pet*
GLODWICK (St Mark w Christ Church) *Man 19* **P** *Bp* **V** M A NARUSAWA
GLOOSTON (St John the Baptist) *see* Gt Bowden w Welham, Glooston and Cranoe *Leic*
GLOSSOP (All Saints) *Derby 6* **P** *Patr Bd* **V** F K WHITEHEAD
GLOUCESTER (St Aldate) Finlay Road *Glouc 5* **P** *Bp* **V** D C SAWYER
GLOUCESTER (St Barnabas) *see* Tuffley *Glouc*
GLOUCESTER (St Catharine) *Glouc 5* **P** *Bp* **V** R J LLEWELYN, **NSM** J R MURPHY
GLOUCESTER (St George) w Whaddon *Glouc 5* **P** *Bp* **V** H D BROAD, **C** D J RUSSELL
GLOUCESTER (St James and All Saints) *Glouc 5* **P** *Bp* **V** M W BUTLER, **C** S A BOWEN, **NSM** V J FRAY
GLOUCESTER (St Mark) *Glouc 5* **P** *Bp* **P-in-c** A M LYNETT
GLOUCESTER (St Mary de Crypt) (St John the Baptist) (Christ Church) (St Mary de Lode and St Nicholas) *Glouc 5* **P** *D&C, Bp, and Ld Chan (by turn)* **C** S B MORRIS, **Hon C** M J P BINGHAM
GLOUCESTER (St Michael) *see* Tuffley *Glouc*
GLOUCESTER (St Oswald) *see* Coney Hill *Glouc*
GLOUCESTER (St Paul) *Glouc 5* **P** *Bp* **V** R C KEY
GLOUCESTER (St Stephen) *Glouc 5* **P** *Bp* **P-in-c** J A L B CATERER
GLOUCESTER DOCKS Mariners' Church Proprietary Chapel *Glouc 5* **P** *Ch Soc Trust,* S G GWILT
GLOUCESTER ROAD (St Stephen) *see* S Kensington St Steph *Lon*
GLUSBURN (All Saints) *see* Sutton *Bradf*
GLYMPTON (St Mary) *see* Wootton w Glympton and Kiddington *Ox*
GLYNDE (St Mary), West Firle and Beddingham *Chich 18* **P** *Bp and D&C Windsor (alt)* **V** P A LYNN
GNOSALL (St Lawrence) *Lich 7* **P** *Bp* **V** M J POPE
GOADBY (St John the Baptist) *see* Billesdon and Skeffington *Leic*
GOADBY MARWOOD (St Denys) *see* Scalford w Goadby Marwood and Wycombe etc *Leic*
GOATHILL (St Peter) *see* Milborne Port w Goathill *B & W*
GOATHLAND (St Mary) *York 23* **P** *Abp* **P-in-c** E NEWLYN
GOATHURST (St Edward the King and Martyr) *see* Spaxton w Charlynch, Goathurst, Enmore etc *B & W*
GOBOWEN (All Saints) *see* Hengoed w Gobowen *Lich*
GOBOWEN ROAD (Mission Room) *see* Oswestry *Lich*
GODALMING (St Peter and St Paul) *Guildf 4* **P** *Bp* **V** F J ASHE, **C** D R TOMLINSON, D G M PRICE, **Hon C** J C TOMLINSON, **NSM** D S MACE
GODINGTON (Holy Trinity) *see* Shelswell *Ox*
GODLEY cum Newton Green (St John the Baptist) *Ches 14* **P** *R Cheadle* **P-in-c** R H WHITE
GODMANCHESTER (St Mary) *Ely 9* **P** *D&C Westmr* **V** N R T FOLLETT, **NSM** J G CRADDOCK
GODMANSTONE (Holy Trinity) *see* Cerne Abbas w Godmanstone and Minterne Magna *Sarum*
GODMERSHAM (St Lawrence the Martyr) *see* Crundale w Godmersham *Cant*
GODNEY (Holy Trinity) *see* Glastonbury w Meare, W Pennard and Godney *B & W*
GODOLPHIN (St John the Baptist) *see* Crowan w Godolphin *Truro*
GODREVY *Truro 5* **P** *Patr Bd* **TR** A T NEAL, **TV** R G HOLLINGS, **C** C C McQUILLEN-WRIGHT, **NSM** A J HANCOCK, J B FOX
GODSHILL (All Saints) *Portsm 7* **P** *Guild of All So* **P-in-c** J M RYDER
GODSHILL (St Giles) *see* Fordingbridge *Win*
GODSTONE (St Nicholas) *S'wark 25* **P** *C K G Hoare Esq* **R** R E WATTS
GOFF'S OAK (St James) *St Alb 20* **P** *V Cheshunt* **V** J W BRIDSTRUP
GOLBORNE (St Thomas) *Liv 16* **P** *Bp* **R** R PLANT
GOLCAR (St John the Evangelist) *Wakef 5* **P** *V Huddersfield* **V** R M F CROMPTON, **NSM** G M DODD
GOLDEN GREEN (Mission) *see* Hadlow *Roch*
GOLDEN VALLEY (St Matthias) *see* Riddings and Ironville *Derby*
GOLDENHILL (St John the Evangelist) *Lich 11* **P** *Bp* **P-in-c** K P SCOTT
GOLDERS GREEN (St Alban the Martyr and St Michael) *Lon 15* **P** *Bp* **V** P G BAKER, **C** S W COOPER
GOLDHANGER (St Peter) w Little Totham *Chelmsf 24* **P** *Ld Chan* **R** D J ALLAN
GOLDINGTON (St Mary the Virgin) *St Alb 10* **P** *Bp* **V** T MAINES, **C** J S REVELEY, **NSM** D G PRESTON, H WORSNIP

GOLDS HILL (St Paul) *see* W Bromwich St Paul Golds Hill *Lich*
GOLDSBOROUGH (St Mary) *see* Knaresborough *Ripon*
GOLDSWORTH PARK (St Andrew) *Guildf 12* **P** *Bp* **V** R J N COOK, **C** S R ALLEN
GOLDTHORPE (St John the Evangelist and St Mary Magdalene) w Hickleton *Sheff 12* **P** *CR (2 turns), Earl of Halifax (1 turn)* **V** A J DELVES, **C** M W OSBORNE
GOMERSAL (St Mary) *Wakef 8* **P** *Bp* **V** M G RAWSON, **C** J L SMITH
GONALSTON (St Laurence) *S'well 11* **P** *Comdr M B P Francklin, Bp, and Ld Chan (by turn)* **R** M J BROCK, **C** T J RENSHAW
GONERBY, GREAT (St Sebastian) *see* Barrowby and Gt Gonerby *Linc*
GOOD EASTER (St Andrew) *see* High and Gd Easter w Margaret Roding *Chelmsf*
GOODERSTONE (St George) *see* Cockley Cley w Gooderstone *Nor*
GOODLEIGH (St Gregory) *see* Barnstaple *Ex*
GOODMANHAM (All Saints) *York 7* **P** *Abp* **R** A CLEMENTS
GOODMAYES (All Saints) *Chelmsf 4* **P** *Hyndman Trustees* **V** C R KEATING
GOODMAYES (St Paul) *Chelmsf 4* **P** *Bp* **V** B J RUTT-FIELD, **NSM** S J BREWSTER
GOODNESTONE (Holy Cross) *see* Nonington w Wymynswold and Goodnestone etc *Cant*
GOODRICH (St Giles) *see* Walford and St John w Bishopswood, Goodrich etc *Heref*
GOODRINGTON (St George) *Ex 10* **P** *Bp* **V** B D PROTHERO, **C** P M J COOMBS
GOODSHAW (St Mary and All Saints) and Crawshawbooth *Man 15* **P** *Bp and Wm Hulme Trustees (jt)* **P-in-c** J A ARMES, **C** E J LOMAX
GOODWORTH CLATFORD (St Peter) *see* Abbotts Ann and Upper and Goodworth Clatford *Win*
GOOLE (St John the Evangelist) (St Mary) (Mariners' Club and Chapel) *Sheff 11* **P** *Bp* **V** G TAYLOR, **NSM** K W SARGEANTSON
GOOSE GREEN (St Paul) *Liv 15* **P** *Bp* **V** J J HARTLEY
GOOSEY (All Saints) *see* Stanford in the Vale w Goosey and Hatford *Ox*
GOOSNARGH (St Mary the Virgin) w Whittingham *Blackb 10* **P** *Bp* **V** B M BEAUMONT
GOOSTREY (St Luke) *Ches 11* **P** *V Sandbach* **V** A G SPARHAM
GORAN HAVEN (St Just) *see* St Goran w St Mich Caerhays *Truro*
GOREFIELD (St Paul) *Ely 19* **P** *Bp* **P-in-c** N A WHITEHOUSE
GORING (St Thomas of Canterbury) w South Stoke *Ox 6* **P** *Ch Ch Ox* **V** P E NIXON
GORING-BY-SEA (St Mary) (St Laurence) *Chich 4* **P** *Bp* **V** M J HORE, **C** C H LOVELESS, **Hon C** P MATTHEWS
GORLESTON (St Andrew) *Nor 6* **P** *Ch Trust Fund Trust* **V** A P WARD, **C** P G McGLINCHEY, D M BENT, **NSM** A T CADMORE, C M UPTON
GORLESTON (St Mary Magdalene) *Nor 6* **P** *Bp and Ch Trust Fund Trust (jt)* **V** T W RIESS
GORNAL, LOWER (St James the Great) *Worc 10* **P** *Bp* **V** P E HUTCHINSON
GORNAL, UPPER (St Peter) *Worc 10* **P** *V Sedgley All SS* **V** M K BATE
GORSLEY (Christ Church) *see* Newent and Gorsley w Cliffords Mesne *Glouc*
GORTON (Emmanuel) (St James) *Man 1* **P** *Bp and D&C (jt)* **R** M R J WILLIAMS, **NSM** D C GRAY
GORTON (Our Lady and St Thomas) *Man 1* **P** *Trustees* **R** R G J HERRON
GORTON (St Philip) *Man 1* **P** *The Crown* **P-in-c** V I MORGAN
GOSBECK (St Mary) *see* Coddenham w Gosbeck and Hemingstone w Henley *St E*
GOSBERTON (St Peter and St Paul), Gosberton Clough and Quadrin *Linc 17* **P** *Bp and D&C (jt)* **V** T G WILLIAMSON, **NSM** A J LITTLEWOOD
GOSBERTON CLOUGH (St Gilbert and St Hugh) *see* Gosberton, Gosberton Clough and Quadrin *Linc*
GOSCOTE, EAST (St Hilda) *see* Syston TM *Leic*
GOSFIELD (St Katherine) *Chelmsf 19* **P** *Mrs G M Lowe and Mrs M A Wilson (jt)* **P-in-c** D E COWIE
GOSFORTH (All Saints) *Newc 5* **P** *Bp* **V** R B HILL, **C** G C EVANS, **NSM** G E SMITH
GOSFORTH (St Hugh) *see* Newc Epiphany *Newc*
GOSFORTH (St Mary) w Nether Wasdale and Wasdale Head *Carl 5* **P** *Bp, Earl of Lonsdale, V St Bees, and PCCs (jt)* **P-in-c** C B GALLOWAY
GOSFORTH (St Nicholas) *Newc 5* **P** *Bp* **V** A M ROFF
GOSFORTH, NORTH (St Columba) *see* Ch the King in the Dio of Newc *Newc*
GOSFORTH VALLEY (St Andrew) *see* Dronfield w Holmesfield *Derby*
GOSPEL END (St Barnabas) *see* Sedgley All SS *Worc*
GOSPEL LANE (St Michael) *Birm 6* **P** *Bp* **V** R K JOHNSON, **C** C A HIBBERD
GOSPEL OAK (All Hallows) *see* Hampstead St Steph w All Hallows *Lon*
GOSPEL OAK (St Martin) *see* Kentish Town St Martin w St Andr *Lon*
GOSPORT (Christ Church) *Portsm 3* **P** *Bp* **P-in-c** E A GOODYER, **C** D A GIBBONS, **NSM** J H ALDOUS
GOSPORT (Holy Trinity) *Portsm 3* **P** *DBP* **V** J R CAPPER
GOSSOPS GREEN (St Alban) *see* Ifield *Chich*
GOTHAM (St Lawrence) *S'well 10* **P** *Bp* **P-in-c** D C GORICK, **NSM** J M GORICK
GOUDHURST (St Mary the Virgin) w Kilndown *Cant 11* **P** *Abp and Prime Min (alt)* **V** R C CAMPBELL-SMITH
GOULCEBY (All Saints) *see* Asterby Gp *Linc*
GOXHILL (All Saints) *see* Barrow and Goxhill *Linc*
GOXHILL (St Giles) *see* Aldbrough, Mappleton w Goxhill and Withernwick *York*
GRADE (St Grada and the Holy Cross) *see* St Ruan w St Grade and Landewednack *Truro*
GRAFFHAM (St Giles) w Woolavington *Chich 11* **P** *Bp* **P-in-c** K F HYDE-DUNN
GRAFFOE GROUP *Linc 18* **P** *Ch Coll Cam, D&C and DBP, Viscountess Chaplin, Or Coll Ox, J C M Fullerton Esq (by turn)* **P-in-c** J A PATRICK
GRAFHAM (All Saints) *Ely 10* **P** *Bp* **P-in-c** J ALFORD
GRAFHAM (St Andrew) *see* Bramley and Grafham *Guildf*
GRAFTON, EAST (St Nicholas) *see* Wexcombe *Sarum*
GRAFTON FLYFORD (St John the Baptist) *see* Abberton, The Flyfords, Naunton Beauchamp etc *Worc*
GRAFTON REGIS (St Mary) *see* Stoke Bruerne w Grafton Regis and Alderton *Pet*
GRAFTON UNDERWOOD (St James the Apostle) *see* Cranford w Grafton Underwood and Twywell *Pet*
GRAHAME PARK (St Augustine) Conventional District *Lon 15 Vacant*
GRAIN (St James) w Stoke *Roch 6* **P** *DBP* **V** W ROBBINS
GRAINSBY (St Nicholas) *see* The North-Chapel Parishes *Linc*
GRAINTHORPE (St Clement) *see* Somercotes and Grainthorpe w Conisholme *Linc*
GRAMPOUND (St Nun) *see* Probus, Ladock and Grampound w Creed and St Erme *Truro*
GRAMPOUND ROAD Mission Church *as above*
GRANBOROUGH (St John the Baptist) *see* Schorne *Ox*
GRANBY (All Saints) *see* Cropwell Bishop w Colston Bassett, Granby etc *S'well*
GRANDBOROUGH (St Peter) w Willoughby and Flecknoe *Cov 6* **P** *Bp* **P-in-c** A J HOBSON
GRANGE (Holy Trinity) *see* Borrowdale *Carl*
GRANGE (St Andrew) *Ches 3* **P** *Bp* **V** D R FELIX, **C** D E WATSON
GRANGE FELL (not known) *see* Grange-over-Sands *Carl*
GRANGE MOOR (St Bartholomew) *see* Kirkheaton *Wakef*
GRANGE-OVER-SANDS (St Paul) *Carl 10* **P** *Bp* **P-in-c** J A H CLEGG
GRANGE PARK (St Peter) *Lon 18* **P** *Bp* **V** S P STARTUP
GRANGE VILLA (St Columba) *see* W Pelton *Dur*
GRANGETOWN (St Aidan) *Dur 16* **P** *V Ryhope* **V** C COLLINS
GRANGETOWN (St Hilda of Whitby) *York 19* **P** *Abp* **V** J RICHARDSON
GRANSDEN, GREAT (St Bartholomew) w LITTLE (St Peter and St Paul) *Ely 12* **P** *Clare Coll Cam* **R** *Vacant* (01767) 677227
GRANTCHESTER (St Andrew and St Mary) *Ely 7* **P** *CCC Cam* **V** *Vacant* (01223) 840460
GRANTHAM (St Anne) (St Wulfram) (Ascension) (Epiphany) *Linc 19* **P** *Bp* **TR** C P ANDREWS, **TV** P J MANDER, M T HURLEY, M K NICHOLAS, **C** D E ALLEN, **NSM** J T FARLEY, F H LONG
GRANVILLES WOOTTON (St Mary the Virgin) *see* Dungeon Hill *Sarum*
GRAPPENHALL (St Wilfrid) *Ches 4* **P** *P G Greenall Esq* **R** M B KELLY, **Hon C** S BECKETT, **NSM** M JONES
GRASBY (All Saints) *Linc 5* **P** *Lord Tennyson* **P-in-c** I ROBINSON
GRASMERE (St Oswald) *Carl 10* **P** *Qu Coll Ox* **P-in-c** W E R WILKINSON
GRASSENDALE (St Mary) *Liv 4* **P** *Trustees* **V** M E GREENWOOD
GRATELEY (St Leonard) *see* Amport, Grateley, Monxton and Quarley *Win*
GRATWICH (St Mary the Virgin) *see* Uttoxeter Area *Lich*

GRAVELEY (St Botolph) w Papworth St Agnes w Yelling and Toseland *Ely 1* **P** *Jes Coll Cam, T J H Sperling Esq, and Ld Chan (by turn)* **R** *Vacant* (01480) 830222
GRAVELEY (St Mary) *see* Gt and Lt Wymondley w Graveley and Chivesfield *St Alb*
GRAVELLY HILL (All Saints) *Birm 8* **P** *Bp* **V** D E NEWSOME, **C** H EDWARDS
GRAVENEY (All Saints) *see* Preston next Faversham, Goodnestone and Graveney *Cant*
GRAVENHURST, UPPER (St Giles) w Lower Gravenhurst *St Alb 16* **P** *Bp* **P-in-c** P J SWINDELLS, **NSM** C M EAGGER
GRAVESEND (Holy Family) w Ifield *Roch 4* **P** *Bp and Lt-Col F B Edmeades (jt)* **R** R J R AMYS, **C** K R HAYES
GRAVESEND (St Aidan) *Roch 4* **P** *Bp* **V** B PEARSON, **NSM** J P LITTLEWOOD
GRAVESEND (St George) *Roch 4* **P** *Bp* **R** D G WILLEY, **C** J P A ELVIN
GRAVESEND (St Mary) *Roch 4* **P** *R Gravesend* **V** *Vacant* (01959) 540482
GRAYINGHAM (St Radegunda) *Linc 6* **P** *Bp* **R** D I WALKER
GRAYRIGG (St John the Evangelist), Old Hutton and New Hutton *Carl 9* **P** *V Kendal* **P-in-c** B PEDDER
GRAYS NORTH (St John the Evangelist) *Chelmsf 14* **P** *Bp* **V** E N P TUFNELL, **C** C B REED
GRAYS THURROCK (St Peter and St Paul) *Chelmsf 14* **P** *DBP* **TR** R J WIGGS, **TV** M IVIN, **C** C P G DICKSON, **NSM** J K EDWARDS
GRAYSHOTT (St Luke) *Guildf 3* **P** *Bp* **V** W J MEYER, **NSM** D J LUSBY
GRAYSWOOD (All Saints) *Guildf 4* **P** *Bp* **P-in-c** A J SHAW
GRAYTHWAITE (Mission Room) *see* Hawkshead and Low Wray w Sawrey *Carl*
GRAZELEY (Holy Trinity) *see* Beech Hill, Grazeley and Spencers Wood *Ox*
GREASBROUGH (St Mary) *Sheff 6* **P** *Sir Stephen Hastings* **V** K E TONES, **C** J HELLEWELL
GREASBY (St Nicholas) *see* Frankby w Greasby *Ches*
GREASLEY (St Mary) *S'well 4* **P** *Bp* **V** T A JOYCE, **C** G CHATFIELD
GREAT *see also under substantive place name*
GREAT CAMBRIDGE ROAD (St John the Baptist and St James) *Lon 19* **P** *D&C St Paul's* **V** P B LYONS
GREAT GLEN (St Cuthbert), Stretton Magna and Wistow cum Newton Harcourt *Leic 5* **P** *Bp and Hon Ann Brooks (jt)* **V** J F WELLINGTON, **NSM** P HEBDEN
GREAT MOOR (St Saviour) *see* Stockport St Sav *Ches*
GREATER *see under substantive place name*
GREATFORD (St Thomas a Becket) *see* Uffington Gp *Linc*
GREATHAM (not known) *see* Amberley w N Stoke and Parham, Wiggonholt etc *Chich*
GREATHAM (St John the Baptist) *Dur 3* **P** *Trustees* **V** D C COULING
GREATHAM w Empshott and Hawkley w Prior's Dean *Portsm 5* **P** *DBP* **R** W C DAY
GREATSTONE (St Peter) *see* Lydd *Cant*
GREATWORTH (St Peter) and Marston St Lawrence w Warkorth and Thenford *Pet 1* **P** *Bp (2 turns), Crown (1 turn)* **R** A E TURNER
GREAVE FOLD (Holy Innocents) *see* Chadkirk *Ches*
GREEN HAMMERTON (St Thomas) *see* Whixley w Green Hammerton *Ripon*
GREEN HAWORTH (St Clement) *see* Accrington *Blackb*
GREEN HEATH (St Saviour) *see* Hednesford *Lich*
GREEN STREET GREEN (St Mary) and Pratts Bottom *Roch 16* **P** *Bp* **V** P MILLER, **C** R M WORSSAM
GREEN VALE (Holy Trinity) *see* Stockton H Trin *Dur*
GREENFIELD (St Mary) *Man 21* **P** *Bp* **V** *Vacant* (01457) 872346
GREENFIELDS (United Church) *see* Shrewsbury All SS w St Mich *Lich*
GREENFORD (Holy Cross) (St Edward the Confessor) *Lon 22* **P** *K Coll Cam* **R** N RICHARDSON, **C** J R BAKER
GREENFORD, NORTH (All Hallows) *Lon 22* **P** *Bp* **Dn-in-c** M WHEELER, **NSM** D C DAVIS
GREENGATES (St John the Evangelist) *Bradf 3* **P** *D&C* **V** T COLLIN
GREENHAM (St Mary the Virgin) *Ox 14* **P** *Bp* **V** J P H CLARKE
GREENHAM (St Peter) *see* Wellington and Distr *B & W*
GREENHEAD (St Cuthbert) *see* Haltwhistle and Greenhead *Newc*
GREENHILL (St John the Baptist) *Lon 23* **P** *Bp, Adn, and V Harrow St Mary (jt)* **V** J F SPINKS
GREENHILL (St Peter) *Sheff 2* **P** *Bp* **V** L C JENKINS
GREENHITHE (St Mary) *Roch 2* **P** *Ch Soc Trust and Canon T L Livermore (jt)* **R** R D BARRON
GREENHOW HILL (St Mary) *see* Upper Nidderdale *Ripon*
GREENLANDS (St Anne) *Blackb 9* **P** *Bp and V Blackpool St Steph (jt)* **V** D M PORTER
GREENLANDS (St John the Evangelist) *see* Ipsley *Worc*
GREENS NORTON (St Bartholomew) w Bradden and Lichborough *Pet 5* **P** *J E Grant-Ives Esq (1 turn), The Crown (3 turns), and Melanesian Miss Trust (1 turn)* **R** *Vacant* (01327) 359508
GREENSIDE (St John) *Dur 13* **P** *R Ryton w Hedgefield* **V** P D SADDINGTON
GREENSTEAD (St Andrew) (St Edmund's Church Hall) (St Matthew) *Chelmsf 16* **P** *Ld Chan* **P-in-c** B L BIRCHMORE, **C** B S RAWLINGS, J H DELFGOU, **NSM** J D MITSON
GREENSTEAD GREEN (St James Apostle) *see* Halstead St Andr w H Trin and Greenstead Green *Chelmsf*
GREENSTED-JUXTA-ONGAR (St Andrew) w Stanford Rivers *Chelmsf 27* **P** *Bp Lon and Duchy of Lanc (alt)* **R** T A GARDINER
GREENWICH (St Alfege w St Peter and St Paul) *S'wark 3* **P** *The Crown* **V** G S HARCOURT, **C** R P H BUCK, B THORLEY
GREENWICH, EAST (Christ Church) (St Andrew w St Michael) (St George) *S'wark 3* **P** *Patr Bd* **TR** M N A TORRY, **TV** C J MORGAN, **NSM** E BOGLE
GREETE (St James) *see* Burford II w Greete and Hope Bagot *Heref*
GREETHAM (All Saints) *see* Fulletby w Greetham and Ashby Puerorum *Linc*
GREETHAM (St Mary the Virgin) and Thistleton w Stretton and Clipsham *Pet 14* **P** *Bp and Sir David Davenport-Handley (alt)* **V** P TOWNSEND
GREETLAND (St Thomas) and West Vale *Wakef 2* **P** *V Halifax* **V** S GOTT
GREETWELL (All Saints) *see* Cherry Willingham w Greetwell *Linc*
GREINTON (St Michael and All Angels) *B & W 5* **P** *Bp* **R** *Vacant*
GRENDON (All Saints) *see* Baddesley Ensor w Grendon *Birm*
GRENDON (St Mary) *see* Yardley Hastings, Denton and Grendon etc *Pet*
GRENDON BISHOP (St John the Baptist) *see* Bredenbury w Grendon Bishop and Wacton etc *Heref*
GRENDON UNDERWOOD (St Leonard) *see* Swan *Ox*
GRENOSIDE (St Mark) *Sheff 3* **P** *Bp and V Ecclesfield (jt)* **V** K THOMPSON, **C** P E BOLD
GRESHAM (All Saints) *Nor 21* **P** *Guild of All So* **P-in-c** D F HAYDEN
GRESLEY (St George and St Mary) *Derby 16* **P** *Simeon's Trustees* **V** W B HERD
GRESSENHALL (Assumption of the Blessed Virgin Mary) w Longham w Wendling and Bittering Parva *Nor 14* **P** *Ld Chan (1 turn), CPAS (2 turns)* **R** J E BELHAM
GRESSINGHAM (St John the Evangelist) *see* Whittington w Arkholme and Gressingham *Blackb*
GRETTON (Christ Church) *see* Winchcombe, Gretton, Sudeley Manor etc *Glouc*
GRETTON (St James the Great) w Rockingham *Pet 9* **P** *Bp (2 turns), Comdr L M M Saunders-Watson (1 turn)* **V** G H RICHMOND
GREWELTHORPE (St James) *see* Fountains Gp *Ripon*
GREYSTOKE (St Andrew), Matterdale, Mungrisdale and Watermillock *Carl 4* **P** *DBP* **TR** R P H FRANK, **C** B J TURNER
GREYSTONES (St Gabriel) *see* Ecclesall *Sheff*
GREYSTONES (St Gabriel) *Sheff 2* **P** *Provost Sheff* **V** P W BECKLEY
GREYWELL (St Mary) *see* Newnham w Nately Scures w Mapledurwell etc *Win*
GRIMEHILLS (St Mary) *see* Darwen St Barn *Blackb*
GRIMETHORPE (St Luke) *Wakef 7* **P** *Bp* **V** C D WHITE
GRIMLEY (St Bartholomew) *see* Hallow and Grimley w Holt *Worc*
GRIMOLDBY (St Edith) *see* Mid Marsh Gp *Linc*
GRIMSARGH (St Michael) *Blackb 14* **P** *R Preston* **V** A J HASLAM
GRIMSBURY (St Leonard) *see* Banbury *Ox*
GRIMSBY (St Augustine of Hippo) *Linc 9* **P** *TR Gt Grimsby SS Mary and Jas* **V** M C KING
GRIMSBY, GREAT (St Andrew w St Luke and All Saints) *Linc 9* **P** *Bp* **V** M M E ISAM, **C** J A MUSTON
GRIMSBY, GREAT (St Mary and St James) (St Hugh) (St Mark) (St Martin) *Linc 9* **P** *Bp* **TR** M O HUNTER, **TV** T A REDFEARN, D M McCORMICK, P C PATRICK, D A MAYO, **Hon C** E MARSHALL, **NSM** A I McCORMICK
GRIMSBY, LITTLE (St Edith) *see* Fotherby *Linc*
GRIMSTEAD, EAST (Holy Trinity) *see* Alderbury Team *Sarum*
GRIMSTEAD, WEST (St John) *as above*

GRIMSTON (St Botolph), Congham and Roydon *Nor 20* **P** *Qu Coll Cam, Bp, and G Howard Esq (jt)* **R** W A HOWARD
GRIMSTON (St John the Baptist) *see* Ab Kettleby Gp *Leic*
GRIMSTON, NORTH (St Nicholas) *see* Settrington w N Grimston, Birdsall w Langton *York*
GRINDALE (St Nicholas) *see* Burton Fleming w Fordon, Grindale etc *York*
GRINDLEFORD (St Helen) *see* Eyam *Derby*
GRINDLETON (St Ambrose) *see* Bolton by Bowland w Grindleton *Bradf*
GRINDON (All Saints) *see* Calton, Cauldon, Grindon and Waterfall *Lich*
GRINDON (St James) and Stillington *Dur 10* **P** *Bp* **V** M GOODALL
GRINDON (St Oswald) *see* Sunderland Pennywell St Thos *Dur*
GRINGLEY-ON-THE-HILL (St Peter and St Paul) *S'well 1* **P** *Bp* **P-in-c** D HOLLIS
GRINSDALE (St Kentigern) *see* Burgh-by-Sands and Kirkbampton w Kirkandrews etc *Carl*
GRINSHILL (All Saints) *see* Astley, Clive, Grinshill and Hadnall *Lich*
GRINSTEAD, EAST (St Mary the Virgin) *Chich 7* **P** *Bp* **V** G BOND
GRINSTEAD, EAST (St Swithun) *Chich 7* **P** *Bp* **V** J R BROWN, **C** A M WINDROSS, S ATTWATER, **NSM** I M EDYE
GRINSTEAD, WEST (St George) *Chich 8* **P** *Bp* **R** W E M HARRIS
GRINTON (St Andrew) *see* Swaledale *Ripon*
GRISTHORPE (St Thomas) *see* Filey *York*
GRISTON (St Peter and St Paul) *see* Caston, Griston, Merton, Thompson etc *Nor*
GRITTLETON (St Mary the Virgin) and Leigh Delamere *Bris 9* **P** *Bp and R W Neeld Esq (jt)* **P-in-c** R V C LEWIS
GRIZEBECK (The Good Shepherd) *see* Kirkby Ireleth *Carl*
GROBY (St Philip and St James) *see* Ratby w Groby *Leic*
GROOMBRIDGE (St John the Evangelist) *see* Speldhurst w Groombridge and Ashurst *Roch*
GROOMBRIDGE, NEW (St Thomas) *Chich 19* **P** *R Withyham* **P-in-c** A B GREEN
GROSMONT (St Matthew) *see* Egton w Grosmont *York*
GROSVENOR CHAPEL (no dedication) Chapel of Ease in the parish of Hanover Square St George w St Mark *Lon 3* **C-in-c** S J HOBBS
GROTON (St Bartholomew) *see* Edwardstone w Groton and Lt Waldingfield *St E*
GROVE (St Helen) *see* E Markham w Askham, Headon w Upton and Grove *S'well*
GROVE (St John the Baptist) *Ox 19* **P** *D&C Windsor* **V** R J FRENCH, **C** R W FRAY
GROVE GREEN (St John) Local Ecumenical Project *Cant 15* **Min** S P WALKER
GROVE PARK (St Augustine) *see* Lee St Aug *S'wark*
GROVEHILL (Resurrection) *see* Hemel Hempstead *St Alb*
GRUNDISBURGH (St Mary the Virgin) *see* Boulge w Burgh and Grundisburgh *St E*
GUARLFORD (St Mary) and Madresfield w Newland *Worc 2* **P** *Bp and Lady Rosalind Morrison (jt)* **P-in-c** J H GREEN
GUERNSEY (Holy Trinity) *Win 14* **P** *Trustees* **V** J BERRY
GUERNSEY L'Islet (St Mary) *see* Guernsey St Sampson *Win*
GUERNSEY (St Andrew de la Pommeraye) *Win 14* **P** *The Crown* **R** J A GUILLE
GUERNSEY (St John the Evangelist) *Win 14* **P** *Trustees* **V** P HENRY
GUERNSEY (St Marguerite de la Foret) *Win 14* **P** *The Crown* **R** *Vacant* (01481) 38392
GUERNSEY (St Martin) *Win 14* **P** *The Crown* **R** F M TRICKEY, **NSM** R G BELLINGER
GUERNSEY (St Matthew) *Win 14* **P** *R Ste Marie du Castel* **V** M R STARR, **NSM** L S LE VASSEUR
GUERNSEY (St Michel du Valle) *Win 14* **P** *The Crown* **R** E J WIDDOWS
GUERNSEY (St Peter Port) *Win 14* **P** *The Crown* **R** J E N ELLISTON
GUERNSEY (St Philippe de Torteval) *Win 14* **P** *The Crown* **R** *Vacant* (01481) 63544
GUERNSEY (St Pierre du Bois) *Win 14* **P** *The Crown* **R** N GRIFFITHS
GUERNSEY (St Sampson) *Win 14* **P** *The Crown* **R** J E IRONSIDE
GUERNSEY (St Saviour) (Chapel of St Apolline) *Win 14* **P** *The Crown* **R** *Vacant* (01481) 63045
GUERNSEY (St Stephen) *Win 14* **P** *R St Peter Port* **V** M C MILLARD, **Hon C** H S RIDGE
GUERNSEY (Ste Marie du Castel) *Win 14* **P** *The Crown* **R** M R STARR, **NSM** L S LE VASSEUR
GUESTLING (St Lawrence) *see* Fairlight, Guestling and Pett *Chich*
GUESTWICK (St Peter) *see* Foulsham w Hindolveston and Guestwick *Nor*
GUILDEN MORDEN (St Mary) *see* Shingay Gp of Par *Ely*
GUILDEN SUTTON (St John the Baptist) *see* Plemstall w Guilden Sutton *Ches*
GUILDFORD (All Saints) *Guildf 5* **P** *Bp* **V** B J COLEMAN
GUILDFORD (Christ Church) *Guildf 5* **P** *Simeon's Trustees* **V** J J R COLLINGWOOD, **C** S J DAUGHTERY, **NSM** D H BEVIS
GUILDFORD (Holy Spirit) *see* Burpham *Guildf*
GUILDFORD (Holy Trinity) (St Mary) (St Michael) *Guildf 5* **P** *Bp* **R** R L COTTON, **C** M J VERNON, **Hon C** A S LEAK, **NSM** J G TODD
GUILDFORD (St Clare) *see* Westborough *Guildf*
GUILDFORD (St Francis) *as above*
GUILDFORD (St Luke) *see* Burpham *Guildf*
GUILDFORD (St Nicolas) *Guildf 5* **P** *Bp* **R** A H NORMAN, **C** P M BLEE
GUILDFORD (St Saviour) *Guildf 5* **P** *Simeon's Trustees* **R** D J BRACEWELL, **C** P M BARON
GUILSBOROUGH (St Ethelreda) w Hollowell and Cold Ashby *Pet 2* **P** *J L Lowther Esq (2 turns) and Bp (1 turn)* **V** W G GIBBS
GUILTCROSS *Nor 11* **P** *Bp, Mrs C Noel, Exors C P B Goldson, and DBP (jt)* **R** A V HEDGES
GUISBOROUGH (St Nicholas) *York 17* **P** *Abp* **R** P L BISHOP, **C** R TAYLOR
GUISELEY (St Oswald King and Martyr) w Esholt *Bradf 4* **P** *Patr Bd* **TR** G B ATHERTON, **NSM** T H BAXTER
GUIST (St Andrew) *see* Twyford, Guist, Bintree, Themelthorpe etc *Nor*
GUITING POWER (St Michael) *see* The Guitings, Cutsdean and Farmcote *Glouc*
GUITINGS, Cutsdean and Farmcote, The *Glouc 15* **P** *E R Cochrane Esq and Ch Ch Ox (alt)* **V** *Vacant* (01451) 850268
GULDEFORD, EAST (St Mary) *see* Rye *Chich*
GULVAL (St Gulval) *Truro 5* **P** *Ld Chan* **V** A K TORRY
GULWORTHY (St Paul) *see* Tavistock and Gulworthy *Ex*
GUMLEY (St Helen) *see* Foxton w Gumley and Laughton and Lubenham *Leic*
GUNBY (St Nicholas) *see* Witham Gp *Linc*
GUNBY (St Peter) *see* Welton-le-Marsh w Gunby *Linc*
GUNHOUSE (otherwise Gunness) (St Barnabas) w Burringham *Linc 4* **P** *Bp Lon* **R** *Vacant* (01724) 783550
GUNN CHAPEL (Holy Name) *see* Swimbridge and W Buckland *Ex*
GUNNESS (St Barnabas) *see* Gunhouse w Burringham *Linc*
GUNNISLAKE (St Anne) *see* Calstock *Truro*
GUNTHORPE (St John the Baptist) *see* Lowdham w Caythorpe, and Gunthorpe *S'well*
GUNTHORPE (St Mary) w Bale w Field Dalling, Saxlingham and Sharrington *Nor 18* **P** *Keble Coll Ox, MMCET, Bp, and DBP (by turn)* **R** M R WARD
GUNTON St Peter (St Benedict) *Nor 9* **P** *CPAS* **R** J A FAIRBAIRN, **NSM** A C W CHAMBERLAIN
GUNWALLOE (St Winwalloe) *see* Cury and Gunwalloe w Mawgan *Truro*
GURNARD (All Saints) *Portsm 8* **P** *Bp* **R** C B BURLAND, **NSM** D M NETHERWAY
GUSSAGE (St Andrew) *see* Handley w Gussage St Andrew and Pentridge *Sarum*
GUSSAGE ALL SAINTS (All Saints) *see* Tollard Royal w Farnham, Gussage St Michael etc *Sarum*
GUSSAGE ST MICHAEL (St Michael) *as above*
GUSTARD WOOD (St Peter) *see* Wheathampstead *St Alb*
GUSTON (St Martin of Tours) *see* Whitfield w Guston *Cant*
GUYHIRN (St Mary Magdalene) w Ring's End *Ely 19* **P** *Bp* **V** *Vacant*
GWEEK (Mission Church) *see* Constantine *Truro*
GWENNAP (St Weneppa) *see* St Stythians w Perranarworthal and Gwennap *Truro*
GWINEAR (St Winnear) *see* Godrevy *Truro*
GWITHIAN (St Gwithian) *as above*
HABBERLEY (St Mary) *Heref 13* **P** *Bp* **P-in-c** W K ROWELL
HABERGHAM (All Saints) *see* W Burnley *Blackb*
HABERGHAM EAVES (St Matthew the Apostle) *see* Burnley (Habergham Eaves) St Matt w H Trin *Blackb*
HABROUGH Group, The (St Margaret) *Linc 10* **P** *DBP* **P-in-c** B A HARRISON
HABTON, GREAT (St Chad) *see* Kirby Misperton w Normanby, Edston and Salton *York*
HACCOMBE (St Blaise) *see* Stoke-in-Teignhead w Combe-in-Teignhead etc *Ex*
HACCONBY (St Andrew) *see* Ringstone in Aveland Gp *Linc*
HACHESTON (St Andrew) *see* Campsea Ashe w Marlesford, Parham and Hacheston *St E*

HACKBRIDGE and North Beddington (All Saints) *S'wark 24* **P** *Bp* **P-in-c** A O ROLAND
HACKENTHORPE (Christ Church) *Sheff 2* **P** *Bp* **V** S J WILLETT, **NSM** I JENNINGS
HACKFORD (St Mary the Virgin) *see* High Oak *Nor*
HACKINGTON (St Stephen) *Cant 3* **P** *Adn Cant* **R** P R DOWN, **C** D CRABTREE
HACKNESS (St Peter) w Harwood Dale *York 16* **P** *Lord Derwent* **V** J W BAKER, **P-in-c** W F CURTIS
HACKNEY Mount Pleasant Lane (St Matthew) *see* Upper Clapton St Matt *Lon*
HACKNEY (St James) (St John) *Lon 5* **P** *Patr Bd* **TR** J S PRIDMORE, **TV** J H SETTIMBA, **C** J P WILKES
HACKNEY (St Luke) Homerton Terrace *see* Homerton St Luke *Lon*
HACKNEY (St Thomas) *see* Stamford Hill St Thos *Lon*
HACKNEY, OVER (Mission Room) *see* Darley *Derby*
HACKNEY, SOUTH (St John) (Christ Church) *Lon 5* **P** *Lord Amherst* **R** N R J FUNNELL, **C** P A FARQUHAR
HACKNEY, SOUTH (St Michael and All Angels) London Fields w Haggerston (St Paul) *Lon 5* **P** *R S Hackney St Jo w Ch Ch* **V** A N EVERETT, **NSM** J M KING, H LODER
HACKNEY, WEST St Barnabas (St Paul) *Lon 5* **P** *Bp* **R** F A PRESTON
HACKNEY MARSH (All Souls) *Lon 5* **P** *Patr Bd* **TR** A P HOBSON, **TV** U D PATEL, **C** R A FAIRHURST
HACKNEY WICK (St Mary of Eton) (St Augustine) *Lon 5* **P** *Eton Coll* **V** E J JONES
HACKTHORN (St Michael and All Angels) w Cold Hanworth *Linc 3* **P** *Mrs B K Eley* **P-in-c** I R HOWITT
HADDENHAM (Holy Trinity) *Ely 14* **P** *Adn Ely* **V** M P WADSWORTH, **NSM** P M DUFFETT-SMITH
HADDENHAM (St Mary the Virgin) w Cuddington, Kingsey and Aston Sandford *Ox 20* **P** *D&C Roch* **V** A C DENHAM, **C** D C CHEDZEY, **NSM** D A R WALLACE
HADDESLEY (St John the Baptist) *see* Haddlesey w Hambleton and Birkin *York*
HADDISCOE (St Mary) *see* The Raveningham Gp *Nor*
HADDLESEY w Hambleton and Birkin *York 6* **P** *Abp and Simeon's Trustees (jt)* **R** A G GREENHOUGH
HADDON (St Mary) *see* Stilton w Denton and Caldecote etc *Ely*
HADDON, EAST (St Mary the Virgin) *see* Church Brampton, Chapel Brampton, Harleston etc *Pet*
HADDON, OVER (St Anne) *see* Bakewell *Derby*
HADDON, WEST (All Saints) w Winwick and Ravensthorpe *Pet 2* **P** *DBP* **V** D STAPLES
HADFIELD (St Andrew) *Derby 6* **P** *Bp* **V** A BUCKLEY
HADHAM, LITTLE (St Cecilia) w Albury *St Alb 18* **P** *Bp Lon* **R** J TAPLIN
HADHAM, MUCH (St Andrew) *St Alb 18* **P** *Bp Lon* **R** N D B ABBOTT
HADLEIGH (St Barnabas) *Chelmsf 10* **P** *Bp* **V** S J HOLMES, **NSM** M A BOYS
HADLEIGH (St James the Less) *Chelmsf 10* **P** *Dr P W M Copeman* **R** M J KETLEY
HADLEIGH (St Mary) *St E 3* **P** *Abp (2 turns), St Jo Coll Cam, St Chad's Coll Dur, and Bp* **R** S C MORRIS, **NSM** J M WILLIS, J H DOSSOR
HADLEY (Holy Trinity) *Lich 22* **P** *Bp, Adn Salop, V Wrockwardine, R Kynnersley, and V Wellington w Eyton (jt)* **P-in-c** V C SWEET
HADLEY WOOD (St Paul) *see* Enfield Ch Ch Trent Park *Lon*
HADLOW (St Mary) *Roch 8* **P** *Exors Miss I N King* **V** M M CAMP
HADLOW DOWN (St Mark) *see* Buxted and Hadlow Down *Chich*
HADNALL (St Mary Magdalene) *see* Astley, Clive, Grinshill and Hadnall *Lich*
HADSTOCK (St Botolph) *see* Ashdon w Hadstock *Chelmsf*
HADZOR w Oddingley (St James) *see* Bowbrook S *Worc*
HAGBOURNE (St Andrew) *see* Blewbury, Hagbourne and Upton *Ox*
HAGGERSTON (All Saints) *Lon 5* **P** *Ld Chan* **C** R J S PEARSON
HAGGERSTON (St Chad) *Lon 5* **P** *The Crown* **P-in-c** J J WESTCOTT
HAGLEY (St John the Baptist) *Worc 12* **P** *Viscount Cobham* **P-in-c** R J C NEWTON
HAGLEY, WEST (St Saviour) *see* Hagley *Worc*
HAGNABY (St Andrew) *see* Marden Hill Gp *Linc*
HAGWORTHINGHAM (Holy Trinity) *as above*
HAIGH (St David) *Liv 14* **P** *R Wigan* **V** G J T TAYLOR
HAIL WESTON (St Nicholas) *Ely 12* **P** *Mert Coll Ox* **V** *Vacant*
HAILE (not known) *see* Egremont and Haile *Carl*
HAILES (Chapel) *see* Toddington, Stanton, Didbrook w Hailes etc *Glouc*
HAILEY (St John the Evangelist) *see* Witney *Ox*
HAILSHAM (St Mary) *Chich 16* **P** *Ch Soc Trust* **V** R G H PORTHOUSE, **C** W K PUGH, J R JAMES
HAINAULT (St Paul) *Chelmsf 4* **P** *Bp* **V** M W LEARMOUTH
HAINFORD (All Saints) *see* Hevingham w Hainford and Stratton Strawless *Nor*
HAINTON (St Mary) *see* Barkwith Gp *Linc*
HALA (St Paul's Centre) *see* Scotforth *Blackb*
HALAM (St Michael) *see* Edingley w Halam *S'well*
HALBERTON (St Andrew) *see* Sampford Peverell, Uplowman, Holcombe Rogus etc *Ex*
HALDEN, HIGH (St Mary the Virgin) *see* Bethersden w High Halden *Cant*
HALDENS (Christ the King) *see* Digswell and Panshanger *St Alb*
HALDENS (Christ the King) *as above*
HALDON *see* Teignmouth, Ideford w Luton, Ashcombe etc *Ex*
HALE (St David) *see* Timperley *Ches*
HALE (St John the Evangelist) *Guildf 3* **P** *Bp* **TR** H I J SOUTHERN, **TV** G D KING, **C** J R REEVE
HALE (St Mary) *Liv 13* **P** *Trustees* **P-in-c** J D ENGEL, **NSM** W O BALMER
HALE (St Mary) w South Charford *Win 8* **P** *P N Hickman Esq* **P-in-c** T E DAYKIN, **NSM** C E ROLFE
HALE (St Peter) and Ashley *Ches 10* **P** *V Bowdon* **V** M J ROBINSON
HALE, GREAT (St John the Baptist) *see* Helpringham w Hale *Linc*
HALE, UPPER (St Mark) *see* Hale *Guildf*
HALEBANK (St Mary Mission) *as above*
HALES (St Mary) *see* Cheswardine, Childs Ercall, Hales, Hinstock etc *Lich*
HALESOWEN (St John the Baptist) *Worc 9* **P** *Patr Bd* **TR** J C EVEREST, **TV** S R BUCKLEY, V J ENEVER, **C** J A PARSONS, **Hon C** C A KENT
HALESWORTH (St Mary) w Linstead, Chediston, Holton St Peter, Blyford, Spexhall, Wissett and Walpole *St E 15* **P** *Ld Chan and DBP (alt)* **TR** L W DOOLAN, **TV** A B NORTON, W M BULMAN, **C** J J VICKERSTAFF, **NSM** F V G BALLENTYNE
HALEWOOD (St Nicholas) (St Mary) *Liv 4* **P** *Bp* **TR** C DOWDLE, **TV** A D J JEWELL, **NSM** C CRITCHLEY
HALFORD (Our Blessed Lady) *see* Alderminster and Halford *Cov*
HALFORD (St Thomas) *see* Sibdon Carwood w Halford *Heref*
HALFWAY (St Peter) *see* Minster in Sheppey *Cant*
HALIFAX Haley Hill (All Souls) *Wakef 4* **P** *Simeon's Trustees* **P-in-c** D J ROBERTSON
HALIFAX (Holy and Undivided Trinity) *Wakef 4* **P** *Bp and V Halifax (jt)* **V** G R CALVERT
HALIFAX (St Anne in the Grove) *Wakef 4* **P** *V Halifax* **V** D BURROWS
HALIFAX (St Augustine) *Wakef 4* **P** *Trustees* **V** P W GOODMAN
HALIFAX (St Hilda) *Wakef 4* **P** *Bp* **P-in-c** P F MILLWARD
HALIFAX (St John the Baptist) *Wakef 4* **P** *The Crown* **V** A A ROSS, **C** W R S LAMB
HALIFAX (St John the Baptist in the Wilderness) *Wakef 3* **P** *V Halifax* **V** *Vacant* (01422) 882572
HALIFAX (St Jude) *Wakef 4* **P** *Trustees* **V** *Vacant* (01422) 354842
HALIFAX (St James and St Mary) *see* Halifax H Trin *Wakef*
HALL GREEN (Ascension) *Birm 6* **P** *Bp, V Yardley, and Vice-Chmn of PCC (jt)* **P-in-c** D J SENIOR
HALL GREEN (St Peter) *Birm 5* **P** *Bp* **C** D E REES
HALL STREET (St Andrew) *see* Stockport St Mary *Ches*
HALLAM, WEST (St Wilfred) and Mapperley *Derby 13* **P** *Bp* **R** E C LYONS, **NSM** S G WATHEN
HALLATON (St Michael and All Angels) w Horninghold and Allexton, Tugby and East Norton and Slawston *Leic 4* **P** *Bp, DBP, and E Brudenell Esq (jt)* **R** J RICHARDSON
HALLING (St John the Baptist) *see* Cuxton and Halling *Roch*
HALLINGBURY, GREAT (St Giles) (St Andrew) and LITTLE (St Mary the Virgin) *Chelmsf 26* **P** *Bp and Govs Charterhouse (jt)* **R** T J G LOW
HALLIWELL (St Luke) *Man 9* **P** *MMCET* **V** A BROWN, **C** P E BERRY
HALLIWELL (St Margaret) *Man 9* **P** *Trustees* **V** D McCOULOUGH
HALLIWELL (St Paul) *Man 9* **P** *Ch Soc Trust* **P-in-c** I BROWN
HALLIWELL (St Peter) (Barrow Bridge Mission) (St Andrew's Mission Church) *Man 9* **P** *Trustees* **V** R F OLDFIELD, **C** G HARPER, M R S SMITH
HALLIWELL (St Thomas) *see* Bolton St Thos *Man*
HALLOUGHTON (St James) *see* Thurgarton w Hoveringham and Bleasby etc *S'well*

HALLOW (St Philip and St James) and Grimley w Holt *Worc 3* **P** *Bp* **R** R N LATHAM
HALLWOOD (St Mark) *Ches 3* **P** *DBP* **V** J C WILKINSON, **C** P B WAINWRIGHT
HALSALL (St Cuthbert) *Liv 11* **P** *Brig D H Blundell-Hollinshead-Blundell* **R** P GOODRICH
HALSE (Mission Church) *see* Brackley St Pet w St Jas *Pet*
HALSE (St James) *see* Milverton w Halse and Fitzhead *B & W*
HALSETOWN (St John's in the Fields) *Truro 5* **P** *D&C* **NSM** J DIBB SMITH
HALSHAM (All Saints) *see* Keyingham w Ottringham, Halsham and Sunk Is *York*
HALSTEAD (St Andrew) w Holy Trinity and Greenstead Green *Chelmsf 19* **P** *Bp* **V** B E ROSE, **C** D J NORFIELD
HALSTEAD (St Margaret) *see* Knockholt w Halstead *Roch*
HALSTOCK (St Mary) *see* Melbury *Sarum*
HALSTOW, HIGH (St Margaret) (All Hallows) and Hoo St Mary *Roch 6* **P** *MMCET and Ch Soc Trust (jt)* **R** P S McVEAGH
HALSTOW, LOWER (St Margaret) *see* Upchurch w Lower Halstow *Cant*
HALTER DEVIL (Mission Room) *see* Mugginton and Kedleston *Derby*
HALTON (St Andrew) *see* Corbridge w Halton and Newton Hall *Newc*
HALTON (St Mary) *Ches 3* **P** *Bp* **V** R J SAMUELS, **C** A E SAMUELS
HALTON (St Michael and All Angels) *Ox 28* **P** *DBF* **P-in-c** H P MARSHALL
HALTON (St Oswald and St Cuthbert and King Alfwald) *see* Corbridge w Halton and Newton Hall *Newc*
HALTON (St Wilfred) w Aughton *Blackb 15* **P** *Exors of R T Sanderson Esq* **R** M P KEIGHLEY
HALTON (St Wilfrid) *see* Leeds Halton St Wilfrid *Ripon*
HALTON, EAST (St Peter) *see* Habrough Gp *Linc*
HALTON, WEST (St Etheldreda) *see* Alkborough *Linc*
HALTON HOLGATE (St Andrew) *Linc 7* **P** *Bp* **R** G ROBSON
HALTON QUAY (St Indract's Chapel) *see* St Dominic, Landulph and St Mellion w Pillaton *Truro*
HALTON WEST (Mission Church) *see* Hellifield *Bradf*
HALTWHISTLE (Holy Cross) and Greenhead *Newc 4* **P** *Bp* **V** G A NEWMAN
HALVERGATE (St Peter and St Paul) *see* Freethorpe w Wickhampton, Halvergate etc *Nor*
HALWELL (St Leonard) w Moreleigh *Ex 13* **P** *Bp (1 turn) and D&C (2 turns)* **V** *Vacant*
HALWILL (St Peter and St James) *see* Ashwater, Halwill, Beaworthy, Clawton etc *Ex*
HAM (All Saints) *see* Wexcombe *Sarum*
HAM (St Andrew) *S'wark 16* **P** *K Coll Cam* **V** D R MOORE, **Hon C** D S MARKWELL
HAM (St Barnabas Mission Church) *see* Combe St Nicholas w Wambrook *B & W*
HAM (St James the Less) *see* Plymouth St Jas Ham *Ex*
HAM (St Richard) *S'wark 17* **P** *Bp* **Hon C** P H BUSS, J R WEBB
HAMBLE LE RICE (St Andrew) *Win 9* **P** *St Mary's Coll Win* **V** J W TRAVERS
HAMBLEDEN VALLEY (St Mary the Virgin) *Ox 29* **P** *Bp, Viscount Hambleden, and Miss M Mackenzie (jt)* **P-in-c** M M FITZWILLIAMS, **C** P R NICOLSON, **NSM** C L WODEHOUSE
HAMBLEDON (St Peter) *Guildf 4* **P** *MMCET* **R** *Vacant* (01428) 682753
HAMBLEDON (St Peter and St Paul) *Portsm 1* **P** *Ld Chan* **V** *Vacant* (01705) 632717
HAMBLETON (Blessed Virgin Mary) w Out Rawcliffe *Blackb 10* **P** *V Kirkham and V St Michaels-on-Wyre (jt)* **V** P P F WARD
HAMBLETON (St Andrew) *see* Oakham, Hambleton, Egleton, Braunston and Brooke *Pet*
HAMBLETON (St Mary) *see* Haddlesey w Hambleton and Birkin *York*
HAMBRIDGE (St James the Less) *see* Kingsbury Episcopi w E Lambrook, Hambridge etc *B & W*
HAMER (All Saints) *Man 20* **P** *Bp* **V** M JONES
HAMERINGHAM (All Saints) w Scrafield and Winceby *Linc 11* **P** *DBP* **R** *Vacant*
HAMERTON (All Saints) *Ely 10* **P** *G R Petherick Esq* **NSM** I D M GIBSON
HAMILTON TERRACE (St Mark) *see* St Marylebone St Mark Hamilton Terrace *Lon*
HAMILTON TERRACE (St Mark) *as above*
HAMMER (St Michael) *see* Lynchmere and Camelsdale *Chich*
HAMMERFIELD (St Francis of Assisi) *see* Boxmoor St Jo *St Alb*
HAMMERSMITH (Holy Innocents) *Lon 9* **P** *Bp* **V** M W GRANT, **NSM** G MORGAN
HAMMERSMITH (St John the Evangelist) *Lon 9* **P** *V Hammersmith St Paul* **P-in-c** M P ANDREW, **NSM** A H MEAD
HAMMERSMITH (St Luke) *Lon 9* **P** *Bp* **P-in-c** R A BLOCK
HAMMERSMITH (St Matthew) *Lon 9* **P** *Trustees* **V** G H CHIPLIN
HAMMERSMITH (St Michael and St George) White City Estate Conventional District *Lon 9* **C-in-c** R A BLOCK, **C** D W CHERRY
HAMMERSMITH (St Paul) *Lon 9* **P** *Bp* **V** R A M THACKER, **NSM** P E BATES
HAMMERSMITH (St Peter) *Lon 9* **P** *Bp* **V** G W F LANG
HAMMERSMITH (St Saviour) *see* Cobbold Road St Sav w St Mary *Lon*
HAMMERSMITH (St Simon) *Lon 9* **P** *Simeon's Trustees* **V** J J CLARK, **C** J TATE
HAMMERSMITH, NORTH (St Katherine) *Lon 9* **P** *Bp* **V** *Vacant* 0181-743 3951
HAMMERWICH (St John the Baptist) *Lich 1* **P** *Hammerwich Ch Lands Trustees* **P-in-c** E M TURNER, **C** M J BUTT
HAMMERWOOD (St Stephen) *see* Cowden w Hammerwood *Chich*
HAMMOON (St Paul) *see* Childe Okeford, Okeford Fitzpaine, Manston etc *Sarum*
HAMNISH (St Dubricius and All Saints) *see* Kimbolton w Hamnish and Middleton-on-the-Hill *Heref*
HAMPDEN, GREAT (St Mary Magdalene) *see* Prestwood and Gt Hampden *Ox*
HAMPDEN, LITTLE (not known) *see* Gt Missenden w Ballinger and Lt Hampden *Ox*
HAMPDEN PARK (St Mary-in-the-Park) *Chich 16* **P** *Bp* **V** F R SEARLE
HAMPNETT (St George) *see* Northleach w Hampnett and Farmington *Glouc*
HAMPRESTON (All Saints) *Sarum 10* **P** *Patr Bd* **TR** R G L LUTHER, **TV** C M STRAIN, M J RAINSBURY, **Hon C** M A BARBER
HAMPSTEAD Belsize Park (St Peter) *see* Belsize Park *Lon*
HAMPSTEAD (Christ Church) *Lon 16* **P** *Trustees* **P-in-c** P D CONRAD
HAMPSTEAD Downshire Hill (St John) Proprietary Chapel *Lon 16* **Min** J G L GOULD
HAMPSTEAD (Emmanuel) West End *Lon 16* **P** *Trustees* **V** P J GALLOWAY
HAMPSTEAD (St John) *Lon 16* **P** *DBP* **V** P J W BUCKLER, **C** I L PHILLIPS
HAMPSTEAD St Stephen w (All Hallows) *Lon 16* **P** *DBP and D&C Cant (jt)* **V** D N C HOULDING, **NSM** S D DEWEY
HAMPSTEAD, SOUTH (St Saviour) *Lon 16* **P** *V Hampstead St Jo* **P-in-c** A C PAVLIBEYI
HAMPSTEAD, WEST (Holy Trinity) *Lon 16* **P** *MMCET* **V** M NOLAN
HAMPSTEAD, WEST (St Cuthbert) *Lon 16* **P** *Ch Trust Fund Trust* **V** C O MASON
HAMPSTEAD, WEST (St James) *Lon 16* **P** *Trustees* **C** D H P BROWN, D A SHERRATT
HAMPSTEAD, WEST (St Luke) *Lon 16* **P** *CPAS* **V** B J MORRISON
HAMPSTEAD GARDEN SUBURB (St Jude on the Hill) *Lon 15* **P** *Bp* **V** A R G WALKER
HAMPSTEAD NORREYS (St Mary) *see* Hermitage and Hampstead Norreys, Cold Ash etc *Ox*
HAMPSTHWAITE (St Thomas a Becket) and Killinghall *Ripon 1* **P** *Sir James Aykroyd Bt, Sir Thomas Ingilby Bt, and Bp (jt)* **V** A G HUDSON
HAMPTON (All Saints) *Lon 10* **P** *Ld Chan* **V** W D F VANSTONE, **C** A C McCOLLUM, **NSM** M R THOMSETT
HAMPTON (St Andrew) *see* Herne Bay Ch Ch *Cant*
HAMPTON (St Andrew) *Worc 1* **P** *Ch Ch Ox* **V** J R N J BOMYER, **NSM** G KNEE
HAMPTON (St Mary the Virgin) *Lon 10* **P** *The Crown* **V** D N WINTERBURN
HAMPTON BISHOP (St Andrew) *see* Tupsley w Hampton Bishop *Heref*
HAMPTON GAY (St Giles) *see* Akeman *Ox*
HAMPTON HILL (St James) *Lon 10* **P** *V Hampton St Mary* **V** B LEATHARD
HAMPTON IN ARDEN (St Mary and St Bartholomew) *Birm 12* **P** *Guild of All So* **P-in-c** J DE WIT
HAMPTON LOVETT (St Mary and All Saints) *see* Elmley Lovett w Hampton Lovett and Elmbridge etc *Worc*
HAMPTON LUCY (St Peter ad Vincula) w Charlecote and Loxley *Cov 8* **P** *Sir Edmund Fairfax-Lucy, Bt (3 turns), Col A M H Gregory-Hood (1 turn)* **P-in-c** H C J M KEEP
HAMPTON POYLE (St Mary the Virgin) *see* Kidlington w Hampton Poyle *Ox*

HAMPTON WICK (St John the Baptist) *see* Teddington St Mark and Hampton Wick St Jo *Lon*
HAMSEY (St Peter) *Chich 18* **P** *Bp* **P-in-c** D BASTIDE
HAMSTALL RIDWARE (St Michael and All Angels) *see* The Ridwares and Kings Bromley *Lich*
HAMSTEAD (St Bernard) *Birm 3* **P** *Bp* **V** A D J COE
HAMSTEAD (St Paul) *Birm 3* **P** *Bp* **V** J W MASDING, **C** J E DOUGLAS
HAMSTEAD MARSHALL (St Mary) *see* W Woodhay w Enborne, Hampstead Marshall etc *Ox*
HAMSTEELS (St John the Baptist) *Dur 4* **P** *The Crown* **NSM** S I WRIGHT
HAMSTERLEY (St James) and Witton-le-Wear *Dur 6* **P** *Bp and The Crown (alt)* **V** G W WEBSTER
HAMWORTHY (St Gabriel) (St Michael) *Sarum 8* **P** *MMCET* **P-in-c** J E WARING, **C** G F PERRYMAN
HANBOROUGH (St Peter and St Paul) and Freeland *Ox 9* **P** *St Jo Coll Ox* **R** C A RANDALL
HANBURY (St Mary the Virgin) *see* Bowbrook N *Worc*
HANBURY (St Werburgh) w Newborough and Rangemore *Lich 14* **P** *DBP and Lord Burton (jt)* **NSM** D C FELIX
HANCHURCH (Chapel of Ease) *see* Trentham *Lich*
HANDCROSS (All Saints) *see* Slaugham *Chich*
HANDFORTH (St Chad) *Ches 17* **P** *R Cheadle* **V** S P ISHERWOOD, **C** P A CARR
HANDLEY (All Saints) *see* Tattenhall and Handley *Ches*
HANDLEY (St John the Baptist) *see* Eckington w Handley and Ridgeway *Derby*
HANDLEY (St Mark) *see* N Wingfield, Clay Cross and Pilsley *Derby*
HANDLEY (St Mary) w Gussage St Andrew and Pentridge *Sarum 7* **P** *D&C Windsor and Earl of Shaftesbury (alt)* **R** R E WOOD
HANDSACRE (St Luke) *see* Armitage *Lich*
HANDSWORTH (St Andrew) *Birm 3* **P** *Bp* **C** J AUSTEN
HANDSWORTH (St James) *Birm 3* **P** *Bp* **V** R J MORRIS, **C** J V MARCH, Q D WARBRICK
HANDSWORTH (St Mary) *Sheff 1* **P** *DBP* **R** I HOLLIN
HANDSWORTH (St Mary) (Epiphany) *Birm 3* **P** *Bp* **R** B A HALL, **C** C M FEAK
HANDSWORTH (St Michael) (St Peter) *Birm 3* **P** *Bp* **V** D HARE
HANDSWORTH Woodhouse (St James) *Sheff 1* **P** *Bp* **V** B R CRANWELL
HANFORD (St Matthias) *Lich 13* **P** *Bp* **P-in-c** J P HARTLEY
HANGER HILL (Ascension) and West Twyford *Lon 22* **P** *Bp and DBP (jt)* **P-in-c** S J REED
HANGER LANE (St Ann) *see* S Tottenham St Ann *Lon*
HANGING HEATON (St Paul) *Wakef 10* **P** *R Dewsbury* **V** M GARSIDE
HANGLETON (St Helen) (St Richard) *Chich 4* **P** *Bp* **V** A G SAGE, **C** J K T ELDRIDGE
HANHAM (Christ Church) (St George) *Bris 2* **P** *Bp* **V** S W COOK
HANKERTON (Holy Cross) *see* Ashley, Crudwell, Hankerton, Long Newnton etc *Bris*
HANLEY (All Saints) *see* Stoke-upon-Trent *Lich*
HANLEY Holy Evangelists (St Luke) *Lich 11* **P** *Bp* **TR** R P OWEN, **TV** R H P THORNBURGH, **C** A C STEWART-SYKES, **NSM** C LOWNDES
HANLEY (St Chad) *see* Hanley H Ev *Lich*
HANLEY CASTLE (St Mary), Hanley Swan and Welland *Worc 5* **P** *Ld Chan and Sir Berwick Lechmere Bt (alt)* **V** S J SWAIN, **NSM** E J BIRKIN
HANLEY CHILD (St Michael and All Angels) *see* Teme Valley S *Worc*
HANLEY SWAN (St Gabriel) *see* Hanley Castle, Hanley Swan and Welland *Worc*
HANLEY WILLIAM (All Saints) *see* Teme Valley S *Worc*
HANNAH (St Andrew) cum Hagnaby w Markby *Linc 8* **P** *Bp and Mrs E Smyth (alt)* **R** A READER-MOORE
HANNEY (St James the Great), Denchworth and East Challow *Ox 19* **P** *Bp (2 turns), Worc Coll Ox (1 turn)* **V** A HOGG
HANNINGFIELD, EAST (All Saints) *Chelmsf 9* **P** *CPAS* **P-in-c** H A MATTY
HANNINGFIELD, WEST (St Mary and St Edward) *Chelmsf 9* **P** *DBP* **P-in-c** B G HALL
HANNINGTON (All Saints) *see* Baughurst, Ramsdell, Wolverton w Ewhurst etc *Win*
HANNINGTON (St John the Baptist) *see* Highworth w Sevenhampton and Inglesham etc *Bris*
HANNINGTON (St Peter and St Paul) *see* Walgrave w Hannington and Wold and Scaldwell *Pet*
HANOVER SQUARE (St George) (St Mark) *Lon 3* **P** *Bp* **R** W M ATKINS, **C** S J HOBBS
HANSLOPE (St James the Great) w Castlethorpe *Ox 27* **P** *Bp* **V** C M G BEAKE
HANWELL (St Mary) (St Christopher) *Lon 22* **P** *Bp* **R** M R GRAYSHON, **C** D J BURGESS, J R LUCAS, **NSM** R WEBB
HANWELL (St Mellitus w St Mark) *Lon 22* **P** *Bp* **P-in-c** J O HEREWARD
HANWELL (St Peter) *see* Ironstone *Ox*
HANWELL (St Thomas) *Lon 22* **P** *The Crown* **V** P A ANDREWS
HANWOOD, GREAT (St Thomas) *Heref 13* **P** *Lt-Col H de Grey-Warter* **R** P TOWNER
HANWORTH (All Saints) *Lon 11* **P** *Bp* **V** J A FLETCHER
HANWORTH (St Bartholomew) *see* Roughton and Felbrigg, Metton, Sustead etc *Nor*
HANWORTH (St George) *Lon 11* **P** *Lee Abbey Trust* **P-in-c** P S WILLIAMSON
HANWORTH (St Richard of Chichester) *Lon 11* **P** *Bp* **V** A JACKSON
HAPPISBURGH (St Mary the Virgin), Walcott, Hempstead w Eccles and Sea Palling w Waxham *Nor 12* **P** *Bp (3 turns), K Coll Cam (2 turns), E C Evans-Lombe Esq andBp (1 turn)* **R** J A LINES, R A HINES, **NSM** E M MELLERUP
HAPTON (St Margaret) *see* Padiham *Blackb*
HAPTON (St Margaret) *see* Wreningham *Nor*
HARBERTON (St Andrew) *see* Diptford, N Huish, Harberton and Harbertonford *Ex*
HARBERTONFORD (St Peter) *as above*
HARBLEDOWN (St Michael and All Angels) *Cant 3* **P** *Abp* **P-in-c** M A MORRIS
HARBORNE (St Faith and St Laurence) *Birm 2* **P** *Bp* **V** I M MICHAEL, **NSM** T R BOTT
HARBORNE (St Peter) *Birm 2* **P** *Bp* **V** C J EVANS
HARBORNE HEATH (St John the Baptist) *Birm 2* **P** *Ch Soc Trust* **V** J P HUGHES, **C** G P LANHAM, W E L SOUTER
HARBOROUGH MAGNA (All Saints) *Cov 6* **P** *A H F W Boughton-Leigh Esq* **R** P S RUSSELL
HARBRIDGE (All Saints) *see* Ellingham and Harbridge and Hyde w Ibsley *Win*
HARBURY (All Saints) and Ladbroke *Cov 10* **P** *Bp* **R** P R BROWN
HARBY (All Saints) w Thorney and North and South Clifton *S'well 3* **P** *Ld Chan and Bp (alt)* **NSM** K B POTTER
HARBY (St Mary the Virgin), Long Clawson and Hose *Leic 3* **P** *Duke of Rutland, Bp and DBP (alt)* **P-in-c** G SPENCER, **C** M TURNER
HARDEN (St Saviour) and Wilsden *Bradf 8* **P** *Bp, Adn, V Bradf, and R Bingley Esq (jt)* **NSM** D P HALLIDAY
HARDENHUISH (St Nicholas) *see* Chippenham St Paul w Hardenhuish etc *Bris*
HARDHAM (St Botolph) *see* Coldwaltham and Hardham *Chich*
HARDINGHAM (St George) *see* Barnham Broom *Nor*
HARDINGSTONE (St Edmund) and Horton and Piddington *Pet 7* **P** *Bp* **V** B H STEVENS
HARDINGTON MANDEVILLE (Blessed Virgin Mary) *see* W Coker w Hardington Mandeville, E Chinnock etc *B & W*
HARDLEY (St Margaret) *see* Chedgrave w Hardley and Langley *Nor*
HARDMEAD (St Mary) *see* Sherington w Chicheley, N Crawley, Astwood etc *Ox*
HARDRAW (St Mary and St John) *see* Hawes and Hardraw *Ripon*
HARDRES, LOWER (St Mary) *see* Petham and Waltham w Lower Hardres etc *Cant*
HARDRES, UPPER (St Peter and St Paul) *as above*
HARDSTOFT (St Peter) *see* Ault Hucknall *Derby*
HARDWICK (St James) *see* Stockton St Jas *Dur*
HARDWICK (St Leonard) *see* Mears Ashby and Hardwick and Sywell etc *Pet*
HARDWICK (St Margaret) *see* Hempnall *Nor*
HARDWICK (St Mary) *Ely 1* **P** *Bp* **R** D G DEBOYS, **NSM** A G WILMAN
HARDWICK, EAST (St Stephen) *Wakef 11* **P** *Cawood Trustees* **P-in-c** S A STACEY
HARDWICK-CUM-TUSMORE (St Mary) *see* Shelswell *Ox*
HARDWICKE (Holy Trinity) *see* Cusop w Clifford, Hardwicke, Bredwardine etc *Heref*
HARDWICKE (St Mary the Virgin) *see* Schorne *Ox*
HARDWICKE (St Nicholas), Quedgeley and Elmore w Longney *Glouc 8* **P** *Adn Glouc and Sir John Guise (1 turn), Bp (2 turns), and Ld Chan (1 turn)* **R** G J B STICKLAND, **NSM** M E C WHATSON
HAREBY (St Peter and St Paul) *see* Marden Hill Gp *Linc*
HAREFIELD (St Mary the Virgin) *Lon 24* **P** *The Hon J E F Newdegate* **V** A J R GANDON, **C** S A GROOM
HARESCOMBE (St John the Baptist) *see* The Edge, Pitchcombe, Harescombe and Brookthorpe *Glouc*
HARESFIELD (St Peter) *see* Standish w Haresfield and Moreton Valence etc *Glouc*

HAREWOOD (Methodist Chapel) *see* Collingham w Harewood *Ripon*
HARFORD (St Petroc) *see* Ivybridge w Harford *Ex*
HARGRAVE (All Saints) *see* Stanwick w Hargrave *Pet*
HARGRAVE (St Edmund) *see* Chevington w Hargrave and Whepstead w Brockley *St E*
HARGRAVE (St Peter) *Ches 5* **P** *Bp* **P-in-c** R M POWLEY
HARKSTEAD (St Mary) *see* Chelmondiston and Erwarton w Harkstead *St E*
HARLASTON (St Matthew) *see* Clifton Campville w Edingale and Harlaston *Lich*
HARLAXTON GROUP, The (St Mary and St Peter) *Linc 19* **P** *Bp, DBP, Sir Richard Welby Bt, D&C, and Duke of Rutland (jt)* **R** F C THORNETT
HARLESCOTT (Holy Spirit) *Lich 21* **P** *Bp* **V** M F WALKER, **C** I M BROTHERSTON, **NSM** D W G UFFINDELL
HARLESDEN (All Souls) *Lon 21* **P** *The Crown* **V** M D MOORHEAD, **NSM** M D ENGLER
HARLESDEN (St Mark) *see* Kensal Rise St Mark and St Martin *Lon*
HARLESTON (St Augustine) *see* Gt Finborough w Onehouse and Harleston *St E*
HARLESTON (St John the Baptist) *see* Redenhall, Harleston, Wortwell and Needham *Nor*
HARLESTONE (St Andrew) *see* Church Brampton, Chapel Brampton, Harleston etc *Pet*
HARLEY (St Mary) *see* Wenlock *Heref*
HARLING, EAST (St Peter and St Paul) w West, Bridgham w Roudham, Larling, Brettenham and Rushford *Nor 11* **P** *Ld Chan (1 turn), DBP, Sir Robin Nugent Bt, C D F Musker Esq, Major E H C Garnier, and Exors Sir John Musker (3 turns)* **R** J HANDLEY
HARLINGTON (Christ Church) Waltham Avenue Conventional District *Lon 24* **C-in-c** R N McCANN
HARLINGTON (St Mary the Virgin) *St Alb 12* **P** *Bp* **V** S J WILLIAMS
HARLINGTON (St Peter and St Paul) *Lon 24* **P** *Bp* **R** D R JENKINS
HARLOW (St Mary and St Hugh w St John the Baptist) *Chelmsf 26* **P** *Simeon's Trustees and Bp (alt)* **V** S P E MOURANT, **C** T W BALL, **NSM** J C MOURANT
HARLOW (St Mary Magdalene) *Chelmsf 26* **P** *V Harlow St Mary and St Hugh etc* **V** G R SMITH, **C** M J HAMPSON, **Hon C** G R NEAVE
HARLOW Town Centre (St Paul) w Little Parndon *Chelmsf 26* **P** *Patr Bd* **TV** A R B HIGGS, A E MELANIPHY
HARLOW GREEN (St Ninian) *see* Gateshead Harlow Green *Dur*
HARLOW HILL (All Saints) *see* Low Harrogate St Mary *Ripon*
HARLSEY, EAST (St Oswald) *see* Osmotherley w Harlsey and Ingleby Arncliffe *York*
HARLTON (Assumption of the Blessed Virgin Mary) *see* Haslingfield w Harlton and Gt and Lt Eversden *Ely*
HARMANSWATER (St Paul) *see* Bracknell *Ox*
HARMER HILL (St Andrew) *see* Myddle *Lich*
HARMONDSWORTH (St Mary) *Lon 24* **P** *DBP* **P-in-c** J P ADAMS
HARMSTON (All Saints) *see* Graffoe Gp *Linc*
HARNHAM (St George) (All Saints) *Sarum 15* **P** *Bp (1 turn), V Britford (2 turns)* **P-in-c** D P SCRACE, **C** J BOULTON-REYNOLDS
HARNHILL (St Michael and All Angels) *see* The Ampneys w Driffield and Poulton *Glouc*
HAROLD HILL (St George) *Chelmsf 2* **P** *Bp* **C** T D HULL
HAROLD HILL (St Paul) *Chelmsf 2* **P** *Bp* **V** E W COCKETT
HAROLD WOOD (St Peter) *Chelmsf 2* **P** *New Coll Ox* **C** P A WILLIAMS, M W LUCAS
HAROME (St Saviour) w Stonegrave, Nunnington and Pockley *York 18* **P** *Lady Clarissa Collin, Abp, Adn Cleveland and V Helmsley (jt), The Crown, and Abp (by turn)* **R** *Vacant* (01439) 70163
HARPENDEN (St John the Baptist) *St Alb 8* **P** *DBP* **V** J P SMITH
HARPENDEN (St Nicholas) (All Saints) *St Alb 8* **P** *Ld Chan* **R** N COLLINGS, **C** R W B ARDILL, D J SWAN, D G WILLIAMS, **NSM** D PRICE
HARPFORD (St Gregory the Great) *see* Newton Poppleford, Harpford and Colaton Raleigh *Ex*
HARPHAM (St John of Beverley) *see* Burton Agnes w Harpham and Lowthorpe etc *York*
HARPLEY (St Lawrence) *see* Gt and Lt Massingham and Harpley *Nor*
HARPOLE (All Saints) *see* Kislingbury and Harpole *Pet*
HARPSDEN (St Margaret) w Bolney *Ox 6* **P** *All So Coll Ox* **P-in-c** P J FOX
HARPSWELL (St Chad) *see* Glentworth Gp *Linc*
HARPTREE, EAST (St Laurence) w WEST (Blessed Virgin Mary) and Hinton Blewett *B & W 10* **P** *Duchy of Cornwall* **R** R G HARVEY
HARPUR HILL (St James) *see* Buxton w Burbage and King Sterndale *Derby*
HARPURHEY cum Moston (Christ Church) *Man 5* **P** *Bp, Dean, K Greenwood Esq, Ms A Greenhalgh, and V Morley Esq (jt)* **R** M D ASHCROFT
HARPURHEY (St Stephen) *Man 5* **P** *Bp* **R** M D ASHCROFT
HARRABY (St Elisabeth) *Carl 3* **P** *Bp* **P-in-c** D C BICKERSTETH, **C** M J MURRAY
HARRIETSHAM (St John the Baptist) w Ulcombe *Cant 15* **P** *The Crown* **R** A C STOCKBRIDGE
HARRINGAY (St Paul) *Lon 19* **P** *Bp* **V** R P P MARTIN
HARRINGTON (St Mary) *Carl 7* **P** *Mrs E H S Thornely* **R** J D HODGKINSON
HARRINGTON (St Mary) *see* S Ormsby Gp *Linc*
HARRINGTON (St Peter and St Paul) *see* Arthingworth, Harrington w Oxendon and E Farndon *Pet*
HARRINGWORTH (St John the Baptist) *see* Bulwick, Blatherwycke w Harringworth and Laxton *Pet*
HARROGATE (St Mark) *Ripon 1* **P** *Peache Trustees* **V** P D G HOOPER, **C** A M GUBBINS
HARROGATE (St Wilfrid) *Ripon 1* **P** *Bp* **V** B R PEARSON, **C** A CALLAN-TRAVIS, **NSM** G P CORNISH
HARROGATE, HIGH (Christ Church) *Ripon 1* **P** *Bp* **V** J E COLSTON, **C** P J CONWAY
HARROGATE, HIGH (St Peter) *Ripon 1* **P** *Ch Patr Trust* **V** A M SHEPHERD, **NSM** L J WASSELL
HARROGATE, LOW (St Mary) *Ripon 4* **P** *Peache Trustees* **V** M W SOAR
HARROLD (St Peter and All Saints) and Carlton w Chellington *St Alb 15* **P** *Bp* **R** *Vacant* (01234) 720262
HARROW (Church of the Holy Spirit) *see* Kenton *Lon*
HARROW (Holy Trinity) (St Michael) *Lon 23* **P** *Bp* **V** T A MAPSTONE, **C** A R SALISBURY, M I BENNETT, A P RUMSEY
HARROW (St John the Baptist) *see* Greenhill St Jo *Lon*
HARROW (St Paul) *see* Roxeth *Lon*
HARROW, NORTH (St Alban) *Lon 23* **P** *Bp* **V** P HEMINGWAY, **Hon C** D S ARDEN
HARROW GREEN (Holy Trinity and St Augustine of Hippo) *see* Leytonstone H Trin Harrow Green *Chelmsf*
HARROW ON THE HILL (St Mary) *Lon 23* **P** *Bp, Adn, and Hd Master Harrow Sch (jt)* **C** J M RUSHTON
HARROW WEALD (All Saints) *Lon 23* **P** *Bp, Adn, V Harrow St Mary, and R Bushey (jt)* **V** F D JAKEMAN, **C** M RAJKOVIC
HARROWBARROW (All Saints) *see* Calstock *Truro*
HARROWBY (The Ascension) *see* Grantham *Linc*
HARROWDEN, GREAT (All Saints) w LITTLE (St Mary the Virgin) and Orlingbury *Pet 6* **P** *Sir Stephen Hastings and Bp (alt)* **V** J E COOPER
HARSTON (All Saints) w Hauxton *Ely 7* **P** *Bp (2 turns), D&C (1 turn)* **P-in-c** J PARR, **NSM** R G HOWELLS
HARSTON (St Michael and All Angels) *see* High Framland Parishes *Leic*
HARSWELL (St Peter) *see* Seaton Ross Gp of Par *York*
HART (St Mary Magdalene) w Elwick Hall *Dur 3* **P** *Bp and DBP (alt)* **V** J E LUND
HART COMMON (not known) *see* Westhoughton and Wingates *Man*
HARTBURN (All Saints) *see* Stockton St Pet *Dur*
HARTBURN (St Andrew) *see* Bolam w Whalton and Hartburn w Meldon *Newc*
HARTCLIFFE (St Andrew) *see* Bris St Andr Hartcliffe *Bris*
HARTEST (All Saints) *see* Glem Valley United Benefice *St E*
HARTFIELD (St Mary) w Coleman's Hatch *Chich 19* **P** *Earl de la Warr* **R** P T CRAIG
HARTFORD (All Saints) *see* Huntingdon *Ely*
HARTFORD (All Souls) *see* Hartley Wintney, Elvetham, Winchfield etc *Win*
HARTFORD (St John the Baptist) *Ches 6* **P** *Mrs I H Wilson, Mrs R H Emmet, and Mrs J M Wearne (jt)* **V** P D GARDNER, **C** R S MUNRO, R A FRANCE
HARTHILL (All Hallows) and Thorpe Salvin *Sheff 5* **P** *Bp* **R** P MORLEY
HARTHILL (All Saints) and Burwardsley *Ches 5* **P** *Bp and A G Barbour Esq (jt)* **P-in-c** D R BUCKLEY
HARTING (St Mary and St Gabriel) w Elsted and Treyford cum Didling *Chich 10* **P** *Bp* **R** D R C GIBBONS
HARTINGTON (St Giles), Biggin and Earl Sterndale *Derby 4* **P** *Duke of Devonshire* **P-in-c** P THOMPSON
HARTISMERE, NORTH *St E 16* **P** *MMCET, K Coll Cam, Bp, and DBP (jt)* **P-in-c** D N STEVENSON
HARTLAND (St Nectan) *see* Parkham, Alwington, Buckland Brewer etc *Ex*
HARTLAND COAST *as above*

HARTLEBURY (St James) *Worc 13* **P** *Bp*
P-in-c M E STANTON-HYDE
HARTLEPOOL (Holy Trinity) (St Mark's Centre) *Dur 3* **P** *Bp* **V** P J NORTH, **C** S J ATKINSON
HARTLEPOOL (St Aidan) (St Columba) *Dur 3* **P** *Bp* **V** M H WHITEHEAD, **C** A C JONES
HARTLEPOOL (St Hilda) *Dur 3* **P** *Bp* **R** P Z KASHOURIS
HARTLEPOOL (St Luke) *Dur 3* **P** *Bp* **V** P TOWNSEND
HARTLEPOOL (St Oswald) *Dur 3* **P** *Bp* **V** B R TURNBULL, **C** C R BATES
HARTLEPOOL (St Paul) *Dur 3* **P** *Bp* **V** R E MASSHEDAR
HARTLEY (All Saints) *see* Fawkham and Hartley *Roch*
HARTLEY, NEW (St Michael and All Angels) *see* Delaval *Newc*
HARTLEY BROOK (Mission Hall) *see* Becontree St Mary *Chelmsf*
HARTLEY MAUDITT (St Leonard) *see* E and W Worldham, Hartley Mauditt w Kingsley etc *Win*
HARTLEY WESPALL (St Mary) *see* Sherfield-on-Loddon and Stratfield Saye etc *Win*
HARTLEY WINTNEY (St John the Evangelist), Elvetham, Winchfield and Dogmersfield *Win 5* **P** *Bp and Sir Euan Anstruther-Gough-Calthorpe, Bt (jt)*
V P E de D WARBURTON, **C** J WATKINS
HARTLIP (St Michael and All Angels) *see* Newington w Hartlip and Stockbury *Cant*
HARTOFT (Mission Room) *see* Lastingham w Appleton-le-Moors, Rosedale etc *York*
HARTON (St Peter) (St Lawrence) *Dur 15* **P** *D&C*
V R O DICK, **C** C A DICK
HARTPLAIN *Portsm 4* **P** *DBP* **V** M S COOPER
HARTPURY (St Mary the Virgin) w Corse and Staunton *Glouc 6* **P** *Bp (2 turns), DBP (1 turn)* **P-in-c** J G EVANS
HARTSHEAD (St Peter) and Hightown *Wakef 8*
P *R Dewsbury* **V** *Vacant* (01274) 873786
HARTSHILL (Holy Trinity) *Cov 5* **P** *V Mancetter*
P-in-c A S MAIRS, **NSM** P DODDS
HARTSHILL (Holy Trinity) *Lich 12* **P** *Bp* **V** J A WALSH
HARTSHORNE (St Peter) *Derby 16* **P** *MMCET*
R I R WILLIAMS-HUNTER
HARTWELL (St John the Baptist) *see* Roade and Ashton w Hartwell *Pet*
HARTWITH (St Jude) *see* Dacre w Hartwith and Darley w Thornthwaite *Ripon*
HARTY (St Thomas Apostle) *see* Eastchurch w Leysdown and Harty *Cant*
HARVINGTON (St James) *Worc 1* **P** *D&C* **R** *Vacant* (01386) 871068
HARWELL (St Matthew) w Chilton *Ox 18* **P** *DBP and CPAS (jt)* **R** C J STOTT, **C** M P CARNEY
HARWICH (St Nicholas) *see* Dovercourt and Parkeston w Harwich *Chelmsf*
HARWOOD (Christ Church) *Man 16* **P** *DBP*
V A R HAZLEHURST, **NSM** H MOLLOY, M J FROST
HARWOOD, GREAT (St Bartholomew) *Blackb 8* **P** *V Blackb*
V J HEIL
HARWOOD, GREAT (St John) *Blackb 8* **P** *Bp and V Gt Harwood St Bart (jt)* **V** B DARBYSHIRE
HARWOOD DALE (St Margaret) *see* Hackness w Harwood Dale *York*
HARWORTH (All Saints) *S'well 1* **P** *Sir James Whitaker, Bt*
V J A BRITTON
HASBURY (St Margaret) *see* Halesowen *Worc*
HASCOMBE (St Peter) *Guildf 2* **P** *SMF*
R R C D MACKENNA
HASELBECH (St Michael) *see* Clipston w Naseby and Haselbech w Kelmarsh *Pet*
HASELBURY PLUCKNETT (St Michael and All Angels), Misterton and North Perrott *B & W 15* **P** *Ld Chan (2 turns), Bp (2 turns), and H W F Hoskyns Esq (1 turn)*
V R D MARTIN
HASELEY (St Mary) *see* Hatton w Haseley, Rowington w Lowsonford etc *Cov*
HASELEY, GREAT (St Peter) *see* Gt w Lt Milton and Gt Haseley *Ox*
HASELOR (St Mary and All Saints) *see* Kinwarton w Gt Alne and Haselor *Cov*
HASELTON (St Andrew) *see* Withington and Compton Abdale w Haselton *Glouc*
HASFIELD (St Mary) w Tirley and Ashleworth *Glouc 6*
P *W G F Meath-Baker Esq, Ld Chan, and Bp (by turn)*
P-in-c G E PARSONS
HASKETON (St Andrew) *see* Ufford w Bredfield and Hasketon *St E*
HASLAND (St Paul) *Derby 5* **P** *V Chesterfield*
R C W D VOGT

HASLEMERE (St Bartholomew) (St Christopher) *Guildf 4*
P *Ld Chan* **R** C EDMONDS, **C** P P LEONARD,
Hon C D C G BROWN
HASLINGDEN (St James) w Grane and Stonefold *Blackb 1*
P *Bp and Hulme Trustees (jt)* **P-in-c** T R SMITH
HASLINGFIELD (All Saints) w Harlton and Eversden, Great w Little *Ely 1* **P** *Qu Coll Cam, Ld Chan, Jes Coll Cam (by turn)*
R P C OWEN-JONES
HASLINGTON (St Matthew) w Crewe Green St Michael *Ches 15* **P** *Bp* **V** P H GEDDES
HASSALL GREEN (St Philip) *see* Wheelock *Ches*
HASSINGHAM (St Mary) *see* Burlingham St Edmund w Lingwood, Strumpshaw etc *Nor*
HASTINGLEIGH (St Mary the Virgin) *see* Elmsted w Hastingleigh *Cant*
HASTINGS (All Souls) Clive Vale *Chich 17* **P** *R Upper St Leon* **V** B TRILL
HASTINGS (Christ Church and St Andrew) *see* Blacklands Hastings Ch Ch and St Andr *Chich*
HASTINGS (Emmanuel and St Mary in the Castle) *Chich 17*
P *MMCET and Hyndman Trustees (alt)* **V** P A O'GORMAN
HASTINGS (Holy Trinity) *Chich 17* **P** *Bp*
V C TOLWORTHY, **NSM** R L TREE
HASTINGS (St Clement) (All Saints) *Chich 17* **P** *Bp*
R C L J RICHARDSON, **C** R HAY, **NSM** D F FENTIMAN
HASWELL (St Paul) *see* S Hetton w Haswell *Dur*
HATCH, WEST (St Andrew) *see* Hatch Beauchamp w Beercrocombe, Curry Mallet etc *B & W*
HATCH BEAUCHAMP (St John the Baptist) w Beercrocombe, Curry Mallet and West Hatch *B & W 18* **P** *Duchy of Cornwall (1 turn), Ch Trust Fund Trust (2 turns), and D&C (1 turn)*
R *Vacant* (01823) 480220
HATCH END (St Anselm) *Lon 23* **P** *Bp* **V** C PEARCE
HATCHAM (St Catherine) *S'wark 3* **P** *Haberdashers' Co*
V F J MAKAMBWE, **C** M J JACKSON, **Hon C** D H HAINES, R M G MORRELL, **NSM** J M L L BOGLE, A C OBIORA, A R TYLER
HATCHAM (St James) (St George) (St Michael) *S'wark 3*
P *Ch Patr Soc* **V** F Y-C HUNG, **C** C LITTLE,
NSM E O ADOYO
HATCHAM PARK (All Saints) *S'wark 3* **P** *Hyndman Trustees (2 turns), Haberdashers' Co (1 turn)* **V** O J BEAMENT,
NSM B E WEST
HATCLIFFE (St Mary) *see* Ravendale Gp *Linc*
HATFIELD (St Etheldreda) (St John) (St Michael and All Angels) (St Luke) *St Alb 21* **P** *Marquess of Salisbury*
R W C D TODD, **C** J A STOBART, J H HORNER
HATFIELD (St Lawrence) *Sheff 11* **P** *Bp* **V** J W SWEED,
NSM G BECKETT
HATFIELD (St Leonard) *see* Leominster *Heref*
HATFIELD BROAD OAK (St Mary the Virgin) and Bush End *Chelmsf 26* **P** *Bp* **V** *Vacant* (01279) 718274
HATFIELD HEATH (Holy Trinity) and Sheering *Chelmsf 26*
P *Ch Ch Ox and V Hatfield Broad Oak (alt)* **R** T J POTTER
HATFIELD HYDE (St Mary Magdalene) *St Alb 21*
P *Marquess of Salisbury* **V** M L BANKS
HATFIELD PEVEREL (St Andrew) w Ulting *Chelmsf 24*
P *Bp* **V** S R NORTHFIELD
HATFIELD REGIS *see* Hatfield Broad Oak and Bush End *Chelmsf*
HATHERDEN (Christ Church) w Tangley and Weyhill and Penton Mewsey *Win 3* **P** *Bp and Qu Coll Ox (jt)*
V R E WHETTINGSTEEL
HATHERLEIGH (St John the Baptist) Meeth, Exbourne and Jacobstowe *Ex 12* **P** *CPAS, Lord Clinton, DBP, and Keble Coll Ox (jt)* **P-in-c** R A L WELBY
HATHERN (St Peter and St Paul), Long Whatton and Diseworth w Belton and Osgathorpe *Leic 7* **P** *Ld Chan, Haberdashers' Co, and Bp (by turn)* **C** S M CHANTRY
HATHEROP (St Nicholas) *see* Coln St Aldwyns, Hatherop, Quenington etc *Glouc*
HATHERSAGE (St Michael and All Angels) *Derby 2* **P** *Duke of Devonshire* **V** J W ALLUM
HATHERTON (St Saviour) *Lich 2* **P** *A R W Littleton Esq*
V *Vacant*
HATLEY ST GEORGE (St George) *see* Gamlingay w Hatley St Geo and E Hatley *Ely*
HATTERS LANE (St Andrew) *see* High Wycombe *Ox*
HATTERSLEY (St Barnabas) *Ches 14* **P** *Bp* **V** P A BROWN,
C J P L WHALLEY
HATTON (All Saints) *see* Marston on Dove w Scropton *Derby*
HATTON (Chapel of Ease) *see* E Bedfont *Lon*
HATTON (Holy Trinity) w Haseley, Rowington w Lowsonford and Honiley and Wroxall *Cov 4* **P** *Bp* **R** *Vacant* (01926) 484332
HATTON (St Stephen) *see* Hemingby *Linc*
HAUGH (St Leonard) *see* S Ormsby Gp *Linc*
HAUGHLEY (St Mary the Virgin) w Wetherden *St E 6*
P *Ld Chan and Bp (alt)* **P-in-c** D J PARMENTER

HAUGHTON (Mission Room) *see* Bunbury and Tilstone Fearnall *Ches*
HAUGHTON (St Anne) *Man 17* **P** *DBP* **P-in-c** I L JOHNSON, **NSM** P A CLARK
HAUGHTON (St Chad) *see* W Felton *Lich*
HAUGHTON (St Giles) *see* Derrington, Haughton and Ranton *Lich*
HAUGHTON (St Mary the Virgin) *Man 17* **P** *Bp* **R** M J DOWLAND
HAUGHTON LE SKERNE (St Andrew) *Dur 8* **P** *Bp* **R** D J KENNEDY, **C** S M ROSSETER, M J NORMAN
HAUTBOIS, GREAT (Holy Trinity) *see* Coltishall w Gt Hautbois and Horstead *Nor*
HAUXTON (St Edmund) *see* Harston w Hauxton *Ely*
HAUXWELL (St Oswald) *see* Spennithorne w Finghall and Hauxwell *Ripon*
HAVANT (St Faith) *Portsm 4* **P** *Bp* **R** D F BROWN
HAVENSTREET (St Peter) *Portsm 7* **P** *SMF* **V** S M CHALONER
HAVERHILL (St Mary the Virgin) w Withersfield, the Wrattings, the Thurlows and the Bradleys *St E 8* **P** *Patr Bd* **TR** E J BETTS, **C** J P T OLANCZUK, **NSM** S A BAREHAM
HAVERIGG (St Luke) *see* Millom *Carl*
HAVERING-ATTE-BOWER (St John) *see* Collier Row St Jas and Havering-atte-Bower *Chelmsf*
HAVERINGLAND (St Peter) *see* Cawston w Booton and Brandiston etc *Nor*
HAVERSHAM (St Mary) *see* Lamp *Ox*
HAVERSTOCK HILL (Holy Trinity) w Kentish Town *Lon 17* **P** *D&C St Paul's* **P-in-c** G C ROWLANDS, **C** N P PAINE DAVEY
HAVERTHWAITE (St Anne) *see* Leven Valley *Carl*
HAWES (St Margaret) and Hardraw *Ripon 4* **P** *Bp, V Aysgarth and Bolton cum Redmire, Mrs R Metcalfe, and W H Willan Esq (jt)* **V** W M SIMMS
HAWES SIDE (St Christopher) *Blackb 9* **P** *Bp* **V** R G RAINFORD, **NSM** M WORSLEY
HAWKCHURCH (St John the Baptist) *see* Marshwood Vale TM *Sarum*
HAWKEDON (St Mary) *see* Chedburgh w Depden, Rede and Hawkedon *St E*
HAWKESBURY (St Mary) *see* Badminton w Lt Badminton, Acton Turville etc *Glouc*
HAWKHURST (St Laurance) *Cant 11* **P** *Ch Ch Ox* **V** J RECORD
HAWKINGE (St Luke) w Acrise and Swingfield *Cant 5* **P** *Abp* **R** C A SPARKES
HAWKLEY (St Peter and St Paul) *see* Greatham w Empshott and Hawkley w Prior's Dean *Portsm*
HAWKRIDGE (St Giles) *see* Exford, Exmoor, Hawkridge and Withypool *B & W*
HAWKSHAW LANE (St Mary) *Man 10* **P** *F Whowell Esq* **V** E A RUEHORN
HAWKSHEAD (St Michael and All Angels) and Low Wray w Sawrey *Carl 10* **P** *Bp* **V** D A SOUTHWARD
HAWKSWOOD *see* Hailsham *Chich*
HAWKSWORTH (St Mary and All Saints) *see* Whatton w Aslockton, Hawksworth, Scarrington etc *S'well*
HAWKSWORTH WOOD (St Mary) *Ripon 7* **P** *Patrons Leeds St Pet* **V** R BROWN, **C** K D JACKSON
HAWKWELL (Emmanuel) (St Mary the Virgin) *Chelmsf 12* **P** *CPAS* **R** A R HIGTON, **C** S F KIMBER
HAWKWOOD (St Francis) *see* Chingford SS Pet and Paul *Chelmsf*
HAWLEY (Holy Trinity) *Guildf 1* **P** *Keble Coll Ox* **C** R A SEABROOK
HAWLEY, SOUTH (All Saints) *see* Hawley H Trin *Guildf*
HAWLING (St Edward) *see* Sevenhampton w Charlton Abbotts and Hawling etc *Glouc*
HAWNBY (All Saints) *see* Upper Ryedale *York*
HAWORTH (St Michael and All Angels) *Bradf 8* **P** *V Bradf and Haworth Ch Lands Trust (jt)* **R** P J SLATER
HAWRIDGE (St Mary) w Cholesbury and St Leonard *Ox 28* **P** *Bp, Chpl Trust, and Neale's Charity (jt)* **NSM** P R BINNS
HAWSKER (All Saints) *see* Fylingdales and Hawsker cum Stainsacre *York*
HAWSTEAD (All Saints) and Nowton w Stanningfield and Bradfield Combust *St E 13* **P** *Mrs J Oakes (2 turns), Bp (3 turns)* **P-in-c** K A FINNIMORE
HAWTHORN (St Michael and All Angels) *Dur 2* **P** *I Pemberton Esq* **P-in-c** A MILNE
HAWTON (All Saints) *see* Farndon w Thorpe, Hawton and Cotham *S'well*
HAXBY (St Mary) w Wigginton *York 8* **P** *Abp and Ld Chan (alt)* **TR** M W ESCRITT, **TV** A A HORSMAN, **NSM** L PERRINS
HAXEY (St Nicholas) *Linc 1* **P** *Ld Chan* **P-in-c** J STAFF
HAY MILL (St Cyprian) *see* Yardley St Cypr Hay Mill *Birm*
HAYDOCK (St James) *Liv 16* **P** *R Ashton-in-Makerfield* **V** R MIDDLETON, **NSM** G J HARDMAN
HAYDOCK (St Mark) *Liv 10* **P** *MMCET* **V** P POTTER
HAYDON BRIDGE (St Cuthbert) *see* Haydon Bridge and Beltingham w Henshaw *Newc*
HAYDON BRIDGE (St Cuthbert) and Beltingham w Henshaw *Newc 4* **P** *Bp and V Haltwhistle and Greenhead (jt)* **V** V G ASHWIN
HAYDON WICK (St John) *see* Rodbourne Cheney *Bris*
HAYES (St Anselm) *Lon 24* **P** *Bp* **V** P McGEARY
HAYES (St Edmund of Canterbury) *Lon 24* **P** *Bp* **V** P J BALL, **C** W A BROOKER, **NSM** J R MOTHERSOLE
HAYES (St Mary) *Lon 24* **P** *Keble Coll Ox* **R** P L de S HOMEWOOD
HAYES (St Mary the Virgin) *Roch 14* **P** *D&C* **R** P G H THOMAS, **C** F L MATTHEWS
HAYES (St Nicholas) Raynton Drive Conventional District *Lon 24* **C-in-c** D M BRADSHAW, **C** J W KNILL-JONES
HAYFIELD (St Matthew) *Derby 6* **P** *Resident Freeholders* **V** D M ROWLEY
HAYLE (St Elwyn) *see* Godrevy *Truro*
HAYLING, NORTH (St Peter) *Portsm 4* **P** *DBP* **V** N R RALPH
HAYLING, SOUTH (St Mary) *Portsm 4* **P** *DBP* **V** *Vacant* (01705) 462914
HAYLING ISLAND (St Andrew) Eastoke *Portsm 4* **P** *DBP* **V** N R RALPH, **NSM** M G BULL
HAYNES (St Mary) (Mission Room) *St Alb 16* **P** *Bp* **V** *Vacant* (01234) 381235 or (01727) 854532
HAYTON (St James) *see* Aspatria w Hayton *Carl*
HAYTON (St Martin) *see* Shiptonthorpe w Hayton *York*
HAYTON (St Mary Magdalene) w Cumwhitton *Carl 2* **P** *D&C* **V** A S PYE
HAYTON (St Peter) *see* Clarborough w Hayton *S'well*
HAYWARDS HEATH (St Richard) *Chich 6* **P** *Bp* **V** C R BEARD
HAYWARDS HEATH (St Wilfrid) (Church of the Ascension) (Church of the Good Shepherd) (Church of the Presentation) *Chich 6* **P** *Bp* **TR** R C W SMITH, **TV** G PIPER, **NSM** D J HOLLIS, J SEDGLEY
HAYWOOD, GREAT (St Stephen) *see* Colwich w Gt Haywood *Lich*
HAZELBURY BRYAN (St Mary and St James) and the Hillside Parishes *Sarum 6* **P** *Duke of Northd (2 turns), M J Scott-Williams Esq, G A L Pitt-Rivers Esq, Exors F N Kent Esq, and Bp (1 turn each)* **R** S GILL
HAZELWELL (St Mary Magdalen) *Birm 5* **P** *Bp* **V** A C PRIESTLEY
HAZELWOOD (St John the Evangelist) *Derby 11* **P** *Bp* **V** *Vacant* (01773) 824974
HAZLEMERE (Holy Trinity) *Ox 29* **P** *Peache Trustees* **V** P C COLLIER, **C** A M RIMMER, G C DOWNES
HEACHAM (St Mary) *Nor 16* **P** *Bp* **V** B S P LEATHERS, **NSM** D LOXLEY
HEADBOURNE WORTHY (St Swithun) *Win 13* **P** *Univ Coll Ox and Lord Northbrook (alt)* **R** *Vacant*
HEADCORN (St Peter and St Paul) *Cant 15* **P** *Abp* **P-in-c** B E LANGMAN
HEADINGLEY (St Chad) *see* Far Headingley St Chad *Ripon*
HEADINGLEY (St Michael and All Angels) *Ripon 7* **P** *V Leeds St Pet* **V** M A CROSS, **C** A D NORWOOD, K A P DOWLING, **NSM** D W PEAT
HEADINGLEY (St Oswald) *see* Far Headingley St Chad *Ripon*
HEADINGTON (St Andrew) *Ox 4* **P** *Keble Coll Ox* **V** W M BREWIN
HEADINGTON (St Mary) *Ox 4* **P** *Bp* **V** C J WALKER
HEADINGTON QUARRY (Holy Trinity) *Ox 4* **P** *Bp* **P-in-c** T D HONEY, **C** R W NICHOLS
HEADLESS CROSS (St Luke) *see* Redditch, The Ridge *Worc*
HEADLEY (All Saints) *Guildf 3* **P** *Patr Bd* **TR** R W WOODGER, **TV** S GOODWIN, **C** P A GODFREY, **NSM** S E GOODWIN
HEADLEY (St Mary the Virgin) w Box Hill (St Andrew) *Guildf 9* **P** *Bp* **R** D A WOTTON, **Hon C** A F TATHAM
HEADLEY (St Peter) *see* Ashford Hill w Headley *Win*
HEADON (St Peter) *see* E Markham w Askham, Headon w Upton and Grove *S'well*
HEADSTONE (St George) *Lon 23* **P** *Bp* **P-in-c** S R KEEBLE
HEAGE (St Luke) *see* Ambergate and Heage *Derby*
HEALAUGH (St John the Baptist) w Wighill, Bilbrough and Askham Richard *York 1* **P** *Abp (3 turns), A G Wailes Fairburn Esq (1 turn)* **P-in-c** P E JARAM
HEALD GREEN (St Catherine) *Ches 17* **P** *Bp* **V** R D CLARKE, **NSM** H M EVANS
HEALEY (Christ Church) *Man 20* **P** *Bp* **P-in-c** J D QUANCE
HEALEY (St John) and Slaley *Newc 3* **P** *Bp and V Bywell St Pet (jt)* **V** *Vacant* (01434) 673609
HEALEY (St Paul) *see* Masham and Healey *Ripon*

HEALEY (War Memorial Mission) *see* S Ossett *Wakef*
HEALING (St Peter and St Paul) and Stallingborough *Linc 10* **P** *Bp* **P-in-c** D E KING
HEAMOOR (St Thomas) *see* Madron *Truro*
HEANOR (St Laurence) *Derby 12* **P** *Wright Trustees* **V** C L BLAKEY, **C** T E BENNETT
HEANTON PUNCHARDON (St Augustine) w Marwood *Ex 15* **P** *CPAS (3 turns), St Jo Coll Cam (1 turn)* **R** J E DYKES
HEAP BRIDGE (St Thomas and St George) *see* Bury Ch King *Man*
HEAPEY (St Barnabas) and Withnell *Blackb 4* **P** *V Leyland* **V** G R LOXHAM
HEAPHAM (All Saints) *see* Lea Gp *Linc*
HEARTSEASE (St Francis) *see* Nor Heartsease St Fran *Nor*
HEATH (All Saints) *Derby 5* **P** *Duke of Devonshire and Simeon's Trustees (jt)* **V** B M SPROSTON
HEATH (Mission Church) *see* Uttoxeter Area *Lich*
HEATH, LITTLE (Christ Church) *St Alb 17* **P** *Ch Patr Trust* **V** I D BROWN, **NSM** A HARDING, R H WIKNER
HEATH, THE (not known) *see* Bitterley w Middleton, Stoke St Milborough etc *Heref*
HEATH AND REACH (St Leonard) *St Alb 12* **P** *V Leighton Buzzard* **P-in-c** D RIDGEWAY
HEATH HAYES (St John) *see* Cannock *Lich*
HEATH TOWN (Holy Trinity) *see* Wednesfield Heath *Lich*
HEATHER (St John the Baptist) *see* Ibstock w Heather *Leic*
HEATHERLANDS (St John) *Sarum 8* **P** *MMCET* **V** G A G LOUGHLIN, **C** D N ANDREW
HEATHERYCLEUGH (St Thomas) *Dur 9* **P** *Bp* **V** D M SKELTON
HEATHFIELD (All Saints) *Chich 15* **P** *Bp* **V** *Vacant* (01435) 862457
HEATHFIELD (St Catherine) *see* Bovey Tracey St John, Chudleigh Knighton etc *Ex*
HEATHFIELD (St John the Baptist) *see* Bradford w Oake, Hillfarrance and Heathfield *B & W*
HEATHFIELD (St Richard) *Chich 15* **P** *Bp* **V** R S CRITTALL
HEATON (Christ Church) *Man 9* **P** *R Deane St Mary* **V** D B GRIFFITHS, **NSM** M E MAYOH
HEATON (St Barnabas) *Bradf 1* **P** *Trustees* **V** R S ANDERSON
HEATON (St Gabriel) *see* Newc St Gabr *Newc*
HEATON (St Martin) *Bradf 1* **P** *Bp* **V** A J BURNISTON
HEATON, HIGH (St Francis) *see* Newc St Fran *Newc*
HEATON CHAPEL (St Thomas) *see* Heaton Norris St Thos *Man*
HEATON MERSEY (St John the Baptist) *Man 3* **P** *Bp* **P-in-c** M H MAXWELL
HEATON MOOR (St Paul) *Man 3* **P** *Trustees* **R** S E W GUY, **Hon C** M A BROWN
HEATON NORRIS (Christ w All Saints) *Man 3* **P** *Bp* **R** M K BOOTH
HEATON NORRIS (St Thomas) *Man 3* **P** *D&C* **P-in-c** A J SERVANT
HEATON REDDISH (St Mary) *Man 3* **P** *Trustees* **R** W J McKAE
HEAVITREE (St Michael and All Angels) (St Lawrence) (St Loye) w Exeter St Paul *Ex 3* **P** *Patr Bd* **TR** M S HART, **TV** J D A WILLIAMS, **NSM** P R MORRELL
HEBBURN (St Cuthbert) *Dur 15* **P** *TR Jarrow* **P-in-c** J B HUNT
HEBBURN (St John) *Dur 15* **P** *Bp* **V** *Vacant* 0191-483 2054
HEBBURN (St Oswald) *Dur 15* **P** *The Crown* **P-in-c** L H SKINNER
HEBDEN (St Peter) *see* Linton in Craven *Bradf*
HEBDEN BRIDGE (St James) *Wakef 3* **P** *V Halifax* **V** M W PARROTT, **NSM** C J WARDMAN
HEBRON (St Cuthbert) *see* Longhorsley and Hebron *Newc*
HECK (St John the Baptist) *see* Gt Snaith *Sheff*
HECKFIELD (St Michael) w Mattingley and Rotherwick *Win 5* **P** *New Coll Ox (2 turns), Bp (1 turn)* **V** A E BENNETT
HECKINGTON (St Andrew) *Linc 22* **P** *Bp (2 turns), Ven A C Foottit (1 turn)* **P-in-c** D F BOUTLE
HECKMONDWIKE (All Souls) (St James) *Wakef 8* **P** *V Birstall* **V** J F LOWE
HEDDINGTON (St Andrew) *see* Oldbury *Sarum*
HEDDON-ON-THE-WALL (St Andrew) *Newc 3* **P** *Ld Chan* **P-in-c** P J BRYARS
HEDENHAM (St Peter) *see* Ditchingham, Hedenham and Broome *Nor*
HEDGE END (St John the Evangelist) *Win 9* **P** *Bp* **V** C J BANNISTER
HEDGE END (St Luke) *Win 9* **P** *Bp* **V** D S FARLEY
HEDGEFIELD (St Hilda) *see* Ryton w Hedgefield *Dur*
HEDGERLEY (St Mary the Virgin) *see* Farnham Royal w Hedgerley *Ox*
HEDNESFORD (St Peter) *Lich 3* **P** *Bp* **V** D J DITCH, **C** B N WHITMORE
HEDON (St Augustine) w Paull *York 13* **P** *Abp* **V** J D HARGREAVE
HEDSOR (St Nicholas) and Bourne End *Ox 29* **P** *Bp* **P-in-c** J E SCLATER, **NSM** R G FORDHAM
HEDWORTH (St Nicholas) *Dur 15* **P** *The Crown* **V** W P B CARLIN, **C** M D ALLSOPP
HEELEY (Christ Church) *Sheff 1* **P** *The Crown* **V** J M STRIDE
HEENE (St Botolph) *Chich 5* **P** *D&C* **R** P R ROBERTS, **C** C G H KASSELL
HEIGHAM (Holy Trinity) *Nor 3* **P** *Ch Trust Fund Trust* **P-in-c** A M STRANGE, **NSM** C J SCOTT
HEIGHAM (St Barnabas) (St Bartholomew) *Nor 3* **P** *Bp* **V** D M JONES
HEIGHAM (St Thomas) *Nor 3* **P** *Bp* **V** N J H GARRARD, **NSM** E HUTCHEON, H M WRIGHT
HEIGHINGTON (not known) *see* Washingborough w Heighington and Canwick *Linc*
HEIGHINGTON (St Michael) *Dur 8* **P** *D&C* **V** P H E THOMAS
HEIGHTINGTON (St Giles) *see* Mamble w Bayton, Rock w Heightington etc *Worc*
HELFORD (St Paul's Mission Church) *see* Manaccan w St Anthony-in-Meneage and St Martin *Truro*
HELHOUGHTON (All Saints) *see* South Raynham, E w W Raynham, Helhoughton, etc *Nor*
HELIDON (St John the Baptist) *see* Daventry, Ashby St Ledgers, Braunston etc *Pet*
HELIONS BUMPSTEAD (St Andrew) *see* Steeple Bumpstead and Helions Bumpstead *Chelmsf*
HELLAND (St Helena) *Truro 10* **P** *MMCET* **P-in-c** R D C WHITEMAN, J L BRENDON-COOK
HELLESDON (St Mary) (St Paul and St Michael) *Nor 2* **P** *Bp* **V** D M HOARE, **C** J M FOLLETT, M W L PICKETT
HELLIFIELD (St Aidan) *Bradf 5* **P** *Ch Ch Ox* **V** G WALKER, **NSM** G L HALL
HELLINGLY (St Peter and St Paul) and Upper Dicker *Chich 15* **P** *Abp and Bp (jt)* **V** R E CHATWIN, **NSM** D J SWANEPOEL
HELMDON (St Mary Magdalene) w Stuchbury and Radstone and Syresham w Whitfield *Pet 1* **P** *Ox Univ, Mert Coll Ox, and Worc Coll Ox (3 turns), Bp (1 turn), and DBP (1 turn)* **P-in-c** J H ROBERTS, **NSM** E W PALMER
HELME (Christ Church) *Wakef 1* **P** *Bp* **P-in-c** M C RUSSELL, **NSM** R T TUCK
HELMINGHAM (St Mary) w Framsden and Pettaugh w Winston *St E 18* **P** *Ld Chan, MMCET, and Lord Tollemache (by turn)* **P-in-c** S RITCHIE
HELMSLEY (All Saints) *York 18* **P** *Lord Feversham* **V** *Vacant* (01439) 770236
HELMSLEY, UPPER (St Peter) *see* Sand Hutton *York*
HELPERTHORPE (St Peter) *see* Weaverthorpe w Helperthorpe, Luttons Ambo etc *York*
HELPRINGHAM (St Andrew) w Hale *Linc 22* **P** *Ld Chan (2 turns), D&C (1 turn), and DBP (1 turn)* **R** *Vacant* (01529) 421435
HELPSTON (St Botolph) *see* Etton w Helpston and Maxey *Pet*
HELSBY (St Paul) and Dunham-on-the-Hill *Ches 3* **P** *Bp* **V** A R RIDLEY, **C** J A KENDALL
HELSINGTON (St John the Baptist) *Carl 9* **P** *V Kendal H Trin* **V** *Vacant*
HELSTON (St Michael) and Wendron *Truro 4* **P** *Patr Bd* **TR** D G MILLER, **C** P D SAYLE, **NSM** D NOAKES
HEMBLINGTON (All Saints) *see* Blofield w Hemblington *Nor*
HEMEL HEMPSTEAD Apsley End (St Mary) *see* Chambersbury (Hemel Hempstead) *St Alb*
HEMEL HEMPSTEAD Bennetts End (St Benedict) *as above*
HEMEL HEMPSTEAD Leverstock Green (Holy Trinity) *as above*
HEMEL HEMPSTEAD (St Mary) *St Alb 3* **P** *Ld Chan* **TR** P J COTTON, **TV** F A JACKSON, V J LAMONT, S J ROGERS, G R KEGG, D J BEVINGTON, **C** U J GERRY, **NSM** T J BARTON
HEMINGBROUGH (St Mary the Virgin) *York 4* **P** *Abp* **P-in-c** M A PASKETT
HEMINGBY (St Margaret) *Linc 11* **P** *Bp (2 turns), Ld Chan (2 turns), and DBP (1 turn)* **R** D J LAWRENCE
HEMINGFORD ABBOTS (St Margaret of Antioch) *Ely 9* **P** *Lord Hemingford* **R** *Vacant* (01480) 698856
HEMINGFORD GREY (St James) *Ely 9* **P** *Mrs G A Scott* **P-in-c** S R TALBOT
HEMINGSTONE (St Gregory) *see* Coddenham w Gosbeck and Hemingstone w Henley *St E*
HEMINGTON (St Peter and St Paul) *see* Polebrook and Lutton w Hemington and Luddington *Pet*
HEMINGTON (The Blessed Virgin Mary) *see* Norton St Philip w Hemington, Hardington etc *B & W*
HEMLEY (All Saints) *see* Waldringfield w Hemley and Newbourn *St E*

HEMLINGTON (St Timothy) *York 22* **P** *Abp* **V** I M GRAHAM
HEMPNALL (St Margaret) *Nor 5* **P** *Ld Chan (1 turn), Patr Bd (5 turns)* **TR** C M MAHONY
HEMPSTEAD (All Saints) *see* Barningham w Matlaske w Baconsthorpe etc *Nor*
HEMPSTEAD (All Saints) *see* S Gillingham *Roch*
HEMPSTEAD (St Andrew) *see* Radwinter w Hempstead *Chelmsf*
HEMPSTEAD (St Andrew) *see* Happisburgh, Walcott, Hempstead w Eccles etc *Nor*
HEMPSTED (St Swithun) *Glouc 5* **P** *Bp* **P-in-c** M W S PARSONS
HEMPTON (Holy Trinity) and Pudding Norton *Nor 15* **P** *The Crown* **V** *Vacant*
HEMPTON (St John the Evangelist) *see* Deddington w Barford, Clifton and Hempton *Ox*
HEMSBY (St Mary) *Nor 6* **P** *Major R A Ferrier* **Hon C** C A POWLES
HEMSWELL (All Saints) *see* Glentworth Gp *Linc*
HEMSWORTH (St Helen) *Wakef 11* **P** *Bp* **R** M DAVIES
HEMYOCK (St Mary) w Culm Davy, Clayhidon and Culmstock *Ex 4* **P** *DBP, SMF, and D&C (jt)* **R** M M CAMERON
HENBURY (St Mary the Virgin) *Bris 8* **P** *Lord Middleton (1 turn), Bp (3 turns)* **V** H B TROTTER
HENBURY (St Thomas) *Ches 13* **P** *Bp* **P-in-c** D S HARRISON
HENDFORD (St Mary the Virgin and All Saints) *see* Yeovil H Trin w Barwick *B & W*
HENDON (All Saints) Childs Hill *Lon 15* **P** *Bp* **V** J P WAINWRIGHT
HENDON (Christ Church) *Lon 15* **P** *Bp* **V** *Vacant* 0181-202 8123
HENDON (St Alphage) *Lon 15* **P** *Bp* **V** H D MOORE, **C** J P CARLISLE
HENDON (St Ignatius) *Dur 16* **P** *Bp* **R** A M BARTLETT
HENDON (St Mary) (St Mary Magdalene) *Lon 15* **P** *Bp* **C** A J WARD
HENDON (St Paul) Mill Hill *Lon 15* **P** *Bp* **V** M D KETTLE, **C** S R J ELLIOTT, **Hon C** P M HUNT
HENDON, WEST (St John) *Lon 15* **P** *Bp* **V** J M WARNER
HENDRED, EAST (St Augustine of Canterbury) *see* Wantage Downs *Ox*
HENDRED, WEST (Holy Trinity) *as above*
HENFIELD (St Peter) w Shermanbury and Woodmancote *Chich 9* **P** *Bp* **V** P C KEFFORD, **C** G J SMITH, **NSM** A McNEIL, C L WILSON
HENGOED w Gobowen *Lich 19* **P** *R Selattyn* **V** C J GROOCOCK
HENGROVE (Christ Church) *Bris 3* **P** *Bp and Simeon's Trustees (alt)* **V** N LAYTON
HENHAM (St Mary the Virgin) and Elsenham w Ugley *Chelmsf 21* **P** *Ch Hosp, Ch Soc Trust, and Bp (jt)* **P-in-c** R W FARR
HENLEAZE (St Peter) *Bris 5* **P** *Bp* **V** F SMITH, **Hon C** S ALLMAN, **NSM** B J PULLAN
HENLEY on Thames w Remenham *Ox 6* **P** *Bp and Jes Coll Ox (jt)* **R** D P PRITCHARD
HENLEY (St Peter) *see* Coddenham w Gosbeck and Hemingstone w Henley *St E*
HENLEY IN ARDEN (St John the Baptist) *see* Beaudesert and Henley-in-Arden w Ullenhall *Cov*
HENLEY-ON-THAMES (Holy Trinity) *see* Rotherfield Greys H Trin *Ox*
HENLOW (St Mary the Virgin) *St Alb 16* **P** *Ld Chan* **V** *Vacant* (01462) 816296
HENNOCK (St Mary) *see* Bovey Tracey SS Pet, Paul and Thos w Hennock *Ex*
HENNY, GREAT (St Mary) and LITTLE w Middleton and Wickam St Paul w Twinstead *Chelmsf 19* **P** *Earl of Verulam, Bp, D&C St Paul's, and Ld Chan (by turn)* **R** B A CAREW
HENSALL (St Paul) *see* Gt Snaith *Sheff*
HENSHAW (All Hallows) *see* Haydon Bridge and Beltingham w Henshaw *Newc*
HENSINGHAM (St John) (Keekle Mission) *Carl 5* **P** *Trustees* **V** I G MAINEY, **C** J H A LEGGETT, M C BEHREND
HENSTEAD (St Mary) *see* Wrentham w Benacre, Covehithe, Frostenden etc *St E*
HENSTRIDGE (St Nicholas) and Charlton Horethorne w Stowell *B & W 7* **P** *Bp (2 turns), K S D Wingfield Digby Esq (1 turn)* **R** P HALLETT
HENTLAND (St Dubricius) *see* How Caple w Sollarshope, Sellack etc *Heref*
HENTON (Christ Church) *see* Coxley, Henton and Wookey *B & W*
HEPPLE (Christ Church) *see* Rothbury *Newc*
HEPTONSTALL (St Thomas a Becket and St Thomas the Apostle) *Wakef 3* **P** *V Halifax* **P-in-c** J C GORE
HEPWORTH (Holy Trinity) *see* Upper Holme Valley *Wakef*
HEPWORTH (St Peter) w Hinderclay, Wattisfield and Thelnetham *St E 9* **P** *Bp, K Coll Cam, MMCET, and P J Holt-Wilson Esq (jt)* **R** J W FULTON
HEREFORD (All Saints) (St Barnabas Church Centre) *Heref 3* **P** *D&C Windsor* **P-in-c** A P MOTTRAM
HEREFORD (Holy Trinity) *Heref 3* **P** *Bp* **P-in-c** R D KING
HEREFORD (St Francis) *see* Heref S Wye *Heref*
HEREFORD (St John the Baptist) *Heref 3* **P** *D&C* **P-in-c** R A WILLIS
HEREFORD (St Martin) *see* Heref S Wye *Heref*
HEREFORD (St Nicholas) *Heref 3* **P** *Ld Chan* **P-in-c** R NORTH
HEREFORD (St Paul) *see* Tupsley w Hampton Bishop *Heref*
HEREFORD (St Peter w St Owen) (St James) *Heref 3* **P** *Simeon's Trustees* **V** P T WOOD, **C** C D PINES, M E THOMPSON
HEREFORD, LITTLE (St Mary Magdalene) *see* Burford III w Lt Heref *Heref*
HEREFORD SOUTH WYE (St Francis) (St Martin) *Heref 3* **P** *Patr Bd* **TV** P G HADDLETON, A J HARDING, **C** R C GREEN, J A DAVIES
HERMITAGE (Holy Trinity) and Hampstead Norreys, Cold Ash and Yattendon w Frilsham *Ox 14* **P** *Patr Bd* **TR** J K COOMBS, **TV** M J WARREN, **NSM** D B WINTER
HERMITAGE (St Mary) *see* Yetminster w Ryme Intrinseca and High Stoy *Sarum*
HERNE (St Martin) *Cant 7* **P** *Abp* **V** P D SALES
HERNE BAY (Christ Church) (St Andrew's Church and Centre) *Cant 7* **P** *Simeon's Trustees* **V** R W COTTON, **C** M S G MORGAN, **Hon C** S A MUST
HERNE BAY (St Bartholomew) *see* Reculver and Herne Bay St Bart *Cant*
HERNE HILL (St John) (St Paul) *S'wark 8* **P** *Bp and Trustees (jt)* **V** A O LADIPO, **C** T J C WARD
HERNER (Chapel) *see* Newport, Bishops Tawton and Tawstock *Ex*
HERNHILL (St Michael) *see* Boughton under Blean w Dunkirk and Hernhill *Cant*
HERODSFOOT (All Saints) *see* Duloe w Herodsfoot *Truro*
HERONSGATE (St John the Evangelist) *see* Mill End and Heronsgate w W Hyde *St Alb*
HERRIARD (St Mary) w Winslade and Long Sutton and South Warnborough and Tunworth and Upton Grey and Weston Patrick *Win 5* **P** *Bp, Qu Coll Ox, St Jo Coll Ox, Exors Viscount Camrose, and J L Jervoise Esq (jt)* **V** T J B JENKYNS, **NSM** B J SMITH
HERRINGFLEET (St Margaret) *see* Somerleyton, Ashby, Fritton, Herringfleet etc *Nor*
HERRINGSWELL (St Ethelbert) *see* Mildenhall *St E*
HERRINGTHORPE (St Cuthbert) *Sheff 6* **P** *Bp* **V** B H COOPER
HERRINGTON *Dur 14* **P** *Bp* **P-in-c** D BODDY
HERSHAM (St Peter) *Guildf 8* **P** *Bp* **V** N J WHITEHEAD, **C** A C JONAS
HERSTMONCEUX (All Saints) and Wartling *Chich 15* **P** *Bp* **R** M R FRANCIS
HERSTON (St Mark) *see* Swanage and Studland *Sarum*
HERTFORD (All Saints) *St Alb 22* **P** *Ld Chan and Marquess Townshend (alt)* **V** W St J KEMM
HERTFORD (St Andrew) *St Alb 22* **P** *Duchy of Lanc* **R** G C EDWARDS
HERTFORD HEATH (Holy Trinity) *see* Lt Amwell *St Alb*
HERTINGFORDBURY (St Mary) *St Alb 22* **P** *The Crown* **P-in-c** J BIRTWISTLE, **C** R A CARUANA
HESKET-IN-THE-FOREST (St Mary the Virgin) and Armathwaite *Carl 4* **P** *D&C and E P Ecroyd Esq (jt)* **V** D C CROOK
HESKETH (All Saints) w Becconsall *Blackb 6* **P** *Trustees* **R** K POWELL
HESLERTON, EAST (St Andrew) *see* Sherburn and W and E Heslerton w Yedingham *York*
HESLERTON, WEST (All Saints) *as above*
HESLINGTON (St Paul) *York 4* **P** *Abp* **V** F G HUNTER
HESSAY (St John the Baptist) *see* Rufforth w Moor Monkton and Hessay *York*
HESSENFORD (St Anne) *see* St Germans *Truro*
HESSETT (St Ethelbert) *see* Rougham, Beyton w Hessett and Rushbrooke *St E*
HESSLE (All Saints) *York 15* **P** *Ld Chan* **V** K A DAVID
HESTER WAY LANE (St Silas) *see* Cheltenham St Mark *Glouc*
HESTON (All Saints) (St Leonard) *Lon 11* **P** *Bp* **V** T J L MAIDMENT, **C** D V WYLIE
HESWALL (Church of the Good Shepherd) (St Peter) *Ches 8* **P** *W A B Davenport Esq* **C** R J RENDALL, K P OWEN
HETHE (St Edmund and St George) *see* Shelswell *Ox*
HETHEL (All Saints) *see* Wreningham *Nor*
HETHERSETT (St Remigius) w Canteloff w Little Melton and Great Melton *Nor 7* **P** *G&C Coll Cam, E C Evans-*

Lombe Esq, and Em Coll Cam (by turn) **R** D B LAMMAS, **NSM** P J UNSWORTH
HETHERSGILL (St Mary) *see* Bewcastle, Stapleton and Kirklinton etc *Carl*
HETTON, SOUTH (Holy Trinity) w Haswell *Dur 2* **P** *Bp* **P-in-c** C TODD
HETTON-LE-HOLE (St Nicholas) *see* Eppleton and Hetton le Hole *Dur*
HEVENINGHAM (St Margaret) *see* Cratfield w Heveningham and Ubbeston etc *St E*
HEVER (St Peter), Four Elms and Mark Beech *Roch 11* **P** *Bp and C Talbot Esq (jt)* **R** P J PLUMLEY
HEVERSHAM (St Peter) and Milnthorpe *Carl 9* **P** *Trin Coll Cam* **V** J C HANCOCK
HEVINGHAM (St Mary and St Botolph) w Hainford and Stratton Strawless *Nor 19* **P** *Bp and Sir Thomas Beevor Bt (jt)* **R** P B FOREMAN
HEWELSFIELD (St Mary Magdalene) *see* St Briavels w Hewelsfield *Glouc*
HEWISH (Good Shepherd) *see* Crewkerne w Wayford *B & W*
HEWORTH (Holy Trinity) (Christ Church) (St Wulstan) *York 8* **P** *Patr Bd* **TR** D ANDREW, **TV** T McDONOUGH, P W WHITE
HEWORTH (St Alban) *Dur 12* **P** *V Heworth St Mary* **P-in-c** C M HOOPER
HEWORTH (St Mary) *Dur 12* **P** *Bp* **P-in-c** W D TAYLOR, **C** V T FENTON
HEXHAM (St Andrew) *Newc 4* **P** *Mercers' Co and Viscount Allendale (alt)* **R** M NELSON, **C** D J IRVINE, **NSM** E M NICHOLAS
HEXTABLE (St Peter) *see* Swanley St Paul *Roch*
HEXTHORPE (St Jude) *see* Doncaster St Jude *Sheff*
HEXTON (St Faith) *see* Barton-le-Cley w Higham Gobion and Hexton *St Alb*
HEY (St John the Baptist) *Man 21* **P** *R Aston-under-Lyne St Mich* **P-in-c** B H LOCKE
HEYBRIDGE (St Andrew) (St George) w Langford *Chelmsf 11* **P** *D&C St Paul's and Lord Byron (alt)* **V** T F BARNFATHER
HEYBROOK BAY (Holy Nativity) *see* Wembury *Ex*
HEYDON (Holy Trinity), Great Chishill and Little Chishill, Chrishall, Elmdon w Wenden Lofts and Strethall *Chelmsf 22* **P** *Patr Bd* **R** J G SIMMONS, **NSM** J D RUSSELL-SMITH, E H G FISHER
HEYDON (St Peter and St Paul) *see* Cawston w Booton and Brandiston etc *Nor*
HEYDOUR (St Michael and All Angels) *see* Ancaster Wilsford Gp *Linc*
HEYFORD (St Peter and St Paul) w Stowe Nine Churches and Flore w Brockhall *Pet 3* **P** *The Revd S Hope, Ch Ch Ox, DPB and Bp (by turn)* **R** D EVANS
HEYFORD, LOWER (St Mary) *see* The Heyfords w Rousham and Somerton *Ox*
HEYFORD, UPPER (St Mary) *as above*
HEYFORDS w Rousham and Somerton, The *Ox 2* **P** *New Coll Ox, CCC Ox, C Cottrell-Dormer Esq, and P W G Barnes Esq (by turn)* **P-in-c** N B W JAMES
HEYHOUSES (St Nicholas) *see* Sabden and Pendleton *Blackb*
HEYHOUSES ON SEA (St Anne) *Blackb 11* **P** *J C Hilton Esq* **V** M S MALKINSON
HEYSHAM (St Peter) (St Andrew) (St James) *Blackb 12* **P** *C E C Royds Esq* **R** E LACEY, **C** S J HUNT
HEYSHOTT (St James) *Chich 10* **P** *Bp* **P-in-c** C BOXLEY
HEYSIDE (St Mark) *Man 22* **P** *Trustees* **V** R MORRIS, **NSM** G F WEIR, S E WARD
HEYTESBURY (St Peter and St Paul) and Sutton Veny *Sarum 14* **P** *Bp* **P-in-c** H G HOSKINS
HEYTHROP (St Nicholas) *see* Enstone and Heythrop *Ox*
HEYWOOD (St James) *Man 18* **P** *Bp* **V** S A EVASON
HEYWOOD (St Luke) (All Souls) *Man 18* **P** *Bp and R Bury St Mary (jt)* **P-in-c** I J STAMP, **C** G TURNER, A L OWENS, **NSM** I TAYLOR, R A J MILLER
HEYWOOD (St Margaret) *Man 18* **P** *Bp* **V** I J STAMP, **NSM** A BROWN, M S THORP
HIBALDSTOW (St Hibald) *see* Scawby, Redbourne and Hibaldstow *Linc*
HICKLETON (St Wilfrid) *see* Goldthorpe w Hickleton *Sheff*
HICKLING (St Luke) w Kinoulton and Broughton Sulney (Upper Broughton) *S'well 9* **P** *Prime Min, Qu Coll Cam, and Bp (by turn)* **P-in-c** S B FAHIE, **NSM** T H KIRKMAN
HICKLING (St Mary) *see* Ludham, Potter Heigham and Hickling *Nor*
HIGH *see also under substantive place name*
HIGH CROSS (St John the Evangelist) *St Alb 22* **P** *DBP* **V** H J SHARMAN
HIGH HAM (St Andrew) *see* Langport Area Chs *B & W*
HIGH LANE (St Thomas) *Ches 16* **P** *R Stockport* **V** I C WATTS, **NSM** C BULL
HIGH OAK *Nor 7* **P** *Bp, D&C Cant, Earl of Kimberley, A E H Heber-Percy Esq, andD&C (jt)* **P-in-c** P J STEPHENS, **NSM** J LYNCH
HIGHAM (St John the Evangelist) *see* Padiham *Blackb*
HIGHAM (St John the Evangelist) and Merston *Roch 6* **P** *St Jo Coll Cam* **V** J F SOUTHWARD
HIGHAM (St Mary), Holton St Mary, Raydon and Stratford St Mary *St E 3* **P** *Duchy of Lanc, Reformation Ch Trust, and Sir Joshua Rowley, Bt (by turn)* **R** T R J WELLS
HIGHAM FERRERS (St Mary the Virgin) w Chelveston *Pet 10* **P** *Bp* **V** *Vacant* (01933) 312433
HIGHAM GOBION (St Margaret) *see* Barton-le-Cley w Higham Gobion and Hexton *St Alb*
HIGHAM GREEN (St Stephen) *see* Barrow w Denham St Mary and Higham Green *St E*
HIGHAM HILL (St Andrew) *see* Walthamstow St Andr *Chelmsf*
HIGHAM-ON-THE-HILL (St Peter) w Fenny Drayton and Witherley *Leic 13* **P** *D&C, and Lord O'Neill (jt)* **P-in-c** M CHARLES
HIGHAMPTON (Holy Cross) *see* Black Torrington, Bradf w Cookbury etc *Ex*
HIGHAMS PARK (All Saints) Hale End *Chelmsf 5* **P** *Bp* **P-in-c** C A McGHIE
HIGHBRIDGE (St John the Evangelist) *B & W 1* **P** *Bp* **V** M F W BOND
HIGHBROOK (All Saints) and West Hoathly *Chich 6* **P** *Ld Chan* **V** A C CARR
HIGHBURY (Christ Church) (St John) (St Saviour) *Lon 6* **P** *Ch Trust Fund Trust and Islington Ch Trust (jt)* **V** J R LITTLEWOOD, **C** N F MASON, **NSM** T J I WITTER
HIGHBURY NEW PARK (St Augustine) *Lon 6* **P** *Trustees* **V** P M ALLCOCK
HIGHCLERE (St Michael and All Angels) and Ashmansworth w Crux Easton *Win 6* **P** *Earl of Carnarvon* **R** T F HORSINGTON
HIGHCLIFFE (St Mark) w Hinton Admiral *Win 8* **P** *Sir George Tapps-Gervis-Meyrick, Bt, and Bp (alt)* **V** J R WILLIAMS, **C** E C BOOTH
HIGHER *see also under substantive place name*
HIGHER FOLD Leigh (St Matthew) *see* Bedford Leigh *Man*
HIGHERTOWN (All Saints) and Baldhu *Truro 6* **P** *Bp and Viscount Falmouth (alt)* **V** G W SMYTH, **NSM** A J STEVENSON
HIGHFIELD (All Saints) *Ox 4* **P** *Bp* **V** J E COCKE
HIGHFIELD (Christ Church) *see* Portswood Ch Ch *Win*
HIGHFIELD (St Catherine) *see* New Bury *Man*
HIGHFIELD (St Mary) *see* Sheff St Mary Bramhall Lane *Sheff*
HIGHFIELD (St Matthew) *Liv 15* **P** *Trustees* **V** W H HARRINGTON
HIGHFIELD (St Paul) *see* Hemel Hempstead *St Alb*
HIGHGATE (All Saints) *Lon 20* **P** *Bp* **V** D H HUBBARD, **Hon C** J S BOWDEN
HIGHGATE (St Alban and St Patrick) *Birm 9* **P** *Keble Coll Ox* **V** J G PENDORF
HIGHGATE (St Augustine) *Lon 20* **P** *Bp* **V** T BUGBY
HIGHGATE (St Michael) *Lon 20* **P** *Bp* **V** J D TRIGG, **C** J BROOKS
HIGHGATE CENTRE *see* Bredbury St Barn *Ches*
HIGHGATE RISE (St Anne) *see* Brookfield St Anne, Highgate Rise *Lon*
HIGHLEY (St Mary) *Heref 9* **P** *MMCET* **V** C G WILLIAMS
HIGHMORE (St Paul) *see* Nettlebed w Bix and Highmore *Ox*
HIGHNAM (Holy Innocents), Lassington, Rudford, Tibberton and Taynton *Glouc 3* **P** *D&C, T J Fenton Esq, and A E Woolley (jt)* **R** M CLARKE, **Hon C** G N CRAGO
HIGHTERS HEATH (Immanuel) *Birm 5* **P** *Bp* **V** *Vacant* 0121-430 7578
HIGHTOWN (St Barnabas) *see* Hartshead and Hightown *Wakef*
HIGHTOWN (St Stephen) *Liv 5* **P** *Bp* **P-in-c** F A BRISCOE
HIGHWEEK (All Saints) (St Mary) and Teigngrace *Ex 11* **P** *Bp* **R** C R KNOTT
HIGHWORTH (St Michael) w Sevenhampton and Inglesham and Hannington *Bris 12* **P** *Bp (4 turns), Mrs M G Hussey-Freke (1 turn)* **V** D J STEVENS, **C** C J WRIGHT
HILBOROUGH (All Saints) w Bodney *Nor 13* **P** *DBP* **P-in-c** G R DRAKE
HILDENBOROUGH (St John the Evangelist) *Roch 11* **P** *V Tonbridge* **V** R J BAWTREE, **C** B S SENIOR, **NSM** E M TOY
HILDERSHAM (Holy Trinity) *Ely 4* **P** *Trustees* **R** *Vacant*
HILDERSTONE (Christ Church) *see* Fulford w Hilderstone *Lich*
HILFIELD (St Nicholas) *see* Yetminster w Ryme Intrinseca and High Stoy *Sarum*
HILGAY (All Saints) *Ely 16* **P** *Hertf Coll Ox* **R** A G COCHRANE

HILL (St James) *Birm 13* **P** *Bp* **V** R D HINDLEY, **C** A M WEAVER
HILL (St Michael) *see* Stone w Woodford and Hill *Glouc*
HILL CROOME (St Mary) *see* Ripple, Earls Croome w Hill Croome and Strensham *Worc*
HILL TOP (Mission Room) *see* Greasley *S'well*
HILLESDEN (All Saints) *see* Lenborough *Ox*
HILLESLEY (St Giles) *see* Kingswood w Alderley and Hillesley *Glouc*
HILLFARRANCE (Holy Cross) *see* Bradford w Oake, Hillfarrance and Heathfield *B & W*
HILLINGDON (All Saints) *Lon 24* **P** *Bp* **V** A P GODSALL, **C** G S THOMAS
HILLINGDON (St John the Baptist) *Lon 24* **P** *Bp* **V** R W HARRISON, **C** R H WORMALD
HILLINGTON (St Mary the Virgin) *Nor 16* **P** *E W Dawnay Esq* **P-in-c** G R HALL
HILLMORTON (St John the Baptist) *Cov 6* **P** *Bp and TR Rugby* **V** A P HAINES
HILLOCK (St Andrew) *Man 14* **P** *Bp and R Stand All SS* **V** K B ASHWORTH
HILLSBOROUGH and Wadsley Bridge (Christ Church) *Sheff 4* **P** *Ch Patr Trust* **V** *Vacant* 0114-231 1576
HILLTOP (Mission Room) *see* Endon w Stanley *Lich*
HILMARTON (St Lawrence) *see* Broad Town, Clyffe Pypard, Hilmarton etc *Sarum*
HILPERTON (St Michael and All Angels) w Whaddon and Staverton w Hilperton Marsh *Sarum 17* **P** *R Trowbridge St Jas and Viscount Long (alt)* **R** R B HICKS
HILPERTON MARSH (St Mary) *see* Hilperton w Whaddon and Staverton etc *Sarum*
HILSTON (St Margaret) *see* Roos and Garton in Holderness w Tunstall etc *York*
HILTON (All Saints) *see* Milton Abbas, Hilton w Cheselbourne etc *Sarum*
HILTON (St Mary Magdalene) *Ely 9* **P** *Bp* **V** P S G CAMERON
HILTON (St Peter) *see* Stainton w Hilton *York*
HIMBLETON (St Mary Magdalen) *see* Bowbrook S *Worc*
HIMLEY (St Michael and All Angels) *Lich 25* **P** *Bp* **P-in-c** H M FULLARTON
HINCASTER (Mission Room) *see* Heversham and Milnthorpe *Carl*
HINCHLEY WOOD (St Christopher) *Guildf 8* **P** *Bp* **V** R D ROBINSON
HINCKLEY (Assumption of St Mary the Virgin) (St Francis) (St Paul) *Leic 13* **P** *Bp* **V** B DAVIS, **C** A S REED, **NSM** B STANTON
HINCKLEY (Holy Trinity) (St John the Evangelist) *Leic 13* **P** *DBP* **TR** G D HAYLES, **TV** J N JEE
HINDERCLAY (St Mary) *see* Hepworth, Hinderclay, Wattisfield and Thelnetham *St E*
HINDERWELL (St Hilda) w Roxby *York 23* **P** *Abp* **R** D J DERMOTT
HINDHEAD (St Alban) *Guildf 3* **P** *Adn Surrey* **V** J N E BUNDOCK
HINDLEY (All Saints) *Liv 14* **P** *R Wigan* **V** D P LUND, **C** W L WHITFORD
HINDLEY (St Peter) *Liv 14* **P** *St Pet Coll Ox* **V** I S CARTER
HINDLEY GREEN (St John) *Liv 14* **P** *Bp* **V** C WARRILOW
HINDLIP (St James) *see* Salwarpe and Hindlip w Martin Hussingtree *Worc*
HINDOLVESTON (St George) *see* Foulsham w Hindolveston and Guestwick *Nor*
HINDON (St John the Baptist) *see* Tisbury *Sarum*
HINDRINGHAM (St Martin) *see* Barney, Fulmodeston w Croxton, Hindringham etc *Nor*
HINDSFORD (St Anne) *Man 13* **P** *Bp* **V** A S WELLS
HINGHAM (St Andrew) w Wood Rising w Scoulton *Nor 7* **P** *Earl of Verulam and Trustees (alt)* **C** P J STEPHENS
HINKSEY, NEW (St John the Evangelist) *see* S Hinksey *Ox*
HINKSEY, NORTH (St Lawrence) and Wytham *Ox 7* **P** *Bp* **P-in-c** R E H BATES
HINKSEY, SOUTH (St Lawrence) *Ox 7* **P** *Bp* **V** E J C DAVIS, **Hon C** B SINGH
HINSTOCK (St Oswald) *see* Cheswardine, Childs Ercall, Hales, Hinstock etc *Lich*
HINTLESHAM (St Nicholas) *see* Hadleigh *St E*
HINTON ADMIRAL (St Michael and All Angels) *see* Highcliffe w Hinton Admiral *Win*
HINTON AMPNER (All Saints) w Bramdean and Kilmeston *Win 1* **P** *D&C and The Crown (alt)* **P-in-c** A R CROAD
HINTON BLEWETT (St Margaret) *see* E w W Harptree and Hinton Blewett *B & W*
HINTON CHARTERHOUSE (St John the Baptist) *see* Freshford, Limpley Stoke and Hinton Charterhouse *B & W*
HINTON-IN-THE-HEDGES (Holy Trinity) *see* Aynho and Croughton w Evenley etc *Pet*
HINTON MARTEL (St John the Evangelist) *see* Horton, Chalbury, Hinton Martel and Holt St Jas *Sarum*
HINTON-ON-THE-GREEN (St Peter) *see* Sedgeberrow w Hinton-on-the-Green *Worc*
HINTON PARVA (St Swithun) *see* Lyddington and Wanborough and Bishopstone etc *Bris*
HINTON ST GEORGE (St George) *see* Merriott w Hinton, Dinnington and Lopen *B & W*
HINTON ST MARY (St Mary) *see* Sturminster Newton and Hinton St Mary *Sarum*
HINTON WALDRIST (St Margaret) *see* Cherbury *Ox*
HINTS (St Bartholomew) *Lich 4* **P** *Personal Reps A E Jones Esq* **P-in-c** H J BAKER
HINXHILL (St Mary) *see* Mersham w Hinxhill *Cant*
HINXTON (St Mary and St John) *Ely 7* **P** *Jes Coll Cam* **V** J E E CHARMAN, **C** B TETLEY, **NSM** P F NEWLAND
HINXWORTH (St Nicholas) *see* Ashwell w Hinxworth and Newnham *St Alb*
HIPSWELL (St John the Evangelist) *Ripon 2* **P** *Bp* **V** C M UPTON
HISTON (St Andrew) *Ely 5* **P** *MMCET* **V** H K McCURDY, **C** J M PRATT
HITCHAM (All Saints) w Little Finborough *St E 10* **P** *Bp and Pemb Coll Ox (alt)* **P-in-c** R S EXCELL
HITCHAM (St Mary) *see* Burnham w Dropmore, Hitcham and Taplow *Ox*
HITCHIN (Holy Saviour) (St Faith) (St Mark) (St Mary) *St Alb 4* **P** *Patr Bd* **TR** L E OGLESBY, **TV** F J C MERCURIO, P J NORTON, **C** R B REYNOLDS
HITTISLEIGH (St Andrew) *Ex 12* **P** *Bp* **V** C J L NAPIER
HIXON (St Peter) w Stowe-by-Chartley *Lich 15* **P** *DBP* **P-in-c** J H STERLING, **C** J M OAKES
HOAR CROSS (Holy Angels) w Newchurch *Lich 14* **P** *Bp and Meynell Ch Trustees* **V** *Vacant*
HOARWITHY (St Catherine) *see* How Caple w Sollarshope, Sellack etc *Heref*
HOATH (Holy Cross) *see* St Nicholas at Wade w Sarre and Chislet w Hoath *Cant*
HOATHLY, EAST (not known) *see* Chiddingly w E Hoathly *Chich*
HOATHLY, WEST (St Margaret) *see* Highbrook and W Hoathly *Chich*
HOBS MOAT (St Mary) *Birm 12* **P** *Bp* **V** D A LEAHY, **C** A W MOORE
HOBY (All Saints) *see* Upper Wreake *Leic*
HOCKERILL (All Saints) *St Alb 18* **P** *Bp Lon* **V** A J ALLSOP, **C** S CONLON
HOCKERING (St Michael), Honingham, East Tuddenham and North Tuddenham *Nor 17* **P** *J V Berney Esq (1 turn), DBP (2 turns)* **R** A R DAWSON
HOCKERTON (St Nicholas) *see* Kirklington w Hockerton *S'well*
HOCKHAM, GREAT (Holy Trinity) *see* Caston, Griston, Merton, Thompson etc *Nor*
HOCKLEY (St Matthew) *see* Wilnecote *Lich*
HOCKLEY (St Peter and St Paul) *Chelmsf 12* **P** *Wadh Coll Ox* **V** *Vacant* (01702) 203668
HOCKLIFFE (St Nicholas) *see* Leighton Buzzard w Eggington, Hockliffe etc *St Alb*
HOCKWOLD (St James) w Wilton *Ely 15* **P** *G&C Coll Cam* **P-in-c** J B ROWSELL
HOCKWORTHY (St Simon and St Jude) *see* Sampford Peverell, Uplowman, Holcombe Rogus etc *Ex*
HODDESDON (St Catherine and St Paul) *St Alb 20* **P** *Peache Trustees* **V** J H SPRINGBETT, **C** A J BAWTREE
HODDLESDEN (St Paul) *see* Darwen St Pet w Hoddlesden *Blackb*
HODGE HILL (St Philip and St James) *Birm 10* **P** *Bp* **TR** R J TAYLOR, **TV** W E DUDLEY, **C** R J YEOMAN
HODNET (St Luke) w Weston under Redcastle *Lich 18* **P** *A E H Heber-Percy Esq* **R** J H GRAHAM
HODTHORPE (St Martin) *see* Whitwell *Derby*
HOE (St Andrew) *see* Swanton Morley w Beetley w E Bilney and Hoe *Nor*
HOE, WEST (St Michael) *see* Plymouth St Andr and St Paul Stonehouse *Ex*
HOE BENHAM (not known) *see* Welford w Wickham and Gt Shefford, Boxford etc *Ox*
HOGGESTON (Holy Cross) *see* Schorne *Ox*
HOGHTON (Holy Trinity) *Blackb 6* **P** *V Leyland* **P-in-c** M SAWLE
HOGNASTON (St Bartholomew) *see* Hulland, Atlow, Bradley and Hognaston *Derby*
HOGSTHORPE (St Mary) *see* Chapel St Leonards w Hogsthorpe *Linc*
HOLBEACH (All Saints) *Linc 16* **P** *Bp* **V** P HILL, **C** C P ROBERTSON
HOLBEACH FEN (St John) *Linc 16* **P** *Bp* **V** D A CARNEY

HOLBEACH MARSH (St Luke) (St Mark) (St Martin) (St Matthew) *Linc 16* **P** *V Holbeach* **P-in-c** M J NOTLEY
HOLBECK (St Luke the Evangelist) *Ripon 6* **P** *Bp, V Leeds St Pet, and Meynell Ch Trust (jt)* **C** J T HODGES
HOLBETON (All Saints) *Ex 20* **P** *The Crown* **P-in-c** T R DEACON, **Hon C** W E WELDON
HOLBORN (St Alban the Martyr) w Saffron Hill St Peter *Lon 1* **P** *D&C St Paul's* **V** H LEVETT
HOLBORN (St George the Martyr) Queen Square (Holy Trinity) (St Bartholomew) Grays Inn Road *Lon 1* **P** *Ch Soc Trust* **R** D K WERNER
HOLBORN (St-Giles-in-the-Fields) *see* St Giles-in-the-Fields *Lon*
HOLBROOK (All Saints) w Freston and Woolverstone *St E 5* **P** *Bp* **P-in-c** A B LEIGHTON, **NSM** A J MARSHALL, C A MARSHALL
HOLBROOK (St Michael) and Little Eaton *Derby 11* **P** *DBP* **V** M J FENTON, **NSM** P J OWEN-JONES
HOLBROOK ROAD (St Swithin) *see* Belper *Derby*
HOLBROOKS (St Luke) *Cov 2* **P** *Bp* **V** C DUNKLEY
HOLBURY (Good Shepherd) *see* Fawley *Win*
HOLCOMBE (Emmanuel) (Canon Lewis Hall) *Man 10* **P** *R Bury St Mary* **R** C R HONOUR
HOLCOMBE (St Andrew) *see* Coleford w Holcombe *B & W*
HOLCOMBE (St George) *see* Dawlish *Ex*
HOLCOMBE BURNELL (St John the Baptist) *see* Tedburn St Mary, Whitestone, Oldridge etc *Ex*
HOLCOMBE ROGUS (All Saints) *see* Sampford Peverell, Uplowman, Holcombe Rogus etc *Ex*
HOLCOT (St Mary and All Saints) *see* Brixworth w Holcot *Pet*
HOLDENHURST (St John the Evangelist) *Win 7* **P** *Bp* **V** *Vacant* (01202) 393438
HOLDGATE (Holy Trinity) *see* Diddlebury w Munslow, Holdgate and Tugford *Heref*
HOLFORD (St Mary the Virgin) *see* Quantoxhead *B & W*
HOLKHAM (St Withiburga) w Egmere w Warham, Wells-next-the-Sea and Wighton *Nor 15* **P** *Viscount Coke (2 turns), M J Beddard Esq (2 turns), and D&C (1 turn)* **R** W A J SAYER
HOLLACOMBE (St Petroc) *see* Holsworthy w Hollacombe and Milton Damerel *Ex*
HOLLAND, GREAT (All Saints) *see* Kirby-le-Soken w Gt Holland *Chelmsf*
HOLLAND, NEW (Christ Church) *see* Barrow and Goxhill *Linc*
HOLLAND FEN (All Saints) *see* Brothertoft Gp *Linc*
HOLLAND-ON-SEA (St Bartholomew) *Chelmsf 23* **P** *Ch Patr Trust* **V** G A CATCHPOLE
HOLLAND ROAD (St John the Baptist) *see* Kensington St Jo *Lon*
HOLLESLEY (All Saints) *see* Boyton w Capel St Andrew and Hollesley *St E*
HOLLINFARE (St Helen) *see* Glazebury w Hollinfare *Liv*
HOLLINGBOURNE (All Saints) and Hucking w Leeds and Broomfield *Cant 15* **P** *Abp* **V** D C BROOKES
HOLLINGDEAN (St Richard) *see* Brighton St Matthias *Chich*
HOLLINGTON (St John the Evangelist) *see* Rocester and Croxden w Hollington *Lich*
HOLLINGTON (St John the Evangelist) (St Peter and St Paul) *Chich 17* **P** *Ch Patr Trust* **V** M G H LACKEY
HOLLINGTON (St Leonard) (St Anne) *Chich 17* **P** *E G Brabazon Esq* **R** A J TURNER, **C** S R NUNN
HOLLINGWOOD (St Francis) *see* Staveley and Barrow Hill *Derby*
HOLLINGWORTH (St Hilda) *see* Milnrow *Man*
HOLLINGWORTH (St Mary) *Ches 14* **P** *Trustees* **V** *Vacant* (01457) 762310
HOLLINSWOOD (not known) *see* Cen Telford *Lich*
HOLLINWOOD (St Margaret) *Man 19* **P** *R Prestwich St Mary* **V** *Vacant* 0161-681 4541
HOLLOWAY (Emmanuel) *see* Tollington *Lon*
HOLLOWAY Hanley Road (St Saviour) *as above*
HOLLOWAY (St Francis of Assisi) *see* W Holloway St Luke *Lon*
HOLLOWAY (St Mary Magdalene) *Lon 6* **P** *Bp and V Islington St Mary (jt)* **V** S J W COX, **C** M D ROGERS, E C M K JONES
HOLLOWAY, UPPER (All Saints) *see* Tufnell Park St Geo and All SS *Lon*
HOLLOWAY, UPPER (St Andrew) (St John) (St Mary) (St Peter) *Lon 6* **P** *Patr Bd* **TV** I D THACKER, **C** F M HINTON
HOLLOWAY, WEST (St Luke) *Lon 6* **P** *Lon Coll Div Trustees* **P-in-c** S F F PARKE, **C** P A THOMSON
HOLLOWELL (St James) *see* Guilsborough w Hollowell and Cold Ashby *Pet*
HOLLY HALL (St Augustine) *see* Dudley St Aug Holly Hall *Worc*
HOLLY HILL (Church Centre) *see* Frankley *Birm*
HOLLYBUSH (All Saints) *see* Berrow w Pendock, Eldersfield, Hollybush etc *Worc*
HOLLYM (St Nicholas) *see* Patrington w Hollym, Welwick and Winestead *York*
HOLMBRIDGE (St David) *see* Upper Holme Valley *Wakef*
HOLMBURY ST MARY (St Mary the Virgin) *see* Wotton and Holmbury St Mary *Guildf*
HOLMCROFT (St Bertelin) *see* Stafford *Lich*
HOLME (Holy Trinity) *see* Burton and Holme *Carl*
HOLME (St Giles) *see* Yaxley and Holme w Conington *Ely*
HOLME (St Giles) *see* Langford w Holme *S'well*
HOLME, EAST (St John the Evangelist) *see* Wareham *Sarum*
HOLME CULTRAM (St Cuthbert) *Carl 3* **P** *V Holme Cultram St Mary* **P-in-c** H GRAINGER
HOLME CULTRAM (St Mary) *Carl 3* **P** *Ox Univ* **P-in-c** H GRAINGER
HOLME EDEN (St Paul) *Carl 2* **P** *DBP* **V** J S CASSON
HOLME HALE (St Andrew) *see* Necton, Holme Hale w N and S Pickenham *Nor*
HOLME-IN-CLIVIGER (St John) *Blackb 3* **P** *Mrs C P Creed* **P-in-c** L LAYCOCK
HOLME-NEXT-THE-SEA (St Mary) *see* Hunstanton St Mary w Ringstead Parva etc *Nor*
HOLME-ON-SPALDING MOOR (All Saints) (Old School Mission Room) *York 7* **P** *St Jo Coll Cam* **V** D S COOK
HOLME PIERREPONT (St Edmund) *see* Radcliffe-on-Trent and Shelford etc *S'well*
HOLME RUNCTON (St James) w South Runcton and Wallington *Ely 16* **P** *Bp* **R** J C W NOLAN
HOLME VALLEY, The UPPER *Wakef 6* **P** *Patr Bd* **TR** J M SAUSBY, **TV** L GREENWOOD, J S ROBERTSHAW, **NSM** M D ELLERTON
HOLME WOOD (St Christopher) *see* Tong *Bradf*
HOLMER (St Bartholomew) (St Mary) w Huntington *Heref 3* **P** *D&C* **P-in-c** P A WILLIAMS
HOLMER GREEN (Christ Church) *see* Penn Street *Ox*
HOLMES CHAPEL (St Luke) *see* Church Hulme *Ches*
HOLMESDALE (St Philip) *see* Dronfield w Holmesfield *Derby*
HOLMESFIELD (St Swithin) *as above*
HOLMEWOOD (St Alban Mission) *see* Heath *Derby*
HOLMFIELD (St Andrew) *Wakef 4* **P** *Bp* **V** G A BANKS
HOLMFIRTH (Holy Trinity) *see* Upper Holme Valley *Wakef*
HOLMPTON (St Nicholas) *see* Easington w Skeffling, Kilnsea and Holmpton *York*
HOLMSIDE (St John the Evangelist) *Dur 4* **P** *The Crown* **P-in-c** B DAVISON
HOLMWOOD (St Mary Magdalene) *Guildf 7* **P** *Bp* **P-in-c** P C KNAPPER
HOLMWOOD, NORTH (St John the Evangelist) *Guildf 12* **P** *Bp* **V** W C FREDERICK
HOLNE (St Mary the Virgin) *see* Widecombe-in-the-Moor, Leusdon, Princetown etc *Ex*
HOLNEST (Church of the Assumption) *see* Dungeon Hill *Sarum*
HOLSWORTHY (St Peter and St Paul) w Hollacombe and Milton Damerel *Ex 9* **P** *DBP and Mrs F M Palmer (jt)* **R** R M REYNOLDS
HOLT (St Andrew) w High Kelling *Nor 18* **P** *St Jo Coll Cam* **R** D L LAWRENCE-MARCH, **NSM** D M HOWELL
HOLT (St James) *see* Horton, Chalbury, Hinton Martel and Holt St Jas *Sarum*
HOLT (St Katharine) *see* Broughton Gifford, Gt Chalfield and Holt *Sarum*
HOLT (St Martin) *see* Hallow and Grimley w Holt *Worc*
HOLTBY (Holy Trinity) *see* Stockton-on-the-Forest w Holtby and Warthill *York*
HOLTON (St Bartholomew) *see* Wheatley *Ox*
HOLTON (St Nicholas) *see* Camelot Par *B & W*
HOLTON (St Peter) *see* Halesworth w Linstead, Chediston, Holton etc *St E*
HOLTON-CUM-BECKERING (All Saints) *see* Wickenby Gp *Linc*
HOLTON-LE-CLAY (St Peter) and Tetney *Linc 10* **P** *Ld Chan (2 turns), Bp (1 turn)* **V** *Vacant* (01472) 824082
HOLTON-LE-MOOR (St Luke) *see* S Kelsey Gp *Linc*
HOLTON ST MARY (St Mary) *see* Higham, Holton St Mary, Raydon and Stratford *St E*
HOLTS (St Hugh) Conventional District *Man 18* **C-in-c** B A HARRISON
HOLTSPUR (St Thomas) *see* Beaconsfield *Ox*
HOLTYE (St Peter) *see* Cowden w Hammerwood *Chich*
HOLWELL (St Laurence) *see* The Caundles w Folke and Holwell *Sarum*
HOLWELL (St Leonard) *see* Ab Kettleby Gp *Leic*
HOLWELL (St Mary the Virgin) *see* Shill Valley and Broadshire *Ox*
HOLWELL (St Peter) *see* Ickleford w Holwell *St Alb*

HOLWORTH (St Catherine by the Sea) *see* Broadmayne, W Knighton, Owermoigne etc *Sarum*
HOLY ISLAND (St Mary the Virgin) *Newc 12* **P** *Bp* **V** D ADAM, **Hon C** C E TRISTRAM
HOLYBOURNE (Holy Rood) *see* Froyle and Holybourne *Win*
HOLYMOORSIDE (St Peter) *see* Brampton St Thos *Derby*
HOLYSTONE (St Mary the Virgin) *see* Alwinton w Holystone and Alnham *Newc*
HOLYWELL (St John the Baptist) w Needingworth *Ely 11* **P** *Bp* **R** O SWAN
HOLYWELL (St Mary) *see* Seghill *Newc*
HOMERSFIELD (St Mary) *see* S Elmham and Ilketshall *St E*
HOMERTON (Christ Church on the Mead) *see* Hackney Marsh *Lon*
HOMERTON (St Barnabas w St Paul) *as above*
HOMERTON (St Luke) *Lon 5* **P** *St Olave Hart Street Trustees* **V** C D HEWITT
HOMINGTON (St Mary the Virgin) *see* Chalke Valley W *Sarum*
HONEYCHURCH (St Mary) *see* N Tawton, Bondleigh, Sampford Courtenay etc *Ex*
HONICKNOWLE (St Francis) *Ex 22* **P** *Ld Chan* **V** P J MORGAN
HONILEY (St John the Baptist) *see* Hatton w Haseley, Rowington w Lowsonford etc *Cov*
HONING (St Peter and St Paul) *see* Smallburgh w Dilham w Honing and Crostwight *Nor*
HONINGHAM (St Andrew) *see* Hockering, Honingham, E and N Tuddenham *Nor*
HONINGTON (All Saints) *see* Shipston-on-Stour w Honington and Idlicote *Cov*
HONINGTON (All Saints) *see* Blackbourne *St E*
HONINGTON (St Wilfred) *see* Barkston and Hough Gp *Linc*
HONITON (St Michael) (St Paul), Gittisham, Combe Raleigh, Monkton and Awliscombe *Ex 5* **P** *DBP* **TR** J W I TREVELYAN, **Hon C** R C H SAUNDERS
HONLEY (St Mary) *Wakef 1* **P** *R Almondbury* **V** R N WHITTINGHAM
HOO (All Hallows) *see* High Halstow w All Hallows and Hoo St Mary *Roch*
HOO (St Andrew and St Eustachius) *see* Charsfield w Debach, Monewden, Hoo etc *St E*
HOO (St Werburgh) *Roch 6* **P** *D&C* **V** D A LOW
HOOBROOK (St Cecilia) *see* Kidderminster St Geo *Worc*
HOOE (St John the Evangelist) *see* Plymstock and Hooe *Ex*
HOOE (St Oswald) *Chich 14* **P** *Bp* **V** P C CLEMENTS
HOOK (St John the Evangelist) *Win 5* **P** *Bp* **P-in-c** N S VIGERS, **NSM** M R M JAGGS
HOOK (St Mary the Virgin) *see* Airmyn, Hook and Rawcliffe *Sheff*
HOOK (St Mary) w Warsash *Portsm 2* **P** *Bp* **V** T A J READER
HOOK (St Paul) *S'wark 16* **P** *The Crown* **V** M C DEARNLEY
HOOK COMMON (Good Shepherd) *see* Upton-upon-Severn *Worc*
HOOK NORTON (St Peter) w Great Rollright, Swerford and Wigginton *Ox 3* **P** *Bp, DBP, BNC Ox, and Jes Coll Ox (jt)* **R** J ACREMAN, **Hon C** C G TURNER
HOOKE (St Giles) *see* Beaminster Area *Sarum*
HOOLE (All Saints) *Ches 2* **P** *Simeon's Trustees* **V** R J KIRKLAND, **C** J F E MANN, **NSM** M S SEARLE
HOOLE (St Michael) *Blackb 6* **P** *Reps of Mrs E A Dunne and Mrs D Downes (jt)* **R** H PUGH
HOOLEY (Mission Hall) *see* Redhill St Jo *S'wark*
HOOTON (St Paul) *Ches 9* **P** *Trustees* **V** R W CAMPBELL
HOOTON PAGNELL (All Saints) *see* Bilham *Sheff*
HOOTON ROBERTS (St John) *see* Bramley and Ravenfield w Hooton Roberts etc *Sheff*
HOPE (Holy Trinity) w Shelve *Heref 13* **P** *New Coll Ox (3 turns), J J C Coldwell Esq (1 turn)* **R** N D MINSHALL
HOPE (St James) *Man 6* **P** *Trustees* **V** D SHARPLES
HOPE (St Peter) and Castleton *Derby 2* **P** *Bp and D&C Lich (jt)* **V** M F COLLIER
HOPE BAGOT (St John the Baptist) *see* Burford II w Greete and Hope Bagot *Heref*
HOPE BOWDLER (St Andrew) w Eaton-under-Heywood *Heref 11* **P** *DBP, Bp Birm, and Mrs R Bell (jt)* **R** M BROMFIELD
HOPE COVE (St Clements) *see* Malborough w S Huish, W Alvington and Churchstow *Ex*
HOPE MANSEL (St Michael) *see* Ross w Brampton Abbotts, Bridstow, Peterstow etc *Heref*
HOPE-UNDER-DINMORE (St Mary the Virgin) *see* Bodenham w Hope-under-Dinmore, Felton etc *Heref*
HOPESAY (St Mary the Virgin) *see* Lydbury N w Hopesay and Edgton *Heref*
HOPTON (All Saints), Market Weston, Barningham and Coney Weston *St E 9* **P** *Ld Chan and Bp (alt)* **R** C P GANE
HOPTON (St Peter) *see* Salt and Sandon w Burston *Lich*
HOPTON w Corton *Nor 9* **P** *Ld Chan and D&C (alt)* **P-in-c** J B SIMPSON
HOPTON, UPPER (St John the Evangelist) *see* Eastthorpe and Upper Hopton *Wakef*
HOPTON CASTLE (St Edward) *see* Clungunford w Clunbury and Clunton, Bedstone etc *Heref*
HOPTON WAFERS (St Michael and All Angels) *see* Cleobury Mortimer w Hopton Wafers etc *Heref*
HOPWAS (St Chad) *see* Tamworth *Lich*
HOPWOOD (St John) *Man 18* **P** *R Bury St Mary* **V** *Vacant* (01706) 369324
HORAM (Christ Church) (St James) *Chich 15* **P** *Bp* **V** K A MEPHAM
HORBLING (St Andrew) *see* Billingborough Gp *Linc*
HORBURY (St Peter and St Leonard) w Horbury Bridge (St John) *Wakef 12* **P** *Provost* **V** O J AISBITT
HORBURY JUNCTION (St Mary) *Wakef 12* **P** *DBP* **P-in-c** S GOLDTHORPE
HORDEN (St Mary) *Dur 2* **P** *Bp* **V** A BOWSER
HORDLE (All Saints) *Win 10* **P** *Bp* **V** M G ANDERSON, **Hon C** D PRICE, **NSM** J G SMITH, P E HEAD
HORDLEY (St Mary the Virgin) *see* Baschurch and Weston Lullingfield w Hordley *Lich*
HORFIELD (Holy Trinity) *Bris 6* **P** *Bp* **R** J N A BRADBURY, **C** D R JOHNSON
HORFIELD (St Gregory) *Bris 6* **P** *Bp* **V** D D HOLLOWAY, **Hon C** R D WALKER
HORHAM (St Mary) *see* Stradbroke, Horham, Athelington and Redlingfield *St E*
HORKESLEY, GREAT (All Saints) (St John) *Chelmsf 17* **P** *Ball Coll Ox* **R** C G A WOODS
HORKESLEY, LITTLE (St Peter and St Paul) *see* Wormingford, Mt Bures and Lt Horkesley *Chelmsf*
HORKSTOW (St Maurice) *Linc 6* **P** *DBP* **P-in-c** G A PLUMB
HORLEY (St Bartholomew) (St Francis) (St Wilfrid) *S'wark 26* **P** *Patr Bd* **TR** P R MAY, **TV** K B ANDERSON, K B ROBINSON
HORLEY (St Etheldreda) *see* Ironstone *Ox*
HORLEY ROW (St Wilfrid) *see* Horley *S'wark*
HORMEAD (St Mary), Wyddial, Anstey, Brent Pelham and Meesden *St Alb 19* **P** *St Jo Coll Cam, Ch Coll Cam, and Bp (by turn)* **V** G A DREW
HORMEAD (St Nicholas) *see* Hormead, Wyddial, Anstey, Brent Pelham etc *St Alb*
HORN HILL (St Paul) *see* Chalfont St Peter *Ox*
HORN PARK (St Francis) *see* Eltham St Jo *S'wark*
HORNBLOTTON (St Peter) *see* Six Pilgrims *B & W*
HORNBY (St Margaret) w Claughton *Blackb 15* **P** *D R Battersby Esq and DBF (alt)* **V** I H RENNIE
HORNBY (St Mary) *Ripon 4* **P** *D&C York* **V** *Vacant*
HORNCASTLE (St Mary the Virgin) w Low Toynton *Linc 11* **P** *Bp (2 turns), Baroness Wiloughby de Eresby (1 turn)* **V** N A THORNLEY, **C** D C PAYNE, **NSM** A C FORD, J F PARKIN
HORNCHURCH Elm Park (St Nicholas) *see* Elm Park St Nic Hornchurch *Chelmsf*
HORNCHURCH (Holy Cross) *Chelmsf 2* **P** *Bp and New Coll Ox (alt)* **V** R B N HAYCRAFT
HORNCHURCH (St Andrew) (St George) (St Matthew and St John) *Chelmsf 2* **P** *New Coll Ox* **V** H R DIBBENS, **C** D C BARNES, P J F GOODEY, **NSM** S M PAPWORTH
HORNCHURCH, SOUTH (St John and St Matthew) *Chelmsf 2* **P** *MMCET* **V** R LOVE
HORNDALE (St Francis) *see* Gt Aycliffe *Dur*
HORNDON EAST (St Francis) and West Horndon w Little Warley and Childerditch *Chelmsf 7* **P** *Sir Antony Browne's Sch and Bp (by turn)* **V** C F WELLS
HORNDON ON THE HILL (St Peter and St Paul) *see* Orsett and Bulphan and Horndon on the Hill *Chelmsf*
HORNE (St Mary) *S'wark 25* **P** *Bp* **R** *Vacant* (01342) 842054
HORNING (St Benedict) w Beeston St Laurence and Ashmanhaugh *Nor 12* **P** *Bp and Sir Ronald Preston, Bt (jt)* **R** K FLETCHER
HORNINGHOLD (St Peter) *see* Hallaton w Horninghold, Allexton, Tugby etc *Leic*
HORNINGLOW (St John the Divine) *Lich 14* **P** *Trustees* **V** P J JEFFERIES
HORNINGSEA (St Peter) *Ely 6* **P** *St Jo Coll Cam* **P-in-c** L A MARSH
HORNINGSHAM (St John the Baptist) *see* Cley Hill Warminster *Sarum*
HORNINGTOFT (St Edmund) *see* Colkirk w Oxwick w Pattesley, Whissonsett etc *Nor*
HORNSEA (St Nicholas) w Atwick *York 12* **P** *Ld Chan* **V** B H WILCOX
HORNSEY (Christ Church) *Lon 20* **P** *Bp* **V** J E TOWNSEND
HORNSEY (Holy Innocents) *Lon 20* **P** *Bp* **P-in-c** N H ASBRIDGE

HORNSEY (St Mary) (St George) *Lon 20* **P** *Bp* **R** G B SEABROOK
HORNSEY RISE (St Mary) *see* Upper Holloway *Lon*
HORNTON (St John the Baptist) *see* Ironstone *Ox*
HORRABRIDGE (St John the Baptist) *see* Sampford Spiney w Horrabridge *Ex*
HORRINGER (St Leonard) cum Ickworth *St E 13* **P** *DBP* **P-in-c** B RAISTRICK
HORSEHEATH (All Saints) *see* Linton *Ely*
HORSELL (St Mary the Virgin) *Guildf 12* **P** *Bp* **V** R JONES, **C** W A PRESCOTT, **NSM** B ASHLEY
HORSENDON (St Michael and All Angels) *see* Bledlow w Saunderton and Horsenden *Ox*
HORSEY (All Saints) *see* Winterton w E and W Somerton and Horsey *Nor*
HORSFORD (All Saints) and Horsham w Newton St Faith *Nor 2* **P** *Bp* **V** J B BOSTON
HORSFORTH (St Margaret) *Ripon 7* **P** *Bp* **V** M E SIDDLE
HORSHAM (Holy Trinity) (St Leonard) (St Mary the Virgin) (St Peter in the Causeway) *Chich 8* **P** *Patr Bd* **TR** D E E TANSILL, **TV** C J CARTER, S J W NORMAND, T R J GODDEN, B E STATHAM, **C** J A C SEWELL, G C PICKERING, **NSM** C SHORT, B SINTON
HORSHAM ST FAITH (St Mary and Andrew) *see* Horsford and Horsham w Newton St Faith *Nor*
HORSINGTON (All Saints) *see* Woodhall Spa Gp *Linc*
HORSINGTON (St John the Baptist) *see* Abbas and Templecombe w Horsington *B & W*
HORSLEY (Holy Trinity) *see* N Tyne and Redesdale Team *Newc*
HORSLEY (St Clement) *Derby 12* **P** *Bp* **P-in-c** P SWALES
HORSLEY (St Martin) and Newington Bagpath w Kingscote *Glouc 16* **P** *Bp (2 turns), DBP (1 turn)* **V** *Vacant* (01453) 833814
HORSLEY, EAST (St Martin) *Guildf 10* **P** *D&C Cant* **R** B J PARADISE
HORSLEY, WEST (St Mary) *Guildf 10* **P** *Col A R N Weston* **R** P E B ROBINSON
HORSLEY HILL South Shields (St Lawrence the Martyr) *Dur 15* **P** *D&C* **V** G BUTTERY
HORSLEY WOODHOUSE (St Susanna) *Derby 12* **P** *Bp* **P-in-c** D J PHYPERS
HORSMONDEN (St Margaret) *Roch 8* **P** *Bp* **P-in-c** J M SAUNDERS
HORSPATH (St Giles) *see* Wheatley *Ox*
HORSTEAD (All Saints) *see* Coltishall w Gt Hautbois and Horstead *Nor*
HORSTED, LITTLE (St Michael and All Angels) *Chich 21* **P** *Rt Revd P J Ball* **NSM** C HOWARTH, R C DALLING
HORSTED KEYNES (St Giles) *Chich 6* **P** *Bp* **R** D A STONEBANKS
HORTON (All Saints) *Bradf 2* **P** *J F Bardsley Esq* **P-in-c** W HOLLIDAY
HORTON (St James the Elder) and Little Sodbury *Glouc 7* **P** *Duke of Beaufort (1 turn), CPAS (2 turns)* **R** K V ENSOR
HORTON (St Mary Magdalene) *see* Hardingstone and Horton and Piddington *Pet*
HORTON (St Mary the Virgin) *Newc 1* **P** *V Woodhorn w Newbiggin* **V** J D HOPKINS
HORTON (St Michael and All Angels) *see* Riverside *Ox*
HORTON (St Michael), Lonsdon and Rushton Spencer *Lich 8* **P** *Bp and R Leek and Meerbrook (jt)* **V** E J TOMLINSON
HORTON (St Peter) *see* Ilminster and District *B & W*
HORTON (St Wolfrida), Chalbury, Hinton Martel and Holt St James *Sarum 10* **P** *Earl of Shaftesbury and Qu Eliz Free Gr Sch (jt)* **P-in-c** J R SINGLETON
HORTON, GREAT (St John the Evangelist) *Bradf 2* **P** *V Bradf* **V** S ALLEN, **C** J D BREWSTER, **NSM** L J SLOW
HORTON-CUM-STUDLEY (St Barnabas) *see* Wheatley *Ox*
HORTON-IN-RIBBLESDALE (St Oswald) *see* Langcliffe w Stainforth and Horton *Bradf*
HORTON KIRBY (St Mary) *Roch 2* **P** *Bp* **V** L E LAKER
HORWICH (Holy Trinity) (St Catherine) (St Elizabeth) and Rivington *Man 11* **P** *Patr Bd* **TR** D W GATENBY, **TV** G C BURROWS, W P BREW, **C** C R DUXBURY, **Hon C** B H CRASTON, **NSM** T LITHERLAND
HORWOOD (St Michael) *see* Newton Tracey, Horwood, Alverdiscott etc *Ex*
HORWOOD, GREAT (St James) *see* Winslow w Gt Horwood and Addington *Ox*
HORWOOD, LITTLE (St Nicholas) *see* Mursley w Swanbourne and Lt Horwood *Ox*
HOSE (St Michael) *see* Harby, Long Clawson and Hose *Leic*
HOTHAM (St Oswald) *York 14* **P** *Ld Chan* **R** P N HAYWARD
HOTHFIELD (St Margaret) *see* Westwell, Hothfield, Eastwell and Boughton Aluph *Cant*
HOUGH GREEN (All Saints) *see* Ditton St Mich *Liv*
HOUGH-ON-THE-HILL (All Saints) *see* Barkston and Hough Gp *Linc*
HOUGHAM (All Saints) *as above*
HOUGHAM (St Laurence) *see* Alkham w Capel le Ferne and Hougham *Cant*
HOUGHTON (All Saints) *see* Broughton, Bossington, Houghton and Mottisfont *Win*
HOUGHTON (St Giles) *see* Walsingham, Houghton and Barsham *Nor*
HOUGHTON (St John the Evangelist) (St Peter) *Carl 3* **P** *Trustees* **V** A M MacLEAY, **C** J P FRITH
HOUGHTON (St Martin) *see* E and W Rudham, Houghton-next-Harpley etc *Nor*
HOUGHTON (St Mary) w Wyton *Ely 9* **P** *Bp* **R** D D BILLINGS
HOUGHTON (St Nicholas) *see* Bury and Houghton *Chich*
HOUGHTON, GREAT (St Mary) *see* Cogenhoe and Gt and Lt Houghton w Brafield *Pet*
HOUGHTON, GREAT (St Michael and All Angels) Conventional District *Sheff 12* **C-in-c** J P MILTON-THOMPSON
HOUGHTON, LITTLE (St Mary the Blessed Virgin) *see* Cogenhoe and Gt and Lt Houghton w Brafield *Pet*
HOUGHTON, NEW (Christ Church) *see* E Scarsdale *Derby*
HOUGHTON CONQUEST (All Saints) *see* Wilshamstead and Houghton Conquest *St Alb*
HOUGHTON LE SPRING (St Michael and All Angels) *Dur 14* **P** *Bp* **R** I G WALLIS, **C** S BURNS
HOUGHTON-ON-THE-HILL (St Catharine) Keyham and Hungarton *Leic 5* **P** *Bp* **R** O S BENNETT
HOUGHTON REGIS (All Saints) (St Thomas) *St Alb 12* **P** *DBP* **V** J F REDVERS HARRIS, **C** C W WOOD
HOUND (St Edward the Confessor) (St Mary the Virgin) *Win 9* **P** *St Mary's Coll Win* **V** R W GOODHEW
HOUNSLOW (Holy Trinity) (St Paul) *Lon 11* **P** *Bp* **V** O C M ROSS, **C** J C McGINLEY, **NSM** N LAWRENCE
HOUNSLOW (St Mary the Virgin) *see* Isleworth St Mary *Lon*
HOUNSLOW (St Stephen) *Lon 11* **P** *Bp* **V** R L RAMSDEN
HOUNSLOW WEST (Good Shepherd) *Lon 11* **P** *Bp* **P-in-c** C S P DOUGLAS LANE
HOVE (All Saints) (St Andrew Old Church) (St John the Baptist) (Holy Trinity) *Chich 4* **P** *Bp* **TR** J M P CALDICOTT, **TV** J S G COTMAN, C R BREEDS, D ACOTT, **C** E J POLLARD, N J MASON, **NSM** H C HELLICAR
HOVE (Bishop Hannington Memorial Church) (Holy Cross) *Chich 4* **P** *Trustees* **V** A P BAKER, **C** S N MIDGLEY, D F P RUTHERFORD, M D REDHOUSE
HOVE (St Barnabas) and St Agnes *Chich 4* **P** *Bp and V Hove (alt)* **V** A R REED, **NSM** T J MacDONALD
HOVE (St Patrick) *Chich 4* **P** *Bp, V Hove, and V Brighton (jt)* **V** A B SHARPE, **NSM** D P WEBBER
HOVE (St Philip) *see* Aldrington *Chich*
HOVERINGHAM (St Michael) *see* Thurgarton w Hoveringham and Bleasby etc *S'well*
HOVETON (St John) *see* Wroxham w Hoveton and Belaugh *Nor*
HOVETON (St Peter) *as above*
HOVINGHAM (All Saints) *see* Street TM *York*
HOW CAPLE (St Andrew and St Mary) w Sollarshope, Sellack, Kings Caple, Foy, Hentland and Hoarwithy *Heref 8* **P** *Bp, D&C, and Brig A F L Clive (jt)* **P-in-c** D J ENOCH
HOWDEN Team Ministry, The (St Peter) *York 14* **P** *Abp (4 turns), Ld Chan (1 turn)* **TR** I M W ELLERY, **TV** M R G SMITH, R HUNTER
HOWDEN-LE-WEAR and Hunwick *Dur 9* **P** *Bp and V Auckland St Andr (alt)* **V** S IRWIN
HOWE (St Mary the Virgin) *see* Poringland *Nor*
HOWE BRIDGE (St Michael and All Angels) *Man 13* **P** *DBP* **V** D H BRACEY
HOWELL (St Oswald) *see* Heckington *Linc*
HOWELL HILL (St Paul) *Guildf 9* **P** *Bp* **V** S A WILCOCKSON, **C** S R BEAK, **NSM** F L McGILL
HOWGILL (Holy Trinity) *see* Firbank, Howgill and Killington *Bradf*
HOWICK (St Michael and All Angels) *see* Longhoughton w Howick *Newc*
HOWLE HILL (St John the Evangelist) *see* Walford and St John w Bishopswood, Goodrich etc *Heref*
HOWSHAM (St John) *see* Sand Hutton *York*
HOXNE (St Peter and St Paul) w Denham, Syleham and Wingfield *St E 17* **P** *Bp and DBP (jt)* **R** A R LOWE, **NSM** R J CLARK
HOXTON (Holy Trinity) (St Mary) *Lon 5* **P** *Bp* **P-in-c** I C YOUNG
HOXTON (St Anne) (St Columba) *Lon 5* **P** *The Crown* **V** G R BUSH
HOXTON (St John the Baptist) *see* Shoreditch St Leon and Hoxton St Jo *Lon*

HOYLAKE (Holy Trinity and St Hildeburgh) *Ches 8* **P** *Bp* **V** J K BALL, **Hon C** D K CHESTER
HOYLAND, HIGH (All Saints), Scissett and Clayton West *Wakef 6* **P** *Bp* **R** *Vacant* (01484) 862321
HOYLAND, NETHER (St Andrew) *Sheff 7* **P** *Bp* **P-in-c** N WILLIAMSON
HOYLAND, NETHER (St Peter) *Sheff 7* **P** *Sir Stephen Hastings* **P-in-c** N P HOLMES
HOYLANDSWAINE (St John the Evangelist) and Silkstone w Stainborough *Wakef 7* **P** *Bp* **V** D BIRCH
HUBBERHOLME (St Michael and All Angels) *see* Kettlewell w Conistone, Hubberholme etc *Bradf*
HUCCABY (St Raphael) *see* Widecombe-in-the-Moor, Leusdon, Princetown etc *Ex*
HUCCLECOTE (St Philip and St James) *Glouc 5* **P** *Bp* **V** P H KENCHINGTON
HUCKING (St Margaret) *see* Hollingbourne and Hucking w Leeds and Broomfield *Cant*
HUCKLOW, GREAT (Mission Room) *see* Bradwell *Derby*
HUCKNALL TORKARD (St Mary Magdalene) (St Peter and St Paul) (St John's Mission Church) *S'well 4* **P** *Bp* **TR** F G GREEN, **TV** C M BROWNE, **C** B V WILL, **NSM** R HALLETT, G KNOWLES
HUDDERSFIELD (Holy Trinity) *Wakef 5* **P** *Simeon's Trustees* **V** E O ROBERTS, **C** E J A McCULLAGH, **NSM** R C SWINDELL, P T WILCOCK
HUDDERSFIELD (St John the Evangelist) *see* N Huddersfield *Wakef*
HUDDERSFIELD (St Peter) *Wakef 5* **P** *DBP* **V** B W MAGUIRE, **C** R A LANE, D A EARL, **NSM** D KENT
HUDDERSFIELD (St Thomas) *Wakef 5* **P** *DBP* **V** R S GILES, **C** T C K SLEDGE
HUDDERSFIELD, NORTH (St Cuthbert) *Wakef 5* **P** *DBP* **TR** M J LOWLES, **TV** J LONGUET-HIGGINS
HUDDINGTON (St James) *see* Bowbrook S *Worc*
HUDSWELL (St Michael and All Angels) *see* Richmond w Hudswell *Ripon*
HUGGATE (St Mary) *see* Pocklington and Owsthorpe and Kilnwick Percy etc *York*
HUGGLESCOTE (St John the Baptist) w Donington, Ellistown and Snibston *Leic 8* **P** *Bp* **TV** M D WEBB
HUGHENDEN (St Michael) *Ox 29* **P** *DBP* **P-in-c** C H OVERTON, **C** M P WYNTER, **NSM** F J FRIEND
HUGHLEY (St John the Baptist) *see* Wenlock *Heref*
HUISH (St James the Less) *see* Shebbear, Buckland Filleigh, Sheepwash etc *Ex*
HUISH (St Nicholas) *see* Swanborough *Sarum*
HUISH, SOUTH (Holy Trinity) *see* Malborough w S Huish, W Alvington and Churchstow *Ex*
HUISH CHAMPFLOWER (St Peter) *see* Wiveliscombe w Chipstable, Huish Champflower etc *B & W*
HUISH EPISCOPI (Blessed Virgin Mary) *see* Langport Area Chs *B & W*
HULCOTE (St Nicholas) *see* Cranfield and Hulcote w Salford *St Alb*
HULCOTT (All Saints) *see* Aylesbury w Bierton and Hulcott *Ox*
HULL (Ascension) *see* Derringham Bank *York*
HULL (Holy Apostles) *see* Kingston upon Hull H Trin *York*
HULL (Most Holy and Undivided Trinity) *as above*
HULL Newland (St John) *York 15* **P** *Abp* **V** M TINKER, **C** C B HOBBS, M C BRAILSFORD
HULL (St Aidan) Southcoates *see* Kingston upon Hull St Aid Southcoates *York*
HULL (St Alban) *see* Kingston upon Hull St Alb *York*
HULL (St Cuthbert) *York 15* **P** *Abp* **V** J D DAGLISH
HULL (St George) *see* Marfleet *York*
HULL (St Giles) *as above*
HULL (St Hilda) *as above*
HULL (St John the Baptist) *see* Newington w Dairycoates *York*
HULL (St Martin) (Transfiguration) *York 15* **P** *Abp* **V** E WILSON, **C** M A HILL
HULL (St Mary) Sculcoates *York 15* **P** *V Sculcoates* **P-in-c** T C GILL
HULL (St Mary the Virgin) Lowgate *see* Kingston upon Hull St Mary *York*
HULL (St Matthew w St Barnabas) *see* Kingston upon Hull St Matt w St Barn *York*
HULL (St Nicholas) *see* Kingston upon Hull St Nic *York*
HULL (St Paul) *see* Sculcoates St Paul w Ch Ch and St Silas *York*
HULL (St Philip) *see* Marfleet *York*
HULL (St Stephen) Sculcoates *York 15* **P** *Ld Chan (2 turns), V Hull H Trin (1 turn), and Abp (1 turn)* **V** F A C S BOWN
HULL (St Thomas) *see* Derringham Bank *York*
HULL, NORTH (St Michael and All Angels) *York 15* **P** *Abp* **V** D A WALKER
HULLAND (Christ Church), Atlow, Bradley and Hognaston *Derby 8* **P** *Bp, D&C Lich, Trustees, and Exors Col I P A M Walker-Okeover (by turn)* **R** *Vacant* (01335) 370605
HULLAVINGTON (St Mary Magdalene), Norton and Stanton St Quintin *Bris 12* **P** *Bp, Eton Coll, and R W Neeld Esq (jt)* **R** J W M MORGAN
HULLBRIDGE (St Thomas of Canterbury) *Chelmsf 12* **P** *Bp* **V** W H REED
HULME (Ascension) *Man 4* **P** *Trustees* **R** M E JACKSON, **C** M THOMPSON, **Hon C** H C WEST
HULME WALFIELD (St Michael) *see* Eaton and Hulme Walfield *Ches*
HULTON, LITTLE (St John the Baptist) *see* Walkden Moor w Lt Hulton *Man*
HULTON, OVER (St Andrew) *see* Deane *Man*
HUMBER (St Mary the Virgin) *see* Leominster *Heref*
HUMBERSTON (St Peter) *Linc 10* **P** *Bp* **V** I H TINKLER
HUMBERSTONE (St Mary) *Leic 1* **P** *DBP* **P-in-c** W J D DOWN, **NSM** A T HELM, H M BENCE
HUMBERSTONE, NEW (St Barnabas) *see* Leic Presentation *Leic*
HUMBLE, WEST (St Michael) *see* Mickleham *Guildf*
HUMBLETON (St Peter) *see* Burton Pidsea and Humbleton w Elsternwick *York*
HUMPHREY PARK (St Clement) *see* Urmston *Man*
HUMSHAUGH (St Peter) w Simonburn and Wark *Newc 2* **P** *Bp* **R** J M THOMPSON
HUNCOAT (St Augustine) *see* Accrington St Jo w Huncoat *Blackb*
HUNCOTE (St James the Greater) *see* Narborough and Huncote *Leic*
HUNDLEBY (St Mary) *see* Spilsby w Hundleby *Linc*
HUNDON (All Saints) w Barnardiston *St E 8* **P** *Jes Coll Cam (2 turns), Ridley Hall Cam (1 turn)* **R** J J COOPER, **NSM** S A BAREHAM
HUNDRED RIVER Benefice, The *St E 14* **P** *DBP, Shadingfield Properties Ltd, Bp, Miss to Seamen, and F D L Barnes Esq (by turn)* **R** C J ATKINSON
HUNGARTON (St John the Baptist) *see* Houghton-on-the-Hill, Keyham and Hungarton *Leic*
HUNGERFORD (St Lawrence) and Denford *Ox 14* **P** *D&C Windsor* **V** A W SAWYER
HUNMANBY (All Saints) w Muston *York 16* **P** *MMCET* **V** J W R HATTAN
HUNNINGHAM (St Margaret) *Cov 10* **P** *Ld Chan* **P-in-c** P J CROOKS, **C** M L D GREIG
HUNSDON (St Dunstan) (St Francis) w Widford and Wareside *St Alb 22* **P** *DBP* **R** J RISBY
HUNSINGORE (St John the Baptist) *see* Lower Nidderdale *Ripon*
HUNSLET (St Mary) *Ripon 6* **P** *Bp (2 turns) and V Leeds St Pet (1 turn)* **V** P GREENWELL
HUNSLET MOOR (St Peter) and St Cuthbert *Ripon 6* **P** *Bp* **V** A J PEARSON
HUNSLEY (St Peter) *see* Rowley w Skidby *York*
HUNSTANTON (St Edmund) w Ringstead *Nor 16* **P** *H Le Strange Esq* **V** M H SELLORS
HUNSTANTON (St Mary) w Ringstead Parva, Holme-next-the-Sea, Thornham, Brancaster, Burnham Deepdaleand Titchwell *Nor 16* **P** *Bp, Exors of the late H le Strange Esq, and Exors of the late H S N Simms-Adams Esq (jt)* **R** L H CAMPBELL, **C** D J ROPER
HUNSTANWORTH (St James) *see* Blanchland w Hunstanworth and Edmundbyers etc *Newc*
HUNSTON (St Leodegar) *see* N Mundham w Hunston and Merston *Chich*
HUNSTON (St Michael) *see* Badwell Ash w Gt Ashfield, Stowlangtoft etc *St E*
HUNTINGDON (All Saints w St John the Baptist) (St Barnabas) (St Mary) *Ely 9* **P** *Bp* **TR** W R KING, **TV** A M GUITE, **C** P SOMERS HESLAM, **NSM** M A GUITE
HUNTINGFIELD (St Mary) *see* Cratfield w Heveningham and Ubbeston etc *St E*
HUNTINGTON (All Saints) *York 8* **P** *Patr Bd* **TR** K J DAVIES, **TV** C J CULLWICK, O J LAMBERT
HUNTINGTON (St Luke) *Ches 2* **P** *Bp* **V** I J HUTCHINGS
HUNTINGTON (St Mary Magdalene) *see* Holmer w Huntington *Heref*
HUNTINGTON (St Thomas) *see* Cannock *Lich*
HUNTINGTON (St Thomas a Becket) *see* Kington w Huntington, Old Radnor, Kinnerton etc *Heref*
HUNTLEY (St John the Baptist) and Longhope *Glouc 3* **P** *Bp* **R** A J MINCHIN, **NSM** C BEATSON
HUNTON (St James) *see* Wonston and Stoke Charity w Hunton *Win*
HUNTON (St Mary) *see* Coxheath w E Farleigh, Hunton and Linton *Roch*
HUNTS CROSS (St Hilda) *Liv 4* **P** *Bp* **V** G A PERERA

HUNTSHAM (All Saints) *see* Sampford Peverell, Uplowman, Holcombe Rogus etc *Ex*
HUNTSHAW (St Mary Magdalene) *see* Newton Tracey, Horwood, Alverdiscott etc *Ex*
HUNTSPILL (St Peter and All Hallows) *B & W 1* **P** *Ball Coll Ox* **R** G M WALSH
HUNWICK (St Paul) *see* Howden-le-Wear and Hunwick *Dur*
HUNWORTH (St Lawrence) *see* Brinton, Briningham, Hunworth, Stody etc *Nor*
HURDSFIELD (Holy Trinity) *Ches 13* **P** *Hyndman Trustees* **V** J G TSIPOURAS
HURLEY (Resurrection) *see* Baxterley w Hurley and Wood End and Merevale etc *Birm*
HURLEY (St Mary the Virgin) and Stubbings *Ox 13* **P** *DBP* **V** S J WELCH, **NSM** M W SKINNER
HURSLEY (All Saints) and Ampfield *Win 11* **P** *T H Faber Esq and Lord Lifford (jt)* **V** R B EDWARDS
HURST *see* Fawkenhurst *Cant*
HURST (St John the Evangelist) *Man 17* **P** *The Crown* **V** I St J FISHER
HURST (St Nicholas) *Ox 16* **P** *Bp* **V** D H LOVERIDGE
HURST GREEN (Holy Trinity) *Chich 15* **P** *Bp* **V** B C GURD
HURST GREEN (St John the Evangelist) *S'wark 25* **P** *Bp* **V** D F G BUTLIN, **NSM** M J SELLER
HURST GREEN (St John the Evangelist) and Mitton *Bradf 5* **P** *Bp and J E R Aspinall Esq (jt)* **V** J T BIRBECK
HURSTBOURNE PRIORS (St Andrew) *see* Barton Stacey and Bullington etc *Win*
HURSTBOURNE TARRANT (St Peter) and Faccombe and Vernham Dean and Linkenholt *Win 3* **P** *Bp* **V** M HARLEY, **NSM** P A MILLS
HURSTPIERPOINT (Holy Trinity) (St George) *Chich 9* **P** *Woodard Schs* **R** D M REEVE
HURSTWOOD, HIGH (Holy Trinity) *Chich 21* **P** *Abp* **P-in-c** I GIBSON, **NSM** M COXHEAD
HURWORTH (All Saints) *Dur 8* **P** *Ch Soc Trust* **R** R R A GRAHAM
HUSBANDS BOSWORTH (All Saints) w Mowsley and Knaptoft and Theddingworth *Leic 4* **P** *DBP (2 turns), Bp (1 turn)* **NSM** R H HUTCHINGS
HUSBORNE CRAWLEY (St Mary Magdalene or St James) *see* Aspley Guise w Husborne Crawley and Ridgmont *St Alb*
HUSTHWAITE (St Nicholas) *see* Coxwold and Husthwaite *York*
HUTHWAITE (All Saints) *S'well 4* **P** *V Sutton-in-Ashfield* **P-in-c** C A K MAIDEN
HUTTOFT (St Margaret) *see* Sutton, Huttoft and Anderby *Linc*
HUTTON (All Saints) (St Peter) *Chelmsf 7* **P** *D&C St Paul's* **R** R WALLACE, **C** B C WALLACE
HUTTON (Blessed Virgin Mary) *B & W 11* **P** *DBP* **R** B N STEVENSON
HUTTON, NEW (St Stephen) *see* Grayrigg, Old Hutton and New Hutton *Carl*
HUTTON, OLD (St John the Evangelist) *as above*
HUTTON BONVILLE (St Laurence) *see* Gt Smeaton w Appleton Wiske and Birkby etc *Ripon*
HUTTON BUSCEL (St Matthew) *see* Wykeham and Hutton Buscel *York*
HUTTON CRANSWICK (St Peter) w Skerne, Watton and Beswick *York 11* **P** *Abp* **V** J McNAUGHTON
HUTTON HENRY (St Francis) *see* Wingate Grange *Dur*
HUTTON-IN-THE-FOREST (St James) *see* Skelton and Hutton-in-the-Forest w Ivegill *Carl*
HUTTON-LE-HOLE (St Chad) *see* Lastingham w Appleton-le-Moors, Rosedale etc *York*
HUTTON MAGNA (St Mary) *see* Barningham w Hutton Magna and Wycliffe *Ripon*
HUTTON ROOF (St John the Divine) *see* Kirkby Lonsdale *Carl*
HUTTON RUDBY (All Saints) *see* Rudby in Cleveland w Middleton *York*
HUTTONS AMBO (St Margaret) *see* Whitwell w Crambe, Flaxton, Foston etc *York*
HUXHAM (St Mary the Virgin) *see* Stoke Canon, Poltimore w Huxham and Rewe etc *Ex*
HUXLEY (St Andrew) *see* Hargrave *Ches*
HUYTON (St George) *Liv 2* **P** *Bp* **V** D G TOWLER
HUYTON (St Michael) *Liv 2* **P** *Lord Derby* **V** J A STANLEY, **C** G C ELSMORE
HUYTON QUARRY (St Gabriel) *Liv 2* **P** *V Huyton St Mich* **V** N F BOON
HYDE (Holy Ascension) *see* Ellingham and Harbridge and Hyde w Ibsley *Win*
HYDE (St George) *Ches 14* **P** *R Stockport St Mary* **V** J H DARCH, **C** J E HARRIES
HYDE (St Thomas) *Ches 14* **P** *Bp* **P-in-c** P J HIBBERT
HYDE, EAST (Holy Trinity) *see* Woodside w E Hyde *St Alb*
HYDE, WEST (St Thomas) *see* Mill End and Heronsgate w W Hyde *St Alb*
HYDE HEATH (Mission Church) *see* Lt Missenden *Ox*
HYDE PARK CRESCENT (St John) *see* Paddington St Jo w St Mich *Lon*
HYDNEYE, THE (St Peter) *Chich 16* **P** *Bp* **V** M G ONIONS
HYKEHAM (All Saints) (St Hugh) (St Michael and All Angels) *Linc 18* **P** *Ld Chan and Bp (alt)* **TR** E L RENNARD, **TV** J FREEBAIRN-SMITH, **C** M R RENNARD
HYLTON, NORTH (St Margaret) Castletown *Dur 16* **P** *Bp* **P-in-c** C P A LOCKHART
HYLTON, SOUTH (St Mary) *Dur 16* **P** *Bp* **V** J E RUSCOE
HYSSINGTON (St Etheldreda) *see* Churchstoke w Hyssington and Sarn *Heref*
HYTHE Butts Ash (St Anne) *see* Hythe *Win*
HYTHE (St John the Baptist) *Win 10* **P** *Bp* **V** P D BAIRD, **Hon C** J M WEBSTER, **NSM** J M MEW
HYTHE (St Leonard) (St Michael and All Angels) *Cant 5* **P** *R Saltwood* **V** N H WOODS, **C** M J RAMSHAW
HYTHE, WEST (St Mary) *see* Sellindge w Monks Horton and Stowting etc *Cant*
IBBERTON (St Eustace) *see* Hazelbury Bryan and the Hillside Par *Sarum*
IBSTOCK (St Denys) w Heather *Leic 8* **P** *Bp and MMCET (jt)* **R** R N EVERETT
IBSTONE (St Nicholas) *see* Stokenchurch and Ibstone *Ox*
ICKBURGH (St Peter) w Langford *Nor 13* **P** *Bp* **P-in-c** G H WHEATLEY
ICKENHAM (St Giles) *Lon 24* **P** *Eton Coll* **P-in-c** P ROBINSON, **NSM** K R TOMBS
ICKFORD (St Nicholas) *see* Worminghall w Ickford, Oakley and Shabbington *Ox*
ICKHAM (St John the Evangelist) *see* Littlebourne and Ickham w Wickhambreaux etc *Cant*
ICKLEFORD (St Katherine) w Holwell *St Alb 4* **P** *DBP* **R** R I OAKLEY
ICKLESHAM (St Nicolas) *see* Winchelsea and Icklesham *Chich*
ICKLETON (St Mary Magdalene) *Ely 7* **P** *Ld Chan* **V** J E E CHARMAN, **C** B TETLEY, **NSM** P F NEWLAND
ICKLINGHAM (All Saints w St James) *see* Mildenhall *St E*
ICKNIELD *Ox 1* **P** *Ld Chan (1 turn), Ch Ch Ox (1 turn), Bp and Earl of Macclesfield (1 turn)* **R** C I EVANS, **C** J M RUSSELL, **NSM** E R M HENDERSON, C R SEAMAN
ICOMB (St Mary) *see* Westcote w Icomb and Bledington *Glouc*
IDBURY (St Nicholas) *see* Shipton-under-Wychwood w Milton-under-Wychwood *Ox*
IDDESLEIGH (St James) w Dowland *Ex 19* **P** *Bp* **P-in-c** R C THORP
IDE (St Ida) *see* Dunchideock and Shillingford St George w Ide *Ex*
IDE HILL (St Mary the Virgin) *see* Sundridge w Ide Hill *Roch*
IDEFORD (St Mary the Virgin) *see* Teignmouth, Ideford w Luton, Ashcombe etc *Ex*
IDEN (All Saints) *see* Rye *Chich*
IDLE (Holy Trinity) *Bradf 3* **P** *V Calverley* **V** D A JOHNSON
IDLICOTE (St James the Great) *see* Shipston-on-Stour w Honington and Idlicote *Cov*
IDRIDGEHAY (St James) *see* Wirksworth *Derby*
IDSWORTH (St Hubert) *see* Blendworth w Chalton w Idsworth *Portsm*
IFFLEY (St Mary the Virgin) *Ox 4* **P** *Ch Ch Ox* **NSM** D G S BARTON
IFIELD (St Margaret) *Chich 7* **P** *Bp* **TR** D L PARKER, **TV** A G LOW, **C** S J PATCH, **NSM** D M GOODWIN
IFIELD (St Margaret) *see* Gravesend H Family w Ifield *Roch*
IFORD (St Nicholas) w Kingston and Rodmell *Chich 18* **P** *Bp* **V** G M DAW, **C** S L PANTER MARSHALL
IFORD (St Saviour) *Win 7* **P** *Bp* **V** I M SCOTT-THOMPSON, **NSM** N M BENCE, W MACDONALD
IGHTFIELD (St John the Baptist) *see* Adderley, Ash, Calverhall, Ightfield etc *Lich*
IGHTHAM (St Peter) *Roch 10* **P** *Sir John Winnifrith* **R** R H WHITTINGTON
IKEN (St Botolph) *see* Orford w Sudbourne, Chillesford, Butley and Iken *St E*
ILAM (Holy Cross) w Blore Ray and Okeover *Lich 5* **P** *Sir Peter Walker-Okeover* **V** *Vacant*
ILCHESTER (St Mary Major) w Northover, Limington, Yeovilton and Podimore *B & W 6* **P** *Bp Lon (7 turns), Bp (1 turn), and Wadh Coll Ox (1 turn)* **R** C F H SUTCLIFFE
ILDERTON (St Michael) *see* Glendale Gp *Newc*
ILFORD, GREAT (St Alban) *Chelmsf 4* **P** *Bp* **V** D I MILNES, **Hon C** M R GRIFFIN
ILFORD, GREAT (St Andrew) *Chelmsf 4* **P** *Bp* **V** P L DEEMING, **C** C S T CANT
ILFORD, GREAT (St Clement) (St Margaret of Antioch) *Chelmsf 4* **P** *Patr Bd* **V** T H SHANNON, **C** C F P McDERMOTT

ILFORD, GREAT (St John the Evangelist) *Chelmsf 4* **P** *Bp* **V** G M TARRY, **C** S G O O OLUKANMI
ILFORD, GREAT (St Luke) *Chelmsf 4* **P** *Bp* **V** M R JUDGE
ILFORD, GREAT (St Mary) *Chelmsf 4* **P** *V Gt Ilford* **V** J B BARNES
ILFORD, LITTLE (St Barnabas) *Chelmsf 3* **P** *Bp* **R** B J ARSCOTT
ILFORD, LITTLE (St Michael and All Angels) *Chelmsf 3* **P** *Hertf Coll Ox* **R** J P WHITWELL, **C** L C WINKETT, **NSM** A C CLARKE
ILFRACOMBE (Holy Trinity) (St Peter), Lee, Woolacombe, Bittadon and Mortehoe *Ex 15* **P** *Patr Bd* **TR** N JACKSON-STEVENS, **TV** G A B KING-SMITH, **C** S C E LAIRD
ILFRACOMBE (St Philip and St James) w West Down *Ex 15* **P** *Bp and Ch Trust Fund Trust (jt)* **V** C E G TENNANT
ILKESTON (Holy Trinity) *Derby 13* **P** *Bp* **NSM** K W G JOHNSON
ILKESTON (St John the Evangelist) *Derby 13* **P** *V Ilkeston St Mary* **P-in-c** E A PALMER
ILKESTON (St Mary the Virgin) *Derby 13* **P** *Bp* **V** J R HENSON
ILKETSHALL ST ANDREW (St Andrew) *see* Wainford *St E*
ILKETSHALL ST JOHN (St John the Baptist) *see* S Elmham and Ilketshall *St E*
ILKETSHALL ST LAWRENCE (St Lawrence) *as above*
ILKETSHALL ST MARGARET (St Margaret) *as above*
ILKLEY (All Saints) *Bradf 4* **P** *Hyndman Trustees* **V** P J C MARSHALL, **NSM** N H TUCKER
ILKLEY (St Margaret) *Bradf 4* **P** *CR* **V** R D HOYAL, **NSM** A G BROWN
ILLINGWORTH (St Mary) *Wakef 4* **P** *V Halifax* **V** L T McKENNA, **C** S H FAIRWEATHER
ILLOGAN (St Illogan) *see* St Illogan *Truro*
ILMER (St Peter) *see* Princes Risborough w Ilmer *Ox*
ILMINGTON (St Mary) and Stretton-on-Fosse and Ditchford w Preston-on-Stour w Whitchurch and Atherstone-on-Stour *Cov 9* **P** *Bp, MMCET, and Ms C A Alston-Roberts-West (jt)* **P-in-c** R J GRIFFITHS
ILMINSTER (Blessed Virgin Mary) and District *B & W 15* **P** *Patr Bd* **TR** J P C REED, **TV** J R J HISCOX, J T TYLER
ILSINGTON (St Michael) *Ex 11* **P** *D&C Windsor* **P-in-c** C J L CURD
ILSLEY, EAST (St Mary) *see* Compton w E Ilsley *Ox*
ILSLEY, WEST (All Saints) *see* Beedon and Peasemore w W Ilsley and Farnborough *Ox*
ILSTON (St Michael and All Angels) *see* Gaulby *Leic*
ILTON (St Peter) *see* Ilminster and District *B & W*
IMMINGHAM (St Andrew) *Linc 10* **P** *DBP* **V** H W P HALL
IMPINGTON (St Andrew) *Ely 5* **P** *Adn Ely* **C** J M PRATT
INCE (St James) *see* Thornton le Moors w Ince and Elton *Ches*
INCE IN MAKERFIELD (Christ Church) (St Christopher) *Liv 14* **P** *Simeon's Trustees* **V** C J CROOKS
INCE IN MAKERFIELD (St Mary) *Liv 14* **P** *Simeon's Trustees* **V** D W LONG
INDIAN QUEEN (St Francis) *see* St Enoder *Truro*
INGATESTONE (St Edmund and St Mary) w Buttsbury *Chelmsf 7* **P** *Bp* **P-in-c** P E COULTON
INGESTRE (St Mary the Virgin) *see* Stafford St Jo and Tixall w Ingestre *Lich*
INGHAM (All Saints) w Cammeringham w Fillingham *Linc 3* **P** *Bp and Ball Coll Ox (jt)* **P-in-c** J HOBBS, **C** C A ZOTOV, **Hon C** D J PRYOR
INGHAM (Holy Trinity) *see* Sutton w Ingham and Catfield *Nor*
INGHAM (St Bartholomew) *see* Blackbourne *St E*
INGLEBY ARNCLIFFE (All Saints) *see* Osmotherley w Harlsey and Ingleby Arncliffe *York*
INGLEBY BARWICK Conventional District *York 22* **C-in-c** J M E COOPER
INGLEBY BARWICK (St Francis) *see* Stainton w Hilton *York*
INGLEBY GREENHOW (St Andrew) w Bilsdale Priory, Kildale and Westerdale *York 22* **P** *Abp, Adn Cleveland, Bp Whitby, Viscount de l'Isle, R G Beckett Esq, and Mrs C M Sutcliffe (jt)* **P-in-c** R F ROWLING
INGLETON (St John the Evangelist) *Dur 8* **P** *Lord Barnard* **P-in-c** D J ELLEANOR
INGLETON (St Mary the Virgin) w Chapel le Dale *Bradf 6* **P** *Bp* **V** T ASHWORTH, **Hon C** V ASHWORTH
INGOL (St Margaret) *Blackb 14* **P** *Bp* **V** *Vacant* (01772) 727208
INGOLDISTHORPE (St Michael) *see* Snettisham w Ingoldisthorpe and Fring *Nor*
INGOLDMELLS (St Peter and St Paul) w Addlethorpe *Linc 8* **P** *Ld Chan and Wadh Coll Ox (alt)* **R** D B WOODS
INGOLDSBY (St Bartholomew) *Linc 14* **P** *Ch Coll Cam, Sir Lyonel Tollemache, Bt, D&C, Bp, and DBP (by turn)* **R** R BURGESS, **NSM** K A C BROWN, I R WALTERS
INGRAM (St Michael) *see* Glendale Gp *Newc*
INGRAVE (St Nicholas) *see* Gt Warley and Ingrave St Nic *Chelmsf*
INGRAVE (St Stephen) Conventional District *Chelmsf 7* **C-in-c** J RYELAND
INGROW (St John the Evangelist) cum Hainworth *Bradf 8* **P** *Bp* **C** S A GRIFFITHS
INGS (St Anne) *see* Staveley, Ings and Kentmere *Carl*
INGWORTH (St Lawrence) *see* Erpingham w Calthorpe, Ingworth, Aldborough etc *Nor*
INHAM NOOK (St Barnabas) *see* Chilwell *S'well*
INKBERROW (St Peter) w Cookhill and Kington w Dormston *Worc 1* **P** *Bp* **R** G S CROSS, **NSM** F M BATTIN
INKERSALL (St Columba) *see* Staveley and Barrow Hill *Derby*
INKPEN (St Michael) *see* W Woodhay w Enborne, Hampstead Marshall etc *Ox*
INSKIP (St Peter) *Blackb 10* **P** *V St Michael's-on-Wyre* **V** G M HILTON-TURVEY
INSTOW (All Saints Chapel) (St John the Baptist) *Ex 16* **P** *Christie Trustees* **R** G A SATTERLY
INTAKE (All Saints) *see* Doncaster Intake *Sheff*
INTWOOD (All Saints) *see* Swardeston w E Carleton, Intwood, Keswick etc *Nor*
INWARDLEIGH (St Petroc) *see* Okehampton w Inwardleigh, Bratton Clovelly etc *Ex*
INWORTH (All Saints) *see* Copford w Easthorpe and Messing w Inworth *Chelmsf*
IPING (St Mary) *see* Stedham w Iping *Chich*
IPPLEPEN (St Andrew) w Torbryan *Ex 10* **P** *D&C Windsor* **V** P W DARBY
IPSDEN (St Mary the Virgin) *see* Langtree *Ox*
IPSLEY (St Peter) *Worc 7* **P** *Patr Bd* **TR** R M ADAMS, **TV** A J KELSO, A E J TOSTEVIN, **C** L CORKE, **NSM** J W DAVEY
IPSTONES (St Leonard) w Berkhamsytch and Onecote w Bradnop *Lich 6* **P** *Bp and R Leek and Meerbrook (jt)* **V** S G PRICE
IPSWICH (All Hallows) *St E 4* **P** *Bp* **V** C A GARRARD, **NSM** R F ALLARD
IPSWICH (All Saints) *St E 4* **P** *Bp* **V** A G WILCOX
IPSWICH (St Andrew) *St E 4* **P** *Bp* **V** G I HOUSE
IPSWICH (St Augustine of Hippo) *St E 4* **P** *Bp* **V** L F SIMPKINS, **C** B A WATKINS
IPSWICH (St Bartholomew) *St E 4* **P** *Bp* **V** J E BURROWS
IPSWICH (St Clement w St Luke) (Holy Trinity) *St E 4* **P** *Ch Patr Trust* **P-in-c** R G WARREN
IPSWICH (St Francis) (St Clare's Church Centre) *St E 4* **P** *Bp* **TV** C G G EVERETT, **C** P R GARBETT
IPSWICH (St Helen) (St James) *St E 4* **P** *Ch Patr Trust* **R** *Vacant* (01473) 232898
IPSWICH (St John the Baptist) *St E 4* **P** *Simeon's Trustees* **V** K WHITE, **C** J N BEAUCHAMP
IPSWICH (St Margaret) *St E 4* **P** *Simeon's Trustees* **V** D CUTTS, **C** J M GOSNEY
IPSWICH (St Mary at Stoke) (St Peter) *St E 4* **P** *Bp* **TR** I D J MORGAN, **TV** C M LACK, J M HUTCHINSON, **C** N J COLE
IPSWICH (St Mary at the Elms) *St E 4* **P** *PCC* **P-in-c** B A TOLL
IPSWICH (St Mary-le-Tower) (St Nicholas) *St E 4* **P** *Bp (3 turns), Ch Patr Trust (1 turn)* **V** P K TOWNLEY
IPSWICH (St Matthew) *St E 4* **P** *Ld Chan* **R** P D HARDINGHAM, **P-in-c** P W GIBBS, **C** H J D WRIGHT
IPSWICH (St Michael) *St E 4* **P** *Simeon's Trustees* **P-in-c** S H COWLEY
IPSWICH (St Thomas) *St E 4* **P** *Bp* **V** J E WALLMAN, **NSM** B F ROSE, E A T ARNOLD
IRBY (St Chad's Mission Church) *see* Thurstaston *Ches*
IRBY-IN-THE-MARSH (All Saints) *see* Bratoft w Irby-in-the-Marsh *Linc*
IRBY ON HUMBER (St Andrew) *see* Laceby *Linc*
IRCHESTER (St Katharine) *Pet 10* **P** *Bp* **V** P A PAYNTON
IRCHESTER, LITTLE (St John) *see* Irchester *Pet*
IREBY (St James) *see* Bolton w Ireby and Uldale *Carl*
IRELAND WOOD (St Paul) *Ripon 7* **P** *R Adel* **V** J SAXTON, **C** D A CALDER
IRELETH w Askam (St Peter) *Carl 8* **P** *V Dalton-in-Furness* **V** D SANDERSON
IRLAM (St John the Baptist) *Man 2* **P** *Trustees* **V** P J P WETZ
IRNHAM (St Andrew) *see* Corby Glen *Linc*
IRON ACTON (St James the Less) *Bris 7* **P** *Ch Ch Ox* **R** *Vacant* (01454) 228412
IRON-BRIDGE (St Luke) *see* Coalbrookdale, Iron-Bridge and Lt Wenlock *Heref*
IRONSTONE: Drayton, Hanwell, Horley, Hornton, Shenington w Alkerton, and Wroxton w Balscote *Ox 5* **P** *Ld Chan (1 turn), Bp, Earl De La Warr, and DBP (1 turn)* **R** R J CHARD, **NSM** D B ADDLEY
IRONVILLE (Christ Church) *see* Riddings and Ironville *Derby*

IRSTEAD (St Michael) *see* Neatishead, Barton Turf and Irstead *Nor*
IRTHINGTON (St Kentigern), Crosby-on-Eden and Scaleby *Carl 2* **P** *Bp* **V** J G PEART
IRTHLINGBOROUGH (St Peter) *Pet 10* **P** *Sir Stephen Hastings* **R** R G KNIGHT
IRTON (St Paul) *see* Eskdale, Irton, Muncaster and Waberthwaite *Carl*
ISEL (St Michael) *see* Bassenthwaite, Isel and Setmurthy *Carl*
ISFIELD (St Margaret) *Chich 21* **P** *Abp* **NSM** C HOWARTH, R C DALLING
ISHAM (St Peter) w Pytchley *Pet 11* **P** *Bp* **R** P R GATENBY
ISLE ABBOTTS (Blessed Virgin Mary) *see* Ilminster and District *B & W*
ISLE BREWERS (All Saints) *as above*
ISLE OF DOGS (Christ Church) (St John) (St Luke) *Lon 7* **P** *Bp* **V** M A SEELEY, **C** C L OWENS, J BRUEK, J BRUECK
ISLEHAM (St Andrew) *Ely 3* **P** *Ld Chan* **V** *Vacant*
ISLES OF SCILLY: St Mary's, St Agnes, St Martin's, Bryher and Tresco *Truro 6* **P** *Duchy of Cornwall* **TR** J C OULD, **NSM** K D CAMPION
ISLEWORTH (All Saints) *Lon 11* **P** *D&C Windsor* **V** W J MORGAN
ISLEWORTH (St Francis of Assisi) *Lon 11* **P** *Bp* **NSM** R J S BURN
ISLEWORTH (St John the Baptist) *Lon 11* **P** *V Isleworth All SS* **P-in-c** P R MYLES, **C** V K LUCAS
ISLEWORTH (St Luke) *see* Spring Grove St Mary *Lon*
ISLEWORTH (St Mary) Osterley Road *as above*
ISLEWORTH (St Mary the Virgin) *Lon 11* **P** *Bp* **V** *Vacant* 0181-560 6166
ISLEY WALTON (All Saints) *see* Breedon cum Isley Walton and Worthington *Leic*
ISLINGTON (St James the Apostle) (St Peter) *Lon 6* **P** *Bp* **V** E H JONES
ISLINGTON (St Jude and St Paul) *see* Mildmay Grove St Jude and St Paul *Lon*
ISLINGTON (St Mary) *Lon 6* **P** *CPAS* **V** G L CLAYDON
ISLINGTON (St Mary Magdalene) *see* Holloway St Mary Magd *Lon*
ISLIP (St Nicholas) *Pet 10* **P** *L G Stopford-Sackville Esq* **P-in-c** F COLEMAN
ISLIP (St Nicholas) w Charlton on Otmoor, Oddington, Noke and Woodeaton *Ox 2* **P** *D&C Westmr, Revd E H W Crusha, and Qu Coll Ox (jt)* **R** R L STURCH, **C** E J JOHNSON
ISTEAD RISE (St Barnabas) *Roch 4* **P** *Bp* **V** S R DYER, **NSM** A C DYER
ITCHEN ABBAS (St John the Baptist) *see* Itchen Valley *Win*
ITCHEN VALLEY, THE *Win 1* **P** *Ld Chan* **R** J M STEVENETTE, **NSM** J B NAPIER
ITCHENOR, WEST (St Nicholas) *see* W Wittering and Birdham w Itchenor *Chich*
ITCHINGFIELD (St Nicholas) w Slinfold *Chich 7* **P** *Bp* **R** D M BEAL, **NSM** P GRAVES
IVEGILL (Christ Church) *see* Skelton and Hutton-in-the-Forest w Ivegill *Carl*
IVER (St Peter) *Ox 23* **P** *Trustees* **V** B A SKINNER, **C** S K TIMMINS
IVER HEATH (St Margaret) *Ox 23* **P** *Trustees* **R** D S REYNISH
IVINGHOE (St Mary the Virgin) w Pitstone and Slapton *Ox 26* **P** *Bp and Ch Ch Ox (jt)* **V** P A LAWRENCE
IVINGTON (St John) *see* Leominster *Heref*
IVY HATCH (not known) *see* Ightham *Roch*
IVY ROW (Mission Room) *see* Roos and Garton in Holderness w Tunstall etc *York*
IVYBRIDGE (St John the Evangelist) w Harford *Ex 20* **P** *Bp* **V** F H COLES, **C** W G HAMILTON, C J BARTON
IVYCHURCH (St George) *see* St Mary's Bay w St Mary-in-the-Marsh etc *Cant*
IWADE (All Saints) *Cant 14* **P-in-c** J P LEFROY, **Hon C** D W WEBB
IWERNE COURTNEY (St Mary) *see* The Iwernes, Sutton Waldron and Fontmell Magna *Sarum*
IWERNE MINSTER (St Mary) *as above*
IWERNES, Sutton Waldron and Fontmell Magna, The *Sarum 7* **P** *Bp, D&C Windsor, DBP, and G A L F Pitt-Rivers Esq (jt)* **V** E A SELLGREN, **NSM** J H SIMMONS
IXWORTH (St Mary) *see* Blackbourne *St E*
IXWORTH THORPE (All Saints) *as above*
JACKFIELD (St Mary) *see* Broseley w Benthall, Jackfield, Linley etc *Heref*
JACOBSTOW (St James) *see* St Gennys, Jacobstow w Warbstow and Treneglos *Truro*
JACOBSTOWE (St James) *see* Hatherleigh, Meeth, Exbourne and Jacobstowe *Ex*
JARROW (St John the Baptist) (St Mark) (St Paul) (St Peter) *Dur 15* **P** *Bp* **TR** K HUNT, **TV** P A BAKER, M G JOHNSON, **C** T THORP, **NSM** A RAINE
JARROW GRANGE (Christ Church) *Dur 15* **P** *Lord Northbourne* **R** N SWAINSON
JARVIS BROOK (St Michael and All Angels) *Chich 19* **P** *Bp* **V** I E MORRISON, **NSM** P K BURNETT
JERSEY (All Saints) *Win 15* **P** *R St Helier, Bp, and The Crown (by turn)* **P-in-c** G J HOUGHTON
JERSEY Gouray (St Martin) *Win 15* **P** *Bp and The Crown (alt)* **V** *Vacant* (01534) 54294
JERSEY Greve d'Azette (St Nicholas) *see* Jersey St Clem *Win*
JERSEY (Holy Trinity) *Win 15* **P** *The Crown* **R** A KEOGH
JERSEY Millbrook (St Matthew) *Win 15* **P** *The Crown* **P-in-c** A G FORMAN
JERSEY (St Andrew) *Win 15* **P** *Dean of Jersey* **V** *Vacant* (01534) 34975
JERSEY (St Brelade) (Communicare Chapel) (St Aubin) *Win 15* **P** *The Crown* **P-in-c** N W CARTER, **C** P J WILKIN, **Hon C** J M GURDON
JERSEY (St Clement) *Win 15* **P** *The Crown* **R** *Vacant* (01534) 851992
JERSEY (St Helier) *Win 15* **P** *The Crown* **R** J N SEAFORD, **NSM** A D WILLIAMS
JERSEY (St James) *Win 15* **P** *Bp* **P-in-c** D R D JONES, **NSM** A F PEARCE
JERSEY (St John) *Win 15* **P** *The Crown* **P-in-c** A J THEWLIS
JERSEY (St Lawrence) *Win 15* **P** *The Crown* **R** *Vacant* (01534) 20934
JERSEY (St Luke) *Win 15* **P** *Bp and The Crown (alt)* **P-in-c** D R D JONES, **NSM** J D DODD, A F PEARCE
JERSEY (St Mark) *Win 15* **P** *Bp* **V** C I BUCKLEY
JERSEY (St Martin) *Win 15* **P** *The Crown* **R** L J TURNER
JERSEY (St Mary) *Win 15* **P** *The Crown* **R** A HART
JERSEY (St Ouen) (St George) *Win 15* **P** *The Crown* **R** R G SPECK
JERSEY (St Paul) Proprietary Chapel *Win 15* **Min** P J BROOKS
JERSEY (St Peter) *Win 15* **P** *The Crown* **R** B J GILES
JERSEY (St Saviour) *Win 15* **P** *The Crown* **R** A C SWINDELL, **NSM** J J ILTON
JERSEY (St Simon) *Win 15* **P** *R St Helier, Bp, and The Crown (by turn)* **V** *Vacant* (01534) 24885
JERSEY DE GROUVILLE (St Martin) (St Peter la Roque) *Win 15* **P** *The Crown* **P-in-c** F R A MASON, **Hon C** M A HALLIWELL
JESMOND (Clayton Memorial Church) *Newc 5* **P** *Trustees* **V** D R J HOLLOWAY, **C** J J S PRYKE, C J P HOBBS
JESMOND (Holy Trinity) *Newc 5* **P** *Trustees* **P-in-c** R L SIMPSON
JESMOND (St Hilda) *see* Newc St Hilda *Newc*
JEVINGTON (St Andrew) *see* E Dean w Friston and Jevington *Chich*
JOYDENS WOOD (St Barnabas) *Roch 17* **P** *Bp* **V** D H HORTON
JURBY (St Patrick) *S & M 4* **P** *Bp* **V** R C GEDDES
KATE'S HILL (St John) *see* Dudley St Jo *Worc*
KEA (All Hallows) (Old Church) *Truro 6* **P** *V St Clement* **V** R J REDRUP
KEAL, EAST (St Helen) *see* Marden Hill Gp *Linc*
KEAL, WEST (St Helen) *as above*
KEARSLEY MOOR (St Stephen) *Man 6* **P** *R E Farnworth and Kearsley* **V** K F WAINWRIGHT
KEASDEN (St Matthew) *see* Clapham-with-Keasden and Austwick *Bradf*
KEDDINGTON (St Margaret) *see* Louth *Linc*
KEDINGTON (St Peter and St Paul) *St E 8* **P** *Walsingham Coll Trust* **P-in-c** J F M WILLIAMS, **NSM** S A BAREHAM
KEEDWELL HILL (Ascension) *see* Long Ashton *B & W*
KEELBY (St Bartholomew) w Riby and Aylesby *Linc 10* **P** *DBP (2 turns), J E Spillman Esq (1 turn)* **V** A S CAVE
KEELE (St John the Baptist) *see* Betley and Keele *Lich*
KEEVIL (St Leonard) *see* Steeple Ashton w Semington and Keevil *Sarum*
KEGWORTH (St Andrew) *Leic 7* **P** *Ch Coll Cam* **R** R L NASH
KEIGHLEY (All Saints) *Bradf 8* **P** *Bp and R Keighley St Andr* **P-in-c** N DANIELS, **Hon C** C P HUTCHINSON
KEIGHLEY (St Andrew) *Bradf 8* **P** *Bp* **TR** M J HARDY
KEINTON MANDEVILLE (St Mary Magdalene) w Lydford-on-Fosse, Barton St David and Kingweston *B & W 3* **P** *Ch Soc Trust and J H Cordle (1 turn), A J Whitehead (2 turns), Bp (1 turn), and Mrs E J Burden (1 turn)* **P-in-c** P N LITTLEWOOD
KELBROOK (St Mary) *Bradf 7* **P** *Bp* **Dn-in-c** J P SMITH
KELBY (St Andrew) *see* Ancaster Wilsford Gp *Linc*
KELHAM (St Wilfrid) *see* Averham w Kelham *S'well*
KELLET, NETHER (St Mark) *see* Bolton le Sands *Blackb*

KELLET, OVER (St Cuthbert) *Blackb 15* **P** *Reformation Ch Trust* **V** K CLAPHAM
KELLING (St Mary) *see* Weybourne Gp *Nor*
KELLINGTON (St Edmund) w Whitley *Wakef 11* **P** *DBP* **P-in-c** M C E BOOTES
KELLOE (St Helen) and Coxhoe *Dur 5* **P** *Bp* **V** M J COOKE
KELLS (St Peter) *Carl 5* **P** *Bp* **V** A D WHIPP, **NSM** W D MAHONEY
KELLY (St Mary the Virgin) w Bradstone *Ex 24* **P** *W F Kelly Esq* **P-in-c** J H HEATH
KELMARSH (St Denys) *see* Clipston w Naseby and Haselbech w Kelmarsh *Pet*
KELMSCOTT (St George) *see* Shill Valley and Broadshire *Ox*
KELSALE (St Peter) *see* Kelsale-cum-Carlton, Middleton-cum-Fordley etc *St E*
KELSALE-CUM-CARLTON, Middleton-cum-Fordley and Theberton w Eastbridge *St E 19* **P** *DBP, Prime Min, and Ch Patr Trust (by turn)* **R** R S SMITH
KELSALL (St Philip) *Ches 2* **P** *V Tarvin* **V** F C CONANT
KELSEY Group, The SOUTH (St Mary) *Linc 5* **P** *Bp (3 turns), J M B Young Esq and S B Young Esq (1 turn)* **P-in-c** K J SAUNDERS
KELSEY, NORTH (All Hallows) *Linc 6* **P** *Bp* **P-in-c** K J SAUNDERS
KELSHALL (St Faith) *see* Therfield w Kelshall *St Alb*
KELSTON (St Nicholas) *see* Bath Weston St Jo w Kelston *B & W*
KELVEDON (St Mary the Virgin) *Chelmsf 24* **P** *Bp* **V** D J D THORNTON
KELVEDON HATCH (St Nicholas) *Chelmsf 7* **P** *Bp* **P-in-c** R A L ROSE
KEMBERTON (St Andrew) *see* Beckbury, Badger, Kemberton, Ryton, Stockton etc *Lich*
KEMBLE (All Saints), Poole Keynes, Somerford Keynes and Sharncote *Glouc 12* **P** *DBP, Duchy of Lanc, and Mrs L R Rank (by turn)* **V** *Vacant* (01285) 770049
KEMERTON (St Nicholas) *see* Woolstone w Gotherington and Oxenton etc *Glouc*
KEMP TOWN (St Mary) *Chich 2* **P** *Bp, Mrs R A Hinton, A C R Elliott Esq, and Canon D Walker (jt)* **V** J E LLOYD-JAMES
KEMPSEY (St Mary the Virgin) and Severn Stoke w Croome d'Abitot *Worc 5* **P** *D&C and Croome Estate Trustees (alt)* **R** F J MUSHEN
KEMPSFORD (St Mary) w Welford *Glouc 13* **P** *Bp* **P-in-c** J F GREGORY
KEMPSHOTT (St Mark) *Win 4* **P** *Bp* **V** K V BATT, **C** P F D TAYLOR, **NSM** J E LEESE
KEMPSTON (All Saints) *St Alb 10* **P** *Bp* **P-in-c** R J SUTTON
KEMPSTON (Transfiguration) *St Alb 10* **P** *Bp* **V** J R BROWN, **C** S T SMITH, **NSM** G A WEBB, V E HOLLIS
KEMSING (St Mary the Virgin) w Woodlands *Roch 10* **P** *DBP* **V** C C HORN, **NSM** J G GOULDING
KENARDINGTON (St Mary) *see* Appledore w Brookland, Fairfield, Brenzett etc *Cant*
KENCHESTER (St Michael) *see* Credenhill w Brinsop and Wormsley etc *Heref*
KENCOT (St George) *see* Shill Valley and Broadshire *Ox*
KENDAL (Holy Trinity) (All Hallows Chapel) *Carl 9* **P** *Trin Coll Cam* **V** G A HOWE, **C** J J RICHARDS, J E MAYCOCK, **NSM** P SMITH
KENDAL (St George) *Carl 9* **P** *V Kendal H Trin* **V** A R BILLINGS, **C** C V TAYLOR
KENDAL (St Thomas) *Carl 9* **P** *CPAS* **V** R A MACHIN, **C** P G BAXENDALE
KENDERCHURCH (St Mary) *see* Ewyas Harold w Dulas, Kenderchurch etc *Heref*
KENDRAY (St Andrew) *Sheff 12* **P** *V Ardsley* **V** S DONALD
KENILWORTH (St John) *Cov 4* **P** *Simeon's Trustees* **V** R D TURNER, **C** I D GOW
KENILWORTH (St Nicholas) (St Barnabas) *Cov 4* **P** *Ld Chan* **V** D J RAKE
KENLEY (All Saints) *S'wark 23* **P** *Abp* **V** R C HAGON, **Hon C** S C CONWAY
KENLEY (St John the Baptist) *see* Wenlock *Heref*
KENN (St Andrew) *see* Exminster and Kenn *Ex*
KENN (St John the Evangelist) *see* Yatton Moor *B & W*
KENNERLEIGH (St John the Baptist) *see* N Creedy *Ex*
KENNET, EAST (Christ Church) *see* Upper Kennet *Sarum*
KENNET, UPPER *Sarum 20* **P** *Bp* **TR** W J SELLERS, **NSM** G M MacKICHAN
KENNETT (St Nicholas) *Ely 3* **P** *Mrs M F de Packh* **P-in-c** A HASELHURST
KENNINGHALL (St Mary) *see* Guiltcross *Nor*
KENNINGTON (St John the Divine w St James the Apostle) *S'wark 10* **P** *Ripon Coll Cuddesdon and Bp (jt)* **V** L DENNEN, **C** B J CUNNINGHAM, **NSM** P ANSDELL-EVANS
KENNINGTON (St Mark) *S'wark 12* **P** *Abp* **V** J M STARR
KENNINGTON (St Mary) *Cant 10* **P** *Abp* **V** C G PREECE, **C** M WRAY
KENNINGTON (St Swithun) *Ox 10* **P** *Bp* **V** H BLOOMFIELD, **Hon C** E A JOHNSON
KENNINGTON CROSS (St Anselm) *see* N Lambeth *S'wark*
KENNINGTON PARK (St Agnes) *S'wark 9* **P** *Trustees* **V** C I PEARSON
KENNY HILL (St James) *see* Mildenhall *St E*
KENSAL GREEN (St John) *Lon 2* **P** *Bp* **V** R D BEAL
KENSAL RISE (St Mark) (St Martin) *Lon 21* **P** *St Olave Hart Street Trustees and Bp (jt)* **V** P W STONE, **C** G P NOYCE
KENSAL TOWN (St Thomas) (St Andrew) (St Philip) *Lon 12* **P** *Hyndman Trustees* **V** D FLETCHER, **Hon C** P J MATHIE
KENSINGTON (St Barnabas) *Lon 12* **P** *V Kensington St Mary Abbots w St Geo and Ch Ch* **V** J D IRVINE, **C** R J G HOVIL
KENSINGTON (St Clement) *see* Notting Dale St Clem w St Mark and St Jas *Lon*
KENSINGTON (St Helen) (Holy Trinity) *Lon 12* **P** *Bp* **V** A SIMPSON
KENSINGTON (St James) *see* Notting Dale St Clem w St Mark and St Jas *Lon*
KENSINGTON (St John the Baptist) *Lon 12* **P** *Trustees* **V** G F BRIGHT, **NSM** A E SPEAKMAN
KENSINGTON (St Mary Abbots) (St George) (Christ Church) *Lon 12* **P** *Bp* **V** I L ROBSON, **C** F J GELLI, M G FULLER
KENSINGTON (St Philip) Earl's Court *Lon 12* **P** *Bp* **V** M B E FORREST
KENSINGTON, SOUTH (Holy Trinity w All Saints) *Lon 3* **P** *D&C Westmr* **V** *Vacant* 0171-370 5160
KENSINGTON, SOUTH (St Augustine) *Lon 3* **P** *Keble Coll Ox* **V** R P MARSHALL
KENSINGTON, SOUTH (St Jude) *Lon 8* **P** *Sir Laurence Magnus Bt* **V** D A STONE, **Hon C** P E P BRICE
KENSINGTON, SOUTH (St Luke) *Lon 8* **P** *Ch Patr Trust* **V** W R HEALD
KENSINGTON, SOUTH (St Stephen) *Lon 12* **P** *Guild of All So* **P-in-c** R F BUSHAU
KENSINGTON, WEST (St Andrew) *see* Fulham St Andr Fulham Fields *Lon*
KENSINGTON, WEST (St Mary) *see* Fulham St Mary N End *Lon*
KENSINGTON, WEST The Boltons (St Mary) *see* W Brompton St Mary w St Pet *Lon*
KENSWORTH (St Mary the Virgin), Studham and Whipsnade *St Alb 12* **P** *Ld Chan and D&C St Paul's (alt)* **V** L M LANE
KENT TOWN *see* E Molesey St Paul *Guildf*
KENTCHURCH (St Mary) *see* Ewyas Harold w Dulas, Kenderchurch etc *Heref*
KENTFORD (St Mary) *see* Gazeley w Dalham, Moulton and Kentford *St E*
KENTISBEARE (St Mary) w Blackborough *Ex 4* **P** *Exors G C Wyndham Esq* **R** *Vacant*
KENTISBURY (St Thomas) *see* Shirwell, Loxhore, Kentisbury, Arlington, etc *Ex*
KENTISH TOWN (St Benet and All Saints) (St Luke) *Lon 17* **P** *Prime Min and D&C St Paul's (alt)* **V** R N ARNOLD, **C** R A HANSON
KENTISH TOWN (St Martin) (St Andrew) *Lon 17* **P** *Exors Dame Jewell Magnus-Allcroft* **V** J A HAYWARD
KENTISH TOWN (St Silas the Martyr) *Lon 17* **P** *Bp* **V** G C ROWLANDS, **C** N P PAINE DAVEY
KENTMERE (St Cuthbert) *see* Staveley, Ings and Kentmere *Carl*
KENTON (All Saints) *see* Debenham w Aspall and Kenton *St E*
KENTON (All Saints), Mamhead, Powderham, Cofton and Starcross *Ex 6* **P** *Earl of Devon, D&C, D&C Sarum, and SMF (jt)* **R** R J WEBBER, **Hon C** P DAWKES
KENTON (Ascension) *Newc 5* **P** *Bp* **V** *Vacant* 0191-285 7803
KENTON (St Mary the Virgin) *Lon 23* **P** *Bp* **V** D J SHERWOOD, **C** C J FLETCHER
KENTON, SOUTH (Annunciation) *see* Wembley Park St Aug *Lon*
KENWYN (St Keyne) w St Allen *Truro 6* **P** *Bp* **R** M S BYROM
KERESLEY (St Thomas) and Coundon *Cov 2* **P** *Bp* **V** K J MOBBERLEY, **C** E A DONALDSON, **NSM** S MOBBERLEY
KERESLEY END (Church of the Ascension) *see* Keresley and Coundon *Cov*
KERRIDGE (Holy Trinity) *see* Bollington St Jo *Ches*
KERSAL, LOWER (St Aidan) *Man 6* **P** *Bp* **V** G D MORRIS
KERSAL MOOR (St Paul) *Man 6* **P** *Trustees* **R** S FLETCHER, **C** S R BULLOCK
KERSEY (St Mary) w Lindsey *St E 3* **P** *Bp* **V** *Vacant*
KERSWELL GREEN (St John the Baptist) *see* Kempsey and Severn Stoke w Croome d'Abitot *Worc*
KESGRAVE (All Saints) *St E 4* **P** *Bp* **V** D R W HARES

KESSINGLAND (St Edmund) w Gisleham *Nor 9* **P** *Ld Chan (1 turn), Bp (2 turns)* **P-in-c** J S HUNT
KESTON (not known) (St Audrey) *Roch 14* **P** *D&C* **R** M R KEIRLE
KESWICK (All Saints) *see* Swardeston w E Carleton, Intwood, Keswick etc *Nor*
KESWICK (St John) *Carl 6* **P** *Trustees* **P-in-c** B SMITH
KESWICK, EAST (St Mary Magdalene) *see* Bardsey *Ripon*
KETLEY (St Mary the Virgin) and Oakengates *Lich 22* **P** *Bp* **V** D P SMITH
KETTERING (All Saints) *Pet 11* **P** *SMF* **V** R T COOK
KETTERING (Christ the King) *Pet 11* **P** *R Barton Seagrave w Warkton* **V** D M TALBOT, **C** J D NAUDE
KETTERING (St Andrew) *Pet 11* **P** *Bp* **V** C ALSBURY
KETTERING (St Mary the Virgin) (St John the Evangelist) *Pet 11* **P** *SMF* **V** S J RAINE
KETTERING (St Peter and St Paul) (St Michael and All Angels) *Pet 11* **P** *Comdr L M M Saunders Watson* **R** G FISHER
KETTERINGHAM (St Peter) *see* Swardeston w E Carleton, Intwood, Keswick etc *Nor*
KETTLEBASTON (St Mary) *see* Monks Eleigh w Chelsworth and Brent Eleigh etc *St E*
KETTLEBROOK (St Andrew) *see* Tamworth *Lich*
KETTLEBURGH (St Andrew) *see* Brandeston w Kettleburgh *St E*
KETTLENESS (St John the Baptist) *see* Lythe w Ugthorpe *York*
KETTLESTONE (All Saints) *see* Barney, Fulmodeston w Croxton, Hindringham etc *Nor*
KETTLETHORPE (St Peter and St Paul) *see* Saxilby Gp *Linc*
KETTLEWELL (St Mary) w Conistone, Hubberholme and Arncliff w Halton Gill *Bradf 7* **P** *Bp, Mrs A M Harries and W R G Bell Esq (jt)* **V** A B KNAPP
KETTON (St Mary the Virgin) w Tinwell *Pet 8* **P** *Bp (3 turns), Burghley Ho Preservation Trust (1 turn)* **R** M W M SAUNDERS
KEW (St Anne) *S'wark 17* **P** *The Crown* **V** P McCRORY
KEW (St Francis of Assisi) *Liv 9* **P** *Bp, Adn Warrington, and V Southport All SS and All So (jt)* **V** A P J GALBRAITH
KEW (St Philip and All Saints) (St Luke) *S'wark 17* **P** *Bp* **V** N P DARBY, **NSM** I K E AHRENS
KEWSTOKE (St Paul) w Wick St Lawrence *B & W 11* **P** *Ld Chan* **V** P A M WEST
KEXBY (St Paul) w Wilberfoss *York 7* **P** *Viscount de Vesci and Lord Egremont (alt)* **C** C W ANKERS
KEYHAM (All Saints) *see* Houghton-on-the-Hill, Keyham and Hungarton *Leic*
KEYHAM, NORTH (St Thomas) *Ex 21* **P** *Bp* **V** *Vacant* (01752) 51102
KEYINGHAM (St Nicholas) w Ottringham, Halsham and Sunk Island *York 13* **P** *Abp (3 turns), DBP (1 turn)* **R** I R S WALKER, **Hon C** S J WALKER
KEYMER (St Cosmas and St Damian) *see* Clayton w Keymer *Chich*
KEYMER (St Francis of Assisi) *as above*
KEYNSHAM (St Francis) (St John the Baptist) *B & W 10* **P** *Patr Bd* **TV** N HAWKINS, S M STEVENETTE, **C** N GANE, **NSM** A A J CLARIDGE, M A SNOOK
KEYSOE (St Mary the Virgin) w Bolnhurst and Little Staughton *St Alb 15* **P** *CCC Ox (1 turn), Bp (2 turns)* **V** J C LAIRD
KEYSTON (St John the Baptist) and Bythorn *Ely 10* **P** *Sir Stephen Hastings (2 turns), Bp (1 turn)* **P-in-c** J HINDLEY, **NSM** B A BEARCROFT, J RAWLINSON
KEYWORTH (St Mary Magdalene) *S'well 9* **P** *Bp* **P-in-c** T SISSON, **C** A D LITTLEWOOD
KIBWORTH (St Wilfrid) and Smeeton Westerby and Saddington *Leic 5* **P** *Mert Coll Ox and Bp (jt)* **P-in-c** S M LEE
KIDBROOKE (St James) (St Nicholas) (Holy Spirit) *S'wark 2* **P** *Patr Bd* **TR** K W HITCH, **TV** I SALONIA, J M WALLACE, **C** T H HULL, **NSM** K F SITCH
KIDDERMINSTER (St George) (St Chad) (St John the Baptist Church Hall) *Worc 11* **P** *Patr Bd* **TR** N J W BARKER, **TV** H A BURTON, **C** C J WINDLEY
KIDDERMINSTER (St John the Baptist) (Holy Innocents) *Worc 11* **P** *Patr Bd* **TR** G H SMITH, **TV** C F RAVEN, **C** K D SHILVOCK
KIDDERMINSTER (St Mary and All Saints) w Trimpley, Franche, Broadwaters and Upper Arley *Worc 11* **P** *Bp* **TR** D O BELL, **TV** P A GOLDSMITH, **C** J L SAMUEL, **NSM** S GOLDSMITH
KIDDINGTON (St Nicholas) *see* Wootton w Glympton and Kiddington *Ox*
KIDLINGTON (St Mary the Virgin) w Hampton Poyle *Ox 7* **P** *Patr Bd* **TR** G C M SMITH, **TV** R G COPPEN, **C** S E BOOYS, **NSM** B DOUBTFIRE, J A TURNER
KIDLINGTON, SOUTH (St John the Baptist) *see* Kidlington w Hampton Poyle *Ox*
KIDMORE END (St John the Baptist) *Ox 6* **P** *Bp* **V** G D FOULIS BROWN
KIDSGROVE (St Thomas) *Lich 9* **P** *MMCET* **V** R FARNWORTH, **C** J J REDFEARN
KILBURN (Mission Room) *see* Horsley *Derby*
KILBURN Priory Road (St Mary w All Souls) *Lon 16* **P** *Bp and Ch Patr Trust (jt)* **V** *Vacant*
KILBURN (St Augustine) (St John) *Lon 2* **P** *SMF* **V** A H YATES, **C** R W C PAGE
KILBURN (St Mary) *see* Thirkleby w Kilburn and Bagby *York*
KILBURN, WEST (St Luke) (St Simon) (St Jude) *Lon 2* **P** *CPAS* **V** R D de BERRY, **C** E J BARRATT
KILBY (St Mary Magdalene) *see* Fleckney and Kilby *Leic*
KILDALE (St Cuthbert) *see* Ingleby Greenhow w Bilsdale Priory, Kildale etc *York*
KILDWICK (St Andrew) *Bradf 8* **P** *Ch Ch Ox* **V** P MOORE
KILHAM (All Saints) *see* Rudston w Boynton and Kilham *York*
KILKHAMPTON (St James the Great) w Morwenstow *Truro 8* **P** *DBP and Bp (jt)* **R** B G DORRINGTON
KILLAMARSH (St Giles) *Derby 3* **P** *The Crown* **R** R J BRADSHAW
KILLERTON (Holy Evangelist) *see* Pinhoe and Broadclyst *Ex*
KILLINGHALL (St Thomas the Apostle) *see* Hampsthwaite and Killinghall *Ripon*
KILLINGHOLME, NORTH AND SOUTH (St Denys) *see* Habrough Gp *Linc*
KILLINGTON (All Saints) *see* Firbank, Howgill and Killington *Bradf*
KILLINGWORTH (St John) *Newc 1* **P** *V Longbenton St Bart* **V** M L MALLESON, **C** M F LAYBOURNE
KILMERSDON (St Peter and St Paul) w Babington *B & W 12* **P** *Lord Hylton* **R** C P J TURNER
KILMESTON (St Andrew) *see* Hinton Ampner w Bramdean and Kilmeston *Win*
KILMINGTON (St Giles) *see* Stockland, Dalwood, Kilmington and Shute *Ex*
KILMINGTON (St Mary the Virgin) *see* Upper Stour *Sarum*
KILNDOWN (Christ Church) *see* Goudhurst w Kilndown *Cant*
KILNGREEN (Diggle Mission Church) *see* Saddleworth *Man*
KILNHURST (St Thomas) *Sheff 12* **P** *Ld Chan* **V** N H ELLIOTT
KILNWICK (All Saints) *see* Bainton w N Dalton, Middleton-on-the-Wolds etc *York*
KILNWICK PERCY (St Helen) *see* Pocklington and Owsthorpe and Kilnwick Percy etc *York*
KILPECK (St Mary and St David) *see* Ewyas Harold w Dulas, Kenderchurch etc *Heref*
KILSBY (St Faith) *see* Barby w Kilsby *Pet*
KILTON (St Nicholas) *see* Quantoxhead *B & W*
KILVERSTONE (St Andrew) *see* Thetford *Nor*
KILVINGTON (St Mary) *S'well 3* **P** *E G Staunton Esq* **P-in-c** J H BATESON
KILVINGTON, SOUTH (St Wilfrid) *see* Thirsk *York*
KILWORTH, NORTH (St Andrew) w SOUTH (St Nicholas) and Misterton *Leic 11* **P** *Ld Chan, R R D Belgrave Esq, and Revd C E N Richards (by turn)* **P-in-c** P J C CLEMENTS
KIMBERLEY (Holy Trinity) *S'well 7* **P** *Bp* **R** D W WILDE
KIMBERLEY (St Peter) *see* Barnham Broom *Nor*
KIMBERWORTH (St Thomas) (St Mark) *Sheff 6* **P** *Bp* **V** P J HUGHES, **C** A T ISAACSON
KIMBERWORTH PARK (St John) *Sheff 6* **P** *Bp* **V** *Vacant* (01709) 552268
KIMBLE, GREAT (St Nicholas) *see* Ellesborough, The Kimbles and Stoke Mandeville *Ox*
KIMBLE, LITTLE (All Saints) *as above*
KIMBLESWORTH (St Philip and St James) *see* Sacriston and Kimblesworth *Dur*
KIMBOLTON (St Andrew) *Ely 10* **P** *Trustees Duke of Man* **V** R A FROST
KIMBOLTON (St James the Great) w Hamnish and Middleton-on-the-Hill *Heref 7* **P** *Bp* **P-in-c** W R PRIDIE
KIMCOTE (All Saints) *see* Gilmorton w Peatling Parva and Kimcote etc *Leic*
KIMMERIDGE (St Nicholas of Myra) *see* Corfe Castle, Church Knowle, Kimmeridge etc *Sarum*
KIMPTON (St Peter and St Paul) *see* Appleshaw, Kimpton, Thruxton and Fyfield *Win*
KIMPTON (St Peter and St Paul) w Ayot St Lawrence *St Alb 8* **P** *Bp* **R** C J WHARTON
KINETON (St Peter) *Cov 8* **P** *Lady Willoughby de Broke* **V** C A HOST
KING CROSS (St Paul) *Wakef 4* **P** *Bp* **V** J VICKERMAN
KING STERNDALE (Christ Church) *see* Buxton w Burbage and King Sterndale *Derby*
KINGHAM (St Andrew) w Churchill, Daylesford and Sarsden *Ox 3* **P** *Ch Soc Trust* **R** J E ANDREWS, **NSM** T J MANN
KINGS BROMLEY (All Saints) *see* The Ridwares and Kings Bromley *Lich*

KING'S CAPLE (St John the Baptist) *see* How Caple w Sollarshope, Sellack etc *Heref*
KING'S CLIFFE (All Saints) *Pet 8* **P** *Bp* **R** J HUMPHRIES
KINGS HEATH (All Saints) *Birm 5* **P** *V Moseley St Mary* **V** J L WILKINSON
KINGS HEATH (St Augustine) *Pet 7* **P** *Bp* **V** O R PAGE, **C** J C MICKLETHWAITE
KING'S HILL (St Andrew) *see* Wednesbury St Bart *Lich*
KINGS LANGLEY (All Saints) *St Alb 2* **P** *Abp* **V** P R STEARN
KING'S LYNN (All Saints) *see* S Lynn *Nor*
KING'S LYNN (St John the Evangelist) *Nor 20* **P** *Bp* **P-in-c** S C STOKES
KING'S LYNN (St Margaret) (St Edmund) w St Nicholas *Nor 20* **P** *D&C* **P-in-c** W R HURDMAN, **C** S R PIRRIE
KING'S LYNN (St Peter) *see* Clenchwarton and W Lynn *Ely*
KINGS NORTON (St John the Baptist) *see* Gaulby *Leic*
KINGS NORTON (St Nicholas) *Birm 4* **P** *Patr Bd* **TR** M F LEIGH, **TV** E I PITTS, R BRISTOW, S C WINTER, **NSM** M G HUDSON
KING'S PYON (St Mary the Virgin) *see* Canon Pyon w Kings Pyon and Birley *Heref*
KINGS RIPTON (St Peter) *Ely 9* **P** *Lord de Ramsey* **P-in-c** B J HYDER-SMITH
KING'S STANLEY (St George) *see* The Stanleys *Glouc*
KING'S SUTTON (St Peter and St Paul) and Newbottle and Charlton *Pet 1* **P** *SMF and Lady Townsend (jt)* **V** J D CORBETT
KING'S WALDEN (St Mary) and Offley w Lilley *St Alb 4* **P** *Sir Thomas Pilkington, Bt (2 turns), St Jo Coll Cam (1 turn), D K C Salusbury-Hughes Esq and Mrs P A L McGrath (2 turns)* **P-in-c** J SCHILD
KING'S WORTHY (St Mary) (St Mary's Chapel) *Win 13* **P** *Univ Coll Ox and Lord Northbrook (alt)* **R** R A CORNE
KINGSBRIDGE (St Edmund the King and Martyr) and Dodbrooke *Ex 14* **P** *Bp* **R** C C ROBINS
KINGSBURY (Holy Innocents) *Lon 21* **P** *D&C St Paul's* **V** D E NENO, **NSM** A J HOPKINS
KINGSBURY (St Andrew) *Lon 21* **P** *The Crown* **V** J T SMITH
KINGSBURY (St Peter and St Paul) *Birm 11* **P** *Bp* **V** M D MARSH
KINGSBURY EPISCOPI (St Martin) w East Lambrook, Hambridge and Earnshill *B & W 15* **P** *Bp (2 turns), D&C (1 turn)* **V** D A BURTON, A R ELWOOD
KINGSCLERE (St Mary) *Win 6* **P** *Bp* **P-in-c** M J BENTON, **NSM** A J ASKEW
KINGSCLERE WOODLANDS (St Paul) *see* Ashford Hill w Headley *Win*
KINGSCOTE (St John the Baptist) *see* Horsley and Newington Bagpath w Kingscote *Glouc*
KINGSDON (All Saints) *see* Somerton w Compton Dundon, the Charltons etc *B & W*
KINGSDOWN (St Edmund the King and Martyr) *Roch 10* **P** *D&C* **R** D P WREN
KINGSDOWN (St John the Evangelist) *see* Ringwould w Kingsdown *Cant*
KINGSEY (St Nicholas) *see* Haddenham w Cuddington, Kingsey etc *Ox*
KINGSHURST (St Barnabas) *Birm 10* **P** *Bp* **P-in-c** J FORTUNE-WOOD
KINGSKERSWELL (St Mary) w Coffinswell *Ex 10* **P** *V St Marychurch* **V** J F LEONARD
KINGSLAND (St Michael and All Angels) w Eardisland, Aymestrey and Leinthall Earles *Heref 7* **P** *DBP (2 turns), Ld Chan (1 turn)* **R** S B THOMAS, **NSM** J W M ROBINSON
KINGSLEY (All Saints) *see* E and W Worldham, Hartley Mauditt w Kingsley etc *Win*
KINGSLEY (St John the Evangelist) *Ches 3* **P** *V Frodsham* **P-in-c** R H N ROBB, **C** J E PEARCE
KINGSLEY (St Werburgh) *Lich 6* **P** *Mrs G I A Dalrymple-Hamilton* **P-in-c** L R PRICE
KINGSLEY MOOR (St John the Baptist) *see* Kingsley *Lich*
KINGSNORTH (St Michael and All Angels) w Shadoxhurst *Cant 10* **P** *Abp* **P-in-c** S E McLACHLAN
KINGSNYMPTON (St James) *see* S Molton w Nymet St George, High Bray etc *Ex*
KINGSTAG (not known) *see* Stock and Lydlinch *Sarum*
KINGSTANDING (St Luke) *Birm 3* **P** *Bp* **V** D J A SMITH, **C** R D WOODWARD, B A I SMART
KINGSTANDING (St Mark) *Birm 3* **P** *Bp* **V** R A FARRELL, **C** R D WOODWARD, **Hon C** A BARTLETT
KINGSTEIGNTON (St Michael) *Ex 11* **P** *Bp* **V** C H BENSON
KINGSTHORPE (St John the Baptist) w Northampton St David *Pet 4* **P** *Patr Bd* **TR** J T SHORT, **TV** R J LEE, L A W SWABY, **Par Dn** C P ROSE-CASEMORE
KINGSTON (All Saints and St Andrew) *see* Bourn and Kingston w Caxton and Longstowe *Ely*
KINGSTON (St Giles) *see* Barham w Bishopsbourne and Kingston *Cant*
KINGSTON (St James) *see* Modbury, Bigbury, Ringmore w Kingston etc *Ex*
KINGSTON (St James) *see* Shorwell w Kingston *Portsm*
KINGSTON (St James), Langton Matravers and Worth Matravers *Sarum 9* **P** *Bp, Lt-Col H E Scott, and R Swanage and Studland (jt)* **R** R N K WATTON
KINGSTON (St Pancras) *see* Iford w Kingston and Rodmell *Chich*
KINGSTON (St Winifred) and Ratcliffe-on-Soar *S'well 10* **P** *Lord Belper* **P-in-c** R A SPRAY, **NSM** J M GORICK
KINGSTON BAGPUIZE (St John the Baptist) *see* Fyfield w Tubney and Kingston Bagpuize *Ox*
KINGSTON BUCI (St Julian) *Chich 4* **P** *Lord Egremont* **R** S C KERSLEY, **C** E K HOWARD
KINGSTON DEVERILL (St Mary) *see* Cley Hill Warminster *Sarum*
KINGSTON HILL (St Paul) *S'wark 16* **P** *DBP* **V** R M de VIAL
KINGSTON LACY (St Stephen) *see* Sturminster Marshall, Kingston Lacy and Shapwick *Sarum*
KINGSTON LISLE (St John the Baptist) *see* Ridgeway *Ox*
KINGSTON PARK (not known) *see* Newc Epiphany *Newc*
KINGSTON SEYMOUR (All Saints) *see* Yatton Moor *B & W*
KINGSTON ST MARY (Blessed Virgin Mary) Broomfield and Cheddon Fitzpaine *B & W 18* **P** *D&C Bris and Bp (alt)* **R** R J EDWARDS, **NSM** M M T DOBLE
KINGSTON UPON HULL (Ascension) *see* Derringham Bank *York*
KINGSTON UPON HULL (Most Holy and Undivided Trinity) *York 15* **P** *H Trin Hull & Distr Ch Patr Soc Ltd* **V** J W WALLER, **C** J M BEADLE, A BASH
KINGSTON UPON HULL (St Aidan) Southcoates *York 15* **P** *Simeon's Trustees* **V** M A FRYER, **C** B S DIXON
KINGSTON UPON HULL (St Alban) *York 15* **P** *Abp* **V** E T FORWARD, **C** C R HILLMAN
KINGSTON UPON HULL (St Cuthbert) *see* Hull St Cuth *York*
KINGSTON UPON HULL (St John the Baptist) *see* Newington w Dairycoates *York*
KINGSTON UPON HULL (St Mary) Sculcoates *see* Hull St Mary Sculcoates *York*
KINGSTON UPON HULL (St Mary the Virgin) *York 15* **P** *Abp* **P-in-c** P A BURKITT
KINGSTON UPON HULL (St Matthew w St Barnabas) *York 15* **P** *V Hull H Trin* **V** J A BAGSHAWE
KINGSTON UPON HULL (St Nicholas) *York 15* **P** *Abp* **V** R A SCRIVENER
KINGSTON UPON HULL (St Paul) *see* Sculcoates St Paul w Ch Ch and St Silas *York*
KINGSTON UPON HULL (St Stephen) *see* Hull St Steph Sculcoates *York*
KINGSTON UPON HULL (St Thomas) *see* Derringham Bank *York*
KINGSTON UPON THAMES (All Saints) (St John the Evangelist) *S'wark 16* **P** *K Coll Cam* **V** J BATES, **C** A MILLS, **Hon C** E J RICHARDSON
KINGSTON UPON THAMES (St Luke) *S'wark 16* **P** *Bp* **P-in-c** I C DAVIES
KINGSTON VALE (St John the Baptist) *S'wark 16* **P** *Bp* **P-in-c** P S HAUGHTON
KINGSTONE (St John and All Saints) *see* Ilminster and District *B & W*
KINGSTONE (St John the Baptist) *see* Uttoxeter Area *Lich*
KINGSTONE (St Michael and All Angels) w Clehonger, Eaton Bishop, Allensmore and Thruxton *Heref 1* **P** *Bp (2 turns), Prime Min (1 turn)* **R** B A M GILLETT
KINGSWEAR (St Thomas of Canterbury) *see* Brixham w Churston Ferrers and Kingswear *Ex*
KINGSWINFORD (St Mary) *Worc 10* **P** *Patr Bd* **TR** J S LUNGLEY
KINGSWOOD (Church of the Ascension) (Holy Trinity) *Bris 2* **P** *Patr Bd* **TR** R NEWTON, **TV** A J HEAGERTY, **C** C J PEARCE
KINGSWOOD (St Andrew) *S'wark 26* **P** *Bp and R&S Ch Trust (jt)* **V** P V FISHER, **Hon C** R F SHAW
KINGSWOOD (St Mary the Virgin) w Alderley and Hillesley *Glouc 7* **P** *Bp, DBP and R M G S Hale Esq (jt)* **P-in-c** S W ELDRIDGE
KINGSWOOD, LOWER (Wisdom of God) *see* Kingswood *S'wark*
KINGTON (St James) *see* Inkberrow w Cookhill and Kington w Dormston *Worc*
KINGTON (St Mary) w Huntington, Old Radnor, Kinnerton and Knill *Heref 5* **P** *Bp, D&C, and D&C Worc (jt)* **P-in-c** P TARLING
KINGTON (St Michael) *Bris 9* **P** *Patr Bd* **V** J A SMITH, **Hon C** G H EDWARDS

KINGTON, WEST (St Mary the Virgin) *Bris 9* **P** *Bp* **P-in-c** R V C LEWIS
KINGTON LANGLEY (St Peter) *see* Draycot *Bris*
KINGTON MAGNA (All Saints) *see* Gillingham *Sarum*
KINGTON UPON HULL (St Martin) *see* Hull St Martin w Transfiguration *York*
KINGWESTON (All Saints) *see* Keinton Mandeville w Lydford-on-Fosse etc *B & W*
KINLET (St John the Baptist) *see* Cleobury Mortimer w Hopton Wafers etc *Heref*
KINNERLEY (St Mary) w Melverley and Knockin w Maesbrook *Lich 19* **R** D N AUSTERBERRY
KINNERSLEY (St James) *see* Lyonshall w Titley, Almeley and Kinnersley *Heref*
KINNERTON (St Mary the Virgin) *see* Kington w Huntington, Old Radnor, Kinnerton etc *Heref*
KINNERTON, HIGHER (All Saints) *see* Dodleston *Ches*
KINNINVIE (Mission Room) *see* Barnard Castle w Whorlton *Dur*
KINOULTON (St Luke) *see* Hickling w Kinoulton and Broughton Sulney *S'well*
KINSBOURNE GREEN (St Mary) *see* Harpenden St Nic *St Alb*
KINSHAM (All Saints) *see* Presteigne w Discoed, Kinsham and Lingen *Heref*
KINSLEY (Ascension) w Wragby *Wakef 11* **P** *Bp and Lord St Oswald (jt)* **V** J F HARPER
KINSON (St Andrew) (St Philip) *Sarum 8* **P** *Patr Bd* **TR** V R BARRON, **TV** R G SAUNDERS, **C** J J MOULD, **NSM** J MOULD
KINTBURY (St Mary the Virgin) w Avington *Ox 14* **P** *DBP (2 turns), Bp (1 turn)* **P-in-c** D A PLUMMER
KINVER (St Peter) and Enville *Lich 25* **P** *Bp, Mrs E Bissill, and DBP (jt)* **R** W F R BATSON, **Hon C** M MORRIS, J H DEAKIN
KINWARTON (St Mary the Virgin) w Great Alne and Haselor *Cov 7* **P** *Bp* **P-in-c** S R BURCH
KIPPAX (St Mary the Virgin) w Allerton Bywater *Ripon 8* **P** *Bp* **TR** K A PAYNE, **TV** J SYKES, **C** G W COOPER
KIPPINGTON (St Mary) *Roch 9* **P** *DBP* **V** S R JONES
KIRBY, WEST (St Andrew) *Ches 8* **P** *D&C* **R** D C KELLY
KIRBY, WEST (St Bridget) *Ches 8* **P** *D&C* **R** D M FERRIDAY, **C** K G LOWE
KIRBY BEDON (St Andrew) *see* Rockland St Mary w Hellington, Bramerton etc *Nor*
KIRBY BELLARS (St Peter) *see* Upper Wreake *Leic*
KIRBY CANE (All Saints) *see* Gillingham w Geldeston, Stockton, Ellingham etc *Nor*
KIRBY GRINDALYTHE (St Andrew) *see* Weaverthorpe w Helperthorpe, Luttons Ambo etc *York*
KIRBY KNOWLE (St Wilfrid) *York 20* **P** *Abp* **P-in-c** P R A R HOARE
KIRBY-LE-SOKEN (St Michael) w Great Holland *Chelmsf 23* **P** *Bp and CPAS (jt)* **R** A H P BEAUCHAMP
KIRBY MISPERTON (St Laurence) w Normanby, Edston and Salton *York 21* **P** *Countess Feversham, Abp, and St Jo Coll Cam (by turn)* **R** D R SAMWAYS
KIRBY MUXLOE (St Bartholomew) *Leic 12* **P** *Bp* **TR** G H SUART, **TV** J A COUTTS
KIRBY-ON-THE-MOOR (All Saints), Cundall w Norton-le-Clay and Skelton-cum-Newby *Ripon 3* **P** *Bp, Sir Arthur Collins, and R E J Compton Esq (jt)* **V** *Vacant* (01423) 2551
KIRBY SIGSTON (St Lawrence) *see* Northallerton w Kirby Sigston *York*
KIRBY UNDERDALE (All Saints) *see* Bishop Wilton w Full Sutton, Kirby Underdale etc *York*
KIRBY WISKE (St John the Baptist) *see* Ainderby Steeple w Yafforth and Kirby Wiske etc *Ripon*
KIRDFORD (St John the Baptist) *Chich 11* **P** *Lord Egremont* **V** *Vacant* (01403) 820605
KIRK BRAMWITH (St Mary) *see* Fishlake w Sykehouse, Kirk Bramwith, Fenwick etc *Sheff*
KIRK DEIGHTON (All Saints) *see* Spofforth w Kirk Deighton *Ripon*
KIRK ELLA (St Andrew) *York 15* **P** *Patr Bd* **TR** J A G SCOTT, **TV** W D NICHOL, **NSM** B S BOWES
KIRK FENTON (St Mary) w Kirkby Wharfe and Ulleskelfe *York 1* **P** *Abp and Trustees of Capt J Fielden* **V** R A CLEGG
KIRK HALLAM (All Saints) *Derby 13* **P** *Bp* **P-in-c** J O GOLDSMITH, **NSM** M L GOLDSMITH
KIRK HAMMERTON (St John the Baptist) *see* Lower Nidderdale *Ripon*
KIRK IRETON (Holy Trinity) *see* Wirksworth *Derby*
KIRK LANGLEY (St Michael) *Derby 11* **P** *G Meynell Esq and J M Clark-Maxwell Esq (alt)* **P-in-c** K JARDIN, **NSM** H M MEYNELL
KIRK MAUGHOLD (St Maughold) *see* Maughold *S & M*
KIRK SANDALL and Edenthorpe (Good Shepherd) *Sheff 9* **P** *Ld Chan* **R** J H MARTIN
KIRK SMEATON (St Peter) *see* Womersley and Kirk Smeaton *Wakef*
KIRKANDREWS ON EDEN (St Mary) *see* Burgh-by-Sands and Kirkbampton w Kirkandrews etc *Carl*
KIRKANDREWS ON ESK (St Andrew) *see* Nicholforest and Kirkandrews on Esk *Carl*
KIRKBAMPTON (St Peter) *see* Burgh-by-Sands and Kirkbampton w Kirkandrews etc *Carl*
KIRKBRIDE (St Bridget) *S & M 4* **P** *The Crown* **R** *Vacant* (0162488) 351
KIRKBRIDE (St Bridget or St Bride) w Newton Arlosh *Carl 3* **P** *Earl of Lonsdale and V Holme Cultram (alt)* **P-in-c** J T SPENCE
KIRKBURN (St Mary) *see* Wetwang and Garton-on-the-Wolds w Kirkburn *York*
KIRKBURTON (All Hallows) *Wakef 6* **P** *Bp* **V** D BARRACLOUGH
KIRKBY (St Andrew) *see* S Kelsey Gp *Linc*
KIRKBY (St Chad) (St Mark) (St Martin) (St Andrew) *Liv 7* **P** *Patr Bd* **TR** A B HAWLEY, **TV** A M DOYLE, J M MORRELL, **C** N G KELLEY, M M THORNTON, P S HUDD
KIRKBY, SOUTH (All Saints) *Wakef 11* **P** *Guild of All So* **V** T H KAYE
KIRKBY FLEETHAM (St Mary) w Langton on Swale and Scruton *Ripon 4* **P** *Bp Ripon and D&C York (jt)* **R** *Vacant* (01609) 748251
KIRKBY GREEN (Holy Cross) *see* Scopwick Gp *Linc*
KIRKBY IN ASHFIELD (St Thomas) *S'well 4* **P** *Bp* **V** M EVANS
KIRKBY IN ASHFIELD (St Wilfrid) *S'well 4* **P** *Bp* **R** A BUTT
KIRKBY-IN-CLEVELAND (St Augustine) *York 22* **P** *Abp* **V** D J BOASE
KIRKBY-IN-MALHAMDALE (St Michael the Archangel) w Coniston Cold *Bradf 5* **P** *Bp and D&C (jt)* **V** *Vacant* (01729) 830215
KIRKBY IRELETH (St Cuthbert) *Carl 8* **P** *D&C York* **V** G MURFET
KIRKBY LAYTHORPE (St Denys) *Linc 22* **P** *Bp and DBP (alt)* **R** R J ABRAHAM
KIRKBY LONSDALE (St Mary the Virgin) *Carl 9* **P** *Patr Bd* **TR** G W BETTRIDGE, **TV** R J A MITCHELL, **C** P S ATKINSON, **NSM** P FINLINSON, K W BATEMAN
KIRKBY MALHAM (St Michael the Archangel) *see* Kirkby-in-Malhamdale w Coniston Cold *Bradf*
KIRKBY MALLORY (All Saints) *see* Newbold de Verdun and Kirkby Mallory *Leic*
KIRKBY MALZEARD (St Andrew) *see* Fountains Gp *Ripon*
KIRKBY-ON-BAIN (St Mary) *see* Thornton Gp *Linc*
KIRKBY OVERBLOW (All Saints) *Ripon 1* **P** *Bp* **R** P A SUMMERS, **NSM** J P F CUMMINS
KIRKBY RAVENSWORTH (St Peter and St Felix) *see* Gilling and Kirkby Ravensworth *Ripon*
KIRKBY STEPHEN (not known) w Mallerstang and Crosby Garrett w Soulby *Carl 1* **P** *Bp, Earl of Lonsdale, and Lord Hothfield (jt)* **C** D B de M LEATHES, **NSM** I F MacDOUGALL, J WRIGHT
KIRKBY THORE (St Michael) w Temple Sowerby and Newbiggin *Carl 1* **P** *Lord Hothfield (3 turns), Major and Mrs Sawrey-Cookson (1 turn)* **R** I L McLOUGHLIN
KIRKBY UNDERWOOD (St Mary and All Saints) *see* Ringstone in Aveland Gp *Linc*
KIRKBY WHARFE (St John the Baptist) *see* Kirk Fenton w Kirkby Wharfe and Ulleskelfe *York*
KIRKBY WOODHOUSE (St John the Evangelist) *S'well 4* **P** *Bp* **V** M J MACDONALD
KIRKBYMOORSIDE (All Saints) w Gillamoor, Farndale and Bransdale *York 18* **P** *Countess Feversham* **V** J D PURDY
KIRKCAMBECK (St Kentigern) *see* Lanercost w Kirkcambeck and Walton *Carl*
KIRKDALE (St Gregory) *York 18* **P** *Ox Univ* **V** J M WARDEN
KIRKDALE (St Lawrence) *Liv 3* **P** *CPAS* **V** *Vacant* 0151-922 5794
KIRKDALE (St Mary and St Athanasius) *Liv 3* **P** *Simeon's Trustees* **P-in-c** J C M BISSEX
KIRKDALE (St Paul) *see* Bootle St Mary w St Paul *Liv*
KIRKHAM (St Michael) *Blackb 11* **P** *Ch Ch Ox* **V** J K BROCKBANK
KIRKHAUGH (Holy Paraclete) *see* Alston Team *Newc*
KIRKHEATON (St Bartholomew) *see* Kirkwhelpington, Kirkharle, Kirkheaton and Cambo *Newc*
KIRKHEATON (St John the Baptist) *Wakef 1* **P** *Ch Trust Fund Trust* **R** W L HALLING, **C** D E MALE
KIRKHOLT (St Thomas) *Man 20* **P** *Bp* **C** J HILDITCH
KIRKLAND (Mission Church) *see* Lamplugh w Ennerdale *Carl*

KIRKLAND (St Lawrence) *see* Skirwith, Ousby and Melmerby w Kirkland *Carl*
KIRKLEATHAM (St Cuthbert) (St Hilda) *York 17* **P** *Abp* **V** C GREENWELL, **C** P J MOTHERSDALE
KIRKLEVINGTON (St Martin) *York 22* **P** *Abp* **V** D MOORE
KIRKLEY (St Peter and St John) *Nor 9* **P** *Bp and DBP (jt)* **R** J T EYRE
KIRKLINGTON (St Michael) w Burneston and Wath and Pickhill *Ripon 4* **P** *Ch Soc Trust, Mrs M St B Anderson, G W Prior-Wandesforde Esq, and DBP (jt)* **R** C N R MANSELL
KIRKLINGTON (St Swithin) w Hockerton *S'well 15* **P** *Bp* **P-in-c** D J BARTLETT
KIRKLINTON (St Cuthbert) *see* Bewcastle, Stapleton and Kirklinton etc *Carl*
KIRKNEWTON (St Gregory) *see* Glendale Gp *Newc*
KIRKOSWALD (St Oswald), Renwick and Ainstable *Carl 4* **P** *Bp and E P Ecroyd Esq (jt)* **V** D M FOWLER
KIRKSTALL (St Stephen) *Ripon 7* **P** *Patrons Leeds St Pet* **V** *Vacant* 0113-278 1007
KIRKSTEAD (St Leonard) *see* Woodhall Spa Gp *Linc*
KIRKTHORPE (St Peter) *see* Warmfield *Wakef*
KIRKWHELPINGTON (St Bartholomew) w Kirkharle, Kirkheaton and Cambo *Newc 11* **P** *Ld Chan (2 turns), J P P Anderson Esq (1 turn), and Bp (1 turn)* **V** R A FERGUSON
KIRMINGTON (St Helen) *see* Brocklesby Park *Linc*
KIRMOND-LE-MIRE (St Martin) *see* Walesby *Linc*
KIRSTEAD (St Margaret) *see* Brooke, Kirstead, Mundham w Seething and Thwaite *Nor*
KIRTLING (All Saints) *Ely 4* **P** *Mrs D A Bowlby and Countess Ellesmere (alt)* **V** C A SINDALL
KIRTLINGTON (St Mary the Virgin) *see* Akeman *Ox*
KIRTON (Holy Trinity) *S'well 3* **P** *SMF* **R** C C LEVY
KIRTON (St Mary and St Martin) w Falkenham *St E 2* **P** *Ld Chan* **P-in-c** G L GRANT
KIRTON HOLME (Christ Church) *see* Brothertoft Gp *Linc*
KIRTON IN HOLLAND (St Peter and St Paul) *see* Frampton w Kirton in Holland *Linc*
KIRTON IN LINDSEY (St Andrew) *Linc 6* **P** *Bp* **V** D I WALKER
KISLINGBURY (St Luke) and Harpole *Pet 3* **P** *Bp and Sir Stephen Hastings (alt)* **R** D G BOND
KITT GREEN (St Francis of Assisi) *see* Pemberton St Fran Kitt Green *Liv*
KITTISFORD (St Nicholas) *see* Wellington and Distr *B & W*
KLIVE (Blessed Virgin Mary) *see* Quantoxhead *B & W*
KNAITH (St Mary) *see* Lea Gp *Linc*
KNAPHILL (Holy Trinity) *Guildf 12* **P** *V Woking St Jo* **V** R B WATSON
KNAPTON (St Peter) *see* Trunch *Nor*
KNAPWELL (All Saints) *see* Elsworth w Knapwell *Ely*
KNARESBOROUGH (Holy Trinity) (St John the Baptist) *Ripon 1* **P** *Bp and Earl of Harewood (jt)* **R** A C BETTS, **C** D J WHEELER, T M TUNLEY
KNARESDALE (St Jude) *see* Alston Team *Newc*
KNEBWORTH (St Martin) (St Mary the Virgin and St Thomas of Canterbury) *St Alb 23* **P** *Hon D A Fromanteel* **R** T W HARFORD
KNEESALL (St Bartholomew) w Laxton and Wellow *S'well 3* **P** *DBP and Bp (jt)* **V** V E RAMPTON
KNEETON (St Helen) *see* E Bridgford and Kneeton *S'well*
KNIGHTLEY (Christ Church) *see* High Offley and Norbury *Lich*
KNIGHTON (St John the Baptist) *see* Clarendon Park St Jo w Knighton St Mich *Leic*
KNIGHTON (St Mary Magdalene) (St Guthlac) *Leic 2* **P** *Bp* **V** C D ALLEN, **C** C M HEBDEN, **NSM** M R SEDEN, R J BONNEY
KNIGHTON (Village Hall) *see* Mucklestone *Lich*
KNIGHTON, WEST (St Peter) *see* Broadmayne, W Knighton, Owermoigne etc *Sarum*
KNIGHTON-ON-TEME (St Michael and All Angels) *see* Teme Valley N *Worc*
KNIGHTS ENHAM (St Michael and All Angels) (St Paul's Church Centre) *Win 3* **P** *Bp* **NSM** J M BENTALL
KNIGHTSBRIDGE (St Paul) Wilton Place *see* Wilton Place St Paul *Lon*
KNIGHTWICK (St Mary) *see* Martley and Wichenford, Knightwick etc *Worc*
KNILL (St Michael and All Angels) *see* Kington w Huntington, Old Radnor, Kinnerton etc *Heref*
KNIPTON (All Saints) *see* High Framland Parishes *Leic*
KNIVETON (St Michael and All Angels) *see* Fenny Bentley, Kniveton, Thorpe and Tissington *Derby*
KNOCKHOLT (St Katharine) w Halstead *Roch 9* **P** *D&C* **R** D M FLAGG
KNOCKIN (St Mary) *see* Kinnerley w Melverley and Knockin w Maesbrook *Lich*
KNODISHALL (St Lawrence) *see* Aldringham w Thorpe, Knodishall w Buxlow etc *St E*
KNOOK (St Margaret) *see* Heytesbury and Sutton Veny *Sarum*
KNOSSINGTON (St Peter) *see* Whatborough Gp of Par *Leic*
KNOTTING (St Margaret) *see* Sharnbrook and Knotting w Souldrop *St Alb*
KNOTTINGLEY (St Botolph) *Wakef 11* **P** *Bp and V Pontefract (alt)* **V** H N LAWRANCE, **C** C D LETHBRIDGE
KNOTTY ASH (St John) *Liv 2* **P** *R W Derby* **V** J G M ROOKE
KNOWBURY (St Paul) *Heref 12* **P** *Bp* **P-in-c** D M BURGESS
KNOWBURY (St Peter's Mission Room) Clee Hill *see* Wigmore Abbey *Heref*
KNOWL HILL (St Peter) w Littlewick *Ox 13* **P** *Bp and Trustees (alt)* **V** P NEWTON
KNOWLE (Holy Nativity) *Bris 3* **P** *Bp* **V** K NEWTON, **C** S D ELLIS, **NSM** J F HOUSE
KNOWLE (Mission Room) *see* Coreley w Doddington *Heref*
KNOWLE (St Barnabas) and Holy Cross Inns Court *Bris 3* **P** *Bp and Bris Ch Trustees (jt)* **V** R K A THOMPSON, **C** B P LUCK, J V THOMPSON
KNOWLE (St Boniface) *see* Crediton and Shobrooke *Ex*
KNOWLE (St John) *see* E Budleigh w Bicton and Otterton *Ex*
KNOWLE (St John the Baptist) (St Lawrence and St Anne) *Birm 12* **P** *Bp* **V** A J M DOW, **C** E W RUSSELL, D M DEWES
KNOWLE (St Martin) *Bris 3* **P** *Bp* **V** R WARD
KNOWSLEY (St Mary) *Liv 2* **P** *Lord Derby* **V** E F H GRIMSHAW, **Hon C** J T LEIGHTON
KNOWSTONE (St Peter) *see* Bishopsnympton, Rose Ash, Mariansleigh etc *Ex*
KNOYLE, EAST (St Mary the Virgin), Semley and Sedgehill *Sarum 13* **P** *Bp and Ch Ch Ox* **P-in-c** P J RIDLEY
KNOYLE, WEST (St Mary the Virgin) *see* Mere w W Knoyle and Maiden Bradley *Sarum*
KNUTSFORD (St Cross) Cross Town *Ches 12* **P** *Mrs J Singer* **V** J R HEATON
KNUTSFORD (St John the Baptist) and Toft *Ches 12* **P** *Bp (3 turns), Mrs L M Anderson (1 turn)* **V** M W WALTERS, **C** D J PAGE
KNUTTON (St Mary) *Lich 9* **P** *Sir Beville Stanier, Bt and T H G Howard-Sneyd Esq (alt)* **V** P G HOUGH, **C** P M JELF, **NSM** K R STABLES
KNUZDEN (St Oswald) *Blackb 2* **P** *Bp* **V** C J NELSON, **NSM** K THOMAS
KNYPERSLEY (St John the Evangelist) *Lich 8* **P** *CPAS* **V** A E BACKHOUSE
KYME, NORTH (St Luke) *see* Kirkby Laythorpe *Linc*
KYME, SOUTH (St Mary and All Saints) *as above*
KYNNERSLEY (St Chad) *see* Edgmond w Kynnersley and Preston Wealdmoors *Lich*
KYRE WYARD (St Mary) *see* Teme Valley S *Worc*
LACEBY (St Margaret) *Linc 10* **P** *Earl of Yarborough and Ridley Hall Cam (jt)* **R** A J ADAMSON
LACEY GREEN (Church Hall) *see* Wilmslow *Ches*
LACEY GREEN (St John the Evangelist) *Ox 21* **P** *R Princes Risborough* **P-in-c** R D S CAINK
LACH DENNIS (All Saints) *see* Lostock Gralam *Ches*
LACHE (St Mark) cum Saltney *Ches 2* **P** *Bp* **V** T G N GREEN, **C** B V GAUGE, S F WALKER, R M HINTON
LACKFORD (St Lawrence) *see* Culford, W Stow and Wordwell w Flempton etc *St E*
LACOCK (St Cyriac) w Bowden Hill *Bris 9* **P** *A M Burnett-Brown Esq (2 turns), Ms Z M Dunlop (1 turn)* **Dn-in-c** C A M MANN
LADBROKE (All Saints) *see* Harbury and Ladbroke *Cov*
LADDINGFORD (St Mary) *see* Yalding w Collier Street *Roch*
LADOCK (St Ladoca) *see* Probus, Ladock and Grampound w Creed and St Erme *Truro*
LADY BAY (All Hallows) *S'well 10* **P** *Bp* **V** R W BRECKLES
LADYBARN (St Chad) *Man 8* **P** *Bp* **R** D K PRYCE
LADYBROOK (St Mary the Virgin) *S'well 2* **P** *Bp* **V** W STOCKTON
LADYWOOD (St John the Evangelist) *see* Birm St Jo Ladywood *Birm*
LAFFORD, SOUTH *Linc 22* **P** *G Heathcote Esq, Bp, J Wilson Esq, D&C, DBP, N Playne Esq, Sir Bruno Welby Bt, and Baroness Willoughby de Eresby (by turn)* **R** S H SPEERS, **C** A C R BALFOUR
LAINDON (St Nicholas) w Dunton *Chelmsf 6* **P** *Bp* **R** N C PAUL
LAIRA (St Augustine) *see* Plymouth Em, St Paul Efford and St Aug *Ex*
LAIRA (St Mary the Virgin) Plymouth *Ex 23* **P** *Bp* **V** *Vacant* (01752) 257284
LAISTERDYKE (St Mary) *Bradf 3* **P** *Simeon's Trustees* **V** A F POPPLEWELL
LAITHKIRK (not known) *see* Romaldkirk w Laithkirk *Ripon*

LAKE (Good Shepherd) *Portsm 7* **P** *Bp* **P-in-c** R M SMITH
LAKENHAM (St Alban) *Nor 3* **P** *D&C* **P-in-c** D K ALEXANDER
LAKENHAM (St John the Baptist and All Saints) *Nor 3* **P** *D&C* **V** A L BEWLEY, **Hon C** G M BRIDGES
LAKENHAM (St Mark) w Trowse *Nor 1* **P** *D&C* **V** J L WILSON
LAKENHEATH (St Mary) *St E 11* **P** *D&C Ely* **V** J W MATHER
LALEHAM (All Saints) *Lon 13* **P** *Earl of Lucan* **V** P R BROWN, **C** G L WARREN
LAMARSH (Holy Innocents) *see* Alphamstone w Lamarsh and Pebmarsh *Chelmsf*
LAMBERHURST (St Mary) and Matfield *Roch 8* **P** *D&C and V Brenchley (jt)* **V** R J MIDDLEWICK
LAMBETH, NORTH (St Anselm) (St Mary's Mission) (St Peter) *S'wark 12* **P** *The Crown (1 turn), Patr Bd (2 turns)* **TR** I HARPER, **TV** K WOOLHOUSE
LAMBETH, SOUTH (St Anne and All Saints) *S'wark 12* **P** *Abp and Bp* **V** G M KENDAL, **Hon C** P A PACKER
LAMBETH, SOUTH (St Stephen) *S'wark 12* **P** *CPAS* **V** I D FARLEY
LAMBLEY (Holy Trinity) *S'well 11* **P** *Revd W J Gull* **P-in-c** N PEYTON
LAMBLEY (St Mary and St Patrick) *see* Alston Team *Newc*
LAMBOURN (St Michael and All Angels) *Ox 14* **P** *Bp* **V** W J STEWART
LAMBOURNE (St Mary and All Saints) w Abridge and Stapleford Abbotts *Chelmsf 25* **P** *CCC Cam and Ld Chan (alt)* **P-in-c** R J HOARE, **NSM** R A WALTERS
LAMBROOK, EAST (St James) *see* Kingsbury Episcopi w E Lambrook, Hambridge etc *B & W*
LAMERTON (St Peter) *see* Milton Abbot, Dunterton, Lamerton etc *Ex*
LAMESLEY (St Andrew) *Dur 12* **P** *Bp* **V** N B WARNER
LAMMAS (St Andrew) *see* Buxton w Oxnead, Lammas and Brampton *Nor*
LAMORBEY (Holy Redeemer) *Roch 17* **P** *Bp* **V** N I KERR
LAMORBEY (Holy Trinity) *Roch 17* **P** *D Malcolm Esq* **V** D V COSSAR
LAMORRAN (Holy Trinity) and Merther *Truro 6* **P** *Viscount Falmouth* **R** *Vacant* (01872) 52431
LAMORRAN Tresillian (Holy Trinity) *see* Lamorran and Merther *Truro*
LAMP *Ox 27* **P** *CPAS* **R** S A WEEDEN
LAMPLUGH (St Michael) w Ennerdale *Carl 5* **P** *Trustees* **R** J P SIMPSON
LAMPORT (All Saints) *see* Maidwell w Draughton, Lamport w Faxton *Pet*
LAMYATT (St Mary and St John) *see* Bruton and Distr *B & W*
LANCASTER (Christ Church) (Christ Church Worship Centre) w St John and St Anne *Blackb 12* **P** *V Lanc and Trustees (alt)* **V** P J BALLARD, **C** A ROUNDHILL, **NSM** B K HARDING
LANCASTER (St Chad) *see* Skerton St Chad *Blackb*
LANCASTER (St Mary) *Blackb 12* **P** *Trustees* **V** M E BARTLETT, **C** G W NELSON, T E A PARK
LANCASTER (St Paul) *see* Scotforth *Blackb*
LANCASTER (St Thomas) *Blackb 12* **P** *CPAS* **V** P G GUINNESS
LANCHESTER (All Saints) *Dur 4* **P** *Ld Chan* **V** P WATERHOUSE
LANCING (St James the Less) w Coombes *Chich 5* **P** *Bp Lon* **R** R G RUSSELL, **C** R T A FARROW
LANCING (St Michael and All Angels) *Chich 5* **P** *Bp* **V** B G CARTER
LANDBEACH (All Saints) *Ely 6* **P** *CCC Cam* **R** D P E REINDORP
LANDCROSS (Holy Trinity) *see* Bideford, Northam, Westward Ho!, Appledore etc *Ex*
LANDEWEDNACK (St Wynwallow) *see* St Ruan w St Grade and Landewednack *Truro*
LANDFORD (St Andrew) *see* Bramshaw and Landford w Plaitford *Sarum*
LANDKEY (St Paul) *see* Barnstaple *Ex*
LANDRAKE (St Michael) w St Erney and Botus Fleming *Truro 11* **P** *Bp and MMCET (jt)* **V** M GRIFFITHS
LANDSCOVE (St Matthew) *see* Broadhempston, Woodland, Staverton etc *Ex*
LANDULPH (St Leonard and St Dilpe) *see* St Dominic, Landulph and St Mellion w Pillaton *Truro*
LANDYWOOD (St Andrew) *see* Gt Wyrley *Lich*
LANE END (Holy Trinity) w Cadmore End *Ox 29* **P** *Bp* **V** R H JENNINGS
LANEAST (St Sidwell and St Gulvat) *see* Altarnon w Bolventor, Laneast and St Clether *Truro*
LANEHAM (St Peter) *see* Rampton w Laneham, Treswell, Cottam and Stokeham *S'well*
LANERCOST (St Mary Magdalene) w Kirkcambeck and Walton *Carl 2* **P** *Bp, Adn, Earl of Carlisle, and PCC Lanercost (jt)* **P-in-c** C J MORRIS
LANESIDE (St Peter) *Blackb 1* **P** *V Haslingden St Jas* **V** J W FINCH
LANGAR (St Andrew) *see* Cropwell Bishop w Colston Bassett, Granby etc *S'well*
LANGCLIFFE (St John the Evangelist) w Stainforth and Horton-in-Ribblesdale *Bradf 5* **P** *Bp, Adn Craven, W R G Bell Esq, N Caton Esq, and Churchwardens of Horton-in-Ribblesdale (jt)* **P-in-c** R G WOOD
LANGDALE (Holy Trinity) (Mission Chapel) *Carl 10* **P** *R Grasmere* **V** *Vacant* (015394) 37267
LANGDALE END (St Peter) *see* Wykeham and Hutton Buscel *York*
LANGDON, EAST (St Augustine) *see* St Margarets-at-Cliffe w Westcliffe etc *Cant*
LANGDON, WEST (St Mary the Virgin) *as above*
LANGDON HILLS (St Mary and All Saints) *Chelmsf 6* **P** *D&C St Paul's* **R** A BARRETT, **C** A P PARSONS
LANGFORD (Blessed Virgin Mary) *see* Burrington and Churchill *B & W*
LANGFORD (St Andrew) *St Alb 16* **P** *Ld Chan* **V** *Vacant* (01462) 700248
LANGFORD (St Bartholomew) w Holme *S'well 3* **P** *Bp* **P-in-c** A K SHAW
LANGFORD (St Giles) *see* Heybridge w Langford *Chelmsf*
LANGFORD (St Matthew) *see* Shill Valley and Broadshire *Ox*
LANGFORD, LITTLE (St Nicholas of Mira) *see* Yarnbury *Sarum*
LANGFORD BUDVILLE (St Peter) *see* Wellington and Distr *B & W*
LANGHAM (not known) *see* Gillingham *Sarum*
LANGHAM (St Mary the Virgin) *see* Boxted w Langham *Chelmsf*
LANGHAM (St Mary the Virgin) *see* Badwell Ash w Gt Ashfield, Stowlangtoft etc *St E*
LANGHAM (St Peter and St Paul) *Pet 14* **P** *Bp* **V** *Vacant* (01572) 722969
LANGHAM EPISCOPI (St Andrew and St Mary) *see* Stiffkey and Cockthorpe w Morston, Langham etc *Nor*
LANGHAM PLACE (All Souls) *Lon 4* **P** *The Crown* **R** R T BEWES, **C** J R M COOK, R M TRIST, A RIDER, P BLACKHAM, R I TICE, **Hon C** J R W STOTT
LANGHO BILLINGTON (St Leonard) *Blackb 8* **P** *V Blackb* **V** Q H WILSON
LANGLEY (All Saints and Martyrs) and Parkfield *Man 18* **P** *Patr Bd* **P-in-c** P H MILLER, **TV** M G CROOK
LANGLEY (St Francis) *see* Fawley *Win*
LANGLEY (St John) *Birm 7* **P** *Bp* **V** R T ETHERIDGE
LANGLEY (St John the Evangelist) *see* Clavering w Langley and Arkesden *Chelmsf*
LANGLEY (St Mary) *see* Otham w Langley *Cant*
LANGLEY (St Mary the Virgin) *see* Wolverton w Norton Lindsey and Langley *Cov*
LANGLEY (St Michael) *see* Chedgrave w Hardley and Langley *Nor*
LANGLEY (St Michael and All Angels) *Birm 7* **P** *The Crown* **P-in-c** R T ETHERIDGE
LANGLEY BURRELL (St Peter) *see* Chippenham St Paul w Hardenhuish etc *Bris*
LANGLEY GREEN (St Leonard) *see* Ifield *Chich*
LANGLEY MARISH (St Mary the Virgin) *Ox 23* **P** *Patr Bd* **TR** J R HURST, **TV** A W CLEEVE, I P S GOODING, **NSM** M E COLEMAN
LANGLEY MARSH (St Luke Mission Church) *see* Wiveliscombe w Chipstable, Huish Champflower etc *B & W*
LANGLEY MILL (St Andrew) *Derby 12* **P** *V Heanor* **P-in-c** C L HUGHES
LANGLEY PARK (All Saints) *see* Esh *Dur*
LANGLEY PARK (St Peter's Church Hall) *see* Beckenham St Barn *Roch*
LANGLEY STREET (Mission Room) *see* Derby St Barn *Derby*
LANGLEYBURY (St Paul) *St Alb 7* **P** *D W A Loyd Esq* **V** F H GIMSON
LANGNEY (St Richard of Chichester) *Chich 16* **P** *Bp* **V** *Vacant* (01323) 761158
LANGOLD (St Luke) *S'well 6* **P** *Bp* **P-in-c** I R LILLEY
LANGPORT Area Churches, The *B & W 6* **P** *Patr Bd* **TV** S J CONNOR, **Hon C** A H G JONES, **NSM** A C PARFITT
LANGRICK (St Margaret of Scotland) *see* Brothertoft Gp *Linc*
LANGRIDGE (St Mary Magdalene) *see* Bath Weston All SS w N Stoke and Langridge *B & W*
LANGRISH (St John the Evangelist) *Portsm 5* **P** *Bp* **V** T E LOUDEN
LANGSTONE (St Nicholas) *see* Havant *Portsm*
LANGTOFT (St Michael) *see* Ness Gp *Linc*

LANGTOFT (St Peter) w Foxholes, Butterwick, Cottam and Thwing *York 11* **P** *Abp and Keble Coll Ox (2 turns), Ld Chan (1 turn)* **V** R EVELEIGH
LANGTON (St Andrew) *see* Settrington w N Grimston, Birdsall w Langton *York*
LANGTON (St Margaret) *see* Woodhall Spa Gp *Linc*
LANGTON (St Peter) *as above*
LANGTON, GREAT (St Wilfrid) *see* Kirkby Fleetham w Langton on Swale and Scruton *Ripon*
LANGTON, GREAT (The Good Shepherd) *as above*
LANGTON BY PARTNEY (St Peter and St Paul) w Sutterby *Linc 7* **P** *Mrs D E P Douglas* **R** G ROBSON
LANGTON-BY-WRAGBY (St Giles) *see* Wragby *Linc*
LANGTON GREEN (All Saints) *Roch 12* **P** *R Speldhurst* **V** B D SIMMONS
LANGTON HERRING (St Peter) *see* Abbotsbury, Portesham and Langton Herring *Sarum*
LANGTON LONG (All Saints) *see* Blandford Forum and Langton Long *Sarum*
LANGTON MATRAVERS (St George) *see* Kingston, Langton Matravers and Worth Matravers *Sarum*
LANGTON ON SWALE (St Wilfrid) *see* Kirkby Fleetham w Langton on Swale and Scruton *Ripon*
LANGTREE *Ox 6* **P** *Patr Bd* **TR** D R OSBORN, **TV** C D ROGERS, **NSM** N E MOSS
LANGTREE (not known) *see* Shebbear, Buckland Filleigh, Sheepwash etc *Ex*
LANGWATHBY (St Peter) *see* Addingham, Edenhall, Langwathby and Culgaith *Carl*
LANGWITH, UPPER (Holy Cross) *see* E Scarsdale *Derby*
LANGWORTH (St Hugh) *see* Barlings *Linc*
LANHYDROCK (St Hydrock) *see* Bodmin w Lanhydrock and Lanivet *Truro*
LANIVET (St Ia) *as above*
LANLIVERY (St Brevita) w Luxulyan *Truro 10* **P** *Bp (1 turn), Adn Bodmin (1 turn), and DBP (2 turns)* **V** D J KEIGHLEY
LANNER (Christ Church) *see* Redruth w Lanner and Treleigh *Truro*
LANREATH (St Marnarck) *Truro 12* **P** *J B Kitson Esq and Mrs S R Parker (alt)* **R** *Vacant* (01503) 220310
LANSALLOS (St Ildierna) *Truro 12* **P** *DBP and W Gundry-Mills Esq (alt)* **R** *Vacant*
LANSDOWN (St Stephen) *see* Charlcombe w Bath St Steph *B & W*
LANTEGLOS BY CAMELFORD (St Julitta) w Advent *Truro 10* **P** *Duchy of Cornwall* **R** S SMITH
LANTEGLOS BY FOWEY (St Wyllow) *Truro 12* **P** *D&C* **P-in-c** J S HALKES
LAPAL (St Peter) *see* Halesowen *Worc*
LAPFORD (St Thomas of Canterbury), Nymet Rowland and Coldridge *Ex 2* **P** *Bp* **P-in-c** D G BACON
LAPLEY (All Saints) w Wheaton Aston *Lich 2* **P** *Keble Coll Ox* **V** J R McMANUS, **Hon C** R C W DAMPIER
LAPWORTH (St Mary the Virgin) *Birm 6* **P** *Mert Coll Ox* **R** A V WILLMONT
LARCHFIELD (St George) *see* Boyne Hill *Ox*
LARKFIELD (Holy Trinity) *Roch 7* **P** *DBP* **V** D J WALKER
LARLING (St Ethelbert) *see* E w W Harling, Bridgham w Roudham, Larling etc *Nor*
LASBOROUGH (St Mary) *see* Shipton Moyne w Westonbirt and Lasborough *Glouc*
LASHAM (St Mary) *see* Bentworth and Shalden and Lasham *Win*
LASHBROOK (Mission Room) *see* Shiplake w Dunsden *Ox*
LASTINGHAM (St Mary) w Appleton-le-Moors, Rosedale and Cropton *York 18* **P** *Abp (2 turns), Ld Chan (1 turn)* **V** D H BRYANT
LATCHFORD (Christ Church) *Ches 4* **P** *R Grappenhall* **V** C J P CRISALL, **NSM** W P POVEY
LATCHFORD (St James) (St Hilda) *Ches 4* **P** *R Grappenhall* **V** J T OWEN
LATCHINGDON (Christ Church) *see* Creeksea w Althorne, Latchingdon and N Fambridge *Chelmsf*
LATHBURY (All Saints) *see* Newport Pagnell w Lathbury and Moulsoe *Ox*
LATHOM PARK (St John) *see* Ormskirk *Liv*
LATIMER (St Mary Magdalene) *see* Chenies and Lt Chalfont, Latimer and Flaunden *Ox*
LATTON (St John the Baptist) *see* Cricklade w Latton *Bris*
LAUGHTON (All Saints) *see* Corringham and Blyton Gp *Linc*
LAUGHTON (All Saints) w Ripe and Chalvington *Chich 18* **P** *Earl of Chich, Hertf Coll Ox, and BNC Ox (by turn)* **R** D M FAREY
LAUGHTON (St Luke) *see* Foxton w Gumley and Laughton and Lubenham *Leic*
LAUGHTON-EN-LE-MORTHEN (All Saints) w Throapham *Sheff 5* **P** *Bp* **V** W MOORE
LAUNCELLS (St Andrew and St Swithin) *see* Stratton and Launcells *Truro*
LAUNCESTON (St Mary Magdalene) (St Thomas the Apostle) *Truro 9* **P** *Bp and PCC (jt)* **V** T J G NEWCOMBE
LAUNCESTON (St Stephen) *see* St Stephen by Launceston *Truro*
LAUNTON (Assumption of the Blessed Virgin Mary) *see* Bicester w Bucknell, Caversfield and Launton *Ox*
LAVANT (St Mary) (St Nicholas) *Chich 3* **P** *Earl of March and Kinrara* **R** *Vacant* (01243) 527313
LAVENDER HILL (Ascension) *S'wark 15* **P** *Keble Coll Ox* **V** *Vacant* 0171-228 5340
LAVENDON (St Michael) w Cold Brayfield, Clifton Reynes and Newton Blossomville *Ox 27* **P** *T V Sutthery Esq, Revd S F Hamill-Stewart, Exors M E FarrerEsq, and Bp (jt)* **R** P J BOYLES
LAVENHAM (St Peter and St Paul) w Preston *St E 10* **P** *G&C Coll Cam, and Em Coll Cam (by turn)* **R** D M STIFF
LAVENHAM (St Peter and St Paul) *see* Lavenham w Preston *St E*
LAVER, HIGH (All Saints) w Magdalen Laver and Little Laver and Matching *Chelmsf 27* **P** *Bp* **P-in-c** P T C MASHEDER
LAVER, LITTLE (St Mary the Virgin) *see* High Laver w Magdalen Laver and Lt Laver etc *Chelmsf*
LAVERSTOCK (St Andrew) *Sarum 15* **P** *D&C* **P-in-c** K ROBINSON
LAVERSTOKE (St Mary) *see* Overton w Laverstoke and Freefolk *Win*
LAVERTON (The Blessed Virgin Mary) *see* Norton St Philip w Hemington, Hardington etc *B & W*
LAVINGTON, WEST and the Cheverells *Sarum 19* **P** *Bp* **R** *Vacant* (01380) 818388
LAVINGTON, WEST (St Mary Magdalene) *see* Cocking, Bepton and W Lavington *Chich*
LAWFORD (St Mary) *Chelmsf 20* **P** *St Jo Coll Cam* **R** P E BALL, **NSM** C M MITSON
LAWHITTON (St Michael) *see* Lezant w Lawhitton and S Petherwin w Trewen *Truro*
LAWLEY (St John the Evangelist) *see* Cen Telford *Lich*
LAWRENCE WESTON (St Peter) *Bris 8* **P** *Bp* **V** H W WARDALE
LAWSHALL (All Saints) w Shimplingthorne and Alpheton *St E 12* **P** *DBP and Lord de Saumarez (alt)* **R** *Vacant* (01284) 830184
LAWTON (All Saints) *see* Church Lawton *Ches*
LAWTON MOOR (St Michael) *Man 8* **P** *Bp* **V** P D ROLFE
LAXEY (Christ Church) *S & M 2* **P** *Bp* **V** W H MARTIN
LAXFIELD (All Saints) *St E 17* **P** *Simeon's Trustees* **P-in-c** M G T WALKEY
LAXTON (All Saints) *see* Bulwick, Blatherwycke w Harringworth and Laxton *Pet*
LAXTON (St Michael) *see* Kneesall w Laxton and Wellow *S'well*
LAXTON (St Peter) *see* Howden TM *York*
LAYER BRETON (St Mary the Virgin) *see* Birch w Layer Breton and Layer Marney *Chelmsf*
LAYER-DE-LA-HAYE (St John the Baptist) *Chelmsf 16* **P** *Bp* **V** M H CLARKE
LAYER MARNEY (St Mary the Virgin) *see* Birch w Layer Breton and Layer Marney *Chelmsf*
LAYHAM (St Andrew) *see* Hadleigh *St E*
LAYSTON W BUNTINGFORD (St Peter) *see* Aspenden, Buntingford and Westmill *St Alb*
LAYTON, EAST (Christ Church) *see* Forcett and Aldbrough and Melsonby *Ripon*
LAZONBY (St Nicholas) *see* Gt Salkeld w Lazonby *Carl*
LEA Group, The (St Helen) *Linc 2* **P** *Bp, DBP, Exors Lt Col J E W G Sandars (jt)* **R** *Vacant* (01427) 613188
LEA (St Christopher) (St Barnabas) *Blackb 14* **P** *Bp* **V** G LEWIS, **NSM** J T RICHARDSON
LEA (St Giles) *see* Garsdon, Lea and Cleverton and Charlton *Bris*
LEA, THE (St John the Baptist) *see* Ross w Brampton Abbotts, Bridstow, Peterstow etc *Heref*
LEA AND HOLLOWAY (Christ Church) *see* Tansley, Dethick, Lea and Holloway *Derby*
LEA CROSS (St Anne) *see* Pontesbury I and II *Heref*
LEA HALL (St Richard) *Birm 14* **P** *Bp* **P-in-c** P M BRACHER
LEA MARSTON (St John the Baptist) *see* The Whitacres and Shustoke *Birm*
LEADEN RODING (St Michael) and Abbess Roding and Beauchamp Roding w White Roding *Chelmsf 18* **P** *Ld Chan, Bp, and Viscount Gough (by turn)* **R** T J PIGREM
LEADENHAM (St Swithin) *Linc 23* **P** *P R Reeve Esq* **R** *Vacant* (01400) 73253
LEADGATE (St Ives) *see* Dipton and Leadgate *Dur*
LEAFIELD (St Michael and All Angels) *see* Ramsden, Finstock and Fawler, Leafield etc *Ox*

LEAGRAVE (St Luke) *St Alb 14* **P** *Bp* **V** M D PETITT, **C** S M HARDWICKE
LEAHOLM (St James' Chapel) *see* Glaisdale *York*
LEAKE (St Mary) w Over and Nether Silton and Kepwick *York 20* **P** *Abp* **P-in-c** P R A R HOARE
LEAKE, EAST (St Mary), WEST (St Helena), Stanford-on-Soar, Rempstone and Costock *S'well 10* **P** *Bp, DBP, Lord Belper, and SS Coll Cam (jt)* **R** S J SMITH, **C** K WAKEFIELD, **NSM** G C HETHERINGTON
LEAKE, NEW (St Jude) *see* Stickney Gp *Linc*
LEAKE, OLD (St Mary) w Wrangle *Linc 20* **P** *Bp and DBP (alt)* **V** *Vacant* (01205) 870130
LEAM LANE (St Andrew) *Dur 12* **P** *Bp* **V** *Vacant* 0191-469 3257
LEAMINGTON, SOUTH (St John the Baptist) *Cov 11* **P** *Bp* **V** D W LAWSON
LEAMINGTON HASTINGS (All Saints) and Birdingbury *Cov 6* **P** *Bp and Mrs H M O Lodder (alt)* **V** *Vacant* (01926) 632455
LEAMINGTON PRIORS (All Saints) *Cov 11* **P** *Bp* **P-in-c** G F WARNER, **C** S J BROWN
LEAMINGTON PRIORS (St Mary) *Cov 11* **P** *Ch Patr Trust* **V** M RODHAM, **C** M WARNES
LEAMINGTON PRIORS (St Paul) *Cov 11* **P** *Ch Patr Trust* **V** B MERRINGTON, **C** M M MILLER
LEAMINGTON SPA (Holy Trinity) and Old Milverton *Cov 11* **P** *Bp and M Heber-Percy Esq (jt)* **P-in-c** G F WARNER, **C** S J BROWN
LEAMINGTON SPA (St Mark New Milverton) *see* New Milverton *Cov*
LEAMORE (St Aidan) *see* Blakenall Heath *Lich*
LEASINGHAM (St Andrew) *Linc 22* **P** *DBP* **P-in-c** C M J THODY
LEASOWE (St Chad) *Ches 7* **P** *Bp* **V** D M SHEPHERD
LEATHERHEAD (All Saints) (St Mary and St Nicholas) *Guildf 10* **P** *D&C Roch* **V** D J EATON, **C** M J PROCTOR
LEATHLEY (St Oswald) w Farnley, Fewston and Blubberhouses *Bradf 4* **P** *Bp and G N le G Horton-Fawkes Esq* **P-in-c** D E CREASER, **NSM** M F CLEVERLEY
LEATON (Holy Trinity) and Albrighton w Battlefield *Lich 21* **P** *Col H Lloyd and J F Sparrow Esq (jt)* **V** P M GOLDTHORPE
LEAVELAND (St Laurence) *see* Selling w Throwley, Sheldwich w Badlesmere etc *Cant*
LEAVENHEATH (St Matthew) *see* Stoke by Nayland w Leavenheath *St E*
LEAVENING (not known) *see* Burythorpe, Acklam and Leavening w Westow *York*
LEAVESDEN (All Saints) *St Alb 7* **P** *Bp* **V** M POWELL, **C** A G CARTER, J A BIRDSEYE
LECHLADE (St Lawrence) *Glouc 13* **P** *Em Coll Cam* **V** S C PARSONS
LECK (St Peter) *see* Tunstall w Melling and Leck *Blackb*
LECKFORD (St Nicholas) *see* Stockbridge and Longstock and Leckford *Win*
LECKHAMPSTEAD (Assumption of the Blessed Virgin Mary) *see* N Buckingham *Ox*
LECKHAMPSTEAD (St James) *see* Brightwalton w Catmore, Leckhampstead etc *Ox*
LECKHAMPTON (St Christopher) *see* Leckhampton SS Phil and Jas w Cheltenham St Jas *Glouc*
LECKHAMPTON (St Peter) *Glouc 11* **P** *Bp* **R** A C BERRY
LECKHAMPTON (St Philip and St James) w Cheltenham (St James) *Glouc 10* **P** *Bp* **V** P L CHICKEN, **C** R C PARRISH, A E COLES
LECONFIELD (St Catherine) *see* Lockington and Lund and Scorborough w Leconfield *York*
LEDBURY (St Michael and All Angels) (St Katherine's Chapel) w Eastnor *Heref 6* **P** *Bp and J F S Hervey-Bathurst Esq (jt)* **P-in-c** C L BEEVERS, **C** R J TRAFFORD-ROBERTS, **NSM** E C REED
LEDGEMOOR (Mission Room) *see* Canon Pyon w Kings Pyon and Birley *Heref*
LEDSHAM (All Saints) w Fairburn *York 6* **P** *G H H Wheler Esq* **V** C J COPLAND
LEDSTON LUCK (not known) *see* Ledsham w Fairburn *York*
LEE (Good Shepherd) (St Peter) *S'wark 4* **P** *R Lee St Marg* **V** J R GILES, **Hon C** A E HOAD, **NSM** M MONK
LEE (St Augustine) Grove Park *S'wark 4* **P** *Bp* **V** G A BERRIMAN
LEE (St John the Baptist) *Ox 28* **P** *Bp* **V** *Vacant* (0124020) 315
LEE (St Margaret) *S'wark 4* **P** *Ld Chan* **R** R C B BUTLER
LEE (St Matthew) *see* Ilfracombe, Lee, Woolacombe, Bittadon etc *Ex*
LEE (St Mildred) Burnt Ash Hill *S'wark 4* **P** *Bp* **V** M C HILL, **Hon C** A D HILL
LEE (St Oswald) *see* St Oswald in Lee w Bingfield *Newc*
LEE BROCKHURST (St Peter) *Lich 23* **P** *Lord Barnard* **V** N MacGREGOR
LEE MOOR (Mission Church) *see* Bickleigh (Roborough) and Shaugh Prior *Ex*
LEE-ON-THE-SOLENT (St Faith) *Portsm 3* **P** *Bp* **V** P A SUTTON, **C** J G P JEFFERY
LEEBOTWOOD (St Mary) *see* Dorrington w Leebotwood, Longnor, Stapleton etc *Heref*
LEEDS (All Hallows) *Ripon 7* **P** *Bp and DBP (jt)* **V** A C JENKINS
LEEDS (All Souls) *Ripon 7* **P** *V Leeds St Pet, Simeon's Trustees, and DBP (jt)* **V** R L A PATERSON
LEEDS Belle Isle (St John and St Barnabas) *Ripon 6* **P** *Bp* **V** D J HOPKINSON, **C** C M DAVEY
LEEDS (Emmanuel) *Ripon 7* **P** *Trustees* **P-in-c** S J ROBINSON
LEEDS Gipton (Church of the Epiphany) *Ripon 5* **P** *Bp* **V** R J U HARINGTON, **C** R G GASTON
LEEDS Halton (St Wilfrid) *Ripon 5* **P** *Bp* **V** N P GEORGE
LEEDS (Parish Church) *see* Leeds City *Ripon*
LEEDS Richmond Hill (All Saints) (St Hilda) (St Saviour) *Ripon 8* **P** *Bp and Keble Coll Ox (jt)* **V** P F HUNT, **C** R G COOPER
LEEDS (St Aidan) *Ripon 5* **P** *V Leeds St Pet* **V** A L TAYLOR, **C** J S WEBB
LEEDS (St Cyprian and St James) Harehills *Ripon 5* **P** *Bp* **V** J W THEOBALD
LEEDS (St Edmund) *see* Roundhay St Edm *Ripon*
LEEDS (St George) *Ripon 7* **P** *Simeon's Trustees* **V** D J L HAWKINS, **C** J E MORRIS, P K ELLEM, **NSM** M B HANSON
LEEDS (St John the Evangelist) *see* Roundhay St Jo *Ripon*
LEEDS (St Nicholas) *see* Hollingbourne and Hucking w Leeds and Broomfield *Cant*
LEEDS (St Wilfrid) *Ripon 5* **P** *Bp* **V** J HILTON
LEEDS CITY (St Peter) (Holy Trinity) *Ripon 5* **P** *DBP* **TV** C R CORNWELL, N S HOWE, **C** D A HUNTLEY
LEEDSTOWN (St James's Mission Church) *see* Crowan w Godolphin *Truro*
LEEK (All Saints) (St Edward the Confessor) (St John the Evangelist) (St Luke) (St Paul) and Meerbrook *Lich 8* **P** *Patr Bd* **TR** K E JONES, **TV** P C GRAY, K R HAYWOOD, **C** R D SPENCER, **NSM** T WARNER
LEEK WOOTTON (All Saints) *Cov 4* **P** *Lord Leigh* **P-in-c** G R CORNWALL-JONES
LEEMING (St John the Baptist) *Ripon 4* **P** *R Kirklington w Burneston etc* **P-in-c** M D EMMEL
LEEMING BAR (St Augustine) *see* Bedale *Ripon*
LEES HILL (Mission Hall) *see* Lanercost w Kirkcambeck and Walton *Carl*
LEESFIELD Knoll's Lane (St Agnes) *see* Leesfield *Man*
LEESFIELD (St Thomas) *Man 19* **P** *Bp* **V** H G SMITH
LEFTWICH (Farm of the Good Shepherd) *see* Davenham *Ches*
LEGBOURNE (All Saints) *Linc 12* **P** *Ch Trust Fund Trust and Bp (jt)* **V** *Vacant* (01507) 602535
LEGBURTHWAITE (Mission Church) *see* St Johns-in-the-Vale w Wythburn *Carl*
LEGH, HIGH (St John) *see* Over Tabley and High Legh *Ches*
LEGSBY (St Thomas) *Linc 5* **P** *Bp* **V** M J CARTWRIGHT, **NSM** D L INKPIN
LEICESTER (Holy Apostles) (St Oswald) *Leic 2* **P** *DBP and Ridley Hall Cam (jt)* **V** J C RAINER, **NSM** R MILLER, P R BERRY
LEICESTER (Holy Spirit) (St Andrew) (St Nicholas) *Leic 2* **P** *Bp* **TR** M G IPGRAVE, **TV** I M McINTOSH, D L CAWLEY, **C** J Z RAY, J D CURTIS
LEICESTER (Holy Trinity w St John the Divine) *Leic 2* **P** *Peache Trustees* **V** R W MORGAN, **C** J M A LEE, **Hon C** F R ENTWISTLE
LEICESTER (Martyrs) *Leic 2* **P** *Bp* **V** R J FREEMAN, **C** B A ROBERTSON, P H RICHMOND
LEICESTER Presentation of Christ (St Barnabas) (St Peter) (St Saviour) *Leic 1* **P** *Bp* **TR** S F BOULD, **TV** S M NYAHWA, **NSM** A D BREAR
LEICESTER Resurrection (St Alban) *Leic 1* **P** *Bp* **TV** M J COURT, M WAGSTAFF
LEICESTER (St Aidan) *Leic 2* **P** *Bp* **C** D P HOWELL
LEICESTER (St Alban) *see* Leic Resurr *Leic*
LEICESTER (St Anne) *Leic 2* **P** *Bp* **V** I W HARRISON, **Hon C** H J CLARKE, **NSM** J M A SEMEONOFF
LEICESTER (St Chad) *Leic 1* **P** *Bp* **P-in-c** T S G VALE
LEICESTER (St Christopher) *Leic 2* **P** *MMCET* **V** A TELFORD
LEICESTER (St James the Greater) *Leic 2* **P** *Bp* **V** G RICHERBY, **C** R R POWELL
LEICESTER (St John the Baptist) *see* Claybrooke cum Wibtoft and Frolesworth *Leic*
LEICESTER (St Mary de Castro) *Leic 2* **P** *Bp* **V** D L CAWLEY

LEICESTER (St Paul) *Leic 2* **P** *Bp* **P-in-c** W A D BERRYMAN
LEICESTER (St Philip) *Leic 1* **P** *Adn Leic, V Evington, V Leic H Trin, G A Cooling Esq, and A S Price Esq (jt)* **P-in-c** C FINCH, **C** L R CURTIS
LEICESTER (St Stephen) *see* N Evington *Leic*
LEICESTER (St Theodore of Canterbury) *Leic 1* **P** *Bp* **V** J J LEONARD
LEICESTER, The Abbey (St Augustine) (St Margaret and All Saints) *Leic 2* **P** *Bp* **TR** W A D BERRYMAN, **TV** M J PEERS
LEICESTER FOREST EAST (St Andrew) *see* Kirby Muxloe *Leic*
LEIGH (All Saints) *see* Ashton Keynes, Leigh and Minety *Bris*
LEIGH (All Saints) *see* Uttoxeter Area *Lich*
LEIGH (All Saints' Mission) *see* Bedford Leigh *Man*
LEIGH or Wimborne (St John the Evangelist) *see* New Borough and Leigh *Sarum*
LEIGH (St Andrew) *see* Yetminster w Ryme Intrinseca and High Stoy *Sarum*
LEIGH (St Bartholomew) *S'wark 26* **P** *N J Charrington Esq* **P-in-c** J M A WILLANS
LEIGH (St Catherine) *see* Twigworth, Down Hatherley, Norton, The Leigh etc *Glouc*
LEIGH (St Clement) *Chelmsf 10* **P** *Bp* **R** S F JONES
LEIGH (St Edburga) *see* Alfrick, Lulsley, Suckley, Leigh and Bransford *Worc*
LEIGH (St John the Evangelist) *Man 13* **P** *Bp* **V** R R USHER
LEIGH (St Mary) *Roch 11* **P** *Ch Trust Fund Trust* **V** T V E OVERTON
LEIGH (St Mary the Virgin) *Man 13* **P** *Bp* **V** *Vacant* (01942) 673546
LEIGH, LITTLE (St Michael and All Angels) and Lower Whitley *Ches 4* **P** *P G Greenall Esq and V Gt Budworth (alt)* **P-in-c** M E REAVIL, **NSM** R BIGGIN
LEIGH, NORTH (St Mary) *Ox 9* **P** *Ld Chan* **P-in-c** R N F COLLINS
LEIGH, SOUTH (St James the Great) *see* Cogges and S Leigh *Ox*
LEIGH, WEST (St Alban) *Portsm 4* **P** *Bp* **V** M J SHEFFIELD, **C** D A WEIR
LEIGH-ON-SEA (St Aidan) the Fairway *Chelmsf 10* **P** *Bp* **V** C J ELLIOTT, **NSM** J M BARHAM
LEIGH-ON-SEA (St James) *Chelmsf 10* **P** *Bp* **V** B J SCHOOLING, **NSM** C R BEECHAM, **Hon Par Dn** E J A INGRAM
LEIGH-ON-SEA (St Margaret) *Chelmsf 10* **P** *Bp* **V** R H S EASTOE, **C** P J GROVES
LEIGH PARK (St Francis) *Portsm 4* **P** *Bp* **V** R C WHITE, **C** R A ORCHIN, **NSM** M S HARPER
LEIGH UPON MENDIP (St Giles) w Stoke St Michael *B & W 4* **P** *DBP and V Doulting (jt)* **V** P D WINKS
LEIGH WOODS (St Mary the Virgin) *see* Abbots Leigh w Leigh Woods *Bris*
LEIGHLAND (St Giles) *see* Old Cleeve, Leighland and Treborough *B & W*
LEIGHS, GREAT (St Mary the Virgin) *Chelmsf 8* **P** *Linc Coll Ox* **P-in-c** H ANSELL
LEIGHS, LITTLE (St John) *Chelmsf 8* **P** *Reformation Ch Trust* **P-in-c** H ANSELL
LEIGHTERTON (St Andrew) *see* Boxwell, Leighterton, Didmarton, Oldbury etc *Glouc*
LEIGHTON (Holy Trinity) *see* Trelystan *Heref*
LEIGHTON (St Mary) *see* Wrockwardine Deanery *Lich*
LEIGHTON BROMSWOLD (St Mary) *Ely 10* **P** *Bp* **P-in-c** C M FURLONG
LEIGHTON BUZZARD (All Saints) w Eggington, Hockliffe and Billington *St Alb 12* **P** *Bp* **V** J A L HULBERT, **C** A T BELL, E M CONSTANTINE, **NSM** V H SMITH
LEIGHTON-CUM-MINSHULL VERNON (St Peter) *Ches 15* **P** *Bp* **V** G D GEDDES
LEINTHALL EARLES (St Andrew) *see* Kingsland w Eardisland, Aymestrey etc *Heref*
LEINTHALL STARKES (St Mary Magdalene) *see* Wigmore Abbey *Heref*
LEINTWARDINE (St Andrew) Adforton *as above*
LEINTWARDINE (St Mary Magdalene) *as above*
LEIRE (St Peter) w Ashby Parva and Dunton Bassett *Leic 11* **P** *Ball Coll Ox, Exors Major T G F Paget, and Adn Loughb (by turn)* **R** C D BRADLEY
LEISTON (St Margaret) *St E 19* **P** *Haberdashers' Co* **V** D C LOWE
LELANT (St Uny) *see* Carbis Bay w Lelant *Truro*
LEMINGTON, LOWER (St Leonard) *see* Moreton-in-Marsh w Batsford, Todenham etc *Glouc*
LEMSFORD (St John the Evangelist) *St Alb 21* **P** *Lord Brocket* **P-in-c** R S INGAMELLS, **NSM** J E FORDHAM
LENBOROUGH *Ox 23* **P** *Ch Ch Ox, Cam Univ, and New Coll Ox (2 turns), Ld Chan (1 turn)* **V** J HUDSON
LENHAM (St Mary) w Boughton Malherbe *Cant 15* **P** *Viscount Chilston and Lord Cornwallis (jt)* **R** D E C WRIGHT
LENTON (Holy Trinity) (Priory Church of St Anthony) *S'well 14* **P** *CPAS* **P-in-c** W R LOVATT, **C** D CHAPMAN
LENTON (St Peter) *see* Ingoldsby *Linc*
LENTON ABBEY (St Barnabas) *S'well 14* **P** *CPAS* **P-in-c** P A WILLIAMS
LENWADE (All Saints) *see* Weston Longville w Morton and the Witchinghams *Nor*
LEOMINSTER (St Peter and St Paul) *Heref 7* **P** *Patr Bd* **TR** M W HOOPER, **TV** G L JONES, P J PRIVETT, **C** O S DALE, **NSM** J E GASPER
LEONARD STANLEY (St Swithun) *see* The Stanleys *Glouc*
LEPTON (St John) *Wakef 6* **P** *R Kirkheaton* **V** G F WHITCROFT
LESBURY (St Mary) w Alnmouth *Newc 9* **P** *Dioc Soc* **V** B COWEN
LESNEWTH (St Michael and All Angels) *see* Boscastle w Davidstow *Truro*
LESSINGHAM (All Saints) *see* Happisburgh, Walcott, Hempstead w Eccles etc *Nor*
LETCHWORTH (St Mary the Virgin) (St Michael) *St Alb 4* **P** *Guild of All So* **R** N M SETTERFIELD
LETCHWORTH (St Paul) w Willian *St Alb 4* **P** *Bp* **V** G E TURNER, **C** S K YOUNG, **NSM** M P DACK
LETCOMBE BASSETT (St Michael and All Angels) *see* Ridgeway *Ox*
LETCOMBE REGIS (St Andrew) *as above*
LETHERINGHAM (St Mary) *see* Charsfield w Debach, Monewden, Hoo etc *St E*
LETHERINGSETT (St Andrew) *see* Blakeney w Cley, Wiveton, Glandford etc *Nor*
LETTON (St John the Baptist) w Staunton, Byford, Mansel Gamage and Monnington *Heref 5* **P** *Sir John Cotterell Bt (2 turns), Exors Mrs Dew (1 turn), Ch Ch Ox (3 turns), and DBP (1 turn)* **P-in-c** R A BIRT, **NSM** G N PRIDAY
LETTY GREEN (St John) *see* Hertingfordbury *St Alb*
LETWELL (St Peter) *see* Firbeck w Letwell *Sheff*
LEUSDON (St John the Baptist) *see* Widecombe-in-the-Moor, Leusdon, Princetown etc *Ex*
LEVEDALE (Mission Church) *see* Penkridge Team *Lich*
LEVEN (Holy Trinity) *see* Brandesburton and Leven w Catwick *York*
LEVEN VALLEY *Carl 10* **P** *Mrs C M Chaplin, V Colton, and Bp (jt)* **P-in-c** G G DOUGLAS
LEVENS (St John the Evangelist) *Carl 9* **P** *Trustees* **P-in-c** A M R STOCKLEY
LEVENSHULME (St Mark) *Man 3* **P** *Bp* **R** N P TAYLOR
LEVENSHULME (St Peter) *Man 3* **P** *Trustees* **R** R A J AXTELL
LEVENSHULME, SOUTH (St Andrew) *Man 3* **P** *Bp* **R** J L CLEGG
LEVER, GREAT (St Michael w St Bartholomew) *Man 12* **P** *Bp* **R** E J HALLIDAY
LEVER, LITTLE (St Matthew) *Man 12* **P** *V Bolton-le-Moors St Pet* **V** S F BRANDES, **NSM** I C ANTHONY
LEVER BRIDGE (St Stephen and All Martyrs) *Man 9* **P** *The Crown* **V** *Vacant* (01204) 528300
LEVERINGTON (St Leonard) *Ely 19* **P** *Bp* **R** F B H WOOLLEY
LEVERTON (St Helen) *see* Benington w Leverton *Linc*
LEVERTON, NORTH and SOUTH (St Martin) (All Saints) *S'well 5* **P** *Bp* **V** R AKERMAN, **NSM** I CARTER
LEVINGTON (St Peter) *see* Nacton and Levington w Bucklesham and Foxhall *St E*
LEVISHAM (St John the Baptist) *see* Pickering w Lockton and Levisham *York*
LEWANNICK (St Martin) *see* North Hill and Lewannick *Truro*
LEWES All Saints (St Mary) (St Anne) (St Michael) (St Thomas at Cliffe) *Chich 18* **P** *Ld Chan (3 turns), Patr Bd (1 turn)* **C** G L LINNEGAR, **NSM** R V C HEBBORN, P D YATES
LEWES (St John sub Castro) *Chich 18* **P** *Bp* **R** R M BELL
LEWES (St John the Baptist) *see* Southover *Chich*
LEWISHAM (St Mary) *S'wark 4* **P** *Earl of Dartmouth* **V** D GARLICK
LEWISHAM (St Stephen) and St Mark *S'wark 4* **P** *Keble Coll Ox* **V** G KIRK, **Hon C** F D GARDOM
LEWISHAM (St Swithun) Hither Green *S'wark 4* **P** *V Lewisham St Mary* **V** R DANIELL, **NSM** E BAKER
LEWKNOR (St Margaret) *see* Tetsworth, Adwell w S Weston, Lewknor etc *Ox*
LEWSEY (St Hugh) *see* Luton Lewsey St Hugh *St Alb*
LEWTRENCHARD (St Peter) *see* Marystowe, Coryton, Stowford, Lewtrenchard etc *Ex*
LEXDEN (St Leonard) *Chelmsf 16* **P** *Bp* **R** S CARTER
LEXHAM, EAST (St Andrew) *see* Litcham w Kempston, E and W Lexham, Mileham etc *Nor*
LEXHAM, WEST (St Nicholas) *as above*

LEYBOURNE (St Peter and St Paul) *Roch 7* **P** *Major Sir David Hawley, Bt* **P-in-c** C D DENCH
LEYBURN (St Matthew) w Bellerby *Ripon 4* **P** *Lord Bolton and Mrs M E Scragg (alt)* **V** J B BLACKMAN
LEYFIELDS (St Francis) *see* Tamworth *Lich*
LEYLAND (St Ambrose) *Blackb 6* **P** *V Leyland* **V** A F RANSON
LEYLAND (St Andrew) *Blackb 6* **P** *CPAS* **V** K HORSFALL, **C** J A DAWSWELL
LEYLAND (St James) *Blackb 6* **P** *Sir Henry Farington, Bt* **V** A HOLLIDAY, **NSM** M H PENMAN
LEYLAND (St John) *Blackb 6* **P** *V Leyland St Andr and CPAS (jt)* **V** I SMITH
LEYSTERS (St Andrew) *see* Bockleton w Leysters *Heref*
LEYTON (All Saints) *Chelmsf 5* **P** *V St Mary's Leyton* **P-in-c** M I HOLMDEN, **NSM** M R NIE
LEYTON (Christ Church) *Chelmsf 5* **P** *Ch Trust Fund Trust* **V** M E BURKILL
LEYTON (Emmanuel) *Chelmsf 5* **P** *Bp* **V** T B JONES
LEYTON (St Catherine) (St Paul) *Chelmsf 5* **P** *V Leyton St Mary w St Edw* **V** A J HOWARD
LEYTON (St Mary w St Edward) *see* Leyton St Mary w St Edw and St Luke *Chelmsf*
LEYTON (St Mary w St Edward) and St Luke *Chelmsf 5* **P** *Simeon's Trustees* **V** D S AINGE, **C** P SHERRING, **Dss** A BUTLER
LEYTONSTONE (Holy Trinity) Harrow Green *Chelmsf 5* **P** *Bp* **V** T C N SCOTT, **NSM** B P MOSS
LEYTONSTONE (St Andrew) *Chelmsf 5* **P** *Bp* **P-in-c** P J W MURPHY
LEYTONSTONE (St John the Baptist) *Chelmsf 5* **P** *Bp* **V** R C FIELD, **C** C J BRIXTON
LEYTONSTONE (St Margaret w St Columba) *Chelmsf 5* **P** *Bp* **V** P J W MURPHY, **C** P A BOSTOCK, J C RAVENSDALE
LEZANT (St Briochus) *see* Stoke Climsland *Truro*
LEZANT (St Briochus) w Lawhitton and South Petherwin w Trewen *Truro 9* **P** *Bp and Ox Univ (jt)* **NSM** J MARSHALL
LEZAYRE (Holy Trinity) *S & M 4* **P** *The Crown* **V** B E SHEPHARD
LEZAYRE (St Olave) Ramsey *S & M 4* **P** *The Crown and Bp (alt)* **V** J H SHEEN, **NSM** A HADWIN
LICHBOROUGH (St Martin) *see* Greens Norton w Bradden and Lichborough *Pet*
LICHFIELD (Christ Church) *Lich 1* **P** *Bp* **V** I W WILLIAMS
LICHFIELD (St Chad) *Lich 1* **P** *D&C* **R** E G H TOWNSHEND, **C** M J HORTON, D D SCEATS, **NSM** B WILLIAMS, D J SHERIDAN
LICHFIELD (St John's Hospital) *Lich 1* **P** *Bp* **I** J HOWE
LICHFIELD (St Michael) (St Mary) and Wall St John *Lich 1* **P** *D&C* **R** D A SMITH, **C** D P BROCKBANK, J G WESSON, M D GELDARD, **NSM** J ANKETELL, J PATTEN
LICKEY, THE (Holy Trinity) *Birm 4* **P** *V Bromsgrove* **P-in-c** P D SWAN
LIDEN (St Timothy) *see* Swindon Dorcan *Bris*
LIDLINGTON (St Margaret) *see* Marston Morteyne w Lidlington *St Alb*
LIFTON (St Mary) *Ex 24* **P** *Countess de Wolovey* **P-in-c** J H HEATH
LIGHTBOWNE (St Luke) *Man 5* **P** *D&C* **R** A J L LEWIS
LIGHTCLIFFE (St Matthew) *Wakef 2* **P** *V Halifax* **V** D WILDING
LIGHTHORNE (St Laurence) *Cov 8* **P** *Lady Willoughby de Broke* **R** J R WILLIAMS
LIGHTWATER (All Saints) *Guildf 6* **P** *Ld Chan and Bp (alt)* **V** M J HORTON
LILBOURNE (All Saints) *see* Crick and Yelvertoft w Clay Coton and Lilbourne *Pet*
LILLESHALL (St John the Evangelist) (St Michael and All Angels) and Sheriffhales *Lich 16* **P** *Bp* **V** D J BUTTERFIELD, **C** D A ACKROYD
LILLEY (St Peter) *see* King's Walden and Offley w Lilley *St Alb*
LILLINGSTONE DAYRELL (St Nicholas) *see* N Buckingham *Ox*
LILLINGSTONE LOVELL (Assumption of the Blessed Virgin Mary) *as above*
LILLINGTON (St Martin) *see* Sherborne w Castleton and Lillington *Sarum*
LILLINGTON (St Mary Magdalene) *Cov 11* **P** *Bp* **V** T M H BOYNS, **C** N MORGAN
LILLIPUT (Holy Angels) *Sarum 8* **P** *Bp* **V** C HODGE
LIMBER, GREAT (St Peter) *see* Brocklesby Park *Linc*
LIMEHOUSE (St Anne) (St Peter) *Lon 7* **P** *BNC Ox* **R** J F D PEARCE, **C** A C TRESIDDER, **Hon Par Dn** A E PEARCE
LIMESIDE (St Chad) *see* Oldham St Chad Limeside *Man*
LIMINGTON (The Blessed Virgin Mary) *see* Ilchester w Northover, Limington, Yeovilton etc *B & W*
LIMPENHOE (St Botolph) *see* Reedham w Cantley w Limpenhoe and Southwood *Nor*
LIMPLEY STOKE (St Mary) *see* Freshford, Limpley Stoke and Hinton Charterhouse *B & W*
LIMPSFIELD (St Andrew) (St Peter) and Titsey *S'wark 25* **P** *Bp* **R** N H THOMPSON, **C** A E HEFFERNAN, M H KELLY
LINBY (St Michael) w Papplewick *S'well 4* **P** *T W A Cundy Esq* **R** K H TURNER
LINCHMERE (St Peter) *see* Lynchmere and Camelsdale *Chich*
LINCOLN Minster Group, The (St Mary Magdalene) (St Michael on the Mount) (St Peter in Eastgate) *Linc 15* **P** *Adn Linc, D&C, and Bp (by turn)* **R** J B BAYLEY
LINCOLN (St Botolph by Bargate) *Linc 15* **P** *Bp* **P-in-c** J P HAYES
LINCOLN (St Faith) (St Martin) (St Peter-at-Arches) *Linc 15* **P** *Bp* **P-in-c** L C ACKLAM, **C** C HILLIAM
LINCOLN (St George) Swallowbeck *Linc 15* **P** *Bp and V Skellingthorpe (jt)* **P-in-c** I G SILK, **NSM** J A DUFF
LINCOLN (St Giles) *Linc 15* **P** *Bp* **V** *Vacant* (01522) 527655
LINCOLN (St John the Baptist) (St John the Evangelist) *Linc 15* **P** *Bp* **V** G WARD
LINCOLN (St Mary-le-Wigford) (St Benedict) (St Mark) *Linc 15* **P** *Bp* **V** K R COOK
LINCOLN (St Nicholas) (St John) Newport *Linc 15* **P** *Bp and D&C (alt)* **V** B L WISKEN, **NSM** S PROSSER
LINCOLN (St Peter-at-Gowts) (St Andrew) *Linc 15* **P** *Bp* **P-in-c** P D GODDEN
LINCOLN (St Swithin) (All Saints) *Linc 15* **P** *Bp* **P-in-c** D G KERRIDGE
LINDAL IN MARTON (St Peter) *see* Pennington and Lindal w Marton and Bardsea *Carl*
LINDALE (St Paul) w Field Broughton *Carl 10* **P** *Bp* **V** *Vacant* (015395) 34717
LINDFIELD (All Saints) *Chich 6* **P** *Ch Soc Trust* **V** D J CLARKE, **C** P V PARKER, R C JACKSON
LINDLEY (St Stephen) *Wakef 5* **P** *V Huddersfield* **V** M T A HAYNES
LINDOW (St John) *Ches 12* **P** *Bp* **V** S R GALES
LINDRIDGE (St Lawrence) *see* Teme Valley N *Worc*
LINDSELL (St Mary the Virgin) *see* Stebbing w Lindsell *Chelmsf*
LINDSEY (St Peter) *see* Kersey w Lindsey *St E*
LINFORD (St Francis) *see* E and W Tilbury and Linford *Chelmsf*
LINFORD, GREAT (St Andrew) *see* Stantonbury and Willen *Ox*
LINFORD, LITTLE (St Leonard) *see* Lamp *Ox*
LINGDALE (Mission Room) *see* Boosbeck w Moorsholm *York*
LINGEN (St Michael and All Angels) *see* Presteigne w Discoed, Kinsham and Lingen *Heref*
LINGFIELD (St Peter and St Paul) and Crowhurst *S'wark 25* **P** *Bp* **V** E J S PLAXTON
LINGWOOD (St Peter) *see* Burlingham St Edmund w Lingwood, Strumpshaw etc *Nor*
LINKENHOLT (St Peter) *see* Hurstbourne Tarrant, Faccombe, Vernham Dean etc *Win*
LINKINHORNE (St Mellor) *Truro 12* **P** *DBP* **V** P R MEDLEY
LINLEY (St Leonard) *see* Broseley w Benthall, Jackfield, Linley etc *Heref*
LINLEY GREEN (not known) *see* Acton Beauchamp and Evesbatch w Stanford Bishop *Heref*
LINSLADE (St Barnabas) (St Mary) *Ox 26* **P** *Bp* **V** C G MATTOCK
LINSTEAD PARVA (St Margaret) *see* Halesworth w Linstead, Chediston, Holton etc *St E*
LINTHORPE (St Barnabas) *York 19* **P** *Abp* **V** I D REID, **C** A M LAIRD, **NSM** R A MORRIS
LINTHWAITE (Christ Church) *Wakef 5* **P** *R Almondbury* **V** *Vacant* (01484) 842591
LINTON (Christ Church) and Castle Gresley *Derby 16* **P** *Bp* **V** W C E ROSE
LINTON (St Aidan) *see* Ashington *Newc*
LINTON (St Mary) *Ely 4* **P** *Patr Bd* **TR** J H THOMSON, **TV** L L RANDALL, **NSM** M W B O'LOUGHLIN
LINTON (St Mary the Virgin) w Upton Bishop and Aston Ingham *Heref 8* **P** *St Jo Coll Ox, D&C, and Preb H L Whatley (jt)* **P-in-c** R STIRRUP
LINTON (St Nicholas) *see* Coxheath w E Farleigh, Hunton and Linton *Roch*
LINTON IN CRAVEN (St Michael) *Bradf 7* **P** *D&C* **R** C J HAYWARD
LINWOOD (St Cornelius) *Linc 5* **P** *MMCET* **R** M J CARTWRIGHT, **NSM** D L INKPIN
LIPHOOK (Church Centre) *see* Bramshott and Liphook *Portsm*
LISCARD (St John) *see* Egremont St Jo *Ches*
LISCARD (St Mary w St Columba) *Ches 7* **P** *Bp* **P-in-c** J A V FLORANCE

LISCARD (St Thomas) *Ches 7* **P** *Bp* **P-in-c** R T NELSON
LISKEARD (St Martin), St Keyne, St Pinnock, Morval and Bradoc *Truro 12* **P** *Patr Bd (2 turns), Ld Chan (1 turn)* **TR** M G SELLIX, **TV** D J BURLEIGH, G M ROBERTS, **C** A W G CHALKLEY
LISS (St Mary) (St Peter) (St Saviour) *Portsm 5* **P** *Bp* **R** B E COOK, **C** M J LANE, **Hon C** D J VARNEY
LISSET (St James of Compostella) *see* Beeford w Frodingham and Foston *York*
LISSINGTON (St John the Baptist) *see* Wickenby Gp *Linc*
LISTON (not known) *see* Pentlow, Foxearth, Liston and Borley *Chelmsf*
LITCHAM (All Saints) w Kempston, East and West Lexham, Mileham, Beeston-next-Mileham, Stanfield, Tittleshall and Godwick *Nor 14* **P** *Bp, Earl of Leic, Ch Soc Tr, DBP, Mrs E M Olesen, and N W D Foster Esq (jt)* **R** *Vacant* (01328) 701223
LITCHFIELD (St James the Less) *see* Whitchurch w Tufton and Litchfield *Win*
LITHERLAND (St Andrew) *Liv 1* **P** *Bp* **P-in-c** C H KIRKE
LITHERLAND (St John and St James) *Liv 1* **P** *CPAS* **P-in-c** R J G PANTER
LITHERLAND (St Paul) Hatton Hill *Liv 1* **P** *Bp* **P-in-c** J W WHITLEY
LITHERLAND (St Philip) *Liv 1* **P** *Trustees* **C** I C COWELL, **Hon C** J T LEIGHTON
LITLINGTON (St Catherine) *see* Shingay Gp of Par *Ely*
LITLINGTON (St Michael the Archangel) *see* Alfriston w Lullington, Litlington and W Dean *Chich*
LITTLE *see also under substantive place name*
LITTLE BIRCH (St Mary) *see* Much Birch w Lt Birch, Much Dewchurch etc *Heref*
LITTLEBOROUGH (Holy Trinity) *Man 20* **P** *TR Rochdale* **V** J B PETTIFER, **Dss** K J OLIVER
LITTLEBOURNE (St Vincent) and Ickham w Wickhambreaux and Stodmarsh *Cant 1* **P** *Abp, D&C, Ch Trust Fund Trust, and Adn Cant (jt)* **R** A J ALLAN
LITTLEBURY (Holy Trinity) *see* Saffron Walden w Wendens Ambo and Littlebury *Chelmsf*
LITTLEBURY GREEN (St Peter) *as above*
LITTLEDEAN (St Ethelbert) *see* Cinderford St Steph w Littledean *Glouc*
LITTLEHAM (St Margaret) w Exmouth *Ex 1* **P** *Patr Bd* **TR** K F MIDDLETON, **C** J E DICKER, **Hon C** E M MORRIS, **NSM** M K WEATHERLEY
LITTLEHAM (St Swithin) *see* Bideford, Northam, Westward Ho!, Appledore etc *Ex*
LITTLEHAMPTON (St James) (St Mary) and Wick *Chich 1* **P** *Bp* **TR** R J CASWELL, **TV** J S A HUDSON, J S BLOOMFIELD
LITTLEHEMPSTON (St John the Baptist) *see* Broadhempston, Woodland, Staverton etc *Ex*
LITTLEMOOR (St Francis of Assisi) *see* Preston w Sutton Poyntz and Osmington w Poxwell *Sarum*
LITTLEMORE (St Mary the Virgin and St Nicholas) *Ox 4* **P** *Or Coll Ox* **P-in-c** B G SCHUNEMANN, **NSM** G SIMPSON
LITTLEOVER (St Peter) *Derby 10* **P** *PCC* **V** W B G MATHER, **C** M J ARCHER, **NSM** E A MATHER
LITTLEPORT (St George) (St Matthew) *Ely 14* **P** *Bp* **V** A G F VILLER
LITTLETON (St Catherine of Alexandria) *see* Crawley and Littleton and Sparsholt w Lainston *Win*
LITTLETON (St Mary Magdalene) *Lon 13* **P** *C W L Barratt Esq* **P-in-c** P V K HOARE
LITTLETON, HIGH (Holy Trinity) *B & W 12* **P** *Hyndman Trustees* **V** P M HAND
LITTLETON, NORTH (St Nicholas) *see* Cleeve Prior and The Littletons *Worc*
LITTLETON, SOUTH (St Michael the Archangel) *as above*
LITTLETON DREW (All Saints) *see* Nettleton w Littleton Drew *Bris*
LITTLETON ON SEVERN (St Mary of Malmesbury) w Elberton *Bris 8* **P** *Bp* **P-in-c** P W ROWE
LITTLEWICK (St John the Evangelist) *see* Knowl Hill w Littlewick *Ox*
LITTLEWICK (St Thomas) *see* Horsell *Guildf*
LITTLEWORTH (Holy Ascension) *Ox 17* **P** *Or Coll Ox* **V** C R RUDD
LITTON (Christ Church) *see* Tideswell *Derby*
LITTON (St Mary the Virgin) *see* Chewton Mendip w Ston Easton, Litton etc *B & W*
LITTON CHENEY (St Mary) *see* Bride Valley *Sarum*
LIVERMERE, GREAT (St Peter) *see* Blackbourne *St E*
LIVERPOOL (All Souls) Springwood *Liv 4* **P** *The Crown* **V** S P WEST
LIVERPOOL (Christ Church) Norris Green *Liv 8* **P** *Bp* **V** P W DAWKIN
LIVERPOOL (Our Lady and St Nicholas w St Anne) *Liv 3* **P** *Patr Bd* **TR** N A FRAYLING, **TV** D R CAPES, S S WILLIAMS, **Hon C** J S WILLIAMS
LIVERPOOL (St Anne) *see* Stanley *Liv*
LIVERPOOL (St Christopher) Norris Green *Liv 8* **P** *Bp* **V** *Vacant* 0151-226 1637
LIVERPOOL (St Luke in the City) (St Bride w St Saviour) (St Michael in the City) (St Stephen w St Catherine) *Liv 6* **P** *Patr Bd* **TR** N BLACK, **TV** S M STARKEY, M J FRY
LIVERPOOL (St Paul) Stoneycroft *Liv 8* **P** *St Chad's Coll Dur* **V** J C BAKER, **NSM** D BENSON
LIVERPOOL (St Philip w St David) *Liv 3* **P** *Bp* **P-in-c** J A GARNETT
LIVERSEDGE (Christ Church) *Wakef 8* **P** *V Birstall* **V** D F HANDLEY
LIVERTON (St Martin) *see* Easington w Liverton *York*
LIVERTON MINES (St Hilda) *as above*
LIVESEY (St Andrew) *Blackb 5* **P** *Trustees* **P-in-c** N J WHETTON, **C** K HOWLES
LLANCILLO (St Peter) *see* Ewyas Harold w Dulas, Kenderchurch etc *Heref*
LLANDINABO (St Junabius) *see* Much Birch w Lt Birch, Much Dewchurch etc *Heref*
LLANFAIR WATERDINE (St Mary) *see* Bucknell w Chapel Lawn, Llanfair Waterdine etc *Heref*
LLANGARRON (St Deinst) w Llangrove, Whitchurch and Ganarew *Heref 8* **P** *Bp, DBP, and D&C (jt)* **R** *Vacant* (01989) 770341
LLANGROVE (Christ Church) *see* Llangarron w Llangrove, Whitchurch and Ganarew *Heref*
LLANGUA (St James) *see* Ewyas Harold w Dulas, Kenderchurch etc *Heref*
LLANVEYNOE (St Beuno and St Peter) *see* Clodock and Longtown w Craswall, Llanveynoe etc *Heref*
LLANWARNE (Christ Church) *see* Much Birch w Lt Birch, Much Dewchurch etc *Heref*
LLANYBLODWEL (St Michael) and Trefonen *Lich 19* **P** *Bp and Earl of Powis (jt)* **R** C R BALL
LLANYMYNECH (St Agatha) *Lich 19* **P** *Bp* **R** T VILLIERS
LOBLEY HILL (All Saints) *Dur 13* **P** *Bp* **V** R K HOPPER
LOCKERLEY (St John) and East Dean w East and West Tytherley *Win 11* **P** *DBP (1 turn), H B G Dalgety Esq (2 turns)* **V** D J PASKINS
LOCKING (St Augustine) *B & W 11* **P** *MMCET* **V** M C COTTERELL
LOCKINGE (All Saints) *see* Wantage Downs *Ox*
LOCKINGE, WEST (All Souls) *as above*
LOCKINGTON (St Mary) and Lund and Scorborough w Leconfield *York 9* **P** *Abp* **R** C M F WHITEHEAD
LOCKINGTON (St Nicholas) *see* Castle Donington and Lockington cum Hemington *Leic*
LOCKS HEATH (St John the Baptist) *Portsm 2* **P** *Bp* **V** P D INGRAMS, **NSM** P A BOGGUST, S MARTIN
LOCKTON (St Giles) *see* Pickering w Lockton and Levisham *York*
LODDINGTON (St Leonard) *see* Broughton w Loddington and Cransley etc *Pet*
LODDINGTON (St Michael and All Angels) *Leic 3* **P** *Bp* **P-in-c** G J JOHNSON
LODDISWELL (St Michael and All Angels) *see* Modbury, Bigbury, Ringmore w Kingston etc *Ex*
LODDON (Holy Trinity), Sisland w Hales and Heckingham *Nor 8* **P** *Bp (3 turns), E G Gilbert Esq (1 turn)* **P-in-c** C R CHAPMAN, **C** E RANDALL
LODE (St James) *see* Bottisham and Lode w Long Meadow *Ely*
LODERS (St Mary Magdalene) *see* Askerswell, Loders and Powerstock *Sarum*
LODGE, THE (St John) *see* Weston Rhyn and Selattyn *Lich*
LODGE MOOR (St Luke) *Sheff 4* **P** *CPAS* **V** J D STRIDE
LODSWORTH (St Peter) *see* Lurgashall, Lodsworth and Selham *Chich*
LOFTHOUSE (Christ Church) *Ripon 8* **P** *DBP* **V** V G UTTLEY
LOFTUS-IN-CLEVELAND (St Leonard) and Carlin How w Skinningrove *York 17* **P** *Ld Chan (2 turns), Abp (1 turn)* **R** J P PAYNE
LOLWORTH (All Saints) *see* Fen Drayton w Conington and Lolworth etc *Ely*
LONAN (All Saints) *S & M 2* **P** *The Crown* **V** W H MARTIN
LONDESBOROUGH (All Saints) *York 7* **P** *R F Ashwin Esq* **P-in-c** J C MELLING
LONDON, LITTLE (St Stephen) *see* Bramley *Win*
LONDON CITY CHURCHES:
All Hallows Berkynchirche-by-the-Tower w St Dunstan-in-the-East *Lon 1* **P** *Abp* **V** P A DELANEY, **Hon C** G R de MELLO, M D C FORRER, S VAN CULIN
St Andrew-by-the-Wardrobe w St Ann, Blackfriars *Lon 1* **P** *PCC and Mercers' Co (jt)* **R** J W PAUL

St Bartholomew the Great, Smithfield *Lon 1* **P** *D&C Westmr* **R** M R DUDLEY, **Hon C** A C WINTER, **NSM** N J GOULDING
St Bartholomew the Less, Smithfield Gate *Lon 1* **P** *St Bart's Hosp* **V** *Vacant*
St Botolph Aldgate w Holy Trinity Minories *Lon 1* **P** *Bp* **V** B J LEE, **C** P WRIGHT, R A DEEDES, **Hon C** J W HOLDEN, F P COLEMAN, **NSM** J PEIRCE, K LEECH
St Botolph without Bishopgate *Lon 1* **P** *D&C St Paul's* **Hon C** H J M TURNER
St Bride Fleet Street w Bridewell and Trinity Gough Square *Lon 1* **P** *D&C Westmr* **R** J OATES
St Clement Eastcheap w St Martin Orgar *Lon 1* **P** *D&C St Paul's* **Hon C** M B KIDDLE
St Edmund the King and St Mary Woolnoth w St Nicholas Acons, All Hallows Lombard Street, St Benet Gracechurch, St Leonard Eastcheap, St Dionis Backchurch and St Mary Woolchurch, Haw *Lon 1* **P** *The Crown (3 turns), D&C Cant (1 turn), Bp (1 turn), and Abp (1 turn)* **R** R HAYES
St Giles Cripplegate w St Bartholomew Moor Lane and St Alphage London Wall and St Luke Old Street w St Mary Charterhouse and St Paul Clerkenwell *Lon 1* **P** *D&C St Paul's* **R** D RHODES, **Hon C** E F TINKER, **NSM** S NIGHTINGALE
St Helen, Bishopsgate w St Andrew Undershaft and St Ethelburga, Bishopsgate and St Martin Outwich and St Mary Axe *Lon 1* **R** R C LUCAS, **C** W T TAYLOR, R M COOMBS, J S JUCKES
St James Garlickhythe w St Michael Queenhithe and Holy Trinity-the-Less *Lon 1* **P** *D&C St Paul's* **R** J W PAUL, **Hon C** W D BAKER
St Magnus the Martyr w St Margaret New Fish Street and St Michael Crooked Lane *Lon 1* **P** *DBP* **R** *Vacant* 0171-626 4481
St Margaret Lothbury and St Stephen Coleman Street w St Christopher-le-Stocks, St Bartholomew-by-the-Exchange, St Olave Old Jewry, St Martin Pomeroy, St Mildred Poultry and St Mary Colechurch *Lon 1* **P** *Simeon's Trustees* **R** T S FARRELL
St Mary at Hill w St Andrew Hubbard, St George Botolph Lane and St Botolph by Billingsgate *Lon 1* **P** *Ball Coll Ox (2 turns), PCC (1 turn), and Abp (1 turn)* **R** B A C KIRK-DUNCAN
St Mary le Bow w St Pancras Soper Lane, All Hallows Honey Lane, All Hallows Bread Street, St John the Evangelist Watling Street, St Augustine w St Faith under St Paul's and St Mildred Bread Street w St Margaret Moyses *Lon 1* **P** *Grocers' Co (1 turn), Abp (2 turns)* **R** V A STOCK, **NSM** J-H D BOWDEN
St Michael Cornhill w St Peter le Poer and St Benet Fink *Lon 1* **P** *Drapers' Co* **P-in-c** W G REID
St Olave Hart Street w All Hallows Staining and St Catherine Coleman *Lon 1* **P** *Trustees* **R** J F COWLING, **Hon Par Dn** P D PERKINS
St Peter Cornhill *Lon 1* **P** *City Corp* **P-in-c** R M COOMBS
St Sepulchre w Christ Church Greyfriars and St Leonard Foster Lane *Lon 1* **P** *St Jo Coll Ox* **R** *Vacant*
St Stephen Walbrook and St Swithun London Stone w St Benet Sherehog and St Mary Bothaw w St Laurence Pountney *Lon 1* **P** *Grocers' Co and Magd Coll Cam (alt)* **R** E C VARAH
St Vedast w St Michael-le-Querne, St Matthew Friday Street, St Peter Cheap, St Alban Wood Street, St Olave Silver Street, St Michael Wood Street, St Mary Staining, St Anne and St Agnes and St John Zachary Gresham Street *Lon 1* **P** *D&C St Paul's* **P-in-c** J D M PATON
LONDON DOCKS (St Peter) w Wapping St John *Lon 7* **P** *Bp* **R** T E JONES, **C** O C G HIGGS
LONDON GUILD CHURCHES:
All Hallows London Wall *Lon 1* **P** *Ld Chan* **V** *Vacant* 0171-588 3388
St Andrew Holborn *Lon 1* **P** *Bp* **V** C YOUNG
St Benet Paul's Wharf *Lon 1* **P** *Bp* **V** A P HAWKINS
St Botolph without Aldersgate *Lon 1* **P** *Bp* **P-in-c** D C L PRIOR
St Dunstan in the West *Lon 1* **P** *Abp* **P-in-c** A T J SALTER
St Katharine Cree *Lon 1* **P** *Bp* **V** *Vacant* 0171-283 5733
St Lawrence Jewry *Lon 1* **P** *City Corp* **V** D J BURGESS
St Margaret Pattens *Lon 1* **P** *Ld Chan* **P-in-c** A G C PEARSON
St Martin Ludgate *Lon 1* **P** *D&C St Paul's* **V** *Vacant* 0171-236 2827
St Mary Abchurch *Lon 1* **P** *CCC Cam* **P-in-c** O R CLARKE
St Mary Aldermary *Lon 1* **P** *The Crown and Ld Chan (alt)* **P-in-c** V A STOCK
St Michael Paternoster Royal *Lon 1* **P** *Bp* **V** G JONES
LONDONDERRY (St Mark) (Holy Trinity) *Birm 7* **P** *Bp* **V** J BIRKETT
LONDONTHORPE (St John the Baptist) *see* Grantham *Linc*
LONG ASHTON (All Saints) *B & W 13* **P** *Bp* **V** H B TASKER
LONG BENNINGTON (St Swithin) *see* Saxonwell *Linc*
LONG BENTON (St Bartholomew) *Newc 6* **P** *Ball Coll Ox* **V** P S RAMSDEN, **C** R J PIMM
LONG BENTON (St Mary Magdalene) *Newc 6* **P** *Ball Coll Ox* **V** J R SINCLAIR
LONG BREDY (St Peter) *see* Bride Valley *Sarum*
LONG BUCKBY (St Lawrence) w Watford *Pet 2* **P** *Bp and Ld Chan (alt)* **V** C R EVANS
LONG BURTON (St James) *see* Dungeon Hill *Sarum*
LONG CLAWSON (St Remigius) *see* Harby, Long Clawson and Hose *Leic*
LONG COMPTON (St Peter and St Paul), Whichford and Barton-on-the-Heath *Cov 9* **P** *Bp, Trin Coll Ox, and Ch Ch Ox (by turn)* **V** R K SMITH, **C** R D HOLDER
LONG CRENDON (St Mary the Virgin) w Chearsley and Nether Winchendon *Ox 21* **P** *Bp and R V Spencer-Bernard Esq (jt)* **P-in-c** R JACKSON
LONG CRICHEL (St Mary) *see* Witchampton, Stanbridge and Long Crichel etc *Sarum*
LONG CROSS (Christ Church) *Guildf 11* **P** *J D Tringham Esq* **V** A B OLSEN
LONG DITTON (St Mary) *S'wark 16* **P** *Bp* **R** D LANKEY, **NSM** P J MALLETT
LONG EATON (St John) *Derby 13* **P** *Bp* **V** G R PERCY, **C** L A DESHPANDE
LONG EATON (St Laurence) *Derby 13* **P** *Bp* **V** G M KNOX
LONG HANBOROUGH (Christ Church) *see* Hanborough and Freeland *Ox*
LONG ITCHINGTON (Holy Trinity) and Marton *Cov 10* **P** *Bp* **V** P J CROOKS, **C** M L D GREIG
LONG LANE (Christ Church) *see* Longford, Long Lane, Dalbury and Radbourne *Derby*
LONG LAWFORD (St John) *see* Newbold on Avon *Cov*
LONG LOAD (Christ Church) *see* Langport Area Chs *B & W*
LONG MARSTON (All Saints) *see* Tring *St Alb*
LONG MARSTON (All Saints) *York 1* **P** *Col E C York* **R** J A RENDALL, **NSM** J E CHAPMAN
LONG MARTON (St Margaret and St James) w Dufton and w Milburn *Carl 1* **P** *Lord Hothfield* **R** A HERBERT
LONG MELFORD (Holy Trinity) (St Catherine) *St E 12* **P** *Bp* **R** C J SANSBURY
LONG NEWNTON (Holy Trinity) *see* Ashley, Crudwell, Hankerton, Long Newnton etc *Bris*
LONG PRESTON (St Mary the Virgin) w Tosside *Bradf 5* **P** *D&C Ch Ch Ox and V Gisburn (alt)* **P-in-c** M R RUSSELL-SMITH
LONG RISTON (St Margaret) *see* Skirlaugh w Long Riston *York*
LONG STANTON (All Saints) w St Michael *Ely 5* **P** *Magd Coll Cam and Bp (alt)* **P-in-c** G A LAY
LONG STANTON (St Michael and All Angels) *see* Wenlock *Heref*
LONG SUTTON (All Saints) *see* Herriard w Winslade and Long Sutton etc *Win*
LONG SUTTON (Holy Trinity) *see* Langport Area Chs *B & W*
LONG SUTTON (St Mary) *see* Sutton St Mary *Linc*
LONG WHATTON (All Saints) *see* Hathern, Long Whatton and Diseworth w Belton etc *Leic*
LONG WITTENHAM (St Mary the Virgin) *see* Dorchester *Ox*
LONGBOROUGH (St James), Sezincote, Condicote and the Swells *Glouc 15* **P** *Lord Leigh, Mrs S Peake, DBP, and Ch Ch Ox (by turn)* **R** E B HYDE
LONGBRIDGE (St John the Baptist) *Birm 4* **P** *Bp* **V** M S BRIDGEN
LONGBRIDGE DEVERILL (St Peter and St Paul) *see* Cley Hill Warminster *Sarum*
LONGCOT (St Mary the Virgin) *see* Ashbury, Compton Beauchamp and Longcot w Fernham *Ox*
LONGDEN (St Ruthen) and Annscroft w Pulverbatch *Heref 13* **P** *Bp and MMCET (jt)* **P-in-c** N J CHARRINGTON, **NSM** J J WADDINGTON-FEATHER
LONGDON (St James) *Lich 1* **P** *Bp* **P-in-c** J W ALLAN
LONGDON (St Mary), Castlemorton, Bushley, Queenhill w Holdfast *Worc 5* **P** *Bp, D&C Westmr, and Ch Union Trustees (jt)* **V** C A MOSS
LONGDON-UPON-TERN (St Bartholomew) *see* Wrockwardine Deanery *Lich*
LONGFIELD (Mission Room) (St Mary Magdalene) *Roch 1* **P** *Ld Chan* **R** J R CHALLICE
LONGFLEET (St Mary) *Sarum 8* **P** *MMCET* **P-in-c** A N PERRY, **C** I B PAUL
LONGFORD (St Chad), Long Lane, Dalbury and Radbourne *Derby 14* **P** *Bp, R Church Broughton, and Mrs I J Chandos-Pole (jt)* **R** *Vacant* (01332) 824560
LONGFORD (St Thomas) *Cov 2* **P** *Bp* **V** D I BRUCE
LONGFRAMLINGTON (St Mary the Virgin) w Brinkburn *Newc 9* **P** *Bp* **P-in-c** P A G ETTERLEY
LONGHAM (St Andrew and St Peter) *see* Gressenhall w Longham w Wendling etc *Nor*
LONGHILL (St Margaret) *see* Sutton St Mich *York*

LONGHIRST (St John the Evangelist) *see* Bothal and Pegswood w Longhirst *Newc*
LONGHOPE (All Saints) *see* Huntley and Longhope *Glouc*
LONGHORSLEY (St Helen) and Hebron *Newc 11* **P** *Ld Chan* **P-in-c** G EVANS, **NSM** J WAIYAKI
LONGHOUGHTON (St Peter and St Paul) w Howick *Newc 9* **P** *Trustees of the late Duke of Northd and Bp (alt)* **V** *Vacant* (01665) 577305
LONGLEVENS (Holy Trinity) *see* Wotton St Mary *Glouc*
LONGNEWTON (St Mary) w Elton *Dur 10* **P** *Bp and St Chad's Coll Dur (alt)* **NSM** A I TRIMBLE
LONGNEY (St Lawrence) *see* Hardwicke, Quedgeley and Elmore w Longney *Glouc*
LONGNOR (St Bartholomew), Quarnford and Sheen *Lich 5* **P** *Bp, V Alstonfield, and Miss A I M Harpur-Crewe (jt)* **V** A C F NICOLL
LONGNOR (St Mary) *see* Dorrington w Leebotwood, Longnor, Stapleton etc *Heref*
LONGPARISH (St Nicholas) *see* Barton Stacey and Bullington etc *Win*
LONGRIDGE (St Lawrence) (St Paul) *Blackb 14* **P** *Trustees* **V** R W E AWRE, **C** A W WILKINSON
LONGSDON (St Chad) *see* Horton, Lonsdon and Rushton Spencer *Lich*
LONGSIGHT (St John w St Cyprian) *see* Birch St Agnes w Longsight St Jo w St Cypr *Man*
LONGSIGHT (St Luke) *Man 1* **P** *D&C and Trustees (jt)* **R** P N CLARK
LONGSLEDDALE (St Mary) *see* Skelsmergh w Selside and Longsleddale *Carl*
LONGSOLE (Mission Room) *see* Barming *Roch*
LONGSTOCK (St Mary) *see* Stockbridge and Longstock and Leckford *Win*
LONGSTONE, GREAT (St Giles) *see* Ashford w Sheldon and Longstone *Derby*
LONGSTOWE (St Mary) *see* Bourn and Kingston w Caxton and Longstowe *Ely*
LONGTHORPE (St Botolph) *Pet 13* **P** *Sir Stephen Hastings* **V** H C SMART, **NSM** L M ELLIOTT
LONGTON (St Andrew) *Blackb 6* **P** *A F Rawstorne Esq* **V** A PARKINSON, **C** W J ROUTH
LONGTON (St James and St John) *Lich 12* **P** *Bp* **R** P N SUCH
LONGTON (St Mark) *see* Edensor *Lich*
LONGTON (St Mary and St Chad) *Lich 12* **P** *Bp* **V** P LOCKETT
LONGTON, NEW (All Saints) *Blackb 6* **P** *Bp* **V** D M ROGERS
LONGWELL GREEN (All Saints) *Bris 2* **P** *Bp* **P-in-c** P S SHIPP
LONGWOOD (St Mark) *Wakef 5* **P** *V Huddersfield* **V** J A HUNT, **NSM** S HOLT
LONGWORTH (St Mary) *see* Cherbury *Ox*
LOOE, WEST (St Nicholas) *see* St Martin w E and W Looe *Truro*
LOOSE (All Saints) *Cant 15* **P** *Abp* **V** R C COATES, **NSM** R G GAMBLE
LOPEN (All Saints) *see* Merriott w Hinton, Dinnington and Lopen *B & W*
LOPHAM NORTH (St Nicholas) *see* Bressingham w N and S Lopham and Fersfield *Nor*
LOPHAM SOUTH (St Andrew) *as above*
LOPPINGTON (St Michael and All Angels) w Newtown *Lich 23* **P** *Bp and R Wem (jt)* **P-in-c** N MacGREGOR, **NSM** K M SOMERVELL
LORD'S HILL Local Ecumenical Project *Win 12* **P** *Bp* **V** J L H PAGE
LORTON (St Cuthbert) and Loweswater w Buttermere *Carl 6* **P** *Bp and Earl of Lonsdale (alt)* **V** M R BRAITHWAITE
LOSCOE (St Luke) *Derby 12* **P** *Bp* **C** A LOVE
LOSTOCK (St Thomas and St John) *Man 11* **P** *Bp and TR Deane St Mary the Virgin (jt)* **V** *Vacant* (01204) 654863
LOSTOCK GRALAM (St John the Evangelist) *Ches 6* **P** *V Witton* **V** H W STRATTON
LOSTOCK HALL (St James) *Blackb 6* **P** *Bp* **V** S BAXTER
LOSTWITHIEL (St Bartholomew), St Winnow w St Nectan's Chapel, St Veep and Boconnoc *Truro 10* **P** *D&C and A D G Fortescue Esq (jt)* **Hon C** F E STUBBINGS
LOTHERSDALE (Christ Church) *see* Carleton and Lothersdale *Bradf*
LOTHERTON (St James) *see* Aberford w Micklefield *York*
LOTTISHAM (The Blessed Virgin Mary) *see* Baltonsborough w Butleigh and W Bradley *B & W*
LOUDWATER (St Peter) *Ox 21* **P** *MMCET* **V** T G BUTLIN
LOUGHBOROUGH (All Saints) (Holy Trinity) *Leic 7* **P** *Bp and Em Coll Cam (jt)* **R** S A CHERRY, **NSM** G MITCHELL, M J MORRIS
LOUGHBOROUGH (Emmanuel) (St Mary in Charnwood) *Leic 7* **P** *Patr Bd* **TR** D M F NEWMAN, **TV** P G DAY, **C** D MACHA, **Hon C** C R ROE, **NSM** R BOOKLESS
LOUGHBOROUGH (Good Shepherd) *Leic 7* **P** *Bp* **P-in-c** K H MLEMETA, **NSM** R J WHITLEY
LOUGHBOROUGH (St Peter) *Leic 7* **P** *Bp* **V** D PATERSON
LOUGHTON (All Saints) *see* Watling Valley *Ox*
LOUGHTON (not known) *see* Ditton Priors w Neenton, Burwarton etc *Heref*
LOUGHTON (St John the Baptist) (St Gabriel) (St Nicholas) *Chelmsf 25* **P** *Patr Bd* **TR** G K WELCH, **TV** J DELFGOU, **C** M E WEST, **Hon C** O B WELLS
LOUGHTON (St Mary the Virgin) *Chelmsf 25* **P** *Bp* **R** D J BROOMFIELD
LOUGHTON (St Michael and All Angels) *Chelmsf 25* **P** *Bp* **V** P A G RAYNER
LOUND (St Anne) *see* Babworth w Sutton-cum-Lound *S'well*
LOUND (St John the Baptist) *see* Somerleyton, Ashby, Fritton, Herringfleet etc *Nor*
LOUNDSLEY GREEN (Church of the Ascension) *see* Old Brampton and Loundsley Green *Derby*
LOUTH (Holy Trinity) (St James) (St Michael) *Linc 12* **P** *Patr Bd* **TR** S D HOLDAWAY, **TV** B A HILL, D R WISE, **C** R L HOWLETT, **NSM** R W MANSFIELD
LOVERSALL (St Katherine) *see* Wadworth w Loversall *Sheff*
LOVINGTON (St Thomas a Becket) *see* Six Pilgrims *B & W*
LOW *see also under substantive place name*
LOW FELL (St Helen) *see* Gateshead St Helen *Dur*
LOW HAM (Chapel) *see* Langport Area Chs *B & W*
LOW HILL (Good Shepherd) *see* Bushbury *Lich*
LOW MOOR (Holy Trinity) *Bradf 2* **P** *V Bradf* **V** *Vacant* (01274) 678859
LOW MOOR (St Mark) *Bradf 2* **P** *Bp* **P-in-c** S J LORD
LOW VALLEY (St Matthew) *see* Darfield *Sheff*
LOWDHAM (St Mary the Virgin) w Caythorpe, and Gunthorpe *S'well 11* **P** *Bp* **V** E ASHBY, **NSM** M A KEENE
LOWER *see also under substantive place name*
LOWER MANOR (St Andrew) *see* Sheff Manor *Sheff*
LOWER WINDRUSH *Ox 8* **P** *Bp, DBP, St Jo Coll Ox, D&C Ex, and B Babington-Smith Esq (jt)* **R** D M MURRAY, **Hon C** P P SYMES
LOWER WYLYE and Till Valley *Sarum 16* **P** *Earl of Pembroke, D&C Windsor, and DBP (by turn)* **P-in-c** P F SMITH
LOWESBY (All Saints) *see* Whatborough Gp of Par *Leic*
LOWESTOFT (Christ Church) *Nor 9* **P** *CPAS* **V** P R MOON
LOWESTOFT (Good Shepherd) *see* Lowestoft St Marg *Nor*
LOWESTOFT (St Andrew) *Nor 9* **P** *Ch Patr Tr* **V** *Vacant* (01502) 511521
LOWESTOFT (St Margaret) *Nor 9* **P** *Patr Bd* **TR** M C GRAY, **C** L F GANDIYA
LOWESWATER (St Bartholomew) *see* Lorton and Loweswater w Buttermere *Carl*
LOWFIELD HEATH (St Michael) *see* Crawley *Chich*
LOWGATE (St Mary) *see* Hexham *Newc*
LOWGATE (St Mary the Virgin) *see* Kingston upon Hull St Mary *York*
LOWICK (St John the Baptist) and Kyloe w Ancroft *Newc 12* **P** *D&C Dur (2 turns), Bp (1 turn)* **V** V T DICKINSON
LOWICK (St Luke) *see* Egton-cum-Newland and Lowick *Carl*
LOWICK (St Peter) *see* Brigstock w Stanion and Lowick and Sudborough *Pet*
LOWSONFORD (St Luke) *see* Hatton w Haseley, Rowington w Lowsonford etc *Cov*
LOWTHER (St Michael) and Askham and Clifton and Brougham *Carl 1* **P** *Earl of Lonsdale* **R** D J RADCLIFFE
LOWTHORPE (St Martin) *see* Burton Agnes w Harpham and Lowthorpe etc *York*
LOWTON (St Luke) *Liv 16* **P** *Bp* **R** J R MACAULAY
LOWTON (St Mary) *Liv 16* **P** *Bp* **V** R BRITTON
LOXBEARE (St Michael and All Angels) *see* Washfield, Stoodleigh, Withleigh etc *Ex*
LOXHORE (St Michael and All Angels) *see* Shirwell, Loxhore, Kentisbury, Arlington, etc *Ex*
LOXLEY (St Nicholas) *see* Hampton Lucy w Charlecote and Loxley *Cov*
LOXTON (St Andrew) *see* Crook Peak *B & W*
LOXWOOD (St John the Baptist) *see* Alfold and Loxwood *Guildf*
LOZELLS (St Paul and St Silas) *Birm 8* **P** *Aston Patr Trust* **P-in-c** J PRASADAM
LUBENHAM (All Saints) *see* Foxton w Gumley and Laughton and Lubenham *Leic*
LUCCOMBE (The Blessed Virgin Mary) *see* Selworthy, Timberscombe, Wootton Courtenay etc *B & W*
LUCKER (St Hilda) *see* Belford and Lucker *Newc*
LUCKINGTON (St Mary) *see* Sherston Magna, Easton Grey, Luckington etc *Bris*

LUDBOROUGH (St Mary) *see* Fotherby *Linc*
LUDDENDEN (St Mary) w Luddenden Foot *Wakef 3* **P** *Bp and V Halifax (alt)* **V** *Vacant* (01422) 882127
LUDDESDOWN (St Peter and St Paul) *see* Cobham w Luddesdowne and Dode *Roch*
LUDDINGTON (All Saints) *see* Stratford-on-Avon w Bishopton *Cov*
LUDDINGTON (St Margaret) *see* Polebrook and Lutton w Hemington and Luddington *Pet*
LUDDINGTON (St Oswald) *see* N Axholme Gp *Linc*
LUDFORD (St Giles) *see* Ludlow, Ludford, Ashford Carbonell etc *Heref*
LUDFORD MAGNA (St Mary) *see* Binbrook Gp *Linc*
LUDGERSHALL (St James) *see* Tidworth, Ludgershall and Faberstown *Sarum*
LUDGERSHALL (St Mary the Virgin) w Wotton Underwood and Ashendon *Ox 24* **P** *CPAS and Bp (jt)* **R** C S JEE
LUDGVAN (St Ludgvan and St Paul) *Truro 5* **P** *Lord St Levan* **R** A PARSONS, **NSM** H M POOLE
LUDHAM (St Catherine), Potter Heigham and Hickling *Nor 12* **P** *Bp and Major J M Mills (jt)* **V** W J CAMERON
LUDLOW (St Laurence) (St John), Ludford, Ashford Carbonell, Ashford Bowdler, Caynham and Richards Castle *Heref 12* **P** *Patr Bd* **TR** B L CURNEW, **TV** J V ROBERTS, **C** M T TOWNSEND, A M BARGE, **NSM** G H EARNEY
LUFFENHAM, NORTH (St John the Baptist) *see* Edith Weston w N Luffenham and Lyndon w Manton *Pet*
LUFFENHAM, SOUTH (St Mary the Virgin) *see* Barrowden and Wakerley w S Luffenham *Pet*
LUFTON (St Peter and St Paul) *see* Odcombe, Brympton, Lufton and Montacute *B & W*
LUGWARDINE (St Peter) w Bartestree, Weston Beggard and Dormington *Heref 4* **P** *D&C (3 turns), and A T Foley Esq (1 turn)* **V** D J BOWEN
LULLINGSTONE (St Botolph) *see* Eynsford w Farningham and Lullingstone *Roch*
LULLINGTON (All Saints) *see* Beckington w Standerwick, Berkley, Rodden etc *B & W*
LULLINGTON (All Saints) *see* Seale and Lullington *Derby*
LULLINGTON (not known) *see* Alfriston w Lullington, Litlington and W Dean *Chich*
LULWORTHS, (St Andrew) (Holy Trinity) Winfrith Newburgh and Chaldon, The *Sarum 9* **P** *Bp (3 turns), Col Sir Joseph Weld (1 turn)* **P-in-c** W A ROGERS
LUMB (St Michael) *see* Newchurch *Man*
LUMLEY (Christ Church) *Dur 11* **P** *Bp* **V** J R STRINGER
LUND (All Saints) *see* Lockington and Lund and Scorborough w Leconfield *York*
LUND (St John the Evangelist) *Blackb 11* **P** *Ch Ch Ox* **V** J K BRIGHAM
LUNDWOOD (St Mary Magdalene) *Wakef 7* **P** *Bp* **V** *Vacant* (01226) 203194
LUNDY ISLAND (St Helen) Extra-Parochial Place *Ex 15* **P-in-c** W G BLAKEY
LUPPITT (St Mary) *see* Dunkeswell, Sheldon and Luppitt *Ex*
LUPSET (St George) *Wakef 12* **P** *Bp* **V** G CLAY, **NSM** G D GREEN
LUPTON (All Saints) *see* Kirkby Lonsdale *Carl*
LURGASHALL (St Laurence), Lodsworth and Selham *Chich 11* **P** *Cowdray Trust and Lord Egremont (alt)* **R** J A LUSTED
LUSBY (St Peter) *see* Marden Hill Gp *Linc*
LUSTLEIGH (St John the Baptist) *see* Moretonhampstead, Manaton, N Bovey and Lustleigh *Ex*
LUTON (All Saints) (St Peter) *St Alb 14* **P** *Bp* **NSM** T SHACKLADY
LUTON (Christ Church) *Roch 5* **P** *R Chatham* **R** C D COLLINS, **C** A J D FOOT
LUTON Lewsey (St Hugh) *St Alb 14* **P** *Bp* **V** P J LAW, **C** D R ELLIOTT
LUTON Limbury (St Augustine of Canterbury) *St Alb 14* **P** *Bp* **V** R I CHEETHAM, **Hon C** J YABSLEY
LUTON (St Andrew) *St Alb 14* **P** *Bp* **V** R J BASS
LUTON (St Anne) *St Alb 14* **P** *Peache Trustees, Bp, and V Luton (jt)* **V** P C BUDGELL, **Hon C** R A BUDGELL
LUTON (St Christopher) Round Green *St Alb 14* **P** *Bp* **V** R B ETHERINGTON, **NSM** F M G ETHERINGTON
LUTON (St Francis) *St Alb 14* **P** *Peache Trustees, Bp, and V Luton (jt)* **V** A T SHARP, **C** J DANIEL
LUTON (St John) *see* Teignmouth, Ideford w Luton, Ashcombe etc *Ex*
LUTON (St Mary) *St Alb 14* **P** *Peache Trustees* **V** N P J BELL, **C** S M HUDSPITH, R C HIBBERT
LUTON (St Matthew) High Town *St Alb 14* **P** *Ch Patr Trust* **V** M J PRITCHARD
LUTON (St Paul) *St Alb 14* **P** *Peache Trustees* **V** A SELLERS, **NSM** C A PULLINGER
LUTON (St Saviour) *St Alb 14* **P** *Bp* **V** D H GOODBURN, **NSM** D C ANDERSON, P J MOSS
LUTTERWORTH (St Mary) w Cotesbach *Leic 11* **P** *The Crown (3 turns), Ld Chan (1 turn)* **R** M H W COUSSENS, **C** M A HAND
LUTTON (St Nicholas) w Gedney Drove End, Dawsmere *Linc 16* **P** *The Crown, Ld Chan, and V Long Sutton (by turn)* **P-in-c** M J NOTLEY
LUTTON (St Peter) *see* Polebrook and Lutton w Hemington and Luddington *Pet*
LUTTONS AMBO (St Mary) *see* Weaverthorpe w Helperthorpe, Luttons Ambo etc *York*
LUXBOROUGH (Blessed Virgin Mary) *see* Exton and Winsford and Cutcombe w Luxborough *B & W*
LUXULYAN (St Cyrus and St Julietta) *see* Lanlivery w Luxulyan *Truro*
LYDBROOK (Holy Jesus) *Glouc 4* **P** *Bp* **V** M J FOSTER
LYDBURY NORTH (St Michael and All Angels) w Hopesay and Edgton *Heref 10* **P** *Earl of Powis (3 turns), Mrs R E Bell (1 turn)* **R** A F DENYER
LYDD (All Saints) *Cant 13* **P** *Abp* **P-in-c** G N STARTIN
LYDDEN (St Mary the Virgin) *see* Temple Ewell w Lydden *Cant*
LYDDINGTON (All Saints) and Wanborough and Bishopstone w Hinton Parva *Bris 11* **P** *Bp and Ld Chan (alt)* **R** R W SANDAY
LYDDINGTON (St Andrew) w Stoke Dry and Seaton w Caldecott *Pet 14* **P** *Bp, Burghley Ho Preservation Trust, and R E M Elborne Esq (by turn)* **V** *Vacant* (01572) 822221
LYDEARD ST LAWRENCE (St Lawrence) w Brompton Ralph, Combe Florey, Ash Priors and Tolland *B & W 19* **P** *Ld Chan (2 turns), W H J Hancock Esq (2 turns), and MMCET (1 turn)* **R** J C F HAWNT
LYDFORD (St Petrock) *see* Peter Tavy, Mary Tavy, Lydford and Brent Tor *Ex*
LYDFORD ON FOSSE (St Peter) *see* Keinton Mandeville w Lydford-on-Fosse etc *B & W*
LYDGATE (St Anne), w (Christ Church), Friezland *Man 21* **P** *Bp* **V** R I S WHITE, **NSM** E OGDEN
LYDGATE (St Mary) *see* Wickhambrook w Lydgate, Ousden and Cowlinge *St E*
LYDHAM (Holy Trinity) *see* Wentnor w Ratlinghope, Myndtown, Norbury etc *Heref*
LYDIARD MILLICENT (All Saints) *see* W Swindon and the Lydiards *Bris*
LYDIARD TREGOZE (St Mary) *as above*
LYDIATE (St Thomas) *Liv 11* **P** *R Halsall* **V** A A DAVIES
LYDLINCH (St Thomas a Beckett) *see* Stock and Lydlinch *Sarum*
LYDNEY (St Mary the Virgin) *Glouc 4* **P** *Ld Chan* **V** D F F EVANS, **NSM** M D MILLER
LYE, THE (Christchurch) and Stambermill *Worc 12* **P** *Bp and CPAS (alt)* **V** D M WOODHOUSE
LYFORD (St Mary) *see* Cherbury *Ox*
LYME REGIS (St Michael the Archangel) *Sarum 3* **P** *Bp* **P-in-c** J G W ANDREWS
LYMINGE (St Mary and St Ethelburga) w Paddlesworth and Stanford w Postling and Radegund *Cant 5* **P** *Abp* **R** F KENT
LYMINGTON (St Thomas the Apostle) *Win 10* **P** *Bp* **V** M H WEAVER, **C** J T McDOWALL
LYMINGTON Woodside (All Saints) *see* Lymington *Win*
LYMINSTER (St Mary Magdalene) *Chich 1* **P** *Eton Coll on nomination of BNC Ox* **V** J E SLEGG
LYMM (St Mary the Virgin) *Ches 4* **P** *Bp* **R** *Vacant* (01925) 752164
LYMPNE (St Stephen) *see* Sellindge w Monks Horton and Stowting etc *Cant*
LYMPSHAM (St Christopher) *see* Brent Knoll, E Brent and Lympsham *B & W*
LYMPSTONE (Nativity of the Blessed Virgin Mary) *Ex 1* **P** *SMF* **P-in-c** J CLAPHAM
LYNCH (St Luke) w Iping Marsh and Milland *Chich 10* **P** *Cowdray Trust and Bp (jt)* **V** M J SMITH
LYNCHMERE (St Peter) and Camelsdale *Chich 10* **P** *Prime Min* **V** W J MUSSON
LYNCOMBE (St Bartholomew) *see* Bath St Bart *B & W*
LYNDHURST (St Michael) and Emery Down *Win 10* **P** *Bp and P J P Green Esq (alt)* **V** P F MURPHY, **NSM** F O BOOT
LYNDON (St Martin) *see* Edith Weston w N Luffenham and Lyndon w Manton *Pet*
LYNEAL (St John the Evangelist) *see* Petton w Cockshutt, Welshampton and Lyneal etc *Lich*
LYNEHAM (St Michael) w Bradenstoke *Sarum 18* **P** *Ld Chan* **V** *Vacant*
LYNEMOUTH (St Aidan) *see* Cresswell and Lynemouth *Newc*
LYNESACK (St John the Evangelist) *Dur 7* **P** *Bp* **V** M J SHEARING
LYNG (St Bartholomew) *see* Stoke St Gregory w Burrowbridge and Lyng *B & W*

LYNG (St Margaret), Sparham, Elsing, Bylaugh, Bawdeswell and Foxley *Nor 22* **P** *DBP, Sir Edward Evans-Lombe, and Bp (by turn)* **R** E A CUNNINGTON
LYNGFORD (St Peter) *see* Taunton Lyngford *B & W*
LYNMOUTH (St John the Baptist) *see* Combe Martin, Berrynarbor, Lynton, Brendon etc *Ex*
LYNN, NORTH (St Edmund) *see* King's Lynn St Marg w St Nic *Nor*
LYNN, SOUTH (All Saints) *Nor 20* **P** *Bp* **P-in-c** K J REEVE
LYNN, WEST (St Peter) *see* Clenchwarton and W Lynn *Ely*
LYNSTED (St Peter and St Paul) *see* Teynham w Lynsted and Kingsdown *Cant*
LYNTON (St Mary the Virgin) *see* Combe Martin, Berrynarbor, Lynton, Brendon etc *Ex*
LYONS (St Michael and All Angels) *Dur 14* **P** *The Crown* **R** G HARRIS
LYONSDOWN (Holy Trinity) *St Alb 17* **P** *Ch Patr Trust* **V** G R HUDDLESTON
LYONSHALL (St Michael and All Angels) w Titley, Almeley and Kinnersley *Heref 5* **P** *Bp, D&C, and Ch Patr Trust (jt)* **V** *Vacant* (01544) 340212
LYSTON (not known) *see* Pentlow, Foxearth, Liston and Borley *Chelmsf*
LYTCHETT MATRAVERS (St Mary the Virgin) *Sarum 8* **P** *DBP* **P-in-c** P J A HASTINGS
LYTCHETT MINSTER (not known) *Sarum 8* **P** *Bp* **V** E C CARDALE, **C** C M ROWBERRY, **NSM** H D PAGE-CLARK
LYTHAM (St Cuthbert) *Blackb 11* **P** *DBP* **V** G I HIRST, **C** A R HODGSON
LYTHAM (St John the Divine) *Blackb 11* **P** *J C Hilton Esq* **V** C J CARLISLE
LYTHE (St Oswald) w Ugthorpe *York 23* **P** *Abp* **V** W SMITH
MABE (St Laudus) *Truro 3* **P** *Bp* **P-in-c** S BROCKLEHURST
MABLETHORPE (St Mary) w Trusthorpe *Linc 8* **P** *Bp Lon (2 turns), Bp Linc (1 turn)* **R** *Vacant* (01507) 473159
MACCLESFIELD (St John the Evangelist) *Ches 13* **P** *Bp* **V** D TAYLOR
MACCLESFIELD (St Paul) *Ches 13* **P** *Bp* **V** S M EAST
MACCLESFIELD Team Parish, The (All Saints) (Christ Church) (St Michael and All Angels) (St Peter) *Ches 13* **P** *Patr Bd* **TR** J BRIGGS, **TV** J C G STALEY, **C** J S BISHOP, J BUCKLEY, **NSM** J A MYNETT
MACKWORTH (All Saints) *Derby 11* **P** *J M Clark-Maxwell Esq* **P-in-c** K JARDIN
MACKWORTH (St Francis) *Derby 9* **P** *Bp* **V** B W G HACKNEY
MADEHURST (St Mary Magdalene) *see* Slindon, Eartham and Madehurst *Chich*
MADELEY (All Saints) *Lich 9* **P** *J C Crewe Esq* **V** *Vacant* (01782) 750205
MADELEY (St Michael) *Heref 14* **P** *Patr Bd* **TR** R L PAMPLIN, **TV** H A SCRIVEN, J A FOX, **C** K S EVANS
MADINGLEY (St Mary Magdalene) *Ely 5* **P** *Bp* **V** *Vacant*
MADLEY (Nativity of the Blessed Virgin Mary) w Tyberton, Preston-on-Wye and Blakemere *Heref 1* **P** *D&C* **V** T R N JONES, **NSM** R S JONES
MADRESFIELD (St Mary) *see* Guarlford and Madresfield w Newland *Worc*
MADRON (St Maddern) *Truro 5* **P** *Bp* **V** J K P S ROBERTSHAW, **NSM** P A T HORDER
MAER (St Peter) *see* Chapel Chorlton, Maer and Whitmore *Lich*
MAESBROOK (St John) *see* Kinnerley w Melverley and Knockin w Maesbrook *Lich*
MAESBURY (St John the Baptist) *Lich 19* **P** *Bp* **P-in-c** A B STRATFORD
MAGDALEN LAVER (St Mary Magdalen) *see* High Laver w Magdalen Laver and Lt Laver etc *Chelmsf*
MAGHAM DOWN (St Mark) *see* Hailsham *Chich*
MAGHULL (St Andrew) (St James) (St Peter) *Liv 11* **P** *Patr Bd* **TR** J M GOODCHILD, **TV** B A MUSK, K DAGGER, **Hon C** W H TULLOCH, **NSM** C R SANDS
MAIDA VALE (St Peter) *see* Paddington St Pet *Lon*
MAIDA VALE (St Saviour) *see* Paddington St Sav *Lon*
MAIDEN BRADLEY (All Saints) *see* Mere w W Knoyle and Maiden Bradley *Sarum*
MAIDEN NEWTON (St Mary) *see* Melbury *Sarum*
MAIDENHEAD (All Saints) *see* Boyne Hill *Ox*
MAIDENHEAD (St Andrew and St Mary Magdalene) *Ox 13* **P** *Peache Trustees* **V** T K PARKIN, **NSM** N W SANDERS, R D MANDERSON
MAIDENHEAD (St Luke) *Ox 13* **P** *Bp* **P-in-c** J R HOLROYD
MAIDENHEAD (St Peter) *see* Furze Platt *Ox*
MAIDFORD (St Peter and St Paul) *see* Blakesley w Adstone and Maidford etc *Pet*
MAIDS MORETON (St Edmund) *see* N Buckingham *Ox*
MAIDSTONE (All Saints) (St Philip) w St Stephen Tovil *Cant 15* **P** *Abp* **V** C J MORGAN-JONES
MAIDSTONE Barming Heath (St Andrew) *see* Barming Heath *Cant*
MAIDSTONE (St Faith) *Cant 15* **P** *Abp* **V** I H CROFTS
MAIDSTONE (St Luke the Evangelist) *Cant 15* **P** *Trustees* **V** E D DELVE
MAIDSTONE (St Martin) *Cant 15* **P** *Abp* **V** E R ROUTH, **TV** D J A POLLARD, **C** R G BROWN
MAIDSTONE (St Michael and All Angels) *Cant 15* **P** *Abp* **V** P J GIBBONS
MAIDSTONE (St Paul) *Cant 15* **P** *Abp* **V** N H TAYLOR, **NSM** E A ATTAWAY
MAIDWELL (St Mary) w Draughton and Lamport w Faxton *Pet 2* **P** *Bp (3 turns), Sir Ian Isham (1 turn)* **P-in-c** W G GIBBS, B LEE
MAINSTONE (St John the Baptist) *see* Bishop's Castle w Mainstone *Heref*
MAISEMORE (St Giles) *Glouc 6* **P** *Bp* **P-in-c** G E PARSONS
MAKER (St Mary and St Julian) w Rame *Truro 11* **P** *The Crown and Earl of Mount Edgcumbe (jt)* **V** R A DOYLE
MALBOROUGH (All Saints) w South Huish, West Alvington and Churchstow *Ex 14* **P** *Bp and D&C (jt)* **P-in-c** J SWEATMAN
MALDEN (St James) *S'wark 16* **P** *Bp* **C** E H LEE, **Hon C** A HARDY, **NSM** O PIGGOTT
MALDEN (St John) *S'wark 16* **P** *Mert Coll Ox* **V** P J KNIGHT
MALDEN, NEW (St John the Divine) and Coombe *S'wark 16* **P** *CPAS* **V** J S DOWNEY, **C** S M BENOY, **NSM** I R L PRIOR
MALDON (All Saints w St Peter) *Chelmsf 11* **P** *Bp* **V** P J MASON, **NSM** K L HACKER HUGHES
MALDON (St Mary) w Mundon *Chelmsf 11* **P** *D&C Westmr* **R** A M A McINTOSH
MALEW Ballasalla (St Mary the Virgin) *see* Malew *S & M*
MALEW (St Mark) (St Moluag or St Lupus) *S & M 1* **P** *The Crown* **V** M ROBERTS, **NSM** G BARKER
MALIN BRIDGE (St Polycarp) *Sheff 4* **P** *Bp* **V** M G COCKAYNE
MALINS LEE (St Leonard) *see* Cen Telford *Lich*
MALLERSTANG (St Mary) *see* Kirkby Stephen w Mallerstang etc *Carl*
MALLING, EAST (St James) *Roch 7* **P** *D&C* **V** P J MILLS
MALLING, SOUTH (St Michael) *Chich 18* **P** *MMCET* **V** A T HINDLEY
MALLING, WEST (St Mary) w Offham *Roch 7* **P** *Ld Chan and DBP (alt)* **V** R B STEVENSON
MALMESBURY (St Peter and St Paul) w Westport and Brokenborough *Bris 12* **P** *Ch Trust Fund Trust* **V** D LITTLEFAIR
MALPAS (St Andrew) *see* Truro St Paul and St Clem *Truro*
MALPAS (St Oswald) and Threapwood *Ches 5* **P** *DBF* **R** T ETHERIDGE
MALTBY (St Bartholomew) (Ascension) (Venerable Bede) *Sheff 5* **P** *Bp* **TR** V J FILER, **TV** H M HOTCHIN
MALTON, NEW (St Michael) *York 3* **P** *Sir Stephen Hastings* **V** R ROGERS
MALTON, OLD (St Mary the Virgin) *York 3* **P** *Sir Stephen Hastings* **V** J C MANCHESTER
MALVERN (Holy Trinity) (St James) *Worc 2* **P** *Bp and D&C Westmr (jt)* **V** P C G BILLINGHAM, **C** A J COOTE
MALVERN (St Andrew) *Worc 2* **P** *Bp* **P-in-c** D J LLOYD
MALVERN, GREAT (Christchurch) *Worc 2* **P** *Bp* **P-in-c** P M J GINEVER
MALVERN, GREAT (St Mary and St Michael) *Worc 2* **P** *Bp* **P-in-c** M J A BARR
MALVERN, LITTLE (St Giles), Malvern Wells and Wyche *Worc 2* **P** *Bp, V Gt Malvern Ch Ch, and Exors T M Berington Esq (jt)* **NSM** E G KNOWLES
MALVERN, WEST (St James) *see* Malvern H Trin and St Jas *Worc*
MALVERN LINK (Church of the Ascension) (St Matthias) w Cowleigh *Worc 2* **P** *Patr Bd* **TR** G LYALL, **TV** D C OSBORNE, **C** A R N WILLIAMS, **Hon Par Dn** R HERBERT
MAMBLE (St John the Baptist) w Bayton, Rock w Heightington w Far Forest *Worc 4* **P** *Ld Chan and R Ribbesford w Bewdley etc (alt)* **P-in-c** L M GIBSON
MAMHEAD (St Thomas the Apostle) *see* Kenton, Mamhead, Powderham, Cofton and Starcross *Ex*
MANACCAN (St Manaccus and St Dunstan) w St Anthony-in-Meneage and St Martin-in-Meneage *Truro 4* **P** *Ld Chan* **P-in-c** T E DOREY
MANATON (St Winifred) *see* Moretonhampstead, Manaton, N Bovey and Lustleigh *Ex*
MANBY (St Mary) *see* Mid Marsh Gp *Linc*
MANCETTER (St Peter) *Cov 5* **P** *Ch Patr Trust* **V** A S MAIRS

MANCHESTER (Apostles) w Miles Platting *Man 1* **P** *DBP* **C** P J CLEMENT
MANCHESTER (Church of the Resurrection) *see* Manchester Gd Shep and St Barn *Man*
MANCHESTER Clayton (St Cross w St Paul) *Man 1* **P** *Bp* **R** N J PRIOR
MANCHESTER Good Shepherd (St Barnabas) (Church of the Resurrection) *Man 1* **P** *Prime Min and Trustees (alt)* **R** T S R CHOW, **C** J HARGREAVES, **NSM** A-M HUMPHREYS
MANCHESTER (St Ann) *Man 4* **P** *Bp* **R** M ARUNDEL
MANCHESTER (St John Chrysostom) Victoria Park *Man 4* **P** *Bp* **P-in-c** J W B TOMLINSON
MANCHESTER Whitworth (not known) *Man 4* **P** *Bp* **TV** A S HAVENS, I D GOMERSALL
MANEA (St Nicholas) *see* Christchurch and Manea and Welney *Ely*
MANEY (St Peter) *Birm 13* **P** *Bp* **V** J C W ROSE
MANFIELD (All Saints) *see* Barton and Manfield and Cleasby w Stapleton *Ripon*
MANGOTSFIELD (St James) *Bris 7* **P** *Peache Trustees* **V** K M BOXALL
MANLEY (St John the Evangelist) *see* Alvanley *Ches*
MANNINGFORD BRUCE (St Peter) *see* Swanborough *Sarum*
MANNINGHAM (St Chad) *see* Toller Lane St Chad *Bradf*
MANNINGHAM (St Mary Magdalene and St Michael and All Angels) (St Paul and St Jude) *Bradf 1* **P** *Patr Bd* **TR** G MOFFAT, **TV** G J PETERS, B W PIERCE
MANNINGS HEATH (Church of the Good Shepherd) *see* Nuthurst *Chich*
MANOR PARK (St Barnabas) *see* Lt Ilford St Barn *Chelmsf*
MANOR PARK (St John the Baptist) *see* W Slough *Ox*
MANOR PARK (St John the Evangelist) *see* Lt Ilford St Mich *Chelmsf*
MANOR PARK (St Mary the Virgin) *as above*
MANOR PARK (St Michael and All Angels) *as above*
MANOR PARK (William Temple) *see* Sheff Manor *Sheff*
MANSEL LACY (St Michael) *see* Credenhill w Brinsop, Mansel Lacey, Yazor etc *Heref*
MANSERGH (St Peter) *see* Kirkby Lonsdale *Carl*
MANSFIELD Oak Tree Lane *S'well 2* **P** *DBP* **P-in-c** P A CHAPMAN
MANSFIELD (St Augustine) *S'well 2* **P** *Bp* **V** J M BURGESS
MANSFIELD (St John the Evangelist) *S'well 2* **P** *Bp* **P-in-c** G K KNOTT, **C** D A MARVIN
MANSFIELD (St Lawrence) *S'well 2* **P** *Bp* **P-in-c** D J HULL
MANSFIELD (St Mark) *S'well 2* **P** *Bp* **P-in-c** M J DOBBS
MANSFIELD (St Peter and St Paul) *S'well 2* **P** *Bp* **V** R T WARBURTON, **C** R J St C HARLOW-TRIGG
MANSFIELD WOODHOUSE (St Edmund King and Martyr) *S'well 2* **P** *Bp* **V** D B STEVEN, **C** J HEATH, G E HOLLOWAY
MANSTON (St Catherine) *see* St Laur in Thanet *Cant*
MANSTON (St James) *Ripon 8* **P** *R Barwick in Elmet* **V** R W SHAW, **C** S J HILL, A J MARRIOTT
MANSTON (St Nicholas) *see* Childe Okeford, Okeford Fitzpaine, Manston etc *Sarum*
MANTHORPE (St John the Evangelist) *see* Grantham *Linc*
MANTON (St Hibald) *Linc 6* **P** *Bp* **R** D I WALKER
MANTON (St Mary the Virgin) *see* Edith Weston w N Luffenham and Lyndon w Manton *Pet*
MANUDEN (St Mary the Virgin) w Berden *Chelmsf 21* **P** *Patr Bd and Ch Hosp (alt)* **P-in-c** C BISHOP
MAPERTON (St Peter and St Paul) *see* Camelot Par *B & W*
MAPLEBECK (St Radegund) *S'well 15* **P** *Sir Stephen Hastings* **P-in-c** H H WILCOX
MAPLEDURHAM (St Margaret) *see* Caversham and Mapledurham *Ox*
MAPLEDURWELL (St Mary) *see* Newnham w Nately Scures w Mapledurwell etc *Win*
MAPLESTEAD, GREAT (St Giles) and Little (St John) w Gestingthorpe *Chelmsf 19* **P** *Bp* **P-in-c** P D DAKIN, **NSM** C E DAKIN
MAPPERLEY (Holy Trinity) *see* W Hallam and Mapperley *Derby*
MAPPERLEY (St Jude) *see* Nottingham St Jude *S'well*
MAPPLEBOROUGH GREEN (Holy Ascension) *see* Studley *Cov*
MAPPLETON (All Saints) *see* Aldbrough, Mappleton w Goxhill and Withernwick *York*
MAPPLETON (St Mary) *see* Ashbourne w Mapleton *Derby*
MAPPOWDER (St Peter and St Paul) *see* Hazelbury Bryan and the Hillside Par *Sarum*
MARAZION (All Saints) *Truro 5* **P** *V St Hilary* **V** A K TORRY
MARBURY (St Michael) *Ches 5* **P** *Bp* **V** G H SANSOME
MARCH (St John) *Ely 18* **P** *Bp* **R** A T SCHOFIELD
MARCH (St Mary) *Ely 18* **P** *Bp* **R** D W SPENCER, **NSM** A CHANDLER
MARCH (St Peter) *Ely 18* **P** *Bp* **R** D W SPENCER, **NSM** A CHANDLER
MARCH (St Wendreda) *Ely 18* **P** *MMCET* **R** P BAXANDALL, **Hon Par Dn** S M BARCLAY
MARCHAM (All Saints) w Garford *Ox 10* **P** *Ch Ch Ox* **P-in-c** R R J LAPWOOD, **NSM** J C COTTERILL
MARCHINGTON (St Peter) *see* Uttoxeter Area *Lich*
MARCHINGTON WOODLANDS (St John) *as above*
MARCHWOOD (St John) *Win 10* **P** *Bp* **R** J D CURTIS
MARCLE, LITTLE (St Michael and All Angels) *Heref 6* **P** *Bp* **R** *Vacant*
MARCLE, MUCH (St Bartholomew) *Heref 6* **P** *E Money-Kyrle Esq* **P-in-c** C L BEEVERS
MARDEN (All Saints) *see* Redhorn *Sarum*
MARDEN (St Hilda) *see* Cullercoats St Geo *Newc*
MARDEN (St Mary the Virgin) w Amberley and Wisteston *Heref 4* **P** *D&C* **P-in-c** U J SUMMERS
MARDEN (St Michael and All Angels) *Cant 11* **P** *Abp* **V** J M BOURNE
MARDEN, EAST (St Peter) *see* Compton, the Mardens, Stoughton and Racton *Chich*
MARDEN, NORTH (St Mary) *as above*
MARDEN ASH (St James) *see* High Ongar w Norton Mandeville *Chelmsf*
MARDEN HILL Group, The *Linc 7* **P** *Bp (2 turns), B Eley Esq & DBP, Baroness Willoughby, Duchy of Lanc, J Pain Esq & M Dudley Hewitt Esq, A Lee Esq (1 each)* **R** A M SULLIVAN
MAREHAM-LE-FEN (St Helen) and Revesby *Linc 11* **P** *Bp and Mrs A D Lee (alt)* **R** S JONES-CRABTREE
MAREHAM ON THE HILL (All Saints) *Linc 11* **P** *Bp* **V** *Vacant*
MARESFIELD (St Bartholomew) *Chich 21* **P** *Ch Trust Fund Trust* **R** M T A BULMAN
MARFLEET (St Giles) (St George) (St Hilda) (St Philip) *York 15* **P** *Patr Bd* **TR** A PATTERSON, **TV** S W OSMAN, J G F GRAHAM-BROWN, S SHERIFF
MARGARET MARSH (St Margaret) *see* Shaston *Sarum*
MARGARET RODING (St Margaret) *see* High and Gd Easter w Margaret Roding *Chelmsf*
MARGARET STREET (All Saints) *see* St Marylebone All SS *Lon*
MARGARETTING (St Margaret) *see* Fryerning w Margaretting *Chelmsf*
MARGATE (All Saints) *Cant 9* **P** *Abp* **V** M J A ANDERSON
MARGATE (Holy Trinity) *Cant 9* **P** *Ch Patr Trust* **V** K M THORPE, **C** T C WILSON, R J MARSDEN, **Hon C** D S HARE, **NSM** E M SHEARCROFT
MARGATE (St John the Baptist in Thanet) *Cant 9* **P** *Abp* **V** B P SHARP, **C** A C NUNN
MARGATE (St Paul) *see* Cliftonville *Cant*
MARHAM (Holy Trinity) *Ely 16* **P** *St Jo Coll Cam* **P-in-c** G PARROTT
MARHAMCHURCH (St Marwenne) *see* Bude Haven and Marhamchurch *Truro*
MARHOLM (St Mary the Virgin) *see* Castor w Sutton and Upton w Marholm *Pet*
MARIANSLEIGH (St Mary) *see* Bishopsnympton, Rose Ash, Mariansleigh etc *Ex*
MARISHES, THE (Chapel) *see* Pickering w Lockton and Levisham *York*
MARK (Holy Cross) w Allerton *B & W 1* **P** *Bp and D&C (jt)* **R** M T PAVEY
MARK BEECH (Holy Trinity) *see* Hever, Four Elms and Mark Beech *Roch*
MARK CROSS (St Mark) *see* Rotherfield w Mark Cross *Chich*
MARKBY (St Peter) *see* Hannah cum Hagnaby w Markby *Linc*
MARKET BOSWORTH (St Peter), Cadeby w Sutton Cheney and Congerstone *Leic 13* **P** *DBP* **TR** J F PLANT, **C** B CAMPBELL
MARKET DEEPING (St Guthlac) *Linc 13* **P** *Ld Chan* **R** S D EARIS
MARKET DRAYTON (St Mary) *see* Drayton in Hales *Lich*
MARKET HARBOROUGH (St Dionysius) *Leic 4* **P** *Bp* **P-in-c** C J E MOODY, **C** S J BISHOP, N P JACOB, **NSM** B M KNIGHT
MARKET HARBOROUGH (Transfiguration) and Little Bowden *Leic 4* **P** *Bp* **P-in-c** C J E MOODY, **C** N P JACOB
MARKET LAVINGTON (St Mary of the Assumption) and Easterton *Sarum 19* **P** *Bp and Ch Ch Ox (alt)* **V** D J GREENMAN
MARKET OVERTON (St Peter and St Paul) *see* Teigh w Whissendine and Market Overton *Pet*
MARKET RASEN (St Thomas the Apostle) *Linc 5* **P** *Ld Chan* **V** M J CARTWRIGHT, **NSM** D L INKPIN
MARKET STAINTON (St Michael and All Angels) *see* Asterby Gp *Linc*

MARKET WEIGHTON (All Saints) *York 7* **P** *Abp* **V** A CLEMENTS
MARKET WESTON (St Mary) *see* Hopton, Market Weston, Barningham etc *St E*
MARKFIELD (St Michael) *Leic 12* **P** *MMCET* **R** G T WILLETT, **NSM** J A DOWNS
MARKHAM, EAST (St John the Baptist) w Askham, Headon w Upton and Grove *S'well 5* **P** *Grove Settled Estate Trustees and SMF (jt)* **R** J H LITTLE
MARKHAM CLINTON (All Saints) *see* Tuxford w Weston and Markham Clinton *S'well*
MARKINGTON (St Michael) w South Stainley and Bishop Thornton *Ripon 3* **P** *Bp, D&C, Sir Thomas Ingilby Bt and N A Hudleston Esq (jt) (by turn)* **V** S J TALBOTT
MARKS GATE (St Mark) Chadwell Heath *Chelmsf 1* **P** *Bp* **V** R K GAYLER
MARKS TEY (St Andrew) w Aldham and Little Tey *Chelmsf 17* **P** *CPAS, Ch Patr Trust and MMCET (jt)* **R** B SNELLING, **Hon C** S G HUCKLE
MARKSBURY (St Peter) *see* Farmborough, Marksbury and Stanton Prior *B & W*
MARKYATE STREET (St John the Baptist) *St Alb 8* **P** *Bp* **V** M J CROW
MARLBOROUGH (St Mary the Virgin) *Sarum 20* **P** *Patr Bd* **TR** H G PEARSON, **TV** J R SARGANT, **C** A MANN, **NSM** P H JOHNS
MARLBROOK (St Luke) *see* Catshill and Dodford *Worc*
MARLDON (St John the Baptist) *Ex 10* **P** *Bp* **V** G L BROCKHOUSE
MARLESFORD (St Andrew) *see* Campsea Ashe w Marlesford, Parham and Hacheston *St E*
MARLEY HILL (St Cuthbert) *Dur 13* **P** *The Crown* **P-in-c** S G RADLEY
MARLINGFORD (Assumption of the Blessed Virgin Mary) *see* Easton w Colton and Marlingford *Nor*
MARLOW, GREAT (All Saints) w Marlow Bottom, Little Marlow and Bisham *Ox 29* **P** *Patr Bd* **TR** N J MOLONY, **TV** M G REED, S E IRWIN
MARLOW, LITTLE (St John the Baptist) *see* Gt Marlow w Marlow Bottom, Lt Marlow and Bisham *Ox*
MARLOW BOTTOM (St Mary the Virgin) *as above*
MARLPIT HILL (St Paulinus) *see* Edenbridge *Roch*
MARLPOOL (All Saints) *Derby 12* **P** *V Heanor* **P-in-c** P BENTLEY
MARLSTON (St Mary) *see* Bucklebury w Marlston *Ox*
MARNHULL (St Gregory) *Sarum 6* **P** *DBF* **P-in-c** R D G WEYMAN, **NSM** M J FICKE
MAROWN (Old Parish Church) (St Runius) *S & M 3* **P** *The Crown* **V** A M CONVERY
MARPLE (All Saints) *Ches 16* **P** *R Stockport St Mary* **V** M A LOWE, **C** P J MACKRIELL, **NSM** B J LOWE, K ELLIS
MARPLE, LOW (St Martin) *Ches 16* **P** *Keble Coll Ox* **V** J H CAM
MARR (St Helen) *see* Bilham *Sheff*
MARSDEN (St Bartholomew) *Wakef 5* **P** *R Almondbury* **V** D MATHERS
MARSDEN, GREAT *Blackb 7* **P** *The Crown* **C** B PARKINSON
MARSDEN, LITTLE (St Paul) *Blackb 7* **P** *Bp* **V** J M HALL, **C** G J HUMPHRYES
MARSH (St George) *see* Lancaster St Mary *Blackb*
MARSH (St James chapel) *see* Huddersfield H Trin *Wakef*
MARSH BALDON (St Peter) *see* Dorchester *Ox*
MARSH FARM (Holy Cross) *St Alb 14* **P** *Bp* **V** J R BELITHER
MARSH GIBBON (St Mary the Virgin) *see* Swan *Ox*
MARSHAM (All Saints) w Burgh-next-Aylsham *Nor 19* **P** *Bp, Mercers of the City of Lon, and J M Roberts Esq (jt)* **R** R J HEWETSON
MARSHCHAPEL (St Mary the Virgin) *see* The North-Chapel Parishes *Linc*
MARSHFIELD (St Mary the Virgin) w Cold Ashton and Tormarton w West Littleton *Bris 2* **P** *New Coll Ox and Bp (alt)* **V** M P WESTLAKE
MARSHLAND, The *Sheff 11* **P** *Ld Chan and Bp (alt)* **V** J I BATTY
MARSHWOOD VALE Team Ministry, The (St Mary) *Sarum 3* **P** *Patr Bd* **TR** R H FAIRBROTHER, **TV** J M DAVEY
MARSKE (St Edmund) *see* Downholme and Marske *Ripon*
MARSKE, NEW (St Thomas) *York 17* **P** *Abp* **V** C M DURNFORD
MARSKE IN CLEVELAND (St Mark) *York 17* **P** *Trustees* **V** D H LAMBERT
MARSTON (St Alban) *see* Stafford *Lich*
MARSTON (St Leonard) *as above*
MARSTON (St Mary) *see* Barkston and Hough Gp *Linc*
MARSTON (St Nicholas) w Elsfield *Ox 4* **P** *Bp and D&C (jt)* **V** A R PRICE
MARSTON, NEW (St Michael and All Angels) *Ox 4* **P** *Bp* **V** E B BARDWELL
MARSTON, NORTH (Assumption of the Blessed Virgin Mary) *see* Schorne *Ox*
MARSTON, SOUTH (St Mary Magdalene) *see* Stratton St Margaret w S Marston etc *Bris*
MARSTON BIGOT (St Leonard) *see* Nunney and Witham Friary, Marston Bigot etc *B & W*
MARSTON GREEN (St Leonard) *Birm 10* **P** *Birm Dioc Trustees* **V** R V ALLEN
MARSTON MAGNA (Blessed Virgin Mary) *see* Chilton Cantelo, Ashington, Mudford, Rimpton etc *B & W*
MARSTON MEYSEY (St James) *see* Meysey Hampton w Marston Meysey and Castle Eaton *Glouc*
MARSTON MONTGOMERY (St Giles) *see* Alkmonton, Cubley, Marston, Montgomery etc *Derby*
MARSTON MORTEYNE (St Mary the Virgin) w Lidlington *St Alb 13* **P** *Bp and St Jo Coll Cam (alt)* **R** *Vacant* (01525) 403687
MARSTON SICCA (St James the Great) *see* Quinton w Marston Sicca *Glouc*
MARSTON ST LAWRENCE (St Lawrence) *see* Greatworth and Marston St Lawrence etc *Pet*
MARSTON TRUSSELL (St Nicholas) *see* Welford w Sibbertoft and Marston Trussell *Pet*
MARSTON UPON DOVE (St Mary) w Scropton *Derby 14* **P** *N J M Spurrier Esq* **C** A G MURPHIE
MARSTOW (St Matthew) *see* Walford and St John w Bishopswood, Goodrich etc *Heref*
MARSWORTH (All Saints) *see* Cheddington w Mentmore and Marsworth *Ox*
MARTHALL (All Saints) *Ches 12* **P** *DBP* **P-in-c** L R THOMAS
MARTHAM (St Mary) and Repps with Bastwick, Thurne and Clippesby *Nor 6* **P** *Bp, D&C, DBP and K Edw VI Gr Sch (jt)* **V** P S PAINE
MARTIN (All Saints) *see* W Downland *Sarum*
MARTIN (Holy Trinity) *see* Scopwick Gp *Linc*
MARTIN (St Michael) *see* Thornton Gp *Linc*
MARTIN HUSSINGTREE (St Michael) *see* Salwarpe and Hindlip w Martin Hussingtree *Worc*
MARTINDALE (Old Church) *see* Barton, Pooley Bridge and Martindale *Carl*
MARTINDALE (St Peter) *as above*
MARTINHOE (St Martin) *see* Combe Martin, Berrynarbor, Lynton, Brendon etc *Ex*
MARTLESHAM (St Mary the Virgin) w Brightwell *St E 2* **P** *Bp* **R** B D LILLISTONE, **C** T P B BREENE
MARTLEY (St Peter) and Wichenford, Knightwick and Doddenham, Broadwas and Cotheridge *Worc 3* **P** *D&C (2 turns), Bp (1 turn)* **R** W N RICHARDS, **C** S A GAZE, **NSM** J C GUISE
MARTOCK (All Saints) w Ash *B & W 6* **P** *Bp* **V** T J FARMILOE, **C** C SNELL, **Hon C** V M WRIGHT
MARTON (Room) *see* Middleton, Newton and Sinnington *York*
MARTON (St Esprit) *see* Long Itchington and Marton *Cov*
MARTON (St James) *see* Capesthorne w Siddington and Marton *Ches*
MARTON (St Margaret of Antioch) *see* Lea Gp *Linc*
MARTON (St Mark) *Heref 13* **P** *V Chirbury* **V** P D HARRATT
MARTON (St Mary) *see* Sheriff Hutton, Farlington, Stillington etc *York*
MARTON (St Paul) *Blackb 9* **P** *V Poulton-le-Fylde* **C** M A GISBOURNE
MARTON-CUM-GRAFTON (Christ Church) *see* Gt and Lt Ouseburn w Marton-cum-Grafton *Ripon*
MARTON-IN-CHIRBURY (St Mark) *see* Marton *Heref*
MARTON-IN-CLEVELAND (St Cuthbert) *York 19* **P** *Abp* **V** J E D CAVE
MARTON IN CRAVEN (St Peter) *see* Broughton, Marton and Thornton *Bradf*
MARTON MOSS (St Nicholas) *Blackb 9* **P** *Bp* **V** A R WOOD
MARTYR WORTHY (St Swithun) *see* Itchen Valley *Win*
MARWOOD (St Michael and All Angels) *see* Heanton Punchardon w Marwood *Ex*
MARY TAVY (St Mary) *see* Peter Tavy, Mary Tavy, Lydford and Brent Tor *Ex*
MARYFIELD (St Philip and St James) *see* Antony w Sheviock *Truro*
MARYPORT (St Mary) (Christ Church) *Carl 7* **P** *Trustees* **V** *Vacant* (01900) 813077
MARYSTOWE (St Mary the Virgin), Coryton, Stowford, Lewtrenchard and Thrushelton *Ex 24* **P** *P T L Newman Esq, Mrs A M Baring-Gould Almond, Air Cdre P L Donkin, and R H Wollocombe Esq (by turn)* **V** G W BALL

MASBROUGH (St Paul) *Sheff 6* **P** *Bp and Ld Chan (alt)* **V** P G HARBORD
MASHAM (St Mary the Virgin) and Healey *Ripon 3* **P** *Trin Coll Cam* **V** B ABELL
MASSINGHAM, GREAT (St Mary) and LITTLE (St Andrew) and Harpley *Nor 14* **P** *Bp, J H Brereton Esq, and DBP (jt)* **R** *Vacant* (01485) 520211
MASTIN MOOR (St Paul) *see* Staveley and Barrow Hill *Derby*
MATCHBOROUGH (Christ Church) *see* Ipsley *Worc*
MATCHING (St Mary) *see* High Laver w Magdalen Laver and Lt Laver etc *Chelmsf*
MATCHING GREEN (St Edmund) *as above*
MATFEN (Holy Trinity) *see* Stamfordham w Matfen *Newc*
MATFIELD (St Luke) *see* Lamberhurst and Matfield *Roch*
MATHON (St John the Baptist) *see* Cradley w Mathon and Storridge *Heref*
MATLASKE (St Peter) *see* Barningham w Matlaske w Baconsthorpe etc *Nor*
MATLOCK (St Giles) (St John the Baptist) *Derby 7* **P** *Bp* **R** J C TOMLINSON
MATLOCK BANK (All Saints) *Derby 7* **P** *Bp* **P-in-c** S I MITCHELL, **NSM** K J ORFORD
MATLOCK BATH (Holy Trinity) and Cromford *Derby 7* **P** *Ch Trust Fund Trust* **V** *Vacant* (01629) 582947
MATSON (St Katherine) *Glouc 5* **P** *D&C* **NSM** A D HAYMAN
MATTERDALE (not known) *see* Greystoke, Matterdale, Mungrisdale etc *Carl*
MATTERSEY (All Saints) *see* Everton and Mattersey w Clayworth *S'well*
MATTINGLEY (not known) *see* Heckfield w Mattingley and Rotherwick *Win*
MATTISHALL (All Saints) w Mattishall Burgh, Welborne and Yaxham *Nor 17* **P** *G&C Coll Cam and Bp (alt)* **R** D PEARSON, **C** I R BENTLEY
MATTISHALL BURGH (St Peter) *see* Mattishall w Mattishall Burgh, Welborne etc *Nor*
MAUGHOLD (St Maughold) *S & M 4* **P** *The Crown* **V** D J GREEN, **NSM** E C B CORLETT
MAULDEN (St Mary) *St Alb 9* **P** *Bp* **R** D LEWTHWAITE
MAUNBY (St Michael) *see* Ainderby Steeple w Yafforth and Kirby Wiske etc *Ripon*
MAUTBY (St Peter and St Paul) *see* Filby, Thrigby, Mautby, Stokesby, Runham etc *Nor*
MAVESYN RIDWARE (St Nicholas) *see* The Ridwares and Kings Bromley *Lich*
MAVIS ENDERBY (St Michael) *see* Marden Hill Gp *Linc*
MAWDESLEY (St Peter) *Blackb 4* **P** *R Croston* **R** D J REYNOLDS
MAWGAN (St Mawgan) *see* Cury and Gunwalloe w Mawgan *Truro*
MAWNAN (St Mawnan) (St Michael) *Truro 3* **P** *Bp* **P-in-c** H F JACKSON
MAXEY (St Peter) *see* Etton w Helpston and Maxey *Pet*
MAXSTOKE (St Michael and All Angels) *Birm 10* **P** *Lord Leigh* **V** R G BOLLARD
MAYBRIDGE (St Richard) *Chich 5* **P** *Bp* **V** R T E B WOODS
MAYBUSH Redbridge (All Saints) *see* Southampton Maybush St Pet *Win*
MAYBUSH (St Peter) *as above*
MAYFAIR (Christ Church) *Lon 3* **P** *Bp* **P-in-c** D C L PRIOR, **Hon C** A M ANSELL
MAYFIELD (St Dunstan) *Chich 15* **P** *Keble Coll Ox* **V** G W HOLMES
MAYFIELD (St John the Baptist) *Lich 15* **P** *Ch Soc Trust* **P-in-c** G L HUMPHRIES
MAYFORD (Emmanuel) *see* Woking St Jo *Guildf*
MAYHILL (All Saints) *see* Huntley and Longhope *Glouc*
MAYLAND (St Barnabas) (St Barnabas Family Centre) *Chelmsf 11* **P** *Bp* **P-in-c** L BLANEY
MEANWOOD (Holy Trinity) *Ripon 7* **P** *Bp* **V** R M WIGGEN
MEARE (Blessed Virgin Mary and All Saints) *see* Glastonbury w Meare, W Pennard and Godney *B & W*
MEARS ASHBY (All Saints) and Hardwick and Sywell w Overstone *Pet 6* **P** *Duchy of Cornwall (2 turns), Bracegirdle Trustees (1 turn), and Mrs C K Edmiston (1 turn)* **R** *Vacant* (01604) 812907
MEASHAM (St Lawrence) *Leic 9* **P** *CPAS* **V** J N PEARSON
MEAVY (St Peter) *see* Yelverton, Meavy, Sheepstor and Walkhampton *Ex*
MEDBOURNE (St Giles) *see* Six Saints circa Holt *Leic*
MEDMENHAM (St Peter and St Paul) *see* Hambleden Valley *Ox*
MEDOMSLEY (St Mary Magdalene) *Dur 4* **P** *Bp* **V** A E HARRISON
MEDSTEAD (St Andrew) cum Wield *Win 2* **P** *The Crown* **R** T SMITH
MEERBROOK (St Matthew) *see* Leek and Meerbrook *Lich*
MEESDEN (St Mary) *see* Hormead, Wyddial, Anstey, Brent Pelham etc *St Alb*
MEETH (St Michael and All Angels) *see* Hatherleigh, Meeth, Exbourne and Jacobstowe *Ex*
MEIR (Holy Trinity) *Lich 6* **P** *Bp* **P-in-c** G W WHITTY
MEIR HEATH (St Francis of Assisi) *Lich 12* **P** *Bp* **V** J W PAWSON
MEIR PARK (St Clare) *see* Meir Heath *Lich*
MELBECKS (Holy Trinity) *see* Swaledale *Ripon*
MELBOURN (All Saints) *Ely 8* **P** *D&C* **P-in-c** A D O'BRIEN
MELBOURNE (St Michael) *Derby 15* **P** *Bp* **V** F ROSS
MELBOURNE (St Monica) *see* Seaton Ross Gp of Par *York*
MELBURY (St Mary the Virgin) (St Osmund) *Sarum 1* **P** *Patr Bd* **TR** T R WEST, **TV** J E CURTIS, R N HUNGERFORD, **NSM** N E de CHAZAL
MELBURY ABBAS (St Thomas) *see* Shaston *Sarum*
MELBURY BUBB (St Mary the Virgin) *see* Melbury *Sarum*
MELBURY OSMUND (St Osmund) *as above*
MELCHBOURNE (St Mary Magdalene) *see* The Stodden Churches *St Alb*
MELCOMBE HORSEY (St Andrew) *see* Milton Abbas, Hilton w Cheselbourne etc *Sarum*
MELDON (St John the Baptist) *see* Bolam w Whalton and Hartburn w Meldon *Newc*
MELDRETH (Holy Trinity) *Ely 8* **P** *D&C* **P-in-c** A D O'BRIEN
MELKSHAM (St Barnabas) (St Michael and All Angels) *Sarum 17* **P** *DBP* **TR** M B G PAIN, **TV** C E SUGDEN, **NSM** K SUGDEN
MELKSHAM FOREST (St Andrew) *see* Melksham *Sarum*
MELLING (St Thomas) *see* Bickerstaffe and Melling *Liv*
MELLING (St Wilfrid) *see* Tunstall w Melling and Leck *Blackb*
MELLIS (St Mary the Virgin) *see* Thornhams Magna and Parva, Gislingham and Mellis *St E*
MELLOR (St Mary) *Blackb 2* **P** *V Blackb* **V** J P HUDSON
MELLOR (St Thomas) *Derby 6* **P** *Bp* **P-in-c** P J JENNER
MELLS (St Andrew) w Buckland Dinham, Elm, Whatley, Vobster and Chantry *B & W 4* **P** *DBP (2 turns), Bp (1 turns)* **R** *Vacant* (01373) 812320
MELMERBY (St John the Baptist) *see* Skirwith, Ousby and Melmerby w Kirkland *Carl*
MELPLASH (Christ Church) *see* Beaminster Area *Sarum*
MELSONBY (St James the Great) *see* Forcett and Aldbrough and Melsonby *Ripon*
MELTHAM Christ the King (St Bartholomew) (St James) *Wakef 5* **P** *R Almondbury w Farnley Tyas, and Simeon's Trustees (jt)* **NSM** P ROLLS
MELTON (St Andrew) *St E 7* **P** *D&C Ely* **R** M SANDERS, **Hon C** H C SANDERS
MELTON, GREAT (All Saints) *see* Hethersett w Canteloff w Lt and Gt Melton *Nor*
MELTON, HIGH (St James) *see* Barnburgh w Melton on the Hill etc *Sheff*
MELTON, LITTLE (All Saints) *see* Hethersett w Canteloff w Lt and Gt Melton *Nor*
MELTON, WEST (St Cuthbert) *see* Brampton Bierlow *Sheff*
MELTON CONSTABLE (St Peter) *see* Briston w Burgh Parva and Melton Constable *Nor*
MELTON MOWBRAY (St Mary) *Leic 3* **P** *Patr Bd* **TR** C A G JENKIN, **TV** A S HUNT, A C DEEGAN, **C** D E HEBBLEWHITE, **Hon C** S A BIRCH
MELTON ROSS (Ascension) *see* Brocklesby Park *Linc*
MELVERLEY (St Peter) *see* Kinnerley w Melverley and Knockin w Maesbrook *Lich*
MEMBURY (St John the Baptist) *see* Yarcombe, Membury, Upottery and Cotleigh *Ex*
MENDHAM (All Saints) *see* Fressingfield, Mendham, Metfield, Weybread etc *St E*
MENDLESHAM (St Mary) *St E 6* **P** *SMF* **V** P T GRAY
MENHENIOT (St Lalluwy and St Antoninus) *Truro 12* **P** *Ex Coll Ox* **V** D J LOEWENDAHL, **Hon C** P C BELLENES
MENITH WOOD (Chapel) *see* Teme Valley N *Worc*
MENSTON (St John the Divine) w Woodhead *Bradf 4* **P** *Bp* **V** C D E CLARKE
MENTMORE (St Mary the Virgin) *see* Cheddington w Mentmore and Marsworth *Ox*
MEOLE BRACE (Holy Trinity) *Lich 21* **P** *J K Bather Esq* **V** K T ROBERTS, **C** C W DEVONISH, **NSM** A M ROBERTS
MEOLS, GREAT (St John the Baptist) *Ches 8* **P** *Bp* **V** K J PRITCHARD
MEOLS, NORTH (St Cuthbert) *Liv 9* **P** *Personal Reps R F Hesketh Esq* **R** *Vacant* (01704) 28325
MEON, EAST (All Saints) *Portsm 5* **P** *Ld Chan* **V** T E LOUDEN
MEON, WEST (St John the Evangelist) and Warnford *Portsm 5* **P** *Bp and DBP (alt)* **P-in-c** H G PRIDEAUX, **NSM** J R BARNETT

MEONSTOKE (St Andrew) w Corhampton cum Exton *Portsm 1* **P** *Bp* **R** D E HENLEY, **NSM** P FLETCHER
MEOPHAM (St John the Baptist) w Nurstead *Roch 1* **P** *D&C and Lt-Col F B Edmeades (jt)* **R** S H DUNN
MEPAL (St Mary) *see* Witcham w Mepal *Ely*
MEPPERSHALL (St Mary the Virgin) w Campton and Stondon *St Alb 16* **P** *St Jo Coll Cam (1 turn), Bp (2 turns)* **R** J H BARRALL, **NSM** S J WHEATLEY
MERE (St Michael the Archangel) w West Knoyle and Maiden Bradley *Sarum 14* **P** *Bp* **V** W H V ELLIOTT, **NSM** S M WOOD
MERESIDE (St Wilfrid) *see* Blackpool St Wilfrid *Blackb*
MEREVALE (St Mary the Virgin) *see* Baxterley w Hurley and Wood End and Merevale etc *Birm*
MEREWORTH (St Lawrence) w West Peckham *Roch 7* **P** *Viscount Falmouth and D&C (alt)* **R** R N McCONACHIE
MERIDEN (St Laurence) *Cov 4* **P** *Chapter Cov Cathl* **R** M H DAWKINS
MERRINGTON (St John the Evangelist) *see* Spennymoor, Whitworth and Merrington *Dur*
MERRIOTT (All Saints) w Hinton, Dinnington and Lopen *B & W 15* **P** *D&C Bris (2 turns), Bp (1 turn)* **R** J C KING
MERROW (St John the Evangelist) *Guildf 5* **P** *Earl of Onslow* **R** A P HODGETTS, **NSM** D E C MATTHEWS
MERRY HILL (St Joseph) *see* Penn Fields *Lich*
MERRYMEET (St Mary) *see* Menheniot *Truro*
MERSEA, WEST (St Peter and St Paul) w East (St Edmund) *Chelmsf 16* **P** *Bp and The Crown (alt)* **P-in-c** R H ELPHICK
MERSHAM (St John the Baptist) w Hinxhill *Cant 12* **P** *Abp* **P-in-c** J W TIPPING
MERSTHAM (St Katharine) (Epiphany) and Gatton *S'wark 26* **P** *Abp* **R** R J M GROSVENOR, **C** C E LATHAM
MERSTHAM, SOUTH (All Saints) *S'wark 26* **P** *Bp* **NSM** D C HUGHES
MERSTON (St Giles) *see* N Mundham w Hunston and Merston *Chich*
MERTON (All Saints) *see* Shebbear, Buckland Filleigh, Sheepwash etc *Ex*
MERTON (St James) *S'wark 13* **P** *Bp and V Merton St Mary (jt)* **V** *Vacant* 0181-540 3122
MERTON (St John the Divine) *S'wark 13* **P** *Bp and V Merton St Mary (jt)* **V** S A ROBERTS
MERTON (St Mary) *S'wark 13* **P** *Bp* **V** T G LEARY, **NSM** D HAGGIE, M J HANCOCK
MERTON (St Peter) *see* Caston, Griston, Merton, Thompson etc *Nor*
MERTON (St Swithun) *see* Ambrosden w Mert and Piddington *Ox*
MESHAW (St John) *see* Witheridge, Thelbridge, Creacombe, Meshaw etc *Ex*
MESSING (All Saints) *see* Copford w Easthorpe and Messing w Inworth *Chelmsf*
MESSINGHAM (Holy Trinity) *Linc 4* **P** *Bp* **V** *Vacant* (01724) 762823
MESTY CROFT (St Luke) *see* Wednesbury St Paul Wood Green *Lich*
METFIELD (St John the Baptist) *see* Fressingfield, Mendham, Metfield, Weybread etc *St E*
METHERINGHAM (St Wilfred) w Blankney and Dunston *Linc 18* **P** *Bp (2 turns), Br Field Products Ltd (1 turn)* **V** J H RICHARDSON
METHLEY (St Oswald) w Mickletown *Ripon 8* **P** *Bp (3 turns), Duchy of Lanc (1 turn)* **P-in-c** G R LURIE
METHWOLD (St George) *Ely 15* **P** *Ld Chan* **P-in-c** D J KIGHTLEY
METTINGHAM (All Saints) *see* Wainford *St E*
METTON (St Andrew) *see* Roughton and Felbrigg, Metton, Sustead etc *Nor*
MEVAGISSEY (St Peter) and St Ewe *Truro 1* **P** *Bp and Penrice Ho (St Austell) Ltd* **R** A E ALLARDICE
MEXBOROUGH (St John the Baptist) *Sheff 12* **P** *Adn York* **C** D S BAILEY
MEYSEY HAMPTON (St Mary) w Marston Meysey and Castle Eaton *Glouc 13* **P** *Ch Soc Trust* **R** H BUSK
MICHAEL (St Michael and All Angels) *S & M 3* **P** *The Crown* **V** *Vacant*
MICHAELCHURCH ESCLEY (St Michael) *see* Clodock and Longtown w Craswall, Llanveynoe etc *Heref*
MICHAELSTOW (St Michael) *see* St Tudy w St Mabyn and Michaelstow *Truro*
MICHELDEVER (St Mary) and East Stratton, Woodmancote and Popham *Win 13* **P** *Lord Northbrook (3 turns), Bp (2 turns)* **V** B R G FLENLEY, **NSM** M J ABSOLON
MICHELMERSH (Our Lady) and Timsbury and Farley Chamberlayne and Braishfield *Win 11* **P** *Bp* **R** D B KINGTON
MICKLEGATE (Holy Trinity) and Bishophill Junior (St Mary) *York 8* **P** *D&C* **R** G S HIGGINSON
MICKLEHAM (St Michael) *Guildf 7* **P** *St Jo Foundn Sch* **P-in-c** J P HARKIN
MICKLEHURST (All Saints) *Ches 14* **P** *Bp* **V** *Vacant* (01457) 832393
MICKLEOVER (All Saints) *Derby 10* **P** *MMCET* **V** A W WARD
MICKLEOVER (St John) *Derby 10* **P** *Bp* **V** B M WILSON, **C** M A PRIDDIN
MICKLETON (St Lawrence) *Glouc 11* **P** *Ld Chan* **P-in-c** D G HUMPHRIES
MICKLEY (St George) *Newc 3* **P** *Bp* **P-in-c** T EMMETT
MICKLEY (St John the Evangelist) *see* Fountains Gp *Ripon*
MID MARSH Group, The *Linc 12* **P** *Rear Admiral G P D Hall, Bp, D&C, and Lord Deramore (by turn)* **R** P G FAULKNER, **NSM** L W CARROLL, J R SELFE
MIDDLE *see also under substantive place name*
MIDDLE RASEN Group, The *Linc 5* **P** *Bp and DBP (jt)* **R** C H LILLEY
MIDDLEHAM (St Mary and St Alkelda) w Coverdale and East Witton *Ripon 4* **P** *Bp, R Craven-Smith-Milnes Esq, and W R Burdon Esq (jt)* **R** D W EYLES
MIDDLESBROUGH (All Saints) *York 19* **P** *Abp* **V** G HOLLAND
MIDDLESBROUGH (Ascension) *York 19* **P** *Abp* **V** D G HODGSON
MIDDLESBROUGH (Holy Trinity) *see* N Ormesby *York*
MIDDLESBROUGH (St Agnes) *York 19* **P** *Abp* **V** G J PACEY
MIDDLESBROUGH (St Barnabas) *see* Linthorpe *York*
MIDDLESBROUGH (St Chad) *York 19* **P** *Abp* **V** *Vacant* (01642) 819854
MIDDLESBROUGH (St Columba w St Paul) *York 19* **P** *Abp* **P-in-c** S COOPER
MIDDLESBROUGH (St Cuthbert) *York 19* **P** *Abp* **NSM** S C CHALLENGER
MIDDLESBROUGH (St John the Evangelist) *York 19* **P** *Abp* **V** A CAMPBELL-WILSON
MIDDLESBROUGH (St Martin of Tours) *York 19* **P** *Abp* **V** P H BURMAN
MIDDLESBROUGH (St Oswald) *York 19* **P** *Abp* **V** G J WOOD, **C** M R NELSON
MIDDLESBROUGH (St Thomas) *York 19* **P** *Abp* **V** *Vacant* (01642) 244908
MIDDLESMOOR (St Chad) *see* Upper Nidderdale *Ripon*
MIDDLESTOWN (St Luke) *Wakef 12* **P** *R Thornhill* **V** L J SHUTT
MIDDLETON (All Saints) *see* Gt and Lt Henny w Middleton, Wickham St Paul etc *Chelmsf*
MIDDLETON (Holy Ghost) *see* Kirkby Lonsdale *Carl*
MIDDLETON (Holy Trinity) *see* Bitterley w Middleton, Stoke St Milborough etc *Heref*
MIDDLETON (Holy Trinity) *Heref 13* **P** *V Chirbury* **V** N D MINSHALL
MIDDLETON (Holy Trinity) *see* Kelsale-cum-Carlton, Middleton-cum-Fordley etc *St E*
MIDDLETON (St Andrew), Newton and Sinnington *York 21* **P** *Abp (2 turns), Simeon's Trustees (1 turn)* **R** T A SMITH
MIDDLETON (St Cross) *Ripon 6* **P** *DBP* **V** M S HATTON
MIDDLETON (St George) (St Laurence) *Dur 8* **P** *Bp* **R** C LINGARD
MIDDLETON (St John the Baptist) *Birm 13* **P** *Bp* **P-in-c** J W WOODWARD
MIDDLETON (St Leonard) (St Margaret) w Thornham *Man 18* **P** *Bp* **TR** N J FEIST, **TV** C FALLONE, **NSM** F JACKSON
MIDDLETON (St Mary the Virgin) *Ripon 6* **P** *V Rothwell* **V** J N O HORTON, **C** S A STUTZ
MIDDLETON (St Mary) w East Winch *Nor 20* **P** *Ld Chan and W O Lancaster Esq (alt)* **P-in-c** P BROWN
MIDDLETON (St Michael and All Angels) *see* Youlgreave, Middleton, Stanton-in-Peak etc *Derby*
MIDDLETON (St Nicholas) *see* Felpham w Middleton *Chich*
MIDDLETON-BY-WIRKSWORTH (Holy Trinity) *see* Wirksworth *Derby*
MIDDLETON CHENEY (All Saints) w Chacombe *Pet 1* **P** *BNC Ox (2 turns), Bp (1 turn)* **R** A VILLAGE
MIDDLETON-IN-CHIRBY (Holy Trinity) *see* Middleton *Heref*
MIDDLETON-IN-TEESDALE (St Mary the Virgin) w Forest and Frith *Dur 7* **P** *Lord Barnard and The Crown (alt)* **R** J E G CLARK
MIDDLETON JUNCTION (St Gabriel) *Man 18* **P** *Bp* **V** I B COOK
MIDDLETON ON LEVEN (St Cuthbert) *see* Rudby in Cleveland w Middleton *York*
MIDDLETON-ON-SEA Conventional District *Chich 1* **C-in-c** W T MARSTON
MIDDLETON-ON-THE-HILL (St Mary the Virgin) *see* Kimbolton w Hamnish and Middleton-on-the-Hill *Heref*

MIDDLETON-ON-THE-WOLDS (St Andrew) *see* Bainton w N Dalton, Middleton-on-the-Wolds etc *York*
MIDDLETON SCRIVEN (St John the Baptist) *see* Billingsley w Sidbury, Middleton Scriven etc *Heref*
MIDDLETON STONEY (All Saints) *see* Akeman *Ox*
MIDDLETON TYAS (St Michael and All Angels) w Croft and Eryholme *Ripon 2* **P** *Prime Min and V Gilling (alt)* **R** J R WRAIGHT
MIDDLETOWN (St John the Baptist) *see* Gt Wollaston *Heref*
MIDDLEWICH (St Michael and All Angels) w Byley *Ches 6* **P** *Bp* **V** S R HAWORTH
MIDDLEZOY (Holy Cross) and Othery and Moorlinch *B & W 5* **P** *Bp Worc (1 turn), Bp (2 turns)* **P-in-c** G WEYMONT
MIDGHAM (St Matthew) *see* Woolhampton w Midgham and Beenham Valance *Ox*
MIDHOPE (St James) *see* Penistone and Thurlstone *Wakef*
MIDHURST (St Mary Magdalene and St Denis) *Chich 10* **P** *Cowdray Trust* **V** A T CUNNINGTON
MIDSOMER NORTON (St John the Baptist) w Clandown *B & W 12* **P** *Ch Ch Ox* **V** C G CHIPLIN
MIDVILLE (St Peter) *see* Stickney Gp *Linc*
MILBER (St Luke) *Ex 11* **P** *Bp* **V** J E POTTER
MILBORNE PORT (St John the Evangelist) w Goathill *B & W 7* **P** *Mrs J E Smith (2 turns), Trustees (1 turn)* **V** B C B WHITWORTH
MILBORNE ST ANDREW (St Andrew) w Dewlish *Sarum 2* **P** *Revd J L Baillie* **P-in-c** R W B THOMSON
MILBORNE WICK (Mission Church) *see* Milborne Port w Goathill *B & W*
MILBOURNE (Holy Saviour) *see* Ponteland *Newc*
MILBURN (St Cuthbert) *see* Long Marton w Dufton and w Milburn *Carl*
MILCOMBE (St Laurence) *see* Bloxham w Milcombe and S Newington *Ox*
MILDEN (St Peter) *see* Monks Eleigh w Chelsworth and Brent Eleigh etc *St E*
MILDENHALL (St John the Baptist) *see* Marlborough *Sarum*
MILDENHALL (St Mary) *St E 11* **P** *Patr Bd (2 turns), Bp (1 turn)* **TR** D S MEIKLE, **TV** M G S WHITCOMBE, G S ANDERSON, D GARDNER, **C** J W HOLLINGSWORTH, **NSM** P W TAMS
MILDMAY GROVE (St Jude and St Paul) *Lon 6* **P** *Islington Ch Trust* **V** D SILVESTER
MILE CROSS (St Catherine) *see* Horsford and Horsham w Newton St Faith *Nor*
MILE CROSS (St Catherine) *Nor 2* **P** *Dr J P English, Canon G F Bridger, Revd K W Habershon, and Revd H Palmer (jt)* **P-in-c** D E COURT, **C** R A BETTS
MILE END Old Town (St Paul) *see* Bow Common *Lon*
MILEHAM (St John the Baptist) *see* Litcham w Kempston, E and W Lexham, Mileham etc *Nor*
MILES PLATTING (St Cuthbert) *see* Man Apostles w Miles Platting *Man*
MILFORD (Holy Trinity) *see* Belper Ch Ch and Milford *Derby*
MILFORD (St John the Evangelist) *Guildf 4* **P** *V Witley* **V** D J MUSKETT
MILFORD, SOUTH (St Mary the Virgin) *see* Monk Fryston and S Milford *York*
MILFORD-ON-SEA (All Saints) *Win 10* **P** *Bp* **V** A M C DUNN, **Hon C** A RIDGE
MILKWALL (St Luke) *see* Coleford w Staunton *Glouc*
MILL END (St Peter) and Heronsgate w West Hyde *St Alb 5* **P** *Bp and V Rickmansworth* **V** A A HORSLEY, **C** J L OSBORNE
MILL HILL (John Keble Church) *Lon 15* **P** *Bp* **V** O R OSMOND, **Hon C** R M HILLS, **NSM** P A JONES
MILL HILL (St Michael and All Angels) *Lon 15* **P** *Bp* **V** D F SHARPE, **NSM** R M HILLS
MILL HILL (St Paul) *see* Hendon St Paul Mill Hill *Lon*
MILLAND (St Luke) *see* Lynch w Iping Marsh and Milland *Chich*
MILLBROOK (All Saints) *see* St John w Millbrook *Truro*
MILLBROOK (Christ the King) *see* Kettering Ch the King *Pet*
MILLBROOK (Holy Trinity) *Win 12* **P** *Bp* **R** R N H HOLYHEAD
MILLBROOK Regents Park (St Clement) *see* Millbrook *Win*
MILLBROOK (St James) *Ches 14* **P** *Bp, V Stalybridge St Paul, and Mrs E Bissill (jt)* **P-in-c** P N BROMILEY
MILLBROOK (St Michael and All Angels) *see* Ampthill w Millbrook and Steppingley *St Alb*
MILLERS DALE (St Anne) *see* Tideswell *Derby*
MILLFIELD (St Mark) and Pallion *Dur 16* **P** *Bp* **V** M R JUDSON, **C** P W JUDSON
MILLFIELD (St Mary) *Dur 16* **P** *The Crown* **V** B SKELTON
MILLHOUSES (Holy Trinity) *Sheff 2* **P** *Bp* **V** K E JONES, **NSM** I W DRAFFAN
MILLHOUSES (St Oswald) *see* Sheff St Oswald *Sheff*
MILLINGTON (St Margaret) *see* Pocklington and Owsthorpe and Kilnwick Percy etc *York*
MILLOM Holburn Hill (Mission) *see* Millom *Carl*
MILLOM (Holy Trinity) (St George) *Carl 8* **P** *Bp and Trustees (jt)* **V** P A GREENHALGH
MILNROW (St James) *Man 20* **P** *TR Rochdale* **V** D BOWERS, **NSM** R WHYBORN, A CUNNINGTON
MILNTHORPE (St Thomas) *see* Heversham and Milnthorpe *Carl*
MILSON (St George) *see* Cleobury Mortimer w Hopton Wafers etc *Heref*
MILSTED (St Mary and the Holy Cross) *see* Bredgar w Bicknor and Frinsted w Wormshill etc *Cant*
MILSTON (St Mary) *see* Avon Valley *Sarum*
MILTON (All Saints) *Ely 6* **P** *K Coll Cam* **R** I M COWLEY
MILTON (St Blaise) *see* Steventon w Milton *Ox*
MILTON (St James) (St Andrew's Church Centre) (St Patrick) *Portsm 6* **P** *V Portsea St Mary* **V** H O ALBY
MILTON (St John the Evangelist) *see* Adderbury w Milton *Ox*
MILTON (St Mary Magdalene) *Win 8* **P** *V Milford* **R** A H BAILEY, **C** J HEARN, C J MURRAY
MILTON (St Peter) w St Jude *B & W 11* **P** *Ld Chan* **V** J N O WILLIAMS, **C** A J FRY
MILTON (St Philip and St James) *Lich 8* **P** *Bp* **V** D M B WILMOT
MILTON (St Simon and St Jude) *see* Gillingham *Sarum*
MILTON, GREAT (St Mary the Virgin) w Little (St James) and Great Haseley *Ox 1* **P** *Bp and D&C Windsor (jt)* **R** N A BRYAN
MILTON, SOUTH (All Saints) *see* Thurlestone w S Milton *Ex*
MILTON ABBAS (St James the Great), Hilton w Cheselbourne and Melcombe Horsey *Sarum 7* **P** *Bp (3 turns) and G A L F Pitt-Rivers Esq (1 turn)* **P-in-c** J M BAILEY
MILTON ABBOT (St Constantine), Dunterton, Lamerton and Sydenham Demerel *Ex 24* **P** *Bp, J W Tremayne Esq, and Bedf Estates (jt)* **V** G J STANTON
MILTON BRYAN (St Peter) *see* Woburn w Eversholt, Milton Bryan, Battlesden etc *St Alb*
MILTON CLEVEDON (St James) *see* Evercreech w Chesterblade and Milton Clevedon *B & W*
MILTON COMBE (Holy Spirit) *see* Buckland Monachorum *Ex*
MILTON DAMEREL (Holy Trinity) *see* Holsworthy w Hollacombe and Milton Damerel *Ex*
MILTON ERNEST (All Saints) *St Alb 15* **P** *Bp* **V** C W GONIN
MILTON KEYNES (Christ the Cornerstone) *Ox 25* **P** *Bp* **V** D GOLDIE, M J BURNS
MILTON KEYNES VILLAGE (All Saints) *see* Walton Milton Keynes *Ox*
MILTON LILBOURNE (St Peter) *see* Pewsey TM *Sarum*
MILTON MALSOR (Holy Cross) *see* Collingtree w Courteenhall and Milton Malsor *Pet*
MILTON NEXT GRAVESEND (Christ Church) *Roch 4* **P** *Bp* **V** J S KING, **Hon C** A P WIBROE
MILTON NEXT GRAVESEND (St Peter and St Paul) w Denton *Roch 4* **P** *Bp* **R** V J LAWRENCE
MILTON NEXT SITTINGBOURNE (Holy Trinity) *Cant 14* **P** *D&C* **V** *Vacant* (01795) 472016
MILTON REGIS (St Mary) *see* Sittingbourne St Mary *Cant*
MILTON-UNDER-WYCHWOOD (St Simon and St Jude) *see* Shipton-under-Wychwood w Milton-under-Wychwood *Ox*
MILVERTON (St Michael) w Halse and Fitzhead *B & W 19* **P** *Adn Taunton (4 turns), Bp and V Wiveliscombe (1 turn)* **R** A D NORRIS, **NSM** A NORRIS
MILVERTON, NEW (St Mark) *Cov 11* **P** *CPAS* **V** A MORT
MILVERTON, OLD (St James) *see* Leamington Spa and Old Milverton *Cov*
MILWICH (All Saints) *see* Fradswell, Gayton, Milwich and Weston *Lich*
MIMMS, NORTH *see* N Mymms *St Alb*
MIMMS, SOUTH (Christ Church) *Lon 14* **P** *Ch Patr Trust* **V** N T W TAYLOR, **C** I M CHAPMAN, **NSM** P W LIDDELOW
MINCHINHAMPTON (Holy Trinity) *Glouc 8* **P** *Bp* **R** M J D IRVING, **Hon C** G P KNOTT
MINEHEAD (St Andrew) (St Michael) (St Peter) *B & W 16* **P** *Lt-Col G W F Luttrell and Bp (jt)* **V** G J WRAYFORD, **C** M H HASLAM, J HASLAM
MINETY (St Leonard) *see* Ashton Keynes, Leigh and Minety *Bris*
MININGSBY WITH EAST KIRKBY (St Nicholas) *see* Marden Hill Gp *Linc*
MINLEY (St Andrew) *Guildf 1* **P** *Bp* **V** *Vacant*
MINNIS BAY (St Thomas) *see* Birchington w Acol and Minnis Bay *Cant*
MINSKIP (Mission Room) *see* Aldborough w Boroughbridge and Roecliffe *Ripon*
MINSTEAD (All Saints) *see* Copythorne and Minstead *Win*

MINSTER (St Mary the Virgin) w Monkton *Cant 9* **P** *Abp* **P-in-c** R R COLES
MINSTER (St Merteriana) *see* Boscastle w Davidstow *Truro*
MINSTER IN SHEPPEY (St Mary and St Sexburga) *Cant 14* **P** *Ch Patr Trust* **V** G H SPENCER, **C** E B DAVIES, **NSM** J G KNELL
MINSTER LOVELL (St Kenelm) and Brize Norton *Ox 8* **P** *Eton Coll and Ch Ch Ox (jt)* **V** A W D GABB-JONES
MINSTERLEY (Holy Trinity) *Heref 13* **P** *DBP and Bp (alt)* **P-in-c** W K ROWELL
MINSTERWORTH (St Peter) *see* Churcham w Bulley and Minsterworth *Glouc*
MINTERNE MAGNA (St Andrew) *see* Cerne Abbas w Godmanstone and Minterne Magna *Sarum*
MINTING (St Andrew) *see* Bardney *Linc*
MIREHOUSE (St Andrew) *Carl 5* **P** *Bp* **V** M BARBER
MIRFIELD (St Mary) *Wakef 10* **P** *Bp* **V** P J CRAIG-WILD, **C** A I G SNOWDEN
MISERDEN (St Andrew) *see* Bisley, Oakridge, Miserden and Edgeworth *Glouc*
MISSENDEN, GREAT (St Peter and St Paul) w Ballinger and Little Hampden *Ox 28* **P** *Bp* **V** D RYDINGS, **NSM** D M DERRICK
MISSENDEN, LITTLE (St John the Baptist) *Ox 28* **P** *Earl Howe* **V** D R HEMSLEY
MISSION (St John the Baptist) *see* Bawtry w Austerfield and Misson *S'well*
MISTERTON (All Saints) and West Stockwith *S'well 1* **P** *D&C York and Bp (alt)* **V** M F B HARDY
MISTERTON (St Leonard) *see* Haselbury Plucknett, Misterton and N Perrott *B & W*
MISTERTON (St Leonard) *see* N w S Kilworth and Misterton *Leic*
MISTLEY (St Mary and St Michael) w Manningtree and Bradfield *Chelmsf 20* **P** *DBP and Bp (jt)* **R** *Vacant* (01206) 392200
MITCHAM (Ascension) Pollards Hill *S'wark 13* **P** *Bp* **V** N J WORN, **C** N C GOLDING, **NSM** P M STEVENSON
MITCHAM (Christ Church) *S'wark 13* **P** *Bp* **V** M J BULL
MITCHAM (St Barnabas) *S'wark 13* **P** *Bp* **V** A D KIRKWOOD, **C** V A ROBERTS
MITCHAM (St Mark) *S'wark 13* **P** *Bp* **V** A B RAMSAY
MITCHAM (St Olave) *S'wark 13* **P** *The Crown* **V** P G ENSOR
MITCHAM (St Peter and St Paul) *S'wark 13* **P** *Keble Coll Ox* **V** J M SHEPHERD, **C** S CARLSSON
MITCHELDEAN (St Michael and All Angels) *see* Abenhall w Mitcheldean *Glouc*
MITFORD (St Mary Magdalene) *Newc 11* **P** *Brig E C Mitford* **V** D F MAYHEW
MITHIAN (St Peter) w Mount Hawke *Truro 6* **P** *Bp* **V** *Vacant* (01209) 890926
MITTON (All Hallows) *see* Hurst Green and Mitton *Bradf*
MIXBURY (All Saints) *see* Shelswell *Ox*
MIXENDEN (Holy Nativity) *Wakef 4* **P** *Bp* **V** *Vacant* (01422) 244761
MOBBERLEY (St Wilfrid) *Ches 12* **P** *Bp* **R** M GRAHAM
MOCCAS (St Michael and All Angels) *see* Cusop w Clifford, Hardwicke, Bredwardine etc *Heref*
MODBURY (St George), Bigbury, Ringmore w Kingston, Aveton Gifford, Woodleigh, Loddiswell and Allington, East *Ex 14* **P** *Patr Bd* **TR** J S COLE, **TV** R D WITHNELL, **NSM** A DROWLEY
MODDERSHALL (All Saints) *see* Stone Ch Ch and Oulton *Lich*
MOGGERHANGER (St John the Evangelist) *see* Northill w Moggerhanger *St Alb*
MOIRA (St Hilda) *see* Donisthorpe and Moira w Stretton-en-le-Field *Leic*
MOLASH (St Peter) *see* Chilham w Challock and Molash *Cant*
MOLDGREEN (Christ Church) *Wakef 1* **P** *R Kirkheaton* **C** A J HUDSON
MOLESCROFT (St Leonard) *see* Beverley Minster *York*
MOLESEY, EAST (St Mary) *Guildf 8* **P** *Bp* **P-in-c** D J ADAMS
MOLESEY, EAST (St Paul) *Guildf 8* **P** *Bp* **P-in-c** A J FACEY
MOLESEY, WEST (St Peter) *Guildf 8* **P** *Canon W K Perry-Gore* **V** W A J YEEND
MOLESWORTH (St Peter) *see* Brington w Molesworth and Old Weston *Ely*
MOLLAND (St Mary) *see* Bishopsnympton, Rose Ash, Mariansleigh etc *Ex*
MOLLINGTON (All Saints) *see* Shires' Edge *Ox*
MOLTON, NORTH (All Saints) *see* S Molton w Nymet St George, High Bray etc *Ex*
MOLTON, SOUTH (St Mary Magdalene) w Nymet St George, High Bray, Charles, Filleigh, East Buckland, Warkleigh, Satterleigh, Chittlehamholt, Kingsnympton, Romansleigh, North Molton, Twitchen and Chittlehampton *Ex 18* **P** *DBP* **TV** S P GIRLING, J H BELL, **C** M WARD
MONEWDEN (St Mary) *see* Charsfield w Debach, Monewden, Hoo etc *St E*
MONGEHAM, GREAT (St Martin) w Ripple and Sutton by Dover *Cant 8* **P** *Abp* **P-in-c** S C TURNER, **Hon C** J A GOSLING, **NSM** R C NELSON
MONK BRETTON (St Paul) *Wakef 7* **P** *V Royston* **P-in-c** J F P MORRISON-WELLS
MONK FRYSTON (St Wilfrid of Ripon) and South Milford *York 6* **P** *Ld Chan and Abp (alt)* **R** D G RICHARDSON, **NSM** A W B AYLMER-KELLY
MONK SHERBORNE (All Saints) *see* The Sherbornes w Pamber *Win*
MONK SOHAM (St Peter) *see* Worlingworth, Southolt, Tannington, Bedfield etc *St E*
MONKEN HADLEY (St Mary the Virgin) *Lon 14* **P** *N A Dove Esq* **R** *Vacant* 0181-449 2414
MONKHESLEDEN (St Mary w St John) *see* Castle Eden w Monkhesleden *Dur*
MONKHOPTON (St Peter) *see* Upton Cressett w Monk Hopton *Heref*
MONKLAND (All Saints) *see* Leominster *Heref*
MONKLEIGH (St George) *Ex 16* **P** *Bp* **P-in-c** G J HANSFORD
MONKOKEHAMPTON (All Saints) *Ex 19* **P** *Bp* **P-in-c** R C THORP
MONKS COPPENHALL (Christ Church) *see* Crewe Ch Ch and St Pet *Ches*
MONKS ELEIGH (St Peter) w Chelsworth and Brent Eleigh w Milden and Kettlebaston *St E 10* **P** *Bp, Guild of All So, Ld Chan (2 turns), and M J Hawkins Esq* **R** R A BIRD
MONKS HORTON (St Peter) *see* Sellindge w Monks Horton and Stowting etc *Cant*
MONKS KIRBY (St Editha) w Pailton and Stretton-under-Fosse *Cov 6* **P** *Trin Coll Cam* **V** P S RUSSELL
MONKS RISBOROUGH (St Dunstan) *Ox 26* **P** *Bp* **P-in-c** A F MEYNELL, **NSM** A A TAYLOR
MONKSEATON (St Mary) *Newc 8* **P** *Bp* **V** J L HALLATT
MONKSEATON (St Peter) *Newc 8* **P** *Bp* **V** J A ROBERTSON, **C** A D BOWDEN
MONKSILVER (All Saints) *see* Stogumber w Nettlecombe and Monksilver *B & W*
MONKTON (St Mary Magdalene) *see* Minster w Monkton *Cant*
MONKTON (St Mary Magdalene) *see* Honiton, Gittisham, Combe Raleigh, Monkton etc *Ex*
MONKTON, WEST (St Augustine) *B & W 18* **P** *Bp* **R** R SCHOFIELD
MONKTON COMBE (St Michael) *see* Combe Down w Monkton Combe and S Stoke *B & W*
MONKTON FARLEIGH (St Peter), South Wraxall and Winsley *Sarum 17* **P** *D&C Bris (2 turns), Bp (1 turn)* **R** D G SMITH, **NSM** M A CLARK
MONKTON WYLD (St Andrew) *see* Marshwood Vale TM *Sarum*
MONKWEARMOUTH (All Saints) (St Andrew) (St Peter) *Dur 16* **P** *Bp* **TV** E G LLOYD
MONKWOOD (Mission Church) *see* Bishop's Sutton and Ropley and W Tisted *Win*
MONNINGTON-ON-WYE (St Mary) *see* Letton w Staunton, Byford, Mansel Gamage etc *Heref*
MONTACUTE (St Catherine of Alexandria) *see* Odcombe, Brympton, Lufton and Montacute *B & W*
MONTFORD (St Chad) *see* Bicton, Montford w Shrawardine and Fitz *Lich*
MONTON (St Paul) *see* Eccles *Man*
MONXTON (St Mary) *see* Amport, Grateley, Monxton and Quarley *Win*
MONYASH (St Leonard) *see* Taddington, Chelmorton and Flagg, and Monyash *Derby*
MOOR (St Thomas) *see* Fladbury, Wyre Piddle and Moor *Worc*
MOOR ALLERTON (St John the Evangelist) (St Stephen) *Ripon 5* **P** *Patr Bd* **TR** J D W KING, **TV** P JACKSON, P H AINSWORTH
MOOR GRANGE (St Andrew) *see* Hawksworth Wood *Ripon*
MOOR MILNER (Church Institute) *see* Daresbury *Ches*
MOOR MONKTON (All Saints) *see* Rufforth w Moor Monkton and Hessay *York*
MOORBRIDGE LANE (St Luke) *see* Stapleford *S'well*
MOORCOURT (St Mary) *see* Pembridge w Moorcourt, Shobdon, Staunton etc *Heref*
MOORDOWN (St John the Baptist) *Win 7* **P** *Bp* **V** W A SWAIN
MOORENDS (St Wilfrith) *Sheff 11* **P** *Bp* **V** K C NORTHOVER
MOORHOUSE (Chantry Chapel) *see* Kneesall w Laxton and Wellow *S'well*
MOORHOUSES (St Lawrence) *see* Mareham-le-Fen and Revesby *Linc*

MOORLAND *see* Widecombe-in-the-Moor, Leusdon, Princetown etc *Ex*
MOORLINCH (Blessed Virgin Mary) *see* Middlezoy and Othery and Moorlinch *B & W*
MOORSHOLM (St Mary) *see* Boosbeck w Moorsholm *York*
MOORSIDE (St Thomas) *see* Oldham Moorside *Man*
MOORSIDE St Wilfrid Conventional District *Dur 12* **C-in-c** P L WALKER
MORBORNE (All Saints) *see* Stilton w Denton and Caldecote etc *Ely*
MORCHARD BISHOP (St Mary) *see* N Creedy *Ex*
MORCOTT (St Mary the Virgin) w Glaston and Bisbrooke *Pet 14* **P** *Mr P W Rowley and Peterho Cam (alt)* **P-in-c** J L HUTCHINSON
MORDEN (Emmanuel Church Hall) (St George) (St Lawrence) (St Martin) *S'wark 13* **P** *Patr Bd* **TR** R F SKINNER, **TV** C A WOOD, A L FLOWERDAY, W MUNCEY, **C** M G KUHRT, **NSM** T A BRYAN
MORDEN (St Mary) *see* Red Post *Sarum*
MORDIFORD (Holy Rood) *see* Fownhope w Mordiford, Brockhampton etc *Heref*
MORE (St Peter) *see* Wentnor w Ratlinghope, Myndtown, Norbury etc *Heref*
MOREBATH (St George) *see* Bampton, Morebath, Clayhanger and Petton *Ex*
MORECAMBE (St Barnabas) *Blackb 12* **P** *R Poulton-le-Sands* **V** N L CUTTS
MORECAMBE (St Christopher) *see* Bare *Blackb*
MORELEIGH (All Saints) *see* Halwell w Moreleigh *Ex*
MORESBY (St Bridget) *Carl 5* **P** *Earl of Lonsdale* **R** G D A THORBURN
MORESBY PARKS (Mission Church) *see* Moresby *Carl*
MORESTEAD (not known) *see* Twyford and Owslebury and Morestead *Win*
MORETON (Christ Church) *Ches 8* **P** *Simeon's Trustees* **R** R A WALTON, **C** E W McLEOD
MORETON (St Mary) *see* Fyfield, Moreton w Bobbingworth etc *Chelmsf*
MORETON (St Mary) *see* Bradeley, Church Eaton and Moreton *Lich*
MORETON (St Nicholas) and Woodsford w Tincleton *Sarum 2* **P** *Hon Mrs M A Bartenk and Miss M B F Frampton (alt)* **R** P D STEVENS
MORETON, SOUTH (St John the Baptist) w North (All Saints), Aston Tirrold and Aston Upthorpe *Ox 18* **P** *Adn Berks, Hertf Coll Ox, and Magd Coll Ox (jt)* **R** A F OTTER
MORETON CORBET (St Bartholomew) *Lich 23* **P** *C C Corbet Esq* **R** *Vacant*
MORETON HALL (Christ Church) *see* Bury St Edmunds Ch Ch *St E*
MORETON-IN-MARSH (St David) w Batsford, Todenham and Lower Lemington *Glouc 15* **P** *Bp and Lord Dulverton (jt)* **R** S M WOOKEY
MORETON JEFFRIES (St Peter and St Paul) *see* Stoke Lacy, Moreton Jeffries w Much Cowarne etc *Heref*
MORETON MORRELL (Holy Cross) *see* Newbold Pacey w Moreton Morrell *Cov*
MORETON-ON-LUGG (St Andrew) *see* Wellington w Pipe-cum-Lyde and Moreton-on-Lugg *Heref*
MORETON PINKNEY (St Mary the Virgin) *see* Weedon Lois w Plumpton and Moreton Pinkney etc *Pet*
MORETON SAY (St Margaret of Antioch) *see* Adderley, Ash, Calverhall, Ightfield etc *Lich*
MORETON VALENCE (St Stephen) *see* Standish w Haresfield and Moreton Valence etc *Glouc*
MORETONHAMPSTEAD (St Andrew), Manaton, North Bovey and Lustleigh *Ex 11* **P** *Bp and DBP (jt)* **R** A R LEIGH, **NSM** K E JACKSON
MORGAN'S VALE (St Birinus) *see* Redlynch and Morgan's Vale *Sarum*
MORLAND (St Lawrence), Thrimby, Gt Strickland and Cliburn *Carl 1* **P** *Lord Hothfield and D&C (jt)* **V** K J COVE
MORLEY (St Botolph) *see* High Oak *Nor*
MORLEY (St Matthew) *Derby 12* **P** *Bp* **P-in-c** V J PRICE
MORLEY (St Paul) Townend *Wakef 8* **P** *V Batley and V Morley St Peter (alt)* **V** *Vacant* (01532) 534530
MORLEY (St Peter) *see* High Oak *Nor*
MORLEY (St Peter) w Churwell *Wakef 8* **P** *Bp* **V** M G WHITTOCK
MORNINGTHORPE (St John the Baptist) *see* Hempnall *Nor*
MORPETH (St Aidan) (St James) (St Mary the Virgin) *Newc 11* **P** *Bp* **R** A S CRAIG, **C** G SOUTH, M L EVANS, **NSM** M O CHESTER
MORSTON (All Saints) *see* Stiffkey and Cockthorpe w Morston, Langham etc *Nor*
MORTEHOE (St Mary Magdalene) *see* Ilfracombe, Lee, Woolacombe, Bittadon etc *Ex*
MORTIMER COMMON (St John) *see* Stratfield Mortimer *Ox*
MORTIMER WEST END (St Saviour) w Padworth *Ox 12* **P** *Englefield Estate Trust and Ld Chan (alt)* **P-in-c** J A ELLIS
MORTLAKE (St Mary) w East Sheen *S'wark 17* **P** *Patr Bd* **TR** B A SAUNDERS, **TV** J C ANSELL, J P KENNINGTON, **C** D M J BARRINGTON, **Hon C** P D KING
MORTOMLEY (St Saviour), High Green *Sheff 7* **P** *Bp* **V** D G RHODES, **C** A MURRAY
MORTON (Holy Cross) and Stonebroom *Derby 1* **P** *Bp (2 turns), St Jo Coll Cam (1 turn)* **R** I N PALLETT
MORTON (St Denis) *see* Rolleston w Fiskerton, Morton and Upton *S'well*
MORTON (St John the Baptist) *see* Ringstone in Aveland Gp *Linc*
MORTON (St Luke) *Bradf 8* **P** *Bp* **V** A M E BROWN
MORTON (St Paul) *Linc 2* **P** *Bp* **V** *Vacant* (01427) 612654
MORTON (St Philip and St James) *Lich 19* **P** *Ld Chan* **V** T VILLIERS
MORTON BAGOT (Holy Trinity) *see* Spernall, Morton Bagot and Oldberrow *Cov*
MORVAH (St Bridget of Sweden) *see* Pendeen w Morvah *Truro*
MORVAL (St Wenna) *see* Liskeard, St Keyne, St Pinnock, Morval etc *Truro*
MORVILLE (St Gregory) w Aston Eyre *Heref 9* **P** *DBP* **Hon C** H J PATTERSON
MORWENSTOW (St John the Baptist) *see* Kilkhampton w Morwenstow *Truro*
MOSBOROUGH (St Mark) *Sheff 1* **P** *Bp* **V** R F BLACKBURN, **C** J E BRADLEY, H A JOWETT
MOSELEY (St Agnes) *Birm 5* **P** *V Moseley St Mary* **V** D J NEW, **Hon C** R C HINGLEY
MOSELEY (St Anne) *Birm 5* **P** *V Moseley St Mary* **V** A T W REYNOLDS, **NSM** A J JOYCE
MOSELEY (St Mary) *Birm 5* **P** *Bp* **V** H J OSBORNE, **C** M J SMALL, **NSM** J A GRIFFIN
MOSLEY COMMON (St John) *Man 13* **P** *Bp* **V** A J LINDOP
MOSS BANK (Mission Church) *see* Carr Mill *Liv*
MOSS SIDE (Christ Church) *Man 4* **P** *Trustees* **P-in-c** S D A KILLWICK
MOSS SIDE (St James w St Clement) *Man 4* **P** *Bp* **R** G A WHEALE
MOSSER (St Philip) (Michael's Chapel) *Carl 6* **P** *Bp* **V** C GODDARD
MOSSLEY (Holy Trinity) *Ches 11* **P** *R Astbury* **V** S WATERS
MOSSLEY (St George) *Man 17* **P** *R Ashton-under-Lyne St Mich* **V** R J LINDSAY, **NSM** P PHILLIPS
MOSSLEY ESTATE (St Thomas Church) *see* Bloxwich *Lich*
MOSSLEY HILL (St Barnabas) *Liv 4* **P** *Bp* **V** K A ROWLANDS
MOSSLEY HILL (St Matthew and St James) *Liv 4* **P** *Trustees* **C** E M STOREY
MOSSWOOD (St Barnabas) *see* Cannock *Lich*
MOSTERTON (St Mary) *see* Beaminster Area *Sarum*
MOSTON (St Chad) *Man 5* **P** *Bp* **R** *Vacant* 0161-681 3203
MOSTON (St John) Ashley Lane *Man 5* **P** *Bp* **R** C S FORD, **C** H J BARBER
MOSTON (St Luke) *see* Lightbowne *Man*
MOSTON (St Mary) *Man 5* **P** *D&C* **R** D J LOW, **NSM** G L CORNISH
MOTCOMBE (St Mary) *see* Shaston *Sarum*
MOTSPUR PARK (Holy Cross) *S'wark 13* **P** *Bp* **V** A P ROBBINS-COLE
MOTTINGHAM (St Andrew) (St Alban Mission Church) *S'wark 2* **P** *Bp* **R** G W DAVIES, **C** Y V CLARKE, **NSM** D WARREN
MOTTINGHAM (St Edward the Confessor) *S'wark 2* **P** *Bp* **V** N J CALVER
MOTTISFONT (St Andrew) *see* Broughton, Bossington, Houghton and Mottisfont *Win*
MOTTISTONE (St Peter and St Paul) *see* Brighstone and Brooke w Mottistone *Portsm*
MOTTRAM IN LONGDENDALE (St Michael) *Ches 14* **P** *Bp* **V** A J REES, **NSM** R L HILLS
MOULSECOOMB (St Andrew) *Chich 2* **P** *Bp* **TR** C R LANSDALE, **TV** D J BIGGS, **C** C R LAWLOR
MOULSFORD (St John the Baptist) *see* Streatley w Moulsford *Ox*
MOULSHAM (St John the Evangelist) *Chelmsf 9* **P** *Provost* **V** J C HASSELL, **NSM** A M OVERTON BENGE
MOULSHAM (St Luke) *Chelmsf 9* **P** *Bp* **V** R E FARRELL, **NSM** P PENNELL
MOULSOE (Assumption of the Blessed Virgin Mary) *see* Streatley w Moulsford *Ox*
MOULTON (All Saints) (St James) (Mission Room) *Linc 17* **P** *DBP* **V** J ADAMS
MOULTON (Mission Church) *see* Middleton Tyas w Croft and Eryholme *Ripon*
MOULTON (St Peter) *see* Gazeley w Dalham, Moulton and Kentford *St E*

MOULTON (St Peter and St Paul) *Pet 4* **P** *Ch Soc Trust* **V** P H BRECKWOLDT
MOULTON (St Stephen the Martyr) *Ches 6* **P** *R Davenham* **P-in-c** S J WILSON
MOULTON, GREAT (St Michael) *see* Bunwell, Carleton Rode, Tibenham, Gt Moulton etc *Nor*
MOUNT BURES (St John) *see* Wormingford, Mt Bures and Lt Horkesley *Chelmsf*
MOUNT HAWKE (St John the Baptist) *see* Mithian w Mt Hawke *Truro*
MOUNT PELLON (Christ Church) *Wakef 4* **P** *Bp* **V** T J E MAYFIELD, **C** A DICK, **NSM** M H NEVILL
MOUNTFIELD (All Saints) *see* Brightling, Dallington, Mountfield etc *Chich*
MOUNTNESSING (St Giles) *see* Doddinghurst and Mountnessing *Chelmsf*
MOUNTSORREL (Christ Church) (St Peter) *Leic 7* **P** *CPAS and Bp* **V** F BRODIE
MOW COP (St Luke's Mission Church) *see* Odd Rode *Ches*
MOW COP (St Thomas) *Lich 11* **P** *Prime Min* **P-in-c** J C WATERS
MOWSLEY (St Nicholas) *see* Husbands Bosworth w Mowsley and Knaptoft etc *Leic*
MOXLEY (All Saints) *Lich 27* **P** *Prime Min* **P-in-c** I H MURRAY
MUCH *see also under substantive place name*
MUCH BIRCH (St Mary and St Thomas a Becket) w Little Birch, Much Dewchurch, Llanwarne and Llandinabo *Heref 8* **P** *A W Twiston-Davies Esq (1 turn), Bp (3 turns), and Ld Chan (1 turn)* **P-in-c** A N JEVONS, **Hon C** K B GARLICK
MUCHELNEY (St Peter and St Paul) *see* Langport Area Chs *B & W*
MUCKLESTONE (St Mary) *Lich 7* **P** *Mrs F F Friend* **P-in-c** D J WILLIAMS
MUDEFORD (All Saints) *see* Christchurch *Win*
MUDFORD (Blessed Virgin Mary) *see* Chilton Cantelo, Ashington, Mudford, Rimpton etc *B & W*
MUGGINTON (All Saints) and Kedleston *Derby 11* **P** *Major J W Chandos-Pole* **P-in-c** K JARDIN
MUGGLESWICK (All Saints) *see* Blanchland w Hunstanworth and Edmundbyers etc *Newc*
MUKER (St Mary) *see* Swaledale *Ripon*
MULBARTON (St Mary Magdalene) w Kenningham *Nor 7* **P** *Mrs R M Watkinson* **P-in-c** J W STUBENBORD
MULLION (St Mellanus) *Truro 4* **P** *Bp* **P-in-c** I J BUTLER
MUMBY (St Thomas of Canterbury) *see* Willoughby *Linc*
MUNCASTER (St Michael) *see* Eskdale, Irton, Muncaster and Waberthwaite *Carl*
MUNDEN, LITTLE (All Saints) *see* The Mundens w Sacombe *St Alb*
MUNDENS, The w Sacombe *St Alb 22* **P** *Ch Trust Fund Trust, K Coll Cam, and R M Abel Smith Esq (jt)* **P-in-c** A E DAVIE
MUNDESLEY (All Saints) *see* Trunch *Nor*
MUNDFORD (St Leonard) w Lynford *Nor 13* **P** *Ch Patr Trust* **P-in-c** G H WHEATLEY
MUNDHAM (St Peter) *see* Brooke, Kirstead, Mundham w Seething and Thwaite *Nor*
MUNDHAM, NORTH (St Stephen) w Hunston and Merston *Chich 3* **P** *St Jo Coll Cam* **R** V C de R MALAN
MUNGRISDALE (St Kentigern) *see* Greystoke, Matterdale, Mungrisdale etc *Carl*
MUNSLEY (St Bartholomew) *see* Tarrington w Stoke Edith, Aylton, Pixley etc *Heref*
MUNSLOW (St Michael) *see* Diddlebury w Munslow, Holdgate and Tugford *Heref*
MUNSTER SQUARE (Christ Church) (St Mary Magdalene) *Lon 17* **P** *Bp* **V** S J GRIGG, **Hon C** J G F KESTER
MUNSTONE (Church Room) *see* Holmer w Huntington *Heref*
MURCOTT (Mission Room) *see* Islip w Charlton on Otmoor, Oddington, Noke etc *Ox*
MURROW (Corpus Christi) *see* Southea w Murrow and Parson Drove *Ely*
MURSLEY (St Mary the Virgin) w Swanbourne and Little Horwood *Ox 26* **P** *Ch Soc Trust, Ch Patr Soc, and Hon J T Fremantle (by turn)* **R** J M KINCHIN-SMITH
MURSTON (All Saints) w Bapchild and Tonge *Cant 14* **P** *Abp and St Jo Coll Cam (jt)* **R** B A SHERSBY
MURTON (St James) *see* Osbaldwick w Murton *York*
MURTON (St John the Baptist) *see* Appleby *Carl*
MUSBURY (St Michael) *see* Colyton, Southleigh, Offwell, Widworthy etc *Ex*
MUSBURY (St Thomas) *Blackb 1* **P** *The Crown* **V** S M AIKEN
MUSGRAVE (St Theobald) *see* Brough w Stainmore, Musgrave and Warcop *Carl*
MUSKHAM, NORTH (St Wilfrid) and SOUTH (St Wilfrid) *S'well 3* **P** *Ld Chan* **P-in-c** A C ARMSTRONG, **NSM** M B ARMSTRONG
MUSTON (All Saints) *see* Hunmanby w Muston *York*
MUSTON (St John the Baptist) *see* Bottesford and Muston *Leic*
MUSWELL HILL (St James) (St Matthew) *Lon 20* **P** *Bp and CPAS (jt)* **V** D A ROSS, **C** P H SUDELL, R P KHAKHRIA, N H GREEN, **Hon C** P F WATSON, **NSM** H C HENDRY
MUTFORD (St Andrew) *see* Carlton Colville w Mutford and Rushmere *Nor*
MYDDELTON SQUARE (St Mark) *see* Clerkenwell H Redeemer and St Mark *Lon*
MYDDLE (St Peter) *Lich 23* **P** *Bp* **P-in-c** E A HADLEY
MYLAND (St Michael) *see* Colchester St Mich Myland *Chelmsf*
MYLOR (St Mylor) w Flushing *Truro 3* **P** *Bp* **V** J C JAMES
MYLOR BRIDGE (All Saints) *see* Mylor w Flushing *Truro*
MYMMS, NORTH (St Mary) (St Michael) *St Alb 21* **P** *Bp* **V** T W J RANSON
MYMMS, SOUTH (King Charles the Martyr) *St Alb 17* **P** *Bp Lon* **V** D M WILLIAMS, **NSM** G J RANDALL
MYMMS, SOUTH (St Giles) and Ridge *St Alb 17* **P** *DBP* **V** *Vacant* (01707) 643142
MYNDTOWN (St John the Baptist) *see* Wentnor w Ratlinghope, Myndtown, Norbury etc *Heref*
MYTHOLM ROYD (St Michael) *Wakef 3* **P** *Bp* **V** *Vacant* (01422) 883130
MYTON ON SWALE (St Mary) *see* Brafferton w Pilmoor, Myton on Swale etc *York*
NABB (Mission Church) *see* Wrockwardine Wood *Lich*
NACKINGTON (St Mary) *see* Petham and Waltham w Lower Hardres etc *Cant*
NACTON (St Martin) and Levington w Bucklesham and Foxhall *St E 2* **P** *DBP* **R** G L GRANT, **NSM** J S FOUNTAIN, D E N KING
NAFFERTON (All Saints) w Wansford *York 11* **P** *Abp* **V** J R BOOTH
NAILSEA (Christ Church) w Tickenham *B & W 13* **P** *CPAS (3 turns), Ld Chan (1 turn)* **R** A Q H WHEELER, **C** S P PHILLIPSON-MASTERS
NAILSEA (Holy Trinity) *B & W 13* **P** *MMCET* **C** J T SIMONS
NAILSTONE (All Saints) and Carlton w Shackerstone *Leic 13* **P** *The Crown and DBP (alt)* **R** W E QUINNEY
NAILSWORTH (St George) *Glouc 16* **P** *Bp* **V** J D STRONG, **C** J A NEWCOMBE
NANPANTAN (St Mary in Charnwood) *see* Loughborough Em and St Mary in Charnwood *Leic*
NANPEAN (St George) *see* St Stephen in Brannel *Truro*
NANSTALLION (St Stephen's Mission Room) *see* Bodmin w Lanhydrock and Lanivet *Truro*
NANTWICH (St Mary) *Ches 15* **P** *Q H Crewe Esq and J C Crewe Esq (jt)* **R** J R PRICE, **C** M A M WOLVERSON
NAPTON-ON-THE-HILL (St Lawrence), Lower Shuckburgh and Stockton *Cov 10* **P** *Ld Chan (2 turns), Sir Rupert Shuckburgh, Bt (1 turn), and New Coll Ox (2 turns)* **R** P L JACKSON
NARBOROUGH (All Saints) and Huncote *Leic 10* **P** *SMF* **R** N J BURTON
NARBOROUGH (All Saints) w Narford *Nor 20* **P** *Bp* **V** S R NAIRN
NARFORD (St Mary) *see* Narborough w Narford *Nor*
NASEBY (All Saints) *see* Clipston w Naseby and Haselbech w Kelmarsh *Pet*
NASH (All Saints) *see* Buckingham *Ox*
NASH (St John the Baptist) *see* Burford I *Heref*
NASSINGTON (St Mary the Virgin and All Saints) w Yarwell and Woodnewton *Pet 12* **P** *Lord Brassey and Bp (alt)* **V** R A LOVELESS
NATELY SCURES (St Swithun) *see* Newnham w Nately Scures w Mapledurwell etc *Win*
NATLAND (St Mark) *Carl 9* **P** *V Kendal H Trin* **P-in-c** T S EVANS, **NSM** M P JAYNE
NAUGHTON (St Mary) *see* Whatfield w Semer, Nedging and Naughton *St E*
NAUNTON (St Andrew) *see* Upper and Lower Slaughter w Eyford and Naunton *Glouc*
NAUNTON BEAUCHAMP (St Bartholomew) *see* Abberton, The Flyfords, Naunton Beauchamp etc *Worc*
NAVENBY (St Peter) *see* Graffoe Gp *Linc*
NAVESTOCK (St Thomas) *Chelmsf 7* **P** *Bp* **P-in-c** R A L ROSE
NAWTON (St Hilda) *see* Kirkdale *York*
NAYLAND (St James) w Wiston *St E 3* **P** *Ld Chan (2 turns) and DBP (1 turn)* **V** D A C STRANACK, **Hon C** B WATLING
NAYLAND DRIVE (Church Centre) *see* Clacton St Jas *Chelmsf*
NAZEING (All Saints) (St Giles) *Chelmsf 26* **P** *Ld Chan* **V** M D WEBSTER, **NSM** G ELLIS
NEASDEN (St Catherine w St Paul) *Lon 21* **P** *Bp and D&C St Paul's (jt)* **V** E E GAUNT

NEATISHEAD (St Peter), Barton Turf and Irstead *Nor 12* **P** *Bp* **P-in-c** M W SMITH, **Hon C** R S M MILLARD
NECHELLS (St Clement) *see* Duddeston w Nechells *Birm*
NECTON (All Saints), Holme Hale w Pickenham, North and South *Nor 13* **P** *Major-Gen R S Broke, Ch Soc Trust, MMCET and S Pickenham Estate Co Ltd (jt)* **R** P J TAYLOR, **C** W A STILLWELL
NEDGING (St Mary) *see* Whatfield w Semer, Nedging and Naughton *St E*
NEEDHAM (St Peter) *see* Redenhall, Harleston, Wortwell and Needham *Nor*
NEEDHAM MARKET (St John the Baptist) w Badley *St E 1* **P** *PCC* **P-in-c** P R DALTRY
NEEN SAVAGE (St Mary) *see* Cleobury Mortimer w Hopton Wafers etc *Heref*
NEEN SOLLARS (All Saints) *as above*
NEENTON (All Saints) *see* Ditton Priors w Neenton, Burwarton etc *Heref*
NEITHROP (St Paul) *see* Banbury *Ox*
NELSON (St Bede) *Blackb 7* **P** *Bp* **V** M A BURGESS
NELSON (St Mary) *see* Nelson in Lt Marsden *Blackb*
NELSON (St Philip) *Blackb 7* **P** *Bp* **V** S J R HARTLEY, **C** T J HOROBIN
NELSON IN LITTLE MARSDEN (St Mary) *Blackb 7* **P** *Trustees* **V** *Vacant* (01282) 614919
NEMPNETT THRUBWELL (The Blessed Virgin Mary) *see* Chew Stoke w Nempnett Thrubwell *B & W*
NENTHEAD (St John) *see* Alston Team *Newc*
NESS Group, The *Linc 13* **P** *Ld Chan (1 turn), Bp and DBP (2 turns)* **V** *Vacant* (01778) 422475
NESS, GREAT (St Andrew) *see* Ruyton XI Towns w Gt and Lt Ness *Lich*
NESS, LITTLE (St Martin) *as above*
NESTON (St Mary and St Helen) *Ches 9* **P** *D&C* **V** A V SHUFFLEBOTHAM, **C** S P C KYLE, **NSM** P A ROW
NESTON (St Phillip and St James) *see* Gtr Corsham *Bris*
NESTON, LITTLE (St Michael and All Angels) *see* Neston *Ches*
NETHER *see also under substantive place name*
NETHER HALL (St Elizabeth) *see* Scraptoft *Leic*
NETHERAVON (All Saints) *see* Avon Valley *Sarum*
NETHERBURY (St Mary) *see* Beaminster Area *Sarum*
NETHEREXE (St John the Baptist) *see* Stoke Canon, Poltimore w Huxham and Rewe etc *Ex*
NETHERFIELD (St George) *S'well 11* **P** *DBP* **R** M H F BEACH
NETHERFIELD (St John the Baptist) *see* Brightling, Dallington, Mountfield etc *Chich*
NETHERHAMPTON (St Katherine) *see* Wilton w Netherhampton and Fugglestone *Sarum*
NETHERLEY (Christ Church) *see* Gateacre *Liv*
NETHERNE (St Luke) *see* Merstham and Gatton *S'wark*
NETHERSEAL (St Peter) *see* Seale and Lullington *Derby*
NETHERTHONG (All Saints) *see* Upper Holme Valley *Wakef*
NETHERTHORPE (St Bartholomew) *see* Sheff St Bart *Sheff*
NETHERTHORPE (St Stephen) *Sheff 4* **P** *Ch Patr Trust and Sheff Ch Burgesses Trust (jt)* **V** N A CLEMAS
NETHERTON (All Souls) *Carl 7* **P** *Bp* **V** *Vacant* (01900) 812200
NETHERTON (St Andrew) *see* Middlestown *Wakef*
NETHERTON (St Andrew) *Worc 9* **P** *V Dudley* **V** M G PRICE
NETHERTON (St Oswald) *Liv 1* **P** *Bp* **V** A J EDWARDS, **C** P D McGRATH
NETHERWITTON (St Giles) *see* Nether Witton *Newc*
NETLEY ABBEY *see* Hound *Win*
NETLEY MARSH (St Matthew) *see* Totton *Win*
NETTLEBED (St Bartholomew) w Bix and Highmore *Ox 6* **P** *Ch Patr Trust, Earl of Macclesfield, DBP, and R RotherfieldGreys (jt)* **R** B J WEAVER
NETTLECOMBE (Blessed Virgin Mary) *see* Stogumber w Nettlecombe and Monksilver *B & W*
NETTLEDEN (Ashridge Chapel) *see* Potten End w Nettleden *St Alb*
NETTLEDEN (St Lawrence) *as above*
NETTLEHAM (All Saints) *Linc 3* **P** *Bp* **V** G F SLEIGHT
NETTLESTEAD (St Mary) *see* Gt and Lt Blakenham w Baylham and Nettlestead *St E*
NETTLESTEAD (St Mary the Virgin) *see* E Peckham and Nettlestead *Roch*
NETTLETON (St John the Baptist) *see* Swallow *Linc*
NETTLETON (St Mary) w Littleton Drew *Bris 9* **P** *Bp and Adn Swindon (alt)* **P-in-c** R V C LEWIS, **Dn-in-c** A MADDOCK
NEVENDON (St Peter) *see* Pitsea w Nevendon *Chelmsf*
NEVILLE'S CROSS (St John) Conventional District *Dur 2* **P** *Bp* **C-in-c** M F RUSK, **NSM** S C BARTON
NEW *see also under substantive place name*
NEW BOROUGH and Leigh (St John the Evangelist) *Sarum 10* **P** *Ch Soc Trust* **V** R J A TULLOCH, **C** J DUDLEY-SMITH
NEW BUILDINGS (Beacon Church) *see* Sandford w Upton Hellions *Ex*
NEW FERRY (St Mark) *Ches 8* **P** *R Bebington* **V** *Vacant* 0151-645 2638
NEW HAW (All Saints) *Guildf 11* **P** *Bp* **V** G J TICKNER, **NSM** R A MILLER
NEW MILL (Christ Church) *see* Upper Holme Valley *Wakef*
NEW MILLS (St George) (St James the Less) *Derby 6* **P** *V Glossop* **P-in-c** D J MURDOCH, **NSM** R J ANDERS
NEW SPRINGS (St John) *Liv 14* **P** *Bp* **P-in-c** J C SHARPLES
NEWALL GREEN (St Francis of Assisi) *Man 8* **P** *Bp* **P-in-c** P J DINES, **NSM** O E MARLOW
NEWARK-UPON-TRENT (St Mary Magdalene) (St Augustine's Mission) (Christ Church) (St Leonard) *S'well 3* **P** *The Crown* **TR** R A J HILL, **TV** P HUTCHINSON, **C** N BURGESS, H J WILD
NEWBALD (St Nicholas) *York 14* **P** *Abp* **P-in-c** P N HAYWARD
NEWBARNS (St Paul) w Hawcoat *Carl 8* **P** *DBP* **R** C C JENKIN, **C** M E DAY
NEWBIGGIN (St Edmund) *see* Kirkby Thore w Temple Sowerby and Newbiggin *Carl*
NEWBIGGIN-BY-THE-SEA (St Bartholomew) *see* Woodhorn w Newbiggin *Newc*
NEWBIGGIN HALL (St Wilfrid) *Newc 7* **P** *Bp* **V** M D TETLEY
NEWBOLD (St John the Evangelist) w Dunston and Great Barlow *Derby 5* **P** *Patr Bd* **P-in-c** G A FRIEND, **NSM** P S RHODES
NEWBOLD (St Peter) *see* Rochdale *Man*
NEWBOLD DE VERDUN (St James) and Kirkby Mallory *Leic 13* **P** *Bp and Trin Coll Ox (jt)* **R** C E FOX
NEWBOLD ON AVON (St Botolph) *Cov 6* **P** *H A F W Boughton Leigh Esq* **V** P M WILKINSON
NEWBOLD ON STOUR (St David) *see* Tredington and Darlingscott w Newbold on Stour *Cov*
NEWBOLD PACEY (St George) w Moreton Morrell *Cov 8* **P** *Qu Coll Ox and Lt-Col J E Little (alt)* **V** J R WILLIAMS
NEWBOROUGH (All Saints) *see* Hanbury w Newborough and Rangemore *Lich*
NEWBOROUGH (St Bartholomew) *Pet 13* **P** *The Crown* **V** K P FITZGIBBON
NEWBOTTLE (St James) *see* King's Sutton and Newbottle and Charlton *Pet*
NEWBOTTLE (St Matthew) *Dur 14* **P** *Bp* **P-in-c** E WILKINSON
NEWBOURN (St Mary) *see* Waldringfield w Hemley and Newbourn *St E*
NEWBROUGH (St Peter) *see* Warden w Newbrough *Newc*
NEWBURGH (Christ Church) w Westhead *Liv 11* **P** *Bp and V Ormskirk (jt)* **NSM** D M BURROWS
NEWBURN (St Michael and All Angels) *Newc 7* **P** *MMCET* **V** R G BATEMAN
NEWBURY (St John the Evangelist) (St Nicholas and St Mary) *Ox 14* **P** *Bp* **TR** D C M COOK, **TV** F T BONHAM, B DAGNALL, M STRANGE, **C** R B MILLER, M A E ASTIN, **NSM** J H G LEWIS, D S CASTLE
NEWBY (St Mark) *York 16* **P** *Abp* **V** M SPENCELEY
NEWCASTLE (Christ Church) (St Ann) *Newc 5* **P** *Bp* **V** A J A ROMANIS
NEWCASTLE (Epiphany) *Newc 5* **P** *Bp* **P-in-c** J E SADLER, **TV** M THOMPSON, **C** P INGHAM, **NSM** P E DAVIES
NEWCASTLE (St Andrew) (St Luke) *Newc 5* **P** *Bp and V Newcastle (jt)* **V** A W J MAGNESS
NEWCASTLE (St John the Evangelist) *see* Clun w Bettws-y-Crwyn and Newcastle *Heref*
NEWCASTLE (St Philip) and St Augustine *Newc 7* **P** *Bp* **P-in-c** I G FALCONER
NEWCASTLE UNDER LYME (St George) *Lich 9* **P** *R Newcastle w Butterton* **P-in-c** K A L DENNIS
NEWCASTLE UNDER LYME (St Giles) w Butterton *Lich 9* **P** *Simeon's Trustees* **R** J G RIDYARD
NEWCASTLE UNDER LYME (St Paul) *Lich 9* **P** *Trustees* **V** M D HARDING
NEWCASTLE UPON TYNE Byker (St Martin) *see* Byker St Martin *Newc*
NEWCASTLE UPON TYNE Byker (St Michael w St Lawrence) *see* Byker St Mich w St Lawr *Newc*
NEWCASTLE UPON TYNE Byker (St Silas) *see* Byker St Silas *Newc*
NEWCASTLE UPON TYNE Fenham (St James and St Basil) *see* Fenham St Jas and St Basil *Newc*
NEWCASTLE UPON TYNE High Elswick (St Paul) *see* High Elswick St Paul *Newc*
NEWCASTLE UPON TYNE (Holy Cross) *Newc 7* **P** *Bp* **C** R HERON

NEWCASTLE UPON TYNE Jesmond *see* Jesmond Clayton Memorial *Newc*
NEWCASTLE UPON TYNE Jesmond (Holy Trinity) *see* Jesmond H Trin *Newc*
NEWCASTLE UPON TYNE Low Elswick (St Stephen) *see* Low Elswick *Newc*
NEWCASTLE UPON TYNE Scotswood (St Margaret) *see* Scotswood *Newc*
NEWCASTLE UPON TYNE (St Anthony) Byker *see* Byker St Ant *Newc*
NEWCASTLE UPON TYNE (St Barnabas and St Jude) *Newc 5* **P** *V Jesmond Clayton Memorial and CPAS (alt)* **P-in-c** R L SIMPSON
NEWCASTLE UPON TYNE (St Francis) High Heaton *Newc 6* **P** *Bp* **V** R FINDLAYSON
NEWCASTLE UPON TYNE (St Gabriel) Heaton *Newc 6* **P** *Bp* **V** M J WEBB, **C** J P HAGGER, **NSM** S E AULD
NEWCASTLE UPON TYNE (St George) *Newc 5* **P** *Bp* **V** F R DEXTER, **C** A JONES
NEWCASTLE UPON TYNE (St Hilda) *Newc 5* **P** *Bp* **P-in-c** F R DEXTER
NEWCASTLE UPON TYNE (St John the Baptist) *Newc 5* **P** *V Newc* **P-in-c** P KENNEY
NEWCASTLE UPON TYNE (St Matthew w St Mary) *Newc 7* **P** *Bp* **P-in-c** I G FALCONER, **C** K L DUNN
NEWCASTLE UPON TYNE (St Thomas) Proprietary Chapel *Newc 5* **P** *Trustees of St Thos Chpl Charity* **C-in-c** J C WIDDOWS
NEWCASTLE UPON TYNE Walker (Christ Church) *see* Walker *Newc*
NEWCASTLE UPON TYNE Walkergate (St Oswald) *see* Byker St Mark and Walkergate St Oswald *Newc*
NEWCASTLE UPON TYNE, WEST Benwell *see* Benwell Team *Newc*
NEWCHAPEL (St James the Apostle) *Lich 11* **P** *CPAS* **V** W E SLATER, **C** N R IRONS
NEWCHURCH (All Saints) *Portsm 7* **P** *Bp* **V** D H HEATLEY
NEWCHURCH (Christ Church) *see* Hoar Cross w Newchurch *Lich*
NEWCHURCH (not known) *Liv 16* **P** *Bp* **R** A LITTON
NEWCHURCH (St Nicholas w St John) *Man 15* **P** *Bp* **R** A T TOOMBS
NEWCHURCH (St Peter and St Paul) *see* Dymchurch w Burmarsh and Newchurch *Cant*
NEWCHURCH-IN-PENDLE (St Mary) *see* Fence and Newchurch-in-Pendle *Blackb*
NEWDIGATE (St Peter) *Guildf 7* **P** *Ld Chan* **R** C J BLISSARD-BARNES
NEWENDEN (St Peter) *see* Sandhurst w Newenden *Cant*
NEWENT (St Mary the Virgin) and Gorsley w Cliffords Mesne *Glouc 3* **P** *Bp* **R** R C SIMPSON, **NSM** R G CHIVERS
NEWHALL (St John) *Derby 16* **P** *Bp* **V** I F R JARVIS
NEWHAVEN (St Michael) *Chich 18* **P** *Ch Patr Trust* **R** N WESTON
NEWHEY (St Thomas) *Man 20* **P** *Bp* **V** S H TOMLINE
NEWICK (St Mary) *Chich 21* **P** *Ch Soc Trust and J H Cordle Esq (jt)* **R** P P FRANCIS
NEWINGTON (St Christopher) *see* St Laur in Thanet *Cant*
NEWINGTON (St Giles) *see* Dorchester *Ox*
NEWINGTON (St John the Baptist) w Dairycoates St Mary and St Peter *York 15* **P** *Abp* **V** M R B HILLS, **NSM** A CRAVEN
NEWINGTON (St Mary) *S'wark 9* **P** *Bp* **R** P C EDWARDS, **Hon C** J WASH
NEWINGTON (St Mary the Virgin) w Hartlip and Stockbury *Cant 14* **P** *Abp* **V** M A MASCALL
NEWINGTON (St Nicholas) *see* Cheriton All So w Newington *Cant*
NEWINGTON (St Paul) *S'wark 9* **P** *Bp* **V** G D SHAW, **NSM** M BREWSTER
NEWINGTON, SOUTH (St Peter ad Vincula) *see* Bloxham w Milcombe and S Newington *Ox*
NEWLAND (All Saints) and Redbrook w Clearwell *Glouc 4* **P** *Bp* **V** D J F ADDISON
NEWLAND (St John) *see* Hull Newland St Jo *York*
NEWLAND (St Leonard) *see* Guarlford and Madresfield w Newland *Worc*
NEWLANDS (not known) *see* Thornthwaite cum Braithwaite and Newlands *Carl*
NEWLAY LANE (St Margaret's Church Hall) *see* Bramley *Ripon*
NEWLYN (St Newlyn) *Truro 5* **P** *Bp* **P-in-c** W FISH
NEWLYN (St Peter) *Truro 5* **P** *Bp* **V** R L STRANGE
NEWMARKET (All Saints) *St E 11* **P** *Bp* **V** J C ROSS
NEWMARKET (St Mary the Virgin) w Exning St Agnes *St E 11* **P** *Bp and DBP (alt)* **R** G C SMITH
NEWNHAM (St Mark) *see* Cambridge St Mark *Ely*
NEWNHAM (St Michael and All Angels) *see* Badby w Newham and Charwelton w Fawsley etc *Pet*
NEWNHAM (St Nicholas) w Nately Scures w Mapledurwell w Up Nateley w Greywell *Win 5* **P** *Bp and Qu Coll Ox (jt)* **R** M R HAWES
NEWNHAM (St Peter and St Paul) *see* Doddington, Newnham and Wychling *Cant*
NEWNHAM (St Peter) w Awre and Blakeney *Glouc 3* **P** *Haberdashers' Co and Bp (alt)* **V** R J SEAMAN
NEWNHAM (St Vincent) *see* Ashwell w Hinxworth and Newnham *St Alb*
NEWNTON, NORTH (St James) *see* Swanborough *Sarum*
NEWPORT (St John the Baptist) *Portsm 8* **P** *Ch Patr Trust* **V** A BROWN, **C** N I BOURNE, **NSM** R J WHATLEY
NEWPORT (St John the Baptist), Bishops Tawton and Tawstock *Ex 15* **P** *Patr Bd* **P-in-c** J P BENSON
NEWPORT (St Mary the Virgin) *Chelmsf 21* **P** *Bp* **V** S SANDERSON
NEWPORT (St Nicholas) w Longford, Chetwynd and Forton *Lich 16* **P** *Bp* **C** D J B ABINGTON
NEWPORT (St Stephen) *see* Howden TM *York*
NEWPORT (St Thomas) *Portsm 8* **P** *Bp* **P-in-c** A BROWN
NEWPORT PAGNELL (St Luke) w Lathbury and Moulsoe *Ox 27* **P** *Bp, Ch Ch Ox, and Lord Carrington (jt)* **R** J H LEWIS, **C** J B RUSSELL
NEWQUAY (St Michael) *Truro 7* **P** *Bp* **V** M H FISHER
NEWSHAM (St Bede) *Newc 1* **P** *Bp* **V** J R PRINGLE
NEWSHOLME (St John) *see* Oakworth *Bradf*
NEWSOME (St John the Evangelist) and Armitage Bridge *Wakef 1* **P** *DBP, V Rashcliffe and Lockwood, and R Almondbury (jt)* **V** I JACKSON
NEWSTEAD (St Mary the Virgin) *see* Annesley w Newstead *S'well*
NEWTIMBER (St John the Evangelist) *see* Poynings w Edburton, Newtimber and Pyecombe *Chich*
NEWTON and TOFT (St Michael) *see* Middle Rasen Gp *Linc*
NEWTON (Church Hall) *see* Blackwell *Derby*
NEWTON (Good Shepherd) *see* Clifton upon Dunsmore and Newton *Cov*
NEWTON (Mission Church) *see* Embleton w Rennington and Rock *Newc*
NEWTON (St Botolph) *see* S Lafford *Linc*
NEWTON (St James) *Ely 7* **P** *Bp* **P-in-c** N A WHITEHOUSE
NEWTON (St John the Baptist) *see* Clodock and Longtown w Craswall, Llanveynoe etc *Heref*
NEWTON (St Luke) *see* Hatfield *St Alb*
NEWTON (St Margaret) *see* Lt Shelford *Ely*
NEWTON (St Michael and All Angels) *Ches 8* **P** *R W Kirby St Bridget* **V** *Vacant* 0151-625 8517
NEWTON (St Oswald) *see* Gt Ayton w Easby and Newton in Cleveland *York*
NEWTON (St Petrock) *see* Shebbear, Buckland Filleigh, Sheepwash etc *Ex*
NEWTON (St Stephen) Flowery Field *Ches 14* **P** *Bp* **P-in-c** P J HIBBERT
NEWTON, NORTH (St Peter) w St Michaelchurch, Thurloxton and Durston *B & W 14* **P** *Bp (3 turns), Sir Benjamin Slade, Bt (1 turn)* **P-in-c** R RADCLIFFE
NEWTON, OLD (St Mary) w Stowupland *St E 6* **P** *Ch Patr Trust and DBP (alt)* **V** *Vacant* (01449) 744551
NEWTON, SOUTH (St Andrew) *see* Lower Wylye and Till Valley *Sarum*
NEWTON, WEST (St Matthew) *Carl 7* **P** *Bp* **P-in-c** P J SWAIN
NEWTON, WEST (St Peter and St Paul) *see* Sandringham w W Newton and Appleton etc *Nor*
NEWTON ABBOT *see* Highweek and Teigngrace *Ex*
NEWTON ABBOT (St Michael) *see* Wolborough w Newton Abbot *Ex*
NEWTON ABBOT (St Paul) *as above*
NEWTON ARLOSH (St John the Evangelist) *see* Kirkbride w Newton Arlosh *Carl*
NEWTON AYCLIFFE (St Clare) *see* Gt Aycliffe *Dur*
NEWTON BLOSSOMVILLE (St Nicolas) *see* Lavendon w Cold Brayfield, Clifton Reynes etc *Ox*
NEWTON BROMSWOLD (St Peter) *see* Rushden w Newton Bromswold *Pet*
NEWTON-BY-CASTLE-ACRE (All Saints) *see* Castle Acre w Newton, Rougham and Southacre *Nor*
NEWTON CAP (St Paul) *see* Auckland St Andr and St Anne *Dur*
NEWTON FERRERS (Holy Cross) w Revelstoke *Ex 20* **P** *Bp and Comdr P E Yonge* **R** T R DEACON
NEWTON FLOTMAN (St Mary the Virgin) *see* Swainsthorpe w Newton Flotman *Nor*
NEWTON GREEN (All Saints) *see* Assington w Newton Green and Lt Cornard *St E*

NEWTON HALL (All Saints) *Dur 1* **P** *D&C* **P-in-c** J D PICKERING
NEWTON HALL (St James) *see* Corbridge w Halton and Newton Hall *Newc*
NEWTON HARCOURT (St Luke) *see* Gt Glen, Stretton Magna and Wistow etc *Leic*
NEWTON HEATH (All Saints) *Man 5* **P** *D&C* **R** *Vacant* 0161-681 3102
NEWTON HEATH (St Wilfrid and St Anne) *Man 5* **P** *The Crown* **P-in-c** G N DOBSON
NEWTON IN MAKERFIELD (Emmanuel) *Liv 16* **P** *Bp* **R** *Vacant* (01925) 224920
NEWTON IN MAKERFIELD (St Peter) *Liv 16* **P** *Lord Newton* **V** G B KEEGAN
NEWTON IN MOTTRAM (St Mary) *Ches 14* **P** *V Mottram* **P-in-c** P ENNION
NEWTON KYME (St Andrew) *see* Tadcaster w Newton Kyme *York*
NEWTON-LE-WILLOWS (All Saints) *Liv 16* **P** *Bp* **V** D HALL
NEWTON LONGVILLE (St Faith) w Stoke Hammond and Whaddon *Ox 26* **P** *Exors R J Dalziel Smith Esq, New Coll Ox, and Cam Univ (by turn)* **P-in-c** D W A GREGG
NEWTON ON OUSE (All Saints) *see* Skelton w Shipton and Newton on Ouse *York*
NEWTON-ON-RAWCLIFFE (St John) *see* Middleton, Newton and Sinnington *York*
NEWTON-ON-TRENT (St Peter) *see* Saxilby Gp *Linc*
NEWTON POPPLEFORD (St Luke), Harpford and Colaton Raleigh *Ex 7* **P** *Bp, I Aylesbeare, Farringdon, Clyst Honiton and Sowton, andDBP (jt)* **V** T W BRIGHTON
NEWTON PURCELL (St Michael) *see* Shelswell *Ox*
NEWTON REGIS (St Mary) w Seckington and Shuttington *Birm 11* **P** *Birm Dioc Trustees and Mrs E V G Inge-Innes-Lillingston (alt)* **R** *Vacant* (01827) 830254
NEWTON REIGNY (St John) *see* Penrith w Newton Reigny and Plumpton Wall *Carl*
NEWTON SOLNEY (St Mary the Virgin) *see* Bretby w Newton Solney *Derby*
NEWTON ST CYRES (St Cyres and St Julitta) *see* Thorverton, Cadbury, Upton Pyne etc *Ex*
NEWTON ST LOE (Holy Trinity) *see* Saltford w Corston and Newton St Loe *B & W*
NEWTON TONY (St Andrew) *see* Bourne Valley *Sarum*
NEWTON TRACEY (St Thomas a Becket), Horwood, Alverdiscott, Huntshaw, Yarnscombe, Tawstock, Atherington, High Bickington, Roborough, St Giles in the Wood and Beaford *Ex 19* **P** *Ld Chan (1 turn), Patr Bd (3 turns)* **TR** R J P ACWORTH, **TV** J C CARVOSSO, S L THORP, H G POLLOCK
NEWTON VALENCE (St Mary) and Selborne and East Tisted w Colemore *Win 2* **P** *Bp, Earl of Selborne, and Exors Lt Col Sir James Scott Bt (jt)* **R** J F W ANDERSON
NEWTOWN (Holy Spirit) *see* Calbourne w Newtown *Portsm*
NEWTOWN (Holy Trinity) *see* Soberton w Newtown *Portsm*
NEWTOWN (King Charles the Martyr) *see* Loppington w Newtown *Lich*
NEWTOWN (St Mary the Virgin) *see* Hungerford and Denford *Ox*
NEWTOWN (St Mary the Virgin and St John the Baptist) *see* Burghclere w Newtown and Ecchinswell w Sydmonton *Win*
NEWTOWN (St Paul) *see* Longnor, Quarnford and Sheen *Lich*
NEWTOWN LINFORD (All Saints) *Leic 12* **P** *Lord Deramore* **P-in-c** A R LEIGHTON, **NSM** P SHERIDAN
NIBLEY, NORTH (St Martin) *see* Wotton-under-Edge w Ozleworth and N Nibley *Glouc*
NICHOLFOREST (St Nicholas) and Kirkandrews on Esk *Carl 2* **P** *Bp, Sir Charles Graham, Bt, and PCC (jt)* **P-in-c** W KELLY
NIDD (St Paul and St Margaret) *Ripon 1* **P** *Viscount Mountgarret and R Knaresborough (alt)* **P-in-c** G K TIBBO
NIDDERDALE, LOWER *Ripon 8* **P** *Trustees K Bell Esq, DBP, and C J Dent Esq (jt)* **R** M P SPURGEON
NIDDERDALE, UPPER *Ripon 3* **P** *D&C and V Masham and Healey (jt)* **V** P L DUNBAR
NINEBANKS (St Mark) *see* Allendale w Whitfield *Newc*
NINEFIELDS (St Lawrence School Worship Centre) *see* Waltham H Cross *Chelmsf*
NINFIELD (St Mary the Virgin) *Chich 14* **P** *D&C Cant* **R** P C CLEMENTS
NITON (St John the Baptist) *Portsm 7* **P** *Qu Coll Ox* **P-in-c** S E LLOYD, **NSM** J A WOOLLEY, M M SLATTERY
NOAK HILL (St Thomas) *see* Harold Hill St Geo *Chelmsf*
NOCTON (All Saints) *see* Branston w Nocton and Potterhanworth *Linc*
NOEL PARK (St Mark) *Lon 19* **P** *Bp* **V** R R ROBINSON
NOKE (St Giles) *see* Islip w Charlton on Otmoor, Oddington, Noke etc *Ox*
NOMANS HEATH (St Mary the Virgin) *Lich 4* **P** *Bp* **P-in-c** A L WHEALE
NONINGTON (St Mary the Virgin) w Wymynswold and Goodnestone w Chillenden and Knowlton *Cant 1* **P** *Abp and Lord Fitzwalter (jt)* **V** P GOODSELL
NORBITON (St Peter) *S'wark 16* **P** *V Kingston All SS* **V** P A HOLMES
NORBURY (All Saints) *see* Wentnor w Ratlinghope, Myndtown, Norbury etc *Heref*
NORBURY (St Mary and St Barlok) w Snelston *Derby 8* **P** *Mrs M F Stanton, L A Clowes Esq, and V Ashbourne (by turn)* **P-in-c** A H HART
NORBURY (St Oswald) *S'wark 24* **P** *Bp* **V** A G STUDDERT-KENNEDY, **Hon C** M K WATTS
NORBURY (St Peter) *see* High Offley and Norbury *Lich*
NORBURY (St Philip) *S'wark 24* **P** *Bp* **V** P L WASHINGTON
NORBURY (St Stephen) and Thornton Heath *S'wark 24* **P** *Bp* **V** F J M POLE
NORBURY (St Thomas) *Ches 16* **P** *Lord Newton* **V** W F M COLLINS, **C** D G SARGENT, R H GREEN
NORDELPH (Holy Trinity) *see* Wimbotsham w Stow Bardolph and Stow Bridge etc *Ely*
NORDEN (St Paul) w Ashworth *Man 20* **P** *Bp* **V** K N PROCTOR
NORFOLK PARK (St Leonard) Conventional District *Sheff 1* **C-in-c** W N CRAFT
NORHAM (St Cuthbert) and Duddo *Newc 12* **P** *D&C (1 turn), D&C Dur (2 turns)* **V** R THOMPSON
NORK (St Paul) *Guildf 9* **P** *The Crown* **V** P J BROOKS
NORLAND (St Luke) *see* Sowerby Bridge w Norland *Wakef*
NORLANDS (St James) *see* Notting Dale St Clem w St Mark and St Jas *Lon*
NORLEY (St John the Evangelist) and Crowton *Ches 3* **P** *Bp and V Weaverham (jt)* **V** R H N ROBB, **C** J E PEARCE
NORMACOT (Holy Evangelists) *Lich 12* **P** *DBP* **P-in-c** H F HARPER
NORMANBY (St Andrew) *see* Kirby Misperton w Normanby, Edston and Salton *York*
NORMANBY (St George) *see* Eston w Normanby *York*
NORMANBY-LE-WOLD (St Peter) *see* Walesby *Linc*
NORMANTON (All Saints) *Wakef 9* **P** *Trin Coll Cam* **V** S M ROSE
NORMANTON (St Giles) *Derby 10* **P** *CPAS* **V** J C GRINHAM, **C** T J HOUGHTON
NORMANTON, SOUTH (St Michael) *Derby 1* **P** *MMCET* **R** E E CHAMBERLAIN
NORMANTON-LE-HEATH (Holy Trinity) *see* Packington w Normanton-le-Heath *Leic*
NORMANTON-ON-SOAR (St James) *see* Sutton Bonington w Normanton-on-Soar *S'well*
NORMANTON-ON-TRENT (St Matthew) *see* Sutton w Carlton and Normanton upon Trent etc *S'well*
NORRIS BANK (St Martin) *Man 3* **P-in-c** T P RYLEY
NORRISTHORPE (All Souls) *see* Heckmondwike *Wakef*
NORTH *see also under substantive place name*
NORTH CAVE (All Saints) w Cliffe *York 14* **P** *P W J Carver Esq* **V** P N HAYWARD
NORTH-CHAPEL Parishes, The *Linc 10* **P** *Mrs W B Ashley, R H C Haigh Esq, and Trustees (1 turn), andDuchy of Lanc (1 turn)* **R** R K EMM
NORTH CHAPEL (St Michael) w Ebernoe *Chich 11* **P** *Lord Egremont* **R** C G F KIRKHAM
NORTH COVE (St Botolph) *see* Worlingham w Barnby and N Cove *St E*
NORTH END (Ascension) *see* Portsea Ascension *Portsm*
NORTH END (Chapel of Ease) *see* Burton Dassett *Cov*
NORTH END (St Francis) *see* Portsea N End St Mark *Portsm*
NORTH END (St Mark) *as above*
NORTH END (St Nicholas) *as above*
NORTH HILL (St Torney) and Lewannick *Truro 9* **P** *Ld Chan and DBP (alt)* **P-in-c** B STAMFORD
NORTH KENN TEAM *see* Tedburn St Mary, Whitestone, Oldridge etc *Ex*
NORTH SHIELDS (Christ Church) *see* N Shields *Newc*
NORTH SHIELDS (St Augustine) (Christ Church) *Newc 5* **P** *Patr Bd* **TR** W N STOCK, **TV** D E CANT, **C** P J A ROBINSON, **NSM** T C DUFF
NORTHALLERTON (All Saints) w Kirby Sigston *York 20* **P** *D&C Dur* **V** I J FOX, **C** P T HARRISON, K M GORHAM
NORTHAM (St Margaret) *see* Bideford, Northam, Westward Ho!, Appledore etc *Ex*
NORTHAMPTON (All Saints w St Katherine) *Pet 4* **P** *Bp* **V** S H M GODFREY
NORTHAMPTON (Christ Church) *Pet 4* **P** *Bp* **V** J D V EVANS
NORTHAMPTON (Emmanuel) *Pet 4* **P** *DBP* **TR** J F A M KNIGHT, **C** M A H JOHNSON

NORTHAMPTON (Holy Sepulchre w St Andrew and St Lawrence) *Pet 4* **P** *Bp* **V** K E ANDERSON
NORTHAMPTON (Holy Trinity) *Pet 4* **P** *Bp* **V** *Vacant* (01604) 711468
NORTHAMPTON (St Alban the Martyr) (Glorious Ascension) *Pet 4* **P** *Bp* **V** G J STEELE, **C** S J M READING
NORTHAMPTON (St Benedict) *Pet 7* **P** *Bp* **C** A SLATER
NORTHAMPTON (St David) *see* Kingsthorpe w Northn St Dav *Pet*
NORTHAMPTON (St Giles) *Pet 4* **P** *Simeon's Trustees* **C** H M CAW
NORTHAMPTON (St James) *Pet 4* **P** *Bp* **V** B B C PROWSE
NORTHAMPTON (St Mary the Virgin) *Pet 4* **P** *Bp* **V** G I BURGON
NORTHAMPTON (St Matthew) *Pet 4* **P** *DBP* **C** B N GORDON-TAYLOR, **Hon C** M M CLARKE
NORTHAMPTON (St Michael and All Angels w St Edmund) *Pet 4* **P** *Bp* **V** J COOPER
NORTHAMPTON St Paul *Pet 4* **P** *Bp* **V** S J EVANS, **Dss** D EVANS
NORTHAMPTON (St Peter) w Upton *Pet 4* **P** *R Foundn of St Kath* **R** *Vacant* (01604) 714015
NORTHAW (St Thomas of Canterbury) *St Alb 20* **P** *Mrs K R Dore* **NSM** M K ROBINS, **Hon Par Dn** B L COOKE
NORTHBOROUGH (St Andrew) *see* Peakirk w Glinton and Northborough *Pet*
NORTHBOURNE (St Augustine) *see* Eastry and Northbourne w Tilmanstone etc *Cant*
NORTHCHURCH (St Mary) *see* Berkhamsted St Mary *St Alb*
NORTHCOURT (Christ Church) *see* Abingdon *Ox*
NORTHENDEN (St Wilfrid) *Man 8* **P** *Bp* **R** G S FORSTER
NORTHFIELD (St Laurence) *Birm 4* **P** *Keble Coll Ox* **R** R I WARREN
NORTHFLEET (All Saints) *see* Perry Street *Roch*
NORTHFLEET (St Botolph) *Roch 4* **P** *The Crown* **V** A C SMITH, **NSM** P M SNOW
NORTHGATE (St Elizabeth) *see* Crawley *Chich*
NORTHIAM (St Mary) *Chich 20* **P** *MMCET* **R** D BOND
NORTHILL (St Mary the Virgin) w Moggerhanger *St Alb 11* **P** *Grocers' Co and Bp (alt)* **NSM** J D LANE
NORTHINGTON (St John the Evangelist) *see* The Candover Valley *Win*
NORTHLEACH (St Peter and St Paul) w Hampnett and Farmington *Glouc 14* **P** *Bp* **P-in-c** D C NYE, **NSM** P G W PRIDGEON
NORTHLEIGH (St Giles) *see* Colyton, Southleigh, Offwell, Widworthy etc *Ex*
NORTHLEW (St Thomas of Canterbury) *see* Okehampton w Inwardleigh, Bratton Clovelly etc *Ex*
NORTHMOOR (St Denys) *see* Lower Windrush *Ox*
NORTHMOOR GREEN (St Peter and St John) *see* N Petherton w Northmoor Green *B & W*
NORTHOLT (St Joseph) W End *Lon 22* **P** *DBP* **V** D M BRADSHAW
NORTHOLT (St Mary) (St Hugh) (St Richard) *Lon 22* **P** *BNC Ox* **R** P S WALKER, **Hon C** M J WALKER
NORTHOLT PARK (St Barnabas) *Lon 22* **P** *Bp* **V** P B DENTON, **C** K B BEST
NORTHORPE (St John the Baptist) *see* Scotton w Northorpe *Linc*
NORTHOWRAM (St Matthew) *Wakef 2* **P** *Bp* **V** J L MARSHALL, **C** J M HOGGARD
NORTHREPPS (St Mary) *see* Overstrand, Northrepps, Sidestrand etc *Nor*
NORTHUMBERLAND HEATH (St Paul) *see* Erith St Paul *Roch*
NORTHWICH (St Helen) *see* Witton *Ches*
NORTHWICH (St Luke) (Holy Trinity) *Ches 6* **P** *Bp* **V** R W CROOK
NORTHWOLD (St Andrew) *Ely 15* **P** *Bp* **P-in-c** N O TUFFNELL
NORTHWOOD (Emmanuel) *Lon 23* **P** *Ch Trust Fund Trust* **V** J A WALLIS, **C** M E BROWN, S JONES, J J WILSON, **NSM** P D O GREENE
NORTHWOOD (Holy Trinity) *see* Hanley H Ev *Lich*
NORTHWOOD (Holy Trinity) *Lon 23* **P** *Trustees* **V** P E FAINT
NORTHWOOD Pinner Road (St Edmund the King) *see* Northwood Hills St Edm *Lon*
NORTHWOOD (St John the Baptist) *Portsm 8* **P** *Bp* **R** C B BURLAND, **NSM** D M NETHERWAY
NORTHWOOD (St Mark) *see* Kirkby *Liv*
NORTHWOOD GREEN (Mission Church) *see* Westbury-on-Severn w Flaxley and Blaisdon *Glouc*
NORTHWOOD HILLS (St Edmund the King) *Lon 23* **P** *Bp* **C** N S MERCER
NORTON (All Saints) *see* Hullavington, Norton and Stanton St Quintin *Bris*
NORTON (All Saints) *see* Brington w Whilton and Norton *Pet*
NORTON (St Andrew) *see* Pakenham w Norton and Tostock *St E*
NORTON (St Berteline and St Christopher) *Ches 3* **P** *DBP* **V** R J GATES
NORTON (St Egwin) *see* Evesham w Norton and Lenchwick *Worc*
NORTON (St George) (St Nicholas) *St Alb 4* **P** *Bp* **V** C R BRIGGS
NORTON (St James) *Sheff 2* **P** *CCC Cam* **R** M J MORGAN, **C** R B PARKER
NORTON (St James) *see* Stoulton w Drake's Broughton and Pirton etc *Worc*
NORTON (St Mary) *Cant 6* **P** *Ld Chan* **R** *Vacant*
NORTON (St Mary) *see* Twigworth, Down Hatherley, Norton, The Leigh etc *Glouc*
NORTON (St Mary the Virgin) *Dur 10* **P** *Bp* **V** S A D FERNS
NORTON (St Michael and All Angels) *Dur 10* **P** *V Norton St Mary* **V** M G T GOBBETT
NORTON (St Michael and All Angels) *see* Stourbridge St Mich Norton *Worc*
NORTON (St Peter) *see* Norton juxta Malton *York*
NORTON, EAST (All Saints) *see* Hallaton w Horninghold, Allexton, Tugby etc *Leic*
NORTON, OVER (St James) *see* Chipping Norton *Ox*
NORTON BAVANT (All Saints) *see* Heytesbury and Sutton Veny *Sarum*
NORTON BRIDGE (St Luke) *see* Chebsey, Ellenhall and Seighford-with-Creswell *Lich*
NORTON CANES (St James) *Lich 3* **P** *Bp* **R** N L HIBBINS
NORTON CANON (St Nicholas) *see* Weobley w Sarnesfield and Norton Canon *Heref*
NORTON CUCKNEY (St Mary) *S'well 6* **P** *Lady Alexandra Cavendish Bentinck* **P-in-c** R F THEODOSIUS
NORTON DISNEY (St Peter) *see* Thurlby w Norton Disney *Linc*
NORTON FITZWARREN (All Saints) *B & W 18* **P** *MMCET* **R** P STEPHENS
NORTON IN HALES (St Chad) *see* Woore and Norton in Hales *Lich*
NORTON IN THE MOORS (St Bartholomew) *Lich 8* **P** *Lord Norton* **P-in-c** P S DAVIES
NORTON JUXTA MALTON (St Peter) *York 2* **P** *Abp* **V** W C HEDLEY, **NSM** M D YEWDALL
NORTON JUXTA TWYCROSS (Holy Trinity) *see* The Appleby Gp *Leic*
NORTON-LE-CLAY (St John the Evangelist) *see* Kirby-on-the-Moor, Cundall w Norton-le-Clay etc *Ripon*
NORTON LEES (St Paul) *see* Norton Woodseats St Paul *Sheff*
NORTON LINDSEY (Holy Trinity) *see* Wolverton w Norton Lindsey and Langley *Cov*
NORTON MALREWARD (Holy Trinity) *B & W 10* **P** *Bp* **R** *Vacant*
NORTON MANDEVILLE (All Saints) *see* High Ongar w Norton Mandeville *Chelmsf*
NORTON ST PHILIP (St Philip and St James) w Hemington, Hardington and Laverton *B & W 4* **P** *Bp and J B Owen-Jones Esq (alt)* **R** J G WILLIAMS
NORTON SUB HAMDON (Blessed Virgin Mary) w West Chinnock, Chiselborough and Middle Chinnock *B & W 6* **P** *Bp* **R** B J DALTON
NORTON SUBCOURSE (St Mary) *see* The Raveningham Gp *Nor*
NORTON WOODSEATS (St Chad) *Sheff 2* **P** *Bp* **V** E HUME
NORTON WOODSEATS (St Paul) *Sheff 2* **P** *R Norton* **V** M P HIRONS
NORWELL (St Laurence), w Ossington, Cromwell and Caunton *S'well 3* **P** *Bp, SMF, and Mrs P Goedhuis (jt)* **P-in-c** A I TUCKER
NORWICH (Christ Church) *see* New Catton Ch Ch *Nor*
NORWICH Heartsease (St Francis) *Nor 1* **P** *Bp* **P-in-c** P L HOWARD
NORWICH (St Andrew) *Nor 1* **P** *PCC* **P-in-c** R ALLINGTON-SMITH
NORWICH (St Augustine) *see* Norwich Over-the-Water *Nor*
NORWICH (St Barnabas) *see* Heigham St Barn w St Bart *Nor*
NORWICH (St George) *see* Norwich Over-the-Water *Nor*
NORWICH (St George) Tombland *Nor 1* **P** *Bp* **NSM** J C MINNS
NORWICH (St Giles) *Nor 1* **P** *Ld Chan and Bp (alt)* **P-in-c** A TYLER
NORWICH (St Helen) *Nor 1* **P** *Gt Hosp Nor* **P-in-c** L WOOD
NORWICH (St Julian) *see* Nor St Pet Parmentergate w St Jo *Nor*
NORWICH (St Luke) *see* New Catton St Luke *Nor*
NORWICH (St Mary in the Marsh) *Nor 1* **P** *D&C* **V** *Vacant*

NORWICH (St Mary Magdalene) *see* Norwich Over-the-Water *Nor*
NORWICH (St Peter Mancroft) (St John Maddermarket) *Nor 1* **P** *PCC* **R** D M SHARP, **C** R D SIMPER, **Hon C** H R G COOKE, **NSM** R J M COLLIER
NORWICH St Peter Parmentergate w St John de Sepulchre (St John) (St Julian) *Nor 1* **P** *Patr Bd* **P-in-c** M D SMITH
NORWICH (St Stephen) *Nor 1* **P** *D&C* **P-in-c** K G BEAKE
NORWICH Timberhill (St John) *see* Nor St Pet Parmentergate w St Jo *Nor*
NORWICH OVER-THE-WATER (St Augustine) (St George) (St Mary Magdalene) *Nor 1* **P** *Patr Bd* **TR** R M S WOODHAM
NORWOOD (St Margaret) *see* Upper Norwood All SS *S'wark*
NORWOOD (St Mary the Virgin) *Lon 23* **P** *SMF* **P-in-c** L LAWRENCE
NORWOOD (St Leonard) *see* Sheff Norwood St Leon *Sheff*
NORWOOD, SOUTH (Holy Innocents) *S'wark 24* **P** *Bp* **V** R D NEWMAN
NORWOOD, SOUTH (St Alban the Martyr) *S'wark 24* **P** *Bp* **P-in-c** I S BROTHWOOD
NORWOOD, SOUTH (St Mark) *S'wark 24* **P** *Bp* **V** P E THROWER
NORWOOD, UPPER (All Saints) *S'wark 24* **P** *V Croydon* **V** A D MIDDLETON, **C** A J PRICE
NORWOOD, UPPER (St John) *S'wark 24* **P** *Bp* **V** D G MARTIN, **NSM** T L DAVIS
NORWOOD, WEST (St Luke) *S'wark 14* **P** *Abp* **V** P H RONAYNE, **C** A R CHRISTIE, **Hon C** B ALLEN
NOTGROVE (St Bartholomew) *see* Cold Aston w Notgrove and Turkdean *Glouc*
NOTTING DALE (St Clement) (St Mark) and Norlands St James *Lon 12* **P** *Bp* **V** H D J RAYMENT-PICKARD, **C** C E SARGENT, **NSM** E J WALLER
NOTTING HILL (All Saints) (St Columb) *Lon 12* **P** *SMF* **V** J K BROWNSELL, **C** A F HILL, **NSM** R E DUGUID, D C CLUES
NOTTING HILL (St John) (St Peter) *Lon 12* **P** *Bp* **V** H J STRINGER, **C** M K HARGREAVES, S E GENT, **Hon C** D O ONSLOW
NOTTING HILL (St Michael and All Angels) (Christ Church) (St Francis) *Lon 12* **P** *Trustees* **V** A B ANDREWS
NOTTINGHAM (All Saints) *S'well 12* **P** *Trustees* **V** D C WHITE, **C** R M M CREIGHTON, J M PILGRIM
NOTTINGHAM (St Andrew) *S'well 12* **P** *Peache Trustees* **V** R M CLARK
NOTTINGHAM (St Ann w Emmanuel) *S'well 12* **P** *Trustees* **V** J P NEILL
NOTTINGHAM (St George w St John the Baptist) *S'well 12* **P** *Bp* **V** D C F TUDOR
NOTTINGHAM (St Jude) *S'well 12* **P** *CPAS* **V** S E DYAS, **C** R KELLETT
NOTTINGHAM (St Mary the Virgin) and St Catharine *S'well 12* **P** *Bp* **V** J E M NEALE, **Hon C** J E LAMB
NOTTINGHAM (St Nicholas) *S'well 12* **P** *CPAS* **R** D J BETTS, **C** S J HELLYER
NOTTINGHAM (St Peter and St James) *S'well 12* **P** *Bp* **R** L J MORLEY, **C** E M McLEAN, J W HUCKLE
NOTTINGHAM (St Saviour) *S'well 12* **P** *CPAS* **V** J W BENTHAM, **C** S P HOLLINGHURST, A E HOLLINGHURST
NOTTINGHAM (St Stephen) *see* Basford w Hyson Green *S'well*
NOWTON (St Peter) *see* Hawstead and Nowton w Stanningfield etc *St E*
NUFFIELD (Holy Trinity) *Ox 6* **P** *MMCET* **R** J F SHEARER
NUN MONKTON (St Mary) *see* Lower Nidderdale *Ripon*
NUNBURNHOLME (St James) and Warter *York 7* **P** *Abp and Marquis of Normanby (jt)* **P-in-c** J C MELLING
NUNEATON (St Mary) *Cov 5* **P** *V Nuneaton* **V** N D ADAMS
NUNEATON (St Nicolas) *Cov 5* **P** *The Crown* **V** D JONES, **C** C B POLLARD
NUNHEAD (St Antony) (St Silas) *S'wark 7* **P** *Bp* **V** *Vacant* 0171-639 4261
NUNNEY (All Saints) and Witham Friary, Marston Bigot, Wanstrow and Cloford *B & W 4* **P** *Bp, SMF, and C N Clarke Esq and Exors Duke of Somerset (jt)* **R** J K HODDER
NUNNINGTON (All Saints) *see* Harome w Stonegrave, Nunnington and Pockley *York*
NUNTHORPE (St Mary the Virgin) (St Mary's Church Hall) *York 22* **P** *Abp* **V** T M THOMPSON, **C** G B USHER, **NSM** P M HARRISON
NUNTON (St Andrew) *see* Chalke Valley W *Sarum*
NURSLING (St Boniface) (St John the Evangelist) and Rownhams *Win 11* **P** *Bp* **R** I D GARDNER
NURSTEAD (St Mildred) *see* Meopham w Nurstead *Roch*
NUTBOURNE (St Wilfrid) *see* Chidham *Chich*
NUTFIELD (St Peter and St Paul) *S'wark 26* **P** *Jes Coll Ox* **R** G I WILLIAMS
NUTFIELD, LOWER (Christ Church) *S'wark 26* **P** *Ch Patr Trust* **P-in-c** A E THOMPSON, **NSM** L M BARLEY
NUTHALL (St Patrick) *S'well 7* **P** *Bp* **R** R PALIN
NUTHURST (St Andrew) *Chich 8* **P** *Bp Lon* **R** J G HAIGH
NUTHURST (St Thomas) *see* Packwood w Hockley Heath *Birm*
NUTLEY (St James the Less) *Chich 21* **P** *R Maresfield* **V** M T A BULMAN
NYMET (St George) *see* S Molton w Nymet St George, High Bray etc *Ex*
NYMET ROWLAND (St Bartholomew) *see* Lapford, Nymet Rowland and Coldridge *Ex*
NYMET TRACEY (St Bartholomew) *see* Bow w Broad Nymet *Ex*
NYMPSFIELD (St Bartholomew) *see* Uley w Owlpen and Nympsfield *Glouc*
NYNEHEAD (All Saints) *see* Wellington and Distr *B & W*
OADBY (St Paul) (St Peter) *Leic 5* **P** *Bp* **R** D H CLARK, **TV** R KANERIA, **C** L MATHIAS, **NSM** G TURNOCK, A J MORGAN
OAKAMOOR (Holy Trinity) *see* Alton w Bradley-le-Moors and Oakamoor w Cotton *Lich*
OAKDALE (St George) *Sarum 8* **P** *Bp* **TR** D K CALLARD, **TV** C G ROBINSON, M G OATES, **C** R MELLOR
OAKE (St Bartholomew) *see* Bradford w Oake, Hillfarrance and Heathfield *B & W*
OAKENGATES (Holy Trinity) *see* Ketley and Oakengates *Lich*
OAKENSHAW (Church of the Good Shepherd) *see* Willington and Sunnybrow *Dur*
OAKENSHAW (St Andrew) cum Woodlands *Bradf 2* **P** *Bp* **P-in-c** P G WALKER
OAKFIELD (St John) *Portsm 7* **P** *V St Helens* **V** H E WRIGHT, **NSM** C A DAVIES
OAKFORD (St Peter) *see* Washfield, Stoodleigh, Withleigh etc *Ex*
OAKHAM (All Saints) w Hambleton and Egleton and Braunston w Brooke *Pet 14* **P** *Dr E R Hanbury (1 turn), D&C Linc (2 turns)* **V** M W R COVINGTON, **C** S J PINNINGTON, **NSM** E B WALKER
OAKHANGER (St Luke's Mission Church) *see* Alsager Ch Ch *Ches*
OAKHANGER (St Mary Magdalene) *see* E and W Worldham, Hartley Mauditt w Kingsley etc *Win*
OAKHILL (All Saints) *see* Ashwick w Oakhill and Binegar *B & W*
OAKHILL Eastwood View (shared church) *see* Clifton St Jas *Sheff*
OAKINGTON (St Andrew) *Ely 5* **P** *Qu Coll Cam* **V** J C ALEXANDER
OAKLEY (St Mary) *see* Worminghall w Ickford, Oakley and Shabbington *Ox*
OAKLEY (St Mary) *see* Bromham w Oakley and Stagsden *St Alb*
OAKLEY (St Nicholas) *see* N Hartismere *St E*
OAKLEY, EAST (St John) *see* Church Oakley and Wootton St Lawrence *Win*
OAKLEY, GREAT (All Saints) w Wix and Wrabness *Chelmsf 20* **P** *Ld Chan, Ch Patr Trust, and St Jo Coll Cam (by turn)* **R** P H WILLIAMS, **NSM** P E H PALMER
OAKLEY, GREAT (St Michael) *see* Corby SS Pet and Andr w Gt and Lt Oakley *Pet*
OAKLEY, LITTLE (St Peter) *as above*
OAKMOOR *see* Bishopsnympton, Rose Ash, Mariansleigh etc *Ex*
OAKRIDGE (St Bartholomew) *see* Bisley, Oakridge, Miserden and Edgeworth *Glouc*
OAKS IN CHARNWOOD (St James the Greater) and Copt Oak *Leic 8* **P** *DBP* **V** G A PADDOCK
OAKSEY (All Saints) *see* Ashley, Crudwell, Hankerton, Long Newnton etc *Bris*
OAKWOOD (no dedication) *Derby 9* **P** *Bp and MMCET (jt)* **P-in-c** P T WALLER
OAKWOOD (St Thomas) *Lon 18* **P** *Bp* **C** N L SHARP
OAKWORTH (Christ Church) *Bradf 8* **P** *Bp* **V** D J SWALES
OARE (Blessed Virgin Mary) w Culbone *B & W 16* **P** *Bp* **P-in-c** A F I NOBLE
OARE (Holy Trinity) *see* Swanborough *Sarum*
OARE (St Bartholomew) *see* Chieveley w Winterbourne and Oare *Ox*
OARE (St Peter) *see* The Brents and Davington w Oare and Luddenham *Cant*
OATLANDS (St Mary) *Guildf 8* **P** *Bp* **V** M ANKER, **C** H WHITEHEAD
OBORNE (St Cuthbert) *see* Queen Thorne *Sarum*
OCCOLD (St Michael) *St E 16* **P** *Lt-Comdr G C Marshall* **R** *Vacant*

OCKBROOK (All Saints) *Derby 13* **P** *Lt-Col T H Pares* **P-in-c** J G KELLY, **C** T M SUMPTER, **NSM** J D BISHOP
OCKENDON, NORTH (St Mary Magdalene) *Chelmsf 2* **P** *Bp* **NSM** J E SKIPPER, P RADLEY
OCKENDON, SOUTH (St Nicholas) *Chelmsf 14* **P** *Guild of All So* **P-in-c** R W SPRINGETT, **C** D J PALMER
OCKER HILL (St Mark) *Lich 27* **P** *Bp* **V** A R BOYD-WILLIAMS
OCKFORD RIDGE (St Mark) *see* Godalming *Guildf*
OCKHAM (All Saints) w Hatchford *Guildf 10* **P** *Bp* **P-in-c** K A ELFORD
OCKLEY (St Margaret), Okewood and Forest Green *Guildf 7* **P** *Bp and J P M H Evelyn Esq (alt)* **R** C de F TICKNER
OCLE PYCHARD (St James the Great) *see* Stoke Lacy, Moreton Jeffries w Much Cowarne etc *Heref*
ODCOMBE (St Peter and St Paul), Brympton, Lufton and Montacute *B & W 6* **P** *Ch Ch Ox (4 turns), C E B Clive-Ponsonby-Fane Esq (1 turn)* **R** J F JENKINS
ODD RODE (All Saints) *Ches 11* **P** *R Astbury* **R** R N W ELBOURNE, **C** P J CLARKE
ODDINGLEY (St James) *see* Bowbrook S *Worc*
ODDINGTON (Holy Ascension) *see* Broadwell, Evenlode, Oddington and Adlestrop *Glouc*
ODDINGTON (St Andrew) *see* Islip w Charlton on Otmoor, Oddington, Noke etc *Ox*
ODDINGTON (St Nicholas) *see* Broadwell, Evenlode, Oddington and Adlestrop *Glouc*
ODELL (All Saints) and Pavenham *St Alb 15* **P** *Lord Luke of Pavenham* **R** J T LIGHTOWLER, **NSM** D R BANNARD-SMITH
ODIHAM (All Saints) *Win 5* **P** *Bp* **P-in-c** M C S BEVER
ODSTOCK (St Mary) *see* Chalke Valley W *Sarum*
OFFCHURCH (St Gregory) *Cov 10* **P** *Bp* **P-in-c** P J CROOKS, **C** M L D GREIG
OFFENHAM (St Mary and St Milburgh) *see* Badsey w Aldington and Offenham and Bretforton *Worc*
OFFERTON (St Alban) (St John) *Ches 18* **P** *Bp* **V** R E READ, **C** J E L ALEXANDER
OFFHAM (Old St Peter) *see* Hamsey *Chich*
OFFHAM (St Michael) *see* W Malling w Offham *Roch*
OFFLEY (St Mary Magdalene) *see* King's Walden and Offley w Lilley *St Alb*
OFFLEY, HIGH (St Mary the Virgin) and Norbury *Lich 7* **P** *Bp* **R** D KNIGHT
OFFLEY HAY (Mission Church) *see* Eccleshall *Lich*
OFFORD D'ARCY (All Saints) w Offord Cluny *Ely 12* **P** *Ld Chan* **R** P J TAYLOR
OFFTON (St Mary) *see* Somersham w Flowton and Offton w Willisham *St E*
OFFWELL (St Mary the Virgin) *see* Colyton, Southleigh, Offwell, Widworthy etc *Ex*
OGBOURNE (St Andrew) *see* Ridgeway *Sarum*
OGBOURNE (St George) *as above*
OGLEY HAY (St James) *Lich 1* **P** *Bp* **V** C N THOMAS, **C** M P BRANSCOMBE, **NSM** P F HARRIS
OGWELL (St Bartholomew) and Denbury *Ex 11* **P** *Bp and SMF (jt)* **R** R G DAVIS
OKEFORD FITZPAINE (St Andrew) *see* Childe Okeford, Okeford Fitzpaine, Manston etc *Sarum*
OKEHAMPTON (All Saints) (St James) w Inwardleigh; Bratton Clovelly w Germansweek; Northlew w Ashbury; and Bridestowe and Sourton *Ex 12* **P** *Patr Bd* **TR** R C CHAMBERLAIN, **TV** R W L VODEN, **Hon C** G D HARRIS
OKEWOOD (St John the Baptist) *see* Ockley, Okewood and Forest Green *Guildf*
OLD *see also under substantive place name*
OLD FORD (St Paul) (St Mark) *Lon 7* **P** *Hyndman Trustees and CPAS (jt)* **P-in-c** P J BOARDMAN
OLD HILL (Holy Trinity) *Worc 9* **P** *Ch Soc Trust* **V** P D J SWANN
OLD LANE (Mission Church) *see* Bloxwich *Lich*
OLD WIVES LEES (Mission Church) *see* Chilham w Challock and Molash *Cant*
OLDBERROW (St Mary) *see* Spernall, Morton Bagot and Oldberrow *Cov*
OLDBROOK (Community Church) *see* Woughton *Ox*
OLDBURY *Birm 7* **P** *Bp* **P-in-c** R T ETHERIDGE
OLDBURY *Sarum 18* **P** *Bp, CPAS, Earl of Shelborne, and E Money-Kyrle Esq (jt)* **P-in-c** J P R SAUNT
OLDBURY (St Nicholas) *see* Bridgnorth, Tasley, Astley Abbotts, Oldbury etc *Heref*
OLDBURY-ON-SEVERN (St Arilda) *Glouc 7* **P** *Ch Ch Ox* **P-in-c** R W MARTIN
OLDCOTES (St Mark's Mission Church) *see* Langold *S'well*
OLDHAM Moorside (St Thomas) *Man 21* **P** *Trustees* **V** J H GRAY
OLDHAM (St Ambrose) *Man 19* **P** *Bp* **V** B P H JAMES
OLDHAM (St Andrew) (St Mary w St Peter) *Man 19* **P** *Patr Bd* **TR** J SYKES, **TV** C H RAZZALL
OLDHAM (St Barnabas) *Man 19* **P** *The Crown* **V** F A CORBIN
OLDHAM (St Chad) Limeside *Man 19* **P** *Bp* **V** *Vacant* 0161-624 0970
OLDHAM (St James) *Man 19* **P** *R Prestwich St Mary* **V** P PLUMPTON
OLDHAM (St Paul) *Man 19* **P** *Bp* **P-in-c** C MARSDEN, **C** D J QUARMBY
OLDHAM (St Stephen and All Martyrs) Lower Moor *Man 19* **P** *Bp* **P-in-c** A KERR
OLDHURST (St Peter) *see* Somersham w Pidley and Oldhurst *Ely*
OLDLAND (St Anne) *Bris 2* **P** *Bp* **V** M H PERRY
OLDRIDGE (St Thomas) *see* Tedburn St Mary, Whitestone, Oldridge etc *Ex*
OLDSWINFORD (St Mary) *see* Old Swinford Stourbridge *Worc*
OLIVER'S BATTERY (St Mark) *see* Stanmore *Win*
OLLERTON (St Giles) (St Paulinus) w Boughton *S'well 6* **P** *Ld Chan and Bp (alt)* **C** A A TOOBY
OLNEY (St Peter and St Paul) *Ox 27* **P** *Bp* **R** N P H POND, **Hon C** C M LOOKER
OLTON (St Margaret) *Birm 12* **P** *Bp and V Bickenhill (jt)* **V** N S DODDS
OLVESTON (St Mary of Malmesbury) *Bris 8* **P** *D&C* **V** *Vacant*
OMBERSLEY (St Andrew) w Doverdale *Worc 8* **P** *Bp and Lord Sandys (alt)* **P-in-c** S P KERR, **NSM** R W WAGSTAFF
ONCHAN (St Peter) *S & M 2* **P** *The Crown* **V** N A WELLS
ONECOTE (St Luke) *see* Ipstones w Berkhamsytch and Onecote w Bradnop *Lich*
ONEHOUSE (St John the Baptist) *see* Gt Finborough w Onehouse and Harleston *St E*
ONGAR, HIGH (St Mary the Virgin) w Norton Mandeville *Chelmsf 27* **P** *Ch Soc Trust* **C** D J EDWARDS
ONIBURY (St Michael and All Angels) *see* Culmington w Onibury, Bromfield etc *Heref*
OPENSHAW (St Barnabas) *see* Manchester Gd Shep and St Barn *Man*
OPENSHAW, HIGHER (St Clement) *Man 1* **P** *Trustees* **R** W NELSON
OPENWOODGATE (St Mark) *see* Belper *Derby*
ORBY (All Saints) *Linc 8* **P** *Bp* **V** T STEELE
ORCHARD (Community Centre) *see* Egglescliffe *Dur*
ORCHARD PORTMAN (St Michael) *see* Staple Fitzpaine, Orchard Portman, Thurlbear etc *B & W*
ORCHARD WAY (St Barnabas) *see* Cheltenham St Mark *Glouc*
ORCHARDLEIGH (Blessed Virgin Mary) *see* Beckington w Standerwick, Berkley, Rodden etc *B & W*
ORCHESTON (St Mary) *see* Tilshead, Orcheston and Chitterne *Sarum*
ORCOP (St John the Baptist) *see* St Weonards w Orcop, Garway, Tretire etc *Heref*
ORDSALL (All Hallows) (St Alban) *S'well 5* **P** *Bp* **P-in-c** P S BAGSHAW
ORDSALL (St Clement) *see* Salford Ordsall St Clem *Man*
ORE (Christ Church) *Chich 17* **P** *Simeon's Trustees* **V** J G PANGBOURNE, **NSM** F ROWSON
ORE (St Barnabas) *Chich 17* **P** *Simeon's Trustees* **R** C H KEY, **C** C G SPENCER, S J GURR, **NSM** D K MOYNAGH
ORESTON (Church of the Good Shepherd) *see* Plymstock and Hooe *Ex*
ORFORD (St Andrew) *Liv 12* **P** *Bp* **V** M RAYNOR
ORFORD (St Bartholomew) w Sudbourne, Chillesford, Butley and Iken *St E 7* **P** *Bp* **P-in-c** R W CLIFTON
ORFORD (St Margaret) *Liv 12* **P** *Bp* **V** M S FINLAY, **NSM** J BROCKLEBANK
ORLESTONE (St Mary) w Snave and Ruckinge w Warehorne *Cant 12* **P** *Abp and Ld Chan (alt)* **P-in-c** R D KING
ORLETON (St George) w Brimfield *Heref 7* **P** *Bp* **P-in-c** J E FOX
ORLINGBURY (St Mary) *see* Gt w Lt Harrowden and Orlingbury *Pet*
ORMESBY (St Cuthbert) *York 19* **P** *Abp* **V** R A SMAILES
ORMESBY, NORTH (Holy Trinity) *York 19* **P** *Abp* **V** T J ROBINSON
ORMESBY ST MARGARET (St Margaret) w Scratby, Ormesby St Michael and Rollesby *Nor 6* **P** *Bp, D&C, DBP and R J H Tacon Esq (jt)* **V** C W COUSINS
ORMESBY ST MICHAEL (St Michael) *see* Ormesby St Marg w Scratby, Ormesby St Mich etc *Nor*
ORMSBY Group, The SOUTH (St Leonard) *Linc 7* **P** *A J Massingberd-Mundy Esq, Sir Thomas Ingilby, Bt, Mert Coll Ox, Bp, and DBP (jt)* **R** *Vacant* (01507) 480236

ORMSGILL (St Francis) *see* Barrow St Matt *Carl*
ORMSIDE (St James) *Carl 1* **P** *Bp and D&C (jt)* **R** P E P NORTON, **NSM** R A COLLINSON
ORMSKIRK (St Peter and St Paul) *Liv 11* **P** *Lord Derby* **V** P M KIRBY, **NSM** C D BENGE
ORPINGTON (All Saints) *Roch 16* **P** *D&C* **V** E H HESELWOOD, **NSM** M T SKINNER
ORPINGTON (Christ Church) *Roch 16* **P** *Ch Trust Fund Trust, Bp, and V Orpington (jt)* **V** A C EAVES, **C** M D WOODCOCK
ORPINGTON (St Andrew) *Roch 16* **P** *Bp* **V** J A GROVES
ORRELL (St Luke) *Liv 15* **P** *Bp* **V** *Vacant* (01695) 623410
ORSETT (St Giles and All Saints) and Bulphan and Horndon on the Hill *Chelmsf 14* **P** *Bp and D&C St Paul's (jt)* **R** V G CATO, **NSM** J M WHITEHORN
ORSTON (St Mary) *see* Whatton w Aslockton, Hawksworth, Scarrington etc *S'well*
ORTON (All Saints) and Tebay w Ravenstonedale and Newbiggin-on-Lune *Carl 1* **P** *Bp and Ravenstonedale Trustees (1 turn), Resident Landowners (1 turn)* **R** C R LEVEY
ORTON (St Giles) *Carl 1* **P** *MMCET* **C** G M HART
ORTON, GREAT *see* Orton St Giles *Carl*
ORTON GOLDHAY (St John) Conventional District *Ely 13 Vacant*
ORTON LONGUEVILLE (Holy Trinity) *see* The Ortons, Alwalton and Chesterton *Ely*
ORTON MALBORNE (not known) *as above*
ORTON-ON-THE-HILL (St Edith of Polesworth) *see* The Sheepy Gp *Leic*
ORTON WATERVILLE (St Mary) *see* The Ortons, Alwalton and Chesterton *Ely*
ORTONS, Alwalton and Chesterton, The *Ely 13* **P** *Patr Bd* **TR** M SOULSBY, **TV** G GOSWELL, R A D STURT, F E G BRAMPTON
ORWELL (St Andrew) *Ely 8* **P** *Bp and DBP (alt)* **R** N A BRICE
OSBALDWICK (St Thomas) w Murton *York 4* **P** *Abp* **V** *Vacant* (01904) 416763
OSBOURNBY (St Peter and St Paul) *see* S Lafford *Linc*
OSCOTT, OLD (All Saints) *see* Kingstanding St Mark *Birm*
OSGATHORPE (St Mary the Virgin) *see* Hathern, Long Whatton and Diseworth w Belton etc *Leic*
OSMASTON (St Martin) *see* Brailsford w Shirley and Osmaston w Edlaston *Derby*
OSMINGTON (St Osmond) *see* Preston w Sutton Poyntz and Osmington w Poxwell *Sarum*
OSMONDTHORPE (St Philip) *Ripon 8* **P** *Bp* **P-in-c** P B STOODLEY
OSMOTHERLEY (St Peter) w Harlsey and Ingleby Arncliffe *York 20* **P** *J B Barnard Esq (1 turn), Ld Chan (2 turns)* **V** A H DODD
OSMOTHERLY (St John) *see* Ulverston St Mary w H Trin *Carl*
OSPRINGE (St Peter and St Paul) *see* Eastling w Ospringe and Stalisfield w Otterden *Cant*
OSSETT (St Oswald's Mission Room) (Holy and Undivided Trinity) cum Gawthorpe *Wakef 10* **P** *R Dewsbury* **V** M GREEN
OSSETT, SOUTH (Christ Church) *Wakef 10* **P** *Bp* **P-in-c** J HARRIS, **C** M J CAREY, **NSM** C BULLIMORE
OSSINGTON (Holy Rood) *see* Norwell w Ossington, Cromwell and Caunton *S'well*
OSTERLEY ROAD (St Mary) *see* Spring Grove St Mary *Lon*
OSWALDKIRK (St Oswald) *see* Ampleforth and Oswaldkirk and Gilling E *York*
OSWALDTWISTLE (Immanuel) (All Saints) *Blackb 1* **P** *Trustees* **V** P W WATSON
OSWALDTWISTLE (St Paul) *Blackb 1* **P** *Trustees* **V** M D RATCLIFFE
OSWESTRY (St Oswald) (Holy Trinity) *Lich 19* **P** *Earl of Powis* **V** D B CROWHURST, **C** T N THOROLD
OTFORD (St Bartholomew) *Roch 10* **P** *D&C Westmr* **V** P M HOPKINS
OTFORD LANE (Mission Hall) *see* Knockholt w Halstead *Roch*
OTHAM (St Nicholas) w Langley *Cant 15* **P** *Abp and CPAS (jt)* **R** D A MUSTON, **NSM** D W BOND
OTHERY (St Michael) *see* Middlezoy and Othery and Moorlinch *B & W*
OTLEY (All Saints) *Bradf 4* **P** *Bp* **V** I T RODLEY, **C** M P SHORT
OTLEY (St Mary) *see* Clopton w Otley, Swilland and Ashbocking *St E*
OTTER VALE *see* Ottery St Mary, Alfington, W Hill, Tipton etc *Ex*
OTTERBOURNE (St Matthew) *see* Compton and Otterbourne *Win*
OTTERBURN (St John the Evangelist) *see* N Tyne and Redesdale Team *Newc*
OTTERFORD (St Leonard) *see* Churchstanton, Buckland St Mary and Otterford *B & W*
OTTERHAM (St Denis) *see* Boscastle w Davidstow *Truro*
OTTERINGTON, NORTH (St Michael and All Angels) *see* The Thorntons and The Otteringtons *York*
OTTERINGTON, SOUTH (St Andrew) *as above*
OTTERSHAW (Christ Church) *Guildf 11* **P** *Bp* **V** J W BATT
OTTERTON (St Michael) *see* E Budleigh w Bicton and Otterton *Ex*
OTTERY ST MARY (St Mary the Virgin), Alfington, West Hill and Tipton St John w Venn Ottery *Ex 7* **P** *Patr Bd* **P-in-c** S G FRANKLIN, **C** A M JORDAN
OTTRINGHAM (St Wilfrid) *see* Keyingham w Ottringham, Halsham and Sunk Is *York*
OUGHTIBRIDGE (Ascension) *Sheff 7* **P** *V Wadsley* **V** L M ATKINSON
OUGHTRINGTON (St Peter) *Ches 10* **P** *Bp* **R** E M BURGESS
OULTON (St John the Evangelist) *see* Stone Ch Ch and Oulton *Lich*
OULTON (St John) w Woodlesford *Ripon 8* **P** *Bp* **V** W J HULSE, **NSM** R N MULKERN
OULTON (St Michael) *Nor 9* **P** *Ch Soc Trust* **R** A R PRITCHARD
OULTON (St Peter and St Paul) *see* Lt Barningham, Blickling, Edgefield etc *Nor*
OULTON BROAD (St Mark) (St Luke the Evangelist) *Nor 9* **P** *Simeon's Trustees* **C** J M BEACH
OUNDLE (St Peter) *Pet 12* **P** *Bp* **V** R L HAWKES, **NSM** D M JARMY
OUSBY (St Luke) *see* Skirwith, Ousby and Melmerby w Kirkland *Carl*
OUSDEN (St Peter) *see* Wickhambrook w Lydgate, Ousden and Cowlinge *St E*
OUSEBURN, GREAT (St Mary) and LITTLE (Holy Trinity) w Marton-cum-Grafton *Ripon 3* **P** *Bp and St Jo Coll Cam (alt)* **NSM** M SAUNDERS
OUT RAWCLIFFE (St John the Evangelist) *see* Hambleton w Out Rawcliffe *Blackb*
OUTLANE (St Mary Magdalene) *see* Stainland *Wakef*
OUTWELL (St Clement) *Ely 19* **P** *Bp* **P-in-c** R J M BLACKALL
OUTWOOD (St Aidan) *see* Ringley w Prestolee *Man*
OUTWOOD (St John) *S'wark 25* **P** *Bp* **V** *Vacant*
OUTWOOD (St Mary Magdalene) *Wakef 12* **P** *V Stanley* **V** J W BUTTERWORTH
OUTWOOD COMMON (St John the Divine) *see* Billericay and Lt Burstead *Chelmsf*
OVAL WAY (All Saints) *see* Chalfont St Peter *Ox*
OVENDEN (St George) *Wakef 4* **P** *V Halifax* **V** D J ROBERTSON, **C** P F HINCKLEY
OVENDEN (St John the Evangelist) *see* Bradshaw *Wakef*
OVER *see also under substantive place name*
OVER (St Chad) *Ches 6* **P** *Bp* **V** J J E SUTTON, **C** M SAVILLE
OVER (St John the Evangelist) *Ches 6* **P** *Lord Delamere and W R Cullimore Esq (jt)* **V** S F HAMILL-STEWART
OVER (St Mary) *Ely 5* **P** *Trin Coll Cam* **V** M WARRICK
OVERBURY (St Faith) w Teddington, Alstone and Little Washbourne w Beckford and Ashton under Hill *Worc 4* **P** *D&C and MMCET (jt)* **V** I BUTCHER, **NSM** H M HUMPHREY
OVERCHURCH (St Mary) *see* Upton (Overchurch) *Ches*
OVERPOOL (St Francis) *see* Ellesmere Port *Ches*
OVERSEAL (St Matthew) *see* Seale and Lullington *Derby*
OVERSTONE (St Nicholas) *see* Mears Ashby and Hardwick and Sywell etc *Pet*
OVERSTRAND (St Martin), Northrepps, Sidestrand and Trimingham *Nor 21* **P** *Duchy of Lanc, DBP, and Bp (by turn)* **R** S HABGOOD
OVERTON (St Helen) *Blackb 12* **P** *V Lanc* **P-in-c** C J ENTWISTLE
OVERTON (St Mary) w Laverstoke and Freefolk *Win 6* **P** *Bp* **R** N P CUMMING
OVERTON (St Michael and All Angels) *see* Upper Kennet *Sarum*
OVING (All Saints) *see* Schorne *Ox*
OVING (St Andrew) *see* Tangmere and Oving *Chich*
OVINGDEAN (St Wulfran) *Chich 2* **P** *SMF* **P-in-c** S R TUCKER
OVINGHAM (St Mary the Virgin) *Newc 3* **P** *Bp* **V** D L GOODACRE
OVINGTON (St John the Evangelist) *see* Watton w Carbrooke and Ovington *Nor*
OVINGTON (St Mary) *see* Belchamp Otten w Belchamp Walter and Bulmer etc *Chelmsf*
OVINGTON (St Peter) *see* New Alresford w Ovington and Itchen Stoke *Win*

OWERMOIGNE (St Michael) *see* Broadmayne, W Knighton, Owermoigne etc *Sarum*
OWERSBY, NORTH (St Martin) *see* S Kelsey Gp *Linc*
OWLERTON (St John the Baptist) *Sheff 4* **P** *Ch Patr Trust* **V** N A DAWSON, **NSM** G COCKAYNE
OWLPEN (Holy Cross) *see* Uley w Owlpen and Nympsfield *Glouc*
OWLSMOOR (St George) *Ox 16* **P** *Bp* **P-in-c** R V PARRETT
OWLSWICK (Chapel) *see* Monks Risborough *Ox*
OWMBY Group, The (St Peter and St Paul) *Linc 3* **P** *Duchy of Lanc, Bp and D&C, and Major-Gen W M Hutton and Earl of Scarbrough (by turn)* **R** I R HOWITT
OWSLEBURY (St Andrew) *see* Twyford and Owslebury and Morestead *Win*
OWSTON (All Saints) *Sheff 8* **P** *DBP* **V** J Y W RITCHIE
OWSTON (St Andrew) *see* Whatborough Gp of Par *Leic*
OWSTON (St Martin) *Linc 1* **P** *The Crown* **P-in-c** J STAFF
OWTHORNE (St Matthew) and Rimswell w Withernsea *York 13* **P** *Ld Chan and Abp (alt)* **V** P I ADDISON
OWTHORPE (St Margaret) *S'well 9* **P** *Trustees Sir Rupert Bromley* **P-in-c** G B BARRODALE
OWTON MANOR (St James) *Dur 3* **P** *Bp* **V** P ANDERTON, **C** T D PIKE
OXBOROUGH (St John the Evangelist) w Foulden and Caldecote *Nor 13* **P** *G&C Coll Cam* **P-in-c** G R DRAKE
OXCLOSE (not known) *Dur 11* **P** *R Washington, TR Usworth, and V Fatfield (jt)* **P-in-c** K H DUNNE
OXENDON (St Helen) *see* Arthingworth, Harrington w Oxendon and E Farndon *Pet*
OXENHALL (St Anne) *see* Redmarley D'Abitot, Bromesberrow w Pauntley etc *Glouc*
OXENHOPE (St Mary the Virgin) *Bradf 8* **P** *Bp* **V** B GRAINGER
OXENTON *see* Woolstone w Gotherington and Oxenton etc *Glouc*
OXFORD Canning Crescent (St Luke) *see* Ox St Aldate *Ox*
OXFORD (St Aldate) *Ox 7* **P** *Simeon's Trustees* **R** D R MACINNES, **C** J S W CHORLTON, A J H BUCKLER, **Hon C** A R WINGFIELD-DIGBY, **NSM** J EDMONDS-SEAL, J SEARS, T BRADSHAW
OXFORD (St Andrew) *Ox 7* **P** *Trustees* **V** R F KEY, **C** D H JACKSON, S D COE
OXFORD (St Barnabas and St Paul) *Ox 7* **P** *Keble Coll Ox* **V** E M WRIGHT, **NSM** D W MASON
OXFORD (St Clement) *Ox 4* **P** *Ox Ch Trust* **R** J B GILLINGHAM, **C** J L MACLAREN, **NSM** A BEETHAM
OXFORD (St Ebbe w Holy Trinity and St Peter-le-Bailey) *Ox 7* **P** *Ox Ch Trust* **R** D C M FLETCHER, **C** D R A GIBB
OXFORD (St Giles) (St Philip) (St James) (St Margaret) *Ox 7* **P** *St Jo Coll Ox* **C** A J E GREEN, **NSM** D R HOLMES, M SCREECH, A ASTON SMITH
OXFORD (St Mary Magdalene) *Ox 7* **P** *Ch Ch Ox* **V** H M WYBREW
OXFORD (St Mary the Virgin) (St Cross or Holywell) (St Peter in the East) *Ox 7* **P** *Or Coll Ox and Mert Coll Ox (jt)* **V** B W MOUNTFORD
OXFORD (St Matthew) *Ox 7* **P** *Ox Ch Trust* **R** J F SAMWAYS
OXFORD (St Michael at the North Gate w St Martin and All Saints) *Ox 7* **P** *Linc Coll Ox* **V** S J PIX
OXFORD (St Thomas the Martyr) (St Frideswide) and Binsey *Ox 7* **P** *Ch Ch Ox* **V** R M SWEENEY, **NSM** R C de V MARTIN
OXHEY (All Saints) *St Alb 7* **P** *Bp* **V** A P DOUGLAS, **C** P I LEECH
OXHEY (St Matthew) *St Alb 7* **P** *DBP* **V** *Vacant* (01923) 241420
OXHILL (St Lawrence) *see* Tysoe w Oxhill and Whatcote *Cov*
OXLEY (Epiphany) *Lich 29* **P** *Bp* **V** G JOHNSON
OXNEAD (St Michael & all Angels) *see* Buxton w Oxnead, Lammas and Brampton *Nor*
OXON and Shelton *Lich 21* **P** *V Shrewsbury SS Chad & Mary* **V** P F T FISHER
OXSHOTT (St Andrew) *Guildf 10* **P** *Bp* **V** J P CRESSWELL
OXSPRING (St Aidan) *see* Penistone and Thurlstone *Wakef*
OXTED (St Mary) and Tandridge *S'wark 24* **P** *Bp* **R** G BENNETT, **C** A J HALE, **NSM** F A HARDING
OXTON (St Peter and St Paul) *S'well 15* **P** *Ld Chan, Bp, and Comdr M B P Francklin (by turn)* **V** M J BROCK, **C** T J RENSHAW
OXTON (St Saviour) *Ches 1* **P** *DBP* **V** I A DAVENPORT, **C** C M KEMP
PACKINGTON (Holy Rood) w Normanton-le-Heath *Leic 9* **P** *MMCET and The Crown (alt)* **Dn-in-c** C M PARKER
PACKWOOD (St Giles) w Hockley Heath *Birm 6* **P** *DBP and Bp (alt)* **V** P H ROE
PADBURY (St Mary the Virgin) *see* Lenborough *Ox*
PADDINGTON (Emmanuel) Harrow Road *Lon 2* **P** *Hyndman Trustees* **V** M M H JONES
PADDINGTON (St David's Welsh Church) Extra-Parochial Place *Lon 2* **P-in-c** A P HAWKINS
PADDINGTON (St James) *Lon 2* **P** *Bp* **V** W G WILSON, **C** A J B MELDRUM
PADDINGTON (St John the Evangelist) (St Michael and All Angels) *Lon 2* **P** *DBP* **V** T J BIRCHARD, **C** J C TERRY, U S MONBERG, **Hon C** C D V RICHARDS
PADDINGTON (St Luke the Evangelist) *see* W Kilburn St Luke w St Simon and St Jude *Lon*
PADDINGTON (St Mary) *Lon 2* **P** *Bp* **P-in-c** G S BRADLEY, **NSM** M GIBSON
PADDINGTON (St Mary Magdalene) *Lon 2* **P** *Keble Coll Ox* **V** *Vacant* 0171-289 1818
PADDINGTON (St Peter) *Lon 2* **P** *Ch Patr Trust* **P-in-c** G M BUCKLE, **NSM** F W WARD
PADDINGTON (St Saviour) *Lon 2* **P** *Bp* **V** G S BRADLEY, **C** W H BAYNES, **NSM** F E BLACKMORE, M GIBSON
PADDINGTON (St Stephen w St Luke) *Lon 2* **P** *Bp* **P-in-c** T A GILLUM
PADDINGTON GREEN (St Mary) *see* Paddington St Mary *Lon*
PADDLESWORTH (St Oswald) *see* Lyminge w Paddlesworth, Stanford w Postling etc *Cant*
PADDOCK WOOD (St Andrew) *Roch 8* **P** *D&C Cant* **V** D G St L WINTER, **C** S C TILLOTSON
PADGATE (Christ Church) *Liv 12* **P** *Bp, Adn, and R Warrington (jt)* **V** N T MOFFATT, **C** J W REED
PADIHAM (St Leonard) (St Anne and St Elizabeth) *Blackb 3* **P** *Bp* **V** J C DUXBURY, **NSM** E J BOOTH
PADSTOW (St Petrock) *Truro 7* **P** *C R Prideaux Brune Esq* **V** M A BOXALL, **Hon C** S H HOFFMAN
PADWORTH (St John the Baptist) *see* Mortimer W End w Padworth *Ox*
PAGANHILL (Holy Spirit) *see* Whiteshill and Randwick *Glouc*
PAGHAM (St Thomas a Becket) *Chich 1* **P** *Abp* **V** J W MAYNARD
PAGLESHAM (St Peter) *see* Canewdon w Paglesham *Chelmsf*
PAIGNTON (Christ Church) (School Room) *Ex 10* **P** *Peache Trustees* **V** R C ADAMS
PAIGNTON (St John the Baptist) (St Andrew) (St Boniface) *Ex 10* **P** *DBP* **V** B R TUBBS, **C** R N LOCKE, R A SEARLE
PAIGNTON (St Paul) Preston *Ex 10* **P** *Bp* **V** M J BURTON
PAILTON (St Denis) *see* Monks Kirby w Pailton and Stretton-under-Fosse *Cov*
PAINSWICK (St Mary the Virgin) w Sheepscombe and Cranham *Glouc 1* **P** *Ld Chan (2 turns), Mrs N Owen (1 turn)* **V** M R MILES, **NSM** M B COLE
PAKEFIELD (All Saints and St Margaret) *Nor 9* **P** *Ch Patr Trust* **R** R J K BAKER
PAKENHAM (St Mary) w Norton and Tostock *St E 9* **P** *Bp and Peterho Cam (jt)* **V** I HOOPER
PALFREY (St Mary and All Saints) *see* Walsall St Mary and All SS Palfrey *Lich*
PALGRAVE (St Peter) *see* N Hartismere *St E*
PALLION (St Luke) *see* Millfield St Mark and Pallion *Dur*
PALMARSH (Holy Cross) *see* Hythe *Cant*
PALMERS GREEN (St John the Evangelist) *Lon 18* **P** *V Southgate Ch Ch* **V** R C KNOWLING, **C** G D ALLEN
PALTERTON (St Luke's Mission Room) *see* E Scarsdale *Derby*
PAMBER (St Mary and St John the Baptist) *see* The Sherbornes w Pamber *Win*
PAMBER HEATH (St Luke) *see* Tadley St Pet *Win*
PAMPISFORD (St John the Baptist) *Ely 7* **P** *Mrs B A Killander* **V** *Vacant*
PANCRASWEEK (St Pancras) *see* Pyworthy, Pancrasweek and Bridgerule *Ex*
PANFIELD (St Mary the Virgin) and Rayne *Chelmsf 15* **P** *Bp and DBP (alt)* **R** P J MEADER
PANGBOURNE (St James the Less) w Tidmarsh and Sulham *Ox 12* **P** *Bp, Ch Soc Trust, and Mrs I E Moon (jt)* **P-in-c** J W STAPLES
PANNAL (St Robert of Knaresborough) w Beckwithshaw *Ripon 1* **P** *Bp and Peache Trustees (jt)* **V** M de la P BERESFORD-PEIRSE
PANSHANGER (United Church) Conventional District *St Alb 7* **Min** S P SAYERS
PAPCASTLE (Mission Church) *see* Bridekirk *Carl*
PAPPLEWICK (St James) *see* Linby w Papplewick *S'well*
PAPWORTH EVERARD (St Peter) *Ely 1* **P** *DBP* **R** P S DUFFETT
PAR (St Mary the Virgin) (Good Shepherd) *Truro 1* **P** *The Crown* **V** W N PRICE
PARHAM (St Mary the Virgin) *see* Campsea Ashe w Marlesford, Parham and Hacheston *St E*
PARHAM (St Peter) *see* Amberley w N Stoke and Parham, Wiggonholt etc *Chich*

PARKEND (St Paul) *see* Dean Forest St Paul *Glouc*
PARKESTON (St Paul) *see* Dovercourt and Parkeston w Harwich *Chelmsf*
PARKFIELD (Holy Trinity) *see* Langley and Parkfield *Man*
PARKGATE (St Thomas) *see* Neston *Ches*
PARKHAM (St James), Alwington, Buckland Brewer, Abbotsham, Hartland, Welcombe, Clovelly, Woolfardisworthy West and Buck Mills *Ex 16* **P** *Patr Bd (4 turns), Crown (1 turn)* **TR** W G BLAKEY, **TV** R D S SANDERS, D J FORD, **Hon C** J A WHEELER, **NSM** S R SANDERS
PARKSTONE (Good Shepherd) *see* Heatherlands St Jo *Sarum*
PARKSTONE (St Barnabas) *see* Branksome St Clem *Sarum*
PARKSTONE (St Clement) *as above*
PARKSTONE (St Luke) *Sarum 8* **P** *Ch Trust Fund Trust* **P-in-c** J W DAVIES
PARKSTONE (St Peter) (St Osmund) w Branksea *Sarum 8* **P** *Patr Bd* **TR** N J C LLOYD, **TV** D J NEWMAN, **C** S G L WOOD
PARKWOOD (Christ Church) Conventional District *Cant 15* **C-in-c** R G DAVIS, **C** D J A POLLARD
PARLAUNT ROAD (Christ the Worker) *see* Langley Marish *Ox*
PARLEY, WEST (All Saints) (St Mark) *Sarum 10* **P** *P E E Prideaux-Brune Esq* **R** A G WATTS, **C** S E HUTTON
PARNDON, GREAT (St Mary) *Chelmsf 26* **P** *Bp* **R** C P BURTON, **C** R J BULLOCK, J M RAGAN
PARNDON, LITTLE (St Mary) *see* Harlow Town Cen w Lt Parndon *Chelmsf*
PARR Blackbrook (St Paul) *see* Parr *Liv*
PARR Derbyshire Hill (St Philip) *as above*
PARR (St Peter) (St Paul) (St Philip) *Liv 10* **P** *Patr Bd* **TR** D A THOMPSON, **TV** P C CATON, **C** P D RATTIGAN
PARR MOUNT (Holy Trinity) *Liv 10* **P** *V St Helens* **V** C S WOODS, **NSM** R J G HOPKINS
PARRACOMBE (Christ Church) *see* Combe Martin, Berrynarbor, Lynton, Brendon etc *Ex*
PARSON CROSS (St Cecilia) *see* Sheff Parson Cross St Cecilia *Sheff*
PARSON'S GREEN (St Dionis) *see* Fulham St Dionis Parson's Green *Lon*
PARTINGTON (St Mary) and Carrington *Ches 10* **P** *Bp and V Bowdon (alt)* **V** P MASON, **C** A Q GREENHOUGH
PARTNEY (St Nicholas) *Linc 7* **P** *DBP, Bp, Baroness Willoughby de Eresby, and Mrs E M V Drake (by turn)* **R** *Vacant* (01790) 53570
PARTRIDGE GREEN (St Michael and All Angels) *see* W Grinstead *Chich*
PARWICH (St Peter) w Alsop en le Dale *Derby 8* **P** *D A G Shields Esq* **P-in-c** C D HARRISON
PASSENHAM (St Guthlac) *Pet 5* **P** *MMCET* **R** C J MURRAY
PASTON (All Saints) *Pet 13* **P** *Bp* **R** M J G TOMPKINS
PASTON (St Margaret) *see* Trunch *Nor*
PATCHAM (All Saints) *Chich 2* **P** *MMCET* **V** N E D MILMINE, **C** A J M SPEAR, C D REDKNAP
PATCHAM, SOUTH (Christ the King) *Chich 2* **P** *Bp* **V** D H HUMPHREY
PATCHING (St John the Divine) *see* Findon w Clapham and Patching *Chich*
PATCHWAY (St Chad) *Bris 6* **P** *Trustees* **V** B E PENN, **C** C D BLAKE
PATELEY BRIDGE (St Cuthbert) *see* Upper Nidderdale *Ripon*
PATRICK (Holy Trinity) *S & M 3* **P** *Bp* **V** P J BENNETT
PATRICK BROMPTON (St Patrick) and Hunton *Ripon 4* **P** *Bp* **V** D J CHRISTIE
PATRICROFT (Christ Church) *see* Eccles *Man*
PATRINGTON (St Patrick) w Hollym, Welwick and Winestead *York 13* **P** *DBP, Ld Chan, and CPAS (by turn)* **R** *Vacant* (01964) 630327
PATRIXBOURNE (St Mary) w Bridge and Bekesbourne *Cant 1* **P** *Abp* **V** R GILBERT
PATTERDALE (St Patrick) *Carl 4* **P** *Trustees* **P-in-c** R P H FRANK
PATTINGHAM (St Chad) w Patshull *Lich 25* **P** *Bp and Lady Kwiatkowska (jt)* **Dn-in-c** G BLOOMFIELD
PATTISHALL (Holy Cross) w Cold Higham and Gayton w Tiffield *Pet 5* **P** *Bp, SS Coll Cam, and SMF (jt)* **R** P J BROADBENT
PAUL (St Pol de Lion) *Truro 5* **P** *Ld Chan* **V** G HARPER
PAULERSPURY (St James the Apostle) *see* Whittlebury w Paulerspury *Pet*
PAULL (St Andrew and St Mary) *see* Hedon w Paull *York*
PAULSGROVE (St Michael and All Angels) *Portsm 6* **P** *Bp* **V** I W RUTHERFORD
PAULTON (Holy Trinity) *B & W 12* **P** *Bp and R Chewton Mendip (alt)* **V** R E INGLESBY
PAUNTLEY (St John the Evangelist) *see* Redmarley D'Abitot, Bromesberrow w Pauntley etc *Glouc*
PAVENHAM (St Peter) *see* Odell and Pavenham *St Alb*
PAWLETT (St John the Baptist) *see* Puriton and Pawlett *B & W*
PAXFORD (Mission Church) *see* Blockley w Aston Magna and Bourton on the Hill *Glouc*
PAXTON, GREAT (Holy Trinity) *Ely 12* **P** *D&C Linc* **V** P J TAYLOR
PAXTON, LITTLE (St James) *Ely 12* **P** *D&C Linc* **V** *Vacant* (01480) 73526
PAYHEMBURY (St Mary the Virgin) *see* Broadhembury, Payhembury and Plymtree *Ex*
PEACEHAVEN (Ascension) *Chich 18* **P** *Bp* **P-in-c** D A HIDER, **C** D L I PERKS
PEAK DALE (Holy Trinity) *see* Wormhill, Peak Forest w Peak Dale and Dove Holes *Derby*
PEAK FOREST (St Charles the King and Martyr) *as above*
PEAKIRK (St Pega) w Glinton and Northborough *Pet 13* **P** *D&C* **R** N E FRY
PEAR TREE (Jesus Chapel) *see* Southampton St Mary Extra *Win*
PEASE POTTAGE (Ascension) *see* Slaugham *Chich*
PEASEDOWN ST JOHN (St John the Baptist) w Wellow *B & W 12* **P** *Bp and R H Horton-Fawkes Esq (jt)* **V** H R L BONSEY
PEASEMORE (St Barnabas) *see* Beedon and Peasemore w W Ilsley and Farnborough *Ox*
PEASENHALL (St Michael) *see* Yoxford and Peasenhall w Sibton *St E*
PEASE'S WEST (St George) *see* Crook *Dur*
PEASLAKE (St Mark) *see* Shere *Guildf*
PEASLEY CROSS (Mission Hall) *see* Parr Mt *Liv*
PEASMARSH (St Michael) *see* Shalford *Guildf*
PEASMARSH (St Peter and St Paul) *see* Beckley and Peasmarsh *Chich*
PEATLING MAGNA (All Saints) *see* Willoughby Waterleys, Peatling Magna etc *Leic*
PEATLING PARVA (St Andrew) *see* Gilmorton w Peatling Parva and Kimcote etc *Leic*
PEBMARSH (St John the Baptist) *see* Alphamstone w Lamarsh and Pebmarsh *Chelmsf*
PEBWORTH (St Peter) w Dorsington and Honeybourne *Glouc 10* **P** *Bp* **R** *Vacant* (01386) 830302
PECKHAM (St John w St Andrew) *S'wark 7* **P** *Bp* **V** M S JOHNSON, **Hon C** J E LANE
PECKHAM (St Mary Magdalene) (St Paul) *S'wark 7* **P** *Ch Patr Soc* **V** M F PAYNE
PECKHAM (St Saviour) *S'wark 8* **P** *Bp* **V** W C HEATLEY
PECKHAM, EAST (Holy Trinity) and Nettlestead *Roch 8* **P** *St Pet Coll Ox and D&C Cant (jt)* **R** A M LEIGH, **NSM** R S LEIGH, S M MORRELL
PECKHAM, WEST (St Dunstan) *see* Mereworth w W Peckham *Roch*
PECKLETON (St Mary Magdalene) *see* Desford and Peckleton w Tooley *Leic*
PEDLINGE (Estate Chapel) *see* Saltwood *Cant*
PEDMORE (St Peter) *Worc 12* **P** *Oldswinford Hosp* **R** A L HAZLEWOOD
PEEL (St Paul) *Man 12* **P** *Patr Bd* **TR** P BRODY, **TV** H BRUNYEE, **NSM** K HOPWOOD OWEN
PEEL GREEN (St Catherine) *see* Barton w Peel Green *Man*
PEEL GREEN (St Michael and All Angels) *as above*
PEGSWOOD (St Margaret) *see* Bothal and Pegswood w Longhirst *Newc*
PELDON (St Mary) w Great and Little Wigborough *Chelmsf 16* **P** *Ch Soc Trust and T Wheatley-Hubbard Esq* **P-in-c** R H ELPHICK
PELSALL (St Michael and All Angels) *Lich 26* **P** *Bp* **V** *Vacant* (01922) 682098
PELTON (Holy Trinity) *Dur 16* **P** *R Chester le Street* **V** *Vacant* 0191-370 2204
PELTON, WEST (St Paul) *Dur 11* **P** *Bp* **P-in-c** J LINTERN
PELYNT (St Nun) *Truro 12* **P** *J B Kitson and Mrs S R Parker (alt)* **Hon C** D A WOODS
PEMBERTON (St Francis of Assisi) Kitt Green *Liv 15* **P** *R Wigan and Bp (jt)* **V** N P ANDERSON
PEMBERTON (St John) *Liv 15* **P** *R Wigan* **V** J A SOUTHERN
PEMBERTON (St Mark) Newtown *Liv 15* **P** *Duke of Sutherland, Bp, and R Pemberton St Jo (jt)* **V** D V ROUCH
PEMBRIDGE (St Mary the Virgin) w Moorcourt, Shobdon, Staunton-on-Arrow and Byton *Heref 5* **P** *Ld Chan (1 turn), J R Whitehead Esq and Miss R Whitehead (jt) (1 turn), and DBP (2 turns)* **R** S HOLLINGHURST
PEMBURY (St Peter) *Roch 8* **P** *Ch Ch Ox* **V** S SEALY
PEN SELWOOD (St Michael) *B & W 2* **P** *Bp* **R** *Vacant*
PENCOMBE (St John) *see* Bredenbury w Grendon Bishop and Wacton etc *Heref*
PENCOYD (St Denys) *see* St Weonards w Orcop, Garway, Tretire etc *Heref*

PENCOYS (St Andrew) *see* Redruth w Lanner and Treleigh *Truro*
PENDEEN (St John the Baptist) w Morvah *Truro 5* **P** *R A H Aitken Esq and C W M Aitken Esq (jt)* **V** A ROWELL, **NSM** J HARPER
PENDEFORD (St Paul) *see* Tettenhall Regis *Lich*
PENDLEBURY (St Augustine) *see* Swinton and Pendlebury *Man*
PENDLEBURY (St John) *Man 6* **P** *Trustees* **P-in-c** T M MALONEY, **C** F E MALONEY
PENDLETON (All Saints) *see* Sabden and Pendleton *Blackb*
PENDLETON (St Ambrose) (St Thomas) *Man 6* **P** *Patr Bd* **TR** W S BRISON, **TV** A BUTLER, A I SALMON, **C** D R PETCH, P BUTLER, **Hon C** D J H KEYTE
PENDOCK CROSS (Holy Redeemer) *see* Berrow w Pendock, Eldersfield, Hollybush etc *Worc*
PENDOMER (St Roch) *see* W Coker w Hardington Mandeville, E Chinnock etc *B & W*
PENGE (Christ Church w Holy Trinity) *see* Anerley *Roch*
PENGE (St John the Evangelist) *Roch 13* **P** *Simeon's Trustees* **V** P R M VENABLES
PENGE (St Paul) *Roch 13* **P** *Ch Patr Trust* **V** D I CHARNOCK
PENGE LANE (Holy Trinity) *Roch 13* **P** *CPAS* **V** A R RUTHERFORD
PENHILL (St Peter) *Bris 10* **P** *Bp* **V** G S COLE, **C** A I FESSEY
PENHURST (St Michael the Archangel) *see* Ashburnham w Penhurst *Chich*
PENISTONE (St John the Baptist) and Thurlstone *Wakef 7* **P** *Bp* **TR** G W MIDGLEY
PENKETH (St Paul) *Liv 13* **P** *Bp* **V** P W HOCKLEY
PENKHULL (St Thomas) *Lich 12* **P** *R Stoke-on-Trent* **V** I MAITIN
PENKRIDGE Team, The (St Michael and All Angels) *Lich 2* **P** *Patr Bd* **TR** G STATON, **TV** C L GILBERT, **C** R B READE, **NSM** C G HEATH
PENN (Holy Trinity) *Ox 20* **P** *Earl Howe* **P-in-c** C J WILLIAMS, **NSM** J H PIERCE
PENN (St Bartholomew) (St Anne) *Lich 25* **P** *Bp* **V** G M F WILLIAMS, **C** M Y CLAYTON, **Hon C** B MORGAN
PENN FIELDS St Philip (St Aidan) *Lich 25* **P** *Ch Trust Fund Trust* **V** W H NASH, **C** M J HUNTER, A M JONES
PENN STREET (Holy Trinity) *Ox 20* **P** *Earl Howe* **V** N J STOWE
PENNARD, EAST (All Saints) *see* Ditcheat w E Pennard and Pylle *B & W*
PENNARD, WEST (St Nicholas) *see* Glastonbury w Meare, W Pennard and Godney *B & W*
PENNINGTON (Christ Church) *Man 13* **P** *Trustees* **V** P W LEAKEY, **C** J G ARMSTRONG, **NSM** W G SPEDDING
PENNINGTON (St Mark) *Win 10* **P** *V Milford* **V** P H RENYARD
PENNINGTON (St Michael and the Holy Angels) and Lindal w Marton and Bardsea *Carl 8* **P** *Bp and DBP (jt)* **P-in-c** S D RUDKIN
PENNYCROSS (St Pancras) *Ex 21* **P** *CPAS* **V** A M M PARKER
PENNYWELL (St Thomas) *see* Sunderland Pennywell St Thos *Dur*
PENPONDS (Holy Trinity) *Truro 2* **P** *The Crown* **P-in-c** J M MATHER
PENRITH (Christ Church) (St Andrew) w Newton Reigny and Plumpton Wall *Carl 4* **P** *Bp* **TV** C E FARRER
PENRUDDOCK (All Saints) *see* Greystoke, Matterdale, Mungrisdale etc *Carl*
PENSAX (St James the Great) *see* Teme Valley N *Worc*
PENSBY (St Michael and All Angels) *see* Barnston *Ches*
PENSHAW (All Saints) *Dur 14* **P** *Bp* **R** K WALKER
PENSHURST (St John the Baptist) and Fordcombe *Roch 12* **P** *Viscount De L'Isle* **P-in-c** T E HOLME
PENSILVA (St John) *see* St Ive and Pensilva w Quethiock *Truro*
PENSNETT (St Mark) *Worc 10* **P** *Bp* **V** J C STALLARD, **NSM** C A HATHORNE
PENTEWAN (All Saints) *see* St Austell *Truro*
PENTLOW (St George and St Gregory), Foxearth, Liston and Borley *Chelmsf 19* **P** *K Foster Esq, Bp, and DBP (by turn)* **P-in-c** B A SAMPSON
PENTNEY (St Mary Magdalene) w West Bilney *Nor 20* **P** *Bp* **V** S R NAIRN
PENTON MEWSEY (Holy Trinity) *see* Hatherden w Tangley, Weyhill and Penton Mewsey *Win*
PENTONVILLE (St Silas w All Saints) (St James) *Lon 6* **P** *Bp* **V** A T J SALTER
PENTRICH (St Matthew) *see* Swanwick and Pentrich *Derby*
PENTRIDGE (St Rumbold) *see* Handley w Gussage St Andrew and Pentridge *Sarum*
PENWERRIS (St Michael and All Angels) (Holy Spirit) *Truro 3* **P** *V St Gluvias* **V** D S SMITH
PENWORTHAM (St Leonard) *Blackb 6* **P** *Bp* **V** T D WILBY, **C** C G LORD
PENWORTHAM (St Mary) *Blackb 6* **P** *Miss A M Rawstorne* **V** D RAITT, **C** W D COOPER
PENZANCE (St John the Baptist) *Truro 5* **P** *Bp* **P-in-c** S M WRIST-KNUDSEN
PENZANCE (St Mary the Virgin) (St Paul) *Truro 5* **P** *Bp* **V** J F WHITLOCK, **C** M R POOLTON
PEOPLETON (St Nicholas) and White Ladies Aston w Churchill and Spetchley and Upton Snodsbury and Broughton Hackett *Worc 4* **P** *Bp, Croom Estate Trustees, and Major R J G Berkley (1 turn), and Ld Chan (1 turn)* **R** H G PHILLIPS
PEOVER, NETHER (St Oswald) *Ches 12* **P** *Man Univ* **V** K M BURGHALL
PEOVER, OVER (St Lawrence) *Ches 12* **P** *DBP* **P-in-c** K M BURGHALL
PEPER HAROW (St Nicholas) *see* Compton w Shackleford and Peper Harow *Guildf*
PEPLOW (The Epiphany) *see* Hodnet w Weston under Redcastle *Lich*
PERIVALE (St Mary w St Nicholas) *Lon 22* **P** *Trustees* **C** A R CORSIE
PERLETHORPE (St John the Evangelist) *S'well 6* **P** *Earl Manvers' Trustees* **V** *Vacant*
PERRANARWORTHAL (St Piran) *see* St Stythians w Perranarworthal and Gwennap *Truro*
PERRANPORTH (St Michael's Mission Church) *see* Perranzabuloe *Truro*
PERRANUTHNOE (St Michael and St Piran) *see* St Hilary w Perranuthnoe *Truro*
PERRANZABULOE (St Piran) *Truro 6* **P** *D&C* **V** J B SAUNDERS
PERROTT, NORTH (St Martin) *see* Haselbury Plucknett, Misterton and N Perrott *B & W*
PERROTT, SOUTH (St Mary) *see* Beaminster Area *Sarum*
PERRY BARR (St John the Evangelist) *Birm 3* **P** *Bp* **V** C S JONES
PERRY BEECHES (St Matthew) *Birm 3* **P** *St Martin's Trustees* **V** S P M MACKENZIE
PERRY COMMON (St Martin) *Birm 8* **P** *Bp* **V** *Vacant* 0121-382 7666
PERRY GREEN (St Thomas) *see* Much Hadham *St Alb*
PERRY HILL (St George) *S'wark 5* **P** *Bp and D&C (alt)* **V** W G GOLBOURNE
PERRY STREET (All Saints) *Roch 4* **P** *Bp* **V** P E WAKELIN
PERSHORE (Holy Cross) w Pinvin, Wick and Birlingham *Worc 4* **P** *Patr Bd* **V** M A TRISTRAM, **C** A P DICKENS, **Hon C** B CHATWIN, **NSM** J WOOLLCOMBE
PERTENHALL (St Peter) *see* The Stodden Churches *St Alb*
PETER TAVY (St Peter), Mary Tavy, Lydford and Brent Tor *Ex 24* **P** *Guild of All So and Bp (1 turn), Duchy of Cornwall (1 turn)* **Hon C** D C ORMSBY, R D ORMSBY
PETERBOROUGH (All Saints) *Pet 13* **P** *Bp* **V** D J T MILLER
PETERBOROUGH (Christ the Carpenter) *Pet 13* **P** *Bp* **V** A P HOLFORD
PETERBOROUGH (Holy Spirit) Bretton *Pet 13* **P** *Bp* **V** P M HAWKINS
PETERBOROUGH (St Barnabas) *Pet 13* **P** *Bp* **P-in-c** M D DAVIES, **NSM** P H SEDGWICK
PETERBOROUGH (St John the Baptist) (Mission Church) *Pet 13* **P** *Bp* **V** P A SPENCE, **NSM** B J WITHINGTON
PETERBOROUGH (St Jude) *Pet 13* **P** *Bp* **V** G J KEATING
PETERBOROUGH (St Mark) *Pet 13* **P** *Bp* **V** C J PEARSON
PETERBOROUGH (St Mary) Boongate *Pet 13* **P** *D&C* **V** A P BROWN, **C** J GOULD, **NSM** C D MASON
PETERBOROUGH (St Paul) *Pet 13* **P** *Bp* **V** B SECKER
PETERCHURCH (St Peter) w Vowchurch, Turnastone and Dorstone *Heref 1* **P** *Bp (2 turns), Bp Birm (1 turn)* **NSM** F M HANCOCK
PETERLEE (St Cuthbert) *Dur 2* **P** *Bp* **V** K I WOODHOUSE, **C** K S CONWAY
PETERSFIELD (St Peter) *Portsm 5* **P** *Bp* **V** C LOWSON, **C** S E ROBERTS, R C HARRISON
PETERSHAM (All Saints) (St Peter) *S'wark 17* **P** *Bp* **P-in-c** F R BENTLEY
PETERSMARLAND (St Peter) *see* Shebbear, Buckland Filleigh, Sheepwash etc *Ex*
PETERSTOW (St Peter) *see* Ross w Brampton Abbotts, Bridstow, Peterstow etc *Heref*
PETHAM (All Saints) and Waltham w Lower Hardres and Nackington w Upper Hardres and Stelling *Cant 2* **P** *Abp, St Jo Coll Ox, and Trustees Lord Tomlin (jt)* **P-in-c** R W BATEMAN, P G COX, **C** P J FILMER

PETHERTON, NORTH (St Mary the Virgin) w Northmoor Green *B & W 14* **P** *D&C Windsor* **V** J T L STILL
PETHERTON, SOUTH (St Peter and St Paul) w the Seavingtons *B & W 15* **P** *D&C* **R** G A RIPLEY
PETHERWIN, NORTH (St Paternus) *see* Egloskerry, N Petherwin, Tremaine and Tresmere *Truro*
PETROCKSTOWE (St Petrock) *see* Shebbear, Buckland Filleigh, Sheepwash etc *Ex*
PETT (St Mary and St Peter) *see* Fairlight, Guestling and Pett *Chich*
PETT LEVEL (St Nicholas) *as above*
PETTAUGH (St Catherine) *see* Helmingham w Framsden and Pettaugh w Winston *St E*
PETTISTREE (St Peter and St Paul) *see* Wickham Market w Pettistree and Easton *St E*
PETTON (not known) w Cockshutt, Welshampton and Lyneal w Colemere *Lich 17* **P** *Bp and R K Mainwaring Esq (jt)* **R** *Vacant* (01939) 270211
PETTON (St Petrock) *see* Bampton, Morebath, Clayhanger and Petton *Ex*
PETTS WOOD (St Francis) *Roch 16* **P** *Bp* **V** J T GUNN
PETWORTH (St Mary) *Chich 11* **P** *Lord Egremont* **R** D S POLLARD
PEVENSEY (St Nicholas) (St Wilfred) *Chich 16* **P** *Bp* **P-in-c** A C H CHRISTIAN
PEWSEY (St John the Baptist) *see* Pewsey TM *Sarum*
PEWSEY Team Ministry, The *Sarum 21* **P** *Patr Bd* **TR** C G FOX, **TV** S J FLATT
PHEASEY (St Chad) *Lich 26* **P** *DBP* **C** M R KINDER
PHILBEACH GARDENS (St Cuthbert) *see* Earl's Court St Cuth w St Matthias *Lon*
PHILLACK (St Felicitas) *see* Godrevy *Truro*
PHILLEIGH (St Philleigh) *see* St Just in Roseland w Philleigh *Truro*
PICCADILLY (St James) *see* Westmr St Jas *Lon*
PICKENHAM, NORTH (St Andrew) *see* Necton, Holme Hale w N and S Pickenham *Nor*
PICKENHAM, SOUTH (All Saints) *as above*
PICKERING (St Peter and St Paul) w Lockton and Levisham *York 21* **P** *Abp* **V** F J A HEWITT, **C** D J MATHER
PICKHILL (All Saints) *see* Kirklington w Burneston and Wath and Pickhill *Ripon*
PICKWELL (All Saints) *see* Burrough Hill Pars *Leic*
PICKWORTH (All Saints) *see* Gt and Lt Casterton w Pickworth and Tickencote *Pet*
PICKWORTH (St Andrew) *see* S Lafford *Linc*
PICTON (St Hilary) *see* Kirklevington *York*
PIDDINGHOE (St John) *see* Telscombe w Piddinghoe and Southease *Chich*
PIDDINGTON (St John the Baptist) *see* Hardingstone and Horton and Piddington *Pet*
PIDDINGTON (St Nicholas) *see* Ambrosden w Mert and Piddington *Ox*
PIDDLE, NORTH (St Michael) *see* Abberton, The Flyfords, Naunton Beauchamp etc *Worc*
PIDDLEHINTON (St Mary the Virgin) *see* Piddletrenthide w Plush, Alton Pancras etc *Sarum*
PIDDLETRENTHIDE (All Saints) w Plush, Alton Pancras and Piddlehinton *Sarum 2* **P** *Eton Coll, D&C, and D&C Win (by turn)* **P-in-c** R W B THOMSON
PIDLEY CUM FENTON (All Saints) *see* Somersham w Pidley and Oldhurst *Ely*
PIERCEBRIDGE (St Mary) *see* Coniscliffe *Dur*
PILHAM (All Saints) *see* Corringham and Blyton Gp *Linc*
PILL (Christ Church) w Easton in Gordano and Portbury *B & W 13* **P** *Bp* **V** R H M LEGG
PILLATON (St Modwen) *see* Penkridge Team *Lich*
PILLATON (St Odolph) *see* St Dominic, Landulph and St Mellion w Pillaton *Truro*
PILLERTON HERSEY (St Mary) *see* Butlers Marston and the Pillertons w Ettington *Cov*
PILLEY (Mission Church) *see* Tankersley, Thurgoland and Wortley *Sheff*
PILLEY (St Nicholas) *see* Boldre w S Baddesley *Win*
PILLING (St John the Baptist) *Blackb 10* **P** *A F Mason-Hornby Esq and H D H Elletson Esq (alt)* **V** *Vacant* (01253) 790231
PILNING (St Peter) w Compton Greenfield *Bris 8* **P** *Bp* **V** D B HARREX, **NSM** A J PARKER
PILSLEY (St Mary the Virgin) *see* N Wingfield, Clay Cross and Pilsley *Derby*
PILTON (All Saints) *see* Aldwincle w Thorpe Achurch, Pilton, Wadenhoe etc *Pet*
PILTON (St John the Baptist) w Croscombe, North Wootton and Dinder *B & W 8* **P** *Bp and Peache Trustees (jt)* **R** D R OSBORNE
PILTON (St Mary the Virgin) w Ashford *Ex 15* **P** *Ld Chan* **V** J C SPEAR, **C** C J HUDSPITH
PILTON (St Nicholas) *see* Preston and Ridlington w Wing and Pilton *Pet*
PIMLICO Bourne Street (St Mary) *see* Pimlico St Mary Graham Terrace *Lon*
PIMLICO (St Barnabas) *Lon 3* **P** *Bp* **V** *Vacant* 0171-730 5054
PIMLICO (St Gabriel) *Lon 3* **P** *Bp* **V** D W SKEOCH, **NSM** W D PATTINSON
PIMLICO (St James the Less) *see* Westminster St Jas the Less *Lon*
PIMLICO (St Mary) Graham Terrace *Lon 3* **P** *Trustees* **V** W S SCOTT, **Hon C** P PILKINGTON of Oxenford, **NSM** S E YOUNG
PIMLICO (St Peter) w Westminster Christ Church *Lon 3* **P** *Bp* **V** D B TILLYER, **C** W P KEYES, **NSM** A R CHIDWICK
Pimlico (St Saviour) *Lon 3* **P** *Bp* **V** *Vacant* 0171-821 9526
PIMPERNE (St Peter), Stourpaine, Durweston and Bryanston *Sarum 7* **P** *DBP (2 turns), D&C (1 turn)* **R** G S M SQUAREY, **NSM** B R SEARLE-BARNES
PINCHBECK (St Mary) *Linc 17* **P** *Mrs B S Corley* **V** D R HILL
PINCHBECK, WEST (St Bartholomew) *see* Surfleet *Linc*
PINHOE (St Michael and All Angels) (Hall) and Broadclyst *Ex 1* **P** *Patr Bd* **TR** A J MORTIMER, **TV** B C BAILEY, **NSM** M GENT
PINNER (St Anselm) *see* Hatch End St Anselm *Lon*
PINNER (St John the Baptist) *Lon 23* **P** *V Harrow* **V** D J TUCK, **C** D M BOURNE, **Hon C** M S NATTRASS, **NSM** I W MURRAY
PINNER VIEW (St George) *see* Headstone St Geo *Lon*
PINVIN (St Nicholas) *see* Pershore w Pinvin, Wick and Birlingham *Worc*
PINXTON (St Helen) (Church Hall) *Derby 1* **P** *Bp* **R** *Vacant* (01773) 580024
PIPE-CUM-LYDE (St Peter) *see* Wellington w Pipe-cum-Lyde and Moreton-on-Lugg *Heref*
PIPEWELL (St Mary) *see* Rothwell w Orton, Rushton w Glendon and Pipewell *Pet*
PIRBRIGHT (St Michael) *Guildf 12* **P** *Ld Chan* **V** R E N STREVENS
PIRNOUGH (All Hallows) *see* Ditchingham, Hedenham and Broome *Nor*
PIRTON (St Mary) *St Alb 4* **P** *D&C Ely* **P-in-c** I S TATTUM, **NSM** F S E GIBBS
PIRTON (St Peter) *see* Stoulton w Drake's Broughton and Pirton etc *Worc*
PISHILL (not known) *see* Nettlebed w Bix and Highmore *Ox*
PITCHCOMBE (St John the Baptist) *see* The Edge, Pitchcombe, Harescombe and Brookthorpe *Glouc*
PITCHFORD (St Michael and All Angels) *see* Condover w Frodesley, Acton Burnell etc *Heref*
PITCOMBE (St Leonard) *see* Bruton and Distr *B & W*
PITMINSTER (St Mary and St Andrew) w Corfe *B & W 18* **P** *DBP and M V Spurway Esq (alt)* **V** R L PARKER
PITNEY (St John the Baptist) *see* Langport Area Chs *B & W*
PITSEA (St Gabriel) w Nevendon *Chelmsf 6* **P** *Bp* **P-in-c** E E McCAFFERTY
PITSFORD (All Saints) w Boughton *Pet 2* **P** *Bp* **R** S J TROTT
PITSMOOR (Christ Church) *Sheff 3* **P** *Ch Patr Trust* **V** J F HARDY
PITTINGTON (St Laurence) *see* Sherburn w Pittington *Dur*
PITTON (St Peter) *see* Alderbury Team *Sarum*
PITTVILLE (All Saints) *see* Cheltenham All SS *Glouc*
PIXHAM (St Mary the Virgin) *see* Dorking w Ranmore *Guildf*
PIXLEY (St Andrew) *see* Tarrington w Stoke Edith, Aylton, Pixley etc *Heref*
PLAISTOW (Holy Trinity) *see* Kirdford *Chich*
PLAISTOW (St Martin) (St Mary) (St Philip and St James) and North Canning Town *Chelmsf 3* **P** *Patr Bd* **TR** C F TURNER, **TV** S D MASON, R J MAGOR, **NSM** L C STEWARD
PLAISTOW (St Mary) *Roch 14* **P** *Bp* **C** W G LLOYD, **Hon C** R B HANDFORTH, **NSM** E J DAVIS
PLAITFORD (St Peter) *see* Bramshaw and Landford w Plaitford *Sarum*
PLALTS HEATH (St Edmund) *see* Lenham w Boughton Malherbe *Cant*
PLAS NEWTON (St Michael) *Ches 2* **P** *Simeon's Trustees* **V** R J KITELEY
PLATT (St Mary the Virgin) *Roch 10* **P** *Bp* **V** D C FRANCIS
PLATT BRIDGE (St Nathaniel) *Liv 14* **P** *Bp* **V** M B DARBY, **C** A D GREENHILL
PLAXTOL (not known) *Roch 10* **P** *Bp* **P-in-c** S M RAMSARAN
PLAYDEN (St Michael) *see* Rye *Chich*
PLAYFORD (St Mary) *see* Gt and Lt Bealings w Playford and Culpho *St E*
PLEASLEY (St Michael) *see* E Scarsdale *Derby*

PLEASLEY HILL (St Barnabas) *S'well 2* **P** *Bp* **V** A M SMYTHE
PLEASLEY VALE (St Chad) *see* Mansfield Woodhouse *S'well*
PLEMSTALL (St Peter) w Guilden Sutton *Ches 2* **P** *Capt P Egerton Warburton* **V** J A MALBON, **NSM** S R MITCHELL
PLESHEY (Holy Trinity) *Chelmsf 8* **P** *Bp* **P-in-c** J T HOWDEN, **NSM** L K SPENDLOVE
PLUCKLEY (St Mary) *see* Egerton w Pluckley *Cant*
PLUCKLEY (St Nicholas) *as above*
PLUMBLAND (St Cuthbert) and Gilcrux *Carl 7* **P** *Mrs E H S Thornely* **R** *Vacant* (016973) 20255
PLUMPTON (All Saints) (St Michael and All Angels) w East Chiltington cum Novington *Chich 18* **P** *Ld Chan* **R** G D BROSTER
PLUMPTON (St John the Baptist) *see* Weedon Lois w Plumpton and Moreton Pinkney etc *Pet*
PLUMPTON WALL (St John the Evangelist) *see* Penrith w Newton Reigny and Plumpton Wall *Carl*
PLUMSTEAD (All Saints) Shooters Hill *S'wark 3* **P** *CPAS* **V** H D OWEN, **Hon C** A L AYRES
PLUMSTEAD (Ascension) *S'wark 3* **P** *Bp* **V** C R WELHAM
PLUMSTEAD (St John the Baptist) w St James and St Paul *S'wark 3* **P** *Simeon's Trustees and CPAS (alt)* **V** P J ROGERS, **C** D J B HAZLEHURST
PLUMSTEAD (St Mark and St Margaret) *S'wark 3* **P** *DBP* **V** R W JAMES
PLUMSTEAD (St Michael) *see* Barningham w Matlaske w Baconsthorpe etc *Nor*
PLUMSTEAD (St Nicholas) *S'wark 3* **P** *V Plumstead St Mark w St Marg* **V** A G STEVENS
PLUMSTEAD, GREAT (St Mary) and LITTLE (St Gervase and Protase) w Thorpe End and Witton *Nor 4* **P** *Bp and D&C (jt)* **R** B W TOMLINSON
PLUMTREE (St Mary) *S'well 9* **P** *DBP* **P-in-c** D M GEE
PLUNGAR (St Helen) *see* Barkestone w Plungar, Redmile and Stathern *Leic*
PLYMOUTH Crownhill (Ascension) *Ex 22* **P** *Bp* **P-in-c** P HANCOCK
PLYMOUTH Emmanuel, St Paul Efford and St Augustine *Ex 23* **P** *Patr Bd* **TV** I J LOVETT, J C WHITE, **C** J C OUGH, **NSM** P A WHITE
PLYMOUTH (St Andrew) and St Paul Stonehouse *Ex 23* **P** *Patr Bd* **TR** N H P McKINNEL, **TV** M T BAILEY, **C** R C H THOMAS, R S WILKINSON
PLYMOUTH (St Augustine) *see* Plymouth Em, St Paul Efford and St Aug *Ex*
PLYMOUTH (St Gabriel) Peverell *Ex 23* **P** *Bp* **V** J J STARK, **NSM** L J HOWARTH
PLYMOUTH (St James the Less) Ham *Ex 21* **P** *Keble Coll Ox* **V** T M S MORLEY
PLYMOUTH (St John the Evangelist) *see* Sutton on Plym *Ex*
PLYMOUTH (St Jude) *Ex 23* **P** *Trustees* **V** S R DINSMORE, **C** D R DAVIS
PLYMOUTH (St Mary the Virgin) *see* Laira *Ex*
PLYMOUTH (St Matthias) *see* Charles w Plymouth St Matthias *Ex*
PLYMOUTH (St Peter) (All Saints) *Ex 21* **P** *Keble Coll Ox* **V** S PHILPOTT, **C** W J JOHNSTONE
PLYMOUTH (St Simon) *Ex 23* **P** *St Simon Trustees* **V** J C STYLER
PLYMPTON (St Mary the Blessed Virgin) *Ex 22* **P** *Bp* **V** J F RICHARDS, **C** J M GIDDINGS, R W BECK, **NSM** M BRIMICOMBE
PLYMPTON (St Maurice) *Ex 22* **P** *D&C Windsor* **R** T E THOMAS
PLYMSTOCK (St Mary and All Saints) and Hooe *Ex 23* **P** *Patr Bd* **TR** P H W HAWKINS, **TV** C H OSBORNE, J J SPEAR, **C** P R SEARLE, **NSM** M CARTER
PLYMTREE (St John the Baptist) *see* Broadhembury, Payhembury and Plymtree *Ex*
POCKLEY (St John the Baptist) *see* Harome w Stonegrave, Nunnington and Pockley *York*
POCKLINGTON (All Saints) and Owsthorpe and Kilnwick Percy w Great Givendale, Huggate and Millington *York 7* **P** *Abp* **R** R H K PROSSER
PODIMORE (St Peter) *see* Ilchester w Northover, Limington, Yeovilton etc *B & W*
PODINGTON (St Mary the Virgin) *see* Wymington w Podington *St Alb*
POINT CLEAR (Mission) *see* St Osyth *Chelmsf*
POINTON (Christ Church) *see* Billingborough Gp *Linc*
POKESDOWN (All Saints) *Win 7* **P** *V Christchurch* **V** B G APPS
POKESDOWN (St James) *Win 7* **P** *Bp* **V** A F J CHAMBERS, **NSM** P M SCHOLLAR
POLDENS, WEST *B & W 5* **P** *Bp* **P-in-c** W B GRAHAM
POLEBROOK (All Saints) and Lutton w Hemington and Luddington *Pet 12* **P** *Bp, Sir Stephen Hastings, and DBP (by turn)* **R** I A LOVETT
POLEGATE (St John) (St Wilfred) *Chich 16* **P** *Bp* **V** D L N GUTSELL, **C** C K MACDONALD
POLESWORTH (St Editha) *Birm 11* **P** *Ld Chan* **V** P A WELLS
POLING (St Nicholas) *Chich 1* **P** *Bp* **V** J E SLEGG
POLLINGTON (St John the Baptist) *see* Gt Snaith *Sheff*
POLPERRO (St John the Baptist) *see* Talland *Truro*
POLRUAN (St Saviour) *see* Lanteglos by Fowey *Truro*
POLSTEAD (St Mary) *St E 3* **P** *St Jo Coll Ox* **P-in-c** D W FINCH
POLTIMORE (St Mary the Virgin) *see* Stoke Canon, Poltimore w Huxham and Rewe etc *Ex*
PONDERS END (St Matthew) *Lon 18* **P** *V Enfield* **V** B G RODFORD
PONDERSBRIDGE (St Thomas) *see* Whittlesey, Pondersbridge and Coates *Ely*
PONSANOOTH (St Michael and All Angels) *see* Mabe *Truro*
PONSBOURNE (St Mary) *see* Lt Berkhamsted and Bayford, Essendon etc *St Alb*
PONSONBY (not known) *see* Beckermet St Jo and St Bridget w Ponsonby *Carl*
PONTEFRACT (All Saints) *Wakef 11* **P** *Bp* **V** K PARTINGTON, **C** J R JONES
PONTEFRACT (St Giles w St Mary) *Wakef 11* **P** *Bp* **V** G HIGGINS
PONTELAND (St Mary the Virgin) *Newc 7* **P** *Mert Coll Ox* **V** M J JACKSON, **Hon C** P G WOLFENDEN, C G THORNE
PONTESBURY First and Second Portions (St George) *Heref 13* **P** *St Chad's Coll Dur* **R** D H ROBERTS
PONTON, GREAT (Holy Cross) *see* Colsterworth Gp *Linc*
PONTON, LITTLE (St Guthlac) *as above*
POOL (St Wilfrid) w Arthington *Ripon 1* **P** *C E W Sheepshanks Esq and V Otley (jt)* **V** D R H de la HOYDE
POOLE (St James w St Paul) *Sarum 8* **P** *Ch Soc Trust and J H Cordle Esq (jt)* **R** S C HOLBROOKE-JONES
POOLE KEYNES (St Michael and All Angels) *see* Kemble, Poole Keynes, Somerford Keynes etc *Glouc*
POOLEY BRIDGE (St Paul) *see* Barton, Pooley Bridge and Martindale *Carl*
POOLSBROOK (St Alban) *see* Staveley and Barrow Hill *Derby*
POORTON, NORTH (St Mary Magdalene) *see* Askerswell, Loders and Powerstock *Sarum*
POPLAR (All Saints) *Lon 7* **P** *Patr Bd* **TR** A J WYNNE, **TV** J E I HAWKINS, **C** M J BROWN, **NSM** T DUNCAN
POPPLETON, NETHER (St Everilda) w Upper (All Saints) *York 1* **P** *Abp* **V** P W THOMAS, **Hon C** M C S FOSSETT
POPPLETON ROAD (Mission Room) *see* York St Paul *York*
PORCHESTER (St James) *S'well 11* **P** *Bp* **C** C J RATTENBERRY
PORINGLAND (All Saints) *Nor 8* **P** *Bp, BNC Ox, J D Alston Esq, and G H Hastings Esq (3 turns) and DBP (1 turn)* **R** R B HEMS
PORLOCK (St Dubricius) w Stoke Pero *B & W 16* **P** *Ld Chan* **R** B E PRIORY
PORLOCK WEIR (St Nicholas) *see* Porlock w Stoke Pero *B & W*
PORT ERIN (St Catherine) *see* Rushen *S & M*
PORT ISAAC (St Peter) *see* St Endellion w Port Isaac and St Kew *Truro*
PORT ST MARY (St Mary) *see* Rushen *S & M*
PORTBURY (Blessed Virgin Mary) *see* Pill w Easton in Gordano and Portbury *B & W*
PORTCHESTER (St Mary) *Portsm 2* **P** *J R Thistlethwaite Esq* **V** M L S THOMAS
PORTESHAM (St Peter) *see* Abbotsbury, Portesham and Langton Herring *Sarum*
PORTHILL (St Andrew) *see* Wolstanton *Lich*
PORTHLEVEN (St Bartholomew) w Sithney *Truro 4* **P** *Bp* **P-in-c** P A A WALKER
PORTHPEAN (St Levan) *see* St Austell *Truro*
PORTINSCALE (Mission) *see* Crosthwaite Keswick *Carl*
PORTISHEAD (St Peter) *B & W 13* **P** *Mrs E Haigh* **R** A C TAYLOR, **C** C L LAWS
PORTKELLIS (St Christopher) *see* Helston and Wendron *Truro*
PORTLAND (All Saints w St Peter) *Sarum 5* **P** *Bp* **P-in-c** A D THORNE
PORTLAND (St John) *Sarum 5* **P** *Hyndman Trustees* **P-in-c** E LEWIS
PORTLEMOUTH, EAST (St Winwaloe Onocaus) *see* Charleton w Buckland Tout Saints etc *Ex*
PORTLOE (All Saints) *see* Veryan w Ruan Lanihorne *Truro*
PORTMAN SQUARE (St Paul) *see* Langham Place All So *Lon*
PORTON (St Nicholas) *see* Bourne Valley *Sarum*

PORTREATH (St Mary) *see* St Illogan *Truro*
PORTSDOWN (Christ Church) *Portsm 4* **P** *Simeon's Trustees* **V** S C PALMER, **NSM** M MORGAN
PORTSEA (All Saints) *Portsm 6* **P** *V Portsea St Mary and Bp (jt)* **P-in-c** L FOX, **NSM** M E TILLMAN
PORTSEA (Ascension) *Portsm 6* **P** *Bp* **P-in-c** S W JONES, **NSM** M S R GOVER
PORTSEA North End (St Mark) *Portsm 6* **P** *V Portsea St Mary* **V** J W BELL, **C** B T WILLIAMS, **NSM** P K PAYNE
PORTSEA (St Alban) *Portsm 6* **P** *Bp* **P-in-c** A DEAN, **Hon C** J W MORTIBOYS
PORTSEA (St Cuthbert) *Portsm 6* **P** *Bp* **V** D M POWER, **NSM** J POWER
PORTSEA (St George) *Portsm 6* **P** *Bp* **P-in-c** D L GAMBLE
PORTSEA (St Luke) *Portsm 6* **P** *Ch Patr Trust* **V** M J SMITHSON
PORTSEA (St Mary) (St Faith and St Barnabas) (St Wilfrid) *Portsm 6* **P** *Win Coll* **V** A R WRIGHT, **C** K R M BRISTOW, R C PEERS, J A D BUXTON, D G BOURNE, **NSM** K H APPLEFORD
PORTSEA (St Saviour) *Portsm 6* **P** *Bp* **P-in-c** P HASTROP
PORTSLADE (Good Shepherd) *Chich 4* **P** *Bp* **V** P D CLEGG
PORTSLADE (St Nicolas) (St Andrew) *Chich 4* **P** *Bp* **V** R H RUSHFORTH
PORTSWOOD (Christ Church) *Win 12* **P** *Bp* **V** D C JAMES, **C** R D TURNBULL, **Hon C** J D BENWELL
PORTSWOOD (St Denys) *Win 12* **P** *Bp* **P-in-c** S FOULKES, **Hon C** C L ATKINS
POSBURY (St Francis Proprietary Chapel) *see* Crediton and Shobrooke *Ex*
POSLINGFORD (St Mary) *see* Clare w Poslingford, Cavendish etc *St E*
POSTBRIDGE (St Gabriel) *see* Widecombe-in-the-Moor, Leusdon, Princetown etc *Ex*
POSTLEBURY *see* Nunney and Witham Friary, Marston Bigot etc *B & W*
POSTLING (St Mary and St Radegund) *see* Lyminge w Paddlesworth, Stanford w Postling etc *Cant*
POSTWICK (All Saints) *see* Brundall w Braydeston and Postwick *Nor*
POTT SHRIGLEY (St Christopher) *Ches 13* **P** *MMCET* **V** G H GREENHOUGH
POTTEN END (Holy Trinity) w Nettleden *St Alb 2* **P** *Bp* **V** J V M KIRKBY
POTTER HEIGHAM (St Nicholas) *see* Ludham, Potter Heigham and Hickling *Nor*
POTTERHANWORTH (St Andrew) *see* Branston w Nocton and Potterhanworth *Linc*
POTTERNE (St Mary the Virgin) w Worton and Marston *Sarum 19* **P** *Bp* **V** P WILKINSON
POTTERNEWTON (St Martin) *Ripon 5* **P** *Trustees* **V** J R W SILLER, **C** N S ROBINSON, **Par Dn** D LEPPINGTON, **NSM** D G RHODES
POTTERS BAR (St Mary and All Saints) *St Alb 17* **P** *Bp Lon* **V** P J BEVAN, **C** J K WILLIAMS
POTTERS GREEN (St Philip Deacon) *Cov 1* **P** *Ld Chan* **V** W J ADAMSON
POTTERS MARSTON (St Mary) *see* Barwell w Potters Marston and Stapleton *Leic*
POTTERSPURY (St Nicholas) w Furtho and Yardley Gobion and Cosgrove *Pet 5* **P** *D&C (2 turns), Jes Coll Ox (1 turn)* **V** M H CHAMPNEYS, **NSM** J ROBINSON
POTTO (St Mary) *see* Whorlton w Carlton and Faceby *York*
POTTON (St Mary the Virgin) w Sutton and Cockayne Hatley *St Alb 11* **P** *The Crown (3 turns), St Jo Coll Ox (1 turn)* **R** V W BEYNON, **NSM** D L SMITH
POUGHILL (St Michael and All Angels) *see* N Creedy *Ex*
POUGHILL (St Olaf King and Martyr) *Truro 8* **P** *Ch Soc Trust* **V** L H KEENAN
POULNER (St John) *see* Ringwood *Win*
POULSHOT (St Peter) *see* Rowde and Poulshot *Sarum*
POULTON (St Luke) *Ches 7* **P** *Bp* **P-in-c** A J MAUNDER
POULTON (St Michael and All Angels) *see* The Ampneys w Driffield and Poulton *Glouc*
POULTON LANCELYN (Holy Trinity) *Ches 8* **P** *R Bebington* **V** G J MOTE
POULTON-LE-FYLDE (St Chad) *Blackb 13* **P** *DBP* **V** C H WILLIAMS, **C** I A HELLYER
POULTON-LE-SANDS (Holy Trinity) w Morecambe St Laurence *Blackb 12* **P** *V Lanc* **C** D J THOMPSON
POUND HILL (St Barnabas) *see* Worth *Chich*
POUNDSBRIDGE (Chapel) *see* Penshurst and Fordcombe *Roch*
POUNDSTOCK (St Winwaloe) *see* Week St Mary w Poundstock and Whitstone *Truro*
POWDERHAM (St Clement Bishop and Martyr) *see* Kenton, Mamhead, Powderham, Cofton and Starcross *Ex*
POWERSTOCK (St Mary the Virgin) *see* Askerswell, Loders and Powerstock *Sarum*
POWICK (St Peter) *see* Powyke *Worc*
POWYKE (St Peter) *Worc 2* **P** *Croome Estate Trustees* **V** *Vacant* (01905) 830270
POYNINGS (Holy Trinity) w Edburton, Newtimber and Pyecombe *Chich 9* **P** *Ld Chan (1 turn), Bp and Abp (1 turn)* **R** *Vacant* (01273) 857375
POYNTINGTON (All Saints) *see* Queen Thorne *Sarum*
POYNTON (St George) *Ches 17* **P** *Bp* **V** J D THOMPSTONE, **C** A M TUCKER, **NSM** R J BROOKE
POYNTON, HIGHER (St Martin) *see* Poynton *Ches*
PRATTS BOTTOM (All Souls) *see* Green Street Green and Pratts Bottom *Roch*
PREES (St Chad) *Lich 23* **P** *Bp* **V** D J TITLEY
PREESALL (St Oswald) *Blackb 10* **P** *Bp* **V** E ANGUS, **NSM** M JENKINSON
PRENTON (St Stephen) *Ches 1* **P** *Bp* **C** D C P MOORE, **NSM** E D O'NEILL
PRENTON DELL (St Alban) *see* Prenton *Ches*
PRESCOT (St Mary) (St Paul) *Liv 10* **P** *K Coll Cam* **V** T M STEEL, **C** A SWIFT
PRESHUTE (St George) *see* Marlborough *Sarum*
PRESTBURY (St Mary) (St Nicholas) *Glouc 11* **P** *Mrs F L Baghot de la Bere Aldendifer* **V** S S GREGORY, **C** M G COZENS
PRESTBURY (St Peter) *Ches 13* **P** *Ms C J C B Legh* **V** D ASHWORTH, **C** J N CLARKE, **Hon C** R OTTLEY
PRESTEIGNE (St Andrew) w Discoed, Kinsham and Lingen *Heref 5* **P** *Bp* **P-in-c** D R P HAYES
PRESTLEIGH (St James Mission Church) *see* Shepton Mallet w Doulting *B & W*
PRESTOLEE (Holy Trinity) *see* Ringley w Prestolee *Man*
PRESTON Acregate Lane (Mission) *see* Preston Risen Lord *Blackb*
PRESTON (All Saints) *Blackb 14* **P** *Trustees* **P-in-c** J D RUSHTON
PRESTON (All Saints) *see* Siddington w Preston *Glouc*
PRESTON (All Saints) and Sproatley in Holderness *York 13* **P** *Abp* **R** S ROBINSON
PRESTON (Church of the Ascension) *Lon 21* **P** *Bp* **V** F C HUMPHRIES, **C** F C PAPANTONIOU, **NSM** N D BIRD
PRESTON (Emmanuel) *Blackb 14* **P** *R Preston* **V** S HUNT
PRESTON (Good Shepherd) *see* Brighton Gd Shep Preston *Chich*
PRESTON (St Alban) *see* Brighton Resurr *Chich*
PRESTON (St Andrew) w Sutton Poyntz and Osmington w Poxwell *Sarum 5* **P** *Patr Bd* **TV** A C MACROW-WOOD, **C** L C STOCK
PRESTON (St Augustine and St Saviour) *see* Brighton St Aug and St Sav *Chich*
PRESTON (St Cuthbert) *Blackb 14* **P** *Bp* **V** D GASKELL
PRESTON (St John) (St George the Martyr) (Christ the King Chapel) *Blackb 14* **P** *DBP* **R** R S LADDS, **C** D P A FEENEY
PRESTON (St John the Baptist) *Glouc 3* **P** *Bp* **P-in-c** R HART
PRESTON (St John the Evangelist) *Chich 2* **P** *Bp* **V** F MITCHINSON
PRESTON (St Jude w St Paul) *Blackb 14* **P** *Bp and V Preston St John* **V** *Vacant* (01772) 52987
PRESTON (St Luke) (St Oswald) *Blackb 14* **P** *Bp and Simeon's Trustees (jt)* **P-in-c** J N MANSFIELD
PRESTON (St Mark) *see* Ashton-on-Ribble St Mich w Preston St Mark *Blackb*
PRESTON (St Martin) *see* King's Walden and Offley w Lilley *St Alb*
PRESTON (St Mary the Virgin) *see* Lavenham w Preston *St E*
PRESTON (St Matthias) *see* Brighton St Matthias *Chich*
PRESTON (St Mildred) *see* Wingham w Elmstone and Preston w Stourmouth *Cant*
PRESTON (St Paul) *see* Paignton St Paul Preston *Ex*
PRESTON (St Peter and St Paul) and Ridlington w Wing and Pilton *Pet 14* **P** *Bp, Baroness Willoughby de Eresby, and DBP (jt)* **R** A M S WILSON
PRESTON (St Stephen) *Blackb 14* **P** *Bp* **V** D BARTON
PRESTON The Risen Lord (St Matthew) (St Hilda) (St James's church hall) *Blackb 14* **P** *Patr Bd* **TR** P N TYERS, **TV** P A BROOKFIELD
PRESTON, EAST (St Mary) w Kingston *Chich 1* **P** *D&C* **V** B J MARSHALL
PRESTON, GREAT (St Aidan) *see* Kippax w Allerton Bywater *Ripon*
PRESTON BAGOT (All Saints) *see* Claverdon w Preston Bagot *Cov*
PRESTON BISSET (St John the Baptist) *see* Swan *Ox*
PRESTON BROOK (St Faith) *see* Daresbury *Ches*
PRESTON CAPES (St Peter and St Paul) *see* Badby w Newham and Charwelton w Fawsley etc *Pet*

PRESTON NEXT FAVERSHAM (St Catherine) w Goodnestone and Graveney *Cant 6* **P** *Abp* **V** S C WILSON, **C** A A G OLD
PRESTON ON STOUR (St Mary) *see* Ilmington w Stretton-on-Fosse etc *Cov*
PRESTON ON TEES (All Saints) *Dur 10* **P** *Bp* **V** D T OSMAN
PRESTON-ON-WYE (St Lawrence) *see* Madley w Tyberton, Preston-on-Wye and Blakemere *Heref*
PRESTON PATRICK (St Patrick) *see* Crosscrake and Preston Patrick *Carl*
PRESTON PLUCKNETT (St James the Great) (St Peter) *B & W 7* **P** *Bp (2 turns), Mrs S W Rawlins (1 turn)* **V** A PERRIS, **C** J G EDWARDS
PRESTON UNDER SCARR (St Margaret) *see* Wensley *Ripon*
PRESTON WEALDMOORS (St Lawrence) *see* Edgmond w Kynnersley and Preston Wealdmoors *Lich*
PRESTON WYNNE (Holy Trinity) *see* Bodenham w Hope-under-Dinmore, Felton etc *Heref*
PRESTONVILLE (St Luke) *Chich 2* **P** *Trustees* **NSM** G B ROBERTS
PRESTWICH (St Gabriel) *Man 14* **P** *Bp* **P-in-c** P RICHARDSON
PRESTWICH (St Hilda) *Man 14* **P** *Trustees* **P-in-c** R CROFT
PRESTWICH (St Margaret) (St George) *Man 14* **P** *R Prestwich St Mary the Virgin* **V** M ASHWORTH
PRESTWICH (St Mary the Virgin) *Man 14* **P** *Trustees* **R** F BIBBY
PRESTWOLD (St Andrew) *see* Wymeswold and Prestwold w Hoton *Leic*
PRESTWOOD (Holy Trinity) and Great Hampden *Ox 28* **P** *Bp and Hon I H Hope-Morley (jt)* **R** J R WHITE, **C** C NICHOLSON
PRICKWILLOW (St Peter) *see* Ely *Ely*
PRIDDY (St Lawrence) *B & W 1* **P** *Bp* **V** E A MACPHERSON
PRIESTWOOD (St Andrew) *see* Bracknell *Ox*
PRIMROSE HILL (Holy Trinity) *see* Lydney *Glouc*
PRIMROSE HILL (St Mary the Virgin) w Avenue Road (St Paul) *Lon 16* **P** *Trustees* **V** J A OVENDEN, **NSM** C L VAN DER PUMP, S V WEBSTER, D J H JONES
PRINCE ALBERT ROAD (St Mark) *see* Regent's Park St Mark *Lon*
PRINCE CONSORT ROAD (Holy Trinity) *see* S Kensington H Trin w All SS *Lon*
PRINCE'S PARK (Christ the King) Conventional District *Roch 5* **C-in-c** J F ELDRIDGE
PRINCE'S PARK (St Paul) *Liv 4* **V** *Vacant*
PRINCES RISBOROUGH (St Mary) w Ilmer *Ox 21* **P** *Ld Chan* **P-in-c** P F B FISKE, **Hon C** R E PEAKE, **NSM** A K PHILLIPS
PRINCETOWN (St Michael and All Angels) *see* Widecombe-in-the-Moor, Leusdon, Princetown etc *Ex*
PRIOR'S DEAN (not known) *see* Greatham w Empshott and Hawkley w Prior's Dean *Portsm*
PRIORS HARDWICK (St Mary the Virgin) w Priors Marston and Wormleighton *Cov 10* **P** *Earl Spencer* **P-in-c** K J PHILLIPS
PRIORS LEE (St Peter) (St Georges) *Lich 22* **P** *Bp and V Shifnal (jt)* **V** G L HANCOX
PRIORS MARSTON (St Leonard) *see* Priors Hardwick, Priors Marston and Wormleighton *Cov*
PRIORS PARK (Mission Hall) *see* Tewkesbury w Walton Cardiff *Glouc*
PRISTON (St Luke) *see* Timsbury and Priston *B & W*
PRITTLEWELL (All Saints) *see* Southend *Chelmsf*
PRITTLEWELL (St Luke) *Chelmsf 13* **P** *Bp* **V** D F C GIRLING
PRITTLEWELL (St Mary the Virgin) *Chelmsf 13* **P** *Bp* **V** R A MASON, **C** M A COHEN, **Hon C** A J MORLEY, **NSM** F M SMITH
PRITTLEWELL (St Peter) w Westcliff St Cedd and the Saints of Essex *Chelmsf 13* **P** *Bp* **V** G R STEEL, **NSM** S M WARING
PRITTLEWELL (St Stephen) *Chelmsf 13* **P** *Bp* **P-in-c** R A MASON
PROBUS (St Probus and St Grace), Ladock and Grampound w Creed and St Erme *Truro 6* **P** *DBP* **TR** I H MORRIS, **TV** D H DIXON, **Hon C** M E RICHARDS
PRUDHOE (St Mary Magdalene) *Newc 3* **P** *Dioc Soc* **P-in-c** D J ELKINGTON, **C** A A ELKINGTON
PUBLOW (All Saints) w Pensford, Compton Dando and Chelwood *B & W 10* **P** *Bp* **P-in-c** G CALWAY
PUCKINGTON (St Andrew) *see* Ilminster and District *B & W*
PUCKLECHURCH (St Thomas a Becket) and Abson *Bris 7* **P** *D&C* **V** I L WILLS
PUDDINGTON (St Thomas a Becket) *see* N Creedy *Ex*
PUDDLETOWN (St Mary the Virgin) and Tolpuddle *Sarum 2* **P** *Trustees, Ch Ch Ox, and Viscount Rothermere (by turn)* **P-in-c** J V WALTON
PUDLESTON (St Peter) *see* Leominster *Heref*
PUDSEY St James (Conventional District) *Bradf 3 Vacant*
PUDSEY (St Lawrence and St Paul) *Bradf 3* **P** *Bp and V Calverley (jt)* **V** P N AYERS
PULBOROUGH (St Mary) *Chich 12* **P** *Lord Egremont* **R** P J BENFIELD
PULFORD (St Mary the Virgin) *see* Eccleston and Pulford *Ches*
PULHAM Market (St Mary Magdalene), Pulham St Mary and Starston *Nor 10* **P** *The Crown (2 turns), Bp (1 turn)* **R** *Vacant* (01379) 676256
PULHAM (St Thomas a Beckett) *see* Dungeon Hill *Sarum*
PULHAM ST MARY (St Mary the Virgin) *see* Pulham Market, Pulham St Mary and Starston *Nor*
PULLOXHILL (St James the Apostle) *see* Silsoe, Pulloxhill and Flitton *St Alb*
PULVERBATCH (St Edith) *see* Longden and Annscroft w Pulverbatch *Heref*
PUNCKNOWLE (St Mary the Blessed Virgin) *see* Bride Valley *Sarum*
PUNNETS TOWN (St Peter) *see* Heathfield *Chich*
PURBROOK (St John the Baptist) *Portsm 4* **P** *Bp* **V** R I P COUTTS, **NSM** M M SHERWIN, B A MOSSE
PUREWELL (St John) *see* Christchurch *Win*
PURFLEET (St Stephen) *see* Aveley and Purfleet *Chelmsf*
PURITON (St Michael and All Angels) and Pawlett *B & W 14* **P** *Ld Chan (1 turn), D&C Windsor (2 turns)* **V** K G J WILLIAMS
PURLEIGH (All Saints), Cold Norton and Stow Maries *Chelmsf 11* **P** *Suttons Hosp, Or Coll Ox, and Bp (jt)* **P-in-c** D W COOLING, **NSM** M D COOLING
PURLEY (Christ Church) *S'wark 23* **P** *Bp* **V** C R TREFUSIS
PURLEY (St Barnabas) *S'wark 23* **P** *Bp* **V** A C WAIT, **Hon C** Y A DAVIS
PURLEY (St Mark) Woodcote *S'wark 23* **P** *Bp* **V** P M SILLS, **C** H RHODES, H J N FULLERTON
PURLEY (St Mary the Virgin) *Ox 12* **P** *Ld Chan* **R** R B HOWELL, **C** B J BAILEY
PURLEY (St Swithun) *S'wark 23* **P** *Bp* **V** J K GREIG
PURLWELL (St Andrew) *Wakef 10* **P** *Bp* **P-in-c** K WILLIAMS
PURSE CAUNDLE (St Peter) *see* The Caundles w Folke and Holwell *Sarum*
PURSTON (St Thomas) cum South Featherstone *Wakef 11* **P** *Bp* **V** A S RAMSDEN
PURTON (St John) *see* Sharpness w Purton and Brookend *Glouc*
PURTON (St Mary) *Bris 13* **P** *Bp* **V** B A FESSEY
PUSEY (All Saints) *Ox 17* **P** *Bp* **R** C R RUDD
PUTFORD (St Stephen) *Ex 9* **P** *Bp* **V** H J ROCHE
PUTLEY (not known) *see* Tarrington w Stoke Edith, Aylton, Pixley etc *Heref*
PUTNEY (St Margaret) *S'wark 19* **P** *Bp* **NSM** R C BENSON
PUTNEY (St Mary) (All Saints) *S'wark 19* **P** *D&C Worc* **V** J L DRAPER, **C** R J C MAJOR, L T FRANCIS-DEHQANI, **Hon C** D PEACOCK, **NSM** T J E MARWOOD
PUTTENHAM (St John the Baptist) *see* Seale, Puttenham and Wanborough *Guildf*
PUTTENHAM (St Mary) *see* Tring *St Alb*
PUXTON (St Saviour) *see* Congresbury w Puxton and Hewish St Ann *B & W*
PYE NEST (St James) *see* King Cross *Wakef*
PYECOMBE (Transfiguration) *see* Poynings w Edburton, Newtimber and Pyecombe *Chich*
PYLLE (St Thomas a Becket) *see* Ditcheat w E Pennard and Pylle *B & W*
PYPE HAYES (St Mary the Virgin) *Birm 8* **P** *Trustees* **V** J F RYAN
PYRFORD (Church of the Good Shepherd) *see* Wisley w Pyrford *Guildf*
PYRFORD (St Nicolas) *as above*
PYRTON (St Mary) *see* Icknield *Ox*
PYTCHLEY (All Saints) *see* Isham w Pytchley *Pet*
PYWORTHY (St Swithun), Pancrasweek and Bridgerule *Ex 9* **P** *DBP* **R** *Vacant* (01409) 254062
QUADRING (St Margaret) *see* Gosberton, Gosberton Clough and Quadrin *Linc*
QUAINTON (Holy Cross and St Mary) *see* Schorne *Ox*
QUANTOXHEAD (Blessed Virgin Mary) (St Ethelreda) *B & W 17* **P** *Bp, Lady Gass, and Lt-Col W Luttrell (jt)* **R** J D A STEVENS, **NSM** P CUFF
QUARLEY (St Michael and All Angels) *see* Amport, Grateley, Monxton and Quarley *Win*
QUARNDON (St Paul) *Derby 11* **P** *Exors Viscount Scarsdale* **V** J D MORISON
QUARNFORD (St Paul) *see* Longnor, Quarnford and Sheen *Lich*
QUARRENDON ESTATE (St Peter) *see* Aylesbury w Bierton and Hulcott *Ox*
QUARRINGTON (St Botolph) w Old Sleaford *Linc 22* **P** *Bp* **R** D J MUSSON

QUARRY BANK (Christ Church) *Worc 10* **P** *Prime Min* **V** T G CHAPMAN
QUARRY HILL (St Mary) *see* Leeds City *Ripon*
QUATFORD (St Mary Magdalene) *see* Bridgnorth, Tasley, Astley Abbotts, Oldbury etc *Heref*
QUATT (St Andrew) *see* Alveley and Quatt *Heref*
QUEDGELEY (St James) *see* Hardwicke, Quedgeley and Elmore w Longney *Glouc*
QUEEN CAMEL (St Barnabas) w West Camel, Corton Denham, Sparkford, Weston Bampfylde and Sutton Montis *B & W 3* **P** *Bp and DBP (2 turns), CPAS, MMCET and Revd G Bennett (1 turn)* **P-in-c** R H AXFORD
QUEEN CHARLTON (St Margaret) *see* Keynsham *B & W*
QUEEN THORNE *Sarum 4* **P** *Bp, Revd J M P Goodden, Major K S D Wingfield Digby, and MMCET (jt)* **P-in-c** A J H EDWARDS, **NSM** I WOODWARD, A J B MONDS
QUEENBOROUGH (Holy Trinity) *Cant 14* **P** *Abp* **V** R N MURCH
QUEENHILL (St Nicholas) *see* Longdon, Castlemorton, Bushley, Queenhill etc *Worc*
QUEENSBURY (All Saints) *Lon 23* **P** *The Crown* **V** J N LUSCOMBE
QUEENSBURY (Holy Trinity) *Bradf 2* **P** *Bp* **V** *Vacant* (01274) 880573
QUENDON (not known) w Rickling and Wicken Bonhunt and Widdington *Chelmsf 21* **P** *Keble Coll Ox and Bp (alt)* **R** A LINDSAY
QUENIBOROUGH (St Mary) *see* Syston TM *Leic*
QUENINGTON (St Swithun) *see* Coln St Aldwyns, Hatherop, Quenington etc *Glouc*
QUERNMORE (St Peter) *see* Dolphinholme w Quernmore *Blackb*
QUETHIOCK (St Hugh) *see* St Ive and Pensilva w Quethiock *Truro*
QUIDENHAM Group, The (St Andrew) *Nor 11* **P** *Ld Chan (1 turn), Bp, Sir Thomas Beevor Bt, Major E H C Garnier, Trustees, and New Buckenham PCC (3 turns)* **V** M A SAVAGE, **C** P M KNIGHT, **NSM** A R WRIGHT
QUINTON and PRESTON DEANERY (St John the Baptist) *see* Wootton w Quinton and Preston Deanery *Pet*
QUINTON (St Swithun) w Marston Sicca *Glouc 10* **P** *D&C Worc and Bp (jt)* **NSM** J P M WILSON
QUINTON, THE (Christ Church) *Birm 2* **P** *Bp* **R** J R BARNETT, **C** A M BUCKNALL, S C CARTER
QUINTON ROAD WEST (St Boniface) *Birm 2* **P** *Bp* **V** W BROWN
QUORN (St Bartholomew) *see* Quorndon *Leic*
QUORNDON (St Bartholomew) *Leic 7* **P** *Bp* **V** D H BOWLER
QUY (St Mary) *see* Stow w Quy *Ely*
RACKENFORD (All Saints) *see* Washfield, Stoodleigh, Withleigh etc *Ex*
RACKHEATH (Holy Trinity) and Salhouse *Nor 4* **P** *Bp* **P-in-c** G HOWELLS
RACTON (St Peter) *see* Compton, the Mardens, Stoughton and Racton *Chich*
RADBOURNE (St Andrew) *see* Longford, Long Lane, Dalbury and Radbourne *Derby*
RADCLIFFE (St Andrew) Black Lane *Man 14* **P** *R Radcliffe St Mary* **V** P N W GRAYSHON
RADCLIFFE (St Mary) (St Thomas and St John) (St Philip Mission Church) *Man 14* **P** *Patr Bd* **TR** C H ELLIS, **TV** B M HACKETT, **C** P D GULLY
RADCLIFFE-ON-TRENT (St Mary) and Shelford w Holme Pierrepont and Adbolton *S'well 8* **P** *DBP (2 turns), Ld Chan (1 turn)* **R** K H NEWCOMBE, **NSM** D E BENNETT
RADCLIVE (St John the Evangelist) *see* Buckingham *Ox*
RADDINGTON (St Michael) *see* Wiveliscombe w Chipstable, Huish Champflower etc *B & W*
RADDON *see* Thorverton, Cadbury, Upton Pyne etc *Ex*
RADFORD (All Souls) w Christ Church and St Michael *S'well 12* **P** *Bp* **V** D A JONES
RADFORD (St Nicholas) *Cov 2* **P** *Bp* **V** G HANDS
RADFORD (St Peter) *S'well 12* **P** *Bp* **V** H J WORSLEY
RADFORD, NORTH (St Francis of Assisi) *see* Cov St Fran N Radford *Cov*
RADFORD SEMELE (St Nicholas) and Ufton *Cov 10* **P** *Bp* **P-in-c** R D ALLON-SMITH
RADIPOLE (Emmanuel) (St Adhelm) (St Ann) and Melcombe Regis *Sarum 5* **P** *Patr Bd* **TR** M P H STEAR, **TV** D N H MAKEPEACE, P W FINCH, **C** S A WOAN, **NSM** G G DRIVER
RADLETT (Christ Church) (St John) *St Alb 1* **P** *V Aldenham* **V** G FELLOWS, **C** M J FLOWERDEW, **Hon C** S M HALMSHAW
RADLEY (St James the Great) and Sunningwell *Ox 10* **P** *Radley Coll and DBP (by turn)* **R** T P GIBBONS, **NSM** P E HEWLINS
RADNAGE (St Mary) *see* W Wycombe w Bledlow Ridge, Bradenham and Radnage *Ox*
RADNOR, OLD (St Stephen) *see* Kington w Huntington, Old Radnor, Kinnerton etc *Heref*
RADSTOCK (St Nicholas) w Writhlington *B & W 12* **P** *Bp* **R** C P J TURNER
RADWAY (St Peter) *see* Warmington w Shotteswell and Radway w Ratley *Cov*
RADWELL (All Saints) *see* Stotfold and Radwell *St Alb*
RADWINTER (St Mary the Virgin) w Hempstead *Chelmsf 22* **P** *Keble Coll Ox* **R** B J MACDONALD-MILNE
RAGDALE (All Saints) *see* Upper Wreake *Leic*
RAINFORD (All Saints) *Liv 11* **P** *V Prescot* **V** F R N MICHELL
RAINHAM (St Helen and St Giles) w Wennington *Chelmsf 2* **P** *MMCET* **R** A C WARD, **C** P H ANSELL, C P SMITH
RAINHAM (St Margaret) *Roch 3* **P** *Bp* **V** B M M O'CONNOR, **C** M R COOPER, E P I WESTBROOK, **NSM** A V SHILLING
RAINHILL (St Ann) *Liv 13* **P** *Trustees* **V** T R EVANS, **C** E COLLISON
RAINOW (Holy Trinity) w Saltersford and Forest *Ches 13* **P** *Bp* **V** L LEWIS
RAINTON (not known) *see* Topcliffe w Baldersby, Dalton, Dishforth etc *York*
RAINTON, EAST (St Cuthbert) *Dur 14* **P** *D&C* **V** D GUEST
RAINTON, WEST (St Mary) *Dur 14* **P** *Bp* **R** D GUEST
RAINWORTH (St Simon and St Jude) *S'well 2* **P** *DBP* **V** *Vacant* (01623) 792293
RAITHBY (Holy Trinity) *Linc 7* **P** *Baroness Willoughby de Eresby* **R** G ROBSON
RAITHBY (St Peter) *Linc 12* **P** *Bp and Viscount Chaplain (alt)* **R** *Vacant*
RAME (St Germanus) *see* Maker w Rame *Truro*
RAMPISHAM (St Michael and All Angels) *see* Melbury *Sarum*
RAMPSIDE (St Michael) *see* Aldingham, Dendron, Rampside and Urswick *Carl*
RAMPTON (All Saints) *Ely 5* **R** E A HUBBARD
RAMPTON (All Saints) w Laneham, Treswell, Cottam and Stokeham *S'well 5* **P** *D&C York and The Crown (alt)* **R** *Vacant* (01777) 248143
RAMSBOTTOM (St Andrew) *Man 10* **P** *Bp* **V** I M ROGERSON
RAMSBOTTOM (St John) (St Paul) *Man 10* **P** *Prime Min and Bp (alt)* **V** J ARCUS
RAMSBURY (Holy Cross) *see* Whitton *Sarum*
RAMSDALE (Christ Church) *see* Baughurst, Ramsdell, Wolverton w Ewhurst etc *Win*
RAMSDEN (Church of Unity) *see* Orpington All SS *Roch*
RAMSDEN (St James), Finstock and Fawler, Leafield w Wychwood and Wilcote *Ox 3* **P** *Bp, V Charlbury, and Sir Mark Norman, Bt (jt)* **V** B J FREETH, **NSM** P FREETH
RAMSDEN BELLHOUSE (St Mary the Virgin) *see* Ramsden Crays w Ramsden Bellhouse *Chelmsf*
RAMSDEN CRAYS w Ramsden Bellhouse *Chelmsf 6* **P** *Reformation Ch Trust* **R** *Vacant* (01268) 521043
RAMSDEN HEATH (St John) *see* Downham w S Hanningfield *Chelmsf*
RAMSEY (St Michael) w Little Oakley and Wrabness *Chelmsf 20* **P** *Ld Chan* **P-in-c** C F SHILLAKER
RAMSEY, NORTH (St Olave) *see* Lezayre St Olave Ramsey *S & M*
RAMSEY, SOUTH (St Paul) *S & M 4* **P** *Bp* **V** P C ROBINSON
RAMSEY ST MARY'S (St Mary) *see* The Ramseys and Upwood *Ely*
RAMSEYS (St Thomas a Becket) (St Mary) and Upwood, The *Ely 11* **P** *Patr Bd* **TR** R H ROLLETT, **TV** J R SIMPSON
RAMSGATE (Christ Church) *Cant 9* **P** *Ch Patr Trust* **V** S YOUNG
RAMSGATE (Holy Trinity) (St George) *Cant 9* **P** *Abp* **R** P A ADAMS
RAMSGATE (St Luke) *Cant 9* **P** *CPAS* **V** V G WILKINS, **NSM** J P BRENCHLEY, S GOLDING
RAMSGATE (St Mark) *Cant 9* **P** *CPAS* **P-in-c** H L BOREHAM
RAMSGILL (St Mary) *see* Upper Nidderdale *Ripon*
RAMSHOLT (All Saints) *see* Alderton w Ramsholt and Bawdsey *St E*
RANBY (St German) *see* Asterby Gp *Linc*
RANBY (St Martin) *see* Babworth w Sutton-cum-Lound *S'well*
RAND (St Oswald) *see* Wragby *Linc*
RANDWICK (St John the Baptist) *see* Whiteshill and Randwick *Glouc*
RANGEMORE (All Saints) *see* Hanbury w Newborough and Rangemore *Lich*
RANGEWORTHY (Holy Trinity) *see* Wickwar w Rangeworthy *Glouc*

RANMOOR (St John the Evangelist) *Sheff 4* **P** *Trustees* **V** R M JARRATT, **Hon C** B C BROOKE
RANMORE (St Barnabas) *see* Dorking w Ranmore *Guildf*
RANSKILL (St Barnabas) *see* Scrooby *S'well*
RANTON (All Saints) *see* Derrington, Haughton and Ranton *Lich*
RANWORTH (St Helen) w Panxworth and Woodbastwick *Nor 4* **P** *Bp and J Cator Esq (jt)* **V** P McFADYEN
RASEN, WEST (All Saints) *see* Middle Rasen Gp *Linc*
RASHCLIFFE (St Stephen) and Lockwood *Wakef 5* **P** *R Almondbury and R Kirkheaton (jt)* **P-in-c** M J ARCHER
RASKELF (St Mary) *see* Easingwold w Raskelfe *York*
RASTRICK (St John the Divine) *Wakef 2* **P** *Bp* **V** S J TYNDALL
RASTRICK (St Matthew) *Wakef 2* **P** *V Halifax* **V** T L SWINHOE
RATBY (St Philip and St James) w Groby *Leic 12* **P** *Patr Bd* **TR** A R LEIGHTON, **TV** M H HARDY, **C** S LEIGHTON, **NSM** P SHERIDAN
RATCLIFFE CULEY (All Saints) *see* The Sheepy Gp *Leic*
RATCLIFFE-ON-SOAR (Holy Trinity) *see* Kingston and Ratcliffe-on-Soar *S'well*
RATCLIFFE ON THE WREAKE (St Botolph) *see* Syston TM *Leic*
RATHMELL (Holy Trinity) *see* Giggleswick and Rathmell w Wigglesworth *Bradf*
RATLEY (St Peter ad Vincula) *see* Warmington w Shotteswell and Radway w Ratley *Cov*
RATLINGHOPE (St Margaret) *see* Wentnor w Ratlinghope, Myndtown, Norbury etc *Heref*
RATTERY (Blessed Virgin Mary) *see* S Brent and Rattery *Ex*
RATTLESDEN (St Nicholas) w Thorpe Morieux and Brettenham *St E 10* **P** *Bp (2 turns), Ld Chan (1 turn)* **R** R S EXCELL
RAUCEBY, NORTH (St Peter) *see* Ancaster Wilsford Gp *Linc*
RAUGHTON HEAD (All Saints) w Gatesgill *Carl 3* **P** *DBP* **P-in-c** P KYBIRD, **C** H J CARTER
RAUNDS (St Peter) *Pet 10* **P** *Bp* **V** W P K KENTIGERN-FOX
RAVENDALE Group, The *Linc 10* **P** *Ld Chan, Trustees of D Parkinson Settled Estates, and Bp (by turn)* **R** *Vacant* (01472) 822980
RAVENDALE, EAST (St Martin) *see* Ravendale Gp *Linc*
RAVENFIELD (St James) *see* Bramley and Ravenfield w Hooton Roberts etc *Sheff*
RAVENGLASS (Mission Room) *see* Eskdale, Irton, Muncaster and Waberthwaite *Carl*
RAVENHEAD (St John) *see* Parr Mt *Liv*
RAVENHEAD (St John the Evangelist) *Liv 10* **P** *V St Helens* **V** E R DORAN, **C** M X THORPE
RAVENINGHAM Group, The (St Andrew) *Nor 8* **P** *Bp, Adn Nor, Sir Nicholas Bacon Bt, Major C A Boycott, D&C, K Coll Cam, and DBP (jt)* **R** C POULARD, **C** M J TALBOT
RAVENSCAR (St Hilda) *see* Cloughton and Burniston w Ravenscar etc *York*
RAVENSDEN (All Saints) *see* Wilden w Colmworth and Ravensden *St Alb*
RAVENSHEAD (St Peter) *S'well 4* **P** *Bp* **V** G O SPEDDING, **NSM** E S STEINER
RAVENSTHORPE (St Denys) *see* W Haddon w Winwick and Ravensthorpe *Pet*
RAVENSTHORPE (St Saviour) *Wakef 10* **P** *V Mirfield* **P-in-c** C S BARTER
RAVENSTONE (All Saints) *see* Gayhurst w Ravenstone, Stoke Goldington etc *Ox*
RAVENSTONE (St Michael and All Angels) and Swannington *Leic 8* **P** *Ld Chan and V Whitwick (alt)* **R** K C EMMETT
RAVENSTONEDALE (St Oswald) *see* Orton and Tebay w Ravenstonedale etc *Carl*
RAWCLIFFE (St James) *see* Airmyn, Hook and Rawcliffe *Sheff*
RAWCLIFFE (St Mark) *see* Clifton *York*
RAWCLIFFE BRIDGE (St Philip) *see* Airmyn, Hook and Rawcliffe *Sheff*
RAWDON (St Peter) *Bradf 4* **P** *Bp and Trustees (jt)* **V** C M MORRIS
RAWMARSH (St Mary the Virgin) w Parkgate *Sheff 6* **P** *Ld Chan* **R** M R H BELLAMY, **C** A P ARNOLD
RAWMARSH (St Nicolas) *see* Ryecroft St Nic *Sheff*
RAWNSLEY (St Michael) *see* Hednesford *Lich*
RAWRETH (St Nicholas) w Rettendon *Chelmsf 12* **P** *Ld Chan and Pemb Coll Cam (alt)* **R** *Vacant* (01268) 766766
RAWTENSTALL (St Mary) *Man 15* **P** *CPAS* **V** G D PARKIN, **NSM** M V MURPHY
RAWTHORPE (St James) *Wakef 1* **P** *DBP* **V** *Vacant* (01484) 428045
RAYDON (St Mary) *see* Higham, Holton St Mary, Raydon and Stratford *St E*
RAYLEIGH (Holy Trinity) (St Michael) *Chelmsf 12* **P** *MMCET* **R** D W PARROTT, **C** J A FISHER, **NSM** I E L LAWRENCE
RAYNE (All Saints) *see* Panfield and Rayne *Chelmsf*
RAYNES PARK (St Saviour) *S'wark 13* **P** *Bp* **V** N A TURNER, **Par Dn** P A TURNER
RAYNHAM, EAST (St Mary) *see* South Raynham, E w W Raynham, Helhoughton, etc *Nor*
RAYNHAM, SOUTH (St Martin), East w West Raynham, Helhoughton, Weasenham and Wellingham *Nor 14* **P** *Bp, Marquess Townshend, and Viscount Coke (by turn)* **R** *Vacant* (0132874) 385
REACH (St Ethelreda) *see* Swaffham Bulbeck and Swaffham Prior w Reach *Ely*
READ IN WHALLEY (St John the Evangelist) *Blackb 8* **P** *V Whalley* **V** H A REID
READING (All Saints) *Ox 15* **P** *Bp* **V** R H EVERETT
READING (Christ Church) *see* Whitley Ch Ch *Ox*
READING Greyfriars (St James) *Ox 15* **P** *Ch Trust Fund Trust* **V** J A de B WILMOT, **C** N J LYNESS
READING (Holy Trinity) *Ox 15* **P** *SMF* **NSM** R H LUSTY
READING (St Agnes w St Paul) *Ox 15* **P** *Bp* **P-in-c** R J COWEN, **C** J P COLWILL
READING (St Barnabas) *Ox 15* **P** *Bp* **P-in-c** W M HETLING, **NSM** G L FRENCH
READING (St Giles w St Saviour) *Ox 15* **P** *Bp* **R** M J G MELROSE, **C** V J A BULLOCK, **Hon C** L J C JOY
READING (St John the Evangelist and St Stephen) *Ox 15* **P** *Simeon's Trustees* **V** A R VIGARS, **C** E MARQUEZ, **NSM** T R ASTIN
READING (St Luke) (St Bartholomew) *Ox 15* **P** *Bp and V Reading St Giles (alt)* **P-in-c** N A B DAVIES, **NSM** B D E BLACKMAN, E M JACKSON, C F PRATT
READING (St Mark) *Ox 15* **P** *Bp* **P-in-c** J M R BAKER
READING (St Mary the Virgin) (St Laurence) *Ox 15* **P** *Bp* **R** B SHENTON
READING (St Matthew) *Ox 15* **P** *Bp* **P-in-c** B SHENTON, **Hon C** D J M JASPER
REAPSMOOR (St John) *see* Longnor, Quarnford and Sheen *Lich*
REARSBY (St Michael and All Angels) *see* Syston TM *Leic*
RECULVER (St Mary the Virgin) and Herne Bay St Bartholomew *Cant 7* **P** *Abp* **V** M C BOWERS
RED HOUSE (St Cuthbert) *see* Sunderland Red Ho *Dur*
RED POST *Sarum 7* **P** *Mrs V M Chattey, H W Plunkett-Ernle-Erle-Drax Esq, and Bp (by turn)* **V** H I M MADDOX
REDBOURN (St Mary) *St Alb 8* **P** *Earl of Verulam* **V** J G PEDLAR, **NSM** A D OSBORNE
REDBROOK (St Saviour) *see* Newland and Redbrook w Clearwell *Glouc*
REDCAR (St Peter) *York 17* **P** *Trustees* **V** S N FISHER
REDCLIFFE BAY (St Nicholas) *see* Portishead *B & W*
REDCLIFFE WAY (St Mary the Virgin) *see* Bris St Mary Redcliffe w Temple etc *Bris*
REDDAL HILL (St Luke) *Worc 9* **P** *The Crown* **V** M F BAYNHAM
REDDISH (St Elisabeth) *Man 3* **P** *Bp* **R** N D HAWLEY, **C** J M PRESTWOOD
REDDISH (St Mary) *see* Heaton Reddish *Man*
REDDISH, NORTH (St Agnes) *Man 3* **P** *The Crown* **R** M P N JEWITT
REDDITCH (St Stephen) *Worc 7* **P** *Bp* **V** D C SALT
REDDITCH, The Ridge: Redditch (St George), Headless Cross, Webheath and Crabbs Cross *Worc 7* **P** *Bp* **TR** B N HALFPENNY, **TV** A J SMITH, M HERBERT, M F BARTLETT
REDE (All Saints) *see* Chedburgh w Depden, Rede and Hawkedon *St E*
REDENHALL (Assumption of the Blessed Virgin Mary), Harleston, Wortwell and Needham *Nor 10* **P** *Bp* **R** P MORRIS
REDFIELD (St Leonard) *see* E Bris *Bris*
REDGRAVE cum Botesdale (St Mary) w Rickinghall *St E 16* **P** *P J H Wilson Esq* **R** K W HOLDER
REDHILL (Christ Church) *see* Wrington w Butcombe *B & W*
REDHILL (Holy Trinity) *S'wark 26* **P** *Simeon's Trustees* **V** D P R SHACKLOCK
REDHILL (St John the Evangelist) (Meadvale Hall) *S'wark 26* **P** *Bp* **C** C M E G TOURNAY
REDHILL (St Matthew) *S'wark 26* **P** *Bp* **NSM** D T BRYANT
REDHORN *Sarum 19* **P** *Patr Bd* **TV** B J SMITH, **NSM** G D BAKER, M J C WHEELER
REDISHAM (St Peter) *see* Wainford *St E*
REDLAND (not known) *Bris 6* **P** *Ch Trust Fund Trust* **V** *Vacant* 0117-923 8202
REDLINGFIELD (St Andrew) *see* Stradbroke, Horham, Athelington and Redlingfield *St E*

REDLYNCH (St Mary) and Morgan's Vale *Sarum 11* **P** *DBF and V Downton (alt)* **P-in-c** I K PROVOST
REDLYNCH (St Peter) *see* Bruton and Distr *B & W*
REDMARLEY D'ABITOT (St Bartholomew) and Bromesberrow w Pauntley, Upleadon and Oxenhall *Glouc 3* **P** *Bp and Revd D J M Niblett (jt)* **R** T WILLIAMS, **Hon C** W E W BARBER, **NSM** A W PERRY
REDMARSHALL (St Cuthbert) *Dur 10* **P** *The Crown* **P-in-c** R WALTER
REDMILE (St Peter) *see* Barkestone w Plungar, Redmile and Stathern *Leic*
REDMIRE (St Mary) *see* Aysgarth and Bolton cum Redmire *Ripon*
REDNAL (St Stephen the Martyr) *Birm 4* **P** *Bp* **V** P W THOMAS
REDRUTH (St Andrew) (St Euny) w Lanner and Treleigh *Truro 2* **P** *DBP* **TR** R C BUSH, **TV** R SELLERS, C B THURSTON
REED (St Mary) *see* Barkway, Reed and Buckland w Barley *St Alb*
REEDHAM (St John the Baptist) w Cantley w Limpenhoe and Southwood *Nor 4* **P** *Lt-Col E R F Gilbert (1 turn), Ch Soc Trust (2 turns)* **P-in-c** R F GIBSON, **Hon C** T J N HULL
REEPHAM (St Mary) and Hackford w Whitwell and Kerdiston, Thurning w Wood Dalling and Salle *Nor 22* **P** *Bp, CCC Cam, Pemb Coll Cam, Trin Coll Cam, and Ch Soc Trust (jt)* **R** M D W PADDISON
REEPHAM (St Peter and St Paul) *see* Fiskerton w Reepham *Linc*
REGENT'S PARK (Christ Church) *see* Munster Square Ch Ch and St Mary Magd *Lon*
REGENT'S PARK (St Mark) *Lon 16* **P** *D&C St Paul's* **V** T P N D JONES
REGIL (St James Mission Church) *see* Winford w Felton Common Hill *B & W*
REIGATE (St Luke) South Park *S'wark 26* **P** *Bp* **V** A J MAYER
REIGATE (St Mark) *S'wark 26* **P** *Bp* **V** I H ROBERTSON
REIGATE (St Mary Magdalene) *S'wark 26* **P** *Trustees* **V** R I THOMSON, **C** P H CUNLIFFE, T D GILES, R A BURNINGHAM, **Hon C** M J H FOX, **NSM** D A HAGGAN
REIGATE (St Philip) *S'wark 26* **P** *Bp* **P-in-c** J P SCOTT
REIGATE HEATH (not known) *see* Reigate St Mary *S'wark*
REIGHTON (St Peter) *see* Bempton w Flamborough, Reighton w Speeton *York*
REKENDYKE (St Jude) *Dur 15* **P** *The Crown and D&C* **V** A J BEALING, **C** P R BEALING
REMENHAM (St Nicholas) *see* Henley on Thames w Remenham *Ox*
REMPSTONE (All Saints) *see* E and W Leake, Stanford-on-Soar, Rempstone etc *S'well*
RENDCOMB (St Peter) *Glouc 12* **P** *Major M T N H Wills* **R** *Vacant* (0128583) 319
RENDHAM (St Michael) w Sweffling *St E 19* **P** *CPAS* **R** *Vacant* (0172878) 495
RENDLESHAM (St Gregory the Great) *see* Eyke w Bromeswell, Rendlesham, Tunstall etc *St E*
RENHOLD (All Saints) *St Alb 10* **P** *MMCET* **P-in-c** L R McDONALD
RENISHAW (St Matthew) *see* Eckington w Handley and Ridgeway *Derby*
RENNINGTON (All Saints) *see* Embleton w Rennington and Rock *Newc*
RENWICK (All Saints) *see* Kirkoswald, Renwick and Ainstable *Carl*
REPPS (St Peter) *see* Martham and Repps with Bastwick, Thurne etc *Nor*
REPTON (St Wystan) *Derby 16* **P** *Mrs M Burdett-Fisher (1 turn), Miss A I M Harpur-Crewe (2 turns)* **V** J R P BARKER
RESTON, NORTH (St Edith) *see* Wold-Marsh Gp *Linc*
RETFORD (St Saviour) *S'well 5* **P** *Simeon's Trustees* **V** A C St J WALKER, **C** A R HUMPHRIES
RETFORD, EAST (St Swithin) *S'well 5* **P** *Bp* **V** J L OTTEY
RETFORD, WEST (St Michael) *S'well 5* **P** *Meynell Ch Trust* **R** J L OTTEY
RETTENDON (All Saints) *see* Rawreth w Rettendon *Chelmsf*
REVELSTOKE (St Peter) *see* Newton Ferrers w Revelstoke *Ex*
REVESBY (St Lawrence) *see* Mareham-le-Fen and Revesby *Linc*
REWE (St Mary the Virgin) *see* Stoke Canon, Poltimore w Huxham and Rewe etc *Ex*
REYDON (St Margaret) *see* Blythburgh w Reydon *St E*
REYMERSTON (St Peter) w Cranworth, Letton, Southburgh, Whinburgh and Westfield *Nor 17* **P** *Ch Soc Trust and MMCET (jt)* **P-in-c** C H MILFORD
RHODES (All Saints) (St Thomas) *Man 18* **P** *R Middleton* **V** G D GARRETT, **NSM** A BROXTON
RHYDYCROESAU (Christ Church) *Lich 19* **P** *Bp* **R** D B CROWHURST
RIBBESFORD (St Leonard) w Bewdley and Dowles *Worc 11* **P** *E J Winnington-Ingram Esq* **R** A G ANDERSON, **NSM** G D MORPHY, L E POCOCK
RIBBLETON (St Mary Magdalene) (St Anne's Church Centre) (Ascension) *Blackb 14* **P** *Patr Bd* **TR** J W GODDARD, **TV** R K HENSHALL, **C** C R SCHAEFER, R MARSH, **NSM** T DE LACEY
RIBBY w Wrea (St Nicholas) *Blackb 11* **P** *V Kirkham* **V** J WIXON
RIBCHESTER (St Wilfred) w Stidd *Blackb 14* **P** *Bp* **R** J FRANCIS
RIBSTON, LITTLE (St Helen) *see* Spofforth w Kirk Deighton *Ripon*
RIBY (St Edmund) *see* Keelby w Riby and Aylesby *Linc*
RICCALL (St Mary) *see* Barlby w Riccall *York*
RICHARDS CASTLE (All Saints) *see* Ludlow, Ludford, Ashford Carbonell etc *Heref*
RICHMOND (Holy Trinity and Christ Church) *S'wark 17* **P** *CPAS* **V** D C CASSON, **NSM** J F HARTERINK
RICHMOND (St Luke) *see* Kew St Phil and All SS w St Luke *S'wark*
RICHMOND (St Mary Magdalene) (St Matthias) (St John the Divine) *S'wark 17* **P** *K Coll Cam* **TR** M C J REINDORP, **TV** W F WARREN, J D S FRENCH, **NSM** H R SCOTT
RICHMOND (St Mary w Holy Trinity) w Hudswell *Ripon 2* **P** *Bp* **R** C N H WHITE, **C** H C STOKER
RICHMOND HILL (All Saints) *see* Leeds Richmond Hill *Ripon*
RICKERSCOTE (St Peter) *Lich 10* **P** *Bp and V Stafford St Paul (jt)* **V** S J HOTCHEN
RICKINGHALL (St Mary) *see* Redgrave cum Botesdale w Rickinghall *St E*
RICKLING (All Saints) *see* Quendon w Rickling and Wicken Bonhunt etc *Chelmsf*
RICKMANSWORTH (St Mary the Virgin) *St Alb 5* **P** *Bp* **V** B L DRIVER, **NSM** A P L SHAW
RIDDINGS (Holy Spirit) *see* Bottesford w Ashby *Linc*
RIDDINGS (St James) and Ironville *Derby 1* **P** *Wright Trustees and V Alfreton (jt)* **V** P J A LEVERTON
RIDDLESDEN (St Mary the Virgin) *Bradf 8* **P** *Bp* **V** *Vacant* (01535) 603419
RIDDLESDOWN (St James) *S'wark 23* **P** *Bp* **V** R St L BROADBERRY, **NSM** J DAGLEISH, D J ROWLAND
RIDDLESWORTH (St Peter) *see* Guiltcross *Nor*
RIDGE (St Margaret) *see* S Mymms and Ridge *St Alb*
RIDGEWAY *Ox 19* **P** *DBP, CCC Ox, and Qu Coll Ox (jt)* **R** A WADGE, **NSM** A P HOPWOOD
RIDGEWAY *Sarum 20* **P** *Patr Bd* **TR** J R H RAILTON
RIDGEWAY (St John the Evangelist) *see* Eckington w Handley and Ridgeway *Derby*
RIDGEWELL (St Laurence) w Ashen, Birdbrook and Sturmer *Chelmsf 19* **P** *Duchy of Lanc, Bp, and DBP (by turn)* **R** M D HEWITT
RIDGMONT (All Saints) *see* Aspley Guise w Husborne Crawley and Ridgmont *St Alb*
RIDING MILL (St James) *Newc 3* **P** *Viscount Allendale* **V** M F FENWICK
RIDLEY (St Peter) *Roch 1* **P** *J R A B Scott Esq* **R** L W G KEVIS
RIDLINGTON (St Mary Magdalene and St Andrew) *see* Preston and Ridlington w Wing and Pilton *Pet*
RIDLINGTON (St Peter) *see* Bacton w Edingthorpe w Witton and Ridlington *Nor*
RIDWARES and Kings Bromley, The *Lich 1* **P** *Bp, Lord Leigh, and D&C (jt)* **R** F FINCH, **C** J G LISTER
RIEVAULX (St Mary) *see* Helmsley *York*
RIGSBY (St James) *see* Alford w Rigsby *Linc*
RIGTON, NORTH (St John) *see* Kirkby Overblow *Ripon*
RILLINGTON (St Andrew) w Scampston, Wintringham and Thorpe Bassett *York 2* **P** *Major G R H Cholmley* **V** F B WILLIAMS
RIMPTON (The Blessed Virgin Mary) *see* Chilton Cantelo, Ashington, Mudford, Rimpton etc *B & W*
RIMSWELL (St Mary) *see* Owthorne and Rimswell w Withernsea *York*
RINGLAND (St Peter) *see* Taverham w Ringland *Nor*
RINGLEY (St Saviour) (St Aidan) w Prestolee *Man 14* **P** *R Prestwich St Mary* **P-in-c** F R COOKE
RINGMER (St Mary the Virgin) *Chich 18* **P** *Abp* **V** H M MOSELEY, **NSM** J R LOWERSON
RINGMORE (All Hallows) *see* Modbury, Bigbury, Ringmore w Kingston etc *Ex*
RINGSFIELD (All Saints) *see* Wainford *St E*
RINGSHALL (St Catherine) w Battisford, Barking w Darmsden and Great Bricett *St E 1* **P** *Bp, Ch Patr Trust, and J C W de la Bere Esq (jt)* **P-in-c** C A GRAY

RINGSTEAD (Nativity of the Blessed Virgin Mary) *see* Denford w Ringstead *Pet*
RINGSTEAD (St Andrew) *see* Hunstanton St Edm w Ringstead *Nor*
RINGSTONE IN AVELAND Group, The *Linc 13* **P** *Bp (2 turns), Baroness Willoughby de Eresby and Charterhouse (1 turn)* **R** G A CURTIS
RINGWAY (All Saints) and St Mary *Ches 10* **P** *Bp* **V** S R MARSH
RINGWOOD (St Peter and St Paul) *Win 8* **P** *K Coll Cam* **V** J R TURPIN, **C** P FURBER
RINGWOULD (St Nicholas) w Kingsdown *Cant 8* **P** *R S C Monins Esq and Ch Patr Trust (jt)* **P-in-c** K F ARVIDSSON
RIPE (St John the Baptist) *see* Laughton w Ripe and Chalvington *Chich*
RIPLEY (All Saints) *Derby 12* **P** *Wright Trustees* **V** R P FULLER
RIPLEY (All Saints) *Ripon 3* **P** *Sir Thomas Ingilby, Bt* **P-in-c** S J BROWN
RIPLEY (St Mary) *Guildf 12* **P** *Bp* **V** C J ELSON
RIPON (Holy Trinity) *Ripon 3* **P** *Simeon's Trustees* **V** D MANN, **NSM** J A MONTGOMERY
RIPON St Peter and St Wilfrid (Cathedral Church) *Ripon 3* **P** *The Crown* **V** *Vacant*
RIPPINGALE (St Andrew) *see* Ringstone in Aveland Gp *Linc*
RIPPLE (St Mary the Virgin) *see* Gt Mongeham w Ripple and Sutton by Dover *Cant*
RIPPLE (St Mary), Earls Croome w Hill Croome and Strensham *Worc 5* **P** *Bp (1 turn), Mrs A J Hyde-Smith and Mrs A L Wynne (1 turn)* **R** C G HARDWICK
RIPPONDEN (St Bartholomew) *Wakef 4* **P** *Bp and V Halifax (jt)* **NSM** M JAMES
RISBY (St Giles) w Great Saxham, Little Saxham and Westley *St E 13* **P** *Ld Chan, Trustees Sir William Stirling, and DBP (by turn)* **R** C J ROGERS
RISE (All Saints) *see* Sigglesthorne and Rise w Nunkeeling and Bewholme *York*
RISEHOLME (St Mary) *see* Nettleham *Linc*
RISELEY (All Saints) w Bletsoe *St Alb 15* **P** *MMCET* **V** D J BOURNE
RISHTON (St Peter and St Paul) *Blackb 8* **P** *Trustees* **V** P A SMITH
RISHWORTH (St John) *see* Ripponden *Wakef*
RISLEY (All Saints) *Derby 13* **P** *Bp* **P-in-c** I E GOODING
RISSINGTONS, The (St John the Baptist) (St Peter) *Glouc 15* **P** *C T R Wingfield Esq, Ld Chan, and DBP (by turn)* **P-in-c** S MOTH
RITCHINGS PARK (St Leonard) *see* Iver *Ox*
RIVENHALL (St Mary the Virgin and All Saints) *Chelmsf 24* **P** *DBP* **R** N S COOPER
RIVER (St Peter and St Paul) *Cant 4* **P** *Abp* **R** P W A BOWERS, **NSM** L R CRUTTENDEN
RIVERHEAD (St Mary) w Dunton Green *Roch 9* **P** *R Sevenoaks and Bp (jt)* **V** G T CUNLIFFE
RIVERSIDE: Colnbrook, Datchet, Dorney, Eton, Eton Wick, Horton, Wraysbury *Ox 23* **P** *Patr Bd* **TR** W L KNIGHT, **TV** P A REYNOLDS, J A HARPER, P W ABRAHAMS
RIVINGTON (not known) *see* Horwich and Rivington *Man*
ROADE (St Mary the Virgin) and Ashton w Hartwell *Pet 5* **P** *Ld Chan and Bp (alt)* **V** H W WEBB
ROADHEAD Kinkry Hill (Mission Room) *see* Bewcastle, Stapleton and Kirklinton etc *Carl*
ROADWATER (St Luke) *see* Old Cleeve, Leighland and Treborough *B & W*
ROBERTSBRIDGE (Mission Room) *see* Salehurst *Chich*
ROBERTTOWN (All Saints) *Wakef 8* **P** *V Birstall* **P-in-c** N H S BERSWEDEN, **NSM** J A BERSWEDEN
ROBOROUGH *see* Bickleigh (Roborough) and Shaugh Prior *Ex*
ROBOROUGH (St Peter) *see* Newton Tracey, Horwood, Alverdiscott etc *Ex*
ROBY (St Bartholomew) *Liv 2* **P** *Bp* **V** G S PEARSON, **C** A J COLMER
ROCESTER (St Michael) and Croxden w Hollington *Lich 15* **P** *Bp and Trustees (jt)* **V** J B HALL
ROCHDALE Deeplish (St Luke) *Man 20* **P** *Bp* **V** R F CUTLER
ROCHDALE (St Chad) (St John the Divine) *Man 20* **P** *Bp* **TV** G C DOBBS, C A POWELL, D FINNEY, **NSM** I G KAY
ROCHDALE (St George w St Alban) *Man 20* **P** *Bp* **V** J B KELLY
ROCHE (St Gomonda of the Rock) and Withiel *Truro 1* **P** *Bp and DBP (jt)* **R** E B L BROWNING
ROCHESTER (St Justus) *Roch 5* **P** *Bp* **V** J G C LAWRENCE
ROCHESTER (St Margaret) (St Peter's Parish Centre) *Roch 5* **P** *Bp and D&C (jt)* **V** R THOMSON, **C** M ILYAS, **NSM** H DAUBNEY
ROCHESTER ROW (St Stephen) *see* Westmr St Steph w St Jo *Lon*
ROCHFORD (St Andrew) *Chelmsf 12* **P** *Bp* **P-in-c** D J WILLIAMS, **NSM** J M HILL
ROCHFORD (St Michael) *see* Teme Valley S *Worc*
ROCK (St Peter and St Paul) *see* Mamble w Bayton, Rock w Heightington etc *Worc*
ROCK (St Philip and St James) *see* Embleton w Rennington and Rock *Newc*
ROCK FERRY (St Peter) *Ches 1* **P** *Bp* **V** R C TOAN, **C** M D HARRIES
ROCKBEARE (St Mary w St Andrew) *see* Aylesbeare, Rockbeare, Farringdon etc *Ex*
ROCKBOURNE (St Andrew) *see* W Downland *Sarum*
ROCKCLIFFE (St Mary the Virgin) and Blackford *Carl 2* **P** *D&C* **V** R D A TANKARD
ROCKHAMPTON (St Oswald) *see* Falfield w Rockhampton *Glouc*
ROCKINGHAM (St Leonard) *see* Gretton w Rockingham *Pet*
ROCKLAND (All Saints) *see* Gt and Lt Ellingham, Rockland and Shropham etc *Nor*
ROCKLAND (St Peter) *as above*
ROCKLAND ST MARY (St Mary) with Hellington, Bramerton, Surlingham, Claxton, Carleton St Peter and Kirby Bedon w Whitlingham *Nor 8* **P** *Bp, Adn Nor, MMCET, and BNC Ox (jt)* **R** C WHEELER
RODBOROUGH (St Mary Magdalene) *Glouc 8* **P** *Bp* **R** S J RIGGS
RODBOURNE (Holy Rood) *see* Gt Somerford, Lt Somerford, Seagry, Corston etc *Bris*
RODBOURNE CHENEY (St Mary) *Bris 10* **P** *Patr Bd* **TR** G W CREES, **TV** R W ADAMS, **NSM** A J DEAN
RODDEN (All Saints) *see* Beckington w Standerwick, Berkley, Rodden etc *B & W*
RODE, NORTH (St Michael) *see* Bosley and N Rode w Wincle and Wildboarclough *Ches*
RODE HEATH (Good Shepherd) *see* Odd Rode *Ches*
RODE MAJOR (Christ Church) *B & W 4* **P** *Bp* **P-in-c** T V COOK
RODHUISH (St Bartholomew) *see* Dunster, Carhampton and Withycombe w Rodhuish *B & W*
RODING, HIGH (All Saints) *see* Gt Canfield w High Roding and Aythorpe Roding *Chelmsf*
RODING, HIGH (Mission Hall) *as above*
RODINGTON (St George) *see* Wrockwardine Deanery *Lich*
RODLEY (Ecumenical Centre) *see* Bramley *Ripon*
RODLEY (Mission Church) *see* Westbury-on-Severn w Flaxley and Blaisdon *Glouc*
RODMARTON (St Peter) *see* Coates, Rodmarton and Sapperton etc *Glouc*
RODMELL (St Peter) *see* Iford w Kingston and Rodmell *Chich*
RODMERSHAM (St Nicholas) *see* Tunstall w Rodmersham *Cant*
RODNEY STOKE (St Leonard) w Draycott *B & W 1* **P** *Bp* **P-in-c** J C HALL
ROEHAMPTON (Holy Trinity) *S'wark 19* **P** *Bp* **V** J A McKINNEY, **C** A N TREDENNICK
ROFFEY (All Saints) *see* Roughey *Chich*
ROGATE (St Bartholomew) w Terwick and Trotton w Chithurst *Chich 10* **P** *Ld Chan* **R** R S STRINGER
ROGERS LANE (St Andrew's Chapel) *see* Stoke Poges *Ox*
ROKEBY (St Mary) *see* Startforth and Bowes and Rokeby w Brignall *Ripon*
ROKER (St Aidan) *see* Monkwearmouth *Dur*
ROLLESBY (St George) w Burgh w Billockby w Ashby w Oby, Thurne and Clippesby *Nor 6* **P** *Bp, R J H Tacon Esq, and DBP (jt)* **R** *Vacant* (01493) 740323
ROLLESTON (Holy Trinity) w Fiskerton, Morton and Upton *S'well 15* **P** *Ld Chan* **V** *Vacant* (01636) 830331
ROLLESTON (St John the Baptist) *see* Billesdon and Skeffington *Leic*
ROLLESTON (St Mary) *Lich 14* **P** *MMCET* **R** M D BIRT
ROLLRIGHT, GREAT (St Andrew) *see* Hook Norton w Gt Rollright, Swerford etc *Ox*
ROLLRIGHT, LITTLE (St Phillip) *see* Lt Compton w Chastleton, Cornwell etc *Ox*
ROLVENDEN (St Mary the Virgin) *Cant 11* **P** *Abp* **P-in-c** A E WILLIAMS
ROMALDKIRK (St Romald) w Laithkirk *Ripon 2* **P** *Bp and Earl of Strathmore's Trustees (alt)* **R** *Vacant* (01833) 650202
ROMANBY (St James) *see* Northallerton w Kirby Sigston *York*
ROMANSLEIGH (St Rumon) *see* S Molton w Nymet St George, High Bray etc *Ex*
ROMFORD (Ascension) Collier Row *Chelmsf 2* **P** *Trustees* **V** G P LAUT
ROMFORD (Good Shepherd) Collier Row *Chelmsf 2* **P** *CPAS* **V** R C SAMME, **C** P J COOK
ROMFORD (St Alban) *Chelmsf 2* **P** *Bp* **V** R S P HINGLEY

ROMFORD (St Andrew) (St Agnes) *Chelmsf 2* **P** *New Coll Ox* **R** B J LEWIS, **C** P A KENNEDY
ROMFORD (St Augustine) Rush Green *see* Rush Green *Chelmsf*
ROMFORD (St Edward the Confessor) *Chelmsf 2* **P** *New Coll Ox* **V** S J WAINE, **C** R HAGGIS, **NSM** B C DENNIS
ROMFORD (St John the Divine) *Chelmsf 2* **P** *Bp* **V** G P LAW
ROMILEY (St Chad) *see* Chadkirk *Ches*
ROMNEY, NEW (St Nicholas) w OLD (St Clement) and Midley *Cant 13* **P** *Abp* **P-in-c** J H COLEMAN, **Hon C** A M CLARKE, **NSM** M A GOOCH
ROMSEY (St Mary and St Ethelflaeda) *Win 11* **P** *Bp* **V** N C JONES, **C** D J SIMPSON, **NSM** D F WILLIAMS
ROMSLEY (St Kenelm) *Worc 9* **P** *R Halesowen* **R** *Vacant* (01562) 710216
ROOKERY, THE (St Saviour) *see* Mow Cop *Lich*
ROOKHOPE (St John the Evangelist) *see* Eastgate w Rookhope *Dur*
ROOS (All Saints) and Garton in Holderness w Tunstall, Grimston and Hilston *York 13* **P** *Abp (1 turn), SMF (2 turns)* **P-in-c** P MOATE
ROOSE (St Perran) *see* Barrow St Geo w St Luke *Carl*
ROPLEY (St Peter) *see* Bishop's Sutton and Ropley and W Tisted *Win*
ROPSLEY (St Peter) *Linc 14* **P** *Bp* **R** *Vacant*
ROSE ASH (St Peter) *see* Bishopsnympton, Rose Ash, Mariansleigh etc *Ex*
ROSEDALE (St Lawrence) *see* Lastingham w Appleton-le-Moors, Rosedale etc *York*
ROSHERVILLE (St Mark) *Roch 4* **P** *DBP* **V** P J DAVIES
ROSLEY (Holy Trinity) *see* Westward, Rosley-w-Woodside and Welton *Carl*
ROSLISTON (St Mary) *see* Walton on Trent w Croxall etc *Derby*
ROSS (St Mary the Virgin) w Brampton Abbotts, Bridstow, Peterstow, Weston-under-Penyard, Hope Mansel and The Lea *Heref 8* **P** *DBP* **TR** R STIRRUP, **TV** T M ALBAN-JONES
ROSSINGTON (St Michael) *Sheff 10* **P** *Bp* **R** M J SECCOMBE
ROSSINGTON, NEW (St Luke) *Sheff 10* **P** *Bp* **V** P F GASCOIGNE
ROSTHERNE (St Mary) w Bollington *Ches 12* **P** *C L S Cornwall-Legh Esq* **V** N D ROGERS
ROTHBURY (All Saints) *Newc 9* **P** *Duchy of Lanc* **R** L F T EDDERSHAW, **Hon C** A E TREWEEKS
ROTHERBY (All Saints) *see* Upper Wreake *Leic*
ROTHERFIELD (St Denys) w Mark Cross *Chich 19* **P** *Bp, Adn Lewes and Hastings, and Ch Patr Trust (jt)* **P-in-c** D J CLEEVES
ROTHERFIELD GREYS (Holy Trinity) *Ox 6* **P** *R Rotherfield Greys St Nich* **V** D R B CARTER
ROTHERFIELD GREYS (St Nicholas) *Ox 6* **P** *Trin Coll Ox* **R** B G BUTLER-SMITH
ROTHERFIELD PEPPARD (All Saints) *Ox 6* **P** *Jes Coll Ox* **R** B G BUTLER-SMITH
ROTHERHAM (All Saints) *Sheff 6* **P** *Bp* **V** R W B ATKINSON, **NSM** M WATERS
ROTHERHAM Ferham Park (St Paul) *see* Masbrough *Sheff*
ROTHERHITHE (Holy Trinity) *S'wark 6* **P** *R Rotherhithe St Mary* **C** J WADSWORTH
ROTHERHITHE (St Katharine) *see* Bermondsey St Kath w St Bart *S'wark*
ROTHERHITHE (St Mary) w All Saints *S'wark 6* **P** *Clare Coll Cam* **R** C E N RICHARDS, **Hon C** P J HINCHEY
ROTHERSTHORPE (St Peter and St Paul) *see* Bugbrooke w Rothersthorpe *Pet*
ROTHERWICK (not known) *see* Heckfield w Mattingley and Rotherwick *Win*
ROTHLEY (St Mary the Virgin and St John the Baptist) *Leic 6* **P** *MMCET* **V** N BAINES, **C** E J SEWELL
ROTHWELL (Holy Trinity) *Ripon 8* **P** *Bp* **V** P R CRESSALL, **C** P A BICKNELL, **NSM** G W SELLERS
ROTHWELL (Holy Trinity) w Orton and Rushton w Glendon and Pipwell *Pet 11* **P** *Hosp of Jes (1 turn), Bp (2 turns), J Hipwell Esq (1 turn),and Mert Coll Ox (1 turn)* **R** P R ROSE
ROTHWELL (St Mary the Virgin) *see* Swallow *Linc*
ROTTINGDEAN (St Margaret) *Chich 2* **P** *Bp* **V** M P MORGAN, **C** D G LLOYD-JAMES
ROUGH CLOSE (St Matthew) *see* Meir Heath *Lich*
ROUGH COMMON (St Gabriel) *see* Harbledown *Cant*
ROUGH HAY (St Christopher) *see* Darlaston St Lawr *Lich*
ROUGH HILLS (St Martin) *Lich 29* **P** *Bp* **V** J C OAKES
ROUGHAM (St Mary) *see* Castle Acre w Newton, Rougham and Southacre *Nor*
ROUGHAM (St Mary), Beyton w Hessett and Rushbrooke *St E 10* **P** *MMCET, CPAS, Ld Chan, Mrs V J Clarke, and Bp (by turn)* **R** G H CLOTHIER, **C** A W SPENCER
ROUGHEY or Roffey (All Saints) *Chich 8* **P** *Bp* **V** *Vacant* (01403) 265333
ROUGHTON (St Margaret) *see* Thornton Gp *Linc*
ROUGHTON (St Mary) and Felbrigg, Metton, Sustead, Bessingham and Gunton w Hanworth *Nor 21* **P** *Bp and Exors G Whately (jt)* **R** K E A JAMES
ROUGHTOWN (St John the Baptist) *Man 17* **P** *Bp* **P-in-c** R A ANDERSON
ROUNDHAY (St Edmund) *Ripon 5* **P** *Bp* **V** S C COWLING, **C** J C TREW
ROUNDHAY (St John the Evangelist) *Ripon 5* **P** *DBF* **V** R G PLACE
ROUNDS GREEN (St James) *Birm 7* **P** *V Langley* **V** J F N ROBINSON
ROUNDSHAW Conventional District *S'wark 25* **C-in-c** J B GOULD
ROUNDSWELL Conventional District *Ex 15* **C-in-c** A C BING
ROUNTON, WEST (St Oswald) and East (St Laurence) w Welbury *York 20* **P** *Ld Chan* **P-in-c** T L JONES
ROUS LENCH (St Peter) *see* Church Lench w Rous Lench and Abbots Morton *Worc*
ROUSHAM (St Leonard and St James) *see* The Heyfords w Rousham and Somerton *Ox*
ROUTH (All Saints) *York 9* **P** *Ch Soc Trust and Reformation Ch Trust (jt)* **R** *Vacant*
ROWBERROW (St Michael and All Angels) *see* Axbridge w Shipham and Rowberrow *B & W*
ROWDE (St Matthew) and Poulshot *Sarum 19* **P** *Bp and DBP (alt)* **P-in-c** R J PRESS
ROWENFIELD (Emmanuel) *see* Cheltenham St Mark *Glouc*
ROWINGTON (St Lawrence) *see* Hatton w Haseley, Rowington w Lowsonford etc *Cov*
ROWLAND LUBBOCK (Memorial Hall) *see* E Horsley *Guildf*
ROWLANDS CASTLE (St John the Baptist) *Portsm 4* **P** *Bp* **R** N STUART-LEE
ROWLANDS GILL (St Barnabas) *see* High Spen and Rowlands Gill *Dur*
ROWLEDGE (St James) *Guildf 3* **P** *Adn Surrey* **V** C J RICHARDSON
ROWLESTONE (St Peter) *see* Ewyas Harold w Dulas, Kenderchurch etc *Heref*
ROWLEY (St Peter) w Skidby *York 9* **P** *Abp and Sir David Hildyard (jt)* **NSM** H McCOUBREY
ROWLEY REGIS (St Giles) *Birm 7* **P** *Ld Chan* **V** J B NIGHTINGALE, **C** E M HATCHMAN
ROWNER (St Mary the Virgin) *Portsm 3* **P** *R J F Prideaux-Brune Esq* **R** J W DRAPER
ROWNEY GREEN (Mission Chapel) *see* Alvechurch *Worc*
ROWSLEY (St Katherine) *Derby 2* **P** *Duke of Rutland* **P-in-c** E D MILROY
ROWSTON (St Clement) *see* Digby *Linc*
ROWTON (All Hallows) *see* Wrockwardine Deanery *Lich*
ROXBOURNE (St Andrew) *Lon 23* **P** *Bp* **V** D J COCKBILL, **C** I A WILLIAMSON
ROXBY (St Mary) *see* Winterton Gp *Linc*
ROXBY (St Nicholas) *see* Hinderwell w Roxby *York*
ROXETH (Christ Church) *Lon 23* **P** *Patr Bd* **TR** B C COLLINS, **TV** A J HULME, R M GOLDENBERG, **C** P S MACKENZIE, H D KENDAL
ROXHOLME *see* Leasingham *Linc*
ROXTON (St Mary Magdalene) w Great Barford *St Alb 11* **P** *Trin Coll Cam* **V** L G BLANCHARD
ROXWELL (St Michael and All Angels) *Chelmsf 8* **P** *New Coll Ox* **P-in-c** V W HYDON
ROYDON (All Saints) *see* Grimston, Congham and Roydon *Nor*
ROYDON (St Peter) *Chelmsf 26* **P** *Earl Cowley* **V** P J COLLINS
ROYDON (St Remigius) *Nor 10* **P** *DBP* **P-in-c** W M C BESTELINK
ROYSTON (St John the Baptist) *St Alb 19* **P** *Bp* **V** L D HARMAN, **C** C E MIER, **NSM** J H FIDLER
ROYSTON (St John the Baptist) *Wakef 7* **P** *Bp* **V** J L HUDSON, **C** J A BOOTH
ROYTON (St Anne) Longsight *Man 22* **P** *Bp* **V** D SHARPLES, **C** W E BRAVINER, **NSM** D J HALFORD
ROYTON (St Paul) *Man 22* **P** *R Prestwich St Mary* **V** D BOOTH
RUAN LANIHORNE (St Rumon) *see* Veryan w Ruan Lanihorne *Truro*
RUAN MINOR (St Rumon) *see* St Ruan w St Grade and Landewednack *Truro*
RUARDEAN (St John the Baptist) *Glouc 4* **P** *Bp* **R** C T DAVIES, **NSM** W J CAMMELL
RUBERY (St Chad) *Birm 4* **P** *The Crown* **V** J J J BARRETT

RUCKINGE (St Mary Magdalene) *see* Orlestone w Snave and Ruckinge w Warehorne *Cant*
RUCKLAND (St Olave) *see* S Ormsby Gp *Linc*
RUDBY IN CLEVELAND (All Saints) w Middleton *York 22* **P** *Abp* **V** D F LICKESS
RUDDINGTON (St Peter) *S'well 10* **P** *Simeon's Trustees* **V** F G HARRISON
RUDFORD (St Mary the Virgin) *see* Highnam, Lassington, Rudford, Tibberton etc *Glouc*
RUDGWICK (Holy Trinity) *Chich 8* **P** *Ld Chan* **V** J D MORRIS
RUDHAM, EAST and WEST (St Mary), Houghton-next-Harpley, Tattersett and Tatterford *Nor 15* **P** *Most Revd G D Hand, Bp, Marquess of Cholmondeley, and Marquess Townshend (by turn)* **R** *Vacant* (01485) 528756
RUDHEATH (Licensed Room) *see* Witton *Ches*
RUDSTON (All Saints) Boynton and Kilham *York 10* **P** *Abp (2 turns), Ld Chan (1 turn)* **V** S V COPE
RUFFORD (St Mary the Virgin) *Blackb 6* **P** *Bp* **R** J D BURNS
RUFFORTH (All Saints) w Moor Monkton and Hessay *York 1* **P** *MMCET and Abp (alt)* **R** J A RENDALL, **P-in-c** P E JARAM, **NSM** J E CHAPMAN
RUGBY (St Andrew) (St George) (St John) (St Peter) (St Philip) *Cov 6* **P** *Bp* **TR** E F CONDRY, **TV** A R STEVENS, E J SMITH, P M de la P BERESFORD, **NSM** P A MARTINDALE, D M CHARLES-EDWARDS, S E ENEVER
RUGBY (St Matthew) *Cov 6* **P** *Ch Trust Fund Trust* **V** M P SAXBY
RUGELEY (St Augustine) (Good Shepherd) *Lich 3* **P** *Patr Bd* **TR** M J NEWMAN
RUISHTON (St George) w Thornfalcon *B & W 18* **P** *Bp and Dr W R Chisholm-Batten (alt)* **V** D F GOODFIELD
RUISLIP (St Martin) *Lon 24* **P** *D&C Windsor* **V** S EVANS, **C** R G THOMPSON
RUISLIP (St Mary) *Lon 24* **P** *Bp* **V** B G COPUS
RUISLIP MANOR (St Paul) *Lon 24* **P** *Bp* **V** A C BALL, **NSM** B C ALLEN
RUMBURGH (St Michael and All Angels and St Felix) *see* S Elmham and Ilketshall *St E*
RUNCORN (All Saints) *Ches 3* **P** *Ch Ch Ox* **P-in-c** J H A HAYES, **C** M D HOCKNULL
RUNCORN (Holy Trinity) *Ches 3* **P** *Bp* **P-in-c** D R FELIX, **C** D E WATSON
RUNCORN (St John the Evangelist) Weston *Ches 3* **P** *Bp* **V** J BRONNERT
RUNCORN (St Michael and All Angels) *Ches 3* **P** *Bp* **P-in-c** J H A HAYES, **C** M D HOCKNULL
RUNCTON, NORTH (All Saints) *see* W Winch w Setchey and N Runcton *Nor*
RUNCTON, SOUTH (St Andrew) *see* Holme Runcton w S Runcton and Wallington *Ely*
RUNCTON HOLME (St James) *as above*
RUNHALL (All Saints) *see* Barnham Broom *Nor*
RUNHAM (St Peter and St Paul) *see* Filby, Thrigby, Mautby, Stokesby, Runham etc *Nor*
RUNNINGTON (St Peter and St Paul) *see* Wellington and Distr *B & W*
RUNTON (Holy Trinity) *see* Aylmerton w Runton *Nor*
RUNTON, EAST (St Andrew) *as above*
RUNWELL (St Mary) *see* Wickford and Runwell *Chelmsf*
RUSCOMBE (St James the Great) and Twyford *Ox 16* **P** *Bp* **V** G R HAMBORG, **NSM** D FOOTE
RUSH GREEN (St Augustine) Romford *Chelmsf 2* **P** *Bp* **V** S SWIFT, **NSM** D HENDERSON
RUSHALL (Christ the King) (St Michael the Archangel) *Lich 26* **P** *Sir Andrew Buchanan, Bt and H C S Buchanan Esq (jt)* **V** D P LINGWOOD
RUSHALL (St Mary) *see* Dickleburgh, Langmere, Shimpling, Thelveton etc *Nor*
RUSHALL (St Matthew) *see* Uphavon w Rushall and Charlton *Sarum*
RUSHBROOKE (St Nicholas) *see* Rougham, Beyton w Hessett and Rushbrooke *St E*
RUSHBURY (St Peter) *Heref 11* **P** *Bp Birm* **R** M BROMFIELD
RUSHDEN (St Mary) *see* Sandon, Wallington and Rushden w Clothall *St Alb*
RUSHDEN (St Mary) (St Peter) (St Mark) w Newton Bromswold *Pet 10* **P** *CPAS* **TV** Q D CHANDLER, **C** A G KAYE, **NSM** E J TYE
RUSHEN Christ Church (Holy Trinity) *S & M 1* **P** *The Crown* **V** F H BIRD
RUSHEY MEAD (St Theodore of Canterbury) *see* Leic St Theodore *Leic*
RUSHFORD (St John the Evangelist) *see* E w W Harling, Bridgham w Roudham, Larling etc *Nor*
RUSHLAKE GREEN (Little St Mary) *see* Warbleton and Bodle Street Green *Chich*
RUSHMERE (St Andrew) *St E 4* **P** *Bp* **V** R B THOMPSON, **C** M BROSNAN
RUSHMERE (St Michael) *see* Carlton Colville w Mutford and Rushmere *Nor*
RUSHMOOR (St Francis) *see* Churt *Guildf*
RUSHOCK (St Michael) *see* Elmley Lovett w Hampton Lovett and Elmbridge etc *Worc*
RUSHOLME (Holy Trinity) *Man 4* **P** *CPAS* **R** A PORTER, **C** J M SHEPHERD
RUSHTON (All Saints) *see* Rothwell w Orton, Rushton w Glendon and Pipewell *Pet*
RUSHTON SPENCER *see* Horton, Lonsdon and Rushton Spencer *Lich*
RUSKIN PARK (St Saviour) *see* Herne Hill *S'wark*
RUSKINGTON (All Saints) *Linc 22* **P** *DBP* **P-in-c** G P WILLIAMS
RUSLAND (St Paul) *Carl 10* **P** *Mrs C M Chaplin* **NSM** D HARRISON
RUSPER (St Mary Magdalene) w Colgate *Chich 8* **P** *Mrs E C Calvert and Bp (alt)* **R** N A FLINT, **C** P H ADDENBROOKE
RUSTHALL (St Paul) (St Paul's Mission Church) *Roch 12* **P** *R Speldhurst* **V** R E WHYTE, **C** A F PLEDGER, **NSM** S E SUDDABY
RUSTINGTON (St Peter and St Paul) *Chich 1* **P** *Bp* **V** K L MASTERS
RUSTON, SOUTH *see* Tunstead w Sco' Ruston *Nor*
RUSTON PARVA (St Nicholas) *see* Burton Agnes w Harpham and Lowthorpe etc *York*
RUSWARP (St Bartholomew) *see* Aislaby and Ruswarp *York*
RUYTON XI TOWNS (St John the Baptist) w Great Ness and Little Ness *Lich 17* **P** *Bp and Guild of All So (jt) and Ld Chan (alt)* **V** R D BRADBURY
RYAL (All Saints) *see* Stamfordham w Matfen *Newc*
RYARSH (St Martin) *see* Birling, Addington, Ryarsh and Trottiscliffe *Roch*
RYBURGH, GREAT (St Andrew) and LITTLE w Gateley and Testerton *Nor 15* **P** *Ch Coll Cam* **R** *Vacant*
RYDAL (St Mary) *Carl 10* **P** *Bp* **P-in-c** M A KITCHENER
RYDE (All Saints) *Portsm 7* **P** *Bp* **V** D W DALE, **NSM** E W BUTCHER, T I CARD
RYDE (Holy Trinity) *Portsm 7* **P** *Bp* **V** M F JONES, **NSM** T F SEAR, M D H JOHNSTON
RYDE (St James) Proprietary Chapel *Portsm 7* **P** *Ch Soc Trust Vacant*
RYDE (St John) *see* Oakfield St Jo *Portsm*
RYE (St Mary the Virgin) *Chich 20* **P** *Patr Bd* **TR** M SHEPPARD, **TV** A V BOWMAN, J A WHITING, **NSM** M N HARPER
RYE HARBOUR (Holy Spirit) *see* Rye *Chich*
RYE PARK (St Cuthbert) *St Alb 20* **P** *DBP* **V** H J SPANNER
RYECROFT (St Nicolas) Rawmarsh *Sheff 6* **P** *Bp* **V** S P PICKERING
RYEDALE, UPPER *York 18* **P** *Abp, Adn Cleveland, R G Beckett Esq, and Exors Capt V M Wombwell (jt)* **R** *Vacant* (01439) 798355
RYHALL (St John the Evangelist) w Essendine and Carlby *Pet 8* **P** *Burghley Ho Preservation Trust* **V** P J McKEE
RYHILL (St James) *Wakef 9* **P** *Bp* **V** A W H ASHDOWN
RYHOPE (St Paul) *Dur 16* **P** *Bp* **NSM** R N TEMPERLEY
RYLSTONE (St Peter) *see* Burnsall w Rylstone *Bradf*
RYME INTRINSECA (St Hypolytus) *see* Yetminster w Ryme Intrinseca and High Stoy *Sarum*
RYPE (St John the Baptist) *see* Laughton w Ripe and Chalvington *Chich*
RYSTON (St Michael) w Roxham *Ely 16* **P** *Bp* **P-in-c** J K ISAACS
RYTHER (All Saints) *York 6* **P** *Ld Chan* **P-in-c** A STOKER
RYTON (Holy Cross) w Hedgefield *Dur 13* **P** *Bp* **R** T L JAMIESON
RYTON (Mission Chapel) *see* Condover w Frodesley, Acton Burnell etc *Heref*
RYTON (St Andrew) *see* Beckbury, Badger, Kemberton, Ryton, Stockton etc *Lich*
RYTON ON DUNSMORE (St Leonard) w Bubbenhall *Cov 6* **P** *Bp (1 turn), Provost & Chapter (2 turns)* **V** J T SYKES
SABDEN (St Nicholas) and Pendleton-in-Whalley (All Saints) *Blackb 8* **P** *Bp and Trustees (jt)* **V** R NICHOLSON
SACKLETON (St George the Martyr) *see* Street TM *York*
SACOMBE (St Catherine) *see* The Mundens w Sacombe *St Alb*
SACRISTON (St Peter) and Kimblesworth *Dur 1* **P** *The Crown* **P-in-c** N M JAY
SADBERGE (St Andrew) *Dur 8* **P** *Bp* **P-in-c** R J COOPER
SADDINGTON (St Helen) *see* Kibworth and Smeeton Westerby and Saddington *Leic*
SADDLEWORTH (St Chad) (Parochial Hall) *Man 21* **P** *Bp* **P-in-c** M J R TINKER, **NSM** G B ADAMS, D RHODES

SAFFRON WALDEN (St Mary) w Wendens Ambo and Littlebury *Chelmsf 22* **P** *Patr Bd* **TR** D J GREEN, **TV** L BOND, **C** R W FINCH
SAHAM TONEY (St George) *see* Ashill w Saham Toney *Nor*
ST AGNES (St Agnes) *Truro 6* **P** *D&C* **V** M J ADAMS
ST AGNES (St Agnes) *see* Is of Scilly *Truro*
ST ALBANS (Christ Church) *St Alb 6* **P** *Trustees* **V** B UNDERWOOD
ST ALBANS (St Luke) *St Alb 6* **P** *DBP* **V** P G RICH, **Par Dn** E G HARLOW
ST ALBANS (St Mary) Marshalswick *St Alb 6* **P** *Bp* **V** R E PYKE
ST ALBANS (St Michael) *St Alb 6* **P** *Earl of Verulam* **V** T M BEAUMONT, **NSM** J A HAYTON
ST ALBANS (St Paul) *St Alb 6* **P** *V St Alb St Pet* **V** A R HURLE, **C** L J BIGGS, **Hon C** G M ABBOTT, **NSM** L M HURLE
ST ALBANS (St Peter) *St Alb 6* **P** *The Crown* **V** D J BRENTNALL, **C** M G GREENSTREET
ST ALBANS (St Saviour) *St Alb 6* **P** *Bp* **V** B P MOORE, **NSM** M R MUGAN
ST ALBANS (St Stephen) *St Alb 6* **P** *J N W Dudley Esq* **V** C D FUTCHER, **NSM** L C HALL
ST ALLEN (St Alleyne) *see* Kenwyn w St Allen *Truro*
ST ANNES-ON-THE-SEA (St Anne) *see* Heyhouses on Sea *Blackb*
ST ANNES-ON-THE-SEA (St Margaret) *Blackb 11* **P** *Bp* **V** J H CATLEY, **NSM** M J THOMAS
ST ANNES-ON-THE-SEA (St Thomas) *Blackb 11* **P** *J C Hilton Esq* **V** P D LAW-JONES, **NSM** T B SCHOLZ
ST ANTHONY-IN-MENEAGE (St Anthony) *see* Manaccan w St Anthony-in-Meneage and St Martin *Truro*
ST AUSTELL (Holy Trinity) *Truro 1* **P** *The Crown* **V** A F MATTHEW, **C** G L BURN, **Hon C** A SYKES
ST BEES (St Mary and St Bega) *Carl 5* **P** *Trustees* **V** P R BRYAN
ST BLAZEY (St Blaise) *Truro 1* **P** *Bp* **V** F M BOWERS
ST BREOKE (St Breoke) and Egloshayle in Wadebridge *Truro 10* **P** *Bp and DBP (jt)* **R** B A ANDERSON
ST BREWARD (St Breward) *see* Blisland w St Breward *Truro*
ST BRIAVELS (St Mary the Virgin) w Hewelsfield *Glouc 4* **P** *D&C Heref* **P-in-c** P E PINKERTON
ST BUDEAUX *see* Devonport St Budeaux *Ex*
ST BURYAN (St Buriana), St Levan and Sennen *Truro 5* **P** *Duchy of Cornwall* **R** A H BURLTON, **NSM** C M JAGO
ST CLEER (St Clarus) *Truro 12* **P** *Ld Chan* **V** M A FRIGGENS
ST CLEMENT (St Clement) *see* Truro St Paul and St Clem *Truro*
ST CLEMENT DANES *see* St Mary le Strand w St Clem Danes *Lon*
ST CLETHER (St Clederus) *see* Altarnon w Bolventor, Laneast and St Clether *Truro*
ST COLAN (St Colan) *see* St Columb Minor and St Colan *Truro*
ST COLUMB MAJOR (St Columba) w St Wenn *Truro 7* **P** *Bp* **R** R F LAW
ST COLUMB MINOR (St Columba) and St Colan *Truro 7* **P** *Bp* **V** J F EDWARDS, **NSM** P G DAVY
ST DAY (Holy Trinity) *see* Chacewater w St Day and Carharrack *Truro*
ST DECUMANS (St Decuman) *B & W 17* **P** *Bp* **V** D C IRESON
ST DENNIS (St Denys) *Truro 1* **P** *Bp* **P-in-c** T J RUSS
ST DEVEREUX (St Dubricius) *see* Ewyas Harold w Dulas, Kenderchurch etc *Heref*
ST DOMINIC (St Dominica), Landulph and St Mellion w Pillaton *Truro 11* **P** *D&C and Trustees Major J Coryton, Duchy of Cornwall, and SMF (by turn)* **R** P R J LAMB
ST EDMUNDS Anchorage Lane Conventional District *Sheff 8* **C-in-c** S TRICKLEBANK
ST ENDELLION (St Endelienta) w Port Isaac and St Kew *Truro 10* **P** *Bp* **R** M G BARTLETT, **NSM** J POLLINGER
ST ENODER (St Enoder) *Truro 7* **P** *Bp* **P-in-c** P A ROBSON
ST ENODOC (St Enodoc) *see* St Minver *Truro*
ST ERME (St Hermes) *see* Probus, Ladock and Grampound w Creed and St Erme *Truro*
ST ERNEY (St Erney) *see* Landrake w St Erney and Botus Fleming *Truro*
ST ERTH (St Erth) *see* Godrevy *Truro*
ST ERVAN (St Ervan) *see* St Mawgan w St Ervan and St Eval *Truro*
ST EVAL (St Uvelas) *as above*
ST EWE (All Saints) *see* Mevagissey and St Ewe *Truro*
ST GENNYS (St Gennys), Jacobstow w Warbstow and Treneglos *Truro 8* **P** *Bp and Earl of St Germans (jt)* **R** *Vacant* (018403) 206
ST GEORGE-IN-THE-EAST (St Mary) *Lon 7* **P** *Bp* **V** *Vacant* 0171-790 0973
ST GEORGE-IN-THE-EAST w St Paul *Lon 7* **P** *Bp* **R** G W CRAIG, **Hon C** M J W COOK
ST GEORGES (St George) *see* Priors Lee and St Georges *Lich*
ST GERMANS (St Germans of Auxerre) *Truro 11* **P** *D&C Windsor* **V** S COFFIN, **NSM** J M LOBB
ST GILES-IN-THE-FIELDS *Lon 3* **P** *Bp* **R** G C TAYLOR, **Hon C** D K JAMESON
ST GILES-IN-THE-HEATH (St Giles) *see* Boyton, N Tamerton, Werrington etc *Truro*
ST GILES IN THE WOOD (St Giles) *see* Newton Tracey, Horwood, Alverdiscott etc *Ex*
ST GLUVIAS (St Gluvias) *Truro 3* **P** *Bp* **V** J HARRIS
ST GORAN (St Goranus) w St Michael Caerhays *Truro 1* **P** *Bp* **NSM** L MASTERS
ST HELENS (St Helen) (Barton Street Mission) (St Andrew) *Liv 10* **P** *Trustees* **TR** C H B BYWORTH, **C** C R SMITH, M NORRIS
ST HELENS (St Helen) (St Catherine by the Green) *Portsm 7* **P** *Bp* **V** J H BARKER
ST HELENS (St Mark) *Liv 10* **P** *Trustees* **P-in-c** J LABDON
ST HELENS (St Matthew) Thatto Heath *Liv 10* **P** *Bp* **V** C L BRAY
ST HELIER (St Peter) (Bishop Andrewes Church) *S'wark 24* **P** *Bp* **V** G J JENKINS, **C** P J DYKES
ST HILARY (St Hilary) w Perranuthnoe *Truro 5* **P** *D&C and Mrs S R Parker (jt)* **R** *Vacant* (01736) 710294
ST ILLOGAN (St Illogan) *Truro 2* **P** *Ch Soc Trust* **C** J S WOOD, **NSM** P I TREMELLING
ST IPPOLYTS (St Ippolyts) *St Alb 4* **P** *Bp* **V** C J N MARTIN, **Hon C** M J BREBNER
ST ISSEY (St Issey) w St Petroc Minor *Truro 7* **P** *Keble Coll Ox* **P-in-c** G C BARRETT
ST IVE (St Ive) and Pensilva w Quethiock *Truro 12* **P** *Bp (1 turn), The Crown (2 turns)* **R** R J LUCAS
ST IVES (All Saints) *Ely 11* **P** *Guild of All So* **V** J D MOORE
ST IVES (St Ia the Virgin) *Truro 5* **P** *V Lelant* **V** A N COUCH
ST JOHN (St John the Baptist) w Millbrook *Truro 11* **P** *Bp and Col Sir John Carew-Pole, Bt (alt)* **R** T W PILKINGTON
ST JOHN IN BEDWARDINE (St John the Baptist) *Worc 3* **P** *D&C* **V** C PULLIN
ST JOHN IN WEARDALE (St John the Baptist) *Dur 9* **P** *Bp* **V** D M SKELTON
ST JOHN LEE (St John of Beverley) *Newc 4* **P** *Viscount Allendale* **R** W RIGBY
ST JOHN ON BETHNAL GREEN *Lon 7* **P** *Patr Bd* **TV** B C RALPH, **NSM** R A VAUGHAN
ST JOHNS-IN-THE-VALE (St John) w Wythburn *Carl 6* **P** *Bp and V Crosthwaite (alt)* **P-in-c** B ROTHWELL
ST JOHN'S WOOD (St John) *Lon 4* **P** *Bp* **V** J SLATER, **C** P GRANDELL
ST JOHN'S WOOD (St Mark) *see* St Marylebone St Mark Hamilton Terrace *Lon*
ST JULIOT (St Julitta) *see* Boscastle w Davidstow *Truro*
ST JUST IN PENWITH (St Just) *Truro 5* **P** *Ld Chan* **V** S W LEACH
ST JUST IN ROSELAND (St Just) w Philleigh *Truro 6* **P** *A M J Galsworthy Esq and MMCET (jt)* **R** E R ANDREWS
ST KEVERNE (St Keverne) *Truro 4* **P** *CPAS* **P-in-c** T St J HAWKINS
ST KEW (St James the Great) *see* St Endellion w Port Isaac and St Kew *Truro*
ST KEYNE (St Keyna) *see* Liskeard, St Keyne, St Pinnock, Morval etc *Truro*
ST LAURENCE in the Isle of Thanet (St Laurence) *Cant 9* **P** *Patr Bd* **TR** P L DEWEY, **TV** N D PERKINSON, M J HUGHES
ST LAWRENCE (Old Church) (St Lawrence) *Portsm 7* **P** *Bp* **NSM** J A WOOLLEY, M M SLATTERY
ST LAWRENCE (St Peter's Chapel) *Chelmsf 10* **P** *Bp* **R** *Vacant*
ST LEONARD (St Leonard) *see* Hawridge w Cholesbury and St Leonard *Ox*
ST LEONARDS and St Ives (All Saints) *Win 8* **P** *Bp* **V** P G H DOORES
ST LEONARDS (Christ Church and St Mary Magdalen) *Chich 17* **P** *Bp and Trustees (jt)* **R** R M HARPER, **C** G J A COOK, **NSM** R G RALPH, D ASHTON
ST LEONARDS, UPPER (St John the Evangelist) *Chich 17* **P** *Trustees* **R** R J H WILLIAMS
ST LEONARDS-ON-SEA (St Ethelburga) *Chich 17* **P** *Hyndman Trustees* **V** B E CROSBY
ST LEONARDS-ON-SEA (St Leonard) *Chich 17* **P** *Hyndman Trustees* **R** J B CROSS
ST LEONARDS-ON-SEA (St Matthew) *see* Silverhill St Matt *Chich*

ST LEONARDS-ON-SEA (St Peter and St Paul) *Chich 17* **P** *Bp* **V** A P-A BROWN
ST LEVAN (St Levan) *see* St Buryan, St Levan and Sennen *Truro*
ST MABYN (St Mabena) *see* St Tudy w St Mabyn and Michaelstow *Truro*
ST MARGARET'S (St Margaret) *see* Clodock and Longtown w Craswall, Llanveynoe etc *Heref*
ST MARGARETS-AT-CLIFFE (St Margaret of Antioch) w Westcliffe and East Langdon w West Langdon *Cant 4* **P** *Abp* **V** A M DURKIN
ST MARGARETS ON THAMES (All Souls) *Lon 11* **P** *Bp* **P-in-c** W J MORGAN, P R TOPHAM
ST MARTHA-ON-THE-HILL (St Martha) *see* Albury w St Martha *Guildf*
ST MARTIN (St Martin) w East and West Looe *Truro 12* **P** *Bp and Revd W M M Picken (jt)* **R** B A McQUILLEN
ST MARTIN-IN-MENEAGE (St Martin) *see* Manaccan w St Anthony-in-Meneage and St Martin *Truro*
ST MARTIN-IN-THE-FIELDS *Lon 3* **P** *Bp* **V** N R HOLTAM, **C** D R M MONTEITH, C M HERBERT, **NSM** G LEE, W J RATCHFORD
ST MARTIN'S (St Martin) *Lich 19* **P** *Lord Trevor* **V** W J WEBB
ST MARTIN'S (St Martin) *see* Is of Scilly *Truro*
ST MARY ABBOTS *see* Kensington St Mary Abbots w St Geo *Lon*
ST MARY-AT-LATTON Harlow *Chelmsf 26* **P** *J L H Arkwright Esq* **V** P J BEECH, **Hon C** G R NEAVE
ST MARY BOURNE (St Peter) and Woodcott *Win 6* **P** *Bp* **V** M A COPPEN
ST MARY CRAY and St Paul's (St Paulinus) Cray *Roch 16* **P** *Bp* **V** A E COOKE
ST MARY LE STRAND w St Clement Danes *Lon 3* **P** *Ld Chan and Burley Ho Preservation Trust (alt)* **P-in-c** D WHITE
ST MARYCHURCH (St Mary the Virgin) *Ex 10* **P** *D&C* **V** K C MOSS, **C** T J HANDLEY
ST MARYLEBONE (All Saints) *Lon 4* **P** *Bp* **V** L A MOSES, **C** I E DAVIES, **Hon C** J A YOUNGER
ST MARYLEBONE (All Souls) *see* Langham Place All So *Lon*
ST MARYLEBONE (Annunciation) Bryanston Street *Lon 4* **P** *Bp* **V** M W BURGESS
ST MARYLEBONE (Holy Trinity) (St Marylebone) *Lon 4* **P** *The Crown* **R** C R GOWER, **NSM** J CALDWELL
ST MARYLEBONE (St Cyprian) *Lon 4* **P** *Bp* **V** P R HARDING, **Hon C** J D WILKINSON
ST MARYLEBONE (St Mark) Hamilton Terrace *Lon 4* **P** *The Crown* **V** J A BARRIE
ST MARYLEBONE (St Mark w St Luke) *see* Bryanston Square St Mary w St Marylebone St Mark *Lon*
ST MARYLEBONE (St Paul) *Lon 4* **P** *Prime Min* **R** J P MAPLE, **C** A R HACK
ST MARYLEBONE (St Peter) *see* Langham Place All So *Lon*
ST MARY'S (St Mary) *see* Is of Scilly *Truro*
ST MARY'S BAY (All Saints) w St Mary-in-the-Marsh (St Mary the Virgin) and Ivychurch *Cant 13* **P** *Abp* **V** J H COLEMAN, **Hon C** A M CLARKE
ST MAWES (St Mawes) *see* St Just in Roseland w Philleigh *Truro*
ST MAWGAN (St Mawgan) w St Ervan and St Eval *Truro 7* **P** *D&C and Bp (alt)* **R** J G SLEE, **C** M L BARRETT, **Hon C** F T SURRIDGE
ST MELLION (St Melanus) *see* St Dominic, Landulph and St Mellion w Pillaton *Truro*
ST MERRYN (St Merryn) *Truro 7* **P** *Bp* **NSM** B B WOODMAN
ST MEWAN (St Mewan) *Truro 1* **P** *A J M Galsworthy Esq (2 turns), Penrice Ho (St Austell) Ltd(1 turn), and DBP (1 turn)* **P-in-c** D G ADAMS, **NSM** M P C ROWETT
ST MEWAN Sticker (St Mark's Mission Church) *see* St Mewan *Truro*
ST MICHAEL PENKEVIL (St Michael) *Truro 6* **P** *Viscount Falmouth* **P-in-c** T M GOULDSTONE
ST MICHAEL ROCK (St Michael) *see* St Minver *Truro*
ST MICHAELCHURCH (St Michael) *see* N Newton w St Michaelchurch, Thurloxton etc *B & W*
ST MICHAELS ON WYRE (St Michael) *Blackb 10* **P** *R P Hornby Esq* **V** K H GIBBONS
ST MINVER (St Menefreda) *Truro 10* **P** *DBP* **V** M E PINNOCK
ST NECTAN (St Nectan) *see* Lostwithiel, St Winnow w St Nectan's Chpl etc *Truro*
ST NEOT (St Neot) and Warleggan *Truro 12* **P** *R G Grylls Esq (2 turns), DBP (1 turn)* **R** H C T OLIVEY
ST NEOTS (St Mary) *Ely 12* **P** *P W Rowley Esq* **V** R H W ARGUILE, **C** S W P HAMPTON, **Hon C** T R HENTHORNE
ST NEWLYN EAST (St Newlina) *see* Newlyn St Newlyn *Truro*
ST NICHOLAS AT WADE (St Nicholas) w Sarre and Chislet w Hoath *Cant 7* **P** *Abp* **P-in-c** R R COLES, **NSM** R D PLANT
ST OSWALD IN LEE w Bingfield (St Mary) *Newc 2* **P** *Bp* **P-in-c** C S PRICE
ST OSYTH (St Peter and St Paul) *Chelmsf 23* **P** *Bp* **V** I T WHITE
ST PANCRAS (Holy Cross) (St Jude) (St Peter) *Lon 17* **P** *Bp* **P-in-c** B D CLOVER, **C** T S P PHELAN
ST PANCRAS (Holy Trinity w St Barnabas) *see* Haverstock Hill H Trin w Kentish Town St Barn *Lon*
ST PANCRAS (Old Church) w Bedford New Town (St Matthew) *Lon 17* **P** *D&C St Paul's* **P-in-c** N P WHEELER
ST PANCRAS (St Martin) *see* Kentish Town St Martin w St Andr *Lon*
ST PANCRAS (St Pancras) (St James) (Christ Church) *Lon 17* **P** *D&C St Paul's* **P-in-c** B D CLOVER, **C** M G C YOUNG, M DAY, **Hon C** R I T JARRETT
ST PAUL'S CRAY (St Barnabas) *Roch 16* **P** *CPAS* **V** G C DAY, **C** S L WILLOUGHBY, **Hon C** J E RAWLING
ST PAUL'S WALDEN (All Saints) *St Alb 4* **P** *D&C St Paul's* **P-in-c** A P WINTON
ST PETER in the Isle of Thanet (St Peter the Apostle) (St Andrew) *Cant 9* **P** *Abp* **V** T J HENDERSON, **C** J A SAGE, J F GANGA
ST PETER-UPON-CORNHILL *see* St Pet Cornhill *Lon*
ST PETROC MINOR (St Petroc) *see* St Issey w St Petroc Minor *Truro*
ST PINNOCK (St Pinnock) *see* Liskeard, St Keyne, St Pinnock, Morval etc *Truro*
ST RUAN w St Grade and Landewednack *Truro 4* **P** *CPAS and A F Vyvyan-Robinson (jt)* **R** G K BENNETT
ST SAMPSON (St Sampson) *Truro 1* **P** *Bp* **R** M J OATEY
ST STEPHEN BY LAUNCESTON *Truro 9* **P** *D&C* **V** *Vacant* (01566) 772974
ST STEPHEN IN BRANNEL (not known) *Truro 1* **P** *Capt J D G Fortescue* **R** *Vacant* (01726) 822236
ST STEPHENS (St Stephen) *see* Saltash *Truro*
ST STYTHIANS w Perranarworthal and Gwennap *Truro 2* **P** *Viscount Falmouth (2 turns), D&C (1 turn)* **V** E J M HOGAN, **NSM** I D T LITTLE, L BARTER
ST TEATH (St Teatha) *Truro 10* **P** *Bp* **P-in-c** S L BRYAN
ST TUDY (St Tudy) w St Mabyn and Michaelstow *Truro 10* **P** *Ch Ch Ox, Viscount Falmouth, and Duchy of Cornwall (by turn)* **P-in-c** R HOWARD
ST VEEP (St Cyricius) *see* Lostwithiel, St Winnow w St Nectan's Chpl etc *Truro*
ST WENN (St Wenna) *see* St Columb Major w St Wenn *Truro*
ST WEONARDS (St Weonard) w Orcop, Garway, Tretire, Michaelchurch, Pencoyd, Welsh Newton and Llanrothal *Heref 8* **P** *Bp, D&C, and MMCET (jt)* **R** S R ASHTON
ST WINNOW (St Winnow) *see* Lostwithiel, St Winnow w St Nectan's Chpl etc *Truro*
SAINTBURY (St Nicholas) *see* Willersey, Saintbury, Weston-sub-Edge etc *Glouc*
SALCOMBE (Holy Trinity) *Ex 7* **P** *Keble Coll Ox* **V** *Vacant* (01548) 842626
SALCOMBE REGIS (St Mary and St Peter) *see* Sidmouth, Woolbrook, Salcombe Regis, Sidbury etc *Ex*
SALCOT VIRLEY (St Mary the Virgin) *see* Tollesbury w Salcot Virley *Chelmsf*
SALE (St Anne) (St Francis's Church Hall) *Ches 10* **P** *DBP* **V** P M POTTER
SALE (St Paul) *Ches 10* **P** *Trustees* **V** R SELWOOD
SALEBY (St Margaret) w Beesby and Maltby *Linc 8* **P** *Bp and DBP* **R** A READER-MOORE
SALEHURST (St Mary) *Chich 15* **P** *Bp* **V** J B LAMBOURNE
SALESBURY (St Peter) *Blackb 2* **P** *V Blackb* **V** J W HARTLEY
SALFORD Ordsall (St Clement) *Man 6* **P** *Bp* **P-in-c** D S C WYATT, E FORRESTER
SALFORD (Sacred Trinity) *Man 6* **P** *Exors Sir Josslyn Gore-Booth, Bt* **P-in-c** G BABB, **NSM** G TURNER
SALFORD (St Ignatius and Stowell Memorial) *Man 6* **P** *Bp* **R** R K S BRACEGIRDLE
SALFORD (St Mary) *see* Lt Compton w Chastleton, Cornwell etc *Ox*
SALFORD (St Mary) *see* Cranfield and Hulcote w Salford *St Alb*
SALFORD (St Paul w Christ Church) *Man 6* **P** *The Crown and Trustees (alt)* **R** D S C WYATT
SALFORD (St Philip w St Stephen) *Man 6* **P** *D&C* **R** *Vacant* 0161-834 2041
SALFORD PRIORS (St Matthew) *Cov 7* **P** *Peache Trustees* **P-in-c** S R TASH
SALFORDS (Christ the King) *S'wark 26* **P** *Bp* **NSM** F PLUMMER
SALHOUSE (All Saints) *see* Rackheath and Salhouse *Nor*

SALING, GREAT (St James) *see* Gt and Lt Bardfield w Gt and Lt Saling *Chelmsf*
SALING, LITTLE (St Peter and St Paul) *as above*
SALISBURY (St Francis) *Sarum 15* **P** *Bp* **V** R E DUNNINGS
SALISBURY (St Mark) *Sarum 15* **P** *Bp* **P-in-c** P J D HAWKSWORTH
SALISBURY (St Martin) *Sarum 15* **P** *Bp* **P-in-c** K ROBINSON
SALISBURY (St Thomas and St Edmund) *Sarum 15* **P** *Bp and D&C (alt)* **P-in-c** J C HATTON
SALKELD, GREAT (St Cuthbert) w Lazonby *Carl 4* **P** *Bp* **P-in-c** K REALE, **NSM** E R RADCLIFFE
SALLE (St Peter and St Paul) *see* Reepham, Hackford w Whitwell, Kerdiston etc *Nor*
SALT (St James the Great) and Sandon w Burston *Lich 10* **P** *Keble Coll Ox and Personal Reps Earl of Harrowby (jt)* **P-in-c** J N GREAVES
SALTASH (St Nicholas and St Faith) *Truro 11* **P** *Patr Bd* **TR** R E B MAYNARD, **TV** A J LING
SALTBURN-BY-THE-SEA (Emmanuel) *York 17* **P** *Abp, Adn Cleveland, Marquis of Zetland, and M Jarratt Esq (jt)* **V** I R PARKINSON
SALTBY (St Peter) *see* High Framland Parishes *Leic*
SALTDEAN (St Nicholas) *Chich 2* **P** *Bp* **V** A D MAYES, **C** M WICKENS
SALTER STREET (St Patrick) *see* Tanworth St Patr Salter Street *Birm*
SALTERHEBBLE (All Saints) *Wakef 4* **P** *Ch Trust Fund Trust* **V** T J WILSON, **C** R D BALDOCK, C SMITH, **NSM** J C K FREEBORN
SALTERSFORD (St John the Baptist) *see* Rainow w Saltersford and Forest *Ches*
SALTFLEETBY (St Peter) *Linc 12* **P** *Or Coll Ox, Bp, and MMCET (jt)* **V** *Vacant* (01507) 338074
SALTFORD (Blessed Virgin Mary) w Corston and Newton St Loe *B & W 10* **P** *DBP (2 turns), Duchy of Cornwall (1 turn)* **R** G R W HALL, **NSM** C S HARE
SALTHOUSE (St Nicholas) *see* Weybourne Gp *Nor*
SALTLEY (St Saviour) and Shaw Hill, Alum Rock *Birm 14* **P** *Bp and Trustees (jt)* **V** *Vacant* 0121-327 0570
SALTNEY FERRY (St Matthew) *see* Lache cum Saltney *Ches*
SALTON (St John of Beverley) *see* Kirby Misperton w Normanby, Edston and Salton *York*
SALTWOOD (St Peter and St Paul) *Cant 5* **P** *Abp* **R** R G HUMPHRISS
SALVINGTON (St Peter) *see* Durrington *Chich*
SALWARPE (St Michael) and Hindlip w Martin Hussingtree *Worc 8* **P** *Bp, D&C, and Exors Lady Hindlip (by turn)* **R** *Vacant* (01905) 778757
SALWAY ASH (Holy Trinity) *see* Beaminster Area *Sarum*
SAMBOURNE (Mission Church) *see* Coughton *Cov*
SAMBROOK (St Luke) *see* Cheswardine, Childs Ercall, Hales, Hinstock etc *Lich*
SAMLESBURY (St Leonard the Less) *see* Walton-le-Dale St Leon w Samlesbury St Leon *Blackb*
SAMPFORD, GREAT (St Michael) *see* The Sampfords *Chelmsf*
SAMPFORD, LITTLE (St Mary) *as above*
SAMPFORD ARUNDEL (Holy Cross) *see* Wellington and Distr *B & W*
SAMPFORD BRETT (St George) *see* Bicknoller w Crowcombe and Sampford Brett *B & W*
SAMPFORD COURTENAY (St Andrew) *see* N Tawton, Bondleigh, Sampford Courtenay etc *Ex*
SAMPFORD PEVERELL (St John the Baptist), Uplowman, Holcombe Rogus, Hockworthy, Burlescombe, Huntsham and Halberton w Ash Thomas *Ex 4* **P** *Patr Bd* **TR** B PETTY, **TV** K G GALE
SAMPFORD SPINEY (St Mary) w Horrabridge *Ex 24* **P** *D&C Windsor* **R** C FURNESS
SAMPFORDS, The *Chelmsf 22* **P** *New Coll Ox (1 turn), Guild of All So (2 turns)* **R** *Vacant*
SANCREED (St Creden) *Truro 5* **P** *D&C* **V** S W LEACH
SANCTON (All Saints) *York 7* **P** *Abp* **V** *Vacant*
SAND HILL (Church of the Good Shepherd) *see* N Farnborough *Guildf*
SAND HUTTON (St Leonard) *see* Thirsk *York*
SAND HUTTON (St Mary) *York 3* **P** *Abp (2 turns), D&C Dur (1 turn)* **V** J W VALENTINE
SANDAL (St Catherine) *Wakef 9* **P** *V Sandal Magna* **V** M P CROFT
SANDAL MAGNA (St Helen) *Wakef 9* **P** *Peache Trustees* **V** R G MARTIN
SANDBACH (St Mary) *Ches 11* **P** *DBP* **V** D W G STOCKER, **NSM** G AGAR
SANDBACH HEATH (St John the Evangelist) *Ches 11* **P** *V Sandwich* **V** E J GORDON
SANDBANKS (St Nicolas) *see* Canford Cliffs and Sandbanks *Sarum*
SANDERSTEAD (All Saints) (St Anthony) (St Edmund the King and Martyr) *S'wark 23* **P** *DBP* **TR** C J SKILTON, **TV** D S HEYWOOD, A M PRINCE
SANDERSTEAD (St Mary) *S'wark 23* **P** *Bp* **V** M W ELFRED, **NSM** M J JOHNSON
SANDFORD (All Saints) *see* Burrington and Churchill *B & W*
SANDFORD (St Martin) *see* Westcote Barton w Steeple Barton, Duns Tew etc *Ox*
SANDFORD (St Martin) *see* Wareham *Sarum*
SANDFORD (St Swithin) w Upton Hellions *Ex 2* **P** *12 Govs of Crediton Ch* **R** *Vacant* (01363) 772530
SANDFORD-ON-THAMES (St Andrew) *Ox 4* **P** *DBP* **P-in-c** R C MORGAN
SANDFORD ORCAS (St Nicholas) *see* Queen Thorne *Sarum*
SANDGATE (St Paul) w Folkestone (St George) *Cant 5* **P** *Abp and Ld Chan (alt)* **C** G MARCH, **NSM** C B HILL
SANDHURST (St Lawrence) *see* Twigworth, Down Hatherley, Norton, The Leigh etc *Glouc*
SANDHURST (St Michael and All Angels) *Ox 16* **P** *Bp* **R** A T L WILSON, **C** A B BULLOCK, **NSM** J F KNOWLES
SANDHURST (St Nicholas) (Mission Church) w Newenden *Cant 11* **P** *Abp* **R** R H DENGATE
SANDHURST, LOWER (St Mary) *see* Sandhurst *Ox*
SANDIACRE (St Giles) *Derby 13* **P** *Ld Chan* **R** W B COONEY
SANDIWAY (St John the Evangelist) *Ches 6* **P** *Bp* **V** J V GRIFFITH
SANDLEHEATH (St Aldhelm) *see* Fordingbridge *Win*
SANDON (All Saints) *see* Salt and Sandon w Burston *Lich*
SANDON (All Saints), Wallington and Rushden w Clothall *St Alb 19* **P** *Duchy of Lanc (1 turn), Marquess of Salisbury (1 turn), andBp (2 turns)* **R** *Vacant* (01763) 287256
SANDON (St Andrew) *Chelmsf 9* **P** *Qu Coll Cam* **P-in-c** H A MATTY
SANDOWN (Christ Church) *Portsm 7* **P** *Ch Patr Trust* **V** H J CUNNINGTON
SANDOWN, LOWER (St John the Evangelist) *Portsm 7* **P** *Bp* **V** *Vacant*
SANDRIDGE (St Leonard) *St Alb 8* **P** *Earl Spencer* **V** P J NELSON
SANDRINGHAM (St Mary Magdalene) w West Newton and Appleton, Wolferton w Babingley and Flitcham *Nor 16* **P** *The Crown* **R** G R HALL
SANDS (Church of the Good Shepherd) *see* Seale, Puttenham and Wanborough *Guildf*
SANDS (St Mary and St George) *see* High Wycombe *Ox*
SANDSEND (St Mary) *see* Lythe w Ugthorpe *York*
SANDWICH (St Clement) *Cant 8* **P** *Adn Cant* **R** J M A ROBERTS, **NSM** J C ROBERTS
SANDY (St Swithun) *St Alb 11* **P** *Lord Pym* **R** E E J ROWLAND
SANDY LANE (St Mary and St Nicholas) *see* Bromham, Chittoe and Sandy Lane *Sarum*
SANDYLANDS (St John) *Blackb 12* **P** *Bp* **V** J G REEVES
SANKEY, GREAT (St Mary) *Liv 13* **P** *Lord Lilford* **V** G McKIBBIN
SANTAN (St Sanctain) *S & M 1* **P** *The Crown* **V** G B CLAYTON
SANTON DOWNHAM (St Mary the Virgin) *see* Brandon and Santon Downham w Elveden *St E*
SAPCOTE (All Saints) and Sharnford w Wigston Parva *Leic 13* **P** *Ld Chan and DBP (alt)* **R** *Vacant* (01455) 272215
SAPEY, UPPER (St Michael) *see* Edvin Loach w Tedstone Delamere etc *Heref*
SAPPERTON (St Kenelm) *see* Coates, Rodmarton and Sapperton etc *Glouc*
SAPPERTON (St Nicholas) w Braceby *Linc 14* **P** *Bp (1 turn), Sir Richard Welby, Bt (3 turns)* **R** *Vacant*
SARISBURY (St Paul) *Portsm 2* **P** *V Titchfield* **V** R H MOSELEY
SARK (St Peter) *Win 14* **P** *Le Seigneur de Sercq* **C** G L LEWORTHY
SARN (Holy Trinity) *see* Churchstoke w Hyssington and Sarn *Heref*
SARNESFIELD (St Mary) *see* Weobley w Sarnesfield and Norton Canon *Heref*
SARRATT (Holy Cross) *St Alb 5* **P** *Bp* **P-in-c** J P HART
SATLEY (St Cuthbert) and Tow Law *Dur 9* **P** *Bp and Ld Chan (alt)* **V** D A WRIGHT
SATTERTHWAITE (All Saints) *Carl 10* **P** *V Hawkshead* **NSM** D HARRISON
SAUGHALL, GREAT (All Saints) *Ches 9* **P** *Bp* **P-in-c** D F HAY
SAUL (St James the Great) *see* Frampton on Severn, Arlingham, Saul etc *Glouc*

SAUNDERTON (St Mary and St Nicholas) *see* Bledlow w Saunderton and Horsenden *Ox*
SAUNTON (St Anne) *see* Braunton *Ex*
SAUSTHORPE (St Andrew) *see* Aswardby w Sausthorpe *Linc*
SAVERNAKE FOREST (St Katharine) *see* Gt and Lt Bedwyn and Savernake Forest *Sarum*
SAW MILLS (St Mary) *see* Ambergate and Heage *Derby*
SAWBRIDGEWORTH (Great St Mary) *St Alb 18* **P** *Bp* **V** T D LEWIS LLOYD, **C** P BRENT
SAWLEY (All Saints) (St Mary) *Derby 13* **P** *D&C Lich* **R** *Vacant* 0115-973 4900
SAWLEY (St Michael) *see* Fountains Gp *Ripon*
SAWREY (St Peter) *see* Hawkshead and Low Wray w Sawrey *Carl*
SAWSTON (St Mary) *Ely 7* **P** *SMF* **V** R L POWELL
SAWTRY (All Saints) and Glatton *Ely 13* **P** *Duke of Devonshire* **R** J R SANSOM
SAXBY (St Helen) *see* Owmby Gp *Linc*
SAXBY (St Peter) *see* Waltham on the Wolds, Stonesby, Saxby etc *Leic*
SAXBY ALL SAINTS (All Saints) *Linc 6* **P** *R H H Barton Esq* **P-in-c** G A PLUMB
SAXELBYE (St Peter) *see* Ab Kettleby Gp *Leic*
SAXHAM, GREAT (St Andrew) *see* Risby w Gt and Lt Saxham and Westley *St E*
SAXHAM, LITTLE (St Nicholas) *as above*
SAXILBY Group, The (St Botolph) *Linc 2* **P** *Bp and DBP (jt)* **P-in-c** R PROSSER
SAXLINGHAM (St Margaret) *see* Gunthorpe w Bale w Field Dalling, Saxlingham etc *Nor*
SAXLINGHAM NETHERGATE (St Mary) and Shotesham *Nor 5* **P** *Adn and Mrs M E Hicks (jt)* **P-in-c** I G BISHOP
SAXMUNDHAM (St John the Baptist) *St E 19* **P** *Exors Mrs A H V Aldous* **R** *Vacant* (01728) 604234
SAXONWELL *Linc 19* **P** *Duchy of Lanc (2 turns), Ld Chan (1 turn)* **R** R S EYRE, **NSM** C C MUNN
SAXTEAD (All Saints) *see* Framlingham w Saxtead *St E*
SAXTHORPE (St Andrew) *see* Lt Barningham, Blickling, Edgefield etc *Nor*
SAXTON (All Saints) *see* Sherburn in Elmet w Saxton *York*
SAYERS COMMON (Christ Church) *see* Albourne w Sayers Common and Twineham *Chich*
SCALBY (St Laurence) *York 16* **P** *Abp* **V** J W BAKER
SCALDWELL (St Peter and St Paul) *see* Walgrave w Hannington and Wold and Scaldwell *Pet*
SCALEBY (All Saints) *see* Irthington, Crosby-on-Eden and Scaleby *Carl*
SCALFORD (St Egelwin) w Goadby Marwood and Wycombe and Chadwell, Eastwell and Eaton *Leic 3* **P** *Ld Chan and Bp (alt)* **R** L N KING
SCAMMONDEN, WEST (St Bartholomew) *see* Barkisland w W Scammonden *Wakef*
SCAMPSTON (St Martin) *see* Rillington w Scampston, Wintringham etc *York*
SCAMPTON (St John the Baptist) *see* Aisthorpe w Scampton w Thorpe le Fallows etc *Linc*
SCARBOROUGH (St Columba) *York 16* **P** *Abp* **V** G R SOUTHEY
SCARBOROUGH (St James w Holy Trinity) *York 16* **P** *Abp and CPAS (jt)* **V** *Vacant* (01723) 361469
SCARBOROUGH (St Luke) *York 16* **P** *Abp* **V** M P CHAPPELL
SCARBOROUGH (St Mark) *see* Newby *York*
SCARBOROUGH (St Martin) *York 16* **P** *Trustees* **V** C J ARMSTRONG, **C** M GREENLAND
SCARBOROUGH (St Mary) w Christ Church and (Holy Apostles) *York 16* **P** *Abp* **V** R W JACKSON, **Hon C** H S WATSON, **NSM** R C WALSER
SCARBOROUGH (St Saviour w All Saints) *York 16* **P** *Abp* **V** A J MILLS
SCARCLIFFE (St Leonard) *see* E Scarsdale *Derby*
SCARISBRICK (St Mark) (Good Shepherd) *Liv 11* **P** *V Ormskirk* **V** A K GOODE
SCARLE, NORTH (All Saints) *see* Swinderby *Linc*
SCARLE, SOUTH (St Helena) *see* Collingham w S Scarle and Besthorpe and Girton *S'well*
SCARNING (St Peter and St Paul) *see* E Dereham and Scarning *Nor*
SCARRINGTON (St John of Beverley) *see* Whatton w Aslockton, Hawksworth, Scarrington etc *S'well*
SCARSDALE, EAST *Derby 3* **P** *Patr Bd* **TR** I E WINTERBOTTOM, **TV** R CHARLES, W J BLAKEMAN
SCARTHO (St Giles) *Linc 9* **P** *Jes Coll Ox* **C** C NORMAN, **NSM** C L BOGGIS
SCAWBY (St Hibald), Redbourne and Hibaldstow *Linc 6* **P** *Lt-Col R Sutton-Nelthorpe (2 turns), Bp (1 turn), and Duke of St Alb (1 turn)* **V** R HARDWICK
SCAWTHORPE (St Luke) *see* Doncaster St Leon and St Jude *Sheff*
SCAWTON (St Mary) *see* Upper Ryedale *York*
SCAYNES HILL (St Augustine) *Chich 6* **P** *Bp* **P-in-c** G B MITCHELL
SCHOLES (St Philip) *see* Barwick in Elmet *Ripon*
SCHOLES (St Philip and St James) *Wakef 8* **P** *Bp* **V** M E SMITH
SCHORNE *Ox 24* **P** *Patr Bd (2 turns), Ld Chan (1 turn)* **TR** T M THORP, **TV** B G KYRIACOU, **NSM** M D W PARTRIDGE
SCILLY, ISLES OF *see* Is of Scilly *Truro*
SCISSETT (St Augustine) *see* High Hoyland, Scissett and Clayton W *Wakef*
SCOFTON (St John the Evangelist) w Osberton *S'well 6* **P** *G M T Foljambe Esq* **V** *Vacant*
SCOLE (St Andrew) w Brockdish, Billingford, Thorpe Abbots and Thorpe Parva *Nor 10* **P** *Bp, Ex Coll Ox, MMCET, Adn Norfolk, and Exors Lady Mann (jt)* **P-in-c** P W RUSHTON
SCOPWICK Group, The (Holy Cross) *Linc 18* **P** *Ld Chan* **P-in-c** T R STOKES
SCORBOROUGH (St Leonard) *see* Lockington and Lund and Scorborough w Leconfield *York*
SCORTON (St Peter) *Blackb 10* **P** *V Lanc* **P-in-c** C R HUGGETT
SCOT HAY (St Paul) *see* Silverdale and Alsagers Bank *Lich*
SCOT WILLOUGHBY (St Andrew) *see* S Lafford *Linc*
SCOTBY (All Saints) *Carl 2* **P** *Trustees* **P-in-c** K G DAVIES
SCOTFORTH (St Paul) *Blackb 12* **P** *Rt Revd J Nicholls* **V** A CLITHEROW, **C** R J PRIESTLEY
SCOTHERN (St Germain) *see* Welton and Dunholme w Scothern *Linc*
SCOTSWOOD (St Margaret) *Newc 7* **P** *Bp* **V** N J HENSHALL
SCOTTER (St Peter) w East Ferry *Linc 4* **P** *Bp* **P-in-c** O G FOLKARD, **NSM** R I WATTS
SCOTTON (St Genewys) w Northorpe *Linc 4* **P** *Ld Chan* **P-in-c** K A WINDSLOW, **NSM** W KEAST, D L LANGFORD
SCOTTON (St Thomas) *see* Farnham w Scotton, Staveley, Copgrove etc *Ripon*
SCOTTOW (All Saints) *see* Worstead, Westwick, Sloley, Swanton Abbot etc *Nor*
SCOULTON (Holy Trinity) *see* Hingham w Wood Rising w Scoulton *Nor*
SCOUTHEAD (St Paul) *see* Dobcross w Scouthead *Man*
SCRAMBLESBY (St Martin) *see* Asterby Gp *Linc*
SCRAPTOFT (All Saints) *Leic 1* **P** *Bp, Dr M J A Sharp, and DBP (jt)* **V** *Vacant* (0116) 241 2318
SCRAYINGHAM (St Peter and St Paul) *see* Stamford Bridge Gp of Par *York*
SCREDINGTON (St Andrew) *see* Helpringham w Hale *Linc*
SCREMBY (St Peter and St Paul) *see* Partney *Linc*
SCREMERSTON (St Peter) *Newc 12* **P** *Bp* **V** J W SHEWAN
SCREVETON (St Wilfrid) *see* Car Colston w Screveton *S'well*
SCRIVELSBY (St Benedict) *see* Thornton Gp *Linc*
SCROOBY (St Wilfrid) *S'well 5* **P** *Bp* **P-in-c** J J VAN DEN BERG
SCROPTON (St Paul) *see* Marston on Dove w Scropton *Derby*
SCRUTON (St Radegund) *see* Kirkby Fleetham w Langton on Swale and Scruton *Ripon*
SCULCOATES (St Mary) *see* Hull St Mary Sculcoates *York*
SCULCOATES (St Paul) w Christ Church and St Silas *York 15* **P** *Abp* **P-in-c** T C GILL
SCULCOATES (St Stephen) *see* Hull St Steph Sculcoates *York*
SCULTHORPE (St Mary and All Saints) *see* N and S Creake w Waterden, Syderstone etc *Nor*
SCUNTHORPE (All Saints) *see* Brumby *Linc*
SCUNTHORPE (Resurrection) Berkeley *Linc 4* **P** *Bp* **P-in-c** A TOWELL
SEA MILLS (St Edyth) *Bris 8* **P** *Bp* **NSM** D J A ADAMS
SEA PALLING (St Margaret) *see* Happisburgh, Walcott, Hempstead w Eccles etc *Nor*
SEA VIEW (St Peter) *Portsm 7* **P** *Bp* **V** J H BARKER
SEABOROUGH (St John) *see* Beaminster Area *Sarum*
SEABROOK (Mission Hall) *see* Cheriton *Cant*
SEACOMBE (St Paul) *Ches 7* **P** *Trustees* **V** *Vacant* 0151-638 3677
SEACROFT (St James) (Church of the Ascension) (St Richard) *Ripon 8* **P** *DBF* **TR** A F BUNDOCK, **TV** A T SHAW, P J LANGFORD, L C PEARSON, D E P WILKINSON, **C** R BROOKE
SEAFORD (St Leonard) w Sutton *Chich 18* **P** *Ld Chan* **V** C H ATHERSTONE, **C** E J DAVIES, A W WEAVER
SEAFORTH (St Thomas) *Liv 1* **P** *Sir William Gladstone, Bt* **V** P A WINN
SEAGRAVE (All Saints) *see* Sileby, Cossington and Seagrave *Leic*

SEAGRY (St Mary the Virgin) *see* Gt Somerford, Lt Somerford, Seagry, Corston etc *Bris*
SEAHAM (St Mary the Virgin) w Seaham Harbour *Dur 2* **P** *Bp* **V** P JOBSON, **NSM** D NEWTON
SEAHAM, NEW (Christ Church) *Dur 2* **P** *Bp* **P-in-c** D A ROBERTS
SEAHAM HARBOUR (St John) *see* Seaham w Seaham Harbour *Dur*
SEAL (St Lawrence) *Roch 9* **P** *Bp* **P-in-c** M D COOKE
SEAL (St Peter and St Paul) *Roch 9* **P** *DBP* **V** K C BLACKBURN
SEALE (St Lawrence) *see* Seale, Puttenham and Wanborough *Guildf*
SEALE (St Lawrence), Puttenham and Wanborough *Guildf 4* **P** *Adn Surrey, T I Perkins Esq, and Ld Chan (by turn)* **R** N S McGREGOR, **NSM** N C EVANS, J A PATERSON
SEALE (St Peter) (St Matthew) and Lullington *Derby 16* **P** *Bp and C W Worthington Esq (alt)* **R** J H LISTER
SEAMER (St Martin) w East Ayton *York 16* **P** *Abp* **V** *Vacant* (01723) 863102
SEAMER IN CLEVELAND (St Martin) *York 22* **P** *Lord Egremont* **P-in-c** M D A DYKES
SEARBY (St Nicholas) w Owmby *Linc 5* **P** *D&C* **P-in-c** I ROBINSON
SEASALTER (St Alphege Old Church) *see* Whitstable *Cant*
SEASCALE (St Cuthbert) and Drigg *Carl 5* **P** *DBP* **V** W J P GRIME
SEATHWAITE (Holy Trinity) *see* Broughton and Duddon *Carl*
SEATON (All Hallows) *see* Lyddington w Stoke Dry and Seaton w Caldecott *Pet*
SEATON (St Gregory) *Ex 5* **P** *DBP* **V** N T SCHOFIELD
SEATON (St Paul) *see* Camerton, Seaton and W Seaton *Carl*
SEATON, WEST (Holy Trinity) *as above*
SEATON CAREW (Holy Trinity) *Dur 3* **P** *Bp* **V** W WORLEY
SEATON HIRST (St John) (St Andrew) *Newc 11* **P** *Bp* **P-in-c** D P PALMER, **TV** M J HILLS
SEATON ROSS Group of Parishes, The (St Edmund) *York 7* **P** *Ld Chan (1 turn), Abp and Schroder Exor & Trustee Co (2 turns)* **R** *Vacant* (01430) 860602
SEATON SLUICE (St Paul) *see* Delaval *Newc*
SEAVIEW *see* Sea View *Portsm*
SEAVINGTON (St Michael and St Mary) *see* S Petherton w the Seavingtons *B & W*
SEBERGHAM (St Mary) *see* Caldbeck, Castle Sowerby and Sebergham *Carl*
SECKINGTON (All Saints) *see* Newton Regis w Seckington and Shuttington *Birm*
SEDBERGH (St Andrew), Cautley and Garsdale *Bradf 6* **P** *Trin Coll Cam* **V** A W FELL, **NSM** F M I'ANSON
SEDGEBERROW (St Mary the Virgin) w Hinton-on-the-Green *Worc 1* **P** *D&C and Laslett's Charity (alt)* **P-in-c** H F GODDARD
SEDGEBROOK (St Lawrence) *see* Saxonwell *Linc*
SEDGEFIELD (St Edmund) *Dur 5* **P** *Bp* **R** M Q KING, **C** E A VARLEY
SEDGEHILL (St Katherine) *see* E Knoyle, Semley and Sedgehill *Sarum*
SEDGFORD (St Mary) *see* Docking, The Birchams, Stanhoe and Sedgeford *Nor*
SEDGLEY (All Saints) *Worc 10* **P** *DBP* **TR** P G ASHBY, **TV** A K LANE, **C** I R PETRIE
SEDGLEY (St Mary the Virgin) *Worc 10* **P** *Bp and V Sedgley All SS (jt)* **V** S M MILLER, **Hon C** J S WATTS
SEDLESCOMBE (St John the Baptist) w Whatlington *Chich 14* **P** *Ld Chan and Bp (alt)* **R** C I PRITCHARD
SEEND (Holy Cross) and Bulkington *Sarum 19* **P** *D&C (3 turns), Bp (1 turn)* **P-in-c** D C FROST
SEER GREEN (Holy Trinity) and Jordans *Ox 20* **P** *Bp* **V** *Vacant* (01494) 675013
SEETHING (St Margaret) *see* Brooke, Kirstead, Mundham w Seething and Thwaite *Nor*
SEFTON (St Helen) *Liv 5* **P** *Bp* **P-in-c** P J E CREAN
SEGHILL (Holy Trinity) *Newc 1* **P** *The Crown* **V** A MURRAY
SEIGHFORD (St Chad) *see* Chebsey, Ellenhall and Seighford-with-Creswell *Lich*
SELATTYN (St Mary) *see* Weston Rhyn and Selattyn *Lich*
SELBORNE (St Mary) *see* Newton Valence, Selborne and E Tisted w Colemore *Win*
SELBY (St James the Apostle) *York 6* **P** *Simeon's Trustees* **V** D J WOOLLARD, **C** M J CUNDIFF
SELBY ABBEY (St Mary and St Germain) (St Richard) *York 6* **P** *Abp* **P-in-c** R I J MATTHEWS, K M JUKES
SELHAM (St James) *see* Lurgashall, Lodsworth and Selham *Chich*
SELLACK (St Tysilio) *see* How Caple w Sollarshope, Sellack etc *Heref*
SELLINDGE (St Mary the Virgin) w Monks Horton and Stowting and Lympne w West Hythe *Cant 12* **P** *Abp* **P-in-c** D R HANCOCK
SELLING (St Mary the Virgin) w Throwley and Sheldwich w Badlesmere and Leaveland *Cant 6* **P** *Abp and D&C (jt)* **P-in-c** J M MASON, **Hon C** M JOHNSON
SELLY OAK (St Mary) *Birm 2* **P** *Bp* **V** C J ALDRIDGE
SELLY PARK (St Stephen) (St Wulstan) (St Stephen's Centre) *Birm 5* **P** *Trustees* **V** C J S TURNER, **C** N A HAND, N J LACEY
SELMESTON (St Mary) *see* Berwick w Selmeston and Alciston *Chich*
SELSDON (St John) (St Francis) *S'wark 21* **P** *Bp* **TR** L A D WATSON, **TV** B A WELLS, **NSM** K HOLT, S MARTIN
SELSEY (St Peter) *Chich 3* **P** *Bp* **R** V R CASSAM, **C** M L CATHERALL
SELSIDE (St Thomas) *see* Skelsmergh w Selside and Longsleddale *Carl*
SELSLEY (All Saints) *see* Cainscross w Selsley *Glouc*
SELSTON (St Helen) *S'well 4* **P** *Wright Trustees* **P-in-c** R W YULE, **NSM** G E HILL
SELWORTHY (All Saints), Timberscombe, Wootton Courtenay and Luccombe *B & W 16* **P** *Bp* **R** P S C WALKER, **Hon C** M J DUVALL
SEMER (All Saints) *see* Whatfield w Semer, Nedging and Naughton *St E*
SEMINGTON (St George) *see* Steeple Ashton w Semington and Keevil *Sarum*
SEMLEY (St Leonard) *see* E Knoyle, Semley and Sedgehill *Sarum*
SEMPRINGHAM (St Andrew) *see* Billingborough Gp *Linc*
SEND (St Mary the Virgin) *Guildf 12* **P** *Bp* **P-in-c** A J SHUTT, **NSM** G H CLAYTON
SENNEN (St Sennen) *see* St Buryan, St Levan and Sennen *Truro*
SENNICOTTS (St Mary) *see* Funtington and Sennicotts *Chich*
SESSAY (St Cuthbert) *York 20* **P** *Viscount Downe* **P-in-c** J H DAVIS
SETCHEY (St Mary) *see* W Winch w Setchey and N Runcton *Nor*
SETMURTHY (St Barnabas) *see* Bassenthwaite, Isel and Setmurthy *Carl*
SETTLE (Holy Ascension) *Bradf 5* **P** *Trustees* **V** S G RIDLEY
SETTRINGTON (All Saints) w North Grimston, Birdsall w Langton *York 2* **P** *Ld Chan (1 turn), Lord Middleton (2 turns), Abp and Lord Middleton (1 turn)* **NSM** J W A WOODS, M D B SINCLAIR
SEVENHAMPTON (St Andrew) w Charlton Abbotts and Hawling w Whittington *Glouc 14* **P** *Bp, T W Bailey Esq, E M Bailey Esq, MMCET, and Mrs J A Stringer (jt)* **P-in-c** R A B MORRIS
SEVENHAMPTON (St James) *see* Highworth w Sevenhampton and Inglesham etc *Bris*
SEVENOAKS (St John the Baptist) *Roch 9* **P** *Guild of All So* **V** R WARD, **NSM** C J R DAWSON
SEVENOAKS (St Luke) *Roch 9* **P** *Bp* **V** R CHAVNER
SEVENOAKS (St Nicholas) *Roch 9* **P** *Trustees* **R** O M THOMSON, **C** P de GREY-WARTER, M J STANDEN, **Hon C** N N HENSHAW, D G MILTON-THOMPSON, **NSM** J W HICKMAN
SEVENOAKS WEALD (St George) *Roch 9* **P** *R Sevenoaks* **P-in-c** M P P HOWARD
SEVERN BEACH (St Nicholas) *see* Pilning w Compton Greenfield *Bris*
SEVERN STOKE (St Dennis) *see* Kempsey and Severn Stoke w Croome d'Abitot *Worc*
SEVINGTON (St Mary) *Cant 10* **P** *Ch Soc Trust* **P-in-c** J W TIPPING
SEWARDS END (not known) *see* Saffron Walden w Wendens Ambo and Littlebury *Chelmsf*
SEWERBY (St John) *see* Bridlington H Trin and Sewerby w Marton *York*
SEWSTERN (Holy Trinity) *see* Wymondham w Edmondthorpe, Buckminster etc *Leic*
SHABBINGTON (St Mary Magdalene) *see* Worminghall w Ickford, Oakley and Shabbington *Ox*
SHACKERSTONE (St Peter) *see* Nailstone and Carlton w Shackerstone *Leic*
SHACKLEFORD (St Mary the Virgin) *see* Compton w Shackleford and Peper Harow *Guildf*
SHADFORTH (St Cuthbert) *Dur 1* **P** *D&C* **R** P E MARTIN, **C** P T ALLINSON
SHADINGFIELD (St John the Baptist) *see* Hundred River *St E*
SHADOXHURST (St Peter and St Paul) *see* Kingsnorth w Shadoxhurst *Cant*
SHADWELL (St Paul) *Ripon 5* **P** *V Thorner* **V** H A THOMPSON

SHADWELL (St Paul) w Ratcliffe St James *Lon 7* **P** *Bp* **P-in-c** R T SIMPSON
SHAFTESBURY (St James) *see* Shaston *Sarum*
SHAFTESBURY (St Peter) *as above*
SHAFTON (St Hugh) *see* Felkirk w Brierley *Wakef*
SHALBOURNE (St Michael and All Angels) *see* Wexcombe *Sarum*
SHALDEN (St Peter and St Paul) *see* Bentworth and Shalden and Lasham *Win*
SHALDON (St Nicholas) (St Peter) *Ex 10* **P** *SMF* **V** A L MANHIRE
SHALFLEET (St Michael the Archangel) *Portsm 8* **P** *Ld Chan* **P-in-c** B M C MORRIS
SHALFORD (St Andrew) *see* Finchingfield and Cornish Hall End etc *Chelmsf*
SHALFORD (St Mary the Virgin) *Guildf 5* **P** *Ld Chan* **V** D N HOBDEN, **NSM** J J SWANTON
SHALSTONE (St Edward the Confessor) *see* Westbury w Turweston, Shalstone and Biddlesden *Ox*
SHAMLEY GREEN (Christ Church) *Guildf 2* **P** *Bp* **V** M C HUGHES
SHANGTON (St Nicholas) *see* Gaulby *Leic*
SHANKLIN (St Blasius) *Portsm 7* **P** *Bp* **P-in-c** A W SWANBOROUGH
SHANKLIN (St Paul) *see* Gatten St Paul *Portsm*
SHANKLIN (St Saviour on the Cliff) *Portsm 7* **P** *Bp* **P-in-c** R M SMITH
SHAP (St Michael) w Swindale and Bampton w Mardale *Carl 1* **P** *Earl of Lonsdale* **V** G G FIELD
SHAPWICK (Blessed Virgin Mary) w Ashcott and Burtle *B & W 5* **P** *Lord Vestey (2 turns), Bp (1 turn)* **P-in-c** J P ROWE
SHAPWICK (St Bartholomew) *see* Sturminster Marshall, Kingston Lacy and Shapwick *Sarum*
SHARD END (All Saints) *Birm 10* **P** *Keble Coll Ox* **V** J F WARD, **P-in-c** C J BOYLE
SHARDLOW (St James) *see* Elvaston and Shardlow *Derby*
SHARESHILL (St Luke and St Mary the Virgin) *Lich 2* **P** *Bp* **P-in-c** P H J THORNEYCROFT
SHARLSTON (St Luke) *Wakef 9* **P** *Bp* **V** R A CHAPMAN
SHARNBROOK (St Peter) and Knotting w Souldrop *St Alb 15* **P** *Bp* **P-in-c** I W ARTHUR
SHARNFORD (St Helen) *see* Sapcote and Sharnford w Wigston Parva *Leic*
SHARPNESS (St Andrew) w Purton and Brookend *Glouc 2* **P** *Bp* **P-in-c** W J BOON
SHARRINGTON (All Saints) *see* Gunthorpe w Bale w Field Dalling, Saxlingham etc *Nor*
SHASTON *Sarum 6* **P** *Patr Bd* **TV** D D BOTTERILL, T TAYLOR, **NSM** T J ORCHARD, I WITCHER
SHAUGH PRIOR (St Edward) *see* Bickleigh (Roborough) and Shaugh Prior *Ex*
SHAVINGTON (St Mark) *see* Weston *Ches*
SHAW (Christchurch) *see* Atworth w Shaw and Whitley *Sarum*
SHAW (Holy Trinity) *Man 22* **P** *R Prestwich St Mary* **V** A N WILSON
SHAW (St Mary) cum Donnington *Ox 14* **P** *DBP* **R** B TAYLOR
SHAW HILL (St Mary and St John) *see* Saltley and Shaw Hill *Birm*
SHAWBURY (St Mary the Virgin) *Lich 23* **P** *C C Corbet Esq* **V** D J HUMPHRIES
SHAWELL (All Saints) *see* Swinford w Catthorpe, Shawell and Stanford *Leic*
SHEARSBY (St Mary Magdalene) *see* Arnesby w Shearsby and Bruntingthorpe *Leic*
SHEBBEAR (St Michael), Buckland Filleigh, Sheepwash, Langtree, Newton St Petrock, Petrockstowe, Petersmarland, Merton and Huish *Ex 19* **P** *Ld Chan (1 turn), Patr Bd (2 turns)* **TV** C HANSON
SHEDFIELD (St John the Baptist) *Portsm 1* **P** *DBP* **V** G B MORRELL, **NSM** B R McHUGH
SHEEN (St Luke) *see* Longnor, Quarnford and Sheen *Lich*
SHEEN, EAST (All Saints) *see* Mortlake w E Sheen *S'wark*
SHEEN, EAST (Christ Church) *as above*
SHEEPSCOMBE (St John the Evangelist) *see* Painswick w Sheepscombe and Cranham *Glouc*
SHEEPSTOR (St Leonard) *see* Yelverton, Meavy, Sheepstor and Walkhampton *Ex*
SHEEPWASH (St Lawrence) *see* Shebbear, Buckland Filleigh, Sheepwash etc *Ex*
SHEEPY GROUP, The *Leic 13* **P** *Ld Chan, Pemb Coll Ox, and MMCET (by turn)* **R** *Vacant* (01827) 880301
SHEERING (St Mary the Virgin) *see* Hatfield Heath and Sheering *Chelmsf*
SHEERNESS (Holy Trinity w St Paul) *Cant 14* **P** *V Minster-in-Sheppey* **V** D WALKER
SHEERWATER (St Michael and All Angels) *see* Woodham *Guildf*
SHEET (St Mary Magdalene) *Portsm 5* **P** *Bp* **V** S J CHAPMAN, **NSM** C M PEEL
SHEFFIELD Norwood (St Leonard) *Sheff 3* **P** *Bp* **V** T W ELLIS, **C** H G SMART
SHEFFIELD Parson Cross (St Cecilia) *Sheff 3* **P** *Bp* **P-in-c** T H CASWELL
SHEFFIELD Sharrow (St Andrew) *Sheff 2* **P** *Trustees* **V** N P A JOWETT
SHEFFIELD (St Aidan w St Luke) *see* Sheff Manor *Sheff*
SHEFFIELD (St Bartholomew) *Sheff 4* **P** *Ch Patr Trust and Sheff Ch Burgesses Trust (jt)* **V** N HELM
SHEFFIELD (St Catherine of Siena) Richmond Road *Sheff 1* **P** *The Crown* **V** H LOXLEY, **C** W J STOKOE
SHEFFIELD (St Cuthbert) *Sheff 3* **P** *Ch Burgesses* **V** *Vacant* 0114-243 6506
SHEFFIELD (St John the Evangelist) *Sheff 1* **P** *Ch Burgesses* **V** C W KEMP, **C** B HICKS
SHEFFIELD (St Mark) Broomhill *Sheff 4* **P** *Ch Burgesses* **V** A ALKER, **C** J E BOLTON
SHEFFIELD (St Mary) Bramhall Lane *Sheff 2* **P** *Ch Burgesses and Provost (alt)* **V** J C SULLIVAN, **C** J W MWANGI, M J BAYLEY
SHEFFIELD (St Matthew) Carver Street *Sheff 2* **P** *Bp* **V** M WAKELY
SHEFFIELD (St Oswald) *Sheff 2* **P** *Ch Burgesses* **V** J K MOORE
SHEFFIELD (St Paul) Wordsworth Avenue *Sheff 3* **P** *DBP* **V** N S KAGGWA
SHEFFIELD (St Peter) Abbeydale *Sheff 2* **P** *Ch Burgesses* **V** R J H BEARD
SHEFFIELD (St Silas) Broomhall *Sheff 2* **P** *Ch Burgesses* **V** M F HOLLAND
SHEFFIELD MANOR (St Swithun) *Sheff 1* **P** *Patr Bd* **TR** P T STEVENS, **TV** N J WRIGHT, C P ARNESEN, H J SMART
SHEFFIELD PARK (St John the Evangelist) *see* Sheff St Jo *Sheff*
SHEFFORD (St Michael) *St Alb 16* **P** *Adn Bedford, R Clifton, and R Campton (jt)* **V** D R SMITH
SHEFFORD, GREAT (St Mary) *see* Welford w Wickham and Gt Shefford, Boxford etc *Ox*
SHEINTON (St Peter and St Paul) *see* Wenlock *Heref*
SHELDON (St Giles) *Birm 10* **P** *K S D Wingfield Digby Esq* **R** B A L CAMP
SHELDON (St James the Greater) *see* Dunkeswell, Sheldon and Luppitt *Ex*
SHELDON (St Michael and All Angels) *see* Ashford w Sheldon and Longstone *Derby*
SHELDWICH (St James) *see* Selling w Throwley, Sheldwich w Badlesmere etc *Cant*
SHELF St Michael w Buttershaw St Aidan *Bradf 2* **P** *Bp* **TR** P G STANNARD, **TV** J A HOLFORD
SHELFANGER (All Saints) *see* Winfarthing w Shelfanger w Burston w Gissing etc *Nor*
SHELFIELD (St Mark) Conventional District *Lich 6* **Min** E A JORDAN
SHELFORD (St Peter and St Paul) *see* Radcliffe-on-Trent and Shelford etc *S'well*
SHELFORD, GREAT (St Mary) *Ely 7* **P** *Bp* **V** *Vacant* (01223) 843274
SHELFORD, LITTLE (All Saints) w Newton *Ely 7* **P** *Bp* **P-in-c** C B G ASH
SHELLAND (King Charles the Martyr) *see* Buxhall w Shelland *St E*
SHELLEY (All Saints) *see* Hadleigh *St E*
SHELLEY (Emmanuel) and Shepley *Wakef 6* **P** *V Kirkburton* **V** A HEZEL
SHELLEY (St Peter) *see* Chipping Ongar w Shelley *Chelmsf*
SHELLINGFORD (St Faith) *see* Uffington, Shellingford, Woolstone and Baulking *Ox*
SHELSLEY BEAUCHAMP (All Saints) *see* Clifton-on-Teme, Lower Sapey and the Shelsleys *Worc*
SHELSLEY WALSH (St Andrew) *as above*
SHELSWELL *Ox 2* **P** *Ld Chan (1 turn) and Ch Ch Ox, CCC Ox, Baroness von Maltzahn, and R J Vallings Esq (1 turn)* **R** W J YATES, **NSM** D WENHAM
SHELTON (Christ Church) *see* Oxon and Shelton *Lich*
SHELTON (St Mark) *see* Hanley H Ev *Lich*
SHELTON (St Mary) *see* Hempnall *Nor*
SHELTON (St Mary) *see* The Stodden Churches *St Alb*
SHELTON (St Mary and All Saints) *S'well 3* **P** *Bp* **R** G A FIRTH
SHELVE (All Saints) *see* Hope w Shelve *Heref*
SHENFIELD (St Mary the Virgin) *Chelmsf 7* **P** *Personal Reps R H Courage* **R** P G BRETT
SHENINGTON (Holy Trinity) *see* Ironstone *Ox*

SHENLEY (St Martin) *St Alb 1* **P** *DBP* **P-in-c** C J TWYCROSS
SHENLEY (St Mary) *see* Watling Valley *Ox*
SHENLEY GREEN (St David) *Birm 4* **P** *Bp* **V** C J W JACKSON, **C** H M FLACK
SHENSTONE (St John the Baptist) *Lich 1* **P** *MMCET* **NSM** J B ASTON
SHENTON (St John the Evangelist) *see* Market Bosworth, Cadeby w Sutton Cheney etc *Leic*
SHEPHERD'S BUSH (St Stephen) (St Thomas) *Lon 9* **P** *Bp* **V** D M H REECE
SHEPLEY (St Paul) *see* Shelley and Shepley *Wakef*
SHEPPERDINE (Chapel) *see* Oldbury-on-Severn *Glouc*
SHEPPERTON (St Nicholas) *Lon 13* **P** *Bp* **R** C J SWIFT, **C** M L TOOGOOD
SHEPRETH (All Saints) *Ely 8* **P** *Bp* **V** M W BAKER
SHEPSHED (St Botolph) *Leic 7* **P** *Lord Crawshaw* **V** S J BOWRING
SHEPTON BEAUCHAMP (St Michael) *see* Ilminster and District *B & W*
SHEPTON MALLET (St Peter and St Paul) w Doulting *B & W 8* **P** *Duchy of Cornwall and Bp (alt)* **R** J S T WOOLMER, **C** M S PERSSON
SHEPTON MONTAGUE (St Peter) *see* Bruton and Distr *B & W*
SHEPWELL GREEN (St Matthias) *see* Willenhall St Giles *Lich*
SHERBORNE (Abbey Church of St Mary) (All Souls) (St Paul) w Castleton and Lillington *Sarum 4* **P** *Major K S D Wingfield Digby* **V** E J WOODS, **C** J W S PATON, R M HORNER
SHERBORNE (St Mary Magdalene), Windrush, the Barringtons and Aldsworth *Glouc 14* **P** *C T R Wingfield Esq, Ch Ch Ox, and DBP (by turn)* **P-in-c** M SELWOOD
SHERBORNES (St Andrew) (Vyne Chapel) w Pamber, The *Win 4* **P** *Bp and Qu Coll Ox (jt)* **R** J N HAMILTON
SHERBOURNE (All Saints) *see* Barford w Wasperton and Sherbourne *Cov*
SHERBURN (St Hilda) and West and East Heslerton w Yedingham *York 2* **P** *D&C (2 turns), The Crown (2 turns), and Sir Stephen Hastings (1 turn)* **P-in-c** D M B SHARPE
SHERBURN (St Mary) w Pittington *Dur 1* **P** *D&C* **V** P E MARTIN, **C** P T ALLINSON
SHERBURN IN ELMET (All Saints) w Saxton *York 1* **P** *Abp* **V** C I COATES, **C** V D CLARKE
SHERE (St James) *Guildf 2* **P** *Mrs H Bray* **P-in-c** H G MEIRION-JONES
SHEREFORD (St Nicholas) *see* Toftrees w Shereford *Nor*
SHERFIELD ENGLISH (St Leonard) *see* Awbridge w Sherfield English *Win*
SHERFIELD-ON-LODDON (St Leonard) and Stratfield Saye w Hartley Wespall w Stratfield Turgis *Win 4* **P** *Bp, Duke of Wellington, and D&C Windsor (jt)* **R** J N THOMAS
SHERFORD (St Martin) *see* Stokenham w Sherford and Beesands, and Slapton *Ex*
SHERIFF HUTTON (St Helen and the Holy Cross), Farlington, Stillington and Marton w Moxby *York 5* **P** *Abp (3 turns), DBP (1 turn)* **V** D W D LEE
SHERIFFHALES (St Mary) *see* Lilleshall and Sheriffhales *Lich*
SHERINGHAM (St Peter) *Nor 21* **P** *Bp* **P-in-c** A C H LATHE
SHERINGHAM, UPPER (All Saints) *see* Weybourne Gp *Nor*
SHERINGTON (St Laud) w Chicheley, North Crawley, Astwood and Hardmead *Ox 27* **P** *Bp (2 turns), MMCET (1 turn), and Major J G B Chester (1 turn)* **R** M C STANTON-SARINGER
SHERMANBURY (St Giles) *see* Henfield w Shermanbury and Woodmancote *Chich*
SHERNBOURNE (St Peter and St Paul) *see* Dersingham w Anmer and Shernborne *Nor*
SHERRARDS GREEN (St Mary the Virgin) *see* Gt Malvern Ch Ch *Worc*
SHERRINGTON (St Cosmo and St Damian) *see* Ashton Gifford *Sarum*
SHERSTON MAGNA (Holy Cross), Easton Grey, Luckington, Alderton and Foxley w Bremilham *Bris 12* **P** *D&C, Bp, Adn Swindon and Lord Lilford (jt)* **V** M H ROSS
SHERWOOD (St Martin) *S'well 13* **P** *Bp* **V** C GALE, **C** P H REISS
SHERWOOD PARK (St Philip) *see* Tunbridge Wells St Jas w St Phil *Roch*
SHEVINGTON (St Anne) *Blackb 4* **P** *R Standish* **V** F A O D DAWSON
SHEVIOCK (Blessed Virgin Mary) *see* Antony w Sheviock *Truro*
SHIFFORD (St Mary) *see* Bampton w Clanfield *Ox*
SHIFNAL (St Andrew) *Lich 20* **P** *R I Legge Esq* **P-in-c** G C FOWELL
SHILBOTEL (St James) *see* Shilbottle *Newc*
SHILBOTTLE (St James) *Newc 9* **P** *Dioc Soc* **V** *Vacant* (01665) 575800
SHILDON (St John) w Eldon *Dur 6* **P** *Bp (2 turns), The Crown (1 turn)* **V** R CUTHBERTSON, **C** L POTTER
SHILDON, NEW (All Saints) *Dur 6* **P** *Bp* **V** *Vacant* (01388) 772785
SHILL VALLEY and Broadshire *Ox 8* **P** *J Heyworth Esq, Mrs P Allen, and Ch Ch Ox (1 turn), Ch Soc Tr, F R Goodenough Esq, and D F Goodenough Esq (1 turn)* **R** R H LLOYD, **Hon C** J M MOUNT, **NSM** C D RAWSON, L N USHER-WILSON
SHILLING OKEFORD (Holy Rood) *Sarum 6* **P** *DBP* **P-in-c** M A TURNER
SHILLINGFORD (St George) *see* Dunchideock and Shillingford St George w Ide *Ex*
SHILLINGSTONE (Holy Rood) *see* Shilling Okeford *Sarum*
SHILLINGTON (All Saints) *St Alb 16* **P** *Bp* **P-in-c** P J SWINDELLS
SHILTON (Holy Rood) *see* Shill Valley and Broadshire *Ox*
SHILTON (St Andrew) *see* Bulkington w Shilton and Ansty *Cov*
SHIMPLINGTHORNE (St George) *see* Lawshall w Shimplingthorne and Alpheton *St E*
SHINCLIFFE (St Mary the Virgin) *Dur 1* **P** *D&C* **R** S M SANDHAM, **NSM** R D THOMSON
SHINEY ROW (St Oswald) *Dur 14* **P** *The Crown* **P-in-c** D BODDY
SHINFIELD (St Mary) *Ox 15* **P** *D&C Heref* **V** S N H BAKER
SHINGAY Group of Parishes, The *Ely 8* **P** *Bp, Mrs E E Sclater, Ch Patr Trust, Down Coll Cam, New CollOx, and Jes Coll Cam (jt)* **V** S F C WILLIAMS
SHIPBOURNE (St Giles) *Roch 11* **P** *E Cazalet Esq* **P-in-c** S M RAMSARAN
SHIPDHAM (All Saints) w East and West Bradenham *Nor 17* **P** *Bp* **R** B J WOOD
SHIPHAM (St Leonard) *see* Axbridge w Shipham and Rowberrow *B & W*
SHIPHAY COLLATON (St John the Baptist) *Ex 10* **P** *Bp* **V** D A PINCHES
SHIPLAKE (St Peter and St Paul) w Dunsden *Ox 6* **P** *D&C Windsor and DBP (jt)* **V** M R C PRICE
SHIPLEY (St Mary the Virgin) *Chich 8* **P** *C R Burrell Esq* **P-in-c** D L POPE
SHIPLEY (St Paul) and Frizinghall St Margaret *Bradf 1* **P** *Patr Bd* **P-in-c** C R PENFOLD, **Hon C** S I PENFOLD
SHIPLEY (St Peter) *Bradf 1* **P** *TR Shipley St Paul and Frizinghall* **V** C P EDMONDSON, **C** S R CAPITANCHIK
SHIPPON (St Mary Magdalene) *Ox 10* **P** *Bp* **V** M A J GOODE
SHIPSTON-ON-STOUR (St Edmund) w Honington and Idlicote *Cov 9* **P** *Jes Coll Ox, D&C Worc, Bp (jt)* **R** A C DE SMET
SHIPTON (Holy Evangelist) *see* Skelton w Shipton and Newton on Ouse *York*
SHIPTON (St James) *see* Wenlock *Heref*
SHIPTON BELLINGER (St Peter) *Win 3* **P** *Bp* **V** A R H MACLEOD
SHIPTON GORGE (St Martin) *see* Bride Valley *Sarum*
SHIPTON MOYNE (St John the Baptist) w Westonbirt and Lasborough *Glouc 16* **P** *Westonbirt Sch and DBP (jt)* **NSM** W I BARBOUR, J L BARBOUR
SHIPTON OLIFFE (St Oswald) *see* Dowdeswell and Andoversford w the Shiptons etc *Glouc*
SHIPTON ON CHERWELL (Holy Cross) *see* Yarnton w Begbroke and Shipton on Cherwell *Ox*
SHIPTON SOLLARS (St Mary) *see* Dowdeswell and Andoversford w the Shiptons etc *Glouc*
SHIPTON-UNDER-WYCHWOOD (St Mary) w Milton-under-Wychwood, Fifield and Idbury *Ox 3* **P** *Bp* **V** G G B CANNING
SHIPTONTHORPE (All Saints) w Hayton *York 7* **P** *Abp* **P-in-c** J C MELLING
SHIREBROOK (Holy Trinity) *see* E Scarsdale *Derby*
SHIREGREEN (St Hilda) *Sheff 3* **P** *Bp* **P-in-c** T W ELLIS, A H MORGAN
SHIREGREEN (St James and St Christopher) *Sheff 3* **P** *Provost* **V** A J P THOMPSON
SHIREHAMPTON (St Mary) *Bris 8* **P** *Bp* **V** F R SYMONS, **NSM** A W WHEELER
SHIREMOOR (St Mark) *Newc 8* **P** *Bp* **V** M C VINE
SHIREOAKS (St Luke) *S'well 6* **P** *Bp* **P-in-c** M P D KENNARD
SHIRES' EDGE *Ox 5* **P** *Bp* **V** P G ATKINSON, **NSM** D B ADDLEY
SHIRESHEAD (St James) *Blackb 12* **P** *V Cockerham* **V** *Vacant*
SHIRLAND (St Leonard) *Derby 1* **P** *Adn Chesterfield and Trustees* **R** *Vacant* (01773) 836003
SHIRLEY (St George) *S'wark 21* **P** *Bp* **V** D J FROST, **Hon C** N N KIRKUP
SHIRLEY (St James) (St John) *Win 12* **P** *Ch Patr Trust* **V** D P HAZLEWOOD, **C** E BUTT

SHIRLEY (St James the Great) (St John the Divine) (Christ the King) (St Luke) (St Mary Magdalene) *Birm 6* **P** *Patr Bd* **TR** M G B C CADDY, **TV** W K McMASTER, **C** N I JONES
SHIRLEY (St John) *S'wark 21* **P** *Bp* **V** A H R QUINN, **Hon C** H G LEWIS, A C COLLIER
SHIRLEY (St Michael) *see* Brailsford w Shirley and Osmaston w Edlaston *Derby*
SHIRLEY WARREN (St Jude) *see* Southampton St Jude *Win*
SHIRWELL (St Peter), Loxhore, Kentisbury, Arlington, East Down, Bratton Fleming, Challacombe and Stoke Rivers *Ex 17* **P** *Patr Bd* **TR** L E AUSTIN, **TV** R D SIMPSON, **NSM** E A SIMPSON
SHOBDON (St John the Evangelist) *see* Pembridge w Moorcourt, Shobdon, Staunton etc *Heref*
SHOBNALL (St Aidan) *Lich 14* **P** *Bp* **P-in-c** D M MORRIS, **C** A R BAILEY
SHOBROOKE (St Swithin) *see* Crediton and Shobrooke *Ex*
SHOCKLACH (St Edith) *see* Tilston and Shocklach *Ches*
SHOEBURY, NORTH (St Mary the Virgin) *Chelmsf 13* **P** *Ld Chan* **V** P G KEARNS
SHOEBURY, SOUTH (St Andrew) (St Peter) *Chelmsf 13* **P** *Hyndman Trustees* **C** M E MILLARD
SHOLDEN (St Nicholas) *see* Deal St Leon and St Rich and Sholden *Cant*
SHOLING (St Francis of Assisi) (St Mary) *Win 12* **P** *Bp* **V** B J HARTNELL, **C** D E CHANDLER, K TAPLIN
SHOOTERS HILL (All Saints) *see* Plumstead All SS *S'wark*
SHOOTERS HILL (Christ Church) *S'wark 3* **P** *Bp* **NSM** J D BROWN
SHORE (St Barnabas) *Man 20* **P** *D&C* **P-in-c** M C HODSON
SHOREDITCH (All Saints) Haggerston Road *see* Haggerston All SS *Lon*
SHOREDITCH (St Anne) Hoxton Street *see* Hoxton St Anne w St Columba *Lon*
SHOREDITCH (St Leonard) and Hoxton St John the Baptist *Lon 5* **P** *Patr Bd* **TR** P R TURP, **TV** W M MACNAUGHTON, **C** E P KAMRAN, J W S COWIE
SHOREHAM (St Giles) *see* Kingston Buci *Chich*
SHOREHAM (St Peter and St Paul) *Roch 10* **P** *D&C Westmr* **V** B J SIMMONS
SHOREHAM, NEW (St Mary de Haura) *Chich 4* **P** *Bp* **V** K KINNAIRD, **C** J M BALDWIN
SHOREHAM, OLD (St Nicholas) *Chich 4* **P** *Bp* **V** K KINNAIRD, **C** J M BALDWIN
SHOREHAM BEACH (Good Shepherd) *Chich 4* **P** *Bp* **V** Q M RONCHETTI
SHORNE (St Peter and St Paul) *Roch 4* **P** *D&C* **V** P E LONGBOTTOM
SHORT HEATH (Holy Trinity) *see* Willenhall H Trin *Lich*
SHORT HEATH (St Margaret) *Birm 8* **P** *Bp* **V** A E POWER
SHORTHAMPTON (All Saints) *see* Charlbury w Shorthampton *Ox*
SHORTLANDS (All Saints' Community Church) *see* Bromley SS Pet and Paul *Roch*
SHORTLANDS (St Mary) *Roch 13* **P** *Bp* **V** D S R REDMAN, **Hon C** P LEUNG, **NSM** J G MEDCALF
SHORTWOOD (All Saints) *see* Nailsworth *Glouc*
SHORWELL (St Peter) w Kingston *Portsm 8* **P** *Bp* **V** J W RUSSELL, **NSM** C SMART, S C HENDERSON
SHOSCOMBE (St Julian) *see* Camerton w Dunkerton, Foxcote and Shoscombe *B & W*
SHOTESHAM (All Saints w St Mary) *see* Saxlingham Nethergate and Shotesham *Nor*
SHOTLEY (St John) *Newc 3* **P** *Lord Crewe's Trustees* **P-in-c** T J ATKINS, **NSM** R VICKERS
SHOTLEY (St Mary) *St E 5* **P** *Bp* **R** R SPITTLE
SHOTTERMILL (St Stephen) *Guildf 4* **P** *Adn Surrey* **V** A C JONES
SHOTTERY (St Andrew) *Cov 8* **P** *Bp* **V** S A BEAKE, **C** D R PATTERSON
SHOTTESBROOKE (St John the Baptist) *see* White Waltham w Shottesbrooke *Ox*
SHOTTESWELL (St Lawrence) *see* Warmington w Shotteswell and Radway w Ratley *Cov*
SHOTTISHAM (St Margaret) w Sutton *St E 7* **P** *Bp* **P-in-c** M H INMAN
SHOTTLE (St Lawrence) *see* Hazelwood *Derby*
SHOTTON (St Saviour) *Dur 2* **P** *Bp* **V** J F MASSHEDAR
SHOTWICK (St Michael) *see* Burton and Shotwick *Ches*
SHOULDHAM (All Saints) *Ely 16* **P** *Bp* **P-in-c** G PARROTT
SHOULDHAM THORPE (St Mary) *Ely 16* **P** *Bp* **P-in-c** G PARROTT
SHRAWARDINE (St Mary) *see* Bicton, Montford w Shrawardine and Fitz *Lich*
SHRAWLEY (St Mary), Witley, Astley and Abberley *Worc 13* **P** *Bp and Guild of All So (jt)* **R** R P HEAPS, **C** D F GUTTERIDGE
SHRED (Mission Church) *see* Slaithwaite w E Scammonden *Wakef*
SHREWSBURY (All Saints and St Michael) *Lich 21* **P** *Bp* **V** A W MARKS
SHREWSBURY (Holy Cross) (St Peter) *Lich 21* **P** *Bp* **V** F I ROSS
SHREWSBURY (Holy Trinity) (St Julian) *Lich 21* **P** *Bp and Ch Patr Trust (jt)* **V** P G FIRMIN
SHREWSBURY (St Alkmund) *Lich 21* **P** *Bp* **P-in-c** C F LILEY
SHREWSBURY (St Chad) w St Mary *Lich 21* **P** *Bp* **V** C F LILEY, **C** M P HOBBS
SHREWSBURY (St George of Cappadocia) *Lich 21* **P** *V Shrewsbury St Chad* **V** R W D BIDDLE, **NSM** S M OWEN
SHREWSBURY (St Giles) w Sutton and Atcham *Lich 21* **P** *Bp and R L Burton Esq (jt)* **R** P J WILLIAMS
SHREWTON (St Mary) *Sarum 16* **P** *Ld Chan* **V** *Vacant* (01980) 620580
SHRIVENHAM (St Andrew) w Watchfield and Bourton *Ox 17* **P** *Ld Chan* **V** T D RAWDON-MOGG, **NSM** E L GUTSELL
SHROPHAM (St Peter) *see* Gt and Lt Ellingham, Rockland and Shropham etc *Nor*
SHROTON (St Mary) *see* The Iwernes, Sutton Waldron and Fontmell Magna *Sarum*
SHRUB END (All Saints) (St Cedd) *Chelmsf 16* **P** *Bp* **V** C W NEWLANDS, **C** A COLEBROOKE
SHUCKBURGH, LOWER (St John the Baptist) *see* Napton-on-the-Hill, Lower Shuckburgh etc *Cov*
SHUDY CAMPS (St Mary) *see* Linton *Ely*
SHURDINGTON (St Paul) *see* Badgeworth, Shurdington and Witcombe w Bentham *Glouc*
SHURLOCK ROW (All Saints) *see* Waltham *Ox*
SHUSTOKE (St Cuthbert) *see* The Whitacres and Shustoke *Birm*
SHUTE (St Michael) *see* Stockland, Dalwood, Kilmington and Shute *Ex*
SHUTFORD (St Martin) *see* Wykeham *Ox*
SHUTTINGTON (St Matthew) *see* Newton Regis w Seckington and Shuttington *Birm*
SHUTTLEWOOD (St Laurence Mission Church) *see* Bolsover *Derby*
SHUTTLEWORTH (St John) *see* Ramsbottom St Jo and St Paul *Man*
SIBBERTOFT (St Helen) *see* Welford w Sibbertoft and Marston Trussell *Pet*
SIBDON CARWOOD (St Michael) w Halford *Heref 11* **P** *Bp and R Holden (alt)* **P-in-c** A N TOOP
SIBERTSWOLD (St Andrew) *see* Eythorne and Elvington w Waldershare etc *Cant*
SIBFORD (Holy Trinity) *see* Wykeham *Ox*
SIBLE HEDINGHAM (St Peter) w Castle Hedingham *Chelmsf 19* **P** *Bp, and Hon T R Lindsay (alt)* **R** D N KELLY
SIBSEY (St Margaret) w Frithville *Linc 20* **P** *Ld Chan* **V** W G PAGE
SIBSON (St Botolph) *see* The Sheepy Gp *Leic*
SIBTHORPE (St Peter) *S'well 3* **P** *Bp* **V** G A FIRTH
SIBTON (St Peter) *see* Yoxford and Peasenhall w Sibton *St E*
SICKLINGHALL (St Peter's Mission Church) *see* Kirkby Overblow *Ripon*
SID VALLEY *see* Sidmouth, Woolbrook, Salcombe Regis, Sidbury etc *Ex*
SIDBURY (Holy Trinity) *see* Billingsley w Sidbury, Middleton Scriven etc *Heref*
SIDBURY (St Giles and St Peter) *see* Sidmouth, Woolbrook, Salcombe Regis, Sidbury etc *Ex*
SIDCUP (Christ Church) Longland *Roch 17* **P** *Ch Trust Fund Trust* **V** A K WILSON, **Hon C** H DYALL
SIDCUP (St Andrew) *Roch 17* **P** *Bp* **V** D HILDRED, **Hon C** B W SHARPE
SIDCUP (St John the Evangelist) *Roch 17* **P** *D&C* **V** B G MIDDLETON, **Hon C** B M VINCENT
SIDDAL (St Mark) *Wakef 4* **P** *Ch Trust Fund Trust* **V** H J R FEREDAY
SIDDINGTON (All Saints) *see* Capesthorne w Siddington and Marton *Ches*
SIDDINGTON (St Peter) w Preston *Glouc 12* **P** *Ld Chan and R T G Chester-Master Esq (alt)* **R** H J MORRIS
SIDESTRAND (St Michael) *see* Overstrand, Northrepps, Sidestrand etc *Nor*
SIDFORD (St Peter) *see* Sidmouth, Woolbrook, Salcombe Regis, Sidbury etc *Ex*
SIDLESHAM (St Mary the Virgin) *Chich 3* **P** *Bp* **P-in-c** A K JENKINS
SIDLEY (All Saints) *Chich 14* **P** *R Bexhill* **V** N A TAYLOR, **NSM** S M TAYLOR
SIDLOW BRIDGE (Emmanuel) *S'wark 26* **P** *DBP* **R** W G CAMPEN

SIDMOUTH (St Nicholas w St Giles), Woolbrook, Salcombe Regis, Sidbury w Sidford, and All Saints Sidmouth *Ex 7* **P** *Patr Bd* **TR** D H JAMES, **TV** R G PECKHAM, J G STONES, J S LEE, **NSM** S W WILLINK
SIGGLESTHORNE (St Lawrence) and Rise w Nunkeeling and Bewholme *York 12* **P** *Prime Min and Ld Chan (alt)* **R** A MAKEL
SILCHESTER (St Mary) *Win 4* **P** *Duke of Wellington* **R** D C McKEEMAN
SILCHESTER COMMON (Mission Church) *see* Silchester *Win*
SILEBY (St Mary), Cossington and Seagrave *Leic 6* **P** *Patr Bd* **TR** A S COSTERTON
SILK WILLOUGHBY (St Denis) *Linc 22* **P** *Sir Lyonel Tollemache, Bt* **R** D J MUSSON
SILKSTONE (All Saints) *see* Hoylandswaine and Silkstone w Stainborough *Wakef*
SILKSTONE COMMON (Mission Room) *as above*
SILKSWORTH (St Matthew) *Dur 16* **P** *Bp* **V** *Vacant* 0191-521 1167
SILLOTH (Christ Church) w Silloth St Paul *Carl 7* **P** *Simeon's Trustees (2 turns), V Holme Cultram St Mary (1 turn)* **V** M A HESLOP
SILSDEN (St James) *Bradf 8* **P** *Bp, Adn Craven, and Trustees (jt)* **V** J COOPER
SILSOE (St James), Pulloxhill and Flitton *St Alb 9* **P** *Ball Coll Ox and Bp (alt)* **V** S C HOLROYD
SILTON (St Nicholas) *Sarum 6* **P** *DBP* **R** *Vacant*
SILTON, NETHER (All Saints) *see* Leake w Over and Nether Silton and Kepwick *York*
SILTON, OVER (St Mary) *as above*
SILVER END (St Francis) *see* Rivenhall *Chelmsf*
SILVERDALE (St John) *Blackb 15* **P** *V Warton* **V** R MASHEDER
SILVERDALE (St Luke) and Alsagers Bank *Lich 9* **P** *Bp and T H G Howard-Sneyd Esq (jt)* **P-in-c** P M JELF
SILVERHILL (St Matthew) *Chich 17* **P** *Simeon's Trustees* **R** R M COMBES
SILVERSTONE (St Michael) and Abthorpe w Slapton *Pet 5* **P** *The Crown, Leeson's Trustees, and T L Langton-Lockton Esq (by turn)* **P-in-c** B M SMITH
SILVERTON (St Mary), Butterleigh, Bickleigh and Cadeleigh *Ex 8* **P** *Bp and Sir Rivers Carew Bt* **R** A H MACDONALD
SILVINGTON (St Michael) *see* Stottesdon w Farlow, Cleeton and Silvington *Heref*
SIMONBURN (St Mungo) *see* Humshaugh w Simonburn and Wark *Newc*
SIMONSTONE (St Peter) *see* Padiham *Blackb*
SIMPSON (St Thomas) *see* Woughton *Ox*
SINFIN (St Stephen) *Derby 10* **P** *CPAS* **V** T F PRICE
SINFIN MOOR (not known) *Derby 10* **P** *Bp* **V** *Vacant* (01332) 760016
SINGLETON (St Anne) w Weeton (St Michael) *Blackb 13* **P** *R Dumbreck and V Kirkham (jt)* **V** D WILLIAMS
SINGLETON (St Mary the Virgin) *Chich 13* **P** *Bp* **R** P M JENKINS
SINNINGTON (All Saints) *see* Middleton, Newton and Sinnington *York*
SISLAND (St Mary) *see* Loddon, Sisland w Hales and Heckingham *Nor*
SISSINGHURST (Holy Trinity) w Frittenden *Cant 11* **P** *CPAS* **V** A E NORRIS
SITHNEY (St Sithney) *see* Porthleven w Sithney *Truro*
SITTINGBOURNE (Holy Trinity) w Bobbing *Cant 14* **P** *Abp* **V** R A LOVE, **NSM** B D FOULGER, E J WILLIAMS
SITTINGBOURNE (St Mary) *Cant 14* **P** *Abp* **P-in-c** N M HALL
SITTINGBOURNE (St Michael) *Cant 14* **P** *Abp* **P-in-c** C R MURRIE
SIX HILLS (Mission) *see* Old Dalby and Nether Broughton *Leic*
SIX MILE BOTTOM (St George) *see* Lt Wilbraham *Ely*
SIX PILGRIMS, The *B & W 3* **P** *Ch Soc Trust, D&C, DBF, and Bp (by turn)* **R** *Vacant* (0196324) 230
SIX SAINTS circa Holt: Bringhurst, Great Easton, Medbourne cum Holt, Stockerston and Blaston *Leic 4* **P** *D&C Pet and Adn Leic (2 turns), St Jo Coll Cam (1 turn)* **R** S R LONG
SIXHILLS (All Saints) *see* Barkwith Gp *Linc*
SKEEBY (St Agatha's District Church) *see* Easby w Brompton on Swale and Bolton on Swale *Ripon*
SKEFFINGTON (St Thomas a Beckett) *see* Billesdon and Skeffington *Leic*
SKEFFLING (St Helen) *see* Easington w Skeffling, Kilnsea and Holmpton *York*
SKEGBY (St Andrew) *S'well 4* **P** *Ld Chan* **P-in-c** J J FLETCHER, **C** B HALL, **NSM** L A CHURCH
SKEGNESS (St Clement) (St Matthew) and Winthorpe *Linc 8* **P** *Earl of Scarbrough and Bp (alt)* **R** G J WICKSTEAD, **C** S C WITCOMBE
SKELBROOKE (St Michael and All Angels) *see* Adwick-le-Street w Skelbrooke *Sheff*
SKELLINGTHORPE (St Lawrence) w Doddington *Linc 18* **P** *MMCET* **R** R G BILLINGHURST
SKELLOW (St Michael and All Angels) *see* Owston *Sheff*
SKELMANTHORPE (St Aidan) *Wakef 6* **P** *Bp* **P-in-c** P D REYNOLDS
SKELMERSDALE (Church at the Centre) *Liv 11* **P** *Bp* **V** P A BARNETT
SKELMERSDALE (St Paul) *Liv 11* **P** *V Ormskirk* **V** G E GREENWOOD, **C** A J TELFER
SKELSMERGH (St John the Baptist) w Selside and Longsleddale *Carl 9* **P** *V Kendal H Trin and DBP (alt)* **V** R D J DEW
SKELTON (All Saints) w Upleatham *York 17* **P** *Abp* **R** T N EVANS, **C** P J THOMAS
SKELTON (St Giles) w Shipton and Newton on Ouse *York 5* **P** *Abp* **R** M HARRISON
SKELTON (St Michael) and Hutton-in-the-Forest w Ivegill *Carl 4* **P** *Bp, D&C, and CCC Ox (jt)* **R** B DAWSON
SKELTON-CUM-NEWBY (St Helen's Old Church) *see* Kirby-on-the-Moor, Cundall w Norton-le-Clay etc *Ripon*
SKENDLEBY (St Peter and St Paul) *see* Partney *Linc*
SKERNE (St Leonard) *see* Hutton Cranswick w Skerne, Watton and Beswick *York*
SKERTON (St Chad) *Blackb 12* **P** *Bp* **V** T A G BILL, **NSM** E Y WILSON
SKERTON (St Luke) *Blackb 12* **P** *Trustees* **V** A J FULLER
SKEYTON (All Saints) *see* Felmingham, Skeyton, Colby, Banningham etc *Nor*
SKIDBY (St Michael) *see* Rowley w Skidby *York*
SKILGATE (St John the Baptist) *see* Brompton Regis w Upton and Skilgate *B & W*
SKILLINGTON (St James) *see* Colsterworth Gp *Linc*
SKIPSEA (All Saints) w Ulrome and Barmston w Fraisthorpe *York 10* **P** *Abp, Hon Susan Cunliffe-Lister and Exors Dr W Kane (jt)* **R** L TRENDER
SKIPTON (Christ Church) *Bradf 7* **P** *R Skipton H Trin* **V** J E PEERS
SKIPTON (Holy Trinity) *Bradf 7* **P** *Ch Ch Ox* **R** A P BOTWRIGHT, **C** J A SHARP
SKIPTON ON SWALE (St John) *see* Topcliffe w Baldersby, Dalton, Dishforth etc *York*
SKIPWITH (St Helen) *see* Bubwith w Skipwith *York*
SKIRBECK (Holy Trinity) *Linc 20* **P** *Trustees* **V** B C OSBORNE, **C** M ALLEN, **NSM** J C COLE
SKIRBECK (St Nicholas) *Linc 20* **P** *DBP* **R** *Vacant* (01205) 362734
SKIRBECK QUARTER (St Thomas) *Linc 20* **P** *DBP* **V** J A BLANCHARD
SKIRLAUGH (St Augustine) w Long Riston *York 12* **P** *Abp* **V** D W PERRY
SKIRPENBECK (St Mary) *see* Stamford Bridge Gp of Par *York*
SKIRWITH (St John the Evangelist), Ousby and Melmerby w Kirkland *Carl 4* **P** *DBP and D&C (jt)* **P-in-c** M H BURDEN
SLAD (Holy Trinity) *see* Stroud and Uplands w Slad *Glouc*
SLADE GREEN (St Augustine) *Roch 15* **P** *Bp* **P-in-c** A M HORTON
SLAIDBURN (St Andrew) *Bradf 5* **P** *Ch Soc Trust* **P-in-c** M R RUSSELL-SMITH
SLAITHWAITE (St James) w East Scammonden *Wakef 5* **P** *V Huddersfield* **V** C R TOWNSEND
SLALEY (St Mary the Virgin) *see* Healey and Slaley *Newc*
SLAPTON (Holy Cross) *see* Ivinghoe w Pitstone and Slapton *Ox*
SLAPTON (St Botolph) *see* Silverstone and Abthorpe w Slapton *Pet*
SLAPTON (St James the Great) *see* Stokenham w Sherford and Beesands, and Slapton *Ex*
SLAUGHAM (St Mary) *Chich 6* **P** *M R Warren Esq* **R** J E POSTILL
SLAUGHTER, UPPER (St Peter) and LOWER (St Mary) w Eyford and Naunton *Glouc 15* **P** *F E B Witts Esq and Bp (alt)* **P-in-c** J W S FIELDGATE
SLAUGHTERFORD (St Nicholas) *see* Biddestone w Slaughterford *Bris*
SLAWSTON (All Saints) *see* Hallaton w Horninghold, Allexton, Tugby etc *Leic*
SLEAFORD (St Denys) *see* New Sleaford *Linc*
SLEAFORD, NEW (St Denys) *Linc 22* **P** *Bp* **V** J S THOROLD, **Hon C** B W LEVICK, **NSM** P G HARDING
SLEDMERE (St Mary) and Cowlam w Fridaythorpe, Fimber and Thixendale *York 11* **P** *Abp and Sir T C M Sykes (jt)* **V** *Vacant* (01377) 226220
SLEEKBURN (St John) *Newc 1* **P** *D&C* **P-in-c** P DAWSON
SLEIGHTS (St John) *see* Eskdaleside w Ugglebarnby and Sneaton *York*
SLIMBRIDGE (St John the Evangelist) *Glouc 2* **P** *Magd Coll Ox* **P-in-c** W J BOON

SLINDON (St Chad) *see* Eccleshall *Lich*
SLINDON (St Mary), Eartham and Madehurst *Chich 1* **P** *Bp, D&C, and Mrs J Izard (jt)* **P-in-c** N M S WATERS, **NSM** H J M COSSAR
SLINFOLD (St Peter) *see* Itchingfield w Slinfold *Chich*
SLINGSBY (All Saints) *see* Street TM *York*
SLIPTON (St John the Baptist) *Pet 11* **P** *L G Stopford Sackville Esq* **V** *Vacant*
SLITTING MILL (St John the Baptist) *see* Rugeley *Lich*
SLOANE STREET (Holy Trinity) *see* Upper Chelsea H Trin w St Jude *Lon*
SLOLEY (St Bartholomew) *see* Worstead, Westwick, Sloley, Swanton Abbot etc *Nor*
SLOUGH (St Paul) (Christ Church) *Ox 23* **P** *Trustees* **V** G T KAYE, **NSM** A R CULLINGWORTH
SLOUGH, WEST *Ox 23* **P** *Patr Bd* **TR** F A WRIGHT, **TV** R J THOMPSON, G A FINLAYSON, C J DYER
SLYNE (St Luke) w Hest *Blackb 15* **P** *Bp* **V** J B SELVEY
SMALL HEATH (St Aidan) (St Oswald of Worcester) *Birm 9* **P** *Patr Bd* **V** G A WILKINSON, **C** D K CHANDA, G S GAKURU
SMALLBRIDGE (St John the Baptist) and Wardle *Man 20* **P** *Bp* **P-in-c** A J HOWELL
SMALLBURGH (St Peter) w Dilham w Honing and Crostwight *Nor 12* **P** *Bp, T R Cubitt Esq, and J C Wickman Esq (jt)* **P-in-c** B M LLEWELLYN
SMALLEY (St John the Baptist) *Derby 12* **P** *Bp* **P-in-c** V J PRICE
SMALLFIELD (Church Room) *see* Burstow *S'wark*
SMALLHYTHE (St John the Baptist) *see* Tenterden St Mildred w Smallhythe *Cant*
SMALLTHORNE (St Saviour) *Lich 11* **P** *R Norton in the Moors* **V** R J S GRIGSON
SMALLWOOD (St John the Baptist) *see* Astbury and Smallwood *Ches*
SMANNELL (Christ Church) w Enham Alamein *Win 3* **P** *Bp* **P-in-c** D F KING
SMARDEN (St Michael) *see* Biddenden and Smarden *Cant*
SMAWTHORPE St Michael *Wakef 11* **P** *Bp* **V** E I CHETWYND
SMEATON, GREAT (St Eloy) w Appleton Wiske and Birkby and Danby Wiske w Hutton Bonville *Ripon 2* **P** *MMCET (2 turns), Abp York (1 turn)* **R** *Vacant* (01609) 881205
SMEETH (St Mary) *see* Brabourne w Smeeth *Cant*
SMEETON WESTERBY (Christ Church) *see* Kibworth and Smeeton Westerby and Saddington *Leic*
SMETHCOTT (St Michael) *see* Dorrington w Leebotwood, Longnor, Stapleton etc *Heref*
SMETHWICK (Old Church) *Birm 7* **P** *Dorothy Parkes Trustees* **V** M C W GORICK, **C** B FLETCHER
SMETHWICK (Resurrection) (St Alban) (St Stephen and St Michael) *Birm 7* **P** *Bp* **V** D RAYNER, **C** J K D FULLJAMES
SMETHWICK (St Matthew w St Chad) *Birm 7* **P** *Bp and V Smethwick (alt)* **V** P E NICHOLSON
SMISBY (St James) *see* Ticknall, Smisby and Stanton by Bridge *Derby*
SMITHILLS HALL (Chapel) *see* Halliwell St Pet *Man*
SMORRALL LANE (St Andrew) *see* Bedworth *Cov*
SNAILBEACH (St Luke) *see* Minsterley *Heref*
SNAILWELL (St Peter) *Ely 3* **P** *Mrs A Crawley* **R** *Vacant*
SNAINTON (St Stephen) *see* Brompton-by-Sawdon w Snainton, Ebberston etc *York*
SNAITH (St Laurence Priory) *see* Gt Snaith *Sheff*
SNAITH, GREAT (Holy Trinity) (St John the Baptist) (St Paul) *Sheff 11* **P** *Bp* **TR** C ROBERTS
SNAPE (St John the Baptist) *see* Sternfield w Benhall and Snape *St E*
SNAPE CASTLE (Chapel of St Mary) *see* W Tanfield and Well w Snape and N Stainley *Ripon*
SNARESTONE (St Bartholomew) *see* The Appleby Gp *Leic*
SNARGATE (St Dunstan) *see* Appledore w Brookland, Fairfield, Brenzett etc *Cant*
SNEAD (St Mary the Virgin) *see* Wentnor w Ratlinghope, Myndtown, Norbury etc *Heref*
SNEATON (St Hilda) *see* Eskdaleside w Ugglebarnby and Sneaton *York*
SNEINTON (St Christopher) w St Philip *S'well 12* **P** *CPAS and Trustees (alt)* **V** I M BLAKE
SNEINTON (St Cyprian) *S'well 12* **P** *Bp* **V** W J GULL
SNEINTON (St Matthias) *S'well 12* **P** *Bp* **V** R F B SMITH
SNEINTON (St Stephen) (St Alban) *S'well 12* **P** *SMF and Bp (alt)* **V** M J THOMPSON
SNELLAND (All Saints) *see* Wickenby Gp *Linc*
SNELSTON (St Peter) *see* Norbury w Snelston *Derby*
SNETTISHAM (St Mary) w Ingoldisthorpe and Fring *Nor 16* **P** *Bp, CPAS, and D&C (jt)* **R** J D GRUNDY, **NSM** J M T M GRUNDY
SNEYD (Holy Trinity) *Lich 11* **P** *Bp* **V** B L WILLIAMS
SNEYD GREEN (St Andrew) *Lich 11* **P** *Bp* **V** B THOMPSON
SNIBSTON (St James) *see* Hugglescote w Donington, Ellistown and Snibston *Leic*
SNITTERBY (St Nicholas) *see* Bishop Norton, Wadingham and Snitterby *Linc*
SNITTERFIELD (St James the Great) w Bearley *Cov 7* **P** *Bp and V Wootton Wawen* **V** R N TREW
SNODLAND (All Saints) (Christ Church) *Roch 1* **P** *Bp and CPAS (jt)* **R** J E TIPP
SNORING, GREAT (St Mary) *see* Barney, Fulmodeston w Croxton, Hindringham etc *Nor*
SNORING, LITTLE (St Andrew) *as above*
SNOWDEN HILL Chapel Farm (not known) *see* Penistone and Thurlstone *Wakef*
SNOWSHILL (St Barnabas) *see* Childswyckham w Aston Somerville, Buckland etc *Glouc*
SOBERTON (St Peter) w Newtown *Portsm 1* **P** *Bp* **V** P J GARRATT
SOCKBURN (All Saints) *see* Dinsdale w Sockburn *Dur*
SODBURY, LITTLE (St Adeline) *see* Horton and Lt Sodbury *Glouc*
SODBURY, OLD (St John the Baptist) *see* Chipping Sodbury and Old Sodbury *Glouc*
SOHAM (St Andrew) *Ely 3* **P** *Pemb Coll Cam* **V** M G F SHEARS
SOHO (St Anne) (St Thomas) (St Peter) *Lon 3* **P** *R Westmr St Jas* **R** F C STEVENS
SOLIHULL (Catherine de Barnes) (St Alphege) (St Helen) (St Michael) *Birm 12* **P** *Patr Bd* **TR** A R WILDS, **TV** A T BULLOCK, **C** F J SMITH
SOLLARS HOPE (St Michael) *see* How Caple w Sollarshope, Sellack etc *Heref*
SOMBORNE w Ashley *Win 11* **P** *Bp* **V** M J M NORTON
SOMERBY (All Saints) *see* Burrough Hill Pars *Leic*
SOMERBY (St Margaret) *see* N Wolds Gp *Linc*
SOMERBY, NEW (St Anne) *see* Grantham *Linc*
SOMERBY, OLD (St Mary Magdalene) *Linc 14* **P** *Baroness Willoughby de Eresby* **R** *Vacant*
SOMERCOTES and Grainthorpe w Conisholme *Linc 12* **P** *Duchy of Lanc (2 turns), Magd Coll Cam and Bp (1 turn)* **P-in-c** M K DAVIES
SOMERCOTES (St Thomas) *Derby 1* **P** *Bp* **P-in-c** J B A COPE
SOMERCOTES, NORTH (St Mary) *see* Somercotes and Grainthorpe w Conisholme *Linc*
SOMERFORD (All Saints) *see* Astbury and Smallwood *Ches*
SOMERFORD (St Mary) *see* Christchurch *Win*
SOMERFORD, GREAT (St Peter and St Paul), Little Somerford, Seagry and Corston w Rodbourne *Bris 12* **P** *Bp, MMCET, and Ex Coll Ox (jt) (3 turns), Ld Chan (2 turns)* **R** J E G OSWALD
SOMERFORD, LITTLE (St John the Baptist) *see* Gt Somerford, Lt Somerford, Seagry, Corston etc *Bris*
SOMERFORD KEYNES (All Saints) *see* Kemble, Poole Keynes, Somerford Keynes etc *Glouc*
SOMERLEYTON (St Mary), Ashby, Fritton, Herringfleet, Blundeston and Lound *Nor 9* **P** *Lord Somerleyton and SMF (jt)* **R** J B V RIVIERE
SOMERS TOWN (St Mary the Virgin) *Lon 17* **P** *D&C St Paul's* **P-in-c** N P WHEELER, **C** R E M DOWLER
SOMERSAL HERBERT (St Peter) *see* Sudbury and Somersal Herbert *Derby*
SOMERSBY (St Margaret) *see* S Ormsby Gp *Linc*
SOMERSHAM (St John the Baptist) w Pidley and Oldhurst *Ely 11* **P** *Bp* **R** D J EVANS
SOMERSHAM (St Mary) w Flowton and Offton w Willisham *St E 1* **P** *Bp and MMCET (jt)* **P-in-c** R J DEDMAN
SOMERTON (St James) *see* The Heyfords w Rousham and Somerton *Ox*
SOMERTON (St Margaret) *see* Glem Valley United Benefice *St E*
SOMERTON (St Michael and All Angels) w Compton Dundon, the Charltons and Kingsdon *B & W 6* **P** *Bp Lon (1 turn), Bp (2 turns), and DBP (1 turn)* **R** C A HADLEY, **C** R O DAVIES
SOMERTON, WEST (St Mary) *see* Winterton w E and W Somerton and Horsey *Nor*
SOMPTING (St Mary the Virgin) (St Peter) *Chich 5* **P** *OStJ* **V** J W RICHARDSON
SONNING (St Andrew) (St Patrick) *Ox 16* **P** *Bp* **P-in-c** C G CLARKE, **Hon C** A C E SANDERS
SONNING COMMON (Christ the King) *see* Kidmore End *Ox*
SOOKHOLME (St Augustine) *see* Warsop *S'well*
SOOTHILL (St Luke) *see* Hanging Heaton *Wakef*
SOPLEY (St Michael and All Angels) *see* Burton and Sopley *Win*
SOPWORTH (St Mary the Virgin) *see* Boxwell, Leighterton, Didmarton, Oldbury etc *Glouc*

SOTHERTON (St Andrew) *see* Uggeshall w Sotherton, Wangford and Henham *St E*
SOTTERLEY (St Margaret) *see* Hundred River *St E*
SOTWELL (St James) *see* Brightwell w Sotwell *Ox*
SOUDLEY (St Michael) *see* Cinderford St Jo *Glouc*
SOULBURY (All Saints) *see* Stewkley w Soulbury and Drayton Parslow *Ox*
SOULBY (St Luke) *see* Kirkby Stephen w Mallerstang etc *Carl*
SOULDERN (Annunciation of the Blessed Virgin Mary) *see* Fritwell w Souldern and Ardley w Fewcott *Ox*
SOULDROP (All Saints) *see* Sharnbrook and Knotting w Souldrop *St Alb*
SOUNDWELL (St Stephen) *Bris 2* **P** *Bp* **V** W R HARRISON
SOURTON (St Thomas of Canterbury) *see* Okehampton w Inwardleigh, Bratton Clovelly etc *Ex*
SOUTH *see also under substantive place name*
SOUTH BANK (St John) *York 19* **P** *Abp* **V** C M BURKE, **C** D JAGO
SOUTH CAVE (All Saints) and Ellerker w Broomfleet *York 14* **P** *CPAS and D&C Dur (jt)* **V** D C BAILEY, **C** H A EDGERTON
SOUTH COVE (St Lawrence) *see* Wrentham w Benacre, Covehithe, Frostenden etc *St E*
SOUTH HILL (St Sampson) w Callington *Truro 11* **P** *PCC* **R** R OAKES, **NSM** D N HATREY
SOUTH MOOR (St George) *Dur 4* **P** *Bp* **P-in-c** M BEBBINGTON
SOUTH POOL (St Nicholas and St Cyriac) *see* Charleton w Buckland Tout Saints etc *Ex*
SOUTH SHIELDS (All Saints) *Dur 15* **P** *Patr Bd* **TR** J D MILLER, **C** J R FOX
SOUTH SHIELDS St Aidan (St Stephen) The Lawe *Dur 15* **P** *Bp and D&C* **R** *Vacant* 0191-456 1831
SOUTH SHIELDS (St Hilda) w St Thomas *Dur 15* **P** *D&C* **V** R L BURR
SOUTH SHIELDS (St Oswin) *Dur 15* **P** *The Crown* **V** G F FINN
SOUTH SHIELDS (St Simon) *Dur 15* **P** *The Crown* **V** R F TOBIN
SOUTH SHORE (Holy Trinity) *Blackb 9* **P** *J C Hilton Esq* **V** B DUNN, **C** P W ALLSOP
SOUTH SHORE (St Peter) *Blackb 9* **P** *Bp* **P-in-c** J BARKER
SOUTHACRE (St George) *see* Castle Acre w Newton, Rougham and Southacre *Nor*
SOUTHACRE (St George) *as above*
SOUTHALL (Christ the Redeemer) *Lon 22* **P** *Bp* **P-in-c** N J ORCHARD
SOUTHALL (Emmanuel) Conventional District *Lon 22* **C-in-c** L B SMILLIE
SOUTHALL (Holy Trinity) *Lon 22* **P** *Ch Patr Trust* **P-in-c** D I BARNES
SOUTHALL (St George) *Lon 22* **P** *D&C St Paul's* **P-in-c** D L E BRONNERT
SOUTHALL GREEN (St John) *Lon 22* **P** *Ch Patr Trust* **V** D L E BRONNERT, **P-in-c** P B DENTON, **C** D J C BOOKLESS, T L WAMBUNYA, R CHRISTOPHER
SOUTHAM (Ascension) *see* Bishop's Cleeve *Glouc*
SOUTHAM (St James) *Cov 10* **P** *The Crown* **R** J P WELBY
SOUTHAMPTON (Christ Church) Portswood *see* Portswood Ch Ch *Win*
SOUTHAMPTON City Centre (St Mary) (St Michael) *Win 12* **P** *Bp* **TR** R R WHEELER, **TV** A R AAGAARD, V J ROCKALL, S W BARTON, R V A MORRISON
SOUTHAMPTON Maybush (St Peter) *Win 12* **P** *Bp* **V** N BOAKES, **C** G R SMITH, B L COX
SOUTHAMPTON (St Alban) *see* Swaythling *Win*
SOUTHAMPTON (St Barnabas) *Win 12* **P** *Bp* **V** B J FRY
SOUTHAMPTON (St Denys) Portswood *see* Portswood St Denys *Win*
SOUTHAMPTON (St Jude) Warren Road *Win 12* **P** *Bp* **V** *Vacant* (01703) 774603
SOUTHAMPTON (St Mark) *Win 12* **P** *Ch Patr Trust* **V** P D COOPER
SOUTHAMPTON (St Mary Extra) *Win 12* **P** *Bp* **V** B P JAMES
SOUTHAMPTON Thornhill (St Christopher) *Win 12* **P** *Bp* **V** G P ANNAS, **C** R J SIMMONDS
SOUTHAMPTON Winkle Street (St Julian) *see* Southampton (City Cen) *Win*
SOUTHBERGH (St Andrew) *see* Reymerston w Cranworth, Letton, Southburgh etc *Nor*
SOUTHBOROUGH (St Peter) (Christ Church) (St Matthew) *Roch 12* **P** *Patr Bd* **TV** C B WICKS, **C** J A CASTLE
SOUTHBOROUGH (St Thomas) *Roch 12* **P** *Bp* **V** S D MASON
SOUTHBOURNE (All Saints) *see* Pokesdown All SS *Win*
SOUTHBOURNE (St Christopher) *Win 7* **P** *Bp* **V** J G BARKER
SOUTHBOURNE (St John the Evangelist) w West Thorney *Chich 13* **P** *Bp* **V** C R JENKINS, **NSM** M BAGGOTT
SOUTHBOURNE (St Katharine) (St Nicholas) *Win 7* **P** *Bp* **V** D V WASTIE
SOUTHBROOM (St James) *Sarum 19* **P** *D&C* **V** M A WARD, **C** R F TOOGOOD, **Hon C** T V F PAPE
SOUTHCHURCH (Christ Church) *Chelmsf 13* **P** *Bp* **V** M J HARRIS
SOUTHCHURCH (Holy Trinity) *Chelmsf 13* **P** *Abp Cant* **R** M A BALLARD, **C** E S ELMES
SOUTHCOATES (St Aidan) *see* Kingston upon Hull St Aid Southcoates *York*
SOUTHCOURT (Good Shepherd) *see* Walton H Trin *Ox*
SOUTHDENE (St Martin) *see* Kirkby *Liv*
SOUTHEA (Emmanuel) w Murrow and Parson Drove *Ely 19* **P** *Bp* **V** *Vacant* (01945) 700426
SOUTHEASE (St Peter) *see* Telscombe w Piddinghoe and Southease *Chich*
SOUTHEND (St John the Baptist) (St Mark) (All Saints) (St Alban) *Chelmsf 13* **P** *Patr Bd* **TR** G R BENNETT, **TV** T S WRIGHT, K K BARRON, **NSM** C R D CHEATLE, J C RAYNER
SOUTHEND (St Peter) *see* Bradfield and Stanford Dingley *Ox*
SOUTHEND-ON-SEA (St Saviour) Westcliff *Chelmsf 13* **P** *Bp, Adn Southend, and Churchwardens (jt)* **V** R H WILLIAMS, **NSM** L M WILLIAMS
SOUTHERY (St Mary) *Ely 16* **P** *Guild of All So* **R** A G COCHRANE
SOUTHFIELDS (St Barnabas) *S'wark 19* **P** *Bp* **V** D E EMMOTT
SOUTHFIELDS (St Michael and All Angels) *see* Wandsworth St Mich *S'wark*
SOUTHFLEET (St Nicholas) *Roch 4* **P** *CPAS* **R** C D GOBLE, **NSM** J C STONE
SOUTHGATE (Christ Church) *Lon 18* **P** *V Edmonton All SS* **V** D M HOYLE, **C** T A DONNELLY
SOUTHGATE Local Ecumenical Project *St E 13* **Min** F SCAMMELL
SOUTHGATE (Shared Church) *see* Grange St Andr *Ches*
SOUTHGATE (St Andrew) *Lon 18* **P** *Bp* **V** P S TAYLOR, **C** R H NORMAN
SOUTHGATE (St Mary) *Chich 7* **P** *Patr Bd* **TR** A F HAWKER, **TV** M D S GREIG, L P R MEERING, J R J BURLEY, **C** J M MORTIMER
SOUTHGATE, NEW (St Paul) *Lon 14* **P** *V Southgate Ch Ch* **V** R M TAYLOR
SOUTHILL (All Saints) *see* Clifton and Southill *St Alb*
SOUTHLAKE (St James's Church Centre) *see* Woodley *Ox*
SOUTHLEIGH (St Lawrence) *see* Colyton, Southleigh, Offwell, Widworthy etc *Ex*
SOUTHMEAD (St Stephen) *Bris 8* **P** *Bp* **V** R T BARKER, **NSM** D V EVANS
SOUTHMINSTER (St Leonard) *Chelmsf 11* **P** *Govs Charterhouse* **V** J E BATEMAN
SOUTHOE (St Leonard) *Ely 12* **P** *Mert Coll Ox* **R** *Vacant*
SOUTHOVER (St John the Baptist) *Chich 18* **P** *CPAS* **R** P J J MARKBY
SOUTHOWRAM (St Anne in the Grove) *see* Halifax St Anne Southowram *Wakef*
SOUTHPORT (All Saints) (All Souls) *Liv 9* **P** *Trustees* **V** J E BASSETT, **NSM** D H MARSTON
SOUTHPORT (Christ Church) *Liv 9* **P** *Trustees* **V** S T REID
SOUTHPORT (Emmanuel) *Liv 9* **P** *PCC* **V** C POPE, **C** P C GREEN
SOUTHPORT (Holy Trinity) *Liv 9* **P** *Trustees* **V** R G GARNER
SOUTHPORT (St Luke) *Liv 9* **P** *V Southport H Trin* **P-in-c** I R SHACKLETON
SOUTHPORT (St Philip) (St Paul) *Liv 9* **P** *V Southport Ch Ch and Trustees (jt)* **V** J M BURGESS, **C** G J BIRCH
SOUTHPORT (St Simon and St Jude) *Liv 9* **P** *Trustees* **V** M J DUERDEN
SOUTHREPPS (St James) *see* Trunch *Nor*
SOUTHREY (St John the Divine) *see* Bardney *Linc*
SOUTHROP (St Peter) *see* Coln St Aldwyns, Hatherop, Quenington etc *Glouc*
SOUTHSEA (Holy Spirit) *Portsm 6* **P** *Bp* **V** M D B LEWIS, **C** G R WADDINGTON
SOUTHSEA (St Jude) *Portsm 6* **P** *Trustees* **V** J V BYRNE, **C** C A BELL
SOUTHSEA (St Luke) *see* Portsea St Luke *Portsm*
SOUTHSEA (St Peter) *Portsm 6* **P** *Bp* **P-in-c** J V BYRNE, **C** G B HILL, **NSM** M R MILLETT
SOUTHSEA (St Simon) *Portsm 6* **P** *Ch Patr Trust* **Hon C** P A LEWIS
SOUTHTOWN (St Mary) *see* Gt Yarmouth *Nor*
SOUTHWARK (Christ Church) *S'wark 9* **P** *Marshall's Charity* **R** J E PAXTON, **NSM** A HURST

SOUTHWARK (Holy Trinity w St Matthew) *S'wark 9* **P** *Bp* **V** N A McKINNON, **C** C S BAINBRIDGE
SOUTHWARK (St George the Martyr) (St Alphege) (St Jude) *S'wark 9* **P** *Lon Corp (1 turn), Ld Chan (4 turns), Walsingham Coll TrustAssn (1 turn)* **R** A S LUCAS
SOUTHWARK (St Hugh) *see* Bermondsey St Hugh CD *S'wark*
SOUTHWATER (Holy Innocents) *Chich 8* **P** *V Horsham* **V** P H JONES
SOUTHWAY (Holy Spirit) *Ex 22* **P** *Ld Chan* **V** D M WOOD, **C** D J HOSKIN, **NSM** M J FAIRALL
SOUTHWELL (Holy Trinity) *S'well 15* **P** *CPAS* **P-in-c** M S TANNER
SOUTHWELL (St Andrew) *see* Portland All SS w St Pet *Sarum*
SOUTHWICK (Holy Trinity) *Dur 16* **P** *D&C* **R** R DIXON
SOUTHWICK (St Columba) *Dur 16* **P** *Bp* **V** J R TROOP
SOUTHWICK (St James) w Boarhunt *Portsm 1* **P-in-c** H S GRIFFITHS
SOUTHWICK (St Mary the Virgin) *see* Benefield and Southwick w Glapthorn *Pet*
SOUTHWICK (St Michael and All Angels) *Chich 4* **P** *Ld Chan* **R** C EVERETT-ALLEN, **C** D G STANIFORD, **Hon C** H F McNEIGHT, **NSM** C A THOMAS
SOUTHWICK (St Peter) *Chich 4* **P** *Bp* **P-in-c** G C CAREY
SOUTHWICK (St Thomas) *see* N Bradley, Southwick and Heywood *Sarum*
SOUTHWOLD (St Edmund King and Martyr) *St E 15* **P** *Simeon's Trustees* **NSM** T HANDLEY MACMATH
SOUTHWOOD (Mission Church) *see* Evercreech w Chesterblade and Milton Clevedon *B & W*
SOWERBY (St Mary) (St Peter) *Wakef 4* **P** *DBP* **V** J W MUIR
SOWERBY (St Oswald) *York 20* **P** *Abp* **V** J H DAVIS
SOWERBY BRIDGE (Christ Church) w Norland *Wakef 4* **P** *V Halifax* **V** P J JEFFERY
SOWTON (St Michael and All Angels) *see* Aylesbeare, Rockbeare, Farringdon etc *Ex*
SPALDING (St John the Baptist) w Deeping St Nicholas *Linc 17* **P** *Bp* **V** K A ALMOND, **C** T STOTT
SPALDING (St Mary and St Nicholas) *Linc 17* **P** *Feoffees* **V** P G F NORWOOD, **C** K STEVENTON, **NSM** A J FIDDYMENT
SPALDING (St Paul) *Linc 17* **P** *Bp and V Spalding (jt)* **P-in-c** D C MAYLOR, **NSM** P W J WINN
SPALDWICK (St James) w Barham and Woolley *Ely 10* **P** *Bp* **P-in-c** J ALFORD
SPARHAM (St Mary) *see* Lyng, Sparham, Elsing, Bylaugh, Bawdeswell etc *Nor*
SPARKBROOK (Christ Church) *Birm 9* **P** *Aston Trustees* **V** S A HOLLOWAY
SPARKBROOK (Emmanuel) *see* Sparkhill w Greet and Sparkbrook *Birm*
SPARKBROOK (St Agatha) w Balsall Heath St Barnabas *Birm 9* **P** *Bp* **V** J A HERVE
SPARKFORD (St Mary Magdalene) *see* Queen Camel w W Camel, Corton Denham etc *B & W*
SPARKHILL (St John the Evangelist) (St Bede and Emmanuel) w Greet St Bede and Sparkbrook *Birm 9* **P** *Dioc Trustees and Aston Trustees (alt)* **V** J A SELF
SPARKWELL (All Saints) *Ex 20* **P** *D&C Windsor* **V** F G DENMAN
SPARSHOLT (Holy Cross) *see* Ridgeway *Ox*
SPARSHOLT (St Stephen) *see* Crawley and Littleton and Sparsholt w Lainston *Win*
SPAXTON (St Margaret) w Charlynch, Goathurst, Enmore and Aisholt *B & W 14* **P** *Bp, MMCET, and Ch Trust Fund Trust (jt)* **R** R R EARNSHAW
SPEEN (St Mary the Virgin) *see* Newbury *Ox*
SPEETON (St Leonard) *see* Bempton w Flamborough, Reighton w Speeton *York*
SPEKE (St Aidan) (All Saints) *Liv 4* **P** *Bp* **TR** M E PLUNKETT
SPELDHURST (St Mary the Virgin) w Groombridge and Ashurst *Roch 12* **P** *DBP* **P-in-c** B C H FORTNUM, **Hon C** B E E MARSHALL
SPELSBURY (All Saints) *see* Chadlington and Spelsbury, Ascott under Wychwood *Ox*
SPEN, HIGH (St Patrick) and Rowlands Gill *Dur 13* **P** *Bp* **V** K A WYLD
SPENCERS WOOD (St Michael and All Angels) *see* Beech Hill, Grazeley and Spencers Wood *Ox*
SPENNITHORNE (St Michael) w Finghall and Hauxwell *Ripon 4* **P** *R J Dalton Esq and M C AWyvill Esq (alt)* **R** D W TORDOFF, **NSM** M G TORDOFF
SPENNYMOOR (St Paul), Whitworth and Merrington *Dur 6* **P** *D&C* **V** J S BAIN, **C** M H J HAMPEL, **NSM** G NICHOLSON
SPERNALL, Morton Bagot and Oldberrow *Cov 7* **P** *Mrs J M Pinney and Bp (alt)* **P-in-c** F J BALLINGER
SPETISBURY (St John the Baptist) w Charlton Marshall and Blandford St Mary *Sarum 7* **P** *Worc Coll Ox (1 turn), Bp (2 turns)* **R** D B PENNAL
SPEXHALL (St Peter) *see* Halesworth w Linstead, Chediston, Holton etc *St E*
SPILSBY (St James) w Hundleby *Linc 7* **P** *Baroness Willoughby de Eresby* **V** G ROBSON
SPITAL (St Agnes) *see* New Windsor *Ox*
SPITAL (St Leonard's Mission Room) *see* Chesterfield St Mary and All SS *Derby*
SPITALFIELDS (Christ Church w All Saints) *Lon 7* **P** *MMCET* **R** P W BOWTELL
SPITALGATE (St John the Evangelist) *see* Grantham *Linc*
SPITTAL (St John) *Newc 12* **P** *Bp and Mercers' Co (alt)* **V** J W SHEWAN
SPIXWORTH (St Peter) w Crostwick and Frettenham *Nor 2* **P** *Bp, Ch Soc Trust, and DBP (jt)* **R** A R GOOD
SPOFFORTH (All Saints) w Kirk Deighton *Ripon 1* **P** *Bp* **R** G JONES
SPONDON (St Werburgh) *Derby 9* **P** *Mrs L B Palmer* **V** R J ANDREWS, **C** P D MAYBURY
SPORLE (St Mary) *see* Gt and Lt Dunham w Gt and Lt Fransham and Sporle *Nor*
SPOTLAND (St Clement) *Man 20* **P** *Bp* **P-in-c** B McNIVEN, **NSM** P R ZUCCA
SPRATTON (St Andrew) *Pet 2* **P** *Bp* **V** B LEE
SPREYTON (St Michael) *Ex 12* **P** *Bp* **V** C J L NAPIER
SPRIDLINGTON (St Hilary) *see* Owmby Gp *Linc*
SPRIGG'S ALLEY (Mission Room) *see* Chinnor w Emmington and Sydenham etc *Ox*
SPRING GROVE (St Mary) *Lon 11* **P** *Ch Patr Trust* **V** D G WILSON
SPRING PARK (All Saints) *S'wark 21* **P** *Bp* **V** *Vacant* 0181-777 4447
SPRINGFIELD (All Saints) *Chelmsf 8* **P** *Air Cdre N S Paynter* **R** R J BROWN, **NSM** J MANN
SPRINGFIELD (Holy Trinity) *Chelmsf 8* **P** *Simeon's Trustees* **V** J K HAYWARD
SPRINGFIELD (St Christopher) *Birm 5* **P** *Trustees* **V** S P CORBETT
SPRINGFIELD, EAST (Church of Our Saviour) (not known) *Chelmsf 8* **P** *Bp* **P-in-c** C E HOPKINSON
SPRINGFIELD, NORTH (St Augustine of Canterbury) *Chelmsf 8* **P** *Bp* **P-in-c** J D HAYWARD
SPRINGFIELDS (St Stephen) *see* Wolverhampton St Steph *Lich*
SPRINGHILL (St Peter) *see* Birm St Pet *Birm*
SPRINGTHORPE (St George and St Laurence) *see* Corringham and Blyton Gp *Linc*
SPRINGWELL (St Mary the Virgin) *see* Sunderland St Mary and St Pet *Dur*
SPROATLEY (St Swithin) *see* Preston and Sproatley in Holderness *York*
SPROTBROUGH (St Mary the Virgin) *Sheff 8* **P** *Bp* **R** S J MATTHEWS
SPROUGHTON (All Saints) w Burstall *St E 5* **P** *D&C Cant (1 turn), Bp (2 turns)* **P-in-c** R F PALLANT
SPROWSTON (St Cuthbert) (St Mary and St Margaret) w Beeston *Nor 2* **P** *D&C* **R** M H STAGG, **C** T P P HEFFER, **NSM** R J BUNN
SPROXTON (St Bartholomew) *see* High Framland Parishes *Leic*
SPROXTON (St Chad) *see* Helmsley *York*
SQUIRRELS HEATH (All Saints) *Chelmsf 2* **P** *Bp* **V** *Vacant* (01708) 446571
STADHAMPTON (St John the Baptist) *see* Dorchester *Ox*
STAFFHURST WOOD (St Silvan) *see* Limpsfield and Titsey *S'wark*
STAFFORD (Christ Church) (St Chad) (St Mary) *Lich 10* **P** *Patr Bd* **TR** A G MURSELL, **TV** A M DAFFERN, P M FREEMAN, **C** D E KENDRICK, B M LEACH, **NSM** M J FISHER
STAFFORD (St John the Baptist) and Tixall w Ingestre *Lich 10* **P** *Bp and Earl of Shrewsbury and Talbot (jt)* **V** R M VAUGHAN
STAFFORD (St Paul) Forebridge *Lich 10* **P** *V Castle Ch* **V** M R METCALF
STAFFORD (St Thomas and St Andrew) Doxey *see* Castle Town *Lich*
STAFFORD, WEST (St Andrew) w Frome Billet *Sarum 2* **P** *Brig S Floyer-Acland* **P-in-c** P C WHEATLEY
STAGSDEN (St Leonard) *see* Bromham w Oakley and Stagsden *St Alb*
STAGSHAW CHAPEL (St Aidan) *see* St John Lee *Newc*
STAINBY (St Peter) *see* Witham Gp *Linc*
STAINCLIFFE (Christ Church) *Wakef 10* **P** *V Batley* **V** C P MORTIMER

STAINCROSS (St John the Divine) *Wakef 7* **P** *Bp* **V** J K BUTTERWORTH
STAINDROP (St Mary) *Dur 7* **P** *Lord Barnard* **V** D R JONES
STAINES (Christ Church) *Lon 13* **P** *Bp* **V** L O LINDO
STAINES (St Mary) (St Peter) *Lon 13* **P** *Ld Chan* **V** M A M ST JOHN-CHANNELL, **C** S SCOTT-HAMBLEN
STAINFIELD (St Andrew) *see* Bardney *Linc*
STAINFORTH (St Mary) *Sheff 11* **P** *Bp* **P-in-c** J E ASHTON
STAINFORTH (St Peter) *see* Langcliffe w Stainforth and Horton *Bradf*
STAINING (St Luke Mission Church) *see* Blackpool St Mich *Blackb*
STAINLAND (St Andrew) *Wakef 2* **P** *V Halifax* **V** S DANDO
STAINLEY, NORTH (St Mary the Virgin) *see* W Tanfield and Well w Snape and N Stainley *Ripon*
STAINLEY, SOUTH (St Wilfrid) *see* Markington w S Stainley and Bishop Thornton *Ripon*
STAINMORE (St Stephen) *see* Brough w Stainmore, Musgrave and Warcop *Carl*
STAINTON (St Peter w St Paul) w Hilton *York 22* **P** *Abp (2 turns), DBP (1 turn)* **V** B A HOPKINSON
STAINTON (St Winifred) *see* Tickhill w Stainton *Sheff*
STAINTON, GREAT (All Saints) *see* Bishopton w Gt Stainton *Dur*
STAINTON BY LANGWORTH (St John the Baptist) *see* Barlings *Linc*
STAINTON DALE (St John the Baptist) *see* Cloughton and Burniston w Ravenscar etc *York*
STAINTON LE VALE (St Andrew) *see* Walesby *Linc*
STAITHES (St Peter) *see* Hinderwell w Roxby *York*
STAKEFORD (Holy Family) *see* Choppington *Newc*
STALBRIDGE (St Mary) *Sarum 6* **P** *CCC Cam* **R** *Vacant* (01963) 362859
STALHAM (St Mary) and East Ruston w Brunstead *Nor 12* **P** *Mrs S F Baker and DBP (alt)* **V** A C BILLETT
STALISFIELD (St Mary) *see* Eastling w Ospringe and Stalisfield w Otterden *Cant*
STALLING BUSK (St Matthew) *see* Askrigg w Stallingbusk *Ripon*
STALLINGBOROUGH (St Peter and St Paul) *see* Healing and Stallingborough *Linc*
STALMINE (St James) *Blackb 10* **P** *V Lanc* **V** T G MIDDLEDITCH
STALYBRIDGE (Holy Trinity and Christ Church) *Ches 14* **P** *Trustees* **NSM** M R CAVANAGH
STALYBRIDGE (St George) *Man 17* **P** *Lord Deramore and R Ashton-under-Lyne St Mich (jt)* **NSM** P BRIERLEY, D BROADBENT, R FOX
STALYBRIDGE (St Paul) *Ches 14* **P** *Trustees* **V** P L ROBINSON, **C** J M MacLEOD
STAMBOURNE (St Peter and St Thomas Becket) *see* Upper Colne *Chelmsf*
STAMBRIDGE (St Mary and All Saints) *Chelmsf 12* **P** *Ld Chan (1 turn), Govs Charterhouse (3 turns)* **P-in-c** F W B KENNY
STAMFORD (All Saints) (St John the Baptist) *Linc 13* **P** *Ld Chan and Burghley Ho Preservation Trust (alt)* **V** N RUSSELL, **C** R J SEAL, **Hon C** D M BOND
STAMFORD (Christ Church) *Linc 13* **P** *Bp* **P-in-c** R J MACKRILL
STAMFORD (St George) (St Paul) *Linc 13* **P** *Burghley Ho Preservation Trust* **R** K S SWITHINBANK, **C** M A N TAYLOR
STAMFORD (St Mary) (St Martin) *Linc 13* **P** *Burghley Ho Preservation Trust* **R** N S D GIBSON
STAMFORD BRIDGE Group of Parishes, The (St John the Baptist) *York 7* **P** *Lord Egremont (2 turns), The Crown (1 turn), and Ld Chan (1 turn)* **R** J HARRISON
STAMFORD HILL (St Bartholomew) *Lon 19* **P** *The Crown* **V** R N S LEECE
STAMFORD HILL (St Thomas) *Lon 19* **P** *R Hackney* **V** E S MORROW
STAMFORDHAM (St Mary the Virgin) w Matfen *Newc 3* **P** *Ld Chan* **V** R CAVAGAN
STANBRIDGE (St John the Baptist) *see* Totternhoe, Stanbridge and Tilsworth *St Alb*
STANBURY (Mission Church) *see* Haworth *Bradf*
STAND (All Saints) *Man 14* **P** *Earl of Wilton* **C** D J FRENCH
STANDISH (St Nicholas) w Haresfield and Moreton Valence w Whitminster *Glouc 8* **P** *Bp and Col Sir Piers Bengough (jt)* **P-in-c** N E L BAKER
STANDISH (St Wilfrid) *Blackb 4* **P** *Bp* **R** P K WARREN, **C** T J COOPER
STANDLAKE (St Giles) *see* Lower Windrush *Ox*
STANDON (All Saints) and Cotes Heath *Lich 7* **P** *Bp and V Eccleshall (jt)* **Dn-in-c** C M WITHERS
STANDON (St Mary) *St Alb 18* **P** *Ch Fund Trust Fund* **V** D L HUMPHREY
STANFIELD (St Margaret) *see* Litcham w Kempston, E and W Lexham, Mileham etc *Nor*
STANFORD (All Saints) *see* Lyminge w Paddlesworth, Stanford w Postling etc *Cant*
STANFORD (All Saints) *Nor 13* **P** *Bp* **V** *Vacant*
STANFORD (St Nicholas) *see* Swinford w Catthorpe, Shawell and Stanford *Leic*
STANFORD BISHOP (St James) *see* Acton Beauchamp and Evesbatch w Stanford Bishop *Heref*
STANFORD DINGLEY (St Denys) *see* Bradfield and Stanford Dingley *Ox*
STANFORD IN THE VALE (St Denys) w Goosey and Hatford *Ox 17* **P** *D&C Westmr (3 turns), Simeon's Trustees (2 turns)* **V** M T WENHAM
STANFORD-LE-HOPE (St Margaret) w Mucking *Chelmsf 14* **P** *MMCET* **P-in-c** J A K GUEST, **C** M J LUNT, **NSM** L R SMITH
STANFORD-ON-SOAR (St John the Baptist) *see* E and W Leake, Stanford-on-Soar, Rempstone etc *S'well*
STANFORD-ON-TEME (St Mary) *see* Teme Valley N *Worc*
STANFORD RIVERS (St Margaret) *see* Greensted-juxta-Ongar w Stanford Rivers *Chelmsf*
STANGROUND (St John the Baptist) (St Michael and All Angels) and Farcet *Ely 13* **P** *Em Coll Cam* **TR** D E S DE SILVA, **TV** I H FIRMSTONE
STANHOE (All Saints) *see* Docking, The Birchams, Stanhoe and Sedgeford *Nor*
STANHOPE (St Thomas) w Frosterley *Dur 9* **P** *Bp and The Crown (alt)* **C** J D F INKPIN, **Hon C** P H JONES
STANION (St Peter) *see* Brigstock w Stanion and Lowick and Sudborough *Pet*
STANLEY (All Saints) (St Andrew) *Derby 13* **P** *Bp* **P-in-c** J C CLARKE
STANLEY (St Agnes) *see* Endon w Stanley *Lich*
STANLEY (St Anne) *Liv 8* **P** *R W Derby* **V** M C DAVIES, **C** G J CUFF
STANLEY (St Peter) *Wakef 12* **P** *Provost* **V** W E HENDERSON, **C** M J BARNES
STANLEY (St Stephen) *Dur 4* **P** *Bp (2 turns), The Crown (1 turn)* **TR** R J WALLACE, **C** G E GLOVER, A P HUTCHINSON
STANLEY (St Thomas) *Dur 9* **P** *R Brancepeth* **V** A FEATHERSTONE
STANLEY PONTLARGE (Chapel) *see* Winchcombe, Gretton, Sudeley Manor etc *Glouc*
STANLEYS, The *Glouc 8* **P** *Mrs L Y K Fisher and Jes Coll Cam (jt)* **P-in-c** H E ALLEN, **NSM** R M BRYANT
STANMER (not known) w Falmer *Chich 2* **P** *Bp* **P-in-c** A N ROBINSON
STANMORE (St Luke) *Win 13* **P** *Bp* **V** N P SEAL, **C** M R GARDNER
STANMORE, GREAT (St John the Evangelist) *Lon 23* **P** *R O Bernays Esq* **R** M H V BOWLES, **NSM** L D MACKENZIE
STANMORE, LITTLE (St Lawrence) *Lon 23* **P** *Bp* **R** P M REECE, **C** J C NEAL
STANNEY (St Andrew) *see* Ellesmere Port *Ches*
STANNINGFIELD (St Nicholas) *see* Hawstead and Nowton w Stanningfield etc *St E*
STANNINGLEY (St Thomas) *Ripon 6* **P** *V Leeds St Pet* **R** S C BROWN, **C** P J COWPER
STANNINGTON (Christ Church) *Sheff 4* **P** *Bp* **V** P W WEST
STANNINGTON (St Mary the Virgin) *Newc 1* **P** *Bp* **V** K R WARD
STANSFIELD (All Saints) *see* Denston w Stradishall and Stansfield *St E*
STANSTEAD (St James) *see* Glem Valley United Benefice *St E*
STANSTEAD ABBOTS (St Andrew) *see* Gt Amwell w St Margaret's and Stanstead Abbots *St Alb*
STANSTEAD ST MARGARET (St Mary the Virgin) *as above*
STANSTED (St Mary) w Fairseat and Vigo *Roch 10* **P** *Bp* **R** D G CLARK, **P-in-c** C J L NOBLE
STANSTED (St Paul) (Christ Church) *Chich 13* **P** *Earl of Bessborough* **C** R F THOMAS
STANSTED MOUNTFITCHET (St John) w Birchanger and Farnham *Chelmsf 21* **P** *Bp, New Coll Ox, and Mrs L A Murphy (jt)* **C** A SPURR
STANTON (All Saints) (St John the Baptist) *St E 9* **P** *The Crown* **R** F T HOWARD
STANTON (St Gabriel) *see* Marshwood Vale TM *Sarum*
STANTON (St Mary) *see* Denstone w Ellastone and Stanton *Lich*
STANTON (St Mary and All Saints) *see* Markfield *Leic*
STANTON (St Michael and All Angels) *see* Toddington, Stanton, Didbrook w Hailes etc *Glouc*
STANTON BY BRIDGE (St Michael) *see* Ticknall, Smisby and Stanton by Bridge *Derby*

STANTON-BY-DALE (St Michael and All Angels) w Dale Abbey *Derby 15* **P** *Bp* **R** I E GOODING
STANTON DREW (Blessed Virgin Mary) *see* Bishop Sutton and Stanton Drew and Stowey *B & W*
STANTON FITZWARREN (St Leonard) *see* Stratton St Margaret w S Marston etc *Bris*
STANTON HARCOURT (St Michael) *see* Lower Windrush *Ox*
STANTON HILL (All Saints) *see* Skegby *S'well*
STANTON-IN-PEAK (Holy Trinity) *see* Youlgreave, Middleton, Stanton-in-Peak etc *Derby*
STANTON LACY (Hayton Bent Hall) *see* Culmington w Onibury, Bromfield etc *Heref*
STANTON LACY (St Peter) *as above*
STANTON ON HINE HEATH (St Andrew) *Lich 23* **P** *Sir Beville Stanier, Bt* **V** D J HUMPHRIES
STANTON-ON-THE-WOLDS (All Saints) *S'well 9* **P** *Trustees of Sir Rupert Bromley* **P-in-c** T SISSON
STANTON PRIOR (St Lawrence) *see* Farmborough, Marksbury and Stanton Prior *B & W*
STANTON ST BERNARD (All Saints) *see* Swanborough *Sarum*
STANTON ST JOHN (St John the Baptist) *see* Wheatley *Ox*
STANTON ST QUINTIN (St Quintin) *see* Hullavington, Norton and Stanton St Quintin *Bris*
STANTONBURY (Christ Church) and Willen *Ox 25* **P** *Patr Bd* **TR** J A PONTER, **TV** P F WORTHEN, J M STOKER, H M BAKER, J M HENRY, **NSM** D B MILLS, J M APPLEBY, C R BAKER
STANWAY (St Albright) (St Andrew) *Chelmsf 17* **P** *Magd Coll Ox* **R** H HEATH
STANWAY (St Peter) *see* Toddington, Stanton, Didbrook w Hailes etc *Glouc*
STANWELL (St Mary the Virgin) *Lon 13* **P** *Ld Chan* **V** D C PEMBERTON, **NSM** H S L NICHOLSON
STANWICK (St Laurence) w Hargrave *Pet 10* **P** *Ld Chan (2 turns), Bp (1 turn)* **P-in-c** E L WOOD
STANWIX (St Michael) *Carl 3* **P** *Bp* **C** W E SANDERS
STAPEHILL (All Saints) *see* Hampreston *Sarum*
STAPENHILL (Immanuel) *Derby 16* **P** *Ch Soc Trust* **V** G D SIMMONS
STAPENHILL (St Peter) w Cauldwell *Derby 16* **P** *Ch Soc Trust* **V** E E LOBB, **C** M P KENDALL
STAPLE (St James) *see* Woodnesborough w Worth and Staple *Cant*
STAPLE FITZPAINE (St Peter) w Orchard Portman, Thurlbear and Stoke St Mary *B & W 18* **P** *Bp* **R** *Vacant* (01823) 443581
STAPLE TYE (St James) *see* Gt Parndon *Chelmsf*
STAPLECROSS (St Mark) *see* Ewhurst *Chich*
STAPLEFIELD COMMON (St Mark) *Chich 6* **P** *V Cuckfield* **P-in-c** T S STRATFORD
STAPLEFORD (All Saints) *see* Carlton-le-Moorland w Stapleford *Linc*
STAPLEFORD (St Andrew) *Ely 7* **P** *D&C* **P-in-c** K F M FISHER
STAPLEFORD (St Andrew's Mission Church) (St Helen) (St Luke) *S'well 7* **P** *CPAS* **C** S M FALSHAW
STAPLEFORD (St Mary) *see* Bramfield w Stapleford and Waterford *St Alb*
STAPLEFORD (St Mary) *see* Lower Wylye and Till Valley *Sarum*
STAPLEFORD ABBOTTS (St Mary) *see* Lambourne w Abridge and Stapleford Abbotts *Chelmsf*
STAPLEFORD TAWNEY (St Mary the Virgin) w Theydon Mount *Chelmsf 27* **P** *DBP* **P-in-c** P H W CHAPMAN
STAPLEGROVE (St John) *B & W 18* **P** *Bp* **R** N C VENNING
STAPLEHURST (All Saints) *Cant 11* **P** *St Jo Coll Cam* **R** B BARNES
STAPLETON (Holy Trinity) *Bris 7* **P** *Bp* **R** J A RISDON, **Hon C** S R EMTAGE
STAPLETON (St John) *see* Dorrington w Leebotwood, Longnor, Stapleton etc *Heref*
STAPLETON (St Martin) *see* Barwell w Potters Marston and Stapleton *Leic*
STAPLETON (St Mary) *see* Bewcastle, Stapleton and Kirklinton etc *Carl*
STARBECK (St Andrew) *Ripon 1* **P** *V Harrogate Ch Ch* **V** M B TAYLOR
STARCROSS (St Paul) *see* Kenton, Mamhead, Powderham, Cofton and Starcross *Ex*
STARSTON (St Margaret) *see* Pulham Market, Pulham St Mary and Starston *Nor*
STARTFORTH (Holy Trinity) and Bowes and Rokeby w Brignall *Ripon 2* **P** *Ld Chan (1 turn), Bp, Earl of Lonsdale and Lords of the Manor of Bowes (2 turns)* **V** G F DEAR
STATFOLD (St Matthew) *see* Clifton Campville w Edingale and Harlaston *Lich*
STATHERN (St Guthlac) *see* Barkestone w Plungar, Redmile and Stathern *Leic*

STAUGHTON, GREAT (St Andrew) *Ely 12* **P** *St Jo Coll Ox* **V** *Vacant* (01480) 861554
STAUGHTON, LITTLE (All Saints) *see* Keysoe w Bolnhurst and Lt Staughton *St Alb*
STAUNTON (All Saints) *see* Coleford w Staunton *Glouc*
STAUNTON (St James) *see* Hartpury w Corse and Staunton *Glouc*
STAUNTON (St Mary) w Flawborough *S'well 3* **P** *E G Staunton Esq* **P-in-c** J H BATESON
STAUNTON HAROLD (Holy Trinity) *see* Breedon cum Isley Walton and Worthington *Leic*
STAUNTON ON ARROW (St Peter) *see* Pembridge w Moorcourt, Shobdon, Staunton etc *Heref*
STAUNTON-ON-WYE (St Mary the Virgin) *see* Letton w Staunton, Byford, Mansel Gamage etc *Heref*
STAVELEY (All Saints) *see* Farnham w Scotton, Staveley, Copgrove etc *Ripon*
STAVELEY (St James), Ings and Kentmere *Carl 9* **P** *V Kendal H Trin* **V** G WATSON
STAVELEY (St John the Baptist) and Barrow Hill *Derby 3* **P** *Bp, Adn Chesterfield, and Duke of Devonshire (jt)* **TR** W A BUTT, **TV** P J O'REILLY, **C** D BOOTH
STAVELEY IN CARTMEL (St Mary) *see* Leven Valley *Carl*
STAVERTON (St Catherine) w Boddington and Tredington w Stoke Orchard and Hardwicke *Glouc 11* **P** *Bp* **V** K R CORLESS
STAVERTON (St Mary the Virgin) *see* Daventry, Ashby St Ledgers, Braunston etc *Pet*
STAVERTON (St Paul) *see* Hilperton w Whaddon and Staverton etc *Sarum*
STAVERTON (St Paul de Leon) *see* Broadhempston, Woodland, Staverton etc *Ex*
STAWELL (St Francis) *see* Middlezoy and Othery and Moorlinch *B & W*
STAWLEY (St Michael and All Angels) *see* Wellington and Distr *B & W*
STEANE (St Peter) *see* Aynho and Croughton w Evenley etc *Pet*
STEART BAY (St Andrew) *see* Cannington, Otterhampton, Combwich and Stockland *B & W*
STEBBING (St Mary the Virgin) w Lindsell *Chelmsf 18* **P** *Bp* **V** J S SUTTON, **NSM** S C BAZLINTON
STECHFORD (All Saints) (St Andrew) *Birm 14* **P** *St Pet Coll Ox* **P-in-c** G C FRANCIS
STEDHAM (St James) w Iping *Chich 10* **P** *Bp* **R** *Vacant* (0173081) 3342
STEEP (All Saints) and Froxfield w Privett *Portsm 5* **P** *Ld Chan and Magd Coll Cam (alt)* **V** D M PINE, **NSM** J C GRACE
STEEPING, GREAT (All Saints) *see* Firsby w Gt Steeping *Linc*
STEEPING, LITTLE (St Andrew) *Linc 7* **P** *Baroness Willoughby de Eresby* **R** G ROBSON
STEEPLE (St Lawrence and All Saints) *Chelmsf 11* **P-in-c** L BLANEY
STEEPLE (St Michael and All Angels) *see* Corfe Castle, Church Knowle, Kimmeridge etc *Sarum*
STEEPLE ASHTON (St Mary the Virgin) w Semington and Keevil *Sarum 17* **P** *D&C Win (1 turn), Magd Coll Cam (3 turns)* **V** D M HART
STEEPLE ASTON (St Peter and St Paul) w North Aston and Tackley *Ox 9* **P** *BNC Ox, St Jo Coll Ox, and Exors Lt-Col A D Taylor (jt)* **R** M A H RODEN
STEEPLE BARTON (St Mary) *see* Westcote Barton w Steeple Barton, Duns Tew etc *Ox*
STEEPLE BUMPSTEAD (St Mary) and Helions Bumpstead *Chelmsf 19* **P** *Ld Chan* **V** G R MANSFIELD
STEEPLE CLAYDON (St Michael) *see* The Claydons *Ox*
STEEPLE LANGFORD (All Saints) *see* Yarnbury *Sarum*
STEEPLE MORDEN (St Peter and St Paul) *see* Shingay Gp of Par *Ely*
STEETLY (All Saints) *see* Whitwell *Derby*
STEETON (St Stephen) *Bradf 8* **P** *V Kildwick* **V** K R OWEN, **C** B M WILKINSON
STELLA (St Cuthbert) *Dur 13* **P** *Bp* **R** A OATES
STELLING (St Mary) *see* Petham and Waltham w Lower Hardres etc *Cant*
STENIGOT (St Nicholas) *see* Asterby Gp *Linc*
STEPNEY (St Dunstan and All Saints) *Lon 7* **P** *Bp* **R** C T J CHESSUN, **C** K J SCULLY, G D IRESON, A M M BISHOP, **Hon C** G G WHITE
STEPPINGLEY (St Lawrence) *see* Ampthill w Millbrook and Steppingley *St Alb*
STERNFIELD (St Mary Magdalene) w Benhall and Snape *St E 19* **P** *Exors Mrs A H V Aldous, Mrs A C V Wentworth, and Mrs M A Bertin (by turn)* **R** N H BEVAN
STERT (St James) *see* Redhorn *Sarum*
STETCHWORTH (St Peter) *Ely 4* **P** *Duke of Sutherland* **P-in-c** J S ASKEY
STEVENAGE (All Saints) Pin Green *St Alb 23* **P** *Bp* **V** S F AUSTIN

STEVENAGE (Holy Trinity) *St Alb 23* **P** *Bp* **V** C E HARDMAN, **C** H K DERHAM, J R CROCKER, **NSM** A MARINER
STEVENAGE (St Andrew and St George) *St Alb 23* **P** *Bp* **R** M BARNSLEY
STEVENAGE (St Hugh) (St John) Chells *St Alb 23* **P** *Bp* **V** J D CAMPBELL, **C** B EBELING
STEVENAGE (St Mary) Sheppall w Aston *St Alb 23* **P** *Bp* **V** G B WHITE, **C** A D MILTON, **NSM** A M GRIEVES
STEVENAGE (St Nicholas) *St Alb 23* **P** *Bp* **V** J R BAINBRIDGE, **C** R H TOTTERDELL
STEVENAGE (St Peter) Broadwater *St Alb 23* **P** *Bp* **V** D H HAGUE
STEVENTON (St Michael and All Angels) w Milton *Ox 10* **P** *Ch Ch Ox and D&C Westmr (jt)* **P-in-c** C J PATCHING
STEVENTON (St Nicholas) *see* N Waltham and Steventon, Ashe and Deane *Win*
STEVINGTON (Church Room) (St Mary the Virgin) *St Alb 15* **P** *Bp* **P-in-c** P N JEFFERY
STEWARDS LANE (St Thomas) *see* Ditton St Mich *Liv*
STEWKLEY (St Michael and All Angels) w Soulbury and Drayton Parslow *Ox 26* **P** *Bp, Earl of Rosebery, and MMCET (jt)* **V** N J COTTON
STEWTON (St Andrew) *see* Louth *Linc*
STEYNING (St Andrew) *Chich 12* **P** *MMCET* **V** P M RAMPTON
STIBBARD (All Saints) *see* Twyford, Guist, Bintree, Themelthorpe etc *Nor*
STIBBINGTON (St John the Baptist) *Ely 13* **P** *Sir Stephen Hastings* **P-in-c** P O POOLEY
STICKFORD (St Helen) *see* Stickney Gp *Linc*
STICKLEPATH (St Mary) *see* S Tawton and Belstone *Ex*
STICKLEPATH (St Paul) *see* Barnstaple *Ex*
STICKNEY Group, The (St Luke) *Linc 7* **P** *DBP, Ld Chan, and Bp (by turn)* **V** J R WORSDALL
STIDD (St Saviour) *see* Ribchester w Stidd *Blackb*
STIFFKEY (St John and St Mary) and Cockthorpe w Morston, Langham and Binham *Nor 18* **P** *Bp, Sir Euan Anstruther-Gough-Calthorpe Bt, and DBP (by turn)* **P-in-c** E J PENNY, **NSM** D E PENNY
STIFFORD (St Cedd) (St Mary) *Chelmsf 14* **P** *Bp* **R** M B WOODMANSEY
STIFFORD, SOUTH (St Mary the Virgin) *see* Grays Thurrock *Chelmsf*
STILLINGFLEET (St Helen) *see* Escrick and Stillingfleet w Naburn *York*
STILLINGTON (St John) *see* Grindon and Stillington *Dur*
STILLINGTON (St Nicholas) *see* Sheriff Hutton, Farlington, Stillington etc *York*
STILTON (St Mary Magdalene) w Denton and Caldectoe and Folkesworth w Morborne and Haddon *Ely 13* **P** *Mrs H R Horne and Bp, Ld Chan (alt)* **R** R LONGFOOT, **NSM** M GRIFFITH
STINCHCOMBE (St Cyr) *see* Cam w Stinchcombe *Glouc*
STINSFORD (St Michael) *see* Charminster and Stinsford *Sarum*
STIRCHLEY (All Saints) *see* Cen Telford *Lich*
STIRCHLEY (Ascension) *Birm 4* **P** *R Kings Norton* **NSM** M HARRIS
STISTED (All Saints) w Bradwell-juxta-Coggeshall and Pattiswick *Chelmsf 15* **P** *Bp, Personal Reps Mrs D E G Keen, and Abp Cant (by turn)* **P-in-c** J MARVELL
STITHIANS (St Stythians) *see* St Stythians w Perranarworthal and Gwennap *Truro*
STIXWOULD (St Peter) *see* Woodhall Spa Gp *Linc*
STOAK (St Lawrence) *see* Ellesmere Port *Ches*
STOCK (St Barnabas) and Lydlinch *Sarum 6* **P** *G A L F Pitt-Rivers Esq (2 turns), Col J L Yeatman (2 turns), and V Iwerne Minster (1 turn)* **P-in-c** J C DAY
STOCK HARVARD (All Saints) *Chelmsf 9* **P** *Guild of All So* **R** R A J BUCKINGHAM
STOCKBRIDGE (Old St Peter) (St Peter) and Longstock and Leckford *Win 11* **P** *Bp and St Jo Coll Ox (jt)* **R** P C AVES
STOCKBURY (St Mary Magdalene) *see* Newington w Hartlip and Stockbury *Cant*
STOCKCROSS (St John) *see* Welford w Wickham and Gt Shefford, Boxford etc *Ox*
STOCKERSTON (St Peter) *see* Six Saints circa Holt *Leic*
STOCKING FARM (St Luke) *Leic 1* **P** *Bp* **V** M J SMITH
STOCKING PELHAM (St Mary) *see* Braughing w Furneux Pelham and Stocking Pelham *St Alb*
STOCKINGFORD (St Paul) *Cov 5* **P** *V Nuneaton* **P-in-c** M F VINCENT
STOCKLAND (St Mary Magdalene) *see* Cannington, Otterhampton, Combwich and Stockland *B & W*
STOCKLAND (St Michael and All Angels), Dalwood, Kilmington and Shute *Ex 5* **P** *Bp, D&C and DBP (jt)* **P-in-c** P E WILSON, **Hon C** J N C GIDDINGS
STOCKLAND GREEN (St Mark) *Birm 8* **P** *The Crown* **P-in-c** P A HINDS
STOCKLEIGH ENGLISH (St Mary the Virgin) *see* N Creedy *Ex*
STOCKLEIGH POMEROY (St Mary the Virgin) *as above*
STOCKLINCH (St Mary Magdalene) *see* Ilminster and District *B & W*
STOCKPORT South West (St George) (St Mark) (St Gabriel) *Ches 18* **P** *Patr Bd* **TR** J M ROFF, **TV** M J PARKER, S I D WHITE, **C** M R CHRISTIAN
STOCKPORT (St Augustine) *see* Cheadle Heath *Ches*
STOCKPORT (St Mary) *Ches 18* **P** *G&C Coll Cam* **R** R P SCOONES, **NSM** H C BRIDGE, J BOWLES
STOCKPORT (St Matthew) *Ches 18* **P** *Bp* **P-in-c** S A FOSTER
STOCKPORT (St Saviour) *Ches 18* **P** *Trustees* **V** D V COOKSON
STOCKPORT (St Thomas) (St Peter) *Ches 18* **P** *Bp and Ch Union (jt)* **R** K D N KENRICK, **C** K R BROOKES
STOCKSBRIDGE (St Matthias) *Sheff 7* **P** *Bp* **V** *Vacant* 0114-288 6964
STOCKSFIELD (St John) *see* Bywell St Pet *Newc*
STOCKTON (Holy Trinity) *Dur 10* **P** *Bp* **P-in-c** N E WATSON
STOCKTON (St Andrew) *see* Teme Valley N *Worc*
STOCKTON (St Chad) *Dur 10* **P** *Bp* **V** J M PERKINS, **NSM** E WALKER
STOCKTON (St Chad) *see* Beckbury, Badger, Kemberton, Ryton, Stockton etc *Lich*
STOCKTON (St John the Baptist) *see* Yarnbury *Sarum*
STOCKTON (St Mark) *Dur 10* **P** *Bp* **NSM** J M THOMAS
STOCKTON (St Michael and All Angels) *see* Napton-on-the-Hill, Lower Shuckburgh etc *Cov*
STOCKTON (St Michael and All Angels) *see* Gillingham w Geldeston, Stockton, Ellingham etc *Nor*
STOCKTON HEATH (St Thomas) *Ches 4* **P** *P G Greenall Esq* **V** T P F KENNY, **NSM** D L MELLOR
STOCKTON-ON-TEES (St Chad) *see* Stockton St Chad *Dur*
STOCKTON ON TEES (St James) *Dur 10* **P** *Bp* **V** W T G GRIFFITHS
STOCKTON-ON-TEES (St John the Baptist) *Dur 10* **P** *Bp* **V** D J STEPHENSON
STOCKTON-ON-TEES (St Mark) *see* Stockton St Mark *Dur*
STOCKTON-ON-TEES (St Paul) *Dur 10* **P** *The Crown* **V** P M HOOD
STOCKTON-ON-TEES (St Peter) *Dur 10* **P** *Bp* **V** M A WHITEHEAD, **C** A JOHNSTON, **NSM** N G BENZIES
STOCKTON-ON-TEES (St Thomas) *Dur 10* **P** *Bp* **V** D J WHITTINGTON, **C** P D ASHDOWN
STOCKTON-ON-THE-FOREST (Holy Trinity) w Holtby and Warthill *York 4* **P** *Abp* **R** B A GIBLIN
STOCKWELL (St Michael) *S'wark 10* **P** *V Kennington St Mark* **V** G S PARFITT
STOCKWELL GREEN (St Andrew) *S'wark 10* **P** *Abp, Bp, and TR N Lambeth (jt)* **V** P R SIMMONDS
STOCKWITH, EAST (St Peter) *see* Corringham and Blyton Gp *Linc*
STOCKWITH, WEST (St Mary the Virgin) *see* Misterton and W Stockwith *S'well*
STOCKWOOD (Christ the Servant) *see* Bris Ch the Servant Stockwood *Bris*
STODDEN Churches, The *St Alb 15* **P** *MMCET and DBP (alt)* **Dn-in-c** S R STEVENSON
STODMARSH (St Mary) *see* Littlebourne and Ickham w Wickhambreaux etc *Cant*
STODY (St Mary) *see* Brinton, Briningham, Hunworth, Stody etc *Nor*
STOGUMBER (Blessed Virgin Mary) w Nettlecombe and Monksilver *B & W 17* **P** *D&C, and D&C Windsor (alt)* **P-in-c** B T LYONS
STOGURSEY (St Andrew) w Fiddington *B & W 17* **P** *Eton Coll and DBP (alt)* **R** A E APPLEGARTH
STOKE (St Mary and St Andrew) *see* Colsterworth Gp *Linc*
STOKE (St Michael) *see* Coventry Caludon *Cov*
STOKE (St Peter and St Paul) *see* Grain w Stoke *Roch*
STOKE, EAST (St Oswald) w Syerston *S'well 3* **P** *Bp* **R** G A FIRTH
STOKE, NORTH (St Martin) *see* Bath Weston All SS w N Stoke and Langridge *B & W*
STOKE, NORTH (St Mary the Virgin) *see* Langtree *Ox*
STOKE, SOUTH (St Andrew) *see* Goring w S Stoke *Ox*
STOKE, SOUTH (St James the Great) *see* Combe Down w Monkton Combe and S Stoke *B & W*
STOKE, SOUTH (St Leonard) *see* Arundel w Tortington and S Stoke *Chich*
STOKE, WEST (St Andrew) *Chich 13* **P** *Bp* **R** D A JOHNSON
STOKE ABBOTT (St Mary) *see* Beaminster Area *Sarum*
STOKE ALBANY (St Botolph) w Wilbarston and Ashley w Weston-by-Welland and Sutton Bassett *Pet 9* **P** *Comdr*

L M M Saunders-Watson (2 turns), Bp (1 turn), DBP (1 turn) **R** R V STAPLETON
STOKE ALDERMOOR (St Catherine) *see* Coventry Caludon *Cov*
STOKE ASH (All Saints) *see* Thorndon w Rishangles, Stoke Ash, Thwaite etc *St E*
STOKE BARDOLPH (St Luke) *see* Gedling *S'well*
STOKE BISHOP (St Mary Magdalene) *Bris 8* **P** *Bp* **V** D J R RITCHIE, **Hon C** C M PILGRIM, **NSM** C A FROUDE
STOKE BLISS (St Peter) *see* Teme Valley S *Worc*
STOKE BRUERNE (St Mary the Virgin) w Grafton Regis and Alderton *Pet 5* **P** *BNC Ox and Ld Chan (alt)* **R** *Vacant* (01604) 862352
STOKE BY CLARE (St John the Baptist) *see* Clare w Poslingford, Cavendish etc *St E*
STOKE BY NAYLAND (St Mary) w Leavenheath *St E 3* **P** *Sir Joshua Rowley, Bt* **P-in-c** D W FINCH
STOKE CANON (St Mary Magdalene), Poltimore w Huxham and Rewe w Netherexe *Ex 2* **P** *D&C, Lady Stucley, and Bp (by turn)* **V** P D L AVIS
STOKE CHARITY (St Mary and St Michael) *see* Wonston and Stoke Charity w Hunton *Win*
STOKE CLIMSLAND (not known) *Truro 9* **P** *Bp and Duchy of Cornwall (alt)* **P-in-c** A R INGLEBY
STOKE D'ABERNON (St Mary the Virgin) *Guildf 10* **P** *K Coll Cam* **R** D C VINCENT
STOKE DAMEREL (St Andrew w St Luke) *Ex 21* **P** *Trustees Lord St Levan* **R** G D CRYER
STOKE DOYLE (St Rumbold) *see* Aldwincle w Thorpe Achurch, Pilton, Wadenhoe etc *Pet*
STOKE DRY (St Andrew) *see* Lyddington w Stoke Dry and Seaton w Caldecott *Pet*
STOKE EDITH (St Mary) *see* Tarrington w Stoke Edith, Aylton, Pixley etc *Heref*
STOKE FERRY (All Saints) w Wretton *Ely 15* **P** *Ld Chan* **P-in-c** N O TUFFNELL
STOKE FLEMING (St Peter), Blackawton and Strete *Ex 14* **P** *Bp and BDP (jt)* **V** R H WHITE
STOKE GABRIEL (St Gabriel) and Collaton *Ex 13* **P** *Bp* **V** R P PRANCE
STOKE GIFFORD (St Michael) *Bris 6* **P** *Bp* **TR** D C R WIDDOWS, **TV** S J SMITH, **NSM** G T D ANGEL
STOKE GOLDING (St Margaret) w Dadlington *Leic 13* **P** *Bp* **P-in-c** C A R GASH
STOKE GOLDINGTON (St Peter) *see* Gayhurst w Ravenstone, Stoke Goldington etc *Ox*
STOKE HAMMOND (St Luke) *see* Newton Longville w Stoke Hammond and Whaddon *Ox*
STOKE HEATH (St Alban) *see* Cov E *Cov*
STOKE HILL (St Peter) *Guildf 5* **P** *Bp* **V** D J FURNESS, **NSM** B J RICH
STOKE HOLY CROSS (Holy Cross) w Dunston, Arminghall and Caistor St Edmunds w Markshall *Nor 8* **P** *D&C and Mrs D Pott (jt)* **R** D C BROOME
STOKE-IN-TEIGNHEAD (St Andrew) w Combe-in-Teignhead and Haccombe *Ex 11* **P** *Sir Rivers Carew, Bt* **R** R A SOUTHWOOD
STOKE LACY (St Peter and St Paul) and Moreton Jeffries w Much Cowarne, Ocle Pychard and Ullingswick *Heref 2* **P** *D&C, Bp Birm, P H G Morgan Esq, and Bp (by turn)* **P-in-c** M R SMITH, **C** D PEARCE, E J BRYANT
STOKE LYNE (St Peter) *see* Shelswell *Ox*
STOKE MANDEVILLE (St Mary the Virgin) *see* Ellesborough, The Kimbles and Stoke Mandeville *Ox*
STOKE NEWINGTON (St Andrew) *Lon 5* **P** *Bp* **V** R K BALLANTINE
STOKE NEWINGTON St Faith (St Matthias) and All Saints *Lon 5* **P** *City Corp* **V** C J FULLER, **NSM** R A FARLEY
STOKE NEWINGTON (St John the Evangelist) *see* Brownswood Park *Lon*
STOKE NEWINGTON (St Mary) (Old Parish Church) *Lon 5* **P** *Bp* **R** A G SCOTT, **C** P C HULLYER
STOKE NEWINGTON (St Olave) *Lon 5* **P** *Ld Chan* **P-in-c** J C E SYLVESTER
STOKE NEWINGTON COMMON (St Michael and All Angels) *Lon 5* **P** *Bp* **V** N R EVANS, **C** J F PORTER-PRYCE
STOKE-NEXT-GUILDFORD (St John the Evangelist) *Guildf 5* **P** *Simeon's Trustees* **NSM** D M WHITWAM
STOKE ORCHARD (St James the Great) *see* Staverton w Boddington and Tredington etc *Glouc*
STOKE PARK (St Peter) *see* Ipswich St Mary at Stoke w St Pet *St E*
STOKE PERO (not known) *see* Porlock w Stoke Pero *B & W*
STOKE POGES (St Giles) *Ox 23* **P** *Trustees Duke of Leeds Trust* **V** C E HARRIS
STOKE PRIOR (St Luke) *see* Leominster *Heref*
STOKE PRIOR (St Michael), Wychbold and Upton Warren *Worc 8* **P** *Bp and D&C (alt)* **R** D M WIGHT, **NSM** S H WIGHT
STOKE RIVERS (St Bartholomew) *see* Shirwell, Loxhore, Kentisbury, Arlington, etc *Ex*
STOKE ROW (St John the Evangelist) *see* Langtree *Ox*
STOKE ST GREGORY (St Gregory) w Burrowbridge and Lyng *B & W 18* **P** *D&C (2 turns), R O Meade-King Esq (1 turn)* **V** C F E ROWLEY
STOKE ST MARY (St Mary) *see* Staple Fitzpaine, Orchard Portman, Thurlbear etc *B & W*
STOKE ST MICHAEL (St Michael) *see* Leigh upon Mendip w Stoke St Michael *B & W*
STOKE ST MILBOROUGH (St Milburgha) *see* Bitterley w Middleton, Stoke St Milborough etc *Heref*
STOKE SUB HAMDON (Blessed Virgin Mary) (All Saints Mission Church) *B & W 6* **P** *Ch Patr Trust* **V** H A HALLETT
STOKE TALMAGE (St Mary Magdalene) *see* Tetsworth, Adwell w S Weston, Lewknor etc *Ox*
STOKE TRISTER (St Andrew) *see* Charlton Musgrove, Cucklington and Stoke Trister *B & W*
STOKE UPON TERN (St Peter) *see* Cheswardine, Childs Ercall, Hales, Hinstock etc *Lich*
STOKE-UPON-TRENT (St Peter-ad-Vincula) (St Paul) *Lich 12* **P** *Bp* **TR** E C RUDDOCK, **TV** W H SMITH, J A GORDON
STOKEHAM (St Peter) *see* Rampton w Laneham, Treswell, Cottam and Stokeham *S'well*
STOKENCHURCH (St Peter and St Paul) and Ibstone *Ox 29* **P** *Bp* **P-in-c** C J P CHADWICK
STOKENHAM (St Michael and All Angels) w Sherford and Beesands, and Slapton *Ex 14* **P** *Prime Min* **R** W A McCOUBREY
STOKESAY (St Christopher) (St John the Baptist) *Heref 11* **P** *T P D La Touche Esq* **P-in-c** A N TOOP
STOKESBY (St Andrew) *see* Filby, Thrigby, Mautby, Stokesby, Runham etc *Nor*
STOKESLEY (St Peter and St Paul) *York 22* **P** *Abp* **R** M D A DYKES, **C** D R WILLIAMS
STOLFORD (St Peter) *see* Stogursey w Fiddington *B & W*
STON EASTON (Blessed Virgin Mary) *see* Chewton Mendip w Ston Easton, Litton etc *B & W*
STONDON (All Saints) *see* Meppershall w Campton and Stondon *St Alb*
STONDON MASSEY (St Peter and St Paul) *see* Blackmore and Stondon Massey *Chelmsf*
STONE (All Saints) w Woodford and Hill *Glouc 2* **P** *Major R Jenner-Fust and V Berkeley (alt)* **V** P C F WOOSTER
STONE (Christ Church) and Oulton-with-Moddershall *Lich 13* **P** *Simeon's Trustees* **V** T J JOHNSON
STONE near Dartford (St Mary) *Roch 2* **P** *Bp* **R** J A RANDALL
STONE (St John the Baptist) w Dinton and Hartwell *Ox 21* **P** *Bp and Grocers' Co (jt)* **R** D J COOKE
STONE (St Mary the Virgin) *see* Chaddesley Corbett and Stone *Worc*
STONE (St Michael) w Aston (St Saviour) *Lich 13* **P** *Bp* **R** J R HARGREAVES, **NSM** B F WILSON
STONE CROSS (St Luke) w Langney, North *Chich 16* **P** *Bp* **V** J M GRAVES
STONE-IN-OXNEY (St Mary the Virgin) *see* Wittersham w Stone-in-Oxney and Ebony *Cant*
STONE QUARRY (St Luke) *see* E Grinstead St Swithun *Chich*
STONEBRIDGE (St Michael and All Angels) *Lon 21* **P** *Bp* **V** R L SMITH, **C** F ADU-BOACHIE
STONEBROOM (St Peter) *see* Morton and Stonebroom *Derby*
STONEFOLD (St John) *see* Haslingden w Grane and Stonefold *Blackb*
STONEGATE (St Peter) *Chich 19* **P** *E J B Hardcastle Esq and M H Reid Esq (jt)* **P-in-c** M G P INSLEY, **C** S W NUTH
STONEGRAVE (Holy Trinity) *see* Harome w Stonegrave, Nunnington and Pockley *York*
STONEHAM, NORTH (All Saints) *Win 9* **P** *R H W Fleming Esq* **R** J E OWEN, **C** L DOLAN, **NSM** D C BRAY
STONEHAM, NORTH (St Nicholas) *see* Valley Park *Win*
STONEHAM, SOUTH (St Mary) *see* Swaythling *Win*
STONEHAM BASSETT, NORTH (St Michael) *see* N Stoneham *Win*
STONEHAM BASSETT GREEN, NORTH (St Christopher) *as above*
STONEHOUSE (St Cyr) *Glouc 8* **P** *The Crown* **V** J N K HARRIS
STONEHOUSE (St Paul) *see* Plymouth St Andr and St Paul Stonehouse *Ex*
STONELEIGH (St John the Baptist) *Guildf 9* **P** *Bp* **V** *Vacant* 0181-393 3738

STONELEIGH (St Mary the Virgin) w Ashow and Baginton *Cov 4* **P** *Lord Leigh and Bp (jt)* **R** D E WEBSTER, **NSM** D JOHNSON, E JOHNSON
STONESBY (St Peter) *see* Waltham on the Wolds, Stonesby, Saxby etc *Leic*
STONESFIELD (St James the Great) w Combe *Ox 9* **P** *Duke of Marlborough* **R** G J H B van der WEEGEN
STONEY MIDDLETON (St Martin) *see* Baslow w Curbar and Stoney Middleton *Derby*
STONEY STANTON (St Michael) *see* Broughton Astley and Croft w Stoney Stanton *Leic*
STONEYCROFT (All Saints) *Liv 8* **P** *Bp* **V** W J STALKER
STONEYCROFT (St Paul) *see* Liv St Paul Stoneycroft *Liv*
STONEYDELPH (St Martin in the Delph) *see* Glascote and Stonydelph *Lich*
STONHAM ASPAL (St Mary and St Lambert) *see* Crowfield w Stonham Aspal and Mickfield *St E*
STONHAM PARVA (St Mary) *see* Creeting St Mary, Creeting St Peter etc *St E*
STONNALL (St Peter) *Lich 1* **P** *V Shenstone* **P-in-c** J R FAGAN
STONTON WYVILLE (St Denys) *see* Church Langton w Tur Langton, Thorpe Langton etc *Leic*
STONY STRATFORD (St Mary and St Giles) *Ox 25* **P** *Bp* **V** C H J CAVELL-NORTHAM
STOODLEIGH (St Margaret) *see* Washfield, Stoodleigh, Withleigh etc *Ex*
STOPHAM (St Mary the Virgin) and Fittleworth *Chich 11* **P** *D&C and Sir Brian Barttelot, Bt (jt)* **R** A I SMYTH
STOPSLEY (St Thomas) *St Alb 14* **P** *Bp* **V** D G ALEXANDER
STORRIDGE (St John the Baptist) *see* Cradley w Mathon and Storridge *Heref*
STORRINGTON (St Mary) *Chich 12* **P** *Keble Coll Ox* **R** J M ACHESON, **C** P A HESS
STORTH (All Saints Mission) *see* Arnside *Carl*
STOTFOLD (St Mary the Virgin) and Radwell *St Alb 16* **P** *Bp* **R** S G PUGH
STOTTESDON (St Mary) w Farlow, Cleeton St Mary and Silvington *Heref 9* **P** *Bp* **R** W J BROMLEY
STOUGHTON (Emmanuel) *Guildf 5* **P** *Simeon's Trustees* **V** J F SALTER, **C** R J SLIPPER
STOUGHTON (St Mary) *see* Compton, the Mardens, Stoughton and Racton *Chich*
STOUGHTON (St Mary and All Saints) *see* Thurnby w Stoughton *Leic*
STOULTON (St Edmund) w Drake's Broughton and Pirton and Norton *Worc 4* **P** *Croome Estate Trustees, D&C, and Bp (jt)* **R** I READ
STOUR, EAST (Christ Church) *see* Gillingham *Sarum*
STOUR, UPPER *Sarum 14* **P** *Exors H P R Hoare (1 turn), Bp (2 turns), and Bourton Chpl Trustees (1 turn)* **R** C A R MOORSOM, **Hon C** P A RUNDLE
STOUR, WEST (St Mary) *see* Gillingham *Sarum*
STOUR PROVOST (St Michael and All Angels) *as above*
STOUR ROW (All Saints) *as above*
STOUR VALLEY Group, The *see* Clare w Poslingford, Cavendish etc *St E*
STOURBRIDGE (St John the Evangelist) *see* Old Swinford Stourbridge *Worc*
STOURBRIDGE (St Mary) *as above*
STOURBRIDGE (St Michael and All Angels) Norton *Worc 12* **P** *Bp* **V** M J BEASLEY
STOURBRIDGE (St Thomas) *Worc 12* **P** *Bp* **V** S HUTCHINSON, **NSM** C S MOORHOUSE
STOURPAINE (Holy Trinity) *see* Pimperne, Stourpaine, Durweston and Bryanston *Sarum*
STOURPORT-ON-SEVERN (St Michael and All Angels) and Wilden *Worc 13* **P** *Earl Baldwin of Bewdley and V Kidderminster St Mary and All SS (jt)* **V** B GILBERT, **C** A E WOOLCOCK, **NSM** S M DATSON
STOURTON (St Peter) *see* Kinver and Enville *Lich*
STOURTON (St Peter) *see* Upper Stour *Sarum*
STOURTON CAUNDLE (St Peter) *see* The Caundles w Folke and Holwell *Sarum*
STOVEN (St Margaret) *see* Hundred River *St E*
STOW Group, The (St Mary the Virgin) *Linc 2* **P** *Bp and DBP (jt)* **R** G S RICHARDSON
STOW w Quy *Ely 6* **P** *Bp* **V** *Vacant* (01223) 811277
STOW, WEST (St Mary) *see* Culford, W Stow and Wordwell w Flempton etc *St E*
STOW BARDOLPH (Holy Trinity) *see* Wimbotsham w Stow Bardolph and Stow Bridge etc *Ely*
STOW BEDON (St Botolph) *see* Caston, Griston, Merton, Thompson etc *Nor*
STOW BRIDGE Mission (St Peter) *see* Wimbotsham w Stow Bardolph and Stow Bridge etc *Ely*
STOW LONGA (St Botolph) *Ely 10* **P** *Bp* **V** R A FROST
STOW MARIES (St Mary and St Margaret) *see* Purleigh, Cold Norton and Stow Maries *Chelmsf*
STOW ON THE WOLD (St Edward) *Glouc 15* **P** *DBP* **R** R F ROTHERY, **NSM** H J GARDNER
STOWE (Assumption of St Mary the Virgin) *Ox 22* **P** *Stowe Sch* **P-in-c** R B JACKSON
STOWE (St Michael and All Angels) *see* Bucknell w Chapel Lawn, Llanfair Waterdine etc *Heref*
STOWE, UPPER (St James) *see* Heyford w Stowe Nine Churches and Flore etc *Pet*
STOWE BY CHARTLEY (St John the Baptist) *see* Hixon w Stowe-by-Chartley *Lich*
STOWE NINE CHURCHES (St Michael) *see* Heyford w Stowe Nine Churches and Flore etc *Pet*
STOWELL (St Leonard) *see* Chedworth, Yanworth and Stowell, Coln Rogers etc *Glouc*
STOWELL (St Mary Magdalene) *see* Henstridge and Charlton Horethorne w Stowell *B & W*
STOWEY (St Nicholas and Blessed Virgin Mary) *see* Bishop Sutton and Stanton Drew and Stowey *B & W*
STOWEY, NETHER (Blessed Virgin Mary) w Over Stowey *B & W 17* **P** *D&C Windsor and MMCET (alt)* **V** P DENISON
STOWEY, OVER (St Peter and St Paul) *see* Nether Stowey w Over Stowey *B & W*
STOWFORD (St John) *see* Marystowe, Coryton, Stowford, Lewtrenchard etc *Ex*
STOWLANGTOFT (St George) *see* Badwell Ash w Gt Ashfield, Stowlangtoft etc *St E*
STOWMARKET (St Peter and St Mary) *St E 6* **P** *Ch Patr Trust* **V** T C JONES, **NSM** R M STRETCH, D WEBB, R F GILBERT
STOWTING (St Mary the Virgin) *see* Sellindge w Monks Horton and Stowting etc *Cant*
STOWUPLAND (Holy Trinity) *see* Old Newton w Stowupland *St E*
STRADBROKE (All Saints) w Horham, Athelington and Redlingfield *St E 17* **P** *Bp (3 turns), Lt-Comdr G C Marshall (1 turn), and Dr G I Soden (1 turn)* **R** D J STREETER
STRADISHALL (St Margaret) *see* Denston w Stradishall and Stansfield *St E*
STRADSETT (St Mary) *see* Crimplesham w Stradsett *Ely*
STRAGGLETHORPE (St Michael) *see* Brant Broughton and Beckingham *Linc*
STRAITS, THE (St Andrew) *see* Sedgley All SS *Worc*
STRAMSHALL (St Michael and All Angels) *see* Uttoxeter Area *Lich*
STRANTON (All Saints) *Dur 3* **P** *St Jo Coll Dur* **V** S R TAYLOR, **C** S BUTLER
STRATFIELD MORTIMER (St Mary) *Ox 12* **P** *Eton Coll* **V** J A ELLIS, **NSM** C G LEA, M J OKE
STRATFIELD SAYE (St Mary) *see* Sherfield-on-Loddon and Stratfield Saye etc *Win*
STRATFORD (St John the Evangelist and Christ Church) w Forest Gate St James *Chelmsf 3* **P** *V W Ham* **V** D A RICHARDS, **C** M OKELLO, **Hon C** J P RICHARDSON, **NSM** J V MEADWAY
STRATFORD NEW TOWN (St Paul) *Chelmsf 3* **P** *Ch Patr Trust* **P-in-c** S M GRIFFITHS
STRATFORD-ON-AVON (Holy Trinity) w Bishopton *Cov 8* **P** *Bp* **R** P L HOLLIDAY, **C** D J TURNER, M TURNER
STRATFORD ST MARY (St Mary) *see* Higham, Holton St Mary, Raydon and Stratford *St E*
STRATFORD SUB CASTLE (St Lawrence) *Sarum 15* **P** *D&C* **P-in-c** B J HOPKINSON
STRATTON (St Andrew) and Launcells *Truro 8* **P** *Duchy of Cornwall and CPAS (alt)* **V** R N STRANACK
STRATTON (St Mary) (St Michael) and Wacton *Nor 5* **P** *G&C Coll Cam, DBP, and New Coll Ox (by turn)* **R** P L COLEY
STRATTON (St Mary the Virgin) *see* Bradford Peverell, Stratton, Frampton etc *Sarum*
STRATTON (St Peter), North Cerney, Baunton and Bagendon *Glouc 12* **P** *R T G Chester Master Esq, Jes Coll Ox, Univ Coll Ox (jt)* **R** H A S COCKS, **NSM** D H S LEESON, D R EADY
STRATTON, EAST (All Saints) *see* Micheldever and E Stratton, Woodmancote etc *Win*
STRATTON, UPPER (St Philip) *Bris 12* **P** *Bp* **V** P J STONE
STRATTON AUDLEY (St Mary and St Edburga) *see* Shelswell *Ox*
STRATTON ON THE FOSSE (St Vigor) *see* Chilcompton w Downside and Stratton on the Fosse *B & W*
STRATTON ST MARGARET (St Margaret) w South Marston and Stanton Fitzwarren *Bris 12* **P** *Patr Bd* **TR** T D HAWKINGS, **TV** R J SNOW, **Hon C** R J BURSTON
STRATTON STRAWLESS (St Margaret) *see* Hevingham w Hainford and Stratton Strawless *Nor*
STREAT (not known) w Westmeston *Chich 9* **P** *Woodard Schs* **NSM** G R WALKER

STREATHAM (Christ Church) *S'wark 14* **P** *R Streatham St Leon* **V** C J IVORY
STREATHAM Furzedown (St Paul) *see* Streatham St Paul *S'wark*
STREATHAM (Immanuel) (St Andrew) *S'wark 14* **P** *Bp, Hyndman Trustees, and R Streatham St Leon (jt)* **V** S BUTLER, **C** J A CARROLL
STREATHAM (St Leonard) *S'wark 14* **P** *Bp* **R** J R WILCOX, **Hon C** L M WRIGHT, **NSM** D W SHACKELL
STREATHAM (St Paul) (St Andrew's Church Hall) *S'wark 18* **P** *Bp* **V** A J R DRIVER, **Hon C** J M DRIVER
STREATHAM (St Peter) *S'wark 14* **P** *St Steph Ho Ox* **V** A S WALKER
STREATHAM (St Thomas) *see* Telford Park St Thos *S'wark*
STREATHAM, WEST (St James) *S'wark 18* **P** *CPAS* **V** P I MOUNSTEPHEN, **C** C T BARKER
STREATHAM HILL (St Margaret the Queen) *S'wark 14* **P** *Bp* **V** G T WILLIAMS
STREATHAM PARK (St Alban) *S'wark 18* **P** *Ch Soc Trust* **V** A W EVERETT
STREATHAM VALE (Holy Redeemer) *S'wark 14* **P** *CPAS* **V** I H GILMOUR
STREATLEY (St Margaret) *St Alb 14* **P** *Bp* **V** R W WOOD
STREATLEY (St Mary) w Moulsford *Ox 18* **P** *Bp* **P-in-c** E R M POLOMSKI, **Hon C** J P MACKNEY, **NSM** C L WINDEBANK
STREET (Holy Trinity) (Mission Church) w Walton *B & W 5* **P** *DBP* **R** F J GREED
STREET Team Ministry, The *York 3* **P** *Patr Bd* **TR** G S SIMPSON, **C** R E LONG
STREETLY (All Saints) *Lich 26* **P** *Bp* **V** P A R HAMMERSLEY, **C** G FRASER, C R SUCH
STRELLEY (All Saints) *see* Bilborough w Strelley *S'well*
STRENSALL (St Mary the Virgin) *York 5* **P** *Abp* **V** G C GALLEY
STRETE (St Michael) *see* Stoke Fleming, Blackawton and Strete *Ex*
STRETFORD (All Saints) *Man 7* **P** *Bp* **P-in-c** A DURRANS
STRETFORD (St Bride) *Man 7* **P** *Trustees* **R** P J RAWLINGS, **NSM** V M ECCLES
STRETFORD (St Matthew) *Man 7* **P** *D&C* **R** H R ENTWISTLE, **NSM** B A DUNN
STRETFORD (St Peter) *Man 7* **P** *The Crown* **R** J S CROSS
STRETHALL (St Mary the Virgin) *see* Heydon, Gt and Lt Chishill, Chrishall etc *Chelmsf*
STRETHAM (St James) *see* Ely *Ely*
STRETTON (St John) *see* Penkridge Team *Lich*
STRETTON (St Mary) w Claymills *Lich 14* **P** *Baroness Gretton* **V** P D HOWARD
STRETTON (St Matthew) and Appleton Thorn *Ches 4* **P** *Mrs P F du Bois Grantham and Dr S P L du Bois Davidson (jt)* **V** R ROWLANDS
STRETTON (St Nicholas) *see* Greetham and Thistleton w Stretton and Clipsham *Pet*
STRETTON, LITTLE (All Saints) *see* Church Stretton *Heref*
STRETTON GRANDISON (St Laurence) *see* Bosbury w Wellington Heath etc *Heref*
STRETTON MAGNA (St Giles) *see* Gt Glen, Stretton Magna and Wistow etc *Leic*
STRETTON ON DUNSMORE (All Saints) *see* Bourton w Frankton and Stretton on Dunsmore etc *Cov*
STRETTON ON DUNSMORE (Mission Church) *as above*
STRETTON ON FOSSE (St Peter) *see* Ilmington w Stretton-on-Fosse etc *Cov*
STRETTON PARVA (St John the Baptist) *see* Gaulby *Leic*
STRETTON SUGWAS (St Mary Magdalene) *Heref 4* **P** *DBP* **P-in-c** J W R MORRISON
STRICKLAND, GREAT (St Barnabas) *see* Morland, Thrimby, Gt Strickland and Cliburn *Carl*
STRINES (St Paul) *see* Marple All SS *Ches*
STRINGSTON (not known) *see* Quantoxhead *B & W*
STRIXTON (St John) *see* Wollaston and Strixton *Pet*
STROOD (St Francis) *Roch 6* **P** *Bp* **V** B R INGRAM
STROOD (St Nicholas) w St Mary *Roch 6* **P** *Bp and D&C (jt)* **V** A A MUSTOE, **C** A C UPHILL
STROUD (Holy Trinity) (St Alban Mission Church) *Glouc 1* **P** *Bp* **P-in-c** D T MERRY, **C** S J EARLEY, **NSM** D E STODDART
STROUD (Mission Church) *see* Steep and Froxfield w Privett *Portsm*
STROUD (St Laurence) and Uplands w Slad *Glouc 1* **P** *Bp* **V** B C E COKER
STROUD GREEN (Holy Trinity) *Lon 20* **P** *Bp* **V** B K LUNN
STROXTON (All Saints) *see* Harlaxton Gp *Linc*
STRUBBY (St Oswald) *see* Wold-Marsh Gp *Linc*
STRUMPSHAW (St Peter) *see* Burlingham St Edmund w Lingwood, Strumpshaw etc *Nor*
STUBBINGS (St James the Less) *see* Hurley and Stubbings *Ox*
STUBBINS (St Philip) *see* Edenfield and Stubbins *Man*
STUBBS CROSS (St Francis) *see* Kingsnorth w Shadoxhurst *Cant*
STUBSHAW CROSS (St Luke) *see* Ashton-in-Makerfield St Thos *Liv*
STUBTON (St Martin) *see* Claypole *Linc*
STUDHAM (St Mary the Virgin) *see* Kensworth, Studham and Whipsnade *St Alb*
STUDLAND (St Nicholas) *see* Swanage and Studland *Sarum*
STUDLEY (Nativity of the Blessed Virgin Mary) *Cov 7* **P** *DBP* **V** R W DEIMEL, **C** T J HARMER, **NSM** M M DEIMEL
STUDLEY (St John the Evangelist) *Sarum 17* **P** *R Trowbridge St Jas* **P-in-c** P N BARNES
STUKELEY, GREAT (St Bartholomew) w Little (St Martin) *Ely 9* **P** *SMF and Bp (jt)* **R** *Vacant* (01480) 453016
STUNTNEY (Holy Cross) *see* Ely *Ely*
STURMER (St Mary) *see* Ridgewell w Ashen, Birdbrook and Sturmer *Chelmsf*
STURMINSTER MARSHALL (St Mary), Kingston Lacy and Shapwick *Sarum 10* **P** *Eton Coll and Nat Trust (alt)* **V** I J MAYO
STURMINSTER NEWTON (St Mary) and Hinton St Mary *Sarum 6* **P** *G A L F Pitt-Rivers Esq (3 turns), Col J L Yeatman (2 turns), and V Iwerne Minster (1 turn)* **P-in-c** J C DAY
STURRY (St Nicholas) w Fordwich and Westbere w Hersden *Cant 3* **P** *Abp, Ld Chan, and St Aug Foundn Cant (by turn)* **R** P J GAUSDEN
STURTON (St Hugh) *see* Stow Gp *Linc*
STURTON, GREAT (All Saints) *see* Hemingby *Linc*
STURTON-LE-STEEPLE (St Peter and St Paul) *see* N Wheatley, W Burton, Bole, Saundby, Sturton etc *S'well*
STUSTON (All Saints) *see* N Hartismere *St E*
STUTTON (St Aidan) *see* Tadcaster w Newton Kyme *York*
STUTTON (St Peter) *see* Brantham w Stutton *St E*
STYVECHALE (St James) *Cov 3* **P** *Col A M H Gregory-Hood* **V** J LEACH, **C** B R WILSON
SUCKLEY (St John the Baptist) *see* Alfrick, Lulsley, Suckley, Leigh and Bransford *Worc*
SUDBOROUGH (All Saints) *see* Brigstock w Stanion and Lowick and Sudborough *Pet*
SUDBOURNE (All Saints) *see* Orford w Sudbourne, Chillesford, Butley and Iken *St E*
SUDBROOKE (St Edward) *see* Barlings *Linc*
SUDBURY (All Saints) and Somersal Herbert *Derby 14* **P** *Bp and DBP (alt)* **P-in-c** D MILNER
SUDBURY (All Saints) w Ballingdon and Brundon *St E 12* **P** *Simeon's Trustees* **P-in-c** A M R PLATT
SUDBURY (St Andrew) *Lon 21* **P** *Bp* **V** A J CHRISTIAN, **NSM** G E HEWLETT
SUDBURY (St Gregory) St Peter and Chilton *St E 12* **P** *Bp (3 turns), Ch Soc Trust (1 turn)* **P-in-c** L R PIZZEY
SUDDEN (St Aidan) *see* Rochdale *Man*
SUDLEY MANOR (St Mary) *see* Winchcombe, Gretton, Sudeley Manor etc *Glouc*
SUFFIELD (St Margaret) *see* Felmingham, Skeyton, Colby, Banningham etc *Nor*
SUFFIELD PARK (St Martin) *see* Cromer *Nor*
SUGLEY (Holy Saviour) *Newc 7* **P** *Bp* **V** S T ROBSON
SULBY (St Stephen's Chapel) *see* Lezayre *S & M*
SULGRAVE (St James the Less) *see* Culworth w Sulgrave and Thorpe Mandeville etc *Pet*
SULHAM (St Nicholas) *see* Pangbourne w Tidmarsh and Sulham *Ox*
SULHAMSTEAD ABBOTS (St Mary) and Bannister w Ufton Nervet *Ox 12* **P** *Qu Coll Ox and Or Coll Ox (alt)* **P-in-c** J P E SIBLEY
SULLINGTON (St Mary) and Thakeham w Warminghurst *Chich 12* **P** *Bp and DBP (alt)* **R** P MESSENGER
SUMMERFIELD (Christ Church) (Cavendish Road Hall) *Birm 2* **P** *R Birm St Martin w Bordesley* **V** J B KNIGHT
SUMMERFIELD (St John's Chapel) *see* Hartlebury *Worc*
SUMMERSDALE (St Michael) *see* Chichester *Chich*
SUMMERSTOWN (St Mary) *S'wark 18* **P** *Ch Soc Trust* **V** R J RYAN
SUMMERTOWN (St Michael and All Angels) *see* Wolvercote w Summertown *Ox*
SUNBURY, UPPER (St Saviour) *Lon 13* **P** *V Sunbury* **V** A F P BROWN
SUNBURY-ON-THAMES (St Mary) *Lon 13* **P** *D&C St Paul's* **V** J R DUDLEY
SUNDERLAND Pennywell (St Thomas) *Dur 16* **P** *Bp* **V** *Vacant* 0191-534 2100
SUNDERLAND Red House (St Cuthbert) *Dur 16* **P** *D&C* **P-in-c** N S GOSSWINN
SUNDERLAND (St Chad) *Dur 16* **P** *Bp* **V** J D CHADD
SUNDERLAND (St Mary the Virgin) (St Peter) *Dur 16* **P** *Bp* **V** K A WALTON, **C** P J NORTH

SUNDERLAND (St Michael) *Dur 16* **P** *Bp* **TR** B HAILS, **TV** D W ROSAMOND, I D HUNTER SMART, **NSM** W HALL, J M M FRANCIS
SUNDERLAND Town End Farm (St Bede) *Dur 16* **P** *Bp* **V** J W POULTER
SUNDERLAND, NORTH (St Paul) *Newc 10* **P** *Lord Crewe's Trustees* **V** D G ROGERSON
SUNDERLAND POINT (Mission Church) *see* Overton *Blackb*
SUNDON (St Mary) *St Alb 14* **P** *Bp* **V** L S PULLAN
SUNDRIDGE (St Mary) w Ide Hill *Roch 9* **P** *Abp* **R** B E S GODFREY, **NSM** A M BOYLE
SUNNINGDALE (Holy Trinity) *Ox 11* **P** *Bp* **V** *Vacant* (01344) 20061
SUNNINGHILL (St Michael and All Angels) *Ox 11* **P** *St Jo Coll Cam* **V** T W GUNTER
SUNNINGWELL (St Leonard) *see* Radley and Sunningwell *Ox*
SUNNYSIDE (St Barnabas) *see* E Grinstead St Swithun *Chich*
SUNNYSIDE (St Michael and All Angels) w Bourne End *St Alb 2* **P** *CPAS* **NSM** R CLARKSON
SURBITON (St Andrew) (St Mark) *S'wark 16* **P** *Bp* **V** J H TIDY, **TV** G N OWEN, **Hon C** T BRAUN
SURBITON (St Matthew) *S'wark 16* **P** *R&S Ch Trust* **V** S A HONES, **C** H D UFFINDELL, M R GILBERTSON
SURBITON HILL (Christ Church) *S'wark 16* **P** *Ch Soc Trust and Trustees (jt)* **V** G WINTLE, **C** C M GREEN, M ANDREYEV, **NSM** D J BENDELL, M L GODIN
SURFLEET (St Lawrence) *Linc 17* **P** *Bp* **P-in-c** T W THOMPSON
SURLINGHAM (St Mary) *see* Rockland St Mary w Hellington, Bramerton etc *Nor*
SUSSEX GARDENS (St James) *see* Paddington St Jas *Lon*
SUSTEAD (St Peter and St Paul) *see* Roughton and Felbrigg, Metton, Sustead etc *Nor*
SUTCOMBE (St Andrew) *Ex 9* **P** *Bp* **R** H J ROCHE
SUTTERBY (not known) *see* Langton w Sutterby *Linc*
SUTTERTON (St Mary) w Fosdyke and Algarkirk *Linc 21* **P** *Prime Min, Bp and DBP (alt)* **P-in-c** H HALL
SUTTON (All Saints) *see* Potton w Sutton and Cockayne Hatley *St Alb*
SUTTON (All Saints) *see* Shottisham w Sutton *St E*
SUTTON (All Saints) w Shopland *Chelmsf 12* **P** *SMF* **P-in-c** G A BISHTON
SUTTON (Christ Church) *S'wark 24* **P** *R Sutton St Nic* **V** C E GALE, **C** M S RANDALL
SUTTON (Mission Room) *see* Felixkirk w Boltby *York*
SUTTON (St Andrew) *Ely 14* **P** *D&C* **V** B SNELL, **NSM** M T COOPER
SUTTON (St Clement), Huttoft and Anderby *Linc 8* **P** *Bp (2 turns), Magd Coll Cam (1 turn)* **R** G J WILCOX
SUTTON (St George) (St Barnabas's Mission Church) *Ches 13* **P** *Trustees* **V** *Vacant* (01625) 423209
SUTTON (St James) *Ches 13* **P** *Trustees* **V** C F EASTWOOD
SUTTON (St James) and Wawne *York 15* **P** *Patr Bd* **TR** T W DOHERTY
SUTTON (St John the Baptist) *see* Barlavington, Burton w Coates, Sutton and Bignor *Chich*
SUTTON (St Mary) *see* Calow and Sutton cum Duckmanton *Derby*
SUTTON (St Michael and All Angels) *see* Castor w Sutton and Upton w Marholm *Pet*
SUTTON (St Michael) w Ingham and Catfield *Nor 12* **P** *Bp* **R** S WESTON
SUTTON (St Nicholas) *S'wark 24* **P** *Hertf Coll Ox* **R** S J H GOATCHER, **C** J A G POPP
SUTTON (St Nicholas) (All Saints) (St Michael and All Angels) *Liv 10* **P** *Patr Bd* **TR** J L HIGHAM, **TV** F E MYATT, **C** K D STILL
SUTTON (St Thomas) *Bradf 8* **P** *Ch Ch Ox* **V** *Vacant* (01535) 633372
SUTTON w Carlton and Normanton upon Trent and Marnham *S'well 3* **P** *Bp* **P-in-c** S DIXON
SUTTON, EAST (St Peter and St Paul) *see* Sutton Valence w E Sutton and Chart Sutton *Cant*
SUTTON, GREAT (St John the Evangelist) *Ches 9* **P** *V Eastham* **V** T J VIRTUE
SUTTON, NORTH *see* Plymouth Em, St Paul Efford and St Aug *Ex*
SUTTON AT HONE (St John the Baptist) *Roch 2* **P** *D&C* **V** F E J WILLOUGHBY
SUTTON BASSETT (All Saints) *see* Stoke Albany w Wilbarston and Ashley etc *Pet*
SUTTON BENGER (All Saints) *see* Draycot *Bris*
SUTTON BONINGTON (St Michael) (St Anne) w Normanton-on-Soar *S'well 10* **P** *Bp* **P-in-c** C B PERKINS
SUTTON BRIDGE (St Matthew) *Linc 16* **P** *Bp* **P-in-c** E J BANGAY
SUTTON BY DOVER (St Peter and St Paul) *see* Gt Mongeham w Ripple and Sutton by Dover *Cant*
SUTTON CHENEY (St James) *see* Market Bosworth, Cadeby w Sutton Cheney etc *Leic*
SUTTON COLDFIELD (Holy Trinity) *Birm 13* **P** *Bp* **R** D CONNOLLY, **C** T D HILL-BROWN
SUTTON COLDFIELD (St Chad) *Birm 13* **P** *Bp* **V** P A W WATTS
SUTTON COLDFIELD (St Columba) *Birm 13* **P** *Bp* **V** *Vacant* 0121-354 5873
SUTTON COURTENAY (All Saints) w Appleford *Ox 10* **P** *D&C Windsor* **P-in-c** A L THOMAS
SUTTON-CUM-LOUND (St Bartholomew) *see* Babworth w Sutton-cum-Lound *S'well*
SUTTON GREEN (All Souls) *see* Woking St Pet *Guildf*
SUTTON HILL (Pastoral Centre) *see* Madeley *Heref*
SUTTON IN ASHFIELD (St Mary Magdalene) *S'well 4* **P** *Bp* **P-in-c** A N EVANS, **C** F H HAWORTH
SUTTON IN ASHFIELD (St Michael and All Angels) *S'well 4* **P** *Bp* **P-in-c** B G DUCKWORTH
SUTTON IN HOLDERNESS (St Michael) *York 15* **P** *Abp* **V** M BURLEY
SUTTON LE MARSH (St Clement) *see* Sutton, Huttoft and Anderby *Linc*
SUTTON MADDOCK (St Mary) *see* Beckbury, Badger, Kemberton, Ryton, Stockton etc *Lich*
SUTTON MANDEVILLE (All Saints) *see* Fovant, Sutton Mandeville and Teffont Evias etc *Sarum*
SUTTON MONTIS (Holy Trinity) *see* Queen Camel w W Camel, Corton Denham etc *B & W*
SUTTON NEW TOWN (St Barnabas) *S'wark 24* **P** *Bp* **V** P A THOMPSON
SUTTON ON DERWENT (St Michael) *see* Elvington w Sutton on Derwent and E Cottingwith *York*
SUTTON ON PLYM (St John the Evangelist) *Ex 23* **P** *Keble Coll Ox* **V** B R LAY
SUTTON-ON-SEA (St Clement) *see* Sutton, Huttoft and Anderby *Linc*
SUTTON ON THE FOREST (All Hallows) *York 5* **P** *Ld Chan* **P-in-c** S E FLETCHER
SUTTON ON THE HILL (St Michael) *see* Ch Broughton w Barton Blount, Boylestone etc *Derby*
SUTTON-ON-TRENT (All Saints) *see* Sutton w Carlton and Normanton upon Trent etc *S'well*
SUTTON PARK (St Andrew) *see* Sutton St Jas and Wawne *York*
SUTTON ST EDMUND (St Edmund King and Martyr) *see* The Suttons w Tydd *Linc*
SUTTON ST JAMES (St James) *as above*
SUTTON ST MARY (otherwise known as Long Sutton) (St Mary) *Linc 16* **P** *Lady McGeoch* **P-in-c** J M LOWEN, **NSM** R SPIVEY
SUTTON ST MICHAEL (St Michael) *see* Sutton St Nicholas w Sutton St Michael *Heref*
SUTTON ST NICHOLAS *see* Lutton w Gedney Drove End, Dawsmere *Linc*
SUTTON ST NICHOLAS (St Nicholas) w Sutton St Michael *Heref 4* **P** *Bp* **P-in-c** N C H VARNON
SUTTON UNDER BRAILES (St Thomas a Becket) *Cov 9* **P** *Bp* **R** N J MORGAN, **NSM** J W ROLFE
SUTTON VALENCE (St Mary the Virgin) w East Sutton and Chart Sutton *Cant 15* **P** *Abp York* **V** D R BARKER
SUTTON VENY (St John the Evangelist) *see* Heytesbury and Sutton Veny *Sarum*
SUTTON WALDRON (St Bartholomew) *see* The Iwernes, Sutton Waldron and Fontmell Magna *Sarum*
SUTTONS w Tydd, The *Linc 16* **P** *Ld Chan (1 turn), V Long Sutton (2 turns)* **V** P V NOBLE
SWABY (St Nicholas) *see* Wold-Marsh Gp *Linc*
SWADLINCOTE (Emmanuel) *Derby 16* **P** *V Gresley* **V** D J HORSFALL
SWAFFHAM (St Peter and St Paul) *Nor 13* **P** *Bp* **V** *Vacant* (01760) 721373
SWAFFHAM BULBECK (St Mary) and Swaffham Prior w Reach *Ely 3* **P** *Bp and D&C (jt)* **V** M N HAWORTH
SWAFFHAM PRIOR (St Mary) *see* Swaffham Bulbeck and Swaffham Prior w Reach *Ely*
SWAFIELD (St Nicholas) *see* Trunch *Nor*
SWAINSTHORPE (St Peter) w Newton Flotman *Nor 7* **P** *Bp* **P-in-c** C J COLLISON
SWAINSWICK (Blessed Virgin Mary) *see* Bath St Sav w Swainswick and Woolley *B & W*
SWALCLIFFE (St Peter and St Paul) *see* Wykeham *Ox*
SWALECLIFFE (St John the Baptist) *see* Whitstable *Cant*
SWALEDALE *Ripon 2* **P** *Bp* **V** P S MIDWOOD
SWALLOW (Holy Trinity) *Linc 5* **P** *Revd J R H and Revd H C Thorold, DBP, Bp, and Earl of Yarborough (by turn)* **R** *Vacant* (01472) 371560
SWALLOWCLIFFE (St Peter) *see* Tisbury *Sarum*

SWALLOWFIELD (All Saints) *Ox 15* **P** *D&C Heref* **P-in-c** P E BANNISTER
SWALWELL (Holy Trinity) *Dur 13* **P** *R Whickham* **V** J M H GIBSON
SWAN *Ox 24* **P** *Patr Bd* **TV** D A HISCOCK
SWANAGE (All Saints) (St Mary the Virgin) and Studland *Sarum 9* **P** *Patr Bd* **TR** D J RACTLIFFE, **TV** W H N WATTS, P G McAVOY, **NSM** A C HIGGINS
SWANBOROUGH *Sarum 9* **P** *Patr Bd* **TR** P J RIVETT, **TV** J D N GRAY
SWANBOURNE (St Swithun) *see* Mursley w Swanbourne and Lt Horwood *Ox*
SWANLAND (St Barnabas) *see* N Ferriby *York*
SWANLEY (St Mary) *Roch 2* **P** *Guild of All So* **V** M R BRUNDLE
SWANLEY (St Paul) *Roch 2* **P** *Merchant Taylors' Co* **V** A D PROCTER
SWANMORE (St Barnabas) *Portsm 1* **P** *DBP* **P-in-c** P H KELLY, **NSM** M MORT
SWANMORE (St Michael and All Angels) *Portsm 7* **P** *SMF* **V** M F JONES, **NSM** T F SEAR, M D H JOHNSTON
SWANNINGTON (St George) *see* Ravenstone and Swannington *Leic*
SWANNINGTON (St Margaret) *see* Alderford w Attlebridge and Swannington *Nor*
SWANSCOMBE (St Peter and St Paul) *Roch 4* **P** *DBP* **R** D SCOTT
SWANTON ABBOT (St Michael) *see* Worstead, Westwick, Sloley, Swanton Abbot etc *Nor*
SWANTON MORLEY (All Saints) w Beetley w East Bilney and Hoe *Nor 14* **P** *G&C Coll Cam, Ld Chan, and DBP (by turn)* **R** L A WILMAN
SWANTON NOVERS (St Edmund) *see* Brinton, Briningham, Hunworth, Stody etc *Nor*
SWANWICK (St Andrew) and Pentrich *Derby 1* **P** *Wright Trustees and Duke of Devonshire (alt)* **P-in-c** D W ASHTON
SWANWICK (St Barnabas) *see* Sarisbury *Portsm*
SWARBY (St Mary and All Saints) *see* S Lafford *Linc*
SWARCLIFFE (St Luke) *see* Seacroft *Ripon*
SWARDESTON (St Mary the Virgin) w East Carleton, Intwood, Keswick and Ketteringham *Nor 7* **P** *Bp, DBP, and Miss M B Unthank (jt)* **R** D J CHAMBERLIN
SWARKESTONE (St James) *see* Barrow-on-Trent w Twyford and Swarkestone *Derby*
SWARTHMORE (Mission Church) *see* Pennington and Lindal w Marton and Bardsea *Carl*
SWATON (St Michael) *see* Helpringham w Hale *Linc*
SWAVESEY (St Andrew) *see* Fen Drayton w Conington and Lolworth etc *Ely*
SWAY (St Luke) *Win 10* **P** *Bp* **V** J S WHITE
SWAYFIELD (St Nicholas) *see* Corby Glen *Linc*
SWAYTHLING (St Mary South Stoneham w St Alban the Martyr) *Win 12* **P** *Bp and TR Southn City Cen (jt)* **V** J M MOORE, **C** M L RICHES
SWEFFLING (St Mary) *see* Rendham w Sweffling *St E*
SWELL (St Catherine) *see* Curry Rivel w Fivehead and Swell *B & W*
SWELL, LOWER (St Mary) *see* Longborough, Sezincote, Condicote and the Swells *Glouc*
SWELL, UPPER (St Mary) *as above*
SWEPSTONE (St Peter) *see* The Appleby Gp *Leic*
SWERFORD (St Mary) *see* Hook Norton w Gt Rollright, Swerford etc *Ox*
SWETTENHAM (St Peter) *see* Brereton w Swettenham *Ches*
SWILLAND (St Mary) *see* Clopton w Otley, Swilland and Ashbocking *St E*
SWILLINGTON (St Mary) *Ripon 8* **P** *Bp* **R** E M JONES
SWIMBRIDGE (St James the Apostle) and West Buckland *Ex 17* **P** *Bp and Trustees Earl Fortescue (jt)* **V** P BOWERS
SWINBROOK (St Mary) *see* Burford w Fulbrook, Taynton, Asthall etc *Ox*
SWINDERBY (All Saints) *Linc 18* **P** *Bp, Ld Chan, E M K Kirk Esq, and D&C (by turn)* **V** G C GOALBY
SWINDON (All Saints) (St Barnabas) *Bris 10* **P** *Bp* **P-in-c** A R STEVENSON
SWINDON (Christ Church) (St Mary) *Bris 13* **P** *Ld Chan* **V** O C BARRACLOUGH, **C** J HOUSE
SWINDON Dorcan *Bris 12* **P** *Bp* **TR** B J DUCKETT, **C** P E H SELLEY, **NSM** D N PARSONS
SWINDON New Town (St Mark) (St Adhelm) (St Luke) (St Saviour) *Bris 13* **P** *Patr Bd* **TV** P D ANDREWS, **NSM** A S PAGETT
SWINDON (St Andrew) (St John the Baptist) *Bris 13* **P** *Ld Chan* **C** R E WALKER
SWINDON (St Augustine) *Bris 10* **P** *Bp* **V** C DOBB
SWINDON (St John the Evangelist) *Lich 25* **P** *H Cooke Esq, A T Jenks Esq, and S King Esq (jt)* **P-in-c** H M FULLARTON
SWINDON (St Lawrence) w Uckington and Elmstone Hardwicke *Glouc 11* **P** *Bp* **R** B HUMPHREY
SWINDON (St Peter) *see* Penhill *Bris*
SWINDON, WEST and the Lydiards *Bris 13* **P** *Patr Bd* **TR** A HETHERINGTON, **TV** P A WALKER, R J BURLES, P M KNIGHT, **Hon C** W H ANDREW
SWINE (St Mary) *York 12* **P** *W J A Wilberforce Esq and Baroness de Stempel (jt)* **V** *Vacant* (01482) 815250
SWINEFLEET (St Margaret) *see* The Marshland *Sheff*
SWINESHEAD (St Mary) *Linc 21* **P** *Bp* **P-in-c** M A BARSLEY
SWINESHEAD (St Nicholas) *see* The Stodden Churches *St Alb*
SWINFORD (All Saints) w Catthorpe, Shawell and Stanford *Leic 11* **P** *DBP and Ld Chan (alt)* **V** P J C CLEMENTS
SWINFORD, OLD Stourbridge (St Mary) *Worc 12* **P** *Bp* **C** J A OLIVER
SWINGFIELD (St Peter) *see* Hawkinge w Acrise and Swingfield *Cant*
SWINHOPE (St Helen) *see* Binbrook Gp *Linc*
SWINNOW (Christ the Saviour) *see* Stanningley St Thos *Ripon*
SWINSTEAD (St Mary) *see* Corby Glen *Linc*
SWINTON (Holy Rood) *Man 2* **P** *TR Swinton and Pendlebury* **V** M W DAGGETT
SWINTON (St Margaret) *Sheff 12* **P** *Sir Stephen Hastings* **V** *Vacant* (01709) 582259
SWINTON (St Peter) and Pendlebury *Man 2* **P** *Patr Bd* **TR** M R GRIFFITHS, **TV** D A DAVIES, P B McEVITT, **C** R T D PARKER
SWITHLAND (St Leonard) *Leic 7* **P** *Ld Chan* **P-in-c** R A HORTON
SWYNCOMBE (St Botolph) *see* Icknield *Ox*
SWYNNERTON (St Mary) and Tittensor *Lich 13* **P** *Bp and Simeon's Trustees (jt)* **R** B J BREWER, **NSM** N M RUSSELL
SWYRE (Holy Trinity) *see* Bride Valley *Sarum*
SYDE (St Mary) *see* Brimpsfield w Birdlip, Syde, Daglingworth, etc *Glouc*
SYDENHAM (All Saints) *S'wark 5* **P** *V Sydenham St Bart* **V** J O ARDLEY
SYDENHAM (Holy Trinity) *S'wark 5* **P** *Simeon's Trustees* **V** R P DORMANDY, **C** M M JONES, **Hon C** V J SHIRLEY
SYDENHAM (St Bartholomew) *S'wark 5* **P** *Earl of Dartmouth* **V** M J KINGSTON, **C** C E ELVEY
SYDENHAM (St Mary) *see* Chinnor w Emmington and Sydenham etc *Ox*
SYDENHAM (St Philip) *S'wark 5* **P** *V Sydenham St Bart* **V** P W TIERNAN
SYDENHAM, LOWER (St Michael and All Angels) Bell Green *S'wark 5* **P** *Bp* **V** S M BURNETT, **NSM** R W POTTIER
SYDENHAM DAMEREL (St Mary) *see* Milton Abbot, Dunterton, Lamerton etc *Ex*
SYDERSTONE (St Mary) *see* N and S Creake w Waterden, Syderstone etc *Nor*
SYDLING (St Nicholas) *see* Bradford Peverell, Stratton, Frampton etc *Sarum*
SYERSTON (All Saints) *see* E Stoke w Syerston *S'well*
SYKEHOUSE (Holy Trinity) *see* Fishlake w Sykehouse, Kirk Bramwith, Fenwick etc *Sheff*
SYLEHAM (St Mary) *see* Hoxne w Denham, Syleham and Wingfield *St E*
SYMONDS GREEN (Christ the King) *see* Stevenage H Trin *St Alb*
SYMONDSBURY (St John the Baptist) and Chideock *Sarum 3* **P** *Bp* **P-in-c** J AYOK-LOEWENBERG
SYRESHAM (St James) *see* Helmdon w Stuchbury and Radstone etc *Pet*
SYSTON (St Mary) *see* Barkston and Hough Gp *Linc*
SYSTON Team Ministry, The (St Peter and St Paul) *Leic 6* **P** *Patr Bd* **TR** K R COURT, **TV** C A FLATTERS, J A HILLMAN, J S HOPEWELL, **C** N J HEALE
SYSTON (St Anne) *see* Warmley, Syston and Bitton *Bris*
SYSTONBY (not known) *see* Melton Mowbray *Leic*
SYWELL (St Peter and St Paul) *see* Mears Ashby and Hardwick and Sywell etc *Pet*
TABLEY, OVER (St Paul) and High Legh *Ches 12* **P** *Bp and Mrs P H Langford-Brooke (1 turn), C L S Cornwall-Legh Esq (1 turn)* **V** *Vacant* (01925) 753612
TACKLEY (St Nicholas) *see* Steeple Aston w N Aston and Tackley *Ox*
TACOLNESTON (All Saints) *see* Wreningham *Nor*
TADCASTER (St Mary) w Newton Kyme *York 1* **P** *Abp* **V** R P BURTON, **C** J CRANE
TADDINGTON (St Michael), Chelmorton and Flagg, and Monyash *Derby 4* **P** *V Bakewell* **V** T H COMLEY
TADDIPORT (St Mary Magdalene) *see* Gt and Lt Torrington and Frithelstock *Ex*
TADLEY (St Peter) (St Paul) *Win 4* **P** *Bp* **R** J M NOCKELS
TADLEY, NORTH (St Mary) *Win 4* **P** *Bp* **V** B J NORRIS, **NSM** S G ARMSTRONG

TADLOW (St Giles) *see* Shingay Gp of Par *Ely*
TADMARTON (St Nicholas) *see* Wykeham *Ox*
TADWORTH (Good Shepherd) *S'wark 26* **P** *V Kingswood St Andr* **V** R H McLEAN
TAKELEY (Holy Trinity) w Little Canfield *Chelmsf 18* **P** *Bp and Ch Coll Cam* **P-in-c** F MILLAR
TALATON (St James the Apostle) *see* Whimple, Talaton and Clyst St Lawr *Ex*
TALBOT VILLAGE (St Mark) *Sarum 8* **P** *Trustees* **V** C J F RUTLEDGE, **C** A C HEYWOOD
TALKE O' THE HILL (St Martin) *Lich 9* **P** *V Audley* **R** J T PYE
TALKIN (not known) *see* Hayton w Cumwhitton *Carl*
TALLAND (St Tallan) *Truro 12* **P** *DBP and W Gundry-Mills Esq (alt)* **V** *Vacant* (01503) 72356
TALLINGTON (St Laurence) *see* Uffington Gp *Linc*
TAMERTON, NORTH (St Denis) *see* Boyton, N Tamerton, Werrington etc *Truro*
TAMERTON FOLIOT (St Mary) *Ex 22* **P** *Ld Chan* **V** C W H GOODWINS
TAMWORTH (St Editha) *Lich 4* **P** *Bp* **C** N A DI CASTIGLIONE, D R W ROBBINS, **NSM** J READ, M J PACEY
TANDRIDGE (St Peter) *see* Oxted and Tandridge *S'wark*
TANFIELD (St Margaret of Antioch) *Dur 4* **P** *Bp* **V** R SHAW
TANFIELD, WEST (St Nicholas) and Well w Snape and North Stainley *Ripon 3* **P** *Bp and Mrs M E Bourne-Arton (alt)* **R** A C CARRUTHERS
TANGLEY (St Thomas of Canterbury) *see* Hatherden w Tangley, Weyhill and Penton Mewsey *Win*
TANGMERE (St Andrew) and Oving *Chich 3* **P** *Bp and Duke of Richmond (jt)* **R** P M GILBERT
TANKERSLEY (St Peter), Thurgoland and Wortley *Sheff 7* **P** *Dowager Countess of Wharncliffe, Sir Stephen Hastings, V Silkstone (jt)* **R** K J E HALE
TANNINGTON (St Ethelbert) *see* Worlingworth, Southolt, Tannington, Bedfield etc *St E*
TANSLEY (Holy Trinity), Dethick, Lea and Holloway *Derby 7* **P** *Bp, V Crich, and DBF (jt)* **P-in-c** R G LAWRENCE
TANSOR (St Mary) *see* Warmington, Tansor, Cotterstock and Fotheringhay *Pet*
TANWORTH (St Mary Magdalene) *Birm 6* **P** *F D Muntz Esq* **V** M W TUNNICLIFFE
TANWORTH (St Patrick) Salter Street *Birm 6* **P** *V Tanworth* **P-in-c** M G B C CADDY
TAPLOW (St Nicholas) *see* Burnham w Dropmore, Hitcham and Taplow *Ox*
TARDEBIGGE (St Bartholomew) *Worc 7* **P** *Earl of Plymouth* **P-in-c** A WHITE
TARLETON (Holy Trinity) *Blackb 6* **P** *St Pet Coll Ox* **R** A J JEYNES
TARLTON (St Osmund) *see* Coates, Rodmarton and Sapperton etc *Glouc*
TARPORLEY (St Helen) *Ches 5* **P** *Bp (4 turns), D&C (1 turn), and Sir John Grey Regerton, Bt (1 turn)* **R** G L COOKSON
TARRANT GUNVILLE (St Mary) *see* Tarrant Valley *Sarum*
TARRANT HINTON (St Mary) *as above*
TARRANT KEYNSTON (All Saints) *as above*
TARRANT MONKTON (All Saints) *as above*
TARRANT RUSHTON (St Mary) *as above*
TARRANT VALLEY *Sarum 7* **P** *Pemb Coll Cam (1 turn), Bp (2 turns), and Univ Coll Ox (1 turn)* **P-in-c** J J HAMILTON-BROWN
TARRING, WEST (St Andrew) *Chich 5* **P** *Abp* **R** W E JERVIS
TARRING NEVILLE (St Mary) *see* Denton w S Heighton and Tarring Neville *Chich*
TARRINGTON (St Philip and St James) w Stoke Edith, Aylton, Pixley, Munsley, Putley and Yarkhill *Heref 6* **P** *A T Foley Esq, D&C, Hopton Trustees, H W Wiggin Esq, and J Hervey-Bathurst Esq (jt)* **R** *Vacant* (01432) 890314
TARVIN (St Andrew) *Ches 2* **P** *Bp* **V** D R HERBERT
TASBURGH (St Mary) w Tharston, Forncett and Flordon *Nor 5* **P** *MMCET, Bp, St Jo Coll Cam, and DBP (by turn)* **P-in-c** S G STEPHENSON
TASLEY (St Peter and St Paul) *see* Bridgnorth, Tasley, Astley Abbotts, Oldbury etc *Heref*
TATENHILL (St Michael and All Angels) *see* Branston w Tatenhill *Lich*
TATHAM (St James the Less) *see* Wray w Tatham and Tatham Fells *Blackb*
TATHAM FELLS (Good Shepherd) *as above*
TATHWELL (St Vedast) *see* Raithby *Linc*
TATSFIELD (St Mary) *S'wark 25* **P** *Bp* **P-in-c** C J CORKE
TATTENHALL (St Alban) and Handley *Ches 5* **P** *Bp and D&C (jt)* **R** G G TURNER
TATTENHAM CORNER (St Mark) and Burgh Heath *Guildf 9* **P** *Bp* **V** G J CLIFTON-SMITH
TATTENHOE (St Giles) *see* Watling Valley *Ox*
TATTERFORD (St Margaret) *see* E and W Rudham, Houghton-next-Harpley etc *Nor*
TATTERSETT (All Saints and St Andrew) *as above*
TATTERSHALL (Holy Trinity) *see* Coningsby w Tattershall *Linc*
TATTINGSTONE (St Mary) *see* Bentley w Tattingstone *St E*
TATWORTH (St John the Evangelist) *B & W 15* **P** *V Chard* **P-in-c** R E MASLEN, **C** M M MASLEN
TAUNTON (All Saints) *B & W 18* **P** *Bp* **P-in-c** D C W FAYLE
TAUNTON (Holy Trinity) *B & W 18* **P** *Bp* **V** J B V LAURENCE
TAUNTON (St Andrew) *B & W 18* **P** *Bp* **V** J SMITH, **C** M J VENABLES, S TUCKER, **NSM** C F CRAGGS
TAUNTON (St James) *B & W 18* **P** *Simeon's Trustees* **V** A P BANNISTER
TAUNTON (St John the Evangelist) *B & W 18* **P** *Bp* **P-in-c** D ROBERTS
TAUNTON (St Mary Magdalene) *B & W 18* **P** *Ch Patr Trust* **V** N R MADDOCK, **C** A L SMITH
TAUNTON (St Peter) Lyngford *B & W 18* **P** *Bp* **V** T J GOSDEN, **C** E C BROWN, **NSM** P A SELF
TAVERHAM (St Edmund) w Ringland *Nor 2* **P** *Bp and Major J M Mills (alt)* **R** *Vacant* (01603) 868217
TAVISTOCK (St Eustachius) and Gulworthy (St Paul) *Ex 24* **P** *Bp* **V** J E F RAWLINGS, **C** G J BOUCHER, **NSM** J NELSON
TAW VALLEY *see* Newport, Bishops Tawton and Tawstock *Ex*
TAWSTOCK (St Peter) *see* Newton Tracey, Horwood, Alverdiscott etc *Ex*
TAWTON, NORTH (St Peter), Bondleigh, Sampford Courtenay and Honeychurch *Ex 12* **P** *MMCET, K Coll Cam, and D&C (jt)* **R** M A BUTCHERS
TAWTON, SOUTH (St Andrew) and Belstone *Ex 12* **P** *D&C Windsor and Bp (jt)* **P-in-c** B WOOD
TAYNTON (St John the Evangelist) *see* Burford w Fulbrook, Taynton, Asthall etc *Ox*
TAYNTON (St Laurence) *see* Highnam, Lassington, Rudford, Tibberton etc *Glouc*
TEALBY (All Saints) *see* Walesby *Linc*
TEAN, UPPER (Christ Church) *Lich 6* **P** *R Checkley* **P-in-c** R M JAMES, **Hon C** E C LAST
TEBAY (St James) *see* Orton and Tebay w Ravenstonedale etc *Carl*
TEDBURN ST MARY (St Mary), Whitestone, Oldridge, Holcombe Burnell, Dunsford, Doddiscombsleigh and Cheriton Bishop *Ex 6* **P** *Patr Bd* **R** V STANDING, **TV** S M HAYNES
TEDDINGTON (St Mark) and Hampton Wick (St John the Baptist) *Lon 11* **P** *Bp* **V** J P WARNER
TEDDINGTON (St Mary) (St Alban the Martyr) *Lon 10* **P** *Bp* **V** J M CLEAVER
TEDDINGTON (St Nicholas) *see* Overbury w Teddington, Alstone etc *Worc*
TEDDINGTON (St Peter and St Paul) and Fulwell (St Michael and St George) *Lon 10* **P** *Bp* **V** P A LOCK, **Hon C** M L NICHOLAS
TEDSTONE DELAMERE (St James) *see* Edvin Loach w Tedstone Delamere etc *Heref*
TEDSTONE WAFER (St Mary) *as above*
TEFFONT EVIAS (St Michael) *see* Fovant, Sutton Mandeville and Teffont Evias etc *Sarum*
TEFFONT MAGNA (St Edward) *as above*
TEIGH (Holy Trinity) Whissendine and Market Overton *Pet 14* **P** *Bp and Lady Gretton (alt)* **R** N P DENHAM
TEIGNGRACE (St Peter and St Paul) *see* Highweek and Teigngrace *Ex*
TEIGNMOUTH (St James) (St Michael the Archangel), Ideford w Luton, Ashcombe and Bishopsteignton *Ex 6* **P** *Patr Bd* **TR** P G LUFF, **TV** T J WRIGHT, **Par Dn** J W DEBENHAM, C M S LUFF
TELFORD, CENTRAL: Dawley, Lawley, Malinslee, Stirchley, Brookside and Hollinswood *Lich 22* **P** *Patr Bd (3 turns), The Crown (1 turn)* **TR** D M R WILLIAMS, **TV** P A CORNISH, P G F LAWLEY, M L COPE
TELFORD PARK (St Thomas) *S'wark 14* **P** *Trustees* **V** S A EVANS
TELLISFORD (All Saints) *see* Rode Major *B & W*
TELSCOMBE (St Laurence) w Piddinghoe and Southease *Chich 18* **P** *Gorham Trustees* **P-in-c** D A HIDER, **C** D L I PERKS
TEME VALLEY NORTH: Knighton-on-Teme, Lindridge, Pensax, Menith Wood, Stanford-on-Teme and Stockton *Worc 13* **P** *Bp and D&C (alt)* **R** R G SMITH
TEME VALLEY SOUTH: Eastham, Rochford, Stoke Bliss, Hanley Child, Hanley William and Kyre Wyard *Worc 13* **P** *Ld Chan, Bp, and Mrs M M Miles (by turn)* **R** M P LACK
TEMPLE (St Catherine) *see* Blisland w St Breward *Truro*

TEMPLE BALSALL (St Mary) *Birm 12* **P** *Lady Leveson Hosp* **V** R H P WATSON WILLIAMS
TEMPLE BRUER (St John the Baptist) *see* Graffoe Gp *Linc*
TEMPLE CLOUD (St Barnabas) *see* Clutton w Cameley *B & W*
TEMPLE EWELL (St Peter and St Paul) w Lydden *Cant 4* **P** *Abp* **R** P CHRISTIAN
TEMPLE GRAFTON (St Andrew) w Binton *Cov 7* **P** *Dioc Trustees* **V** E F WILLIAMS
TEMPLE GUITING (St Mary) *see* The Guitings, Cutsdean and Farmcote *Glouc*
TEMPLE HIRST (St John the Baptist) *see* Haddlesey w Hambleton and Birkin *York*
TEMPLE NORMANTON (St James the Apostle) *Derby 5* **P** *Bp* **V** C W D VOGT
TEMPLE SOWERBY (St James) *see* Kirkby Thore w Temple Sowerby and Newbiggin *Carl*
TEMPLECOMBE (Blessed Virgin Mary) *see* Abbas and Templecombe w Horsington *B & W*
TEMPLETON (St Margaret) *see* Washfield, Stoodleigh, Withleigh etc *Ex*
TEMPSFORD (St Peter) *see* Blunham w Tempsford and Lt Barford *St Alb*
TEN MILE BANK (St Mark) *see* Hilgay *Ely*
TENBURY (St Mary) *Heref 12* **P** *Revd F J Evans* **TR** D S DORMOR, **TV** C V HUTT, **C** J GROVES
TENBURY (St Michael and All Angels) *Heref 12* **P** *St Mich Coll* **V** D S DORMOR
TENDRING (St Edmund King and Martyr) and Little Bentley w Beaufort cum Moze *Chelmsf 20* **P** *Em Coll Cam, DBP, and Ball Coll Ox (by turn)* **R** C J A HARVEY
TENTERDEN (St Michael and All Angels) *Cant 11* **P** *Abp* **P-in-c** J K BUTTERWORTH, **Hon C** J C L EMMOTT
TENTERDEN (St Mildred) w Smallhythe *Cant 11* **P** *D&C* **V** D G TRUSTRAM, **NSM** M ROYLANCE
TERLING (All Saints) *see* Fairstead w Terling and White Notley etc *Chelmsf*
TERRIERS (St Francis) *Ox 29* **P** *V High Wycombe* **P-in-c** A W DICKINSON
TERRINGTON (All Saints) *see* Bulmer w Dalby, Terrington and Welburn *York*
TERRINGTON ST CLEMENT (St Clement) *Ely 17* **P** *The Crown* **V** J F WILSON
TERRINGTON ST JOHN (St John) *Ely 17* **P** *The Crown* **V** C A BARBER
TERWICK (St Peter) *see* Rogate w Terwick and Trotton w Chithurst *Chich*
TESTON (St Peter and St Paul) *see* Wateringbury w Teston and W Farleigh *Roch*
TESTWOOD (St Winfrid) *see* Totton *Win*
TETBURY (St Mary the Virgin) w Beverston *Glouc 16* **P** *Lt-Col J J B Pope (5 turns), The Crown (1 turn)* **R** J W HAWTHORNE
TETCOTT (Holy Cross) *see* Ashwater, Halwill, Beaworthy, Clawton etc *Ex*
TETFORD (St Mary) *see* S Ormsby Gp *Linc*
TETNEY (St Peter and St Paul) *see* The North-Chapel Parishes *Linc*
TETSWORTH (St Giles), Adwell w South Weston, Lewknor and Stoke Talmage w Wheatfield *Ox 1* **P** *Bp, Peache Trustees, W R A Birch Reynardson Esq, Earl of Macclesfield, and Mrs D C H Mann (jt)* **P-in-c** S F L BRIGNALL
TETTENHALL REGIS (St Michael and All Angels) *Lich 25* **P** *Patr Bd* **TR** J D MAKEPEACE, **TV** G R HARPER, J J N QUIN, **C** N A MPUNZI, **NSM** V A BARNSLEY
TETTENHALL WOOD (Christ Church) *Lich 25* **P** *Patr Bd* **TR** C R GOUGH, **TV** M A SMALLMAN, S H CARTER, **C** M L E LAST
TEVERSAL (St Katherine) *S'well 4* **P** *DBP* **P-in-c** J J FLETCHER
TEVERSHAM (All Saints) *Ely 6* **P** *Bp* **P-in-c** C D BOULTON
TEW, GREAT (St Michael and All Angels) w Little (St John the Evangelist) *Ox 3* **P** *Bp and J M Johnston Esq (jt)* **P-in-c** R A DENNISTON
TEWIN (St Peter) *see* Datchworth w Tewin *St Alb*
TEWKESBURY (Holy Trinity) *Glouc 9* **P** *Ch Soc Trust* **V** P L SIBLEY
TEWKESBURY (St Mary the Virgin) w Walton Cardiff *Glouc 9* **P** *Ld Chan* **V** M E TAVINOR, **C** P F QUINNELL
TEY, GREAT (St Barnabas) and Wakes Colne w Chappel *Chelmsf 17* **P** *DBP, PCC Chappel and Bp (jt)* **R** J RICHARDSON
TEY, LITTLE (St James the Less) *see* Marks Tey w Aldham and Lt Tey *Chelmsf*
TEYNHAM (St Mary) (Primary School Worship Centre) w Lynsted and Kingsdown *Cant 6* **P** *Adn Cant* **V** *Vacant* (01795) 522510
THAKEHAM (St Mary) *see* Sullington and Thakeham w Warminghurst *Chich*
THAME (All Saints) (St Mary the Virgin) w Towersey *Ox 1* **P** *Peache Trustees* **V** C C NEAL, **C** C D STIRLING, I R ADAMS, **NSM** J E M HULETT
THAMES DITTON (St Nicholas) *Guildf 8* **P** *K Coll Cam* **V** J A SILK
THAMES VIEW (Christ Church) *see* Barking St Marg w St Patr *Chelmsf*
THAMESMEAD (Church of the Cross) (St Paul's Ecumenical Centre) *S'wark 3* **P** *Bp* **TR** C M BYERS, **TV** M GODDARD, J KOTHARE, **C** W J SAUNDERS
THANET (St Laurence) *see* St Laur in Thanet *Cant*
THANINGTON (St Nicholas) (St Faith's Mission Church) *Cant 3* **P** *Abp* **P-in-c** T D HERBERT
THARSTON (St Mary) *see* Tasburgh w Tharston, Forncett and Flordon *Nor*
THATCHAM (St Mary) *Ox 14* **P** *Patr Bd* **TR** P L SEAR, **TV** J M P HEDGES, **C** C DALE
THATTO HEATH (St Matthew) *see* St Helens St Matt Thatto Heath *Liv*
THAXTED (St John the Baptist, Our Lady and St Laurence) *Chelmsf 22* **P** *Bp* **V** R N ROWE
THE *see under substantive place name*
THEALE (Christ Church) *see* Wedmore w Theale and Blackford *B & W*
THEALE (Holy Trinity) and Englefield *Ox 12* **P** *Magd Coll Ox and Englefield Est Trust (jt)* **R** D RICE
THEBERTON (St Peter) *see* Kelsale-cum-Carlton, Middleton-cum-Fordley etc *St E*
THEDDINGWORTH (All Saints) *see* Husbands Bosworth w Mowsley and Knaptoft etc *Leic*
THEDDLETHORPE (St Helen) *Linc 12* **P** *Baroness Willoughby de Eresby (2 turns), Bp (1 turn)* **R** *Vacant*
THELBRIDGE (St David) *see* Witheridge, Thelbridge, Creacombe, Meshaw etc *Ex*
THELNETHAM (St Nicholas) *see* Hepworth, Hinderclay, Wattisfield and Thelnetham *St E*
THELVETON (St Andrew) *see* Dickleburgh, Langmere, Shimpling, Thelveton etc *Nor*
THELWALL (All Saints) *Ches 4* **P** *Keble Coll Ox* **V** A G BROWN
THEMELTHORPE (St Andrew) *see* Twyford, Guist, Bintree, Themelthorpe etc *Nor*
THENFORD (St Mary the Virgin) *see* Greatworth and Marston St Lawrence etc *Pet*
THERFIELD (St Mary the Virgin) w Kelshall *St Alb 19* **P** *Ld Chan and D&C St Paul's (alt)* **R** R M MORGAN
THETFORD (St Cuthbert) (St Peter) *Nor 11* **P** *Patr Bd* **TR** C J HALL, **TV** M J M HUGHES, K WILSON, **Hon C** B R HOGWOOD
THETFORD, LITTLE (St George) *see* Ely *Ely*
THEYDON BOIS (St Mary) *Chelmsf 25* **P** *M G E N Buxton Esq* **V** D DRISCOLL, **NSM** M CHAPMAN
THEYDON GARNON (All Saints) *see* Epping Distr *Chelmsf*
THEYDON MOUNT (St Michael) *see* Stapleford Tawney w Theydon Mt *Chelmsf*
THIMBLEBY (St Margaret) *see* Thornton Gp *Linc*
THIRKLEBY (All Saints) w Kilburn and Bagby *York 20* **P** *Abp* **V** D G BILES
THIRSK (St Mary) *York 20* **P** *Abp* **TR** E R NORRIS, **TV** N C SINCLAIR, **C** E M BAXTER, **NSM** S R BAXTER
THISTLETON (St Nicholas) *see* Greetham and Thistleton w Stretton and Clipsham *Pet*
THIXENDALE (St Mary) *see* Sledmere and Cowlam w Fridaythorpe, Fimer etc *York*
THOCKRINGTON (St Aidan) *see* Chollerton w Birtley and Thockrington *Newc*
THOMPSON (St Martin) *see* Caston, Griston, Merton, Thompson etc *Nor*
THONGSBRIDGE (St Andrew) *see* Upper Holme Valley *Wakef*
THORESBY, NORTH (St Helen) *see* The North-Chapel Parishes *Linc*
THORESBY, SOUTH (St Andrew) *see* Wold-Marsh Gp *Linc*
THORESWAY (St Mary) *see* Swallow *Linc*
THORGANBY (All Saints) *see* Binbrook Gp *Linc*
THORGANBY (St Helen) *see* Wheldrake w Thorganby *York*
THORINGTON (St Peter) w Wenhaston, Bramfield and Walberswick *St E 15* **P** *Ld Chan (3 turns), Ch Patr Trust (1 turn), and Sir Charles Blois Bt (1 turn)* **V** *Vacant* (01502) 722118
THORLEY (St James the Great) *St Alb 18* **P** *Bp* **R** C P SLAUGHTER, **C** J BURROWS
THORLEY (St Swithun) *Portsm 8* **P** *Bp* **V** J A YORKE, **P-in-c** J A YORKE
THORMANBY (St Mary Magdalene) *see* Brafferton w Pilmoor, Myton on Swale etc *York*

THORNABY, NORTH (St Luke) (St Paul) *York 19* **P** *Abp* **V** H C HOPKINS
THORNABY, SOUTH (St Mark) (St Peter ad Vincula) *York 19* **P** *Abp* **V** D HAWTHORN
THORNAGE (All Saints) *see* Brinton, Briningham, Hunworth, Stody etc *Nor*
THORNBOROUGH (St Mary) *see* Buckingham *Ox*
THORNBURY (St Anna) *see* Bredenbury w Grendon Bishop and Wacton etc *Heref*
THORNBURY (St Margaret) *Bradf 3* **P** *Vs Bradf, Calverley, and Laisterdyke (jt)* **V** P C HACKWOOD, **C** P A HEDGE
THORNBURY (St Mary) (St Paul) *Glouc 7* **P** *Ch Ch Ox* **V** M G P VOOGHT, **C** J T PERRY
THORNBURY (St Peter) *see* Black Torrington, Bradf w Cookbury etc *Ex*
THORNBY (St Helen) *see* Cottesbrooke w Gt Creaton and Thornby *Pet*
THORNCOMBE (Blessed Virgin Mary) w Winsham and Cricket St Thomas *B & W 15* **P** *Bp Worc and C G S Eyre Esq (jt)* **V** B R SUTTON
THORNDON (All Saints) w Rishangles, Stoke Ash, Thwaite and Wetheringsett cum Brockford *St E 16* **P** *Bp, Capt F P Brooke-Popham, MMCET, and Ch Soc Trust (jt)* **P-in-c** F G BURNINGHAM
THORNE (St Nicholas) *Sheff 11* **P** *Bp* **V** P M BROWN, **C** J BARNES
THORNE COFFIN (St Andrew) *see* Tintinhull w Chilthorne Domer, Yeovil Marsh etc *B & W*
THORNE ST MARGARET (St Margaret) *see* Wellington and Distr *B & W*
THORNER (St Peter) *Ripon 8* **P** *Earl of Mexborough* **V** D R GRICE, **NSM** A B HAIGH
THORNES (St James) w Christ Church *Wakef 12* **P** *DBP* **P-in-c** C W DIXON
THORNEY (St Helen) *see* Harby w Thorney and N and S Clifton *S'well*
THORNEY, WEST (St Nicholas) *see* Southbourne w W Thorney *Chich*
THORNEY ABBEY (St Mary and St Botolph) *Ely 19* **P** *Bp* **P-in-c** A J MILTON
THORNEY CLOSE (St Peter) *see* Sunderland St Mary and St Pet *Dur*
THORNEY HILL (All Saints) *see* Bransgore *Win*
THORNEYBURN (St Aidan) *see* N Tyne and Redesdale Team *Newc*
THORNFALCON (Holy Cross) *see* Ruishton w Thornfalcon *B & W*
THORNFORD (St Mary Magdalene) *see* Bradford Abbas and Thornford w Beer Hackett *Sarum*
THORNGUMBALD (St Mary) *see* Burstwick w Thorngumbald *York*
THORNHAM (All Saints) *see* Hunstanton St Mary w Ringstead Parva etc *Nor*
THORNHAM (St James) *Man 22* **P** *Bp* **V** P N BARRATT
THORNHAM (St John) *see* Middleton w Thornham *Man*
THORNHAM MAGNA (St Mary Magdalene) w Thornham Parva, Gislingham and Mellis *St E 16* **P** *Bp, Lord Henniker, and MMCET (jt)* **R** *Vacant* (01379) 783652
THORNHAM PARVA (St Mary) *see* Thornhams Magna and Parva, Gislingham and Mellis *St E*
THORNHAUGH (St Andrew) *see* Wittering w Thornhaugh and Wansford *Pet*
THORNHILL (Mission Church) *see* Beckermet St Jo and St Bridget w Ponsonby *Carl*
THORNHILL (St Christopher) *see* Southampton Thornhill St Chris *Win*
THORNHILL (St Michael and All Angels) and Whitley Lower *Wakef 10* **P** *Lord Savile* **R** L C DEW, **NSM** M HARRISON
THORNHILL LEES (Holy Innocents w St Mary) *Wakef 10* **P** *Bp* **V** J R ASHWORTH
THORNLEY (St Bartholomew) *Dur 11* **P** *Bp* **P-in-c** S WARD
THORNLEY (St Bartholomew) *see* Wolsingham and Thornley *Dur*
THORNTHWAITE (St Mary the Virgin) cum Braithwaite and Newlands *Carl 6* **P** *V Crosthwaite and V Keswick St Jo (alt)* **P-in-c** C T MATTHEWS, **NSM** J M BLAKEMAN
THORNTHWAITE (St Saviour) *see* Dacre w Hartwith and Darley w Thornthwaite *Ripon*
THORNTON Group, The (St Wilfrid) *Linc 11* **P** *R H Spurrier Esq, Bp, SMF, and Lt Col J L M Dymoke (2 turns), Ld Chan (1 turn)* **R** *Vacant* (01507) 526456
THORNTON (St Frideswyde) *Liv 5* **P** *R Sefton* **V** *Vacant* 0151-931 4676
THORNTON (St James) *Bradf 1* **P** *V Bradf* **V** S P HACKING, **Hon C** A HOLLIDAY
THORNTON (St Michael) *see* Seaton Ross Gp of Par *York*
THORNTON (St Peter), Bagworth and Stanton *Leic 12* **P** *MMCET* **V** A S COSTERTON, **P-in-c** G T WILLETT, **NSM** J A DOWNS
THORNTON, LITTLE (St John) *Blackb 13* **P** *Bp* **V** P R F CLEMENCE
THORNTON CURTIS (St Laurence) *see* Ulceby Gp *Linc*
THORNTON DALE (All Saints) w Ellerburne and Wilton *York 21* **P** *Mrs E M Morgan and Abp (alt)* **R** J D S CLARK
THORNTON HEATH (St Jude w St Aidan) *S'wark 24* **P** *Bp* **V** C H A GARRETT
THORNTON HEATH (St Paul) *S'wark 24* **P** *The Crown* **V** G PADDICK
THORNTON HOUGH (All Saints) *Ches 9* **P** *Simeon's Trustees* **V** *Vacant* 0151-336 3429
THORNTON IN CRAVEN (St Mary) *see* Broughton, Marton and Thornton *Bradf*
THORNTON IN LONSDALE (St Oswald) w Burton in Lonsdale *Bradf 6* **P** *Bp* **V** M J BAMFORTH
THORNTON LE FEN (St Peter) *see* Brothertoft Gp *Linc*
THORNTON-LE-FYLDE (Christ Church) *Blackb 13* **P** *Trustees* **V** J F FAIRCLOUGH, **C** P W BENNETT
THORNTON-LE-MOOR (All Saints) *see* S Kelsey Gp *Linc*
THORNTON LE MOORS (St Mary) w Ince and Elton *Ches 3* **P** *Bp* **P-in-c** K W DAVEY
THORNTON LE STREET (St Leonard) *see* The Thorntons and The Otteringtons *York*
THORNTON RUST (Mission Room) *see* Aysgarth and Bolton cum Redmire *Ripon*
THORNTON STEWARD (St Oswald) *see* Thornton Watlass w Thornton Steward *Ripon*
THORNTON WATLASS (St Mary the Virgin) w Thornton Steward *Ripon 4* **P** *Bp and D S Dodsworth Esq (jt)* **P-in-c** D W EYLES
THORNTONS and The Otteringtons, The *York 20* **P** *Ch Ch Ox, Linc Coll Ox, and Abp (by turn)* **R** E W SPILLER
THOROTON (St Helena) *see* Whatton w Aslockton, Hawksworth, Scarrington etc *S'well*
THORP ARCH (All Saints) w Walton *York 1* **P** *G H H Wheler Esq and G Lane Fox Esq (alt)* **P-in-c** T ELBOURNE
THORPE (St Andrew) (Good Shepherd) *Nor 1* **P** *Trustees W J Birkbeck Esq* **R** A J SNASDELL, **C** S J COLLIER, **Hon C** W H MOORE
Thorpe (St Laurence) *see* Farndon w Thorpe, Hawton and Cotham *S'well*
THORPE (St Leonard) *see* Fenny Bentley, Kniveton, Thorpe and Tissington *Derby*
THORPE (St Mary) *Guildf 11* **P** *Keble Coll Ox* **V** M J H ROTHWELL
THORPE (St Matthew) *Nor 1* **P** *R Thorpe St Andr* **V** D A ABRAHAM, **C** E J CARTER
THORPE (St Peter) *see* The Wainfleet Gp *Linc*
THORPE ABBOTS (All Saints) *see* Scole, Brockdish, Billingford, Thorpe Abbots etc *Nor*
THORPE ACHURCH (St John the Baptist) *see* Aldwincle w Thorpe Achurch, Pilton, Wadenhoe etc *Pet*
THORPE ACRE w Dishley (All Saints) *Leic 7* **P** *Bp* **V** E K WHITLEY, **C** G A O JESSON
THORPE ARNOLD (St Mary the Virgin) *see* Melton Mowbray *Leic*
THORPE AUDIN (Mission Room) *see* Badsworth *Wakef*
THORPE BASSETT (All Saints) *see* Rillington w Scampston, Wintringham etc *York*
THORPE BAY (St Augustine) *Chelmsf 13* **P** *Bp* **V** E H BEAVAN, **NSM** T E C SHARPE
THORPE CONSTANTINE (St Constantine) *Lich 4* **P** *Mrs E V G Inge-Innes* **P-in-c** A L WHEALE
THORPE EDGE (St John the Divine) *Bradf 3* **P** *Vs Bradf, Calverley, and Idle (jt)* **V** C SPIVEY, **C** S C R PONSONBY
THORPE END (St David) *see* Gt and Lt Plumstead w Thorpe End and Witton *Nor*
THORPE EPISCOPI (St Andrew) *see* Thorpe *Nor*
THORPE HAMLET (St Matthew) *see* Thorpe St Matt *Nor*
THORPE HESLEY (Holy Trinity) *Sheff 6* **P** *Sir Stephen Hastings* **V** A J LACEY
THORPE LANGTON (St Leonard) *see* Church Langton w Tur Langton, Thorpe Langton etc *Leic*
THORPE-LE-SOKEN (St Michael) *Chelmsf 23* **P** *Bp* **V** P J CARTER
THORPE MALSOR (All Saints) *see* Broughton w Loddington and Cransley etc *Pet*
THORPE MANDEVILLE (St John the Baptist) *see* Culworth w Sulgrave and Thorpe Mandeville etc *Pet*
THORPE MARKET (St Margaret) *see* Trunch *Nor*
THORPE MORIEUX (St Mary the Virgin) *see* Rattlesden w Thorpe Morieux and Brettenham *St E*
THORPE-NEXT-HADDISCOE (St Matthias) *see* The Raveningham Gp *Nor*

THORPE-ON-THE-HILL (St Michael) *see* Swinderby *Linc*
THORPE SALVIN (St Peter) *see* Harthill and Thorpe Salvin *Sheff*
THORPE SATCHVILLE (St Michael and All Angels) *see* S Croxton Gp *Leic*
THORPE WILLOUGHBY (St Francis of Assisi) *see* Brayton *York*
THORRINGTON (St Mary Magdalene) *see* Gt Bentley and Frating w Thorrington *Chelmsf*
THORVERTON (St Thomas of Canterbury), Cadbury, Upton Pyne, Brampford Speke and Newton St Cyres *Ex 2* **P** *Ld Chan (1 turn), Patr Bd (3 turns)* **TR** L J YEO, **TV** R E N WESTON
THRANDESTON (St Margaret) *see* N Hartismere *St E*
THRAPSTON (St James) *Pet 10* **P** *Ld Chan* **R** D R BIRD
THREAPWOOD (St John) *see* Malpas and Threapwood *Ches*
THRECKINGHAM (St Peter) *see* S Lafford *Linc*
THREE LEGGED CROSS (All Saints) *see* Verwood *Sarum*
THRELKELD (St Mary) *Carl 6* **P** *Trustees* **R** *Vacant* (017687) 72130
THREXTON (All Saints) *see* Gt and Lt Cressingham w Threxton *Nor*
THRIGBY (St Mary) *see* Filby, Thrigby, Mautby, Stokesby, Runham etc *Nor*
THRIMBY (St Mary) *see* Morland, Thrimby, Gt Strickland and Cliburn *Carl*
THRINGSTONE (St Andrew) *Leic 8* **P** *Duchy of Lanc* **V** B MATTHEWS
THRIPLOW (St George) *Ely 8* **P** *Bp* **P-in-c** J B MYNORS
THROCKING (Holy Trinity) *see* Cottered w Broadfield and Throcking *St Alb*
THROCKLEY (St Mary the Virgin) *see* Newburn *Newc*
THROCKMORTON (Chapelry) *see* Abberton, The Flyfords, Naunton Beauchamp etc *Worc*
THROOP (St Paul) *Win 7* **P** *Ch Soc Trust* **V** R D PETERS
THROPTON (St Andrew) *see* Rothbury *Newc*
THROWLEIGH (St Mary the Virgin) *see* Chagford w Gidleigh and Throwleigh *Ex*
THROWLEY (St Michael and All Angels) *see* Selling w Throwley, Sheldwich w Badlesmere etc *Cant*
THRUMPTON (All Saints) *S'well 10* **P** *Mrs M Gottlieb* **P-in-c** R A SPRAY, **NSM** J M GORICK
THRUSCROSS (no dedication) *see* Dacre w Hartwith and Darley w Thornthwaite *Ripon*
THRUSHELTON (St George) *see* Marystowe, Coryton, Stowford, Lewtrenchard etc *Ex*
THRUSSINGTON (Holy Trinity) *see* Syston TM *Leic*
THRUXTON (St Bartholomew) *see* Kingstone w Clehonger, Eaton Bishop etc *Heref*
THRUXTON (St Peter and St Paul) *see* Appleshaw, Kimpton, Thruxton and Fyfield *Win*
THRYBERGH (St Leonard) *Sheff 6* **P** *J C M Fullerton Esq* **R** B E LENG
THUNDERSLEY (St Michael and All Angels) (St Peter) *Chelmsf 10* **P** *Bp* **R** P J SANDBERG
THUNDERSLEY, NEW (St George) *Chelmsf 10* **P** *Bp* **V** J R D KEMP
THUNDRIDGE (St Mary) *St Alb 22* **P** *Bp* **V** H J SHARMAN
THURCASTON (All Saints) w Cropston *Leic 12* **P** *Em Coll Cam* **R** D F BREWIN
THURCROFT (St Simon and St Jude) *Sheff 5* **P** *Bp* **V** P HUNTER, **NSM** R GOMERSALL
THURGARTON (St Peter) w Hoveringham and Bleasby w Halloughton *S'well 15* **P** *Ld Chan and Trin Coll Cam (alt)* **V** A P de BERRY
THURGOLAND (Holy Trinity) *see* Tankersley, Thurgoland and Wortley *Sheff*
THURLASTON (All Saints) *see* Enderby w Lubbesthorpe and Thurlaston *Leic*
THURLASTON (St Edmund) *see* Dunchurch *Cov*
THURLBY (St Firmin) *see* Ness Gp *Linc*
THURLBY (St Germain) w Norton Disney *Linc 18* **P** *Bp and W R S Brown Esq (alt)* **R** M J N HOWES, **NSM** J R D SCARBOROUGH
THURLEIGH (St Peter) *St Alb 15* **P** *Bp* **V** C W GONIN
THURLESTONE (All Saints) w South Milton *Ex 14* **P** *D&C* **R** P S STEPHENS
THURLOW, GREAT (All Saints) *see* Haverhill w Withersfield, the Wrattings etc *St E*
THURLOW, LITTLE (St Peter) *as above*
THURLOXTON (St Giles) *see* N Newton w St Michaelchurch, Thurloxton etc *B & W*
THURLSTONE (St Saviour) *see* Penistone and Thurlstone *Wakef*
THURLTON (All Saints) *see* The Raveningham Gp *Nor*
THURMASTON (St Michael and All Angels) *Leic 6* **P** *Bp* **V** T R MARTIN, **C** D SHENTON
THURNBY (St Luke) w Stoughton *Leic 5* **P** *MMCET* **V** G W DUNSETH
THURNBY LODGE (Christ Church) *Leic 1* **P** *Bp* **P-in-c** P A TAILBY, **NSM** I M HILL
THURNE (St Edmund) *see* Rollesby w Burgh w Billockby w Ashby w Oby etc *Nor*
THURNHAM (St Mary the Virgin) *see* Bearsted w Thurnham *Cant*
THURNING (St Andrew) *see* Reepham, Hackford w Whitwell, Kerdiston etc *Nor*
THURNING (St James the Great) *see* Barnwell w Tichmarsh, Thurning and Clapton *Pet*
THURNSCOE (St Helen) *Sheff 12* **P** *Sir Stephen Hastings* **R** I A DAVIS
THURNSCOE (St Hilda) *Sheff 12* **P** *Bp* **V** M P THOMPSON
THURROCK, LITTLE (St John the Evangelist) *see* Grays North *Chelmsf*
THURROCK, LITTLE (St Mary the Virgin) *see* Grays Thurrock *Chelmsf*
THURROCK, WEST (Church Centre) *as above*
THURSBY (St Andrew) *Carl 3* **P** *D&C* **V** *Vacant* (01228) 710303
THURSFORD (St Andrew) *see* Barney, Fulmodeston w Croxton, Hindringham etc *Nor*
THURSLEY (St Michael and All Angels) *Guildf 4* **P** *V Witley* **V** W D LANG
THURSTASTON (St Bartholomew) *Ches 8* **P** *D&C* **R** J B HARRIS
THURSTON (St Peter) *St E 9* **P** *Bp* **V** D M B MATHERS
THURSTONLAND (St Thomas) *see* Upper Holme Valley *Wakef*
THURTON (St Ethelbert) w Ashby Saint Mary, Bergh Apton w Yelverton and Framingham Pigot *Nor 8* **P** *Bp and Major J H Thursby, Bp and MMCET, and Ld Chan (by turn)* **R** *Vacant* (01508) 480738
THUXTON (St Paul) *see* Barnham Broom *Nor*
THWAITE (All Saints) *see* Erpingham w Calthorpe, Ingworth, Aldborough etc *Nor*
THWAITE (St George) *see* Thorndon w Rishangles, Stoke Ash, Thwaite etc *St E*
THWAITE (St Mary) *see* Brooke, Kirstead, Mundham w Seething and Thwaite *Nor*
THWAITES (St Anne) *see* Millom *Carl*
THWAITES BROW (St Barnabas) *Bradf 8* **P** *DBP* **V** P J ENDALL, **NSM** D J GRIFFITHS
THWING (All Saints) *see* Langtoft w Foxholes, Butterwick, Cottam etc *York*
TIBBERTON (All Saints) w Bolas Magna and Waters Upton *Lich 16* **P** *R Edgmond w Kynnersley etc, MMCET, and A B Davies Esq (jt)* **P-in-c** R F DABORN
TIBBERTON (Holy Trinity) *see* Highnam, Lassington, Rudford, Tibberton etc *Glouc*
TIBBERTON (St Peter ad Vincula) *see* Bowbrook S *Worc*
TIBENHAM (All Saints) *see* Bunwell, Carleton Rode, Tibenham, Gt Moulton etc *Nor*
TIBSHELF (St John the Baptist) *Derby 1* **P** *MMCET* **V** E J ABLETT
TICEHURST (St Mary) and Flimwell *Chich 19* **P** *Bp, E J B Harcastle Esq, and A F Drewe Esq (jt)* **V** R J GOODCHILD
TICHBORNE (St Andrew) *see* Cheriton w Tichborne and Beauworth *Win*
TICHMARSH (St Mary the Virgin) *see* Barnwell w Tichmarsh, Thurning and Clapton *Pet*
TICKENCOTE (St Peter) *see* Gt and Lt Casterton w Pickworth and Tickencote *Pet*
TICKENHAM (St Quiricus and St Julietta) *see* Nailsea Ch Ch w Tickenham *B & W*
TICKHILL (St Mary) w Stainton *Sheff 10* **P** *Bp* **V** A R TEAL
TICKNALL (St George), Smisby and Stanton by Bridge *Derby 15* **P** *Bp and Miss A I M Harpur-Crewe (jt)* **P-in-c** R HILL
TICKTON (St Paul) *see* Beverley Minster *York*
TIDCOMBE (St Michael) *see* Wexcombe *Sarum*
TIDDINGTON *see* Wheatley *Ox*
TIDDINGTON (St Peter) *see* Alveston *Cov*
TIDEBROOK (St John the Baptist) *Chich 19* **P** *V Wadhurst and V Mayfield (alt)* **V** M G P INSLEY
TIDEFORD (St Luke) *see* St Germans *Truro*
TIDENHAM (St Mary) w Beachley and Lancaut *Glouc 4* **P** *Bp* **V** *Vacant* (01291) 622442
TIDENHAM CHASE (St Michael and All Angels) *see* Tidenham w Beachley and Lancaut *Glouc*
TIDESWELL (St John the Baptist) *Derby 4* **P** *D&C Lich* **V** M F H HULBERT
TIDMARSH (St Laurence) *see* Pangbourne w Tidmarsh and Sulham *Ox*

TIDMINGTON (not known) *see* Shipston-on-Stour w Honington and Idlicote *Cov*
TIDWORTH (Holy Trinity), Ludgershall and Faberstown *Sarum 12* **P** *Ld Chan and DBP (alt)* **R** M J BRIDGER, **C** D JONES
TIFFIELD (St John the Baptist) *see* Pattishall w Cold Higham and Gayton w Tiffield *Pet*
TILBROOK (All Saints) *Ely 10* **P** *SMF* **P-in-c** J HINDLEY, **NSM** B A BEARCROFT, J RAWLINSON
TILBURY, EAST (St Katherine) and West Tilbury and Linford *Chelmsf 14* **P** *Ld Chan* **R** E R LITTLER
TILBURY DOCKS (St John the Baptist) *Chelmsf 14* **P** *Bp* **V** T M CODLING
TILBURY-JUXTA-CLARE (St Margaret) *see* Upper Colne *Chelmsf*
TILE CROSS (St Peter) *Birm 10* **P** *Bp* **NSM** M MacLACHLAN
TILE HILL (St Oswald) *Cov 3* **P** *Bp* **V** B REGAN, **NSM** P MARTIN-SMITH
TILEHURST (St Catherine of Siena) *Ox 15* **P** *Magd Coll Ox* **V** A R BEEVER
TILEHURST (St George) *Ox 15* **P** *Bp* **V** J J GILL
TILEHURST (St Mary Magdalen) *Ox 15* **P** *Bp* **V** *Vacant* 0118-942 7234
TILEHURST (St Michael) *Ox 15* **P** *Magd Coll Ox* **R** F W DAWSON, **C** B SCOTT
TILFORD (All Saints) *Guildf 3* **P** *Bp* **P-in-c** D EDE
TILGATE (Holy Trinity) *see* Southgate *Chich*
TILLINGHAM (St Nicholas) *Chelmsf 11* **P** *D&C St Paul's* **P-in-c** I M FINN
TILLINGTON (All Hallows) *Chich 11* **P** *Lord Egremont* **P-in-c** C D BIDDELL
TILMANSTONE (St Andrew) *see* Eastry and Northbourne w Tilmanstone etc *Cant*
TILNEY ALL SAINTS (All Saints) *Ely 17* **P** *Pemb Coll Cam* **V** C A BARBER
TILNEY ST LAWRENCE (St Lawrence) *Ely 17* **P** *Pemb Coll Cam* **V** *Vacant*
TILSHEAD (St Thomas a Becket), Orcheston and Chitterne *Sarum 16* **P** *Bp (3 turns), D&C (1 turn)* **R** *Vacant* (01980) 620517
TILSTOCK (Christ Church), Edstaston and Whixall *Lich 23* **P** *V Prees, R Wem, and R Whitchurch (jt)* **V** A T BARTLAM
TILSTON (St Mary) and Shocklach *Ches 5* **P** *Bp* **P-in-c** J M HUNT
TILSTONE FEARNALL (St Jude) *see* Bunbury and Tilstone Fearnall *Ches*
TILSWORTH (All Saints) *see* Totternhoe, Stanbridge and Tilsworth *St Alb*
TILTON ON THE HILL (St Peter) *see* Whatborough Gp of Par *Leic*
TILTY (St Mary the Virgin) *see* Broxted w Chickney and Tilty etc *Chelmsf*
TIMBERLAND (St Andrew) *see* Scopwick Gp *Linc*
TIMBERSCOMBE (St Petroc) *see* Selworthy, Timberscombe, Wootton Courtenay etc *B & W*
TIMPERLEY (Christ Church) (St Andrew) (St Catherine) *Ches 10* **P** *Trustees* **V** J SUTTON, **C** A J MANNINGS, **Hon C** M E HEPWORTH, **NSM** G M GILL
TIMSBURY (Blessed Virgin Mary) and Priston *B & W 9* **P** *Ball Coll Ox (3 turns), R W Lovegrove Esq (1 turn)* **R** C C BROWN
TIMSBURY (St Andrew) *see* Michelmersh, Timsbury, Farley Chamberlayne etc *Win*
TIMWORTH (St Andrew) *see* Fornham All SS and Fornham St Martin w Timworth *St E*
TINCLETON (St John the Evangelist) *see* Moreton and Woodsford w Tincleton *Sarum*
TINDALE (Mission Church) *see* Gilsland w Nether Denton *Carl*
TINGEWICK (St Mary Magdalene) *see* Lenborough *Ox*
TINGRITH (St Nicholas) *see* Westoning w Tingrith *St Alb*
TINSLEY (St Lawrence) *see* Attercliffe, Darnall and Tinsley *Sheff*
TINTAGEL (St Materiana) *Truro 10* **P** *D&C Windsor* **P-in-c** R THOMAS
TINTINHULL (St Margaret) w Chilthorne Domer, Yeovil Marsh and Thorne Coffin *B & W 6* **P** *Guild of All So* **R** T R BONIWELL, **NSM** A J YOUNG
TINTWISTLE (Christ Church) *Ches 14* **P** *Trustees* **P-in-c** J R WATTS
TINWELL (All Saints) *see* Ketton w Tinwell *Pet*
TIPTOE (St Andrew) *see* Hordle *Win*
TIPTON Great Bridge (St Luke) *see* Tipton St Martin and St Paul *Lich*
TIPTON (St John) *see* Ottery St Mary, Alfington, W Hill, Tipton etc *Ex*
TIPTON (St John the Evangelist) *Lich 27* **P** *V W Bromwich St Jas* **V** J C GREATBATCH
TIPTON (St Mark) *see* Ocker Hill *Lich*
TIPTON (St Martin) (St Paul) *Lich 27* **P** *MMCET* **V** J H ALGAR
TIPTON (St Matthew) *Lich 27* **P** *Simeon's Trustees* **V** M S PHILPS
TIPTREE (St Luke) *see* Tolleshunt Knights w Tiptree and Gt Braxted *Chelmsf*
TIRLEY (St Michael) *see* Hasfield w Tirley and Ashleworth *Glouc*
TISBURY (St John the Baptist) *Sarum 13* **P** *Patr Bd (3 turns), Ld Chan (1 turn)* **TR** C J MEYRICK, **C** J M STAPLES, **NSM** M A SHALLCROSS, R WREN
TISMANS COMMON (St John the Baptist) *see* Rudgwick *Chich*
TISSINGTON (St Mary) *see* Fenny Bentley, Kniveton, Thorpe and Tissington *Derby*
TISTED, EAST w Colemore (St James) *see* Newton Valence, Selborne and E Tisted w Colemore *Win*
TISTED, WEST (St Mary Magdalene) *see* Bishop's Sutton and Ropley and W Tisted *Win*
TITCHFIELD (St Peter) *Portsm 2* **P** *D&C Win* **V** J A MITCHELL-INNES
TITCHWELL (St Mary) *see* Hunstanton St Mary w Ringstead Parva etc *Nor*
TITLEY (St Peter) *see* Lyonshall w Titley, Almeley and Kinnersley *Heref*
TITTENSOR (St Luke) *see* Swynnerton and Tittensor *Lich*
TITTLESHALL (St Mary) *see* Litcham w Kempston, E and W Lexham, Mileham etc *Nor*
TIVERTON (St Andrew) *Ex 8* **P** *Bp* **P-in-c** D M FLETCHER, **Hon C** B STRANGE
TIVERTON (St George) *Ex 8* **P** *MMCET* **V** C G H DUNN
TIVERTON (St Paul) *see* W Exe *Ex*
TIVERTON (St Peter) and Chevithorne w Cove *Ex 8* **P** *Peache Trustees (3 turns), Ld Chan (1 turn)* **P-in-c** A R GIBSON, **NSM** D A LYDDON
TIVETSHALL (St Mary and St Margaret) *see* Winfarthing w Shelfanger w Burston w Gissing etc *Nor*
TIVIDALE (St Michael the Archangel) (Holy Cross) (St Augustine) *Lich 27* **P** *Bp* **V** D F MAWSON, **C** A H TOWNSEND
TIVINGTON (St Leonard) *see* Selworthy, Timberscombe, Wootton Courtenay etc *B & W*
TIXALL (St John the Baptist) *see* Stafford St Jo and Tixall w Ingestre *Lich*
TIXOVER (St Luke) *see* Easton on the Hill, Collyweston w Duddington etc *Pet*
TOCKENHAM (St Giles) *see* Broad Town, Clyffe Pypard, Hilmarton etc *Sarum*
TOCKHOLES (St Stephen) *see* Darwen St Cuth w Tockholes St Steph *Blackb*
TOCKWITH (Epiphany) and Bilton w Bickerton *York 1* **P** *Abp and D&C (jt)* **V** *Vacant* (01423) 358338
TODBER (St Andrew) *see* Gillingham *Sarum*
TODDINGTON (St Andrew), Stanton, Didbrook w Hailes and Stanway *Glouc 17* **P** *DBP, Lord Neidpath, and Bp (by turn)* **R** M E BENNETT
TODDINGTON (St George of England) *St Alb 12* **P** *Bp* **R** W T A MATTHEWS
TODENHAM (St Thomas of Canterbury) *see* Moreton-in-Marsh w Batsford, Todenham etc *Glouc*
TODMORDEN (St Mary) (Christ Church) *Wakef 3* **P** *Bp* **V** P N CALVERT
TODWICK (St Peter and St Paul) *see* Aston cum Aughton w Swallownest, Todwick etc *Sheff*
TOFT (St Andrew) w Caldecote and Childerley *Ely 1* **P** *Ch Coll Cam* **R** D G DEBOYS, **NSM** A G WILMAN, D A J WILMAN
TOFT (St John the Evangelist) *see* Knutsford St Jo and Toft *Ches*
TOFT MONKS (St Margaret) *see* The Raveningham Gp *Nor*
TOFT NEXT NEWTON (St Peter and St Paul) *see* Middle Rasen Gp *Linc*
TOFTREES (All Saints) w Shereford *Nor 15* **P** *Marquess Townshend* **V** *Vacant*
TOFTS, WEST and Buckenham Parva *Nor 13* **P** *Guild of All So* **R** *Vacant*
TOKYNGTON (St Michael) *Lon 21* **P** *Bp* **V** R J METIVIER
TOLLADINE (Christ Church) *see* Worc St Barn w Ch Ch *Worc*
TOLLAND (St John the Baptist) *see* Lydeard St Lawrence w Brompton Ralph etc *B & W*
TOLLARD ROYAL (St Peter ad Vincula) w Farnham, Gussage St Michael and Gussage All Saints, Ashmore and Chettle *Sarum 7* **P** *Bp, Adn Dorset, Ch Soc Trust, A C L Sturge Esq, and J P C Bourke Esq (2 turns), Ld Chan (1 turn)* **R** *Vacant* (01725) 516221
TOLLER FRATRUM (St Basil) *see* Melbury *Sarum*

TOLLER LANE St Chad *Bradf 1* **P** *Keble Coll Ox* **V** S R CROWE
TOLLER PORCORUM (St Andrew) *see* Beaminster Area *Sarum*
TOLLER WHELME (St John) *see* Melbury *Sarum*
TOLLERTON (St Michael) *see* Alne *York*
TOLLERTON (St Peter) *S'well 9* **P** *Ld Chan* **P-in-c** P E GRIFFITHS
TOLLESBURY (St Mary) w Salcot Virley *Chelmsf 24* **P** *Bp (1 turn), Ex Coll Ox (3 turns)* **V** K M B LOVELL
TOLLESHUNT D'ARCY (St Nicholas) w Tolleshunt Major (St Nicholas) *Chelmsf 24* **P** *Mrs E A Comerford MMCET, and Ld Chan (by turn)* **P-in-c** P R SOUTHERN
TOLLESHUNT KNIGHTS w Tiptree and Great Braxted *Chelmsf 24* **P** *Bp (2 turns), Ld Chan (2 turns), and CCC Cam (1 turn)* **R** J A PRATT
TOLLINGTON (St Mark) *Lon 6* **P** *Patr Bd* **TR** R S CAMPBELL, **TV** S J HANCE, D E CLAYDEN, **C** W K DORGU, **NSM** E McCARTNEY
TOLPUDDLE (St John the Evangelist) *see* Puddletown and Tolpuddle *Sarum*
TOLWORTH (Emmanuel) *see* Surbiton Hill Ch Ch *S'wark*
TOLWORTH (St George) *see* Surbiton St Matt *S'wark*
TONBRIDGE (St Peter and St Paul) (St Saviour) *Roch 11* **P** *Mabledon Trust* **C** R E T FOXWELL, J AUSTIN, A SAVILLE, G E TOVAR, **NSM** B P ADAMS
TONBRIDGE (St Stephen) (St Eanswythe Mission Church) *Roch 11* **P** *CPAS* **V** W D MACDOUGALL, **C** R J M BYRNE, J C CHANDLER
TONG (St Bartholomew) *Lich 20* **P** *Bp* **V** G FROST
TONG (St James) *Bradf 3* **P** *CR* **TR** C G N DEY, **C** P DEO
TONGE (St Giles) *see* Murston w Bapchild and Tonge *Cant*
TONGE (St Michael) w Alkrington *Man 18* **P** *R Middleton St Leon* **V** G F JOYCE, **C** P R HOLLEY, **NSM** A MATTHEWS
TONGE FOLD (St Chad) *Man 9* **P** *Bp and Wm Hulme Trustees (alt)* **V** A J BUTTERWORTH
TONGE MOOR (St Augustine) (St Aidan) *Man 16* **P** *Keble Coll Ox* **V** B J FINDLAY, **C** A R HEYES, **Hon C** J M DRUMMOND
TONGHAM (St Paul) *Guildf 1* **P** *Adn Surrey* **V** P S J GARLAND
TONWELL (St Mary the Virgin) *see* Bengeo *St Alb*
TOOT BALDON (St Lawrence) *see* Dorchester *Ox*
TOOTING (All Saints) *S'wark 18* **P** *Bp* **V** P D MAURICE
TOOTING (St Augustine) *S'wark 18* **P** *Bp* **V** S J LOPEZ-FERREIRO
TOOTING, UPPER (Holy Trinity) *S'wark 18* **P** *R Streatham St Leon* **V** B M C BROGGIO
TOOTING GRAVENEY (St Nicholas) *S'wark 18* **P** *MMCET* **R** J B HALL
TOP VALLEY (St Philip) *see* Bestwood *S'well*
TOPCLIFFE (St Columba) w Baldersby, Dalton, Dishforth and Skipton on Swale *York 20* **P** *Abp, Viscount Downe, and D&C (jt)* **V** C M HADDON-REECE
TOPCROFT (St Margaret) *see* Hempnall *Nor*
TOPPESFIELD (St Margaret) *see* Upper Colne *Chelmsf*
TOPSHAM (St Margaret) *Ex 1* **P** *D&C* **V** R W C JEFFERY
TORBRYAN (Holy Trinity) *see* Ipplepen w Torbryan *Ex*
TORKSEY (St Peter) *see* Stow Gp *Linc*
TORMARTON (St Mary Magdalene) *see* Marshfield w Cold Ashton and Tormarton etc *Bris*
TORPENHOW (St Michael and All Angels) *Carl 7* **P** *Bp* **P-in-c** C S SIMS
TORPOINT (St James) *Truro 11* **P** *R Antony* **V** J R WARREN
TORQUAY (St John) and Ellacombe *Ex 10* **P** *Ch Patr Trust and Bp (jt)* **P-in-c** R W TAYLOR
TORQUAY (St Luke) *Ex 10* **P** *D&C* **P-in-c** M J A BARR, **NSM** M E BARR
TORQUAY (St Martin) Barton *Ex 10* **P** *V St Marychurch* **V** G CHAPMAN
TORQUAY (St Mary Magdalene) *see* Upton *Ex*
TORQUAY (St Matthias) (St Mark) (Holy Trinity) *Ex 10* **P** *Ch Patr Trust, Bp and Torwood Trustees (jt)* **R** P J LARKIN, **C** A C EDMUNDS, **Hon C** J M PRINGLE, **NSM** P G H COOKE
TORRE (All Saints) *Ex 10* **P** *Bp* **V** R I McDOWALL
TORRIDGE *see* Shebbear, Buckland Filleigh, Sheepwash etc *Ex*
TORRINGTON, EAST (St Michael) *see* Barkwith Gp *Linc*
TORRINGTON, GREAT (St Michael), Little Torrington and Frithelstock *Ex 19* **P** *Ch Ch Ox (8 turns), Lord Clinton (1 turn), J de C Stevens-Guille Esq (1 turn)* **V** J D HUMMERSTONE
TORRINGTON, LITTLE (St Giles) *see* Gt and Lt Torrington and Frithelstock *Ex*
TORRINGTON, WEST (St Michael) *see* Barkwith Gp *Linc*
TORRISHOLME (Ascension) *Blackb 12* **P** *Bp* **V** B H PITHERS, **C** N L STIMPSON
TORTWORTH (St Leonard) *see* Cromhall w Tortworth and Tytherington *Glouc*
TORVER (St Luke) *Carl 8* **P** *Peache Trustees* **P-in-c** M H CANNON
TOSELAND (St Michael) *see* Graveley w Papworth St Agnes w Yelling etc *Ely*
TOSSIDE (St Bartholomew) *see* Long Preston w Tosside *Bradf*
TOSTOCK (St Andrew) *see* Pakenham w Norton and Tostock *St E*
TOTHAM, GREAT (St Peter) *Chelmsf 24* **P** *Bp* **V** M J HATCHETT
TOTHAM, LITTLE (All Saints) *see* Goldhanger w Lt Totham *Chelmsf*
TOTLAND BAY (Christ Church) *Portsm 8* **P** *Ch Patr Trust* **V** J A YORKE
TOTLEY (All Saints) *Sheff 2* **P** *Bp* **V** J D BENSON
TOTNES (St Mary), Bridgetown and Berry Pomeroy and Dartington *Ex 13* **P** *Patr Bd* **TV** N J C PIGOTT, P WIMSETT, **NSM** R E YEO, J M YEO
TOTON (St Peter) *see* Attenborough *S'well*
TOTTENHAM (All Hallows) *Lon 19* **P** *D&C St Paul's* **V** R B PEARSON
TOTTENHAM (Holy Trinity) *Lon 19* **P** *Bp* **V** I C THURSTON
TOTTENHAM (St Bartholomew) *see* Stamford Hill St Bart *Lon*
TOTTENHAM (St Benet Fink) *Lon 19* **P** *D&C St Paul's* **V** M A DAVENPORT
TOTTENHAM (St Cuthbert) *see* Chitts Hill St Cuth *Lon*
TOTTENHAM (St Mary) *Lon 19* **P** *Bp* **V** L J MILLER
TOTTENHAM (St Paul) *Lon 19* **P** *V Tottenham All Hallows* **V** A K DANGERFIELD, **C** M C ELLIOTT SMITH
TOTTENHAM (St Philip the Apostle) *Lon 19* **P** *Bp* **P-in-c** K EVANS
TOTTENHAM, SOUTH (St Ann) *Lon 19* **P** *D&C St Paul's* **P-in-c** J M WOOD
TOTTENHILL (St Botolph) w Wormegay *Ely 16* **P** *Bp* **V** J C W NOLAN
TOTTERIDGE (St Andrew) *St Alb 17* **P** *R Hatfield* **V** C P HUITSON
TOTTERNHOE (St Giles), Stanbridge and Tilsworth *St Alb 12* **P** *Bp* **V** P C HOLLAND
TOTTINGTON (St Anne) *Man 10* **P** *R Bury St Mary* **V** H W BEARN, **Hon C** S G MARTIN
TOTTON *Win 10* **P** *Bp* **TR** P BAYES, **TV** E J WETHERELL, A G RIVETT, D BROAD, **C** G D ROBINSON
TOW LAW (St Philip and St James) *see* Satley and Tow Law *Dur*
TOWCESTER (St Lawrence) w Easton Neston *Pet 5* **P** *Bp and Lord Hesketh (alt)* **V** M R H BAKER
TOWEDNACK (St Tewinock) *Truro 5* **P** *Bp* **V** *Vacant*
TOWER CHAPEL (St Nicholas) *see* Whitehaven *Carl*
TOWERSEY (St Catherine) *see* Thame w Towersey *Ox*
TOWN END FARM (St Bede) *see* Sunderland Town End Farm *Dur*
TOWNSTAL (St Clement) *see* Dartmouth *Ex*
TOXTETH (St Bede) *see* Toxteth Park Ch Ch w St Bede *Liv*
TOXTETH (St Cyprian w Christ Church) *Liv 3* **P** *Simeon's Trustees* **V** D A LEWIS, **C** S NICHOLSON
TOXTETH (St Margaret) *Liv 6* **P** *St Chad's Coll Dur* **V** R GALLAGHER
TOXTETH (St Philemon) (St Gabriel) St Cleopas *Liv 6* **P** *Patr Bd* **TR** D C KIRKWOOD, **TV** R V STOCK, D G GAVIN
TOXTETH PARK (Christ Church) (St Bede) *Liv 6* **P** *Simeon's Trustees and Trustees (jt)* **V** *Vacant* 0151-727 2827
TOXTETH PARK (St Agnes and St Pancras) *Liv 6* **P** *St Chad's Coll Dur* **V** D H McKITTRICK
TOXTETH PARK (St Clement) *Liv 6* **P** *Trustees* **P-in-c** F R CAIN
TOXTETH PARK (St Michael-in-the-Hamlet) (St Andrew) *Liv 6* **P** *Simeon's Trustees* **V** S FORBES
TOYNTON, HIGH (St John the Baptist) *Linc 11* **P** *Bp* **NSM** A C FORD, J F PARKIN
TOYNTON ALL SAINTS (All Saints) *see* Marden Hill Gp *Linc*
TOYNTON ST PETER (St Peter) *as above*
TOYS HILL (Hall) *see* Hever, Four Elms and Mark Beech *Roch*
TRAFALGAR SQUARE (St Martin-in-the-Fields) *see* St Martin-in-the-Fields *Lon*
TRAFFORD, OLD (St Bride) *see* Stretford St Bride *Man*
TRAFFORD, OLD (St Hilda) *Man 7* **P** *The Crown* **R** D G BARNETT
TRAFFORD, OLD (St John the Evangelist) *Man 7* **P** *The Crown* **R** D I WHEELER
TRANMERE (St Catherine) *Ches 1* **P** *R Bebington* **V** S R BECKLEY
TRANMERE (St Paul w St Luke) *Ches 1* **P** *Bp* **V** D J JOHNSON

TRANMERE PARK (St Peter's Hall) *see* Guiseley w Esholt *Bradf*
TRAWDEN (St Mary the Virgin) *Blackb 7* **P** *Bp* **P-in-c** R L ALLEN
TREALES (Christ Church) *Blackb 11* **P** *V Kirkham* **V** *Vacant* (01772) 682219
TREBOROUGH (St Peter) *see* Old Cleeve, Leighland and Treborough *B & W*
TREDINGTON (St Gregory) and Darlingscott w Newbold on Stour *Cov 9* **P** *Jes Coll Ox* **R** *Vacant* (01608) 661264
TREDINGTON (St John the Baptist) *see* Staverton w Boddington and Tredington etc *Glouc*
TREETON (St Helen) *see* Brinsworth w Catcliffe and Treeton *Sheff*
TREFONEN (All Saints) *see* Llanyblodwel and Trefonen *Lich*
TREGADILLET (St Mary's Mission) *see* Launceston *Truro*
TREGONY (not known) w St Cuby and Cornelly *Truro 6* **P** *Bp* **R** *Vacant* (01872) 530507
TREKNOW (Holy Family) *see* Tintagel *Truro*
TRELEIGH (St Stephen) *see* Redruth w Lanner and Treleigh *Truro*
TRELYSTAN (St Mary the Virgin) *Heref 13* **P** *Bp* **V** P D HARRATT
TREMAINE (St Winwalo) *see* Egloskerry, N Petherwin, Tremaine and Tresmere *Truro*
TRENDLEWOOD *see* Nailsea H Trin *B & W*
TRENEGLOS (St Gregory) *see* St Gennys, Jacobstow w Warbstow and Treneglos *Truro*
TRENT (St Andrew) *see* Queen Thorne *Sarum*
TRENT VALE (St John the Evangelist) *Lich 12* **P** *R Stoke-on-Trent* **V** D W WATKIN
TRENTHAM (St Mary and All Saints) *Lich 13* **P** *Countess of Sutherland* **C** R M GLADSTONE
TRENTISHOE (St Peter) *see* Combe Martin, Berrynarbor, Lynton, Brendon etc *Ex*
TRESCO (St Nicholas) *see* Is of Scilly *Truro*
TRESHAM (Chapel) *see* Kingswood w Alderley and Hillesley *Glouc*
TRESLOTHAN (St John the Evangelist) *Truro 2* **P** *Mrs W A Pendarves* **C** D G EVERETT, **NSM** D L HOLLINGDALE
TRESMERE (St Nicholas) *see* Egloskerry, N Petherwin, Tremaine and Tresmere *Truro*
TRESWELL (St John the Baptist) *see* Rampton w Laneham, Treswell, Cottam and Stokeham *S'well*
TRETHEVY (St Piran) *see* Tintagel *Truro*
TRETIRE (St Mary) *see* St Weonards w Orcop, Garway, Tretire etc *Heref*
TREVALGA (St Petroc) *see* Boscastle w Davidstow *Truro*
TREVENSON (St Illogan) *see* St Illogan *Truro*
TREVERBYN (St Peter) *Truro 1* **P** *The Crown* **V** W M CARTWRIGHT
TREVONE (St Saviour) *see* Padstow *Truro*
TREWEN (St Michael) *see* Lezant w Lawhitton and S Petherwin w Trewen *Truro*
TREYFORD CUM DIDLING (St Andrew) *see* Harting w Elsted and Treyford cum Didling *Chich*
TRIMDON GRANGE (St Alban) *see* The Trimdons *Dur*
TRIMDON STATION (St Paul) *as above*
TRIMDONS, The (St Mary Magdalene) (St Alban) (St Paul) *Dur 5* **P** *Bp* **V** P A BALDWIN
TRIMINGHAM (St John the Baptist) *see* Overstrand, Northrepps, Sidestrand etc *Nor*
TRIMLEY (St Martin) (St Mary the Virgin) *St E 2* **P** *Bp and Ld Chan (alt)* **R** C LEFFLER, **C** L J PAYNE
TRIMPLEY (Holy Trinity) *see* Kidderminster St Mary and All SS w Trimpley etc *Worc*
TRING (St Martha) (St Peter and St Paul) (St Mary) *St Alb 2* **P** *Bp* **TR** J A S PAYNE COOK, **TV** R VARTY, M M NATHANAEL, **Hon C** J E K RIDGWAY, **NSM** E INALL
TROSTON (St Mary the Virgin) *see* Blackbourne *St E*
TROTTISCLIFFE (St Peter and St Paul) *see* Birling, Addington, Ryarsh and Trottiscliffe *Roch*
TROTTON (St George) *see* Rogate w Terwick and Trotton w Chithurst *Chich*
TROUTBECK (Jesus Church) *see* Windermere St Mary and Troutbeck *Carl*
TROWBRIDGE (Holy Trinity) *Sarum 17* **P** *Patr Bd* **TR** B C ATKINSON, **TV** D J COOPER
TROWBRIDGE (St James) *Sarum 17* **P** *Ch Patr Trust* **R** C F BROWN
TROWBRIDGE (St Thomas) and West Ashton *Sarum 17* **P** *CPAS* **P-in-c** F SEARS, **Hon C** A S REYNOLDS, **NSM** J DARLING
TROWELL (St Helen) *S'well 7* **P** *Lord Middleton* **P-in-c** G R BOOTH, **Hon C** C E HART
TROWSE (St Andrew) *see* Lakenham St Mark w Trowse *Nor*
TRULL (All Saints) w Angersleigh *B & W 18* **P** *DBP and M V Spurway Esq (jt)* **R** R A HATHWAY
TRUMPINGTON (St Mary and St Michael) *Ely 2* **P** *Trin Coll Cam* **V** N J THISTLETHWAITE
TRUNCH (St Botolph) *Nor 21* **P** *Duchy of Lanc (3 turns), Patr Bd (1 turn)* **TR** P B ALLAN, **TV** B N CARLING, **C** J A NASH, **Hon C** P M FAWCETT, **NSM** R H MacPHEE
TRURO (St George the Martyr) (St John the Evangelist) *Truro 6* **P** *Prime Min and V Kenwyn St Cuby (alt)* **V** I L J FROOM
TRURO (St Mary's Cathedral and Parish Church) *Truro 6* **P** *The Crown* **R** D J SHEARLOCK, **C** I F FRITH
TRURO (St Paul) (St Clement) *Truro 6* **P** *Bp* **V** P B STAPLES, **NSM** W C H STRIBLEY
TRUSHAM (St Michael and All Angels) *see* Christow, Ashton, Trusham and Bridford *Ex*
TRUSLEY (All Saints) *see* Ch Broughton w Barton Blount, Boylestone etc *Derby*
TRUSTHORPE (St Peter) *see* Mablethorpe w Trusthorpe *Linc*
TRYSULL (All Saints) *see* Wombourne w Trysull and Bobbington *Lich*
TRYTHALL (Mission Church) *see* Gulval *Truro*
TUBNEY (St Lawrence) *see* Fyfield w Tubney and Kingston Bagpuize *Ox*
TUCKHILL (Holy Innocents) *see* Claverley w Tuckhill *Heref*
TUCKINGMILL (All Saints) *Truro 2* **P** *Bp* **V** A N STRINGER, **NSM** E C WOON
TUCKSWOOD (St Paul) *Nor 3* **P** *Bp* **V** *Vacant* (01603) 53739
TUDDENHAM (St Martin) *see* Westerfield and Tuddenham w Witnesham *St E*
TUDDENHAM (St Mary) *see* Mildenhall *St E*
TUDDENHAM, EAST (All Saints) *see* Hockering, Honingham, E and N Tuddenham *Nor*
TUDDENHAM, NORTH (St Mary the Virgin) *as above*
TUDELEY (All Saints) w Capel *Roch 11* **P** *Bp* **V** S D RILEY
TUDHOE (St David) *see* Croxdale and Tudhoe *Dur*
TUDHOE GRANGE (St Andrew) *Dur 6* **P** *Bp* **V** N D BAKER
TUEBROOK (St John) *see* W Derby (or Tuebrook) St Jo *Liv*
TUFFLEY (St Barnabas) *Glouc 5* **P** *Bp* **C** M J ROBSON
TUFNELL PARK (St George and All Saints) *Lon 6* **P** *Trustees and CPAS (jt)* **V** S F F PARKE, **C** R MONTGOMERY, **NSM** J S B TODD
TUFTON (St Mary) *see* Whitchurch w Tufton and Litchfield *Win*
TUGBY (St Thomas a Becket) *see* Hallaton w Horninghold, Allexton, Tugby etc *Leic*
TUGFORD (St Catherine) *see* Diddlebury w Munslow, Holdgate and Tugford *Heref*
TULSE HILL (Holy Trinity and St Matthias) *S'wark 11* **P** *Simeon's Trustees and Peache Trustees (jt)* **Hon C** G E McWATT, **NSM** M B POOLE, D J LUBBOCK
TUNBRIDGE WELLS (Holy Trinity w Christ Church) *Roch 12* **P** *Mabledon Trust and CPAS (jt)* **V** J W BANNER
TUNBRIDGE WELLS (King Charles the Martyr) *Roch 12* **P** *Trustees* **V** M J HANCOCK
TUNBRIDGE WELLS (St Barnabas) *Roch 12* **P** *Guild of All So* **V** M S NICHOLLS
TUNBRIDGE WELLS (St James) w (St Philip) *Roch 12* **P** *Patr Bd* **TV** D J ABBOTT, **C** A D JENKINS
TUNBRIDGE WELLS (St John) *Roch 12* **P** *CPAS and V H Trin Tunbridge Wells (jt)* **V** G R WALTER, **C** M P WARREN, **NSM** I D HARRISON
TUNBRIDGE WELLS (St Luke) *Roch 12* **P** *Five Trustees* **P-in-c** J A WHEELER
TUNBRIDGE WELLS (St Mark) Broadwater Down *Roch 12* **P** *Bp Chich* **V** F R CUMBERLEGE, **C** N I VESEY
TUNBRIDGE WELLS (St Peter) Windmill Fields *Roch 12* **P** *Trustees and CPAS (jt)* **V** P R PAYN
TUNSTALL (All Saints) *see* Roos and Garton in Holderness w Tunstall etc *York*
TUNSTALL (Christ Church) *Lich 11* **P** *Bp* **V** A D BUIK, **C** M JEAVONS
TUNSTALL (Holy Trinity) *see* Catterick *Ripon*
TUNSTALL (St John the Baptist) w Melling and Leck *Blackb 15* **P** *Bp, Lord Shuttleworth, Judge E S Temple, and Ripon Coll Cuddesdon (jt)* **V** F PARR
TUNSTALL (St John the Baptist) w Rodmersham *Cant 14* **P** *D&C and G L Doubleday Esq (jt)* **R** D MATTHIAE
TUNSTALL (St Michael and All Angels) *see* Eyke w Bromeswell, Rendlesham, Tunstall etc *St E*
TUNSTEAD (Holy Trinity) *Man 15* **P** *Bp and Dioc Chan (jt)* **V** *Vacant* (01706) 874508
TUNSTEAD (St Mary) w Sco' Ruston *Nor 12* **P** *Bp* **P-in-c** A R LONG
TUNWORTH (All Saints) *see* Herriard w Winslade and Long Sutton etc *Win*
TUPSLEY (St Paul) w Hampton Bishop *Heref 3* **P** *Bp* **V** J D REESE, **C** C M SYKES, E C GARRETT, **NSM** R S MURRIN

TUPTON (St John) *see* N Wingfield, Clay Cross and Pilsley *Derby*
TUR LANGTON (St Andrew) *see* Church Langton w Tur Langton, Thorpe Langton etc *Leic*
TURKDEAN (All Saints) *see* Cold Aston w Notgrove and Turkdean *Glouc*
TURNASTONE (St Mary Magdalene) *see* Peterchurch w Vowchurch, Turnastone and Dorstone *Heref*
TURNDITCH (All Saints) *Derby 11* **P** *Bp* **P-in-c** D PERKINS
TURNERS HILL (St Leonard) *Chich 7* **P** *Bp* **V** *Vacant* (01342) 715278
TURNFORD (St Clement) Conventional District *St Alb 6* **P-in-c** S R MEPHAM
TURNHAM GREEN (Christ Church) *Lon 11* **P** *Bp* **P-in-c** J E DAINTY
TURNWORTH (St Mary) *see* Winterbourne Stickland and Turnworth etc *Sarum*
TURTON (St Anne) (St James) *Man 16* **P** *Bp* **V** J H DAULMAN, **Hon C** R LADDS
TURVEY (All Saints) *St Alb 15* **P** *Mrs P K C Hanbury* **R** P N JEFFERY
TURVILLE (St Mary) *see* Hambleden Valley *Ox*
TURWESTON (Assumption of the Blessed Virgin Mary) *see* Westbury w Turweston, Shalstone and Biddlesden *Ox*
TUSHINGHAM (St Chad) and Whitewell (St Mary) *Ches 5* **P** *MMCET* **R** P WINCHESTER
TUTBURY (St Mary the Virgin) *Lich 14* **P** *Duchy of Lanc* **V** T J GANZ
TUTSHILL (St Luke) *see* Tidenham w Beachley and Lancaut *Glouc*
TUTTINGTON (St Peter and St Paul) *see* Felmingham, Skeyton, Colby, Banningham etc *Nor*
TUXFORD (St Nicholas) w Weston and Markham Clinton *S'well 3* **P** *Ld Chan and Bp (alt)* **V** J E MARTIN
TWEEDMOUTH (St Bartholomew) *Newc 12* **P** *D&C Dur* **V** A S ADAMSON
TWERTON-ON-AVON *see* Bath Twerton-on-Avon *B & W*
TWICKENHAM (All Hallows) *Lon 10* **P** *D&C St Paul's* **P-in-c** G A BARBER, **NSM** V F FRAY
TWICKENHAM (All Saints) *Lon 10* **P** *Bp* **P-in-c** P L BUSTIN
TWICKENHAM (St Mary the Virgin) *Lon 10* **P** *D&C Windsor* **V** A GLYN-JONES, **Hon C** A F B ROGERS, D J ELLIOTT, **NSM** M H WINDRIDGE
TWICKENHAM, EAST (St Stephen) (St Paul) *Lon 10* **P** *CPAS* **V** A J WATSON, **C** D R McDOUGALL, R P FOTHERGILL, H C MACINNES
TWICKENHAM COMMON (Holy Trinity) *Lon 10* **P** *Bp* **V** D A WALTER
TWIGWORTH (St Matthew), Down Hatherley, Norton, The Leigh, Evington and Sandhurst *Glouc 6* **P** *Bp (1 turn), Ld Chan (2 turns), and D&C Bris (1 turn)* **V** J O'BRIEN, **C** J S MOESEL
TWINEHAM (St Peter) *see* Albourne w Sayers Common and Twineham *Chich*
TWINSTEAD (St John the Evangelist) *see* Gt and Lt Henny w Middleton, Wickham St Paul etc *Chelmsf*
TWITCHEN (St Peter) *see* S Molton w Nymet St George, High Bray etc *Ex*
TWO GATES (St Peter) *see* Wilnecote *Lich*
TWO MILE ASH (not known) *see* Watling Valley *Ox*
TWO MILE HILL (St Michael) *Bris 2* **P** *Prime Min* **V** *Vacant* 0117-967 1371
TWYCROSS (St James) *see* The Sheepy Gp *Leic*
TWYFORD (Assumption of the Blessed Virgin Mary) *see* Swan *Ox*
TWYFORD (St Andrew) *see* Barrow-on-Trent w Twyford and Swarkestone *Derby*
TWYFORD (St Andrew) *see* S Croxton Gp *Leic*
TWYFORD (St Mary) and Owslebury and Morestead *Win 13* **P** *Em Coll Cam and Bp (alt)* **V** P V LIPPIETT, **NSM** J D MORRIS
TWYFORD (St Mary the Virgin) *see* Ruscombe and Twyford *Ox*
TWYFORD (St Nicholas), Guist, Bintree, Themelthorpe, Wood Norton and Stibbard *Nor 22* **P** *Bp, and Mrs H M Cook (2 turns), DBP (1 turn)* **R** A K GREENHOUGH
TWYNING (St Mary Magdalene) *Glouc 9* **P** *Ch Ch Ox* **P-in-c** H E MONTAGUE-YOUENS
TWYWELL (St Nicholas) *see* Cranford w Grafton Underwood and Twywell *Pet*
TYBERTON (St Mary) *see* Madley w Tyberton, Preston-on-Wye and Blakemere *Heref*
TYDD (St Mary) *see* The Suttons w Tydd *Linc*
TYDD ST GILES (St Giles) *Ely 19* **P** *Bp* **P-in-c** N A WHITEHOUSE
TYE GREEN (St Barnabas) *see* Fairstead w Terling and White Notley etc *Chelmsf*
TYE GREEN (St Stephen) w St Andrew Netteswell *Chelmsf 26* **P** *J L H Arkwright Esq* **R** A V WATSON, **NSM** P A VOSS
TYLDESLEY (St George) w Shakerley *Man 13* **P** *Bp* **V** R I McCALLA
TYLER HILL (St Francis) *see* Hackington *Cant*
TYLERS GREEN (St Margaret) *Ox 29* **P** *Earl Howe* **V** M E HALL
TYLER'S HILL (St George) *see* Gt Chesham *Ox*
TYNE, NORTH and Redesdale Team *Newc 2* **P** *Patr Bd* **TR** T R HARPER, **TV** B A McKAY, P ADAMSON
TYNEMOUTH Balkwell (St Peter) *see* Balkwell *Newc*
TYNEMOUTH Cullercoats (St Paul) *Newc 8* **P** *Dioc Soc* **V** N BANKS, **C** B T BELL, **Hon C** C G BELLAMY, **NSM** D F TITTLEY
TYNEMOUTH Shiremoor (St Mark) *see* Shiremoor *Newc*
TYNEMOUTH (St John Percy) *Newc 8* **P** *Dioc Soc* **V** C H HOPE
TYNEMOUTH PRIORY (Holy Saviour) *Newc 8* **P** *Dioc Soc* **V** R G FORD
TYNINGS LANE (St Mary's Mission Church) *see* Aldridge *Lich*
TYRINGHAM (St Peter) *see* Lamp *Ox*
TYRLEY (Mission Room) *see* Drayton in Hales *Lich*
TYSELEY (St Edmund) *Birm 9* **P** *The Crown* **V** P A EVENS
TYSOE (Assumption of the Blessed Virgin Mary) w Oxhill and Whatcote *Cov 9* **P** *Marquess of Northn and DBP (jt)* **V** D A KNIGHT
TYTHBY (Holy Trinity) *see* Cropwell Bishop w Colston Bassett, Granby etc *S'well*
TYTHERINGTON (St James) *see* Cromhall w Tortworth and Tytherington *Glouc*
TYTHERINGTON (St James) *see* Heytesbury and Sutton Veny *Sarum*
TYTHERLEY, EAST (St Peter) *see* Lockerley and E Dean w E and W Tytherley *Win*
TYTHERLEY, WEST (St Peter) *as above*
TYTHERTON KELLAWAYS (St Giles) *see* Draycot *Bris*
TYTHERTON LUCAS (St Nicholas) *see* Chippenham St Andr w Tytherton Lucas *Bris*
TYWARDREATH (St Andrew) w Tregaminion *Truro 1* **P** *DBP* **V** M J OATEY
UBLEY (St Bartholomew) *see* Blagdon w Compton Martin and Ubley *B & W*
UCKFIELD (Holy Cross) (St Saviour) *Chich 21* **P** *Abp* **C** A J CARLILL, **Hon C** C G STABLES, **NSM** C HOWARTH, R C DALLING
UDIMORE (St Mary) *see* Brede w Udimore *Chich*
UFFCULME (St Mary the Virgin) *Ex 4* **P** *Bp* **V** J P BIRD
UFFINGTON Group, The (St Michael and All Angels) *Linc 13* **P** *Ld Chan (2 turns), Bp (2 turns), D&C (1 turn)* **R** T R SHEPHERD
UFFINGTON (Holy Trinity) *see* Wrockwardine Deanery *Lich*
UFFINGTON (St Mary), Shellingford, Woolstone and Baulking *Ox 17* **P** *Bp (2 turns), J J Twynam Esq (1 turn)* **R** J GAWNE-CAIN, **Hon C** J J H PAYNE
UFFORD (Assumption of the Blessed Virgin Mary) w Bredfield and Hasketon *St E 7* **P** *Bp, Ld Chan, and Exors T E Bloise-Brooke Esq (by turn)* **R** P BOURNER
UFFORD (St Andrew) *see* Barnack w Ufford and Bainton *Pet*
UFTON (St Michael and All Angels) *see* Radford Semele and Ufton *Cov*
UGBOROUGH (St Peter) *see* Ermington and Ugborough *Ex*
UGGESHALL (St Mary) w Sotherton, Wangford and Henham *St E 15* **P** *Exors Earl of Stradbroke* **R** *Vacant* (0150278) 235
UGGLEBARNBY (All Saints) *see* Eskdaleside w Ugglebarnby and Sneaton *York*
UGLEY (St Peter) *see* Henham and Elsenham w Ugley *Chelmsf*
UGTHORPE (Christ Church) *see* Lythe w Ugthorpe *York*
ULCEBY (All Saints) *see* Willoughby *Linc*
ULCEBY Group, The (St Nicholas) *Linc 6* **P** *Ld Chan* **V** A R MARSDEN
ULCOMBE (All Saints) *see* Harrietsham w Ulcombe *Cant*
ULDALE (St James) *see* Bolton w Ireby and Uldale *Carl*
ULEY (St Giles) w Owlpen and Nympsfield *Glouc 2* **P** *Ld Chan* **R** C RAWLINSON
ULGHAM (St John the Baptist) *Newc 11* **P** *Bp* **V** R L VERNON
ULLENHALL (St Mary the Virgin) *see* Beaudesert and Henley-in-Arden w Ullenhall *Cov*
ULLESKELFE (St Saviour) *see* Kirk Fenton w Kirkby Wharfe and Ulleskelfe *York*
ULLEY (Holy Trinity) *see* Aston cum Aughton w Swallownest, Todwick etc *Sheff*
ULLINGSWICK (St Luke) *see* Stoke Lacy, Moreton Jeffries w Much Cowarne etc *Heref*
ULPHA (St John) *see* Broughton and Duddon *Carl*
ULROME (St Andrew) *see* Skipsea w Ulrome and Barmston w Fraisthorpe *York*

ULTING (All Saints) *see* Hatfield Peverel w Ulting *Chelmsf*
ULVERSTON (St Mary w Holy Trinity) (St Jude) *Carl 8* **P** *Peache Trustees* **R** J HOLDEN
UMBERLEIGH (Church of the Good Shepherd) *see* S Molton w Nymet St George, High Bray etc *Ex*
UNDERBARROW (All Saints) *Carl 9* **P** *V Kendal H Trin* **V** *Vacant*
UNDERRIVER (St Margaret) *Roch 9* **P** *Bp* **P-in-c** M D COOKE
UNDERSKIDDAW (Parish Room) *see* Crosthwaite Keswick *Carl*
UNDERWOOD (St Michael and All Angels) *see* Brinsley w Underwood *S'well*
UNSTONE (St Mary) *see* Dronfield w Holmesfield *Derby*
UNSWORTH (St George) *Man 10* **P** *R Prestwich St Mary* **V** R E MALLINSON
UP HATHERLEY (St Philip and St James) *Glouc 11* **P** *Ch Union* **V** K M WRAY, **C** R NORTHING, **NSM** H R WOOD
UP MARDEN (St Michael) *see* Compton, the Mardens, Stoughton and Racton *Chich*
UP NATELY (St Stephen) *see* Newnham w Nately Scures w Mapledurwell etc *Win*
UP WALTHAM (St Mary the Virgin) *Chich 11* **P** *Lord Egremont* **P-in-c** C D BIDDELL
UPCHURCH (St Mary the Virgin) w Lower Halstow *Cant 14* **P** *D&C* **V** J P LEFROY, **NSM** R W PARTRIDGE
UPHAM (All Saints) (Blessed Mary of Upham) *Portsm 1* **P** *Ld Chan* **R** S E WILKINSON, **C** G E D HITCHINS
UPHAVON (St Mary the Virgin) w Rushall and Charlton *Sarum 12* **P** *Mert Coll Ox, Ld Chan, and Ch Ch Ox (by turn)* **R** D G SLOGGETT
UPHILL (St Nicholas) (St Barnabas Mission Church) *B & W 11* **P** *Patr Bd* **TR** D N MITCHELL, **TV** M J NORMAN, **C** G P EALES
UPHOLLAND (St Thomas the Martyr) *Liv 11* **P** *Patr Bd* **TR** P D D BRADLEY, **TV** K D CRINKS, **C** P L ROBINSON
UPLANDS (All Saints) *see* Stroud and Uplands w Slad *Glouc*
UPLEADON (St Mary the Virgin) *see* Redmarley D'Abitot, Bromesberrow w Pauntley etc *Glouc*
UPLOWMAN (St Peter) *see* Sampford Peverell, Uplowman, Holcombe Rogus etc *Ex*
UPLYME (St Peter and St Paul) w Axmouth *Ex 5* **P** *CPAS and Hyndman Trustees (jt)* **R** F S WORTH
UPMINSTER (St Laurence) *Chelmsf 2* **P** *Revd W R Holden* **R** C J MANN, **C** B RHODES
UPNOR (St Philip and St James) *see* Frindsbury w Upnor *Roch*
UPOTTERY (St Mary the Virgin) *see* Yarcombe, Membury, Upottery and Cotleigh *Ex*
UPPER *see also under substantive place name*
UPPERBY (St John the Baptist) *Carl 3* **P** *D&C* **V** T J HYSLOP, **C** A D CORDINER
UPPERTHONG (St John the Evangelist) *see* Upper Holme Valley *Wakef*
UPPINGHAM (St Peter and St Paul) w Ayston and Wardley w Belton *Pet 14* **P** *Bp* **R** J I WILLETT
UPPINGTON (Holy Trinity) *see* Wrockwardine Deanery *Lich*
UPSHIRE (St Thomas) *see* Waltham H Cross *Chelmsf*
UPTON (All Saints) *see* Lea Gp *Linc*
UPTON (Holy Ascension) *Ches 2* **P** *Duke of Westmr* **V** G H CONWAY, **NSM** G J WELCH
UPTON (St Dunstan) *see* Lytchett Minster *Sarum*
UPTON (St James) *see* Brompton Regis w Upton and Skilgate *B & W*
UPTON (St John the Baptist) *see* Castor w Sutton and Upton w Marholm *Pet*
UPTON (St Laurence) *see* Upton cum Chalvey *Ox*
UPTON (St Margaret) *see* S Walsham and Upton *Nor*
UPTON (St Margaret) and Copmanford *Ely 10* **P** *Bp* **NSM** I D M GIBSON
UPTON (St Mary) *Ches 8* **P** *Simeon's Trustees* **V** R J SHIMWELL, **C** D N LEAVER, J J CLARK
UPTON (St Mary Magdalene) *Ex 10* **P** *Simeon's Trustees and Ch Patr Trust (alt)* **R** B J R GERRY
UPTON (St Mary the Virgin) *see* Blewbury, Hagbourne and Upton *Ox*
UPTON (St Peter and St Paul) *see* Rolleston w Fiskerton, Morton and Upton *S'well*
UPTON BISHOP (St John the Baptist) *see* Linton w Upton Bishop and Aston Ingham *Heref*
UPTON CRESSETT w Monk Hopton *Heref 9* **P** *DBP and Miss E A Bird (alt)* **Hon C** H J PATTERSON
UPTON CROSS (St Paul) *see* Linkinhorne *Truro*
UPTON CUM CHALVEY (St Mary) *Ox 23* **P** *Bp* **TR** D K MIELL, **TV** D E WEST, **C** T NORWOOD
UPTON GREY (St Mary) *see* Herriard w Winslade and Long Sutton etc *Win*
UPTON HELLIONS (St Mary the Virgin) *see* Sandford w Upton Hellions *Ex*
UPTON LOVELL (St Augustine of Canterbury) *see* Ashton Gifford *Sarum*
UPTON MAGNA (St Lucia) *see* Wrockwardine Deanery *Lich*
UPTON NOBLE (St Mary Magdalene) *see* Bruton and Distr *B & W*
UPTON PARK (St Alban) *see* E Ham w Upton Park St Alb *Chelmsf*
UPTON PRIORY (Church of the Resurrection) *Ches 13* **P** *Bp* **V** D J SAMBELL, **NSM** U B GAMBLES
UPTON PYNE (Our Lady) *see* Thorverton, Cadbury, Upton Pyne etc *Ex*
UPTON SCUDAMORE (St Mary the Virgin) *see* Cley Hill Warminster *Sarum*
UPTON SNODSBURY (St Kenelm) *see* Peopleton and White Ladies Aston w Churchill etc *Worc*
UPTON ST LEONARDS (St Leonard) *Glouc 6* **P** *Bp* **P-in-c** R N MANN
UPTON-UPON-SEVERN (St Peter and Paul) *Worc 5* **P** *Bp* **R** A R KING, **NSM** J A FRASER
UPTON WARREN (St Michael) *see* Stoke Prior, Wychbold and Upton Warren *Worc*
UPWELL (St Peter) *Ely 19* **P** *R T Townley Esq* **P-in-c** R J M BLACKALL
UPWELL CHRISTCHURCH (Christ Church) *see* Christchurch and Manea and Welney *Ely*
UPWEY (St Laurence) *see* Bincombe w Broadwey, Upwey and Buckland Ripers *Sarum*
UPWOOD (St Peter) *see* The Ramseys and Upwood *Ely*
URCHFONT (St Michael and All Angels) *see* Redhorn *Sarum*
URMSTON (St Clement) *Man 7* **P** *Bp* **V** A M TILTMAN, **C** W J GASH
URSWICK (St Mary the Virgin and St Michael) *see* Aldingham, Dendron, Rampside and Urswick *Carl*
USHAW MOOR (St Luke) *see* Bearpark and Ushaw Moor *Dur*
USSELBY (St Margaret) *see* S Kelsey Gp *Linc*
USWORTH (Holy Trinity) (St Michael and All Angels) *Dur 11* **P** *Patr Bd* **TR** A MELTON, **TV** J H LAWSON, **C** S G HILL
UTKINTON (St Paul) *see* Tarporley *Ches*
UTLEY (St Mark) *Bradf 8* **P** *Bp and R Keighley St Andr (jt)* **V** W D JAMIESON, **C** D WALMSLEY, **NSM** W GREEN
UTTERBY (St Andrew) *see* Fotherby *Linc*
UTTOXETER AREA (St Mary the Virgin) *Lich 15* **P** *Patr Bd* **TR** A G SADLER, **TV** R M VIDAL-HALL, A O L HODGSON, **C** D F B BALDWIN
UXBRIDGE (St Andrew) (St Margaret) (St Peter) *Lon 24* **P** *Bp* **TR** J J WITCOMBE, **TV** S B ROBERTS, A F SHEARD
VALLEY END (St Saviour) *see* Chobham w Valley End *Guildf*
VALLEY PARK (St Francis) *Win 9* **P** *Bp* **V** P F HUTCHINSON
VANGE (St Chad) *Chelmsf 6* **P** *MMCET* **P-in-c** D A EATON, **C** L ELLIS
VAUXHALL (St Peter) *see* N Lambeth *S'wark*
VENN OTTERY (St Gregory) *see* Ottery St Mary, Alfington, W Hill, Tipton etc *Ex*
VENTA Group, The *see* Stoke H Cross w Dunston, Arminghall etc *Nor*
VENTNOR (Holy Trinity) *Portsm 7* **P** *Bp* **P-in-c** D H LAURIE
VENTNOR (St Alban) *see* Godshill *Portsm*
VENTNOR (St Catherine) *Portsm 7* **P** *Ch Patr Trust* **P-in-c** D H LAURIE
VERNHAM DEAN (St Mary the Virgin) *see* Hurstbourne Tarrant, Faccombe, Vernham Dean etc *Win*
VERWOOD (St Michael and All Angels) *Sarum 10* **P** *Bp* **V** A G GILL, **C** C R ARDAGH-WALTER
VERYAN (St Symphorian) w Ruan Lanihorne *Truro 6* **P** *D&C and DBP (jt)* **R** *Vacant* (01872) 501618
VICTORIA DOCKS (Ascension) *Chelmsf 3* **P** *Bp* **P-in-c** J A W BRICE
VICTORIA DOCKS St Luke *Chelmsf 3* **P** *Ld Chan* **V** D P WADE
VICTORIA PARK (St John Chrysostom) *see* Man Victoria Park *Man*
VICTORIA PARK (St Mark) *see* Old Ford St Paul and St Mark *Lon*
VIGO (Village Hall) *see* Stansted w Fairseat and Vigo *Roch*
VINEY HILL (All Saints) *Glouc 4* **P** *Univ Coll Ox* **P-in-c** I L DAVIES
VIRGINIA WATER (Christ Church) *Guildf 11* **P** *Simeon's Trustees* **V** S R SIZER
VIRGINSTOW (St Bridget) *see* Boyton, N Tamerton, Werrington etc *Truro*
VOWCHURCH (St Bartholomew) *see* Peterchurch w Vowchurch, Turnastone and Dorstone *Heref*
WABERTHWAITE (St John) *see* Eskdale, Irton, Muncaster and Waberthwaite *Carl*

WACTON (All Saints) *see* Stratton St Mary w Stratton St Michael etc *Nor*
WADDESDON (St Michael and All Angels) w Over Winchendon and Fleet Marston *Ox 24* **P** *Duke of Marlborough* **R** C M HUTCHINGS
WADDINGHAM (St Mary and St Peter) *see* Bishop Norton, Wadingham and Snitterby *Linc*
WADDINGTON (St Helen) *Bradf 5* **P** *E C Parker Esq* **V** A G BAILEY
WADDINGTON (St Michael) *Linc 18* **P** *Linc Coll Ox* **P-in-c** R J G PARKER, **NSM** S E KIDDLE
WADDON (St George) *see* Croydon St Jo *S'wark*
WADEBRIDGE *see* St Breoke and Egloshayle *Truro*
WADENHOE (St Michael and All Angels) *see* Aldwincle w Thorpe Achurch, Pilton, Wadenhoe etc *Pet*
WADHURST (St Peter and St Paul) *Chich 19* **P** *J M Hardcastle Esq and M R Toynbee Esq (jt)* **V** M G P INSLEY, **C** S W NUTH
WADINGHAM (St Mary and St Peter) *see* Bishop Norton, Wadingham and Snitterby *Linc*
WADSHELF (Mission Room) *see* Old Brampton and Loundsley Green *Derby*
WADSLEY (no dedication) *Sheff 4* **P** *Ch Patr Trust* **V** G J HUTCHISON
WADWORTH (St John the Baptist) w Loversall *Sheff 10* **P** *V Doncaster and DBP (alt)* **V** R W IVELL
WAINCLIFFE (St David) *see* Beeston *Ripon*
WAINFLEET (All Saints) *see* The Wainfleet Gp *Linc*
WAINFLEET Group, The (All Saints) (St Mary) (St Michael) *Linc 8* **P** *Ld Chan, Bp and T E Pitts Esq (alt)* **R** P F COATES
WAINFLEET (St Mary) *see* The Wainfleet Gp *Linc*
WAINFLEET (St Michael) *as above*
WAINFORD *St E 14* **P** *Bp, Mrs B I T Suckling, CPAS, Magd Coll Cam, and Ch Soc Trust (jt)* **R** F GEORGE, **NSM** R C B ALLEN, J F W BUCHANAN, N H SIMISTER
WAITHE (St Martin) *see* The North-Chapel Parishes *Linc*
WAKEFIELD Chantry Bridge (St Mary) *see* Wakef St Andr and St Mary *Wakef*
WAKEFIELD (St Andrew and St Mary) (St Swithun) *Wakef 12* **P** *Peache Trustees* **V** B S ELLIS
WAKEFIELD (St John the Baptist) *Wakef 12* **P** *Provost* **V** P M DOWLING, **Hon C** R B GRAINGER
WAKEFIELD (St Michael the Archangel) *see* Westgate Common *Wakef*
WAKERING, GREAT (St Nicholas) w Foulness *Chelmsf 13* **P** *Bp* **V** B J SHANNON
WAKERING, LITTLE (St Mary the Virgin) *see* Barling w Lt Wakering *Chelmsf*
WAKERLEY (St John the Baptist) *see* Barrowden and Wakerley w S Luffenham *Pet*
WAKES COLNE (All Saints) *see* Gt Tey and Wakes Colne w Chappel *Chelmsf*
WALBERSWICK (St Andrew) *see* Thorington w Wenhaston, Bramfield etc *St E*
WALBERTON (St Mary) w Binsted *Chich 21* **P** *Bp* **V** M J SULLY
WALBROOK Epiphany *Derby 10* **P** *Patr Bd* **TR** D E WILLS, **TV** D N GOUGH, M R FUTERS, **C** N R M ELLIOT
WALCOT *see* Bath Walcot *B & W*
WALCOT (All Saints) *see* Happisburgh, Walcott, Hempstead w Eccles etc *Nor*
WALCOT (St Nicholas) *see* S Lafford *Linc*
WALCOT (St Oswald) *see* Billinghay *Linc*
WALDEN, LITTLE (St John) *see* Saffron Walden w Wendens Ambo and Littlebury *Chelmsf*
WALDERSLADE (St William) *see* Chatham St Wm *Roch*
WALDINGFIELD, GREAT (St Lawrence) *see* Acton w Gt Waldingfield *St E*
WALDINGFIELD, LITTLE (St Lawrence) *see* Edwardstone w Groton and Lt Waldingfield *St E*
WALDITCH (St Mary) *see* Bridport *Sarum*
WALDRINGFIELD (All Saints) w Hemley and Newbourn *St E 2* **P** *Canon T Waller and Revd A H N Waller, Ld Chan, and Sir Joshua Rowley Bt (by turn)* **R** J P WALLER
WALDRON (All Saints) *Chich 15* **P** *Ex Coll Ox* **R** R W GREENLAND
WALES (St John the Baptist) *Sheff 5* **P** *Bp* **V** H J PATRICK
WALESBY (St Edmund) *S'well 3* **P** *DBP* **V** C C LEVY
WALESBY (St Mary and All Saints) *Linc 5* **P** *Bp, DBP, and W Drake Esq (jt)* **R** B M DODDS
WALFORD (St Michael and All Angels) and St John, w Bishopswood, Goodrich, Marstow and Welsh Bicknor *Heref 8* **P** *Bp and Ld Chan (alt)* **P-in-c** M A KELK, **NSM** P B BARLOW
WALGRAVE (St Peter) w Hannington and Wold and Scaldwell *Pet 2* **P** *Bp (2 turns), BNC Ox (1 turn)* **R** D G THOMAS
WALHAM GREEN (St John) (St James) *Lon 9* **P** *Bp* **P-in-c** K D MOULE
WALKDEN MOOR (St Paul) (St Barnabas' Mission) w Little Hulton *Man 12* **P** *Bp* **TR** A E BALLARD, **TV** A N BATEMAN, **C** H J GRAHAM
WALKER (Christ Church) *Newc 6* **P** *Bp* **V** R BEST, **C** D M IND, A J MILLER
WALKERGATE (St Oswald) *see* Byker St Mark and Walkergate St Oswald *Newc*
WALKERINGHAM (St Mary Magdalene) *see* Beckingham w Walkeringham *S'well*
WALKERN (St Mary the Virgin) *see* Benington w Walkern *St Alb*
WALKHAMPTON (St Mary the Virgin) *see* Yelverton, Meavy, Sheepstor and Walkhampton *Ex*
WALKINGTON (All Hallows) *see* Bishop Burton w Walkington *York*
WALKLEY (St Mary) *Sheff 4* **P** *Bp* **V** I K DUFFIELD
WALL (St George) *see* St Oswald in Lee w Bingfield *Newc*
WALL (St John the Baptist) *see* Lich St Mich w St Mary and Wall *Lich*
WALLASEY (St Hilary) *Ches 7* **P** *Bp* **R** R ORTON, **C** L P EDEN
WALLASEY (St Nicholas) *Ches 7* **P** *Bp* **V** E J BENTLEY
WALLINGFORD (St Mary le More w All Hallows) (St Leonard) and St Peter w Crowmarsh Gifford and Newnham Murren *Ox 18* **P** *Bp* **TR** J MORLEY, **TV** S HAYTER, **C** J M COATES
WALLINGTON (Holy Trinity) (St Patrick) *S'wark 24* **P** *Ch Soc Trust* **V** D V LEWIS, **C** R L WILLIAMS, B E BROWN
WALLINGTON (St Mary) *see* Sandon, Wallington and Rushden w Clothall *St Alb*
WALLISDOWN (St Saviour) *see* Talbot Village *Sarum*
WALLOP, NETHER (St Andrew) *see* Over Wallop w Nether Wallop *Win*
WALLOP, OVER (St Peter) w Nether Wallop *Win 3* **P** *D&C York and Earl of Portsm (alt)* **P-in-c** A R GRAHAM
WALLSEND (St John the Evangelist) *Newc 8* **P** *Bp* **V** F WILSON
WALLSEND (St Luke) *Newc 8* **P** *Bp* **V** R G S DEADMAN, **NSM** A J ELDER, S HAMIL
WALLSEND (St Peter) *Newc 8* **P** *Bp* **P-in-c** J ROSS, A A CLEMENTS
WALMER (St Mary) (St Saviour) (Blessed Virgin Mary) *Cant 8* **P** *Abp* **V** B A HAWKINS, **C** M R GRIFFIN, **NSM** S M LEE
WALMERSLEY (Christ Church) *Man 10* **P** *Trustees* **V** B STANNARD
WALMLEY (St John the Evangelist) *Birm 13* **P** *Trustess* **V** M B HARPER, **C** K D N CHANDRA
WALMSLEY (Christ Church) *Man 16* **P** *V Bolton-le-Moors St Pet* **V** D J BRIERLEY, **C** W L OLIVER, **NSM** R E IDDON
WALNEY ISLAND (St Mary the Virgin) *Carl 8* **P** *V Dalton-in-Furness* **V** R J WILLIAMSON
WALPOLE (St Mary the Virgin) *see* Halesworth w Linstead, Chediston, Holton etc *St E*
WALPOLE ST PETER (St Peter and St Paul) w Walpole St Andrew *Ely 17* **P** *The Crown and DBP (alt)* **R** A R TREEN
WALSALL (Annunciation of Our Lady) *see* Walsall St Gabr Fulbrook *Lich*
WALSALL (St Andrew) *Lich 26* **P** *Bp* **P-in-c** A P MITCHELL
WALSALL (St Gabriel) Fulbrook *Lich 26* **P** *Bp* **V** T R H COYNE, **NSM** W H POULTNEY
WALSALL (St Mary and All Saints) Palfrey *Lich 26* **P** *Bp* **C** F R MILLER
WALSALL (St Matthew) (St Luke) (St Martin) *Lich 26* **P** *Patr Bd* **TR** M B SANDERS, **TV** A P L SMITH, A G C SMITH, P O HART, **C** P HOWELL-JONES, J S OAKLEY
WALSALL (St Michael and All Angels) *see* Caldmore *Lich*
WALSALL St Paul *Lich 26* **P** *R Walsall* **V** *Vacant* (01922) 24963
WALSALL (St Peter) *Lich 26* **P** *R Walsall* **P-in-c** S R KIRBY
WALSALL THE PLECK (St John) and Bescot *Lich 26* **P** *V Walsall* **V** J REID, **C** M L CHAMBERLAIN
WALSALL WOOD (St John) *Lich 26* **P** *R Walsall* **V** J A WIDDAS, **C** M R GILBERT
WALSDEN (St Peter) *Wakef 3* **P** *Bp* **V** *Vacant* (01706) 817776
WALSGRAVE ON SOWE (St Mary) *Cov 1* **P** *Ld Chan* **V** M TYLER, **NSM** F E TYLER
WALSHAM, NORTH (St Nicholas) w Antingham *Nor 12* **P** *Bp* **V** M W SMITH, **C** R B STAINER, **NSM** V A WATTS
WALSHAM, SOUTH (St Laurence w St Mary) and Upton *Nor 4* **P** *Qu Coll Cam and Bp (jt)* **R** G A HENDY

WALSHAM LE WILLOWS (St Mary) and Finningham w Westhorpe *St E 9* **P** *R M Martineau Esq, DBP, and Ch Union (jt)* **P-in-c** M G CLARKE
WALSHAW (Christ Church) *Man 10* **P** *Simeon's Trustees* **V** S FOSTER, **C** I J HALSALL
WALSINGHAM (St Mary and All Saints) (St Peter), Houghton and Barsham *Nor 15* **P** *J Gurney Esq and Capt J D A Keith (jt)* **P-in-c** K F HAYDON
WALSOKEN (All Saints) *Ely 19* **P** *DBP* **R** J DAVIS
WALTERSTONE (St Mary) *see* Ewyas Harold w Dulas, Kenderchurch etc *Heref*
WALTHAM (All Saints) *Linc 10* **P** *The Crown* **P-in-c** I R SHELTON
WALTHAM (Holy Cross) *Chelmsf 25* **P** *Patr Bd* **TR** P J B HOBSON, **TV** J PEARCE, R A D ENEVER, **C** A J P GARROW, **NSM** J W ENEVER
WALTHAM (St Bartholomew) *see* Petham and Waltham w Lower Hardres etc *Cant*
WALTHAM (St Lawrence) *Ox 13* **P** *Lord Braybrooke* **NSM** D CHERRY
WALTHAM, GREAT (St Mary and St Lawrence) w Ford End *Chelmsf 8* **P** *Trin Coll Ox* **P-in-c** M T PROCTOR
WALTHAM, LITTLE (St Martin) *Chelmsf 8* **P** *Ex Coll Ox* **R** H ANSELL
WALTHAM, NEW (St Matthew) *Linc 10* **P** *The Crown* **P-in-c** M E THORNE
WALTHAM, NORTH (St Michael) and Steventon, Ashe and Deane *Win 6* **P** *DBP* **R** M S KENNING
WALTHAM ABBEY (Holy Cross) *see* Waltham H Cross *Chelmsf*
WALTHAM CROSS (Christ Church) *St Alb 20* **P** *V Cheshunt* **V** M J BANISTER, **C** R C WINSLADE
WALTHAM ON THE WOLDS (St Mary Magdalene), Stonesby, Saxby w Stapleford and Wyfordby *Leic 3* **P** *Duke of Rutland, Lady Gretton, and Sir Lyonel Tollemache, Bt (jt)* **P-in-c** S SAMUEL
WALTHAMSTOW (St Andrew) *Chelmsf 5* **P** *Bp* **V** M R J LAND
WALTHAMSTOW (St Barnabas and St James the Great) *Chelmsf 5* **P** *Bp* **V** A D COUCHMAN
WALTHAMSTOW (St Gabriel) (St Luke) (St Mary) (St Stephen) *Chelmsf 5* **P** *Patr Bd* **TR** P R BUTLER, **TV** N J ANSTEY, L A CURRELL
WALTHAMSTOW (St John) *Chelmsf 5* **P** *TR Walthamstow* **P-in-c** A J BISHOP
WALTHAMSTOW (St Michael and All Angels) *Chelmsf 5* **P** *Bp* **V** *Vacant* 0181-520 6328
WALTHAMSTOW (St Peter-in-the-Forest) *Chelmsf 5* **P** *Bp* **V** K M ELBOURNE, **C** L K NEWTON, **NSM** W S ROBINS, **Hon Par Dn** D E P PALK
WALTHAMSTOW (St Saviour) *Chelmsf 5* **P** *Bp* **V** P D D JAMES, **C** K H BALL
WALTON (Holy Trinity) *see* Street w Walton *B & W*
WALTON (Holy Trinity) *Ox 21* **P** *Patr Bd and DBP (jt)* **TR** A K ROYLE, **C** S C WILLIAMS, J A EVANS
WALTON Milton Keynes *Ox 25* **P** *Patr Bd* **TR** D LUNN, **TV** S STAFF
WALTON (not known) *see* Gilmorton w Peatling Parva and Kimcote etc *Leic*
WALTON (St John) *see* Brampton St Thos *Derby*
WALTON (St John the Evangelist) *Ches 4* **P** *P G Greenall Esq* **V** W J HIGHTON
WALTON (St Mary) *see* Lanercost w Kirkcambeck and Walton *Carl*
WALTON (St Mary) (St Philip) *St E 2* **P** *Ch Trust Fund Trust* **P-in-c** G J ARCHER, **C** M E OSBORNE, R G CORKE, **NSM** I W BARLEY, A C BARLEY, J K B FOWLER, B PERCY
WALTON (St Paul) *see* Sandal St Helen *Wakef*
WALTON (St Peter) *see* Thorp Arch w Walton *York*
WALTON (St Thomas) *see* Baswich *Lich*
WALTON, EAST (St Mary) *see* Gayton Gp of Par *Nor*
WALTON, HIGHER (All Saints) *Blackb 6* **P** *V Blackb* **V** J HANNA
WALTON, WEST (St Mary) *Ely 17* **P** *Ld Chan* **P-in-c** A R TREEN, **NSM** L D FYSH
WALTON BRECK (Christ Church) *Liv 7* **P** *Simeon's Trustees* **V** S B PIERCE
WALTON BRECK (Holy Trinity) *Liv 7* **P** *Simeon's Trustees* **V** *Vacant* 0151-263 1538
WALTON D'EIVILLE (St James) *Cov 8* **P** *Sir Richard Hamilton Bt* **R** N V HOWES
WALTON IN GORDANO (St Mary) *see* E Clevedon and Walton w Weston w Clapton *B & W*
WALTON IN GORDANO (St Paul) *as above*
WALTON-LE-DALE (St Leonard) w Samlesbury St Leonard the Less *Blackb 6* **P** *V Blackb St Mary and St Paul* **V** R McCULLOUGH
WALTON LE SOKEN (All Saints) (St George) *Chelmsf 23* **P** *Bp* **V** G D A BENNET
WALTON LE WOLDS (St Mary) *see* Barrow upon Soar w Walton le Wolds *Leic*
WALTON-ON-THAMES (St Mary) *Guildf 8* **P** *Bp* **V** T J SEDGLEY, **C** K W SCOTT, M P STOKES, **NSM** G L HORREX
WALTON ON THE HILL (St John) *Liv 7* **P** *Bp, Adn, and R Walton (jt)* **P-in-c** J M WATERMAN
WALTON ON THE HILL (St Luke) *Liv 7* **P** *Bp* **V** H E ROSS
WALTON-ON-THE-HILL (St Mary) (St Aidan) *Liv 5* **P** *Bp* **TR** P R TILLEY, **TV** T H ALLEN, **C** P GARTSIDE, K L F PITT
WALTON-ON-THE-HILL (St Peter) *Guildf 9* **P** *Bp* **R** J S HARRIS
WALTON ON TRENT (St Lawrence) w Croxall and Coton in the Elms w Rosliston *Derby 16* **P** *Bp and D W H Neilson Esq (jt)* **P-in-c** E J THOMPSON
WALWORTH (St Christopher) *S'wark 9* **P** *Bp and Pemb Coll Miss* **V** M DURRAN
WALWORTH (St John w the Lady Margaret) *S'wark 9* **P** *Bp* **V** J F WALKER, **C** B M D OLIVIER, **Hon C** E DAWSON
WALWORTH (St Peter) *S'wark 9* **P** *Bp* **TR** G S MURRAY, **NSM** A J WILD
WAMBROOK (Blessed Virgin Mary) *see* Combe St Nicholas w Wambrook *B & W*
WANBOROUGH (St Andrew) *see* Lyddington and Wanborough and Bishopstone etc *Bris*
WANBOROUGH (St Bartholomew) *see* Seale, Puttenham and Wanborough *Guildf*
WANDSWORTH (All Saints) (Holy Trinity) *S'wark 19* **P** *Ch Soc Trust* **V** G L WINCHESTER, **C** C A COTTON
WANDSWORTH (St Anne) *S'wark 19* **P** *Bp* **V** M H CLARK
WANDSWORTH (St Faith) *S'wark 19* **P** *Bp* **P-in-c** G D SWINTON
WANDSWORTH (St Michael and All Angels) Southfields *S'wark 19* **P** *Ch Soc Trust* **V** D J CASIOT
WANDSWORTH (St Paul) Wimbledon Park *S'wark 19* **P** *Bp* **V** W A J ALLBERRY, **NSM** G E D BONHAM-CARTER, A J TOWNSEND
WANDSWORTH (St Stephen) *S'wark 19* **P** *CPAS* **V** S MELLUISH, **Hon C** J H FREEMAN
WANDSWORTH COMMON (St Mary Magdalene) *S'wark 18* **P** *Bp* **V** I KITTERINGHAM, **NSM** B STEWART
WANDSWORTH COMMON (St Michael) *see* Battersea St Mich *S'wark*
WANGFORD (St Peter) *see* Uggeshall w Sotherton, Wangford and Henham *St E*
WANLIP (Our Lady and St Nicholas) *see* Birstall and Wanlip *Leic*
WANSFORD (St Mary) *see* Nafferton w Wansford *York*
WANSFORD (St Mary the Virgin) *see* Wittering w Thornhaugh and Wansford *Pet*
WANSTEAD (Holy Trinity) Hermon Hill *Chelmsf 4* **P** *Bp* **V** A H ASHDOWN, **Hon Par Dn** D E P PALK
WANSTEAD (St Mary) (Christ Church) *Chelmsf 4* **P** *Bp* **R** S F FOSTER, **C** M K LAWRENCE
WANSTROW (Blessed Virgin Mary) *see* Nunney and Witham Friary, Marston Bigot etc *B & W*
WANTAGE (St Peter and St Paul) *Ox 19* **P** *D&C Windsor* **V** J L SALTER, **C** C M SMITH
WANTAGE DOWNS *Ox 19* **P** *Bp, CCC Ox, and C L Loyd Esq (jt)* **R** E G ADLEY, **NSM** C J KING, M G D ENDEAN, D J PAGE
WANTISDEN (St John the Baptist) *see* Eyke w Bromeswell, Rendlesham, Tunstall etc *St E*
WAPLEY (St Peter) *see* Yate New Town *Bris*
WAPPENBURY (St John the Baptist) w Weston under Wetherley *Cov 10* **P** *Bp* **P-in-c** P J CROOKS, **C** M L D GREIG
WAPPENHAM (St Mary the Virgin) *see* Weedon Lois w Plumpton and Moreton Pinkney etc *Pet*
WARBLETON (St Mary) and Bodle Street Green *Chich 15* **P** *Revd E S Haviland* **R** G FRANCE
WARBLINGTON (St Thomas a Becket) and Emsworth *Portsm 4* **P** *Bp and J H Norris Esq (alt)* **R** D J F PARTRIDGE, **NSM** L H MORRIS
WARBOROUGH (St Lawrence) *Ox 1* **P** *CCC Ox* **V** *Vacant* (01867) 328381
WARBOYS (St Mary Magdelene) w Broughton and Bury w Wistow *Ely 11* **P** *Bp and Ch Soc Trust (jt)* **R** S O LEEKE, **C** C HURST
WARBSTOW (St Werburgh) *see* St Gennys, Jacobstow w Warbstow and Treneglos *Truro*
WARBURTON (St Werburgh) *Ches 10* **P** *Hon M L W Flower* **P-in-c** E M BURGESS
WARCOP (St Columba) *see* Brough w Stainmore, Musgrave and Warcop *Carl*
WARD END (Christ Church) *see* Burney Lane *Birm*

WARD END (St Margaret) *Birm 14* **P** *Aston Trustees* **P-in-c** J C WELLER
WARDEN (St Michael and All Angels) w Newbrough *Newc 4* **P** *Bp* **V** J W GLEDHILL
WARDEN, OLD (St Leonard) *St Alb 11* **P** *R O Shuttleworth Trustees* **P-in-c** R J DOULTON
WARDINGTON (St Mary Magdalene) *see* Shires' Edge *Ox*
WARDLEWORTH (St Mary w St James) *see* Rochdale *Man*
WARDLEY (All Saints) *see* Swinton and Pendlebury *Man*
WARDLEY (St Botolph) *see* Uppingham w Ayston and Wardley w Belton *Pet*
WARDLOW (Good Shepherd) *see* Ashford w Sheldon and Longstone *Derby*
WARE (Christ Church) *St Alb 22* **P** *CPAS* **V** D J PROUD, **C** D A WILLIAMS
WARE (St Mary the Virgin) *St Alb 22* **P** *Trin Coll Cam* **V** H E WILCOX, **NSM** M S E M BEAZLEY
WAREHAM (Lady St Mary) (St Martin) *Sarum 9* **P** *Patr Bd* **TR** P G HARDMAN, **TV** A C ASHCROFT, **C** R C BARTLETT, **NSM** J CLEATON
WAREHORNE (St Matthew) *see* Orlestone w Snave and Ruckinge w Warehorne *Cant*
WARESIDE (Holy Trinity) *see* Hunsdon w Widford and Wareside *St Alb*
WARESLEY (St James) *Ely 12* **P** *Pemb Coll Cam* **P-in-c** B CURRY
WARFIELD (St Michael the Archangel) *Ox 11* **P** *DBP* **V** B H MEARDON, **P-in-c** M T J SMITH
WARGRAVE (St Mary the Virgin) *Ox 16* **P** *Lord Remnant* **V** J W RATINGS
WARHAM (All Saints) *see* Holkham w Egmere w Warham, Wells and Wighton *Nor*
WARK (St Michael) *see* Humshaugh w Simonburn and Wark *Newc*
WARKLEIGH (St John) *see* S Molton w Nymet St George, High Bray etc *Ex*
WARKTON (St Edmund) *see* Barton Seagrave w Warkton *Pet*
WARKWORTH (St Lawrence) and Acklington *Newc 9* **P** *Bp and Trustees of the late Duke of Northd (alt)* **V** J M BREARLEY, **NSM** J A RICHARDSON
WARKWORTH (St Mary the Virgin) *see* Greatworth and Marston St Lawrence etc *Pet*
WARLEGGAN (St Bartholomew) *see* St Neot and Warleggan *Truro*
WARLEY (St John the Evangelist) *Wakef 4* **P** *V Halifax* **P-in-c** A J STREET, **NSM** J S BRADBERRY
WARLEY, GREAT (Christ Church) *Chelmsf 7* **P** *Bp* **P-in-c** A J PUGSLEY
WARLEY, GREAT (St Mary the Virgin) and Ingrave St Nicholas *Chelmsf 7* **P** *Hon G C D Jeffreys and Ch Patr Trust (jt)* **Hon C** C J TRAVERS
WARLEY, LITTLE (St Peter) *see* E and W Horndon w Lt Warley and Childerditch *Chelmsf*
WARLEY WOODS (St Hilda) *Birm 7* **P** *Bp* **V** M R DUNK
WARLINGHAM (All Saints) w Chelsham and Farleigh *S'wark 25* **P** *Patr Bd* **TR** R D W HAWKINS, **TV** I A COUTTS, **C** S M SOKOLOWSKI
WARMFIELD (St Peter) *Wakef 9* **P** *Oley Trustees Clare Coll Cam* **P-in-c** G S S WATTS
WARMINGHAM (St Leonard) *see* Elworth and Warmingham *Ches*
WARMINGTON (St Mary the Blessed Virgin), Tansor w Cotterstock and Fotheringhay *Pet 12* **P** *Bp and D&C Linc (alt)* **P-in-c** B V ROGERS
WARMINGTON (St Michael) w Shotteswell and Radway w Ratley *Cov 8* **P** *Bp* **R** R P PAUL
WARMINSTER (Christ Church) *Sarum 14* **P** *R Warminster St Denys etc* **P-in-c** P W HUNTER
WARMINSTER (St Denys) *see* Cley Hill Warminster *Sarum*
WARMLEY (St Barnabas), Syston and Bitton *Bris 2* **P** *Bp* **R** D G MITCHELL, **C** J M CARPENTER, **Hon C** J E NORMAN
WARMSWORTH (St Peter) *Sheff 10* **P** *Bp* **R** J M RICHARDS
WARMWELL (Holy Trinity) *see* Broadmayne, W Knighton, Owermoigne etc *Sarum*
WARNBOROUGH, SOUTH (St Andrew) *see* Herriard w Winslade and Long Sutton etc *Win*
WARNDON (St Nicholas) *Worc 6* **P** *Bp* **P-in-c** K I CRAWFORD
WARNDON (St Wulstan) *see* Worc St Wulstan *Worc*
WARNERS END (St Alban) *see* Hemel Hempstead *St Alb*
WARNFORD (Our Lady) *see* W Meon and Warnford *Portsm*
WARNHAM (St Margaret) *Chich 8* **P** *J C Lucas Esq* **V** J R TAYLOR
WARNINGLID (St Andrew) *see* Slaugham *Chich*
WARREN PARK (St Clare) *Portsm 4* **P** *Bp* **V** R C WHITE, **C** R A ORCHIN, **NSM** M S HARPER
WARREN ROW (St Paul) *see* Knowl Hill w Littlewick *Ox*
WARRINGTON (Holy Trinity) *Liv 12* **P** *R Warrington* **V** I D ELLIOTT, **NSM** R E LICHTENBERGER
WARRINGTON St Ann *Liv 12* **P** *Simeon's Trustees* **V** S R PARISH
WARRINGTON (St Barnabas) Bank Quay *Liv 12* **P** *R Warrington and Bp (jt)* **V** *Vacant* (01925) 633556
WARRINGTON (St Elphin) (St John) *Liv 12* **P** *Lord Lilford* **R** J O COLLING, **C** M D CHILCOTT
WARSLOW (St Lawrence) *see* Alstonfield, Butterton, Warslow w Elkstone etc *Lich*
WARSOP (St Peter and St Paul) *S'well 2* **P** *Trustees* **R** C W BOWMAN, **C** P J STEAD, **Hon C** J V SHARPE
WARTER (St James) *see* Nunburnholme and Warter *York*
WARTHILL (St Mary) *see* Stockton-on-the-Forest w Holtby and Warthill *York*
WARTLING (St Mary Magdalene) *see* Herstmonceux and Wartling *Chich*
WARTNABY (St Michael) *see* Ab Kettleby Gp *Leic*
WARTON (Holy Trinity) *see* Austrey and Warton *Birm*
WARTON (St Oswald or Holy Trinity) w Yealand Conyers *Blackb 15* **P** *Bp* **V** F B ODDY
WARTON (St Paul) *Blackb 11* **P** *Ch Ch Ox* **V** G WORTHINGTON
WARWICK (St Leonard) *see* Wetheral w Warw *Carl*
WARWICK (St Mary) (St Nicholas) *Cov 11* **P** *Ld Chan and Patr Bd (alt)* **TR** D C BRINDLEY, **TV** K M ROBERTS, G SANDERSON
WARWICK (St Paul) *Cov 11* **P** *TR Warw* **V** S W HEWITT
WARWICK SQUARE (St Gabriel) *see* Pimlico St Gabr *Lon*
WASDALE, NETHER (St Michael) *see* Gosforth w Nether Wasdale and Wasdale Head *Carl*
WASDALE HEAD (not known) *as above*
WASH COMMON (St George) *see* Newbury *Ox*
WASHBOURNE, GREAT (St Mary) *see* Alderton, Gt Washbourne, Dumbleton etc *Glouc*
WASHFIELD (St Mary the Virgin), Stoodleigh, Withleigh, Calverleigh, Oakford, Templeton, Loxbeare, Rackenford, and Cruwys Morchard *Ex 8* **P** *Patr Bd* **TR** C H MEE, **TV** G B BELL, **NSM** J C W ROBERTS
WASHFORD (St Mary) *see* Old Cleeve, Leighland and Treborough *B & W*
WASHFORD PYNE (St Peter) *see* N Creedy *Ex*
WASHINGBOROUGH (St John) w Heighington and Canwick *Linc 18* **P** *DBP and Mercers' Co (jt)* **R** A C BELL
WASHINGTON (Holy Trinity) *Dur 11* **P** *Bp* **R** J G A ROBERTS, **C** A PATTMAN, R L FERGUSON
WASHINGTON (St Mary) *see* Ashington, Washington and Wiston with Buncton *Chich*
WASHWOOD HEATH (St Mark) *Birm 14* **P** *V Saltley* **V** R E CRANE
WASING (St Nicholas) *see* Aldermaston w Wasing and Brimpton *Ox*
WASKERLEY (St Andrew) *see* Blanchland w Hunstanworth and Edmundbyers etc *Newc*
WASPERTON (St John the Baptist) *see* Barford w Wasperton and Sherbourne *Cov*
WASS (St Thomas) *see* Coxwold and Husthwaite *York*
WATCHET (Holy Cross Chapel) *see* St Decumans *B & W*
WATCHET (St Decuman) *as above*
WATCHFIELD (St Thomas's Chapel) *see* Shrivenham w Watchfield and Bourton *Ox*
WATER EATON (St Frideswide) *Ox 25* **P** *Bp* **V** P A SMITH
WATER NEWTON (St Remigius) *Ely 13* **P** *Keble Coll Ox* **P-in-c** P O POOLEY
WATER ORTON (St Peter and St Paul) *Birm 10* **P** *Patr Bd* **V** S T MAYES
WATER STRATFORD (St Giles) *Ox 22* **P** *DBP* **P-in-c** J HUDSON
WATERBEACH (St John) *Ely 6* **P** *Bp* **V** D P E REINDORP
WATERDEN (All Saints) *see* N and S Creake w Waterden, Syderstone etc *Nor*
WATERFALL (St James and St Bartholomew) *see* Calton, Cauldon, Grindon and Waterfall *Lich*
WATERFOOT (St James the Great) *Man 15* **P** *Trustees* **V** *Vacant* (01706) 215959
WATERFORD (St Michael and All Angels) *see* Bramfield w Stapleford and Waterford *St Alb*
WATERHEAD (Holy Trinity) *Man 21* **P** *The Crown* **P-in-c** G WHITTAKER
WATERHOUSES (St Paul) *Dur 1* **P** *R Brancepeth Esq* **P-in-c** P R MURRAY
WATERINGBURY (St John the Baptist) w Teston and West Farleigh *Roch 7* **P** *Peache Trustees and D&C (jt)* **R** D V GOWER
WATERLOO (Christ Church) (St Mary) *Liv 1* **P** *Trustees* **NSM** D C M TAYLOR
WATERLOO (St John) *Liv 1* **P** *Trustees* **P-in-c** P W DEARNLEY

WATERLOO (St John the Evangelist) (St Andrew) *S'wark 12* **P** *Abp and CPAS (jt)* **V** C R TRUSS, **C** K M RUMENS
WATERLOOVILLE (St George the Martyr) *Portsm 4* **P** *Bp* **V** M FERRIER
WATERMILLOCK (All Saints) *see* Greystoke, Matterdale, Mungrisdale etc *Carl*
WATERMOOR (Holy Trinity) *see* Cirencester *Glouc*
WATERPERRY (St Mary the Virgin) *see* Wheatley *Ox*
WATERS UPTON (St Michael) *see* Tibberton w Bolas Magna and Waters Upton *Lich*
WATERSTOCK (St Leonard) *see* Wheatley *Ox*
WATERTHORPE (Emmanuel) *see* Mosborough *Sheff*
WATFORD (Christ Church) (St Mark) *St Alb 7* **P** *Bp, V Watford, and Churchwardens (jt)* **V** R C LEWIS, **C** C M PUNSHON, **NSM** C THORP
WATFORD (St Andrew) *St Alb 7* **P** *Bp and Churchwardens (jt)* **V** G R WARREN
WATFORD (St John) *St Alb 7* **P** *Bp* **V** R SALTER
WATFORD (St Luke) *St Alb 7* **P** *Bp, Adn St Alb, V Watford, and Ch Trust Fund Trust (jt)* **V** J KIDDLE, **C** S A STARKEY
WATFORD (St Mary) *St Alb 7* **P** *Ch Trust Fund Trust* **V** J M WOODGER, **C** D C WEAVER
WATFORD (St Michael and All Angels) *St Alb 7* **P** *Bp* **V** J B BROWN, **C** O MURPHY
WATFORD (St Peter) *St Alb 7* **P** *Bp* **V** C P COTTEE
WATFORD (St Peter and St Paul) *see* Long Buckby w Watford *Pet*
WATH (St Mary) *see* Kirklington w Burneston and Wath and Pickhill *Ripon*
WATH BROW (Mission Church) *see* Cleator Moor w Cleator *Carl*
WATH-UPON-DEARNE (All Saints) *Sheff 12* **P** *Ch Ch Ox* **V** T E LEACH
WATLING VALLEY, Milton Keynes (not known) *Ox 25* **P** *Patr Bd* **TR** J WALLER, **TV** S F MORRIS, V E W RUSHTON, D YATES, **C** S D GODDARD
WATLINGTON (St Leonard) *see* Icknield *Ox*
WATLINGTON (St Peter and St Paul) *Ely 16* **P** *Bp* **R** J C W NOLAN
WATTISFIELD (St Margaret) *see* Hepworth, Hinderclay, Wattisfield and Thelnetham *St E*
WATTLESBOROUGH (St Margaret) *see* Alberbury w Cardeston *Heref*
WATTON (St Mary) *see* Hutton Cranswick w Skerne, Watton and Beswick *York*
WATTON (St Mary) w Carbrooke and Ovington *Nor 13* **P** *Ld Chan (3 turns), Cam Univ (1 turn), and SMF (2 turns)* **V** R J BOWETT, **NSM** R J BROUGHALL
WATTON AT STONE (St Mary and St Andrew) *St Alb 22* **P** *R M A Smith Esq* **P-in-c** B H GWINN
WAVENDON (Assumption of the Blessed Virgin Mary) *see* Walton Milton Keynes *Ox*
WAVERTON (Christ Church) *see* Bromfield w Waverton *Carl*
WAVERTON (St Peter) *Ches 5* **P** *Bp* **R** J M G DAVIES, **NSM** E T DAVIES
WAVERTREE (Holy Trinity) *Liv 6* **P** *Bp* **R** J EASTWOOD, **C** P HRYZIUK, **NSM** L B BRUCE
WAVERTREE (St Bridget) (St Thomas) *Liv 6* **P** *Simeon's Trustees and R Wavertree H Trin (jt)* **V** W J SANDERS
WAVERTREE (St Mary) *Liv 6* **P** *Bp* **R** J M MATTHEWS
WAWNE (St Peter) *see* Sutton St Jas and Wawne *York*
WAXHAM, GREAT (St John) *see* Happisburgh, Walcott, Hempstead w Eccles etc *Nor*
WAYFORD (St Michael and All Angels) *see* Crewkerne w Wayford *B & W*
WEALD (St George) *see* Sevenoaks Weald *Roch*
WEALD, NORTH Bassett (St Andrew) *Chelmsf 27* **P** *Bp* **V** T C THORPE
WEALD, SOUTH (St Peter) *Chelmsf 7* **P** *Bp* **P-in-c** I H JORYSZ
WEAR (St Luke) *see* Countess Wear *Ex*
WEARE (St Gregory) *see* Crook Peak *B & W*
WEARE GIFFARD (Holy Trinity) *see* Bideford, Northam, Westward Ho!, Appledore etc *Ex*
WEASENHAM (All Saints) *see* South Raynham, E w W Raynham, Helhoughton, etc *Nor*
WEASENHAM (St Peter) *as above*
WEASTE (St Luke w All Saints) *Man 6* **P** *Bp and V Eccles (jt)* **V** K M ARCHER
WEAVERHAM (St Mary the Virgin) *Ches 6* **P** *Bp* **V** M L RIDLEY
WEAVERTHORPE (St Andrew) w Helperthorpe, Luttons Ambo and Kirby Grindalythe w Wharram *York 2* **P** *Abp and D&C (jt)* **V** B A ARMITAGE
WEBHEATH (St Philip) *see* Redditch, The Ridge *Worc*
WEDDINGTON (St James) and Caldecote *Cov 5* **P** *Bp* **R** A J ADAMS, **C** M C HATHAWAY
WEDMORE (St Mary) w Theale and Blackford *B & W 1* **P** *Bp* **V** E M CROSS, **C** T J BELL
WEDNESBURY (St Bartholomew) *Lich 27* **P** *Bp* **V** D K BEEDON, **NSM** D MARSH
WEDNESBURY (St James and St John) *Lich 27* **P** *Trustees* **R** I B COOK, **NSM** R C GILBERT
WEDNESBURY (St Paul) Wood Green *Lich 27* **P** *Bp* **V** J D POINTS, **C** G E TOWLSON
WEDNESFIELD (St Augustine and St Chad) *Lich 29* **P** *Patr Bd* **TR** J D D PORTER, **TV** C W J STYLES, C R DUNCAN, **C** V E DUNCAN
WEDNESFIELD (St Gregory) *Lich 29* **P** *Bp* **V** D MELVILLE
WEDNESFIELD HEATH (Holy Trinity) *Lich 29* **P** *CPAS* **V** S R J FRENCH, **C** D C WELLER
WEEDON (School Chapel) *see* Schorne *Ox*
WEEDON BEC (St Peter and St Paul) w Everdon and Dodford *Pet 3* **P** *Bp* **V** *Vacant* (01327) 340359
WEEDON LOIS (St Mary and St Peter) w Plumpton and Moreton Pinkney and Wappenham *Pet 1* **P** *Bp, Jes Coll Ox, and Or Coll Ox (by turn)* **P-in-c** F E PICKARD
WEEFORD (St Mary the Virgin) *see* Whittington w Weeford *Lich*
WEEK ST MARY (St Mary the Virgin) w Poundstock and Whitstone *Truro 8* **P** *SS Coll Cam, Walsingham Coll, and Guild of All So (jt)* **P-in-c** W I MEADS, **NSM** R C W DICKENSON
WEEKE *see* Win St Matt *Win*
WEEKLEY (St Mary the Virgin) *see* Geddington w Weekley *Pet*
WEELEY (St Andrew) and Little Clacton *Chelmsf 23* **P** *Bp and BNC Ox (alt)* **R** D M NEWMAN
WEETHLEY (St James) *see* Alcester and Arrow w Oversley and Weethley *Cov*
WEETING (St Mary) *Ely 15* **P** *G&C Coll Cam* **P-in-c** J B ROWSELL
WEETON (St Barnabas) *see* Kirkby Overblow *Ripon*
WEETON (St Michael) *see* Singleton w Weeton *Blackb*
WEETSLADE (St Paul) *Newc 1* **P** *Bp* **V** *Vacant* 0191-268 9366
WELBORNE (All Saints) *see* Mattishall w Mattishall Burgh, Welborne etc *Nor*
WELBOURN (St Chad) *Linc 23* **P** *Hyndman Trustees* **R** *Vacant*
WELBURN (St John the Evangelist) *see* Bulmer w Dalby, Terrington and Welburn *York*
WELBURY (St Leonard) *see* Rounton w Welbury *York*
WELBY (not known) *see* Melton Mowbray *Leic*
WELBY (St Bartholemew) *see* Ancaster Wilsford Gp *Linc*
WELCOMBE (St Nectan) *see* Parkham, Alwington, Buckland Brewer etc *Ex*
WELDON (St Mary the Virgin) w Deene *Pet 9* **P** *DBP and E Brudenell Esq (jt)* **R** *Vacant* (01536) 203671
WELFORD (St Gregory) w Wickham and Great Shefford, Boxford and Stockcross *Ox 14* **P** *Bp and BNC Ox (jt)* **R** N C SANDS
WELFORD (St Mary the Virgin) w Sibbertoft and Marston Trussell *Pet 2* **P** *Bp* **V** R J CATTLE, **NSM** K W BAKER
WELFORD (St Peter) w Weston and Clifford Chambers *Glouc 10* **P** *DBP* **R** R D WYATT
WELHAM (St Andrew) *see* Gt Bowden w Welham, Glooston and Cranoe *Leic*
WELL (St Margaret) *Linc 8* **P** *J Reeve Esq* **R** A READER-MOORE
WELL (St Michael) *see* W Tanfield and Well w Snape and N Stainley *Ripon*
WELL HILL (Mission) *see* Chelsfield *Roch*
WELLAND (St James) *see* Hanley Castle, Hanley Swan and Welland *Worc*
WELLESBOURNE (St Peter) *Cov 8* **P** *Ld Chan* **V** N V HOWES
WELLING (St John the Evangelist) *Roch 15* **P** *Bp* **V** M G KICHENSIDE, **C** B W ROWLAND
WELLING (St Mary the Virgin) *S'wark 3* **P** *Bp* **V** C E BLANKENSHIP, **C** L C GALE
WELLINGBOROUGH (All Hallows) *Pet 6* **P** *Exors Major E C S Byng-Maddick* **V** I C HUNT
WELLINGBOROUGH (All Saints) *Pet 6* **P** *V Wellingborough* **V** P B WELCH
WELLINGBOROUGH (St Andrew) *Pet 6* **P** *Bp* **V** J R WESTWOOD, **NSM** C J MOGRIDGE
WELLINGBOROUGH (St Barnabas) *Pet 6* **P** *Bp* **V** D W WITCHELL
WELLINGBOROUGH (St Mark) *Pet 6* **P** *Bp* **V** I R LOWELL
WELLINGBOROUGH (St Mary the Virgin) *Pet 6* **P** *Guild of All So* **P-in-c** R J FARMER
WELLINGHAM (St Andrew) *see* South Raynham, E w W Raynham, Helhoughton, etc *Nor*
WELLINGORE (All Saints) *see* Graffoe Gp *Linc*

WELLINGTON (All Saints) (St John the Baptist) and District *B & W 19* **P** *Patr Bd* **TR** T W STOKES, **TV** R P LODGE, L H COLTON, D P RANDELL, **NSM** C I BRIERLEY
WELLINGTON (All Saints) w Eyton (St Catherine) *Lich 22* **P** *Ch Trust Fund Trust* **V** M E POTTER, **C** N M A TRAYNOR
WELLINGTON (Christ Church) *Lich 22* **P** *V Wellington w Eyton* **V** M J CLARIDGE
WELLINGTON (St Margaret of Antioch) w Pipe-cum-Lyde and Moreton-on-Lugg *Heref 4* **P** *Bp, Ch Union, and D&C (by turn)* **P-in-c** C M BURKE
WELLINGTON HEATH (Christ Church) *see* Bosbury w Wellington Heath etc *Heref*
WELLOW (St Julian the Hospitaller) *see* Peasedown St John w Wellow *B & W*
WELLOW (St Margaret) *Win 11* **P** *Bp* **V** G R BIGGS, **NSM** N M HARRISON
WELLOW (St Swithun) *see* Kneesall w Laxton and Wellow *S'well*
WELLS (St Cuthbert) w Wookey Hole *B & W 8* **P** *D&C* **V** C D TAYLOR
WELLS (St Thomas) w Horrington *B & W 8* **P** *D&C* **V** C T TOOKEY, **C** M P LEE, **NSM** A L BIRBECK
WELLS-NEXT-THE-SEA (St Nicholas) *see* Holkham w Egmere w Warham, Wells and Wighton *Nor*
WELNEY (St Mary) *see* Christchurch and Manea and Welney *Ely*
WELSH BICKNOR (St Margaret) *see* Walford and St John w Bishopswood, Goodrich etc *Heref*
WELSH FRANKTON (St Andrew) *see* Criftins w Dudleston and Welsh Frankton *Lich*
WELSH NEWTON (St Mary the Virgin) *see* St Weonards w Orcop, Garway, Tretire etc *Heref*
WELSH NEWTON COMMON (St Faith) *as above*
WELSHAMPTON (St Michael) *see* Petton w Cockshutt, Welshampton and Lyneal etc *Lich*
WELTON (St Helen) w Melton *York 15* **P** *DBP* **P-in-c** A F RABLEN
WELTON (St James) *see* Westward, Rosley-w-Woodside and Welton *Carl*
WELTON (St Martin) *see* Daventry, Ashby St Ledgers, Braunston etc *Pet*
WELTON (St Mary) and Dunholme w Scothern *Linc 3* **P** *Bp and DBP (jt)* **V** G S DARLISON
WELTON-LE-MARSH (St Martin) w Gunby *Linc 8* **P** *J M Montgomery-Massingberd Esq* **R** T STEELE
WELTON-LE-WOLD (St Martin) *see* Louth *Linc*
WELWICK (St Mary) *see* Patrington w Hollym, Welwick and Winestead *York*
WELWYN (St Mary the Virgin) (St Michael) w Ayot (St Peter) *St Alb 21* **P** *All So Coll Ox* **R** G R TRISTRAM
WELWYN GARDEN CITY (St Francis of Assisi) *St Alb 21* **P** *Bp* **V** P A LOUIS, **NSM** D M WEBSTER
WEM (St Peter and St Paul) *Lich 23* **P** *Lord Barnard* **R** N MacGREGOR
WEMBDON (St George) *B & W 14* **P** *Ch Soc Trust* **V** J S BARKS
WEMBLEY (Church of the Ascension) Preston Road *see* Preston Ascension *Lon*
WEMBLEY (St John the Evangelist) *Lon 21* **P** *Ch Patr Trust* **P-in-c** D B WADLAND, **C** A L LEE
WEMBLEY, NORTH (St Cuthbert) *Lon 21* **P** *Bp* **P-in-c** M STEWART, **NSM** F A MEADOWS
WEMBLEY PARK (St Augustine) *Lon 21* **P** *Bp* **C** J S FOULDS, **NSM** A C BAYLEY
WEMBURY (St Werburgh) *Ex 20* **P** *D&C Windsor* **V** T FREEMAN
WEMBWORTHY (St Michael) *see* Chulmleigh, Chawleigh w Cheldon, Wembworthy etc *Ex*
WENDENS AMBO (St Mary the Virgin) *see* Saffron Walden w Wendens Ambo and Littlebury *Chelmsf*
WENDLEBURY (St Giles) *see* Akeman *Ox*
WENDLING (St Peter and St Paul) *see* Gressenhall w Longham w Wendling etc *Nor*
WENDOVER (St Agnes's Chapel) (St Mary) *Ox 28* **P** *Ld Chan* **V** H P MARSHALL, **NSM** B J ROBERTS, H W HESLOP
WENDRON(St Wendron) *see* Helston and Wendron *Truro*
WENDY (All Saints) *see* Shingay Gp of Par *Ely*
WENHAM, GREAT (St John) *see* Capel St Mary w Lt and Gt Wenham *St E*
WENHASTON (St Peter) *see* Thorington w Wenhaston, Bramfield etc *St E*
WENLOCK *Heref 11* **P** *Patr Bd* **TR** R B DAVIES, **TV** W A BUCK, M C CLUETT
WENLOCK, LITTLE (St Lawrence) *see* Coalbrookdale, Iron-Bridge and Lt Wenlock *Heref*
WENLOCK, MUCH (Holy Trinity) *see* Wenlock *Heref*
WENNINGTON (St Mary and St Peter) *see* Rainham w Wennington *Chelmsf*
WENSLEY (Holy Trinity) *Ripon 4* **P** *Lord Bolton* **R** H F K CHEALL
WENTBRIDGE (St John) *see* Darrington w Wentbridge *Wakef*
WENTNOR (St Michael and All Angels) w Ratlinghope, Myndtown, Norbury, More, Lydham and Snead *Heref 10* **P** *Ch Ch Ox (4 turns) and J J C Coldwell Esq (1 turn)* **R** R T FRANCE
WENTWORTH (Harley Mission Church) (Holy Trinity) *Sheff 12* **P** *Sir Stephen Hastings* **V** R J BUCKLEY
WENTWORTH (St Peter) *see* Witchford w Wentworth *Ely*
WEOBLEY (St Peter and St Paul) w Sarnesfield and Norton Canon *Heref 5* **P** *Bp (2 turns), R A Marshall Esq (1 turn)* **V** R A BIRT
WEOLEY CASTLE (St Gabriel) *Birm 2* **P** *Bp* **V** M D CASTLE, **C** D N MILLER
WEREHAM (St Margaret) *Ely 16* **P** *Bp* **P-in-c** M TUCKER
WERNETH (St Paul) *Ches 16* **P** *Trustees* **P-in-c** B S PERCIVAL
WERNETH (St Thomas) *Man 19* **P** *Bp* **V** J HUNTER
WERRINGTON (St John the Baptist w Emmanuel) *Pet 13* **P** *Bp* **V** J B BATTMAN, **C** P R LARCOMBE
WERRINGTON (St Martin of Tours) *see* Boyton, N Tamerton, Werrington etc *Truro*
WERRINGTON (St Philip) *Lich 6* **P** *V Caverswall* **V** J L HUMPHREYS
WESHAM (Christ Church) *Blackb 11* **P** *V Kirkham* **V** A J WHYTE
WESSINGTON (Christ Church) *see* S Wingfield and Wessington *Derby*
WEST *see also under substantive place name*
WEST BAY (St John) *see* Bridport *Sarum*
WEST DEAN (St Andrew) *Chich 13* **P** *D&C* **V** P M JENKINS
WEST DOWN (St Calixtus) *see* Ilfracombe SS Phil and Jas w W Down *Ex*
WEST END (Holy Trinity) *see* Bisley and W End *Guildf*
WEST END (St George) *see* Esher *Guildf*
WEST END (St James) *Win 9* **P** *Bp* **V** J M PRESTON, **C** D S BENNETT
WEST END (St John the Evangelist) *see* High Wycombe *Ox*
WEST GREEN (Christ Church w St Peter) *Lon 19* **P** *Bp* **V** M O BRACKLEY
WEST GREEN (St Peter) *see* Crawley *Chich*
WEST HAM (All Saints) *Chelmsf 3* **P** *The Crown* **V** U E E J SCHARF, **TV** R A LEWIS, **C** M J WYLIE-SMITH
WEST HAM (St Matthew) *see* Forest Gate St Sav w W Ham St Matt *Chelmsf*
WEST HEATH (St Anne) *Birm 4* **P** *Bp* **V** S P MAYOSS-HURD
WEST HILL (St Michael the Archangel) *see* Ottery St Mary, Alfington, W Hill, Tipton etc *Ex*
WEST MOORS (St Mary the Virgin) (St John the Evangelist) *Sarum 10* **P** *Bp* **V** I K CHISHOLM, **C** R J H MAGILL
WEST ORCHARD (St Luke) *see* Shaston *Sarum*
WEST ROW (St Peter) *see* Mildenhall *St E*
WESTACRE (All Saints) *see* Gayton Gp of Par *Nor*
WESTBERE (All Saints) *see* Sturry w Fordwich and Westbere w Hersden *Cant*
WESTBOROUGH (All Saints) *see* Claypole *Linc*
WESTBOROUGH (St Clare) (St Francis) *Guildf 5* **P** *Bp* **TR** G P READ, **TV** C G POTTER
WESTBOURNE Christ Church Conventional District *Win 7* **Min** B C RUFF
WESTBOURNE (St John the Baptist) *Chich 13* **P** *Bp* **R** R J WELLS
WESTBROOK (St James) Hood Manor *Liv 12* **P** *Bp, R Warrington, and V Gt Sankey (jt)* **P-in-c** D MARSHALL
WESTBROOK (St Philip) Old Hall and Callands *Liv 12* **P** *Bp and R Warrington (jt)* **V** L BENTLEY
WESTBURY (All Saints) *Sarum 14* **P** *Bp* **V** M J FLIGHT, **NSM** M A DAVIES
WESTBURY (St Augustine) w Turweston, Shalstone and Biddlesden *Ox 22* **P** *Bp, D&C Westmr, Mrs M L G Purefoy, and Exors Mrs E M Gordon (jt)* **R** R LEIGH
WESTBURY (St Mary) *Heref 13* **P** *Bp* **P-in-c** C B BULL
WESTBURY-ON-SEVERN (St Peter and St Paul) w Flaxley and Blaisdon *Glouc 3* **P** *Sir Thomas Crawley-Boevey Bt (1 turn), D&C Heref (2 turns), and Trustees late T Place Esq (1 turn)* **V** D A COLBY, **NSM** M WHITE
WESTBURY-ON-TRYM (Holy Trinity) *Bris 8* **P** *SMF* **V** G M COLLINS, **C** C P LUNT
WESTBURY-ON-TRYM (St Alban) *Bris 8* **P** *Bp* **V** J A H BOWES
WESTBURY PARK (St Alban) *see* Westbury-on-Trym St Alb *Bris*
WESTBURY SUB MENDIP (St Lawrence) w Easton *B & W 1* **P** *Bp* **V** E A MACPHERSON
WESTCLIFF (Church of Reconciliation) *see* Brumby *Linc*

WESTCLIFF (St Alban) *see* Southend *Chelmsf*
WESTCLIFF (St Andrew) *Chelmsf 13* **P** *Bp* **V** E SMITH
WESTCLIFF (St Cedd and the Saints of Essex) *see* Prittlewell w Westcliff *Chelmsf*
WESTCLIFF (St Michael and All Angels) *Chelmsf 13* **P** *Bp* **V** P C NICHOLSON
WESTCLIFF (St Paul) *see* Prittlewell *Chelmsf*
WESTCLIFF (St Saviour) *see* Southend St Sav Westcliff *Chelmsf*
WESTCLIFFE (St Peter) *see* St Margarets-at-Cliffe w Westcliffe etc *Cant*
WESTCOMBE PARK (St George) *see* E Greenwich *S'wark*
WESTCOTE (St Mary the Virgin) w Icomb and Bledington *Glouc 15* **P** *D&C Worc, Ch Ch Ox, and Bp (by turn)* **NSM** G R H SMITH
WESTCOTE BARTON (St Edward the Confessor) w Steeple Barton, Duns Tew and Sandford St Martin *Ox 9* **P** *Duke of Marlborough, Exors Mrs Rittson-Thomas, DBP, D C D Webb Esq, and Bp (jt)* **NSM** H R B WHITE
WESTCOTT (Holy Trinity) *Guildf 7* **P** *Bp* **V** J D H WEYMAN
WESTCOTT (St Mary) *see* Waddesdon w Over Winchendon and Fleet Marston *Ox*
WESTDENE (The Ascension) *see* Patcham *Chich*
WESTERDALE (Christ Church) *see* Ingleby Greenhow w Bilsdale Priory, Kildale etc *York*
WESTERFIELD (St Mary Magdalene) and Tuddenham w Witnesham *St E 4* **P** *Bp, Peterho Cam, and DBP (alt)* **R** H LUNNEY
WESTERHAM (St Mary the Virgin) *Roch 9* **P** *J St A Warde Esq* **V** P A BIRD
WESTERLEIGH (St James the Great) *see* Yate New Town *Bris*
WESTERN DOWNLAND *Sarum 13* **P** *Hyndman Trustees, Sir William van Straubenzee, and W J Purvis Esq (jt)* **R** M E RIDLEY
WESTFIELD (St Andrew) *see* Reymerston w Cranworth, Letton, Southburgh etc *Nor*
WESTFIELD (St John the Baptist) *Chich 20* **P** *Bp* **V** E N L FRANCE
WESTFIELD (St Mark) *see* Woking St Pet *Guildf*
WESTFIELD (St Mary) *Carl 7* **P** *Bp* **V** A MITCHELL, **C** J E CROSSLEY, **NSM** M T STILWELL
WESTFIELD (St Peter) *B & W 12* **P** *Bp* **V** J B THICKE, **NSM** D R BARGE
WESTGATE (St Andrew) *Dur 9* **P** *Bp* **V** D M SKELTON
WESTGATE (St James) *Cant 9* **P** *Abp* **V** J A CHEESEMAN
WESTGATE (St Martin) *see* Torrisholme *Blackb*
WESTGATE COMMON (St Michael the Archangel) *Wakef 12* **P** *V Alverthorpe* **V** A S MACPHERSON
WESTGATE-ON-SEA (St Saviour) *Cant 9* **P** *Abp* **V** S M EVANS
WESTHALL (St Andrew) *see* Hundred River *St E*
WESTHAM (St Mary) *Chich 16* **P** *Duke of Devonshire* **P-in-c** G J BARRETT
WESTHAMPNETT (St Peter) *see* Chichester *Chich*
WESTHEAD (St James) *see* Newburgh w Westhead *Liv*
WESTHIDE (St Bartholomew) *see* Withington w Westhide *Heref*
WESTHOPE (Mission Room) *see* Canon Pyon w Kings Pyon and Birley *Heref*
WESTHORPE (St Margaret) *see* Walsham le Willows and Finningham w Westhorpe *St E*
WESTHOUGHTON (St Bartholomew) and Wingates *Man 11* **P** *Patr Bd* **TR** S C TATTON-BROWN, **TV** S J BEACH, **C** T P HUMPHRY, **NSM** G J SMETHURST
WESTHOUGHTON (St James) *see* Daisy Hill *Man*
WESTHOUSES (St Saviour) *see* Blackwell *Derby*
WESTLANDS (St Andrew) *Lich 9* **P** *Simeon's Trustees* **V** W G H GARDINER
WESTLEIGH (St Paul) *Man 13* **P** *V Leigh St Mary* **V** T D HARGREAVES-STEAD
WESTLEIGH (St Peter) *Ex 16* **P** *D&C* **V** G A SATTERLY
WESTLEIGH (St Peter) *Man 13* **P** *Bp, Dioc Chan, and V Leigh St Mary (jt)* **V** R COOKE
WESTLETON (St Peter) w Dunwich *St E 19* **P** *Ch Patr Trust (2 turns), Shadingfield Properties Ltd (1 turn)* **V** R J GINN
WESTLEY (St Mary) *see* Risby w Gt and Lt Saxham and Westley *St E*
WESTLEY WATERLESS (St Mary the Less) *Ely 4* **P** *Exors C L Thomas Esq* **P-in-c** J S ASKEY
WESTMEADS (St Michael and All Angels) *see* Aldwick *Chich*
WESTMESTON (St Martin) *see* Streat w Westmeston *Chich*
WESTMILL (St Mary the Virgin) *see* Aspenden, Buntingford and Westmill *St Alb*
WESTMINSTER Hanover Square (St George) *see* Hanover Square St Geo w St Mark *Lon*
WESTMINSTER (St James) Piccadilly *Lon 3* **P** *Bp (2 turns), Ld Chan (1 turn)* **R** D St J REEVES, **Hon C** S B CATHIE, **NSM** H W J VALENTINE
WESTMINSTER (St James the Less) *Lon 3* **P** *D&C Westmr* **V** W J H CROSSLEY, **C** C A KEIGHLEY
WESTMINSTER (St Mary le Strand) *see* St Mary le Strand w St Clem Danes *Lon*
WESTMINSTER (St Matthew) *Lon 3* **P** *D&C Westmr* **P-in-c** P A E CHESTER, **Hon C** R CRAWFORD, R E BALLARD
WESTMINSTER (St Michael) *see* Ches Square St Mich w St Phil *Lon*
WESTMINSTER (St Saviour) *see* Pimlico St Sav *Lon*
WESTMINSTER (St Stephen) w St John *Lon 3* **P** *The Crown* **V** R C GODSALL, **C** A S BISHOP, **Hon C** R St J J MARSH
WESTOE, SOUTH (St Michael and All Angels) *Dur 15* **P** *Bp* **V** J M HANCOCK
WESTON (All Saints) *see* Bath Weston All SS w N Stoke and Langridge *B & W*
WESTON (All Saints) *Ches 15* **P** *Bp* **P-in-c** W HODSON
WESTON (All Saints) *see* Welford w Weston and Clifford Chambers *Glouc*
WESTON (All Saints) *Guildf 8* **P** *Bp* **V** B M SHAND, **C** C A CORRY
WESTON (All Saints) *see* Tuxford w Weston and Markham Clinton *S'well*
WESTON (All Saints) w Denton *Bradf 4* **P** *Lt-Col H V Dawson and C Wyvill Esq (jt)* **V** D E CREASER
WESTON (Holy Trinity) *St Alb 23* **P** *Mrs A M Pryor* **V** *Vacant* (01462) 790330
WESTON (Holy Trinity) *Win 12* **P** *Bp* **V** A L McPHERSON, **C** I A PULLINGER
WESTON (St Mary) *see* Cowbit *Linc*
WESTON (St Peter) *see* Hundred River *St E*
WESTON, OLD (St Swithun) *see* Brington w Molesworth and Old Weston *Ely*
WESTON, SOUTH (St Lawrence) *see* Tetsworth, Adwell w S Weston, Lewknor etc *Ox*
WESTON BAMPFLYDE (Holy Cross) *see* Queen Camel w W Camel, Corton Denham etc *B & W*
WESTON BEGGARD (St John the Baptist) *see* Lugwardine w Bartestree, Weston Beggard etc *Heref*
WESTON BY WELLAND (St Mary) *see* Stoke Albany w Wilbarston and Ashley etc *Pet*
WESTON COLVILLE (St Mary) *Ely 4* **P** *D&C* **NSM** L R WICKHAM
WESTON COYNEY (St Andrew) *see* Caverswall and Weston Coyney w Dilhorne *Lich*
WESTON ESTATE CHURCH (not known) *see* Otley *Bradf*
WESTON FAVELL (St Peter) *Pet 4* **P** *DBP* **R** C W WAKE, **C** M M STRANGE, **NSM** G C RUMBOLD
WESTON HILLS (St John) *see* Cowbit *Linc*
WESTON IN GORDANO (St Peter and St Paul) *see* E Clevedon and Walton w Weston w Clapton *B & W*
WESTON LONGVILLE (All Saints) w Morton on the Hill w Great w Little Witchingham *Nor 22* **P** *J V Berney Esq (1 turn), New Coll Ox (3 turns)* **R** J P P ILLINGWORTH
WESTON LULLINGFIELD (Holy Trinity) *see* Baschurch and Weston Lullingfield w Hordley *Lich*
WESTON MILL (St Philip) *see* Devonport St Boniface and St Phil *Ex*
WESTON-ON-THE-GREEN (St Mary) *see* Akeman *Ox*
WESTON-ON-TRENT (St Mary the Virgin) *see* Aston-on-Trent and Weston-on-Trent *Derby*
WESTON PATRICK (St Lawrence) *see* Herriard w Winslade and Long Sutton etc *Win*
WESTON POINT (Christ Church) *see* Runcorn St Jo Weston *Ches*
WESTON RHYN (St John) and Selattyn *Lich 19* **P** *Bp and Mrs A F Hamilton-Hill (jt)* **R** N G COATSWORTH
WESTON-SUB-EDGE (St Lawrence) *see* Willersey, Saintbury, Weston-sub-Edge etc *Glouc*
WESTON SUPER MARE (All Saints) and St Saviour *B & W 11* **P** *Bp* **V** P G CLARKE
WESTON-SUPER-MARE (Christ Church) *B & W 11* **P** *Trustees* **V** G W HOBDEN
WESTON SUPER MARE (Emmanuel) *B & W 11* **P** *Trustees* **P-in-c** E T PETTENGELL
WESTON-SUPER-MARE (St Andrew) Bournville *B & W 11* **P** *Bp* **V** H M WILLIAMS
WESTON SUPER MARE (St John the Baptist) *B & W 11* **P** *Bp and Trustees (jt)* **R** B IRONS
WESTON-SUPER-MARE (St Paul) *B & W 11* **P** *Bp* **V** P H DAVIES
WESTON TURVILLE (St Mary the Virgin) *Ox 28* **P** *All So Coll Ox* **P-in-c** D N WALES, **NSM** N TAYLOR
WESTON-UNDER-LIZARD (St Andrew) *see* Blymhill w Weston-under-Lizard *Lich*
WESTON-UNDER-PENYARD (St Lawrence) *see* Ross w Brampton Abbotts, Bridstow, Peterstow etc *Heref*
WESTON UNDER REDCASTLE (St Luke) *see* Hodnet w Weston under Redcastle *Lich*

WESTON UNDER WETHERLEY (St Michael) *see* Wappenbury w Weston under Wetherley *Cov*
WESTON UNDERWOOD (St Laurence) *see* Gayhurst w Ravenstone, Stoke Goldington etc *Ox*
WESTON UPON TRENT (St Andrew) *see* Fradswell, Gayton, Milwich and Weston *Lich*
WESTON ZOYLAND (Blessed Virgin Mary) w Chedzoy *B & W 14* **P** *Bp* **P-in-c** P J RICHMOND, **C** S F LACY
WESTONBIRT (St Catherine) *see* Shipton Moyne w Westonbirt and Lasborough *Glouc*
WESTONING (St Mary Magdalene) w Tingrith *St Alb 9* **P** *Ld Chan* **V** M J BETTIS
WESTOW (St Mary) *see* Burythorpe, Acklam and Leavening w Westow *York*
WESTWARD (St Hilda), Rosley-with-Woodside and Welton *Carl 3* **P** *D&C* **P-in-c** N L ROBINSON
WESTWARD HO! (Holy Trinity) *see* Bideford, Northam, Westward Ho!, Appledore etc *Ex*
WESTWAY (St Katherine) *see* N Hammersmith St Kath *Lon*
WESTWELL (St Mary) *see* Shill Valley and Broadshire *Ox*
WESTWELL (St Mary) w Hothfield and Eastwell w Boughton Aluph *Cant 10* **P** *Abp and Lord Hothfield (jt)* **V** J F GLEADALL
WESTWICK (St Botolph) *see* Worstead, Westwick, Sloley, Swanton Abbot etc *Nor*
WESTWOOD Jacksdale (St Mary) *see* Selston *S'well*
WESTWOOD (Mission Church) *see* Golcar *Wakef*
WESTWOOD (St John the Baptist) *Cov 3* **P** *Bp* **V** P FINDLEY
WESTWOOD (St Mary the Virgin) and Wingfield *Sarum 17* **P** *D&C Bris, CPAS, and Bp (jt)* **R** R M LOWRIE
WESTWOOD (St Paul) *see* Pinhoe and Broadclyst *Ex*
WESTWOOD, LOW (Christ Church) *see* Ebchester *Dur*
WETHERAL (Holy Trinity and St Constantine) w Warwick *Carl 2* **P** *D&C* **P-in-c** C H COWPER, **NSM** P TIPLADY
WETHERBY (St James) *Ripon 1* **P** *Bp* **V** A M BARTON, **C** C A JAMES
WETHERDEN (St Mary the Virgin) *see* Haughley w Wetherden *St E*
WETHERINGSETT (All Saints) *see* Thorndon w Rishangles, Stoke Ash, Thwaite etc *St E*
WETHERSFIELD (St Mary Magdalene) *see* Finchingfield and Cornish Hall End etc *Chelmsf*
WETLEY ROCKS (St John the Baptist) *Lich 8* **P** *Bp* **V** *Vacant* (01782) 550251
WETTENHALL (St David) *see* Acton and Worleston, Church Minshull etc *Ches*
WETTON (St Margaret) *see* Alstonfield, Butterton, Warslow w Elkstone etc *Lich*
WETWANG (St Nicholas) and Garton-on-the-Wolds w Kirkburn *York 11* **P** *Ld Chan* **V** R I JONES
WEXCOMBE *Sarum 21* **P** *DBP* **TR** D M RYDER, **TV** S F EVERETT, N A LEIGH-HUNT, **NSM** A J DEBOO
WEXHAM (St Mary) *Ox 26* **P** *Ld Chan* **R** G W FARMER
WEYBOURNE (All Saints), Upper Sheringham, Kelling, Salthouse, Bodham and East and West Beckham (The Weybourne Group) *Nor 18* **P** *Bp (2 turns), Sir Charles Mott-Radclyffe (1 turn), D&C (1 turn), and Lord Walpole (1 turn)* **R** P J G BARNES-CLAY
WEYBREAD (St Andrew) *see* Fressingfield, Mendham, Metfield, Weybread etc *St E*
WEYBRIDGE (St James) *Guildf 8* **P** *Ld Chan* **R** S D BROOKES, **C** D W PECK
WEYHILL (St Michael and All Angels) *see* Hatherden w Tangley, Weyhill and Penton Mewsey *Win*
WEYMOUTH (Holy Trinity) (St Nicholas) *Sarum 5* **P** *Bp* **V** R H FRANKLIN, **C** R W HAWKINS, **NSM** R E MILVERTON
WEYMOUTH (St Edmund) *Sarum 5* **P** *R Wyke Regis* **P-in-c** P S THOMAS
WEYMOUTH (St John) *see* Radipole and Melcombe Regis *Sarum*
WEYMOUTH (St Mary) *as above*
WEYMOUTH (St Paul) *Sarum 5* **P** *Bp* **P-in-c** D LASHBROOKE
WHADDON (St Margaret) *see* Glouc St Geo w Whaddon *Glouc*
WHADDON (St Mary) *Ely 8* **P** *D&C Windsor* **P-in-c** J E ARMSTRONG
WHADDON (St Mary) *see* Newton Longville w Stoke Hammond and Whaddon *Ox*
WHADDON (St Mary) *see* Alderbury Team *Sarum*
WHADDON (St Mary the Virgin) *see* Hilperton w Whaddon and Staverton etc *Sarum*
WHALEY BRIDGE (St James) *Ches 16* **P** *Bp and Bp Derby (alt)* **R** D C SPEEDY
WHALEY THORNS (St Luke) *see* E Scarsdale *Derby*
WHALLEY (St Mary and All Saints) *Blackb 8* **P** *Hulme Trustees* **V** J M ACKROYD
WHALLEY RANGE St Edmund *Man 4* **P** *Simeon's Trustees* **R** R J HORROCKS, **C** J A HORROCKS
WHALLEY RANGE (St Margaret) *Man 4* **P** *Trustees* **R** R G BOULTER
WHALTON (St Mary Magdalene) *see* Bolam w Whalton and Hartburn w Meldon *Newc*
WHAPLODE (St Mary) *Linc 16* **P** *Ld Chan* **V** D A CARNEY
WHAPLODE DROVE (St John the Baptist) *Linc 16* **P** *Feoffees* **P-in-c** J MONTAGUE
WHARNCLIFFE SIDE (not known) *see* Oughtibridge *Sheff*
WHARRAM (St Mary) *see* Weaverthorpe w Helperthorpe, Luttons Ambo etc *York*
WHARTON (Christ Church) *Ches 6* **P** *R Davenham* **V** M A PICKLES
WHATBOROUGH Group of Parishes, The *Leic 4* **P** *Bp* **V** H R BROAD
WHATCOTE (St Peter) *see* Tysoe w Oxhill and Whatcote *Cov*
WHATFIELD (St Margaret) w Semer, Nedging and Naughton *St E 3* **P** *Bp, Jes Coll Cam, and Reformation Ch Trust (jt)* **P-in-c** H J CRELLIN
WHATLEY (St George) *see* Mells w Buckland Dinham, Elm, Whatley etc *B & W*
WHATLINGTON (St Mary Magdalene) *see* Sedlescombe w Whatlington *Chich*
WHATSTANDWELL (Mission Room) *see* Crich *Derby*
WHATTON (St John of Beverley) w Aslockton, Hawksworth, Scarrington, Orston and Thoroton *S'well 8* **P** *Trustees* **V** D H BRIDGE-COLLYNS
WHEATACRE (All Saints) *see* The Raveningham Gp *Nor*
WHEATCROFT (St Michael and All Angels) *see* Scarborough St Martin *York*
WHEATFIELD (St Andrew) *see* Tetsworth, Adwell w S Weston, Lewknor etc *Ox*
WHEATHAMPSTEAD (St Helen) *St Alb 8* **P** *Bp* **R** T PURCHAS, **Hon C** C P A PURCHAS, **NSM** J HAZELWOOD, R B EARDLEY
WHEATHILL (Holy Trinity) *see* Ditton Priors w Neenton, Burwarton etc *Heref*
WHEATLEY (St Mary) *see* Doncaster St Mary *Sheff*
WHEATLEY (St Mary the Virgin) *Ox 1* **P** *Patr Bd* **TR** J J FULLER, **TV** W D BRIERLEY, R M COWLES, P N TOVEY, **NSM** J C H M LEE, A E BUTLER, C N KING
WHEATLEY, NORTH (St Peter and St Paul) and West Burton w Bole and Saundby and Sturton w Littleborough *S'well 5* **P** *Lord Middleton and G M T Foljambe Esq (alt)* **R** M W BRIGGS
WHEATLEY HILL (All Saints) *Dur 2* **P** *Bp* **V** *Vacant* (01429) 820496
WHEATLEY HILLS (St Aidan) *Sheff 9* **P** *Bp* **V** D J GOSS
WHEATLEY PARK (St Paul) *Sheff 9* **P** *Bp* **V** D R SHERWIN
WHEATON ASTON (St Mary) *see* Lapley w Wheaton Aston *Lich*
WHEELOCK (Christ Church) *Ches 11* **P** *V Sandbach* **P-in-c** E J GORDON
WHELDRAKE (St Helen) w Thorganby *York 4* **P** *Abp and Sir Mervyn Dunnington-Jefferson (jt)* **R** D C W POST
WHELFORD (St Anne) *see* Kempsford w Welford *Glouc*
WHELNETHAM, GREAT (St Thomas a Becket) and Little (St Mary) w Bradfield St George *St E 10* **P** *Bp* **P-in-c** J E SWAIN
WHELPLEY HILL (St Michael and All Angels) *see* Gt Chesham *Ox*
WHENBY (St Martin) *see* Bulmer w Dalby, Terrington and Welburn *York*
WHEPSTEAD (St Petronilla) *see* Chevington w Hargrave and Whepstead w Brockley *St E*
WHERSTEAD (St Mary) *St E 5* **P** *MMCET* **P-in-c** A B LEIGHTON, **NSM** A J MARSHALL, C A MARSHALL
WHERWELL (St Peter and Holy Cross) *see* Chilbolton cum Wherwell *Win*
WHETSTONE (St John the Apostle) *Lon 14* **P** *Bp* **V** K MITCHELL
WHETSTONE (St Peter) *Leic 10* **P** *Bp* **P-in-c** V T GOODMAN
WHICHAM (St Mary) *see* Bootle, Corney, Whicham and Whitbeck *Carl*
WHICHFORD (St Michael) *see* Long Compton, Whichford and Barton-on-the-Heath *Cov*
WHICKHAM (St Mary the Virgin) *Dur 13* **P** *Ld Chan* **R** D E B REED, **C** J N J C DUSSEK
WHILTON (St Andrew) *see* Brington w Whilton and Norton *Pet*
WHIMPLE (St Mary), Talaton and Clyst St Lawrence *Ex 7* **P** *DBP, D&C and MMCET (jt)* **P-in-c** K FELTHAM
WHINBURGH (St Mary) *see* Reymerston w Cranworth, Letton, Southburgh etc *Nor*
WHINMOOR (St Paul) *see* Seacroft *Ripon*
WHINNEY HILL (St Peter) *see* Thrybergh *Sheff*

WHIPPINGHAM (St Mildred) w East Cowes *Portsm 8* **P** *Ld Chan* **P-in-c** S D CLEAVER, **NSM** G L LONG
WHIPSNADE (St Mary Magdalene) *see* Kensworth, Studham and Whipsnade *St Alb*
WHIPTON (St Boniface) *Ex 3* **P** *Bp* **V** C P BARRETT
WHISSENDINE (St Andrew) *see* Teigh w Whissendine and Market Overton *Pet*
WHISSONSETT (St Mary) *see* Colkirk w Oxwick w Pattesley, Whissonsett etc *Nor*
WHISTON (St Mary Magdalene) *Sheff 6* **P** *Bp* **R** G C M MILLS
WHISTON (St Mary the Virgin) *see* Yardley Hastings, Denton and Grendon etc *Pet*
WHISTON (St Mildred) *see* Foxt w Whiston *Lich*
WHISTON (St Nicholas) *Liv 2* **P** *V Prescot* **V** G G AMEY
WHITACRE, NETHER (St Giles) *see* The Whitacres and Shustoke *Birm*
WHITACRE, OVER (St Leonard) *as above*
WHITACRES and Shustoke, The *Birm 10* **P** *S W Digby Esq (1 turn), Bp (2 turns), and Ld Chan (1 turn)* **R** J D WATERSTREET
WHITBECK (St Mary) *see* Bootle, Corney, Whicham and Whitbeck *Carl*
WHITBOURNE (Bringsty Iron Church) *see* Edvin Loach w Tedstone Delamere etc *Heref*
WHITBOURNE (St John the Baptist) *as above*
WHITBURN (no dedication) *Dur 16* **P** *Bp* **R** K R SMITH, **C** J A BRADSHAW
WHITBY (St Hilda) (St John) (St Mary) *York 23* **P** *Abp* **R** M AISBITT, **C** G P TAYLOR
WHITBY (St Thomas) *see* Ellesmere Port *Ches*
WHITBY ROAD (St Michael) *see* W Slough *Ox*
WHITCHURCH (All Hallows) w Tufton and Litchfield *Win 6* **P** *Bp* **V** M J GRYLLS
WHITCHURCH (St Alkmund) *Lich 23* **P** *Bp* **R** R D JENKINS
WHITCHURCH (St Andrew) *Ex 24* **P** *Bp* **V** S G MAY
WHITCHURCH (St Augustine) (St Nicholas) *Bris 3* **P** *Bp* **V** R A D'V THORN, **C** D G OWEN, **NSM** E A J CHIVERS
WHITCHURCH (St Dubricius) *see* Llangarron w Llangrove, Whitchurch and Ganarew *Heref*
WHITCHURCH (St John the Evangelist) *see* Schorne *Ox*
WHITCHURCH (St Lawrence) *see* Lt Stanmore St Lawr *Lon*
WHITCHURCH (St Mary the Virgin) *see* Ilmington w Stretton-on-Fosse etc *Cov*
WHITCHURCH (St Mary the Virgin) *Ox 6* **P** *Bp* **R** R M HUGHES
WHITCHURCH CANONICORUM (St Candida and Holy Cross) *see* Marshwood Vale TM *Sarum*
WHITCHURCH HILL (St John the Baptist) *see* Whitchurch St Mary *Ox*
WHITE COLNE (St Andrew) *see* Earls Colne w White Colne and Colne Engaine *Chelmsf*
WHITE LADIES ASTON (St John) *see* Peopleton and White Ladies Aston w Churchill etc *Worc*
WHITE NOTLEY (St Etheldreda) *see* Fairstead w Terling and White Notley etc *Chelmsf*
WHITE RODING (St Martin) *see* Leaden Roding and Abbess Roding etc *Chelmsf*
WHITE WALTHAM (St Mary the Virgin) w Shottesbrooke *Ox 13* **P** *Sir John Smith* **R** T E F COULSON
WHITE WELL (St Mary) *see* St Paul's Walden *St Alb*
WHITECHAPEL (St James) w Admarsh-in-Bleasdale *Blackb 10* **P** *Bp and V Lanc (alt)* **V** G CONNOR, **NSM** G K HENWOOD
WHITEFIELD (St Andrew) *see* Hillock *Man*
WHITEGATE (St Mary) w Little Budworth *Ches 6* **P** *Bp, Lord Delamere and W R Cullimore Esq (alt)* **V** C P BURKETT
WHITEHALL PARK (St Andrew) *see* Upper Holloway *Lon*
WHITEHAVEN (St James) *Carl 5* **P** *Patr Bd* **V** J H BAKER, **NSM** D TEMBEY
WHITEHAWK (St Cuthman) *Chich 2* **P** *Bp* **P-in-c** J D WRIGHT
WHITEHILLS (St Mark) *see* Kingsthorpe w Northn St Dav *Pet*
WHITELACKINGTON (The Blessed Virgin Mary) *see* Ilminster and District *B & W*
WHITELEAS (St Mary and St Martin) *see* Horsley Hill S Shields *Dur*
WHITEPARISH (All Saints) *see* Alderbury Team *Sarum*
WHITESHILL (St Paul) and Randwick *Glouc 1* **P** *Bp* **V** M F JEFFERY, **NSM** I C GOBEY
WHITESTAUNTON (St Andrew) *B & W 15* **P** *Personal Reps Gp Capt N W D Marwood-Elton* **P-in-c** P REGAN
WHITESTONE (St Catherine) *see* Tedburn St Mary, Whitestone, Oldridge etc *Ex*
WHITESTONE PATHFINDER (St John the Evangelist) *as above*
WHITEWELL (St Mary) *see* Tushingham and Whitewell *Ches*
WHITEWELL (St Michael) *see* Chipping and Whitewell *Blackb*
WHITFIELD (Holy Trinity) *see* Allendale w Whitfield *Newc*
WHITFIELD (St James) (St Luke) *Derby 6* **P** *Bp* **V** C COOPER, **C** W R EARDLEY
WHITFIELD (St John) *see* Allendale w Whitfield *Newc*
WHITFIELD (St John the Evangelist) *see* Helmdon w Stuchbury and Radstone etc *Pet*
WHITFIELD (St Peter) w Guston *Cant 4* **P** *Abp and D&C (alt)* **V** J W PHILPOTT
WHITFORD (St Mary at the Cross) *see* Stockland, Dalwood, Kilmington and Shute *Ex*
WHITGIFT (St Mary Magdalene) *see* The Marshland *Sheff*
WHITGREAVE (St John the Evangelist) *see* Stafford *Lich*
WHITKIRK (St Mary) *Ripon 8* **P** *Meynell Trustees* **V** J K DAY
WHITLEIGH (St Chad) *Ex 22* **P** *Bp* **P-in-c** J C DOWDING
WHITLEY (Christ Church) *Ox 15* **P** *Bp* **V** E A ESSERY, **C** D M WEST
WHITLEY (St Helen) *Newc 4* **P** *Bp* **V** A J PATTERSON
WHITLEY (St James) *Cov 1* **P** *Bp* **P-in-c** M R PEATMAN, **NSM** D A PEATMAN
WHITLEY, LOWER or NETHER (St Luke) *see* Lt Leigh and Lower Whitley *Ches*
WHITLEY BRIDGE (All Saints) *see* Kellington w Whitley *Wakef*
WHITLEY LOWER (St Mary and St Michael) *see* Thornhill and Whitley Lower *Wakef*
WHITMINSTER (St Andrew) *see* Standish w Haresfield and Moreton Valence etc *Glouc*
WHITMORE (St Mary and All Saints) *see* Chapel Chorlton, Maer and Whitmore *Lich*
WHITNASH (St Margaret) *Cov 11* **P** *Lord Leigh* **R** A B GARDNER, **C** I R WHITEHEAD
WHITNEY (St Peter and St Paul) *see* Eardisley w Bollingham, Willersley, Brilley etc *Heref*
WHITSBURY (St Leonard) *see* W Downland *Sarum*
WHITSTABLE (All Saints) *Cant 7* **P** *DBP* **TR** J S WOOD, **TV** G T ARNOLD, S J CONEYS, **C** S J TURNER
WHITSTONE (St Anne) *see* Week St Mary w Poundstock and Whitstone *Truro*
WHITTINGHAM (St Bartholomew) and Edlingham w Bolton Chapel *Newc 9* **P** *D&C Carl and D&C Dur (alt)* **V** R J GLOVER
WHITTINGTON (Christ Church) *Ely 15* **P** *Ch Patr Trust* **P-in-c** N O TUFFNELL
WHITTINGTON (St Bartholomew) *Derby 5* **P** *Bp* **R** D C PICKERING
WHITTINGTON (St Bartholomew) *see* Sevenhampton w Charlton Abbotts and Hawling etc *Glouc*
WHITTINGTON (St Giles) w Weeford *Lich 1* **P** *Bp* **V** J H MARTIN, **Hon C** C M J IBALL
WHITTINGTON (St John the Baptist) *Lich 19* **P** *Mrs P Hamilton Hill* **R** D R NORTH
WHITTINGTON (St Michael the Archangel) w Arkholme and Gressingham *Blackb 15* **P** *Ch Ch Ox, V Lanc, and V Melling (by turn)* **V** W G BOWNESS
WHITTINGTON (St Philip and St James) *see* Worc SE *Worc*
WHITTINGTON, NEW (St Barnabas) *Derby 5* **P** *Bp* **V** J PINDER-PACKARD
WHITTLE-LE-WOODS (St John the Evangelist) *Blackb 4* **P** *V Leyland* **V** D M GILKES, **C** C J WADE, C A BELL, **NSM** D M LUTES
WHITTLEBURY (St Mary) w Paulerspury *Pet 5* **P** *The Crown and New Coll Ox (alt)* **V** E D HOUSTON
WHITTLESEY (St Andrew) (St Mary), Pondersbridge and Coates *Ely 18* **P** *Ld Chan (2 turns), Patr Bd (1 turn)* **TR** P H N COLLINS, **TV** B E WAY, **C** A R M MARSHALL
WHITTLESFORD (St Mary and St Andrew) *Ely 7* **P** *Jes Coll Cam* **V** *Vacant* (01223) 833382
WHITTON *Sarum 20* **P** *Patr Bd* **TR** R K HYATT, **TV** P R HYSON, **C** P H C KINGMAN, **NSM** J PROUT
WHITTON (St Augustine of Canterbury) *Lon 10* **P** *Bp* **V** R J COSH, **C** J E M UDAL
WHITTON (St John the Baptist) *see* Alkborough *Linc*
WHITTON (St Mary) *see* Burford II w Greete and Hope Bagot *Heref*
WHITTON (St Mary) (Ascension) and Thurleston w Akenham *St E 4* **P** *Bp (2 turns), Exors G K Drury Esq (1 turn)* **R** G G BAULCOMB, **C** A S F BENNETT
WHITTON (St Philip and St James) *Lon 10* **P** *V Twickenham St Mary* **V** J L VINCENT
WHITTONSTALL (St Philip and St James) *Newc 3* **P** *D&C* **P-in-c** M F FENWICK
WHITWELL (St John the Evangelist) w Crambe, Flaxton, Foston and Huttons Ambo *York 3* **P** *Abp and D&C Dur (jt)* **R** *Vacant* (0165381) 647
WHITWELL (St Lawrence) *Derby 3* **P** *Bp* **P-in-c** A JENNINGS
WHITWELL (St Mary) *see* St Paul's Walden *St Alb*

WHITWELL (St Mary and St Rhadegunde) *Portsm 7* **P** *Bp* **V** S E LLOYD, **NSM** J A WOOLLEY, M M SLATTERY
WHITWELL (St Michael and All Angels) *see* Reepham, Hackford w Whitwell, Kerdiston etc *Nor*
WHITWELL (St Michael and All Angels) *see* Empingham and Exton w Horn w Whitwell *Pet*
WHITWICK (St John the Baptist) *Leic 8* **P** *Duchy of Lanc* **V** *Vacant* (01530) 836904
WHITWOOD (All Saints) *Wakef 11* **P** *Bp* **R** *Vacant* (01977) 559215
WHITWORTH (not known) *see* Spennymoor, Whitworth and Merrington *Dur*
WHITWORTH (not known) *see* Man Whitworth *Man*
WHITWORTH (St Bartholomew) *Man 20* **P** *Keble Coll Ox* **V** D H HUGHES
WHIXALL (St Mary) *see* Tilstock, Edstaston and Whixall *Lich*
WHIXLEY (Ascension) w Green Hammerton *Ripon 3* **P** *DBP and R Knaresborough (alt)* **V** *Vacant* (01423) 330269
WHORLTON (Holy Cross Old Church) w Carlton and Faceby *York 22* **P** *Mrs H J F L Steel and Mrs K F L Davies (jt)* **V** W J FORD
WHORLTON (St John the Evangelist) *Newc 7* **P** *Bp* **V** D J TULLY, **NSM** J L JACKSON, A E MARR
WHORLTON (St Mary) *see* Barnard Castle w Whorlton *Dur*
WHYKE (St George) w Rumboldswhyke St Mary and Portfield All Saints *Chich 3* **P** *Bp* **R** P R SEAMAN, **Hon C** J RHODES-WRIGLEY
WHYTELEAFE (St Luke) *S'wark 25* **P** *Bp* **P-in-c** J E SMITH
WIBTOFT (Assumption of Our Lady) *see* Claybrooke cum Wibtoft and Frolesworth *Leic*
WICHENFORD (St Lawrence) *see* Martley and Wichenford, Knightwick etc *Worc*
WICK (All Saints) *see* Littlehampton and Wick *Chich*
WICK (St Bartholomew) w Doynton and Dyrham *Bris 2* **P** *Simeon's Trustees, Ld Chan, and M H W Blaythwayt Esq (by turn)* **V** P F YACOMENI
WICK (St Mary) *see* Pershore w Pinvin, Wick and Birlingham *Worc*
WICK ST LAWRENCE (St Lawrence) *see* Kewstoke w Wick St Lawrence *B & W*
WICKEN (St John the Evangelist) *Pet 5* **P** *Soc Merchant Venturers Bris* **P-in-c** E D HOUSTON
WICKEN (St Laurence) *Ely 3* **P** *Ch Patr Trust* **V** R F BELOE
WICKEN BONHUNT (St Margaret) *see* Quendon w Rickling and Wicken Bonhunt etc *Chelmsf*
WICKENBY Group, The (St Peter and St Laurence) *Linc 5* **P** *DBP, D&C York, Bp, and Charterhouse (by turn)* **R** M J CARTWRIGHT
WICKERSLEY (St Alban) *Sheff 6* **P** *DBP* **R** R J DRAPER, **NSM** M J WHIPP
WICKFORD (St Andrew) (St Catherine) and Runwell *Chelmsf 6* **P** *Patr Bd* **TR** C A McCAFFERTY, **TV** W P WATERS, M S PUDGE, **C** T F CLAY, **NSM** R V GOODWIN
WICKHAM (St Nicholas) *Portsm 1* **P** *Sir Richard Rashleigh Bt* **R** R A A HIRST
WICKHAM (St Paul and All Saints) *see* Gt and Lt Henny w Middleton, Wickham St Paul etc *Chelmsf*
WICKHAM (St Swithun) *see* Welford w Wickham and Gt Shefford, Boxford etc *Ox*
WICKHAM, EAST (St Michael) *S'wark 3* **P** *Provost and Chapter* **V** D W FRITH, **Hon C** C HEARD
WICKHAM, WEST (St Francis) *S'wark 21* **P** *Bp* **V** O N EVERSON
WICKHAM, WEST (St John) *S'wark 21* **P** *Bp* **V** J D B POOLE, **C** K J D GAVED
WICKHAM, WEST (St Mary) *Ely 4* **P** *Bp* **P-in-c** W N C GIRARD
WICKHAM, WEST (St Mary of Nazareth) *S'wark 21* **P** *Bp* **V** F S MADGE
WICKHAM BISHOPS (St Bartholomew) w Little Braxted *Chelmsf 24* **P** *Bp (3 turns), CCC Cam (1 turn)* **R** C J SLY
WICKHAM MARKET (All Saints) w Pettistree and Easton *St E 18* **P** *Ch Trust Fund Trust, MMCET, and Ld Chan (by turn)* **V** G D R BELL
WICKHAM SKEITH (St Andrew) *St E 6* **P** *Ch Patr Trust* **P-in-c** P T GRAY
WICKHAMBREAUX (St Andrew) *see* Littlebourne and Ickham w Wickhambreaux etc *Cant*
WICKHAMBROOK (All Saints) w Lydgate, Ousden and Cowlinge *St E 8* **P** *DBP, and Ld Chan (alt)* **R** *Vacant* (01440) 820288
WICKHAMFORD (St John the Baptist) *see* Broadway w Wickhamford *Worc*
WICKHAMPTON (St Andrew) *see* Freethorpe w Wickhampton, Halvergate etc *Nor*
WICKLEWOOD (All Saints) *see* High Oak *Nor*
WICKMERE (St Andrew) *see* Lt Barningham, Blickling, Edgefield etc *Nor*
WICKWAR (Holy Trinity) w Rangeworthy *Glouc 7* **P** *Bp and Earl of Ducie (jt)* **R** D B SMALL
WIDCOMBE *see* Bath Widcombe *B & W*
WIDDINGTON (St Mary) *see* Quendon w Rickling and Wicken Bonhunt etc *Chelmsf*
WIDDRINGTON (Holy Trinity) *Newc 11* **P** *Bp* **V** R L VERNON
WIDDRINGTON STATION (St Mary) *see* Ulgham *Newc*
WIDECOMBE-IN-THE-MOOR (St Pancras), Leusdon, Princetown, Postbridge, Huccaby and Holne *Ex 11* **P** *Duchy of Cornwall (1 turn), Patr Bd (2 turns)* **TR** D J NEWPORT, **C** A J SMITH
WIDEMOUTH BAY (Our Lady and St Anne) *see* Week St Mary w Poundstock and Whitstone *Truro*
WIDFORD (St John the Baptist) *see* Hunsdon w Widford and Wareside *St Alb*
WIDFORD (St Mary) (Holy Spirit) *Chelmsf 9* **P** *CPAS* **R** N J HAY
WIDFORD (St Oswald) *see* Burford w Fulbrook, Taynton, Asthall etc *Ox*
WIDLEY w Wymering *Portsm 6* **P** *E G Nugee Esq* **P-in-c** M L HILL-TOUT
WIDMER END (Good Shepherd) *see* Hazlemere *Ox*
WIDMERPOOL (St Peter) *see* Willoughby-on-the-Wolds w Wysall and Widmerpool *S'well*
WIDNES (St Ambrose) *Liv 13* **P** *Trustees* **V** P T JONES
WIDNES (St John) *Liv 13* **P** *Bp and V Farnworth (jt)* **V** D J GAIT
WIDNES (St Mary) *Liv 13* **P** *Bp* **P-in-c** B ROBINSON
WIDNES (St Paul) *Liv 13* **P** *Bp* **P-in-c** A HODGE
WIDWORTHY (St Cuthbert) *see* Colyton, Southleigh, Offwell, Widworthy etc *Ex*
WIELD (St James) *see* Medstead cum Wield *Win*
WIGAN (All Saints) *Liv 14* **P** *Bp* **R** K M FORREST, **C** R C THOMPSON
WIGAN New Springs (St John) *see* New Springs *Liv*
WIGAN (St Andrew) *Liv 15* **P** *R Wigan* **V** C HURST
WIGAN (St Anne) *Liv 15* **P** *Bp* **V** R CRANKSHAW, **C** L McCLUSKEY
WIGAN (St Barnabas) Marsh Green *Liv 15* **P** *V Pemberton St Mark Newtown and Bp (jt)* **V** J WINNARD
WIGAN (St Catherine) *Liv 14* **P** *R Wigan* **V** J T CLEGG
WIGAN (St George) *Liv 14* **P** *R Wigan* **V** B C HARRISON
WIGAN (St James) (St Thomas) *Liv 15* **P** *R Wigan and Bp (jt)* **V** J A TAYLOR, **C** S E DRAPER
WIGAN (St Michael and All Angels) *Liv 15* **P** *R Wigan* **V** D G CLAWSON
WIGAN (St Stephen) *Liv 14* **P** *Bp* **V** E P TODD
WIGAN Whelley (St Stephen) *see* Wigan St Steph *Liv*
WIGBOROUGH, GREAT (St Stephen) *see* Peldon w Gt and Lt Wigborough *Chelmsf*
WIGBOROUGH, LITTLE (St Nicholas) *as above*
WIGGATON (St Edward the Confessor) *see* Ottery St Mary, Alfington, W Hill, Tipton etc *Ex*
WIGGENHALL (St Mary Magdalen) *Ely 17* **P** *MMCET* **V** *Vacant*
WIGGENHALL ST GERMANS (St Mary the Virgin) and Islington St Mary *Ely 17* **P** *Ld Chan (2 turns), Bp (1 turn)* **V** *Vacant* (0155385) 371
WIGGINTON (St Bartholomew) *St Alb 2* **P** *Bp* **P-in-c** R VARTY
WIGGINTON (St Giles) *see* Hook Norton w Gt Rollright, Swerford etc *Ox*
WIGGINTON (St Leonard) (St James) *Lich 4* **P** *V Tamworth* **P-in-c** I R CARDINAL
WIGGINTON (St Mary and St Nicholas) *see* Haxby w Wigginton *York*
WIGGLESWORTH (School) *see* Giggleswick and Rathmell w Wigglesworth *Bradf*
WIGGONHOLT (not known) *see* Amberley w N Stoke and Parham, Wiggonholt etc *Chich*
WIGHILL (All Saints) *see* Healaugh w Wighill, Bilbrough and Askham Richard *York*
WIGHTON (All Saints) *see* Holkham w Egmere w Warham, Wells and Wighton *Nor*
WIGMORE (St James the Apostle) *see* Wigmore Abbey *Heref*
WIGMORE ABBEY *Heref 7* **P** *Trustees* **R** A TALBOT-PONSONBY, **NSM** G TALBOT-PONSONBY, D W G VICKERS
WIGSLEY *see* Harby w Thorney and N and S Clifton *S'well*
WIGSTON, SOUTH (St Thomas) *see* Glen Parva and S Wigston *Leic*
WIGSTON MAGNA (All Saints) (St Wistan) *Leic 5* **P** *Haberdashers' Co* **V** E J GREEN
WIGSTON PARVA (St Mary the Virgin) *see* Sapcote and Sharnford w Wigston Parva *Leic*
WIGTOFT (St Peter and St Paul) *see* Bicker and Wigtoft *Linc*
WIGTON (St Mary) *Carl 3* **P** *Bp* **V** G P RAVALDE, **C** R P BLACKETT

WIKE (School Room) *see* Bardsey *Ripon*
WILBARSTON (All Saints) *see* Stoke Albany w Wilbarston and Ashley etc *Pet*
WILBERFOSS (St John the Baptist) *see* Kexby w Wilberfoss *York*
WILBRAHAM, GREAT (St Nicholas) *Ely 6* **P** *DBP* **P-in-c** B E KERLEY
WILBRAHAM, LITTLE (St John) *Ely 6* **P** *CCC Cam* **P-in-c** B E KERLEY
WILBURTON (St Peter) *Ely 14* **P** *Adn Ely* **V** M P WADSWORTH
WILBURY (St Thomas) *St Alb 4* **P** *Bp* **V** D E DOWLING
WILBY (All Saints) *see* Quidenham Gp *Nor*
WILBY (St Mary the Virgin) *see* Gt Doddington and Wilby *Pet*
WILBY (St Mary) w Brundish *St E 17* **P** *Dr F H C Marriott and Miss A W G Marriott (3 turns), Bp (1 turn)* **R** *Vacant* (01379) 84333
WILCOT (Holy Cross) *see* Swanborough *Sarum*
WILCOTE (St Peter) *see* Ramsden, Finstock and Fawler, Leafield etc *Ox*
WILDBOARCLOUGH (St Saviour) *see* Bosley and N Rode w Wincle and Wildboarclough *Ches*
WILDEN (All Saints) *see* Stourport and Wilden *Worc*
WILDEN (St Nicholas) w Colmworth and Ravensden *St Alb 15* **P** *Ld Chan, Bp, and DBP (by turn)* **R** J R ROGERS
WILFORD (St Wilfrid) *S'well 10* **P** *Lt Col Peter Clifton* **R** P NEWTON
WILFORD HILL (St Paul) *S'well 10* **P** *DBP* **V** G J PIGOTT, **NSM** B M GRIFFITHS, K BATTE
WILKSBY (All Saints) *see* Mareham-le-Fen and Revesby *Linc*
WILLAND (St Mary the Virgin) *Ex 4* **P** *CPAS* **R** K D AGNEW
WILLASTON (Christ Church) *Ches 9* **P** *DBF* **V** R W DENT
WILLASTON (St Luke) *see* Wistaston *Ches*
WILLEN (St Mary Magdalene) *see* Stantonbury and Willen *Ox*
WILLENHALL (Holy Trinity) *Lich 29* **P** *Patr Bd* **TV** T J LEYLAND, S A CHAPMAN, **C** M I RHODES
WILLENHALL (St Anne) *Lich 29* **P** *Mrs L Grant-Wilson* **V** C A St A RAMSAY
WILLENHALL (St Giles) *Lich 29* **P** *Trustees* **V** C R MARSHALL
WILLENHALL (St John the Divine) *Cov 1* **P** *V Cov H Trin* **V** T J COLLING, **C** D R TILLEY
WILLENHALL (St Stephen) *Lich 29* **P** *Bp* **V** D R HARTLAND
WILLERBY (St Luke) *see* Kirk Ella *York*
WILLERBY (St Peter) w Ganton and Folkton *York 16* **P** *M H Wrigley Esq, MMCET, and Revd G C Day (by turn)* **P-in-c** J H HARKER
WILLERSEY (St Peter), Saintbury, Weston-sub-Edge and Aston-sub-Edge *Glouc 10* **P** *Gen Sir John Gibbon and Major G B Gibbon, Earl of Harrowby, and Bp (by turn)* **R** D E VINCE
WILLESBOROUGH (St Mary the Virgin) *Cant 10* **P** *D&C* **R** M J McENERY, **C** T R WHATELEY
WILLESDEN (St Mark) *see* Kensal Rise St Mark and St Martin *Lon*
WILLESDEN (St Martin) *as above*
WILLESDEN (St Mary) *Lon 21* **P** *D&C St Paul's* **V** I G BOOTH, **Hon C** J L McKENZIE
WILLESDEN (St Matthew) *Lon 21* **P** *Bp* **P-in-c** M D MOORHEAD, **C** K A ROBUS
WILLESDEN (St Michael and All Angels) *see* Stonebridge St Mich *Lon*
WILLESDEN GREEN (St Andrew) (St Francis of Assisi) *Lon 21* **P** *Bp* **V** P S ANDERSON, **C** S RICHARDS
WILLEY (St Leonard) *see* Churchover w Willey *Cov*
WILLIAN (All Saints) *see* Letchworth St Paul w Willian *St Alb*
WILLINGALE (St Christopher) *see* Fyfield, Moreton w Bobbingworth etc *Chelmsf*
WILLINGDON (St Mary the Virgin) *Chich 16* **P** *D&C* **V** J R P ASHBY, **C** P BENNETT
WILLINGHAM (St Mary and All Saints) *Ely 5* **P** *Bp* **R** E A HUBBARD
WILLINGHAM, NORTH (St Thomas) *see* Walesby *Linc*
WILLINGHAM, SOUTH (St Martin) *see* Barkwith Gp *Linc*
WILLINGHAM BY STOW (St Helen) *see* Stow Gp *Linc*
WILLINGTON (St Lawrence) *see* Cople w Willington *St Alb*
WILLINGTON (St Michael) *Derby 16* **P** *CPAS* **P-in-c** D J T RYMER
WILLINGTON (St Stephen) and Sunnybrow *Dur 9* **P** *R Brancepeth* **R** P GRUNDY
WILLINGTON Team, The (Good Shepherd) (St Mary the Virgin) (St Paul) *Newc 8* **P** *Prime Min* **TR** J M DOTCHIN, **TV** R A STONE, **C** A W MARKS, A MAUGHAN
WILLINGTON QUAY (St Paul) *see* Willington Team *Newc*
WILLISHAM (St Mary) *see* Somersham w Flowton and Offton w Willisham *St E*
WILLITON (St Peter) *B & W 17* **P** *V Watchet* **V** R J ALLEN
WILLOUGHBY (St Helen) *Linc 8* **P** *Baroness Willoughby de Eresby, Ball Coll Ox, and Bp (jt)* **R** D C ROBINSON
WILLOUGHBY (St Nicholas) *see* Grandborough w Willoughby and Flecknoe *Cov*
WILLOUGHBY-ON-THE-WOLDS (St Mary and All Saints) w Wysall and Widerpool *S'well 9* **P** *MMCET* **V** J M PROTHERO
WILLOUGHBY WATERLEYS (St Mary), Peatling Magna and Ashby Magna *Leic 10* **P** *Bp* **P-in-c** C W DOIDGE
WILLOUGHTON (St Andrew) *see* Glentworth Gp *Linc*
WILMCOTE (St Andrew) *see* Aston Cantlow and Wilmcote w Billesley *Cov*
WILMINGTON (St Mary and St Peter) *see* Arlington, Folkington and Wilmington *Chich*
WILMINGTON (St Michael) *Roch 2* **P** *D&C* **V** R ARDING, **Hon C** P J IVESON
WILMSLOW (St Bartholomew) *Ches 12* **P** *Bp* **R** P J HUNT, **C** S T COLLIS, **NSM** R A YATES, N J WALTHEW
WILNE (St Chad) and Draycott w Breaston *Derby 13* **P** *Bp* **R** G K G GRIFFITH
WILNECOTE (Holy Trinity) *Lich 4* **P** *V Tamworth* **V** A P HARPER, **C** G J THOMPSON, S M HEMSLEY, **NSM** G THOMPSON
WILSDEN (St Matthew) *see* Harden and Wilsden *Bradf*
WILSFORD (St Mary) *see* Ancaster Wilsford Gp *Linc*
WILSFORD (St Michael) *see* Woodford Valley *Sarum*
WILSFORD (St Nicholas) *see* Redhorn *Sarum*
WILSHAMSTEAD (All Saints) and Houghton Conquest *St Alb 13* **P** *St Jo Coll Cam and Bp (alt)* **V** D R PALMER, **NSM** R C WHITE
WILSHAW (St Mary) *see* Meltham *Wakef*
WILSILL (St Michael and All Angels) *see* Upper Nidderdale *Ripon*
WILSTHORPE (St Faith) *see* Uffington Gp *Linc*
WILSTONE (St Cross) *see* Tring *St Alb*
WILTON (St Cuthbert) *York 17* **P** *Abp* **V** *Vacant*
WILTON (St George) *B & W 18* **P** *Mrs E C Cutbush* **TR** N J TAYLOR, **TV** M D CLARK, **Hon C** R W COLWILL
WILTON (St George) *see* Thornton Dale w Ellerburne and Wilton *York*
WILTON (St Mary and St Nicholas) w Netherhampton and Fugglestone *Sarum 16* **P** *Earl of Pembroke* **R** B R COOPER
WILTON PLACE (St Paul) *Lon 3* **P** *Bp* **V** A C C COURTAULD, **NSM** N DAWSON
WIMBISH (All Saints) *see* Debden and Wimbish w Thunderley *Chelmsf*
WIMBLEDON (Emmanuel) Ridgway Proprietary Chapel *S'wark 12* **Min** J J M FLETCHER, **C** M C CAIN, N WILSON-BROWN, **Hon C** D L JOHNSON, R J COEKIN, **NSM** R A S THOMSON
WIMBLEDON (St Luke) *S'wark 13* **P** *Simeon's Trustees* **V** D J WILES
WIMBLEDON (St Mary) (St Matthew) (St Mark) (St John the Baptist) *S'wark 13* **P** *Patr Bd* **TR** C J DAVIES, **TV** P J H DUNN, C D EYDEN, **C** E A MORSE, **NSM** H A JOHNSON, C JACKSON
WIMBLEDON, SOUTH (All Saints) *S'wark 13* **P** *Bp* **V** K J BALE, **Hon C** I P GREGORY
WIMBLEDON, SOUTH (Holy Trinity and St Peter) *S'wark 13* **P** *Bp and TR Wimbledon St Mary (jt)* **V** D S GATLIFFE, **C** A P WHITE
WIMBLEDON, SOUTH (St Andrew) *S'wark 13* **P** *Bp* **P-in-c** A D WAKEFIELD
WIMBLEDON, WEST (Christ Church) *S'wark 13* **P** *TR Wimbledon* **V** C S M THOMSON
WIMBLEDON PARK *see* Wimbledon St Luke *S'wark*
WIMBLEDON PARK (St Paul) *see* Wandsworth St Paul *S'wark*
WIMBLINGTON (St Peter) *see* Doddington w Benwick and Wimblington *Ely*
WIMBORNE (St Giles) *see* Cranborne w Boveridge, Edmondsham etc *Sarum*
WIMBORNE (St John the Evangelist) *see* New Borough and Leigh *Sarum*
WIMBORNE MINSTER (St Cuthberga) *Sarum 10* **P** *Qu Eliz Free Gr Sch* **R** D R PRICE
WIMBOTSHAM (St Mary) w Stow Bardolph and Stow Bridge w Nordelph *Ely 16* **P** *Bp and R T Townley Esq (jt)* **R** R D TOMKINSON
WIMPOLE (St Andrew) *Ely 8* **P** *Bp* **R** N A BRICE
WINCANTON (St Peter and St Paul) *B & W 2* **P** *D&C* **R** *Vacant* (01963) 33367
WINCH, EAST (All Saints) *see* Middleton w E Winch *Nor*
WINCH, WEST (St Mary) w Setchey and North Runcton *Nor 20* **P** *H N D Gurney Esq (1 turn), Ld Chan (2 turns)* **P-in-c** P BROWN
WINCHAM (St Andrew) *see* Lostock Gralam *Ches*

WINCHCOMBE (St Peter), Gretton, Sudeley Manor and Stanley Pontlarge *Glouc 17* **P** *Lady Ashcombe* **V** M J PAGE, **NSM** P M RAGBOURNE, J C CORNELL
WINCHELSEA (St Thomas) (St Richard) and Icklesham *Chich 20* **P** *Bp and Guild of All So (jt)* **R** K WOOD, **NSM** G F PEGG
WINCHENDON, NETHER (St Nicholas) *see* Long Crendon w Chearsley and Nether Winchendon *Ox*
WINCHENDON, OVER (St Mary Magdalene) *see* Waddesdon w Over Winchendon and Fleet Marston *Ox*
WINCHESTER (All Saints), Chilcomb (St Andrew), Chesil St Peter *Win 13* **P** *Bp and Ld Chan (alt)* **R** C BASTON, **Hon C** T E HEMMING
WINCHESTER (Christ Church) *Win 13* **P** *Simeon's Trustees* **V** E S SHIRRAS, **C** A JONES
WINCHESTER (Holy Trinity) *see* Winnall *Win*
WINCHESTER (St Barnabas) *Win 13* **P** *Bp* **V** R C STONE, **NSM** W J WILSON
WINCHESTER (St Cross Hospital w St Faith) *Win 13* **P** *Bp* **V** S A OUTHWAITE
WINCHESTER (St John the Baptist w St Martin Winnall) *see* Winnall *Win*
WINCHESTER (St Lawrence and St Maurice) (St Swithun-upon-Kingsgate) *Win 13* **P** *Ld Chan* **R** D V SCOTT, **Hon C** J M KERR, **NSM** N H de la MOUETTE
WINCHESTER St Matthew (St Paul's Mission Church) *Win 13* **P** *Bp* **R** C N WRIGHT, **NSM** N W BIRKETT
WINCHESTER Stanmore (St Luke) *see* Stanmore *Win*
WINCHESTER HYDE (St Bartholomew) *Win 13* **P** *Ld Chan* **V** G M ARMSTEAD, **NSM** J A FOREMAN
WINCHFIELD (St Mary the Virgin) *see* Hartley Wintney, Elvetham, Winchfield etc *Win*
WINCHMORE HILL (Holy Trinity) *Lon 18* **P** *V Winchmore Hill St Paul* **V** C M GRAY
WINCHMORE HILL (St Andrew) *see* Amersham *Ox*
WINCHMORE HILL (St Paul) *Lon 18* **P** *V Edmonton* **V** D J NASH, **C** S SHAHZAD, C M MORTON
WINCLE (St Michael) *see* Bosley and N Rode w Wincle and Wildboarclough *Ches*
WINCOBANK (St Thomas) *see* Brightside w Wincobank *Sheff*
WINDERMERE (St Martin) *Carl 10* **P** *Bp and Trustees (jt)* **P-in-c** C M BUTT, **NSM** C FORD
WINDERMERE (St Mary) Applethwaite and Troutbeck *Carl 10* **P** *Bp* **V** D R JACKSON, **NSM** D G GODDARD
WINDHILL (Christ Church) *Bradf 1* **P** *Bp* **V** G PERCIVAL
WINDLESHAM (St John the Baptist) *Guildf 6* **P** *Ld Chan* **R** P W MICKLETHWAITE, **C** D G NEWSTEAD
WINDRUSH (St Peter) *see* Sherborne, Windrush, the Barringtons etc *Glouc*
WINDSOR, NEW (Holy Trinity) (St John the Baptist w All Saints) *Ox 13* **P** *Ld Chan* **TR** J W G WHALE, **TV** A W H BUNCH, J G CRUICKSHANK, **C** A S PEBERDY
WINDSOR, OLD (St Luke's Mission Room) (St Peter and St Andrew) *Ox 13* **P** *Ld Chan* **V** *Vacant* (01753) 865778
WINESTEAD (St German) *see* Patrington w Hollym, Welwick and Winestead *York*
WINFARTHING (St Mary) w Shelfanger w Burston w Gissing and Tivetshall *Nor 10* **P** *Ld Chan, Bp, and DBP (jt), Hertf Coll Ox (alt)* **R** D V WHALE
WINFORD (Blessed Virgin Mary and St Peter) w Felton Common Hill *B & W 10* **P** *Worc Coll Ox and Mrs H D Pullman (jt)* **R** J BOLTON
WINFORTON (St Michael and All Angels) *see* Eardisley w Bollingham, Willersley, Brilley etc *Heref*
WINFRITH NEWBURGH (St Christopher) *see* The Lulworths, Winfrith Newburgh and Chaldon *Sarum*
WING (St Peter and St Paul) *see* Preston and Ridlington w Wing and Pilton *Pet*
WING w Grove (All Saints) *Ox 26* **P** *Bp* **V** B SAGAR
WINGATE GRANGE (Holy Trinity) *Dur 2* **P** *Bp* **P-in-c** M J VAIZEY
WINGATES (St John the Evangelist) *see* Westhoughton and Wingates *Man*
WINGERWORTH (All Saints) *Derby 5* **P** *Bp* **R** S MILLINGTON, **NSM** R E SMITH
WINGFIELD (St Andrew) *see* Fressingfield, Mendham, Metfield, Weybread etc *St E*
WINGFIELD (St Mary) *see* Westwood and Wingfield *Sarum*
WINGFIELD, NORTH (St Lawrence), Clay Cross and Pilsley *Derby 5* **P** *Bp* **TR** H L ORMEROD, **TV** B DALE, N S ATKINS, P G BYSOUTH
WINGFIELD, SOUTH (All Saints) and Wessington *Derby 1* **P** *Duke of Devonshire and V Crich (jt)* **V** W M RUMBALL
WINGHAM (St Mary the Virgin) w Elmstone and Preston w Stourmouth *Cant 1* **P** *Lord Fitzwalter and D&C (alt)* **V** P J BROWNBRIDGE
WINGRAVE (St Peter and St Paul) w Rowsham, Aston Abbotts and Cublington *Ox 26* **P** *Bp and Linc Coll Ox (jt)* **R** R O N WILLMOTT, **NSM** P R BINNS
WINKBURN (St John of Jerusalem) *S'well 15* **P** *Bp* **P-in-c** H H WILCOX
WINKFIELD (St Mary the Virgin) and Cranbourne *Ox 11* **P** *Bp* **V** S H BAYNES
WINKLEBURY (Good Shepherd) *Win 4* **P** *MMCET* **V** D T PERRETT, **NSM** R P BOWSKILL
WINKLEIGH (All Saints) *Ex 19* **P** *D&C* **V** P J NORMAN, **Hon C** G A HAMEY
WINKSLEY (St Cuthbert and St Oswald) *see* Fountains Gp *Ripon*
WINLATON (St Paul) *Dur 13* **P** *Bp* **R** E JONES
WINMARLEIGH (St Luke) *see* Cockerham w Winmarleigh and Glasson *Blackb*
WINNALL (Holy Trinity) (St John the Baptist w St Martin) *Win 13* **P** *Bp* **R** R J H TEARE
WINNERSH (St Mary the Virgin) *see* Hurst *Ox*
WINSCOMBE (St James) *B & W 11* **P** *D&C* **V** I M HUBBARD, **NSM** C NELMES
WINSFORD (St Mary Magdalene) *see* Exton and Winsford and Cutcombe w Luxborough *B & W*
WINSHAM (St Stephen) *see* Thorncombe w Winsham and Cricket St Thomas *B & W*
WINSHILL (St Mark) *Derby 16* **P** *Lady H M Gretton and Baroness Gretton (jt)* **V** K C JONES
WINSLEY (St Nicholas) *see* Monkton Farleigh, S Wraxall and Winsley *Sarum*
WINSLOW (St Laurence) w Great Horwood and Addington *Ox 24* **P** *Ld Chan (3 turns), New Coll Ox (2 turns), and DBP (1 turn)* **R** A A WHALLEY, **C** J M REES, **NSM** P A HOWARD
WINSON (St Michael) *see* Bibury w Winson and Barnsley *Glouc*
WINSTER (Holy Trinity) *Carl 9* **P** *V Kendal H Trin* **P-in-c** W F GREETHAM
WINSTER (St John the Baptist) *see* S Darley, Elton and Winster *Derby*
WINSTON (St Andrew) *Dur 7* **P** *Bp* **R** T J D OLLIER
WINSTON (St Andrew) *see* Helmingham w Framsden and Pettaugh w Winston *St E*
WINSTONE (St Bartholomew) *see* Brimpsfield w Birdlip, Syde, Daglingworth, etc *Glouc*
WINTERBOURNE (St James) *see* Chieveley w Winterbourne and Oare *Ox*
WINTERBOURNE (St Michael the Archangel) *Bris 7* **P** *St Jo Coll Ox* **R** E I BAILEY, **Hon C** W J DEIGHTON
WINTERBOURNE ABBAS (St Mary) *see* The Winterbournes and Compton Valence *Sarum*
WINTERBOURNE BASSETT (St Katharine) *see* Upper Kennet *Sarum*
WINTERBOURNE CLENSTON (St Nicholas) *see* Winterbourne Stickland and Turnworth etc *Sarum*
WINTERBOURNE DOWN (All Saints) *see* Frenchay and Winterbourne Down *Bris*
WINTERBOURNE EARLS (St Michael and All Angels) *see* Bourne Valley *Sarum*
WINTERBOURNE GUNNER (St Mary) *as above*
WINTERBOURNE HOUGHTON (St Andrew) *see* Winterbourne Stickland and Turnworth etc *Sarum*
WINTERBOURNE KINGSTON (St Nicholas) *see* Red Post *Sarum*
WINTERBOURNE MONKTON (St Mary Magdalene) *see* Upper Kennet *Sarum*
WINTERBOURNE MONKTON (St Simon and St Jude) *see* Dorchester *Sarum*
WINTERBOURNE ST MARTIN (St Martin) *see* The Winterbournes and Compton Valence *Sarum*
WINTERBOURNE STEEPLETON (St Michael) *as above*
WINTERBOURNE STICKLAND (St Mary) and Turnworth, Winterbourne Houghton, Winterbourne Whitechurch and Winterbourne Clenston *Sarum 7* **P** *Bp (3 turns), P D H Chichester Esq and Exors Mrs V P Railston (1 turn)* **R** R S GREEN, **NSM** A M F HALL
WINTERBOURNE STOKE (St Peter) *see* Lower Wylye and Till Valley *Sarum*
WINTERBOURNE WHITECHURCH (St Mary) *see* Winterbourne Stickland and Turnworth etc *Sarum*
WINTERBOURNE ZELSTONE (St Mary) *see* Red Post *Sarum*
WINTERBOURNES and Compton Valence, The *Sarum 2* **P** *Adn Sherborne, Linc Coll Ox, and Sir Robert Williams, Bt (by turn)* **P-in-c** J R ADAMS
WINTERBURN (Chapel of Ease) *see* Gargrave *Bradf*
WINTERINGHAM (All Saints) *see* Alkborough *Linc*
WINTERSLOW (All Saints) (St John) *Sarum 11* **P** *St Jo Coll Ox* **R** C R F COHEN

WINTERTON Group, The (All Saints) *Linc 4* **P** *Lord St Oswald, Bp, and Capt J G G P Elwes (jt)* **V** D EDGAR
WINTERTON (Holy Trinity and All Saints) w East and West Somerton and Horsey *Nor 6* **P** *Bp, SMF, and D&C (jt)* **NSM** A T CADMORE
WINTHORPE (All Saints) *S'well 3* **P** *Keble Coll Ox* **P-in-c** A K SHAW
WINTHORPE (St Mary) *see* Skegness and Winthorpe *Linc*
WINTON (St Mary Magdalene) *Man 2* **P** *Trustees* **V** D R SUTTON
WINTRINGHAM (St Peter) *see* Rillington w Scampston, Wintringham etc *York*
WINWICK (All Saints) *Ely 10* **P** *Bp* **P-in-c** C M FURLONG, **NSM** I D M GIBSON
WINWICK (St Michael and All Angels) *see* W Haddon w Winwick and Ravensthorpe *Pet*
WINWICK (St Oswald) *Liv 16* **P** *Bp* **R** R G LEWIS
WIRKSWORTH (St Mary) *Derby 7* **P** *Bp* **TR** R S CANEY, **TV** J D HAYWARD, M SMITH, **C** D J ADAMS
WISBECH (St Augustine) *Ely 19* **P** *Bp* **V** R D BULL, **C** D L MASON, **NSM** G G A WARING
WISBECH (St Peter and St Paul) *Ely 19* **P** *Bp* **V** W A L ZWALF, **C** J E PHILLIPS
WISBECH ST MARY (St Mary) *Ely 19* **P** *Bp* **P-in-c** F B H WOOLLEY
WISBOROUGH GREEN (St Peter ad Vincula) *Chich 11* **P** *Bp Lon* **V** D F PIKE
WISHAW (St Chad) *Birm 13* **P** *Bp* **P-in-c** J W WOODWARD
WISHFORD, GREAT (St Giles) *see* Lower Wylye and Till Valley *Sarum*
WISLEY (not known) w Pyrford *Guildf 12* **P** *Bp* **R** N J AIKEN, **C** R W NEILL, **NSM** K R CROOKS
WISSETT (St Andrew) *see* Halesworth w Linstead, Chediston, Holton etc *St E*
WISSINGTON (St Mary the Virgin) *see* Nayland w Wiston *St E*
WISTANSTOW (Holy Trinity) *Heref 11* **P** *Bp* **P-in-c** G M SUMNER
WISTASTON (St Mary) *Ches 15* **P** *Trustees* **R** W J WHITE
WISTON (St Mary) *see* Ashington, Washington and Wiston with Buncton *Chich*
WISTOW (All Saints) *York 6* **P** *Abp* **P-in-c** A STOKER, **NSM** M J CUNDIFF
WISTOW (St John the Baptist) *see* Warboys w Broughton and Bury w Wistow *Ely*
WISTOW (St Wistan) *see* Gt Glen, Stretton Magna and Wistow etc *Leic*
WITCHAM (St Martin) w Mepal *Ely 14* **P** *D&C* **R** B SNELL, **NSM** M T COOPER
WITCHAMPTON (St Mary and St Cuthberga and All Saints), Stanbridge and Long Crichel w More Crichel *Sarum 10* **P** *Hon Mrs M A S E Marten* **V** G E WALTON
WITCHFORD (St Andrew) w Wentworth *Ely 14* **P** *D&C* **P-in-c** T AMBROSE
WITCHINGHAM GREAT (St Mary) *see* Weston Longville w Morton and the Witchinghams *Nor*
WITCOMBE, GREAT (St Mary) *see* Badgeworth, Shurdington and Witcombe w Bentham *Glouc*
WITHAM Group, The *Linc 14* **P** *Sir Lyonel Tollemache Bt, Revd J R H and Revd H C Thorold, and Bp (jt)* **R** N S F ALLDRIT
WITHAM (St Nicholas) *Chelmsf 24* **P** *Patr Bd* **TR** D SHERLOCK, **TV** B J MAPLEY, **C** K R PLAISTER
WITHAM, NORTH (St Mary) *see* Witham Gp *Linc*
WITHAM, SOUTH (St John the Baptist) *as above*
WITHAM FRIARY (Blessed Virgin Mary and St John the Baptist and All Saints) *see* Nunney and Witham Friary, Marston Bigot etc *B*
WITHAM-ON-THE-HILL (St Andrew) *see* Edenham w Witham-on-the-Hill *Linc*
WITHCALL (St Martin) *see* Raithby *Linc*
WITHERIDGE (St John the Baptist), Thelbridge, Creacombe, Meshaw, East and West Worlington *Ex 18* **P** *Bp, Sir Hugh Stucley Bt, A M O Bruton Esq and MMCET (jt)* **P-in-c** V ROSS
WITHERLEY (St Peter) *see* Higham-on-the-Hill w Fenny Drayton and Witherley *Leic*
WITHERNSEA (St Nicholas) *see* Owthorne and Rimswell w Withernsea *York*
WITHERNWICK (St Alban) *see* Aldbrough, Mappleton w Goxhill and Withernwick *York*
WITHERSDALE (St Mary Magdalene) *see* Fressingfield, Mendham, Metfield, Weybread etc *St E*
WITHERSFIELD (St Mary the Virgin) *see* Haverhill w Withersfield, the Wrattings etc *St E*
WITHERSLACK (St Paul) *Carl 9* **P** *DBP* **P-in-c** W F GREETHAM
WITHIEL (St Clement) *see* Roche and Withiel *Truro*
WITHIEL FLOREY (St Mary Magdalene) *see* Brompton Regis w Upton and Skilgate *B & W*
WITHINGTON (St Christopher) *Man 8* **P** *The Crown* **Dn-in-c** G R RAINES
WITHINGTON (St Crispin) *Man 4* **P** *Bp* **R** S J DOBSON
WITHINGTON (St John the Baptist) *see* Wrockwardine Deanery *Lich*
WITHINGTON (St Michael and All Angels) and Compton Abdale w Haselton *Glouc 14* **P** *Bp (2 turns), Ld Chan (1 turn)* **P-in-c** C D J G BURSLEM
WITHINGTON (St Paul) *Man 8* **P** *Trustees* **R** N W DAWSON
WITHINGTON (St Peter) w Westhide *Heref 4* **P** *Bp* **P-in-c** N C H VARNON
WITHINGTON, LOWER (St Peter) *see* Chelford w Lower Withington *Ches*
WITHLEIGH (St Catherine) *see* Washfield, Stoodleigh, Withleigh etc *Ex*
WITHNELL (St Paul) *see* Heapey St Barnabas and Withnell St Paul *Blackb*
WITHYBROOK (All Saints) *see* Wolvey w Burton Hastings, Copston Magna etc *Cov*
WITHYCOMBE (St Nicholas) *see* Dunster, Carhampton and Withycombe w Rodhuish *B & W*
WITHYCOMBE RALEIGH (All Saints) *see* Withycombe Raleigh *Ex*
WITHYCOMBE RALEIGH (St John the Evangelist) (St John in the Wilderness) (All Saints) *Ex 1* **P** *Patr Bd* **TR** F A OSWIN, **TV** J D H CLEMENTS
WITHYHAM (St John the Evangelist) *Chich 19* **P** *Guild of All So* **V** R L FEATHERSTONE
WITHYHAM (St Michael and All Angels) *Chich 19* **P** *Earl de la Warr* **P-in-c** G R PARISH
WITHYPOOL (St Andrew) *see* Exford, Exmoor, Hawkridge and Withypool *B & W*
WITHYWOOD (shared church) *Bris 1* **P** *Bp* **V** B E PEARCE, **C** D A PARRY
WITLEY (All Saints) *Guildf 4* **P** *Mrs C M Chandler and R D Chandler Esq (jt)* **V** I C S FENTON
WITLEY, GREAT (St Michael) *see* Shrawley, Witley, Astley and Abberley *Worc*
WITLEY, LITTLE (St Michael) *as above*
WITNESHAM (St Mary) *see* Westerfield and Tuddenham w Witnesham *St E*
WITNEY (St Mary the Virgin) (Holy Trinity) *Ox 8* **P** *Patr Bd* **TR** C J BUTLAND, **TV** T P EDGE, **C** G R ARTHUR, W J ADAM, L R F COLLINS, **Hon C** J H COOK
WITTENHAM, LITTLE (St Peter) *see* Dorchester *Ox*
WITTERING (All Saints) w Thornhaugh and Wansford *Pet 8* **P** *Burghley Ho Preservation Trust (2 turns), Bp (1 turn)* **R** H R WATSON
WITTERING, EAST (St Anne) *see* Earnley and E Wittering *Chich*
WITTERING, WEST (St Peter and St Paul) and Birdham w Itchenor *Chich 3* **P** *Bp* **R** J B WILLIAMS, **Hon C** C J HANKINS
WITTERSHAM (St John the Baptist) w Stone-in-Oxney and Ebony *Cant 13* **P** *Abp* **Hon C** M S WING, D C BINDON
WITTON (St Helen) *Ches 6* **P** *Bp* **V** A A LONG, **C** P WAIN, **NSM** B R K PERKES
WITTON (St Margaret) *see* Bacton w Edingthorpe w Witton and Ridlington *Nor*
WITTON (St Margaret) *see* Gt and Lt Plumstead w Thorpe End and Witton *Nor*
WITTON (St Mark) *Blackb 2* **P** *V Blackb* **V** C L ALBIN
WITTON, EAST (St John the Evangelist) *see* Middleham w Coverdale and E Witton *Ripon*
WITTON, NETHER (St Giles) *Newc 11* **P** *Ld Chan* **V** G F REVETT
WITTON, WEST (St Bartholomew) *Ripon 4* **P** *Lord Bolton* **V** H F K CHEALL
WITTON GILBERT (St Michael and All Angels) *Dur 1* **P** *D&C* **R** *Vacant* 0191-371 0376
WITTON LE WEAR (St Philip and St James) *see* Hamsterley and Witton-le-Wear *Dur*
WITTON PARK (St Paul) *Dur 6* **P** *Bp* **V** N M J-W BEDDOW
WIVELISCOMBE (St Andrew) w Chipstable, Huish Champflower and Clatworthy *B & W 19* **P** *Bp and A H Trollope-Bellew Esq (jt)* **R** P A EAST, **C** G A OWEN, **NSM** S M GREEN
WIVELSFIELD (St Peter and St John the Baptist) *Chich 6* **P** *DBP* **V** S A FALLOWS
WIVENHOE (St Mary) *Chelmsf 16* **P** *Bp* **R** D G THOMAS
WIVETON (St Mary) *see* Blakeney w Cley, Wiveton, Glandford etc *Nor*
WIX (St Mary the Virgin) *see* Gt Oakley w Wix and Wrabness *Chelmsf*
WIXFORD (St Milburga) *see* Exhall w Wixford *Cov*

WIXOE (St Leonard) *see* Clare w Poslingford, Cavendish etc *St E*
WOBURN (St Mary) w Eversholt, Milton Bryan, Battlesden and Pottesgrove *St Alb 9* **P** *Bedf Estates Trustees* **V** P R MILLER
WOBURN SANDS (St Michael) *St Alb 9* **P** *Bp* **V** N JEFFERY, **NSM** N J PARKINSON
WOBURN SQUARE (Christ Church) *see* Bloomsbury St Geo w Woburn Square Ch Ch *Lon*
WOKING (Christ Church) *Guildf 12* **P** *Ridley Hall Cam* **V** M F HERBERT, **C** J A HUGHMAN, **NSM** J A M VICKERS
WOKING (St John the Baptist) *Guildf 12* **P** *V Woking St Pet* **V** G P WILLIAMS, **C** P J PARTINGTON, K B ATKINSON
WOKING (St Mary of Bethany) *Guildf 12* **P** *V Woking Ch Ch* **V** R DERBRIDGE
WOKING (St Paul) *Guildf 12* **P** *Ridley Hall Cam* **V** S C PITTIS
WOKING (St Peter) *Guildf 12* **P** *Ch Soc Trust* **V** B J GRIMSTER, **C** T C LING
WOKINGHAM (All Saints) *Ox 16* **P** *Bp* **R** D P HODGSON, **C** A DUFF, **NSM** C R JAMES
WOKINGHAM (St Paul) *Ox 16* **P** *DBP* **P-in-c** R J STILLMAN, **C** P CHAPLIN, **NSM** R G HOLMES
WOKINGHAM (St Sebastian) *Ox 16* **P** *Bp* **NSM** E C FUDGE
WOLBOROUGH (St Mary) w Newton Abbot *Ex 11* **P** *Earl of Devon* **P-in-c** A P G FRAMPTON-MORGAN, **NSM** A K CLARKE
WOLD (St Andrew) *see* Walgrave w Hannington and Wold and Scaldwell *Pet*
WOLD-MARSH Group, The *Linc 8* **P** *Ld Chan (1 turn), Bp, D&C, and DBP (2 turns), and Duchy of Lanc (1 turn)* **P-in-c** M A PARSONS
WOLD NEWTON (All Saints) *see* Binbrook Gp *Linc*
WOLD NEWTON (All Saints) *see* Burton Fleming w Fordon, Grindale etc *York*
WOLDINGHAM (St Agatha) (St Paul) *S'wark 25* **P** *Bp* **P-in-c** E B WOOD, **NSM** M C JOHNSON
WOLDS, NORTH Group *Linc 6* **P** *Bp, DBP, and D&C (jt)* **V** M A BATTY
WOLFERLOW (St Andrew) *see* Edvin Loach w Tedstone Delamere etc *Heref*
WOLFERTON (St Peter) *see* Sandringham w W Newton and Appleton etc *Nor*
WOLFORD (St Michael and All Angels) w Burmington *Cov 9* **P** *Mert Coll Ox* **P-in-c** R K SMITH, **C** R D HOLDER
WOLLASTON (St James) *Worc 12* **P** *Bp* **V** M J WILLOWS
WOLLASTON (St Mary) and Strixton *Pet 6* **P** *Bp* **V** A SMITH
WOLLASTON, GREAT (All Saints) (St John the Baptist) *Heref 13* **P** *Bp* **P-in-c** C B BULL
WOLLATON (St Leonard) *S'well 14* **P** *Lord Middleton* **R** D W S JAMES, **C** K HERROD, **NSM** P D C BROWN
WOLLATON PARK (St Mary) *S'well 14* **P** *CPAS* **P-in-c** A R HOWE
WOLLESCOTE (St Andrew) *Worc 12* **P** *Bp* **V** R A BROADBENT
WOLSINGHAM (St Mary and St Stephen) and Thornley *Dur 9* **P** *Bp* **R** R L WELSH
WOLSTANTON (St Margaret) *Lich 9* **P** *Bp* **TR** J P EADES, **TV** D A AKKER, **C** R M McINTYRE
WOLSTON (St Margaret) and Church Lawford *Cov 6* **P** *DBP (2 turns), Bp (1 turn)* **V** P WATKINS, **C** P A H SIMMONDS, **NSM** E M COWLEY
WOLVERCOTE (St Peter) w Summertown *Ox 7* **P** *Patr Bd* **TR** A M GANN, **TV** D A E MICHAELS, **NSM** W L A PRYOR, G G WRIGHT
WOLVERHAMPTON Pond Lane (Mission Hall) *see* Wolverhampton St Luke *Lich*
WOLVERHAMPTON (St Andrew) *Lich 29* **P** *Bp* **V** J L SMITH, **NSM** T B FYFFE
WOLVERHAMPTON (St Chad) (St Mark's Centre) (St Peter) *Lich 29* **P** *Patr Bd* **TR** J C B HALL-MATTHEWS, **TV** O SMITH, D GHOSH, **C** J R HOPCRAFT, D J DORMOR
WOLVERHAMPTON (St John) *Lich 29* **P** *Bp* **P-in-c** J R HOPCRAFT
WOLVERHAMPTON (St Jude) *Lich 29* **P** *CPAS* **V** R E CARTER
WOLVERHAMPTON (St Luke) Blakenhall *Lich 29* **P** *Trustees* **P-in-c** T G ANDERSON, **C** G J STRAIN
WOLVERHAMPTON (St Martin) *see* Rough Hills *Lich*
WOLVERHAMPTON (St Matthew) *Lich 29* **P** *Baldwin Pugh Trustees* **V** L P BEARD, **C** J C BRYAN
WOLVERHAMPTON (St Stephen) *Lich 29* **P** *Bp* **P-in-c** J C OAKES, **C** G BUCKBY
WOLVERLEY (St John the Baptist) and Cookley *Worc 11* **P** *D&C and Bp (jt)* **V** G SHILVOCK
WOLVERTON (Holy Trinity) (St George the Martyr) *Ox 25* **P** *Bp* **R** R G RHODES, **TV** J M TRIGG
WOLVERTON (St Katherine) *see* Baughurst, Ramsdell, Wolverton w Ewhurst etc *Win*
WOLVERTON (St Mary the Virgin) w Norton Lindsey and Langley *Cov 7* **P** *Bp* **P-in-c** R LIVINGSTON, **NSM** M WEBSTER
WOLVEY (St John the Baptist) w Burton Hastings, Copston Magna and Withybrook *Cov 5* **P** *Bp* **V** R J JAMES
WOLVISTON (St Peter) *Dur 10* **P** *D&C* **R** G W R HARPER
WOMBOURNE (St Benedict) w Trysull and Bobbington *Lich 25* **P** *Patr Bd* **TR** C HUGHES, **TV** M J G BINNEY, **NSM** D LUMB
WOMBRIDGE (St Mary and St Leonard) *Lich 22* **V** R W BAILEY
WOMBWELL (St Mary) (St George) *Sheff 12* **P** *Trin Coll Cam* **R** E MITCHELL
WOMERSLEY (St Martin) and Kirk Smeaton *Wakef 11* **P-in-c** W T HICKS
WONERSH (St John the Baptist) *Guildf 2* **P** *Selw Coll Cam* **V** J R WATTLEY, **C** P M C KETTLE, **NSM** C V SOWTER
WONSTON (Holy Trinity) and Stoke Charity w Hunton *Win 13* **P** *Bp and D&C (jt)* **R** A JARDINE, **NSM** R C CLARKSON
WONSTON, SOUTH (St Margaret) *see* Wonston and Stoke Charity w Hunton *Win*
WOOBURN (St Paul) *Ox 29* **P** *Bp* **P-in-c** D R BURDEN
WOOD DALLING (St Andrew) *see* Reepham, Hackford w Whitwell, Kerdiston etc *Nor*
WOOD DITTON (St Mary) w Saxon Street *Ely 4* **P** *Duke of Sutherland* **V** C A SINDALL
WOOD END (St Chad) *Cov 1* **P** *Ld Chan* **V** M N A JONES, **C** C C PRENTIS
WOOD END (St Michael and All Angels) *see* Baxterley w Hurley and Wood End and Merevale etc *Birm*
WOOD GREEN (St Michael) w Bounds Green (St Gabriel) (St Michael-at-Bowes) *Lon 19* **P** *Patr Bd* **TR** C W COPPEN, **TV** K JEFFRIES, **C** R L WHITEHEAD
WOOD GREEN (St Paul) *see* Wednesbury St Paul Wood Green *Lich*
WOOD NORTON (All Saints) *see* Twyford, Guist, Bintree, Themelthorpe etc *Nor*
WOOD STREET (St Alban) *see* Worplesdon *Guildf*
WOODBASTWICK (St Fabian and St Sebastian) *see* Ranworth w Panxworth and Woodbastwick *Nor*
WOODBERRY DOWN (St Olave) *see* Stoke Newington St Olave *Lon*
WOODBOROUGH (St Mary Magdalene) *see* Swanborough *Sarum*
WOODBOROUGH (St Swithun) *S'well 11* **P** *Bp* **V** W G CALTHROP-OWEN
WOODBRIDGE (St John the Evangelist) *St E 7* **P** *Ch Patr Trust* **P-in-c** R F WEBB
WOODBRIDGE (St Mary the Virgin) *St E 7* **P** *Bp* **R** D J PITCHER
WOODBURY (Holy Cross) *see* Axminster, Chardstock, Combe Pyne and Rousdon *Ex*
WOODBURY (St Swithun) *Ex 1* **P** *D&C* **P-in-c** P J McGEE
WOODBURY SALTERTON (Holy Trinity) *see* Clyst St Mary, Clyst St George etc *Ex*
WOODCHESTER (St Mary) and Brimscombe *Glouc 8* **P** *Simeon's Trustees* **R** *Vacant* (01453) 882204
WOODCHURCH (All Saints) *Cant 10* **P** *Abp* **P-in-c** C A TOMKINS
WOODCHURCH (Holy Cross) *Ches 1* **P** *DBP* **R** A D DEAN
WOODCOTE (St Leonard) *see* Langtree *Ox*
WOODCOTE (St Peter) *see* Lilleshall and Sheriffhales *Lich*
WOODCOTT (St James) *see* St Mary Bourne and Woodcott *Win*
WOODDITTON (St Mary) *see* Wood Ditton w Saxon Street *Ely*
WOODEATON (Holy Rood) *see* Islip w Charlton on Otmoor, Oddington, Noke etc *Ox*
WOODFORD (Christ Church) *Ches 12* **P** *W A B Davenport Esq* **P-in-c** F H BARKER
WOODFORD (St Barnabas) *Chelmsf 4* **P** *Bp* **V** A CROSS
WOODFORD (St Mary the Virgin) *see* Gt w Lt Addington and Woodford *Pet*
WOODFORD (St Mary w St Philip and St James) *Chelmsf 4* **P** *Bp* **R** *Vacant* 0181-504 3472
WOODFORD, SOUTH Hermon Hill (Holy Trinity) *see* Wanstead H Trin Hermon Hill *Chelmsf*
WOODFORD BRIDGE (St Paul) *Chelmsf 4* **P** *R Woodford* **V** R C MATTHEWS, **NSM** I K MONKS
WOODFORD HALSE (St Mary the Virgin) w Eydon *Pet 1* **P** *Ld Chan (2 turns), Bp (1 turn)* **V** J M COURTIE
WOODFORD VALLEY (All Saints) *Sarum 12* **P** *Bp* **V** J L REYNOLDS
WOODFORD WELLS (All Saints) (St Andrew) *Chelmsf 4* **P** *Trustees* **V** M J COLE, **C** L S RAYFIELD, P G HARCOURT, **NSM** D J BLACKLEDGE

WOODGATE VALLEY Conventional District *Birm 2 Vacant*
WOODGREEN (St Boniface) *see* Hale w S Charford *Win*
WOODHALL (St James the Great) *Bradf 3* **P** *Bp* **V** S BAILEY, **C** K S TROMANS
WOODHALL, OLD *see* Woodhall Spa Gp *Linc*
WOODHALL SPA Group *Linc 11* **P** *Bp and DBP (jt)* **R** R I McMASTER
WOODHAM (All Saints) *Guildf 12* **P** *Bp* **V** P G P FARRELL, **NSM** A J K MACKENZIE
WOODHAM (St Elizabeth of Hungary) *see* Gt Aycliffe *Dur*
WOODHAM FERRERS (St Mary) and Bicknacre *Chelmsf 9* **P** *Lord Fitzwalter* **NSM** M J COTTEE
WOODHAM FERRERS, SOUTH (Holy Trinity) (St Mary) *Chelmsf 9* **P** *Bp* **P-in-c** M L LANGAN, **C** A M WARD, **NSM** E S LANGAN
WOODHAM MORTIMER (St Margaret) w Hazeleigh *Chelmsf 11* **P** *Bp* **P-in-c** K I DUNSTAN
WOODHAM WALTER (St Michael) *Chelmsf 11* **P** *Ch Soc Trust* **R** *Vacant*
WOODHAY, EAST (St Martin) and Woolton Hill *Win 6* **P** *Bp* **R** D J CARTER
WOODHAY, WEST (St Laurence) w Enborne, Hampstead Marshall, Inkpen and Combe *Ox 14* **P** *Bp, D&C Windsor, and J R Henderson Esq (jt)* **R** J F RAMSBOTTOM, **NSM** R M GRIFFITHS
WOODHORN w Newbiggin *Newc 11* **P** *Bp* **V** *Vacant* (01670) 817220
WOODHOUSE (Christ Church) *Wakef 5* **P** *Bp* **V** S K M HENRY
WOODHOUSE (St Mark) and Wrangthorn *Ripon 7* **P** *DBP* **V** T G MUNRO
WOODHOUSE (St Mary in the Elms) and Woodhouse Eaves *Leic 7* **P** *DBP* **V** D M BUXTON
WOODHOUSE CLOSE (not known) *see* Bishop Auckland Woodhouse Close CD *Dur*
WOODHOUSE EAVES (St Paul) *see* Woodhouse and Woodhouse Eaves *Leic*
WOODHOUSE MILL (St James) *see* Handsworth Woodhouse *Sheff*
WOODHOUSE PARK (Wm Temple Church) *see* Wythenshawe Wm Temple Ch *Man*
WOODHOUSES (not known) *see* Bardsley *Man*
WOODHOUSES (St John the Divine) *see* Dunham Massey St Marg and St Mark *Ches*
WOODHURST (St John the Baptist) *see* Bluntisham cum Earith w Colne and Woodhurst *Ely*
WOODINGDEAN (Holy Cross) *Chich 2* **P** *Bp* **V** R A BROMFIELD
WOODKIRK (St Mary) *see* W Ardsley *Wakef*
WOODLAND (St John the Baptist) *see* Broadhempston, Woodland, Staverton etc *Ex*
WOODLAND (St John the Evangelist) *see* Broughton and Duddon *Carl*
WOODLAND (St Mary) *see* Lynesack *Dur*
WOODLANDS (All Saints) *Sheff 8* **P** *Bp* **V** M J GODFREY
WOODLANDS (Ascension) *see* Cranborne w Boveridge, Edmondsham etc *Sarum*
WOODLANDS (Mission Chapel) *see* W Meon and Warnford *Portsm*
WOODLANDS (St Katherine) *B & W 4* **P** *DBP* **V** J G PESCOD
WOODLANDS (St Mary) *see* Kemsing w Woodlands *Roch*
WOODLANDS (St Stephen) *see* Welford w Wickham and Gt Shefford, Boxford etc *Ox*
WOODLEIGH (St Mary the Virgin) *see* Modbury, Bigbury, Ringmore w Kingston etc *Ex*
WOODLEY (St John the Evangelist) *Ox 15* **P** *DBP* **TR** F J WOODS, **TV** P C ROBERTS, D R BYRNE
WOODMANCOTE (Mission Church) *see* Westbourne *Chich*
WOODMANCOTE (St James) *see* Micheldever and E Stratton, Woodmancote etc *Win*
WOODMANCOTE (St Mark) *see* Dursley *Glouc*
WOODMANCOTE (St Peter) *see* Henfield w Shermanbury and Woodmancote *Chich*
WOODMANSEY (St Peter) *see* Beverley Minster *York*
WOODMANSTERNE (St Peter) *S'wark 27* **P** *Ld Chan* **R** N A BARKER
WOODNESBOROUGH (St Mary the Blessed Virgin) w Worth and Staple *Cant 8* **P** *Abp* **V** J G K BATSON, **Hon C** D G WILLIS, **NSM** K I HAGGAR
WOODNEWTON (St Mary) *see* Nassington w Yarwell and Woodnewton *Pet*
WOODPLUMPTON (St Anne) *Blackb 10* **P** *V St Michael's-on-Wyre* **P-in-c** I W FORBES
WOODRISING (St Nicholas) *see* Hingham w Wood Rising w Scoulton *Nor*
WOODSETTS (St George) *Sheff 5* **P** *Bp* **V** P IRESON
WOODSFORD (St John the Baptist) *see* Moreton and Woodsford w Tincleton *Sarum*
WOODSIDE (St Andrew) w East Hyde *St Alb 14* **P** *D&C St Paul's* **V** D R BOLSTER, **NSM** G N CRAPNELL
WOODSIDE (St James) *Ripon 7* **P** *Bp* **V** P Q TUDGE
WOODSIDE (St Luke) *see* Croydon Woodside *S'wark*
WOODSIDE GREEN (St Andrew) *see* Gt Hallingbury and Lt Hallingbury *Chelmsf*
WOODSIDE PARK (St Barnabas) *Lon 14* **P** *Ch Patr Trust* **V** J S H COLES, **C** G BOLAND
WOODSTOCK (St Mary Magdalene) *see* Bladon w Woodstock *Ox*
WOODSTON (St Augustine of Canterbury) (Mission Church) *Ely 13* **P** *Bp* **R** D G STEVENS
WOODTHORPE (St Mark) *S'well 11* **P** *Bp* **V** F W BRIDGER, **NSM** R W BRIDGER
WOODTHORPE (St Peter) *see* Staveley and Barrow Hill *Derby*
WOODTON (All Saints) *see* Hempnall *Nor*
WOODVILLE (St Stephen) *see* Blackfordby and Woodville *Leic*
WOOKEY (St Matthew) *see* Coxley, Henton and Wookey *B & W*
WOOKEY HOLE (St Mary Magdalene) *see* Wells St Cuth w Wookey Hole *B & W*
WOOL (Holy Rood) and East Stoke *Sarum 9* **P** *Bp (3 turns), Keble Coll Ox (1 turn)* **P-in-c** J P TOWNEND
WOOLACOMBE (St Sabinus) *see* Ilfracombe, Lee, Woolacombe, Bittadon etc *Ex*
WOOLASTON (St Andrew) w Alvington and Aylburton *Glouc 4* **P** *DBP and Ld Chan (by turn)* **R** J E TAYLOR
WOOLAVINGTON (Blessed Virgin Mary) w Cossington and Bawdrip *B & W 14* **P** *D&C Windsor and J A Church Esq (alt)* **V** N W STEEL
WOOLBEDING (All Hallows) *Chich 10* **P** *Cowdray Trust* **R** A T CUNNINGTON
WOOLBROOK (St Francis of Assisi) *see* Sidmouth, Woolbrook, Salcombe Regis, Sidbury etc *Ex*
WOOLER (St Mary) *see* Glendale Gp *Newc*
WOOLFARDISWORTHY (Holy Trinity) *see* Parkham, Alwington, Buckland Brewer etc *Ex*
WOOLFARDISWORTHY EAST (St Mary) *see* N Creedy *Ex*
WOOLFOLD (St James) *Man 10* **P** *R Bury St Mary* **P-in-c** E A CARNELLEY
WOOLHAMPTON (St Peter) w Midgham and Beenham Valance *Ox 12* **P** *Bp, Keble Coll Ox, and CPAS (jt)* **P-in-c** C H REDGRAVE
WOOLHOPE (St George) *see* Fownhope w Mordiford, Brockhampton etc *Heref*
WOOLLAND (not known) *see* Hazelbury Bryan and the Hillside Par *Sarum*
WOOLLEY (All Saints) *see* Bath St Sav w Swainswick and Woolley *B & W*
WOOLLEY (St Peter) *Wakef 9* **P** *Bp* **P-in-c** C OGLE
WOOLMER GREEN (St Michael) *see* Welwyn w Ayot St Peter *St Alb*
WOOLPIT (Blessed Virgin Mary) w Drinkstone *St E 10* **P** *Bp and A Harvie-Clark Esq (alt)* **R** A G TAYLOR
WOOLSTASTON (St Michael and All Angels) *see* Dorrington w Leebotwood, Longnor, Stapleton etc *Heref*
WOOLSTHORPE (St James) *see* Harlaxton Gp *Linc*
WOOLSTON (Ascension) *Liv 12* **P** *Bp, Adn, and R Warrington (jt)* **V** R L PEARSON
WOOLSTON (St Mark) *Win 12* **P** *Bp* **V** F P MATTHEWS, **NSM** A R BEVIS
WOOLSTONE (All Saints) *see* Uffington, Shellingford, Woolstone and Baulking *Ox*
WOOLSTONE (not known) *see* Woughton *Ox*
WOOLSTONE (St Martin) w Gotherington and Oxenton, and Kemerton *Glouc 9* **P** *DBP and Croome Estate* **R** J BUTLER
WOOLTON, MUCH (St Peter) *Liv 4* **P** *Bp* **R** J V ROBERTS, **C** J MARSDEN, J P LEFFLER
WOOLTON HILL (St Thomas) *see* E Woodhay and Woolton Hill *Win*
WOOLVERSTONE (St Michael) *see* Holbrook w Freston and Woolverstone *St E*
WOOLVERTON (St Lawrence) *see* Rode Major *B & W*
WOOLWICH (St Mary Magdelene and St Andrew) (St Michael and All Angels) *S'wark 3* **P** *Bp and Keble Coll Ox (jt)* **R** J van der VALK
WOOLWICH (St Thomas) *S'wark 3* **P** *Bp* **R** I M PAGE
WOOLWICH, NORTH (St John) w Silvertown *Chelmsf 3* **P** *Bp and Lon Corp (alt)* **P-in-c** R J A HAMER
WOONTON (Mission Room) *see* Lyonshall w Titley, Almeley and Kinnersley *Heref*
WOORE (St Leonard) and Norton in Hales *Lich 18* **P** *Bp and CPAS (jt)* **P-in-c** P M JAMES
WOOSEHILL (Community Church) *see* Bearwood *Ox*
WOOTTON Boars Hill (St Peter) *Ox 10* **P** *Bp* **V** P N CHALLENGER

WOOTTON (St Andrew) *see* Ulceby Gp *Linc*
WOOTTON (St Edmund) *Portsm 8* **P** *DBP* **P-in-c** A W FROUD
WOOTTON (St George the Martyr) w Quinton and Preston Deanery *Pet 7* **P** *Ex Coll Ox and Bp (alt)* **R** D SCHOLEY
WOOTTON (St Martin) *see* Elham w Denton and Wootton *Cant*
WOOTTON (St Mary the Virgin) *St Alb 13* **P** *MMCET* **V** C P STRONG, **NSM** R J ROBY
WOOTTON (St Mary) w Glympton and Kiddington *Ox 9* **P** *New Coll Ox (2 turns), Bp (1 turn), and Exors E W Towler Esq (1 turn)* **R** R J FARMAN, **Hon Par Dn** R FARMAN
WOOTTON, NORTH (All Saints) w SOUTH (St Mary) *Nor 20* **P** *Ld Chan and G Howard Esq (alt)* **R** B R OAKE, **C** R L N HARRISON
WOOTTON, NORTH (St Peter) *see* Pilton w Croscombe, N Wootton and Dinder *B & W*
WOOTTON BASSETT (St Bartholomew and All Saints) *Sarum 18* **P** *DBP* **V** B J GARRATT
WOOTTON BRIDGE (St Mark) *see* Wootton *Portsm*
WOOTTON COURTENAY (All Saints) *see* Selworthy, Timberscombe, Wootton Courtenay etc *B & W*
WOOTTON FITZPAINE (not known) *see* Marshwood Vale TM *Sarum*
WOOTTON RIVERS (St Andrew) *see* Pewsey TM *Sarum*
WOOTTON ST LAWRENCE (St Lawrence) *see* Church Oakley and Wootton St Lawrence *Win*
WOOTTON WAWEN (St Peter) *Cov 7* **P** *K Coll Cam* **P-in-c** L G MORTIMER
WORCESTER (St Andrew and All Saints w St Helen) *see* Worc City St Paul and Old St Martin etc *Worc*
WORCESTER (St Barnabas) (Christ Church) *Worc 6* **P** *Bp* **TR** R G JONES, **C** C J SELBY
WORCESTER (St Clement) *Worc 6* **P** *D&C* **R** D A CHAPLIN
WORCESTER (St George w St Mary Magdalene) *Worc 6* **P** *Bp and V Claines (alt)* **V** S LOWE
WORCESTER (St John in Bedwardine) *see* St Jo in Bedwardine *Worc*
WORCESTER (St Martin in the Cornmarket) *see* Worc City St Paul and Old St Martin etc *Worc*
WORCESTER (St Michael) *Worc 3* **P** *Bp* **V** P R HOLZAPFEL
WORCESTER (St Stephen) *see* Barbourne *Worc*
WORCESTER (St Wulstan) *Worc 6* **P** *Bp* **V** M J STRANGE, **Hon C** J W BAINBRIDGE
WORCESTER (St Wulstan) *see* Warndon St Nic *Worc*
WORCESTER CITY (St Paul) (Old St Martin w St Swithun) (St Nicholas and All Saints) *Worc 6* **P** *Bp and D&C (jt)* **R** P D A COLLINS, **C** B J PYKE
WORCESTER SOUTH EAST (St Martin w St Peter) (St Mark in the Cherry Orchard) (Holy Trinity w St Matthew) *Worc 6* **P** *Patr Bd* **TR** M A O LEWIS, **TV** N M WRIGHT, A J HAWKER, P E JONES, **C** S M SHARPLES
WORDSLEY (Holy Trinity) *Worc 10* **P** *Patr Bd* **TR** D A PICKEN, **TV** H C HANKE, B J RUMBOLD, **NSM** G HODGSON
WORFIELD (St Peter) *Heref 9* **P** *Trustees of the late J R S Greenshields Esq* **P-in-c** G FLEMING
WORKINGTON (St John) *Carl 7* **P** *R Workington* **V** J M COOK
WORKINGTON (St Michael) *Carl 7* **P** *Mrs E H S Thornely* **R** T H M SAMPSON
WORKSOP (St Anne) *S'well 6* **P** *Bp* **V** F T BEECH
WORKSOP (St John the Evangelist) *S'well 6* **P** *CPAS* **V** G E JONES, **C** D W BARTLETT
WORKSOP (St Paul) *S'well 6* **P** *Bp* **V** B C B BROWN
WORKSOP PRIORY (St Mary and St Cuthbert) *S'well 6* **P** *St Steph Ho Ox* **V** A R WAGSTAFF, **C** A HOWARD
WORLABY (St Clement) *Linc 6* **P** *DBP* **P-in-c** G A PLUMB
WORLDHAM, EAST (St Mary the Virgin) and WEST (St Nicholas), Hartley Mauditt w Kingsley and Oakhanger *Win 2* **P** *D&C and Bp (alt)* **V** P BRADFORD
WORLE (St Martin) (St Mark's Church Centre) *B & W 11* **P** *Ld Chan* **TR** N KENT, **TV** S S WILKINS, **NSM** J E G ANGLE
WORLESTON (St Oswald) *see* Acton and Worleston, Church Minshull etc *Ches*
WORLINGHAM (All Saints) w Barnby and North Cove *St E 14* **P** *Ld Chan* **R** A A B JONES
WORLINGTON (All Saints) *see* Mildenhall *St E*
WORLINGTON, EAST (St Mary) *see* Witheridge, Thelbridge, Creacombe, Meshaw etc *Ex*
WORLINGTON, WEST (St Mary) *as above*
WORLINGWORTH (St Mary) w Southolt, Tannington, Bedfield and Monk Soham *St E 17* **P** *Lord Henniker, R C Rous Esq and Bp, and DBP (by turn)* **R** *Vacant* (01728) 768102
WORMBRIDGE (St Peter) *see* Ewyas Harold w Dulas, Kenderchurch etc *Heref*
WORMEGAY (St Michael and All Angels and Holy Cross) *see* Tottenhill w Wormegay *Ely*
WORMHILL (St Margaret) and Peak Forest w Peak Dale and Dove Holes *Derby 4* **P** *Bp and Duke of Devonshire (jt)* **V** O J POST
WORMINGFORD (St Andrew), Mount Bures and Little Horkesley *Chelmsf 17* **P** *J J Tufnell Esq, Mrs F Reynolds, and Keble Coll Ox (jt)* **P-in-c** A M WHAWELL
WORMINGHALL (St Peter and St Paul) w Ickford, Oakley and Shabbington *Ox 21* **P** *Bp and Guild of All So (jt)* **P-in-c** A R NIXON, **NSM** E A MASON
WORMINGTON (St Katharine) *see* Alderton, Gt Washbourne, Dumbleton etc *Glouc*
WORMLEIGHTON (St Peter) *see* Priors Hardwick, Priors Marston and Wormleighton *Cov*
WORMLEY (Church Room) *see* Broxbourne w Wormley *St Alb*
WORMLEY (St Laurence) *as above*
WORMSHILL (St Giles) *see* Bredgar w Bicknor and Frinsted w Wormshill etc *Cant*
WORPLESDON (St Mary the Virgin) *Guildf 5* **P** *Eton Coll* **R** R P ROBINS, **C** H M WOODHEAD, **NSM** J BUSBY
WORSALL, HIGH AND LOW (All Saints) *York 22* **P** *Abp (3 turns), V Northallerton (1 turn)* **V** D MOORE
WORSBROUGH (St Mary) *Sheff 7* **P** *DBP* **V** D WARNER
WORSBROUGH (St Thomas) (St James) *Sheff 7* **P** *Bp and The Crown (alt)* **V** D C GAY
WORSBROUGH COMMON (St Luke) *Sheff 7* **P** *Bp* **V** J TRICKETT
WORSLEY (St Mark) *Man 2* **P** *Bp* **TR** M R AINSWORTH
WORSLEY MESNES (not known) *see* Wigan St Jas w St Thos *Liv*
WORSTEAD (St Mary), Westwick, Sloley, Swanton Abbot and Scottow *Nor 12* **P** *DBP, J T D Shaw Esq, D&C, and Bp (by turn)* **R** A R LONG
WORSTHORNE (St John the Evangelist) *Blackb 3* **P** *Trustees* **P-in-c** L LAYCOCK
WORTH (St Nicholas) *Chich 7* **P** *DBP* **TR** A PIPER, **TV** S W BARNES, G V RICKETTS
WORTH (St Peter and St Paul) *see* Woodnesborough w Worth and Staple *Cant*
WORTH MATRAVERS (St Aldhelm) *see* Kingston, Langton Matravers and Worth Matravers *Sarum*
WORTH MATRAVERS (St Nicholas) *as above*
WORTHAM (St Mary the Virgin) *see* N Hartismere *St E*
WORTHEN (All Saints) *Heref 13* **P** *New Coll Ox (8 turns), J J C Coldwell Esq (1 turn), I Chirbury (1 turn)* **R** N D MINSHALL
WORTHING Christ the King (Christ Church) (Holy Trinity) (St Matthew) (St Paul) *Chich 5* **P** *Patr Bd* **TR** G G GUINNESS, **TV** V H J GILLETT, **NSM** M E PARGETER
WORTHING (St Andrew) *Chich 5* **P** *Keble Coll Ox* **V** E J R CHOWN, **Hon C** E G OGDEN
WORTHING (St George) (Emmanuel) *Chich 5* **P** *Ch Soc Trust* **V** D E A MARROW
WORTHING (St Margaret) *see* N Elmham w Billingford and Worthing *Nor*
WORTHING, WEST (St John the Divine) *Chich 5* **P** *Bp* **V** A M MITCHAM
WORTHINGTON (St Matthew) *see* Breedon cum Isley Walton and Worthington *Leic*
WORTING (St Thomas of Canterbury) *Win 4* **P** *MMCET* **R** C J M VAUGHAN, **NSM** A J MACGREGOR
WORTLEY (St Leonard) *see* Tankersley, Thurgoland and Wortley *Sheff*
WORTLEY, NEW (St Mary's Parish Centre) *see* Armley w New Wortley *Ripon*
WORTLEY DE LEEDS (St John the Evangelist) *Ripon 6* **P** *Trustees* **V** T G WARR
WORTON (Christ Church) *see* Potterne w Worton and Marston *Sarum*
WORTON, NETHER (St James) *see* Over w Nether Worton *Ox*
WORTON, OVER (Holy Trinity) w Nether Worton *Ox 5* **P** *Exors J B Schuster Esq* **P-in-c** R A DENNISTON
WOTTON (St John the Evangelist) and Holmbury St Mary *Guildf 7* **P** *Bp and J P M H Evelyn Esq (jt)* **R** P R FLEMING
WOTTON ST MARY WITHOUT (Holy Trinity) *Glouc 5* **P** *Bp* **V** P M NUNN, **C** B V EAST
WOTTON-UNDER-EDGE (St Mary the Virgin) w Ozleworth and North Nibley *Glouc 2* **P** *Ch Ch Ox* **V** J A C MAY, **C** D M SHAW, **NSM** E M CHAPPELL
WOTTON UNDERWOOD (All Saints) *see* Ludgershall w Wotton Underwood and Ashendon *Ox*
WOUGHTON *Ox 25* **P** *Patr Bd* **TR** F J BEVERIDGE, **TV** M J KIPPAX, M A HOUSTON, **NSM** D J RUDIGER
WOUGHTON-ON-THE-GREEN (St Mary) *see* Woughton *Ox*

WOULDHAM (All Saints) *see* Burham and Wouldham *Roch*
WRABNESS (All Saints) *see* Gt Oakley w Wix and Wrabness *Chelmsf*
WRAGBY (All Saints) *Linc 11* **P-in-c** P A McCULLOCK
WRAGBY (St Michael and Our Lady) *see* Kinsley w Wragby *Wakef*
WRAMPLINGHAM (St Peter and St Paul) *see* Barnham Broom *Nor*
WRANGBROOK (St Michael) *see* Badsworth *Wakef*
WRANGLE (St Mary and St Nicholas) *see* Old Leake w Wrangle *Linc*
WRANGTHORN (St Augustine of Hippo) *see* Woodhouse and Wrangthorn *Ripon*
WRATTING, GREAT (St Mary) *see* Haverhill w Withersfield, the Wrattings etc *St E*
WRATTING, LITTLE (St Mary) *as above*
WRATTING, WEST (St Andrew) *Ely 4* **P** *D&C* **NSM** L R WICKHAM
WRAWBY (St Mary the Virgin) *see* Brigg, Wrawby and Cadney cum Howsham *Linc*
WRAXALL (All Saints) *B & W 13* **P** *Trustees* **P-in-c** C V CLARKE, **NSM** R D WATLING
WRAXALL (St Mary) *see* Melbury *Sarum*
WRAXALL, NORTH (St James) *see* Colerne w N Wraxall *Bris*
WRAXALL, SOUTH (St James) *see* Monkton Farleigh, S Wraxall and Winsley *Sarum*
WRAY (Holy Trinity) w Tatham and Tatham Fells *Blackb 15* **P** *Bp, Trustees and PCCs (jt)* **V** R F JACKSON
WRAY, LOW (St Margaret) *see* Hawkshead and Low Wray w Sawrey *Carl*
WRAYSBURY (St Andrew) *see* Riverside *Ox*
WREAKE, UPPER *Leic 3* **P** *Bp and DBP (jt)* **V** G L SPENCER
WREAY (St Mary) *Carl 3* **P** *D&C* **P-in-c** P KYBIRD, **C** H J CARTER
WRECCLESHAM (St Peter) *Guildf 3* **P** *Bp* **V** S E FORD
WRENBURY (St Margaret) *see* Baddiley and Wrenbury w Burleydam *Ches*
WRENINGHAM (All Saints) *Nor 7* **P** *Ld Chan (1 turn), Patr Bd (4 turns)* **P-in-c** J W STUBENBORD, **TV** S G STEPHENSON,
WRENTHAM (St Nicholas) w Benacre, Covehithe, Frostenden, South Cove and Henstead *St E 15* **P** *Sir John Gooch Bt* **R** C E HALLIWELL
WRENTHORPE (St Anne) *Wakef 12* **P** *Bp* **V** P WHITTINGHAM
WRESSLE (St John of Beverly) *see* Howden TM *York*
WRESTLINGWORTH (St Peter) *see* Dunton w Wrestlingworth and Eyeworth *St Alb*
WRETHAM (St Ethelbert) *see* Thetford *Nor*
WRETTON (All Saints) *see* Stoke Ferry w Wretton *Ely*
WRIBBENHALL (All Saints) *Worc 11* **P** *V Kidderminster* **P-in-c** H HUGHES
WRIGHTINGTON (St James the Great) *Blackb 4* **P** *Bp* **V** R TOWNLEY
WRINGTON (All Saints) w Butcombe *B & W 11* **P** *SMF* **R** N A HECTOR
WRITTLE (All Saints) w Highwood *Chelmsf 8* **P** *New Coll Ox* **V** R P LANE
WROCKWARDINE, The Deanery of (St Peter) *Lich 24* **P** *Patr Bd* **TR** C S COOKE, **TV** D K B HAWKINS, G HORNER, **C** P J BENTHAM, **NSM** P M MILLICHAMP
WROCKWARDINE WOOD (Holy Trinity) *Lich 22* **P** *Bp* **P-in-c** C M CASE
WROOT (St Pancras) *see* Epworth and Wroot *Linc*
WROSE (St Cuthbert) *Bradf 3* **P** *The Crown* **V** *Vacant* (01274) 611631
WROTHAM (St George) *Roch 10* **P** *D&C* **P-in-c** H W TURNER
WROUGHTON (St John the Baptist) *Bris 13* **P** *Bp* **R** M A JOHNSON, **C** J C G BROMLEY
WROXALL (St John the Evangelist) *Portsm 7* **P** *Bp* **V** A TEDMAN
WROXALL (St Leonard) *see* Hatton w Haseley, Rowington w Lowsonford etc *Cov*
WROXETER (St Mary) *see* Wrockwardine Deanery *Lich*
WROXHAM (St Mary) w Hoveton St John w Hoveton St Peter and Belaugh *Nor 12* **P** *Bp* **R** A D PARSONS
WROXTON (All Saints) *see* Ironstone *Ox*
WYBERTON (St Leodegar) *Linc 21* **P** *DBP* **R** R H IRESON
WYBUNBURY (St Chad) w Doddington (St John) *Ches 15* **P** *Bp and Sir Evelyn Broughton, Bt (jt)* **V** *Vacant* (01270) 841178
WYCH, HIGH (St James) and Gilston w Eastwick *St Alb 18* **P** *V Sawbridgeworth (2 turns), P T S Bowlby Esq (1 turn)* **R** D C CLARKE
WYCHBOLD (St Mary de Wyche) *see* Stoke Prior, Wychbold and Upton Warren *Worc*
WYCHE (All Saints) *see* Lt Malvern, Malvern Wells and Wyche *Worc*
WYCHLING (St Margaret) *see* Doddington, Newnham and Wychling *Cant*
WYCHNOR (St Leonard) *Lich 1* **P** *Personal Reps W H Harrison Esq* **V** S J MORRIS
WYCK RISSINGTON (St Laurence) *see* The Rissingtons *Glouc*
WYCLIFFE (St Mary) *see* Barningham w Hutton Magna and Wycliffe *Ripon*
WYCOMBE, HIGH (All Saints) (St Peter) *Ox 29* **P** *Patr Bd* **TR** F D HILLEBRAND, **TV** S A WHITMORE, J M WILKINSON, C J BARLEY, D B FOSTER, **C** C E WILSON, B I de la T HARTLESS, **NSM** P VINEY, M J PRAGNELL, V J BEAUMONT, M H CLEMENTS
WYCOMBE, WEST (St Laurence) (St Paul) w Bledlow Ridge, Bradenham and Radnage *Ox 29* **P** *Bp, DBP, Peache Trustees, and Sir Francis Dashwood (jt)* **P-in-c** M J GILLHAM, **C** P A GILLHAM, E M DYKE, **NSM** A C WOODS
WYCOMBE AND CHADWELL (St Mary) *see* Scalford w Goadby Marwood and Wycombe etc *Leic*
WYCOMBE LANE (St Mary) *see* Wooburn *Ox*
WYCOMBE MARSH (St Anne) *see* High Wycombe *Ox*
WYDDIAL (St Giles) *see* Hormead, Wyddial, Anstey, Brent Pelham etc *St Alb*
WYE (St Gregory and St Martin) w Brook *Cant 2* **P** *Abp* **P-in-c** D STUART-SMITH
WYE, SOUTH Team Ministry *see* Heref S Wye *Heref*
WYESHAM (St James) *see* Dixton *Heref*
WYFORDBY (St Mary) *see* Waltham on the Wolds, Stonesby, Saxby etc *Leic*
WYKE *see* Win St Matt *Win*
WYKE (Holy Trinity) *see* Bruton and Distr *B & W*
WYKE (St Mark) *Guildf 5* **P** *Bp* **V** A W A KNOWLES
WYKE (St Mary the Virgin) *Bradf 2* **P** *Bp* **P-in-c** G H COLES
WYKE REGIS (All Saints) *Sarum 5* **P** *D&C* **R** K A HUGO
WYKEHAM (All Saints) and Hutton Buscel *York 21* **P** *Viscount Downe and Sir Stephen Hastings (alt)* **V** E RICHARDS
WYKEHAM (St Nicholas) *see* Wickham *Portsm*
WYKEHAM: Broughton w North Newington, Epwell w Sibford, Shutford, Swalcliffe, and Tadmarton *Ox 5* **P** *New Coll, Worc Coll, and Lord Saye and Sele (jt)* **R** T WIMBUSH, **NSM** K WALKLATE
WYKEN (Church of Risen Christ) *see* Coventry Caludon *Cov*
WYKEN (Holy Cross) *as above*
WYKEN (St Mary Magdalene) *as above*
WYLAM (St Oswin) *Newc 3* **P** *Bp* **V** *Vacant* (01661) 853254
WYLDE GREEN (Emmanuel) *Birm 13* **P** *Bp* **V** H J PITCHFORD
WYLYE (St Mary the Virgin) *see* Yarnbury *Sarum*
WYMERING (St Peter and St Paul) *see* Widley w Wymering *Portsm*
WYMESWOLD (St Mary) and Prestwold w Hoton *Leic 7* **P** *S J Packe-Drury-Lowe Esq and Bp (by turn)* **V** *Vacant* (01509) 880275
WYMINGTON (St Lawrence) w Podington *St Alb 15* **P** *R M Orlebar Esq (1 turn), DBP (3 turns)* **R** A R H WOODWARD
WYMONDHAM (St Mary and St Thomas) *Nor 7* **P** *Bp* **V** B L GANT, **C** A C COLES
WYMONDHAM (St Peter) w Edmondthorpe, Buckminster w Sewstern, Coston and Garthorpe *Leic 3* **P** *Ld Chan and Sir Lyonel Tollemache, Bt (alt)* **P-in-c** S SAMUEL
WYMONDLEY, GREAT (St Mary the Virgin) and Little (St Mary the Virgin) w Graveley and Chivesfield *St Alb 4* **P** *Bp and MMCET (jt)* **P-in-c** M H SABELL
WYMYNSWOLD (St Margaret) *see* Nonington w Wymynswold and Goodnestone etc *Cant*
WYNYARD PARK (Chapel) *see* Grindon and Stillington *Dur*
WYRE PIDDLE (not known) *see* Fladbury, Wyre Piddle and Moor *Worc*
WYRESDALE, OVER (Christ Church) *Blackb 12* **P** *Bp* **V** *Vacant* (01524) 792393
WYRLEY, GREAT (St Mark) *Lich 3* **P** *R Cannock* **V** A F CREBER, **C** N S TODD, R BIDDLE
WYSALL (Holy Trinity) *see* Willoughby-on-the-Wolds w Wysall and Widmerpool *S'well*
WYTHALL *Birm 4* **P** *R Kings Norton* **V** P M THOMSON
WYTHAM (All Saints) *see* N Hinksey and Wytham *Ox*
WYTHBURN (not known) *see* St Johns-in-the-Vale w Wythburn *Carl*
WYTHENSHAWE Lawton Moor (St Michael and All Angels) *see* Lawton Moor *Man*
WYTHENSHAWE (St Martin) *Man 8* **P** *Bp* **V** P J DINES, **C** S G TALBOT
WYTHENSHAWE (St Richard of Chichester) *Man 8* **P** *Bp* **V** G A LAWSON
WYTHENSHAWE (William Temple Church) *Man 8* **P** *Bp* **P-in-c** A PILKINGTON

WYTHER (Venerable Bede) *Ripon 6* **P** *Bp* **V** V E JOHNSON
WYTHOP (St Margaret) *see* Cockermouth w Embleton and Wythop *Carl*
WYVERSTONE (St George) *see* Bacton w Wyverstone and Cotton *St E*
WYVILL (St Catherine) *see* Harlaxton Gp *Linc*
YAFFORTH (All Saints) *see* Ainderby Steeple w Yafforth and Kirby Wiske etc *Ripon*
YALDING (St Peter and St Paul) w Collier Street *Roch 8* **P** *Ld Chan* **V** *Vacant* (01622) 814182
YANWORTH (St Michael) *see* Chedworth, Yanworth and Stowell, Coln Rogers etc *Glouc*
YAPHAM (St Martin) *see* Barmby Moor w Allerthorpe, Fangfoss and Yapham *York*
YAPTON (St Mary) *see* Clymping and Yapton w Ford *Chich*
YARCOMBE (St John the Baptist), Membury, Upottery and Cotleigh *Ex 5* **P** *The Crown (1 turn), Bp and D&C (1 turn)* **V** A J STONE
YARDLEY (St Cyprian) Hay Mill *Birm 14* **P** *Bp* **P-in-c** M ALDERSON
YARDLEY (St Edburgha) *Birm 14* **P** *St Pet Coll Ox* **P-in-c** J H TYNDALL, **C** M E LEIGH
YARDLEY (St Lawrence) *see* Ardeley *St Alb*
YARDLEY, SOUTH (St Michael and All Angels) *Birm 14* **P** *Bp* **P-in-c** C G GRAHAM, **NSM** G R PIKE
YARDLEY GOBION (St Leonard) *see* Potterspury, Furtho, Yardley Gobion and Cosgrove *Pet*
YARDLEY HASTINGS (St Andrew), Denton and Grendon w Castle Ashby and Whiston *Pet 7* **P** *Marquess of Northampton and Bp (alt)* **R** M R RYALL
YARDLEY WOOD (Christ Church) *Birm 5* **P** *Bp* **P-in-c** J G RICHARDS
YARKHILL (St John the Baptist) *see* Tarrington w Stoke Edith, Aylton, Pixley etc *Heref*
YARLINGTON (Blessed Virgin Mary) *see* Camelot Par *B & W*
YARM (St Mary Magdalene) *York 22* **P** *Abp* **R** D W SMITH, **NSM** P W ELLIOTT, M LOCKEY
YARMOUTH (St James) *Portsm 8* **P** *Keble Coll Ox* **R** B W E BANKS, **P-in-c** B W E BANKS, **NSM** D K BELLAMY
YARMOUTH, GREAT (St John) (St Nicholas) (St Paul) (St Luke) (St Mary) *Nor 6* **P** *Patr Bd* **TR** M S WOODS, **TV** P T S KERLEY, **NSM** A W BOWLES, J M GREENWAY
YARNBURY *Sarum 16* **P** *Bp, CCC Ox, and D&C (by turn)* **R** B THOMAS
YARNFIELD (Mission Room St Barnabas) *see* Swynnerton and Tittensor *Lich*
YARNSCOMBE (St Andrew) *see* Newton Tracey, Horwood, Alverdiscott etc *Ex*
YARNTON (St Bartholomew) w Begbroke and Shipton on Cherwell *Ox 9* **P** *BNC Ox, Duke of Marlborough, and C Wolfson Trust (jt)* **R** E CRAIG
YARPOLE (St Leonard) *see* Eye, Croft w Yarpole and Lucton *Heref*
YARWELL (St Mary Magdalene) *see* Nassington w Yarwell and Woodnewton *Pet*
YATE New Town (St Mary) *Bris 7* **P** *Bp* **TR** C D SUTCH, **TV** D T R WILCOX, D G BAINBRIDGE, **C** M A CLACKER
YATELEY (St Peter) *Win 5* **P** *Bp* **V** N D BEAMER, **C** D J STRATHIE, D J CHILLMAN, **NSM** R L THOMAS, B R LILLINGTON
YATESBURY (All Saints) *see* Oldbury *Sarum*
YATTENDON (St Peter and St Paul) *see* Hermitage and Hampstead Norreys, Cold Ash etc *Ox*
YATTON (All Saints) *see* Much Marcle *Heref*
YATTON KEYNELL (St Margaret) *Bris 9* **P** *Bp* **P-in-c** R V C LEWIS, **NSM** J M HARRISON
YATTON MOOR (Blessed Virgin Mary) *B & W 13* **P** *DBF* **TR** J L RUFFLE, **TV** J J CRUSE, C M HORSEMAN
YAVERLAND (St John the Baptist) *see* Brading w Yaverland *Portsm*
YAXHAM (St Peter) *see* Mattishall w Mattishall Burgh, Welborne etc *Nor*
YAXLEY (St Mary the Virgin) *see* Eye w Braiseworth and Yaxley *St E*
YAXLEY (St Peter) and Holme w Conington *Ely 13* **P** *Ld Chan (2 turns), J H B Heathcote Esq (1 turn)* **V** T J HEGGS, **Hon C** G LIMBRICK
YEADON (St Andrew) *Bradf 4* **P** *Bp* **V** K C POTTER
YEADON (St John the Evangelist) *Bradf 4* **P** *R Guiseley w Esholt* **V** H M WIGLEY
YEALAND CONYERS (St John the Evangelist) *see* Warton St Oswald w Yealand Conyers *Blackb*
YEALMPTON (St Bartholomew) and Brixton *Ex 20* **P** *D&C Windsor and Bp (jt)* **V** *Vacant* (01752) 880229
YEARSLEY (Holy Trinity) *see* Crayke w Brandsby and Yearsley *York*
YEAVELEY (Holy Trinity) *see* Alkmonton, Cubley, Marston, Montgomery etc *Derby*
YEDINGHAM (St John the Baptist) *see* Sherburn and W and E Heslerton w Yedingham *York*
YELDEN (St Mary) *see* The Stodden Churches *St Alb*
YELDHAM, GREAT (St Andrew) *see* Upper Colne *Chelmsf*
YELDHAM, LITTLE (St John the Baptist) *as above*
YELFORD (St Nicholas and St Swithin) *see* Lower Windrush *Ox*
YELLING (Holy Cross) *see* Graveley w Papworth St Agnes w Yelling etc *Ely*
YELVERTOFT (All Saints) *see* Crick and Yelvertoft w Clay Coton and Lilbourne *Pet*
YELVERTON (St Mary) *see* Thurton *Nor*
YELVERTON (St Paul), Meavy, Sheepstor and Walkhampton *Ex 24* **P** *Patr Bd* **TR** R H TEBBS, **TV** M J LEVERTON, **NSM** J W M WEIR, M SALMON, N S SHUTT
YEOFORD CHAPEL (Holy Trinity) *see* Crediton and Shobrooke *Ex*
YEOVIL (Holy Trinity) w Barwick *B & W 7* **P** *Ms Y L Bennett and Ms R S Mullen (1 turn), The Crown (3 turns)* **R** J D BENNETT
YEOVIL (St Andrew) (St John the Baptist) w Kingston Pitney *B & W 7* **P** *Mrs S W Rawlins (3 turns), DBP (1 turn)* **R** I G HUGHES, **C** H F THOMAS
YEOVIL (St Michael and All Angels) *B & W 7* **P** *Bp* **V** M D ELLIS, **C** N P A PNEMATICATOS
YEOVIL (St Peter) *see* Preston Plucknett *B & W*
YEOVIL MARSH (All Saints) *see* Tintinhull w Chilthorne Domer, Yeovil Marsh etc *B & W*
YETMINSTER (St Andrew) w Ryme Intrinseca and High Stoy *Sarum 4* **P** *Duchy of Cornwall (1 turn), Bp (3 turns)* **P-in-c** S R BATTY
YIEWSLEY (St Matthew) *Lon 24* **P** *V Hillingdon* **P-in-c** D J WALLER
YOCKLETON (Holy Trinity) *Heref 13* **P** *Bp* **P-in-c** C B BULL
YORK Acomb (St Aidan) *see* Acomb St Steph *York*
YORK (All Saints) *see* Huntington *York*
YORK (All Saints) North Street *York 8* **P** *D&C* **P-in-c** E E S JONES
YORK (All Saints) Pavement w St Crux (St Martin) (St Helen) (St Denys) *York 8* **P** *Abp* **TR** D M PORTER
YORK (Christ Church) *see* Heworth *York*
YORK (Holy Redeemer) *see* Acomb H Redeemer *York*
YORK (Holy Trinity) *see* Heworth *York*
YORK Holy Trinity Goodramgate w St Maurice *York* **V** *Vacant*
YORK (Holy Trinity) Micklegate *see* Micklegate H Trin and Bishophill Junior St Mary *York*
YORK (James the Deacon) *see* Acomb Moor *York*
YORK (St Barnabas) *York 8* **P** *CPAS* **P-in-c** S R STANLEY, **NSM** K BURNETT-HALL
YORK (St Chad) *York 8* **P** *Abp* **V** D B EMMOTT
YORK (St Clement w St Mary) Bishophill Senior *York 8* **P** *Abp* **R** E E S JONES
YORK (St Edward the Confessor) *see* Dringhouses *York*
YORK (St Hilda) *York 8* **P** *Abp* **V** M LOCKHART
YORK (St Lawrence w St Nicholas) *York 8* **P** *D&C* **V** P S THORNTON
YORK (St Luke) *York 8* **P** *Abp* **V** J McGRATH
YORK (St Martin-cum-Gregory) *see* Micklegate H Trin and Bishophill Junior St Mary *York*
YORK (St Mary) Bishophill Junior *as above*
YORK (St Michael-le-Belfrey) (St Cuthbert) *York 8* **P** *Abp* **V** D P WHITE, **C** F S K WAINAINA, **NSM** W J ROBERTS
YORK (St Olave w St Giles) *York 8* **P** *Abp* **V** A C HODGE, **NSM** R M OWEN, P J CUNNINGHAM
YORK (St Oswald) *see* Fulford *York*
YORK (St Paul) Holgate Road *York 8* **P** *CPAS* **R** D R WOOLDRIDGE, **C** B HERITAGE
YORK (St Philip and St James) *see* Clifton *York*
YORK (St Stephen) *see* Acomb St Steph *York*
YORK (St Thomas w St Maurice) *York 8* **P** *Abp* **V** P WORDSWORTH
YORK (St Wulstan) *see* Heworth *York*
YORKLEY, LOWER (St Luke's Church Centre) *see* Dean Forest St Paul *Glouc*
YOULGREAVE (All Saints), Middleton, Stanton-in-Peak and Birchover *Derby 2* **P** *Duke of Devonshire and N B B Davie-Thornhill Esq (jt)* **V** R TAYLOR
YOXALL (St Peter) *Lich 1* **P** *Bp* **P-in-c** J G LISTER
YOXFORD (St Peter) and Peasenhall w Sibton *St E 19* **P** *Bp, Exors Lt Col J A Brooke and CPAS (jt) (alt)* **V** P H MILLER
ZEAL, SOUTH (St Mary) *see* S Tawton and Belstone *Ex*
ZEAL MONACHORUM (St Peter) *Ex 2* **P** *DBP* **R** J C HALL, **Hon C** G SAUNDERS
ZEALS (St Martin) *see* Upper Stour *Sarum*
ZENNOR (St Senera) *Truro 5* **P** *Bp* **V** *Vacant* (01736) 796955

WELSH BENEFICES AND CHURCHES

An index of the benefices of the Church in Wales (shown in bold type) together with entries for churches and other licensed places of worship. Where the church name is the same as the benefice (or the first place name in the benefice), the church entry is omitted. Church dedications are indicated in brackets.

The benefice entry gives the full legal name, followed by the diocese, the deanery number (page 842), and the name(s) and appointment(s) of the clergy serving there (if there are none, the telephone number of the parsonage house is given). The following are the main abbreviations used; for others see the full list of abbreviations.

C	Curate	**P-in-c**	Priest-in-charge
C-in-c	Curate-in-charge	**Par Dn**	Parish Deacon
Dn-in-c	Deacon-in-charge	**R**	Rector
Dss	Deaconess	**TM**	Team Minister
Hon C	Honorary Curate	**TV**	Team Vicar
NSM	Non-stipendiary Minister	**V**	Vicar

ABBEY CWMHIR (St Mary the Virgin) *see* Llanbadarn Fawr, Llandegley and Llanfihangel etc *S & B*

ABERAERON (Holy Trinity) *see* Henfynyw w Aberaeron and Llanddewi Aberarth *St D*

ABERAMAN (St Margaret) and Abercwmboi w Cwmaman *Llan 7* **V** R DONKIN, **NSM** B L JONES

ABERAVON (Holy Trinity) *Llan 8* **V** P R GOULD

ABERAVON (St Mary) (St Paul) *Llan 8* **V** S BARNES, **C** M A STARK

ABERBARGOED (St Peter) *see* Bedwellty *Mon*

ABERCANAID (St Peter) *Llan 9* **P-in-c** G G FOSTER

ABERCARN *Mon 7* **V** N J HODGE

ABERCRAF (St David) w Callwen w Capel Coelbren *S & B 7* **I** D J PHIPPS

ABERCWMBOI *see* Aberaman and Abercwmboi w Cwmaman *Llan*

ABERCYNON (St Donat) (St Gwynno) *Llan 7* **V** P S WEEDING

ABERDARE (St Fagan) *Llan 7* **V** S J RYAN

ABERDARE (St John the Baptist) (St Elvan) (St Matthew) (St John the Evangelist) *Llan 7* **V** R E DAVIES, **C** B TAYLOR

ABERDARON (St Hywyn) w Rhiw and Llanfaelrhys w Llangwnnadl and Penllech *Ban 11* **R** C J R ARMSTRONG

ABERDYFI (St Peter) *see* Llanegryn w Aberdyfi w Tywyn *Ban*

ABEREDW (St Cewydd) w Llandeilo Graban and Llanbadarn-y-Garreg w Crickadarn and Gwenddwr *S & B 2* **V** A C CHARTERS

ABERERCH (St Cawrdaf) *see* Denio w Abererch *Ban*

ABERFFRAW (St Beuno) *see* Trefdraeth w Aberffraw and Llangwyfan etc *Ban*

ABERGAVENNY (Holy Trinity) (Christ Church) *Mon 1* **V** R P MATTHEWS

ABERGAVENNY (St Mary) (Christchurch) w Llanwenarth Citra *Mon 1* **V** J H WINSTON, **C** J S BRAY, **NSM** P F COLEMAN

ABERGELE (St Michael) (St David) *St As 6* **V** D J ROBERTS, **C** P A RIMMER

ABERGORLECH (St David) *see* Brechfa w Abergorlech etc *St D*

ABERGWILI (St David) w Llanfihangel-uwch-Gwili and Capel-y-Groes *St D 11* **V** J K DAVIES

ABERGWYNFI (St Thomas) *see* Glyncorrwg w Afan Vale and Cymmer Afan *Llan*

ABERGWYNGREGYN (St Bodfan) *see* Llanfairfechan w Abergwyngregyn *Ban*

ABERGYNOLWYN *see* Llanegryn w Aberdyfi w Tywyn *Ban*

ABERHAFESP (St Gwynog) *see* Newtown w Llanllwchaiarn w Aberhafesp *St As*

ABERKENFIG (St John) *see* Penyfai w Tondu *Llan*

ABERNANT (St Lucia) *see* Tre-lech a'r Betws w Abernant and Llanwinio *St D*

ABERNANT (St Matthew) *see* Aberdare St Jo *Llan*

ABERPERGWM (St Cadoc) and Blaengwrach *Llan 10* **V** R A ANGEL

ABERPORTH (St Cynwyl) w Tremain w Blaenporth and Betws Ifan *St D 6* **V** E J EDMUNDS

ABERSYCHAN and Garndiffaith *Mon 10* **V** A W TYLER

ABERTILLERY (St Michael) w Cwmtillery w Six Bells *Mon 8* **V** D NICHOLSON, **C** T R PRESCOTT

ABERTYSSWG (St Paul) *see* New Tredegar *Mon*

ABERYSKIR (St Mary and St Cynidr) *see* Trallwng, Bettws Penpont w Aberyskir etc *S & B*

ABERYSTWYTH (St Michael) (Holy Trinity) (St Mary) (St Anne) *St D 10* **R** S R BELL, **TV** A T G JOHN, C HUGHES, **C** H N L LATHAM, E M GREEN, **NSM** J WIGLEY

AFAN VALE *see* Glyncorrwg w Afan Vale and Cymmer Afan *Llan*

ALLTMAWR (St Mauritius) *see* Builth and Llanddewi'r Cwm w Llangynog etc *S & B*

ALLTWEN (St John the Baptist) *see* Cilybebyll *Llan*

AMBLESTON (St Mary) *see* Spittal w Trefgarn and Ambleston w St Dogwells *St D*

AMLWCH (St Eleth) (St Peter) (St Gwenllwyfo) (St Eilian) *Ban 6* **P-in-c** R W TOWNSEND

AMMANFORD (All Saints) *see* Betws w Ammanford *St D*

AMMANFORD (St Michael) *as above*

AMROTH (St Elidyr) *see* St Issell's and Amroth *St D*

ANGLE (St Mary) *see* Castlemartin w Warren and Angle etc *St D*

ARTHOG (St Catherine) w Fairbourne w Llangelynnin w Rhoslefain *Ban 12* **V** *Vacant* (01341) 250737

BAGILLT (St Mary) (St Peter) *St As 4* **V** B TAYLOR

BAGLAN (St Catherine) (St Baglan) *Llan 8* **V** D W LEWIS, **C** G H GREEN

BALA (Christ Church) *see* Llanycil w Bala and Frongoch and Llangower etc *St As*

BANGOR (Cathedral of St Deiniol) (St Mary) (Eglwys y Groes) (St James) (St David) (St Peter) *Ban 1* **R** A J HAWKINS, **TV** W ROBERTS, **P-in-c** K L SANDELLS-REES, **C** L J PERRY

BANGOR MONACHORUM (St Dunawd) and Worthenbury *St As 11* **R** P R OWENS

BANGOR TEIFI (St David) w Henllan and Llanfairorllwyn w Llangynllo *St D 7* **R** *Vacant* (01559) 370463

BARGOED (St Gwladys) and Deri w Brithdir *Llan 2* **V** *Vacant* (01443) 831069

BARMOUTH *see* Llanaber w Caerdeon *Ban*

BARRY (All Saints) (St John w St Baruc) *Llan 6* **R** J G D OEPPEN, **C** C R LEWIS-JENKINS, P N THOMPSON

BARRY (St Paul) *see* Merthyr Dyfan *Llan*

BASSALEG (St Basil) *Mon 6* **TR** J T LEWIS, **TV** V J PAYNE, **C** O HARRIS, **NSM** P D CROCKER

BATTLE (St Cynog) *see* Brecon St Mary and Battle w Llanddew *S & B*

BEAUFORT (St Andrew) *see* Ebbw Vale *Mon*

BEAUFORT (St David) *as above*

BEAUMARIS (St Mary and St Nicholas) (St Catherine) (St Seiriol) (St Cawrdaf) (St Michael) *Ban 5* **R** G M HUGHES

BEDDGELERT (St Mary) *see* Penrhyndeudraeth w Llanfrothen w Beddgelert *Ban*

BEDLINOG (St Cadoc) *see* Treharris w Bedlinog *Llan*

BEDLINOG (St Mary) *as above*

BEDWAS (St Barrwg) and Rudry *Mon 6* **R** R JEFFORD

BEDWELLTY (St Sannan) *Mon 7* **V** D J CARPENTER

BEGELLY (St Mary) w Ludchurch and Crunwere *St D 4* **R** N CALE

BEGUILDY (St Michael and All Angels) (St Peter) and Heyope *S & B 5* **V** G L J WARRINGTON

BENLLECH (St Andrew) *see* Llanfair Mathafarn Eithaf w Llanbedrgoch *Ban*

BERRIEW (St Beuno) and Manafon *St As 10* **V** T W PRITCHARD

BERSE (Parish Church) and Southsea *St As 16* **V** D T B LEWIS

BETTISFIELD (St John the Baptist) *see* Hanmer, Bronington, Bettisfield, Tallarn Green *St As*

BETTWS *see* Trallwng, Bettws Penpont w Aberyskir etc *S & B*

BETTWS (St David) *see* St Brides Minor w Bettws *Llan*

BETTWS (St David) *Mon 9* **V** P H VIVASH

BETTWS CHAPEL *see* Llantillio Pertholey w Bettws Chpl etc *Mon*

BETTWS DISSERTH (St Mary) *see* Llanelwedd w Llanfaredd w Llansantffraed etc *S & B*

BETTWS NEWYDD (not known) w Trostrey and Kemeys Commander and Llanfihangel Gobion w Llanfair Kilgeddin *Mon 5* **R** T G CLEMENT

BETWS (Holy Trinity) *see* Glasbury and Llowes w Clyro and Betws *S & B*

BETWS (St David) w Ammanford *St D 13* **V** A F HERRICK, **C** J B DAVIES

BETWS BLEDRWS (St Bledrws or St Michael) *St D 9* **R** *Vacant*

BETWS CEDEWAIN (St Beuno) and Tregynon and Llanwyddelan *St As 7* **V** J R GUY
BETWS GARMON (St Garmon) *see* Llanbeblig w Caernarfon and Betws Garmon etc *Ban*
BETWS GWERFUL GOCH (St Mary) *see* Cerrigydrudion w Llanfihangel etc *St As*
BETWS LEUCU (St Lucia) *see* Llangeitho and Blaenpennal w Betws Leucu etc *St D*
BETWS-Y-COED (St Mary) and Capel Curig w Penmachno w Dolwyddelan *Ban 2* **V** C J D PROBERT
BETWS-YN-RHOS (St Michael) *see* Llanelian and Betws-yn-Rhos *St As*
BEULAH *see* Llanwrtyd w Llanddulas in Tir Abad etc *S & B*
BIRCHGROVE (St John) *see* Llansamlet *S & B*
BISHOPSTON (St Teilo) *S & B 8* **R** C G LEE
BISHTON (St Cadwaladr) *Mon 4* **R** P K WALKER
BISTRE (Emmanuel) (All Saints) (St Cecilia) *St As 14* **V** J R KENNETT-ORPWOOD, **NSM** C R JAMES, P A WALKER
BLACKWOOD (St Margaret) *Mon 7* **V** D JONES
BLAENAU FFESTINIOG (St David) *see* Ffestiniog w Blaenau Ffestiniog *Ban*
BLAENAVON (St Peter) w Capel Newydd *Mon 10* **V** P C JONES
BLAENCELYN (St David) *see* Llangrannog w Llandysiliogogo w Penbryn *St D*
BLAENGARW (St James) *see* Pontycymer and Blaengarw *Llan*
BLAENGWRACH (St Mary) *see* Aberpergwm and Blaengwrach *Llan*
BLAENLLECHAU (St Thomas) *see* Ferndale w Maerdy *Llan*
BLAENPENNAL (St David) *see* Llangeitho and Blaenpennal w Betws Leucu etc *St D*
BLAENPORTH (St David) *see* Aberporth w Tremain w Blaenporth and Betws Ifan *St D*
BLAINA (St Peter) and Nantyglo *Mon 8* **R** M N PREVETT
BLEDDFA (St Mary Magdalene) *see* Whitton and Pilleth and Cascob etc *S & B*
BLETHERSTON (St Mary) *see* Llawhaden w Bletherston and Llanycefn *St D*
BODEDERN (St Edern) w Llechgynfarwy and Llechylched w Ceirchiog w Llanfihangel-yn-Nhywyn w Caergeiliog *Ban 3* **P-in-c** C M EVANS
BODELYWDDAN (St Margaret) *St As 1* **V** G B HUGHES
BODEWRYD (St Mary) *see* Llanfechell w Bodewryd w Rhosbeirio etc *Ban*
BODFARI (St Stephen) *see* Caerwys and Bodfari *St As*
BODWROG (St Twrog) *see* Llandrygarn w Bodwrog and Heneglwys etc *Ban*
BONTDDU *see* Llanaber w Caerdeon *Ban*
BONVILSTON (St Mary) *see* St Nicholas w Bonvilston and St George-super-Ely *Llan*
BONYMAEN (St Margaret) *see* Glantawe *S & B*
BORTH (St Matthew) and Eglwys-fach w Llangynfelyn *St D 10* **V** D E B FRANCIS
BORTH Y GEST *see* Ynyscynhaearn w Penmorfa and Porthmadog *Ban*
BOSHERSTON (St Michael) *see* St Petrox w Stackpole Elidor and Bosherston etc *St D*
BOTWNNOG (St Beuno) w Bryncroes (St Mary) *Ban 11* **R** P D JAMES
BOUGHROOD (St Cynog) *see* Llandefalle and Llyswen w Boughrood etc *S & B*
BOULSTON *see* Slebech and Uzmaston w Boulston *St D*
BRAWDY (St David) *see* Whitchurch w Solva and St Elvis w Brawdy etc *St D*
BRECHFA (St Teilo) w Abergorlech and Llanfihangel Rhos-y-corn *St D 14* **R** P H B THOMAS
BRECON (Cathedral of St John the Evangelist) (St Mary) and Battle w Llanddew *S & B 1* **V** E C JOHN, **C** N HOOK
BRECON (St David) w Llanspyddid and Llanilltyd *S & B 1* **V** D E THOMAS
BRIDELL (St David) *see* Cilgerran w Bridell and Llantwyd *St D*
BRIDGEND (St Illtud) *see* Newcastle *Llan*
BRIDGEND (St Mary) *see* Coity w Nolton *Llan*
BRIGHTON, NEW (St James) *see* Mold *St As*
BRITHDIR (St David) *see* Bargoed and Deri w Brithdir *Llan*
BRITHDIR (St Mark) *see* Dolgellau w Llanfachreth and Brithdir etc *Ban*
BRITHDIR (St Mary) *see* Llanrhaeadr-ym-Mochnant and Llanarmon etc *St As*
BRITON FERRY (St Clement) *see* Llansawel w Briton Ferry *Llan*
BRONGWYN (St Mary) *see* Newcastle Emlyn w Llandyfriog etc *St D*
BRONINGTON (Holy Trinity) *see* Hanmer, Bronington, Bettisfield, Tallarn Green *St As*
BRONLLYS (St Mary) and Llanfilo w Llandefaelog Tre'graig *S & B 4* **V** P DIXON
BRONWYDD (St Celynnin) *see* Llanpumsaint w Llanllawddog *St D*
BROUGHTON (St Mary) *see* Hawarden *St As*
BROUGHTON (St Paul) (St Peter) *St As 16* **V** R G OWEN
BRYMBO (St Mary) *St As 16* **V** R P BILLINGSLEY
BRYN (St Tydfil) *see* Llangynwyd w Maesteg *Llan*
BRYNAMAN (St Catherine) w Cwmllynfell *St D 13* **V** A TEALE
BRYNCETHIN *see* St Brides Minor w Bettws *Llan*
BRYNCOEDIFOR (St Paul) *see* Dolgellau w Llanfachreth and Brithdir etc *Ban*
BRYNCROES (St Mary) *see* Botwnnog w Bryncroes *Ban*
BRYNEGLWYS (St Tysilio) *St As 12* **D-in-c** M C HARVEY
BRYNFORD (St Michael) *see* Gorsedd w Brynford and Ysgeifiog *St As*
BRYNGWRAN *see* Bodedern w Llechgynfarwy and Llechylched etc *Ban*
BRYNGWYN (St Mary) *see* Newcastle Emlyn w Llandyfriog etc *St D*
BRYNGWYN (St Michael) and Newchurch and Llanbedr Painscastle and Llanddewi Fach *S & B 4* **P-in-c** T J WILLIAMS, **NSM** H J FISHER
BRYNGWYN (St Peter) *see* Raglan w Llandenny and Bryngwyn *Mon*
BRYNMAWR (St Mary the Virgin) *S & B 3* **V** N JONES
BRYNNA *see* Llanharan w Peterston-super-Montem *Llan*
BRYNYMAEN (Christ Church) w Trofarth *St As 6* **V** J M WILLIAMS
BUCKHOLT *see* Penallt and Trellech *Mon*
BUCKHOLT (St John the Baptist) *see* Monmouth *Mon*
BUCKLEY (St Matthew) (Good Shepherd) *St As 14* **V** J T HUGHES
BUILTH (St Mary) and Llanddewi'r Cwm w Llangynog and Maesmynis and Llanynys and Alltmawr *S & B 2* **V** N D HALL
BULWARK (St Christopher) *see* Chepstow *Mon*
BURRY PORT (St Mary) and Pwll *St D 12* **V** G D HARRIES, **NSM** E J W ROBERTS
BURTON (St Mary) and Rosemarket *St D 5* **R** J HALE
BUTE TOWN (St Aidan) *see* Pontlottyn w Fochriw *Llan*
BUTTINGTON (All Saints) *St As 10* **V** *Vacant* (01938) 554245
BWLCH (All Saints) *see* Llangorse, Cathedine, Llanfihangel Talyllyn etc *S & B*
BWLCHGWYN (Christ Church) *St As 16* **V** E B WILLIAMS
BWLCHYCIBAU (Christ Church) *see* Llanfyllin and Bwlchycibau *St As*
BYLCHAU (St Thomas) *see* Henllan and Llannefydd and Bylchau *St As*
CADOXTON-JUXTA-BARRY (St Cadoc) (St Mary) *Llan 6* **R** J M HUGHES
CADOXTON-JUXTA-NEATH (St Catwg) *Llan 10* **V** N LEA
CAERAU (St Cynfelin) (St Peter) *Llan 8* **V** P A DEROY-JONES, **NSM** C E LASKEY
CAERAU w Ely (St David) (St Timothy) *Llan 3* **V** J C BUTTIMORE, **C** A C N BUCKLEY
CAERDEON (St Philip) *see* Llanaber w Caerdeon *Ban*
CAEREITHIN (St Teilo) *S & B 10* **V** R P PITCHER
CAERFALLWCH (St Paul) *see* Halkyn w Caerfallwch w Rhesycae *St As*
CAERGEILIOG *see* Bodedern w Llechgynfarwy and Llechylched etc *Ban*
CAERGYBI *see* Holyhead *Ban*
CAERHUN (St Mary) w Llangelynin w Llanbedr-y-Cennin *Ban 2* **V** W BYNON
CAERLEON (St Cadoc) *Mon 9* **V** A J EDWARDS, **C** J V MOLE
CAERLEON-ULTRA-PONTEM (Holy Spirit) *see* Newport Ch Ch *Mon*
CAERNARFON (St Mary) *see* Llanbeblig w Caernarfon and Betws Garmon etc *Ban*
CAERPHILLY (St Martin) (St Catherine) (St Andrew) *Llan 2* **R** M J SHORT, **C** D K WATERS, H H E SIMON
CAERSWS (St Mary) *see* Llanwnnog and Caersws w Carno *Ban*
CAERWENT (St Stephen and St Tathan) w Dinham and Llanfair Discoed and Shirenewton w Newchurch *Mon 2* **V** H TRENCHARD, **NSM** S J HOWELLS
CAERWYS (St Michael) and Bodfari *St As 2* **R** J K MUSSON
CALDICOT (St Mary) *Mon 4* **V** P J S EDWARDS, **C** R H A JAONA, **NSM** D WOOD
CALLWEN (St John the Baptist) *see* Abercraf w Callwen w Capel Coelbren *S & B*
CAMROSE (St Ishmael) and St Lawrence w Ford and Haycastle *St D 5* **V** B JONES
CANTON (St Catherine) *Llan 3* **V** A D HUNTER
CANTON (St John) *Llan 3* **R** M W SSERUNKUMA
CANTON (St Luke) *Llan 3* **V** G F HORWOOD
CANTREF (St Mary) *see* Llanfrynach and Cantref w Llanhamlach *S & B*
CAPEL (Dewi Sant) *see* Llansadwrn w Llanwrda and Manordeilo *St D*

CAPEL BANGOR (Church) *see* Elerch w Penrhyncoch w Capel Bangor and Goginan *St D*
CAPEL COELBREN (Capel Coelbren) *see* Abercraf w Callwen w Capel Coelbren *S & B*
CAPEL COLMAN (St Colman) *see* Maenordeifi and Capel Colman w Llanfihangel etc *St D*
CAPEL CYNON (St Cynon) *see* Llanarth and Capel Cynon w Talgarreg etc *St D*
CAPEL DEWI (St David) *see* Llanfihangel-ar-arth w Capel Dewi *St D*
CAPEL GARMON *see* Llanrwst and Llanddoget and Capel Garmon *St As*
CAPEL IFAN (St John the Baptist) *see* Pontyberem *St D*
CAPEL LLANILLTERN (St Ellteyrn) *see* Llan w Capel Llanilltern *Llan*
CAPEL MAIR *see* Llangeler w Pen-Boyr *St D*
CAPEL NANTDDU *see* Cefn Coed and Capel Nantddu w Vaynor etc *S & B*
CAPEL NEWYDD (St Paul) *see* Blaenavon w Capel Newydd *Mon*
CAPEL TAFFECHAN *see* Cefn Coed and Capel Nantddu w Vaynor etc *S & B*
CAPEL TYGWYDD *see* Llandygwydd and Cenarth w Cilrhedyn etc *St D*
CAPEL-Y-FFIN (St Mary) *see* Hay w Llanigon and Capel-y-Ffin *S & B*
CAPEL-Y-GROES *see* Abergwili w Llanfihangel-uwch-Gwili etc *St D*
CARDIFF (Dewi Sant) *Llan 3* **V** A EDWARDS
CARDIFF (St Andrew and St Teilo) *Llan 3* **V** *Vacant* (01222) 32407
CARDIFF (St John the Baptist) (St James the Great) (St Michael) *Llan 3* **V** M R ELLIS, **C** A H STEVENS, M A R HILL
CARDIFF (St Mary) (St Stephen) w Cardiff (St Dyfrig and St Samson) *Llan 3* **V** K J JORDAN, **C** D C WAY
CARDIGAN (St Mary) and Mwnt and Y Ferwig *St D 6* **V** W H RICHARDS, **C** P A LEWIS
CAREW (St Mary) *see* Lamphey w Hodgeston and Carew *St D*
CARMARTHEN (St David) (Christ Church) *St D 11* **V** T G JONES
CARMARTHEN (St Peter) (St John the Evangelist) *St D 11* **V** A J R THOMAS, **C** L L RICHARDSON
CARMEL (Eglwys Fair) *see* Gors-las *St D*
CARNHEDRYN *see* Llanrhian w Llanhywel and Carnhedryn etc *St D*
CARNO (St John) *see* Llanwnnog and Caersws w Carno *Ban*
CARROG (St Ffraid) *see* Glyndyfrdwy and Llansantfraid Glyn Dyfrdwy *St As*
CASCOB (St Michael) *see* Whitton and Pilleth and Cascob etc *S & B*
CASTELL DWYRAN *see* Llanfallteg w Clunderwen and Castell Dwyran *St D*
CASTELLAN *see* Maenordeifi and Capel Colman w Llanfihangel etc *St D*
CASTLE BYTHE *see* Letterston w Llanfair Nant-y-Gof etc *St D*
CASTLE CAEREINION (St Garmon) *see* Welshpool w Castle Caereinion *St As*
CASTLEMARTIN (St Michael and All Angels) w Warren and Angle and Rhoscrowther and Pwllcrochan *St D 1* **R** A J TURNER
CATBROOK (St John the Baptist) *see* Penallt and Trellech *Mon*
CATHEDINE (St Michael) *see* Llangorse, Cathedine, Llanfihangel Talyllyn etc *S & B*
CEFN (St Mary) (All Saints) *St As 1* **R** *Vacant*
CEFN COED (St John the Baptist) and Capel Nantddu w Vaynor and Capel Taffechan *S & B 1* **V** B H JOHN
CEFN CRIBWR (St Colman) *see* Kenfig Hill *Llan*
CEFN FOREST (St Thomas) *see* Fleur-de-Lis *Mon*
CEFN HENGOED (St Anne) *see* Gelligaer *Llan*
CEFN PENNAR (St Illtyd) *see* Mountain Ash *Llan*
CEFNLLYS (St Michael) *see* Llandrindod w Cefnllys and Disserth *S & B*
CEIRCHIOG (St David) *see* Bodedern w Llechgynfarwy and Llechylched etc *Ban*
CELLAN (All Saints) *see* Llanddewi Brefi w Llanbadarn Odwyn, Cellan etc *St D*
CEMAES *see* Llanfechell w Bodewryd w Rhosbeirio etc *Ban*
CEMAIS (St Tydecho) *see* Mallwyd w Cemais, Llanymawddwy, Darowen etc *Ban*
CENARTH (St Llawddog) *see* Llandygwydd and Cenarth w Cilrhedyn etc *St D*
CERRIGCEINWEN (St Ceinwen) *see* Llangefni w Tregaean and Llangristiolus etc *Ban*
CERRIGYDRUDION (St Mary Magdalene) w Llanfihangel Glyn Myfyr and Llangwm w Ysbyty Ifan and Pentrevoelas and Betws Gwerful Goch and Dinmael *St As 12* **R** S BRUSH
CHEPSTOW (St Mary) *Mon 2* **V** J P HARRIS
CHERITON *see* St Petrox w Stackpole Elidor and Bosherston etc *St D*
CHERITON (St Cadoc) *see* Llanrhidian w Llanmadoc and Cheriton *S & B*
CHIRK (St Mary) *St As 13* **V** M B ROBERTS
CIL-Y-CWM (St Michael) and Ystrad-ffin w Rhandirmwyn Llanfair-ar-y-Bryn *St D 14* **V** J T WILLIAMS
CILCAIN (St Mary) and Nannerch and Rhyd-y-mwyn *St As 14* **R** R C PULLEN
CILCENNIN (Holy Trinity) *see* Llanfihangel Ystrad and Cilcennin w Trefilan etc *St D*
CILFYNYDD (St Luke) *Llan 11* **P-in-c** N J K COURT
CILGERRAN (St Llawddog) w Bridell and Llantwyd *St D 6* **R** E L THOMAS
CILGWYN (St Mary) *see* Newport w Cilgwyn and Dinas w Llanllawer *St D*
CILIAU AERON (St Michael) *see* Llanerch Aeron w Ciliau Aeron and Dihewyd etc *St D*
CILRHEDYN *see* Llandygwydd and Cenarth w Cilrhedyn etc *St D*
CILYBEBYLL (St John the Evangelist) *Llan 10* **R** N R SANDFORD
CILYMAENLLWYD (St Philip and St James) *see* Llandysilio w Egremont and Llanglydwen etc *St D*
CLARBESTON (St Martin of Tours) *see* Wiston w Walton E and Clarbeston *St D*
CLOCAENOG (St Foddhyd) *see* Llanfwrog and Clocaenog and Gyffylliog *St As*
CLUNDERWEN (St David) *see* Llanfallteg w Clunderwen and Castell Dwyran *St D*
CLYDACH (St John the Evangelist) (St Mary) (St Michael) *S & B 7* **V** D H E MOSFORD, **C** A K HOLMES, **NSM** J M PHILLIPS
CLYDACH VALE (St Thomas) *see* Tonypandy w Clydach Vale *Llan*
CLYDAU (St Clydai) *see* Maenordeifi and Capel Colman w Llanfihangel etc *St D*
CLYNNOG FAWR (St Beuno) *see* Llanaelhaearn w Clynnog Fawr *Ban*
CLYRO (St Michael and All Angels) *see* Glasbury and Llowes w Clyro and Betws *S & B*
CLYTHA *see* Llanddewi Rhydderch and Llangattock etc *Mon*
COCKETT (St Peter) *see* Swansea St Pet *S & B*
COEDKERNEW *see* Marshfield and Peterstone Wentloog etc *Mon*
COEDYPAEN (Christchurch) *see* Llangybi and Coedypaen w Llanbadoc *Mon*
COETMOR (Church) *see* Glanogwen *Ban*
COITY (St Mary) w Nolton *Llan 1* **R** D YEOMAN, **C** P K McMULLEN, R W H ALLEN
COLVA (St David) *see* New Radnor and Llanfihangel Nantmelan etc *S & B*
COLWINSTON (St Michael) w Llandow and Llysworney *Llan 4* **R** P M LEONARD
COLWYN (St Catherine) (St John the Baptist) *St As 6* **V** D V GRIFFITH
COLWYN BAY (St Paul) (St Andrew) (St David) *St As 6* **V** J T EVANS, **C** S M EDWARDS
COMINS COCH *see* Llanbadarn Fawr *St D*
CONNAH'S QUAY (St Mark) (St David's Mission Church) *St As 14* **V** P H VARAH
CONWY (St Mary and All Saints) w Gyffin *Ban 2* **V** P R JONES
CORRIS (Holy Trinity) *see* Pennal w Corris and Esgairgeiliog *Ban*
CORWEN (St Mael and St Sulien) and Llangar w Gwyddelwern and Llawrybetws *St As 12* **C** H FENTON
COSHESTON (St Michael) w Nash and Upton *St D 1* **R** R A GORDON
COWBRIDGE (Holy Cross) *Llan 4* **R** R M E PATERSON, **TV** D Y L HELLARD, G MILLAR, **C** V L PARKINSON
COYCHURCH (St Crallo) w Llangan and St Mary Hill *Llan 1* **R** K ANDREWS
COYTREAHEN (St Thomas) *see* Penyfai w Tondu *Llan*
CRAI (St Ilid) *see* Llywel and Traean-glas w Llanulid *S & B*
CREGRINA (St David) *see* Llanelwedd w Llanfaredd w Llansantffraed etc *S & B*
CRIBYN (St Silin) *see* Llanfihangel Ystrad and Cilcennin w Trefilan etc *St D*
CRICCIETH (St Catherine) w Treflys *Ban 10* **R** F J S DAVIES, **NSM** S WILLIAMS
CRICKADARN (St Mary) *see* Aberedw w Llandeilo Graban and Llanbadarn etc *S & B*
CRICKHOWELL (St Edmund) w Cwmdu and Tretower *S & B 3* **V** J L VICKERY
CRIGGION (St Michael) *see* Llandysilio and Penrhos and Llandrinio etc *St As*
CRINDAU (All Saints) *see* Newport All SS *Mon*

CRINOW (St Teilo) *see* Narberth w Mounton w Robeston Wathen and Crinow *St D*
CROESCEILIOG (St Mary) *see* Cwmbran *Mon*
CROESERW (St Clare) *see* Glyncorrwg w Afan Vale and Cymmer Afan *Llan*
CROSS HANDS (St Anne) *see* Gors-las *St D*
CROSS INN (Holy Trinity) *see* Llanllwchaearn and Llanina *St D*
CROSS KEYS (St Catherine) *see* Risca *Mon*
CRUGYBYDDAR (St Peter) *see* Beguildy and Heyope *S & B*
CRUMLIN (St Mary) *see* Penmaen and Crumlin *Mon*
CRUNWERE (St Elidyr) *see* Begelly w Ludchurch and Crunwere *St D*
CRYNANT (St Margaret) (Chapel of Ease) *Llan 10* **V** S F MINTY
CWM (St Mael and St Sulien) *see* Dyserth and Trelawnyd and Cwm *St As*
CWM (St Paul) *see* Ebbw Vale *Mon*
CWM-COCH (St Mark) *see* Llandybie *St D*
CWMAMAN (Christ Church) *St D 13* **V** J L W WILLIAMS
CWMAMAN (St Joseph) *see* Aberaman and Abercwmboi w Cwmaman *Llan*
CWMANN (St James) *see* Pencarreg and Llanycrwys *St D*
CWMAVON (St Michael) *Llan 8* **V** K W CHANT
CWMBACH (St Mary Magdalene) *Llan 7* **V** B H SHARP
CWMBACH LLECHRYD (St John the Divine) *see* Newbridge-on-Wye and Llanfihangel Brynpabuan etc *S & B*
CWMBRAN (St Gabriel) *Mon 10* **R** M J PHILLIPS, **TV** C H A PRINCE, D V R HARVEY, **C** D RICHARDS, **NSM** J M JENKINS, E J MARTIN
CWMBWRLA (St Luke) *see* Swansea St Luke *S & B*
CWMCARN (St John the Evangelist) *Mon 7* **V** A DILWORTH
CWMCARVAN (St Clement) *see* Dingestow and Llangovan w Penyclawdd etc *Mon*
CWMDARE (St Luke) *see* Aberdare St Fagan *Llan*
CWMDDAUDDWR (St Winifred) (St Bride) w St Harmon's and Llanwrthwl *S & B 5* **V** D T HURLEY
CWMDU (St Michael the Archangel) *see* Crickhowell w Cwmdu and Tretower *S & B*
CWMDUAD (St Alban) *see* Cynwil Elfed and Newchurch *St D*
CWMFFRWD (St Anne) *see* Llangynnwr and Cwmffrwd *St D*
CWMFFRWDOER (All Saints) *see* Pontypool *Mon*
CWMLLYNFELL (St Margaret) *see* Brynaman w Cwmllynfell *St D*
CWMPARC (St George) *Llan 12* **NSM** P G COUSINS
CWMTILLERY (St Paul) *see* Abertillery w Cwmtillery w Six Bells *Mon*
CWMYOY (St Martin) *see* Llanfihangel Crucorney w Oldcastle etc *Mon*
CWRT-HENRI (St Mary) *see* Llangathen w Llanfihangel Cilfargen etc *St D*
CYDWELI (St Mary) (St Teilo) and Llandyfaelog *St D 12* **V** D T W PRICE
CYFFIG (St Cyffig) *see* Whitland w Cyffig and Henllan Amgoed etc *St D*
CYMAU (All Saints) *see* Llanfynydd *St As*
CYMMER (St John the Evangelist) and Porth *Llan 12* **V** R G LLOYD, **NSM** M J MAUND
CYMMER AFAN (St John the Evangelist) *see* Glyncorrwg w Afan Vale and Cymmer Afan *Llan*
CYNCOED (All Saints) (St Edeyrn) *Mon 6* **R** J C WOODWARD, **TV** C D CLARKE, S G CARBY
CYNWIL ELFED (St Cynwyl) and Newchurch *St D 11* **V** I D JOHN
CYNWYL GAEO (St Cynwyl) w Llansawel and Talley *St D 14* **V** D R OLIVER
DAFEN (St Michael and All Angels) *St D 12* **V** D M C DAVIES, **C** C S WEBB
DALE (St James) and St Brides w Marloes *St D 5* **V** M BEYNON
DAROWEN (St Tudur) *see* Mallwyd w Cemais, Llanymawddwy, Darowen etc *Ban*
DEFYNNOG (St Cynog) w Rhydybriw and Llandilo'r-fan *S & B 1* **V** M P WILDING
DEGANWY (All Saints) *see* Llanrhos *St As*
DENBIGH (St Mary) (St Marcella) (St David) and Nantglyn *St As 2* **R** J H C DAVIES, **C** N H WILLIAMS
DENIO (St Peter) w Abererch *Ban 11* **V** M L WILLIAMS
DERI (St Peter) *see* Bargoed and Deri w Brithdir *Llan*
DERWEN (St Mary) *see* Llanfair, Derwen, Llanelidan and Efenechtyd *St As*
DEVAUDEN (St James) *see* Itton and St Arvans w Penterry and Kilgwrrwg etc *Mon*
DIHEWYD (St Vitalis) *see* Llanerch Aeron w Ciliau Aeron and Dihewyd etc *St D*
DINAS (Mission) and Penygraig w Williamstown *Llan 12* **V** S J BODYCOMBE
DINAS (St Brynach) *see* Newport w Cilgwyn and Dinas w Llanllawer *St D*
DINGESTOW (St Dingad) and Llangovan w Penyclawdd and Tregaer and Cwmcarvan *Mon 3* **V** P M SCRIVEN
DINHAM *see* Caerwent w Dinham and Llanfair Discoed etc *Mon*
DINMAEL (St Catherine) *see* Cerrigydrudion w Llanfihangel etc *St As*
DISSERTH (St Cewydd) *see* Llandrindod w Cefnllys and Disserth *S & B*
DOLBENMAEN (St Mary) w Llanystymdwy w Llangybi and Llanarmon *Ban 10* **R** W JONES
DOLFOR (St Paul) *see* Kerry and Llanmerewig and Dolfor *St As*
DOLGARROG (St Mary) *see* Caerhun w Llangelynin w Llanbedr-y-Cennin *Ban*
DOLGELLAU (St Mary) w Llanfachreth and Brithdir and Bryncoedifor and Llanelltud *Ban 12* **R** C N COOPER, **C** K THOMPSON
DOLWYDDELAN (St Gwyddelan) *see* Betws-y-Coed and Capel Curig w Penmachno etc *Ban*
DOWLAIS (St John the Baptist) (Christ Church) *Llan 9* **R** M L WISHART
DWYGYFYLCHI or Penmaenmawr (St Gwynin) (St Seiriol) (St David) *Ban 2* **V** J POWELL
DYFFRYN *see* Llanenddwyn w Llanddwywe, Llanbedr w Llandanwg *Ban*
DYFFRYN (St Matthew) *Llan 10* **V** T G SMITH
DYFFRYN HONDDU (St Cynog) *see* Merthyr Cynog and Dyffryn Honddu etc *S & B*
DYSERTH (St Bridget) (St Michael) (St Mael and St Sulien) and Trelawnyd and Cwm *St As 1* **V** R W ROWLAND
EBBW VALE (Christchurch) (St John the Baptist) *Mon 8* **R** D J JONES, **TV** L HARRISON, B W IRESON, J M HARRIS
EDERN (St Edern) *see* Nefyn w Pistyll w Tudweiliog w Llandudwen etc *Ban*
EFENECHTYD (St Michael) *see* Llanfair, Derwen, Llanelidan and Efenechtyd *St As*
EGLWYS-FACH (St Michael) *see* Borth and Eglwys-fach w Llangynfelyn *St D*
EGLWYS FAIR GLYN-TAF *see* Whitland w Cyffig and Henllan Amgoed etc *St D*
EGLWYS GYMYN (St Margaret) *see* Pendine w Llanmiloe and Eglwys Gymyn w Marros *St D*
EGLWYS NEWYDD *see* Ysbyty Cynfyn w Llantrisant and Eglwys Newydd *St D*
EGLWYS OEN DUW *see* Llanwrtyd w Llanddulas in Tir Abad etc *S & B*
EGLWYSBREWIS (St Brewis) w St Athan w Gileston *Llan 4* **R** J W BINNY
EGLWYSFACH *see* Llansantffraid Glan Conway and Eglwysfach *St As*
EGLWYSILAN (St Ilan) *Llan 2* **R** J E PARKIN, **C** J E DAVIES
EGLWYSRHOS (St Eleri and St Mary) *see* Llanrhos *St As*
EGLWYSWEN (St Michael) *see* Nevern and Y Beifil w Eglwyswrw and Meline etc *St D*
EGLWYSWRW (St Cristiolus) *as above*
EGREMONT *see* Llandysilio w Egremont and Llanglydwen etc *St D*
ELERCH (St Peter) w Penrhyncoch w Capel Bangor and Goginan *St D 10* **V** N FAIRLAMB
ELY (St David) *see* Caerau w Ely *Llan*
ELY (St Timothy) *as above*
ERBISTOCK (St Hilary) *see* Overton and Erbistock and Penley *St As*
ESCLUSHAM (Holy Trinity) *St As 16* **V** P T ALLSWORTH
ESGAIRGEILIOG *see* Pennal w Corris and Esgairgeiliog *Ban*
EVANCOYD (St Peter) *see* New Radnor and Llanfihangel Nantmelan etc *S & B*
EWENNY (St Michael) w St Brides Major *Llan 1* **R** M R PREECE
EYTON (St Deiniol) *see* Ban Monachorum and Worthenbury *St As*
FAIRBOURNE (St Cynon) *see* Arthog w Fairbourne w Llangelynnin w Rhoslefain *Ban*
FAIRHILL *see* Cwmbran *Mon*
FAIRWATER (St Peter) *Llan 5* **V** N CAHILL
FAIRWATER (St Peter) *see* Cwmbran *Mon*
FAWR *see* Llandeilo and Taliaris *St D*
FELIN-FOEL (Holy Trinity) *St D 12* **V** A J MEATS
FELIN-GWM (St John) *see* Llanegwad w Llanfynydd *St D*
FELINDRE (St Barnabas) *see* Llangeler w Pen-Boyr *St D*
FERNDALE (St Dunstan) (St Thomas) w Maerdy *Llan 12* **V** E E DAVIES, **C** S I DAVIES
FERRYSIDE (St Thomas) *see* St Ishmael's w Llan-saint and Ferryside *St D*
FFESTINIOG (St Michael) w Blaenau Ffestiniog *Ban 7* **V** *Vacant* (01341) 247207
FFYNNONGROYW (All Saints) *see* Mostyn w Ffynnongroyw *St As*

FISHGUARD (St Mary) w Llanychar and Pontfaen w Morfil and Llanychlwydog *St D 3* **V** R M GRIFFITHS
FLEMINGSTON (St Michael) *see* Cowbridge *Llan*
FLEUR-DE-LIS (St David) *Mon 7* **V** P M WINCHESTER
FLINT (St Mary) (St Thomas) (St David) *St As 4* **R** G R JONES, **NSM** M M GRAHAM
FOCHRIW (St Mary and St Andrew) *see* Pontlottyn w Fochriw *Llan*
FORD (Church) *see* Camrose and St Lawrence w Ford and Haycastle *St D*
FORDEN (St Michael) *see* Montgomery and Forden and Llandyssil *St As*
FREYSTROP (St Justinian) *see* Llangwm w Freystrop and Johnston *St D*
FRON (Mission Church) *see* Berriew and Manafon *St As*
FRONCYSYLLTE (St David) *see* Chirk *St As*
FRONGOCH *see* Llanycil w Bala and Frongoch and Llangower etc *St As*
FURNACE (Mission Church) *see* Llanelli *St D*
GABALFA (St Mark) (Highfields Centre and Mynachdy Institute) *Llan 5* **V** W G R LEWIS
GAERWEN *see* Llanfihangel Ysgeifiog and Llanffinan etc *Ban*
GARNDIFFAITH (St John the Evangelist) *see* Abersychan and Garndiffaith *Mon*
GARTHBEIBIO (St Tydecho) and Llanerfyl and Llangadfan *St As 8* **R** *Vacant* (01938) 500231
GARTHBRENGY (St David) *see* Merthyr Cynog and Dyffryn Honddu etc *S & B*
GARTHELI (St Gartheli) *see* Llangeitho and Blaenpennal w Betws Leucu etc *St D*
GAUFRON (St David) *see* Rhayader and Nantmel *S & B*
GELLIGAER (St Catwg) (St Margaret) (St Anne) *Llan 2* **R** R S EVANS
GILESTON (St Giles) *see* Eglwysbrewis w St Athan w Gileston *Llan*
GILFACH GOCH (St Barnabas) *see* Tonyrefail w Gilfach Goch and Llandyfodwg *Llan*
GILVACH (St Margaret) *see* Gelligaer *Llan*
GLADWESTRY (St Mary) *see* New Radnor and Llanfihangel Nantmelan etc *S & B*
GLAIS (St Paul) *see* Llansamlet *S & B*
GLAN ELY (Resurrection) *Llan 3* **V** S LISK, **C** R E MOVERLEY
GLANAMAN (St Margaret) *see* Cwmaman *St D*
GLANGWRYNE (Mission Church) *see* Llangenni and Llanbedr Ystrad Yw w Patricio *S & B*
GLANOGWEN (Christ Church) *Ban 2* **V** *Vacant* (01492) 593402
GLANTAWE (St Margaret) (St Peter) *S & B 11* **V** H M LERVY
GLASBURY (St Peter) (All Saints) and Llowes w Clyro and Betws *S & B 4* **V** G M REED
GLASCOED (St Michael) *see* Usk and Monkswood w Glascoed Chpl and Gwehelog *Mon*
GLASCOMBE (St David) *see* Llanelwedd w Llanfaredd w Llansantffraed etc *S & B*
GLYN *see* Brecon St David w Llanspyddid and Llanilltyd *S & B*
GLYNCOLLWNG *see* Llanfeugan and Llanthetty and Glyncollwng etc *S & B*
GLYNCORRWG (St John the Baptist) (St Clare) (St Thomas) w Afan Vale and Cymmer Afan *Llan 8* **R** G J WAGGETT, J P W REES
GLYNDYFRDWY (St Thomas) and Llansantfraid Glyn Dyfrdwy *St As 12* **P-in-c** C A PELL
GLYNTAFF (St Mary) *Llan 11* **V** K D LERRY
GOETRE (St Peter) w Llanover *Mon 5* **R** C R F CALE
GOGINAN (Church) *see* Elerch w Penrhyncoch w Capel Bangor and Goginan *St D*
GOLDCLIFFE (St Mary Magdalen) and Whiston and Nash *Mon 4* **V** T F L GRIFFITHS
GOODWICK (St Peter) *see* Llanwnda, Goodwick, w Manorowen and Llanstinan *St D*
GORS-LAS (St Lleian) *St D 13* **V** N JOHN
GORSEDD (St Paul) w Brynford and Ysgeifiog *St As 4* **V** J W K SOMERVILLE
GORSEINON (St Catherine) *S & B 9* **V** J I HOLDSWORTH, **NSM** W G G JAMES
GOVILON (Christchurch) w Llanfoist w Llanelen *Mon 1* **R** R T GREY, **NSM** D W F ROSSITER
GOWERTON (St John the Evangelist) *S & B 9* **V** C J COLEBROOK
GRAIG (St John) *Llan 11* **V** N J K COURT
GRANDSTON (St Catherine) *see* Mathry w St Edren's and Grandston etc *St D*
GRANGETOWN (St Paul) *Llan 3* **V** L V DAVIES
GREENHILL *see* Swansea St Matt w Greenhill *S & B*
GREENWAY (St Hilary) *see* St Hilary Greenway *Mon*
GRESFORD (All Saints) *St As 16* **V** D GRIFFITHS, **NSM** V C T TUCKER, E C H OWEN
GRIFFITHSTOWN (St Hilda) *Mon 10* **V** C J WILCOX, **C** A F PYE
GROESWEN (St David) *see* Pentyrch *Llan*
GRONANT (St Winifred) *see* Llanasa *St As*
GROSMONT (St Nicholas) and Skenfrith and Llangattock Lingoed and Llanfair Chapel *Mon 1* **R** D K POPE
GUILSFIELD (St Aelhaiarn) w Pool Quay *St As 10* **R** R A BIRD
GUMFRESTON (St Lawrence) *see* Tenby *St D*
GWAENYSGOR *see* Meliden and Gwaenysgor *St As*
GWAUN-CAE-GURWEN *St D 13* **V** J G M LADD
GWEHELOG *see* Usk and Monkswood w Glascoed Chpl and Gwehelog *Mon*
GWENDDWR (St Dubricius) *see* Aberedw w Llandeilo Graban and Llanbadarn etc *S & B*
GWENLLI (St Mark) *see* Llanarth and Capel Cynon w Talgarreg etc *St D*
GWERNAFFIELD (Holy Trinity) and Llanferres *St As 14* **V** S CAWLEY, **NSM** J STEPHENS
GWERNAMYNYDD (St Mark) *see* Mold *St As*
GWERNESNEY (St Michael) *see* Llangwm Uchaf w Llangwm Isaf w Gwernesney etc *Mon*
GWERNFFRWD (St David) *see* Llanyrnewydd *S & B*
GWERSYLLT (Holy Trinity) *St As 16* **V** R J PEARCE
GWYDDELWERN (St Beuno) *see* Corwen and Llangar w Gwyddelwern and Llawrybetws *St As*
GWYNFE (All Saints) *see* Llangadog and Gwynfe w Llanddeusant *St D*
GWYTHERIN (St Winifred) *see* Llanfair Talhaearn and Llansannan etc *St As*
GYFFIN (St Benedict) *see* Conwy w Gyffin *Ban*
GYFFYLLIOG (St Mary) *see* Llanfwrog and Clocaenog and Gyffylliog *St As*
HAFOD (St John) *see* Swansea St Mark and St Jo *S & B*
HAKIN (St Mary) *see* Hubbertson *St D*
HALKYN (St Mary the Virgin) w Caerfallwch w Rhesycae *St As 4* **R** K R SOUTHERTON
HANMER (St Chad) and Bronington and Bettisfield and Tallarn Green *St As 11* **V** T J BLEWETT
HARLECH (St Tanwg) and Llanfair-juxta-Harlech w Llanfihangel-y-Traethau and Llandecwyn *Ban 7* **V** R E-G HUGHES
HAROLDSTON ST ISSELLS (St Issell) *see* Haverfordwest St Mary and St Thos w Haroldston *St D*
HAROLDSTON WEST (St Madog) *see* Walton W w Talbenny and Haroldston W *St D*
HAVERFORDWEST (St Martin) w Lambston *St D 5* **V** D J R LEAN
HAVERFORDWEST (St Mary) and St Thomas w Haroldston St Issells *St D 5* **R** D EVANS
HAWARDEN (St Deiniol) (Holy Spirit) *St As 14* **R** J B THELWELL, **TV** N BALL, M W HILL, **C** N R KING, **NSM** M QUINN
HAY (St Mary) (St John) w Llanigon and Capel-y-Ffin *S & B 4* **V** D E REES
HAYCASTLE (St Mary) *see* Camrose and St Lawrence w Ford and Haycastle *St D*
HENDY (St David) *see* Llangennech and Hendy *St D*
HENEGLWYS (St Llwydian) *see* Llandrygarn w Bodwrog and Heneglwys etc *Ban*
HENFYNYW (St David) w Aberaeron and Llanddewi Aberarth *St D 8* **V** M L REES, **C** J W SMITH, **NSM** H G LEWIS
HENLLAN (St David) *see* Bangor Teifi w Henllan and Llanfairorllwyn etc *St D*
HENLLAN (St Sadwrn) and Llannefydd and Bylchau *St As 2* **R** J P P WILLIAMS
HENLLAN AMGOED (St David) *see* Whitland w Cyffig and Henllan Amgoed etc *St D*
HENLLYS (St Peter) *see* Cwmbran *Mon*
HENRY'S MOAT (St Bernard) *see* Maenclochog and New Moat etc *St D*
HEOL-Y-CYW (St Paul) *see* Llanilid w Pencoed *Llan*
HERBRANDSTON (St Mary) and Hasguard w St Ishmael's *St D 5* **R** D PARRY
HEYOPE (St David) *see* Beguildy and Heyope *S & B*
HIGH CROSS (St Anne) *see* Bassaleg *Mon*
HIRWAUN (St Lleurwg) (St Winifred) *Llan 7* **V** H M WILLIAMS, **C** H YAHAYA
HODGESTON (Church) *see* Lamphey w Hodgeston and Carew *St D*
HOLT (St Chad) *St As 16* **V** *Vacant* (01978) 852236
HOLYHEAD (St Cybi) (Morawelon) (St Ffraid) (St Gwenfaen) *Ban 3* **R** J E NICE, **TV** C A LLEWELLYN, **C** J G PARRY
HOLYWELL (St James) (Holy Trinity) *St As 4* **V** R N PARRY, **NSM** P G TAYLOR
HOPE (Parish Church) *St As 14* **R** G L GRIFFITHS
HOWEY (St David) *see* Llandrindod w Cefnllys and Disserth *S & B*

HUBBERTSON (St David) (Holy Spirit) *St D 5* **R** P BROWN
HUNDLETON (St David) *see* Monkton *St D*
ILSTON (St Illtyd) w Pennard *S & B 8* **V** D J WILKINSON
ISYCOED (St Paul) *see* Marchwiel and Isycoed *St As*
ITTON (St Deiniol) and St Arvans w Penterry and Kilgwrrwg w Devauden *Mon 2* **V** M J GOLLOP, **NSM** M E ZORAB
JAMESTON *see* Manobier and St Florence w Redberth *St D*
JEFFREYSTON (St Jeffrey) w Reynoldston and East Williamston and Loveston *St D 4* **R** N P DAVIES
JOHNSTON (St Peter) *see* Llangwm w Freystrop and Johnston *St D*
JORDANSTON (St Cawrda) *see* Mathry w St Edren's and Grandston etc *St D*
KEMEYS COMMANDER (All Saints) *see* Bettws Newydd w Trostrey etc *Mon*
KEMEYS INFERIOR *see* Tredunnoc and Llantrisant w Llanhennock etc *Mon*
KENFIG *see* Pyle w Kenfig *Llan*
KENFIG HILL (St Theodore) (St Colman) *Llan 8* **V** G W JAMES
KERRY (St Michael) and Llanmerewig and Dolfor *St As 7* **V** M J WALKER
KILGETTY *see* Begelly w Ludchurch and Crunwere *St D*
KILGWRRWG (Holy Cross) *see* Itton and St Arvans w Penterry and Kilgwrrwg etc *Mon*
KILLAY (St Hilary) (St Martin) *S & B 6* **V** B H JONES
KILVEY (All Saints) *see* Swansea St Thos and Kilvey *S & B*
KNELSTON *see* Port Eynon w Rhosili and Llanddewi and Knelston *S & B*
KNIGHTON (St Edward) and Norton *S & B 5* **V** T J WILLIAMS, **NSM** K I WARRINGTON
LALESTON (St David) w Tythegston and Merthyr Mawr *Llan 1* **V** E J EVANS
LAMBSTON (St Ishmael) *see* Haverfordwest St Martin w Lambston *St D*
LAMPETER PONT STEFFAN (St Peter) w Silian *St D 9* **V** W S T MORGAN, **C** J L JONES, I D FORSTER
LAMPETER VELFREY (St Peter) and Llanddewi Velfrey *St D 15* **R** M G R MORRIS
LAMPHEY (St Faith and St Tyfei) w Hodgeston and Carew *St D 1* **V** G A DAVIES
LANDORE (St Paul) *S & B 10* **V** R J COSSLETT
LANGSTONE (not known) *see* Bishton *Mon*
LANKNANSH (St Mary) *see* Llantwit Major *Llan*
LAUGHARNE (St Martin) w Llansadwrnen and Llandawke *St D 15* **V** D B G DAVIES
LAVERNOCK (St Lawrence) *see* Penarth w Lavernock *Llan*
LAWRENNY (St Caradog) *see* Martletwy w Lawrenny and Minwear etc *St D*
LECKWITH *see* Llandough w Leckwith *Llan*
LETTERSTON (St Giles) w Llanfair Nant-y-Gof and Puncheston w Little Newcastle and Castle Bythe *St D 3* **R** R GRIFFITHS, **NSM** M C CHARLES
LISVANE (St Denys) *Llan 2* **V** G E WILLIAMS, **NSM** M J PRICE
LISWERRY *see* Newport St Andr *Mon*
LITTLE NEWCASTLE (St Peter) *see* Letterston w Llanfair Nant-y-Gof etc *St D*
LLAN-GAN *see* Whitland w Cyffig and Henllan Amgoed etc *St D*
LLAN-LLWCH (St Mary) w Llangain and Llangynog *St D 11* **V** R I PROTHEROE
LLAN-NON (St Non) *St D 12* **P-in-c** T J HEWITT
LLAN-SAINT (All Saints) *see* St Ishmael's w Llan-saint and Ferryside *St D*
LLAN-Y-BRI (Holy Trinity) *see* Llansteffan and Llan-y-bri etc *St D*
LLANABER (St Mary) (St John) (St David) w Caerdeon *Ban 7* **R** P W D FLAVELL
LLANAELHAEARN (St Aelhaiarn) w Clynnog Fawr *Ban 1* **R** I THOMAS
LLANAFAN FAWR (St Afan) *see* Newbridge-on-Wye and Llanfihangel Brynpabuan etc *S & B*
LLANAFAN-Y-TRAWSCOED (St Afan) *see* Llanfihangel w Llanafan and Llanwnnws etc *St D*
LLANALLGO (St Gallo) *see* Llaneugrad w Llanallgo and Penrhosllugwy etc *Ban*
LLANANNO (St Anno) *see* Llanbister and Llanbadarn Fynydd w Llananno etc *S & B*
LLANARMON (St Garmon) *see* Dolbenmaen w Llanystymdwy w Llangybi etc *Ban*
LLANARMON DYFFRYN CEIRIOG (St Garmon) *see* Llansantffraid and Llanarmon and Pontfadog *St As*
LLANARMON MYNYD (St Garmon) *see* Llanrhaeadr-ym-Mochnant and Llanarmon etc *St As*
LLANARMON YN IAL (St Garmon) *see* Llandegla and Llanarmon yn Ial *St As*
LLANARTH (St David) (St Teilo) and Capel Cynon w Talgarreg and (St Mark) *St D 8* **V** C L BOLTON
LLANARTH (St Teilo) *see* Llanddewi Rhydderch and Llangattock etc *Mon*
LLANARTHNE (St David) and Llanddarog *St D 11* **V** H M THOMAS
LLANASA (St Asaph and St Cyndeyrn) (St Winifred) *St As 4* **V** G H TRIMBY
LLANBABO (St Pabo) *see* Valley w Llanfachraeth *Ban*
LLANBADARN FAWR (St Padarn) *St D 10* **V** R H WILLIAMS
LLANBADARN FAWR (St Padarn) and Llandegley and Llanfihangel Rhydithon w Abbey Cwmhir *S & B 5* **R** D M GRIFFITHS
LLANBADARN FYNYDD (St Padarn) *see* Llanbister and Llanbadarn Fynydd w Llananno etc *S & B*
LLANBADARN ODWYN (St Padarn) *see* Llanddewi Brefi w Llanbadarn Odwyn, Cellan etc *St D*
LLANBADARN TREFEGLWYS (St Padarn) *see* Llansantffraed and Llanbadarn Trefeglwys etc *St D*
LLANBADARN-Y-GARREG (St Padarn) *see* Aberedw w Llandeilo Graban and Llanbadarn etc *S & B*
LLANBADOC (St Madog) *see* Llangybi and Coedypaen w Llanbadoc *Mon*
LLANBADRIG (St Padrig) *see* Llanfechell w Bodewryd w Rhosbeirio etc *Ban*
LLANBEBLIG (St Peblig) w Caernarfon and Betws Garmon w Waunfawr *Ban 1* **R** R F DONALDSON, R J HUGHES
LLANBEDR (St Peter) *see* Llanenddwyn w Llanddwywe, Llanbedr w Llandanwg *Ban*
LLANBEDR DYFFRYN CLWYD (St Peter) *see* Llangynhafal and Llanbedr Dyffryn Clwyd *St As*
LLANBEDR PAINSCASTLE (St Peter) *see* Bryngwyn and Newchurch and Llanbedr etc *S & B*
LLANBEDR-Y-CENNIN (St Peter) *see* Caerhun w Llangelynin w Llanbedr-y-Cennin *Ban*
LLANBEDR YSTRAD YW (St Peter) *see* Llangenni and Llanbedr Ystrad Yw w Patricio *S & B*
LLANBEDRGOCH (St Peter) *see* Llanfair Mathafarn Eithaf w Llanbedrgoch *Ban*
LLANBEDROG (St Pedrog) w Llannor w Llanfihangel Bachellaeth w Bodfuan *Ban 11* **R** A JONES
LLANBERIS (St Peris) (St Padarn) w Llanrug *Ban 1* **R** P HUGHES, **C** E OWEN
LLANBISTER (St Cynllo) and Llanbadarn Fynydd w Llananno and Llanddewi Ystradenni *S & B 5* **V** V C HODGSON
LLANBLETHIAN (St Blethian) *see* Cowbridge *Llan*
LLANBOIDY (St Brynach) *see* Meidrim and Llanboidy and Merthyr *St D*
LLANBRADACH (All Saints) *see* Ystrad Mynach w Llanbradach *Llan*
LLANBRYN-MAIR (St Mary) *see* Mallwyd w Cemais, Llanymawddwy, Darowen etc *Ban*
LLANCARFAN (St Cadoc) w Llantrithyd *Llan 4* **V** M DAVIES
LLANDAFF (Cathedral of St Peter and St Paul w St Dyfrig, St Teilo and St Euddogwy) w Capel Llanilltern *Llan 5* **V** J ROGERS, **NSM** R L FORD
LLANDAFF North (All Saints) *Llan 5* **V** T J G S COOPER
LLANDANWG *see* Llanenddwyn w Llanddwywe, Llanbedr w Llandanwg *Ban*
LLANDAVENNY *see* Penhow, St Brides Netherwent w Llandavenny etc *Mon*
LLANDAWKE (St Odoceus) *see* Laugharne w Llansadwrnen and Llandawke *St D*
LLANDDANIEL-FAB (St Deiniolfab) *see* Llanfihangel Ysgeifiog and Llanffinan etc *Ban*
LLANDDAROG (St Twrog) *see* Llanarthne and Llanddarog *St D*
LLANDDEINIOL (St Deiniol) *see* Llanychaearn w Llanddeiniol *St D*
LLANDDEINIOLEN (St Deiniol) *see* Llanfair-is-gaer and Llanddeiniolen *Ban*
LLANDDERFEL (St Derfel) *see* Llandrillo and Llandderfel *St As*
LLANDDEW (St David) *see* Brecon St Mary and Battle w Llanddew *S & B*
LLANDDEWI *see* Llanwrtyd w Llanddulas in Tir Abad etc *S & B*
LLANDDEWI (St David) *see* Port Eynon w Rhosili and Llanddewi and Knelston *S & B*
LLANDDEWI ABERARTH (St David) *see* Henfynyw w Aberaeron and Llanddewi Aberarth *St D*
LLANDDEWI BREFI (St David) w Llanbadarn Odwyn and Cellan w Llanfair Clydogau and Llangybi *St D 9* **V** A W WILLIAMS
LLANDDEWI FACH (St David) *see* Bryngwyn and Newchurch and Llanbedr etc *S & B*
LLANDDEWI RHONDDA (St Barnabas) *see* Pwllgwaun w Llanddewi Rhondda *Llan*
LLANDDEWI RHONDDA (St David) *as above*

LLANDDEWI RHYDDERCH (St David) and Llangattock-juxta-Usk and Llanarth w Clytha and Llansantffraed *Mon 1* **V** M S SADLER
LLANDDEWI YSTRADENNI (St David) *see* Llanbister and Llanbadarn Fynydd w Llananno etc *S & B*
LLANDDEWI'R CWM (St David) *see* Builth and Llanddewi'r Cwm w Llangynog etc *S & B*
LLANDDOGET (St Doged) *see* Llanrwst and Llanddoget and Capel Garmon *St As*
LLANDDONA (St Dona) *see* Llansadwrn w Llanddona and Llaniestyn etc *Ban*
LLANDDOWROR (St Teilo) *see* St Clears w Llangynin and Llanddowror etc *St D*
LLANDDULAS (St Cynfryd) and Llysfaen *St As 6* **R** V E LEWIS
LLANDDWYWE (St Ddwywe) *see* Llanenddwyn w Llanddwywe, Llanbedr w Llandanwg *Ban*
LLANDDYFNAN (St Ddyfnan) *see* Llansadwrn w Llanddona and Llaniestyn etc *Ban*
LLANDDYFNAN (St Deiniol) *as above*
LLANDECWYN (St Tecwyn) *see* Harlech and Llanfair-juxta-Harlech etc *Ban*
LLANDEFAELOG-FACH (St Maelog) *see* Merthyr Cynog and Dyffryn Honddu etc *S & B*
LLANDEFAELOG TRE'GRAIG *see* Bronllys and Llanfilo w Llandefaelog Tre'graig *S & B*
LLANDEFALLE (St Matthew) and Llyswen w Boughrood and Llanstephen w Talachddu *S & B 4* **R** I P CHARLESWORTH
LLANDEGFAN (St Tegfan) w Llandysilio *Ban 5* **V** J N GILLIBRAND, **Hon C** P A G WESTLAKE
LLANDEGLA (St Tecla) and Llanarmon yn Ial *St As 3* **R** C B HALL
LLANDEGLEY (St Tecla) *see* Llanbadarn Fawr, Llandegley and Llanfihangel etc *S & B*
LLANDEGVETH (St Tegfeth) *see* Llanfrechfa and Llanddewi Fach w Llandegveth *Mon*
LLANDEILO *see* Maenclochog and New Moat etc *St D*
LLANDEILO (St Teilo) and Taliaris *St D 14* **V** P J BEMENT
LLANDEILO ABERCYWYN *see* Llansteffan and Llan-y-bri etc *St D*
LLANDEILO GRABAN (St Teilo) *see* Aberedw w Llandeilo Graban and Llanbadarn etc *S & B*
LLANDEILO TAL-Y-BONT (St Teilo) (St Michael) *S & B 9* **V** J P H WALTERS
LLANDELOY (St Teilo) *see* Whitchurch w Solva and St Elvis w Brawdy etc *St D*
LLANDENNY (St John the Apostle) *see* Raglan w Llandenny and Bryngwyn *Mon*
LLANDEUSSANT (St Simon and St Jude) *see* Llangadog and Gwynfe w Llanddeusant *St D*
LLANDEVAUD (St Peter) *see* Penhow, St Brides Netherwent w Llandavenny etc *Mon*
LLANDEWI FACH *see* Llanfrechfa and Llanddewi Fach w Llandegveth *Mon*
LLANDEWI SKIRRID (St David) *see* Llantillio Pertholey w Bettws Chpl etc *Mon*
LLANDEWI VELFREY (St David) *see* Lamp Velfrey and Llanddewi Velfrey *St D*
LLANDILO'R-FAN (St Teilo) *see* Defynnog w Rhydybriw and Llandilo'r-fan *S & B*
LLANDINAM (St Llonio) w Trefeglwys w Penstrowed *Ban 8* **V** M G H B TUDOR
LLANDINGAT (St Dingad) w Myddfai *St D 14* **V** B T RICE
LLANDINORWIG (Christ Church) (St Mary) w Penisa'r-waen *Ban 1* **NSM** T ROBERTS
LLANDOGO (St Oudoceus) and Tintern *Mon 2* **R** J E L WHITE
LLANDOUGH (St Dochdwy) w Leckwith *Llan 6* **R** B M LODWICK
LLANDOUGH (St Dochwy) *see* Cowbridge *Llan*
LLANDOVERY *see* Llandingat w Myddfai *St D*
LLANDOW (Holy Trinity) *see* Colwinston w Llandow and Llysworney *Llan*
LLANDRILLO (St Trilio) (St Derfel) and Llandderfel *St As 15* **V** M JONES
LLANDRILLO-YN-RHOS (St Trillo) (St George) *St As 6* **V** E G PRICE, **C** J R MATTHIAS
LLANDRINDOD (Holy Trinity) (Old Parish Church) w Cefnllys and Disserth *S & B 5* **R** G M H HUGHES, **NSM** A TWEED
LLANDRINIO (St Trinio, St Peter and St Paul) *see* Llandysilio and Penrhos and Llandrinio etc *St As*
LLANDRYGARN (St Trygarn) w Bodwrog and Heneglwys and Trewalchmai *Ban 4* **NSM** E D JERMAN
LLANDUDNO (St George) (St Tudno) (Holy Trinity) (Our Saviour) *Ban 2* **R** P J COUSINS, **C** M C PARRY, D J L ROBERTS
LLANDUDWEN (St Tudwen) *see* Nefyn w Pistyll w Tudweiliog w Llandudwen etc *Ban*
LLANDULAIS IN TIR ABAD (St David) *see* Llanwrtyd w Llanddulas in Tir Abad etc *S & B*
LLANDWROG (St Twrog) and Llanwnda *Ban 1* **V** D C BRYANT
LLANDYBIE (St Tybie) *St D 13* **V** J H GRAVELL
LLANDYFAELOG (St Maelog) *see* Cydweli and Llandyfaelog *St D*
LLANDYFAN (Church) *see* Llandybie *St D*
LLANDYFODWG (St Tyfodwg) *see* Tonyrefail w Gilfach Goch and Llandyfodwg *Llan*
LLANDYFRIOG (St Tyfriog) *see* Newcastle Emlyn w Llandyfriog etc *St D*
LLANDYFRYDOG (St Tyfrydog) *see* Llanerch-y-medd *Ban*
LLANDYGAI (St Tegai) (St Ann) w Tregarth *Ban 2* **V** M PRICE-ROBERTS
LLANDYGWNNIN (St Gwyninin) *see* Botwnnog w Bryncroes *Ban*
LLANDYGWYDD (St Tygwydd) (Capel Tygwydd) and Cenarth w Cilrhedyn and Llangoedmor w Llechryd *St D 7* **V** D M MORRIS
LLANDYRNOG (St Tyrnog) (St Cwyfan) and Llangwyfan *St As 2* **R** J S DAVIES
LLANDYRY (Church) *see* Pen-bre *St D*
LLANDYSILIO (St Tysilio) *see* Llandegfan w Llandysilio *Ban*
LLANDYSILIO (St Tysilio) (St Mary) and Penrhos and Llandrinio w Criggion *St As 10* **R** H G A JALLAND
LLANDYSILIO (St Tysilio) w Egremont and Llanglydwen w Cilymaenllwyd and Llanfyrnach *St D 15* **P-in-c** A BAILEY
LLANDYSILIOGOGO (St Tysilio) *see* Llangrannog w Llandysiliogogo w Penbryn *St D*
LLANDYSSIL (St Tyssil) *see* Montgomery and Forden and Llandyssil *St As*
LLANDYSUL (St Tysul) *St D 7* **V** J H ROWLANDS, **C** P W DAVIES
LLANEDEYRN (All Saints) *see* Cyncoed *Mon*
LLANEDI (St Edith) w Tycroes and Saron *St D 13* **V** T J WILLIAMS
LLANEDWEN (St Edwen) *see* Llanfihangel Ysgeifiog and Llanffinan etc *Ban*
LLANEGRYN (St Mary and St Egryn) w Aberdyfi w Tywyn *Ban 12* **V** J M RILEY
LLANEGWAD (St Egwad) w Llanfynydd *St D 14* **V** P S JOHNES
LLANEILIAN (St Eilian) *see* Amlwch *Ban*
LLANELEN (St Helen) *see* Govilon w Llanfoist w Llanelen *Mon*
LLANELIAN (St Elian) and Betws-yn-Rhos *St As 6* **R** R H KENDRICK
LLANELIDAN (St Elidan) *see* Llanfair, Derwen, Llanelidan and Efenechtyd *St As*
LLANELLI (Christ Church) (St David) *St D 12* **V** D A WALKER
LLANELLI (St Elli) *S & B 3* **V** J R ELLIS, **NSM** J M ELLIS
LLANELLI (St Elli) (All Saints) (St Alban) *St D 12* **V** A R WILLIAMS, **C** D B DAVIES, E L MATHIAS-JONES
LLANELLI St Paul (St Peter) (St John) *St D 12* **V** M T DAVIES
LLANELLTUD (St Illtyd) *see* Dolgellau w Llanfachreth and Brithdir etc *Ban*
LLANELWEDD (St Matthew) w Llanfaredd w Llansantffraed-in-Elwell w Bettws Disserth and Cregrina w Glascombe and Rhulen *S & B 2* **V** P A C PEARCEY
LLANENDDWYN (St Enddwyn) w Llanddwywe and Llanbedr w Llandanwg *Ban 7* **R** R A BEACON, **NSM** S BEACON
LLANENGAN (St Engan) and Llangian *Ban 11* **R** W L JONES
LLANERCH AERON (St Non) w Ciliau Aeron and Dihewyd and Mydroilyn *St D 8* **R** *Vacant* (01545) 570433
LLANERCH-Y-MEDD (St Mair) (Eglwys Crist) *Ban 6* **V** *Vacant* (01248) 470585
LLANERFYL (St Erfyl) *see* Garthbeibio and Llanerfyl and Llangadfan *St As*
LLANEUGRAD (St Eugrad) w Llanallgo and Penrhosllugwy w Llanfihangel Tre'r Beirdd *Ban 6* **C** G D LOVELUCK
LLANFABON (St Mabon) (St John the Baptist) *Llan 2* **R** D S LEE
LLANFACHRAETH (St Machraeth) *see* Valley w Llanfachraeth *Ban*
LLANFACHRETH (St Machreth) *see* Dolgellau w Llanfachreth and Brithdir etc *Ban*
LLANFAELOG (St Maelog) *Ban 3* **P-in-c** M M BRADY
LLANFAELRHYS (St Maelrhys) *see* Aberdaron w Rhiw and Llanfaelrhys etc *Ban*
LLANFAES *see* Brecon St David w Llanspyddid and Llanilltyd *S & B*
LLANFAETHLU (St Maethlu) w Llanfwrog and Llanrhuddlad w Llanfair-yng-Nghornwy w Llanrhwydrus *Ban 3* **R** P H PRITCHARD
LLANFAGLAN (St Mary) *see* Llandwrog and Llanwnda *Ban*
LLANFAIR (Church) *see* Gwaun-cae-Gurwen *St D*

LLANFAIR (Church) *see* Llandingat w Myddfai *St D*
LLANFAIR (St Mary) *see* Grosmont and Skenfrith and Llangattock etc *Mon*
LLANFAIR-AR-Y-BRYN (St Mary) *see* Cil-y-Cwm and Ystrad-ffin w Rhandir-mwyn etc *St D*
LLANFAIR CAEREINION (St Mary) w Llanllugan *St As 8* **V** P K D EVANS
LLANFAIR CLYDOGAU (St Mary) *see* Llanddewi Brefi w Llanbadarn Odwyn, Cellan etc *St D*
LLANFAIR DISCOED (St Mary) *see* Caerwent w Dinham and Llanfair Discoed etc *Mon*
LLANFAIR DYFFRYN CLWYD (St Cynfarch and St Mary) (Jesus Chapel) and Derwen and Llanelidan and Efenechtyd *St As 3* **V** C N L POTTER
LLANFAIR-IS-GAER (St Mary) (Old Parish Church) and Llanddeiniolen *Ban 1* **V** *Vacant* (01286) 660547
LLANFAIR-JUXTA-HARLECH (St Mary) *see* Harlech and Llanfair-juxta-Harlech etc *Ban*
LLANFAIR KILGEDDIN *see* Bettws Newydd w Trostrey etc *Mon*
LLANFAIR MATHAFARN EITHAF (St Mary) w Llanbedrgoch *Ban 5* **R** *Vacant* (01248) 852348
LLANFAIR NANT-GWYN (St Mary) *see* Nevern and Y Beifil w Eglwyswrw and Meline etc *St D*
LLANFAIR NANT-Y-GOF (St Mary) *see* Letterston w Llanfair Nant-y-Gof etc *St D*
LLANFAIR TALHAEARN (St Mary) and Llansannan w Llangernyw and Gwytherin *St As 6* **R** *Vacant* (0174584) 273
LLANFAIR-YN-NEUBWLL *see* Holyhead *Ban*
LLANFAIR-YN-Y-CWMWD (St Mary) *see* Newborough w Llangeinwen w Llangaffo etc *Ban*
LLANFAIR-YNG-NGHORNWY (St Mary) *see* Llanfaethlu w Llanfwrog and Llanrhuddlad etc *Ban*
LLANFAIRFECHAN (St Mary) (Christ Church) w Abergwyngregyn *Ban 2* **R** *Vacant* (01492) 593402
LLANFAIRORLLWYN (St Mary) *see* Bangor Teifi w Henllan and Llanfairorllwyn etc *St D*
LLANFAIRPWLL (St Mary) w Penmynydd *Ban 5* **R** T O EVANS
LLANFALLTEG (St Mallteg) w Clunderwen and Castell Dwyran *St D 15* **P-in-c** G R RENOWDEN
LLANFAREDD (St Mary) *see* Llanelwedd w Llanfaredd w Llansantffraed etc *S & B*
LLANFECHAIN (St Garmon) *see* Llansantffraid-ym-Mechain and Llanfechain *St As*
LLANFECHAN (St Afan) *see* Llanganten and Llangammarch and Llanfechan etc *S & B*
LLANFECHELL (St Mechell) w Bodewryd w Rhosbeirio w Llanfflewin and Llanbadrig *Ban 6* **R** G W EDWARDS
LLANFERRES (St Berres) *see* Gwernaffield and Llanferres *St As*
LLANFEUGAN (St Meugan) and Llanthetty and Glyncollwng w Llansantffraed-juxta-Usk *S & B 3* **V** W S P JACKSON
LLANFFINAN (St Ffinan) *see* Llanfihangel Ysgeifiog and Llanffinan etc *Ban*
LLANFFLEWIN (St Fflewin) *see* Llanfechell w Bodewryd w Rhosbeirio etc *Ban*
LLANFIHANGEL (St Michael) *see* Llantwit Major *Llan*
LLANFIHANGEL ABERCYWYN (St Michael) *see* St Clears w Llangynin and Llanddowror etc *St D*
LLANFIHANGEL ABERGWESSIN *see* Llanwrtyd w Llanddulas in Tir Abad etc *S & B*
LLANFIHANGEL ABERYTHYCH (St Michael) *see* Llangathen w Llanfihangel Cilfargen etc *St D*
LLANFIHANGEL-AR-ARTH (St Michael) w Capel Dewi *St D 7* **V** J H A JAMES
LLANFIHANGEL BRYNPABUAN (St Michael and All Angels) *see* Newbridge-on-Wye and Llanfihangel Brynpabuan etc *S & B*
LLANFIHANGEL CILFARGEN *see* Llangathen w Llanfihangel Cilfargen etc *St D*
LLANFIHANGEL CRUCORNEY (St Michael) w Oldcastle and Cwmyoy and Llanthony *Mon 1* **V** D W T DUNN
LLANFIHANGEL FECHAN (St Michael) *see* Merthyr Cynog and Dyffryn Honddu etc *S & B*
LLANFIHANGEL GENAU'R-GLYN (St Michael) and Llangorwen *St D 10* **V** D B THOMAS
LLANFIHANGEL GLYN MYFYR (St Michael) *see* Cerrigydrudion w Llanfihangel etc *St As*
LLANFIHANGEL GOBION (St Michael) *see* Bettws Newydd w Trostrey etc *Mon*
LLANFIHANGEL HELYGEN (St Michael) *see* Llanllyr-yn-Rhos w Llanfihangel Helygen *S & B*
LLANFIHANGEL LLEDROD (St Michael) *see* Llanilar w Rhostie and Llangwyryfon etc *St D*
LLANFIHANGEL NANTBRAN (St Michael) *see* Trallwng, Bettws Penpont w Aberyskir etc *S & B*
LLANFIHANGEL NANTMELAN (St Michael) *see* New Radnor and Llanfihangel Nantmelan etc *S & B*
LLANFIHANGEL PENBEDW *see* Maenordeifi and Capel Colman w Llanfihangel etc *St D*
LLANFIHANGEL PONTYMOILE (St Michael) *see* Mamhilad and Llanfihangel Pontymoile *Mon*
LLANFIHANGEL RHOS-Y-CORN (St Michael) *see* Brechfa w Abergorlech etc *St D*
LLANFIHANGEL RHYDITHON (St Michael) *see* Llanbadarn Fawr, Llandegley and Llanfihangel etc *S & B*
LLANFIHANGEL ROGIET *see* Portskewett and Roggiett w Llanfihangel Rogiet *Mon*
LLANFIHANGEL TALYLLYN (St Michael) *see* Llangorse, Cathedine, Llanfihangel Talyllyn etc *S & B*
LLANFIHANGEL-TOR-Y-MYNYDD (St Michael) *see* Llanishen w Trellech Grange and Llanfihangel etc *Mon*
LLANFIHANGEL TRE'R BEIRDD (St Mihangel) *see* Llaneugrad w Llanallgo and Penrhosllugwy etc *Ban*
LLANFIHANGEL-UWCH-GWILI (St Michael) *see* Abergwili w Llanfihangel-uwch-Gwili etc *St D*
LLANFIHANGEL-Y-CREUDDYN (St Michael) w Llanafan-y-Trawscoed and Llanwnnws and Ysbyty Ystwyth *St D 10* **V** A C SULLY
LLANFIHANGEL-Y-PENNANT (St Michael) *see* Llanegryn w Aberdyfi w Tywyn *Ban*
LLANFIHANGEL-Y-TRAETHAU (St Michael) *see* Harlech and Llanfair-juxta-Harlech etc *Ban*
LLANFIHANGEL-YN-NHYWYN *see* Bodedern w Llechgynfarwy and Llechylched etc *Ban*
LLANFIHANGEL-YNG-NGHWYNFA (St Michael) *see* Llanwddyn and Llanfihangel and Llwydiarth *St As*
LLANFIHANGEL YSGEIFIOG (St Michael) and Llanffinan w Llanidan and Llanddaniel-fab and Llanedwen *Ban 4* **NSM** I JONES
LLANFIHANGEL-YSTERN-LLEWERN (St Michael) *see* Rockfield and St Maughen's w Llangattock etc *Mon*
LLANFIHANGEL YSTRAD (St Michael) and Cilcennin w Trefilan and Nantcwnlle *St D 8* **V** D P DAVIES, **NSM** J D E JONES
LLANFILO (St Bilo) *see* Bronllys and Llanfilo w Llandefaelog Tre'graig *S & B*
LLANFOIST (St Ffwyst) *see* Govilon w Llanfoist w Llanelen *Mon*
LLANFOR (St Mor and St Deiniol) w Rhosygwaliau *St As 15* **R** *Vacant*
LLANFRECHFA (All Saints) and Llanddewi Fach w Llandegveth *Mon 10* **V** A SILVERTHORN
LLANFROTHEN (St Brothen) *see* Penrhyndeudraeth w Llanfrothen w Beddgelert *Ban*
LLANFRYNACH (St Brynach) *see* Llandysilio w Egremont and Llanglydwen etc *St D*
LLANFRYNACH (St Brynach) *see* Cowbridge *Llan*
LLANFRYNACH (St Brynach) and Cantref w Llanhamlach *S & B 3* **V** P G R SIMS
LLANFUGAIL (St Migail) *see* Valley w Llanfachraeth *Ban*
LLANFWROG (St Mwrog and St Mary) and Clocaenog and Gyffylliog *St As 3* **R** J B DAVIES
LLANFYLLIN (St Myllin) and Bwlchycibau *St As 9* **R** M R BALKWILL
LLANFYNYDD (St Egwad) *see* Llanegwad w Llanfynydd *St D*
LLANFYNYDD (St Michael) (St Egwad) *St As 16* **R** A J POOLMAN
LLANGADFAN (St Cadfan) *see* Garthbeibio and Llanerfyl and Llangadfan *St As*
LLANGADOG (St Cadog) and Gwynfe w Llanddeusant *St D 14* **V** K M D COTTAM
LLANGADWALADR (St Cadwaladr) *see* Llansilin w Llangadwaladr and Llangedwyn *St As*
LLANGADWALADR (St Cadwaladr) *see* Trefdraeth w Aberffraw and Llangwyfan etc *Ban*
LLANGAFFO (St Caffo) *see* Newborough w Llangeinwen w Llangaffo etc *Ban*
LLANGAIN (St Cain) *see* Llan-llwch w Llangain and Llangynog *St D*
LLANGAMMARCH (St Cadmarch) *see* Llanganten and Llangammarch and Llanfechan etc *S & B*
LLANGAN (St Canna) *see* Coychurch w Llangan and St Mary Hill *Llan*
LLANGANTEN (St Cannen) and Llangammarch and Llanfechan and Llanlleonfel *S & B 2* **V** J P SMITH
LLANGAR (St John the Evangelist) *see* Corwen and Llangar w Gwyddelwern and Llawrybetws *St As*
LLANGASTY TALYLLYN (St Gastyn) *see* Llangorse, Cathedine, Llanfihangel Talyllyn etc *S & B*
LLANGATHEN (St Cathen) w Llanfihangel Cilfargen and Llanfihangel Aberythych *St D 14* **V** W R HUGHES
LLANGATTOCK (St Cattwg) and Llangyndir *S & B 3* **V** K RICHARDS, **NSM** A S ROBINSON

LLANGATTOCK-JUXTA-USK (St Cadoc) *see* Llanddewi Rhydderch and Llangattock etc *Mon*
LLANGATTOCK LINGOED (St Cadoc) *see* Grosmont and Skenfrith and Llangattock etc *Mon*
LLANGATTOCK-VIBON-AVEL (St Cadoc) *see* Rockfield and St Maughen's w Llangattock etc *Mon*
LLANGEDWYN (St Cedwyn) *see* Llansilin w Llangadwaladr and Llangedwyn *St As*
LLANGEFNI (St Cyngar) w Tregaean and Llangristiolus w Cerrigceinwen *Ban 4* **C** E J JONES
LLANGEINOR (St Ceinor) (St John the Baptist) *Llan 1* **V** C J SANDERSON
LLANGEINWEN (St Ceinwen) *see* Newborough w Llangeinwen w Llangaffo etc *Ban*
LLANGEITHO (St Ceitho) and Blaenpennal w Betws Leucu and Gartheli *St D 9* **R** *Vacant* (01974) 298937
LLANGELER (St Celer) w Pen-Boyr *St D 7* **V** E HOWELLS
LLANGELYNIN (St Celynnin) *see* Caerhun w Llangelynin w Llanbedr-y-Cennin *Ban*
LLANGELYNNIN (St Celynin) *see* Arthog w Fairbourne w Llangelynnin w Rhoslefain *Ban*
LLANGENNECH (St Gwynog) and Hendy *St D 12* **V** B D WITT
LLANGENNI (St Cenau) and Llanbedr Ystrad Yw w Patricio *S & B 3* **V** C J BLANCHARD, **NSM** R O MULLIS
LLANGENNITH (St Cenydd) *see* Reynoldston w Penrice and Llangennith *S & B*
LLANGERNYW (St Digain) *see* Llanfair Talhaearn and Llansannan etc *St As*
LLANGEVIEW (St David) *see* Llangwm Uchaf w Llangwm Isaf w Gwernesney etc *Mon*
LLANGIAN (St Gian) *see* Llanengan and Llangian *Ban*
LLANGIWG (St Ciwg) *S & B 7* **V** D T JENKINS
LLANGLYDWEN (St Cledwyn) *see* Llandysilio w Egremont and Llanglydwen etc *St D*
LLANGOEDMOR (St Cynllo) *see* Llandygwydd and Cenarth w Cilrhedyn etc *St D*
LLANGOLLEN (St Collen) (St John) w Trevor and Llantysilio *St As 13* **V** W L JONES, **C** S L BLOOMER, **NSM** D EVANS
LLANGOLMAN (St Colman) *see* Maenclochog and New Moat etc *St D*
LLANGORSE (St Paulinus), Cathedine, Llanfihangel Talyllyn, Llanywern and Llangasty Talyllyn *S & B 4* **V** R T EDWARDS, **NSM** M J F WILLETT
LLANGORWEN (All Saints) *see* Llanfihangel Genau'r-glyn and Llangorwen *St D*
LLANGOWER (St Cywair) *see* Llanycil w Bala and Frongoch and Llangower etc *St As*
LLANGRANNOG (St Carannog) w Llandysiliogogo w Penbryn *St D 8* **V** J C HARVEY
LLANGRISTIOLUS (St Cristiolus) *see* Llangefni w Tregaean and Llangristiolus etc *Ban*
LLANGUNNOG *see* Llanishen w Trellech Grange and Llanfihangel etc *Mon*
LLANGURIG (St Curig) *see* Llanidloes w Llangurig *Ban*
LLANGWLLOG (St Cwyllog) *see* Llanerch-y-medd *Ban*
LLANGWLLONG (St Anau) *as above*
LLANGWM *see* Cerrigydrudion w Llanfihangel etc *St As*
LLANGWM (St Jerome) w Freystrop and Johnston *St D 5* **R** W G HOOPER
LLANGWM ISAF (St John) *see* Llangwm Uchaf w Llangwm Isaf w Gwernesney etc *Mon*
LLANGWM UCHAF (St Jerome) w Llangwm Isaf w Gwernesney and Llangeview and Wolvesnewton *Mon 5* **V** G ASTON
LLANGWNNADL (St Gwynhoedl) *see* Aberdaron w Rhiw and Llanfaelrhys etc *Ban*
LLANGWYFAN *see* Llandyrnog and Llangwyfan *St As*
LLANGWYFAN (St Cwyfan) *see* Trefdraeth w Aberffraw and Llangwyfan etc *Ban*
LLANGWYFAN (St Cwyfan Old Church) *as above*
LLANGWYRYFON (St Ursula) *see* Llanilar w Rhostie and Llangwyryfon etc *St D*
LLANGYBI (St Cybi) *see* Dolbenmaen w Llanystymdwy w Llangybi etc *Ban*
LLANGYBI (St Cybi) *see* Llanddewi Brefi w Llanbadarn Odwyn, Cellan etc *St D*
LLANGYBI (St Cybi) and Coedypaen w Llanbadoc *Mon 5* **R** A E MORTON, **NSM** P A BRYANT
LLANGYFELACH (St David and St Cyfelach) (St Teilo-on-the-Clase) *S & B 7* **P-in-c** S SARAPUK
LLANGYNDEYRN (St Cyndeyrn) *see* Pontyates and Llangyndeyrn *St D*
LLANGYNDIR (St Cynidr and St Mary) *see* Llangattock and Llangyndir *S & B*
LLANGYNFELYN (St Cynfelyn) *see* Borth and Eglwys-fach w Llangynfelyn *St D*
LLANGYNHAFAL (St Cynhafal) and Llanbedr Dyffryn Clwyd *St As 3* **R** P R OWEN
LLANGYNIN (St Cynin) *see* St Clears w Llangynin and Llanddowror etc *St D*
LLANGYNLLO (St Cynllo) *see* Bangor Teifi w Henllan and Llanfairorllwyn etc *St D*
LLANGYNLLO (St Cynllo) *see* Whitton and Pilleth and Cascob etc *S & B*
LLANGYNNWR (St Ceinwr) and Cwmffrwd *St D 11* **V** W D A GRIFFITHS
LLANGYNOG *see* Builth and Llanddewi'r Cwm w Llangynog etc *S & B*
LLANGYNOG (St Cynog) *see* Llan-llwch w Llangain and Llangynog *St D*
LLANGYNOG (St Cynog) (St Melangel) *St As 9* **NSM** E D DAVIES
LLANGYNWYD (St Cynwyd) (St Stephen) (St Tydfil) w Maesteg *Llan 8* **V** E B THOMAS, **C** A P BOOKLESS
LLANGYNYW (St Cynyw) *see* Meifod and Llangynyw *St As*
LLANGYSTENNIN (St Cystenin) (St Michael) (St Katherine) (St Mary) *St As 5* **R** T E MART
LLANHAMLACH (St Peter and St Illtyd) *see* Llanfrynach and Cantref w Llanhamlach *S & B*
LLANHARAN (St Julius and St Aaron) w Peterston-super-Montem *Llan 1* **V** *Vacant* (01443) 226307
LLANHARRY (St Illtud) *Llan 4* **P-in-c** J G WILLIAMS
LLANHENNOCK (St John) *see* Tredunnoc and Llantrisant w Llanhennock etc *Mon*
LLANHILLETH (Christchurch) (St Mark) *Mon 8* **V** A J WAY
LLANHYWEL (St Hywel) *see* Llanrhian w Llanhywel and Carnhedryn etc *St D*
LLANIDAN (St Nidan) *see* Llanfihangel Ysgeifiog and Llanffinan etc *Ban*
LLANIDLOES (St Idloes) w Llangurig *Ban 8* **V** D J PARRY, **NSM** K FERGUSON
LLANIESTYN (St Iestyn) *see* Llansadwrn w Llanddona and Llaniestyn etc *Ban*
LLANIESTYN (St Iestyn) *see* Botwnnog w Bryncroes *Ban*
LLANIGON (St Eigon) *see* Hay w Llanigon and Capel-y-Ffin *S & B*
LLANILAR (St Hilary) w Rhostie and Llangwyryfon w Llanfihangel Lledrod *St D 10* **V** E G JONES
LLANILID (St Illid and St Curig) w Pencoed *Llan 1* **R** N P JONES
LLANILLTYD (St John) *see* Brecon St David w Llanspyddid and Llanilltyd *S & B*
LLANINA (St Ina) *see* Llanllwchaearn and Llanina *St D*
LLANISHEN (Christ Church) *Llan 2* **V** A W EVANS
LLANISHEN (St Dennis) w Trellech Grange and Llanfihangel Tor-y-Mynydd w Llangunnog and Llansoy *Mon 3* **V** G M DAVIES
LLANISHEN (St Isan) (St Faith) *Llan 2* **V** N G JONES
LLANLLAWDDOG (St Llawddog) *see* Llanpumsaint w Llanllawddog *St D*
LLANLLAWER *see* Newport w Cilgwyn and Dinas w Llanllawer *St D*
LLANLLECHID (St Llechid) (St Cross) *Ban 2* **R** D J DREDGE
LLANLLEONFEL (Parish Church) *see* Llanganten and Llangammarch and Llanfechan etc *S & B*
LLANLLIBIO *see* Valley w Llanfachraeth *Ban*
LLANLLOWELL (St Llywel) *see* Tredunnoc and Llantrisant w Llanhennock etc *Mon*
LLANLLUGAN (St Mary) *see* Llanfair Caereinion w Llanllugan *St As*
LLANLLWCHAEARN (St Llwchaiarn) and Llanina *St D 8* **R** M J NEEDS
LLANLLWCHAIARN (All Saints) *see* Newtown w Llanllwchaiarn w Aberhafesp *St As*
LLANLLWCHAIARN (St Llwchaiarn) *as above*
LLANLLWNI (St Luke or St Llonio) *see* Llanybydder and Llanwenog w Llanllwni *St D*
LLANLLYFNI (St Rhedyw) (St John) (Christ Church) *Ban 1* **R** E ROBERTS
LLANLLYR-YN-RHOS (St Llyr) w Llanfihangel Helygen *S & B 5* **P-in-c** D B JAMES
LLANMADOC (St Madoc) *see* Llanrhidian w Llanmadoc and Cheriton *S & B*
LLANMAES (St Catwg) *see* Llantwit Major *Llan*
LLANMARTIN (St Martin) *see* Bishton *Mon*
LLANMEREWIG (St Llwchaiarn) *see* Kerry and Llanmerewig and Dolfor *St As*
LLANMILOE (St Barbara) *see* Pendine w Llanmiloe and Eglwys Gymyn w Marros *St D*
LLANNEFYDD (St Nefydd and St Mary) *see* Henllan and Llannefydd and Bylchau *St As*
LLANNOR (Holy Cross) *see* Llanbedrog w Llannor w Llanfihangel etc *Ban*
LLANOVER (St Bartholomew) *see* Goetre w Llanover *Mon*
LLANPUMSAINT (Five Saints) w Llanllawddog *St D 11* **V** J O ESAU

LLANRHAEADR-YM-MOCHNANT (St Dogfan) and Llanarmon Mynyd and Pennant and Hirnant *St As 9* **V** *Vacant* (01691) 791209
LLANRHAEADR-YNG-NGHINMEIRCH (St Dyfnog) and Prion *St As 2* **V** C W EVANS
LLANRHEITHAN (St Rheithan) *see* Llanrhian w Llanhywel and Carnhedryn etc *St D*
LLANRHIAN (St Rhian) w Llanhywel and Carnhedryn w Llanrheithan *St D 3* **V** D R REES
LLANRHIDIAN (St Rhidian and St Illtyd) w Llanmadoc and Cheriton *S & B 8* **V** J W GRIFFIN
LLANRHOS (St Paul) *St As 5* **V** R H GRIFFITHS, **NSM** J H ECCLES
LLANRHUDDLAD (St Rhuddlad) *see* Llanfaethlu w Llanfwrog and Llanrhuddlad etc *Ban*
LLANRHWYDRUS *as above*
LLANRHYCHWYN (St Rhychwyn) *see* Caerhun w Llangelynin w Llanbedr-y-Cennin *Ban*
LLANRHYDD (St Meugan) *see* Ruthin w Llanrhydd *St As*
LLANRHYSTUD (St Restitutis) *see* Llansantffraed and Llanbadarn Trefeglwys etc *St D*
LLANRUG (St Gabriel) *see* Llanberis w Llanrug *Ban*
LLANRUG (St Michael) *as above*
LLANRUMNEY (St Dyfrig) *Mon 6* **V** S W FLETCHER
LLANRWST (St Grwst) and Llanddoget and Capel Garmon *St As 5* **R** *Vacant* (01492) 583579
LLANSADWRN (St Sadwrn) w Llanddona and Llaniestyn w Pentraeth w Llanddyfnan *Ban 5* **R** D PRYS
LLANSADWRN (St Sadwrn) w Llanwrda and Manordeilo *St D 14* **V** A J LEGG
LLANSADWRNEN (St Sadwrnen) *see* Laugharne w Llansadwrnen and Llandawke *St D*
LLANSAMLET (St Samlet) (St John) (St Paul) *S & B 7* **V** C M DARVILL, **C** A J PEARCE
LLANSANNAN (St Sannan) *see* Llanfair Talhaearn and Llansannan etc *St As*
LLANSANNOR (St Senwyr) *see* Cowbridge *Llan*
LLANSANTFFRAED (St Bridget) *see* Llanddewi Rhydderch and Llangattock etc *Mon*
LLANSANTFFRAED (St Bridget) and Llanbadarn Trefeglwys w Llanrhystud *St D 8* **V** M S TAYLOR
LLANSANTFFRAED-IN-ELWELL (St Bridget) *see* Llanelwedd w Llanfaredd w Llansantffraed etc *S & B*
LLANSANTFFRAED-JUXTA-USK (St Bride) *see* Llanfeugan and Llanthetty and Glyncollwng etc *S & B*
LLANSANTFFRAID GLAN CONWAY (St Ffraid) (St Martin) and Eglwysfach *St As 5* **R** K HOWARD
LLANSANTFFRAID GLYN CEIRIOG (St Ffraid) and Llanarmon Dyffryn Ceiriog and Pontfadog *St As 13* **V** M V JONES
LLANSANTFFRAID-YM-MECHAIN (St Ffraid) and Llanfechain *St As 9* **V** L ROGERS
LLANSANTFRAID GLYN DYFRDWY (St Ffraid) *see* Glyndyfrdwy and Llansantfraid Glyn Dyfrdwy *St As*
LLANSAWEL (St Mary) w Briton Ferry *Llan 10* **V** I D HAMER
LLANSAWEL (St Sawyl) *see* Cynwyl Gaeo w Llansawel and Talley *St D*
LLANSILIN (St Silin) w Llangadwaladr and Llangedwyn *St As 9* **V** C F CARTER
LLANSOY (St Tysoi) *see* Llanishen w Trellech Grange and Llanfihangel etc *Mon*
LLANSPYDDID (St Cattwg) *see* Brecon St David w Llanspyddid and Llanilltyd *S & B*
LLANSTADWEL (St Tudwal) *St D 5* **V** M K LIKEMAN
LLANSTEFFAN (St Ystyffan) and Llan-y-bri and Llandeilo Abercywyn *St D 11* **V** S E JONES
LLANSTEPHEN (St Steffan) *see* Llandefalle and Llyswen w Boughrood etc *S & B*
LLANSTINAN (St Justinian) *see* Llanwnda, Goodwick, w Manorowen and Llanstinan *St D*
LLANTARNAM (St Michael) *see* Cwmbran *Mon*
LLANTHETTY (St Tetti) *see* Llanfeugan and Llanthetty and Glyncollwng etc *S & B*
LLANTHONY (St David) *see* Llanfihangel Crucorney w Oldcastle etc *Mon*
LLANTILIO CROSSENNY (St Teilo) and Penrhos w Llanvetherine and Llanvapley *Mon 1* **V** *Vacant* (01600) 85240
LLANTILLIO PERTHOLEY (St Teilo) w Bettws Chapel and Llanddewi Skirrid *Mon 1* **V** M D VINE
LLANTOOD *see* Cilgerran w Bridell and Llantwyd *St D*
LLANTRISANT (Church) *see* Ysbyty Cynfyn w Llantrisant and Eglwys Newydd *St D*
LLANTRISANT (St Afran, St Ieuan and St Sanan) *see* Valley w Llanfachraeth *Ban*
LLANTRISANT (St Illtyd, St Gwynno and St Dyfodwg) (St Michael) (St David) *Llan 11* **C** G A BLYTH
LLANTRISANT (St Peter, St Paul and St John) *see* Tredunnoc and Llantrisant w Llanhennock etc *Mon*
LLANTRITHYD (St Illtyd) *see* Llancarfan w Llantrithyd *Llan*
LLANTWIT (St Illtyd) *see* Neath w Llantwit *Llan*
LLANTWIT FADRE (St Illtyd) (St Andrew) *Llan 11* **V** M K JONES, **C** H BUTLER
LLANTWIT MAJOR (St Illtud) (St Donat) *Llan 4* **R** D M JENKINS, **TV** P G MORRIS, M KOMOR, **C** C M HAYNES, **NSM** D V GINN
LLANTWYD (St Illtud) *see* Cilgerran w Bridell and Llantwyd *St D*
LLANTYSILIO (St Tysilio) *see* Llangollen w Trevor and Llantysilio *St As*
LLANULID (St Ilid) *see* Llywel and Traean-glas w Llanulid *S & B*
LLANUWCHLLYN (St Deiniol) *see* Llanycil w Bala and Frongoch and Llangower etc *St As*
LLANVACHES (St Dyfrig) *see* Penhow, St Brides Netherwent w Llandavenny etc *Mon*
LLANVAPLEY (St Mable) *see* Llantilio Crossenny w Penrhos, Llanvetherine etc *Mon*
LLANVETHERINE (St James the Elder) *as above*
LLANWDDYN (St Wyddyn) and Llanfihangel-yng-Nghwynfa and Llwydiarth *St As 9* **V** *Vacant* (01691) 791209
LLANWELLWYFO (St Gwenllwyfo) *see* Amlwch *Ban*
LLANWENARTH CITRA (St Peter) *see* Abergavenny St Mary w Llanwenarth Citra *Mon*
LLANWENOG (St Gwenog) *see* Llanybydder and Llanwenog w Llanllwni *St D*
LLANWERN (St Mary) *see* Bishton *Mon*
LLANWINIO (St Gwynio) *see* Tre-lech a'r Betws w Abernant and Llanwinio *St D*
LLANWNDA (St Baglan Old Church) *see* Llandwrog and Llanwnda *Ban*
LLANWNDA (St Gwyndaf) *as above*
LLANWNDA (St Gwyndaf) and Goodwick (St Peter) w Manorowen and Llanstinan *St D 3* **V** B BARNES
LLANWNNEN (St Lucia) *see* Llanybydder and Llanwenog w Llanllwni *St D*
LLANWNNOG (St Gwynog) and Caersws w Carno *Ban 8* **V** D J CHAPMAN
LLANWNNWS (St Gwnnws) *see* Llanfihangel w Llanafan and Llanwnnws etc *St D*
LLANWRDA (St Cwrdaf) *see* Llansadwrn w Llanwrda and Manordeilo *St D*
LLANWRIN (St Ust and St Dyfrig) *see* Machynlleth w Llanwrin and Penegoes *Ban*
LLANWRTHWL (St Gwrthwl) *see* Cwmddauddwr w St Harmon's and Llanwrthwl *S & B*
LLANWRTYD (St James) (St David) w Llanddulas in Tir Abad and Eglwys Oen Duw and Llanfihangel Abergwessin and Llanddewi *S & B 2* **V** I B BESSANT
LLANWYDDELAN (St Gwyddelan) *see* Betws Cedewain and Tregynon and Llanwyddelan *St As*
LLANWYNNO (St Gwynno) (Christ Church) *Llan 11* **V** P J BENNETT
LLANYBYDDER (St Peter) and Llanwenog w Llanllwni *St D 9* **V** D BOWEN
LLANYCEFN (Church) *see* Llawhaden w Bletherston and Llanycefn *St D*
LLANYCHAEARN (St Llwchaiarn) w Llanddeiniol *St D 10* **V** B J H JONES
LLANYCHAN (St Hychan) *see* Llanynys w Llanychan *St As*
LLANYCHAR (Church) *see* Fishguard w Llanychar and Pontfaen w Morfil etc *St D*
LLANYCHLWYDOG *as above*
LLANYCIL (St Beuno) w Bala and Frongoch and Llangower w Llanuwchllyn *St As 15* **R** G THOMAS
LLANYCRWYS (St David) *see* Pencarreg and Llanycrwys *St D*
LLANYMAWDDWY (St Tydecho) *see* Mallwyd w Cemais, Llanymawddwy, Darowen etc *Ban*
LLANYNGHENEDL VALLEY (St Michael) *see* Valley w Llanfachraeth *Ban*
LLANYNYS *see* Builth and Llanddewi'r Cwm w Llangynog etc *S & B*
LLANYNYS (St Saeran) w Llanychan *St As 3* **V** *Vacant* (01824) 704866
LLANYRE *see* Llanllyr-yn-Rhos w Llanfihangel Helygen *S & B*
LLANYRNEWYDD (St Gwynour) *S & B 8* **V** T EVANS
LLANYSTYMDWY (St John the Baptist) *see* Dolbenmaen w Llanystymdwy w Llangybi etc *Ban*
LLANYWERN (St Mary the Virgin) *see* Llangorse, Cathedine, Llanfihangel Talyllyn etc *S & B*
LLAWHADEN (St Aidan) w Bletherston and Llanycefn *St D 2* **V** D E FAULKNER
LLAWRYBETWS (St James) *see* Corwen and Llangar w Gwyddelwern and Llawrybetws *St As*
LLAY (St Martin) *St As 16* **V** D Q BELLAMY
LLECHGYNFARWY (St Cynfarwy) *see* Bodedern w Llechgynfarwy and Llechylched etc *Ban*

LLECHRYD (St Tydfil) *see* Llandygwydd and Cenarth w Cilrhedyn etc *St D*
LLECHYLCHED (Holy Trinity) *see* Bodedern w Llechgynfarwy and Llechylched etc *Ban*
LLOWES (St Meilig) *see* Glasbury and Llowes w Clyro and Betws *S & B*
LLWYDCOED (St James) *see* Aberdare St Fagan *Llan*
LLWYDIARTH (St Mary) *see* Llanwddyn and Llanfihangel and Llwydiarth *St As*
LLWYNCELLYN (St Luke) *see* Cymmer and Porth *Llan*
LLWYNDERW (Holy Cross) (Clyne Chapel) *S & B 6* **V** G E BENNETT, **C** E M DOYLE
LLWYNGWRIL *see* Arthog w Fairbourne w Llangelynnin w Rhoslefain *Ban*
LLWYNHENDY (St David) *St D 12* **V** A M GRAY
LLWYNYPIA *see* Ystrad Rhondda w Ynyscynon *Llan*
LLYS-Y-FRAN (St Meilyr) *see* Maenclochog and New Moat etc *St D*
LLYSDINAM *see* Newbridge-on-Wye and Llanfihangel Brynpabuan etc *S & B*
LLYSFAEN (St Cynfran) *see* Llanddulas and Llysfaen *St As*
LLYSWEN (St Gwendoline) *see* Llandefalle and Llyswen w Boughrood etc *S & B*
LLYSWORNEY (St Tydfil) *see* Colwinston w Llandow and Llysworney *Llan*
LLYWEL (St David) and Traean-glas w Llanulid *S & B 1* **V** *Vacant* (0187482) 481
LOUGHER (St Michael) (St David) (St Paul) *S & B 9* **V** D ROBERTS, **NSM** K MORGAN
LOVESTON (St Leonard) *see* Jeffreyston w Reynoldston and E Williamston etc *St D*
LUDCHURCH (St Elidyr) *see* Begelly w Ludchurch and Crunwere *St D*
MACHEN (St Michael) (St John the Baptist) *Mon 6* **R** P VANN
MACHYNLLETH (St Peter) w Llanwrin and Penegoes *Ban 9* **R** E W ROWLANDS, **NSM** B V GRIFFITH
MAENCLOCHOG (St Mary) and Llandeilo w Henry's Moat w Mynachlogddu w Llangolman w New Moat w Llys y Fran *St D 2* **V** M N H GRAINGER, **NSM** J P LIVINGSTONE
MAENORDEIFI (St David) (Old Parish Church) and Capel Colman w Llanfihangel Penbedw and Clydau w Penrhydd and Castellan *St D 6* **R** G WATKINS
MAENTWROG (St Twrog) w Trawsfynydd *Ban 7* **R** B EVANS
MAERDY (All Saints) *see* Ferndale w Maerdy *Llan*
MAESGLAS and Duffryn *Mon* **I** A B WATERS
MAESMYNIS AND LLANYNYS (St David) *see* Builth and Llanddewi'r Cwm w Llangynog etc *S & B*
MAESTEG (St David) *see* Llangynwyd w Maesteg *Llan*
MAESTEG (St Michael) *as above*
MAESTEILO (St John) *see* Llandeilo and Taliaris *St D*
MAESTIR (St Mary) *see* Lampeter Pont Steffan w Silian *St D*
MAGOR (St Mary) w Redwick and Undy *Mon 4* **V** B J PARFITT, **C** P A WHYBROW
MAINDEE (St John the Evangelist) (St Mary) *Mon 9* **V** J D E DAVIES, **NSM** J K BEARDMORE
MALLWYD (St Tydecho) w Cemais, Llanymawddwy, Darowen and Llanbryn-Mair *Ban 9* **R** G ap GWILYM
MALPAS (St Mary) *Mon 9* **V** R M CAPPER, **C** D G PARFITT
MAMHILAD (St Illtud) and Llanfihangel Pontymoile *Mon 5* **V** P W WOODMAN
MANAFON (St Michael) *see* Berriew and Manafon *St As*
MANCOT (St Michael) *see* Hawarden *St As*
MANOBIER (St James) and St Florence w Redberth *St D 1* **V** V F MILLGATE
MANORDEILO (St Paul) *see* Llansadwrn w Llanwrda and Manordeilo *St D*
MANOROWEN (St Mary) *see* Llanwnda, Goodwick, w Manorowen and Llanstinan *St D*
MANSELTON (St Michael and All Angels) *S & B 10* **V** T H JONES
MARCHWIEL (St Marcella) and Isycoed *St As 11* **R** D A SLIM
MARCROSS (Holy Trinity) *see* Llantwit Major *Llan*
MARGAM (St Mary) (St David) *Llan 8* **V** D G BELCHER
MARLOES (St Peter) *see* Dale and St Brides w Marloes *St D*
MARROS (St Lawrence) *see* Pendine w Llanmiloe and Eglwys Gymyn w Marros *St D*
MARSHFIELD (St Mary) and Peterstone Wentloog and Coedkernew w St Bride's Wentloog *Mon 6* **V** J S WILLIAMS
MARTLETWY (St Marcellus) w Lawrenny and Minwear and Yerbeston w Templeton *St D 4* **V** M H ROWLANDS
MATHERN (St Tewdric) and Mounton w St Pierre *Mon 2* **V** A R WILLIE
MATHRY (Holy Martyrs) w St Edren's and Grandston w St Nicholas and Jordanston *St D 3* **V** G O ASSON
MATTHEWSTOWN (All Saints) *see* Penrhiwceiber w Matthewstown and Ynysboeth *Llan*
MAUDLAM (St Mary Magdalene) *see* Pyle w Kenfig *Llan*
MEIDRIM (St David) and Llanboidy and Merthyr *St D 15* **V** J GAINER
MEIFOD (St Tysilio and St Mary) and Llangynyw *St As 8* **V** G MORGAN
MELIDEN (St Melyd) (St Mary Magdalene) and Gwaenysgor *St As 1* **V** D P D H REES
MELINE (St Dogmael) *see* Nevern and Y Beifil w Eglwyswrw and Meline etc *St D*
MENAI BRIDGE (St Mary) *see* Llandegfan w Llandysilio *Ban*
MERLIN'S BRIDGE (St Mark) *see* Haverfordwest St Mary and St Thos w Haroldston *St D*
MERTHYR (St Martin) *see* Meidrim and Llanboidy and Merthyr *St D*
MERTHYR CYNOG (St Cynog) and Dyffryn Honddu w Garthbrengy w Llandefaelog-Fach and Llanfihangel Fechan *S & B 1* **V** T C JOHNS
MERTHYR DYFAN (St Dyfan and St Teilo) *Llan 6* **R** T A DOHERTY, **C** D J ATKINS
MERTHYR MAWR (St Teilo) *see* Laleston w Tythegston and Merthyr Mawr *Llan*
MERTHYR TYDFIL (Christ Church) (St Luke) *Llan 9* **V** S S MORGAN
MERTHYR TYDFIL (St David) (St Tydfil's Well) *Llan 9* **R** M J MARSDEN
MERTHYR VALE (St Mary and Holy Innocents) *see* Troedyrhiw w Merthyr Vale *Llan*
MICHAELSTON-LE-PIT (St Michael and All Angels) *see* St Andrew's Major and Michaelston-le-Pit *Llan*
MICHAELSTON-SUPER-AVON *see* Cwmavon *Llan*
MICHAELSTON-SUPER-ELY (St Michael) *see* St Fagans w Michaelston-super-Ely *Llan*
MICHAELSTON-Y-FEDW (St Michael) *Mon 6* **P-in-c** B RICHARDS
MICHEL TROY (St Michael) *see* Overmonnow w Wonastow and Michel Troy *Mon*
MILFORD HAVEN (St Katherine) (St Peter) (St Thomas a Becket) *St D 5* **V** J H M DAVIES
MINERA (St Mary) (St Tudfil) (St Andrew) (St David) *St As 16* **V** J G CANHAM
MINWEAR (St Womar) *see* Martletwy w Lawrenny and Minwear etc *St D*
MISKIN (St John the Baptist) *Llan 7* **V** N C H BROWN
MOCHDRE (All Saints) *St As 7* **V** *Vacant* (01686) 650345
MOLD (St Mary) *St As 14* **V** C I DAY, **C** A F C KEULEMANS, P McLEAN
MONINGTON (St Nicholas) *see* St Dogmael's w Moylgrove and Monington *St D*
MONKSWOOD (St Matthew) *see* Usk and Monkswood w Glascoed Chpl and Gwehelog *Mon*
MONKTON (St Nicholas and St John) *St D 1* **V** M L COX
MONMOUTH (St Mary the Virgin) *Mon 3* **V** J W C COUTTS, **Par Dn** U M P KROLL
MONTGOMERY (St Nicholas) and Forden and Llandyssil *St As 10* **R** A M HIRST
MORFIL *see* Fishguard w Llanychar and Pontfaen w Morfil etc *St D*
MORRISTON (St David) (St John) *S & B 7* **V** A J KNIGHT, **C** E A SMITHAM, C W G DOBBIE
MOSTYN (Christ Church) w Ffynnongroyw *St As 4* **V** S D GREEN
MOUNTAIN ASH (St Margaret) (St Illtyd) *Llan 7* **V** B LETSON, **C** M WILLIAMS
MOUNTON *see* Narberth w Mounton w Robeston Wathen and Crinow *St D*
MOUNTON (St Andoenus) *see* Mathern and Mounton w St Pierre *Mon*
MOYLGROVE (St Mynno, St David and St Andrew) *see* St Dogmael's w Moylgrove and Monington *St D*
MWNT (Holy Cross) *see* Cardigan and Mwnt and Y Ferwig *St D*
MYDDFAI (St Michael) *see* Llandingat w Myddfai *St D*
MYDROILYN (Holy Trinity) *see* Llanerch Aeron w Ciliau Aeron and Dihewyd etc *St D*
MYNACHLOGDDU (St Dogmael) *see* Maenclochog and New Moat etc *St D*
MYNYDDISLWYN (St Tudor) *Mon 7* **TR** R J SUMMERS, **TV** A C EDWARDS, L A F C WATKINS
NANNERCH (St Michael) *see* Cilcain and Nannerch and Rhyd-y-mwyn *St As*
NANTCWNLLE (St Cynllo) *see* Llanfihangel Ystrad and Cilcennin w Trefilan etc *St D*
NANTGLYN (St James) *see* Denbigh and Nantglyn *St As*
NANTMEL (St Cynllo) *see* Rhayader and Nantmel *S & B*
NANTYGLO (Holy Trinity and St Anne) *see* Blaina and Nantyglo *Mon*
NANTYMOEL (St Peter and St Paul) w Wyndham *Llan 1* **V** *Vacant* (01656) 840248

NARBERTH (St Andrew) w Mounton w Robeston Wathen and Crinow *St D 4* **R** H A CHIPLIN
NASH (St Mary) *see* Cosheston w Nash and Upton *St D*
NASH (St Mary) *see* Goldcliffe and Whiston and Nash *Mon*
NEATH (St Thomas) (St David) (St Catherine) (St Peter and StPaul) w Llantwit *Llan 10* **R** W P THOMAS, **C** P J ABBOTT, **NSM** C MULLIGAN
NEBO (Dewi Sant) *see* Llansantffraed and Llanbadarn Trefeglwys etc *St D*
NEFYN (St David) (St Mary) w Pistyll w Tudweiliog w Llandudwen w Edern *Ban 11* **V** E W THOMAS
NELSON (St John the Baptist) *see* Llanfabon *Llan*
NERCWYS (St Mary) *see* Treuddyn w Nercwys *St As*
NEVERN (St Brynach) and Y Beifil w Eglwyswrw and Meline and Eglwyswen and Llanfair Nant-gwyn *St D 6* **V** J P LEWIS
NEW HEDGES (St Anne) *see* Tenby *St D*
NEW MOAT (St Nicholas) *see* Maenclochog and New Moat etc *St D*
NEW RADNOR (St Mary) and Llanfihangel Nantmelan and Evancoyd w Gladwestry and Colva *S & B 5* **V** S B THATCHER
NEW TREDEGAR (St Dingat) *Mon 7* **V** D J YOUNG
NEWBOROUGH (St Peter) w Llangeinwen w Llangaffo and Llanfair-yn-y-Cwmwd *Ban 4* **R** R L NEWALL
NEWBRIDGE (St Paul) (St Peter) *Mon 7* **V** T N COLEMAN, **NSM** J J WILKINS
NEWBRIDGE-ON-WYE (All Saints) and Llanfihangel Brynpabuan w Cwmbach Llechryd and Llanafan Fawr *S & B 2* **V** B WOOLLASTON
NEWCASTLE (St Illtud) *Llan 1* **V** M D WITCOMBE, **NSM** O M PARRY
NEWCASTLE EMLYN (Holy Trinity) w Llandyfriog and Troed-yr-aur w Brongwyn *St D 7* **V** M H JOHN
NEWCHURCH (St Mary) *see* Cynwil Elfed and Newchurch *St D*
NEWCHURCH (St Mary) *see* Bryngwyn and Newchurch and Llanbedr etc *S & B*
NEWCHURCH (St Michael) *see* Cynwil Elfed and Newchurch *St D*
NEWCHURCH (St Peter) *as above*
NEWCHURCH (St Peter) *see* Caerwent w Dinham and Llanfair Discoed etc *Mon*
NEWMARKET *see* Dyserth and Trelawnyd and Cwm *St As*
NEWPORT (All Saints) *Mon 9* **P-in-c** I S DOULL
NEWPORT (Cathedral of St Woolos) (St Martin) *Mon 9* **V** R D FENWICK
NEWPORT (Christ Church) *Mon 9* **V** R G HACKETT
NEWPORT (St Andrew) (St Philip) *Mon 9* **V** H J DAVIES, **NSM** J M DRAPER
NEWPORT (St John Baptist) *Mon 9* **V** C D WESTBROOK
NEWPORT (St John the Evangelist) *see* Maindee *Mon*
NEWPORT St Julian (St Julius and St Aaron) *Mon 9* **V** D R WILLIAMS
NEWPORT (St Mark) *Mon 9* **V** K W SHARPE
NEWPORT (St Mary) *see* Maindee *Mon*
NEWPORT (St Mary) w Cilgwyn and Dinas w Llanllawer *St D 6* **R** R C JONES, **NSM** P L DAVIES
NEWPORT (St Matthew) *Mon 9* **P-in-c** P MUSINDI
NEWPORT St Paul *Mon 9* **V** W E KELLY
NEWPORT (St Stephen) and Holy Trinity *Mon 9* **V** M R AINSCOUGH
NEWPORT (St Teilo) *Mon 9* **V** C J NICKLESS, **NSM** I R GALT
NEWQUAY (St Llwchaiarn) *see* Llanllwchaearn and Llanina *St D*
NEWTON (St Peter) *S & B 6* **V** C M P JONES, **C** D S COSSLETT
NEWTON NORTH *see* Slebech and Uzmaston w Boulston *St D*
NEWTON NOTTAGE (St John the Baptist) (All Saints) (St David) *Llan 8* **R** P R MASSON, **C** M D GABLE, J G DAVIS
NEWTOWN (St David) w Llanllwchaiarn w Aberhafesp *St As 7* **R** P B JONES, **NSM** A R MARSHALL, G K MARSHALL
NEYLAND (St Clement) *see* Llanstadwel *St D*
NICHOLASTON (St Nicholas) *see* Oxwich w Penmaen and Nicholaston *S & B*
NOLTON (St Madog) w Roch *St D 5* **R** A CRAVEN
NOLTON (St Mary) *see* Coity w Nolton *Llan*
NORTHOP (St Eurgain and St Peter) (St Mary) *St As 14* **V** G L JONES
NORTON (Mission Church) *see* Oystermouth *S & B*
NORTON (St Andrew) *see* Knighton and Norton *S & B*
NOTTAGE (St David) *see* Newton Nottage *Llan*
OAKWOOD (St John) *see* Port Talbot St Agnes w Oakwood *Llan*
OAKWOOD (St Teilo) *as above*
OGMORE VALE (St John the Baptist) *see* Llangeinor *Llan*
OVERMONNOW (St Thomas) w Wonastow and Michel Troy *Mon 3* **V** J F GRAY
OVERTON (St Mary the Virgin) and Erbistock and Penley *St As 11* **R** P A CROWE
OXWICH (St Illtyd) w Penmaen and Nicholaston *S & B 8* **V** R H MORGAN
OYSTERMOUTH (All Saints) *S & B 6* **V** G H THOMAS, **NSM** D J H WATKINS
PANTEG (St Mary) *Mon 10* **R** D G BRUNNING
PANTYFFRID (Mission Church) *see* Berriew and Manafon *St As*
PATRICIO (St Issui the Martyr) *see* Llangenni and Llanbedr Ystrad Yw w Patricio *S & B*
PEMBROKE (St Mary) (St Michael) (St Daniel) *St D 1* **V** C W BOWEN
PEMBROKE DOCK (St John) (St Patrick) (St Teilo) *St D 1* **V** A THOMAS
PEN-BOYR (St Llawddog) *see* Llangeler w Pen-Boyr *St D*
PEN-BRE (St Illtud) *St D 12* **V** V P ROBERTS
PENALLT (Old Church) and Trellech *Mon 3* **V** J K C DENERLEY
PENALLY (St Nicholas) *see* Tenby *St D*
PENARTH (All Saints) (St Peter) (St Luke) *Llan 6* **V** P A COX, **C** I H AVESON
PENARTH (St Augustine) (Holy Nativity) w Lavernock *Llan 6* **R** N H COLLINS, **C** A P JOHNSON
PENBRYN (St Michael) *see* Llangrannog w Llandysiliogogo w Penbryn *St D*
PENCADER (St Mary) *see* Llanfihangel-ar-arth w Capel Dewi *St D*
PENCARREG (St Patrick) and Llanycrwys *St D 9* **V** B E MORRIS
PENCLAWDD *see* Llanyrnewydd *S & B*
PENCOED (St David) *see* Llanilid w Pencoed *Llan*
PENCOED (St Paul) *as above*
PENCOEDCAE (Mission) *see* Graig *Llan*
PENDERYN (St Cynog) w Ystradfellte and Pontneathvaughan *S & B 1* **R** J H SCOTT
PENDINE (St Margaret) w Llanmiloe and Eglwys Gymyn w Marros *St D 15* **R** K T LITTLER
PENDOYLAN (St Cadoc) and Welsh St Donats *Llan 5* **V** E C R COUNSELL
PENEGOES (St Cadfarch) *see* Machynlleth w Llanwrin and Penegoes *Ban*
PENHOW (St John the Baptist) and St Brides Netherwent w Llandavenny and Llanvaches and Llandevaud *Mon 4* **V** J HEALES
PENISA'R-WAEN (St Helen) *see* Llandinorwig w Penisa'r-waen *Ban*
PENLEY (St Mary Magdalene) *see* Overton and Erbistock and Penley *St As*
PENLLECH *see* Aberdaron w Rhiw and Llanfaelrhys etc *Ban*
PENLLERGAER (St David) *S & B 9* **V** D R PAYNE
PENLLWYN (St Mary the Virgin) *see* Mynyddislwyn *Mon*
PENLLYN (Chapel of Ease) *see* Cowbridge *Llan*
PENMACHNO (St Tudclud) *see* Betws-y-Coed and Capel Curig w Penmachno etc *Ban*
PENMAEN (St David) and Crumlin *Mon 7* **V** R E HIGGINS
PENMAEN (St John the Baptist) *see* Oxwich w Penmaen and Nicholaston *S & B*
PENMAENMAWR *see* Dwygyfylchi *Ban*
PENMARK (St Mary) w Porthkerry *Llan 6* **V** S C PARE
PENMORFA *see* Ynyscynhaearn w Penmorfa and Porthmadog *Ban*
PENMYNYDD (St Credifael) *see* Llanfairpwll w Penmynydd *Ban*
PENNAL (St Peter ad Vincula) w Corris and Esgairgeiliog *Ban 9* **R** G ap IORWERTH
PENNANT (St Thomas) *see* Llanrhaeadr-ym-Mochnant and Llanarmon etc *St As*
PENNANT MELANGELL (St Melangel) *see* Llangynog *St As*
PENNARD (St Mary) *see* Ilston w Pennard *S & B*
PENPONT (no dedication) *see* Trallwng, Bettws Penpont w Aberyskir etc *S & B*
PENRHIWCEIBER (St Winifred) w Matthewstown and Ynysboeth *Llan 7* **V** G J FRANCIS
PENRHOS (Holy Trinity) *see* Llandysilio and Penrhos and Llandrinio etc *St As*
PENRHOS (St Cadoc) *see* Llantilio Crossenny w Penrhos, Llanvetherine etc *Mon*
PENRHOSLLUGWY (St Michael) *see* Llaneugrad w Llanallgo and Penrhosllugwy etc *Ban*
PENRHYDD *see* Maenordeifi and Capel Colman w Llanfihangel etc *St D*
PENRHYN-COCH (St John) *see* Elerch w Penrhyncoch w Capel Bangor and Goginan *St D*
PENRHYNDEUDRAETH (Holy Trinity) w Llanfrothen w Beddgelert *Ban 7* **V** J ASHLEY-ROBERTS
PENRHYNSIDE (St Sannan) *see* Llanrhos *St As*
PENRHYNSIDE BAY (St David) *as above*

PENRICE (St Andrew) *see* Reynoldston w Penrice and Llangennith *S & B*
PENSARN (St David) *see* Abergele *St As*
PENSTROWED (St Gwrhai) *see* Llandinam w Trefeglwys w Penstrowed *Ban*
PENTERRY (St Mary) *see* Itton and St Arvans w Penterry and Kilgwrrwg etc *Mon*
PENTIR (St Cedol) (St Elizabeth) *Ban 1* **P-in-c** G W HEWITT
PENTRAETH (St Mary) *see* Llansadwrn w Llanddona and Llaniestyn etc *Ban*
PENTRE (St Peter) *Llan 12* **V** P H MORGANS
PENTRECHWYTH (St Peter) *see* Glantawe *S & B*
PENTREFELIN *see* Ynyscynhaearn w Penmorfa and Porthmadog *Ban*
PENTREVOELAS (Parish Church) *see* Cerrigydrudion w Llanfihangel etc *St As*
PENTROBIN (St John) *see* Hawarden *St As*
PENTWYN (St David) *see* Cyncoed *Mon*
PENTWYN (St Mary) *see* Penallt and Trellech *Mon*
PENTYRCH (St Cadwg) (St David) *Llan 5* **V** G W A HOLCOMBE
PENYBONTFAWR *see* Llanrhaeadr-ym-Mochnant and Llanarmon etc *St As*
PENYCAE (St Thomas) *St As 16* **V** G PITT, **NSM** B A PITT
PENYCLAWDD (St Martin) *see* Dingestow and Llangovan w Penyclawdd etc *Mon*
PENYDARREN (St John the Baptist) *Llan 9* **V** M I WILLIAMS
PENYFAI (All Saints) w Tondu *Llan 1* **V** J F SEWARD
PENYFFORDD (Emmanuel) *see* Hope *St As*
PENYGRAIG (St Barnabas) *see* Dinas and Penygraig w Williamstown *Llan*
PENYWAUN (St Winifred) *see* Hirwaun *Llan*
PETERSTON-SUPER-ELY (St Peter) w St Brides-super-Ely *Llan 5* **R** R E YOUNG, **NSM** S P TOMS
PETERSTON-SUPER-MONTEM (St Peter) *see* Llanharan w Peterston-super-Montem *Llan*
PETERSTONE WENTLOOG (St Peter) *see* Marshfield and Peterstone Wentloog etc *Mon*
PILLETH (Our Lady of Pilleth) *see* Whitton and Pilleth and Cascob etc *S & B*
PISTYLL (St Beuno) *see* Nefyn w Pistyll w Tudweiliog w Llandudwen etc *Ban*
PLAS POWER (St Mary) *see* Wrexham *St As*
PONT AMAN (St Thomas) *see* Betws w Ammanford *St D*
PONT DOLANOG (St John the Evangelist) *see* Pont Robert and Pont Dolanog *St As*
PONT-IETS *see* Pontyates and Llangyndeyrn *St D*
PONT ROBERT (St John the Evangelist) and Pont Dolanog *St As 8* **R** J ROCK
PONTARDAWE (All Saints) *see* Llangiwg *S & B*
PONTARDAWE (St Peter) *as above*
PONTARDDULAIS *see* Llandeilo Tal-y-bont *S & B*
PONTARFYNACH *see* Ysbyty Cynfyn w Llantrisant and Eglwys Newydd *St D*
PONTARGOTHI (Holy Trinity) *see* Llanegwad w Llanfynydd *St D*
PONTBLYDDYN (Christ Church) *St As 14* **V** C O BENNETT
PONTERWYD *see* Ysbyty Cynfyn w Llantrisant and Eglwys Newydd *St D*
PONTFADOG (St John) *see* Llansantffraid and Llanarmon and Pontfadog *St As*
PONTFAEN (St Brynach) *see* Fishguard w Llanychar and Pontfaen w Morfil etc *St D*
PONTLANIO *see* Llanychaearn w Llanddeiniol *St D*
PONTLLANFRAITH (St Augustine) *see* Mynyddislwyn *Mon*
PONTLLIW (St Anne) *see* Penllergaer *S & B*
PONTLOTTYN (St Tyfaelog) (St Michael) (St Aidan) w Fochriw *Llan 2* **V** M PERRY
PONTNEATHVAUGHAN (St John) *see* Penderyn w Ystradfellte and Pontneathvaughan *S & B*
PONTNEWYDD (Holy Trinity) *Mon 10* **V** D J DUNN, **NSM** M ENDICOTT
PONTNEWYNYDD (All Saints) *see* Pontypool *Mon*
PONTRHYDFENDIGAID (St David) *see* Tregaron w Ystrad Meurig and Strata Florida *St D*
PONTSIAN (St John) *see* Llandysul *St D*
PONTYATES (St Mary) and Llangyndeyrn *St D 12* **V** D I DAVIES
PONTYBEREM (St John) *St D 12* **V** S R THOMAS
PONTYCLUN (St Paul) w Talygarn *Llan 4* **V** R G AUSTIN
PONTYCYMER (St David) and Blaengarw *Llan 1* **V** M H BOIT
PONTYGWAITH (St Mary Magdalene) *see* Tylorstown w Ynyshir *Llan*
PONTYMISTER (St Margaret) *see* Risca *Mon*
PONTYPOOL (St James) (St Matthew) *Mon 10* **R** B R PIPPEN, **C** J M T CARLYON, D G BATE
PONTYPRIDD (St Catherine) (All Saints) (St David) (St Matthew) *Llan 11* **V** J H S THOMAS, **NSM** G TUCK
POOL QUAY (St John the Evangelist) *see* Guilsfield w Pool Quay *St As*
PORT EYNON (St Cattwg) w Rhosili and Llanddewi and Knelston *S & B 8* **V** D J MOSFORD
PORT TALBOT (St Agnes) w Oakwood *Llan 8* **V** S P KIRK
PORT TALBOT (St David) *see* Margam *Llan*
PORT TALBOT (St Theodore) (Holy Cross) (St Peter) *Llan 8* **V** C J AMOS
PORTH *see* Cymmer and Porth *Llan*
PORTH (St Paul) w Trealaw *Llan 12* **V** M J DAVIES
PORTHCAWL (All Saints) *see* Newton Nottage *Llan*
PORTHKERRY (Rhoose Mission Church) *see* Penmark w Porthkerry *Llan*
PORTHKERRY (St Curig) *as above*
PORTHMADOG (St John) *see* Ynyscynhaearn w Penmorfa and Porthmadog *Ban*
PORTMADOC (St Cyngar) *as above*
PORTSKEWETT (St Mary) and Roggiett w Llanfihangel Rogiet *Mon 4* **R** T H J PALMER
PRENDERGAST (St David) w Rudbaxton *St D 2* **R** G D GWYTHER
PRESTATYN (Christ Church) (Church of Holy Spirit) *St As 1* **V** P C SOUTHERTON
PRINCES GATE (St Catherine) *see* Lamp Velfrey and Llanddewi Velfrey *St D*
PRION (St James) *see* Llanrhaeadr-yng-Nghinmeirch and Prion *St As*
PUNCHESTON (St Mary) *see* Letterston w Llanfair Nant-y-Gof etc *St D*
PUNCHSTON *see* Fishguard w Llanychar and Pontfaen w Morfil etc *St D*
PWLL (Holy Trinity) *see* Burry Port and Pwll *St D*
PWLLCROCHAN *see* Castlemartin w Warren and Angle etc *St D*
PWLLGWAUN (St Mark) w Llanddewi Rhondda *Llan 11* **V** M L CHIPLIN
PWLLHELI *see* Denio w Abererch *Ban*
PYLE (St James) (St Mary Magdalene) w Kenfig *Llan 8* **V** P G WHITE
QUAR, THE (St Tydfil's Well) *see* Merthyr Tydfil St Dav *Llan*
QUEENSFERRY (St Andrew) *see* Shotton *St As*
RADYR (St John the Baptist) (Christ Church) *Llan 5* **R** W G BARLOW, **C** B JOHN
RAGLAN (St Cadoc) w Llandenny and Bryngwyn *Mon 5* **V** S L GUEST
REDBERTH (Church) *see* Manobier and St Florence w Redberth *St D*
REDWICK (St Thomas) *see* Magor w Redwick and Undy *Mon*
RESOLVEN (St David) w Tonna *Llan 10* **V** N HADFIELD, **NSM** D O JONES
REYNOLDSTON (Church) *see* Jeffreyston w Reynoldston and E Williamston etc *St D*
REYNOLDSTON (St George) w Penrice and Llangennith *S & B 8* **R** P J WILLIAMS
RHANDIRMWYN (St Barnabas) *see* Cil-y-Cwm and Ystrad-ffin w Rhandir-mwyn etc *St D*
RHAYADER (St Clement) and Nantmel *S & B 5* **V** L A MARSHALL
RHESYCAE (Christ Church) *see* Halkyn w Caerfallwch w Rhesycae *St As*
RHEWL (Church) *see* Llanynys w Llanychan *St As*
RHIWLAS (Mission Church) *see* Llansilin w Llangadwaladr and Llangedwyn *St As*
RHOS (St James) *see* Llangeler w Pen-Boyr *St D*
RHOSBEIRIO *see* Llanfechell w Bodewryd w Rhosbeirio etc *Ban*
RHOSCOLYN *see* Holyhead *Ban*
RHOSCROWTHER (St Decumanus) *see* Castlemartin w Warren and Angle etc *St D*
RHOSDDU *see* Wrexham *St As*
RHOSESEMOR *see* Halkyn w Caerfallwch w Rhesycae *St As*
RHOSILI (St Mary the Virgin) *see* Port Eynon w Rhosili and Llanddewi and Knelston *S & B*
RHOSLEFAIN (St Mary) *see* Arthog w Fairbourne w Llangelynnin w Rhoslefain *Ban*
RHOSLLANNERCHRUGOG (St John the Evangelist) (St David) (St Mary) *St As 16* **V** D J HART
RHOSTIE *see* Llanilar w Rhostie and Llangwyryfon etc *St D*
RHOSYGWALIAU (Holy Trinity) *see* Llanfor w Rhosygwaliau *St As*
RHOSYMEDRE (St John the Evangelist) *St As 13* **V** R EVANS
RHUDDLAN (St Mary) *St As 1* **V** J G GRIFFITHS
RHULEN (St David) *see* Llanelwedd w Llanfaredd w Llansantffraed etc *S & B*
RHYD-Y-MWYN (St John the Evangelist) *see* Cilcain and Nannerch and Rhyd-y-mwyn *St As*
RHYDYBRIW (Capel Rhydybriw) *see* Defynnog w Rhydybriw and Llandilo'r-fan *S & B*

RHYDYFELIN (St Luke) *Llan 11* **V** C P SUTTON
RHYL (Holy Trinity) (St Thomas) (St John) (St Ann) *St As 1* **V** J GLOVER, **C** J D LOMAS, C J HEYCOCKS
RHYMNEY (St David) *Mon 7* **V** A E PAYNE
RISCA (St Mary) *Mon 6* **V** R E PAIN, **C** M J JEFFORD, J R CONNELL, **NSM** J A WELSH
ROATH (St German) *Llan 3* **V** R D DOXSEY, **NSM** R L FANTHORPE
ROATH (St Margaret) (St Anne) (St Edward) (St Philip) (St Teilo's School) *Llan 3* **V** P I REID, **C** G C POWELL, G REEVES
ROATH (St Martin) *Llan 3* **V** H G CLARKE, **NSM** T G WATKIN
ROATH (St Saviour) *Llan 3* **V** A RABJOHNS
ROBERTSTOWN (St John the Evangelist) *see* Aberdare St Jo *Llan*
ROBESTON WATHEN (Church) *see* Narberth w Mounton w Robeston Wathen and Crinow *St D*
ROBESTON WEST (St Andrew) *see* Walwyn's Castle w Robeston W *St D*
ROCH (St Mary) *see* Nolton w Roch *St D*
ROCKFIELD (St Cenedlon) and St Maughen's w Llangattock-vibon-Avel and Llanfihangel-ystern-Llewern *Mon 3* **V** P M BOND
ROGERSTONE (St John the Baptist) *see* Bassaleg *Mon*
ROGGIETT (St Mary) *see* Portskewett and Roggiett w Llanfihangel Rogiet *Mon*
ROSEMARKET (St Ishmael) *see* Burton and Rosemarket *St D*
ROSSETT (Christ Church) *St As 16* **V** R A SUTER
RUABON (St Mary) (All Saints) *St As 13* **V** G C JONES
RUDBAXTON (St Michael) *see* Prendergast w Rudbaxton *St D*
RUDRY (St James) *see* Bedwas and Rudry *Mon*
RUMNEY (St Augustine) *Mon 6* **V** D A G HATHAWAY
RUTHIN (St Peter) w Llanrhydd *St As 3* **R** R BAYLEY
ST ANDREW'S MAJOR (St Andrew) (St Peter) and Michaelston-le-Pit *Llan 6* **R** D H RHYDDERCH
ST ARVANS (St Arvan) *see* Itton and St Arvans w Penterry and Kilgwrrwg etc *Mon*
ST ASAPH (Cathedral of St Asaph and St Cyndeyrn) and Tremeirchion *St As 1* **V** *Vacant* (01745) 583597
ST ATHAN (St Tathan) *see* Eglwysbrewis w St Athan w Gileston *Llan*
ST BRIDES (St Bridget) *see* Dale and St Brides w Marloes *St D*
ST BRIDES MAJOR (St Bridget) *see* Ewenny w St Brides Major *Llan*
ST BRIDES MINOR (St Bride) w Bettws *Llan 1* **R** D J A BURTON
ST BRIDES NETHERWENT (St Bridget) *see* Penhow, St Brides Netherwent w Llandavenny etc *Mon*
ST BRIDES-SUPER-ELY (St Bride) *see* Peterston-super-Ely w St Brides-super-Ely *Llan*
ST BRIDE'S WENTLOOG *see* Marshfield and Peterstone Wentloog etc *Mon*
ST CLEARS (St Mary Magdalene) w Llangynin and Llanddowror and Llanfihangel Abercywyn *St D 15* **V** R THOMAS
ST DAVIDS (Cathedral of St David and St Andrew) *St D 3* **V** J W EVANS
ST DOGMAEL'S (St Thomas) w Moylgrove and Monington *St D 6* **V** E R WILLIAMS
ST DOGWELLS (St Dogfael) *see* Spittal w Trefgarn and Ambleston w St Dogwells *St D*
ST EDREN'S *see* Mathry w St Edren's and Grandston etc *St D*
ST ELVIS *see* Whitchurch w Solva and St Elvis w Brawdy etc *St D*
ST FAGANS (St Mary) w Michaelston-super-Ely *Llan 5* **R** A R WINTLE
ST FLORENCE (St Florentius) *see* Manobier and St Florence w Redberth *St D*
ST GEORGE (St George) *see* Towyn and St George *St As*
ST GEORGE-SUPER-ELY (St George) *see* St Nicholas w Bonvilston and St George-super-Ely *Llan*
ST HARMON'S (St Garmon) *see* Cwmddauddwr w St Harmon's and Llanwrthwl *S & B*
ST HILARY Greenway (St Hilary) *Mon 6* **V** T H WOOD
ST HILARY (St Hilary) *see* Cowbridge *Llan*
ST ISHMAEL'S (St Ishmael) *see* Herbrandston and Hasguard w St Ishmael's *St D*
ST ISHMAEL'S (St Ishmael) w Llan-saint and Ferryside *St D 12* **V** R M JENKINS
ST ISSELL'S (St Issell) and Amroth *St D 4* **V** M BUTLER
ST LAWRENCE (St Lawrence) *see* Camrose and St Lawrence w Ford and Haycastle *St D*
ST LYTHANS (St Bleiddian) *see* Wenvoe and St Lythans *Llan*
ST MARY CHURCH (St Mary) *see* Cowbridge *Llan*
ST MARY HILL (St Mary) *see* Coychurch w Llangan and St Mary Hill *Llan*
ST MAUGHEN'S (St Meugan) *see* Rockfield and St Maughen's w Llangattock etc *Mon*
ST MELLONS (St Mellon) *Mon 6* **V** D KELLEN, **C** M I R DOWSETT, **NSM** G R DAVIES
ST NICHOLAS (St Nicholas) *see* Mathry w St Edren's and Grandston etc *St D*
ST NICHOLAS (St Nicholas) w Bonvilston and St George-super-Ely *Llan 6* **R** E T WILSON
ST PETROX (St Pedrog) w Stackpole Elidor and Bosherston w St Twynnells *St D 1* **R** J H RICHARDS
ST PIERRE (St Peter) *see* Mathern and Mounton w St Pierre *Mon*
ST THOMAS *see* Haverfordwest St Mary and St Thos w Haroldston *St D*
ST TWYNNELLS (St Gwynog) *see* St Petrox w Stackpole Elidor and Bosherston etc *St D*
SANDFIELDS *see* Aberavon H Trin *Llan*
SANDYCROFT (Holy Spirit) *see* Hawarden *St As*
SANDYCROFT (St Francis) *as above*
SARON (St David) *see* Llanedi w Tycroes and Saron *St D*
SAUNDERSFOOT *see* St Issell's and Amroth *St D*
SEALAND (St Barth) *see* Hawarden *St As*
SEBASTOPOL (St Oswald) *see* Griffithstown *Mon*
SENGHENYDD (St Peter) *see* Eglwysilan *Llan*
SEVEN SISTERS (St Mary) (St David) *Llan 10* **V** R I BLACKMORE
SHIRENEWTON (St Thomas a Becket) *see* Caerwent w Dinham and Llanfair Discoed etc *Mon*
SHOTTON (St Ethelwold) *St As 14* **V** D P MORRIS, **C** G R ROWLANDS
SILIAN (St Sulien) *see* Lampeter Pont Steffan w Silian *St D*
SINAN (All Saints) *see* Cefn *St As*
SIX BELLS (St John) *see* Abertillery w Cwmtillery w Six Bells *Mon*
SKENFRITH (St Bride) *see* Grosmont and Skenfrith and Llangattock etc *Mon*
SKETTY (St Paul) (Holy Trinity) *S & B 6* **V** R J WILLIAMS, **C** M J BATCHELOR, **NSM** S H JONES
SKEWEN (St John) (All Saints) (St Mary) *Llan 10* **V** P RAIKES, **C** S J H DUNWOODY
SLEBECH (St John the Baptist Parish Centre) and Uzmaston w Boulston *St D 2* **V** W H WATKINS
SOLVA (St Aidan) *see* Whitchurch w Solva and St Elvis w Brawdy etc *St D*
SOUTHERNDOWN (All Saints) *see* Ewenny w St Brides Major *Llan*
SOUTHSEA (All Saints) *see* Berse and Southsea *St As*
SOUTHSEA (St Alban) *as above*
SPITTAL (St Mary) w Trefgarn and Ambleston w St Dogwells *St D 2* **V** R D WHITE
STACKPOLE ELIDOR (St James and St Elidyr) *see* St Petrox w Stackpole Elidor and Bosherston etc *St D*
STEYNTON (St Cewydd and St Peter) *St D 5* **V** G J DAVIES
STRATA FLORIDA (St Mary) *see* Tregaron w Ystrad Meurig and Strata Florida *St D*
SULLY (St John the Baptist) *Llan 6* **R** E B DOWDING, **NSM** B BUTLER
SWANSEA (Christ Church) *S & B 11* **P-in-c** L HOPKINS
SWANSEA (St Barnabas) *S & B 11* **P-in-c** P C FRENCH
SWANSEA (St Gabriel) *S & B 6* **V** E M WASTELL
SWANSEA (St James) *S & B 11* **V** A G HOWELLS, **C** C D BROWN
SWANSEA (St Jude) *S & B 11* **V** D W WHITE
SWANSEA (St Luke) *S & B 10* **P-in-c** R J HANNEN
SWANSEA (St Mark) (St John) *S & B 10* **P-in-c** S J COLEMAN
SWANSEA (St Mary) (Holy Trinity) *S & B 11* **V** A E PIERCE, **NSM** P WARD
SWANSEA (St Matthew) w Greenhill *S & B 11* **P-in-c** L O WARD
SWANSEA (St Nicholas-on-the-Hill) *S & B 11* **V** D M GRIFFITHS, **C** L J TAYLOR
SWANSEA (St Peter) *S & B 10* **V** A G LEE, **C** A FRANCIS
SWANSEA (St Thomas) (St Stephen) and Kilvey *S & B 11* **V** P J GWYNN, **C** H V PARSELL
TAI'RGWAITH (St David) *see* Gwaun-cae-Gurwen *St D*
TAL-Y-LLYN (St David) *see* Llanegryn w Aberdyfi w Tywyn *Ban*
TALACHDDU (St Mary) *see* Llandefalle and Llyswen w Boughrood etc *S & B*
TALBENNY (St Mary) *see* Walton W w Talbenny and Haroldston W *St D*
TALGARREG (St David) *see* Llanarth and Capel Cynon w Talgarreg etc *St D*
TALGARTH (St Gwendoline) and Llanelieu *S & B 4* **V** D T WALTERS
TALIARIS (Holy Trinity) *see* Llandeilo and Taliaris *St D*
TALLARN GREEN (St Mary Magdalene) *see* Hanmer, Bronington, Bettisfield, Tallarn Green *St As*
TALLEY (St Michael) *see* Cynwyl Gaeo w Llansawel and Talley *St D*

TALYBONT (St David) *see* Llanfihangel Genau'r-glyn and Llangorwen *St D*
TALYGARN (St Anne) *see* Pontyclun w Talygarn *Llan*
TALYLLYN *see* Pennal w Corris and Esgairgeiliog *Ban*
TALYLLYN (St Mary) *see* Llanegryn w Aberdyfi w Tywyn *Ban*
TEMPLETON (St John) *see* Martletwy w Lawrenny and Minwear etc *St D*
TENBY (St Mary) (St Julian's Chapel) *St D 4* **TR** W D JENKINS, **TV** W J JONES, **C** M SOADY, **NSM** S M TEMPLE
TINTERN (St Michael) *see* Llandogo and Tintern *Mon*
TIRABAD (St David) *see* Llanwrtyd w Llanddulas in Tir Abad etc *S & B*
TIRTHIL (St Michael) *see* Pontlottyn w Fochriw *Llan*
TON-YR-YWEN (School) *see* Llanishen *Llan*
TONDU (St John) *see* Penyfai w Tondu *Llan*
TONDU (St Thomas) *as above*
TONGWYNLAIS (St Michael) (St James) *Llan 5* **V** C B W SMITH
TONMAWR (St Teilo) *see* Port Talbot St Agnes w Oakwood *Llan*
TONNA (St Anne) *see* Resolven w Tonna *Llan*
TONPENTRE *see* Ystradyfodwg *Llan*
TONYPANDY (St Andrew) w Clydach Vale *Llan 12* **V** M J GILL
TONYREFAIL (St Alban) *see* Tonyrefail w Gilfach Goch and Llandyfodwg *Llan*
TONYREFAIL (St David) *as above*
TONYREFAIL (St David) (St Alban) w Gilfach Goch and Llandyfodwg *Llan 12* **V** E HASTEY, **C** G H J BALL
TOWNHILL *see* Swansea St Nic *S & B*
TOWYN (St Mary) and St George *St As 1* **V** J W JAUNDRILL
TRAEAN-GLAS (St Mary) *see* Llywel and Traean-glas w Llanulid *S & B*
TRALLWNG (St David) and Bettws, Penpont w Aberyskir and Llanfihangel Nantbran *S & B 1* **V** B M JONES
TRAWSFYNYDD (St Madryn) *see* Maentwrog w Trawsfynydd *Ban*
TRE-GROES (St Ffraid) *see* Llandysul *St D*
TRE-LECH A'R BETWS (St Teilo) w Abernant and Llanwinio *St D 11* **V** D E EVANS
TREALAW (All Saints) *see* Porth w Trealaw *Llan*
TREBANOS (St Michael) *see* Clydach *S & B*
TREBOETH (St Alban) (Penlan Church) *S & B 10* **V** N J SHEARD, **NSM** R G JONES
TREDEGAR (St George) *Mon 7* **V** S M JOHN
TREDEGAR (St James) *Mon 7* **V** D S TURNER
TREDUNNOC (St Andrew) and Llantrisant w Llanhennock and Llanllowell *Mon 5* **V** R D WILLIAMS
TREFDRAETH (St Beuno) (Eglwys Crist y Brenin) w Aberffraw and Llangwyfan and Llangadwaladr *Ban 4* **R** J E T YENDALL
TREFEGLWYS (St Michael) *see* Llandinam w Trefeglwys w Penstrowed *Ban*
TREFGARN (St Michael) *see* Spittal w Trefgarn and Ambleston w St Dogwells *St D*
TREFILAN (St Hilary) *see* Llanfihangel Ystrad and Cilcennin w Trefilan etc *St D*
TREFLYS (St Michael) *see* Criccieth w Treflys *Ban*
TREFNANT (Holy Trinity) *St As 2* **R** W T C LACKEY
TREFOR (St George) *see* Llanaelhaearn w Clynnog Fawr *Ban*
TREFRIW (St Mary) *see* Caerhun w Llangelynin w Llanbedr-y-Cennin *Ban*
TREGAEAN (St Caian) *see* Llangefni w Tregaean and Llangristiolus etc *Ban*
TREGAER (St Mary) *see* Dingestow and Llangovan w Penyclawdd etc *Mon*
TREGARON (St Caron) w Ystrad Meurig and Strata Florida *St D 9* **V** *Vacant* (01974) 298937
TREGARTH (St Mair) *see* Llandygai w Tregarth *Ban*
TREGYNON (St Cynon) *see* Betws Cedewain and Tregynon and Llanwyddelan *St As*
TREHARRIS (St Matthias) w Bedlinog *Llan 9* **V** P M N GULLIDGE
TREHERBERT (St Alban) (St Mary Communion Centre) w Treorchy *Llan 12* **V** C T REANEY
TRELAWNYD (St Michael) *see* Dyserth and Trelawnyd and Cwm *St As*
TRELEWIS *see* Treharris w Bedlinog *Llan*
TRELLECH (St Nicholas) *see* Penallt and Trellech *Mon*
TRELLECH GRANGE (not known) *see* Llanishen w Trellech Grange and Llanfihangel etc *Mon*
TREMADOC *see* Ynyscynhaearn w Penmorfa and Porthmadog *Ban*
TREMAIN (St Michael) *see* Aberporth w Tremain w Blaenporth and Betws Ifan *St D*
TREMEIRCHION (Corpus Christi) *see* St As and Tremeirchion *St As*
TREORCHY (St Matthew) *see* Treherbert w Treorchy *Llan*
TRETHOMAS (St Thomas) *see* Bedwas and Rudry *Mon*
TRETOWER (St John the Evangelist) *see* Crickhowell w Cwmdu and Tretower *S & B*
TREUDDYN (St Mary) w Nercwys *St As 14* **V** J B JONES
TREVETHIN (St Cadoc) *see* Pontypool *Mon*
TREVETHIN (St John the Divine) *as above*
TREVOR (Church) *see* Llangollen w Trevor and Llantysilio *St As*
TREWALCHMAI (St Morhaiarn) *see* Llandrygarn w Bodwrog and Heneglwys etc *Ban*
TROED-YR-AUR (St Michael) *see* Newcastle Emlyn w Llandyfriog etc *St D*
TROEDRHIWGARTH (St Mary the Virgin) *Llan 8* **V** D G MORRIS
TROEDYRHIW (St John) w Merthyr Vale *Llan 9* **V** S J BARNES
TROFARTH (St John) *see* Brynymaen w Trofarth *St As*
TROSTEY (St David) *see* Bettws Newydd w Trostrey etc *Mon*
TUDWEILIOG (St Cwyfan) *see* Nefyn w Pistyll w Tudweiliog w Llandudwen etc *Ban*
TUMBLE (Dewi Sant) *see* Llan-non *St D*
TY SIGN (St David) *see* Risca *Mon*
TYCOCH (All Souls) *S & B 6* **V** R BRITTON, **NSM** I JONES
TYCROES (St Edmund) *see* Llanedi w Tycroes and Saron *St D*
TYLORSTOWN (Holy Trinity) (St Mary Magdalene) w Ynyshir *Llan 12* **V** *Vacant* (01443) 434201
TYNANT (Mission Church) *see* Maentwrog w Trawsfynydd *Ban*
TYTHEGSTON (St Tydwg) *see* Laleston w Tythegston and Merthyr Mawr *Llan*
TYWYN (St Cadfan) *see* Llanegryn w Aberdyfi w Tywyn *Ban*
TYWYN (St Matthew) *as above*
UNDY (St Mary) *see* Magor w Redwick and Undy *Mon*
UPTON *see* Cosheston w Nash and Upton *St D*
USK (St Mary) and Monkswood w Glascoed Chapel and Gwehelog *Mon 5* **V** R L DAVIES
UZMASTON (St Ismael) *see* Slebech and Uzmaston w Boulston *St D*
VALLEY (St Michael) w Llanfachraeth *Ban 3* **R** T BONNET
VAYNOR (St Gwynno) *see* Cefn Coed and Capel Nantddu w Vaynor etc *S & B*
WALTON EAST (St Mary) *see* Wiston w Walton E and Clarbeston *St D*
WALTON WEST (All Saints) w Talbenny and Haroldston West *St D 5* **R** B D B O'MALLEY
WALWYN'S CASTLE (St James the Great) w Robeston West *St D 5* **R** D J LOWEN
WARREN *see* Castlemartin w Warren and Angle etc *St D*
WATERSTON *see* Llanstadwel *St D*
WATTSTOWN (St Thomas) *see* Tylorstown w Ynyshir *Llan*
WAUNARLLWYDD (St Barnabas) *S & B 9* **V** A J M MEREDITH
WAUNFAWR (St John the Evangelist) *see* Llanbeblig w Caernarfon and Betws Garmon etc *Ban*
WAUNFELIN (St John the Divine) *see* Pontypool *Mon*
WAUNWEN (St Mark) *see* Swansea St Mark and St Jo *S & B*
WELSH ST DONATS (St Donat) *see* Pendoylan and Welsh St Donats *Llan*
WELSHPOOL (St Mary) (Christ Church) w Castle Caereinion *St As 10* **R** R L BROWN
WENVOE (St Mary) and St Lythans *Llan 6* **R** B T JOHNS
WHISTON (not known) *see* Goldcliffe and Whiston and Nash *Mon*
WHITCHURCH (St David) w Solva and St Elvis w Brawdy and Llandeloy *St D 3* **V** R J E W REES
WHITCHURCH (St Mary) (St Thomas) (All Saints) *Llan 5* **V** J H L ROWLANDS, **C** S F AMBANI, R L HEWETT, R M M JOHNSON, D J ADLINGTON
WHITEBROOK (Holy Trinity) *see* Llandogo and Tintern *Mon*
WHITECHURCH IN KEMES *see* Nevern and Y Beifil w Eglwyswrw and Meline etc *St D*
WHITFORD (St Mary and St Beuno) *St As 4* **V** R E KILGOUR
WHITLAND (St Mary) w Cyffig and Henllan Amgoed and Llan-gan *St D 15* **V** K G TAYLOR
WHITTON (St David) and Pilleth and Cascob w Llangynllo and Bleddfa *S & B 5* **V** A G LOAT
WICK (St James) *see* Llantwit Major *Llan*
WILCRICK (St Mary) *see* Bishton *Mon*
WILLIAMSTON, EAST (Church) *see* Jeffreyston w Reynoldston and E Williamston etc *St D*
WILLIAMSTOWN (St Illtud) *see* Dinas and Penygraig w Williamstown *Llan*
WISTON (St Mary Magdalene) w Walton East and Clarbeston *St D 2* **V** R JONES
WOLVESNEWTON (St Thomas a Becket) *see* Llangwm Uchaf w Llangwm Isaf w Gwernesney etc *Mon*
WONASTOW (St Wonnow) *see* Overmonnow w Wonastow and Michel Troy *Mon*

WORTHENBURY (St Deiniol) *see* Ban Monachorum and Worthenbury *St As*
WREXHAM (St Giles's Parish Church) (St David) (St Mark) (St Mary) (All Saints) (St Margaret) (St James) (St John) *St As 16* **R** M SQUIRES, **TV** M K SNELLGROVE, M J BENNETT, **TD** S M HUYTON, **C** D J BLACK, **NSM** J G AYLWARD
WYNDHAM (St David) *see* Nantymoel w Wyndham *Llan*
Y BEIFIL (St Andrew) *see* Nevern and Y Beifil w Eglwyswrw and Meline etc *St D*
Y FERWIG (St Pedrog) *see* Cardigan and Mwnt and Y Ferwig *St D*
YERBESTON *see* Martletwy w Lawrenny and Minwear etc *St D*
YNYSBOETH *see* Penrhiwceiber w Matthewstown and Ynysboeth *Llan*
YNYSCYNHAEARN (St Cynhaearn) (Mission Church) w Penmorfa and Porthmadog *Ban 10* **V** A J WILLIAMS
YNYSCYNON (St Cynon) *see* Ystrad Rhondda w Ynyscynon *Llan*
YNYSDDU (St Theodore) *see* Mynyddislwyn *Mon*
YNYSHIR (St Anne) *see* Tylorstown w Ynyshir *Llan*
YNYSHIR (St Thomas) *as above*
YNYSMEUDW (St Mary) *see* Llangiwg *S & B*
YSBYTY CYNFYN (St John the Baptist) w Llantrisant and Eglwys Newydd *St D 10* **V** M K R STALLARD
YSBYTY YSTWYTH (St John the Baptist) *see* Llanfihangel w Llanafan and Llanwnnws etc *St D*
YSFA (St Mark) *see* Rhayader and Nantmel *S & B*
YSGEIFIOG (St Mary) *see* Gorsedd w Brynford and Ysgeifiog *St As*
YSPYTY IFAN (St John the Baptist) *see* Cerrigydrudion w Llanfihangel etc *St As*
YSTALYFERA (St David) *S & B 7* **V** G TURNER
YSTRAD-FFIN (St Paulinus) *see* Cil-y-Cwm and Ystrad-ffin w Rhandir-mwyn etc *St D*
YSTRAD MEURIG (St John the Baptist) *see* Tregaron w Ystrad Meurig and Strata Florida *St D*
YSTRAD MYNACH (Holy Trinity) w Llanbradach *Llan 2* **V** M D BROOKS
YSTRAD RHONDDA (St Stephen) w Ynyscynon *Llan 12* **V** P S GALE
YSTRAD ROAD (St Illtyd) *see* Swansea St Pet *S & B*
YSTRADFELLTE (St Mary) *see* Penderyn w Ystradfellte and Pontneathvaughan *S & B*
YSTRADGYNLAIS (St Cynog) *S & B 7* **R** K EVANS, **NSM** J E PHILLIPS
YSTRADOWEN (St Owain) *see* Cowbridge *Llan*
YSTRADYFODWG (St John the Baptist) *Llan 12* **V** P N COLEMAN, **NSM** E M JONES

SCOTTISH INCUMBENCIES

An index of the incumbencies of the Scottish Episcopal Church. The incumbency entry gives the full legal name, followed by the diocese, name(s) and appointment(s) of the clergy serving there (if there are none, the telephone number of the parsonage house is given). Church dedications are indicated in brackets. The following are the main abbreviations used; for others see the full list of abbreviations.

C	Curate
C-in-c	Curate-in-charge
Dn-in-c	Deacon-in-charge
Dss	Deaconess
Hon C	Honorary Curate
NSM	Non-stipendiary Minister
P-in-c	Priest-in-charge
Par Dn	Parish Deacon
R	Rector
TM	Team Minister

ABERCHIRDER (St Marnan) *Mor* **R** H M LOPDELL-BRADSHAW
ABERDEEN (Cathedral of St Andrew) *Ab* **R** W D WIGHTMAN, **NSM** R FINNIE
ABERDEEN (St Clement) *Ab* **R** *Vacant* (01224) 662247
ABERDEEN (St James) *Ab* **R** M C PATERNOSTER
ABERDEEN (St John the Evangelist) *Ab* **R** A B ALLAN
ABERDEEN (St Margaret of Scotland) *Ab* **R** A E NIMMO, **NSM** A J MURPHY
ABERDEEN (St Mary) *Ab* **R** I M THOMPSON
ABERDEEN (St Ninian) *Ab* **P-in-c** W D WIGHTMAN, **NSM** R FINNIE
ABERDEEN (St Peter) *Ab* **R** D N CALVIN-THOMAS
ABERDOUR (St Columba) - West Fife Team Ministry *St And* **P-in-c** E J COOK
ABERFOYLE (St Mary) *St And* **R** A BUNNELL, **NSM** S M COATES
ABERLOUR (St Margaret of Scotland) *Mor* **R** J M DUNCAN
ABOYNE (St Peter) *Ab* **R** C S GIBSON, **NSM** A F R FENNELL
AIRDRIE (St Paul) *Glas* **R** D S MUNGAVIN
ALEXANDRIA (St Mungo) *Glas* **P-in-c** D J GORDON
ALFORD (St Andrew) *Ab* **R** J WALKER, **NSM** J BURCHILL
ALLOA (St John the Evangelist) *St And* **R** A H D KNOCK, **NSM** D FINLAYSON, E FORGAN, R E MURRAY
ALYTH (St Ninian) *St And* **R** K W RATHBAND, **C** J I CAMERON, **NSM** P S FERNANDO, D A CAMERON, R G SOMMERVILLE
ANNAN (St John the Evangelist) *Glas* **P-in-c** D J B FOSTEKEW
APPIN *see* Portnacrois *Arg*
ARBROATH (St Mary) *Bre* **R** W F WARD, **Hon C** M T BONE
ARDBRECKNISH (St James) *Arg* **R** A M MACLEAN
ARDCHATTAN (Holy Spirit) *Arg* **R** A M MACLEAN
ARDROSSAN (St Andrew) *Glas* **P-in-c** S ROBERTSON, **NSM** A MONTGOMERIE
ARPAFEELIE (St John the Evangelist) *Mor* **R** R F BURKITT
ARRAN, ISLE OF *Arg* **NSM** T A PRINGLE
AUCHENBLAE *see* Drumtochty *Bre*
AUCHINDOIR (St Mary) *Ab* **R** J WALKER, **NSM** J BURCHILL
AUCHMITHIE (St Peter) *Bre* **R** S FOX, **NSM** S G LETTON
AUCHTERARDER (St Kessog) *St And* **R** A C RUSSELL, **NSM** W B ROOTES
AYR (Holy Trinity) *Glas* **R** I JONES, **C** G B FYFE, **NSM** J A MASON
BAILLIESTON (St John) *Glas* **TV** J M McLUCKIE, **C** J B LENNOX
BALERNO (St Mungo) *Edin* **R** M J H ROUND, **NSM** N F HALLAM
BALLACHULISH (St John) *Arg* **R** J R BETTELEY
BALLATER (St Kentigern) *Ab* **R** C S GIBSON, **NSM** A F R FENNELL
BANCHORY (St Ternan) *Ab* **R** R E ROYDEN
BANFF (St Andrew) *Ab* **R** *Vacant*
BARROWFIELD (St John the Baptist) *Glas* **NSM** A W WINSPER
BATHGATE (St Columba) *Edin* **P-in-c** S C BONNEY, **NSM** P F KIRK
BEARSDEN (All Saints) *Glas* **TR** K T ROACH, **TV** E M FARROW
BELLS WYND *see* Douglas *Glas*
BIELDSIDE (St Devenick) *Ab* **R** K D GORDON, **NSM** P W BRUNT, **Dss** J E MACCORMACK
BIRNAM *see* Dunkeld *St And*
BISHOPBRIGGS (St James-the-Less) *Glas* **P-in-c** S R PAISLEY
BLAIR ATHOLL *see* Kilmaveonaig *St And*
BLAIRGOWRIE (St Catherine) *St And* **R** K W RATHBAND, **C** J I CAMERON, **NSM** P S FERNANDO, D A CAMERON, R G SOMMERVILLE
BO'NESS (St Catharine) *Edin* **P-in-c** N D MacCALLUM, **Hon C** T J LENNARD, E J M P LENNARD
BRAEMAR (St Margaret) *Ab* **P-in-c** C S GIBSON, **NSM** A F R FENNELL
BRECHIN (St Andrew) *Bre* **R** S FOX, **NSM** S G LETTON
BRIDGE OF ALLAN (St Saviour) *St And* **R** J M CROOK, **NSM** D FINLAYSON, S J HARRISON
BRIDGE OF WEIR (St Mary) *Glas* **R** E G LINDSAY
BRIDGEND *see* Islay *Arg*
BRORA (St Columba) *Mor* **P-in-c** A R GORDON
BROUGHTY FERRY (St Mary) *Bre* **R** R W BREADEN
BUCKIE (All Saints) *Ab* **P-in-c** J M PAISEY, **NSM** P J LEES
BUCKSBURN (St Machar) *Ab* **P-in-c** D HEDDLE
BURNSIDE *see* Moffat *Glas*
BURNTISLAND (St Serf) - West Fife Team Ministry *St And* **R** *Vacant*
BURRAVOE (St Colman) *Ab* **R** L S SMITH, **NSM** E H McNAB
CALLANDER (St Andrew) *St And* **R** A BUNNELL
CAMBUSLANG (St Cuthbert) *Glas* **R** A M BURN-MURDOCH, **NSM** M A DANSON
CAMPBELTOWN (St Kiaran) *Arg* **R** K V PAGAN
CARNOUSTIE (Holy Rood) *Bre* **R** D B MACKAY, **Hon C** J B HARDIE
CASTLE DOUGLAS (St Ninian) *Glas* **R** *Vacant* (01556) 3818
CATTERLINE (St Philip) *Bre* **NSM** G H J PAISEY
CHALLOCH (All Saints) w Newton Stewart *Glas* **P-in-c** N E H NEWTON, **Hon C** R C CUTLER
CHAPELHILL *see* Cruden Bay *Ab*
CLARKSTON (St Aidan) *Glas* **P-in-c** D J NORWOOD, **Hon C** K R BREWIN, C CURTIS
CLERMISTON *see* Edin Clermiston Em *Edin*
CLYDEBANK (St Columba) *Glas* **R** R J A HASLAM, **NSM** G L NICOLL
COATBRIDGE (St John the Evangelist) *Glas* **R** D S MUNGAVIN
COLDSTREAM (St Mary and All Souls) *Edin* **P-in-c** G T C TAMS
COLINTON *see* Edin St Cuth *Edin*
COMRIE (St Serf) *St And* **R** H G C LEE
COUPAR ANGUS (St Anne) *St And* **R** K W RATHBAND, **C** J I CAMERON, **NSM** P S FERNANDO, D A CAMERON, R G SOMMERVILLE
COURTHILL Chapel *see* Kishorn *Mor*
COVE BAY (St Mary) *Ab* **P-in-c** D N CALVIN-THOMAS
CRAIGHALL *see* Ellon *Ab*
CRIEFF (St Columba) *St And* **R** H G C LEE
CROACHY *see* Strathnairn St Paul *Mor*
CROMARTY (St Regulus) *Mor* **R** R F BURKITT
CRUDEN BAY (St James the Less) *Ab* **R** G H STRANRAER-MULL, **NSM** J F F SHEPHERD, G P WHALLEY, J F F STENHOUSE, D E F FIRMIN, A L JAMES, R SPENCER
CULLODEN (St Mary-in-the-Fields) *Mor* **P-in-c** M E GRANT, A A SINCLAIR
CUMBERNAULD (Holy Name) *Glas* **P-in-c** D A COOK
CUMBRAE (Cathedral of The Isles and Collegiate Church of the Holy Spirit) *Arg* **P-in-c** D A GRAY
CUMINESTOWN (St Luke) *Ab* **R** *Vacant*
CUPAR (St James the Great) *St And* **R** M C ALDCROFT, **Par Dn** M D HERVEY
DALBEATTIE (Christ Church) *Glas* **R** J F C WOODLEY
DALKEITH (St Mary) *Edin* **R** M A S GOODMAN
DALMAHOY (St Mary) *Edin* **R** *Vacant* 0131-333 1683
DALRY (St Peter) *Glas* **P-in-c** I BOFFEY, S ROBERTSON
DINGWALL (St James the Great) *Mor* **P-in-c** M F HICKFORD
DOLLAR (St James the Great) *St And* **R** C P SHERLOCK, **NSM** D FINLAYSON, F A M LAWRY, H I SOGA
DORNOCH (St Finnbarr) *Mor* **P-in-c** A R GORDON
DOUGLAS (Sancta Sophia) *Glas* **R** B H C GORDON
DOUNE (St Modoc) *St And* **NSM** S M COATES
DRUMLITHIE (St John the Baptist) *Bre* **R** M J R TURNER
DRUMTOCHTY (St Palladius) *Bre* **R** M J R TURNER, **NSM** D P STEEL
DUFFTOWN (St Michael and All Angels) *Ab* **C** R E TAIT

DUMBARTON (St Augustine) *Glas* **P-in-c** M A F BYRNE, **NSM** J M LOCOCK
DUMFRIES (St John the Evangelist) *Glas* **R** D W BAYNE, **C** G A F HINCHCLIFFE
DUNBAR (St Anne) *Edin* **R** I J PATON, **C** G J GRUNEWALD, **NSM** J WOOD
DUNBLANE (St Mary) *St And* **R** G TELLINI, **NSM** J W ALLAN
DUNDEE (Cathedral of St Paul) *Bre* **NSM** G J H PONT, G M GREIG
DUNDEE (St John the Baptist) *Bre* **P-in-c** J J MORROW, **Hon C** J P FORBES
DUNDEE (St Luke) *Bre* **R** K J CAVANAGH, **NSM** L STEVENSON
DUNDEE (St Margaret) *Bre* **R** W J McAUSLAND, **C** P M BALFOUR
DUNDEE (St Martin) *Bre* **P-in-c** D ELDER
DUNDEE (St Mary Magdalene) *Bre* **R** D SHEPHERD, **Hon C** M T BONE
DUNDEE (St Ninian) *Bre* **P-in-c** E M FAULKES
DUNDEE (St Salvador) *Bre* **R** P J HARVIE
DUNFERMLINE (Holy Trinity) - West Fife Team Ministry *St And* **R** H B FARQUHARSON, **NSM** V A NELLIST, E J COOK, J A RANDALL
DUNKELD (St Mary) w Birnam *St And* **R** R F PATERSON, **NSM** I ATKINSON
DUNOON (Holy Trinity) *Arg* **R** G A GUINNESS
DUNS (Christ Church) *Edin* **R** C J MARTIN, **Hon C** A J TABRAHAM, M E JONES, **NSM** E S JONES
DUROR (St Adamnan) *Arg* **R** D W DAY
EAST KILBRIDE (St Mark) *Glas* **R** K G G GIBSON, **NSM** M M COLEMAN
EASTGATE (St Peter) *see* Peebles *Edin*
EASTRIGGS (St John the Evangelist) *Glas* **P-in-c** M P CALLAGHAN
EDINBURGH (Cathedral of St Mary) *Edin* **R** G J T FORBES, **C** J CUTHBERT, J A CONWAY, **NSM** J M MILLARD, I RYRIE
EDINBURGH (Christ Church) *Edin* **R** J A MEIN, **TV** D L COLLINGWOOD, **Min** P D SKELTON, **NSM** R H PROCTER
EDINBURGH (Emmanuel) *Edin* **P-in-c** P J WARREN
EDINBURGH (Good Shepherd) *Edin* **R** D H RIMMER
EDINBURGH (Holy Cross) *Edin* **R** W D KORNAHRENS, **C** T J HARKIN, **NSM** M F HARRISON
EDINBURGH (Old St Paul) *Edin* **Hon C** C S DAVIES-COLE, D A B JOWITT, **NSM** R G W STRONG, C NAISMITH
EDINBURGH (St Andrew and St Aidan) *Edin* **R** T G ENGH, **NSM** I C McKENZIE
EDINBURGH (St Barnabas) *Edin* **P-in-c** P D DIXON, **NSM** A C ANDERSON
EDINBURGH (St Columba) *Edin* **R** A J FULLER, **TV** R O GOULD, J S RICHARDSON
EDINBURGH (St Cuthbert) *Edin* **R** M C GOLDSMITH, **C** D YEOMAN, G R HART
EDINBURGH (St David of Scotland) *Edin* **P-in-c** J N WYNN-EVANS
EDINBURGH (St Fillan) *Edin* **R** F W TOMLINSON, **NSM** D EMERSON, D L COLLINGWOOD
EDINBURGH (St Hilda) *Edin* **R** F W TOMLINSON, **NSM** D EMERSON, D L COLLINGWOOD
EDINBURGH (St James the Less) *Edin* **R** A J BAIN
EDINBURGH (St John the Evangelist) *Edin* **R** M J FULLER, **NSM** P J BRAND, C A HUME
EDINBURGH (St Luke) *see* Wester Hailes St Luke *Edin*
EDINBURGH (St Margaret of Scotland) *Edin* **TV** M S NORTHCOTT, **P-in-c** A J BAIN, **NSM** H L WILLIAMSON, C NAISMITH
EDINBURGH (St Mark) *Edin* **R** T G ENGH, **NSM** I C McKENZIE
EDINBURGH (St Martin of Tours) *Edin* **R** W J T BROCKIE, **NSM** S KILBEY
EDINBURGH (St Michael and All Saints) *Edin* **R** K PEARSON, **NSM** J E ROULSTON
EDINBURGH (St Ninian) *Edin* **P-in-c** P J D ALLEN, **NSM** R T PERCIVAL, D DARLING
EDINBURGH (St Paul and St George) *Edin* **R** M P MAUDSLEY, **C** D G RICHARDS
EDINBURGH (St Peter) *Edin* **R** I D ZASS-OGILVIE, **C** I M POOBALAN, **Hon C** C T UPTON
EDINBURGH (St Philip and St James) *Edin* **R** K F SCOTT
EDINBURGH (St Salvador) *Edin* **P-in-c** G R HART
EDINBURGH (St Thomas) Private Chapel *Edin* **Chapl** M J PARKER, **C** R P HARLEY
EDINBURGH (St Vincent) Private Chapel *Edin* **Chapl** M A CLARK
ELGIN (Holy Trinity) w Lossiemouth (St Margaret) *Mor* **R** G S BROWN
ELIE AND EARLSFERRY (St Michael and All Angels) *St And* **R** S G HALL
ELLON (St Mary on the Rock) *Ab* **R** G H STRANRAER-MULL, **NSM** J F F SHEPHERD, G P WHALLEY, J F F STENHOUSE, D E F FIRMIN, A L JAMES, R SPENCER
EORRAPAIDH (St Moluag) *Arg* **R** S J G BENNIE, **Hon C** J R BULLAMORE, **NSM** B A MORRISON
ERSKINE *see* Renfrew *Glas*
EYEMOUTH (St Ebba) *Edin* **P-in-c** S A BULL
FALKIRK (Christ Church) *Edin* **P-in-c** D I McCOSH
FASQUE (St Andrew) *Bre* **R** M J R TURNER
FETTERCAIRN *see* Fasque *Bre*
FOCHABERS Gordon Chapel *Mor* **R** J M DUNCAN
FORFAR (St John the Evangelist) *St And* **R** J M RICHARDSON, **C** E N RAMSAY, **NSM** J M PRIOR, D A ROBERTSON
FORRES (St John the Evangelist) *Mor* **R** R W FORREST
FORT WILLIAM (St Andrew) *Arg* **R** J H J MACLEAY, **NSM** D N CLIFFORD
FORTROSE (St Andrew) *Mor* **R** R F BURKITT
FRASERBURGH (St Peter) w New Pitsligo *Ab* **R** A O COUSLAND
FYVIE (All Saints) *Ab* **R** A B MacGILLIVRAY
GALASHIELS (St Peter) *Edin* **R** T D MORRIS, **Hon C** O L S DOVER
GALLOWGATE *see* Aberdeen St Marg *Ab*
GARTCOSH (St Andrew) *Glas* **R** D S MUNGAVIN
GATEHOUSE OF FLEET (St Mary) *Glas* **R** *Vacant*
GIRVAN (St John) *Glas* **C** G B FYFE, **NSM** B H G COLLIE, J A MASON
GLASGOW (All Saints) *Glas* **P-in-c** V J PERRICONE
GLASGOW (Cathedral of St Mary the Virgin) *Glas* **C** K H MARSHALL
GLASGOW (Good Shepherd and Ascension) *Glas* **R** *Vacant*
GLASGOW (Holy Cross) *Glas* **NSM** D D KEEBLE
GLASGOW (St Bride) *Glas* **R** G M M THOMSON, **P-in-c** I T DRAPER
GLASGOW (St Gabriel) *Glas* **R** *Vacant*
GLASGOW (St George) *Glas* **Hon C** S M P MAITLAND
GLASGOW (St Kentigern) *Glas* **Hon C** J GRAHAM
Glasgow St Luke *Glas* **I** *Vacant*
GLASGOW (St Margaret) *Glas* **R** T C O MONTGOMERY
GLASGOW (St Matthew) *Glas* **P-in-c** M N OXLEY
GLASGOW (St Ninian) *Glas* **R** D W J REID, **Hon C** R F GRAHAM
GLASGOW (St Oswald) *Glas* **R** P J TAYLOR
GLASGOW (St Serf) *Glas* **R** *Vacant*
GLASGOW (St Silas) Private Chapel *Glas* **R** D W McCARTHY
GLENCARSE (All Saints) *Bre* **P-in-c** K E WRIGHT
GLENCOE (St Mary) *Arg* **R** J R BETTELEY
GLENROTHES (St Luke the Evangelist) - Cen Fife Team Ministry *St And* **TV** J D MARTIN, **C** A M H ROBERTSON
GLENURQUHART (St Ninian) *Mor* **NSM** J A HUTTON
GOUROCK (St Bartholomew) *Glas* **C** J F LYON
GOVAN *see* Glas St Gabr *Glas*
GRANGEMOUTH (St Mary) *Edin* **R** N D MacCALLUM, **Hon C** T J LENNARD, E J M P LENNARD
GRANTOWN-ON-SPEY (St Columba) *Mor* **P-in-c** A WHEATLEY, D H BENNETT
GREENOCK (St John the Evangelist) *Glas* **R** C D LYON, **C** J F LYON
GRETNA (All Saints) *Glas* **P-in-c** M P CALLAGHAN
GREYFRIARS *see* Kircudbright *Glas*
GRULINE (St Columba) *Arg* **P-in-c** D W DAY
GULLANE (St Adrian) *Edin* **R** J C LINDSAY
HADDINGTON (Holy Trinity) *Edin* **R** I J PATON, **NSM** J WOOD
HAMILTON (St Mary the Virgin) *Glas* **R** I D BARCROFT
HARRIS, ISLE OF *see* Leverburgh *Arg*
HAWICK (St Cuthbert) *Edin* **R** S M PATERSON
HAY DRIVE *see* Edin St Andr and St Aid *Edin*
HELENSBURGH (St Michael and All Angels) *Glas* **R** A B LAING, **NSM** A J MANN, B M THATCHER
HUNTLY (Christ Church) *Mor* **R** H M LOPDELL-BRADSHAW
INNERLEITHEN (St Andrew) *Edin* **P-in-c** R D LEE, **NSM** C B AITCHISON
INSCH (St Drostan) *Ab* **R** A B MacGILLIVRAY
INVERARAY (All Saints) *Arg* **R** *Vacant*
INVERBERVIE (St David) *Bre* **P-in-c** I G STEWART
INVERGORDON (St Ninian) *Mor* **R** C H CLAPSON
INVERGOWRIE (All Souls) *Bre* **P-in-c** A W CUMMINS
INVERKEITHING (St Peter) - West Fife Team Ministry *St And* **R** *Vacant*
INVERNESS (Cathedral of St Andrew) *Mor* **R** M E GRANT, **C** G S P C NAPIER, **Hon C** J W L TAYLOR
INVERNESS (St John the Evangelist) *Mor* **P-in-c** A A SINCLAIR
INVERNESS (St Michael and All Angels) *Mor* **R** L A BLACK

INVERURIE (St Mary) *Ab* **R** J WALKER, **NSM** J BURCHILL
IONA (St Columba) *Arg* **R** *Vacant*
IRVINE (St Andrew) Local Ecumenical Project *Glas* **P-in-c** S ROBERTSON, **NSM** A MONTGOMERIE
ISLAY (St Columba) *Arg* **R** K V PAGAN
JEDBURGH (St John the Evangelist) *Edin* **R** R M WATTS, **Hon C** W J GROVER, **NSM** S E WIFFEN
JOHNSTONE (St John) *Glas* **P-in-c** S A MARSH
KEITH (Holy Trinity) *Mor* **R** H M LOPDELL-BRADSHAW
KELSO (St Andrew) *Edin* **R** D R H EDWARDSON
KEMNAY (St Anne) *Ab* **R** J WALKER, **NSM** J BURCHILL
KENTALLEN (St Moluag) *Arg* **P-in-c** D W DAY
KESSOCK-TORE *see* Arpafeelie *Mor*
KILLIN (St Fillan) *St And* **R** *Vacant*
KILMACOLM (St Fillan) *Glas* **R** E G LINDSAY
KILMARNOCK (Holy Trinity) *Glas* **R** K G STEPHEN
KILMARTIN (St Columba) *Arg* **R** R F F FLATT
KILMAVEONAIG (St Adamnan) *St And* **R** R G DEVONSHIRE
KINCARDINE O'NEIL (Christ Church) *Ab* **R** R E ROYDEN
KINGHORN (St Mary and St Leonard) *St And* **R** J R LEIGH, **NSM** G N BENSON
KINLOCH RANNOCH (All Saints) *St And* **P-in-c** J L L FAGERSON
KINLOCHLEVEN (St Paul) *Arg* **P-in-c** D W DAY
KINLOCHMOIDART (St Finian) *Arg* **P-in-c** D W DAY, **NSM** D N CLIFFORD
KINROSS (St Paul) *St And* **R** K S NICHOLSON
KIRCUDBRIGHT (St Francis of Assisi) *Glas* **R** *Vacant* (01557) 30580
KIRKCALDY (St Peter) *St And* **R** J R LEIGH, **NSM** G N BENSON
KIRKWALL (St Olaf) *Ab* **R** J MORSON, **NSM** E MORSON
KIRRIEMUIR (St Mary) *St And* **P-in-c** I M TEMPLETON, **C** E N RAMSAY, **NSM** D MACLEAN, J M PRIOR, P D WILLIAMS
KISHORN Chapel *Mor* **P-in-c** C R DORMER
LADYBANK (St Mary) *St And* **R** M C ALDCROFT
LADYCROFT *see* Balerno *Edin*
LANARK (Christ Church) *Glas* **R** B H C GORDON
LANGHOLM (All Saints) *Glas* **R** *Vacant* (01461) 38268
LARGS (St Columba) *Glas* **R** G D DUNCAN, **Hon C** J POW
LASSWADE (St Leonard) *Edin* **R** M A S GOODMAN
LAURENCEKIRK (St Laurence) *Bre* **R** M J R TURNER, **NSM** D P STEEL
LEITH (St James the Less) *see* Edin St Jas *Edin*
LENZIE (St Cyprian) *Glas* **R** K J SHAW, **Hon C** B A OGUGUO, **NSM** S H B GORTON
LERWICK (St Magnus) *Ab* **R** L S SMITH, **NSM** E H McNAB
LEVEN (St Margaret) - Cen Fife Team Ministry *St And* **TV** J D MARTIN, **C** A M H ROBERTSON, T SHARPUS-JONES
LEVERBURGH *Arg* **P-in-c** J H DOWNIE
LEWIS, ISLE OF *see* Stornoway *Arg*
LINLITHGOW (St Peter) *Edin* **P-in-c** S C BONNEY
LIVINGSTON Local Ecumenical Project *Edin* **TV** P C J BURGESS, **NSM** M KESTON
LOCHALSH (St Donnan) *Mor* **P-in-c** C R DORMER
LOCHBUIE (St Kilda) *Arg* **P-in-c** D W DAY
LOCHEARNHEAD (St Angus) *St And* **P-in-c** H G C LEE
LOCHGELLY (St Finnian) - Cen Fife Team Ministry *St And* **TV** J D MARTIN, **C** A M H ROBERTSON
LOCHGILPHEAD (Christ Church) *Arg* **R** R F F FLATT
LOCKERBIE (All Saints) *Glas* **P-in-c** D J B FOSTEKEW
LONGSIDE (St John) *Ab* **R** *Vacant*
LOSSIEMOUTH (St Margaret) *see* Elgin w Lossiemouth *Mor*
LUNAN HEAD (St Margaret) *St And* **R** *Vacant*
MARYGATE *see* Pittenweem *St And*
MAYBOLE (St Oswald) *Glas* **C** G B FYFE, **NSM** B H G COLLIE, J A MASON
MELROSE (Holy Trinity) *Edin* **R** P A BURT, **NSM** D W WOOD
MILLPORT *see* Cumbrae (or Millport) *Arg*
MILNGAVIE (St Andrew) *Glas* **P-in-c** P G M FLETCHER
MOFFAT (St John the Evangelist) *Glas* **Par Dn** J M MARR, **Hon C** R J AMES, J K TOWERS
MONIFIETH (Holy Trinity) *Bre* **R** R JONES
MONKSTOWN *see* Ladybank *St And*
MONTROSE (St Mary and St Peter) *Bre* **R** I G STEWART
MOTHERWELL (Holy Trinity) *Glas* **R** M C REED
MUCHALLS (St Ternan) *Bre* **P-in-c** K R A DALL, **Par Dn** J NELSON
MULL, ISLE OF *see* Gruline *Arg*
MULL, ISLE OF *see* Lochbuie *Arg*
MUSSELBURGH (St Peter) *Edin* **R** J M JONES, **NSM** D R BUNYAN
MUTHILL (St James) *St And* **R** A C RUSSELL, **NSM** W B ROOTES
NAIRN (St Columba) *Mor* **P-in-c** D McALISTER
NETHER LOCHABER (St Bride) *Arg* **R** *Vacant*
NEW GALLOWAY (St Margaret of Scotland) *Glas* **P-in-c** D JELLEY
NEW PITSLIGO (St John the Evangelist) *see* Fraserburgh w New Pitsligo *Ab*
NEWBURGH (St Katherine) *St And* **P-in-c** A P PEEBLES
NEWPORT-ON-TAY (St Mary) *St And* **P-in-c** D CAMPBELL
NEWTON STEWART *see* Challoch w Newton Stewart *Glas*
NORTH BALLACHULISH *see* Onich *Arg*
NORTH BERWICK (St Baldred) *Edin* **R** J C LINDSAY
OBAN (Cathedral of St John) *Arg* **R** A M MACLEAN
OLD DEER (St Drostan) *Ab* **R** *Vacant* (01771) 2344
OLDMELDRUM (St Matthew) *Ab* **R** A B MacGILLIVRAY
ONICH (St Bride) *Arg* **R** J R BETTELEY
PAISLEY (Holy Trinity) *Glas* **R** B A HUTTON, **NSM** A G BOYD
PAISLEY (St Barnabas) *Glas* **R** B A HUTTON, **NSM** A G BOYD
PEEBLES (St Peter) *Edin* **R** R D LEE, **NSM** C B AITCHISON
PENICUIK (St James the Less) *Edin* **R** G J SCOTT, **NSM** N F SUTTLE, F E McLEAN, T A BRAMLEY
PERTH (Cathedral of St Ninian) *St And*, V A NELLIST **R** K G FRANZ, **C** M D ROBSON, K HOLDSWORTH, **NSM** R F SAUNDERS, M D ROBSON
PERTH (St John the Baptist) *St And* **R** R C FYFFE, **C** D F L PETZSCH, **Hon C** H L YOUNG, R H DARROCH, W F HARRIS
PETERHEAD (St Peter) *Ab* **R** J H BOOKER
PINMORE *Glas* **NSM** B H G COLLIE
PITLOCHRY (Holy Trinity) *St And* **R** R G DEVONSHIRE
PITTENWEEM (St John the Evangelist) *St And* **R** S G HALL
POLTALLOCH *see* Kilmartin *Arg*
POOLEWE (St Maelrubha) *Mor* **P-in-c** C R DORMER, **NSM** H S WIDDOWS
PORT GLASGOW (St Mary the Virgin) *Glas* **P-in-c** S D N BARRETT
PORTNACROIS (Holy Cross) *Arg* **P-in-c** D W DAY
PORTPATRICK (St Ninian) *Glas* **R** *Vacant*
PORTREE (St Columba) *Arg* **P-in-c** J M PORTEUS, **NSM** J O LEAWORTHY
PORTSOY (St John the Baptist) *Ab* **P-in-c** J M PAISEY
PRESTONPANS (St Andrew) *Edin* **R** J M JONES, **NSM** D R BUNYAN
PRESTWICK (St Ninian) *Glas* **R** P D NOBLE, **Hon C** P M DOUGLAS
RENFREW (St Margaret) w Erskine *Glas* **P-in-c** S A MARSH
ROSLIN (Collegiate Church of St Matthew) *Edin* **NSM** M J FASS
ROTHESAY (St Paul) *Arg* **R** *Vacant*
ROTHIEMURCHUS (St John the Baptist) *Mor* **P-in-c** A WHEATLEY, C K RACE, **C** H COOK, **Hon C** R K SHAW
ST ANDREWS (All Saints) *St And* **R** J P MASON, **C** M-L MOFFETT
ST ANDREWS (St Andrew) - Cen Fife Team Ministry *St And* **R** R A GILLIES, **C** P B ROBERTSON, T SHARPUS-JONES, **Hon C** G D WHITE, **NSM** D A BEADLE, R T EVANS, J H BRUCE
ST FILLANS (Church of the Holy Spirit) *St And* **R** *Vacant*
SANDYLOAN *see* Gullane *Edin*
SELKIRK (St John the Evangelist) *Edin* **R** W B ELLIOT, **NSM** E S JONES
SKYE, ISLE OF *see* Portree *Arg*
SOUTH QUEENSFERRY (Priory Church St Mary of Mount Carmel) *Edin* **C** T J HARKIN, **NSM** A V SMITH
STANLEY (St Columba) *St And* **NSM** R F SAUNDERS, J M HARRISON
STIRLING (Holy Trinity) *Edin* **R** C JARMAN
STONEHAVEN (St James) *Bre* **NSM** G H J PAISEY
STORNOWAY (St Peter) *Arg* **R** S J G BENNIE
STRANRAER (St John the Evangelist) *Glas* **R** *Vacant*
STRATHNAIRN (St Paul) *Mor* **R** M E GRANT, **Hon C** S A T MALLIN
STRATHPEFFER (St Anne) *Mor* **P-in-c** M F HICKFORD
STRATHTAY (St Andrew) *St And* **R** R F PATERSON
STRICHEN (All Saints) *Ab* **R** *Vacant*
STROMNESS (St Mary) *Ab* **R** J MORSON, **NSM** I St C COSBY
STRONTIAN *Arg* **P-in-c** D W DAY, **NSM** D N CLIFFORD
TAIN (St Andrew) *Mor* **P-in-c** M F HUNT, **NSM** C J PIPER
TARFSIDE (St Drostan) *Bre* **R** S FOX, **NSM** S G LETTON
TAYPORT (St Margaret of Scotland) *St And* **P-in-c** D CAMPBELL
TEINDHILLGREEN *see* Duns *Edin*
THURSO (St Peter and Holy Rood) *Mor* **P-in-c** R MARTIN, **Hon C** F E DAVIES, G R TYLER
TIGHNABRUAICH *Arg* **R** *Vacant*

TOFTS *see* Dalry *Glas*
TORRY *see* Aberdeen St Pet *Ab*
TROON (St Ninian) *Glas* **R** J A TRIMBLE
TURRIFF (St Congan) *Ab* **NSM** P J LEES, S M DYER
UDDINGSTON (St Andrew) *Glas* **R** A M BURN-MURDOCH, **NSM** M A DANSON
ULLAPOOL (St Mary the Virgin) *Mor* **P-in-c** C R DORMER
West Coast Joint Congregations Moray *Mor* **Hon C** G J WILLEY
WEST FIFE Team Ministry - See ABERDOUR; BURNTISLAND; DUNFERMLINE; INVERKEITHING and LOCHGELLY *St And* **NSM** V A NELLIST
WEST LINTON (St Mungo) *Edin* **R** G J SCOTT, **NSM** F E McLEAN, T A BRAMLEY
WESTER HAILES (St Luke) *Edin* , K R WHITEFIELD
WESTGATE *see* Dunbar *Edin*
WESTHILL (Trinity) *Ab* **R** I J FERGUSON
WHITERASHES (All Saints) *Ab* **R** A B MacGILLIVRAY
WHITING BAY *see* Is of Arran *Arg*
WICK (St John the Evangelist) *Mor* **R** R MARTIN, **Hon C** F E DAVIES, G R TYLER
WISHAW (St Andrew) *Glas* **R** M C REED
WOODHEAD OF FETTERLETTER *see* Fyvie *Ab*
YELL *see* Burravoe *Ab*

IRISH BENEFICES AND CHURCHES

An index of the benefices of the Church of Ireland (shown in bold type), together with entries for churches and other licensed places of worship. Where the church name is the same as that of the benefice (or the first placed name in the benefice), the church entry is omitted. Church dedications are indicated in brackets.

The benefice entry gives the full legal name, together with the diocese and the name(s) and appointment(s) of clergy serving there (if there are none, the telephone number of the parsonage house is given). The following are the main abbreviations used; for others see the full list of abbreviations.

Bp's C	Bishop's Curate	**Hon C**	Honorary Curate
C	Curate	**I**	Incumbent (includes Rector or Vicar)
C-in-c	Curate-in-charge	**NSM**	Non-stipendiary Minister

AASLEAGH (St John the Baptist) *see* Tuam w Cong and Aasleagh *T, K & A*

ABBEYLEIX (no dedication) w The Old Church, Ballyroan, Ballinakill, Killermogh, Aughmacart, Durrow and Attanagh *C & O* **I** P A HARVEY, **NSM** A WALLACE

ABBEYSTREWRY (no dedication) w Creagh, Tullagh, Castlehaven and Caheragh *C, C & R* **I** T R LESTER

ABINGDON (no dedication) *see* Killaloe w Stradbally *L & K*

ACHILL (Holy Trinity) *see* Aughaval w Achill, Knappagh, Dugort etc *T, K & A*

ACHONRY (Cathedral of St Crumnathy) w Tubbercurry and Killoran *T, K & A* **I** S F GILLMOR

ACTON (no dedication) w Drumbanagher *Arm* **I** *Vacant*

ADARE (St Nicholas) w Kilpeacon and Croom *L & K* **I** M J B NUTTALL, **P-in-c** P C JOHANSEN

AGHABOG (no dedication) *see* Ematris w Rockcorry, Aghabog and Aughnamullan *Clogh*

AGHADE (All Saints) *see* Fenagh w Myshall, Aghade and Ardoyne *C & O*

AGHADERG (St Mellan) w Donaghmore and Scarva *D & D* **I** G N LITTLE

AGHADOE *see* Killarney w Aghadoe and Muckross *L & K*

AGHADOWEY (St Guaire) w Kilrea *D & R* **I** J R D SLATER

AGHADOWN (Church Cross) *see* Ballydehob w Aghadown *C, C & R*

AGHADOWN (St Matthew) *as above*

AGHADRUMSEE (no dedication) w Clogh and Drumsnatt *Clogh* **I** V E KILLE

AGHALEE (Holy Trinity) *D & D* **I** J A HARRON

AGHALURCHER (no dedication) w Tattykeeran, Cooneen and Mullaghfad *Clogh* **I** R T GILLIAN

AGHANAGH (no dedication) *see* Boyle and Elphin w Aghanagh, Kilbryan etc *K, E & A*

AGHANCON (no dedication) *see* Shinrone w Aghancon etc *L & K*

AGHANLOO (St Lugha) *see* Tamlaghtard w Aghanloo *D & R*

AGHAVEA (no dedication) *Clogh* **I** *Vacant*

AGHAVILLY (St Mary) *see* Arm St Mark w Aghavilly *Arm*

AGHAVOE (no dedication) *see* Rathdowney w Castlefleming, Donaghmore etc *C & O*

AGHER (no dedication) *see* Rathmolyon w Castlerickard, Rathcore and Agher *M & K*

AGHERTON (St John the Baptist) *Conn* **I** P W ROOKE, **C** M R K FERRY

AGHOLD (no dedication) *see* Tullow w Shillelagh, Aghold and Mullinacuff *C & O*

AGHOUR (St Lachtan) *see* Kilkenny w Aghour and Kilmanagh *C & O*

AHASCRAGH *see* Aughrim w Ballinasloe etc *L & K*

AHERLA *see* Moviddy Union *C, C & R*

AHOGHILL (St Colmanell) w Portglenone *Conn* **I** W K M BREW

ALDERGROVE *see* Killead w Gartree *Conn*

ALMORITIA (St Nicholas) *see* Mullingar, Portnashangan, Moyliscar, Kilbixy etc *M & K*

ALTEDESERT (no dedication) *see* Kildress w Altedesert *Arm*

ANNACLONE (Christ Church) *see* Magherally w Annaclone *D & D*

ANNACREVY *see* Powerscourt w Kilbride and Annacrevy *D & G*

ANNADUFF (St Ann) *see* Kiltoghart w Drumshambo, Annaduff and Kilronan *K, E & A*

ANNAGH (St Andrew) w Drumaloor, Cloverhill, Drumgoon, Dernakesh, Ashfield and Killesherdoney *K, E & A* **I** W D JOHNSTON, **C** E C O'REILLY

ANNAGHMORE (St Francis) *Arm* **I** R J N PORTEUS

ANNAHILT (Ascension) w Magherahamlet *D & D* **I** J R HOWARD

ANNALONG (no dedication) *D & D* **I** W T LONG

ANNESTOWN *see* Waterford w Killea, Drumcannon and Dunhill *C & O*

ANTRIM (All Saints) *Conn* **I** S R McBRIDE

ANTRIM (St Patrick) *see* Connor w Antrim St Patr *Conn*

ARBOE (no dedication) *see* Ballinderry w Tamlaght and Arboe *Arm*

ARDAGH (St Patrick) w Tashinny, Shrule and Kilcommick *K, E & A* **Bp's C** A W KINGSTON

ARDAMINE (St John the Evangelist) w Kiltennel, Glascarrig, Kilnamanagh, Kilmuckridge and Monamolin *C & O* **I** J JACOB

ARDARA (St Connall) w Glencolumbkille, Inniskeel, Glenties and Lettermacaward *D & R* **I** M S HARTE, **NSM** M C CLASSON

ARDCARNE (no dedication) *see* Boyle and Elphin w Aghanagh, Kilbryan etc *K, E & A*

ARDCLINIS (St Mary) and Tickmacrevan w Layde and Cushendun *Conn* **I** K B de S SCOTT

ARDCOLM (no dedication) *see* Wexford w Ardcolm and Killurin *C & O*

ARDEE (St Mary) *see* Drogheda w Ardee, Collon and Termonfeckin *Arm*

ARDGLASS (St Nicholas) *see* Lecale Gp *D & D*

ARDKEEN (Christ Church) *see* Ballyhalbert w Ardkeen *D & D*

ARDMORE (no dedication) w Craigavon *D & D* **I** D M COLLINS

ARDMORE (St Paul) *see* Youghal Union *C, C & R*

ARDNAGEEHY (no dedication) *see* Fermoy Union *C, C & R*

ARDOYNE (Holy Trinity) *see* Fenagh w Myshall, Aghade and Ardoyne *C & O*

ARDOYNE (Immanuel) *see* Belfast H Trin and Ardoyne *Conn*

ARDQUIN (no dedication) *see* Ballyphilip w Ardquin *D & D*

ARDRAHAN *see* Aughrim w Ballinasloe etc *L & K*

ARDSTRAW (St Eugene) w Baronscourt, Badoney Lower and Badoney Upper and Greenan *D & R* **I** W C McNEE

ARDTREA (St Andrew) w Desertcreat *Arm* **I** E P DUNDAS

ARKLOW (St Saviour) w Inch and Kilbride *D & G* **I** N J W SHERWOOD

ARMAGH (Cathedral of St Patrick) *Arm* **I** H CASSIDY

ARMAGH (St Mark) w Aghavilly *Arm* **I** J W McKEGNEY, C G WYLIE, **Bp's C** C G WYLIE

ARMAGHBREAGUE (no dedication) *see* Keady w Armaghbreague and Derrynoose *Arm*

ARMOY (St Patrick) w Loughguile and Drumtullagh *Conn* **I** W E McCRORY

ARVAGH (no dedication) w Carrigallen, Gowna and Columbkille *K, E & A* **I** J R T WATSON

ASHFIELD (no dedication) *see* Annagh w Drumgoon, Ashfield etc *K, E & A*

ASKEATON (St Mary) *see* Rathkeale w Askeaton and Kilcornan *L & K*

ATHBOY (St James) *see* Trim and Athboy Gp *M & K*

ATHLONE (St Mary) w Benown, Kiltoom and Forgney *M & K* **I** I J POWER

ATHY (St Michael) w Kilberry, Fontstown and Kilkea *D & G* **I** J L CRAMPTON

ATTANAGH *see* Abbeyleix w Old Church, Ballyroan etc *C & O*

AUGHANUNSHIN *see* Conwal Union w Gartan *D & R*

AUGHAVAL (no dedication) w Achill, Knappagh, Dugort, Castlebar and Turlough *T, K & A* **I** G L HASTINGS

AUGHAVAS (no dedication) *see* Mohill w Farnaught, Aughavas, Oughteragh etc *K, E & A*

AUGHER (no dedication) w Newtownsaville and Eskrahoole *Clogh* **I** B M BOWER

AUGHMACART (St Tighernagh) *see* Abbeyleix w Old Church, Ballyroan etc *C & O*

AUGHNACLIFFE *see* Arvagh w Carrigallen, Gowna and Columbkille *K, E & A*

AUGHNACLOY *see* Carnteel and Crilly *Arm*

AUGHNAMULLAN (Christ Church) *see* Ematris w Rockcorry, Aghabog and Aughnamullan *Clogh*

AUGHRIM (Holy Trinity) w Ballinasloe, Clontuskert, Ahascragh, Woodlawn, Kilmacduagh and Ardrahan *L & K* **I** T A SULLIVAN

AUGHRIM (St John the Evangelist) *see* Castlemacadam w Ballinaclash, Aughrim etc *D & G*

BADONEY LOWER (St Patrick) *see* Ardstraw w Baronscourt, Badoney Lower etc *D & R*

BADONEY UPPER (St Aichen) *as above*
BAGENALSTOWN *see* Dunleckney w Nurney, Lorum and Kiltennel *C & O*
BAILIEBOROUGH (no dedication) w Knockbride, Shercock and Mullagh *K, E & A* **I** B R RUSSELL, **NSM** A J LINDSAY
BALBRIGGAN (St George) *see* Holmpatrick w Balbriggan and Kenure *D & G*
BALGRIFFIN (St Doulagh) *see* Malahide w Balgriffin *D & G*
BALLAGHTOBIN (no dedication) *see* Kells Union *C & O*
BALLEE (no dedication) *see* Bright w Ballee and Killough *D & D*
BALLIGAN *see* Ballywalter w Inishargie *D & D*
BALLINACLASH (no dedication) *see* Castlemacadam w Ballinaclash, Aughrim etc *D & G*
BALLINADEE (no dedication) *see* Bandon Union *C, C & R*
BALLINAFAD *see* Boyle and Elphin w Aghanagh, Kilbryan etc *K, E & A*
BALLINALEA *see* Mostrim w Granard, Clonbroney, Killoe etc *K, E & A*
BALLINALECK *see* Cleenish w Mullaghdun *Clogh*
BALLINAMALLARD *see* Magheracross *Clogh*
BALLINAMORE *see* Mohill w Farnaught, Aughavas, Oughteragh etc *K, E & A*
BALLINASLOE (St John the Evangelist) *see* Aughrim w Ballinasloe etc *L & K*
BALLINATONE *see* Castlemacadam w Ballinaclash, Aughrim etc *D & G*
BALLINDERRY (no dedication) *Conn* **I** E J HARRIS
BALLINDERRY (St John) w Tamlaght and Arboe *Arm* **I** H J W MOORE
BALLINEEN *see* Kinneigh Union *C, C & R*
BALLINGARRY (no dedication) *see* Cloughjordan w Borrisokane etc *L & K*
BALLINLOUGH *see* Roscommon w Donamon, Rathcline, Kilkeevin etc *K, E & A*
BALLINROBE (St Mary) *see* Tuam w Cong and Aasleagh *T, K & A*
BALLINTEMPLE (no dedication) *see* Kilmore w Ballintemple, Kildallon etc *K, E & A*
BALLINTEMPLE (St Mary) *see* Cashel w Magorban, Tipperary, Clonbeg etc *C & O*
BALLINTOGHER *see* Taunagh w Kilmactranny, Ballysumaghan etc *K, E & A*
BALLINTOY (no dedication) w Rathlin and Dunseverick *Conn* **I** J N PATTERSON
BALLINTUBBERT (St Brigid) *see* Stradbally w Ballintubbert, Coraclone etc *C & O*
BALLISODARE (Holy Trinity) w Collooney and Emlaghfad *T, K & A* **I** R M STRATFORD
BALLIVOR *see* Trim and Athboy Gp *M & K*
BALLNACARGY *see* Mullingar, Portnashangan, Moyliscar, Kilbixy etc *M & K*
BALLYBAY (Christ Church) w Mucknoe and Clontibret *Clogh* **I** *Vacant* Castleblayney (42) 41102
BALLYBEEN (St Mary) *D & D* **I** J M WHITE
BALLYBRACK *see* Killiney Ballybrack *D & G*
BALLYBUNNION *see* Tralee w Ballymacelligott, Kilnaughtin etc *L & K*
BALLYCANEW (no dedication) *see* Gorey w Kilnahue, Leskinfere and Ballycanew *C & O*
BALLYCARNEY (no dedication) *see* Ferns w Kilbride, Toombe, Kilcormack etc *C & O*
BALLYCARRY *see* Kilroot and Templecorran *Conn*
BALLYCASTLE (Holy Trinity) *see* Ramoan w Ballycastle and Culfeightrin *Conn*
BALLYCLARE *see* Ballynure and Ballyeaston *Conn*
BALLYCLOG (St Patrick) *see* Brackaville w Donaghendry and Ballyclog *Arm*
BALLYCLUG (St Patrick) *see* Ballymena w Ballyclug *Conn*
BALLYCOMMON *see* Geashill w Killeigh and Ballycommon *M & K*
BALLYCONNELL *see* Swanlinbar w Tomregan, Kinawley, Drumlane etc *K, E & A*
BALLYCOTTON *see* Youghal Union *C, C & R*
BALLYCULTER (Christ Church) *see* Lecale Gp *D & D*
BALLYDEHOB (St Matthias) w Aghadown *C, C & R* **I** P R DRAPER
BALLYEASTON (St John the Evangelist) *see* Ballynure and Ballyeaston *Conn*
BALLYEGLISH (St Matthias) *see* Desertlyn w Ballyeglish *Arm*
BALLYFIN (no dedication) *see* Maryborough w Dysart Enos and Ballyfin *C & O*
BALLYGAWLEY (no dedication) *see* Errigle Keerogue w Ballygawley and Killeshil *Arm*
BALLYHAISE *see* Drung w Castleterra, Larah and Lavey etc *K, E & A*
BALLYHALBERT (St Andrew) w Ardkeen *D & D* **I** J M BATCHELOR
BALLYHOLME (St Columbanus) *D & D* **I** A F ABERNETHY, **C** W C S WRIGHT
BALLYHOOLEY (no dedication) *see* Fermoy Union *C, C & R*
BALLYJAMESDUFF (no dedication) *see* Kildrumferton w Ballymachugh and Ballyjamesduff *K, E & A*
BALLYKELLY *see* Tamlaghtfinlagan w Myroe *D & R*
BALLYLESSON *see* Drumbo *D & D*
BALLYMACARRETT (St Martin) *D & D* **Bp's C** I R BETTS
BALLYMACARRETT (St Patrick) *D & D* **I** D COE
BALLYMACASH (St Mark) *Conn* **I** W G IRWIN, **C** P G HEAK
BALLYMACELLIGOTT (no dedication) *see* Tralee w Ballymacelligott, Kilnaughtin etc *L & K*
BALLYMACHUGH (St Paul) *see* Kildrumferton w Ballymachugh and Ballyjamesduff *K, E & A*
BALLYMACKEY (St Michael) *see* Nenagh *L & K*
BALLYMACORMACK (no dedication) *see* Templemichael w Clongish, Clooncumber etc *K, E & A*
BALLYMAGLASSON *see* Dunboyne w Kilcock, Maynooth, Moyglare etc *M & K*
BALLYMAHON *see* Ardagh w Tashinny, Shrule and Kilcommick *K, E & A*
BALLYMARTLE (no dedication) *see* Kinsale Union *C, C & R*
BALLYMASCANLAN (St Mary) w Creggan and Rathcor *Arm* **I** G M KINGSTON
BALLYMENA (St Patrick) w Ballyclug *Conn* **I** S G E LLOYD, **C** T H PRIESTLY, P L STOREY
BALLYMONEY *see* Kinneigh Union *C, C & R*
BALLYMONEY (St Patrick) w Finvoy and Rasharkin *Conn* **I** E R LAVERY, **C** G M S WATSON
BALLYMORE *see* Clondehorkey w Cashel *D & R*
BALLYMORE (St Mark) *Arm* **I** S J BLACK
BALLYMORE EUSTACE (St John) *see* Blessington w Kilbride, Ballymore Eustace etc *D & G*
BALLYMOTE *see* Ballisodare w Collooney and Emlaghfad *T, K & A*
BALLYMOYER (St Luke) *see* Newtownhamilton w Ballymoyer and Belleck *Arm*
BALLYNAFEIGH (St Jude) *D & D* **I** W M MOORE
BALLYNAHINCH *see* Magheradroll *D & D*
BALLYNAKILL (All Saints) *see* Abbeyleix w Old Church, Ballyroan etc *C & O*
BALLYNAKILL (St Thomas) *see* Omey w Ballynakill, Errislannan and Roundstone *T, K & A*
BALLYNASCREEN *see* Kilcronaghan w Draperstown and Sixtowns *D & R*
BALLYNURE (Ascension) *see* Baltinglass w Ballynure etc *C & O*
BALLYNURE (Christ Church) and Ballyeaston *Conn* **I** J F A BOND
BALLYPHILIP (no dedication) w Ardquin *D & D* **I** S McCULLOUGH
BALLYRASHANE (St John the Baptist) w Kildollagh *Conn* **I** N C SHORTT
BALLYROAN (no dedication) *see* Abbeyleix w Old Church, Ballyroan etc *C & O*
BALLYSALLY (St Andrew) *see* Coleraine *Conn*
BALLYSCULLION (no dedication) *see* Drummaul w Duneane and Ballyscullion *Conn*
BALLYSCULLION (St Tida) *D & R* **I** F J REILLY
BALLYSEEDY (no dedication) *see* Tralee w Ballymacelligott, Kilnaughtin etc *L & K*
BALLYSHANNON *see* Kilbarron w Rossnowlagh and Drumholm *D & R*
BALLYSILLAN *see* Belfast St Mark *Conn*
BALLYSUMAGHAN (no dedication) *see* Taunagh w Kilmactranny, Ballysumaghan etc *K, E & A*
BALLYWALTER (Holy Trinity) w Inishargie *D & D* **I** J R L BOWLEY
BALLYWARD *see* Drumgath w Drumgooland and Clonduff *D & D*
BALLYWILLAN (Holy Trinity) *Conn* **I** G E GRAHAM, **NSM** D J STEELE
BALRATHBOYNE *see* Kells w Balrathboyne, Moynalty etc *M & K*
BALTEAGH (St Canice) w Carrick *D & R* **I** J J HEMPHILL
BALTIMORE *see* Abbeystrewry Union *C, C & R*
BALTINGLASS (St Mary) w Ballynure, Stratford-on-Slaney and Rathvilly *C & O* **I** M A McCULLAGH
BANAGHER (St Moresuis) *see* Cumber Lower w Banagher *D & R*
BANAGHER (St Paul) *see* Clonfert Gp of Par *L & K*
BANBRIDGE *see* Seapatrick *D & D*
BANDON (St Peter) w Rathclaren, Innishannon, Ballinadee and Brinny *C, C & R* **I** M A J BURROWS, **C** O DONOHOE
BANGOR Primacy (Christ Church) *D & D* **P-in-c** J E C RUTTER
BANGOR (St Comgall) *D & D* **I** W R D McCREERY

BANGOR ABBEY (Bangor Abbey) *D & D* **I** R NESBITT, **C** S D LOGAN
BANNOW (no dedication) *see* Taghmon w Horetown and Bannow *C & O*
BANTRY *see* Kilmocomogue Union *C, C & R*
BARONSCOURT (no dedication) *see* Ardstraw w Baronscourt, Badoney Lower etc *D & R*
BARR (no dedication) *see* Donacavey w Barr *Clogh*
BEARA (St Peter) *C, C & R* **I** *Vacant* Cork (21) 63036
BECTIVE *see* Trim w Bective and Galtrim *M & K*
BELFAST (All Saints) *Conn* **I** C WEST
BELFAST (Cathedral of St Anne) *Conn* , N C SHORTT **I** J SHEARER
BELFAST (Christ Church) *Conn* **I** S N M BAYLY
BELFAST (Holy Trinity) and Ardoyne *Conn* **I** S S HEANEY, **C** T A DUNLOP
BELFAST Malone (St John) *Conn* **I** A E T HARPER
BELFAST (St Aidan) *Conn* **I** *Vacant* (01232) 666741
BELFAST (St Andrew) *Conn* **NSM** S K HOUSTON
BELFAST (St Bartholomew) *Conn* **I** G B MOLLER
BELFAST (St Brendan) *D & D* **I** F McCREA
BELFAST (St Christopher) *D & D* **Bp's C** E M JOHNSTON
BELFAST (St Clement) *D & D* **I** *Vacant*
BELFAST (St Donard) *D & D* **I** H N PEDLOW, **C** T D B PIERCE
BELFAST (St George) *Conn* **I** B STEWART, **NSM** G W ODLING-SMEE
BELFAST (St James) (St Silas) *Conn* **I** *Vacant*
BELFAST (St Jude) *see* Ballynafeigh St Jude *D & D*
BELFAST (St Katharine) *Conn* **I** W J TAGGART
BELFAST (St Mark) *Conn* **I** P REDFERN
BELFAST (St Mary) (Holy Redeemer) *Conn* **I** J P WALKER
BELFAST (St Mary Magdalene) *Conn* **Bp's C** A MALLON
BELFAST (St Matthew) *Conn* **I** G J O DUNSTAN, **C** K E SUTTON
BELFAST (St Michael) *Conn* **I** N B DODDS
BELFAST (St Nicholas) *Conn* **I** F J RUSK
BELFAST (St Ninian) *Conn* **I** *Vacant*
BELFAST (St Paul) (St Barnabas) *Conn* **I** K M YOUNG
BELFAST (St Peter) *Conn* **I** C J McCOLLUM, **NSM** R MAXWELL
BELFAST (St Simon) (St Philip) *Conn* **I** W T HOEY
BELFAST (St Stephen) (St Luke) *Conn* **I** D LOCKHART
BELFAST (St Thomas) *Conn* **I** W A LEWIS
BELFAST Upper Falls (St John the Baptist) *Conn* **I** C J ATKINSON
BELFAST Upper Malone (Epiphany) *Conn* **I** J I CARSON
BELFAST Whiterock (St Columba) *Conn* **Bp's C** I R GAMBLE
BELLAGHY *see* Ballyscullion *D & R*
BELLEEK (no dedication) *see* Garrison w Slavin and Belleek *Clogh*
BELLEEK (St Luke) *see* Newtownhamilton w Ballymoyer and Belleek *Arm*
BELLERENA *see* Tamlaghtard w Aghanloo *D & R*
BELMONT (St Peter) *see* Culmore w Muff and Belmont *D & R*
BELTURBET *see* Annagh w Drumgoon, Ashfield etc *K, E & A*
BELVOIR (Transfiguration) *D & D* **I** T KEIGHTLEY
BENOWN (no dedication) *see* Athlone w Benown, Kiltoom and Forgney *M & K*
BILBO (no dedication) *see* Castlecomer w Colliery Ch, Mothel and Bilbo *C & O*
BILLIS (no dedication) *see* Lurgan w Billis, Killinkere and Munterconnaught *K, E & A*
BILLY (no dedication) w Derrykeighan *Conn* **I** A A JOHNS, **NSM** W J HOLMES
BIRR (St Brendan) w Eglish, Lorrha, Dorrha and Lockeen *L & K* **I** D L KEEGAN
BLACKLION *see* Killinagh w Kiltyclogher and Innismagrath *K, E & A*
BLACKROCK (All Saints) *see* Stillorgan w Blackrock *D & G*
BLACKROCK (St Michael) *see* Douglas Union w Frankfield *C, C & R*
BLARNEY *see* Carrigrohane Union *C, C & R*
BLESSINGTON (St Mary) w Kilbride, Ballymore Eustace and Holywood *D & G* **I** N K DUNNE
BOHO (no dedication) *see* Devenish w Boho *Clogh*
BOOTERSTOWN *see* Dublin Booterstown *D & G*
BORNACOOLA *see* Templemichael w Clongish, Clooncumber etc *K, E & A*
BORRIS Clonagoose *see* Leighlin w Grange Sylvae, Shankill etc *C & O*
BORRIS Littleton *see* Kilcooley w Littleon, Crohane and Fertagh *C & O*
BORRIS-IN-OSSORY (no dedication) *see* Clonenagh w Offerlane, Borris-in-Ossory etc *C & O*
BORRISNAFARNEY (no dedication) *see* Cloughjordan w Borrisokane etc *L & K*
BORRISOKANE (no dedication) *as above*
BOURNEY (St Burchin) *see* Roscrea w Kyle, Bourney and Corbally *L & K*
BOVEVAGH (St Eugenius) *see* Dungiven w Bovevagh *D & R*
BOYLE (no dedication) and Elphin w Aghanagh, Kilbryan, Ardcarne and Croghan *K, E & A* **NSM** S JOHNSON
BRACKAVILLE (Holy Trinity) w Donaghendry and Ballyclog *Arm* **I** *Vacant* (018687) 40424
BRANTRY (Holy Trinity) *see* Caledon w Brantry *Arm*
BRAY (Christ Church) *D & G* **NSM** S A KINGSTON
BRIGHT (no dedication) w Ballee and Killough *D & D* **I** J SCOTT
BRIGOWN (St George) *see* Fermoy Union *C, C & R*
BRINNY (no dedication) *see* Bandon Union *C, C & R*
BROOKEBOROUGH *see* Aghavea *Clogh*
BROOMHEDGE (St Matthew) *Conn* **I** P J GALBRAITH
BROUGHSHANE *see* Skerry w Rathcavan and Newtowncrommelin *Conn*
BRUFF *see* Kilmallock w Kilflynn, Kilfinane, Knockaney etc *L & K*
BRYANSFORD *see* Castlewellan w Kilcoo *D & D*
BUNBEG *see* Gweedore, Carrickfin and Templecrone *D & R*
BUNCLODY (St Mary) w Kildavin, Clonegal and Kilrush *C & O* **I** N J W WAUGH
BUNCRANA *see* Fahan Lower and Upper *D & R*
BUNDORAN *see* Cloonclare w Killasnett, Lurganboy and Drumlease *K, E & A*
BUSH *see* Ballymascanlan w Creggan and Rathcor *Arm*
BUSHMILLS *see* Dunluce *Conn*
CAHERAGH (St Mary) *see* Abbeystrewry Union *C, C & R*
CAHERCONLISH (St Ailbe) *see* Kilmallock w Kilflynn, Kilfinane, Knockaney etc *L & K*
CAHIR (St Paul) *see* Clonmel w Innislounagh, Tullaghmelan etc *C & O*
CAIRNCASTLE (St Patrick) *see* Kilwaughter w Cairncastle and Craigy Hill *Conn*
CALARY (no dedication) *see* Newcastle w Newtownmountkennedy and Calary *D & G*
CALEDON (St John) w Brantry *Arm* **I** D B WILSON
CALRY (no dedication) *K, E & A* **Bp's C** D GRISCOME
CAMLOUGH (Christ the Redeemer) w Mullaglass *Arm* **I** R G HOEY
CAMP *see* Dingle w Killiney and Kilgobbin *L & K*
CAMUS-JUXTA-BANN (St Mary) *D & R* **I** A I GALLAGHER
CAMUS-JUXTA-MOURNE (Christ Church) *D & R* **I** F W FAWCETT
CAPPAGH (St Eugene) w Lislimnaghan *D & R* **I** D J QUINN
CAPPOQUIN (St Anne) *see* Lismore w Cappoquin, Kilwatermoy, Dungarvan etc *C & O*
CARBURY (no dedication) *see* Clonsast w Rathangan, Thomastown etc *M & K*
CARLOW (St Mary) w Urglin and Staplestown *C & O* **I** G G DOWD
CARNALEA (St Gall) *D & D* **I** W P HOUSTON
CARNALWAY (St Patrick) *see* Newbridge w Carnalway and Kilcullen *M & K*
CARNDONAGH *see* Moville w Greencastle, Donagh, Cloncha etc *D & R*
CARNEW (All Saints) *see* Crosspatrick Gp *C & O*
CARNLOUGH *see* Ardclinis and Tickmacrevan w Layde and Cushendun *Conn*
CARNMONEY (Holy Evangelists) *Conn* **I** N P BAYLOR
CARNTEEL (St James) and Crilly *Arm* **I** G P BRIDLE
CARRICK (no dedication) *see* Balteagh w Carrick *D & R*
CARRICK-ON-SHANNON *see* Kiltoghart w Drumshambo, Annaduff and Kilronan *K, E & A*
CARRICKFERGUS (St Nicholas) *Conn* **I** J A McMASTER, **C** T A G McCANN, D S McVEIGH
CARRICKFIN (St Andrew) *see* Gweedore, Carrickfin and Templecrone *D & R*
CARRICKMACROSS (St Fin Barre) w Magheracloone *Clogh* **I** J L SUTCLIFFE
CARRIGALINE (St Mary) w Killanully and Monkstown *C, C & R* **I** A J HOUSTON
CARRIGALLEN (no dedication) *see* Arvagh w Carrigallen, Gowna and Columbkille *K, E & A*
CARRIGANS *see* Taughboyne, Craigadooish, Newtowncunningham etc *D & R*
CARRIGART *see* Mevagh w Glenalla *D & R*
CARRIGROHANE (St Peter) w Garrycloyne, Inniscarra and Magourney *C, C & R* **I** *Vacant*
CARRIGTWOHILL (St David) *see* Rathcooney Union *C, C & R*
CARROWDORE (Christ Church) w Millisle *D & D* **I** T R CONWAY
CARRYDUFF (St Ignatius) *see* Killaney w Carryduff *D & D*
CASHEL (Cathedral of St John the Baptist) w Magorban, Tipperary, Clonbeg and Ballintemple *C & O* **I** P J KNOWLES
CASHEL (no dedication) *see* Clondehorkey w Cashel *D & R*

CASTLEARCHDALE (St Patrick) *see* Derryvullen N w Castlearchdale *Clogh*
CASTLEBAR (Christ Church) *see* Aughaval w Achill, Knappagh, Dugort etc *T, K & A*
CASTLEBLAYNEY *see* Ballybay w Mucknoe and Clontibret *Clogh*
CASTLECOMER (St Mary) w the Colliery Church, Mothel and Bilbo *C & O* **I** A D H ORR
CASTLECONNELL *see* Killaloe w Stradbally *L & K*
CASTLECONNOR (no dedication) *see* Killala w Dunfeeny, Crossmolina, Kilmoremoy etc *T, K & A*
CASTLEDAWSON (Christ Church) *D & R* **I** R J STEWART
CASTLEDERG *see* Derg w Termonamongan *D & R*
CASTLEDERMOT (St James) *see* Narraghmore w Timolin, Castledermot and Kinneagh *D & G*
CASTLEFLEMING (no dedication) *see* Rathdowney w Castlefleming, Donaghmore etc *C & O*
CASTLEGREGORY *see* Dingle w Killiney and Kilgobbin *L & K*
CASTLEHAVEN (no dedication) *see* Abbeystrewry Union *C, C & R*
CASTLEKNOCK (St Brigid) and Mulhuddart, w Clonsilla *D & G* **I** W P COLTON, **C** L E A PEILOW
CASTLELOST *see* Mullingar, Portnashangan, Moyliscar, Kilbixy etc *M & K*
CASTLEMACADAM (Holy Trinity) w Ballinaclash, Aughrim and Macreddin *D & G* **I** G W BUTLER
CASTLEMAINE *see* Kilcolman w Kiltallagh, Killorglin, Knockane etc *L & K*
CASTLEMARTYR (St Anne) *see* Youghal Union *C, C & R*
CASTLEPOLLARD (St Michael) and Oldcastle w Loughcrew, Mount Nugent, Mayne and Drumcree *M & K* **I** G A R MILNE
CASTLEREA *see* Roscommon w Donamon, Rathcline, Kilkeevin etc *K, E & A*
CASTLERICKARD *see* Rathmolyon w Castlerickard, Rathcore and Agher *M & K*
CASTLEROCK (Christ Church) w Dunboe and Fermoyle *D & R* **I** W B JOHNSTON
CASTLETERRA (no dedication) *see* Drung w Castleterra, Larah and Lavey etc *K, E & A*
CASTLETOWN *see* Killeshin w Cloydagh and Killabban *C & O*
CASTLETOWN *see* Rathkeale w Askeaton and Kilcornan *L & K*
CASTLETOWN *see* Kells w Balrathboyne, Moynalty etc *M & K*
CASTLETOWNBERE *see* Beara *C, C & R*
CASTLETOWNROCHE (no dedication) *see* Mallow Union *C, C & R*
CASTLETOWNSEND *see* Abbeystrewry Union *C, C & R*
CASTLEVENTRY (no dedication) *see* Ross Union *C, C & R*
CASTLEWELLAN (St Paul) w Kilcoo *D & D* **I** R F GREER
CAVAN *see* Urney w Denn and Derryheen *K, E & A*
CELBRIDGE (Christ Church) w Straffan and Newcastle-Lyons *D & G* **I** D H BOYLAND
CHAPELIZOD (St Laurence) *see* Dublin Crumlin w Chapelizod *D & G*
CHARLEMONT (no dedication) *see* Moy w Charlemont *Arm*
CLABBY (St Margaret) *see* Tempo and Clabby *Clogh*
CLANABOGAN (no dedication) *see* Edenderry w Clanabogan *D & R*
CLANE (St Michael and All Angels) w Donadea and Coolcarrigan *M & K* **I** D FRAZER, **NSM** D HUTTON-BURY
CLARA (St Brigid) w Liss, Moate and Clonmacnoise *M & K* **NSM** M M S GRAY-STACK
CLARE (no dedication) *see* Loughgilly w Clare *Arm*
CLAUDY *see* Cumber Upper w Learmount *D & R*
CLEENISH (no dedication) w Mullaghdun *Clogh* **I** W S WRIGHT
CLIFDEN *see* Omey w Ballynakill, Errislannan and Roundstone *T, K & A*
CLOGH (Holy Trinity) *see* Aghadrumsee w Clogh and Drumsnatt *Clogh*
CLOGHER (Cathedral of St Macartan) w Errigal Portclare *Clogh* **I** T R MOORE
CLOGHERNEY (St Partick) w Seskinore and Drumnakilly *Arm* **I** *Vacant*
CLONAGOOSE (St Moling) *see* Leighlin w Grange Sylvae, Shankill etc *C & O*
CLONAKILTY *see* Kilgariffe Union *C, C & R*
CLONALLON (no dedication) w Warrenpoint *D & D* **I** *Vacant* (01693) 772267
CLONARD *see* Mullingar, Portnashangan, Moyliscar, Kilbixy etc *M & K*
CLONASLEE *see* Mountmellick w Coolbanagher, Rosenallis etc *M & K*
CLONBEG (St Sedna) *see* Cashel w Magorban, Tipperary, Clonbeg etc *C & O*
CLONBRONEY (St John) *see* Mostrim w Granard, Clonbroney, Killoe etc *K, E & A*
CLONBULLOGUE *see* Clonsast w Rathangan, Thomastown etc *M & K*
CLONCHA (no dedication) *see* Moville w Greencastle, Donagh, Cloncha etc *D & R*
CLONDALKIN (St John) w Rathcoole *D & G* **I** J E McCULLAGH, **NSM** O BOOTHMAN
CLONDEHORKEY (St John) w Cashel *D & R* **I** P D THORNBURY
CLONDEVADDOCK (Christ the Redeemer) w Portsalon and Leatbeg *D & R* **P-in-c** A H KERR
CLONDUFF (St John) *see* Drumgath w Drumgooland and Clonduff *D & D*
CLONE (St Paul) *see* Enniscorthy w Clone, Clonmore, Monart etc *C & O*
CLONEGAL (no dedication) *see* Bunclody w Kildavin, Clonegal and Kilrush *C & O*
CLONEGAM (Holy Trinity) *see* Fiddown w Clonegam, Guilcagh and Kilmeaden *C & O*
CLONENAGH (no dedication) w Offerlane, Borris-in-Ossory, Seirkieran and Roskelton *C & O* **I** *Vacant* Portlaoise (502) 32146
CLONES (St Tighernach) w Killeevan *Clogh* **I** *Vacant*
CLONEYHURKE (no dedication) *see* Portarlington w Cloneyhurke and Lea *M & K*
CLONFADFORAN *see* Tullamore w Durrow, Newtownfertullagh, Rahan etc *M & K*
CLONFEACLE (St Patrick) w Derrygortreavy *Arm* **I** A J PARKHILL
CLONFERT (Cathedral of St Brendan) w Donanaughta, Banagher and Lickmolassy *L & K* **Bp's C** R W CARNEY
CLONGISH (St Paul) *see* Templemichael w Clongish, Clooncumber etc *K, E & A*
CLONLARA *see* Killaloe w Stradbally *L & K*
CLONLEIGH (St Lugadius) *see* Raphoe w Raymochy and Clonleigh *D & R*
CLONMACNOISE (St Kieran) *see* Clara w Liss, Moate and Clonmacnoise *M & K*
CLONMEL (St Mary) w Innislounagh, Tullaghmelan, Fethard, Kilvemnon and Cahir *C & O* **I** G A KNOWD, **C** A CARTER
CLONMEL UNION (Christ Church) *C, C & R* **I** P J ANDERSON
CLONMELLON *see* Trim and Athboy Gp *M & K*
CLONMORE (St John) *see* Enniscorthy w Clone, Clonmore, Monart etc *C & O*
CLONMORE (St John) *see* Kiltegan w Hacketstown, Clonmore and Moyne *C & O*
CLONOE (St Michael) *see* Tullaniskin w Clonoe *Arm*
CLONSAST (no dedication) w Rathangan, Thomastown, Monasteroris, Carbury and Rahan *M & K* **I** R W DEANE
CLONSILLA (St Mary) *see* Castleknock and Mulhuddart, w Clonsilla *D & G*
CLONTARF *see* Dublin Clontarf *D & G*
CLONTIBRET (St Colman) *see* Ballybay w Mucknoe and Clontibret *Clogh*
CLONTUSKERT (St Matthew) *see* Aughrim w Ballinasloe etc *L & K*
CLOONCLARE (no dedication) w Killasnett, Lurganboy and Drumlease *K, E & A* **Bp's C** C J STEVENSON
CLOONCUMBER (no dedication) *see* Templemichael w Clongish, Clooncumber etc *K, E & A*
CLOONEY (All Saints) w Strathfoyle *D & R* **I** J C D MAYES, **C** R J GRAY
CLOUGH *see* Craigs w Dunaghy and Killagan *Conn*
CLOUGHFERN (Ascension) *Conn* **I** J O MANN, **NSM** J M ELSDON
CLOUGHJORDAN (St Kieran) w Borrisokane, Ballingary, Borrisnafarney and Templeharry *L & K* **I** *Vacant*
CLOUGHMILLS *see* Craigs w Dunaghy and Killagan *Conn*
CLOVERHILL (St John) *see* Annagh w Drumgoon, Ashfield etc *K, E & A*
CLOYDAGH (no dedication) *see* Killeshin w Cloydagh and Killabban *C & O*
CLOYNE (Cathedral of St Colman) w Inch, Corkbeg, Midleton and Gurranekennefeake *C, C & R* **I** G P St J HILLIARD
COACHFORD *see* Carrigrohane Union *C, C & R*
COALISLAND *see* Brackaville w Donaghendry and Ballyclog *Arm*
COBH *see* Clonmel Union *C, C & R*
COLAGHTY *see* Lack *Clogh*
COLEBROOK *see* Aghalurcher w Tattykeeran, Cooneen etc *Clogh*
COLERAINE *see* Killowen *D & R*
COLERAINE (St Patrick) *Conn* **I** K H CLARKE, **C** M J ELLIOTT, D J BELL
COLIN (St Andrew) *see* Derriaghy w Colin *Conn*

COLLIERY CHURCH, THE *see* Castlecomer w Colliery Ch, Mothel and Bilbo *C & O*
COLLON (no dedication) *see* Drogheda w Ardee, Collon and Termonfeckin *Arm*
COLLOONEY (St Paul) *see* Ballisodare w Collooney and Emlaghfad *T, K & A*
COLPE (St Columba) *see* Julianstown and Colpe w Drogheda and Duleek *M & K*
COLUMBKILLE (St Thomas) *see* Arvagh w Carrigallen, Gowna and Columbkille *K, E & A*
COMBER (St Mary) *D & D* **I** J P O BARRY
COMERAGH *see* Lismore w Cappoquin, Kilwatermoy, Dungarvan etc *C & O*
CONARY (St Bartholomew) *see* Dunganstown w Redcross and Conary *D & G*
CONG (St Mary) *see* Tuam w Cong and Aasleagh *T, K & A*
CONNOR (St Saviour) w Antrim St Patrick *Conn* **I** S GILCHRIST
CONVOY (St Ninian) w Monellan and Donaghmore *D & R* **I** M COMBER
CONWAL (no dedication) w Aughanunshin and Gartan *D & R* **I** W W MORTON
COOKSTOWN *see* Derryloran *Arm*
COOLBANAGHER (St John) *see* Mountmellick w Coolbanagher, Rosenallis etc *M & K*
COOLCARRIGAN (no dedication) *see* Clane w Donadea and Coolcarrigan *M & K*
COOLKELLURE (St Edmund) *see* Fanlobbus Union *C, C & R*
COOLOCK (St John) *see* Raheny w Coolock *D & G*
COONEEN (no dedication) *see* Aghalurcher w Tattykeeran, Cooneen etc *Clogh*
COOTEHILL *see* Annagh w Drumgoon, Ashfield etc *K, E & A*
CORACLONE (St Peter) *see* Stradbally w Ballintubbert, Coraclone etc *C & O*
CORBALLY (Christ Church) *see* Roscrea w Kyle, Bourney and Corbally *L & K*
CORK (Cathedral of St Fin Barre) (St Nicholas) *C, C & R* **I** M G St A JACKSON, **C** M GRAHAM, **NSM** E W HUNTER
CORK (St Luke) w Shandon (St Ann) w St Mary *C, C & R* **I** W J HEASLIP
CORKBEG (St Michael and All Angels) *see* Cloyne Union *C, C & R*
CORRAWALLEN (no dedication) *see* Kilmore w Ballintemple, Kildallon etc *K, E & A*
COURTMACSHERRY (St John the Evangelist) *see* Kilgariffe Union *C, C & R*
CRAIGADOOISH (no dedication) *see* Taughboyne, Craigadooish, Newtowncunningham etc *D & R*
CRAIGAVAD *see* Glencraig *D & D*
CRAIGAVON (St Saviour) *see* Ardmore w Craigavon *D & D*
CRAIGS (no dedication) w Dunaghy and Killagan *Conn* **I** *Vacant*
CRAIGY HILL (All Saints) *see* Kilwaughter w Cairncastle and Craigy Hill *Conn*
CREAGH *see* Abbeystrewry Union *C, C & R*
CREAGH *see* Aughrim w Ballinasloe etc *L & K*
CRECORA *see* Adare w Kilpeacon and Croom *L & K*
CREGAGH (St Finnian) *D & D* **I** J N BATTYE, **C** S E DOOGAN
CREGGAN (no dedication) *see* Ballymascanlan w Creggan and Rathcor *Arm*
CRILLY (St George) *see* Carnteel and Crilly *Arm*
CRINKEN (St James) *D & G* **I** G FYLES
CROGHAN (Holy Trinity) *see* Boyle and Elphin w Aghanagh, Kilbryan etc *K, E & A*
CROHANE (no dedication) *see* Kilcooley w Littleon, Crohane and Fertagh *C & O*
CROM (Holy Trinity) *see* Kinawley w H Trin *K, E & A*
CROOKHAVEN (St Brendan) *see* Kilmoe Union *C, C & R*
CROOM (no dedication) *see* Adare w Kilpeacon and Croom *L & K*
CROSSGAR *see* Kilmore w Inch *D & D*
CROSSHAVEN *see* Templebreedy w Tracton and Nohoval *C, C & R*
CROSSMOLINA (no dedication) *see* Killala w Dunfeeny, Crossmolina, Kilmoremoy etc *T, K & A*
CROSSPATRICK Group (no dedication) w Kilcommon, Kilpipe, Preban and Carnew, The *C & O* **I** P P HALLIDAY
CRUMLIN *see* Dublin Crumlin w Chapelizod *D & G*
CRUMLIN (St John) *see* Glenavy w Tunny and Crumlin *Conn*
CRUMLIN ROAD *see* Belfast St Mary w H Redeemer *Conn*
CULDAFF (no dedication) *see* Moville w Greencastle, Donagh, Cloncha etc *D & R*
CULFEIGHTRIN (no dedication) *see* Ramoan w Ballycastle and Culfeightrin *Conn*
CULLYBACKEY *see* Craigs w Dunaghy and Killagan *Conn*
CULMORE (Holy Trinity) w Muff and Belmont *D & R* **I** M E G MOORE
CUMBER LOWER (Holy Trinity) w Banagher *D & R* **I** *Vacant*
CUMBER UPPER (no dedication) w Learmount *D & R* **I** J A MARTIN
CURRAGH (Garrison Church of St Paul) *see* Kildare w Kilmeague and Curragh *M & K*
CURRIN (St Andrew) w Drum and Newbliss *Clogh* **I** T B GOLDING
CUSHENDALL *see* Ardclinis and Tickmacrevan w Layde and Cushendun *Conn*
CUSHENDUN (no dedication) *as above*
DALKEY (St Patrick) *D & G* **C** T F BLENNERHASSETT
DARTREY *see* Ematris w Rockcorry, Aghabog and Aughnamullan *Clogh*
DELGANY (Christ Church) *D & G* **I** D T MUIR
DENN (no dedication) *see* Urney w Denn and Derryheen *K, E & A*
DERG (no dedication) w Termonamongan *D & R* **I** W P QUILL
DERNAKESH (Chapel of Ease) *see* Annagh w Drumgoon, Ashfield etc *K, E & A*
DERRALOSSARY *see* Rathdrum w Glenealy, Derralossary and Laragh *D & G*
DERRIAGHY (Christ Church) w Colin *Conn* **I** J C BUDD
DERRYBRUSK (St Michael) *see* Maguiresbridge w Derrybrusk *Clogh*
DERRYGONNELLY *see* Inishmacsaint *Clogh*
DERRYGORTREAVY (St Columba) *see* Clonfeacle w Derrygortreavy *Arm*
DERRYHEEN (no dedication) *see* Urney w Denn and Derryheen *K, E & A*
DERRYKIGHAN (St Colman) *see* Billy w Derrykeighan *Conn*
DERRYLANE (no dedication) *see* Killeshandra w Killegar and Derrylane *K, E & A*
DERRYLIN *see* Kinawley w H Trin *K, E & A*
DERRYLORAN (St Luran) *Arm* **I** J M BARTON, **C** S R T BOYD
DERRYNOOSE (St John) *see* Keady w Armaghbreague and Derrynoose *Arm*
DERRYVOLGIE (St Columba) *Conn* **I** C J POLLOCK
DERRYVULLEN NORTH (St Tighernach) w Castlearchdale *Clogh* **I** R C THOMPSON
DERRYVULLEN SOUTH (St Tighernach) w Garvary *Clogh* **I** J W STEWART
DERVOCK *see* Billy w Derrykeighan *Conn*
DESERTCREAT (no dedication) *see* Ardtrea w Desertcreat *Arm*
DESERTLYN (St John) w Ballyeglish *Arm* **I** J CLYDE
DESERTMARTIN (St Conghall) w Termoneeny *D & R* **I** K R KINGSTON
DESERTOGHILL (no dedication) *see* Errigal w Garvagh *D & R*
DESERTSERGES (no dedication) *see* Kinneigh Union *C, C & R*
DEVENISH (St Molaise) w Boho *Clogh* **I** D P KERR
DIAMOND (St Paul) *see* Tartaraghan w Diamond *Arm*
DINGLE (St James) w Killiney and Kilgobbin *L & K* **I** *Vacant*
DIOC C *C & O Vacant*
DOAGH *see* Kilbride *Conn*
DOLLINGSTOWN (St Saviour) *see* Magheralin w Dollingstown *D & D*
DONABATE (St Patrick) *see* Swords w Donabate and Killsallaghan *D & G*
DONACAVEY (no dedication) w Barr *Clogh* **I** J HAY
DONADEA (St Peter) *see* Clane w Donadea and Coolcarrigan *M & K*
DONAGH (no dedication) *see* Moville w Greencastle, Donagh, Cloncha etc *D & R*
DONAGH (St Salvator) w Tyholland and Errigal Truagh *Clogh* **I** I F R PATTERSON
DONAGHADEE (no dedication) *D & D* **I** L T C STEVENSON
DONAGHCLONEY (St Patrick) w Waringstown *D & D* **I** J C MOORE
DONAGHEADY (St James) *D & R* **I** F L GRAHAM
DONAGHENDRY (St Patrick) *see* Brackaville w Donaghendry and Ballyclog *Arm*
DONAGHMORE (no dedication) *see* Rathdowney w Castlefleming, Donaghmore etc *C & O*
DONAGHMORE (St Bartholomew) *see* Aghaderg w Donaghmore and Scarva *D & D*
DONAGHMORE (St Michael) w Upper Donaghmore *Arm* **I** R D LAWRENSON
DONAGHMORE (St Patrick) *see* Convoy w Monellan and Donaghmore *D & R*
DONAGHMORE, UPPER (St Patrick) *see* Donaghmore w Upper Donaghmore *Arm*
DONAGHPATRICK (St Patrick) *see* Kells w Balrathboyne, Moynalty etc *M & K*
DONAMON (no dedication) *see* Roscommon w Donamon, Rathcline, Kilkeevin etc *K, E & A*

DONANAUGHTA (St John the Baptist) *see* Clonfert Gp of Par *L & K*
DONARD (no dedication) *see* Donoughmore and Donard w Dunlavin *D & G*
DONEGAL (no dedication) w Killymard, Lough Eske and Laghey *D & R* **I** T H TRIMBLE
DONEGORE (St John) *see* Templepatrick w Donegore *Conn*
DONEMANA *see* Donagheady *D & R*
DONERAILE (St Mary) *see* Mallow Union *C, C & R*
DONNYBROOK (St Mary) *see* Dublin Irishtown w Donnybrook *D & G*
DONOUGHMORE (no dedication) and Donard w Dunlavin *D & G* **I** R W M BOWDER
DORRHA (no dedication) *see* Birr w Lorrha, Dorrha and Lockeen *L & K*
DOUGLAS (St Luke) w Blackrock, Frankfield and Marmullane *C, C & R* **I** R E B WHITE, **C** E E M LYNCH, **NSM** A D KINGSTON
DOWN (Cathedral of the Holy and Undivided Trinity) *D & D* **I** *Vacant*
DOWN (St Margaret) w Hollymount *D & D* **I** S M J DICKSON
DOWNPATRICK *see* Down H Trin w Hollymount *D & D*
DOWNPATRICK *see* Down Cathl *D & D*
DRAPERSTOWN (St Columb) *see* Kilcronaghan w Draperstown and Sixtowns *D & R*
DREW MEMORIAL *see* Belfast St Simon w St Phil *Conn*
DRIMOLEAGUE (St Matthew) *see* Fanlobbus Union *C, C & R*
DRINAGH (Christ Church) *as above*
DROGHEDA (St Mary) *see* Julianstown and Colpe w Drogheda and Duleek *M & K*
DROGHEDA (St Peter) w Ardee, Collon and Termonfeckin *Arm* **I** C J G BEVAN
DROMAHAIR *see* Cloonclare w Killasnett, Lurganboy and Drumlease *K, E & A*
DROMARA (St John) w Garvaghy *D & D* **I** *Vacant*
DROMARD (Christ Church) *see* Skreen w Kilmacshalgan and Dromard *T, K & A*
DROMOD (St Michael and All Angels) *see* Kenmare w Sneem, Waterville etc *L & K*
DROMORE (Cathedral of Christ the Redeemer) *D & D* **I** W B NEILL
DROMORE (Holy Trinity) *Clogh* **I** D W GAMBLE
DRUM (no dedication) *see* Currin w Drum and Newbliss *Clogh*
DRUMACHOSE (Christ Church) *D & R* **I** S McVEIGH
DRUMALOOR (St Andrew) *see* Annagh w Drumgoon, Ashfield etc *K, E & A*
DRUMANY (Christ Church) *see* Kinawley w H Trin *K, E & A*
DRUMBANAGHER (St Mary) *see* Acton w Drumbanagher *Arm*
DRUMBEG (St Patrick) *D & D* **I** C W M COOPER
DRUMBO (Holy Trinity) *D & D* **I** J C BELL
DRUMCANNON (Christ Church) *see* Waterford w Killea, Drumcannon and Dunhill *C & O*
DRUMCAR *see* Kilsaran w Drumcar, Dunleer and Dunany *Arm*
DRUMCLAMPH (no dedication) w Lower Langfield and Upper Langfield *D & R* **I** F D CREIGHTON
DRUMCLIFFE (St Columba) w Kilrush, Kilfenora, Kilfarboy, Kilnasoolagh, Shannon and Kilferagh *L & K* **I** R C HANNA
DRUMCLIFFE (St Columba) w Lissadell and Munninane *K, E & A* **I** I GALLAGHER
DRUMCONDRA *see* Dublin Drumcondra w N Strand *D & G*
DRUMCONRATH (St Peter) *see* Kingscourt w Drumconrath, Syddan and Moybologue *M & K*
DRUMCREE (Ascension) *Arm* **I** J A PICKERING
DRUMCREE (St John) *see* Castlepollard and Oldcastle w Loughcrew etc *M & K*
DRUMGATH (St John) w Drumgooland and Clonduff *D & D* **I** W A SEALE
DRUMGLASS (St Anne) w Moygashel *Arm* **I** F D SWANN, **C** T S FORSTER
DRUMGOOLAND (no dedication) *see* Drumgath w Drumgooland and Clonduff *D & D*
DRUMGOON (All Saints) *see* Annagh w Drumgoon, Ashfield etc *K, E & A*
DRUMHOLM (no dedication) *see* Kilbarron w Rossnowlagh and Drumholm *D & R*
DRUMINISKILL (Chapel of Ease) *see* Killesher *K, E & A*
DRUMKEERAN *see* Killinagh w Kiltyclogher and Innismagrath *K, E & A*
DRUMKEERAN (no dedication) w Templecarne and Muckross *Clogh* **I** P F TIZZARD
DRUMLANE (no dedication) *see* Annagh w Drumgoon, Ashfield etc *K, E & A*
DRUMLEASE (no dedication) *see* Cloonclare w Killasnett, Lurganboy and Drumlease *K, E & A*
DRUMMAUL (St Brigid) w Duneane and Ballyscullion *Conn* **I** J R WILSON
DRUMMULLY (no dedication) *see* Galloon w Drummully *Clogh*
DRUMNAKILLY (Holy Trinity) *see* Clogherney w Seskinore and Drumnakilly *Arm*
DRUMQUIN *see* Drumclamph w Lower and Upper Langfield *D & R*
DRUMRAGH (St Columba) w Mountfield *D & R* **I** C B LEEKE, **C** R H ADAMS
DRUMREILLY (no dedication) *see* Mohill w Farnaught, Aughavas, Oughteragh etc *K, E & A*
DRUMSHAMBO (St John) *see* Kiltoghart w Drumshambo, Annaduff and Kilronan *K, E & A*
DRUMSNATT (St Molua) *see* Aghadrumsee w Clogh and Drumsnatt *Clogh*
DRUMTALLAGH (no dedication) *see* Armoy w Loughguile and Drumtullagh *Conn*
DRUNG (no dedication) w Castleterra, Larah and Lavey and Killoughter *K, E & A* **I** J M CATTERALL
DUBLIN Booterstown (St Philip and St James) *D & G* **I** S B FORDE
DUBLIN (Christ Church Cathedral) Group: (St Andrew) (St Werburgh) (St Michan) St Paul and Grangegorman *D & G* **I** J T F PATERSON, D A PIERPOINT, **Min** W J STEWART, **C** V H ROGERS, A T McLELLAN
DUBLIN Clontarf (St John the Baptist) *D & G* **I** T HASKINS
DUBLIN Crumlin (St Mary) w Chapelizod *D & G* **I** W S LAING
DUBLIN Drumcondra (no dedication) w North Strand *D & G* **I** R K BROOKES
DUBLIN (Irish Church Missions) and St Thomas *D & G*, W J BRIDCUT
DUBLIN Irishtown (St Matthew) w Donnybrook *D & G* **I** R H BERTRAM, **NSM** J M GORDON
DUBLIN Mount Merrion (St Thomas) *D & G* **I** *Vacant*
DUBLIN Rathfarnham (no dedication) *D & G* **I** E C J WOODS, **C** A E TAYLOR
DUBLIN Rathmines (Holy Trinity) w Harold's Cross *D & G* **I** N G McENDOO
DUBLIN Sandford (no dedication) w Milltown *D & G* **I** R D HARMAN, **NSM** C E BAKER
DUBLIN Sandymount (St John the Evangelist) *D & G* **P-in-c** J M G CAREY, **C** G P IRVINE
DUBLIN Santry (St Pappan) w Glasnevin and Finglas *D & G* **I** M D GARDNER, **NSM** M A GILBERT
DUBLIN (St Ann) (St Stephen) *D & G* **I** C A EMPEY, **C** W H BLACK
DUBLIN (St Bartholomew) w Leeson Park *D & G* **I** J A McKAY
DUBLIN (St George and St Thomas) *D & G* **Bp's C** S P SEMPLE
DUBLIN (St Patrick's Cathedral) Group: (St Catherine and St James) (St Audoen) *D & G* **I** M E STEWART, **TV** J W R CRAWFORD
DUBLIN Whitechurch (no dedication) *D & G* **I** A H N McKINLEY, **NSM** H E A LEW
DUBLIN (Zion Church) *D & G* **I** W R J GOURLEY
DUGORT (St Thomas) *see* Aughaval w Achill, Knappagh, Dugort etc *T, K & A*
DULEEK *see* Julianstown and Colpe w Drogheda and Duleek *M & K*
DUN LAOGHAIRE (Christ Church) *D & G* **I** V G STACEY
DUNAGHY (St James) *see* Craigs w Dunaghy and Killagan *Conn*
DUNANY *see* Kilsaran w Drumcar, Dunleer and Dunany *Arm*
DUNBOE (St Paul) *see* Castlerock w Dunboe and Fermoyle *D & R*
DUNBOYNE Union (St Peter and St Paul) w Kilcock, Maynooth, Moyglare, Dunshaughlin and Ballymaglasson *M & K* **I** A M WILKINSON
DUNDALK (St Nicholas) w Heynestown *Arm* **I** M A J WILSON
DUNDELA (St Mark) *D & D* **I** J N T CAMPBELL, **C** M A PARKER
DUNDONALD (St Elizabeth) *D & D* **I** E CROOKS, **C** C D BELL
DUNDRUM *see* Cashel w Magorban, Tipperary, Clonbeg etc *C & O*
DUNDRUM (St Donard) *see* Kilmegan w Maghera *D & D*
DUNEANE (no dedication) *see* Drummaul w Duneane and Ballyscullion *Conn*
DUNFANAGHY (Holy Trinity), Raymunterdoney and Tullaghbegley *D & R* **I** *Vacant* Letterkenny (74) 36187
DUNFEENY (no dedication) *see* Killala w Dunfeeny, Crossmolina, Kilmoremoy etc *T, K & A*
DUNGANNON *see* Drumglass w Moygashel *Arm*
DUNGANSTOWN (St Kevin) w Redcross and Conary *D & G* **I** J R HEANEY
DUNGARVAN (St Mary) *see* Lismore w Cappoquin, Kilwatermoy, Dungarvan etc *C & O*

DUNGIVEN (no dedication) w Bovevagh *D & R* **I** G P McADAM
DUNGLOE *see* Gweedore, Carrickfin and Templecrone *D & R*
DUNHILL (St John the Baptist) *see* Waterford w Killea, Drumcannon and Dunhill *C & O*
DUNKERRIN (no dedication) *see* Shinrone w Aghancon etc *L & K*
DUNLAVIN (St Nicholas) *see* Donoughmore and Donard w Dunlavin *D & G*
DUNLECKNEY (St Mary) w Nurney, Lorum and Kiltennel *C & O* **I** F J G WYNNE
DUNLEER (no dedication) *see* Kilsaran w Drumcar, Dunleer and Dunany *Arm*
DUNLUCE (St John the Baptist) *Conn* **I** S D HAZLETT
DUNMANWAY *see* Fanlobbus Union *C, C & R*
DUNMORE EAST *see* Waterford w Killea, Drumcannon and Dunhill *C & O*
DUNMURRY (St Colman) *Conn* **I** M J McCANN
DUNNALONG (St John) *see* Leckpatrick w Dunnalong *D & R*
DUNSEVERICK (no dedication) *see* Ballintoy w Rathlin and Dunseverick *Conn*
DUNSFORD (St Mary) *see* Lecale Gp *D & D*
DUNSHAUGHLIN (St Seachnal) *see* Dunboyne w Kilcock, Maynooth, Moyglare etc *M & K*
DURROW (St Columba) *see* Tullamore w Durrow, Newtownfertullagh, Rahan etc *M & K*
DURROW (St Fintan) *see* Abbeyleix w Old Church, Ballyroan etc *C & O*
DURRUS (St James the Apostle) *see* Kilmocomogue Union *C, C & R*
DYSART ENOS (Holy Trinity) *see* Maryborough w Dysart Enos and Ballyfin *C & O*
EASKEY (St Anne) *see* Killala w Dunfeeny, Crossmolina, Kilmoremoy etc *T, K & A*
EDENDERRY *see* Clonsast w Rathangan, Thomastown etc *M & K*
EDENDERRY (no dedication) w Clanabogan *D & R* **I** R W CLARKE
EDGEWORTHSTOWN *see* Mostrim w Granard, Clonbroney, Killoe etc *K, E & A*
EGLANTINE (All Saints) *Conn* **I** C W BELL
EGLINTON *see* Faughanvale *D & R*
EGLISH *see* Birr w Lorrha, Dorrha and Lockeen *L & K*
EGLISH (Holy Trinity) w Killylea *Arm* **I** J R AUCHMUTY
ELPHIN (no dedication) *see* Boyle and Elphin w Aghanagh, Kilbryan etc *K, E & A*
EMATRIS (St John the Evangelist) w Rockcorry, Aghabog and Aughnamullan *Clogh* **I** J T A MERRY
EMLAGHFAD (no dedication) *see* Ballisodare w Collooney and Emlaghfad *T, K & A*
ENNIS *see* Drumcliffe w Kilnasoolagh *L & K*
ENNISCORTHY (St Mary) w Clone, Clonmore, Monart and Templescobin *C & O* **I** K S WILKINSON, **NSM** J DEACON
ENNISKEEN *see* Kingscourt w Drumconrath, Syddan and Moybologue *M & K*
ENNISKERRY *see* Powerscourt w Kilbride and Annacrevy *D & G*
ENNISKILLEN *see* Rossory *Clogh*
ENNISKILLEN (Cathedral of St Macartin) *Clogh* **I** B J COURTNEY, **C** B T KERR
ENNISNAG (St Peter) *see* Kells Union *C & O*
ERRIGAL (St Paul) w Garvagh *D & R* **I** *Vacant*
ERRIGAL PORTCLARE (no dedication) *see* Clogh w Errigal Portclare *Clogh*
ERRIGAL TRUAGH (St Muadhan) *see* Donagh w Tyholland and Errigal Truagh *Clogh*
ERRIGLE KEEROGUE (no dedication) w Ballygawley and Killeshil *Arm* **I** G J WHITEHEAD
ERRISLANNNAN (no dedication) *see* Omey w Ballynakill, Errislannan and Roundstone *T, K & A*
ESKRAHOOLE (no dedication) *see* Augher w Newtownsaville and Eskrahoole *Clogh*
EYRECOURT *see* Clonfert Gp of Par *L & K*
FAHAN LOWER (Christ Church) and UPPER (St Mura) *D & R* **Bp's C** S D BARTON
FALLS, LOWER (St Luke) *see* Belfast St Steph w St Luke *Conn*
FALLS, UPPER *see* Belfast Upper Falls *Conn*
FANLOBBUS (St Mary) w Drimoleague, Drinagh and Coolkellure *C, C & R* **I** W P HEWITT
FARNAUGHT (no dedication) *see* Mohill w Farnaught, Aughavas, Oughteragh etc *K, E & A*
FAUGHANVALE (St Canice) *D & R* **I** *Vacant*
FENAGH (All Saints) w Myshall, Aghade and Ardoyne *C & O* **I** L D D SCOTT
FERMOY (Christ Church) w Ballyhooley, Knockmourne, Ardnageehy and Brigown *C, C & R* **I** A G MARLEY
FERMOYLE (no dedication) *see* Castlerock w Dunboe and Fermoyle *D & R*
FERNS (Cathedral of St Edan) w Kilbride, Toombe, Kilcormack and Ballycarney *C & O* **I** L D A FORREST
FERRY, EAST *see* Cloyne Union *C, C & R*
FERTAGH (no dedication) *see* Kilcooley w Littleon, Crohane and Fertagh *C & O*
FETHARD (Holy Trinity) *see* Clonmel w Innislounagh, Tullaghmelan etc *C & O*
FETHARD (St Mogue) *see* New w Old Ross, Whitechurch, Fethard etc *C & O*
FIDDOWN (no dedication) w Clonegam, Guilcagh and Kilmeaden *C & O* **C** C G CLIFFE
FINAGHY (St Polycarp) *Conn* **I** J C T SKILLEN
FINGLAS (St Canice) *see* Dublin Santry w Glasnevin and Finglas *D & G*
FINNER (Christ Church) *see* Killinagh w Kiltyclogher and Innismagrath *K, E & A*
FINTONA *see* Donacavey w Barr *Clogh*
FINVOY (no dedication) *see* Ballymoney w Finvoy and Rasharkin *Conn*
FIVEMILETOWN (St John) *Clogh* **I** R J RIDDEL
FLORENCECOURT *see* Killesher *K, E & A*
FONTSTOWN (St John the Evangelist) *see* Athy w Kilberry, Fontstown and Kilkea *D & G*
FORGNEY (St Munis) *see* Athlone w Benown, Kiltoom and Forgney *M & K*
FOUNTAINS *see* Lismore w Cappoquin, Kilwatermoy, Dungarvan etc *C & O*
FOXFORD *see* Straid *T, K & A*
FOYNES *see* Rathkeale w Askeaton and Kilcornan *L & K*
FRANKFIELD (Holy Trinity) *see* Douglas Union w Frankfield *C, C & R*
FRENCH CHURCH *see* Portarlington w Cloneyhurke and Lea *M & K*
FRENCHPARK *see* Roscommon w Donamon, Rathcline, Kilkeevin etc *K, E & A*
GALLOON (St Comgall) w Drummully *Clogh* **I** A P S SYNNOTT
GALWAY (St Nicholas) w Kilcummin *T, K & A* **I** R B MacCARTHY, **C** P G MOONEY
GARRISON (no dedication) w Slavin and Belleek *Clogh* **I** *Vacant* (01365) 685372
GARRYCLOYNE (no dedication) *see* Carrigrohane Union *C, C & R*
GARTAN (St Columba) *see* Conwal Union w Gartan *D & R*
GARTREE (no dedication) *see* Killead w Gartree *Conn*
GARVAGH *see* Errigal w Garvagh *D & R*
GARVAGHY (no dedication) *see* Dromara w Garvaghy *D & D*
GARVARY (Holy Trinity) *see* Derryvullen S w Garvary *Clogh*
GEASHILL (St Mary) w Killeigh and Ballycommon *M & K* **I** P H A LAWRENCE
GILFORD *see* Tullylish *D & D*
GILFORD (St Paul) *D & D* **I** A P PATTERSON
GILNAHIRK (St Dorothea) *D & D* **I** T C KINAHAN
GLANDORE *see* Ross Union *C, C & R*
GLANMIRE *see* Rathcooney Union *C, C & R*
GLASCARRIG (no dedication) *see* Ardamine w Kiltennel, Glascarrig etc *C & O*
GLASLOUGH *see* Donagh w Tyholland and Errigal Truagh *Clogh*
GLASNEVIN (St Mobhi) *see* Dublin Santry w Glasnevin and Finglas *D & G*
GLENAGEARY (St Paul) *D & G* **I** G C S LINNEY, **C** D M PALMER
GLENALLA (St Columbkille) *see* Mevagh w Glenalla *D & R*
GLENARM *see* Ardclinis and Tickmacrevan w Layde and Cushendun *Conn*
GLENAVY (St Aidan) w Tunny and Crumlin *Conn* **I** T WRIGHT
GLENBEIGH (St John) *see* Kilcolman w Kiltallagh, Killorglin, Knockane etc *L & K*
GLENCAIRN *see* Belfast St Andr *Conn*
GLENCAR *see* Cloonclare w Killasnett, Lurganboy and Drumlease *K, E & A*
GLENCOLUMBKILLE (St Columba) *see* Ardara w Glencolumbkille, Inniskeel etc *D & R*
GLENCRAIG (Holy Trinity) *D & D* **I** P S P HEWITT
GLENDERMOTT (no dedication) *D & R* **I** R N MOORE, **C** G S A WILSON, **NSM** H J K McLAUGHLIN
GLENEALY (no dedication) *see* Rathdrum w Glenealy, Derralossary and Laragh *D & G*
GLENOE *see* Glynn w Raloo *Conn*
GLENTIES (no dedication) *see* Ardara w Glencolumbkille, Inniskeel etc *D & R*
GLENVILLE *see* Fermoy Union *C, C & R*
GLYNN (St John) w Raloo *Conn* **C** F M BACH
GORESBRIDGE *see* Leighlin w Grange Sylvae, Shankill etc *C & O*
GOREY (Christ Church) w Kilnahue, Leskinfere and Ballycanew *C & O* **I** C W MULLEN, **NSM** J F FORBES

GORTIN *see* Ardstraw w Baronscourt, Badoney Lower etc *D & R*
GOWNA (no dedication) *see* Arvagh w Carrigallen, Gowna and Columbkille *K, E & A*
GRACEFIELD (no dedication) *see* Woodschapel w Gracefield *Arm*
GRANARD (St Patrick) *see* Mostrim w Granard, Clonbroney, Killoe etc *K, E & A*
GRANGE (St Aidan) *see* Loughgall w Grange *Arm*
GRANGE SYLVAE (St George) *see* Leighlin w Grange Sylvae, Shankill etc *C & O*
GRANGEGORMAN (All Saints) *see* Dublin Ch Ch Cathl Gp *D & G*
GREENAN (no dedication) *see* Ardstraw w Baronscourt, Badoney Lower etc *D & R*
GREENCASTLE (St Finian) *see* Moville w Greencastle, Donagh, Cloncha etc *D & R*
GREENISLAND (Holy Name) *Conn* **I** S H LOWRY
GREY ABBEY (St Saviour) w Kircubbin *D & D* **I** W A McMONAGLE
GREYSTONES (St Patrick) *D & G* **I** E J SWANN, **C** D W McFARLAND
GROOMSPORT (no dedication) *D & D* **I** J D TYNEY
GUILCAGH (St John the Evangelist) *see* Fiddown w Clonegam, Guilcagh and Kilmeaden *C & O*
GURRANEKENNEFEAKE (no dedication) *see* Cloyne Union *C, C & R*
GWEEDORE (St Patrick), Carrickfin and Templecrone *D & R* **C** R P KELLY
HACKETSTOWN (St John the Baptist) *see* Kiltegan w Hacketstown, Clonmore and Moyne *C & O*
HAROLD'S CROSS (no dedication) *see* Dublin Rathmines w Harold's Cross *D & G*
HELEN'S BAY (St John the Baptist) *D & D* **I** L J MEDHURST
HEYNESTOWN (St Paul) *see* Dundalk w Heynestown *Arm*
HIGHFIELD *see* Belfast Whiterock *Conn*
HILLSBOROUGH (St Malachi) *D & D* **I** J F DINNEN
HILLTOWN *see* Drumgath w Drumgooland and Clonduff *D & D*
HOLLYFORT *see* Gorey w Kilnahue, Leskinfere and Ballycanew *C & O*
HOLLYMOUNT (no dedication) *see* Down H Trin w Hollymount *D & D*
HOLMPATRICK (St Patrick) w Balbriggan and Kenure *D & G* **I** R H WATTS
HOLYCROSS *see* Templemore w Thurles and Kilfithmone *C & O*
HOLYWOOD (St Kevin) *see* Blessington w Kilbride, Ballymore Eustace etc *D & G*
HOLYWOOD (St Philip and St James) *D & D* **I** J A MONROE, **C** D I BLAKELY, N H PARKER
HORETOWN (St James) *see* Taghmon w Horetown and Bannow *C & O*
HORSELEAP *see* Clara w Liss, Moate and Clonmacnoise *M & K*
HOWTH (St Mary) *D & G* **I** C G HYLAND
INCH *see* Cloyne Union *C, C & R*
INCH (no dedication) *see* Kilmore w Inch *D & D*
INCH (no dedication) *see* Arklow w Inch and Kilbride *D & G*
INISHARGIE (St Andrew) *see* Ballywalter w Inishargie *D & D*
INISHMACSAINT (St Ninnidh) *Clogh* **I** M A JONES
INISTIOGE (St Mary) *see* Kells Union *C & O*
INNISCALTRA (St Caimin) *see* Killaloe w Stradbally *L & K*
INNISCARRA (no dedication) *see* Carrigrohane Union *C, C & R*
INNISHANNON (Christ Church) *see* Bandon Union *C, C & R*
INNISKEEL (no dedication) *see* Ardara w Glencolumbkille, Inniskeel etc *D & R*
INNISLOUNAGH (St Patrick) *see* Clonmel w Innislounagh, Tullaghmelan etc *C & O*
INNISMAGRATH (no dedication) *see* Killinagh w Kiltyclogher and Innismagrath *K, E & A*
INVER *see* Larne and Inver *Conn*
INVER (St John the Evangelist) w Mountcharles, Killaghtee and Killybegs *D & R* **I** *Vacant* Donegal (73) 36013
INVER, Mountcharles and Killaghtee *D & R* **I** *Vacant*
IRISHTOWN *see* Dublin Irishtown w Donnybrook *D & G*
IRVINESTOWN *see* Derryvullen N w Castlearchdale *Clogh*
ISLANDMAGEE (St John) *see* Whitehead w Islandmagee *Conn*
JOANMOUNT *see* Belfast H Trin and Ardoyne *Conn*
JOHNSTOWN *see* Kilcooley w Littleon, Crohane and Fertagh *C & O*
JORDANSTOWN (St Patrick) *Conn* **I** E J MOORE, **C** M A MALCOLM
JULIANSTOWN (St Mary) and Colpe w Drogheda and Duleek *M & K* **I** A J NELSON
KEADY (St Matthew) w Armaghbreague and Derrynoose *Arm* **I** W G NEELY
KELLS (St Columba) w Balrathboyne, Moynalty, Donaghpatrick and Castletown *M & K* **I** W J RITCHIE
KELLS (St Mary) w Ballaghtobin, Kilmoganny, Ennisnag, Inistioge and Kilfane *C & O* **I** D L SANDES
KENAGH *see* Ardagh w Tashinny, Shrule and Kilcommick *K, E & A*
KENMARE (St Patrick) w Sneem, Dromod and Valentia *L & K* **NSM** A W SHAW
KENTSTOWN (St Mary) *see* Navan w Kentstown, Tara, Slane, Painestown etc *M & K*
KENURE (no dedication) *see* Holmpatrick w Balbriggan and Kenure *D & G*
KESH *see* Magheraculmoney *Clogh*
KILBARRON (St Anne) w Rossnowlagh and Drumholm *D & R* **I** D SKUCE
KILBERRY (no dedication) *see* Athy w Kilberry, Fontstown and Kilkea *D & G*
KILBIXY (St Bigseach) *see* Mullingar, Portnashangan, Moyliscar, Kilbixy etc *M & K*
KILBONANE (St Mark) *see* Moviddy Union *C, C & R*
KILBRIDE (Holy Trinity) *see* Ferns w Kilbride, Toombe, Kilcormack etc *C & O*
KILBRIDE (no dedication) *see* Blessington w Kilbride, Ballymore Eustace etc *D & G*
KILBRIDE (St Bride) *Conn* **I** C L HALL-THOMPSON
KILBRIDE (St Brigid) *see* Arklow w Inch and Kilbride *D & G*
KILBRIDE BRAY (no dedication) *see* Powerscourt w Kilbride and Annacrevy *D & G*
KILBRONEY (no dedication) *D & D* **Bp's C** J H SIMS
KILBRYAN (no dedication) *see* Boyle and Elphin w Aghanagh, Kilbryan etc *K, E & A*
KILCLEAGH *see* Clara w Liss, Moate and Clonmacnoise *M & K*
KILCLIEF (no dedication) *see* Lecale Gp *D & D*
KILCLUNEY (St John) *see* Mullabrack w Markethill and Kilcluney *Arm*
KILCOCK *see* Dunboyne w Kilcock, Maynooth, Moyglare etc *M & K*
KILCOLMAN (no dedication) w Kiltallagh, Killorglin, Knockane and Glenbeigh *L & K* **I** M J D SHANNON, **C** J C STEPHENS
KILCOMMICK (no dedication) *see* Ardagh w Tashinny, Shrule and Kilcommick *K, E & A*
KILCOMMON (no dedication) *see* Crosspatrick Gp *C & O*
KILCOO (no dedication) *see* Castlewellan w Kilcoo *D & D*
KILCOOLEY (no dedication) w Littleton, Crohane and Fertagh *C & O* **C** B Y FRYDAY
KILCOOLEY (St Columba) *see* Bangor Abbey *D & D*
KILCORMACK (St Cormac) *see* Ferns w Kilbride, Toombe, Kilcormack etc *C & O*
KILCORNAN (no dedication) *see* Rathkeale w Askeaton and Kilcornan *L & K*
KILCROHANE *see* Kenmare w Sneem, Waterville etc *L & K*
KILCRONAGHAN (no dedication) w Draperstown and Sixtowns *D & R* **I** S J CAMPBELL
KILCULLEN (St John) *see* Newbridge w Carnalway and Kilcullen *M & K*
KILCUMMIN (no dedication) *see* Galway w Kilcummin *T, K & A*
KILDALLON (no dedication) *see* Kilmore w Ballintemple, Kildallon etc *K, E & A*
KILDARE (Cathedral of St Brigid) w Kilmeague and Curragh Garrison Church *M & K* **I** *Vacant* Curragh (45) 41654
KILDARTON (no dedication) *see* Lisnadill w Kildarton *Arm*
KILDAVIN (St Paul) *see* Bunclody w Kildavin, Clonegal and Kilrush *C & O*
KILDOLLAGH (St Paul) *see* Ballyrashane w Kildollagh *Conn*
KILDRESS (St Patrick) w Altedesert *Arm* **I** B J A CRUISE
KILDRUMFERTON (St Patrick) w Ballymachugh and Ballyjamesduff *K, E & A* **I** J R SIDES
KILFANE (no dedication) *see* Kells Union *C & O*
KILFARBOY (Christ Church) *see* Drumcliffe w Kilnasoolagh *L & K*
KILFAUGHNABEG (Christ Church) *see* Ross Union *C, C & R*
KILFENORA (Cathedral of St Fachan) *see* Drumcliffe w Kilnasoolagh *L & K*
KILFERAGH (no dedication) *as above*
KILFINANE (St Andrew) *see* Kilmallock w Kilflynn, Kilfinane, Knockaney etc *L & K*
KILFITHMONE (no dedication) *see* Templemore w Thurles and Kilfithmone *C & O*
KILFLYNN (no dedication) *see* Kilmallock w Kilflynn, Kilfinane, Knockaney etc *L & K*
KILGARIFFE (no dedication) w Kilmalooda, Kilnagross, Timoleague and Courtmacsherry *C, C & R* **I** I R JONAS
KILGLASS (no dedication) *see* Killala w Dunfeeny, Crossmolina, Kilmoremoy etc *T, K & A*

KILGLASS (St Anne) *see* Mostrim w Granard, Clonbroney, Killoe etc *K, E & A*
KILGOBBIN (no dedication) *see* Dingle w Killiney and Kilgobbin *L & K*
KILHORNE *see* Annalong *D & D*
KILKEA (no dedication) *see* Athy w Kilberry, Fontstown and Kilkea *D & G*
KILKEE *see* Drumcliffe w Kilnasoolagh *L & K*
KILKEEL (Christ Church) *D & D* **I** D A McCLAY
KILKEEVIN (Holy Trinity) *see* Roscommon w Donamon, Rathcline, Kilkeevin etc *K, E & A*
KILKENNY (Cathedral of St Canice) (St John), Aghour and Kilmanagh *C & O* **I** N N LYNAS
KILKENNY WEST *see* Athlone w Benown, Kiltoom and Forgney *M & K*
KILL (no dedication) *D & G* **I** S F GLENFIELD, **NSM** A W YOUNG
KILL (St John) *see* Naas w Kill and Rathmore *M & K*
KILL O' THE GRANGE *see* Kill *D & G*
KILLABBAN (no dedication) *see* Killeshin w Cloydagh and Killabban *C & O*
KILLADEAS (Priory Church) *see* Trory w Killadeas *Clogh*
KILLAGAN (no dedication) *see* Craigs w Dunaghy and Killagan *Conn*
KILLAGHTEE (St Peter) *see* Inver w Mountcharles, Killaghtee and Killybegs *D & R*
KILLALA (Cathedral of St Patrick) w Dunfeeny, Crossmolina, Kilmoremoy, Castleconnor, Easkey and Kilglass *T, K & A* **I** E G ARDIS, **C** A M O'S FERGUSON, **NSM** D T S CLEMENTS
KILLALLON (St John) *see* Trim and Athboy Gp *M & K*
KILLALOE (Cathedral of St Flannan) w Stradbally, Clonlara, Mountshannon, Abingdon and Tuomgraney *L & K* **I** N M CUMMINS
KILLANEY (St Andrew) w Carryduff *D & D* **I** R FOX
KILLANNE (St Anne) w Killegney, Rossdroit and Templeshanbo *C & O* **I** A M JACKSON
KILLANULLY *see* Carrigaline Union *C, C & R*
KILLARGUE (no dedication) *see* Killinagh w Kiltyclogher and Innismagrath *K, E & A*
KILLARNEY (St Mary) w Aghadoe and Muckross *L & K* **I** B F B LOUGHEED
KILLASHEE (St Paul) *see* Templemichael w Clongish, Clooncumber etc *K, E & A*
KILLASNETT (no dedication) *see* Clooncla re w Killasnett, Lurganboy and Drumlease *K, E & A*
KILLCONNELL *see* Aughrim w Ballinasloe etc *L & K*
KILLEA (St Andrew) *see* Waterford w Killea, Drumcannon and Dunhill *C & O*
KILLEA (St Fiach) *see* Taughboyne, Craigadooish, Newtowncunningham etc *D & R*
KILLEAD (St Catherine) w Gartree *Conn* **I** *Vacant*
KILLEDMOND *see* Dunleckney w Nurney, Lorum and Kiltennel *C & O*
KILLEEVAN (no dedication) *see* Clones w Killeevan *Clogh*
KILLEGAR (no dedication) *see* Killeshandra w Killegar and Derrylane *K, E & A*
KILLEGNEY (no dedication) *see* Killanne w Killegney, Rossdroit and Templeshanbo *C & O*
KILLEIGH (no dedication) *see* Geashill w Killeigh and Ballycommon *M & K*
KILLELAGH (no dedication) *see* Maghera w Killelagh *D & R*
KILLENAULE (no dedication) *see* Kilcooley w Littleon, Crohane and Fertagh *C & O*
KILLERMOGH (no dedication) *see* Abbeyleix w Old Church, Ballyroan etc *C & O*
KILLERY *see* Taunagh w Kilmactranny, Ballysumaghan etc *K, E & A*
KILLESHANDRA (no dedication) w Killegar and Derrylane *K, E & A* **NSM** C LINDSAY
KILLESHER (St John) *K, E & A* **I** *Vacant*
KILLESHERDONEY (St Mark) *see* Annagh w Drumgoon, Ashfield etc *K, E & A*
KILLESHIL (St Paul) *see* Errigle Keerogue w Ballygawley and Killeshil *Arm*
KILLESHIN (no dedication) w Cloydagh and Killabban *C & O* **I** C CHALLENDER
KILLESK (All Saints) *see* New w Old Ross, Whitechurch, Fethard etc *C & O*
KILLETER *see* Derg w Termonamongan *D & R*
KILLINAGH (no dedication) w Kiltyclogher and Innismagrath *K, E & A* **I** R S P RICHEY
KILLINCHY (no dedication) w Kilmood and Tullynakill *D & D* **I** R R W DEVENNEY
KILLINEY Ballybrack (no dedication) *D & G* **I** *Vacant* Dublin (1) 285-6180
KILLINEY (Holy Trinity) *D & G* **I** C L PETERS
KILLINEY (St Brendan) *see* Dingle w Killiney and Kilgobbin *L & K*
KILLINICK (no dedication) *see* Kilscoran w Killinick and Mulrankin *C & O*
KILLINKERE (no dedication) *see* Lurgan w Billis, Killinkere and Munterconnaught *K, E & A*
KILLISKEY (no dedication) *see* Wicklow w Killiskey *D & G*
KILLODIERNAN (no dedication) *see* Nenagh *L & K*
KILLOE (St Catherine) *see* Mostrim w Granard, Clonbroney, Killoe etc *K, E & A*
KILLORAN (no dedication) *see* Achonry w Tubbercurry and Killoran *T, K & A*
KILLORGLIN (no dedication) *see* Kilcolman w Kiltallagh, Killorglin, Knockane etc *L & K*
KILLOUGH (St Anne) *see* Bright w Ballee and Killough *D & D*
KILLOUGHTER (no dedication) *see* Drung w Castleterra, Larah and Lavey etc *K, E & A*
KILLOUGHY *see* Tullamore w Durrow, Newtownfertullagh, Rahan etc *M & K*
KILLOWEN *see* Kinneigh Union *C, C & R*
KILLOWEN (St John) *D & R* **I** I H McDONALD, **C** K P WHITTAKER
KILLSALLAGHAN (St David) *see* Swords w Donabate and Killsallaghan *D & G*
KILLUCAN (St Etchen) *see* Mullingar, Portnashangan, Moyliscar, Kilbixy etc *M & K*
KILLURIN (no dedication) *see* Wexford w Ardcolm and Killurin *C & O*
KILLYBEGS (no dedication) *see* Inver w Mountcharles, Killaghtee and Killybegs *D & R*
KILLYGARVAN (St Columb) *see* Tullyaughnish w Kilmacrennan and Killygarvan *D & R*
KILLYLEA (St Mark) *see* Eglish w Killylea *Arm*
KILLYLEAGH (St John the Evangelist) *D & D* **I** R M McCONNELL
KILLYMAN (St Andrew) *Arm* **I** A S J WARKE, **C** E O'BRIEN
KILLYMARD (no dedication) *see* Donegal w Killymard, Lough Eske and Laghey *D & R*
KILMACABEA (no dedication) *see* Ross Union *C, C & R*
KILMACDUAGH (no dedication) *see* Aughrim w Ballinasloe etc *L & K*
KILMACRENNAN (St Finnian and St Mark) *see* Tullyaughnish w Kilmacrennan and Killygarvan *D & R*
KILMACSHALGAN (St Mary) *see* Skreen w Kilmacshalgan and Dromard *T, K & A*
KILMACTHOMAS (no dedication) *see* Lismore w Cappoquin, Kilwatermoy, Dungarvan etc *C & O*
KILMACTRANNY (no dedication) *see* Taunagh w Kilmactranny, Ballysumaghan etc *K, E & A*
KILMAKEE (St Hilda) *Conn* **I** F G RUTLEDGE, **NSM** R MOORE
KILMALLOCK (St Peter and St Paul) w Kilflynn, Kilfinane, Knockaney, Bruff and Caherconlish *L & K* **I** *Vacant*
KILMALOODA (All Saints) *see* Kilgariffe Union *C, C & R*
KILMANAGH (no dedication) *see* Kilkenny w Aghour and Kilmanagh *C & O*
KILMEADEN (St Mary) *see* Fiddown w Clonegam, Guilcagh and Kilmeaden *C & O*
KILMEAGUE (no dedication) *see* Kildare w Kilmeague and Curragh *M & K*
KILMEEN (Christ Church) *see* Kinneigh Union *C, C & R*
KILMEGAN (no dedication) w Maghera *D & D* **Bp's C** C J CARSON
KILMOCOMOGUE Union (no dedication) *C, C & R* **I** P M WILLOUGHBY
KILMOE (no dedication) w Teampol-na-mbocht, Schull and Crookhaven *C, C & R* **I** H M WAKEMAN
KILMOGANNY (St Matthew) *see* Kells Union *C & O*
KILMOOD (St Mary) *see* Killinchy w Kilmood and Tullynakill *D & D*
KILMORE (Cathedral of St Fethlimidh) w Ballintemple, Kildallon, Newtowngore and Corrawallen *K, E & A* **I** D S G GODFREY
KILMORE (Christ Church) w Inch *D & D* **I** M F TAYLOR
KILMORE (no dedication) *see* Monaghan w Tydavnet and Kilmore *Clogh*
KILMORE (no dedication) *see* Kiltoghart w Drumshambo, Annaduff and Kilronan *K, E & A*
KILMORE (St Aidan) (St Saviour) *Arm* **I** E T DUNDAS
KILMOREROY (St Michael) *see* Killala w Dunfeeny, Crossmolina, Kilmoremoy etc *T, K & A*
KILMOYLEY *see* Tralee w Ballymacelligott, Kilnaughtin etc *L & K*
KILMUCKRIDGE (no dedication) *see* Ardamine w Kiltennel, Glascarrig etc *C & O*
KILMURRY (St Andrew) *see* Moviddy Union *C, C & R*
KILNAGROSS (no dedication) *see* Kilgariffe Union *C, C & R*
KILNAHUE (St John the Evangelist) *see* Gorey w Kilnahue, Leskinfere and Ballycanew *C & O*

KILNALECK *see* Kildrumferton w Ballymachugh and Ballyjamesduff *K, E & A*
KILNAMANAGH (St John) *see* Ardamine w Kiltennel, Glascarrig etc *C & O*
KILNASOOLAGH (no dedication) *see* Drumcliffe w Kilnasoolagh *L & K*
KILNAUGHTIN (St Brendan) *see* Tralee w Ballymacelligott, Kilnaughtin etc *L & K*
KILPEACON (St Beacon) *see* Adare w Kilpeacon and Croom *L & K*
KILPIPE (no dedication) *see* Crosspatrick Gp *C & O*
KILREA (St Patrick) *see* Aghadowey w Kilrea *D & R*
KILRONAN (St Thomas) *see* Kiltoghart w Drumshambo, Annaduff and Kilronan *K, E & A*
KILROOT (St Colman) and Templecorran *Conn* **I** R HENDERSON
KILROSSANTY (no dedication) *see* Lismore w Cappoquin, Kilwatermoy, Dungarvan etc *C & O*
KILRUSH *see* Drumcliffe w Kilnasoolagh *L & K*
KILRUSH (St Brigid) *see* Bunclody w Kildavin, Clonegal and Kilrush *C & O*
KILSARAN (St Mary) w Drumcar, Dunleer and Dunany *Arm* **I** A V G FLYNN
KILSCORAN (no dedication) w Killinick and Mulrankin *C & O* **I** H J KEOGH
KILSKEERY (no dedication) w Trillick *Clogh* **I** W J JOHNSTON
KILTALLAGH (St Carthage) *see* Kilcolman w Kiltallagh, Killorglin, Knockane etc *L & K*
KILTEEVOGUE (St John) *see* Stranorlar w Meenglas and Kilteevogue *D & R*
KILTEGAN (St Peter) w Hacketstown, Clonmore and Moyne *C & O* **I** S A CROWTHER
KILTENNEL (no dedication) *see* Ardamine w Kiltennel, Glascarrig etc *C & O*
KILTENNEL (St Peter) *see* Dunleckney w Nurney, Lorum and Kiltennel *C & O*
KILTERNAN (St Kiernan) *D & G* **I** D G MOYNAN, **NSM** C C WEST
KILTINANLEA (no dedication) *see* Killaloe w Stradbally *L & K*
KILTOGHART (St George) w Drumshambo, Anaduff and Kilronan *K, E & A* **I** *Vacant* Shannon (61) 20053
KILTOOM *see* Athlone w Benown, Kiltoom and Forgney *M & K*
KILTUBRIDE (St Brigid) *see* Mohill w Farnaught, Aughavas, Oughteragh etc *K, E & A*
KILTULLAGH (no dedication) *see* Roscommon w Donamon, Rathcline, Kilkeevin etc *K, E & A*
KILTYCLOGHER (no dedication) *see* Killinagh w Kiltyclogher and Innismagrath *K, E & A*
KILVEMNON (St Hugh) *see* Clonmel w Innislounagh, Tullaghmelan etc *C & O*
KILWARLIN UPPER (St John) w LOWER (St James) *D & D* **I** W FENTON
KILWATERMOY (St Mary) *see* Lismore w Cappoquin, Kilwatermoy, Dungarvan etc *C & O*
KILWAUGHTER (no dedication) w Cairncastle and Craigy Hill *Conn* **I** R W JONES, **C** K M POULTON
KINAWLEY (no dedication) w Holy Trinity *K, E & A* **I** G T W DAVISON
KINAWLEY (St Paul) *see* Swanlinbar w Tomregan, Kinawley, Drumlane etc *K, E & A*
KINGSCOURT (St Ernan) w Drumconrath, Syddan and Moybologue *M & K* **I** R S J BOURKE
KINLOUGH *see* Killinagh w Kiltyclogher and Innismagrath *K, E & A*
KINNEAGH (no dedication) *see* Narraghmore w Timolin, Castledermot and Kinneagh *D & G*
KINNEIGH (St Bartholomew) w Ballymoney, Kilmeen, Desertserges, Killowen and Murragh *C, C & R* **I** D COLE
KINNITTY (St Trinnian) *see* Shinrone w Aghancon etc *L & K*
KINSALE (St Multose) w Runcurran, Ballymartle and Templetrine *C, C & R* **I** D WILLIAMS
KIRCONRIOLA *see* Ballymena w Ballyclug *Conn*
KIRCUBBIN (Holy Trinity) *see* Grey Abbey w Kircubbin *D & D*
KNAPPAGH (St Thomas) *see* Aughaval w Achill, Knappagh, Dugort etc *T, K & A*
KNOCK (St Columba) *D & D* **I** G A McCAMLEY, **C** A W McCORMACK
KNOCKANE (no dedication) *see* Kilcolman w Kiltallagh, Killorglin, Knockane etc *L & K*
KNOCKANEY (St John) *see* Kilmallock w Kilflynn, Kilfinane, Knockaney etc *L & K*
KNOCKBREDA (no dedication) *D & D* **I** P F PATTERSON, **C** J D M PIERCE
KNOCKBRIDE (no dedication) *see* Bailieborough w Knockbride, Shercock and Mullagh *K, E & A*
KNOCKLOUGHRIM *see* Desertmartin w Termoneeny *D & R*
KNOCKMOURNE (no dedication) *see* Fermoy Union *C, C & R*
KNOCKNAGONEY (Annunciation) *D & D* **Bp's C** D L BROWN
KNOCKNAMUCKLEY (St Matthias) *D & D* **I** B T BLACOE
KNOCKNAREA (St Anne) *see* Sligo w Knocknarea and Rosses Pt *K, E & A*
KYLE (no dedication) *see* Roscrea w Kyle, Bourney and Corbally *L & K*
LACK (no dedication) *Clogh* **I** R J JOHNSTON
LAGHEY (no dedication) *see* Donegal w Killymard, Lough Eske and Laghey *D & R*
LAMBEG (no dedication) *Conn* **I** K A McREYNOLDS
LANESBOROUGH *see* Roscommon w Donamon, Rathcline, Kilkeevin etc *K, E & A*
LANGFIELD, LOWER (no dedication) *see* Drumclamph w Lower and Upper Langfield *D & R*
LANGFIELD, UPPER (no dedication) *as above*
LARAGH (St John) *see* Rathdrum w Glenealy, Derralossary and Laragh *D & G*
LARAH AND LAVEY (no dedication) *see* Drung w Castleterra, Larah and Lavey etc *K, E & A*
LARNE AND INVER (St Cedma) *Conn* **I** I P POULTON, **C** F M BACH
LAVEY *see* Drung w Castleterra, Larah and Lavey etc *K, E & A*
LAYDE (no dedication) *see* Ardclinis and Tickmacrevan w Layde and Cushendun *Conn*
LEA (no dedication) *see* Portarlington w Cloneyhurke and Lea *M & K*
LEAP *see* Ross Union *C, C & R*
LEARMOUNT (no dedication) *see* Cumber Upper w Learmount *D & R*
LEATBEG (no dedication) *see* Clondevaddock w Portsalon and Leatbeg *D & R*
LECALE Group *see* Down Cathl *D & D*
LECALE Group: Saul, Loughinisland, Ardglass, Dunsford, Ballyculter and Kilclief *D & D* **I** J A B MAYNE, **C** G B FREEMAN
LECKPATRICK (St Patrick) w Dunnalong *D & R* **I** D H J FERRY
LEESON PARK (Christ Church) *see* Dublin St Bart w Leeson Park *D & G*
LEIGHLIN (Catherdal of St Laserian) w Grange Sylvae, Shankill, Clonagoose and Gowran *C & O* **P-in-c** C A FAULL, **NSM** K H SHERWOOD
LEIXLIP (St Mary) *see* Lucan w Leixlip *D & G*
LESKINFERE (no dedication) *see* Gorey w Kilnahue, Leskinfere and Ballycanew *C & O*
LETTERKENNY *see* Conwal Union w Gartan *D & R*
LETTERMACAWARD (no dedication) *see* Ardara w Glencolumbkille, Inniskeel etc *D & R*
LICKMOLASSY *see* Clonfert Gp of Par *L & K*
LIFFORD *see* Raphoe w Raymochy and Clonleigh *D & R*
LIMAVADY *see* Drumachose *D & R*
LIMAVADY *see* Tamlaghtfinlagan w Myroe *D & R*
LIMERICK CITY (Cathedral of St Mary) (St Michael) *L & K* **I** J M G SIRR, **C** S M NEILL
LISBELLAW (no dedication) *Clogh* **I** E R G WEST
LISBURN (Christ Church) *Conn* **I** S McCOMB, **C** T CLELAND
LISBURN (Christ Church Cathedral) *Conn* **I** J T McCAMMON, **C** J HALES
LISBURN (St Paul) *Conn* **I** K W COCHRANE, **C** P K McDOWELL
LISLIMNAGHAN (Holy Trinity) *see* Cappagh w Lislimnaghan *D & R*
LISMORE (Cathedral of St Carthage) w Cappoquin, Kilwatermoy, Dungarvan, Kilrossanty, Stradbally and Kilmacthomas *C & O* **I** J C HEALEY
LISNADILL (St John) w Kildarton *Arm* **I** M C KENNEDY
LISNASKEA (Holy Trinity) *Clogh* **I** W L BENNETT
LISS (no dedication) *see* Clara w Liss, Moate and Clonmacnoise *M & K*
LISSADELL (no dedication) *see* Drumcliffe w Lissadell and Munninane *K, E & A*
LISSAN (no dedication) *Arm* **I** R H BOYD
LISTOWEL *see* Tralee w Ballymacelligott, Kilnaughtin etc *L & K*
LITTLE ISLAND (St Lappan) *see* Rathcooney Union *C, C & R*
LITTLETON (no dedication) *see* Kilcooley w Littleon, Crohane and Fertagh *C & O*
LOCKEEN (no dedication) *see* Birr w Lorrha, Dorrha and Lockeen *L & K*
LONDONDERRY *see* Templemore *D & R*
LONDONDERRY (Christ Church) *D & R* **I** D S McLEAN
LONDONDERRY (St Augustine) *D & R* **I** R C LOGUE

LONGFORD *see* Templemichael w Clongish, Clooncumber etc *K, E & A*
LORRHA (St Ruadhan) *see* Birr w Lorrha, Dorrha and Lockeen *L & K*
LORUM (no dedication) *see* Dunleckney w Nurney, Lorum and Kiltennel *C & O*
LOUGH ESKE (Christ Church) *see* Donegal w Killymard, Lough Eske and Laghey *D & R*
LOUGHBRICKLAND *see* Aghaderg w Donaghmore and Scarva *D & D*
LOUGHCREW *see* Castlepollard and Oldcastle w Loughcrew etc *M & K*
LOUGHGALL (St Luke) w Grange *Arm* **I** I W ELLIS
LOUGHGILLY (St Patrick) w Clare *Arm* **I** J L WILSON
LOUGHGUILE (All Saints) *see* Armoy w Loughguile and Drumtullagh *Conn*
LOUGHINISLAND (no dedication) *see* Lecale Gp *D & D*
LUCAN (St Andrew) w Leixlip *D & G* **I** B A PIERCE, **C** G V WHARTON
LUGGACURREN (Resurrection) *see* Stradbally w Ballintubbert, Coraclone etc *C & O*
LURGAN (Christ the Redeemer) (St Andrew) *D & D* **I** K R GOOD, **C** T J CADDEN
LURGAN (no dedication) w Billis, Killinkere and Munterconnaught *K, E & A* **I** W D NELSON
LURGAN (St John the Evangelist) *D & D* **I** S G BOURKE
LURGANBOY (Chapel of Ease) *see* Clooncl are w Killasnett, Lurganboy and Drumlease *K, E & A*
MACOSQUIN *see* Camus-juxta-Bann *D & R*
MACREDDIN *see* Castlemacadam w Ballinaclash, Aughrim etc *D & G*
MACROOM *see* Moviddy Union *C, C & R*
MAGHERA (no dedication) *see* Kilmegan w Maghera *D & D*
MAGHERA (St Lurach) w Killelagh *D & R* **I** T D ALLEN
MAGHERACLOONE (St Molua) *see* Carrickmacross w Magheracloone *Clogh*
MAGHERACROSS (no dedication) *Clogh* **I** D P HOEY
MAGHERACULMONEY (St Mary) *Clogh* **I** W E McGIRR
MAGHERADROLL (no dedication) *D & D* **I** W W RUSSELL
MAGHERAFELT (St Swithin) *Arm* **I** T SCOTT
MAGHERAGALL (no dedication) *Conn* **I** G A CHEEVERS
MAGHERAHAMLET (no dedication) *see* Annahilt w Magherahamlet *D & D*
MAGHERALIN (Holy and Undivided Trinity) w Dollingstown *D & D* **I** C R A EASTON, **C** M E E McELHINNEY
MAGHERALLY (St John the Evangelist) w Annaclone *D & D* **I** C R J RUDD
MAGORBAN (no dedication) *see* Cashel w Magorban, Tipperary, Clonbeg etc *C & O*
MAGOURNEY *see* Carrigrohane Union *C, C & R*
MAGUIRESBRIDGE (Christ Church) w Derrybrusk *Clogh* **I** P S WILSON
MALAHIDE (St Andrew) w Balgriffin *D & G* **I** N E C GAMBLE
MALIN *see* Moville w Greencastle, Donagh, Cloncha etc *D & R*
MALLOW (St James) w Doneraile and Castletownroche *C, C & R* **I** A G S WHITING
MALLUSK (St Brigid) *Conn* **I** I C BALLENTINE
MALONE *see* Belfast Malone St Jo *Conn*
MALONE, UPPER *see* Belfast Upper Malone (Epiphany) *Conn*
MANORCUNNINGHAM *see* Raphoe w Raymochy and Clonleigh *D & R*
MANORHAMILTON *see* Clooncl are w Killasnett, Lurganboy and Drumlease *K, E & A*
MARKETHILL (no dedication) *see* Mullabrack w Markethill and Kilcluney *Arm*
MARMULLANE (St Mary) *see* Douglas Union w Frankfield *C, C & R*
MARYBOROUGH (St Peter) w Dysart Enos and Ballyfin *C & O* **I** R J HARMSWORTH
MAYNE *see* Castlepollard and Oldcastle w Loughcrew etc *M & K*
MAYNOOTH (St Mary) *see* Dunboyne w Kilcock, Maynooth, Moyglare etc *M & K*
MAYO (no dedication) *see* Killeshin w Cloydagh and Killabban *C & O*
MEALIFFE *see* Templemore w Thurles and Kilfithmone *C & O*
MEENGLASS (Ascension) *see* Stranorlar w Meenglas and Kilteevogue *D & R*
MEVAGH (Holy Trinity) w Glenalla *D & R* **I** P D THORNBURY
MIDDLE CHURCH (no dedication) *see* Ballinderry *Conn*
MIDDLETOWN (St John) *see* Tynan w Middletown *Arm*
MIDLETON (St John the Baptist) *see* Cloyne Union *C, C & R*
MILLISLE (St Patrick) *see* Carrowdore w Millisle *D & D*
MILLTOWN *see* Kilcolman w Kiltallagh, Killorglin, Knockane etc *L & K*
MILLTOWN (St Andrew) *Arm* **I** E J COULTER
MILLTOWN (St Philip) *see* Dublin Sandford w Milltown *D & G*
MILLTOWN MALBAY *see* Drumcliffe w Kilnasoolagh *L & K*
MITCHELSTOWN *see* Fermoy Union *C, C & R*
MOATE (St Mary) *see* Clara w Liss, Moate and Clonmacnoise *M & K*
MOHILL (St Mary) w Farnaught, Aughavas, Oughteragh, Kiltubride and Drumreilly *K, E & A* **I** J T P TWOMEY
MOIRA (St John) *D & D* **I** T R WEST
MONAGHAN (St Patrick) w Tydavnet and Kilmore *Clogh* **I** J M HARVEY
MONAMOLIN (St Molig) *see* Ardamine w Kiltennel, Glascarrig etc *C & O*
MONART (St Peter) *see* Enniscorthy w Clone, Clonmore, Monart etc *C & O*
MONASTEREVAN (St John the Evangelist) w Nurney and Rathdaire *M & K* **I** *Vacant* Monasterevan (45) 25411
MONASTERORIS (no dedication) *see* Clonsast w Rathangan, Thomastown etc *M & K*
MONELLAN (no dedication) *see* Convoy w Monellan and Donaghmore *D & R*
MONEYMORE *see* Desertlyn w Ballyeglish *Arm*
MONEYREAGH (no dedication) *see* Orangefield w Moneyreagh *D & D*
MONKSTOWN (Good Shepherd) *Conn* **I** G E WITHERS
MONKSTOWN (no dedication) *D & G* **I** K DALTON
MONKSTOWN (St John) *see* Carrigaline Union *C, C & R*
MOSSLEY (Holy Spirit) *Conn* **I** N R CUTCLIFFE, **NSM** G WITHERS
MOSTRIM (St John) w Granard, Clonbroney, Killoe, Rathaspeck and Streete *K, E & A* **I** T G HUDSON
MOTHEL (no dedication) *see* Castlecomer w Colliery Ch, Mothel and Bilbo *C & O*
MOUNT MERRION *see* Dublin Mt Merrion *D & G*
MOUNT MERRION (Pentecost) *D & D* **I** R C NEILL
MOUNT NUGENT (St Bride) *see* Castlepollard and Oldcastle w Loughcrew etc *M & K*
MOUNTCHARLES (Christ Church) *see* Inver w Mountcharles, Killaghtee and Killybegs *D & R*
MOUNTFIELD (no dedication) *see* Drumragh w Mountfield *D & R*
MOUNTMELLICK (St Paul) w Coolbanagher, Rosenallis and Clonaslee *M & K* **I** *Vacant*
MOUNTRATH *see* Clonenagh w Offerlane, Borris-in-Ossory etc *C & O*
MOUNTSHANNON *see* Killaloe w Stradbally *L & K*
MOVIDDY (no dedication), Kilbonane, Kilmurry, Templemartin and Macroom *C, C & R* **NSM** J E FENNING
MOVILLA (no dedication) *D & D* **Bp's C** K HIGGINS
MOVILLE (St Columb) w Greencastle, Donagh, Cloncha and Culdaff *D & R* **I** H GILMORE
MOY (St James) w Charlemont *Arm* **I** J STEWART
MOYBOLOGUE *see* Kingscourt w Drumconrath, Syddan and Moybologue *M & K*
MOYDOW (no dedication) *see* Ardagh w Tashinny, Shrule and Kilcommick *K, E & A*
MOYGASHEL (no dedication) *see* Drumglass w Moygashel *Arm*
MOYGLARE (All Saints) *see* Dunboyne w Kilcock, Maynooth, Moyglare etc *M & K*
MOYLISCAR *see* Mullingar, Portnashangan, Moyliscar, Kilbixy etc *M & K*
MOYNALTY (St Mary) *see* Kells w Balrathboyne, Moynalty etc *M & K*
MOYNE (St John) *see* Kiltegan w Hacketstown, Clonmore and Moyne *C & O*
MOYNTAGHS *see* Ardmore w Craigavon *D & D*
MOYRUS *see* Omey w Ballynakill, Errislannan and Roundstone *T, K & A*
MUCKAMORE (St Jude) (St Matthias) *Conn* **I** B S CADDEN
MUCKNOE (St Maeldoid) *see* Ballybay w Mucknoe and Clontibret *Clogh*
MUCKROSS (Holy Trinity) *see* Killarney w Aghadoe and Muckross *L & K*
MUCKROSS (St John) *see* Drumkeeran w Templecarne and Muckross *Clogh*
MUFF (no dedication) *see* Culmore w Muff and Belmont *D & R*
MULHUDDART (St Thomas) *see* Castleknock and Mulhuddart, w Clonsilla *D & G*
MULLABRACK (no dedication) w Markethill and Kilcluney *Arm* **I** W R FERGUSON, **NSM** N J HUGHES
MULLAGH (no dedication) *see* Bailieborough w Knockbride, Shercock and Mullagh *K, E & A*
MULLAGHDUN (no dedication) *see* Cleenish w Mullaghdun *Clogh*
MULLAGHFAD (All Saints) *see* Aghalurcher w Tattykeeran, Cooneen etc *Clogh*
MULLAGLASS (St Luke) *see* Camlough w Mullaglass *Arm*

MULLAVILLY (no dedication) *Arm* **I** B J HARPER
MULLINACUFF (no dedication) *see* Tullow w Shillelagh, Aghold and Mullinacuff *C & O*
MULLINGAR (All Saints) w Portnashangan, Moyliscar, Kilbixy, Almoritia, Killucan, Clonard and Castlelost *M & K* **I** D P R CARMODY, **C** A V STEWART
MULRANKIN (St David) *see* Kilscoran w Killinick and Mulrankin *C & O*
MUNNINANE (St Kevin) *see* Drumcliffe w Lissadell and Munninane *K, E & A*
MUNTERCONNAUGHT (no dedication) *see* Lurgan w Billis, Killinkere and Munterconnaught *K, E & A*
MURRAGH (no dedication) *see* Kinneigh Union *C, C & R*
MYROE (St John) *see* Tamlaghtfinlagan w Myroe *D & R*
MYROSS *see* Ross Union *C, C & R*
MYSHALL (Christ the Redeemer) *see* Fenagh w Myshall, Aghade and Ardoyne *C & O*
NAAS (St David) w Kill and Rathmore *M & K* **I** M G WOODERSON
NARRAGHMORE (Holy Saviour) w Timolin, Castledermot and Kinneagh *D & G* **I** K V KENNERLEY
NAVAN (St Mary) w Kentstown, Tara, Slane, Painestown and Stackallen *M & K* **I** J D M CLARKE
NENAGH (St Mary) w Ballymackey, Templederry and Killodiernan *L & K* **I** P L TOWERS
NEWBLISS (no dedication) *see* Currin w Drum and Newbliss *Clogh*
NEWBRIDGE (St Patrick) w Carnalway and Kilcullen *M & K* **I** *Vacant*
NEWCASTLE (no dedication) w Newtownmountkennedy and Calary *D & G* **Bp's C** B J G O'ROURKE
NEWCASTLE (St John) *D & D* **I** I M ELLIS
NEWCASTLE-LYONS (no dedication) *see* Celbridge w Straffan and Newcastle-Lyons *D & G*
NEWCESTOWN *see* Kinneigh Union *C, C & R*
NEWMARKET-ON-FERGUS *see* Drumcliffe w Kilnasoolagh *L & K*
NEWRY (St Mary) (St Patrick) *D & D* **I** T H W DUNWOODY
NEWTOWNARDS (St Mark) *D & D* **I** K J SMYTH, **C** G CLUNIE, **Hon C** N L WHITE
NEWTOWNBARRY *see* Bunclody w Kildavin, Clonegal and Kilrush *C & O*
NEWTOWNBUTLER *see* Galloon w Drummully *Clogh*
NEWTOWNCROMMELIN (no dedication) *see* Skerry w Rathcavan and Newtowncrommelin *Conn*
NEWTOWNCUNNINGHAM (All Saints) *see* Taughboyne, Craigadooish, Newtowncunningham etc *D & R*
NEWTOWNFERTULLAGH *see* Tullamore w Durrow, Newtownfertullagh, Rahan etc *M & K*
NEWTOWNFORBES *see* Templemichael w Clongish, Clooncumber etc *K, E & A*
NEWTOWNGORE (no dedication) *see* Kilmore w Ballintemple, Kildallon etc *K, E & A*
NEWTOWNHAMILTON (St John) w Ballymoyer and Belleck *Arm* **I** C F MOORE
NEWTOWNMOUNTKENNEDY (St Matthew) *see* Newcastle w Newtownmountkennedy and Calary *D & G*
NEWTOWNSAVILLE (no dedication) *see* Augher w Newtownsaville and Eskrahoole *Clogh*
NEWTOWNSTEWART *see* Ardstraw w Baronscourt, Badoney Lower etc *D & R*
NOHOVAL (no dedication) *see* Templebreedy w Tracton and Nohoval *C, C & R*
NURNEY (no dedication) *see* Monasterevan w Nurney and Rathdaire *M & K*
NURNEY (St John) *see* Dunleckney w Nurney, Lorum and Kiltennel *C & O*
OFFERLANE (no dedication) *see* Clonenagh w Offerlane, Borris-in-Ossory etc *C & O*
OLD CHURCH, THE *see* Abbeyleix w Old Church, Ballyroan etc *C & O*
OLD LEIGHLIN *see* Leighlin w Grange Sylvae, Shankill etc *C & O*
OLDCASTLE (St Bride) *see* Castlepollard and Oldcastle w Loughcrew etc *M & K*
OMAGH *see* Drumragh w Mountfield *D & R*
OMEY (Christ Church) w Ballynakill, Errislannan and Roundstone *T, K & A* **I** A M A PREVITE
ORANGEFIELD (St John the Evangelist) w Moneyreagh *D & D* **I** W J R LAVERTY
OSSORY *see* Kilcooley w Littleon, Crohane and Fertagh *C & O*
OUGHTERAGH (no dedication) *see* Mohill w Farnaught, Aughavas, Oughteragh etc *K, E & A*
OUGHTERARD *see* Galway w Kilcummin *T, K & A*
PACKANE *see* Nenagh *L & K*
PAINESTOWN *see* Navan w Kentstown, Tara, Slane, Painestown etc *M & K*
PALLASKENRY *see* Rathkeale w Askeaton and Kilcornan *L & K*
PASSAGE WEST *see* Douglas Union w Frankfield *C, C & R*
PAULSTOWN *see* Leighlin w Grange Sylvae, Shankill etc *C & O*
PETTIGO *see* Drumkeeran w Templecarne and Muckross *Clogh*
PILTOWN *see* Fiddown w Clonegam, Guilcagh and Kilmeaden *C & O*
POMEROY (no dedication) *Arm* **NSM** W J A DAWSON
PORT LAOIS *see* Maryborough w Dysart Enos and Ballyfin *C & O*
PORTADOWN (St Columba) *Arm* **I** W M ADAIR, **C** N D J KIRKPATRICK
PORTADOWN (St Mark) *Arm* **I** W R TWADDELL, **C** D W ROBINSON, A MOORE
PORTAFERRY *see* Ballyphilip w Ardquin *D & D*
PORTARLINGTON (St Paul) w Cloneyhurke and Lea *M & K* **I** J S PEOPLES
PORTGLENONE (no dedication) *see* Ahoghill w Portglenone *Conn*
PORTLAW *see* Fiddown w Clonegam, Guilcagh and Kilmeaden *C & O*
PORTNASHANGAN *see* Mullingar, Portnashangan, Moyliscar, Kilbixy etc *M & K*
PORTRUSH *see* Ballywillan *Conn*
PORTSALON (All Saints) *see* Clondevaddock w Portsalon and Leatbeg *D & R*
PORTSTEWART *see* Agherton *Conn*
PORTUMNA (Christ Church) *see* Clonfert Gp of Par *L & K*
POWERSCOURT (St Patrick) w Kilbride and Annacrevy *D & G* **I** R B ROUNTREE
PREBAN (St John) *see* Crosspatrick Gp *C & O*
RAHAN *see* Clonsast w Rathangan, Thomastown etc *M & K*
RAHAN (St Carthach) *see* Tullamore w Durrow, Newtownfertullagh, Rahan etc *M & K*
RAHENY (All Saints) w Coolock *D & G* **I** J T CARROLL
RALOO (no dedication) *see* Glynn w Raloo *Conn*
RAMELTON *see* Tullyaughnish w Kilmacrennan and Killygarvan *D & R*
RAMOAN (St James) w Ballycastle and Culfeightrin *Conn* **I** P THOMPSON
RANDALSTOWN *see* Drummaul w Duneane and Ballyscullion *Conn*
RAPHOE (Cathedral of St Eunan) w Raymochy and Clonleigh *D & R* **I** S R WHITE
RASHARKIN (St Andrew) *see* Ballymoney w Finvoy and Rasharkin *Conn*
RATHANGAN (no dedication) *see* Clonsast w Rathangan, Thomastown etc *M & K*
RATHASPECK (St Thomas) *see* Mostrim w Granard, Clonbroney, Killoe etc *K, E & A*
RATHBARRON *see* Achonry w Tubbercurry and Killoran *T, K & A*
RATHCAVAN (no dedication) *see* Skerry w Rathcavan and Newtowncrommelin *Conn*
RATHCLAREN (Holy Trinity) *see* Bandon Union *C, C & R*
RATHCLINE (no dedication) *see* Roscommon w Donamon, Rathcline, Kilkeevin etc *K, E & A*
RATHCOOLE (no dedication) *see* Clondalkin w Rathcoole *D & G*
RATHCOOLE (St Comgall) *Conn* **I** A J RUFLI
RATHCOONEY (St Mary and All Saints) w Little Island and Carrigtwohill *C, C & R* **I** P J ANDERSON
RATHCOR (no dedication) *see* Ballymascanlan w Creggan and Rathcor *Arm*
RATHCORE (St Ultan) *see* Rathmolyon w Castlerickard, Rathcore and Agher *M & K*
RATHDAIRE (Ascension) *see* Monasterevan w Nurney and Rathdaire *M & K*
RATHDOWNEY (no dedication) w Castlefleming, Donaghmore, Rathsaran and Aghavoe *C & O* **I** J G MURRAY
RATHDRUM (St Saviour) w Glenealy, Derralossary and Laragh *D & G* **I** C N R HALLIDAY
RATHFARNHAM *see* Dublin Rathfarnham *D & G*
RATHFRILAND *see* Drumgath w Drumgooland and Clonduff *D & D*
RATHGAR *see* Dublin Zion Ch *D & G*
RATHKEALE (Holy Trinity) w Askeaton, Foynes and Kilcornan *L & K* **I** S E MOURANT
RATHLIN (St Thomas) *see* Ballintoy w Rathlin and Dunseverick *Conn*
RATHMICHAEL (no dedication) *D & G* **I** F C APPELBE
RATHMINES *see* Dublin Rathmines w Harold's Cross *D & G*
RATHMOLYON (St Michael and All Angels) w Castlerickard, Rathcore and Agher *M & K* **Bp's C** J C WILSON
RATHMORE (St Columbkille) *see* Naas w Kill and Rathmore *M & K*

RATHMULLAN *see* Tullyaughnish w Kilmacrennan and Killygarvan *D & R*
RATHMULLAN (no dedication) w Tyrella *D & D* **I** *Vacant* (0139685) 237
RATHOWEN *see* Mostrim w Granard, Clonbroney, Killoe etc *K, E & A*
RATHSARAN (no dedication) *see* Rathdowney w Castlefleming, Donaghmore etc *C & O*
RATHVILLY (St Mary) *see* Baltinglass w Ballynure etc *C & O*
RAYMOCHY (no dedication) *see* Raphoe w Raymochy and Clonleigh *D & R*
RAYMUNTERDONEY (St Paul) *see* Dunfanaghy, Raymunterdoney and Tullaghbegley *D & R*
REDCROSS (Holy Trinity) *see* Dunganstown w Redcross and Conary *D & G*
REDHILLS *see* Drung w Castleterra, Larah and Lavey etc *K, E & A*
RICHHILL (St Matthew) *Arm* **I** M A ARMSTRONG
RIVERSTOWN *see* Taunagh w Kilmactranny, Ballysumaghan etc *K, E & A*
ROCHFORT BRIDGE *see* Mullingar, Portnashangan, Moyliscar, Kilbixy etc *M & K*
ROCKCORRY (no dedication) *see* Ematris w Rockcorry, Aghabog and Aughnamullan *Clogh*
ROSCOMMON (St Colman) w Donamon, Rathcline, Kilkeevin, Kiltullagh and Tybohine *K, E & A* **NSM** S JOHNSON
ROSCREA (St Cronan) w Kyle, Bourney and Corbally *L & K* **I** J A A CONDELL, **NSM** L W RUDDOCK
ROSENALLIS (St Brigid) *see* Mountmellick w Coolbanagher, Rosenallis etc *M & K*
ROSKELTON (no dedication) *see* Clonenagh w Offerlane, Borris-in-Ossory etc *C & O*
ROSS (Cathedral of St Fachtna) w Kilmacabea, Myross, Kilfaughnabeg and Castleventry *C, C & R* **I** R C A HENDERSON
ROSS, NEW (St Mary) w OLD (St Mary), Whitechurch, Fethard, Killesk and Tintern *C & O* **I** *Vacant* New Ross (51) 21391
ROSSCARBERY *see* Ross Union *C, C & R*
ROSSDROIT (St Peter) *see* Killanne w Killegney, Rossdroit and Templeshanbo *C & O*
ROSSES POINT (no dedication) *see* Sligo w Knocknarea and Rosses Pt *K, E & A*
ROSSINVER (no dedication) *see* Killinagh w Kiltyclogher and Innismagrath *K, E & A*
ROSSMIRE *see* Lismore w Cappoquin, Kilwatermoy, Dungarvan etc *C & O*
ROSSNAKILL *see* Clondevaddock w Portsalon and Leatbeg *D & R*
ROSSNOWLAGH (St John) *see* Kilbarron w Rossnowlagh and Drumholm *D & R*
ROSSORY (no dedication) *Clogh* **I** C T PRINGLE, **NSM** F I NIXON
ROSTREVOR *see* Kilbroney *D & D*
ROUNDSTONE (no dedication) *see* Omey w Ballynakill, Errislannan and Roundstone *T, K & A*
RUNCURRAN *see* Kinsale Union *C, C & R*
RUSHBROOKE *see* Clonmel Union *C, C & R*
RUTLAND *see* Carlow w Urglin and Staplestown *C & O*
RYNAGH *see* Clonfert Gp of Par *L & K*
SAINTFIELD (no dedication) *D & D* **I** A S DELAMERE
SALLAGHY (no dedication) *Clogh* **I** *Vacant*
SANDFORD *see* Dublin Sandford w Milltown *D & G*
SANDHILL *see* Sligo w Knocknarea and Rosses Pt *K, E & A*
SANDYMOUNT *see* Dublin Sandymount *D & G*
SANTRY *see* Dublin Santry w Glasnevin and Finglas *D & G*
SAUL (St Patrick) *see* Lecale Gp *D & D*
SCARVA (St Matthew) *see* Aghaderg w Donaghmore and Scarva *D & D*
SCHULL (Holy Trinity) *see* Kilmoe Union *C, C & R*
SCOTSHOUSE *see* Currin w Drum and Newbliss *Clogh*
SEAFORDE *see* Lecale Gp *D & D*
SEAGOE (St Gobhan) *D & D* **I** D R CHILLINGWORTH, **NSM** K A L BARRETT
SEAPATRICK (Holy Trinity) (St Patrick) *D & D* **I** W J SCOTT, **C** B T STANLEY, **NSM** R M McCLEAN, G G GRAHAM
SEIRKIERAN (St Kieran) *see* Clonenagh w Offerlane, Borris-in-Ossory etc *C & O*
SESKINORE (no dedication) *see* Clogherney w Seskinore and Drumnakilly *Arm*
SEYMOUR HILL *see* Kilmakee *Conn*
SHANDON (St Ann) *see* Cork St Luke Union *C, C & R*
SHANKILL *see* Belfast St Matt *Conn*
SHANKILL *see* Lurgan Ch the Redeemer *D & D*
SHANKILL (St John) *see* Leighlin w Grange Sylvae, Shankill etc *C & O*
SHANNON (Christ Church) *see* Drumcliffe w Kilnasoolagh *L & K*
SHERCOCK (no dedication) *see* Bailieborough w Knockbride, Shercock and Mullagh *K, E & A*
SHILLELAGH (no dedication) *see* Tullow w Shillelagh, Aghold and Mullinacuff *C & O*
SHINRONE (St Mary) w Aghancon, Dunkerrin and Kinnitty *L & K* **I** R B HAYTHORNTHWAITE, **NSM** J J WHITE SPUNNER
SHRULE (no dedication) *see* Ardagh w Tashinny, Shrule and Kilcommick *K, E & A*
SION MILLS (Good Shepherd) *see* Urney w Sion Mills *D & R*
SIXMILECROSS (St Michael) w Termonmaguirke *Arm* **I** W R H DEVERELL
SIXMILECROSS w Dunmoyle *Arm* **I** *Vacant*
SIXTOWNS (St Anne) *see* Kilcronaghan w Draperstown and Sixtowns *D & R*
SKERRIES *see* Holmpatrick w Balbriggan and Kenure *D & G*
SKERRY (St Patrick) w Rathcavan and Newtowncrommelin *Conn* **I** J ROONEY
SKIBBEREEN *see* Abbeystrewry Union *C, C & R*
SKREEN (no dedication) w Kilmacshalgan and Dromard *T, K & A* **Bp's C** A G MITCHELL
SLANE (St Patrick) *see* Navan w Kentstown, Tara, Slane, Painestown etc *M & K*
SLAVIN (no dedication) *see* Garrison w Slavin and Belleek *Clogh*
SLIGO (Cathedral of St Mary and St John the Baptist) w Knocknarea and Rosses Point *K, E & A* **I** S I McGEE
SNEEM (Transfiguration) *see* Kenmare w Sneem, Waterville etc *L & K*
SPANISH POINT *see* Drumcliffe w Kilnasoolagh *L & K*
STACKALLEN *see* Navan w Kentstown, Tara, Slane, Painestown etc *M & K*
STAPLESTOWN (no dedication) *see* Carlow w Urglin and Staplestown *C & O*
STEWARTSTOWN *see* Brackaville w Donaghendry and Ballyclog *Arm*
STILLORGAN (St Brigid) w Blackrock *D & G* **I** M A GRAHAM
STONEYFORD (St John) *Conn* **Bp's C** G R SHAW
STORMONT (St Molua) *D & D* **I** W D HUMPHRIES
STRABANE *see* Camus-juxta-Mourne *D & R*
STRADBALLY (All Saints) *see* Killaloe w Stradbally *L & K*
STRADBALLY (St James) *see* Lismore w Cappoquin, Kilwatermoy, Dungarvan etc *C & O*
STRADBALLY (St Patrick) w Ballintubbert, Coraclone, Timogue and Luggacurren *C & O* **I** W BEARE
STRAFFAN (no dedication) *see* Celbridge w Straffan and Newcastle-Lyons *D & G*
STRAID (no dedication) *T, K & A* **I** *Vacant*
STRAND, NORTH (no dedication) *see* Dublin Drumcondra w N Strand *D & G*
STRANGFORD *see* Lecale Gp *D & D*
STRANORLAR (no dedication) w Meenglas and Kilteevogue *D & R* **I** S IRVINE
STRATFORD-ON-SLANEY (St John the Baptist) *see* Baltinglass w Ballynure etc *C & O*
STRATHFOYLE (no dedication) *see* Clooney w Strathfoyle *D & R*
STREETE (no dedication) *see* Mostrim w Granard, Clonbroney, Killoe etc *K, E & A*
SUMMER COVE *see* Kinsale Union *C, C & R*
SWANLINBAR (St Augustine) w Tomregan, Kinawley, Drumlane and Templeport *K, E & A* **I** R G KEOGH
SWATRAGH *see* Maghera w Killelagh *D & R*
SWORDS (St Columba) w Donabate and Killsallaghan *D & G* **I** W S BAIRD, **NSM** K E LONG
SYDDAN (St David) *see* Kingscourt w Drumconrath, Syddan and Moybologue *M & K*
SYDENHAM *see* Belfast St Brendan *D & D*
TAGHMON (St Munn) w Horetown and Bannow *C & O* **I** *Vacant*
TALLAGHT (St Maelruain) *D & G* **I** R G KINGSTON, **NSM** O E HENDERSON
TAMLAGHT *see* Derryvullen S w Garvary *Clogh*
TAMLAGHT (St Luke) *see* Ballinderry w Tamlaght and Arboe *Arm*
TAMLAGHT O'CRILLY UPPER (no dedication) w LOWER (no dedication) *D & R* **I** *Vacant* (012665) 40296
TAMLAGHTARD (St Gedanus) w Aghanloo *D & R* **I** *Vacant* (015047) 239
TAMLAGHTFINLAGAN (St Findlunganus) w Myroe *D & R* **I** H R GIVEN
TANEY (Christ Church) (St Nahi) *D & G* **I** W D SINNAMON, I MOORE, **C** P R CAMPION, B DALY, **NSM** R C REED
TARA *see* Navan w Kentstown, Tara, Slane, Painestown etc *M & K*
TARBERT *see* Tralee w Ballymacelligott, Kilnaughtin etc *L & K*

TARTARAGHAN (St Paul) w Diamond *Arm* **I** D HILLIARD
TASHINNY (no dedication) *see* Ardagh w Tashinny, Shrule and Kilcommick *K, E & A*
TATTYKEERAN (no dedication) *see* Aghalurcher w Tattykeeran, Cooneen etc *Clogh*
TAUGHBOYNE (St Baithan) w Craigadooish, Newtowncunningham and Killea *D & R* **I** D W T CROOKS
TAUNAGH (no dedication) w Kilmactranny, Ballysumaghan and Killery *K, E & A* **I** A MINION
TEAMPOL-NA-MBOCHT (Altar) *see* Kilmoe Union *C, C & R*
TEMPLEBREEDY (Holy Trinity) w Tracton and Nohoval *C, C & R* **I** L J MACKEY
TEMPLECARNE (no dedication) *see* Drumkeeran w Templecarne and Muckross *Clogh*
TEMPLECORRAN (St John) *see* Kilroot and Templecorran *Conn*
TEMPLECRONE (St Crone) *see* Gweedore, Carrickfin and Templecrone *D & R*
TEMPLEDERRY (no dedication) *see* Nenagh *L & K*
TEMPLEHARRY (no dedication) *see* Cloughjordan w Borrisokane etc *L & K*
TEMPLEMARTIN (St Martin) *see* Moviddy Union *C, C & R*
TEMPLEMICHAEL (St John) w Clongish, Clooncumber, Killashee and Ballymacormack *K, E & A* **I** S JOHNSON
TEMPLEMORE Londonderry (Cathedral of St Columb) *D & R* **I** *Vacant*
TEMPLEMORE (St Mary) w Thurles and Kilfithmone *C & O* **C** T A SHERLOCK
TEMPLEPATRICK (St Patrick) w Donegore *Conn* **I** S A FIELDING
TEMPLEPORT (St Peter) *see* Swanlinbar w Tomregan, Kinawley, Drumlane etc *K, E & A*
TEMPLESCOBIN (St Paul) *see* Enniscorthy w Clone, Clonmore, Monart etc *C & O*
TEMPLESHANBO (St Colman) *see* Killanne w Killegney, Rossdroit and Templeshanbo *C & O*
TEMPLETRINE (no dedication) *see* Kinsale Union *C, C & R*
TEMPO (no dedication) and Clabby *Clogh* **I** D MORROW
TERMONAMONGAN (St Bestius) *see* Derg w Termonamongan *D & R*
TERMONEENY (no dedication) *see* Desertmartin w Termoneeny *D & R*
TERMONFECKIN (St Feckin) *see* Drogheda w Ardee, Collon and Termonfeckin *Arm*
TERMONMAGUIRKE (St Columbkille) *see* Sixmilecross w Termonmaguirke *Arm*
THOMASTOWN (no dedication) *see* Clonsast w Rathangan, Thomastown etc *M & K*
THURLES (no dedication) *see* Templemore w Thurles and Kilfithmone *C & O*
TICKMACREVAN (St Patrick) *see* Ardclinis and Tickmacrevan w Layde and Cushendun *Conn*
TIMOGUE (St Mogue) *see* Stradbally w Ballintubbert, Coraclone etc *C & O*
TIMOLEAGUE (Ascension) *see* Kilgariffe Union *C, C & R*
TIMOLIN (St Mullin) *see* Narraghmore w Timolin, Castledermot and Kinneagh *D & G*
TINTERN (St Mary) *see* New w Old Ross, Whitechurch, Fethard etc *C & O*
TIPPERARY (St Mary) *see* Cashel w Magorban, Tipperary, Clonbeg etc *C & O*
TOBERMORE *see* Kilcronaghan w Draperstown and Sixtowns *D & R*
TOMREGAN (no dedication) *see* Swanlinbar w Tomregan, Kinawley, Drumlane etc *K, E & A*
TOOMBE (St Catherine) *see* Ferns w Kilbride, Toombe, Kilcormack etc *C & O*
TOOMNA (no dedication) *see* Kiltoghart w Drumshambo, Annaduff and Kilronan *K, E & A*
TOORMORE *see* Kilmoe Union *C, C & R*
TRACTON *see* Templebreedy w Tracton and Nohoval *C, C & R*
TRALEE (St John the Evangelist) w Kilmoyley, Ballymacelligott, Ballyseedy, Kilnaughtin, Listowel and Ballybunnion *L & K* **I** R WARREN, **NSM** H A P STEPHENS
TRAMORE *see* Waterford w Killea, Drumcannon and Dunhill *C & O*
TREAS Lisburn Ch Ch Cathl *Conn* , J R WILSON
TRILLICK (Christ Church) *see* Kilskeery w Trillick *Clogh*
TRIM (Cathedral of St Patrick) and Athboy Group, The *M & K* **I** A W U FURLONG
TRORY (St Michael) w Killadeas *Clogh* **I** V E S McKEON
TUAM (Cathedral of St Mary) w Cong and Aasleagh *T, K & A* **I** I D CORBETT
TUAMGRANEY (St Cronan) *see* Killaloe w Stradbally *L & K*
TUBBERCURRY (St George) *see* Achonry w Tubbercurry and Killoran *T, K & A*
TUBRID *see* Drumkeeran w Templecarne and Muckross *Clogh*
TULLAGH (no dedication) *see* Abbeystrewry Union *C, C & R*
TULLAGHBEGLEY (St Ann) *see* Dunfanaghy, Raymunterdoney and Tullaghbegley *D & R*
TULLAGHMELAN (no dedication) *see* Clonmel w Innislounagh, Tullaghmelan etc *C & O*
TULLAMORE (St Catherine) w Durrow, Newtownfertullagh, Rahan, Tyrellspass and Killoughy *M & K* **I** A J GRIMASON
TULLANISKIN (Holy Trinity) w Clonoe *Arm* **I** E M CULBERTSON
TULLOW (no dedication) *D & G* **I** K A KEARON
TULLOW (St Columba) w Shillelagh, Aghold and Mullinacuff *C & O* **I** D W OXLEY
TULLYAUGHNISH (St Paul) w Kilmacrennan and Killygarvan *D & R* **I** W B A SMEATON
TULLYLISH (All Saints) *D & D* **I** D WILSON
TULLYNAKILL (no dedication) *see* Killinchy w Kilmood and Tullynakill *D & D*
TUNNY (St Andrew) *see* Glenavy w Tunny and Crumlin *Conn*
TURLOUGH (no dedication) *see* Aughaval w Achill, Knappagh, Dugort etc *T, K & A*
TYBOHINE (no dedication) *see* Roscommon w Donamon, Rathcline, Kilkeevin etc *K, E & A*
TYDAVNET (St Davnet) *see* Monaghan w Tydavnet and Kilmore *Clogh*
TYHOLLAND (St Sillian) *see* Donagh w Tyholland and Errigal Truagh *Clogh*
TYNAN (St Vindic) w Middletown *Arm* **I** *Vacant* (01861) 568619
TYRELLA (St John) *see* Rathmullan w Tyrella *D & D*
TYRELLSPASS (St Sinian) *see* Tullamore w Durrow, Newtownfertullagh, Rahan etc *M & K*
UPPER DONAGHMORE (St Patrick) *see* Donaghmore w Upper Donaghmore *Arm*
URGLIN (no dedication) *see* Carlow w Urglin and Staplestown *C & O*
URNEY (Christ Church) w Sion Mills *D & R* **I** J I H STAFFORD
URNEY (no dedication) w Denn and Derryheen *K, E & A* **I** M R LIDWILL
VALENTIA (St John the Baptist) *see* Kenmare w Sneem, Waterville etc *L & K*
VIRGINIA *see* Lurgan w Billis, Killinkere and Munterconnaught *K, E & A*
WARINGSTOWN (Holy Trinity) *see* Donaghcloney w Waringstown *D & D*
WARRENPOINT (no dedication) *see* Clonallon w Warrenpoint *D & D*
WATERFORD (Christ Church Cathedral) w Killea, Drumcannon and Dunhill *C & O* **I** W B A NEILL, **C** A J NEVIN
WATERVILLE *see* Kenmare w Sneem, Waterville etc *L & K*
WESTPORT *see* Aughaval w Achill, Knappagh, Dugort etc *T, K & A*
WEXFORD (St Iberius) w Ardcolm and Killurin *C & O* **I** N T RUDDOCK, **NSM** R G GRAHAM
WHITECHURCH *see* Dublin Whitechurch *D & G*
WHITECHURCH (no dedication) *see* New w Old Ross, Whitechurch, Fethard etc *C & O*
WHITEGATE *see* Cloyne Union *C, C & R*
WHITEHEAD (St Patrick) w Islandmagee *Conn* **I** S JONES
WHITEHOUSE (St John) *Conn* **I** R H MOORE
WHITEROCK *see* Belfast Whiterock *Conn*
WICKLOW (no dedication) w Killiskey *D & G* **I** J P CLARKE
WILLOWFIELD (no dedication) *D & D* **I** N JARDINE, **C** G A HARRON
WOODLAWN (no dedication) *see* Aughrim w Ballinasloe etc *L & K*
WOODSCHAPEL (St John) w Gracefield *Arm* **I** *Vacant*
YOUGHAL (St Mary's Collegiate) w Ardmore, Castlemartyr and Ballycotton *C, C & R* **I** P R THOMAS
ZION *see* Dublin Zion Ch *D & G*

THE DIOCESE OF GIBRALTAR IN EUROPE

Vicar General and Archdeacon in Europe: The Ven W G REID
14 Tufton Street, London SW1P 3QZ
Tel 0171-976 8001 Fax 976 8002

ARCHDEACONS
Eastern S J B PEAKE
North West Europe G G ALLEN
France M P DRAPER
Gibraltar and Iberia J K ROBINSON
Italy and Malta *Vacant*
Scandinavia and Germany D W RATCLIFF
Switzerland P J HAWKER

In places with more than one chaplain the names are listed in order of seniority. Further information, including a detailed leaflet, may be obtained from the Vicar General.

Albania

Served from Naples

Andorra

Served from Barcelona

Armenia

C R C COUSSMAKER, P STORR VENTER

Austria

Vienna (Christ Church) S J B PEAKE, S WELLS

Belgium

Antwerp (St Boniface) D W VAN LEEUWEN, D J COLLIN
Antwerp Seafarers' Centre *Vacant*
Brussels (Pro-Cathedral of the Holy Trinity) N M WALKER (Chan), M R BOUTAN
Charleroi D W VAN LEEUWEN, C FILBERT-ULLMANN
Ghent (St John the Divine) J C WALKER
Ostend w Knokke (St George) and Bruges (St Peter) D E H MOLE
Tervuren w Liege S J G SEAMER, R YATES
Ypres (St George) D W VAN LEEUWEN, G F OLIVER

Bosnia and Herzegovina

Served from Vienna

Bulgaria

Sofia E J POOLE

Croatia

Served from Vienna

Czech Republic

Prague S J B PEAKE, R A E KENT

Denmark

Copenhagen (St Alban) w Aarhus T O MENDEL

Estonia

Tallinn F A E CHADWICK

Finland

Helsinki F A E CHADWICK

France

Aix-en-Provence *see* Marseille w Aix-en-Provence
Aquitaine (Bordeaux, Chancelade, Cognac, Limeuil, Monteton and Tocane) D V GERRISH
Beaulieu-sur-Mer (St Michael) G GRANT
Biarritz J M LIVINGSTONE
Boulogne-sur-Mer *see* Nord Pas de Calais
Calais *see* Nord Pas de Calais
Cannes (Holy Trinity) A E MATHERS
Chantilly (St Peter) J A WILKINSON
Chevry *see* Versailles w Chevry
Dunkerque Missions to Seamen A R W RIMMER
Fontainebleau W A WILSON
Grenoble J R BALL
Lille (Christ Church) W SCOTT
Lyon J E PERRYMAN
Maisons-Laffitte (Holy Trinity) O B EATON, D M R FLACH
Marseille (All Saints) w Aix-en-Provence P N CASSIDY
Menton (St John) A B WODEHOUSE
Montauroux (Chapel of the Glorious Ascension) C HARRISON
Nice (Holy Trinity) w Vence K J LETTS
Nord Pas de Calais D A RUDDLE
Paris (St George) M P DRAPER, M H HARRISON
Paris (St Michael) A W K BROWN, A NORMAN
Pau (St Andrew) D B EVANS
Rouen All Saints *Vacant*
Rouen Missions to Seamen *Vacant*
St Raphael (St John the Evangelist) *Vacant*
Sophia Antipolis R G L McALISTER
Strasbourg A J L BARNETT, J L MURRAY
Toulouse I L MORT
Vence (St Hugh) *see* Nice w Vence
Versailles (St Mark) w Chevry D C MARSHALL, A MARSHALL

Georgia

C R C COUSSMAKER, P STORR VENTER

Germany

Berlin (St George) C W JAGE-BOWLER
Bonn w Cologne P M S CURRAN, S J MILES
Düsseldorf (Christ Church) R E SEED
Freiburg-im-Breisgau J R GIBBS
Hamburg (St Thomas à Becket) J K NEWSOME
Heidelberg *Vacant*
Leipzig G M REAKES-WILLIAMS
Stuttgart M S NAIDU
Wiesbaden (St Augustine of Canterbury) K E BELL

Gibraltar

Gibraltar (Cathedral of the Holy Trinity) B W HORLOCK (Dean), M T COOMBE, D A S HOARE

Greece

Athens (St Paul) w Kifissia, Patras (St Andrew), Thessaloniki and Voula P K HARRISON
Corfu (Holy Trinity) W ELLIOT

Hungary

Budapest S J B PEAKE, D MOSS

Italy

Florence (St Mark) w Siena (St Peter) *Vacant*
Milan (All Saints) w Genoa (The Holy Ghost), Cadenabbia (The Ascension) and Varese G S BEHEYDT, M J GOUGH
Naples (Christ Church) w Sorrento, Capri and Bari M BULLOCK

Palermo (Holy Cross) *see* Sicily
Rome (All Saints) G B EVANS
San Remo *Vacant*
Sicily *Vacant*
Taormina (St George) *see* Sicily
Venice (St George) w Trieste J R HARKINS

Latvia

Riga (St Saviour) *Vacant*

Lithuania

Served from Warsaw

Luxembourg

Luxembourg C G POOLE

Macedonia, Former Yugoslav Republic of

Skopje S J B PEAKE, P J ANDERSEN

Malta

Sliema (Holy Trinity) *Vacant*
Valletta (Pro-Cathedral of St Paul) A G WOODS (Chan), N lo POLITO

Monaco

Monte Carlo (St Paul) B W THOMAS

Montenegro see *Yugoslavia*

Morocco

Casablanca (St John the Evangelist) P A LETFORD
Tangier (St Andrew) *Vacant*

The Netherlands

Amsterdam (Christ Church) w Den Helder and Heiloo I L S WATSON, B J H PORTER
Arnhem *see* East Netherlands
East Netherlands G G ALLEN
Eindhoven R A LENS VAN RIJN
Haarlem G G ALLEN
Hague, The (St John and St Philip) M B LEA, R W G DE MURALT, O HARRISON
Nijmegen *see* East Netherlands
Rotterdam (St Mary) D L E BERRY
Rotterdam Missions to Seamen P W LEITCH
Schiedam Missions to Seamen M K SPARROW
Twente (St Mary) *see* East Netherlands
Utrecht (Holy Trinity) w Amersfoort, Harderwijk and Zwolle T WHITFIELD
Vlissingen Missions to Seamen V L STORY
Voorschoten P J BOURNE

Norway

Oslo (St Edmund) w Bergen, Trondheim and Stavanger T PARK, D T LEWIS

Poland

Warsaw D H WILLIAMS

Portugal

Algarve St Vincent D W HEAL
Lisbon (St George) w Estoril (St Paul) J K ROBINSON, N P HORTA
Madeira (Holy Trinity) J F A FARRANT
Porto (or Oporto) (St James) H C SASSER

Romania

Bucharest (The Resurrection) E J POOLE, S P HUGHES

Russian Federation

Moscow (St Andrew) C R C COUSSMAKER, J J FRAIS

Serbia see *Yugoslavia*

Slovakia

Served from Vienna

Slovenia

Served from Vienna

Spain

Barcelona (St George) R W SEWELL
Costa Blanca R R J MORETON
Costa del Sol West M A HORSEY
Fuengirola (St Andrew) R T JONES
Ibiza C J M MAXWELL
Lanzarote *Vacant*
Las Palmas (Holy Trinity) *Vacant*
Madrid (St George) R L HODSON
Malaga (St George) *Vacant*
Menorca W J HAWTHORNE, S E STEPHENS
Mojacar B A CRADDOCK
Nerja *Vacant*
Palma de Mallorca (St Philip and St James) W J HAWTHORNE
Playa de Las Americas, Tenerife *Vacant*
Puerto de la Cruz, Tenerife (All Saints) C FOWLER
Puerto Pollensa, Mallorca C A C COOPER
Torrevieja G WAKEHAM

Sweden

Gothenburg (St Andrew) w Halmstad, Jönköping and Uddevalla M D S COCKS
Stockholm (St Peter and St Sigfrid) w Gävle and Västerås B J CUMBERLAND

Switzerland

Basle J R GIBBS
Berne (St Ursula) w Neuchatel D C WOTHERSPOON
Geneva (Holy Trinity) J K KIMBER
Lausanne (Christ Church) *Vacant*
Lugano (St Edward the Confessor) E A SIMMONDS
Montreux (St John) w Gstaad C DIZERENS
Vevey (All Saints) w Château d'Oex and Villars D J FRANK
Zürich (St Andrew) w Winterthur P J HAWKER, M J HAZELTON

Turkey

Ankara (St Nicholas) R E INGHAM
Istanbul (Christ Church) (Chapel of St Helena) w Moda (All Saints) I W L SHERWOOD
Izmir (Smyrna) (St John the Evangelist) w Bornova (St Mary Magdalene) R J ROGERS

Yugoslavia, Federal Republic of

Belgrade *Vacant*

CHAPLAINS TO HER MAJESTY'S SERVICES

ROYAL NAVY

Chaplain of the Fleet and Archdeacon for the Royal Navy
Director Naval Chaplaincy Service (Manning)
The Ven S J GOLDING QHC
Royal Navy Chaplaincy Service, Room 203, Victory Building, HM Naval Base, Portsmouth PO1 3LS
Tel (01705) 727903 Fax 727112

Chaplains RN

J P AMES
D BARLOW
R D BAXENDALE
S A R BEVERIDGE
K C BROMAGE
M BROTHERTON
R F BUCKLEY
A M CALLON
B R CLARKE
R COATES
R C CUTLER
I EGLIN
G M ELMORE
B D S FAIRBANK
W H FRANKLIN
J GREEN
B K HAMMETT
M J HARMAN
J A HEMPENSTALL
J HILL
R G HILLIARD
C W W HOWARD
M H JACKSON
E W JONES
N J KELLY
T J LEWIS
C J LUCKRAFT
A J F METTERS
J O MORRIS
I F NAYLOR
R NURTON
G S PETZER
M G POLL
R L PYNE
E D J-B RENFREY
P J D S SCOTT
S P SPRINGETT
B F SWABEY
S M THEAKSTON
D W W THOMAS
I J WHEATLEY
M L WISHART
N E WOODCOCK

ARMY

Chaplain-General to the Forces
The Rev V DOBBIN MBE, QHC
(The present Chaplain-General is a Minister of the Presbyterian Church of Ireland)

Deputy Chaplain-General and Archdeacon for the Army
The Ven J J HOLLIMAN QHC
Ministry of Defence, Chaplains (Army), Trenchard Lines, Upavon, Pewsey, Wilts SN9 6BE
Tel (01980) 615802 Fax 615800

Chaplains to the Forces

W G ASHTON
J L ASTON
K P ATHERLEY
J BALL
K G BARRY
K D BELL
J BLACKBURN
P R BOSHER
A J BOYD
K M BRETEL
C S T BRODDLE
A J BROWN
L H BRYAN
M A G BRYCE
R M BURT
P J CABLE
P M CARTER
P T CLEMETT
T A R COLE
G L COLLINGWOOD
F COLLINS
J C D COOK
N L COOK
A J COOPER
A A COSLETT
N N CROSSEY
A W CUMBERLIDGE
D W DAVIES
R J DOWNES
V R DUNSTAN-MEADOWS
P A EAGLES
B ELLIOTT
S A FRANKLIN
J R B GOUGH
R L GREEN
S E GRIFFITH
G F HADFIELD
R J HALL
M J HALSALL
R W HAYTER
D C HEAVER
R A HEMMINGS
L T J HILLARY
J P HOOLEY
P A IRWIN
M V JONES
K R JOYCE
P J A KENNEDY
N A KNIGHTS JOHNSON
R LANDALL
C M LANGSTON
W B LISTER
N A LLEWELLYN
R A LOCKE
J M LOVEDAY
R C McCARTNEY
C MACDONALD
R A McDOWALL
K F McGARAHAN
T R McKNIGHT
N A MAXTED
D J MERCERON
R M MITCHELL
M P MORTON
R G W NOCK
R A OWEN
W B PAINE
S P PARSELLE
D J PEACHELL
K J PILLAR
T R PLACE
R PLUCK
J A H POLLARD
D J M POLLOCK
A H PRICE
J R PRICE
R M PRIEST
S ROBBINS
J H E ROSKELLY
P M RUTHERFORD
P F A SPRINGFORD
R W STEVENS
M R N STEVENSON
J TEE
A H THOMAS
P THOMPSON
D A TICKNER
A J TOTTEN
P VICKERS
C J A WALKER
S M M WALKER
D M T WALTERS
B WALTON
R E WILLIAMS
P S WRIGHT

ROYAL AIR FORCE

Chaplain-in-Chief
The Ven P R TURNER QHC

Command Chaplains
A P BISHOP, I M THOMAS
Chaplaincy Services (RAF), HQ, Personnel and Training Command, RAF Innsworth, Gloucester GL3 1EZ
Tel (01452) 712612 ext 5164 Fax 510828

Chaplains RAF

P J ABELL
R W BAILEY
N B P BARRY
J P M CHAFFEY
L E D CLARK
A T COATES
I R COLSON
E CORE
J E COYNE
A J DAVIES
C W K DAVIES
M J ELLIOTT
A P R FLETCHER
A C GATRILL
A J D GILBERT
I F GREENHALGH
N P HERON
R D HESKETH
J C HETHERINGTON
A D HEWETT
C E HEWITT
J F HUDGHTON
J W G HUGHES
S P IREDALE
I A JONES
I A LAMBERT
T R LEE
C W LONG
M F LOVELESS
D J McKAVANAGH
D S MACKENZIE
A B McMULLON
K MADDY
W L F MOUNSEY
R NOBLE
D T OSBORN
C PARNELL-HOPKINSON
R J PENTLAND
M P ROEMMELE
P SLADEN
L E SPICER
J W K TAYLOR
A J TURNER
I S WARD
R A P WARD
S J WARE
I J WESTON
G WILLIAMS
A L WILLIS
J K WILSON
D WYNNE-JONES

PRISON CHAPLAINS

HOME OFFICE PRISON SERVICE

(England and Wales)

Chaplain General of Prisons
The Ven D FLEMING
Assistant Chaplain General (HQ)
T M JOHNS
HM Prison Service Chaplaincy, Abell House, John Islip Street, London SW1P 4LH
0171-217 5817   Fax 217 5090

Assistant Chaplains General
J R HARGREAVES, R C PAYNE, P J TAYLOR
HM Prison Service Chaplaincy, PO Box 349, Stafford ST16 3DL
Tel (01785) 54421   Fax 227734

At institutions with more than one chaplain the names are listed in order of seniority.

Prisons

Acklington E M DIXON, S A JONES, G EVANS
Albany J D BIRD
Aldington P FOSTER
Altcourse M T RANDALL
Ashwell J RIDLEY
Askham Grange R A CLEGG
Bedford R A WILLCOX
Belmarsh A D HILL
Birmingham B J GRACIE
Blakenhurst M L PALMER
Blantyre House J M BOURNE
Blundeston W J SALMON
Brinsford P C ROBSON
Bristol A D HAMILTON, M PETERS, S J GILES
Brixton S W P ROSHEUVEL, J R GRIFFITHS
Brockhill R F LODGE
Buckley Hall D W HIRST
Bullingdon W M CAREY, S P HALL
Bullwood Hall J R D KEMP
Camp Hill R HIGGINBOTTOM
Canterbury H J CROWIE
Cardiff M J KIDDLE
Channings Wood C V L CURD
Chelmsford J K HAYWARD
Coldingley G CLARKSON
Cookham Wood J KING
Dartmoor W H BIRDWOOD
Doncaster J E BLAND
Dorchester P F TURNBULL
Downview P A NEWMAN
Drake Hall D E TWISS
Durham F A ELTRINGHAM
Eastwood Park V I WOODS
Elmley T G JACQUET
Everthorpe M R ESCRITT
Exeter D K HASTINGS
Featherstone A M BALL, K L WASSALL
Ford B BARNES-CEENEY
Frankland E CUMMINGS
Full Sutton W A NOBLETT, C W ANKERS
Gartree M T PHILLIPS
Gloucester A M LYNETT
Grendon and Spring Hill K S POUND
Haslar P A SUTTON
Haverigg I C SMITH, J M SKINNER
Hewell Grange R F LODGE
Highdown A R BODDY
Highpoint J M N HUNT
Holloway P D DERBYSHIRE, M L KEARNS
Holme House T A McCARTHY, I JELLEY, M FERGUSON
Hull C B DICK
Kingston (Portsmouth) E H O'CONNOR
Kirkham A P HARVEY
Lancaster Castle G W NELSON
Latchmere House F R BENTLEY
Leeds C H CHEESEMAN, G JONES
Lewes D J H POWE
Leyhill A K SWANN
Lincoln A R DUCE, C C MUNN
Lindholme P TARLETON
Littlehey R C BUNYAN
Liverpool F SUDWORTH, P A RENNIE, P M L PHILLIPS, I R SHACKLETON
Long Lartin J W GEEN
Maidstone S EDWARDS
Manchester B JOHNSON
Moorland P J WALKER
Morton Hall M R RENNARD
Mount, The J C HONOUR, J P HART
New Hall E J CLAY
North Sea Camp K M TOMLIN
Nottingham J E FITZGERALD
Oxford H D DUPREE
Parkhurst M L STEER
Pentonville W St C COLLINS
Preston A J B KEITH, S E MASKREY, W DRAIN
Ranby D G WAKEFIELD, R GOODHAND
Reading A K BUSH
Rochester D J BURTON, J G C LAWRENCE
Send A J FORAN
Shepton Mallet M S PERSSON
Shrewsbury M L COPE, J J WADDINGTON-FEATHER
Stafford J M DIXON, G E PYE
Standford Hill C E N DAVIS, R M WILTSHIRE
Stocken P MOORHOUSE
Styal D J WOODLEY
Sudbury P A GOWER
Swaleside R T GREEN
Swansea L HOPKINS, N R SANDFORD
Verne, The J M BLOOMFIELD, E S MITCHELL
Wellingborough K R BROWN
Wakefield A HIRST
Wandsworth P G W MEADEN
Wayland P D STELL, C I GREEN
Whatton J PULMAN
Winchester R J GUYMER
Woodhill P GREEN
Wormwood Scrubs P WESTWOOD, G E STEVENSON
Wymott L S ROSE

Young Offender Institutions

Deerbolt S BINDOFF
Dover B M W STARES
Erlestoke House G D BAKER
Feltham M REDFEARN
Foston Hall A J TARPER, P A GOWER
Glen Parva L H COOPER, H K DODHIA
Guys Marsh S C LISTON
Hatfield J M TOMLINSON
Hindley M J SMEATON, R N ARBERY
Hollesley Bay Colony J A WILSON
Huntercombe and Finnamore Wood E SUTHERLAND
Kirklevington Grange D MOORE
Lancaster Farms B J MAYNE
Northallerton T L JONES
Onley G DARVILL
Pennington N E H NEWTON
Portland P W TULLETT
Stoke Heath B K COOPER, N C PEDLEY
Swinfen Hall J B ASTON, J R FAGAN
Thorn Cross D L MELLOR
Usk and Prescoed M C JOHN
Wealstun F FLETCHER
Werrington House J L HUMPHREYS

Remand Centres

Low Newton S A WATSON
Risley R GIBBARD

Channel Islands

Jersey C I BUCKLEY

SCOTTISH PRISON SERVICE

Scottish Prison Service, Calton House, 5 Redheughs Rigg, Edinburgh E12 9HW
0131-556 8400 Fax 244 8774

Aberdeen J D ALEXANDER
Glasgow (Barlinnie) S D N BARRETT
Glenochil F A M LAWRY
Inverness A WHEATLEY
Perth M LAWRENSON
Peterhead J H BOOKER
Polmont M C REED

NORTHERN IRELAND PRISON SERVICE

Northern Ireland Office, Dundonald House, Upper Newtownards Road, Belfast BT4 3SU
Tel (01232) 520700 Fax 525327

Belfast N B DODDS
Belfast, Young Offender Centre J C BELL
Maghaberry J A HARRON
Maze, The W A MURPHY

IRISH PRISON SERVICE

Department of Justice, 72–76 St Stephen's Green, Dublin 2, Irish Republic
Dublin (1) 678 9711 Fax 676 4718

Arbour Hill W J BRIDCUT
Fort Mitchel C L HALL-THOMPSON
Limerick J M G SIRR

HOSPITAL CHAPLAINS

An index of whole-time and part-time hospital chaplains

Secretary to the Hospital Chaplaincies Council
The Revd R S CLARKE
Fielden House, Little College Street, London SW1P 3SH
Tel 0171-222 5090 Fax 222 5156

At institutions with more than one chaplain the names are listed in order of seniority.

ABERBARGOED D J CARPENTER
ADDENBROOKE'S NHS TRUST Cambridge J M LAW, I J P MORRIS, C E HOUGH
AIREDALE GENERAL K R OWEN, B M WILKINSON
ALDER HEY Liverpool M E J ABREY
ALEXANDRA Redditch *see* Alexandra Healthcare NHS Trust Redditch
ALEXANDRA HEALTHCARE NHS TRUST Redditch B M JONES
ALL SAINTS Birmingham *see* N Birm Mental Health Services NHS Trust
ALLTYRYN Gwent K W SHARPE
ALTON COMMUNITY *see* Loddon Trust Hants
ALTRINCHAM GENERAL J BEANEY
ARROWE PARK *see* Wirral Hosp NHS Trust
ASHFORD *see* S Kent Hosps NHS Trust
ASHWORTH J C COSSINS, G A PERERA
ASTON HALL Derby B H MUNRO
ATHERLEIGH R I McCALLA
ATKINSON MORLEY London I M AINSWORTH-SMITH
AYCLIFFE Darlington B SELMES
AYLESBURY VALE COMMUNITY HEALTHCARE NHS TRUST N TAYLOR
BABINGTON Belper D PERKINS
BARNET GENERAL *see* Wellhouse NHS Trust
BARNSLEY DISTRICT GENERAL *see* Barnsley Distr Gen Hosp NHS Trust
BARNSLEY DISTRICT GENERAL HOSPITAL NHS TRUST M P YATES
BARROW N G MARTIN
BASFORD Nottingham J MORTON
BASSETLAW HOSPITAL AND COMMUNITY SERVICES NHS TRUST R D BENNETT
BATTLE Reading *see* R Berks and Battle Hosps NHS Trust
BEBINGTON M B KELLY
BECKENHAM *see* Bromley Hosps NHS Trust
BEDFORD HOSPITAL NHS TRUST P N S GIBSON
BEIGHTON CENTRE Sheffield *see* Community Health Sheff NHS Trust
BENSHAM Gateshead *see* Gateshead Hosps NHS Trust
BETHLEM AND MAUDSLEY NHS TRUST London M R SUTHERLAND
BETHLEM ROYAL Beckenham *see* Bethlem and Maudsley NHS Trust Lon
BILLINGE Wigan S E DRAPER
BIRCH HILL C A POWELL
BIRMINGHAM All Saints *see* N Birm Mental Health Services NHS Trust
BIRMINGHAM Monyhull Learning Disabilities Service *see* S Birm Mental Health NHS Trust
BIRMINGHAM AND MIDLAND EYE *see* City Hosp NHS Trust Birm
BIRMINGHAM CHILDREN'S HOSPITAL NHS TRUST K M RICKETTS
BIRMINGHAM CITY *see* City Hosp NHS Trust Birm
BIRMINGHAM HEARTLANDS AND SOLIHULL NHS TRUST TEACHING S R RESTALL, D P BYRNE
BIRMINGHAM SKIN *see* City Hosp NHS Trust Birm
BIRMINGHAM WOMEN'S HEALTH CARE NHS TRUST D MAWBEY, P M BRACHER
BISHOP AUCKLAND GENERAL J MARSHALL
BISHOPSTOKE St Paul *see* Win and Eastleigh Healthcare NHS Trust
BISHOPSTOKE The Mount *as above*
BLACKBURN, HYNDBURN AND RIBBLE VALLEY HEALTHCARE NHS TRUST J R L CLARK
BLACKBURN ROYAL INFIRMARY *see* Blackb, Hyndburn and Ribble Valley NHS Trust
BLOXWICH (Community Unit) Walsall *see* Walsall Community Health Trust
BLYTH Community Hosp Northd B BENISON
BOLTON GENERAL *see* Bolton Hosps NHS Trust
BOLTON HOSPITALS NHS TRUST N K GRAY, I BROWN, G F WEIR
BOOTH HALL CHILDREN'S Manchester *see* N Man Healthcare NHS Trust
BORDERS GENERAL P A BURT
BOURNE HOSPITALS Lincs J M WARWICK
BOURNEMOUTH, ROYAL GENERAL *see* R Bournemouth and Christchurch Hosps NHS Trust
BRADFORD HOSPITALS NHS TRUST D J POOLE
BRIDLINGTON DISTRICT GENERAL T J DAVIDSON
BRIDPORT R W SHAMBROOK
BRIGHTON HEALTHCARE NHS TRUST G S JOHNSON
BRISTOL GENERAL *see* United Bris Healthcare NHS Trust
BRISTOL MATERNITY *as above*
BRISTOL ROYAL FOR SICK CHILDREN *as above*
BRISTOL ROYAL INFIRMARY *as above*
BROADGREEN HOSPITAL NHS TRUST Liverpool A H P BAILLIE
BROADMOOR Crowthorne T WALT
BROCKHALL Blackburn Q H WILSON
BROMLEY HOSPITALS NHS TRUST A T VOUSDEN, I NASH, T J MERCER
BROMYARD D W GOULD
BROOKWOOD Woking *see* Heathlands Mental Health Trust Surrey
BROOMFIELD Chelmsford *see* Mid Essex Hosp Services NHS Trust
BRYNTIRION Llanelli A R WILLIAMS
BUCKLAND Dover G G GILL
BURNLEY HEALTHCARE NHS TRUST S TURNER
CALDERSTONES Blackburn J M ACKROYD
CAMDEN AND ISLINGTON COMMUNITY AND HEALTH NHS TRUST P W A WHELAN
CANE HILL SECURE UNIT N J BUNKER
CANNOCK CHASE *see* Mid Staffs Gen Hosps NHS Trust
CANTERBURY St Martin's *see* Cant and Thanet Community Health Trust
CANTERBURY AND THANET COMMUNITY HEALTH CARE TRUST G W P WILTON, J M HALL
CANTERBURY AND THANET MENTAL HEALTH UNIT D J VENABLES
CARDIFF ROYAL INFIRMARY D R LLOYD-RICHARDS, E J BURKE
CARLISLE GENERAL P J BYE
CARLTON HAYES Narborough *see* Leics Mental Health Services NHS Trust
CARSHALTON St Helier *see* St Helier NHS Trust Surrey
CASTLE HILL Cottingham *see* E Yorkshire Hosps NHS Trust
CATERHAM LIFECARE NHS TRUST R LAMONT
CATISFIELD Hove J M P CALDICOTT
CELL BARNES St Albans *see* St Albans and Hemel Hempstead NHS Trust
CENTRAL MANCHESTER HEALTHCARE NHS TRUST M W FOLLAND, A M RHODES, A-M HUMPHREYS, O E MARLOW
CENTRAL MIDDLESEX NHS TRUST N J ROBERTS
CENTRAL SHEFFIELD UNIVERSITY HOSPITALS NHS TRUST M J KELLAM, C M KING
CHADWELL HEATH J A A FLETCHER
CHARING CROSS *see* Hammersmith Hosps NHS Trust
CHASE, THE Bordon *see* Loddon Trust Hants
CHASE FARM HOSPITALS NHS TRUST Enfield T M BARON, J H NODDINGS
CHEDDON ROAD *see* Taunton and Somerset NHS Trust
CHELMSFORD Broomfield *see* Mid Essex Hosp Services NHS Trust
CHELMSLEY Birmingham P A SILLITOE

CHELTENHAM GENERAL *see* E Glos NHS Trust
CHERRY KNOWLE Sunderland *see* Priority Healthcare Wearside NHS Trust
CHESTERFIELD AND NORTH DERBYSHIRE NHS TRUST J K BUTTERFIELD
CHESTERTON Cambridge *see* Addenbrooke's NHS Trust Cam
CHICHESTER St Richard's *see* R W Sussex NHS Trust
CHICHESTER PRIORITY CARE SERVICES NHS TRUST C A ASHLEY
CHORLEY AND SOUTH RIBBLE NHS TRUST C G HOUGHTON
CHRISTCHURCH T J SPONG
CITY AND HACKNEY COMMUNITY SERVICES NHS TRUST A J MARCETTI
CITY HOSPITAL NHS TRUST Birmingham G DOWNS
CITY HOSPITALS SUNDERLAND NHS TRUST P H WEBB, M A MILLWARD
CLACTON GENERAL *see* Essex Rivers Healthcare NHS Trust
CLATTERBRIDGE Wirral H J ALDRIDGE
CLAYBURY Woodford Bridge *see* Forest Healthcare NHS Trust Lon
CLAYTON Wakefield *see* Pinderfields Hosps NHS Trust
COLCHESTER GENERAL *see* Essex Rivers Healthcare NHS Trust
COLCHESTER MATERNITY *as above*
COLMAN Norwich *see* Norfolk and Nor Healthcare NHS Trust
COMMUNITY HEALTH SHEFFIELD NHS TRUST J W BROWNING
CONQUEST, THE Bexhill *see* Hastings and Rother NHS Trust
CORNWALL HEALTHCARE TRUST M E RICHARDS
COUNTESS MOUNTBATTEN HOSPICE Southampton *see* Southn Univ Hosps NHS Trust
COUNTESS OF CHESTER HOSPITAL NHS TRUST E T DAVIES
COVENTRY AND WARWICKSHIRE D E KERR
CRANAGE HALL J EARDLEY
CROMER AND DISTRICT Norfolk D F HAYDEN
CROYDON COMMUNITY MENTAL HEALTH UNIT A A WILSON
CYNTHIA SPENCER UNIT MANFIELD HOSPITAL G C RUMBOLD
DARLINGTON MEMORIAL HOSPITAL NHS TRUST B SELMES
DARTFORD AND GRAVESHAM NHS TRUST N J BUNKER
DELANCEY Cheltenham *see* E Glos NHS Trust
DELLWOOD Reading *see* R Berks and Battle Hosps NHS Trust
DERBY CITY GENERAL HOSPITAL NHS TRUST S TURNBULL
DERBYSHIRE CHILDREN'S S TURNBULL
DERBYSHIRE ROYAL INFIRMARY NHS TRUST K J SKIPPON, M R COBB
DERRIFORD Plymouth P S MACPHERSON
DEWSBURY HEALTH CARE NHS TRUST P L BENSON
DODDINGTON COMMUNITY K G PRATT
DONCASTER Tickhill Road *see* Doncaster Health Care NHS Trust
DONCASTER HEALTH CARE NHS TRUST J E PALIN
DONCASTER ROYAL INFIRMARY AND MONTAGUE HOSPITAL NHS TRUST M C WRIGHT, S TRICKLEBANK
DORSET HEALTHCARE NHS TRUST K S TIMBRELL
DRYBURN Durham *see* N Dur Acute Hosps NHS Trust
DUCHY Truro G V BENNETTS
DUDLEY GROUP OF HOSPITALS NHS TRUST B J RUMBOLD
DUDLEY PRIORITY HEALTH NHS TRUST M K BATE
DUNDEE HOSPITALS W J McAUSLAND
DUNSTON HILL Durham J M H GIBSON
EALING HOSPITAL NHS TRUST P ROWNTREE
EAST BERKSHIRE COMMUNITY HEALTH NHS TRUST G F THEOBALD
EAST GLOUCESTERSHIRE NHS TRUST W B IRVINE
EAST HAM MEMORIAL *see* Newham Healthcare NHS Trust Lon
EAST SUFFOLK LOCAL HEALTH SERVICES NHS TRUST G J ARCHER
EAST SURREY HOSPITAL AND COMMUNITY HEALTHCARE NHS TRUST P M HARTLEY
EAST SURREY LEARNING DISABILITY AND MENTAL HEALTH SERVICES NHS TRUST N J COPSEY, C E LATHAM
EAST YORKSHIRE HOSPITALS NHS TRUST P L DODD
EASTBOURNE HOSPITALS NHS TRUST J H KIMBERLEY, V M STEADY
EASTRY *see* Cant and Thanet Community Health Trust
EDGWARE GENERAL H D MOORE
EDINBURGH HEALTHCARE NHS TRUST J D R WHITLEY
EDITH CAVELL Peterborough *see* Pet Hosps NHS Trust
ELY Cardiff J C BUTTIMORE
ENFIELD COMMUNITY CARE TRUST T M BARON
EPSOM St Ebba's *see* Surrey Heartlands NHS Trust
EPSOM GENERAL *see* Epsom Healthcare NHS Trust
EPSOM HEALTHCARE NHS TRUST C VALLINS
ERITH AND DISTRICT J A PEAL
ESSEX COUNTY *see* Essex Rivers Healthcare NHS Trust
ESSEX RIVERS HEALTHCARE NHS TRUST R SMITH, M W THOMPSON, P S LANSLEY
EXETER AND DISTRICT COMMUNITY HEALTH SERVICE NHS TRUST D J WALFORD
EXETER HEALTH AUTHORITY (Mental Health/ Handicap) D J WALFORD
FAIRFIELD Hitchin *see* S Beds Community Healthcare Trust
FAIRFIELD GENERAL Bury A R BROCKBANK
FALMOUTH *see* R Cornwall Hosps NHS Trust
FARLEIGH Avon N G MARTIN
FARNBOROUGH AND ORPINGTON HOSPITALS N J BUNKER
FARNHAM Guildford A K TUCK
FIELDHEAD Wakefield *see* Wakef and Pontefract Community NHS Trust
FIELDHEAD ELDERLY CARE Wakefield *see* Pinderfields Hosps NHS Trust
FINCHLEY MEMORIAL T D ATKINS
FLETCHER Norfolk D F HAYDEN
FOREST HEALTHCARE NHS TRUST London M O PRITCHARD, M R GODSON
FOSSE HEALTH NHS TRUST G B McAVOY
FOUNDATION NHS TRUST Stafford G E O'BRIEN
FRENCHAY HEALTHCARE NHS TRUST Bristol D B HEWLETT, C A G LEGGATE
FRIARAGE AND DISTRICT Northallerton I J FOX
FRIMLEY PARK HOSPITAL NHS TRUST A W WARNER
FULBOURN Cambridge *see* Addenbrooke's NHS Trust Cam
FURNESS GENERAL Barrow-in-Furness *see* Furness Hosps NHS Trust
FURNESS HOSPITALS NHS TRUST G GARBUTT
GARLANDS Carlisle M J MURRAY
GATESHEAD HOSPITALS NHS TRUST J R PERRY, R L FERGUSON
GEORGE ELIOT HOSPITAL NHS TRUST Nuneaton E C POGMORE, C ADAMS
GLASGOW ROYAL INFIRMARY J GRAHAM
GLENFIELD NHS TRUST Leicester T H GIRLING, M T SHARPE
GLENSIDE Bristol *see* Frenchay Healthcare NHS Trust Bris
GLOUCESTERSHIRE ROYAL HOSPITAL NHS TRUST D H GODWIN
GOGARBURN D YEOMAN
GOOD HOPE HOSPITAL NHS TRUST Sutton Coldfield A T BALL
GRAMPIAN HEALTH CARE J NELSON
GRAYLINGWELL Chichester C A ASHLEY
GREAT ORMOND STREET HOSPITAL FOR CHILDREN NHS TRUST N WALTER
GREENBANK AND FREEDOM FIELDS Exeter P W WARLAND
GREENWICH DISTRICT *see* Greenwich Healthcare NHS Trust
GREENWICH HEALTHCARE NHS TRUST C F A B J LE VAY, N C M SALTER
GRIMSBY DISTRICT GENERAL *see* Grimsby Health NHS Trust
GRIMSBY HEALTH NHS TRUST H D TER BLANCHE, P RUSSELL
GUILDFORD St Luke's *see* R Surrey County and St Luke's Hosps NHS Trust
GUY'S AND ST THOMAS' HOSPITALS NHS TRUST London A M HARLEY

GWENT ROYAL R G HACKETT
GWYNEDD Bangor K L SANDELLS-REES
HAINE Ramsgate *see* Cant and Thanet Community Health Trust
HALSTEAD COMMUNITY *see* Essex Rivers Healthcare NHS Trust
HALTON GENERAL D R FELIX
HAM GREEN Bristol *see* Southmead Health Services NHS Trust Bris
HAMMERSMITH HOSPITALS NHS TRUST A H BORTHWICK, E MORRIS, N SPICER
HARESTONE Marie Curie Centre Caterham H A EVE
HAROLD WOOD *see* Havering Hosps NHS Trust
HARPERBURY Radlett *see* Horizon NHS Trust Herts
HARROGATE HEALTH CARE NHS TRUST R R WATSON
HARROW *see* Northwick Park and St Mark's NHS Trust Harrow
HARTLEPOOL GENERAL A C JONES
HARTSHILL ORTHOPAEDIC *see* N Staffs Hosp NHS Trust
HARWICH COMMUNITY *see* Essex Rivers Healthcare NHS Trust
HASTINGS AND ROTHER NHS TRUST D J JEFFREYS
HAVERING HOSPITALS NHS TRUST G LAKER, S B SMITH
HEANOR, LANGLEY MILL AND DISTRICT P BENTLEY
HEATHERWOOD AND WEXHAM PARK HOSPITAL NHS TRUST F G GODBER, D S JONES, R A CHEEK
HEATHLANDS MENTAL HEALTH TRUST SURREY R R WYNNE-GREEN, R D C STEELE-PERKINS
HELLESDON Norfolk *see* Norfolk Mental Health Care NHS Trust
HELLINGLY AND AMBERSTONE HOSPITALS Hailsham M J ELWIS
HEMEL HEMPSTEAD GENERAL *see* St Albans and Hemel Hempstead NHS Trust
HEREFORD HOSPITALS NHS TRUST P A ROBERTS, P T WOOD, L C RHODES
HERTFORDSHIRE AND ESSEX Bishop's Stortford A J ALLSOP
HEXHAM GENERAL A J PATTERSON
HIGHBURY Nottingham D R L WHITE
HIGHCROFT *see* N Birm Mental Health Services NHS Trust
HILL END *see* Horizon NHS Trust Herts
HILLINGDON Uxbridge R CHRISTIAN
HINCHINGBROOKE HEALTHCARE NHS TRUST K G T COOK
HITCHIN Fairfield *see* S Beds Community Healthcare Trust
HITHER GREEN A L SHAW
HOMELANDS Durham G G GRAHAM
HOMERTON HOSPITAL NHS TRUST Lon A J MARCETTI, I McDOWELL
HOPE Salford *see* Salford R Hosps NHS Trust
HORIZON NHS TRUST Herts J D JOHNSON
HORSHAM GENERAL B E STATHAM
HORTON Epsom C VALLINS
HUDDERSFIELD NHS TRUST J WESTON
HULL MATERNITY *see* R Hull Hosps NHS Trust
HULL ROYAL INFIRMARY *as above*
HULTON R B JACKSON
HURSTWOOD PARK *see* Mid Sussex NHS Trust
IDA DARWIN Cambridge *see* Addenbrooke's NHS Trust Cam
ILKESTON COMMUNITY J D HOLT
IPSWICH M W THORPE, G T MELVIN
IPSWICH ST CLEMENTS *see* E Suffolk Local Health Services NHS Trust
JAMES PAGET HOSPITAL NHS TRUST Gorleston W CURRIE, S COX
JOHN COUPLAND Gainsborough D F BOUTLE
JOHN RADCLIFFE Oxford *see* Ox Radcliffe Hosp NHS Trust
KENT AND CANTERBURY HOSPITALS NHS TRUST H D CONNOLL
KENT AND SUSSEX WEALD NHS TRUST A P AYLING
KETTERING GENERAL HOSPITAL NHS TRUST L S McCORMACK
KEYCOL Kent *see* N Kent Health Care NHS Trust
KEYNSHAM S M STEVENETTE
KIDDERMINSTER HEALTH CARE NHS TRUST P D BROTHWELL
KING EDWARD VII Midhurst M C JUDGE
KING EDWARD VII Windsor *see* E Berks Community Health NHS Trust
KING GEORGE Redbridge *see* Redbridge Healthcare NHS Trust
KING'S HEALTHCARE NHS TRUST S T MEYER, R A SHAW
KING'S LYNN AND WISBECH HOSPITALS NHS TRUST A L HAIG, K M LEES
KINGS MILL CENTRE FOR HEALTH CARE SERVICES NHS TRUST J A S WOOD
KINGSTON GENERAL Hull *see* R Hull Hosps NHS Trust
KINGSTON HOSPITAL NHS TRUST Surrey A GRIFFITHS
KINGSWAY Derby *see* S Derbys Mental Health NHS Trust
KNARESBOROUGH A C BETTS
LADYWELL Salford *see* Salford R Hosps NHS Trust
LANCASTER MOOR Lancaster D V A BROWN
LANCASTER ROYAL INFIRMARY D V A BROWN
LEA CASTLE Kidderminster *see* Kidderminster Health Care NHS Trust
LEEDS St James's University *see* St Jas Univ Hosp NHS Trust Leeds
LEEDS GENERAL INFIRMARY *see* United Leeds Teaching Hosps NHS Trust
LEICESTER Glenfield *see* Glenfield Hosp NHS Trust Leic
LEICESTER GENERAL HOSPITAL NHS TRUST P J HARBORD
LEICESTER ROYAL INFIRMARY NHS TRUST C S RUSHFORTH
LEICESTERSHIRE MENTAL HEALTH SERVICES NHS TRUST P F GREEN
LEICESTERSHIRE MENTAL HEALTH SERVICE UNIT P F GREEN, L J BUTLER
LEIGHTON Crewe G D GEDDES, S J WILSON
LEWISHAM HOSPITAL NHS TRUST A L SHAW
LEYTONSTONE HOUSE M J COLE
LINCOLN St Barnabas' Hospice *see* Linc Distr Health Services and Hosps NHS Trust
LINCOLN St George's *as above*
LINCOLN Witham Court ESMI Unit *see* Linc Distr Healthcare NHS Trust
LINCOLN COUNTY *see* Linc Distr Health Services and Hosps NHS Trust
LINCOLN DISTRICT HEALTH SERVICES NHS TRUST AND LINCOLN HOSPITALS NHS TRUST D X LOMAS
LINCOLN DISTRICT HEALTHCARE NHS TRUST D YOUNG
LISTER Stevenage *see* N Herts NHS Trust
LITTLE PLUMSTEAD T J N HULL
LITTLEHAMPTON R J CASWELL
LITTLEMORE Oxford F B STEVENSON, D K WILLOWS
LIVERPOOL St Helen's *see* St Helen's and Knowsley Hosps Trust
LIVERPOOL WOMEN'S N BLACK
LLANDUDNO GENERAL R H GRIFFITHS
LODDON TRUST Hampshire P J GOOLD, A J ASKEW
LONDON Middlesex, Mortimer Street *see* Univ Coll Lon Hosps NHS Trust
LONDON Paddington Community *see* Parkside Community NHS Trust Lon
LONDON Princess Louise, Kensington *as above*
LONDON Springfield *see* Wandsworth HA Mental Health Unit
LONDON St Charles Community, Exmoor Street *see* Parkside Community NHS Trust Lon
LONDON University College *see* Univ Coll Lon Hosps NHS Trust
LONDON AND SURREY *see* R Marsden NHS Trust Lon and Surrey
LOTHINGLAND M C GRAY
LOUTH COUNTY B A HILL
MAIDSTONE *see* Mid Kent Healthcare NHS Trust
MALMESBURY L F GRIMWADE
MANCHESTER St Mary's *see* Cen Man Healthcare NHS Trust
MANCHESTER AND SALFORD SKIN *see* Salford R Hosps NHS Trust
MANCHESTER ROYAL EYE *see* Cen Man Healthcare NHS Trust
MANCHESTER ROYAL INFIRMARY *as above*
MANOR Walsall *see* Walsall Hosps NHS Trust
MANYGATES MATERNITY Wakefield M P CROFT
MASTER GREATHAM D C COULING

MAUDSLEY Denmark Hill *see* Bethlem and Maudsley NHS Trust Lon
MAYDAY HEALTHCARE NHS TRUST Thornton Heath H A EVE, P L GIBBS
MAYDAY UNIVERSITY *see* Mayday Healthcare NHS Trust Thornton Heath
MAYFLOWER Billericay P D ASHTON
MEDWAY NHS TRUST A J AMOS
MELKSHAM M B G PAIN
MERTON AND SUTTON COMMUNITY NHS TRUST H A SMITH
MID ESSEX HOSPITAL SERVICES NHS TRUST E S BRITT
MID KENT HEALTHCARE NHS TRUST D A PORTER, N G STARTIN
MID STAFFORDSHIRE GENERAL HOSPITALS NHS TRUST I S VAUGHAN, P J GRAYSMITH
MID SUSSEX NHS TRUST L D POODHUN
MIDDLESBROUGH GENERAL S COOPER
MIDDLESEX Mortimer Street, London *see* Univ Coll Lon Hosps NHS Trust
MILDMAY MISSION N E D SCHIBILD
MILL HILL Huddersfield W L HALLING
MILTON KEYNES COMMUNITY NHS TRUST M R SAUNDERS
MILTON KEYNES GENERAL NHS TRUST M R SAUNDERS, N P H POND
MONKTON AND PRIMROSE HILL K HUNT, M G JOHNSON
MONYHULL LEARNING DISABILITIES SERVICE Birmingham *see* S Birm Mental Health NHS Trust
MOORGREEN West End Southampton A R BEVIS
MORRISTON Swansea N R GRIFFIN, C W G DOBBIE
MOSS SIDE Liverpool J C COSSINS
MOUNT GOULD Plymouth J C STYLER
MOUNT VERNON AND WATFORD HOSPITALS NHS TRUST M J CARTER
MUSGROVE PARK Taunton *see* Taunton and Somerset NHS Trust
N DURHAM NHS TRUST W M GOLIGHTLY
NATIONAL HOSPITAL FOR NEUROLOGY AND NEUROSURGERY London P W LEWIS
NEW CROSS Wolverhampton *see* R Wolv Hosps NHS Trust
NEWCASTLE Royal Victoria Infirmary *see* R Victoria Infirmary and Assoc Hosps NHS Trust
NEWCASTLE St Nicholas *see* Newc City Health NHS Trust
NEWCASTLE CITY HEALTH NHS TRUST F B ALLEN
NEWCASTLE GENERAL *see* R Victoria Infirmary and Assoc Hosps NHS Trust
NEWCASTLE MENTAL HEALTH UNIT F B ALLEN
NEWHAM HEALTHCARE NHS TRUST London L C STEWARD
NEWMARKET GENERAL C T CATTON
NEWTON STEWART N E H NEWTON
NORFOLK AND NORWICH HEALTHCARE NHS TRUST L A J WARD, S F NUNNEY
NORFOLK MENTAL HEALTH CARE NHS TRUST I J BAILEY, M J TALBOT
NORTH DEVON DISTRICT Barnstaple J R ILSON, P D PILDITCH
NORTH DURHAM ACUTE HOSPITALS NHS TRUST K ALLISON
NORTH HAMPSHIRE HOSPITALS NHS TRUST P J GOOLD, A J ASKEW
NORTH HERTFORDSHIRE NHS TRUST P J B HINDLE
NORTH KENT HEALTH CARE NHS TRUST D L WILLIAMS
NORTH LINCOLNSHIRE MENTAL HEALTH UNIT D YOUNG
NORTH MANCHESTER HEALTHCARE NHS TRUST M R MORGAN, G N DOBSON
NORTH STAFFORDSHIRE HOSPITAL NHS TRUST D J HAWKINS
NORTH TEES HEALTH NHS TRUST Stockton-on-Tees P O BENNISON
NORTH TYNESIDE HEALTHCARE NHS TRUST G M BASS
NORTHAMPTON GENERAL HOSPITAL NHS TRUST R L INSTRELL
NORTHAMPTON HEALTHCARE NHS TRUST C R GOODLEY, G A SARMEZEY
NORTHERN BIRMINGHAM MENTAL HEALTH SERVICES NHS TRUST D L HART
NORTHERN GENERAL HOSPITAL NHS TRUST Sheffield D E R EQUEALL, W WATSON, J A FRYER
NORTHFIELD Aldershot S A ZEAL
NORTHGATE MENTAL HANDICAP UNIT Morpeth D F MAYHEW
NORTHUMBERLAND HEALTH AUTHORITY J M PENNINGTON, G A NEWMAN
NORTHWICK PARK AND ST MARK'S NHS TRUST Harrow A J ANDREWS
NORWICH, WEST *see* Norfolk and Nor Healthcare NHS Trust
NOTTINGHAM Wells Road Centre *see* Nottm Healthcare NHS Trust
NOTTINGHAM CITY HOSPITAL NHS TRUST M J KERRY, J MORTON, C BROWN
NOTTINGHAM GENERAL D J STOTER
NOTTINGHAM HEALTHCARE NHS TRUST K D WILLIAMS
NOTTINGHAM MENTAL ILLNESS AND PSYCHIATRIC UNIT K R EVANS
NUFFIELD ORTHOPAEDIC CENTRE OXFORD J E COCKE
NUNNERY FIELDS Canterbury *see* Kent and Cant Hosps NHS Trust
OAKDALE Gwent D J YOUNG
ODIHAM COTTAGE *see* Loddon Trust Hants
OLDCHURCH Romford *see* Havering Hosps NHS Trust
OLDHAM NHS TRUST F D STUART
ORMSKIRK Liverpool E BRAMHALL
ORSETT E R LITTLER
OXFORD Churchill *see* Ox Radcliffe Hosp NHS Trust
OXFORD RADCLIFFE HOSPITAL NHS TRUST V R SLATER, N P FENNEMORE, P F SUTTON, S C BULLOCK
OXLEAS NHS TRUST N J BUNKER
PAPWORTH HOSPITALS P S DUFFETT
PARK LANE Liverpool J C COSSINS
PARK LEE Blackburn *see* Blackb, Hyndburn and Ribble Valley NHS Trust
PARK PREWETT *see* Loddon Trust Hants
PARKSIDE Chester U B GAMBLES
PARKSIDE COMMUNITY NHS TRUST London O A A O OLUMIDE
PEMBURY Tunbridge Wells *see* Kent and Sussex Weald NHS Trust
PETER HODGKINSON CENTRE Lincoln *see* Linc Distr Healthcare NHS Trust
PETERBOROUGH HOSPITALS NHS TRUST J E SHEPHERD
PILGRIM HEALTH NHS TRUST BOSTON C M BONNEYWELL
PINDERFIELDS HOSPITALS NHS TRUST Wakefield R W CRESSEY, M J WINBOLT LEWIS
PLAISTOW *see* Newham Healthcare NHS Trust Lon
PONTEFRACT HOSPITALS NHS TRUST G DRIVER
POOLE St Ann's *see* Dorset Healthcare NHS Trust
POOLE HOSPITAL NHS TRUST E J LLOYD, S C PARRETT
PORTLAND Weymouth E LEWIS
PORTSMOUTH HOSPITALS NHS TRUST A P BURR, S A SMITH, G A BARKER
PRESTON North Shields *see* N Tyneside Healthcare NHS Trust
PRESTON ACUTE HOSPITALS NHS TRUST J M TURNER, S HUNT
PRINCESS ALICE Eastbourne *see* Eastbourne Hosps NHS Trust
PRINCESS ANNE Southampton *see* Southn Univ Hosps NHS Trust
PRINCESS MARGARET Swindon *see* Swindon and Marlborough NHS Trust
PRINCESS MARINA Northampton *see* Northn Healthcare NHS Trust
PRINCESS ROYAL Haywards Heath *see* Mid Sussex NHS Trust
PRINCESS ROYAL Hull *see* R Hull Hosps NHS Trust
PRINCESS ROYAL HOSPITAL NHS TRUST Telford R G R SMITH
PRIORITY HEALTHCARE WEARSIDE NHS TRUST C J WORSFOLD
PRUDHOE Northumberland M H WHEELWRIGHT
QUEEN ALEXANDRA Portsmouth *see* Portsm Hosps NHS Trust
QUEEN ALEXANDRA'S HOSPITAL HOME Worthing D S FARRANT
QUEEN CHARLOTTE Hammersmith *see* Hammersmith Hosps NHS Trust
QUEEN ELIZABETH Birmingham *see* Univ Hosp Birm NHS Trust

QUEEN ELIZABETH Gateshead *see* Gateshead Hosps NHS Trust
QUEEN ELIZABETH King's Lynn *see* K Lynn and Wisbech Hosps NHS Trust
QUEEN ELIZABETH HOSPITAL FOR CHILDREN London J M V WEIR
QUEEN ELIZABETH II Welwyn Garden City G N BUSTARD
QUEEN ELIZABETH PSYCHIATRIC Birmingham *see* S Birm Mental Health NHS Trust
QUEEN ELIZABETH THE QUEEN MOTHER *see* Thanet Healthcare NHS Trust
QUEEN MARY'S NHS TRUST Sidcup L A SHIPTON
QUEEN MARY'S UNIVERSITY Roehampton Lane *see* Richmond, Twickenham and Roehampton NHS Trust
QUEEN VICTORIA'S East Grinstead J R BROWN
QUEEN VICTORIA'S Morecambe J BARKER
QUEEN'S MEDICAL CENTRE NOTTINGHAM UNIVERSITY HOSPITAL NHS TRUST D J STOTER, D R L WHITE, C TURNER, J HEMSTOCK, S M CUMMING, B M S CHAMBERS
QUEEN'S PARK Blackburn *see* Blackb, Hyndburn and Ribble Valley NHS Trust
RADCLIFFE INFIRMARY NHS TRUST A C McGOWAN, M D A WILLIAMS
RAIGMORE Inverness A A SINCLAIR
RAMPTON Retford G F COOKE, J CALVERT
RAMSGATE GENERAL *see* Thanet Healthcare NHS Trust
RATHBONE Liverpool M C DAVIES
RAUCEBY Lincolnshire F H BAILEY
RAVENSBOURNE NHS TRUST N J BUNKER
REDBRIDGE HEALTHCARE NHS TRUST P MARTIN
REDDITCH Alexandra *see* Alexandra Healthcare NHS Trust Redditch
RICHMOND, TWICKENHAM AND ROEHAMPTON HEALTHCARE NHS TRUST, A N JOHNSTON, C C M COWARD
RIDGE LEA Lancaster D V A BROWN
RIPLEY AND DISTRICT COTTAGE R P FULLER
ROBERT JONES AND AGNES HUNT ORTHOPAEDIC A B STRATFORD
ROCHFORD S M WARING, F W B KENNY
ROEHAMPTON LANE Queen Mary's University *see* Richmond, Twickenham and Roehampton NHS Trust
ROSSENDALE GENERAL D ALTHAM
ROTHERHAM GENERAL HOSPITALS NHS TRUST A J ATKINS
ROUNDWAY Devizes P WILKINSON
ROYAL BERKSHIRE AND BATTLE HOSPITALS NHS TRUST P H WOOD, E M JACKSON
ROYAL BOURNEMOUTH AND CHRISTCHURCH HOSPITALS NHS TRUST M J JOINT
ROYAL CHELSEA T B F HINEY
ROYAL CORNWALL HOSPITALS NHS TRUST D G HOLLANDS, J B SEWELL
ROYAL DEVON AND EXETER HEALTH CARE NHS TRUST D J WALFORD
ROYAL EARLSWOOD Redhill *see* E Surrey Learning Disability NHS Trust
ROYAL FREE HAMPSTEAD NHS TRUST R H MITCHELL, M A TREMBATH
ROYAL HALLAMSHIRE Sheffield *see* Cen Sheff Univ Hosps NHS Trust
ROYAL HAMPSHIRE COUNTY Winchester *see* Win and Eastleigh Healthcare NHS Trust
ROYAL HOSPITAL AND HOME Putney G E D BONHAM-CARTER
ROYAL HULL HOSPITALS NHS TRUST M P PICKERING, B S BOWES
ROYAL LIVERPOOL UNIVERSITY HOSPITAL NHS TRUST S C PRATT
ROYAL LONDON HOSPITALS NHS TRUST P J COWELL, F C CLARINGBULL
ROYAL MARSDEN NHS TRUST London and Surrey D F BROWN, A R MIR
ROYAL NATIONAL ORTHOPAEDIC P M REECE
ROYAL OLDHAM *see* Oldham NHS Trust
ROYAL PRESTON *see* Preston Acute Hosps NHS Trust
ROYAL SEA BATHING *see* Thanet Healthcare NHS Trust
ROYAL SHREWSBURY D W JOHNSON
ROYAL SOUTH HAMPSHIRE *see* Southn Univ Hosps NHS Trust
ROYAL SURREY COUNTY AND ST LUKE'S HOSPITALS NHS TRUST R R WYNNE-GREEN, R D C STEELE-PERKINS
ROYAL SUSSEX COUNTY Brighton S C WALLS
ROYAL UNITED HOSPITAL BATH NHS TRUST C M ROBERTS, M R ATKINSON
ROYAL VICTORIA Folkestone *see* S Kent Hosps NHS Trust
ROYAL VICTORIA INFIRMARY AND ASSOCIATED HOSPITALS NHS TRUST Newcastle A MAUDE, M J SHIPTON, M WARNER
ROYAL WEST SUSSEX NHS TRUST C A ASHLEY
ROYAL WOLVERHAMPTON HOSPITALS NHS TRUST R H MARTIN
RUNWELL Essex W P WATERS
RUSH GREEN Romford *see* Havering Hosps NHS Trust
RUSSELLS HALL Dudley F M TRETHEWEY
ST ALBANS AND HEMEL HEMPSTEAD NHS TRUST C L SMITH
ST ALBANS CITY *see* St Albans and Hemel Hempstead NHS Trust
ST ANDREW'S Billericay P D ASHTON, J E EATON
ST ANDREW'S Northampton J E CAMP
ST ANN'S Poole *see* Dorset Healthcare NHS Trust
ST BARNABAS Saltash R E B MAYNARD
ST BARNABAS' HOSPICE Lincoln *see* Linc Distr Health Services and Hosps NHS Trust
ST BARTHOLOMEW'S London M J STEVENS, V H GOSHAI
ST BARTHOLOMEW'S Rochester R THOMSON
ST BARTHOLOMEW'S Sandwich R A GARDEN
ST CATHERINE'S Doncaster *see* Doncaster Health Care NHS Trust
ST CHARLES COMMUNITY Exmoor Street, London *see* Parkside Community NHS Trust Lon
ST CHRISTOPHER'S Fareham R A WHITE
ST CLEMENT'S HOSPITAL AND ST ELIZABETH HOSPICE Ipswich J C CASSELTON
ST EBBA'S Epsom *see* Surrey Heartlands NHS Trust
ST EDMUND'S Northampton *see* Northn Gen Hosp NHS Trust
ST GEORGE'S Lincoln *see* Linc Distr Health Services and Hosps NHS Trust
ST GEORGE'S Stafford *see* Foundation NHS Trust Stafford
ST GEORGE'S AND COTTAGE Morpeth A S CRAIG
ST GEORGE'S HEALTHCARE NHS TRUST London H A JOHNSON, I M AINSWORTH-SMITH
ST HELEN'S AND KNOWSLEY HOSPITALS TRUST M THOMAS, G SPENCER, C L CARTER
ST HELIER GENERAL Jersey M INMAN
ST HELIER NHS TRUST Surrey C J MARSHALL, R O L LOWNDES
ST JAMES'S UNIVERSITY HOSPITAL NHS TRUST Leeds P R EVANS
ST JOHN'S Axbridge J SMITH
ST JOHN'S Canterbury A A W DAWKINS
ST JOHN'S Trowbridge F SEARS
ST MARGARET'S Epping J M GLASSPOOL
ST MARTIN'S Bath H ANDREWES UTHWATT
ST MARTIN'S Canterbury *see* Cant and Thanet Community Health Trust
ST MARY'S Manchester *see* Cen Man Healthcare NHS Trust
ST MARY'S Newport (Isle of Wight) C SMART
ST MARY'S NHS TRUST Paddington B A NEWTON
ST MICHAEL'S Aylsham N J A PUMPHREY
ST NICHOLAS Canterbury M A MORRIS
ST NICHOLAS Newcastle *see* Newc City Health NHS Trust
ST OSWALD'S Ashbourne A H HART
ST PETER'S HOSPITAL NHS TRUST Chertsey J M ALLFORD
ST RICHARD'S Chichester *see* R W Sussex NHS Trust
ST THOMAS' London *see* Guy's and St Thos' Hosps NHS Trust Lon
SALFORD MENTAL HEALTH SERVICES NHS TRUST N BARNES, D R SUTTON
SALFORD ROYAL *see* Salford R Hosps NHS Trust
SALFORD ROYAL HOSPITALS NHS TRUST F N HOLMAN, J B F GRANT, C J BROWN
SALISBURY HEALTHCARE NHS TRUST G M EVANS, C RENYARD
SAVERNAKE Marlborough H G PEARSON
SCARBOROUGH GENERAL M P CHAPPELL
SCARBOROUGH HOSPITALS D W RENSHAW
SELLY OAK *see* Univ Hosp Birm NHS Trust

SEVENOAKS G A R SWANNELL
SEVERALLS Colchester *see* Essex Rivers Healthcare NHS Trust
SHAROE GREEN Preston *see* Preston Acute Hosps NHS Trust
SHEFFIELD Beighton Centre *see* Community Health Sheff NHS Trust
SHEFFIELD Royal Hallamshire *see* Cen Sheff Univ Hosps NHS Trust
SHEFFIELD CHILDREN'S *as above*
SHEFFIELD NORTHERN GENERAL *see* N Gen Hosp NHS Trust Sheff
SHEFFIELD (SOUTH) MENTAL HEALTH CENTRES J W BROWNING
SHENLEY Radlett C J TWYCROSS
SHEPPEY GENERAL G H SPENCER
SHIRE HILL Glossop F K WHITEHEAD
SHOTLEY BRIDGE Consett *see* N Dur Acute Hosps NHS Trust
SOLIHULL DISTRICT A M BOYD
SOUTH BEDFORDSHIRE COMMUNITY HEALTHCARE TRUST J N RAPLEY
SOUTH BIRMINGHAM ACUTE UNIT D WRAPSON
SOUTH BIRMINGHAM MENTAL HEALTH NHS TRUST B J B EASTER, R G GLEESON
SOUTH BUCKINGHAMSHIRE NHS TRUST J A GREEN
SOUTH CLEVELAND Middlesbrough P J CARRINGTON
SOUTH DERBYSHIRE MENTAL HEALTH NHS TRUST G MARTIN
SOUTH DEVON HEALTHCARE NHS TRUST G S KENDALL, J M PRINGLE
SOUTH DOWNS HEALTH NHS TRUST G S JOHNSON
SOUTH KENT HOSPITALS NHS TRUST V E PERRY, J W EVERETT
SOUTH MANCHESTER UNIVERSITY HOSPITALS NHS TRUST J F C PERRYMAN, S GROSSCURTH, J A HORROCKS, P BUTLER
SOUTH PEMBROKESHIRE A THOMAS
SOUTH TYNESIDE DISTRICT P R BEALING, A J BEALING
SOUTH WARWICKSHIRE HEALTH CARE NHS TRUST P S KNIGHT
SOUTH WESTERN London W F BAZELY
SOUTHAMPTON COMMUNITY SERVICES NHS TRUST A D MACDONALD
SOUTHAMPTON GENERAL *see* Southn Univ Hosps NHS Trust
SOUTHAMPTON UNIVERSITY HOSPITALS NHS TRUST G HANCOCKS, P W SPECK, J V RICHARDS, V F D NAYLOR
SOUTHEND HEALTH CARE NHS TRUST G L CROOK, L M WILLIAMS
SOUTHMEAD HEALTH SERVICES NHS TRUST Bristol D C DAVIES, A R GOOD, W B M DOWIE
SOUTHPORT AND FORMBY NHS TRUST A P J GALBRAITH
SPRINGFIELD London *see* Wandsworth HA Mental Health Unit
STAFFORD St George's *see* Foundation NHS Trust Stafford
STAFFORD DISTRICT GENERAL *see* Mid Staffs Gen Hosps NHS Trust
STANDISH Gloucester J N K HARRIS
STANLEY ROYD Wakefield *see* Wakef and Pontefract Community NHS Trust
STOBHILL NHS TRUST S R PAISLEY
STOKE MANDEVILLE Aylesbury *see* Aylesbury Vale Community Healthcare NHS Trust
STOKE MANDEVILLE HOSPITAL NHS TRUST S F SEWELL
STOKE-ON-TRENT CITY GENERAL *see* N Staffs Hosp NHS Trust
STROUD GENERAL D T MERRY
SUNDERLAND DISTRICT GENERAL *see* City Hosps Sunderland NHS Trust
SURREY HEARTLANDS NHS TRUST R N T MOORE
SWINDON AND MARLBOROUGH NHS TRUST A BUCKNALL
TAMESIDE AND GLOSSOP COMMUNITY AND PRIORITY SERVICES NHS TRUST J M AUSTERBERRY, J H KERSHAW
TAUNTON AND SOMERSET NHS TRUST P R HUXHAM, P CUFF
TELFORD Princess Royal *see* Princess R Hosp NHS Trust Telford
THAMESLINK NHS TRUST N J BUNKER
THANET HEALTHCARE NHS TRUST E M SHEARCROFT
THETFORD COTTAGE DAY *see* W Suffolk Hosps NHS Trust
THURROCK Essex E N P TUFNELL
TICKHILL ROAD Doncaster *see* Doncaster Health Care NHS Trust
TINDAL CENTRE Aylesbury *see* Aylesbury Vale Community Healthcare NHS Trust
TINDALE CRESCENT R I McTEER
TONE VALE *see* Taunton and Somerset NHS Trust
TOOTING BEC London W F BAZELY
TORBAY *see* S Devon Healthcare NHS Trust
TOWERS Humberstone L J BUTLER
TOWNLEYS Bolton R LADDS
TRINITY Retford P W WIGGINTON
TRINITY Somerset *see* Taunton and Somerset NHS Trust
TROWBRIDGE COMMUNITY F SEARS
TYNTALA, LLWYNYPIA AND PORTH AND DISTRICT R E YOUNG
UNITED BRISTOL HEALTHCARE NHS TRUST R J YEOMANS, H M A WILLIAMS, P C BROWNE, S E RUSHTON
UNITED LEEDS TEACHING HOSPITALS NHS TRUST D J RIVERS, C P JOHNSON
UNIVERSITY Nottingham *see* Qu Medical Cen Nottm Univ Hosp NHS Trust
UNIVERSITY COLLEGE LONDON HOSPITALS NHS TRUST T MORLEY, P KINSEY
UNIVERSITY HOSPITAL BIRMINGHAM NHS TRUST E F BUXTON
UNIVERSITY HOSPITAL OF WALES Cardiff D R LLOYD-RICHARDS, E J BURKE
VICTORIA Frome P E LAWLESS
WAKEFIELD AND PONTEFRACT COMMUNITY NHS TRUST C M GARTLAND
WAKEFIELD HEALTH AUTHORITY (Mental Health Services) C M GARTLAND
WALSALL COMMUNITY HEALTH TRUST E J LEWIS
WALSALL HOSPITALS NHS TRUST E J LEWIS, S PETTY
WALSGRAVE HOSPITAL NHS TRUST Coventry D H ROBINSON, A BEECH
WALTON F E WILLETT
WANDSWORTH HEALTH AUTHORITY MENTAL HEALTH UNIT E W CARDEN
WAREHAM P G HARDMAN
WARLEY Brentwood J C TADMAN
WARLINGHAM PARK Croydon A A WILSON
WARMINSTER D R A BRETT
WARNEFORD Leamington Spa *see* S Warks Health Care NHS Trust
WARNEFORD PARK Oxford D K WILLOWS
WARRINGTON COMMUNITY HEALTHCARE NHS TRUST P G HOUGHTON
WARRINGTON DISTRICT GENERAL P D MEARS, W HITCHMOUGH
WARWICKSHIRE, SOUTH *see* S Warks Health Care NHS Trust
WATFORD GENERAL *see* Mt Vernon and Watford Hosps NHS Trust
WAYLAND Norfolk J C MALLETT
WELLHOUSE NHS TRUST C J SWIFT
WESHAM PARK Blackburn A J WHYTE
WEST CHESHIRE NHS TRUST J A ROBERTS
WEST CORNWALL *see* R Cornwall Hosps NHS Trust
WEST DORSET GENERAL HOSPITALS NHS TRUST N D TOOTH
WEST HILL Dartford P J IVESON
WEST LONDON HEALTH CARE NHS TRUST P ROWNTREE
WEST MIDDLESEX UNIVERSITY HOSPITAL NHS TRUST P M BESTLEY
WEST PARK Macclesfield J BRIGGS
WEST SUFFOLK HOSPITALS NHS TRUST D CRAWLEY
WESTBURY S F TREEBY
WESTERN COMMUNITY Southampton A R BEVIS
WESTHAVEN Weymouth P S THOMAS
WESTMINSTER MEMORIAL Shaftesbury T TAYLOR
WESTMORLAND HOSPITALS NHS TRUST G GARBUTT
WESTON PARK Sheffield W WATSON
WESTON-SUPER-MARE GENERAL D N MITCHELL
WESTWOOD Bradford R M LOWRIE

WEXHAM PARK Slough *see* Heatherwood and Wexham Park Hosp NHS Trust
WHIPPS CROSS *see* Forest Healthcare NHS Trust Lon
WHISTON Prescot *see* St Helen's and Knowsley Hosps Trust
WHITCHURCH Cardiff J H L ROWLANDS
WHITTINGTON HALL J PINDER-PACKARD
WHITTINGTON HOSPITAL NHS TRUST P W A WHELAN
WIGAN AND LEIGH HEALTH SERVICES NHS TRUST R J HUTCHINSON
WILLIAM HARVEY Ashford *see* S Kent Hosps NHS Trust
WINCHESTER AND EASTLEIGH HEALTHCARE NHS TRUST N R FLOOD
WINWICK Warrington *see* Warrington Community Healthcare NHS Trust
WIRRAL HOSPITAL NHS TRUST A SCAIFE, D TURNER
WITHAM COURT ESMI UNIT Lincoln *see* Linc Distr Healthcare NHS Trust
WITHINGTON Manchester *see* S Man Univ Hosps NHS Trust
WOKINGHAM R J STILLMAN
WORCESTER ROYAL INFIRMARY NHS TRUST L R D RYDER, J M HUGHES
WORDSLEY *see* Dudley Gp of Hosps NHS Trust
WYCOMBE GENERAL *see* S Bucks NHS Trust
WYGGESTON'S Leics R SAUNDERS
WYTHENSHAWE Manchester *see* S Man Univ Hosps NHS Trust
YARE AND NORVIC CLINICS AND ST ANDREW'S HOSPITAL Norwich P D VARNEY
YEATMAN E J WOODS
YORK HEALTH SERVICES NHS TRUST G H WEBSTER

HOSPICE CHAPLAINS

ARDGOWAN J F LYON
ARTHUR RANK Cambridge G C MILLS
AYRSHIRE J JENKINS
COMPTON HALL HOSPICE Wolverhampton S H CARTER
DERIAN HOUSE CHILDREN'S HOSPICE Ormskirk D J REYNOLDS
DOROTHY HOUSE FOUNDATION Winsley G P HARRISON
EAST HERTFORDSHIRE HOSPICE CARE G G BROWN
EDEN VALLEY HOSPICE Carlisle D C DONALD
KEMP Kidderminster R S MURRIN
LOROS J V CHAPMAN
MARTIN HOUSE FOR CHILDREN Boston Spa R M C SEED
MILTON CHILDREN'S D M OSBORN
MOUNT EDGCUMBE D G ADAMS
MYTON HAMLET G BAISLEY
PRINCESS ALICE Esher D N HEAD
RUSHDEN SANATORIUM A SMITH
ST BARNABAS' Worthing J H McCORMACK, R N AITON
ST CATHERINE'S Scarborough D W RENSHAW, W F CURTIS
ST CHRISTOPHER'S London M C GARDNER
ST ELIZABETH Ipswich J C CASSELTON
ST HELENA'S Colchester M D THAYER
ST JOHN'S Wirral P B PRITCHARD
ST LUKE'S Plymouth P W WARLAND
ST LUKE'S Sheffield J SANKEY
SIR MICHAEL SOBELL HOUSE V R SLATER
ST PETER'S Bristol R H TORRENS
ST WILFRID'S Eastbourne J M GRAVES
SHROPSHIRE AND MID-WALES H J EDWARDS
STRATHCARRON Denny S M COATES

EDUCATIONAL CHAPLAINS

This index only lists deans and chaplains, and does not aim to provide a comprehensive list of clergy serving at educational institutions. Those institutions which do not currently have Anglican chaplains are not recorded.

General Synod Board of Education: Secretary Mr G Duncan
Church House, Great Smith Street, London SW1P 3NZ
Tel 0171-222 9011 Fax 799 2714

UNIVERSITIES

ABERDEEN D HEDDLE
ABERTAY P M BALFOUR
ANGLIA POLYTECHNIC I R MOODY, E M PERCY
ASTON T F PYKE
BATH B F CHAPMAN, J W LLOYD
BIRMINGHAM H C BENSON, E D COOMBES, A A GORHAM
BRADFORD M R HARRISON
BRIGHTON A W N S CANE
BRIGHTON *Eastbourne Campus* G T RIDEOUT
BRISTOL A F STUART, S M WATTERSON
BRUNEL *Osterley and Isleworth Campus* D G WILSON
BRUNEL *Uxbridge Campus* M D WITCOMBE
CAMBRIDGE
Churchill B D SPINKS
Clare N SAGOVSKY, J B WELLS
Corpus Christi R M PRYCE
Downing B R L KINSEY
Emmanuel J L CADDICK
Fitzwilliam J B QUASH
Girton J N CLARK-KING
Gonville and Caius J D McDONALD
King's E S HEBBLETHWAITE, G L PATTISON
Magdalene H E FINLAY
Newnham N W S CRANFIELD
Pembroke B WATCHORN
Peterhouse G J WARD
Queens' J M HOLMES
Selwyn N W S CRANFIELD
Sidney Sussex E J CLARK-KING
St Catharine's D J GOODHEW
St John's A A MACINTOSH, N I MOIR
Trinity A S BROWNE, A H STEVENS
Trinity Hall C M ELLIOTT (Dean), W F CLOCKSIN, D A J WILMAN
Wolfson C M FARRINGTON
CENTRAL ENGLAND IN BIRMINGHAM M HARRIS
CENTRAL LANCASHIRE W E TURNER
CITY L S A MARSH
CORK *University College* R L CLARKE
COVENTRY C R KENNEDY
CRANFIELD H K SYMES-THOMPSON
DE MONTFORT J D CURTIS, M R SEDEN
DERBY D A HESLOP
DUBLIN
Trinity College P F BARRETT
University College (Dean of Residence) S B FORDE
DUNDEE A W CUMMINS
DURHAM
Collingwood B J H de la MARE
Hatfield D C GLOVER
St Aidan's R D THOMSON
St Chad's M P KENT, C W RYLAND
St Hild and St Bede F A BAYES
St John's N G EVANS
St Mary's M PARKER
Trevelyan K ANDERSON
University P D ASHDOWN, C YEATS
Van Mildert K ANDERSON
EAST LONDON J P RICHARDSON
EDINBURGH A J FULLER
ESSEX I M KENWAY, P J MOSSOP
EXETER J T LAW, D J NIXON
GALWAY *University College* R B MacCARTHY
GLAMORGAN G W WILLIAMS
GLASGOW D REID
GLASGOW CALEDONIAN D REID
HERTFORDSHIRE G H BOLT, M V BOLT, W R de C TAYLOR
HUDDERSFIELD J T ALLISON
HULL A BAILEY
KEELE J S WHITEHEAD
KENT D CRABTREE
KINGSTON H D SHILSON-THOMAS
LANCASTER D P WILLIAMS
LEEDS C BARRETT, S J ROBINSON
LEEDS METROPOLITAN M P BENWELL
LEICESTER I M McINTOSH
LIMERICK R B A BYRNE
LINCOLNSHIRE AND HUMBERSIDE
Cottingham Road Campus L C ACKLAM
LIVERPOOL M J CARTLEDGE, E M STOREY
LIVERPOOL JOHN MOORES R E DICKINSON
LONDON J CALDWELL
Central Chaplaincies S G WILLIAMS
Goldsmiths' College F Y-C HUNG
Imperial College of Science, Technology and Medicine D G BANNOCKS
King's (Dean) R A BURRIDGE
King's T F DITCHFIELD
London School of Economics and Political Science N D R NICHOLLS
Queen Mary and Westfield J M KING, D T PEEBLES
Royal Free Hospital School of Medicine G L LEGOOD
Royal Holloway and Bedford New A D TAYLOR
Royal Veterinary College G L LEGOOD
University College Medical School G L LEGOOD
Wye D STUART-SMITH
LOUGHBOROUGH S E FIELD
LUTON R M LILLINGTON
MANCHESTER A S HAVENS
MANCHESTER METROPOLITAN I D GOMERSHALL
MIDDLESEX J M BEER
NAPIER D L COLLINGWOOD
NEWCASTLE R C MILLS
NORTH LONDON J D CLARK, B K SHIPSIDES
NORTHUMBRIA AT NEWCASTLE A J SHIPTON, D J WILSON
NOTTINGHAM R G A RIEM
NOTTINGHAM TRENT D G CANTRELL, T HATTON
OXFORD
All Souls J McMANNERS
Balliol H D DUPREE
Brasenose R C SMAIL
Christ Church J H DRURY (Dean), R J WILLIAMSON
Corpus Christi J D MALTBY
Exeter D E MARSHALL
Hertford R M CHANTRY
Jesus A J MOORE
Keble J H DAVIES
Lady Margaret Hall A G DOIG
Linacre R C MORGAN
Lincoln R G GRIFFITH-JONES
Magdalen J C HARDY, M J PIRET

Mansfield J B MUDDIMAN
Merton M EVERITT
New R G HARNISH
Oriel N J BIGGAR
Pembroke J E PLATT
Queen's P J M SOUTHWELL
St Edmund Hall D A S MacLAREN
St Hilda's B W MOUNTFORD
St Hugh's J D GILPIN
St John's E D H CARMICHAEL
St Peter's C M JONES
Somerville R M CHANTRY, R H WATTS
Trinity T S M WILLIAMS
University W G D SYKES
Wadham R H WATTS
Worcester A J E GREEN
OXFORD BROOKES A M COLEBY
PLYMOUTH C H BENSON, J E DICKER, R S WILLIAMS
PORTSMOUTH F L STEWART-DARLING
QUEEN'S Belfast *(Dean of Residence)* A J FORSTER
READING H A N PLATTS, G N RAINEY
ROYAL COLLEGE OF ART D G BANNOCKS
ST ANDREWS M D HERVEY, G F McPHATE
SALFORD J H FIFE
SHEFFIELD C A COLLINS
SHEFFIELD HALLAM R J H BEARD, M R GOATER
SOUTH BANK S J KNOWERS, R W MAYO
SOUTHAMPTON D E HALE
STAFFORDSHIRE A L HUGHES, W G McNAMEE
STIRLING R E MURRAY
STRATHCLYDE D REID
SUNDERLAND C A DICK, I D HUNTER SMART
SUSSEX G R P ASHENDEN, J R LOWERSON, A N ROBINSON
THAMES VALLEY
Ealing Campus J E PETERSEN
Slough Campus J R HURST
ULSTER J E G BACH, J R HOWARD
WALES
College of Cardiff P OVEREND
College of Swansea S H JONES
St David's University College, Lampeter M A FARAH
University College of North Wales, Bangor M M BRADY, J P BUTLER
University College of Wales, Aberystwyth S R BELL
WARWICK C M GREGORY
WEST OF ENGLAND S M J CROSSMAN, S A N DARLEY
WESTMINSTER A CLARK
WOLVERHAMPTON H J PATTERSON, G WYNNE
YORK J C ROBERTSON

COLLEGES OF HIGHER EDUCATION

This index only includes those establishments known to have Anglican chaplains. It is not intended to be comprehensive.

BATH G R W HALL
BISHOP GROSSETESTE Lincoln S J FOSTER
BOLTON INSTITUTE C E VANN
BUCKINGHAMSHIRE M H ATKINSON
CHELTENHAM AND GLOUCESTER G A POLLITT
CHESTER M A FRENCH
CHICHESTER INSTITUTE S M GRIFFITHS
CHRIST CHURCH Canterbury B E KELLY
HARPER ADAMS W E WARD
KING ALFRED'S Winchester M A BARTON
LIVERPOOL INSTITUTE L E J LEAVER
NORWICH CITY D K ALEXANDER
RICHMOND-UPON-THAMES G A BARBER
RIPON AND YORK ST JOHN J G HOYLAND, D G PATON-WILLIAMS
ROEHAMPTON INSTITUTE D A HART
ST MARTIN'S Lancaster M G SMITH
ST PATRICK'S Maynooth A M WILKINSON
SWANSEA INSTITUTE D M GRIFFITHS
TRINITY Carmarthen L J FRANCIS, J E PHILLIPS, A C WILLIAMS-POTTER
WELSH COLLEGE OF MUSIC AND DRAMA S LISK
WESTMINSTER Oxford P J BUDD

COLLEGES OF FURTHER EDUCATION

This index only includes those establishments known to have Anglican chaplains. It is not intended to be comprehensive.

BASINGSTOKE COLLEGE OF TECHNOLOGY C M SAVAGE
BATH, CITY OF A R HAWKINS
BISHOP BURTON COLLEGE OF AGRICULTURE York E A CULLING
BLACKBURN J R CREE
BOSTON J S KNEE
BOURNEMOUTH AND POOLE A F DAWTRY, J H S STEVEN
BRADFORD AND ILKLEY COMMUNITY M R HARRISON
CANNINGTON P MARTIN
CENTRAL LIVERPOOL J S WILLIAMS
DUDLEY COLLEGE OF TECHNOLOGY M C BRAIN
EVESHAM J R N J BOMYER
FARNBOROUGH COLLEGE OF TECHNOLOGY P S J GARLAND, P P MOYSE
HALTON A HODGE
HAVERING T D HULL
HULL R EVELEIGH, S J WALKER
MERRIST WOOD COLLEGE OF AGRICULTURE AND HORTICULTURE R P ROBINS
NELSON AND COLNE G S INGRAM
NEW COLLEGE Swindon D ORMSTON
NORTH EAST WORCESTERSHIRE M HERBERT
NORTH WEST LONDON F B CAPIE
OAKLANDS P A LOUIS
PENDLETON A BUTLER
ST MARK AND ST JOHN Plymouth K F FREEMAN
SHUTTLEWORTH AGRICULTURAL J A TERRY
SOMERSET COLLEGE OF ARTS AND TECHNOLOGY D ROBERTS
TYNEMOUTH D E CANT
WEALD F D JAKEMAN
WESTMINSTER, CITY OF R D de BERRY
WEYMOUTH G J MUGRIDGE, M P H STEAR
WORCESTER COLLEGE OF TECHNOLOGY P D A COLLINS
YARMOUTH, GREAT E M TOLLER

SCHOOLS

This index only includes those schools known to have Anglican chaplains. It is not intended to be comprehensive.

ABBERLEY HALL Worcester D F GUTTERIDGE
ABBEY GRANGE HIGH Leeds M C DOE
ABBOT'S HILL Herts C L TERRY
ABINGDON T P LEWIS
AGNES STEWART Leeds N P GEORGE
ALDENHAM Hertfordshire A M STEAD
ARCHBISHOP TENISON'S GRAMMAR Kennington A J REID
ARDINGLY COLLEGE Haywards Heath K I GOSS, R K HARRISON
ARNOLD Blackpool B DUNN
BANCROFT'S Woodford Green M J WALKER
BARNARD CASTLE J A MOORE, S J RIDLEY
BEARWOOD COLLEGE Wokingham J R PEEK
BEDFORD A P MANNING, D M STEVENSON
BEDGEBURY Kent N R GALLAGHER
BEECHWOOD PARK St Albans D J KERR
BENENDEN Kent P C M PRESTNEY
BENNETT MEMORIAL Tunbridge Wells J P CAPERON, C J S GILL
BERKHAMSTED COLLEGIATE Hertfordshire P L TAIT
BETHANY Goudhurst C J ROOKWOOD
BIRKENHEAD Merseyside H L KIRK
BISHOP OF LLANDAFF HIGH D ALLEN
BISHOP RAWSTORNE Preston R J BRUNSWICK
BISHOP WORDSWORTH Salisbury C M CUTHBERTSON
BISHOP'S STORTFORD COLLEGE J HART
BLOXHAM D J DUNCANSON
BLUE COAT Birmingham J H D JENKINS
BLUE COAT Nottingham S KRZEMINSKI
BLUE COAT Reading N J BENNETT
BLUE COAT COMPREHENSIVE Walsall A J WILLIAMS
BLUNDELL'S Tiverton D H HAMER
BOX HILL Surrey J P HARKIN
BRADFIELD Berkshire D R MULLINER
BRENTWOOD Essex D J GILCHRIST
BRIGHTON COLLEGE A K BURTT
BRISTOL CATHEDRAL T J WHITE
BROMSGROVE S M AGNEW
BRUTON Somerset D PARSONS
BRYANSTON Dorset R E A ADAMSON, A J DAYNES
CANFORD Wimborne C JERVIS
CANON SLADE Bolton D R EVANS
CASTERTON Lancashire P S ATKINSON
CHARTERHOUSE Godalming S J HARKER, C J O'NEILL
CHELTENHAM COLLEGE N G LOWTON, R de la BAT SMIT
CHELTENHAM LADIES' COLLEGE A D BARLOW, H R WOOD
CHRIST'S COLLEGE Brecon R M LLEWELLYN
CHRIST'S HOSPITAL Horsham G DOBBIE, C P M DUNCAN, A MITRA, N J MITRA
CLIFTON COLLEGE Bristol P W DILL
CRANBROOK Kent D COOK
CRANLEIGH Surrey A J KEEP, N A T MENON
CROFT HOUSE Shillingstone M A TURNER
DAME ALLAN'S Newcastle J HAZELTON
DAUNTSEY'S Devizes O J D BAYLEY
DEAN CLOSE Cheltenham D G H YOUNG
DENSTONE COLLEGE Uttoxeter R M D ORAM
DERBY HIGH G O MARSHALL
DOVER COLLEGE G M CALVER
DUKE OF YORK'S ROYAL MILITARY Dover J R BROUGHTON
DURHAM T J E FERNYHOUGH
EASTBOURNE COLLEGE R JOHNSON
ELIZABETH COLLEGE Guernsey S A BAKER
ELLESMERE COLLEGE Shropshire J C VERNON
ELMHURST BALLET Camberley J H G CARTER
EMMANUEL Wandsworth E M HILL
EMSCOTE LAWN Warwick R C GARRATT
EPSOM COLLEGE S L GREEN, B R ROBERTS
ETON COLLEGE Berkshire D COOPER, C M JONES, C W MITCHELL-INNES, T D MULLINS
EXETER I H BLYDE
EXETER CATHEDRAL G DAXTER
FELSTED Essex C D GRIFFIN
FETTES COLLEGE Edinburgh R MARSDEN
FOREMARK PREPARATORY Derby N A BAILEY
FRAMLINGHAM COLLEGE Suffolk M C BOOKER, R J DIXON
GIGGLESWICK T H MORDECAI
GLENALMOND COLLEGE H M D PETZSCH
GODOLPHIN Salisbury F C CARPENTER
GRESHAM'S Holt R N MYERSCOUGH
HABERDASHERS' ASKE'S Elstree D M LINDSAY
HAILEYBURY COLLEGE Hertfordshire S M BEAUMONT, J S PULLEN
HARROW V L BARON, P J E JACKSON, J E POWER
HAWTREY'S Marlborough J ROUNDHILL
HEATHFIELD Ascot K G O'DONNELL, W B PUGH
HEREFORD CATHEDRAL A C HUTCHINSON, A P LAW
HIGHGATE London P J J KNIGHT
HOLMEWOOD HOUSE Tunbridge Wells C K CHANNER
HURSTPIERPOINT COLLEGE Hassocks S C EVERSON
HYMERS COLLEGE Hull J J PAGE
IAN RAMSEY Stockton N E WATSON
IPSWICH P M HAMLET
JOHN NIGHTINGALE West Molesley D GODDARD
KIMBOLTON Cambridgeshire A P GOODCHILD
KING EDWARD VI Norwich P W BUTCHER
KING EDWARD'S Birmingham D H RAYNOR
KING EDWARD'S Witley R W E MILLINGTON, C J SUMNERS
KING'S Bruton W H M CAMERON
KING'S Gloucester J B P J HADFIELD
KING'S Rochester P L F ALLSOP, S R ALLSOPP, G J KIRK
KING'S Tynemouth W D MILLER
KING'S COLLEGE Taunton A C SMITH
KING'S COLLEGE SCHOOL Wimbledon R G STEVENS
KING'S, THE Canterbury J A THACKRAY
KING'S, THE Ely T AMBROSE, R G HUGHES
KING'S, THE Macclesfield R J CRAIG
LANCING COLLEGE I M FORRESTER, S J HEANS, J W HUNWICKE
LEEDS GRAMMAR M B HANSON
LIVERPOOL COLLEGE M D J McCREADY
LLANDOVERY COLLEGE S LEYSHON
LORD MAYOR TRELOAR COLLEGE Alton E B PRUEN
LORD WANDSWORTH COLLEGE Basingstoke B KEMP
LOUGHBOROUGH GRAMMAR A J S COX
LUCKLEY-OAKFIELD Wokingham J WAKELING
MAGDALEN COLLEGE SCHOOL Oxford R C de V MARTIN
MALVERN COLLEGE B E CLOSE
MALVERN GIRLS' COLLEGE F L MIDDLEMISS
MARLBOROUGH COLLEGE D J DALES, J G W DICKIE
MERCHANT TAYLORS' Crosby D A SMITH
MERCHANT TAYLORS' Northwood R D E BOLTON
MILL HILL London P M HUNT
MILLFIELD Somerset S F BLOXAM-ROSE
MOIRA HOUSE East Sussex G T RIDEOUT
MONKTON COMBE Bath G P HERBERT
MONMOUTH J B HENCHER, N F M MORRIS
MORETON HALL A B STRATFORD
NEW HALL Essex R E TURNER
NORTH FORELAND LODGE Basingstoke R W POLITT
OAKHAM J N DARRALL, J J N SYKES
OUNDLE Peterborough A C V ALDOUS, I C BROWNE, A K THOMSON
PANGBOURNE COLLEGE Berkshire J D R SPRIGGS
PETERBOROUGH HIGH R P FLINDALL
POCKLINGTON York M A SMITH
PORTORA ROYAL Enniskillen J D G KINGSTON
PORTSMOUTH GRAMMAR J M GRINDELL
PREBENDAL Chichester D NASON
QUAINTON HALL Harrow R H M FLETCHER
QUEEN ANNE'S Caversham T P NICHOLSON
QUEEN MARGARET'S York R L OWEN

RADLEY COLLEGE Oxfordshire P F BOYDEN, D S COULTON
RANBY HOUSE Retford R A WHITTAKER
RANNOCH Perthshire J L L FAGERSON
REED'S Cobham T D PAGE
REIGATE GRAMMAR M J H FOX
REPTON Derby R L SHORT
RIDDLESWORTH HALL Norwich A V HEDGES
ROSSALL Fleetwood A D T RICHARDS
ROYAL HOSPITAL Holbrook K S McCORMACK
ROYAL MASONIC FOR GIRLS Rickmansworth D F THOMPSON
ROYAL RUSSELL Croydon J A B PADDOCK
ROYAL WOLVERHAMPTON P C ATKINSON
ROYAL, THE Bath J P KNOTT
RUTHIN C W EVANS
ST AIDAN'S Harrogate W A WILBY
ST ALBANS HIGH SCHOOL FOR GIRLS M A McLEAN
ST ANDREW'S Croydon P D HENDRY
ST BEDE'S ECUMENICAL Reigate J P SCOTT
ST BEES Cumbria P R BRYAN
ST CATHERINE'S Bramley E M V BOUGHTON
ST COLUMBA'S Dublin M R HEANEY
ST DAVID'S COLLEGE Llandudno T R HALL
ST DUNSTAN'S ABBEY Plymouth G D CRYER
ST EDMUND'S Canterbury R H ELLIS
ST EDWARD'S Oxford D S WIPPELL, A D G WRIGHT
ST ELPHIN'S Matlock S F JONES
ST FELIX Southwold A K E SORENSEN
ST FRANCIS XAVIER Richmond C N H WHITE
ST GEORGE'S Harpenden J F H GREEN
ST GEORGE'S Windsor T J HARVEY
ST HELEN'S AND ST KATHARINE'S Abingdon P E HEWLINS
ST HILDA'S Whitby B WILLIAMS
ST JAMES AND THE ABBEY Malvern C N H ATTWOOD
ST JOHN'S Leatherhead M J LAWSON
ST JOHN'S COLLEGE SCHOOL Cambridge O R SPENCER-THOMAS
ST LAWRENCE COLLEGE Ramsgate D D R BLACKWALL, S GOLDING, D J PEAT
ST MARGARET'S Bushey J C SYKES
ST MARGARET'S Exeter I H BLYDE
ST MARY AND ST ANNE Abbots Bromley J R HOUGHTON
ST MARY'S Calne S P V CADE, M T B EVANS
ST MARY'S Cheshunt L S DRAKE
ST MARY'S Wantage R F CLAYTON-JONES
ST MARY'S HALL Brighton D C PAIN
ST OLAVE'S GRAMMAR Orpington H P C BROADBENT
ST PAUL'S Barnes S E YOUNG
ST PAUL'S GIRLS' Hammersmith A FORD
ST PETER'S York J DALY
ST PETER'S COLLEGIATE Wolverhampton C CHAPMAN
ST PETER'S HIGH Exeter A J CLARKE
ST SWITHUN'S Winchester T E HEMMING
SCARBOROUGH COLLEGE A J RICHARDSON
SEDBERGH R G LAIRD
SEVENOAKS N N HENSHAW, G A R SWANNELL
SHERBORNE C W M AITKEN, D J DUNNING
SHIPLAKE Henley-on-Thames E W D TILDESLEY
SHREWSBURY G J WILLIAMS
SMALLWOOD MANOR Uttoxeter C J CANN
STAMFORD M R RUFF
STOCKPORT GRAMMAR M J PARKER, S I D WHITE
STOWE Bucks T M HASTIE-SMITH, R B JACKSON
SUMMER FIELDS Oxford B S A GADD
TALBOT HEATH Bournemouth K J RANDALL
TAUNTON G D EVANS
TIFFIN Kingston-upon-Thames I C DAVIES
TONBRIDGE J S BELL, A W SWINDELLS
TRENT COLLEGE Nottingham T R HAGGIS
UPPER CHINE Shanklin A W SWANBOROUGH
UPPINGHAM Leicestershire A J MEGAHEY
WARWICK A W GOUGH
WELLINGBOROUGH P W LOCKYER
WELLINGTON Somerset J P HELLIER
WELLINGTON COLLEGE Berkshire R A STIDOLPH
WELLS CATHEDRAL P S HOGG
WEST BUCKLAND Barnstaple A M KETTLE
WEST HEATH Sevenoaks G A R SWANNELL
WESTMINSTER R E BALLARD
WESTONBIRT P DIXON
WINCHESTER COLLEGE R G A FERGUSON, J D SMITH, N C A VON MALAISE
WOODBRIDGE M E PERCIVAL
WORKSOP COLLEGE Nottinghamshire P M KONIG
WYCOMBE ABBEY High Wycombe R J WARDEN

THEOLOGICAL COLLEGES AND COURSES

This index includes the name of the principal or warden and the names of staff members who are Anglican clergy and whose appointments are at least half-time.

Theological Colleges

Church of Ireland Theological College Braemor Park, Dublin 14, Irish Republic
Tel Dublin (1) 492 3506 Fax 492 3082
PRIN J R BARTLETT VICE-PRIN W J MARSHALL
TUTORS/LECTS J J MARSDEN, T W GORDON, J M YOUNG, N McCAUSLAND

College of the Resurrection Stocksbank Road, Mirfield, W Yorkshire WF14 0BW
Tel (01924) 490441 Fax 492738
ACTING PRIN P A G GUIVER CR DIR STUDIES P ALLAN CR
TUTOR/LECT J GRIBBEN CR

Cranmer Hall St John's College, 3 South Bailey, Durham DH1 3RJ
Tel 0191-374 3579 Fax 374 3573
PRIN St John's D V DAY[1] WARDEN Cranmer Hall S J L CROFT
DIR PAST STUDIES A M WHITE
TUTORS/LECTS M R VASEY, R N INNES, A B BARTLETT

Oak Hill Theological College Chase Side, London N14 4PS
Tel 0181-449 0467 Fax 441 5996
PRIN D PETERSON VICE-PRIN P D A WESTON
ACADEMIC REGISTRAR A M BUTLER TUTORS/LECTS G M ABBOTT, M J HANSEN, H C HENDRY, R W HEINZE

The Queen's College Somerset Road, Edgbaston, Birmingham B15 2QH
Tel 0121-454 1527 Fax 454 8171
PRIN P T FISHER TUTOR/LECT D J BRYAN

Ridley Hall Cambridge CB3 9HG
Tel (01223) 353040 Fax 301287
PRIN G A CRAY VICE-PRIN J S BEGBIE
DIR STUDIES M B THOMPSON
DIR PAST STUDIES M P M BOOKER

Ripon College Cuddesdon, Oxford OX44 9EX
Tel (01865) 874427 Fax 875431
PRIN J M CLARKE VICE-PRIN AND DIR STUDIES B C CASTLE
TUTORS/LECTS R B EDWARDS, M CHAPMAN

St John's College Bramcote, Nottingham NG9 3DS
Tel 0115-925 1114 Fax 943 6438
PRIN C BAXTER[2] DIR STUDIES G A COOPER
TUTORS/LECTS J R BOWEN, A F CHATFIELD, C E HART, J HENDERSON, D M MUIR, S J WALTON, I AVEYARD, R W BRIDGER

St Michael and All Angels' College 54 Cardiff Road, Llandaff, Cardiff CF5 2YJ
Tel (01222) 563379 or 576377
WARDEN J HOLDSWORTH SUB-WARDEN G P JEANES
TUTORS/LECTS R H SPENCER, A EDWARDS

St Stephen's House 16 Marston Street, Oxford OX4 1JX
Tel (01865) 247874 Fax 794338
PRIN J SHEEHY VICE-PRIN A BURNHAM DIR STUDIES D G MOSS

Theological Institute of the Scottish Episcopal Church 21 Inverleith Terrace, Edinburgh EH3 5NS
Tel 0131-343 2038 Fax 315 3754
PRIN R A NIXON DIR STUDIES M N OXLEY
PASTORAL DIR I R JONES
DIR LITURG STUDIES I PATON COURSE DIR M KESTON

Trinity College Stoke Hill, Bristol BS9 1JP
Tel 0117-968 2803 Fax 968 7470
PRIN D K GILLETT VICE-PRIN J L NOLLAND
DIR STUDIES D J E ATTWOOD
TUTORS/LECTS P P JENSON, R H PESKETT, P J ROBERTS, S M PATTERSON, J A SEARLE

Westcott House Jesus Lane, Cambridge CB5 8BP
Tel (01223) 350074 Fax 301512
PRIN M G V ROBERTS VICE-PRIN J N MORRIS

Wycliffe Hall 54 Banbury Road, Oxford OX2 6PW
Tel (01865) 274200 Fax 274215
PRIN A MCGRATH VICE-PRIN W G CHALLIS
SEN TUTOR P J M SOUTHWELL
TUTORS/LECTS V M SINTON, G S TOMLIN, D WENHAM, C J HEADLEY, P W L WALKER

Part-Time Courses

Carlisle and Blackburn Diocesan Training Institute Church House, West Walls, Carlisle CA3 8UE
Tel (01228) 22573
PRIN M S LANGLEY TUTORS/LECTS P J PIKE, G E MARRISON

East Anglian Ministerial Training Course EAMTC Office, 5 Pound Hill, Cambridge CB3 0AE
Tel (01223) 741026 Fax 741027
PRIN J D TETLEY VICE-PRIN AND DIR STUDIES A J TODD
TUTOR/LECT J R KEELEY

East Midlands Ministry Training Course Department of Continuing Education, The University, Nottingham NG7 2RD
Tel 0115-951 4854 E-mail emmtc@nottingham.ac.uk
PRIN M J TAYLOR LECT G A COOPER

North East Ordination Course Carter House, Pelaw Leazes Lane, Durham DH1 1TB
Tel 0191-384 8317 Fax 384 7529
PRIN T PITT DIR PRACTICAL TH P H JONES
TUTORS/LECTS M SAUNDERS, P K LEE

Northern Ordination Course Luther King House, Brighton Grove, Rusholme, Manchester M14 5JP
Tel 0161-225 6668 Fax 248 9201
E-mail office@noc.u-net.com
PRIN M J WILLIAMS DIR PAST STUDIES M TUNNICLIFFE
TUTOR/LECT M E LEIGH

North Thames Ministerial Training Course Chase Side, London N14 4PS
Tel 0181-364 9442 Fax 364 8889
PRIN T M THORNTON TUTOR A OSBORN
LON DIOC CO-ORD R T SIMPSON
CHELMSF DIOC CO-ORD C J TRAVERS

St Albans and Oxford Ministry Course Church House, North Hinksey, Oxford OX2 0NB
Tel (01865) 244566 or 790084
PRIN G M BUTTERWORTH ASSOC PRIN G V GILLARD
DIR STUDIES S MOYISE[3]

The South East Institute for Theological Education Deanery Gate, The Precinct, Rochester, Kent ME1 1SJ, and 27 Blackfriars Road, London SE1 8NY
Tel (01634) 832299 and 0171-928 4793
PRIN A LE GRYS COURSE/TUTOR J GLEDHILL S'WARK
TUTOR G M HESKINS

Southern Theological Education Training Scheme 19 The Close, Salisbury SP1 2EE
Tel (01722) 412996
PRIN C J COCKSWORTH VICE-PRIN AND MINL DEVELOPMENT OFFICER M B CRAMERI

South West Ministry Training Course SWMTC Office, The Whisperings, Petherwin Gate, North Petherwin, Launceston, Cornwall PL15 8LW
Tel (01566) 785545 Fax as telephone
PRIN D J P HEWLETT TUTOR/LECT G C H WATSON

West Midlands Ministerial Training Course The Queen's College, Somerset Road, Edgbaston, Birmingham B15 2QH
Tel 0121-454 8597
PRIN D STAMPS TUTORS/LECTS C A WORSLEY, J L HUGHES

West of England Ministerial Training Course 7C College Green, Gloucester GL1 2LX
Tel (01452) 300494 Fax as telephone
PRIN R CLUTTERBUCK[4] DIR STUDIES M DAVIES[5]

Pre-Theological Training Courses

The Simon of Cyrene Theological Institute 2 St Ann's Crescent, London SW18 2LR
Tel 0181-874 1353
PRIN A KASIBANTE

[1] Mr Day is a lay person.
[2] Dr Baxter is a lay person.
[3] Dr Moyise is a lay person.
[4] Dr Clutterbuck is a Methodist.
[5] Dr Davies is a Roman Catholic lay person.

BISHOPS OF ANGLICAN DIOCESES OVERSEAS

AUSTRALIA

PROVINCE OF NEW SOUTH WALES

Armidale	Peter Chiswell PO Box 198, Armidale, NSW, Australia 2350 Fax (67) 729261
Bathurst	Bruce Winston Wilson PO Box 23, Bathurst, NSW, Australia 2795 Fax (63) 322772
Canberra and Goulburn	George Victor Browning GPO Box 1981, Canberra, ACT, Australia 2601 Fax (6) 247 6829
(Assistant)	John Richard Randerson address and fax as above
Grafton	Bruce Allan Schultz PO Box 4, Grafton, NSW, Australia 2460 Fax (66) 431814
Newcastle	Roger Adrian Herft Bishopscourt, Brown Street, Newcastle, NSW, Australia 2300 Fax (49) 294867
Riverina	Bruce Quinton Clark PO Box 10, Narrandera, NSW, Australia 2700 Fax (69) 592903
Sydney (Archbishop and Metropolitan)	Richard Henry Goodhew PO Box Q190, Queen Victoria Buildings, Sydney, NSW, Australia 1230 Fax (2) 9265 1504
(Assistants)	Raymond George Smith (Liverpool) address as above Fax (2) 9265 1543
	Paul William Barnett (North Sydney) address as above Fax (2) 9265 1543
	Brian Franklin Vernon King (Parramatta) PO Box 1443, Parramatta, NSW, Australia 2124 Fax (2) 9633 3636
	Peter Robert Watson (South Sydney) PO Box Q190, Queen Victoria Buildings, Sydney, NSW, Australia 1230 Fax (2) 9265 1543
	Reginald John Piper (Wollongong) 74 Church Street, Wollongong, NSW, Australia 2500 Fax (42) 284296

PROVINCE OF QUEENSLAND

Brisbane (Archbishop)	Peter John Hollingworth PO Box 421, Brisbane, Queensland, Australia 4001 Fax (7) 3832 5030
(Assistants)	John Ashley Noble (Northern Region) address and fax as above
	Ronald John Chantler Williams (Southern Region) address and fax as above
	Raymond Bruce Smith (Western Region) PO Box 2600, Toowomba, Queensland, Australia 4350 Fax (76) 326882
Carpentaria	Anthony F B Hall-Matthews PO Box 180, Earlville, Queensland, Australia 4871
North Queensland	Clyde Maurice Wood PO Box 1244, Townsville, Queensland, Australia 4810 Fax (76) 326882
(Assistants)	Ian Campbell Stuart PO Box 235, Charters Towers, Queensland, Australia 4820 Fax (77) 873049
	Arthur Alistair Malcolm 178 Smith Street, Yarrabah, North Queensland, Australia 4871 Fax (89) 480585
	Morrison Edward Mosby (Torres Strait) PO Box 1244, Townsville, Queensland, Australia 4810 Fax (76) 326882
Northern Territory	Richard Franklin Appleby PO Box 6, Nightcliff, NT, Australia 0810 Fax (8) 8948 0585
Rockhampton	Ronald Francis Stone PO Box 6158, Rockhampton Mail Centre, Queensland, Australia 4702 Fax (79) 224562

PROVINCE OF SOUTH AUSTRALIA

Adelaide (Archbishop)	Ian Gordon Combe George PO Box 2667, Adelaide, S Australia 5001 Fax (8) 8211 8748
(Assistant)	Stuart Meldrum Smith address as above Fax (8) 8211 8748
The Murray	Graham Howard Walden PO Box 269, Murray Bridge, S Australia 5253 Fax (8) 8532 5760
Willochra	William David Hair McCall Bishop's House, Gladstone, S Australia 5473 Fax (8) 8662 2027

PROVINCE OF VICTORIA

Ballarat	Robert David Silk PO Box 89, Ballarat, Victoria, Australia 3350 Fax (53) 322982
Bendigo	Raymond David Bowden PO Box 2, Bendigo, Victoria, Australia 3552 Fax (3) 5441 2173
Gippsland	Arthur Lucas Vivian Jones PO Box 28, Sale, Victoria, Australia 3850 Fax (51) 447183
Melbourne (Archbishop and Primate)	Keith Rayner Bishopscourt, 120 Clarendon Street, Melbourne, Victoria, Australia 3002 Fax (3) 9650 2184
(Assistants)	Andrew Reginald St John (Western Region in Geelong) The Bishop's House, 364 Shannon Avenue, Newtown, Victoria, Australia 3220 Fax (52) 222378
	John Warwick Wilson (Southern Region) St Paul's Cathedral Buildings, 209 Flinders Lane, Melbourne, Victoria, Australia 3000 Fax (3) 9650 2184
	Andrew William Curnow (Northern Region) address and fax as above
	James Alexander Grant address and fax as above
	John Craig Stewart (Eastern Region) address and fax as above
Wangaratta	Paul Richardson PO Box 457, Wangaratta, Victoria, Australia 3677 Fax (3) 5722 1427

PROVINCE OF WESTERN AUSTRALIA

Bunbury	Hamish Thomas Umphelby Jamieson Bishopscourt, PO Box 15, Bunbury, W Australia 6230 Fax (8) 9791 2300
North West Australia	Anthony Howard Nichols PO Box 171, Geraldton, W Australia 6530 Fax (99) 642220
Perth (Archbishop)	Peter Frederick Carnley GPO Box W2067, Perth, W Australia 6001 Fax (8) 9325 6741
(Assistants)	Philip James Huggins (Northern Region) PO Box 42, Joondalup, W Australia 6027 Fax (8) 9300 0893
	David Owen Murray (Fremantle) 3rd Floor, 26 Queen Street, Fremantle, W Australia 6160 Fax (8) 9336 3374
	Brian George Farran (Goldfields Region) PO Box 439, Kalgoorlie, W Australia 6430 Fax (90) 912757

DIOCESE OF TASMANIA

Tasmania	Phillip Keith Newell GPO Box 748H, Hobart, Tasmania, Australia 7001 Fax (3) 6223 8968

BRAZIL

Brasilia	Almir dos Santos Caixa Postal 00515, 70359-970 Brasilia, DF, Brazil Fax (61) 243 8074
Pelotas	Luiz Osorio Prado Caixa Postal 791, Pelotas, RS 96.001-970, Brazil Fax (532) 221347
Recife (formerly Northern Brazil)	Edward Robinson de Barros Cavalcanti Caixa Postal 04704, Recife, PE 51.012-970, Brazil Fax (81) 325 2089
Rio de Janeiro (formerly Central Brazil)	Sydney Alcoba Ruiz Av Rio Branco 277/907, Cinelândia, Rio de Janeiro, RJ 20.047-900, Brazil Fax (21) 220 2705
São Paulo (Primate)	Glauco Soares de Lima Rua Comendador Elias Zarzur 1239, São Paulo, 04736-002, Brazil Fax (11) 246 2180
Southern Brazil	Claudio Vinicius De Senna Gastal Caixa Postal 11504, Porto Alegre, RS 9 1700-150, Brazil Fax (51) 336 3531
South Western Brazil	Jubal Pereira Neves Caixa Postal 98, Santa Maria, RS 97001-970, Brazil Fax (55) 223 1196

BURMA *see* **MYANMAR**

BURUNDI

Bujumbura	Pie Ntukamazina BP 1300, Bujumbura, Burundi Fax (2) 29275
Buye	Samuel Ndayisenga Eglise Episcopale du Burundi, BP 94, Ngozi, Burundi Fax (30) 2317
Gitega	Jean Nduwayo BP 23, Gitega, Burundi
Matana (Archbishop)	Samuel Sindamuka BP 2098, Bujumbura, Burundi Fax (2) 29129
(Coadjutor)	Bernard Ntahoturi address and fax as above
Makambo	Martin Blaise Nyaboho BP 96, Makamba, Burundi Fax (2) 29129

CANADA

Primate of Canada	Michael Geoffrey Peers 600 Jarvis Street, Toronto, ON, Canada, M4Y 2J6 Fax (416) 924 0211

PROVINCE OF BRITISH COLUMBIA

British Columbia	R Barry Jenks 912 Vancouver Street, Victoria, BC, Canada, V8V 3V7 Fax (250) 386 4013
Caledonia	John E Hannen PO Box 278, Prince Rupert, BC, Canada, V8J 3P6 Fax (250) 624 4299
Cariboo	James D Cruickshank 5-618 Tranquille Road, Kamloops, BC, Canada, V2B 3H6 Fax (250) 376 1984
Kootenay (Archbishop and Metropolitan)	David P Crawley 1876 Richter Street, Kelowna, BC, Canada, V1Y 2M9 Fax (250) 763 5507
New Westminster	Michael C Ingham 580 401 W Georgia Street, Vancouver, BC, Canada, V6B 5A1 Fax (604) 684 7017
Yukon	Terrence O Buckle PO Box 4247, Whitehorse, Yukon, Canada, Y1A 3T3 Fax (403) 667 6125

PROVINCE OF CANADA

Central Newfoundland	Edward F Marsh 34 Fraser Road, Gander, NF, Canada, A1V 2E8 Fax (709) 256 2396
Eastern Newfoundland and Labrador	Donald F Harvey 19 King's Bridge Road, St John's, NF, Canada, A1C 3K4 Fax (709) 576 7122
Fredericton	George Colborne Lemmon 115 Church Street, Fredericton, NB, Canada, E3B 4C8 Fax (506) 459 8475
Montreal	Andrew Sandford Hutchison 1444 Union Avenue, Montreal, QC, Canada, H3A 2B8 Fax (514) 843 3221
Nova Scotia	Arthur G Peters 5732 College Street, Halifax, NS, Canada, B3H 1X3 Fax (902) 425 0717
(Suffragan)	Frederick J Hiltz address and fax as above
Quebec	A Bruce Stavert 31 rue des Jardins, Quebec, QC, Canada, G1R 4L6 Fax (418) 692 3876
Western Newfoundland	Leonard Whitten 25 Main Street, Corner Brook, NF, Canada, A2H 1C2 Fax (709) 639 1636

PROVINCE OF ONTARIO

Algoma	Ronald C Ferris PO Box 1168, Sault Ste Marie, ON, Canada, P6A 5N7 Fax (705) 946 1860
Huron (Archbishop and Metropolitan)	Percy O'Driscoll 4-220 Dundas Street, London, ON, Canada, N6A 1H3 Fax (519) 673 4151
(Suffragan)	C Robert Townshend address and fax as above
Moosonee	Caleb J Lawrence Box 841, Schumacher, ON, Canada, P0N 1G0 Fax (705) 360 1120
Niagara	Walter G Asbil Cathedral Place, 252 James Street N, Hamilton, ON, Canada, L8N 2S8 Fax (905) 527 1281
(Coadjutor)	D Ralph Spence address and fax as above
Ontario	Peter R Mason 90 Johnson Street, Kingston, ON, Canada, K7L 1X7 Fax (613) 547 3745
Ottawa	John A Baycroft 71 Bronson Avenue, Ottawa, ON, Canada, K1R 6G6 Fax (613) 232 7088
Toronto	Terence E Finlay 135 Adelaide Street East, Toronto, ON, Canada, M5C 1L8 Fax (416) 363 3683
(Suffragans)	Anne Tottenham (Credit Valley) address and fax as above
	Douglas C Blackwell (Trent-Durham) 300 Dundas Street West, Whitby, ON, Canada, L1N 2M5 Fax (416) 668 8216
	Michael H H Bedford-Jones (York-Scarborough) 3333 Finch Avenue East, Scarborough, ON, Canada, M1W 2R9 Fax (416) 497 4103
	J Taylor Pryce (York-Simcoe) 8 Pinehurst Court, Aurora, ON, Canada, L4G 6B2 Fax (905) 727 4937

PROVINCE OF RUPERT'S LAND

The Arctic	J Christopher R Williams PO Box 164, Iqaluit, NWT, Canada, X0A 0H0 Fax (819) 979 2481

(Suffragan)	Paul O Idlout PO Box 129, Cape Dorset, NT, Canada, X0A 0C0 Fax (819) 897 8580
Athabasca	John R Clarke Box 6868, Peace River, Alberta, Canada, T8S 1S6 Fax (403) 624 2365
Brandon	Malcolm A W Harding 341-13th Street, Brandon, MB, Canada, R7A 4P8 Fax (204) 727 4135
Calgary (Archbishop and Metropolitan)	John B Curtis 3015 Glencoe Road SW, Calgary, AB, Canada, T2S 2L9 Fax (403) 243 2182
(Assistant)	Gary F Woolsey St Peter's Anglican Church, 903-75th Avenue SW, Calgary, AB, Canada, T2V 0S7 Fax (403) 255 0752
Edmonton	Victoria Matthews 10033-84th Avenue, Edmonton, AB, Canada, T6E 2G6 Fax (403) 439 6549
Keewatin	Gordon Beardy 915 Ottawa Street, Keewatin, ON, Canada, P0X 1C0 Fax (807) 547 3356
Qu'Appelle	Eric Bays 1501 College Avenue, Regina, SK, Canada, S4P 1B8 Fax (306) 352 6808
Rupert's Land	Patrick Vaughan Lee 935 Nesbitt Bay, Winnipeg, MB, Canada, R3T 1W6 Fax (204) 452 3915
Saskatchewan	Anthony J Burton 427 21st Street W, Prince Albert, SK, Canada, S6V 5S6 Fax (306) 764 5172
(Suffragan)	Charles J Arthurson Box 96, Lac La Ronge, Saskatchewan, Canada, S0J 1L0
Saskatoon	Thomas O Morgan PO Box 1965, Saskatoon, SK, Canada, S7K 3S5 Fax (306) 665 0244

CENTRAL AFRICA

Botswana (Archbishop)	Walter Paul Khotso Makhulu PO Box 769, Gaborone, Botswana Fax 313015
Central Zambia	Clement W Hlanya-Shaba PO Box 70172, Ndola, Zambia Fax (2) 615954
Central Zimbabwe	Titus Zhenje PO Box 25, Gweru, Zimbabwe Fax (54) 3416
Eastern Zambia	John Osmers PO Box 510154, Chipata, Zambia Fax (1) 262379
Harare	Jonathon Siyachitema Bishopsmount Close, PO Box UA7, Harare, Zimbabwe Fax (4) 700419
Lake Malawi	Peter Nathaniel Nyanja PO Box 30349, Lilongwe 3, Malawi Fax 731966
Lusaka	*Vacant* Bishop's Lodge, PO Box 30183 Lusaka, Zambia Fax (1) 262379
Manicaland	Elijah Musekiwa Peter Masuko 115 Herbert Chitepo Street, Mutare, Zimbabwe Fax (20) 63076
Matabeleland	Theophilus Tswere Naledi PO Box 2422, Bulawayo, Zimbabwe Fax (9) 68353
Northern Malawi	Jackson Cunningham Biggers PO Box 120, Mzuzu, Malawi
Northern Zambia	Bernard Amos Malango PO Box 20173, Kitwe, Zambia Fax (2) 224778
Southern Malawi	*Vacant* PO Box Chilema, Zomba, Malawi Fax 531243

CENTRAL AMERICA

A new Province of Central America will come into existence on 1 January 1998, and will comprise those dioceses which currently form Province IX of the Episcopal Church of the United States of America.

CEYLON (SRI LANKA)

Colombo	Kenneth Michael James Fernando Bishop's House, 368/2 Bauddhaloka Mawatha, Colombo 7, Sri Lanka Fax (1) 684811
Kurunagala	Andrew O Kumarage Bishop's House, Kandy Road, Kurunagala, Sri Lanka

INDIAN OCEAN

Antananarivo (Archbishop)	Remi Joseph Rabenirina Evêché Anglican, Ambohimanoro, 101 Antananarivo, Madagascar Fax (2) 33749
Antsiranana	Keith J Benzies Evêché Anglican, BP 278, 201 Antsiranana, Madagascar
Mahajanga	Jean-Claude Andrianjafimanana BP 169, Mahajanga 401, Madagascar
Mauritius	Rex Donat Bishop's House, Phoenix, Mauritius Fax 697 1096
Seychelles	French Kitchener Chang-Him PO Box 44, Victoria, Seychelles Fax 224296
Toamasina	Donald Westwood Smith Evêché Anglican, BP 531, Toamasina 501, Madagascar

JAPAN

Chubu	Samuel Wataru Hoyo 1-47 Yamawaki-cho, Showa-ku, Nagoya 466, Japan Fax (52) 731 6222
Hokkaido	Nathaniel Makoto Uematsu Kita 15jo, 20 Nishi 5-chome, Kita-ku, Sapporo 001, Japan Fax (11) 736 8377
Kita Kanto (Archbishop)	James Takashi Yashiro 2-172 Sakuragi-cho, Omiya 300, Japan Fax (48) 648 0358
Kobe	John Junichiro Furumoto 5-11-1 Shimoyamate Dori, Chuo-ku, Kobe 650, Japan Fax (78) 382 1095
Kyoto	Barnabas Mutsuji Muto Shimotachiuri-agaru, Karasumadori, Kamikyo-ku, Kyoto 602, Japan Fax (75) 441 4238
Kyushu	Joseph Noriaki Iida 2-9-22 Kusagae, Chuo-ku, Fukuoka 810, Japan Fax (92) 771 9857
Okinawa	*Vacant* 101 Aza Yoshihara, Chatan-cho, Okinawa-Ken 904-01, Japan Fax (98) 936 3019
Osaka	Augustine Koichi Takano 2-1-8 Matsuzakicho, Abenoku, Osaka 545, Japan Fax (6) 621 3097
Tohoku	John Tadao Sato 2-13-15 Kokobun-cho, Sendai 980, Japan Fax (22) 223 2349
Tokyo	John Makoto Takeda 3-6-18 Shiba-koen, Minato-ku, Tokyo 105, Japan Fax (3) 3433 8678
Yokohama	Raphael Shiro Kajiwara 14-57 Mitsuzawa Shimo-cho, Kanagawa-ku, Yokohama 221, Japan Fax (45) 323 2763

JERUSALEM AND THE MIDDLE EAST

Cyprus and the Gulf (Bishop *in*)	George Clive Handford 2 Grigori Afxentiou Street, PO Box 2075, Nicosia, Cyprus Fax (2) 466553

JERUSALEM AND THE MIDDLE EAST

Egypt (Bishop *in*)	Ghais Abdel Malik Diocesan Office, PO Box 87, Zamalek, Cairo, Egypt Fax (2) 340 8941
Iran (Bishop *in*)	Iraj Mottahedeh PO Box 135, Postal Code 81465, Isfahan, Iran
Jerusalem (Bishop *in*)	Samir Kafity PO Box 19122, Jerusalem 91191, Israel Fax (2) 627 3847
(Coadjutor)	Riah Hanna Abu el-Assal Christ Church, PO Box 75, Nazareth, Israel Fax (6) 563649

KENYA

Bungoma	Eliud Wabukala PO Box 2392, Bungoma, Kenya
Butere	Horace Etemesi PO Box 54, Butere, Kenya Fax (2) 714752
Eldoret	*Vacant* PO Box 3404, Eldoret, Kenya Fax (321) 33477
(Assistant)	Thomas K Kogo address and fax as above
Embu	Moses S N Njue PO Box 189, Embu, Kenya Fax (161) 30468
Kajiado	Jermiah John Mutua Taama PO Box 21, Kajiado, Kenya
Katakwa	Eluid O Okiring PO Box 68, Amagoro, Kenya
Kirinyaga	*Vacant* PO Box 95, Kutus, Kenya Fax (163) 44020
Kitale	Stephen Kewasis Nyorsok PO Box 245, Kitale, Kenya
Kitui	Benjamin M P Nzimbi PO Box 1054, Kitui, Kenya Fax (141) 22119
Machakos	Joseph M Kanuku PO Box 282, Machakos, Kenya Fax (145) 20178
Maseno North	Simon M Oketch PO Box 416, Kakemega, Kenya
Maseno South	Francis Mwayi-Abiero PO Box 114, Kisumu, Kenya Fax (35) 43384
Maseno West	Joseph Otieno Wasonga PO Box 793, Siaya, Kenya Tel (334) 21483
Mbeere	*Vacant*
Meru	*Vacant*
Mombasa	Julius Robert Katoi Kalu PO Box 80072, Mombasa, Kenya Fax (11) 311105
Mt Kenya Central	Julius Gatambo Gachuche PO Box 121, Murang'a, Kenya Fax (156) 22642
Mt Kenya South	Peter Karioki Njenga PO Box 23031, Lower Kabete, Kenya Fax (2) 580758
Mt Kenya West	Alfred Charles Chipman PO Box 229, Nyeri, Kenya
Mumias	William Wesa PO Box 213, Mumias, Kenya
Nairobi (Archbishop)	David Mukuba Gitari PO Box 40502, Nairobi, Kenya Fax (2) 718442
Nakuru	Stephen Njihia Mwangi PO Box 56, Nakuru, Kenya Fax (37) 44379
Nambale	Josiah Makhandia Were PO Box 4, Nambale, Kenya
Nyahururu	*Vacant*
Southern Nyanza	Haggai Nyang' PO Box 7, Homa Bay, Kenya
Taita Taveta	Samson Mwaluda PO Box 75, Voi, Kenya

KOREA

Pusan (Primate)	Bundo Chae Hon Kim PO Box 103, Tongrae-Ku, Pusan, 607-600, Republic of Korea Fax (51) 553 9643
Seoul	Matthew Chul Bum Chung 3 Chong Dong, Chung Ku, Seoul 100-120, Republic of Korea Fax (2) 723 2640
Taejon	Paul Hwan Yoon PO Box 22, Taejon 300-600, Republic of Korea Fax (42) 255 8918

MELANESIA

Banks and Torres (formerly North Vanuatu)	Charles Welchman Ling Bishop's House, Sola, Vanualava, Torba Province, Vanuatu
Central Melanesia (Archbishop)	Ellison Leslie Pogo PO Box 19, Honiara, Solomon Islands Fax 21098
Central Solomons	Charles Koete PO Box 52, Tulagia Solomon Islands
Hanuato'o	James Philip Mason c/o PO Kirakira, Makira/Ulawa Province, Solomon Islands Fax 50128
Malaita	Terry M Brown Bishop's House, PO Box 7, Auki, Malaita Province, Solomon Islands Fax 40027
Temotu	Lazarus S Munamua c/o PO Luesalo, Lata, Santa Cruz, Temotu Province, Solomon Islands Fax 53092
Vanuatu	Michael Henry Tavoa Bishop's House, PO Box 238, Luganville, Santo, Vanuatu Fax 36026
Ysabel	Walter Siba PO Box 6, Buala, Jejevo, Ysabel Province, Solomon Islands Fax 37071

MEXICO

Cuernavaca	Martiniano Garcia-Montiel Apartado Postal 192, Admon 4, CP 62431 Cuernavaca, Morelos, Mexico Fax (73) 152870
Mexico	Sergio Carranza-Gomez Ave San Jeronimo 117, Col S Angel, Deleg A Obregon, 01000, Mexico Fax (5) 616 2205
Northern Mexico	German Martínez-Márquez Simón Bolivar 2005 Norte, Mitras Centro CP 64460, Monterrey NL, Mexico Fax (8) 348 7362
Southeastern Mexico (Acting Primate)	Claro Huerta Ramos Avenue de Las Americas, #73 Col Aguacatal 91130, Jalapa, Veracruz, Mexico Fax (28) 144387
Western Mexico	Samuel Espinoza Apartado 2-366 (CP44280) 44100 Guadalajara, Jalisco, Mexico

MYANMAR (formerly BURMA)

Hpa-an	Daniel Hoi Kyin c/o Church of the Province of Myanmar, 140 Pyidaungsu Yeiktha Road, Dagon PO (11191), Yangon, Myanmar Fax (1) 77512
Mandalay	Andrew Hla Aung Bishopscourt, 22nd Street, 'C' Road (between 85-86 Road), Mandalay, Myanmar

Mytikyina	John Shan Lum Diocesan Office, Tha Kin Nat Pe Road, Thida Ya, Mytikyina, Myanmar
Sittwe	Barnabas Theaung Hawi St John's Church, Paletwa, Southern Chin State, via Sittwe, Myanmar
(Assistant)	Aung Tha Tun address as above
Toungoo	Saw John Wilme Diocesan Office, Nat-shin-Naung Road, Toungoo, Myanmar
Yangon (Archbishop)	Andrew Mya Han Bishopscourt, 140 Pyidaungsu Yeiktha Road, Dagon PO (11191), Yangon, Myanmar Fax (1) 251405
(Assistant)	Joseph Than Pe address as above Fax (1) 77512

NEW ZEALAND (AOTEAROA, NEW ZEALAND AND POLYNESIA)

Aotearoa	Whakahuihui Vercoe PO Box 146, Rotorua, New Zealand Fax (7) 348 6091
(East Coast Region)	William Brown Turei (Bishop in Tairawhiti) PO Box 1128, Napier, New Zealand Fax (6) 835 7467
(Northern Region)	Waiohau Rui Te Haara (Bishop in Tai Tokerau) PO Box 25, Paihia, Bay of Islands, New Zealand Fax (9) 402 6663
(Wellington/ Taranaki)	Muru Walters (Bishop in Te Upoko O Te Ika) 11 Hobson Street, Levin, New Zealand Fax (6) 368 1462
(South Island)	John Robert Kuru Gray (Bishop in Waipounamu) PO Box 10 086, Christchurch, New Zealand Fax (3) 389 0912
Auckland	John Campbell Paterson PO Box 37 242, Parnell, Auckland 1001, New Zealand Fax (9) 366 0703
(Assistant)	Bruce MacGregor Moore 4 Lemonwood Place, Manurewa, Auckland, New Zealand Fax (9) 268 1905
Christchurch	David John Coles PO Box 8471, Riccarton, Christchurch 8034, New Zealand Fax (3) 348 3827
Dunedin	Penelope Ann Bansall Jamieson PO Box 5445, Dunedin, New Zealand Fax (3) 477 4932
Nelson	Derek Lionel Eaton PO Box l00, Nelson, New Zealand Fax (3) 548 2125
Polynesia (Acting Primate)	Jabez Leslie Bryce Box 35, Suva, Fiji Fax 302687
(Assistant)	Viliami Maealiuaki Lausi'a Finau Hala'api'api address as above Fax 302152
Waiapu	Murray John Mills PO Box 227, Napier, Hawkes Bay, New Zealand Fax (6) 835 0680
(Regional Bishop in the Bay of Plenty)	George Howard Douglas Connor 60 Judea Road, Tauranga, Aotearoa, New Zealand Fax (7) 577 0684
(Regional Bishop of Hawke's Bay and Eastland)	Murray John Mills PO Box 227, Napier, Hawkes Bay, New Zealand Fax (6) 835 0680
Waikato	David John Moxon PO Box 21, Hamilton, Waikato, New Zealand Fax (7) 838 0052
Wellington	*Vacant* PO Box 12 046, Wellington, New Zealand Fax (4) 499 1360
(Assistants)	Thomas John Brown address and fax as above Brian Ruane Carrell PO Box 442, Palmerston North, New Zealand Fax (6) 359 3264

NIGERIA

The roman numerals indicate to which of the three provinces the diocese belongs

Aba (II)	Augustine Onyeyrichukwu Iwuagwu Bishopscourt, PO Box 212, Aba, Nigeria
Abakaliki (II)	*Vacant*
Abuja (Archbishop of Province III)	Peter Jasper Akinola Bishopscourt, PO Box 212, ADCP, Abuja, Nigeria Fax (9) 523 0986
Akoko (I)	Jacob O K Olowokure Bishopscourt, Lennon Hill, PO Box 572, Ikare-Akoko, Ondo State, Nigeria
Akure (I)	Emmanuel B Gbonigi Bishopscourt, PO Box 1622, Akure, Nigeria
Asaba (II)	Roland N Chukwunweike Nwosu Bishopscourt, Cable Point, PO Box 216, Asaba, Delta State, Nigeria
Awka (II)	Maxwell Samuel Chike Anikwenwa Bishopscourt, Ifite Road, PO Box 130, Awka, Anambra State, Nigeria Fax (42) 336224
Bauchi (III)	Emmanuel O Chukwuma Bishop's House, 2 Hospital Road, PO Box 2450, Bauchi, Nigeria
Benin (I)	Peter Imhona Onekpe St Andrew's Church, PO Box 82, Benin City, Edo State, Nigeria
Calabar (II)	Wilfred George Ekprikpo Bishopscourt, PO Box 74, Calabar, Cross River State, Nigeria Fax (88) 220835
Damaturu (III)	Daniel Abu Yisa PO Box 312, Damaturu, Yobe State, Nigeria
Dutse (III)	Yesufu Ibrahim Lumu PO Box 15, Dutse, Jigawa State, Nigeria
Egba (I)	Matthew Oluremi Owadayo Bishopscourt, Onikolobo, PO Box 267, Ibara, Abeokuta, Nigeria
Egbu (II)	Emmanuel U Iheagwam PO Box 1967, Owerri, Imo State, Nigeria
Ekiti (I)	Clement A Akinbola Bishopscourt, PO Box 12, Ado-Ekiti, Nigeria
Enugu (II)	Gideon N Otubelu Bishop's House-Uwani, PO Box 418, Enugu, Nigeria
Ibadan (I)	Gideon I O Olajide Bishopscourt, Arigidi Street, Bodija Estate, PO Box 3075, Mapo, Ibadan, Nigeria Fax (2) 810 1413
Ife (I)	Gabriel B Oloniyo Bishopscourt, PO Box 312, Ile-Ife, Osun State, Nigeria
Ijebu (I)	Abraham O Olowoyo Bishopscourt, Ejirin Road, PO Box 112, Ijebu-Ode, Nigeria
Ikale-Ilaje (I)	Joseph Akinyele Omoyajowo Bishopscourt, Ikoya Road, PMB 3, Ilutitun, Ondo State, Nigeria
Ilesha (I)	Ephraim Adebola Ademowo Bishopscourt, Oke-Ooye, PO Box 237, Ilesha, Nigeria
Jalingo (III)	Tanimu Samari Aduda PO Box 4, Jalingo, Taraba State, Nigeria
Jos (III)	Benjamin Argak Kwashi Bishopscourt, PO Box 6283, Jos, Plateau State, Nigeria
Kabba (I)	Solomon Olaife Oyelade Bishopscourt, Obaro Way, PO Box 62, Kabba, Kogi State, Nigeria
Kaduna (III)	Titus Ogbonyomi Bishopscourt, 4 Kanta Road, PO Box 72, Kaduna, Nigeria
Kafanchan (III)	William Weh Diya Bishopscourt, 5B Jemma'a Street, PO Box 29, Kafanchan, Kaduna State, Nigeria
Kano (III)	*Vacant* Bishopscourt, PO Box 362, Kano, Nigeria Fax (64) 627816

Katsina (III)	James S Kwasu Bishop's Lodge, PO Box 904, Katsina, Nigeria
Kebbi (III)	Edmund Efoyikeye Akanya PO Box 701, Birnin Kebbi, Kebbi State, Nigeria
Kwara (I)	Jeremiah Olagbamigbe A Fabuluje Bishopscourt, Fate Road, PO Box 1884, Ilorin, Kwara State, Nigeria
Lagos (Archbishop of Province I)	Joseph Abiodun Adetiloye Archbishop's Palace, 29 Marina, PO Box 13, Lagos, Nigeria Fax (1) 263 6026
Lokoja (I)	George Bako PO Box 11, Lokoja, Kogi State, Nigeria Fax (58) 220588
Maiduguri (III)	Emmanuel K Mani Bishopscourt, Off Lagos Street, GRA PO Box 1693, Maiduguri, Borno State, Nigeria
Makurdi (III)	Nathaniel N Inyom Bishopscourt, PO Box 1, Makurdi, Nigeria
Mbaise (II)	Cyril Chukwuka Anyanwu Bishop's Court, PO Box 10, Ife, Ezinihitte Mbaise, Imo State, Nigeria
Minna (III)	Nathaniel Yisa Bishopscourt, Dutsen Kura, PO Box 2469, Minna, Nigeria
The Niger (II) (Bishop *on*)	Jonathan Onyemelukwe Bishopscourt, PO Box 42, Onitsha, Nigeria
Niger Delta The (II)	Gabriel H Pepple Bishopcourt, PO Box 115, Port Harcourt, Rivers State, Nigeria
Niger Delta North (II)	Samuel Onyuku Elenwo Bishop's Court, St Paul's Cathedral, Diobu, PO Box 53, Port Harcourt, Rivers State, Nigeria
Nnewi (II)	Godwin Okpala St Mary's Pro-Cathedral, Uruagu, Nnewi, Anambra State, Nigeria
Nsukka (II)	Jonah Chukwuemeka Ilonuba St Paul's Cathedral, PO Box 16, Nsukka, Enugu State, Nigeria
Oji River (II)	*Vacant*
Oke-Osun (I)	Abraham O Awosan Bishopscourt, PO Box 251, Gbongan, Osun State, Nigeria
Okigwe North (II)	Alfred Nwaizuzu PO Box 156, Okigwe, Imo State, Nigeria
Okigwe South (II)	Bennett C I Okoro Bishopscourt, Ezeoke Nsu, PO Box 235, Nsu, Ehime Mbano LGA, Imo State, Nigeria
Ondo (I)	Samuel O Aderin Bishopscourt, College Road, PO Box 265, Ondo, Nigeria
Orlu (II)	Samuel Chukuma N Ebo Bishop's House, PO Box 260, Nkwerre, Imo State, Nigeria
Osun (I)	Seth Oni Fagbemi Bishopscourt, Isale-Aro, PO Box 285, Osogbo, Nigeria
Oturkpo (III)	Ityobee Ugede c/o Provincial Secretariat, 29 Marina, PO Box 78, Lagos, Nigeria
Owerri (Archbishop of Province II)	Benjamin Nwankiti Archbishop's Palace, Transfiguration Hills, PO Box 31, Owerri, Imo State, Nigeria
Owo (I)	Peter Adebiyi Bishopscourt, PO Box 472, Owo, Ondo State, Nigeria
Remo (I)	*Vacant* Bishopscourt, Ewusi Street, PO Box 522, Sagamu, Ogun State, Nigeria
Sabongidda-Ora (I)	Albert Agbaje Bishopscourt, PO Box 13, Sabongidda-Ora, Edo State, Nigeria
Sokoto (III)	Josiah Idowu-Fearon Bishop's Lodge, PO Box 3489, Sokoto, Nigeria
Ukwa (II)	Uju Otuokwesiri Wachukwu Obinya PO Box 20468, Aba, Nigeria
Umuahia (II)	Ugochukwu U Ezuoke St Stephen's Cathedral Church Compound, PO Box 96, Umuahia, Nigeria
Uyo (II)	Emmanuel E Nglass Bishopscourt, PO Box 70, Uyo, Akwa Ibom State, Nigeria Fax (85) 200451
Warri (I)	Nathaniel A Enuku Bishopscourt, PO Box 760, Ughelli, Delta State, Nigeria
Yewa (I)	*Vacant* Bishopscourt, PO Box 484, Ilaro, Ogun State, Nigeria
Yola (III)	Christian Ogochukwu Efobi PO Box 601, Yola, Adamawa State, Nigeria

PAPUA NEW GUINEA

Aipo Rongo (Archbishop)	James Simon Ayong PO Box 893, Mount Hagen, Western Highlands Province, Papua New Guinea Fax 542 1181
Dogura	Tevita Talanoa PO Box 19, Dogura, MBP, Papua New Guinea Fax 641 1129
The New Guinea Islands	Michael George Hough Bishop's House, PO Box 806, Kimbe, WNBP, Papua New Guinea Fax 935492
(Assistant)	Rhynold Ewaruba Sanana PO Box 198, Kimbe, WNBP, Papua New Guinea
Popondota	Reuben Barago Tariambari PO Box 26, Popondetta, Oro Province, Papua New Guinea Fax 729 7476
Port Moresby	*Vacant* PO Box 6491, Boroko, NCD, Papua New Guinea Fax 326 1073

THE PHILIPPINES

Prime Bishop	Ignacio Capuyan Soliba PO Box 10321, Broadway Centrum 1112, Quezon City, Philippines Fax (2) 721 1923
Central Philippines	Benjamin Gayno Botengan PO Box 655, Manila 2081, Philippines Fax (2) 721 1923
North Central Philippines	Joel A Pachao PO Box 403, Baguio City 2600, Philippines Fax (74) 442 3638
Northern Luzon	Renato M Abibico Bulanao, Tabuk, Kalinga-Apayao 3800, Philippines Fax 721 1923
Northern Philippines	Edward P Malecdan St Andrew's Theological Seminary, PO Box 3167, Manila, Philippines
(Suffragan)	Miguel Paredes Yamoyam Diocesan Office, Bontoc, Mt Province 0601, Philippines Fax (2) 721 1923
Southern Philippines	James Buanda Manguramas PO Box 113, Cotabato City 9600, Philippines

RWANDA

Butare	Venuste Mutiganda BP 255, Butare, Rwanda Fax 30504
Byumba	Onesphore Rwaje BP 17, Byumba, Rwanda Fax 64242
Cyangugu	Kenneth Lawrence Barham Rosewood, Canadia Road, Battle, E Sussex TN33 0LR Fax (01424) 773073
Gahini (formerly Umutara)	Alexis Bilindabagabo BP 2507, Kigali, Rwanda Fax 77831
Kibungo	Prudence Ngarambe BP 18, Kibungo, Rwanda
Kigali (Archbishop)	Jonathan Ruhumuliza BP 61, Kigali, Rwanda Fax 73213

Kigeme — Norman Kayumba
BP 67, Gikongoro, Rwanda
Fax 34011

Shyira — John Rucyahana
BP 275, Kigali, Rwanda
Fax 46449

Shyogwe — Jered Karimba
BP 27, Gitarama, Rwanda
Fax 62460

Umutara — *see* Gahini

SOUTH EAST ASIA

Kuching — Made Katib
Bishop's House, PO Box 347,
Kuching, Sarawak, Malaysia
Fax (82) 426488

Sabah — Datuk Ping Chung Yong
PO Box 10811, 88809 Kota Kinabalu,
Sabah, Malaysia
Fax (88) 245942

Singapore (Archbishop) — Moses Tay
4 Bishopsgate, Singapore 1024
Fax 479 5482

(Assistant) — John Tan
address and fax as above

West Malaysia — Cheng Ean Lim
Rumah Bishop, 14 Pesiaran Stonor,
50450 Kuala Lumpur, Malaysia
Fax (3) 201 3225

(Assistant) — Moses Elisha Ponniah
St Christopher's Church, Johor Bahru,
No 5 Jalan Mustaffa,
80100 Johor Bahru, Johor, Malysia

SOUTHERN AFRICA

Bloemfontein — Elistan Patrick Glover
PO Box 411, Bloemfontein,
9300 South Africa
Fax (51) 475874

Cape Town (Primate) — Winston Hugh Njongonkulu Ndungane
Bishopscourt, Claremont, 7700 South Africa
Fax (21) 761 4193

(Suffragans) — Merwyn Edwin Castle
Bishopsholme, 18 Rue Ursula,
Glenhaven, Bellville, 7530 South Africa
Fax (21) 951 4314

Alan Geoff Quinlan
79 Kildare Road, Newlands, 7700 South Africa
Fax (21) 611921

Edward MacKenzie
39 Paradise Road, Newlands, 7700 South Africa

Christ the King — Peter John Lee
PO Box 1653, Rosettenville, 2130 South Africa
Fax (11) 435 2868

George — Derek George Damant
PO Box 227, George, 6530 South Africa
Fax (441) 735680

Grahamstown — David Patrick Hamilton Russell
PO Box 162, Grahamstown, 6140 South Africa
Fax (461) 25231

Johannesburg — Duncan Buchanan
PO Box 1131, Johannesburg, 2000 South Africa
Fax (11) 333 3051

Kimberley and Kuruman — Itumeleng Baldwin Moseki
PO Box 45, Kimberley, 8300 South Africa
Fax (531) 812730

Klerksdorp — David Cecil Tapi Nkwe
PO Box 11417, Klerksdorp, 2570 South Africa
Fax (18) 462 4939

Lebombo — Dinis Salomao Sengulane
CP 120, Maputo, Mozambique
Fax 140 1093

Lesotho — Philip S Mokuku
PO Box 87, Maseru 100, Lesotho
Fax 310161

(Suffragan) — Andrew Thabo Duma
address and fax as above

Namibia — James Hamupanda Kauluma
PO Box 57, Windhoek, Namibia
Fax (61) 225903

(Suffragan) — Petrus Hidulika Hilukiluah
address and fax as above

Natal — Michael Nuttall
PO Box 899, Pietermaritzburg, 3200 South Africa
Fax (331) 948785

(Suffragans) — Rubin Phillip
PO Box 47439, Greyville, 4023 South Africa
Fax (31) 309 6963

Matthew Mandlenkosi Makhaye
PO Box 463, Ladysmith 3370, South Africa
Fax (361) 24949

Niassa — Paulino T Manhique
Missao Anglicana de Messumba,
CP 264, Lichinga, Niassa, Mozambique

Order of Ethiopia (Bishop of the) — Sigqibo Dwane
508A Lansdowne Road, Lansdowne, 7700 South Africa
Fax (21) 762 7220

Port Elizabeth — Eric Pike
PO Box 7109, Newton Park,
Port Elizabeth, 6055 South Africa
Fax (41) 352049

Pretoria — Richard Austin Kraft
PO Box 1032, Pretoria, 0001 South Africa
Fax (12) 322 9411

(Suffragan) — Robin Campbell Rawdon Briggs
PO Box 187, White River, 1240 South Africa
Fax (13) 750 0773

St Helena — John Harry Gerald Ruston
Bishopsholme, PO Box 62,
St Helena Island, South Atlantic Ocean
Fax 4330

St John's — Jacoh Zambuhle Dlamini
PO Box 163, Umtata, Transkei, South Africa
Fax (471) 22895

St Mark the Evangelist — Philip John Le Feuvre PO Box 643,
Pietersburg, 0700 South Africa
Fax (152) 297 0408

South Eastern Transvaal — David Albert Beetge
PO Box 2025, Trekker, Brakpan, 1547 South Africa
Fax (11) 740 9156

Swaziland — Lawrence Bekisia Zulu
PO Box 118, Mbabane, Swaziland
Fax 46759

Umzimvubu — Geoffrey Francis Davies
PO Box 644, Kokstad, 4700 South Africa
Fax (37) 727 4117

Zululand — Anthony Thembinkosi B Mdletshe
PO Box 147, Eshowe,
Zululand, 3815 South Africa
Fax (354) 42047

SOUTHERN CONE OF AMERICA

Argentina — David Leake
Casilla de Correo 4293, 1000 Correo Centro,
Buenos Aires, Argentina
Fax (1) 331 0234

Bolivia — Gregory James Venables
Casilla 9574, La Paz, Bolivia
Fax (2) 371414

Chile — Colin Frederick Bazley
Casilla 50675, Correo Central, Santiago, Chile
Fax (2) 639 4581

(Assistant) — Abelino Apeleo
Casilla de Correo 26-D, Temuco, Chile
Fax (45) 211130

Northern Argentina (Primate) — Maurice Walter Sinclair
Casilla de Correo 187, 4400 Salta, Argentina
Fax (87) 312622

(Assistants) — Mario L Marino
Casilla 19, CP 3636 Ingeniero Juarez,
FCNGB Formosa, Argentina

Humberto Axt
Casilla de Correo 187, 4400 Salta, Argentina
Fax (87) 312622

Paraguay — John Alexander Ellison
Iglesia Anglicana Paraguya,
Casilla de Correo 1124, Asuncion, Paraguay
Fax (21) 214328

Peru	*Vacant* Apartado 18-1032, Miraflores, Lima 18, Peru Fax (14) 453044
Uruguay	Harold William Godfrey Casilla 6108, 11000 Montevideo, Uruguay Fax (2) 962519

SUDAN

Bor	Nathaniel Garang c/o NSCC, PO Box 52802, Nairobi, Kenya
Cueibet	Reuben Maciir Makoi c/o ACROSS, PO Box 21033, Nairobi, Kenya Fax (2) 726509
El-Obeid	Ismail Gabriel PO Box 65, Omdurman, Dem Rep Sudan
Ezo	Benjamin Ruati c/o NSCC, PO Box 52802, Nairobi, Kenya Fax 447015
Iba	Levi Hassan PO Box 110, Juba, Dem Rep Sudan
Juba (Archbishop)	Benjamina Wani Yugusuk PO Box 110, Juba, Dem Rep Sudan
Kadugli and Nuba Mountains	Kuthurdu Peter ElBersh Kowa PO Box 65, Omdurman, Dem Rep Sudan
Kajo Keji	Manasseh Binyi Dawidi c/o NSCC, PO Box 52802, Nairobi, Kenya
Khartoum	Bulus T Idris Tia PO Box 65, Omdurman, Dem Rep Sudan
Lainya	Eliaba L Menasona PO Box 110, Juba, Dem Rep Sudan
Lui	Ephraim Natana PO Box 3364, Khartoum, Dem Rep Sudan
Malakal	Kedhekia Mabior c/o NSCC, PO Box 52802, Nairobi, Kenya
Maridi	Joseph Marona PO Box 676, Arua, Uganda Fax 447015
Mundri	Eluzai Munda PO Box 110, Juba, Dem Rep Sudan
Port Sudan	Yousif Abdalla Kuku PO Box 65, Omdurman, Dem Rep Sudan
Rejaf	Michael Sokiri Lugör PO Box 110, Juba, Dem Rep Sudan
Renk	Daniel Deng PO Box 3364, Khartoum, Dem Rep Sudan
Rokon	Francis Loyo PO Box 110, Juba, Dem Rep Sudan
Rumbek	Gabriel Roric Jur PO Box 65, Omdurman, Dem Rep Sudan Fax 77100
Torit	Wilson Arop c/o Church of Uganda, PO Box 14123, Kampala, Uganda Fax (41) 254423
Wau	Henry Riak PO Box 135, Khartoum, Dem Rep Sudan
Yambio	Daniel Zindo c/o NSCC, PO Box 52802, Nairobi, Kenya
(Suffragan)	Benjamin J Ruate (Bishop of Ezzo Area) address as above
Yei	Seme L Solomona PO Box 370, Arua, Uganda
Yirol	Benjamin Mangar Mamur PO Box 3364, Khartoum, Dem Rep Sudan

TANZANIA

Central Tanganyika	Godfrey Mdimi Mhogolo PO Box 15, Dodoma, Tanzania
(Assistant)	John Martin Ball address as above
Dar es Salaam	Basil M Sambano PO Box 25016, Ilala, Dar es Salaam, Tanzania
Kagera	Edwin Alan Gakobe Nyamubi PO Box 18, Ngara, Tanzania Fax (871) 176 0266
Mara	Hilkiah Omindo PO Box 131, Musoma, Tanzania
Masasi	Patrick Mwachiko Private Bag, PO Masasi, Mtwara Region, Tanzania
Morogoro	Dudley Mageni PO Box 320, Morogoro, Tanzania
Mount Kilimanjaro	Simon Makundi PO Box 1057, Arusha, Tanzania
Mpwapwa	Simon Chiwanga PO Box 2, Mpwapwa, Tanzania
The Rift Valley	Alpha Mohamed PO Box 16, Manyoni, Tanzania Fax (61) 24565
Ruaha	Donald Mtetemela Box 1028, Iringa, Tanzania Fax (64) 2479
Ruvuma	Stanford S Shauri PO Box 1, Liuli, Mbinga District, Tanzania
South West Tanganyika	Charles J Mwaigoga PO Box 32, Njombe, Tanzania
Tabora	Francis Ntiruka, PO Box 1408, Tabora, Tanzania
Victoria Nyanza	John Paul Changae PO Box 278, Mwanza, Tanzania
Western Tanganyika	Gerard E Mpango PO Box 13, Kasulu, Tanzania Fax 695 3434
Zanzibar and Tanga (Archbishop)	John Acland Ramadhani PO Box 35, Korogwe, Tanga Region, Tanzania Fax (61) 24565

UGANDA

Bukedi	Nicodemus Okille PO Box 170, Tororo, Uganda
Bunyoro-Kitara	Wilson Nkuna Turumanya PO Box 20, Hoima, Uganda Fax 231671
Busoga	*Vacant* PO Box 1658, Jinja, Uganda Fax (43) 20547
Central Buganda	George Sinabulya PO Box 1200, Karoni-Gomba, Mpigi, Uganda Fax (41) 242742
East Ankole	Elisha Kyamugambi PO Box 14, Mbarara, Ankole, Uganda
Kampala (Archbishop)	Livingstone Mpalanyi-Nkoyoyo PO Box 14123, Kampala, Uganda Fax (41) 251925
(Assistant)	Lucas Gonahasa PO Box 335, Kampala, Uganda Fax (41) 242601
Karamoja	Peter Lomongin PO Box 1, Kampala, Uganda
Kigezi	George Katwesigwe PO Box 14123, Kampala, Uganda Fax (41) 250922
Kinkizi	John Ntegyereize PO Box 77, Karuhinda, Rukungiri, Uganda
Kitgum	*Vacant* PO Box 187, Kitgum, Uganda
Lango	Melchizedek Otim PO Box 6, Lira, Uganda
Luwero	Evans Mukasa Kisekka PO Box 125, Luwero, Uganda
Madi and West Nile	Enock Lee Drati PO Box 370, Arua, Uganda
Mbale	Israel Koboyi Bishop's House, PO Box 473, Mbale, Uganda
Mityana	Wilson Mutebi PO Box 102, Mityana, Uganda
Muhabura	Ernest Shalita Church of Uganda, PO Box 22, Kisoro, Uganda
Mukono	Michael Senyimba PO Box 39, Mukono, Uganda
Namirembe	Samuel Balagadde Ssekkadde PO Box 14297, Kampala, Uganda
Nebbi	Henry Orombi PO Box 27, Nebbi, Uganda
North Kigezi	John Wilson Kahigwa PO Box 23, Rukungiri, Uganda
North Mbale	Nathan Muwombi PO Box 1837, Mbale, Uganda Fax (41) 254576

Northern Uganda	Gideon Oboma PO Box 232, Gulu, Uganda
Ruwenzori	Eustace Kamanyire Bishop's House, PO Box 37, Fort Portal, Uganda Fax (493) 22636
Soroti	Geresom Ilukor PO Box 107, Soroti, Uganda
South Ruwenzori	Zebedee K Masereka PO Box 142, Kasese, Uganda
West Ankole	William Magambo PO Box 140, Bushenyi, Uganda
West Buganda	Christopher D Senyonjo PO Box 242, Masaka, Uganda

UNITED STATES OF AMERICA

The roman numerals indicate to which of the nine provinces of ECUSA the diocese belongs

Presiding Bishop	Frank Tracy Griswold Episcopal Church Center, 815 Second Avenue, New York, NY 10017, USA Fax (212) 490 3298
Alabama (IV)	Robert Oran Miller Carpenter House, 521 N 20th Street, Birmingham, AL 35203, USA Fax (205) 715 2066
(Coadjutor)	Henry Nutt Parsley address and fax as above
Alaska (VIII)	Mark Lawrence MacDonald 1205 Denali Way, Fairbanks, AK 99701-4178, USA Fax (907) 456 6552
Albany (II)	David Standish Ball 68 South Swan Street, Albany, NY 12210-2301, USA Fax (518) 436 1182
(Coadjutor)	Daniel William Herzog address and fax as above
Arizona (VIII)	Robert Reed Shahan 114 West Roosevelt Street, Phoenix, AZ 85003, USA Fax (602) 495 6603
Arkansas (VII)	Larry Maze Cathedral House, PO Box 164668, Little Rock, AR 72216, USA Fax (501) 372 2147
Atlanta (IV)	Frank Kellogg Allan 2744 Peachtree Road NW, Atlanta, GA 30363-0701, USA Fax (404) 261 2515
(Assistant)	Onell Asiselo Soto address and fax as above
Bethlehem (III)	Paul Victor Marshall 333 Wyandotte Street, Bethlehem, PA 18015, USA Fax (610) 691 1682
California (VIII)	William Edwin Swing 1055 Taylor Street, San Francisco, CA 94108, USA Fax (415) 673 9268
(Assistants)	George Richard Millard 502 Portola Road, Box 8107, Portola Valley, CA 94028-7603, USA
	Charles Ellesworth Bennison 2331 Warner Range Avenue, Menlo Park, CA 94025, USA
Central Florida (IV)	John Wadsworth Howe Diocesan Office, 1017 E Robinson Street, Orlando, FL 32801, USA Fax (407) 872 0006
(Assistants)	Reginald Hollis Anglican Fellowship of Prayer, PO Box 31 Orlando, FL 32802, USA
	Herbert DaCosta Edmondson 1404 Ruthbern Road, Daytona Beach, FL 32014, USA
	Hugo Luis Pina-Lopez Diocesan Office, 1017 E Robinson Street, Orlando, FL 32801, USA Fax (407) 872 0096
Central Gulf Coast (IV)	Charles Farmer Duvall Box 13330, Pensacola, FL 32591-3330, USA Fax (904) 434 8577

Central New York (II)	David Bruce Joslin 310 Montgomery Street, Suite 200, Syracuse, NY 13202-2093, USA Fax (315) 478 1632
Central Pennsylvania (III)	Michael Whittington Creighton Box 11937, Harrisburg, PA 17108-1937, USA Fax (717) 236 6448
Chicago (V) (Presiding Bishop Elect)	*Vacant* 65 East Huron Street, Chicago, IL 60611, USA Fax (312) 787 4534
Colombia (IX)	Bernardo Merino-Botero Apartado Aereo 52964, Bogota 2, Colombia Fax (1) 288 3248
Colorado (VI)	William Jerry Winterrowd 1300 Washington Street, Denver, CO 80203, USA Fax (303) 837 1311
Connecticut (I)	Clarence Nicholas Coleridge 1335 Asylum Avenue, Hartford, CT 06105-2295, USA Fax (203) 523 1410
(Suffragan)	Andrew Donnan Smith address and fax as above
Dallas (VII)	James Monte Stanton 1630 Garrett Street, Dallas, TX 75206, USA Fax (214) 826 5968
(Assistant)	Harry Woolston Shipps 715 Washington Avenue, Savannah, GA 31405, USA
Delaware (III)	Calvin Cabell Tennis 2020 Tatnall Street, Wilmington, DE 19802, USA Fax (302) 656 7342
Dominican Republic (IX)	Julio Cesar Holguin Lynx Air, PO Box 5600-DR-Sto.Dgo, Ft Lauderdale, FL 33340, USA Fax (809) 686 6364
East Carolina (IV)	Clifton Daniel 705 Doctors Drive, (Box 1336), Kinston, NC 28503, USA Fax (919) 523 5272
East Tennessee (IV)	Robert Gould Tharp 401 Cumberland Avenue, Knoxville, TN 37902-2302, USA Fax (615) 521 2905
Eastern Michigan (V)	Edwin Max Leidel Diocesan Office, 4611 Swede Avenue, Midland, MI 48642-3861, USA Fax (517) 835 6302
Eastern Oregon (VIII)	Rustin Ray Kimsey PO Box 620, The Dalles, OR 97058, USA Fax (503) 298 7875
Easton (III)	Martin Gough Townsend Box 1027, Easton, MD 21601, USA Fax (410) 820 6578
Eau Claire (V)	William Charles Wantland 510 South Farwell Street, Eau Claire, WI 54701, USA Fax (715) 835 9212
Ecuador (IX)	Jose Neptali Larrea-Moreno PO Box 17-03 - 353-A, Quito, Ecuador Fax (2) 252225
El Camino Real (VIII)	Richard Lester Shimpfky PO Box 1903, Monterey, CA 93940, USA Fax (408) 394 7133
El Salvador (IX)	Martin Barahona 47 Avenida Sur, 723 Col. Flor Blanca, Apt Postal (01), 274 San Salvador, El Salvador Fax 223 7952
Europe, Convocation of American Churches in	Jeffery William Rowthorn 23 Avenue George V, 75008 Paris, France Fax (1) 47 23 95 30
Florida (IV)	Stephen Hays Jecko 325 Market Street, Jacksonville, FL 32202, USA Fax (904) 355 1934
Fond du Lac (V)	Russell Edward Jacobus PO Box 149, Fond du Lac, WI 54936-0149, USA Fax (414) 921 8761

Fort Worth (VII)	Jack Leo Iker 6300 Ridglea Place, Suite 1100, Fort Worth, TX 76116, USA Fax (817) 738 9955
Georgia (IV)	Henry Irving Louttit 611 E Bay Street, Savannah, GA 31401-1296, USA Fax (912) 236 2007
Guatemala (IX)	Armando Roman Guerra-Soria Apartado 58A, Guatemala City, Guatemala Fax (2) 720764
Haiti (II)	Jean Zache Duracin PO Box 1309, Port-au-Prince, Haiti Fax 573412
Hawaii (VIII)	Richard Sui On Chang 229 Queen Emma Square, Honolulu, HI 96813, USA Fax (808) 538 7194
Honduras (IX)	Leopold Frade Apartado 586, San Pedro Sula, Honduras, Central America Fax 566467
Idaho (VIII)	John Stuart Thornton PO Box 936, Boise, ID 83701, USA Fax (208) 345 9735
Indianapolis (V)	Edward Witker Jones 1100 West 42nd Street, Indianapolis, IN 46208, USA Fax (317) 926 5456
(Coadjutor)	Catherine Elizabeth Maples Waynick 6111 Meridian West Drive, Indianapolis, IN 46208, USA Fax (317) 926 5456
Iowa (VI)	Carl Christopher Epting 225 37th Street, Des Moines, IA 50312, USA Fax (515) 277 0273
Kansas (VII)	William Edward Smalley 835 Polk Street, Topeka, KS 66612, USA Fax (913) 235 2449
Kentucky (IV)	Edwin Funsten Gulick 600 East Main Street, Louisville, KY 40202, USA Fax (502) 587 8123
Lexington (IV)	Don Adgar Wimberley PO Box 610, Lexington, KY 40586, USA Fax (606) 231 9077
Litoral Diocese of Ecuador (IX)	Alfredo Morante-Arevalo Box 0901-5250, Amarilis Fuentesentre V Trusillo, y La 'D', Guayaquil, Equador Fax (4) 443088
Long Island (II)	Orris George Walker 36 Cathedral Avenue, Garden City, NY 11530, USA Fax (516) 248 4883
(Suffragan)	Rodney Rae Michel address as above Fax (516) 248 1616
Los Angeles (VIII)	Frederick Houk Borsch Box 2164, Los Angeles, CA 90051, USA Fax (213) 482 5304
(Suffragan)	Chester Lovelle Talton address and fax as above
Louisiana (IV)	James Barrow Brown 1623 Seventh Street, New Orleans, LA 70115-4111, USA Fax (504) 895 6637
Maine (I)	*Vacant* Loring House, 143 State Street, Portland, ME 04101, USA Fax (207) 773 0095
Maryland (III)	Robert Wilkes Ihloff 4 East University Parkway, Baltimore, MD 21218, USA Fax (410) 554 6387
(Suffragan)	Charles Lindsay Longest address and fax as above
Massachusetts (I)	Marvil Thomas Shaw Society of St John the Evangelist, 980 Memorial Drive, Cambridge, MA 02138, USA Fax (617) 482 8431
(Suffragan)	Barbara Clementine Harris 138 Tremont Street, Boston, MA 02111, USA Fax (617) 482 8431
Michigan (V)	Raymond Stewart Wood 4800 Woodward Avenue, Detroit, MI 48201, USA Fax (313) 831 0259
Milwaukee (V)	Roger John White 804 East Juneau Street, Milwaukee, WI 53202, USA Fax (414) 272 7790
Minnesota (VI)	James Louis Jelinek 430 Oak Grove Street, Suite 306, Minneapolis, MN 55403, USA Fax (612) 871 0552
Mississippi (IV)	Alfred Clark Marble St Andrew Cathedral, PO Box 23107, Jackson, MS 39225-3107, USA Fax (601) 354 3401
Missouri (V)	Hays Hamilton Rockwell 1210 Locust Street, St Louis, MO 63103, USA Fax (314) 231 3373
Montana (VI)	Charles Irving Jones 515 North Park Avenue, Helena, MT 59601, USA Fax (406) 442 2238
Navajoland Area Mission (VIII)	Steven Tsosie Plummer Diocesan Office, Box 720, Farmington, NM 87499, USA Fax (505) 327 6904
Nebraska (VIII)	James Edward Krotz 200 North 62nd Street, Omaha, NE 68132-6357, USA Fax (402) 558 0094
Nevada (VIII)	Stewart Clark Zabriskie 2100 South Maryland Parkway, Suite 4, Las Vegas, NV 89104, USA Fax (702) 737 6488
New Hampshire (I)	Douglas Edwin Theuner 63 Green Street, Concord, NH 03301, USA Fax (603) 225 7884
New Jersey (II)	Joe Morris Doss 808 West State Street, Trenton, NJ 08618, USA Fax (603) 394 9546
New York (II)	Richard Frank Grein Synod House, 1047 Amsterdam Avenue, Cathedral Heights, New York, NY 10025, USA Fax (212) 932 7312
(Suffragans)	Walter Decoster Dennis address as above Fax (212) 316 7405
	Catherine Scimeca Roskam address and fax as above
(Assistant)	Egbert Don Taylor address and fax as above
Newark (II)	John Shelby Spong 24 Rector Street, Newark, NJ 07102, USA Fax (201) 622 3503
(Suffragan)	Jack McKelvey address and fax as above
Nicaragua (IX)	Sturdie Downs Apartado 1207, Managua, Nicaragua Fax (505) 226701
North Carolina (IV)	Robert Carroll Johnson PO Box 17025, 201 St Alban's Drive, Raleigh, NC 27619-7025, USA Fax (919) 787 0156
(Suffragan)	James Gary Gloster address and fax as above
North Dakota (VI)	Andrew Hedtler Fairfield 3600 25th Street, Box 10337, Fargo, ND 58106-0337, USA Fax (701) 232 3077
Northern California (VIII)	Jerry Alban Lamb Box 161268, 1318 27th Street, Sacramento, CA 95816, USA Fax (916) 442 6927
Northern Indiana (V)	Francis Campbell Gray Cathedral House, 117 North Lafayette Boulevard, South Bend, IN 46601, USA Fax (219) 287 7914
Northern Michigan (V)	Thomas Kreider Ray 131 East Ridge Street, Marquette, MI 49855, USA Fax (906) 228 7171

Northwest Texas (VII)	C Wallis Ohl The Episcopal Church Center, 1802 Broadway, Lubbock, TX 79408, USA Fax (806) 763 2026
Northwestern Pennsylvania (III)	Robert Deane Rowley 145 West 6th Street, Erie, PA 16501, USA Fax (814) 454 8703
Ohio (V)	Joseph Clark Grew 2230 Euclid Avenue, Cleveland, OH 441155-2499, USA Fax (216) 623 0735
(Suffragan)	Arthur Benjamin Williams address and fax as above
Oklahoma (VII)	Robert Manning Moody 924 North Robinson, Oklahoma City, OK 73102, USA Fax (405) 232 4912
Olympia (VIII)	Vincent Waydell Warner PO Box 12126, Seattle, WA 98102, USA Fax (206) 325 4631
(Assistant)	Sanford Zangwill Kaye Hampton address and fax as above
Oregon (VIII)	Robert Louis Ladehoff PO Box 467, Lake Oswego, OR 97034-0467, USA Fax (503) 636 5616
Panama (IX)	Clarence Wallace Hayes Box R, Balboa, Republic of Panama Fax (507) 262 2097
Pennsylvania (III)	Charles Ellesworth Bennison 240 South 4th Street, Philadelphia, PA 19106, USA Fax (215) 627 7550
(Suffragan)	Franklin Delton Turner address and fax as above
Pittsburgh (III)	Robert William Duncan 325 Oliver Avenue, Pittsburgh, PA 15222-2467, USA Fax (412) 471 5591
Quincy (V)	Keith Lynn Ackerman 3601 N North Street, Peoria, IL 61604, USA Fax (309) 688 8229
Rhode Island (I)	Geralyn Wolf 275 North Main Street, Providence, RI 02903, USA Fax (401) 331 9430
Rio Grande (VII)	Terence Kelshaw 4304 Carlisle Boulevard North East, Albuquerque, NM 87107-4811, USA Fax (505) 883 9048
Rochester (II)	William George Burrill 935 East Avenue, Rochester, NY 14607, USA Fax (716) 473 3195
San Diego (VIII)	Gethin Benwil Hughes 2728 Sixth Avenue, San Diego, CA 92103-6397, USA Fax (619) 291 8362
San Joaquin (VIII)	John-David Mercer Schofield 4159 East Dakota Avenue, Fresno, CA 93726, USA Fax (209) 244 4832
South Carolina (IV)	Edward Lloyd Salmon Box 20127, 126 Coming Street, Charleston, SC 294133-0127, USA Fax (803) 723 7628
(Suffragan)	William Jones Skilton address and fax as above
South Dakota (VI)	Creighton Leland Robertson 500 South Main Street, Sioux Falls, SD 57102-0914, USA Fax (605) 336 6243
Southeast Florida (IV)	Calvin Onderdonk Schofield 525 North East 15th Street, Miami, FL 33132, USA Fax (305) 375 8054
(Suffragan)	John Lewis Said address and fax as above
Southern Ohio (V)	Herbert Thompson 412 Sycamore Street, Cincinnati, OH 45202, USA Fax (513) 421 0315
(Suffragan)	Kenneth Lester Price 125 East Broad Street, Columbus, OH 43215, USA Fax (614) 461 1015
Southern Virginia (III)	Frank Harris Vest 600 Talbot Hall Road, Norfolk, VA 23505, USA Fax (804) 440 5354
(Assistant)	O'Kelley Whitaker 306 Sycamore Road, Portsmouth, VA 23707-1217, USA
Southwest Florida (IV)	Rogers Sanders Harris PO Box 491, St Petersburg, FL 33731, USA Fax (813) 821 9254
(Coadjutor)	John Bailey Lipscomb address and fax as above
Southwestern Virginia (III)	Frank Neff Powell PO Box 2279, Roanoke, VA 24009-2279, USA Fax (703) 343 9114
Spokane (VIII)	Frank Jeff Terry 245 East 13th Avenue, Spokane, WA 99202, USA Fax (509) 747 0049
Springfield (VIII)	Peter Hess Beckwith 821 South 2nd Street, Springfield, IL 62704, USA Fax (217) 525 1877
Taiwan (VIII)	John Chieh-Tsung Chien Friendship House, 1-105-7 Hangchow South Road, Taipei, Taiwan 10044, Republic of China Fax (2) 396 2014
Tennessee (IV)	Bertram Nelson Herlong 1 LeFleur Boulevard - Suite 100, 50 Vantage Way, Nashville, TN 37228-1504, USA Fax (615) 251 8010
Texas (VII)	Claude Edward Payne 3203 West Alabama Street, Houston, TX 77098, USA Fax (713) 520 5723
(Suffragans)	William Elwood Sterling address and fax as above Leopoldo Jesus Alard address and fax as above
Upper South Carolina (IV)	Dorsey Felix Henderson 1115 Marion Street, Columbia, SC 29201, USA Fax (803) 799 5119
(Assistant)	William Franklin Carr address and fax as above
Utah (VIII)	Carolyn Tanner Irish 80 South 300 East Street, PO Box 3090, Salt Lake City, UT 84110-3090, USA Fax (801) 322 5096
Vermont (I)	Mary Adelia Rosamond McLeod 5 Rock Point Road, Burlington, VT 05401-2735, USA Fax (802) 860 1562
Virgin Islands (II)	Theodore Athelbert Daniels Box 7488, St Thomas, VI 00801, USA Fax (809) 777 8485
Virginia (III)	Peter James Lee 110 West Franklin Street, Richmond, VA 23220, USA Fax (804) 644 6928
(Suffragans)	Frank Clayton Matthews address and fax as above David Colin Jones 6043 Burnside Landing Drive, Burke, VA 22015, USA Fax (703) 823 9524
Washington (III)	Ronald Haywood Haines Episcopal Church House, Mount St Alban, Washington, DC 20016, USA Fax (202) 364 6605
(Suffragan)	Jane Holmes Dixon address and fax as above
West Missouri (VII)	John Clark Buchanan PO Box 413227, Kansas City, MO 64141-3227, USA Fax (816) 471 0379
(Coadjutor)	Barry Robert Howe address and fax as above
West Tennessee (IV)	James Malone Coleman 692 Poplar Avenue, Memphis, TN 38105, USA Fax (901) 526 1555
West Texas (VII)	James Edward Folts PO Box 6885, San Antonio, TX 78209, USA Fax (210) 822 8779

(Suffragan)	Robert Boyd Hibbs address and fax as above
West Virginia (III)	John Henry Smith PO Box 5400, Charleston, WV 25361-5400, USA Fax (304) 343 3295
Western Kansas (VII)	Vernon Edward Strickland Box 2507, Salina, KS 67402-2507, USA Fax (913) 825 0974
Western Louisiana (VII)	Robert Jefferson Hargrove PO Box 2031, Alexandria, LA 71309, USA Fax (318) 442 8712
Western Massachusetts (I)	Gordon Paul Scruton 37 Chestnut Street, Springfield, MA 01103, USA Fax (413) 746 9873
Western Michigan (V)	Edward Lewis Lee 2600 Vincent Avenue, Kalamazoo, MI 49008, USA Fax (616) 381 7067
Western New York (II)	David Charles Bowman 1114 Delaware Avenue, Buffalo, NY 14209, USA Fax (716) 881 1724
Western North Carolina (IV)	Robert Hodges Johnson Box 369, Vance Avenue, Black Mountain, NC 28711, USA Fax (704) 669 2756
Wyoming (VI)	Bruce Edward Caldwell 104 South Fourth Street, Laramie, WY 82070, USA Fax (307) 742 6782

WEST AFRICA

Accra	Justice Ofei Akrofi Bishopscourt, PO Box 8, Accra, Ghana Fax (21) 669125
Bo	Samuel Sao Gbonda PO Box 21, MacRobert Street, Bo, Southern Province, Sierra Leone
Cape Coast	Kobina Adduah Quashie Bishopscourt, PO Box A233, Adisadel Estates, Cape Coast, Ghana Fax (42) 2637
Freetown	Julius Olotu Prince Lynch Bishopscourt, PO Box 128, Freetown, Sierra Leone
The Gambia	Solomon Tilewa E W Johnson Bishopscourt, PO Box 51, Banjul, The Gambia Fax (220) 229495
Guinea	*Vacant* BP 105, Conakry, Guinea Bissau, West Africa
Koforidua (Archbishop)	Robert Garshong Allotey Okine PO Box 980, Koforidua, Ghana Fax (21) 669125
Kumasi	Edmund Yeboah St Cyprian's Church House, PO Box 144, Kumasi, Ghana Fax (51) 24117
Liberia	Edward Neufville PO Box 10-0277, 1000 Monrovia 10, Liberia Fax 227579
Sekondi	Theophilus S A Annobil PO Box 85, Sekondi, Ghana Fax (21) 669125
Sunyani	Thomas A Brient PO Box 23, Sunyani, Ghana Fax (61) 7283
Tamale	Emmanuel A Arongo Bishop's House, PO Box 110, Tamale NR, Ghana Fax (71) 22849

WEST INDIES

Barbados	Rufus Theophilus Brome Leyland, Philip Drive, Pine Gardens, St Michael, Barbados, West Indies Fax 426 0871
Belize	Sylvestre Donato Romero-Palma Bishopsthorpe, Southern Foreshore, PO Box 535, Belize City, Belize Fax (2) 76898

Guyana	Randolph O George Austin House, 49 George Street, Georgetown 1, Guyana Fax (2) 64183
Jamaica	Neville Wordsworth de Souza Church House, 2 Caledonia Avenue, Kingston 5, Jamaica Fax (809) 968 0618
(Suffragans)	Herman Spence (Bishop of Kingston) Church House, 2 Caledonia Avenue, Kingston 5, Jamaica Fax 968 0618
	William A Murray (Bishop of Mandeville) PO Box 159, Mandeville, Jamaica
	Alfred C Reid (Bishop of Montego Bay) PO Box 346, Montego Bay, St James, Jamaica
Nassau and the Bahamas	Drexel Gomez Church House, PO Box N-7107, Nassau, Bahamas Fax 322 7943
North Eastern Caribbean and Aruba (Archbishop)	Orland U Lindsay Bishop's Lodge, PO Box 23, St John's, Antigua, West Indies Fax (268) 462 2090
Trinidad and Tobago	Rawle E Douglin Hayes Court, 21 Maraval Road, Port of Spain, Trinidad, West Indies Fax 628 1319
Windward Islands	Sehon S Goodridge Bishop's Court, PO Box 520, St Vincent, West Indies Fax (809) 456 2591

ZAIRE

Boga-Zaïre (Archbishop)	Patrice Byankya Njojo CAZ - Boga-Zaire, PO Box 21285, Nairobi, Kenya
Bukavu	Fidéle Balufuga Dirokpa CAZ - Bukavu, PO Box 53435, Nairobi, Kenya
Kindu	Zecharie Masimango Katanda address as above
Kisangani	Sylvestre Mugera Tibafa CAZ - Kisangani, BP 861, Kisangani, Dem Rep Congo
Nord Kivu	Methusela Musubaho Munzenda CAZ - Butembo, PO Box 21285, Nairobi, Kenya Fax (871) 166 1121
Shaba	Isingoma Kahwa CAZ - Lubumbashi, c/o United Methodist Mission, PO Box 22037, Kitwe, Zambia Fax (2) 711032

EXTRA-PROVINCIAL DIOCESES

Bermuda (Canterbury)	Alexander Ewen Ratteray Bishop's Lodge, PO Box HM 769, Hamilton HM CX, Bermuda Fax 292 5421
Costa Rica (Extra-Provincial to IX, USA)	Cornelius J Wilson Apartado 2773, 1000 San José, Costa Rica Fax (506) 253 8331
Cuba (Canterbury)	Jorge Perera Hurtado Calle 6, No 273 Vedado, Havana 4, 10400 Cuba Fax (7) 615330
§Hong Kong	Peter Kwong Bishop's House, 1 Lower Albert Road, Hong Kong Fax 2525 2537
§Kowloon East	Louis Tsui address as above Fax 2521 2199
§Kowloon West	Thomas Yee-po Soo address and fax as above
Lusitanian Church (Canterbury)	Fernando Soares Secretaria Diocesana, Apartado 392, P-4430 Vila Nova de Gaia, Portugal Fax (2) 302016

§ Also members of the Council of the Churches of East Asia

Puerto Rico (Extra-Provincial to IX, USA)	David Alvarez PO Box 902, Saint Just, Puerto Rico 00978 Fax 761 0320
Spanish Reformed Episcopal Church (Canterbury)	Carlos López-Lozano Calle Beneficencia 18, 28004 Madrid, Spain Fax (1) 594 4572
Venezuela (Extra-Provincial to IX, USA)	Orlando Guerrero Apartado 49-143, Avenida Caroni 100, Colinas de Bello Monte, Caracas 1042-A, Venezuela Fax (2) 751 3180

BISHOPS OF CHURCHES WHERE ANGLICANS HAVE UNITED WITH CHRISTIANS OF OTHER TRADITIONS

NORTH INDIA

Agra	Morris Andrews Bishop's House, St Paul's Church, 4/116-B Church Road, Civil Lines, Agra, 287007 UP, India Fax (562) 350244
Amritsar	Anand Chandu Lal 26 R B Prakash Chand Road, Amritsar 143 001, India Fax (183) 222910
Andaman and Car Nicobar Islands	Edmund Matthew Cathedral Church Compound, House No 1, Staging Post, Car Nicobar 744 301, Andaman and Nicobar Islands
Barrackpore	Brojen Malakar Bishop's Lodge, 86 Middle Road, Barrackpore, West Bengal 743 101, India
Bhopal	Manohar B Singh 7 Old Sehore Road, Indore 452 001 MP, India
Bombay	Samuel Bright Joshua St John's House, Duxbury Lane, Colaba, Bombay 400 005, India Fax (22) 202 4162
Calcutta	Dinesh C Gorai Bishop's House, 51 Chowringhee Road, Calcutta, WB 700 071, India Fax (33) 242 6340
Chandigarh	Joel Vidyasagar Mal Bishop's House, Mission Compound, Brown Road, Ludhiana 141 008, Punjab, India
Chotanagpur	Zechariah James Terom Bishop's Lodge, PO Box 1, Church Road, Ranchi 834 001, Bihar, India
Cuttack (Moderator)	Dhirendra Kumar Mohanty Bishop's House, Madhusudan Road, Cuttack 753 001, Orissa, India Fax (671) 602206
Delhi	Pritam B Santram Bishop's House, 1 Church Lane, off North Avenue, New Delhi 110 001, India
Durgapur	Onil Kumar Tirkey Bishop's House, PO Box 20, South East Railway, Bankura 722 101, West Bengal, India Fax (343) 5123
Eastern Himalayas	Gerald Augustine Andrews Bishop's House, PO Box 4, Darjeeling 734 101, West Bengal, India Fax (354) 54264
Gujarat	Vinod Kumar Mathushellah Malaviya Bishop's House, Ellis Bridge, Ahmedabad 380 006, Gujarat State, India Fax (79) 272 6561 950
Jabalpur	Sunil Cak Bishop's House, 2131 Napier Town, Jabalpur, MP 482 001, India
Kolhapur	MacDonald Claudius Bishop's House, EP School Compound, Kolhapur, Maharashtra 416 003, India Fax (231) 654832
Lucknow	Anil R Stephen Bishop's House, 25 Mahatma Gandhi Marg, Allahabad, UP 211 001, India Fax (532) 624637
Nagpur	Vinod A R Peter Cathedral House, Civil Lines, Sadar, Nagpur 440 001, Maharashtra, India Fax (712) 523089
Nasik	George A Ninan Bishop's House, Tarakur, 1 Outram Road, Ahmednagar, Maharashtra 414 001, India Fax (241) 28682
North East India	Purely Lyngdoh Bishop's Kuti, Shillong 1, Meghalaya 793 001, India Fax (364) 223155
Patna	Philip Phembuar Marandih Bishop's House, Christ Church Compound, Bhagalpur 812 001, Bihar, India Fax (641) 400314
Rajasthan	Emmanuel Christopher Anthony 62/X Savitri Girls' College Road, Civil Lines, Ajmer 305 001, Rajasthan, India
Sambalpur	Lingaraj Tandy Mission Compound, Bolangir 767 001, Orissa, India

SOUTH INDIA

Coimbatore (Bishop *in*)	William Moses Bishop's House, 204 Race Course Road, Coimbatore 641018, TN1, India
Dornakal (Bishop *in*)	A Rajarathnam Bishop's House, Cathedral Compound, Dornakal, Andhra Pradesh 506 381, India
East Kerala (Bishop *in*)	Kunnumpurathu Joseph Samuel Bishop's House, Melukavumattom 686 652, Kerala, India
Jaffna (Bishop *in*)	Subramaniam Jebanesan Bishop's House, 17 Frances Road, Wellawatte, Colombo 6, Sri Lanka Fax (1) 582015
Kanyakumari (Bishop *in*)	Messiadhas Kesari 71-A Dennis Street, Nagercoil 629 001, India Fax (4652) 25800
Karimnagar (Bishop *in*)	Sanki John Theodore Bishop's House, Mukarampura PO, Karimnagar, Andhra Pradesh 505 002, India
Karnataka Central	S Vasanthkumar Diocesan Office, 20 Third Cross, CSI Compound, Bangalore, Karnataka 560 027, India
Karnataka North (Bishop *in*) (Moderator)	Vasant P Dandin Bishop's House, Haliyal Road, Dharwad 508 008, Karnataka State, India Fax (836) 42604
Karnataka South (Bishop *in*)	Christopher L Furtado Bishop's House, Balmatta, Mangalore 575 002, India Fax (824) 422363
Krishna-Godavari (Bishop *in*)	T B D Prakasha Rao Bishop Azariah High School Compound, Vijayawada, AP 520 002, India
Madhya Kerala (Bishop *in*)	Sam Mathew Bishop's House, Cathedral Road, Kottayam 686 001, Kerala State, India
Madras (Bishop *in*)	Mazilimani Azariah Diocesan Office, PO Box 4914, Cathedral PO, Madras 600 086, TN, India
Madurai-Ramnad	Thavaraj David Eames New Mission Compound, Thirumangalam 625 706, Madurai District, Tamil Nadu, India
Medak	B Peter Sugandhar CSI Cathedral Compound, Medak, Andhra Pradesh 502 110, India Fax (40) 833151

Nandyal (Bishop *in*)	Abraham Theodore Gondi Bishop's House, RS 518 502, Kurnool District, Nandyal, Andhra Pradesh, India Fax (8514) 42255
North Kerala (Bishop *in*)	P G Kuruvilla Diocesan Office, PO Box No 104, Shoranur 679 121, Kerala State, India
Rayalaseema (Bishop *in*)	Moses Fredericks CSI Compound, Gooty 515 401, Andhra Pradesh, India
South Kerala (Bishop *in*)	Samuel Amirtham Bishop's House, LMS Compound, Trivandrum 695 033, Kerala, India Fax (471) 446859
Tirunelveli (Bishop *in*) (Deputy Moderator)	Jason S Dharmaraj Bishopstowe, Box 18, Palayamkottai, Tirunelveli, T Nadu 627 002, India Fax (462) 574525
Trichy-Tanjore (Bishop *in*)	R Paulraj PO Box 31, Tiruchirapalli 620 001, Tamil Nadu, India
Vellore (Bishop *in*)	R Trinity Baskeran Ashram Bungalow, 13 Filterbed Road, Vellore, North Arcot District 632 001, India Fax (416) 27490

BANGLADESH

Dhaka (Moderator)	Barnabas Dwijen Mondal St Thomas's Church, 54 Johnson Road, Dhaka-1, Bangladesh Fax (2) 238218
Kushtia	Michael S Baroi 94 N S Road, Thanapara, Kushtia, Bangladesh

PAKISTAN

Arabian Peninsula (Area Bishop)	Azad Marshall PO Box 3192, Gulberg-1, Lahore, Punjab 54660, Pakistan Fax (42) 5220 591
Faisalabad (Deputy Moderator)	John Samuel Bishop's House, PO Box 27, Mission Road, Gojra, Toba Tek Sing, Faisalabad, Pakistan Fax (411) 4651 2747
Hyderabad	S K Dass Church House, Jacob Road, Hyderabad 71000, Sind, Pakistan Fax (221) 780018
Karachi	*Vacant* Bishop's House, Trinity Close, Karachi 0405, Pakistan
Lahore	Alexander John Malik Bishopsbourne, Cathedral Close, The Mall, Lahore 54000, Pakistan Fax (42) 722 1270
Multan	John Victor Mall 113 Qasim Road, PO Box 204, Multan Cantt, Pakistan
Peshawar	Mano K Rumalshah St John's Cathedral, 1 Sir-Syed Road, Peshawar 25000, Pakistan Fax (521) 277499
Rawind	Samuel Azariah 17 Warris Road, PO Box 2319, Lahore 3, Pakistan Fax (42) 757 7255
Sialkot	Samuel Pervez Lal Kothi, Barah Patthar, Sialkot 2, Punjab, Pakistan Fax (432) 264828

PROVINCIAL OFFICES

From which further information may be sought

Anglican Communion Office Partnership House, 157 Waterloo Road, London SE1 8UT, UK

Australia PO Box Q190, Queen Victoria PO, Sydney, NSW, Australia 2000

Bangladesh St Thomas's Church, 54 Johnson Road, Dhaka 1100, Bangladesh

Brazil Caixa Postal 11510, Porto Alegre, RS 9 0841-970, Brazil

Burundi BP 2098, Bujumbura, Burundi

Canada 600 Jarvis Street, Toronto, Ontario, Canada, M4Y 2J6

Central Africa PO Box 769, Gaborone, Botswana

Ceylon 368/2 Bauddhaloka Mawatha, Colombo 7, Sri Lanka

England Church House, Great Smith Street, London SW1P 3NZ, UK

Indian Ocean Lot IVD 101 L ler Ambat Omisangana, Ankadifotsy, 101-Antananarivo, Madagascar

Ireland Church of Ireland House, Church Avenue, Rathmines, Dublin 6, Irish Republic

Japan 65 Yarai-cho, Shinjuku-ku, Tokyo 162, Japan

Jerusalem and the Middle East Christ Church, PO Box 75, Nazareth, Israel

Kenya PO Box 40502, Nairobi, Kenya

Korea 3 Chong-dong, Chung-ku, Seoul 100-120, South Korea

Melanesia PO Box 19, Honiara, Solomon Islands

Mexico Apartado Postal 192, Admon 4, CP 62431, Cuernavaca, Morelos, Mexico

Myanmar (formerly Burma) 140 Pyidaungsu-Yeiktha Road, Dagon PO (11191), Yangon, Myanmar

New Zealand (Aotearoa, New Zealand and Polynesia) PO Box 885, Hastings, New Zealand

Nigeria PO Box 78, Lagos, Nigeria

North India CNI, 16 Pandit Pant Marg, New Delhi 110001, India

Pakistan Cathedral Close, The Mall, Lahore 3, Pakistan

Papua New Guinea Box 673, Lae, MP, Papua New Guinea

Philippines c/o Prime Bishop of the Philippines, PO Box 10321, Broadway Centrum, 1112 Quezon City, Philippines

Rwanda BP 566, Butare, Rwanda

Scotland 21 Grosvenor Crescent, Edinburgh EH12 5EE, UK

South East Asia PO Box 347, Kuching, 93704 Sarawak, East Malaysia

South India CSI Centre, 5 Whites Road, Royapettah, Madras 600041, India

Southern Africa Bishopscourt, Claremont, 7700 South Africa

South America Casilla 6108, 11000 Montevideo, Uruguay

Sudan PO Box 110, Juba, Sudan

Tanzania PO Box 899, Dodoma, Tanzania

Uganda PO Box 14123, Kampala, Uganda

USA 815 Second Avenue, New York, NY 10017, USA

Wales 39 Cathedral Road, Cardiff CF1 9XF, UK

West Africa PO Box 8, Accra, Ghana

West Indies PO Box N-7107, Nassau, Bahamas

Zaire CAZ-Bunia, PO Box 21285, Nairobi, Kenya

DIRECTORIES OF THE ANGLICAN PROVINCES

The following provinces of the Anglican Communion are known to publish directories of their clergy. These may be ordered through Church House Bookshop, 31 Great Smith Street, London SW1P 3BN, which has information on the cost and availability of current and future editions.

Australia *The Australian Anglican Directory* Published annually
Angela Grutzner & Associates Pty Ltd, PO Box 306, Malvern, Victoria, Australia 3144

Canada *The Anglican Year Book* Published annually
Anglican Book Centre, 600 Jarvis Street, Toronto, Ontario, Canada, M4Y 2J6

Ireland *Church of Ireland Directory* Published annually
Styletype Publishing Co (Ireland) Ltd, Sheldon House, 60 Pembroke Road, Dublin 4, Irish Republic

Japan (in Japanese) *Seikokai Yearbook* Published annually
Nippon Sei Ko Kai Provincial Office, 4-21 Higashi 1-chome, Shibuya-Ku, Tokyo, Japan 150

Jerusalem and the Middle East *A Provincial Directory*
Provincial Office, Box 1248, 20 Nablus Road, Jerusalem

New Zealand *Clerical Directory* Published annually
Provincial Secretary, PO Box 885, Hastings, New Zealand

Nigeria *Nigeria Churchman's Year Book*
Church House, 29 Marina, PO Box 78, Lagos, Nigeria

Scotland *Scottish Episcopal Church Directory* Published annually
Secretary General and Treasurer, 21 Grosvenor Crescent, Edinburgh EH12 5EE

Southern Africa *Clerical Directory* Published annually
Provincial Office, Bishopscourt, Claremont, 7700 South Africa

Southern Cone of America *Directorio Provincial* Published every three years
Casilla 50675, Santiago, Chile

United States *Episcopal Clerical Directory* Published annually
Church Hymnal Corporation, 800 Second Avenue, New York, NY 10017, USA

Diocesan lists are the source of information for the Churches of Brazil, Central Africa and Ceylon. In the West Indies, the Diocese of Jamaica publishes a *Clerical Directory*.

Close links with many overseas provinces are maintained by the United Society for the Propagation of the Gospel and by the Church Mission Society, both at Partnership House, 157 Waterloo Road, London SE1 8XA (for USPG), and SE1 8UU (for CMS).

Crosslinks (formerly the Bible Churchmen's Missionary Society) at 251 Lewisham Way, London SE4 1XF also has contacts with many provinces overseas.

The South American Mission Society, serving not only that sub-continent but also the Iberian peninsula, is at Allen Gardiner House, Pembury Road, Tunbridge Wells, Kent TN2 3QU.

For the provinces not listed above, information should be sought from the provincial secretary or from dioceses. Details of other Anglican missionary societies may be found in *The Church of England Year Book*.

ADDRESSES UNKNOWN

The following are clergy whose addresses are currently unknown. Fuller details are contained in the biographical section. We should be grateful for any information to help us complete our records in respect of these clergy.

AFFLECK, Stuart John. b 47. **d** 70. Warden Pilsdon Community 80-94
ANSTICE, John Neville. b 39. **d** 71. Perm to Offic *Chich* from 80
BELL, Bryan Bland. b 07. **d** 40. rtd 72; Perm to Offic *Ex* from 81
BELL, Jeremy Aidan. b 46. **d** 82. Perm to Offic *Ex* from 83
BLUNDELL, Peter Grahame. b 61. **d** 94. Zimbabwe from 97
BOWYER, Dr Richard Astley. b 55. **d** 84. USA from 95
BURKE, Jonathan. b 53. **d** 82. R Bere Regis and Affpuddle w Turnerspuddle *Sarum* 85-92
BURTON, Frank Victor. b 10. **d** 76. Perm to Offic *Linc* from 80
BUXTON, Edward Brian. b 41. **d** 66. Perm to Offic *Chelmsf* 76-85
CALDWELL, Robert McKinley. b 20. **d** 64. USA from 97; rtd 97
CAPPER, William Alan. **d** 88. I Tamlaght O'Crilly Upper w Lower *D & R* 94-96
CHALMERS, Robert Alan. b 66. **d** 91. Bp's C Boyle and Elphin w Aghanagh, Kilbryan etc *K, E & A* 96-97
COKER, Alexander Bryan (Alex). b 48. **d** 86. C Cheam Common St Phil *S'wark* 93-94
COMBE, Edward Charles. b 40. **d** 89. USA from 94
COOKE, Charles James. b 31. **d** 56. Perm to Offic *Derby* 65-94
COTTON, Patrick Arthur William. b 46. **d** 71. rtd 95
CROSSMAN, Mrs Charmian Jeanette. b 27. **d** 91. P-in-c Thursby *Carl* 95-97
DANSKIN, William Campbell. b 35. **d** 80. R Challoch w Newton Stewart *Glas* 87-95
DUFFIELD, Ronald Bertram Charles (Ron). b 26. **d** 92. rtd 95
DURANT, Stanton Vincent. b 42. **d** 72. Adn Liv 91-93; V Stoneycroft All SS 91-93; Hon Can Liv Cathl 91-93
FARRANT, Jonathan. b 44. **d** 73. Lic to Offic *Heref* 78-80
FOX, Norman Stanley. b 39. **d** 64. V Pensnett *Lich* 91-93
FROSTICK, Paul Andrew. b 52. **d** 77
GATES, John Richard. b 47. **d** 73. V Cosby *Leic* 82-86
GHINN, Edward. b 45. **d** 74. Brazil from 96
GODFREY, Michael. b 49. **d** 72. Ind Chapl *Lich* 79-93; TV Wolverhampton 86-93
GOLDEN, Stephen Gerard. b 61. **d** 86. CF 90-94
GOLTON, Alan Victor. b 29. **d** 85. Perm to Offic *Birm* 95-96
GREEN, Stuart. b 57. **d** 85. R Bardney *Linc* 88-96
HAMILTON, Richard Alexander. b 46. **d** 85. P-in-c Tottenham H Trin *Lon* 91-96
HAMPTON, Terence Alastair Godfrey Macpherson. b 38. **d** 64. R Jersey Grouville *Win* 83-94
HARRIS, James Philip. b 59. **d** 86. V Newport St Matt *Mon* 91-96
HARRISON, Ernest Wilfrid. b 17. **d** 40. Canada from 52.
HARTLEY, Nigel Rogers. b 65. **d** 89. R Foundn of St Kath in Ratcliffe 93-94
HENSON, Ms Carolyn. b 44. **d** 87. Adult Educn and Tr Officer *Ely* 89-91
HENWOOD (née OAKLEY), Mrs Susan Mary. b 55. **d** 87. C Howell Hill *Guildf* 91-96
HERON. Alexander Francis. b 28. **d** 52. Canada from 77.
HIPPLE, Maureen Atlee. b 53. **d** 94. USA from 97
HOLDSWORTH, Ian Scott. b 52. **d** 81. P-in-c S Leigh *Ox* 84-89
HOLMES, Roger Cockburn. b 46. **d** 84. V Helmsley *York* 93-97
HOWARD, David William. b 43. **d** 67. Jamaica from 72
JAMES, Dewi Hirwaun. b 41. **d** 70. C Holyhead *Ban* 95-96
JAMES, Gareth Hugh. b 40. **d** 66. rtd 93
JARVIS, Graham Michael. b 60. **d** 91. Sweden from 94
JEFFERIES, Cecil Arthur. b 11. **d** 69. rtd 89
JENKINS, John Raymond. b 26. **d** 53. rtd 91
JONES, Ioan Wynne. b 66. **d** 91. P-in-c Glanogwen *Ban* 95-97
KESTERTON, David William. b 59. **d** 88. TV Dunstable *St Alb* 92-97; Chapl Dunstable Coll 92-97
LLOYD, Michael Francis. b 57. **d** 84. Chapl Ch Coll Cam 90-94
LOVELL, David John. b 38. **d** 60. Australia from 73
LYNN, Jeffrey. b 39. **d** 79. rtd 96
McCULLOCH, Alistair John. b 59. **d** 87. V Reading St Matt *Ox* 94-95
McINTOSH, David Henry. b 45. **d** 70. P-in-c Barnton *Ches* 94-97
MARTIN, Robin Hugh. b 35. **d** 58. rtd 93
MOUNTFORD, John. b 55. **d** 78. Australia 91-94
PARTRIDGE, Ronald Malcolm. b 49. **d** 75. Asst Chapl Gt Ormond Street Hosp for Sick Children Lon 91-97
PEARSON, Fergus Tom. b 58. **d** 92. Australia from 96
PEASTON, Canon Monroe. b 14. **d** 38. Hon Can Montreal from 66; rtd 84; USA from 84
PECK, Trevor Paul Owen. b 47. **d** 72. V Burgh le Marsh *Linc* 86-87; R Bratoft w Irby-in-the-Marsh 86-87
PHILLIPS, Andrew Graham. b 58. **d** 87. CF 92-97
✠PONNIAH, The Rt Revd Jacob Samuel. b 22. **d** 52. Miss Partner CMS from 91
PRIESTNER, Hugh. b 45. **d** 75. Chapl Stafford Distr Gen Hosp 88-91; Chapl Stafford Distr Infirmary 88-91
PRITCHARD, Miss Kathryn Anne. b 60. **d** 87. Perm to Offic *Cov* 92-95
QUINN, Mrs Helen Elizabeth. b 46. **d** 95. Hon C Old Catton *Nor* 95-96
REUSS, John Christopher Edward. b 1900. **d** 38. Canada from 52
RICHARDS, Jonathan Berry Hillacre. b 52. **d** 86. P-in-c Shebbear, Buckland Filleigh, Sheepwash etc *Ex* 96-97
ROGERS, John Iorwerth. b 17. **d** 41. rtd 87
SAUNDERS, David Anthony. b 48. **d** 78. USA from 97
SKILTON, Joseph Laurence. b 41. **d** 70. Australia from 80
STEPHENS, Simon Edward. b 41. **d** 67. Asst Chapl Menorca *Eur* from 97
STEPHENS-WILKINSON, Patricia Ann. b 45. **d** 89. NSM Machen *Mon* 89-93
STEVENSON, John. b 39. **d** 87. Israel from 95
STOCKWELL, John Nicholas. b 49. **d** 82. P-in-c Burwash Weald *Chich* 93-97
STRICKLAND (née CUTTS), Mrs Elizabeth Joan Gabrielle. b 61. **d** 90. NSM Biggin Hill *Roch* 93-96
SWALLOW, Robert Andrew (Bob). b 52. **d** 78. TV Fareham H Trin *Portsm* 90-92
THOMAS, Canon Ernest Keith. b 49. **d** 76. S Africa from 96
THOMPSON, John Wilfred. b 44. **d** 85. R Fritwell w Souldern and Ardley w Fewcott *Ox* 87-97
TILLER, Charles Edgar Gregory. b 61. **d** 89. C Crediton and Shobrooke *Ex* 93-95
TRICKETT, Stanley Mervyn Wood. b 27. **d** 66. V Shrewton *Sarum* 81-97
TYLER, Paul Graham Edward. b 58. **d** 83. V Esh *Dur* 89-92; V Hamsteels 89-92
VAN GORDER, Lloyd Franklin. b 11. **d** 73. Perm to Offic *Portsm* 79-94
VINCENT, Canon William Alfred Leslie. b 11. **d** 39. Lic to Offic *Mon* from 42; Lic to Offic *Ches* from 52
WAITE, Julian Henry. b 47. **d** 72
WALKER, Mark Robert Joseph George. b 66. **d** 92. C Larne and Inver *Conn* 92-95
WALTERS, Peter Shane. b 54. **d** 87. Colombia from 93
WARBURTON, Andrew James. b 44. **d** 69. Chapl Paris St Mich *Eur* 94-97
WESTERN, Robert Geoffrey. b 37. **d** 62. Hd Master Linc Cathl Sch 74-97; Can and Preb Linc Cathl *Linc* 74-97
WILKINSON, John Stoddart. b 47. **d** 70. Sub-Chapl HM Young Offender Inst Hewell Grange 89-90; Sub-Chapl HM Rem Cen Brockhill 89-90
WILLIAMS, Malcolm Kendra. b 34. **d** 85. Zimbabwe from 95

ORDINATIONS TO THE DIACONATE AT MICHAELMAS 1997

ADAMS, Mrs Jayne Maxine. b 57. Westhill Coll Birm CertEd78. WMMTC 94. **d** 97. NSM Cotteridge *Birm* from 97. *6A Kings Gardens, Kings Norton, Birmingham B30 1DX* Tel 0121-451 1961

ADAMS, Richard John. b 48. Leeds Univ BA70. St Alb and Ox Min Course 94. **d** 97. C N Hinksey and Wytham *Ox* from 97. *10 Rochester Place, Charlbury, Oxford OX7 3SF* Tel (01608) 811397

ATKINS, Robert Brian (Bob). b 49. CIPFA78 Open Univ BA94. St Alb and Ox Min Course 94. **d** 97. NSM Bicester w Bucknell, Caversfield and Launton *Ox* from 97. *8 Tubb Close, Bicester, Oxon OX6 8BN* Tel (01869) 253448 Mobile 0973-713149

BALL, Mrs Rita Enid. b 49. Sheff Univ LLB69. **d** 97. NSM Newbury *Ox* from 97. *42 Meyrick Drive, Newbury, Berks RG14 6SX* Tel (01635) 46705

BONHAM, Mrs Valerie. b 47. ALA94. St Alb and Ox Min Course 94. **d** 97. NSM Newbury *Ox* from 97. *St Mary's Vicarage, 14 Strawberry Hill, Newbury, Berks RG14 1XJ* Tel (01635) 40889

BOWMAN, Ivelaw Alexander. b 46. LNSM course 94. **d** 97. NSM Stockwell Green St Andr *S'wark* from 97. *16 Horsford Road, London SW2 5BN* Tel 0171-733 2309

CALLAGHAN, Michael James. b 63. Clare Coll Cam BA85. SEITE 94. **d** 97. C Blackheath Park St Mich *S'wark* from 97. *3 Willowcroft, London SE3 9HH* Tel 0181-318 7561 E-mail mikecall@netcomuk.co.uk

CAPPLEMAN, Graham Robert (Sam). b 56. Chelsea Coll Lon BSc79 Sheff Univ PhD83. ADipR92 St Alb and Ox Min Course 94. **d** 97. NSM Bedf St Mark *St Alb* from 97. *107 Dover Crescent, Bedford MK41 8QR* Tel (01234) 266952 Mobile 0836-784051 Fax 402624 E-mail sam_cappleman@hp.com

CLARKE, Nicholas John. b 57. Lon Univ BA78 Lon Inst of Educn PGCE80. Ridley Hall Cam 95. **d** 97. C Attleborough *Cov* from 97. *87 Shakespeare Drive, Whitestone, Nuneaton, Warks CV11 6NW* Tel (01203) 353068

CRAGG, Mrs Sandra Anne (Sandy). b 45. St Hugh's Coll Ox BA67. SEITE 94. **d** 97. C Kingston All SS w St Jo *S'wark* from 97. *10 Lingfield Avenue, Kingston upon Thames, Surrey KT1 2TN* Tel 0181-546 1997 Fax 541 5281

CURRIE, John Stuart. b 47. SEITE 94. **d** 97. C Chatham St Wm *Roch* from 97. *15 Oaksdene, Walderslade, Chatham, Kent ME5 9HN* Tel 0370-363876 (mobile) E-mail j.s.currie @compuserve.com

DICKINSON, Simon Braithwaite Vincent. b 34. St Alb and Ox Min Course 94. **d** 97. NSM Waddesdon w Over Winchendon and Fleet Marston *Ox* from 97. *The White House, Waddesdon, Aylesbury, Bucks HP18 0JA* Tel (01296) 651693

DOUGLAS, Richard Norman Henry (Dick). b 37. St Alb and Ox Min Course 94. **d** 97. NSM Broadmayne, W Knighton, Owermoigne etc *Sarum* from 97. *St Edmund's Vicarage, Lynch Road, Weymouth, Dorset DT4 0SJ* Tel (01305) 782408 Fax as telephone

DOYLE, Mrs Tracey Elizabeth. b 58. St Alb and Ox Min Course 94. **d** 97. NSM Winslow w Gt Horwood and Addington *Ox* from 97. *53 Spring Lane, Great Horwood, Bucks MK17 0QP* Tel (01296) 714319 Mobile 0976-980093

ELLACOTT, David. SW Minl Tr Course. **d** 97. NSM Fremington *Ex* from 97. *92 Yelland Road, Fremington, Barnstaple, Devon EX31 3EF* Tel (01271) 860843

ERRINGTON, Mrs Sarah. b 67. UEA BA90. Wycliffe Hall Ox BTh94. **d** 97. C Gateacre *Liv* from 97. *24 Lee Vale Road, Liverpool L25 3RW* Tel 0151-487 9391

FIELD, James Lewis (Jim). b 46. Open Univ BSc96 DMS79 HNC70. SEITE 94. **d** 97. NSM Chatham St Mary w St Jo *Roch* from 97. *45 Beacon Road, Chatham, Kent ME5 7BW* Tel (01634) 400371

FIFE, Miss Yvonne Holborn. b 48. SS Hild & Bede Coll Dur BA90. Cranmer Hall Dur 95. **d** 97. C Gt Aycliffe *Dur* from 97. *35 Beechfield, Newton Aycliffe, Co Durham DL5 7AX* Tel (01325) 311090

FROST, Richard. SW Minl Tr Course. **d** 97. NSM Shebbear, Buckland Filleigh, Sheepwash etc *Ex* from 97. *Shalom, Mount Raleigh Avenue, Bideford, Devon EX39 3NR* Tel (01237) 476749

GALLON, Mrs Audrey Kay. b 41. SEITE 94. **d** 97. C Gt Mongeham w Ripple and Sutton by Dover *Cant* from 97; C Eastry and Northbourne w Tilmanstone etc from 97. *14 White Acre Drive, Walmer, Deal, Kent CT14 7TP* Tel (01304) 363424

GODDARD, Derek George. b 38. St Martin's Coll Lanc BA97 CEng FIMechE FIMarE FIMgt. Cranmer Hall Dur 94 Carl and Blackb Tr Inst DipTh95. **d** 97. NSM Windermere St Mary and Troutbeck *Carl* from 97. *1 Ferney Green Drive, Bowness-on-Windermere, Cumbria LA23 3HS* Tel (01539) 442830

GOURLEY, Malcolm Samuel. b 37. MRPharmS58. NE Ord Course DipHE94. **d** 97. C Gt Smeaton w Appleton Wiske and Birkby etc *Ripon* from 97. *15 Church Garth, Great Smeaton, Yorkshire DL6 2HW* Tel (01609) 881551

GRAHAM, Ms Olivia Josephine. b 56. UEA BA84. St Alb and Ox Min Course 94. **d** 97. C Wheatley *Ox* from 97. *60 Church Road, Wheatley, Oxford OX33 1LZ* Tel (01865) 874963

GRATTON, Ms Patricia Margaret. b 46. Leeds Univ BTh94 MA96 SRN67 TCert84 CertEd88. EMMTC 89 N Ord Course 96. **d** 97. C Shipley St Pet *Bradf* from 97. *22 Hirst Wood Road, Shipley, W Yorkshire BD18 4BS* Tel (01274) 585314

GREGORY, Andrew Forsythe. b 71. St Jo Coll Dur BA92. Wycliffe Hall Ox BA96 DipMin97. **d** 97. C E Acton St Dunstan w St Thos *Lon* from 97; Asst Chapl Keble Coll Ox from 97. *4 Mall Court, 30 The Mall, London W5 2PZ* Tel 0181-566 2196

GRIFFITHS, Prof Richard Mathias. b 35. K Coll Cam BA57 MA61 PhD62 BNC Ox MA66 FKC95. Ox Min Course 89 St Alb and Ox Min Course 96. **d** 97. NSM W Woodhay w Enborne, Hampstead Marshall etc *Ox* from 97. *Tregarthen, Ravensworth Road, Mortimer West End, Reading RG7 3UD* Tel 0118-933 3729 Fax 933 3131

HADJIOANNOU, John. b 56. Cam Univ BA78 MA81. St Alb and Ox Min Course 95. **d** 97. C Linslade *Ox* from 97. *Minster Cottage, Sandford Lane, Woodley, Reading RG5 4SY* Tel 0118-944 1939 Mobile 0850-000105 Fax 944 0823 E-mail john@minster.co.uk

HARDY, Stephen John Arundell. b 49. Lon Univ DipTh74. SEITE 95. **d** 97. NSM Marden *Cant* from 97. *1 Jubilee Cottages, Goudhurst Road, Marden, Tonbridge, Kent TN12 9JT* Tel (01622) 831912

HARRIS, Stuart. b 40. St Alb and Ox Min Course 94. **d** 97. NSM Wokingham St Sebastian *Ox* from 97. *Maple Cottage, 38 The Avenue, Crowthorne, Berks RG45 6PG* Tel (01344) 761894

HINDER, Doreen Paterson. **d** 97. C Stanwix *Carl* from 97. *8 Etterby Lea Crescent, Stanwix, Carlisle CA3 9LG* Tel (01228) 33277

HINKS, Mrs Marion. SW Minl Tr Course. **d** 97. NSM Plymstock and Hooe *Ex* from 97. *52 Southland Park Road, Wembury, Plymouth PL9 0HQ* Tel (01752) 862439

HORTON, Mrs Joy. b 52. SEITE 94. **d** 97. C Dartford St Edm *Roch* from 97. *St Augustine's Vicarage, Slade Green Road, Erith, Kent DA8 2HX* Tel (01322) 333970 or 225335

JOHNSON, Michael. **d** 97. C E Greenwich *S'wark* from 97. *37 Chevening Road, London SE10 0LA* Tel 0181-858 6936

LANG, Nicholas (Nick). b 45. SEITE 94. **d** 97. NSM Beckenham St Jo *Roch* from 97. *63 St James's Avenue, Beckenham, Kent BR3 4HE* Tel 0181-650 6151

LOVERIDGE (née RODEN), Ms Joan Margaretha Holland (Jo). b 57. K Coll Lon BD78 AKC78 Ox Univ MTh98. St Alb and Ox Min Course 95. **d** 97. C Caversham St Jo *Ox* from 97. *The Vicarage, Hurst, Berks RG10 0SJ* Tel 0118-934 0017

LYONS, Graham Selby. b 29. MBE84. Open Univ BA79. LNSM course 94. **d** 97. NSM New Eltham All SS *S'wark* from 97. *56 Cadwallon Road, London SE9 3PY* Tel 0181-850 6576

McCAFFERTY, William Andrew (Andy). SW Minl Tr Course. **d** 97. NSM Lapford, Nymet Rowland and Coldridge *Ex* from 97. *37 Highfield, Lapford, Crediton, Devon EX17 6PY* Tel (01363) 83326

NASH, Paul. b 59. WMMTC 94. **d** 97. C Aston SS Pet and Paul *Birm* from 97. *68 Manor Road, Aston, Birmingham B6 6QT* Tel 0121-326 7390 E-mail 10451,252@compuserve.com

PEILOW, Lynda Elizabeth Anne. b 74. CITC BTh97. **d** 97. C Castleknock and Mulhuddart, w Clonsilla *D & G* from 97. *Alderborough, Geashill, Co Offaly, Irish Republic* Tel Tullamore (506) 43632

RAVEN, Tony. b 39. MIEE72 CEng72 Garnett Coll Lon CertEd65. St Alb and Ox Min Course 94. **d** 97. NSM Lt Berkhamsted and Bayford, Essendon etc *St Alb* from 97. *26 The Avenue, Bengeo, Hertford, Herts SG14 3DS* Tel (01992) 584505

ROBINSON, Eric Charles. **d** 97. C Carl St Cuth w St Mary *Carl* from 97. *15 The Maltings, Carlisle CA2 5SW* Tel (01228) 819307

SMITH, Mrs Corinne Anne. b 52. St Andr Univ MTh91. St Alb and Ox Min Course 95. **d** 97. C Abingdon *Ox* from 97. *72 Hanson Road, Abingdon, Oxon OX14 1YL* Tel (01235) 550946

SMITH, Jeremy John Hawthorn. b 52. Birm Univ BSc73. Carl and Blackb Tr Inst 94. **d** 97. C Long Marton w Dufton and w Milburn *Carl* from 97. *10 Castle View Road, Appleby, Cumbria CA16 6HH* Tel (01768) 352786

SMITH, John Sydney. **d** 97. C Arthuret *Carl* from 97; C Nicholforest and Kirkandrews on Esk from 97. *The Jays, 3 White House, Walton, Brampton, Carlisle CA8 2DJ* Tel (016977) 41114

SMITH, Mrs Susan Jennifer (Sue). b 52. MITD90 MIPD94 DipTM90. St Alb and Ox Min Course 94. **d** 97. C Ascot Heath

Ox from 97. *11 Maple Close, Little Sandhurst, Berks GU47 8HX* Tel (01252) 875489 Mobile 0589-244174 Fax as telephone

SOWDEN, Charles William Bartholomew. b 47. DipADO68. Local Minl Tr Course 90 LNSM course 96. **d** 97. NSM Saxonwell *Linc* from 97. *River View, 7 The Meadows, Long Bennington, Newark, Notts NG23 5EL* Tel (01400) 281596

SOWDEN, Geoffrey David. b 57. Kingston Poly BA79. Wycliffe Hall Ox DipMin95. **d** 97. C Ware Ch Ch *St Alb* from 97. *10 Cromwell Road, Ware, Herts SG12 7SZ* Tel (01920) 467918

STACE, Michael John. b 44. Open Univ BA80 BEng MIMgt. SEITE 94. **d** 97. C Cant St Dunstan w H Cross *Cant* from 97. *124 St Stephen's Road, Canterbury, Kent CT2 7JS* Tel (01227) 451169 Mobile 0831-174900 Fax as telephone

STEVENSON, Miss Pamela Mary. b 35. Lon Univ CQSW74. LNSM course 94. **d** 97. NSM Mitcham Ascension *S'wark* from 97. *7 Robin Hood Close, Mitcham, Surrey CR4 1JN* Tel 0181-764 8331 Mobile 0402-928204

STILL, Mrs Gill. SW Minl Tr Course. **d** 97. NSM Peter Tavy, Mary Tavy, Lydford and Brent Tor *Ex* from 97. *2 North Park, Brentor, Tavistock, Devon PL19 0LY* Tel (01822) 810489

STRANGE, Michael Paul (Mike). b 46. Univ of Wales (Ban) BSc67 MSc71. SEITE 94. **d** 97. C Clapham TM *S'wark* from 97. *33 Ilminster Gardens, London SW11 1PJ* Tel 0171-978 4519 or 228 2086

STRUTT, Peter Edward. b 40. St Alb and Ox Min Course 94. **d** 97. NSM Penn Street *Ox* from 97. *59 King's Ride, Tyler's Green, High Wycombe, Bucks HP10 8BP* Tel (01494) 812418

TALLON, Jonathan Robert Roe. b 66. Rob Coll Cam BA88 Cam Univ MA92. St Jo Coll Nottm BTh94. **d** 97. NSM Bury St Jo w St Mark *Man* from 97. *St Mark's House, 150 Walmersley Road, Bury, Manchester BL9 6LL* Tel 0161-764 6928

TAYLOR, Mrs Maureen. b 36. Lon Bible Coll BTh90 MA94. **d** 97. NSM Borehamwood *St Alb* from 97. *57A Loom Lane, Radlett, Herts WD7 8NX* Tel (01923) 855197

THOMAS, Nigel Bruce. b 63. St Jo Coll Nottm BD. **d** 97. C Millom *Carl* from 97. *24 Salthouse Road, Millom, Cumbria LA18 5AD*

THOMPSON, Ian David. b 51. Hull Univ BSc72. N Ord Course 94. **d** 97. C Blackley St Andr *Man* from 97. *54 Tweedlehill Road, Higher Slackley, Manchester M9 8LG* Tel 0161-740 6774

THOMPSON, Patricia. b 60. SRN. NE Ord Course 94. **d** 97. NSM Sunderland St Chad *Dur* from 97. *11 Friarsfield Close, Chapelgarth, Sunderland SR3 2RZ* Tel 0191-522 7911

TOPLEY, Mrs Caren Teresa. b 59. Avery Hill Coll BEd81. SEITE 94. **d** 97. C Arlesey w Astwick *St Alb* from 97. *3 Sears Close, Clifton, Shefford, Beds SG17 5HG* Tel (01462) 816307

TUNNICLIFFE, Mrs Siv. b 33. Stockholm Univ MPhil58. St Alb and Ox Min Course 94. **d** 97. NSM Wingrave w Rowsham, Aston Abbotts and Cublington *Ox* from 97. *Baldway House, Wingrave, Aylesbury, Bucks HP22 4PA* Tel (01296) 681374 Fax as telephone

TURPIN, Raymond Gerald. b 35. LNSM course 94. **d** 97. NSM Brockley Hill St Sav *S'wark* from 97. *60 Bankhurst Road, London SE6 4XN* Tel 0181-690 6877

WALTON, Luke. b 64. Leeds Univ LLB87. Cranmer Hall Dur BA94. **d** 97. C Didsbury St Jas and Em *Man* from 97. *99 Mellington Avenue, East Didsbury, Manchester M20 5NF* Tel 0161-445 9758

WELTERS, Mrs Elizabeth Ann (Liz). b 49. Bris Univ BSc70 Reading Univ PGCE71. St Alb and Ox Min Course 94. **d** 97. NSM Aylesbury w Bierton and Hulcott *Ox* from 97. *235 Bicester Road, Aylesbury, Bucks HP19 3BE* Tel (01296) 21200

WESTHAVER, George. **d** 97. C Cherry Hinton St Andr *Ely* from 97. *39 Eland Way, Cherry Hinton, Cambridge CB1 4XQ*

WILD, Alan James. b 46. LNSM course 94. **d** 97. NSM Walworth St Pet *S'wark* from 97. *67 Liverpool Grove, London SE17 2HP* Tel 0171-708 1216

WILLIAMS, Hugh Marshall. b 38. Lon Univ MB, BS62 FRCS70. St Alb and Ox Min Course 95. **d** 97. NSM Lt Compton w Chastleton, Cornwell etc *Ox* from 97. *7 Rivington Glebe, Little Compton, Moreton-in-Marsh, Glos GL56 0TD* Tel (01608) 674563 or (01484) 428392 Mobile 0378-923018 Fax (01484) 428392

WILSON, Stuart. SW Minl Tr Course. **d** 97. NSM Monkokehampton *Ex* from 97. *Red Spider Cottage, Bratton Clovelly, Okehampton, Devon EX20 4JD* Tel (01837) 87248 Mobile 0831-407345

WOOKEY, Mrs Frances Anne. b 52. ACII73. W of England Minl Tr Course 94. **d** 97. C Glouc St Jas and All SS *Glouc* from 97. *16 Derby Road, Gloucester GL1 4AE* Tel (01452) 308951 Mobile 0589-221631 E-mail fwookey@fides.demon.co.uk

CLERGY WHO HAVE DIED SINCE THE LAST EDITION

A list of clergy who have died since 31 July 1995, when the compilation of the 1995/96 edition was completed. The month and year of death (if known) are recorded with each entry.

ABBOTT, Leslie Leonard 08/96
ADAMS, Arthur White 03/97
ADAMS, Douglass Arthur 11/96
ADAMS, John Peregrine 11/95
ADAMS, Richard 09/95
ADLINGTON, Kenneth Leonard 11/95
AGLEN, Elizabeth Senga 04/97
AITCHISON, John Frederick 06/97
ALBANY, Edric George 11/96
ALLAN, Arthur Ashford 12/96
ALLCOCK, David 02/97
ALLEN, Bruce Owen 08/97
ALLSOPP, Edmund Gibson 09/95
AMES, Henry George 12/95
ANDERSON, Thomas 08/97
ANDREWS, Alfred Vincent 01/96
ANDREWS, Walford Brian 08/97
ANNELY, Maurice James Leonard 01/96
ANSTEY, Christopher Robin Paul 06/97
ASHCROFT, Lawrence 05/96
ASHFOLD, Sidney Sayer 10/95
AUSTERBERRY, Sidney Denham 03/96
AWDRY, Wilbert Vere 03/97
AWRE, Edward Francis Wintour 05/97
BADHAM, Herbert William 04/96
BAGNALL, John Thomas 07/97
BAILEY, Ronald George Bainton 05/97
BAILEY, Simon Paul 11/95
BAILLIE, John Launcelot 12/96
BAILY, Rodney Alexander 12/95
BALES, Charles Noel 10/96
BALL, Albert Bernard 12/96
BALL, Michael Gordon 07/96
BARDELL, Frank Stanley 06/96
BARDSLEY, Edwin Roy 06/97
BARFORD, Valerie Anne 07/97
BARKER, Donald Charles 10/95
BARKER, John Frederic Waller 04/96
BARLOW, Arthur Stanley 11/95
BARNARD, Harold Reginald 03/97
BARNBY, Bertram Louis 11/96
BARNES, John Kenneth 02/97
BARR JOHNSTON, Charles Walter 01/96
BARRETT, John Alan Gardiner 07/96
BARRETT, John Edward 12/96
BARTON, Alfred Ernest 02/97
BARTON, Sydney Gerald 03/96
BASTIN, Edward James 04/96
BATE, Bernard Percival 06/97
BATES, Wilfred Abel 09/95
BAYLEY, Barbara Alice 09/96
BAYLISS, Joan Edith 12/96
BAYLISS, Maurice Selwyn 04/96
BEALL, John 03/97
BEEVOR, Michael Branthwayt 02/96
BELL, Derek Arthur 02/96
BELLAIRS-COX, Diana Geraldine 03/97
BELOE, Archibald John Martin 11/95
BENNETT, Dennis Stanley 04/96
BENTINCK, Richard 03/97
BENTLEY, Geoffrey Bryan 09/96
BESS, Cyril Henry George 11/95
BEST, Frank Milner 03/97
BEYNON, Sidney James 08/96
BIGBY, John Harman 04/97
BILLINGHURST, Peter John 04/96
BIRD, Archibald Brian 10/95
BISHOP, Arthur Jack 09/95
BISHOP, Malcolm Geoffrey 02/97
BISHOP, Mark Wreford 04/96
BLACKBURN, Donald 11/96
✠BLACKBURNE, Hugh Charles 10/95
BLADES, Joseph Henry 03/96
BLAIN, Alexander Francis John 12/96
BLORE, Robert William 04/96
BOARDMAN, William (Bill) 05/96
BODDY, William Kenneth 05/97
BOLLOM, David 03/97
BOLSIN, Cyril Edward 01/97
BOLTON, William 11/96
BONE, Trevor Hubert 05/97
✠BOOTH-CLIBBORN, Stanley Eric Francis 03/96
BOOTY, John Robert 12/95
BOUNDS, John Henry 12/96
BOURNE, Michael 03/96
BOWDEN, Frank James 03/96
BOWEN, Philip Jackson 07/96
BOYCE, Kenneth 06/96
BRADSHAW, Gordon George 09/96
BRANDON, Dennis Ralph 04/97
BRANDON, Ernest Arthur 12/95
BRANDON, Owen Rupert 03/96
BRANDWOOD, Herbert 02/97
BRANSON, Charles Stanley 05/97
BRASNETT, Leslie Stanley 06/97
BRAZINGTON, David Albert 05/97
BREAY, John 03/96
BREUKELMAN, Stephen Peter 02/97
BREWSTER, Lester Arnold 03/96
BRIDLE, Reginald 12/95
BRIGGS, John Arthur 06/97
BRISCOE, Henry Ellis 05/96
BRITTON, Basil 08/96
BROOKER, David George 02/97
BROOME, Gordon Alty 11/95
BROWN, Alexander Thomas 03/97
BROWN, Arthur Henry 08/96
BROWN, Arthur William Neville 01/97
BROWN, Cyril James 01/97
BROWN, Shelagh Margaret 06/97
BROWNE, Cyril Theodore Martin 07/96
BRUCE, Lewis Stewart 08/96
BRUNDRITT, Cyril 10/96
BRYAN, Charles Rigney 01/97
BRYANT, Max Gordon 05/97
BUCKLEY, Basil Foster 12/95
BUCKLEY, Wyndham Awdry 05/97
BUCKS, Michael William 07/97
BUDGETT, Robert Brackenbury 07/96
BULL, Frank Spencer 10/96
BULL, Robert Humphrey 10/96
BULLIVANT, Ronald 09/95
BURBIDGE, Edward Humphrey 12/96
BURGESS, Colin 09/96
BURGESS, James Graham 07/97
BURGOYNE, Edward Geoffrey 02/96
BURNE, Wilfrid Durnford Elvis 03/97
BURROWS, Leonard Ernest 06/97
BURTON, Cecil John 02/96
BURTON, Geoffrey Robert William 08/96
BURTON, Harold Alban 02/97
BUTCHER, Francis Walter Lowndes 05/96
BUTLER, Sidney 08/97
BUTLER, William Hamilton Arthur 10/95
CAINE (née BALDWIN), Joyce Gertrude 12/95
CALDERBANK, Geoffrey Randall 04/97
CAMM, Joseph Arnold 01/97
CAMPBELL, Nelson James 08/97
CANNING, Richard Dandridge 11/95
CARBUTT, George Maurice 11/96
CARLILE, Edward Wilson 06/96
CARTER, Hector Thomas 04/97
✠CARTWRIGHT, Edward David 04/97
CARTY, Hilton Manasseh 10/95
CASHMORE, Cyril 02/96
CASTERTON, Michael John 08/97
CASTLE, Charles 07/97
CATO, Percy William Frederick 01/97
CHALLIS, James Dobb 12/96
CHAPPELL, Henry Pegg 05/97
CHARLES, John Hugo Audley 04/96
CHARLTON, Colin 03/97
CHASE, Frank Selby Mason 11/95
CHEAL, Kenneth Herbert 03/96
CHOULES, Edward Frank 09/95
CLARK, Charles Gordon Froggatt 11/96
CLARK, Hugh Lockhart 11/96
CLARKE, John Cecil 06/96
CLARKE, Royston James 08/97
CLAYTON, Michael John 03/97
CLAYTON, Wilfred 08/96
CLOUGH, Harry 07/97
COATES, Raymond Frederick William 03/96
COATES, Robert James 08/97
COATHAM, Sydney 11/95
✠COCKIN, George Eyles Irwin 11/96
COHEN, John Arthur 07/96
COLE, John Wilfrid 11/96
COLE, Melvin George Merriman 01/97
COLE, Norman George 05/97
COLE, Ronald Berkeley 07/96
✠COLIN, Gerald Fitzmaurice 12/95
COLLETT, Maurice John 05/97
COLLIN, Anthony Garth 02/96
COLLISHAW, Arthur Beecroft 06/97
COLLYER, John Gordon Llewellyn 12/96
COLQUHOUN, Frank 04/97
COMPTON, Frank Edward 05/96
CONWAY, Reginald Henry 07/97
COOKE, Samuel 02/96
COON, Clayton Hollis 12/96
COOPER, Christopher 07/97
COOPER, George Frank 11/95
COOPER, Leslie Martin 02/97
CORNWALL, John Whitmore 12/96
CORREY, William Henry 10/95
COSSAR, John Robert Mackenzie 04/96
COTGROVE, Norman James 06/97
COULING, Albert James 06/97
COULSON, Robert Gustavus 12/95
COVE, Tom Griffiths William 01/96
COX, William Arthur Moncrieff 10/95
COYLE, Matthew Ernest 12/96
CRANE, Bryant Frederick Francis 08/96
CRANE, Robert Bartlett 02/96
CRANSTON, Robert William 10/96
CRAWFORD, Arthur Edward 10/95
CRAWSHAW, Charles Barritt 08/96
CRINGLE, William Edward James 08/97
CRITCHLEY, Ronald John 06/96
CRUST, John Allen 09/96

CRUTTWELL, Norman Edward Garry 10/95
CRYER, Percival 12/96
CUMMINGS, George Osmond 02/97
CUTLER, Francis Bert 12/95
✠CUTTS, Richard Stanley 04/97
DALLING, Antony Fraser 09/96
DALTON, Lawrence Richard 02/96
DANIEL, Isaac Thomas 06/96
DANIELS, Hubert Frederick 03/96
DARE, Charles Gilbert Francis 10/96
DARLINGTON, David John 06/96
DAVEY, William Edwin 01/97
DAVIES, Anthony William (Tony) 04/97
DAVIES, Arthur Cecil Francis 03/96
DAVIES, John Rees 06/97
DAVIES, Joseph Henry 10/96
DAVIES, Joseph Thomas 10/95
DAVIES, Ronald 02/96
DAVIES, Tommy 09/96
DAVIS, Allan 08/97
DAVIS, Ivor Leslie 05/96
DAVIS, James Raymond 03/97
DAVIS, Kenneth Gordon 10/96
DAWKINS, Cuthbert Howard 05/97
DAWSON, George Cuming 10/95
DAWSON, John Thomas Merrilees 09/95
DAY, Fergus William 03/96
DEACON, Edwin William Frederick 06/97
DEAN, Maurice 02/97
DELIGHT, Paul Charles 02/96
DENHOLM, Edward Godfrey Denholm 11/95
DEWAR, Michael Willoughby 11/96
DIAMOND, Gordon Ernest 12/95
DICKINSON, John Frederick 02/96
DICKINSON, Matthew Lewis 10/96
DINGLE, John Rodger 11/95
DIXON, Guy Kenneth 05/97
DOBBS, John Hedley 09/97
DOBSON, Robert William 04/96
DOCKRELL, George Thomas 12/96
DODD, Walter Herbert 01/96
DONALDSON, John Colvin 09/95
DOUGLAS, Robert Vernon 04/96
DOWMAN, John Frederick 04/96
DOWN, Wilfred Samuel 07/97
DRAKE-BROCKMAN, Archibald David 03/97
du HEAUME, Cecil Cabot 03/97
DUCKER, Vere Townshend 03/96
DUFF, Harold Patterson 08/95
DUGDALE, Dennis 03/97
DUNCAN, George Ballie 04/97
DUNCAN, Harold Norton 11/95
DUNFORD, Evelyn Cecil Braley 01/96
DUNN, John Samuel 03/97
DUNNING, George Henry John 11/95
EADE, Stephen David 02/96
EAGLES, Anthony Arthur 04/97
EASTWOOD, Irvine Thomas 02/96
EDE, Albert Alfred 04/96
EDMONDS, John Herbert 03/96
EDMONDS, Richard Henry 12/95
EDWARDS, Jonathan Gilbert 10/95
EDWARDS, Stephen Zachary 01/96
EDWARDS, William Emrys 01/96
ELIOT, Peter Charles 12/95
EPPINGSTONE, Rudolph Oscar Herbert 05/97
EVANS, David Eifion 05/97
EVANS, David Thomas Pugh 10/96
✠EVANS, Edward Lewis 12/96
EVANS, Elwyn Thomas 12/95
EVANS, Evan Austin 01/96
EVANS, Hugh Arfon 11/95
EVANS, Hywel Victor 10/95
EVANS, John Mascal 02/96
EVANS, Kenneth Percy 10/96
EVANS, Kenwyn Harries Price 07/96
EVANS, Percy 06/97
EVANS, Thomas Eric 08/96
EYRES, Leslie 07/96
FAIR, James Alexander (Lex) 11/95
FARMER, Kenneth William 02/97
FAUNCH, Paul 09/95
FEARN, Hugh 06/97
FEDDEN, Patrick Vincent 06/96
FERGUSON, James Paterson 10/95
FERLEY, John Harold 10/95
FERNSBY, Jack 01/96
FISHER, Ernest George Reginald 01/97
FISHER, John Bertie 03/97
FISHER, John Douglas Close 12/96
FLETCHER, Timothy 09/96
FLOWERDAY, Edward Arthur 01/96
FLOWERDEW, George Douglas Hugh 01/97
FOLLAND, Ronald George 01/97
FOOTITT, John Michael 01/97
FOOTTIT, John Guy 02/97
FORD, Douglas William Cleverley 05/96
FORD, John 06/96
FORDER, Harry Walter 10/95
FORSTER, Brian John 08/96
FOSTER, Phillip Deighton 02/97
FOTHERGILL, Leslie Gurth 02/97
FOWKE. Walter Henry 08/97
FOWLES, Peter 08/96
FOX, Joseph Denis 11/96
FOX, Michael Storrs 02/96
FOXCROFT, James 10/96
FRANCIS, Kenneth Edgar 08/95
FRANKHAM, Harold Edward 01/96
FRANKLAND, John Ashlin 11/95
FRANKLIN, Arthur Harrington 03/96
FRANKLIN, Kenneth Douglas 10/95
FRANKS, Dennis Leslie 03/97
FRAYNE, Derek Arthur Vivian 01/96
FREEMAN, Douglas Charles 01/97
FROST, Thomas Laurence 05/96
FRY, David John 10/95
FRYER, Kenneth Wesley 02/96
FUSSELL, Laurence Walkling 07/96
GALE, Edwin Donald 08/96
GARDINER, Arthur John 04/97
GARDINER, John Kingsmill 05/97
GARDNER, Christopher John 08/97
GARNETT, Joseph William 08/97
GARWELL, John Arthur 01/96
GASKILL, Ernest Raymond 01/96
GELL, Reginald Arthur Patrick 04/97
GENOWER, Arthur Herbert 02/96
GEORGE, William Havard 02/97
GERRARD, Brian James 03/97
GETHYN-JONES, John Eric 11/95
GIBBARD, Sydney Mark 02/97
GIBBS, Roderick Harold 03/96
GIBSON, Alan Gordon 10/96
GICK, Alan Gladney 10/96
GILDING, Richard Herbert 12/95
GILLIES, Eric Robert 09/96
GILLINGHAM, Peter Llewellyn 04/96
GILMORE, Norman 03/96
GIRLING, William Havelock 04/96
GIVEN, John Thornton 11/96
GLEED, Roy Edward 06/97
GODFREY, Robert Bernard 10/95
GODWIN, Noel 05/97
GOODWIN, Deryck William 03/97
GORIN, Walter 01/97
GOSS, Arthur John Knill 06/96
GOUGE, Frank 12/95
GOULD, Jack 04/97
GOW, William Connell 10/96
GOWER, Peter Charles Gwynne 10/96
GOWING, John Ellis 06/97
GRAVES, Eric Arthur 02/97
GRAY, Christopher John 08/96
GRAY, Christopher John 05/97
GRAY, David Kenneth 06/97
GRAY, George Francis Selby 04/96
GREATHEAD, Edwin Bateson 11/95
GREEN, Charles Clisby 05/96
GREEN, David John 01/96
GREEN, Leslie James 01/97
GREEN, Nicholas Eliot 02/96
GREENING, Nigella May 03/97
GREENUP, Basil William 07/97
GREER, John Edmund 08/96
GRESSWELL, George Gilbert 09/95
GRIFFIN, Robert Maurice 10/96
GRIFFITHS, Evan David 11/95
GRIFFITHS, George Francis 12/96
GRIFFITHS, Jack 04/96
GRIFFITHS, Thomas Elwyn 01/97
GWILLIAM, Oswald Neol 02/97
HABGOOD, John Gerald Peace 05/96
HALE, Richard Laurence 01/96
HALFORD, Harry William 03/97
HALL, John Wintour 02/97
HALLETT, Ronald Walter 10/96
HAMER, Andrew Frank 01/96
HAMILTON, James 03/97
HAMMOND, James Francis 03/97
HANSCOMBE, Derek George 06/96
HARDAKER, Leonard 12/95
HARDCASTLE, Richard 05/97
HARDIE, Archibald George 02/97
HARPER, Paul 10/95
HARRIS, Basil George 08/96
HARRIS, Charles Edwin Laurence 05/96
HARRIS, Donald Bertram 01/96
HARRIS, Leslie Ernest 03/97
HARRIS, Robert William 02/97
HARRIS, William Ernest 06/96
HARRISON, Walter Edward 01/96
HARROD, Victor Ralph (Vic) 10/96
HARTIN, James 08/96
HARTLESS, Gordon Frederick James 09/96
HARVEY, Frank Chivas 03/97
HARVEY, Leslie Francis 01/96
HARVEY, Oliver Douglas 11/95
HARVEY, Peter Harold Noel 02/96
HARVEY, Stephen George Kay 11/95
HARWOOD, Leslie Thomas Prosser 09/96
HAWKEN, Michael Vaughan 12/95
HAWKINS, Arthur Herbert 01/97
HAWKINS, David Frederick Cox 01/97
HAYMAN, Perceval Ecroyd Cobham 05/97
HAYNES, Kenneth Gordon 02/96
HAYTER, John Charles Edwin 09/95
HAYWOOD, Frank 02/96
HEAP, Edward Jocelyne Fortrey 08/97
HEARN, Thomas Michael 02/96
HEATHCOTE, Edgar 08/97
HEATON, Eric William 08/96
HEATON-RENSHAW, Squire Heaton 03/97
HENCKEN, Alfred David 12/96
✠HENDERSON, George Kennedy Buchanan 09/96
HENNELL, Michael Murray 08/96
HENRY, Trevor 02/97
HERBERT, John William 11/95
HERITAGE, Thomas Charles 09/95
HERRETT, Graham 03/97
HESKETH, John Arthur 01/97
HEYGATE, Jack Lincoln 08/97
HEYWOOD, John 03/96
HEYWOOD-WADDINGTON, Roger 07/97
HICKIN, Leonard Charles 12/96
HILES, Douglas Arthur 05/96
HILL, Raymond William 10/95
HILL, Sidney John 11/95
HINCHLIFF, Peter Bingham 10/95
HINDLEY, Godfrey Talbot 10/96
HINGLEY, Bernadette 10/95
HIPWELL, Trevor Senior 09/95
HIRST, Roland Geoffrey 08/96
HISCOX, Edward 10/95
HODKIN, Hedley 12/95
HOFMEESTER, Adrian Sidney 05/96

HOLDEN, Jack Hatherley 02/96
HOLDEN, Richard Davis 04/96
HOLEHOUSE, Ernest William 05/97
HOLLAND, Jack Newton Charles 06/97
HOLLINS, Peter Charles 02/96
HOLLINSHEAD, Cyril Wyndham 10/96
HOLMES, George Henry 01/97
HOLTAM, Ralph 10/96
HONEYBALL, Mark George 04/96
✠HOOK, Ross Sydney 06/96
HOPKINS, Aubrey Lionel Evan 11/95
HOPKINS, Reginald Evan 01/97
✠HORAN, Forbes Trevor 05/96
HORWOOD, Thomas Gilbert 12/95
HOSKINS, James Paul 11/95
HOUGH, John Francis 04/96
HOULDEN, Kenneth Harry 09/95
HOWARD, Alban Caldicott Morton 09/95
HOWARTH, Benjamin Wrigley 12/95
HOWARTH, Gerald Simeon 12/96
HOWDEN, Arthur Travis 08/97
HOWE, Alfred William 10/96
HOWELL-EVERSON, Douglas Norman 01/97
HOWITT, Alan John 02/97
HOWSON, David James 11/95
HUDSON, Edmund John 08/97
HUDSON, Thomas Bernard 08/97
HUELIN, Gordon 02/97
HUGHES, David Harwood 08/97
HUGHES, Evan Thomas 02/96
HUMBLE, Joseph Francis 02/96
HUNT, Jessie 01/97
HURLEY, Patrick Norman 04/96
HURST, John Wilton 11/96
HUTCHINSON, Charles William Aldersey 05/96
IBALL, Charles Herbert 05/96
IBALL, Glyn 01/96
ILIFF, Hugh Graham 01/96
IRESON, Arthur Stanley (John) 12/95
IRVINE, Yvonne Patricia 08/96
IRWIN, Alexander John 09/95
IRWIN, Francis William 06/96
ISAAC, Philip Davies 02/97
JACKSON, Hubert Edwyn Alston 03/97
JACKSON, Michael James 10/95
JACKSON, Neil Lawrence 03/96
JAMES, Alan Raymond 06/96
JAMES, Billie 07/97
JAMES, Edmund Pollard 07/96
JAMES, Martyn Howard 11/95
JARVIS, Kenneth Eric 09/95
JARVIS, Wilfrid Harry 03/97
JARVIS, William Grantham 12/95
JEFFERY, Robert Michael 07/96
JELLY, James Hugh 12/95
JENKINS, John Alfred Morgan 11/96
JENKINS, Thomas Edward 08/96
JENNINGS, Francis Kingston 01/97
JEROME, Charles Stephen 07/97
JERVIS, Clement Frank Cooper 08/97
JOHN, Daniel Francis 01/96
JOHNSON, Harold Everard 03/97
JOHNSON, Kenneth Reginald 01/96
JOHNSON, Thomas Wyndham Page 06/96
JOHNSTON, Albert Richard 04/97
JOHNSTON, George Ralph Harden 10/95
JOHNSTON, Walter Barr 09/96
JONES, Arthur Howard Glyn (Tim) 03/96
JONES, Arthur Kenneth Hughes 12/96
JONES, Arthur Leslie 10/96
JONES, Gareth Thomas 12/95
JONES, Gordon Rowland 09/96
JONES, Hywel Tudor 10/96
JONES, James Morgan 07/97
JONES, John Jenkin 07/96
JONES, Ronald Albert 12/95
JONES, Thomas Jenkin 10/96
JONES, Thomas Madoc 10/95
JONES, Thomas William Warren 04/96
JONES, Walter 12/96
JONES, Warwick 06/96
JONES, William Hugh 01/97
JONES-EVANS, Thomas Dewi Theodore 04/97
KARNEY, Gilbert Henry Peter 05/96
KEATES, Frederick 10/95
KEE, David 05/96
KEEN, Charles William Ernest 09/95
KELLY, John Norman Davidson 03/97
KEMP, Allan James 02/96
KEMP, Michael Rouse 08/97
KENDALL, Cosmo Norman 03/96
KENNEDY, Brian McMahon 12/96
KENNEDY, John Wilkinson 08/97
KESTELL-CORNISH, Geoffrey 12/96
KILPIN, Stanley Leonard 08/96
KING, Thomas George 07/96
KITCHEN, Harold Malcolm 12/96
KNIGHT, Alan Keith 01/96
KNIGHT, Herbert John 10/96
KNOWLES, John 11/95
LACEY, Clifford George 02/97
LAING, James 07/96
LANGDON, Eric 08/95
LAURENCE, William Gregory (Bill) 09/96
LAVENDER, Cyril Norman 12/96
LAW, Timothy Robert Kelway 10/96
LAWTON, John Stewart 01/96
LEACH, William Howard 09/95
LEAK, David 02/96
LEATHLEY, Hubert Brian 03/96
LEE, Francis George (Frank) 10/95
LEE, Reginald Wilfred 02/97
LEWIS, Christopher Thomas Samuel 01/97
LEWIS, David Austin 05/96
LEWIS, David Gareth 05/97
LEWIS, Peter Graham 12/96
LEWIS, Thomas James 03/97
LIDDON, Alfred James 10/95
LILLEY, John 01/96
LINN, John David Alan 11/95
LISTER, Frederick William 08/97
LLEWELLIN DAVIES, Lawrence John David 05/96
LLOYD, Glenys Elizabeth Barrett 09/97
LLOYD, Rex Edward Ambrose 04/96
LLOYD, Samuel 04/97
LLOYD-JONES (formerly JONES), Thomas (Tom) 10/96
LOASBY, Edgar Harold 10/95
LOVEJOY, James Allan 10/95
LOVELL, Frederick Arthur 09/96
LYNN, Edward Brown 10/95
LYTH, Richard Francis 01/97
McARDLE, Thomas 07/96
MACARTNEY, William Horne 07/96
McCAY, Alexander Wilson Michael 08/97
McCLATCHIE, Donald William 10/95
McDONALD, James Stewart 06/97
MACDONALD-STEELE, Arthur Henry 09/95
McDOWELL, Charles 01/97
McGOWAN, James Rutherford 07/97
MACKENZIE, Alan George Kett Fairbairn 03/97
MACKEY, William John Noel 02/96
McKINNEY, Richard William Alexander 11/96
MACLURE, Andrew Seaton 09/96
MADDOCK, Eric John 08/96
MADDOCK, Norman 07/97
MADDOX, David Morgan 01/97
MALE, John 07/97
MALLETT, Peter 06/96
MANN, David Peter 03/97
MANN, Robert Francis Christopher Stephen 10/96
MANSEL, James Seymour Denis 09/95
MANTON, Peter Geoffrey Kevitt 03/97
MARKHAM, David Christopher 12/96
MARKHAM, John William 04/97
MARSH, Bazil Roland 05/97
MARSH, Peter Derek 03/96
MARSHALL, Arthur 04/96
MARSHALL-TAYLOR, Aubrey 03/97
MARTIN, John 05/96
MARTIN, John William 11/95
MARTINSON, Peter Stephen Douglas 10/96
MASON, David John 04/97
MASSEY, Frederick 04/97
MATTHEWS, Brian Benjamin 06/97
MEED, Henry Robert (Harry) 12/95
MELLOR, Robert Frederick 02/97
MERCHANT, William Moelwyn 04/97
MEREDITH, Claison Charles Evans 05/96
MESSER, Ralph Edwin 12/95
MICHELL, Jocelyn Ralph Stamerham 03/96
MILLER, John Stephen Corfield 01/97
MILLER, Kenneth Huitson 11/96
MILLS, Clifford James Holden 11/96
MILLS, John 04/96
MINSHALL, Neville David 09/97
MINTER, Richard Arthur 03/97
MINTON, Richard Reginald 12/95
MITCHELL, Wilfred Christopher 07/96
MOFFATT, Percy Elliott 05/97
MONCUR, Henry Alexander 12/96
MOOR, Maurice Albert Charles 12/95
MOORE, Ronald Spencer 07/96
MORGAN, Bernard Spencer Trevor 08/96
MORGAN, Edgar Francis Andrew 02/97
MORLEY, Leonard 09/96
✠MORRELL, James Herbert Lloyd 03/96
MORRIS, Thomas Ernest Gilbert 02/96
MORRISON, Walter Edward 08/96
MORT, John Ernest Llewelyn 07/97
MORTON, Alfred Bruce 12/95
MORTON, Arthur 03/96
MORTON, John Peter Sargeson 02/96
MOSELEY, Colin Francis 01/97
MOSES, Norman 11/96
MOSS, Clement Frederick 11/96
MOULE, George William Henry 05/96
MUNDY, Katherine Ann 12/96
MUNRO, Louis Cecil Garth 01/97
MURPHY, David 03/96
MUSSELWHITE, Edward Charles 11/96
MUXLOW, George 01/97
NAZER, Raymond 11/96
NEEDHAM, George Oswald 10/95
NEIL, Richard Wilfred 06/96
NEIL-SMITH, John Christopher 11/95
NEILL, Charles Christopher Stanley 08/96
NELSON, Nelson John 05/97
NEVELL, Frederick George 06/96
NEW, John Bingley 03/96
NEWTON, Derek Lewis 07/97
NICHOLLS, David Gwyn 06/96
✠NICHOLLS, Vernon Sampson 02/96
NIGHTINGALE, William Hirst 04/96
NIXON, Bernard Lawrence 03/96
NOCKELS, Donald Reginald 01/97

NORTH, George Lewis 09/95
OGDEN-SWIFT, Geoffrey William 11/95
OLLIER, Cecil Rupert 07/97
ORRELL, Joseph Albert (Joe) 09/96
OVENDEN, Edward Clifford Lewis 06/96
OVERTHROW, Terence Reginald Charles (Terry) 05/96
OWEN, John Peregrine 05/96
OWENS, Tuddyd 07/97
OWENS, Ashby 10/96
OXFORD, Victor Thomas 09/96
PANTING, John 08/96
PARKE, George Reginald 11/96
PARKER, Frank Maxwell Lewis 06/97
PARKER, John William 08/96
PARKES, Norman John 03/96
PARSONS, Martin 02/97
PARSONS, Victor 10/95
PASLEY, Charles Victor 11/96
PASSINGHAM, Eric Albert 11/96
PATERSON, William John McCallum 04/97
PAULEY, Denniss Franklyn 12/96
PAXTON, Cyril 10/96
PAYNE, Victor Harold 05/96
PEARCE, Alfred Edward 01/97
PEARCE, Ronald Edgar John 09/97
PEARCE, Stephen Wilson 01/97
PEARS, John Barbour 05/97
PEASE, John Alfred 01/97
PECK, William Gerard 12/96
PECKETT, John Freeman 04/96
PENNELL, James Henry Leslie 02/96
PENNIE, Gibb Niven 05/96
PENNOCK, John Harding Lovell 05/96
PERFECT, Leslie Charles 12/95
PERRETT-JONES, Reginald James Archibald 04/96
PERRY, Geoffrey 04/97
PERRY, Michael Arnold 12/96
PETERS, Richard Paul 12/96
PHAIR, Henry Lloyd 03/97
PHALO, Arthur (Ramoabi) 06/97
PHILLIPS, Ivor Lloyd 01/97
PHILLIPS, William Ufelgwyn Maundy 11/96
PIBWORTH, John David 03/97
PIERCY, Henry Graham 06/96
PILL, Hugh Godfrey Reginald 11/96
PIRIE, John Henry 12/95
PITT, Mervyn George Mottram 12/95
PLUMMER, Charles Henry 04/97
POCKLINGTON, Eric Charles 06/96
POLWIN, Peggy Yvonne 08/96
POOLE, Ronald John Ajax 05/96
PORTER, Geoffrey Ernest 02/97
PORTEUS, Matthew Thomas 11/95
POTTER, Guy Anthony 10/95
POWNALL, Tom Basil 05/97
PRATT, Eric 07/96
PREBBLE, Frederick John 07/97
PRESTON, Joseph Arthur 10/96
PRICE, Philip Roger 02/97
PRICE-JONES, Haydn 04/97
PRITCHARD, John Richard 08/96
PROCTOR, Hugh Gordon 05/96
PUGH, John 07/96
PUMFREY, John Lawrence 03/97
PUSEY, Robert Guy 04/97
QUIN, Cosslett William Charles 12/95
RABAN, James Peter Caplin Priaulx 06/96
RABBETTS, Reginald Douglas Cyprian 01/96
RADFORD, Donald George 11/96
RADFORD, Samuel 04/96
RADLEY, Roy Taylor 12/96
RALPH-BOWMAN, Murray Peter 01/97
RAMELL, Arthur Lewis 05/96
RAMSAY, John Leslie 12/95
RAMSDEN, Francis Samuel Lloyd 01/97
RANDALL, David William 08/96
RANDALL, John Randall 06/97
RANDALL, Philip Joseph 03/97
RANDOLPH, Michael Richard Spencer 06/97
RATCLIFF, Richard Charles 01/97
RAWLINS, Douglas Royston 02/96
RAYMOND, George William 04/97
RAYNOR, Robert Ernest 01/96
READ, John Charles 01/96
REAKES-WILLIAMS, John Michael Reakes Andrew 07/97
REAY, John 02/96
REBERT, Nicholas Aubrey Russell 12/95
REDMOND, Ernest Wilkinson 12/96
REED, Albert 12/96
REES, James Arthur 06/97
REES, John Harold 12/96
REES, Philip William Watkins 02/96
RENDELL, Peter Vivian 02/96
RHODES, Maurice Arthur 06/97
RHYMES, Douglas Alfred 01/96
RHYS, Trevor William 02/96
RICHARDS, Peter Lane Campling 08/96
RICHARDSON, Stephen 12/95
RICHARDSON, Thomas Warner 05/96
RIDLEY, John Sidney 06/97
RIGLER, Edgar Henry (Tony) 08/96
ROBERTS, Arthur Stansfield 03/97
✠ROBERTS, Eric Matthias 03/97
ROBERTS, Hugh Godfrey Lloyd 10/96
ROBERTS, John Robert 10/96
ROBERTS, John William Melton 12/95
ROBERTS, Thomas 10/96
ROBINSON, Francis George 04/96
ROBINSON, Gordon Stanislaus 06/96
ROBSON, Bernard John 10/96
ROBSON, Thomas George Harry 11/96
RODERICK, John Howard 04/97
ROEBUCK, John William 01/96
ROGERS, John Iorweth ?/96
ROGERS, Richard George 08/97
ROSENTHALL, Henry David 05/97
ROWE, Edward Nelson 12/96
ROWLAND, Henry Rees 06/96
RUMALSHAH, Inayat 01/97
RUMSEY, Philip Charles 02/97
RUSSON, Joseph Kenneth 06/96
SADLER, John Harvey 03/96
SAMBROOK, Ernest 12/96
SAMPSON, Everard Archbold 01/97
SANDERS, Frederick Alvin Oliver 09/96
SAVAGE, William Humphrey 02/97
SAVIGE, John Sydney 07/97
SAWLE, William John 10/95
SCAMMELL, John James Frank 03/97
SCOTT, David 08/96
SCOTT, Hedley 05/97
SCOTT, Peter Lawrence 02/97
SCUTT, John Melville 10/95
SEALE, Daisy Elaine 08/97
SEARIGHT, Mervyn Warren 01/96
SECRETAN, Paul Lawrence 11/96
SELL, John Lewis 09/96
SEMPER, Cecil Michael 03/97
SERCOMBE, Theodore Friend 05/97
SERGEANT, John Middlemore 03/97
SERJEANTSON, Eric William 08/96
✠SESSFORD, George Minshull 07/96
SHANNON, William Patrick 10/95
SHARP, Ralph Norman 09/95
SHAW, Basil Earle 05/97
SHAW, Cuthbert Charles 01/97
SHAW, Denis Walter 05/97
SHAW-HAMILTON, Janet Elizabeth (Jan) 02/97
SHEPHERD, Philip Reginald 08/96
SHORT, Terence 02/97
SHORTHOUSE, Stephen Arthur 03/96
SHORTLAND, Thomas (Tom) 11/96
SIMON, Ulrich Ernst 08/97
SIMPSON, Brian Shepherd Tinley 02/97
SIMPSON, Clarence 05/97
SIMPSON, Rennie 01/97
SLADE, Harold Godfrey Rex 01/96
SLATER, Gilbert Leonard 02/96
SLATER, Ronald Spencer 04/97
SMALLBONE, Denys George 11/96
SMALLWOOD, Graham Marten 10/96
SMERDON, Stanley William 05/97
SMITH, Edward Leonard Richard 06/97
SMITH, Eric Alfred Norman 12/95
SMITH, John Edward Allin 09/97
SMITH, Philip Morell 03/96
SMITH, Ronald George (Ron) 04/96
SMITH, Sydney Robert 10/95
SMITHIES, Edwin Henry 02/96
SMYTH, James Desmond 07/96
SMYTHE, Paul Rodney 02/97
SNELLGROVE, Frederic Mortimer 06/97
SNELLING, Stanley Alfred 05/97
SNOW, William George Sinclair 05/96
SORENSEN, Arthur Frank 03/97
SPARKES, Richard Graham Brabant 07/97
SPARKS, Hedley Frederick Davis 01/96
SPEERS, Albert Edward 03/96
SPENCER, Robert 03/97
SPENCER, Stanley 09/96
SPENCER, William Lowbridge 03/96
STACEY, John Roderick (Jack) 03/97
STAFFORD, John James 06/97
STANDLEY, Leslie Gordon 02/96
STARK, Edwin George John 06/97
STEAD, Leslie Cawthorn 07/96
STEVENSEN, Albert 02/96
STEWART, John 06/97
STOKES, Godfrey Julian Fenwick 07/97
STRANEX, Douglas 05/96
STRANGE, Edward Stanley 12/95
STRONG, George Noel 04/96
STURDY, John Vivian Mortland 07/96
SUDBURY, Peter John 05/96
SUGDEN, Andrew Neville Burn 12/95
SUTCLIFFE, Maurice 07/97
SUTCLIFFE, Thomas Henry 02/96
SUTTON, Christopher Hope 06/96
SWABEY, Henry Sandys 11/95
SWALLOW, Arnold Birkett 06/96
SWINNEY, Thomas 10/95
SYER, George Vivian 12/95
SYKES, Frederick Drummond 01/96
TAIT, Henry Alexander 05/97
TAYLOR, Frank Leslie 10/96
TAYLOR, Herbert Cyril 04/96
TEBBOTH, Alfred Thomas Henderson 10/96
TEMPLETON (née McCUTCHEON), Irene 10/95
TENNICK, Edward 06/96
THACKER, Charles Kent 01/96
THATCHER, Rodney David (Rod) 07/97
THOMAS, Arthur George 01/96
THOMAS, John Degwel 01/97
THOMAS, Joseph Neville 08/97
THOMAS, Lewis Llewellyn 11/96
THOMAS, Trevor Wilson 03/96
THURSFIELD, John Richard 05/97
TICQUET, Cyril Edward 04/96
TILLYARD, James Donald 04/97
TIMMS, Robert Newell 10/95
TINDALL, Frederick Cryer 12/95
TODD, John Lindsay 08/97
TODD, Leslie Alwill 10/95
TONGUE, Denis Harold 05/96
TOONE, Lawrence Raymond 12/96
TORLACH, Charles Emil 12/95

TOSTEVIN, Ronald Edwin 07/96
TREADWELL, Albert Frederick 11/95
TRUBRIDGE, George Ernest Samuel 07/97
TRUMAN, John Malcolm 08/96
TUCKWELL, Paul 08/96
TURNER, Eric Gurney Hammond 06/96
TURNER, Henry Ernest William 12/95
TURNER, John Girvan 12/96
TURNER, Noel Macdonald Muncaster 04/97
TYSON, John Wood Worsley 10/96
✠ud-DIN, Khair- 01/97
VASEY, David 10/95
VAUGHAN, Richard John 08/96
VAUGHAN-JONES, Frederick Edward Cecil 08/96
VEAR, Frank Henry 06/96
VERNON, Reginald Joseph (Reg) 11/95
VERNON, William Bradney 05/97
VICKERS, Allan Frederick 01/96
VINCE, Edwin George 06/96
VOKES-DUDGEON, Thomas Pierre 10/96
WAKELING, Stanley George 05/96
WAKER, Anthony Francis 11/96
WALKER, Eric Henry 05/96
WALKER, Thomas 06/97
WALL, Charles William 11/96
WALLACE, Edgar Walker 10/96
WALLBANK, Newell Eddius 03/96
WALLER, Gordon Hamilton 05/96
WALLER, Trevor 12/95
WALMSLEY, Alexander David 07/96
WALSH, William Arthur 09/95
WALTER, Arthur Reginald 04/96
WALTERS, David Miles Ivor 01/97
WARD-ANDREWS, Lewes 01/96
WARDLE-HARPUR, Charles Noel 12/96
WARE, John Franklin Jones 04/97
WARING, Wilfrid Harold 08/97
WARNER, Thomas Edward 03/96
WATERSON, John Hayden Lionel 04/97
WATKIN, Stephen Roy 12/96
WATLING, Arthur Edward 10/95
WATSON, Cecil Henry Barrett 05/96
WATSON, George 11/96
WATTS, Michael 07/96
WATTS, Michael 06/96
WATTS-JONES, William Vyvyan Francis Kynaston 06/97
WEAVER, George Edward 11/95
WEAVER, Thomas James 02/97
WEDDERBURN, John Alroy 01/97
WEDGWOOD, Peter John 02/96
WELCH, Alice 09/96
WELLS, Charles 06/96
WENHAM, John William 02/96
WENSLEY, John Ettery 03/97
WEST, Thomas 08/95
WHILD, James Edward 09/95
WHITE, Egbert Douglas 02/97
WHITE, Harold Kent 03/96
WHITE-THOMSON, Ian Hugh 01/97
WHITFIELD, Benjamin Owen 03/96
WHITLEY, Charles Francis 03/96
WHITTAKER, Ivan Harrison 06/96
WHITTON, Norman 01/97
WILD, Robert David Fergusson 11/95
WILDRIDGE, Peter 05/96
WILKINSON, Norman Ellis 05/97
WILKINSON, Raymond Stewart 10/95
WILLCOCK, Donald Thomas 10/95
WILLIAMS, Frederick Vivian 11/95
WILLIAMS, Howard Graham (Brother Anthony) 10/95
WILLIAMS, Leslie Arthur 07/96
WILLIAMS, Michael John 12/96
WILLIAMS, Richard Pierce 05/97
WILLIAMS, Robert Wilfred Callard 01/96
WILLIAMS, Roger Arthur 12/96
WILLIS, Christopher Rawdon 07/97
WILLMINGTON, John Henry William 08/96
WILLMOTT, Oliver Leonard 05/96
WILLOUGHBY, Bernard Digby 03/97
WILLS, Kenneth Charles Austen 12/95
WILSON, Allen 02/97
WILSON, Arthur 04/97
WILSON, Spencer William 08/96
WILSON, Stanley 06/97
WILSON, William Hubert 04/97
WINGFIELD-DIGBY, Stephen Basil 01/96
WISE, Geoffrey John 09/96
WITTEY, William Francis George 03/96
WITTS, Cyril Charles 11/96
WOOD, George John Edmund 06/97
WOOD, Jack Barrington 10/95
WOOD, Jane 10/96
WOODD, Basil John 02/97
WOODERSON, Timothy George Arthur 06/97
WOODHEAD, Alan Howard 02/97
WOODHOUSE, Samuel Mostyn Forbes 10/95
WOODS, Howard Charles 02/97
WORTH, Douglas Albert Victor 07/96
WRIGHT, Samuel John 12/96
WRIGLEY, Philip Arthur 11/96
YANDELL, Owen James 01/97
YEOMANS, Thomas Henry 12/95
YEULETT, George Eric 01/97
YORKE, Edward Frederick 05/97
YORKE, Leslie Henry 08/96
YOULE, Peter William 10/95
YOUNG, Katharine Jane (Katie) 01/97
YOUNG, Paul Goodwin 06/97
YOUNGMAN, Frank Arthur 06/97

SCOTLAND
0 10 20 30 40 50miles
0 20 40 60 80km
Provincial Boundary
Diocesan Boundary
Location of Cathedral
ABERDEEN AND ORKNEY
ABERDEEN AND ORKNEY
SHETLAND ISLANDS
MORAY, ROSS AND CAITHNESS
Inverness
ABERDEEN AND ORKNEY
Aberdeen
ARGYLL AND THE ISLES
Oban
BRECHIN
ST ANDREWS, DUNKELD AND DUNBLANE
Perth
Dundee
Glasgow
Edinburgh
GLASGOW AND GALLOWAY
EDINBURGH
IRELAND
ENGLAND

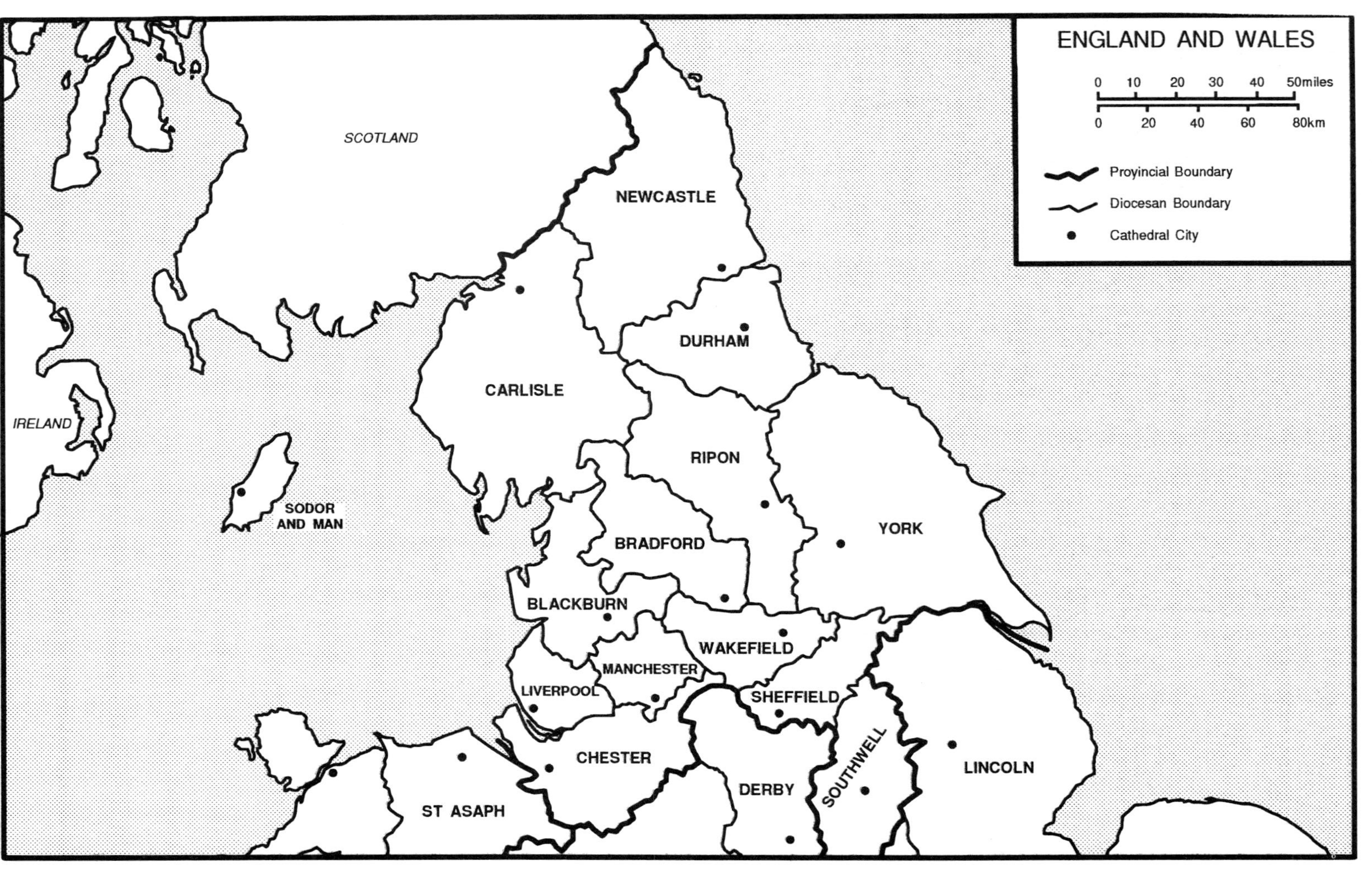
ENGLAND AND WALES
0 10 20 30 40 50miles
0 20 40 60 80km
Provincial Boundary
Diocesan Boundary
Cathedral City
SCOTLAND
IRELAND
NEWCASTLE
DURHAM
CARLISLE
RIPON
YORK
SODOR AND MAN
BRADFORD
BLACKBURN
WAKEFIELD
MANCHESTER
LIVERPOOL
SHEFFIELD
CHESTER
SOUTHWELL
LINCOLN
DERBY
ST ASAPH

LICHFIELD
BANGOR
LEICESTER
NORWICH
BIRMINGHAM
PETERBOROUGH
ELY
ST EDMUNDSBURY AND IPSWICH
WORCESTER
COVENTRY
SWANSEA AND BRECON
HEREFORD
ST DAVIDS
ST ALBANS
GLOUCESTER
CHELMSFORD
MONMOUTH
OXFORD
LONDON
LLANDAFF
BRISTOL
SOUTHWARK
ROCHESTER
CANTERBURY
GUILDFORD
WINCHESTER
BATH AND WELLS
SALISBURY
CHICHESTER
PORTSMOUTH
EXETER
The Channel Islands are annexed to the Diocese of Winchester
TRURO
The Isles of Scilly are included in the Diocese of Truro

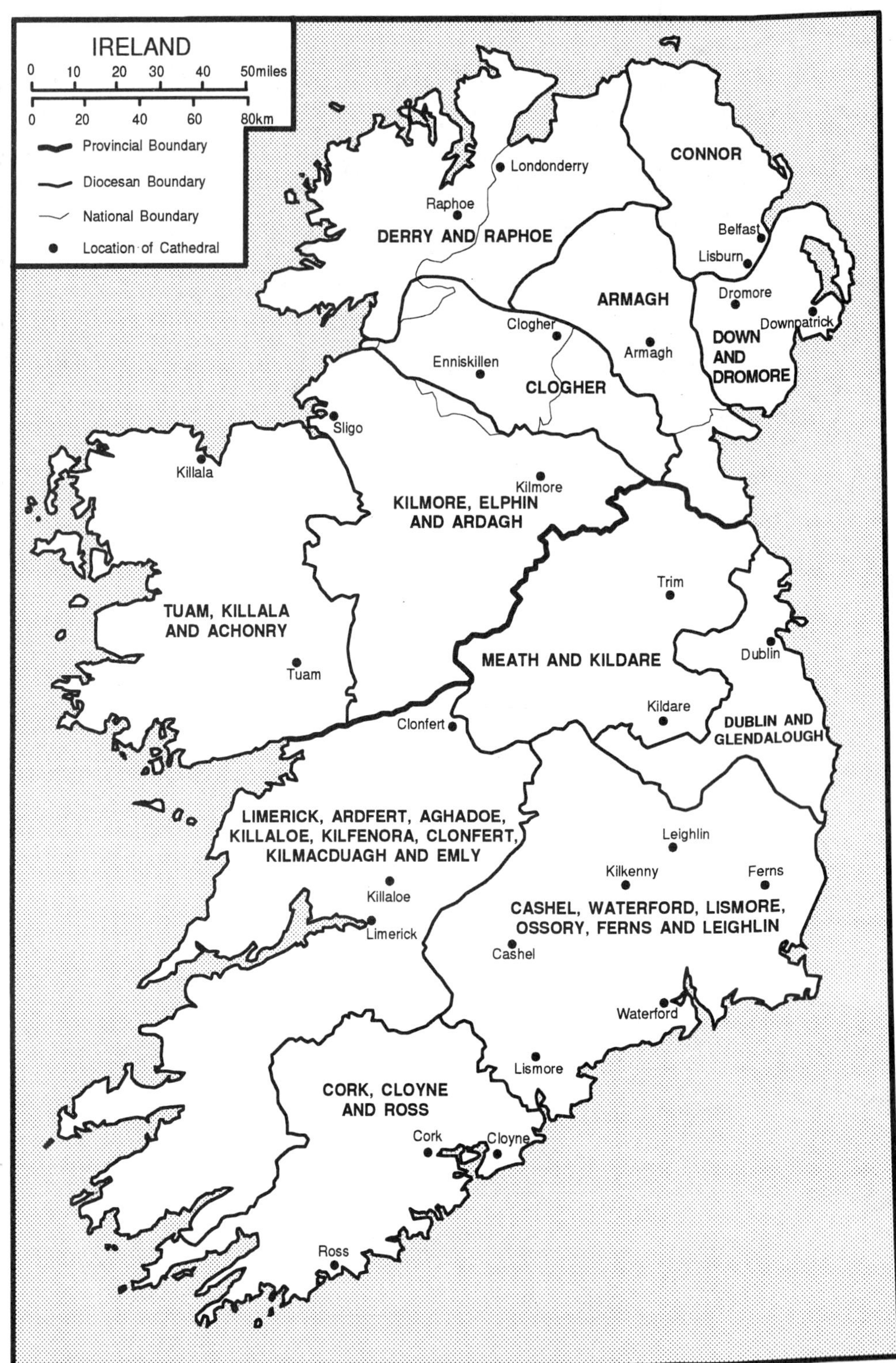

IRELAND
0
10
20
30
40
50miles
0
20
40
60
80km
Provincial Boundary
Diocesan Boundary
National Boundary
Location of Cathedral
Londonderry
Raphoe
DERRY AND RAPHOE
CONNOR
Belfast
Lisburn
Dromore
ARMAGH
DOWN AND DROMORE
Downpatrick
Clogher
Armagh
Enniskillen
CLOGHER
Sligo
Killala
Kilmore
KILMORE, ELPHIN AND ARDAGH
TUAM, KILLALA AND ACHONRY
Tuam
Trim
MEATH AND KILDARE
Dublin
Kildare
DUBLIN AND GLENDALOUGH
Clonfert
LIMERICK, ARDFERT, AGHADOE, KILLALOE, KILFENORA, CLONFERT, KILMACDUAGH AND EMLY
Leighlin
Kilkenny
Ferns
Killaloe
Limerick
CASHEL, WATERFORD, LISMORE, OSSORY, FERNS AND LEIGHLIN
Cashel
Waterford
Lismore
CORK, CLOYNE AND ROSS
Cork
Cloyne
Ross